PrincetonReview.com

THE COMPLETE BOOK OF COLLEGES

2021 Edition

Penguin
Random
House

The Princeton Review
110 East 42nd Street, 7th Floor
New York, NY 10017
Email: editorialsupport@review.com

Published in the United States by Penguin Random House LLC, New York, and
in Canada by Random House of Canada, a division of Penguin Random House
Ltd.,Toronto.

Terms of Service: The Princeton Review Online Companion Tools ("Student
Tools") for retail books are available for only the two most recent editions of that
book. Student Tools may be activated only twice per eligible book purchased for
two consecutive 12-month periods, for a total of 24 months of access. Activation
of Student Tools more than twice per book is in direct violation of these Terms of
Service and may result in discontinuation of access to Student Tools Services.

ISBN: 978-0-525-56941-1
ISSN: 1088-8594

The Princeton Review is not affiliated with Princeton University.

Editors: Aaron Riccio and Brian Saladino
Production Editor: Liz Dacey
Production Artist: Deborah Weber

Printed in the United States of America.

9 8 7 6 5 4 3 2 1

2021 Edition

Editorial
Robert Franek, Editor-in-Chief
David Soto, Director of Content Development
Stephen Koch, Student Survey Manager
Deborah Weber, Director of Production
Gabriel Berlin, Production Design Manager
Selena Coppock, Managing Editor
Aaron Riccio, Senior Editor
Meave Shelton, Senior Editor
Chris Chimera, Editor
Eleanor Green, Editor
Orion McBean, Editor
Brian Saladino, Editor
Patricia Murphy, Editorial Assistant

Penguin Random House Publishing Team
Tom Russell, VP, Publisher
Alison Stoltzfus, Publishing Director
Amanda Yee, Associate Managing Editor
Ellen L. Reed, Production Manager
Suzanne Lee, Designer

ACKNOWLEDGMENTS

Each year we assemble an awe-inspiringly talented group of colleagues who work together to produce our guidebooks; this year is no exception. Everyone involved in this effort—authors, editors, data collectors, production specialists, and designers—gives so much more than is required to make *The Complete Book of Colleges* an exceptional student resource guide.

My sincere thanks go to the many who contributed to this tremendous project. Very special thanks go to Aaron Riccio and Brian Saladino for their editorial commitment and vision. A warm and special thank you goes to our Student Survey expert, Stephen Koch, who continues to work in partnership with school administrators and students alike. My continued thanks go to our data collection pro, David Soto, for his successful efforts in collecting and accurately representing the statistical data that appear with each college profile and to Liz Dacey for her dedication to reading through the massive amounts of data. Likewise, we owe a debt to Deborah Weber for calmly sifting through all of that data and those ever-shifting deadline constraints so as to fully assemble this book. Special thanks also go to publicist Jeanne Krier, for the dedicated work she continues to do on this book and the overall series since its inception. Jeanne continues to be my trusted colleague, media advisor, and friend. I would also like to make special mention of Tom Russell and Alison Stoltzfus, our Random House publishing team, for their continuous investment and faith in our ideas. Again, to all who contributed so much to this publication, thank you for your efforts; they do not go unnoticed.

Robert Franek
Editor-in-Chief

CONTENTS

Get More (Free) Content
at **PrincetonReview.com/guidebook**

As easy as 1·2·3

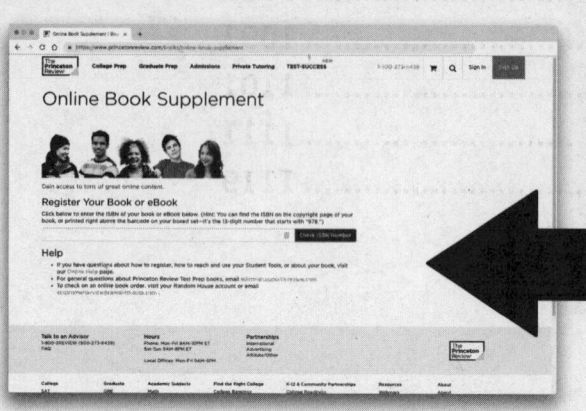

1 Go to PrincetonReview.com/ guidebooks and enter the following ISBN for your book:

9780525569411

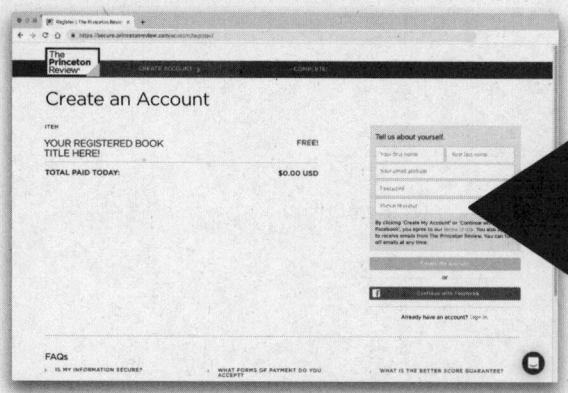

2 Answer a few simple questions to set up an exclusive Princeton Review account. *(If you already have one, you can just log in.)*

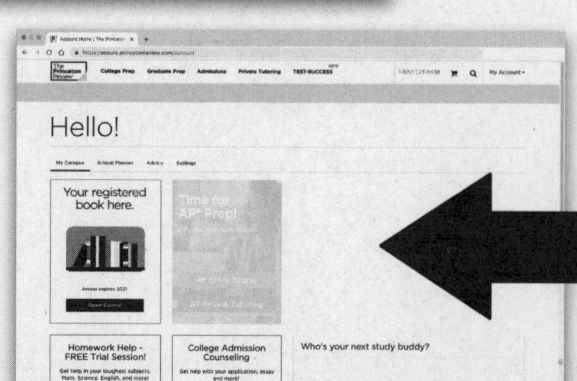

3 Enjoy access to your **FREE** content!

Once you've registered, you can...

- Access a printable version of the indexes for this book, so that you can more easily sort and find the schools you're looking for by tuition, size, and more

- Get valuable advice about the college application process, including tips for writing a great essay and where to apply for financial aid

- Check to see if there have been any corrections or updates to this edition

Need to report a potential **content** issue?

Contact **EditorialSupport@review.com** and include:

- full title of the book
- ISBN
- page number

Need to report a **technical** issue?

Contact **TPRStudentTech@review.com** and provide:

- your full name
- email address used to register the book
- full book title and ISBN
- Operating system (Mac/PC) and browser (Firefox, Safari, etc.)

FOREWORD

Welcome. You have found the best place to begin, fine-tune, and execute the search for your perfect college. With the understanding that choosing a school wisely is a top priority for each prospective student, we have provided a significant breadth of information in this text to help you navigate the exciting, amazing, and sometimes confusing process of choosing the right college.

The design of this guidebook will allow you to narrow your search of colleges from 1,349 to a few dozen. Here you'll find all the individual college statistics you'll need to make informed choices about the competitiveness, size, location, and academic offerings of the schools available to you. In addition, you can find even more information about individual schools at The Princeton Review's website, PrincetonReview.com. The site includes college search tools, college profiles, college advice, a college majors search engine, and much more.

By using this book, you can search for, choose, and apply to colleges with the confidence of a pro—or at the very least a well-informed undergraduate hopeful! We supply the information and guidance, and you ultimately make your own decision.

The college selection, application, and interview processes can be overwhelming at times. They can also be rewarding experiences. For most, choosing a college is the first major life decision. I know it was mine. Remember that your college decision is yours alone, so arm yourself with the best available information. Reach out to teachers, friends, high school and college admissions counselors, brothers, sisters, and parents; ask them how they chose their colleges and why. The more you know when beginning the process, the more in control of the situation you'll feel.

Whatever it is that you choose as your path in life, your college selection will forever be your first step in that direction. The friends you make, the professors you meet, and the classes you take are all springboards to the next phase of your life.

I wish you much luck and success at whichever college you decide to attend. My sincere hope is that this publication and other tools from The Princeton Review will be helpful in the process.

Robert Franek
Editor-in-Chief

INTRODUCTION

Before you dive into *The Complete Book of Colleges*, we want to give you some tips for your college search—especially on how to get the most out of this book and what to do once you've made your choices and are ready to apply. Since the most important thing for you to do now is to start your search, we want to start right off by revealing the secret to getting admitted to the college of your choice.

A crucial, and often overlooked, element to getting into college is compatibility: that is, finding colleges that have the educational and social environments you're looking for, where you are well-suited academically, and have something the college is looking for in return. You have a lot more control over where you end up going to college than you might think.

Finding your college fit is a two-step process. You should begin with a thorough self-examination or personal inventory. Your personal inventory is best structured in the form of a chart, so that when you begin to consider your options, you can check off those colleges that satisfy the various needs or wants you've identified. In this way, your best college choices will gradually begin to identify themselves.

Divide your inventory into two sections. One section should be biographical, including your high school course selection, GPA, SAT and/or ACT scores, class rank, and personal information like extracurricular activities—especially those you plan to continue in college. This will help you to assess how you stack up against each college's admissions standards and student body. The second section is a listing of the characteristics you need or want in the college you'll choose to attend. This list should include anything and everything you consider important, such as location, size of the student body, availability of scholarships, dormitory options, clubs and activities, even school colors if you want. This part of your inventory should grow continuously as you become more and more aware of what is important to you in your choice of colleges.

Armed with your personal inventory, you can begin to take advantage of the numerous resources available to help you narrow your choices of where to apply. There are five sources for information and advice that have become standard for most college-bound students:

1. ***College websites, social media feeds, videos, brochures, catalogs...***

   If you are a junior or senior in high school, you probably know more about the information these materials should include than the people who are responsible for designing and writing them. College marketing material will give you an overview of the academic offerings and the basic admissions requirements. You will never see anything but the most appealing architecture and the best-looking students on campus, nor will you hear about the recent tuition increases that were greater than the rate of inflation. Look these materials over, but don't make any decisions based solely on what you read or see.

2. Your friends

The experts on specific colleges and universities are the students who currently attend them. Seek out any and all of your friends, offspring of your parents' friends, and recent graduates of your high school who attend colleges that you are considering. Talk to them when they come home. Arrange to stay with them when you visit their colleges. Pick their brains for everything they know. It doesn't get any more direct and honest than this.

3. Books and college guides

There are two types of books that can be helpful to you in your search: those that discuss specific aspects of going to college and those that serve as college guides. A great narrative guide that stresses students' own opinions of colleges is our own annual *Best Colleges* guide. In addition, look at other guides for good second opinions. As for comprehensive guides—those that emphasize data over narrative content—you're holding the most up-to-date and useful one in your hands.

4. The Internet

Beyond a college's own website and social media presence, there are many publications and communities online dedicated to college admissions. Our site, PrincetonReview.com, provides a wide range of resources to help you research colleges, prepare for standardized tests, raise your grades, and complete your college application.

5. Your counselor

Since it's *critically* important, we'll say it again: Once you've developed some ideas about your personal inventory and college options, schedule a meeting with your school counselor. The more research you've done before you get together, the more help you're likely to get. Good advice comes out of thoughtful discussion, not from the expectation that your counselor will do your work. Many students and families opt to work with a professional college counselor, such as the expert College Admission Counselors at The Princeton Review, to supplement the support they receive from their high schools. When it comes time to file applications, look over the materials and requirements together, and allow plenty of time to craft your best application.

Using College Information in The Complete Book of Colleges *and Elsewhere*

Throughout the course of your college search, you'll confront an amazing array of statistics and other data related to every college you consider. In order for all of this information to be helpful, you need to have some sense of how to interpret it. We've included a detailed key to the college entries in this book a few pages deeper into this introduction. Almost all the statistics we've compiled are self-explanatory, but there are a few that will be more useful with some elaboration.

Let's start with **student/teacher ratio**. Don't use it to assess average class size; they are not interchangeable terms. At almost every college, the average class size is larger than its student/teacher ratio. At many big universities, it is considerably larger. What is useful about the ratio is that it can give you an idea of how accessible your professors will be outside of the classroom. Once you are in college, you'll grow to realize just how important this is.

In the same way, the **percentage of faculty that holds PhDs** is useful information. When you're paying thousands of dollars in tuition each year, there's something comforting about knowing that your professors have a considerably broader and deeper grasp of what you're studying than you do. In contrast, teaching assistants (TAs) may often be just one or two steps ahead of you.

Another interesting group of statistics deals with the **percentage of students who go on to graduate or professional school**. Never allow yourself to be swayed by such statistics, unless you've taken the time to ponder their meaning and visited the college in question. High percentages almost always mean one of two things: that the college is an intellectual enclave that inspires students onward to further their education, or that it is a pre-professional bastion of aggressive careerists. There isn't anything inherently wrong with either scenario, but neither has universal appeal to prospective students. Colleges that are exceptions to this rule are rare and precious. The most misleading figures provided to prospective students are those for medical school acceptance rates. Virtually every college in the country can boast of high acceptance rates to medical school for its graduates; pre-med programs are designed to weed out those who will not be strong candidates before they even get to apply! If you're thinking about medical school, ask colleges how many of their students apply to medical school each year. Also, try to get a sense of the attrition rate within the pre-med program.

One final piece of advice about statistics relates to the **Freshman Admission Statistics**. Simply knowing the percentage of applicants who are admitted each year is helpful, but it is even more helpful if you also know how many applied. When you compare these figures to the first-year profile, you have the most accurate picture of just how tough it is to get in. An 80 percent acceptance rate doesn't mean there's an open door if you don't match up well to the academic achievements of the college's typical first-year. Beyond this, keep an eye out for colleges that have relatively self-selecting applicant pools. In these cases, high acceptance rates may be misleading. When evaluating highly selective public colleges as an out-of-state applicant, remember that you will likely face a more selective evaluation than state residents.

A Few Final Thoughts

Once you've narrowed down your options and decided where to apply, get to work filling out applications. The admissions process is stressful enough without putting extra pressure on yourself by waiting until the last minute. The first thing you should do when you receive the necessary forms is go over them with your school counselor. Immediately remove the recommendation forms (if they are required) and give them to the teachers and counselor(s) who will be completing them for you. They'll have a better opportunity to write a thorough and supportive recommendation if you give them enough time to complete them. This is also the time to make your request for official transcripts. Again, it takes time to do these things. Plan ahead.

As for completing the applications, organize yourself and all the materials. Keep everything in folders (physically, on your computer, or in the cloud) and accessible in case you need to speak with an admissions officer over the telephone. When essays and information on your extracurricular activities are required, do some outlining and rough draft-writing before you commit yourself to the actual forms or online tools, and make sure you ask someone you trust to proofread your work.

Paying for college requires some work on your part, too. While this book is not dedicated to the subject, it's very important that you get to work on your financial circumstances right away. Keep in mind that while college is expensive, few people pay the full "sticker price." You have to have your finances in order before you can get the most financial aid possible. Visit fafsa.gov for the latest on the Free Application for Federal Student Aid. You can also find the most exhaustive strategies for financing your education in our book *Paying for College*.

Last but not least, **don't take it easy during your senior year!** Colleges routinely request mid-year grades, and they expect you to continue taking challenging academic courses and keep your grades up throughout your high school career. Doing so takes you one step closer to getting good news. On behalf of The Princeton Review, have a good time, and good luck. See you on campus!

Nota Bene

The data reported in this book, unless otherwise noted, was collected from the profiled colleges from the fall of 2019 through the winter of 2020. In some cases, we were unable to publish the most recent data because schools did not report the necessary statistics to us in time, despite our repeated outreach efforts. Because enrollment and financial statistics as well as application and financial aid deadlines fluctuate from one year to another, we recommend that you check to make sure you have the most current information before applying. Best of luck!

HOW THE COMPLETE BOOK
OF COLLEGES *IS ORGANIZED*

There are two types of profiles in this book. Not every school listed will have both. All of the 1,349 colleges and universities included in this book have their own informational profiles, and each entry follows the same basic format. Some of the institutions also have special two-page spreads located at the back of the book. These are written by the colleges and universities that wanted to present detailed descriptions of their campuses and programs.

Unless noted in the descriptions below, the Admissions Services Division of The Princeton Review collected all of the data presented in the informational profiles. As is customary with college guides, all data reflect figures for the academic year prior to publication, unless otherwise indicated. Since college offerings and demographics vary significantly from one institution to another and some colleges report data more thoroughly than others, few entries will include all of the individual data points described below.

The Heading

This section includes school name, address, telephone number, fax number, e-mail address, website, financial aid telephone number, and college code numbers for both the College Board (CEEB) and the American College Testing Program (ACT) when applicable. All website addresses were accurate and functioning at the time of publication. Check PrincetonReview.com for the most up-to-date links to colleges.

The Best Colleges Icon

 Indicates whether the school can be found in our annual book, The Best Colleges. In that book, each school has a detailed profile that includes the results of our surveys regarding student opinion about many aspects of their schools and their educations.

The Blurb

Describes the college or university. Includes all available data that relate to the date of founding of the school, religious affiliation, whether the school is public or private, and campus size.

Ratings

This section includes the school's Fire Safety Rating, its Admissions Selectivity Rating, and its Green Rating.

Admissions Selectivity Rating

This rating measures how competitive admissions are at the school. This rating is determined by several institutionally reported factors, including: the class rank, standardized test scores, and high school GPA of entering freshmen; the percentage of students who hail from out-of-state; and the percentage of applicants accepted and those deciding to enroll. This rating is given on a scale of 60–99. Please note that if a school has an Admissions Selectivity Rating of 60* (sixty with an asterisk), it means that the school did not report to us enough of the statistics that go into the rating in order for us to accurately measure its admissions selectivity.

Fire Safety

We asked all the schools from which we collect data annually to answer several questions about their efforts to ensure fire safety for campus residents. Each school's responses to nine of those questions were considered when calculating its Fire Safety Rating. The questions were developed in consultation with the Center for Campus Fire Safety (www.campusfire.org), and they cover: 1) The percentage of student housing sleeping rooms protected by an automatic fire sprinkler system with a fire sprinkler head located in the individual sleeping rooms; 2) The percentage of student housing sleeping rooms equipped with a smoke detector connected to a supervised fire alarm system; 3) The number of malicious fire alarms that occur in student housing per year; 4) The number of unwanted fire alarms that occur in student housing per year; 5) The banning of certain hazardous items and activities in residence halls, like candles, smoking, halogen lamps, etc.; 6) The percentage of student housing building fire alarm systems that, if activated, result in a signal being transmitted to a monitored location on campus or the fire department.

Schools that did not report answers to any of the above questions receive a Fire Safety Rating of 60*. The schools have an opportunity to update their fire safety data every year and will have their fire safety ratings re-calculated and published annually.

Each individual rating places a college on a continuum for purposes of comparing all colleges within this academic year only. Though similar, these ratings are not intended to be compared directly to those that appeared on PrincetonReview .com in any prior academic year or within any Princeton Review print publication, except for *The Best 386 Colleges, 2021 Edition*. Our ratings computations are refined and change annually.

Green

This rating, on a scale of 60–99, provides a comprehensive measure of a school's performance as an environmentally aware and prepared institution. Specifically, it includes 1) whether students have a campus quality of life that is both healthy and sustainable, 2) how well a school is preparing students for employment in the clean-energy economy of the 21st century as well as for citizenship in a world now defined by environmental concerns and opportunities and 3) how environmentally responsible a school's policies are. Colleges that did not supply answers to a sufficient number of the questions for us to fairly compare them to other schools received a Green Rating of 60*.

Students & Faculty

Enrollment

The total number of full-time undergraduates.

Student Body

The percentage of male, female, out-of-state, and international students, and the number of foreign countries represented.

Ethnic Representation

By percentage according to ethnic group. Figures may not add up to 100 percent, as student reporting of ethnicity is voluntary by law.

Retention and Graduation

The percentage of first-year undergraduate students who return for sophomore year. The percentage of last year's seniors who entered as first-years and graduated in four years, and who graduated in six years. The percentage of graduates who pursue further study within one year, and the percentage of those graduates who pursue further study for arts and sciences, law, medical, or business degrees.

Faculty

The ratio of undergraduates to full-time faculty. The number of full-time instructional faculty. The percentage of faculty who hold PhDs. The percentage of faculty members who belong to minority groups and the percentage of those who are women. The percentage of classes taught by a teaching assistant.

Academics

Degrees
The types of degrees awarded to students.

Classes
Number of students in an average regular class and an average lab/discussion section.

Most Popular Majors
The majors with the highest enrollment.

Special Study Options
May include accelerated programs, cross registration, cooperative (work-study) program, distance learning, double majors, dual enrollment, English as a Second Language, student exchange programs (domestic), external degree programs, honors programs, independent study, internships, liberal arts/career combinations, student-designed majors, study abroad, teacher certification programs, weekend college, and other options as specified by each school.

Disability Services Offered
A list of any services provided for those with disabilities.

Career Services
A list of career-specific services, such as job search classes and internships, provided through the school.

Facilities

Housing
Types of school-owned or affiliated housing available. May include coed dorms, women's dorms, men's dorms, apartments for married students, apartments for single students, special housing for disabled students, special housing for international students, fraternity/sorority housing, cooperative housing, and other options as specified by the school. The availability of assistance in finding off-campus housing. Any housing requirements that may exist, such as required on-campus residence for first-years.

Special Academic Facilities/Equipment
Other facilities and equipment of note (e.g., nuclear reactor, on-campus elementary school for student teachers, scanning electron microscopes, and so forth).

Campus Network
The percentage of locations on campus—such as classrooms, dining areas, libraries—that have wireless network access.

Campus Life

Environment
There are several categories of school environments. Here's the breakdown for each category:

- Rural (In or near a rural community, pop. under 5,000)
- Village (In a small town, pop. 5,000–24,999, or near a small town)
- Town (In a large town, pop. 25,000–74,999, or near a large town)
- City (In a small/medium city, pop. 75,000–299,999, or within its metropolitan area)
- Metropolis (In a major city, pop. 300,000 or more, or within its metropolitan area)

Activities
Standard activities available. May include campus ministries, choral groups, concert band, dance, drama/theater, international student organization, jazz band, literary magazine, Model UN, musical ensembles, musical theater, opera, pep band, radio station, student film society, student government, student newspaper, symphony orchestra, television station, and yearbook.

Organizations
Total number of registered organizations, honor societies, religious organizations, fraternities, sororities.

Athletics
Intercollegiate athletics available, listed by sex.

On-Campus Highlights
Any notable buildings.

Environmental Initiatives
Any notable eco-friendly programs.

Admissions

Freshman Academic Profile

Average high school GPA. Class rank distribution. The percentage from public high schools. Median range of SAT (Math, Critical Reading, and Writing sections) and/or ACT composite scores. Middle 50 percent score range of SAT (Math and Evidence-Based Reading and Writing sections) and/or ACT composite scores. Test of English as a Foreign Language (TOEFL) requirements for international students.

Basis for Candidate Selection

The criteria considered by the admissions committee in evaluating candidates. May include secondary school record, class rank, recommendations, standardized test scores, essay, interview, extracurricular activities, talent/ability, character/personal qualities, alumni/-ae relations, geographic residence, state residency, religious affiliation/commitment, minority status, volunteer work, work experience.

Freshman Admission Requirements

High school diploma/GED requirements. The number of academic units required or recommended in total and by academic subject. (Individual subject totals may not equal the complete sum of academic units required; in most cases, the difference is made up with electives. Check with the admissions office for any additional requirements.)

Freshman Admissions Statistics

The number of students who applied, the percentage of applicants who were accepted, and the percentage of those accepted who ultimately enrolled.

Transfer Admissions Requirements

Application requirements (may include high school transcript, college transcript, essay, interview, standardized tests, statement of good standing from prior school). Minimum high school GPA required. Minimum college GPA required. Lowest course grade transferable.

General Admissions Information

Application fee. Application deadlines. Admission notification date. "Rolling" indicates that decisions are sent to candidates as they are made, rather than held for a common notification date. Registration policy for terms other than the fall term. Common Application participation. Credit policies for College Entrance Examination Board Advanced Placement tests. Deferred admission policy.

Costs and Financial Aid

Tuition, room & board, fees, and books.

Required Forms and Deadlines

Forms that applicants for financial aid must file and their respective deadlines. May include FAFSA, institution's own financial aid form, CSS Profile, business/farm supplement, state aid form, noncustodial (divorced/separated) parent statement, and other forms specified by the school. Deadlines for filing financial aid forms.

Notification of Awards

The date that notification of financial aid awards occurs. "Rolling" indicates that notification is ongoing—the sooner you complete all of your required financial aid paperwork, the sooner you'll hear about your package.

Types of Aid

Need-based scholarships and grants may include Federal Pell, SEOG, state scholarships/grants, private scholarships, college/university gift aid from institutional funds, United Negro College Fund, Federal Nursing Scholarship, and other resources as specified by the school. Loans may include Direct Subsidized Loans, Direct Unsubsidized Loans, Direct PLUS Loans, Federal Perkins Loans, Federal Nursing Loans, state loans, college/university loans from institutional funds, and other resources as specified by the school.

Also includes a listing of any opportunities for student employment on campus, specifically Federal Work-Study (which is need-based), but also any part-time jobs direct from the college, and the college's assessment of potential off-campus employment opportunities.

Financial Aid Statistics

The percentage of first-years who received some form of need-based financial aid. The percentage of undergraduates who received some form of need-based financial aid. The number of first-years and undergrads who received an athletic scholarship or grant. The average amount of first-year scholarships and grants. The average amount of first-year loans. The average income from an on-campus job.

COLLEGE DIRECTORY

ABILENE CHRISTIAN UNIVERSITY

ACU Box 29000, Abilene, TX 79699
Phone: 325-674-2650 **Financial Aid Phone:** 325-674-2300
E-mail: info@admissions.acu.edu **CEEB Code:** 6001
Fax: 325-674-2130 **Website:** www.acu.edu **ACT Code:** 4050

This private school, affiliated with the Church of Christ, was founded in 1906. It has a 208 acre campus.

RATINGS

Admissions Selectivity Rating: 85 **Fire Safety Rating:** 88 **Green Rating:** 68

STUDENTS AND FACULTY

Enrollment: 3,524. **Student Body:** 60% female, 40% male, 11% out-of-state, 4% international (35 countries represented). Asian 1%, African American 9%, Caucasian 64%, Hispanic 17%, Native American <1%, Pacific Islander <1%, Two or more races 5%, Race unknown <1%.
Retention and Graduation: 77% freshmen return for sophomore year. 53% freshmen graduate within 4 years. 67% freshmen graduate within 6 years. 33% grads go on to further study within 1 year. 20% grads pursue arts and sciences degrees. 1% grads pursue law degrees. 5% grads pursue business degrees. 3% grads pursue medical degrees. **Faculty:** Student/faculty ratio 14:1. 266 full-time faculty, 77% hold PhDs, 11% are members of minority groups, 41% are women. 1% of classes are taught by teaching assistants.

ACADEMICS

Degrees: Associate; Bachelor's; Certificate; Doctoral degree—other; Doctoral degree research/scholarship; Master's; Post-bachelor's certificate; Post-master's certificate. **Classes:** Most classes have 10–19 students. Most lab/discussion sessions have 10–19 students. **Most popular majors:** Sport and Fitness Administration/Management; Business Administration and Management, General; Registered Nursing/Registered Nurse. **Special Study Options:** Accelerated program; Cross-registration; Distance learning; Double major; Dual enrollment; English as a Second Language (ESL); Honors program; Independent study; Internships; Student-designed major; Study abroad; Teacher certification program. **Honors programs:** The Honors College offers highly motivated students stimulating classes, opportunities to work with select faculty members, travel-based experiential learning and the chance to do research projects in their major field. **Disability Services offered:** Note-taking services; Reader services; Tape recorders. **Career services:** Alumni network; Alumni services; Career assessment; Career/job search classes; Internships.

FACILITIES

Housing: Apartments for single students; Men's dorms; Special housing for disabled students; Women's dorms; 95% of campus accessible to physically disabled. **Special Academic Facilities/Equipment:** Center for Christian Service and Leadership; Writing Center; Speaking Center; AT&T learning studio; Maker Lab; Shore Art Gallery; converged media newsroom; Center for Speech, Language and Learning; School of Nursing high-fidelity simulation labs; Rhoden Field lab and observatory.

CAMPUS LIFE

Environment: City. **Activities:** Campus Ministries; Choral groups; Concert band; Dance; Drama/theater; International Student Organization; Jazz band; Literary magazine; Marching band; Model UN; Music ensembles; Musical theater; Opera; Pep band; Radio station; Student government; Student newspaper; Symphony orchestra; Television station. 114 registered organizations, 9 honor societies, 6 religious organizations, 7 fraternities, 7 sororities, on campus. **Athletics (Intercollegiate):** *Men:* baseball, basketball, cross-country, football, tennis, track/field (outdoor), track/field (indoor). *Women:* basketball, cross-country, soccer, softball, tennis, track/field (outdoor), track/field (indoor), volleyball. **On-Campus Highlights:** Student Recreation and Wellness Center. **Environmental Initiatives:** Campus grounds: Bee Campus USA, Tree Campus USA, The Feral Cat Initiative.

ADMISSIONS

Freshman Academic Profile: Average high school GPA 3.6. 24% in top 10% of high school class, 56% in top 25% of high school class, 86% in top 50% of high school class. 60% from public high schools. **Test Scores:** SAT Math middle 50% range 510–610. SAT EBRW middle 50% range 530–620. ACT middle 50% range 21–27. **Basis for Candidate Selection:** *Very important factors include:* rigor of secondary school record, class rank, academic GPA, standardized test scores. *Important factors include:* talent/ability, character/personal qualities. *Other factors include:* application essay, recommendation(s),

extracurricular activities, first generation, alumni/ae relation, volunteer work, work experience, level of applicant's interest. **Freshman Admission Requirements:** High school diploma is required and GED is accepted. *Academic units required:* 4 English, 3 math, 3 science, 2 science labs, 2 foreign language, 1 history. *Academic units recommended:* 4 English, 3 math, 3 science, 2 science labs, 2 foreign language, 1 history. **Freshman Admission Statistics:** 11,569 applied, 57% admitted, 14% enrolled. **Transfer Admission Requirements:** High school transcript, college transcript(s), interview, Minimum college GPA of 2.0 required. Lowest grade transferable 2. **General Admission Information:** Application fee $50. Regular application deadline 2/15. Non-fall registration accepted.

COSTS AND FINANCIAL AID

Annual tuition $33,280. Room and board $10,378. Required fees $50. Average book and supplies expense $1,250. **Required Forms and Deadlines:** FAFSA. **Notification of Awards:** Applicants will be notified of awards on a rolling basis beginning 4/1. **Types of Aid:** *Need-based scholarships/grants:* College/university scholarship or grant aid from institutional funds; Federal Pell; Private scholarships; SEOG; State scholarships/grants. *Loans:* Direct PLUS loans; Direct Subsidized Stafford Loans; Direct Unsubsidized Stafford Loans. **Student Employment:** Federal Work-Study Program available. Institutional employment available. **Financial Aid Statistics:** 100% needy freshmen, 99% needy undergrads receive need-based scholarship or grant aid. 100% freshmen, 99% undergrads receive non-need-based scholarship or grant aid. 65% freshmen, 67% undergrads receive need-based self-help aid. 4% freshmen, 7% undergrads receive athletic scholarships. 100% freshmen, 97% undergrads receive any aid. **Criteria awarding aid:** *Non-need-based:* Academics, Art, Athletics, Leadership, Minority status, Music/drama, Religious affiliation, State/district residency.

ACADEMY OF ART UNIVERSITY

79 New Montgomery St, San Francisco, CA 94105
Phone: 415-274-2222 **Financial Aid Phone:** 800-544-2787
E-mail: info@academyart.edu
Fax: 415-618-6287 **Website:** www.academyart.edu **ACT Code:** 155

This proprietary school was founded in 1929. It has a 20 acre campus.

RATINGS

Admissions Selectivity Rating: 63 **Fire Safety Rating:** 91 **Green Rating:** 60*

STUDENTS AND FACULTY

Enrollment: 6,570. **Student Body:** 57% female, 43% male, 39% out-of-state, 26% international (95 countries represented). Asian 5%, African American 6%, Caucasian 15%, Hispanic 11%, Native American <1%, Pacific Islander 1%, Two or more races 3%, Race unknown 33%.
Retention and Graduation: 72% freshmen return for sophomore year. 10% freshmen graduate within 4 years. **Faculty:** Student/faculty ratio 14:1. 219 full-time faculty, 16% hold PhDs, 7% are members of minority groups, 43% are women. 0% of classes are taught by teaching assistants.

ACADEMICS

Degrees: Associate; Bachelor's; Certificate; Master's; Post-bachelor's certificate. **Classes:** Most classes have 10–19 students. **Most popular majors:** Animation, Interactive Technology, Video Graphics and Special Effects; Modeling, Virtual Environments and Simulation; Fashion/Apparel Design. **Special Study Options:** Distance learning; English as a Second Language (ESL); Independent study; Internships; Study abroad; Teacher certification program. **Disability Services offered:** Note-taking services; Reader services; Tape recorders. **Career services:** Alumni services; Career assessment; Career/job search classes; Internships.

FACILITIES

Housing: Apartments for single students; Coed dorms; Men's dorms; Women's dorms. 40% of campus accessible to physically disabled. **Special Academic Facilities/Equipment:** 3 Art Galleries for display of student work and 1 Fashion Retail Store.

CAMPUS LIFE

Environment: Metropolis. **Activities:** Choral groups; Dance; Drama/theater; International Student Organization; Model UN; Pep band; Radio station; Student government; Student newspaper; Student-run film society; Television station. 20 registered organizations, 1 religious organization, 1 fraternity, 1 sorority, on campus. **Athletics (Intercollegiate):** *Men:* baseball, basketball, cross-country, golf, soccer, tennis, track/field (outdoor). *Women:* basketball, cross-country, golf, soccer, softball, tennis, track/field (outdoor), volleyball. **On-Campus Highlights:** Urban Knight Kafe.

ADMISSIONS

Freshman Admission Requirements: High school diploma is required and GED is accepted. **Freshman Admission Statistics:** 2,396 applied, 100% admitted, 33% enrolled. **Transfer Admission Requirements:** High school transcript, college transcript(s), Minimum college GPA of 2.0 required. Lowest grade transferable C. **General Admission Information:** Application fee $50. Non-fall registration accepted.

COSTS AND FINANCIAL AID

Annual tuition $30,330. Room and board $18,386. Required fees $300. Average book and supplies expense $1,080. **Required Forms and Deadlines:** FAFSA; Institution's own financial aid form. **Notification of Awards:** Applicants will be notified of awards on a rolling basis beginning 3/15. **Types of Aid:** *Need-based scholarships/grants:* College/university scholarship or grant aid from institutional funds; Federal Pell; Private scholarships; SEOG; State scholarships/grants. *Loans:* Direct PLUS loans; Direct Subsidized Stafford Loans; Direct Unsubsidized Stafford Loans. **Student Employment:** Federal Work-Study Program available. **Financial Aid Statistics:** 84% needy freshmen, 82% needy undergrads receive need-based scholarship or grant aid. 8% freshmen, 10% undergrads receive non-need-based scholarship or grant aid. 76% freshmen, 78% undergrads receive need-based self-help aid. 5% freshmen, 3% undergrads receive athletic scholarships. 73% freshmen, 64% undergrads receive any aid. 57% undergrads borrow to pay for school. Average cumulative indebtedness $31,361. **Criteria awarding aid:** *Non-need-based:* Academics, Art, Athletics.

ACADIA UNIVERSITY

Admissions Office, Wolfville, NS B4P 2R6
Phone: 1-902-585-1446 **Financial Aid Phone:** 902-585-1016
E-mail: pam.dimock@acadiau.ca
Fax: 902-585-1092 **Website:** www.acadiau.ca

This public school was founded in 1838. It has a 200 acre campus.

RATINGS

Admissions Selectivity Rating: 74   **Fire Safety Rating:** 60*   **Green Rating:** 60*

STUDENTS AND FACULTY

Enrollment: 2,928. **Student Body:** 55% female, 45% male, 42% out-of-state. **Retention and Graduation:** 83% freshmen return for sophomore year. **Faculty:** Student/faculty ratio 10:1. 243 full-time faculty, 0% hold PhDs, 0% are members of minority groups, 36% are women. 0% of classes are taught by teaching assistants.

ACADEMICS

Degrees: Bachelor's; Certificate; Diploma; Master's. **Special Study Options:** Cooperative education program; Distance learning; Double major; English as a Second Language (ESL); Exchange student program (domestic); Honors program; Independent study; Internships; Study abroad. **Career services:** Career assessment; Career/job search classes; Internships.

FACILITIES

Housing: Apartments for single students; Coed dorms; Men's dorms; Special housing for disabled students; Women's dorms. **Campus network:** 100% of classrooms, 100% of dorms, 100% of student union, 100% of libraries, 100% of dining areas, 100% of common outdoor areas, have wireless network access.

CAMPUS LIFE

Environment: Rural. **Activities:** Campus Ministries; Choral groups; Concert band; Dance; Drama/theater; International Student Organization; Jazz band; Literary magazine; Music ensembles; Musical theater; Opera; Pep band; Radio station; Student government; Student newspaper; Symphony orchestra; Yearbook. 60 registered organizations, 3 religious organizations, on campus. **Athletics (Intercollegiate):** *Men:* basketball, cheerleading, cross-country, football, ice hockey, rugby, soccer, track/field (outdoor), volleyball. W*omen:* basketball, cheerleading, cross-country, ice hockey, rugby, soccer, track/field (outdoor), volleyball. **On-Campus Highlights:** KC Irving Environmental Science Centre.

ADMISSIONS

Freshman Academic Profile: 80% from public high schools. **Basis for Candidate Selection:** *Very important factors include:* rigor of secondary school record, academic GPA. *Important factors include:* recommendation(s), talent/ability. *Other factors include:* class rank, standardized test scores, extracurricular activities, character/personal qualities, geographical residence, volunteer work, work experience. **Freshman Admission Requirements:** High school diploma is required and GED is not accepted *Academic units required:* 1 English, 1 math. *Academic units recommended:* 1 English, 2 math, 1 science, 1 foreign language, 1 social studies, 1 history, 2 academic electives. **Freshman Admission Statistics:** 1,600 applied, 49% admitted, 68% enrolled. **Transfer Admission Requirements:** college transcript(s). **General Admission Information:** Application fee $25. Priority deadline 3/15. Non-fall registration accepted.

COSTS AND FINANCIAL AID

Annual in-state tuition $8,062. Annual out-of-state tuition $8,062. Room and board $8,284. Average book and supplies expense $1,200. **Notification of Awards:** Applicants will be notified of awards on or about 4/15. **Types of Aid:** *Loans:* Direct PLUS loans; Direct Subsidized Stafford Loans; Direct Unsubsidized Stafford Loans. **Criteria awarding aid:** *Need-based:* Leadership. *Non-need-based:* Academics, Leadership, Music/drama, State/district residency.

ADAMS STATE UNIVERSITY

208 Edgemont Blvd, Alamosa, CO 81102
Phone: 719-587-7712 **Financial Aid Phone:** 719-587-7306
E-mail: ascadmit@adams.edu **CEEB Code:** 4001
Fax: 719-587-7522 **ACT Code:** 496

This public school was founded in 1921. It has a 90 acre campus.

RATINGS

Admissions Selectivity Rating: 72   **Fire Safety Rating:** 60*   **Green Rating:** 60*

STUDENTS AND FACULTY

Enrollment: 1,882. **Student Body:** 44% female, 56% male, 39% out-of-state, 1% international (10 countries represented). Asian 1%, African American 8%, Caucasian 40%, Hispanic 35%, Native American 1%, Pacific Islander 1%, Two or more races 3%, Race unknown 10%.
Retention and Graduation: 54% freshmen return for sophomore year. 24% freshmen graduate within 4 years. 35% freshmen graduate within 6 years. **Faculty:** Student/faculty ratio 16:1. 98 full-time faculty, 58% hold PhDs, 20% are members of minority groups, 50% are women. 0% of classes are taught by teaching assistants.

ACADEMICS

Degrees: Associate; Bachelor's; Master's. **Classes:** Most classes have 10–19 students. Most lab/discussion sessions have fewer than 10 students. **Most popular majors:** Business Administration and Management, General; Exercise Science and Kinesiology; Teacher Education, Multiple Levels. **Special Study Options:** Accelerated program; Distance learning; Double major; Exchange student program (domestic); External degree program; Independent study; Internships; Student-designed major; Study abroad; Teacher certification program; Weekend college. **Disability Services offered:** Note-taking services; Reader services; Tutors. **Career services:** Alumni network; Career assessment; Career/job search classes; Internships.

FACILITIES

Housing: Apartments for married students; Apartments for single students; Coed dorms; Men's dorms; Women's dorms 95% of campus accessible to physically disabled. **Special Academic Facilities/Equipment:** Luther Bean Museum, Hatfield Gallery, Gallery 114, Leon Memorial Music Hall, Zacheis Planetarium, Ryan Geology Museum

CAMPUS LIFE

Environment: Village. **Activities:** Campus Ministries; Choral groups; Concert band; Drama/theater; Literary magazine; Model UN; Music ensembles; Radio station; Student government; Student newspaper. 27 registered organizations, on campus. **Athletics (Intercollegiate):** *Men:* basketball, cross-country, football, golf, soccer, track/field (outdoor), track/field (indoor), wrestling. Wo*Men:* basketball, cross-country, golf, soccer, softball, swimming, track/field (outdoor), track/field (indoor), volleyball. **On-Campus Highlights:** Leon Memorial Concert Hall. **Environmental Initiatives:** Establishment of EARTH (Environmental Action for Resources, Transportation, & Health) group on campus.

ADMISSIONS

Freshman Academic Profile: Average high school GPA 3.2. 7% in top 10% of high school class, 26% in top 25% of high school class, 56% in top 50% of high school class. **Test Scores:** SAT Math middle 50% range 430–530. SAT EBRW middle 50% range 440–550. ACT middle 50% range 17–22. **Basis for Candidate Selection:** *Very important factors include:* academic GPA, standardized test scores. *Important factors include:* rigor of secondary school record. *Other factors include:* class rank, application essay, recommendation(s), interview, extracurricular activities, character/personal qualities, geographical residence, volunteer work, work experience. **Freshman Admission Requirements:** High school diploma is required and GED is accepted. *Academic units required:* 4 English, 3 math, 3 science, 2 science labs, 1 foreign language, 2 academic electives. **Freshman Admission Statistics:** 1,698 applied, 99% admitted, 27% enrolled. **Transfer Admission Requirements:** college transcript(s), Minimum college GPA of 2.0 required. Lowest grade transferable D. **General Admission Information:** Application fee $30. Priority deadline 8/1. Non-fall registration accepted.2 years.

COSTS AND FINANCIAL AID

Required Forms and Deadlines: FAFSA. **Notification of Awards:** Applicants will be notified of awards on a rolling basis beginning 1/1. **Types of Aid:** *Need-based scholarships/grants:* College/university scholarship or grant aid from institutional funds; Federal Pell; Private scholarships; SEOG; State scholarships/grants. *Loans:* Direct PLUS loans; Direct Subsidized Stafford Loans; Direct Unsubsidized Stafford Loans. **Student Employment:** Federal Work-Study Program available. Institutional employment available. **Financial Aid Statistics:** 97% needy freshmen, 94% needy undergrads receive need-based scholarship or grant aid. 50% freshmen, 31% undergrads receive non-need-based scholarship or grant aid. 70% freshmen, 75% undergrads receive need-based self-help aid. 0% freshmen, 0% undergrads receive athletic scholarships. 82% undergrads borrow to pay for school. Average cumulative indebtedness $22,822. **Criteria awarding aid:** *Need-based:* Academics, Alumni affiliation, Art, Athletics, Leadership, Minority status, Music/drama. *Non-need-based:* Academics, Alumni affiliation, Art, Athletics, Leadership, Minority status, Music/drama, State/district residency.

ADELPHI UNIVERSITY

Nexus Building, Room 111, Garden City, NY 11530
Phone: 516-877-3050 **Financial Aid Phone:** 516-877-3080
E-mail: admissions@adelphi.edu **CEEB Code:** 2003
Fax: 516-877-3039 **Website:** www.adelphi.edu **ACT Code:** 2664

This private school was founded in 1896. It has a 75 acre campus.

RATINGS

Admissions Selectivity Rating: 78   **Fire Safety Rating:** 99   **Green Rating:** 66

STUDENTS AND FACULTY

Enrollment: 5,275. **Student Body:** 69% female, 31% male, 6% out-of-state, 4% international (46 countries represented). Asian 11%, African American 9%, Caucasian 50%, Hispanic 17%, Native American <1%, Pacific Islander <1%, Two or more races 3%, Race unknown 6%.
Retention and Graduation: 81% freshmen return for sophomore year. 55% freshmen graduate within 4 years. 68% freshmen graduate within 6 years. 28% grads go on to further study within 1 year. 1% grads pursue law degrees. 5% grads pursue business degrees. 1% grads pursue medical degrees. **Faculty:** Student/faculty ratio 11:1. 352 full-time faculty, 86% hold PhDs, 26% are members of minority groups, 54% are women. 0% of classes are taught by teaching assistants.

ACADEMICS

Degrees: Associate; Bachelor's; Certificate; Doctoral degree—professional practice; Doctoral degree research/scholarship; Master's; Post-bachelor's certificate; Post-master's certificate; Terminal Associate. **Classes:** Most classes have 10–19 students. Most lab/discussion sessions have 20–29 students. **Most popular majors:** Biology/Biological Sciences, General; Registered Nursing/Registered Nurse; Business/Commerce, General. **Special Study Options:** Accelerated program; Cross-registration; Distance learning; Double major; Dual enrollment; English as a Second Language (ESL); Honors program; Independent study; Internships; Liberal arts/career combination; Student-designed major; Study abroad; Teacher certification program; Weekend college. **Honors programs:** The Honors College seeks to prepare highly talented

and motivated students to face the 21st century by providing them with the intellectual perspectives and critical skills necessary to exercise responsible leadership. It involves an intense curricular and extracurricular program that asks students to view themselves and their work with integrity, passion, and seriousness. **Combined degree programs:** BA/DDS; BA/JD; BA/MA; BA/MD; BA/MEng. **Disability Services offered:** Note-taking services; Reader services; Tape recorders; Tutors. **Career services:** Alumni network; Alumni services; Career assessment; Career/job search classes; Internships; Regional alumni.

FACILITIES

Housing: Coed dorms; Special housing for disabled students; Theme housing; 95% of campus accessible to physically disabled.

CAMPUS LIFE

Environment: Metropolis. **Activities:** Campus Ministries; Choral groups; Concert band; Dance; Drama/theater; International Student Organization; Jazz band; Literary magazine; Model UN; Music ensembles; Musical theater; Opera; Radio station; Student government; Student newspaper; Student-run film society; Symphony orchestra; Yearbook. 80 registered organizations, 33 honor societies, 5 religious organizations, 8 fraternities, 10 sororities, on campus. **Athletics (Intercollegiate):** *Men:* baseball, basketball, cross-country, golf, lacrosse, soccer, swimming, tennis, track/field (outdoor), track/field (indoor). *Women:* basketball, bowling, cross-country, field hockey, lacrosse, soccer, softball, swimming, tennis, track/field (outdoor), track/field (indoor), volleyball. **On-Campus Highlights:** Ruth S. Harley University Center. **Environmental Initiatives:** LEED rating for the CSPA project.

ADMISSIONS

Freshman Academic Profile: Average high school GPA 3.5. 26% in top 10% of high school class, 59% in top 25% of high school class, 89% in top 50% of high school class. 75% from public high schools. **Test Scores:** SAT Math middle 50% range 530–620. SAT EBRW middle 50% range 530–630. ACT middle 50% range 21–27. **Basis for Candidate Selection:** *Very important factors include:* rigor of secondary school record. *Important factors include:* class rank, academic GPA, application essay, standardized test scores, recommendation(s), extracurricular activities, talent/ability, character/personal qualities, volunteer work. *Other factors include:* interview, first generation, alumni/ae relation, work experience, level of applicant's interest. **Freshman Admission Requirements:** High school diploma is required and GED is accepted. *Academic units recommended:* 4 English, 3 math, 3 science, 2 foreign language. **Freshman Admission Statistics:** 13,919 applied, 74% admitted, 11% enrolled. **Transfer Admission Requirements:** college transcript(s), essay or personal statement, Minimum college GPA of 2.3 required. **General Admission Information:** Application fee $40. Priority deadline 3/1. Non-fall registration accepted.

COSTS AND FINANCIAL AID

Annual tuition $36,920. Room and board $16,030. Required fees $1,740. Average book and supplies expense $1,020. **Required Forms and Deadlines:** FAFSA; State aid form. **Notification of Awards:** Applicants will be notified of awards on a rolling basis beginning 12/15. **Types of Aid:** *Need-based scholarships/grants:* College/university scholarship or grant aid from institutional funds; Federal Pell; Private scholarships; SEOG; State scholarships/grants; United Negro College Fund. *Loans:* Direct PLUS loans; Direct Subsidized Stafford Loans; Direct Unsubsidized Stafford Loans. **Student Employment:** Federal Work-Study Program available. Institutional employment available. **Financial Aid Statistics:** 97% needy freshmen, 95% needy undergrads receive need-based scholarship or grant aid. 94% freshmen, 92% undergrads receive non-need-based scholarship or grant aid. 88% freshmen, 87% undergrads receive need-based self-help aid. 1% freshmen, 2% undergrads receive athletic scholarships. 98.9% freshmen, 94.6% undergrads receive any aid. 62% undergrads borrow to pay for school. Average cumulative indebtedness $34,980. **Criteria awarding aid:** *Need-based:* Job skills. *Non-need-based:* Academics, Alumni affiliation, Art, Athletics, Leadership, Minority status, Music/drama, Religious affiliation, State/district residency.

ADRIAN COLLEGE

110 South Madison Street, Adrian, MI 49221
Phone: 517-265-5161 **Financial Aid Phone:** 517-265-5161
E-mail: admissions@adrian.edu **CEEB Code:** 1001
Fax: 517-264-3331 **Website:** www.adrian.edu **ACT Code:** 1954

This private school, affiliated with the Methodist Church, was founded in 1859. It has a 100 acre campus.

RATINGS

Admissions Selectivity Rating: 79   **Fire Safety Rating:** 69   **Green Rating:** 60*

STUDENTS AND FACULTY

Enrollment: 1,308. **Student Body:** 47% female, 53% male, 24% out-of-state, 4% international (6 countries represented). Asian 1%, African American 4%, Caucasian 77%, Hispanic 2%, Native American <1%, Pacific Islander , Two or more races , Race unknown 12%.
Retention and Graduation: 73% freshmen return for sophomore year. 25% grads go on to further study within 1 year. 51% grads pursue arts and sciences degrees. 9% grads pursue law degrees. 9% grads pursue business degrees. 22% grads pursue medical degrees. **Faculty:** Student/faculty ratio 12:1. 78 full-time faculty, 82% hold PhDs, 9% are members of minority groups, 41% are women. 0% of classes are taught by teaching assistants.

ACADEMICS

Degrees: Associate; Bachelor's; Transfer Associate. **Classes:** Most classes have 10–19 students. Most lab/discussion sessions have 10–19 students. **Most popular majors:** English Language and Literature, General; Business/Commerce, General; Exercise Science and Kinesiology. **Special Study Options:** Double major; Dual enrollment; Honors program; Independent study; Internships; Student-designed major; Study abroad; Teacher certification program. **Combined degree programs:** BA/MEng. **Disability Services offered:** Note-taking services; Reader services; Tape recorders; Tutors. **Career services:** Alumni network; Alumni services; Career assessment; Internships; Regional alumni.

FACILITIES

Housing: Apartments for single students; Coed dorms; Fraternity/sorority housing; Men's dorms; Women's dorms 50% of campus accessible to physically disabled. **Special Academic Facilities/Equipment:** Art gallery, studio theatre, arboretum, education resource center, language lab, observatory, planetarium, solar greenhouse, nuclear magnetic resonance spectrometer, differential scanning calorimeter. **Campus network:** 100% of classrooms, 90% of dorms, 100% of student union, 100% of libraries, 100% of dining areas, 100% of common outdoor areas, have wireless network access.

CAMPUS LIFE

Environment: Town. **Activities:** Campus Ministries; Choral groups; Concert band; Dance; Drama/theater; International Student Organization; Jazz band; Literary magazine; Marching band; Music ensembles; Musical theater; Pep band; Radio station; Student government; Student newspaper; Symphony orchestra; Yearbook. 68 registered organizations, 13 honor societies, 8 religious organizations, 4 fraternities, 3 sororities, on campus. **Athletics (Intercollegiate):** *Men:* baseball, basketball, cross-country, football, golf, ice hockey, lacrosse, soccer, tennis, track/field (outdoor). *Women:* basketball, bowling, cross-country, golf, ice hockey, lacrosse, soccer, softball, tennis, track/field (outdoor), volleyball. **On-Campus Highlights:** Caine Student Center.

ADMISSIONS

Freshman Academic Profile: Average high school GPA 3.3. 17% in top 10% of high school class, 46% in top 25% of high school class, 81% in top 50% of high school class. **Test Scores:** SAT Math middle 50% range 410–535. SAT EBRW middle 50% range 430–515. ACT middle 50% range 20–25. **Basis for Candidate Selection:** *Very important factors include:* rigor of secondary school record, class rank. *Important factors include:* academic GPA, standardized test scores, talent/ability. *Other factors include:* interview, extracurricular activities, character/personal qualities, alumni/ae relation, volunteer work, work experience, level of applicant's interest. **Freshman Admission Requirements:** High school diploma is required and GED is accepted. *Academic units recommended:* 4 English, 3 math, 2 science, 1 science labs, 2 foreign language, 1 social studies, 1 history, 2 academic electives. **Freshman Admission Statistics:** 3,709 applied, 64% admitted, 21% enrolled. **Transfer Admission Requirements:** High school transcript, college transcript(s), Minimum college GPA of 2.7 required. Lowest grade transferable C. **General**

Admission Information: Priority deadline 3/15. Admission may be deferred for a maximum of 1 year.

COSTS AND FINANCIAL AID

Annual tuition $23,090. Room and board $7,600. Required fees $300. Average book and supplies expense $400. **Required Forms and Deadlines:** FAFSA. **Notification of Awards:** Applicants will be notified of awards on a rolling basis beginning 3/15. **Types of Aid:** *Need-based scholarships/grants:* College/university scholarship or grant aid from institutional funds; Federal Pell; Private scholarships; SEOG; State scholarships/grants. **Student Employment:** Federal Work-Study Program available. Institutional employment available. **Financial Aid Statistics:** 87% needy freshmen, 86% needy undergrads receive need-based scholarship or grant aid. 88% freshmen, 86% undergrads receive non-need-based scholarship or grant aid. 89% freshmen, 88% undergrads receive need-based self-help aid. 0% freshmen, 0% undergrads receive athletic scholarships. 98% freshmen, 92% undergrads receive any aid. **Criteria awarding aid:** *Non-need-based:* Academics, Alumni affiliation, Art, Leadership, Music/drama, Religious affiliation.

AGNES SCOTT COLLEGE

141 E. College Ave., Decatur, GA 30030-3770
Phone: 404-471-6285 **Financial Aid Phone:** 404-471-6395
E-mail: https://www.agnesscott.edu/admission/index.html **CEEB Code:** 5002
Fax: 404-471-6414 **Website:** www.agnesscott.edu **ACT Code:** 780

This private school, affiliated with the Presbyterian Church, was founded in 1889. It has a 100 acre campus.

RATINGS

Admissions Selectivity Rating: 86   **Fire Safety Rating:** 96   **Green Rating:** 96

STUDENTS AND FACULTY

Enrollment: 974. **Student Body:** 100% female, 0% male, 40% out-of-state, 6% international (28 countries represented). Asian 8%, African American 32%, Caucasian 31%, Hispanic 14%, Native American <1%, Pacific Islander <1%, Two or more races 6%, Race unknown 3%.
Retention and Graduation: 85% freshmen return for sophomore year. 70% freshmen graduate within 4 years. 73% freshmen graduate within 6 years. 20% grads go on to further study within 1 year. **Faculty:** Student/faculty ratio 10:1. 92 full-time faculty, 97% hold PhDs, 28% are members of minority groups, 70% are women. 0% of classes are taught by teaching assistants.

ACADEMICS

Degrees: Bachelor's; Master's; Post-bachelor's certificate. **Classes:** Most classes have 10–19 students. Most lab/discussion sessions have 10–19 students. **Most popular majors:** Psychology, General; Public Health, General; Business Administration and Management, General. **Special Study Options:** Accelerated program; Cross-registration; Distance learning; Double major; Dual enrollment; Exchange student program (domestic); Independent study; Internships; Liberal arts/career combination; Student-designed major; Study abroad. **Honors programs:** SUMMIT at Agnes Scott reinvents a liberal arts education for the twenty-first century by preparing every student to be an effective change agent in a global society Guided by a personal board of advisors, every student, regardless of major, designs an individualized course of study and co-curricular experiences that develop leadership abilities and an understanding of complex global dynamics. All students: • Complete a core curriculum suffused with leadership development and global learning • Kick-off their college career with a three-day leadership immersion • Participate in a faculty-led global study tour in the Spring of their first year • Build a personalized board of advisors consisting of a SUMMIT advisor, a peer advisor, a major advisor, and a career mentor to guide them in crafting their unique educational journey • Create a digital portfolio in which they collect, reflect upon and showcase their achievements • Engage a cutting edge leadership curriculum that includes coursework, practica and opportunities to meet extraordinary leaders from all walks of life and a global curriculum that builds inter-cultural understanding and grapples with global issues at home and abroad • Complete a culminating project that synthesizes and contextualizes their four years of learning at Agnes Scott College • Have the opportunity to complete a specialization in leadership development or global learning and earn a notation on their transcript Equipped with a rigorous liberal arts and sciences education, an understanding of complex global issues and the ability to lead strategically and honorably, Agnes Scott graduates are ready to scale the next SUMMIT. **Disability Services offered:** Note-taking services; Reader services; Tape recorders; Tutors. **Career services:** Alumni network; Alumni services; Career assessment; Career/job search classes; Internships; Regional alumni.

FACILITIES

Housing: Apartments for single students; Theme housing; Women's dorms 90% of campus accessible to physically disabled. **Special Academic Facilities/ Equipment:** Art galleries,tracking LEED Gold and recently renovated Campbell Hall, collaborative learning centers, language lab, electron microscope, observatory, 30-inch Beck telescope, planetarium, interactive learning center, multimedia presentation classrooms, instructional technology center, multi-media production facility. **Campus network:** 100% of dorms, 100% of student union, 100% of libraries, have wireless network access.

CAMPUS LIFE

Environment: Metropolis. **Activities:** Campus Ministries; Choral groups; Dance; Drama/theater; International Student Organization; Jazz band; Literary magazine; Marching band; Model UN; Music ensembles; Musical theater; Radio station; Student government; Student newspaper; Symphony orchestra; Yearbook. 79 registered organizations, 11 honor societies, 12 religious organizations, on campus. **Athletics (Intercollegiate):** *Women:* basketball, lacrosse, soccer, softball, tennis, volleyball. **On-Campus Highlights:** Campbell Hall (Tracking LEED Gold, newly renovated) **Environmental Initiatives:** Converted to campus-wide single stream recycling and composting. Agnes Scott is committed to Zero Waste and has already achieved a 62% waste diversion rate.

ADMISSIONS

Freshman Academic Profile: Average high school GPA 3.8. 32% in top 10% of high school class, 67% in top 25% of high school class, 95% in top 50% of high school class. 75% from public high schools. **Test Scores:** SAT Math middle 50% range 540–650. SAT EBRW middle 50% range 590–690. ACT middle 50% range 24–30. **Basis for Candidate Selection:** *Very important factors include:* rigor of secondary school record, academic GPA, talent/ ability, character/personal qualities. *Important factors include:* application essay, standardized test scores, recommendation(s), extracurricular activities. *Other factors include:* class rank, interview, first generation, alumni/ae relation, geographical residence, state residency, work experience, level of applicant's interest. **Freshman Admission Requirements:** High school diploma is required and GED is accepted. *Academic units recommended:* 4 English, 3 math, 2 science, 2 science labs, 2 foreign language, 2 social studies. **Freshman Admission Statistics:** 1,751 applied, 65% admitted, 26% enrolled. **Transfer Admission Requirements:** High school transcript, college transcript(s), essay or personal statement, statement of good standing from prior institution(s). Minimum college GPA of 3.0 required. Lowest grade transferable C. **General Admission Information:** Priority deadline 1/15. Regular application deadline 5/1. Admission may be deferred for a maximum of 1 year.

COSTS AND FINANCIAL AID

Annual tuition $43,920. Room and board $13,050. Required fees $330. Average book and supplies expense $1,000. **Required Forms and Deadlines:** FAFSA. **Notification of Awards:** Applicants will be notified of awards on a rolling basis beginning 3/1. **Types of Aid:** *Need-based scholarships/grants:* College/university scholarship or grant aid from institutional funds; Federal Pell; Private scholarships; SEOG; State scholarships/grants. *Loans:* Direct PLUS loans; Direct Subsidized Stafford Loans; Direct Unsubsidized Stafford Loans. **Student Employment:** Federal Work-Study Program available. Institutional employment available. **Financial Aid Statistics:** 100% needy freshmen, 100% needy undergrads receive need-based scholarship or grant aid. 25% freshmen, 21% undergrads receive non-need-based scholarship or grant aid. 75% freshmen, 82% undergrads receive need-based self-help aid. 0% freshmen, 0% undergrads receive athletic scholarships. 100% freshmen, 99% undergrads receive any aid. 64% undergrads borrow to pay for school. Average cumulative indebtedness $31,271. **Criteria awarding aid:** *Non-need-based:* Academics, Leadership, Minority status, Music/drama, Religious affiliation.

ALABAMA A&M UNIVERSITY

P.O. Box 908, Normal, AL 35762
Phone: 256-851-5245
E-mail: juan.alexander@aamu.edu **CEEB Code:** 1003
Fax: 256-851-5249 **ACT Code:** 2

This public school was founded in 1875. It has a 880 acre campus.

RATINGS

Admissions Selectivity Rating: 86   **Fire Safety Rating:** 60*   **Green Rating:** 60*

STUDENTS AND FACULTY

Enrollment: 4,489. **Student Body:** 52% female, 48% male, 31% out-of-state, 1% international (42 countries represented). Asian <1%, African American 96%, Caucasian 2%, Hispanic <1%, Native American <1%, Race unknown <1%. **Retention and Graduation:** 77% grads go on to further study within 1 year. 40% grads pursue arts and sciences degrees. 2% grads pursue law degrees. 45% grads pursue business degrees. 11% grads pursue medical degrees. **Faculty:** Student/faculty ratio 14:1. 314 full-time faculty, 45% hold PhDs, 55% are members of minority groups, 39% are women. 1% of classes are taught by teaching assistants.

ACADEMICS

Degrees: Bachelor's; Master's; Post-master's certificate. **Classes:** Most classes have fewer than 10 students. Most lab/discussion sessions have 20–29 students. **Most popular majors:** Biology/Biological Sciences, General; Mechanical Engineering Related Technologies/Technicians, Other; Elementary Education and Teaching. **Special Study Options:** Accelerated program; Cooperative education program; Distance learning; Double major; Dual enrollment; Exchange student program (domestic); Honors program; Independent study; Internships; Study abroad; Teacher certification program; Weekend college. **Disability Services offered:** Note-taking services; Reader services; Tape recorders; Tutors. **Career services:** Career assessment; Career/job search classes; Internships; Regional alumni.

FACILITIES

Housing: Apartments for single students; Men's dorms; Women's dorms; 65% of campus accessible to physically disabled. **Special Academic Facilities/ Equipment:** State Black Archives.

CAMPUS LIFE

Environment: City. **Activities:** Campus Ministries; Choral groups; Concert band; Dance; Drama/theater; International Student Organization; Jazz band; Literary magazine; Marching band; Music ensembles; Pep band; Radio station; Student government; Student newspaper; Symphony orchestra; Television station; Yearbook. 76 registered organizations, 14 honor societies, 3 religious organizations, 4 fraternities, 4 sororities, on campus. **Athletics (Intercollegiate):** *Men:* baseball, basketball, cross-country, football, golf, soccer, track/field (outdoor). *Women:* basketball, cross-country, soccer, softball, track/ field (outdoor), volleyball. **On-Campus Highlights:** Engineering Building.

ADMISSIONS

Test Scores: SAT Math middle 50% range 380–470. SAT EBRW middle 50% range 400–470. ACT middle 50% range 16–19. **Basis for Candidate Selection:** *Very important factors include:* standardized test scores, alumni/ae relation, geographical residence, state residency. *Important factors include:* racial/ ethnic status. *Other factors include:* class rank, recommendation(s). **Freshman Admission Requirements:** High school diploma is required and GED is accepted. *Academic units required:* 4 English, 4 math, 4 science, 2 science labs, 4 social studies, 4 history. **Freshman Admission Statistics:** 5,697 applied, 47% admitted, 39% enrolled. **Transfer Admission Requirements:** High school transcript, college transcript(s), standardized test scores, statement of good standing from prior institution(s). Minimum college GPA of 2.5 required. Lowest grade transferable C. **General Admission Information:** Application fee $10. Priority deadline 4/1. Regular application deadline 7/1. Non-fall registration accepted. Admission may be deferred for a maximum of 12 months.

COSTS AND FINANCIAL AID

Annual in-state tuition $3,948. Annual out-of-state tuition $7,896. Room and board $5,350. Required fees $744. **Required Forms and Deadlines:** FAFSA; Institution's own financial aid form. **Types of Aid:** *Need-based scholarships/ grants:* College/university scholarship or grant aid from institutional funds; Federal Pell; Private scholarships; SEOG; State scholarships/grants; United Negro College Fund. *Loans:* Direct PLUS loans; Direct Subsidized Stafford Loans; Direct Unsubsidized Stafford Loans.

ALASKA PACIFIC UNIVERSITY

4101 University Drive, Anchorage, AK 99508-4625
Phone: 907-564-8248 **Financial Aid Phone:** 907-564-8341
E-mail: admissions@alaskapacific.edu **CEEB Code:** 4201
Fax: 907-564-8317 **Website:** http://www.alaskapacific.edu **ACT Code:** 0062

This private school, affiliated with the Methodist Church, was founded in 1957.
It has a 170 acre campus.

RATINGS
Admissions Selectivity Rating: 88   **Fire Safety Rating:** 91   **Green Rating:** 60*

STUDENTS AND FACULTY
Enrollment: 455. **Student Body:** 65% female, 35% male, 32% out-of-state, <1% international (3 countries represented). Asian 2%, African American 3%, Caucasian 58%, Hispanic 3%, Native American 15%, Pacific Islander <1%, Two or more races 0%, Race unknown 18%.
Retention and Graduation: 67% freshmen return for sophomore year.
Faculty: Student/faculty ratio 10:1. 50 full-time faculty, 64% hold PhDs, 4% are members of minority groups, 58% are women. 0% of classes are taught by teaching assistants.

ACADEMICS
Degrees: Associate; Bachelor's; Certificate; Doctoral degree—other; Doctoral degree—professional practice; Master's; Post-bachelor's certificate; Terminal Associate. **Classes:** Most classes have 10–19 students. Most lab/discussion sessions have fewer than 10 students. **Most popular majors:** Business Administration and Management, General; Elementary Education and Teaching; Marine Biology and Biological Oceanography. **Special Study Options:** Distance learning; Double major; Exchange student program (domestic); Independent study; Internships; Student-designed major; Study abroad; Teacher certification program. **Disability Services offered:** Note-taking services; Tape recorders; Tutors. **Career services:** Career assessment; Career/job search classes; Internships.

FACILITIES
Housing: Coed dorms; Cooperative housing; 75% of campus accessible to physically disabled. **Special Academic Facilities/Equipment:** Alaskana collection GIS lab gym with pool Student Center with weight room and indoor climbing wall Outdoor recreation center with classes and rental equipment Lake for canoeing and kayaking trails for running, skiing, hiking, biking, etc., connected to city's trail system.

CAMPUS LIFE
Environment: City. **Activities:** Drama/theater; Literary magazine; Music ensembles; Student government; Student newspaper; Yearbook. 15 registered organizations, 1 religious organizations, on campus. **On-Campus Highlights:** Student Center. **Environmental Initiatives:** Kellogg Farm dedicated to organic and sustainable enterprises.

ADMISSIONS
Freshman Academic Profile: Average high school GPA 3.3. 17% in top 10% of high school class, 31% in top 25% of high school class, 72% in top 50% of high school class. 95% from public high schools. **Test Scores:** SAT Math middle 50% range 470–560. SAT EBRW middle 50% range 490–600. ACT middle 50% range 21–27. **Basis for Candidate Selection:** *Very important factors include:* rigor of secondary school record, academic GPA, application essay. *Important factors include:* standardized test scores, recommendation(s), alumni/ae relation. *Other factors include:* extracurricular activities, talent/ability, volunteer work, work experience. **Freshman Admission Requirements:** High school diploma is required and GED is accepted. *Academic units recommended:* 4 English, 3 math, 2 science, 1 science labs, 2 foreign language, 1 social studies, 1 history. **Freshman Admission Statistics:** 245 applied, 48% admitted, 43% enrolled. **Transfer Admission Requirements:** College transcript(s), essay or personal statement, statement of good standing from prior institution(s). Minimum college GPA of 2.0 required. Lowest grade transferable C. **General Admission Information:** Application fee $25. Priority deadline 12/1. Regular application deadline 8/15. Non-fall registration accepted. Admission may be deferred for a maximum of 12 months.

COSTS AND FINANCIAL AID
Annual tuition $26,250. Room and board $9,300. Required fees $110. Average book and supplies expense $1,000. **Required Forms and Deadlines:** FAFSA. **Notification of Awards:** Applicants will be notified of awards on a rolling basis beginning 2/1. **Types of Aid:** *Need-based scholarships/grants:* College/ university scholarship or grant aid from institutional funds; Federal Pell; Private scholarships; SEOG; State scholarships/grants. *Loans:* Direct PLUS loans; Direct Subsidized Stafford Loans; Direct Unsubsidized Stafford Loans. **Student Employment:** Federal Work-Study Program available. Institutional employment available. **Financial Aid Statistics:** 47% needy freshmen, 55% needy undergrads receive need-based scholarship or grant aid. 100% freshmen, 48% undergrads receive non-need-based scholarship or grant aid. 68% freshmen, 42% undergrads receive need-based self-help aid. 0% freshmen, 0% undergrads receive athletic scholarships. 88% freshmen, 92% undergrads receive any aid. **Criteria awarding aid:** *Need-based:* Academics, Alumni affiliation, Leadership, Minority status, Religious affiliation. *Non-need-based:* Academics, Alumni affiliation, Leadership, Religious affiliation, State/district residency.

ALBANY COLLEGE OF PHARMACY

106 New Scotland Avenue, Albany, NY 12208
Phone: 518-694-7221 **Financial Aid Phone:** 518-694-7256
E-mail: admissions@acp.edu **CEEB Code:** 2013
Fax: 518-694-7322 **Website:** www.acp.edu **ACT Code:** 2672

This private school was founded in 1881. It has a 21 acre campus.

RATINGS
Admissions Selectivity Rating: 88   **Fire Safety Rating:** 70   **Green Rating:** 70

STUDENTS AND FACULTY
Enrollment: 1,015. **Student Body:** 58% female, 42% male, 10% out-of-state, 8% international (6 countries represented). Asian 13%, African American 2%, Caucasian 73%, Hispanic 1%, Native American <1%, Race unknown 3%.
Retention and Graduation: 79% freshmen return for sophomore year.
Faculty: Student/faculty ratio 16:1. 82 full-time faculty, 74% hold PhDs, 12% are members of minority groups, 49% are women. 0% of classes are taught by teaching assistants.

ACADEMICS
Degrees: Bachelor's; Certificate. **Classes:** Most classes have 20–29 students. Most lab/discussion sessions have 20–29 students. **Most popular majors:** Pharmacy. **Special Study Options:** Accelerated program; Cross-registration. **Combined degree programs:** BA/JD. **Disability Services offered:** Tutors. **Career services:** Career assessment; Career/job search classes.

FACILITIES
Housing: Apartments for single students; Coed dorms; 100% of campus accessible to physically disabled. **Special Academic Facilities/Equipment:** Throop Pharmaceutical Museum.

CAMPUS LIFE
Environment: City. **Activities:** Choral groups; Concert band; Dance; International Student Organization; Literary magazine; Student government; Student newspaper; Yearbook. 2 honor societies, 1 religious organizations, on campus. **Athletics (Intercollegiate):** *Men:* basketball, soccer. *Women:* basketball, soccer. **On-Campus Highlights:** NEW—ACP Student Center.

ADMISSIONS
Freshman Academic Profile: 47% in top 10% of high school class, 86% in top 25% of high school class, 99% in top 50% of high school class. **Test Scores:** SAT Math middle 50% range 570–650. SAT EBRW middle 50% range 530–620. ACT middle 50% range 23–28. **Basis for Candidate Selection:** *Very important factors include:* academic GPA, standardized test scores. *Important factors include:* rigor of secondary school record, class rank. *Other factors include:* application essay, recommendation(s), extracurricular activities, talent/ability, character/personal qualities, alumni/ae relation, geographical residence, volunteer work, work experience, level of applicant's interest. **Freshman Admission Requirements:** High school diploma is required and GED is accepted. *Academic units required:* 4 English, 4 math, 3 science, 3 science labs, 4 social studies. *Academic units recommended:* 4 science, 4 science labs, 4 foreign language. **Freshman Admission Statistics:** 1,049 applied, 61% admitted, 38% enrolled. **Transfer Admission Requirements:** College transcript(s), essay or personal statement, statement of good standing from prior institution(s). Minimum college GPA of 3.2 required. Lowest grade transferable B. **General Admission Information:** Application fee $75. Priority deadline 2/1. Regular application deadline 3/1. Admission may be deferred for a maximum of 1 year.

COSTS AND FINANCIAL AID

Required Forms and Deadlines: FAFSA. **Notification of Awards:** Applicants will be notified of awards on a rolling basis beginning 3/25. **Types of Aid:** *Need-based scholarships/grants:* College/university scholarship or grant aid from institutional funds; Federal Pell; Private scholarships; SEOG; State scholarships/grants. **Financial Aid Statistics:** 92% needy freshmen, 80% needy undergrads receive need-based scholarship or grant aid. 12% freshmen, 6% undergrads receive non-need-based scholarship or grant aid. 84% freshmen, 90% undergrads receive need-based self-help aid. 0% freshmen, 0% undergrads receive athletic scholarships. **Criteria awarding aid:** *Need-based:* Academics, Alumni affiliation, Leadership. *Non-need-based:* Academics, Alumni affiliation, Leadership.

ALBANY STATE UNIVERSITY

504 College Drive, Albany, GA 31705
Phone: 229-430-4646 **Financial Aid Phone:** 229-430-4650
E-mail: enrollmentservices@asurams.edu **CEEB Code:** 5004
Fax: 229-430-4105 **Website:** http://www.asurams.edu **ACT Code:** 0782

This public school was founded in 1903. It has a 232 acre campus.

RATINGS

Admissions Selectivity Rating: 91 · **Fire Safety Rating:** 91 **Green Rating:** 60*

STUDENTS AND FACULTY

Enrollment: 4,173. **Student Body:** 66% female, 34% male, 4% out-of-state, <1% international (22 countries represented). Asian <1%, African American 83%, Caucasian 4%, Hispanic 1%, Native American <1%, Pacific Islander <1%, Two or more races <1%, Race unknown 11%.
Retention and Graduation: 65% freshmen return for sophomore year.
Faculty: Student/faculty ratio 21:1. 164 full-time faculty, 77% hold PhDs, 78% are members of minority groups, 45% are women. 0% of classes are taught by teaching assistants.

ACADEMICS

Degrees: Bachelor's; Master's; Post-master's certificate. **Classes:** Most classes have 20–29 students. Most lab/discussion sessions have 20–29 students. **Most popular majors:** Criminal Justice/Safety Studies; Business Administration and Management, General; Early Childhood Education and Teaching. **Special Study Options:** Cooperative education program; Cross-registration; Distance learning; Double major; Dual enrollment; Honors program; Independent study; Internships; Study abroad; Teacher certification program; Weekend college. **Honors programs:** The Velma Fudge Grant Honors Program represents a commitment made by Albany State University (ASU) to broaden and enrich educational experiences of bright, highly motivated and creative students. Honors Program students are provided opportunities for scholarships, access to special extracurricular programs, a chance to pursue independent projects and research interests, professional experience through internship programs and special service options. Through its specially designed curriculum, the University provides the opportunity for faculty to teach academically talented students in inventive, interdisciplinary, small class settings designed to fulfill core curriculum requirements, as well as in advanced or intensive classes in particular disciplines. The Honors Program is specifically designed for academic scholarship recipients, academically talented students and entering freshman and transfer students with a proven dedication to academic excellence and scholarship. The Honors Program student must reach beyond good grades for success and have the courage to demonstrate superior ethical leadership in his/her chosen field of study. **Combined degree programs:** BA/MEng. **Disability Services offered:** Note-taking services; Reader services; Tape recorders; Tutors. **Career services:** Alumni network; Alumni services; Career assessment; Internships; Regional alumni.

FACILITIES

Housing: Coed dorms; Men's dorms; Women's dorms; 98% of campus accessible to physically disabled. **Campus network:** 100% of classrooms, 100% of dorms, 100% of student union, 100% of libraries, 100% of dining areas, 100% of common outdoor areas, have wireless network access.

CAMPUS LIFE

Environment: City. **Activities:** Choral groups; Concert band; Dance; Drama/theater; Jazz band; Marching band; Model UN; Music ensembles; Opera; Pep band; Radio station; Student government; Student newspaper; Television station; Yearbook. 87 registered organizations, 10 honor societies, 2 religious organizations, 8 fraternities, 5 sororities, on campus. **Athletics (Intercollegiate):** *Men:* baseball, basketball, cross-country, football, track/field (outdoor). *Women:* basketball, cross-country, softball, tennis, track/field (outdoor), volleyball. **On-Campus Highlights:** New Student Center. **Environmental Initiatives:** 1. Hazardous Waste Lab, 2. Paint shops and carpentry, 3. Universal Waste.

ADMISSIONS

Freshman Academic Profile: 10% in top 10% of high school class, 30% in top 25% of high school class, 67% in top 50% of high school class. **Test Scores:** SAT Math middle 50% range 390–460. SAT EBRW middle 50% range 390–450. ACT middle 50% range 16–19. **Basis for Candidate Selection:** *Very important factors include:* academic GPA, standardized test scores. *Other factors include:* rigor of secondary school record, class rank, application essay, recommendation(s). **Freshman Admission Requirements:** High school diploma is required and GED is accepted. *Academic units required:* 4 English, 4 math, 3 science, 2 science labs, 2 foreign language, 3 social studies. **Freshman Admission Statistics:** 6,554 applied, 29% admitted, 57% enrolled. **Transfer Admission Requirements:** College transcript(s). Minimum college GPA of 2.0 required. Lowest grade transferable D. **General Admission Information:** Application fee $20. Priority deadline 5/1. Regular application deadline 6/1. Non-fall registration accepted. Admission may be deferred for a maximum of one year.

COSTS AND FINANCIAL AID

Required Forms and Deadlines: FAFSA; State aid form. **Notification of Awards:** Applicants will be notified of awards on a rolling basis beginning 1/7. **Student Employment:** Federal Work-Study Program available. Institutional employment available. **Criteria awarding aid:** *Non-need-based:* Academics, Alumni affiliation, Art, Athletics.

ALBERTA COLLEGE OF ART + DESIGN

1407 14 Avenue NW, Calgary, AB T2N 4R3
Phone: 403-284-7617 **Financial Aid Phone:** 403-284-7600
E-mail: admissions@acad.ca
Fax: 403-284-7644 **Website:** www.acad.ca

This public school was founded in 1926.

RATINGS

Admissions Selectivity Rating: 71 **Fire Safety Rating:** 60* **Green Rating:** 60*

STUDENTS AND FACULTY

Enrollment: 1,112. **Student Body:** 73% female, 27% male, 11% out-of-state, 5% international (49 countries represented). Asian 0%, African American 0%, Caucasian 0%, Hispanic 0%, Native American 0%, Pacific Islander 0%, Two or more races 0%, Race unknown 95%.
Retention and Graduation: 64% freshmen return for sophomore year.
Faculty: Student/faculty ratio 15:1. 46 full-time faculty, 0% hold PhDs, 0% are members of minority groups, 0% are women.

ACADEMICS

Degrees: Bachelor's. **Most popular majors:** Painting; Drawing; Sculpture. **Special Study Options:** Cross-registration; Exchange student program (domestic); Internships; Study abroad. **Disability Services offered:** Reader services; Tutors.

FACILITIES

Housing: Coed dorms; 100% of campus accessible to physically disabled. **Special Academic Facilities/Equipment:** 2 Art Galleries.

CAMPUS LIFE

Environment: Metropolis. **Activities:** Student government. **Athletics (Intercollegiate):** *Men:* basketball, ice hockey, volleyball. *Women:* basketball, volleyball.

ADMISSIONS

Freshman Academic Profile: 91% from public high schools. **Basis for Candidate Selection:** *Very important factors include:* academic GPA, application essay, talent/ability, level of applicant's interest. *Other factors include:* standardized test scores, recommendation(s), extracurricular activities, character/personal qualities, work experience. **Freshman Admission Requirements:** High school diploma is required and GED is accepted. *Academic units required:* 4 English. **Freshman Admission Statistics:** 576 applied, 65% admitted, 73%

enrolled. **Transfer Admission Requirements:** College transcript(s), essay or personal statement. **General Admission Information:** Application fee $85. Regular application deadline 4/1. Non-fall registration accepted.

COSTS AND FINANCIAL AID
Annual in-state tuition $4,435. Annual out-of-state tuition $4,435. Room and board $5,904. Average book and supplies expense $3,150. **Required Forms and Deadlines:** FAFSA. **Criteria awarding aid:** *Need-based:* Academics, Art. *Non-need-based:* Academics, Art.

ALBERTUS MAGNUS COLLEGE

700 Prospect Street, New Haven, CT 06511
Phone: 203-773-8501 **Financial Aid Phone:** 203-773-8508
E-mail: admissions@albertus.edu **CEEB Code:** 3001
Fax: 203-773-5248 **Website:** www.albertus.edu **ACT Code:** 549

This private school, affiliated with the Roman Catholic Church, was founded in 1925. It has a 50 acre campus.

RATINGS
Admissions Selectivity Rating: 75   Fire Safety Rating: 85   Green Rating: 60*

STUDENTS AND FACULTY
Enrollment: 1,682. **Student Body:** 68% female, 32% male, 15% out-of-state, <1% international. Asian 1%, African American 27%, Caucasian 55%, Hispanic 10%, Native American <1%, Race unknown 7%.
Retention and Graduation: 78% freshmen return for sophomore year.
Faculty: Student/faculty ratio 13:1. 42 full-time faculty, 79% hold PhDs, 0% are members of minority groups, 43% are women. 0% of classes are taught by teaching assistants.

ACADEMICS
Degrees: Associate; Bachelor's; Certificate; Master's. **Classes:** Most classes have 10–19 students. **Most popular majors:** Education, General; Business/Commerce, General; Psychology, General. **Special Study Options:** Accelerated program; Double major; Honors program; Independent study; Internships; Student-designed major; Teacher certification program. **Honors programs:** Students may apply to follow the Honors Program, which involves work in special courses designated each semester as honors courses and the development of individual projects designed in consultation with faculty mentors. Entering qualified students are assigned to special honors courses and returning students interested in such a program should consult, by the spring of their sophomore year or earlier, with their advisor and the Director of the Honors Program. **Disability Services offered:** Note-taking services; Reader services; Tape recorders; Tutors. **Career services:** Alumni network; Career assessment; Career/job search classes; Internships.

FACILITIES
Housing: Coed dorms; Women's dorms; 70% of campus accessible to physically disabled. **Special Academic Facilities/Equipment:** Margaret McDonough Art Gallery.

CAMPUS LIFE
Environment: City. **Activities:** Campus Ministries; Choral groups; Dance; Drama/theater; Literary magazine; Musical theater; Student government; Yearbook. 1 honor societies, 1 religious organizations, on campus. **Athletics (Intercollegiate):** *Men:* baseball, basketball, cross-country, lacrosse, soccer, tennis, volleyball. *Women:* basketball, cross-country, lacrosse, soccer, softball, tennis, volleyball. **On-Campus Highlights:** Center for Science, Art and Technology.

ADMISSIONS
Freshman Academic Profile: Average high school GPA 3.0. 10% in top 10% of high school class, 29% in top 25% of high school class, 68% in top 50% of high school class. 70% from public high schools. **Test Scores:** SAT Math middle 50% range 470–500. SAT EBRW middle 50% range 490–560. **Basis for Candidate Selection:** *Very important factors include:* rigor of secondary school record, academic GPA. *Important factors include:* standardized test scores, recommendation(s). *Other factors include:* class rank, application essay, interview, extracurricular activities, talent/ability, character/personal qualities, first generation, alumni/ae relation, volunteer work, work experience, level of applicant's interest. **Freshman Admission Requirements:** High school diploma is required and GED is accepted. *Academic units required:* 4 English, 2 math, 2 science, 2 foreign language, 2 social studies, 2 history, 2 academic electives.

Academic units recommended: 3 math, 3 science, 1 science labs, 3 foreign language, 1 social studies, 2 history. **Freshman Admission Statistics:** 556 applied, 84% admitted, 22% enrolled. **Transfer Admission Requirements:** College transcript(s). Minimum college GPA of 2.0 required. Lowest grade transferable C. **General Admission Information:** Application fee $35. Non-fall registration accepted.

COSTS AND FINANCIAL AID
Annual tuition $20,166. Room and board $8,907. Required fees $908. Average book and supplies expense $920. **Required Forms and Deadlines:** FAFSA; Institution's own financial aid form. **Notification of Awards:** Applicants will be notified of awards on a rolling basis beginning 3/1. **Types of Aid:** *Need-based scholarships/grants:* College/university scholarship or grant aid from institutional funds; Federal Pell; SEOG; State scholarships/grants. *Loans:* Direct PLUS loans; Direct Subsidized Stafford Loans; Direct Unsubsidized Stafford Loans. **Student Employment:** Federal Work-Study Program available. **Financial Aid Statistics:** 89% needy freshmen, 93% needy undergrads receive need-based scholarship or grant aid. 60% freshmen, 65% undergrads receive non-need-based scholarship or grant aid. 37% freshmen, 39% undergrads receive need-based self-help aid. freshmen, undergrads receive athletic scholarships. 87% freshmen, 75% undergrads receive any aid. **Criteria awarding aid:** *Need-based:* Academics *Non-need-based:* Academics, Leadership, Religious affiliation.

ALBION COLLEGE

611 East Porter, Albion, MI 49224
Phone: 517-629-0321 **Financial Aid Phone:** 517-629-0440
E-mail: admission@albion.edu **CEEB Code:** 1007
Fax: 517-629-0569 **Website:** www.albion.edu **ACT Code:** 1956

This private school, affiliated with the Methodist Church, was founded in 1835. It has a 585 acre campus.

RATINGS
Admissions Selectivity Rating: 80   Fire Safety Rating: 86   Green Rating: 70

STUDENTS AND FACULTY
Enrollment: 1,512. **Student Body:** 54% female, 46% male, 26% out-of-state, 2% international (11 countries represented). Asian 2%, African American 15%, Caucasian 63%, Hispanic 10%, Native American <1%, Pacific Islander 0%, Two or more races 3%, Race unknown 5%.
Retention and Graduation: 75% freshmen return for sophomore year. 46% freshmen graduate within 4 years. 57% freshmen graduate within 6 years. 29% grads go on to further study within 1 year. 21% grads pursue arts and sciences degrees. 2% grads pursue law degrees. 1% grads pursue business degrees. 3% grads pursue medical degrees. **Faculty:** Student/faculty ratio 11:1. 117 full-time faculty, 94% hold PhDs, 10% are members of minority groups, 49% are women. 0% of classes are taught by teaching assistants.

ACADEMICS
Degrees: Bachelor's. **Classes:** Most classes have 10–19 students. Most lab/discussion sessions have 10–19 students. **Most popular majors:** Biology/Biological Sciences, General; Psychology, General; Economics, General. **Special Study Options:** Distance learning; Double major; Dual enrollment; English as a Second Language (ESL); Honors program; Independent study; Internships; Liberal arts/career combination; Student-designed major; Study abroad; Teacher certification program. **Honors programs:** The Honors Program at Albion was founded in 1976, and in August of 2004 it was renamed The Prentiss M. Brown Honors Program. We provide an exciting and unique variety of academic experiences for highly motivated and talented students. The Program's mix of small discussion classes, independent research, academic rigor, and personal attention provides Honors students with special challenges and opportunities for growth. Many of the College's finest teachers and scholars regularly contribute to the program's curriculum. **Disability Services offered:** Note-taking services; Reader services; Tape recorders; Tutors. **Career services:** Alumni network; Alumni services; Career assessment; Career/job search classes; Internships; Regional alumni.

FACILITIES

Housing: Apartments for married students; Apartments for single students; Coed dorms; Cooperative housing; Fraternity/sorority housing; Special housing for disabled students; Theme housing; 95% of campus accessible to physically disabled. **Special Academic Facilities/Equipment:** Visual arts museum; nature center; equestrian center; science complex museum; greenhouse; geographic information systems/computer-aided mapping lab; observatory; a Dow analytical science laboratory; see website for much more, listed by department/facility: https://www.albion.edu/academics/departments/geological-sciences/campus-facilities. **Campus network:** 100% of classrooms, 100% of dorms, 100% of student union, 100% of libraries, 100% of dining areas, 85% of common outdoor areas, have wireless network access.

CAMPUS LIFE

Environment: Village. **Activities:** Campus Ministries; Choral groups; Concert band; Dance; Drama/theater; International Student Organization; Jazz band; Literary magazine; Marching band; Model UN; Music ensembles; Musical theater; Opera; Radio station; Student government; Student newspaper; Student-run film society; Symphony orchestra; Yearbook. 110 registered organizations, 27 honor societies, 8 religious organizations, 6 fraternities, 6 sororities, on campus. **Athletics (Intercollegiate):** *Men:* baseball, basketball, cross-country, diving, equestrian sports, football, golf, soccer, swimming, tennis, track/field (outdoor), track/field (indoor). *Women:* basketball, cross-country, diving, equestrian sports, golf, soccer, softball, swimming, tennis, track/field (outdoor), track/field (indoor), volleyball. **On-Campus Highlights:** Kellogg Center- Student Center **Environmental Initiatives:** Development of Center for Sustainability and the Environment, which fosters involvement and projects by students. Examples include establishment of residential E-House (2006-present), E.P.A. P3 grant (2006–07), two National Wildlife Federation Sustainability Fellows (2008), active "Focus the Nation" and "Step it Up" participation (2007–08), and starting a student organic farm (2010).

ADMISSIONS

Freshman Academic Profile: Average high school GPA 3.5. **Test Scores:** SAT Math middle 50% range 500–610. SAT EBRW middle 50% range 510–630. ACT middle 50% range 20–26. **Basis for Candidate Selection:** *Very important factors include:* rigor of secondary school record, academic GPA, standardized test scores. *Important factors include:* class rank. *Other factors include:* application essay, recommendation(s), interview, extracurricular activities, talent/ability, character/personal qualities, alumni/ae relation, geographical residence, state residency, racial/ethnic status, volunteer work, work experience. **Freshman Admission Requirements:** High school diploma is required and GED is accepted. *Academic units recommended:* 4 English, 5 math, 3 science, 2 science labs, 2 foreign language, 2 social studies. **Freshman Admission Statistics:** 4,226 applied, 68% admitted, 15% enrolled. **Transfer Admission Requirements:** High school transcript, college transcript(s), essay or personal statement, interview, standardized test scores, statement of good standing from prior institution(s). Minimum college GPA of 2.5 required. Lowest grade transferable C. **General Admission Information:** Non-fall registration accepted. Admission may be deferred for a maximum of 1 year.

COSTS AND FINANCIAL AID

Annual tuition $47,570. Room and board $12,380. Required fees $705. Average book and supplies expense $700. **Required Forms and Deadlines:** FAFSA. **Notification of Awards:** Applicants will be notified of awards on a rolling basis beginning 12/1. **Types of Aid:** *Need-based scholarships/grants:* College/university scholarship or grant aid from institutional funds; Federal Pell; Private scholarships; SEOG; State scholarships/grants. *Loans:* Direct PLUS loans; Direct Subsidized Stafford Loans; Direct Unsubsidized Stafford Loans. **Student Employment:** Federal Work-Study Program available. Institutional employment available. **Financial Aid Statistics:** 100% needy freshmen, 100% needy undergrads receive need-based scholarship or grant aid. 99% freshmen, 99% undergrads receive non-need-based scholarship or grant aid. 86% freshmen, 86% undergrads receive need-based self-help aid. 0% freshmen, 0% undergrads receive athletic scholarships. 100% freshmen, 100% undergrads receive any aid. 72% undergrads borrow to pay for school. Average cumulative indebtedness $40,347. **Criteria awarding aid:** *Need-based:* Academics, Alumni affiliation, Art, Leadership, Music/drama, Religious affiliation. *Non-need-based:* Academics, Alumni affiliation, Art, Leadership, Music/drama.

ALBRIGHT COLLEGE

PO Box 15234, Reading, PA 19612-5234
Phone: 610-921-7799 **Financial Aid Phone:** 610-921-7264
E-mail: admission@albright.edu **CEEB Code:** 2004
Fax: 610-921-7729 **Website:** www.albright.edu **ACT Code:** 2004

This private school, affiliated with the Methodist Church, was founded in 1856. It has a 118 acre campus.

RATINGS

Admissions Selectivity Rating: 84   **Fire Safety Rating:** 61   **Green Rating:** 60*

STUDENTS AND FACULTY

Enrollment: 1,897. **Student Body:** 60% female, 40% male, 42% out-of-state, 2% international (15 countries represented). Asian 2%, African American 23%, Caucasian 50%, Hispanic 15%, Native American 1%, Pacific Islander 0%, Two or more races 2%, Race unknown 4%.

Retention and Graduation: 68% freshmen return for sophomore year. 44% freshmen graduate within 4 years. 53% freshmen graduate within 6 years. 19% grads go on to further study within 1 year. **Faculty:** Student/faculty ratio 14:1. 97 full-time faculty, 85% hold PhDs, 18% are members of minority groups, 47% are women. 0% of classes are taught by teaching assistants.

ACADEMICS

Degrees: Bachelor's; Certificate; Master's. **Classes:** Most classes have 10–19 students. Most lab/discussion sessions have 10–19 students. **Most popular majors:** Biology/Biological Sciences, General; Business, Management, Marketing, And Related Support Services; Fashion Merchandising. **Special Study Options:** Accelerated program; Cross-registration; Distance learning; Double major; Dual enrollment; Exchange student program (domestic); Honors program; Independent study; Internships; Liberal arts/career combination; Student-designed major; Study abroad; Teacher certification program. **Combined degree programs:** BA/MA. **Disability Services offered:** Tape recorders. **Career services:** Alumni network; Alumni services; Career assessment; Career/job search classes; Internships; Regional alumni.

FACILITIES

Housing: Apartments for single students; Coed dorms; Special housing for disabled students; Theme housing. **Special Academic Facilities/Equipment:** Freedman Art Gallery.

CAMPUS LIFE

Environment: City. **Activities:** Campus Ministries; Choral groups; Concert band; Dance; Drama/theater; International Student Organization; Jazz band; Literary magazine; Music ensembles; Musical theater; Radio station; Student government; Student newspaper; Student-run film society; Symphony orchestra; Television station; Yearbook. 84 registered organizations, 3 honor societies, 3 religious organizations, 4 fraternities, 3 sororities, on campus. **Athletics (Intercollegiate):** *Men:* baseball, basketball, cheerleading, cross-country, football, golf, soccer, swimming, tennis, track/field (outdoor), track/field (indoor), wrestling. *Women:* badminton, basketball, cheerleading, cross-country, field hockey, soccer, softball, swimming, tennis, track/field (outdoor), track/field (indoor), volleyball. **On-Campus Highlights:** Student Center.

ADMISSIONS

Freshman Academic Profile: Average high school GPA 3.1. 14% in top 10% of high school class, 40% in top 25% of high school class, 76% in top 50% of high school class. 77% from public high schools. **Test Scores:** SAT Math middle 50% range 503–590. SAT EBRW middle 50% range 520–610. ACT middle 50% range 20–24. **Basis for Candidate Selection:** *Very important factors include:* rigor of secondary school record, academic GPA. *Important factors include:* class rank, character/personal qualities. *Other factors include:* application essay, standardized test scores, recommendation(s), interview, extracurricular activities, talent/ability, alumni/ae relation, volunteer work, work experience, level of applicant's interest. **Freshman Admission Requirements:** High school diploma is required and GED is accepted. *Academic units required:* 4 English, 3 math, 3 science, 1 science labs, 2 foreign language, 2 social studies, 1 history. *Academic units recommended:* 4 English, 3 math, 4 science, 2 science labs, 2 foreign language, 2 social studies, 1 history, 1 academic electives. **Freshman Admission Statistics:** 6,755 applied, 62% admitted, 14% enrolled. **Transfer Admission Requirements:** college transcript(s), essay or personal statement, statement of good standing from prior institution(s). Minimum college GPA of 2.0 required. Lowest grade transferable C-. **General Admission Information:** Application fee $35. Priority deadline 3/1.

COSTS AND FINANCIAL AID

Annual tuition $24,500. Room and board $12,480. Required fees $1,142. Average book and supplies expense $1,000. **Required Forms and Deadlines:** FAFSA. **Notification of Awards:** Applicants will be notified of awards on a rolling basis beginning 11/15. **Types of Aid:** *Need-based scholarships/grants:* College/university scholarship or grant aid from institutional funds; Federal Pell; Private scholarships; SEOG; State scholarships/grants; United Negro College Fund. *Loans:* Direct PLUS loans; Direct Subsidized Stafford Loans; Direct Unsubsidized Stafford Loans. **Student Employment:** Federal Work-Study Program available. Institutional employment available. **Financial Aid Statistics:** 100% needy freshmen, 99% needy undergrads receive need-based scholarship or grant aid. 11% freshmen, 9% undergrads receive non-need-based scholarship or grant aid. 100% freshmen, 88% undergrads receive need-based self-help aid. 0% freshmen, 0% undergrads receive athletic scholarships. 91% undergrads borrow to pay for school. Average cumulative indebtedness $36,422. **Criteria awarding aid:** *Non-need-based:* Academics, Art, Music/drama, Religious affiliation, State/district residency.

ALCORN STATE UNIVERSITY

1000 ASU Drive #300, Lorman, MS 39096
Phone: 601-877-6147
E-mail: ksampson@alcorn.edu **CEEB Code:** 1008
Fax: 601-877-6347 **Website:** www.alcorn.edu **ACT Code:** 2176

This public school was founded in 1871. It has a 1756 acre campus.

RATINGS

Admissions Selectivity Rating: 75   **Fire Safety Rating:** 60*   **Green Rating:** 60*

STUDENTS AND FACULTY

Enrollment: 3,006. **Student Body:** 64% female, 36% male, 13% out-of-state, 1% international (14 countries represented). Asian <1%, African American 94%, Caucasian 2%, Hispanic <1%, Native American <1%, Pacific Islander <1%, Two or more races 2%, Race unknown 0%.
Retention and Graduation: 76% freshmen return for sophomore year. 38% grads go on to further study within 1 year. **Faculty:** Student/faculty ratio 17:1. 163 full-time faculty, 66% hold PhDs, 80% are members of minority groups, 45% are women.

ACADEMICS

Degrees: Associate; Bachelor's; Master's; Post-master's certificate. **Classes:** Most classes have 10–19 students. Most lab/discussion sessions have fewer than 10 students. **Most popular majors:** Liberal Arts and Sciences/Liberal Studies; Elementary Education and Teaching. **Special Study Options:** Accelerated program; Cooperative education program; Distance learning; Double major; Dual enrollment; Honors program; Independent study; Internships; Liberal arts/career combination; Study abroad; Teacher certification program. **Career services:** Internships.

FACILITIES

Housing: Men's dorms; Women's dorms; 0% of campus accessible to physically disabled. **Special Academic Facilities/Equipment:** Honor's Resident Hall. **Campus network:** 100% of classrooms, 100% of dorms, 100% of student union, 100% of libraries, 100% of dining areas, 90% of common outdoor areas, have wireless network access.

CAMPUS LIFE

Environment: Rural. **Activities:** Choral groups; Concert band; Dance; Drama/theater; International Student Organization; Jazz band; Marching band; Music ensembles; Radio station; Student government; Student newspaper; Television station; Yearbook. 120 registered organizations, 10 honor societies, 8 religious organizations, 8 fraternities, 7 sororities, on campus. **Athletics (Intercollegiate):** *Men:* baseball, basketball, cross-country, football, golf, tennis, track/field (outdoor). *Women:* basketball, cross-country, golf, soccer, softball, tennis, track/field (outdoor), volleyball.

ADMISSIONS

Freshman Academic Profile: Average high school GPA 3.0. 68% in top 50% of high school class. 99% from public high schools. **Test Scores:** SAT Math middle 50% range 405–500. SAT EBRW middle 50% range 390–485. ACT middle 50% range 16–20. **Basis for Candidate Selection:** *Very important factors include:* rigor of secondary school record, class rank, academic GPA. *Important factors include:* standardized test scores. *Other factors include:* recommendation(s), interview. **Freshman Admission Requirements:** High school diploma is required

and GED is accepted. *Academic units required:* 4 English, 3 math, 3 science, 2 science labs, 1 foreign language, 3 social studies, 1 academic electives, 2 computer science. *Academic units recommended:* 4 English, 4 math, 4 science, 2 science labs, 1 foreign language, 4 social studies, 1 academic electives, 2 computer science, 1 visual/performing arts. **Freshman Admission Statistics:** 2,078 applied, 78% admitted, 32% enrolled. **Transfer Admission Requirements:** College transcript(s), statement of good standing from prior institution(s). Minimum college GPA of 2.0 required. Lowest grade transferable C. **General Admission Information:** Non-fall registration accepted.

COSTS AND FINANCIAL AID

Required Forms and Deadlines: FAFSA; Institution's own financial aid form. **Notification of Awards:** Applicants will be notified of awards on a rolling basis beginning 4/1. **Types of Aid:** *Need-based scholarships/grants:* College/university scholarship or grant aid from institutional funds; Federal Pell; Private scholarships; SEOG; State scholarships/grants. *Loans:* Direct PLUS loans; Direct Subsidized Stafford Loans; Direct Unsubsidized Stafford Loans. **Student Employment:** Federal Work-Study Program available. Institutional employment available. **Financial Aid Statistics:** 95% needy freshmen, 93% needy undergrads receive need-based scholarship or grant aid. 33% freshmen, 24% undergrads receive non-need-based scholarship or grant aid. 75% freshmen, 84% undergrads receive need-based self-help aid. 10% freshmen, 8% undergrads receive athletic scholarships. **Criteria awarding aid:** *Need-based:* Academics, Alumni affiliation, Athletics, Leadership, Minority status, Music/drama *Non-need-based:* Academics, Athletics, Leadership.

ALDERSON BROADDUS UNIVERSITY

101 College Hill Drive, Philippi, WV 26416
Phone: 800-263-1549 **Financial Aid Phone:** 304-457-6354
E-mail: admissions@ab.edu **CEEB Code:** 5005
Fax: 304-457-6239 **Website:** www.ab.edu **ACT Code:** 4508

This private school, affiliated with the American Baptist Church, was founded in 1871. It has a 170 acre campus.

RATINGS

Admissions Selectivity Rating: 83   **Fire Safety Rating:** 83   **Green Rating:** 60*

STUDENTS AND FACULTY

Enrollment: 1,066. **Student Body:** 46% female, 54% male, 63% out-of-state, 5% international (15 countries represented). Asian 1%, African American 16%, Caucasian 73%, Hispanic 4%, Native American <1%, Pacific Islander <1%, Two or more races 1%, Race unknown 0%.
Retention and Graduation: 55% freshmen return for sophomore year. 7% grads go on to further study within 1 year. 1% grads pursue arts and sciences degrees. 0% grads pursue law degrees. 7% grads pursue business degrees. **Faculty:** Student/faculty ratio 17:1. 62 full-time faculty, 47% hold PhDs, 6% are members of minority groups, 55% are women. 0% of classes are taught by teaching assistants.

ACADEMICS

Degrees: Associate; Bachelor's; Master's. **Classes:** Most classes have fewer than 10 students. Most lab/discussion sessions have 10–19 students. **Most popular majors:** Registered Nursing/Registered Nurse; Biology/Biological Sciences, General; Athletic Training/Trainer. **Special Study Options:** Accelerated program; Distance learning; Double major; Honors program; Independent study; Internships; Liberal arts/career combination; Study abroad; Teacher certification program. **Disability Services offered:** Note-taking services; Reader services; Tape recorders; Tutors. **Career services:** Alumni network; Career assessment; Career/job search classes; Internships.

FACILITIES

Housing: Coed dorms; Special housing for disabled students 70% of campus accessible to physically disabled. **Special Academic Facilities/Equipment:** Art Gallery in Burbick Hall. Campbell School House **Campus network:** 75% of classrooms, 100% of dorms, 100% of student union, 100% of libraries, 100% of dining areas, 100% of common outdoor areas, have wireless network access.

CAMPUS LIFE

Environment: Rural. **Activities:** Campus Ministries; Choral groups; Concert band; Dance; Drama/theater; Jazz band; Literary magazine; Marching band; Music ensembles; Musical theater; Pep band; Radio station; Student government; Student newspaper; Television station; Yearbook. 30 registered organizations, 2 honor societies, 4 religious organizations, 3 fraternities, 3 sororities, on campus. **Athletics (Intercollegiate):** *Men:* baseball, basketball, cross-country, soccer, track/field (outdoor), track/field (indoor). *Women:* basketball, cross-country, soccer, softball, track/field (outdoor), track/field (indoor), volleyball. **On-Campus Highlights:** Rex Pyles Arena. **Environmental Initiatives:** Recycling efforts.

ADMISSIONS

Freshman Academic Profile: Average high school GPA 3.2. 11% in top 10% of high school class, 31% in top 25% of high school class, 69% in top 50% of high school class. 97% from public high schools. **Test Scores:** SAT Math middle 50% range 450–530. SAT EBRW middle 50% range 440–510. ACT middle 50% range 19–23. **Basis for Candidate Selection:** *Very important factors include:* rigor of secondary school record, academic GPA, standardized test scores. *Important factors include:* application essay, *Other factors include:* recommendation(s), interview, talent/ability, first generation, alumni/ae relation, level of applicant's interest. **Freshman Admission Requirements:** High school diploma is required and GED is accepted. *Academic units required:* 4 English, 3 math, 3 science, 1 science labs, 1 social studies. *Academic units recommended:* 3 science labs, 1 foreign language, 3 social studies. **Freshman Admission Statistics:** 4,206 applied, 54% admitted, 15% enrolled. **Transfer Admission Requirements:** High school transcript, college transcript(s), statement of good standing from prior institution(s). Minimum college GPA of 2.0 required. Lowest grade transferable C. **General Admission Information:** Non-fall registration accepted. Admission may be deferred for a maximum of 1 year.

COSTS AND FINANCIAL AID

Annual tuition $23,930. Room and board $7,606. Required fees $210. Average book and supplies expense $800. **Required Forms and Deadlines:** FAFSA; State aid form. **Notification of Awards:** Applicants will be notified of awards on a rolling basis beginning 3/1. **Types of Aid:** *Need-based scholarships/ grants:* College/university scholarship or grant aid from institutional funds; Federal Nursing Scholarships; Federal Pell; Private scholarships; SEOG; State scholarships/grants. *Loans:* Direct PLUS loans; Direct Subsidized Stafford Loans; Direct Unsubsidized Stafford Loans. **Student Employment:** Federal Work-Study Program available. **Financial Aid Statistics:** 100% needy freshmen, 99% needy undergrads receive need-based scholarship or grant aid. 10% freshmen, 13% undergrads receive non-need-based scholarship or grant aid. 96% freshmen, 84% undergrads receive need-based self-help aid. 5% freshmen, 5% undergrads receive athletic scholarships. 100% freshmen, 99% undergrads receive any aid. 88% undergrads borrow to pay for school. Average cumulative indebtedness $23,715. **Criteria awarding aid:** *Need-based:* Academics, Athletics, Music/drama, Religious affiliation. *Non-need-based:* Academics, Athletics, Music/drama.

ALFRED UNIVERSITY

Alumni Hall, Alfred, NY 14802-1205
Phone: 607-871-2115 **Financial Aid Phone:** 607-871-2159
E-mail: admissions@alfred.edu **CEEB Code:** 2005
Fax: 607-871-2198 **Website:** www.alfred.edu **ACT Code:** 2666

This private school was founded in 1836. It has a 600 acre campus.

RATINGS

Admissions Selectivity Rating: 82 **Fire Safety Rating:** 89 **Green Rating:** 60*

STUDENTS AND FACULTY

Enrollment: 1,668. **Student Body:** 47% female, 53% male, 24% out-of-state, 7% international (9 countries represented). Asian 2%, African American 13%, Caucasian 58%, Hispanic 9%, Native American <1%, Pacific Islander 0%, Two or more races 3%, Race unknown 8%.
Retention and Graduation: 73% freshmen return for sophomore year. 57% freshmen graduate within 6 years. 30% grads go on to further study within 1 year.
Faculty: Student/faculty ratio 11:1. 163 full-time faculty, 97% hold PhDs, 6% are members of minority groups, 45% are women. 0% of classes are taught by teaching assistants.

ACADEMICS

Degrees: Bachelor's; Doctoral degree research/scholarship; Master's; Post-master's certificate. **Classes:** Most classes have 10–19 students. Most lab/ discussion sessions have 10–19 students. **Most popular majors:** Psychology, General; Business/Commerce, General; Fine/Studio Arts, General. **Special Study Options:** Cooperative education program; Cross-registration; Double major; Exchange student program (domestic); Honors program; Independent study; Internships; Liberal arts/career combination; Student-designed major; Study abroad; Teacher certification program. **Honors programs:** The Alfred University Honors Program is designed to enrich the lives of exceptional students. It has two components: an honors seminar—meets one evening a week and the senior thesis. **Disability Services offered:** Note-taking services; Tape recorders; Tutors. **Career services:** Alumni network; Alumni services; Career assessment; Internships.

FACILITIES

Housing: Apartments for single students; Coed dorms; Special housing for international students; Theme housing; Wellness housing; 90% of campus accessible to physically disabled. **Special Academic Facilities/Equipment:** Art museums, carillon, language labs, electron microscope, observatory, extensive engineering equipment, performing arts center.

CAMPUS LIFE

Environment: Rural. **Activities:** Campus Ministries; Choral groups; Concert band; Dance; Drama/theater; International Student Organization; Jazz band; Literary magazine; Music ensembles; Musical theater; Pep band; Radio station; Student government; Student newspaper; Student-run film society; Yearbook. 80 registered organizations, 6 honor societies, 6 religious organizations, on campus. **Athletics (Intercollegiate):** *Men:* basketball, cross-country, diving, equestrian sports, football, lacrosse, skiing (downhill/Alpine), soccer, swimming, tennis, track/field (outdoor), track/field (indoor). *Women:* basketball, cross-country, diving, equestrian sports, lacrosse, skiing (downhill/Alpine), soccer, softball, swimming, tennis, track/field (outdoor), track/field (indoor), volleyball. **On-Campus Highlights:** Powell Campus Center **Environmental Initiatives:** Campus-wide recycling program (paper, glass, plastic, electronics, printer/toner cartridges).

ADMISSIONS

Freshman Academic Profile: Average high school GPA 3.1. **Test Scores:** SAT Math middle 50% range 470–590. SAT EBRW middle 50% range 470–590. ACT middle 50% range 19–26. **Basis for Candidate Selection:** *Very important factors include:* rigor of secondary school record, class rank, academic GPA, extracurricular activities, character/personal qualities. *Important factors include:* application essay, standardized test scores, recommendation(s), volunteer work, work experience. *Other factors include:* interview, talent/ability, first generation, racial/ethnic status, level of applicant's interest. **Freshman Admission Requirements:** High school diploma is required and GED is accepted. *Academic units required:* 4 English, 4 math, 3 science, 3 science labs, 3 social studies. *Academic units recommended:* 4 English, 4 math, 3 science, 3 science labs, 1 foreign language, 3 social studies. **Freshman Admission Statistics:** 4,485 applied, 62% admitted, 16% enrolled. **Transfer Admission Requirements:** College transcript(s), statement of good standing from prior institution(s). Minimum college GPA of 2.5 required. Lowest grade transferable C. **General Admission Information:** Application fee $50. Priority deadline 2/1. Regular application deadline 8/1. Non-fall registration accepted. Admission may be deferred for a maximum of 1 year.

COSTS AND FINANCIAL AID

Annual tuition $35,076. Room and board $12,924. Required fees $1,200. Average book and supplies expense $1,300. **Required Forms and Deadlines:** FAFSA; State aid form. **Notification of Awards:** Applicants will be notified of awards on a rolling basis beginning 2/15. **Types of Aid:** *Need-based scholarships/ grants:* College/university scholarship or grant aid from institutional funds; Federal Pell; Private scholarships; SEOG; State scholarships/grants. *Loans:* Direct PLUS loans; Direct Subsidized Stafford Loans; Direct Unsubsidized Stafford Loans. **Student Employment:** Federal Work-Study Program available. Institutional employment available. **Financial Aid Statistics:** 99% needy freshmen, 99% needy undergrads receive need-based scholarship or grant aid. 53% freshmen, 55% undergrads receive non-need-based scholarship or grant aid. 89% freshmen, 87% undergrads receive need-based self-help aid. 0% freshmen, 0% undergrads receive athletic scholarships. 96% freshmen, 92% undergrads receive any aid. 86% undergrads borrow to pay for school. Average cumulative indebtedness $34,224. **Criteria awarding aid:** *Need-based:* Academics, Art *Non-need-based:* Academics, Art, Leadership, Music/drama.

ALICE LLOYD COLLEGE

100 Purpose Road, Pippa Passes, KY 41844
Phone: 606-368-6036
E-mail: admissions@alc.edu **CEEB Code:** 1098
Fax: 606-368-6215 **Website:** www.alc.edu **ACT Code:** 1502

This private school was founded in 1923. It has a 225 acre campus.

RATINGS
Admissions Selectivity Rating: 86   Fire Safety Rating: 93   Green Rating: 60*

STUDENTS AND FACULTY
Enrollment: 607. **Student Body:** 51% female, 49% male, 13% out-of-state, <1% international (1 countries represented). Asian <1%, African American 1%, Caucasian 99%, Hispanic 0%, Native American 0%, Race unknown 0%. **Retention and Graduation:** 63% freshmen return for sophomore year. 55% grads go on to further study within 1 year. 35% grads pursue arts and sciences degrees. 5% grads pursue law degrees. 10% grads pursue business degrees. 5% grads pursue medical degrees. **Faculty:** Student/faculty ratio 18:1. 29 full-time faculty, 59% hold PhDs, 10% are members of minority groups, 41% are women. 0% of classes are taught by teaching assistants.

ACADEMICS
Degrees: Bachelor's. **Classes:** Most classes have 20–29 students. **Most popular majors:** Education, General; Business/Commerce, General; Biology/Biological Sciences, General. **Special Study Options:** Cooperative education program; Double major; Honors program; Independent study; Internships; Liberal arts/career combination; Study abroad; Teacher certification program. **Disability Services offered:** Reader services; Tutors. **Career services:** Alumni network; Alumni services; Career assessment; Internships; Regional alumni.

FACILITIES
Housing: Men's dorms; Women's dorms; 90% of campus accessible to physically disabled. **Special Academic Facilities/Equipment:** Photographic archives, oral history museum, Appalachian collection, on-campus day care center, kindergarten, elementary, and secondary school. **Campus network:** 50% of classrooms, 100% of student union, 100% of libraries, 30% of common outdoor areas, have wireless network access.

CAMPUS LIFE
Environment: Rural. **Activities:** Choral groups; Drama/theater; Music ensembles; Musical theater; Pep band; Radio station; Student government; Student newspaper; Yearbook. 19 registered organizations, 2 honor societies, 1 religious organizations, on campus. **Athletics (Intercollegiate):** *Men:* baseball, basketball, cheerleading, cross-country, golf, tennis. *Women:* basketball, cheerleading, cross-country, golf, softball, tennis. **On-Campus Highlights:** Jerry Davis Student Center.

ADMISSIONS
Freshman Academic Profile: Average high school GPA 3.4. 30% in top 10% of high school class, 58% in top 25% of high school class, 86% in top 50% of high school class. 90% from public high schools. **Test Scores:** SAT Math middle 50% range 480–570. SAT EBRW middle 50% range 440–590. ACT middle 50% range 17–23. **Basis for Candidate Selection:** *Very important factors include:* rigor of secondary school record, standardized test scores, character/personal qualities, geographical residence. *Important factors include:* class rank, recommendation(s), alumni/ae relation, state residency. *Other factors include:* application essay, interview, extracurricular activities, talent/ability, volunteer work, work experience. **Freshman Admission Requirements:** High school diploma is required and GED is accepted. *Academic units required:* 4 English, 3 math, 2 science, 2 social studies, 1 history. *Academic units recommended:* 4 English, 3 math, 2 science, 2 foreign language, 2 social studies. **Freshman Admission Statistics:** 994 applied, 56% admitted, 32% enrolled. **Transfer Admission Requirements:** High school transcript, college transcript(s), standardized test scores, statement of good standing from prior institution(s). Minimum college GPA of 2.0 required. Lowest grade transferable C. **General Admission Information:** Priority deadline 6/1. Regular application deadline 5/1. Non-fall registration accepted.

COSTS AND FINANCIAL AID
Room and board $4,250. Required fees $1,300. Average book and supplies expense $850. **Required Forms and Deadlines:** FAFSA. **Notification of Awards:** Applicants will be notified of awards on a rolling basis beginning 4/1. **Types of Aid:** *Need-based scholarships/grants:* College/university scholarship or grant aid from institutional funds; Federal Pell; Private scholarships; SEOG;

State scholarships/grants. **Student Employment:** Federal Work-Study Program available. Institutional employment available. **Financial Aid Statistics:** 99% needy freshmen, 99% needy undergrads receive need-based scholarship or grant aid. 11% freshmen, 16% undergrads receive non-need-based scholarship or grant aid. 89% freshmen, 84% undergrads receive need-based self-help aid. 7% freshmen, 5% undergrads receive athletic scholarships. 100% freshmen, 100% undergrads receive any aid. **Criteria awarding aid:** *Non-need-based:* Athletics, Minority status, State/district residency.

ALLEGHENY COLLEGE

Allegheny College, Meadville, PA 16335
Phone: 814-332-4351 **Financial Aid Phone:** 800-835-7780
E-mail: admissions@allegheny.edu **CEEB Code:** 2006
Fax: 814-337-0431 **Website:** https://allegheny.edu **ACT Code:** 3520

This private school was founded in 1815. It has a 566 acre campus.

RATINGS
Admissions Selectivity Rating: 87   Fire Safety Rating: 85   Green Rating: 60*

STUDENTS AND FACULTY
Enrollment: 1,726. **Student Body:** 56% female, 44% male, 48% out-of-state, 3% international (58 countries represented). Asian 4%, African American 8%, Caucasian 68%, Hispanic 9%, Native American <1%, Pacific Islander 0%, Two or more races 4%, Race unknown 3%. **Retention and Graduation:** 86% freshmen return for sophomore year. 66% freshmen graduate within 4 years. 74% freshmen graduate within 6 years. 22% grads go on to further study within 1 year. 3% grads pursue arts and sciences degrees. 1% grads pursue law degrees. 0% grads pursue business degrees. 5% grads pursue medical degrees. **Faculty:** Student/faculty ratio 11:1. 148 full-time faculty, 93% hold PhDs, 14% are members of minority groups, 53% are women. 0% of classes are taught by teaching assistants.

ACADEMICS
Degrees: Bachelor's. **Classes:** Most classes have 10–19 students. Most lab/discussion sessions have 10–19 students. **Most popular majors:** Biology/Biological Sciences, General; Psychology, General; Economics, General. **Special Study Options:** Double major; Dual enrollment; Honors program; Independent study; Internships; Student-designed major; Study abroad. **Combined degree programs:** BA/MA; BA/MD; BA/MEng. **Disability Services offered:** Note-taking services; Tape recorders; Tutors. **Career services:** Alumni network; Alumni services; Career assessment; Career/job search classes; Internships; Regional alumni.

FACILITIES
Housing: Apartments for single students; Coed dorms; Fraternity/sorority housing; Men's dorms; Special housing for disabled students; Theme housing; Women's dorms; 50% of campus accessible to physically disabled. **Special Academic Facilities/Equipment:** Center For Communication Arts with a trap stage and green and blue screen room; radio and television stations; state-of-the-art, nationally acclaimed science complex; video conference facilities; planetarium; observatory; GIS lab; state-of-the-art language-learning center; smart classrooms; dance studios and performance spaces; art studios & galleries; world's largest solid-volume glass sculpture grouping; 283-acre Environmental Research Reserve; 80-acre protected forest; sustainable luminescent solar concentrator roof greenhouse; alumni center; comprehensive sports and fitness center; seismographic network station; Center for Political Participation; Center for Business & Economics; environmental roof garden; Living & Learning Residential Communities; Richard J. Cook Center for Environmental Science; Allegheny Gateway: Connecting classroom learning to real-world experience; Augmented Reality Sandbox; Creek Connections; 17 acre sustainable forest; state-of-the-art neuroscience & psychology research facility; Lab for Innovation & Creativity.

CAMPUS LIFE
Environment: Town. **Activities:** Campus Ministries; Choral groups; Concert band; Dance; Drama/theater; International Student Organization; Jazz band; Literary magazine; Model UN; Music ensembles; Musical theater; Opera; Pep band; Radio station; Student government; Student newspaper; Symphony

orchestra; Television station; Yearbook. 116 registered organizations, 14 honor societies, 9 religious organizations, 6 fraternities, 6 sororities, on campus. **Athletics (Intercollegiate):** *Men:* baseball, basketball, cross-country, diving, football, golf, soccer, swimming, tennis, track/field (outdoor), track/field (indoor). *Women:* basketball, cross-country, diving, golf, lacrosse, soccer, softball, swimming, tennis, track/field (outdoor), track/field (indoor), volleyball. **On-Campus Highlights:** Rustic Bridge. **Environmental Initiatives:** Climate action plan.

ADMISSIONS

Freshman Academic Profile: Average high school GPA 3.5. 40% in top 10% of high school class, 63% in top 25% of high school class, 85% in top 50% of high school class. 84% from public high schools. **Test Scores:** SAT Math middle 50% range 580–680. SAT EBRW middle 50% range 590–680. ACT middle 50% range 24–30. **Basis for Candidate Selection** *Very important factors include:* rigor of secondary school record, class rank, academic GPA. *Important factors include:* recommendation(s), interview, extracurricular activities, character/personal qualities. *Other factors include:* application essay, standardized test scores, talent/ability, first generation, alumni/ae relation, geographical residence, racial/ethnic status, volunteer work. **Freshman Admission Requirements:** High school diploma is required and GED is accepted. *Academic units required:* 4 English, 3 math, 3 science, 2 foreign language, 3 social studies, 1 academic electives. **Freshman Admission Statistics:** 5,208 applied, 62% admitted, 15% enrolled. **Transfer Admission Requirements:** High school transcript, college transcript(s), essay or personal statement, standardized test scores. Minimum college GPA of 2.5 required. Lowest grade transferable C. **General Admission Information:** Regular application deadline 2/15. Non-fall registration accepted. Admission may be deferred for a maximum of 1 year.

COSTS AND FINANCIAL AID

Annual tuition $50,480. Room and board $13,080. Required fees $500. Average book and supplies expense $1,000. **Required Forms and Deadlines:** FAFSA. **Notification of Awards:** Applicants will be notified of awards on a rolling basis beginning 12/1. **Types of Aid:** *Need-based scholarships/grants:* College/university scholarship or grant aid from institutional funds; Federal Pell; Private scholarships; SEOG; State scholarships/grants. *Loans:* Direct PLUS loans; Direct Subsidized Stafford Loans; Direct Unsubsidized Stafford Loans. **Student Employment:** Federal Work-Study Program available. Institutional employment available. **Financial Aid Statistics:** 100% needy freshmen, 100% needy undergrads receive need-based scholarship or grant aid. 32% freshmen, 19% undergrads receive non-need-based scholarship or grant aid. 71% freshmen, 81% undergrads receive need-based self-help aid. 0% freshmen, 0% undergrads receive athletic scholarships. 100% freshmen, 99% undergrads receive any aid. **Criteria awarding aid:** *Need-based:* Academics, Minority status. *Non-need-based:* Academics, Leadership, Minority status, State/district residency.

ALLEN COLLEGE

1825 Logan Avenue, Waterloo, IA 50703
Phone: 319-226-2000 **Financial Aid Phone:** 319-226-2514
E-mail: Admissions@AllenCollege.edu
Fax: 319-226-2051 **Website:** www.allencollege.edu **ACT Code:** 30691

This private school was founded in 1989.

RATINGS

Admissions Selectivity Rating: 60*   **Fire Safety Rating:** 63   **Green Rating:** 60*

STUDENTS AND FACULTY

Enrollment: 341. **Student Body:** 92% female, 8% male, 7% out-of-state, 1% international (4 countries represented). Asian 1%, African American 1%, Caucasian 88%, Hispanic 1%, Native American <1%, Pacific Islander 0%, Two or more races 2%, Race unknown 6%.
Retention and Graduation: 86% freshmen return for sophomore year. 10% grads go on to further study within 1 year. **Faculty:** Student/faculty ratio 11:1. 41 full-time faculty, 59% hold PhDs, 0% are members of minority groups, 95% are women. 0% of classes are taught by teaching assistants.

ACADEMICS

Degrees: Associate; Bachelor's; Certificate; Master's; Post-master's certificate. **Classes:** Most classes have 20–29 students. Most lab/discussion sessions have fewer than 10 students. **Most popular majors:** Health Professions And Related

Programs; Health Professions And Related Programs; Health Professions And Related Programs. **Special Study Options:** Accelerated program; Cooperative education program; Distance learning; Honors program; Independent study; Internships. **Disability Services offered:** Tutors.

FACILITIES

Housing: 100% of campus accessible to physically disabled.

CAMPUS LIFE

Environment: City. **Activities:** Choral groups; Student government. 3 registered organizations, 2 honor societies, 1 religious organizations, on campus.

ADMISSIONS

Basis for Candidate Selection: *Important factors include:* rigor of secondary school record, class rank, academic GPA, application essay, standardized test scores, recommendation(s), extracurricular activities, character/personal qualities. *Other factors include:* interview, talent/ability, first generation, alumni/ae relation, racial/ethnic status, volunteer work, work experience, level of applicant's interest. **Freshman Admission Requirements:** High school diploma is required and GED is accepted. *Academic units required:* 8 English, 6 math, 6 science, 6 social studies. **Freshman Admission Statistics:** applied, admitted, enrolled. **Transfer Admission Requirements:** High school transcript, college transcript(s), essay or personal statement, standardized test scores. Minimum college GPA of 2.7 required. Lowest grade transferable C. **General Admission Information:** Application fee $50. Priority deadline 2/1. Non-fall registration accepted.

COSTS AND FINANCIAL AID

Annual tuition $18,540. Required fees $1,430. Average book and supplies expense $1,200. **Required Forms and Deadlines:** FAFSA; Institution's own financial aid form. **Notification of Awards:** Applicants will be notified of awards on a rolling basis beginning 4/1. **Types of Aid:** *Need-based scholarships/grants:* College/university scholarship or grant aid from institutional funds; Federal Nursing Scholarships; Federal Pell; Private scholarships; SEOG; State scholarships/grants. *Loans:* Direct PLUS loans; Direct Subsidized Stafford Loans; Direct Unsubsidized Stafford Loans. **Student Employment:** Federal Work-Study Program available. **Financial Aid Statistics:** 90% needy undergrads receive need-based scholarship or grant aid. 0% undergrads receive non-need-based scholarship or grant aid. 92% undergrads receive need-based self-help aid. 0% undergrads receive athletic scholarships. 94.7% undergrads receive any aid. 0% undergrads borrow to pay for school. **Criteria awarding aid:** *Need-based:* Academics, Alumni affiliation, Leadership, Minority status. *Non-need-based:* Academics, Alumni affiliation, Leadership, Minority status, State/district residency.

ALMA COLLEGE

614 West Superior Street, Alma, MI 48801-1599
Phone: 989-463-7139 **Financial Aid Phone:** 989-463-7347
E-mail: admissions@alma.edu **CEEB Code:** 1010
Fax: 989-463-7057 **Website:** www.alma.edu **ACT Code:** 1958

This private school, affiliated with the Presbyterian Church, was founded in 1886. It has a 125 acre campus.

RATINGS

Admissions Selectivity Rating: 83   **Fire Safety Rating:** 73   **Green Rating:** 60*

STUDENTS AND FACULTY

Enrollment: 1,396. **Student Body:** 58% female, 42% male, 9% out-of-state, 1% international (10 countries represented). Asian 1%, African American 3%, Caucasian 79%, Hispanic 5%, Native American 1%, Pacific Islander <1%, Two or more races 4%, Race unknown 6%.
Retention and Graduation: 79% freshmen return for sophomore year. 56% freshmen graduate within 4 years. 68% freshmen graduate within 6 years. 29% grads go on to further study within 1 year. **Faculty:** Student/faculty ratio 12:1. 100 full-time faculty, 84% hold PhDs, 15% are members of minority groups, 48% are women. 0% of classes are taught by teaching assistants.

ACADEMICS

Degrees: Bachelor's. **Classes:** Most classes have 10–19 students. Most lab/discussion sessions have fewer than 10 students. **Most popular majors:** Education, General; Health and Wellness, General; Biology, General. **Special Study Options:** Double major; Dual enrollment; Honors program; Independent study; Internships; Student-designed major; Study abroad; Teacher certification program. **Honors programs:** Students in the Presidential Honors Program participate in special seminar opportunities and enroll in courses designed for honors scholars. **Disability Services offered:** Note-taking services; Reader services; Tape recorders; Tutors. **Career services:** Alumni services; Career assessment; Internships.

FACILITIES

Housing: Apartments for single students; Coed dorms; Fraternity/sorority housing; Special housing for disabled students; Special housing for international students; Theme housing; Wellness housing; 75% of campus accessible to physically disabled. **Special Academic Facilities/Equipment:** Performing arts center, art gallery, science labs, planetarium, 200-acre ecological tract. **Campus network:** 100% of classrooms, 100% of dorms, 100% of student union, 100% of libraries, 100% of dining areas, 100% of common outdoor areas, have wireless network access.

CAMPUS LIFE

Environment: Village. **Activities:** Campus Ministries; Choral groups; Concert band; Dance; Drama/theater; International Student Organization; Jazz band; Literary magazine; Marching band; Model UN; Music ensembles; Student government; Student newspaper; Student-run film society; Symphony orchestra; Yearbook. 81 registered organizations, 22 honor societies, 4 religious organizations, 6 fraternities, 5 sororities, on campus. **Athletics (Intercollegiate):** *Men:* baseball, basketball, cross-country, diving, football, golf, soccer, swimming, tennis, track/field (outdoor). *Women:* basketball, cross-country, diving, golf, soccer, softball, swimming, tennis, track/field (outdoor), volleyball. **On-Campus Highlights:** Library **Environmental Initiatives:** The Hogan Center is the first official LEED-certified building for green construction at Alma College and Gratiot County. The renovated Hogan Center and new Art Smith Arena were awarded LEED certification at the Silver level by the U.S. Green Building Council (USGBC) and verified by the Green Building Certification Institute (GBCI). LEED is the nation's preeminent program for the design, construction and operation of high performance green buildings. The arena serves as the primary venue for commencement, convocations, major speakers, concerts, athletics and other major events.

ADMISSIONS

Freshman Academic Profile: Average high school GPA 3.6. 20% in top 10% of high school class, 29% in top 25% of high school class, 83% in top 50% of high school class. **Test Scores:** SAT Math middle 50% range 520–600. SAT EBRW middle 50% range 520–620. ACT middle 50% range 20–27. **Basis for Candidate Selection:** *Very important factors include:* academic GPA, application essay, standardized test scores. *Important factors include:* rigor of secondary school record. *Other factors include:* recommendation(s), interview, extracurricular activities, character/personal qualities, alumni/ae relation, volunteer work, work experience. **Freshman Admission Requirements:** High school diploma is required and GED is accepted. *Academic units required:* 4 English, 3 math, 3 science, 3 social studies. *Academic units recommended:* 2 foreign language. **Freshman Admission Statistics:** 4,833 applied, 64% admitted, 13% enrolled. **Transfer Admission Requirements:** High school transcript, college transcript(s), statement of good standing from prior institution(s). Minimum college GPA of 3.0 required. Lowest grade transferable C. **General Admission Information:** Application fee $25. Non-fall registration accepted. Admission may be deferred for a maximum of 1 year.

COSTS AND FINANCIAL AID

Annual tuition $39,998. Required fees $260. **Required Forms and Deadlines:** FAFSA. **Notification of Awards:** Applicants will be notified of awards on a rolling basis beginning 12/15. **Types of Aid:** *Need-based scholarships/grants:* College/university scholarship or grant aid from institutional funds; Federal Pell; Private scholarships; SEOG; State scholarships/grants. *Loans:* Direct PLUS loans; Direct Subsidized Stafford Loans; Direct Unsubsidized Stafford Loans. **Student Employment:** Federal Work-Study Program available. Institutional employment available. **Financial Aid Statistics:** 99% needy freshmen, 99% needy undergrads receive need-based scholarship or grant aid. 14% freshmen, 11% undergrads receive non-need-based scholarship or grant aid. 83% freshmen, 81% undergrads receive need-based self-help aid. 0% freshmen, 0% undergrads receive athletic scholarships. 98% freshmen, 91% undergrads receive any aid. 84% undergrads borrow to pay for school. Average cumulative indebtedness $39,801. **Criteria awarding aid:** *Non-need-based:* Academics, Alumni affiliation, Art, Minority status, Music/drama, Religious affiliation.

ALVERNIA UNIVERSITY

400 St. Bernardine Street, Reading, PA 19607
Phone: 610-790-2873 **Financial Aid Phone:** 610-796-8356
E-mail: admissions@alvernia.edu
Fax: 610-790-2873 **Website:** www.alvernia.edu

RATINGS

Admissions Selectivity Rating: 79   **Fire Safety Rating:** 81   **Green Rating:** 60*

STUDENTS AND FACULTY

Enrollment: 2,176. **Student Body:** 70% female, 30% male, 26% out-of-state, <1% international (9 countries represented). Asian 2%, African American 12%, Caucasian 68%, Hispanic 11%, Native American <1%, Pacific Islander 0%, Two or more races 3%, Race unknown 4%.
Retention and Graduation: 74% freshmen return for sophomore year. 44% freshmen graduate within 4 years. 60% freshmen graduate within 6 years. **Faculty:** Student/faculty ratio 13:1. 114 full-time faculty, 75% hold PhDs, 11% are members of minority groups, 59% are women. 0% of classes are taught by teaching assistants.

ACADEMICS

Degrees: Associate; Bachelor's; Doctoral degree—professional practice; Doctoral degree research/scholarship; Master's. **Classes:** Most classes have 10–19 students. Most lab/discussion sessions have 10–19 students. **Most popular majors:** Criminal Justice/Law Enforcement Administration; Substance Abuse/Addiction Counseling; Elementary Education and Teaching. **Special Study Options:** Accelerated program; Cross-registration; Distance learning; Double major; Dual enrollment; Honors program; Independent study; Internships; Student-designed major; Study abroad; Teacher certification program. **Honors programs:** Alvernia College Honors Program. **Combined degree programs:** BA/MA. **Disability Services offered:** Note-taking services; Tape recorders; Tutors. **Career services:** Career assessment; Career/job search classes; Internships.

FACILITIES

Housing: Apartments for single students; Coed dorms; Special housing for disabled students; Theme housing; 90% of campus accessible to physically disabled.

CAMPUS LIFE

Environment: Village. **Activities:** Campus Ministries; Choral groups; Concert band; Dance; Drama/theater; Literary magazine; Pep band; Student government; Student newspaper. 35 registered organizations, 5 honor societies, 5 religious organizations, on campus. **On-Campus Highlights:** Student Center.

ADMISSIONS

Freshman Academic Profile: Average high school GPA 3.3. 74% from public high schools. **Test Scores:** SAT Math middle 50% range 470–560. SAT EBRW middle 50% range 480–570. **Basis for Candidate Selection:** *Very important factors include:* academic GPA, standardized test scores. *Important factors include:* rigor of secondary school record, class rank, application essay, extracurricular activities, character/personal qualities, alumni/ae relation, volunteer work. *Other factors include:* recommendation(s), interview, talent/ability, first generation. **Freshman Admission Requirements:** High school diploma is required and GED is accepted. **Freshman Admission Statistics:** 2,628 applied, 68% admitted, 21% enrolled. **General Admission Information:** Non-fall registration accepted. Admission may be deferred for a maximum of 12 months.

COSTS AND FINANCIAL AID

Annual tuition $34,070. Room and board $12,130. Required fees $830. Average book and supplies expense $1,500. **Required Forms and Deadlines:** FAFSA. **Types of Aid:** *Need-based scholarships/grants:* College/university scholarship or grant aid from institutional funds; Federal Pell; Private scholarships; SEOG; State scholarships/grants. *Loans:* Direct PLUS loans; Direct Subsidized Stafford Loans; Direct Unsubsidized Stafford Loans. **Financial Aid Statistics:** 94% freshmen, 98% undergrads receive any aid.

ALVERNO COLLEGE

3400 South 43rd Street, Milwaukee, WI 53234-3922
Phone: 414-382-6101 **Financial Aid Phone:** 414-382-6046
E-mail: admissions@alverno.edu **CEEB Code:** 1012
Fax: 414-382-6055 **Website:** www.alverno.edu **ACT Code:** 4558

This private school, affiliated with the Roman Catholic Church, was founded in 1887. It has a 47 acre campus.

RATINGS

Admissions Selectivity Rating: 77 **Fire Safety Rating:** 82 **Green Rating:** 66

STUDENTS AND FACULTY

Enrollment: 1,090. **Student Body:** 99% female, 1% male, 9% out-of-state, <1% international (3 countries represented). Asian 5%, African American 14%, Caucasian 43%, Hispanic 33%, Native American 1%, Pacific Islander 0%, Two or more races 5%, Race unknown <1%.
Retention and Graduation: 71% freshmen return for sophomore year. 22% freshmen graduate within 4 years. 49% freshmen graduate within 6 years. **Faculty:** Student/faculty ratio 9:1. 88 full-time faculty, 64% hold PhDs, 9% are members of minority groups, 78% are women. 0% of classes are taught by teaching assistants.

ACADEMICS

Degrees: Associate; Bachelor's; Doctoral degree—professional practice; Master's; Post-bachelor's certificate; Post-master's certificate. **Classes:** Most classes have 10–19 students. **Most popular majors:** Education, General; Registered Nursing/Registered Nurse; Business Administration and Management, General. **Special Study Options:** Accelerated program; Distance learning; Double major; Honors program; Independent study; Internships; Student-designed major; Study abroad; Teacher certification program. **Disability Services offered:** Note-taking services; Reader services; Tape recorders; Tutors. **Career services:** Alumni services; Career assessment; Career/job search classes.

FACILITIES

Housing: Theme housing; Women's dorms; 95% of campus accessible to physically disabled. **Special Academic Facilities/Equipment:** Art & Culture Gallery, Career Center, Fitness center, Reiman Gymnasium, Nursing Skills Lab, Student centered multi-media production facility, Diagnostic Digital Portfolio, computer center, science labs, theatre venue **Campus network:** 95% of classrooms, 100% of dorms, 100% of student union, 100% of libraries, 100% of dining areas, 85% of common outdoor areas, have wireless network access.

CAMPUS LIFE

Environment: Metropolis. **Activities:** Campus Ministries; Choral groups; Dance; Drama/theater; International Student Organization; Literary magazine; Model UN; Music ensembles; Radio station; Student government; Student newspaper. 36 registered organizations, 1 honor societies, 2 religious organizations, 2 sororities, on campus. **Athletics (Intercollegiate):** *Women:* basketball, cross-country, soccer, softball, tennis, volleyball. **On-Campus Highlights:** Inferno Cafe. **Environmental Initiatives:** Renovated and new construction totaling 13,000 sq ft utilizing LED lighting throughout project.

ADMISSIONS

Freshman Academic Profile: Average high school GPA 3.2. 67% from public high schools. **Test Scores:** ACT middle 50% range 18–21. **Basis for Candidate Selection:** *Very important factors include:* academic GPA, standardized test scores. *Important factors include:* rigor of secondary school record. *Other factors include:* application essay, recommendation(s), interview, extracurricular activities, talent/ability, character/personal qualities, volunteer work, work experience, level of applicant's interest. **Freshman Admission Requirements:** High school diploma is required and GED is accepted. *Academic units required:* 4 English, 3 math, 3 science, 3 social studies, 4 academic electives. *Academic units recommended:* 2 foreign language. **Freshman Admission Statistics:** 800 applied, 67% admitted, 32% enrolled. **Transfer Admission Requirements:** High school transcript, college transcript(s), essay or personal statement, Minimum college GPA of 2.0 required. Lowest grade transferable C. **General Admission Information:** Non-fall registration accepted. Admission may be deferred for a maximum of 1 year.

COSTS AND FINANCIAL AID

Average book and supplies expense $768. **Required Forms and Deadlines:** FAFSA. **Notification of Awards:** Applicants will be notified of awards on a rolling basis beginning 11/1. **Types of Aid:** *Need-based scholarships/grants:* College/university scholarship or grant aid from institutional funds; Federal Pell; Private

scholarships; SEOG; State scholarships/grants. *Loans:* Direct PLUS loans; Direct Subsidized Stafford Loans; Direct Unsubsidized Stafford Loans. **Student Employment:** Federal Work-Study Program available. Institutional employment available. **Financial Aid Statistics:** 100% needy freshmen, 98% needy undergrads receive need-based scholarship or grant aid. 82% freshmen, 87% undergrads receive non-need-based scholarship or grant aid. 96% freshmen, 84% undergrads receive need-based self-help aid. 0% freshmen, 0% undergrads receive athletic scholarships. 100% freshmen, 99.6% undergrads receive any aid. 85% undergrads borrow to pay for school. Average cumulative indebtedness $38,959. **Criteria awarding aid:** *Non-need-based:* Academics, Alumni affiliation.

AMERICAN INTERNATIONAL COLLEGE

1000 State Street, Springfield, MA 01109-3184
Phone: 413-205-3201 **Financial Aid Phone:** (413) 205-3270
E-mail: inquiry@aic.edu **CEEB Code:** 3002
Fax: 413-205-3051 **Website:** www.aic.edu **ACT Code:** 1772

This private school was founded in 1885. It has a 58 acre campus.

RATINGS

Admissions Selectivity Rating: 73 **Fire Safety Rating:** 89 **Green Rating:** 61

STUDENTS AND FACULTY

Enrollment: 1,478. **Student Body:** 60% female, 40% male, 39% out-of-state, 3% international (27 countries represented). Asian 1%, African American 25%, Caucasian 39%, Hispanic 14%, Native American <1%, Pacific Islander <1%, Two or more races 3%, Race unknown 14%.
Retention and Graduation: 72% freshmen return for sophomore year. 34% grads go on to further study within 1 year. **Faculty:** Student/faculty ratio 14:1. 74 full-time faculty, 64% hold PhDs, 16% are members of minority groups, 58% are women. 0% of classes are taught by teaching assistants.

ACADEMICS

Degrees: Associate; Bachelor's; Doctoral degree—professional practice; Doctoral degree research/scholarship; Master's; Post-bachelor's certificate; Post-master's certificate; Terminal Associate. **Classes:** Most classes have 20–29 students. Most lab/discussion sessions have 10–19 students. **Most popular majors:** Criminal Justice and Corrections; Registered Nursing/Registered Nurse; Psychology, General. **Special Study Options:** Accelerated program; Cross-registration; Distance learning; Double major; Dual enrollment; Honors program; Independent study; Internships; Study abroad; Teacher certification program. **Honors programs:** Four Year Honors program open to students in any major with appropriate credentials. **Combined degree programs:** BA/MA. **Disability Services offered:** Note-taking services; Reader services; Tape recorders; Tutors. **Career services:** Alumni services; Career assessment; Career/job search classes; Internships.

FACILITIES

Housing: Apartments for single students; Coed dorms; Theme housing; Women's dorms; 90% of campus accessible to physically disabled.

CAMPUS LIFE

Environment: City. **Activities:** Campus Ministries; Dance; Drama/theater; International Student Organization; Literary magazine; Model UN; Pep band; Student government; Student newspaper; Yearbook. 45 registered organizations, 5 honor societies, 1 religious organizations, 3 fraternities, 3 sororities, on campus. **Athletics (Intercollegiate):** *Men:* baseball, basketball, cheerleading, cross-country, football, golf, ice hockey, lacrosse, soccer, tennis, track/field (outdoor), track/field (indoor), wrestling. *Women:* basketball, cheerleading, cross-country, field hockey, lacrosse, soccer, softball, tennis, track/field (outdoor), track/field (indoor), volleyball. **On-Campus Highlights:** Courniotes Hall, Health Sciences.

ADMISSIONS

Freshman Academic Profile: Average high school GPA 2.8. **Test Scores:** SAT Math middle 50% range 400–500. SAT EBRW middle 50% range 390–480. ACT middle 50% range 16–23. **Basis for Candidate Selection:** *Very important factors include:* academic GPA, standardized test scores. *Important factors include:* rigor of secondary school record. *Other factors include:* application essay, recommendation(s), extracurricular activities, talent/ability, character/personal qualities, first generation, alumni/ae relation, volunteer work, work experience, level of applicant's interest. **Freshman Admission Requirements:** High school diploma is required and GED is accepted. *Academic units recommended:* 4 English, 3 math, 2 science, 2 science labs, 1 foreign language, 2 social studies,

4 academic electives. **Freshman Admission Statistics:** 1,522 applied, 86% admitted, 26% enrolled. **Transfer Admission Requirements:** High school transcript, college transcript(s), Minimum college GPA of 2.0 required. Lowest grade transferable C. **General Admission Information:** Non-fall registration accepted. Admission may be deferred for a maximum of 1 year.

COSTS AND FINANCIAL AID

Annual tuition $33,140. Room and board $13,590. Required fees $60. Average book and supplies expense $1,235. **Required Forms and Deadlines:** FAFSA. **Notification of Awards:** Applicants will be notified of awards on a rolling basis beginning 3/1. **Types of Aid:** *Need-based scholarships/grants:* College/university scholarship or grant aid from institutional funds; Federal Nursing Scholarships; Federal Pell; Private scholarships; SEOG; State scholarships/grants. *Loans:* Direct PLUS loans; Direct Subsidized Stafford Loans; Direct Unsubsidized Stafford Loans. **Student Employment:** Federal Work-Study Program available. Institutional employment available. **Financial Aid Statistics:** 100% needy freshmen, 100% needy undergrads receive need-based scholarship or grant aid. 10% freshmen, 10% undergrads receive non-need-based scholarship or grant aid. 89% freshmen, 89% undergrads receive need-based self-help aid. 7% freshmen, 9% undergrads receive athletic scholarships. 99% freshmen, 95% undergrads receive any aid. 91% undergrads borrow to pay for school. Average cumulative indebtedness $22,976. **Criteria awarding aid:** *Non-need-based:* Academics, Athletics.

AMERICAN PUBLIC UNIVERSITY SYSTEM

111 W Congress St., Charles Town, WV 25414
Website: www.apus.edu

This proprietary school was founded in 1991.

RATINGS

Admissions Selectivity Rating: 60*   **Fire Safety Rating:** 60*   **Green Rating:** 60*

STUDENTS AND FACULTY

Enrollment: 35,656. **Student Body:** 36% female, 64% male, 1% international. Asian 2%, African American 16%, Caucasian 53%, Hispanic 14%, Native American 1%, Pacific Islander 1%, Two or more races 4%, Race unknown 7%.

ACADEMICS

Degrees: Associate; Bachelor's; Certificate; Doctoral degree research/scholarship; Master's; Post-bachelor's certificate. **Special Study Options:** Distance learning. **Career services:** Alumni network; Alumni services; Career assessment; Internships; Regional alumni.

CAMPUS LIFE

Environment: Rural.

ADMISSIONS

Freshman Admission Requirements: High school diploma is required and GED is accepted.

AMERICAN UNIVERSITY

4400 Massachusetts Ave, NW, Washington, DC 20016-8001
Phone: 202-885-6000 **Financial Aid Phone:** 202-885-6500
E-mail: admissions@american.edu **CEEB Code:** 5007
Fax: 202-885-1025 **Website:** www.american.edu **ACT Code:** 648

This private school, affiliated with the Methodist Church, was founded in 1893. It has a 84 acre campus.

RATINGS

Admissions Selectivity Rating: 92   **Fire Safety Rating:** 90   **Green Rating:** 98

STUDENTS AND FACULTY

Enrollment: 7,659. **Student Body:** 62% female, 38% male, 80% out-of-state, 10% international (109 countries represented). Asian 6%, African American

7%, Caucasian 55%, Hispanic 13%, Native American 1%, Pacific Islander 1%, Two or more races 5%, Race unknown 4%.
Retention and Graduation: 87% freshmen return for sophomore year. 75% freshmen graduate within 4 years. 79% freshmen graduate within 6 years.
Faculty: Student/faculty ratio 12:1. 818 full-time faculty, 94% hold PhDs, 21% are members of minority groups, 49% are women. 0% of classes are taught by teaching assistants.

ACADEMICS

Degrees: Associate; Bachelor's; Certificate; Doctoral degree—professional practice; Doctoral degree research/scholarship; Master's; Post-bachelor's certificate. **Classes:** Most classes have 10–19 students. **Most popular majors:** International Relations and Affairs; Political Science and Government, General; Business Administration and Management, General. **Special Study Options:** Accelerated program; Distance learning; Double major; Dual enrollment; English as a Second Language (ESL); Honors program; Independent study; Internships; Liberal arts/career combination; Student-designed major; Study abroad; Teacher certification program. **Honors programs:** The American University Honors Program (AU Honors) is a rigorous, hands-on, four-year program dedicated to exploring real world issues through an interdisciplinary lens. AU Honors students are dedicated, hard-working, intelligent, and committed to expanding their worldview. Enrolling small cohorts of talented students each year, the program is designed to challenge students with the desire and ability to perform at the highest level. AU Honors students receive a $30,000 undergraduate merit award each year—a $20,000 Presidential Scholarship and a $10,000 AU Honors Scholarship. **Combined degree programs:** BA/MA. **Disability Services offered:** Note-taking services; Reader services; Tape recorders; Tutors. **Career services:** Alumni network; Alumni services; Career assessment; Career/job search classes; Internships; Regional alumni.

FACILITIES

Housing: Coed dorms; Special housing for disabled students; Theme housing; 95% of campus accessible to physically disabled. **Special Academic Facilities/Equipment:** Student-run Radio and TV Facilities, Watkins Art Gallery, Katzen Arts Center, Experimental Theater,Greenberg Theater, Friedheim Journalism Center, William I Jacobs Fitness Center, Game Lab, Kay Spiritual Life Center (interdenominational), Language Resource Center, Multimedia Center.

CAMPUS LIFE

Environment: Metropolis. **Activities:** Campus Ministries; Choral groups; Concert band; Dance; Drama/theater; International Student Organization; Jazz band; Literary magazine; Model UN; Music ensembles; Musical theater; Opera; Pep band; Radio station; Student government; Student newspaper; Student-run film society; Symphony orchestra; Television station; Yearbook. 200 registered organizations, 12 honor societies, 17 religious organizations, on campus. **Athletics (Intercollegiate):** *Men:* basketball, cross-country, diving, soccer, swimming, track/field (outdoor), track/field (indoor), wrestling. *Women:* basketball, cross-country, diving, field hockey, lacrosse, soccer, swimming, track/field (outdoor), track/field (indoor), volleyball. **On-Campus Highlights:** Mary Graydon Center (student activties hub and dining venues). **Environmental Initiatives:** A Climate Action Plan which calls for achieving carbon neutrality by 2020.

ADMISSIONS

Test Scores: SAT Math middle 50% range 590–690. SAT EBRW middle 50% range 620–700. ACT middle 50% range 27–31. **Basis for Candidate Selection:** *Very important factors include:* rigor of secondary school record, academic GPA, level of applicant's interest. *Important factors include:* application essay, recommendation(s), extracurricular activities, talent/ability, character/personal qualities, volunteer work. *Other factors include:* standardized test scores, first generation, alumni/ae relation, geographical residence, racial/ethnic status, work experience. **Freshman Admission Requirements:** High school diploma is required and GED is accepted. *Academic units required:* 4 English, 3 math, 3 science, 2 science labs, 2 foreign language, 2 social studies, 3 academic electives. *Academic units recommended:* 4 English, 4 math, 4 science, 3 foreign language, 4 social studies, 4 academic electives. **Freshman Admission Statistics:** 18,545 applied, 36% admitted, 26% enrolled. **Transfer Admission Requirements:** College transcript(s), essay or personal statement. Minimum college GPA of 2.5 required. Lowest grade transferable C. **General Admission Information:** Application fee $75. Regular application deadline 1/15. Non-fall registration accepted. Admission may be deferred for a maximum of 1 year.

COSTS AND FINANCIAL AID

Annual tuition $50,542. Room and board $14,980. Required fees $819. Average book and supplies expense $800. **Required Forms and Deadlines:** CSS/Financial Aid PROFILE; FAFSA. **Notification of Awards:** Applicants will be notified of awards on or about 4/1. **Types of Aid:** *Need-based scholarships/grants:* College/university scholarship or grant aid from institutional funds; Federal Pell; Private scholarships; SEOG. *Loans:* Direct PLUS loans; Direct Subsidized Stafford Loans; Direct Unsubsidized Stafford Loans. **Student Employment:** Federal Work-Study Program available. Institutional employment available. **Financial Aid Statistics:** 93% needy freshmen, 90% needy undergrads receive need-based scholarship or grant aid. 24% freshmen, 26% undergrads receive non-need-based scholarship or grant aid. 89% freshmen, 90% undergrads receive need-based self-help aid. 2% freshmen, 2% undergrads receive athletic scholarships. 76% freshmen, 67% undergrads receive any aid. 63% undergrads borrow to pay for school. Average cumulative indebtedness $35,122. **Criteria awarding aid:** *Need-based:* Academics, Leadership. *Non-need-based:* Academics, Alumni affiliation, Athletics, Leadership, Minority status, Music/drama, Religious affiliation, State/district residency.

AMERICAN UNIVERSITY IN CAIRO

AUC Avenue, P.O. Box 74 New Cairo 11835, New Cairo,
Phone: 20.2.26151459 **Financial Aid Phone:** 2.02.2615-3865
E-mail: enrolauc@aucegypt.edu
Website: www.aucegypt.edu

This private school was founded in 1919. It has a 260 acre campus.

RATINGS
Admissions Selectivity Rating: 91   **Fire Safety Rating:** 94   **Green Rating:** 67

STUDENTS AND FACULTY
Enrollment: 5,586. **Student Body:** 55% female, 45% male.
Retention and Graduation: 92% freshmen return for sophomore year. 28% freshmen graduate within 4 years. **Faculty:** Student/faculty ratio 10:1. 425 full-time faculty, 73% hold PhDs, 0% are members of minority groups, 48% are women. 0% of classes are taught by teaching assistants.

ACADEMICS
Degrees: Bachelor's; Diploma; Master's. **Classes:** Most classes have 20–29 students. **Most popular majors:** Business Administration, Management and Operations, Other; Construction Engineering; Mechanical Engineering. **Special Study Options:** Double major; English as a Second Language (ESL); Independent study; Internships; Liberal arts/career combination; Study abroad. **Honors programs:** Honors Program in Political Science (BA). **Combined degree programs:** BA/MA. **Disability Services offered:** Note-taking services; Reader services. **Career services:** Alumni network; Alumni services; Career assessment; Career/job search classes; Internships; Regional alumni.

FACILITIES
Housing: Apartments for single students; Men's dorms; Special housing for disabled students; Theme housing; Women's dorms; 100% of campus accessible to physically disabled. **Special Academic Facilities/Equipment:** Rare Books and Special Collections Library http://library.aucegypt.edu/rbscl/index.html.

CAMPUS LIFE
Environment: Metropolis. **Activities:** Choral groups; Concert band; Dance; Drama/theater; International Student Organization; Model UN; Music ensembles; Student government; Student newspaper; Student-run film society. 60 registered organizations, on campus. **Athletics (Intercollegiate):** *Men:* basketball, boxing, fencing, football, gymnastics, handball, rugby, soccer, squash, swimming, table tennis, tennis, track/field (outdoor), volleyball, water polo, wrestling. *Women:* basketball, fencing, football, gymnastics, handball, soccer, squash, swimming, table tennis, tennis, track/field (outdoor), volleyball. **On-Campus Highlights:** Food Court. **Environmental Initiatives:** United Nations Global Compact: The UN Global Compact is the world's largest sustainability initiative, and it calls on global organizations to align their operations with 10 principles on human rights, labor, the environment and anti-corruption. The Office of Sustainability submitted AUC's first Communication on Engagement to the United Nations Global Compact headquarters in New York City. The report is inclusive of the state of operations of the Office and future initiatives. Further details on the work of the Office of Sustainability to integrate environmental and social sustainability into the culture and structure of the University referenced in the website. (https://www.unglobalcompact.org/participation/report/cop/create-and submit/detail/281861)

ADMISSIONS
Test Scores: SAT Math middle 50% range 540–630. SAT EBRW middle 50% range 510–590. **Basis for Candidate Selection:** *Very important factors include:* academic GPA, standardized test scores. *Important factors include:* recommendation(s), alumni/ae relation. *Other factors include:* application essay, extracurricular activities, character/personal qualities, geographical residence, volunteer work, work experience. **Freshman Admission Requirements:** High school diploma is required and GED is accepted. *Academic units recommended:* 3 English, 3 math, 2 science, 2 foreign language, 3 social studies. **Freshman Admission Statistics:** 2,933 applied, 53% admitted, 72% enrolled. **Transfer Admission Requirements:** High school transcript, college transcript(s), essay or personal statement, standardized test scores, statement of good standing from prior institution(s). Minimum college GPA of 2.0 required. Lowest grade transferable C. **General Admission Information:** Application fee $85. Regular application deadline 1/3. Non-fall registration accepted. Admission may be deferred for a maximum of one semester.

COSTS AND FINANCIAL AID
Required Forms and Deadlines: Institution's own financial aid form. **Types of Aid:** *Need-based scholarships/grants:* College/university scholarship or grant aid from institutional funds; Federal Pell; SEOG; State scholarships/grants. *Loans:* Direct PLUS loans; Direct Subsidized Stafford Loans; Direct Unsubsidized Stafford Loans. **Criteria awarding aid:** *Need-based:* Academics, Leadership. *Non-need-based:* Academics, Athletics, Music/drama.

AMHERST COLLEGE

220 South Pleasant Street, Amherst, MA 01002
Phone: 413-542-2328 **Financial Aid Phone:** 413-542-2296
E-mail: admission@amherst.edu **CEEB Code:** 3003
Fax: 413-542-2040 **Website:** www.amherst.edu **ACT Code:** 1774

This private school was founded in 1821. It has a 1020 acre campus.

RATINGS
Admissions Selectivity Rating: 98   **Fire Safety Rating:** 60*   **Green Rating:** 81

STUDENTS AND FACULTY
Enrollment: 1,839. **Student Body:** 50% female, 50% male, 86% out-of-state, 9% international (61 countries represented). Asian 15%, African American 10%, Caucasian 43%, Hispanic 13%, Native American <1%, Pacific Islander <1%, Two or more races 7%, Race unknown 3%.
Retention and Graduation: 97% freshmen return for sophomore year. 88% freshmen graduate within 4 years. 95% freshmen graduate within 6 years. **Faculty:** Student/faculty ratio 7:1. 231 full-time faculty, 95% hold PhDs, 24% are members of minority groups, 49% are women. 0% of classes are taught by teaching assistants.

ACADEMICS
Degrees: Bachelor's. **Classes:** Most classes have 10–19 students. Most lab/discussion sessions have 10–19 students. **Most popular majors:** Mathematics, General; Econometrics and Quantitative Economics. **Special Study Options:** Cross-registration; Double major; Exchange student program (domestic); Independent study; Internships; Student-designed major; Study abroad; Teacher certification program. **Honors programs:** Senior Honors Thesis: an opportunity to engage in extensive research with a professor as the student's adviser. **Career services:** Alumni network; Alumni services; Career assessment; Career/job search classes; Internships; Regional alumni.

FACILITIES
Housing: Coed dorms; Cooperative housing; Theme housing; Wellness housing. **Special Academic Facilities/Equipment:** Mead Art Museum, Beneski Museum of Natural History, Eli Marsh Gallery, Russian Center Art Gallery, Emily Dickinson Museum, Bassett Planetarium, Wilder Observatory, Wildlife Sanctuary.

CAMPUS LIFE
Environment: Town. **Activities:** Campus Ministries; Choral groups; Concert band; Dance; Drama/theater; International Student Organization; Jazz band; Literary magazine; Model UN; Music ensembles; Musical theater; Opera; Pep

band; Radio station; Student government; Student newspaper; Student-run film society; Symphony orchestra; Yearbook. 230 registered organizations, 8 religious organizations, on campus. **Athletics (Intercollegiate):** *Men:* baseball, basketball, cross-country, diving, football, golf, ice hockey, lacrosse, soccer, squash, swimming, tennis, track/field (outdoor), track/field (indoor). *Women:* basketball, cross-country, diving, field hockey, golf, ice hockey, lacrosse, soccer, softball, squash, swimming, tennis, track/field (outdoor), track/field (indoor), volleyball. **On-Campus Highlights:** Mead Art Museum.

ADMISSIONS

Freshman Academic Profile: 88% in top 10% of high school class, 98% in top 25% of high school class, 100% in top 50% of high school class. 60% from public high schools. **Test Scores:** SAT Math middle 50% range 720–790. SAT EBRW middle 50% range 690–760. ACT middle 50% range 31–34. **Basis for Candidate Selection:** *Very important factors include:* rigor of secondary school record, academic GPA, application essay, standardized test scores, recommendation(s), extracurricular activities, talent/ability, character/personal qualities. *Important factors include:* class rank, first generation, volunteer work. *Other factors include:* alumni/ae relation, geographical residence, racial/ethnic status. **Freshman Admission Requirements:** High school diploma or equivalent is not required. *Academic units recommended:* 4 English, 4 math, 3 science, 1 science labs, 3 foreign language, 2 social studies, 2 history. **Freshman Admission Statistics:** 10,569 applied, 11% admitted, 39% enrolled. **Transfer Admission Requirements:** High school transcript, college transcript(s), essay or personal statement, statement of good standing from prior institution(s). Minimum college GPA of 3.5 required. Lowest grade transferable C. **General Admission Information:** Application fee $65. Regular application deadline 1/1. Admission may be deferred for a maximum of 2 years.

COSTS AND FINANCIAL AID

Annual tuition $57,640. Room and board $15,310. Required fees $1,000. Average book and supplies expense $1,000. **Required Forms and Deadlines:** CSS/Financial Aid PROFILE; FAFSA; Noncustodial PROFILE. **Notification of Awards:** Applicants will be notified of awards on or about 4/1. **Types of Aid:** *Need-based scholarships/grants:* College/university scholarship or grant aid from institutional funds; Federal Pell; Private scholarships; SEOG; State scholarships/grants. *Loans:* Direct PLUS loans; Direct Subsidized Stafford Loans; Direct Unsubsidized Stafford Loans. **Student Employment:** Federal Work-Study Program available. Institutional employment available. **Financial Aid Statistics:** 99% needy freshmen, 99% needy undergrads receive need-based scholarship or grant aid. 0% freshmen, 0% undergrads receive non-need-based scholarship or grant aid. 86% freshmen, 88% undergrads receive need-based self-help aid. 0% freshmen, 0% undergrads receive athletic scholarships. 57% freshmen, 57% undergrads receive any aid. 28% undergrads borrow to pay for school. Average cumulative indebtedness $22,629.

ANDERSON UNIVERSITY (IN)

1100 East Fifth Street, Anderson, IN 46012-3495
Phone: 765-641-4080 **Financial Aid Phone:** 765-641-4182
E-mail: info@anderson.edu **CEEB Code:** 1016
Fax: 765-641-4091 **Website:** www.anderson.edu **ACT Code:** 1174

This private school, affiliated with the Church of God, was founded in 1917. It has a 163 acre campus.

RATINGS

Admissions Selectivity Rating: 82   **Fire Safety Rating:** 85   **Green Rating:** 71

STUDENTS AND FACULTY

Enrollment: 1,392. **Student Body:** 60% female, 40% male, 23% out-of-state, 2% international (11 countries represented). Asian <1%, African American 7%, Caucasian 81%, Hispanic 4%, Native American <1%, Pacific Islander <1%, Two or more races 5%, Race unknown 1%.
Retention and Graduation: 65% freshmen return for sophomore year. 48% freshmen graduate within 4 years. 57% freshmen graduate within 6 years.
Faculty: Student/faculty ratio 10:1. 105 full-time faculty, 68% hold PhDs, 9% are members of minority groups, 45% are women. 0% of classes are taught by teaching assistants.

ACADEMICS

Degrees: Associate; Bachelor's; Master's. **Classes:** Most classes have 10–19 students. Most lab/discussion sessions have fewer than 10 students. **Most popular majors:** Elementary Education and Teaching; Registered Nursing/

Registered Nurse; Marketing/Marketing Management, General. **Special Study Options:** Accelerated program; Cross-registration; Distance learning; Double major; Dual enrollment; Honors program; Independent study; Internships; Student-designed major; Study abroad; Teacher certification program.
Honors programs: The Honors Program at Anderson University is devoted to fostering within its honors scholars a passionate dedication to intellectual inquiry and spiritual development so that they may serve as vibrant leaders in their professions and in their communities. **Disability Services offered:** Note-taking services; Reader services; Tape recorders; Tutors. **Career services:** Alumni network; Alumni services; Career assessment; Career/job search classes; Internships.

FACILITIES

Housing: Apartments for married students; Apartments for single students; Coed dorms; Men's dorms; Wellness housing; Women's dorms; 95% of campus accessible to physically disabled. **Special Academic Facilities/Equipment:** Gustav Jeeninga Museum of Bible and Near Eastern Studies, Wilson Galleries, Archives of the Church of God. **Campus network:** 100% of classrooms, 100% of dorms, 100% of student union, 100% of libraries, 100% of dining areas, 90% of common outdoor areas, have wireless network access.

CAMPUS LIFE

Environment: Town. **Activities:** Campus Ministries; Choral groups; Concert band; Dance; Drama/theater; International Student Organization; Jazz band; Literary magazine; Model UN; Music ensembles; Musical theater; Opera; Pep band; Radio station; Student government; Student newspaper; Symphony orchestra; Yearbook. 42 registered organizations, 16 honor societies, 15 religious organizations, on campus. **Athletics (Intercollegiate):** *Men:* baseball, basketball, cheerleading, cross-country, football, golf, soccer, tennis, track/field (outdoor). *Women:* basketball, cheerleading, cross-country, golf, soccer, softball, tennis, track/field (outdoor), volleyball. **On-Campus Highlights:** Kardatzke Wellness Center. **Environmental Initiatives:** Recycling.

ADMISSIONS

Freshman Academic Profile: Average high school GPA 3.4. 20% in top 10% of high school class, 50% in top 25% of high school class, 74% in top 50% of high school class. 95% from public high schools. **Test Scores:** SAT Math middle 50% range 500–570. SAT EBRW middle 50% range 500–590. ACT middle 50% range 19–25. **Basis for Candidate Selection:** *Very important factors include:* rigor of secondary school record, recommendation(s), religious affiliation/commitment. *Important factors include:* class rank, academic GPA, standardized test scores, interview, extracurricular activities, character/personal qualities, volunteer work. *Other factors include:* application essay, talent/ability, first generation, alumni/ae relation, racial/ethnic status, level of applicant's interest. **Freshman Admission Requirements:** High school diploma is required and GED is accepted. *Academic units required:* 4 English, 3 math, 3 science, 3 science labs, 2 foreign language, 1 social studies, 1 history. *Academic units recommended:* 4 English, 4 math, 4 science, 4 science labs, 3 foreign language, 2 social studies, 2 history, 5 academic electives, 1 computer science, 1 visual/performing arts. **Freshman Admission Statistics:** 3,834 applied, 65% admitted, 16% enrolled. **Transfer Admission Requirements:** High school transcript, college transcript(s), standardized test scores, statement of good standing from prior institution(s). Minimum college GPA of 2.0 required. Lowest grade transferable C-. **General Admission Information:** Application fee $25. Priority deadline 1/1. Regular application deadline 7/1. Non-fall registration accepted. Admission may be deferred for a maximum of 1 year.

COSTS AND FINANCIAL AID

Annual tuition $29,950. Room and board $9,890. Required fees $500. Average book and supplies expense $1,200. **Required Forms and Deadlines:** FAFSA. **Notification of Awards:** Applicants will be notified of awards on a rolling basis beginning 2/15. **Types of Aid:** *Need-based scholarships/grants:* College/university scholarship or grant aid from institutional funds; Federal Pell; Private scholarships; SEOG; State scholarships/grants. *Loans:* Direct PLUS loans; Direct Subsidized Stafford Loans; Direct Unsubsidized Stafford Loans. **Student Employment:** Federal Work-Study Program available. **Financial Aid Statistics:** 82% needy freshmen, 78% needy undergrads receive need-based scholarship or grant aid. 100% freshmen, 93% undergrads receive non-need-based scholarship or grant aid. 76% freshmen, 78% undergrads receive need-based self-help aid. 0% freshmen, 0% undergrads receive athletic scholarships. **Criteria awarding aid:** *Need-based:* Religious affiliation. *Non-need-based:* Academics.

ANDERSON UNIVERSITY (SC)

316 Boulevard, Anderson, SC 29621
Phone: 864-231-2030 **Financial Aid Phone:** 864-231-2070
E-mail: admission@andersonuniversity.edu **CEEB Code:** 5008
Fax: 864-231-2033 **Website:** www.andersonuniversity.edu **ACT Code:** 3832

This private school, affiliated with the Southern Baptist Church, was founded in 1911. It has a 271 acre campus.

RATINGS
Admissions Selectivity Rating: 83   Fire Safety Rating: 84   Green Rating: 60*

STUDENTS AND FACULTY
Enrollment: 2,676. **Student Body:** 68% female, 32% male, 20% out-of-state, 2% international (29 countries represented). Asian 1%, African American 6%, Caucasian 83%, Hispanic 4%, Native American <1%, Pacific Islander <1%, Two or more races 2%, Race unknown 2%.
Retention and Graduation: 80% freshmen return for sophomore year. 59% freshmen graduate within 4 years. 66% freshmen graduate within 6 years. 40% grads go on to further study within 1 year. 13% grads pursue arts and sciences degrees. 1% grads pursue law degrees. 9% grads pursue business degrees. 3% grads pursue medical degrees. **Faculty:** Student/faculty ratio 14:1. 158 full-time faculty, 67% hold PhDs, 9% are members of minority groups, 54% are women. 0% of classes are taught by teaching assistants.

ACADEMICS
Degrees: Bachelor's; Doctoral degree—other; Doctoral degree—professional practice; Doctoral degree research/scholarship; Master's; Post-bachelor's certificate; Post-master's certificate. **Classes:** Most classes have 10–19 students. Most lab/discussion sessions have 10–19 students. **Most popular majors:** Business Administration and Management, General; Elementary Education and Teaching; Exercise Science and Kinesiology. **Special Study Options:** Accelerated program; Distance learning; Double major; Dual enrollment; Honors program; Independent study; Internships; Liberal arts/career combination; Study abroad; Teacher certification program. **Disability Services offered:** Note-taking services; Reader services; Tape recorders; Tutors. **Career services:** Alumni services; Career assessment; Internships; Regional alumni.

FACILITIES
Housing: Apartments for single students; Men's dorms; Women's dorms
Campus network: 98% of classrooms, 100% of dorms, 100% of libraries, have wireless network access.

CAMPUS LIFE
Environment: Town. **Activities:** Campus Ministries; Choral groups; Concert band; Dance; Drama/theater; International Student Organization; Jazz band; Literary magazine; Music ensembles; Musical theater; Student government. 42 registered organizations, 6 honor societies, 6 religious organizations, on campus. **Athletics (Intercollegiate):** *Men:* baseball, basketball, cross-country, equestrian sports, golf, soccer, tennis, track/field (outdoor), wrestling. *Women:* basketball, cheerleading, cross-country, equestrian sports, golf, soccer, softball, tennis, track/field (outdoor), volleyball. **On-Campus Highlights:** Java City.

ADMISSIONS
Freshman Academic Profile: Average high school GPA 3.7. 41% in top 10% of high school class, 62% in top 25% of high school class, 85% in top 50% of high school class. **Test Scores:** SAT Math middle 50% range 410–590. SAT EBRW middle 50% range 450–620. ACT middle 50% range 20–26. **Basis for Candidate Selection:** *Very important factors include:* rigor of secondary school record. *Important factors include:* class rank, academic GPA, standardized test scores, character/personal qualities. *Other factors include:* application essay, recommendation(s), extracurricular activities, talent/ability, volunteer work. **Freshman Admission Requirements:** High school diploma is required and GED is accepted. *Academic units required:* 4 English, 3 math, 3 science, 2 science labs, 2 foreign language. **Freshman Admission Statistics:** 2,277 applied, 69% admitted, 41% enrolled. **Transfer Admission Requirements:** College transcript(s). Minimum college GPA of 2.0 required. Lowest grade transferable C. **General Admission Information:** Application fee $40. Regular application deadline 8/1. Non-fall registration accepted. Admission may be deferred for a maximum of 1 year.

COSTS AND FINANCIAL AID
Annual tuition $26,820. Room and board $10,640. Required fees $3,160. Average book and supplies expense $1,200. **Required Forms and Deadlines:** FAFSA. **Notification of Awards:** Applicants will be notified of awards on a rolling basis beginning 3/1. **Types of Aid:** *Need-based scholarships/grants:* College/university scholarship or grant aid from institutional funds; Federal Pell; Private scholarships; SEOG; State scholarships/grants. *Loans:* Direct PLUS loans; Direct Subsidized Stafford Loans; Direct Unsubsidized Stafford Loans. **Student Employment:** Federal Work-Study Program available. Institutional employment available. **Financial Aid Statistics:** 100% needy freshmen, 97% needy undergrads receive need-based scholarship or grant aid. 32% freshmen, 27% undergrads receive non-need-based scholarship or grant aid. 52% freshmen, 62% undergrads receive need-based self-help aid. 6% freshmen, 6% undergrads receive athletic scholarships. 69% undergrads borrow to pay for school. Average cumulative indebtedness $32,609. **Criteria awarding aid:** *Need-based:* Academics, Art, Leadership, Minority status, Music/drama. *Non-need-based:* Academics, Art, Athletics, Leadership, Minority status, Music/drama, Religious affiliation, State/district residency.

ANGELO STATE UNIVERSITY

ASU Station #11014, San Angelo, TX 76909-1014
Phone: 325-942-2041 **Financial Aid Phone:** 325-942-2246
E-mail: admissions@angelo.edu **CEEB Code:** 6644
Fax: 325-942-2078 **Website:** www.angelo.edu **ACT Code:** 4164

This public school was founded in 1928. It has a 268 acre campus.

RATINGS
Admissions Selectivity Rating: 79   Fire Safety Rating: 96   Green Rating: 83

STUDENTS AND FACULTY
Enrollment: 6,031. **Student Body:** 57% female, 43% male, 3% out-of-state, 4% international (26 countries represented). Asian 1%, African American 7%, Caucasian 46%, Hispanic 38%, Native American <1%, Pacific Islander <1%, Two or more races 3%, Race unknown <1%.
Retention and Graduation: 69% freshmen return for sophomore year. 28% freshmen graduate within 4 years. **Faculty:** Student/faculty ratio 20:1. 309 full-time faculty, 77% hold PhDs, 19% are members of minority groups, 47% are women. 1% of classes are taught by teaching assistants.

ACADEMICS
Degrees: Bachelor's; Certificate; Doctoral degree—professional practice; Master's; Post-bachelor's certificate; Post-master's certificate. **Classes:** Most classes have 20–29 students. Most lab/discussion sessions have 20–29 students. **Most popular majors:** Multi-/Interdisciplinary Studies, Other; Business Administration and Management, General; Registered Nursing/Registered Nurse. **Special Study Options:** Distance learning; Double major; Dual enrollment; English as a Second Language (ESL); Honors program; Independent study; Internships; Study abroad; Teacher certification program. **Honors programs:** http://www.angelo.edu/dept/honors/index.php. **Disability Services offered:** Note-taking services; Reader services; Tape recorders; Tutors. **Career services:** Alumni services; Career assessment; Internships.

FACILITIES
Housing: Apartments for single students; Coed dorms; Special housing for disabled students; Theme housing; 99% of campus accessible to physically disabled. **Special Academic Facilities/Equipment:** Global Immersion Center—Combining the technology of an domed theater and a planetarium; West Texas Collection; Management, Instruction, and Research (Agricultural) Center; Food Safety and Product Development Lab; 6,000 acre ranch/farmland; Newly constructed greenhouse; New university museum finishing construction.

CAMPUS LIFE
Environment: City. **Activities:** Campus Ministries; Choral groups; Concert band; Dance; Drama/theater; International Student Organization; Jazz band; Literary magazine; Marching band; Music ensembles; Musical theater; Pep band; Radio station; Student government; Student newspaper; Symphony orchestra; Television station. 91 registered organizations, 16 honor societies, 7 religious organizations, 4 fraternities, 2 sororities, on campus. **Athletics (Intercollegiate):** *Men:* baseball, basketball, cross-country, football, track/field (outdoor). *Women:* basketball, cross-country, golf, soccer, softball, track/field (outdoor), volleyball. **On-Campus Highlights:** Houston Harte University Center. **Environmental Initiatives:** LEED Certification initiataives in all new buildings.

ADMISSIONS

Freshman Academic Profile: 13% in top 10% of high school class, 38% in top 25% of high school class, 72% in top 50% of high school class. **Test Scores:** SAT Math middle 50% range 460–550. SAT EBRW middle 50% range 470–570. ACT middle 50% range 17–23. **Basis for Candidate Selection:** *Very important factors include:* class rank, standardized test scores. *Important factors include:* rigor of secondary school record. *Other factors include:* academic GPA, extracurricular activities, talent/ability, character/personal qualities, first generation, geographical residence, state residency, volunteer work, work experience, level of applicant's interest. **Freshman Admission Requirements:** High school diploma is required and GED is accepted. *Academic units recommended:* 4 English, 4 math, 4 science, 2 foreign language, 3.5 social studies, 5.5 academic electives, 1 visual/performing arts. **Freshman Admission Statistics:** 3,913 applied, 77% admitted, 48% enrolled. **Transfer Admission Requirements:** College transcript(s), statement of good standing from prior institution(s). Minimum college GPA of 2.0 required. Lowest grade transferable D. **General Admission Information:** Application fee $40. Non-fall registration accepted. Admission may be deferred for a maximum of 1 Semester (Excluding Summer Terms).

COSTS AND FINANCIAL AID

Annual in-state tuition $5,516. Annual out-of-state tuition $17,786. Room and board $9,630. Required fees $3,495. Average book and supplies expense $1,200. **Required Forms and Deadlines:** FAFSA. **Notification of Awards:** Applicants will be notified of awards on a rolling basis beginning 4/1. **Types of Aid:** *Need-based scholarships/grants:* College/university scholarship or grant aid from institutional funds; Federal Nursing Scholarships; Federal Pell; Private scholarships; SEOG; State scholarships/grants. *Loans:* Direct PLUS loans; Direct Subsidized Stafford Loans; Direct Unsubsidized Stafford Loans. **Student Employment:** Federal Work-Study Program available. Institutional employment available. **Financial Aid Statistics:** 90% needy freshmen, 89% needy undergrads receive need-based scholarship or grant aid. 59% freshmen, 54% undergrads receive non-need-based scholarship or grant aid. 61% freshmen, 63% undergrads receive need-based self-help aid. 5% freshmen, 5% undergrads receive athletic scholarships. 71% freshmen, 64% undergrads receive any aid. 58% undergrads borrow to pay for school. Average cumulative indebtedness $24,269. **Criteria awarding aid:** *Need-based:* Academics. *Non-need-based:* Academics, Art, Athletics, Leadership, Music/drama, State/district residency.

ANNA MARIA COLLEGE

50 Sunset Lane, Paxton, MA 01612-1198
Phone: 508-849-3360 **Financial Aid Phone:** 508-849-3366
E-mail: admission@annamaria.edu **CEEB Code:** 3005
Fax: 508-849-3362 **Website:** www.annamaria.edu **ACT Code:** 3232

This private school, affiliated with the Roman Catholic Church, was founded in 1946. It has a 190 acre campus.

RATINGS

Admissions Selectivity Rating: 74   **Fire Safety Rating:** 83   **Green Rating:** 60*

STUDENTS AND FACULTY

Enrollment: 978. **Student Body:** 56% female, 44% male, 12% out-of-state, 1% international. Asian 1%, African American 6%, Caucasian 73%, Hispanic 5%, Native American <1%, Race unknown 14%.
Retention and Graduation: 70% freshmen return for sophomore year. 47% grads go on to further study within 1 year. 19% grads pursue arts and sciences degrees. 2% grads pursue law degrees. 1% grads pursue business degrees. 0% grads pursue medical degrees. **Faculty:** Student/faculty ratio 10:1. 50 full-time faculty, 72% hold PhDs, 0% are members of minority groups, 66% are women. 0% of classes are taught by teaching assistants.

ACADEMICS

Degrees: Associate; Bachelor's; Certificate; Master's; Post-bachelor's certificate; Post-master's certificate. **Classes:** Most classes have 10–19 students. Most lab/discussion sessions have fewer than 10 students. **Most popular majors:** Criminal Justice/Safety Studies; Business Administration and Management, General; Fire Science/Fire-fighting. **Special Study Options:** Accelerated program; Cooperative education program; Cross-registration; Double major; Independent study; Internships; Liberal arts/career combination; Student-designed major; Study abroad; Teacher certification program. **Honors**

programs: The Honors Program at Anna Maria College is designed to intellectually challenge highly motivated scholastic achievers. The Program is now a member of "National Collegiate Honors Programs," the national association of Honors Programs. Each Honors Program participant will have the opportunity to engage directly in foreign culture through interesting study abroad programs, such as a semester abroad experience, or a focused Urban Seminar that meets in a city like Paris, Vienna, Rome or Berlin that is sponsored by the College and supervised by a professor who oversees the program. **Combined degree programs:** BA/MA. **Disability Services offered:** Note-taking services; Reader services; Tape recorders; Tutors. **Career services:** Alumni services; Career assessment; Internships.

FACILITIES

Housing: Coed dorms; Special housing for disabled students; Wellness housing. **Special Academic Facilities/Equipment:** The Mondor-Eagan Library houses Anna Maria College's volumes, stacks, periodicals, study rooms, computer center, resource centers, and language laboratory. Classrooms are located in Trinity Hall, Cardinal Cushing Hall, and Foundress Hall. Foundress Hall houses the Zecco Performing Arts Center. Trinity Hall also houses the learning center. Among the other buildings are Madore Chapel, St. Joseph's Hall for sciences and Miriam Hall for music, performance, and art.

CAMPUS LIFE

Environment: Rural. **Activities:** Campus Ministries; Choral groups; Dance; Drama/theater; Jazz band; Pep band; Student government; Student newspaper; Yearbook. 17 registered organizations, 5 honor societies, 1 religious organizations, on campus. **Athletics (Intercollegiate):** *Men:* baseball, basketball, cross-country, football, golf, lacrosse, soccer, tennis. *Women:* basketball, field hockey, lacrosse, soccer, softball, tennis, volleyball. **On-Campus Highlights:** NEW: Residence Hall. **Environmental Initiatives:** There is a "Green Committee" that meets regularly to discuss environmental issues and ways that the college can be be more sustainable.

ADMISSIONS

Freshman Academic Profile: Average high school GPA 2.6. 2% in top 10% of high school class, 13% in top 25% of high school class, 41% in top 50% of high school class. **Test Scores:** SAT Math middle 50% range 378–480. SAT EBRW middle 50% range 378–490. ACT middle 50% range 18–21. **Basis for Candidate Selection:** *Very important factors include:* academic GPA, standardized test scores. *Other factors include:* rigor of secondary school record, application essay, recommendation(s), extracurricular activities, volunteer work, work experience, level of applicant's interest. **Freshman Admission Requirements:** High school diploma is required and GED is accepted. *Academic units required:* 4 English, 3 math, 3 science, 1 science labs, 2 foreign language, 2 social studies, 2 history, 4 academic electives. **Freshman Admission Statistics:** 712 applied, 87% admitted, 41% enrolled. **Transfer Admission Requirements:** High school transcript, college transcript(s), essay or personal statement, statement of good standing from prior institution(s). Minimum college GPA of 2.0 required. Lowest grade transferable C. **General Admission Information:** Application fee $40. Priority deadline 3/1. Non-fall registration accepted. Admission may be deferred for a maximum of 1 year.

COSTS AND FINANCIAL AID

Annual tuition $23,500. Room and board $9,350. Required fees $2,350. Average book and supplies expense $800. **Required Forms and Deadlines:** FAFSA; State aid form. **Notification of Awards:** Applicants will be notified of awards on a rolling basis beginning 4/1. **Types of Aid:** *Need-based scholarships/grants:* College/university scholarship or grant aid from institutional funds; Federal Pell; Private scholarships; SEOG; State scholarships/grants; United Negro College Fund. **Student Employment:** Federal Work-Study Program available. **Financial Aid Statistics:** 99% needy freshmen, 98% needy undergrads receive need-based scholarship or grant aid. 99% freshmen, 98% undergrads receive non-need-based scholarship or grant aid. 92% freshmen, 92% undergrads receive need-based self-help aid. 0% freshmen, 0% undergrads receive athletic scholarships. 98% freshmen, 95% undergrads receive any aid. **Criteria awarding aid:** *Non-need-based:* Academics, Alumni affiliation, Music/drama, Religious affiliation, State/district residency.

ANTIOCH COLLEGE

1 Morgan Place, Yellow Springs, OH 45387
Phone: 937-319-6082 Financial Aid Phone: 937-319-6016
E-mail: admission@antiochcollege.edu
Fax: 937-319-6085 Website: www.antiochcollege.edu ACT Code: 3232

This private school was founded in 1852. It has a 1100 acre campus.

RATINGS

Admissions Selectivity Rating: 77   Fire Safety Rating: 91   Green Rating: 90

STUDENTS AND FACULTY

Enrollment: 102. **Student Body:** 62% female, 38% male, 28% out-of-state, 0% international (3 countries represented). Asian 2%, African American 17%, Caucasian 54%, Hispanic 16%, Native American 1%, Pacific Islander 0%, Two or more races 6%, Race unknown 5%. **Retention and Graduation:** 47% freshmen return for sophomore year. 66% freshmen graduate within 4 years. 13% grads go on to further study within 1 year. 9% grads pursue arts and sciences degrees. **Faculty:** Student/faculty ratio 4:1. 24 full-time faculty, 71% hold PhDs, 33% are members of minority groups, 50% are women. 0% of classes are taught by teaching assistants.

ACADEMICS

Degrees: Bachelor's. **Classes:** Most classes have 10–19 students. **Most popular majors:** Liberal Arts and Sciences, General Studies and Humanities, Other; Psychology, General; Political Economy. **Special Study Options:** Cooperative education program; Cross-registration; Distance learning; Independent study; Internships; Liberal arts/career combination; Student-designed major; Study abroad. **Disability Services offered:** Note-taking services; Reader services; Tape recorders; Tutors. **Career services:** Alumni network; Alumni services; Career/job search classes; Internships; Regional alumni.

FACILITIES

Housing: Coed dorms; 86% of campus accessible to physically disabled. **Special Academic Facilities/Equipment:** Glen Helen—1,000-acre nature preserve WYSO—National Public Radio station Coretta Scott King Center for Cultural and Intellectual Freedom Wellness Center with competition-length, indoor swimming pool. **Campus network:** 100% of classrooms, 100% of dorms, 100% of student union, 100% of libraries, 100% of dining areas, 100% of common outdoor areas, have wireless network access.

CAMPUS LIFE

Environment: Rural. **Activities:** Literary magazine; Radio station; Student government; Student newspaper; Yearbook. 5 registered organizations, on campus. **On-Campus Highlights:** Wellness Center. **Environmental Initiatives:** Antioch College is committed to sustainable energy and building design and demonstrates this commitment in a variety of ways. Antioch College has an on-campus, five-acre solar farm of 3,300 solar panels that produces 1.2 million kilowatt hours of energy annually. This solar array provides enough power to offset the electrical consumption of the College's Central Geothermal Plant. The Central Geothermal Plant, which heats and cools campus buildings, offsets 2,900 tons of CO_2 when compared with traditional heating and cooling methods. The College tracks and monitors all energy consumption at 66% of campus buildings and provides real-time updates of that energy consumption through online data dashboards.

ADMISSIONS

Freshman Academic Profile: Average high school GPA 3.1. 68% from public high schools. **Test Scores:** SAT Math middle 50% range 490–680. SAT EBRW middle 50% range 575–670. ACT middle 50% range 26–31. **Basis for Candidate Selection:** *Very important factors include:* rigor of secondary school record, academic GPA, application essay, recommendation(s), talent/ability, character/personal qualities, level of applicant's interest. *Important factors include:* interview, extracurricular activities, volunteer work. *Other factors include:* class rank, standardized test scores, first generation, alumni/ae relation, racial/ethnic status. **Freshman Admission Requirements:** High school diploma is required and GED is accepted. *Academic units required:* 4 English, 3 math, 3 science, 4 social studies, 2 history. *Academic units recommended:* 4 math, 4 science, 2 foreign language, 4 academic electives. **Freshman Admission Statistics:** 134 applied, 84% admitted, 16% enrolled. **Transfer Admission Requirements:** High school transcript, college transcript(s), essay or personal statement, statement of good standing from prior institution(s). **General Admission Information:** Priority deadline 2/1. Admission may be deferred for a maximum of 1 year.

COSTS AND FINANCIAL AID

Annual tuition $35,949. Room and board $7,640. Required fees $1,149. Average book and supplies expense $1,200. **Required Forms and Deadlines:** FAFSA. **Types of Aid:** *Need-based scholarships/grants:* College/university scholarship or grant aid from institutional funds; Federal Pell; Private scholarships; State scholarships/grants. *Loans:* Direct PLUS loans; Direct Subsidized Stafford Loans; Direct Unsubsidized Stafford Loans. **Student Employment:** Institutional employment available. **Financial Aid Statistics:** 100% needy freshmen, 100% needy undergrads receive need-based scholarship or grant aid. 10% freshmen, 12% undergrads receive non-need-based scholarship or grant aid. 74% freshmen, 62% undergrads receive need-based self-help aid. 0% freshmen, 0% undergrads receive athletic scholarships. 100% freshmen, 100% undergrads receive any aid. 30% undergrads borrow to pay for school. Average cumulative indebtedness $17,000. **Criteria awarding aid:** *Need-based:* Academics, Minority status. *Non-need-based:* Academics.

ANTIOCH UNIVERSITY SANTA BARBARA

801 Garden Street, Santa Barbara, CA 93101
Phone: 805-962-8179 Financial Aid Phone: 805-962-8179
E-mail: admissions@antiochsb.edu
Fax: 805-962-4786 Website: www.antiochsb.edu

This private school was founded in 1852.

RATINGS

Admissions Selectivity Rating: 60*   Fire Safety Rating: 60*   Green Rating: 60*

STUDENTS AND FACULTY

Enrollment: 105. **Student Body:** 75% female, 25% male. **Faculty:** 16 full-time faculty, 0% hold PhDs, 0% are members of minority groups, 69% are women.

ACADEMICS

Degrees: Bachelor's; Master's. **Special Study Options:** Cross-registration; Double major; Independent study; Internships; Liberal arts/career combination; Study abroad; Teacher certification program; Weekend college.

CAMPUS LIFE

Environment: City.

ADMISSIONS

Freshman Admission Requirements: High school diploma is required and GED is accepted. **Transfer Admission Requirements:** High school transcript, college transcript(s), essay or personal statement, interview, statement of good standing from prior institution(s). Minimum college GPA of 2.0 required. Lowest grade transferable C. **General Admission Information:** Application fee $60.

COSTS AND FINANCIAL AID

Annual tuition $15,375. **Required Forms and Deadlines:** FAFSA; Institution's own financial aid form. **Notification of Awards: Types of Aid:** *Need-based scholarships/grants:* College/university scholarship or grant aid from institutional funds; Federal Pell; Private scholarships; SEOG; State scholarships/grants. **Financial Aid Statistics:** 54% needy undergrads receive need-based scholarship or grant aid. 0% undergrads receive non-need-based scholarship or grant aid. 54% undergrads receive need-based self-help aid. **Criteria awarding aid:** *Need-based:* Minority status.

APPALACHIAN STATE UNIVERSITY

Office of Admissions, Boone, NC 28608-2004
Phone: 828-262-2120 Financial Aid Phone: 828-262-2190
E-mail: admissions@appstate.edu CEEB Code: 5010
Fax: 828-262-3296 Website: www.appstate.edu ACT Code: 3062

This public school was founded in 1899. It has a 415 acre campus.

RATINGS

Admissions Selectivity Rating: 84   Fire Safety Rating: 95   Green Rating: 97

STUDENTS AND FACULTY

Enrollment: 17,266. **Student Body:** 56% female, 44% male, 8% out-of-state, <1% international (62 countries represented). Asian 2%, African American 3%,

Caucasian 83%, Hispanic 6%, Native American <1%, Pacific Islander <1%, Two or more races 4%, Race unknown 1%.
Retention and Graduation: 87% freshmen return for sophomore year. 52% freshmen graduate within 4 years. % freshmen graduate within 6 years. **Faculty:** Student/faculty ratio 16:1. 1,004 full-time faculty, 98% hold PhDs, 6% are members of minority groups, 48% are women. 1% of classes are taught by teaching assistants.

ACADEMICS
Degrees: Bachelor's; Doctoral degree research/scholarship; Master's; Post-bachelor's certificate; Post-master's certificate. **Classes:** Most classes have 20–29 students. Most lab/discussion sessions have 10–19 students. **Most popular majors:** Exercise Science and Kinesiology; Psychology, General; Registered Nursing/Registered Nurse. **Special Study Options:** Cross-registration; Distance learning; Double major; English as a Second Language (ESL); Exchange student program (domestic); Honors program; Independent study; Internships; Liberal arts/career combination; Student-designed major; Study abroad; Teacher certification program. **Honors programs:** Heltzer Honors College offers promising and highly motivated students opportunities by providing honors classes in many fields. **Disability Services offered:** Note-taking services; Reader services; Tape recorders; Tutors. **Career services:** Alumni network; Alumni services; Career assessment; Career/job search classes; Internships; Regional alumni.

FACILITIES
Housing: Apartments for single students; Coed dorms; Special housing for disabled students; Theme housing; Women's dorms; 100% of campus accessible to physically disabled. **Special Academic Facilities/Equipment:** NPHC Plots & Garden, Exercise Science Human Performance Lab, Dark Sky Observatory, Turchin Center for the Visual Arts, Living Learning Center, Beech Mountain Small Wind Research and Demonstration Site, Center for Judaic, Holocaust, and Peace Studies, Appalachian Special Collections, Biodiesel Research and Education Projects, Catherine J. Smith Gallery, F. Kenneth & Marjorie J. McKinney Geology Teaching Museum, Looking Glass Gallery, Outdoor Geology Lab, Rosen Outdoor Sculpture, AppalAir Meteorological Reporting Station, Solar Research and Teaching Lab, Sustainable Development Civic Garden, Language Lab.

CAMPUS LIFE
Environment: Village. **Activities:** Campus Ministries; Choral groups; Concert band; Dance; Drama/theater; International Student Organization; Jazz band; Literary magazine; Marching band; Model UN; Music ensembles; Musical theater; Opera; Pep band; Radio station; Student government; Student newspaper; Student-run film society; Symphony orchestra; Television station. 383 registered organizations, 18 honor societies, 26 religious organizations, 18 fraternities, 14 sororities, on campus. **Athletics (Intercollegiate):** *Men:* baseball, basketball, cross-country, football, golf, soccer, tennis, track/field (outdoor), track/field (indoor), wrestling. *Women:* basketball, cross-country, field hockey, golf, soccer, softball, tennis, track/field (outdoor), track/field (indoor), volleyball. **On-Campus Highlights:** Plemmons Student Union. **Environmental Initiatives:** Signatory of the American College and University Presidents Climate Commitment. On track with the target requirements. Climate Action Plan completed 2010. Climate neutrality date of 2050.

ADMISSIONS
Freshman Academic Profile: Average high school GPA 4.3. 19% in top 10% of high school class, 59% in top 25% of high school class, 93% in top 50% of high school class. 91% from public high schools. **Test Scores:** SAT Math middle 50% range 540–630. SAT EBRW middle 50% range 560–640. ACT middle 50% range 23–28. **Basis for Candidate Selection:** *Very important factors include:* rigor of secondary school record, class rank, academic GPA, standardized test scores. *Important factors include:* application essay, extracurricular activities, talent/ability, character/personal qualities, volunteer work. *Other factors include:* first generation, alumni/ae relation. **Freshman Admission Requirements:** High school diploma is required and GED is accepted. *Academic units required:* 4 English, 4 math, 3 science, 1 science labs, 2 foreign language, 1 social studies, 1 history. **Freshman Admission Statistics:** 16,154 applied, 69% admitted, 31% enrolled. **Transfer Admission Requirements:** High school transcript, college transcript(s). Minimum college GPA of 2.0 required. Lowest grade transferable C. **General Admission Information:** Application fee $65. Priority deadline 11/1. Regular application deadline 3/1. Non-fall registration accepted. Admission may be deferred for a maximum of 2 terms with approval of the Director.

COSTS AND FINANCIAL AID
Annual in-state tuition $4,242. Annual out-of-state tuition $19,049. Room and board $8,304. Required fees $3,122. Average book and supplies expense $700.

Required Forms and Deadlines: FAFSA. **Notification of Awards:** Applicants will be notified of awards on a rolling basis beginning 3/15. **Types of Aid:** *Need-based scholarships/grants:* College/university scholarship or grant aid from institutional funds; Federal Pell; Private scholarships; SEOG; State scholarships/grants. *Loans:* Direct PLUS loans; Direct Subsidized Stafford Loans; Direct Unsubsidized Stafford Loans. **Student Employment:** Federal Work-Study Program available. Institutional employment available. **Financial Aid Statistics:** 71% needy freshmen, 73% needy undergrads receive need-based scholarship or grant aid. 5% freshmen, 3% undergrads receive non-need-based scholarship or grant aid. 70% freshmen, 73% undergrads receive need-based self-help aid. 2% freshmen, 1% undergrads receive athletic scholarships. 69% freshmen, 66% undergrads receive any aid. 58% undergrads borrow to pay for school. Average cumulative indebtedness $23,230. **Criteria awarding aid:** *Non-need-based:* Academics, Alumni affiliation, Art, Athletics, Job skills, Leadership, Minority status, Music/drama, Religious affiliation, State/district residency.

AQUINAS COLLEGE

1607 Robinson Road SE, Grand Rapids, MI 49506-1799
Phone: 616-632-2900 **Financial Aid Phone:** 616-632-2893
E-mail: admissions@aquinas.edu **CEEB Code:** 1018
Fax: 616-732-4469 **Website:** www.aquinas.edu **ACT Code:** 1962

This private school was founded in 1886. It has a 107 acre campus.

RATINGS
Admissions Selectivity Rating: 72   **Fire Safety Rating:** 97   **Green Rating:** 98

STUDENTS AND FACULTY
Enrollment: 1,851. **Student Body:** 62% female, 38% male, 6% out-of-state, 1% international (8 countries represented). Asian 1%, African American 3%, Caucasian 85%, Hispanic 5%, Native American <1%, Pacific Islander 0%, Two or more races 2%, Race unknown 3%.
Retention and Graduation: 76% freshmen return for sophomore year. 17% grads go on to further study within 1 year. 7% grads pursue arts and sciences degrees. 3% grads pursue law degrees. 3% grads pursue business degrees. 2% grads pursue medical degrees. **Faculty:** Student/faculty ratio 13:1. 86 full-time faculty, 78% hold PhDs, 9% are members of minority groups, 44% are women.

ACADEMICS
Degrees: Associate; Bachelor's; Master's. **Classes:** Most classes have 10–19 students. Most lab/discussion sessions have 20–29 students. **Most popular majors:** Liberal Arts and Sciences/Liberal Studies. **Special Study Options:** Accelerated program; Cooperative education program; Cross-registration; Distance learning; Double major; Dual enrollment; Exchange student program (domestic); Honors program; Independent study; Internships; Liberal arts/career combination; Student-designed major; Study abroad; Teacher certification program. **Honors programs:** Insignis Honors Program. **Disability Services offered:** Note-taking services; Reader services; Tape recorders; Tutors. **Career services:** Alumni network; Alumni services; Career assessment; Career/job search classes; Internships.

FACILITIES
Housing: Apartments for single students; Coed dorms; Theme housing; Wellness housing; 95% of campus accessible to physically disabled. **Special Academic Facilities/Equipment:** Observatory and Jarecki Center for Advanced Learning featuring high-speed, two-way interactive video conferencing for courses and a virtual connection for external experts to interact with classes (sound, video, graphics) using a laptop computer equipped with a camera that is housed in a self-contained briefcase. The package includes all the technology needed to accomplish the connection through a standard phone jack. This "virtual faculty briefcase" can be shipped to a guest lecturer at another location anywhere in the world and they are able to conduct an interactive lecture or discussion with an Aquinas classroom. **Campus network:** 100% of classrooms, 100% of dorms, 100% of student union, 100% of libraries, 100% of dining areas, 30% of common outdoor areas, have wireless network access.

CAMPUS LIFE
Environment: Metropolis. **Activities:** Campus Ministries; Choral groups; Dance; Drama/theater; International Student Organization; Jazz band; Literary magazine; Model UN; Music ensembles; Radio station; Student government; Student newspaper. 63 registered organizations, 4 honor societies, 2 religious organizations, on campus. **Athletics (Intercollegiate):** *Men:* baseball, basketball, cheerleading, cross-country, golf, lacrosse, soccer, tennis, track/

field (outdoor), track/field (indoor). *Women:* basketball, cheerleading, cross-country, golf, lacrosse, soccer, softball, tennis, track/field (outdoor), track/field (indoor), volleyball. **On-Campus Highlights:** Sturrus Sports & Fitness Center. **Environmental Initiatives:** Sustainable Business practices restore environmental quality, promote stable and healthy communities, and increase long-term profitability. The Aquinas Sustainable Business Degree program fosters ecological and social intelligence in all business decisions and is the only undergraduate program of its kind in Michigan and possibly the United States. Aquinas also offers a Master of Sustainable Business.

ADMISSIONS

Freshman Academic Profile: Average high school GPA 3.5. 19% in top 10% of high school class, 45% in top 25% of high school class, 77% in top 50% of high school class. 80% from public high schools. **Test Scores:** ACT middle 50% range 21–26. **Basis for Candidate Selection:** *Very important factors include:* rigor of secondary school record, academic GPA, standardized test scores. *Other factors include:* class rank, application essay, recommendation(s), interview, extracurricular activities, talent/ability, character/personal qualities, first generation, volunteer work, work experience, level of applicant's interest. **Freshman Admission Requirements:** High school diploma is required and GED is not accepted. *Academic units recommended:* 4 English, 4 math, 3 science, 2 foreign language, 3 social studies. **Freshman Admission Statistics:** 1,842 applied, 100% admitted, 21% enrolled. **Transfer Admission Requirements:** High school transcript, college transcript(s). Minimum college GPA of 2.0 required. Lowest grade transferable D. **General Admission Information:** Priority deadline 5/1. Non-fall registration accepted. Admission may be deferred for a maximum of one year.

COSTS AND FINANCIAL AID

Annual tuition $27,332. Room and board $8,350. Required fees $394. Average book and supplies expense $800. **Required Forms and Deadlines:** FAFSA. **Notification of Awards:** Applicants will be notified of awards on a rolling basis beginning 3/1. **Types of Aid:** *Need-based scholarships/grants:* College/university scholarship or grant aid from institutional funds; Federal Pell; Private scholarships; SEOG; State scholarships/grants. *Loans:* Direct PLUS loans; Direct Subsidized Stafford Loans; Direct Unsubsidized Stafford Loans. **Student Employment:** Federal Work-Study Program available. Institutional employment available. **Financial Aid Statistics:** 100% needy freshmen, 100% needy undergrads receive need-based scholarship or grant aid. 74% freshmen, 69% undergrads receive non-need-based scholarship or grant aid. 100% freshmen, 100% undergrads receive need-based self-help aid. 2% freshmen, 6% undergrads receive athletic scholarships. 95% freshmen, 90% undergrads receive any aid. **Criteria awarding aid:** *Non-need-based:* Academics, Alumni affiliation, Art, Athletics, Leadership, Music/drama.

ARCADIA UNIVERSITY

450 South Easton Road, Glenside, PA 19038
Phone: 215-572-2910 **Financial Aid Phone:** 215-572-2980
E-mail: admiss@arcadia.edu **CEEB Code:** 2039
Fax: 215-572-4049 **Website:** www.arcadia.edu

This private school, affiliated with the Presbyterian Church, was founded in 1853. It has a 76 acre campus.

RATINGS

Admissions Selectivity Rating: 83   **Fire Safety Rating:** 60*   **Green Rating:** 60*

STUDENTS AND FACULTY

Enrollment: 2,003. **Student Body:** 68% female, 32% male, 41% out-of-state, 4% international. Asian 5%, African American 9%, Caucasian 65%, Hispanic 10%, Native American <1%, Pacific Islander <1%, Two or more races 5%, Race unknown 3%.
Retention and Graduation: 78% freshmen return for sophomore year. 63% freshmen graduate within 4 years. 66% freshmen graduate within 6 years.
Faculty: Student/faculty ratio 12:1. 165 full-time faculty, 90% hold PhDs, 15% are members of minority groups, 61% are women. 0% of classes are taught by teaching assistants.

ACADEMICS

Degrees: Bachelor's; Certificate; Doctoral degree—professional practice; Doctoral degree research/scholarship; Master's; Post-bachelor's certificate; Post-master's certificate. **Classes:** Most classes have 10–19 students. Most lab/discussion sessions have 10–19 students. **Most popular majors:** English

Language and Literature, General; Biology/Biological Sciences, General; Psychology, General. **Special Study Options:** Accelerated program; Cooperative education program; Cross-registration; Distance learning; Double major; Dual enrollment; Exchange student program (domestic); Honors program; Independent study; Internships; Liberal arts/career combination; Student-designed major; Study abroad; Teacher certification program. **Honors programs:** Honors program for invited students. Specialized opportunities for professional-level scholarship, co-curricular experiences, mentoring, academic service learning, and presentations are provided to ready these students for their professional careers and maximize their marketability. **Combined degree programs:** BA/MA. **Disability Services offered:** Reader services; Tape recorders; Tutors. **Career services:** Alumni network; Alumni services; Career assessment; Career/job search classes; Internships.

FACILITIES

Housing: Apartments for single students; Coed dorms; Special housing for disabled students; Wellness housing; Women's dorms; 99% of campus accessible to physically disabled. **Special Academic Facilities/Equipment:** Art gallery, language lab, observatory.

CAMPUS LIFE

Environment: Town. **Activities:** Choral groups; Dance; Drama/theater; Literary magazine; Music ensembles; Musical theater; Pep band; Radio station; Student government; Student newspaper; Television station; Yearbook. 11 honor societies, 4 religious organizations, on campus. **Athletics (Intercollegiate):** *Men:* baseball, basketball, cheerleading, golf, soccer, swimming, tennis. *Women:* basketball, cheerleading, field hockey, lacrosse, soccer, softball, swimming, tennis, volleyball. **On-Campus Highlights:** Student Commons.

ADMISSIONS

Freshman Academic Profile: Average high school GPA 3.7. 21% in top 10% of high school class, 50% in top 25% of high school class, 83% in top 50% of high school class. **Test Scores:** SAT Math middle 50% range 510–610. SAT EBRW middle 50% range 540–640. ACT middle 50% range 21–27. **Basis for Candidate Selection:** *Very important factors include:* rigor of secondary school record, academic GPA, standardized test scores, recommendation(s). *Important factors include:* class rank, application essay, extracurricular activities, alumni/ae relation. *Other factors include:* interview, talent/ability, character/personal qualities, volunteer work, work experience, level of applicant's interest. **Freshman Admission Requirements:** High school diploma is required and GED is accepted. *Academic units recommended:* 4 English, 3 math, 3 science, 3 science labs, 2 foreign language, 2 social studies, 2 history. **Freshman Admission Statistics:** 9,243 applied, 64% admitted, 8% enrolled. **Transfer Admission Requirements:** College transcript(s), essay or personal statement. Minimum college GPA of 2.5 required. Lowest grade transferable C-. **General Admission Information:** Application fee $30. Priority deadline 1/15. Regular application deadline 3/1. Non-fall registration accepted. Admission may be deferred for a maximum of 12 months.

COSTS AND FINANCIAL AID

Annual tuition $42,880. Room and board $13,800. Average book and supplies expense $1,500. **Required Forms and Deadlines:** FAFSA; Institution's own financial aid form. **Notification of Awards:** Applicants will be notified of awards on or about 11/20. **Types of Aid:** *Need-based scholarships/grants:* College/university scholarship or grant aid from institutional funds; Federal Pell; Private scholarships; SEOG; State scholarships/grants. *Loans:* Direct PLUS loans; Direct Subsidized Stafford Loans; Direct Unsubsidized Stafford Loans. **Student Employment:** Federal Work-Study Program available. **Criteria awarding aid:** *Non-need-based:* Academics, Alumni affiliation, Art, Leadership, Music/drama.

ARIZONA CHRISTIAN UNIVERSITY

2625 East Cactus Road, Phoenix, AZ 85032
Phone: 602-386-4100 **Financial Aid Phone:** (602) 386-4106
E-mail: admissions@arizonachristian.edu
Fax: 602-404-2159 **Website:** www.arizonachristian.edu

This private school was founded in 1960. It has a 17 acre campus.

RATINGS

Admissions Selectivity Rating: 83   **Fire Safety Rating:** 85   **Green Rating:** 60*

STUDENTS AND FACULTY

Enrollment: 175. **Student Body:** 57% female, 43% male, 27% out-of-state, 2% international. Asian 2%, African American 8%, Caucasian 79%, Hispanic

8%, Native American 1%, Pacific Islander 0%, Two or more races 0%, Race unknown <1%.
Retention and Graduation: 56% freshmen return for sophomore year. **Faculty:** Student/faculty ratio 16:1. 13 full-time faculty, 69% hold PhDs, 0% are members of minority groups, 0% are women.

ACADEMICS
Degrees: Associate; Bachelor's. **Special Study Options:** Dual enrollment; Independent study; Internships; Teacher certification program. **Disability Services offered:** Tutors.

FACILITIES
Housing: Apartments for single students; Men's dorms; Women's dorms. **Campus network:** 100% of classrooms, 90% of student union, 100% of libraries, have wireless network access.

CAMPUS LIFE
Environment: Metropolis. **Activities:** Campus Ministries; Choral groups; Drama/theater; Jazz band; Music ensembles; Musical theater; Yearbook. **Athletics (Intercollegiate):** *Men:* basketball. *Women:* basketball, volleyball.

ADMISSIONS
Freshman Academic Profile: 72% from public high schools. **Test Scores:** SAT Math middle 50% range 450–560. SAT EBRW middle 50% range 460–570. ACT middle 50% range 19–24. **Basis for Candidate Selection:** *Very important factors include:* rigor of secondary school record, academic GPA, application essay, standardized test scores, recommendation(s), religious affiliation/commitment. *Important factors include:* class rank, character/personal qualities, level of applicant's interest. *Other factors include:* interview, extracurricular activities, talent/ability. **Freshman Admission Requirements:** High school diploma is required and GED is accepted. **Freshman Admission Statistics:** 223 applied, 74% admitted, 61% enrolled. **Transfer Admission Requirements:** High school transcript, college transcript(s), essay or personal statement, statement of good standing from prior institution(s). Minimum college GPA of 2.0 required. Lowest grade transferable C. **General Admission Information:** Application fee $30. Priority deadline 3/1. Non-fall registration accepted. Admission may be deferred for a maximum of 1 semester.

COSTS AND FINANCIAL AID
Annual tuition $17,982. Room and board $7,374. Average book and supplies expense $1,600. **Required Forms and Deadlines:** FAFSA; Institution's own financial aid form. **Notification of Awards:** Applicants will be notified of awards on a rolling basis beginning 5/1. **Types of Aid:** *Need-based scholarships/grants:* College/university scholarship or grant aid from institutional funds; Federal Pell; Private scholarships; SEOG; State scholarships/grants. *Loans:* Direct PLUS loans; Direct Subsidized Stafford Loans; Direct Unsubsidized Stafford Loans. **Student Employment:** Federal Work-Study Program available. Institutional employment available. **Financial Aid Statistics:** 0% freshmen, 0% undergrads receive athletic scholarships. **Criteria awarding aid:** *Need-based:* Minority status. *Non-need-based:* Academics, Alumni affiliation, Athletics, Leadership, Music/drama, Religious affiliation.

ARIZONA STATE UNIVERSITY

Admissions Services Applicant Processing, Tempe, AZ 85287-1004
Phone: 480-965-7788 **Financial Aid Phone:** 855-278-5080
E-mail: admissions@asu.edu **CEEB Code:** 4007
Fax: 480-965-3610 **Website:** www.asu.edu **ACT Code:** 88

This public school was founded in 1885. It has a 661 acre campus.

RATINGS
Admissions Selectivity Rating: 80   **Fire Safety Rating:** 84   **Green Rating:** 98

STUDENTS AND FACULTY
Enrollment: 44,038. **Student Body:** 45% female, 55% male, 27% out-of-state, 9% international (99 countries represented). Asian 9%, African American 4%, Caucasian 49%, Hispanic 23%, Native American 1%, Pacific Islander <1%, Two or more races 5%, Race unknown 1%.

Retention and Graduation: 52% freshmen graduate within 4 years. 22% grads go on to further study within 1 year. 22% grads pursue arts and sciences degrees. <1% grads pursue law degrees. <1% grads pursue business degrees. <1% grads pursue medical degrees.

ACADEMICS
Degrees: Bachelor's; Certificate; Doctoral degree research/scholarship; Master's; Post-bachelor's certificate. **Most popular majors:** Computer Science; Biology/Biological Sciences, General; Business, Management, Marketing, and Related Support Services, Other. **Special Study Options:** Accelerated program; Cooperative education program; Distance learning; Double major; English as a Second Language (ESL); Honors program; Independent study; Internships; Liberal arts/career combination; Student-designed major; Study abroad; Teacher certification program. **Honors programs:** Barrett, the Honors College at ASU, is a selective, residential college that recruits academically outstanding undergraduates across the nation. Students enrolled in Barrett are part of both the honors college community and an ASU disciplinary college of their choice. They may major in any field offered on one of the four metropolitan Phoenix ASU campuses. Honors courses are taught by honors faculty within the college and within a variety of departments and programs. **Combined degree programs:** BA/MA; BA/MEng. **Disability Services offered:** Note-taking services; Reader services; Tape recorders; Tutors. **Career services:** Alumni network; Alumni services; Career assessment; Career/job search classes; Internships; Regional alumni.

FACILITIES
Housing: Apartments for single students; Coed dorms; Fraternity/sorority housing; Special housing for disabled students; 99% of campus accessible to physically disabled. **Special Academic Facilities/Equipment:** art, anthropology, geology, history, and sports museums, herbarium, planetarium, galleries, collections, biodesign institute, student pavilion, assorted research labs and facilities, digital labs, art, dance and development studios. **Campus network:** 100% of classrooms, 100% of dorms, 100% of student union, 100% of libraries, 100% of dining areas, 100% of common outdoor areas, have wireless network access.

CAMPUS LIFE
Environment: Metropolis. **Activities:** Campus Ministries; Choral groups; Concert band; Dance; Drama/theater; International Student Organization; Jazz band; Literary magazine; Marching band; Model UN; Music ensembles; Musical theater; Opera; Student government; Student newspaper; Student-run film society; Symphony orchestra. 847 registered organizations, 19 honor societies, 69 religious organizations, 42 fraternities, 33 sororities, on campus. **Athletics (Intercollegiate):** *Men:* baseball, basketball, cross-country, diving, football, golf, swimming, track/field (outdoor), wrestling. *Women:* basketball, cross-country, diving, golf, gymnastics, soccer, softball, swimming, tennis, track/field (outdoor), volleyball, water polo. **On-Campus Highlights:** ASU Memorial Union. **Environmental Initiatives:** The Carbon Project Launched in June 2018, the ASU Carbon Project purchases and generates carbon offsets for difficult to mitigate ASU carbon emissions. The Project is partially funded by a price on carbon for ASU-sponsored air travel. ASU is reducing its carbon footprint, reducing the need to acquire offsets in the future, telling the ASU story and connecting to local communities while also supporting academics and research through these efforts. The Project is currently offsetting over 45,000 MTCDE of air travel emissions through Community Offset Bundles. These bundles are market offsets coupled with local tree plantings. Trees are being planted throughout Phoenix and Tempe to combat urban heat island, improve walkability and shade, and improve air quality. When the trees mature, ASU will use a protocol, that will provide classroom experiences, to claim offsets from the trees.

ADMISSIONS
Freshman Academic Profile: Average high school GPA 3.5. 31% in top 10% of high school class, 61% in top 25% of high school class, 88% in top 50% of high school class. **Test Scores:** SAT Math middle 50% range 560–690. SAT EBRW middle 50% range 560–670. ACT middle 50% range 22–28. **Basis for Candidate Selection:** *Very important factors include:* class rank, academic GPA, standardized test scores. *Important factors include:* rigor of secondary school record. *Other factors include:* state residency. **Freshman Admission Requirements:** High school diploma is required and GED is accepted. *Academic units required:* 4 English, 4 math, 3 science, 3 science labs, 2 foreign language, 1 social studies, 1 history, 1 unit from above areas or other academic areas. **Freshman Admission Statistics:** 34,188 applied, 86% admitted, 34% enrolled. **Transfer Admission Requirements:** College transcript(s), standardized test scores. Minimum college GPA of 2.0 required. Lowest grade transferable C. **General Admission Information:** Application fee $50. Priority

deadline 1/15. Non-fall registration accepted. Admission may be deferred for a maximum of 2 years.

COSTS AND FINANCIAL AID

Annual in-state tuition $10,710. Annual out-of-state tuition $28,800. Room and board $13,164. Required fees $628. Average book and supplies expense $1,171. **Required Forms and Deadlines:** FAFSA. **Notification of Awards:** Applicants will be notified of awards on a rolling basis beginning 3/1. **Types of Aid:** *Need-based scholarships/grants:* College/university scholarship or grant aid from institutional funds; Federal Pell; Private scholarships; SEOG; State scholarships/grants; United Negro College Fund. *Loans:* Direct PLUS loans; Direct Subsidized Stafford Loans; Direct Unsubsidized Stafford Loans. **Student Employment:** Federal Work-Study Program available. Institutional employment available. **Financial Aid Statistics:** 99% needy freshmen, 94% needy undergrads receive need-based scholarship or grant aid. 16% freshmen, 10% undergrads receive non-need-based scholarship or grant aid. 46% freshmen, 59% undergrads receive need-based self-help aid. 1% freshmen, 1% undergrads receive athletic scholarships. 96.5% freshmen, 86.3% undergrads receive any aid. 45% undergrads borrow to pay for school. Average cumulative indebtedness $23,711. **Criteria awarding aid:** *Need-based:* Academics. *Non-need-based:* Academics, Art, Athletics, Leadership, Music/drama, State/district residency.

ARIZONA STATE UNIVERSITY AT THE DOWNTOWN PHOENIX CAMPUS

Admissions Services Applicant Processing, Tempe, AZ 85287-1004
Phone: (480) 965-7788 **Financial Aid Phone:** 855-278-5080
E-mail: admissions@asu.edu
Fax: (480) 965-3610 **Website:** https://campus.asu.edu/downtown/

This public school was founded in 2006. It has a 18 acre campus.

RATINGS

Admissions Selectivity Rating: 78   **Fire Safety Rating:** 84   **Green Rating:** 60*

STUDENTS AND FACULTY

Enrollment: 8,509. **Student Body:** 69% female, 31% male, 26% out-of-state, 2% international (31 countries represented). Asian 6%, African American 6%, Caucasian 44%, Hispanic 34%, Native American 2%, Pacific Islander <1%, Two or more races 5%, Race unknown 1%.
Retention and Graduation: 59% freshmen graduate within 4 years. 24% grads go on to further study within 1 year. 24% grads pursue arts and sciences degrees. <1% grads pursue medical degrees.

ACADEMICS

Degrees: Bachelor's; Certificate; Doctoral degree—professional practice; Doctoral degree research/scholarship; Master's; Post-bachelor's certificate; Post-master's certificate. **Most popular majors:** Journalism, Other; Criminal Justice/Law Enforcement Administration; Registered Nursing/Registered Nurse. **Special Study Options:** Accelerated program; Cooperative education program; Distance learning; Double major; Honors program; Independent study; Internships; Liberal arts/career combination; Student-designed major; Study abroad; Teacher certification program. **Honors programs:** Barrett, the Honors College at ASU, is a selective, residential college that recruits academically outstanding undergraduates across the nation. Students enrolled in Barrett are part of both the honors college community and an ASU disciplinary college of their choice. They may major in any field offered on one of the four metropolitan Phoenix ASU campuses. Honors courses are taught by honors faculty within the college and within a variety of departments and programs. **Combined degree programs:** BA/MA. **Disability Services offered:** Note-taking services; Reader services; Tape recorders; Tutors. **Career services:** Alumni network; Alumni services; Career assessment; Career/job search classes; Internships; Regional alumni.

FACILITIES

Housing: Apartments for single students; Coed dorms; Special housing for disabled students 99% of campus accessible to physically disabled. **Special Academic Facilities/Equipment:** Radio station, TV station, writing labs, tutoring, research labs, instructional kitchen, news studio, news museum.

CAMPUS LIFE

Environment: Metropolis. **Activities:** Campus Ministries; International Student Organization; Literary magazine; Radio station; Student government; Student newspaper; Television station. 110 registered organizations, 2 honor societies, 8 religious organizations, on campus. **On-Campus Highlights:** Sun Devil Fitness Center. **Environmental Initiatives:** The Carbon Project Launched in June 2018, the ASU Carbon Project purchases and generates carbon offsets for difficult to mitigate ASU carbon emissions. The Project is partially funded by a price on carbon for ASU-sponsored air travel. ASU is reducing its carbon footprint, reducing the need to acquire offsets in the future, telling the ASU story and connecting to local communities while also supporting academics and research through these efforts. The Project is currently offsetting over 45,000 MTCDE of air travel emissions through Community Offset Bundles. These bundles are market offsets coupled with local tree plantings. Trees are being planted throughout Phoenix and Tempe to combat urban heat island, improve walkability and shade, and improve air quality. When the trees mature, ASU will use a protocol, that will provide classroom experiences, to claim offsets from the trees.

ADMISSIONS

Freshman Academic Profile: Average high school GPA 3.5. 30% in top 10% of high school class, 65% in top 25% of high school class, 92% in top 50% of high school class. **Test Scores:** SAT Math middle 50% range 530–630. SAT EBRW middle 50% range 550–640. ACT middle 50% range 20–26. **Basis for Candidate Selection:** *Very important factors include:* class rank, academic GPA, standardized test scores. *Important factors include:* rigor of secondary school record. *Other factors include:* state residency. **Freshman Admission Requirements:** High school diploma is required and GED is accepted. *Academic units required:* 4 English, 4 math, 3 science, 3 science labs, 2 foreign language, 1 social studies, 1 history, 1 unit from above areas or other academic areas. **Freshman Admission Statistics:** 7,752 applied, 82% admitted, 26% enrolled. **General Admission Information:** Application fee $50. Priority deadline 1/15. Non-fall registration accepted. Admission may be deferred for a maximum of 2 years.

COSTS AND FINANCIAL AID

Annual in-state tuition $10,710. Annual out-of-state tuition $28,800. Room and board $14,924. Required fees $628. Average book and supplies expense $1,171. **Required Forms and Deadlines:** FAFSA. **Notification of Awards:** Applicants will be notified of awards on a rolling basis beginning 3/1. **Types of Aid:** *Need-based scholarships/grants:* College/university scholarship or grant aid from institutional funds; Federal Nursing Scholarships; Federal Pell; Private scholarships; SEOG; State scholarships/grants; United Negro College Fund. *Loans:* Direct PLUS loans; Direct Subsidized Stafford Loans; Direct Unsubsidized Stafford Loans. **Student Employment:** Federal Work-Study Program available. Institutional employment available. **Financial Aid Statistics:** 98% needy freshmen, 93% needy undergrads receive need-based scholarship or grant aid. 14% freshmen, 8% undergrads receive non-need-based scholarship or grant aid. 47% freshmen, 62% undergrads receive need-based self-help aid. 0% freshmen, 1% undergrads receive athletic scholarships. 98.5% freshmen, 90.1% undergrads receive any aid. 61% undergrads borrow to pay for school. Average cumulative indebtedness $25,136. **Criteria awarding aid:** *Need-based:* Academics. *Non-need-based:* Academics, Athletics, Leadership, State/district residency.

ARIZONA STATE UNIVERSITY AT THE WEST CAMPUS

Admissions Services Applicant Processing, Tempe, AZ 85287-1004
Phone: (480) 965-7788 **Financial Aid Phone:** 855-278-5080
E-mail: admissions@asu.edu **CEEB Code:** 4007
Fax: (480) 965-3610 **Website:** https://campus.asu.edu/west **ACT Code:** 880

This public school was founded in 1984. It has a 278 acre campus.

RATINGS

Admissions Selectivity Rating: 79   **Fire Safety Rating:** 84   **Green Rating:** 60*

STUDENTS AND FACULTY

Enrollment: 4,540. **Student Body:** 63% female, 37% male, 14% out-of-state, 4% international (33 countries represented). Asian 6%, African American 5%, Caucasian 41%, Hispanic 38%, Native American 1%, Pacific Islander <1%, Two or more races 3%, Race unknown 1%.

Retention and Graduation: 57% freshmen graduate within 4 years. % freshmen graduate within 6 years. 22% grads go on to further study within 1 year. 22% grads pursue arts and sciences degrees.

ACADEMICS

Degrees: Bachelor's; Certificate; Doctoral degree research/scholarship; Master's; Post-bachelor's certificate. **Most popular majors:** Biology/Biological Sciences, General; Psychology, General; Business, Management, Marketing, and Related Support Services, Other. **Special Study Options:** Accelerated program; Cooperative education program; Distance learning; Double major; English as a Second Language (ESL); Honors program; Independent study; Internships; Liberal arts/career combination; Student-designed major; Study abroad; Teacher certification program. **Honors programs:** Barrett, the Honors College at ASU, is a selective, residential college that recruits academically outstanding undergraduates across the nation. Students enrolled in Barrett are part of both the honors college community and an ASU disciplinary college of their choice. They may major in any field offered on one of the four metropolitan Phoenix ASU campuses. Honors courses are taught by honors faculty within the college and within a variety of departments and programs. **Combined degree programs:** BA/MA. **Disability Services offered:** Note-taking services; Reader services; Tape recorders; Tutors. **Career services:** Alumni network; Alumni services; Career assessment; Career/job search classes; Internships; Regional alumni.

FACILITIES

Housing: Apartments for single students; Coed dorms; Special housing for disabled students; 99% of campus accessible to physically disabled. **Special Academic Facilities/Equipment:** Herberger Young Scholars Academy-school for 7th grade thru 12th grade, art collections/galleries, dance studios, Little Theatre/black box, communication assessment learning lab, research labs, digital labs, music labs, cooking labs, performing arts studios, writing labs. **Campus network:** 100% of classrooms, 100% of dorms, 100% of student union, 100% of libraries, 100% of dining areas, 75% of common outdoor areas, have wireless network access.

CAMPUS LIFE

Environment: Metropolis. **Activities:** Campus Ministries; Choral groups; Dance; Drama/theater; International Student Organization; Musical theater; Student government; Student newspaper. 95 registered organizations, 5 honor societies, 3 religious organizations, on campus. **On-Campus Highlights:** Fletcher Library. **Environmental Initiatives:** The Carbon Project Launched in June 2018, the ASU Carbon Project purchases and generates carbon offsets for difficult to mitigate ASU carbon emissions. The Project is partially funded by a price on carbon for ASU-sponsored air travel. ASU is reducing its carbon footprint, reducing the need to acquire offsets in the future, telling the ASU story and connecting to local communities while also supporting academics and research through these efforts. The Project is currently offsetting over 45,000 MTCDE of air travel emissions through Community Offset Bundles. These bundles are market offsets coupled with local tree plantings. Trees are being planted throughout Phoenix and Tempe to combat urban heat island, improve walkability and shade, and improve air quality. When the trees mature, ASU will use a protocol, that will provide classroom experiences, to claim offsets from the trees.

ADMISSIONS

Freshman Academic Profile: Average high school GPA 3.5. 32% in top 10% of high school class, 66% in top 25% of high school class, 92% in top 50% of high school class. **Test Scores:** SAT Math middle 50% range 510–630. SAT EBRW middle 50% range 530–640. ACT middle 50% range 19–25. **Basis for Candidate Selection:** *Very important factors include:* class rank, academic GPA, standardized test scores. *Important factors include:* rigor of secondary school record. *Other factors include:* state residency. **Freshman Admission Requirements:** High school diploma is required and GED is accepted. *Academic units required:* 4 English, 4 math, 3 science, 3 science labs, 2 foreign language, 1 social studies, 1 history, 1 unit from above areas or other academic areas. **Freshman Admission Statistics:** 3,376 applied, 82% admitted, 29% enrolled. **General Admission Information:** Application fee $50. Priority deadline 1/15. Non-fall registration accepted. Admission may be deferred for a maximum of 2 years.

COSTS AND FINANCIAL AID

Annual in-state tuition $10,175. Annual out-of-state tuition $27,360. Room and board $11,914. Required fees $628. Average book and supplies expense $1,171. **Required Forms and Deadlines:** FAFSA. **Notification of Awards:** Applicants will be notified of awards on a rolling basis beginning 3/1. **Types of Aid:** *Need-based scholarships/grants:* College/university scholarship or grant aid from institutional funds; Federal Pell; Private scholarships; SEOG;

State scholarships/grants; United Negro College Fund. *Loans:* Direct PLUS loans; Direct Subsidized Stafford Loans; Direct Unsubsidized Stafford Loans. **Student Employment:** Federal Work-Study Program available. Institutional employment available. **Financial Aid Statistics:** 99% needy freshmen, 94% needy undergrads receive need-based scholarship or grant aid. 7% freshmen, 6% undergrads receive non-need-based scholarship or grant aid. 38% freshmen, 60% undergrads receive need-based self-help aid. 0% freshmen, 0% undergrads receive athletic scholarships. 97.9% freshmen, 89% undergrads receive any aid. 56% undergrads borrow to pay for school. Average cumulative indebtedness $25,021. **Criteria awarding aid:** *Need-based:* Academics. *Non-need-based:* Academics, Athletics, Leadership, State/district residency.

ARIZONA STATE UNIVERSITY POLYTECHNIC CAMPUS

Admissions Services Applicant Processing, Tempe, AZ 85287-1004
Phone: 480-965-7788 **Financial Aid Phone:** 855-278-5080
E-mail: admissions@asu.edu **CEEB Code:** 4007
Fax: (480) 965-3610 **Website:** https://campus.asu.edu/polytechnic **ACT Code:** 88

This public school was founded in 1996. It has a 575 acre campus.

RATINGS
Admissions Selectivity Rating: 77   **Fire Safety Rating:** 84   **Green Rating:** 60*

STUDENTS AND FACULTY
Enrollment: 4,606. **Student Body:** 33% female, 67% male, 21% out-of-state, 6% international (45 countries represented). Asian 7%, African American 5%, Caucasian 50%, Hispanic 24%, Native American 2%, Pacific Islander <1%, Two or more races 4%, Race unknown 1%.
Retention and Graduation: 42% freshmen graduate within 4 years. % freshmen graduate within 6 years. 27% grads go on to further study within 1 year. 27% grads pursue arts and sciences degrees.

ACADEMICS
Degrees: Bachelor's; Certificate; Doctoral degree research/scholarship; Master's; Post-bachelor's certificate. **Most popular majors:** Engineering, General; Biology/Biological Sciences, General; Business, Management, Marketing, and Related Support Services, Other. **Special Study Options:** Accelerated program; Cooperative education program; Distance learning; Double major; Honors program; Independent study; Internships; Liberal arts/career combination; Student-designed major; Study abroad; Teacher certification program. **Honors programs:** Barrett, the Honors College at ASU, is a selective, residential college that recruits academically outstanding undergraduates across the nation. Students enrolled in Barrett are part of both the honors college community and an ASU disciplinary college of their choice. They may major in any field offered on one of the four metropolitan Phoenix ASU campuses. Honors courses are taught by honors faculty within the college and within a variety of departments and programs. **Combined degree programs:** BA/MA; BA/MEng. **Disability Services offered:** Note-taking services; Reader services; Tape recorders; Tutors. **Career services:** Alumni network; Alumni services; Career assessment; Career/job search classes; Internships; Regional alumni.

FACILITIES
Housing: Apartments for single students; Coed dorms; Special housing for disabled students 99% of campus accessible to physically disabled. **Special Academic Facilities/Equipment:** variety of labs—fuel cell, perception, print and imaging, automation, technology, engineering, I3DEA, robotics, laser, photography, device and usability lab; 3-D printing technology, King Air simulator, tower simulator; altitude chamber **Campus network:** 100% of classrooms, 100% of dorms, 100% of student union, 100% of libraries, 100% of dining areas, 30% of common outdoor areas, have wireless network access.

CAMPUS LIFE
Environment: Metropolis. **Activities:** Campus Ministries; Dance; Model UN; Student government; Student newspaper. 77 registered organizations, 9 honor societies, 8 religious organizations, on campus. **On-Campus Highlights:** Sun Devil Fitness Center. **Environmental Initiatives:** The Carbon Project Launched in June 2018, the ASU Carbon Project purchases and generates carbon offsets for difficult to mitigate ASU carbon emissions. The Project is partially funded by a price on carbon for ASU-sponsored air travel. ASU is reducing its carbon footprint, reducing the need to acquire offsets in the future, telling the ASU story and connecting to local communities while also supporting academics and research through these efforts. The Project is currently offsetting over 45,000 MTCDE of air travel emissions through Community Offset Bundles. These

bundles are market offsets coupled with local tree plantings. Trees are being planted throughout Phoenix and Tempe to combat urban heat island, improve walkability and shade, and improve air quality. When the trees mature, ASU will use a protocol, that will provide classroom experiences, to claim offsets from the trees.

ADMISSIONS

Freshman Academic Profile: Average high school GPA 3.5. 25% in top 10% of high school class, 59% in top 25% of high school class, 90% in top 50% of high school class. **Test Scores:** SAT Math middle 50% range 570–660. SAT EBRW middle 50% range 550–640. ACT middle 50% range 21–27. **Basis for Candidate Selection:** *Very important factors include:* class rank, academic GPA, standardized test scores. *Important factors include:* rigor of secondary school record. *Other factors include:* state residency. **Freshman Admission Requirements:** High school diploma is required and GED is accepted. *Academic units required:* 4 English, 4 math, 3 science, 3 science labs, 2 foreign language, 1 social studies, 1 history, 1 unit from above areas or other academic areas. **Freshman Admission Statistics:** 3,328 applied, 84% admitted, 24% enrolled. **General Admission Information:** Application fee $50. Priority deadline 1/15. Non-fall registration accepted. Admission may be deferred for a maximum of 2 years.

COSTS AND FINANCIAL AID

Annual in-state tuition $10,175. Annual out-of-state tuition $27,360. Room and board $12,728. Required fees $628. Average book and supplies expense $1,171. **Required Forms and Deadlines:** FAFSA. **Notification of Awards:** Applicants will be notified of awards on a rolling basis beginning 3/1. **Types of Aid:** *Need-based scholarships/grants:* College/university scholarship or grant aid from institutional funds; Federal Pell; Private scholarships; SEOG; State scholarships/grants; United Negro College Fund. *Loans:* Direct PLUS loans; Direct Subsidized Stafford Loans; Direct Unsubsidized Stafford Loans. **Student Employment:** Federal Work-Study Program available. Institutional employment available. **Financial Aid Statistics:** 97% needy freshmen, 91% needy undergrads receive need-based scholarship or grant aid. 13% freshmen, 8% undergrads receive non-need-based scholarship or grant aid. 46% freshmen, 65% undergrads receive need-based self-help aid. 0% freshmen, 1% undergrads receive athletic scholarships. 95.1% freshmen, 85.2% undergrads receive any aid. 56% undergrads borrow to pay for school. Average cumulative indebtedness $26,096. **Criteria awarding aid:** *Need-based:* Academics. *Non-need-based:* Academics, Athletics, Leadership, State/district residency.

ARKANSAS STATE UNIVERSITY

PO Box 1570, State University, AR 72467
Phone: 870-972-3024 **Financial Aid Phone:** 870-972-2310
E-mail: admissions@astate.edu **CEEB Code:** 6011
Fax: 870-972-3406 **Website:** www.astate.edu **ACT Code:** 116

This public school was founded in 1909. It has a 1376 acre campus.

RATINGS

Admissions Selectivity Rating: 82   **Fire Safety Rating:** 90   **Green Rating:** 60*

STUDENTS AND FACULTY

Enrollment: 8,909. **Student Body:** 57% female, 43% male, 11% out-of-state, 6% international (50 countries represented). Asian 1%, African American 14%, Caucasian 74%, Hispanic 2%, Native American <1%, Pacific Islander <1%, Two or more races 2%, Race unknown 1%.
Retention and Graduation: 76% freshmen return for sophomore year. 22% grads go on to further study within 1 year. 15% grads pursue arts and sciences degrees. 1% grads pursue law degrees. 20% grads pursue business degrees. 24% grads pursue medical degrees. **Faculty:** Student/faculty ratio 17:1. 505 full-time faculty, 69% hold PhDs, 16% are members of minority groups, 53% are women. 4% of classes are taught by teaching assistants.

ACADEMICS

Degrees: Associate; Bachelor's; Doctoral degree—professional practice; Doctoral degree research/scholarship; Master's; Post-bachelor's certificate; Post-master's certificate. **Classes:** Most classes have 20–29 students. Most lab/discussion sessions have 10–19 students. **Most popular majors:** Registered Nursing/Registered Nurse; Early Childhood Education and Teaching; General Studies. **Special Study Options:** Accelerated program; Distance learning; Double major; Dual enrollment; English as a Second Language (ESL); Exchange student program (domestic); Honors program; Independent study; Internships; Study abroad; Teacher certification program. **Disability Services offered:** Note-taking

services; Reader services; Tape recorders; Tutors. **Career services:** Alumni services; Career assessment; Career/job search classes; Internships.

FACILITIES

Housing: Apartments for married students; Apartments for single students; Coed dorms; Fraternity/sorority housing; Men's dorms; Theme housing; Women's dorms; 90% of campus accessible to physically disabled. **Special Academic Facilities/Equipment:** Art gallery, museum of Native American cultures and Arkansas artifacts. Ecotoxicology research facility, electron microscope facility, geographic information system facility. Equine center.

CAMPUS LIFE

Environment: Town. **Activities:** Campus Ministries; Choral groups; Concert band; Dance; Drama/theater; International Student Organization; Jazz band; Marching band; Model UN; Music ensembles; Musical theater; Opera; Pep band; Radio station; Student government; Student newspaper; Symphony orchestra; Television station; Yearbook. 175 registered organizations, 10 honor societies, 25 religious organizations, 13 fraternities, 7 sororities, on campus. **Athletics (Intercollegiate):** *Men:* baseball, basketball, cross-country, football, golf, track/field (outdoor), track/field (indoor). *Women:* basketball, cross-country, golf, soccer, tennis, track/field (outdoor), track/field (indoor), volleyball. **On-Campus Highlights:** Student Union. **Environmental Initiatives:** Recycling.

ADMISSIONS

Freshman Academic Profile: Average high school GPA 3.5. 27% in top 10% of high school class, 49% in top 25% of high school class, 74% in top 50% of high school class. 93% from public high schools. **Test Scores:** SAT Math middle 50% range 470–540. SAT EBRW middle 50% range 400–540. ACT middle 50% range 21–26. **Basis for Candidate Selection:** *Very important factors include:* rigor of secondary school record, standardized test scores. *Important factors include:* class rank. *Other factors include:* recommendation(s), talent/ability. **Freshman Admission Requirements:** High school diploma is required and GED is accepted. *Academic units required:* 4 English, 4 math, 3 science, 3 science labs, 1 social studies, 2 history. *Academic units recommended:* 2 foreign language. **Freshman Admission Statistics:** 5,346 applied, 70% admitted, 42% enrolled. **Transfer Admission Requirements:** College transcript(s). Minimum college GPA of 2.0 required. Lowest grade transferable C. **General Admission Information:** Application fee $15. Regular application deadline 8/24. Non-fall registration accepted.no maximum.

COSTS AND FINANCIAL AID

Annual in-state tuition $6,060. Annual out-of-state tuition $12,120. Room and board $8,540. Required fees $2,140. Average book and supplies expense $1,000. **Required Forms and Deadlines:** FAFSA; Institution's own financial aid form. **Notification of Awards:** Applicants will be notified of awards on a rolling basis beginning 6/1. **Types of Aid:** *Need-based scholarships/grants:* College/university scholarship or grant aid from institutional funds; Federal Pell; Private scholarships; SEOG; State scholarships/grants. *Loans:* Direct PLUS loans; Direct Subsidized Stafford Loans; Direct Unsubsidized Stafford Loans. **Student Employment:** Federal Work-Study Program available. Institutional employment available. **Financial Aid Statistics:** 98% needy freshmen, 96% needy undergrads receive need-based scholarship or grant aid. 46% freshmen, 54% undergrads receive non-need-based scholarship or grant aid. 52% freshmen, 63% undergrads receive need-based self-help aid. 5% freshmen, 4% undergrads receive athletic scholarships. 92% freshmen, 79% undergrads receive any aid. 67% undergrads borrow to pay for school. Average cumulative indebtedness $27,400. **Criteria awarding aid:** *Need-based:* Academics. *Non-need-based:* Academics, Alumni affiliation, Art, Athletics, Leadership, Minority status, Music/drama, State/district residency.

ARKANSAS TECH UNIVERSITY

Doc Bryan; 1605 Coliseum Dr, Russellville, AR 72801
Phone: 479-968-0343 **Financial Aid Phone:** 479-968-0399
E-mail: tech.enroll@atu.edu **CEEB Code:** 6010
Fax: 479-964-0522 **Website:** http://www.atu.edu/ **ACT Code:** 0114

This public school was founded in 1909. It has a 559 acre campus.

RATINGS

Admissions Selectivity Rating: 76   **Fire Safety Rating:** 91   **Green Rating:** 60*

STUDENTS AND FACULTY

Enrollment: 8,799. **Student Body:** 55% female, 45% male, 4% out-of-state, 4% international (36 countries represented). Asian 1%, African American 10%,

Caucasian 76%, Hispanic 6%, Native American 1%, Pacific Islander <1%, Two or more races 3%, Race unknown 0%.
Retention and Graduation: 71% freshmen return for sophomore year.
Faculty: Student/faculty ratio 19:1. 349 full-time faculty, 62% hold PhDs, 9% are members of minority groups, 50% are women. 1% of classes are taught by teaching assistants.

ACADEMICS
Degrees: Associate; Bachelor's; Certificate; Master's; Post-master's certificate; Terminal Associate. **Classes:** Most classes have 20–29 students. Most lab/discussion sessions have 10–19 students. **Special Study Options:** Accelerated program; Distance learning; Double major; Dual enrollment; English as a Second Language (ESL); Honors program; Independent study; Internships; Study abroad; Teacher certification program; Weekend college. **Honors programs:** Arkansas Tech University's Honors Program is designed to elevate the college learning experience. To maintain a sense of community and enhance personal learning skills, honors courses are conscientiously designed to be small in size and to promote interaction, not only with peers, but with professors as well. Students admitted into the Honors program are not only educated for their university years, they are educated for life. **Disability Services offered:** Note-taking services; Reader services; Tape recorders; Tutors. **Career services:** Career assessment; Career/job search classes; Internships.

FACILITIES
Housing: Apartments for single students; Coed dorms; Fraternity/sorority housing; Men's dorms; Special housing for disabled students; Theme housing; Women's dorms; 100% of campus accessible to physically disabled. **Special Academic Facilities/Equipment:** 1. Arkansas Center for Energy, Natural Resources, and Environmental Studies. 2. Crabaugh Communications Center. 3. Arkansas Tech Museum. 4. Technology Center.

CAMPUS LIFE
Environment: Town. **Activities:** Campus Ministries; Choral groups; Concert band; Dance; Drama/theater; International Student Organization; Jazz band; Literary magazine; Marching band; Model UN; Music ensembles; Radio station; Student government; Student newspaper; Symphony orchestra; Television station. 110 registered organizations, 4 honor societies, 14 religious organizations, 7 fraternities, 4 sororities, on campus. **Athletics (Intercollegiate):** *Men:* baseball, basketball, cheerleading, football, golf. *Women:* basketball, cheerleading, cross-country, golf, softball, tennis, volleyball. **On-Campus Highlights:** Ross Pendergraft Library and Technology Center.

ADMISSIONS
Freshman Academic Profile: Average high school GPA 3.2. 13% in top 10% of high school class, 34% in top 25% of high school class, 65% in top 50% of high school class. **Test Scores:** SAT Math middle 50% range 440–590. SAT EBRW middle 50% range 440–530. ACT middle 50% range 18–25. **Basis for Candidate Selection:** *Very important factors include:* academic GPA, standardized test scores. *Important factors include:* rigor of secondary school record. *Other factors include:* class rank. **Freshman Admission Requirements:** High school diploma is required and GED is accepted. *Academic units required:* 4 English, 4 math, 3 science, 3 science labs, 2 foreign language, 3 social studies, 1 history, 4.5 academic electives, 0.5 visual/performing arts, 2 unit from above areas or other academic areas. **Freshman Admission Statistics:** 4,619 applied, 89% admitted, 49% enrolled. **Transfer Admission Requirements:** College transcript(s). Minimum college GPA of 2.0 required. Lowest grade transferable D. **General Admission Information:** Non-fall registration accepted. Admission may be deferred for a maximum of 1 semester.

COSTS AND FINANCIAL AID
Annual in-state tuition $6,450. Annual out-of-state tuition $12,900. Room and board $7,098. Required fees $1,290. Average book and supplies expense $1,410. **Required Forms and Deadlines:** FAFSA; Institution's own financial aid form. **Notification of Awards:** Applicants will be notified of awards on a rolling basis beginning 3/15. **Types of Aid:** *Need-based scholarships/grants:* Federal Pell; Private scholarships; SEOG; State scholarships/grants. *Loans:* Direct PLUS loans; Direct Subsidized Stafford Loans; Direct Unsubsidized Stafford Loans. **Student Employment:** Federal Work-Study Program available. Institutional employment available. **Financial Aid Statistics:** 84% needy freshmen, 82% needy undergrads receive need-based scholarship or grant aid. 70% freshmen, 49% undergrads receive non-need-based scholarship or grant aid. 63% freshmen, 69% undergrads receive need-based self-help aid. 4% freshmen, 3% undergrads receive athletic scholarships. **Criteria awarding aid:** *Non-need-based:* Academics, Athletics, Leadership, Music/drama, State/district residency.

ARLINGTON BAPTIST COLLEGE

Admissions Office, Arlington, TX 76012
Phone: 817-461-8741 **Financial Aid Phone:** 817-461-8741, ext 110
E-mail: jtaylor@arlingtonbaptistcollege.edu
Fax: 817-274-1138 **Website:** www.arlingtonbaptistcollege.edu **ACT Code:** 4163

This private school, affiliated with the Baptist Church, was founded in 1939. It has a 35 acre campus.

RATINGS
Admissions Selectivity Rating: 66   **Fire Safety Rating:** 94   **Green Rating:** 60*

STUDENTS AND FACULTY
Enrollment: 220. **Student Body:** 45% female, 55% male, 17% out-of-state, 1% international (1 country represented). Asian 0%, African American 18%, Caucasian 71%, Hispanic 8%, Native American 2%, Pacific Islander 0%, Two or more races 0%, Race unknown 0%.
Retention and Graduation: 51% freshmen return for sophomore year. 15% grads go on to further study within 1 year. **Faculty:** Student/faculty ratio 16:1. 12 full-time faculty, 17% hold PhDs, 0% are members of minority groups, 25% are women.

ACADEMICS
Degrees: Bachelor's; Certificate; Diploma; Master's. **Classes:** Most classes have fewer than 10 students. Most lab/discussion sessions have 20–29 students. **Most popular majors:** Pastoral Studies/Counseling; Religious Education; Theological and Ministerial Studies, Other. **Special Study Options:** Distance learning; Double major; Dual enrollment; External degree program; Teacher certification program.

FACILITIES
Housing: Men's dorms; Wellness housing; Women's dorms. **Special Academic Facilities/Equipment:** Heritage Collection. **Campus network:** 100% of classrooms, 100% of dorms, 100% of student union, 100% of libraries, 100% of dining areas, 100% of common outdoor areas, have wireless network access.

CAMPUS LIFE
Environment: Metropolis. **Activities:** Campus Ministries; Choral groups; Drama/theater; Student government; Yearbook. 2 religious organizations, on campus. **Athletics (Intercollegiate):** *Men:* baseball, basketball. *Women:* basketball, cheerleading, volleyball. **On-Campus Highlights:** Student Union Building.

ADMISSIONS
Freshman Academic Profile: Average high school GPA 2.9. 2% in top 10% of high school class, 21% in top 25% of high school class, 47% in top 50% of high school class. 80% from public high schools. **Basis for Candidate Selection:** *Very important factors include:* application essay, recommendation(s), religious affiliation/commitment. *Important factors include:* interview, level of applicant's interest. *Other factors include:* character/personal qualities. **Freshman Admission Requirements:** High school diploma is required and GED is accepted. *Academic units required:* 3 English, 2 math, 1 science, 2 social studies. **Freshman Admission Statistics:** 86 applied, 100% admitted, 63% enrolled. **Transfer Admission Requirements:** High school transcript, college transcript(s), essay or personal statement. Lowest grade transferable C. **General Admission Information:** Application fee $15. Priority deadline 8/1. Non-fall registration accepted. Admission may be deferred for a maximum of three semesters.

COSTS AND FINANCIAL AID
Annual tuition $7,100. Room and board $4,800. Required fees $740. Average book and supplies expense $750. **Required Forms and Deadlines:** FAFSA. **Notification of Awards:** Applicants will be notified of awards on a rolling basis beginning 12/1. **Types of Aid:** *Need-based scholarships/grants:* College/university scholarship or grant aid from institutional funds; Federal Pell; Private scholarships. *Loans:* Direct PLUS loans; Direct Subsidized Stafford Loans; Direct Unsubsidized Stafford Loans. **Student Employment:** Institutional employment available. **Financial Aid Statistics:** 100% needy freshmen, 100% needy undergrads receive need-based scholarship or grant aid. 0% freshmen, 0% undergrads receive non-need-based scholarship or grant aid. 0% freshmen, 0% undergrads receive need-based self-help aid. 0% freshmen, 0% undergrads receive athletic scholarships. 80% freshmen, 80% undergrads receive any aid. **Criteria awarding aid:** *Need-based:* Academics, Alumni affiliation, Leadership, Religious affiliation. *Non-need-based:* Academics, Leadership, Religious affiliation.

ART ACADEMY OF CINCINNATI

1212 Jackson Street, Cincinnati, OH 45202
Phone: 513-562-8740 **Financial Aid Phone:** 513-562-8751
E-mail: admissions@artacademy.edu
Fax: 513-562-8778 **Website:** www.artacademy.edu **ACT Code:** 003011

This private school was founded in 1887.

RATINGS
Admissions Selectivity Rating: 87   Fire Safety Rating: 60*   Green Rating: 60*

STUDENTS AND FACULTY
Enrollment: 159. **Student Body:** 64% female, 36% male, 1% international (2 countries represented). Asian 1%, African American 4%, Caucasian 90%, Hispanic 1%, Native American 0%, Race unknown 2%.
Faculty: Student/faculty ratio 6:1. 14 full-time faculty, 100% hold PhDs, 7% are members of minority groups, 57% are women. 0% of classes are taught by teaching assistants.

ACADEMICS
Degrees: Associate; Bachelor's; Master's. **Most popular majors:** Illustration; Graphic Design; Painting. **Special Study Options:** Cooperative education program; Cross-registration; Double major; Internships. **Disability Services offered:** Note-taking services; Tape recorders; Tutors.

FACILITIES
Housing: Coed dorms. **Campus network:** 100% of classrooms, 100% of dorms, 100% of student union, 100% of libraries, 100% of dining areas, 100% of common outdoor areas, have wireless network access.

CAMPUS LIFE
Environment: Metropolis. **Activities:** Literary magazine; Student government; Student-run film society; Yearbook. **On-Campus Highlights:** New Building. **Environmental Initiatives:** Received Leadership in Energy and Environmental Design (LEED) Green Building certification by the United States Green Building Council.

ADMISSIONS
Test Scores: SAT Math middle 50% range 420–570. SAT EBRW middle 50% range 480–600. ACT middle 50% range 18–24. **Basis for Candidate Selection:** *Very important factors include:* rigor of secondary school record, interview, talent/ability. *Important factors include:* academic GPA, application essay, *Other factors include:* standardized test scores, recommendation(s), extracurricular activities, character/personal qualities. **Freshman Admission Requirements:** High school diploma is required and GED is accepted. *Academic units recommended:* 4 English, 3 math, 2 science, 1 social studies. **Freshman Admission Statistics:** 192 applied, 57% admitted, 45% enrolled. **Transfer Admission Requirements:** High school transcript, college transcript(s), essay or personal statement, interview. Minimum college GPA of 2.0 required. Lowest grade transferable C. **General Admission Information:** Priority deadline 3/1. Regular application deadline 6/30. Non-fall registration accepted. Admission may be deferred for a maximum of one year.

COSTS AND FINANCIAL AID
Annual tuition $21,500. Room and board $6,000. Required fees $380. Average book and supplies expense $1,200. **Required Forms and Deadlines:** FAFSA; State aid form. **Notification of Awards:** Applicants will be notified of awards on a rolling basis beginning 3/1. **Types of Aid:** *Need-based scholarships/grants:* College/university scholarship or grant aid from institutional funds; Federal Pell; Private scholarships; SEOG; State scholarships/grants. *Loans:* Direct PLUS loans; Direct Subsidized Stafford Loans; Direct Unsubsidized Stafford Loans. **Student Employment:** Federal Work-Study Program available. Institutional employment available. **Financial Aid Statistics:** 95% undergrads receive any aid. **Criteria awarding aid:** *Non-need-based:* Academics, Art.

ART CENTER COLLEGE OF DESIGN

1700 Lida Street, Pasadena, CA 91103-1999
Phone: 626-396-2373 **Financial Aid Phone:** 626-396-2215
E-mail: admissions@artcenter.edu **CEEB Code:** 4009
Fax: 626-795-0578 **Website:** www.artcenter.edu **ACT Code:** 0164

This private school was founded in 1930. It has a 162.62 acre campus.

RATINGS
Admissions Selectivity Rating: 60*   Fire Safety Rating: 60*   Green Rating: 71

STUDENTS AND FACULTY
Enrollment: 2,003. **Student Body:** 54% female, 46% male, 35% international (51 countries represented). Asian 33%, African American 1%, Caucasian 14%, Hispanic 11%, Native American <1%, Pacific Islander <1%, Two or more races 4%, Race unknown <1%.
Retention and Graduation: 80% freshmen return for sophomore year. 30% freshmen graduate within 4 years. **Faculty:** Student/faculty ratio 9:1. 0% of classes are taught by teaching assistants.

ACADEMICS
Degrees: Bachelor's; Master's. **Classes:** Most classes have 10–19 students. **Most popular majors:** Engineering-Related Fields, Other; Illustration; Graphic Design. **Special Study Options:** Cross-registration; Exchange student program (domestic); Independent study; Internships; Study abroad. **Honors programs:** Semester of study following graduation for undergraduates—project focused. **Disability Services offered:** Note-taking services; Reader services; Tape recorders; Tutors. **Career services:** Alumni network; Alumni services; Career assessment; Career/job search classes; Internships; Regional alumni.

FACILITIES
98% of campus accessible to physically disabled. **Special Academic Facilities/ Equipment:** Sinclair Pavilion, Alyce de Roulet Williamson Gallery, Peter and Merle Mullin Gallery, The Hoffmitz Milken Center for Typography, Hutto-Patterson Exhibition Hall.

CAMPUS LIFE
Environment: City. **Activities:** Campus Ministries; International Student Organization; Student government; Student-run film society. 62 registered organizations, 1 religious organizations, on campus. **On-Campus Highlights:** Student Gallery. **Environmental Initiatives:** All building projects comply with CALGreen.

ADMISSIONS
Basis for Candidate Selection: *Very important factors include:* rigor of secondary school record, application essay, talent/ability. *Important factors include:* class rank, academic GPA, standardized test scores, character/personal qualities. *Other factors include:* recommendation(s), extracurricular activities, first generation, geographical residence, volunteer work, work experience. **Freshman Admission Requirements:** High school diploma is required and GED is accepted. **Transfer Admission Requirements:** College transcript(s), essay or personal statement. Lowest grade transferable C. **General Admission Information:** Application fee $50. Priority deadline 2/15. Non-fall registration accepted. Admission may be deferred for a maximum of 1 consecutive term.

COSTS AND FINANCIAL AID
Annual tuition $44,272. Average book and supplies expense $4,000. **Required Forms and Deadlines:** FAFSA; State aid form. **Notification of Awards:** Applicants will be notified of awards on a rolling basis beginning 4/1. **Types of Aid:** *Need-based scholarships/grants:* College/university scholarship or grant aid from institutional funds; Federal Pell; Private scholarships; SEOG; State scholarships/grants. *Loans:* Direct PLUS loans; Direct Subsidized Stafford Loans; Direct Unsubsidized Stafford Loans. **Student Employment:** Federal Work-Study Program available. Institutional employment available. **Criteria awarding aid:** *Need-based:* Art. *Non-need-based:* Art.

THE ART INSTITUTE OF ATLANTA

6600 Peachtree Dunwoody Road, Atlanta, GA 30328
Phone: (770) 394-8300 **Financial Aid Phone:** 770-689-4824
E-mail: aia-admis@aii.edu
Fax: (770) 394-0008 **Website:** http://www.artinstitutes.edu/atlanta/ **ACT Code:** 859

This proprietary school was founded in 1949. It has a 7 acre campus.

RATINGS

Admissions Selectivity Rating: 60*   **Fire Safety Rating:** 60*   **Green Rating:** 60*

STUDENTS AND FACULTY

Enrollment: 3,839. **Student Body:** 44% female, 56% male, <1% international (33 countries represented). Asian 1%, African American 36%, Caucasian 30%, Hispanic 3%, Native American <1%, Race unknown 30%. **Faculty:** Student/faculty ratio 21:1. 131 full-time faculty, 48% hold PhDs, 21% are members of minority groups, 45% are women.

ACADEMICS

Degrees: Associate; Bachelor's; Certificate; Diploma. **Classes:** Most classes have 10–19 students. **Most popular majors:** Culinary Arts/Chef Training; Interior Design; Commercial and Advertising Art. **Special Study Options:** Accelerated program; Distance learning; Dual enrollment; Honors program; Independent study; Internships; Study abroad; Weekend college. **Honors programs:** Design Honors Studio for graphic design students: students work with clients in the community. **Disability Services offered:** Note-taking services; Reader services; Tape recorders; Tutors. **Career services:** Alumni network; Alumni services; Career/job search classes; Internships.

FACILITIES

Housing: Coed dorms; 100% of campus accessible to physically disabled. **Special Academic Facilities/Equipment:** Art gallery, multi-camera video studio with digital and non-linear video editing suites, and an audio studio and control room featuring Protools stations. Professional photography studios with traditional and digital darkroom facilities containing high-end professional equipment such as the Imacon scanner, Cone Piezograph BandW printers, Epson 5500 printer, and Epson 10000 printer. Photographic video editing stations consist of Dual Processor G4s with cinema displays that are color managed with Greytag MacBeth equipment. Culinary facilities with five teaching kitchens and a dining lab.

CAMPUS LIFE

Environment: Metropolis. **Activities:** International Student Organization; Student government. 16 registered organizations, on campus. **On-Campus Highlights:** Gallery.

ADMISSIONS

Freshman Academic Profile: 97% from public high schools. **Basis for Candidate Selection:** *Very important factors include:* academic GPA, application essay, standardized test scores, recommendation(s). *Important factors include:* interview. **Freshman Admission Requirements:** High school diploma is required and GED is accepted. **Transfer Admission Requirements:** High school transcript, college transcript(s), essay or personal statement, interview, standardized test scores, statement of good standing from prior institution(s). Lowest grade transferable C. **General Admission Information:** Application fee $50. Non-fall registration accepted. Admission may be deferred for a maximum of 4 quarters.

COSTS AND FINANCIAL AID

Annual tuition $23,535. Room and board $9,984. Average book and supplies expense $1,700. **Required Forms and Deadlines:** FAFSA; State aid form. **Notification of Awards:** Applicants will be notified of awards on a rolling basis beginning 3/15. **Types of Aid:** *Need-based scholarships/grants:* College/university scholarship or grant aid from institutional funds; Federal Pell; Private scholarships; SEOG; State scholarships/grants. *Loans:* Direct PLUS loans; Direct Subsidized Stafford Loans; Direct Unsubsidized Stafford Loans. **Student Employment:** Federal Work-Study Program available. Institutional employment available. **Financial Aid Statistics:** 52% needy freshmen, 72% needy undergrads receive need-based scholarship or grant aid. 39% freshmen, 8% undergrads receive non-need-based scholarship or grant aid. 100% freshmen, 100% undergrads receive need-based self-help aid. 0% freshmen, 0% undergrads receive athletic scholarships. 19% freshmen, 81% undergrads receive any aid. **Criteria awarding aid:** *Non-need-based:* Academics, Art, State/district residency.

THE ART INSTITUTE OF BOSTON AT LESLEY UNIVERSITY

700 Beacon Street, Boston, MA 02215-2598
Phone: 617.585.6710 **Financial Aid Phone:** 617-349-8710
E-mail: admissions@aiboston.edu **CEEB Code:** 3777
Fax: 617.585.6720 **Website:** aiboston.edu **ACT Code:** 1850

This private school was founded in 1912. It has a 1 acre campus.

RATINGS

Admissions Selectivity Rating: 81   **Fire Safety Rating:** 89   **Green Rating:** 60*

STUDENTS AND FACULTY

Enrollment: 1,261. **Student Body:** 75% female, 25% male, 44% out-of-state, 3% international (15 countries represented). Asian 3%, African American 4%, Caucasian 63%, Hispanic 5%, Native American <1%, Race unknown 21%. **Retention and Graduation:** 66% freshmen return for sophomore year. **Faculty:** Student/faculty ratio 10:1. 73 full-time faculty, 68% hold PhDs, 12% are members of minority groups, 55% are women. 0% of classes are taught by teaching assistants.

ACADEMICS

Degrees: Associate; Bachelor's; Master's; Post-master's certificate. **Classes:** Most classes have 10–19 students. **Most popular majors:** Illustration; Photography; Graphic Design. **Special Study Options:** Accelerated program; Cross-registration; Distance learning; Double major; Dual enrollment; Exchange student program (domestic); Honors program; Independent study; Internships; Liberal arts/career combination; Student-designed major; Study abroad; Teacher certification program. **Honors programs:** First year foundation students are eligible for advanced placement, foundation studio exemptions, and enrolling in Honors Studio and Honors English. **Disability Services offered:** Note-taking services; Reader services; Tape recorders; Tutors. **Career services:** Alumni network; Alumni services; Career assessment; Career/job search classes; Internships; Regional alumni.

FACILITIES

Housing: Coed dorms; Women's dorms; 90% of campus accessible to physically disabled. **Special Academic Facilities/Equipment:** Art Gallery with regular shows of prominant artists; art library; applied art facilities, including state of the art photo and computer labs, annimation studio, ceramics studio, wood shop, metals studio, and printmaking studio. **Campus network:** 100% of classrooms, 100% of dorms, 100% of student union, 100% of libraries, 100% of dining areas, 50% of common outdoor areas, have wireless network access.

CAMPUS LIFE

Environment: Metropolis. **Activities:** Campus Ministries; Choral groups; Dance; Drama/theater; International Student Organization; Literary magazine; Musical theater; Student government; Student newspaper. 25 registered organizations, 2 honor societies, 2 religious organizations, on campus. **Athletics (Intercollegiate):** *Men:* basketball, cross-country, soccer, tennis, volleyball. *Women:* basketball, crew/rowing, cross-country, soccer, softball, tennis, volleyball. **On-Campus Highlights:** Gallery. **Environmental Initiatives:** Continual enhancement of recycling, waste management and composting programs on campus.

ADMISSIONS

Freshman Academic Profile: Average high school GPA 3.0. 12% in top 10% of high school class, 38% in top 25% of high school class, 70% in top 50% of high school class. 84% from public high schools. **Test Scores:** SAT Math middle 50% range 460–560. SAT EBRW middle 50% range 490–600. ACT middle 50% range 19–26. **Basis for Candidate Selection:** *Very important factors include:* rigor of secondary school record, academic GPA. *Important factors include:* class rank, application essay, standardized test scores, recommendation(s), interview, extracurricular activities, talent/ability, character/personal qualities. *Other factors include:* first generation, alumni/ae relation, geographical residence, racial/ethnic status, volunteer work, work experience, level of applicant's interest. **Freshman Admission Requirements:** High school diploma is required and GED is accepted. *Academic units required:* 4 English. *Academic units recommended:* 4 English, 1 math, 1 science, 1 foreign language, 2 social studies, 2 history, 2 academic electives, 2 unit from above areas or other academic areas. **Freshman Admission Statistics:** 2,523 applied, 65% admitted, 20% enrolled. **Transfer Admission Requirements:** High school transcript, college transcript(s), essay or personal statement, interview, statement of good standing from prior institution(s). Minimum college GPA of 2.0 required.

Lowest grade transferable C. **General Admission Information:** Application fee $50. Priority deadline 2/15. Non-fall registration accepted. Admission may be deferred for a maximum of 1 year.

COSTS AND FINANCIAL AID
Annual tuition $28,000. Room and board $13,250. Required fees $750. Average book and supplies expense $1,575. **Required Forms and Deadlines:** FAFSA. **Notification of Awards:** Applicants will be notified of awards on a rolling basis beginning 2/15. *Types of Aid: Need-based scholarships/grants:* College/university scholarship or grant aid from institutional funds; Federal Pell; Private scholarships; SEOG; State scholarships/grants. *Loans:* Direct PLUS loans; Direct Subsidized Stafford Loans; Direct Unsubsidized Stafford Loans. **Student Employment:** Federal Work-Study Program available. Institutional employment available. **Financial Aid Statistics:** 98% needy freshmen, 96% needy undergrads receive need-based scholarship or grant aid. 24% freshmen, 64% undergrads receive non-need-based scholarship or grant aid. 0% freshmen, 0% undergrads receive athletic scholarships. 70% freshmen, 70% undergrads receive any aid. **Criteria awarding aid:** *Need-based:* Academics, Art, Minority status. *Non-need-based:* Academics, Art, Leadership, Minority status, State/district residency.

THE ART INSTITUTE OF LAS VEGAS

2350 Corporate Cir., Henderson, NV 89074
Phone: 702.369.9944
E-mail: ailvadm@aii.edu
Fax: 702.992.8458 **Website:** http://www.artinstitutes.edu/lasvegas/

This proprietary school has a 1.5 acre campus.

RATINGS
Admissions Selectivity Rating: 71   **Fire Safety Rating:** 71   **Green Rating:** 60*

STUDENTS AND FACULTY
Enrollment: 1,301. **Student Body:** 48% female, 52% male, 0% international. Asian 12%, African American 9%, Caucasian 35%, Hispanic 14%, Native American 1%, Race unknown 28%.
Retention and Graduation: 54% freshmen return for sophomore year.
Faculty: Student/faculty ratio 17:1. 27 full-time faculty, 7% hold PhDs, 0% are members of minority groups, 22% are women. 0% of classes are taught by teaching assistants.

ACADEMICS
Degrees: Associate; Bachelor's. **Classes:** Most classes have 10–19 students. **Most popular majors:** Digital Communication and Media/Multimedia; Culinary Arts/Chef Training. **Special Study Options:** Distance learning; Independent study; Internships; Study abroad. **Disability Services offered:** Note-taking services; Reader services; Tape recorders; Tutors. **Career services:** Alumni network; Alumni services; Career assessment; Career/job search classes; Internships; Regional alumni.

FACILITIES
Housing: Apartments for single students; Wellness housing.

CAMPUS LIFE
Environment: City. **Activities:** Student-run film society. **On-Campus Highlights:** Student Lounge.

ADMISSIONS
Freshman Academic Profile: Average high school GPA 2.6. **Basis for Candidate Selection:** *Very important factors include:* application essay, interview. *Important factors include:* talent/ability, level of applicant's interest. *Other factors include:* academic GPA, standardized test scores, character/personal qualities. **Freshman Admission Requirements:** High school diploma is required and GED is accepted. **Freshman Admission Statistics:** 436 applied, 68% admitted, 78% enrolled. **Transfer Admission Requirements:** High school transcript, college transcript(s), essay or personal statement, interview, statement of good standing from prior institution(s). Minimum college GPA of 2.0 required. Lowest grade transferable 2. **General Admission Information:** Application fee $150. Non-fall registration accepted.

COSTS AND FINANCIAL AID
Annual tuition $21,552. **Student Employment:** Federal Work-Study Program available.

THE ART INSTITUTES INTERNATIONAL MINNESOTA

15 South 9th Street, Minneapolis, mn 55402
Phone: 612-332-3361 **Financial Aid Phone:** 612-332-3361
E-mail: aimadm@aii.edu
Fax: 612-332-3934 **Website:** www.artinstitutes.edu/minneapolis

This proprietary school was founded in 1997.

RATINGS
Admissions Selectivity Rating: 60*   **Fire Safety Rating:** 85   **Green Rating:** 60*

STUDENTS AND FACULTY
Enrollment: 1,974. **Student Body:** 61% female, 39% male, 20% out-of-state. **Retention and Graduation:** 60% freshmen return for sophomore year. **Faculty:** Student/faculty ratio 20:1. 56 full-time faculty, 0% hold PhDs, 0% are members of minority groups, 36% are women.

ACADEMICS
Degrees: Associate; Bachelor's; Certificate. **Special Study Options:** Distance learning; Independent study; Internships; Study abroad. **Disability Services offered:** Note-taking services; Tape recorders; Tutors. **Career services:** Alumni network; Alumni services; Career/job search classes; Internships; Regional alumni.

FACILITIES
Housing: Apartments for single students; 100% of campus accessible to physically disabled.

CAMPUS LIFE
Environment: Metropolis. **Activities:** Campus Ministries; International Student Organization; Literary magazine; Student newspaper. 16 registered organizations, 1 honor societies, on campus. **On-Campus Highlights:** School dining lab.

ADMISSIONS
Basis for Candidate Selection: *Very important factors include:* application essay, interview. *Important factors include:* talent/ability. *Other factors include:* academic GPA, standardized test scores, extracurricular activities, character/personal qualities, level of applicant's interest. **Freshman Admission Requirements:** High school diploma is required and GED is accepted. **Transfer Admission Requirements:** High school transcript, college transcript(s). **General Admission Information:** Application fee $50. Non-fall registration accepted.

COSTS AND FINANCIAL AID
Annual tuition $22,416. **Required Forms and Deadlines:** FAFSA. **Types of Aid:** *Need-based scholarships/grants:* College/university scholarship or grant aid from institutional funds; Federal Pell; Private scholarships; SEOG; State scholarships/grants; United Negro College Fund. *Loans:* Direct PLUS loans; Direct Subsidized Stafford Loans; Direct Unsubsidized Stafford Loans. **Student Employment:** Federal Work-Study Program available. Institutional employment available. **Criteria awarding aid:** *Need-based:* Academics.

ASHLAND UNIVERSITY

401 College Ave, Ashland, OH 44805
Phone: 419-289-5052 **Financial Aid Phone:** 419-289-5944
E-mail: enrollme@ashland.edu **CEEB Code:** 1021
Fax: 419-289-5999 **Website:** www.ashland.edu **ACT Code:** 3234

This private school, affiliated with the Church of Brethren, was founded in 1878. It has a 12 acre campus.

RATINGS
Admissions Selectivity Rating: 66   **Fire Safety Rating:** 73   **Green Rating:** 60*

STUDENTS AND FACULTY
Enrollment: 3,232. **Student Body:** 51% female, 49% male, 2% international (24 countries represented). Asian <1%, African American 13%, Caucasian 78%, Hispanic 3%, Native American <1%, Pacific Islander <1%, Two or more races 1%, Race unknown 2%.
Retention and Graduation: 77% freshmen return for sophomore year.
Faculty: 0% of classes are taught by teaching assistants.

ACADEMICS

Degrees: Associate; Bachelor's; Certificate; Diploma; Doctoral degree—professional practice; Master's; Post-master's certificate; Terminal Associate; Transfer Associate. **Most popular majors:** Education, General; Business/Commerce, General. **Special Study Options:** Accelerated program; Distance learning; Double major; Dual enrollment; English as a Second Language (ESL); Honors program; Independent study; Internships; Student-designed major; Study abroad; Teacher certification program. **Honors programs:** Ashland University Honors Program. **Disability Services offered:** Note-taking services; Reader services; Tape recorders; Tutors. **Career services:** Alumni network; Alumni services; Career assessment; Career/job search classes; Internships.

FACILITIES

Housing: Coed dorms; Fraternity/sorority housing; Special housing for disabled students; Theme housing; Women's dorms. **Special Academic Facilities/Equipment:** Numismatic Center, Patterson Technology Center, Coburn Art Gallery, Hugo Young Theatre, Studio Theatre, Instructional Resource Center, Ashbrook Center, and the Simulation Center at the College of Nursing and Health Sciences. **Campus network:** 100% of classrooms, 100% of dorms, 100% of student union, 100% of libraries, 100% of dining areas, 20% of common outdoor areas, have wireless network access.

CAMPUS LIFE

Environment: Town. **Activities:** Campus Ministries; Choral groups; Concert band; Dance; Drama/theater; International Student Organization; Jazz band; Marching band; Music ensembles; Musical theater; Pep band; Radio station; Student government; Student newspaper; Symphony orchestra; Television station. 102 registered organizations, 10 religious organizations, 4 fraternities, 4 sororities, on campus. **Athletics (Intercollegiate):** *Men:* baseball, basketball, cross-country, diving, football, golf, soccer, swimming, track/field (outdoor), track/field (indoor), wrestling. *Women:* basketball, cheerleading, cross-country, diving, golf, soccer, softball, swimming, tennis, track/field (outdoor), track/field (indoor), volleyball. **On-Campus Highlights:** Dwight Schar College of Education.

ADMISSIONS

Basis for Candidate Selection: *Very important factors include:* rigor of secondary school record, academic GPA, standardized test scores. *Important factors include:* class rank, extracurricular activities. *Other factors include:* application essay, recommendation(s), talent/ability, character/personal qualities, first generation, alumni/ae relation, religious affiliation/commitment, volunteer work, work experience. **Freshman Admission Requirements:** High school diploma is required and GED is accepted. **Freshman Admission Statistics:** 4,480 applied, 69% admitted, 19% enrolled. **Transfer Admission Requirements:** College transcript(s), essay or personal statement. Minimum college GPA of 2.5 required. Lowest grade transferable C-. **General Admission Information:** Non-fall registration accepted. Admission may be deferred for a maximum of 1 semester.

COSTS AND FINANCIAL AID

Annual tuition $20,332. Room and board $9,942. Required fees $1,010. **Required Forms and Deadlines:** FAFSA. *Types of Aid: Need-based scholarships/grants:* College/university scholarship or grant aid from institutional funds; Federal Pell; Private scholarships; SEOG; State scholarships/grants. *Loans:* Direct PLUS loans; Direct Subsidized Stafford Loans; Direct Unsubsidized Stafford Loans. **Student Employment:** Federal Work-Study Program available. Institutional employment available. **Criteria awarding aid:** *Need-based:* Academics, Job skills, Minority status. *Non-need-based:* Academics, Alumni affiliation, Art, Athletics, Job skills, Leadership, Minority status, Music/drama, Religious affiliation.

ASSUMPTION COLLEGE

The Office of Undergraduate Admissions, Assumption College,, Worcester, MA 01609-1296
Phone: 508-767-7285 **Financial Aid Phone:** 508-767-7158
E-mail: admiss@assumption.edu **CEEB Code:** 3009
Fax: (508) 799-4412 **Website:** http://www.assumption.edu **ACT Code:** 1782

This private school, affiliated with the Roman Catholic Church, was founded in 1904. It has a 180 acre campus.

RATINGS

Admissions Selectivity Rating: 77 **Fire Safety Rating:** 82 **Green Rating:** 60*

STUDENTS AND FACULTY

Enrollment: 1,955. **Student Body:** 56% female, 44% male, 34% out-of-state, 1% international (23 countries represented). Asian 3%, African American 5%, Caucasian 77%, Hispanic 7%, Native American <1%, Pacific Islander <1%, Two or more races 3%, Race unknown 4%.
Retention and Graduation: 85% freshmen return for sophomore year. 68% freshmen graduate within 4 years. 70% freshmen graduate within 6 years. 25% grads go on to further study within 1 year. 15% grads pursue arts and sciences degrees. 2% grads pursue law degrees. 3% grads pursue business degrees. 1% grads pursue medical degrees. **Faculty:** Student/faculty ratio 12:1. 137 full-time faculty, 92% hold PhDs, 7% are members of minority groups, 43% are women. 0% of classes are taught by teaching assistants.

ACADEMICS

Degrees: Bachelor's; Master's; Post-bachelor's certificate; Post-master's certificate. **Classes:** Most classes have 20–29 students. Most lab/discussion sessions have 10–19 students. **Most popular majors:** Accounting; Rehabilitation and Therapeutic Professions; Psychology, General. **Special Study Options:** Cross-registration; Double major; Honors program; Independent study; Internships; Student-designed major; Study abroad; Teacher certification program. **Honors programs:** The Assumption College Honors Program is a selective program designed to foster academic engagement inside and outside the classroom. The program promotes intellectual friendship and discourse while providing a common, intensive learning experience in small seminar classes. **Combined degree programs:** BA/MA. **Disability Services offered:** Note-taking services; Reader services; Tape recorders; Tutors. **Career services:** Alumni network; Career assessment; Career/job search classes; Internships; Regional alumni.

FACILITIES

Housing: Coed dorms; Special housing for disabled students; Theme housing; Wellness housing; Women's dorms; 71% of campus accessible to physically disabled. **Special Academic Facilities/Equipment:** French Institute museum, Institute for Social and Rehabilitation Services, language lab, media center Living/Learning Center Testa Science Center Information Technology Center.

CAMPUS LIFE

Environment: City. **Activities:** Campus Ministries; Choral groups; Concert band; Dance; Drama/theater; Jazz band; Literary magazine; Music ensembles; Musical theater; Pep band; Student government; Student newspaper; Student-run film society; Television station; Yearbook. 60 registered organizations, 12 honor societies, 1 religious organizations, on campus. **Athletics (Intercollegiate):** *Men:* baseball, basketball, cross-country, football, golf, ice hockey, lacrosse, soccer, tennis, track/field (outdoor), track/field (indoor). *Women:* basketball, crew/rowing, cross-country, field hockey, lacrosse, soccer, softball, swimming, tennis, track/field (outdoor), track/field (indoor), volleyball. **On-Campus Highlights:** Testa Science Center.

ADMISSIONS

Freshman Academic Profile: Average high school GPA 3.4. 14% in top 10% of high school class, 41% in top 25% of high school class, 76% in top 50% of high school class. 68% from public high schools. **Test Scores:** SAT Math middle 50% range 540–610. SAT EBRW middle 50% range 550–628. ACT middle 50% range 23–28. **Basis for Candidate Selection:** *Very important factors include:* academic GPA, application essay. *Important factors include:* rigor of secondary school record, recommendation(s), interview, volunteer work. *Other factors include:* class rank, standardized test scores, extracurricular activities, talent/ability, character/personal qualities, first generation, alumni/ae relation, racial/ethnic status. **Freshman Admission Requirements:** High school diploma is required and GED is accepted. *Academic units required:* 4 English, 3 math, 2 science, 2 foreign language, 2 history, 5 academic electives. **Freshman Admission Statistics:** 4,465 applied, 81% admitted, 16% enrolled. **Transfer Admission Requirements:** High school transcript, college transcript(s), essay or personal statement, statement of good standing from prior institution(s). Minimum college GPA of 2.5 required. Lowest grade transferable C. **General Admission Information:** Application fee $50. Regular application deadline 2/15. Non-fall registration accepted. Admission may be deferred for a maximum of 1 year.

COSTS AND FINANCIAL AID

Annual tuition $41,516. Room and board $13,128. Required fees $800. Average book and supplies expense $1,000. **Required Forms and Deadlines:** FAFSA. **Notification of Awards:** Applicants will be notified of awards on a rolling basis beginning 2/16. **Types of Aid:** *Need-based scholarships/grants:* College/university scholarship or grant aid from institutional funds; Federal Pell; Private scholarships; SEOG; State scholarships/grants. *Loans:* Direct PLUS loans; Direct Subsidized Stafford Loans; Direct Unsubsidized Stafford Loans. **Student Employment:** Federal Work-Study Program available. Institutional employment available. **Financial Aid Statistics:** 100% needy freshmen, 100% needy undergrads receive need-based scholarship or grant aid. 24% freshmen, 20% undergrads receive non-need-based scholarship or grant aid. 74% freshmen, 79% undergrads receive need-based self-help aid. 4% freshmen, 5% undergrads receive athletic scholarships. 98.4% freshmen, 98% undergrads receive any aid. **Criteria awarding aid:** *Need-based:* Academics, Athletics. *Non-need-based:* Academics, Athletics, Music/drama.

ATHABASCA UNIVERSITY

1 University Drive, Athabasca, AB T9S 3A3
Phone: 800-788-9041 **Financial Aid Phone:** 780-675-6147
Fax: 780-675-6145 **Website:** www.athabascau.ca

This public school was founded in 1970.

RATINGS
Admissions Selectivity Rating: 68   **Fire Safety Rating:** 60*   **Green Rating:** 60*

STUDENTS AND FACULTY
Enrollment: 35,071. **Student Body:** 61% out-of-state, 90 countries represented.

ACADEMICS
Degrees: Bachelor's; Certificate; Diploma; Master's; Post-bachelor's certificate; Post-master's certificate. **Most popular majors:** Criminal Justice/Safety Studies; Elementary Education and Teaching. **Special Study Options:** Accelerated program; Cross-registration; Distance learning; Double major; English as a Second Language (ESL); External degree program. **Disability Services offered:** Tape recorders; Tutors.

CAMPUS LIFE
Environment: Rural. **Activities:** Student government.

ADMISSIONS
Freshman Admission Statistics: 38,876 applied, 100% admitted, 100% enrolled. **Transfer Admission Requirements:** High school transcript, college transcript(s). **General Admission Information:** Application fee $100. Non-fall registration accepted. Admission may be deferred for a maximum of 1 year.

COSTS AND FINANCIAL AID
Annual in-state tuition $657. Annual out-of-state tuition $762.

AUBURN UNIVERSITY

The Quad Center, Auburn, AL 36849-5149
Phone: 334-844-6425 **Financial Aid Phone:** 334-844-4634
E-mail: admissions@auburn.edu **CEEB Code:** 1005
Fax: 334-844-6436 **Website:** www.auburn.edu **ACT Code:** 11

This public school was founded in 1856. It has a 1875 acre campus.

RATINGS
Admissions Selectivity Rating: 83   **Fire Safety Rating:** 94   **Green Rating:** 87

STUDENTS AND FACULTY
Enrollment: 24,209. **Student Body:** 48% female, 52% male, 37% out-of-state, 6% international (66 countries represented). Asian 2%, African American 5%, Caucasian 80%, Hispanic 3%, Native American <1%, Pacific Islander <1%, Two or more races 3%, Race unknown <1%.
Retention and Graduation: 91% freshmen return for sophomore year. 50% freshmen graduate within 4 years. 79% freshmen graduate within 6 years. 18% grads go on to further study within 1 year. 4% grads pursue arts and sciences degrees. 1% grads pursue law degrees. 2% grads pursue business degrees. 4% grads pursue medical degrees. **Faculty:** Student/faculty ratio 20:1. 1,426 full-time faculty, 89% hold PhDs, 22% are members of minority groups, 41% are women.

ACADEMICS
Degrees: Bachelor's; Certificate; Doctoral degree—professional practice; Doctoral degree research/scholarship; Master's; Post-bachelor's certificate; Post-master's certificate. **Classes:** Most classes have 20–29 students. Most lab/discussion sessions have 20–29 students. **Most popular majors:** Secondary Education and Teaching; Mechanical Engineering; Business Administration and Management, General. **Special Study Options:** Accelerated program; Cooperative education program; Distance learning; Double major; Dual enrollment; English as a Second Language (ESL); Exchange student program (domestic); Honors program; Independent study; Internships; Liberal arts/career combination; Study abroad; Teacher certification program. **Honors programs:** The Auburn University's Honors College offers qualified students a unique academic experience, designed to provide many of the advantages of a small college in the midst of the many diverse opportunities available at a large university. It is designed for students capable of academic excellence. The program selects 200 entering freshmen each year, who may be enrolled in any College or School of the University which has undergraduate programs or offerings. Students already enrolled at Auburn can also qualify for the Honors College. **Disability Services offered:** Note-taking services; Reader services; Tape recorders; Tutors. **Career services:** Alumni network; Alumni services; Career assessment; Career/job search classes; Internships.

FACILITIES
Housing: Apartments for married students; Apartments for single students; Coed dorms; Fraternity/sorority housing; Men's dorms; Special housing for disabled students; Women's dorms; 100% of campus accessible to physically disabled. **Special Academic Facilities/Equipment:** Nuclear Science Center; Hybridoma Facility; Freeman Herbarium; Jule Collins Smith Art Museum; Hypervelocity Impact Facility; Advanced Microscopy & Imaging Laboratory; Alabama Microelectronics Science & Technology Center; Alabama Water Resources Research Institute; AU Airport with single/multi-engine aircraft and flight simulators; Center for Forest Sustainability; Center for Governmental Services; Center for Pharmacy Operations & Designs; Drug Information & Learning Resources Center; Economic & Community Development Institute; Fish Molecular Genetics & Biotechnology Laboratory; Forest Policy Center; Forest Products Development Center; Fusion Lab; Harris Early Learning Center; Dept of Psychology Health Behavior Assessment Center; Highway Research Center; Marriage & Family Therapy Center; Microfibrous Materials Manufacturing Center; Dept of Kinesiology Biomechanics Lab, and Motor Behavior Center; Plasma Sciences Lab; Veterinary Medicine Radiology Clinic, Scott-Ritchey Research Center; Southeastern Raptor Rehabilitation Center; Small & Large Animal Health Clinics. **Campus network:** 100% of classrooms, 100% of dorms, 100% of libraries, 20% of dining areas, 15% of common outdoor areas, have wireless network access.

CAMPUS LIFE

Environment: Town. **Activities:** Campus Ministries; Choral groups; Concert band; Dance; Drama/theater; International Student Organization; Jazz band; Literary magazine; Marching band; Music ensembles; Musical theater; Opera; Pep band; Radio station; Student government; Student newspaper; Student-run film society; Symphony orchestra; Television station; Yearbook. 579 registered organizations, 45 honor societies, 42 religious organizations, 34 fraternities, 20 sororities, on campus. **Athletics (Intercollegiate):** *Men:* baseball, basketball, cheerleading, cross-country, diving, football, golf, swimming, tennis, track/field (outdoor), track/field (indoor). *Women:* basketball, cheerleading, cross-country, diving, equestrian sports, golf, gymnastics, soccer, softball, swimming, tennis, track/field (outdoor), track/field (indoor), volleyball. **On-Campus Highlights:** Recreation and Wellness Center. **Environmental Initiatives:** Adopted in 2011, Auburn University's Sustainability Policy (https://sites.auburn.edu/admin/universitypolicies/Policies/SustainabilityPolicy.pdf) affirms the university's commitment to sustainability as a core value and guiding principle for its operations, instruction, research, and outreach. It also outlines key sustainability goals, and commits to using a tracking and assessment system to measure progress.

ADMISSIONS

Freshman Academic Profile: Average high school GPA 3.9. 33% in top 10% of high school class, 63% in top 25% of high school class, 89% in top 50% of high school class. 86% from public high schools. **Test Scores:** SAT Math middle 50% range 570–670. SAT EBRW middle 50% range 580–650. ACT middle 50% range 25–31. **Basis for Candidate Selection:** *Very important factors include:* academic GPA, application essay, standardized test scores. *Important factors include:* rigor of secondary school record, extracurricular activities, talent/ability, character/personal qualities, first generation, alumni/ae relation, geographical residence, state residency, volunteer work. *Other factors include:* recommendation(s). **Freshman Admission Requirements:** High school diploma is required and GED is accepted. *Academic units required:* 4 English, 3 math, 2 science, 1 science labs, 3 social studies. *Academic units recommended:* 2 science labs, 1 foreign language, 4 social studies. **Freshman Admission Statistics:** 20,205 applied, 81% admitted, 29% enrolled. **Transfer Admission Requirements:** College transcript(s). Minimum college GPA of 2.5 required. Lowest grade transferable C. **General Admission Information:** Application fee $50. Priority deadline 11/1. Regular application deadline 2/3. Non-fall registration accepted.

COSTS AND FINANCIAL AID

Annual in-state tuition $9,816. Annual out-of-state tuition $29,448. Room and board $13,600. Required fees $1,676. Average book and supplies expense $1,200. **Required Forms and Deadlines:** FAFSA. **Notification of Awards:** Applicants will be notified of awards on a rolling basis beginning 10/2. **Types of Aid:** *Need-based scholarships/grants:* College/university scholarship or grant aid from institutional funds; Federal Pell; Private scholarships; SEOG; State scholarships/grants. *Loans:* Direct PLUS loans; Direct Subsidized Stafford Loans; Direct Unsubsidized Stafford Loans. **Student Employment:** Federal Work-Study Program available. Institutional employment available. **Financial Aid Statistics:** 86% needy freshmen, 75% needy undergrads receive need-based scholarship or grant aid. 13% freshmen, 9% undergrads receive non-need-based scholarship or grant aid. 57% freshmen, 74% undergrads receive need-based self-help aid. 1% freshmen, 2% undergrads receive athletic scholarships. 51% freshmen, 45% undergrads receive any aid. 39% undergrads borrow to pay for school. Average cumulative indebtedness $31,732.

AUBURN UNIVERSITY AT MONTGOMERY

P.O. Box 244023, Montgomery, AL 36124-4023
Phone: 334-244-3615 **Financial Aid Phone:** (334) 244-3571
E-mail: admissions@aum.edu
Fax: 334-244-3795 **Website:** www.aum.edu **ACT Code:** 0057

This public school was founded in 1967. It has a 500 acre campus.

RATINGS

Admissions Selectivity Rating: 73   **Fire Safety Rating:** 88   **Green Rating:** 60*

STUDENTS AND FACULTY

Enrollment: 4,435. **Student Body:** 64% female, 36% male, 6% out-of-state, 6% international (37 countries represented). Asian 2%, African American 42%, Caucasian 44%, Hispanic 1%, Native American <1%, Pacific Islander <1%, Two or more races 4%, Race unknown 1%.

Retention and Graduation: 66% freshmen return for sophomore year. 9% freshmen graduate within 4 years. 34% freshmen graduate within 6 years. **Faculty:** Student/faculty ratio 16:1. 221 full-time faculty, 79% hold PhDs, 18% are members of minority groups, 48% are women. 3% of classes are taught by teaching assistants.

ACADEMICS

Degrees: Bachelor's; Certificate; Doctoral degree research/scholarship; Master's; Post-bachelor's certificate; Post-master's certificate. **Classes:** Most classes have 20–29 students. Most lab/discussion sessions have 20–29 students. **Most popular majors:** Elementary Education and Teaching; Biology/Biological Sciences, General; Nursing Practice. **Special Study Options:** Accelerated program; Cross-registration; Distance learning; Double major; Dual enrollment; English as a Second Language (ESL); Honors program; Independent study; Internships; Liberal arts/career combination; Study abroad; Teacher certification program. **Honors programs:** Since 1981, the University Honors Program (UHP) has been open to qualified students in any major at AUM. The mission of the University Honors Program is to attract highly motivated AUM students and to recruit potential AUM students with qualifying ACT scores and GPAs, and to provide those students with a stimulating intellectual, scholarly, and social environment in which they can participate as part of a diverse community in which high achievement is the norm. **Disability Services offered:** Note-taking services; Reader services; Tape recorders; Tutors. **Career services:** Alumni services; Career assessment; Career/job search classes; Internships.

FACILITIES

Housing: Apartments for married students; Apartments for single students; Coed dorms; Special housing for international students; Theme housing; 90% of campus accessible to physically disabled. **Special Academic Facilities/Equipment:** Graphic arts center, mass communications lab, geographic information systems and computer cartography lab, multimedia television studio and other computer labs in various buildings across campus with different disciplinary areas. The Wellness Center, Warhawk Academic Success Center, Office of Global Initiatives. **Campus network:** 100% of classrooms, 100% of dorms, 100% of student union, 100% of libraries, 100% of dining areas, 100% of common outdoor areas, have wireless network access.

CAMPUS LIFE

Environment: City. **Activities:** Campus Ministries; Choral groups; Dance; Drama/theater; International Student Organization; Literary magazine; Musical theater; Student government; Student newspaper. 52 registered organizations, 12 honor societies, 6 religious organizations, 3 fraternities, 6 sororities, on campus. **Athletics (Intercollegiate):** *Men:* baseball, basketball, cheerleading, soccer, tennis. *Women:* basketball, cheerleading, soccer, softball, tennis. **On-Campus Highlights:** Wellness Center. **Environmental Initiatives:** Recycling.

ADMISSIONS

Freshman Academic Profile: Average high school GPA 3.4. 20% in top 10% of high school class, 46% in top 25% of high school class, 78% in top 50% of high school class. 80% from public high schools. **Test Scores:** SAT Math middle 50% range 470–550. SAT EBRW middle 50% range 485–560. ACT middle 50% range 19–23. **Basis for Candidate Selection:** *Very important factors include:* rigor of secondary school record, academic GPA, standardized test scores. **Freshman Admission Requirements:** High school diploma is required and GED is accepted. *Academic units recommended:* 3 English, 3 math, 2 science, 2 science labs, 2 foreign language, 2 social studies, 2 history, 2 academic electives. **Freshman Admission Statistics:** 4,109 applied, 90% admitted, 17% enrolled. **Transfer Admission Requirements:** College transcript(s). Minimum college GPA of 2.0 required. Lowest grade transferable D. **General Admission Information:** Regular application deadline 8/1. Non-fall registration accepted.

COSTS AND FINANCIAL AID

Annual in-state tuition $7,992. Annual out-of-state tuition $17,952. Required fees $868. Average book and supplies expense $1,200. **Required Forms and Deadlines:** FAFSA. **Notification of Awards:** Applicants will be notified of awards on a rolling basis beginning 4/15. **Types of Aid:** *Need-based scholarships/grants:* College/university scholarship or grant aid from institutional funds; Federal Pell; Private scholarships; SEOG; State scholarships/grants. *Loans:* Direct PLUS loans; Direct Subsidized Stafford Loans; Direct Unsubsidized Stafford Loans. **Student Employment:** Federal Work-Study Program available. Institutional employment available. **Financial Aid Statistics:** 93% needy freshmen, 85% needy undergrads receive need-based scholarship or grant aid. 95% freshmen, 50% undergrads receive non-need-based scholarship or grant aid. 94% freshmen, 91% undergrads receive need-based self-help aid. 5% freshmen, 5% undergrads receive athletic scholarships. 95% freshmen, 67% undergrads receive any aid. 68% undergrads borrow to pay for school. Average cumulative indebtedness $30,138.

AUGSBURG UNIVERSITY

2211 Riverside Avenue South, Minneapolis, MN 55454
Phone: 612-330-1001 **Financial Aid Phone:** 612-330-1046
E-mail: admissions@augsburg.edu **CEEB Code:** 6014
Fax: 612-330-1590 **Website:** www.augsburg.edu **ACT Code:** 2080

This private school, affiliated with the Lutheran Church, was founded in 1869. It has a 23 acre campus.

RATINGS
Admissions Selectivity Rating: 87   **Fire Safety Rating:** 83   **Green Rating:** 60*

STUDENTS AND FACULTY
Enrollment: 3,014. **Student Body:** 55% female, 45% male, 13% out-of-state, 2% international (24 countries represented). Asian 7%, African American 9%, Caucasian 68%, Hispanic 3%, Native American 2%, Pacific Islander <1%, Two or more races 2%, Race unknown 6%.
Retention and Graduation: 83% freshmen return for sophomore year. 27% grads go on to further study within 1 year. 15% grads pursue arts and sciences degrees. 2% grads pursue law degrees. 4% grads pursue business degrees. 5% grads pursue medical degrees. **Faculty:** Student/faculty ratio 16:1. 195 full-time faculty, 75% hold PhDs, 8% are members of minority groups, 51% are women. 0% of classes are taught by teaching assistants.

ACADEMICS
Degrees: Bachelor's; Certificate; Doctoral degree—professional practice; Master's. **Classes:** Most classes have 10–19 students. Most lab/discussion sessions have 10–19 students. **Most popular majors:** Education, General; Business/Commerce, General. **Special Study Options:** Cooperative education program; Cross-registration; Double major; Dual enrollment; Honors program; Independent study; Internships; Liberal arts/career combination; Student-designed major; Study abroad; Teacher certification program; Weekend college. **Honors programs:** First, the Honors Signature Courses, based on the medieval divisions of knowledge, automatically satisfy all of the College's general education requirements (except health/physical education and modern language) in a simple sequence of challenging courses, created just for Honors students. Second, Student-Created Courses allow students to design their own coursesÂ—as either a replacement or supplement to the established Honors courses. Students can learn through one-on-one tutoring, small reading groups, or out-of-classroom experiences. Third, Honors Leadership Activities give Honors students access to the The Augsburg Review, Honors Debate League, Faculty/Student Research Collaboration, and the Honors Houses. Through these activities, students can engage in travel abroad, service-learning, social justice activities, political activism, leadership, research, and social gatherings with their friends. **Disability Services offered:** Note-taking services; Reader services; Tape recorders; Tutors. **Career services:** Alumni network; Career/job search classes; Internships; Regional alumni.

FACILITIES
Housing: Coed dorms; Special housing for disabled students; 99% of campus accessible to physically disabled. **Special Academic Facilities/Equipment:** Electron microscope, center for atmospheric science research, theatre, pipe organ. **Campus network:** 100% of classrooms, 100% of dorms, 100% of student union, 100% of libraries, 100% of dining areas, 100% of common outdoor areas, have wireless network access.

CAMPUS LIFE
Environment: Metropolis. **Activities:** Campus Ministries; Choral groups; Concert band; Dance; Drama/theater; International Student Organization; Jazz band; Literary magazine; Music ensembles; Opera; Radio station; Student government; Student newspaper; Yearbook. 35 registered organizations, 1 honor societies, 1 religious organizations, on campus. **Athletics (Intercollegiate):** *Men:* baseball, basketball, cross-country, football, golf, ice hockey, soccer, tennis, track/field (outdoor), track/field (indoor), wrestling. *Women:* basketball, cheerleading, cross-country, golf, ice hockey, soccer, softball, swimming, tennis, track/field (outdoor), track/field (indoor), volleyball. **On-Campus Highlights:** Christensen Center/Starbucks Coffee Shop.

ADMISSIONS
Freshman Academic Profile: Average high school GPA 3.3. 11% in top 10% of high school class, 37% in top 25% of high school class, 69% in top 50% of high school class. **Test Scores:** SAT Math middle 50% range 500–640. SAT EBRW middle 50% range 510–640. ACT middle 50% range 19–25. **Basis for Candidate Selection:** *Very important factors include:* rigor of secondary school record, class rank, academic GPA, application essay, recommendation(s). *Important factors include:* standardized test scores, extracurricular activities, alumni/ae relation. *Other factors include:* interview, talent/ability, first generation, volunteer work, work experience. **Freshman Admission Requirements:** High school diploma is required and GED is accepted. *Academic units required:* 4 English, 3 math, 3 science, 2 foreign language, 2 social studies. *Academic units recommended:* 4 social studies, 2 history. **Freshman Admission Statistics:** 2,192 applied, 54% admitted, 35% enrolled. **Transfer Admission Requirements:** College transcript(s), statement of good standing from prior institution(s). Minimum college GPA of 2.5 required. Lowest grade transferable B. **General Admission Information:** Application fee $25. Priority deadline 5/1. Regular application deadline 8/15. Non-fall registration accepted. Admission may be deferred for a maximum of 24 months.

COSTS AND FINANCIAL AID
Annual tuition $29,794. Room and board $8,072. Required fees $624. Average book and supplies expense $1,000. **Required Forms and Deadlines:** FAFSA. **Notification of Awards:** Applicants will be notified of awards on a rolling basis beginning 3/1. **Types of Aid:** *Need-based scholarships/grants:* College/ university scholarship or grant aid from institutional funds; Federal Pell; Private scholarships; SEOG; State scholarships/grants. *Loans:* Direct PLUS loans; Direct Subsidized Stafford Loans; Direct Unsubsidized Stafford Loans. **Student Employment:** Institutional employment available. **Financial Aid Statistics:** 99% needy freshmen, 91% needy undergrads receive need-based scholarship or grant aid. 19% freshmen, 17% undergrads receive non-need-based scholarship or grant aid. 94% freshmen, 92% undergrads receive need-based self-help aid. 0% freshmen, 0% undergrads receive athletic scholarships. 93% freshmen, 86% undergrads receive any aid. **Criteria awarding aid:** *Need-based:* Academics, Minority status. *Non-need-based:* Academics, Alumni affiliation, Art, Leadership, Minority status, Music/drama, Religious affiliation.

AUGUSTANA COLLEGE (IL)

639 38th Street, Rock Island, IL 61201-2296
Phone: (309) 794-7341 **Financial Aid Phone:** 309-794-7207
E-mail: admissions@augustana.edu **CEEB Code:** 1025
Fax: (309) 794-7422 **Website:** www.augustana.edu **ACT Code:** 0946

This private school, affiliated with the Lutheran Church, was founded in 1860. It has a 115 acre campus.

RATINGS
Admissions Selectivity Rating: 86   **Fire Safety Rating:** 94   **Green Rating:** 60*

STUDENTS AND FACULTY
Enrollment: 2,634. **Student Body:** 58% female, 42% male, 15% out-of-state, 7% international (42 countries represented). Asian 2%, African American 4%, Caucasian 72%, Hispanic 10%, Native American <1%, Pacific Islander <1%, Two or more races 3%, Race unknown 1%.
Retention and Graduation: 87% freshmen return for sophomore year. 71% freshmen graduate within 4 years. 77% freshmen graduate within 6 years. 33% grads go on to further study within 1 year. 18% grads pursue arts and sciences degrees. 3% grads pursue law degrees. 1% grads pursue business degrees. 10% grads pursue medical degrees. **Faculty:** Student/faculty ratio 12:1. 195 full-time faculty, 92% hold PhDs, 14% are members of minority groups, 48% are women. 0% of classes are taught by teaching assistants.

ACADEMICS
Degrees: Bachelor's. **Classes:** Most classes have 10–19 students. Most lab/discussion sessions have 10–19 students. **Most popular majors:** Biology/Biological Sciences, General; Psychology, General; Business Administration and Management, General. **Special Study Options:** Double major; Honors program; Independent study; Internships; Liberal arts/career combination; Student-designed major; Study abroad; Teacher certification program. **Honors programs:** Augustana has two tracks in first-year honors studies, Foundations and Logos. The Foundations program is a challenging interdisciplinary honors curriculum offering an intensive examination of the basic questions that have perplexed humans for centuries, and focuses on integrated learning and the development of critical thinking and writing skills. Logos is a challenging interdisciplinary honors curriculum with a special focus on how science has evolved across the centuries, how science has been used and viewed at particular historical moments, and how we live with the fruits of science today. **Disability**

Services offered: Tape recorders; Tutors. **Career services:** Alumni network; Alumni services; Career assessment; Career/job search classes; Internships.

FACILITIES

Housing: Apartments for single students; Coed dorms; Special housing for disabled students; Wellness housing; 95% of campus accessible to physically disabled. **Special Academic Facilities/Equipment:** Educational technology building, art gallery, black culture house, Hispanic culture house, geology museum, on-campus preschool, immigration research center, scanning and transmission electron microscopes, nuclear magnetic resonance, atomic absorption, and diode array mass spectrophotometers, 3D printer, planetarium, observatory with celestron telescope, environmental field stations. **Campus network:** 80% of classrooms, 100% of dorms, 100% of student union, 100% of libraries, 100% of dining areas, 5% of common outdoor areas, have wireless network access.

CAMPUS LIFE

Environment: City. **Activities:** Campus Ministries; Choral groups; Concert band; Dance; Drama/theater; International Student Organization; Jazz band; Literary magazine; Model UN; Music ensembles; Musical theater; Opera; Pep band; Radio station; Student government; Student newspaper; Symphony orchestra. 208 registered organizations, 16 honor societies, 10 religious organizations, 7 fraternities, 7 sororities, on campus. **Athletics (Intercollegiate):** *Men:* baseball, basketball, cross-country, diving, football, golf, soccer, swimming, tennis, track/field (outdoor), track/field (indoor), wrestling. *Women:* basketball, cross-country, diving, golf, lacrosse, soccer, softball, swimming, tennis, track/field (outdoor), track/field (indoor), volleyball. **On-Campus Highlights:** Gerber Center for Student Life and Thomas Tredway Libarary. **Environmental Initiatives:** Recycling Program.

ADMISSIONS

Freshman Academic Profile: Average high school GPA 3.3. 36% in top 10% of high school class, 64% in top 25% of high school class, 90% in top 50% of high school class. **Test Scores:** SAT Math middle 50% range 570–700. SAT EBRW middle 50% range 530–640. ACT middle 50% range 23–28. **Basis for Candidate Selection:** *Very important factors include:* rigor of secondary school record, class rank, academic GPA. *Important factors include:* application essay, standardized test scores, recommendation(s), interview, extracurricular activities, talent/ability, character/personal qualities. *Other factors include:* alumni/ae relation, geographical residence, religious affiliation/commitment, racial/ethnic status, volunteer work, work experience. **Freshman Admission Requirements:** High school diploma is required and GED is accepted. *Academic units required:* 3 English, 3 math, 3 science, 2 science labs, 1 foreign language, 1 social studies, 1 history. *Academic units recommended:* 4 English, 4 math, 4 science, 2 science labs, 2 foreign language, 2 social studies, 1 history, 4 academic electives. **Freshman Admission Statistics:** 6,750 applied, 59% admitted, 18% enrolled. **Transfer Admission Requirements:** High school transcript, college transcript(s), statement of good standing from prior institution(s). Minimum college GPA of 2.0 required. Lowest grade transferable D. **General Admission Information:** Priority deadline 2/1. Non-fall registration accepted.

COSTS AND FINANCIAL AID

Annual tuition $42,135. Room and board $10,572. Average book and supplies expense $1,000. **Required Forms and Deadlines:** FAFSA; Institution's own financial aid form. **Notification of Awards:** Applicants will be notified of awards on a rolling basis beginning 3/1. **Types of Aid:** *Need-based scholarships/grants:* College/university scholarship or grant aid from institutional funds; Federal Pell; Private scholarships; SEOG; State scholarships/grants. *Loans:* Direct PLUS loans; Direct Subsidized Stafford Loans; Direct Unsubsidized Stafford Loans. **Student Employment:** Federal Work-Study Program available. Institutional employment available. **Financial Aid Statistics:** 100% needy freshmen, 98% needy undergrads receive need-based scholarship or grant aid. 19% freshmen, 17% undergrads receive non-need-based scholarship or grant aid. 76% freshmen, 77% undergrads receive need-based self-help aid. 0% freshmen, 0% undergrads receive athletic scholarships. 91.5% freshmen, 89.5% undergrads receive any aid. 73% undergrads borrow to pay for school. Average cumulative indebtedness $34,964. **Criteria awarding aid:** *Need-based:* Minority status. *Non-need-based:* Academics, Alumni affiliation, Art, Leadership, Music/drama, Religious affiliation.

AUGUSTANA UNIVERSITY

2001 South Summit Avenue, Sioux Falls, SD 57197
Phone: 605-274-5516 **Financial Aid Phone:** 605-274-5216
E-mail: admission@augie.edu **CEEB Code:** 6015
Fax: 605-274-5518 **Website:** www.augie.edu **ACT Code:** 3902

This private school, affiliated with the Lutheran Church, was founded in 1860. It has a 100 acre campus.

RATINGS

Admissions Selectivity Rating: 85   **Fire Safety Rating:** 94   **Green Rating:** 87

STUDENTS AND FACULTY

Enrollment: 1,765. **Student Body:** 64% female, 36% male, 49% out-of-state, 6% international (35 countries represented). Asian 2%, African American 2%, Caucasian 85%, Hispanic 3%, Native American 1%, Pacific Islander <1%, Two or more races 2%, Race unknown <1%.
Retention and Graduation: 82% freshmen return for sophomore year. 45% freshmen graduate within 4 years. 58% freshmen graduate within 6 years. 22% grads go on to further study within 1 year. **Faculty:** Student/faculty ratio 11:1. 150 full-time faculty, 83% hold PhDs, 6% are members of minority groups, 52% are women. 0% of classes are taught by teaching assistants.

ACADEMICS

Degrees: Bachelor's; Master's. **Classes:** Most classes have 10–19 students. Most lab/discussion sessions have 10–19 students. **Most popular majors:** Education, General; Business Administration, Management and Operations, Other; Registered Nursing/Registered Nurse. **Special Study Options:** Accelerated program; Cross-registration; Distance learning; Double major; Dual enrollment; Exchange student program (domestic); External degree program; Honors program; Independent study; Internships; Liberal arts/career combination; Student-designed major; Study abroad; Teacher certification program. **Honors programs:** Our campus-wide, interdisciplinary Honors program is called Civitas (citizenship). Specific majors also offer departmental honors programs for students willing to accept academic challenges that go well beyond those required for graduation. **Combined degree programs:** BA/MEng. **Disability Services offered:** Note-taking services; Reader services; Tape recorders; Tutors. **Career services:** Alumni network; Alumni services; Career assessment; Career/job search classes; Internships; Regional alumni.

FACILITIES

Housing: Apartments for married students; Apartments for single students; Coed dorms; Special housing for disabled students; Theme housing; 85% of campus accessible to physically disabled. **Special Academic Facilities/Equipment:** Center for Western Studies, Archeology Lab, Eide/Dalrymple Art Gallery, Center for Liturgical Art.

CAMPUS LIFE

Environment: City. **Activities:** Campus Ministries; Choral groups; Concert band; Dance; Drama/theater; International Student Organization; Jazz band; Literary magazine; Music ensembles; Musical theater; Pep band; Student government; Student newspaper; Symphony orchestra; Yearbook. 83 registered organizations, 16 honor societies, 8 religious organizations, on campus. **Athletics (Intercollegiate):** *Men:* baseball, basketball, cross-country, football, golf, tennis, track/field (outdoor), track/field (indoor), wrestling. *Women:* basketball, cheerleading, cross-country, golf, soccer, softball, tennis, track/field (outdoor), track/field (indoor), volleyball. **On-Campus Highlights:** Sports Complex. **Environmental Initiatives:** Most recent building (120,000 square feet) is at least LEED silver, the first LEED building on campus.

ADMISSIONS

Freshman Academic Profile: Average high school GPA 3.7. 32% in top 10% of high school class, 64% in top 25% of high school class, 90% in top 50% of high school class. 89% from public high schools. **Test Scores:** SAT Math middle 50% range 540–700. SAT EBRW middle 50% range 550–660. ACT middle 50% range 23–29. **Basis for Candidate Selection:** *Important factors include:* rigor of secondary school record, academic GPA, standardized test scores. *Other factors include:* class rank, application essay, recommendation(s), interview, extracurricular activities, character/personal qualities, alumni/ae relation, volunteer work, work experience, level of applicant's interest. **Freshman Admission Requirements:** High school diploma is required and GED is accepted. *Academic units recommended:* 4 English, 4 math, 4 science, 2 foreign language, 3 social studies, 3 visual/performing arts. **Freshman**

Admission Statistics: 2,224 applied, 67% admitted, 29% enrolled. **Transfer Admission Requirements:** High school transcript, college transcript(s), essay or personal statement. Minimum college GPA of 2.2 required. Lowest grade transferable C-. **General Admission Information:** Priority deadline 1/15. Non-fall registration accepted. Admission may be deferred for a maximum of 1 year.

COSTS AND FINANCIAL AID

Annual tuition $34,934. Room and board $8,616. Required fees $950. Average book and supplies expense $1,000. **Required Forms and Deadlines:** FAFSA. **Notification of Awards:** Applicants will be notified of awards on a rolling basis beginning 4/1. **Types of Aid:** *Need-based scholarships/grants:* College/university scholarship or grant aid from institutional funds; Federal Pell; Private scholarships; SEOG; State scholarships/grants. *Loans:* Direct PLUS loans; Direct Subsidized Stafford Loans; Direct Unsubsidized Stafford Loans. **Student Employment:** Federal Work-Study Program available. Institutional employment available. **Financial Aid Statistics:** 100% needy freshmen, 98% needy undergrads receive need-based scholarship or grant aid. 99% freshmen, 97% undergrads receive non-need-based scholarship or grant aid. 70% freshmen, 76% undergrads receive need-based self-help aid. 2% freshmen, 20% undergrads receive athletic scholarships. 100% freshmen, 100% undergrads receive any aid. 69% undergrads borrow to pay for school. Average cumulative indebtedness $37,647. **Criteria awarding aid:** *Need-based:* Academics, Athletics, Leadership, Minority status, Music/drama, Religious affiliation. *Non-need-based:* Academics, Alumni affiliation, Art, Athletics, Leadership, Minority status, Music/drama, Religious affiliation, State/district residency.

AUGUSTA STATE UNIVERSITY

2500 Walton Way, Augusta, GA 30904-2200
Phone: 706-737-1632 **Financial Aid Phone:** 706-737-1431
E-mail: admissio@aug.edu **CEEB Code:** 5336
Fax: 706-667-4355 **ACT Code:** 796

This public school was founded in 1925. It has a 76 acre campus.

RATINGS

Admissions Selectivity Rating: 89   **Fire Safety Rating:** 73   **Green Rating:** 60*

STUDENTS AND FACULTY

Enrollment: 5,394. **Student Body:** 64% female, 36% male, 9% out-of-state, 1% international (60 countries represented). Asian 3%, African American 28%, Caucasian 59%, Hispanic 3%, Native American <1%, Race unknown 5%. **Retention and Graduation:** 69% freshmen return for sophomore year. **Faculty:** Student/faculty ratio 18:1. 236 full-time faculty, 64% hold PhDs, 16% are members of minority groups, 51% are women. 0% of classes are taught by teaching assistants.

ACADEMICS

Degrees: Associate; Bachelor's; Master's; Post-master's certificate; Terminal Associate; Transfer Associate. **Classes:** Most classes have 20–29 students. Most lab/discussion sessions have 20–29 students. **Most popular majors:** Biology/Biological Sciences, General; Elementary Education and Teaching; Psychology, General. **Special Study Options:** Cooperative education program; Cross-registration; Distance learning; Double major; Dual enrollment; English as a Second Language (ESL); Honors program; Independent study; Internships; Study abroad; Teacher certification program. **Honors programs:** Augusta State University's Honors Program provides about 100 of our best students with special sections of classes in the core curriculum. Those classes are usually smaller, involve much closer interaction with the professor, and encourage more independent and collaborative work than non-honors sections of these courses. In their Junior and Senior years, Honors students take two interdisciplinary courses, prepare, write, and defend a thesis, and conclude their undergraduate program with a Capstone course. **Disability Services offered:** Note-taking services; Reader services; Tape recorders; Tutors. **Career services:** Alumni services.

FACILITIES

Housing: Apartments for single students; 90% of campus accessible to physically disabled. **Special Academic Facilities/Equipment:** Performing Arts Theatre, Christenberry Field House, Forest Hill Golf Course. **Campus network:** 100% of classrooms, 100% of dorms, 100% of student union, 100% of libraries, 100% of dining areas, 0% of common outdoor areas, have wireless network access.

CAMPUS LIFE

Environment: City. **Activities:** Choral groups; Concert band; Drama/theater; Jazz band; Literary magazine; Pep band; Radio station; Student government; Student newspaper. 60 registered organizations, 5 honor societies, 5 religious organizations, 3 fraternities, 3 sororities, on campus. **Athletics (Intercollegiate):** *Men:* baseball, basketball, golf, tennis. *Women:* basketball, golf, softball, tennis, volleyball. **On-Campus Highlights:** Allgood Hall.

ADMISSIONS

Freshman Academic Profile: Average high school GPA 2.9. 95% from public high schools. **Test Scores:** SAT Math middle 50% range 430–540. SAT EBRW middle 50% range 440–540. ACT middle 50% range 17–21. **Basis for Candidate Selection:** *Important factors include:* rigor of secondary school record, academic GPA, standardized test scores. **Freshman Admission Requirements:** High school diploma is required and GED is accepted. *Academic units required:* 4 English, 4 math, 3 science, 2 foreign language, 3 social studies. **Freshman Admission Statistics:** 2,401 applied, 52% admitted, 75% enrolled. **Transfer Admission Requirements:** College transcript(s). Minimum college GPA of 2.0 required. Lowest grade transferable D. **General Admission Information:** Application fee $20. Priority deadline 7/1. Non-fall registration accepted. Admission may be deferred for a maximum of Period is not limite.

COSTS AND FINANCIAL AID

Average book and supplies expense $1,000. **Required Forms and Deadlines:** FAFSA; State aid form. **Notification of Awards:** Applicants will be notified of awards on or about 6/1. **Types of Aid:** *Need-based scholarships/grants:* College/university scholarship or grant aid from institutional funds; Federal Pell; Private scholarships; SEOG; State scholarships/grants. **Financial Aid Statistics:** 73% needy freshmen, 67% needy undergrads receive need-based scholarship or grant aid. 25% freshmen, 29% undergrads receive non-need-based scholarship or grant aid. 67% freshmen, 65% undergrads receive need-based self-help aid. 0% freshmen, 2% undergrads receive athletic scholarships. **Criteria awarding aid:** *Need-based:* Academics, Art, Leadership, Music/drama. *Non-need-based:* Academics, Alumni affiliation, Art, Athletics, Job skills, Leadership, Minority status, Music/drama, State/district residency.

AURORA UNIVERSITY

347 South Gladstone Ave, Aurora, IL 60506
Phone: 630-844-5533 **Financial Aid Phone:** 630-844-6190
E-mail: admission@aurora.edu **CEEB Code:** 1027
Fax: 630-844-6191 **Website:** www.aurora.edu **ACT Code:** 950

This private school was founded in 1893. It has a 30 acre campus.

RATINGS

Admissions Selectivity Rating: 76   **Fire Safety Rating:** 91   **Green Rating:** 60*

STUDENTS AND FACULTY

Enrollment: 3,944. **Student Body:** 65% female, 35% male, 11% out-of-state, <1% international (2 countries represented). Asian 2%, African American 7%, Caucasian 48%, Hispanic 32%, Native American <1%, Pacific Islander <1%, Two or more races 3%, Race unknown 6%. **Retention and Graduation:** 75% freshmen return for sophomore year. 37% freshmen graduate within 4 years. **Faculty:** Student/faculty ratio 19:1. 139 full-time faculty, 0% hold PhDs, 7% are members of minority groups, 54% are women. 0% of classes are taught by teaching assistants.

ACADEMICS

Degrees: Bachelor's; Doctoral degree research/scholarship; Master's; Post-master's certificate. **Classes:** Most classes have 20–29 students. Most lab/discussion sessions have 10–19 students. **Most popular majors:** Business Administration and Management, General; Elementary Education and Teaching; Nursing/Registered Nurse (Rn, Asn, Bsn, Msn). **Special Study Options:** Accelerated program; Cross-registration; Distance learning; Double major; Dual enrollment; Independent study; Internships; Liberal arts/career combination; Student-designed major; Study abroad; Teacher certification program. **Honors programs:** Honors Program including honors seminars, honors section of some general education courses and a senior honors project. **Disability Services offered:** Note-taking services; Reader services; Tape recorders; Tutors. **Career services:** Alumni network; Alumni services; Career assessment; Career/job search classes; Internships.

FACILITIES

Housing: Coed dorms; 95% of campus accessible to physically disabled.
Special Academic Facilities/Equipment: Schingoethe Center for Native American Culture Downstairs Dunham Gallery Center For Faith And Action Perry Theatre in the Aurora Foundation Center for Community Education.
Campus network: 100% of classrooms, 100% of dorms, 100% of student union, 100% of libraries, 100% of dining areas, 25% of common outdoor areas, have wireless network access.

CAMPUS LIFE

Environment: City. **Activities:** Campus Ministries; Choral groups; Dance; Drama/theater; Literary magazine; Music ensembles; Musical theater; Opera; Pep band; Radio station; Student government; Student newspaper; Television station. 50 registered organizations, 2 honor societies, 1 religious organizations, 1 fraternities, 4 sororities, on campus. **Athletics (Intercollegiate):** *Men:* baseball, basketball, cross-country, football, golf, soccer, tennis, track/field (outdoor), track/field (indoor). *Women:* basketball, cross-country, golf, soccer, softball, tennis, track/field (outdoor), track/field (indoor), volleyball. **On-Campus Highlights:** The Spartan Spot. **Environmental Initiatives:** Campus-wide recycling.

ADMISSIONS

Freshman Academic Profile: Average high school GPA 3.4. 92% from public high schools. **Test Scores:** SAT Math middle 50% range 480–570. SAT EBRW middle 50% range 490–580. ACT middle 50% range 19–23. **Basis for Candidate Selection:** *Very important factors include:* rigor of secondary school record, class rank, academic GPA, standardized test scores. *Important factors include:* extracurricular activities, character/personal qualities. *Other factors include:* application essay, recommendation(s), interview, talent/ability, first generation, alumni/ae relation, volunteer work, work experience, level of applicant's interest. **Freshman Admission Requirements:** High school diploma is required and GED is accepted. *Academic units required:* 4 English, 3 math, 3 science, 3 social studies, 3 academic electives. **Freshman Admission Statistics:** 3,296 applied, 81% admitted, 28% enrolled. **Transfer Admission Requirements:** College transcript(s), statement of good standing from prior institution(s). Minimum college GPA of 2.0 required. Lowest grade transferable C. **General Admission Information:** Non-fall registration accepted.

COSTS AND FINANCIAL AID

Annual tuition $24,800. Room and board $11,700. Required fees $260. Average book and supplies expense $1,000. **Required Forms and Deadlines:** FAFSA. **Notification of Awards:** Applicants will be notified of awards on a rolling basis beginning 11/15. **Types of Aid:** *Need-based scholarships/grants:* College/university scholarship or grant aid from institutional funds; Federal Pell; Private scholarships; SEOG; State scholarships/grants. *Loans:* Direct PLUS loans; Direct Subsidized Stafford Loans; Direct Unsubsidized Stafford Loans. **Student Employment:** Federal Work-Study Program available. Institutional employment available. **Financial Aid Statistics:** 96% needy freshmen, 94% needy undergrads receive need-based scholarship or grant aid. 17% freshmen, 16% undergrads receive non-need-based scholarship or grant aid. 88% freshmen, 89% undergrads receive need-based self-help aid. 0% freshmen, 0% undergrads receive athletic scholarships. 100% freshmen, 98% undergrads receive any aid. 78% undergrads borrow to pay for school. Average cumulative indebtedness $28,373. **Criteria awarding aid:** *Need-based:* Leadership, Religious affiliation. *Non-need-based:* Academics, Alumni affiliation, Art, Music/drama, Religious affiliation, State/district residency.

AUSTIN COLLEGE

900 N. Grand Avenue, Sherman, TX 75090
Phone: 903-813-3000 **Financial Aid Phone:** 903-813-2900
E-mail: admission@austincollege.edu **CEEB Code:** 6016
Fax: 903-813-3198 **Website:** www.austincollege.edu **ACT Code:** 4058

This private school, affiliated with the Presbyterian Church, was founded in 1849. It has a 70 acre campus.

RATINGS

Admissions Selectivity Rating: 88   **Fire Safety Rating:** 84   **Green Rating:** 85

STUDENTS AND FACULTY

Enrollment: 1,223. **Student Body:** 51% female, 49% male, 8% out-of-state, 3% international (15 countries represented). Asian 13%, African American 9%, Caucasian 49%, Hispanic 21%, Native American 1%, Pacific Islander <1%, Two or more races 4%, Race unknown <1%.
Retention and Graduation: 81% freshmen return for sophomore year. 71% freshmen graduate within 4 years. 75% freshmen graduate within 6 years. 35% grads go on to further study within 1 year. 3% grads pursue law degrees. <1% grads pursue business degrees. 9% grads pursue medical degrees. **Faculty:** Student/faculty ratio 13:1. 77 full-time faculty, 95% hold PhDs, 22% are members of minority groups, 38% are women. 0% of classes are taught by teaching assistants.

ACADEMICS

Degrees: Bachelor's; Master's. **Classes:** Most classes have 20–29 students. Most lab/discussion sessions have 10–19 students. **Most popular majors:** Business/Commerce, General; Biology/Biological Sciences, General; Psychology, General. **Special Study Options:** Double major; Exchange student program (domestic); Independent study; Internships; Student-designed major; Study abroad; Teacher certification program. **Disability Services offered:** Tutors. **Career services:** Alumni network; Alumni services; Career assessment; Career/job search classes; Internships.

FACILITIES

Housing: Apartments for single students; Men's dorms; Special housing for disabled students; Special housing for international students; Women's dorms; 99% of campus accessible to physically disabled. **Special Academic Facilities/Equipment:** Idea Center, moot court program, student-managed investment fund.

CAMPUS LIFE

Environment: Town. **Activities:** Campus Ministries; Choral groups; Concert band; Dance; Drama/theater; International Student Organization; Jazz band; Literary magazine; Model UN; Music ensembles; Musical theater; Pep band; Student government; Student newspaper; Symphony orchestra; Yearbook. 60 registered organizations, 16 honor societies, 9 religious organizations, 10 fraternities, 5 sororities, on campus. **Athletics (Intercollegiate):** *Men:* baseball, basketball, football, soccer, swimming, tennis. *Women:* basketball, soccer, softball, swimming, tennis, volleyball. **On-Campus Highlights:** Wright Campus Center (WCC). **Environmental Initiatives:** Board approval of Climate Action Plan to reduce emissions to 0 and well established Center for Envronmental Studies that offers a major and minor.

ADMISSIONS

Freshman Academic Profile: Average high school GPA 3.5. 41% in top 10% of high school class, 35% in top 25% of high school class, 96% in top 50% of high school class. 77% from public high schools. **Test Scores:** SAT Math middle 50% range 570–680. SAT EBRW middle 50% range 590–680. ACT middle 50% range 23–29. **Basis for Candidate Selection:** *Very important factors include:* rigor of secondary school record, class rank, academic GPA, application essay, standardized test scores, recommendation(s). *Important factors include:* interview, talent/ability, character/personal qualities. *Other factors include:* extracurricular activities, first generation, alumni/ae relation, geographical residence, state residency, religious affiliation/commitment, volunteer work, work experience. **Freshman Admission Requirements:** High school diploma is required and GED is accepted. *Academic units required:* 4 English, 3 math, 3 science, 1 science labs, 2 foreign language, 2 social studies, 1 history, 1 visual/performing arts. *Academic units recommended:* 4 English, 4 math, 4 science, 2 science labs, 4 foreign language, 3 social studies, 1 history, 2 visual/performing arts. **Freshman Admission Statistics:** 3,545 applied, 52% admitted, 18% enrolled. **Transfer Admission Requirements:** College transcript(s), essay or personal statement, statement of good standing from prior institution(s). Minimum college GPA of 3.0 required. Lowest grade transferable C. **General Admission Information:** Priority deadline 12/1. Regular application deadline 3/1.

COSTS AND FINANCIAL AID

Annual tuition $40,970. Room and board $12,752. Required fees $185. Average book and supplies expense $1,250. **Required Forms and Deadlines:** FAFSA. **Notification of Awards:** Applicants will be notified of awards on a rolling basis beginning 12/1. **Types of Aid:** *Need-based scholarships/grants:* College/university scholarship or grant aid from institutional funds; Federal Pell; Private scholarships; SEOG; State scholarships/grants. *Loans:* Direct PLUS loans; Direct Subsidized Stafford Loans; Direct Unsubsidized Stafford Loans. **Student Employment:** Federal Work-Study Program available. Institutional employment available. **Financial Aid Statistics:** 100% needy freshmen, 100% needy undergrads receive need-based scholarship or grant aid. 19% freshmen, 18% undergrads receive non-need-based scholarship or grant aid. 67% freshmen, 71% undergrads receive need-based self-help aid. 0% freshmen, 0% undergrads receive athletic scholarships. 97% freshmen, 98% undergrads receive any aid. **Criteria awarding aid:** *Non-need-based:* Academics, Alumni affiliation, Art, Leadership, Music/drama, Religious affiliation.

AUSTIN PEAY STATE UNIVERSITY

P.O. Box 4548, Clarksville, TN 37044
Phone: (931) 221-7661
E-mail: admissions@apsu.edu **CEEB Code:** 1028
Fax: (931) 221-6168 **Website:** www.apsu.edu **ACT Code:** 3944

This public school was founded in 1927. It has a 210 acre campus.

RATINGS
Admissions Selectivity Rating: 74   **Fire Safety Rating:** 60*   **Green Rating:** 60*

STUDENTS AND FACULTY
Enrollment: 8,935. **Student Body:** 58% female, 42% male, 16% out-of-state, 1% international (13 countries represented). Asian 2%, African American 23%, Caucasian 57%, Hispanic 9%, Native American <1%, Pacific Islander <1%, Two or more races 7%, Race unknown 2%.
Retention and Graduation: 63% freshmen return for sophomore year. 23% freshmen graduate within 4 years. 41% freshmen graduate within 6 years.
Faculty: Student/faculty ratio 17:1. 385 full-time faculty, 0% hold PhDs, 16% are members of minority groups, 49% are women. 0% of classes are taught by teaching assistants.

ACADEMICS
Degrees: Associate; Bachelor's; Doctoral degree—professional practice; Master's; Post-bachelor's certificate; Post-master's certificate; Terminal Associate; Transfer Associate. **Classes:** Most classes have 20–29 students. Most lab/discussion sessions have 20–29 students. **Special Study Options:** Accelerated program; Cooperative education program; Distance learning; Double major; Dual enrollment; English as a Second Language (ESL); Honors program; Independent study; Internships; Study abroad; Teacher certification program.
Disability Services offered: Note-taking services; Reader services; Tutors.
Career services: Career assessment; Career/job search classes; Internships.

FACILITIES
Housing: Apartments for married students; Apartments for single students; Coed dorms; Fraternity/sorority housing; Men's dorms; Special housing for disabled students; Women's dorms; 100% of campus accessible to physically disabled. **Special Academic Facilities/Equipment:** Art museum, biology museum, language lab, demonstration farm, 21st century classroom.

CAMPUS LIFE
Environment: Village. **Activities:** Campus Ministries; Choral groups; Concert band; Dance; Drama/theater; International Student Organization; Jazz band; Literary magazine; Marching band; Music ensembles; Musical theater; Opera; Pep band; Radio station; Student government; Student newspaper; Student-run film society; Symphony orchestra; Television station; Yearbook. 50 registered organizations, 13 honor societies, 10 religious organizations, 8

fraternities, 6 sororities, on campus. **Athletics (Intercollegiate):** *Men:* baseball, basketball, cheerleading, cross-country, football, golf, tennis. *Women:* basketball, cheerleading, cross-country, golf, riflery, soccer, softball, tennis, track/field (outdoor), volleyball. **On-Campus Highlights:** University Center.

ADMISSIONS
Freshman Academic Profile: Average high school GPA 3.2. 12% in top 10% of high school class, 34% in top 25% of high school class, 68% in top 50% of high school class. 95% from public high schools. **Test Scores:** SAT Math middle 50% range 470–600. SAT EBRW middle 50% range 490–570. ACT middle 50% range 19–24. **Basis for Candidate Selection:** *Very important factors include:* academic GPA, standardized test scores. *Other factors include:* rigor of secondary school record. **Freshman Admission Requirements:** High school diploma is required and GED is accepted. *Academic units required:* 4 English, 3 math, 2 science, 1 science labs, 2 foreign language, 1 social studies, 1 history, 1 visual/performing arts. **Freshman Admission Statistics:** 7,416 applied, 95% admitted, 24% enrolled. **Transfer Admission Requirements:** College transcript(s). Lowest grade transferable D. **General Admission Information:** Application fee $25. Regular application deadline 8/21. Non-fall registration accepted. Admission may be deferred for a maximum of 12 months.

COSTS AND FINANCIAL AID
Annual in-state tuition $7,044. Annual out-of-state tuition $12,588. Room and board $9,994. Average book and supplies expense $1,250. **Required Forms and Deadlines:** FAFSA. **Notification of Awards:** Applicants will be notified of awards on a rolling basis beginning 2/1. **Types of Aid:** *Need-based scholarships/grants:* College/university scholarship or grant aid from institutional funds; Federal Pell; Private scholarships; SEOG; State scholarships/grants. *Loans:* Direct PLUS loans; Direct Subsidized Stafford Loans; Direct Unsubsidized Stafford Loans. **Student Employment:** Federal Work-Study Program available. Institutional employment available. **Financial Aid Statistics:** 70% needy freshmen, 68% needy undergrads receive need-based scholarship or grant aid. 85% freshmen, 65% undergrads receive non-need-based scholarship or grant aid. 58% freshmen, 60% undergrads receive need-based self-help aid. 3% freshmen, 4% undergrads receive athletic scholarships. 68% undergrads borrow to pay for school. Average cumulative indebtedness $25,938. **Criteria awarding aid:** *Non-need-based:* Academics, Alumni affiliation, Art, Athletics, Leadership, Music/drama, State/district residency.

AVERETT UNIVERSITY

420 West Main Street, Danville, VA 24541
Phone: 434-791-5600 **Financial Aid Phone:** 434-791-5890
CEEB Code: 5017
Fax: 434-797-2784 **Website:** www.averett.edu **ACT Code:** 4338

This private school, affiliated with the Baptist General Association of Virginia Church, was founded in 1859. It has a 185 acre campus.

RATINGS
Admissions Selectivity Rating: 77   **Fire Safety Rating:** 93   **Green Rating:** 61

STUDENTS AND FACULTY
Enrollment: 892. **Student Body:** 44% female, 56% male, 40% out-of-state, 7% international (19 countries represented). Asian 1%, African American 28%, Caucasian 55%, Hispanic 4%, Native American 1%, Pacific Islander 1%, Two or more races 4%, Race unknown 1%.
Retention and Graduation: 69% freshmen return for sophomore year. 35% freshmen graduate within 4 years. 41% freshmen graduate within 6 years. 24% grads go on to further study within 1 year. 2% grads pursue arts and sciences degrees. 0% grads pursue law degrees. 3% grads pursue business degrees. 2% grads pursue medical degrees. **Faculty:** Student/faculty ratio 10:1. 54 full-time faculty, 61% hold PhDs, 11% are members of minority groups, 52% are women. 0% of classes are taught by teaching assistants.

ACADEMICS
Degrees: Associate; Bachelor's. **Classes:** Most classes have fewer than 10 students. **Most popular majors:** Flight Instructor; Pre-Medicine/Pre-Medical Studies; Sociology, General. **Special Study Options:** Cross-registration; Distance learning; Double major; Dual enrollment; Honors program; Independent study; Internships; Student-designed major; Study abroad; Teacher certification program. **Honors programs:** Our Honors Program gives students the opportunity to go a step beyond regular classroom study. Students explore, in-depth, selected areas of academics. Participation in the Honors Program

For more free content, visit PrincetonReview.com

demonstrates a commitment to scholarship and will give students an edge in graduate study or in the job market. To earn the honors distinction students would be required to complete 9 credit hours in Honors courses [This would include one 3-credit interdisciplinary Honors course (taken in either the sophomore year or fall semester of junior year) and then the completion of an Honors project, taking place in the spring semester of one's junior year (Honors 401–3 credits) and the fall of senior year (Honors 402–3 credits).] and have an overall GPA of 3.4 or better. Honors Program students may also participate in the Honors Association and attend conferences, social activities and cultural performances. **Disability Services offered:** Note-taking services; Reader services; Tutors. **Career services:** Alumni services; Career assessment; Career/job search classes; Internships; Regional alumni.

FACILITIES

Housing: Apartments for single students; Coed dorms; Men's dorms; Special housing for disabled students; Women's dorms; 73% of campus accessible to physically disabled. **Special Academic Facilities/Equipment:** Averett's Flight Center located 4 miles from the main campus at Danville Regional Airport has two runways (one with ILS approach), automated weather system, and UNICOM service. Averett's facility houses aircraft, areas for ground instruction, simulator rooms, technology center. Averett's 100-acre Equestrian Center is a 15-minute drive from the main campus. It houses an indoor ring, 40 stalls with removable partitions, 3 tack rooms, wash room for horses and equipment, breeding area, offices, and a laboratory. The outdoor facilities include a round pen, riding ring, jumping area, pastures, and cross-country trails.

CAMPUS LIFE

Environment: Town. **Activities:** Campus Ministries; Choral groups; Concert band; Dance; Drama/theater; International Student Organization; Literary magazine; Music ensembles; Musical theater; Pep band; Student government. 16 registered organizations, 8 honor societies, 2 religious organizations, 2 fraternities, 1 sororities, on campus. **Athletics (Intercollegiate):** *Men:* baseball, basketball, cheerleading, cross-country, equestrian sports, football, golf, soccer, tennis. *Women:* basketball, cheerleading, cross-country, equestrian sports, soccer, softball, tennis, volleyball. **On-Campus Highlights:** Student Center.

ADMISSIONS

Freshman Academic Profile: Average high school GPA 3.2. 4% in top 10% of high school class, 19% in top 25% of high school class, 58% in top 50% of high school class. 87% from public high schools. **Test Scores:** SAT Math middle 50% range 430–530. SAT EBRW middle 50% range 430–530. ACT middle 50% range 15–20. **Basis for Candidate Selection:** *Very important factors include:* rigor of secondary school record, class rank, academic GPA, standardized test scores. *Other factors include:* application essay, recommendation(s), interview, extracurricular activities, character/personal qualities, alumni/ae relation, volunteer work, work experience, level of applicant's interest. **Freshman Admission Requirements:** High school diploma is required and GED is accepted. *Academic units required:* 4 English, 3 math, 3 science, 2 science labs, 3 social studies, 3 history. *Academic units recommended:* 2 foreign language. **Freshman Admission Statistics:** 2,745 applied, 65% admitted, 13% enrolled. **Transfer Admission Requirements:** College transcript(s), statement of good standing from prior institution(s). Minimum college GPA of 2.0 required. Lowest grade transferable C. **General Admission Information:** Non-fall registration accepted. Admission may be deferred for a maximum of 2 years.

COSTS AND FINANCIAL AID

Annual tuition $35,450. Room and board $10,560. Required fees $150. Average book and supplies expense $1,000. **Required Forms and Deadlines:** FAFSA; State aid form. **Types of Aid:** *Need-based scholarships/grants:* College/university scholarship or grant aid from institutional funds; Federal Pell; Private scholarships; SEOG; State scholarships/grants. *Loans:* Direct PLUS loans; Direct Subsidized Stafford Loans; Direct Unsubsidized Stafford Loans. **Student Employment:** Federal Work-Study Program available. Institutional employment available. **Financial Aid Statistics:** 100% needy freshmen, 100% needy undergrads receive need-based scholarship or grant aid. 9% freshmen, 9% undergrads receive non-need-based scholarship or grant aid. 83% freshmen, 84% undergrads receive need-based self-help aid. 0% freshmen, 0% undergrads receive athletic scholarships. 99% freshmen, 99% undergrads receive any aid. 75% undergrads borrow to pay for school. Average cumulative indebtedness $33,711. **Criteria awarding aid:** *Need-based:* Academics, Art, Job skills, Leadership, Minority status, Music/drama, Religious affiliation. *Non-need-based:* Academics, Alumni affiliation, Art, Job skills, Leadership, Minority status, Music/drama, Religious affiliation, State/district residency.

AZUSA PACIFIC UNIVERSITY

PO Box 7000, Azusa, CA 91702-7000
Phone: 626-812-3016 **Financial Aid Phone:** (626) 815-2020
E-mail: admissions@apu.edu **CEEB Code:** 4596
Fax: 626-812-3096 **Website:** www.apu.edu **ACT Code:** 0166

This private school, affiliated with the Christian (Nondenominational) Church, was founded in 1899. It has a 105 acre campus.

RATINGS

Admissions Selectivity Rating: 75 **Fire Safety Rating:** 64 **Green Rating:** 60*

STUDENTS AND FACULTY

Enrollment: 5,762. **Student Body:** 66% female, 34% male, 19% out-of-state, 3% international. Asian 9%, African American 5%, Caucasian 41%, Hispanic 31%, Native American <1%, Pacific Islander 1%, Two or more races 8%, Race unknown 2%.
Retention and Graduation: 86% freshmen return for sophomore year.
Faculty: Student/faculty ratio 12:1. 458 full-time faculty, 63% hold PhDs, 28% are members of minority groups, 52% are women.

ACADEMICS

Degrees: Bachelor's; Certificate; Doctoral degree—professional practice; Doctoral degree research/scholarship; Master's; Post-bachelor's certificate; Post-master's certificate. **Classes:** Most classes have 10–19 students. Most lab/discussion sessions have 10–19 students. **Most popular majors:** Business, Management, Marketing, and Related Support Services, Other; Psychology, General. **Special Study Options:** Accelerated program; Cooperative education program; Distance learning; Double major; English as a Second Language (ESL); Exchange student program (domestic); Honors program; Independent study; Internships; Study abroad; Teacher certification program. **Honors programs:** Every year, Azusa Pacific University attracts increasing numbers of the country's best students seeking a rigorous academic experience grounded in the Christian faith. The university has expanded the institution's investment in academically gifted students by establishing an Honors College. Today's top-performing students are tomorrow's leaders. The Honors College telos—its aim, purpose, end—is to liberally educate the next generation of intellectually gifted Christian leaders, helping them develop the moral and intellectual virtue, the right habits of the heart and of the mind, to become global leaders. **Combined degree programs:** BA/MA. **Disability Services offered:** Note-taking services; Tape recorders. **Career services:** Alumni services; Career assessment; Career/job search classes; Internships.

FACILITIES

Housing: Apartments for single students; Coed dorms; Men's dorms; Theme housing; Women's dorms; 100% of campus accessible to physically disabled. **Special Academic Facilities/Equipment:** Electron microscope.

CAMPUS LIFE

Environment: Town. **Activities:** Campus Ministries; Choral groups; Concert band; Dance; Drama/theater; International Student Organization; Jazz band; Literary magazine; Marching band; Music ensembles; Musical theater; Opera; Pep band; Radio station; Student government; Student newspaper; Student-run film society; Symphony orchestra; Television station; Yearbook. 47 registered organizations, 7 honor societies, on campus. **Athletics (Intercollegiate):** *Men:* baseball, basketball, cross-country, football, soccer, tennis, track/field (outdoor), volleyball. *Women:* basketball, cheerleading, cross-country, diving, soccer, softball, swimming, tennis, track/field (outdoor), volleyball, water polo. **On-Campus Highlights:** Coffee Shops.

ADMISSIONS

Freshman Academic Profile: Average high school GPA 3.7. **Test Scores:** SAT Math middle 50% range 460–580. SAT EBRW middle 50% range 470–580. ACT middle 50% range 21–26. **Basis for Candidate Selection:** *Very important factors include:* class rank, academic GPA, application essay, standardized test scores, character/personal qualities. *Important factors include:* recommendation(s), religious affiliation/commitment. *Other factors include:* rigor of secondary school record, interview, extracurricular activities, talent/ability, first generation, alumni/ae relation, racial/ethnic status, volunteer work, level of applicant's interest. **Freshman Admission Requirements:** High school diploma is required and GED is accepted. *Academic units recommended:* 4 English, 3 math, 2 science, 3 foreign language, 1 social studies, 2 history. **Freshman Admission Statistics:** 6,605 applied, 84% admitted, 21% enrolled. **Transfer Admission Requirements:** College transcript(s), essay or personal statement, statement of good standing from prior institution(s). Minimum college GPA of 2.2 required. Lowest grade transferable C. **General Admission Information:** Priority deadline 2/15. Regular application deadline 6/1.

COSTS AND FINANCIAL AID
Annual tuition $35,540. Room and board $9,492. Required fees $580. Average book and supplies expense $1,792. **Student Employment:** Federal Work-Study Program available. Institutional employment available. **Financial Aid Statistics:** 98% needy freshmen, 98% needy undergrads receive need-based scholarship or grant aid. 10% freshmen, 7% undergrads receive non-need-based scholarship or grant aid. 71% freshmen, 78% undergrads receive need-based self-help aid. 5% freshmen, 5% undergrads receive athletic scholarships. 35.3% freshmen, 38% undergrads receive any aid. 66% undergrads borrow to pay for school. Average cumulative indebtedness $24,338.

BABSON COLLEGE

Best Colleges

Lunder Hall, Babson Park, MA 02457
Phone: 781-239-5522 **Financial Aid Phone:** 781.239.4219
E-mail: ugradadmission@babson.edu **CEEB Code:** 2121
Fax: 781-239-4006 **Website:** www.babson.edu **ACT Code:** 1780

This private school was founded in 1919. It has a 370 acre campus.

RATINGS
Admissions Selectivity Rating: 95   **Fire Safety Rating:** 95   **Green Rating:** 91

STUDENTS AND FACULTY
Enrollment: 2,361. **Student Body:** 48% female, 52% male, 71% out-of-state, 28% international (81 countries represented). Asian 12%, African American 4%, Caucasian 36%, Hispanic 11%, Native American <1%, Pacific Islander <1%, Two or more races 2%, Race unknown 5%.
Retention and Graduation: 95% freshmen return for sophomore year. 90% freshmen graduate within 4 years. 92% freshmen graduate within 6 years. 4% grads go on to further study within 1 year. 1% grads pursue arts and sciences degrees. <1% grads pursue law degrees. 2% grads pursue business degrees.
Faculty: Student/faculty ratio 14:1. 195 full-time faculty, 88% hold PhDs, 19% are members of minority groups, 41% are women. 0% of classes are taught by teaching assistants.

ACADEMICS
Degrees: Bachelor's; Master's; Post-bachelor's certificate. **Classes:** Most classes have 20–29 students. **Most popular majors:** Business Administration and Management, General. **Special Study Options:** Accelerated program; Cross-registration; Honors program; Independent study; Internships; Study abroad. **Honors programs:** This Honors Program has three main components in which students add to their academic and personal development. This includes an Honors seminar, an Honors thesis and a required international experience. **Disability Services offered:** Note-taking services; Reader services; Tape recorders; Tutors. **Career services:** Alumni network; Alumni services; Career assessment; Career/job search classes; Internships; Regional alumni.

FACILITIES
Housing: Coed dorms; Fraternity/sorority housing; Theme housing; Wellness housing. **Special Academic Facilities/Equipment:** The Babson World Globe, Roger Babson Museum, Isaac Newton Museum, Arthur M. Blank Center for Entrepreneurship, Center for Women's Entrepreneurial Leadership, Media and Design Studio, Babson TV, Babson Radio, Stephen D. Cutler Center for Investments & Finance, Leonard A. Schlesinger Innovation Center.

CAMPUS LIFE
Environment: Village. **Activities:** Campus Ministries; Choral groups; Dance; Drama/theater; International Student Organization; Literary magazine; Model UN; Music ensembles; Musical theater; Radio station; Student government; Student newspaper; Student-run film society. 120 registered organizations, 2 honor societies, 8 religious organizations, 4 fraternities, 3 sororities, on campus. **Athletics (Intercollegiate):** *Men:* baseball, basketball, cross-country, diving, golf, ice hockey, lacrosse, skiing (downhill/Alpine), soccer, swimming, tennis, track/field (outdoor), track/field (indoor). *Women:* basketball, cross-country, diving, field hockey, lacrosse, skiing (downhill/Alpine), soccer, softball,

swimming, tennis, track/field (outdoor), track/field (indoor), volleyball. **On-Campus Highlights:** Reynolds Campus Center. **Environmental Initiatives:** Investment of $4 million into energy efficiency and capital improvements to save energy.

ADMISSIONS
Freshman Academic Profile: 63% in top 10% of high school class, 84% in top 25% of high school class. **Test Scores:** SAT Math middle 50% range 650–760. SAT EBRW middle 50% range 620–690. ACT middle 50% range 28–32. **Basis for Candidate Selection:** *Very important factors include:* rigor of secondary school record, class rank, academic GPA, application essay, standardized test scores, recommendation(s), extracurricular activities, character/personal qualities. *Other factors include:* interview, talent/ability, first generation, alumni/ae relation, geographical residence, state residency, racial/ethnic status, volunteer work, work experience, level of applicant's interest. **Freshman Admission Requirements:** High school diploma is required and GED is accepted. *Academic units required:* 4 English, 4 math, 3 science, 4 social studies. *Academic units recommended:* 4 English, 4 math, 3 science, 4 foreign language, 4 social studies. **Freshman Admission Statistics:** 6,383 applied, 24% admitted, 35% enrolled. **Transfer Admission Requirements:** High school transcript, college transcript(s), essay or personal statement, statement of good standing from prior institution(s). Lowest grade transferable C. **General Admission Information:** Application fee $75. Priority deadline 11/1. Regular application deadline 1/2. Non-fall registration accepted. Admission may be deferred for a maximum of 2 years.

COSTS AND FINANCIAL AID
Annual tuition $52,608. Room and board $16,776. Average book and supplies expense $1,144. **Required Forms and Deadlines:** CSS/Financial Aid PROFILE; FAFSA; Noncustodial PROFILE. **Notification of Awards:** Applicants will be notified of awards on or about 4/1. **Types of Aid:** *Need-based scholarships/grants:* College/university scholarship or grant aid from institutional funds; Federal Pell; Private scholarships; SEOG; State scholarships/grants. *Loans:* Direct PLUS loans; Direct Subsidized Stafford Loans; Direct Unsubsidized Stafford Loans. **Student Employment:** Federal Work-Study Program available. Institutional employment available. **Financial Aid Statistics:** 93% needy freshmen, 96% needy undergrads receive need-based scholarship or grant aid. 14% freshmen, 15% undergrads receive non-need-based scholarship or grant aid. 90% freshmen, 80% undergrads receive need-based self-help aid. 0% freshmen, 0% undergrads receive athletic scholarships. 46% freshmen, 47% undergrads receive any aid. 40% undergrads borrow to pay for school. Average cumulative indebtedness $37,866. **Criteria awarding aid:** *Non-need-based:* Academics, Leadership.

BAKER UNIVERSITY

P.O. Box 65, Baldwin City, KS 66006
Phone: 785-594-8325 **Financial Aid Phone:** 785-594-4595
E-mail: admissions@bakeru.edu **CEEB Code:** 6031
Fax: 785-594-8353 **Website:** www.bakerU.edu **ACT Code:** 1386

This private school, affiliated with the Methodist Church, was founded in 1858. It has a 36 acre campus.

RATINGS
Admissions Selectivity Rating: 74   **Fire Safety Rating:** 94   **Green Rating:** 60*

STUDENTS AND FACULTY
Enrollment: 854. **Student Body:** 49% female, 51% male, 28% out-of-state, 3% international (15 countries represented). Asian 1%, African American 8%, Caucasian 70%, Hispanic 10%, Native American 1%, Pacific Islander 1%, Two or more races 6%, Race unknown 1%.
Retention and Graduation: 75% freshmen return for sophomore year. 45% freshmen graduate within 4 years. 64% freshmen graduate within 6 years. 25% grads go on to further study within 1 year. 7% grads pursue arts and sciences degrees. 0% grads pursue law degrees. 4% grads pursue business degrees. 1% grads pursue medical degrees. **Faculty:** Student/faculty ratio 11:1. 60 full-time faculty, 90% hold PhDs, 5% are members of minority groups, 52% are women. 0% of classes are taught by teaching assistants.

ACADEMICS
Degrees: Bachelor's. **Classes:** Most classes have 10–19 students. Most lab/discussion sessions have fewer than 10 students. **Most popular majors:** Exercise Science and Kinesiology; Business/Commerce, General; Sport and Fitness

Administration/Management. **Special Study Options:** Accelerated program; Double major; Dual enrollment; Honors program; Independent study; Internships; Liberal arts/career combination; Student-designed major; Study abroad; Teacher certification program. **Honors programs:** Promising Scholars Honors Program, Bronston Fellows Program. **Disability Services offered:** Note-taking services; Reader services; Tape recorders; Tutors. **Career services:** Alumni services; Career assessment; Career/job search classes; Internships.

FACILITIES

Housing: Apartments for single students; Coed dorms; Fraternity/sorority housing; Men's dorms; Special housing for disabled students; Women's dorms; 85% of campus accessible to physically disabled. **Special Academic Facilities/Equipment:** Old Castle Museum, Quayle Bible Collection. **Campus network:** 100% of classrooms, 100% of dorms, 100% of student union, 100% of libraries, 100% of dining areas, 100% of common outdoor areas, have wireless network access.

CAMPUS LIFE

Environment: Rural. **Activities:** Campus Ministries; Choral groups; Concert band; Dance; Drama/theater; International Student Organization; Jazz band; Literary magazine; Music ensembles; Musical theater; Pep band; Radio station; Student government; Student newspaper; Symphony orchestra; Television station. 75 registered organizations, 12 honor societies, 3 religious organizations, 4 fraternities, 4 sororities, on campus. **Athletics (Intercollegiate):** *Men:* baseball, basketball, cheerleading, cross-country, football, golf, soccer, tennis, track/field (outdoor), track/field (indoor), wrestling. *Women:* basketball, bowling, cheerleading, cross-country, golf, soccer, softball, tennis, track/field (outdoor), track/field (indoor), volleyball. **On-Campus Highlights:** Library.

ADMISSIONS

Freshman Academic Profile: Average high school GPA 3.5. 21% in top 10% of high school class, 44% in top 25% of high school class, 73% in top 50% of high school class. 95% from public high schools. **Test Scores:** ACT middle 50% range 20–25. **Basis for Candidate Selection:** *Very important factors include:* rigor of secondary school record, academic GPA, standardized test scores, level of applicant's interest. *Other factors include:* class rank, application essay, recommendation(s), interview, extracurricular activities, talent/ability, character/personal qualities, alumni/ae relation, geographical residence, volunteer work, work experience. **Freshman Admission Requirements:** High school diploma is required and GED is accepted. *Academic units recommended:* 4 English, 3 math, 3 science, 1 science labs, 2 foreign language, 3 social studies, 1 visual/performing arts. **Freshman Admission Statistics:** 839 applied, 88% admitted, 33% enrolled. **Transfer Admission Requirements:** High school transcript, college transcript(s), standardized test scores. Minimum college GPA of 2.3 required. Lowest grade transferable C. **General Admission Information:** Priority deadline 3/1. Non-fall registration accepted. Admission may be deferred for a maximum of 1 year.

COSTS AND FINANCIAL AID

Annual tuition $30,170. Room and board $9,150. Required fees $600. Average book and supplies expense $1,200. **Required Forms and Deadlines:** FAFSA. **Notification of Awards:** Applicants will be notified of awards on a rolling basis beginning 1/1. **Types of Aid:** *Need-based scholarships/grants:* College/university scholarship or grant aid from institutional funds; Federal Pell; Private scholarships; SEOG; State scholarships/grants. *Loans:* Direct PLUS loans; Direct Subsidized Stafford Loans; Direct Unsubsidized Stafford Loans. **Student Employment:** Federal Work-Study Program available. Institutional employment available. **Financial Aid Statistics:** 65% needy freshmen, 72% needy undergrads receive need-based scholarship or grant aid. 100% freshmen, 99% undergrads receive non-need-based scholarship or grant aid. 75% freshmen, 65% undergrads receive need-based self-help aid. 72% freshmen, 66% undergrads receive athletic scholarships. 100% freshmen, 92% undergrads receive any aid. 65% undergrads borrow to pay for school. Average cumulative indebtedness $33,046. **Criteria awarding aid:** *Need-based:* Minority status. *Non-need-based:* Academics, Alumni affiliation, Art, Athletics, Music/drama, Religious affiliation.

BALDWIN WALLACE UNIVERSITY

275 Eastland Rd, Berea, OH 44017
Phone: 440-826-2222 **Financial Aid Phone:** 440-826-2108
E-mail: admission@bw.edu **CEEB Code:** 1050
Fax: 440-826-3830 **Website:** www.bw.edu **ACT Code:** 3236

This private school, affiliated with the United Methodist Church, was founded in 1845. It has a 153 acre campus.

RATINGS

Admissions Selectivity Rating: 81 **Fire Safety Rating:** 86 **Green Rating:** 80

STUDENTS AND FACULTY

Enrollment: 2,925. **Student Body:** 54% female, 46% male, 26% out-of-state, 1% international (12 countries represented). Asian 1%, African American 8%, Caucasian 79%, Hispanic 6%, Native American <1%, Pacific Islander <1%, Two or more races 5%, Race unknown <1%.
Retention and Graduation: 81% freshmen return for sophomore year. 51% freshmen graduate within 4 years. 65% freshmen graduate within 6 years. 16% grads go on to further study within 1 year. 3% grads pursue arts and sciences degrees. 0% grads pursue law degrees. 1% grads pursue business degrees. 0% grads pursue medical degrees. **Faculty:** Student/faculty ratio 11:1. 225 full-time faculty, 74% hold PhDs, 12% are members of minority groups, 52% are women. 0% of classes are taught by teaching assistants.

ACADEMICS

Degrees: Bachelor's; Certificate; Master's; Post-master's certificate. **Classes:** Most classes have 10–19 students. Most lab/discussion sessions have 10–19 students. **Most popular majors:** Psychology, General; Accounting; Biology/Biological Sciences, General. **Special Study Options:** Accelerated program; Cross-registration; Distance learning; Double major; Dual enrollment; English as a Second Language (ESL); Exchange student program (domestic); Honors program; Independent study; Internships; Liberal arts/career combination; Student-designed major; Study abroad; Teacher certification program; Weekend college. **Honors programs:** The Honors Program at Baldwin Wallace University provides students with an enriched liberal arts curriculum characterized by interdisciplinary courses and an emphasis on experiential learning. Both curricular and co-curricular in nature, the Honors Program offers opportunities to live in Honors-specific housing; annual programming related to leadership development, community service, and career preparation; and numerous community-building activities that begin with a first-year student overnight orientation prior to the start of fall classes. Other special opportunities and privileges include subsidized domestic and international travel experiences; annual trips to regional Honors conferences; priority registration; and mini-scholarships to help fund study abroad, service trips, and the purchase of research supplies. **Disability Services offered:** Note-taking services; Reader services; Tutors. **Career services:** Alumni network; Alumni services; Career assessment; Career/job search classes; Internships.

FACILITIES

Housing: Apartments for single students; Coed dorms; Fraternity/sorority housing; Special housing for disabled students; Special housing for international students; Theme housing; 80% of campus accessible to physically disabled. **Special Academic Facilities/Equipment:** Art gallery, electron microscope, observatory. **Campus network:** 100% of classrooms, 100% of dorms, 100% of student union, 100% of libraries, 100% of dining areas, have wireless network access.

CAMPUS LIFE

Environment: Village. **Activities:** Campus Ministries; Choral groups; Concert band; Dance; Drama/theater; Jazz band; Literary magazine; Marching band; Model UN; Music ensembles; Musical theater; Opera; Pep band; Radio station; Student government; Student newspaper; Student-run film society; Symphony orchestra; Television station. 120 registered organizations, 26 honor societies, 6 religious organizations, 8 fraternities, 6 sororities, on campus. **Athletics (Intercollegiate):** *Men:* baseball, basketball, cross-country, diving, football, golf, soccer, swimming, tennis, track/field (outdoor), track/field (indoor), wrestling. *Women:* basketball, cross-country, diving, golf, soccer, softball, swimming, tennis, track/field (outdoor), track/field (indoor), volleyball. **On-Campus Highlights:** Hive Cafe. **Environmental Initiatives:** Commitment to geo-thermal energy with all new buildings and major renovations.

ADMISSIONS

Freshman Academic Profile: Average high school GPA 3.6. 16% in top 10% of high school class, 48% in top 25% of high school class, 82% in top 50% of high school class. 80% from public high schools. **Test Scores:** SAT Math middle 50% range 520–620. SAT EBRW middle 50% range 520–633. ACT middle 50% range 21–27. **Basis for Candidate Selection:** *Very important factors include:* rigor of secondary school record, academic GPA. *Important factors include:* class rank, application essay, standardized test scores, extracurricular activities, talent/ability, character/personal qualities. *Other factors include:* recommendation(s), interview, first generation, alumni/ae relation, geographical residence, state residency, racial/ethnic status, volunteer work, work experience, level of applicant's interest. **Freshman Admission Requirements:** High school diploma is required and GED is accepted. *Academic units required:* 4 English, 4 math, 3 science, 2 science labs, 1 foreign language, 2 social studies, 1 history. *Academic units recommended:* 4 English, 4 math, 4 science, 2 science labs, 2 foreign language, 3 social studies, 1 history, 3 academic electives. **Freshman Admission Statistics:** 3,922 applied, 73% admitted, 23% enrolled. **Transfer Admission Requirements:** High school transcript, college transcript(s), statement of good standing from prior institution(s). Minimum college GPA of 2.5 required. Lowest grade transferable C. **General Admission Information:** Application fee $25. Priority deadline 3/1. Non-fall registration accepted. Admission may be deferred for a maximum of 1 year.

COSTS AND FINANCIAL AID

Annual tuition $34,504. Room and board $11,946. Average book and supplies expense $1,500. **Required Forms and Deadlines:** FAFSA. **Notification of Awards:** Applicants will be notified of awards on a rolling basis beginning 12/4. **Types of Aid:** *Need-based scholarships/grants:* College/university scholarship or grant aid from institutional funds; Federal Pell; Private scholarships; SEOG; State scholarships/grants. *Loans:* Direct PLUS loans; Direct Subsidized Stafford Loans; Direct Unsubsidized Stafford Loans. **Student Employment:** Federal Work-Study Program available. Institutional employment available. **Financial Aid Statistics:** 100% needy freshmen, 98% needy undergrads receive need-based scholarship or grant aid. 21% freshmen, 21% undergrads receive non-need-based scholarship or grant aid. 100% freshmen, 79% undergrads receive need-based self-help aid. 0% freshmen, 0% undergrads receive athletic scholarships. 100% freshmen, 98% undergrads receive any aid. 76% undergrads borrow to pay for school. Average cumulative indebtedness $33,919. **Criteria awarding aid:** *Need-based:* Academics, Minority status, Music/drama, Religious affiliation. *Non-need-based:* Academics, Alumni affiliation, Art, Minority status, Music/drama, Religious affiliation, State/district residency.

BALL STATE UNIVERSITY

Admissions Office, Ball State University, Muncie, IN 47306-0855
Phone: 765-285-8300 **Financial Aid Phone:** (765) 285-5600
E-mail: askus@bsu.edu **CEEB Code:** 1051
Fax: 765-285-1632 **Website:** www.bsu.edu **ACT Code:** 1176

This public school was founded in 1918. It has a 1140 acre campus.

RATINGS

Admissions Selectivity Rating: 85 **Fire Safety Rating:** 89 **Green Rating:** 91

STUDENTS AND FACULTY

Enrollment: 15,689. **Student Body:** 59% female, 41% male, 13% out-of-state, 2% international (44 countries represented). Asian 1%, African American 7%, Caucasian 80%, Hispanic 4%, Native American <1%, Pacific Islander <1%, Two or more races 3%, Race unknown 2%. **Retention and Graduation:** 82% freshmen return for sophomore year. **Faculty:** Student/faculty ratio 14:1. 1,017 full-time faculty, 74% hold PhDs, 7% are members of minority groups, 47% are women.

ACADEMICS

Degrees: Associate; Bachelor's; Certificate; Doctoral degree—professional practice; Doctoral degree research/scholarship; Master's; Post-bachelor's certificate; Post-master's certificate. **Classes:** Most classes have 20–29 students. **Most popular majors:** Radio and Television; Elementary Education and Teaching; General Studies. **Special Study Options:** Accelerated program; Cooperative education program; Distance learning; Double major; Dual enrollment; English as a Second Language (ESL); External degree program; Honors program; Independent study; Internships; Liberal arts/career combination; Student-designed major; Study abroad; Teacher certification

program. **Honors programs:** BSU offers an Honors College which has its own curriculum, undergraduate research fellowships and study abroad programs. **Disability Services offered:** Note-taking services; Reader services; Tape recorders; Tutors. **Career services:** Alumni services; Career assessment; Career/job search classes; Internships; Regional alumni.

FACILITIES

Housing: Apartments for married students; Apartments for single students; Coed dorms; Fraternity/sorority housing; Men's dorms; Special housing for disabled students; Special housing for international students; Theme housing; Women's dorms; 95% of campus accessible to physically disabled. **Special Academic Facilities/Equipment:** Art gallery, museum, on-campus school (K-12), learning center, weather station, physical therapy lab, human performance lab, student wellness and recreation center including rock climbing wall, planetarium/observatory, wildlife and nature preserve. **Campus network:** 75% of classrooms, 90% of dorms, 85% of student union, 100% of libraries, 85% of dining areas, 50% of common outdoor areas, have wireless network access.

CAMPUS LIFE

Environment: City. **Activities:** Campus Ministries; Choral groups; Concert band; Dance; Drama/theater; International Student Organization; Jazz band; Literary magazine; Marching band; Music ensembles; Opera; Pep band; Radio station; Student government; Student newspaper; Student-run film society; Symphony orchestra; Television station. 369 registered organizations, 33 honor societies, 27 religious organizations, 16 fraternities, 15 sororities, on campus. **Athletics (Intercollegiate):** *Men:* baseball, basketball, cheerleading, cross-country, diving, football, golf, swimming, tennis, volleyball. *Women:* basketball, cheerleading, cross-country, diving, field hockey, golf, gymnastics, soccer, softball, swimming, tennis, track/field (outdoor), volleyball. **On-Campus Highlights:** Student Recreation and Wellness Facility. **Environmental Initiatives:** Installing a district-scale ground-source heating and cooling system to serve all 45 campus buildings and eliminate four coal-fired boilers and reduce our GHG emissions by nearly 50%.

ADMISSIONS

Freshman Academic Profile: Average high school GPA 3.5. 19% in top 10% of high school class, 50% in top 25% of high school class, 90% in top 50% of high school class. 93% from public high schools. **Test Scores:** SAT Math middle 50% range 500–590. SAT EBRW middle 50% range 510–600. ACT middle 50% range 20–24. **Basis for Candidate Selection:** *Very important factors include:* rigor of secondary school record, academic GPA, standardized test scores. *Other factors include:* application essay, recommendation(s), extracurricular activities, talent/ability, volunteer work, work experience. **Freshman Admission Requirements:** High school diploma is required and GED is accepted. *Academic units required:* 4 English, 3 math, 3 science, 2 science labs, 2 social studies, 1 history. *Academic units recommended:* 4 math, 3 foreign language. **Freshman Admission Statistics:** 22,147 applied, 61% admitted, 26% enrolled. **Transfer Admission Requirements:** College transcript(s). Minimum college GPA of 2.0 required. Lowest grade transferable C. **General Admission Information:** Application fee $55. Priority deadline 3/1. Regular application deadline 8/10. Non-fall registration accepted.

COSTS AND FINANCIAL AID

Annual in-state tuition $8,992. Annual out-of-state tuition $24,766. Room and board $9,936. Required fees $602. Average book and supplies expense $1,320. **Required Forms and Deadlines:** FAFSA. **Notification of Awards:** Applicants will be notified of awards on a rolling basis beginning 4/1. **Types of Aid:** *Need-based scholarships/grants:* College/university scholarship or grant aid from institutional funds; Federal Pell; Private scholarships; SEOG; State scholarships/grants. *Loans:* Direct PLUS loans; Direct Subsidized Stafford Loans; Direct Unsubsidized Stafford Loans. **Student Employment:** Federal Work-Study Program available. Institutional employment available. **Financial Aid Statistics:** 55% needy freshmen, 60% needy undergrads receive need-based scholarship or grant aid. 71% freshmen, 53% undergrads receive non-need-based scholarship or grant aid. 92% freshmen, 90% undergrads receive need-based self-help aid. 2% freshmen, 2% undergrads receive athletic scholarships. 82% freshmen, 78% undergrads receive any aid. 72% undergrads borrow to pay for school. Average cumulative indebtedness $27,732. **Criteria awarding aid:** *Need-based:* Academics, Alumni affiliation, Art, Leadership, Minority status, Music/drama. *Non-need-based:* Academics, Athletics, Leadership, Minority status, Music/drama, State/district residency.

BAPTIST COLLEGE OF FLORIDA

5400 College Drive, Graceville, FL 32440-1898
Phone: 850-263-3261 **Financial Aid Phone:** 18003282660 ext. 461
E-mail: admissions@baptistcollege.edu
Fax: 850-263-9026 **Website:** www.baptistcollege.edu **ACT Code:** 6870

This private school, affiliated with the Southern Baptist Church, was founded in 1943. It has a 250 acre campus.

RATINGS
Admissions Selectivity Rating: 74   **Fire Safety Rating:** 81   **Green Rating:** 60*

STUDENTS AND FACULTY
Enrollment: 296. **Student Body:** 43% female, 57% male, 27% out-of-state, <1% international (1 countries represented). Asian 1%, African American 7%, Caucasian 77%, Hispanic 2%, Native American 1%, Pacific Islander <1%, Two or more races 1%, Race unknown 10%.
Retention and Graduation: 47% freshmen return for sophomore year. 27% freshmen graduate within 4 years. 63% freshmen graduate within 6 years. 50% grads go on to further study within 1 year. **Faculty:** Student/faculty ratio 8:1. 23 full-time faculty, 65% hold PhDs, 4% are members of minority groups, 30% are women. 0% of classes are taught by teaching assistants.

ACADEMICS
Degrees: Associate; Bachelor's; Master's. **Classes:** Most classes have fewer than 10 students. **Most popular majors:** Pastoral Studies/Counseling; Religious Education; Theology/Theological Studies. **Special Study Options:** Distance learning; Double major; Dual enrollment; Independent study; Internships; Liberal arts/career combination. **Disability Services offered:** Note-taking services; Reader services; Tape recorders; Tutors. **Career services:** Alumni services; Internships.

FACILITIES
Housing: Apartments for married students; Apartments for single students; Men's dorms; Special housing for disabled students; Women's dorms; 100% of campus accessible to physically disabled. **Special Academic Facilities/Equipment:** Florida Baptist Historical Society; Heritage Village; Weight Rooms in Wellness Center. **Campus network:** 100% of classrooms, 100% of dorms, 100% of student union, 100% of libraries, 100% of dining areas, have wireless network access.

CAMPUS LIFE
Environment: Rural. **Activities:** Campus Ministries; Choral groups; Concert band; Drama/theater; Jazz band; Music ensembles; Musical theater; Radio station. 1 registered organizations, 2 religious organizations, on campus. **Athletics (Intercollegiate):** *Men:* golf. *Women:* volleyball. **On-Campus Highlights:** Athletic Center.

ADMISSIONS
Test Scores: SAT Math middle 50% range 393–555. SAT EBRW middle 50% range 465–600. ACT middle 50% range 15–21. **Basis for Candidate Selection:** *Very important factors include:* recommendation(s), character/personal qualities, religious affiliation/commitment, level of applicant's interest. *Important factors include:* academic GPA, talent/ability, alumni/ae relation. *Other factors include:* rigor of secondary school record, standardized test scores, interview, extracurricular activities, volunteer work. **Freshman Admission Requirements:** High school diploma is required and GED is accepted. *Academic units recommended:* 4 English, 4 math, 3 science, 1 social studies, 2 history. **Freshman Admission Statistics:** 78 applied, 94% admitted, 38% enrolled. **Transfer Admission Requirements:** High school transcript, college transcript(s), essay or personal statement. Minimum college GPA of 2.0 required. Lowest grade transferable C. **General Admission Information:** Application fee $25. Regular application deadline 8/15. Non-fall registration accepted. Admission may be deferred for a maximum of 2 semesters.

COSTS AND FINANCIAL AID
Annual tuition $10,500. Room and board $4,612. Required fees $900. Average book and supplies expense $1,050. **Required Forms and Deadlines:** Business/Farm Supplement; FAFSA; Institution's own financial aid form; State aid form. **Notification of Awards:** Applicants will be notified of awards on a rolling basis beginning 6/15. **Types of Aid:** *Need-based scholarships/grants:* Federal Pell; Private scholarships; SEOG; State scholarships/grants. *Loans:* Direct PLUS loans; Direct Subsidized Stafford Loans; Direct Unsubsidized Stafford Loans. **Student Employment:** Federal Work-Study Program available. Institutional employment available. **Financial Aid Statistics:** 48% needy freshmen, 71%

needy undergrads receive need-based scholarship or grant aid. 2% freshmen, 2% undergrads receive non-need-based scholarship or grant aid. 21% freshmen, 44% undergrads receive need-based self-help aid. 0% freshmen, 0% undergrads receive athletic scholarships. 66% undergrads borrow to pay for school. Average cumulative indebtedness $15,465. **Criteria awarding aid:** *Need-based:* Academics, Minority status, Music/drama, Religious affiliation. *Non-need-based:* Academics, Minority status, Music/drama, Religious affiliation.

BARD COLLEGE

Office of Admissions, Annandale-on-Hudson, NY 12504
Phone: 845-758-7472 **Financial Aid Phone:** 845-758-7526
E-mail: admissions@bard.edu **CEEB Code:** 2037
Fax: 845-758-5208 **Website:** www.bard.edu **ACT Code:** 2674

This private school was founded in 1860. It has a 1000 acre campus.

RATINGS
Admissions Selectivity Rating: 86   **Fire Safety Rating:** 97   **Green Rating:** 92

STUDENTS AND FACULTY
Enrollment: 1,804. **Student Body:** 59% female, 41% male, 66% out-of-state, 11% international (57 countries represented). Asian 4%, African American 6%, Caucasian 57%, Hispanic 10%, Native American <1%, Pacific Islander 0%, Two or more races 5%, Race unknown 6%.
Retention and Graduation: 85% freshmen return for sophomore year. 62% freshmen graduate within 4 years. 74% freshmen graduate within 6 years. **Faculty:** Student/faculty ratio 10:1. 156 full-time faculty, 90% hold PhDs, 20% are members of minority groups, 42% are women. 0% of classes are taught by teaching assistants.

ACADEMICS
Degrees: Associate; Bachelor's; Doctoral degree research/scholarship; Master's. **Classes:** Most classes have 10–19 students. **Most popular majors:** English Language and Literature, General; Visual and Performing Arts, General; Social Sciences, General. **Special Study Options:** Cross-registration; Double major; Dual enrollment; English as a Second Language (ESL); Independent study; Internships; Student-designed major; Study abroad. **Combined degree programs:** BA/MA; BA/MEng. **Disability Services offered:** Note-taking services; Reader services; Tape recorders; Tutors. **Career services:** Alumni network; Alumni services; Career assessment; Career/job search classes; Internships; Regional alumni.

FACILITIES
Housing: Coed dorms; Cooperative housing; Special housing for disabled students; Theme housing; Wellness housing; Women's dorms; 70% of campus accessible to physically disabled. **Special Academic Facilities/Equipment:** Performing arts center, gallery, art museum, collection of contemporary art, center for curatorial studies, language lab, nursery school, ecology field station, archaeology field school, economics institute.

CAMPUS LIFE
Environment: Rural. **Activities:** Campus Ministries; Choral groups; Concert band; Dance; Drama/theater; International Student Organization; Jazz band; Literary magazine; Model UN; Music ensembles; Musical theater; Opera; Radio station; Student government; Student newspaper; Student-run film society; Symphony orchestra. 150 registered organizations, 5 religious organizations, on campus. **Athletics (Intercollegiate):** *Men:* basketball, cross-country, soccer, squash, tennis, track/field (outdoor), volleyball. *Women:* basketball, cross-country, soccer, tennis, track/field (outdoor), volleyball. **On-Campus Highlights:** Richard B Fisher Center for the Performing Arts **Environmental Initiatives:** 40% of the total building square footages utilizes geothermal heat-exchange for space heating and cooling

ADMISSIONS
Freshman Academic Profile: 41% in top 10% of high school class, 69% in top 25% of high school class, 94% in top 50% of high school class. 58% from public high schools. **Test Scores:** ACT middle 50% range 27–31. **Basis for Candidate Selection:** *Very important factors include:* rigor of secondary school record, academic GPA, application essay, recommendation(s), extracurricular

activities, talent/ability, character/personal qualities. *Other factors include:* class rank, standardized test scores, interview, first generation, alumni/ae relation, geographical residence, state residency, religious affiliation/commitment, racial/ethnic status, level of applicant's interest. **Freshman Admission Requirements:** High school diploma is required and GED is accepted. *Academic units recommended:* 4 English, 4 math, 4 science, 3 science labs, 4 foreign language, 4 social studies, 4 history. **Freshman Admission Statistics:** 5,141 applied, 65% admitted, 15% enrolled. **Transfer Admission Requirements:** College transcript(s), essay or personal statement, statement of good standing from prior institution(s). Minimum college GPA of 3.0 required. Lowest grade transferable C. **General Admission Information:** Application fee $50. Regular application deadline 1/1. Admission may be deferred for a maximum of 1 year.

COSTS AND FINANCIAL AID
Annual tuition $55,566. Room and board $15,876. Required fees $470. Average book and supplies expense $1,100. **Required Forms and Deadlines:** CSS/Financial Aid PROFILE; FAFSA; Noncustodial PROFILE. **Notification of Awards:** Applicants will be notified of awards on or about 4/1. **Types of Aid:** *Need-based scholarships/grants:* College/university scholarship or grant aid from institutional funds; Federal Pell; Private scholarships; SEOG; State scholarships/grants. *Loans:* Direct PLUS loans; Direct Subsidized Stafford Loans; Direct Unsubsidized Stafford Loans. **Student Employment:** Federal Work-Study Program available. Institutional employment available. **Financial Aid Statistics:** 97% needy freshmen, 96% needy undergrads receive need-based scholarship or grant aid. 0% freshmen, 0% undergrads receive non-need-based scholarship or grant aid. 82% freshmen, 81% undergrads receive need-based self-help aid. 0% freshmen, 0% undergrads receive athletic scholarships. 69% freshmen, 68% undergrads receive any aid. 57% undergrads borrow to pay for school. Average cumulative indebtedness $27,726. **Criteria awarding aid:** *Need-based:* Academics. *Non-need-based:* Academics.

BARD COLLEGE AT SIMON'S ROCK

84 Alford Road, Great Barrington, MA 01230
Phone: 413-528-7228 **Financial Aid Phone:** 413-528-7297
E-mail: admit@simons-rock.edu **CEEB Code:** 3795
Fax: 413-541-0081 **Website:** www.simons-rock.edu **ACT Code:** 1893

This private school was founded in 1964. It has a 275 acre campus.

RATINGS
Admissions Selectivity Rating: 79 **Fire Safety Rating:** 95 **Green Rating:** 78

STUDENTS AND FACULTY
Enrollment: 391. **Student Body:** 60% female, 40% male, 66% out-of-state, 37% international (18 countries represented). Asian 14%, African American 12%, Caucasian 12%, Hispanic 5%, Native American 1%, Pacific Islander 1%, Two or more races 6%, Race unknown 12%.
Retention and Graduation: 77% freshmen return for sophomore year.
Faculty: Student/faculty ratio 6:1. 46 full-time faculty, 93% hold PhDs, 13% are members of minority groups, 46% are women. 0% of classes are taught by teaching assistants.

ACADEMICS
Degrees: Associate; Bachelor's. **Classes:** Most classes have 10–19 students. Most lab/discussion sessions have 10–19 students. **Most popular majors:** Computer Science; General Literature; Psychology, General. **Special Study Options:** Double major; External degree program; Independent study; Internships; Student-designed major; Study abroad. **Disability Services offered:** Note-taking services; Reader services; Tape recorders; Tutors. **Career services:** Alumni network; Alumni services; Career assessment; Career/job search classes; Internships; Regional alumni.

FACILITIES
Housing: Coed dorms; Men's dorms; Special housing for disabled students; Women's dorms; 80% of campus accessible to physically disabled. **Special Academic Facilities/Equipment:** Kellogg Music Center Daniel Arts Center Hillman/Jackson Gallery Fisher Science Center Liebowitz Center for International Studies.

CAMPUS LIFE
Environment: Village. **Activities:** Choral groups; Dance; Drama/theater; International Student Organization; Jazz band; Literary magazine; Model UN; Music ensembles; Student government; Student newspaper; Yearbook.

25 registered organizations, on campus. **Athletics (Intercollegiate):** *Men:* basketball, soccer, swimming, tennis. *Women:* basketball, soccer, swimming, tennis. **On-Campus Highlights:** Fisher Science and Academic Center. **Environmental Initiatives:** The College is currently expanding renewable energy sources. This month, solar panels will be lit which will generate 12% of our electricity use annually.

ADMISSIONS
Freshman Academic Profile: Average high school GPA 3.5. 50% in top 10% of high school class, 72% in top 25% of high school class, 97% in top 50% of high school class. 58% from public high schools. **Basis for Candidate Selection:** *Very important factors include:* rigor of secondary school record, academic GPA, application essay, interview, talent/ability. *Important factors include:* recommendation(s), character/personal qualities. *Other factors include:* class rank, standardized test scores, extracurricular activities, first generation, alumni/ae relation, volunteer work, work experience, level of applicant's interest. **Freshman Admission Requirements:** High school diploma or equivalent is not required *Academic units recommended:* 2 English, 2 math, 2 science, 2 foreign language, 2 social studies, 2 history. **Freshman Admission Statistics:** 244 applied, 93% admitted, 66% enrolled. **Transfer Admission Requirements:** College transcript(s), essay or personal statement, interview. Minimum college GPA of 2.0 required. Lowest grade transferable C. **General Admission Information:** Non-fall registration accepted.

COSTS AND FINANCIAL AID
Annual tuition $56,398. Room and board $15,672. Required fees $2,109. Average book and supplies expense $1,000. **Required Forms and Deadlines:** CSS/Financial Aid PROFILE; FAFSA; Noncustodial PROFILE; State aid form. **Types of Aid:** *Need-based scholarships/grants:* College/university scholarship or grant aid from institutional funds; Federal Pell; Private scholarships; SEOG; State scholarships/grants. *Loans:* Direct PLUS loans; Direct Subsidized Stafford Loans; Direct Unsubsidized Stafford Loans. **Student Employment:** Federal Work-Study Program available. Institutional employment available. **Financial Aid Statistics:** 100% needy freshmen, 87% needy undergrads receive need-based scholarship or grant aid. 0% freshmen, 0% undergrads receive non-need-based scholarship or grant aid. 68% freshmen, 62% undergrads receive need-based self-help aid. freshmen, undergrads receive athletic scholarships. 90% freshmen, 88% undergrads receive any aid. 38% undergrads borrow to pay for school. Average cumulative indebtedness $16,700. **Criteria awarding aid:** *Need-based:* Academics, Minority status. *Non-need-based:* Academics, Alumni affiliation, Minority status, State/district residency.

BARNARD COLLEGE

3009 Broadway, New York, NY 10027
Phone: 212-854-2014 **Financial Aid Phone:** 212-854-2154
E-mail: admissions@barnard.edu **CEEB Code:** 2038
Fax: 212-280-8797 **Website:** www.barnard.edu **ACT Code:** 2718

This private school was founded in 1889. It has a 4 acre campus.

RATINGS
Admissions Selectivity Rating: 98 **Fire Safety Rating:** 79 **Green Rating:** 89

STUDENTS AND FACULTY
Enrollment: 2,557. **Student Body:** 100% female, 0% male, 72% out-of-state, 10% international (58 countries represented). Asian 15%, African American 6%, Caucasian 52%, Hispanic 12%, Native American <1%, Pacific Islander <1%, Two or more races 6%, Race unknown <1%.
Retention and Graduation: 96% freshmen return for sophomore year. 87% freshmen graduate within 4 years. 93% freshmen graduate within 6 years.
Faculty: Student/faculty ratio 9:1. 239 full-time faculty, 98% hold PhDs, 25% are members of minority groups, 62% are women. 0% of classes are taught by teaching assistants.

ACADEMICS
Degrees: Bachelor's. **Classes:** Most classes have 10–19 students. **Most popular majors:** English Language and Literature, General; Economics, General; Psychology, General. **Special Study Options:** Cross-registration; Double major; Dual enrollment; Exchange student program (domestic); Independent

study; Internships; Student-designed major; Study abroad; Teacher certification program. **Honors programs:** The Athena Center for Leadership Studies was launched in September of 2009 and offers a range of academic courses that examines all aspects of women's leadership, sponsored lectures, mentoring and leadership opportunities and a lab which offers a wide range of workshops designed to teach practical elements of leadership to students, alums and other leaders in New York. **Combined degree programs:** BA/DDS; BA/JD; BA/MA; BA/MEng. **Disability Services offered:** Note-taking services; Reader services; Tape recorders; Tutors. **Career services:** Alumni network; Alumni services; Career assessment; Career/job search classes; Internships; Regional alumni.

FACILITIES

Housing: Coed dorms; Fraternity/sorority housing; Special housing for disabled students; Women's dorms; 100% of campus accessible to physically disabled. **Special Academic Facilities/Equipment:** Black Box and full theaters, infant-toddler center, greenhouse, academic computer center,art gallery space, advanced architecture labs.

CAMPUS LIFE

Environment: Metropolis. **Activities:** Campus Ministries; Choral groups; Concert band; Dance; Drama/theater; International Student Organization; Jazz band; Literary magazine; Marching band; Model UN; Music ensembles; Musical theater; Opera; Pep band; Radio station; Student government; Student newspaper; Student-run film society; Symphony orchestra; Yearbook. 100 registered organizations, 1 honor societies, 75 religious organizations, 10 sororities, on campus. **Athletics (Intercollegiate):** *Women:* archery, basketball, crew/rowing, cross-country, diving, fencing, field hockey, golf, lacrosse, soccer, softball, swimming, tennis, track/field (outdoor), volleyball. **On-Campus Highlights:** Milstein Center (opening late summer 2018). **Environmental Initiatives:** Barnard is partnered with other New York City organizations as part of Mayor deBlasio's "PlanNYC 2030 Challenge" to reduce the City's greenhouse gas footprint and improve the urban infrastructure and environment.

ADMISSIONS

Freshman Academic Profile: 84% in top 10% of high school class, 97% in top 25% of high school class, 100% in top 50% of high school class. 45% from public high schools. **Test Scores:** SAT Math middle 50% range 660–760. SAT EBRW middle 50% range 670–740. ACT middle 50% range 30–33. **Basis for Candidate Selection:** *Very important factors include:* rigor of secondary school record, academic GPA, application essay, recommendation(s), character/personal qualities. *Important factors include:* class rank, standardized test scores, extracurricular activities, talent/ability, volunteer work. *Other factors include:* interview, first generation, alumni/ae relation, geographical residence, racial/ethnic status, level of applicant's interest. **Freshman Admission Requirements:** High school diploma is required and GED is accepted. *Academic units recommended:* 4 English, 3 math, 3 science, 3 foreign language, 3 history. **Freshman Admission Statistics:** 7,897 applied, 14% admitted, 55% enrolled. **Transfer Admission Requirements:** High school transcript, college transcript(s), essay or personal statement, standardized test scores, statement of good standing from prior institution(s). Lowest grade transferable C-. **General Admission Information:** Application fee $75. Regular application deadline 1/1. Admission may be deferred for a maximum of 1 year.

COSTS AND FINANCIAL AID

Annual tuition $53,252. Room and board $17,525. Required fees $1,780. Average book and supplies expense $1,150. **Required Forms and Deadlines:** CSS/Financial Aid PROFILE; FAFSA; Noncustodial PROFILE; State aid form. **Notification of Awards:** Applicants will be notified of awards on or about 3/31. **Types of Aid:** *Need-based scholarships/grants:* College/university scholarship or grant aid from institutional funds; Federal Pell; Private scholarships; SEOG; State scholarships/grants. *Loans:* Direct PLUS loans; Direct Subsidized Stafford Loans; Direct Unsubsidized Stafford Loans. **Student Employment:** Federal Work-Study Program available. Institutional employment available. **Financial Aid Statistics:** 0% freshmen, 0% undergrads receive athletic scholarships. 51% freshmen, 47% undergrads receive any aid.

BARRY UNIVERSITY

11300 NE 2nd Avenue, Miami Shores, FL 33161-6695
Phone: 305-899-3100 **Financial Aid Phone:** 305-899-3673
E-mail: admissions@barry.edu **CEEB Code:** 5053
Fax: 305-899-2971 **Website:** www.barry.edu **ACT Code:** 0718

This private school, affiliated with the Roman Catholic Church, was founded in 1940.

RATINGS

Admissions Selectivity Rating: 73   **Fire Safety Rating:** 60*   **Green Rating:** 60*

STUDENTS AND FACULTY

Enrollment: 3,368. **Student Body:** 62% female, 38% male, 20% out-of-state, 8% international (69 countries represented). Asian 1%, African American 33%, Caucasian 17%, Hispanic 34%, Native American <1%, Pacific Islander <1%, Two or more races 2%, Race unknown 4%.
Retention and Graduation: 62% freshmen return for sophomore year. 15% freshmen graduate within 4 years. 35% freshmen graduate within 6 years. **Faculty:** Student/faculty ratio 11:1. 310 full-time faculty, 0% hold PhDs, 30% are members of minority groups, 57% are women.

ACADEMICS

Degrees: Bachelor's; Doctoral degree—professional practice; Doctoral degree research/scholarship; Master's; Post-master's certificate. **Classes:** Most classes have 10–19 students. Most lab/discussion sessions have 10–19 students. **Most popular majors:** Business, Management, Marketing, And Related Support Services; Business Administration, Management and Operations; Registered Nursing/Registered Nurse. **Special Study Options:** Accelerated program; Distance learning; Double major; Dual enrollment; English as a Second Language (ESL); Honors program; Internships; Study abroad; Teacher certification program. **Honors programs:** Honors program—Designed to push the best and brightest toward a lifetime of learning, Barry University's Honors Program challenges, enriches, and prepares especially motivated students to pursue their fullest potential. Participants will face a rigorous curriculum, more complicated issues, and tougher questions. Those selected will benefit from exploring the entire spectrum of humanity, the competition of their brightest peers, smaller classes with fewer lectures and more discussions, individualized study (with a senior honors thesis), and hands-on learning. **Disability Services offered:** Note-taking services; Reader services; Tape recorders; Tutors. **Career services:** Career assessment; Career/job search classes; Internships.

FACILITIES

Housing: Coed dorms; Special housing for disabled students; Theme housing. **Special Academic Facilities/Equipment:** Human performance lab, broadcasting studio, radio station, athletic training room, cell biology/biotechnology labs, Classroom of Tomorrow, Biomechanics lab,Photogrpahy lab, darkroom, and studio, Language lab, athletic training room. **Campus network:** 100% of classrooms, 100% of dorms, 100% of student union, 100% of libraries, 100% of dining areas, 100% of common outdoor areas, have wireless network access.

CAMPUS LIFE

Environment: Metropolis. **Activities:** Campus Ministries; Dance; Drama/theater; International Student Organization; Literary magazine; Music ensembles; Musical theater; Opera; Radio station; Student government; Student newspaper; Television station; Yearbook. 58 registered organizations, 20 honor societies, 1 religious organizations, 2 fraternities, 2 sororities, on campus. **Athletics (Intercollegiate):** *Men:* baseball, basketball, golf, soccer, tennis. *Women:* basketball, crew/rowing, golf, soccer, softball, tennis, volleyball. **On-Campus Highlights:** R. Kirk Landon Student Union.

ADMISSIONS

Freshman Academic Profile: Average high school GPA 3.4. **Test Scores:** SAT Math middle 50% range 460–540. SAT EBRW middle 50% range 480–560. ACT middle 50% range 17–22. **Basis for Candidate Selection:** *Very important factors include:* academic GPA, standardized test scores. *Important factors include:* talent/ability, character/personal qualities. *Other factors include:* rigor of secondary school record, class rank, recommendation(s), extracurricular activities, first generation, volunteer work, level of applicant's interest. **Freshman Admission Requirements:** High school diploma is required and GED is accepted. *Academic units recommended:* 4 English, 3 math, 3 science, 3 social studies. **Freshman Admission Statistics:** 5,255 applied, 91% admitted, 13% enrolled. **Transfer Admission Requirements:** College transcript(s).

Minimum college GPA of 2.0 required. Lowest grade transferable C. **General Admission Information:** Non-fall registration accepted. Admission may be deferred for a maximum of 1 year.

COSTS AND FINANCIAL AID
Annual tuition $29,700. Room and board $11,100. Required fees $150. Average book and supplies expense $1,500. **Required Forms and Deadlines:** FAFSA. **Notification of Awards:** Applicants will be notified of awards on or about 10/15. **Types of Aid:** *Need-based scholarships/grants:* College/university scholarship or grant aid from institutional funds; Federal Nursing Scholarships; Federal Pell; Private scholarships; SEOG; State scholarships/grants. *Loans:* Direct PLUS loans; Direct Subsidized Stafford Loans; Direct Unsubsidized Stafford Loans. **Student Employment:** Federal Work-Study Program available. Institutional employment available. **Financial Aid Statistics:** 86% needy freshmen, 81% needy undergrads receive need-based scholarship or grant aid. 100% freshmen, 94% undergrads receive non-need-based scholarship or grant aid. 85% freshmen, 78% undergrads receive need-based self-help aid. 7% freshmen, 6% undergrads receive athletic scholarships. 100% freshmen, 81% undergrads receive any aid. 74% undergrads borrow to pay for school. Average cumulative indebtedness $41,293. **Criteria awarding aid:** *Non-need-based:* Academics, Art, Athletics, Music/drama.

BARTON COLLEGE

Box 5000, Wilson, NC 27893-7000
Phone: 252-399-6317 **Financial Aid Phone:** 252-399-6316
E-mail: enroll@barton.edu **CEEB Code:** 5016
Fax: 252-399-6572 **Website:** www.barton.edu **ACT Code:** 3066

This private school, affiliated with the Disciples of Christ Church, was founded in 1902. It has a 76 acre campus.

RATINGS
Admissions Selectivity Rating: 86   Fire Safety Rating: 88   Green Rating: 60*

STUDENTS AND FACULTY
Enrollment: 1,076. **Student Body:** 69% female, 31% male, 11% out-of-state, 3% international (8 countries represented). Asian 1%, African American 27%, Caucasian 59%, Hispanic 3%, Native American 1%, Pacific Islander <1%, Two or more races 4%, Race unknown 2%.
Retention and Graduation: 71% freshmen return for sophomore year.
Faculty: Student/faculty ratio 12:1. 69 full-time faculty, 68% hold PhDs, 13% are members of minority groups, 49% are women. 0% of classes are taught by teaching assistants.

ACADEMICS
Degrees: Bachelor's; Master's. **Classes:** Most classes have 10–19 students. **Most popular majors:** Business Administration and Management, General; Elementary Education and Teaching; Nursing/Registered Nurse (Rn, Asn, Bsn, Msn). **Special Study Options:** Accelerated program; Cooperative education program; Double major; Honors program; Independent study; Internships; Liberal arts/career combination; Study abroad; Teacher certification program; Weekend college. **Honors programs:** Three competitive international travel scholarships awarded to entering honors students. **Disability Services offered:** Note-taking services; Reader services; Tape recorders; Tutors. **Career services:** Alumni services; Career assessment; Career/job search classes; Internships.

FACILITIES
Housing: Coed dorms; Fraternity/sorority housing; Special housing for disabled students; Women's dorms; 90% of campus accessible to physically disabled. **Special Academic Facilities/Equipment:** TV station, art museum, music recording studio, greenhouse. **Campus network:** 100% of classrooms, 20% of dorms, 100% of student union, 100% of libraries, 100% of dining areas, 50% of common outdoor areas, have wireless network access.

CAMPUS LIFE
Environment: Town. **Activities:** Campus Ministries; Choral groups; Dance; Drama/theater; Musical theater; Pep band; Student government; Student newspaper; Symphony orchestra. 51 registered organizations, 7 honor societies, 4 religious organizations, 3 fraternities, 3 sororities, on campus. **Athletics (Intercollegiate):** *Men:* baseball, basketball, cross-country, golf, soccer, tennis. *Women:* basketball, cross-country, soccer, softball, tennis, volleyball. **On-Campus Highlights:** Hamlin Student Center.

ADMISSIONS
Freshman Academic Profile: Average high school GPA 3.0. 12% in top 10% of high school class, 35% in top 25% of high school class, 73% in top 50% of high school class. 87% from public high schools. **Test Scores:** SAT Math middle 50% range 430–540. SAT EBRW middle 50% range 420–520. **Basis for Candidate Selection:** *Very important factors include:* academic GPA, standardized test scores. *Other factors include:* rigor of secondary school record, class rank, recommendation(s), interview, extracurricular activities, volunteer work, work experience. **Freshman Admission Requirements:** High school diploma is required and GED is accepted. *Academic units required:* 4 English, 3 math, 2 science, 1 science labs, 1 academic electives. *Academic units recommended:* 2 foreign language. **Freshman Admission Statistics:** 3,017 applied, 44% admitted, 15% enrolled. **Transfer Admission Requirements:** College transcript(s), statement of good standing from prior institution(s). Minimum college GPA of 2.0 required. Lowest grade transferable C. **General Admission Information:** Application fee $25. Non-fall registration accepted. Admission may be deferred for a maximum of 1 year.

COSTS AND FINANCIAL AID
Annual tuition $22,278. Room and board $7,940. Required fees $1,902. Average book and supplies expense $1,200. **Required Forms and Deadlines:** FAFSA. **Notification of Awards:** Applicants will be notified of awards on a rolling basis beginning 2/1. **Types of Aid:** *Need-based scholarships/grants:* College/university scholarship or grant aid from institutional funds; Federal Pell; Private scholarships; SEOG; State scholarships/grants. **Student Employment:** Federal Work-Study Program available. Institutional employment available. **Financial Aid Statistics:** 99% needy freshmen, 96% needy undergrads receive need-based scholarship or grant aid. 10% freshmen, 6% undergrads receive non-need-based scholarship or grant aid. 86% freshmen, 85% undergrads receive need-based self-help aid. 9% freshmen, 6% undergrads receive athletic scholarships. 98% freshmen, 93% undergrads receive any aid. **Criteria awarding aid:** *Need-based:* Minority status, Religious affiliation. *Non-need-based:* Academics, Alumni affiliation, Art, Athletics, Leadership, Minority status, Music/drama, Religious affiliation, State/district residency.

BASTYR UNIVERSITY

14500 Juanita Drive NE, Kenmore, WA 98028
Phone: 4256023330 **Financial Aid Phone:** 425-602-3083
E-mail: admissions@bastyr.edu
Fax: 4256023090 **Website:** www.bastyr.edu

This private school was founded in 1978. It has a 51 acre campus.

RATINGS
Admissions Selectivity Rating: 60*   Fire Safety Rating: 88   Green Rating: 60*

STUDENTS AND FACULTY
Enrollment: 227. **Student Body:** 87% female, 13% male, 5% out-of-state, 3% international (31 countries represented). Asian 8%, African American 4%, Caucasian 71%, Hispanic 5%, Native American 2%, Pacific Islander 1%, Two or more races 4%, Race unknown 3%.
Faculty: 43 full-time faculty, 0% hold PhDs, 19% are members of minority groups, 63% are women. 0% of classes are taught by teaching assistants.

ACADEMICS
Degrees: Bachelor's; Certificate; Doctoral degree—professional practice; Master's; Post-master's certificate. **Most popular majors:** Herbalism/Herbalist; Nutrition Sciences; Acupuncture and Oriental Medicine. **Special Study Options:** Double major; Independent study; Internships; Study abroad; Weekend college. **Honors programs:** N/A. **Disability Services offered:** Note-taking services; Tape recorders; Tutors. **Career services:** Alumni services; Career assessment; Career/job search classes; Internships.

FACILITIES
Housing: Apartments for single students; Coed dorms; Special housing for disabled students; 100% of campus accessible to physically disabled. **Special Academic Facilities/Equipment:** Library, Tierney Basic Sciences Research Laboratory, Clinical Research Center. **Campus network:** 60% of classrooms, 100% of dorms, 100% of student union, 100% of libraries, 100% of dining areas, 0% of common outdoor areas, have wireless network access.

CAMPUS LIFE

Environment: Town. **Activities:** Campus Ministries; Choral groups; Dance; International Student Organization; Music ensembles; Student government. 79 registered organizations, 2 religious organizations, on campus. **On-Campus Highlights:** Critically lauded Dining Commons. **Environmental Initiatives:** Our 11-building Student Village has earned LEED Platinum-certification (the first student housing project on the West Coast to receive this honor) and the U.S. Green Building Council's (USGBC) Outstanding Multifamily Project in the 2010 LEED for Homes Awards. The buildings feature "butterfly" roofs to capture rainwater, high efficiency water heaters and gas boilers, energy-efficient appliances and light fixtures, low-flow plumbing, natural ventilation, radiant-heat flooring made of finished concrete, sustainable landscaping, and bicycle storage.

ADMISSIONS

Transfer Admission Requirements: College transcript(s), essay or personal statement. Minimum college GPA of 2.25 required. Lowest grade transferable 2. **General Admission Information:** Application fee $75. Regular application deadline 3/15.

COSTS AND FINANCIAL AID

Annual tuition $24,273. Room and board $6,975. Average book and supplies expense $2,250. **Required Forms and Deadlines:** FAFSA; Institution's own financial aid form. **Notification of Awards:** Applicants will be notified of awards on a rolling basis beginning 2/1. **Types of Aid:** *Need-based scholarships/grants:* College/university scholarship or grant aid from institutional funds; Federal Pell; Private scholarships; SEOG; State scholarships/grants. *Loans:* Direct PLUS loans; Direct Subsidized Stafford Loans; Direct Unsubsidized Stafford Loans. **Student Employment:** Federal Work-Study Program available. Institutional employment available. **Financial Aid Statistics:** 91% needy undergrads receive need-based scholarship or grant aid. freshmen, 2% undergrads receive non-need-based scholarship or grant aid. freshmen, 0% undergrads receive need-based self-help aid. freshmen, 0% undergrads receive athletic scholarships. 87% undergrads receive any aid. **Criteria awarding aid:** *Need-based:* Academics, Alumni affiliation, Job skills, Leadership. *Non-need-based:* Academics, Alumni affiliation, Job skills, Leadership.

BATES COLLEGE

23 Campus Avenue, Lewiston, ME 04240
Phone: 207-786-6000 **Financial Aid Phone:** 207-786-6096
E-mail: admission@bates.edu **CEEB Code:** 3076
Fax: 207-786-6025 **Website:** www.bates.edu **ACT Code:** 1634

This private school was founded in 1855. It has a 133 acre campus.

RATINGS

Admissions Selectivity Rating: 96   **Fire Safety Rating:** 98   **Green Rating:** 97

STUDENTS AND FACULTY

Enrollment: 1,787. **Student Body:** 51% female, 49% male, 7% international (71 countries represented). Asian 4%, African American 5%, Caucasian 70%, Hispanic 9%, Native American <1%, Pacific Islander <1%, Two or more races 5%, Race unknown <1%.
Retention and Graduation: 95% freshmen return for sophomore year. 84% freshmen graduate within 4 years. 88% freshmen graduate within 6 years. **Faculty:** Student/faculty ratio 10:1. 179 full-time faculty, 97% hold PhDs, 17% are members of minority groups, 50% are women. 0% of classes are taught by teaching assistants.

ACADEMICS

Degrees: Bachelor's. **Classes:** Most classes have 10–19 students. **Most popular majors:** History, General; Political Science and Government, General; Psychology, General. **Special Study Options:** Accelerated program; Cross-registration; Double major; Exchange student program (domestic); Honors program; Independent study; Internships; Liberal arts/career combination; Student-designed major; Study abroad; Teacher certification program. **Honors**

programs: The Honors Thesis Program. **Disability Services offered:** Note-taking services; Reader services; Tape recorders; Tutors. **Career services:** Alumni network; Alumni services; Career assessment; Career/job search classes; Internships; Regional alumni.

FACILITIES

Housing: Coed dorms; Men's dorms; Theme housing; Wellness housing; Women's dorms; 60% of campus accessible to physically disabled. **Special Academic Facilities/Equipment:** Art gallery, Edmund S. Muskie Archives, language labs, planetarium, 600-acre conservation area on seacoast for environmental studies, scanning electron microscope, Imaging Center.

CAMPUS LIFE

Environment: Town. **Activities:** Campus Ministries; Choral groups; Concert band; Dance; Drama/theater; International Student Organization; Jazz band; Literary magazine; Model UN; Music ensembles; Musical theater; Radio station; Student government; Student newspaper; Student-run film society; Symphony orchestra; Yearbook. 111 registered organizations, 3 honor societies, 11 religious organizations, on campus. **Athletics (Intercollegiate):** *Men:* baseball, basketball, crew/rowing, cross-country, diving, football, golf, lacrosse, skiing (downhill/Alpine), skiing (Nordic/cross-country), soccer, squash, swimming, tennis, track/field (outdoor), track/field (indoor). *Women:* basketball, crew/rowing, cross-country, diving, field hockey, golf, lacrosse, skiing (downhill/Alpine), skiing (Nordic/cross-country), soccer, softball, squash, swimming, tennis, track/field (outdoor), track/field (indoor), volleyball. **On-Campus Highlights:** Pettengill Hall. **Environmental Initiatives:** Developing sustainable building guidelines and campus energy goals.

ADMISSIONS

Freshman Academic Profile: 63% in top 10% of high school class, 86% in top 25% of high school class, 97% in top 50% of high school class. 53% from public high schools. **Test Scores:** SAT Math middle 50% range 630–720. SAT EBRW middle 50% range 640–730. ACT middle 50% range 29–32. **Basis for Candidate Selection:** *Very important factors include:* rigor of secondary school record, class rank, academic GPA, application essay, recommendation(s), extracurricular activities, talent/ability, character/personal qualities, level of applicant's interest. *Important factors include:* first generation, geographical residence, state residency. *Other factors include:* standardized test scores, interview, alumni/ae relation, racial/ethnic status, volunteer work, work experience. **Freshman Admission Requirements:** High school diploma is required and GED is not accepted *Academic units required:* 4 English, 3 math, 3 science, 2 science labs, 2 foreign language, 3 social studies, 3 history. *Academic units recommended:* 4 English, 4 math, 4 science, 3 science labs, 4 foreign language, 4 social studies, 4 history. **Freshman Admission Statistics:** 5,316 applied, 22% admitted, 42% enrolled. **Transfer Admission Requirements:** High school transcript, college transcript(s), essay or personal statement, statement of good standing from prior institution(s). Lowest grade transferable C. **General Admission Information:** Application fee $60. Regular application deadline 1/1.

COSTS AND FINANCIAL AID

Annual tuition $55,683. Room and board $15,705. Average book and supplies expense $900. **Required Forms and Deadlines:** CSS/Financial Aid PROFILE; FAFSA; Noncustodial PROFILE. **Notification of Awards:** Applicants will be notified of awards on or about 4/1. **Types of Aid:** *Need-based scholarships/grants:* College/university scholarship or grant aid from institutional funds; Federal Pell; Private scholarships; SEOG; State scholarships/grants. *Loans:* Direct PLUS loans; Direct Subsidized Stafford Loans; Direct Unsubsidized Stafford Loans. **Student Employment:** Federal Work-Study Program available. Institutional employment available. **Financial Aid Statistics:** 100% needy freshmen, 100% needy undergrads receive need-based scholarship or grant aid. 0% freshmen, 0% undergrads receive non-need-based scholarship or grant aid. 98% freshmen, 99% undergrads receive need-based self-help aid. 0% freshmen, 0% undergrads receive athletic scholarships. 41.6% freshmen, 42.4% undergrads receive any aid. 35% undergrads borrow to pay for school. Average cumulative indebtedness $21,525.

BAYLOR UNIVERSITY

One Bear Place #97056, Waco, TX 76798-7056
Phone: 254-710-3435 **Financial Aid Phone:** 254-710-2611
E-mail: admissions@baylor.edu **CEEB Code:** 6032
Fax: 254-710-3436 **Website:** www.baylor.edu **ACT Code:** 4062

This private school, affiliated with the Baptist Church, was founded in 1845. It has a 1000 acre campus.

RATINGS

Admissions Selectivity Rating: 90   Fire Safety Rating: 91   Green Rating: 60*

STUDENTS AND FACULTY

Enrollment: 13,948. **Student Body:** 60% female, 40% male, 33% out-of-state, 4% international (75 countries represented). Asian 7%, African American 6%, Caucasian 62%, Hispanic 16%, Native American <1%, Pacific Islander <1%, Two or more races 5%, Race unknown 1%.
Retention and Graduation: 88% freshmen return for sophomore year. 63% freshmen graduate within 4 years. 78% freshmen graduate within 6 years.
Faculty: Student/faculty ratio 13:1. 1,134 full-time faculty, 85% hold PhDs, 17% are members of minority groups, 44% are women.

ACADEMICS

Degrees: Bachelor's; Doctoral degree—professional practice; Doctoral degree research/scholarship; Master's; Post-master's certificate. **Classes:** Most classes have 10–19 students. Most lab/discussion sessions have 10–19 students. **Most popular majors:** Biology/Biological Sciences, General; Registered Nursing/Registered Nurse; Accounting. **Special Study Options:** Accelerated program; Double major; Exchange student program (domestic); Honors program; Internships; Student-designed major; Study abroad; Teacher certification program. **Honors programs:** Honors Program, University Scholars Program, Great Texts Program. **Combined degree programs:** BA/MA. **Disability Services offered:** Note-taking services; Reader services; Tape recorders; Tutors. **Career services:** Alumni network; Alumni services; Career assessment; Career/job search classes; Internships.

FACILITIES

Housing: Apartments for married students; Apartments for single students; Coed dorms; Cooperative housing; Men's dorms; Special housing for disabled students; Special housing for international students; Theme housing; Wellness housing; Women's dorms; 98% of campus accessible to physically disabled.
Special Academic Facilities/Equipment: Baylor Research and Innovation Collaborative: Baylor Advanced Research Institute (a catalyst for creating new and emerging research clusters, interdisciplinary research programs and industrial collaborations), LAUNCH (innovative business accelerator), Baylor Institute for Air Science, Center for Astrophysics, Space Physics and Engineering Research (CASPER), Center for Spatial Research, Veterans Health Research Program of the Baylor Institute of Biomedical Studies, Quantum Optics Laboratory, Laser Spectroscopy Laboratory, and Advanced Composite Technology (ACT) Laboratory; Baylor Sciences Building (500,000-sf of classrooms, laboratories and offices); Paul L. Foster Success Center; Umphrey Law Center; Mayborn Museum Complex (includes the Jeanes Discovery Center, the Daniel Historic Village and the Strecker Museum Collection); Armstrong Browning Library; The Texas Collection; Black Gospel Music Restoration Project (Royce-Darden Collection); Allbritton Art Institute; W.R. Poage Legislative Library; Baylor University Press; Martin Museum of Art; McMullen-Connally Family Collection; J.M. Dawson Institute of Church-State Studies; Academy for Teaching and Learning; Center for Business and Economic Research; Institute for Faith and Learning; Institute for Oral History; Institute for Studies of Religion; Center for Christian Education; Center for Christian Ethics; Center for Christian Music Studies; Center for Community Learning and Enrichment; Center for Family and Community Ministries; Center for International Education; Center for Ministry Effectiveness and Educational Leadership; Center for Nonprofit Leadership and Service; Keston Center for Religion, Politics and Society; Kyle Lake Center for Effective Preaching; Institute of Biblical and Related Languages; language and environmental studies labs; high definition television; radio station.

CAMPUS LIFE

Environment: City. **Activities:** Campus Ministries; Choral groups; Concert band; Dance; Drama/theater; International Student Organization; Jazz band; Literary magazine; Marching band; Model UN; Music ensembles; Musical theater; Opera; Pep band; Radio station; Student government; Student newspaper; Symphony orchestra; Television station; Yearbook. 316 registered organizations, 10 honor societies, 14 religious organizations, 20 fraternities, 23 sororities, on campus.
Athletics (Intercollegiate): *Men:* baseball, basketball, cheerleading, cross-country, football, golf, tennis, track/field (outdoor), track/field (indoor). *Women:* basketball, cheerleading, cross-country, equestrian sports, golf, soccer, softball, tennis, track/field (outdoor), track/field (indoor), volleyball. **On-Campus Highlights:** Bear Habitat. **Environmental Initiatives:** Campus wide recycling, with over 700 locations on campus to recycle in which to recycle and collaboration with Athletics Department to recycle at all university sporting events.

ADMISSIONS

Freshman Academic Profile: 44% in top 10% of high school class, 76% in top 25% of high school class, 96% in top 50% of high school class. **Test Scores:** SAT Math middle 50% range 600–700. SAT EBRW middle 50% range 600–680. ACT middle 50% range 26–32. **Basis for Candidate Selection:** *Very important factors include:* rigor of secondary school record, class rank, standardized test scores. *Important factors include:* academic GPA. *Other factors include:* application essay, recommendation(s), extracurricular activities, talent/ability, character/personal qualities, alumni/ae relation, volunteer work, work experience, level of applicant's interest. **Freshman Admission Requirements:** High school diploma is required and GED is accepted. *Academic units recommended:* 4 English, 4 math, 4 science, 2 science labs, 2 foreign language, 2 social studies, 1 history. **Freshman Admission Statistics:** 34,582 applied, 45% admitted, 21% enrolled. **Transfer Admission Requirements:** College transcript(s). Minimum college GPA of 2.5 required. Lowest grade transferable C. **General Admission Information:** Regular application deadline 2/1. Non-fall registration accepted. Admission may be deferred for a maximum of 1 year.

COSTS AND FINANCIAL AID

Annual tuition $44,544. Room and board $14,324. Required fees $4,892. Average book and supplies expense $1,284. **Required Forms and Deadlines:** CSS/Financial Aid PROFILE. **Notification of Awards:** Applicants will be notified of awards on a rolling basis beginning 12/15. **Types of Aid:** *Need-based scholarships/grants:* College/university scholarship or grant aid from institutional funds; Federal Pell; Private scholarships; SEOG; State scholarships/grants. *Loans:* Direct PLUS loans; Direct Subsidized Stafford Loans; Direct Unsubsidized Stafford Loans. **Student Employment:** Federal Work-Study Program available. Institutional employment available. **Financial Aid Statistics:** 98% needy freshmen, 96% needy undergrads receive need-based scholarship or grant aid. 96% freshmen, 93% undergrads receive non-need-based scholarship or grant aid. 75% freshmen, 80% undergrads receive need-based self-help aid. 2% freshmen, 2% undergrads receive athletic scholarships. 51% undergrads borrow to pay for school. Average cumulative indebtedness $49,610. **Criteria awarding aid:** *Need-based:* Academics, Art, Athletics, Leadership, Music/drama, Religious affiliation. *Non-need-based:* Academics, Art, Athletics, Leadership, Music/drama, Religious affiliation.

BAY PATH UNIVERSITY

588 Longmeadow Street, Longmeadow, MA 01106-2292
Phone: 413-565-1331 **Financial Aid Phone:** 413-565-1345
E-mail: admiss@baypath.edu **CEEB Code:** 2122
Fax: 413-565-1105 **Website:** www.baypath.edu **ACT Code:** 1785

This private school was founded in 1897. It has a 48 acre campus.

RATINGS

Admissions Selectivity Rating: 84   Fire Safety Rating: 99   Green Rating: 60*

STUDENTS AND FACULTY

Enrollment: 1,924. **Student Body:** 100% female, 0% male, 40% out-of-state, <1% international (5 countries represented). Asian 2%, African American 15%, Caucasian 55%, Hispanic 20%, Native American <1%, Pacific Islander <1%, Two or more races 3%, Race unknown 4%.
Retention and Graduation: 80% freshmen return for sophomore year. 81% freshmen graduate within 4 years. 89% freshmen graduate within 6 years.
Faculty: Student/faculty ratio 12:1. 70 full-time faculty, 71% hold PhDs, 14% are members of minority groups, 79% are women. 0% of classes are taught by teaching assistants.

ACADEMICS

Degrees: Associate; Bachelor's; Certificate; Doctoral degree—professional practice; Master's; Post-bachelor's certificate; Post-master's certificate. **Classes:** Most classes have 10–19 students. **Most popular majors:** Business Administration, Management and Operations, Other; Liberal Arts and Sciences/Liberal Studies; Psychology, General. **Special Study Options:** Accelerated program; Cooperative education program; Cross-registration; Distance learning; Double major; English as a Second Language (ESL); Exchange student program (domestic); External degree program; Honors program; Independent study; Internships; Liberal arts/career combination; Student-designed major; Study abroad; Teacher certification program; Weekend college. **Honors programs:** The Bay Path Honors Program provides academically talented and exceptionally motivated student with uniquely challenging and intellectually stimulating educational opportunities beyond the traditional curriculum. Under the guidance of faculty known for their excellence in teaching and scholarship, students investigate special topics in interdisciplinary honors seminars. The Honors Program culminates in a major independent creative or research project, or other departmental requirement. Women in Science Honors (WiSH) offers a four-year curriculum consisting of integrated and advanced study and research for dedicated future scientists. **Disability Services offered:** Note-taking services; Reader services; Tape recorders; Tutors. **Career services:** Alumni network; Alumni services; Career assessment; Career/job search classes; Internships; Regional alumni.

FACILITIES

Housing: Theme housing; Wellness housing; Women's dorms; 50% of campus accessible to physically disabled. **Special Academic Facilities/Equipment:** Blake Student Commons, Bashevkin Academic Development Center, Breck Fitness Center, occupational therapy laboratory, physician's assistant laboratory, and D'Amour Hall for Business, Communications and Technology. **Campus network:** 100% of classrooms, 100% of dorms, 100% of student union, 100% of libraries, 100% of dining areas, 100% of common outdoor areas, have wireless network access.

CAMPUS LIFE

Environment: Village. **Activities:** Choral groups; Dance; Drama/theater; International Student Organization; Model UN; Music ensembles; Musical theater; Student government. 32 registered organizations, 4 honor societies, 1 religious organizations, on campus. **Athletics (Intercollegiate):** *Women:* basketball, cross-country, field hockey, soccer, softball, tennis, volleyball. **On-Campus Highlights:** Carpe Diem Cafe. **Environmental Initiatives:** Recycling program.

ADMISSIONS

Freshman Academic Profile: Average high school GPA 3.4. 29% in top 10% of high school class, 43% in top 25% of high school class, 57% in top 50% of high school class. **Test Scores:** SAT Math middle 50% range 428–520. SAT EBRW middle 50% range 460–570. ACT middle 50% range 24–26. **Basis for Candidate Selection:** *Very important factors include:* rigor of secondary school record, academic GPA, application essay, recommendation(s), interview. *Important factors include:* extracurricular activities, talent/ability. *Other factors include:* class rank, standardized test scores, character/personal qualities, first generation, alumni/ae relation, geographical residence, volunteer work, work experience. **Freshman Admission Requirements:** High school diploma is required and GED is accepted. *Academic units required:* 4 English, 3 math, 2 science, 2 history. **Freshman Admission Statistics:** 1,513 applied, 60% admitted, 15% enrolled. **Transfer Admission Requirements:** College transcript(s). Minimum college GPA of 2.0 required. Lowest grade transferable C-. **General Admission Information:** Application fee $25. Non-fall registration accepted. Admission may be deferred for a maximum of 1 year.

COSTS AND FINANCIAL AID

Required Forms and Deadlines: FAFSA. **Notification of Awards:** Applicants will be notified of awards on a rolling basis beginning 1/15. **Types of Aid:** *Need-based scholarships/grants:* College/university scholarship or grant aid from institutional funds; Federal Pell; Private scholarships; SEOG; State scholarships/grants. *Loans:* Direct PLUS loans; Direct Subsidized Stafford Loans; Direct Unsubsidized Stafford Loans. **Student Employment:** Federal Work-Study Program available. Institutional employment available. **Financial Aid Statistics:** 100% needy freshmen, 100% needy undergrads receive need-based scholarship or grant aid. 4% freshmen, 4% undergrads receive non-need-based scholarship or grant aid. 93% freshmen, 93% undergrads receive need-based self-help aid. 0% freshmen, 0% undergrads receive athletic scholarships. 97% freshmen, 90% undergrads receive any aid. 90% undergrads borrow to pay for school. Average cumulative indebtedness $41,594. **Criteria awarding aid:** *Non-need-based:* Academics.

BEACON COLLEGE

105 E. Main Street, Leesburg, FL 34748
Phone: 352-638-9731 **Financial Aid Phone:** 352-787-6306
E-mail: admissions@beaconcollege.edu
Fax: 352-787-0721 **Website:** www.beaconcollege.edu **ACT Code:** 704

This private school was founded in 1989.

RATINGS

Admissions Selectivity Rating: 67   **Fire Safety Rating:** 94   **Green Rating:** 60*

STUDENTS AND FACULTY

Enrollment: 128. **Student Body:** 38% female, 63% male, 80% out-of-state, 0% international (2 countries represented). Asian 2%, African American 10%, Caucasian 85%, Hispanic 3%, Native American 0%, Race unknown 0%. **Retention and Graduation:** 73% freshmen return for sophomore year. **Faculty:** 17 full-time faculty, 65% hold PhDs, 6% are members of minority groups, 59% are women. 0% of classes are taught by teaching assistants.

ACADEMICS

Degrees: Associate; Bachelor's. **Classes:** Most classes have 10–19 students. **Special Study Options:** Cooperative education program; Independent study; Internships; Study abroad. **Honors programs:** Psi Tau Omega is the academic honor society at Beacon College. **Disability Services offered:** Note-taking services; Reader services; Tape recorders; Tutors.

FACILITIES

Housing: Apartments for single students; Special housing for disabled students.

CAMPUS LIFE

Environment: Village. **Activities:** Choral groups; Drama/theater; Literary magazine; Student government; Student newspaper; Yearbook. 13 registered organizations, 1 honor societies, 1 fraternities, 1 sororities, on campus. **On-Campus Highlights:** New Resident Apartment Complex.

ADMISSIONS

Freshman Academic Profile: Average high school GPA 2.8. **Basis for Candidate Selection:** *Very important factors include:* recommendation(s). *Important factors include:* rigor of secondary school record, application essay, standardized test scores, talent/ability, character/personal qualities. *Other factors include:* class rank, academic GPA, interview, extracurricular activities, volunteer work, work experience. **Freshman Admission Requirements:** High school diploma is required and GED is accepted. *Academic units required:* 4 English, 1 math, 1 science, 1 social studies, 2 history, 3 academic electives. **Freshman Admission Statistics:** 53 applied, 92% admitted, 59% enrolled. **Transfer Admission Requirements:** High school transcript, college transcript(s), essay or personal statement, interview. Lowest grade transferable C. **General Admission Information:** Application fee $50. Priority deadline 6/1. Regular application deadline 8/1. Non-fall registration accepted.

COSTS AND FINANCIAL AID

Annual tuition $27,000. Room and board $8,150. Required fees $700. Average book and supplies expense $900. **Required Forms and Deadlines:** FAFSA; Institution's own financial aid form; State aid form. **Notification of Awards:** Applicants will be notified of awards on or about 2/1. **Types of Aid:** *Need-based scholarships/grants:* College/university scholarship or grant aid from institutional funds; Federal Pell; Private scholarships; SEOG; State scholarships/grants. **Student Employment:** Federal Work-Study Program available. **Financial Aid Statistics:** 60% needy freshmen, 22% needy undergrads receive need-based scholarship or grant aid. 0% freshmen, 0% undergrads receive non-need-based scholarship or grant aid. 60% freshmen, 22% undergrads receive need-based self-help aid. 0% freshmen, 0% undergrads receive athletic scholarships.

BECKER COLLEGE

61 Sever Street, Worcester, MA 01609
Phone: 508-373-9400 **Financial Aid Phone:** 508-373-9440
E-mail: admissions@becker.edu **CEEB Code:** 3079
Fax: 508-890-1500 **Website:** www.becker.edu **ACT Code:** 1784

This private school was founded in 1784. It has a 100 acre campus.

RATINGS
Admissions Selectivity Rating: 77 **Fire Safety Rating:** 93 **Green Rating:** 60*

STUDENTS AND FACULTY
Enrollment: 1,590. **Student Body:** 57% female, 43% male, 34% out-of-state, 1% international (15 countries represented). Asian 3%, African American 8%, Caucasian 62%, Hispanic 10%, Native American <1%, Pacific Islander <1%, Two or more races 3%, Race unknown 12%.
Retention and Graduation: 78% freshmen return for sophomore year. 37% freshmen graduate within 4 years. 45% freshmen graduate within 6 years. **Faculty:** Student/faculty ratio 12:1. 50 full-time faculty, 66% hold PhDs, 6% are members of minority groups, 54% are women. 0% of classes are taught by teaching assistants.

ACADEMICS
Degrees: Associate; Bachelor's; Certificate; Master's. **Classes:** Most classes have 10–19 students. Most lab/discussion sessions have 10–19 students. **Most popular majors:** Business Administration and Management, General; Registered Nursing/Registered Nurse; Animation, Interactive Technology, Video Graphics and Special Effects. **Special Study Options:** Accelerated program; Cooperative education program; Cross-registration; Distance learning; Double major; Dual enrollment; Independent study; Internships; Study abroad. **Honors programs:** N/A. **Combined degree programs:** BA/JD; BA/MA. **Disability Services offered:** Note-taking services; Reader services; Tape recorders; Tutors. **Career services:** Alumni network; Alumni services; Career assessment; Career/job search classes; Internships; Regional alumni.

FACILITIES
Housing: Apartments for single students; Coed dorms; Special housing for disabled students; Theme housing. **Special Academic Facilities/Equipment:** Massachusetts Digital Games Institute (MassDiGI), Community Counseling Clinic @ Becker College, AR/VR Lab, Live Game Studio, Colleen C. Barrett Center, Crime Scene and Evidence Lab, Lenfest Animal Health Center.

CAMPUS LIFE
Environment: City. **Activities:** Dance; Drama/theater; Music ensembles; Musical theater; Student government. 30 registered organizations, 5 honor societies, on campus. **On-Campus Highlights:** Fuller Campus Center in Leicester.

ADMISSIONS
Freshman Academic Profile: Average high school GPA 3.2. **Test Scores:** SAT Math middle 50% range 470–580. SAT EBRW middle 50% range 480–590. ACT middle 50% range 17–24. **Basis for Candidate Selection:** *Very important factors include:* rigor of secondary school record, academic GPA. *Other factors include:* class rank, application essay, standardized test scores, recommendation(s), interview, extracurricular activities, first generation, alumni/ae relation, volunteer work, work experience, level of applicant's interest. **Freshman Admission Requirements:** High school diploma is required and GED is accepted. *Academic units recommended:* 4 English, 3 math, 3 science, 2 science labs, 2 foreign language, 2 social studies, 2 history. **Freshman Admission Statistics:** 2,902 applied, 70% admitted, 13% enrolled. **Transfer Admission Requirements:** College transcript(s). Minimum college GPA of 2.00 required. Lowest grade transferable C. **General Admission Information:** Priority deadline 2/15. Non-fall registration accepted.

COSTS AND FINANCIAL AID
Annual tuition $36,300. Room and board $13,800. Required fees $3,850. Average book and supplies expense $960. **Required Forms and Deadlines:** FAFSA. **Notification of Awards:** Applicants will be notified of awards on a rolling basis beginning 12/15. **Types of Aid:** *Need-based scholarships/grants:* College/university scholarship or grant aid from institutional funds; Federal Pell; Private scholarships; SEOG; State scholarships/grants. *Loans:* Direct PLUS loans; Direct Subsidized Stafford Loans; Direct Unsubsidized Stafford Loans. **Student Employment:** Federal Work-Study Program available. Institutional employment available. **Financial Aid Statistics:** 100% needy freshmen, 97% needy undergrads receive need-based scholarship or grant aid. 0% freshmen, 9% undergrads receive non-need-based scholarship or grant aid. 100% freshmen, 100% undergrads receive need-based self-help aid. 0% freshmen, 0% undergrads receive athletic scholarships. 99% freshmen, 99% undergrads receive any aid. **Criteria awarding aid:** *Non-need-based:* Academics, State/district residency.

BELHAVEN UNIVERSITY

1500 Peachtree Street, Jackson, MS 39202
Phone: 601-968-5940 **Financial Aid Phone:** (601) 968-5920
E-mail: admission@belhaven.edu **CEEB Code:** 1055
Fax: 601-968-8946 **Website:** www.belhaven.edu **ACT Code:** 2180

This private school, affiliated with the Presbyterian Church, was founded in 1883. It has a 42 acre campus.

RATINGS
Admissions Selectivity Rating: 86 **Fire Safety Rating:** 97 **Green Rating:** 60*

STUDENTS AND FACULTY
Enrollment: 2,224. **Student Body:** 66% female, 34% male, 32% out-of-state, 2% international (21 countries represented). Asian 1%, African American 42%, Caucasian 40%, Hispanic 5%, Native American <1%, Pacific Islander <1%, Two or more races 3%, Race unknown 6%.
Retention and Graduation: 67% freshmen return for sophomore year. 34% freshmen graduate within 4 years. % freshmen graduate within 6 years. **Faculty:** Student/faculty ratio 10:1. 109 full-time faculty, 51% hold PhDs, 50% are women. 0% of classes are taught by teaching assistants.

ACADEMICS
Degrees: Associate; Bachelor's; Certificate; Doctoral degree—other; Master's; Post-bachelor's certificate. **Classes:** Most classes have fewer than 10 students. **Most popular majors:** Business/Commerce, General; Dance, General; Social Sciences, General. **Special Study Options:** Accelerated program; Distance learning; Double major; Dual enrollment; English as a Second Language (ESL); Honors program; Independent study; Internships; Student-designed major; Study abroad; Teacher certification program. **Honors programs:** Honors Program: The Honors College at Belhaven College gives academically advanced, highly motivated students a forum in which to deepen and expand their college education, both intellectually and spiritually. Enrollment in the Honors College is limited to students who demonstrate a past record of academic achievement, seriousness about their calling, and enthusiasm for challenging dialogue with students and scholars from a variety of fields. **Career services:** Career/job search classes; Internships.

FACILITIES
Housing: Apartments for single students; Men's dorms; Women's dorms; 100% of campus accessible to physically disabled. **Special Academic Facilities/Equipment:** Bitsy Irby art gallery. **Campus network:** 100% of classrooms, 100% of dorms, 100% of student union, 100% of libraries, 100% of dining areas, 80% of common outdoor areas, have wireless network access.

CAMPUS LIFE
Environment: City. **Activities:** Choral groups; Dance; Drama/theater; International Student Organization; Jazz band; Literary magazine; Marching band; Music ensembles; Musical theater; Pep band; Student government; Student newspaper; Yearbook. 30 registered organizations, 7 honor societies, 4 religious organizations, on campus. **Athletics (Intercollegiate):** *Men:* baseball, basketball, cheerleading, cross-country, football, golf, soccer, tennis. *Women:* basketball, cheerleading, cross-country, golf, soccer, softball, tennis, volleyball. **On-Campus Highlights:** McCravey-Triplett Student Center.

ADMISSIONS
Freshman Academic Profile: Average high school GPA 3.4. 9% in top 10% of high school class, 42% in top 25% of high school class, 72% in top 50% of high school class. **Test Scores:** SAT Math middle 50% range 510–620. SAT EBRW middle 50% range 485–565. ACT middle 50% range 20–24. **Basis for Candidate Selection:** *Very important factors include:* academic GPA, standardized test scores. *Other factors include:* rigor of secondary school record, application essay, recommendation(s), interview, extracurricular activities,

talent/ability, character/personal qualities, alumni/ae relation, level of applicant's interest. **Freshman Admission Requirements:** High school diploma is required and GED is accepted. *Academic units required:* 4 English, 2 math, 1 science, 1 history, 8 academic electives. *Academic units recommended:* 1 computer science. **Freshman Admission Statistics:** 1,961 applied, 52% admitted, 22% enrolled. **Transfer Admission Requirements:** College transcript(s). Minimum college GPA of 2.0 required. Lowest grade transferable D. **General Admission Information:** Application fee $25. Non-fall registration accepted.

COSTS AND FINANCIAL AID

Annual tuition $24,950. Room and board $7,500. Required fees $350. Average book and supplies expense $650. **Required Forms and Deadlines:** FAFSA. **Notification of Awards:** Applicants will be notified of awards on a rolling basis beginning 2/1. **Types of Aid:** *Need-based scholarships/grants:* College/university scholarship or grant aid from institutional funds; Federal Pell; Private scholarships; SEOG; State scholarships/grants. **Student Employment:** Federal Work-Study Program available. **Financial Aid Statistics:** 99% needy freshmen, 96% needy undergrads receive need-based scholarship or grant aid. 0% freshmen, 0% undergrads receive non-need-based scholarship or grant aid. 80% freshmen, 83% undergrads receive need-based self-help aid. 4% freshmen, 11% undergrads receive athletic scholarships. 100% freshmen, 73% undergrads receive any aid. 74% undergrads borrow to pay for school. Average cumulative indebtedness $8,654. **Criteria awarding aid:** *Non-need-based:* Academics, Alumni affiliation, Art, Music/drama.

BELLARMINE UNIVERSITY

2001 Newburg Road, Louisville, KY 40205
Phone: 502-272-8131 **Financial Aid Phone:** 502-272-4723
E-mail: admissions@bellarmine.edu **CEEB Code:** 1056
Fax: 502-272-8002 **Website:** http://www.bellarmine.edu **ACT Code:** 1490

This private school, affiliated with the Roman Catholic Church, was founded in 1950. It has a 144 acre campus.

RATINGS

Admissions Selectivity Rating: 75   **Fire Safety Rating:** 96   **Green Rating:** 60*

STUDENTS AND FACULTY

Enrollment: 2,488. **Student Body:** 64% female, 36% male, 29% out-of-state, 1% international (17 countries represented). Asian 2%, African American 5%, Caucasian 80%, Hispanic 4%, Native American <1%, Pacific Islander <1%, Two or more races 4%, Race unknown 4%.
Retention and Graduation: 79% freshmen return for sophomore year. 50% freshmen graduate within 4 years. 65% freshmen graduate within 6 years. 24% grads go on to further study within 1 year. **Faculty:** Student/faculty ratio 11:1. 176 full-time faculty, 86% hold PhDs, 11% are members of minority groups, 56% are women. 0% of classes are taught by teaching assistants.

ACADEMICS

Degrees: Bachelor's; Certificate; Doctoral degree—other; Doctoral degree—professional practice; Doctoral degree research/scholarship; Master's; Post-bachelor's certificate. **Classes:** Most classes have 10–19 students. Most lab/discussion sessions have fewer than 10 students. **Most popular majors:** Registered Nursing/Registered Nurse; Exercise Science and Kinesiology; Psychology, General. **Special Study Options:** Accelerated program; Cross-registration; Distance learning; Double major; Dual enrollment; Honors program; Independent study; Internships; Liberal arts/career combination; Student-designed major; Study abroad; Teacher certification program. **Honors programs:** Bellarmine Honors Program. **Disability Services offered:** Note-taking services; Reader services; Tutors. **Career services:** Alumni network; Alumni services; Career assessment; Career/job search classes; Internships; Regional alumni.

FACILITIES

Housing: Coed dorms; Fraternity/sorority housing; Men's dorms; Special housing for disabled students; Special housing for international students; Theme housing; Women's dorms. **Special Academic Facilities/Equipment:** McGrath Art Gallery; Thomas Merton Center.

CAMPUS LIFE

Environment: Metropolis. **Activities:** Campus Ministries; Choral groups; Concert band; Dance; Drama/theater; International Student Organization; Jazz band; Literary magazine; Music ensembles; Musical theater; Pep band; Radio station; Student government; Student newspaper; Student-run film society; Yearbook. 75 registered organizations, 5 honor societies, 4 religious organizations, 1 fraternities, 1 sororities, on campus. **Athletics (Intercollegiate):** *Men:* baseball, basketball, bowling, cross-country, golf, lacrosse, soccer, tennis, track/field (outdoor). *Women:* basketball, bowling, cheerleading, cross-country, field hockey, golf, soccer, softball, tennis, track/field (outdoor), volleyball. **On-Campus Highlights:** Norton Health Science Center. **Environmental Initiatives:** Development of an on-campus fruit/vegetable garden.

ADMISSIONS

Freshman Academic Profile: Average high school GPA 3.6. 67% from public high schools. **Test Scores:** SAT Math middle 50% range 520–630. SAT EBRW middle 50% range 540–640. ACT middle 50% range 22–28. **Basis for Candidate Selection:** *Very important factors include:* rigor of secondary school record, academic GPA, standardized test scores, recommendation(s), character/personal qualities, level of applicant's interest. *Important factors include:* class rank, extracurricular activities. *Other factors include:* application essay, interview, talent/ability, first generation, alumni/ae relation, geographical residence, state residency, racial/ethnic status, volunteer work, work experience. **Freshman Admission Requirements:** High school diploma is required and GED is accepted. *Academic units required:* 4 English, 3 math, 3 science, 2 science labs, 2 foreign language, 2 social studies, 1 history, 5 academic electives. *Academic units recommended:* 4 English, 4 math, 4 science, 2 science labs, 2 foreign language, 3 social studies, 2 history, 7 academic electives. **Freshman Admission Statistics:** 5,535 applied, 86% admitted, 14% enrolled. **Transfer Admission Requirements:** College transcript(s). Minimum college GPA of 2.0 required. Lowest grade transferable D. **General Admission Information:** Application fee $25. Priority deadline 2/1. Regular application deadline 8/15. Non-fall registration accepted. Admission may be deferred for a maximum of 12 months.

COSTS AND FINANCIAL AID

Annual tuition $40,880. Room and board $9,420. Required fees $1,950. Average book and supplies expense $752. **Required Forms and Deadlines:** FAFSA. **Notification of Awards:** Applicants will be notified of awards on a rolling basis beginning 1/31. **Types of Aid:** *Need-based scholarships/grants:* College/university scholarship or grant aid from institutional funds; Federal Pell; Private scholarships; SEOG; State scholarships/grants. *Loans:* Direct PLUS loans; Direct Subsidized Stafford Loans; Direct Unsubsidized Stafford Loans. **Student Employment:** Federal Work-Study Program available. Institutional employment available. **Financial Aid Statistics:** 100% needy freshmen, 98% needy undergrads receive need-based scholarship or grant aid. 32% freshmen, 30% undergrads receive non-need-based scholarship or grant aid. 72% freshmen, 69% undergrads receive need-based self-help aid. 5% freshmen, 7% undergrads receive athletic scholarships. 71% undergrads borrow to pay for school. Average cumulative indebtedness $29,095. **Criteria awarding aid:** *Non-need-based:* Academics, Alumni affiliation, Art, Athletics, Leadership, Minority status, Music/drama, Religious affiliation, State/district residency.

BELMONT ABBEY COLLEGE

100 Belmont-Mount Holly Road, Belmont, NC 28012
Financial Aid Phone: 704-461-6718
E-mail: admissions@bac.edu **CEEB Code:** 5055
Website: www.belmontabbeycollege.edu **ACT Code:** 3070

This private school, affiliated with the Roman Catholic Church, was founded in 1876. It has a 650 acre campus.

RATINGS

Admissions Selectivity Rating: 77   **Fire Safety Rating:** 87   **Green Rating:** 60*

STUDENTS AND FACULTY

Enrollment: 1,545. **Student Body:** 57% female, 43% male, 28% out-of-state, 1% international (13 countries represented). Asian 1%, African American 25%, Caucasian 41%, Hispanic 1%, Native American <1%, Pacific Islander 0%, Two or more races <1%, Race unknown 30%.
Retention and Graduation: 63% freshmen return for sophomore year.
Faculty: Student/faculty ratio 17:1. 75 full-time faculty, 69% hold PhDs, 5%

are members of minority groups, 47% are women. 0% of classes are taught by teaching assistants.

ACADEMICS

Degrees: Bachelor's. **Classes:** Most classes have 10–19 students. Most lab/discussion sessions have 10–19 students. **Most popular majors:** Education, General; Business Administration and Management, General; Elementary Education and Teaching. **Special Study Options:** Double major; Dual enrollment; Honors program; Independent study; Internships; Study abroad; Teacher certification program; Weekend college. **Honors programs:** The Hintemeyer program is designed to foster the leadership potential of a select group of Catholic men and women. The program requires exemplary character; serious commitment to the truth and life of Catholicism; exceptionally strong self-motivation, initiative, and creativity; academic diligence and accomplishment; and employment of these qualities and abilities in the service of others. Throughout their four years in the program, Hintemeyer scholars strive to grow together in faith, virtue, and knowledge, and to discern through reflection and practice the nature of authentic Catholic leadership. Central to each participantÂ's experience will be seminars on a variety of leadership and faith topics, communal prayer and participation in the sacraments, and regular student-generated service and leadership activities on and off campus, culminating junior year in a large-scale project of the student's own design. **Disability Services offered:** Note-taking services; Reader services; Tape recorders; Tutors. **Career services:** Alumni services; Career assessment; Career/job search classes; Internships; Regional alumni.

FACILITIES

Housing: Apartments for single students; Coed dorms; Men's dorms; Special housing for disabled students; Women's dorms; 85% of campus accessible to physically disabled. **Special Academic Facilities/Equipment:** The Abbey Theater, Monastery, Basilica, Adoration Chapel, and Rare Book Museum. **Campus network:** 100% of classrooms, 100% of dorms, 100% of student union, 100% of libraries, 100% of dining areas, 100% of common outdoor areas, have wireless network access.

CAMPUS LIFE

Environment: Village. **Activities:** Campus Ministries; Choral groups; Dance; Drama/theater; International Student Organization; Literary magazine; Musical theater; Pep band; Student government; Student newspaper; Yearbook. 30 registered organizations, 2 honor societies, 10 religious organizations, 2 fraternities, 3 sororities, on campus. **Athletics (Intercollegiate):** *Men:* baseball, basketball, cross-country, golf, soccer, tennis, wrestling. *Women:* basketball, cross-country, soccer, softball, tennis, volleyball. **On-Campus Highlights:** Church/Basillica.

ADMISSIONS

Freshman Academic Profile: Average high school GPA 3.1. 5% in top 10% of high school class, 15% in top 25% of high school class, 61% in top 50% of high school class. **Test Scores:** SAT Math middle 50% range 450–570. SAT EBRW middle 50% range 440–550. ACT middle 50% range 18–24. **Basis for Candidate Selection:** *Very important factors include:* rigor of secondary school record, academic GPA, standardized test scores. *Important factors include:* class rank, interview. *Other factors include:* application essay, recommendation(s), extracurricular activities, talent/ability, volunteer work, work experience, level of applicant's interest. **Freshman Admission Requirements:** High school diploma is required and GED is accepted. *Academic units required:* 4 English, 3 math, 2 science, 2 foreign language, 1 social studies, 1 history, 3 academic electives. *Academic units recommended:* 4 math, 3 foreign language. **Freshman Admission Statistics:** 1,950 applied, 69% admitted, 22% enrolled. **Transfer Admission Requirements:** college transcript(s), Minimum college GPA of 2.0 required. Lowest grade transferable C. **General Admission Information:** Application fee $35. Regular application deadline 8/1. Non-fall registration accepted. Admission may be deferred for a maximum of 2 semesters.

COSTS AND FINANCIAL AID

Annual tuition $18,500. Room and board $10,094. Average book and supplies expense $1,200. **Required Forms and Deadlines:** FAFSA. **Notification of Awards:** Applicants will be notified of awards on a rolling basis beginning 3/15. **Types of Aid:** *Need-based scholarships/grants:* College/university scholarship or grant aid from institutional funds; Federal Pell; SEOG; State scholarships/grants. *Loans:* Direct PLUS loans; Direct Subsidized Stafford Loans; Direct Unsubsidized Stafford Loans. **Student Employment:** Federal Work-Study Program available. Institutional employment available. **Financial Aid Statistics:** 99% needy freshmen, 95% needy undergrads receive need-based scholarship or grant aid. 11% freshmen, 5% undergrads receive non-need-based scholarship or grant aid. 87% freshmen, 94% undergrads receive need-based self-help aid. 13% freshmen, 7% undergrads receive athletic scholarships. 98% freshmen,

90% undergrads receive any aid. **Criteria awarding aid:** *Need-based:* Religious affiliation. *Non-need-based:* Academics, Athletics, Religious affiliation, State/district residency.

BELMONT UNIVERSITY

1900 Belmont Blvd, Nashville, TN 37212
Phone: 615-460-6785 **Financial Aid Phone:** 615-460-6403
E-mail: admissions@belmont.edu **CEEB Code:** 1058
Fax: 615-460-5434 **Website:** http://www.belmont.edu/ **ACT Code:** 3946

This private school, affiliated with the Christian (Nondenominational) Church, was founded in 1860. It has a 76 acre campus.

RATINGS

Admissions Selectivity Rating: 80   **Fire Safety Rating:** 91   **Green Rating:** 81

STUDENTS AND FACULTY

Enrollment: 6,783. **Student Body:** 65% female, 35% male, 71% out-of-state, 1% international (30 countries represented). Asian 2%, African American 5%, Caucasian 80%, Hispanic 6%, Native American <1%, Pacific Islander <1%, Two or more races 4%, Race unknown 1%. **Retention and Graduation:** 83% freshmen return for sophomore year. 60% freshmen graduate within 4 years. 72% freshmen graduate within 6 years. 17% grads go on to further study within 1 year. **Faculty:** Student/faculty ratio 14:1. 386 full-time faculty, 88% hold PhDs, 12% are members of minority groups, 50% are women.

ACADEMICS

Degrees: Bachelor's; Doctoral degree—professional practice; Master's. **Classes:** Most classes have 20–29 students. Most lab/discussion sessions have fewer than 10 students. **Most popular majors:** Music, General; Recording Arts Technology/Technician; Music Management. **Special Study Options:** Accelerated program; Cooperative education program; Cross-registration; Distance learning; Double major; Dual enrollment; English as a Second Language (ESL); Honors program; Independent study; Internships; Liberal arts/career combination; Student-designed major; Study abroad; Teacher certification program. **Career services:** Alumni network; Alumni services; Career assessment; Career/job search classes; Internships; Regional alumni.

FACILITIES

Housing: Apartments for single students; Coed dorms; Men's dorms; Special housing for international students; Women's dorms; 98% of campus accessible to physically disabled. **Special Academic Facilities/Equipment:** Language lab, recording studio, the Belmont Mansion, The Gallery of Iconic Guitars. **Campus network:** 100% of classrooms, 100% of dorms, 100% of student union, 100% of libraries, 100% of dining areas, 50% of common outdoor areas, have wireless network access.

CAMPUS LIFE

Environment: Metropolis. **Activities:** Campus Ministries; Choral groups; Concert band; Dance; Drama/theater; International Student Organization; Jazz band; Literary magazine; Marching band; Music ensembles; Musical theater; Opera; Pep band; Student government; Student newspaper; Symphony orchestra; Television station. 108 registered organizations, 15 honor societies, 11 religious organizations, 3 fraternities, 5 sororities, on campus. **Athletics (Intercollegiate):** *Men:* baseball, basketball, cross-country, golf, soccer, tennis, track/field (outdoor). *Women:* basketball, cross-country, golf, soccer, softball, tennis, track/field (outdoor), volleyball. **On-Campus Highlights:** Beaman Student Life Center. **Environmental Initiatives:** Recycle.

ADMISSIONS

Freshman Academic Profile: Average high school GPA 3.5. 32% in top 10% of high school class, 61% in top 25% of high school class, 91% in top 50% of high school class. **Test Scores:** SAT Math middle 50% range 550–650. SAT EBRW middle 50% range 580–670. ACT middle 50% range 24–29. **Basis for Candidate Selection:** *Very important factors include:* rigor of secondary school record, academic GPA, standardized test scores. *Important factors include:* application essay, recommendation(s). *Other factors include:* class rank, extracurricular activities, talent/ability, character/personal qualities, first generation, alumni/ae relation, religious affiliation/commitment, racial/ethnic status, volunteer work, work experience. **Freshman Admission Requirements:** High school diploma is required and GED is accepted. *Academic units required:* 4 English, 3 math, 3 science, 2 foreign language, 3 social studies, 3 academic electives. *Academic units recommended:* 4 English, 4 math, 4 science, 2 foreign language, 3 social studies, 3 academic electives. **Freshman Admission Statistics:** 7,965 applied, 84% admitted, 25% enrolled. **Transfer Admission Requirements:** High school transcript, college transcript(s), essay or personal statement, standardized test scores, Minimum college GPA of 2.0 required. Lowest grade transferable C. **General Admission Information:** Application fee $50. Priority deadline 12/1. Regular application deadline 8/1. Non-fall registration accepted. Admission may be deferred for a maximum of 1 year.

COSTS AND FINANCIAL AID
Annual tuition $31,300. Room and board $11,680. Required fees $1,520. Average book and supplies expense $1,400. **Required Forms and Deadlines:** FAFSA. **Notification of Awards:** Applicants will be notified of awards on a rolling basis beginning 3/15. *Types of Aid: Need-based scholarships/grants:* College/university scholarship or grant aid from institutional funds; Federal Pell; Private scholarships; SEOG; State scholarships/grants. *Loans:* Direct PLUS loans; Direct Subsidized Stafford Loans; Direct Unsubsidized Stafford Loans. **Student Employment:** Federal Work-Study Program available. **Financial Aid Statistics:** 98% needy freshmen, 92% needy undergrads receive need-based scholarship or grant aid. 15% freshmen, 10% undergrads receive non-need-based scholarship or grant aid. 73% freshmen, 73% undergrads receive need-based self-help aid. 1% freshmen, 2% undergrads receive athletic scholarships. 50% undergrads borrow to pay for school. Average cumulative indebtedness $29,702. **Criteria awarding aid:** *Non-need-based:* Academics, Art, Athletics, Leadership, Music/drama, Religious affiliation, State/district residency.

BELOIT COLLEGE

700 College St., Beloit, WI 53511
Phone: 608-363-2500 **Financial Aid Phone:** (608)363-2663
E-mail: admiss@beloit.edu **CEEB Code:** 1059
Fax: 608-363-2075 **Website:** www.beloit.edu **ACT Code:** 4564

This private school was founded in 1846. It has a 75 acre campus.

RATINGS
Admissions Selectivity Rating: 86   **Fire Safety Rating:** 85   **Green Rating:** 76

STUDENTS AND FACULTY
Enrollment: 1,212. **Student Body:** 54% female, 46% male, 84% out-of-state, 17% international (28 countries represented). Asian 4%, African American 7%, Caucasian 52%, Hispanic 11%, Native American <1%, Pacific Islander <1%, Two or more races 4%, Race unknown 4%.
Retention and Graduation: 78% freshmen return for sophomore year. 75% freshmen graduate within 4 years. 86% freshmen graduate within 6 years.
Faculty: Student/faculty ratio 10:1. 117 full-time faculty, 95% hold PhDs, 22% are members of minority groups, 58% are women. 0% of classes are taught by teaching assistants.

ACADEMICS
Degrees: Bachelor's. **Classes:** Most classes have 10–19 students. **Most popular majors:** Science, Technology and Society; Psychology, General; Anthropology, General. **Special Study Options:** Double major; English as a Second Language (ESL); Exchange student program (domestic); Independent study; Internships; Liberal arts/career combination; Student-designed major; Study abroad; Teacher certification program. **Combined degree programs:** BA/MEng. **Disability Services offered:** Note-taking services; Reader services; Tape recorders; Tutors. **Career services:** Alumni network; Alumni services; Career assessment; Career/job search classes; Internships; Regional alumni.

FACILITIES
Housing: Apartments for single students; Coed dorms; Fraternity/sorority housing; Theme housing; Women's dorms; 50% of campus accessible to physically disabled. **Special Academic Facilities/Equipment:** Wright Museum of Art Logan Museum of Anthropology Center for Language Study Student Run Market Research Company (BELMARK) Center for Entrepreneurial Leadership (CELEB) Hendricks Center for the Arts LEED Platinum Certified Science Building.

CAMPUS LIFE
Environment: Town. **Activities:** Campus Ministries; Choral groups; Dance; Drama/theater; International Student Organization; Jazz band; Literary magazine; Model UN; Music ensembles; Musical theater; Radio station; Student government; Student newspaper; Television station. 113 registered organizations, 6 honor societies, 3 religious organizations, 3 fraternities, 3 sororities, on campus. **Athletics (Intercollegiate):** *Men:* baseball, basketball, cross-country, football, golf, soccer, swimming, tennis, track/field (outdoor), track/field (indoor). *Women:* basketball, cross-country, soccer, softball, swimming, tennis, track/field (outdoor), track/field (indoor), volleyball. **On-Campus Highlights:** Logan Museum of Anthropology. **Environmental Initiatives:** New Science Center has been platinum-level LEED certified, one of only three such buildings in the state.

ADMISSIONS
Freshman Academic Profile: Average high school GPA 3.3. 15% in top 10% of high school class, 56% in top 25% of high school class, 87% in top 50% of high school class. 75% from public high schools. **Test Scores:** SAT Math middle 50% range 550–690. SAT EBRW middle 50% range 570–670. ACT middle 50% range 21–29. **Basis for Candidate Selection:** *Very important factors include:* rigor of secondary school record, academic GPA, application essay, recommendation(s). *Important factors include:* extracurricular activities, talent/ability. *Other factors include:* class rank, standardized test scores, interview, character/personal qualities, first generation, alumni/ae relation, racial/ethnic status, volunteer work, work experience, level of applicant's interest. **Freshman Admission Requirements:** High school diploma is required and GED is accepted. *Academic units recommended:* 4 English, 3 math, 3 science, 3 science labs, 2 foreign language, 3 social studies. **Freshman Admission Statistics:** 4,200 applied, 56% admitted, 11% enrolled. **Transfer Admission Requirements:** College transcript(s), essay or personal statement, statement of good standing from prior institution(s). Minimum college GPA of 3.00 required. Lowest grade transferable C. **General Admission Information:** Priority deadline 1/15. Non-fall registration accepted. Admission may be deferred for a maximum of 1 year.

COSTS AND FINANCIAL AID
Annual tuition $51,050. Room and board $9,360. Required fees $482. Average book and supplies expense $1,000. **Required Forms and Deadlines:** FAFSA. *Types of Aid: Need-based scholarships/grants:* College/university scholarship or grant aid from institutional funds; Federal Pell; Private scholarships; SEOG; State scholarships/grants. *Loans:* Direct PLUS loans; Direct Subsidized Stafford Loans; Direct Unsubsidized Stafford Loans. **Student Employment:** Federal Work-Study Program available. Institutional employment available. **Financial Aid Statistics:** 98% needy freshmen, 98% needy undergrads receive need-based scholarship or grant aid. 54% freshmen, 49% undergrads receive non-need-based scholarship or grant aid. 80% freshmen, 83% undergrads receive need-based self-help aid. 0% freshmen, 0% undergrads receive athletic scholarships. 99% freshmen, 99% undergrads receive any aid. 56% undergrads borrow to pay for school. Average cumulative indebtedness $31,675. **Criteria awarding aid:** *Need-based:* Academics. *Non-need-based:* Academics, Leadership, Minority status, Music/drama.

BEMIDJI STATE UNIVERSITY

1500 Birchmont Dr. NE, Bemidji, MN 56601
Phone: 218-755-2040 **Financial Aid Phone:** 218-755-2034
E-mail: admissions@bemidjistate.edu **CEEB Code:** 6676
Fax: 218-755-2390 **Website:** http://www.bemidjistate.edu/ **ACT Code:** 2084

This public school was founded in 1919. It has a 90 acre campus.

RATINGS
Admissions Selectivity Rating: 73   **Fire Safety Rating:** 72   **Green Rating:** 79

STUDENTS AND FACULTY
Enrollment: 4,393. **Student Body:** 57% female, 43% male, 10% out-of-state, 2% international (35 countries represented). Asian 1%, African American 2%, Caucasian 85%, Hispanic 2%, Native American 3%, Pacific Islander 0%, Two or more races 3%, Race unknown 2%.
Retention and Graduation: 66% freshmen return for sophomore year.
Faculty: Student/faculty ratio 19:1. 174 full-time faculty, 68% hold PhDs, 9% are members of minority groups, 44% are women. 5% of classes are taught by teaching assistants.

ACADEMICS

Degrees: Associate; Bachelor's; Certificate; Master's; Post-bachelor's certificate. **Classes:** Most classes have 20–29 students. **Most popular majors:** Education, General; Business/Commerce, General; Industrial Production Technologies/Technicians, Other. **Special Study Options:** Cooperative education program; Cross-registration; Distance learning; Double major; Dual enrollment; English as a Second Language (ESL); External degree program; Honors program; Independent study; Internships; Study abroad; Teacher certification program. **Honors programs:** Honors Program. **Disability Services offered:** Note-taking services; Reader services; Tutors. **Career services:** Alumni services; Career assessment; Career/job search classes; Internships; Regional alumni.

FACILITIES

Housing: Apartments for single students; Coed dorms; Special housing for disabled students; Special housing for international students; Theme housing; 95% of campus accessible to physically disabled. **Special Academic Facilities/Equipment:** Outdoor Program Center Boathouse. C.V. Hobson Forest. American Indian Resource Center. **Campus network:** 100% of classrooms, 100% of dorms, 100% of student union, 100% of libraries, 100% of dining areas, 85% of common outdoor areas, have wireless network access.

CAMPUS LIFE

Environment: Village. **Activities:** Campus Ministries; Choral groups; Concert band; Dance; Drama/theater; International Student Organization; Jazz band; Literary magazine; Music ensembles; Musical theater; Opera; Pep band; Radio station; Student government; Student newspaper; Symphony orchestra; Television station. 93 registered organizations, 1 honor societies, 8 religious organizations, 2 fraternities, 1 sororities, on campus. **Athletics (Intercollegiate):** *Men:* baseball, basketball, cross-country, football, golf, ice hockey, soccer, softball, tennis, track/field (outdoor), track/field (indoor), volleyball. *Women:* basketball, cross-country, golf, ice hockey, soccer, softball, tennis, track/field (outdoor), track/field (indoor), volleyball. **On-Campus Highlights:** Recreation Center. **Environmental Initiatives:** Signature theme of Environmental Stewardship.

ADMISSIONS

Freshman Academic Profile: Average high school GPA 3.1. 7% in top 10% of high school class, 23% in top 25% of high school class, 56% in top 50% of high school class. 95% from public high schools. **Test Scores:** ACT middle 50% range 19–24. **Basis for Candidate Selection:** *Very important factors include:* class rank, standardized test scores. *Important factors include:* rigor of secondary school record. *Other factors include:* academic GPA, application essay, recommendation(s), extracurricular activities, first generation. **Freshman Admission Requirements:** High school diploma is required and GED is accepted. *Academic units required:* 4 English, 3 math, 3 science, 2 foreign language, 3 social studies, 1 academic electives. **Freshman Admission Statistics:** 2,566 applied, 94% admitted, 31% enrolled. Minimum college GPA of 2.0 required. Lowest grade transferable C. **General Admission Information:** Application fee $20. Priority deadline 2/1. Non-fall registration accepted. Admission may be deferred for a maximum of 1 year.

COSTS AND FINANCIAL AID

Annual in-state tuition $7,360. Annual out-of-state tuition $7,360. Room and board $8,500. Required fees $950. **Required Forms and Deadlines:** FAFSA; Institution's own financial aid form. **Notification of Awards:** Applicants will be notified of awards on or about 3/15. **Types of Aid:** *Need-based scholarships/grants:* College/university scholarship or grant aid from institutional funds; Federal Pell; Private scholarships; SEOG; State scholarships/grants. *Loans:* Direct PLUS loans; Direct Subsidized Stafford Loans; Direct Unsubsidized Stafford Loans. **Student Employment:** Federal Work-Study Program available. Institutional employment available. **Financial Aid Statistics:** 70% needy freshmen, 72% needy undergrads receive need-based scholarship or grant aid. 78% freshmen, 76% undergrads receive non-need-based scholarship or grant aid. 82% freshmen, 81% undergrads receive need-based self-help aid. 6% freshmen, 6% undergrads receive athletic scholarships. 62% freshmen, 65% undergrads receive any aid. **Criteria awarding aid:** *Non-need-based:* Academics, Alumni affiliation, Art, Athletics, Job skills, Leadership, Minority status, Music/drama, Religious affiliation.

BENEDICT COLLEGE

1600 Harden St, Columbia, SC 29204
Phone: 803-705-4491
E-mail: thompso@benedict.edu
Fax: 803-253-5167 **Website:** www.benedict.edu

This private school, affiliated with the Baptist Church, was founded in 1870. It has a 110 acre campus.

RATINGS

Admissions Selectivity Rating: 71   **Fire Safety Rating:** 60*   **Green Rating:** 60*

STUDENTS AND FACULTY

Enrollment: 2,641. **Student Body:** 51% female, 49% male, 40% out-of-state, 0% international. Asian <1%, African American 99%, Caucasian <1%, Hispanic 1%, Native American <1%, Race unknown <1%.
Retention and Graduation: 53% freshmen return for sophomore year.
Faculty: Student/faculty ratio 19:1. 117 full-time faculty, 65% hold PhDs, 95% are members of minority groups, 58% are women.

ACADEMICS

Degrees: Bachelor's. **Classes:** Most classes have fewer than 10 students. Most lab/discussion sessions have fewer than 10 students. **Special Study Options:** Accelerated program; Double major; Dual enrollment; External degree program; Honors program; Internships; Teacher certification program; Weekend college.

FACILITIES

Housing: Men's dorms; Women's dorms. **Campus network:** 90% of classrooms, 100% of dorms, 100% of student union, 90% of libraries, 100% of dining areas, 60% of common outdoor areas, have wireless network access.

CAMPUS LIFE

Environment: City. **Activities:** Campus Ministries; Choral groups; Concert band; International Student Organization; Marching band; Student government; Student newspaper.

ADMISSIONS

Freshman Academic Profile: Average high school GPA 2.5. 5% in top 10% of high school class, 15% in top 25% of high school class, 39% in top 50% of high school class. 69% from public high schools. **Test Scores:** SAT Math middle 50% range 320–430. SAT EBRW middle 50% range 320–430. ACT middle 50% range 13–17. **Basis for Candidate Selection: Freshman Admission Requirements:** High school diploma is required and GED is accepted. *Academic units recommended:* 4 English, 3 math, 2 science, 3 social studies. **Freshman Admission Statistics:** 4,624 applied, 83% admitted, 17% enrolled. **Transfer Admission Requirements:** High school transcript, college transcript(s), statement of good standing from prior institution(s). Minimum college GPA of 2.0 required. Lowest grade transferable C. **General Admission Information:** Application fee $25. Non-fall registration accepted.

COSTS AND FINANCIAL AID

Annual tuition $12,516. Room and board $6,444. Average book and supplies expense $1,000. **Required Forms and Deadlines:** FAFSA. **Types of Aid:** *Need-based scholarships/grants:* College/university scholarship or grant aid from institutional funds; Federal Pell; Private scholarships; SEOG; State scholarships/grants; United Negro College Fund. *Loans:* Direct PLUS loans; Direct Subsidized Stafford Loans; Direct Unsubsidized Stafford Loans. **Criteria awarding aid:** *Need-based:* Academics, Alumni affiliation, Athletics, Music/drama, Religious affiliation.

BENEDICTINE COLLEGE

1020 North Second Street, Atchison, KS 66002
Phone: 800-467-5340 **Financial Aid Phone:** 913-360-7480
E-mail: bcadmiss@benedictine.edu **CEEB Code:** 6056
Fax: 913-367-5462 **Website:** www.benedictine.edu **ACT Code:** 1444

This private school, affiliated with the Roman Catholic Church, was founded in 1859. It has a 225 acre campus.

RATINGS

Admissions Selectivity Rating: 74 **Fire Safety Rating:** 64 **Green Rating:** 60*

STUDENTS AND FACULTY

Enrollment: 1,823. **Student Body:** 54% female, 46% male, 76% out-of-state, 2% international (17 countries represented). Asian 1%, African American 3%, Caucasian 79%, Hispanic 7%, Native American 1%, Pacific Islander <1%, Two or more races <1%, Race unknown 7%.
Retention and Graduation: 79% freshmen return for sophomore year. 49% freshmen graduate within 4 years. 63% freshmen graduate within 6 years. 12% grads go on to further study within 1 year. 2% grads pursue law degrees. 2% grads pursue medical degrees. **Faculty:** Student/faculty ratio 13:1. 116 full-time faculty, 71% hold PhDs, 10% are members of minority groups, 28% are women. 0% of classes are taught by teaching assistants.

ACADEMICS

Degrees: Bachelor's; Master's. **Classes:** Most classes have 20–29 students. Most lab/discussion sessions have fewer than 10 students. **Most popular majors:** Theological and Ministerial Studies, Other; Business Administration and Management, General; Elementary Education and Teaching. **Special Study Options:** Distance learning; Double major; Dual enrollment; English as a Second Language (ESL); Honors program; Independent study; Internships; Student-designed major; Study abroad; Teacher certification program. **Honors programs:** Honors Program, Gregorian Fellows. **Disability Services offered:** Note-taking services; Tape recorders; Tutors. **Career services:** Alumni network; Career assessment; Career/job search classes; Internships.

FACILITIES

Housing: Apartments for single students; Men's dorms; Women's dorms 95% of campus accessible to physically disabled. **Campus network:** 80% of classrooms, 100% of dorms, 100% of student union, 100% of libraries, 100% of dining areas, 100% of common outdoor areas, have wireless network access.

CAMPUS LIFE

Environment: Town. **Activities:** Campus Ministries; Choral groups; Concert band; Dance; Drama/theater; International Student Organization; Jazz band; Literary magazine; Marching band; Music ensembles; Musical theater; Opera; Pep band; Student government; Student newspaper; Symphony orchestra; Yearbook. 46 registered organizations, on campus. **Athletics (Intercollegiate):** *Men:* baseball, basketball, cheerleading, cross-country, football, golf, soccer, tennis, track/field (outdoor), track/field (indoor). *Women:* basketball, cheerleading, cross-country, golf, soccer, softball, tennis, track/field (outdoor), track/field (indoor), volleyball. **On-Campus Highlights:** Raven Roost.

ADMISSIONS

Freshman Academic Profile: Average high school GPA 3.5. 19% in top 10% of high school class, 42% in top 25% of high school class, 67% in top 50% of high school class. 43% from public high schools. **Test Scores:** ACT middle 50% range 22–28. **Basis for Candidate Selection:** *Very important factors include:* rigor of secondary school record, academic GPA. *Important factors include:* class rank, standardized test scores. *Other factors include:* recommendation(s), interview, extracurricular activities, talent/ability, character/personal qualities, first generation, volunteer work, work experience. **Freshman Admission Requirements:** High school diploma is required and GED is accepted. *Academic units required:* 3 math, 2 science, 2 foreign language. *Academic units recommended:* 4 English, 4 math, 4 science, 4 foreign language, 2 social studies, 1 history. **Freshman Admission Statistics:** 2,367 applied, 97% admitted, 19% enrolled. **Transfer Admission Requirements:** College transcript(s). Minimum college GPA of 2.0 required. Lowest grade transferable C. **General Admission Information:** Application fee $50. Non-fall registration accepted. Admission may be deferred for a maximum of 1 year.

COSTS AND FINANCIAL AID

Average book and supplies expense $1,200. **Required Forms and Deadlines:** FAFSA. **Notification of Awards:** Applicants will be notified of awards on a rolling basis beginning 12/15. **Types of Aid:** *Need-based scholarships/grants:*

College/university scholarship or grant aid from institutional funds; Federal Pell; Private scholarships; SEOG; State scholarships/grants. *Loans:* Direct PLUS loans; Direct Subsidized Stafford Loans; Direct Unsubsidized Stafford Loans. **Student Employment:** Federal Work-Study Program available. Institutional employment available. **Financial Aid Statistics:** 100% needy freshmen, 100% needy undergrads receive need-based scholarship or grant aid. 20% freshmen, 18% undergrads receive non-need-based scholarship or grant aid. 62% freshmen, 68% undergrads receive need-based self-help aid. 12% freshmen, 12% undergrads receive athletic scholarships. 78% freshmen, 79.5% undergrads receive any aid. 69% undergrads borrow to pay for school. Average cumulative indebtedness $29,196. **Criteria awarding aid:** *Need-based:* Minority status, Religious affiliation. *Non-need-based:* Academics, Alumni affiliation, Art, Athletics, Job skills, Leadership, Minority status, Music/drama, Religious affiliation, State/district residency.

BENEDICTINE UNIVERSITY

5700 College Road, Lisle, IL 60532-0900
Phone: 630-829-6300 **Financial Aid Phone:** (630) 829-6100
E-mail: admissions@ben.edu **CEEB Code:** 1707
Fax: 630-829-6301 **Website:** www.ben.edu **ACT Code:** 1132

This private school, affiliated with the Roman Catholic Church, was founded in 1887. It has a 108 acre campus.

RATINGS

Admissions Selectivity Rating: 80 **Fire Safety Rating:** 96 **Green Rating:** 60*

STUDENTS AND FACULTY

Enrollment: 2,903. **Student Body:** 58% female, 42% male, 8% out-of-state, 1% international (17 countries represented). Asian 18%, African American 8%, Caucasian 44%, Hispanic 10%, Native American <1%, Pacific Islander <1%, Two or more races 0%, Race unknown 19%.
Retention and Graduation: 74% freshmen return for sophomore year. **Faculty:** Student/faculty ratio 18:1. 128 full-time faculty, 88% hold PhDs, 16% are members of minority groups, 48% are women. 0% of classes are taught by teaching assistants.

ACADEMICS

Degrees: Associate; Bachelor's; Certificate; Doctoral degree research/scholarship; Master's; Post-bachelor's certificate; Transfer Associate. **Classes:** Most classes have 10–19 students. Most lab/discussion sessions have 10–19 students. **Most popular majors:** Organizational Behavior Studies; Biology/Biological Sciences, General; Psychology, General. **Special Study Options:** Accelerated program; Cross-registration; Distance learning; Double major; Dual enrollment; English as a Second Language (ESL); Honors program; Independent study; Internships; Study abroad; Teacher certification program; Weekend college. **Honors programs:** University Scholars Program. **Disability Services offered:** Note-taking services; Reader services; Tape recorders; Tutors. **Career services:** Alumni network; Alumni services; Career assessment; Career/job search classes; Internships.

FACILITIES

Housing: Apartments for married students; Apartments for single students; Coed dorms; Men's dorms; Special housing for international students; Wellness housing; Women's dorms; 100% of campus accessible to physically disabled. **Special Academic Facilities/Equipment:** Natural science and history museums, http://www.ben.edu/museum/. Exercise physiology lab. **Campus network:** 100% of classrooms, 100% of dorms, 100% of student union, 100% of libraries, 100% of dining areas, 90% of common outdoor areas, have wireless network access.

CAMPUS LIFE

Environment: Town. **Activities:** Campus Ministries; Choral groups; Concert band; Dance; Drama/theater; International Student Organization; Jazz band; Literary magazine; Model UN; Music ensembles; Pep band; Student government; Student newspaper; Student-run film society; Symphony orchestra; Television station. 40 registered organizations, 1 honor societies, 3 religious organizations, on campus. **Athletics (Intercollegiate):** *Men:* baseball, basketball, cross-country, football, golf, soccer, track/field (outdoor), track/field (indoor). *Women:* basketball, cross-country, golf, soccer, softball, tennis, track/field (outdoor), track/field (indoor), volleyball. **On-Campus Highlights:** Jurica Nature Museum **Environmental Initiatives:** Energy reduction.

ADMISSIONS

Freshman Academic Profile: Average high school GPA 3.4. 21% in top 10% of high school class, 48% in top 25% of high school class, 79% in top 50% of high school class. 85% from public high schools. **Test Scores:** ACT middle 50% range 20–26. **Basis for Candidate Selection:** *Very important factors include:* rigor of secondary school record, class rank, academic GPA, standardized test scores. *Other factors include:* application essay, recommendation(s), interview, extracurricular activities. **Freshman Admission Requirements:** High school diploma is required and GED is accepted. *Academic units required:* 4 English, 3 math, 2 science, 1 science labs, 2 foreign language, 3 social studies, 1 history. *Academic units recommended:* 4 math, 3 science, 2 science labs. **Freshman Admission Statistics:** 2,108 applied, 69% admitted, 32% enrolled. **Transfer Admission Requirements:** College transcript(s), statement of good standing from prior institution(s). Minimum college GPA of 2.0 required. Lowest grade transferable D. **General Admission Information:** Application fee $40. Regular application deadline 8/30. Non-fall registration accepted.

COSTS AND FINANCIAL AID

Annual tuition $25,950. Room and board $8,280. Average book and supplies expense $1,450. **Required Forms and Deadlines:** FAFSA. **Notification of Awards:** Applicants will be notified of awards on a rolling basis beginning 2/1. **Types of Aid:** *Need-based scholarships/grants:* College/university scholarship or grant aid from institutional funds; Federal Pell; Private scholarships; SEOG; State scholarships/grants. *Loans:* Direct PLUS loans; Direct Subsidized Stafford Loans; Direct Unsubsidized Stafford Loans. **Student Employment:** Federal Work-Study Program available. Institutional employment available. **Financial Aid Statistics:** 63% needy freshmen, 62% needy undergrads receive need-based scholarship or grant aid. 98% freshmen, 84% undergrads receive non-need-based scholarship or grant aid. 76% freshmen, 89% undergrads receive need-based self-help aid. 0% freshmen, 0% undergrads receive athletic scholarships. 98% freshmen, 89% undergrads receive any aid. **Criteria awarding aid:** *Non-need-based:* Academics, Alumni affiliation, Leadership, Music/drama, State/district residency.

BENNETT COLLEGE

900 East Washington Street, Greensboro, NC 27401
Phone: 336-370-8624 **Financial Aid Phone:** 336-517-2220
E-mail: admiss@bennett.edu **CEEB Code:** 5058
Fax: 336-370-8653 **Website:** www.bennett.edu **ACT Code:** 3072

This private school, affiliated with the Methodist Church, was founded in 1873. It has a 55 acre campus.

RATINGS

Admissions Selectivity Rating: 76   **Fire Safety Rating:** 80   **Green Rating:** 60*

STUDENTS AND FACULTY

Enrollment: 651. **Student Body:** 100% female, 0% male, 62% out-of-state, <1% international (2 countries represented). Asian 0%, African American 94%, Caucasian <1%, Hispanic 2%, Native American <1%, Pacific Islander 0%, Two or more races 2%, Race unknown 2%.
Retention and Graduation: 58% freshmen return for sophomore year.
Faculty: Student/faculty ratio 10:1. 61 full-time faculty, 64% hold PhDs, 70% are members of minority groups, 77% are women. 0% of classes are taught by teaching assistants.

ACADEMICS

Degrees: Bachelor's. **Classes:** Most classes have 10–19 students. Most lab/discussion sessions have fewer than 10 students. **Most popular majors:** Communication and Media Studies, Other; Biological and Physical Sciences; Psychology, General. **Special Study Options:** Accelerated program; Cooperative education program; Cross-registration; Double major; Dual enrollment; Exchange student program (domestic); Honors program; Independent study; Internships; Student-designed major; Study abroad; Teacher certification program. **Disability Services offered:** Tape recorders; Tutors. **Career services:** Alumni network; Alumni services; Career/job search classes; Internships; Regional alumni.

FACILITIES

Housing: Wellness housing; Women's dorms. **Special Academic Facilities/Equipment:** Intergenerational Center Global Learning Center. **Campus network:** 100% of classrooms, 100% of dorms, 100% of student union, 100% of libraries, 100% of dining areas, have wireless network access.

CAMPUS LIFE

Environment: City. **Activities:** Campus Ministries; Choral groups; Dance; Drama/theater; International Student Organization; Literary magazine; Model UN; Student government; Student newspaper. 34 registered organizations, 5 honor societies, 1 religious organizations, 3 sororities, on campus. **Athletics (Intercollegiate):** *Women:* basketball, cheerleading, cross-country, softball, swimming, tennis, track/field (outdoor), volleyball. **On-Campus Highlights:** Student Union.

ADMISSIONS

Freshman Academic Profile: 8% in top 10% of high school class, 12% in top 25% of high school class, 50% in top 50% of high school class. **Test Scores:** SAT Math middle 50% range 350–420. SAT EBRW middle 50% range 350–430. **Basis for Candidate Selection:** *Very important factors include:* rigor of secondary school record, academic GPA, recommendation(s), talent/ability. *Important factors include:* class rank, application essay, *Other factors include:* standardized test scores, interview, extracurricular activities, character/personal qualities, first generation, alumni/ae relation, geographical residence, state residency, religious affiliation/commitment, racial/ethnic status, volunteer work, work experience, level of applicant's interest. **Freshman Admission Requirements:** High school diploma is required and GED is accepted. *Academic units required:* 4 English, 3 math, 2 science, 2 foreign language, 2 social studies, 5 academic electives. **Freshman Admission Statistics:** 1,433 applied, 63% admitted, 18% enrolled. **Transfer Admission Requirements:** College transcript(s), essay or personal statement. Minimum college GPA of 2.0 required. Lowest grade transferable C. **General Admission Information:** Application fee $35. Non-fall registration accepted. Admission may be deferred for a maximum of 1 year.

COSTS AND FINANCIAL AID

Annual tuition $14,614. Room and board $7,428. Required fees $2,180. Average book and supplies expense $1,500. **Required Forms and Deadlines:** FAFSA; Institution's own financial aid form. **Notification of Awards:** Applicants will be notified of awards on or about 7/15. **Types of Aid:** *Need-based scholarships/grants:* College/university scholarship or grant aid from institutional funds; Federal Nursing Scholarships; Federal Pell; Private scholarships; SEOG; State scholarships/grants; United Negro College Fund. *Loans:* Direct Subsidized Stafford Loans; Direct Unsubsidized Stafford Loans. **Student Employment:** Federal Work-Study Program available. **Financial Aid Statistics:** 96% needy freshmen, 93% needy undergrads receive need-based scholarship or grant aid. 1% freshmen, 2% undergrads receive non-need-based scholarship or grant aid. 96% freshmen, 94% undergrads receive need-based self-help aid. 0% freshmen, 0% undergrads receive athletic scholarships. **Criteria awarding aid:** *Need-based:* Academics, Alumni affiliation, Leadership, Minority status, Religious affiliation. *Non-need-based:* Academics, Alumni affiliation, Leadership, Minority status, Religious affiliation, State/district residency.

BENNINGTON COLLEGE

One College Drive, Bennington, VT 05201
Phone: 802-440-4312 **Financial Aid Phone:** 800-833-6845
E-mail: admissions@bennington.edu **CEEB Code:** 3080
Fax: 802-440-4320 **Website:** www.bennington.edu **ACT Code:** 4296

This private school was founded in 1932. It has a 440 acre campus.

RATINGS

Admissions Selectivity Rating: 88   **Fire Safety Rating:** 96   **Green Rating:** 60*

STUDENTS AND FACULTY

Enrollment: 702. **Student Body:** 65% female, 35% male, 96% out-of-state, 20% international (60 countries represented). Asian 1%, African American 4%, Caucasian 58%, Hispanic 10%, Native American <1%, Pacific Islander <1%, Two or more races 4%, Race unknown 3%.
Retention and Graduation: 83% freshmen return for sophomore year. 66% freshmen graduate within 4 years. 76% freshmen graduate within 6 years. 8% grads go on to further study within 1 year. 7% grads pursue arts and sciences

degrees. **Faculty:** Student/faculty ratio 10:1. 58 full-time faculty, 83% hold PhDs, 21% are members of minority groups, 52% are women.

ACADEMICS

Degrees: Bachelor's; Master's. **Classes:** Most classes have 10–19 students. **Most popular majors:** English Language and Literature, General; Visual and Performing Arts, General; Social Sciences, General. **Special Study Options:** Cross-registration; Dual enrollment; English as a Second Language (ESL); Exchange student program (domestic); Independent study; Internships; Student-designed major; Study abroad. **Disability Services offered:** Note-taking services; Reader services; Tape recorders. **Career services:** Alumni network; Alumni services; Career assessment; Career/job search classes; Internships.

FACILITIES

Housing: Coed dorms; 75% of campus accessible to physically disabled. **Special Academic Facilities/Equipment:** Center for the Advancement of Public Action; observatory; student garden and greenhouse; labs for chemistry, physics, and microbiology; digital arts lab; art gallery; architecture, drawing, painting, printmaking, and sculpture studios; ceramics studio and kilns; photography darkrooms; film and video editing studio; fully equipped professional theaters; dance studios and archives; scripts library; costume shop; electronic music and sound recording studios; music practice rooms and music library; fitness center; student center with cafe and bar; greenhouse; and 440 acres of forest, ponds, wetlands, and fields for recreation and scientific study.

CAMPUS LIFE

Environment: Village. **Activities:** Choral groups; Dance; Drama/theater; Jazz band; Literary magazine; Music ensembles; Musical theater; Radio station; Student-run film society. 44 registered organizations, on campus. **On-Campus Highlights:** Center for the Advancement of Public Action.

ADMISSIONS

Freshman Academic Profile: Average high school GPA 3.5. 29% in top 10% of high school class, 69% in top 25% of high school class, 91% in top 50% of high school class. 59% from public high schools. **Test Scores:** SAT Math middle 50% range 590–700. SAT EBRW middle 50% range 660–740. ACT middle 50% range 29–32. **Basis for Candidate Selection:** *Very important factors include:* rigor of secondary school record, academic GPA, application essay, recommendation(s), interview, talent/ability, character/personal qualities. *Other factors include:* class rank, standardized test scores, extracurricular activities, first generation, racial/ethnic status, volunteer work, work experience. **Freshman Admission Requirements:** High school diploma is required and GED is accepted. *Academic units required:* 4 English. *Academic units recommended:* 4 math, 4 science, 3 science labs, 4 foreign language, 4 social studies. **Freshman Admission Statistics:** 1,344 applied, 61% admitted, 22% enrolled. **Transfer Admission Requirements:** High school transcript, college transcript(s), essay or personal statement, statement of good standing from prior institution(s). Lowest grade transferable C. **General Admission Information:** Regular application deadline 1/15. Non-fall registration accepted. Admission may be deferred for a maximum of one year.

COSTS AND FINANCIAL AID

Annual tuition $57,350. Room and board $16,840. Required fees $1,349. Average book and supplies expense $1,000. **Required Forms and Deadlines:** CSS/Financial Aid PROFILE; FAFSA; Institution's own financial aid form; Noncustodial PROFILE. **Notification of Awards:** Applicants will be notified of awards on or about 3/27. **Types of Aid:** *Need-based scholarships/grants:* College/university scholarship or grant aid from institutional funds; Federal Pell; Private scholarships; SEOG; State scholarships/grants. *Loans:* Direct PLUS loans; Direct Subsidized Stafford Loans; Direct Unsubsidized Stafford Loans. **Student Employment:** Federal Work-Study Program available. Institutional employment available. **Financial Aid Statistics:** 93% needy freshmen, 92% needy undergrads receive need-based scholarship or grant aid. 10% freshmen, 8% undergrads receive non-need-based scholarship or grant aid. 80% freshmen, 80% undergrads receive need-based self-help aid. 0% freshmen, 0% undergrads receive athletic scholarships. 93% freshmen, 91% undergrads receive any aid. 61% undergrads borrow to pay for school. Average cumulative indebtedness $29,443. **Criteria awarding aid:** *Need-based:* Academics, Alumni affiliation, Art, Leadership, Minority status, Music/drama. *Non-need-based:* Academics, Alumni affiliation, Art, Leadership, Minority status, Music/drama, State/district residency.

BENTLEY UNIVERSITY

175 Forest Street, Waltham, MA 02452
Phone: 781-891-2244 **Financial Aid Phone:** 781-891-3441
E-mail: ugadmission@bentley.edu **CEEB Code:** 3096
Fax: 781-891-3414 **Website:** https://www.bentley.edu **ACT Code:** 1783

This private school was founded in 1917. It has a 163 acre campus.

RATINGS

Admissions Selectivity Rating: 90   **Fire Safety Rating:** 99   **Green Rating:** 98

STUDENTS AND FACULTY

Enrollment: 4,159. **Student Body:** 41% female, 59% male, 58% out-of-state, 15% international (68 countries represented). Asian 9%, African American 4%, Caucasian 58%, Hispanic 7%, Native American <1%, Pacific Islander <1%, Two or more races 3%, Race unknown 4%.
Retention and Graduation: 92% freshmen return for sophomore year. 85% freshmen graduate within 4 years. 90% freshmen graduate within 6 years. 10% grads go on to further study within 1 year. **Faculty:** Student/faculty ratio 11:1. 292 full-time faculty, 83% hold PhDs, 16% are members of minority groups, 44% are women. 0% of classes are taught by teaching assistants.

ACADEMICS

Degrees: Bachelor's; Doctoral degree research/scholarship; Master's; Post-bachelor's certificate; Post-master's certificate. **Classes:** Most classes have 20–29 students. **Most popular majors:** Finance, General; Business, Management, Marketing, and Related Support Services, Other; Business Administration and Management, General. **Special Study Options:** Cross-registration; Double major; Exchange student program (domestic); Honors program; Independent study; Internships; Liberal arts/career combination; Study abroad. **Honors programs:** Limited to the top 10% of each entering class, the Bentley Honors Program offers you access to: • Small, highly interactive Honors courses • Dedicated faculty advisors supporting the Honors capstone project • Honors Learning Community • Co-curricular activities including field trips, internships and more • Getting published in peer-reviewed undergraduate research journals Honors Program Mission The Bentley University Honors Program offers a distinctive learning experience to a diverse community of highly motivated students who are passionate about exploring the world, invigorated by inquiry, and driven to expand their horizons while giving back to their community, both within and beyond Bentley. Vision The Honors Program provides participating students with an interdisciplinary curriculum designed to foster advanced intellectual growth and lays a foundation for life-long learning. In a unique business school that values a strong liberal arts education, honors students are enriched by their exposure to interdisciplinary approaches, experiential learning, and academic research. Honors students are expected to demonstrate leadership and initiative in their curricular and extra-curricular endeavors. Honors students have opportunities to integrate their academic life with an array of experiences that enhance their broader individualized learning experience. Benefits Essential benefits to all Bentley University honor students include: • Smaller classes, advanced and specialized courses, and the opportunity to work closely with faculty on research projects • Participation in undergraduate research • Opportunity to participate in various honors committees • Availability of research funding • Dedicated honors lounge in Residential Center • Early class registration • Opportunities to travel to regional honors conferences • Honors specific career service counseling. **Disability Services offered:** Note-taking services; Reader services; Tape recorders; Tutors. **Career services:** Alumni network; Alumni services; Career assessment; Career/job search classes; Internships; Regional alumni.

FACILITIES

Housing: Apartments for single students; Coed dorms; Special housing for disabled students; Theme housing; 80% of campus accessible to physically disabled. **Special Academic Facilities/Equipment:** Academic Technology Center, ACE Lab, Alliance for Ethics and Social Responsibility, Art Gallery, Bentley Library, Center for Business Ethics, Center for International Students and Scholars, Center for Languages and International Collaboration, Center for Marketing Technology, Center for Quantitative Analysis, Center for Women in Business, Cronin International Center, Cyberlaw Center, Design and Usability Center, Enterprise Risk Management Program, ESOL Center, Financial Trading

Room, Hughey Center for Financial Services, Math Learning Center, Media & Culture labs and studio, Service Learning Center, Spiritual Life Center, Valente Center for Arts and Sciences, Winer Accounting Center, Writing Center.

CAMPUS LIFE

Environment: Town. **Activities:** Campus Ministries; Choral groups; Dance; Drama/theater; International Student Organization; Jazz band; Literary magazine; Model UN; Music ensembles; Musical theater; Pep band; Radio station; Student government; Student newspaper; Student-run film society; Symphony orchestra; Yearbook. 115 registered organizations, 4 honor societies, 5 religious organizations, 7 fraternities, 4 sororities, on campus. **Athletics (Intercollegiate):** *Men:* baseball, basketball, cross-country, diving, football, golf, ice hockey, lacrosse, soccer, swimming, tennis, track/field (outdoor), track/field (indoor). *Women:* basketball, cross-country, diving, field hockey, lacrosse, soccer, softball, swimming, tennis, track/field (outdoor), track/field (indoor), volleyball. **On-Campus Highlights:** Harry's Pub. **Environmental Initiatives:** GHG Reduction Commitment: As of January 1, 2020 Bentley University has achieved a 70% reduction in greenhouse gas emissions and is committed to reducing its carbon footprint (compared to a 2008 baseline) by 100% by 2030.

ADMISSIONS

Freshman Academic Profile: 37% in top 10% of high school class, 73% in top 25% of high school class, 97% in top 50% of high school class. 64% from public high schools. **Test Scores:** SAT Math middle 50% range 630–730. SAT EBRW middle 50% range 600–680. ACT middle 50% range 27–31. **Basis for Candidate Selection:** *Very important factors include:* rigor of secondary school record, academic GPA, standardized test scores. *Important factors include:* application essay, recommendation(s), extracurricular activities, talent/ability, character/personal qualities. *Other factors include:* class rank, interview, first generation, alumni/ae relation, geographical residence, state residency, racial/ethnic status, work experience. **Freshman Admission Requirements:** High school diploma is required and GED is accepted. *Academic units required:* 4 English, 4 math, 3 science, 2 science labs, 3 foreign language, 3 social studies. *Academic units recommended:* 4 English, 4 math, 3 science, 2 science labs, 3 foreign language, 4 social studies. **Freshman Admission Statistics:** 9,017 applied, 47% admitted, 22% enrolled. **Transfer Admission Requirements:** High school transcript, college transcript(s), essay or personal statement, statement of good standing from prior institution(s). Lowest grade transferable C. **General Admission Information:** Application fee $75. Priority deadline 11/15. Regular application deadline 1/7. Non-fall registration accepted. Admission may be deferred for a maximum of one year.

COSTS AND FINANCIAL AID

Annual tuition $50,060. Room and board $16,960. Required fees $1,770. Average book and supplies expense $1,300. **Required Forms and Deadlines:** Business/Farm Supplement; CSS/Financial Aid PROFILE; FAFSA; Noncustodial PROFILE. **Notification of Awards:** Applicants will be notified of awards on or about 3/31. **Types of Aid:** *Need-based scholarships/grants:* College/university scholarship or grant aid from institutional funds; Federal Pell; Private scholarships; SEOG; State scholarships/grants. *Loans:* Direct PLUS loans; Direct Subsidized Stafford Loans; Direct Unsubsidized Stafford Loans. **Student Employment:** Federal Work-Study Program available. Institutional employment available. **Financial Aid Statistics:** 100% needy freshmen, 99% needy undergrads receive need-based scholarship or grant aid. 21% freshmen, 17% undergrads receive non-need-based scholarship or grant aid. 93% freshmen, 95% undergrads receive need-based self-help aid. 3% freshmen, 2% undergrads receive athletic scholarships. 75% freshmen, 67% undergrads receive any aid. 57% undergrads borrow to pay for school. Average cumulative indebtedness $30,997. **Criteria awarding aid:** *Need-based:* Academics, Athletics, Minority status. *Non-need-based:* Academics, Athletics, Leadership, Minority status.

BEREA COLLEGE

CPO 2220, Berea, KY 40404
Phone: 859-985-3500 **Financial Aid Phone:** 859-985-3310
E-mail: admissions@berea.edu **CEEB Code:** 1060
Fax: 859-985-3512 **Website:** www.berea.edu **ACT Code:** 1492

This private school was founded in 1855. It has a 140 acre campus.

RATINGS

Admissions Selectivity Rating: 94   **Fire Safety Rating:** 96   **Green Rating:** 93

STUDENTS AND FACULTY

Enrollment: 1,630. **Student Body:** 57% female, 43% male, 55% out-of-state, 8% international (74 countries represented). Asian 3%, African American 16%, Caucasian 54%, Hispanic 12%, Native American <1%, Pacific Islander <1%, Two or more races 7%, Race unknown 1%.
Retention and Graduation: 83% freshmen return for sophomore year. 49% freshmen graduate within 4 years. 66% freshmen graduate within 6 years. **Faculty:** Student/faculty ratio 10:1. 137 full-time faculty, 93% hold PhDs, 13% are members of minority groups, 50% are women. 0% of classes are taught by teaching assistants.

ACADEMICS

Degrees: Bachelor's. **Classes:** Most classes have 10–19 students. **Most popular majors:** Biology/Biological Sciences, General; Business/Commerce, General; Computer and Information Sciences, General. **Special Study Options:** Double major; English as a Second Language (ESL); Exchange student program (domestic); Honors program; Independent study; Internships; Student-designed major; Study abroad; Teacher certification program. **Disability Services offered:** Note-taking services; Reader services; Tape recorders. **Career services:** Alumni network; Alumni services; Career assessment; Career/job search classes; Internships.

FACILITIES

Housing: Apartments for married students; Apartments for single students; Men's dorms; Women's dorms; 75% of campus accessible to physically disabled. **Special Academic Facilities/Equipment:** Appalachian Gallery, Special Collections and Sound Archives in the Hutchins Library, Planetarium and Observatory, Geology Museum, The Ecovillage, the Child Development Laboratory, extensive acreage of farmland and forestland, and the Monty Saulmon Early Technology Lab. **Campus network:** 80% of classrooms, 100% of dorms, 100% of student union, 100% of libraries, 100% of dining areas, 75% of common outdoor areas, have wireless network access.

CAMPUS LIFE

Environment: Village. **Activities:** Campus Ministries; Choral groups; Dance; Drama/theater; International Student Organization; Jazz band; Literary magazine; Music ensembles; Pep band; Student government; Student newspaper; Yearbook. 75 registered organizations, 14 honor societies, 5 religious organizations, on campus. **Athletics (Intercollegiate):** *Men:* baseball, basketball, cross-country, golf, soccer, swimming, tennis, track/field (outdoor). *Women:* basketball, cross-country, soccer, softball, swimming, tennis, track/field (outdoor), volleyball. **On-Campus Highlights:** Woods-Penn Complex (post office, cafe, etc). **Environmental Initiatives:** 1. Sustainability and Environmental Studies academic program.

ADMISSIONS

Freshman Academic Profile: Average high school GPA 3.5. 22% in top 10% of high school class, 69% in top 25% of high school class, 96% in top 50% of high school class. **Test Scores:** SAT Math middle 50% range 510–623. SAT EBRW middle 50% range 520–590. ACT middle 50% range 22–27. **Basis for Candidate Selection:** *Very important factors include:* interview. *Important factors include:* rigor of secondary school record, class rank, academic GPA, application essay, standardized test scores, character/personal qualities. *Other factors include:* recommendation(s), extracurricular activities, talent/ability, first generation, geographical residence, state residency, racial/ethnic status, volunteer work, work experience, level of applicant's interest. **Freshman Admission Requirements:** High school diploma is required and GED is accepted. *Academic units recommended:* 4 English, 3 math, 2 science, 2 science labs, 2 foreign language, 2 social studies. **Freshman Admission Statistics:** 1,576 applied, 38% admitted, 73% enrolled. **Transfer Admission Requirements:**

High school transcript, college transcript(s), interview, Minimum college GPA of 2.0 required. Lowest grade transferable C. **General Admission Information:** Priority deadline 10/31. Regular application deadline 3/31.

COSTS AND FINANCIAL AID
Room and board $6,966. Required fees $600. Average book and supplies expense $700. **Required Forms and Deadlines:** FAFSA. **Notification of Awards:** Applicants will be notified of awards on a rolling basis beginning 11/15. **Types of Aid:** *Need-based scholarships/grants:* College/university scholarship or grant aid from institutional funds; Federal Pell; Private scholarships; SEOG; State scholarships/grants. *Loans:* Direct PLUS loans; Direct Subsidized Stafford Loans; Direct Unsubsidized Stafford Loans. **Student Employment:** Federal Work-Study Program available. **Financial Aid Statistics:** 100% needy freshmen, 100% needy undergrads receive need-based scholarship or grant aid. 0% freshmen, 0% undergrads receive non-need-based scholarship or grant aid. 100% freshmen, 100% undergrads receive need-based self-help aid. 0% freshmen, 0% undergrads receive athletic scholarships. 100% freshmen, 100% undergrads receive any aid. 56% undergrads borrow to pay for school. Average cumulative indebtedness $6,405.

BERKELEY COLLEGE

44 Rifle Camp Road, Woodland Park, NJ 07424
Phone: 1-800-446-5400 xG26
E-mail: info@berkeleycollege.edu **CEEB Code:** 2061
ACT Code: 2576

This proprietary school was founded in 1931. It has a 25 acre campus.

RATINGS
Admissions Selectivity Rating: 60*   **Fire Safety Rating:** 60*   **Green Rating:** 60*

STUDENTS AND FACULTY
Enrollment: 3,806. **Student Body:** 73% female, 27% male, 4% out-of-state, <1% international. Asian 2%, African American 21%, Caucasian 15%, Hispanic 34%, Native American <1%, Pacific Islander <1%, Two or more races 0%, Race unknown 26%.
Retention and Graduation: 68% freshmen return for sophomore year.
Faculty: Student/faculty ratio 17:1. 137 full-time faculty, 0% hold PhDs, 47% are members of minority groups, 0% are women.

ACADEMICS
Degrees: Associate; Bachelor's; Certificate; Master's; Terminal Associate; Transfer Associate. **Classes:** Most classes have 20–29 students. Most lab/discussion sessions have fewer than 10 students. **Most popular majors:** Accounting; Fashion Merchandising; Business Administration and Management, General. **Special Study Options:** Accelerated program; Distance learning; Internships; Study abroad. **Disability Services offered:** Tutors.

FACILITIES
Housing: Coed dorms.

CAMPUS LIFE
Environment: City. **Activities:** Choral groups; Literary magazine; Student government; Student newspaper. 8 registered organizations, 1 honor societies, on campus.

ADMISSIONS
Basis for Candidate Selection: *Very important factors include:* rigor of secondary school record, interview. *Important factors include:* standardized test scores. *Other factors include:* class rank, academic GPA, recommendation(s), extracurricular activities, talent/ability, character/personal qualities, volunteer work, work experience. **Freshman Admission Requirements:** High school diploma is required and GED is accepted. **Transfer Admission Requirements:** College transcript(s). Lowest grade transferable C. **General Admission Information:** Application fee $50. Non-fall registration accepted.

COSTS AND FINANCIAL AID
Annual tuition $17,400. Room and board $12,500. Required fees $750. Average book and supplies expense $1,200. **Required Forms and Deadlines:** FAFSA. **Notification of Awards:** Applicants will be notified of awards on a rolling basis beginning 3/1. **Types of Aid:** *Need-based scholarships/grants:* College/university scholarship or grant aid from institutional funds; Federal Pell; Private scholarships; SEOG; State scholarships/grants. **Financial Aid Statistics:** 85% freshmen receive any aid. **Criteria awarding aid:** *Non-need-based:* Academics, Alumni affiliation.

BERKLEE COLLEGE OF MUSIC

1140 Boylston Street, Boston, MA 02215-3693
Phone: 617-747-2222 **Financial Aid Phone:** 617-747-2274
E-mail: admissions@berklee.edu **CEEB Code:** 3107
Fax: 617-747-2047 **Website:** www.berklee.edu **ACT Code:** 1789

This private school was founded in 1945.

RATINGS
Admissions Selectivity Rating: 87   **Fire Safety Rating:** 60*   **Green Rating:** 60*

STUDENTS AND FACULTY
Enrollment: 3,846. **Student Body:** 31% female, 69% male, 84% out-of-state, 25% international (70 countries represented). Asian 3%, African American 6%, Caucasian 45%, Hispanic 10%, Native American <1%, Pacific Islander <1%, Two or more races 3%, Race unknown 8%.
Retention and Graduation: 79% freshmen return for sophomore year.
Faculty: Student/faculty ratio 13:1. 240 full-time faculty, 15% hold PhDs, 0% are members of minority groups, 23% are women.

ACADEMICS
Degrees: Bachelor's; Diploma; Master's. **Classes:** Most classes have 10–19 students. **Most popular majors:** Music Performance, General; Music, Other. **Special Study Options:** Cooperative education program; Cross-registration; Distance learning; Double major; Dual enrollment; English as a Second Language (ESL); Internships; Student-designed major; Study abroad; Teacher certification program. **Disability Services offered:** Reader services; Tape recorders; Tutors. **Career services:** Alumni services; Career/job search classes; Internships.

FACILITIES
Housing: Coed dorms; 80% of campus accessible to physically disabled.
Special Academic Facilities/Equipment: Ensemble library, 10 professional recording studios, film scoring and editing studio, analog and digital music synthesis labs, 1,200-seat performance center, learning center.

CAMPUS LIFE
Environment: Metropolis. **Activities:** Campus Ministries; Choral groups; Concert band; Dance; Drama/theater; International Student Organization; Jazz band; Literary magazine; Marching band; Music ensembles; Musical theater; Opera; Radio station; Student government; Student newspaper; Student-run film society; Symphony orchestra. 47 registered organizations, 2 honor societies, 4 religious organizations, on campus. **On-Campus Highlights:** Student Activities Center.

ADMISSIONS
Basis for Candidate Selection: *Very important factors include:* interview, talent/ability. *Important factors include:* rigor of secondary school record, academic GPA, character/personal qualities. *Other factors include:* class rank, application essay, standardized test scores, recommendation(s), extracurricular activities, first generation, geographical residence, volunteer work, work experience. **Freshman Admission Requirements:** High school diploma is required and GED is accepted. **Freshman Admission Statistics:** 5,538 applied, 19% admitted, 84% enrolled. **Transfer Admission Requirements:** High school transcript, college transcript(s), essay or personal statement, interview. Lowest grade transferable C. **General Admission Information:** Application fee $150. Priority deadline 11/1. Regular application deadline 1/15. Non-fall registration accepted. Admission may be deferred for a maximum of 1 year.

COSTS AND FINANCIAL AID
Room and board $17,200. Required fees $5,132. Average book and supplies expense $474. **Student Employment:** Federal Work-Study Program available. **Financial Aid Statistics:** 50% needy freshmen, 50% needy undergrads receive need-based scholarship or grant aid. 48% freshmen, 49% undergrads receive non-need-based scholarship or grant aid. 97% freshmen, 97% undergrads receive need-based self-help aid. 0% freshmen, 0% undergrads receive athletic scholarships. 57% freshmen, 38% undergrads receive any aid.

BERRY COLLEGE

P.O. Box 490159, Mount Berry, GA 30149-0159
Phone: 706-236-2215 **Financial Aid Phone:** 706-236-1714
E-mail: admissions@berry.edu **CEEB Code:** 5059
Fax: 706-290-2178 **Website:** https://www.berry.edu/ **ACT Code:** 798

This private school was founded in 1902. It has a 27,000 acre campus.

RATINGS
Admissions Selectivity Rating: 83   **Fire Safety Rating:** 95   **Green Rating:** 89

STUDENTS AND FACULTY
Enrollment: 1,918. **Student Body:** 61% female, 39% male, 30% out-of-state, 1% international (18 countries represented). Asian 2%, African American 7%, Caucasian 78%, Hispanic 7%, Native American <1%, Pacific Islander 0%, Two or more races 4%, Race unknown 1%.
Retention and Graduation: 83% freshmen return for sophomore year. 63% freshmen graduate within 4 years. 69% freshmen graduate within 6 years. 20% grads go on to further study within 1 year. **Faculty:** Student/faculty ratio 11:1. 163 full-time faculty, 92% hold PhDs, 10% are members of minority groups, 47% are women.

ACADEMICS
Degrees: Bachelor's; Master's. **Classes:** Most classes have 10–19 students. Most lab/discussion sessions have 10–19 students. **Most popular majors:** Zoology/Animal Biology; Exercise Science and Kinesiology; Psychology, General.
Special Study Options: Cross-registration; Double major; Dual enrollment; Honors program; Independent study; Internships; Student-designed major; Study abroad; Teacher certification program. **Honors programs:** The Berry College Honors Program provides students with an opportunity to learn within an intellectually challenging community of peers and instructors. Honors courses familiarize students with works that have been central to our past and contemporary intellectual traditions, while encouraging them to examine issues or themes from multiple and conflicting perspectives. Honors courses are typically taught as seminars that provide an ideal environment for the development of effective communication and critical-thinking skills. All Honors students also complete an Honors thesis that allows them to deeply engage with their major field or explore connections between different areas of interest. Additionally, the Berry College Honors Program offers a unique education abroad opportunity in conjunction with the University of Glasgow in Scotland and Berry College International Programs. **Disability Services offered:** Note-taking services; Reader services; Tutors. **Career services:** Alumni network; Alumni services; Career assessment; Career/job search classes; Internships; Regional alumni.

FACILITIES
Housing: Apartments for single students; Coed dorms; Men's dorms; Special housing for disabled students; Theme housing; Wellness housing; Women's dorms; 80% of campus accessible to physically disabled. **Special Academic Facilities/Equipment:** Gunby Equine Center, new 9,226 sq. ft. theatre featuring black-box stage with seating for 276, Memorial Library with nearly 1 million books and e-books, and over 173,000 government documents, Oak Hill and Martha Berry Museum, newly renovated music performance auditorium with high-performance acoustics, Dewey and Irene Large Science Museum, Rollins dairy and beef cattle research center, on-campus lab preschool, elementary and middle school, 60-foot Foucault pendulum and Pew Observatory. **Campus network:** 70% of classrooms, 90% of dorms, 90% of student union, 100% of libraries, 90% of dining areas, 20% of common outdoor areas, have wireless network access.

CAMPUS LIFE
Environment: Town. **Activities:** Campus Ministries; Choral groups; Concert band; Dance; Drama/theater; International Student Organization; Jazz band; Literary magazine; Model UN; Music ensembles; Musical theater; Pep band; Student government; Student newspaper; Symphony orchestra; Yearbook. 65 registered organizations, 12 honor societies, 9 religious organizations, on campus. **Athletics (Intercollegiate):** *Men:* baseball, basketball, cross-country, diving, golf, lacrosse, soccer, swimming, tennis. *Women:* basketball, cross-country, diving, equestrian sports, golf, lacrosse, soccer, softball, swimming, tennis, volleyball. **On-Campus Highlights:** 131,000 sq ft Athletic and Recreation Center. **Environmental Initiatives:** Tree Campus USA award seven years running.

ADMISSIONS
Freshman Academic Profile: Average high school GPA 3.7. 32% in top 10% of high school class, 61% in top 25% of high school class, 87% in top 50% of high school class. 71% from public high schools. **Test Scores:** SAT Math middle 50% range 530–650. SAT EBRW middle 50% range 560–670. ACT middle 50% range 24–30. **Basis for Candidate Selection:** *Very important factors include:* rigor of secondary school record, academic GPA, standardized test scores. *Important factors include:* extracurricular activities. *Other factors include:* application essay, recommendation(s), interview, volunteer work, work experience. **Freshman Admission Requirements:** High school diploma is required and GED is accepted. *Academic units required:* 4 English, 4 math, 3 science, 2 foreign language, 3 social studies, 4 academic electives. **Freshman Admission Statistics:** 4,328 applied, 71% admitted, 19% enrolled. **Transfer Admission Requirements:** College transcript(s), statement of good standing from prior institution(s). Minimum college GPA of 2.5 required. Lowest grade transferable C. **General Admission Information:** Priority deadline 1/15. Regular application deadline 7/24. Non-fall registration accepted.

COSTS AND FINANCIAL AID
Annual tuition $37,020. Room and board $13,070. Required fees $226. Average book and supplies expense $1,000. **Required Forms and Deadlines:** CSS/Financial Aid PROFILE; FAFSA; State aid form. **Notification of Awards:** Applicants will be notified of awards on a rolling basis beginning 11/1. **Types of Aid:** *Need-based scholarships/grants:* College/university scholarship or grant aid from institutional funds; Federal Pell; Private scholarships; SEOG. *Loans:* Direct PLUS loans; Direct Subsidized Stafford Loans; Direct Unsubsidized Stafford Loans. **Student Employment:** Federal Work-Study Program available. Institutional employment available. **Financial Aid Statistics:** 100% needy freshmen, 100% needy undergrads receive need-based scholarship or grant aid. 27% freshmen, 23% undergrads receive non-need-based scholarship or grant aid. 60% freshmen, 67% undergrads receive need-based self-help aid. 0% freshmen, 0% undergrads receive athletic scholarships. 100% freshmen, 99.5% undergrads receive any aid. 61% undergrads borrow to pay for school. Average cumulative indebtedness $31,336. **Criteria awarding aid:** *Need-based:* Academics, Job skills, Leadership, Minority status, Music/drama. *Non-need-based:* Academics, Art, Leadership, Minority status, Music/drama, Religious affiliation.

BETHANY COLLEGE (KS)

335 E Swensson, Lindsborg, KS 67456-1897
Phone: 785-227-3311 **Financial Aid Phone:** 785-227-3311
E-mail: admissions@bethanylb.edu **CEEB Code:** 6034
Fax: 785-227-8993 **Website:** www.bethanylb.edu **ACT Code:** 1388

This private school, affiliated with the Lutheran Church, was founded in 1881. It has a 62 acre campus.

RATINGS
Admissions Selectivity Rating: 80   **Fire Safety Rating:** 96   **Green Rating:** 60*

STUDENTS AND FACULTY
Enrollment: 569. **Student Body:** 48% female, 52% male, 49% out-of-state, 6% international (29 countries represented). Asian 1%, African American 11%, Caucasian 71%, Hispanic 7%, Native American 1%, Race unknown 4%.
Retention and Graduation: 61% freshmen return for sophomore year. 20% grads go on to further study within 1 year. 1% grads pursue law degrees. 3% grads pursue medical degrees. **Faculty:** Student/faculty ratio 9:1. 44 full-time faculty, 57% hold PhDs, 5% are members of minority groups, 36% are women. 0% of classes are taught by teaching assistants.

ACADEMICS
Degrees: Bachelor's. **Classes:** Most classes have 10–19 students. Most lab/discussion sessions have fewer than 10 students. **Most popular majors:** Biology/Biological Sciences, General; Business Administration and Management, General; Elementary Education and Teaching. **Special Study Options:** Accelerated program; Cross-registration; Double major; Dual enrollment; Exchange student program (domestic); Honors program; Independent study; Internships; Liberal arts/career combination; Student-designed major; Study abroad; Teacher certification program. **Honors programs:** Honors program offered. **Combined degree programs:** BA/MEng. **Disability Services offered:**

Note-taking services; Reader services; Tape recorders; Tutors. **Career services:** Alumni network; Alumni services; Career assessment; Career/job search classes; Internships; Regional alumni.

FACILITIES
Housing: Apartments for single students; Coed dorms; Women's dorms; 80% of campus accessible to physically disabled. **Special Academic Facilities/Equipment:** Mingenback Gallery, Bethany College Archives, Plym Gallery, Sandzen Gallery.

CAMPUS LIFE
Environment: Rural. **Activities:** Campus Ministries; Choral groups; Concert band; Dance; Drama/theater; International Student Organization; Jazz band; Music ensembles; Musical theater; Pep band; Student government; Student newspaper; Symphony orchestra; Yearbook. 49 registered organizations, 8 honor societies, 9 religious organizations, 3 fraternities, 3 sororities, on campus. **Athletics (Intercollegiate):** *Men:* baseball, basketball, cheerleading, cross-country, football, golf, soccer, tennis, track/field (outdoor), track/field (indoor). *Women:* basketball, cheerleading, cross-country, golf, soccer, softball, tennis, track/field (outdoor), track/field (indoor), volleyball. **On-Campus Highlights:** Student Union.

ADMISSIONS
Freshman Academic Profile: Average high school GPA 3.3. 15% in top 10% of high school class, 42% in top 25% of high school class, 76% in top 50% of high school class. 97% from public high schools. **Test Scores:** SAT Math middle 50% range 420–560. SAT EBRW middle 50% range 370–500. ACT middle 50% range 19–24. **Basis for Candidate Selection:** *Very important factors include:* rigor of secondary school record, academic GPA, standardized test scores. *Other factors include:* application essay, recommendation(s), extracurricular activities, talent/ability, character/personal qualities, racial/ethnic status, volunteer work. **Freshman Admission Requirements:** High school diploma is required and GED is accepted. *Academic units recommended:* 4 English, 3 math, 3 science, 2 science labs, 2 foreign language, 3 social studies. **Freshman Admission Statistics:** 811 applied, 65% admitted, 34% enrolled. **Transfer Admission Requirements:** College transcript(s), statement of good standing from prior institution(s). Minimum college GPA of 2.3 required. Lowest grade transferable D. **General Admission Information:** Application fee $20. Priority deadline 2/1. Regular application deadline 7/1. Non-fall registration accepted.

COSTS AND FINANCIAL AID
Annual tuition $17,824. Room and board $5,650. Required fees $300. Average book and supplies expense $1,000. **Required Forms and Deadlines:** FAFSA. **Notification of Awards:** Applicants will be notified of awards on a rolling basis beginning 3/1. **Types of Aid:** *Need-based scholarships/grants:* College/university scholarship or grant aid from institutional funds; Federal Pell; Private scholarships; SEOG; State scholarships/grants. **Student Employment:** Federal Work-Study Program available. Institutional employment available. **Financial Aid Statistics:** 85% needy freshmen, 84% needy undergrads receive need-based scholarship or grant aid. 40% freshmen, 32% undergrads receive non-need-based scholarship or grant aid. 76% freshmen, 78% undergrads receive need-based self-help aid. 0% freshmen, 7% undergrads receive athletic scholarships. 100% freshmen, 98% undergrads receive any aid. **Criteria awarding aid:** *Non-need-based:* Academics, Alumni affiliation, Art, Athletics, Leadership, Music/drama, Religious affiliation.

BETHANY COLLEGE (WV)

31 E Campus Dr, Bethany, WV 26032
Phone: 304-829-7611 **Financial Aid Phone:** 304-829-7611
E-mail: enrollment@bethanywv.edu **CEEB Code:** 5060
Fax: 304-829-7142 **Website:** www.bethanywv.edu **ACT Code:** 4512

This private school, affiliated with the Disciples of Christ Church, was founded in 1840. It has a 1300 acre campus.

RATINGS
Admissions Selectivity Rating: 80   **Fire Safety Rating:** 88   **Green Rating:** 60*

STUDENTS AND FACULTY
Enrollment: 716. **Student Body:** 41% female, 59% male, 68% out-of-state, 2% international (11 countries represented). Asian <1%, African American 20%, Caucasian 54%, Hispanic 4%, Native American 1%, Pacific Islander <1%, Two or more races 3%, Race unknown 16%.

Retention and Graduation: 70% freshmen return for sophomore year. **Faculty:** Student/faculty ratio 12:1. 48 full-time faculty, 79% hold PhDs, 4% are members of minority groups, 44% are women. 0% of classes are taught by teaching assistants.

ACADEMICS
Degrees: Bachelor's; Master's. **Classes:** Most classes have fewer than 10 students. Most lab/discussion sessions have 10–19 students. **Most popular majors:** Elementary Education and Teaching; Psychology, General; Speech Communication and Rhetoric. **Special Study Options:** Accelerated program; Distance learning; Double major; Dual enrollment; English as a Second Language (ESL); Independent study; Internships; Liberal arts/career combination; Student-designed major; Study abroad; Teacher certification program. **Combined degree programs:** BA/JD; BA/MA. **Disability Services offered:** Note-taking services; Reader services; Tape recorders; Tutors. **Career services:** Alumni network; Alumni services; Career assessment; Internships; Regional alumni.

FACILITIES
Housing: Apartments for married students; Apartments for single students; Coed dorms; Fraternity/sorority housing; Men's dorms; Special housing for disabled students; Women's dorms. **Special Academic Facilities/Equipment:** Renner Art Gallery, outdoor classroom. **Campus network:** 100% of classrooms, 100% of dorms, 100% of student union, 100% of libraries, 100% of dining areas, 0% of common outdoor areas, have wireless network access.

CAMPUS LIFE
Environment: Rural. **Activities:** Campus Ministries; Choral groups; Concert band; Dance; Drama/theater; International Student Organization; Literary magazine; Marching band; Music ensembles; Musical theater; Pep band; Radio station; Student government; Student newspaper; Television station. 34 registered organizations, 25 honor societies, 4 religious organizations, 5 fraternities, 3 sororities, on campus. **Athletics (Intercollegiate):** *Men:* baseball, basketball, cross-country, diving, football, golf, soccer, swimming, tennis, track/field (outdoor), track/field (indoor). *Women:* basketball, cross-country, diving, golf, soccer, softball, swimming, tennis, track/field (outdoor), track/field (indoor), volleyball. **On-Campus Highlights:** Old Main.

ADMISSIONS
Freshman Academic Profile: Average high school GPA 2.9. 6% in top 10% of high school class, 20% in top 25% of high school class, 49% in top 50% of high school class. 90% from public high schools. **Test Scores:** SAT Math middle 50% range 390–490. SAT EBRW middle 50% range 370–500. ACT middle 50% range 17–23. **Basis for Candidate Selection:** *Very important factors include:* rigor of secondary school record, academic GPA, application essay, standardized test scores, recommendation(s), character/personal qualities. *Important factors include:* class rank. *Other factors include:* interview, extracurricular activities, talent/ability, alumni/ae relation, volunteer work, work experience. **Freshman Admission Requirements:** High school diploma is required and GED is accepted. *Academic units recommended:* 4 English, 3 math, 3 science, 2 foreign language, 3 social studies. **Freshman Admission Statistics:** 1,394 applied, 62% admitted, 28% enrolled. **Transfer Admission Requirements:** College transcript(s), essay or personal statement, statement of good standing from prior institution(s). Minimum college GPA of 2.0 required. Lowest grade transferable D. **General Admission Information:** Priority deadline 3/1. Non-fall registration accepted. Admission may be deferred for a maximum of 1 year.

COSTS AND FINANCIAL AID
Annual tuition $24,836. Room and board $9,636. Required fees $900. Average book and supplies expense $1,200. **Required Forms and Deadlines:** FAFSA. **Notification of Awards:** Applicants will be notified of awards on a rolling basis beginning 2/15. **Types of Aid:** *Need-based scholarships/grants:* College/university scholarship or grant aid from institutional funds; Federal Pell; Private scholarships; SEOG; State scholarships/grants. *Loans:* Direct PLUS loans; Direct Subsidized Stafford Loans; Direct Unsubsidized Stafford Loans. **Student Employment:** Federal Work-Study Program available. Institutional employment available. **Financial Aid Statistics:** 80% needy freshmen, 79% needy undergrads receive need-based scholarship or grant aid. 100% freshmen, 99% undergrads receive non-need-based scholarship or grant aid. 77% freshmen, 79% undergrads receive need-based self-help aid. 0% freshmen, 0% undergrads receive athletic scholarships. 99% freshmen, 99% undergrads receive any aid. **Criteria awarding aid:** *Need-based:* Academics, Alumni affiliation, Leadership, Music/drama, Religious affiliation. *Non-need-based:* Academics, Alumni affiliation, Leadership, Music/drama, Religious affiliation, State/district residency.

BETHEL COLLEGE (KS)

300 E 27th Street, North Newton, KS 67117
Phone: 316-284-5230 **Financial Aid Phone:** 316-284-5232
E-mail: admissions@bethelks.edu **CEEB Code:** 6037
Fax: 316-284-5870 **Website:** www.bethelks.edu **ACT Code:** 1390

This private school, affiliated with the Mennonite Church USA, was founded in 1887. It has a 60 acre campus.

RATINGS
Admissions Selectivity Rating: 86   **Fire Safety Rating:** 82   **Green Rating:** 60*

STUDENTS AND FACULTY
Enrollment: 484. **Student Body:** 51% female, 49% male, 38% out-of-state, 2% international (13 countries represented). Asian <1%, African American 15%, Caucasian 71%, Hispanic 10%, Native American <1%, Pacific Islander 0%, Two or more races 2%, Race unknown 0%.
Retention and Graduation: 63% freshmen return for sophomore year.
Faculty: Student/faculty ratio 10:1. 38 full-time faculty, 66% hold PhDs, 5% are members of minority groups, 55% are women. 0% of classes are taught by teaching assistants.

ACADEMICS
Degrees: Bachelor's; Certificate. **Classes:** Most classes have 10–19 students. Most lab/discussion sessions have 10–19 students. **Most popular majors:** Business/Commerce, General; Biology/Biological Sciences, General; Nursing/Registered Nurse (Rn, Asn, Bsn, Msn). **Special Study Options:** Cross-registration; Double major; Dual enrollment; Exchange student program (domestic); Independent study; Internships; Liberal arts/career combination; Student-designed major; Study abroad; Teacher certification program. **Combined degree programs:** BA/MEng. **Disability Services offered:** Note-taking services; Reader services; Tape recorders; Tutors. **Career services:** Alumni network; Career assessment; Career/job search classes.

FACILITIES
Housing: Coed dorms; Special housing for international students; 75% of campus accessible to physically disabled. **Special Academic Facilities/Equipment:** Art gallery, natural history and midwestern/Kansas history museums, 80 acre natural history field laboratory for biological studies, Mennonite Historical Library and Archives, Institute for Peace and Conflict Resolution, observatory.

CAMPUS LIFE
Environment: Village. **Activities:** Campus Ministries; Choral groups; Concert band; Drama/theater; International Student Organization; Jazz band; Literary magazine; Music ensembles; Radio station; Student government; Student newspaper; Symphony orchestra; Television station; Yearbook. 50 registered organizations, 2 religious organizations, on campus. **Athletics (Intercollegiate):** *Men:* basketball, cross-country, football, golf, soccer, tennis, track/field (outdoor), track/field (indoor). *Women:* basketball, cross-country, golf, soccer, tennis, track/field (outdoor), track/field (indoor), volleyball. **On-Campus Highlights:** Student Center.

ADMISSIONS
Freshman Academic Profile: Average high school GPA 3.4. 17% in top 10% of high school class, 38% in top 25% of high school class, 73% in top 50% of high school class. 97% from public high schools. **Test Scores:** SAT Math middle 50% range 425–475. SAT EBRW middle 50% range 380–435. ACT middle 50% range 19–25. **Basis for Candidate Selection** *Very important factors include:* academic GPA, standardized test scores, level of applicant's interest. *Important factors include:* class rank, extracurricular activities, character/personal qualities, alumni/ae relation. *Other factors include:* rigor of secondary school record, recommendation(s). **Freshman Admission Requirements:** High school diploma is required and GED is accepted. *Academic units recommended:* 4 English, 4 math, 3 science, 2 foreign language, 3 social studies. **Freshman Admission Statistics:** 833 applied, 49% admitted, 27% enrolled. **Transfer Admission Requirements:** High school transcript, college transcript(s), statement of good standing from prior institution(s). Lowest grade transferable D-. **General Admission Information:** Application fee $20. Regular application deadline 8/1. Non-fall registration accepted. Admission may be deferred for a maximum of 1 year.

COSTS AND FINANCIAL AID
Annual tuition $23,500. Room and board $7,980. Average book and supplies expense $900. **Required Forms and Deadlines:** FAFSA. **Notification of Awards:** Applicants will be notified of awards on a rolling basis beginning 2/1. **Types of Aid:** *Need-based scholarships/grants:* College/university scholarship or grant aid from institutional funds; Federal Nursing Scholarships; Federal Pell; Private scholarships; SEOG; State scholarships/grants. *Loans:* Direct PLUS loans; Direct Subsidized Stafford Loans; Direct Unsubsidized Stafford Loans. **Student Employment:** Federal Work-Study Program available. Institutional employment available. **Financial Aid Statistics:** 88% needy freshmen, 85% needy undergrads receive need-based scholarship or grant aid. 100% freshmen, 100% undergrads receive non-need-based scholarship or grant aid. 89% freshmen, 90% undergrads receive need-based self-help aid. 66% freshmen, 48% undergrads receive athletic scholarships. 100% freshmen, 94% undergrads receive any aid. **Criteria awarding aid:** *Non-need-based:* Academics, Alumni affiliation, Art, Athletics, Minority status, Music/drama, Religious affiliation, State/district residency.

BETHEL UNIVERSITY (IN)

1001 Bethel Circle, Mishawaka, IN 46545
Phone: 574-807-7600 **Financial Aid Phone:** 574-807-7415
E-mail: admissions@betheluniversity.edu **CEEB Code:** 1079
Fax: 574-807-7650 **Website:** https://www.betheluniversity.edu **ACT Code:** 1178

This private school, affiliated with the Missionary Church, was founded in 1947. It has a 75 acre campus.

RATINGS
Admissions Selectivity Rating: 74   **Fire Safety Rating:** 83   **Green Rating:** 60*

STUDENTS AND FACULTY
Enrollment: 1,254. **Student Body:** 63% female, 37% male, 27% out-of-state, 2% international (15 countries represented). Asian 2%, African American 10%, Caucasian 72%, Hispanic 9%, Native American <1%, Pacific Islander 0%, Two or more races 5%, Race unknown 1%.
Retention and Graduation: 78% freshmen return for sophomore year. 53% freshmen graduate within 4 years. % freshmen graduate within 6 years. 17% grads go on to further study within 1 year. **Faculty:** Student/faculty ratio 12:1. 67 full-time faculty, 61% hold PhDs, 12% are members of minority groups, 46% are women. 0% of classes are taught by teaching assistants.

ACADEMICS
Degrees: Associate; Bachelor's; Master's. **Classes:** Most classes have 10–19 students. Most lab/discussion sessions have 10–19 students. **Most popular majors:** Registered Nursing/Registered Nurse; Business Administration and Management, General; Elementary Education and Teaching. **Special Study Options:** Accelerated program; Cross-registration; Distance learning; Double major; Exchange student program (domestic); Honors program; Independent study; Internships; Liberal arts/career combination; Student-designed major; Study abroad; Teacher certification program. **Combined degree programs:** BA/MEng. **Disability Services offered:** Note-taking services; Reader services; Tape recorders; Tutors. **Career services:** Alumni services; Career assessment; Career/job search classes; Internships.

FACILITIES
Housing: Apartments for married students; Apartments for single students; Men's dorms; Special housing for disabled students; Theme housing; Women's dorms; 90% of campus accessible to physically disabled. **Special Academic Facilities/Equipment:** Bowen Museum Weaver Gallery.

CAMPUS LIFE
Environment: City. **Activities:** Campus Ministries; Choral groups; Concert band; Drama/theater; International Student Organization; Jazz band; Literary magazine; Music ensembles; Musical theater; Pep band; Radio station; Student government; Student newspaper; Yearbook. 11 registered organizations, 1 honor societies, on campus. **Athletics (Intercollegiate):** *Men:* baseball, basketball, cheerleading, cross-country, golf, soccer, tennis, track/field (outdoor), track/field (indoor). *Women:* basketball, cheerleading, cross-country, golf, soccer, softball, tennis, track/field (outdoor), track/field (indoor), volleyball. **On-Campus Highlights:** The Acorn Snack Shop.

ADMISSIONS

Freshman Academic Profile: Average high school GPA 3.4. 14% in top 10% of high school class, 41% in top 25% of high school class, 72% in top 50% of high school class. 78% from public high schools. **Test Scores:** SAT Math middle 50% range 470–570. SAT EBRW middle 50% range 480–590. ACT middle 50% range 19–25. **Basis for Candidate Selection:** *Very important factors include:* academic GPA, standardized test scores. *Important factors include:* rigor of secondary school record, recommendation(s), character/personal qualities. *Other factors include:* class rank, application essay, interview, extracurricular activities, talent/ability, alumni/ae relation, religious affiliation/commitment, racial/ethnic status, volunteer work, work experience. **Freshman Admission Requirements:** High school diploma is required and GED is accepted. *Academic units recommended:* 4 English, 3 math, 1 science, 1 science labs, 2 foreign language, 1 social studies, 2 history, 3 academic electives. **Freshman Admission Statistics:** 1,065 applied, 90% admitted, 24% enrolled. **Transfer Admission Requirements:** High school transcript, college transcript(s), essay or personal statement, standardized test scores, statement of good standing from prior institution(s). Minimum college GPA of 2.0 required. Lowest grade transferable C-. **General Admission Information:** Priority deadline 12/1. Regular application deadline 8/15. Non-fall registration accepted. Admission may be deferred for a maximum of 1 year.

COSTS AND FINANCIAL AID

Annual tuition $28,140. Room and board $9,000. Required fees $450. Average book and supplies expense $1,230. **Required Forms and Deadlines:** FAFSA. **Notification of Awards:** Applicants will be notified of awards on a rolling basis beginning 12/1. **Types of Aid:** *Need-based scholarships/grants:* College/university scholarship or grant aid from institutional funds; Federal Nursing Scholarships; Federal Pell; Private scholarships; SEOG; State scholarships/grants. *Loans:* Direct PLUS loans; Direct Subsidized Stafford Loans; Direct Unsubsidized Stafford Loans. **Student Employment:** Federal Work-Study Program available. Institutional employment available. **Financial Aid Statistics:** 4% freshmen, 3% undergrads receive athletic scholarships. 99% freshmen, 93% undergrads receive any aid. 68% undergrads borrow to pay for school. Average cumulative indebtedness $33,565. **Criteria awarding aid:** *Non-need-based:* Academics, Art, Athletics, Leadership, Minority status, Music/drama, Religious affiliation.

BETHEL UNIVERSITY (MN)

Office of Admissions - CAS, Saint Paul, MN 55112
Phone: 651-638-6242 **Financial Aid Phone:** 651-638-6241
E-mail: undergrad-admissions@bethel.edu **CEEB Code:** 6038
Fax: 651-635-1490 **Website:** www.bethel.edu **ACT Code:** 2088

This private school, affiliated with the Converge Worldwide (former Baptist General Conference) Church, was founded in 1871. It has a 289 acre campus.

RATINGS

Admissions Selectivity Rating: 84   **Fire Safety Rating:** 69   **Green Rating:** 61

STUDENTS AND FACULTY

Enrollment: 2,723. **Student Body:** 62% female, 38% male, 18% out-of-state, 1% international (9 countries represented). Asian 4%, African American 5%, Caucasian 78%, Hispanic 5%, Native American <1%, Pacific Islander <1%, Two or more races 4%, Race unknown 3%. **Retention and Graduation:** 85% freshmen return for sophomore year. 61% freshmen graduate within 4 years. 70% freshmen graduate within 6 years. 21% grads go on to further study within 1 year. 8% grads pursue arts and sciences degrees. 0% grads pursue law degrees. 0% grads pursue business degrees. 10% grads pursue medical degrees. **Faculty:** Student/faculty ratio 12:1. 206 full-time faculty, 79% hold PhDs, 11% are members of minority groups, 53% are women. 0% of classes are taught by teaching assistants.

ACADEMICS

Degrees: Associate; Bachelor's; Certificate; Doctoral degree—professional practice; Doctoral degree research/scholarship; Master's; Post-bachelor's certificate; Post-master's certificate. **Classes:** Most classes have 10–19 students. Most lab/discussion sessions have 10–19 students. **Most popular majors:** Education, General; Registered Nursing/Registered Nurse; Business Administration and Management, General. **Special Study Options:** Cross-registration; Distance learning; Double major; Dual enrollment; Exchange student program (domestic); Honors program; Independent study; Internships; Liberal arts/career combination; Student-designed major; Study abroad; Teacher certification program. **Honors programs:** The program consists of two honors courses in the freshman year, one in the sophomore year and one in the junior year. In their senior year the student will complete an Honors Senior Project. The two courses in the sophomore year and junior year, as well as the Honors Senior Project are geared toward a discipline of the students choosing. This program also consists of other Honors classes and Honors Forums throughout all four years. **Disability Services offered:** Note-taking services; Reader services; Tape recorders; Tutors. **Career services:** Alumni services; Career assessment; Career/job search classes; Internships.

FACILITIES

Housing: Apartments for single students; Cooperative housing; Special housing for disabled students; 99% of campus accessible to physically disabled. **Special Academic Facilities/Equipment:** Two Art galleries, media center, closed circuit TV, television studio, and radio station, cadaver lab. **Campus network:** 100% of dorms, 100% of libraries, 0% of dining areas, 0% of common outdoor areas, have wireless network access.

CAMPUS LIFE

Environment: Metropolis. **Activities:** Campus Ministries; Choral groups; Concert band; Dance; Drama/theater; International Student Organization; Jazz band; Literary magazine; Music ensembles; Musical theater; Radio station; Student government; Student newspaper; Student-run film society; Symphony orchestra. 55 registered organizations, 3 honor societies, 20 religious organizations, on campus. **Athletics (Intercollegiate):** *Men:* baseball, basketball, cross-country, football, golf, ice hockey, soccer, tennis, track/field (outdoor), track/field (indoor). *Women:* basketball, cross-country, golf, ice hockey, soccer, softball, tennis, track/field (outdoor), track/field (indoor), volleyball. **On-Campus Highlights:** Brushaber Commons/Student Life Building. **Environmental Initiatives:** Green Roof and Permeable Pavers for Brushaber Commons.

ADMISSIONS

Freshman Academic Profile: Average high school GPA 3.6. 25% in top 10% of high school class, 55% in top 25% of high school class, 84% in top 50% of high school class. 76% from public high schools. **Test Scores:** ACT middle 50% range 22–28. **Basis for Candidate Selection:** *Very important factors include:* rigor of secondary school record, academic GPA, standardized test scores, character/personal qualities, alumni/ae relation, religious affiliation/commitment. *Important factors include:* application essay, volunteer work, level of applicant's interest. *Other factors include:* class rank, recommendation(s), interview, extracurricular activities, talent/ability, first generation, racial/ethnic status. **Freshman Admission Requirements:** High school diploma is required and GED is accepted. *Academic units required:* 4 English, 3 math, 3 science, 2 science labs, 4 social studies. *Academic units recommended:* 2 foreign language, 2 history, 1 computer science, 1 visual/performing arts. **Freshman Admission Statistics:** 2,184 applied, 71% admitted, 40% enrolled. **Transfer Admission Requirements:** College transcript(s), essay or personal statement. Minimum college GPA of 2.5 required. Lowest grade transferable C. **General Admission Information:** Priority deadline 1/1. Non-fall registration accepted. Admission may be deferred for a maximum of 1 semester.

COSTS AND FINANCIAL AID

Annual tuition $38,300. Room and board $10,780. Required fees $160. Average book and supplies expense $1,270. **Required Forms and Deadlines:** FAFSA. **Notification of Awards:** Applicants will be notified of awards on a rolling basis beginning 12/15. **Types of Aid:** *Need-based scholarships/grants:* College/university scholarship or grant aid from institutional funds; Federal Pell; Private scholarships; SEOG; State scholarships/grants. *Loans:* Direct PLUS loans; Direct Subsidized Stafford Loans; Direct Unsubsidized Stafford Loans. **Student Employment:** Federal Work-Study Program available. Institutional employment available. **Financial Aid Statistics:** 100% needy freshmen, 100% needy undergrads receive need-based scholarship or grant aid. 15% freshmen, 14% undergrads receive non-need-based scholarship or grant aid. 83% freshmen, 83% undergrads receive need-based self-help aid. 0% freshmen, 0% undergrads receive athletic scholarships. 100% freshmen, 87% undergrads receive any aid. 72% undergrads borrow to pay for school. Average cumulative indebtedness $37,883. **Criteria awarding aid:** *Need-based:* Minority status. *Non-need-based:* Academics, Alumni affiliation, Art, Leadership, Music/drama, State/district residency.

BIOLA UNIVERSITY

13800 Biola Avenue, La Mirada, CA 90639
Phone: 1-800-OK-BIOLA **Financial Aid Phone:** 562-903-4744
E-mail: admissions@biola.edu **CEEB Code:** 4017
Fax: 562-903-4709 **Website:** www.biola.edu **ACT Code:** 172

This private school, affiliated with the Christian (Nondenominational) Church, was founded in 1908. It has a 95 acre campus.

RATINGS
Admissions Selectivity Rating: 76 **Fire Safety Rating:** 90 **Green Rating:** 70

STUDENTS AND FACULTY
Enrollment: 4,005. **Student Body:** 63% female, 37% male, 24% out-of-state, 3% international (40 countries represented). Asian 17%, African American 3%, Caucasian 45%, Hispanic 21%, Native American <1%, Pacific Islander 1%, Two or more races 6%, Race unknown 3%.
Retention and Graduation: 87% freshmen return for sophomore year. 55% freshmen graduate within 4 years. 73% freshmen graduate within 6 years.
Faculty: Student/faculty ratio 14:1. 279 full-time faculty, 83% hold PhDs, 25% are members of minority groups, 36% are women. 0% of classes are taught by teaching assistants.

ACADEMICS
Degrees: Bachelor's; Certificate; Doctoral degree—other; Doctoral degree—professional practice; Doctoral degree research/scholarship; Master's; Post-bachelor's certificate; Post-master's certificate. **Classes:** Most classes have 10–19 students. Most lab/discussion sessions have 10–19 students. **Most popular majors:** Business/Commerce, General; Elementary Education and Teaching; Psychology, General. **Special Study Options:** Distance learning; Double major; English as a Second Language (ESL); Exchange student program (domestic); Honors program; Independent study; Internships; Study abroad; Teacher certification program. **Honors programs:** Biola's Torrey Honors Program which is a nationally recognized great books program. The Stewart Science Honors Program offers a unique opportunity for a small cohort of exceptional students in STEM programs. **Disability Services offered:** Note-taking services; Reader services; Tape recorders; Tutors. **Career services:** Alumni services; Career assessment; Internships.

FACILITIES
Housing: Apartments for married students; Apartments for single students; Coed dorms; Men's dorms; Special housing for disabled students; Women's dorms; 90% of campus accessible to physically disabled. **Special Academic Facilities/Equipment:** Art gallery, electron microscope, TV and Film Production Center, Integrated Media Room, film editing facility, media center, writing center, Student Ministry Union and tutoring services.

CAMPUS LIFE
Environment: Town. **Activities:** Campus Ministries; Choral groups; Concert band; Dance; Drama/theater; International Student Organization; Jazz band; Music ensembles; Musical theater; Opera; Radio station; Student government; Student newspaper; Student-run film society; Symphony orchestra; Television station; Yearbook. 57 registered organizations, 2 honor societies, on campus. **Athletics (Intercollegiate):** *Men:* baseball, basketball, cross-country, golf, soccer, swimming, tennis, track/field (outdoor). *Women:* basketball, cross-country, golf, soccer, softball, swimming, tennis, track/field (outdoor), volleyball. **On-Campus Highlights:** Common Grounds Coffee Shop. **Environmental Initiatives:** Cogen—We produce clean power on campus and use clean waste heat. A certain percentage of this is also used towards cooling purposes.

ADMISSIONS
Freshman Academic Profile: Average high school GPA 3.6. 59% from public high schools. **Test Scores:** SAT Math middle 50% range 520–620. SAT EBRW middle 50% range 520–640. ACT middle 50% range 21–27. **Basis for Candidate Selection:** *Important factors include:* academic GPA, application essay, standardized test scores, religious affiliation/commitment. *Other factors include:* rigor of secondary school record, class rank, recommendation(s), interview, extracurricular activities, talent/ability, character/personal qualities, first generation, alumni/ae relation, racial/ethnic status, volunteer work, work experience, level of applicant's interest. **Freshman Admission Requirements:** High school diploma is required and GED is accepted. *Academic units recommended:* 4 English, 3 math, 2 science, 2 foreign language, 2 social studies. **Freshman Admission Statistics:** 3,784 applied, 87% admitted, 26% enrolled. **Transfer Admission Requirements:** High school transcript, college

transcript(s), essay or personal statement, statement of good standing from prior institution(s). Minimum college GPA of 2.0 required. Lowest grade transferable C. **General Admission Information:** Application fee $45. Priority deadline 3/1. Non-fall registration accepted. Admission may be deferred for a maximum of 2 years.

COSTS AND FINANCIAL AID
Annual tuition $40,488. Room and board $11,312. Average book and supplies expense $1,916. **Required Forms and Deadlines:** FAFSA. **Notification of Awards:** Applicants will be notified of awards on a rolling basis beginning 12/1. **Types of Aid:** *Need-based scholarships/grants:* College/university scholarship or grant aid from institutional funds; Federal Pell; Private scholarships; SEOG; State scholarships/grants; United Negro College Fund. *Loans:* Direct PLUS loans; Direct Subsidized Stafford Loans; Direct Unsubsidized Stafford Loans. **Student Employment:** Federal Work-Study Program available. Institutional employment available. **Financial Aid Statistics:** 100% needy freshmen, 99% needy undergrads receive need-based scholarship or grant aid. 9% freshmen, 6% undergrads receive non-need-based scholarship or grant aid. 75% freshmen, 81% undergrads receive need-based self-help aid. 3% freshmen, 3% undergrads receive athletic scholarships. 87% freshmen, 91% undergrads receive any aid. 66% undergrads borrow to pay for school. Average cumulative indebtedness $34,687. **Criteria awarding aid:** *Non-need-based:* Academics, Alumni affiliation, Art, Athletics, Leadership, Minority status, Music/drama.

BIRMINGHAM-SOUTHERN COLLEGE

Box 549008, Birmingham, AL 35254
Phone: 205-226-4696 **Financial Aid Phone:** 205-226-4688
E-mail: admission@bsc.edu **CEEB Code:** 1064
Fax: 205-226-3074 **Website:** www.bsc.edu **ACT Code:** 1012

This private school, affiliated with the Methodist Church, was founded in 1856. It has a 196 acre campus.

RATINGS
Admissions Selectivity Rating: 85 **Fire Safety Rating:** 87 **Green Rating:** 60*

STUDENTS AND FACULTY
Enrollment: 1,226. **Student Body:** 47% female, 53% male, 41% out-of-state, 0% international (12 countries represented). Asian 4%, African American 8%, Caucasian 84%, Hispanic 3%, Native American 1%, Pacific Islander 0%, Two or more races 0%, Race unknown 1%.
Retention and Graduation: 81% freshmen return for sophomore year. 42% grads go on to further study within 1 year. 27% grads pursue arts and sciences degrees. 17% grads pursue law degrees. 13% grads pursue business degrees. 24% grads pursue medical degrees. **Faculty:** Student/faculty ratio 13:1. 86 full-time faculty, 97% hold PhDs, 3% are members of minority groups, 38% are women. 0% of classes are taught by teaching assistants.

ACADEMICS
Degrees: Bachelor's. **Classes:** Most classes have 10–19 students. Most lab/discussion sessions have 10–19 students. **Most popular majors:** Business/Commerce, General; Biology/Biological Sciences, General; Psychology, General. **Special Study Options:** Accelerated program; Cross-registration; Double major; Exchange student program (domestic); Honors program; Independent study; Internships; Student-designed major; Study abroad; Teacher certification program. **Honors programs:** The Honors Program at Birmingham-Southern is designed to engage students' intellectual curiosity, enhance their oral and written communications skills, and further develop their ability to think and study independently. The importance of viewing issues from interdisciplinary perspectives and of integrating—as well as analyzing—knowledge is a special focus of the program's courses and requirements. The program addresses its mission through small, interdisciplinary seminars developed specifically for Honors students and through upper-level courses with an interdisciplinary focus. The Honors Program serves as a complementary approach to fulfilling the requirements of the College's Foundations Plan for General Education. Honors students are open to new ideas, aware of expanding horizons, and willing to change their own ideas to make room for the knowledge that they gain. They incorporate, embrace, and encourage differences. "Honors" is not synonymous with straight A's and valedictorians. Ideal Honors students would participate in the program even if it did not appear on their transcripts.—Excerpted from "The Ideal Student in the Honors Program" as adopted by the Honors Committee 2002. The Honors Program component of Honors student's

general education consists of five units of Honors seminars and one unit of independent study, known as the Honors Project. The specific general education requirements met by Honors courses and those met by regular courses will vary from student to student, depending on which Honors courses the student elects to take. Students may take one January Interim Term Honors project which will count toward the five units of Honors seminars. Students who participate in study abroad programs that include interdisciplinary courses also may petition to count one such course toward their Honors requirements. Honors students' remaining general education coursework is completed in the regular curriculum of the College. The student's sixth unit in independent study is typically taken over two terms. One-half unit is taken while the project is being designed by the student, the program director, and a faculty sponsor. The project must be interdisciplinary in nature and outside the student's major. Once approved by the Honors Program Committee, the independent study is completed the next term, giving the second half-unit of credit. All Honors Senior, or independent study, projects are presented publicly as part of the program's requirements. **Combined degree programs:** BA/MEng. **Career services:** Alumni network; Alumni services; Career assessment; Career/job search classes; Internships; Regional alumni.

FACILITIES
Housing: Apartments for married students; Apartments for single students; Coed dorms; Fraternity/sorority housing; Men's dorms; Special housing for disabled students; Theme housing; Women's dorms; 90% of campus accessible to physically disabled. **Special Academic Facilities/Equipment:** Theatre planetarium Environmental Center Urban Environmental Park Kennedy Art Center Ropes Course for Leadership Training. **Campus network:** 100% of classrooms, 100% of dorms, 100% of student union, 100% of libraries, 100% of dining areas, 0% of common outdoor areas, have wireless network access.

CAMPUS LIFE
Environment: Metropolis. **Activities:** Campus Ministries; Choral groups; Concert band; Drama/theater; International Student Organization; Jazz band; Literary magazine; Marching band; Model UN; Music ensembles; Musical theater; Opera; Pep band; Student government; Student newspaper; Yearbook. 70 registered organizations, 18 honor societies, 5 religious organizations, 6 fraternities, 6 sororities, on campus. **Athletics (Intercollegiate):** *Men:* baseball, basketball, cheerleading, cross-country, football, golf, lacrosse, soccer, tennis, track/field (outdoor), track/field (indoor). *Women:* basketball, cheerleading, cross-country, golf, lacrosse, riflery, soccer, softball, tennis, track/field (outdoor), track/field (indoor), volleyball. **On-Campus Highlights:** Urban Environmental Park. **Environmental Initiatives:** 10 compressed natural gas operations vehicles will come on line this spring. Campus police vehicles are hybrids.

ADMISSIONS
Freshman Academic Profile: Average high school GPA 3.5. 29% in top 10% of high school class, 61% in top 25% of high school class, 82% in top 50% of high school class. 65% from public high schools. **Test Scores:** SAT Math middle 50% range 510–610. SAT EBRW middle 50% range 500–610. ACT middle 50% range 23–29. **Basis for Candidate Selection:** *Very important factors include:* academic GPA, application essay, standardized test scores, recommendation(s). *Important factors include:* rigor of secondary school record, class rank, extracurricular activities, character/personal qualities. *Other factors include:* interview, talent/ability, work experience. **Freshman Admission Requirements:** High school diploma is required and GED is accepted. *Academic units required:* 4 English. *Academic units recommended:* 2 math, 2 science, 1 science labs, 2 foreign language, 2 social studies, 2 history, 2 academic electives. **Freshman Admission Statistics:** 1,846 applied, 65% admitted, 27% enrolled. **Transfer Admission Requirements:** High school transcript, college transcript(s), essay or personal statement, standardized test scores, statement of good standing from prior institution(s). Minimum college GPA of 2.0 required. Lowest grade transferable D. **General Admission Information:** Application fee $40. Regular application deadline 2/1. Non-fall registration accepted. Admission may be deferred for a maximum of 1 year.

COSTS AND FINANCIAL AID
Annual tuition $31,954. Room and board $11,350. Required fees $1,174. Average book and supplies expense $1,300. **Required Forms and Deadlines:** FAFSA; State aid form. **Notification of Awards:** Applicants will be notified of awards on a rolling basis beginning 3/1. **Types of Aid:** *Need-based scholarships/ grants:* College/university scholarship or grant aid from institutional funds; Federal Pell; Private scholarships; SEOG; State scholarships/grants. *Loans:* Direct PLUS loans; Direct Subsidized Stafford Loans; Direct Unsubsidized Stafford Loans. **Student Employment:** Federal Work-Study Program available. Institutional employment available. **Financial Aid Statistics:** 76% needy freshmen, 82% needy undergrads receive need-based scholarship or grant aid. 92% freshmen, 89% undergrads receive non-need-based scholarship or grant

aid. 99% freshmen, 82% undergrads receive need-based self-help aid. 0% freshmen, 0% undergrads receive athletic scholarships. 99% freshmen, 98% undergrads receive any aid. **Criteria awarding aid:** *Non-need-based:* Academics, Alumni affiliation, Art, Leadership, Music/drama, Religious affiliation, State/ district residency.

BLACKBURN COLLEGE

700 College Ave., Carlinville, Il 62626
Phone: 217-854-3231
E-mail: admit@blackburn.edu
Fax: 217-854-3713 **Website:** www.blackburn.edu **ACT Code:** 0958

This private school, affiliated with the Presbyterian Church, was founded in 1837. It has a 80 acre campus.

RATINGS
Admissions Selectivity Rating: 70   **Fire Safety Rating:** 60*   **Green Rating:** 60*

STUDENTS AND FACULTY
Enrollment: 603. **Student Body:** 59% female, 41% male. **Faculty:** Student/ faculty ratio 17:1. 31 full-time faculty, 0% hold PhDs, 6% are members of minority groups, 35% are women.

ACADEMICS
Degrees: Bachelor's. **Special Study Options:** Double major; Exchange student program (domestic); Honors program; Independent study; Internships; Liberal arts/career combination; Student-designed major; Study abroad; Teacher certification program.

FACILITIES
Housing: Coed dorms; Men's dorms; Theme housing; Women's dorms. **Campus network:** 100% of classrooms, 100% of dorms, 100% of student union, 100% of libraries, 100% of dining areas, 50% of common outdoor areas, have wireless network access.

CAMPUS LIFE
Environment: Village. **Activities:** Campus Ministries; Choral groups; Dance; Drama/theater; International Student Organization; Jazz band; Literary magazine; Music ensembles; Musical theater; Radio station; Student government; Student newspaper; Student-run film society; Yearbook.

ADMISSIONS
Freshman Academic Profile: Average high school GPA 3.5. 16% in top 10% of high school class, 22% in top 25% of high school class, 37% in top 50% of high school class. 81% from public high schools. **Basis for Candidate Selection:** *Very important factors include:* rigor of secondary school record, academic GPA, standardized test scores. *Important factors include:* class rank. *Other factors include:* application essay, recommendation(s), extracurricular activities, talent/ability, character/personal qualities, alumni/ae relation, volunteer work, work experience. **Freshman Admission Requirements:** High school diploma is required and GED is accepted. *Academic units recommended:* 4 English, 3 math, 3 science, 2 foreign language, 3 social studies. **Freshman Admission Statistics:** 893 applied, 64% admitted, 26% enrolled. **Transfer Admission Requirements:** High school transcript, college transcript(s), standardized test scores, Minimum college GPA of 2.0 required. Lowest grade transferable C. **General Admission Information:** Non-fall registration accepted.

COSTS AND FINANCIAL AID
Annual tuition $14,176. Room and board $4,581. Required fees $110. Average book and supplies expense $1,000.

BLOOMFIELD COLLEGE

One Park Place, Bloomfield, NJ 07003
Phone: 973-748-9000 (x1230) **Financial Aid Phone:** 973-748-9000 x1212
E-mail: admission@bloomfield.edu **CEEB Code:** 2044
Fax: 973-748-0916 **Website:** www.bloomfield.edu **ACT Code:** 2540

This private school, affiliated with the Presbyterian Church, was founded in 1868. It has a 12.5 acre campus.

RATINGS
Admissions Selectivity Rating: 77   **Fire Safety Rating:** 99   **Green Rating:** 60*

STUDENTS AND FACULTY
Enrollment: 1,941. **Student Body:** 62% female, 38% male, 6% out-of-state, 4% international (6 countries represented). Asian 2%, African American 50%, Caucasian 9%, Hispanic 28%, Native American <1%, Pacific Islander 1%, Two or more races 1%, Race unknown 5%.
Retention and Graduation: 65% freshmen return for sophomore year. 27% grads go on to further study within 1 year. **Faculty:** Student/faculty ratio 16:1. 70 full-time faculty, 81% hold PhDs, 24% are members of minority groups, 60% are women. 0% of classes are taught by teaching assistants.

ACADEMICS
Degrees: Bachelor's; Certificate; Master's; Post-bachelor's certificate. **Classes:** Most classes have 10–19 students. Most lab/discussion sessions have fewer than 10 students. **Most popular majors:** Visual and Performing Arts, General; Business Administration and Management, General; Sociology, General. **Special Study Options:** Accelerated program; Distance learning; Double major; Dual enrollment; English as a Second Language (ESL); Honors program; Independent study; Internships; Liberal arts/career combination; Student-designed major; Study abroad; Teacher certification program. **Honors programs:** Honors program open to new and enrolled students consisting of interdisciplinary courses, Honors seminars in the arts and sciences, special courses, and honors capstone projects. **Combined degree programs:** BA/MA. **Disability Services offered:** Note-taking services; Reader services; Tape recorders; Tutors. **Career services:** Alumni network; Alumni services; Career assessment; Career/job search classes; Internships; Regional alumni.

FACILITIES
Housing: Apartments for single students; Coed dorms; 78% of campus accessible to physically disabled. **Special Academic Facilities/Equipment:** Westminster Theatre, Art Gallery, State-of-the-Art Library.

CAMPUS LIFE
Environment: Town. **Activities:** Campus Ministries; Dance; International Student Organization; Radio station; Student government. 47 registered organizations, 5 honor societies, 1 religious organizations, 8 fraternities, 9 sororities, on campus. **Athletics (Intercollegiate):** *Men:* baseball, basketball, cross-country, soccer, tennis. *Women:* basketball, cross-country, soccer, softball, volleyball. **On-Campus Highlights:** Center for Technology + Creativity **Environmental Initiatives:** Campus-wide recycling program of all materials, including cooking oil from the campus kitchen.

ADMISSIONS
Freshman Academic Profile: Average high school GPA 2.7. 7% in top 10% of high school class, 20% in top 25% of high school class, 50% in top 50% of high school class. 82% from public high schools. **Test Scores:** SAT Math middle 50% range 380–480. SAT EBRW middle 50% range 380–460. ACT middle 50% range 15–20. **Basis for Candidate Selection:** *Very important factors include:* rigor of secondary school record, academic GPA, recommendation(s). *Important factors include:* class rank, application essay, interview, extracurricular activities. *Other factors include:* standardized test scores, talent/ability, character/personal qualities, first generation, alumni/ae relation, geographical residence, state residency, work experience, level of applicant's interest. **Freshman Admission Requirements:** High school diploma is required and GED is accepted. **Freshman Admission Statistics:** 3,623 applied, 62% admitted, 23% enrolled. **Transfer Admission Requirements:** college transcript(s), Minimum college GPA of 2.0 required. Lowest grade transferable 2. **General Admission Information:** Application fee $40. Priority deadline 3/15. Regular application deadline 8/1. Non-fall registration accepted. Admission may be deferred for a maximum of 1 year.

COSTS AND FINANCIAL AID
Annual tuition $29,300. Room and board $11,700. Average book and supplies expense $1,250. **Required Forms and Deadlines:** FAFSA. **Notification of Awards:** Applicants will be notified of awards on a rolling basis beginning 4/15. **Types of Aid:** *Need-based scholarships/grants:* College/university scholarship or grant aid from institutional funds; Federal Pell; Private scholarships; SEOG; State scholarships/grants. *Loans:* Direct PLUS loans; Direct Subsidized Stafford Loans; Direct Unsubsidized Stafford Loans. **Student Employment:** Federal Work-Study Program available. Institutional employment available. **Financial Aid Statistics:** 95% needy freshmen, 95% needy undergrads receive need-based scholarship or grant aid. 43% freshmen, 46% undergrads receive non-need-based scholarship or grant aid. 82% freshmen, 83% undergrads receive need-based self-help aid. 10% freshmen, 10% undergrads receive athletic scholarships. 98% freshmen, 99% undergrads receive any aid. 0% undergrads borrow to pay for school. **Criteria awarding aid:** *Need-based:* Academics, Alumni affiliation, Religious affiliation. *Non-need-based:* Academics, Alumni affiliation, Athletics, Leadership.

BLOOMSBURG UNIVERSITY OF PENNSYLVANIA

104 Student Services Center, Bloomsburg, PA 17815
Phone: 570-389-4316 **Financial Aid Phone:** (570) 389-4279
CEEB Code: 2646
Fax: 570-389-4741 **Website:** www.bloomu.edu **ACT Code:** 3692

This public school was founded in 1839. It has a 366 acre campus.

RATINGS
Admissions Selectivity Rating: 76   **Fire Safety Rating:** 97   **Green Rating:** 60*

STUDENTS AND FACULTY
Enrollment: 7,661. **Student Body:** 58% female, 42% male, 8% out-of-state, 0% international (18 countries represented). Asian 1%, African American 7%, Caucasian 77%, Hispanic 8%, Native American <1%, Pacific Islander <1%, Two or more races 2%, Race unknown 5%.
Retention and Graduation: 74% freshmen return for sophomore year. 40% freshmen graduate within 4 years. 60% freshmen graduate within 6 years. 20% grads go on to further study within 1 year. **Faculty:** 439 full-time faculty, 8% are members of minority groups, 44% are women. 0% of classes are taught by teaching assistants.

ACADEMICS
Degrees: Bachelor's; Certificate; Doctoral degree—other; Doctoral degree—professional practice; Master's; Post-bachelor's certificate. **Classes:** Most classes have 20–29 students. Most lab/discussion sessions have 10–19 students. **Most popular majors:** Psychology, General; Business Administration and Management, General; Registered Nursing/Registered Nurse. **Special Study Options:** Cooperative education program; Cross-registration; Distance learning; Double major; Dual enrollment; English as a Second Language (ESL); Honors program; Independent study; Internships; Liberal arts/career combination; Student-designed major; Study abroad; Teacher certification program. **Honors programs:** Bloomsburg University's Honors Program provides unique educational opportunities and experiences for academically talented students. The program challenges students to aspire to high academic standards and to achieve more professionally and personally. Students engage in various service activities that foster cooperation and altruism. Students conduct independent research in your major, become part of a community of ambitious scholars, have opportunities to explore the world, and more. » Work in your field on individual research — Choose a research topic within your field of study and, with the help of a dedicated faculty mentor, complete a written thesis and presentation to the Honors community. This independent study project allows every Honors student the opportunity to present their research at the annual meeting of the National Collegiate Honors Council, attended by students and faculty of Honors Programs across the country. Your hard work and presentation skills at this event show your dedication, commitment, and skill within your field, and your ability to work independently. » Get involved in the local community — Become involved in BU and community service projects, and make a difference with groups like the Bloomsburg Fire Department, Relay for Life, TreeFest, Balanced Care, and Habitat for Humanity. These projects enrich the community, provide a great sense of satisfaction, and help you discover other talents and skills. » Enjoy smaller classes — Smaller classes allow you to receive more attention from your professors and cover topics in greater depth and breadth. Build professional and personal relationships with your

teachers so that you can create a strong network of academic references and contacts for the future. » Get settled early on campus — Move onto campus a day early and be welcomed by current Honors students. The Move-In Crew will help you ease into your dorm and get acclimated to campus, Bloomsburg, and the surrounding areas. Making immediate connections with experienced Honors students gives you an honest, inside perspective on classes, campus life, and prospective jobs after college. » Travel! — The Honors Program offers several trips for students every year. Honors students visit exciting places from other states to other countries. Expand your worldview and learn about other cultures. The Bloomsburg Honors Program plans annual trips to New York City in the fall and Washington D.C. in the spring. We are also trying to establish an annual service trip to Jamaica. **Disability Services offered:** Note-taking services; Reader services; Tape recorders; Tutors. **Career services:** Alumni network; Career assessment; Career/job search classes; Internships.

FACILITIES
Housing: Apartments for single students; Coed dorms; 100% of campus accessible to physically disabled. **Special Academic Facilities/Equipment:** Art gallery, language lab, TV studio, radio station.

CAMPUS LIFE
Environment: Village. **Activities:** Campus Ministries; Choral groups; Concert band; Dance; Drama/theater; International Student Organization; Jazz band; Literary magazine; Marching band; Model UN; Music ensembles; Pep band; Radio station; Student government; Student newspaper; Symphony orchestra; Television station; Yearbook. 250 registered organizations, 8 honor societies, 10 religious organizations, 13 fraternities, 11 sororities, on campus. **Athletics (Intercollegiate):** *Men:* baseball, basketball, cheerleading, cross-country, football, soccer, swimming, tennis, track/field (outdoor), track/field (indoor), wrestling. *Women:* basketball, cheerleading, cross-country, field hockey, lacrosse, soccer, softball, swimming, tennis, track/field (outdoor), track/field (indoor). **On-Campus Highlights:** Kehr Student Union. **Environmental Initiatives:** A kiosk was designed to educate the BU community about solar energy and the university's energy consumption using Lucid Design Group's Building Dashboard software. The project ultimately aims to develop energy-saving strategies for the university. The Building Dashboard touchscreen software will also allow users to take an in-depth look at energy use in five campus buildings: Hartline Science Center, Student Recreation Center, Nelson Field House, Columbia Residence Hall and Elwell Residence Hall. These buildings were chosen because they are popular with students or large consumers of energy.

ADMISSIONS
Freshman Academic Profile: Average high school GPA 3.4. 10% in top 10% of high school class, 27% in top 25% of high school class, 60% in top 50% of high school class. 87% from public high schools. **Test Scores:** SAT Math middle 50% range 470–570. SAT EBRW middle 50% range 480–580. ACT middle 50% range 18–23. **Basis for Candidate Selection:** *Very important factors include:* rigor of secondary school record, class rank, academic GPA, standardized test scores. *Other factors include:* application essay, recommendation(s), interview, extracurricular activities, talent/ability, character/personal qualities, geographical residence, state residency, volunteer work, work experience, level of applicant's interest. **Freshman Admission Requirements:** High school diploma is required and GED is accepted. *Academic units required:* 4 English, 3 math, 3 science, 2 social studies, 2 history, 2 academic electives, 2 unit from above areas or other academic areas. *Academic units recommended:* 4 English, 4 math, 4 science, 2 foreign language, 2 social studies, 2 history, 2 academic electives, 1 computer science. **Freshman Admission Statistics:** 16,291 applied, 84% admitted, 29% enrolled. **Transfer Admission Requirements:** High school transcript, college transcript(s). Minimum college GPA of 2.0 required. Lowest grade transferable C. **General Admission Information:** Application fee $35. Non-fall registration accepted. Admission may be deferred for a maximum of 1 year.

COSTS AND FINANCIAL AID
Annual in-state tuition $7,716. Annual out-of-state tuition $19,290. Room and board $10,162. Required fees $3,242. Average book and supplies expense $1,200. **Required Forms and Deadlines:** FAFSA. **Types of Aid:** *Need-based scholarships/grants:* College/university scholarship or grant aid from institutional funds; Federal Pell; Private scholarships; SEOG; State scholarships/grants. *Loans:* Direct PLUS loans; Direct Subsidized Stafford Loans; Direct Unsubsidized Stafford Loans. **Student Employment:** Federal Work-Study Program available. Institutional employment available. **Financial Aid Statistics:** 64% needy freshmen, 62% needy undergrads receive need-based scholarship or grant aid. 40% freshmen, 29% undergrads receive non-need-based scholarship or grant aid. 93% freshmen, 90% undergrads receive need-based self-help aid. 3% freshmen, 3% undergrads receive athletic scholarships. 87% freshmen, 84% undergrads receive any aid. 83% undergrads borrow to pay for school.

Average cumulative indebtedness $38,013. **Criteria awarding aid:** *Need-based:* Academics, Alumni affiliation, Leadership, Minority status. *Non-need-based:* Academics, Art, Athletics, Job skills, Leadership, Minority status, Music/drama, State/district residency.

BLUE MOUNTAIN COLLEGE

PO Box 160, Blue Mountain, MS 38610
Phone: 662-685-4771 **Financial Aid Phone:** 662-685-4771
E-mail: admissions@bmc.edu
Fax: 662-685-4776 **Website:** bmc.edu

This private school, affiliated with the Baptist Church, was founded in 1873. It has a 44 acre campus.

RATINGS
Admissions Selectivity Rating: 88   **Fire Safety Rating:** 71   **Green Rating:** 60*

STUDENTS AND FACULTY
Enrollment: 406. **Student Body:** 64% female, 36% male, 12% out-of-state, <1% international (1 countries represented). Asian <1%, African American 12%, Caucasian 87%, Hispanic <1%, Native American 0%, Race unknown 0%.
Retention and Graduation: 72% freshmen return for sophomore year. 14% grads go on to further study within 1 year. 14% grads pursue arts and sciences degrees. 0% grads pursue law degrees. 1% grads pursue business degrees. 2% grads pursue medical degrees. **Faculty:** Student/faculty ratio 13:1. 24 full-time faculty, 67% hold PhDs, 0% are members of minority groups, 54% are women. 0% of classes are taught by teaching assistants.

ACADEMICS
Degrees: Bachelor's; Master's. **Classes:** Most classes have 10–19 students. Most lab/discussion sessions have 10–19 students. **Most popular majors:** Bible/Biblical Studies; Elementary Education and Teaching; Psychology, General. **Special Study Options:** Double major; Honors program; Internships; Teacher certification program. **Honors programs:** Academic Honors Program. **Disability Services offered:** Note-taking services; Tutors.

FACILITIES
Housing: Men's dorms; Women's dorms; 50% of campus accessible to physically disabled. **Campus network:** 100% of classrooms, 100% of dorms, 100% of student union, 100% of libraries, 100% of dining areas, have wireless network access.

CAMPUS LIFE
Environment: Rural. **Activities:** Choral groups; Drama/theater; Literary magazine; Musical theater; Student government; Yearbook. 28 registered organizations, 4 honor societies, 2 religious organizations, on campus. **Athletics (Intercollegiate):** *Women:* basketball, tennis. **On-Campus Highlights:** Johnnie Armstrong Gal-ry.

ADMISSIONS
Freshman Academic Profile: Average high school GPA 3.3. 19% in top 10% of high school class, 50% in top 25% of high school class, 86% in top 50% of high school class. 73% from public high schools. **Test Scores:** ACT middle 50% range 18–23. **Basis for Candidate Selection:** *Important factors include:* rigor of secondary school record, class rank, academic GPA, standardized test scores. *Other factors include:* recommendation(s), character/personal qualities, alumni/ae relation. **Freshman Admission Requirements:** High school diploma is required and GED is accepted. *Academic units required:* 4 English, 3 math, 3 science, 2 science labs, 2 foreign language, 1 social studies, 2 history. *Academic units recommended:* 4 English, 3 math, 3 science, 2 science labs, 2 foreign language, 1 social studies, 2 history. **Freshman Admission Statistics:** 146 applied, 47% admitted, 87% enrolled. **Transfer Admission Requirements:** College transcript(s). Lowest grade transferable C. **General Admission Information:** Application fee $10. Non-fall registration accepted. Admission may be deferred for a maximum of semester.

COSTS AND FINANCIAL AID
Annual tuition $6,900. Room and board $3,766. Average book and supplies expense $650. **Required Forms and Deadlines:** FAFSA; Institution's own financial aid form. **Notification of Awards:** Applicants will be notified of awards on a rolling basis beginning 4/1. **Types of Aid:** *Need-based scholarships/grants:* Federal Pell; Private scholarships; SEOG; State scholarships/grants. **Student Employment:** Federal Work-Study Program available. Institutional

employment available. **Financial Aid Statistics:** 81% needy freshmen, 64% needy undergrads receive need-based scholarship or grant aid. 81% freshmen, 100% undergrads receive non-need-based scholarship or grant aid. 62% freshmen, 18% undergrads receive need-based self-help aid. 8% freshmen, 6% undergrads receive athletic scholarships. 95% freshmen, 96% undergrads receive any aid. **Criteria awarding aid:** *Need-based:* Alumni affiliation. *Non-need-based:* Academics, Alumni affiliation, Athletics, Religious affiliation, State/district residency.

BLUFFTON UNIVERSITY

Office of Admissions, Bluffton, OH 45817
Phone: 419-358-3257 **Financial Aid Phone:** (419) 358-3409
E-mail: admissions@bluffton.edu **CEEB Code:** 1067
Fax: 419-358-3081 **Website:** www.bluffton.edu **ACT Code:** 3238

This private school, affiliated with the Mennonite Church, was founded in 1899. It has a 65 acre campus.

RATINGS
Admissions Selectivity Rating: 84   **Fire Safety Rating:** 60*   **Green Rating:** 60*

STUDENTS AND FACULTY
Enrollment: 833. **Student Body:** 51% female, 49% male, 12% out-of-state, <1% international. Asian <1%, African American 6%, Caucasian 85%, Hispanic 4%, Native American 0%, Pacific Islander 0%, Two or more races 3%, Race unknown 2%.
Retention and Graduation: 72% freshmen return for sophomore year.
Faculty: Student/faculty ratio 12:1. 56 full-time faculty, 80% hold PhDs, 2% are members of minority groups, 39% are women. 0% of classes are taught by teaching assistants.

ACADEMICS
Degrees: Bachelor's; Master's; Post-bachelor's certificate. **Classes:** Most classes have 10–19 students. Most lab/discussion sessions have fewer than 10 students. **Most popular majors:** Social Work; Business Administration and Management, General; Early Childhood Education and Teaching. **Special Study Options:** Accelerated program; Distance learning; Double major; Dual enrollment; English as a Second Language (ESL); Honors program; Independent study; Internships; Student-designed major; Study abroad; Teacher certification program. **Disability Services offered:** Note-taking services; Reader services; Tape recorders; Tutors. **Career services:** Alumni services; Career/job search classes.

FACILITIES
Housing: Coed dorms; Men's dorms; Women's dorms; 99% of campus accessible to physically disabled. **Special Academic Facilities/Equipment:** Mennonite historical library, peace arts center, nature preserve. **Campus network:** 60% of classrooms, 0% of dorms, 100% of student union, 100% of libraries, 0% of dining areas, 20% of common outdoor areas, have wireless network access.

CAMPUS LIFE
Environment: Rural. **Activities:** Campus Ministries; Choral groups; Drama/theater; International Student Organization; Music ensembles; Pep band; Radio station; Student government; Student newspaper. 50 registered organizations, 19 honor societies, 10 religious organizations, on campus. **Athletics (Intercollegiate):** *Men:* baseball, basketball, cheerleading, cross-country, football, golf, soccer, tennis, track/field (outdoor), track/field (indoor). *Women:* basketball, cheerleading, cross-country, golf, soccer, softball, tennis, track/field (outdoor), track/field (indoor), volleyball. **On-Campus Highlights:** Centennial Hall-academic center.

ADMISSIONS
Freshman Academic Profile: Average high school GPA 3.2. 12% in top 10% of high school class, 25% in top 25% of high school class, 67% in top 50% of high school class. 98% from public high schools. **Test Scores:** SAT Math middle 50% range 430–560. SAT EBRW middle 50% range 410–580. ACT middle 50% range 18–23. **Basis for Candidate Selection:** *Very important factors include:* class rank, academic GPA, standardized test scores. *Other factors include:* interview, extracurricular activities, talent/ability, character/personal qualities. **Freshman Admission Requirements:** High school diploma is required and GED is accepted. *Academic units recommended:* 4 English, 3 math, 3 science, 3 foreign language, 3 social studies. **Freshman Admission**

Statistics: 1,652 applied, 54% admitted, 25% enrolled. **Transfer Admission Requirements:** High school transcript, college transcript(s), statement of good standing from prior institution(s). Minimum college GPA of 2.0 required. Lowest grade transferable C-. **General Admission Information:** Application fee $20. Non-fall registration accepted. Admission may be deferred for a maximum of two years.

COSTS AND FINANCIAL AID
Required Forms and Deadlines: FAFSA. **Notification of Awards:** Applicants will be notified of awards on a rolling basis beginning 3/1. **Types of Aid:** *Need-based scholarships/grants:* Federal Pell; Private scholarships; SEOG; State scholarships/grants. *Loans:* Direct PLUS loans; Direct Subsidized Stafford Loans; Direct Unsubsidized Stafford Loans. **Student Employment:** Federal Work-Study Program available. Institutional employment available. **Financial Aid Statistics:** 99% needy freshmen, 99% needy undergrads receive need-based scholarship or grant aid. 11% freshmen, 11% undergrads receive non-need-based scholarship or grant aid. 91% freshmen, 90% undergrads receive need-based self-help aid. 0% freshmen, 0% undergrads receive athletic scholarships. **Criteria awarding aid:** *Need-based:* Job skills. *Non-need-based:* Academics, Art, Job skills, Minority status, Music/drama, Religious affiliation, State/district residency.

BOB JONES UNIVERSITY

1700 Wade Hampton Blvd, Greenville, SC 29614
Phone: 800-252-6363 **Financial Aid Phone:** 864-242-5100 Ext 3040
E-mail: admission@bju.edu **CEEB Code:** 5065
Fax: 800-232-9258 **Website:** www.bju.edu **ACT Code:** 3836

This private school, affiliated with the Evangelical Christian Church, was founded in 1927. It has a 225 acre campus.

RATINGS
Admissions Selectivity Rating: 77   **Fire Safety Rating:** 87   **Green Rating:** 60*

STUDENTS AND FACULTY
Enrollment: 2,371. **Student Body:** 55% female, 45% male, 68% out-of-state, 7% international (45 countries represented). Asian 2%, African American 2%, Caucasian 77%, Hispanic 6%, Native American <1%, Pacific Islander 1%, Two or more races 3%, Race unknown 2%.
Retention and Graduation: 82% freshmen return for sophomore year. 60% freshmen graduate within 6 years. 23% grads go on to further study within 1 year. **Faculty:** Student/faculty ratio 13:1. 186 full-time faculty, 66% hold PhDs, 5% are members of minority groups, 37% are women. 1% of classes are taught by teaching assistants.

ACADEMICS
Degrees: Associate; Bachelor's; Doctoral degree—professional practice; Master's. **Classes:** Most classes have 10–19 students. Most lab/discussion sessions have fewer than 10 students. **Most popular majors:** Registered Nursing/Registered Nurse; Business Administration and Management, General; Accounting. **Special Study Options:** Distance learning; Double major; Dual enrollment; English as a Second Language (ESL); Internships; Liberal arts/career combination; Student-designed major; Teacher certification program. **Disability Services offered:** Note-taking services; Reader services; Tape recorders; Tutors. **Career services:** Alumni services; Career assessment; Career/job search classes; Internships.

FACILITIES
Housing: Men's dorms; Special housing for disabled students; Women's dorms; 90% of campus accessible to physically disabled. **Special Academic Facilities/Equipment:** Alumni Building, Alumni Stadium, BJU Museum & Gallery, Davis Field House, Fremont Fitness Center, Founder's Memorial Amphitorium, Grace Haight Nursing Building, Gustafson Fine Arts Center, Howell Memorial Science Building, Performance Hall, Rodeheaver Auditorium, Sargent Art Building, Bob Jones Jr. Memorial Seminary and Graduate School of Religion, Stratton Hall, Student Center, War Memorial Chapel.

CAMPUS LIFE
Environment: City. **Activities:** Campus Ministries; Choral groups; Concert band; Drama/theater; International Student Organization; Music ensembles; Opera; Pep band; Radio station; Student government; Student newspaper; Symphony orchestra; Television station; Yearbook. 35 registered organizations,

2 religious organizations, on campus. **On-Campus Highlights:** University Student Center.

ADMISSIONS

Freshman Academic Profile: Average high school GPA 3.2. 13% in top 10% of high school class, 35% in top 25% of high school class, 62% in top 50% of high school class. 4% from public high schools. **Test Scores:** ACT middle 50% range 20–27. **Basis for Candidate Selection:** *Very important factors include:* character/personal qualities, religious affiliation/commitment. *Important factors include:* recommendation(s). *Other factors include:* rigor of secondary school record, class rank, academic GPA, application essay, standardized test scores, extracurricular activities, talent/ability, volunteer work, level of applicant's interest. **Freshman Admission Requirements:** High school diploma is required and GED is accepted. *Academic units required:* 3 English, 2 math, 1 science, 2 social studies, 6 academic electives. *Academic units recommended:* 2 foreign language. **Freshman Admission Statistics:** 1,062 applied, 86% admitted, 65% enrolled. **Transfer Admission Requirements:** College transcript(s). Minimum college GPA of 2.0 required. Lowest grade transferable D-. **General Admission Information:** Non-fall registration accepted. Admission may be deferred for a maximum of one year.

COSTS AND FINANCIAL AID

Annual tuition $17,250. Room and board $6,976. Required fees $900. Average book and supplies expense $1,200. **Required Forms and Deadlines:** FAFSA. **Notification of Awards:** Applicants will be notified of awards on a rolling basis beginning 4/1. **Types of Aid:** *Need-based scholarships/grants:* College/university scholarship or grant aid from institutional funds; Federal Pell; Private scholarships; SEOG; State scholarships/grants. *Loans:* Direct PLUS loans; Direct Subsidized Stafford Loans; Direct Unsubsidized Stafford Loans. **Student Employment:** Federal Work-Study Program available. Institutional employment available. **Financial Aid Statistics:** 99% needy freshmen, 98% needy undergrads receive need-based scholarship or grant aid. 12% freshmen, 12% undergrads receive non-need-based scholarship or grant aid. 41% freshmen, 51% undergrads receive need-based self-help aid. freshmen, undergrads receive athletic scholarships. **Criteria awarding aid:** *Need-based:* Academics, Alumni affiliation, Leadership. *Non-need-based:* State/district residency.

BOISE STATE UNIVERSITY

1910 University Drive, Boise, ID 83725
Phone: 208-426-1156 **Financial Aid Phone:** 208-426-1664
E-mail: bsuinfo@boisestate.edu **CEEB Code:** 4018
Fax: 208-426-3765 **Website:** www.boisestate.edu **ACT Code:** 914

This public school was founded in 1932. It has a 286 acre campus.

RATINGS
Admissions Selectivity Rating: 76   **Fire Safety Rating:** 65   **Green Rating:** 62

STUDENTS AND FACULTY
Enrollment: 16,537. **Student Body:** 56% female, 44% male, 34% out-of-state, 2% international. Asian 2%, African American 2%, Caucasian 73%, Hispanic 14%, Native American <1%, Pacific Islander 1%, Two or more races 5%, Race unknown 2%.
Retention and Graduation: 80% freshmen return for sophomore year. 19% freshmen graduate within 4 years. 43% freshmen graduate within 6 years.
Faculty: Student/faculty ratio 17:1. 769 full-time faculty, 77% hold PhDs, 11% are members of minority groups, 49% are women.

ACADEMICS
Degrees: Associate; Bachelor's; Certificate; Doctoral degree—professional practice; Doctoral degree research/scholarship; Master's; Post-bachelor's certificate; Post-master's certificate; Terminal Associate. **Classes:** Most classes have 20–29 students. Most lab/discussion sessions have 20–29 students. **Most popular majors:** Business/Commerce, General; Registered Nursing/Registered Nurse; Speech Communication and Rhetoric. **Special Study Options:** Distance learning; Double major; Dual enrollment; Exchange student program (domestic); Honors program; Independent study; Internships; Student-designed major; Study abroad; Teacher certification program; Weekend college. **Disability Services offered:** Note-taking services; Reader services; Tape recorders; Tutors. **Career services:** Alumni network; Alumni services; Career assessment; Career/job search classes; Internships.

FACILITIES
Housing: Apartments for married students; Apartments for single students; Coed dorms; 95% of campus accessible to physically disabled.

CAMPUS LIFE
Environment: City. **Activities:** Choral groups; Concert band; Dance; Drama/theater; International Student Organization; Jazz band; Literary magazine; Marching band; Music ensembles; Musical theater; Pep band; Radio station; Student government; Student newspaper; Student-run film society; Symphony orchestra. 300 registered organizations, 12 honor societies, 11 fraternities, 10 sororities, on campus. **Athletics (Intercollegiate):** *Men:* basketball, cheerleading, cross-country, football, golf, tennis, track/field (outdoor), track/field (indoor), wrestling. *Women:* basketball, cheerleading, cross-country, golf, gymnastics, skiing (downhill/Alpine), soccer, tennis, track/field (outdoor), track/field (indoor), volleyball. **On-Campus Highlights:** Student Union Building.

ADMISSIONS
Freshman Academic Profile: Average high school GPA 3.5. 16% in top 10% of high school class, 39% in top 25% of high school class, 74% in top 50% of high school class. **Test Scores:** SAT Math middle 50% range 440–560. SAT EBRW middle 50% range –560. ACT middle 50% range 21–26. **Basis for Candidate Selection:** *Other factors include:* academic GPA, standardized test scores. **Freshman Admission Requirements:** High school diploma is required and GED is accepted. *Academic units recommended:* 8 English, 6 math, 6 science, 2 foreign language, 5 social studies, 1 visual/performing arts. **Freshman Admission Statistics:** 10,788 applied, 81% admitted, 33% enrolled. **Transfer Admission Requirements:** College transcript(s). Minimum college GPA of 2.0 required. Lowest grade transferable C. **General Admission Information:** Application fee $50. Regular application deadline 5/15. Non-fall registration accepted.

COSTS AND FINANCIAL AID
Annual in-state tuition $5,259. Annual out-of-state tuition $21,341. Room and board $8,835. Required fees $2,435. Average book and supplies expense $1,200. **Required Forms and Deadlines:** FAFSA. **Notification of Awards:** Applicants will be notified of awards on a rolling basis beginning 3/15. **Types of Aid:** *Need-based scholarships/grants:* College/university scholarship or grant aid from institutional funds; Federal Nursing Scholarships; Federal Pell; Private scholarships; SEOG; State scholarships/grants. *Loans:* Direct PLUS loans; Direct Subsidized Stafford Loans; Direct Unsubsidized Stafford Loans. **Student Employment:** Federal Work-Study Program available. Institutional employment available. **Financial Aid Statistics:** 63% needy freshmen, 67% needy undergrads receive need-based scholarship or grant aid. 6% freshmen, 3% undergrads receive non-need-based scholarship or grant aid. 56% freshmen, 63% undergrads receive need-based self-help aid. 1% freshmen, 0% undergrads receive athletic scholarships. 60% undergrads borrow to pay for school. Average cumulative indebtedness $27,870. **Criteria awarding aid:** *Need-based:* Athletics, Music/drama. *Non-need-based:* Academics, Alumni affiliation, Art, Athletics, Music/drama.

BOSTON COLLEGE

140 Commonwealth Avenue, Chestnut Hill, MA 02467-3809
Phone: 617-552-3100 **Financial Aid Phone:** 617-552-3300
CEEB Code: 3083
Fax: 617-552-0798 **Website:** www.bc.edu **ACT Code:** 1788

This private school, affiliated with the Roman Catholic Church, was founded in 1863. It has a 227 acre campus.

RATINGS
Admissions Selectivity Rating: 96   **Fire Safety Rating:** 98   **Green Rating:** 88

STUDENTS AND FACULTY
Enrollment: 9,370. **Student Body:** 53% female, 47% male, 73% out-of-state, 8% international (68 countries represented). Asian 11%, African American 4%, Caucasian 58%, Hispanic 12%, Native American <1%, Pacific Islander <1%, Two or more races 4%, Race unknown 4%.

Retention and Graduation: 95% freshmen return for sophomore year. 88% freshmen graduate within 4 years. 92% freshmen graduate within 6 years. 19% grads go on to further study within 1 year. 17% grads pursue law degrees. 13% grads pursue business degrees. 6% grads pursue medical degrees. **Faculty:** Student/faculty ratio 11:1. 860 full-time faculty, 95% hold PhDs, 19% are members of minority groups, 41% are women.

ACADEMICS

Degrees: Bachelor's; Doctoral degree—other; Doctoral degree—professional practice; Doctoral degree research/scholarship; Master's; Post-master's certificate. **Classes:** Most classes have 10–19 students. Most lab/discussion sessions have 10–19 students. **Most popular majors:** Economics, General; Finance, General; Biology, General. **Special Study Options:** Accelerated program; Cross-registration; Distance learning; Double major; English as a Second Language (ESL); Exchange student program (domestic); Honors program; Independent study; Internships; Liberal arts/career combination; Student-designed major; Study abroad; Teacher certification program. **Honors programs:** The Gabelli Presidential Scholars Program is an undergraduate academic, merit program that annually awards full-tuition scholarships and fully-funded, GPSP-sponsored summer programs to 15 incoming freshman students. The Presidential Scholars Program works in tandem with the University's rigorous curricula, challenging Scholars over four years through summer programs focusing on service learning, international experience, and professional internships. During the academic year, Scholars interact with one another on a weekly basis. Each Tuesday night the Scholars gather to attend a cultural event, meet to discuss their academic disciplines, discuss career discernment, or to work on special projects. These gatherings are intended to nurture their development into the nation's future leaders. Presidential Scholars are also required to enroll in one of the University's departmental honors programs, all of which require writing an Honors Thesis. Complete information is available: https://www.bc.edu/content/bc-web/academics/sites/gabelli-presidential-scholars-program.html. **Combined degree programs:** BA/MA; BA/MD. **Disability Services offered:** Note-taking services; Reader services; Tape recorders; Tutors. **Career services:** Alumni network; Alumni services; Career assessment; Career/job search classes; Internships; Regional alumni.

FACILITIES

Housing: Apartments for single students; Coed dorms; Special housing for disabled students; Wellness housing; Women's dorms; 95% of campus accessible to physically disabled. **Special Academic Facilities/Equipment:** Boston College opened the Margot Connell Recreation Center, a 244,000 square-foot, four-story Boston gym in the Fall of 2019. In the Fall of 2018, BC opened the Fish Field House which features 115,700 square-foot of indoor practice fields for student athletes. In 2016, BC opened the new three-story McMullen Museum of Art which features permanent and rotating art exhibits open to faculty, students, staff and the public free of charge.

CAMPUS LIFE

Environment: City. **Activities:** Campus Ministries; Choral groups; Concert band; Dance; Drama/theater; International Student Organization; Jazz band; Literary magazine; Marching band; Music ensembles; Musical theater; Pep band; Radio station; Student government; Student newspaper; Student-run film society; Symphony orchestra; Television station; Yearbook. 300 registered organizations, 12 honor societies, 14 religious organizations, on campus. **Athletics (Intercollegiate):** *Men:* baseball, basketball, cross-country, diving, fencing, football, golf, ice hockey, lacrosse, sailing, skiing (downhill/Alpine), soccer, swimming, tennis, track/field (outdoor), track/field (indoor). *Women:* basketball, crew/rowing, cross-country, diving, fencing, field hockey, golf, ice hockey, lacrosse, sailing, skiing (downhill/Alpine), soccer, softball, swimming, tennis, track/field (outdoor), track/field (indoor), volleyball. **On-Campus Highlights:** Alumni Stadium/Conte Forum.

ADMISSIONS

Freshman Academic Profile: 82% in top 10% of high school class, 93% in top 25% of high school class, 98% in top 50% of high school class. 48% from public high schools. **Test Scores:** SAT Math middle 50% range 680–770. SAT EBRW middle 50% range 660–730. ACT middle 50% range 31–34. **Basis for Candidate Selection:** *Very important factors include:* rigor of secondary school record, academic GPA, standardized test scores. *Important factors include:* class rank, application essay, recommendation(s), extracurricular activities, talent/ability, character/personal qualities, alumni/ae relation, religious affiliation/commitment, volunteer work. *Other factors include:* first generation, racial/ethnic status, work experience. **Freshman Admission Requirements:** High school diploma is required and GED is accepted. *Academic units recommended:* 4 English, 4 math, 4 science, 4 science labs, 4 foreign language, 4 social studies, 4 history. **Freshman Admission Statistics:** 35,552 applied, 27% admitted, 24% enrolled. **Transfer Admission Requirements:** High school transcript, college transcript(s), essay or personal statement, standardized test scores, statement of good standing from prior institution(s). Minimum college GPA of 3.0 required. Lowest grade transferable C. **General Admission Information:** Application fee $80. Regular application deadline 1/1. Non-fall registration accepted. Admission may be deferred for a maximum of 1 years.

COSTS AND FINANCIAL AID

Annual tuition $56,780. Room and board $14,826. Required fees $1,130. Average book and supplies expense $1,250. **Required Forms and Deadlines:** Business/Farm Supplement; CSS/Financial Aid PROFILE; FAFSA; Noncustodial PROFILE. **Notification of Awards:** Applicants will be notified of awards on or about 4/1. *Types of Aid: Need-based scholarships/grants:* College/university scholarship or grant aid from institutional funds; Federal Pell; Private scholarships; SEOG; State scholarships/grants. *Loans:* Direct PLUS loans; Direct Subsidized Stafford Loans; Direct Unsubsidized Stafford Loans. **Student Employment:** Federal Work-Study Program available. Institutional employment available. **Financial Aid Statistics:** 87% needy freshmen, 90% needy undergrads receive need-based scholarship or grant aid. 3% freshmen, 2% undergrads receive non-need-based scholarship or grant aid. 91% freshmen, 93% undergrads receive need-based self-help aid. 3% freshmen, 3% undergrads receive athletic scholarships. 68% undergrads receive any aid. 50% undergrads borrow to pay for school. Average cumulative indebtedness $21,421. **Criteria awarding aid:** *Need-based:* Academics. *Non-need-based:* Academics, Athletics, Leadership.

BOSTON CONSERVATORY

8 The Fenway, Boston, MA 02215
Phone: 617-912-9153
E-mail: admissions@bostonconservatory.edu **CEEB Code:** 3084
Fax: 617-247-3159 **Website:** www.bostonconservatory.edu **ACT Code:** 1790

This private school was founded in 1867.

RATINGS
Admissions Selectivity Rating: 73   **Fire Safety Rating:** 60*   **Green Rating:** 60*

STUDENTS AND FACULTY
Enrollment: 565. **Student Body:** 63% female, 37% male, 60% out-of-state, 9% international (26 countries represented). Asian 2%, African American 4%, Caucasian 50%, Hispanic 9%, Native American 0%, Pacific Islander 0%, Two or more races 2%, Race unknown 25%.
Faculty: Student/faculty ratio 4:1. 74 full-time faculty, 0% hold PhDs, 0% are members of minority groups, 0% are women. 0% of classes are taught by teaching assistants.

ACADEMICS
Degrees: Bachelor's; Master's; Post-bachelor's certificate; Post-master's certificate. **Classes:** Most classes have 10–19 students. **Special Study Options:** Cross-registration; Double major; English as a Second Language (ESL); Independent study; Teacher certification program. **Career services:** Alumni services; Career assessment; Career/job search classes; Internships.

FACILITIES
Housing: Coed dorms; Women's dorms. **Campus network:** 100% of classrooms, 100% of dorms, 100% of student union, 100% of libraries, 100% of dining areas, 100% of common outdoor areas, have wireless network access.

CAMPUS LIFE
Activities: International Student Organization; Literary magazine; Student government; Student newspaper. 11 registered organizations, 1 honor societies, 1 religious organizations, on campus.

ADMISSIONS
Basis for Candidate Selection: *Very important factors include:* recommendation(s), talent/ability, character/personal qualities. *Important factors include:* rigor of secondary school record, class rank, academic GPA, application essay, level of applicant's interest. *Other factors include:* interview, extracurricular activities. **Freshman Admission Requirements:** High school diploma is required and GED is accepted. *Academic units required:* 4 English, 3 math, 2 science, 2 foreign language, 2 social studies, 2 history. **Freshman Admission Statistics:** 1,216 applied, 46% admitted, 33% enrolled. **Transfer Admission Requirements:** High school transcript, college transcript(s), essay or personal statement. Minimum college GPA of 2.5 required. Lowest grade transferable C. **General Admission Information:** Application fee $110. Priority deadline 12/15. Non-fall registration accepted.

COSTS AND FINANCIAL AID

Required Forms and Deadlines: FAFSA. **Notification of Awards:** Applicants will be notified of awards on or about 4/1. **Types of Aid:** *Need-based scholarships/grants:* College/university scholarship or grant aid from institutional funds; Federal Pell; Private scholarships; SEOG; State scholarships/grants. *Loans:* Direct PLUS loans; Direct Subsidized Stafford Loans; Direct Unsubsidized Stafford Loans. **Student Employment:** Federal Work-Study Program available. Institutional employment available. **Financial Aid Statistics:** 75% needy freshmen, 90% needy undergrads receive need-based scholarship or grant aid. 10% freshmen, 7% undergrads receive non-need-based scholarship or grant aid. 90% freshmen, 89% undergrads receive need-based self-help aid. 0% freshmen, 0% undergrads receive athletic scholarships. 61% undergrads borrow to pay for school. Average cumulative indebtedness $49,000. **Criteria awarding aid:** *Need-based:* Music/drama. *Non-need-based:* Music/drama.

BOSTON UNIVERSITY

233 Bay State Road, Boston, MA 02215
Phone: 617-353-2300 **Financial Aid Phone:** 617-353-4176
E-mail: admissions@bu.edu; intadmis@bu.edu **CEEB Code:** 3087
Website: www.bu.edu **ACT Code:** 1794

This private school was founded in 1839. It has a 134 acre campus.

RATINGS

Admissions Selectivity Rating: 96   **Fire Safety Rating:** 95   **Green Rating:** 92

STUDENTS AND FACULTY

Enrollment: 16,891. **Student Body:** 59% female, 41% male, 72% out-of-state, 22% international (125 countries represented). Asian 17%, African American 4%, Caucasian 36%, Hispanic 12%, Native American <1%, Pacific Islander <1%, Two or more races 4%, Race unknown 4%.
Retention and Graduation: 94% freshmen return for sophomore year. 84% freshmen graduate within 4 years. 88% freshmen graduate within 6 years. 19% grads go on to further study within 1 year. 16% grads pursue arts and sciences degrees. 1% grads pursue law degrees. 1% grads pursue business degrees. 1% grads pursue medical degrees. **Faculty:** Student/faculty ratio 10:1. 1,893 full-time faculty, 91% hold PhDs, 17% are members of minority groups, 44% are women. 6% of classes are taught by teaching assistants.

ACADEMICS

Degrees: Bachelor's; Certificate; Doctoral degree—professional practice; Doctoral degree research/scholarship; Master's; Post-bachelor's certificate; Post-master's certificate. **Classes:** Most classes have 10–19 students. Most lab/discussion sessions have 20–29 students. **Most popular majors:** Business Administration and Management, General; Communication and Media Studies; Economics, General. **Special Study Options:** Accelerated program; Cooperative education program; Cross-registration; Distance learning; Double major; Dual enrollment; English as a Second Language (ESL); Exchange student program (domestic); Honors program; Independent study; Internships; Liberal arts/career combination; Student-designed major; Study abroad; Teacher certification program. **Honors programs:** Kilachand Honors College for undergraduates, Questrom School of Business Honors Program, CAS Honors in the Major Program. **Combined degree programs:** BA/MA; BA/MD. **Disability Services offered:** Note-taking services; Reader services; Tape recorders; Tutors. **Career services:** Career assessment; Career/job search classes; Internships.

FACILITIES

Housing: Apartments for single students; Coed dorms; Cooperative housing; Special housing for disabled students; Theme housing; Wellness housing; Women's dorms 95%; of campus accessible to physically disabled. **Special Academic Facilities/Equipment:** Center for Computational Science, Center for Advanced Biotechnology, Center for Photonics Research, art galleries, planetarium, commercial TV station, National Public Radio station, 20th century archives, professional theatre and theatre company, Center for Remote Sensing, Geddes Language Laboratory, speech, language and hearing clinic, Culinary Center, Metcalf Center for Science and Engineering, Tsai Performance Center, College of Communication Multimedia Lab, Engineering

Product Innovation Center (EPIC), Joan & Edgar Booth Theatre, BUildLab student innovation center, Kilachand Center for Integrated Life Sciences & Engineering, and Yawkey Center for Student Services.

CAMPUS LIFE

Environment: Metropolis. **Activities:** Campus Ministries; Choral groups; Concert band; Dance; Drama/theater; International Student Organization; Jazz band; Literary magazine; Marching band; Model UN; Music ensembles; Musical theater; Opera; Pep band; Radio station; Student government; Student newspaper; Student-run film society; Symphony orchestra; Television station; Yearbook. 450 registered organizations, 10 honor societies, 19 religious organizations, 8 fraternities, 13 sororities, on campus. **Athletics (Intercollegiate):** *Men:* basketball, crew/rowing, cross-country, diving, golf, ice hockey, soccer, swimming, tennis, track/field (outdoor), track/field (indoor), wrestling. *Women:* basketball, crew/rowing, cross-country, diving, field hockey, golf, ice hockey, lacrosse, soccer, softball, swimming, tennis, track/field (outdoor), track/field (indoor). **On-Campus Highlights:** George Sherman Student Union. **Environmental Initiatives:** Climate Action Plan http://www.bu.edu/climateactionplan/.

ADMISSIONS

Freshman Academic Profile: Average high school GPA 3.7. 64% in top 10% of high school class, 92% in top 25% of high school class, 100% in top 50% of high school class. 61% from public high schools. **Test Scores:** SAT Math middle 50% range 690–790. SAT EBRW middle 50% range 650–720. ACT middle 50% range 30–34. **Basis for Candidate Selection:** *Very important factors include:* rigor of secondary school record. *Important factors include:* class rank, academic GPA, application essay, standardized test scores, recommendation(s), extracurricular activities, character/personal qualities, alumni/ae relation. *Other factors include:* first generation, geographical residence, state residency, racial/ethnic status, volunteer work, work experience. **Freshman Admission Requirements:** High school diploma is required and GED is accepted. *Academic units required:* 4 English, 3 math, 3 science, 3 science labs, 2 foreign language, 3 social studies. *Academic units recommended:* 4 English, 4 math, 4 science, 4 science labs, 4 foreign language, 4 social studies. **Freshman Admission Statistics:** 62,224 applied, 19% admitted, 27% enrolled. **Transfer Admission Requirements:** High school transcript, college transcript(s), essay or personal statement, standardized test scores, statement of good standing from prior institution(s). Minimum college GPA of 3.5 required. Lowest grade transferable C. **General Admission Information:** Application fee $80. Regular application deadline 1/4. Non-fall registration accepted. Admission may be deferred for a maximum of 1 year.

COSTS AND FINANCIAL AID

Annual tuition $54,720. Room and board $16,160. Required fees $1,172. Average book and supplies expense $1,000. **Required Forms and Deadlines:** CSS/Financial Aid PROFILE; FAFSA; Noncustodial PROFILE. **Notification of Awards:** Applicants will be notified of awards on a rolling basis beginning 4/1. **Types of Aid:** *Need-based scholarships/grants:* College/university scholarship or grant aid from institutional funds; Federal Pell; Private scholarships; SEOG; State scholarships/grants. *Loans:* Direct PLUS loans; Direct Subsidized Stafford Loans; Direct Unsubsidized Stafford Loans. **Student Employment:** Federal Work-Study Program available. Institutional employment available. **Financial Aid Statistics:** 99% needy freshmen, 98% needy undergrads receive need-based scholarship or grant aid. 24% freshmen, 19% undergrads receive non-need-based scholarship or grant aid. 75% freshmen, 75% undergrads receive need-based self-help aid. 2% freshmen, 2% undergrads receive athletic scholarships. 53% freshmen, 55% undergrads receive any aid. 46% undergrads borrow to pay for school. Average cumulative indebtedness $40,349. **Criteria awarding aid:** *Need-based:* Academics, Alumni affiliation, Art, Leadership, Minority status, Music/drama, Religious affiliation. *Non-need-based:* Academics, Alumni affiliation, Art, Athletics, Leadership, Music/drama, Religious affiliation, State/district residency.

BOWDOIN COLLEGE

5000 College Station, Brunswick, ME 04011-8441
Phone: 207-725-3100 **Financial Aid Phone:** (207) 725-3146
E-mail: admissions@bowdoin.edu **CEEB Code:** 3089
Fax: 207-725-3101 **Website:** www.bowdoin.edu **ACT Code:** 1636

This private school was founded in 1794. It has a 207 acre campus.

RATINGS
Admissions Selectivity Rating: 98   **Fire Safety Rating:** 95   **Green Rating:** 97

STUDENTS AND FACULTY
Enrollment: 1,825. **Student Body:** 51% female, 49% male, 89% out-of-state, 6% international (42 countries represented). Asian 8%, African American 8%, Caucasian 61%, Hispanic 10%, Native American <1%, Pacific Islander <1%, Two or more races 6%, Race unknown 1%.
Retention and Graduation: 98% freshmen return for sophomore year. 88% freshmen graduate within 4 years. 17% grads go on to further study within 1 year. 12% grads pursue arts and sciences degrees. 2% grads pursue law degrees. 1% grads pursue business degrees. 2% grads pursue medical degrees. **Faculty:** Student/faculty ratio 9:1. 199 full-time faculty, 100% hold PhDs, 16% are members of minority groups, 55% are women. 0% of classes are taught by teaching assistants.

ACADEMICS
Degrees: Bachelor's. **Classes:** Most classes have 10–19 students. Most lab/discussion sessions have 10–19 students. **Most popular majors:** Mathematics, General; Economics, General; Political Science and Government, General.
Special Study Options: Accelerated program; Double major; Exchange student program (domestic); Independent study; Liberal arts/career combination; Student-designed major; Study abroad; Teacher certification program.
Combined degree programs: BA/JD; BA/MEng. **Disability Services offered:** Note-taking services; Reader services; Tape recorders; Tutors. **Career services:** Alumni network; Alumni services; Career assessment; Career/job search classes; Internships; Regional alumni.

FACILITIES
Housing: Apartments for single students; Coed dorms; Wellness housing; 72% of campus accessible to physically disabled. **Special Academic Facilities/Equipment:** Bowdoin College Museum of Art; Peary-MacMillan Arctic Museum and Arctic Studies Center; Roux Center for the Environment; Massachusetts Hall (the oldest college building in Maine, which now houses the English department); Pickard Theater, Wish Theater (black box); Visual Arts Center (includes the William Pierce Art Library and Kresge Auditorium); Harvey-Dow Gibson Hall of Music (houses electronic music labs); Hawthorne-Longfellow Library (houses the Media Commons, telepresence classroom, the College test center, and the George J. Mitchell Department of Special Collections and Archives); Chapel (houses the Joseph McKeen Center for the Common Good and the THRIVE program); Studzinski Recital Hall; Schwartz Outdoor Leadership Center; Kanbar Hall (houses the Center for Learning and Teaching, which includes the Baldwin Program for Academic Development, the Quantitative Reasoning Program, the Writing Project, English for Multi-Lingual Speakers, and Writing and Rhetoric); Edwards Center for Art and Dance; Harriet Beecher Stowe House, Schiller Coastal Studies Center; Bowdoin Scientific Station on Kent Island; Crafts Center; Druckenmiller Hall (includes the Hatch Science Library); Searles Science Building (houses the Machine Shop and a Class 1000 clean room).

CAMPUS LIFE
Environment: Village. **Activities:** Choral groups; Concert band; Dance; Drama/theater; International Student Organization; Jazz band; Literary magazine; Model UN; Music ensembles; Musical theater; Radio station; Student government; Student newspaper; Student-run film society; Symphony orchestra. 130 registered organizations, 1 honor societies, 6 religious organizations, on campus. **Athletics (Intercollegiate):** *Men:* baseball, basketball, cross-country, diving, football, golf, ice hockey, lacrosse, sailing, skiing (Nordic/cross-country), soccer, squash, swimming, tennis, track/field (outdoor), track/field (indoor). *Women:* basketball, cross-country, diving, field hockey, golf, ice hockey, lacrosse, rugby, sailing, skiing (Nordic/cross-country), soccer, softball, squash, swimming, tennis, track/field (outdoor), track/field (indoor), volleyball.

On-Campus Highlights: Bowdoin College Museum of Art. **Environmental Initiatives:** Bowdoin has committed to becoming a carbon-neutral campus by 2020 and provided a detailed Climate Action Plan to help achieve the goal. As part of this plan, Bowdoin installed a co-generation system at its campus steam plant, along with a 1,920-square-foot solar hot water system, and most recently installed a 1.2-megawatt solar power complex that went live in fall 2014 and includes approximately 4,420 solar panels roof-mounted on three major athletic buildings along with a 654-kW ground-mount installation on three acres owned by the College at the former Naval Air Station Brunswick. These panels collectively provided about 8% of the College's electricity load annually. Combined with the electricity produced by the co-generation turbine at the heating plant, approximately 14% of the College's electricity is now generated on site from renewable or efficient sources.

ADMISSIONS
Freshman Academic Profile: 80% in top 10% of high school class, 96% in top 25% of high school class, 100% in top 50% of high school class. 53% from public high schools. **Test Scores:** SAT Math middle 50% range 650–770. SAT EBRW middle 50% range 650–740. ACT middle 50% range 30–34. **Basis for Candidate Selection:** *Very important factors include:* rigor of secondary school record, class rank, academic GPA, application essay, recommendation(s), extracurricular activities, talent/ability, character/personal qualities. *Important factors include:* standardized test scores. *Other factors include:* interview, first generation, alumni/ae relation, geographical residence, state residency, racial/ethnic status, volunteer work, work experience. **Freshman Admission Requirements:** High school diploma is required and GED is not accepted. *Academic units recommended:* 4 English, 4 math, 4 science, 3 science labs, 4 foreign language, 4 social studies. **Freshman Admission Statistics:** 9,081 applied, 10% admitted, 55% enrolled. **Transfer Admission Requirements:** High school transcript, college transcript(s), essay or personal statement, statement of good standing from prior institution(s). Minimum college GPA of 3.0 required. Lowest grade transferable C-. **General Admission Information:** Application fee $65. Regular application deadline 1/1. Admission may be deferred for a maximum of 12 months.

COSTS AND FINANCIAL AID
Annual tuition $53,418. Room and board $14,698. Required fees $504. Average book and supplies expense $840. **Required Forms and Deadlines:** Business/Farm Supplement; CSS/Financial Aid PROFILE; FAFSA; Noncustodial PROFILE. **Types of Aid:** *Need-based scholarships/grants:* College/university scholarship or grant aid from institutional funds; Federal Pell; Private scholarships; SEOG; State scholarships/grants. *Loans:* Direct Subsidized Stafford Loans; Direct Unsubsidized Stafford Loans. **Student Employment:** Federal Work-Study Program available. Institutional employment available. **Financial Aid Statistics:** 100% needy freshmen, 100% needy undergrads receive need-based scholarship or grant aid. 0% freshmen, 0% undergrads receive non-need-based scholarship or grant aid. 98% freshmen, 99% undergrads receive need-based self-help aid. 0% freshmen, 0% undergrads receive athletic scholarships. 52% freshmen, 50% undergrads receive any aid. 27% undergrads borrow to pay for school. Average cumulative indebtedness $25,482. **Criteria awarding aid:** *Non-need-based:* Academics, Leadership.

BOWLING GREEN STATE UNIVERSITY

200 University Hall, Bowling Green, OH 43403-0085
Phone: 419-372-2478 **Financial Aid Phone:** 419-372-2651
E-mail: choosebgsu@bgsu.edu **CEEB Code:** 1069
Fax: 419-372-6955 **Website:** http://www.bgsu.edu **ACT Code:** 3240

This public school was founded in 1910. It has a 1338 acre campus.

RATINGS
Admissions Selectivity Rating: 81   **Fire Safety Rating:** 91   **Green Rating:** 98

STUDENTS AND FACULTY
Enrollment: 13,772. **Student Body:** 56% female, 44% male, 11% out-of-state, 2% international (43 countries represented). Asian 1%, African American 8%, Caucasian 79%, Hispanic 4%, Native American <1%, Pacific Islander <1%, Two or more races 3%, Race unknown 2%.
Retention and Graduation: 77% freshmen return for sophomore year. 42% freshmen graduate within 4 years. 60% freshmen graduate within 6 years. **Faculty:** Student/faculty ratio 17:1. 760 full-time faculty, 79% hold PhDs, 17% are members of minority groups, 50% are women.

ACADEMICS

Degrees: Bachelor's; Certificate; Doctoral degree research/scholarship; Master's; Post-bachelor's certificate; Post-master's certificate. **Classes:** Most classes have 20–29 students. **Most popular majors:** Education/Teaching of Individuals in Early Childhood Special Education Programs; Biology/Biological Sciences, General; Psychology, General. **Special Study Options:** Accelerated program; Cooperative education program; Cross-registration; Distance learning; Double major; Dual enrollment; English as a Second Language (ESL); Exchange student program (domestic); Honors program; Independent study; Internships; Liberal arts/career combination; Student-designed major; Study abroad; Teacher certification program. **Honors programs:** http://www.bgsu.edu/honors-college.html. **Disability Services offered:** Note-taking services; Reader services; Tape recorders; Tutors. **Career services:** Alumni network; Alumni services; Career assessment; Career/job search classes; Internships; Regional alumni.

FACILITIES

Housing: Apartments for single students; Coed dorms; Fraternity/sorority housing; Special housing for disabled students. **Campus network:** 40% of classrooms, 0% of dorms, 90% of student union, 100% of libraries, 50% of dining areas, 10% of common outdoor areas, have wireless network access.

CAMPUS LIFE

Environment: Town. **Activities:** Campus Ministries; Choral groups; Concert band; Dance; Drama/theater; International Student Organization; Jazz band; Literary magazine; Marching band; Model UN; Music ensembles; Musical theater; Opera; Pep band; Radio station; Student government; Student newspaper; Student-run film society; Symphony orchestra; Television station; Yearbook. 335 registered organizations, 12 honor societies, 14 religious organizations, 20 fraternities, 17 sororities, on campus. **Athletics (Intercollegiate):** *Men:* baseball, basketball, cross-country, football, golf, ice hockey, soccer. *Women:* basketball, cross-country, golf, gymnastics, soccer, softball, swimming, tennis, track/field (outdoor), track/field (indoor), volleyball. **On-Campus Highlights:** Bowen Thompson Student Union. **Environmental Initiatives:** Completion of the Climate Action Plan by the ACUPCC Working Group, under the leadership of the Office of Campus Sustainability, its public filing in January, 2015 and immediate reduction in electricity conservation through several very large LED lighting conversion projects.

ADMISSIONS

Freshman Academic Profile: Average high school GPA 3.5. 16% in top 10% of high school class, 42% in top 25% of high school class, 75% in top 50% of high school class. 89% from public high schools. **Test Scores:** SAT Math middle 50% range 510–600. SAT EBRW middle 50% range 500–610. ACT middle 50% range 20–25. **Basis for Candidate Selection:** *Very important factors include:* rigor of secondary school record, academic GPA, standardized test scores. *Important factors include:* class rank. *Other factors include:* application essay, recommendation(s), interview, extracurricular activities, talent/ability, character/personal qualities, first generation, alumni/ae relation, racial/ethnic status, volunteer work, work experience, level of applicant's interest. **Freshman Admission Requirements:** High school diploma is required and GED is accepted. *Academic units recommended:* 4 English, 3 math, 3 science, 2 science labs, 2 foreign language, 3 social studies, 1 visual/performing arts. **Freshman Admission Statistics:** 17,179 applied, 72% admitted, 27% enrolled. Minimum college GPA of 2.5 required. Lowest grade transferable C. **General Admission Information:** Application fee $45. Priority deadline 2/1. Regular application deadline 7/15. Non-fall registration accepted.

COSTS AND FINANCIAL AID

Annual in-state tuition $9,973. Annual out-of-state tuition $17,962. Room and board $10,396. Required fees $2,154. Average book and supplies expense $728. **Required Forms and Deadlines:** FAFSA. **Notification of Awards:** Applicants will be notified of awards on a rolling basis beginning 2/1. **Types of Aid:** *Need-based scholarships/grants:* College/university scholarship or grant aid from institutional funds; Federal Pell; Private scholarships; SEOG; State scholarships/grants. *Loans:* Direct PLUS loans; Direct Subsidized Stafford Loans; Direct Unsubsidized Stafford Loans. **Student Employment:** Federal Work-Study Program available. Institutional employment available. **Financial Aid Statistics:** 88% needy freshmen, 82% needy undergrads receive need-based scholarship or grant aid. 10% freshmen, 9% undergrads receive non-need-based scholarship or grant aid. 75% freshmen, 78% undergrads receive need-based self-help aid. 3% freshmen, 3% undergrads receive athletic scholarships. 95% freshmen, 83% undergrads receive any aid. 74% undergrads borrow to pay for school. Average cumulative indebtedness $30,603. **Criteria awarding aid:** *Need-based:* Academics, Minority status. *Non-need-based:* Academics, Alumni affiliation, Art, Athletics, Leadership, Minority status, Music/drama, State/district residency.

BRADLEY UNIVERSITY

1501 W. Bradley Avenue, Peoria, IL 61625
Phone: 309-677-1000 **Financial Aid Phone:** 309-677-3089
E-mail: admissions@bradley.edu **CEEB Code:** 1070
Fax: 309-677-2797 **Website:** www.bradley.edu **ACT Code:** 960

This private school was founded in 1897. It has a 85 acre campus.

RATINGS

Admissions Selectivity Rating: 84   **Fire Safety Rating:** 97   **Green Rating:** 69

STUDENTS AND FACULTY

Enrollment: 4,598. **Student Body:** 51% female, 49% male, 18% out-of-state, 2% international (38 countries represented). Asian 3%, African American 7%, Caucasian 73%, Hispanic 10%, Native American <1%, Pacific Islander 0%, Two or more races 3%, Race unknown 2%.
Retention and Graduation: 82% freshmen return for sophomore year. 28% freshmen graduate within 4 years. 72% freshmen graduate within 6 years.
Faculty: Student/faculty ratio 12:1. 354 full-time faculty, 81% hold PhDs, 20% are members of minority groups, 42% are women. 0% of classes are taught by teaching assistants.

ACADEMICS

Degrees: Bachelor's; Doctoral degree—professional practice; Master's; Post-bachelor's certificate; Post-master's certificate. **Classes:** Most classes have 10–19 students. **Most popular majors:** Engineering; Health Professions And Related Programs; Business, Management, Marketing, And Related Support Services. **Special Study Options:** Accelerated program; Cooperative education program; Distance learning; Double major; Honors program; Independent study; Internships; Student-designed major; Study abroad; Teacher certification program. **Honors programs:** The Honors Program is structured so that students majoring in any department are eligible to participate. The program builds progressively through a student's four years, beginning with special honors sections of Bradley Core Curriculum courses and leading to interdisciplinary seminars and possibilities for independent research. Students in the Honors Program also may select housing in a dedicated honors floor within one of our residence halls. **Disability Services offered:** Note-taking services; Reader services; Tutors. **Career services:** Alumni network; Alumni services; Career assessment; Career/job search classes; Internships; Regional alumni.

FACILITIES

Housing: Apartments for single students; Coed dorms; Fraternity/sorority housing; Theme housing; 75% of campus accessible to physically disabled. **Special Academic Facilities/Equipment:** Caterpillar Global Communication Center, Hartmann Center Gallery, Heuser Art Center Gallery, Hayden-Clark Alumni Center, Athletics Hall of Fame in Renaissance Coliseum. **Campus network:** 100% of classrooms, 100% of dorms, 100% of student union, 100% of libraries, 100% of dining areas, 100% of common outdoor areas, have wireless network access.

CAMPUS LIFE

Environment: City. **Activities:** Campus Ministries; Choral groups; Concert band; Dance; Drama/theater; International Student Organization; Jazz band; Literary magazine; Music ensembles; Musical theater; Pep band; Radio station; Student government; Student newspaper; Student-run film society; Symphony orchestra; Television station. 245 registered organizations, 33 honor societies, 12 religious organizations, 15 fraternities, 12 sororities, on campus. **Athletics (Intercollegiate):** *Men:* baseball, basketball, cross-country, golf, soccer, tennis. *Women:* basketball, cross-country, golf, softball, tennis, track/field (outdoor), track/field (indoor), volleyball. **On-Campus Highlights:** Markin Family Student Recreation Center

ADMISSIONS

Freshman Academic Profile: Average high school GPA 3.8. 32% in top 10% of high school class, 64% in top 25% of high school class, 92% in top 50% of high school class. 85% from public high schools. **Test Scores:** SAT Math middle 50% range 540–650. SAT EBRW middle 50% range 550–640. ACT middle 50% range 23–28. **Basis for Candidate Selection:** *Very important factors include:* rigor of secondary school record, academic GPA. *Important factors include:* class rank, standardized test scores. *Other factors include:*

application essay, recommendation(s), interview, extracurricular activities, talent/ability, character/personal qualities, first generation, alumni/ae relation, geographical residence, racial/ethnic status, volunteer work, work experience, level of applicant's interest. **Freshman Admission Requirements:** High school diploma is required and GED is accepted. *Academic units required:* 4 English, 3 math, 2 science, 2 science labs, 2 social studies. *Academic units recommended:* 5 English, 4 math, 3 science, 3 science labs, 2 foreign language, 3 social studies, 2 history. **Freshman Admission Statistics:** 11,209 applied, 67% admitted, 15% enrolled. **Transfer Admission Requirements:** College transcript(s). statement of good standing from prior institution(s). Minimum college GPA of 2.0 required. Lowest grade transferable C. **General Admission Information:** Priority deadline 12/1. Non-fall registration accepted. Admission may be deferred for a maximum of 12 months.

COSTS AND FINANCIAL AID

Annual tuition $34,200. Room and board $10,940. Required fees $410. Average book and supplies expense $1,200. **Required Forms and Deadlines:** FAFSA. **Notification of Awards:** Applicants will be notified of awards on a rolling basis beginning 11/15. *Types of Aid: Need-based scholarships/grants:* College/university scholarship or grant aid from institutional funds; Federal Pell; Private scholarships; SEOG; State scholarships/grants; United Negro College Fund. *Loans:* Direct PLUS loans; Direct Subsidized Stafford Loans; Direct Unsubsidized Stafford Loans. **Student Employment:** Federal Work-Study Program available. Institutional employment available. **Financial Aid Statistics:** 100% needy freshmen, 96% needy undergrads receive need-based scholarship or grant aid. 11% freshmen, 11% undergrads receive non-need-based scholarship or grant aid. 80% freshmen, 81% undergrads receive need-based self-help aid. 2% freshmen, 3% undergrads receive athletic scholarships. **Criteria awarding aid:** *Need-based:* Academics. *Non-need-based:* Academics, Alumni affiliation, Art, Athletics, Leadership, Minority status, Music/drama.

BRANDEIS UNIVERSITY

415 South St., Waltham, MA 02454-9110
Phone: 781-736-3500 **Financial Aid Phone:** (781) 736-3700
E-mail: admissions@brandeis.edu **CEEB Code:** 3092
Fax: 781-736-3536 **Website:** http://www.brandeis.edu/ **ACT Code:** 1802

This private school was founded in 1948. It has a 235 acre campus.

RATINGS

Admissions Selectivity Rating: 95   **Fire Safety Rating:** 98   **Green Rating:** 80

STUDENTS AND FACULTY

Enrollment: 3,678. **Student Body:** 61% female, 39% male, 70% out-of-state, 20% international (56 countries represented). Asian 14%, African American 5%, Caucasian 46%, Hispanic 8%, Native American <1%, Pacific Islander <1%, Two or more races 4%, Race unknown 2%.
Retention and Graduation: 93% freshmen return for sophomore year. 81% freshmen graduate within 4 years. 87% freshmen graduate within 6 years. 36% grads go on to further study within 1 year. 15% grads pursue arts and sciences degrees. 2% grads pursue law degrees. 6% grads pursue business degrees. 6% grads pursue medical degrees. **Faculty:** Student/faculty ratio 10:1. 369 full-time faculty, 94% hold PhDs, 12% are members of minority groups, 46% are women.

ACADEMICS

Degrees: Bachelor's; Doctoral degree research/scholarship; Master's; Post-master's certificate. **Classes:** Most classes have 10–19 students. **Most popular majors:** Biology/Biological Sciences, General; Economics, General; Business/Commerce, General. **Special Study Options:** Accelerated program; Cross-registration; Distance learning; Double major; Exchange student program (domestic); Independent study; Internships; Student-designed major; Study abroad; Teacher certification program. **Combined degree programs:** BA/MA. **Disability Services offered:** Note-taking services; Tape recorders. **Career services:** Alumni network; Alumni services; Career assessment; Career/job search classes; Internships; Regional alumni.

FACILITIES

Housing: Apartments for single students; Coed dorms; Special housing for disabled students; 78% of campus accessible to physically disabled. **Special Academic Facilities/Equipment:** Rose Art Museum, Spingold Theater. **Campus network:** 100% of classrooms, 100% of dorms, 100% of student union, 100% of libraries, 100% of dining areas, 80% of common outdoor areas, have wireless network access.

CAMPUS LIFE

Environment: Metropolis. **Activities:** Campus Ministries; Choral groups; Dance; Drama/theater; International Student Organization; Jazz band; Literary magazine; Model UN; Music ensembles; Musical theater; Pep band; Radio station; Student government; Student newspaper; Student-run film society; Symphony orchestra; Television station; Yearbook. 224 registered organizations, 3 honor societies, 15 religious organizations, on campus.
Athletics (Intercollegiate): *Men:* baseball, basketball, cross-country, diving, fencing, soccer, tennis, track/field (outdoor), track/field (indoor), wrestling. *Women:* basketball, cheerleading, cross-country, diving, fencing, soccer, softball, tennis, track/field (outdoor), track/field (indoor), volleyball, wrestling. **On-Campus Highlights:** Shapiro Science Center. **Environmental Initiatives:** In 2018, Brandeis will burn approximately of 160,000 gallons of renewable fuel oil in its central heating plant. The fuel is made from cooking oil from hundreds of restaurants, schools, hotels and food manufacturers throughout New England. The renewable fuel will displace up to 10% of our natural gas use during winter. If this pilot goes well, we hope to increase the amount we use in the future.

ADMISSIONS

Freshman Academic Profile: Average high school GPA 3.8. 56% in top 10% of high school class, 83% in top 25% of high school class, 97% in top 50% of high school class. 65% from public high schools. **Test Scores:** SAT Math middle 50% range 690–790. SAT EBRW middle 50% range 660–730. ACT middle 50% range 30–33. **Basis for Candidate Selection:** *Very important factors include:* rigor of secondary school record, class rank, academic GPA, character/personal qualities. *Important factors include:* application essay, recommendation(s), extracurricular activities, talent/ability. *Other factors include:* standardized test scores, interview, first generation, alumni/ae relation, geographical residence, state residency, religious affiliation/commitment, racial/ethnic status, volunteer work, work experience, level of applicant's interest. **Freshman Admission Requirements:** High school diploma is required and GED is accepted. *Academic units recommended:* 4 English, 4 math, 4 science, 2 science labs, 4 foreign language, 4 social studies. **Freshman Admission Statistics:** 11,343 applied, 30% admitted, 25% enrolled. **Transfer Admission Requirements:** High school transcript, college transcript(s), essay or personal statement, standardized test scores, statement of good standing from prior institution(s). Minimum college GPA of 3.20 required. Lowest grade transferable C-. **General Admission Information:** Application fee $80. Regular application deadline 1/1. Non-fall registration accepted. Admission may be deferred for a maximum of 1 year.

COSTS AND FINANCIAL AID

Annual tuition $55,340. Room and board $16,080. Required fees $2,596. Average book and supplies expense $1,000. **Required Forms and Deadlines:** CSS/Financial Aid PROFILE; FAFSA; Noncustodial PROFILE. **Types of Aid:** *Need-based scholarships/grants:* College/university scholarship or grant aid from institutional funds; Federal Pell; Private scholarships; SEOG; State scholarships/grants. *Loans:* Direct PLUS loans; Direct Subsidized Stafford Loans; Direct Unsubsidized Stafford Loans. **Student Employment:** Federal Work-Study Program available. Institutional employment available. **Financial Aid Statistics:** 96% needy freshmen, 95% needy undergrads receive need-based scholarship or grant aid. 10% freshmen, 6% undergrads receive non-need-based scholarship or grant aid. 86% freshmen, 92% undergrads receive need-based self-help aid. 0% freshmen, 0% undergrads receive athletic scholarships. 65% freshmen, 67% undergrads receive any aid. 46% undergrads borrow to pay for school. Average cumulative indebtedness $32,158. **Criteria awarding aid:** *Non-need-based:* Academics.

BRENAU UNIVERSITY

500 Washington St SE, Gainesville, GA 30501
Phone: 770-534-6100 **Financial Aid Phone:** 770-534-6152
E-mail: admissions@brenau.edu **CEEB Code:** 5066
Fax: 770-538-4306 **Website:** www.brenau.edu **ACT Code:** 800

This private school was founded in 1878. It has a 56 acre campus.

RATINGS
Admissions Selectivity Rating: 78   **Fire Safety Rating:** 99   **Green Rating:** 64

STUDENTS AND FACULTY
Enrollment: 1,671. **Student Body:** 91% female, 9% male, 5% out-of-state, 6% international (15 countries represented). Asian 2%, African American 29%, Caucasian 46%, Hispanic 11%, Native American <1%, Pacific Islander 0%, Two or more races 2%, Race unknown 4%.
Retention and Graduation: 55% freshmen return for sophomore year. 41% freshmen graduate within 4 years. 47% freshmen graduate within 6 years. **Faculty:** Student/faculty ratio 9:1. 68 full-time faculty, 84% hold PhDs, 16% are members of minority groups, 68% are women. 0% of classes are taught by teaching assistants.

ACADEMICS
Degrees: Associate; Bachelor's; Certificate; Doctoral degree—other; Doctoral degree—professional practice; Master's; Post-bachelor's certificate; Post-master's certificate. **Classes:** Most classes have 10–19 students. Most lab/discussion sessions have 10–19 students. **Most popular majors:** Elementary Education and Teaching; Nursing Practice; Health and Medical Administrative Services, Other. **Special Study Options:** Cross-registration; Distance learning; Double major; Dual enrollment; Honors program; Independent study; Internships; Liberal arts/career combination; Study abroad; Teacher certification program; Weekend college. **Honors programs:** The Honors Program at the Women's College of Brenau University begins in the freshman year and is followed throughout the student's entire college career at Brenau. Special classes reserved for honors students are taught in an enriched manner, affording these students an approach to their general education courses which enables them to study these subjects at an advanced level. **Disability Services offered:** Reader services; Tutors. **Career services:** Alumni network; Alumni services; Career assessment; Career/job search classes; Internships.

FACILITIES
Housing: Apartments for single students; Fraternity/sorority housing; Men's dorms; Special housing for disabled students; Women's dorms; 90% of campus accessible to physically disabled. **Special Academic Facilities/Equipment:** Simmons Art Gallery, Wages House, Whitepath House, Natatorium Physical Fitness Center, Leo Castelli Art Gallery, Northeast Georgia History Center.

CAMPUS LIFE
Environment: Town. **Activities:** Campus Ministries; Choral groups; Concert band; Dance; Drama/theater; International Student Organization; Jazz band; Literary magazine; Music ensembles; Musical theater; Opera; Pep band; Radio station; Student government; Student newspaper; Yearbook. 46 registered organizations, 20 honor societies, 2 religious organizations, 8 sororities, on campus. **Athletics (Intercollegiate):** *Women:* basketball, cross-country, soccer, softball, swimming, tennis, volleyball. **On-Campus Highlights:** Pearce Auditorium.

ADMISSIONS
Freshman Academic Profile: Average high school GPA 3.5. 14% in top 10% of high school class, 37% in top 25% of high school class, 72% in top 50% of high school class. **Test Scores:** SAT Math middle 50% range 440–550. SAT EBRW middle 50% range 460–560. ACT middle 50% range 16–23. **Basis for Candidate Selection:** *Very important factors include:* academic GPA. *Important factors include:* rigor of secondary school record. *Other factors include:* class rank, application essay, standardized test scores, recommendation(s), interview, extracurricular activities, talent/ability, character/personal qualities, first generation, alumni/ae relation, volunteer work, work experience. **Freshman Admission Requirements:** High school diploma is required and GED is accepted. *Academic units required:* 4 English, 4 math, 3 science, 2 foreign language, 3 social studies. **Freshman Admission Statistics:** 1,912 applied, 64% admitted, 13% enrolled. **Transfer Admission Requirements:** College transcript(s). Minimum college GPA of 2.0 required. Lowest grade transferable C. **General Admission Information:** Priority deadline 5/1. Non-fall registration accepted. Admission may be deferred for a maximum of 1 year.

COSTS AND FINANCIAL AID
Annual tuition $29,370. Room and board $12,500. Required fees $1,714. Average book and supplies expense $1,300. **Required Forms and Deadlines:** FAFSA; State aid form. **Notification of Awards:** Applicants will be notified of awards on a rolling basis beginning 1/15. **Types of Aid:** *Need-based scholarships/grants:* College/university scholarship or grant aid from institutional funds; Federal Pell; Private scholarships; SEOG; State scholarships/grants. *Loans:* Direct PLUS loans; Direct Subsidized Stafford Loans; Direct Unsubsidized Stafford Loans. **Student Employment:** Federal Work-Study Program available. Institutional employment available. **Financial Aid Statistics:** 100% needy freshmen, 98% needy undergrads receive need-based scholarship or grant aid. 11% freshmen, 9% undergrads receive non-need-based scholarship or grant aid. 75% freshmen, 81% undergrads receive need-based self-help aid. 2% freshmen, 1% undergrads receive athletic scholarships. 93.78% freshmen, 90.88% undergrads receive any aid. 81% undergrads borrow to pay for school. Average cumulative indebtedness $35,719. **Criteria awarding aid:** *Need-based:* Minority status. *Non-need-based:* Academics, Art, Athletics, Leadership, Music/drama.

BRESCIA UNIVERSITY

717 Frederica Street, Owensboro, KY 42301-3023
Phone: 270-686-4241 **Financial Aid Phone:** 1-877-BRESCIA
E-mail: admissions@brescia.edu **CEEB Code:** 1071
Fax: 270-686-4314 **Website:** www.brescia.edu **ACT Code:** 14980

This private school, affiliated with the Roman Catholic Church, was founded in 1950. It has a 9 acre campus.

RATINGS
Admissions Selectivity Rating: 84   **Fire Safety Rating:** 94   **Green Rating:** 60*

STUDENTS AND FACULTY
Enrollment: 1,007. **Student Body:** 74% female, 26% male, 29% out-of-state, 1% international (17 countries represented). Asian <1%, African American 13%, Caucasian 69%, Hispanic 3%, Native American 1%, Pacific Islander 1%, Two or more races 0%, Race unknown 12%.
Retention and Graduation: 64% freshmen return for sophomore year.
Faculty: Student/faculty ratio 13:1. 37 full-time faculty, 70% hold PhDs, 16% are members of minority groups, 51% are women. 0% of classes are taught by teaching assistants.

ACADEMICS
Degrees: Associate; Bachelor's; Master's; Post-bachelor's certificate. **Classes:** Most classes have fewer than 10 students. Most lab/discussion sessions have fewer than 10 students. **Most popular majors:** Social Work, Other; Elementary Education and Teaching; General Studies. **Special Study Options:** Accelerated program; Cross-registration; Distance learning; Double major; English as a Second Language (ESL); Exchange student program (domestic); Honors program; Independent study; Internships; Liberal arts/career combination; Study abroad; Teacher certification program; Weekend college. **Honors programs:** The Honors Program at Brescia University is intended to challenge and recognize talented and motivated students. Through the program, students will participate in a range of multidisciplinary experiences aimed at extending their inteelectual capabilities and developing public speaking and research skills needed for personal enrichment and/or graduate study. **Disability Services offered:** Note-taking services; Tape recorders; Tutors. **Career services:** Alumni services; Career assessment; Career/job search classes; Internships.

FACILITIES
Housing: Apartments for single students; Coed dorms; Men's dorms; Special housing for disabled students; Theme housing; Women's dorms; 87% of campus accessible to physically disabled. **Special Academic Facilities/Equipment:** Art Gallery, computer labs, campus center, greenhouse, observatory, science building. **Campus network:** 100% of classrooms, 100% of dorms, 100% of student union, 100% of libraries, 100% of dining areas, 20% of common outdoor areas, have wireless network access.

CAMPUS LIFE
Environment: City. **Activities:** Campus Ministries; Choral groups; Drama/theater; International Student Organization; Literary magazine; Pep band; Student government; Student newspaper. 22 registered organizations, 3 honor societies, 2 religious organizations, on campus. **Athletics (Intercollegiate):** *Men:* baseball, basketball, cross-country, golf, soccer, tennis, track/field (outdoor). *Women:* basketball, cross-country, golf, soccer, softball, tennis, track/field (outdoor), volleyball. **Environmental Initiatives:** Recycling.

ADMISSIONS

Freshman Academic Profile: Average high school GPA 3.3. 61% from public high schools. **Test Scores:** SAT Math middle 50% range 400–580. SAT EBRW middle 50% range 440–480. ACT middle 50% range 20–25. **Basis for Candidate Selection:** *Very important factors include:* academic GPA, standardized test scores. **Freshman Admission Requirements:** High school diploma is required and GED is accepted. *Academic units recommended:* 4 English, 3 math, 2 science, 2 foreign language, 2 social studies, 2 history, 2 academic electives. **Freshman Admission Statistics:** 3,757 applied, 49% admitted, 9% enrolled. **Transfer Admission Requirements:** High school transcript, college transcript(s), Minimum college GPA of 2.0 required. Lowest grade transferable C. **General Admission Information:** Application fee $25. Non-fall registration accepted. Admission may be deferred for a maximum of 1 year.

COSTS AND FINANCIAL AID

Annual tuition $19,500. Room and board $8,000. Required fees $490. **Required Forms and Deadlines:** FAFSA. **Notification of Awards:** Applicants will be notified of awards on a rolling basis beginning 3/1. **Types of Aid:** *Need-based scholarships/grants:* College/university scholarship or grant aid from institutional funds; Federal Pell; Private scholarships; SEOG; State scholarships/grants. *Loans:* Direct PLUS loans; Direct Subsidized Stafford Loans; Direct Unsubsidized Stafford Loans. **Student Employment:** Federal Work-Study Program available. Institutional employment available. **Financial Aid Statistics:** needy freshmen, needy undergrads receive need-based scholarship or grant aid. freshmen, undergrads receive non-need-based scholarship or grant aid. freshmen, undergrads receive need-based self-help aid. 0% freshmen, 0% undergrads receive athletic scholarships. 99% freshmen, 98% undergrads receive any aid. **Criteria awarding aid:** *Non-need-based:* Academics, Alumni affiliation, Art, Athletics, Minority status, Music/drama, Religious affiliation, State/district residency.

BREVARD COLLEGE

One Brevard College Drive, Brevard, NC 28712
Phone: 828-884-8300 **Financial Aid Phone:** 828-884-8261
E-mail: admissions@brevard.edu **CEEB Code:** 5067
Fax: 828-884-3790 **ACT Code:** 3074

This private school, affiliated with the Methodist Church, was founded in 1853. It has a 120 acre campus.

RATINGS

Admissions Selectivity Rating: 86   **Fire Safety Rating:** 81   **Green Rating:** 60*

STUDENTS AND FACULTY

Enrollment: 696. **Student Body:** 42% female, 58% male, 42% out-of-state, 6% international (17 countries represented). Asian 1%, African American 10%, Caucasian 71%, Hispanic 2%, Native American 1%, Pacific Islander <1%, Two or more races 3%, Race unknown 6%.
Retention and Graduation: 59% freshmen return for sophomore year.
Faculty: Student/faculty ratio 11:1. 51 full-time faculty, 84% hold PhDs, 0% are members of minority groups, 47% are women. 0% of classes are taught by teaching assistants.

ACADEMICS

Degrees: Bachelor's. **Classes:** Most classes have fewer than 10 students. Most lab/discussion sessions have 10–19 students. **Most popular majors:** Multi-/Interdisciplinary Studies, Other; Parks, Recreation and Leisure Studies; Business Administration and Management, General. **Special Study Options:** Double major; Dual enrollment; Honors program; Independent study; Internships; Student-designed major; Study abroad; Teacher certification program.
Honors programs: To complete the Honors Program, students must take a minimum of 19 s.h. in honors courses during the typical 4-year period of their enrollment at Brevard College. These hours include honors enrichment seminar courses, honors-designated sections of courses, and a senior project. The only coursework of these 19 hours that is not directly attributable to core or major requirements is 4 s.h. of ENR (Enrichment) seminars. **Disability Services offered:** Note-taking services; Reader services; Tape recorders; Tutors. **Career services:** Career assessment; Career/job search classes; Internships.

FACILITIES

Housing: Coed dorms; Men's dorms; Special housing for disabled students; Women's dorms; 100% of campus accessible to physically disabled. **Special**

Academic Facilities/Equipment: Porter Center for Performing Arts; Sims Art Center; Morrison Playhouse; Fitness Appraisal Laboratory; Academic Enrichment Center; Center for Career, Service, and Learning; Medical Services Building; Stamey Counseling Center; 24-hour computer lab; Library with wireless connection; Moore Science Annex Building. **Campus network:** 100% of classrooms, 100% of dorms, 100% of student union, 100% of libraries, 100% of dining areas, 100% of common outdoor areas, have wireless network access.

CAMPUS LIFE

Environment: Village. **Activities:** Campus Ministries; Choral groups; Concert band; Dance; Drama/theater; Jazz band; Literary magazine; Music ensembles; Musical theater; Opera; Pep band; Student government; Student newspaper; Yearbook. 32 registered organizations, 3 honor societies, 1 religious organizations, on campus. **Athletics (Intercollegiate):** *Men:* baseball, basketball, cheerleading, cross-country, cycling, football, golf, soccer, tennis, track/field (outdoor). *Women:* basketball, cheerleading, cross-country, cycling, golf, soccer, softball, tennis, track/field (outdoor), volleyball. **On-Campus Highlights:** Food Court & Dining Hall. **Environmental Initiatives:** Campus-wide recycling program.

ADMISSIONS

Freshman Academic Profile: Average high school GPA 3.1. 6% in top 10% of high school class, 24% in top 25% of high school class, 62% in top 50% of high school class. 82% from public high schools. **Test Scores:** SAT Math middle 50% range 420–530. SAT EBRW middle 50% range 420–520. ACT middle 50% range 17–22. **Basis for Candidate Selection:** *Very important factors include:* rigor of secondary school record, academic GPA, level of applicant's interest. *Important factors include:* class rank, application essay, interview, extracurricular activities, talent/ability, character/personal qualities, volunteer work. *Other factors include:* standardized test scores, recommendation(s), alumni/ae relation, work experience. **Freshman Admission Requirements:** High school diploma is required and GED is accepted. *Academic units recommended:* 4 English, 3 math, 3 science, 1 science labs, 2 foreign language, 4 social studies, 1 history, 4 academic electives. **Freshman Admission Statistics:** 2,858 applied, 43% admitted, 18% enrolled. **Transfer Admission Requirements:** High school transcript, college transcript(s), essay or personal statement, standardized test scores, statement of good standing from prior institution(s). Minimum college GPA of 2.0 required. Lowest grade transferable C-. **General Admission Information:** Non-fall registration accepted. Admission may be deferred for a maximum of one semester.

COSTS AND FINANCIAL AID

Required Forms and Deadlines: FAFSA. **Notification of Awards:** Applicants will be notified of awards on a rolling basis beginning 2/1. **Types of Aid:** *Need-based scholarships/grants:* College/university scholarship or grant aid from institutional funds; Federal Pell; Private scholarships; SEOG; State scholarships/grants. *Loans:* Direct PLUS loans; Direct Subsidized Stafford Loans; Direct Unsubsidized Stafford Loans. **Student Employment:** Federal Work-Study Program available. Institutional employment available. **Financial Aid Statistics:** 82% needy freshmen, 80% needy undergrads receive need-based scholarship or grant aid. 100% freshmen, 60% undergrads receive non-need-based scholarship or grant aid. 82% freshmen, 80% undergrads receive need-based self-help aid. 7% freshmen, 7% undergrads receive athletic scholarships. **Criteria awarding aid:** *Non-need-based:* Academics, Art, Athletics, Leadership, Music/drama, Religious affiliation, State/district residency.

BRIAR CLIFF UNIVERSITY

3303 Rebecca Street, Sioux City, IA 51104
Phone: 712-279-5200 **Financial Aid Phone:** 712-279-5239
E-mail: admissions@briarcliff.edu **CEEB Code:** 1846
Fax: 712-279-1632 **Website:** www.briarcliff.edu **ACT Code:** 1276

This private school, affiliated with the Roman Catholic Church, was founded in 1930. It has a 70 acre campus.

RATINGS

Admissions Selectivity Rating: 81   **Fire Safety Rating:** 88   **Green Rating:** 69

STUDENTS AND FACULTY

Enrollment: 972. **Student Body:** 55% female, 45% male, 40% out-of-state, 5% international (16 countries represented). Asian 1%, African American 9%, Caucasian 66%, Hispanic 15%, Native American 2%, Pacific Islander 1%, Two or more races 1%, Race unknown 0%.

Retention and Graduation: 79% freshmen return for sophomore year. 21% grads go on to further study within 1 year. 16% grads pursue arts and sciences degrees. 1% grads pursue law degrees. 2% grads pursue business degrees. 0% grads pursue medical degrees. **Faculty:** Student/faculty ratio 14:1. 64 full-time faculty, 73% hold PhDs, 8% are members of minority groups, 45% are women. 0% of classes are taught by teaching assistants.

ACADEMICS
Degrees: Associate; Bachelor's; Doctoral degree—professional practice; Master's; Post-bachelor's certificate; Post-master's certificate. **Classes:** Most classes have 10–19 students. Most lab/discussion sessions have 10–19 students. **Most popular majors:** Registered Nursing/Registered Nurse; Biology/Biological Sciences, General; Business Administration and Management, General. **Special Study Options:** Accelerated program; Cross-registration; Distance learning; Double major; Dual enrollment; Honors program; Independent study; Internships; Liberal arts/career combination; Student-designed major; Study abroad; Teacher certification program; Weekend college. **Honors programs:** Briar Cliff's Honor Program involves elements of leadership, service and character as well as academics, and is led by the Student Honors Executive Board. In addition to talking Honors courses with small enrollments, Honors students perform individual research work with faculty at the upper levels. **Combined degree programs:** BA/MA. **Disability Services offered:** Note-taking services; Reader services; Tape recorders; Tutors. **Career services:** Alumni services; Career assessment; Career/job search classes; Internships.

FACILITIES
Housing: Coed dorms; Theme housing; 90% of campus accessible to physically disabled. **Special Academic Facilities/Equipment:** Nursing Simulation Lab Integrated Multimedia Center Human Anatomy Lab Clausen Art Gallery. **Campus network:** 100% of classrooms, 100% of dorms, 100% of student union, 100% of libraries, 100% of dining areas, 100% of common outdoor areas, have wireless network access.

CAMPUS LIFE
Environment: City. **Activities:** Campus Ministries; Choral groups; Dance; Drama/theater; International Student Organization; Jazz band; Literary magazine; Music ensembles; Radio station; Student government; Student newspaper; Television station. 35 registered organizations, 3 honor societies, 2 religious organizations, on campus. **Athletics (Intercollegiate): Men:** baseball, basketball, cross-country, football, golf, soccer, tennis, track/field (outdoor), track/field (indoor), wrestling. **Women:** basketball, cross-country, golf, soccer, softball, tennis, track/field (outdoor), track/field (indoor), volleyball. **On-Campus Highlights:** Java City. **Environmental Initiatives:** Recycling.

ADMISSIONS
Freshman Academic Profile: Average high school GPA 3.2. 11% in top 10% of high school class, 25% in top 25% of high school class, 72% in top 50% of high school class. 86% from public high schools. **Test Scores:** SAT Math middle 50% range 440–540. SAT EBRW middle 50% range 420–490. ACT middle 50% range 18–24. **Basis for Candidate Selection:** *Very important factors include:* academic GPA, standardized test scores. *Important factors include:* rigor of secondary school record, talent/ability, character/personal qualities. *Other factors include:* class rank, application essay, recommendation(s), extracurricular activities. **Freshman Admission Requirements:** High school diploma is required and GED is accepted. *Academic units required:* 4 English, 4 math, 3 science, 2 foreign language, 3 social studies. **Freshman Admission Statistics:** 1,491 applied, 60% admitted, 24% enrolled. **Transfer Admission Requirements:** High school transcript, college transcript(s), statement of good standing from prior institution(s). Minimum college GPA of 2.0 required. Lowest grade transferable D. **General Admission Information:** Application fee $20. Non-fall registration accepted.

COSTS AND FINANCIAL AID
Annual tuition $28,650. Room and board $9,086. Required fees $1,136. Average book and supplies expense $1,339. **Required Forms and Deadlines:** FAFSA; State aid form. **Notification of Awards:** Applicants will be notified of awards on a rolling basis beginning 2/1. **Types of Aid:** *Need-based scholarships/ grants:* College/university scholarship or grant aid from institutional funds; Federal Pell; Private scholarships; SEOG; State scholarships/grants. *Loans:* Direct PLUS loans; Direct Subsidized Stafford Loans; Direct Unsubsidized Stafford Loans. **Student Employment:** Federal Work-Study Program available. Institutional employment available. **Financial Aid Statistics:** 99% needy freshmen, 99% needy undergrads receive need-based scholarship or grant aid. 24% freshmen, 24% undergrads receive non-need-based scholarship or grant aid. 82% freshmen, 86% undergrads receive need-based self-help aid. 75% freshmen, 57% undergrads receive athletic scholarships. 100% freshmen, 97% undergrads receive any aid. 92% undergrads borrow to pay for school.

Average cumulative indebtedness $29,484. **Criteria awarding aid:** *Need-based:* Academics, Minority status. *Non-need-based:* Academics, Alumni affiliation, Art, Athletics, Leadership, Music/drama, Religious affiliation, State/district residency.

BRIDGEWATER COLLEGE

402 East College Street, Bridgewater, VA 22812-1599
Phone: 540-828-5375 **Financial Aid Phone:** 540-828-5376
E-mail: admissions@bridgewater.edu **CEEB Code:** 5069
Fax: 540-828-5481 **Website:** www.bridgewater.edu **ACT Code:** 4342

This private school, affiliated with the Church of Brethren, was founded in 1880. It has a 300 acre campus.

RATINGS
Admissions Selectivity Rating: 80   **Fire Safety Rating:** 97   **Green Rating:** 60*

STUDENTS AND FACULTY
Enrollment: 1,709. **Student Body:** 55% female, 45% male, 23% out-of-state, 2% international (14 countries represented). Asian 1%, African American 15%, Caucasian 65%, Hispanic 7%, Native American <1%, Pacific Islander <1%, Two or more races 6%, Race unknown 3%.
Retention and Graduation: 72% freshmen return for sophomore year. 53% freshmen graduate within 4 years. 59% freshmen graduate within 6 years. 18% grads go on to further study within 1 year. 29% grads pursue arts and sciences degrees. 5% grads pursue law degrees. 5% grads pursue business degrees. 2% grads pursue medical degrees. **Faculty:** Student/faculty ratio 13:1. 116 full-time faculty, 84% hold PhDs, 14% are members of minority groups, 52% are women. 0% of classes are taught by teaching assistants.

ACADEMICS
Degrees: Bachelor's; Master's. **Classes:** Most classes have 10–19 students. Most lab/discussion sessions have 10–19 students. **Most popular majors:** Sports, Kinesiology, and Physical Education/Fitness, General; Business Administration and Management, General; Psychology, General. **Special Study Options:** Distance learning; Double major; Honors program; Independent study; Internships; Liberal arts/career combination; Study abroad; Teacher certification program. **Honors programs:** The Flory Honors Program consists of stimulating and interesting opportunities both inside and outside the classroom. In the curricular element of the program, students take a minimum of five honors designated courses, plus an honors project and capstone seminar, for a total of seven courses. Program participants may also work with faculty to build an additional honors component to a non-honors course. **Combined degree programs:** BA/MA. **Disability Services offered:** Note-taking services; Reader services; Tutors. **Career services:** Alumni network; Alumni services; Career assessment; Internships; Regional alumni.

FACILITIES
Housing: Apartments for single students; Coed dorms; Special housing for disabled students; Women's dorms; 95% of campus accessible to physically disabled. **Campus network:** 100% of classrooms, 100% of dorms, 100% of student union, 100% of libraries, 100% of dining areas, 90% of common outdoor areas, have wireless network access.

CAMPUS LIFE
Environment: Village. **Activities:** Campus Ministries; Choral groups; Concert band; Dance; Drama/theater; International Student Organization; Jazz band; Literary magazine; Music ensembles; Pep band; Radio station; Student government; Student newspaper. 86 registered organizations, 10 honor societies, 12 religious organizations, on campus. **Athletics (Intercollegiate): Men:** baseball, basketball, cross-country, equestrian sports, football, golf, soccer, tennis, track/field (outdoor), track/field (indoor). **Women:** basketball, cross-country, equestrian sports, field hockey, lacrosse, soccer, softball, swimming, tennis, track/field (outdoor), track/field (indoor), volleyball. **On-Campus Highlights:** Forrer Learning Commons. **Environmental Initiatives:** Energy and water conservation.

ADMISSIONS
Freshman Academic Profile: Average high school GPA 3.6. 14% in top 10% of high school class, 40% in top 25% of high school class, 74% in top 50% of high school class. 94% from public high schools. **Test Scores:** SAT Math middle 50% range 470–580. SAT EBRW middle 50% range 490–600. ACT middle 50% range 18–25. **Basis for Candidate Selection:** *Very important*

factors include: rigor of secondary school record, academic GPA, standardized test scores. *Important factors include:* recommendation(s), interview, extracurricular activities, talent/ability, character/personal qualities. *Other factors include:* volunteer work, work experience, level of applicant's interest. **Freshman Admission Requirements:** High school diploma is required and GED is accepted. *Academic units required:* 4 English, 3 math, 3 science, 3 science labs, 4 academic electives, 3 unit from above areas or other academic areas. *Academic units recommended:* 4 English, 3 math, 3 science, 3 science labs, 2 foreign language, 4 academic electives, 3 unit from above areas or other academic areas. **Freshman Admission Statistics:** 6,279 applied, 67% admitted, 12% enrolled. **Transfer Admission Requirements:** High school transcript, college transcript(s), standardized test scores, statement of good standing from prior institution(s). Minimum college GPA of 2.2 required. Lowest grade transferable C. **General Admission Information:** Regular application deadline 5/1. Non-fall registration accepted. Admission may be deferred for a maximum of 1 year.

COSTS AND FINANCIAL AID

Annual tuition $36,800. Room and board $13,360. Required fees $920. Average book and supplies expense $1,150. **Required Forms and Deadlines:** FAFSA; State aid form. **Notification of Awards:** Applicants will be notified of awards on a rolling basis beginning 2/1. **Types of Aid:** *Need-based scholarships/grants:* College/university scholarship or grant aid from institutional funds; Federal Pell; Private scholarships; SEOG; State scholarships/grants. *Loans:* Direct PLUS loans; Direct Subsidized Stafford Loans; Direct Unsubsidized Stafford Loans. **Student Employment:** Federal Work-Study Program available. Institutional employment available. **Financial Aid Statistics:** 100% needy freshmen, 100% needy undergrads receive need-based scholarship or grant aid. 100% freshmen, 100% undergrads receive non-need-based scholarship or grant aid. 69% freshmen, 71% undergrads receive need-based self-help aid. 0% freshmen, 0% undergrads receive athletic scholarships. 100% freshmen, 100% undergrads receive any aid. 80% undergrads borrow to pay for school. Average cumulative indebtedness $31,871. **Criteria awarding aid:** *Non-need-based:* Academics, Minority status, Music/drama, Religious affiliation, State/district residency.

BRIDGEWATER STATE UNIVERSITY

131 Summer Street, Bridgewater, MA 02325
Phone: 508-531-1237 **Financial Aid Phone:** 508-531-1341
E-mail: admission@bridgew.edu **CEEB Code:** 3517
Fax: 508-531-1746 **Website:** www.bridgew.edu **ACT Code:** 1900

This public school was founded in 1840. It has a 235 acre campus.

RATINGS
Admissions Selectivity Rating: 75   **Fire Safety Rating:** 60*   **Green Rating:** 60*

STUDENTS AND FACULTY
Enrollment: 9,312. **Student Body:** 59% female, 41% male, 4% out-of-state, <1% international (37 countries represented). Asian 2%, African American 9%, Caucasian 75%, Hispanic 7%, Native American <1%, Pacific Islander <1%, Two or more races 5%, Race unknown 1%.
Retention and Graduation: 78% freshmen return for sophomore year. 33% freshmen graduate within 4 years. 59 16% grads go on to further study within 1 year. 2% grads pursue law degrees. 1% grads pursue business degrees. **Faculty:** Student/faculty ratio 18:1. 355 full-time faculty, 94% hold PhDs, 17% are members of minority groups, 54% are women. 0% of classes are taught by teaching assistants.

ACADEMICS
Degrees: Bachelor's; Master's; Post-bachelor's certificate; Post-master's certificate. **Classes:** Most classes have 20–29 students. Most lab/discussion sessions have 10–19 students. **Most popular majors:** Business/Commerce, General; Elementary Education and Teaching; Psychology, General. **Special Study Options:** Accelerated program; Cross-registration; Distance learning; Double major; Dual enrollment; English as a Second Language (ESL); Exchange student program (domestic); Honors program; Independent study; Internships; Study abroad; Teacher certification program; Weekend college. **Disability Services offered:** Note-taking services; Reader services; Tape recorders; Tutors. **Career services:** Alumni services; Career assessment; Career/job search classes; Internships.

FACILITIES
Housing: Apartments for single students; Coed dorms; Special housing for disabled students; Theme housing; 95% of campus accessible to physically disabled. **Special Academic Facilities/Equipment:** On-campus school, children's physical development clinic, human performance lab, TV studio, observatory, flight simulators, electron microscope, Moakley Technology Center.

CAMPUS LIFE
Environment: Village. **Activities:** Campus Ministries; Choral groups; Concert band; Dance; Drama/theater; International Student Organization; Jazz band; Literary magazine; Music ensembles; Musical theater; Pep band; Radio station; Student government; Student newspaper; Student-run film society. 67 registered organizations, 11 honor societies, 1 religious organizations, on campus. **Athletics (Intercollegiate):** *Men:* baseball, basketball, cross-country, football, soccer, swimming, tennis, track/field (outdoor), wrestling. *Women:* basketball, cross-country, field hockey, lacrosse, soccer, softball, swimming, tennis, track/field (outdoor), volleyball.

ADMISSIONS
Freshman Academic Profile: Average high school GPA 3.1. **Test Scores:** SAT Math middle 50% range 490–570. SAT EBRW middle 50% range 500–580. ACT middle 50% range 19–25. **Basis for Candidate Selection:** *Very important factors include:* rigor of secondary school record, academic GPA. *Important factors include:* standardized test scores. *Other factors include:* application essay, recommendation(s), extracurricular activities, talent/ability, character/personal qualities, first generation, alumni/ae relation, racial/ethnic status, volunteer work, work experience, level of applicant's interest. **Freshman Admission Requirements:** High school diploma is required and GED is accepted. *Academic units required:* 4 English, 3 math, 3 science, 2 science labs, 2 foreign language, 1 social studies, 1 history, 2 academic electives. *Academic units recommended:* 4 English, 3 math, 3 science, 2 science labs, 2 foreign language, 1 social studies, 1 history, 2 academic electives. **Freshman Admission Statistics:** 6,806 applied, 90% admitted, 25% enrolled. **Transfer Admission Requirements:** college transcript(s), essay or personal statement, Minimum college GPA of 2.0 required. Lowest grade transferable C-. **General Admission Information:** Application fee $50. Priority deadline 2/15. Non-fall registration accepted. Admission may be deferred for a maximum of 1 year.

COSTS AND FINANCIAL AID
Annual in-state tuition $910. Annual out-of-state tuition $7,050. Room and board $12,750. Required fees $9,457. Average book and supplies expense $800. **Required Forms and Deadlines:** FAFSA. **Types of Aid:** *Need-based scholarships/grants:* College/university scholarship or grant aid from institutional funds; Federal Pell; Private scholarships; SEOG; State scholarships/grants. *Loans:* Direct PLUS loans; Direct Subsidized Stafford Loans; Direct Unsubsidized Stafford Loans. **Student Employment:** Federal Work-Study Program available. Institutional employment available. **Financial Aid Statistics:** 82% needy freshmen, 74% needy undergrads receive need-based scholarship or grant aid. 17% freshmen, 16% undergrads receive non-need-based scholarship or grant aid. 91% freshmen, 94% undergrads receive need-based self-help aid. 0% freshmen, 0% undergrads receive athletic scholarships. 79% undergrads borrow to pay for school. Average cumulative indebtedness $31,349. **Criteria awarding aid:** *Non-need-based:* Academics, Leadership, Minority status, State/district residency.

BRIERCREST COLLEGE AND SEMINARY

510 College Drive, Caronport, SK S0H 0S0
Phone: 1-800-667-5199
E-mail: admissions@briercrest.ca
Fax: 800-667-5500 **Website:** www.briercrest.ca

This private school was founded in 1935. It has a 160 acre campus.

RATINGS
Admissions Selectivity Rating: 60*   **Fire Safety Rating:** 60*   **Green Rating:** 60*

STUDENTS AND FACULTY
Enrollment: 632. **Student Body:** 4% out-of-state.
Faculty: Student/faculty ratio 18:1. 31 full-time faculty, 0% hold PhDs, 0% are members of minority groups, 0% are women.

ACADEMICS
Degrees: Associate; Bachelor's; Certificate; Master's; Post-bachelor's certificate. **Special Study Options:** Distance learning; English as a Second Language (ESL); External degree program; Independent study; Internships; Liberal arts/career combination; Study abroad. **Career services:** Alumni services; Career assessment.

FACILITIES

Housing: Apartments for single students; Coed dorms; Fraternity/sorority housing; Special housing for disabled students; Special housing for international students; Theme housing; Wellness housing.

CAMPUS LIFE

Environment: Rural. **Activities:** Campus Ministries; Choral groups; Concert band; Dance; Drama/theater; International Student Organization; Jazz band; Literary magazine; Music ensembles; Musical theater; Radio station; Student government; Student newspaper; Symphony orchestra; Yearbook. **Athletics (Intercollegiate):** *Men:* basketball, ice hockey, volleyball. *Women:* basketball, volleyball.

ADMISSIONS

Basis for Candidate Selection: *Very important factors include:* academic GPA, application essay, recommendation(s), character/personal qualities, religious affiliation/commitment, level of applicant's interest. *Other factors include:* standardized test scores, interview, volunteer work. **Freshman Admission Requirements:** High school diploma is required and GED is accepted. **Transfer Admission Requirements:** High school transcript, college transcript(s), essay or personal statement, **General Admission Information:** Application fee $50. Priority deadline 4/1. Non-fall registration accepted. Admission may be deferred for a maximum of 1 year.

COSTS AND FINANCIAL AID

Annual tuition $7,470. Room and board $2,810. Required fees $250. Average book and supplies expense $500. **Required Forms and Deadlines:** Institution's own financial aid form; State aid form. **Types of Aid:** *Need-based scholarships/ grants:* College/university scholarship or grant aid from institutional funds; Private scholarships.

BRIGHAM YOUNG UNIVERSITY (UT)

A-153 ASB, Provo, UT 84602-1110
Phone: 801-422-2507 **Financial Aid Phone:** (801) 378-4104
E-mail: admissions@byu.edu **CEEB Code:** 4019
Fax: 801-422-0005 **Website:** www.byu.edu **ACT Code:** 4266

This private school, affiliated with the Church of Jesus Christ of Latter-day Saints, was founded in 1875. It has a 557 acre campus.

RATINGS

Admissions Selectivity Rating: 91   **Fire Safety Rating:** 76   **Green Rating:** 60*

STUDENTS AND FACULTY

Enrollment: 31,292. **Student Body:** 50% female, 50% male, 68% out-of-state, 4% international (121 countries represented). Asian 2%, African American <1%, Caucasian 80%, Hispanic 7%, Native American <1%, Pacific Islander 1%, Two or more races 4%, Race unknown 1%.
Retention and Graduation: 90% freshmen return for sophomore year. 22% freshmen graduate within 4 years. 78% freshmen graduate within 6 years.
Faculty: Student/faculty ratio 20:1. 1,268 full-time faculty, 92% hold PhDs, 6% are members of minority groups, 21% are women.

ACADEMICS

Degrees: Bachelor's; Doctoral degree—professional practice; Doctoral degree research/scholarship; Master's; Post-bachelor's certificate; Post-master's certificate. **Classes:** Most classes have 20–29 students. **Most popular majors:** Business/Commerce, General; Elementary Education and Teaching; Exercise Physiology and Kinesiology. **Special Study Options:** Accelerated program; Cooperative education program; Cross-registration; Distance learning; Double major; English as a Second Language (ESL); External degree program; Honors program; Independent study; Internships; Liberal arts/career combination; Study abroad; Teacher certification program. **Honors programs:** The Honors Program, participation in which is open to all BYU students, complements the university's expansive educational agenda by providing the benefits of a small liberal arts learning community. These benefits include offering small classes with high-quality teaching and learning that challenge students to reach their highest potential; fostering a spirit of ongoing inquiry that includes undergraduate research in a mentored environment; and underscoring the importance of combining personal excellence, faithful discipleship, and

meaningful service. **Combined degree programs:** BA/JD; BA/MA. **Disability Services offered:** Note-taking services; Reader services; Tape recorders; Tutors.

FACILITIES

Housing: Apartments for married students; Apartments for single students; Men's dorms; Special housing for disabled students; Women's dorms; 97% of campus accessible to physically disabled. **Special Academic Facilities/ Equipment:** Art, peoples/cultures, life science, and earth science museums, film studio, on-campus nursery school, language research center, seismography equipment, electron microscope.

CAMPUS LIFE

Environment: City. **Activities:** Choral groups; Concert band; Dance; Drama/ theater; Jazz band; Literary magazine; Marching band; Music ensembles; Musical theater; Opera; Pep band; Radio station; Student government; Student newspaper; Student-run film society; Symphony orchestra; Television station. 390 registered organizations, 22 honor societies, 25 religious organizations, on campus. **Athletics (Intercollegiate):** *Men:* baseball, basketball, cheerleading, cross-country, diving, football, golf, swimming, tennis, track/field (outdoor), track/field (indoor), volleyball. *Women:* basketball, cheerleading, cross-country, diving, golf, gymnastics, soccer, softball, swimming, tennis, track/field (outdoor), track/field (indoor), volleyball. **On-Campus Highlights:** Monte L. Bean Life Science Museum.

ADMISSIONS

Freshman Academic Profile: Average high school GPA 3.9. **Test Scores:** SAT Math middle 50% range 600–710. SAT EBRW middle 50% range 610–710. ACT middle 50% range 26–31. **Basis for Candidate Selection:** *Very important factors include:* rigor of secondary school record, academic GPA, application essay, standardized test scores, recommendation(s), extracurricular activities, talent/ ability, character/personal qualities, religious affiliation/commitment, volunteer work, work experience. *Important factors include:* first generation, racial/ethnic status. *Other factors include:* level of applicant's interest. **Freshman Admission Requirements:** High school diploma is required and GED is accepted. *Academic units recommended:* 4 English, 4 math, 3 science, 2 foreign language, 2 history. **Freshman Admission Statistics:** 10,500 applied, 67% admitted, 81% enrolled. **Transfer Admission Requirements:** College transcript(s), essay or personal statement, interview. Minimum college GPA of 3.0 required. Lowest grade transferable C–. **General Admission Information:** Application fee $35. Regular application deadline 12/15. Non-fall registration accepted.

COSTS AND FINANCIAL AID

Annual tuition $5,790. Room and board $7,915. Average book and supplies expense $872. **Required Forms and Deadlines:** FAFSA. **Types of Aid:** *Need-based scholarships/grants:* College/university scholarship or grant aid from institutional funds; Federal Pell; Private scholarships; State scholarships/ grants. *Loans:* Direct PLUS loans; Direct Subsidized Stafford Loans; Direct Unsubsidized Stafford Loans. **Financial Aid Statistics:** 51% needy freshmen, 79% needy undergrads receive need-based scholarship or grant aid. 63% freshmen, 53% undergrads receive non-need-based scholarship or grant aid. 25% freshmen, 22% undergrads receive need-based self-help aid. 2% freshmen, 2% undergrads receive athletic scholarships. 53% freshmen, 64% undergrads receive any aid. 24% undergrads borrow to pay for school. Average cumulative indebtedness $14,672. **Criteria awarding aid:** *Need-based:* Academics, Alumni affiliation, Minority status, Religious affiliation *Non-need-based:* Academics, Art, Athletics, Leadership, Minority status, Music/drama, Religious affiliation, State/ district residency.

BRIGHAM YOUNG UNIVERSITY—HAWAII

BYU- Hawaii # 1973, Laie, HI 96762
Phone: (808) 675- 3738 **Financial Aid Phone:** 808-293-3530
E-mail: admissions@byuh.edu **CEEB Code:** 4106
Fax: 808-675-3741 **ACT Code:** 899

This private school, affiliated with the Church of Jesus Christ of Latter-day Saints, was founded in 1955. It has a 60 acre campus.

RATINGS

Admissions Selectivity Rating: 90   **Fire Safety Rating:** 73   **Green Rating:** 60*

STUDENTS AND FACULTY

Enrollment: 2,312. **Student Body:** 56% female, 44% male, 68% out-of-state, 44% international (67 countries represented). Asian 22%, African American 1%, Caucasian 29%, Hispanic 2%, Native American 1%, Race unknown 1%.

Retention and Graduation: 57% freshmen return for sophomore year.
Faculty: Student/faculty ratio 14:1. 122 full-time faculty, 80% hold PhDs, 23% are members of minority groups, 21% are women. 0% of classes are taught by teaching assistants.

ACADEMICS

Degrees: Bachelor's. **Classes:** Most classes have 10–19 students. Most lab/discussion sessions have 10–19 students. **Most popular majors:** Information Science/Studies; International Business/Trade/Commerce; Intercultural/Multicultural and Diversity Studies. **Special Study Options:** Accelerated program; Cooperative education program; Distance learning; English as a Second Language (ESL); Exchange student program (domestic); Honors program; Independent study; Internships; Student-designed major; Teacher certification program. **Honors programs:** The University Honors Program is open to all interested students who feel they are capable of accepting the challenge of an Honors Education. You will have the opportunity to participate in a stimulating class environment with other top students and the best professors. **Disability Services offered:** Note-taking services; Reader services; Tape recorders; Tutors.

FACILITIES

Housing: Apartments for married students; Men's dorms; Women's dorms; 90% of campus accessible to physically disabled. **Special Academic Facilities/Equipment:** Museum of Natural History Media Lab.

CAMPUS LIFE

Environment: Village. **Activities:** Choral groups; Concert band; Dance; Jazz band; Literary magazine; Music ensembles; Pep band; Student government; Student newspaper; Student-run film society. 52 registered organizations, 3 honor societies, on campus. **Athletics (Intercollegiate):** *Men:* basketball, cross-country, golf, soccer, tennis. *Women:* basketball, cross-country, soccer, softball, tennis, volleyball. **On-Campus Highlights:** Joseph F. Smith Library.

ADMISSIONS

Freshman Academic Profile: Average high school GPA 3.4. **Test Scores:** SAT Math middle 50% range 480–600. SAT EBRW middle 50% range 460–580. ACT middle 50% range 20–27. **Basis for Candidate Selection:** *Very important factors include:* rigor of secondary school record, application essay, standardized test scores, recommendation(s), interview, extracurricular activities, character/personal qualities, geographical residence, religious affiliation/commitment. *Important factors include:* class rank, talent/ability, alumni/ae relation. *Other factors include:* state residency. **Freshman Admission Requirements:** High school diploma is required and GED is not accepted *Academic units recommended:* 4 English, 2 math, 2 science, 2 science labs, 2 foreign language, 2 history. **Freshman Admission Statistics:** 2,078 applied, 19% admitted, 76% enrolled. **Transfer Admission Requirements:** College transcript(s), essay or personal statement, statement of good standing from prior institution(s). Minimum college GPA of 3.0 required. Lowest grade transferable C-. **General Admission Information:** Application fee $30. Regular application deadline 2/15. Non-fall registration accepted. Admission may be deferred for a maximum of 1 semester.

COSTS AND FINANCIAL AID

Annual tuition $3,600. Room and board $5,568. Average book and supplies expense $900. **Required Forms and Deadlines:** FAFSA; Institution's own financial aid form. **Notification of Awards:** Applicants will be notified of awards on or about 6/30. **Types of Aid:** *Need-based scholarships/grants:* College/university scholarship or grant aid from institutional funds; Federal Pell; Private scholarships. **Student Employment:** Institutional employment available. **Financial Aid Statistics:** 88% needy freshmen, 64% needy undergrads receive need-based scholarship or grant aid. 23% freshmen, 41% undergrads receive non-need-based scholarship or grant aid. 70% freshmen, 41% undergrads receive need-based self-help aid. 13% freshmen, 7% undergrads receive athletic scholarships. 70% freshmen, 72% undergrads receive any aid. **Criteria awarding aid:** *Non-need-based:* Academics, Art, Athletics, Leadership, Music/drama, State/district residency.

BROCK UNIVERSITY

500 Glenridge Avenue, St. Catharines, ON L2S 3A1
Phone: 905-688-5550
E-mail: admissns@brocku.ca
Fax: 905-988-5488 **Website:** www.brocku.ca

This public school was founded in 1964. It has a 457 acre campus.

RATINGS
Admissions Selectivity Rating: 60* **Fire Safety Rating:** 85 **Green Rating:** 60*

STUDENTS AND FACULTY
Enrollment: 16,284. **Student Body:** 8% out-of-state, 80 countries represented.
Faculty: Student/faculty ratio 27:1. 577 full-time faculty, 0% hold PhDs, 0% are members of minority groups, 43% are women. 0% of classes are taught by teaching assistants.

ACADEMICS

Degrees: Bachelor's; Certificate; Master's. **Most popular majors:** Education, General; Business/Commerce, General; Health Professions and Related Clinical Sciences, Other. **Special Study Options:** Cooperative education program; Double major; English as a Second Language (ESL); Exchange student program (domestic); Honors program; Internships; Liberal arts/career combination; Student-designed major; Study abroad; Teacher certification program. **Disability Services offered:** Note-taking services; Reader services; Tape recorders; Tutors. **Career services:** Career/job search classes; Internships.

FACILITIES

Housing: Coed dorms; Special housing for disabled students; Women's dorms; 100% of campus accessible to physically disabled. **Special Academic Facilities/Equipment:** Cool Climate Oenology and Viticulture Institute Map Library Intructional Resource Centre Rodman Hall Arts Centre Cypriote Museum. **Campus network:** 100% of classrooms, 100% of dorms, 100% of student union, 100% of libraries, 100% of dining areas, have wireless network access.

CAMPUS LIFE

Environment: City. **Activities:** Campus Ministries; Choral groups; Concert band; Dance; Drama/theater; Literary magazine; Music ensembles; Musical theater; Radio station; Student government; Student newspaper; Student-run film society; Symphony orchestra; Television station; Yearbook. 40 registered organizations, 6 religious organizations, on campus. **Athletics (Intercollegiate):** *Men:* baseball, basketball, cheerleading, crew/rowing, cross-country, curling, fencing, ice hockey, lacrosse, rugby, soccer, squash, swimming, wrestling. *Women:* basketball, cheerleading, crew/rowing, cross-country, curling, fencing, ice hockey, rugby, soccer, swimming, volleyball, wrestling. **On-Campus Highlights:** Residences. **Environmental Initiatives:** Our newest building earned LEED Silver Certification. The energy cost performance is almost 43 per cent better than the Model National Energy Code.

ADMISSIONS

Basis for Candidate Selection: *Very important factors include:* rigor of secondary school record, academic GPA. *Important factors include:* standardized test scores. *Other factors include:* class rank, recommendation(s), talent/ability. **Freshman Admission Requirements:** High school diploma is required and GED is accepted. **Freshman Admission Statistics:** 16,870 applied, admitted, enrolled. **Transfer Admission Requirements:** High school transcript, college transcript(s). **General Admission Information:** Application fee $155. Regular application deadline 4/1.

COSTS AND FINANCIAL AID

Annual in-state tuition $4,852. Room and board $8,215. Average book and supplies expense $900. **Required Forms and Deadlines:** Institution's own financial aid form;. **Types of Aid:** *Need-based scholarships/grants:* College/university scholarship or grant aid from institutional funds. **Student Employment:** Federal Work-Study Program available. Institutional employment available. **Financial Aid Statistics:** 29% needy undergrads receive need-based scholarship or grant aid. freshmen, 0% undergrads receive non-need-based scholarship or grant aid. freshmen, 0% undergrads receive need-based self-help aid. freshmen, 0% undergrads receive athletic scholarships. 39% undergrads receive any aid. **Criteria awarding aid:** *Need-based:* Academics, Athletics, Leadership. *Non-need-based:* Academics, Athletics, Leadership.

BROWN UNIVERSITY

Box 1876, Providence, RI 02912
Phone: 401-863-2378 **Financial Aid Phone:** 401-863-2721
E-mail: admission@brown.edu **CEEB Code:** 3094
Fax: 401-863-9300 **Website:** www.brown.edu **ACT Code:** 3800

This private school was founded in 1764. It has a 146 acre campus.

RATINGS

Admissions Selectivity Rating: 99   **Fire Safety Rating:** 90   **Green Rating:** 89

STUDENTS AND FACULTY

Enrollment: 6,834. **Student Body:** 52% female, 48% male, 95% out-of-state, 11% international (109 countries represented). Asian 17%, African American 7%, Caucasian 43%, Hispanic 11%, Native American <1%, Pacific Islander <1%, Two or more races 6%, Race unknown 5%.
Retention and Graduation: 98% freshmen return for sophomore year. 83% freshmen graduate within 4 years. 96% freshmen graduate within 6 years. 22% grads go on to further study within 1 year. 14% grads pursue arts and sciences degrees. 1% grads pursue law degrees. 1% grads pursue business degrees. 4% grads pursue medical degrees. **Faculty:** Student/faculty ratio 6:1. 851 full-time faculty, 95% hold PhDs, 22% are members of minority groups, 35% are women.

ACADEMICS

Degrees: Bachelor's; Doctoral degree—professional practice; Doctoral degree research/scholarship; Master's; Post-bachelor's certificate. **Classes:** Most classes have 10–19 students. **Most popular majors:** Computer and Information Sciences, General; Biology/Biological Sciences, General; Econometrics and Quantitative Economics. **Special Study Options:** Cross-registration; Double major; Exchange student program (domestic); Honors program; Independent study; Internships; Student-designed major; Study abroad; Teacher certification program. **Combined degree programs:** BA/MA; BA/MD. **Disability Services offered:** Note-taking services; Reader services; Tape recorders; Tutors. **Career services:** Alumni network; Career assessment; Career/job search classes; Internships; Regional alumni.

FACILITIES

Housing: Apartments for single students; Coed dorms; Cooperative housing; Fraternity/sorority housing; Special housing for disabled students; Theme housing; Wellness housing. **Special Academic Facilities/Equipment:** Haffenreffer Museum of Anthropology Forbes Center for Culture and Media Studies John Nicholas Brown Center for Public Humanities John Hay Library Joukowsky Institute for Archaeology and the Ancient World Granoff Center for the Creative Arts Annmary Brown Memorial David Winton Bell Gallery Brown Design Workshop Center for Digital Scholarship Language Resource Center Digital Learning and Design Teaching Lab Science Center Sidney Frank Digital Studio Center for Computation and Visualization Multimedia Labs Yurt (virtual reality theater) Humanity Centered Robotics Lab Nanofabrication Central Facility Electron Microscopy Facility NanoTools Facility Mass Spectrometry Facility Environmental Chemistry Facility Magnetic Resonance Imaging Facility Leduc Bioimaging Facility Genomics Facility Flow Cytometry and Sorting Facility Mouse Transgenic and Gene Targeting Facility Plant Environmental Center Rodent Neurodevelopmental Behavioral Testing Facility Structural Biology Core Facility X-Ray Reconstruction of Moving Morphology Facility.

CAMPUS LIFE

Environment: City. **Activities:** Campus Ministries; Choral groups; Concert band; Dance; Drama/theater; International Student Organization; Jazz band; Literary magazine; Marching band; Model UN; Music ensembles; Musical theater; Opera; Pep band; Radio station; Student government; Student newspaper; Student-run film society; Symphony orchestra; Television station; Yearbook. 527 registered organizations, 3 honor societies, 25 religious organizations, 9 fraternities, 5 sororities, on campus. **Athletics (Intercollegiate):** *Men:* baseball, basketball, crew/rowing, cross-country, diving, fencing, football, golf, ice hockey, lacrosse, soccer, squash, swimming, tennis, track/field (outdoor), track/field (indoor), water polo, wrestling. *Women:* basketball, crew/rowing, cross-country, diving, equestrian sports, fencing, field hockey, golf, gymnastics, ice hockey, lacrosse, skiing (downhill/Alpine), soccer, softball, squash, swimming, tennis, track/field (outdoor), track/field (indoor), volleyball, water polo. **On-Campus Highlights:** The College Green (Main Green). **Environmental Initiatives:** Reduce GHG emissions to 42% (15% below 1990) below 2007 for existing buildings by 2020.

ADMISSIONS

Freshman Academic Profile: 94% in top 10% of high school class, 98% in top 25% of high school class, 100% in top 50% of high school class. 55% from public high schools. **Test Scores:** SAT Math middle 50% range 740–800. SAT EBRW middle 50% range 700–770. ACT middle 50% range 33–35. **Basis for Candidate Selection:** *Very important factors include:* rigor of secondary school record, class rank, academic GPA, application essay, standardized test scores, recommendation(s), talent/ability, character/personal qualities. *Important factors include:* extracurricular activities. *Other factors include:* interview, first generation, alumni/ae relation, geographical residence, state residency, racial/ethnic status, volunteer work, work experience. **Freshman Admission Requirements:** High school diploma is required and GED is accepted. *Academic units required:* 4 English, 3 math, 3 science, 2 science labs, 3 foreign language, 2 history, 1 academic electives. *Academic units recommended:* 4 English, 4 math, 4 science, 3 science labs, 4 foreign language, 1 social studies, 2 history, 1 academic electives, 1 visual/performing arts. **Freshman Admission Statistics:** 38,674 applied, 7% admitted, 61% enrolled. **Transfer Admission Requirements:** High school transcript, college transcript(s), essay or personal statement, standardized test scores, statement of good standing from prior institution(s). Lowest grade transferable C. **General Admission Information:** Application fee $75. Regular application deadline 1/1. Admission may be deferred for a maximum of 1 year.

COSTS AND FINANCIAL AID

Annual tuition $57,112. Room and board $15,332. Required fees $1,292. Average book and supplies expense $1,632. **Required Forms and Deadlines:** CSS/Financial Aid PROFILE; FAFSA; Noncustodial PROFILE. **Notification of Awards:** Applicants will be notified of awards on or about 4/1. **Types of Aid:** *Need-based scholarships/grants:* College/university scholarship or grant aid from institutional funds; Federal Pell; Private scholarships; SEOG; State scholarships/grants. *Loans:* Direct PLUS loans; Direct Subsidized Stafford Loans; Direct Unsubsidized Stafford Loans. **Student Employment:** Federal Work-Study Program available. Institutional employment available. **Financial Aid Statistics:** 100% needy freshmen, 100% needy undergrads receive need-based scholarship or grant aid. 0% freshmen, 0% undergrads receive non-need-based scholarship or grant aid. 84% freshmen, 87% undergrads receive need-based self-help aid. 0% freshmen, 0% undergrads receive athletic scholarships. 58% freshmen, 49% undergrads receive any aid. 31% undergrads borrow to pay for school. Average cumulative indebtedness $24,304.

BRYAN COLLEGE

Bryan College Office of Admissions, Dayton, TN 37321
Phone: (423) 775-7158 **Financial Aid Phone:** 423-775-7339
E-mail: admissions@bryan.edu **CEEB Code:** 1908
Fax: 423-775-7199 **Website:** www.bryan.edu **ACT Code:** 4038

This private school, affiliated with the Christian (Nondenominational) Church, was founded in 1930. It has a 125 acre campus.

RATINGS

Admissions Selectivity Rating: 89   **Fire Safety Rating:** 97   **Green Rating:** 60*

STUDENTS AND FACULTY

Enrollment: 605. **Student Body:** 53% female, 47% male, 66% out-of-state, 5% international (22 countries represented). Asian <1%, African American 3%, Caucasian 87%, Hispanic 3%, Native American 0%, Pacific Islander 0%, Two or more races 3%, Race unknown 0%.
Retention and Graduation: 60% freshmen return for sophomore year.
Faculty: Student/faculty ratio 15:1. 36 full-time faculty, 64% hold PhDs, 0% are members of minority groups, 28% are women. 0% of classes are taught by teaching assistants.

ACADEMICS

Degrees: Associate; Bachelor's; Master's. **Classes:** Most classes have 10–19 students. **Most popular majors:** Communication, Journalism, and Related Programs, Other; Business Administration and Management, General; Sports, Kinesiology, and Physical Education/Fitness, General. **Special Study**

Options: Distance learning; Double major; Dual enrollment; Honors program; Independent study; Internships; Study abroad; Teacher certification program. **Honors programs:** Bryan Center for Undergraduate Research http://bryancollege.wpengine.com/bcur; Sigma Beta Delta Honor Society for students in business, management, and administration; Center for Leadership & Justice http://www.bryan.edu/clj. **Disability Services offered:** Note-taking services; Reader services; Tape recorders; Tutors. **Career services:** Alumni network; Alumni services; Career assessment; Career/job search classes; Internships.

FACILITIES

Housing: Apartments for married students; Apartments for single students; Men's dorms; Women's dorms. **Special Academic Facilities/Equipment:** Willard Henning Natural History Museum. **Campus network:** 100% of classrooms, 100% of dorms, 100% of student union, 100% of libraries, 100% of dining areas, 85% of common outdoor areas, have wireless network access.

CAMPUS LIFE

Environment: Town. **Activities:** Campus Ministries; Choral groups; Drama/theater; International Student Organization; Music ensembles; Musical theater; Opera; Student government; Student newspaper; Yearbook. 14 registered organizations, 7 religious organizations, on campus. **Athletics (Intercollegiate):** *Men:* baseball, basketball, cross-country, golf, soccer, track/field (outdoor), track/field (indoor). *Women:* basketball, cross-country, golf, soccer, softball, track/field (outdoor), track/field (indoor). **On-Campus Highlights:** Student Center.

ADMISSIONS

Freshman Academic Profile: Average high school GPA 3.6. 16% in top 10% of high school class, 48% in top 25% of high school class, 76% in top 50% of high school class. 55% from public high schools. **Test Scores:** SAT Math middle 50% range 450–580. SAT EBRW middle 50% range 450–600. ACT middle 50% range 20–26. **Basis for Candidate Selection:** *Very important factors include:* rigor of secondary school record, academic GPA, application essay, standardized test scores. *Important factors include:* recommendation(s), interview, character/personal qualities, religious affiliation/commitment. *Other factors include:* class rank, extracurricular activities, talent/ability, alumni/ae relation, volunteer work. **Freshman Admission Requirements:** High school diploma is required and GED is accepted. *Academic units recommended:* 4 English, 3 math, 3 science, 2 foreign language, 3 social studies. **Freshman Admission Statistics:** 760 applied, 48% admitted, 50% enrolled. **Transfer Admission Requirements:** College transcript(s), essay or personal statement, standardized test scores. Minimum college GPA of 2.75 required. Lowest grade transferable 2. **General Admission Information:** Application fee $35. Priority deadline 5/5. Non-fall registration accepted.

COSTS AND FINANCIAL AID

Annual tuition $22,200. Room and board $6,550. Average book and supplies expense $1,250. **Required Forms and Deadlines:** FAFSA. **Types of Aid:** *Need-based scholarships/grants:* College/university scholarship or grant aid from institutional funds; Federal Pell; Private scholarships; SEOG; State scholarships/grants. *Loans:* Direct PLUS loans; Direct Subsidized Stafford Loans; Direct Unsubsidized Stafford Loans. **Student Employment:** Federal Work-Study Program available. Institutional employment available. **Financial Aid Statistics:** 0% freshmen, 2% undergrads receive athletic scholarships. 100% freshmen, 98% undergrads receive any aid. **Criteria awarding aid:** *Need-based:* Academics, Minority status. *Non-need-based:* Academics, Alumni affiliation, Athletics, Leadership, Minority status, Music/drama, State/district residency.

BRYANT UNIVERSITY

Office of Admission; 1150 Douglas Pike, Smithfield, RI 02917-1291
Phone: 401-232-6100 **Financial Aid Phone:** 401-232-6020
E-mail: http://www.bryant.edu/admissions/request **CEEB Code:** 3095
Fax: 401-232-6731 **Website:** http://www.bryant.edu/ **ACT Code:** 3802

This private school was founded in 1863. It has a 435 acre campus.

RATINGS
Admissions Selectivity Rating: 81   **Fire Safety Rating:** 89   **Green Rating:** 83

STUDENTS AND FACULTY
Enrollment: 3,471. **Student Body:** 38% female, 62% male, 87% out-of-state, 8% international (53 countries represented). Asian 4%, African American 3%, Caucasian 75%, Hispanic 7%, Native American <1%, Pacific Islander <1%, Two or more races 2%, Race unknown 2%.
Retention and Graduation: 90% freshmen return for sophomore year. 73% freshmen graduate within 4 years. 79% freshmen graduate within 6 years. 21% grads go on to further study within 1 year. 3% grads pursue arts and sciences degrees. 1% grads pursue law degrees. 16% grads pursue business degrees.
Faculty: Student/faculty ratio 13:1. 170 full-time faculty, 81% hold PhDs, 19% are members of minority groups, 40% are women. 0% of classes are taught by teaching assistants.

ACADEMICS
Degrees: Bachelor's; Master's; Post-bachelor's certificate. **Classes:** Most classes have 30–39 students. Most lab/discussion sessions have fewer than 10 students. **Most popular majors:** Accounting; Finance, General; Marketing/Marketing Management, General. **Special Study Options:** Accelerated program; Distance learning; Double major; Dual enrollment; English as a Second Language (ESL); Honors program; Independent study; Internships; Liberal arts/career combination; Study abroad; Teacher certification program. **Honors programs:** The Bryant University Honors Program offers its members a personalized, distinctive experience that enriches their academic, social, cultural and professional talents in a mentor-oriented environment. Academically-talented students with a proven record of achievement are invited to join the Bryant University Honors Program. These exceptional students along with dedicated faculty comprise a community of scholars who are committed to pursuing an enriched educational experience. Successful completion of the program results in the student being recognized as an Honors Program graduate, a distinction that is noted on his or her Bryant University diploma and official academic transcript. More than twenty courses have been designed specifically for The Honors Program. While some of the Honors courses are adapted from standard courses and others are developed around unique topics, all are enhanced by additional course material, group projects, stimulating discussions and/or special assignments. These honors-designated courses are intentionally scheduled with smaller class sizes to afford students opportunities to interact with peers and professors. **Disability Services offered:** Note-taking services; Tape recorders; Tutors. **Career services:** Alumni network; Alumni services; Career assessment; Career/job search classes; Internships; Regional alumni.

FACILITIES
Housing: Apartments for single students; Coed dorms; Special housing for disabled students; Theme housing; 90% of campus accessible to physically disabled. **Special Academic Facilities/Equipment:** George E. Bello Center for Information & Technology, C.V. Star Financial Markets Center, Heidi and Walter Stepan Grand Hall, Linday and Jerry Cerce Multi Media Wall, Douglas & Judith Krupp Library, Jane E. & Keith S. Mahre Periodical Center, Koffler Center & Communications Complex, WJMF Radio Station, TV Production Studio, Janikies Memorial Autditorium, Koffler Rotunda multimedia exhibition space, Shu Fang Zhai (replica of Beijing's Forbidden City, home to U.S.-China Institute, in planning), John H Chafee Center for International Business, Center for Global and Regional Economic Studies, Intercultural Center, Gertrude Meth Hochberg Women's Center, Ronald K. & Kati C. Machtley Interfaith Center, Center for Student Involvement, Center for Teaching & Learning, ACE (Academic Center for Excellence), Writing Center, Amica Center for Career Education, Hassenfeld Institute for Public Leadership, Executive Development Center.

CAMPUS LIFE

Environment: Village. **Activities:** Campus Ministries; Choral groups; Dance; Drama/theater; International Student Organization; Jazz band; Literary magazine; Music ensembles; Musical theater; Pep band; Radio station; Student government; Student newspaper; Television station; Yearbook. 114 registered organizations, 14 honor societies, 6 religious organizations, 4 fraternities, 4 sororities, on campus. **Athletics (Intercollegiate):** *Men:* baseball, basketball, cross-country, football, golf, lacrosse, soccer, swimming, tennis, track/field (outdoor), track/field (indoor). *Women:* basketball, cross-country, field hockey, lacrosse, soccer, softball, swimming, tennis, track/field (outdoor), track/field (indoor), volleyball. **On-Campus Highlights:** Fisher Student Center **Environmental Initiatives:** Recycling Program.

ADMISSIONS

Freshman Academic Profile: Average high school GPA 3.4. 26% in top 10% of high school class, 55% in top 25% of high school class, 88% in top 50% of high school class. 74% from public high schools. **Test Scores:** SAT Math middle 50% range 570–660. SAT EBRW middle 50% range 560–640. ACT middle 50% range 24–28. **Basis for Candidate Selection:** *Very important factors include:* rigor of secondary school record, academic GPA. *Important factors include:* class rank, application essay, standardized test scores, recommendation(s). *Other factors include:* interview, extracurricular activities, talent/ability, character/personal qualities, first generation, alumni/ae relation, geographical residence, state residency, racial/ethnic status, volunteer work, work experience, level of applicant's interest. **Freshman Admission Requirements:** High school diploma is required and GED is accepted. *Academic units required:* 4 English, 4 math, 2 science, 2 science labs, 2 foreign language, 2 history. *Academic units recommended:* 4 English, 4 math, 3 science, 2 science labs, 2 foreign language, 3 history. **Freshman Admission Statistics:** 7,235 applied, 76% admitted, 16% enrolled. **Transfer Admission Requirements:** High school transcript, college transcript(s), essay or personal statement. Minimum college GPA of 2.5 required. Lowest grade transferable C. **General Admission Information:** Application fee $50. Regular application deadline 2/1. Non-fall registration accepted. Admission may be deferred for a maximum of 1 year.

COSTS AND FINANCIAL AID

Annual tuition $44,498. Room and board $16,016. Required fees $897. Average book and supplies expense $1,400. **Required Forms and Deadlines:** FAFSA. **Notification of Awards:** Applicants will be notified of awards on or about 3/24. **Types of Aid:** *Need-based scholarships/grants:* College/university scholarship or grant aid from institutional funds; Federal Pell; Private scholarships; SEOG; State scholarships/grants. *Loans:* Direct PLUS loans; Direct Subsidized Stafford Loans; Direct Unsubsidized Stafford Loans. **Student Employment:** Federal Work-Study Program available. Institutional employment available. **Financial Aid Statistics:** 61% needy freshmen, 63% needy undergrads receive need-based scholarship or grant aid. 79% freshmen, 73% undergrads receive non-need-based scholarship or grant aid. 82% freshmen, 82% undergrads receive need-based self-help aid. 1% freshmen, 1% undergrads receive athletic scholarships. 94% freshmen, 89% undergrads receive any aid. 70% undergrads borrow to pay for school. Average cumulative indebtedness $54,067. **Criteria awarding aid:** *Need-based:* Minority status. *Non-need-based:* Academics, Athletics, Minority status.

BRYN ATHYN COLLEGE OF THE NEW CHURCH

P.O. Box 462, Bryn Athyn, PA 19009
Phone: 267-502-6000 **Financial Aid Phone:** 267-502-6034
E-mail: admissions@brynathyn.edu **CEEB Code:** 2002
Fax: 267-502-2593 **Website:** www.brynathyn.edu **ACT Code:** 3228

This private school, affiliated with the General Church of the New Jerusalem/ Swedenborgian, was founded in 1877. It has a 130 acre campus.

RATINGS

Admissions Selectivity Rating: 88   Fire Safety Rating: 95   Green Rating: 60*

STUDENTS AND FACULTY

Enrollment: 273. **Student Body:** 47% female, 53% male, 41% out-of-state, 4% international (8 countries represented). Asian 3%, African American 20%, Caucasian 62%, Hispanic 10%, Native American 0%, Pacific Islander <1%, Two or more races <1%, Race unknown 1%.

Retention and Graduation: 64% freshmen return for sophomore year. 5% grads go on to further study within 1 year. 5% grads pursue arts and sciences degrees. 5% grads pursue business degrees. 10% grads pursue medical degrees. **Faculty:** Student/faculty ratio 8:1. 28 full-time faculty, 61% hold PhDs, 4% are members of minority groups, 39% are women. 0% of classes are taught by teaching assistants.

ACADEMICS

Degrees: Associate; Bachelor's; Master's. **Classes:** Most classes have 10–19 students. Most lab/discussion sessions have 10–19 students. **Most popular majors:** Business/Commerce, General; Multi-/Interdisciplinary Studies, Other; Psychology, General. **Special Study Options:** Accelerated program; Cooperative education program; Cross-registration; Dual enrollment; English as a Second Language (ESL); Independent study; Internships; Student-designed major; Study abroad; Teacher certification program. **Honors programs:** None. **Disability Services offered:** Tape recorders; Tutors. **Career services:** Alumni network; Alumni services; Career assessment; Internships; Regional alumni.

FACILITIES

Housing: Men's dorms; Women's dorms; 70% of campus accessible to physically disabled. **Special Academic Facilities/Equipment:** Glencairn Museum Swedenborg Library Swedenborgiana Academy of the New Church Archives John Pitcairn Archives Raymond and Mildred Pitcairn Archives.

CAMPUS LIFE

Environment: Village. **Activities:** Choral groups; Dance; Drama/theater; International Student Organization; Literary magazine; Music ensembles; Student government. 15 registered organizations, on campus. **On-Campus Highlights:** Doering Science Center. **Environmental Initiatives:** Chemical purchase, storage and disposal plan, Recycling program for glass and paper in all buildings.

ADMISSIONS

Freshman Academic Profile: Average high school GPA 3.1. **Test Scores:** SAT Math middle 50% range 395–550. SAT EBRW middle 50% range 390–555. ACT middle 50% range 18–23. **Basis for Candidate Selection:** *Very important factors include:* rigor of secondary school record, academic GPA, application essay, standardized test scores, recommendation(s). *Important factors include:* character/personal qualities. *Other factors include:* interview, extracurricular activities, talent/ability, alumni/ae relation, religious affiliation/commitment, racial/ethnic status, volunteer work, work experience, level of applicant's interest. **Freshman Admission Requirements:** High school diploma is required and GED is accepted. *Academic units required:* 4 English, 3 math, 3 science, 2 foreign language, 3 social studies, 3 history. *Academic units recommended:* 3 science labs. **Freshman Admission Statistics:** 439 applied, 42% admitted, 42% enrolled. **Transfer Admission Requirements:** High school transcript, college transcript(s), essay or personal statement. Minimum college GPA of 2.0 required. Lowest grade transferable C. **General Admission Information:** Non-fall registration accepted. Admission may be deferred for a maximum of 1 year.

COSTS AND FINANCIAL AID

Annual tuition $18,558. Room and board $11,538. Required fees $1,324. Average book and supplies expense $750. **Required Forms and Deadlines:** FAFSA; State aid form. **Notification of Awards:** Applicants will be notified of awards on a rolling basis beginning 3/1. **Types of Aid:** *Need-based scholarships/grants:* College/university scholarship or grant aid from institutional funds; Federal Pell; Private scholarships; SEOG; State scholarships/grants. *Loans:* Direct PLUS loans; Direct Subsidized Stafford Loans; Direct Unsubsidized Stafford Loans. **Student Employment:** Federal Work-Study Program available. Institutional employment available. **Financial Aid Statistics:** 88% needy freshmen, 85% needy undergrads receive need-based scholarship or grant aid. 48% freshmen, 51% undergrads receive non-need-based scholarship or grant aid. 78% freshmen, 79% undergrads receive need-based self-help aid. 0% freshmen, 0% undergrads receive athletic scholarships. 71% freshmen, 65% undergrads receive any aid. 77% undergrads borrow to pay for school. Average cumulative indebtedness $23,625. **Criteria awarding aid:** *Non-need-based:* Academics, Religious affiliation.

BRYN MAWR COLLEGE

101 North Merion Avenue, Bryn Mawr, PA 19010-2859
Phone: 610-526-5152 **Financial Aid Phone:** 610-526-5245
E-mail: admissions@brynmawr.edu **CEEB Code:** 2049
Fax: 610-526-7471 **Website:** www.brynmawr.edu **ACT Code:** 3526

This private school was founded in 1885. It has a 111 acre campus.

RATINGS
Admissions Selectivity Rating: 95   **Fire Safety Rating:** 87   **Green Rating:** 93

STUDENTS AND FACULTY
Enrollment: 1,353. **Student Body:** 100% female, 0% male, 85% out-of-state, 22% international (42 countries represented). Asian 13%, African American 6%, Caucasian 39%, Hispanic 10%, Native American 0%, Pacific Islander <1%, Two or more races 6%, Race unknown 6%.
Retention and Graduation: 92% freshmen return for sophomore year. 76% freshmen graduate within 4 years. 83% freshmen graduate within 6 years. 29% grads go on to further study within 1 year. 14% grads pursue arts and sciences degrees. 1% grads pursue law degrees. 1% grads pursue business degrees. 3% grads pursue medical degrees. **Faculty:** Student/faculty ratio 9:1. 156 full-time faculty, 97% hold PhDs, 26% are members of minority groups, 62% are women. 0% of classes are taught by teaching assistants.

ACADEMICS
Degrees: Bachelor's; Doctoral degree research/scholarship; Master's; Post-bachelor's certificate. **Classes:** Most classes have 10–19 students. **Most popular majors:** Biology/Biological Sciences, General; Mathematics, General; Psychology, General. **Special Study Options:** Accelerated program; Cross-registration; Double major; Exchange student program (domestic); Independent study; Internships; Student-designed major; Study abroad; Teacher certification program. **Combined degree programs:** BA/MA. **Career services:** Alumni network; Alumni services; Career assessment; Internships; Regional alumni.

FACILITIES
Housing: Apartments for single students; Coed dorms; Cooperative housing; Women's dorms. **Special Academic Facilities/Equipment:** Museum of classical and Near Eastern archaeology, mineral collection, Neufeld Collection of African Art, Language Learning Center.

CAMPUS LIFE
Environment: Metropolis. **Activities:** Campus Ministries; Choral groups; Dance; Drama/theater; International Student Organization; Literary magazine; Music ensembles; Musical theater; Radio station; Student government; Student newspaper; Student-run film society. 130 registered organizations, 10 religious organizations, on campus. **Athletics (Intercollegiate):** *Women:* badminton, basketball, crew/rowing, cross-country, field hockey, lacrosse, soccer, swimming, tennis, track/field (outdoor), track/field (indoor), volleyball. **On-Campus Highlights:** Great Hall (National Historic Landmark).

ADMISSIONS
Freshman Academic Profile: 59% in top 10% of high school class, 91% in top 25% of high school class, 99% in top 50% of high school class. 64% from public high schools. **Test Scores:** SAT Math middle 50% range 640–770. SAT EBRW middle 50% range 660–730. ACT middle 50% range 28–33. **Basis for Candidate Selection:** *Very important factors include:* rigor of secondary school record, recommendation(s). *Important factors include:* class rank, academic GPA, application essay, extracurricular activities, character/personal qualities. *Other factors include:* standardized test scores, interview, talent/ability, first generation, alumni/ae relation, geographical residence, state residency, racial/ethnic status, volunteer work, work experience. **Freshman Admission Requirements:** High school diploma is required and GED is accepted. *Academic units recommended:* 4 English, 4 math, 4 science, 1 science labs, 3 foreign language, 2 social studies, 2 history, 2 academic electives. **Freshman Admission Statistics:** 3,166 applied, 34% admitted, 36% enrolled. **Transfer Admission Requirements:** High school transcript, college transcript(s), essay or personal statement, standardized test scores, statement of good standing from prior institution(s). Lowest grade transferable C. **General Admission Information:** Application fee $50. Regular application deadline 1/15. Admission may be deferred for a maximum of 12 months.

COSTS AND FINANCIAL AID
Annual tuition $53,180. Room and board $17,100. Required fees $1,260. Average book and supplies expense $1,000. **Required Forms and Deadlines:** CSS/Financial Aid PROFILE; FAFSA; Noncustodial PROFILE. **Types of Aid:** *Need-based scholarships/grants:* College/university scholarship or grant aid from institutional funds; Federal Pell; Private scholarships; SEOG; State scholarships/grants. *Loans:* Direct PLUS loans; Direct Subsidized Stafford Loans; Direct Unsubsidized Stafford Loans. **Student Employment:** Federal Work-Study Program available. Institutional employment available. **Financial Aid Statistics:** 100% needy freshmen, 100% needy undergrads receive need-based scholarship or grant aid. 15% freshmen, 11% undergrads receive non-need-based scholarship or grant aid. 89% freshmen, 92% undergrads receive need-based self-help aid. 0% freshmen, 0% undergrads receive athletic scholarships. 78% freshmen, 73% undergrads receive any aid. 51% undergrads borrow to pay for school. Average cumulative indebtedness $25,682. **Criteria awarding aid:** *Non-need-based:* Academics, Leadership.

BUCKNELL UNIVERSITY

Office of Admissions, 1 Dent Drive, Lewisburg, PA 17837
Phone: 570-577-3000 **Financial Aid Phone:** 570-577-1331
E-mail: admissions@bucknell.edu **CEEB Code:** 2050
Fax: 570-577-3538 **Website:** www.bucknell.edu **ACT Code:** 3528

This private school was founded in 1846. It has a 446 acre campus.

RATINGS
Admissions Selectivity Rating: 94   **Fire Safety Rating:** 94   **Green Rating:** 97

STUDENTS AND FACULTY
Enrollment: 3,608. **Student Body:** 51% female, 49% male, 79% out-of-state, 6% international (49 countries represented). Asian 5%, African American 3%, Caucasian 74%, Hispanic 7%, Native American <1%, Pacific Islander <1%, Two or more races 4%, Race unknown <1%.
Retention and Graduation: 92% freshmen return for sophomore year. 86% freshmen graduate within 4 years. 90% freshmen graduate within 6 years. 17% grads go on to further study within 1 year. 6% grads pursue arts and sciences degrees. 2% grads pursue law degrees. 1% grads pursue business degrees. 2% grads pursue medical degrees. **Faculty:** Student/faculty ratio 9:1. 390 full-time faculty, 95% hold PhDs, 16% are members of minority groups, 42% are women. 0% of classes are taught by teaching assistants.

ACADEMICS
Degrees: Bachelor's; Master's. **Classes:** Most classes have 10–19 students. Most lab/discussion sessions have 10–19 students. **Most popular majors:** Economics, General; Accounting and Finance; Psychology, General. **Special Study Options:** Double major; Dual enrollment; Honors program; Independent study; Internships; Liberal arts/career combination; Student-designed major; Study abroad; Teacher certification program. **Disability Services offered:** Note-taking services; Reader services; Tape recorders; Tutors. **Career services:** Alumni network; Alumni services; Career assessment; Career/job search classes; Internships; Regional alumni.

FACILITIES
Housing: Apartments for single students; Coed dorms; Cooperative housing; Fraternity/sorority housing; Special housing for disabled students; Special housing for international students; Theme housing; Wellness housing; Women's dorms; 80% of campus accessible to physically disabled. **Special Academic Facilities/Equipment:** Art gallery, center for performing arts, poetry center, photography lab, observatory, 63-acre nature site, greenhouse, primate facility, gas chromatograph/mass spectrometer, electron microscope, herbarium, engineering structural test lab, nuclear magnetic resonance spectrometer, environmental center, 18-hole golf course, conference center, high ropes course, crafts center.

CAMPUS LIFE
Environment: Village. **Activities:** Campus Ministries; Choral groups; Concert band; Dance; Drama/theater; International Student Organization; Jazz band; Literary magazine; Model UN; Music ensembles; Musical theater; Opera; Pep band; Radio station; Student government; Student newspaper; Student-run

film society; Symphony orchestra; Yearbook. 190 registered organizations, 12 honor societies, 9 religious organizations, 9 fraternities, 9 sororities, on campus. **Athletics (Intercollegiate):** *Men:* baseball, basketball, cross-country, diving, football, golf, lacrosse, soccer, swimming, tennis, track/field (outdoor), track/field (indoor), water polo, wrestling. *Women:* basketball, crew/rowing, cross-country, diving, field hockey, golf, lacrosse, soccer, softball, swimming, tennis, track/field (outdoor), track/field (indoor), volleyball, water polo. **On-Campus Highlights:** Weis Center for the Performing Arts.

ADMISSIONS

Freshman Academic Profile: Average high school GPA 3.6. 58% in top 10% of high school class, 83% in top 25% of high school class, 98% in top 50% of high school class. 54% from public high schools. **Test Scores:** SAT Math middle 50% range 635–730. SAT EBRW middle 50% range 620–700. ACT middle 50% range 28–32. **Basis for Candidate Selection:** *Very important factors include:* rigor of secondary school record, academic GPA, application essay, standardized test scores, talent/ability, character/personal qualities. *Important factors include:* recommendation(s), extracurricular activities, volunteer work. *Other factors include:* class rank, first generation, alumni/ae relation, geographical residence, religious affiliation/commitment, racial/ethnic status. **Freshman Admission Requirements:** High school diploma is required and GED is accepted. *Academic units required:* 4 English, 3 math, 2 science, 2 foreign language, 2 social studies, 2 history, 1 academic electives. *Academic units recommended:* 4 English, 4 math, 2 science, 2 science labs, 4 foreign language, 2 social studies, 2 history, 1 academic electives. **Freshman Admission Statistics:** 9,845 applied, 34% admitted, 29% enrolled. **Transfer Admission Requirements:** High school transcript, college transcript(s), essay or personal statement, standardized test scores, statement of good standing from prior institution(s). Minimum college GPA of 2.5 required. Lowest grade transferable C. **General Admission Information:** Application fee $40. Regular application deadline 1/15. Admission may be deferred for a maximum of 2 years.

COSTS AND FINANCIAL AID

Annual tuition $57,882. Room and board $14,174. Required fees $314. Average book and supplies expense $900. **Required Forms and Deadlines:** CSS/Financial Aid PROFILE; FAFSA;. **Notification of Awards:** Applicants will be notified of awards on or about 4/1. **Types of Aid:** *Need-based scholarships/grants:* College/university scholarship or grant aid from institutional funds; Federal Pell; Private scholarships; SEOG; State scholarships/grants. *Loans:* Direct PLUS loans; Direct Subsidized Stafford Loans; Direct Unsubsidized Stafford Loans. **Student Employment:** Federal Work-Study Program available. Institutional employment available. **Financial Aid Statistics:** 86% needy freshmen, 87% needy undergrads receive need-based scholarship or grant aid. 33% freshmen, 29% undergrads receive non-need-based scholarship or grant aid. 100% freshmen, 100% undergrads receive need-based self-help aid. 4% freshmen, 5% undergrads receive athletic scholarships. 48% freshmen, 60% undergrads receive any aid. 46% undergrads borrow to pay for school. Average cumulative indebtedness $31,000. **Criteria awarding aid:** *Need-based:* Academics, Athletics, Minority status. *Non-need-based:* Academics, Art, Athletics, Leadership, Music/drama.

BUENA VISTA UNIVERSITY

610 West Fourth Street, Storm Lake, IA 50588-1798
Phone: 712-749-2235 **Financial Aid Phone:** 712-749-2164
E-mail: admissions@bvu.edu **CEEB Code:** 6047
Fax: 712-749-2035 **Website:** www.bvu.edu **ACT Code:** 1278

This private school, affiliated with the Presbyterian Church, was founded in 1891. It has a 60 acre campus.

RATINGS

   Admissions Selectivity Rating: 83   **Fire Safety Rating:** 62   **Green Rating:** 60*

STUDENTS AND FACULTY

Enrollment: 708. **Student Body:** 47% female, 53% male, 30% out-of-state, 1% international (5 countries represented). Asian 1%, African American 4%, Caucasian 73%, Hispanic 12%, Native American 1%, Pacific Islander 0%, Two or more races 4%, Race unknown 5%.
Retention and Graduation: 70% freshmen return for sophomore year. 52% freshmen graduate within 4 years. 60% freshmen graduate within 6 years. 15% grads go on to further study within 1 year. **Faculty:** Student/faculty ratio 8:1. 85 full-time faculty, 72% hold PhDs, 8% are members of minority groups, 55% are women. 0% of classes are taught by teaching assistants.

ACADEMICS

Degrees: Bachelor's; Master's. **Classes:** Most classes have 10–19 students. Most lab/discussion sessions have fewer than 10 students. **Most popular majors:** Elementary Education and Teaching; Biology/Biological Sciences, General; Business/Commerce, General. **Special Study Options:** Distance learning; Double major; Dual enrollment; English as a Second Language (ESL); External degree program; Honors program; Independent study; Internships; Student-designed major; Study abroad; Teacher certification program. **Honors programs:** The honors program at BVU encourages students to develop their academic talents beyond the regular programs at the university and is designed to provide greater depth to the student's regular academic program through specialized intellectual exploration courses, dialogue and research work. The program is especially suited for students contemplating graduate or professional school, and honors recognition will appear on the transcripts of those students who successfully complete the program. **Disability Services offered:** Note-taking services; Reader services; Tape recorders; Tutors. **Career services:** Alumni network; Alumni services; Career assessment; Career/job search classes; Internships.

FACILITIES

Housing: Coed dorms; Special housing for disabled students; Wellness housing **Special Academic Facilities/Equipment:** Art gallery, language lab, television station, radio station, satellite telecommunications system, computer labs/centers, electron microscope. **Campus network:** 100% of classrooms, 100% of dorms, 100% of student union, 100% of libraries, 100% of dining areas, 100% of common outdoor areas, have wireless network access.

CAMPUS LIFE

Environment: Village. **Activities:** Campus Ministries; Choral groups; Concert band; Dance; Drama/theater; International Student Organization; Jazz band; Marching band; Music ensembles; Musical theater; Pep band; Radio station; Student government; Student newspaper; Television station. 50 registered organizations, 6 honor societies, 1 religious organizations, on campus. **Athletics (Intercollegiate):** *Men:* baseball, basketball, cross-country, football, golf, soccer, tennis, track/field (outdoor), track/field (indoor), wrestling. *Women:* basketball, cross-country, golf, soccer, softball, tennis, track/field (outdoor), track/field (indoor), volleyball. **On-Campus Highlights:** Recreation Center for all your working-out needs.

ADMISSIONS

Freshman Academic Profile: Average high school GPA 3.5. 16% in top 10% of high school class, 43% in top 25% of high school class, 77% in top 50% of high school class. 85% from public high schools. **Test Scores:** ACT middle 50% range 19–25. **Basis for Candidate Selection:** *Very important factors include:* academic GPA, standardized test scores, recommendation(s). *Important factors include:* extracurricular activities, character/personal qualities. *Other factors include:* rigor of secondary school record, class rank, application essay, interview, talent/ability, alumni/ae relation, volunteer work, work experience. **Freshman Admission Requirements:** High school diploma is required and GED is accepted. *Academic units recommended:* 4 English, 4 math, 3 science, 1 science labs, 3 social studies. **Freshman Admission Statistics:** 2,101 applied, 57% admitted, 19% enrolled. **Transfer Admission Requirements:** College transcript(s), statement of good standing from prior institution(s). Minimum college GPA of 2.0 required. Lowest grade transferable D. **General Admission Information:** Non-fall registration accepted. Admission may be deferred for a maximum of 1 year.

COSTS AND FINANCIAL AID

Annual tuition $36,426. Room and board $10,218. Average book and supplies expense $1,190. **Required Forms and Deadlines:** FAFSA. **Types of Aid:** *Need-based scholarships/grants:* College/university scholarship or grant aid from institutional funds; Federal Pell; Private scholarships; SEOG; State scholarships/grants. *Loans:* Direct PLUS loans; Direct Subsidized Stafford Loans; Direct Unsubsidized Stafford Loans. **Student Employment:** Federal Work-Study Program available. Institutional employment available. **Financial Aid Statistics:** 100% needy freshmen, 99% needy undergrads receive need-based scholarship or grant aid. 12% freshmen, 11% undergrads receive non-need-based scholarship or grant aid. 86% freshmen, 90% undergrads receive need-based self-help aid. 0% freshmen, 0% undergrads receive athletic scholarships. 99% freshmen, 98% undergrads receive any aid. 85% undergrads borrow to pay for school. Average cumulative indebtedness $35,267. **Criteria awarding aid:** *Non-need-based:* Academics, Art, Minority status, Music/drama.

BUTLER UNIVERSITY

Robertson Hall, 4600 Sunset Avenue, Indianapolis, IN 46208
Phone: 317-940-8100 **Financial Aid Phone:** 317-940-8200
E-mail: admission@butler.edu **CEEB Code:** 1073
Fax: 317-940-8150 **Website:** www.butler.edu **ACT Code:** 1180

This private school was founded in 1855. It has a 295 acre campus.

RATINGS

Admissions Selectivity Rating: 87   Fire Safety Rating: 78   Green Rating: 88

STUDENTS AND FACULTY

Enrollment: 4,553. **Student Body:** 59% female, 41% male, 55% out-of-state, 1% international (40 countries represented). Asian 3%, African American 4%, Caucasian 82%, Hispanic 4%, Native American <1%, Pacific Islander <1%, Two or more races 3%, Race unknown 2%.
Retention and Graduation: 89% freshmen return for sophomore year. 73% freshmen graduate within 4 years. % freshmen graduate within 6 years. 25% grads go on to further study within 1 year. 24% grads pursue arts and sciences degrees. 7% grads pursue law degrees. 5% grads pursue business degrees. 20% grads pursue medical degrees. **Faculty:** Student/faculty ratio 11:1. 377 full-time faculty, 82% hold PhDs, 14% are members of minority groups, 50% are women. 0% of classes are taught by teaching assistants.

ACADEMICS

Degrees: Associate; Bachelor's; Certificate; Doctoral degree—professional practice; Master's; Post-bachelor's certificate. **Classes:** Most classes have 20–29 students. Most lab/discussion sessions have 10–19 students. **Most popular majors:** Marketing/Marketing Management, General; Finance, General; Public Relations, Advertising, and Applied Communication, Other. **Special Study Options:** Accelerated program; Cross-registration; Distance learning; Double major; Dual enrollment; English as a Second Language (ESL); Exchange student program (domestic); Honors program; Independent study; Internships; Liberal arts/career combination; Student-designed major; Study abroad; Teacher certification program. **Honors programs:** The Butler University Honors Program exists to meet the expectations of academically outstanding students in all colleges and majors who wish to develop their talents and potential to the fullest. Through a combination of honors courses, cultural events, independent study, creative activity and research, it is designed to foster a diverse and challenging intellectual environment for honors students and to enhance our academic community by adding a distinctive note of innovative thinking and interdisciplinary dialogue. **Disability Services offered:** Note-taking services; Reader services; Tape recorders; Tutors. **Career services:** Alumni network; Alumni services; Career assessment; Career/job search classes; Internships; Regional alumni.

FACILITIES

Housing: Apartments for single students; Coed dorms; Fraternity/sorority housing; Theme housing; 100% of campus accessible to physically disabled. **Special Academic Facilities/Equipment:** Holcomb Observatory, Clowes Memorial Hall (performing arts theatre), Schrott Center for the Arts. **Campus network:** 100% of classrooms, 100% of dorms, 100% of student union, 100% of libraries, 100% of dining areas, 100% of common outdoor areas, have wireless network access.

CAMPUS LIFE

Environment: Metropolis. **Activities:** Campus Ministries; Choral groups; Concert band; Dance; Drama/theater; International Student Organization; Jazz band; Literary magazine; Marching band; Model UN; Music ensembles; Musical theater; Opera; Pep band; Radio station; Student government; Student newspaper; Student-run film society; Symphony orchestra; Television station; Yearbook. 160 registered organizations, 9 honor societies, 15 religious organizations, 5 fraternities, 7 sororities, on campus. **Athletics (Intercollegiate):** *Men:* baseball, basketball, cross-country, football, golf, soccer, tennis, track/field (outdoor), track/field (indoor). *Women:* basketball, cross-country, golf, soccer, softball, swimming, tennis, track/field (outdoor), track/field (indoor), volleyball. **On-Campus Highlights:** Starbucks in the Union. **Environmental Initiatives:** College of Pharmacy and Health Sciences building will be "Leed Certified-Silver."

ADMISSIONS

Freshman Academic Profile: Average high school GPA 3.9. 45% in top 10% of high school class, 76% in top 25% of high school class, 96% in top 50% of high school class. 66% from public high schools. **Test Scores:** SAT Math middle 50% range 580–670. SAT EBRW middle 50% range 590–660. ACT middle 50% range 25–30. **Basis for Candidate Selection:** *Very important factors include:* rigor of secondary school record, academic GPA, standardized test scores, character/personal qualities. *Important factors include:* application essay, recommendation(s), extracurricular activities, talent/ability. *Other factors include:* class rank, first generation, alumni/ae relation, geographical residence, racial/ethnic status, volunteer work, work experience. **Freshman Admission Requirements:** High school diploma is required and GED is accepted. *Academic units required:* 4 English, 3 math, 3 science, 3 science labs, 2 foreign language, 2 social studies, 2 history. *Academic units recommended:* 4 science, 4 science labs. **Freshman Admission Statistics:** 16,418 applied, 68% admitted, 12% enrolled. **Transfer Admission Requirements:** College transcript(s), essay or personal statement, statement of good standing from prior institution(s). Minimum college GPA of 2.0 required. Lowest grade transferable C. **General Admission Information:** Non-fall registration accepted.

COSTS AND FINANCIAL AID

Annual tuition $41,370. Room and board $15,540. Required fees $990. Average book and supplies expense $1,000. **Required Forms and Deadlines:** FAFSA. **Notification of Awards:** Applicants will be notified of awards on a rolling basis beginning 1/15. **Types of Aid:** *Need-based scholarships/grants:* College/university scholarship or grant aid from institutional funds; Federal Pell; Private scholarships; SEOG; State scholarships/grants. *Loans:* Direct PLUS loans; Direct Subsidized Stafford Loans; Direct Unsubsidized Stafford Loans. **Student Employment:** Federal Work-Study Program available. Institutional employment available. **Financial Aid Statistics:** 99% needy freshmen, 25% needy undergrads receive need-based scholarship or grant aid. 22% freshmen, 16% undergrads receive non-need-based scholarship or grant aid. 64% freshmen, 70% undergrads receive need-based self-help aid. 1% freshmen, 1% undergrads receive athletic scholarships. 97.4% freshmen, 94.9% undergrads receive any aid. 58% undergrads borrow to pay for school. Average cumulative indebtedness $38,191. **Criteria awarding aid:** *Non-need-based:* Academics, Alumni affiliation, Athletics, Leadership, Music/drama.

CABRINI COLLEGE

610 King of Prussia Road, Radnor, PA 19087-3698
Phone: 610-902-8552 **Financial Aid Phone:** (610) 902-8420
E-mail: admit@cabrini.edu **CEEB Code:** 2071
Fax: 610-902-8508 **Website:** www.cabrini.edu **ACT Code:** 3532

This private school, affiliated with the Roman Catholic Church, was founded in 1957. It has a 112 acre campus.

RATINGS

Admissions Selectivity Rating: 74   Fire Safety Rating: 96   Green Rating: 60*

STUDENTS AND FACULTY

Enrollment: 1,820. **Student Body:** 66% female, 34% male, 34% out-of-state, 1% international (34 countries represented). Asian 2%, African American 6%, Caucasian 83%, Hispanic 3%, Native American <1%, Race unknown 6%. **Retention and Graduation:** 66% freshmen return for sophomore year. 21% grads go on to further study within 1 year. 16% grads pursue arts and sciences degrees. 1% grads pursue law degrees. 3% grads pursue business degrees. 1% grads pursue medical degrees. **Faculty:** Student/faculty ratio 16:1. 64 full-time faculty, 80% hold PhDs, 5% are members of minority groups, 55% are women. 0% of classes are taught by teaching assistants.

ACADEMICS

Degrees: Bachelor's; Certificate; Master's; Post-bachelor's certificate. **Classes:** Most classes have 20–29 students. Most lab/discussion sessions have 10–19 students. **Most popular majors:** Business, Management, Marketing, and Related Support Services, Other; Elementary Education and Teaching. **Special Study Options:** Accelerated program; Cooperative education program; Cross-registration; Double major; Honors program; Independent study; Internships; Liberal arts/career combination; Student-designed major; Study abroad; Teacher certification program. **Honors programs:** Cabrini College Honors Program; Honors in the major. **Disability Services offered:** Note-taking services; Reader

FACILITIES

Housing: Coed dorms; Special housing for disabled students; Women's dorms; 97% of campus accessible to physically disabled. **Special Academic Facilities/ Equipment:** Exercise Science Lab; Communications center (includes a graphic design lab, radio station, newsroom, and television studio); Science Education and Technology building with state-of-the-art biology, chemistry, and physics labs; Instructional Technology labs, and research space.

CAMPUS LIFE

Environment: Town. **Activities:** Campus Ministries; Choral groups; Dance; Drama/theater; International Student Organization; Literary magazine; Radio station; Student government; Student newspaper; Student-run film society; Television station; Yearbook. 32 registered organizations, 18 honor societies, 1 religious organizations, on campus. **Athletics (Intercollegiate):** *Men:* basketball, cross-country, golf, lacrosse, soccer, swimming, tennis, track/field (outdoor). *Women:* basketball, cross-country, field hockey, lacrosse, soccer, softball, swimming, tennis, track/field (outdoor), volleyball. **On-Campus Highlights:** Dixon Center- Athletic/Recreation facility.

ADMISSIONS

Freshman Academic Profile: Average high school GPA 3.1. 6% in top 10% of high school class, 20% in top 25% of high school class, 49% in top 50% of high school class. 56% from public high schools. **Test Scores:** SAT Math middle 50% range 430–520. SAT EBRW middle 50% range 440–530. **Basis for Candidate Selection:** *Very important factors include:* academic GPA, standardized test scores. *Other factors include:* rigor of secondary school record, class rank, application essay, recommendation(s), interview, extracurricular activities, talent/ability, character/personal qualities, alumni/ae relation, volunteer work, work experience. **Freshman Admission Requirements:** High school diploma is required and GED is accepted. *Academic units required:* 4 English, 3 math, 3 science, 2 foreign language, 3 social studies, 3 history. *Academic units recommended:* 4 English, 4 math, 3 science, 2 foreign language, 3 social studies, 3 history, 2 academic electives. **Freshman Admission Statistics:** 2,374 applied, 87% admitted, 25% enrolled. **Transfer Admission Requirements:** College transcript(s). Minimum college GPA of 2.2 required. Lowest grade transferable C–. **General Admission Information:** Application fee $35. Priority deadline 5/1. Non-fall registration accepted. Admission may be deferred for a maximum of one year.

COSTS AND FINANCIAL AID

Average book and supplies expense $960. **Required Forms and Deadlines:** FAFSA. **Notification of Awards:** Applicants will be notified of awards on a rolling basis beginning 2/20. **Types of Aid:** *Need-based scholarships/grants:* College/university scholarship or grant aid from institutional funds; Federal Pell; Private scholarships; SEOG; State scholarships/grants. **Financial Aid Statistics:** 81% needy freshmen, 78% needy undergrads receive need-based scholarship or grant aid. 92% freshmen, 94% undergrads receive non-need-based scholarship or grant aid. 80% freshmen, 84% undergrads receive need-based self-help aid. 0% freshmen, 0% undergrads receive athletic scholarships. 98% freshmen, 97% undergrads receive any aid. **Criteria awarding aid:** *Non-need-based:* Academics, Alumni affiliation.

CAIRN UNIVERSITY

200 Manor Avenue, Langhorne, PA 19047
Phone: 215-702-4235 **Financial Aid Phone:** 215-702-4246
E-mail: admissions@cairn.edu
Fax: 215-702-4248 **Website:** www.cairn.edu **ACT Code:** 3658

This private school, affiliated with the Protestant Church, was founded in 1913. It has a 114 acre campus.

RATINGS

Admissions Selectivity Rating: 80   **Fire Safety Rating:** 82   **Green Rating:** 60*

STUDENTS AND FACULTY

Enrollment: 937. **Student Body:** 53% female, 47% male, 44% out-of-state, 2% international (31 countries represented). Asian 4%, African American 14%, Caucasian 72%, Hispanic 5%, Native American 1%, Pacific Islander 0%, Two or more races 2%, Race unknown 1%.

Retention and Graduation: 78% freshmen return for sophomore year. 40% grads go on to further study within 1 year. **Faculty:** Student/faculty ratio 13:1. 50 full-time faculty, 70% hold PhDs, 18% are members of minority groups, 30% are women. 0% of classes are taught by teaching assistants.

ACADEMICS

Degrees: Bachelor's; Certificate; Master's; Post-bachelor's certificate. **Classes:** Most classes have 10–19 students. **Most popular majors:** Bible/Biblical Studies; Social Work; Elementary Education and Teaching. **Special Study Options:** Accelerated program; Double major; Honors program; Internships; Study abroad; Teacher certification program. **Disability Services offered:** Note-taking services; Reader services; Tape recorders; Tutors. **Career services:** Alumni network; Alumni services; Career assessment; Career/job search classes; Internships.

FACILITIES

Housing: Apartments for married students; Apartments for single students; Men's dorms; Special housing for disabled students; Special housing for international students; Women's dorms; 99% of campus accessible to physically disabled. **Special Academic Facilities/Equipment:** Biblical Learning Center Museum area.

CAMPUS LIFE

Environment: Village. **Activities:** Campus Ministries; Choral groups; Concert band; Drama/theater; International Student Organization; Music ensembles; Musical theater; Opera; Student government; Student newspaper; Symphony orchestra; Yearbook. 25 registered organizations, 4 honor societies, 3 religious organizations, on campus. **Athletics (Intercollegiate):** *Men:* baseball, basketball, cross-country, golf, soccer, volleyball. *Women:* basketball, cross-country, soccer, softball, tennis, volleyball. **On-Campus Highlights:** The Cafe.

ADMISSIONS

Freshman Academic Profile: Average high school GPA 3.3. 18% in top 10% of high school class, 39% in top 25% of high school class, 17% in top 50% of high school class. 60% from public high schools. **Test Scores:** SAT Math middle 50% range 450–580. SAT EBRW middle 50% range 470–590. ACT middle 50% range 17–24. **Basis for Candidate Selection:** *Very important factors include:* academic GPA, standardized test scores, interview, character/personal qualities, religious affiliation/commitment, level of applicant's interest. *Important factors include:* rigor of secondary school record, application essay, *Other factors include:* class rank, recommendation(s), extracurricular activities. **Freshman Admission Requirements:** High school diploma is required and GED is accepted. *Academic units recommended:* 4 English, 1 math, 2 science, 2 foreign language, 3 social studies. **Freshman Admission Statistics:** 482 applied, 74% admitted, 41% enrolled. **Transfer Admission Requirements:** College transcript(s), essay or personal statement, interview. Minimum college GPA of 2.2 required. Lowest grade transferable C. **General Admission Information:** Application fee $25. Non-fall registration accepted. Admission may be deferred for a maximum of 1 year.

COSTS AND FINANCIAL AID

Annual tuition $21,500. Room and board $8,525. Required fees $205. Average book and supplies expense $1,200. **Required Forms and Deadlines:** FAFSA. **Notification of Awards:** Applicants will be notified of awards on a rolling basis beginning 2/15. **Types of Aid:** *Need-based scholarships/grants:* College/university scholarship or grant aid from institutional funds; Federal Pell; Private scholarships; SEOG; State scholarships/grants. *Loans:* Direct PLUS loans; Direct Subsidized Stafford Loans; Direct Unsubsidized Stafford Loans. **Student Employment:** Federal Work-Study Program available. Institutional employment available. **Financial Aid Statistics:** 99% needy freshmen, 96% needy undergrads receive need-based scholarship or grant aid. 6% freshmen, 6% undergrads receive non-need-based scholarship or grant aid. 98% freshmen, 96% undergrads receive need-based self-help aid. 0% freshmen, 0% undergrads receive athletic scholarships. 84% freshmen, 82% undergrads receive any aid. **Criteria awarding aid:** *Non-need-based:* Academics, Leadership, Music/drama.

CALIFORNIA BAPTIST UNIVERSITY

8432 Magnolia Ave, Riverside, CA 92504
Phone: 951-343-4212 **Financial Aid Phone:** 951-343-4236
E-mail: admissions@calbaptist.edu **CEEB Code:** 4094
Fax: 951-343-4525 **Website:** www.calbaptist.edu **ACT Code:** 4094

This private school, affiliated with the Southern Baptist Church, was founded in 1950. It has a 160 acre campus.

RATINGS
Admissions Selectivity Rating: 82   **Fire Safety Rating:** 64   **Green Rating:** 60*

STUDENTS AND FACULTY
Enrollment: 6,904. **Student Body:** 63% female, 37% male, 7% out-of-state, 2% international (25 countries represented). Asian 5%, African American 8%, Caucasian 38%, Hispanic 36%, Native American 1%, Pacific Islander 1%, Two or more races 6%, Race unknown 4%.
Retention and Graduation: 75% freshmen return for sophomore year.
Faculty: Student/faculty ratio 18:1. 315 full-time faculty, 75% hold PhDs, 29% are members of minority groups, 47% are women. 0% of classes are taught by teaching assistants.

ACADEMICS
Degrees: Associate; Bachelor's; Doctoral degree research/scholarship; Master's.
Classes: Most classes have 10–19 students. Most lab/discussion sessions have 10–19 students. **Most popular majors:** Business/Commerce, General; Registered Nursing/Registered Nurse; Psychology, General. **Special Study Options:** Accelerated program; Distance learning; Double major; English as a Second Language (ESL); Exchange student program (domestic); Honors program; Internships; Liberal arts/career combination; Study abroad; Teacher certification program; Weekend college. **Honors programs:** The Honors program offers students from all major areas of study the opportunity to participate in rigorous study, requiring diligence in reading primary sources and writing original essays through 6 intensive seminars. Honors students progressively investigate a single generative idea using primary texts, drawing upon the expertise of leading faculty. These seminars may be used to fulfill elective unit requirements and specially selected general education requirements. Successful completion of the Honors Program will be posted on the academic transcript and students will be designated as Honors Program graduates at commencement. **Disability Services offered:** Note-taking services; Tutors. **Career services:** Alumni network; Alumni services; Career assessment; Career/job search classes; Internships.

FACILITIES
Housing: Apartments for married students; Apartments for single students; Cooperative housing; Men's dorms; Theme housing; Women's dorms; 95% of campus accessible to physically disabled. **Special Academic Facilities/Equipment:** Metcalf Art Gallery, Annie Gabriel Library, Wallace Theater, P. Boyd Smith Hymnology Collection, Music Production and Recording Studios, Digital Design and Photography Studio, Theater Arts stage production workshop, Nie Wieder!Holocaust Collection, prayer chapel, Nursing Patient Simulation Laboratory.

CAMPUS LIFE
Environment: Metropolis. **Activities:** Campus Ministries; Choral groups; Concert band; Drama/theater; International Student Organization; Jazz band; Literary magazine; Music ensembles; Musical theater; Student government; Student newspaper; Student-run film society; Symphony orchestra; Yearbook. 81 registered organizations, 6 honor societies, 6 religious organizations, on campus. **Athletics (Intercollegiate):** *Men:* baseball, basketball, cheerleading, cross-country, diving, golf, soccer, swimming, volleyball, water polo, wrestling. *Women:* basketball, cheerleading, cross-country, diving, golf, soccer, softball, swimming, volleyball, water polo. **On-Campus Highlights:** Recreation Center. **Environmental Initiatives:** Energy Efficient Lighting.

ADMISSIONS
Freshman Academic Profile: Average high school GPA 3.4. 15% in top 10% of high school class, 41% in top 25% of high school class, 76% in top 50% of high school class. 77% from public high schools. **Test Scores:** SAT Math middle 50% range 420–550. SAT EBRW middle 50% range 430–550. ACT middle 50% range 19–24. **Basis for Candidate Selection:** *Very important factors include:* rigor of secondary school record, academic GPA, application essay, standardized test scores, recommendation(s), character/personal qualities. *Important factors include:* level of applicant's interest. *Other factors include:* class rank, extracurricular activities, talent/ability, volunteer work. **Freshman Admission Requirements:** High school diploma is required and GED is accepted. *Academic units required:* 4 English, 3 math, 2 science, 2 science labs, 2 foreign language, 2 social studies, 2 history. *Academic units recommended:* 4 English, 4 math, 3 science, 3 science labs, 3 foreign language, 2 social studies, 2 history, 3 academic electives, 1 visual/performing arts. **Freshman Admission Statistics:** 4,971 applied, 64% admitted, 36% enrolled. **Transfer Admission Requirements:** College transcript(s), essay or personal statement, statement of good standing from prior institution(s). Minimum college GPA of 2.0 required. Lowest grade transferable C. **General Admission Information:** Application fee $45. Non-fall registration accepted. Admission may be deferred for a maximum of 1 year.

COSTS AND FINANCIAL AID
Annual tuition $30,446. Room and board $11,540. Required fees $2,120. Average book and supplies expense $1,790. **Required Forms and Deadlines:** FAFSA; State aid form. **Notification of Awards:** Applicants will be notified of awards on a rolling basis beginning 3/2. **Types of Aid:** *Need-based scholarships/grants:* College/university scholarship or grant aid from institutional funds; Federal Nursing Scholarships; Federal Pell; Private scholarships; SEOG; State scholarships/grants. *Loans:* Direct PLUS loans; Direct Subsidized Stafford Loans; Direct Unsubsidized Stafford Loans. **Student Employment:** Federal Work-Study Program available. Institutional employment available. **Financial Aid Statistics:** 93% needy freshmen, 75% needy undergrads receive need-based scholarship or grant aid. 84% freshmen, 58% undergrads receive non-need-based scholarship or grant aid. 63% freshmen, 60% undergrads receive need-based self-help aid. 5% freshmen, 4% undergrads receive athletic scholarships. 92% freshmen, 89% undergrads receive any aid. 77% undergrads borrow to pay for school. Average cumulative indebtedness $20,693. **Criteria awarding aid:** *Need-based:* Academics, Art, Athletics, Music/drama, Religious affiliation. *Non-need-based:* Academics, Art, Athletics, Music/drama, Religious affiliation.

CALIFORNIA COLLEGE OF THE ARTS

1111 Eighth Street, San Francisco, CA 94107
Phone: 415-703-9523 **Financial Aid Phone:** 415-703-9528
E-mail: enroll@cca.edu **CEEB Code:** 4031
Fax: 415-703-9539 **Website:** www.cca.edu **ACT Code:** 176

This private school was founded in 1907. It has a 12.4 acre campus.

RATINGS
Admissions Selectivity Rating: 75   **Fire Safety Rating:** 97   **Green Rating:** 91

STUDENTS AND FACULTY
Enrollment: 1,515. **Student Body:** 64% female, 36% male, 35% out-of-state, 35% international (60 countries represented). Asian 18%, African American 6%, Caucasian 23%, Hispanic 12%, Native American <1%, Pacific Islander 1%, Two or more races 0%, Race unknown 6%.
Retention and Graduation: 82% freshmen return for sophomore year.
Faculty: 100 full-time faculty, 64% hold PhDs, 32% are members of minority groups, 48% are women. 0% of classes are taught by teaching assistants.

ACADEMICS
Degrees: Bachelor's; Master's. **Classes:** Most classes have 10–19 students. **Most popular majors:** Illustration; Graphic Design; Industrial and Product Design. **Special Study Options:** Cross-registration; Double major; English as a Second Language (ESL); Exchange student program (domestic); Independent study; Internships; Student-designed major; Study abroad. **Honors programs:** The First Year Honors Program enhances student's entry-level college experience by providing additional and rigorous critique as well as an introduction to available resources at the college and throughout the Bay Area. **Disability Services offered:** Note-taking services; Reader services; Tape recorders; Tutors. **Career services:** Alumni services; Career assessment; Career/job search classes; Internships.

FACILITIES
Housing: Apartments for single students; Coed dorms; Special housing for disabled students; 95% of campus accessible to physically disabled. **Special Academic Facilities/Equipment:** Wattis Institute for Contemporary Art.

CAMPUS LIFE
Environment: Metropolis. **Activities:** International Student Organization. 30 registered organizations, 1 fraternities, 1 sororities, on campus. **On-Campus**

Highlights: The Nave- San Francisco campus. **Environmental Initiatives:** Largest solar heated facility in San Francisco, named Top Ten Green Building on Earth Day 2001.

ADMISSIONS

Freshman Academic Profile: Average high school GPA 3.3. **Test Scores:** SAT Math middle 50% range 450–620. SAT EBRW middle 50% range 445–580. ACT middle 50% range 20–27. **Basis for Candidate Selection:** *Very important factors include:* academic GPA, application essay, talent/ability. *Important factors include:* recommendation(s). *Other factors include:* rigor of secondary school record, standardized test scores, interview, extracurricular activities, character/personal qualities, first generation, alumni/ae relation, racial/ethnic status, volunteer work, work experience, level of applicant's interest. **Freshman Admission Requirements:** High school diploma is required and GED is accepted. **Freshman Admission Statistics:** 1,896 applied, 81% admitted, 17% enrolled. **Transfer Admission Requirements:** College transcript(s), essay or personal statement. Minimum college GPA of 2.0 required. Lowest grade transferable C. **General Admission Information:** Application fee $70. Priority deadline 2/1. Non-fall registration accepted. Admission may be deferred for a maximum of one semester.

COSTS AND FINANCIAL AID

Annual tuition $44,976. Room and board $9,370. Required fees $460. Average book and supplies expense $1,500. **Required Forms and Deadlines:** FAFSA; State aid form. **Notification of Awards:** Applicants will be notified of awards on a rolling basis beginning 3/15. *Types of Aid: Need-based scholarships/grants:* College/university scholarship or grant aid from institutional funds; Federal Pell; Private scholarships; SEOG; State scholarships/grants. *Loans:* Direct PLUS loans; Direct Subsidized Stafford Loans; Direct Unsubsidized Stafford Loans. **Student Employment:** Federal Work-Study Program available. Institutional employment available. **Financial Aid Statistics:** 100% needy freshmen, 100% needy undergrads receive need-based scholarship or grant aid. 88% freshmen, 61% undergrads receive non-need-based scholarship or grant aid. 95% freshmen, 96% undergrads receive need-based self-help aid. 0% freshmen, 0% undergrads receive athletic scholarships. 78% freshmen, 73% undergrads receive any aid. **Criteria awarding aid:** *Non-need-based:* Academics, Art.

CALIFORNIA INSTITUTE OF TECHNOLOGY

Caltech Office of Undergrad Admissions, Pasadena, CA 91125
Phone: 626-395-6341 **Financial Aid Phone:** 626-395-6280
E-mail: ugadmissions@caltech.edu **CEEB Code:** 4034
Fax: 626-683-3026 **Website:** www.caltech.edu **ACT Code:** 182

This private school was founded in 1891. It has a 124 acre campus.

RATINGS

Admissions Selectivity Rating: 99   **Fire Safety Rating:** 89   **Green Rating:** 60*

STUDENTS AND FACULTY

Enrollment: 938. **Student Body:** 45% female, 55% male, 64% out-of-state, 8% international (25 countries represented). Asian 37%, African American 2%, Caucasian 27%, Hispanic 17%, Native American 0%, Pacific Islander <1%, Two or more races 9%, Race unknown <1%.
Retention and Graduation: 98% freshmen return for sophomore year. 84% freshmen graduate within 4 years. 94% freshmen graduate within 6 years. 48% grads go on to further study within 1 year. **Faculty:** Student/faculty ratio 3:1. 340 full-time faculty, 98% hold PhDs, 23% are members of minority groups, 23% are women. 0% of classes are taught by teaching assistants.

ACADEMICS

Degrees: Bachelor's; Doctoral degree research/scholarship; Master's. **Classes:** Most classes have 10–19 students. Most lab/discussion sessions have 10–19 students. **Most popular majors:** Computer and Information Sciences, General; Physics, General; Electrical and Electronics Engineering. **Special Study Options:** Cooperative education program; Cross-registration; Double major; English as a Second Language (ESL); Exchange student program (domestic); Independent study; Student-designed major; Study abroad. **Disability Services offered:** Note-taking services; Reader services; Tape recorders; Tutors. **Career services:** Alumni network; Alumni services; Career/job search classes; Internships; Regional alumni.

FACILITIES

Housing: Apartments for married students; Coed dorms; Special housing for disabled students; 95% of campus accessible to physically disabled. **Special Academic Facilities/Equipment:** Jet Propulsion Laboratory, Palomar Observatory, Seismological Laboratory, Beckman Institute for Fundamental Research in Biology and Chemistry, Mead Chemistry Laboratory, Moore Laboratory.

CAMPUS LIFE

Environment: City. **Activities:** Campus Ministries; Choral groups; Concert band; Dance; Drama/theater; International Student Organization; Jazz band; Literary magazine; Music ensembles; Musical theater; Student government; Student newspaper; Symphony orchestra; Yearbook. 100 registered organizations, 2 honor societies, 7 religious organizations, on campus. **Athletics (Intercollegiate):** *Men:* baseball, basketball, cross-country, diving, fencing, soccer, swimming, tennis, track/field (outdoor), water polo. *Women:* basketball, cross-country, diving, fencing, swimming, tennis, track/field (outdoor), volleyball, water polo. **On-Campus Highlights:** Hammeetman Center. **Environmental Initiatives:** Energy efficiency and retro-commissioning programs finances through the use of a green revolving loan fund (http://sustainability.caltech.edu/energy/CECIP).

ADMISSIONS

Freshman Academic Profile: 99% in top 10% of high school class, 100% in top 25% of high school class. 74% from public high schools. **Test Scores:** SAT Math middle 50% range 790–800. SAT EBRW middle 50% range 740–760. ACT middle 50% range 35–36. **Basis for Candidate Selection:** *Very important factors include:* rigor of secondary school record, application essay, standardized test scores, recommendation(s), character/personal qualities. *Important factors include:* class rank, academic GPA, extracurricular activities. *Other factors include:* talent/ability, first generation, racial/ethnic status, volunteer work, work experience. **Freshman Admission Requirements:** High school diploma or equivalent is not required. *Academic units required:* 3 English, 4 math, 2 science, 1 science labs, 1 history. *Academic units recommended:* 4 English, 4 science. **Freshman Admission Statistics:** 8,367 applied, 6% admitted, 44% enrolled. **Transfer Admission Requirements:** High school transcript, college transcript(s), essay or personal statement, statement of good standing from prior institution(s). **General Admission Information:** Application fee $75. Regular application deadline 1/3. Admission may be deferred for a maximum of 2 years.

COSTS AND FINANCIAL AID

Annual tuition $52,506. Room and board $16,644. Required fees $2,594. Average book and supplies expense $1,428. **Required Forms and Deadlines:** Business/Farm Supplement; CSS/Financial Aid PROFILE; FAFSA; Institution's own financial aid form; Noncustodial PROFILE; State aid form. **Notification of Awards:** Applicants will be notified of awards on or about 4/15. *Types of Aid: Need-based scholarships/grants:* College/university scholarship or grant aid from institutional funds; Federal Pell; Private scholarships; SEOG; State scholarships/grants. *Loans:* Direct PLUS loans; Direct Subsidized Stafford Loans; Direct Unsubsidized Stafford Loans. **Student Employment:** Federal Work-Study Program available. Institutional employment available. **Financial Aid Statistics:** 100% needy freshmen, 100% needy undergrads receive need-based scholarship or grant aid. 0% freshmen, 0% undergrads receive non-need-based scholarship or grant aid. 46% freshmen, 57% undergrads receive need-based self-help aid. 0% freshmen, 0% undergrads receive athletic scholarships. 57% freshmen, 50% undergrads receive any aid. 30% undergrads borrow to pay for school. Average cumulative indebtedness $20,192. **Criteria awarding aid:** *Need-based:* Academics, Leadership.

CALIFORNIA INSTITUTE OF THE ARTS

24700 McBean Parkway, Valencia, CA 91355
Phone: 661-255-1050 **Financial Aid Phone:** 661-253-7869
E-mail: admissions@calarts.edu **CEEB Code:** 4049
Fax: 661-253-7710 **Website:** www.calarts.edu **ACT Code:** 121

This private school was founded in 1961. It has a 60 acre campus.

RATINGS

Admissions Selectivity Rating: 76   **Fire Safety Rating:** 76   **Green Rating:** 60*

STUDENTS AND FACULTY

Enrollment: 888. **Student Body:** 49% female, 51% male, 49% out-of-state, 8% international (34 countries represented). Asian 12%, African American 8%, Caucasian 58%, Hispanic 12%, Native American 1%, Race unknown 1%.

Retention and Graduation: 75% freshmen return for sophomore year. **Faculty:** Student/faculty ratio 7:1. 160 full-time faculty, 100% hold PhDs, 18% are members of minority groups, 44% are women. 0% of classes are taught by teaching assistants.

ACADEMICS

Degrees: Bachelor's; Certificate; Master's; Post-bachelor's certificate. **Classes:** Most classes have 10–19 students. **Most popular majors:** Music Performance, General. **Special Study Options:** Independent study; Internships; Student-designed major; Study abroad. **Disability Services offered:** Note-taking services; Reader services; Tape recorders; Tutors. **Career services:** Career assessment; Career/job search classes; Internships.

FACILITIES

Housing: Apartments for single students; Coed dorms; Special housing for disabled students; 98% of campus accessible to physically disabled. **Special Academic Facilities/Equipment:** 7 Art galleries, TV studio, Walt Disney Theater, Roy Disney Music Hall, Sharon Disney Lund Dance Theater, Bijou Film Theater.

CAMPUS LIFE

Environment: City. **Activities:** Choral groups; Dance; Drama/theater; Jazz band; Literary magazine; Music ensembles; Opera; Radio station; Student government; Student newspaper; Student-run film society; Symphony orchestra; Television station. 5 registered organizations, on campus. **On-Campus Highlights:** Modular Theater. **Environmental Initiatives:** Recycling Program.

ADMISSIONS

Basis for Candidate Selection: *Very important factors include:* application essay, talent/ability. *Important factors include:* recommendation(s), extracurricular activities. *Other factors include:* rigor of secondary school record, academic GPA, interview, character/personal qualities, level of applicant's interest. **Freshman Admission Requirements:** High school diploma is required and GED is accepted. *Academic units recommended:* 4 English, 3 math, 3 science, 2 foreign language, 3 social studies, 2 academic electives, 1 computer science, 4 visual/performing arts. **Freshman Admission Statistics:** 1,186 applied, 33% admitted, 40% enrolled. **Transfer Admission Requirements:** High school transcript, college transcript(s), essay or personal statement. Lowest grade transferable C. **General Admission Information:** Application fee $70. Priority deadline 12/1. Regular application deadline 1/5. Non-fall registration accepted.

COSTS AND FINANCIAL AID

Annual tuition $36,166. Room and board $9,293. Required fees $576. Average book and supplies expense $1,500. **Required Forms and Deadlines:** FAFSA. **Notification of Awards:** Applicants will be notified of awards on a rolling basis beginning 4/1. **Types of Aid:** *Need-based scholarships/grants:* College/university scholarship or grant aid from institutional funds; Federal Pell; Private scholarships; SEOG; State scholarships/grants. **Student Employment:** Federal Work-Study Program available. Institutional employment available. **Financial Aid Statistics:** 92% needy freshmen, 93% needy undergrads receive need-based scholarship or grant aid. 0% freshmen, 0% undergrads receive non-need-based scholarship or grant aid. 85% freshmen, 89% undergrads receive need-based self-help aid. 0% freshmen, 0% undergrads receive athletic scholarships. 71% freshmen, 77% undergrads receive any aid. **Criteria awarding aid:** *Need-based:* Art, Minority status, Music/drama. *Non-need-based:* Art, Minority status, Music/drama.

CALIFORNIA LUTHERAN UNIVERSITY

60 West Olsen Road, Thousand Oaks, CA 91360
Phone: 805-493-3135 **Financial Aid Phone:** (805) 493-3115
E-mail: admissions@callutheran.edu **CEEB Code:** 4088
Fax: 805-493-3645 **Website:** www.callutheran.edu **ACT Code:** 183

This private school, affiliated with the Lutheran Church, was founded in 1959. It has a 290 acre campus.

RATINGS

Admissions Selectivity Rating: 83   **Fire Safety Rating:** 92   **Green Rating:** 60*

STUDENTS AND FACULTY

Enrollment: 2,802. **Student Body:** 57% female, 43% male, 13% out-of-state, 3% international (52 countries represented). Asian 6%, African American 4%, Caucasian 49%, Hispanic 27%, Native American 1%, Pacific Islander 1%, Two or more races 6%, Race unknown 4%.

Retention and Graduation: 84% freshmen return for sophomore year. 28% grads go on to further study within 1 year. 35% grads pursue arts and sciences degrees. 3% grads pursue law degrees. 7% grads pursue business degrees. 4% grads pursue medical degrees. **Faculty:** Student/faculty ratio 15:1. 193 full-time faculty, 85% hold PhDs, 17% are members of minority groups, 48% are women. 0% of classes are taught by teaching assistants.

ACADEMICS

Degrees: Bachelor's; Doctoral degree—professional practice; Master's; Post-bachelor's certificate; Post-master's certificate. **Classes:** Most classes have 10–19 students. Most lab/discussion sessions have 10–19 students. **Most popular majors:** Business/Commerce, General; Liberal Arts and Sciences/Liberal Studies; Psychology, General. **Special Study Options:** Accelerated program; Cooperative education program; Double major; Dual enrollment; Exchange student program (domestic); Honors program; Independent study; Internships; Student-designed major; Study abroad; Teacher certification program. **Honors programs:** Honors Program. **Disability Services offered:** Note-taking services; Reader services; Tape recorders; Tutors. **Career services:** Alumni network; Alumni services; Career assessment; Career/job search classes; Internships; Regional alumni.

FACILITIES

Housing: Coed dorms; Special housing for disabled students; 95% of campus accessible to physically disabled. **Special Academic Facilities/Equipment:** Human Performance Laboratory; bioengineering, optics and other science laboratories; radio broadcasting, TV production, multimedia and photography labs; Blackbox Theatre; Center for Economic Research and Forecasting; Center for Equality and Justice; Center for Teaching and Learning; Community Counseling & Parent-Child Study center; Community Service Center; Kwan Fong Gallery of Art and Culture; Office for Undergraduate Research; Scandinavian Center; and Segerhammar Center for Faith and Culture.

CAMPUS LIFE

Environment: Town. **Activities:** Campus Ministries; Choral groups; Concert band; Dance; Drama/theater; International Student Organization; Jazz band; Literary magazine; Model UN; Music ensembles; Musical theater; Pep band; Radio station; Student government; Student newspaper; Student-run film society; Symphony orchestra; Television station. 80 registered organizations, 9 honor societies, 5 religious organizations, on campus. **Athletics (Intercollegiate):** *Men:* baseball, basketball, cheerleading, cross-country, diving, football, golf, soccer, swimming, tennis, track/field (outdoor), water polo. *Women:* basketball, cheerleading, cross-country, diving, soccer, softball, swimming, tennis, track/field (outdoor), volleyball, water polo. **On-Campus Highlights:** Gilbert Sports and Fitness Center.

ADMISSIONS

Freshman Academic Profile: Average high school GPA 3.7. 30% in top 10% of high school class, 72% in top 25% of high school class, 93% in top 50% of high school class. 75% from public high schools. **Test Scores:** SAT Math middle 50% range 500–600. SAT EBRW middle 50% range 500–600. ACT middle 50% range 22–27. **Basis for Candidate Selection:** *Very important factors include:* rigor of secondary school record, academic GPA, application essay, standardized test scores, recommendation(s). *Important factors include:* class rank, extracurricular activities, talent/ability, alumni/ae relation. *Other factors include:* interview, character/personal qualities, first generation, geographical residence, state residency, religious affiliation/commitment, racial/ethnic status, volunteer work, work experience. **Freshman Admission Requirements:** High school diploma is required and GED is accepted. *Academic units required:* 4 English, 3 math, 3 science, 2 science labs, 2 foreign language, 2 social studies. *Academic units recommended:* 4 English, 4 math, 3 science. **Freshman Admission Statistics:** 6,569 applied, 62% admitted, 15% enrolled. **Transfer Admission Requirements:** College transcript(s), essay or personal statement, statement of good standing from prior institution(s). Minimum college GPA of 2.8 required. Lowest grade transferable D. **General Admission Information:** Application fee $25. Priority deadline 11/1. Regular application deadline 1/1. Non-fall registration accepted. Admission may be deferred for a maximum of 1 year.

COSTS AND FINANCIAL AID

Annual tuition $39,310. Room and board $12,740. Required fees $450. Average book and supplies expense $1,764. **Required Forms and Deadlines:** FAFSA; State aid form. **Notification of Awards:** Applicants will be notified of awards on a rolling basis beginning 2/15. **Types of Aid:** *Need-based scholarships/grants:* College/university scholarship or grant aid from institutional funds; Federal Pell; Private scholarships; SEOG; State scholarships/grants; United Negro College Fund. *Loans:* Direct PLUS loans; Direct Subsidized Stafford Loans; Direct Unsubsidized Stafford Loans. **Student Employment:** Federal

Work-Study Program available. Institutional employment available. **Financial Aid Statistics:** 100% needy freshmen, 100% needy undergrads receive need-based scholarship or grant aid. 38% freshmen, 49% undergrads receive non-need-based scholarship or grant aid. 77% freshmen, 76% undergrads receive need-based self-help aid. 0% freshmen, 0% undergrads receive athletic scholarships. 96% freshmen, 95% undergrads receive any aid. 62% undergrads borrow to pay for school. Average cumulative indebtedness $28,186. **Criteria awarding aid:** *Need-based:* Academics, Alumni affiliation, Art, Leadership, Minority status, Music/drama, Religious affiliation. *Non-need-based:* Academics, Alumni affiliation, Art, Leadership, Minority status, Music/drama, Religious affiliation, State/district residency.

CALIFORNIA POLYTECHNIC STATE UNIVERSITY

Admissions Office, San Luis Obispo, CA 93407-0031
Phone: 805-756-2311 **Financial Aid Phone:** (805) 756-2927
E-mail: admissions@calpoly.edu **CEEB Code:** 4038
Fax: 805-756-5400 **Website:** www.calpoly.edu **ACT Code:** 188

This public school was founded in 1901. It has a 9678 acre campus.

RATINGS
Admissions Selectivity Rating: 95 **Fire Safety Rating:** 65 **Green Rating:** 96

STUDENTS AND FACULTY
Enrollment: 20,401. **Student Body:** 48% female, 52% male, 7% out-of-state, 2% international. Asian 14%, African American 1%, Caucasian 54%, Hispanic 18%, Native American <1%, Pacific Islander <1%, Two or more races 8%, Race unknown 4%.
Retention and Graduation: 94% freshmen return for sophomore year. 51% freshmen graduate within 4 years. 83% freshmen graduate within 6 years.
Faculty: Student/faculty ratio 18:1. 975 full-time faculty, 75% hold PhDs, 0% are members of minority groups, 38% are women.

ACADEMICS
Degrees: Bachelor's; Master's; Post-bachelor's certificate. **Classes:** Most classes have 20–29 students. Most lab/discussion sessions have 10–19 students. **Special Study Options:** Cooperative education program; Distance learning; Double major; Exchange student program (domestic); Honors program; Independent study; Internships; Liberal arts/career combination; Study abroad; Teacher certification program. **Disability Services offered:** Note-taking services; Reader services; Tape recorders; Tutors. **Career services:** Alumni network; Alumni services; Career assessment; Career/job search classes; Internships; Regional alumni.

FACILITIES
Housing: Apartments for single students; Coed dorms; Special housing for disabled students; Special housing for international students; Theme housing; Wellness housing. **Special Academic Facilities/Equipment:** Dairy, veterinary clinic, printing museum, art gallery.

CAMPUS LIFE
Environment: Town. **Activities:** Campus Ministries; Choral groups; Concert band; Dance; Drama/theater; International Student Organization; Jazz band; Literary magazine; Marching band; Model UN; Music ensembles; Musical theater; Opera; Pep band; Radio station; Student government; Student newspaper; Student-run film society; Symphony orchestra; Television station. 386 registered organizations, 20 honor societies, 19 religious organizations, 19 fraternities, 16 sororities, on campus. **Athletics (Intercollegiate):** *Men:* baseball, basketball, cross-country, football, golf, soccer, swimming, tennis, track/field (outdoor), wrestling. *Women:* basketball, cross-country, golf, soccer, softball, swimming, tennis, track/field (outdoor), track/field (indoor), volleyball. **On-Campus Highlights:** Performing Arts Center.

ADMISSIONS
Freshman Academic Profile: Average high school GPA 4.0. 54% in top 10% of high school class, 85% in top 25% of high school class, 98% in top 50% of high school class. **Test Scores:** SAT Math middle 50% range 620–740. SAT EBRW middle 50% range 620–700. ACT middle 50% range 26–32. **Basis for Candidate Selection:** *Very important factors include:* rigor of secondary school record, academic GPA, standardized test scores. *Other factors include:* extracurricular activities, talent/ability, first generation, geographical residence, volunteer work, work experience. **Freshman Admission Requirements:** High school diploma is required and GED is accepted. *Academic units required:*

4 English, 3 math, 2 science, 2 science labs, 2 foreign language, 1 social studies, 1 history, 1 academic electives, 1 visual/performing arts. *Academic units recommended:* 4 English, 4 math, 4 science, 2 science labs, 4 foreign language, 1 social studies, 1 history, 1 academic electives, 2 visual/performing arts. **Freshman Admission Statistics:** 54,049 applied, 28% admitted, 30% enrolled. **Transfer Admission Requirements:** College transcript(s). Minimum college GPA of 2.0 required. Lowest grade transferable D. **General Admission Information:** Application fee $55. Regular application deadline 11/30.

COSTS AND FINANCIAL AID
Annual in-state tuition $5,742. Annual out-of-state tuition $264. Room and board $14,209. Required fees $4,206. Average book and supplies expense $1,941. **Required Forms and Deadlines:** FAFSA. **Notification of Awards:** Applicants will be notified of awards on a rolling basis beginning 3/15. **Types of Aid:** *Need-based scholarships/grants:* College/university scholarship or grant aid from institutional funds; Federal Pell; Private scholarships; SEOG; State scholarships/grants. *Loans:* Direct PLUS loans; Direct Subsidized Stafford Loans; Direct Unsubsidized Stafford Loans. **Student Employment:** Federal Work-Study Program available. Institutional employment available. **Financial Aid Statistics:** 89% needy freshmen, 87% needy undergrads receive need-based scholarship or grant aid. 39% freshmen, 34% undergrads receive non-need-based scholarship or grant aid. 56% freshmen, 57% undergrads receive need-based self-help aid. 2% freshmen, 2% undergrads receive athletic scholarships. 41% undergrads borrow to pay for school. Average cumulative indebtedness $22,411. **Criteria awarding aid:** *Need-based:* Academics, Art, Job skills, Leadership, Music/drama. *Non-need-based:* Academics, Alumni affiliation, Art, Athletics, Job skills, Leadership, Music/drama, State/district residency.

CALIFORNIA STATE POLYTECHNIC UNIVERSITY, POMONA

3801 W Temple Ave, Pomona, CA 91768
Phone: 909-869-5299 **Financial Aid Phone:** 909-869-3700
E-mail: admissions@cpp.edu **CEEB Code:** 4082
Fax: 909-869-4529 **Website:** www.cpp.edu **ACT Code:** 0202

This public school was founded in 1938. It has a 1437 acre campus.

RATINGS
Admissions Selectivity Rating: 86 **Fire Safety Rating:** 92 **Green Rating:** 92

STUDENTS AND FACULTY
Enrollment: 26,368. **Student Body:** 47% female, 53% male, 2% out-of-state, 6% international (101 countries represented). Asian 22%, African American 3%, Caucasian 15%, Hispanic 47%, Native American <1%, Pacific Islander <1%, Two or more races 4%, Race unknown 3%.
Retention and Graduation: 89% freshmen return for sophomore year. 23% freshmen graduate within 4 years. 69% freshmen graduate within 6 years.
Faculty: Student/faculty ratio 24:1. 638 full-time faculty, 82% hold PhDs, 40% are members of minority groups, 42% are women.

ACADEMICS
Degrees: Bachelor's; Doctoral degree—professional practice; Master's. **Classes:** Most classes have 30–39 students. Most lab/discussion sessions have 20–29 students. **Most popular majors:** Civil Engineering, General; Mechanical Engineering, Psychology, General. **Special Study Options:** Cooperative education program; Cross-registration; Distance learning; Double major; Dual enrollment; English as a Second Language (ESL); Exchange student program (domestic); External degree program; Honors program; Internships; Study abroad; Teacher certification program. **Honors programs:** See web site for complete information about The Kellogg Honors College: http://www.cpp.edu/~honorscollege/. **Disability Services offered:** Note-taking services; Reader services; Tape recorders; Tutors. **Career services:** Alumni network; Alumni services; Career assessment; Career/job search classes; Internships; Regional alumni.

FACILITIES
Housing: Apartments for single students; Coed dorms; Theme housing; 95% of campus accessible to physically disabled. **Special Academic Facilities/Equipment:** Center for Hospitality Management; Restaurant at Kellogg Ranch; W. Keith & Janet Kellogg University Art Gallery; Don B. Huntley Gallery; Voorhis Ecological Reserve; John T. Lyle Center for Regenerative Studies; citrus-packing house; meat-processing building; poultry plant; feed mill; beef and sheep/swine units; W.K. Kellogg Arabian Horse Library & Arabian Horse Center; horse show arena; and aerospace wind tunnel.

CAMPUS LIFE

Environment: City. **Activities:** Campus Ministries; Choral groups; Concert band; Dance; Drama/theater; International Student Organization; Jazz band; Literary magazine; Model UN; Music ensembles; Musical theater; Opera; Pep band; Student government; Student newspaper; Symphony orchestra; Yearbook. 429 registered organizations, 36 honor societies, 13 religious organizations, 10 fraternities, 6 sororities, on campus. **Athletics (Intercollegiate):** *Men:* baseball, basketball, cheerleading, cross-country, soccer, tennis, track/field (outdoor). *Women:* basketball, cheerleading, cross-country, soccer, tennis, track/field (outdoor), volleyball. **On-Campus Highlights:** Centerpointe Dining Commons.

ADMISSIONS

Freshman Academic Profile: Average high school GPA 3.6. 90% from public high schools. **Test Scores:** SAT Math middle 50% range 510–650. SAT EBRW middle 50% range 500–620. ACT middle 50% range 19–27. **Basis for Candidate Selection:** *Very important factors include:* rigor of secondary school record, academic GPA, standardized test scores. **Freshman Admission Requirements:** High school diploma is required and GED is accepted. *Academic units required:* 4 English, 3 math, 2 science, 2 science labs, 2 foreign language, 1 social studies, 1 history, 1 academic electives, 1 visual/performing arts. *Academic units recommended:* 4 math. **Freshman Admission Statistics:** 39,727 applied, 55% admitted, 17% enrolled. **Transfer Admission Requirements:** College transcript(s), statement of good standing from prior institution(s). Minimum college GPA of 2.0 required. **General Admission Information:** Application fee $70. Priority deadline 11/30. Regular application deadline 11/30.

COSTS AND FINANCIAL AID

Annual in-state tuition $5,742. Annual out-of-state tuition $17,622. Room and board $15,791. Required fees $1,654. Average book and supplies expense $1,800. **Required Forms and Deadlines:** FAFSA. **Notification of Awards:** Applicants will be notified of awards on a rolling basis beginning 4/1. **Types of Aid:** *Need-based scholarships/grants:* College/university scholarship or grant aid from institutional funds; Federal Pell; Private scholarships; SEOG; State scholarships/grants. *Loans:* Direct PLUS loans; Direct Subsidized Stafford Loans; Direct Unsubsidized Stafford Loans. **Student Employment:** Federal Work-Study Program available. Institutional employment available. **Financial Aid Statistics:** 80% needy freshmen, 80% needy undergrads receive need-based scholarship or grant aid. 18% freshmen, 17% undergrads receive non-need-based scholarship or grant aid. 46% freshmen, 43% undergrads receive need-based self-help aid. 0% freshmen, 0% undergrads receive athletic scholarships. 77% freshmen, 76% undergrads receive any aid. 52% undergrads borrow to pay for school. Average cumulative indebtedness $21,252. **Criteria awarding aid:** *Need-based:* Academics. *Non-need-based:* Academics, Alumni affiliation, Athletics, Leadership, State/district residency.

CALIFORNIA STATE UNIVERSITY, CHICO

---

400 West First Street, Chico, CA 95929-0722
Phone: 530-898-4428 **Financial Aid Phone:** (530) 898-6451
E-mail: info@csuchico.edu **CEEB Code:** 4048
Fax: 530-898-6456 **Website:** www.csuchico.edu **ACT Code:** 212

This public school was founded in 1887. It has a 119 acre campus.

RATINGS

Admissions Selectivity Rating: 83 **Fire Safety Rating:** 86 **Green Rating:** 98

STUDENTS AND FACULTY

Enrollment: 16,420. **Student Body:** 53% female, 47% male, 1% out-of-state, 3% international (38 countries represented). Asian 5%, African American 3%, Caucasian 41%, Hispanic 34%, Native American <1%, Pacific Islander <1%, Two or more races 5%, Race unknown 8%.
Retention and Graduation: 85% freshmen return for sophomore year. 27% freshmen graduate within 4 years. % freshmen graduate within 6 years. **Faculty:** Student/faculty ratio 23:1. 503 full-time faculty, 85% hold PhDs, 16% are members of minority groups, 48% are women. 1% of classes are taught by teaching assistants.

ACADEMICS

Degrees: Bachelor's; Certificate; Master's; Post-bachelor's certificate; Post-master's certificate. **Classes:** Most classes have 20–29 students. Most lab/discussion sessions have 10–19 students. **Most popular majors:** Psychology, General; Criminal Justice/Safety Studies; Business Administration and Management, General. **Special Study Options:** Cooperative education program; Cross-registration; Distance learning; Double major; Dual enrollment; English as a Second Language (ESL); Exchange student program (domestic); External degree program; Honors program; Independent study; Internships; Student-designed major; Study abroad; Teacher certification program. **Honors programs:** Honors in General Education (HGE) Honors in the Major (HIM). **Disability Services offered:** Note-taking services; Reader services; Tape recorders; Tutors. **Career services:** Alumni network; Alumni services; Career assessment; Career/job search classes; Internships.

FACILITIES

Housing: Apartments for single students; Coed dorms; Fraternity/sorority housing; Special housing for disabled students; Special housing for international students; Theme housing; 95% of campus accessible to physically disabled. **Special Academic Facilities/Equipment:** Anthropology museum, center for intercultural studies, satellite communication dishes, biological field station, university farm, electron microscope.

CAMPUS LIFE

Environment: City. **Activities:** Choral groups; Concert band; Dance; Drama/theater; International Student Organization; Jazz band; Literary magazine; Model UN; Music ensembles; Musical theater; Opera; Pep band; Radio station; Student government; Student newspaper; Student-run film society; Symphony orchestra. 174 registered organizations, 15 honor societies, 10 religious organizations, 12 fraternities, 7 sororities, on campus. **Athletics (Intercollegiate):** *Men:* baseball, basketball, cross-country, golf, soccer, track/field (outdoor). *Women:* basketball, cross-country, golf, soccer, softball, track/field (outdoor), volleyball. **On-Campus Highlights:** Bell Memorial Union. **Environmental Initiatives:** This Way to Sustainability Conference.

ADMISSIONS

Freshman Academic Profile: Average high school GPA 3.4. 35% in top 10% of high school class, 76% in top 25% of high school class, 100% in top 50% of high school class. 93% from public high schools. **Test Scores:** SAT Math middle 50% range 500–590. SAT EBRW middle 50% range 500–600. ACT middle 50% range 18–24. **Basis for Candidate Selection:** *Very important factors include:* academic GPA, standardized test scores. *Important factors include:* geographical residence, state residency. **Freshman Admission Requirements:** High school diploma is required and GED is accepted. *Academic units required:* 4 English, 3 math, 2 science, 2 science labs, 2 foreign language, 2 social studies, 1 academic electives, 1 visual/performing arts. **Freshman Admission Statistics:** 23,964 applied, 65% admitted, 17% enrolled. **Transfer Admission Requirements:** College transcript(s), statement of good standing from prior institution(s). Minimum college GPA of 2.0 required. Lowest grade transferable D. **General Admission Information:** Application fee $55. Priority deadline 10/1. Regular application deadline 11/30. Admission may be deferred for a maximum of 1 year.

COSTS AND FINANCIAL AID

Annual in-state tuition $7,044. Annual out-of-state tuition $18,204. Room and board $12,824. Required fees $1,572. Average book and supplies expense $1,719. **Required Forms and Deadlines:** FAFSA. **Notification of Awards:** Applicants will be notified of awards on a rolling basis beginning 3/2. **Types of Aid:** *Need-based scholarships/grants:* College/university scholarship or grant aid from institutional funds; Federal Pell; Private scholarships; SEOG; State scholarships/grants. *Loans:* Direct PLUS loans; Direct Subsidized Stafford Loans; Direct Unsubsidized Stafford Loans. **Student Employment:** Federal Work-Study Program available. Institutional employment available. **Financial Aid Statistics:** 76% needy freshmen, 78% needy undergrads receive need-based scholarship or grant aid. 22% freshmen, 12% undergrads receive non-need-based scholarship or grant aid. 65% freshmen, 65% undergrads receive need-based self-help aid. freshmen, undergrads receive athletic scholarships. 79% freshmen, 76% undergrads receive any aid. **Criteria awarding aid:** *Need-based:* Academics, Minority status. *Non-need-based:* Academics, Art, Athletics, Leadership, Minority status, Music/drama, Religious affiliation.

CALIFORNIA STATE UNIVERSITY, DOMINGUEZ HILLS

100 East Victoria Street, Carson, CA 90747
Phone: 310-243-3645 **Financial Aid Phone:** 310-243-3189
E-mail: info@csudh.edu **CEEB Code:** 4098
Fax: 310-516-3609 **Website:** www.csudh.edu **ACT Code:** 0203

This public school was founded in 1960. It has a 346 acre campus.

RATINGS
Admissions Selectivity Rating: 74 **Fire Safety Rating:** 72 **Green Rating:** 85

STUDENTS AND FACULTY
Enrollment: 12,613. **Student Body:** 63% female, 37% male, 0% out-of-state, 4% international (41 countries represented). Asian 10%, African American 13%, Caucasian 7%, Hispanic 60%, Native American <1%, Pacific Islander <1%, Two or more races 3%, Race unknown 3%.
Retention and Graduation: 82% freshmen return for sophomore year.
Faculty: Student/faculty ratio 21:1. 277 full-time faculty, 73% hold PhDs, 41% are members of minority groups, 56% are women. 0% of classes are taught by teaching assistants.

ACADEMICS
Degrees: Bachelor's; Master's; Post-bachelor's certificate; Post-master's certificate. **Classes:** Most classes have 20–29 students. Most lab/discussion sessions have 20–29 students. **Most popular majors:** Criminal Justice/Safety Studies; Business Administration and Management, General; Psychology, General. **Special Study Options:** Accelerated program; Cross-registration; Distance learning; Double major; Dual enrollment; External degree program; Honors program; Independent study; Internships; Student-designed major; Study abroad; Teacher certification program; Weekend college. **Honors programs:** University Honors Program is currently on hiatus, while we reorganize to bring back an improved program in 2017–18. **Disability Services offered:** Note-taking services; Reader services; Tape recorders; Tutors. **Career services:** Alumni services; Career assessment; Career/job search classes; Internships.

FACILITIES
Housing: Apartments for married students; Apartments for single students; Special housing for disabled students; 100% of campus accessible to physically disabled. **Special Academic Facilities/Equipment:** University Art Gallery, University Library, University Theater.

CAMPUS LIFE
Environment: City. **Activities:** Choral groups; Concert band; Dance; Drama/theater; International Student Organization; Jazz band; Literary magazine; Music ensembles; Musical theater; Radio station; Student government; Student newspaper; Television station. 115 registered organizations, 5 honor societies, 6 religious organizations, 9 fraternities, 9 sororities, on campus. **Athletics (Intercollegiate):** *Men:* baseball, basketball, golf, soccer. *Women:* basketball, cross-country, soccer, softball, tennis, track/field (outdoor), volleyball. **On-Campus Highlights:** Welch Hall.

ADMISSIONS
Freshman Academic Profile: Average high school GPA 3.1. 93% from public high schools. **Test Scores:** SAT Math middle 50% range 380–470. SAT EBRW middle 50% range 380–470. ACT middle 50% range 15–19. **Basis for Candidate Selection:** *Other factors include:* academic GPA, standardized test scores. **Freshman Admission Requirements:** High school diploma is required and GED is accepted. *Academic units required:* 4 English, 3 math, 2 science, 2 science labs, 2 foreign language, 1 social studies, 1 history, 1 academic electives, 1 visual/performing arts. **Freshman Admission Statistics:** 10,615 applied, 75% admitted, 16% enrolled. **Transfer Admission Requirements:** High school transcript, college transcript(s). Minimum college GPA of 2.0 required. Lowest grade transferable C. **General Admission Information:** Application fee $55. Priority deadline 11/30. Non-fall registration accepted.

COSTS AND FINANCIAL AID
Annual in-state tuition $5,472. Annual out-of-state tuition $16,632. Average book and supplies expense $1,850. **Required Forms and Deadlines:** FAFSA. **Notification of Awards:** Applicants will be notified of awards on a rolling basis beginning 2/28. **Types of Aid:** *Need-based scholarships/grants:* College/university scholarship or grant aid from institutional funds; Federal Pell; Private scholarships; SEOG; State scholarships/grants. *Loans:* Direct PLUS loans; Direct Subsidized Stafford Loans; Direct Unsubsidized Stafford Loans.

Student Employment: Federal Work-Study Program available. Institutional employment available. **Financial Aid Statistics:** 89% needy freshmen, 86% needy undergrads receive need-based scholarship or grant aid. 16% freshmen, 24% undergrads receive non-need-based scholarship or grant aid. 1% freshmen, 2% undergrads receive need-based self-help aid. 0% freshmen, 0% undergrads receive athletic scholarships. 87% freshmen, 82% undergrads receive any aid. 58% undergrads borrow to pay for school. Average cumulative indebtedness $16,370. **Criteria awarding aid:** *Need-based:* Academics, Athletics. *Non-need-based:* Academics, Alumni affiliation, Art, Athletics, Leadership, Music/drama.

CALIFORNIA STATE UNIVERSITY, EAST BAY

25800 Carlos Bee Blvd., Hayward, CA 94542-3035
Phone: 510-885-2784 **Financial Aid Phone:** 510-885-2784
E-mail: admissions@csueastbay.edu **CEEB Code:** 4011
Fax: 510-885-3505 **Website:** www.csueastbay.edu **ACT Code:** 154

This public school was founded in 1957. It has a 342 acre campus.

RATINGS
Admissions Selectivity Rating: 88 **Fire Safety Rating:** 75 **Green Rating:** 60*

STUDENTS AND FACULTY
Enrollment: 9,788. **Student Body:** 60% female, 40% male, 1% out-of-state, 8% international (86 countries represented). Asian 20%, African American 10%, Caucasian 22%, Hispanic 19%, Native American <1%, Pacific Islander 3%, Two or more races 3%, Race unknown 14%.
Retention and Graduation: 76% freshmen return for sophomore year.
Faculty: Student/faculty ratio 26:1. 322 full-time faculty, 0% hold PhDs, 34% are members of minority groups, 49% are women. 5% of classes are taught by teaching assistants.

ACADEMICS
Degrees: Bachelor's; Certificate; Master's; Post-bachelor's certificate; Post-master's certificate. **Classes:** Most classes have 20–29 students. Most lab/discussion sessions have 20–29 students. **Special Study Options:** Cooperative education program; Cross-registration; Distance learning; Double major; Dual enrollment; English as a Second Language (ESL); Exchange student program (domestic); External degree program; Honors program; Independent study; Internships; Liberal arts/career combination; Student-designed major; Study abroad; Teacher certification program; Weekend college. **Disability Services offered:** Note-taking services; Reader services; Tape recorders; Tutors. **Career services:** Alumni services; Career assessment; Career/job search classes; Internships.

FACILITIES
Housing: Apartments for single students; 95% of campus accessible to physically disabled. **Special Academic Facilities/Equipment:** Anthropology museum, art gallery, scanning electron microsope facility, marine lab, ecological field station, geology summer camp.

CAMPUS LIFE
Environment: City. **Activities:** Choral groups; Concert band; Dance; Drama/theater; Jazz band; Literary magazine; Music ensembles; Musical theater; Opera; Pep band; Radio station; Student government; Student newspaper; Symphony orchestra; Television station. 100 registered organizations, 2 honor societies, 2 religious organizations, 7 fraternities, 7 sororities, on campus. **Athletics (Intercollegiate):** *Men:* baseball, basketball, cross-country, golf, soccer. *Women:* basketball, cross-country, golf, soccer, softball, swimming, volleyball, water polo. **On-Campus Highlights:** University Union.

ADMISSIONS
Freshman Academic Profile: Average high school GPA 3.1. **Test Scores:** SAT Math middle 50% range 400–510. SAT EBRW middle 50% range 400–500. ACT middle 50% range 16–21. **Basis for Candidate Selection:** *Very important factors include:* rigor of secondary school record, academic GPA, standardized test scores. *Other factors include:* recommendation(s), state residency. **Freshman Admission Requirements:** High school diploma is required and GED is accepted. *Academic units required:* 4 English, 3 math, 2 science, 2 science labs, 2 foreign language, 1 social studies, 1 history, 1 academic electives, 1 unit from above areas or other academic areas. **Freshman Admission Statistics:** 10,778 applied, 36% admitted, 32% enrolled. **Transfer Admission Requirements:** College transcript(s), statement of good standing from prior institution(s). Minimum college GPA of 2.0 required. Lowest grade transferable D. **General**

Admission Information: Application fee $55. Priority deadline 11/30. Regular application deadline 6/30. Non-fall registration accepted. Admission may be deferred for a maximum of 2 quarters.

COSTS AND FINANCIAL AID
Annual in-state tuition $5,091. Annual out-of-state tuition $14,019. Room and board $11,042. Average book and supplies expense $1,734. **Required Forms and Deadlines:** FAFSA. **Notification of Awards:** Applicants will be notified of awards on a rolling basis beginning 3/15. **Types of Aid:** *Need-based scholarships/grants:* College/university scholarship or grant aid from institutional funds; Federal Pell; Private scholarships; SEOG; State scholarships/grants. **Student Employment:** Federal Work-Study Program available. Institutional employment available. **Financial Aid Statistics:** 83% needy freshmen, 83% needy undergrads receive need-based scholarship or grant aid. 0% freshmen, 0% undergrads receive non-need-based scholarship or grant aid. 61% freshmen, 61% undergrads receive need-based self-help aid. 0% freshmen, 0% undergrads receive athletic scholarships. 43% freshmen, 42% undergrads receive any aid. **Criteria awarding aid:** *Need-based:* Academics. *Non-need-based:* Academics.

CALIFORNIA STATE UNIVERSITY, FRESNO

5150 North Maple Ave. M/S JA 57, Fresno, CA 93740-8026
Phone: 559-278-2261 **Financial Aid Phone:** 559-278-2182
E-mail: admissions@csufresno.edu **CEEB Code:** 4312
Fax: 559-278-4812 **Website:** www.csufresno.edu **ACT Code:** 266

This public school was founded in 1911. It has a 388 acre campus.

RATINGS
Admissions Selectivity Rating: 83   **Fire Safety Rating:** 78   **Green Rating:** 60*

STUDENTS AND FACULTY
Enrollment: 18,784. **Student Body:** 57% female, 43% male, <1% out-of-state, 3% international (116 countries represented). Asian 15%, African American 5%, Caucasian 30%, Hispanic 38%, Native American 1%, Pacific Islander <1%, Two or more races 3%, Race unknown 6%.
Retention and Graduation: 86% freshmen return for sophomore year.
Faculty: Student/faculty ratio 22:1. 624 full-time faculty, 95% hold PhDs, 29% are members of minority groups, 42% are women. 8% of classes are taught by teaching assistants.

ACADEMICS
Degrees: Bachelor's; Doctoral degree research/scholarship; Master's; Post-bachelor's certificate; Post-master's certificate. **Classes:** Most classes have 20–29 students. Most lab/discussion sessions have 20–29 students. **Most popular majors:** Liberal Arts and Sciences/Liberal Studies; Psychology, General; Health Professions And Related Programs. **Special Study Options:** Accelerated program; Cooperative education program; Cross-registration; Distance learning; Double major; Dual enrollment; English as a Second Language (ESL); Exchange student program (domestic); Honors program; Independent study; Internships; Student-designed major; Study abroad; Teacher certification program. **Honors programs:** The Smittcamp Family Honors College (Smittcamp Honors College) was founded in the fall of 1999 to attract high-quality students to the university. These students are recruited from the entire state through solicitations of high school principals, scholarship advisers and California Scholarship Federation advisers, in addition to direct mail to high PSAT scorers. Successful students are selected based on their grades, SAT scores, rigor of their classes, community service, awards, reference letters, and two essays. High school students satisfying any one of the following criteria are eligible to apply: 1200 SAT scores, 3.6 grade point average, or top 10% of their high school class. A large percentage of applicants who are not selected also choose to enroll at the university. Currently, there are 50 seniors, 50 juniors, 75 sophomores, and 75 freshmen in the Honors College. Classes of 75 will be selected in the future. Students in the Honors College take 36 of their 51 general education units in specifically designed honors courses, two courses in each of their first four semesters, then three upper-division general education courses. Classes go through the program as a cohort. All honors students take the Honors Colloquium for five semesters of their career. Students in the Honors College receive a four-year President's Scholarship that includes all registration fees and on-campus housing. The Residence Hall administration attempts to cluster the students in several residence halls. Students also receive free parking, special library privileges, use of a laptop computer, use of the Honors College computer lab, and use of the Honors College Office. Students

must maintain escalating (3.0, 3.25, and 3.4) grade point averages during their attendance. Students perform community service as part of their status in the Honors College. **Disability Services offered:** Note-taking services; Reader services; Tape recorders; Tutors.

FACILITIES
Housing: Coed dorms; Fraternity/sorority housing; Men's dorms; Women's dorms; 100% of campus accessible to physically disabled. **Special Academic Facilities/Equipment:** Marine lab, Downing Planeterium.

CAMPUS LIFE
Environment: Metropolis. **Activities:** Choral groups; Concert band; Dance; Drama/theater; International Student Organization; Jazz band; Marching band; Music ensembles; Musical theater; Radio station; Student government; Student newspaper; Symphony orchestra; Television station; Yearbook. 250 registered organizations, 21 honor societies, 11 religious organizations, 19 fraternities, 13 sororities, on campus. **Athletics (Intercollegiate):** *Men:* baseball, basketball, cheerleading, cross-country, football, golf, tennis, track/field (outdoor). *Women:* basketball, cheerleading, cross-country, diving, equestrian sports, golf, lacrosse, light weight football, soccer, softball, swimming, tennis, track/field (outdoor), volleyball. **On-Campus Highlights:** Savemart Events Center. **Environmental Initiatives:** Solar Photovoltaic Canopy Parking Structure (Lot V) This structure is a 1.1 megawatt solar system, making it the largest photovoltaic paneled parting installation at a U.S. university. Completed in the fall of 2007, the structure was estimated to provide 20% of the core campus power. The system offsets approximately 950 metric tons of carbon monoxide emissions—that is equivalent to planting over 24,300 trees or eliminating from our road systems over 200 vehicles a year!

ADMISSIONS
Freshman Academic Profile: Average high school GPA 3.3. 15% in top 10% of high school class, 80% in top 25% of high school class, 100% in top 50% of high school class. 99% from public high schools. **Test Scores:** SAT Math middle 50% range 410–530. SAT EBRW middle 50% range 400–510. ACT middle 50% range 16–22. **Basis for Candidate Selection:** *Very important factors include:* rigor of secondary school record, academic GPA, standardized test scores. **Freshman Admission Requirements:** High school diploma is required and GED is accepted. *Academic units required:* 4 English, 3 math, 1 science, 1 science labs, 2 foreign language, 1 social studies, 1 history, 1 academic electives, 1 visual/performing arts. **Freshman Admission Statistics:** 15,482 applied, 60% admitted, 31% enrolled. **Transfer Admission Requirements:** College transcript(s). Minimum college GPA of 2.4 required. Lowest grade transferable D. **General Admission Information:** Application fee $55. Regular application deadline 11/30.

COSTS AND FINANCIAL AID
Annual in-state tuition $5,472. Annual out-of-state tuition $11,160. Room and board $12,833. Required fees $790. Average book and supplies expense $1,256. **Required Forms and Deadlines:** FAFSA. **Notification of Awards:** Applicants will be notified of awards on a rolling basis beginning 4/1. **Types of Aid:** *Need-based scholarships/grants:* College/university scholarship or grant aid from institutional funds; Federal Pell; Private scholarships; SEOG; State scholarships/grants. *Loans:* Direct PLUS loans; Direct Subsidized Stafford Loans; Direct Unsubsidized Stafford Loans. **Student Employment:** Federal Work-Study Program available. Institutional employment available. **Financial Aid Statistics:** 83% needy freshmen, 80% needy undergrads receive need-based scholarship or grant aid. 2% freshmen, 9% undergrads receive non-need-based scholarship or grant aid. 67% freshmen, 79% undergrads receive need-based self-help aid. 3% freshmen, 2% undergrads receive athletic scholarships. 76% freshmen, 78% undergrads receive any aid. **Criteria awarding aid:** *Need-based:* Academics, Athletics. *Non-need-based:* Academics, Art, Athletics, Leadership, Music/drama, State/district residency.

CALIFORNIA STATE UNIVERSITY, FULLERTON

P.O. Box 6900, Fullerton, CA 92834-6900
Phone: 657-278-7788 **Financial Aid Phone:** 657-278-3125
E-mail: admissions@fullerton.edu **CEEB Code:** 4589
Fax: 657-278-7699 **Website:** www.fullerton.edu **ACT Code:** 0355

This public school was founded in 1957. It has a 240 acre campus.

RATINGS
Admissions Selectivity Rating: 87   **Fire Safety Rating:** 84   **Green Rating:** 89

STUDENTS AND FACULTY
Enrollment: 34,921. **Student Body:** 57% female, 43% male, 1% out-of-state, 6% international (77 countries represented). Asian 21%, African American 2%, Caucasian 18%, Hispanic 46%, Native American <1%, Pacific Islander <1%, Two or more races 4%, Race unknown 3%.
Retention and Graduation: 89% freshmen return for sophomore year. 23% freshmen graduate within 4 years. 70% freshmen graduate within 6 years.
Faculty: Student/faculty ratio 25:1. 1,007 full-time faculty, 85% hold PhDs, 35% are members of minority groups, 51% are women. 0% of classes are taught by teaching assistants.

ACADEMICS
Degrees: Bachelor's; Certificate; Doctoral degree—professional practice; Doctoral degree research/scholarship; Master's; Post-bachelor's certificate; Post-master's certificate. **Classes:** Most classes have 20–29 students. **Most popular majors:** English Language and Literature, General; Liberal Arts and Sciences/Liberal Studies; Biology/Biological Sciences, General. **Special Study Options:** Cooperative education program; Distance learning; Double major; Honors program; Internships; Study abroad. **Honors programs:** University Honors Program President's Scholars Program. **Disability Services offered:** Note-taking services; Reader services; Tape recorders; Tutors. **Career services:** Alumni network; Alumni services; Career assessment; Career/job search classes; Internships; Regional alumni.

FACILITIES
Housing: Apartments for single students; Coed dorms; Fraternity/sorority housing; Men's dorms; Theme housing; Women's dorms; 100% of campus accessible to physically disabled. **Special Academic Facilities/Equipment:** W.M. Keck Foundation Center for Molecular Structure; Museum of Anthropology; Art Gallery; Fullerton Arboretum; Grand Central Art Center; Herbarium; Speech, Language/Hearing Clinic; Titan Communications; Foreign Language Laboratory; Art Gallery; Sport and Movement Institute; Institute of Gerontology; Institute for Molecular Biology and Nutrition; Center for Molecular Structure; Center for Demographic Research; Social Science Research Center; CA Public Archeology Center. **Campus network:** 100% of classrooms, 100% of dorms, 100% of student union, 100% of libraries, 100% of dining areas, 0% of common outdoor areas, have wireless network access.

CAMPUS LIFE
Environment: City. **Activities:** Choral groups; Concert band; Dance; Drama/theater; International Student Organization; Jazz band; Model UN; Music ensembles; Musical theater; Radio station; Student government; Student newspaper; Symphony orchestra. 374 registered organizations, 17 honor societies, 29 religious organizations, 14 fraternities, 11 sororities, on campus. **Athletics (Intercollegiate):** *Men:* baseball, basketball, cross-country, fencing, soccer, track/field (outdoor), wrestling. *Women:* basketball, cross-country, fencing, gymnastics, soccer, softball, tennis, track/field (outdoor), volleyball. **On-Campus Highlights:** Student Recreation Center.

ADMISSIONS
Freshman Academic Profile: Average high school GPA 3.7. 22% in top 10% of high school class, 63% in top 25% of high school class, 93% in top 50% of high school class. 83% from public high schools. **Test Scores:** SAT Math middle 50% range 520–600. SAT EBRW middle 50% range 510–600. ACT middle 50% range 19–24. **Basis for Candidate Selection:** *Very important factors include:* academic GPA, standardized test scores, geographical residence, state residency. **Freshman Admission Requirements:** High school diploma is required and GED is accepted. *Academic units required:* 4 English, 3 math, 2 science, 2 science labs, 2 foreign language, 1 social studies, 1 history, 1 academic electives, 1 visual/performing arts. *Academic units recommended:* 4 English, 3 math, 2 science, 2 science labs, 3 foreign language, 1 social studies, 1 history, 1 academic electives, 1 visual/performing arts. **Freshman Admission Statistics:** 50,105 applied, 53% admitted, 18% enrolled. **Transfer Admission**

Requirements: College transcript(s), statement of good standing from prior institution(s). Minimum college GPA of 2.0 required. Lowest grade transferable C. **General Admission Information:** Application fee $70. Priority deadline 10/30. Regular application deadline 11/30.

COSTS AND FINANCIAL AID
Annual in-state tuition $6,927. Annual out-of-state tuition $16,431. Required fees $1,181. Average book and supplies expense $2,002. **Types of Aid:** *Need-based scholarships/grants:* College/university scholarship or grant aid from institutional funds; Federal Pell; Private scholarships; SEOG; State scholarships/grants. *Loans:* Direct PLUS loans; Direct Subsidized Stafford Loans; Direct Unsubsidized Stafford Loans. **Student Employment:** Federal Work-Study Program available. Institutional employment available. **Financial Aid Statistics:** 93% needy freshmen, 93% needy undergrads receive need-based scholarship or grant aid. 20% freshmen, 17% undergrads receive non-need-based scholarship or grant aid. 36% freshmen, 37% undergrads receive need-based self-help aid. 1% freshmen, 1% undergrads receive athletic scholarships. 60% freshmen, 65% undergrads receive any aid. 42% undergrads borrow to pay for school. Average cumulative indebtedness $7,665. **Criteria awarding aid:** *Need-based:* Academics, Art, Athletics, Music/drama. *Non-need-based:* Academics, Art, Athletics, Leadership, Music/drama.

CALIFORNIA STATE UNIVERSITY, LONG BEACH

1250 Bellflower Boulevard, Long Beach, CA 90840
Phone: 562-985-5471
E-mail: eslb@csulb.edu **CEEB Code:** 4389
Fax: 562-985-4973 **Website:** www.csulb.edu

This public school was founded in 1949. It has a 322 acre campus.

RATINGS
Admissions Selectivity Rating: 89   **Fire Safety Rating:** 67   **Green Rating:** 89

STUDENTS AND FACULTY
Enrollment: 32,079. **Student Body:** 56% female, 44% male, 1% out-of-state, 7% international. Asian 23%, African American 4%, Caucasian 19%, Hispanic 39%, Native American <1%, Pacific Islander <1%, Two or more races 5%, Race unknown 4%.
Retention and Graduation: 91% freshmen return for sophomore year.
Faculty: Student/faculty ratio 24:1. 960 full-time faculty, 85% hold PhDs, 34% are members of minority groups, 48% are women. 8% of classes are taught by teaching assistants.

ACADEMICS
Degrees: Bachelor's; Doctoral degree—professional practice; Doctoral degree research/scholarship; Master's; Post-bachelor's certificate. **Classes:** Most classes have 20–29 students. **Most popular majors:** Corrections and Criminal Justice, Other; Management Information Systems, General; Psychology, General. **Special Study Options:** Double major; Dual enrollment; English as a Second Language (ESL); Honors program; Independent study; Internships; Student-designed major; Study abroad; Teacher certification program. **Disability Services offered:** Note-taking services; Reader services. **Career services:** Alumni services; Career assessment; Internships.

FACILITIES
Housing: Coed dorms; Special housing for international students; 98% of campus accessible to physically disabled. **Special Academic Facilities/Equipment:** Art and science museums, Japanese garden, special events arena with meeting facilities.

CAMPUS LIFE
Activities: Choral groups; Concert band; Dance; Drama/theater; Jazz band; Literary magazine; Music ensembles; Musical theater; Opera; Radio station; Student government; Student newspaper; Student-run film society; Symphony orchestra; Television station; Yearbook. 300 registered organizations, 25 honor societies, 20 religious organizations, 16 fraternities, 15 sororities, on campus. **Athletics (Intercollegiate):** *Men:* baseball, basketball, cross-country, golf, track/field (outdoor), volleyball, water polo. *Women:* basketball, cross-country, golf, soccer, softball, tennis, track/field (outdoor), volleyball, water polo.

ADMISSIONS
Freshman Academic Profile: Average high school GPA 3.5. 82% from public high schools. **Test Scores:** SAT Math middle 50% range 470–600. SAT EBRW middle 50% range 460–570. **Basis for Candidate Selection:** *Very important*

factors include: academic GPA, standardized test scores, geographical residence, state residency. Important factors include: talent/ability. Other factors include: rigor of secondary school record, application essay, recommendation(s), extracurricular activities, character/personal qualities, volunteer work, work experience. **Freshman Admission Requirements:** High school diploma is required and GED is accepted. Academic units required: 4 English, 3 math, 2 science, 2 science labs, 2 foreign language, 1 social studies, 1 history, 1 academic electives, 1 unit from above areas or other academic areas. **Freshman Admission Statistics:** 56,975 applied, 34% admitted, 23% enrolled. **Transfer Admission Requirements:** College transcript(s), Minimum college GPA of 2.0 required. Lowest grade transferable C. **General Admission Information:** Regular application deadline 11/30.

COSTS AND FINANCIAL AID

Annual in-state tuition $5,472. Annual out-of-state tuition $15,144. Room and board $12,382. Required fees $980. Average book and supplies expense $1,898. **Required Forms and Deadlines:** FAFSA. **Notification of Awards:** Applicants will be notified of awards on a rolling basis beginning 3/25. **Types of Aid:** Need-based scholarships/grants: College/university scholarship or grant aid from institutional funds; Federal Pell; Private scholarships; SEOG; State scholarships/grants. Loans: Direct PLUS loans; Direct Subsidized Stafford Loans; Direct Unsubsidized Stafford Loans. **Student Employment:** Federal Work-Study Program available. Institutional employment available. **Financial Aid Statistics:** 77% needy freshmen, 80% needy undergrads receive need-based scholarship or grant aid. 19% freshmen, 26% undergrads receive non-need-based scholarship or grant aid. 69% freshmen, 79% undergrads receive need-based self-help aid. 1% freshmen, 1% undergrads receive athletic scholarships. 42% undergrads borrow to pay for school. Average cumulative indebtedness $16,077. **Criteria awarding aid:** Need-based: Academics, Art. Non-need-based: Academics, Art, Athletics, Job skills, Leadership, Music/drama, State/district residency.

CALIFORNIA STATE UNIVERSITY, LOS ANGELES

5151 State University Drive, Los Angeles, CA 90032
Phone: 323-343-3901 **Financial Aid Phone:** 323-343-6260
E-mail: admission@calstatela.edu **CEEB Code:** 4399
Fax: 323-343-6306 **ACT Code:** 320

This public school was founded in 1947. It has a 175 acre campus.

RATINGS

Admissions Selectivity Rating: 85   **Fire Safety Rating:** 84   **Green Rating:** 87

STUDENTS AND FACULTY

Enrollment: 22,561. **Student Body:** 58% female, 42% male, 1% out-of-state, 6% international (121 countries represented). Asian 12%, African American 3%, Caucasian 5%, Hispanic 70%, Native American <1%, Pacific Islander <1%, Two or more races 1%, Race unknown 2%.
Retention and Graduation: 81% freshmen return for sophomore year. 8% freshmen graduate within 4 years. 51% freshmen graduate within 6 years.
Faculty: Student/faculty ratio 23:1. 652 full-time faculty, 78% hold PhDs, 49% are members of minority groups, 52% are women. 14% of classes are taught by teaching assistants.

ACADEMICS

Degrees: Bachelor's; Certificate; Doctoral degree—other; Doctoral degree—professional practice; Doctoral degree research/scholarship; Master's; Post-bachelor's certificate; Post-master's certificate. **Classes:** Most classes have 20–29 students. Most lab/discussion sessions have 20–29 students. **Most popular majors:** Criminal Justice/Law Enforcement Administration; Business Administration and Management, General; Psychology, General. **Special Study Options:** Accelerated program; Cooperative education program; Cross-registration; Distance learning; Double major; Dual enrollment; English as a Second Language (ESL); Exchange student program (domestic); Honors program; Independent study; Internships; Student-designed major; Study abroad; Teacher certification program. **Honors programs:** The Honors College provides an academically enriched and socially supportive environment that inspires students in all disciplines to become creative and critical thinkers as well as leaders in their fields. With core learning goals focused on knowledge creation, social innovation, and global citizenship, it prepares students to address the most pressing challenges of the 21st century. **Disability Services offered:** Note-taking services; Reader services. **Career services:** Career/job search classes; Internships.

FACILITIES

Housing: Apartments for single students; Fraternity/sorority housing; Special housing for disabled students; Special housing for international students; 99% of campus accessible to physically disabled. **Special Academic Facilities/Equipment:** Baroque pipe organ, bilingual center, entrepreneurship and small business institutes, center for study of armament and disarmament, Van de Graaff accelerator.

CAMPUS LIFE

Environment: Metropolis. **Activities:** Choral groups; Dance; Drama/theater; Jazz band; Literary magazine; Music ensembles; Musical theater; Opera; Student government; Student newspaper; Student-run film society; Symphony orchestra; Yearbook. 130 registered organizations, 3 religious organizations, 7 fraternities, 4 sororities, on campus. **Athletics (Intercollegiate):** Men: baseball, basketball, cross-country, soccer, track/field (outdoor). Women: basketball, cross-country, soccer, tennis, track/field (outdoor), volleyball. **On-Campus Highlights:** University Student Union.

ADMISSIONS

Freshman Academic Profile: Average high school GPA 3.2. **Test Scores:** SAT Math middle 50% range 390–510. SAT EBRW middle 50% range 380–480. ACT middle 50% range 15–20. **Basis for Candidate Selection:** Very important factors include: rigor of secondary school record, academic GPA, standardized test scores. Other factors include: geographical residence, state residency. **Freshman Admission Requirements:** High school diploma is required and GED is accepted. Academic units required: 4 English, 3 math, 2 science, 2 science labs, 2 foreign language, 1 social studies, 1 academic electives, 1 visual/performing arts. Academic units recommended: 4 English, 3 math, 2 science, 2 science labs, 2 foreign language, 1 social studies, 1 history, 1 academic electives, 1 visual/performing arts. **Freshman Admission Statistics:** 33,641 applied, 48% admitted, 20% enrolled. **Transfer Admission Requirements:** College transcript(s). Minimum college GPA of 2.0 required. Lowest grade transferable C. **General Admission Information:** Application fee $55. Regular application deadline 11/30. Non-fall registration accepted.

COSTS AND FINANCIAL AID

Annual in-state tuition $5,742. Annual out-of-state tuition $17,622. Room and board $15,992. Required fees $1,026. Average book and supplies expense $2,058. **Required Forms and Deadlines:** FAFSA. **Notification of Awards:** Applicants will be notified of awards on or about 4/1. **Types of Aid:** Need-based scholarships/grants: College/university scholarship or grant aid from institutional funds; Federal Pell; Private scholarships; SEOG; State scholarships/grants. Loans: Direct PLUS loans; Direct Subsidized Stafford Loans; Direct Unsubsidized Stafford Loans. **Student Employment:** Federal Work-Study Program available. Institutional employment available. **Financial Aid Statistics:** 54% needy freshmen, 58% needy undergrads receive need-based scholarship or grant aid. 0% freshmen, 0% undergrads receive non-need-based scholarship or grant aid. 39% freshmen, 53% undergrads receive need-based self-help aid. 0% freshmen, 0% undergrads receive athletic scholarships. 76% freshmen, 77% undergrads receive any aid.

CALIFORNIA STATE UNIVERSITY, MARITIME ACADEMY

200 Maritime Academy, Vallejo, CA 94590-0644
Phone: 707-654-1330 **Financial Aid Phone:** (707) 654-1276
E-mail: admission@csum.edu **CEEB Code:** 4035
Fax: 707-654-1336 **Website:** www.csum.edu **ACT Code:** 0184

This public school was founded in 1929. It has a 67 acre campus.

RATINGS

Admissions Selectivity Rating: 76   **Fire Safety Rating:** 60*   **Green Rating:** 60*

STUDENTS AND FACULTY

Enrollment: 1,072. **Student Body:** 15% female, 85% male, 1% international. Asian 10%, African American 2%, Caucasian 53%, Hispanic 17%, Native American <1%, Pacific Islander <1%, Two or more races 11%, Race unknown 6%.
Retention and Graduation: 82% freshmen return for sophomore year.
Faculty: Student/faculty ratio 15:1. 64 full-time faculty, 63% hold PhDs, 6% are members of minority groups, 20% are women. 0% of classes are taught by teaching assistants.

ACADEMICS

Degrees: Bachelor's; Master's. **Classes:** Most classes have 20–29 students. Most lab/discussion sessions have 10–19 students. **Most popular majors:** International Relations and Affairs; Mechanical Engineering; Marine Science/Merchant Marine Officer. **Special Study Options:** Cooperative education program; Double major; Honors program; Internships;. **Disability Services offered:** Tutors. **Career services:** Alumni services; Career/job search classes; Internships.

FACILITIES

Housing: Coed dorms; Special housing for international students; Theme housing; 70% of campus accessible to physically disabled. **Special Academic Facilities/Equipment:** Bookstore, Library, Gym, Swimming Pool.

CAMPUS LIFE

Activities: Choral groups; Student government. 16 registered organizations, on campus. **Athletics (Intercollegiate):** *Men:* basketball, crew/rowing, golf, sailing, soccer, water polo. *Women:* crew/rowing, sailing, volleyball.

ADMISSIONS

Freshman Academic Profile: Average high school GPA 3.3. 80% from public high schools. **Test Scores:** SAT Math middle 50% range 510–610. SAT EBRW middle 50% range 490–600. ACT middle 50% range 21–27. **Basis for Candidate Selection:** *Very important factors include:* academic GPA, standardized test scores. *Important factors include:* rigor of secondary school record. *Other factors include:* extracurricular activities, talent/ability, geographical residence, state residency, volunteer work, work experience. **Freshman Admission Requirements:** High school diploma is required and GED is accepted. *Academic units required:* 4 English, 3 math, 2 science, 2 science labs, 2 foreign language, 1 social studies, 1 history, 1 academic electives, 1 visual/performing arts. *Academic units recommended:* 4 English, 4 math, 3 science, 3 science labs, 2 foreign language, 1 social studies, 1 history, 1 academic electives, 1 visual/performing arts. **Freshman Admission Statistics:** 1,206 applied, 82% admitted, 23% enrolled. **Transfer Admission Requirements:** College transcript(s), statement of good standing from prior institution(s). Minimum college GPA of 2.0 required. Lowest grade transferable C. **General Admission Information:** Application fee $55. Priority deadline 11/30.

COSTS AND FINANCIAL AID

Annual in-state tuition $9,960. Room and board $11,756. Required fees $1,314. Average book and supplies expense $1,336. **Required Forms and Deadlines:** FAFSA. **Notification of Awards:** Applicants will be notified of awards on a rolling basis beginning 4/15. **Types of Aid:** *Need-based scholarships/grants:* College/university scholarship or grant aid from institutional funds; Federal Pell; Private scholarships; SEOG; State scholarships/grants. *Loans:* Direct PLUS loans; Direct Subsidized Stafford Loans; Direct Unsubsidized Stafford Loans. **Financial Aid Statistics:** 87% needy freshmen, 84% needy undergrads receive need-based scholarship or grant aid. 0% freshmen, 0% undergrads receive non-need-based scholarship or grant aid. 80% freshmen, 17% undergrads receive need-based self-help aid. 0% freshmen, 0% undergrads receive athletic scholarships. **Criteria awarding aid:** *Need-based:* Academics, Leadership.

CALIFORNIA STATE UNIVERSITY, MONTEREY BAY

100 Campus Center, Seaside, CA 93955
Phone: 831-582-3738 **Financial Aid Phone:** 831-582-5100
E-mail: admissions@csumb.edu **CEEB Code:** 1945
Fax: 831-582-3738 **Website:** https://www.csumb.edu/ **ACT Code:** 0321

This public school was founded in 1994. It has a 1387 acre campus.

RATINGS

Admissions Selectivity Rating: 76   **Fire Safety Rating:** 87   **Green Rating:** 98

STUDENTS AND FACULTY

Enrollment: 6,794. **Student Body:** 61% female, 39% male, 2% out-of-state, 6% international (20 countries represented). Asian 6%, African American 4%, Caucasian 27%, Hispanic 42%, Native American 1%, Pacific Islander 1%, Two or more races 8%, Race unknown 5%.
Retention and Graduation: 80% freshmen return for sophomore year. 30% freshmen graduate within 4 years. 63% freshmen graduate within 6 years.
Faculty: Student/faculty ratio 25:1. 184 full-time faculty, 90% hold PhDs, 40%

are members of minority groups, 53% are women. 0% of classes are taught by teaching assistants.

ACADEMICS

Degrees: Bachelor's; Master's; Post-bachelor's certificate. **Classes:** Most classes have 20–29 students. Most lab/discussion sessions have 20–29 students. **Most popular majors:** Business Administration and Management, General; Sports, Kinesiology, and Physical Education/Fitness, General; Psychology, General. **Special Study Options:** Accelerated program; Cross-registration; Distance learning; Double major; English as a Second Language (ESL); Exchange student program (domestic); Independent study; Internships; Student-designed major; Study abroad; Teacher certification program. **Disability Services offered:** Note-taking services; Reader services; Tape recorders. **Career services:** Alumni services; Career assessment; Career/job search classes; Internships.

FACILITIES

Housing: Apartments for married students; Apartments for single students; Coed dorms; Special housing for disabled students; Special housing for international students; Theme housing; Wellness housing; 85% of campus accessible to physically disabled. **Special Academic Facilities/Equipment:** Panetta Institute, Tanimura & Antle Family Memorial Library.

CAMPUS LIFE

Environment: Village. **Activities:** Campus Ministries; Dance; Drama/theater; International Student Organization; Radio station; Student government; Student newspaper; Student-run film society; Television station. 76 registered organizations, 3 religious organizations, 6 fraternities, 7 sororities, on campus. **Athletics (Intercollegiate):** *Men:* baseball, basketball, cross-country, golf, sailing, soccer. *Women:* basketball, cross-country, golf, sailing, soccer, softball, volleyball, water polo. **On-Campus Highlights:** Black Box Cabaret. **Environmental Initiatives:** We are an early signatory to the Presidents Climate Commitment.

ADMISSIONS

Freshman Academic Profile: 12% in top 10% of high school class, 44% in top 25% of high school class, 86% in top 50% of high school class. 89% from public high schools. **Test Scores:** SAT Math middle 50% range 470–570. SAT EBRW middle 50% range 490–600. ACT middle 50% range 17–23. **Basis for Candidate Selection:** *Very important factors include:* academic GPA, standardized test scores. *Important factors include:* rigor of secondary school record. *Other factors include:* state residency. **Freshman Admission Requirements:** High school diploma is required and GED is accepted. *Academic units required:* 4 English, 3 math, 2 science, 1 science labs, 2 foreign language, 1 social studies, 1 history, 1 academic electives, 1 visual/performing arts. **Freshman Admission Statistics:** 12,316 applied, 75% admitted, 11% enrolled. **Transfer Admission Requirements:** High school transcript, essay or personal statement, standardized test scores, Minimum college GPA of 2.5 required. Lowest grade transferable C. **General Admission Information:** Application fee $70. Priority deadline 11/30. Regular application deadline 11/30.

COSTS AND FINANCIAL AID

Annual in-state tuition $5,742. Annual out-of-state tuition $17,622. Room and board $13,711. Required fees $1,401. Average book and supplies expense $1,854. **Required Forms and Deadlines:** FAFSA; State aid form. **Notification of Awards:** Applicants will be notified of awards on a rolling basis beginning 2/1. **Types of Aid:** *Need-based scholarships/grants:* College/university scholarship or grant aid from institutional funds; Federal Pell; Private scholarships; SEOG; State scholarships/grants. *Loans:* Direct PLUS loans; Direct Subsidized Stafford Loans; Direct Unsubsidized Stafford Loans. **Student Employment:** Federal Work-Study Program available. Institutional employment available. **Financial Aid Statistics:** 77% needy freshmen, 77% needy undergrads receive need-based scholarship or grant aid. 19% freshmen, 15% undergrads receive non-need-based scholarship or grant aid. 50% freshmen, 49% undergrads receive need-based self-help aid. 4% freshmen, 3% undergrads receive athletic scholarships. 49% freshmen, 59% undergrads receive any aid. 65% undergrads borrow to pay for school. Average cumulative indebtedness $19,859. **Criteria awarding aid:** *Non-need-based:* Academics, Athletics, Leadership, State/district residency.

CALIFORNIA STATE UNIVERSITY, NORTHRIDGE

Admissions and Records, CSU Northridge, Northridge, CA 91330-8207
Phone: 818-677-3700 **Financial Aid Phone:** 818-677-4085
E-mail: admissions.records@csun.edu **CEEB Code:** 4707
Fax: 818-677-3766 **Website:** www.csun.edu **ACT Code:** 400

This public school was founded in 1956. It has a 350 acre campus.

RATINGS
Admissions Selectivity Rating: 73 **Fire Safety Rating:** 60* **Green Rating:** 96

STUDENTS AND FACULTY
Enrollment: 36,917. **Student Body:** 54% female, 46% male, 1% out-of-state, 6% international. Asian 12%, African American 5%, Caucasian 23%, Hispanic 46%, Native American <1%, Pacific Islander <1%, Two or more races 3%, Race unknown 5%.
Retention and Graduation: 78% freshmen return for sophomore year.
Faculty: 917 full-time faculty, 0% hold PhDs, 0% are members of minority groups, 0% are women.

ACADEMICS
Degrees: Bachelor's; Doctoral degree—professional practice; Master's. **Most popular majors:** Psychology, General; Sociology. **Special Study Options:** Accelerated program; Double major; English as a Second Language (ESL); Exchange student program (domestic); Honors program; Independent study; Internships; Student-designed major; Study abroad; Teacher certification program; Weekend college. **Disability Services offered:** Note-taking services; Reader services; Tape recorders; Tutors. **Career services:** Alumni network; Alumni services; Career/job search classes.

FACILITIES
Housing: Apartments for married students; Apartments for single students; Coed dorms; Fraternity/sorority housing; Special housing for international students; Theme housing. **Special Academic Facilities/Equipment:** Anthropology museum, art galleries, deafness center, urban archives, map library, cancer research/developmental biology center, planetarium, observatory.

CAMPUS LIFE
Environment: City. **Activities:** Choral groups; Concert band; Dance; Drama/theater; International Student Organization; Jazz band; Literary magazine; Marching band; Music ensembles; Musical theater; Radio station; Student government; Student newspaper; Yearbook. 323 registered organizations, 15 honor societies, 17 religious organizations, 24 fraternities, 12 sororities, on campus. **Athletics (Intercollegiate):** *Men:* baseball, basketball, cross-country, diving, football, golf, soccer, swimming, track/field (outdoor), track/field (indoor), volleyball. *Women:* basketball, cross-country, diving, football, golf, soccer, softball, swimming, tennis, track/field (outdoor), track/field (indoor), volleyball. **On-Campus Highlights:** Valley Performing Arts Center.

ADMISSIONS
Basis for Candidate Selection: *Very important factors include:* standardized test scores. **Freshman Admission Requirements:** High school diploma is required and GED is accepted. High school diploma is required and GED is not accepted. *Academic units required:* 4 English, 3 math, 1 science, 2 science labs, 2 foreign language, 2 history, 1 academic electives, 1 unit from above areas or other academic areas. **Freshman Admission Statistics:** 32,743 applied, 28% admitted. Lowest grade transferable D. **General Admission Information:** Application fee $55. Non-fall registration accepted.

COSTS AND FINANCIAL AID
Annual in-state tuition $6,564. Annual out-of-state tuition $11,028. Room and board $9,962. Average book and supplies expense $1,860. **Required Forms and Deadlines:** FAFSA. **Types of Aid:** *Need-based scholarships/grants:* College/university scholarship or grant aid from institutional funds; Federal Nursing Scholarships; Federal Pell; Private scholarships; SEOG; State scholarships/grants. **Student Employment:** Federal Work-Study Program available. Institutional employment available.

CALIFORNIA STATE UNIVERSITY, SACRAMENTO

6000 J Street, Sacramento, CA 95819-2694
Phone: 916-278-7766 **Financial Aid Phone:** 916-278-6554
E-mail: outreach@csus.edu **CEEB Code:** 4671
Fax: 916-278-5603 **Website:** www.csus.edu **ACT Code:** 382

This public school was founded in 1947. It has a 300 acre campus.

RATINGS
Admissions Selectivity Rating: 76 **Fire Safety Rating:** 73 **Green Rating:** 60*

STUDENTS AND FACULTY
Enrollment: 25,457. **Student Body:** 57% female, 43% male, 1% out-of-state, 1% international (122 countries represented). Asian 21%, African American 6%, Caucasian 39%, Hispanic 19%, Native American 1%, Pacific Islander 1%, Two or more races 4%, Race unknown 7%.
Retention and Graduation: 81% freshmen return for sophomore year.
Faculty: Student/faculty ratio 28:1. 558 full-time faculty, 87% hold PhDs, 31% are members of minority groups, 47% are women. 0% of classes are taught by teaching assistants.

ACADEMICS
Degrees: Bachelor's; Doctoral degree research/scholarship; Master's. **Classes:** Most classes have 20–29 students. Most lab/discussion sessions have 20–29 students. **Most popular majors:** Business/Commerce, General; Criminal Justice/Law Enforcement Administration; Nursing/Registered Nurse (Rn, Asn, Bsn, Msn). **Special Study Options:** Accelerated program; Cooperative education program; Cross-registration; Distance learning; Double major; Dual enrollment; English as a Second Language (ESL); Honors program; Independent study; Internships; Student-designed major; Study abroad; Teacher certification program. **Combined degree programs:** BA/MA. **Disability Services offered:** Note-taking services; Reader services; Tape recorders; Tutors. **Career services:** Alumni network; Alumni services; Career assessment; Internships; Regional alumni.

FACILITIES
Housing: Apartments for single students; Coed dorms; Special housing for disabled students; Theme housing; 95% of campus accessible to physically disabled. **Special Academic Facilities/Equipment:** CSUS Museum of Anthropology University Library Gallery (Art) Else Gallery (Art) Witt Gallery (Art).

CAMPUS LIFE
Environment: Metropolis. Activities: Concert band; Dance; Drama/theater; International Student Organization; Jazz band; Literary magazine; Marching band; Music ensembles; Musical theater; Opera; Pep band; Radio station; Student government; Student newspaper; Student-run film society; Symphony orchestra. 222 registered organizations, 7 honor societies, 13 religious organizations, 19 fraternities, 20 sororities, on campus. Athletics (Intercollegiate): Men: baseball, basketball, cheerleading, cross-country, football, golf, soccer, tennis, track/field (outdoor). Women: basketball, cheerleading, crew/rowing, cross-country, golf, gymnastics, soccer, softball, tennis, track/field (outdoor), volleyball. On-Campus Highlights: University Union.

ADMISSIONS
Freshman Academic Profile: Average high school GPA 3.3. 89% from public high schools. **Test Scores:** SAT Math middle 50% range 430–540. SAT EBRW middle 50% range 410–520. ACT middle 50% range 17–22. **Basis for Candidate Selection:** *Very important factors include:* academic GPA, standardized test scores. *Other factors include:* recommendation(s), state residency. **Freshman Admission Requirements:** High school diploma is required and GED is accepted. *Academic units required:* 4 English, 3 math, 2 science, 2 science labs, 2 foreign language, 2 history, 1 academic electives, 1 visual/performing arts. **Freshman Admission Statistics:** 19,702 applied, 70% admitted, 23% enrolled. **Transfer Admission Requirements:** College transcript(s), statement of good standing from prior institution(s). Minimum college GPA of 2.0 required. Lowest grade transferable D. **General Admission Information:** Application fee $55. Priority deadline 10/1. Regular application deadline 11/30. Non-fall registration accepted. Admission may be deferred for a maximum of one semester.

COSTS AND FINANCIAL AID
Annual in-state tuition $5,472. Annual out-of-state tuition $16,632. Room and board $10,370. Required fees $1,130. Average book and supplies expense $1,754. **Required Forms and Deadlines:** FAFSA. **Notification of Awards:**

Applicants will be notified of awards on a rolling basis beginning 4/27. **Types of Aid:** *Need-based scholarships/grants:* Federal Nursing Scholarships; Federal Pell; Private scholarships; SEOG; State scholarships/grants. *Loans:* Direct PLUS loans; Direct Subsidized Stafford Loans; Direct Unsubsidized Stafford Loans. **Student Employment:** Federal Work-Study Program available. Institutional employment available. **Financial Aid Statistics:** 77% needy freshmen, 78% needy undergrads receive need-based scholarship or grant aid. 15% freshmen, 7% undergrads receive non-need-based scholarship or grant aid. 92% freshmen, 93% undergrads receive need-based self-help aid. 0% freshmen, 0% undergrads receive athletic scholarships.

CALIFORNIA STATE UNIVERSITY, SAN BERNARDINO

5500 University Parkway, San Bernardino, CA 92407-2397
Phone: 909-537-5188 **Financial Aid Phone:** 909-537-3435
E-mail: moreinfo@mail.csusb.edu **CEEB Code:** 4099
Fax: 909-537-7034 **Website:** www.csusb.edu **ACT Code:** 0205

This public school was founded in 1965. It has a 441 acre campus.

RATINGS
 Admissions Selectivity Rating: 78 Fire Safety Rating: 60* Green Rating: 60*

STUDENTS AND FACULTY
Enrollment: 18,114. **Student Body:** 61% female, 39% male, <1% out-of-state, 7% international (80 countries represented). Asian 5%, African American 5%, Caucasian 11%, Hispanic 66%, Native American <1%, Pacific Islander <1%, Two or more races 2%, Race unknown 4%.
Retention and Graduation: 86% freshmen return for sophomore year. 14% freshmen graduate within 4 years. 55% freshmen graduate within 6 years.
Faculty: Student/faculty ratio 28:1. 467 full-time faculty, 77% hold PhDs, 35% are members of minority groups, 47% are women.

ACADEMICS
Degrees: Bachelor's; Certificate; Doctoral degree—other; Master's; Post-bachelor's certificate. **Classes:** Most classes have 20–29 students. Most lab/discussion sessions have 20–29 students. **Most popular majors:** Business Administration and Management, General; Psychology, General; Social Sciences, General. **Special Study Options:** Accelerated program; Cooperative education program; Cross-registration; Distance learning; Double major; Dual enrollment; English as a Second Language (ESL); Exchange student program (domestic); External degree program; Honors program; Independent study; Internships; Liberal arts/career combination; Student-designed major; Study abroad; Teacher certification program. **Honors programs:** The University Honors Program is a community of students who share a passion for learning and embrace intellectual, creative, and personal challenges as opportunities to grow. The program encourages and supports Honors students' intellectual, creative, and personal growth throughout their undergraduate education by providing challenging coursework, enriching colloquia and seminars, a diverse range of cultural events, and rigorous senior research and scholarship experiences. **Disability Services offered:** Note-taking services; Reader services; Tape recorders. **Career services:** Alumni services; Career assessment; Career/job search classes; Internships.

FACILITIES
Housing: Apartments for single students; Coed dorms; Special housing for disabled students; Theme housing. **Special Academic Facilities/Equipment:** Simulation labs, electronic music studios, language lab, desert studies center, Robert V. Fullerton Art Museum, and Anthropology Museum.

CAMPUS LIFE
Environment: City. **Activities:** Campus Ministries; Choral groups; Concert band; Dance; Drama/theater; International Student Organization; Jazz band; Model UN; Music ensembles; Musical theater; Radio station; Student government; Student newspaper; Television station. 100 registered organizations, 6 honor societies, on campus. **Athletics (Intercollegiate):** *Men:* baseball, basketball, golf, soccer, swimming, water polo. *Women:* basketball, cross-country, soccer, softball, swimming, tennis, volleyball, water polo. **On-Campus Highlights:** Coussoulis Arena.

ADMISSIONS
Freshman Academic Profile: Average high school GPA 3.4. 98% from public high schools. **Test Scores:** SAT Math middle 50% range 450–540. SAT EBRW middle 50% range 460–550. ACT middle 50% range 15–19.

Basis for Candidate Selection: *Very important factors include:* academic GPA, standardized test scores. *Important factors include:* geographical residence. **Freshman Admission Requirements:** High school diploma is required and GED is accepted. *Academic units required:* 4 English, 3 math, 2 science, 2 science labs, 2 foreign language, 1 social studies, 1 history, 1 academic electives, 1 visual/performing arts. **Freshman Admission Statistics:** 16,307 applied, 69% admitted, 25% enrolled. **Transfer Admission Requirements:** College transcript(s). Minimum college GPA of 2.0 required. Lowest grade transferable C. **General Admission Information:** Application fee $55. Priority deadline 11/30. Non-fall registration accepted.

COSTS AND FINANCIAL AID
Annual in-state tuition $5,742. Room and board $13,435. Required fees $1,214. Average book and supplies expense $1,971. **Required Forms and Deadlines:** FAFSA. **Notification of Awards:** Applicants will be notified of awards on a rolling basis beginning 4/1. **Types of Aid:** *Need-based scholarships/grants:* College/university scholarship or grant aid from institutional funds; Federal Pell; Private scholarships; SEOG; State scholarships/grants. *Loans:* Direct PLUS loans; Direct Subsidized Stafford Loans; Direct Unsubsidized Stafford Loans. **Student Employment:** Federal Work-Study Program available. Institutional employment available. **Financial Aid Statistics:** 97% needy freshmen, 95% needy undergrads receive need-based scholarship or grant aid. 79% freshmen, 47% undergrads receive non-need-based scholarship or grant aid. 22% freshmen, 31% undergrads receive need-based self-help aid. 0% freshmen, 0% undergrads receive athletic scholarships. 62.4% freshmen, 60.9% undergrads receive any aid. 56% undergrads borrow to pay for school. Average cumulative indebtedness $18,294. **Criteria awarding aid:** *Need-based:* Academics, Alumni affiliation, Art, Athletics, Job skills, Leadership, Minority status, Music/drama, Religious affiliation.

CALIFORNIA STATE UNIVERSITY, SAN MARCOS

Office of Admission, San Marcos, CA 92096-0001
Phone: 760-750-4848 **Financial Aid Phone:** 760-750-4850
E-mail: apply@csusm.edu **CEEB Code:** 5677
Fax: 760-750-3248 **Website:** www.csusm.edu

This public school was founded in 1989. It has a 304 acre campus.

RATINGS
 Admissions Selectivity Rating: 77 Fire Safety Rating: 60* Green Rating: 94

STUDENTS AND FACULTY
Enrollment: 12,096. **Student Body:** 61% female, 39% male, 1% out-of-state, 2% international. Asian 10%, African American 3%, Caucasian 30%, Hispanic 42%, Native American <1%, Pacific Islander <1%, Two or more races 6%, Race unknown 5%.
Retention and Graduation: 82% freshmen return for sophomore year.
Faculty: Student/faculty ratio 25:1. 254 full-time faculty, 0% hold PhDs, 32% are members of minority groups, 50% are women.

ACADEMICS
Degrees: Bachelor's; Master's. **Classes:** Most classes have 30–39 students. **Special Study Options:** Accelerated program; Cross-registration; Distance learning; Double major; Dual enrollment; English as a Second Language (ESL); Independent study; Internships; Student-designed major; Study abroad; Teacher certification program; Weekend college. **Disability Services offered:** Note-taking services; Reader services; Tape recorders; Tutors. **Career services:** Alumni services; Career assessment; Internships.

FACILITIES
Housing: Apartments for single students. **Campus network:** 90% of classrooms, 100% of dorms, 100% of student union, 100% of libraries, 100% of dining areas, 45% of common outdoor areas, have wireless network access.

CAMPUS LIFE
Environment: Town. **Activities:** Dance; Music ensembles; Student newspaper. 70 registered organizations, 5 honor societies, 2 religious organizations, 2 fraternities, 2 sororities, on campus. **Athletics (Intercollegiate):** *Men:* baseball, cross-country, golf, soccer, track/field (outdoor). *Women:* cross-country, golf, soccer, softball, track/field (outdoor).

ADMISSIONS
Freshman Academic Profile: Average high school GPA 3.3. **Test Scores:** SAT Math middle 50% range 430–530. SAT EBRW middle 50% range 420–520.

Basis for Candidate Selection: *Very important factors include:* academic GPA, standardized test scores. *Other factors include:* geographical residence, state residency. **Freshman Admission Requirements:** High school diploma is required and GED is accepted. *Academic units required:* 4 English, 3 math, 2 science, 2 science labs, 2 foreign language, 1 social studies, 1 history, 1 academic electives, 1 visual/performing arts. *Academic units recommended:* 4 English, 4 math, 2 science, 2 foreign language, 1 social studies, 1 history, 1 academic electives, 1 visual/performing arts. **Freshman Admission Statistics:** 11,560 applied, 67% admitted, 28% enrolled. **Transfer Admission Requirements:** College transcript(s). Minimum college GPA of 2.0 required. Lowest grade transferable C. **General Admission Information:** Application fee $55. Regular application deadline 11/30.

COSTS AND FINANCIAL AID
Annual in-state tuition $5,472. Annual out-of-state tuition $14,400. Room and board $13,240. Required fees $1,792. Average book and supplies expense $1,764. **Required Forms and Deadlines:** FAFSA. **Notification of Awards:** Applicants will be notified of awards on or about 4/15. **Types of Aid:** *Need-based scholarships/grants:* College/university scholarship or grant aid from institutional funds; Federal Pell; Private scholarships; SEOG; State scholarships/grants. *Loans:* Direct PLUS loans; Direct Subsidized Stafford Loans; Direct Unsubsidized Stafford Loans. **Criteria awarding aid:** *Need-based:* Academics, Athletics, Leadership. *Non-need-based:* Academics, Athletics, Leadership, State/district residency.

CALIFORNIA STATE UNIVERSITY, STANISLAUS

One University Circle, Turlock, CA 95382
Phone: 209-667-3070 **Financial Aid Phone:** 209-667-3336
E-mail: Outreach_help_desk@csustan.edu **CEEB Code:** 4713
Fax: 209-667-3788 **Website:** www.csustan.edu **ACT Code:** 435

This public school was founded in 1957. It has a 228 acre campus.

RATINGS
Admissions Selectivity Rating: 73   **Fire Safety Rating:** 97   **Green Rating:** 82

STUDENTS AND FACULTY
Enrollment: 9,685. **Student Body:** 65% female, 35% male, <1% out-of-state, 4% international (24 countries represented). Asian 9%, African American 2%, Caucasian 20%, Hispanic 56%, Native American <1%, Pacific Islander <1%, Two or more races 3%, Race unknown 5%.
Retention and Graduation: 83% freshmen return for sophomore year. 19% freshmen graduate within 4 years. 60% freshmen graduate within 6 years. **Faculty:** Student/faculty ratio 20:1. 355 full-time faculty, 78% hold PhDs, 30% are members of minority groups, 46% are women.

ACADEMICS
Degrees: Bachelor's; Doctoral degree—other; Master's. **Classes:** Most classes have 20–29 students. Most lab/discussion sessions have 20–29 students. **Special Study Options:** Accelerated program; Cooperative education program; Cross-registration; Distance learning; Double major; Dual enrollment; English as a Second Language (ESL); External degree program; Honors program; Independent study; Internships; Liberal arts/career combination; Student-designed major; Study abroad; Teacher certification program. **Honors programs:** University Honors Program. **Disability Services offered:** Note-taking services; Reader services; Tape recorders; Tutors. **Career services:** Alumni network; Alumni services; Career assessment; Career/job search classes; Internships; Regional alumni.

FACILITIES
Housing: Coed dorms; Theme housing; 100% of campus accessible to physically disabled. **Special Academic Facilities/Equipment:** Marine sciences station, laser lab, greenhouse, art gallery, mainstage theatre, recital hall, observatory, science building, art complex, distance learning studios, BioAg Eco building.

CAMPUS LIFE
Environment: City. **Activities:** Campus Ministries; Choral groups; Drama/theater; International Student Organization; Model UN; Music ensembles;

Musical theater; Opera; Radio station; Student government; Student newspaper; Student-run film society; Symphony orchestra. 102 registered organizations, 5 honor societies, 5 religious organizations, 6 fraternities, 10 sororities, on campus. **Athletics (Intercollegiate):** *Men:* baseball, basketball, cross-country, golf, soccer, track/field (outdoor), track/field (indoor). *Women:* basketball, cross-country, soccer, softball, tennis, track/field (outdoor), track/field (indoor), volleyball. **On-Campus Highlights:** Naraghi Hall of Science.

ADMISSIONS
Freshman Academic Profile: Average high school GPA 3.4. 97% from public high schools. **Test Scores:** SAT Math middle 50% range 440–530. SAT EBRW middle 50% range 450–540. ACT middle 50% range 15–21. **Basis for Candidate Selection:** *Very important factors include:* rigor of secondary school record, academic GPA, standardized test scores. *Important factors include:* class rank. **Freshman Admission Requirements:** High school diploma is required and GED is accepted. *Academic units required:* 4 English, 3 math, 2 science, 2 science labs, 2 foreign language, 1 social studies, 1 history, 1 academic electives, 1 visual/performing arts. *Academic units recommended:* 4 English, 3 math, 2 science, 2 science labs, 2 foreign language, 1 social studies, 1 history, 1 academic electives, 1 visual/performing arts. **Freshman Admission Statistics:** 8,764 applied, 89% admitted, 20% enrolled. **Transfer Admission Requirements:** College transcript(s), statement of good standing from prior institution(s). Minimum college GPA of 2.0 required. Lowest grade transferable D. **General Admission Information:** Application fee $55. Priority deadline 11/30. Regular application deadline 11/30. Non-fall registration accepted.

COSTS AND FINANCIAL AID
Annual in-state tuition $5,742. Annual out-of-state tuition $17,622. Room and board $10,950. Required fees $1,842. Average book and supplies expense $1,160. **Required Forms and Deadlines:** FAFSA; Institution's own financial aid form; State aid form. **Notification of Awards:** Applicants will be notified of awards on a rolling basis beginning 4/1. **Types of Aid:** *Need-based scholarships/grants:* College/university scholarship or grant aid from institutional funds; Federal Pell; Private scholarships; SEOG; State scholarships/grants. *Loans:* Direct PLUS loans; Direct Subsidized Stafford Loans; Direct Unsubsidized Stafford Loans. **Student Employment:** Federal Work-Study Program available. Institutional employment available. **Financial Aid Statistics:** 98% needy freshmen, 97% needy undergrads receive need-based scholarship or grant aid. 7% freshmen, 6% undergrads receive non-need-based scholarship or grant aid. 77% freshmen, 87% undergrads receive need-based self-help aid. 1% freshmen, 0% undergrads receive athletic scholarships. 93% freshmen, 87% undergrads receive any aid. 49% undergrads borrow to pay for school. Average cumulative indebtedness $17,952. **Criteria awarding aid:** *Need-based:* Academics, Alumni affiliation, Art, Leadership, Music/drama. *Non-need-based:* Academics, Alumni affiliation, Art, Athletics, Leadership, Music/drama, State/district residency.

CALIFORNIA UNIVERSITY OF PENNSYLVANIA

250 University Avenue, California, PA 15419
Phone: 724-938-4404 **Financial Aid Phone:** 724-938-4415
E-mail: inquiry@cup.edu **CEEB Code:** 2647
Fax: 724-938-4564 **Website:** www.calu.edu **ACT Code:** 3694

This public school was founded in 1852. It has a 188 acre campus.

RATINGS
Admissions Selectivity Rating: 73   **Fire Safety Rating:** 97   **Green Rating:** 70

STUDENTS AND FACULTY
Enrollment: 4,676. **Student Body:** 54% female, 46% male, 10% out-of-state, 1% international (29 countries represented). Asian 1%, African American 12%, Caucasian 75%, Hispanic 4%, Native American <1%, Pacific Islander <1%, Two or more races 4%, Race unknown 3%.
Retention and Graduation: 72% freshmen return for sophomore year. 36% freshmen graduate within 4 years. 50% freshmen graduate within 6 years. 10% grads go on to further study within 1 year. **Faculty:** Student/faculty ratio 17:1. 263 full-time faculty, 76% hold PhDs, 14% are members of minority groups, 51% are women. 0% of classes are taught by teaching assistants.

ACADEMICS
Degrees: Associate; Bachelor's; Certificate; Doctoral degree—professional practice; Master's; Post-bachelor's certificate; Post-master's certificate. **Classes:** Most classes have 20–29 students. **Most popular majors:** Criminal Justice/

Safety Studies; Registered Nursing/Registered Nurse; Business Administration and Management, General. **Special Study Options:** Accelerated program; Cooperative education program; Cross-registration; Distance learning; Double major; Dual enrollment; English as a Second Language (ESL); Exchange student program (domestic); Honors program; Independent study; Internships; Liberal arts/career combination; Study abroad; Teacher certification program. **Disability Services offered:** Note-taking services; Reader services; Tape recorders; Tutors. **Career services:** Alumni network; Alumni services; Career assessment; Career/job search classes; Internships; Regional alumni.

FACILITIES

Housing: Apartments for single students; Coed dorms; Special housing for disabled students; Theme housing; 90% of campus accessible to physically disabled. **Special Academic Facilities/Equipment:** Manderino Gallery of Fine Arts, hosts top 40 corporate art collections in the world.

CAMPUS LIFE

Environment: Village. **Activities:** Campus Ministries; Choral groups; Concert band; Dance; Drama/theater; International Student Organization; Jazz band; Literary magazine; Marching band; Music ensembles; Musical theater; Opera; Pep band; Radio station; Student government; Student newspaper; Symphony orchestra; Television station; Yearbook. 179 registered organizations, 12 honor societies, 4 religious organizations, 6 fraternities, 7 sororities, on campus. **Athletics (Intercollegiate):** *Men:* baseball, basketball, cheerleading, cross-country, football, golf, rugby, soccer, softball, track/field (outdoor), track/field (indoor), volleyball. *Women:* basketball, cheerleading, cross-country, diving, golf, rugby, soccer, softball, swimming, tennis, track/field (outdoor), track/field (indoor), volleyball. **On-Campus Highlights:** Residence Halls. **Environmental Initiatives:** Multimillion Dollar Geothermal project plus replacing ALL residence halls in less than 5 years with Green buildings.

ADMISSIONS

Freshman Academic Profile: Average high school GPA 3.3. 7% in top 10% of high school class, 25% in top 25% of high school class, 61% in top 50% of high school class. 88% from public high schools. **Test Scores:** SAT Math middle 50% range 450–540. SAT EBRW middle 50% range 460–560. ACT middle 50% range 17–23. **Basis for Candidate Selection:** *Very important factors include:* academic GPA, standardized test scores. *Important factors include:* rigor of secondary school record. *Other factors include:* class rank, application essay, recommendation(s), interview, extracurricular activities, talent/ability, character/personal qualities, volunteer work, work experience, level of applicant's interest. **Freshman Admission Requirements:** High school diploma is required and GED is accepted. **Freshman Admission Statistics:** 3,083 applied, 97% admitted, 32% enrolled. **Transfer Admission Requirements:** High school transcript, college transcript(s), statement of good standing from prior institution(s). Minimum college GPA of 2.3 required. Lowest grade transferable C. **General Admission Information:** Application fee $35. Priority deadline 8/21. Non-fall registration accepted. Admission may be deferred for a maximum of 3 years.

COSTS AND FINANCIAL AID

Annual in-state tuition $7,716. Annual out-of-state tuition $11,574. Room and board $10,186. Required fees $3,392. Average book and supplies expense $1,000. **Required Forms and Deadlines:** FAFSA. **Notification of Awards:** Applicants will be notified of awards on a rolling basis beginning 12/1. **Types of Aid:** *Need-based scholarships/grants:* College/university scholarship or grant aid from institutional funds; Federal Pell; Private scholarships; SEOG; State scholarships/grants. *Loans:* Direct PLUS loans; Direct Subsidized Stafford Loans; Direct Unsubsidized Stafford Loans. **Student Employment:** Federal Work-Study Program available. Institutional employment available. **Financial Aid Statistics:** 80% needy freshmen, 80% needy undergrads receive need-based scholarship or grant aid. 33% freshmen, 19% undergrads receive non-need-based scholarship or grant aid. 92% freshmen, 93% undergrads receive need-based self-help aid. 3% freshmen, 2% undergrads receive athletic scholarships. 81% freshmen, 77% undergrads receive any aid. 91% undergrads borrow to pay for school. Average cumulative indebtedness $26,242. **Criteria awarding aid:** *Need-based:* Academics, Leadership, Minority status, Music/drama. *Non-need-based:* Academics, Athletics, Leadership, Minority status, Music/drama, State/district residency.

CALVARY BIBLE COLLEGE AND THEOLOGICAL SEMINARY

15800 Calvary Rd., Kansas City, MO 64147
Phone: 816-322-3960 **Financial Aid Phone:** 816-322-0110
E-mail: admissions@calvary.edu
Fax: 816-331-4474 **Website:** http://www.college.calvary.edu/ **ACT Code:** 2312

This private school, affiliated with the Christian (Nondenominational) Church, was founded in 1932. It has a 56.3 acre campus.

RATINGS

Admissions Selectivity Rating: 76   **Fire Safety Rating:** 83   **Green Rating:** 60*

STUDENTS AND FACULTY

Enrollment: 226. **Student Body:** 50% female, 50% male, 65% out-of-state, 0% international (1 countries represented). Asian 2%, African American 11%, Caucasian 80%, Hispanic 3%, Native American 1%, Pacific Islander 0%, Two or more races 3%, Race unknown 0%.
Retention and Graduation: 69% freshmen return for sophomore year.
Faculty: Student/faculty ratio 7:1. 17 full-time faculty, 71% hold PhDs, 12% are members of minority groups, 41% are women. 0% of classes are taught by teaching assistants.

ACADEMICS

Degrees: Associate; Bachelor's; Certificate; Master's. **Most popular majors:** Bible/Biblical Studies; Pastoral Studies/Counseling; Music, Other. **Special Study Options:** Accelerated program; Distance learning; Double major; Dual enrollment; Independent study; Internships; Teacher certification program. **Disability Services offered:** Reader services; Tape recorders; Tutors.

FACILITIES

Housing: Apartments for married students; Apartments for single students; Men's dorms; Women's dorms; 50% of campus accessible to physically disabled. **Special Academic Facilities/Equipment:** The Learning Center K-Bar Cafe Gym.

CAMPUS LIFE

Environment: Metropolis. **Activities:** Campus Ministries; Choral groups; Concert band; Drama/theater; Music ensembles; Musical theater; Student government. **Athletics (Intercollegiate):** *Men:* basketball, soccer. *Women:* basketball, volleyball. **On-Campus Highlights:** Student Lounge.

ADMISSIONS

Freshman Academic Profile: Average high school GPA 3.4. **Test Scores:** SAT Math middle 50% range 498–518. SAT EBRW middle 50% range 445–518. ACT middle 50% range 19–24. **Basis for Candidate Selection:** *Very important factors include:* academic GPA, application essay, recommendation(s), character/personal qualities, religious affiliation/commitment, level of applicant's interest. *Important factors include:* standardized test scores. *Other factors include:* class rank, interview, extracurricular activities, talent/ability, alumni/ae relation, volunteer work, work experience. **Freshman Admission Requirements:** High school diploma is required and GED is accepted. **Freshman Admission Statistics:** 52 applied, 94% admitted, 67% enrolled. **Transfer Admission Requirements:** College transcript(s), essay or personal statement, Minimum college GPA of 2.0 required. Lowest grade transferable C-. **General Admission Information:** Non-fall registration accepted. Admission may be deferred for a maximum of one year.

COSTS AND FINANCIAL AID

Average book and supplies expense $794. **Required Forms and Deadlines:** FAFSA. **Types of Aid:** *Need-based scholarships/grants:* College/university scholarship or grant aid from institutional funds; Federal Pell; SEOG. *Loans:* Direct PLUS loans; Direct Subsidized Stafford Loans; Direct Unsubsidized Stafford Loans. **Student Employment:** Federal Work-Study Program available. Institutional employment available. **Financial Aid Statistics:** 100% needy freshmen, 91% needy undergrads receive need-based scholarship or grant aid. 19% freshmen, 10% undergrads receive non-need-based scholarship or grant aid. 100% freshmen, 88% undergrads receive need-based self-help aid. 0% freshmen, 0% undergrads receive athletic scholarships. 75% freshmen, 76.44% undergrads receive any aid. 63% undergrads borrow to pay for school. Average cumulative indebtedness $15,498. **Criteria awarding aid:** *Non-need-based:* Academics, Alumni affiliation, Music/drama, Religious affiliation.

CALVIN UNIVERSITY

3201 Burton Street S.E., Grand Rapids, MI 49546
Phone: 616-526-6106 **Financial Aid Phone:** 800-688-0122
E-mail: admissions@calvin.edu **CEEB Code:** 1095
Fax: 616-526-6777 **Website:** www.calvin.edu **ACT Code:** 1968

This private school, affiliated with the Christian Reformed Church, was founded in 1876. It has a 400 acre campus.

RATINGS
Admissions Selectivity Rating: 81   **Fire Safety Rating:** 83   **Green Rating:** 85

STUDENTS AND FACULTY
Enrollment: 3,550. **Student Body:** 53% female, 47% male, 42% out-of-state, 13% international (70 countries represented). Asian 5%, African American 4%, Caucasian 69%, Hispanic 5%, Native American <1%, Pacific Islander 0%, Two or more races 3%, Race unknown 2%.
Retention and Graduation: 87% freshmen return for sophomore year. 59% freshmen graduate within 4 years. 72% freshmen graduate within 6 years. 18% grads go on to further study within 1 year. 14% grads pursue arts and sciences degrees. 1% grads pursue law degrees. 2% grads pursue business degrees. 2% grads pursue medical degrees. **Faculty:** Student/faculty ratio 13:1. 232 full-time faculty, 90% hold PhDs, 9% are members of minority groups, 36% are women. 0% of classes are taught by teaching assistants.

ACADEMICS
Degrees: Associate; Bachelor's; Certificate; Master's. **Classes:** Most classes have 20–29 students. Most lab/discussion sessions have 20–29 students. **Most popular majors:** Engineering, General; Registered Nursing/Registered Nurse; Business Administration and Management, General. **Special Study Options:** Distance learning; Double major; Dual enrollment; Honors program; Independent study; Internships; Student-designed major; Study abroad; Teacher certification program. **Honors programs:** Students can develop their minds and deepen their character at Calvin through the Honors Scholars and Collegiate Scholars Programs. These two programs challenge students to embrace advanced academic options and offer them distinct opportunities that match their strengths and interests. Students who participate in one of these programs receive academic scholarships up to the college's top scholarship of $18,000 per year. In the Honors Scholars program, students experience college with a dynamic cohort of committed learners. In this collaborative community, a student will investigate ideas with peers and faculty, and pursue the connections between subject areas. A student will meet half of the core requirements in interdisciplinary, team-taught courses, and in their third and fourth years, a student will take a themed discussion-based course alongside their major coursework and complete an honors thesis or project with a faculty mentor. In the Collegiate Scholars program, students pour their energy into what they love. Students in this program are encouraged to lead and are dedicated to meeting the challenges inside and outside the classroom. They also participate in four advanced academic leadership or community engagement activities and, like the Honors Scholars, get priority consideration for Calvin Student Research Fellowships and access to honors advising. In addition, many students in these two programs apply to live in the Honors Living-Learning community, a residence hall floor where students develop strong relationships with peers and faculty mentors. **Combined degree programs:** BA/MA. **Disability Services offered:** Note-taking services; Reader services; Tape recorders; Tutors. **Career services:** Alumni network; Alumni services; Career assessment; Career/job search classes; Internships; Regional alumni.

FACILITIES
Housing: Apartments for single students; Men's dorms; Special housing for disabled students; Theme housing; Wellness housing; Women's dorms; 95% of campus accessible to physically disabled. **Special Academic Facilities/ Equipment:** Art gallery, observatory, ecosystem preserve, electron microscope, seismograph lab, mineralogical museum. **Campus network:** 100% of classrooms, 100% of dorms, 100% of student union, 100% of libraries, 100% of dining areas, 20% of common outdoor areas, have wireless network access.

CAMPUS LIFE
Environment: Metropolis. **Activities:** Campus Ministries; Choral groups; Concert band; Dance; Drama/theater; International Student Organization; Jazz band; Literary magazine; Music ensembles; Pep band; Student government; Student newspaper; Student-run film society; Symphony orchestra; Yearbook. 80 registered organizations, 6 honor societies, 5 religious organizations, on campus. **Athletics (Intercollegiate):** *Men:* baseball, basketball, cross-country, diving, golf, soccer, swimming, tennis, track/field (outdoor). *Women:* basketball, cross-country, diving, golf, soccer, softball, swimming, tennis, track/field (outdoor), volleyball. **On-Campus Highlights:** Spoelhof Fieldhouse Complex. **Environmental Initiatives:** The Calvin Energy Recovery Fund, a green revolving fund (http://www.calvin.edu/admin/development/cerf).

ADMISSIONS
Freshman Academic Profile: Average high school GPA 3.8. 31% in top 10% of high school class, 58% in top 25% of high school class, 83% in top 50% of high school class. 40% from public high schools. **Test Scores:** SAT Math middle 50% range 580–690. SAT EBRW middle 50% range 570–680. ACT middle 50% range 24–30. **Basis for Candidate Selection:** *Very important factors include:* rigor of secondary school record, academic GPA, standardized test scores, religious affiliation/commitment. *Important factors include:* application essay, recommendation(s), extracurricular activities, character/personal qualities. *Other factors include:* class rank, volunteer work, work experience, level of applicant's interest. **Freshman Admission Requirements:** High school diploma is required and GED is accepted. *Academic units required:* 3 English, 3 math, 2 science, 2 social studies, 3 academic electives. *Academic units recommended:* 4 English, 3 math, 2 science, 1 science labs, 2 foreign language, 3 social studies, 3 academic electives. **Freshman Admission Statistics:** 3,847 applied, 79% admitted, 27% enrolled. **Transfer Admission Requirements:** High school transcript, college transcript(s), essay or personal statement, statement of good standing from prior institution(s). Minimum college GPA of 2.5 required. Lowest grade transferable C. **General Admission Information:** Application fee $35. Regular application deadline 8/15. Non-fall registration accepted. Admission may be deferred for a maximum of 1 year.

COSTS AND FINANCIAL AID
Annual tuition $36,100. Room and board $10,600. Required fees $200. Average book and supplies expense $1,300. **Required Forms and Deadlines:** FAFSA. **Notification of Awards:** Applicants will be notified of awards on a rolling basis beginning 12/15. **Types of Aid:** *Need-based scholarships/grants:* College/university scholarship or grant aid from institutional funds; Federal Pell; Private scholarships; SEOG; State scholarships/grants. *Loans:* Direct PLUS loans; Direct Subsidized Stafford Loans; Direct Unsubsidized Stafford Loans. **Student Employment:** Federal Work-Study Program available. Institutional employment available. **Financial Aid Statistics:** 100% needy freshmen, 100% needy undergrads receive need-based scholarship or grant aid. 13% freshmen, 12% undergrads receive non-need-based scholarship or grant aid. 85% freshmen, 86% undergrads receive need-based self-help aid. 0% freshmen, 0% undergrads receive athletic scholarships. 100% freshmen, 97% undergrads receive any aid. 60% undergrads borrow to pay for school. Average cumulative indebtedness $29,768. **Criteria awarding aid:** *Need-based:* Academics, Alumni affiliation, Leadership, Minority status. *Non-need-based:* Academics, Alumni affiliation, Art, Leadership, Minority status, Music/drama, Religious affiliation, State/district residency.

CAMBRIDGE COLLEGE

1000 Massachusetts Avenue, Cambridge, MA 02138-5304
Phone: (617) 868-1000 **Financial Aid Phone:** 800-877-4723 ext. 1440
E-mail: admit@cambridgecollege.edu
Fax: (617) 349-3561 **Website:** www.cambridgecollege.edu

This private school was founded in 1971.

RATINGS
Admissions Selectivity Rating: 60*   **Fire Safety Rating:** 60*   **Green Rating:** 60*

STUDENTS AND FACULTY
Enrollment: 1,002. **Student Body:** 75% female, 25% male, 18% out-of-state, 9% international. Asian 3%, African American 30%, Caucasian 18%, Hispanic 22%, Native American <1%, Pacific Islander <1%, Two or more races 1%, Race unknown 16%.
Retention and Graduation: 21% freshmen return for sophomore year.
Faculty: Student/faculty ratio 16:1. 19 full-time faculty, 68% hold PhDs, 26% are members of minority groups, 47% are women.

ACADEMICS

Degrees: Bachelor's; Certificate; Doctoral degree research/scholarship; Master's; Post-bachelor's certificate; Post-master's certificate. **Classes:** Most classes have 10–19 students. **Special Study Options:** Accelerated program; Distance learning; Double major; Independent study; Internships; Weekend college. **Disability Services offered:** Note-taking services; Reader services; Tape recorders; Tutors.

FACILITIES

Campus network: 100% of classrooms, 100% of dorms, 100% of student union, 100% of libraries, 100% of dining areas, 100% of common outdoor areas, have wireless network access.

CAMPUS LIFE

Environment: Metropolis. **Activities:** Student government.

ADMISSIONS

Basis for Candidate Selection: *Other factors include:* class rank, academic GPA, application essay, recommendation(s), interview, character/personal qualities, work experience, level of applicant's interest. **Freshman Admission Requirements:** High school diploma is required and GED is accepted. **General Admission Information:** Non-fall registration accepted. Admission may be deferred for a maximum of 1 year.

COSTS AND FINANCIAL AID

Annual tuition $13,140. Required fees $140. **Required Forms and Deadlines:** FAFSA; Institution's own financial aid form. **Types of Aid:** *Need-based scholarships/grants:* College/university scholarship or grant aid from institutional funds; Federal Pell; Private scholarships; SEOG; State scholarships/grants. *Loans:* Direct PLUS loans; Direct Subsidized Stafford Loans. **Student Employment:** Federal Work-Study Program available. Institutional employment available. **Financial Aid Statistics:** 0% needy freshmen, 1% needy undergrads receive need-based scholarship or grant aid. 0% freshmen, 0% undergrads receive non-need-based scholarship or grant aid. 0% freshmen, 0% undergrads receive need-based self-help aid. 0% freshmen, 0% undergrads receive athletic scholarships. **Criteria awarding aid:** *Need-based:* Academics, Religious affiliation.

CAMPBELLSVILLE UNIVERSITY

1 University Drive, Campbellsville, KY 42718-2799
Phone: 270-789-5220 **Financial Aid Phone:** 270-789-5013
E-mail: admissions@campbellsville.edu **CEEB Code:** 1097
Fax: 270-789-5071 **ACT Code:** 1500

This private school, affiliated with the Baptist Church, was founded in 1906. It has a 90 acre campus.

RATINGS

Admissions Selectivity Rating: 82   Fire Safety Rating: 75   Green Rating: 60*

STUDENTS AND FACULTY

Enrollment: 2,250. **Student Body:** 58% female, 42% male, 12% out-of-state, 7% international. Asian <1%, African American 15%, Caucasian 74%, Hispanic 1%, Native American <1%, Pacific Islander <1%, Two or more races 1%, Race unknown 2%.
Retention and Graduation: 65% freshmen return for sophomore year. 20% grads go on to further study within 1 year. 25% grads pursue arts and sciences degrees. 1% grads pursue law degrees. 15% grads pursue business degrees. 1% grads pursue medical degrees. **Faculty:** Student/faculty ratio 13:1. 146 full-time faculty, 62% hold PhDs, 10% are members of minority groups, 49% are women. 0% of classes are taught by teaching assistants.

ACADEMICS

Degrees: Associate; Bachelor's; Certificate; Master's. **Classes:** Most classes have fewer than 10 students. **Most popular majors:** Business, Management, Marketing, and Related Support Services, Other; Registered Nursing/Registered Nurse; Junior High/Intermediate/Middle School Education and Teaching. **Special Study Options:** Cooperative education program; Distance learning; Double major; Dual enrollment; English as a Second Language (ESL); Honors program; Independent study; Internships; Liberal arts/career combination; Study abroad; Teacher certification program; Weekend college. **Disability Services offered:** Tutors. **Career services:** Alumni services; Career assessment; Internships.

FACILITIES

Housing: Apartments for married students; Apartments for single students; Men's dorms; Women's dorms; 70% of campus accessible to physically disabled. **Special Academic Facilities/Equipment:** Computer labs: Technology lab. **Campus network:** 100% of classrooms, 100% of dorms, 100% of student union, 100% of libraries, 100% of dining areas, 100% of common outdoor areas, have wireless network access.

CAMPUS LIFE

Environment: Rural. **Activities:** Campus Ministries; Choral groups; Concert band; Dance; Drama/theater; International Student Organization; Jazz band; Literary magazine; Marching band; Music ensembles; Musical theater; Pep band; Radio station; Student government; Student newspaper; Television station. 49 registered organizations, 1 honor societies, 7 religious organizations, on campus. **Athletics (Intercollegiate):** *Men:* baseball, basketball, bowling, cheerleading, cross-country, football, golf, soccer, tennis, track/field (outdoor), wrestling. *Women:* basketball, bowling, cheerleading, cross-country, golf, soccer, softball, swimming, tennis, track/field (outdoor), volleyball. **On-Campus Highlights:** Technology Center.

ADMISSIONS

Freshman Academic Profile: Average high school GPA 3.2. 17% in top 10% of high school class, 38% in top 25% of high school class, 69% in top 50% of high school class. 90% from public high schools. **Test Scores:** SAT Math middle 50% range 430–580. SAT EBRW middle 50% range 420–590. ACT middle 50% range 18–23. **Basis for Candidate Selection:** *Very important factors include:* rigor of secondary school record. *Important factors include:* class rank, standardized test scores, recommendation(s), interview, character/personal qualities. *Other factors include:* application essay, extracurricular activities, talent/ability, alumni/ae relation, religious affiliation/commitment, volunteer work, work experience. **Freshman Admission Requirements:** High school diploma is required and GED is accepted. **Academic units recommended:** 4 English, 3 math, 3 science, 1 science labs, 2 social studies, 1 history, 6 academic electives, 1 unit from above areas or other academic areas. **Freshman Admission Statistics:** 2,477 applied, 67% admitted, 35% enrolled. **Transfer Admission Requirements:** college transcript(s), Lowest grade transferable C. **General Admission Information:** Application fee $20. Priority deadline 4/15. Regular application deadline 8/15. Non-fall registration accepted.

COSTS AND FINANCIAL AID

Annual tuition $21,100. Room and board $7,120. Required fees $500. Average book and supplies expense $1,000. **Required Forms and Deadlines:** FAFSA. **Notification of Awards:** Applicants will be notified of awards on a rolling basis beginning 2/15. **Types of Aid:** *Need-based scholarships/grants:* College/university scholarship or grant aid from institutional funds; Federal Pell; Private scholarships; SEOG; State scholarships/grants. **Student Employment:** Federal Work-Study Program available. Institutional employment available. **Financial Aid Statistics:** 100% needy freshmen, 97% needy undergrads receive need-based scholarship or grant aid. 14% freshmen, 10% undergrads receive non-need-based scholarship or grant aid. 74% freshmen, 77% undergrads receive need-based self-help aid. 5% freshmen, 6% undergrads receive athletic scholarships. 95% freshmen, 92% undergrads receive any aid. **Criteria awarding aid:** *Need-based:* Academics, Art, Athletics, Leadership, Minority status, Music/drama, Religious affiliation. *Non-need-based:* Academics, Art, Athletics, Leadership, Minority status, Music/drama, Religious affiliation, State/district residency.

CAMPBELL UNIVERSITY

Post Office Box 546, Buies Creek, NC 27506
Phone: 910-893-1200
E-mail: admissions@campbell.edu **CEEB Code:** 5100
Website: www.campbell.edu **ACT Code:** 3076

This private school, affiliated with the Southern Baptist Church, was founded in 1887. It has a 850 acre campus.

RATINGS

Admissions Selectivity Rating: 79   Fire Safety Rating: 75   Green Rating: 60*

STUDENTS AND FACULTY

Enrollment: 4,236. **Student Body:** 52% female, 48% male, 22% out-of-state, 2% international. Asian 2%, African American 18%, Caucasian 57%, Hispanic 7%, Native American 1%, Pacific Islander <1%, Two or more races 2%, Race unknown 11%.

Retention and Graduation: 72% freshmen return for sophomore year. 23% grads go on to further study within 1 year. 5% grads pursue arts and sciences degrees. 4% grads pursue law degrees. 7% grads pursue business degrees. **Faculty:** Student/faculty ratio 14:1. 196 full-time faculty, 91% hold PhDs, 0% are members of minority groups, 33% are women. 0% of classes are taught by teaching assistants.

ACADEMICS

Degrees: Bachelor's; Doctoral degree—professional practice; Doctoral degree research/scholarship; Master's; Post-bachelor's certificate. **Classes:** Most classes have fewer than 10 students. **Special Study Options:** Distance learning; Double major; Dual enrollment; Independent study; Internships; Study abroad; Teacher certification program. **Combined degree programs:** BA/JD; BA/MA. **Disability Services offered:** Note-taking services; Tape recorders. **Career services:** Career assessment; Career/job search classes; Internships.

FACILITIES

Housing: Apartments for married students; Apartments for single students; Men's dorms; Special housing for disabled students; Women's dorms; 75% of campus accessible to physically disabled. **Special Academic Facilities/Equipment:** Taylor Bott-Rogers Fine Arts Bldg. Lundy-Fetterman School of Business museum and exhibit hall School of Pharmacy Clinical Research Facility. **Campus network:** 100% of classrooms, 100% of dorms, 100% of student union, 100% of libraries, 100% of dining areas, 100% of common outdoor areas, have wireless network access.

CAMPUS LIFE

Environment: Rural. **Activities:** Campus Ministries; Choral groups; Concert band; Drama/theater; International Student Organization; Jazz band; Literary magazine; Music ensembles; Musical theater; Pep band; Radio station; Student government; Student newspaper; Yearbook. 44 registered organizations, 14 honor societies, 20 religious organizations, on campus. **Athletics (Intercollegiate):** *Men:* baseball, basketball, cross-country, golf, soccer, tennis, track/field (outdoor), wrestling. *Women:* basketball, cheerleading, cross-country, golf, soccer, softball, swimming, tennis, track/field (outdoor), volleyball. **On-Campus Highlights:** Lundy-Fetterman School of Business.

ADMISSIONS

Freshman Academic Profile: Average high school GPA 3.4. 38% in top 10% of high school class, 80% in top 25% of high school class, 92% in top 50% of high school class. 85% from public high schools. **Basis for Candidate Selection:** *Very important factors include:* rigor of secondary school record, academic GPA, standardized test scores. *Important factors include:* class rank, interview, talent/ability. *Other factors include:* application essay, recommendation(s), extracurricular activities, character/personal qualities, alumni/ae relation, volunteer work, work experience, level of applicant's interest. **Freshman Admission Requirements:** High school diploma is required and GED is accepted. *Academic units required:* 4 English, 3 math, 2 science, 1 science labs, 2 foreign language, 2 unit from above areas or other academic areas. **Freshman Admission Statistics:** 3,014 applied, 60% admitted, 50% enrolled. **Transfer Admission Requirements:** High school transcript, college transcript(s), standardized test scores, statement of good standing from prior institution(s). Minimum college GPA of 2.5 required. Lowest grade transferable C. **General Admission Information:** Application fee $35. Regular application deadline 8/19. Non-fall registration accepted.

COSTS AND FINANCIAL AID

Annual tuition $19,650. Room and board $6,830. Required fees $700. Average book and supplies expense $1,100. **Required Forms and Deadlines:** FAFSA. **Notification of Awards:** Applicants will be notified of awards on a rolling basis beginning 2/1. **Types of Aid:** *Need-based scholarships/grants:* College/university scholarship or grant aid from institutional funds; Federal Pell; Private scholarships; SEOG; State scholarships/grants. *Loans:* Direct PLUS loans; Direct Subsidized Stafford Loans; Direct Unsubsidized Stafford Loans. **Student Employment:** Federal Work-Study Program available. Institutional employment available. **Financial Aid Statistics:** 69% needy freshmen, 73% needy undergrads receive need-based scholarship or grant aid. 95% freshmen, 77% undergrads receive non-need-based scholarship or grant aid. 87% freshmen, 88% undergrads receive need-based self-help aid. 4% freshmen, 3% undergrads receive athletic scholarships. 97% freshmen, 92% undergrads receive any aid. **Criteria awarding aid:** *Non-need-based:* Academics, Athletics, Music/drama, Religious affiliation, State/district residency.

CANISIUS COLLEGE

2001 Main Street, Buffalo, NY 14208
Phone: 716-888-2200 **Financial Aid Phone:** (716) 888-2300
E-mail: admissions@canisius.edu **CEEB Code:** 2073
Fax: 716-888-3230 **Website:** http://www.canisius.edu **ACT Code:** 2690

This private school, affiliated with the Roman Catholic-Jesuit Church, was founded in 1870. It has a 72 acre campus.

RATINGS

Admissions Selectivity Rating: 77   **Fire Safety Rating:** 89   **Green Rating:** 65

STUDENTS AND FACULTY

Enrollment: 2,325. **Student Body:** 50% female, 50% male, 11% out-of-state, 4% international (21 countries represented). Asian 3%, African American 8%, Caucasian 73%, Hispanic 6%, Native American <1%, Pacific Islander <1%, Two or more races 2%, Race unknown 3%.
Retention and Graduation: 83% freshmen return for sophomore year. 64% freshmen graduate within 4 years. 71% freshmen graduate within 6 years.
Faculty: Student/faculty ratio 11:1. 174 full-time faculty, 98% hold PhDs, 10% are members of minority groups, 41% are women. 0% of classes are taught by teaching assistants.

ACADEMICS

Degrees: Associate; Bachelor's; Master's; Post-bachelor's certificate. **Classes:** Most classes have 10–19 students. Most lab/discussion sessions have 10–19 students. **Most popular majors:** Biology/Biological Sciences, General; Psychology, General; Business Administration and Management, General. **Special Study Options:** Cross-registration; Distance learning; Double major; Dual enrollment; English as a Second Language (ESL); Exchange student program (domestic); External degree program; Honors program; Independent study; Internships; Student-designed major; Study abroad; Teacher certification program. **Honors programs:** The All–College Honors Program is a learning community of Canisius College's top students who have excelled academically in high school and in college entrance exams. These students represent the top 10 percent of applicants to Canisius. These select students enter a program that provides a challenging and adventurous academic atmosphere that provides myriad benefits, including: A rigorous curriculum including interdisciplinary Liberal Arts courses mixed with special seminars that lead to an independent research project and thesis. Small, enriched classes of 20 or fewer students that allow for in-depth discussions between students and faculty. Close interaction with Canisius faculty in one-on-one opportunities. Out-of-classroom scholarly travel that gives students a broader "real life" view of classroom topics. **Disability Services offered:** Note-taking services; Reader services; Tape recorders; Tutors. **Career services:** Alumni network; Alumni services; Career assessment; Career/job search classes; Internships; Regional alumni.

FACILITIES

Housing: Apartments for single students; Special housing for disabled students; Special housing for international students; Theme housing; Wellness housing; 95% of campus accessible to physically disabled. **Special Academic Facilities/Equipment:** TV studio, electron microscope, seismograph, language lab, digital lab, human performance lab, molecular biology and physics labs, mini-planetarium. **Campus network:** 100% of classrooms, 100% of dorms, 100% of student union, 100% of libraries, 100% of dining areas, 100% of common outdoor areas, have wireless network access.

CAMPUS LIFE

Environment: Metropolis. **Activities:** Campus Ministries; Choral groups; Concert band; Dance; Drama/theater; International Student Organization; Jazz band; Literary magazine; Marching band; Model UN; Music ensembles; Musical theater; Pep band; Radio station; Student government; Student newspaper; Student-run film society; Symphony orchestra; Television station; Yearbook. 140 registered organizations, 17 honor societies, 2 religious organizations, 1 fraternities, 1 sororities, on campus. **Athletics (Intercollegiate):** *Men:* baseball, basketball, cross-country, diving, golf, ice hockey, lacrosse, soccer, swimming. *Women:* basketball, cross-country, diving, lacrosse, soccer, softball, swimming, synchronized swimming, volleyball. **On-Campus Highlights:** Montante Cultural Center. **Environmental Initiatives:** Canisius College is deeply committed to utility conservation and the sustainability of our natural resources. This is accomplished in part through our development of policies and practices which are designed to promote sound energy management, and the economic, social and environmental well-being of our students and staff. Canisius College is working with Ecology and

114

Environment, Inc. (E & E) to develop and implement an energy conservation program. The overall goal of the program is to reduce the college's annual electric consumption by five percent, based on historical consumption during the last three academic years. A web page is being designed to explain how Canisius College conserves and supports sustainable use of our natural resources

ADMISSIONS

Freshman Academic Profile: 22% in top 10% of high school class, 47% in top 25% of high school class, 79% in top 50% of high school class. 70% from public high schools. **Test Scores:** SAT Math middle 50% range 520–630. SAT EBRW middle 50% range 520–630. ACT middle 50% range 22–28. **Basis for Candidate Selection:** *Very important factors include:* rigor of secondary school record, academic GPA, standardized test scores. *Important factors include:* application essay, recommendation(s), extracurricular activities, volunteer work. *Other factors include:* class rank, interview, talent/ability, character/personal qualities, first generation, alumni/ae relation, work experience, level of applicant's interest. **Freshman Admission Requirements:** High school diploma is required and GED is accepted. *Academic units required:* 4 English, 3 math, 3 science, 2 science labs, 2 foreign language, 4 social studies. *Academic units recommended:* 4 English, 4 math, 4 science, 2 science labs, 4 foreign language, 4 social studies, 4 academic electives. **Freshman Admission Statistics:** 4,488 applied, 78% admitted, 16% enrolled. **Transfer Admission Requirements:** College transcript(s), statement of good standing from prior institution(s). Minimum college GPA of 2.0 required. Lowest grade transferable C. **General Admission Information:** Non-fall registration accepted. Admission may be deferred for a maximum of 1 year.

COSTS AND FINANCIAL AID

Annual tuition $27,000. Room and board $11,340. Required fees $1,488. Average book and supplies expense $1,000. **Required Forms and Deadlines:** FAFSA; State aid form. **Notification of Awards:** Applicants will be notified of awards on a rolling basis beginning 12/20. **Types of Aid:** *Need-based scholarships/grants:* College/university scholarship or grant aid from institutional funds; Federal Pell; Private scholarships; SEOG; State scholarships/grants; United Negro College Fund. *Loans:* Direct PLUS loans; Direct Subsidized Stafford Loans; Direct Unsubsidized Stafford Loans. **Student Employment:** Federal Work-Study Program available. Institutional employment available. **Financial Aid Statistics:** 26% freshmen, 23% undergrads receive non-need-based scholarship or grant aid. 75% freshmen, 79% undergrads receive need-based self-help aid. 4% freshmen, 5% undergrads receive athletic scholarships. 99% freshmen, 96% undergrads receive any aid. 77% undergrads borrow to pay for school. Average cumulative indebtedness $33,694. **Criteria awarding aid:** *Non-need-based:* Academics, Alumni affiliation, Art, Athletics, Job skills, Music/drama.

CAPITAL UNIVERSITY

Admission Office, Columbus, OH 43209
Phone: 614-236-6101 **Financial Aid Phone:** 614-236-6511
E-mail: admission@capital.edu **CEEB Code:** 1099
Fax: 614-236-6926 **Website:** www.capital.edu **ACT Code:** 3242

This private school, affiliated with the Lutheran Church, was founded in 1830. It has a 48 acre campus.

RATINGS

Admissions Selectivity Rating: 80 **Fire Safety Rating:** 66 **Green Rating:** 60*

STUDENTS AND FACULTY

Enrollment: 2,654. **Student Body:** 58% female, 42% male, 10% out-of-state, 2% international (18 countries represented). Asian 1%, African American 10%, Caucasian 75%, Hispanic 4%, Native American <1%, Pacific Islander 0%, Two or more races 5%, Race unknown 3%. **Retention and Graduation:** 76% freshmen return for sophomore year. **Faculty:** Student/faculty ratio 12:1. 159 full-time faculty, 77% hold PhDs, 9% are members of minority groups, 49% are women. 0% of classes are taught by teaching assistants.

ACADEMICS

Degrees: Bachelor's; Doctoral degree—professional practice; Master's; Post-bachelor's certificate. **Classes:** Most classes have 20–29 students. Most lab/discussion sessions have 10–19 students. **Most popular majors:** Education, General; Registered Nursing/Registered Nurse; Business Administration and Management, General. **Special Study Options:** Accelerated program;

Cooperative education program; Cross-registration; Double major; Dual enrollment; English as a Second Language (ESL); Exchange student program (domestic); External degree program; Honors program; Independent study; Internships; Liberal arts/career combination; Student-designed major; Study abroad; Teacher certification program. **Honors programs:** Capital University Honors Program. **Disability Services offered:** Tape recorders; Tutors. **Career services:** Alumni network; Alumni services; Career assessment; Career/job search classes; Internships.

FACILITIES

Housing: Apartments for single students; Coed dorms; Special housing for disabled students; Theme housing; Wellness housing; 100% of campus accessible to physically disabled. **Special Academic Facilities/Equipment:** Art gallery, Conservatory of Music. **Campus network:** 100% of classrooms, 100% of dorms, 100% of student union, 100% of libraries, 100% of dining areas, 100% of common outdoor areas, have wireless network access.

CAMPUS LIFE

Environment: Metropolis. **Activities:** Campus Ministries; Choral groups; Concert band; Dance; Drama/theater; International Student Organization; Jazz band; Literary magazine; Music ensembles; Musical theater; Radio station; Student government; Student newspaper; Student-run film society; Symphony orchestra; Television station. 63 registered organizations, 16 honor societies, 5 religious organizations, 5 fraternities, 5 sororities, on campus. **Athletics (Intercollegiate):** *Men:* baseball, basketball, cross-country, football, golf, soccer, tennis, track/field (outdoor), track/field (indoor). *Women:* basketball, cross-country, golf, soccer, softball, tennis, track/field (outdoor), track/field (indoor), volleyball. **On-Campus Highlights:** Capital Center. **Environmental Initiatives:** Energy management.

ADMISSIONS

Freshman Academic Profile: Average high school GPA 3.5. 16% in top 10% of high school class, 47% in top 25% of high school class, 81% in top 50% of high school class. 92% from public high schools. **Test Scores:** SAT Math middle 50% range 480–580. SAT EBRW middle 50% range 480–610. ACT middle 50% range 22–28. **Basis for Candidate Selection:** *Very important factors include:* academic GPA, standardized test scores, talent/ability. *Other factors include:* rigor of secondary school record, recommendation(s), interview, extracurricular activities, alumni/ae relation, geographical residence, state residency, religious affiliation/commitment, racial/ethnic status, level of applicant's interest. **Freshman Admission Requirements:** High school diploma is required and GED is accepted. *Academic units recommended:* 4 English, 3 math, 3 science, 2 science labs, 2 foreign language, 3 social studies, 1 visual/performing arts. **Freshman Admission Statistics:** 3,718 applied, 72% admitted, 25% enrolled. **Transfer Admission Requirements:** College transcript(s). Minimum college GPA of 2.5 required. Lowest grade transferable C-. **General Admission Information:** Application fee $25. Priority deadline 12/1. Regular application deadline 5/1. Non-fall registration accepted. Admission may be deferred for a maximum of 1 year.

COSTS AND FINANCIAL AID

Annual tuition $32,630. Room and board $9,250. Required fees $200. Average book and supplies expense $1,550. **Required Forms and Deadlines:** FAFSA. **Notification of Awards:** Applicants will be notified of awards on a rolling basis beginning 3/15. **Types of Aid:** *Need-based scholarships/grants:* College/university scholarship or grant aid from institutional funds; Federal Pell; Private scholarships; SEOG; State scholarships/grants. *Loans:* Direct PLUS loans; Direct Subsidized Stafford Loans; Direct Unsubsidized Stafford Loans. **Student Employment:** Federal Work-Study Program available. Institutional employment available. **Financial Aid Statistics:** 99% needy freshmen, 95% needy undergrads receive need-based scholarship or grant aid. 98% freshmen, 93% undergrads receive non-need-based scholarship or grant aid. 75% freshmen, 78% undergrads receive need-based self-help aid. 0% freshmen, 0% undergrads receive athletic scholarships. 99% freshmen receive any aid. 82% undergrads borrow to pay for school. Average cumulative indebtedness $31,563. **Criteria awarding aid:** *Non-need-based:* Academics, Alumni affiliation, Art, Leadership, Minority status, Music/drama, Religious affiliation, State/district residency.

CARLETON COLLEGE

Best Colleges

100 South College Street, Northfield, MN 55057
Phone: 507-222-4190 **Financial Aid Phone:** 507-222-4138
E-mail: admissions@carleton.edu **CEEB Code:** 6081
Fax: 507-222-4526 **Website:** www.carleton.edu **ACT Code:** 2092

This private school was founded in 1866. It has a 955 acre campus.

RATINGS
Admissions Selectivity Rating: 97   **Fire Safety Rating:** 98   **Green Rating:** 90

STUDENTS AND FACULTY
Enrollment: 2,046. **Student Body:** 50% female, 50% male, 84% out-of-state, 11% international (42 countries represented). Asian 8%, African American 5%, Caucasian 60%, Hispanic 8%, Native American <1%, Pacific Islander 0%, Two or more races 7%, Race unknown 1%.
Retention and Graduation: 97% freshmen return for sophomore year. 89% freshmen graduate within 4 years. 94% freshmen graduate within 6 years. 21% grads go on to further study within 1 year. **Faculty:** Student/faculty ratio 9:1. 212 full-time faculty, 98% hold PhDs, 28% are members of minority groups, 46% are women. 0% of classes are taught by teaching assistants.

ACADEMICS
Degrees: Bachelor's. **Classes:** Most classes have 10–19 students. Most lab/discussion sessions have 10–19 students. **Most popular majors:** Computer and Information Sciences, General; Biology/Biological Sciences, General; Economics, General. **Special Study Options:** Accelerated program; Cross-registration; Double major; Dual enrollment; Independent study; Internships; Student-designed major; Study abroad; Teacher certification program. **Combined degree programs:** BA/JD. **Disability Services offered:** Note-taking services; Reader services; Tape recorders; Tutors. **Career services:** Alumni network; Alumni services; Career assessment; Career/job search classes; Internships; Regional alumni.

FACILITIES
Housing: Apartments for single students; Coed dorms; Cooperative housing; Special housing for disabled students; Theme housing; Wellness housing; 39% of campus accessible to physically disabled. **Special Academic Facilities/Equipment:** Arboretum, greenhouse, observatory, scanning and transmission electron microscopes, refractor and reflector telescopes, nuclear magnetic resonance spectrometer, Weitz Center for Creativity. **Campus network:** 100% of classrooms, 100% of dorms, 100% of student union, 100% of libraries, 100% of dining areas, 90% of common outdoor areas, have wireless network access.

CAMPUS LIFE
Environment: Village. **Activities:** Campus Ministries; Choral groups; Concert band; Dance; Drama/theater; International Student Organization; Jazz band; Literary magazine; Model UN; Music ensembles; Musical theater; Radio station; Student government; Student newspaper; Student-run film society; Symphony orchestra; Yearbook. 328 registered organizations, 3 honor societies, 15 religious organizations, on campus. **Athletics (Intercollegiate):** *Men:* baseball, basketball, cross-country, diving, football, golf, soccer, swimming, tennis, track/field (outdoor), track/field (indoor). *Women:* basketball, cross-country, diving, golf, soccer, softball, swimming, synchronized swimming, tennis, track/field (outdoor), track/field (indoor), volleyball. **On-Campus Highlights:** Cowling Arboretum. **Environmental Initiatives:** 2nd Wind Turbine provided power directly to the campus grid.

ADMISSIONS
Freshman Academic Profile: 79% in top 10% of high school class, 96% in top 25% of high school class, 100% in top 50% of high school class. 60% from public high schools. **Test Scores:** SAT Math middle 50% range 680–780. SAT EBRW middle 50% range 670–750. ACT middle 50% range 31–34. **Basis for Candidate Selection:** *Very important factors include:* rigor of secondary school record, class rank, academic GPA. *Important factors include:* application essay, standardized test scores, recommendation(s), extracurricular activities, talent/ability, character/personal qualities, alumni/ae relation. *Other factors include:* interview, first generation, geographical residence, state residency. **Freshman Admission Requirements:** High school diploma is required and GED is

accepted. *Academic units recommended:* 4 English, 3 math, 3 science, 1 science labs, 3 foreign language, 3 social studies. **Freshman Admission Statistics:** 7,092 applied, 20% admitted, 38% enrolled. **Transfer Admission Requirements:** High school transcript, college transcript(s), essay or personal statement, standardized test scores, statement of good standing from prior institution(s). Minimum college GPA of 2.0 required. Lowest grade transferable C-. **General Admission Information:** Application fee $30. Regular application deadline 1/15. Admission may be deferred for a maximum of 1 year.

COSTS AND FINANCIAL AID
Annual tuition $56,778. Room and board $14,658. Required fees $333. Average book and supplies expense $866. **Required Forms and Deadlines:** CSS/Financial Aid PROFILE; FAFSA; Noncustodial PROFILE. **Notification of Awards:** Applicants will be notified of awards on or about 3/31. **Types of Aid:** *Need-based scholarships/grants:* College/university scholarship or grant aid from institutional funds; Federal Pell; Private scholarships; SEOG; State scholarships/grants. *Loans:* Direct PLUS loans; Direct Subsidized Stafford Loans; Direct Unsubsidized Stafford Loans. **Student Employment:** Federal Work-Study Program available. Institutional employment available. **Financial Aid Statistics:** 100% needy freshmen, 100% needy undergrads receive need-based scholarship or grant aid. 10% freshmen, 13% undergrads receive non-need-based scholarship or grant aid. 99% freshmen, 98% undergrads receive need-based self-help aid. 0% freshmen, 0% undergrads receive athletic scholarships. 55% freshmen, 55% undergrads receive any aid. 12% undergrads borrow to pay for school. Average cumulative indebtedness $21,020. **Criteria awarding aid:** *Non-need-based:* Academics.

CARLOW UNIVERSITY

3333 Fifth Avenue, Pittsburgh, PA 15213-3165
Phone: 412-578-6059 **Financial Aid Phone:** 412-578-6389
E-mail: admissions@carlow.edu **CEEB Code:** 2421
Fax: 412-578-6321 **Website:** www.carlow.edu **ACT Code:** 2421

This private school, affiliated with the Roman Catholic Church, was founded in 1929. It has a 17 acre campus.

RATINGS
Admissions Selectivity Rating: 74   **Fire Safety Rating:** 72   **Green Rating:** 60*

STUDENTS AND FACULTY
Enrollment: 1,288. **Student Body:** 83% female, 17% male, 5% out-of-state, <1% international (4 countries represented). Asian 3%, African American 18%, Caucasian 69%, Hispanic 2%, Native American <1%, Pacific Islander 0%, Two or more races 4%, Race unknown 3%.
Retention and Graduation: 78% freshmen return for sophomore year. 45% freshmen graduate within 4 years. 57% freshmen graduate within 6 years. **Faculty:** Student/faculty ratio 11:1. 108 full-time faculty, 75% hold PhDs, 5% are members of minority groups, 77% are women. 0% of classes are taught by teaching assistants.

ACADEMICS
Degrees: Bachelor's; Certificate; Doctoral degree—professional practice; Master's; Post-bachelor's certificate; Post-master's certificate. **Classes:** Most classes have 10–19 students. Most lab/discussion sessions have 10–19 students. **Most popular majors:** Biology/Biological Sciences, General; Psychology, General; Registered Nursing/Registered Nurse. **Special Study Options:** Accelerated program; Cross-registration; Distance learning; Double major; Dual enrollment; Honors program; Independent study; Internships; Liberal arts/career combination; Study abroad; Teacher certification program; Weekend college. **Honors programs:** Undergraduate Honor Program. **Career services:** Alumni network; Alumni services; Career assessment; Career/job search classes; Internships; Regional alumni.

FACILITIES
Housing: Coed dorms; Men's dorms; Women's dorms

CAMPUS LIFE
Environment: City. **Activities:** Campus Ministries; Choral groups; Dance; Drama/theater; Literary magazine; Musical theater; Student government; Student newspaper. 29 registered organizations, 1 religious organizations, 1 sororities, on campus. **Athletics (Intercollegiate):** *Women:* basketball, soccer, softball, tennis, volleyball. **On-Campus Highlights:** University Commons.

ADMISSIONS

Freshman Academic Profile: Average high school GPA 3.6. **Test Scores:** SAT Math middle 50% range 480–563. SAT EBRW middle 50% range 500–590. ACT middle 50% range 19–24. **Basis for Candidate Selection:** *Very important factors include:* rigor of secondary school record, academic GPA, standardized test scores. *Other factors include:* class rank, application essay, recommendation(s), interview, extracurricular activities, talent/ability, character/personal qualities, first generation, alumni/ae relation, volunteer work, work experience, level of applicant's interest. **Freshman Admission Requirements:** High school diploma is required and GED is accepted. *Academic units required:* 4 English, 3 math, 3 science, 2 social studies, 2 history, 4 academic electives. *Academic units recommended:* 4 math, 4 science, 2 science labs. **Freshman Admission Statistics:** 722 applied, 92% admitted, 25% enrolled. **Transfer Admission Requirements:** College transcript(s). Minimum college GPA of 2.0 required. Lowest grade transferable C. **General Admission Information:** Non-fall registration accepted. Admission may be deferred for a maximum of 1 year.

COSTS AND FINANCIAL AID

Annual tuition $29,652. Room and board $11,902. Required fees $876. Average book and supplies expense $1,400. **Required Forms and Deadlines:** FAFSA; State aid form. **Notification of Awards:** Applicants will be notified of awards on a rolling basis beginning 12/1. **Types of Aid:** *Need-based scholarships/grants:* College/university scholarship or grant aid from institutional funds; Federal Pell; Private scholarships; SEOG; State scholarships/grants. *Loans:* Direct PLUS loans; Direct Subsidized Stafford Loans; Direct Unsubsidized Stafford Loans. **Student Employment:** Federal Work-Study Program available. **Financial Aid Statistics:** 100% needy freshmen, 100% needy undergrads receive need-based scholarship or grant aid. 36% freshmen, 33% undergrads receive non-need-based scholarship or grant aid. 91% freshmen, 92% undergrads receive need-based self-help aid. 4% freshmen, 3% undergrads receive athletic scholarships. 86% undergrads borrow to pay for school. Average cumulative indebtedness $40,958. **Criteria awarding aid:** *Non-need-based:* Academics, Alumni affiliation, Art, Athletics, Job skills, State/district residency.

CARNEGIE MELLON UNIVERSITY

Best Colleges

5000 Forbes Avenue, Pittsburgh, PA 15213
Phone: 412-268-2082 **Financial Aid Phone:** 412-268-8186
E-mail: admission@andrew.cmu.edu **CEEB Code:** 2074
Fax: 412-268-7838 **Website:** www.cmu.edu **ACT Code:** 3534

This private school was founded in 1900. It has a 152.5 acre campus.

RATINGS

Admissions Selectivity Rating: 98   **Fire Safety Rating:** 90   **Green Rating:** 99

STUDENTS AND FACULTY

Enrollment: 6,929. **Student Body:** 50% female, 50% male, 86% out-of-state, 22% international (57 countries represented). Asian 31%, African American 4%, Caucasian 25%, Hispanic 9%, Native American <1%, Pacific Islander <1%, Two or more races 4%, Race unknown 6%. **Retention and Graduation:** 97% freshmen return for sophomore year. 76% freshmen graduate within 4 years. 91% freshmen graduate within 6 years. 27% grads go on to further study within 1 year. 5% grads pursue arts and sciences degrees. <1% grads pursue law degrees. 1% grads pursue business degrees. 1% grads pursue medical degrees. **Faculty:** Student/faculty ratio 7:1. 1,080 full-time faculty, 93% hold PhDs, 17% are members of minority groups, 31% are women.

ACADEMICS

Degrees: Bachelor's; Doctoral degree research/scholarship; Master's; Post-bachelor's certificate; Post-master's certificate. **Classes:** Most classes have 10–19 students. Most lab/discussion sessions have 20–29 students. **Most popular majors:** Computer Science; Electrical and Electronics Engineering; Business Administration and Management, General. **Special Study Options:** Accelerated program; Cooperative education program; Cross-registration; Distance learning; Double major; Independent study; Internships; Liberal arts/career combination; Student-designed major; Study abroad; Teacher certification program. **Combined degree programs:** BA/MA; BA/MEng. **Disability Services offered:**

Note-taking services; Reader services; Tape recorders; Tutors. **Career services:** Alumni services; Career assessment; Career/job search classes; Internships; Regional alumni.

FACILITIES

Housing: Apartments for single students; Coed dorms; Fraternity/sorority housing; Men's dorms; Special housing for disabled students; Theme housing; Wellness housing; Women's dorms; 99% of campus accessible to physically disabled. **Special Academic Facilities/Equipment:** Rare books collection, Entertainment Technology Center, Art galleries, Theatres, Botanical Institute, Extensive lab facilities and equipment, Recording studio, Robotics Institute, Design studios, Photo shoot studio and darkrooms, Radio station, Collaborative Innovation Center, LEED-certified green residence hall, Campo Garden, Observatory, Wood shops, maker spaces, Tepper Quad.

CAMPUS LIFE

Environment: Metropolis. **Activities:** Campus Ministries; Choral groups; Concert band; Dance; Drama/theater; International Student Organization; Jazz band; Literary magazine; Marching band; Model UN; Music ensembles; Musical theater; Pep band; Radio station; Student government; Student newspaper; Student-run film society; Symphony orchestra; Yearbook. 409 registered organizations, 29 religious organizations, 13 fraternities, 11 sororities, on campus. **Athletics (Intercollegiate):** *Men:* basketball, cheerleading, cross-country, diving, football, golf, soccer, swimming, tennis, track/field (outdoor). *Women:* basketball, cheerleading, cross-country, diving, soccer, swimming, tennis, track/field (outdoor), volleyball. **On-Campus Highlights:** Cohon University Center (Student Center). **Environmental Initiatives:** 1. PRACTICE: We purchase renewable electricity certificates for 100% of our campus electricity use and, at minimum, USGBC LEED Silver guidelines are required for all building projects and most renovations. The majority of our projects are LEED Gold Certified. The Scotty Goes Green Office Certification program promotes sustainable office practices in several administrative and academic departments. https://www.cmu.edu/environment/

ADMISSIONS

Freshman Academic Profile: Average high school GPA 3.9. 88% in top 10% of high school class, 96% in top 25% of high school class, 99% in top 50% of high school class. **Test Scores:** SAT Math middle 50% range 760–800. SAT EBRW middle 50% range 700–760. ACT middle 50% range 33–35. **Basis for Candidate Selection:** *Very important factors include:* rigor of secondary school record, class rank, academic GPA, standardized test scores, extracurricular activities, volunteer work, work experience. *Important factors include:* application essay, recommendation(s), talent/ability, character/personal qualities, first generation, alumni/ae relation, racial/ethnic status. **Freshman Admission Requirements:** High school diploma is required and GED is accepted. *Academic units required:* 4 English, 4 math, 3 science, 2 foreign language, 3 academic electives. *Academic units recommended:* 4 English, 4 math, 3 science, 2 foreign language, 3 academic electives. **Freshman Admission Statistics:** 27,634 applied, 15% admitted, 37% enrolled. **Transfer Admission Requirements:** High school transcript, college transcript(s), essay or personal statement, standardized test scores, statement of good standing from prior institution(s). **General Admission Information:** Application fee $75. Regular application deadline 1/1. Admission may be deferred for a maximum of 1 year.

COSTS AND FINANCIAL AID

Annual tuition $57,560. Room and board $15,550. Required fees $1,364. Average book and supplies expense $2,400. **Required Forms and Deadlines:** CSS/Financial Aid PROFILE; FAFSA; Noncustodial PROFILE. **Notification of Awards:** Applicants will be notified of awards on or about 4/15. **Types of Aid:** *Need-based scholarships/grants:* College/university scholarship or grant aid from institutional funds; Federal Pell; Private scholarships; SEOG; State scholarships/grants. *Loans:* Direct PLUS loans; Direct Subsidized Stafford Loans; Direct Unsubsidized Stafford Loans. **Student Employment:** Federal Work-Study Program available. Institutional employment available. **Financial Aid Statistics:** 96% needy freshmen, 97% needy undergrads receive need-based scholarship or grant aid. 33% freshmen, 27% undergrads receive non-need-based scholarship or grant aid. 95% freshmen, 95% undergrads receive need-based self-help aid. 0% freshmen, 0% undergrads receive athletic scholarships. 55.6% freshmen, 52.5% undergrads receive any aid. 52% undergrads borrow to pay for school. Average cumulative indebtedness $31,342. **Criteria awarding aid:** *Need-based:* Academics, Art, Music/drama. *Non-need-based:* Academics, Art, Leadership, Minority status, Music/drama, State/district residency.

CARROLL COLLEGE (MT)

1601 North Benton Avenue, Helena, MT 59625
Phone: 406-447-4384 **Financial Aid Phone:** 406-447-5423
E-mail: admission@carroll.edu **CEEB Code:** 4041
Fax: 406-447-4533 **Website:** www.carroll.edu **ACT Code:** 2408

This private school, affiliated with the Roman Catholic Church, was founded in 1909. It has a 63 acre campus.

RATINGS

Admissions Selectivity Rating: 88   **Fire Safety Rating:** 68   **Green Rating:** 60*

STUDENTS AND FACULTY

Enrollment: 1,376. **Student Body:** 58% female, 42% male, 54% out-of-state, 1% international (15 countries represented). Asian 1%, African American 1%, Caucasian 81%, Hispanic 4%, Native American 1%, Pacific Islander <1%, Two or more races 1%, Race unknown 8%.
Retention and Graduation: 81% freshmen return for sophomore year. 22% grads go on to further study within 1 year. **Faculty:** 0% of classes are taught by teaching assistants.

ACADEMICS

Degrees: Associate; Bachelor's; Certificate; Master's; Transfer Associate. **Most popular majors:** Biology/Biological Sciences, General; Registered Nursing, Nursing Administration, Nursing Research and Clinical Nursing; Psychology, General. **Special Study Options:** Cooperative education program; Double major; Dual enrollment; English as a Second Language (ESL); Exchange student program (domestic); Honors program; Independent study; Internships; Liberal arts/career combination; Student-designed major; Study abroad; Teacher certification program. **Disability Services offered:** Tutors. **Career services:** Career assessment; Career/job search classes; Internships.

FACILITIES

Housing: Apartments for married students; Apartments for single students; Coed dorms; Special housing for international students; Theme housing; 75% of campus accessible to physically disabled. **Special Academic Facilities/Equipment:** Arts lab, observatory, seismograph station, engineering lab.

CAMPUS LIFE

Environment: Village. **Activities:** Campus Ministries; Choral groups; Dance; Drama/theater; International Student Organization; Literary magazine; Music ensembles; Musical theater; Pep band; Radio station; Student government; Student newspaper; Student-run film society; Yearbook. 34 registered organizations, 10 honor societies, 4 religious organizations, on campus. **Athletics (Intercollegiate):** *Men:* basketball, cheerleading, football, golf. *Women:* basketball, cheerleading, golf, soccer, volleyball. **On-Campus Highlights:** Science and Technology Center.

ADMISSIONS

Freshman Academic Profile: Average high school GPA 3.5. 25% in top 10% of high school class, 61% in top 25% of high school class, 90% in top 50% of high school class. 75% from public high schools. **Test Scores:** SAT Math middle 50% range 510–610. SAT EBRW middle 50% range 490–620. ACT middle 50% range 22–27. **Basis for Candidate Selection:** *Very important factors include:* rigor of secondary school record, academic GPA. *Important factors include:* standardized test scores, talent/ability, character/personal qualities. *Other factors include:* class rank, application essay, recommendation(s), interview, extracurricular activities, first generation, volunteer work, work experience, level of applicant's interest. **Freshman Admission Requirements:** High school diploma is required and GED is accepted. *Academic units recommended:* 4 English, 3 math, 2 science, 1 science labs, 2 social studies, 2 history, 2 academic electives, 1 visual/performing arts. **Freshman Admission Statistics:** 13 applied, 18% enrolled. **Transfer Admission Requirements:** College transcript(s), essay or personal statement, statement of good standing from prior institution(s). Minimum college GPA of 2.5 required. Lowest grade transferable C. **General Admission Information:** Application fee $35. Priority deadline 3/1. Regular application deadline 6/1. Non-fall registration accepted. Admission may be deferred for a maximum of 1 year.

COSTS AND FINANCIAL AID

Annual tuition $27,304. Room and board $8,668. Required fees $610. Average book and supplies expense $1,000. **Required Forms and Deadlines:** FAFSA. **Notification of Awards:** Applicants will be notified of awards on a rolling basis beginning 3/1. **Types of Aid:** *Need-based scholarships/grants:* College/university scholarship or grant aid from institutional funds; Federal Pell; Private scholarships; SEOG; State scholarships/grants. **Student Employment:** Federal Work-Study Program available. Institutional employment available. **Financial Aid Statistics:** 99% needy freshmen, 99% needy undergrads receive need-based scholarship or grant aid. 17% freshmen, 14% undergrads receive non-need-based scholarship or grant aid. 81% freshmen, 85% undergrads receive need-based self-help aid. 20% freshmen, 19% undergrads receive athletic scholarships. 98% freshmen, 98% undergrads receive any aid. **Criteria awarding aid:** *Need-based:* Academics, Art, Athletics, Minority status, Religious affiliation. *Non-need-based:* Academics, Art, Athletics, Leadership, Minority status, Music/drama, Religious affiliation.

CARROLL UNIVERSITY (WI)

100 North East Avenue, Waukesha, WI 53186
Phone: 262-524-7220 **Financial Aid Phone:** 262-524-7297
CEEB Code: 1101
Fax: 262-951-3037 **Website:** www.carrollu.edu **ACT Code:** 4570

This private school, affiliated with the Presbyterian Church, was founded in 1846. It has a 53 acre campus.

RATINGS

Admissions Selectivity Rating: 76   **Fire Safety Rating:** 80   **Green Rating:** 60*

STUDENTS AND FACULTY

Enrollment: 3,124. **Student Body:** 31% out-of-state, 2% international (39 countries represented). Asian 1%, African American 2%, Caucasian 87%, Hispanic 3%, Native American <1%, Pacific Islander 0%, Two or more races 0%, Race unknown 4%.
Retention and Graduation: 13% grads go on to further study within 1 year. **Faculty:** Student/faculty ratio 14:1. 139 full-time faculty, 0% hold PhDs, 0% are members of minority groups, 0% are women. 0% of classes are taught by teaching assistants.

ACADEMICS

Degrees: Bachelor's; Master's; Post-bachelor's certificate. **Most popular majors:** Biology/Biological Sciences, General; Business Administration and Management, General; Psychology, General. **Special Study Options:** Distance learning; Double major; Exchange student program (domestic); Honors program; Independent study; Internships; Liberal arts/career combination; Student-designed major; Study abroad; Teacher certification program. **Disability Services offered:** Note-taking services; Tape recorders; Tutors. **Career services:** Alumni network; Career assessment; Career/job search classes; Internships.

FACILITIES

Housing: Apartments for single students; Coed dorms; Women's dorms; 50% of campus accessible to physically disabled. **Special Academic Facilities/Equipment:** A 60 acre scientific study and conservancy area with a class 1 trout stream and associated wetland and upland habitats. **Campus network:** 100% of classrooms, 100% of dorms, 100% of student union, 100% of libraries, 100% of dining areas, 100% of common outdoor areas, have wireless network access.

CAMPUS LIFE

Environment: Town. **Activities:** Choral groups; Concert band; Dance; Drama/theater; International Student Organization; Jazz band; Literary magazine; Music ensembles; Pep band; Radio station; Student government; Student newspaper. 50 registered organizations, 2 religious organizations, 2 fraternities, 4 sororities, on campus. **Athletics (Intercollegiate):** *Men:* baseball, basketball, cross-country, football, golf, soccer, swimming, tennis, track/field (outdoor), track/field (indoor). *Women:* basketball, cross-country, golf, soccer, softball, swimming, tennis, track/field (outdoor), track/field (indoor), volleyball. **On-Campus Highlights:** Main Hall.

ADMISSIONS

Freshman Academic Profile: 38% in top 10% of high school class, 62% in top 25% of high school class, 83% in top 50% of high school class. 87% from public high schools. **Test Scores:** ACT middle 50% range 21–26. **Basis for Candidate Selection:** *Very important factors include:* rigor of secondary school record, class rank, academic GPA. *Important factors include:* standardized test scores. *Other factors include:* application essay, recommendation(s), interview, extracurricular activities, talent/ability, character/personal qualities, alumni/ae relation, geographical residence, state residency, racial/ethnic status, work experience. **Freshman Admission Requirements:** High school diploma is required and GED is accepted. *Academic units recommended:* 4 English, 4 math, 3 science, 2 science labs, 3 social studies, 3 history. **Freshman Admission Statistics:** 2,868 applied, 83% admitted. **Transfer Admission Requirements:** High school transcript, college transcript(s), Minimum college GPA of 2.0 required. Lowest grade transferable C. **General Admission Information:** Non-fall registration accepted.

COSTS AND FINANCIAL AID
Annual tuition $27,850. Room and board $8,513. **Required Forms and Deadlines:** FAFSA. **Notification of Awards:** Applicants will be notified of awards on a rolling basis beginning 2/15. **Types of Aid:** *Need-based scholarships/ grants:* College/university scholarship or grant aid from institutional funds; Federal Nursing Scholarships; Federal Pell; Private scholarships; SEOG; State scholarships/grants. **Student Employment:** Federal Work-Study Program available. Institutional employment available. **Financial Aid Statistics:** 100% needy freshmen, 100% needy undergrads receive need-based scholarship or grant aid. 91% freshmen, 91% undergrads receive non-need-based scholarship or grant aid. 73% freshmen, 79% undergrads receive need-based self-help aid. 0% freshmen, 0% undergrads receive athletic scholarships. 98% freshmen, 98% undergrads receive any aid. **Criteria awarding aid:** *Need-based:* Academics, Art, Leadership, Religious affiliation. *Non-need-based:* Academics, Alumni affiliation, Art, Leadership, Minority status, Religious affiliation.

CARSON-NEWMAN UNIVERSITY

1646 Russell Avenue, Jefferson City, TN 37760
Phone: 865-471-3223 **Financial Aid Phone:** 865-471-3247
E-mail: admitme@cn.edu **CEEB Code:** 1102
Fax: 865-471-4817 **Website:** www.cn.edu **ACT Code:** 3950

This private school, affiliated with the Baptist Church, was founded in 1851. It has a 90 acre campus.

RATINGS
Admissions Selectivity Rating: 79   **Fire Safety Rating:** 85   **Green Rating:** 60*

STUDENTS AND FACULTY
Enrollment: 1,769. **Student Body:** 60% female, 40% male, 19% out-of-state, 3% international (19 countries represented). Asian 1%, African American 9%, Caucasian 78%, Hispanic 4%, Native American 1%, Pacific Islander <1%, Two or more races 2%, Race unknown 1%.
Retention and Graduation: 67% freshmen return for sophomore year. 49% freshmen graduate within 4 years. 56% freshmen graduate within 6 years. 25% grads go on to further study within 1 year. 20% grads pursue arts and sciences degrees. 3% grads pursue law degrees. 1% grads pursue business degrees. 2% grads pursue medical degrees. **Faculty:** Student/faculty ratio 14:1. 122 full-time faculty, 78% hold PhDs, 4% are members of minority groups, 49% are women. 0% of classes are taught by teaching assistants.

ACADEMICS
Degrees: Associate; Bachelor's; Doctoral degree research/scholarship; Master's; Post-master's certificate. **Classes:** Most classes have 10–19 students. Most lab/ discussion sessions have 10–19 students. **Most popular majors:** Registered Nursing/Registered Nurse; Business Administration and Management, General; Exercise Science and Kinesiology. **Special Study Options:** Accelerated program; Distance learning; Double major; Dual enrollment; English as a Second Language (ESL); Exchange student program (domestic); Honors program; Independent study; Internships; Liberal arts/career combination; Student-designed major; Study abroad; Teacher certification program. **Honors programs:** We have an Honors Program, though which high-ability students are given the ability to participate in specialized social and cultural activities, engage specialized coursework designed to encourage critical thinking, and write a thesis project or other special capstone project at the end of their college careers. **Disability Services offered:** Note-taking services; Reader services; Tape recorders; Tutors. **Career services:** Alumni network; Alumni services; Career assessment; Career/job search classes; Internships; Regional alumni.

FACILITIES
Housing: Apartments for single students; Men's dorms; Special housing for disabled students; Women's dorms; 80% of campus accessible to physically disabled. **Special Academic Facilities/Equipment:** Art galleries, Appalachian history museum, home management house, language lab and Saint Johns Bible Exhibit. **Campus network:** 100% of classrooms, 100% of dorms, 100%

of student union, 100% of libraries, 100% of dining areas, 95% of common outdoor areas, have wireless network access.

CAMPUS LIFE
Environment: Village. **Activities:** Campus Ministries; Choral groups; Concert band; Dance; Drama/theater; International Student Organization; Jazz band; Literary magazine; Marching band; Music ensembles; Musical theater; Pep band; Student government; Student newspaper; Student-run film society; Symphony orchestra. 52 registered organizations, 14 honor societies, 7 religious organizations, on campus. **Athletics (Intercollegiate):** *Men:* baseball, basketball, cheerleading, cross-country, football, golf, soccer, tennis, track/field (outdoor), wrestling. *Women:* basketball, cheerleading, cross-country, soccer, softball, tennis, track/field (outdoor), volleyball. **On-Campus Highlights:** Maddox Student Activities Center.

ADMISSIONS
Freshman Academic Profile: Average high school GPA 3.5. **Test Scores:** SAT Math middle 50% range 443–608. SAT EBRW middle 50% range 480–570. ACT middle 50% range 19–29. **Basis for Candidate Selection:** *Very important factors include:* academic GPA, standardized test scores, character/ personal qualities. *Important factors include:* rigor of secondary school record, class rank, extracurricular activities. *Other factors include:* application essay, recommendation(s), interview, talent/ability, volunteer work. **Freshman Admission Requirements:** High school diploma is required and GED is accepted. *Academic units required:* 4 English, 3 math, 3 science, 2 social studies, 1 history, 6 academic electives, 1 unit from above areas or other academic areas. *Academic units recommended:* 2 foreign language. **Freshman Admission Statistics:** 3,862 applied, 69% admitted, 21% enrolled. **Transfer Admission Requirements:** College transcript(s). Minimum college GPA of 2.0 required. Lowest grade transferable D. **General Admission Information:** Non-fall registration accepted. Admission may be deferred for a maximum of 1 year.

COSTS AND FINANCIAL AID
Annual tuition $28,200. Room and board $8,150. Required fees $1,300. Average book and supplies expense $1,600. **Required Forms and Deadlines:** FAFSA. **Notification of Awards:** Applicants will be notified of awards on a rolling basis beginning 3/1. **Types of Aid:** *Need-based scholarships/grants:* College/university scholarship or grant aid from institutional funds; Federal Nursing Scholarships; Federal Pell; Private scholarships; SEOG; State scholarships/grants. *Loans:* Direct PLUS loans; Direct Subsidized Stafford Loans; Direct Unsubsidized Stafford Loans. **Student Employment:** Federal Work-Study Program available. Institutional employment available. **Financial Aid Statistics:** 100% needy freshmen, 98% needy undergrads receive need-based scholarship or grant aid. 12% freshmen, 15% undergrads receive non-need-based scholarship or grant aid. 76% freshmen, 77% undergrads receive need-based self-help aid. 4% freshmen, 7% undergrads receive athletic scholarships. 98% freshmen, 97% undergrads receive any aid. 76% undergrads borrow to pay for school. Average cumulative indebtedness $28,014. **Criteria awarding aid:** *Need-based:* Art, Music/drama, Religious affiliation. *Non-need-based:* Academics, Art, Athletics, Leadership, Music/drama, Religious affiliation, State/district residency.

CARTHAGE COLLEGE

2001 Alford Park Drive, Kenosha WI, WI 53140
Phone: 262-551-6000 **Financial Aid Phone:** 262-551-6001
E-mail: admissions@carthage.edu **CEEB Code:** 1103
Fax: 262-551-5762 **Website:** www.carthage.edu **ACT Code:** 4571

This private school, affiliated with the Lutheran Church, was founded in 1847. It has a 95 acre campus.

RATINGS
Admissions Selectivity Rating: 79   **Fire Safety Rating:** 81   **Green Rating:** 60*

STUDENTS AND FACULTY
Enrollment: 2,874. **Student Body:** 54% female, 46% male, 68% out-of-state, <1% international (16 countries represented). Asian 1%, African American 5%, Caucasian 77%, Hispanic 4%, Native American <1%, Pacific Islander <1%, Two or more races 2%, Race unknown 10%.
Retention and Graduation: 78% freshmen return for sophomore year. 16% grads go on to further study within 1 year. 4% grads pursue arts and sciences degrees. 2% grads pursue law degrees. 1% grads pursue business degrees. 1% grads pursue medical degrees. **Faculty:** Student/faculty ratio 8:1. 149 full-time

faculty, 91% hold PhDs, 7% are members of minority groups, 40% are women. 0% of classes are taught by teaching assistants.

ACADEMICS

Degrees: Bachelor's; Master's. **Classes:** Most classes have 10–19 students. Most lab/discussion sessions have 10–19 students. **Most popular majors:** Biology/Biological Sciences, General; Business Administration and Management, General; Elementary Education and Teaching. **Special Study Options:** Accelerated program; Cooperative education program; Cross-registration; Double major; Honors program; Independent study; Internships; Student-designed major; Study abroad; Teacher certification program. **Honors programs:** We offer All College Honors as well as Honors in the Major. **Combined degree programs:** BA/MA. **Disability Services offered:** Note-taking services; Reader services; Tape recorders; Tutors. **Career services:** Career assessment; Career/job search classes; Internships.

FACILITIES

Housing: Coed dorms; Women's dorms; 99% of campus accessible to physically disabled. **Special Academic Facilities/Equipment:** H.F. Johnson Art Gallery, Center for Children's Literature, planetarium, undergraduate science research lab, graphic design lab, greenhouse, computer/math research lab, physics research lab, ScienceWorks lab, A.W. Clausen Center Boardroom. **Campus network:** 100% of classrooms, 100% of dorms, 100% of student union, 100% of libraries, 100% of dining areas, 70% of common outdoor areas, have wireless network access.

CAMPUS LIFE

Environment: City. **Activities:** Campus Ministries; Choral groups; Concert band; Dance; Drama/theater; International Student Organization; Jazz band; Literary magazine; Model UN; Music ensembles; Musical theater; Pep band; Radio station; Student government; Student newspaper; Student-run film society; Symphony orchestra; Yearbook. 90 registered organizations, 20 honor societies, 7 religious organizations, 8 fraternities, 7 sororities, on campus. **Athletics (Intercollegiate):** *Men:* baseball, basketball, cross-country, football, golf, soccer, swimming, tennis, track/field (outdoor), track/field (indoor), volleyball. *Women:* basketball, cross-country, golf, soccer, softball, swimming, tennis, track/field (outdoor), track/field (indoor), volleyball, water polo. **On-Campus Highlights:** Tarble Athletic and Recreation Center.

ADMISSIONS

Freshman Academic Profile: Average high school GPA 3.3. 21% in top 10% of high school class, 44% in top 25% of high school class, 75% in top 50% of high school class. 91% from public high schools. **Test Scores:** SAT Math middle 50% range 490–620. SAT EBRW middle 50% range 480–610. ACT middle 50% range 21–27. **Basis for Candidate Selection:** *Very important factors include:* rigor of secondary school record, academic GPA, standardized test scores. *Other factors include:* class rank, application essay, recommendation(s), interview, extracurricular activities, talent/ability, character/personal qualities, volunteer work, work experience. **Freshman Admission Requirements:** High school diploma is required and GED is accepted. *Academic units recommended:* 4 English, 3 math, 3 science, 2 foreign language, 3 social studies, 3 academic electives. **Freshman Admission Statistics:** 7,174 applied, 70% admitted, 14% enrolled. **Transfer Admission Requirements:** College transcript(s), statement of good standing from prior institution(s). Minimum college GPA of 2.0 required. Lowest grade transferable C-. **General Admission Information:** Application fee $35. Non-fall registration accepted. Admission may be deferred for a maximum of one year.

COSTS AND FINANCIAL AID

Annual tuition $31,000. Room and board $12,400. Average book and supplies expense $1,600. **Required Forms and Deadlines:** FAFSA. **Notification of Awards:** Applicants will be notified of awards on a rolling basis beginning 2/1. **Types of Aid:** *Need-based scholarships/grants:* College/university scholarship or grant aid from institutional funds; Federal Pell; Private scholarships; SEOG; State scholarships/grants. *Loans:* Direct PLUS loans; Direct Subsidized Stafford Loans; Direct Unsubsidized Stafford Loans. **Financial Aid Statistics:** 100% needy freshmen, 100% needy undergrads receive need-based scholarship or grant aid. 13% freshmen, 11% undergrads receive non-need-based scholarship or grant aid. 83% freshmen, 84% undergrads receive need-based self-help aid. 0% freshmen, 0% undergrads receive athletic scholarships. 97% freshmen, 97% undergrads receive any aid. **Criteria awarding aid:** *Need-based:* Academics, Alumni affiliation, Art, Leadership, Music/drama, Religious affiliation. *Non-need-based:* Academics, Alumni affiliation, Art, Leadership, Music/drama, Religious affiliation, State/district residency.

CASCADE COLLEGE

9101 East Burnside Street, Portland, OR 97216-1515
Phone: 503-257-1202 **Financial Aid Phone:** 503-257-1241
E-mail: admissions@cascade.edu
Fax: 503-257-1222 **Website:** www.cascade.edu **ACT Code:** 3459

This private school, affiliated with the Church of Christ, was founded in 1993. It has a 12 acre campus.

RATINGS

Admissions Selectivity Rating: 73   **Fire Safety Rating:** 70   **Green Rating:** 60*

STUDENTS AND FACULTY

Enrollment: 262. **Student Body:** 59% female, 41% male, 64% out-of-state, 2% international (8 countries represented). Asian 7%, African American 11%, Caucasian 64%, Hispanic 12%, Native American 1%, Pacific Islander , Two or more races , Race unknown 3%.
Retention and Graduation: 46% freshmen return for sophomore year. 15% grads go on to further study within 1 year. 10% grads pursue arts and sciences degrees. 2% grads pursue law degrees. 1% grads pursue business degrees. 0% grads pursue medical degrees. **Faculty:** Student/faculty ratio 12:1. 15 full-time faculty, 60% hold PhDs, 13% are members of minority groups, 27% are women. 0% of classes are taught by teaching assistants.

ACADEMICS

Degrees: Bachelor's. **Classes:** Most classes have 10–19 students. Most lab/discussion sessions have fewer than 10 students. **Most popular majors:** Business/Commerce, General; Psychology, General; Teacher Education, Multiple Levels. **Special Study Options:** Double major; Dual enrollment; Independent study; Internships; Student-designed major; Study abroad; Teacher certification program. **Disability Services offered:** Note-taking services; Reader services; Tutors.

FACILITIES

Housing: Apartments for married students; Men's dorms; Special housing for disabled students; Women's dorms; 70% of campus accessible to physically disabled.

CAMPUS LIFE

Environment: Metropolis. **Activities:** Choral groups; Drama/theater; Jazz band; Literary magazine; Music ensembles; Musical theater; Student government; Yearbook. 16 registered organizations, 2 honor societies, on campus. **Athletics (Intercollegiate):** *Men:* basketball, cross-country, soccer, track/field (outdoor), track/field (indoor). *Women:* basketball, cross-country, soccer, track/field (outdoor), track/field (indoor), volleyball. **On-Campus Highlights:** Classrooms.

ADMISSIONS

Freshman Academic Profile: Average high school GPA 3.0. 85% from public high schools. **Basis for Candidate Selection:** *Other factors include:* academic GPA, standardized test scores, recommendation(s). **Freshman Admission Requirements:** High school diploma is required and GED is accepted. *Academic units recommended:* 4 English, 3 math, 2 science, 1 science labs, 2 foreign language, 4 social studies, 2 history, 1 computer science. **Freshman Admission Statistics:** 204 applied, 57% admitted, 56% enrolled. **Transfer Admission Requirements:** High school transcript, college transcript(s). Minimum college GPA of 2.0 required. Lowest grade transferable D. **General Admission Information:** Application fee $25. Non-fall registration accepted. Admission may be deferred for a maximum of 1 year.

COSTS AND FINANCIAL AID

Average book and supplies expense $900. **Required Forms and Deadlines:** FAFSA; Institution's own financial aid form. **Notification of Awards:** Applicants will be notified of awards on a rolling basis beginning 2/15. **Types of Aid:** *Need-based scholarships/grants:* College/university scholarship or grant aid from institutional funds; Federal Pell; Private scholarships; SEOG. **Student Employment:** Federal Work-Study Program available. Institutional employment available. **Financial Aid Statistics:** 100% needy freshmen, 63% needy undergrads receive need-based scholarship or grant aid. 19% freshmen, 92% undergrads receive non-need-based scholarship or grant aid. 87% freshmen, 84% undergrads receive need-based self-help aid. 48% freshmen, 36% undergrads receive athletic scholarships. 100% freshmen, 99% undergrads receive any aid. **Criteria awarding aid:** *Need-based:* Leadership. *Non-need-based:* Academics, Athletics, Leadership, Music/drama, Religious affiliation, State/district residency.

CASE WESTERN RESERVE UNIVERSITY

Wolstein Hall, Cleveland, OH 44106-7055
Phone: 216-368-4450 **Financial Aid Phone:** 216-368-4530
E-mail: admission@case.edu **CEEB Code:** 1105
Fax: 216-368-5111 **Website:** www.case.edu **ACT Code:** 3244

This private school was founded in 1826. It has a 267 acre campus.

RATINGS

Admissions Selectivity Rating: 95   **Fire Safety Rating:** 88   **Green Rating:** 95

STUDENTS AND FACULTY

Enrollment: 5,269. **Student Body:** 46% female, 54% male, 72% out-of-state, 14% international (46 countries represented). Asian 21%, African American 5%, Caucasian 45%, Hispanic 9%, Native American <1%, Pacific Islander <1%, Two or more races 5%, Race unknown 1%.
Retention and Graduation: 93% freshmen return for sophomore year. 68% freshmen graduate within 4 years. 84% freshmen graduate within 6 years. 38% grads go on to further study within 1 year. 31% grads pursue arts and sciences degrees. 6% grads pursue law degrees. 12% grads pursue business degrees. 21% grads pursue medical degrees. **Faculty:** Student/faculty ratio 11:1. 780 full-time faculty, 91% hold PhDs, 20% are members of minority groups, 44% are women. 5% of classes are taught by teaching assistants.

ACADEMICS

Degrees: Bachelor's; Doctoral degree—professional practice; Doctoral degree research/scholarship; Master's; Post-bachelor's certificate; Post-master's certificate. **Classes:** Most classes have 10–19 students. Most lab/discussion sessions have 10–19 students. **Most popular majors:** Bioengineering and Biomedical Engineering; Mechanical Engineering; Biology/Biological Sciences, General. **Special Study Options:** Accelerated program; Cooperative education program; Cross-registration; Double major; Dual enrollment; English as a Second Language (ESL); Exchange student program (domestic); Honors program; Independent study; Internships; Liberal arts/career combination; Student-designed major; Study abroad; Teacher certification program. **Combined degree programs:** BA/DDS; BA/MA. **Disability Services offered:** Note-taking services; Reader services; Tape recorders; Tutors. **Career services:** Alumni network; Alumni services; Career assessment; Career/job search classes; Internships; Regional alumni.

FACILITIES

Housing: Apartments for married students; Apartments for single students; Coed dorms; Fraternity/sorority housing; Wellness housing; 90% of campus accessible to physically disabled. **Special Academic Facilities/Equipment:** Art, natural history, and auto-aviation museums, historical society, botanical garden, biology field stations, observatory.

CAMPUS LIFE

Environment: Metropolis. **Activities:** Campus Ministries; Choral groups; Concert band; Dance; Drama/theater; International Student Organization; Jazz band; Literary magazine; Marching band; Model UN; Music ensembles; Musical theater; Pep band; Radio station; Student government; Student newspaper; Student-run film society; Symphony orchestra; Yearbook. 249 registered organizations, 8 honor societies, 7 religious organizations, 18 fraternities, 9 sororities, on campus. **Athletics (Intercollegiate):** *Men:* baseball, basketball, cross-country, football, soccer, swimming, tennis, track/field (outdoor), track/field (indoor), wrestling. *Women:* basketball, cross-country, soccer, softball, swimming, tennis, track/field (outdoor), track/field (indoor), volleyball. **On-Campus Highlights:** Kelvin Smith Library. **Environmental Initiatives:** In 2008 President Barbara Snyder signed the American and College and University President's Climate Commitment, now called the Carbon Commitment which is a public declaration that CWRU will aim to be a carbon neutral campus by 2050. The commitment requires public reporting of CWRU's greenhouse gas inventory and other sustainability metrics. CWRU is proud to be a community steward and leader on this vital topic and works with the City of Cleveland and other entries to share strategies and best practices. The University is making progress towards the goal through energy efficiency investments, green buildings and behavior change campaigns.

ADMISSIONS

Freshman Academic Profile: 70% in top 10% of high school class, 92% in top 25% of high school class, 99% in top 50% of high school class. 70% from public high schools. **Test Scores:** SAT Math middle 50% range 700–790. SAT EBRW middle 50% range 640–720. ACT middle 50% range 30–34. **Basis for Candidate Selection:** *Very important factors include:* rigor of secondary school record, class rank, academic GPA, standardized test scores, extracurricular activities. *Important factors include:* application essay, recommendation(s), interview, talent/ability, character/personal qualities, racial/ethnic status, volunteer work. *Other factors include:* first generation, alumni/ae relation, work experience, level of applicant's interest. **Freshman Admission Requirements:** High school diploma is required and GED is accepted. *Academic units required:* 4 English, 3 math, 3 science, 2 science labs, 2 foreign language, 3 social studies. *Academic units recommended:* 4 math, 3 science labs, 3 foreign language, 4 social studies. **Freshman Admission Statistics:** 28,786 applied, 27% admitted, 17% enrolled. **Transfer Admission Requirements:** High school transcript, college transcript(s), essay or personal statement, statement of good standing from prior institution(s). Minimum college GPA of 3.2 required. Lowest grade transferable C. **General Admission Information:** Application fee $70. Regular application deadline 1/15. Non-fall registration accepted. Admission may be deferred for a maximum of 1 year.

COSTS AND FINANCIAL AID

Annual tuition $50,450. Room and board $16,874. Required fees $1,049. Average book and supplies expense $1,200. **Required Forms and Deadlines:** CSS/Financial Aid PROFILE; FAFSA; Institution's own financial aid form; Noncustodial PROFILE. **Notification of Awards:** Applicants will be notified of awards on a rolling basis beginning 3/20. **Types of Aid:** *Need-based scholarships/ grants:* College/university scholarship or grant aid from institutional funds; Federal Pell; Private scholarships; SEOG; State scholarships/grants. *Loans:* Direct PLUS loans; Direct Subsidized Stafford Loans; Direct Unsubsidized Stafford Loans. **Student Employment:** Federal Work-Study Program available. Institutional employment available. **Financial Aid Statistics:** 98% needy freshmen, 97% needy undergrads receive need-based scholarship or grant aid. 32% freshmen, 19% undergrads receive non-need-based scholarship or grant aid. 93% freshmen, 95% undergrads receive need-based self-help aid. 0% freshmen, 0% undergrads receive athletic scholarships. 87% freshmen, 85% undergrads receive any aid. 44% undergrads borrow to pay for school. Average cumulative indebtedness $33,946. **Criteria awarding aid:** *Non-need-based:* Academics, Alumni affiliation, Art, Leadership, Music/drama.

CASTLETON STATE COLLEGE

Office of Admissions, Castleton, VT 05735
Phone: 802-468-1213 **Financial Aid Phone:** 802-468-6070
E-mail: info@castleton.edu **CEEB Code:** 3765
Fax: 802-468-1476 **Website:** www.castleton.edu **ACT Code:** 4314

This public school was founded in 1787. It has a 165 acre campus.

RATINGS

Admissions Selectivity Rating: 75   **Fire Safety Rating:** 87   **Green Rating:** 60*

STUDENTS AND FACULTY

Enrollment: 1,890. **Student Body:** 52% female, 48% male, 30% out-of-state, 2% international (16 countries represented). Asian 1%, African American 2%, Caucasian 85%, Hispanic 2%, Native American <1%, Pacific Islander 0%, Two or more races 2%, Race unknown 6%.
Retention and Graduation: 70% freshmen return for sophomore year.
Faculty: Student/faculty ratio 10:1. 102 full-time faculty, 93% hold PhDs, 6% are members of minority groups, 51% are women. 0% of classes are taught by teaching assistants.

ACADEMICS

Degrees: Associate; Bachelor's; Master's; Post-master's certificate. **Classes:** Most classes have 10–19 students. Most lab/discussion sessions have 10–19 students. **Most popular majors:** Business/Commerce, General; Psychology, General. **Special Study Options:** Cross-registration; Double major; Dual enrollment; English as a Second Language (ESL); Honors program; Independent study; Internships; Liberal arts/career combination; Student-designed major; Study abroad; Teacher certification program. **Honors programs:** Honors programs available in History, Literature, Psychology, and Sociology. **Combined degree programs:** BA/MA. **Disability Services offered:** Note-taking services; Reader services; Tape recorders; Tutors. **Career services:** Alumni network; Career assessment; Internships.

FACILITIES

Housing: Coed dorms; Theme housing; Wellness housing; 100% of campus accessible to physically disabled. **Special Academic Facilities/Equipment:** Historical/medical museum.

CAMPUS LIFE

Environment: Rural. **Activities:** Campus Ministries; Choral groups; Concert band; Dance; Drama/theater; International Student Organization; Jazz band; Literary magazine; Marching band; Music ensembles; Musical theater; Pep band; Radio station; Student government; Student newspaper; Television station; Yearbook. 40 registered organizations, 7 honor societies, 1 religious organizations, on campus. **Athletics (Intercollegiate):** *Men:* baseball, basketball, cross-country, football, ice hockey, lacrosse, skiing (downhill/Alpine), soccer, tennis. *Women:* basketball, cross-country, field hockey, ice hockey, lacrosse, skiing (downhill/Alpine), soccer, softball, tennis. **On-Campus Highlights:** Fireside Cafe. **Environmental Initiatives:** Student-driven recycling effort.

ADMISSIONS

Freshman Academic Profile: Average high school GPA 3.0. 6% in top 10% of high school class, 29% in top 25% of high school class, 61% in top 50% of high school class. **Test Scores:** SAT Math middle 50% range 430–540. SAT EBRW middle 50% range 420–530. ACT middle 50% range 18–22. **Basis for Candidate Selection:** *Very important factors include:* rigor of secondary school record, class rank, academic GPA, application essay, recommendation(s), character/personal qualities. *Other factors include:* standardized test scores, interview, extracurricular activities, volunteer work, level of applicant's interest. **Freshman Admission Requirements:** High school diploma is required and GED is accepted. *Academic units required:* 4 English, 3 math, 3 science, 2 science labs, 3 social studies, 3 history. *Academic units recommended:* 2 foreign language. **Freshman Admission Statistics:** 2,397 applied, 78% admitted, 20% enrolled. **Transfer Admission Requirements:** College transcript(s), essay or personal statement, Minimum college GPA of 2.0 required. Lowest grade transferable C-. **General Admission Information:** Application fee $40. Priority deadline 5/1. Non-fall registration accepted. Admission may be deferred for a maximum of 1 year.

COSTS AND FINANCIAL AID

Annual in-state tuition $9,768. Annual out-of-state tuition $24,432. Room and board $9,414. Required fees $1,224. Average book and supplies expense $1,000. **Required Forms and Deadlines:** FAFSA. **Notification of Awards:** Applicants will be notified of awards on a rolling basis beginning 2/15. **Types of Aid:** *Need-based scholarships/grants:* College/university scholarship or grant aid from institutional funds; Federal Pell; Private scholarships; SEOG; State scholarships/grants. *Loans:* Direct PLUS loans; Direct Subsidized Stafford Loans; Direct Unsubsidized Stafford Loans. **Student Employment:** Federal Work-Study Program available. Institutional employment available. **Criteria awarding aid:** *Need-based:* Academics, Music/drama. *Non-need-based:* Academics, Alumni affiliation, Music/drama, State/district residency.

CATAWBA COLLEGE

Best Colleges

2300 West Innes Street, Salisbury, NC 28144
Phone: 704-637-4402 **Financial Aid Phone:** 704-637-4416
E-mail: admission@catawba.edu **CEEB Code:** 5103
Fax: 704-637-4222 **Website:** www.catawba.edu **ACT Code:** 3080

This private school, affiliated with the United Church of Christ, was founded in 1851. It has a 276 acre campus.

RATINGS

| Admissions Selectivity Rating: 87 | Fire Safety Rating: 89 | Green Rating: 97 |

STUDENTS AND FACULTY

Enrollment: 1,307. **Student Body:** 54% female, 46% male, 19% out-of-state, 4% international (15 countries represented). Asian 1%, African American 19%, Caucasian 65%, Hispanic 7%, Native American <1%, Pacific Islander <1%, Two or more races 3%, Race unknown <1%.

Retention and Graduation: 73% freshmen return for sophomore year. 39% freshmen graduate within 4 years. 52% freshmen graduate within 6 years. **Faculty:** Student/faculty ratio 12:1. 86 full-time faculty, 78% hold PhDs, 9% are members of minority groups, 48% are women. 0% of classes are taught by teaching assistants.

ACADEMICS

Degrees: Bachelor's; Master's. **Classes:** Most classes have 10–19 students. Most lab/discussion sessions have fewer than 10 students. **Most popular majors:** Sport and Fitness Administration/Management; Business Administration and Management, General; Kindergarten/Preschool Education and Teaching. **Special Study Options:** Cross-registration; Distance learning; Double major; Dual enrollment; Honors program; Independent study; Internships; Student-designed major; Study abroad; Teacher certification program. **Honors programs:** The Catawba Honors Program cultivates a community of academically gifted students who pursue challenging educational experiences with outstanding faculty. Through interdisciplinary, provocative, and intellectually demanding courses, e Honors Program piques the curiosity of students, encouraging them to become life-long learners whose lives are enriched by their experiences. http://www.catawba.edu/programs/honors/. **Disability Services offered:** Note-taking services; Tape recorders; Tutors. **Career services:** Alumni network; Career assessment; Career/job search classes; Internships.

FACILITIES

Housing: Apartments for single students; Coed dorms; Men's dorms; Women's dorms; 95% of campus accessible to physically disabled. **Special Academic Facilities/Equipment:** *189 acre Ecological Preserve *300 acre Wildlife Preserve *Center for the Environment & Environmental Programs; completed in 2000 (prior to LEED certification program), and in process of certifying through LEED for existing buildings. **Campus network:** 90% of classrooms, 90% of dorms, 100% of libraries, 100% of dining areas, 80% of common outdoor areas, have wireless network access.

CAMPUS LIFE

Environment: Town. **Activities:** Campus Ministries; Choral groups; Concert band; Dance; Drama/theater; Literary magazine; Marching band; Music ensembles; Musical theater; Pep band; Radio station; Student government; Student newspaper; Yearbook. 49 registered organizations, 13 honor societies, 4 religious organizations, on campus. **Athletics (Intercollegiate):** *Men:* baseball, basketball, cheerleading, cross-country, football, golf, lacrosse, soccer, swimming, tennis. *Women:* basketball, cheerleading, cross-country, golf, soccer, softball, swimming, tennis, volleyball. **On-Campus Highlights:** Center for the Environment **Environmental Initiatives:** Center for the Environment, along with its national, regional, and community environmental outreach. The Center for the Environment at Catawba College sets us apart from other environmental programs. We offer value-added education that goes well beyond classroom teaching, providing many real-world opportunities for our students. See: http://catawba.edu/academics/schools/arts-sciences/environmental-science-studies/ The Center for the Environment at Catawba College has assumed the leadership of the N.C. Green Schools program, a nonprofit organization that promotes sustainability in the state's schools from pre-kindergarten through 12th grade.

ADMISSIONS

Freshman Academic Profile: Average high school GPA 3.8. 13% in top 10% of high school class, 44% in top 25% of high school class, 77% in top 50% of high school class. 88% from public high schools. **Test Scores:** SAT Math middle 50% range 470–580. SAT EBRW middle 50% range 460–520. ACT middle 50% range 18–23. **Basis for Candidate Selection:** *Very important factors include:* academic GPA, recommendation(s), extracurricular activities, talent/ability, character/personal qualities, geographical residence. *Important factors include:* rigor of secondary school record, standardized test scores. *Other factors include:* class rank, application essay, interview, first generation, alumni/ae relation, state residency, religious affiliation/commitment, racial/ethnic status, level of applicant's interest. **Freshman Admission Requirements:** High school diploma is required and GED is accepted. *Academic units required:* 4 English, 3 math, 3 science, 3 social studies. *Academic units recommended:* 2 foreign language. **Freshman Admission Statistics:** 3,125 applied, 42% admitted, 25% enrolled. **Transfer Admission Requirements:** High school transcript, college transcript(s), essay or personal statement, statement of good standing from prior institution(s). Minimum college GPA of 2.0 required. Lowest grade transferable C. **General Admission Information:** Non-fall registration accepted. Admission may be deferred for a maximum of 1 year.

COSTS AND FINANCIAL AID

Annual tuition $30,520. Room and board $10,488. Average book and supplies expense $1,400. **Required Forms and Deadlines:** FAFSA; State aid form.

Notification of Awards: Applicants will be notified of awards on a rolling basis beginning 1/15. **Types of Aid:** *Need-based scholarships/grants:* College/university scholarship or grant aid from institutional funds; Federal Pell; Private scholarships; SEOG; State scholarships/grants. *Loans:* Direct PLUS loans; Direct Subsidized Stafford Loans; Direct Unsubsidized Stafford Loans. **Student Employment:** Federal Work-Study Program available. Institutional employment available. **Financial Aid Statistics:** 68% needy freshmen, 75% needy undergrads receive need-based scholarship or grant aid. 99% freshmen, 88% undergrads receive non-need-based scholarship or grant aid. 70% freshmen, 78% undergrads receive need-based self-help aid. 29% freshmen, 26% undergrads receive athletic scholarships. 99% freshmen, 99% undergrads receive any aid. 79% undergrads borrow to pay for school. Average cumulative indebtedness $31,471. **Criteria awarding aid:** *Non-need-based:* Academics, Athletics, Leadership, Music/drama, Religious affiliation, State/district residency.

THE CATHOLIC UNIVERSITY OF AMERICA

Best Colleges

Office of Undergraduate Admissions, Washington, DC 20064
Phone: 202-319-5305 **Financial Aid Phone:** 202-319-5307
E-mail: cua-admissions@cua.edu **CEEB Code:** 5104
Fax: 202-319-6533 **Website:** www.catholic.edu **ACT Code:** 654

This private school, affiliated with the Roman Catholic Church, was founded in 1887. It has a 176 acre campus.

RATINGS

Admissions Selectivity Rating: 77 **Fire Safety Rating:** 94 **Green Rating:** 85

STUDENTS AND FACULTY

Enrollment: 3,237. **Student Body:** 55% female, 45% male, 96% out-of-state, 5% international (31 countries represented). Asian 3%, African American 4%, Caucasian 67%, Hispanic 14%, Native American <1%, Pacific Islander <1%, Two or more races 4%, Race unknown 2%.
Retention and Graduation: 88% freshmen return for sophomore year. 72% freshmen graduate within 4 years. 71% freshmen graduate within 6 years. 20% grads go on to further study within 1 year. 56% grads pursue arts and sciences degrees. 15% grads pursue law degrees. **Faculty:** Student/faculty ratio 10:1. 381 full-time faculty, 87% hold PhDs, 14% are members of minority groups, 37% are women. 14% of classes are taught by teaching assistants.

ACADEMICS

Degrees: Associate; Bachelor's; Certificate; Doctoral degree—professional practice; Doctoral degree research/scholarship; Master's; Post-bachelor's certificate; Post-master's certificate. **Classes:** Most classes have 10–19 students. Most lab/discussion sessions have 10–19 students. **Most popular majors:** Architecture; Registered Nursing/Registered Nurse; Political Science and Government, General. **Special Study Options:** Accelerated program; Cross-registration; Distance learning; Double major; Dual enrollment; English as a Second Language (ESL); Honors program; Independent study; Internships; Study abroad; Teacher certification program. **Honors programs:** The University Honors Program offers classes in the classical liberal arts and contemporary social and environmental sciences to compliment studentsÂ' major studies. Students take small, rigorous, discussion-based courses from offerings in philosophy, theology, history and literature, social science, environmental science, and liberal studies. Students completing any of these six tracks receive distinction at graduation. Special lectures, symposia, social events, and trips are organized for students in the program. The University Honors Program also provides a special residential community for its students. **Combined degree programs:** BA/MA. **Disability Services offered:** Note-taking services; Reader services; Tape recorders; Tutors. **Career services:** Alumni network; Alumni services; Career assessment; Career/job search classes; Internships; Regional alumni.

FACILITIES

Housing: Apartments for single students; Men's dorms; Special housing for disabled students; Theme housing; Women's dorms; 60% of campus accessible to physically disabled. **Special Academic Facilities/Equipment:** Facilities available on the university campus include an art department gallery; the John

K. Mullen of Denver Memorial Library, which features a rare book collection containing 65,000 volumes that range from medieval documents to first editions of 20th-century authors; the university archives, which has nearly 9,000 feet of records and manuscripts; the Vitreous State Laboratory, which engages some of the world's leading glass scientists to help research and develop methods for safe containment of disposed radioactive materials, primarily by converting nuclear waste into solid glass using vitrification techniques. In 2008, the university dedicated Opus Hall, the first LEED (Leadership in Energy and Environmental Design)-compliant residence hall among colleges and universities in Washington, D.C. The Edward J. Pryzbyla University Center includes nine meeting spaces, two separate dining facilities, a convenience store, the campus bookstore, offices, various atrium and lounge spaces and a 7,500-square-foot great room, where Pope Benedict XVI delivered a speech in April 2008. Adjacent to the campus is the Roman Catholic Basilica of the National Shrine of the Immaculate Conception, the largest church in the Western hemisphere. University Masses and commencement are held every year at the National Shrine. Directly across the street from the university is the Pope John Paul II Cultural Center, a major Catholic museum.

CAMPUS LIFE

Environment: Metropolis. **Activities:** Campus Ministries; Choral groups; Concert band; Dance; Drama/theater; International Student Organization; Jazz band; Literary magazine; Model UN; Music ensembles; Musical theater; Opera; Radio station; Student government; Student newspaper; Student-run film society; Symphony orchestra. 109 registered organizations, 16 honor societies, 10 religious organizations, 1 fraternities, 1 sororities, on campus. **Athletics (Intercollegiate):** *Men:* baseball, basketball, cross-country, football, lacrosse, soccer, swimming, tennis, track/field (outdoor), track/field (indoor). *Women:* basketball, cross-country, field hockey, lacrosse, soccer, softball, swimming, tennis, track/field (outdoor), track/field (indoor), volleyball. **On-Campus Highlights:** Edward J. Pryzbyla University Center **Environmental Initiatives:** Catholic University has been a proponent of sustainable practices for many years. One hundred percent of its electricity is purchased with Green e-Certificates, and the University is halfway through an energy project that will update heating and cooling systems. When complete, the University's gas usage will drop by 23%, and electric usage will be down by 2.2% a year.

ADMISSIONS

Freshman Academic Profile: Average high school GPA 3.5. **Test Scores:** SAT Math middle 50% range 550–660. SAT EBRW middle 50% range 580–670. ACT middle 50% range 24–29. **Basis for Candidate Selection:** *Very important factors include:* rigor of secondary school record, academic GPA, character/personal qualities. *Important factors include:* application essay, recommendation(s), extracurricular activities, first generation. *Other factors include:* class rank, standardized test scores, interview, talent/ability, alumni/ae relation, geographical residence, racial/ethnic status, volunteer work, work experience, level of applicant's interest. **Freshman Admission Requirements:** High school diploma is required and GED is accepted. *Academic units recommended:* 4 English, 4 math, 3 science, 2 science labs, 3 foreign language, 4 social studies. **Freshman Admission Statistics:** 5,668 applied, 85% admitted, 17% enrolled. **Transfer Admission Requirements:** High school transcript, college transcript(s), essay or personal statement, standardized test scores, Minimum college GPA of 2.8 required. Lowest grade transferable C. **General Admission Information:** Regular application deadline 1/15. Non-fall registration accepted. Admission may be deferred for a maximum of 1 year.

COSTS AND FINANCIAL AID

Annual tuition $48,600. Room and board $15,820. Required fees $816. Average book and supplies expense $1,000. **Required Forms and Deadlines:** CSS/Financial Aid PROFILE; FAFSA; Noncustodial PROFILE. **Notification of Awards:** Applicants will be notified of awards on a rolling basis beginning 2/15. **Types of Aid:** *Need-based scholarships/grants:* College/university scholarship or grant aid from institutional funds; Federal Pell; Private scholarships; SEOG; State scholarships/grants. *Loans:* Direct PLUS loans; Direct Subsidized Stafford Loans; Direct Unsubsidized Stafford Loans. **Student Employment:** Federal Work-Study Program available. Institutional employment available. **Financial Aid Statistics:** 98% needy freshmen, 99% needy undergrads receive need-based scholarship or grant aid. 0% freshmen, 0% undergrads receive non-need-based scholarship or grant aid. 78% freshmen, 81% undergrads receive need-based self-help aid. 0% freshmen, 0% undergrads receive athletic scholarships. 94% freshmen, 90% undergrads receive any aid. Average cumulative indebtedness $46,702. **Criteria awarding aid:** *Need-based:* Academics. *Non-need-based:* Academics, Alumni affiliation, Music/drama, Religious affiliation.

CAZENOVIA COLLEGE

3 Sullivan Street, Cazenovia, NY 13035
Phone: 315-655-7208 **Financial Aid Phone:** 315-655-7887
E-mail: admission@cazenovia.edu
Fax: 315-655-4860 **Website:** www.cazenovia.edu

This private school was founded in 1824. It has a 20 acre campus.

RATINGS
Admissions Selectivity Rating: 75   **Fire Safety Rating:** 99   **Green Rating:** 60*

STUDENTS AND FACULTY
Enrollment: 1,067. **Student Body:** 72% female, 28% male, 15% out-of-state, 0% international (3 countries represented). Asian 1%, African American 7%, Caucasian 67%, Hispanic 6%, Native American 1%, Pacific Islander <1%, Two or more races 4%, Race unknown 14%.
Retention and Graduation: 73% freshmen return for sophomore year. 20% grads go on to further study within 1 year. **Faculty:** Student/faculty ratio 12:1. 57 full-time faculty, 77% hold PhDs, 0% are members of minority groups, 68% are women. 0% of classes are taught by teaching assistants.

ACADEMICS
Degrees: Associate; Bachelor's; Certificate. **Classes:** Most classes have 10–19 students. **Most popular majors:** Business Administration, Management and Operations, Other; Interior Design; Fine/Studio Arts, General. **Special Study Options:** Double major; Dual enrollment; Honors program; Independent study; Internships; Liberal arts/career combination; Study abroad; Teacher certification program. **Honors programs:** The All-College Honors Program at Cazenovia College offers to outstanding students in all majors (in the liberal arts and in the professional studies) a stimulating learning environment beyond that found in standard classroom coursework, and fosters their exceptional academic talents and intellectual curiosity. Demanding curriculum, independent research opportunities and co-curricular activities challenge students to achieve their full educational potential not only through encouraging academic excellence but also through promoting social responsibilities in the global community. An honors degree certifies that students have produced academic work that meets the highest standards of academic rigor in both general education and in their career field. **Disability Services offered:** Note-taking services; Reader services; Tape recorders; Tutors. **Career services:** Alumni network; Alumni services; Career assessment; Career/job search classes; Internships; Regional alumni.

FACILITIES
Housing: Apartments for single students; Coed dorms; Men's dorms; Special housing for disabled students; Theme housing; Wellness housing; Women's dorms. **Special Academic Facilities/Equipment:** Reisman Hall is a state-of-the-art Art and Design facility and gallery; 243-acre Equine Education Center; historic Catherine Cummings Theatre.

CAMPUS LIFE
Environment: Village. **Activities:** Campus Ministries; Choral groups; Dance; Drama/theater; International Student Organization; Musical theater; Radio station; Student government; Student newspaper; Yearbook. 54 registered organizations, 5 honor societies, 1 religious organizations, on campus. **Athletics (Intercollegiate):** *Men:* baseball, basketball, cheerleading, crew/rowing, cross-country, equestrian sports, golf, horseback riding, lacrosse, soccer, swimming. *Women:* basketball, cheerleading, crew/rowing, cross-country, equestrian sports, horseback riding, lacrosse, soccer, softball, swimming, volleyball. **On-Campus Highlights:** Residence Halls. **Environmental Initiatives:** Environmental Studies education programs; Look Again program—sustainability in fashion.

ADMISSIONS
Freshman Academic Profile: Average high school GPA 3.3. 14% in top 10% of high school class, 40% in top 25% of high school class, 78% in top 50% of high school class. 90% from public high schools. **Test Scores:** SAT Math middle 50% range 430–530. SAT EBRW middle 50% range 430–540. ACT middle 50% range 19–24. **Basis for Candidate Selection:** *Very important factors include:* rigor of secondary school record, talent/ability. *Important factors include:* class rank, academic GPA, standardized test scores, recommendation(s), interview, extracurricular activities. *Other factors include:* application essay, character/personal qualities, alumni/ae relation, volunteer work, work experience, level of applicant's interest. **Freshman Admission Requirements:** High school diploma is required and GED is accepted. *Academic units recommended:* 4 English, 2 math, 2 science, 4 social studies. **Freshman Admission Statistics:** 2,382 applied, 76% admitted, 15% enrolled. **Transfer Admission Requirements:** High school transcript, college transcript(s).

Minimum college GPA of 2.0 required. Lowest grade transferable C. **General Admission Information:** Application fee $30. Priority deadline 3/1. Non-fall registration accepted. Admission may be deferred for a maximum of 1 year.

COSTS AND FINANCIAL AID
Annual tuition $30,028. Room and board $11,880. Required fees $532. **Required Forms and Deadlines:** FAFSA; State aid form. **Notification of Awards:** Applicants will be notified of awards on a rolling basis beginning 11/1. **Types of Aid:** *Need-based scholarships/grants:* College/university scholarship or grant aid from institutional funds; Federal Pell; Private scholarships; SEOG; State scholarships/grants. *Loans:* Direct PLUS loans; Direct Subsidized Stafford Loans; Direct Unsubsidized Stafford Loans. **Student Employment:** Federal Work-Study Program available. **Financial Aid Statistics:** 100% needy freshmen, 96% needy undergrads receive need-based scholarship or grant aid. 9% freshmen, 12% undergrads receive non-need-based scholarship or grant aid. 100% freshmen, 96% undergrads receive need-based self-help aid. 0% freshmen, 0% undergrads receive athletic scholarships. 92% freshmen, 91% undergrads receive any aid. **Criteria awarding aid:** *Need-based:* Academics, Leadership. *Non-need-based:* Academics, Leadership.

CEDAR CREST COLLEGE

100 College Drive, Allentown, PA 18104
Financial Aid Phone: 610-606-4602
E-mail: admissions@cedarcrest.edu **CEEB Code:** 2079
Website: http://www.cedarcrest.edu **ACT Code:** 3536

This private school was founded in 1867. It has a 84 acre campus.

RATINGS
Admissions Selectivity Rating: 83   **Fire Safety Rating:** 85   **Green Rating:** 60*

STUDENTS AND FACULTY
Enrollment: 1,413. **Student Body:** 88% female, 12% male, 15% out-of-state, 9% international (26 countries represented). Asian 3%, African American 9%, Caucasian 59%, Hispanic 15%, Native American <1%, Pacific Islander <1%, Two or more races 1%, Race unknown 3%.
Retention and Graduation: 82% freshmen return for sophomore year. 40% freshmen graduate within 4 years. 56% freshmen graduate within 6 years. 65% grads go on to further study within 1 year. 55% grads pursue arts and sciences degrees. 1% grads pursue law degrees. 2% grads pursue business degrees. 3% grads pursue medical degrees. **Faculty:** Student/faculty ratio 10:1. 77 full-time faculty, 71% hold PhDs, 0% are members of minority groups, 70% are women. 0% of classes are taught by teaching assistants.

ACADEMICS
Degrees: Bachelor's; Certificate; Master's; Post-bachelor's certificate; Post-master's certificate. **Classes:** Most classes have 10–19 students. Most lab/discussion sessions have 30–39 students. **Most popular majors:** Registered Nursing/Registered Nurse. **Special Study Options:** Accelerated program; Cross-registration; Distance learning; Double major; Honors program; Independent study; Internships; Liberal arts/career combination; Student-designed major; Study abroad; Teacher certification program; Weekend college. **Honors programs:** Special courses reserved for Honors Students, undergraduate research opportunities, including Honors Thesis. **Disability Services offered:** Note-taking services; Reader services; Tape recorders; Tutors. **Career services:** Alumni network; Alumni services; Career assessment; Career/job search classes; Internships; Regional alumni.

FACILITIES
Housing: Theme housing; Women's dorms; 90% of campus accessible to physically disabled. **Special Academic Facilities/Equipment:** Alumnae Museum.

CAMPUS LIFE
Environment: City. **Activities:** Choral groups; Dance; Drama/theater; International Student Organization; Literary magazine; Musical theater; Radio station; Student government; Student newspaper. 61 registered organizations, 15 honor societies, 3 religious organizations, 1 fraternities, on campus. **Athletics (Intercollegiate):** *Women:* basketball, cross-country, field hockey, lacrosse, soccer, softball, tennis, volleyball. **On-Campus Highlights:** Bistro. **Environmental Initiatives:** Recycling: participating in national Recyclemania.

ADMISSIONS

Freshman Academic Profile: Average high school GPA 3.4. 20% in top 10% of high school class, 44% in top 25% of high school class, 80% in top 50% of high school class. 84% from public high schools. **Test Scores:** SAT Math middle 50% range 460–570. SAT EBRW middle 50% range 480–600. ACT middle 50% range 19–26. **Basis for Candidate Selection:** *Very important factors include:* rigor of secondary school record, class rank, academic GPA, application essay, standardized test scores, recommendation(s). *Other factors include:* interview, extracurricular activities, alumni/ae relation, volunteer work, work experience, level of applicant's interest. **Freshman Admission Requirements:** High school diploma is required and GED is accepted. *Academic units required:* 4 English, 3 math, 2 science, 2 science labs, 2 foreign language, 3 social studies, 3 history, 3 academic electives. **Freshman Admission Statistics:** 1,208 applied, 63% admitted, 28% enrolled. **Transfer Admission Requirements:** High school transcript, college transcript(s), Minimum college GPA of 2.00 required. Lowest grade transferable C. **General Admission Information:** Non-fall registration accepted.

COSTS AND FINANCIAL AID

Annual tuition $38,616. Room and board $11,544. Required fees $600. Average book and supplies expense $2,000. **Required Forms and Deadlines:** FAFSA. **Notification of Awards:** Applicants will be notified of awards on a rolling basis beginning 9/15. **Types of Aid:** *Need-based scholarships/grants:* College/university scholarship or grant aid from institutional funds; Federal Pell; Private scholarships; SEOG; State scholarships/grants. *Loans:* Direct PLUS loans; Direct Subsidized Stafford Loans; Direct Unsubsidized Stafford Loans. **Student Employment:** Federal Work-Study Program available. Institutional employment available. **Financial Aid Statistics:** 100% needy freshmen, 100% needy undergrads receive need-based scholarship or grant aid. 13% freshmen, 10% undergrads receive non-need-based scholarship or grant aid. 82% freshmen, 85% undergrads receive need-based self-help aid. 0% freshmen, 0% undergrads receive athletic scholarships. 97% freshmen, 99% undergrads receive any aid. 92% undergrads borrow to pay for school. Average cumulative indebtedness $44,031. **Criteria awarding aid:** *Non-need-based:* Academics, Alumni affiliation, Art, Music/drama.

CEDARVILLE UNIVERSITY

251 N.Main Street, Cedarville, OH 45314
Phone: 937-766-7700 **Financial Aid Phone:** 937-766-7866
E-mail: admiss@cedarville.edu **CEEB Code:** 1151
Fax: 937-766-7575 **Website:** www.cedarville.edu **ACT Code:** 3245

This private school, affiliated with the Baptist Church, was founded in 1887. It has a 441 acre campus.

RATINGS

Admissions Selectivity Rating: 85   **Fire Safety Rating:** 95   **Green Rating:** 60*

STUDENTS AND FACULTY

Enrollment: 3,317. **Student Body:** 53% female, 47% male, 57% out-of-state, 2% international (38 countries represented). Asian 2%, African American 1%, Caucasian 88%, Hispanic 2%, Native American <1%, Pacific Islander <1%, Two or more races 4%, Race unknown 1%.
Retention and Graduation: 87% freshmen return for sophomore year. 61% freshmen graduate within 4 years. 72% freshmen graduate within 6 years. 19% grads go on to further study within 1 year. 13% grads pursue arts and sciences degrees. 2% grads pursue law degrees. 7% grads pursue business degrees. 6% grads pursue medical degrees. **Faculty:** Student/faculty ratio 16:1. 185 full-time faculty, 74% hold PhDs, 10% are members of minority groups, 36% are women. 0% of classes are taught by teaching assistants.

ACADEMICS

Degrees: Bachelor's; Certificate; Doctoral degree—professional practice; Master's; Post-bachelor's certificate; Post-master's certificate. **Classes:** Most classes have 10–19 students. Most lab/discussion sessions have 10–19 students. **Most popular majors:** Early Childhood Education and Teaching; Mechanical Engineering; Registered Nursing/Registered Nurse. **Special Study Options:** Cooperative education program; Cross-registration; Distance learning; Double major; Dual enrollment; English as a Second Language (ESL); Honors program; Independent study; Internships; Liberal arts/career combination; Student-designed major; Study abroad; Teacher certification program. **Honors programs:** Cedarville University's honors programs offer a nationally recognized

curriculum, a community of inquiring minds, seminars discussing classical and innovative knowledge, and one-on-one interaction with top professors. **Disability Services offered:** Note-taking services; Reader services; Tape recorders; Tutors. **Career services:** Alumni network; Alumni services; Career assessment; Career/job search classes; Internships; Regional alumni.

FACILITIES

Housing: Apartments for married students; Apartments for single students; Men's dorms; Women's dorms; 85% of campus accessible to physically disabled. **Special Academic Facilities/Equipment:** Centennial Library, Observatory, Engineering Projects Laboratory, Science/Nursing/Allied Health Labs, Apple Technology Center, Computer Labs, DeVries Theatre. **Campus network:** 100% of classrooms, 100% of dorms, 100% of student union, 100% of libraries, 100% of dining areas, 100% of common outdoor areas, have wireless network access.

CAMPUS LIFE

Environment: Rural. **Activities:** Campus Ministries; Choral groups; Concert band; Dance; Drama/theater; International Student Organization; Jazz band; Model UN; Music ensembles; Musical theater; Pep band; Radio station; Student government; Student newspaper; Student-run film society; Symphony orchestra; Yearbook. 144 registered organizations, 5 honor societies, 12 religious organizations, on campus. **Athletics (Intercollegiate):** *Men:* baseball, basketball, cheerleading, cross-country, golf, soccer, tennis, track/field (outdoor), track/field (indoor). *Women:* basketball, cheerleading, cross-country, soccer, softball, tennis, track/field (outdoor), track/field (indoor), volleyball. **On-Campus Highlights:** Fitness and Recreation Center

ADMISSIONS

Freshman Academic Profile: Average high school GPA 3.8. 29% in top 10% of high school class, 60% in top 25% of high school class, 88% in top 50% of high school class. 53% from public high schools. **Test Scores:** SAT Math middle 50% range 550–670. SAT EBRW middle 50% range 580–680. ACT middle 50% range 23–29. **Basis for Candidate Selection:** *Very important factors include:* rigor of secondary school record, academic GPA, standardized test scores, recommendation(s), character/personal qualities. *Important factors include:* class rank, application essay, alumni/ae relation. *Other factors include:* extracurricular activities, talent/ability, first generation, geographical residence, state residency, volunteer work, work experience. **Freshman Admission Requirements:** High school diploma is required and GED is accepted. *Academic units recommended:* 4 English, 3 math, 3 science, 2 science labs, 3 foreign language, 2 social studies, 2 history. **Freshman Admission Statistics:** 4,039 applied, 71% admitted, 32% enrolled. **Transfer Admission Requirements:** High school transcript, college transcript(s), essay or personal statement, statement of good standing from prior institution(s). Minimum college GPA of 3.0 required. Lowest grade transferable C-. **General Admission Information:** Application fee $30. Priority deadline 11/1. Regular application deadline 8/1. Non-fall registration accepted. Admission may be deferred for a maximum of 1 year.

COSTS AND FINANCIAL AID

Annual tuition $31,122. Room and board $7,618. Required fees $200. Average book and supplies expense $1,248. **Required Forms and Deadlines:** FAFSA. **Notification of Awards:** Applicants will be notified of awards on a rolling basis beginning 3/1. **Types of Aid:** *Need-based scholarships/grants:* College/university scholarship or grant aid from institutional funds; Federal Nursing Scholarships; Federal Pell; Private scholarships; SEOG; State scholarships/grants. *Loans:* Direct PLUS loans; Direct Subsidized Stafford Loans; Direct Unsubsidized Stafford Loans. **Student Employment:** Federal Work-Study Program available. Institutional employment available. **Financial Aid Statistics:** 72% needy freshmen, 75% needy undergrads receive need-based scholarship or grant aid. 98% freshmen, 96% undergrads receive non-need-based scholarship or grant aid. 84% freshmen, 87% undergrads receive need-based self-help aid. 7% freshmen, 7% undergrads receive athletic scholarships. 100% freshmen, 100% undergrads receive any aid. 63% undergrads borrow to pay for school. Average cumulative indebtedness $23,822. **Criteria awarding aid:** *Need-based:* Academics. *Non-need-based:* Academics, Athletics, Minority status, Music/drama.

CENTENARY COLLEGE

400 Jefferson Street, Hackettstown, NJ 07840
Phone: 800-236-8679 **Financial Aid Phone:** (1800) 236-8679
E-mail: admissions@centenarycollege.edu **CEEB Code:** 2080
Fax: 908-852-3454 **Website:** www.centenarycollege.edu **ACT Code:** 2544

This private school, affiliated with the Methodist Church, was founded in 1867. It has a 42 acre campus.

RATINGS
Admissions Selectivity Rating: 73   **Fire Safety Rating:** 60*   **Green Rating:** 60*

STUDENTS AND FACULTY
Enrollment: 1,708. **Student Body:** 60% female, 40% male, 20% out-of-state, 5% international (17 countries represented). Asian 1%, African American 10%, Caucasian 60%, Hispanic 9%, Native American 1%, Pacific Islander 0%, Two or more races 1%, Race unknown 13%.
Retention and Graduation: 71% freshmen return for sophomore year. 18% grads go on to further study within 1 year. 8% grads pursue arts and sciences degrees. 0% grads pursue law degrees. 8% grads pursue business degrees. **Faculty:** Student/faculty ratio 17:1. 79 full-time faculty, 62% hold PhDs, 8% are members of minority groups, 54% are women. 0% of classes are taught by teaching assistants.

ACADEMICS
Degrees: Associate; Bachelor's; Master's; Post-bachelor's certificate; Terminal Associate; Transfer Associate. **Classes:** Most classes have 10–19 students. Most lab/discussion sessions have fewer than 10 students. **Most popular majors:** Criminal Justice/Police Science; Business Administration and Management, General; Elementary Education and Teaching. **Special Study Options:** Accelerated program; Cross-registration; Distance learning; Double major; Dual enrollment; English as a Second Language (ESL); Independent study; Internships; Liberal arts/career combination; Student-designed major; Study abroad; Teacher certification program; Weekend college. **Disability Services offered:** Note-taking services; Reader services; Tutors. **Career services:** Alumni network; Alumni services; Career assessment; Career/job search classes; Internships; Regional alumni.

FACILITIES
Housing: Apartments for single students; Coed dorms; 70% of campus accessible to physically disabled. **Special Academic Facilities/Equipment:** Art gallery, radio station WNTI 91.9FM, equity-status theater, equestrian center.

CAMPUS LIFE
Environment: Town. **Activities:** Campus Ministries; Choral groups; Dance; Drama/theater; International Student Organization; Literary magazine; Model UN; Musical theater; Radio station; Student government; Student newspaper; Student-run film society; Television station; Yearbook. 30 registered organizations, 2 honor societies, 1 sororities, on campus. **Athletics (Intercollegiate):** *Men:* baseball, basketball, cross-country, golf, lacrosse, soccer, wrestling. *Women:* basketball, cross-country, golf, lacrosse, soccer, softball, volleyball. **On-Campus Highlights:** David and Carol Lackland Center.

ADMISSIONS
Freshman Academic Profile: Average high school GPA 3.0. 11% in top 10% of high school class, 28% in top 25% of high school class, 55% in top 50% of high school class. 85% from public high schools. **Test Scores:** SAT Math middle 50% range 410–550. SAT EBRW middle 50% range 410–540. ACT middle 50% range 18–23. **Basis for Candidate Selection:** *Very important factors include:* rigor of secondary school record, academic GPA, standardized test scores. *Important factors include:* application essay, recommendation(s), interview, extracurricular activities. *Other factors include:* class rank, talent/ability, character/personal qualities, alumni/ae relation, religious affiliation/commitment, volunteer work, work experience, level of applicant's interest. **Freshman Admission Requirements:** High school diploma is required and GED is accepted. *Academic units required:* 4 English, 3 math, 2 science, 1 science labs. *Academic units recommended:* 4 English, 4 math, 3 science, 1 science labs, 2 foreign language, 4 social studies. **Freshman Admission Statistics:** 1,038 applied, 91% admitted, 22% enrolled. **Transfer Admission Requirements:** High school transcript, college transcript(s), essay or personal statement. Minimum college GPA of 2.0 required. Lowest grade transferable C-. **General Admission Information:** Application fee $30. Priority deadline 3/1. Non-fall registration accepted. Admission may be deferred for a maximum of 1 semester.

COSTS AND FINANCIAL AID
Annual tuition $15,700. Room and board $6,850. Required fees $1,100. Average book and supplies expense $666. **Required Forms and Deadlines:** FAFSA. **Notification of Awards:** Applicants will be notified of awards on a rolling basis beginning 3/15. **Types of Aid:** *Need-based scholarships/grants:* College/university scholarship or grant aid from institutional funds; Federal Pell; Private scholarships; SEOG; State scholarships/grants. **Financial Aid Statistics:** 100% needy freshmen, 99% needy undergrads receive need-based scholarship or grant aid. 10% freshmen, 7% undergrads receive non-need-based scholarship or grant aid. 90% freshmen, 92% undergrads receive need-based self-help aid. 0% freshmen, 0% undergrads receive athletic scholarships. 98% freshmen receive any aid. **Criteria awarding aid:** *Non-need-based:* Academics, Alumni affiliation, Art, Leadership, Minority status, Music/drama, Religious affiliation, State/district residency.

CENTENARY COLLEGE OF LOUISIANA

Best Colleges

2911 Centenary Blvd, Shreveport, LA 71104
Phone: 3188695131 **Financial Aid Phone:** 318-869-5137
E-mail: admission@centenary.edu
Fax: 318-869-5005 **Website:** https://www.centenary.edu/ **ACT Code:** 1576

This private school, affiliated with the United Methodist Church, was founded in 1825. It has a 65 acre campus.

RATINGS
Admissions Selectivity Rating: 86   **Fire Safety Rating:** 78   **Green Rating:** 60*

STUDENTS AND FACULTY
Enrollment: 544. **Student Body:** 57% female, 43% male, 43% out-of-state, 1% international (7 countries represented). Asian 2%, African American 14%, Caucasian 65%, Hispanic 10%, Native American 1%, Pacific Islander <1%, Two or more races 6%, Race unknown 0%.
Retention and Graduation: 76% freshmen return for sophomore year. 48% freshmen graduate within 6 years. **Faculty:** Student/faculty ratio 9:1. 0% of classes are taught by teaching assistants.

ACADEMICS
Degrees: Bachelor's; Master's. **Classes:** Most classes have fewer than 10 students. Most lab/discussion sessions have 10–19 students. **Most popular majors:** Biology/Biological Sciences, General; Psychology, General; Business Administration and Management, General. **Special Study Options:** Double major; Honors program; Independent study; Internships; Student-designed major; Study abroad; Teacher certification program. **Disability Services offered:** Note-taking services; Reader services; Tape recorders; Tutors. **Career services:** Alumni services; Career assessment; Career/job search classes; Internships.

FACILITIES
Housing: Coed dorms; Fraternity/sorority housing; Special housing for disabled students; 95% of campus accessible to physically disabled. **Special Academic Facilities/Equipment:** Meadows Art Museum, Leuck Arboretum, Marjorie Lyons Playhouse, School of Music recording studio, Science Hall multimedia auditorium. **Campus network:** 100% of classrooms, 100% of dorms, 100% of student union, 100% of libraries, 100% of dining areas, 100% of common outdoor areas, have wireless network access.

CAMPUS LIFE
Environment: Metropolis. **Activities:** Campus Ministries; Choral groups; Drama/theater; International Student Organization; Literary magazine; Model UN; Music ensembles; Musical theater; Radio station; Student government; Student newspaper; Student-run film society; Symphony orchestra; Yearbook. 58 registered organizations, 4 fraternities, 2 sororities, on campus. **Athletics (Intercollegiate):** *Men:* baseball, basketball, cross-country, golf, soccer, swimming, tennis. *Women:* basketball, cross-country, golf, gymnastics, soccer, softball, swimming, tennis, volleyball. **On-Campus Highlights:** Meadows Museum of Art.

ADMISSIONS

Freshman Academic Profile: Average high school GPA 3.5. **Test Scores:** SAT Math middle 50% range 520–610. SAT EBRW middle 50% range 530–610. ACT middle 50% range 21–28. **Basis for Candidate Selection:** *Very important factors include:* rigor of secondary school record, academic GPA, application essay, standardized test scores. *Important factors include:* class rank, extracurricular activities, volunteer work. *Other factors include:* recommendation(s), interview, talent/ability, character/personal qualities, alumni/ae relation, work experience. **Freshman Admission Requirements:** High school diploma is required and GED is accepted. *Academic units recommended:* 4 English, 3 math, 3 science, 2 foreign language, 3 social studies. **Freshman Admission Statistics:** 893 applied, 60% admitted, 32% enrolled. **Transfer Admission Requirements:** High school transcript, college transcript(s), essay or personal statement, statement of good standing from prior institution(s). Minimum college GPA of 2.0 required. Lowest grade transferable C. **General Admission Information:** Priority deadline 2/15. Regular application deadline 8/1. Non-fall registration accepted.

COSTS AND FINANCIAL AID

Annual tuition $37,310. Room and board $13,670. **Required Forms and Deadlines:** FAFSA. **Notification of Awards:** Applicants will be notified of awards on a rolling basis beginning 3/15. **Types of Aid:** *Need-based scholarships/grants:* College/university scholarship or grant aid from institutional funds; Federal Pell; SEOG; State scholarships/grants. *Loans:* Direct PLUS loans; Direct Subsidized Stafford Loans; Direct Unsubsidized Stafford Loans. **Student Employment:** Federal Work-Study Program available. Institutional employment available. **Financial Aid Statistics:** 100% needy freshmen, 100% needy undergrads receive need-based scholarship or grant aid. 22% freshmen, 19% undergrads receive non-need-based scholarship or grant aid. 62% freshmen, 68% undergrads receive need-based self-help aid. 0% freshmen, 0% undergrads receive athletic scholarships. 75% undergrads borrow to pay for school. Average cumulative indebtedness $32,900. **Criteria awarding aid:** *Non-need-based:* Academics, Alumni affiliation, Art, Music/drama, Religious affiliation, State/district residency.

CENTRAL COLLEGE

812 University Street, Pella, IA 50219-1999
Phone: 641-628-5286 **Financial Aid Phone:** 641-628-5336
E-mail: admission@central.edu **CEEB Code:** 6087
Fax: 641-628-5983 **Website:** www.central.edu **ACT Code:** 1284

This private school, affiliated with the Reformed Church, was founded in 1853. It has a 169 acre campus.

RATINGS

Admissions Selectivity Rating: 80　　**Fire Safety Rating:** 89　　**Green Rating:** 60*

STUDENTS AND FACULTY

Enrollment: 1,225. **Student Body:** 52% female, 48% male, 21% out-of-state, <1% international (6 countries represented). Asian 1%, African American 2%, Caucasian 87%, Hispanic 4%, Native American <1%, Pacific Islander <1%, Two or more races 1%, Race unknown 3%. **Retention and Graduation:** 78% freshmen return for sophomore year. 27% grads go on to further study within 1 year. 17% grads pursue arts and sciences degrees. 2% grads pursue law degrees. 2% grads pursue business degrees. 4% grads pursue medical degrees. **Faculty:** Student/faculty ratio 12:1. 100 full-time faculty, 88% hold PhDs, 12% are members of minority groups, 45% are women. 0% of classes are taught by teaching assistants.

ACADEMICS

Degrees: Bachelor's. **Classes:** Most classes have 10–19 students. Most lab/discussion sessions have 10–19 students. **Most popular majors:** Business/Commerce, General; Biology/Biological Sciences, General; Exercise Physiology and Kinesiology. **Special Study Options:** Cooperative education program; Distance learning; Double major; Dual enrollment; Honors program; Independent study; Internships; Student-designed major; Study abroad; Teacher certification program. **Honors programs:** The Honors Program at Central College encourages student creativity, intellectual engagement and independent thinking. The program aims to be developmental: beginning with opportunities for broad exploration, the program helps students move toward greater independence, more advanced work in a discipline, and increased opportunities for personal initiative. The centerpiece of Honors at Central College is the Emerging Scholars Program, which culminates in a Senior Honors Thesis. **Disability Services offered:** Note-taking services; Reader services; Tape recorders; Tutors. **Career services:** Alumni network; Alumni services; Career assessment; Career/job search classes; Internships; Regional alumni.

FACILITIES

Housing: Coed dorms; Fraternity/sorority housing; Men's dorms; Special housing for disabled students; Theme housing; Women's dorms; 95% of campus accessible to physically disabled. **Special Academic Facilities/Equipment:** Two LEED rated academic buildings: Roe Center (platinum) and Vermeer Science Center (silver); Weller Center for Business; Geisler Library with cafe, Ron Schipper Fitness Center, Lubbers Center for the Visual Arts which includes a Glass-blowing studio (only one of two in the state of Iowa). **Campus network:** 100% of classrooms, 100% of dorms, 100% of student union, 100% of libraries, 100% of dining areas, 100% of common outdoor areas, have wireless network access.

CAMPUS LIFE

Environment: Village. **Activities:** Campus Ministries; Choral groups; Concert band; Dance; Drama/theater; Jazz band; Literary magazine; Music ensembles; Pep band; Student government; Symphony orchestra. 80 registered organizations, 9 honor societies, 5 religious organizations, 4 fraternities, 3 sororities, on campus. **Athletics (Intercollegiate):** *Men:* baseball, basketball, football, golf, soccer, tennis, track/field (outdoor), track/field (indoor), wrestling. *Women:* basketball, cross-country, golf, softball, tennis, track/field (outdoor), track/field (indoor), volleyball. **On-Campus Highlights:** Geisler Cafe.

ADMISSIONS

Freshman Academic Profile: Average high school GPA 3.6. 23% in top 10% of high school class, 54% in top 25% of high school class, 85% in top 50% of high school class. 95% from public high schools. **Test Scores:** SAT Math middle 50% range 470–600. SAT EBRW middle 50% range 410–560. ACT middle 50% range 20–26. **Basis for Candidate Selection:** *Very important factors include:* rigor of secondary school record, academic GPA, standardized test scores. *Important factors include:* class rank. *Other factors include:* application essay, recommendation(s), interview, extracurricular activities, talent/ability, character/personal qualities, first generation, alumni/ae relation, volunteer work, work experience, level of applicant's interest. **Freshman Admission Requirements:** High school diploma is required and GED is accepted. *Academic units recommended:* 4 English, 2 math, 2 science, 2 science labs, 2 foreign language, 3 social studies. **Freshman Admission Statistics:** 3,071 applied, 64% admitted, 16% enrolled. **Transfer Admission Requirements:** High school transcript, college transcript(s), standardized test scores, statement of good standing from prior institution(s). Minimum college GPA of 2.5 required. Lowest grade transferable C-. **General Admission Information:** Application fee $25. Regular application deadline 8/15. Non-fall registration accepted. Admission may be deferred for a maximum of 1 year.

COSTS AND FINANCIAL AID

Required Forms and Deadlines: FAFSA. **Notification of Awards:** Applicants will be notified of awards on a rolling basis beginning 3/1. **Types of Aid:** *Need-based scholarships/grants:* College/university scholarship or grant aid from institutional funds; Federal Pell; Private scholarships; SEOG; State scholarships/grants. *Loans:* Direct PLUS loans; Direct Subsidized Stafford Loans; Direct Unsubsidized Stafford Loans. **Student Employment:** Federal Work-Study Program available. Institutional employment available. **Financial Aid Statistics:** 100% needy freshmen, 100% needy undergrads receive need-based scholarship or grant aid. 83% freshmen, 12% undergrads receive non-need-based scholarship or grant aid. 100% freshmen, 89% undergrads receive need-based self-help aid. 0% freshmen, 0% undergrads receive athletic scholarships. 100% freshmen, 99% undergrads receive any aid. 78% undergrads borrow to pay for school. Average cumulative indebtedness $37,169. **Criteria awarding aid:** *Need-based:* Academics, Minority status, Music/drama. *Non-need-based:* Academics, Alumni affiliation, Art, Minority status, Music/drama, Religious affiliation, State/district residency.

CENTRAL CONNECTICUT STATE UNIVERSITY

1615 Stanley Street, New Britain, CT 06050
Phone: 860-832-2278 **Financial Aid Phone:** 860-832-2200
E-mail: admissions@ccsu.edu **CEEB Code:** 3898
Fax: 862-832-2295 **Website:** www.ccsu.edu **ACT Code:** 596

This public school was founded in 1849. It has a 314 acre campus.

RATINGS
Admissions Selectivity Rating: 83   **Fire Safety Rating:** 92   **Green Rating:** 86

STUDENTS AND FACULTY
Enrollment: 8,817. **Student Body:** 47% female, 53% male, 4% out-of-state, 1% international (30 countries represented). Asian 4%, African American 12%, Caucasian 58%, Hispanic 16%, Native American <1%, Pacific Islander <1%, Two or more races 3%, Race unknown 3%.
Retention and Graduation: 74% freshmen return for sophomore year. 30% freshmen graduate within 4 years. 57% freshmen graduate within 6 years. **Faculty:** Student/faculty ratio 14:1. 440 full-time faculty, 85% hold PhDs, 23% are members of minority groups, 44% are women. 0% of classes are taught by teaching assistants.

ACADEMICS
Degrees: Bachelor's; Doctoral degree—professional practice; Doctoral degree research/scholarship; Master's; Post-bachelor's certificate; Post-master's certificate. **Classes:** Most classes have 20–29 students. Most lab/discussion sessions have 10–19 students. **Most popular majors:** Psychology, General; Criminology; Accounting. **Special Study Options:** Cooperative education program; Cross-registration; Distance learning; Double major; Dual enrollment; English as a Second Language (ESL); Honors program; Independent study; Internships; Student-designed major; Study abroad; Teacher certification program. **Honors programs:** Interdisciplinary writing/reading program for undergraduates with strong academic skills. Areas of study: Western Culture, Science and Society, and World Culture, capstone honors thesis in junior year. Scholarship available. **Disability Services offered:** Note-taking services; Reader services; Tape recorders; Tutors. **Career services:** Alumni services; Career assessment; Career/job search classes; Internships.

FACILITIES
Housing: Coed dorms; Special housing for disabled students; Theme housing; Wellness housing; Women's dorms; 100% of campus accessible to physically disabled. **Special Academic Facilities/Equipment:** Art gallery, language lab, childhood center, planetarium and space science center, center for economic education, TV studio and a Fitness Studio, eSports Center.

CAMPUS LIFE
Environment: Town. **Activities:** Campus Ministries; Choral groups; Concert band; Dance; Drama/theater; International Student Organization; Jazz band; Literary magazine; Marching band; Music ensembles; Musical theater; Radio station; Student government; Student newspaper; Student-run film society; Symphony orchestra; Television station. 135 registered organizations, 5 honor societies, 4 religious organizations, 3 fraternities, 2 sororities, on campus. **Athletics (Intercollegiate):** *Men:* baseball, basketball, cross-country, football, golf, soccer, track/field (outdoor), track/field (indoor). *Women:* basketball, cross-country, diving, golf, lacrosse, soccer, softball, swimming, track/field (outdoor), track/field (indoor), volleyball. **On-Campus Highlights:** Student Center. **Environmental Initiatives:** Fuel cell, Class schedule for carpool ease, Building use in summer.

ADMISSIONS
Freshman Academic Profile: Average high school GPA 3.2. 7% in top 10% of high school class, 28% in top 25% of high school class, 64% in top 50% of high school class. 95% from public high schools. **Test Scores:** SAT Math middle 50% range 480–570. SAT EBRW middle 50% range 490–590. ACT middle 50% range 17–23. **Basis for Candidate Selection:** *Very important factors include:* rigor of secondary school record, class rank, academic GPA, standardized test scores, recommendation(s). *Important factors include:* application essay, *Other factors include:* interview, extracurricular activities, talent/ability, first generation, alumni/ae relation, geographical residence, state residency, racial/ethnic status, level of applicant's interest. **Freshman Admission Requirements:** High school diploma is required and GED is accepted. *Academic units required:* 4 English, 3 math, 2 science, 1 science labs, 2 social studies, 1 history. *Academic units recommended:* 3 foreign language. **Freshman Admission Statistics:** 7,807 applied, 66% admitted, 27% enrolled. **Transfer Admission Requirements:** High school transcript, college transcript(s),

statement of good standing from prior institution(s). Minimum college GPA of 2.0 required. Lowest grade transferable C. **General Admission Information:** Application fee $50. Regular application deadline 5/1. Non-fall registration accepted.

COSTS AND FINANCIAL AID
Annual in-state tuition $5,924. Annual out-of-state tuition $17,726. Room and board $12,528. Required fees $5,144. Average book and supplies expense $1,050. **Required Forms and Deadlines:** FAFSA. **Notification of Awards:** Applicants will be notified of awards on a rolling basis beginning 10/31. **Types of Aid:** *Need-based scholarships/grants:* College/university scholarship or grant aid from institutional funds; Federal Pell; Private scholarships; SEOG; State scholarships/grants. *Loans:* Direct PLUS loans; Direct Subsidized Stafford Loans; Direct Unsubsidized Stafford Loans. **Student Employment:** Federal Work-Study Program available. Institutional employment available. **Financial Aid Statistics:** 89% needy freshmen, 81% needy undergrads receive need-based scholarship or grant aid. 53% freshmen, 27% undergrads receive non-need-based scholarship or grant aid. 71% freshmen, 71% undergrads receive need-based self-help aid. 4% freshmen, 4% undergrads receive athletic scholarships. 78% freshmen, 59% undergrads receive any aid. 67% undergrads borrow to pay for school. Average cumulative indebtedness $29,709. **Criteria awarding aid:** *Non-need-based:* Academics, Alumni affiliation, Athletics.

CENTRAL MICHIGAN UNIVERSITY

102 Warriner Hall, Mount Pleasant, MI 48859
Phone: 989-774-3076 **Financial Aid Phone:** 888-392-0007
E-mail: cmuadmit@cmich.edu **CEEB Code:** 1106
Fax: 989-774-7267 **Website:** www.cmich.edu **ACT Code:** 1972

This public school was founded in 1892. It has a 854 acre campus.

RATINGS
Admissions Selectivity Rating: 80   **Fire Safety Rating:** 68   **Green Rating:** 89

STUDENTS AND FACULTY
Enrollment: 14,409. **Student Body:** 59% female, 41% male, 10% out-of-state, 2% international (35 countries represented). Asian 1%, African American 10%, Caucasian 76%, Hispanic 5%, Native American 1%, Pacific Islander <1%, Two or more races 4%, Race unknown 1%.
Retention and Graduation: 74% freshmen return for sophomore year. 28% freshmen graduate within 4 years. 61% freshmen graduate within 6 years. **Faculty:** Student/faculty ratio 19:1. 724 full-time faculty, 82% hold PhDs, 19% are members of minority groups, 43% are women.

ACADEMICS
Degrees: Bachelor's; Doctoral degree—other; Doctoral degree—professional practice; Doctoral degree research/scholarship; Master's; Post-bachelor's certificate; Post-master's certificate. **Classes:** Most classes have 20–29 students. Most lab/discussion sessions have 10–19 students. **Most popular majors:** Exercise Science and Kinesiology; Psychology, General; Marketing/Marketing Management, General. **Special Study Options:** Accelerated program; Distance learning; Double major; Dual enrollment; English as a Second Language (ESL); Honors program; Independent study; Internships; Student-designed major; Study abroad; Teacher certification program. **Honors programs:** The Honors Program, Centralis Program. **Combined degree programs:** BA/MA. **Disability Services offered:** Note-taking services; Reader services; Tape recorders; Tutors. **Career services:** Alumni network; Alumni services; Career assessment; Career/job search classes; Internships; Regional alumni.

FACILITIES
Housing: Apartments for married students; Apartments for single students; Coed dorms; Special housing for disabled students; Special housing for international students; Theme housing; 99% of campus accessible to physically disabled. **Special Academic Facilities/Equipment:** Clarke Historical Library, Central Michigan University Museum of Cultural and Natural History, Gerald L. Poor School Museum, Brooks Astronomical Observatory, University Art Gallery, University Theater, Public Broadcasting, Student Activity Center, Charles V. Park Library, body scanner.

CAMPUS LIFE
Environment: Town. **Activities:** Choral groups; Concert band; Dance; Drama/theater; International Student Organization; Jazz band; Literary magazine; Marching band; Model UN; Music ensembles; Musical theater; Opera; Pep

band; Radio station; Student government; Student newspaper; Student-run film society; Symphony orchestra; Television station. 336 registered organizations, 17 honor societies, 11 religious organizations, 14 fraternities, 14 sororities, on campus. **Athletics (Intercollegiate):** *Men:* baseball, basketball, cross-country, football, track/field (outdoor), track/field (indoor), wrestling. *Women:* basketball, cross-country, field hockey, gymnastics, soccer, softball, track/field (outdoor), track/field (indoor), volleyball. **On-Campus Highlights:** CMU Events Center. **Environmental Initiatives:** Food Recovery.

ADMISSIONS

Freshman Academic Profile: Average high school GPA 3.4. 18% in top 10% of high school class, 39% in top 25% of high school class, 72% in top 50% of high school class. 88% from public high schools. **Test Scores:** SAT Math middle 50% range 490–590. SAT EBRW middle 50% range 500–610. ACT middle 50% range 20–26. **Basis for Candidate Selection:** *Very important factors include:* rigor of secondary school record, academic GPA, standardized test scores. *Important factors include:* talent/ability. *Other factors include:* class rank, application essay, recommendation(s), interview, extracurricular activities, character/personal qualities, alumni/ae relation, geographical residence, volunteer work, work experience, level of applicant's interest. **Freshman Admission Requirements:** High school diploma is required and GED is accepted. *Academic units recommended:* 4 English, 4 math, 4 science, 1 science labs, 2 foreign language, 2 social studies, 2 history, 1 computer science, 2 visual/performing arts. **Freshman Admission Statistics:** 16,411 applied, 70% admitted, 22% enrolled. **Transfer Admission Requirements:** College transcript(s), statement of good standing from prior institution(s). Minimum college GPA of 2.00 required. Lowest grade transferable C-. **General Admission Information:** Application fee $40. Priority deadline 12/1. Regular application deadline 7/1. Non-fall registration accepted. Admission may be deferred for a maximum of 1 year.

COSTS AND FINANCIAL AID

Annual in-state tuition $12,810. Annual out-of-state tuition $12,810. Room and board $10,328. Required fees $450. Average book and supplies expense $1,000. **Required Forms and Deadlines:** FAFSA. **Notification of Awards:** Applicants will be notified of awards on a rolling basis beginning 12/1. **Types of Aid:** *Need-based scholarships/grants:* College/university scholarship or grant aid from institutional funds; Federal Pell; Private scholarships; SEOG; State scholarships/grants. *Loans:* Direct PLUS loans; Direct Subsidized Stafford Loans; Direct Unsubsidized Stafford Loans. **Student Employment:** Federal Work-Study Program available. Institutional employment available. **Financial Aid Statistics:** 95% needy freshmen, 83% needy undergrads receive need-based scholarship or grant aid. 38% freshmen, 3% undergrads receive non-need-based scholarship or grant aid. 71% freshmen, 81% undergrads receive need-based self-help aid. 1% freshmen, 1% undergrads receive athletic scholarships. 89% freshmen, 73% undergrads receive any aid. 74% undergrads borrow to pay for school. Average cumulative indebtedness $31,683. **Criteria awarding aid:** *Need-based:* Leadership. *Non-need-based:* Academics, Alumni affiliation, Art, Athletics, Leadership, Minority status, Music/drama, State/district residency.

CENTRAL OHIO TECHNICAL COLLEGE

1179 University Drive, Newark, OH 43055
Phone: 740-366-9494
E-mail: cotcadmissions@cotc.edu
Fax: 740-366-9290 **Website:** www.cotc.edu

This is a public school.

RATINGS
Admissions Selectivity Rating: 60*   **Fire Safety Rating:** 60*   **Green Rating:** 60*

STUDENTS AND FACULTY
Enrollment: 3,513. **Student Body:** 71% female, 29% male, 1% out-of-state, 0% international. Asian 1%, African American 9%, Caucasian 82%, Hispanic 1%, Native American <1%, Pacific Islander <1%, Two or more races 2%, Race unknown 4%.

ACADEMICS
Degrees: Associate; Certificate. **Special Study Options:** Cooperative education program; Distance learning; Double major; Dual enrollment; English as a Second Language (ESL); Internships; Weekend college.

FACILITIES
Housing: Apartments for single students.

CAMPUS LIFE
Activities: Choral groups; Drama/theater; Music ensembles; Student government; Student newspaper.

ADMISSIONS
Freshman Admission Requirements: High school diploma is required and GED is accepted. **General Admission Information:** Application fee $20. Non-fall registration accepted.

COSTS AND FINANCIAL AID
Annual in-state tuition $4,200. Annual out-of-state tuition $6,960. Average book and supplies expense $1,800.

CENTRAL STATE UNIVERSITY

PO Box 1004, Wilberforce, OH 45384
Phone: 937-376-6348
E-mail: admissions@centralstate.edu **CEEB Code:** 1107
Fax: 937-376-6648 **Website:** www.centralstate.edu **ACT Code:** 3246

This public school was founded in 1887. It has a 60 acre campus.

RATINGS
Admissions Selectivity Rating: 83   **Fire Safety Rating:** 60*   **Green Rating:** 60*

STUDENTS AND FACULTY
Enrollment: 1,701. **Student Body:** 55% female, 45% male, 45% out-of-state, 1% international. Asian <1%, African American 94%, Caucasian 1%, Hispanic 1%, Native American <1%, Pacific Islander 0%, Two or more races 1%, Race unknown 2%.
Retention and Graduation: 40% freshmen return for sophomore year. 32% grads go on to further study within 1 year. 50% grads pursue arts and sciences degrees. 7% grads pursue law degrees. 29% grads pursue business degrees. **Faculty:** Student/faculty ratio 13:1. 97 full-time faculty, 74% hold PhDs, 78% are members of minority groups, 36% are women.

ACADEMICS
Degrees: Bachelor's; Master's. **Classes:** Most classes have 20–29 students. Most lab/discussion sessions have fewer than 10 students. **Most popular majors:** Business/Commerce, General. **Special Study Options:** Cooperative education program; Cross-registration; Distance learning; Double major; Honors program; Independent study; Internships; Study abroad; Teacher certification program; Weekend college. **Disability Services offered:** Note-taking services; Reader services; Tape recorders; Tutors. **Career services:** Alumni services; Career assessment; Career/job search classes; Internships; Regional alumni.

FACILITIES
Housing: Coed dorms; Men's dorms; Women's dorms. **Special Academic Facilities/Equipment:** National Afro-American Museum and Cultural Center; CJ McLin International Center for Water Resources Management; Center for Integrated Manufacturing Protocols Architectures and Logistics Laboratory; Biology Technique Laboratory; Electrochemistry Research Laboratory; Cosby Mass Communication Center; Paul Robeson Cultural and Performing Arts Center. **Campus network:** 22% of classrooms, 26% of dorms, 70% of student union, 100% of libraries, 100% of dining areas, 8% of common outdoor areas, have wireless network access.

CAMPUS LIFE
Environment: Rural. **Activities:** Campus Ministries; Choral groups; Concert band; Dance; Drama/theater; Jazz band; Marching band; Music ensembles; Pep band; Radio station; Student government; Student newspaper; Television station. 30 registered organizations, 3 honor societies, 4 religious organizations, 1 fraternities, 3 sororities, on campus. **Athletics (Intercollegiate):** *Men:* basketball, cheerleading, cross-country, golf, track/field (outdoor). *Women:* basketball, cheerleading, cross-country, golf, track/field (outdoor), volleyball.

ADMISSIONS
Freshman Academic Profile: Average high school GPA 2.5. 5% in top 10% of high school class, 20% in top 25% of high school class, 49% in top 50% of high school class. **Test Scores:** SAT Math middle 50% range 340–430. SAT EBRW middle 50% range 340–430. ACT middle 50% range 15–18. **Basis for Candidate Selection:** *Very important factors include:* rigor of secondary school record, academic GPA, standardized test scores. *Important factors include:* class

rank, application essay, character/personal qualities, geographical residence, state residency. *Other factors include:* recommendation(s), interview, extracurricular activities, talent/ability. **Freshman Admission Requirements:** High school diploma is required and GED is accepted. *Academic units recommended:* 4 English, 3 math, 3 science, 2 foreign language, 3 social studies. **Freshman Admission Statistics:** 7,669 applied, 42% admitted, 20% enrolled. **Transfer Admission Requirements:** college transcript(s), statement of good standing from prior institution(s). Minimum college GPA of 2.0 required. Lowest grade transferable D. **General Admission Information:** Application fee $20. Non-fall registration accepted.

COSTS AND FINANCIAL AID

Annual in-state tuition $3,926. Annual out-of-state tuition $5,776. Room and board $9,934. Average book and supplies expense $1,200. **Required Forms and Deadlines:** FAFSA. **Notification of Awards:** Applicants will be notified of awards on a rolling basis beginning 4/15. **Types of Aid:** *Need-based scholarships/grants:* College/university scholarship or grant aid from institutional funds; Federal Pell; Private scholarships; SEOG; State scholarships/grants. *Loans:* Direct PLUS loans; Direct Subsidized Stafford Loans; Direct Unsubsidized Stafford Loans. **Student Employment:** Federal Work-Study Program available. Institutional employment available. **Financial Aid Statistics:** 100% needy freshmen, 100% needy undergrads receive need-based scholarship or grant aid. 0% freshmen, 0% undergrads receive non-need-based scholarship or grant aid. 0% freshmen, 0% undergrads receive need-based self-help aid. 0% freshmen, 0% undergrads receive athletic scholarships. **Criteria awarding aid:** *Need-based:* Academics. *Non-need-based:* Academics, Alumni affiliation, Art, Athletics, Leadership, Music/drama.

CENTRAL WASHINGTON UNIVERSITY

Admissions Office, Ellensburg, WA 98926-7463
Phone: 509-963-1211 Financial Aid Phone: 509-963-1611
E-mail: cwuadmis@cwu.edu CEEB Code: 4044
Fax: 509-963-3022 Website: www.cwu.edu ACT Code: 4444

This public school was founded in 1891. It has a 350 acre campus.

RATINGS

Admissions Selectivity Rating: 76   Fire Safety Rating: 76   Green Rating: 75

STUDENTS AND FACULTY

Enrollment: 9,688. **Student Body:** 51% female, 49% male, 2% out-of-state, 2% international (60 countries represented). Asian 7%, African American 3%, Caucasian 75%, Hispanic 8%, Native American 3%, Race unknown 3%. **Retention and Graduation:** 75% freshmen return for sophomore year. **Faculty:** Student/faculty ratio 20:1. 432 full-time faculty, 0% hold PhDs, 12% are members of minority groups, 39% are women. 3% of classes are taught by teaching assistants.

ACADEMICS

Degrees: Bachelor's; Master's; Post-bachelor's certificate. **Classes:** Most classes have 20–29 students. Most lab/discussion sessions have 10–19 students. **Most popular majors:** Business/Commerce, General; Elementary Education and Teaching; Social Sciences, General. **Special Study Options:** Cooperative education program; Distance learning; Double major; Dual enrollment; English as a Second Language (ESL); Exchange student program (domestic); Honors program; Independent study; Internships; Liberal arts/career combination; Student-designed major; Study abroad; Teacher certification program. **Honors programs:** The Douglas Honors College student is expected to maintain a grade point average above 3.0. A student will be placed on probation if the grade point average falls below 3.0, and will be dismissed from the Douglas Honors College if the cumulative grade point average is below 3.0 for two consecutive quarters. This policy does not affect academic standing as a student of Central Washington University. **Disability Services offered:** Note-taking services; Reader services; Tape recorders; Tutors. **Career services:** Alumni network; Alumni services; Career assessment; Career/job search classes; Internships; Regional alumni.

FACILITIES

Housing: Apartments for married students; Apartments for single students; Coed dorms; Special housing for disabled students; Special housing for international students; Theme housing; Women's dorms; 100% of campus accessible to physically disabled. **Special Academic Facilities/Equipment:** —Chimpanzee and Human Communication Institute—Geodesy Laboratory,

a data analysis facility of the Pacific Northwest Geodetic Array –Educational Technology Center –Museum collection of NW Native Amer and Circum-Pacific artifacts for teaching and research –regional site of the National Consortium for Rural Geospatial Innovations –Sarah Spugeon Art Gallery –Science Facility Building. **Campus network:** 100% of classrooms, 100% of dorms, 100% of student union, 100% of libraries, 100% of dining areas, 100% of common outdoor areas, have wireless network access.

CAMPUS LIFE

Environment: Village. **Activities:** Campus Ministries; Choral groups; Concert band; Dance; Drama/theater; International Student Organization; Jazz band; Literary magazine; Marching band; Music ensembles; Musical theater; Opera; Pep band; Radio station; Student government; Student newspaper; Student-run film society; Symphony orchestra; Television station. 96 registered organizations, 3 honor societies, 9 religious organizations, on campus. **Athletics (Intercollegiate):** *Men:* baseball, basketball, cheerleading, cross-country, football, track/field (outdoor), track/field (indoor). *Women:* basketball, cheerleading, cross-country, soccer, softball, track/field (outdoor), track/field (indoor), volleyball. **On-Campus Highlights:** Award-winning Student Union Recreation Center. **Environmental Initiatives:** Carbon Reduction.

ADMISSIONS

Freshman Academic Profile: Average high school GPA 3.2. 4% in top 10% of high school class, 23% in top 25% of high school class, 65% in top 50% of high school class. **Test Scores:** SAT Math middle 50% range 440–550. SAT EBRW middle 50% range 440–540. ACT middle 50% range 18–23. **Basis for Candidate Selection:** *Very important factors include:* rigor of secondary school record, academic GPA. *Important factors include:* application essay, standardized test scores. *Other factors include:* class rank, recommendation(s), interview, extracurricular activities, talent/ability, character/personal qualities, first generation, volunteer work, work experience, level of applicant's interest. **Freshman Admission Requirements:** High school diploma is required and GED is accepted. *Academic units required:* 4 English, 3 math, 2 science, 1 science labs, 2 foreign language, 3 social studies. *Academic units recommended:* 4 English, 4 math, 3 science, 2 science labs, 2 foreign language, 3 social studies. **Freshman Admission Statistics:** 5,013 applied, 79% admitted, 40% enrolled. **Transfer Admission Requirements:** College transcript(s), statement of good standing from prior institution(s). Minimum college GPA of 2.5 required. Lowest grade transferable D-. **General Admission Information:** Application fee $55. Regular application deadline 4/1. Non-fall registration accepted.

COSTS AND FINANCIAL AID

Annual in-state tuition $4,842. Annual out-of-state tuition $14,013. Room and board $8,052. Required fees $882. Average book and supplies expense $924. **Required Forms and Deadlines:** FAFSA. **Notification of Awards:** Applicants will be notified of awards on a rolling basis beginning 4/15. **Types of Aid:** *Need-based scholarships/grants:* College/university scholarship or grant aid from institutional funds; Federal Pell; Private scholarships; SEOG; State scholarships/grants. *Loans:* Direct PLUS loans; Direct Subsidized Stafford Loans; Direct Unsubsidized Stafford Loans. **Financial Aid Statistics:** 68% freshmen, 68% undergrads receive any aid. **Criteria awarding aid:** *Need-based:* Academics. *Non-need-based:* Academics, Alumni affiliation, Art, Athletics, Job skills, Leadership, Minority status, Music/drama, Religious affiliation, State/district residency.

CENTRAL WYOMING COLLEGE

2660 Peck Avenue, Riverton, WY 82501
Phone: 307-855-2000 Financial Aid Phone: 307-855-2150
E-mail: admit@cwc.edu CEEB Code: 4115
Fax: 307-855-2065 Website: www.cwc.edu ACT Code: 514999

This public school was founded in 1966. It has a 200 acre campus.

RATINGS

Admissions Selectivity Rating: 74   Fire Safety Rating: 84   Green Rating: 60*

STUDENTS AND FACULTY

Enrollment: 1,045. **Student Body:** 60% female, 40% male, 13% out-of-state, <1% international (6 countries represented). Asian 1%, African American 2%, Caucasian 71%, Hispanic 10%, Native American 11%, Pacific Islander <1%, Two or more races 4%, Race unknown 1%. **Retention and Graduation:** 52% freshmen return for sophomore year. **Faculty:** Student/faculty ratio 12:1. 58 full-time faculty, 78% hold PhDs, 5%

are members of minority groups, 55% are women. 0% of classes are taught by teaching assistants.

ACADEMICS

Degrees: Associate; Certificate; Diploma; Terminal Associate; Transfer Associate. **Classes:** Most classes have 10–19 students. **Most popular majors:** General Studies; Parks, Recreation and Leisure Facilities Management, General. **Special Study Options:** Cooperative education program; Cross-registration; Distance learning; Double major; Dual enrollment; External degree program; Honors program; Independent study; Student-designed major; Teacher certification program. **Disability Services offered:** Note-taking services; Reader services; Tape recorders; Tutors. **Career services:** Career assessment; Career/job search classes; Internships.

FACILITIES

Housing: Apartments for married students; Apartments for single students; Coed dorms; 100% of campus accessible to physically disabled. **Special Academic Facilities/Equipment:** Fine Arts Center, Microsoft training lab, Cisco training lab, Wyoming Public Television Station and Radio station, Stewart Collection (Native American Artifacts), Sinks Canyon Center, Rodeo Arena, Library, Arts Gallery.

CAMPUS LIFE

Environment: Village. **Activities:** Choral groups; Concert band; Dance; Drama/theater; International Student Organization; Jazz band; Music ensembles; Musical theater; Radio station; Student government; Television station. 16 registered organizations, 2 honor societies, 2 religious organizations, on campus. **Athletics (Intercollegiate):** *Men:* basketball, rodeo. *Women:* basketball, rodeo, volleyball. **On-Campus Highlights:** Arts Center.

ADMISSIONS

Freshman Academic Profile: Average high school GPA 3.1. 5% in top 10% of high school class, 17% in top 25% of high school class, 45% in top 50% of high school class. 89% from public high schools. **Test Scores:** SAT Math middle 50% range 400–490. SAT EBRW middle 50% range 400–620. ACT middle 50% range 17–22. **Freshman Admission Requirements:** High school diploma or equivalent is not required. **Freshman Admission Statistics:** 516 applied, 100% admitted, 53% enrolled. **General Admission Information:** Non-fall registration accepted. Admission may be deferred for a maximum of as long as needed.

COSTS AND FINANCIAL AID

Annual in-state tuition $1,992. Annual out-of-state tuition $5,976. Room and board $5,130. Required fees $720. Average book and supplies expense $1,200. **Required Forms and Deadlines:** FAFSA; Institution's own financial aid form. **Notification of Awards:** Applicants will be notified of awards on a rolling basis beginning 5/1. **Types of Aid:** *Need-based scholarships/grants:* College/university scholarship or grant aid from institutional funds; Federal Pell; Private scholarships; SEOG; State scholarships/grants. *Loans:* Direct PLUS loans; Direct Subsidized Stafford Loans; Direct Unsubsidized Stafford Loans. **Student Employment:** Federal Work-Study Program available. Institutional employment available. **Financial Aid Statistics:** 77% needy freshmen, 75% needy undergrads receive need-based scholarship or grant aid. 89% freshmen, 84% undergrads receive non-need-based scholarship or grant aid. 37% freshmen, 42% undergrads receive need-based self-help aid. 0% freshmen, 0% undergrads receive athletic scholarships. 34% freshmen, 43% undergrads receive any aid. **Criteria awarding aid:** *Non-need-based:* Academics, Alumni affiliation, Art, Athletics, Leadership, Minority status, Music/drama, State/district residency.

CENTRE COLLEGE

Best Colleges

600 West Walnut Street, Danville, KY 40422
Phone: 859-238-5350 **Financial Aid Phone:** 800.423.6236
E-mail: admission@centre.edu **CEEB Code:** 1109
Fax: 859-238-5373 **Website:** www.centre.edu **ACT Code:** 1506

This private school, affiliated with the Presbyterian Church, was founded in 1819. It has a 160 acre campus.

RATINGS

Admissions Selectivity Rating: 87   **Fire Safety Rating:** 84   **Green Rating:** 77

STUDENTS AND FACULTY

Enrollment: 1,425. **Student Body:** 51% female, 49% male, 43% out-of-state, 6% international (15 countries represented). Asian 5%, African American 5%, Caucasian 72%, Hispanic 7%, Native American <1%, Pacific Islander <1%, Two or more races 3%, Race unknown 1%.
Retention and Graduation: 90% freshmen return for sophomore year. 85% freshmen graduate within 4 years. 86% freshmen graduate within 6 years. 36% grads go on to further study within 1 year. 26% grads pursue arts and sciences degrees. 5% grads pursue law degrees. 3% grads pursue business degrees. 2% grads pursue medical degrees. **Faculty:** Student/faculty ratio 10:1. 128 full-time faculty, 99% hold PhDs, 8% are members of minority groups, 45% are women. 0% of classes are taught by teaching assistants.

ACADEMICS

Degrees: Bachelor's. **Classes:** Most classes have 10–19 students. Most lab/discussion sessions have 10–19 students. **Most popular majors:** Economics, General; Biology/Biological Sciences, General; Economics, Other. **Special Study Options:** Cross-registration; Double major; Honors program; Independent study; Internships; Student-designed major; Study abroad. **Honors programs:** In partnership with the James Graham Brown Foundation, Centre launched the Brown Fellows Program in 2009. The initiative is the premier scholarship and enrichment program in Kentucky and is one of the nation's elite fellowship programs. Centre is the only private college in Kentucky selected for a Brown Fellows Program. The foundation has also initiated a Brown Fellows Program at the University of Louisville. The program was established as an individualized course of development in which outstanding students build leadership skills through independent study, community service, and experiential learning. Brown Fellows are awarded "full-ride-plus" scholarships and are provided four summer enrichment experiences, beginning the summer before their first year at Centre. Summer enrichment experiences in subsequent years will be organized around themes of service, research, international study, and leadership. The scholarship and enrichment program includes: Full tuition Room and board Summer enrichment programs, which allow students to focus on their areas of interest On-campus program mentors Field-based experimental learning opportunities Customized Leadership Projects that span the student's collegiate career. **Disability Services offered:** Note-taking services; Reader services; Tape recorders; Tutors. **Career services:** Alumni network; Alumni services; Career assessment; Career/job search classes; Internships; Regional alumni.

FACILITIES

Housing: Apartments for single students; Coed dorms; Fraternity/sorority housing; Men's dorms; Special housing for disabled students; Theme housing; Women's dorms; 80% of campus accessible to physically disabled. **Special Academic Facilities/Equipment:** Arts center, physical science and math facility, electron microscope, visible and infrared mass spectroscopy equipment, visual arts center. **Campus network:** 95% of classrooms, 100% of dorms, 100% of libraries, 100% of dining areas, 60% of common outdoor areas, have wireless network access.

CAMPUS LIFE

Environment: Village. **Activities:** Campus Ministries; Choral groups; Concert band; Dance; Drama/theater; International Student Organization; Jazz band; Literary magazine; Music ensembles; Musical theater; Opera; Pep band; Student government; Student newspaper; Student-run film society; Symphony orchestra. 70 registered organizations, 13 honor societies, 5 religious organizations, 6 fraternities, 5 sororities, on campus. **Athletics (Intercollegiate):** *Men:* baseball, basketball, cheerleading, cross-country, diving, football, golf, soccer, swimming, tennis, track/field (outdoor). *Women:* basketball, cheerleading, cross-country, diving, field hockey, golf, soccer, softball, swimming, tennis, track/field (outdoor), volleyball. **On-Campus Highlights:** Norton Center for the Arts. **Environmental Initiatives:** All new buildings and major renovations will be designed and built to conserve energy and enhance the human environment as evaluated by LEED silver standards or equivalent. Certification through U.S.G.B.C. will be pursued as appropriate.

ADMISSIONS

Freshman Academic Profile: Average high school GPA 3.6. 55% in top 10% of high school class, 85% in top 25% of high school class, 99% in top 50% of high school class. 66% from public high schools. **Test Scores:** SAT Math middle 50% range 600–715. SAT EBRW middle 50% range 590–705. ACT middle 50% range 27–32. **Basis for Candidate Selection:** *Very important factors include:* rigor of secondary school record, academic GPA. *Important factors include:* class rank, application essay, standardized test scores, recommendation(s). *Other factors include:* interview, extracurricular activities, talent/ability, character/personal qualities, first generation, alumni/ae relation, geographical residence, racial/ethnic status, volunteer work, work experience. **Freshman Admission Requirements:** High school diploma or equivalent is not required. *Academic units required:* 4 English, 3 math, 2 science, 2 science labs, 2 foreign language, 2 history. *Academic units recommended:* 4 math, 4 science, 4 foreign language, 2 social studies, 2 history, 1 visual/performing arts. **Freshman Admission Statistics:** 2,457 applied, 73% admitted, 20% enrolled. **Transfer Admission Requirements:** High school transcript, college transcript(s), essay or personal statement, standardized test scores, statement of good standing from prior institution(s). Lowest grade transferable C. **General Admission Information:** Regular application deadline 1/15. Admission may be deferred for a maximum of typically 1 year.

COSTS AND FINANCIAL AID

Annual tuition $41,700. Room and board $10,480. Average book and supplies expense $1,500. **Required Forms and Deadlines:** FAFSA; Institution's own financial aid form. **Notification of Awards:** Applicants will be notified of awards on or about 1/10. **Types of Aid:** *Need-based scholarships/grants:* College/university scholarship or grant aid from institutional funds; Federal Pell; Private scholarships; SEOG; State scholarships/grants. *Loans:* Direct PLUS loans; Direct Subsidized Stafford Loans; Direct Unsubsidized Stafford Loans. **Student Employment:** Federal Work-Study Program available. Institutional employment available. **Financial Aid Statistics:** 100% needy freshmen, 100% needy undergrads receive need-based scholarship or grant aid. 0% freshmen, 0% undergrads receive non-need-based scholarship or grant aid. 64% freshmen, 66% undergrads receive need-based self-help aid. 0% freshmen, 0% undergrads receive athletic scholarships. 97% freshmen, 96% undergrads receive any aid. 50% undergrads borrow to pay for school. Average cumulative indebtedness $26,313. **Criteria awarding aid:** *Need-based:* Academics, Leadership. *Non-need-based:* Academics, Alumni affiliation, Art, Leadership, Music/drama.

CHAMINADE UNIVERSITY OF HONOLULU

3140 Waialae Avenue, Honolulu, HI 96816-1578
Phone: 808-735-8340 **Financial Aid Phone:** 808-735-4780
E-mail: admissions@chaminade.edu **CEEB Code:** 4105
Fax: 808-735-4647 **Website:** www.chaminade.edu **ACT Code:** 0898

This private school, affiliated with the Roman Catholic Church, was founded in 1955. It has a 65 acre campus.

RATINGS

Admissions Selectivity Rating: 73   **Fire Safety Rating:** 62   **Green Rating:** 60*

STUDENTS AND FACULTY

Enrollment: 1,084. **Student Body:** 74% female, 26% male, 26% out-of-state, 1% international (10 countries represented). Asian 38%, African American 3%, Caucasian 13%, Hispanic 4%, Native American <1%, Pacific Islander 28%, Two or more races 8%, Race unknown 4%.
Retention and Graduation: 79% freshmen return for sophomore year. 38% freshmen graduate within 4 years. 53% freshmen graduate within 6 years.
Faculty: Student/faculty ratio 11:1. 83 full-time faculty, 0% hold PhDs, 31% are members of minority groups, 47% are women. 0% of classes are taught by teaching assistants.

ACADEMICS

Degrees: Associate; Bachelor's; Master's; Post-bachelor's certificate; Post-master's certificate. **Classes:** Most classes have 10–19 students. Most lab/discussion sessions have 10–19 students. **Most popular majors:** Criminal Justice/Safety Studies; Registered Nursing/Registered Nurse; Business Administration and Management, General. **Special Study Options:** Accelerated program; Distance learning; Double major; Dual enrollment; Exchange student program (domestic); Independent study; Internships; Study abroad; Teacher certification program. **Disability Services offered:** Note-taking services; Reader services; Tape recorders. **Career services:** Alumni network; Career assessment; Career/job search classes; Internships.

FACILITIES

Housing: Apartments for single students; Coed dorms; Special housing for disabled students; Women's dorms; 100% of campus accessible to physically disabled. **Special Academic Facilities/Equipment:** Montessori lab school, observatory, black box theatre.

CAMPUS LIFE

Environment: Metropolis. **Activities:** Campus Ministries; Choral groups; Drama/theater; Musical theater; Radio station; Student government; Student newspaper. 35 registered organizations, 8 honor societies, 1 religious organizations, on campus. **Athletics (Intercollegiate):** *Men:* basketball, cross-country, golf, tennis, water polo. *Women:* cross-country, golf, softball, tennis, volleyball. **On-Campus Highlights:** Jean E. Rolles Sculpture Center.

ADMISSIONS

Freshman Academic Profile: Average high school GPA 3.5. 21% in top 10% of high school class, 40% in top 25% of high school class, 82% in top 50% of high school class. **Test Scores:** SAT Math middle 50% range 480–560. SAT EBRW middle 50% range 490–570. ACT middle 50% range 20–23. **Basis for Candidate Selection:** *Very important factors include:* academic GPA, standardized test scores. *Important factors include:* rigor of secondary school record. *Other factors include:* class rank, application essay, character/personal qualities, first generation, state residency. **Freshman Admission Requirements:** High school diploma is required and GED is accepted. *Academic units recommended:* 4 English, 3 math, 2 science, 3 social studies, 4 academic electives. **Freshman Admission Statistics:** 764 applied, 97% admitted, 25% enrolled. **Transfer Admission Requirements:** College transcript(s), essay or personal statement, statement of good standing from prior institution(s). Minimum college GPA of 2.0 required. Lowest grade transferable C. **General Admission Information:** Application fee $25. Non-fall registration accepted. Admission may be deferred for a maximum of 1 year.

COSTS AND FINANCIAL AID

Annual tuition $26,020. Room and board $14,184. Required fees $114. Average book and supplies expense $1,600. **Required Forms and Deadlines:** FAFSA. **Notification of Awards: Types of Aid:** *Need-based scholarships/grants:* College/university scholarship or grant aid from institutional funds; Federal Pell; Private scholarships; SEOG. *Loans:* Direct PLUS loans; Direct Subsidized Stafford Loans; Direct Unsubsidized Stafford Loans. Federal Work-Study Program available. Institutional employment available. **Financial Aid Statistics:** 91% needy freshmen, 93% needy undergrads receive need-based scholarship or grant aid. 99% freshmen, 97% undergrads receive non-need-based scholarship or grant aid. 55% freshmen, 63% undergrads receive need-based self-help aid. 6% freshmen, 6% undergrads receive athletic scholarships. 99% freshmen, 97% undergrads receive any aid. 62% undergrads borrow to pay for school. Average cumulative indebtedness $23,933. **Criteria awarding aid:** *Need-based:* Academics. *Non-need-based:* Academics, Athletics, Minority status, Religious affiliation, State/district residency.

For more free content, visit PrincetonReview.com

CHAMPLAIN COLLEGE

163 South Willard Street Box 670, Burlington, VT 05402-0670
Phone: 802-860-2727 **Financial Aid Phone:** 802-860-2730
E-mail: admission@champlain.edu **CEEB Code:** 3291
Fax: 802-860-2767 **Website:** www.champlain.edu/ **ACT Code:** 3291

This private school was founded in 1878. It has a 22 acre campus.

RATINGS
Admissions Selectivity Rating: 77 **Fire Safety Rating:** 98 **Green Rating:** 95

STUDENTS AND FACULTY
Enrollment: 2,060. **Student Body:** 36% female, 64% male, 78% out-of-state, 1% international (18 countries represented). Asian 3%, African American 3%, Caucasian 75%, Hispanic 7%, Native American <1%, Pacific Islander <1%, Two or more races 4%, Race unknown 7%.
Retention and Graduation: 83% freshmen return for sophomore year. 57% freshmen graduate within 4 years. 65% freshmen graduate within 6 years.
Faculty: Student/faculty ratio 12:1. 115 full-time faculty, 70% hold PhDs, 10% are members of minority groups, 39% are women. 0% of classes are taught by teaching assistants.

ACADEMICS
Degrees: Associate; Bachelor's; Certificate; Master's; Post-bachelor's certificate. **Classes:** Most classes have 10–19 students. Most lab/discussion sessions have 10–19 students. **Special Study Options:** Accelerated program; Cross-registration; Distance learning; Double major; Independent study; Internships; Liberal arts/career combination; Study abroad; Teacher certification program. **Combined degree programs:** BA/MA. **Disability Services offered:** Note-taking services; Reader services; Tape recorders; Tutors. **Career services:** Alumni network; Alumni services; Career assessment; Career/job search classes; Internships.

FACILITIES
Housing: Apartments for single students; Coed dorms; Special housing for disabled students; Special housing for international students; Women's dorms; 79% of campus accessible to physically disabled. **Special Academic Facilities/Equipment:** Emergent Media Center Miller Information Commons Global Business Center Senator Leahy Center for Digital Investigation Center for Communication and Creative Media. **Campus network:** 100% of classrooms, 100% of dorms, 100% of student union, 100% of libraries, 100% of dining areas, have wireless network access.

CAMPUS LIFE
Environment: Town. **Activities:** Choral groups; Dance; Drama/theater; International Student Organization; Literary magazine; Musical theater; Radio station; Student government; Student newspaper. 50 registered organizations, on campus. **On-Campus Highlights:** Sr. Leahy Center for Digital Forensics. **Environmental Initiatives:** Green Buildings (Master Plan).

ADMISSIONS
Freshman Academic Profile: Average high school GPA 3.4. 14% in top 10% of high school class, 39% in top 25% of high school class, 74% in top 50% of high school class. **Test Scores:** SAT Math middle 50% range 540–650. SAT EBRW middle 50% range 570–670. ACT middle 50% range 24–29. **Basis for Candidate Selection:** *Very important factors include:* rigor of secondary school record, academic GPA, talent/ability. *Important factors include:* application essay, recommendation(s), extracurricular activities, character/personal qualities, first generation, racial/ethnic status. *Other factors include:* class rank, standardized test scores, interview, alumni/ae relation, volunteer work, work experience. **Freshman Admission Requirements:** High school diploma is required and GED is accepted. *Academic units required:* 4 English, 3 math, 3 science, 2 science labs, 2 foreign language, 3 history, 5 academic electives. *Academic units recommended:* 4 math, 4 science, 4 foreign language, 4 history. **Freshman Admission Statistics:** 3,629 applied, 85% admitted, 17% enrolled. **Transfer Admission Requirements:** High school transcript, college transcript(s), essay or personal statement, Minimum college GPA of 2.0 required. Lowest grade transferable C. **General Admission Information:** Priority deadline 11/15. Regular application deadline 1/15. Non-fall registration accepted. Admission may be deferred for a maximum of 1 year.

COSTS AND FINANCIAL AID
Annual tuition $41,728. Room and board $15,766. Required fees $200. Average book and supplies expense $1,000. **Required Forms and Deadlines:** FAFSA. **Notification of Awards:** Applicants will be notified of awards on a rolling basis beginning 3/1. **Types of Aid:** *Need-based scholarships/grants:* College/university scholarship or grant aid from institutional funds; Federal Pell; Private scholarships; SEOG; State scholarships/grants; United Negro College Fund. *Loans:* Direct PLUS loans; Direct Subsidized Stafford Loans; Direct Unsubsidized Stafford Loans. **Student Employment:** Federal Work-Study Program available. Institutional employment available. **Financial Aid Statistics:** 99% needy freshmen, 99% needy undergrads receive need-based scholarship or grant aid. 20% freshmen, 14% undergrads receive non-need-based scholarship or grant aid. 80% freshmen, 82% undergrads receive need-based self-help aid. 0% freshmen, 0% undergrads receive athletic scholarships. 76% undergrads borrow to pay for school. Average cumulative indebtedness $36,976. **Criteria awarding aid:** *Need-based:* Academics, Leadership, Minority status. *Non-need-based:* Academics, Alumni affiliation, Leadership, Minority status.

CHAPMAN UNIVERSITY

One University Drive, Orange, CA 92866
Phone: 714-997-6711 **Financial Aid Phone:** 714-997-6741
E-mail: admit@chapman.edu **CEEB Code:** 4047
Fax: 714-997-6713 **Website:** www.chapman.edu **ACT Code:** 0210

This private school, affiliated with the Disciples of Christ Church, was founded in 1861. It has a 78 acre campus.

RATINGS
Admissions Selectivity Rating: 88 **Fire Safety Rating:** 79 **Green Rating:** 63

STUDENTS AND FACULTY
Enrollment: 7,294. **Student Body:** 61% female, 39% male, 30% out-of-state, 4% international (62 countries represented). Asian 14%, African American 2%, Caucasian 52%, Hispanic 16%, Native American <1%, Pacific Islander <1%, Two or more races 8%, Race unknown 4%.
Retention and Graduation: 91% freshmen return for sophomore year. 72% freshmen graduate within 4 years. 81% freshmen graduate within 6 years.
Faculty: Student/faculty ratio 13:1. 536 full-time faculty, 86% hold PhDs, 43% are women. 3% of classes are taught by teaching assistants.

ACADEMICS
Degrees: Bachelor's; Certificate; Doctoral degree—professional practice; Doctoral degree research/scholarship; Master's. **Classes:** Most classes have 10–19 students. Most lab/discussion sessions have 10–19 students. **Most popular majors:** Cinematography and Film/Video Production; Business Administration and Management, General; Public Relations/Image Management. **Special Study Options:** Distance learning; Double major; Dual enrollment; Honors program; Independent study; Internships; Liberal arts/career combination; Student-designed major; Study abroad; Teacher certification program. **Honors programs:** University Honors Program. **Combined degree programs:** BA/MA. **Disability Services offered:** Note-taking services; Reader services; Tutors. **Career services:** Alumni network; Alumni services; Career assessment; Career/job search classes; Internships.

FACILITIES
Housing: Apartments for married students; Apartments for single students; Coed dorms; Special housing for disabled students. **Special Academic Facilities/Equipment:** Anderson Center for Economic Research, Leatherby Center for Entrepreneurship and Business Ethics, Schmid Center for International Business, Law and organizational Economics Center, Center for Cold War Studies, Henley Social Science Research Laboratory, Guggenheim Art gallery, TV studio, film and television production and digital editing studios, Waltmer Theatre, Albert Schweitzer Collection.

CAMPUS LIFE
Environment: Metropolis. **Activities:** Campus Ministries; Choral groups; Concert band; Dance; Drama/theater; International Student Organization; Jazz band; Literary magazine; Model UN; Music ensembles; Musical theater;

Opera; Pep band; Radio station; Student government; Student newspaper; Student-run film society; Symphony orchestra; Yearbook. 289 registered organizations, 16 honor societies, 20 religious organizations, 8 fraternities, 8 sororities, on campus. **Athletics (Intercollegiate):** *Men:* baseball, basketball, cross-country, football, golf, soccer, tennis, water polo. *Women:* basketball, crew/rowing, cross-country, soccer, softball, swimming, tennis, track/field (outdoor), volleyball, water polo. **On-Campus Highlights:** Marion Knott Film Studios. **Environmental Initiatives:** Adoption of LEED standards in new building projects.

ADMISSIONS

Freshman Academic Profile: 36% in top 10% of high school class, 75% in top 25% of high school class, 94% in top 50% of high school class. **Test Scores:** SAT Math middle 50% range 590–700. SAT EBRW middle 50% range 600–680. ACT middle 50% range 25–31. **Basis for Candidate Selection:** *Very important factors include:* rigor of secondary school record, class rank, academic GPA, application essay, standardized test scores, character/personal qualities. *Important factors include:* extracurricular activities, talent/ability. *Other factors include:* recommendation(s), interview, first generation, alumni/ae relation, geographical residence, state residency, racial/ethnic status, volunteer work, work experience, level of applicant's interest. **Freshman Admission Requirements:** High school diploma is required and GED is accepted. *Academic units required:* 4 English, 3 math, 2 science, 1 science labs, 2 foreign language, 2 social studies, 2 history. *Academic units recommended:* 4 English, 4 math, 4 science, 2 science labs, 4 foreign language, 2 social studies, 2 history, 2 academic electives. **Freshman Admission Statistics:** 14,273 applied, 56% admitted, 22% enrolled. **Transfer Admission Requirements:** college transcript(s), essay or personal statement, Minimum college GPA of 2.5 required. Lowest grade transferable C-. **General Admission Information:** Application fee $70. Priority deadline 11/1. Regular application deadline 4/1. Non-fall registration accepted. Admission may be deferred for a maximum of up to one year and certain majors are not elibigle for deferrment unless on a military service mission. If on a military deferrment, we honor a defer up to two.

COSTS AND FINANCIAL AID

Annual tuition $56,830. Room and board $18,530. Required fees $384. Average book and supplies expense $1,600. **Required Forms and Deadlines:** FAFSA; State aid form. **Notification of Awards:** Applicants will be notified of awards on a rolling basis beginning 3/15. **Types of Aid:** *Need-based scholarships/grants:* College/university scholarship or grant aid from institutional funds; Federal Pell; Private scholarships; SEOG; State scholarships/grants. *Loans:* Direct PLUS loans; Direct Subsidized Stafford Loans; Direct Unsubsidized Stafford Loans. **Student Employment:** Federal Work-Study Program available. Institutional employment available. **Financial Aid Statistics:** 92% needy freshmen, 91% needy undergrads receive need-based scholarship or grant aid. 78% freshmen, 70% undergrads receive non-need-based scholarship or grant aid. 88% freshmen, 90% undergrads receive need-based self-help aid. 0% freshmen, 0% undergrads receive athletic scholarships. 87% freshmen, 84% undergrads receive any aid. 50% undergrads borrow to pay for school. Average cumulative indebtedness $27,117. **Criteria awarding aid:** *Non-need-based:* Academics, Alumni affiliation, Art, Music/drama, Religious affiliation.

CHARTER OAK STATE COLLEGE

55 Paul Manafort Drive, New Britain, CT 06053
Phone: 860-515-3701 **Financial Aid Phone:** 860-515-3703
E-mail: admissions@charteroak.edu
Website: www.charteroak.edu

This public school was founded in 1973.

RATINGS

Admissions Selectivity Rating: 60*   **Fire Safety Rating:** 60*   **Green Rating:** 60*

STUDENTS AND FACULTY

Enrollment: 1,352. **Student Body:** 68% female, 32% male, 19% out-of-state, 1% international. Asian 2%, African American 17%, Caucasian 56%, Hispanic 16%, Native American <1%, Pacific Islander 0%, Two or more races 3%, Race unknown 5%.
Faculty: Student/faculty ratio 12:1.

ACADEMICS

Degrees: Associate; Bachelor's; Certificate; Master's. **Classes:** Most classes have fewer than 10 students. **Special Study Options:** Accelerated program; Distance learning; Double major; External degree program; Independent study; Liberal arts/career combination; Student-designed major.

FACILITIES

100% of campus accessible to physically disabled. **Campus network:** 100% of classrooms, 100% of dorms, 100% of student union, 100% of libraries, 100% of dining areas, have wireless network access.

CAMPUS LIFE

Environment: Town. **Activities:** Student government.

ADMISSIONS

Freshman Admission Requirements: High school diploma or equivalent is not required. **Transfer Admission Requirements:** College transcript(s). Lowest grade transferable D. **General Admission Information:** Application fee $75. Priority deadline 7/1. Non-fall registration accepted. Admission may be deferred for a maximum of One 8-week term.

COSTS AND FINANCIAL AID

Required Forms and Deadlines: FAFSA. **Types of Aid:** *Need-based scholarships/grants:* College/university scholarship or grant aid from institutional funds; Federal Pell; Private scholarships; SEOG; State scholarships/grants. *Loans:* Direct PLUS loans; Direct Subsidized Stafford Loans; Direct Unsubsidized Stafford Loans. **Financial Aid Statistics:** 83% needy undergrads receive need-based scholarship or grant aid. 0% undergrads receive non-need-based scholarship or grant aid. 81% undergrads receive need-based self-help aid. 0% undergrads receive athletic scholarships.

CHATHAM UNIVERSITY

1 Woodland Road, Pittsburgh, PA 15232
Phone: 412-365-1825 **Financial Aid Phone:** 412-365-2797
E-mail: admission@chatham.edu **CEEB Code:** 2081
Fax: 412-365-1609 **Website:** www.chatham.edu **ACT Code:** 3538

This private school was founded in 1869. It has a 427 acre campus.

RATINGS

Admissions Selectivity Rating: 85   **Fire Safety Rating:** 84   **Green Rating:** 99

STUDENTS AND FACULTY

Enrollment: 1,152. **Student Body:** 71% female, 29% male, 23% out-of-state, 2% international (19 countries represented). Asian 3%, African American 5%, Caucasian 78%, Hispanic 5%, Native American 0%, Pacific Islander <1%, Two or more races 3%, Race unknown 4%.
Retention and Graduation: 80% freshmen return for sophomore year. 66% freshmen graduate within 4 years. 70% freshmen graduate within 6 years. 33% grads go on to further study within 1 year. 25% grads pursue arts and sciences degrees. 2% grads pursue law degrees. 2% grads pursue business degrees. 2% grads pursue medical degrees. **Faculty:** Student/faculty ratio 10:1. 126 full-time faculty, 90% hold PhDs, 10% are members of minority groups, 66% are women. 0% of classes are taught by teaching assistants.

ACADEMICS

Degrees: Bachelor's; Doctoral degree—professional practice; Master's; Post-bachelor's certificate. **Classes:** Most classes have 10–19 students. Most lab/discussion sessions have 10–19 students. **Most popular majors:** Biology/Biological Sciences, General; Exercise Science and Kinesiology; Psychology, General. **Special Study Options:** Accelerated program; Cooperative education program; Cross-registration; Distance learning; Double major; Dual enrollment; English as a Second Language (ESL); Exchange student program (domestic); Honors program; Independent study; Internships; Liberal arts/career combination; Student-designed major; Study abroad; Teacher certification program. **Honors programs:** The Chatham Scholars Program offers students a challenging, integrated curriculum with special opportunities for enrichment, mentoring, and networking. **Combined degree programs:** BA/MA. **Disability Services offered:** Note-taking services; Reader services; Tape recorders; Tutors. **Career services:** Alumni network; Alumni services; Career assessment; Career/job search classes; Internships; Regional alumni.

FACILITIES

Housing: Apartments for married students; Apartments for single students; Coed dorms; Special housing for disabled students; Special housing for international students; Theme housing; Women's dorms; 83% of campus accessible to physically disabled. **Special Academic Facilities/Equipment:** Athletic and Fitness Center; Art and Design Center; broadcast studio; art gallery, classroom space, and coffee shop; campus arboretum and greenhouse; proscenium theater.

CAMPUS LIFE

Environment: Metropolis. **Activities:** Campus Ministries; Choral groups; Drama/theater; International Student Organization; Literary magazine; Student government; Student newspaper; Symphony orchestra. 56 registered organizations, 10 honor societies, 4 religious organizations, on campus. **Athletics (Intercollegiate):** *Men:* baseball, basketball, cross-country, diving, ice hockey, lacrosse, soccer, squash, swimming, track/field (outdoor), track/field (indoor). *Women:* basketball, cross-country, ice hockey, soccer, softball, swimming, tennis, volleyball, water polo. **On-Campus Highlights:** Cafe Rachel coffee shop and art gallery. **Environmental Initiatives:** The creation of the Falk School of Sustainability and the Environment. The Falk School provides innovative, interdisciplinary education and research opportunities for undergraduate, graduate and professional students to better prepare them to identify and solve challenges related to the environment and sustainability. The school is located at Eden Hall Campus, on a 300-acre farm with forest. Phases 1A and B of the Master Plan are constructed, and our first group of residents is in place at Orchard Hall. The Eden Hall campus is designed to be a net-zero energy campus upon completion.

ADMISSIONS

Freshman Academic Profile: Average high school GPA 3.7. 24% in top 10% of high school class, 52% in top 25% of high school class, 84% in top 50% of high school class. **Test Scores:** SAT Math middle 50% range 520–620. SAT EBRW middle 50% range 530–650. ACT middle 50% range 23–28. **Basis for Candidate Selection:** *Very important factors include:* rigor of secondary school record. *Important factors include:* academic GPA, application essay, *Other factors include:* class rank, standardized test scores, recommendation(s), interview, extracurricular activities, talent/ability, character/personal qualities, first generation, alumni/ae relation, geographical residence, volunteer work, work experience, level of applicant's interest. **Freshman Admission Requirements:** High school diploma is required and GED is accepted. *Academic units required:* 4 English, 2 math, 2 science, 3 unit from above areas or other academic areas. *Academic units recommended:* 4 English, 3 math, 3 science, 2 foreign language, 3 social studies. **Freshman Admission Statistics:** 2,531 applied, 62% admitted, 20% enrolled. **Transfer Admission Requirements:** College transcript(s), essay or personal statement. Minimum college GPA of 2.0 required. Lowest grade transferable C-. **General Admission Information:** Application fee $35. Priority deadline 3/1. Regular application deadline 8/1. Non-fall registration accepted. Admission may be deferred for a maximum of 1 year.

COSTS AND FINANCIAL AID

Average book and supplies expense $1,000. **Required Forms and Deadlines:** FAFSA. **Notification of Awards:** Applicants will be notified of awards on a rolling basis beginning 12/1. **Types of Aid:** *Need-based scholarships/grants:* College/university scholarship or grant aid from institutional funds; Federal Pell; Private scholarships; SEOG; State scholarships/grants. *Loans:* Direct PLUS loans; Direct Subsidized Stafford Loans; Direct Unsubsidized Stafford Loans. **Student Employment:** Federal Work-Study Program available. Institutional employment available. **Financial Aid Statistics:** 94% needy freshmen, 85% needy undergrads receive need-based scholarship or grant aid. 100% freshmen, 100% undergrads receive non-need-based scholarship or grant aid. 94% freshmen, 86% undergrads receive need-based self-help aid. 0% freshmen, 0% undergrads receive athletic scholarships. 100% freshmen, 99% undergrads receive any aid. 76% undergrads borrow to pay for school. Average cumulative indebtedness $35,199. **Criteria awarding aid:** *Need-based:* Academics. *Non-need-based:* Academics, Alumni affiliation, Art, Music/drama.

CHESTNUT HILL COLLEGE

9601 Germantown Avenue, Philadelphia, PA 19118-2693
Phone: 215-248-7001 **Financial Aid Phone:** 215-248-7182
E-mail: chcapply@chc.edu **CEEB Code:** 2082
Fax: 215-248-7082 **Website:** www.chc.edu **ACT Code:** 3540

This private school, affiliated with the Roman Catholic Church, was founded in 1924. It has a 75 acre campus.

RATINGS

Admissions Selectivity Rating: 81 **Fire Safety Rating:** 91 **Green Rating:** 60*

STUDENTS AND FACULTY

Enrollment: 1,174. **Student Body:** 59% female, 41% male, 21% out-of-state, 3% international (23 countries represented). Asian 1%, African American 32%, Caucasian 40%, Hispanic 12%, Native American <1%, Pacific Islander <1%, Two or more races 4%, Race unknown 7%.
Retention and Graduation: 68% freshmen return for sophomore year. 47% freshmen graduate within 4 years. 56% freshmen graduate within 6 years. **Faculty:** Student/faculty ratio 9:1. 78 full-time faculty, 79% hold PhDs, 17% are members of minority groups, 65% are women. 0% of classes are taught by teaching assistants.

ACADEMICS

Degrees: Associate; Bachelor's; Certificate; Doctoral degree—professional practice; Master's; Post-bachelor's certificate; Post-master's certificate; Transfer Associate. **Classes:** Most classes have 10–19 students. Most lab/discussion sessions have 10–19 students. **Most popular majors:** Public Administration And Social Service Professions; Business Administration and Management, General; Psychology, General. **Special Study Options:** Cross-registration; Distance learning; Double major; Dual enrollment; English as a Second Language (ESL); Exchange student program (domestic); Honors program; Independent study; Internships; Student-designed major; Study abroad; Teacher certification program. **Honors programs:** Interdisciplinary Honors Program for outstanding incoming first year students offers team-taught interdisciplinary seminars which emphasize discussion and writing and which satisfy general education requirements. Departmental Honors challenges students in the junior and senior year to complete an independent research project in their major field. **Combined degree programs:** BA/MA. **Disability Services offered:** Reader services; Tutors. **Career services:** Alumni network; Career assessment; Career/job search classes; Internships.

FACILITIES

Housing: Apartments for single students; Coed dorms; 80% of campus accessible to physically disabled. **Special Academic Facilities/Equipment:** Rare book collection, Irish literature collection, Religion and Science book collection, observatory, planetarium.

CAMPUS LIFE

Environment: Metropolis. **Activities:** Campus Ministries; Choral groups; Concert band; Dance; Drama/theater; International Student Organization; Jazz band; Literary magazine; Music ensembles; Musical theater; Opera; Pep band; Radio station; Student government; Student newspaper; Student-run film society; Television station; Yearbook. 36 registered organizations, 19 honor societies, 1 religious organizations, on campus. **Athletics (Intercollegiate):** *Men:* baseball, basketball, cross-country, golf, lacrosse, soccer, tennis. *Women:* basketball, cross-country, golf, lacrosse, soccer, softball, tennis, volleyball. **On-Campus Highlights:** McCaffrey Lounge and Snack Bar. **Environmental Initiatives:** Recycling program.

ADMISSIONS

Freshman Academic Profile: Average high school GPA 3.2. 4% in top 10% of high school class, 22% in top 25% of high school class, 50% in top 50% of high school class. **Test Scores:** SAT Math middle 50% range 450–540. SAT EBRW middle 50% range 468–560. ACT middle 50% range 26–26. **Basis for Candidate Selection:** *Very important factors include:* academic GPA, standardized test scores. *Important factors include:* character/personal qualities, geographical residence, state residency, volunteer work. *Other factors include:* rigor of secondary school record, class rank, application essay, recommendation(s), interview, extracurricular activities, talent/ability, first generation, alumni/ae relation, level of applicant's interest. **Freshman Admission Requirements:** High school diploma is required and GED is accepted. *Academic units recommended:* 4 English, 3 math, 3 science, 2 foreign language, 4 social studies, 4 history. **Freshman Admission Statistics:** 1,440 applied, 65% admitted, 24% enrolled. **Transfer Admission Requirements:** College transcript(s), essay or personal statement. Minimum college GPA of 2.0 required. Lowest grade transferable C. **General Admission Information:** Application fee $35. Non-fall registration accepted. Admission may be deferred for a maximum of 1 year.

COSTS AND FINANCIAL AID

Annual tuition $37,950. Room and board $11,200. Required fees $320. Average book and supplies expense $1,400. **Required Forms and Deadlines:** Business/Farm Supplement; FAFSA; State aid form. **Notification of Awards:** Applicants will be notified of awards on a rolling basis beginning 10/1. **Types of Aid:** *Need-based scholarships/grants:* College/university scholarship or grant aid from institutional funds; Federal Pell; Private scholarships; SEOG; State scholarships/grants. *Loans:* Direct PLUS loans; Direct Subsidized Stafford Loans; Direct Unsubsidized Stafford Loans. **Student Employment:** Federal Work-Study Program available. Institutional employment available. **Financial Aid Statistics:** 84% needy freshmen, 80% needy undergrads receive need-based scholarship or grant aid. 98% freshmen, 81% undergrads receive non-need-based scholarship or grant aid. 100% freshmen, 99% undergrads receive need-based self-help aid. 6% freshmen, 6% undergrads receive athletic scholarships. 98% freshmen, 63% undergrads receive any aid. 88% undergrads borrow to pay for school. Average cumulative indebtedness $47,542. **Criteria awarding aid:** *Non-need-based:* Academics, Alumni affiliation, Athletics, Leadership, Music/drama.

CHEYNEY UNIVERSITY OF PENNSYLVANIA

1837 University Circle, Cheyney, PA 19319
Phone: 610-399-2275 **Financial Aid Phone:** (610) 399-2302
E-mail: abrown@cheyney.edu **CEEB Code:** 2648
Fax: 610-399-2099 **Website:** www.cheyney.edu

This public school was founded in 1837. It has a 275 acre campus.

RATINGS

Admissions Selectivity Rating: 83   Fire Safety Rating: 98   Green Rating: 60*

STUDENTS AND FACULTY

Enrollment: 1,339. **Student Body:** 53% female, 47% male, 22% out-of-state, <1% international (4 countries represented). Asian <1%, African American 92%, Caucasian 1%, Hispanic 1%, Native American <1%, Race unknown 6%. **Retention and Graduation:** 60% freshmen return for sophomore year. **Faculty:** Student/faculty ratio 15:1. 75 full-time faculty, 0% hold PhDs, 79% are members of minority groups, 48% are women. 0% of classes are taught by teaching assistants.

ACADEMICS

Degrees: Associate; Bachelor's; Master's; Post-bachelor's certificate. **Most popular majors:** Business Administration and Management, General; Social Sciences, General; Speech Communication and Rhetoric. **Special Study Options:** Cooperative education program; Cross-registration; Distance learning; Double major; Honors program; Independent study; Internships; Study abroad; Teacher certification program. **Honors programs:** Keystone Honors Program. **Disability Services offered:** Note-taking services; Tape recorders; Tutors. **Career services:** Alumni services; Career/job search classes; Internships.

FACILITIES

Housing: Coed dorms; Men's dorms; Women's dorms; 60% of campus accessible to physically disabled. **Special Academic Facilities/Equipment:** Afro-American history/culture collection, planetarium, weather station, satellite communication network.

CAMPUS LIFE

Environment: Village. **Activities:** Choral groups; Drama/theater; Jazz band; Marching band; Music ensembles; Radio station; Student government; Student newspaper; Student-run film society; Television station; Yearbook. 30 registered organizations, 12 honor societies, 1 religious organizations, 5 fraternities, 4 sororities, on campus. **Athletics (Intercollegiate):** *Men:* basketball, cross-country, football, tennis, track/field (outdoor), wrestling. *Women:* basketball, bowling, cross-country, tennis, track/field (outdoor), volleyball. **On-Campus Highlights:** Athletics. **Environmental Initiatives:** Recycling.

ADMISSIONS

Freshman Academic Profile: Average high school GPA 2.4. 6% in top 10% of high school class, 15% in top 25% of high school class, 46% in top 50%

---

of high school class. **Test Scores:** SAT Math middle 50% range 320–410. SAT EBRW middle 50% range 330–420. ACT middle 50% range 14–21. **Basis for Candidate Selection:** *Very important factors include:* rigor of secondary school record, recommendation(s). *Important factors include:* class rank, application essay, standardized test scores, interview, extracurricular activities, state residency. *Other factors include:* talent/ability, racial/ethnic status. **Freshman Admission Requirements:** High school diploma is required and GED is accepted. *Academic units required:* 4 English, 3 math, 2 science, 2 foreign language, 2 history. **Freshman Admission Statistics:** 3,298 applied, 50% admitted, 37% enrolled. **Transfer Admission Requirements:** College transcript(s), interview, statement of good standing from prior institution(s). Minimum college GPA of 2.0 required. Lowest grade transferable C. **General Admission Information:** Application fee $20. Priority deadline 6/15. Regular application deadline 3/31. Non-fall registration accepted. Admission may be deferred for a maximum of 1 year.

COSTS AND FINANCIAL AID

Required Forms and Deadlines: FAFSA. **Notification of Awards:** Applicants will be notified of awards on a rolling basis beginning 3/15. **Types of Aid:** *Need-based scholarships/grants:* College/university scholarship or grant aid from institutional funds; Federal Pell; Private scholarships; SEOG; State scholarships/grants. **Student Employment:** Federal Work-Study Program available. Institutional employment available. **Financial Aid Statistics:** 82% needy freshmen, 94% needy undergrads receive need-based scholarship or grant aid. 30% freshmen, 37% undergrads receive non-need-based scholarship or grant aid. 79% freshmen, 95% undergrads receive need-based self-help aid. 0% freshmen, 0% undergrads receive athletic scholarships. **Criteria awarding aid:** *Need-based:* Academics, Alumni affiliation, Athletics, Minority status. *Non-need-based:* Academics, Alumni affiliation, Athletics, Minority status.

CHRISTENDOM COLLEGE

134 Christendom Drive, Front Royal, VA 22630
Phone: 540-636-2900 **Financial Aid Phone:** 800-877-5456
E-mail: admissions@christendom.edu **CEEB Code:** 5691
Fax: 540-636-1655 **Website:** www.christendom.edu **ACT Code:** 4339

This private school, affiliated with the Roman Catholic Church, was founded in 1977. It has a 200 acre campus.

RATINGS

Admissions Selectivity Rating: 79   Fire Safety Rating: 62   Green Rating: 60*

STUDENTS AND FACULTY

Enrollment: 493. **Student Body:** 55% female, 45% male, 63% out-of-state, 100% international (4 countries represented). Asian 0%, African American 0%, Caucasian 0%, Hispanic 0%, Native American 0%, Pacific Islander 0%, Two or more races 0%, Race unknown 0%. **Retention and Graduation:** 90% freshmen return for sophomore year. 18% grads go on to further study within 1 year. 0% grads pursue medical degrees. **Faculty:** Student/faculty ratio 14:1. 29 full-time faculty, 90% hold PhDs, 0% are members of minority groups, 14% are women. 0% of classes are taught by teaching assistants.

ACADEMICS

Degrees: Associate; Bachelor's; Master's. **Classes:** Most classes have 20–29 students. **Most popular majors:** Philosophy; Political Science and Government, General; History, General. **Special Study Options:** Double major; Honors program; Independent study; Internships; Study abroad. **Honors programs:** Advanced Studies program. **Career services:** Alumni network; Career assessment; Internships.

FACILITIES

Housing: Men's dorms; Women's dorms.

CAMPUS LIFE

Environment: Rural. **Activities:** Campus Ministries; Choral groups; Dance; Drama/theater; Literary magazine; Music ensembles; Musical theater; Radio station; Student government; Student newspaper; Student-run film society; Yearbook. 5 registered organizations, 4 religious organizations, on campus. **Athletics (Intercollegiate):** *Men:* baseball, basketball, soccer. *Women:* basketball, soccer, softball, volleyball. **On-Campus Highlights:** St. John the Evangelist Library.

ADMISSIONS

Freshman Academic Profile: Average high school GPA 3.7. 8% from public high schools. **Test Scores:** SAT Math middle 50% range 550–670. SAT EBRW middle 50% range 610–690. ACT middle 50% range 25–29. **Basis for Candidate Selection:** *Very important factors include:* academic GPA, application essay, standardized test scores, recommendation(s), character/personal qualities, level of applicant's interest. *Important factors include:* rigor of secondary school record, religious affiliation/commitment. *Other factors include:* class rank, interview, extracurricular activities, talent/ability, alumni/ae relation, volunteer work, work experience. **Freshman Admission Requirements:** High school diploma or equivalent is not required. *Academic units recommended:* 4 English, 2 math, 2 science, 2 foreign language, 1 social studies, 2 history, 1 academic electives. **Freshman Admission Statistics:** 392 applied, 91% admitted, 47% enrolled. **Transfer Admission Requirements:** College transcript(s), essay or personal statement. Minimum college GPA of 2.8 required. Lowest grade transferable C. **General Admission Information:** Application fee $25. Priority deadline 3/1. Non-fall registration accepted.

COSTS AND FINANCIAL AID

Annual tuition $27,000. Room and board $11,250. Required fees $980. Average book and supplies expense $750. **Required Forms and Deadlines:** Institution's own financial aid form. **Notification of Awards:** Applicants will be notified of awards on a rolling basis beginning 1/15. **Types of Aid:** *Need-based scholarships/grants:* College/university scholarship or grant aid from institutional funds; Private scholarships. **Student Employment:** Institutional employment available. **Financial Aid Statistics:** 100% needy freshmen, 99% needy undergrads receive need-based scholarship or grant aid. 11% freshmen, 4% undergrads receive non-need-based scholarship or grant aid. 66% freshmen, 77% undergrads receive need-based self-help aid. 0% freshmen, 0% undergrads receive athletic scholarships. 80% freshmen, 65% undergrads receive any aid. 68% undergrads borrow to pay for school. Average cumulative indebtedness $32,750. **Criteria awarding aid:** *Non-need-based:* Academics.

CHRISTIAN BROTHERS UNIVERSITY

Admissions, Box T-6, Memphis, TN 38104-5519
Phone: 901-321-3205 **Financial Aid Phone:** 901-321-3306
E-mail: admissions@cbu.edu **CEEB Code:** 1121
Fax: 901-321-3202 **Website:** www.cbu.edu **ACT Code:** 3952

This private school, affiliated with the Roman Catholic Church, was founded in 1871. It has a 75 acre campus.

RATINGS

Admissions Selectivity Rating: 87   **Fire Safety Rating:** 63   **Green Rating:** 68

STUDENTS AND FACULTY

Enrollment: 1,521. **Student Body:** 53% female, 47% male, 20% out-of-state, 3% international (22 countries represented). Asian 5%, African American 27%, Caucasian 40%, Hispanic 9%, Native American 1%, Pacific Islander 0%, Two or more races 3%, Race unknown 12%.
Retention and Graduation: 80% freshmen return for sophomore year. 25% freshmen graduate within 4 years. 23% grads go on to further study within 1 year. 5% grads pursue arts and sciences degrees. 4% grads pursue law degrees. 5% grads pursue business degrees. 6% grads pursue medical degrees. **Faculty:** Student/faculty ratio 10:1. 104 full-time faculty, 88% hold PhDs, 12% are members of minority groups, 38% are women. 0% of classes are taught by teaching assistants.

ACADEMICS

Degrees: Associate; Bachelor's; Master's. **Classes:** Most classes have 10–19 students. Most lab/discussion sessions have 10–19 students. **Most popular majors:** Accounting and Related Services; Biology/Biological Sciences, General; Psychology, General. **Special Study Options:** Accelerated program; Distance learning; Double major; Dual enrollment; Honors program; Independent study; Internships; Student-designed major; Study abroad; Teacher certification program. **Honors programs:** The Honors Program at Christian Brothers University is designed to serve the capacities and needs of students with proven academic abilities who seek a more intensive and challenging educational experience. Students accepted into the Honors Program will be allowed each semester to take at least one special-topics course offered only to a limited number of Honors students by an instructor carefully chosen for his or her teaching expertise. These Honors courses will explore important topics in

depth, often through a multi-disciplinary approach, and while the pace and the workload will demand self-motivated students, the small size of each Honors class will insure ample group discussion and individual interaction with the instructor. Besides taking honors classes, members of the Honors Program will participate in various extra-curricular activities, including outings to cultural events and regional honors conferences. **Disability Services offered:** Note-taking services; Reader services; Tape recorders; Tutors. **Career services:** Alumni network; Alumni services; Career assessment; Career/job search classes; Internships.

FACILITIES

Housing: Apartments for single students; Coed dorms; Men's dorms; Theme housing; Women's dorms. **Special Academic Facilities/Equipment:** Art exhibits and gallery, audiovisual lab, MAC graphics lab, engineering graphics lab, Facing History and Ourselves.

CAMPUS LIFE

Environment: Metropolis. **Activities:** Campus Ministries; Choral groups; Drama/theater; International Student Organization; Literary magazine; Student government. 41 registered organizations, 6 honor societies, 1 religious organizations, 6 fraternities, 4 sororities, on campus. **Athletics (Intercollegiate):** *Men:* baseball, basketball, cross-country, golf, soccer, tennis. *Women:* basketball, cross-country, golf, soccer, softball, tennis, volleyball. **On-Campus Highlights:** Thomas Center (cafeteria, snack bar). **Environmental Initiatives:** Building a new "green" dorm that has 90+ beds.

ADMISSIONS

Freshman Academic Profile: Average high school GPA 3.7. 28% in top 10% of high school class, 60% in top 25% of high school class, 93% in top 50% of high school class. 69% from public high schools. **Test Scores:** ACT middle 50% range 21–27. **Basis for Candidate Selection:** *Very important factors include:* rigor of secondary school record, academic GPA, standardized test scores. *Important factors include:* class rank, application essay, recommendation(s), interview, extracurricular activities, talent/ability, alumni/ae relation, volunteer work. **Freshman Admission Requirements:** High school diploma is required and GED is accepted. *Academic units recommended:* 4 English, 4 math, 4 science. **Freshman Admission Statistics:** 2,229 applied, 50% admitted, 32% enrolled. **Transfer Admission Requirements:** College transcript(s). Minimum college GPA of 2.5 required. Lowest grade transferable C. **General Admission Information:** Application fee $25. Priority deadline 12/1. Non-fall registration accepted. Admission may be deferred for a maximum of 1 year.

COSTS AND FINANCIAL AID

Annual tuition $29,316. Room and board $7,000. Average book and supplies expense $1,000. **Required Forms and Deadlines:** FAFSA. **Notification of Awards:** Applicants will be notified of awards on a rolling basis beginning 3/1. **Types of Aid:** *Need-based scholarships/grants:* College/university scholarship or grant aid from institutional funds; Federal Pell; Private scholarships; SEOG; State scholarships/grants. *Loans:* Direct PLUS loans; Direct Subsidized Stafford Loans; Direct Unsubsidized Stafford Loans. **Student Employment:** Federal Work-Study Program available. Institutional employment available. **Financial Aid Statistics:** 100% needy freshmen, 98% needy undergrads receive need-based scholarship or grant aid. 17% freshmen, 15% undergrads receive non-need-based scholarship or grant aid. 70% freshmen, 75% undergrads receive need-based self-help aid. 17% freshmen, 11% undergrads receive athletic scholarships. **Criteria awarding aid:** *Need-based:* Minority status. *Non-need-based:* Academics, Alumni affiliation, Athletics, Leadership, Music/drama, State/district residency.

CHRISTOPHER NEWPORT UNIVERSITY

1 Avenue of the Arts, Newport News, VA 23606-3072
Phone: 757-594-7015 **Financial Aid Phone:** 757-594-7170
E-mail: admit@cnu.edu **CEEB Code:** 5128
Fax: 757-594-7333 **Website:** www.cnu.edu **ACT Code:** 4345

This public school was founded in 1960. It has a 260 acre campus.

RATINGS
Admissions Selectivity Rating: 83   **Fire Safety Rating:** 93   **Green Rating:** 60*

STUDENTS AND FACULTY
Enrollment: 4,826. **Student Body:** 55% female, 45% male, 8% out-of-state, <1% international (35 countries represented). Asian 3%, African American 6%, Caucasian 77%, Hispanic 6%, Native American <1%, Pacific Islander <1%, Two or more races 5%, Race unknown 2%.
Retention and Graduation: 84% freshmen return for sophomore year. 68% freshmen graduate within 4 years. 78% freshmen graduate within 6 years.
Faculty: Student/faculty ratio 14:1. 291 full-time faculty, 93% hold PhDs, 13% are members of minority groups, 43% are women. 0% of classes are taught by teaching assistants.

ACADEMICS
Degrees: Bachelor's; Master's. **Classes:** Most classes have 10–19 students. **Most popular majors:** Cell/Cellular and Molecular Biology; Psychology, General; Speech Communication and Rhetoric. **Special Study Options:** Cross-registration; Double major; Dual enrollment; Honors program; Independent study; Internships; Student-designed major; Study abroad. **Honors programs:** The CNU Honors Program invites high-ability students to fashion unique academic programs to prepare for post-graduate success. **Disability Services offered:** Note-taking services; Tape recorders; Tutors. **Career services:** Alumni network; Alumni services; Career assessment; Career/job search classes; Internships; Regional alumni.

FACILITIES
Housing: Apartments for single students; Coed dorms; Fraternity/sorority housing; Theme housing; 96% of campus accessible to physically disabled. **Special Academic Facilities/Equipment:** Falk Art Gallery, The Freeman Center, The Ferguson Center for the Arts, Trible Library. **Campus network:** 20% of classrooms, 100% of libraries, 100% of dining areas, 20% of common outdoor areas, have wireless network access.

CAMPUS LIFE
Environment: City. **Activities:** Campus Ministries; Choral groups; Concert band; Dance; Drama/theater; International Student Organization; Jazz band; Literary magazine; Marching band; Model UN; Music ensembles; Musical theater; Opera; Pep band; Radio station; Student government; Student newspaper; Symphony orchestra; Television station. 192 registered organizations, 30 honor societies, 13 religious organizations, 11 fraternities, 9 sororities, on campus. **Athletics (Intercollegiate):** *Men:* baseball, basketball, cheerleading, cross-country, football, golf, lacrosse, sailing, soccer, tennis, track/field (outdoor), track/field (indoor). *Women:* basketball, cheerleading, cross-country, field hockey, lacrosse, sailing, soccer, softball, tennis, track/field (outdoor), track/field (indoor), volleyball. **On-Campus Highlights:** Trible Library.

ADMISSIONS
Freshman Academic Profile: Average high school GPA 3.8. 16% in top 10% of high school class, 48% in top 25% of high school class, 87% in top 50% of high school class. 80% from public high schools. **Test Scores:** SAT Math middle 50% range 540–630. SAT EBRW middle 50% range 570–650. ACT middle 50% range 22–27. **Basis for Candidate Selection:** *Very important factors include:* rigor of secondary school record, academic GPA. *Important factors include:* class rank, application essay, standardized test scores, recommendation(s), interview, extracurricular activities, talent/ability, character/personal qualities. *Other factors include:* first generation, alumni/ae relation, geographical residence, state residency, volunteer work, work experience. **Freshman Admission Requirements:** High school diploma is required and GED is not accepted. *Academic units required:* 4 English, 4 math, 4 science, 4 science labs, 3 foreign language, 4 social studies, 2 academic electives, 1 visual/

performing arts, 4 unit from above areas or other academic areas. *Academic units recommended:* 4 English, 4 math, 4 science, 4 science labs, 3 foreign language, 4 social studies, 2 academic electives, 1 visual/performing arts. **Freshman Admission Statistics:** 7,204 applied, 72% admitted, 24% enrolled. **Transfer Admission Requirements:** High school transcript, college transcript(s), statement of good standing from prior institution(s). Minimum college GPA of 3.0 required. Lowest grade transferable C. **General Admission Information:** Application fee $65. Priority deadline 2/1. Regular application deadline 2/1. Non-fall registration accepted. Admission may be deferred for a maximum of 12 months.

COSTS AND FINANCIAL AID
Required Forms and Deadlines: FAFSA. **Notification of Awards:** Applicants will be notified of awards on a rolling basis beginning 3/1. **Types of Aid:** *Need-based scholarships/grants:* College/university scholarship or grant aid from institutional funds; Federal Pell; Private scholarships; SEOG; State scholarships/grants. *Loans:* Direct PLUS loans; Direct Subsidized Stafford Loans; Direct Unsubsidized Stafford Loans. **Student Employment:** Federal Work-Study Program available. Institutional employment available. **Financial Aid Statistics:** 72% needy freshmen, 69% needy undergrads receive need-based scholarship or grant aid. 41% freshmen, 34% undergrads receive non-need-based scholarship or grant aid. 69% freshmen, 81% undergrads receive need-based self-help aid. 0% freshmen, 0% undergrads receive athletic scholarships. 74% freshmen, 69% undergrads receive any aid. 61% undergrads borrow to pay for school. Average cumulative indebtedness $32,878. **Criteria awarding aid:** *Need-based:* Academics, Leadership. *Non-need-based:* Academics, Alumni affiliation, Art, Leadership, Music/drama, State/district residency.

THE CITADEL, THE MILITARY COLLEGE OF SOUTH CAROLINA

171 Moultrie Street, Charleston, SC 29409
Phone: 843-953-5230 **Financial Aid Phone:** 843-953-5187
E-mail: admissions@citadel.edu **CEEB Code:** 5108
Fax: 843-953-7036 **Website:** www.citadel.edu **ACT Code:** 3838

This public school was founded in 1842. It has a 300 acre campus.

RATINGS
Admissions Selectivity Rating: 81   **Fire Safety Rating:** 97   **Green Rating:** 66

STUDENTS AND FACULTY
Enrollment: 2,905. **Student Body:** 13% female, 87% male, 33% out-of-state, 1% international (9 countries represented). Asian 2%, African American 7%, Caucasian 76%, Hispanic 7%, Native American <1%, Pacific Islander <1%, Two or more races 5%, Race unknown 1%.
Retention and Graduation: 86% freshmen return for sophomore year. 63% freshmen graduate within 4 years. **Faculty:** Student/faculty ratio 12:1. 204 full-time faculty, 94% hold PhDs, 16% are members of minority groups, 36% are women. 0% of classes are taught by teaching assistants.

ACADEMICS
Degrees: Bachelor's; Master's; Post-bachelor's certificate; Post-master's certificate. **Classes:** Most classes have 20–29 students. Most lab/discussion sessions have 10–19 students. **Most popular majors:** Criminal Justice/Law Enforcement Administration; Business Administration and Management, General; Mechanical Engineering. **Special Study Options:** Cooperative education program; Distance learning; Double major; English as a Second Language (ESL); Honors program; Independent study; Internships; Study abroad; Teacher certification program. **Honors programs:** The Citadel Honors Program is a specially designed educational experience meeting the needs of students with an outstanding record of academic achievement and a sense of intellectual adventure. While pursuing majors and minors within any of the degree programs offered by The Citadel, Honors Students have the opportunity to participate in engaging Honors Program courses. These courses are both Citadel General Education Core Curriculum classes--for example, studies based in literature and writing, history, social science, and mathematics-- as well as Honors Program special topics and research. **Disability Services offered:** Note-taking services; Tape recorders. **Career services:** Alumni services; Career assessment; Career/job search classes; Internships.

FACILITIES
Housing: Coed dorms. **Special Academic Facilities/Equipment:** The Citadel Museum. **Campus network:** 10% of classrooms, 0% of dorms, 100% of

student union, 100% of libraries, 100% of dining areas, 0% of common outdoor areas, have wireless network access.

CAMPUS LIFE

Environment: City. **Activities:** Campus Ministries; Choral groups; Concert band; International Student Organization; Literary magazine; Marching band; Pep band; Student government; Student newspaper; Yearbook. 95 registered organizations, 9 honor societies, 15 religious organizations, on campus. **Athletics (Intercollegiate):** *Men:* baseball, basketball, cross-country, football, riflery, tennis, track/field (outdoor), track/field (indoor), wrestling. *Women:* cross-country, golf, riflery, soccer, track/field (outdoor), track/field (indoor), volleyball. **On-Campus Highlights:** Summerall Chapel.

ADMISSIONS

Freshman Academic Profile: Average high school GPA 3.8. 11% in top 10% of high school class, 31% in top 25% of high school class, 71% in top 50% of high school class. **Test Scores:** SAT Math middle 50% range 520–610. SAT EBRW middle 50% range 530–620. ACT middle 50% range 20–25. **Basis for Candidate Selection:** *Very important factors include:* rigor of secondary school record, academic GPA, standardized test scores, level of applicant's interest. *Important factors include:* extracurricular activities, talent/ability, character/personal qualities, state residency. *Other factors include:* class rank, recommendation(s), interview, first generation, alumni/ae relation, geographical residence, volunteer work. **Freshman Admission Requirements:** High school diploma is required and GED is accepted. *Academic units required:* 4 English, 4 math, 3 science, 3 science labs, 2 foreign language, 2 social studies, 1 history, 1 academic electives, 1 visual/performing arts, 1 unit from above areas or other academic areas. **Freshman Admission Statistics:** 2,742 applied, 75% admitted, 31% enrolled. **Transfer Admission Requirements:** High school transcript, college transcript(s), standardized test scores, statement of good standing from prior institution(s). Minimum college GPA of 2.0 required. Lowest grade transferable C. **General Admission Information:** Application fee $40.

COSTS AND FINANCIAL AID

Annual in-state tuition $14,643. Annual out-of-state tuition $38,528. Room and board $7,957. Average book and supplies expense $8,144. **Required Forms and Deadlines:** FAFSA. **Notification of Awards:** Applicants will be notified of awards on a rolling basis beginning 4/1. **Types of Aid:** *Need-based scholarships/grants:* College/university scholarship or grant aid from institutional funds; Federal Pell; Private scholarships; SEOG; State scholarships/grants. *Loans:* Direct PLUS loans; Direct Subsidized Stafford Loans; Direct Unsubsidized Stafford Loans. **Student Employment:** Federal Work-Study Program available. Institutional employment available. **Financial Aid Statistics:** 85% needy freshmen, 84% needy undergrads receive need-based scholarship or grant aid. 18% freshmen, 22% undergrads receive non-need-based scholarship or grant aid. 71% freshmen, 71% undergrads receive need-based self-help aid. 12% freshmen, 11% undergrads receive athletic scholarships. 93.6% freshmen, 86.6% undergrads receive any aid. 60% undergrads borrow to pay for school. Average cumulative indebtedness $28,159. **Criteria awarding aid:** *Need-based:* Academics, Alumni affiliation, Leadership, Minority status, Religious affiliation. *Non-need-based:* Academics, Alumni affiliation, Athletics, Leadership, Minority status, Music/drama, Religious affiliation, State/district residency.

CITY UNIVERSITY OF NEW YORK—BARUCH COLLEGE

One Bernard Baruch Way, New York, NY 10010
Phone: 646-312-1400 **Financial Aid Phone:** 646-312-1390
E-mail: admissions@baruch.cuny.edu **CEEB Code:** 2034
Fax: 646-312-1361 **Website:** www.baruch.cuny.edu

This public school was founded in 1909. It has a 3.5 acre campus.

RATINGS

Admissions Selectivity Rating: 91   **Fire Safety Rating:** 60*   **Green Rating:** 60*

STUDENTS AND FACULTY

Enrollment: 14,629. **Student Body:** 48% female, 52% male, 3% out-of-state, 11% international (168 countries represented). Asian 32%, African American 9%, Caucasian 20%, Hispanic 26%, Native American <1%, Pacific Islander <1%, Two or more races 1%, Race unknown 0%.

Retention and Graduation: 89% freshmen return for sophomore year. 41% freshmen graduate within 4 years. 70% freshmen graduate within 6 years. **Faculty:** Student/faculty ratio 18:1. 493 full-time faculty, 92% hold PhDs, 30% are members of minority groups, 39% are women.

ACADEMICS

Degrees: Bachelor's; Master's; Post-master's certificate. **Classes:** Most classes have 20–29 students. Most lab/discussion sessions have 10–19 students. **Most popular majors:** Accounting; Finance, General. **Special Study Options:** Accelerated program; Cross-registration; Distance learning; Double major; English as a Second Language (ESL); Exchange student program (domestic); Honors program; Independent study; Internships; Liberal arts/career combination; Student-designed major; Study abroad. **Honors programs:** Macaulay Honors College, Baruch Scholar Dean's Scholar. **Combined degree programs:** BA/MA. **Disability Services offered:** Note-taking services; Reader services; Tape recorders; Tutors. **Career services:** Alumni network; Alumni services; Career assessment; Career/job search classes; Internships.

FACILITIES

Housing: Coed dorms; 100% of campus accessible to physically disabled. **Special Academic Facilities/Equipment:** Art gallery, Subotnik Financial Services Center and Wasserman Trading Floor. **Campus network:** 100% of classrooms, 100% of dorms, 100% of student union, 100% of libraries, 100% of dining areas, 100% of common outdoor areas, have wireless network access.

CAMPUS LIFE

Environment: Metropolis. **Activities:** Campus Ministries; Choral groups; Dance; Drama/theater; Literary magazine; Model UN; Musical theater; Radio station; Student government; Student newspaper; Yearbook. 120 registered organizations, 9 honor societies, 7 religious organizations, on campus. **Athletics (Intercollegiate):** *Men:* baseball, basketball, cross-country, soccer, swimming, tennis, volleyball. *Women:* basketball, cheerleading, cross-country, softball, swimming, tennis, volleyball. **On-Campus Highlights:** Student Club Area-Vertical Campus Build.

ADMISSIONS

Freshman Academic Profile: Average high school GPA 3.3. 50% in top 10% of high school class, 77% in top 25% of high school class, 95% in top 50% of high school class. 90% from public high schools. **Test Scores:** SAT Math middle 50% range 630–720. SAT EBRW middle 50% range 590–670. **Basis for Candidate Selection:** *Very important factors include:* rigor of secondary school record, academic GPA, standardized test scores. *Important factors include:* application essay, recommendation(s). *Other factors include:* interview, extracurricular activities, talent/ability, character/personal qualities, work experience. **Freshman Admission Requirements:** High school diploma is required and GED is accepted. *Academic units required:* 4 English, 3 math, 2 science, 2 science labs, 2 foreign language, 4 social studies. *Academic units recommended:* 2 foreign language, 1 academic electives. **Freshman Admission Statistics:** 21,469 applied, 39% admitted, 20% enrolled. **Transfer Admission Requirements:** High school transcript, college transcript(s), statement of good standing from prior institution(s). Minimum college GPA of 2.7 required. Lowest grade transferable C. **General Admission Information:** Application fee $65. Priority deadline 12/1. Regular application deadline 2/1. Non-fall registration accepted.

COSTS AND FINANCIAL AID

Annual in-state tuition $6,930. Annual out-of-state tuition $18,600. Room and board $12,880. Required fees $531. Average book and supplies expense $1,364. **Required Forms and Deadlines:** FAFSA; State aid form. **Notification of Awards:** Applicants will be notified of awards on a rolling basis beginning 4/15. **Types of Aid:** *Need-based scholarships/grants:* College/university scholarship or grant aid from institutional funds; Federal Pell; Private scholarships; SEOG; State scholarships/grants. *Loans:* Direct PLUS loans; Direct Subsidized Stafford Loans; Direct Unsubsidized Stafford Loans. **Student Employment:** Federal Work-Study Program available. Institutional employment available. **Financial Aid Statistics:** 96% needy freshmen, 92% needy undergrads receive need-based scholarship or grant aid. 1% freshmen, 2% undergrads receive non-need-based scholarship or grant aid. 13% freshmen, 21% undergrads receive need-based self-help aid. 0% freshmen, 0% undergrads receive athletic scholarships. 64% freshmen, 62% undergrads receive any aid. 13% undergrads borrow to pay for school. Average cumulative indebtedness $9,182. **Criteria awarding aid:** *Need-based:* Academics. *Non-need-based:* Academics, State/district residency.

CITY UNIVERSITY OF NEW YORK—BROOKLYN COLLEGE

2900 Bedford Avenue, Brooklyn, NY 11210
Phone: 718-951-5001 **Financial Aid Phone:** 718-951-51
Fax: 718-951-4506 **Website:** www.brooklyn.cuny.edu **ACT Code:** 20169

This public school was founded in 1930. It has a 35 acre campus.

RATINGS
Admissions Selectivity Rating: 90   **Fire Safety Rating:** 60*   **Green Rating:** 80

STUDENTS AND FACULTY
Enrollment: 13,953. **Student Body:** 57% female, 43% male, 2% out-of-state, 3% international. Asian 21%, African American 20%, Caucasian 28%, Hispanic 25%, Native American <1%, Pacific Islander <1%, Two or more races 2%, Race unknown 0%. **Retention and Graduation:** 80% freshmen return for sophomore year. 27% freshmen graduate within 4 years. 54% freshmen graduate within 6 years. **Faculty:** Student/faculty ratio 18:1. 504 full-time faculty, 92% hold PhDs, 27% are members of minority groups, 46% are women.

ACADEMICS
Degrees: Bachelor's; Certificate; Master's; Post-bachelor's certificate; Post-master's certificate. **Classes:** Most classes have 20–29 students. **Most popular majors:** Accounting; Computer and Information Sciences, General; Psychology, General. **Special Study Options:** Accelerated program; Distance learning; Double major; Dual enrollment; English as a Second Language (ESL); Honors program; Independent study; Internships; Liberal arts/career combination; Study abroad; Teacher certification program; Weekend college. **Honors programs:** See the URL for more information: http://www.brooklyn.cuny.edu/pub/1654.htm. **Combined degree programs:** BA/MD. **Disability Services offered:** Note-taking services; Reader services; Tutors. **Career services:** Alumni network; Alumni services; Career assessment; Career/job search classes; Internships.

FACILITIES
100% of campus accessible to physically disabled. **Special Academic Facilities/Equipment:** Art museum. language lab, TV studios, speech clinic, research centers and institutes, particle accelerator, physical education and exercise labs, archeology labs, aquatic research center, theaters, music and art studios.

CAMPUS LIFE
Environment: Metropolis. **Activities:** Dance; Drama/theater; International Student Organization; Literary magazine; Music ensembles; Musical theater; Radio station; Student government; Student newspaper; Student-run film society; Symphony orchestra; Television station; Yearbook. 171 registered organizations, 7 honor societies, 7 fraternities, 9 sororities, on campus. **Athletics (Intercollegiate):** *Men:* basketball, cross-country, soccer, tennis, track/field (outdoor), track/field (indoor), volleyball. *Women:* basketball, cross-country, softball, tennis, track/field (outdoor), track/field (indoor), volleyball. **On-Campus Highlights:** Library. **Environmental Initiatives:** The Center for the Performing Arts is the first LEED-certified, sustainable building on the campus incorporating low water-use toilets, recycled materials and highly efficient HVAC and lighting systems.

ADMISSIONS
Freshman Academic Profile: Average high school GPA 3.3. **Test Scores:** SAT Math middle 50% range 530–620. SAT EBRW middle 50% range 510–600. **Basis for Candidate Selection:** *Very important factors include:* rigor of secondary school record, academic GPA, standardized test scores. **Freshman Admission Requirements:** High school diploma is required and GED is accepted. *Academic units recommended:* 4 English, 3 math, 3 science, 3 foreign language, 4 social studies, 4 academic electives. **Freshman Admission Statistics:** 135,973 applied, 9% admitted, 16% enrolled. **Transfer Admission Requirements:** College transcript(s). Minimum college GPA of 2.3 required. Lowest grade transferable C-. **General Admission Information:** Application fee $65. Priority deadline 2/1. Non-fall registration accepted.

COSTS AND FINANCIAL AID
Annual in-state tuition $6,930. Annual out-of-state tuition $18,600. Required fees $510. **Required Forms and Deadlines:** FAFSA; State aid form. **Notification of Awards:** Applicants will be notified of awards on a rolling basis beginning 5/1. **Types of Aid:** *Need-based scholarships/grants:* College/university scholarship or grant aid from institutional funds; Federal Pell; Private scholarships; SEOG; State scholarships/grants. *Loans:* Direct PLUS loans; Direct Subsidized Stafford Loans; Direct Unsubsidized Stafford Loans. **Student Employment:** Federal Work-Study Program available. Institutional employment available. **Financial Aid Statistics:** 80% needy freshmen, 86% needy undergrads receive need-based scholarship or grant aid. 57% freshmen, 27% undergrads receive non-need-based scholarship or grant aid. 11% freshmen, 29% undergrads receive need-based self-help aid. 0% freshmen, 0% undergrads receive athletic scholarships. 14% undergrads borrow to pay for school. Average cumulative indebtedness $12,587. **Criteria awarding aid:** *Non-need-based:* Academics, Art, Leadership, Music/drama, State/district residency.

CITY UNIVERSITY OF NEW YORK—CITY COLLEGE

160 Convent Avenue, Wille Admin. Bldg., New York, NY 10031
Phone: 212-650-6977 **Financial Aid Phone:** 212-650-5824
E-mail: admissions@ccny.cuny.edu **CEEB Code:** 2083
Fax: 212 650 6417 **Website:** www.ccny.cuny.edu **ACT Code:** 2950

This public school was founded in 1847. It has a 36 acre campus.

RATINGS
Admissions Selectivity Rating: 87   **Fire Safety Rating:** 97   **Green Rating:** 95

STUDENTS AND FACULTY
Enrollment: 12,359. **Student Body:** 52% female, 48% male, 4% out-of-state, 7% international (155 countries represented). Asian 22%, African American 16%, Caucasian 17%, Hispanic 36%, Native American <1%, Pacific Islander <1%, Two or more races 2%, Race unknown 0%. **Retention and Graduation:** 92% freshmen return for sophomore year. 5% freshmen graduate within 4 years. 48% freshmen graduate within 6 years. 18% grads go on to further study within 1 year. 1% grads pursue law degrees. 2% grads pursue business degrees. 27% grads pursue medical degrees. **Faculty:** Student/faculty ratio 12:1. 573 full-time faculty, 83% hold PhDs, 35% are members of minority groups, 39% are women.

ACADEMICS
Degrees: Bachelor's; Doctoral degree—professional practice; Doctoral degree research/scholarship; Master's; Post-master's certificate. **Classes:** Most classes have 20–29 students. Most lab/discussion sessions have 10–19 students. **Most popular majors:** Communication and Media Studies, Other; Mechanical/Mechanical Engineering Technology/Technician; Psychology, General. **Special Study Options:** Accelerated program; Cross-registration; Double major; English as a Second Language (ESL); Honors program; Independent study; Internships; Study abroad; Teacher certification program. **Honors programs:** CUNY Macauley College and City College Honors Program. **Combined degree programs:** BA/MA; BA/MD. **Disability Services offered:** Note-taking services; Reader services; Tape recorders; Tutors. **Career services:** Alumni network; Alumni services; Career assessment; Career/job search classes; Internships.

FACILITIES
Housing: Coed dorms. **Special Academic Facilities/Equipment:** Planetarium, NYC Structural Biological Center, Aaron Davis Hall/Harlem Stage Gatehouse, Landmark Neo-Gothic original campus buildings.

CAMPUS LIFE
Environment: Metropolis. **Activities:** Choral groups; Dance; Drama/theater; International Student Organization; Jazz band; Literary magazine; Model UN; Radio station; Student government; Student newspaper; Student-run film society; Yearbook. 170 registered organizations, 8 religious organizations, 6 fraternities, 5 sororities, on campus. **Athletics (Intercollegiate):** *Men:* baseball, basketball, cross-country, soccer, tennis, track/field (outdoor), track/field (indoor), volleyball. *Women:* basketball, fencing, soccer, tennis, track/field (outdoor), track/field (indoor), volleyball. **On-Campus Highlights:** City College Center for Discovery and Innovation. **Environmental Initiatives:** Signed on to ACUPCC and NYC Mayor's Campus 30in10 Challenge to reduce GHG emissions.

ADMISSIONS
Freshman Academic Profile: Average high school GPA 3.4. 85% from public high schools. **Test Scores:** SAT Math middle 50% range 500–620. SAT EBRW middle 50% range 480–570. **Basis for Candidate Selection:** *Very important*

factors include: academic GPA. *Important factors include:* standardized test scores. **Freshman Admission Requirements:** High school diploma is required and GED is accepted. *Academic units recommended:* 4 English, 3 math, 2 science, 2 science labs, 3 foreign language, 4 social studies, 1 visual/performing arts. **Freshman Admission Statistics:** 27,788 applied, 47% admitted, 16% enrolled. **Transfer Admission Requirements:** College transcript(s). Minimum college GPA of 2.0 required. Lowest grade transferable C. **General Admission Information:** Application fee $65. Priority deadline 2/1. Non-fall registration accepted. Admission may be deferred for a maximum of 1 year.

COSTS AND FINANCIAL AID

Annual in-state tuition $6,930. Annual out-of-state tuition $18,600. Room and board $15,577. Required fees $410. Average book and supplies expense $1,364. **Required Forms and Deadlines:** FAFSA; State aid form. **Notification of Awards:** Applicants will be notified of awards on a rolling basis beginning 4/1. **Types of Aid:** *Need-based scholarships/grants:* College/university scholarship or grant aid from institutional funds; Federal Pell; Private scholarships; SEOG; State scholarships/grants. *Loans:* Direct PLUS loans; Direct Subsidized Stafford Loans; Direct Unsubsidized Stafford Loans. **Student Employment:** Federal Work-Study Program available. Institutional employment available. **Financial Aid Statistics:** 100% needy freshmen, 100% needy undergrads receive need-based scholarship or grant aid. 21% freshmen, 33% undergrads receive non-need-based scholarship or grant aid. 11% freshmen, 18% undergrads receive need-based self-help aid. 0% freshmen, 0% undergrads receive athletic scholarships. 80% freshmen, 79% undergrads receive any aid. **Criteria awarding aid:** *Need-based:* Academics, Alumni affiliation, Art, Leadership, Minority status. *Non-need-based:* Academics, Alumni affiliation, Art, Leadership, Minority status, Music/drama.

CITY UNIVERSITY OF NEW YORK—HUNTER COLLEGE

695 Park Ave, Room N203, New York, NY 10065
Phone: 212-772-4490 **Financial Aid Phone:** 212-772-4820
E-mail: admissions@hunter.cuny.edu **CEEB Code:** 2301
Website: www.hunter.cuny.edu/main/

This public school was founded in 1870.

RATINGS

Admissions Selectivity Rating: 92   **Fire Safety Rating:** 93   **Green Rating:** 81

STUDENTS AND FACULTY

Enrollment: 16,081. **Student Body:** 64% female, 36% male, 4% out-of-state, 5% international (158 countries represented). Asian 32%, African American 12%, Caucasian 28%, Hispanic 24%, Native American <1%, Pacific Islander 0%, Two or more races 0%, Race unknown 0%.
Retention and Graduation: 87% freshmen return for sophomore year. 25% freshmen graduate within 4 years. 57% freshmen graduate within 6 years.
Faculty: Student/faculty ratio 13:1. 655 full-time faculty, 87% hold PhDs, 22% are members of minority groups, 54% are women.

ACADEMICS

Degrees: Bachelor's; Doctoral degree—professional practice; Master's; Post-bachelor's certificate; Post-master's certificate. **Classes:** Most classes have 20–29 students. **Most popular majors:** Computer Science; English Language and Literature, General; Psychology, General. **Special Study Options:** Accelerated program; Cross-registration; Distance learning; Double major; Dual enrollment; Exchange student program (domestic); Honors program; Independent study; Internships; Liberal arts/career combination; Student-designed major; Study abroad; Teacher certification program. **Honors programs:** Maccaulay Honors College. **Combined degree programs:** BA/MA. **Disability Services offered:** Note-taking services; Reader services; Tape recorders; Tutors. **Career services:** Alumni network; Alumni services; Career/job search classes; Internships.

FACILITIES

Housing: Coed dorms; 100% of campus accessible to physically disabled. **Special Academic Facilities/Equipment:** Art Gallery, theatre, geology club, on-campus elementary and secondary schools.

CAMPUS LIFE

Environment: Metropolis. **Activities:** Choral groups; Concert band; Dance; Drama/theater; Jazz band; Literary magazine; Model UN; Music ensembles; Musical theater; Radio station; Student government; Student newspaper; Student-run film society; Symphony orchestra; Television station; Yearbook. 150 registered organizations, 20 honor societies, 2 fraternities, 2 sororities, on campus. **Athletics (Intercollegiate):** *Men:* basketball, cross-country, fencing, soccer, tennis, track/field (outdoor), track/field (indoor), volleyball, wrestling. *Women:* basketball, cross-country, diving, fencing, softball, swimming, tennis, track/field (outdoor), track/field (indoor), volleyball. **On-Campus Highlights:** Over 100 Campus Clubs. **Environmental Initiatives:** Annual Hunter Goes Green Week—Every year, Hunter organizes and hosts a Hunter Goes Green Week that culminates on Earth Day. The event is managed by student members of the Hunter Sustainability Project (HSP) student group and provides an opportunity to educate and inform the campus community on environmentally-related issues.

ADMISSIONS

Freshman Academic Profile: Average high school GPA 3.5. 78% from public high schools. **Test Scores:** SAT Math middle 50% range 590–690. SAT EBRW middle 50% range 580–660. **Basis for Candidate Selection:** *Very important factors include:* rigor of secondary school record, class rank, academic GPA. **Freshman Admission Requirements:** High school diploma is required and GED is accepted. *Academic units required:* 2 English, 2 math, 1 science, 1 science labs. *Academic units recommended:* 4 English, 3 math, 2 science, 2 foreign language, 4 social studies, 1 academic electives, 1 visual/performing arts. **Freshman Admission Statistics:** 33,750 applied, 35% admitted, 22% enrolled. **Transfer Admission Requirements:** College transcript(s). Minimum college GPA of 2.3 required. Lowest grade transferable C. **General Admission Information:** Application fee $65. Regular application deadline 2/1.

COSTS AND FINANCIAL AID

Annual in-state tuition $6,930. Annual out-of-state tuition $18,000. Room and board $4,857. Required fees $450. Average book and supplies expense $1,364. **Required Forms and Deadlines:** FAFSA; State aid form. **Notification of Awards:** Applicants will be notified of awards on a rolling basis beginning 5/15. **Types of Aid:** *Need-based scholarships/grants:* College/university scholarship or grant aid from institutional funds; Federal Pell; State scholarships/grants. *Loans:* Direct PLUS loans; Direct Subsidized Stafford Loans; Direct Unsubsidized Stafford Loans. **Student Employment:** Federal Work-Study Program available. Institutional employment available. **Financial Aid Statistics:** 89% needy freshmen, 88% needy undergrads receive need-based scholarship or grant aid. 76% freshmen, 46% undergrads receive non-need-based scholarship or grant aid. 6% freshmen, 11% undergrads receive need-based self-help aid. 0% freshmen, 0% undergrads receive athletic scholarships. 80% freshmen, 73% undergrads receive any aid. 15% undergrads borrow to pay for school. Average cumulative indebtedness $16,272. **Criteria awarding aid:** *Need-based:* Academics. *Non-need-based:* Academics.

CITY UNIVERSITY OF NEW YORK—KINGSBOROUGH COMMUNITY COLLEGE

2001 Oriental Blvd., Brooklyn, NY 11235
Phone: (718)368-4600 **Financial Aid Phone:** (718) 368-4644
E-mail: info@kbcc.cuny.edu **Fax:** (718) 368-5356

This public school was founded in 1963. It has a 72 acre campus.

RATINGS

Admissions Selectivity Rating: 60*   **Fire Safety Rating:** 60*   **Green Rating:** 65

STUDENTS AND FACULTY

Enrollment: 10,889. **Student Body:** 55% female, 45% male, 5% international (137 countries represented). Asian 14%, African American 32%, Caucasian 32%, Hispanic 17%, Native American <1%, Pacific Islander 0%, Two or more races 0%, Race unknown 0%.
Retention and Graduation: 70% freshmen return for sophomore year.
Faculty: Student/faculty ratio 23:1. 333 full-time faculty, 57% hold PhDs, 28% are members of minority groups, 55% are women. 0% of classes are taught by teaching assistants.

ACADEMICS

Degrees: Associate; Certificate; Terminal Associate; Transfer Associate. **Classes:** Most classes have 20–29 students. **Most popular majors:** Business/Commerce, General; Biology/Biological Sciences, General; Liberal Arts and Sciences/Liberal Studies. **Special Study Options:** Accelerated program; Cross-registration; Distance learning; Dual enrollment; English as a Second Language (ESL); Honors program; Independent study; Internships.

CAMPUS LIFE

Environment: Metropolis. **Activities:** Musical theater; Radio station; Student government; Student newspaper.

ADMISSIONS

Freshman Admission Requirements: High school diploma is required and GED is accepted. *Academic units recommended:* 4 English, 3 math, 2 science, 2 foreign language, 4 social studies. **Transfer Admission Requirements:** College transcript(s), essay or personal statement, interview. Lowest grade transferable C. **General Admission Information:** Application fee $65. Priority deadline 7/15. Regular application deadline 8/15. Non-fall registration accepted.

COSTS AND FINANCIAL AID

Annual in-state tuition $4,800. Annual out-of-state tuition $9,600. Required fees $226.

CITY UNIVERSITY OF NEW YORK—LEHMAN COLLEGE

250 Bedford Park Boulevard West, Bronx, NY 10468
Phone: 718-960-8000 **Financial Aid Phone:** (718)960-8545
E-mail: wilkes@alpha.lehman.cuny.edu **CEEB Code:** 2950
Fax: 718-960-8712

This public school was founded in 1968. It has a 38 acre campus.

RATINGS

Admissions Selectivity Rating: 90   **Fire Safety Rating:** 60*   **Green Rating:** 60*

STUDENTS AND FACULTY

Enrollment: 8,236. **Student Body:** 71% female, 29% male, 1% out-of-state, 5% international (123 countries represented). Asian 4%, African American 32%, Caucasian 10%, Hispanic 49%, Native American <1%, Race unknown 0%.
Retention and Graduation: 77% freshmen return for sophomore year.
Faculty: Student/faculty ratio 15:1. 368 full-time faculty, 75% hold PhDs, 27% are members of minority groups, 52% are women.

ACADEMICS

Degrees: Bachelor's; Certificate; Diploma; Master's. **Classes:** Most classes have 20–29 students. **Most popular majors:** Social Work; Sociology, General; Nursing/Registered Nurse (Rn, Asn, Bsn, Msn). **Special Study Options:** Accelerated program; Cooperative education program; Cross-registration; Distance learning; Double major; Dual enrollment; English as a Second Language (ESL); Exchange student program (domestic); Honors program; Independent study; Internships; Student-designed major; Study abroad; Teacher certification program; Weekend college. **Honors programs:** Lehman Scholars Program. Students receive full tuition, stipends, an expense account to use for academically enriching experiences and a laptop computer. **Combined degree programs:** BA/MA. **Disability Services offered:** Note-taking services; Reader services; Tape recorders; Tutors.

FACILITIES

80% of campus accessible to physically disabled. **Special Academic Facilities/ Equipment:** Art gallery, concert hall, sports complex. **Campus network:** 100% of classrooms, 100% of dorms, 100% of student union, 100% of libraries, 100% of dining areas, 50% of common outdoor areas, have wireless network access.

CAMPUS LIFE

Environment: Metropolis. **Activities:** Choral groups; Concert band; Dance; Drama/theater; International Student Organization; Jazz band; Literary magazine; Music ensembles; Musical theater; Opera; Radio station; Student government; Student newspaper; Student-run film society; Symphony orchestra; Television station; Yearbook. 3 honor societies, 1 religious organizations, 1 fraternities, 1 sororities, on campus. **Athletics (Intercollegiate):** *Men:* badminton, baseball, basketball, cross-country, diving, swimming, tennis, track/field (outdoor), volleyball. *Women:* badminton, basketball, cross-country,

diving, softball, swimming, tennis, track/field (outdoor), volleyball. **On-Campus Highlights:** APEX athletic facility.

ADMISSIONS

Freshman Academic Profile: Average high school GPA 2.7. 74% from public high schools. **Test Scores:** SAT Math middle 50% range 400–500. SAT EBRW middle 50% range 400–490. **Basis for Candidate Selection:** *Very important factors include:* rigor of secondary school record, standardized test scores. *Important factors include:* academic GPA. *Other factors include:* application essay, recommendation(s), interview, extracurricular activities, talent/ability. **Freshman Admission Requirements:** High school diploma is required and GED is accepted. *Academic units required:* 4 English, 2 math, 2 science, 1 science labs, 2 foreign language, 1 social studies, 1 history. *Academic units recommended:* 4 English, 3 math, 3 science, 2 foreign language, 2 social studies, 2 history, 1 visual/performing arts. **Freshman Admission Statistics:** 14,155 applied, 32% admitted, 58% enrolled. **Transfer Admission Requirements:** College transcript(s). Minimum college GPA of 2 required. Lowest grade transferable C. **General Admission Information:** Application fee $65. Priority deadline 1/15. Regular application deadline 8/15. Non-fall registration accepted. Admission may be deferred for a maximum of 1 semester.

COSTS AND FINANCIAL AID

Annual in-state tuition $4,000. Annual out-of-state tuition $10,800. Required fees $290. Average book and supplies expense $938. **Required Forms and Deadlines:** FAFSA; State aid form. **Notification of Awards:** Applicants will be notified of awards on a rolling basis beginning 3/1. **Types of Aid:** *Need-based scholarships/grants:* College/university scholarship or grant aid from institutional funds; Federal Pell; Private scholarships; SEOG; State scholarships/grants. *Loans:* Direct PLUS loans; Direct Subsidized Stafford Loans; Direct Unsubsidized Stafford Loans. **Student Employment:** Federal Work-Study Program available. Institutional employment available. **Financial Aid Statistics:** 88% needy freshmen, 90% needy undergrads receive need-based scholarship or grant aid. 42% freshmen, 15% undergrads receive non-need-based scholarship or grant aid. 19% freshmen, 44% undergrads receive need-based self-help aid. 0% freshmen, 0% undergrads receive athletic scholarships. 83% freshmen, 80% undergrads receive any aid. **Criteria awarding aid:** *Need-based:* Academics. *Non-need-based:* Academics.

CITY UNIVERSITY OF NEW YORK— MEDGAR EVERS COLLEGE

1665 Bedford Avenue, Brooklyn, NY 11225
Phone: 718-270-6024 **Financial Aid Phone:** 718-270-6133
E-mail: applytomec@mec.cuny.edu
Fax: 718-270-6411 **Website:** http://www.mec.cuny.edu/

This public school was founded in 1970. It has a 7 acre campus.

RATINGS

Admissions Selectivity Rating: 71   **Fire Safety Rating:** 60*   **Green Rating:** 60*

STUDENTS AND FACULTY

Enrollment: 5,313. **Student Body:** 72% female, 28% male, 1% out-of-state, 1% international. Asian 3%, African American 66%, Caucasian 1%, Hispanic 14%, Native American <1%, Pacific Islander 0%, Two or more races 0%, Race unknown 15%.
Retention and Graduation: 67% freshmen return for sophomore year.
Faculty: Student/faculty ratio 14:1. 182 full-time faculty, 58% hold PhDs, 82% are members of minority groups, 48% are women. 0% of classes are taught by teaching assistants.

ACADEMICS

Degrees: Associate; Bachelor's; Certificate. **Classes:** Most classes have 30–39 students. Most lab/discussion sessions have 30–39 students. **Most popular majors:** Biology/Biological Sciences, General; Business Administration and Management, General; Liberal Arts and Sciences/Liberal Studies. **Special Study Options:** Accelerated program; Cross-registration; Distance learning; Double major; English as a Second Language (ESL); Honors program; Independent study; Internships; Study abroad; Teacher certification program; Weekend college. **Disability Services offered:** Note-taking services; Reader services; Tape recorders; Tutors. **Career services:** Alumni services; Career assessment; Career/ job search classes; Internships.

FACILITIES

100% of campus accessible to physically disabled. **Campus network:** 100% of classrooms, 100% of dorms, 100% of student union, 100% of libraries, 100% of dining areas, 100% of common outdoor areas, have wireless network access.

CAMPUS LIFE

Environment: Metropolis. **Activities:** Choral groups; Dance; Drama/theater; Jazz band; Literary magazine; Radio station; Student government; Student newspaper; Television station; Yearbook. 32 registered organizations, 4 honor societies, on campus. **Athletics (Intercollegiate):** *Men:* basketball, cross-country, soccer, swimming, track/field (outdoor), track/field (indoor), volleyball. *Women:* basketball, cheerleading, cross-country, soccer, softball, swimming, tennis, track/field (outdoor), track/field (indoor), volleyball. **On-Campus Highlights:** Amphitheater.

ADMISSIONS

Freshman Academic Profile: Average high school GPA 2.3. **Test Scores:** SAT Math middle 50% range 390–490. SAT EBRW middle 50% range 420–510. **Basis for Candidate Selection:** *Other factors include:* rigor of secondary school record, academic GPA, standardized test scores. **Freshman Admission Requirements:** High school diploma is required and GED is accepted. *Academic units recommended:* 4 English, 3 math, 2 science, 2 foreign language, 4 social studies, 2 academic electives. **Freshman Admission Statistics:** 13,709 applied, 90% admitted, 7% enrolled. **Transfer Admission Requirements:** College transcript(s). Minimum college GPA of 2.0 required. Lowest grade transferable C. **General Admission Information:** Application fee $65. Non-fall registration accepted. Admission may be deferred for a maximum of one semester.

COSTS AND FINANCIAL AID

Annual in-state tuition $6,930. Annual out-of-state tuition $18,600. Required fees $200. Average book and supplies expense $1,364. **Required Forms and Deadlines:** FAFSA; State aid form. **Notification of Awards:** Applicants will be notified of awards on a rolling basis beginning 5/1. **Types of Aid:** *Need-based scholarships/grants:* Federal Pell; SEOG; State scholarships/grants. *Loans:* Direct PLUS loans; Direct Subsidized Stafford Loans; Direct Unsubsidized Stafford Loans. **Student Employment:** Federal Work-Study Program available. Institutional employment available. **Financial Aid Statistics:** 89% needy freshmen, 92% needy undergrads receive need-based scholarship or grant aid. 49% freshmen, 38% undergrads receive non-need-based scholarship or grant aid. 9% freshmen, 26% undergrads receive need-based self-help aid. 0% freshmen, 0% undergrads receive athletic scholarships. **Criteria awarding aid:** *Non-need-based:* Academics, Leadership.

CITY UNIVERSITY OF NEW YORK—NEW YORK CITY COLLEGE OF TECHNOLOGY

300 Jay Street, Brooklyn, NY 11201
Phone: (718) 260-5500 **Financial Aid Phone:** 718-260-5700
E-mail: admissions@citytech.cuny.edu **CEEB Code:** 2550
Fax: (718) 260-5504 **Website:** http://www.citytech.cuny.edu/ **ACT Code:** 2950

This public school was founded in 1946. It has a 3 acre campus.

RATINGS

Admissions Selectivity Rating: 66   **Fire Safety Rating:** 60*   **Green Rating:** 60*

STUDENTS AND FACULTY

Enrollment: 15,917. **Student Body:** 44% female, 56% male, 1% out-of-state, 5% international (106 countries represented). Asian 18%, African American 32%, Caucasian 13%, Hispanic 31%, Native American <1%, Pacific Islander <1%, Two or more races 1%, Race unknown 0%.
Retention and Graduation: 77% freshmen return for sophomore year.
Faculty: Student/faculty ratio 17:1. 433 full-time faculty, 63% hold PhDs, 45% are members of minority groups, 48% are women. 0% of classes are taught by teaching assistants.

ACADEMICS

Degrees: Associate; Bachelor's; Certificate. **Classes:** Most classes have 20–29 students. Most lab/discussion sessions have 20–29 students. **Most popular majors:** Information Science/Studies; Hospitality Administration/Management, General; Design and Visual Communications, General. **Special Study Options:** Distance learning; Dual enrollment; English as a Second Language (ESL);

Honors program; Independent study; Internships; Student-designed major; Study abroad; Teacher certification program; Weekend college. **Disability Services offered:** Note-taking services; Reader services; Tape recorders; Tutors. **Career services:** Alumni network; Alumni services; Career assessment; Career/job search classes; Internships.

FACILITIES

100% of campus accessible to physically disabled.

CAMPUS LIFE

Environment: Metropolis. **Activities:** Drama/theater; International Student Organization; Literary magazine; Musical theater; Student government; Student newspaper. 60 registered organizations, 1 honor societies, on campus. **Athletics (Intercollegiate):** *Men:* basketball, tennis, track/field (outdoor). *Women:* basketball, tennis, track/field (outdoor). **On-Campus Highlights:** Nursing Department **Environmental Initiatives:** Reducing the amount of waste produced by our purchasing and procurement system.

ADMISSIONS

Basis for Candidate Selection: *Important factors include:* rigor of secondary school record, academic GPA. *Other factors include:* class rank, application essay, standardized test scores, recommendation(s). **Freshman Admission Requirements:** High school diploma is required and GED is accepted. *Academic units required:* 4 English, 3 math, 2 science, 2 science labs, 2 foreign language, 3 social studies, 1 visual/performing arts. *Academic units recommended:* 4 English, 4 math, 3 science, 3 science labs, 2 foreign language, 4 social studies, 1 visual/performing arts. **Freshman Admission Statistics:** 17,465 applied, 71% admitted, 27% enrolled. **Transfer Admission Requirements:** High school transcript, college transcript(s), statement of good standing from prior institution(s). Minimum college GPA of 2.0 required. Lowest grade transferable C. **General Admission Information:** Application fee $65. Priority deadline 2/1. Regular application deadline 2/1. Non-fall registration accepted. Admission may be deferred for a maximum of 1 semester.

COSTS AND FINANCIAL AID

Annual in-state tuition $5,730. Annual out-of-state tuition $15,300. Required fees $339. **Required Forms and Deadlines:** FAFSA; State aid form. **Types of Aid:** *Need-based scholarships/grants:* Federal Nursing Scholarships; Federal Pell; SEOG; State scholarships/grants. *Loans:* Direct PLUS loans; Direct Subsidized Stafford Loans; Direct Unsubsidized Stafford Loans. **Student Employment:** Federal Work-Study Program available. Institutional employment available. **Criteria awarding aid:** *Need-based:* Academics. *Non-need-based:* State/district residency.

CITY UNIVERSITY OF NEW YORK—QUEENS COLLEGE

6530 Kissena Blvd, Queens, NY 11367
Phone: 718 9975600 **Financial Aid Phone:** (718) 997-5123
E-mail: vincent.angrisani@qc.cuny.edu **CEEB Code:** 2750
Fax: 7189975617 **Website:** www.qc.cuny.edu **ACT Code:** 20173

This public school was founded in 1937. It has a 80 acre campus.

RATINGS

Admissions Selectivity Rating: 88   **Fire Safety Rating:** 97   **Green Rating:** 91

STUDENTS AND FACULTY

Enrollment: 15,762. **Student Body:** 54% female, 46% male, 1% out-of-state, 5% international (143 countries represented). Asian 28%, African American 9%, Caucasian 26%, Hispanic 29%, Native American <1%, Pacific Islander <1%, Two or more races 1%, Race unknown 0%.
Retention and Graduation: 84% freshmen return for sophomore year. 31% freshmen graduate within 4 years. 60% freshmen graduate within 6 years. 35% grads go on to further study within 1 year. 10% grads pursue arts and sciences degrees. 2% grads pursue law degrees. 1% grads pursue business degrees. 1% grads pursue medical degrees. **Faculty:** Student/faculty ratio 15:1. 592 full-time faculty, 86% hold PhDs, 23% are members of minority groups, 46% are women. 1% of classes are taught by teaching assistants.

ACADEMICS

Degrees: Bachelor's; Master's; Post-bachelor's certificate; Post-master's certificate. **Classes:** Most classes have 20–29 students. **Most popular majors:** Accounting; Computer Science; Psychology, General. **Special Study Options:** Accelerated program; Double major; Dual enrollment; English as a Second Language (ESL); Exchange student program (domestic); Honors program; Independent study; Internships; Liberal arts/career combination; Study abroad; Teacher certification program; Weekend college. **Honors programs:** Queens College participates in the CUNY Honors College—a highly selective program that offers a challenging curriculum and a full tuition scholarship plus other financial support. The program accepts first-time freshmen in the fall semester only. **Combined degree programs:** BA/MA. **Disability Services offered:** Note-taking services; Reader services; Tape recorders; Tutors. **Career services:** Alumni network; Alumni services; Career assessment; Career/job search classes; Internships.

FACILITIES

Housing: Apartments for single students; 100% of campus accessible to physically disabled. **Special Academic Facilities/Equipment:** Godwin-Ternbach Museum, Louis Armstrong House Museum & Archieves, Colden Auditorium, Kupferberg Center for the Performing Arts, Art Library. **Campus network:** 100% of classrooms, 95% of dorms, 95% of student union, 100% of libraries, 100% of dining areas, 10% of common outdoor areas, have wireless network access.

CAMPUS LIFE

Environment: Metropolis. **Activities:** Campus Ministries; Choral groups; Dance; Drama/theater; International Student Organization; Jazz band; Literary magazine; Model UN; Music ensembles; Musical theater; Opera; Radio station; Student government; Student newspaper; Symphony orchestra; Yearbook. 118 registered organizations, 3 honor societies, 10 religious organizations, 6 fraternities, 5 sororities, on campus. **Athletics (Intercollegiate):** *Men:* baseball, basketball, cross-country, diving, soccer, swimming, tennis, track/field (outdoor), water polo. *Women:* basketball, cross-country, diving, fencing, lacrosse, soccer, softball, swimming, tennis, track/field (outdoor), volleyball, water polo. **On-Campus Highlights:** Rosenthal Library. **Environmental Initiatives:** Retrofit and completion of mechanical upgrade 27M for the new Science Building that will significantly reduce the energy consumption.

ADMISSIONS

Freshman Academic Profile: Average high school GPA 3.5. 75% from public high schools. **Test Scores:** SAT Math middle 50% range 540–620. SAT EBRW middle 50% range 520–600. **Basis for Candidate Selection:** *Very important factors include:* rigor of secondary school record, academic GPA, standardized test scores. *Other factors include:* application essay, recommendation(s). **Freshman Admission Requirements:** High school diploma is required and GED is accepted. *Academic units required:* 4 English, 3 math, 2 science, 2 science labs, 3 foreign language, 4 social studies. *Academic units recommended:* 4 English, 3 math, 3 science, 3 science labs, 3 foreign language, 4 social studies. **Freshman Admission Statistics:** 18,180 applied, 43% admitted, 22% enrolled. **Transfer Admission Requirements:** High school transcript, college transcript(s), standardized test scores. Minimum college GPA of 2.25 required. Lowest grade transferable 2. **General Admission Information:** Application fee $65. Priority deadline 2/1. Non-fall registration accepted. Admission may be deferred for a maximum of 1 semester.

COSTS AND FINANCIAL AID

Annual in-state tuition $6,930. Annual out-of-state tuition $18,600. Room and board $15,992. Required fees $608. Average book and supplies expense $1,364. **Required Forms and Deadlines:** FAFSA; State aid form. **Types of Aid:** *Need-based scholarships/grants:* College/university scholarship or grant aid from institutional funds; Federal Pell; Private scholarships; SEOG; State scholarships/grants. *Loans:* Direct PLUS loans; Direct Subsidized Stafford Loans; Direct Unsubsidized Stafford Loans. **Student Employment:** Federal Work-Study Program available. Institutional employment available. **Financial Aid Statistics:** 88% needy freshmen, 88% needy undergrads receive need-based scholarship or grant aid. 71% freshmen, 32% undergrads receive non-need-based scholarship or grant aid. 7% freshmen, 15% undergrads receive need-based self-help aid. 2% freshmen, 1% undergrads receive athletic scholarships. 76% freshmen, 51% undergrads receive any aid. 15% undergrads borrow to pay for school. Average cumulative indebtedness $16,104. **Criteria awarding aid:** *Non-need-based:* Academics, Athletics.

CITY UNIVERSITY OF NEW YORK— THE COLLEGE OF STATEN ISLAND

2800 Victory Boulevard, Staten Island, NY 10314
Phone: 718-982-2010 **Financial Aid Phone:** 718-982-2030
E-mail: admissions@csi.cuny.edu **CEEB Code:** 2778
Fax: 718-982-2500 **Website:** www.csi.cuny.edu **ACT Code:** 2950

This public school was founded in 1976. It has a 204 acre campus.

RATINGS
Admissions Selectivity Rating: 73   **Fire Safety Rating:** 90   **Green Rating:** 84

STUDENTS AND FACULTY
Enrollment: 11,288. **Student Body:** 54% female, 46% male, 2% out-of-state, 3% international (107 countries represented). Asian 11%, African American 14%, Caucasian 42%, Hispanic 27%, Native American <1%, Pacific Islander <1%, Two or more races 2%.
Retention and Graduation: 75% freshmen return for sophomore year. 48% freshmen graduate within 6 years. **Faculty:** Student/faculty ratio 19:1. 371 full-time faculty, 88% hold PhDs, 27% are members of minority groups, 47% are women.

ACADEMICS
Degrees: Associate; Bachelor's; Certificate; Doctoral degree—professional practice; Master's; Post-bachelor's certificate; Post-master's certificate; Terminal Associate; Transfer Associate. **Classes:** Most classes have 30–39 students. **Most popular majors:** Psychology, General; Business/Commerce, General; Social Sciences, Other. **Special Study Options:** Cross-registration; Double major; English as a Second Language (ESL); Exchange student program (domestic); Honors program; Independent study; Internships; Study abroad; Teacher certification program. **Honors programs:** The University Scholars Program at the College of Staten Island, one of eight CUNY Macaulay programs, is designed to provide an outstanding educational opportunity for academically gifted students. Special features include full financial support and access to exceptional academic and cultural activities. **Combined degree programs:** BA/MA. **Disability Services offered:** Note-taking services; Reader services; Tape recorders; Tutors. **Career services:** Alumni network; Alumni services; Career assessment; Career/job search classes; Internships; Regional alumni.

FACILITIES
Housing: Apartments for single students; Coed dorms; Special housing for disabled students; 100% of campus accessible to physically disabled. **Special Academic Facilities/Equipment:** Art Gallery, Radio Station, Astrophysical Observatory, Tech Incubator, Archives & Special Collections, Center for Engineered Polymeric Materials, Advanced Imaging Facility, Center for the Arts, Center for Developmental Neuroscience, CUNY High Performance Computational Facility, Intelligent Robotics Lab. **Campus network:** 100% of classrooms, 100% of dorms, 100% of student union, 100% of libraries, 100% of dining areas, 100% of common outdoor areas, have wireless network access.

CAMPUS LIFE
Environment: Metropolis. **Activities:** Campus Ministries; Choral groups; Dance; Drama/theater; International Student Organization; Jazz band; Literary magazine; Music ensembles; Radio station; Student government; Student newspaper; Student-run film society. 45 registered organizations, 11 honor societies, 4 religious organizations, on campus. **Athletics (Intercollegiate):** *Men:* baseball, basketball, cross-country, diving, soccer, swimming, tennis. *Women:* basketball, cross-country, diving, soccer, softball, swimming, tennis, volleyball. **On-Campus Highlights:** Campus Center including cafeteria and lounge.

ADMISSIONS
Freshman Academic Profile: Average high school GPA 3.1. 86% from public high schools. **Test Scores:** SAT Math middle 50% range 510–600. SAT EBRW middle 50% range 500–590. **Basis for Candidate Selection:** *Very important factors include:* rigor of secondary school record. *Important factors include:* academic GPA, standardized test scores. *Other factors include:* class rank, application essay, recommendation(s), interview, extracurricular activities, volunteer work, level of applicant's interest. **Freshman Admission Requirements:** High school diploma is required and GED is accepted. *Academic units required:* 4 English, 2 math, 2 science, 2 foreign language, 4 social studies, 0.5 visual/performing arts. *Academic units recommended:* 4 English, 3 math, 3 science, 3 foreign language, 4 social studies, 0.5 visual/performing arts. **Freshman Admission Statistics:** 14,466 applied, 93%

admitted, 18% enrolled. **Transfer Admission Requirements:** College transcript(s). Minimum college GPA of 2.0 required. Lowest grade transferable C. **General Admission Information:** Application fee $65. Priority deadline 2/1. Non-fall registration accepted. Admission may be deferred for a maximum of 1 year.

COSTS AND FINANCIAL AID
Annual in-state tuition $6,930. Annual out-of-state tuition $18,600. Room and board $18,695. Required fees $559. Average book and supplies expense $1,364. **Required Forms and Deadlines:** FAFSA; State aid form. **Notification of Awards:** Applicants will be notified of awards on a rolling basis beginning 2/15. **Types of Aid:** *Need-based scholarships/grants:* College/university scholarship or grant aid from institutional funds; Federal Pell; Private scholarships; SEOG; State scholarships/grants. *Loans:* Direct PLUS loans; Direct Subsidized Stafford Loans; Direct Unsubsidized Stafford Loans. **Student Employment:** Federal Work-Study Program available. Institutional employment available. **Financial Aid Statistics:** 87% needy freshmen, 87% needy undergrads receive need-based scholarship or grant aid. 36% freshmen, 25% undergrads receive non-need-based scholarship or grant aid. 18% freshmen, 23% undergrads receive need-based self-help aid. 1% freshmen, 1% undergrads receive athletic scholarships. 79.4% freshmen, 71.5% undergrads receive any aid. **Criteria awarding aid:** *Need-based:* Academics, Alumni affiliation, Art, Leadership, Minority status, Music/drama. *Non-need-based:* Academics, Alumni affiliation, Art, Leadership, Minority status, Music/drama, State/district residency.

CLAFLIN UNIVERSITY

400 Magnolia Street, Orangeburg, SC 29115
Phone: 803-535-5340 **Financial Aid Phone:** 803-535-5720
E-mail: admissions@claflin.edu **CEEB Code:** 5109
Fax: 803-535-5387 **ACT Code:** 3840

This private school, affiliated with the Methodist Church, was founded in 1869. It has a 46 acre campus.

RATINGS
Admissions Selectivity Rating: 82   **Fire Safety Rating:** 88   **Green Rating:** 85

STUDENTS AND FACULTY
Enrollment: 1,784. **Student Body:** 65% female, 35% male, 19% out-of-state, 3% international (15 countries represented). Asian 1%, African American 92%, Caucasian 1%, Hispanic 2%, Native American 1%, Pacific Islander 0%, Two or more races <1%, Race unknown 0%.
Retention and Graduation: 73% freshmen return for sophomore year.
Faculty: Student/faculty ratio 13:1. 119 full-time faculty, 84% hold PhDs, 76% are members of minority groups, 43% are women.

ACADEMICS
Degrees: Bachelor's; Master's. **Classes:** Most classes have fewer than 10 students. Most lab/discussion sessions have fewer than 10 students. **Most popular majors:** Biology/Biological Sciences, General; Business Administration and Management, General; Sociology, General. **Special Study Options:** Accelerated program; Cooperative education program; Cross-registration; Double major; Dual enrollment; English as a Second Language (ESL); Exchange student program (domestic); Honors program; Independent study; Internships; Study abroad; Teacher certification program. **Honors programs:** The Alice Carson Tisdale Honors College. **Disability Services offered:** Note-taking services. **Career services:** Career assessment; Career/job search classes; Internships.

FACILITIES
Housing: Men's dorms; Women's dorms; 90% of campus accessible to physically disabled. **Special Academic Facilities/Equipment:** T.V. studio, NMR Wilbur R. Gregg collection, Aruther Rose Museum. **Campus network:** 100% of classrooms, 100% of dorms, 100% of student union, 100% of libraries, 100% of dining areas, 75% of common outdoor areas, have wireless network access.

CAMPUS LIFE
Environment: Village. **Activities:** Choral groups; Concert band; Dance; Drama/theater; International Student Organization; Jazz band; Literary magazine; Music ensembles; Radio station; Student government; Student newspaper; Student-run film society; Television station; Yearbook. 64 registered organizations, 3 honor societies, 4 fraternities, 4 sororities, on campus.

Athletics (Intercollegiate): *Men:* baseball, basketball, cross-country, track/field (outdoor), track/field (indoor). *Women:* basketball, cross-country, softball, track/field (outdoor), track/field (indoor), volleyball. **On-Campus Highlights:** Student Life Center. **Environmental Initiatives:** Recycling Program.

ADMISSIONS
Freshman Academic Profile: Average high school GPA 2.7. 10% in top 10% of high school class, 26% in top 25% of high school class, 63% in top 50% of high school class. **Test Scores:** SAT Math middle 50% range 350–440. SAT EBRW middle 50% range 350–440. ACT middle 50% range 15–19. **Basis for Candidate Selection:** *Very important factors include:* rigor of secondary school record, class rank, academic GPA, standardized test scores, character/personal qualities, first generation. *Important factors include:* application essay, extracurricular activities, talent/ability, alumni/ae relation. *Other factors include:* recommendation(s), state residency, volunteer work, work experience. **Freshman Admission Requirements:** High school diploma is required and GED is accepted. *Academic units required:* 4 English; 3 math, 3 science, 1 foreign language, 1 social studies, 1 history, 7 academic electives, 1 computer science, 2 unit from above areas or other academic areas. **Freshman Admission Statistics:** 5,237 applied, 44% admitted, 17% enrolled. **Transfer Admission Requirements:** College transcript(s), statement of good standing from prior institution(s). Minimum college GPA of 2.0 required. Lowest grade transferable C. **General Admission Information:** Application fee $30. Priority deadline 1/15. Regular application deadline 8/1. Non-fall registration accepted.

COSTS AND FINANCIAL AID
Annual tuition $14,640. Room and board $8,420. Required fees $370. Average book and supplies expense $1,750. **Required Forms and Deadlines:** FAFSA; Institution's own financial aid form. **Notification of Awards:** Applicants will be notified of awards on a rolling basis beginning 5/3. **Types of Aid:** *Need-based scholarships/grants:* College/university scholarship or grant aid from institutional funds; Federal Pell; Private scholarships; SEOG; State scholarships/grants; United Negro College Fund. **Student Employment:** Federal Work-Study Program available. Institutional employment available. **Financial Aid Statistics:** 88% needy freshmen, 95% needy undergrads receive need-based scholarship or grant aid. 6% freshmen, 6% undergrads receive non-need-based scholarship or grant aid. 67% freshmen, 0% undergrads receive need-based self-help aid. 0% freshmen, 0% undergrads receive athletic scholarships. **Criteria awarding aid:** *Need-based:* Academics, Alumni affiliation, Art, Athletics, Leadership, Music/drama, Religious affiliation.

CLAREMONT MCKENNA COLLEGE

888 Columbia Avenue, Claremont, CA 91711
Phone: (909) 621-8088 **Financial Aid Phone:** (909) 621-8356
E-mail: admission@cmc.edu **CEEB Code:** 4054
Fax: (909) 621-8516 **Website:** www.claremontmckenna.edu **ACT Code:** 0224

This private school was founded in 1946. It has a 69 acre campus.

RATINGS
Admissions Selectivity Rating: 98   **Fire Safety Rating:** 89   **Green Rating:** 86

STUDENTS AND FACULTY
Enrollment: 1,335. **Student Body:** 50% female, 50% male, 55% out-of-state, 16% international (46 countries represented). Asian 12%, African American 4%, Caucasian 41%, Hispanic 15%, Native American <1%, Pacific Islander <1%, Two or more races 7%, Race unknown 5%.
Retention and Graduation: 95% freshmen return for sophomore year. 84% freshmen graduate within 4 years. 91% freshmen graduate within 6 years.
Faculty: Student/faculty ratio 8:1. 149 full-time faculty, 99% hold PhDs, 19% are members of minority groups, 37% are women. 0% of classes are taught by teaching assistants.

ACADEMICS
Degrees: Bachelor's; Master's. **Classes:** Most classes have 10–19 students. **Special Study Options:** Cross-registration; Double major; Exchange student program (domestic); Honors program; Independent study; Internships; Student-designed major; Study abroad. **Combined degree programs:** BA/MA. **Disability Services offered:** Note-taking services; Reader services;

Tape recorders. **Career services:** Alumni network; Alumni services; Career assessment; Career/job search classes; Internships; Regional alumni.

FACILITIES

Housing: Apartments for single students; Coed dorms; Wellness housing

CAMPUS LIFE

Environment: Town. **Activities:** Campus Ministries; Choral groups; Concert band; Dance; Drama/theater; International Student Organization; Jazz band; Literary magazine; Model UN; Music ensembles; Musical theater; Radio station; Student government; Student newspaper; Symphony orchestra; Yearbook. 70 registered organizations, on campus. **Athletics (Intercollegiate):** *Men:* baseball, basketball, cross-country, diving, football, golf, soccer, swimming, tennis, track/field (outdoor), water polo. *Women:* basketball, cross-country, diving, golf, lacrosse, soccer, softball, swimming, tennis, track/field (outdoor), volleyball, water polo. **On-Campus Highlights:** Marian Miner Cook Athenaeum.

ADMISSIONS

Freshman Academic Profile: 83% in top 10% of high school class, 100% in top 25% of high school class, 100% in top 50% of high school class. **Test Scores:** SAT Math middle 50% range 690–780. SAT EBRW middle 50% range 670–730. ACT middle 50% range 31–34. **Basis for Candidate Selection:** *Very important factors include:* rigor of secondary school record, class rank, academic GPA, standardized test scores, recommendation(s), extracurricular activities, character/personal qualities. *Important factors include:* application essay, interview, talent/ability. *Other factors include:* first generation, alumni/ae relation, geographical residence, racial/ethnic status, volunteer work, work experience. **Freshman Admission Requirements:** High school diploma is required and GED is accepted. *Academic units required:* 4 English, 3 math, 2 science, 2 science labs, 3 foreign language, 1 social studies, 1 history. *Academic units recommended:* 4 English, 4 math, 3 science, 3 science labs, 3 foreign language, 1 social studies, 1 history. **Freshman Admission Statistics:** 6,066 applied, 10% admitted, 52% enrolled. **Transfer Admission Requirements:** High school transcript, college transcript(s), essay or personal statement, statement of good standing from prior institution(s). Lowest grade transferable C. **General Admission Information:** Application fee $70. Regular application deadline 1/5. Admission may be deferred for a maximum of 2 years.

COSTS AND FINANCIAL AID

Annual tuition $56,190. Room and board $17,300. **Required Forms and Deadlines:** Business/Farm Supplement; CSS/Financial Aid PROFILE; FAFSA; Noncustodial PROFILE; State aid form. **Notification of Awards:** Applicants will be notified of awards on or about 4/1. **Types of Aid:** *Need-based scholarships/grants:* College/university scholarship or grant aid from institutional funds; Federal Pell; Private scholarships; SEOG; State scholarships/grants. *Loans:* Direct PLUS loans; Direct Subsidized Stafford Loans; Direct Unsubsidized Stafford Loans. **Student Employment:** Federal Work-Study Program available. Institutional employment available. **Financial Aid Statistics:** 98% needy freshmen, 98% needy undergrads receive need-based scholarship or grant aid. 39% freshmen, 44% undergrads receive non-need-based scholarship or grant aid. 92% freshmen, 94% undergrads receive need-based self-help aid. 0% freshmen, 0% undergrads receive athletic scholarships. 43% freshmen, 42% undergrads receive any aid. 36% undergrads borrow to pay for school. Average cumulative indebtedness $21,450. **Criteria awarding aid:** *Need-based:* Academics. *Non-need-based:* Academics, Leadership.

CLARION UNIVERSITY OF PA

Admissions Office, Clarion, PA 16214
Phone: 814-393-2306 **Financial Aid Phone:** 814-393-2315
E-mail: admissions@clarion.edu **CEEB Code:** 2649
Fax: 814-393-2030 **Website:** www.clarion.edu **ACT Code:** 3698

This public school was founded in 1867. It has a 192 acre campus.

RATINGS

Admissions Selectivity Rating: 74   **Fire Safety Rating:** 93   **Green Rating:** 60*

STUDENTS AND FACULTY

Enrollment: 5,046. **Student Body:** 62% female, 38% male, 10% out-of-state, 1% international (35 countries represented). Asian <1%, African American 7%, Caucasian 88%, Hispanic 1%, Native American <1%, Pacific Islander <1%, Two or more races 2%, Race unknown 2%.

Faculty: Student/faculty ratio 20:1. 222 full-time faculty, 87% hold PhDs, 14% are members of minority groups, 49% are women. 0% of classes are taught by teaching assistants.

ACADEMICS

Degrees: Associate; Bachelor's; Certificate; Master's; Post-bachelor's certificate; Post-master's certificate. **Classes:** Most classes have 20–29 students. Most lab/discussion sessions have 10–19 students. **Most popular majors:** Business Administration and Management, General; Elementary Education and Teaching. **Special Study Options:** Cooperative education program; Distance learning; Double major; Dual enrollment; Honors program; Independent study; Internships; Liberal arts/career combination; Student-designed major; Study abroad; Teacher certification program; Weekend college. **Honors programs:** Clarion University's Honors Program is a close-knit group of talented students preparing for the future. Honors courses satisfy general educational requirements and include field experiences. The 21-credit curriculum promotes development of essential life skills targeted for successful career outcomes. The Honors experience extends beyond the walls of the traditional classroom. Students may spend time with archaeologists in Italy, with anthropologists at a primate center, with large corporate firms and in small businesses, and with molecular biologists in laboratories. Studies have included 20th-century music, learning the art of problem solving, and pondered the ethical implications of research. Co-curricular themes prepare Honors Program students to assume leadership roles. The Honors Program is not for all students—only those individuals who desire professional success, demand academic excellence, and expect to create the future. Each year 50 freshmen are selected for the Honors Program. Courses are taught as special topics and faculty instructors are recruited for their scholarly expertise. Honors students major in every department within the university and receive pre-professional advisement. Students take a six-credit linked English and Speech class and a three-credit Humanities course in the Freshman year. In the sophomore year, students take a three-credit mathematics or science class and a three-credit social sciences course. As juniors, students take a Junior Seminar that culminates in a project prospectus for the capstone experience. Honors 450 is the Senior Presentation delivered in a university-wide presentation. The following program standards must be maintained at the end of each academic year: Freshman Year 3.0 QPA 9 program credits Sophomore Year 3.25 QPA 15 program credits Junior Year 3.4 QPA 18 program credits Senior Year 3.4 QPA 21 program credits To be considered for Honors Program admission, entering freshman must have a minimum SAT score of 1150 or equivalent ACT scores, graduate in the top 15 percent of high school class, and successful completion of an interview. Undergraduate students already enrolled or transfer students may also apply. If a student should fail to residence at Clarion University. Candidates for graduation with an associate degree must complete a minimum of 30 credit hours in residence at the Venango Campus in Oil City, Pennsylvania. maintain the required QPA and course progression, the student will be placed on probation and have one semester to meet the requirements. A student who fails to achieve the required QPA and course progression by the end of the probationary semester will not be allowed to continue in the Honors Program or to continue to receive an Honors scholarship. **Disability Services offered:** Note-taking services; Reader services; Tape recorders; Tutors. **Career services:** Career assessment; Career/job search classes; Internships.

FACILITIES

Housing: Apartments for single students; Coed dorms; Men's dorms; Special housing for disabled students; Women's dorms; 98% of campus accessible to physically disabled. **Special Academic Facilities/Equipment:** Planetarium, Art Gallery.

CAMPUS LIFE

Environment: Village. **Activities:** Campus Ministries; Choral groups; Concert band; Dance; Drama/theater; International Student Organization; Jazz band; Literary magazine; Marching band; Music ensembles; Musical theater; Pep band; Radio station; Student government; Student newspaper; Student-run film society; Symphony orchestra; Television station. 150 registered organizations, 17 honor societies, 4 religious organizations, 5 fraternities, 8 sororities, on campus. **Athletics (Intercollegiate):** *Men:* baseball, basketball, diving, football, golf, swimming, wrestling. *Women:* basketball, cross-country, diving, soccer, softball, swimming, tennis, track/field (outdoor), volleyball. **On-Campus Highlights:** Recreation Center.

ADMISSIONS

Freshman Academic Profile: Average high school GPA 3.2. 2% in top 10% of high school class, 9% in top 25% of high school class, 39% in top 50% of high school class. 87% from public high schools. **Test Scores:** SAT Math middle 50% range 420–520. SAT EBRW middle 50% range 420–510. ACT middle 50% range 17–22. **Basis for Candidate Selection:** *Very* *important factors include:* rigor of secondary school record, academic GPA, standardized test scores. *Important factors include:* class rank, application essay, recommendation(s). *Other factors include:* interview, extracurricular activities, talent/ability, character/personal qualities, first generation, racial/ethnic status, volunteer work, work experience, level of applicant's interest. **Freshman Admission Requirements:** High school diploma is required and GED is accepted. *Academic units required:* 4 English, 3 math, 3 science, 3 social studies. *Academic units recommended:* 4 English, 4 math, 4 science, 1 science labs, 2 foreign language, 4 social studies, 1 history. **Freshman Admission Statistics:** 2,071 applied, 93% admitted, 55% enrolled. **Transfer Admission Requirements:** High school transcript, college transcript(s), statement of good standing from prior institution(s). Minimum college GPA of 2.0 required. Lowest grade transferable C. **General Admission Information:** Application fee $40. Priority deadline 2/15. Regular application deadline 8/1. Non-fall registration accepted.

COSTS AND FINANCIAL AID

Annual in-state tuition $5,554. Annual out-of-state tuition $11,108. Room and board $6,390. Required fees $1,826. Average book and supplies expense $900. **Required Forms and Deadlines:** FAFSA; State aid form. **Notification of Awards:** Applicants will be notified of awards on a rolling basis beginning 3/30. **Types of Aid:** *Need-based scholarships/grants:* College/university scholarship or grant aid from institutional funds; Federal Pell; Private scholarships; SEOG; State scholarships/grants; United Negro College Fund. *Loans:* Direct PLUS loans; Direct Subsidized Stafford Loans; Direct Unsubsidized Stafford Loans. **Student Employment:** Federal Work-Study Program available. Institutional employment available. **Financial Aid Statistics:** 78% needy freshmen, 75% needy undergrads receive need-based scholarship or grant aid. 38% freshmen, 25% undergrads receive non-need-based scholarship or grant aid. 87% freshmen, 60% undergrads receive need-based self-help aid. 4% freshmen, 3% undergrads receive athletic scholarships. 78% freshmen, 75% undergrads receive any aid. **Criteria awarding aid:** *Need-based:* Academics, Alumni affiliation, Art, Leadership, Minority status, Music/drama. *Non-need-based:* Academics, Alumni affiliation, Art, Athletics, Job skills, Leadership, Minority status, Music/drama, State/district residency.

CLARK ATLANTA UNIVERSITY

223 James P. Brawley Dr., SW, Atlanta, GA 30314-4391
Phone: 404-880-8784 **Financial Aid Phone:** 404-880-8992
E-mail: cauadmissions@cau.edu **CEEB Code:** 5110
Fax: 404-880-6605 **Website:** www.cau.edu **ACT Code:** 804

This private school, affiliated with the Methodist Church, was founded in 1988. It has a 126 acre campus.

RATINGS

Admissions Selectivity Rating: 75 **Fire Safety Rating:** 97 **Green Rating:** 60*

STUDENTS AND FACULTY

Enrollment: 3,093. **Student Body:** 71% female, 29% male, 65% out-of-state, 4% international (10 countries represented). Asian <1%, African American 83%, Caucasian <1%, Hispanic <1%, Native American <1%, Pacific Islander 0%, Two or more races 0%, Race unknown 12%.
Retention and Graduation: 67% freshmen return for sophomore year. 27% grads go on to further study within 1 year. 24% grads pursue arts and sciences degrees. 2% grads pursue business degrees. **Faculty:** Student/faculty ratio 19:1. 176 full-time faculty, 85% hold PhDs, 90% are members of minority groups, 43% are women. 0% of classes are taught by teaching assistants.

ACADEMICS

Degrees: Bachelor's; Doctoral degree research/scholarship; Master's; Post-bachelor's certificate; Post-master's certificate. **Classes:** Most classes have 20–29 students. Most lab/discussion sessions have fewer than 10 students. **Most popular majors:** Radio, Television, and Digital Communication, Other; Biology/Biological Sciences, General; Business Administration and Management, General. **Special Study Options:** Accelerated program; Cooperative education program; Cross-registration; Double major; Dual enrollment; Exchange student program (domestic); Honors program; Independent study; Internships; Study abroad; Teacher certification program; Weekend college. **Combined degree programs:** BA/MA. **Disability Services offered:** Note-taking services; Reader services; Tape recorders; Tutors. **Career services:** Career assessment; Career/job search classes; Internships.

FACILITIES

Housing: Apartments for single students; Coed dorms; Men's dorms; Women's dorms; 80% of campus accessible to physically disabled. **Campus network:** 100% of classrooms, 100% of dorms, 100% of student union, 100% of libraries, 100% of dining areas, 100% of common outdoor areas, have wireless network access.

CAMPUS LIFE

Environment: Metropolis. **Activities:** Campus Ministries; Choral groups; Concert band; Dance; Drama/theater; International Student Organization; Marching band; Music ensembles; Musical theater; Opera; Pep band; Radio station; Student government; Student newspaper; Student-run film society; Symphony orchestra; Television station; Yearbook. 80 registered organizations, 12 honor societies, 5 religious organizations, 4 fraternities, 4 sororities, on campus. **Athletics (Intercollegiate):** *Men:* baseball, basketball, cross-country, football, track/field (outdoor). *Women:* basketball, cross-country, softball, tennis, track/field (outdoor), volleyball. **On-Campus Highlights:** Robert W. Woodruff Library.

ADMISSIONS

Freshman Academic Profile: Average high school GPA 3.2. 9% in top 10% of high school class, 30% in top 25% of high school class, 69% in top 50% of high school class. 90% from public high schools. **Test Scores:** SAT Math middle 50% range 400–480. SAT EBRW middle 50% range 420–490. ACT middle 50% range 18–21. **Basis for Candidate Selection:** *Very important factors include:* rigor of secondary school record, academic GPA, standardized test scores, character/personal qualities. *Important factors include:* application essay, recommendation(s), talent/ability. *Other factors include:* alumni/ae relation, work experience, level of applicant's interest. **Freshman Admission Requirements:** High school diploma is required and GED is accepted. *Academic units required:* 4 English, 3 math, 3 science, 1 science labs, 2 foreign language, 3 social studies, 3 academic electives. **Freshman Admission Statistics:** 10,733 applied, 72% admitted, 13% enrolled. **Transfer Admission Requirements:** College transcript(s), statement of good standing from prior institution(s). Minimum college GPA of 2.5 required. Lowest grade transferable C. **General Admission Information:** Application fee $35. Priority deadline 3/1. Regular application deadline 6/1. Non-fall registration accepted. Admission may be deferred for a maximum of one year.

COSTS AND FINANCIAL AID

Annual tuition $20,476. Room and board $10,878. Required fees $2,606. Average book and supplies expense $1,500. **Required Forms and Deadlines:** FAFSA; State aid form. **Notification of Awards:** Applicants will be notified of awards on a rolling basis beginning 4/1. **Types of Aid:** *Need-based scholarships/grants:* College/university scholarship or grant aid from institutional funds; Federal Pell; Private scholarships; SEOG; State scholarships/grants; United Negro College Fund. *Loans:* Direct PLUS loans; Direct Subsidized Stafford Loans; Direct Unsubsidized Stafford Loans. **Student Employment:** Federal Work-Study Program available. Institutional employment available. **Financial Aid Statistics:** 92% needy freshmen, 90% needy undergrads receive need-based scholarship or grant aid. 16% freshmen, 15% undergrads receive non-need-based scholarship or grant aid. 95% freshmen, 95% undergrads receive need-based self-help aid. 0% freshmen, 0% undergrads receive athletic scholarships. 88% freshmen, 91% undergrads receive any aid. 91% undergrads borrow to pay for school. Average cumulative indebtedness $40,393. **Criteria awarding aid:** *Non-need-based:* Academics, Art, Athletics, Leadership, Minority status, Music/drama, Religious affiliation, State/district residency.

CLARKE UNIVERSITY

1550 Clarke Drive, Dubuque, IA 52001-3198
Phone: 563-588-6316
E-mail: admissions@clarke.edu **CEEB Code:** 6099
Fax: 563-588-6789 **Website:** www.clarke.edu **ACT Code:** 1290

This private school, affiliated with the Roman Catholic Church, was founded in 1843. It has a 55 acre campus.

RATINGS

Admissions Selectivity Rating: 77 **Fire Safety Rating:** 60* **Green Rating:** 60*

STUDENTS AND FACULTY

Enrollment: 933. **Student Body:** 69% female, 31% male, 38% out-of-state, 1% international (8 countries represented). Asian 1%, African American 4%,

Caucasian 89%, Hispanic 5%, Native American <1%, Pacific Islander 0%, Two or more races <1%, Race unknown 0%.
Retention and Graduation: 73% freshmen return for sophomore year. 25% grads go on to further study within 1 year. 23% grads pursue arts and sciences degrees. 0% grads pursue law degrees. 2% grads pursue business degrees. 0% grads pursue medical degrees. **Faculty:** Student/faculty ratio 10:1. 89 full-time faculty, 67% hold PhDs, 3% are members of minority groups, 67% are women. 0% of classes are taught by teaching assistants.

ACADEMICS

Degrees: Associate; Bachelor's; Doctoral degree—professional practice; Master's. **Classes:** Most classes have fewer than 10 students. Most lab/discussion sessions have fewer than 10 students. **Most popular majors:** Business/Commerce, General; Psychology, General; Nursing/Registered Nurse (Rn, Asn, Bsn, Msn). **Special Study Options:** Accelerated program; Cross-registration; Distance learning; Double major; Honors program; Independent study; Internships; Student-designed major; Study abroad; Teacher certification program. **Disability Services offered:** Note-taking services; Reader services; Tape recorders; Tutors. **Career services:** Alumni services; Career assessment; Career/job search classes; Internships.

FACILITIES

Housing: Apartments for single students; Coed dorms; Men's dorms; Women's dorms; 90% of campus accessible to physically disabled. **Special Academic Facilities/Equipment:** Art gallery, computer classrooms for math, biology, and computer science, computer-interfaced chemistry lab, human gross anatomy and nursing labs, electron microscope, music performance hall, foreign language lab, distance learning classroom. **Campus network:** 100% of classrooms, 100% of dorms, 100% of student union, 100% of libraries, 100% of dining areas, 80% of common outdoor areas, have wireless network access.

CAMPUS LIFE

Environment: Town. **Activities:** Campus Ministries; Choral groups; Concert band; Dance; Drama/theater; Jazz band; Literary magazine; Music ensembles; Musical theater; Radio station; Student government; Student newspaper; Yearbook. 48 registered organizations, 5 honor societies, 1 religious organizations, on campus. **Athletics (Intercollegiate):** *Men:* baseball, basketball, cheerleading, cross-country, golf, soccer, tennis, volleyball. *Women:* basketball, cheerleading, cross-country, golf, soccer, softball, tennis, volleyball.

ADMISSIONS

Freshman Academic Profile: Average high school GPA 3.5. 13% in top 10% of high school class, 55% in top 25% of high school class, 84% in top 50% of high school class. 81% from public high schools. **Test Scores:** SAT Math middle 50% range 475–550. SAT EBRW middle 50% range 470–530. ACT middle 50% range 20–24. **Basis for Candidate Selection:** *Very important factors include:* rigor of secondary school record, academic GPA, standardized test scores, talent/ability. *Important factors include:* class rank. *Other factors include:* interview, extracurricular activities, racial/ethnic status, volunteer work. **Freshman Admission Requirements:** High school diploma is required and GED is accepted. *Academic units required:* 4 English, 3 math, 3 science, 2 science labs, 2 foreign language, 2 social studies, 4 academic electives. *Academic units recommended:* 4 math, 4 science. **Freshman Admission Statistics:** 1,359 applied, 70% admitted, 19% enrolled. **Transfer Admission Requirements:** High school transcript, college transcript(s), standardized test scores, statement of good standing from prior institution(s). Minimum college GPA of 2.0 required. Lowest grade transferable C. **General Admission Information:** Application fee $25. Non-fall registration accepted. Admission may be deferred for a maximum of 12 months.

COSTS AND FINANCIAL AID

Annual tuition $28,000. Room and board $8,700. Average book and supplies expense $1,160. **Notification of Awards:** Applicants will be notified of awards on a rolling basis beginning 3/15. **Types of Aid:** *Need-based scholarships/grants:* College/university scholarship or grant aid from institutional funds; Federal Nursing Scholarships; Federal Pell; Private scholarships; SEOG; State scholarships/grants. *Loans:* Direct PLUS loans; Direct Subsidized Stafford Loans; Direct Unsubsidized Stafford Loans. **Student Employment:** Federal Work-Study Program available. Institutional employment available. **Financial Aid Statistics:** 100% needy freshmen, 100% needy undergrads receive need-based scholarship or grant aid. 99% freshmen, 95% undergrads receive non-need-based scholarship or grant aid. 90% freshmen, 89% undergrads receive need-based self-help aid. 41% freshmen, 33% undergrads receive athletic scholarships. **Criteria awarding aid:** *Need-based:* Academics. *Non-need-based:* Academics, Art, Athletics, Leadership, Music/drama.

CLARKSON UNIVERSITY

Best Colleges

Holcroft House, Potsdam, NY 13699
Phone: 315-268-6480 **Financial Aid Phone:** 315-268-6480
E-mail: admissions@clarkson.edu **CEEB Code:** 2084
Fax: 315-268-7647 **Website:** https://www.clarkson.edu

This private school was founded in 1896. It has a 640 acre campus.

RATINGS

Admissions Selectivity Rating: 85   **Fire Safety Rating:** 96   **Green Rating:** 91

STUDENTS AND FACULTY

Enrollment: 2,982. **Student Body:** 31% female, 69% male, 31% out-of-state, 3% international (30 countries represented). Asian 4%, African American 3%, Caucasian 79%, Hispanic 5%, Native American <1%, Pacific Islander <1%, Two or more races 4%, Race unknown 2%.
Retention and Graduation: 91% freshmen return for sophomore year. 63% freshmen graduate within 4 years. 81% freshmen graduate within 6 years. 11% grads go on to further study within 1 year. 3% grads pursue arts and sciences degrees. 0% grads pursue law degrees. 3% grads pursue business degrees. 0% grads pursue medical degrees. **Faculty:** Student/faculty ratio 14:1. 246 full-time faculty, 84% hold PhDs, 28% are members of minority groups, 35% are women. 0% of classes are taught by teaching assistants.

ACADEMICS

Degrees: Bachelor's; Doctoral degree—professional practice; Doctoral degree research/scholarship; Master's; Post-bachelor's certificate. **Classes:** Most classes have 10–19 students. Most lab/discussion sessions have 10–19 students. **Most popular majors:** Mechanical Engineering; Engineering/Industrial Management; Civil Engineering, General. **Special Study Options:** Accelerated program; Cooperative education program; Cross-registration; Distance learning; Double major; Dual enrollment; English as a Second Language (ESL); Honors program; Independent study; Internships; Liberal arts/career combination; Student-designed major; Study abroad. **Honors programs:** Built upon current and emerging problems in science, technology and society, the Clarkson University Honors Program offers unique academic challenges and opportunities for Clarkson's most promising students. The program is a gateway to a multitude of opportunities that include internships, research experience, fellowships, graduate schools, study abroad, and jobs. **Disability Services offered:** Note-taking services; Reader services; Tape recorders; Tutors. **Career services:** Alumni network; Alumni services; Career assessment; Career/job search classes; Internships; Regional alumni.

FACILITIES

Housing: Apartments for single students; Coed dorms; Fraternity/sorority housing; Men's dorms; Special housing for disabled students; Special housing for international students; Theme housing; Women's dorms; 85% of campus accessible to physically disabled. **Special Academic Facilities/Equipment:** The Student Center is a place where students can come to spend time between classes, study, and hold meetings and late night events. In it is the Forum, an innovative auditorium in the form of a stairwell equipped with a massive video wall. The Deneka Family Fitness Center offers a full workout facility with an assortment of cardiovascular machines, a weight room and classes. The Denny Brown Adirondack Lodge is home to the Outing Club and the starting point for outdoor adventures. The Outing Club also maintains the Canoe House on the Raquette River, housing canoes and kayaks for student use. Glass walkways connect all hill campus academic buildings, so students need not venture out if there is inclement weather between classes.

CAMPUS LIFE

Environment: Village. **Activities:** Choral groups; Concert band; Dance; Drama/theater; International Student Organization; Jazz band; Model UN; Music ensembles; Musical theater; Pep band; Radio station; Student government; Student newspaper; Student-run film society; Symphony orchestra; Television station; Yearbook. 231 registered organizations, 24 honor societies, 5 religious organizations, 9 fraternities, 4 sororities, on campus. **Athletics (Intercollegiate):** *Men:* baseball, basketball, cross-country, diving, golf, ice hockey, lacrosse, skiing (downhill/Alpine), skiing (Nordic/cross-country), soccer, swimming. *Women:* basketball, cross-country, diving, ice hockey, lacrosse, skiing (downhill/Alpine), skiing (Nordic/cross-country), soccer, swimming, volleyball.

On-Campus Highlights: Student Center Forum & Starbucks Coffee in the ERC. **Environmental Initiatives:** Clarkson has undertaken many activities to integrate sustainability into facilities and campus life. For example, as part of a significant renovation of the Woodstock Village Apartments to increase its energy efficiency, four of the buildings were modified to create the campus' Smart Housing Project. These buildings have a high density of water, electricity and air quality sensors that are used for building energy modeling, advanced building automation and feedback to students about their utility use. Research on feedback and motivation strategies has shown significant conservation, with as much as 21% savings in electricity and hot water use.

ADMISSIONS

Freshman Academic Profile: Average high school GPA 3.7. 37% in top 10% of high school class, 69% in top 25% of high school class, 94% in top 50% of high school class. 86% from public high schools. **Test Scores:** SAT Math middle 50% range 600–690. SAT EBRW middle 50% range 560–660. ACT middle 50% range 23–30. **Basis for Candidate Selection:** *Very important factors include:* rigor of secondary school record, academic GPA. *Important factors include:* class rank, standardized test scores, recommendation(s), extracurricular activities, volunteer work. *Other factors include:* application essay, talent/ ability, character/personal qualities, first generation, alumni/ae relation, work experience, level of applicant's interest. **Freshman Admission Requirements:** High school diploma is required and GED is accepted. *Academic units required:* 4 English, 3 math, 1 science, 4 unit from above areas or other academic areas. *Academic units recommended:* 4 math, 4 science. **Freshman Admission Statistics:** 6,673 applied, 75% admitted, 16% enrolled. **Transfer Admission Requirements:** College transcript(s). Minimum college GPA of 2.75 required. Lowest grade transferable 2. **General Admission Information:** Application fee $50. Regular application deadline 1/15. Non-fall registration accepted. Admission may be deferred for a maximum of 12 months.

COSTS AND FINANCIAL AID

Annual tuition $51,454. Room and board $17,118. Required fees $1,270. Average book and supplies expense $1,446. **Required Forms and Deadlines:** FAFSA; State aid form. **Notification of Awards:** Applicants will be notified of awards on a rolling basis beginning 2/15. **Types of Aid:** *Need-based scholarships/ grants:* College/university scholarship or grant aid from institutional funds; Federal Pell; Private scholarships; SEOG; State scholarships/grants. *Loans:* Direct PLUS loans; Direct Subsidized Stafford Loans; Direct Unsubsidized Stafford Loans. **Student Employment:** Federal Work-Study Program available. Institutional employment available. **Financial Aid Statistics:** 99% needy freshmen, 99% needy undergrads receive need-based scholarship or grant aid. 20% freshmen, 17% undergrads receive non-need-based scholarship or grant aid. 74% freshmen, 77% undergrads receive need-based self-help aid. 1% freshmen, 2% undergrads receive athletic scholarships. 97% freshmen, 97% undergrads receive any aid. 100% undergrads borrow to pay for school. Average cumulative indebtedness $29,000. **Criteria awarding aid:** *Need-based:* Academics, Minority status. *Non-need-based:* Academics, Alumni affiliation, Leadership, Minority status.

CLARKS SUMMIT UNIVERSITY

38 Venard Rd., Clarks Summit, PA
Phone: 570-586-2400 **Financial Aid Phone:** 570-585-9206
E-mail: admissions@SummitU.edu **CEEB Code:** 2036
Fax: 570-585-9299 **Website:** www.SummitU.edu **ACT Code:** 3523

This private school, affiliated with the Baptist Church, was founded in 1932. It has a 121 acre campus.

RATINGS

Admissions Selectivity Rating: 79   **Fire Safety Rating:** 67   **Green Rating:** 61

STUDENTS AND FACULTY

Enrollment: 668. **Student Body:** 59% female, 41% male, 68% out-of-state, 2% international (7 countries represented). Asian 1%, African American 1%, Caucasian 94%, Hispanic 2%, Native American <1%, Race unknown 1%. **Retention and Graduation:** 69% freshmen return for sophomore year. **Faculty:** 35 full-time faculty, 57% hold PhDs, 3% are members of minority groups, 29% are women. 0% of classes are taught by teaching assistants.

ACADEMICS

Degrees: Associate; Bachelor's; Certificate; Doctoral degree—professional practice; Master's. **Classes:** Most classes have 10–19 students. **Most popular**

majors: Counseling Psychology; Theology and Religious Vocations, Other; Elementary Education and Teaching. **Special Study Options:** Distance learning; Double major; Dual enrollment; Independent study; Internships; Study abroad; Teacher certification program. **Career services:** Alumni services; Internships.

FACILITIES

Housing: Men's dorms; Women's dorms.

CAMPUS LIFE

Environment: Town. **Activities:** Campus Ministries; Choral groups; Concert band; Drama/theater; Music ensembles; Student government; Yearbook. **Athletics (Intercollegiate):** *Men:* baseball, basketball, cross-country, golf, soccer. *Women:* basketball, cross-country, soccer, softball, tennis, volleyball. **On-Campus Highlights:** Underground Cafe.

ADMISSIONS

Freshman Academic Profile: 40% from public high schools. **Test Scores:** SAT Math middle 50% range 430–560. SAT EBRW middle 50% range 460–570. ACT middle 50% range 20–24. **Basis for Candidate Selection:** *Very important factors include:* rigor of secondary school record, application essay, standardized test scores, recommendation(s), character/personal qualities, religious affiliation/ commitment. *Important factors include:* academic GPA. *Other factors include:* interview, extracurricular activities, talent/ability, volunteer work, work experience, level of applicant's interest. **Freshman Admission Requirements:** High school diploma is required and GED is accepted. **Freshman Admission Statistics:** 452 applied, 76% admitted, 48% enrolled. **Transfer Admission Requirements:** High school transcript, college transcript(s), essay or personal statement, Minimum college GPA of 2 required. Lowest grade transferable 2. **General Admission Information:** Application fee $30. Priority deadline 5/1. Regular application deadline 8/15. Non-fall registration accepted.

COSTS AND FINANCIAL AID

Annual tuition $6,840. Room and board $5,900. Required fees $468. **Required Forms and Deadlines:** FAFSA; Institution's own financial aid form. **Notification of Awards:** Applicants will be notified of awards on a rolling basis beginning 10/1. **Types of Aid:** *Need-based scholarships/grants:* College/university scholarship or grant aid from institutional funds; Federal Pell; State scholarships/grants. *Loans:* Direct Unsubsidized Stafford Loans. **Student Employment:** Federal Work-Study Program available. Institutional employment available. **Financial Aid Statistics:** 100% freshmen, 96% undergrads receive any aid. **Criteria awarding aid:** *Need-based:* Academics. *Non-need-based:* Academics, Leadership.

CLARK UNIVERSITY

950 Main Street, Worcester, MA 01610-1477
Phone: 508-793-7431 **Financial Aid Phone:** 508-793-7519
E-mail: admissions@clarku.edu **CEEB Code:** 3279
Fax: 508-793-8821 **Website:** www.clarku.edu **ACT Code:** 1808

This private school was founded in 1887. It has a 50 acre campus.

RATINGS

Admissions Selectivity Rating: 88   **Fire Safety Rating:** 98   **Green Rating:** 92

STUDENTS AND FACULTY

Enrollment: 2,283. **Student Body:** 61% female, 39% male, 61% out-of-state, 11% international (53 countries represented). Asian 8%, African American 4%, Caucasian 60%, Hispanic 9%, Native American <1%, Pacific Islander <1%, Two or more races 3%, Race unknown 5%. **Retention and Graduation:** 86% freshmen return for sophomore year. 75% freshmen graduate within 4 years. 79% freshmen graduate within 6 years. 42% grads go on to further study within 1 year. 25% grads pursue arts and sciences degrees. 1% grads pursue law degrees. 5% grads pursue business degrees. 1% grads pursue medical degrees. **Faculty:** Student/faculty ratio 11:1. 173 full-time faculty, 95% hold PhDs, 20% are members of minority groups, 45% are women. 1% of classes are taught by teaching assistants.

ACADEMICS

Degrees: Bachelor's; Certificate; Doctoral degree research/scholarship; Master's; Post-bachelor's certificate; Post-master's certificate. **Classes:** Most classes have 10–19 students. Most lab/discussion sessions have 10–19 students. **Most popular majors:** Political Science and Government, General. **Special Study Options:** Cross-registration; Double major; English as a Second Language (ESL); Independent study; Internships; Liberal arts/career combination; Student-designed major; Study abroad; Teacher certification program. **Combined degree programs:** BA/MA. **Disability Services offered:** Note-taking services; Tape recorders. **Career services:** Alumni network; Alumni services; Career assessment; Career/job search classes; Internships; Regional alumni.

FACILITIES

Housing: Apartments for single students; Coed dorms; Special housing for disabled students; Wellness housing; Women's dorms **Special Academic Facilities/Equipment:** Galleries, 3 full theatres, concert hall, machine shop, near zero lab, Kasperson environmental library, Robert H. Goddard historical exhibition, rare book room, rare map collection, Freud archives, craft center, music rehearsal space, map library, IDRISI GIS lab, Holocaust library & center, arboretum, herbarium, extensive darkroom facilities, radio station, satellite dish for international program reception, electron microscope, nuclear magnetic resonance spectrometer, astronomy observatory.

CAMPUS LIFE

Environment: City. **Activities:** Campus Ministries; Choral groups; Concert band; Dance; Drama/theater; International Student Organization; Jazz band; Literary magazine; Marching band; Model UN; Music ensembles; Musical theater; Pep band; Radio station; Student government; Student newspaper; Student-run film society; Symphony orchestra; Television station; Yearbook. 130 registered organizations, 10 honor societies, 7 religious organizations, on campus. **Athletics (Intercollegiate):** *Men:* baseball, basketball, crew/rowing, cross-country, diving, lacrosse, soccer, swimming, tennis. *Women:* basketball, crew/rowing, cross-country, diving, field hockey, soccer, softball, swimming, tennis, volleyball. **On-Campus Highlights:** Academic Commons at Goddard Library. **Environmental Initiatives:** Becoming Climate Neutral—Zero Emissions—by 2030.

ADMISSIONS

Freshman Academic Profile: Average high school GPA 3.7. 27% in top 10% of high school class, 67% in top 25% of high school class, 94% in top 50% of high school class. 75% from public high schools. **Test Scores:** SAT Math middle 50% range 580–690. SAT EBRW middle 50% range 600–60. ACT middle 50% range 27–31. **Basis for Candidate Selection:** *Very important factors include:* rigor of secondary school record, academic GPA, recommendation(s). *Important factors include:* application essay, extracurricular activities, talent/ability, character/personal qualities, volunteer work. *Other factors include:* class rank, standardized test scores, interview, first generation, alumni/ae relation, geographical residence, racial/ethnic status, work experience, level of applicant's interest. **Freshman Admission Requirements:** High school diploma is required and GED is accepted. *Academic units recommended:* 4 English, 3 math, 3 science, 2 science labs, 2 foreign language, 2 social studies, 2 history. **Freshman Admission Statistics:** 7,639 applied, 53% admitted, 16% enrolled. **Transfer Admission Requirements:** High school transcript, college transcript(s), essay or personal statement, standardized test scores, statement of good standing from prior institution(s). Minimum college GPA of 2.8 required. **General Admission Information:** Application fee $60. Regular application deadline 1/15. Non-fall registration accepted. Admission may be deferred for a maximum of 1 year.

COSTS AND FINANCIAL AID

Required Forms and Deadlines: CSS/Financial Aid PROFILE; FAFSA; Noncustodial PROFILE. **Notification of Awards:** Applicants will be notified of awards on or about 3/31. **Types of Aid:** *Need-based scholarships/grants:* College/university scholarship or grant aid from institutional funds; Federal Pell; SEOG; State scholarships/grants. *Loans:* Direct PLUS loans; Direct Subsidized Stafford Loans; Direct Unsubsidized Stafford Loans. **Student Employment:** Federal Work-Study Program available. Institutional employment available. **Financial Aid Statistics:** 98% needy freshmen, 98% needy undergrads receive need-based scholarship or grant aid. 23% freshmen, 22% undergrads receive non-need-based scholarship or grant aid. 77% freshmen, 70% undergrads receive need-based self-help aid. 0% freshmen, 0% undergrads receive athletic scholarships. 95% freshmen, 91% undergrads receive any aid. 61% undergrads borrow to pay for school. Average cumulative indebtedness $34,390. **Criteria awarding aid:** *Non-need-based:* Academics, Leadership.

CLAYTON STATE UNIVERSITY

2000 Clayton State Blvd., Morrow, GA 30206-0285
Phone: 678-466-4115
E-mail: ccsu-info@mail.clayton.edu
Fax: 678-466-4149 **Website:** www.clayton.edu

This is a public school.

RATINGS

Admissions Selectivity Rating: 84   **Fire Safety Rating:** 60*   **Green Rating:** 60*

STUDENTS AND FACULTY

Enrollment: 5,661. **Student Body:** 69% female, 31% male, 5% out-of-state, 2% international. Asian 4%, African American 48%, Caucasian 43%, Hispanic 3%, Native American 1%, Race unknown 0%.
Retention and Graduation: 61% freshmen return for sophomore year.
Faculty: Student/faculty ratio 28:1. 157 full-time faculty, 57% hold PhDs, 15% are members of minority groups, 59% are women.

ACADEMICS

Degrees: Associate; Bachelor's; Certificate; Master's; Terminal Associate; Transfer Associate. **Classes:** Most classes have 20–29 students. Most lab/discussion sessions have fewer than 10 students. **Special Study Options:** Cooperative education program; Cross-registration; Distance learning; Double major; Dual enrollment; Exchange student program (domestic); Honors program; Independent study; Internships; Liberal arts/career combination; Study abroad; Teacher certification program.

FACILITIES

Housing: Apartments for single students. **Campus network:** 100% of classrooms, 100% of dorms, 100% of student union, 100% of libraries, 100% of dining areas, 100% of common outdoor areas, have wireless network access.

CAMPUS LIFE

Activities: Choral groups; Drama/theater; Jazz band; Literary magazine; Music ensembles; Musical theater; Opera; Pep band; Student government; Student newspaper.

ADMISSIONS

Freshman Academic Profile: Average high school GPA 2.9. **Test Scores:** SAT Math middle 50% range 440–550. SAT EBRW middle 50% range 450–550. ACT middle 50% range 17–21. **Basis for Candidate Selection:** *Very important factors include:* rigor of secondary school record, academic GPA, standardized test scores. *Other factors include:* class rank, extracurricular activities, talent/ability. **Freshman Admission Requirements:** High school diploma is required and GED is not accepted. *Academic units required:* 4 English, 4 math, 3 science, 2 foreign language, 3 social studies. **Freshman Admission Statistics:** 2,920 applied, 71% admitted, 63% enrolled. **Transfer Admission Requirements:** College transcript(s), statement of good standing from prior institution(s). Minimum college GPA of 2.0 required. Lowest grade transferable D. **General Admission Information:** Application fee $40. Priority deadline 2/1. Regular application deadline 7/1. Non-fall registration accepted.

COSTS AND FINANCIAL AID

Annual in-state tuition $2,212. Annual out-of-state tuition $8,848. Average book and supplies expense $1,000. **Required Forms and Deadlines:** FAFSA; State aid form. **Types of Aid:** *Need-based scholarships/grants:* College/university scholarship or grant aid from institutional funds; Federal Nursing Scholarships; Federal Pell; Private scholarships; SEOG; State scholarships/grants. **Financial Aid Statistics:** 65% needy freshmen, 67% needy undergrads receive need-based scholarship or grant aid. 75% freshmen, 43% undergrads receive non-need-based scholarship or grant aid. 45% freshmen, 62% undergrads receive need-based self-help aid. 1% freshmen, 3% undergrads receive athletic scholarships. **Criteria awarding aid:** *Need-based:* Academics. *Non-need-based:* Academics.

CLEAR CREEK BAPTIST BIBLE COLLEGE

300 Clear Creek Road, Pineville, KY 40977-9754
Phone: 606-337-3196 **Financial Aid Phone:** (606) 337-1457
E-mail: ccbbc@ccbbc.edu
Fax: 606-337-2372 **Website:** www.ccbbc.edu

This private school, affiliated with the Southern Baptist Church, was founded in 1926. It has a 700 acre campus.

RATINGS
Admissions Selectivity Rating: 68   **Fire Safety Rating:** 72   **Green Rating:** 60*

STUDENTS AND FACULTY
Enrollment: 160. **Student Body:** 22% female, 78% male, 60% out-of-state, 0% international (0 countries represented). Asian 1%, African American 1%, Caucasian 95%, Hispanic 2%, Native American 0%, Pacific Islander 0%, Two or more races 0%, Race unknown 1%.
Retention and Graduation: 93% freshmen return for sophomore year. 30% grads go on to further study within 1 year. **Faculty:** Student/faculty ratio 10:1. 6 full-time faculty, 83% hold PhDs, 0% are members of minority groups, 0% are women.

ACADEMICS
Degrees: Associate; Bachelor's; Certificate. **Classes:** Most classes have 10–19 students. Most lab/discussion sessions have 10–19 students. **Most popular majors:** Bible/Biblical Studies. **Special Study Options:** Distance learning; Double major; Independent study; Internships. **Career services:** Alumni network.

FACILITIES
Housing: Apartments for married students; Apartments for single students; Men's dorms; Wellness housing; Women's dorms; 95% of campus accessible to physically disabled. **Special Academic Facilities/Equipment:** Jerusalem model. **Campus network:** 100% of classrooms, 100% of dorms, 100% of student union, 100% of libraries, 100% of dining areas, have wireless network access.

CAMPUS LIFE
Environment: Rural. **Activities:** Campus Ministries; Choral groups; Music ensembles; Radio station; Student government; Student newspaper. **On-Campus Highlights:** Kelly Hall.

ADMISSIONS
Basis for Candidate Selection: *Very important factors include:* application essay, recommendation(s), character/personal qualities, religious affiliation/commitment. *Important factors include:* interview. *Other factors include:* talent/ability, alumni/ae relation, level of applicant's interest. **Freshman Admission Requirements:** High school diploma is required and GED is accepted. **Freshman Admission Statistics:** 14 applied, 93% admitted, 85% enrolled. **Transfer Admission Requirements:** High school transcript, college transcript(s), essay or personal statement, interview. Minimum college GPA of 2.0 required. Lowest grade transferable C. **General Admission Information:** Application fee $40. Priority deadline 7/15. Regular application deadline 8/2. Non-fall registration accepted. Admission may be deferred for a maximum of 2 years.

COSTS AND FINANCIAL AID
Annual tuition $5,482. Room and board $3,470. Required fees $400. Average book and supplies expense $1,200. **Required Forms and Deadlines:** FAFSA; Institution's own financial aid form. **Notification of Awards:** Applicants will be notified of awards on a rolling basis beginning 5/1. **Types of Aid:** *Need-based scholarships/grants:* College/university scholarship or grant aid from institutional funds; Federal Pell; Private scholarships; SEOG. **Student Employment:** Federal Work-Study Program available. Institutional employment available. **Financial Aid Statistics:** 100% needy freshmen, 100% needy undergrads receive need-based scholarship or grant aid. 22% freshmen, 42% undergrads receive non-need-based scholarship or grant aid. 33% freshmen, 37% undergrads receive need-based self-help aid. 0% freshmen, 0% undergrads receive athletic scholarships. 81% freshmen, 75% undergrads receive any aid. **Criteria awarding aid:** *Need-based:* Academics, Alumni affiliation, Leadership, Religious affiliation. *Non-need-based:* Academics, Leadership, Religious affiliation, State/district residency.

CLEARWATER CHRISTIAN COLLEGE

3400 Gulf-to-Bay Boulevard, Clearwater, FL 33759-4595
Phone: 727-726-1153 **Financial Aid Phone:** (727) 726-1153
E-mail: admissions@clearwater.edu
Fax: 727-726-8597 **Website:** www.clearwater.edu **ACT Code:** 715

This private school, affiliated with the Christian (Nondenominational) Church, was founded in 1966. It has a 138 acre campus.

RATINGS
Admissions Selectivity Rating: 82   **Fire Safety Rating:** 96   **Green Rating:** 60*

STUDENTS AND FACULTY
Enrollment: 546. **Student Body:** 50% female, 50% male, 52% out-of-state, <1% international (2 countries represented). Asian 1%, African American 5%, Caucasian 82%, Hispanic 4%, Native American <1%, Pacific Islander 0%, Two or more races 0%, Race unknown 8%.
Retention and Graduation: 70% freshmen return for sophomore year. 26% grads go on to further study within 1 year. 16% grads pursue arts and sciences degrees. 1% grads pursue law degrees. 2% grads pursue business degrees. 4% grads pursue medical degrees. **Faculty:** 28 full-time faculty, 68% hold PhDs, 4% are members of minority groups, 32% are women. 0% of classes are taught by teaching assistants.

ACADEMICS
Degrees: Associate; Bachelor's; Certificate; Master's. **Classes:** Most classes have fewer than 10 students. **Most popular majors:** Business Administration and Management, General; Elementary Education and Teaching; Exercise Science and Kinesiology. **Special Study Options:** Cooperative education program; Distance learning; Double major; Dual enrollment; Honors program; Independent study; Internships; Liberal arts/career combination; Student-designed major; Study abroad; Teacher certification program. **Honors programs:** Interdisciplinary Studies, a self-designed multidisciplinary program for students with exceptional ability and focus. **Disability Services offered:** Tape recorders; Tutors. **Career services:** Alumni services; Career/job search classes; Internships.

FACILITIES
Housing: Men's dorms; Women's dorms. **Campus network:** 90% of classrooms, 95% of dorms, 100% of student union, 100% of libraries, 80% of dining areas, 65% of common outdoor areas, have wireless network access.

CAMPUS LIFE
Environment: City. **Activities:** Campus Ministries; Choral groups; Concert band; Drama/theater; Music ensembles; Pep band; Student government; Student newspaper; Student-run film society; Symphony orchestra; Yearbook. 17 registered organizations, 1 honor societies, 1 religious organizations, 5 fraternities, 6 sororities, on campus. **Athletics (Intercollegiate):** *Men:* baseball, basketball, golf, soccer. *Women:* basketball, golf, soccer, softball, volleyball. **On-Campus Highlights:** The Cove.

ADMISSIONS
Test Scores: SAT Math middle 50% range 450–530. SAT EBRW middle 50% range 470–560. ACT middle 50% range 21–23. **Basis for Candidate Selection:** *Very important factors include:* application essay, standardized test scores, recommendation(s), character/personal qualities, religious affiliation/commitment. *Important factors include:* rigor of secondary school record, academic GPA, interview. *Other factors include:* alumni/ae relation, volunteer work, level of applicant's interest. **Freshman Admission Requirements:** High school diploma is required and GED is accepted. *Academic units required:* 4 English, 3 math, 3 science, 2 foreign language, 3 social studies. **Freshman Admission Statistics:** 341 applied, 74% admitted, 56% enrolled. **Transfer Admission Requirements:** High school transcript, college transcript(s), essay or personal statement, standardized test scores, statement of good standing from prior institution(s). Minimum college GPA of 2.0 required. Lowest grade transferable C-. **General Admission Information:** Application fee $35. Regular application deadline 8/1. Admission may be deferred for a maximum of 1 year.

COSTS AND FINANCIAL AID
Annual tuition $16,250. Room and board $7,470. Required fees $95. Average book and supplies expense $1,000. **Required Forms and Deadlines:** FAFSA; Institution's own financial aid form; State aid form. **Notification of Awards:** Applicants will be notified of awards on a rolling basis beginning 3/15. **Types of Aid:** *Need-based scholarships/grants:* College/university scholarship or grant aid from institutional funds; Federal Pell; Private scholarships; SEOG; State

scholarships/grants. *Loans:* Direct PLUS loans; Direct Subsidized Stafford Loans; Direct Unsubsidized Stafford Loans. **Student Employment:** Federal Work-Study Program available. Institutional employment available. **Financial Aid Statistics:** 100% needy freshmen, 99% needy undergrads receive need-based scholarship or grant aid. 9% freshmen, 9% undergrads receive non-need-based scholarship or grant aid. 63% freshmen, 63% undergrads receive need-based self-help aid. 0% freshmen, 0% undergrads receive athletic scholarships. 97% freshmen, 94% undergrads receive any aid. **Criteria awarding aid:** *Need-based:* Academics, Alumni affiliation, Music/drama, Religious affiliation. *Non-need-based:* Academics, Alumni affiliation, Leadership, Music/drama, Religious affiliation.

CLEMSON UNIVERSITY

105 Sikes Hall, Clemson, SC 29634-5124
Phone: 864-656-2287 **Financial Aid Phone:** (864) 656-2280
E-mail: cuadmissions@clemson.edu **CEEB Code:** 5111
Fax: 864-656-2464 **Website:** www.clemson.edu **ACT Code:** 3842

This public school was founded in 1889. It has a 17000 acre campus.

RATINGS
Admissions Selectivity Rating: 91   **Fire Safety Rating:** 97   **Green Rating:** 80

STUDENTS AND FACULTY
Enrollment: 20,074. **Student Body:** 50% female, 50% male, 34% out-of-state, 1% international (84 countries represented). Asian 3%, African American 6%, Caucasian 81%, Hispanic 6%, Native American <1%, Pacific Islander <1%, Two or more races 4%, Race unknown <1%.
Retention and Graduation: 93% freshmen return for sophomore year. 59% freshmen graduate within 4 years. 82% freshmen graduate within 6 years. 28% grads go on to further study within 1 year. 25% grads pursue arts and sciences degrees. 5% grads pursue law degrees. 21% grads pursue business degrees. 8% grads pursue medical degrees. **Faculty:** Student/faculty ratio 16:1. 1,300 full-time faculty, 87% hold PhDs, 21% are members of minority groups, 40% are women. 7% of classes are taught by teaching assistants.

ACADEMICS
Degrees: Bachelor's; Doctoral degree research/scholarship; Master's; Post-bachelor's certificate; Post-master's certificate. **Classes:** Most classes have 10–19 students. **Most popular majors:** Business/Commerce, General; Engineering, General; Biology/Biological Sciences, General. **Special Study Options:** Cooperative education program; Distance learning; Double major; Dual enrollment; Honors program; Independent study; Internships; Study abroad; Teacher certification program. **Honors programs:** The National Scholars Program. Please visit: http://www.clemson.edu/national_scholars/. **Combined degree programs:** BA/MEng. **Disability Services offered:** Note-taking services; Reader services; Tape recorders; Tutors. **Career services:** Alumni network; Alumni services; Career assessment; Career/job search classes; Internships; Regional alumni.

FACILITIES
Housing: Apartments for single students; Coed dorms; Fraternity/sorority housing; Men's dorms; Special housing for disabled students; Special housing for international students; Theme housing; Wellness housing; Women's dorms. **Special Academic Facilities/Equipment:** The South Carolina Botanical Gardens, the Campbell Geology Museum, the Brooks Center for the Performing Arts, the Rudolph Lee Art Gallery, The Garrison Livestock Arena, The John C. Calhoun Home. **Campus network:** 100% of classrooms, 100% of dorms, 100% of student union, 100% of libraries, 100% of dining areas, 100% of common outdoor areas, have wireless network access.

CAMPUS LIFE
Environment: Village. **Activities:** Campus Ministries; Choral groups; Concert band; Dance; Drama/theater; International Student Organization; Jazz band; Literary magazine; Marching band; Model UN; Music ensembles; Pep band; Radio station; Student government; Student newspaper; Television station; Yearbook. 292 registered organizations, 23 honor societies, 24 religious organizations, 26 fraternities, 17 sororities, on campus. **Athletics (Intercollegiate):** *Men:* baseball, basketball, cheerleading, cross-country, diving,

football, golf, soccer, swimming, tennis, track/field (outdoor), track/field (indoor). *Women:* basketball, cheerleading, crew/rowing, cross-country, diving, soccer, swimming, tennis, track/field (outdoor), track/field (indoor), volleyball. **On-Campus Highlights:** SC Botanical Garden/Discovery Center/Geology Muse. **Environmental Initiatives:** LEED.

ADMISSIONS
Freshman Academic Profile: Average high school GPA 4.4. 56% in top 10% of high school class, 87% in top 25% of high school class, 98% in top 50% of high school class. 89% from public high schools. **Test Scores:** SAT Math middle 50% range 610–710. SAT EBRW middle 50% range 610–690. ACT middle 50% range 27–32. **Basis for Candidate Selection:** *Very important factors include:* rigor of secondary school record, class rank, academic GPA, standardized test scores, state residency. *Other factors include:* application essay, recommendation(s), extracurricular activities, talent/ability, alumni/ae relation. **Freshman Admission Requirements:** High school diploma is required and GED is accepted. *Academic units required:* 4 English, 4 math, 3 science, 3 science labs, 2 foreign language, 1 social studies, 1 history, 2 academic electives, 1 computer science, 1 visual/performing arts, 1 unit from above areas or other academic areas. *Academic units recommended:* 4 science labs, 3 foreign language. **Freshman Admission Statistics:** 28,845 applied, 47% admitted, 28% enrolled. **Transfer Admission Requirements:** college transcript(s), Minimum college GPA of 2.5 required. Lowest grade transferable C. **General Admission Information:** Application fee $70. Priority deadline 12/1. Regular application deadline 5/1. Non-fall registration accepted. Admission may be deferred for a maximum of 1 year.

COSTS AND FINANCIAL AID
Annual in-state tuition $13,702. Annual out-of-state tuition $35,056. Room and board $10,832. Required fees $1,268. Average book and supplies expense $1,392. **Required Forms and Deadlines:** FAFSA. **Notification of Awards:** Applicants will be notified of awards on a rolling basis beginning 3/1. **Types of Aid:** *Need-based scholarships/grants:* College/university scholarship or grant aid from institutional funds; Federal Pell; Private scholarships; SEOG; State scholarships/grants. *Loans:* Direct PLUS loans; Direct Subsidized Stafford Loans; Direct Unsubsidized Stafford Loans. **Student Employment:** Federal Work-Study Program available. Institutional employment available. **Financial Aid Statistics:** 94% needy freshmen, 82% needy undergrads receive need-based scholarship or grant aid. 94% freshmen, 82% undergrads receive non-need-based scholarship or grant aid. 71% freshmen, 74% undergrads receive need-based self-help aid. 2% freshmen, 2% undergrads receive athletic scholarships. 87% freshmen, 71% undergrads receive any aid. 47% undergrads borrow to pay for school. Average cumulative indebtedness $32,285. **Criteria awarding aid:** *Need-based:* Academics, Leadership, Minority status, Music/drama. *Non-need-based:* Academics, Art, Athletics, Leadership, Minority status, Music/drama, State/district residency.

THE CLEVELAND INSTITUTE OF ART

11610 Euclid Avenue, Cleveland, OH 44106
Phone: 216-421-7418 **Financial Aid Phone:** 216-421-7425
E-mail: admissions@cia.edu **CEEB Code:** 1152
Fax: 216-754-3634 **Website:** www.cia.edu **ACT Code:** 3243

This private school was founded in 1882. It has a 1 acre campus.

RATINGS
Admissions Selectivity Rating: 80   **Fire Safety Rating:** 95   **Green Rating:** 69

STUDENTS AND FACULTY
Enrollment: 658. **Student Body:** 67% female, 33% male, 32% out-of-state, 6% international (8 countries represented). Asian 3%, African American 11%, Caucasian 67%, Hispanic 8%, Native American <1%, Pacific Islander <1%, Two or more races 5%, Race unknown 0%.
Retention and Graduation: 86% freshmen return for sophomore year. 59% freshmen graduate within 4 years. 3% grads go on to further study within 1 year. 3% grads pursue arts and sciences degrees. 0% grads pursue law degrees. 0% grads pursue business degrees. 0% grads pursue medical degrees. **Faculty:** Student/faculty ratio 8:1. 51 full-time faculty, 71% hold PhDs, 14% are members of minority groups, 67% are women. 0% of classes are taught by teaching assistants.

ACADEMICS

Degrees: Bachelor's. **Classes:** Most classes have 10–19 students. **Most popular majors:** Illustration; Animation, Interactive Technology, Video Graphics and Special Effects; Industrial and Product Design. **Special Study Options:** Cross-registration; Distance learning; Double major; Independent study; Internships; Study abroad. **Disability Services offered:** Note-taking services; Tape recorders; Tutors. **Career services:** Alumni network; Alumni services; Career assessment; Career/job search classes; Internships.

FACILITIES

Housing: Apartments for single students; Coed dorms; Fraternity/sorority housing; Special housing for disabled students; Wellness housing; 100% of campus accessible to physically disabled. **Special Academic Facilities/Equipment:** The Reinberger Galleries **Campus network:** 100% of classrooms, 100% of dorms, 100% of student union, 100% of libraries, 100% of dining areas, 60% of common outdoor areas, have wireless network access.

CAMPUS LIFE

Environment: Metropolis. **Activities:** Campus Ministries; International Student Organization; Marching band; Musical theater; Radio station; Student government; Student-run film society. 7 registered organizations, 2 religious organizations, 14 fraternities, 7 sororities, on campus. **On-Campus Highlights:** University Coffee Shop. **Environmental Initiatives:** Recycling.

ADMISSIONS

Freshman Academic Profile: Average high school GPA 3.4. 9% in top 10% of high school class, 32% in top 25% of high school class, 64% in top 50% of high school class. **Test Scores:** SAT Math middle 50% range 510–590. SAT EBRW middle 50% range 550–640. ACT middle 50% range 19–25. **Basis for Candidate Selection:** *Very important factors include:* talent/ability. *Important factors include:* academic GPA, interview. *Other factors include:* rigor of secondary school record, application essay, standardized test scores, recommendation(s), extracurricular activities, character/personal qualities, level of applicant's interest. **Freshman Admission Requirements:** High school diploma is required and GED is accepted. *Academic units recommended:* 4 English, 3 math, 3 science, 3 social studies, 6 academic electives. **Freshman Admission Statistics:** 1,025 applied, 73% admitted, 23% enrolled. **Transfer Admission Requirements:** College transcript(s), essay or personal statement. Minimum college GPA of 2.0 required. Lowest grade transferable C. **General Admission Information:** Application fee $40. Priority deadline 3/1. Admission may be deferred for a maximum of 1 year.

COSTS AND FINANCIAL AID

Annual tuition $40,480. Room and board $11,330. Required fees $2,825. Average book and supplies expense $2,200. **Required Forms and Deadlines:** FAFSA. **Types of Aid:** *Need-based scholarships/grants:* College/university scholarship or grant aid from institutional funds; Federal Pell; Private scholarships; SEOG; State scholarships/grants. *Loans:* Direct PLUS loans; Direct Subsidized Stafford Loans; Direct Unsubsidized Stafford Loans. **Student Employment:** Federal Work-Study Program available. Institutional employment available. **Financial Aid Statistics:** 100% needy freshmen, 100% needy undergrads receive need-based scholarship or grant aid. 7% freshmen, 8% undergrads receive non-need-based scholarship or grant aid. 86% freshmen, 86% undergrads receive need-based self-help aid. 0% freshmen, 0% undergrads receive athletic scholarships. 80% freshmen, 94.8% undergrads receive any aid. 96% undergrads borrow to pay for school. Average cumulative indebtedness $41,326. **Criteria awarding aid:** *Need-based:* Academics, Art. *Non-need-based:* Academics, Art.

CLEVELAND STATE UNIVERSITY

2121 Euclid Avenue, Cleveland, OH 44115-2214
Phone: 216-523-7416 **Financial Aid Phone:** 216-687-5594
E-mail: admissions@csuohio.edu **CEEB Code:** 3032
Fax: 216-687-5501 **Website:** www.csuohio.edu **ACT Code:** 1221

This public school was founded in 1964. It has a 85 acre campus.

RATINGS

Admissions Selectivity Rating: 74   **Fire Safety Rating:** 60*   **Green Rating:** 85

STUDENTS AND FACULTY

Enrollment: 11,669. **Student Body:** 53% female, 47% male, 4% out-of-state, 5% international (85 countries represented). Asian 3%, African American 17%,

Caucasian 64%, Hispanic 5%, Native American <1%, Pacific Islander <1%, Two or more races 3%, Race unknown 2%. **Retention and Graduation:** 71% freshmen return for sophomore year. **Faculty:** Student/faculty ratio 24:1. 524 full-time faculty, 89% hold PhDs, 14% are members of minority groups, 43% are women. 1% of classes are taught by teaching assistants.

ACADEMICS

Degrees: Bachelor's; Doctoral degree—professional practice; Doctoral degree research/scholarship; Master's; Post-bachelor's certificate; Post-master's certificate. **Classes:** Most classes have 20–29 students. **Most popular majors:** Business Administration, Management and Operations, Other; Accounting; Psychology, General. **Special Study Options:** Accelerated program; Cooperative education program; Cross-registration; Distance learning; Double major; Dual enrollment; English as a Second Language (ESL); Exchange student program (domestic); Honors program; Independent study; Internships; Liberal arts/career combination; Study abroad; Teacher certification program; Weekend college. **Honors programs:** Each year the University Honors Program accepts a very limited number of students based on the scholarship attached to the academic program. Approximately 40 first-year college students (lower division) and 20 college juniors (upper division) enter the program each fall. The Honors Program receives anywhere from 200 to 250 applications each given year. Thus, the Honors Program is very competitive. **Disability Services offered:** Note-taking services; Reader services; Tape recorders; Tutors. **Career services:** Alumni services; Career assessment; Career/job search classes; Internships.

FACILITIES

Housing: Coed dorms; Special housing for disabled students; 90% of campus accessible to physically disabled. **Campus network:** 100% of classrooms, 100% of dorms, 100% of student union, 100% of libraries, 100% of dining areas, 50% of common outdoor areas, have wireless network access.

CAMPUS LIFE

Environment: Metropolis. **Activities:** Campus Ministries; Choral groups; Concert band; Dance; Drama/theater; International Student Organization; Jazz band; Literary magazine; Model UN; Music ensembles; Radio station; Student government; Student newspaper; Symphony orchestra. 246 registered organizations, 9 honor societies, 10 religious organizations, 8 fraternities, 7 sororities, on campus. **Athletics (Intercollegiate):** *Men:* baseball, basketball, fencing, golf, soccer, swimming, wrestling. *Women:* basketball, cross-country, fencing, softball, swimming, tennis, track/field (outdoor), track/field (indoor), volleyball. **On-Campus Highlights:** Recreation Center.

ADMISSIONS

Freshman Academic Profile: Average high school GPA 3.3. 15% in top 10% of high school class, 39% in top 25% of high school class, 71% in top 50% of high school class. **Test Scores:** SAT Math middle 50% range 450–570. SAT EBRW middle 50% range 440–570. ACT middle 50% range 19–25. **Basis for Candidate Selection:** *Very important factors include:* rigor of secondary school record, academic GPA, standardized test scores. *Important factors include:* class rank. **Freshman Admission Requirements:** High school diploma is required and GED is accepted. *Academic units required:* 4 English, 3 math, 3 science, 3 social studies. *Academic units recommended:* 2 foreign language, 1 visual/performing arts. **Freshman Admission Statistics:** 7,544 applied, 91% admitted, 28% enrolled. **Transfer Admission Requirements:** College transcript(s). Minimum college GPA of 2.0 required. Lowest grade transferable D. **General Admission Information:** Application fee $30. Priority deadline 7/15. Regular application deadline 8/15. Non-fall registration accepted. Admission may be deferred for a maximum of 1 year.

COSTS AND FINANCIAL AID

Annual in-state tuition $9,636. Annual out-of-state tuition $12,878. Room and board $12,500. Average book and supplies expense $800. **Required Forms and Deadlines:** FAFSA. **Notification of Awards:** Applicants will be notified of awards on a rolling basis beginning 3/15. **Types of Aid:** *Need-based scholarships/grants:* College/university scholarship or grant aid from institutional funds; Federal Pell; Private scholarships; SEOG; State scholarships/grants. *Loans:* Direct PLUS loans; Direct Subsidized Stafford Loans; Direct Unsubsidized Stafford Loans. **Student Employment:** Federal Work-Study Program available. Institutional employment available. **Financial Aid Statistics:** 80% needy freshmen, 75% needy undergrads receive need-based scholarship or grant aid. 4% freshmen, 3% undergrads receive non-need-based scholarship or grant aid. 72% freshmen, 78% undergrads receive need-based self-help aid. 2% freshmen, 2% undergrads receive athletic scholarships. **Criteria awarding aid:** *Non-need-based:* Academics, Alumni affiliation, Art, Athletics, Leadership, Music/drama.

COASTAL CAROLINA UNIVERSITY

PO Box 261954, Conway, SC 29528-6054
Phone: 843-349-2170 **Financial Aid Phone:** 843-349-2313
E-mail: admissions@coastal.edu **CEEB Code:** 5837
Fax: 843-349-2127 **Website:** www.coastal.edu **ACT Code:** 3843

This public school was founded in 1954. It has a 633 acre campus.

RATINGS

Admissions Selectivity Rating: 80   **Fire Safety Rating:** 94   **Green Rating:** 75

STUDENTS AND FACULTY

Enrollment: 9,321. **Student Body:** 55% female, 45% male, 50% out-of-state, 1% international (54 countries represented). Asian 1%, African American 18%, Caucasian 67%, Hispanic 5%, Native American <1%, Pacific Islander <1%, Two or more races 5%, Race unknown 2%.
Retention and Graduation: 68% freshmen return for sophomore year. 33% freshmen graduate within 4 years. 47% freshmen graduate within 6 years. **Faculty:** Student/faculty ratio 16:1. 488 full-time faculty, 77% hold PhDs, 12% are members of minority groups, 46% are women. 0% of classes are taught by teaching assistants.

ACADEMICS

Degrees: Bachelor's; Certificate; Doctoral degree research/scholarship; Master's; Post-bachelor's certificate; Post-master's certificate. **Classes:** Most classes have 20–29 students. Most lab/discussion sessions have 20–29 students. **Most popular majors:** Marine Biology and Biological Oceanography; Exercise Science and Kinesiology; Business Administration and Management, General. **Special Study Options:** Accelerated program; Cooperative education program; Distance learning; Double major; Dual enrollment; Honors program; Independent study; Internships; Liberal arts/career combination; Student-designed major; Study abroad; Teacher certification program. **Honors programs:** The Honors Program at Coastal Carolina University is design to encourage intellectual curiosity and ability in highly motivated and academically-gifted students. Students enjoy multiple benefits for participating in the Honors Program including high levels of personal attention from faculty, priority registration, and designated housing. **Disability Services offered:** Note-taking services; Reader services; Tape recorders; Tutors. **Career services:** Alumni network; Alumni services; Career assessment; Career/job search classes; Internships; Regional alumni.

FACILITIES

Housing: Apartments for single students; Coed dorms; Special housing for disabled students; Special housing for international students; Theme housing; Wellness housing; 98% of campus accessible to physically disabled. **Campus network:** 20% of classrooms, 20% of dorms, 100% of student union, 100% of libraries, 80% of dining areas, 50% of common outdoor areas, have wireless network access.

CAMPUS LIFE

Environment: Town. **Activities:** Campus Ministries; Choral groups; Concert band; Dance; Drama/theater; International Student Organization; Jazz band; Literary magazine; Marching band; Model UN; Music ensembles; Musical theater; Pep band; Radio station; Student government; Student newspaper. 123 registered organizations, 13 honor societies, 12 religious organizations, 10 fraternities, 11 sororities, on campus. **Athletics (Intercollegiate):** *Men:* baseball, basketball, cheerleading, cross-country, football, golf, soccer, tennis, track/field (outdoor). *Women:* basketball, cheerleading, cross-country, golf, soccer, softball, tennis, track/field (outdoor), volleyball. **On-Campus Highlights:** Swain Science Annex / Science Annex II. **Environmental Initiatives:** Sustainable Transportation including: Zip Car, 600 in the bike sharing fleet, 2 bike fix stations, shuttles and EV stations.

ADMISSIONS

Freshman Academic Profile: Average high school GPA 3.6. 12% in top 10% of high school class, 35% in top 25% of high school class, 69% in top 50% of high school class. 80% from public high schools. **Test Scores:** SAT Math middle 50% range 500–580. SAT EBRW middle 50% range 510–590. ACT middle 50% range 19–24. **Basis for Candidate Selection:** *Very important factors include:* rigor of secondary school record, academic GPA. *Important factors include:* class rank, standardized test scores. *Other factors include:* application essay, recommendation(s), extracurricular activities, talent/ability, character/personal qualities, first generation, alumni/ae relation, geographical residence, state residency, racial/ethnic status. **Freshman Admission Requirements:** High school diploma is required and GED is accepted. *Academic units required:* 4 English, 4 math, 3 science, 3 science labs, 2 foreign language, 2 social studies, 1 history, 1 academic electives, 1 visual/performing arts, 1 unit from above areas or other academic areas. *Academic units recommended:* 1 computer science. **Freshman Admission Statistics:** 15,061 applied, 69% admitted, 22% enrolled. **Transfer Admission Requirements:** College transcript(s), statement of good standing from prior institution(s). Minimum college GPA of 2.0 required. Lowest grade transferable C-. **General Admission Information:** Application fee $45. Priority deadline 12/1. Non-fall registration accepted. Admission may be deferred for a maximum of 1 year.

COSTS AND FINANCIAL AID

Annual in-state tuition $11,460. Annual out-of-state tuition $27,214. Room and board $9,290. Required fees $180. Average book and supplies expense $1,082. **Required Forms and Deadlines:** FAFSA. **Notification of Awards:** Applicants will be notified of awards on a rolling basis beginning 3/1. **Types of Aid:** *Need-based scholarships/grants:* College/university scholarship or grant aid from institutional funds; Federal Pell; Private scholarships; SEOG; State scholarships/grants. *Loans:* Direct PLUS loans; Direct Subsidized Stafford Loans; Direct Unsubsidized Stafford Loans. **Student Employment:** Federal Work-Study Program available. Institutional employment available. **Financial Aid Statistics:** 50% needy freshmen, 53% needy undergrads receive need-based scholarship or grant aid. 45% freshmen, 35% undergrads receive non-need-based scholarship or grant aid. 93% freshmen, 91% undergrads receive need-based self-help aid. 3% freshmen, 4% undergrads receive athletic scholarships. 90% freshmen, 96% undergrads receive any aid. 76% undergrads borrow to pay for school. Average cumulative indebtedness $37,717. **Criteria awarding aid:** *Non-need-based:* Academics, Art, Athletics, Leadership.

COE COLLEGE

Best Colleges

1220 First Avenue NE, Cedar Rapids, IA 52402
Phone: 319-399-8500 **Financial Aid Phone:** 319-399-8540
E-mail: admission@coe.edu **CEEB Code:** 6101
Fax: 319-399-8816 **Website:** www.coe.edu **ACT Code:** 1294

This private school, affiliated with the Presbyterian Church, was founded in 1851. It has a 53 acre campus.

RATINGS

Admissions Selectivity Rating: 86   **Fire Safety Rating:** 88   **Green Rating:** 80

STUDENTS AND FACULTY

Enrollment: 1,323. **Student Body:** 57% female, 43% male, 53% out-of-state, 3% international (12 countries represented). Asian 2%, African American 7%, Caucasian 73%, Hispanic 9%, Native American <1%, Pacific Islander <1%, Two or more races 3%, Race unknown 3%.
Retention and Graduation: 75% freshmen return for sophomore year. 19% grads go on to further study within 1 year. **Faculty:** Student/faculty ratio 11:1. 96 full-time faculty, 91% hold PhDs, 7% are members of minority groups, 40% are women. 0% of classes are taught by teaching assistants.

ACADEMICS

Degrees: Bachelor's. **Classes:** Most classes have 10–19 students. Most lab/discussion sessions have 10–19 students. **Most popular majors:** Biology/Biological Sciences, General; Business Administration and Management, General; Psychology, General. **Special Study Options:** Cross-registration; Double major; Dual enrollment; English as a Second Language (ESL); Exchange student program (domestic); Honors program; Independent study; Internships; Liberal arts/career combination; Student-designed major; Study abroad; Teacher certification program. **Honors programs:** College scholars program consisting of five honors seminars. **Combined degree programs:** BA/JD; BA/MEng. **Disability Services offered:** Note-taking services; Tape recorders; Tutors. **Career services:** Alumni network; Alumni services; Career assessment; Career/job search classes; Internships; Regional alumni.

FACILITIES

Housing: Apartments for single students; Coed dorms; Fraternity/sorority housing; Men's dorms; Special housing for disabled students; Theme housing; Wellness housing; Women's dorms; 70% of campus accessible to physically disabled. **Special Academic Facilities/Equipment:** Ornithological museum, writing lab, theatre. **Campus network:** 65% of classrooms, 50% of dorms, 100% of student union, 100% of libraries, 100% of dining areas, 50% of common outdoor areas, have wireless network access.

CAMPUS LIFE

Environment: City. **Activities:** Campus Ministries; Choral groups; Concert band; Dance; Drama/theater; International Student Organization; Jazz band; Literary magazine; Model UN; Music ensembles; Musical theater; Radio station; Student government; Student newspaper; Student-run film society; Symphony orchestra. 60 registered organizations, 8 honor societies, 4 religious organizations, 5 fraternities, 3 sororities, on campus. **Athletics (Intercollegiate):** *Men:* baseball, basketball, cross-country, diving, football, golf, soccer, swimming, tennis, track/field (outdoor), track/field (indoor), wrestling. *Women:* basketball, cheerleading, cross-country, diving, golf, soccer, softball, swimming, tennis, track/field (outdoor), track/field (indoor), volleyball. **On-Campus Highlights:** Student Union/Coffee Shop. **Environmental Initiatives:** Coe College has embarked on a $3.45m major energy reduction program that will decrease the institution's electricity use by 25 percent and natural gas consumption by almost 50 percent, and deliver approximately $220,000 in guaranteed energy and operational savings each year.

ADMISSIONS

Freshman Academic Profile: Average high school GPA 3.6. 30% in top 10% of high school class, 65% in top 25% of high school class, 89% in top 50% of high school class. **Test Scores:** SAT Math middle 50% range 510–650. SAT EBRW middle 50% range 510–620. ACT middle 50% range 22–28. **Basis for Candidate Selection:** *Very important factors include:* academic GPA, standardized test scores. *Important factors include:* class rank. *Other factors include:* rigor of secondary school record, application essay, recommendation(s), interview, extracurricular activities, talent/ability, character/personal qualities, first generation, alumni/ae relation, volunteer work, level of applicant's interest. **Freshman Admission Requirements:** High school diploma is required and GED is accepted. *Academic units recommended:* 4 English, 3 math, 3 science, 1 science labs, 2 foreign language, 3 social studies, 2 academic electives. **Freshman Admission Statistics:** 6,725 applied, 50% admitted, 11% enrolled. **Transfer Admission Requirements:** High school transcript, college transcript(s), essay or personal statement, statement of good standing from prior institution(s). Minimum college GPA of 2.5 required. Lowest grade transferable C. **General Admission Information:** Application fee $30. Priority deadline 12/10. Regular application deadline 3/1. Non-fall registration accepted. Admission may be deferred for a maximum of 2 years.

COSTS AND FINANCIAL AID

Annual tuition $42,090. Room and board $9,140. Required fees $340. Average book and supplies expense $1,000. **Required Forms and Deadlines:** FAFSA. **Notification of Awards:** Applicants will be notified of awards on a rolling basis beginning 12/15. **Types of Aid:** *Need-based scholarships/grants:* College/university scholarship or grant aid from institutional funds; Federal Pell; Private scholarships; SEOG; State scholarships/grants. *Loans:* Direct PLUS loans; Direct Subsidized Stafford Loans; Direct Unsubsidized Stafford Loans. **Student Employment:** Federal Work-Study Program available. Institutional employment available. **Financial Aid Statistics:** 100% needy freshmen, 100% needy undergrads receive need-based scholarship or grant aid. 14% freshmen, 14% undergrads receive non-need-based scholarship or grant aid. 85% freshmen, 82% undergrads receive need-based self-help aid. 0% freshmen, 0% undergrads receive athletic scholarships. 99% freshmen, 99% undergrads receive any aid. 82% undergrads borrow to pay for school. Average cumulative indebtedness $35,782. **Criteria awarding aid:** *Non-need-based:* Academics, Alumni affiliation, Art, Minority status, Music/drama, State/district residency.

COGSWELL COLLEGE

191 Baypointe Parkway, San Jose, CA 95134
Phone: 408-498-5160 **Financial Aid Phone:** 408.498.5145
E-mail: admissions@cogswell.edu **CEEB Code:** 1177
Fax: 408-747-0764 **ACT Code:** 1177

This proprietary school was founded in 1887. It has a 5 acre campus.

RATINGS

Admissions Selectivity Rating: 90   **Fire Safety Rating:** 96   **Green Rating:** 61

STUDENTS AND FACULTY

Enrollment: 589. **Student Body:** 31% female, 69% male, 8% out-of-state, 2% international (11 countries represented). Asian 21%, African American 6%, Caucasian 33%, Hispanic 22%, Native American 1%, Pacific Islander 1%, Two or more races 5%, Race unknown 10%.
Retention and Graduation: 78% freshmen return for sophomore year. 1% grads pursue business degrees. **Faculty:** Student/faculty ratio 12:1. 19 full-time faculty, 37% hold PhDs, 47% are members of minority groups, 37% are women. 0% of classes are taught by teaching assistants.

ACADEMICS

Degrees: Bachelor's; Master's. **Classes:** Most classes have 10–19 students. **Most popular majors:** Animation, Interactive Technology, Video Graphics and Special Effects; Game and Interactive Media Design; Music Technology. **Special Study Options:** Cooperative education program; Distance learning; Double major; Independent study; Internships; Student-designed major. **Disability Services offered:** Note-taking services; Tutors. **Career services:** Alumni network; Alumni services; Career/job search classes; Internships.

FACILITIES

Housing: Apartments for single students; 100% of campus accessible to physically disabled.

CAMPUS LIFE

Environment: Town. **Activities:** Literary magazine; Student government; Student newspaper. 17 registered organizations, on campus. **On-Campus Highlights:** 3D Animation Studio. **Environmental Initiatives:** Saving energy.

ADMISSIONS

Test Scores: SAT Math middle 50% range 570–620. SAT EBRW middle 50% range 500–640. ACT middle 50% range 25–29. **Basis for Candidate Selection:** *Very important factors include:* academic GPA, application essay, interview, talent/ability, level of applicant's interest. *Important factors include:* rigor of secondary school record, recommendation(s), character/personal qualities. *Other factors include:* class rank, standardized test scores, extracurricular activities, volunteer work, work experience. **Freshman Admission Requirements:** High school diploma is required and GED is accepted. *Academic units required:* 3 English, 3 math, 1 science, 1 science labs. *Academic units recommended:* 1 computer science, 1 visual/performing arts. **Freshman Admission Statistics:** 860 applied, 39% admitted, 29% enrolled. **Transfer Admission Requirements:** High school transcript, college transcript(s), essay or personal statement, Minimum college GPA of 2.5 required. Lowest grade transferable C. **General Admission Information:** Regular application deadline 8/15. Non-fall registration accepted. Admission may be deferred for a maximum of 1 year.

COSTS AND FINANCIAL AID

Annual tuition $19,056. Room and board $11,000. Required fees $1,000. Average book and supplies expense $1,791. **Required Forms and Deadlines:** FAFSA. **Notification of Awards:** Applicants will be notified of awards on a rolling basis beginning 4/1. **Types of Aid:** *Need-based scholarships/grants:* College/university scholarship or grant aid from institutional funds; Federal Pell; Private scholarships; SEOG; State scholarships/grants. *Loans:* Direct PLUS loans; Direct Subsidized Stafford Loans; Direct Unsubsidized Stafford Loans. **Student Employment:** Federal Work-Study Program available. Institutional employment available. **Criteria awarding aid:** *Need-based:* Academics, Alumni affiliation, Music/drama. *Non-need-based:* Academics, Alumni affiliation, Art, Music/drama.

COKER UNIVERSITY

300 East College Avenue, Hartsville, SC 29550
Phone: 843-383-8050
E-mail: admissions@coker.edu
Fax: 843-383-8056 **Website:** www.coker.edu

This is a private school.

RATINGS
Admissions Selectivity Rating: 85   **Fire Safety Rating:** 60*   **Green Rating:** 60*

STUDENTS AND FACULTY
Enrollment: 674. **Student Body:** 63% female, 37% male, 19% out-of-state, 3% international. Asian <1%, African American 27%, Caucasian 67%, Hispanic 2%, Native American 1%, Pacific Islander <1%, Two or more races 0%, Race unknown <1%.
Retention and Graduation: 71% freshmen return for sophomore year.
Faculty: Student/faculty ratio 10:1. 58 full-time faculty, 81% hold PhDs, 12% are members of minority groups, 47% are women. 0% of classes are taught by teaching assistants.

ACADEMICS
Degrees: Bachelor's. **Classes:** Most classes have 10–19 students. Most lab/discussion sessions have 10–19 students. **Most popular majors:** Business/Commerce, General; Graphic Design; Psychology, General. **Special Study Options:** Distance learning; Double major; Dual enrollment; Honors program; Independent study; Internships; Student-designed major; Study abroad; Teacher certification program. **Disability Services offered:** Tape recorders; Tutors. **Career services:** Career assessment; Career/job search classes; Internships.

FACILITIES
Housing: Coed dorms; Special housing for international students; 80% of campus accessible to physically disabled. **Special Academic Facilities/Equipment:** Art gallery, state-of-the-art performing arts center, dark rooms, botanical gardens, graduate-level science equipment. **Campus network:** 100% of classrooms, 100% of dorms, 100% of student union, 100% of libraries, 100% of dining areas, 99% of common outdoor areas, have wireless network access.

CAMPUS LIFE
Activities: Campus Ministries; Choral groups; Dance; Drama/theater; International Student Organization; Literary magazine; Music ensembles; Musical theater; Student government. 27 registered organizations, 4 honor societies, 2 religious organizations, on campus. **Athletics (Intercollegiate):** *Men:* baseball, basketball, cheerleading, cross-country, golf, soccer, tennis. *Women:* basketball, cheerleading, cross-country, soccer, softball, tennis, volleyball. **On-Campus Highlights:** The Cobra Den.

ADMISSIONS
Freshman Academic Profile: Average high school GPA 3.4. 1% in top 10% of high school class, 28% in top 25% of high school class, 70% in top 50% of high school class. **Test Scores:** SAT Math middle 50% range 440–570. SAT EBRW middle 50% range 420–570. ACT middle 50% range 17–22. **Basis for Candidate Selection:** *Very important factors include:* standardized test scores. *Important factors include:* rigor of secondary school record, class rank. *Other factors include:* application essay, recommendation(s), interview, extracurricular activities, talent/ability, character/personal qualities, alumni/ae relation, volunteer work, work experience. **Freshman Admission Requirements:** High school diploma is required and GED is accepted. *Academic units required:* 4 English, 3 math, 3 science, 1 science labs, 2 foreign language, 3 social studies. **Freshman Admission Statistics:** 1,112 applied, 56% admitted, 25% enrolled. **Transfer Admission Requirements:** High school transcript, college transcript(s), statement of good standing from prior institution(s). Minimum college GPA of 2.0 required. Lowest grade transferable C. **General Admission Information:** Application fee $15. Priority deadline 5/1. Regular application deadline 8/1. Non-fall registration accepted. Admission may be deferred for a maximum of 1 year.

COSTS AND FINANCIAL AID
Annual tuition $22,200. Room and board $6,950. Average book and supplies expense $1,500. **Required Forms and Deadlines:** FAFSA. **Notification of Awards:** Applicants will be notified of awards on a rolling basis beginning 3/1. **Types of Aid:** *Need-based scholarships/grants:* College/university scholarship or grant aid from institutional funds; Federal Pell; Private scholarships; SEOG; State scholarships/grants. *Loans:* Direct PLUS loans; Direct Subsidized Stafford

Loans; Direct Unsubsidized Stafford Loans. **Student Employment:** Federal Work-Study Program available. Institutional employment available. **Financial Aid Statistics:** 96% needy freshmen, 96% needy undergrads receive need-based scholarship or grant aid. 100% freshmen, 93% undergrads receive non-need-based scholarship or grant aid. 78% freshmen, 80% undergrads receive need-based self-help aid. 5% freshmen, 6% undergrads receive athletic scholarships. 100% freshmen, 100% undergrads receive any aid. **Criteria awarding aid:** *Need-based:* Academics, Job skills, Minority status, Music/drama, Religious affiliation. *Non-need-based:* Academics, Alumni affiliation, Art, Athletics, Job skills, Leadership, Minority status, Music/drama, Religious affiliation, State/district residency.

COLBY COLLEGE

4800 Mayflower Hill, Waterville, ME 04901
Phone: 207-859-4828 **Financial Aid Phone:** (207) 859-4124
E-mail: admissions@colby.edu **CEEB Code:** 3280
Fax: 207-859-4828 **Website:** www.colby.edu **ACT Code:** 1638

This private school was founded in 1813. It has a 714 acre campus.

RATINGS
Admissions Selectivity Rating: 97   **Fire Safety Rating:** 98   **Green Rating:** 99

STUDENTS AND FACULTY
Enrollment: 2,000. **Student Body:** 52% female, 48% male, 89% out-of-state, 10% international (74 countries represented). Asian 8%, African American 4%, Caucasian 63%, Hispanic 7%, Native American <1%, Pacific Islander <1%, Two or more races 5%, Race unknown 3%.
Retention and Graduation: 94% freshmen return for sophomore year. 89% freshmen graduate within 4 years. 92% freshmen graduate within 6 years. 29% grads go on to further study within 1 year. 20% grads pursue arts and sciences degrees. 3% grads pursue law degrees. 0% grads pursue business degrees. 3% grads pursue medical degrees. **Faculty:** Student/faculty ratio 10:1. 203 full-time faculty, 100% hold PhDs, 14% are members of minority groups, 48% are women. 0% of classes are taught by teaching assistants.

ACADEMICS
Degrees: Bachelor's. **Classes:** Most classes have 10–19 students. **Most popular majors:** English Language and Literature, General; Economics, General; Biology/Biological Sciences, General. **Special Study Options:** Cross-registration; Double major; Dual enrollment; Exchange student program (domestic); Independent study; Internships; Student-designed major; Study abroad; Teacher certification program. **Disability Services offered:** Note-taking services; Reader services; Tape recorders; Tutors. **Career services:** Alumni network; Alumni services; Career assessment; Career/job search classes; Internships; Regional alumni.

FACILITIES
Housing: Apartments for single students; Coed dorms; Cooperative housing; Special housing for disabled students; Theme housing; Wellness housing; 88% of campus accessible to physically disabled. **Special Academic Facilities/Equipment:** Comprising five wings, nearly 8,000 works, and more than 38,000 square feet of exhibition space, the Colby College Museum of Art is considered the finest college art museum in the country. Additional academic spaces on campus include the Goldfarb Center for Public Affairs and Civic Engagement, the Oak Institute for the Study of International Human Rights, the Center for Teaching and Learning, the Center for the Arts and Humanities, and the Pugh Center, a campus multicultural center. Unique facilities include state-of-the-art photography and sculpture studios, an art and music library, an electronic music center, an astronomical observatory with a 35-cm (14-inch) telescope on a research-grade computer-controlled mount with liquid-nitrogen cooled CCD camera, a four-capillary genetic analyzer, a microscopy suite with multiple epifluorescence microscopes and imaging cameras and software, a microscopy suite with Nikon E800 research grade microscope interfaced with MBF Neuroscience Neurolucida and Stereo Investigator software systems for computerized 3-D imaging and reconstruction of brain tissue slices in behavioral and neuroanatomical investigations, magneto-optical trap (MOT) apparatuses, high-powered pulsed laser systems, an astrophysics research

lab, an x-ray fluorescence spectrometer, a 500 MHz NMR, a LC-TOF mass spectrometer, an inductively coupled plasma-atomic emissions spectrometer, a single-crystal x-ray defractometer, a GIS lab, two high-performance Linux computer clusters for computational research, research greenhouses, a research vessel and remote-sensing buoy for biogeochemical lake research, and an organic garden. Most of Colby's 714-acre campus is a wildlife sanctuary that includes the 128-acre Perkins Arboretum and Bird Sanctuary. The College also owns a nearby kettle-hole research bog.

CAMPUS LIFE

Environment: Village. **Activities:** Campus Ministries; Choral groups; Concert band; Dance; Drama/theater; International Student Organization; Jazz band; Literary magazine; Music ensembles; Musical theater; Radio station; Student government; Student newspaper; Symphony orchestra. 153 registered organizations, 7 honor societies, 11 religious organizations, on campus. **Athletics (Intercollegiate):** *Men:* baseball, basketball, crew/rowing, cross-country, diving, football, golf, ice hockey, lacrosse, skiing (downhill/Alpine), skiing (Nordic/cross-country), soccer, squash, swimming, tennis, track/field (outdoor), track/field (indoor). *Women:* basketball, crew/rowing, cross-country, diving, field hockey, golf, ice hockey, lacrosse, skiing (downhill/Alpine), skiing (Nordic/cross-country), soccer, softball, squash, swimming, tennis, track/field (outdoor), track/field (indoor). **On-Campus Highlights:** Museum of Art: lounge, sculpture terrace, evening concerts and events. **Environmental Initiatives:** In April 2013, Colby College became the fourth institution of higher education in the world to achieve carbon neutrality.

ADMISSIONS

Freshman Academic Profile: 79% in top 10% of high school class, 94% in top 25% of high school class, 100% in top 50% of high school class. 52% from public high schools. **Test Scores:** SAT Math middle 50% range 680–770. SAT EBRW middle 50% range 670–740. ACT middle 50% range 31–33. **Basis for Candidate Selection:** *Very important factors include:* rigor of secondary school record, academic GPA, recommendation(s), character/personal qualities. *Important factors include:* class rank, application essay, extracurricular activities, talent/ability. *Other factors include:* standardized test scores, interview, first generation, alumni/ae relation, geographical residence, state residency, racial/ethnic status, volunteer work, work experience, level of applicant's interest. **Freshman Admission Requirements:** High school diploma is required and GED is not accepted. *Academic units recommended:* 4 English, 3 math, 2 science, 2 science labs, 3 foreign language, 2 social studies. **Freshman Admission Statistics:** 12,313 applied, 13% admitted, 36% enrolled. **Transfer Admission Requirements:** High school transcript, college transcript(s), essay or personal statement, standardized test scores, statement of good standing from prior institution(s). Minimum college GPA of 3.0 required. Lowest grade transferable C. **General Admission Information:** Regular application deadline 1/1. Non-fall registration accepted.

COSTS AND FINANCIAL AID

Annual tuition $54,870. Room and board $14,720. Required fees $2,410. Average book and supplies expense $800. **Required Forms and Deadlines:** Business/Farm Supplement; CSS/Financial Aid PROFILE; FAFSA. **Notification of Awards:** Applicants will be notified of awards on or about 4/1. **Types of Aid:** *Need-based scholarships/grants:* College/university scholarship or grant aid from institutional funds; Federal Pell; SEOG; State scholarships/grants. *Loans:* Direct PLUS loans; Direct Subsidized Stafford Loans; Direct Unsubsidized Stafford Loans. **Student Employment:** Federal Work-Study Program available. Institutional employment available. **Financial Aid Statistics:** 100% needy freshmen, 100% needy undergrads receive need-based scholarship or grant aid. 6% freshmen, 6% undergrads receive non-need-based scholarship or grant aid. 42% freshmen, 45% undergrads receive need-based self-help aid. 0% freshmen, 0% undergrads receive athletic scholarships. 47% freshmen, 42% undergrads receive any aid. 25% undergrads borrow to pay for school. Average cumulative indebtedness $24,437.

COLBY-SAWYER COLLEGE

541Main Street, New London, NH 03257-7835
Phone: 603-526-3700 **Financial Aid Phone:** 603-526-3717
E-mail: admissions@colbysawyer.edu **CEEB Code:** 3281
Fax: 603-526-3452 **Website:** www.colby-sawyer.edu **ACT Code:** 2506

This private school was founded in 1837. It has a 200 acre campus.

RATINGS
Admissions Selectivity Rating: 74   **Fire Safety Rating:** 75   **Green Rating:** 60*

STUDENTS AND FACULTY
Enrollment: 942. **Student Body:** 65% female, 35% male, 68% out-of-state, 1% international (11 countries represented). Asian 1%, African American 1%, Caucasian 90%, Hispanic 1%, Native American <1%, Race unknown 5%. **Retention and Graduation:** 71% freshmen return for sophomore year. **Faculty:** Student/faculty ratio 11:1. 60 full-time faculty, 73% hold PhDs, 2% are members of minority groups, 52% are women. 0% of classes are taught by teaching assistants.

ACADEMICS
Degrees: Associate; Bachelor's; Transfer Associate. **Classes:** Most classes have 10–19 students. Most lab/discussion sessions have 10–19 students. **Most popular majors:** Sport and Fitness Administration/Management; Business Administration and Management, General; Nursing/Registered Nurse (Rn, Asn, Bsn, Msn). **Special Study Options:** Accelerated program; Cross-registration; Double major; Dual enrollment; English as a Second Language (ESL); Exchange student program (domestic); Honors program; Independent study; Internships; Student-designed major; Study abroad; Teacher certification program. **Honors programs:** The Wesson Honors Program is designed to provide highly motivated students with an optional intensive experience in the liberal arts. By creating academic, cultural, and social opportunities for integrative and interdisciplinary intellectual discovery, the program challenges students not only to widen their own avenues of intellectual exploration, but to take leadership in a community of scholars and participate as catalysts for inquiry and discussion across the college. **Disability Services offered:** Tape recorders; Tutors.

FACILITIES
Housing: Coed dorms; Special housing for disabled students; Women's dorms; 50% of campus accessible to physically disabled. **Special Academic Facilities/Equipment:** Sawyer Fine Arts Center, Windy Hill School (pre-school- grade 3 laboratory school), Ivey Science Center, Hogan Sports Center, Video Studio and Editing Room, Radio Station (WSCS 90.9 FM).

CAMPUS LIFE
Environment: Rural. **Activities:** Choral groups; Dance; Drama/theater; Literary magazine; Musical theater; Radio station; Student government; Student newspaper; Yearbook. 40 registered organizations, 5 honor societies, 1 religious organizations, on campus. **Athletics (Intercollegiate):** *Men:* baseball, basketball, diving, equestrian sports, skiing (downhill/Alpine), soccer, swimming, tennis, track/field (outdoor). *Women:* basketball, diving, equestrian sports, lacrosse, skiing (downhill/Alpine), soccer, swimming, tennis, track/field (outdoor), volleyball. **On-Campus Highlights:** Dan and Kathleen Hogan Sports Center.

ADMISSIONS
Freshman Academic Profile: Average high school GPA 3.0. 83% from public high schools. **Test Scores:** SAT Math middle 50% range 440–530. SAT EBRW middle 50% range 440–540. ACT middle 50% range 18–22. **Basis for Candidate Selection:** *Very important factors include:* rigor of secondary school record, academic GPA, interview. *Important factors include:* class rank, application essay, standardized test scores, recommendation(s), extracurricular activities, talent/ability, alumni/ae relation. *Other factors include:* first generation, geographical residence, state residency. **Freshman Admission Requirements:** High school diploma is required and GED is accepted. *Academic units recommended:* 4 English, 3 math, 3 science, 3 science labs, 2 foreign language, 3 social studies. **Freshman Admission Statistics:** 1,402 applied, 88% admitted, 29% enrolled. **Transfer Admission Requirements:** College transcript(s), essay or personal statement. Minimum college GPA of 2.0 required. Lowest grade transferable C. **General Admission Information:** Application fee $45. Regular application deadline 4/1. Non-fall registration accepted. Admission may be deferred for a maximum of 1 year.

COSTS AND FINANCIAL AID

Annual tuition $29,620. Room and board $10,340. Average book and supplies expense $750. **Required Forms and Deadlines:** FAFSA. **Notification of Awards:** Applicants will be notified of awards on a rolling basis beginning 3/1. **Types of Aid:** *Need-based scholarships/grants:* College/university scholarship or grant aid from institutional funds; Federal Pell; Private scholarships; SEOG; State scholarships/grants. **Student Employment:** Federal Work-Study Program available. Institutional employment available. **Financial Aid Statistics:** 100% needy freshmen, 95% needy undergrads receive need-based scholarship or grant aid. 4% freshmen, 5% undergrads receive non-need-based scholarship or grant aid. 93% freshmen, 96% undergrads receive need-based self-help aid. 0% freshmen, 0% undergrads receive athletic scholarships. 83% freshmen, 83% undergrads receive any aid. **Criteria awarding aid:** *Need-based:* Academics. *Non-need-based:* Academics, Alumni affiliation, Art, Leadership, Music/drama.

COLGATE UNIVERSITY

Best Colleges

13 Oak Drive, Hamilton, NY 13346
Phone: 315-228-7401 **Financial Aid Phone:** 315-228-7431
E-mail: admission@colgate.edu **CEEB Code:** 2086
Fax: 315-228-7524 **Website:** www.colgate.edu **ACT Code:** 2702

This private school was founded in 1819. It has a 515 acre campus.

RATINGS

Admissions Selectivity Rating: 97   **Fire Safety Rating:** 97   **Green Rating:** 99

STUDENTS AND FACULTY

Enrollment: 2,934. **Student Body:** 55% female, 45% male, 74% out-of-state, 9% international (49 countries represented). Asian 5%, African American 5%, Caucasian 65%, Hispanic 9%, Native American <1%, Pacific Islander <1%, Two or more races 4%, Race unknown 3%.
Retention and Graduation: 94% freshmen return for sophomore year. 88% freshmen graduate within 4 years. 91% freshmen graduate within 6 years. 14% grads go on to further study within 1 year. 4% grads pursue arts and sciences degrees. 2% grads pursue law degrees. 1% grads pursue business degrees. 2% grads pursue medical degrees. **Faculty:** Student/faculty ratio 9:1. 314 full-time faculty, 97% hold PhDs, 25% are members of minority groups, 45% are women.

ACADEMICS

Degrees: Bachelor's; Master's. **Most popular majors:** English Language and Literature, General; Economics, General; Political Science and Government, General. **Special Study Options:** Cross-registration; Double major; Independent study; Internships; Student-designed major; Study abroad; Teacher certification program. **Honors programs:** Colgate University honors top applicants in our pool as Alumni Memorial Scholars (AMS) and Benton Scholars. Acceptance to the AMS Program is the highest honor within the admission process, and an indication of an excellent match, both academically and personally, with Colgate. The cornerstone of the AMS program is the opportunity for each student to apply, at any point before graduating, for grants totaling up to $6,000 to fund independent research, attendance at academic conferences, and internships. Though not a "merit scholarship," the award does recognize academic merit and achievement combined with leadership and accomplishment in top candidates regardless of financial aid status. Selection by the admission staff is based on academic performance, demonstrated talents, and the respect a student has earned from both teachers and counselors. The Benton Scholars program infuses the curriculum of its students with an even greater focus on leadership and global themes. While Benton scholars are free to craft their own majors, courses of study, and extracurricular priorities, they receive unique opportunities to learn on and off campus, and are given the responsibility of sharing the knowledge they acquire with the greater Colgate community. **Disability Services offered:** Note-taking services; Reader services; Tape recorders; Tutors. **Career services:** Alumni network; Alumni services; Career assessment; Career/job search classes; Internships.

FACILITIES

Housing: Apartments for single students; Coed dorms; Cooperative housing; Fraternity/sorority housing; Special housing for disabled students; Theme housing; Wellness housing. **Special Academic Facilities/Equipment:** Clifford Gallery Picker Gallery Longyear Museum of Anthropology Robert M. Linsley Geology Museum Ho Tung Visualization Laboratory Digital Learning and Media Center W.M. Keck Center for Language Study Foggy Bottom Observatory WRCU Radio Station Audio and video recording studios Greenhouse Brehmer Theater.

CAMPUS LIFE

Environment: Rural. **Activities:** Campus Ministries; Choral groups; Concert band; Dance; Drama/theater; International Student Organization; Jazz band; Literary magazine; Model UN; Music ensembles; Musical theater; Opera; Pep band; Radio station; Student government; Student newspaper; Symphony orchestra; Yearbook. 167 registered organizations, 12 honor societies, 10 religious organizations, 5 fraternities, 3 sororities, on campus. **Athletics (Intercollegiate):** *Men:* basketball, crew/rowing, cross-country, diving, football, golf, ice hockey, lacrosse, soccer, swimming, tennis, track/field (outdoor). *Women:* basketball, crew/rowing, cross-country, diving, field hockey, ice hockey, lacrosse, soccer, softball, swimming, tennis, track/field (outdoor), volleyball. **On-Campus Highlights:** O'Connor Campus Center. **Environmental Initiatives:** All electricity used on campus is hydroelectric, with some supplemental nuclear power. Colgate's wood-chip-burning heating plant utilizes a renewable energy source to provide about 70 percent of our total requirement.

ADMISSIONS

Freshman Academic Profile: Average high school GPA 3.7. 77% in top 10% of high school class, 94% in top 25% of high school class, 100% in top 50% of high school class. 56% from public high schools. **Test Scores:** SAT Math middle 50% range 670–780. SAT EBRW middle 50% range 650–730. ACT middle 50% range 31–34. **Basis for Candidate Selection:** *Very important factors include:* rigor of secondary school record, class rank, academic GPA. *Important factors include:* application essay, standardized test scores, recommendation(s), extracurricular activities, talent/ability, character/personal qualities. *Other factors include:* first generation, alumni/ae relation, geographical residence, racial/ethnic status, volunteer work, work experience. **Freshman Admission Requirements:** High school diploma is required and GED is accepted. *Academic units required:* 4 English, 3 math, 3 science, 2 science labs, 3 foreign language, 3 social studies. *Academic units recommended:* 4 English, 4 math, 4 science, 4 science labs, 4 foreign language, 4 social studies. **Freshman Admission Statistics:** 9,716 applied, 25% admitted, 34% enrolled. **Transfer Admission Requirements:** High school transcript, college transcript(s), essay or personal statement, standardized test scores, statement of good standing from prior institution(s). Minimum college GPA of 3.00 required. Lowest grade transferable C. **General Admission Information:** Application fee $60. Regular application deadline 1/15. Admission may be deferred for a maximum of 1 year.

COSTS AND FINANCIAL AID

Annual tuition $57,695. Room and board $14,540. Required fees $350. Average book and supplies expense $2,130. **Required Forms and Deadlines:** CSS/Financial Aid PROFILE; FAFSA; Noncustodial PROFILE. **Notification of Awards:** Applicants will be notified of awards on or about 3/25. **Types of Aid:** *Need-based scholarships/grants:* College/university scholarship or grant aid from institutional funds; Federal Pell; SEOG. *Loans:* Direct PLUS loans; Direct Subsidized Stafford Loans; Direct Unsubsidized Stafford Loans. **Student Employment:** Federal Work-Study Program available. Institutional employment available. **Financial Aid Statistics:** 100% needy freshmen, 100% needy undergrads receive need-based scholarship or grant aid. 0% freshmen, 0% undergrads receive non-need-based scholarship or grant aid. 93% freshmen, 82% undergrads receive need-based self-help aid. 8% freshmen, 10% undergrads receive athletic scholarships. 51.3% freshmen, 51.4% undergrads receive any aid. 32% undergrads borrow to pay for school. Average cumulative indebtedness $24,243. **Criteria awarding aid:** *Non-need-based:* Athletics.

201 East Kirby, Detroit, MI 48202
Phone: 313-664-7425 **Financial Aid Phone:** 313-664-7495
E-mail: admissions@collegeforcreativestudies.edu **CEEB Code:** 1035
Fax: 313-872-2739 **Website:** www.collegeforcreativestudies.edu **ACT Code:** 1989

This private school was founded in 1906. It has a 11 acre campus.

RATINGS
Admissions Selectivity Rating: 88   **Fire Safety Rating:** 87   **Green Rating:** 60*

STUDENTS AND FACULTY
Enrollment: 1,307. **Student Body:** 17% out-of-state, 4% international (15 countries represented). Asian 4%, African American 6%, Caucasian 71%, Hispanic 5%, Native American 1%, Race unknown 10%.
Retention and Graduation: 73% freshmen return for sophomore year.
Faculty: Student/faculty ratio 8:1. 51 full-time faculty, 61% hold PhDs, 14% are members of minority groups, 31% are women. 0% of classes are taught by teaching assistants.

ACADEMICS
Degrees: Bachelor's; Master's; Post-bachelor's certificate. **Most popular majors:** Film/Video and Photographic Arts, Other; Commercial and Advertising Art; Industrial and Product Design. **Special Study Options:** Cooperative education program; Double major; Dual enrollment; English as a Second Language (ESL); Exchange student program (domestic); Independent study; Internships; Study abroad; Teacher certification program. **Disability Services offered:** Reader services; Tape recorders; Tutors. **Career services:** Alumni network; Alumni services; Career assessment; Career/job search classes; Internships; Regional alumni.

FACILITIES
Housing: Coed dorms; 95% of campus accessible to physically disabled.
Special Academic Facilities/Equipment: Top-of-the-line technology for design, animation and audiovisual editing. Wood and Metal shops, hot glass studio, gallery, private studios.

CAMPUS LIFE
Environment: Metropolis. **Activities:** Student government. 5 registered organizations, on campus. **On-Campus Highlights:** Center Galleries.

ADMISSIONS
Test Scores: ACT middle 50% range 18–23. **Basis for Candidate Selection:** *Very important factors include:* talent/ability. *Important factors include:* academic GPA, standardized test scores. *Other factors include:* level of applicant's interest. **Freshman Admission Requirements:** High school diploma is required and GED is accepted. **Freshman Admission Statistics:** 1,260 applied, 39% admitted, 51% enrolled. **Transfer Admission Requirements:** High school transcript, college transcript(s). Minimum college GPA of 2.0 required. Lowest grade transferable C. **General Admission Information:** Application fee $35. Priority deadline 3/1. Regular application deadline 8/1. Non-fall registration accepted. Admission may be deferred for a maximum of 4 semesters.

COSTS AND FINANCIAL AID
Annual tuition $27,090. Room and board $4,300. Required fees $1,185. Average book and supplies expense $2,500. **Required Forms and Deadlines:** FAFSA. **Notification of Awards:** Applicants will be notified of awards on a rolling basis beginning 3/15. **Types of Aid:** *Need-based scholarships/grants:* College/university scholarship or grant aid from institutional funds; Federal Pell; Private scholarships; SEOG; State scholarships/grants. **Criteria awarding aid:** *Non-need-based:* Academics, Art, Minority status.

66 George Street, Charleston, SC 29424
Phone: 843-953-5670 **Financial Aid Phone:** (843) 953-5540
E-mail: admissions@cofc.edu **CEEB Code:** 5113
Fax: 843-953-6322 **Website:** http://cofc.edu **ACT Code:** 3846

This public school was founded in 1770. It has a 52 acre campus.

RATINGS
Admissions Selectivity Rating: 78   **Fire Safety Rating:** 95   **Green Rating:** 85

STUDENTS AND FACULTY
Enrollment: 9,622. **Student Body:** 64% female, 36% male, 34% out-of-state, 1% international (61 countries represented). Asian 2%, African American 8%, Caucasian 78%, Hispanic 6%, Native American <1%, Pacific Islander <1%, Two or more races 4%, Race unknown 1%.
Retention and Graduation: 79% freshmen return for sophomore year. 62% freshmen graduate within 4 years. **Faculty:** Student/faculty ratio 15:1. 558 full-time faculty, 90% hold PhDs, 15% are members of minority groups, 47% are women. 0% of classes are taught by teaching assistants.

ACADEMICS
Degrees: Bachelor's; Certificate; Master's; Post-bachelor's certificate; Post-master's certificate. **Classes:** Most classes have 20–29 students. Most lab/discussion sessions have 20–29 students. **Most popular majors:** Biology/Biological Sciences, General; Psychology, General; Business Administration and Management, General. **Special Study Options:** Accelerated program; Cooperative education program; Cross-registration; Distance learning; Double major; Dual enrollment; English as a Second Language (ESL); Exchange student program (domestic); Honors program; Independent study; Internships; Liberal arts/career combination; Study abroad; Teacher certification program. **Honors programs:** The College of Charleston Honors College began as an Honors Program in 1967 as a "new course of study designed to attract superior students irrespective of their departmental majors and to guide them toward a fuller, more substantial liberal arts education." It has since provided a program and a community for talented and motivated students who enjoy active participation in small stimulating classes and want to be involved in a meaningful way in undergraduate research. In order to better serve the needs of the students, it became an Honors College in 2005, with new positions to provide academic advising and assistance in applying for postgraduate fellowships and additional funding to support its mission. The Honors College is dedicated to providing these students with a place where they can flourish and grow, a true learning community of teachers and students. In addition to receiving exciting and unique educational experiences, students can participate with their fellow Honors students in social, cultural, and intellectual events on the campus and in historic Charleston, SC. The Honors College challenges students to make the most of the opportunities available to them, to become actively involved in their own education, and to prepare themselves to excel in graduate programs, medical or law school, or in whatever comes after they complete their undergraduate education. In Honors classes, students take responsibility for their own learning through class discussions, through interaction with faculty and fellow students, and through independent research. Honors students are advised by specially chosen faculty mentors, receive priority registration, and have the opportunity to room with other Honors students in an Honors living-learning community. **Disability Services offered:** Note-taking services; Reader services; Tape recorders; Tutors. **Career services:** Alumni network; Alumni services; Career assessment; Career/job search classes; Internships; Regional alumni.

FACILITIES
Housing: Apartments for single students; Coed dorms; Fraternity/sorority housing; Men's dorms; Special housing for disabled students; Theme housing; Women's dorms; 70% of campus accessible to physically disabled. **Special Academic Facilities/Equipment:** Halsey Institute of Contemporary Art, sculpture facility, Miles Early Childhood Development Center, Avery Institute for African-American History and Culture, physics and astronomy observatory, Tate Center for Entrepreneurship, Grice Marine Laboratory, Patriots Point Athletics Complex (includes softball, baseball, tennis, soccer and sailing), Natural History Museum. **Campus network:** 98% of classrooms, 85% of

dorms, 100% of student union, 100% of libraries, 100% of dining areas, 75% of common outdoor areas, have wireless network access.

CAMPUS LIFE
Environment: City. **Activities:** Campus Ministries; Choral groups; Dance; Drama/theater; International Student Organization; Jazz band; Literary magazine; Model UN; Music ensembles; Musical theater; Pep band; Radio station; Student government; Student newspaper; Symphony orchestra. 225 registered organizations, 11 honor societies, 19 religious organizations, 12 fraternities, 14 sororities, on campus. **Athletics (Intercollegiate):** *Men:* baseball, basketball, cross-country, diving, golf, sailing, soccer, swimming, tennis. *Women:* basketball, cross-country, diving, equestrian sports, golf, sailing, soccer, softball, swimming, tennis, track/field (outdoor), track/field (indoor), volleyball. **On-Campus Highlights:** The Cistern Yard.

ADMISSIONS
Freshman Academic Profile: Average high school GPA 3.9. 20% in top 10% of high school class, 51% in top 25% of high school class, 87% in top 50% of high school class. 77% from public high schools. **Test Scores:** SAT Math middle 50% range 520–610. SAT EBRW middle 50% range 550–640. ACT middle 50% range 22–28. **Basis for Candidate Selection:** *Very important factors include:* rigor of secondary school record, academic GPA, standardized test scores. *Important factors include:* class rank, talent/ability, character/personal qualities, first generation, state residency. *Other factors include:* application essay, recommendation(s), extracurricular activities, alumni/ae relation, geographical residence, volunteer work, work experience, level of applicant's interest. **Freshman Admission Requirements:** High school diploma is required and GED is accepted. *Academic units required:* 4 English, 4 math, 3 science, 3 science labs, 3 foreign language, 2 social studies, 1 history, 3 academic electives, 1 visual/performing arts, 1 unit from above areas or other academic areas. *Academic units recommended:* 4 English, 4 math, 2 history, 1 computer science. **Freshman Admission Statistics:** 11,675 applied, 79% admitted, 24% enrolled. **Transfer Admission Requirements:** College transcript(s). Minimum college GPA of 2.6 required. Lowest grade transferable C. **General Admission Information:** Application fee $50. Priority deadline 2/15. Regular application deadline 2/15. Non-fall registration accepted. Admission may be deferred for a maximum of 1 or 2 semesters.

COSTS AND FINANCIAL AID
Annual in-state tuition $12,418. Annual out-of-state tuition $31,600. Room and board $12,166. Required fees $320. Average book and supplies expense $1,218. **Required Forms and Deadlines:** FAFSA. **Notification of Awards:** Applicants will be notified of awards on a rolling basis beginning 4/10. **Types of Aid:** *Need-based scholarships/grants:* College/university scholarship or grant aid from institutional funds; Federal Pell; Private scholarships; SEOG; State scholarships/grants. *Loans:* Direct PLUS loans; Direct Subsidized Stafford Loans; Direct Unsubsidized Stafford Loans. **Student Employment:** Federal Work-Study Program available. Institutional employment available. **Financial Aid Statistics:** 76% needy freshmen, 71% needy undergrads receive need-based scholarship or grant aid. 73% freshmen, 47% undergrads receive non-need-based scholarship or grant aid. 69% freshmen, 77% undergrads receive need-based self-help aid. 1% freshmen, 1% undergrads receive athletic scholarships. 53% freshmen, 49% undergrads receive any aid. 51% undergrads borrow to pay for school. Average cumulative indebtedness $27,256. **Criteria awarding aid:** *Non-need-based:* Academics, Alumni affiliation, Art, Athletics, Music/drama.

THE COLLEGE OF IDAHO

2112 Cleveland Blvd, Caldwell, ID 83605-4432
Phone: 208-459-5305 **Financial Aid Phone:** 208-459-5307
E-mail: admissions@collegeofidaho.edu **CEEB Code:** 4060
Fax: 208-459-5757 **Website:** www.collegeofidaho.edu **ACT Code:** 916

This private school was founded in 1891. It has a 50 acre campus.

RATINGS
Admissions Selectivity Rating: 80 **Fire Safety Rating:** 93 **Green Rating:** 69

STUDENTS AND FACULTY
Enrollment: 939. **Student Body:** 52% female, 48% male, 36% out-of-state, 13% international (46 countries represented). Asian 2%, African American 2%, Caucasian 60%, Hispanic 14%, Native American <1%, Pacific Islander 1%, Two or more races 5%, Race unknown 2%.

Retention and Graduation: 79% freshmen return for sophomore year. 58% freshmen graduate within 4 years. 69% freshmen graduate within 6 years. **Faculty:** Student/faculty ratio 9:1. 81 full-time faculty, 83% hold PhDs, 7% are members of minority groups, 41% are women. 0% of classes are taught by teaching assistants.

ACADEMICS
Degrees: Bachelor's; Master's. **Classes:** Most classes have 10–19 students. Most lab/discussion sessions have 10–19 students. **Most popular majors:** Biology/Biological Sciences, General; Psychology, General; Business Administration and Management, General. **Special Study Options:** Cross-registration; Double major; Dual enrollment; English as a Second Language (ESL); Honors program; Independent study; Internships; Study abroad; Teacher certification program. **Honors programs:** Heritage Scholars Program Gipson Honors Program. **Disability Services offered:** Note-taking services; Reader services; Tape recorders; Tutors. **Career services:** Alumni network; Alumni services; Career assessment; Career/job search classes; Internships; Regional alumni.

FACILITIES
Housing: Apartments for married students; Apartments for single students; Coed dorms; Fraternity/sorority housing; Special housing for disabled students; Theme housing; Wellness housing; 95% of campus accessible to physically disabled. **Special Academic Facilities/Equipment:** Museum of Natural History Art Gallery Planetarium Herbarium.

CAMPUS LIFE
Environment: Town. **Activities:** Campus Ministries; Choral groups; Concert band; Dance; Drama/theater; International Student Organization; Jazz band; Literary magazine; Marching band; Model UN; Music ensembles; Musical theater; Opera; Pep band; Student government; Student newspaper; Student-run film society; Symphony orchestra; Yearbook. 33 registered organizations, 4 honor societies, 3 fraternities, 4 sororities, on campus. **Athletics (Intercollegiate):** *Men:* baseball, cheerleading, cross-country, golf, skiing (downhill/Alpine), skiing (Nordic/cross-country), snowboarding, soccer, swimming, tennis, track/field (outdoor). *Women:* basketball, cheerleading, cross-country, golf, skiing (downhill/Alpine), skiing (Nordic/cross-country), snowboarding, soccer, softball, swimming, tennis, track/field (outdoor), volleyball. **On-Campus Highlights:** J.A. Albertson Activity Center. **Environmental Initiatives:** Student Sustainability Steward Position.

ADMISSIONS
Freshman Academic Profile: Average high school GPA 3.7. **Test Scores:** SAT Math middle 50% range 510–600. SAT EBRW middle 50% range 520–613. ACT middle 50% range 21–27. **Basis for Candidate Selection:** *Very important factors include:* academic GPA. *Important factors include:* rigor of secondary school record, application essay, recommendation(s), character/personal qualities, alumni/ae relation. *Other factors include:* class rank, standardized test scores, interview, extracurricular activities, talent/ability, first generation, volunteer work, work experience, level of applicant's interest. **Freshman Admission Requirements:** High school diploma is required and GED is accepted. *Academic units recommended:* 4 English, 3 math, 2 science, 2 foreign language, 2 social studies, 2 history, 4 academic electives. **Freshman Admission Statistics:** 2,754 applied, 49% admitted, 21% enrolled. **Transfer Admission Requirements:** College transcript(s), essay or personal statement. Minimum college GPA of 2.2 required. Lowest grade transferable D-. **General Admission Information:** Priority deadline 11/15. Regular application deadline 8/15. Non-fall registration accepted.

COSTS AND FINANCIAL AID
Annual tuition $31,000. Room and board $9,788. Required fees $755. Average book and supplies expense $1,200. **Required Forms and Deadlines:** FAFSA. **Notification of Awards:** Applicants will be notified of awards on a rolling basis beginning 1/25. **Types of Aid:** *Need-based scholarships/grants:* College/university scholarship or grant aid from institutional funds; Federal Pell; Private scholarships; SEOG; State scholarships/grants. *Loans:* Direct PLUS loans; Direct Subsidized Stafford Loans; Direct Unsubsidized Stafford Loans. **Student Employment:** Federal Work-Study Program available. Institutional employment available. **Financial Aid Statistics:** 71% needy freshmen, 58% needy undergrads receive need-based scholarship or grant aid. 100% freshmen, 100% undergrads receive non-need-based scholarship or grant aid. 82% freshmen, 83% undergrads receive need-based self-help aid. 8% freshmen, 12% undergrads receive athletic scholarships. 100% freshmen, 100% undergrads receive any aid. 72% undergrads borrow to pay for school. Average cumulative indebtedness $30,422. **Criteria awarding aid:** *Need-based:* Art, Athletics, Job skills, Leadership, Minority status, Music/drama, Religious affiliation. *Non-need-based:* Academics, Alumni affiliation, Athletics, Job skills.

COLLEGE OF MOUNT SAINT VINCENT

6301 Riverdale Avenue, Riverdale, NY 10471
Phone: 718-405-3267 **Financial Aid Phone:** 718-405-3349
E-mail: admissions@mountsaintvincent.edu **CEEB Code:** 2088
Fax: 718-549-7945 **Website:** www.mountsaintvincent.edu

This private school, affiliated with the Roman Catholic Church, was founded in 1847. It has a 70 acre campus.

RATINGS

Admissions Selectivity Rating: 71   **Fire Safety Rating:** 90   **Green Rating:** 60*

STUDENTS AND FACULTY

Enrollment: 1,683. **Student Body:** 70% female, 30% male, 12% out-of-state, 2% international (6 countries represented). Asian 9%, African American 14%, Caucasian 25%, Hispanic 41%, Native American <1%, Pacific Islander 0%, Two or more races 4%, Race unknown 4%.
Retention and Graduation: 78% freshmen return for sophomore year.
Faculty: Student/faculty ratio 13:1. 80 full-time faculty, 90% hold PhDs, 13% are members of minority groups, 58% are women. 0% of classes are taught by teaching assistants.

ACADEMICS

Degrees: Associate; Bachelor's; Master's; Post-master's certificate. **Classes:** Most classes have 10–19 students. Most lab/discussion sessions have 10–19 students. **Most popular majors:** Business/Commerce, General; Registered Nursing/Registered Nurse; Sociology, General. **Special Study Options:** Double major; Honors program; Independent study; Internships; Liberal arts/career combination; Study abroad; Teacher certification program. **Honors programs:** The Honors Program at the College of Mount Saint Vincent provides our most competent and motivated students with a stimulating environment in which to maximize their intellectual and personal development. The Honors Curriculum is designed to challenge students through all four years of their undergraduate experience while ensuring that they are exposed to academic experiences that fit the mission of the College. The Honors Curriculum combines unique Honors Courses with select elements of the traditional core curriculum for a baccalaureate degree. The Honors Program allows students the freedom to develop an educational experience suited to their academic and intellectual interests and may be completed while pursuing any of the majors offered by the College. The program's features include small classes and innovative teaching methods (seminars, group projects, individual mentoring, field trips). **Disability Services offered:** Note-taking services; Tape recorders; Tutors. **Career services:** Career assessment; Career/job search classes; Internships; Regional alumni.

FACILITIES

Housing: Coed dorms; Special housing for disabled students 90% of campus accessible to physically disabled. **Special Academic Facilities/Equipment:** Nursing lab, TV studio, radio station, Elizabeth Seton Travelling Museum, Forensic Laboratory equipment.

CAMPUS LIFE

Environment: Metropolis. **Activities:** Campus Ministries; Choral groups; Dance; Drama/theater; International Student Organization; Literary magazine; Model UN; Musical theater; Radio station; Student government; Student newspaper; Television station. 30 registered organizations, 15 honor societies, 2 religious organizations, on campus. **Athletics (Intercollegiate):** *Men:* baseball, basketball, cross-country, lacrosse, soccer, swimming, tennis, volleyball. *Women:* basketball, cross-country, lacrosse, soccer, softball, swimming, tennis, track/field (outdoor), volleyball. **On-Campus Highlights:** Alumnae Pavillion. **Environmental Initiatives:** Recycling.

ADMISSIONS

Freshman Academic Profile: Average high school GPA 3.0. 8% in top 10% of high school class, 28% in top 25% of high school class, 62% in top 50% of high school class. 58% from public high schools. **Test Scores:** SAT Math middle 50% range 380–490. SAT EBRW middle 50% range 400–490. ACT middle 50% range 17–22. **Basis for Candidate Selection:** *Very important factors include:* rigor of secondary school record, academic GPA, character/personal qualities. *Important factors include:* application essay, standardized test scores, recommendation(s), extracurricular activities. *Other factors include:* class rank, interview, alumni/ae relation, geographical residence, state residency, volunteer work, work experience, level of applicant's interest. **Freshman Admission Requirements:** High school diploma is required and GED is

accepted. *Academic units required:* 4 English, 3 math, 3 science, 3 science labs, 2 foreign language, 2 social studies, 2 academic electives. *Academic units recommended:* 4 English, 4 math, 4 science, 4 science labs, 4 foreign language, 4 social studies, 3 academic electives. **Freshman Admission Statistics:** 2,667 applied, 93% admitted, 18% enrolled. **Transfer Admission Requirements:** College transcript(s), essay or personal statement. Minimum college GPA of 2.0 required. Lowest grade transferable C. **General Admission Information:** Application fee $35. Priority deadline 3/1. Non-fall registration accepted. Admission may be deferred for a maximum of 1 year.

COSTS AND FINANCIAL AID

Annual tuition $35,620. Required fees $920. Average book and supplies expense $1,185. **Required Forms and Deadlines:** FAFSA; State aid form. **Notification of Awards:** Applicants will be notified of awards on a rolling basis beginning 3/1. **Types of Aid:** *Need-based scholarships/grants:* College/university scholarship or grant aid from institutional funds; Federal Pell; Private scholarships; SEOG; State scholarships/grants. **Student Employment:** Federal Work-Study Program available. Institutional employment available. **Financial Aid Statistics:** 100% needy freshmen, 100% needy undergrads receive need-based scholarship or grant aid. 0% freshmen, 0% undergrads receive non-need-based scholarship or grant aid. 100% freshmen, 100% undergrads receive need-based self-help aid. 0% freshmen, 0% undergrads receive athletic scholarships. 87% freshmen, 86% undergrads receive any aid. **Criteria awarding aid:** *Non-need-based:* Academics, Alumni affiliation, Leadership.

THE COLLEGE OF NEW JERSEY

PO Box 7718, Ewing, NJ 08628-0718
Phone: 609-771-2131 **Financial Aid Phone:** 609-771-2211
E-mail: tcnjinfo@tcnj.edu **CEEB Code:** 2519
Fax: 609-637-5174 **Website:** www.tcnj.edu **ACT Code:** 2614

This public school was founded in 1855. It has a 289 acre campus.

RATINGS

Admissions Selectivity Rating: 89   **Fire Safety Rating:** 98   **Green Rating:** 84

STUDENTS AND FACULTY

Enrollment: 6,850. **Student Body:** 58% female, 42% male, 6% out-of-state, <1% international (32 countries represented). Asian 11%, African American 6%, Caucasian 66%, Hispanic 12%, Native American <1%, Pacific Islander <1%, Two or more races <1%, Race unknown 3%.
Retention and Graduation: 94% freshmen return for sophomore year. 75% freshmen graduate within 4 years. 87% freshmen graduate within 6 years. 25% grads go on to further study within 1 year. 16% grads pursue arts and sciences degrees. 3% grads pursue law degrees. 0% grads pursue business degrees. 3% grads pursue medical degrees. **Faculty:** Student/faculty ratio 13:1. 365 full-time faculty, 89% hold PhDs, 25% are members of minority groups, 53% are women. 0% of classes are taught by teaching assistants.

ACADEMICS

Degrees: Bachelor's; Master's; Post-bachelor's certificate; Post-master's certificate. **Classes:** Most classes have 20–29 students. Most lab/discussion sessions have 10–19 students. **Most popular majors:** Education, General; Marketing; Psychology, General. **Special Study Options:** Accelerated program; Distance learning; Double major; Dual enrollment; English as a Second Language (ESL); Exchange student program (domestic); Honors program; Independent study; Internships; Liberal arts/career combination; Student-designed major; Study abroad; Teacher certification program. **Honors programs:** The College of New Jersey Honors Program provides a high level of challenge and stimulation to talented students who seek a broad educational experience. TCNJ College Honors is not a departmental program. It serves students in all majors in all schools of the college. Graduates of the program receive special recognition on their official transcript. Completion of the Honors Program is a mark of distinction that is valued by professional schools and graduate schools, as well as by prospective employers. **Combined degree programs:** BA/MD. **Disability Services offered:** Note-taking services; Reader services; Tape recorders; Tutors. **Career services:** Alumni services; Career assessment; Career/job search classes; Internships.

FACILITIES

Housing: Apartments for single students; Coed dorms; Special housing for international students; Theme housing; Wellness housing; Women's dorms; 90% of campus accessible to physically disabled. **Special Academic Facilities/ Equipment:** Art gallery, concert hall, greenhouse, observatory, planetarium, nuclear magnetic resonance lab, optical spectroscopy lab, scanning and transmission electron microscopes.

CAMPUS LIFE

Environment: Town. **Activities:** Campus Ministries; Choral groups; Concert band; Dance; Drama/theater; International Student Organization; Jazz band; Literary magazine; Model UN; Music ensembles; Musical theater; Opera; Pep band; Radio station; Student government; Student newspaper; Student-run film society; Television station; Yearbook. 230 registered organizations, 17 honor societies, 12 religious organizations, 14 fraternities, 14 sororities, on campus. **Athletics (Intercollegiate):** *Men:* baseball, basketball, cross-country, diving, football, soccer, swimming, tennis, track/field (outdoor), track/field (indoor). *Women:* basketball, cross-country, diving, field hockey, lacrosse, soccer, softball, swimming, tennis, track/field (outdoor), track/field (indoor). **On-Campus Highlights:** New Library. **Environmental Initiatives:** Commitment to sustainability being incorporated into the curriculum at TCNJ. This may include Freshman seminars, liberal learning programs, research and possible new minor or major degrees. The College's Municipal Land Use Center is authoring the State's sustainabilty and climate neutrality plans.

ADMISSIONS

Freshman Academic Profile: 36% in top 10% of high school class, 73% in top 25% of high school class, 98% in top 50% of high school class. 70% from public high schools. **Test Scores:** SAT Math middle 50% range 580–670. SAT EBRW middle 50% range 590–660. ACT middle 50% range 25–30. **Basis for Candidate Selection:** *Very important factors include:* rigor of secondary school record, class rank, standardized test scores, extracurricular activities, volunteer work. *Important factors include:* application essay, recommendation(s), talent/ ability, character/personal qualities, geographical residence, state residency. *Other factors include:* academic GPA, first generation, alumni/ae relation, racial/ethnic status, work experience, level of applicant's interest. **Freshman Admission Requirements:** High school diploma is required and GED is accepted. *Academic units required:* 4 English, 4 math, 4 science, 2 science labs, 2 foreign language, 2 social studies, 2 academic electives. *Academic units recommended:* 4 English, 4 math, 4 science, 2 science labs, 2 foreign language, 2 social studies, 4 academic electives. **Freshman Admission Statistics:** 12,898 applied, 48% admitted, 25% enrolled. **Transfer Admission Requirements:** High school transcript, college transcript(s), essay or personal statement, standardized test scores, statement of good standing from prior institution(s). Minimum college GPA of 2.5 required. Lowest grade transferable C. **General Admission Information:** Application fee $75. Priority deadline 11/1. Regular application deadline 2/1. Non-fall registration accepted. Admission may be deferred for a maximum of 2 semesters.

COSTS AND FINANCIAL AID

Annual in-state tuition $13,239. Annual out-of-state tuition $25,217. Room and board $14,048. Required fees $3,684. Average book and supplies expense $1,200. **Required Forms and Deadlines:** FAFSA. **Notification of Awards:** Applicants will be notified of awards on a rolling basis beginning 6/1. **Types of Aid:** *Need-based scholarships/grants:* College/university scholarship or grant aid from institutional funds; Federal Nursing Scholarships; Federal Pell; Private scholarships; SEOG; State scholarships/grants. *Loans:* Direct PLUS loans; Direct Subsidized Stafford Loans; Direct Unsubsidized Stafford Loans. **Student Employment:** Federal Work-Study Program available. Institutional employment available. **Financial Aid Statistics:** 46% needy freshmen, 42% needy undergrads receive need-based scholarship or grant aid. 38% freshmen, 29% undergrads receive non-need-based scholarship or grant aid. 67% freshmen, 76% undergrads receive need-based self-help aid. 0% freshmen, 0% undergrads receive athletic scholarships. 70% freshmen, 62% undergrads receive any aid. 62% undergrads borrow to pay for school. Average cumulative indebtedness $38,937. **Criteria awarding aid:** *Need-based:* Academics. *Non-need-based:* Academics, Art, Music/drama.

COLLEGE OF PERFORMING ARTS AT THE NEW SCHOOL

79 Fifth Avenue, 5th Floor, New York, NY 10003
Phone: 212.580.0210x4862 **Financial Aid Phone:** 212.229.8930
E-mail: performingarts@newschool.edu **CEEB Code:** 2398, 6153, 7336
Website: http://www.newschool.edu/performing-arts/ **ACT Code:** 2828

This private school was founded in 1916.

RATINGS

Admissions Selectivity Rating: 88   **Fire Safety Rating:** 89   **Green Rating:** 90

STUDENTS AND FACULTY

Enrollment: 609. **Student Body:** 48% female, 52% male, 78% out-of-state, 29% international (46 countries represented). Asian 5%, African American 1%, Caucasian 39%, Hispanic 9%, Native American 0%, Pacific Islander <1%, Two or more races 5%, Race unknown 5%.
Retention and Graduation: 76% freshmen return for sophomore year. 61% freshmen graduate within 4 years. 68% freshmen graduate within 6 years.
Faculty: Student/faculty ratio 7:1. 16 full-time faculty, 69% hold PhDs, 19% are members of minority groups, 50% are women. 0% of classes are taught by teaching assistants.

ACADEMICS

Degrees: Bachelor's; Diploma; Master's. **Classes:** Most classes have 10–19 students. Most lab/discussion sessions have fewer than 10 students. **Most popular majors:** Drama and Dramatics/Theatre Arts, General; Jazz/Jazz Studies; Music Performance, General. **Special Study Options:** Accelerated program; Double major; English as a Second Language (ESL); Exchange student program (domestic); Independent study; Internships; Liberal arts/career combination; Study abroad. **Disability Services offered:** Note-taking services; Reader services; Tape recorders. **Career services:** Alumni services; Career assessment; Career/job search classes; Internships.

FACILITIES

Housing: Coed dorms; Special housing for disabled students; 99% of campus accessible to physically disabled. **Special Academic Facilities/Equipment:** Art gallery, photography gallery, extensive collections of contemporary art, concert hall, public lectures, conferences, cultural and intellectual events.

CAMPUS LIFE

Environment: Metropolis. **Activities:** Dance; Drama/theater; International Student Organization; Jazz band; Literary magazine; Music ensembles; Musical theater; Radio station; Student government; Student newspaper; Student-run film society; Symphony orchestra. 42 registered organizations, 4 religious organizations, on campus. **On-Campus Highlights:** Stiefel Hall. **Environmental Initiatives:** Lighting Retrofits: 2W 13th St. and 66 5th Ave are in the midst of an ongoing replacement of all non-LED fixtures. The majority of the building's T8 fluorescent bulbs are being replaced with LED, stairwells are being replaced with dimming-occupancy based bi-level fixtures, and all rooms will be equiped with vacancy sensors. The main lobby and gallery spaces will also recieve significant upgrades as well. These same upgrades are being applied to 2 other large buildings, with a goal of completing the entire campus by early 2017.

ADMISSIONS

Freshman Academic Profile: Average high school GPA 3.3. 22% in top 10% of high school class, 44% in top 25% of high school class, 72% in top 50% of high school class. 48% from public high schools. **Test Scores:** SAT Math middle 50% range 560–640. SAT EBRW middle 50% range 620–700. ACT middle 50% range 24–31. **Basis for Candidate Selection:** *Very important factors include:* academic GPA, application essay, extracurricular activities. *Important factors include:* rigor of secondary school record, recommendation(s), character/personal qualities. *Other factors include:* class rank, standardized test scores, interview, talent/ability, volunteer work, work experience, level of applicant's interest. **Freshman Admission Requirements:** High school diploma is required and GED is accepted. *Academic units required:* 4 English. *Academic units recommended:* 4 math, 4 science, 4 foreign language, 4 social studies, 4 history. **Freshman Admission Statistics:** 1,279 applied, 49% admitted, 21% enrolled. **Transfer Admission Requirements:** College transcript(s), essay or personal statement. Minimum college GPA of 2.0 required. Lowest grade transferable C. **General Admission Information:** Application fee $50. Priority deadline 1/15. Regular application deadline 8/1. Non-fall registration accepted. Admission may be deferred for a maximum of 1 year.

COSTS AND FINANCIAL AID

Annual tuition $48,760. Room and board $17,600. Required fees $1,216. Average book and supplies expense $2,050. **Required Forms and Deadlines:** FAFSA. **Notification of Awards:** Applicants will be notified of awards on a rolling basis beginning 4/1. **Types of Aid:** *Need-based scholarships/grants:* College/university scholarship or grant aid from institutional funds; Federal Pell; Private scholarships; SEOG; State scholarships/grants; United Negro College Fund. *Loans:* Direct PLUS loans; Direct Subsidized Stafford Loans; Direct Unsubsidized Stafford Loans. **Student Employment:** Federal Work-Study Program available. Institutional employment available. **Financial Aid Statistics:** 34% needy freshmen, 47% needy undergrads receive need-based scholarship or grant aid. 87% freshmen, 83% undergrads receive non-need-based scholarship or grant aid. 17% freshmen, 14% undergrads receive need-based self-help aid. 0% freshmen, 0% undergrads receive athletic scholarships. 64% freshmen, 40% undergrads receive any aid. 38% undergrads borrow to pay for school. Average cumulative indebtedness $31,723. **Criteria awarding aid:** *Need-based:* Academics, Art, Leadership, Minority status, Music/drama. *Non-need-based:* Academics, Art, Leadership, Minority status, Music/drama, State/district residency.

COLLEGE OF SAINT BENEDICT/SAINT JOHN'S UNIVERSITY

College of Saint Benedict/Saint John's University, St. Joseph, MN 56321-7155
Phone: 320-363-5060 **Financial Aid Phone:** 320-363-5388
E-mail: admissions@csbsju.edu **CEEB Code:** 6624
Fax: 320-363-5650 **Website:** www.csbsju.edu **ACT Code:** 2146

This private school, affiliated with the Roman Catholic Church, was founded in 1857. It has a 2800 acre campus.

RATINGS

Admissions Selectivity Rating: 77   **Fire Safety Rating:** 98   **Green Rating:** 89

STUDENTS AND FACULTY

Enrollment: 3,329. **Student Body:** 52% female, 48% male, 18% out-of-state, 4% international (18 countries represented). Asian 4%, African American 3%, Caucasian 79%, Hispanic 8%, Native American 1%, Pacific Islander <1%, Two or more races 0%, Race unknown 0%.
Retention and Graduation: 85% freshmen return for sophomore year. 72% freshmen graduate within 4 years. 77% freshmen graduate within 6 years. 16% grads go on to further study within 1 year. **Faculty:** Student/faculty ratio 11:1. 280 full-time faculty, 11% are members of minority groups, 51% are women. 0% of classes are taught by teaching assistants.

ACADEMICS

Degrees: Bachelor's; Master's. **Most popular majors:** Biology/Biological Sciences, General; Business Administration and Management, General; Accounting. **Special Study Options:** Cross-registration; Distance learning; Double major; Dual enrollment; English as a Second Language (ESL); Honors program; Independent study; Internships; Student-designed major; Study abroad; Teacher certification program. **Honors programs:** The Honors Program is a select group of students who explore an exciting world of challenging ideas together. All departments may contribute courses to our honors program. Students in all majors may participate in the Honors Program and receive honors distinction inside the major. **Disability Services offered:** Note-taking services; Reader services; Tape recorders; Tutors. **Career services:** Alumni network; Alumni services; Career assessment; Internships; Regional alumni.

FACILITIES

Housing: Apartments for single students; Men's dorms; Special housing for disabled students; Theme housing; Wellness housing; Women's dorms 90% of campus accessible to physically disabled. **Special Academic Facilities/ Equipment:** Hill Museum and Manuscript Library, art galleries, natural science museum, Saint John's Outdoor University, Benedicta Arts Center, Sommers Digital Video Studio, observatory, greenhouses, pottery kilns

CAMPUS LIFE

Environment: Village. **Activities:** Campus Ministries; Choral groups; Concert band; Dance; Drama/theater; International Student Organization; Jazz band; Literary magazine; Model UN; Music ensembles; Musical theater; Opera;

Radio station; Student government; Student newspaper; Symphony orchestra; Television station. 100 registered organizations, 7 honor societies, 6 religious organizations, on campus. **Athletics (Intercollegiate):** *Men:* baseball, basketball, cross-country, diving, football, golf, ice hockey, skiing (Nordic/cross-country), soccer, swimming, tennis, track/field (outdoor), track/field (indoor), wrestling. *Women:* basketball, cross-country, diving, golf, ice hockey, skiing (Nordic/cross-country), soccer, softball, swimming, tennis, track/field (outdoor), track/field (indoor), volleyball. **On-Campus Highlights:** Gorecki Dining Center/Sexton Commons **Environmental Initiatives:** Renewable Energy/Carbon Neutrality.

ADMISSIONS

Freshman Academic Profile: Average high school GPA 3.6. 26% in top 10% of high school class, 55% in top 25% of high school class, 84% in top 50% of high school class. 74% from public high schools. **Test scores:** SAT Math middle 50% range 510–610. SAT EBRW middle 50% range 520–620. ACT middle 50% range 22–28. **Basis for Candidate Selection:** *Very important factors include:* rigor of secondary school record, academic GPA, standardized test scores, extracurricular activities. *Important factors include:* alumni/ae relation. *Other factors include:* application essay, recommendation(s), interview, talent/ ability, character/personal qualities, first generation, geographical residence, volunteer work, work experience. **Freshman Admission Requirements:** High school diploma is required and GED is accepted. *Academic units required:* 4 English, 3 math, 2 science, 2 science labs, 2 social studies, 4 academic electives. *Academic units recommended:* 4 English, 3 math, 2 science, 2 science labs, 2 foreign language, 2 social studies, 4 academic electives. **Freshman Admission Statistics:** 3,798 applied, 79% admitted, 28% enrolled. **Transfer Admission Requirements:** High school transcript, college transcript(s), essay or personal statement, statement of good standing from prior institution(s). Minimum college GPA of 2.75 required. Lowest grade transferable C. **General Admission Information:** Non-fall registration accepted. Admission may be deferred for a maximum of one year.

COSTS AND FINANCIAL AID

Annual tuition $45,730. Room and board $11,684. Required fees $1,090. Average book and supplies expense $1,000. **Required Forms and Deadlines:** FAFSA. **Notification of Awards:** Applicants will be notified of awards on a rolling basis beginning 12/15. **Types of Aid:** *Need-based scholarships/grants:* College/university scholarship or grant aid from institutional funds; Federal Pell; Private scholarships; SEOG; State scholarships/grants. *Loans:* Direct PLUS loans; Direct Subsidized Stafford Loans; Direct Unsubsidized Stafford Loans. **Student Employment:** Federal Work-Study Program available. Institutional employment available. **Financial Aid Statistics:** 98% needy freshmen, 97% needy undergrads receive need-based scholarship or grant aid. 95% freshmen, 93% undergrads receive non-need-based scholarship or grant aid. 98% freshmen, 95% undergrads receive need-based self-help aid. 0% freshmen, 0% undergrads receive athletic scholarships. 96% freshmen, 97% undergrads receive any aid. 72% undergrads borrow to pay for school. Average cumulative indebtedness $40,434. **Criteria awarding aid:** *Non-Need-based:* Academics, Alumni affiliation, Art, Leadership, Music/drama.

COLLEGE OF SAINT ELIZABETH

Admissions Office, Morristown, NJ 07960-6989
Phone: 973-290-4700 **Financial Aid Phone:** 973-290-4432
E-mail: apply@cse.edu **CEEB Code:** 2090
Fax: 973-290-4710

This private school, affiliated with the Roman Catholic Church, was founded in 1899. It has a 200 acre campus.

RATINGS

Admissions Selectivity Rating: 82   **Fire Safety Rating:** 96   **Green Rating:** 63

STUDENTS AND FACULTY

Enrollment: 852. **Student Body:** 94% female, 6% male, 4% out-of-state, 4% international (8 countries represented). Asian 2%, African American 41%, Caucasian 26%, Hispanic 20%, Native American 1%, Pacific Islander 0%, Two or more races 2%, Race unknown 4%.
Retention and Graduation: 69% freshmen return for sophomore year.
Faculty: Student/faculty ratio 12:1. 52 full-time faculty, 83% hold PhDs, 8% are members of minority groups, 65% are women. 0% of classes are taught by teaching assistants.

ACADEMICS

Degrees: Bachelor's; Certificate; Master's; Post-bachelor's certificate; Post-master's certificate. **Classes:** Most classes have 10–19 students. **Most popular majors:** Criminal Justice/Safety Studies; Registered Nursing/Registered Nurse; Psychology, General. **Special Study Options:** Accelerated program; Cross-registration; Distance learning; Double major; Dual enrollment; English as a Second Language (ESL); Exchange student program (domestic); Honors program; Independent study; Internships; Student-designed major; Study abroad; Teacher certification program; Weekend college. **Combined degree programs:** BA/MA. **Disability Services offered:** Note-taking services; Reader services; Tape recorders; Tutors. **Career services:** Alumni network; Career assessment; Career/job search classes; Internships.

FACILITIES

Housing: Women's dorms 85% of campus accessible to physically disabled. **Special Academic Facilities/Equipment:** Dolan Performance Hall,Greek Theater, Octagon Theater,Mahoney Library,Smart Classrooms,Hyland Lecture Hall

CAMPUS LIFE

Environment: Town. **Activities:** Campus Ministries; Choral groups; Dance; Drama/theater; International Student Organization; Literary magazine; Music ensembles; Student government; Student newspaper; Yearbook. 28 registered organizations, 9 honor societies, 1 religious organizations, on campus. **Athletics (Intercollegiate):** *Women:* basketball, equestrian sports, soccer, softball, swimming, tennis. **On-Campus Highlights:** St. Joesph's Hall-Student Center **Environmental Initiatives:** Hazardous Waste Management process exists.

ADMISSIONS

Freshman Academic Profile: 81% from public high schools. **Test scores:** SAT Math middle 50% range 370–465. SAT EBRW middle 50% range 380–470. **Basis for Candidate Selection:** *Very important factors include:* rigor of secondary school record, class rank, academic GPA, standardized test scores, recommendation(s). *Important factors include:* application essay, character/personal qualities. *Other factors include:* interview, extracurricular activities, talent/ability, first generation, alumni/ae relation, geographical residence, volunteer work, work experience, level of applicant's interest. **Freshman Admission Requirements:** High school diploma is required and GED is accepted. *Academic units required:* 3 English, 2 math, 1 science, 1 science labs, 2 foreign language, 1 history, 7 academic electives. *Academic units recommended:* 3 English, 3 math, 1 science, 2 science labs, 1 history, 8 academic electives. **Freshman Admission Statistics:** 2,496 applied, 48% admitted, 10% enrolled. **Transfer Admission Requirements:** college transcript(s), essay or personal statement, Minimum college GPA of 2.0 required. Lowest grade transferable C. **General Admission Information:** Application fee $35. Priority deadline 3/1. Regular application deadline 8/15. Non-fall registration accepted. Admission may be deferred for a maximum of 1 year.

COSTS AND FINANCIAL AID

Annual tuition $29,148. Room and board $12,744. Required fees $1,947. Average book and supplies expense $1,300. **Required Forms and Deadlines:** FAFSA. **Notification of Awards:** Applicants will be notified of awards on a rolling basis beginning 11/15. **Types of Aid:** *Need-based scholarships/grants:* College/university scholarship or grant aid from institutional funds; Federal Pell; Private scholarships; SEOG; State scholarships/grants. *Loans:* Direct PLUS loans; Direct Subsidized Stafford Loans; Direct Unsubsidized Stafford Loans. **Student Employment:** Federal Work-Study Program available. Institutional employment available. **Financial Aid Statistics:** 89% needy freshmen, 81% needy undergrads receive need-based scholarship or grant aid. 100% freshmen, 88% undergrads receive non-need-based scholarship or grant aid. 93% freshmen, 91% undergrads receive need-based self-help aid. 0% freshmen, 0% undergrads receive athletic scholarships. 87% freshmen, 98% undergrads receive any aid. **Criteria awarding aid:** *Need-based:* Academics, Minority status. *Non-Need-based:* Academics, Alumni affiliation, Art, Leadership, Religious affiliation, State/district residency.

COLLEGE OF SAINT MARY

7000 Mercy Rd., Omaha, NE 68106
Phone: 402-399-2355 **Financial Aid Phone:** 402-399-2362
E-mail: enroll@csm.edu **CEEB Code:** 6106
Fax: 402-399-2412 **Website:** www.csm.edu **ACT Code:** 2440

This private school, affiliated with the Roman Catholic Church, was founded in 1923. It has a 40 acre campus.

RATINGS

Admissions Selectivity Rating: 87   **Fire Safety Rating:** 97   **Green Rating:** 73

STUDENTS AND FACULTY

Enrollment: 810. **Student Body:** 100% female, 0% male, 24% out-of-state, 1% international (8 countries represented). Asian 3%, African American 8%, Caucasian 69%, Hispanic 12%, Native American 1%, Pacific Islander <1%, Two or more races 6%, Race unknown 0%. **Retention and Graduation:** 75% freshmen return for sophomore year. 35% freshmen graduate within 4 years. 47% freshmen graduate within 6 years. 51% grads go on to further study within 1 year. **Faculty:** Student/faculty ratio 10:1. 72 full-time faculty, 75% hold PhDs, 13% are members of minority groups, 89% are women. 0% of classes are taught by teaching assistants.

ACADEMICS

Degrees: Associate; Bachelor's; Certificate; Doctoral degree research/scholarship; Master's; Post-bachelor's certificate; Terminal Associate. **Classes:** Most classes have 20–29 students. Most lab/discussion sessions have 10–19 students. **Most popular majors:** Elementary Education and Teaching; Registered Nursing/Registered Nurse; Biology, General. **Special Study Options:** Accelerated program; Cooperative education program; Distance learning; Double major; Dual enrollment; Honors program; Independent study; Internships; Study abroad; Teacher certification program; Weekend college. **Honors programs:** Walk Tall Honors Program. **Disability Services offered:** Note-taking services; Reader services; Tape recorders; Tutors. **Career services:** Alumni services; Career assessment; Career/job search classes; Internships.

FACILITIES

Housing:; Special housing for disabled students; Women's dorms 100% of campus accessible to physically disabled. **Special Academic Facilities/Equipment:** Hillmer Art Gallery Gross Auditorium

CAMPUS LIFE

Environment: Metropolis. **Activities:** Campus Ministries; Choral groups; Drama/theater; International Student Organization; Music ensembles; Student government. 22 registered organizations, 2 honor societies, 2 religious organizations, on campus. **Athletics (Intercollegiate):** *Women:* basketball, cross-country, soccer, softball, swimming, volleyball. **On-Campus Highlights:** Christina's Place—Coffee Shop/Deli/student gathering place **Environmental Initiatives:** Lower temperature set points in the summer time as well as work without lights to reduce energy during peak hours.

ADMISSIONS

Freshman Academic Profile: Average high school GPA 3.4. 15% in top 10% of high school class, 40% in top 25% of high school class, 72% in top 50% of high school class. 80% from public high schools. **Test scores:** ACT middle 50% range 18–24. **Basis for Candidate Selection:** *Very important factors include:* academic GPA, standardized test scores. *Important factors include:* class rank. *Other factors include:* recommendation(s), extracurricular activities. **Freshman Admission Requirements:** High school diploma is required and GED is accepted. *Academic units required:* 4 English, 2 math, 2 science, 2 social studies. *Academic units recommended:* 3 math, 3 science. **Freshman Admission Statistics:** 428 applied, 52% admitted, 53% enrolled. **Transfer Admission Requirements:** High school transcript, college transcript(s), Minimum college GPA of 2.0 required. Lowest grade transferable C. **General Admission Information:** Application fee $30. Non-fall registration accepted. Admission may be deferred for a maximum of 12 months.

COSTS AND FINANCIAL AID

Annual tuition $20,750. Room and board $7,850. Average book and supplies expense $848. **Required Forms and Deadlines:** FAFSA. **Notification of Awards:** Applicants will be notified of awards on a rolling basis beginning 12/15. **Types of Aid:** *Need-based scholarships/grants:* College/university scholarship or grant aid from institutional funds; Federal Nursing Scholarships; Federal Pell; Private scholarships; SEOG; State scholarships/grants. *Loans:* Direct PLUS loans; Direct Subsidized Stafford Loans; Direct Unsubsidized

Stafford Loans. **Student Employment:** Federal Work-Study Program available. Institutional employment available. **Financial Aid Statistics:** 100% needy freshmen, 96% needy undergrads receive need-based scholarship or grant aid. 18% freshmen, 6% undergrads receive non-need-based scholarship or grant aid. 74% freshmen, 89% undergrads receive need-based self-help aid. 19% freshmen, 9% undergrads receive athletic scholarships. 100% freshmen, 98% undergrads receive any aid. 85% undergrads borrow to pay for school. Average cumulative indebtedness $36,309. **Criteria awarding aid:** *Non-Need-based:* Academics, Athletics.

THE COLLEGE OF SAINT ROSE

432 Western Avenue, Albany, NY 12203
Phone: 518-454-5150 **Financial Aid Phone:** 518-458-5464
E-mail: admit@strose.edu **CEEB Code:** 2091
Fax: 518-454-2013 **Website:** www.strose.edu **ACT Code:** 2714

This private school was founded in 1920. It has a 49 acre campus.

RATINGS
Admissions Selectivity Rating: 74   **Fire Safety Rating:** 95   **Green Rating:** 65

STUDENTS AND FACULTY
Enrollment: 2,409. **Student Body:** 66% female, 34% male, 14% out-of-state, 3% international (36 countries represented). Asian 3%, African American 18%, Caucasian 55%, Hispanic 6%, Native American <1%, Pacific Islander <1%, Two or more races 12%, Race unknown 3%.
Retention and Graduation: 70% freshmen return for sophomore year. 46% freshmen graduate within 4 years. 61% freshmen graduate within 6 years. 32% grads go on to further study within 1 year. **Faculty:** Student/faculty ratio 14:1. 172 full-time faculty, 91% hold PhDs, 15% are members of minority groups, 56% are women. 0% of classes are taught by teaching assistants.

ACADEMICS
Degrees: Bachelor's; Certificate; Master's; Post-bachelor's certificate; Post-master's certificate. **Classes:** Most classes have 10–19 students. Most lab/discussion sessions have 10–19 students. **Most popular majors:** Elementary Education and Teaching; Business Administration and Management, General; Criminal Justice/Law Enforcement Administration. **Special Study Options:** Accelerated program; Cross-registration; Distance learning; Double major; Dual enrollment; English as a Second Language (ESL); Exchange student program (domestic); Independent study; Internships; Liberal arts/career combination; Student-designed major; Study abroad; Teacher certification program.
Combined degree programs: BA/JD; BA/MA. **Disability Services offered:** Note-taking services; Reader services; Tape recorders; Tutors. **Career services:** Alumni network; Alumni services; Career assessment; Career/job search classes; Internships; Regional alumni.

FACILITIES
Housing: Apartments for single students; Coed dorms; Men's dorms; Special housing for disabled students; Theme housing; Wellness housing; Women's dorms 90% of campus accessible to physically disabled. **Special Academic Facilities/Equipment:** The Center for Art and Design houses the Saint Rose Art Gallery, the venue for student art shows and home to one of the largest screen printing facilities in the state of New York. The Esther Massry Gallery features exhibits by acclaimed visiting artists. The College's full-scale television studio is where communications students produce three 30-minute weekly television shows aired on Time Warner Cable. The Music Center features the Saints and Sinners Sound Studio, a 16-track professional recording studio, in addition to a music library. Athletic Facilities include the College's Fitness Center, swimming pool, regulation NCAA basketball court and the Plumeri Sports Complex. The Hubbard Interfaith Sanctuary is home to Campus Ministry and hosts a variety of interfaith lectures, concerts and poetry readings. With private meditation rooms and an indoor serenity garden, this interreligious space provides a place to escape for a few minutes of quiet prayer. The Center for Cultural Diversity provides academic, social, and cultural support in an effort to enhance the quality of experiences for our diverse student population.

CAMPUS LIFE
Environment: City. **Activities:** Campus Ministries; Choral groups; Concert band; Dance; Drama/theater; International Student Organization; Jazz band; Literary magazine; Music ensembles; Musical theater; Pep band; Radio station; Student government; Student newspaper; Symphony orchestra; Television

station. 36 registered organizations, 5 honor societies, 1 religious organizations, on campus. **Athletics (Intercollegiate):** *Men:* baseball, basketball, cross-country, golf, soccer, swimming, track/field (outdoor). *Women:* basketball, cross-country, soccer, softball, swimming, tennis, track/field (outdoor), volleyball. **On-Campus Highlights:** Lally School of Education.

ADMISSIONS
Freshman Academic Profile: 15% in top 10% of high school class, 37% in top 25% of high school class, 72% in top 50% of high school class. **Test scores:** SAT Math middle 50% range 490–600. SAT EBRW middle 50% range 500–610. ACT middle 50% range 21–26. **Basis for Candidate Selection:** *Very important factors include:* rigor of secondary school record, academic GPA. *Important factors include:* recommendation(s), extracurricular activities, talent/ability, character/personal qualities, first generation. *Other factors include:* class rank, application essay, standardized test scores, interview, alumni/ae relation, volunteer work, work experience. **Freshman Admission Requirements:** High school diploma is required and GED is accepted. *Academic units required:* 4 English, 3 math, 3 science, 2 science labs, 1 foreign language, 2 social studies, 2 history. *Academic units recommended:* 4 English, 4 math, 4 science, 2 science labs, 2 foreign language, 4 social studies, 4 history, 4 academic electives. **Freshman Admission Statistics:** 6,576 applied, 87% admitted, 11% enrolled. **Transfer Admission Requirements:** High school transcript, college transcript(s), statement of good standing from prior institution(s). Minimum college GPA of 2.5 required. Lowest grade transferable C-. **General Admission Information:** Priority deadline 12/1. Regular application deadline 5/1. Non-fall registration accepted. Admission may be deferred for a maximum of 1 semester.

COSTS AND FINANCIAL AID
Required Forms and Deadlines: FAFSA; State aid form. **Notification of Awards:** Applicants will be notified of awards on a rolling basis beginning 12/15. **Types of Aid:** *Need-based scholarships/grants:* College/university scholarship or grant aid from institutional funds; Federal Pell; Private scholarships; SEOG; State scholarships/grants. *Loans:* Direct PLUS loans; Direct Subsidized Stafford Loans; Direct Unsubsidized Stafford Loans. **Student Employment:** Federal Work-Study Program available. Institutional employment available. **Financial Aid Statistics:** 83% needy freshmen, 76% needy undergrads receive need-based scholarship or grant aid. 99% freshmen, 86% undergrads receive non-need-based scholarship or grant aid. 100% freshmen, 100% undergrads receive need-based self-help aid. 2% freshmen, 3% undergrads receive athletic scholarships. 99% freshmen, 98% undergrads receive any aid. 86% undergrads borrow to pay for school. Average cumulative indebtedness $36,596. **Criteria awarding aid:** *Need-based:* Academics. *Non-Need-based:* Academics, Alumni affiliation, Art, Athletics, Music/drama.

THE COLLEGE OF SAINT SCHOLASTICA

1200 Kenwood Avenue, Duluth, MN 55811-4199
Phone: 218-723-6046 **Financial Aid Phone:** 218-723-7027
E-mail: admissions@css.edu **CEEB Code:** 6107
Fax: 218-723-5991 **Website:** www.css.edu **ACT Code:** 2098

This private school, affiliated with the Roman Catholic Church, was founded in 1912. It has a 186 acre campus.

RATINGS
Admissions Selectivity Rating: 77   **Fire Safety Rating:** 62   **Green Rating:** 63

STUDENTS AND FACULTY
Enrollment: 2,441. **Student Body:** 71% female, 29% male, 12% out-of-state, 2% international (26 countries represented). Asian 3%, African American 3%, Caucasian 83%, Hispanic 4%, Native American 1%, Pacific Islander <1%, Two or more races 3%, Race unknown 1%.
Retention and Graduation: 81% freshmen return for sophomore year. 60% freshmen graduate within 4 years. 69% freshmen graduate within 6 years. **Faculty:** Student/faculty ratio 14:1. 215 full-time faculty, 59% hold PhDs, 10% are members of minority groups, 68% are women. 0% of classes are taught by teaching assistants.

ACADEMICS
Degrees: Bachelor's; Certificate; Doctoral degree—professional practice; Master's; Post-bachelor's certificate; Post-master's certificate. **Classes:** Most classes have 10–19 students. Most lab/discussion sessions have fewer than 10 students. **Most popular majors:** Registered Nursing/Registered Nurse; Business Administration and Management, General; Social Work. **Special**

Study Options: Accelerated program; Cross-registration; Distance learning; Double major; Dual enrollment; Honors program; Independent study; Internships; Liberal arts/career combination; Student-designed major; Study abroad; Teacher certification program. **Honors programs:** The Honors Program prepares civic scholars committed to the pursuit of knowledge that leads to ethical action in their communities and beyond. Our courses are designed to challenge students intellectually for the purpose of becoming engaged in civic life beyond the walls of the classroom. We ask students to become responsible for their own education and to pay it forward by promoting quality of life for all people. **Combined degree programs:** BA/MA. **Disability Services offered:** Note-taking services; Reader services; Tape recorders; Tutors. **Career services:** Alumni network; Alumni services; Career assessment; Career/job search classes; Internships; Regional alumni.

FACILITIES

Housing: Apartments for single students; Coed dorms; Special housing for disabled students; Special housing for international students 95% of campus accessible to physically disabled. **Campus Network:** 100% of classrooms, 100% of dorms, 100% of student union, 100% of libraries, 100% of dining areas, 100% of common outdoor areas, have wireless network access.

CAMPUS LIFE

Environment: City. **Activities:** Campus Ministries; Choral groups; Concert band; Dance; Drama/theater; International Student Organization; Jazz band; Literary magazine; Model UN; Music ensembles; Musical theater; Student government; Student newspaper; Symphony orchestra; Yearbook. 67 registered organizations, 3 honor societies, 3 religious organizations, on campus. **Athletics (Intercollegiate):** *Men:* baseball, basketball, cross-country, ice hockey, skiing (Nordic/cross-country), soccer, tennis, track/field (outdoor), track/field (indoor). *Women:* basketball, cross-country, skiing (Nordic/cross-country), soccer, softball, tennis, track/field (outdoor), track/field (indoor), volleyball. **On-Campus Highlights:** Wellness Center

ADMISSIONS

Freshman Academic Profile: Average high school GPA 3.5. 23% in top 10% of high school class, 48% in top 25% of high school class, 77% in top 50% of high school class. ACT middle 50% range 22–26. **Basis for Candidate Selection:** *Very important factors include:* rigor of secondary school record, academic GPA. *Other factors include:* application essay, standardized test scores, interview, extracurricular activities, talent/ability, character/personal qualities, first generation, volunteer work. **Freshman Admission Requirements:** High school diploma is required and GED is accepted. *Academic units recommended:* 4 English, 2 math, 3 science, 3 foreign language, 3 social studies, 3 history. **Freshman Admission Statistics:** 1,956 applied, 76% admitted, 30% enrolled. **Transfer Admission Requirements:** college transcript(s), Minimum college GPA of 1.5 required. Lowest grade transferable C. **General Admission Information:** Priority deadline 2/1. Non-fall registration accepted. Admission may be deferred for a maximum of 1 year.

COSTS AND FINANCIAL AID

Annual tuition $38,750. Room and board $10,340. Required fees $660. Average book and supplies expense $1,150. **Required Forms and Deadlines:** FAFSA. **Notification of Awards:** Applicants will be notified of awards on a rolling basis beginning 3/1. **Types of Aid:** *Need-based scholarships/grants:* College/university scholarship or grant aid from institutional funds; Federal Pell; Private scholarships; SEOG; State scholarships/grants. *Loans:* Direct PLUS loans; Direct Subsidized Stafford Loans; Direct Unsubsidized Stafford Loans. **Student Employment:** Federal Work-Study Program available. Institutional employment available. **Financial Aid Statistics:** 66% needy freshmen, 70% needy undergrads receive need-based scholarship or grant aid. 100% freshmen, 80% undergrads receive non-need-based scholarship or grant aid. 63% freshmen, 71% undergrads receive need-based self-help aid. 0% freshmen, 0% undergrads receive athletic scholarships. 80% freshmen, 79% undergrads receive any aid. 74% undergrads borrow to pay for school. Average cumulative indebtedness $41,577. **Criteria awarding aid:** *Non-Need-based:* Academics, Alumni affiliation, Music/drama, Religious affiliation, State/district residency.

COLLEGE OF THE ATLANTIC

105 Eden Street, Bar Harbor, ME 04609
Phone: 207-288-5015 **Financial Aid Phone:** 207-801-5645
E-mail: inquiry@coa.edu **CEEB Code:** 3305
Fax: 207-288-4126 **Website:** www.coa.edu **ACT Code:** 1637

This private school was founded in 1969. It has a 38 acre campus.

RATINGS

Admissions Selectivity Rating: 87   **Fire Safety Rating:** 97   **Green Rating:** 99

STUDENTS AND FACULTY

Enrollment: 327. **Student Body:** 76% female, 24% male, 77% out-of-state, 24% international (47 countries represented). Asian 1%, African American 2%, Caucasian 65%, Hispanic 4%, Native American 0%, Pacific Islander 0%, Two or more races 2%, Race unknown 3%.
Retention and Graduation: 81% freshmen return for sophomore year. 53% freshmen graduate within 4 years. 66% freshmen graduate within 6 years. 25% grads go on to further study within 1 year. 25% grads pursue arts and sciences degrees. 0% grads pursue law degrees. 0% grads pursue business degrees. 0% grads pursue medical degrees. **Faculty:** Student/faculty ratio 9:1. 27 full-time faculty, 96% hold PhDs, 4% are members of minority groups, 41% are women. 0% of classes are taught by teaching assistants.

ACADEMICS

Degrees: Bachelor's; Master's. **Classes:** Most classes have 10–19 students. **Most popular majors:** Humanities/Humanistic Studies; Multi-/Interdisciplinary Studies, Other; Ecology. **Special Study Options:** Cross-registration; Exchange student program (domestic); Independent study; Internships; Liberal arts/career combination; Student-designed major; Study abroad; Teacher certification program. **Honors programs:** We consider all our students to be capable of honors work, which is why all students finish their time at COA with a term-long capstone, or senior project. **Disability Services offered:** Note-taking services; Reader services; Tape recorders; Tutors. **Career services:** Alumni network; Alumni services; Career assessment; Internships; Regional alumni.

FACILITIES

Housing: Coed dorms; Special housing for disabled students; Wellness housing 70% of campus accessible to physically disabled. **Special Academic Facilities/Equipment:** George B. Dorr Natural History Museum, Ethel H. Blum Art Gallery, Beech Hill Farm, Peggy Rockefeller Farms, Edward McC. Blair Marine Research Station at Mount Desert Rock, Alice Eno Field Research Station at Great Duck Island, Diana Davis Spencer Hatchery (business incubator), pottery studio, greenhouse, Geographic Information Systems lab, Green Media & Graphics Lab, Deering Common Community Center with cafe, organic community garden, Beatrix Farrand Gardens. Outdoor equipment includes two ocean-going vessels, sailboats, and several canoes and kayaks, bicycles for loan, plus gear for outdoor activities. We also have a protected wilderness area, the 100-acre Cox Protectorate.

CAMPUS LIFE

Environment: Rural. **Activities:** Choral groups; Concert band; Dance; Drama/theater; International Student Organization; Jazz band; Literary magazine; Music ensembles; Student government; Student newspaper; Student-run film society; Yearbook. 12 registered organizations, on campus. **On-Campus Highlights:** Thorndike Library. **Environmental Initiatives:** Energy Framework: In March of 2013 the college adopted an Energy Framework that seeks to make the college fossil fuel-free by 2030. The framework includes interim goals for 2020 that the college is working on now to achieve. The framework focuses on reducing fossil fuel use and pursuing renewable sources of energy on campus and at our two nearby farms. Integral to the policy is the requirement that our students be involved in creating a fossil fuel-free campus through our hands-on curriculum. We have purchased an electric van and lease an electric Ford Focus for student transportation and have established three solar/electric charging stations for them on campus and at our two farms. These will also be used for additional electric vehicles we expect to bring into service.

ADMISSIONS

Freshman Academic Profile: Average high school GPA 3.6. 35% in top 10% of high school class, 59% in top 25% of high school class, 82% in top 50% of

high school class. 43% from public high schools. **Test scores:** SAT Math middle 50% range 580–670. SAT EBRW middle 50% range 630–730. ACT middle 50% range 30–33. **Basis for Candidate Selection:** *Very important factors include:* rigor of secondary school record, application essay, recommendation(s). *Important factors include:* class rank, academic GPA, interview, extracurricular activities, talent/ability, character/personal qualities. *Other factors include:* standardized test scores, first generation, alumni/ae relation, geographical residence, state residency, racial/ethnic status, level of applicant's interest. **Freshman Admission Requirements:** High school diploma is required and GED is accepted. *Academic units required:* 4 English, 3 math, 2 science, 2 science labs, 2 social studies. *Academic units recommended:* 4 math, 3 science, 2 foreign language, 2 history, 1 academic electives. **Freshman Admission Statistics:** 459 applied, 67% admitted, 27% enrolled. **Transfer Admission Requirements:** High school transcript, college transcript(s), essay or personal statement, Minimum college GPA of 3.0 required. Lowest grade transferable C. **General Admission Information:** Application fee $50. Regular application deadline 2/1. Non-fall registration accepted. Admission may be deferred for a maximum of 1 year.

COSTS AND FINANCIAL AID
Annual tuition $42,993. Room and board $9,747. Required fees $549. Average book and supplies expense $600. **Required Forms and Deadlines:** Business/Farm Supplement; FAFSA; Institution's own financial aid form; Noncustodial PROFILE. **Notification of Awards:** Applicants will be notified of awards on or about 4/1. **Types of Aid:** *Need-based scholarships/grants:* College/university scholarship or grant aid from institutional funds; Federal Pell; Private scholarships; SEOG; State scholarships/grants. *Loans:* Direct PLUS loans; Direct Subsidized Stafford Loans; Direct Unsubsidized Stafford Loans. **Student Employment:** Federal Work-Study Program available. Institutional employment available. **Financial Aid Statistics:** 100% needy freshmen, 100% needy undergrads receive need-based scholarship or grant aid. 2% freshmen, 2% undergrads receive non-need-based scholarship or grant aid. 95% freshmen, 95% undergrads receive need-based self-help aid. 0% freshmen, 0% undergrads receive athletic scholarships. 100% freshmen, 97% undergrads receive any aid. 66% undergrads borrow to pay for school. Average cumulative indebtedness $24,496. **Criteria awarding aid:** *Need-based:* Academics, Art, Leadership, Music/drama *Non-Need-based:* Academics, Art, Leadership, Music/drama.

COLLEGE OF THE HOLY CROSS

1 College Street, Worcester, MA 01610-2395
Phone: 508-793-2443 **Financial Aid Phone:** (508) 793-2265
E-mail: admissions@holycross.edu **CEEB Code:** 3282
Fax: 508-793-3888 **Website:** www.holycross.edu **ACT Code:** 1810

This private school, affiliated with the Roman Catholic Church, was founded in 1843. It has a 174 acre campus.

RATINGS
Admissions Selectivity Rating: 93   Fire Safety Rating: 97   Green Rating: 88

STUDENTS AND FACULTY
Enrollment: 3,102. **Student Body:** 52% female, 48% male, 58% out-of-state, 3% international (24 countries represented). Asian 4%, African American 4%, Caucasian 72%, Hispanic 10%, Native American <1%, Pacific Islander <1%, Two or more races 3%, Race unknown 3%.
Retention and Graduation: 95% freshmen return for sophomore year. 91% freshmen graduate within 4 years. 92% freshmen graduate within 6 years. 13% grads go on to further study within 1 year. **Faculty:** Student/faculty ratio 10:1. 290 full-time faculty, 96% hold PhDs, 15% are members of minority groups, 48% are women. 0% of classes are taught by teaching assistants.

ACADEMICS
Degrees: Bachelor's. **Classes:** Most classes have 10–19 students. Most lab/discussion sessions have 10–19 students. **Most popular majors:** Psychology, General; Economics, General; Political Science and Government, General. **Special Study Options:** Accelerated program; Cross-registration; Double major; Dual enrollment; Exchange student program (domestic); Honors program; Independent study; Internships; Liberal arts/career combination;

Student-designed major; Study abroad; Teacher certification program. **Honors programs:** Fenwick Scholar Program, College Honors Program, departmental honors programs. **Disability Services offered:** Note-taking services; Reader services; Tape recorders; Tutors. **Career services:** Alumni network; Alumni services; Career assessment; Career/job search classes; Internships; Regional alumni.

FACILITIES
Housing: Apartments for single students; Coed dorms; Special housing for disabled students; Wellness housing 85% of campus accessible to physically disabled. **Special Academic Facilities/Equipment:** Art gallery, Concert Hall, Taylor and Boody tracker organ, O'Callahan Science Library, Rehm Library, Multimedia Resource Center, Wellness Center; scientific equipment on par with the best research universities

CAMPUS LIFE
Environment: City. **Activities:** Campus Ministries; Choral groups; Concert band; Dance; Drama/theater; International Student Organization; Jazz band; Literary magazine; Model UN; Music ensembles; Musical theater; Pep band; Radio station; Student government; Student newspaper; Yearbook. 103 registered organizations, 20 honor societies, 4 religious organizations, on campus. **Athletics (Intercollegiate):** *Men:* baseball, basketball, crew/rowing, cross-country, diving, football, golf, ice hockey, lacrosse, soccer, swimming, tennis, track/field (outdoor), track/field (indoor). *Women:* basketball, crew/rowing, cross-country, diving, field hockey, golf, ice hockey, lacrosse, soccer, softball, swimming, tennis, track/field (outdoor), track/field (indoor), volleyball. **On-Campus Highlights:** Library **Environmental Initiatives:** The college has focused investments on energy efficiency in comparison with renewable energy generation. The college has reduced the campus energy consumption by 2,300,000 KWh/year through these investments since 2013. As of 2018, this was an increase of 400,000 kwh.

ADMISSIONS
Freshman Academic Profile: 58% in top 10% of high school class, 88% in top 25% of high school class, 100% in top 50% of high school class. 50% from public high schools. **Test scores:** SAT Math middle 50% range 640–710. SAT EBRW middle 50% range 640–710. ACT middle 50% range 28–32. **Basis for Candidate Selection:** *Very important factors include:* rigor of secondary school record, academic GPA, application essay, recommendation(s), interview, character/personal qualities. *Important factors include:* extracurricular activities, talent/ability. *Other factors include:* class rank, standardized test scores, first generation, alumni/ae relation, geographical residence, state residency, religious affiliation/commitment, racial/ethnic status, volunteer work, work experience, level of applicant's interest. **Freshman Admission Requirements:** High school diploma is required and GED is accepted. *Academic units recommended:* 4 English, 4 math, 4 science, 2 science labs, 4 foreign language, 2 social studies, 2 history. **Freshman Admission Statistics:** 7,054 applied, 38% admitted, 32% enrolled. **Transfer Admission Requirements:** High school transcript, college transcript(s), essay or personal statement, statement of good standing from prior institution(s). Lowest grade transferable C. **General Admission Information:** Application fee $60. Regular application deadline 1/15. Admission may be deferred for a maximum of 12 months.

COSTS AND FINANCIAL AID
Annual tuition $54,050. Room and board $15,070. Required fees $690. Average book and supplies expense $1,000. **Required Forms and Deadlines:** Business/Farm Supplement; CSS/Financial Aid PROFILE; FAFSA; Noncustodial PROFILE;. **Types of Aid:** *Need-based scholarships/grants:* College/university scholarship or grant aid from institutional funds; Federal Pell; Private scholarships; SEOG; State scholarships/grants. *Loans:* Direct PLUS loans; Direct Subsidized Stafford Loans; Direct Unsubsidized Stafford Loans. **Student Employment:** Federal Work-Study Program available. Institutional employment available. **Financial Aid Statistics:** 86% needy freshmen, 85% needy undergrads receive need-based scholarship or grant aid. 19% freshmen, 7% undergrads receive non-need-based scholarship or grant aid. 81% freshmen, 86% undergrads receive need-based self-help aid. 6% freshmen, 7% undergrads receive athletic scholarships. 67% freshmen, 62% undergrads receive any aid. 60% undergrads borrow to pay for school. Average cumulative indebtedness $25,260. **Criteria awarding aid:** *Need-based:* Athletics *Non-Need-based:* Academics, Athletics, Music/drama, State/district residency.

COLLEGE OF THE OZARKS

Office of Admissions, Point Lookout, MO 65726
Phone: 417-690-2636 **Financial Aid Phone:** (417)690-3292
E-mail: admissions@cofo.edu **CEEB Code:** 6713
Fax: 417-690-2635 **Website:** www.cofo.edu **ACT Code:** 023640

This private school, affiliated with the Evangelical Christian Interdenominational, was founded in 1906. It has a 1000 acre campus.

RATINGS

Admissions Selectivity Rating: 97   **Fire Safety Rating:** 83   **Green Rating:** 68

STUDENTS AND FACULTY

Enrollment: 1,491. **Student Body:** 55% female, 45% male, 24% out-of-state, 1% international (17 countries represented). Asian 1%, African American 1%, Caucasian 90%, Hispanic 2%, Native American <1%, Pacific Islander <1%, Two or more races 2%, Race unknown 2%.
Retention and Graduation: 73% freshmen return for sophomore year. 55% freshmen graduate within 4 years. % freshmen graduate within 6 years. 14% grads go on to further study within 1 year. 3% grads pursue arts and sciences degrees. 0% grads pursue law degrees. 2% grads pursue business degrees. 1% grads pursue medical degrees. **Faculty:** Student/faculty ratio 14:1. 91 full-time faculty, 62% hold PhDs, 1% are members of minority groups, 44% are women. 0% of classes are taught by teaching assistants.

ACADEMICS

Degrees: Bachelor's. **Classes:** Most classes have 10–19 students. Most lab/discussion sessions have 10–19 students. **Most popular majors:** AGRICULTURAL/ANIMAL/PLANT/VETERINARY SCIENCE AND RELATED FIELDS; Elementary Education and Teaching; Business Administration and Management, General. **Special Study Options:** Double major; Dual enrollment; Independent study; Internships; Student-designed major; Teacher certification program. **Combined degree programs:** BA/JD. **Disability Services offered:** Note-taking services; Reader services; Tape recorders; Tutors. **Career services:** Career assessment; Career/job search classes; Internships.

FACILITIES

Housing: Men's dorms; Wellness housing; Women's dorms 85% of campus accessible to physically disabled. **Special Academic Facilities/Equipment:** The Missouri Vietnam Veterans Memorial, "Lest We Forget" 911 Memorial, The Missouri Gold Star Families Memorial, Ralph Foster Museum Edwards Mill (working grist mill), The Keeter Center (hotel and restaurant), Fruitcake and Jelly Kitchen, greenhouses, print shop, Gaetz Tractor Museum, Ozarkian room (periodicals and pictures of the Ozarks).

CAMPUS LIFE

Environment: Rural. **Activities:** Campus Ministries; Choral groups; Concert band; Drama/theater; International Student Organization; Jazz band; Music ensembles; Musical theater; Pep band; Radio station; Student government; Student newspaper; Student-run film society; Yearbook. 53 registered organizations, 9 honor societies, 6 religious organizations, on campus. **Athletics (Intercollegiate):** *Men:* baseball, basketball, cheerleading. *Women:* basketball, cheerleading, volleyball. **On-Campus Highlights:** Howell W. Keeter Athletic Complex **Environmental Initiatives:** 1. The College ensures proper management of hazardous, special and universal waste. There is campus-wide recycling: plastic bottles, corrugated cardboard, aluminum cans, tin cans, batteries, tires, light bulbs and electronic products. Light bulb reclamation (recycle of bulbs) and energy efficient lights.

ADMISSIONS

Freshman Academic Profile: Average high school GPA 3.7. 25% in top 10% of high school class, 62% in top 25% of high school class, 96% in top 50% of high school class. 78% from public high schools. **Test scores:** SAT Math middle 50% range 543–605. SAT EBRW middle 50% range 560–625. ACT middle 50% range 21–26. **Basis for Candidate Selection:** *Very important factors include:* rigor of secondary school record, class rank, interview, character/personal qualities. *Important factors include:* academic GPA, standardized test scores, recommendation(s), geographical residence. *Other factors include:* extracurricular activities, talent/ability, first generation, alumni/ae relation, state residency, religious affiliation/commitment. **Freshman Admission**

Requirements: High school diploma is required and GED is accepted. *Academic units required:* 4 English, 3 math, 2 science, 1 science labs, 3 history. *Academic units recommended:* 2 foreign language, 3 social studies. **Freshman Admission Statistics:** 2,879 applied, 16% admitted, 84% enrolled. **Transfer Admission Requirements:** college transcript(s), interview, statement of good standing from prior institution(s). Minimum college GPA of 3.0 required. Lowest grade transferable D-. **General Admission Information:** Priority deadline 12/31. Non-fall registration accepted.

COSTS AND FINANCIAL AID

Room and board $7,400. Required fees $460. Average book and supplies expense $1,100. **Required Forms and Deadlines:** FAFSA. **Notification of Awards:** Applicants will be notified of awards on or about 7/1. **Types of Aid:** *Need-based scholarships/grants:* College/university scholarship or grant aid from institutional funds; Federal Pell; Private scholarships; SEOG; State scholarships/grants. **Student Employment:** Federal Work-Study Program available. Institutional employment available. **Financial Aid Statistics:** 100% needy freshmen, 100% needy undergrads receive need-based scholarship or grant aid. 36% freshmen, 94% undergrads receive non-need-based scholarship or grant aid. 64% freshmen, 94% undergrads receive need-based self-help aid. 0% freshmen, 2% undergrads receive athletic scholarships. 100% freshmen, 100% undergrads receive any aid. 0% undergrads borrow to pay for school. **Criteria awarding aid:** *Need-based:* Academics, Alumni affiliation, Leadership, Minority status. *Non-Need-based:* Academics, Art, Athletics, Leadership, Music/drama, State/district residency.

THE COLLEGE OF WOOSTER

847 College Avenue, Wooster, OH 44691
Phone: 330-263-2322 **Financial Aid Phone:** 330-263-2317
E-mail: admissions@wooster.edu **CEEB Code:** 1134
Fax: 330-263-2621 **Website:** www.wooster.edu **ACT Code:** 3260

This private school, affiliated with the Presbyterian Church, was founded in 1866. It has a 240 acre campus.

RATINGS

Admissions Selectivity Rating: 88   **Fire Safety Rating:** 64   **Green Rating:** 78

STUDENTS AND FACULTY

Enrollment: 1,942. **Student Body:** 54% female, 46% male, 65% out-of-state, 16% international (58 countries represented). Asian 4%, African American 9%, Caucasian 61%, Hispanic 6%, Native American <1%, Pacific Islander 0%, Two or more races 4%, Race unknown 1%.
Retention and Graduation: 86% freshmen return for sophomore year. 75% freshmen graduate within 4 years. 77% freshmen graduate within 6 years. 27% grads go on to further study within 1 year. 10% grads pursue law degrees. 12% grads pursue medical degrees. **Faculty:** Student/faculty ratio 10:1. 173 full-time faculty, 98% hold PhDs, 21% are members of minority groups, 50% are women. 0% of classes are taught by teaching assistants.

ACADEMICS

Degrees: Bachelor's. **Classes:** Most classes have fewer than 10 students. Most lab/discussion sessions have 10–19 students. **Most popular majors:** Biological And Biomedical Sciences; Physical Sciences; Social Sciences. **Special Study Options:** Double major; Exchange student program (domestic); Independent study; Internships; Student-designed major; Study abroad; Teacher certification program. **Combined degree programs:** BA/DDS; BA/MA; BA/MEng. **Disability Services offered:** Note-taking services; Reader services; Tape recorders; Tutors. **Career services:** Alumni network; Alumni services; Career assessment; Career/job search classes; Internships; Regional alumni.

FACILITIES

Housing: Apartments for single students; Coed dorms; Fraternity/sorority housing; Theme housing 95% of campus accessible to physically disabled. **Special Academic Facilities/Equipment:** Art museum, language lab, on-campus nursery school, science library, Collaborative Research Center, Advising, Planning, & Experiential Learning Center (APEX). **Campus Network:** 100% of classrooms, 100% of dorms, 100% of student union, 100% of libraries, 100% of dining areas, have wireless network access.

CAMPUS LIFE

Environment: Town. **Activities:** Campus Ministries; Choral groups; Concert band; Dance; Drama/theater; International Student Organization; Jazz band; Literary magazine; Marching band; Model UN; Music ensembles; Musical theater; Radio station; Student government; Student newspaper; Student-run film society; Symphony orchestra; Yearbook. 125 registered organizations, 5 honor societies, 8 religious organizations, 4 fraternities, 7 sororities, on campus. **Athletics (Intercollegiate):** *Men:* baseball, basketball, cross-country, diving, football, golf, lacrosse, soccer, swimming, tennis, track/field (outdoor), track/field (indoor). *Women:* basketball, cross-country, diving, field hockey, lacrosse, soccer, softball, swimming, tennis, track/field (outdoor), track/field (indoor), volleyball. **On-Campus Highlights:** Kauke Hall **Environmental Initiatives:** Completed $5M Energy Performance Contract that reduced the College's carbon footprint by 36% through lighting and water conservation, building automation system upgrades, and the installation of two new electric chillers and a steam condensor at the Power Plant.

ADMISSIONS

Freshman Academic Profile: Average high school GPA 3.7. 46% in top 10% of high school class, 72% in top 25% of high school class, 92% in top 50% of high school class. 61% from public high schools. **Test scores:** SAT Math middle 50% range 570–700. SAT EBRW middle 50% range 580–680. ACT middle 50% range 24–31. **Basis for Candidate Selection:** *Very important factors include:* rigor of secondary school record, academic GPA. *Important factors include:* class rank, application essay, standardized test scores, recommendation(s), interview, extracurricular activities, character/personal qualities. *Other factors include:* talent/ability, first generation, alumni/ae relation, geographical residence, state residency, racial/ethnic status, volunteer work, work experience. **Freshman Admission Requirements:** High school diploma is required and GED is accepted. *Academic units required:* 4 English, 3 math, 3 science, 2 science labs, 2 foreign language, 3 social studies, 1 academic electives. **Freshman Admission Statistics:** 6,352 applied, 55% admitted, 16% enrolled. **Transfer Admission Requirements:** High school transcript, college transcript(s), essay or personal statement, standardized test scores, statement of good standing from prior institution(s). Minimum college GPA of 2.5 required. Lowest grade transferable C. **General Admission Information:** Priority deadline 2/15. Regular application deadline 2/15. Non-fall registration accepted. Admission may be deferred for a maximum of 1 year.

COSTS AND FINANCIAL AID

Annual tuition $49,810. Room and board $11,850. Required fees $440. Average book and supplies expense $1,000. **Required Forms and Deadlines:** CSS/Financial Aid PROFILE; FAFSA; Institution's own financial aid form. **Notification of Awards:** Applicants will be notified of awards on a rolling basis beginning 1/1. **Types of Aid:** *Need-based scholarships/grants:* College/university scholarship or grant aid from institutional funds; Federal Pell; Private scholarships; SEOG; State scholarships/grants. *Loans:* Direct PLUS loans; Direct Subsidized Stafford Loans; Direct Unsubsidized Stafford Loans. **Student Employment:** Federal Work-Study Program available. Institutional employment available. **Financial Aid Statistics:** 97% needy freshmen, 97% needy undergrads receive need-based scholarship or grant aid. 34% freshmen, 31% undergrads receive non-need-based scholarship or grant aid. 65% freshmen, 67% undergrads receive need-based self-help aid. 0% freshmen, 0% undergrads receive athletic scholarships. 96% freshmen, 96% undergrads receive any aid. 53% undergrads borrow to pay for school. Average cumulative indebtedness $32,194. **Criteria awarding aid:** *Need-based:* Academics, Minority status. *Non-Need-based:* Academics, Minority status, Music/drama, Religious affiliation.

COLORADO CHRISTIAN UNIVERSITY

8787 W. Alameda Ave., Lakewood, CO 80226
Phone: 303-963-3200 **Financial Aid Phone:** 303-963-3233
E-mail: ccuadmissions@ccu.edu **CEEB Code:** 4659
Fax: 303-963-3201 **Website:** www.ccu.edu **ACT Code:** 523

This private school, affiliated with the Christian (Nondenominational) Church, was founded in 1914. It has a 26 acre campus.

RATINGS

Admissions Selectivity Rating: 78   **Fire Safety Rating:** 61   **Green Rating:** 60*

STUDENTS AND FACULTY

Enrollment: 1,849. **Student Body:** 60% female, 40% male, 56% out-of-state, 1% international. Asian 1%, African American 4%, Caucasian 76%, Hispanic 9%, Native American 1%, Race unknown 8%.

Retention and Graduation: 86% freshmen return for sophomore year. **Faculty:** Student/faculty ratio 21:1. 41 full-time faculty, 68% hold PhDs, 5% are members of minority groups, 46% are women. 0% of classes are taught by teaching assistants.

ACADEMICS

Degrees: Associate; Bachelor's; Master's. **Classes:** Most classes have 10–19 students. Most lab/discussion sessions have 10–19 students. **Most popular majors:** Liberal Arts and Sciences/Liberal Studies; Management Information Systems, General; Computer/Information Technology Services Administration and Management, Other. **Special Study Options:** Accelerated program; Cooperative education program; Distance learning; Double major; Honors program; Independent study; Internships; Student-designed major; Study abroad; Teacher certification program; Weekend college. **Disability Services offered:** Tutors. **Career services:** Alumni services; Career assessment; Career/job search classes; Internships.

FACILITIES

Housing: Apartments for single students; Coed dorms; Men's dorms; Special housing for disabled students; Women's dorms 85% of campus accessible to physically disabled. **Special Academic Facilities/Equipment:** Music recording studio, electron microscope.

CAMPUS LIFE

Activities: Choral groups; Concert band; Drama/theater; Jazz band; Literary magazine; Music ensembles; Musical theater; Student government; Student newspaper; Symphony orchestra. 21 registered organizations, 3 honor societies, 14 religious organizations, on campus. **Athletics (Intercollegiate):** *Men:* basketball, cross-country, golf, soccer, tennis. *Women:* basketball, cross-country, soccer, tennis, volleyball.

ADMISSIONS

Freshman Academic Profile: Average high school GPA 3.4. 22% in top 10% of high school class, 46% in top 25% of high school class, 79% in top 50% of high school class. **Test scores:** SAT Math middle 50% range 480–90. SAT EBRW middle 50% range 510–630. ACT middle 50% range 20–26. **Basis for Candidate Selection:** *Very important factors include:* rigor of secondary school record, application essay, standardized test scores, talent/ability, character/personal qualities, first generation, religious affiliation/commitment. *Important factors include:* class rank, academic GPA, recommendation(s), extracurricular activities, racial/ethnic status, volunteer work. *Other factors include:* interview, alumni/ae relation, work experience. **Freshman Admission Requirements:** High school diploma is required and GED is accepted. *Academic units recommended:* 4 English, 3 math, 3 science, 2 science labs, 3 foreign language, 1 social studies, 2 history. **Freshman Admission Statistics:** 946 applied, 77% admitted, 33% enrolled. **Transfer Admission Requirements:** college transcript(s), essay or personal statement, statement of good standing from prior institution(s). Minimum college GPA of 2.0 required. Lowest grade transferable C. **General Admission Information:** Application fee $50. Priority deadline 3/1. Regular application deadline 8/21. Non-fall registration accepted. Admission may be deferred for a maximum of 1 year.

COSTS AND FINANCIAL AID

Annual tuition $18,850. Room and board $9,706. Required fees $150. Average book and supplies expense $1,188. **Required Forms and Deadlines:** FAFSA. **Notification of Awards:** Applicants will be notified of awards on a rolling basis beginning 4/1. **Types of Aid:** *Need-based scholarships/grants:* College/university scholarship or grant aid from institutional funds; Federal Pell; Private scholarships; SEOG. **Student Employment:** Federal Work-Study Program available. Institutional employment available. **Financial Aid Statistics:** 97% needy freshmen, 88% needy undergrads receive need-based scholarship or grant aid. 85% freshmen, 72% undergrads receive non-need-based scholarship or grant aid. 97% freshmen, 88% undergrads receive need-based self-help aid. 14% freshmen, 7% undergrads receive athletic scholarships. **Criteria awarding aid:** *Non-Need-based:* Academics, Athletics, Leadership, Minority status.

COLORADO COLLEGE

14 East Cache la Poudre Street, Colorado Springs, CO 80903
Phone: 719-389-6344 **Financial Aid Phone:** (719) 389-6779
E-mail: admission@coloradocollege.edu **CEEB Code:** 4072
Fax: 719-389-6816 **Website:** www.coloradocollege.edu **ACT Code:** 498

This private school was founded in 1874. It has a 90 acre campus.

RATINGS
Admissions Selectivity Rating: 97　　**Fire Safety Rating:** 96　　**Green Rating:** 93

STUDENTS AND FACULTY
Enrollment: 2,089. **Student Body:** 55% female, 45% male, 83% out-of-state, 8% international (53 countries represented). Asian 5%, African American 3%, Caucasian 65%, Hispanic 9%, Native American <1%, Pacific Islander <1%, Two or more races 8%, Race unknown 2%.
Retention and Graduation: 96% freshmen return for sophomore year. 80% freshmen graduate within 4 years. 83% freshmen graduate within 6 years.
Faculty: Student/faculty ratio 10:1. 209 full-time faculty, 98% hold PhDs, 26% are members of minority groups, 49% are women. 0% of classes are taught by teaching assistants.

ACADEMICS
Degrees: Bachelor's; Master's. **Classes:** Most classes have 10–19 students. **Most popular majors:** Economics, General; Political Science and Government, General; Sociology, General. **Special Study Options:** Double major; English as a Second Language (ESL); Exchange student program (domestic); Independent study; Internships; Liberal arts/career combination; Student-designed major; Study abroad; Teacher certification program. **Disability Services offered:** Note-taking services; Reader services; Tape recorders. **Career services:** Alumni network; Alumni services; Career assessment; Career/job search classes; Internships; Regional alumni.

FACILITIES
Housing: Apartments for single students; Coed dorms; Fraternity/sorority housing; Theme housing; Wellness housing; Women's dorms **Special Academic Facilities/Equipment:** Electronic music studio, telescope dome, multimedia computer laboratory, Balinese orchestras, The Colorado Electronic music studio, Observatory, Extensive herbarium collection 4 greenhouses Environmental Science van equipped for field research Fourier transform nuclear magnetic resonance spectrometer Packard Hall, 300 seat concert/lecture hall Photography darkrooms Drama/Dance: Armstrong Theatre, 740 seat proscenium theatre Armstrong 32, 100 seat experimental theatre 4 dance studios w/Marley, variable speed cd players Drama computer lab Geology: Petrographic microscopes X-ray diffractometer Sedimentology lab El Pomar Sports Center: Metabolic Equipment (COSMED Quark PFT Ergo) Hydrostatic Weighing Equipment Cadaver study in Sports Science Biology: Scanning electron microscope Transmission electron microscope Students amy also engage with local theater, opera, and orchestra.

CAMPUS LIFE
Environment: Metropolis. **Activities:** Campus Ministries; Choral groups; Concert band; Dance; Drama/theater; International Student Organization; Jazz band; Literary magazine; Model UN; Music ensembles; Musical theater; Opera; Radio station; Student government; Student newspaper; Student-run film society; Yearbook. 135 registered organizations, 12 honor societies, 15 religious organizations, 3 fraternities, 3 sororities, on campus. **Athletics (Intercollegiate):** *Men:* basketball, cross-country, ice hockey, lacrosse, soccer, swimming, tennis, track/field (outdoor). *Women:* basketball, cross-country, lacrosse, soccer, swimming, tennis, track/field (outdoor), track/field (indoor), volleyball. **On-Campus Highlights:** Worner Student Center. **Environmental Initiatives:** The College is committed to achieving carbon neutrality by 2020. The plan includes an efficiency target in all campus buildings that will reduce energy intensity by 30%, along with a 20% reduction target through behavior change and conservation, and a strategy to derive 100% of electricity from renewable sources.

ADMISSIONS
Freshman Academic Profile: 82% in top 10% of high school class, 98% in top 25% of high school class, 100% in top 50% of high school class. **Test scores:** SAT Math middle 50% range 650–750. SAT EBRW middle 50% range 650–730. ACT middle 50% range 29–33. **Basis for Candidate Selection:** *Very important factors include:* rigor of secondary school record. *Important factors include:* academic GPA, application essay, recommendation(s), interview, extracurricular activities. *Other factors include:* class rank, standardized test scores, talent/ability, character/personal qualities, first generation, alumni/ae relation, geographical residence, state residency, religious affiliation/commitment, racial/ethnic status, volunteer work, work experience, level of applicant's interest. **Freshman Admission Requirements:** High school diploma or equivalent is not required *Academic units required:* 4 English. *Academic units recommended:* 4 English. **Freshman Admission Statistics:** 9,456 applied, 14% admitted, 42% enrolled. **Transfer Admission Requirements:** High school transcript, college transcript(s), essay or personal statement, standardized test scores, statement of good standing from prior institution(s). Lowest grade transferable C. **General Admission Information:** Priority deadline 1/15. Regular application deadline 1/15. Non-fall registration accepted. Admission may be deferred for a maximum of 2 years.

COSTS AND FINANCIAL AID
Required Forms and Deadlines: CSS/Financial Aid PROFILE; FAFSA; Noncustodial PROFILE; State aid form. **Notification of Awards:** Applicants will be notified of awards on or about 2/15. **Types of Aid:** *Need-based scholarships/grants:* College/university scholarship or grant aid from institutional funds; Federal Pell; Private scholarships; SEOG; State scholarships/grants. *Loans:* Direct PLUS loans; Direct Subsidized Stafford Loans; Direct Unsubsidized Stafford Loans. **Student Employment:** Federal Work-Study Program available. Institutional employment available. **Financial Aid Statistics:** 100% needy freshmen, 90% needy undergrads receive need-based scholarship or grant aid. 5% freshmen, 9% undergrads receive non-need-based scholarship or grant aid. 92% freshmen, 73% undergrads receive need-based self-help aid. 1% freshmen, 2% undergrads receive athletic scholarships. 52% freshmen, 47% undergrads receive any aid. 33% undergrads borrow to pay for school. Average cumulative indebtedness $23,579. **Criteria awarding aid:** *Non-Need-based:* Academics, Athletics, Leadership.

COLORADO MESA UNIVERSITY

1100 North Avenue, Grand Junction, CO 81501
Phone: 970-248-1875 **Financial Aid Phone:** 970.248.1177
E-mail: admissions@coloradomesa.edu **CEEB Code:** 4484
Fax: 970-248-1973 **Website:** www.coloradomesa.edu **ACT Code:** 0518

This is a public school.

RATINGS
Admissions Selectivity Rating: 77　　**Fire Safety Rating:** 81　　**Green Rating:** 60*

STUDENTS AND FACULTY
Enrollment: 8,260. **Student Body:** 54% female, 46% male, 14% out-of-state, 1% international (25 countries represented). Asian 1%, African American 2%, Caucasian 67%, Hispanic 21%, Native American 1%, Pacific Islander 1%, Two or more races 4%, Race unknown 2%.
Retention and Graduation: 75% freshmen return for sophomore year. 22% freshmen graduate within 4 years. 43% freshmen graduate within 6 years.
Faculty: Student/faculty ratio 20:1. 304 full-time faculty, 0% hold PhDs, 47% are women.

ACADEMICS
Degrees: Associate; Bachelor's; Certificate; Doctoral degree—professional practice; Master's; Post-bachelor's certificate; Terminal Associate; Transfer Associate. **Classes:** Most classes have 20–29 students. Most lab/discussion sessions have 20–29 students. **Most popular majors:** Criminal Justice/Safety Studies; Biology/Biological Sciences, General; Liberal Arts and Sciences/Liberal Studies. **Special Study Options:** Accelerated program; Distance learning; Double major; Dual enrollment; Honors program; Internships; Study abroad; Teacher certification program. **Disability Services offered:** Note-taking services; Tape recorders; Tutors.

FACILITIES
Housing: Apartments for single students; Coed dorms; Special housing for disabled students.

CAMPUS LIFE
Environment: Town. **Activities:** Campus Ministries; Choral groups; Concert band; Dance; Drama/theater; International Student Organization; Literary

magazine; Marching band; Music ensembles; Musical theater; Radio station; Student government; Student newspaper; Symphony orchestra; Television station. 78 registered organizations, 5 honor societies, 7 religious organizations, 1 fraternities, 1 sororities, on campus. **On-Campus Highlights:** University Center.

ADMISSIONS

Freshman Academic Profile: Average high school GPA 3.2. 12% in top 10% of high school class, 29% in top 25% of high school class, 59% in top 50% of high school class. **Test score**s: SAT Math middle 50% range 460–580. SAT EBRW middle 50% range 470–590. ACT middle 50% range 18–25. **Basis for Candidate Selection:** *Very important factors include:* academic GPA, standardized test scores. *Important factors include:* rigor of secondary school record, class rank. *Other factors include:* application essay, recommendation(s), interview, extracurricular activities, talent/ability, character/personal qualities, first generation, alumni/ae relation, geographical residence, state residency, volunteer work, work experience, level of applicant's interest. **Freshman Admission Requirements:** High school diploma is required and GED is accepted. *Academic units required:* 4 English, 4 math, 3 science, 2 science labs, 1 foreign language, 2 social studies, 1 history, 2 academic electives. **Freshman Admission Statistics:** 8,845 applied, 78% admitted, 30% enrolled. **General Admission Information:** Application fee $30. Non-fall registration accepted. Admission may be deferred for a maximum of 1 year.

COSTS AND FINANCIAL AID

Average book and supplies expense $1,560. **Required Forms and Deadlines:** FAFSA. **Types of Aid:** *Need-based scholarships/grants:* College/university scholarship or grant aid from institutional funds; Federal Pell; Private scholarships; SEOG; State scholarships/grants. *Loans:* Direct PLUS loans; Direct Subsidized Stafford Loans; Direct Unsubsidized Stafford Loans. **Student Employment:** Federal Work-Study Program available. Institutional employment available. **Financial Aid Statistics:** 89% needy freshmen, 86% needy undergrads receive need-based scholarship or grant aid. 15% freshmen, 10% undergrads receive non-need-based scholarship or grant aid. 82% freshmen, 85% undergrads receive need-based self-help aid. 3% freshmen, 2% undergrads receive athletic scholarships. 64% undergrads borrow to pay for school. Average cumulative indebtedness $27,269.

COLORADO SCHOOL OF MINES

1812 Illinois Street, Golden, CO 80401
Phone: 303-273-3220 **Financial Aid Phone:** (303) 273-3220
E-mail: admissions@mines.edu **CEEB Code:** 4073
Fax: 303-273-3509 **Website:** www.mines.edu **ACT Code:** 500

This public school was founded in 1874. It has a 499 acre campus.

RATINGS

Admissions Selectivity Rating: 92   **Fire Safety Rating:** 93   **Green Rating:** 66

STUDENTS AND FACULTY

Enrollment: 4,908. **Student Body:** 30% female, 70% male, 41% out-of-state, 5% international (43 countries represented). Asian 4%, African American 1%, Caucasian 72%, Hispanic 9%, Native American <1%, Pacific Islander <1%, Two or more races 6%, Race unknown 1%.
Retention and Graduation: 92% freshmen return for sophomore year. 55% freshmen graduate within 4 years. 79% freshmen graduate within 6 years. 20% grads go on to further study within 1 year. 4% grads pursue arts and sciences degrees. 1% grads pursue law degrees. 2% grads pursue business degrees. 1% grads pursue medical degrees. **Faculty:** Student/faculty ratio 15:1. 304 full-time faculty, 92% hold PhDs, 19% are members of minority groups, 29% are women. 2% of classes are taught by teaching assistants.

ACADEMICS

Degrees: Bachelor's; Doctoral degree research/scholarship; Master's; Post-master's certificate. **Classes:** Most classes have 20–29 students. Most lab/discussion sessions have 20–29 students. **Most popular majors:** Petroleum Engineering; Chemical Engineering; Mechanical Engineering. **Special Study Options:** Accelerated program; Cooperative education program; Double major; Dual enrollment; Exchange student program (domestic); Honors program; Independent study; Internships; Study abroad; Teacher certification program. **Honors programs:** The THORSON FIRST YEAR HONORS EXPERIENCE: offers a gateway into the McBride Honors Program. It prepares

students for success in McBride, in their major coursework, and beyond. But First Year Honors is a lot more. It offers an exciting and collaborative approach to learning that uses real-world problems to introduce students to the role of engineers and scientists in a fast-changing world. Working closely with some of the best teachers at Mines, students come to see how the global challenges of the future require innovative and creative thinking. Even better, the First Year Honors Experience includes a supportive and diverse community of students who want to be challenged and want to explore our world. In First Year Honors, professors welcome students as colleagues, they mentor and support them, and they push them to see the world differently. McBRIDE HONORS PROGRAM: instituted in 1978 through a grant from the National Endowment for the Humanities, is a 21 semester-hour program of seminars and off-campus activities that has as its primary goal: To provide a select community of Mines students the enhanced opportunity to explore the interfaces between their areas of technical expertise and the humanities and social sciences; to gain the sensitivity to project and test the moral and social implications of their future professional judgments and activities; and to foster their leadership abilities in preparation for managing change and promoting the general welfare in an evolving technological and global context. To achieve this goal, the program seeks to bring themes from the humanities and the social sciences into the engineering curriculum that will encourage in students the habits of thought necessary for effective management and enlightened leadership. **Disability Services offered:** Tutors. **Career services:** Alumni services; Career assessment; Career/job search classes; Internships.

FACILITIES

Housing: Apartments for married students; Apartments for single students; Coed dorms; Fraternity/sorority housing; Theme housing 95% of campus accessible to physically disabled. **Special Academic Facilities/Equipment:** Center for Entrepreneurship and Innovation; Edgar Experimental Mine; General Research Lab (GRL); Geology Museum; International Center for Multiscale Characterization (ICMC); Nuclear Science and Engineering Center (NUSEC); The Alliance for the Development of Additive Processing Technologies (ADAPT); Ultrafast Science Research Lab; US Geological Survey & Earthquake Center.

CAMPUS LIFE

Environment: Metropolis. **Activities:** Campus Ministries; Choral groups; Concert band; Dance; Drama/theater; International Student Organization; Jazz band; Literary magazine; Marching band; Music ensembles; Musical theater; Pep band; Radio station; Student government; Student newspaper; Symphony orchestra; Yearbook. 255 registered organizations, 9 honor societies, 11 religious organizations, 7 fraternities, 4 sororities, on campus. **Athletics (Intercollegiate):** *Men:* baseball, basketball, cross-country, diving, football, golf, soccer, swimming, track/field (outdoor), track/field (indoor), wrestling. *Women:* basketball, cross-country, diving, soccer, softball, swimming, track/field (outdoor), track/field (indoor), volleyball. **On-Campus Highlights:** Student Recreation Center.

ADMISSIONS

Freshman Academic Profile: Average high school GPA 3.8. 59% in top 10% of high school class, 85% in top 25% of high school class, 100% in top 50% of high school class. 77% from public high schools. **Test scores:** SAT Math middle 50% range 660–740. SAT EBRW middle 50% range 630–710. ACT middle 50% range 28–33. **Basis for Candidate Selection:** *Very important factors include:* rigor of secondary school record, class rank, academic GPA, standardized test scores. *Other factors include:* application essay, recommendation(s), interview, extracurricular activities, talent/ability, character/personal qualities, first generation, alumni/ae relation, geographical residence, state residency, volunteer work, work experience, level of applicant's interest. **Freshman Admission Requirements:** High school diploma is required and GED is accepted. *Academic units required:* 4 English, 4 math, 3 science, 3 science labs, 1 foreign language, 3 social studies, 2 history. **Freshman Admission Statistics:** 12,661 applied, 49% admitted, 19% enrolled. **Transfer Admission Requirements:** High school transcript, college transcript(s), statement of good standing from prior institution(s). Minimum college GPA of 2.75 required. Lowest grade transferable C. **General Admission Information:** Application fee $45. Priority deadline 11/1. Regular application deadline 5/1. Admission may be deferred for a maximum of 12 months.

COSTS AND FINANCIAL AID

Annual in-state tuition $16,650. Annual out-of-state tuition $36,270. Room and board $13,169. Required fees $2,314. Average book and supplies expense $1,500. **Required Forms and Deadlines:** FAFSA. **Notification of Awards:** Applicants will be notified of awards on a rolling basis beginning 1/1. **Types of Aid:** *Need-based scholarships/grants:* College/university scholarship or grant aid from institutional funds; Federal Pell; Private scholarships; SEOG; State scholarships/grants. *Loans:* Direct PLUS loans; Direct Subsidized Stafford Loans; Direct Unsubsidized Stafford Loans. **Student Employment:** Federal Work-Study Program available. Institutional employment available. **Financial Aid Statistics:** 60% needy freshmen, 56% needy undergrads receive need-based scholarship or grant aid. 83% freshmen, 73% undergrads receive non-need-based scholarship or grant aid. 87% freshmen, 90% undergrads receive need-based self-help aid. 8% freshmen, 8% undergrads receive athletic scholarships. 85% freshmen, 74% undergrads receive any aid. 53% undergrads borrow to pay for school. Average cumulative indebtedness $32,482. **Criteria awarding aid:** *Need-based:* Academics, Alumni affiliation. *Non-Need-based:* Academics, Alumni affiliation, Athletics, Music/drama.

COLORADO STATE UNIVERSITY

1062 Campus Delivery, Fort Collins, CO 80523-1062
Phone: 970-491-6909 **Financial Aid Phone:** 970-491-6321
E-mail: admissions@colostate.edu **CEEB Code:** 4075
Fax: 970-491-7799 **Website:** www.colostate.edu/ **ACT Code:** 504

This public school was founded in 1870. It has a 4773 acre campus.

RATINGS

Admissions Selectivity Rating: 77   **Fire Safety Rating:** 65   **Green Rating:** 99

STUDENTS AND FACULTY

Enrollment: 25,542. **Student Body:** 52% female, 48% male, 28% out-of-state, 4% international (76 countries represented). Asian 3%, African American 2%, Caucasian 70%, Hispanic 15%, Native American <1%, Pacific Islander <1%, Two or more races 5%, Race unknown 1%.
Retention and Graduation: 86% freshmen return for sophomore year. 46% freshmen graduate within 4 years. 70% freshmen graduate within 6 years. 17% grads go on to further study within 1 year. **Faculty:** Student/faculty ratio 16:1. 1,380 full-time faculty, 90% hold PhDs, 15% are members of minority groups, 44% are women. 9% of classes are taught by teaching assistants.

ACADEMICS

Degrees: Bachelor's; Doctoral degree—professional practice; Doctoral degree research/scholarship; Master's; Post-bachelor's certificate. **Classes:** Most classes have 20–29 students. Most lab/discussion sessions have 20–29 students. **Most popular majors:** Mechanical Engineering; Biology/Biological Sciences, General; Psychology, General. **Special Study Options:** Cooperative education program; Distance learning; Double major; Honors program; Independent study; Internships; Study abroad; Teacher certification program. **Honors programs:** University Honors Program. **Disability Services offered:** Note-taking services; Reader services; Tape recorders; Tutors. **Career services:** Alumni network; Alumni services; Career assessment; Career/job search classes; Internships; Regional alumni.

FACILITIES

Housing: Apartments for married students; Apartments for single students; Coed dorms; Fraternity/sorority housing; Special housing for international students; Theme housing; Wellness housing 98% of campus accessible to physically disabled. **Special Academic Facilities/Equipment:** International Poster collection Gustafson Gallery--historic clothing Curfman Gallery-- Art Student Recreation Center Ropes Course University Center for the Arts (performance hall, thrust theater,art museum) Avenir Museum of Design and Merchandising (Costumes, Textiles, Interior Artifacts) Engines and Energy Conversion Laboratory.

CAMPUS LIFE

Environment: City. **Activities:** Campus Ministries; Choral groups; Concert band; Dance; Drama/theater; International Student Organization; Jazz band; Literary magazine; Marching band; Music ensembles; Musical theater; Pep band; Radio station; Student government; Student newspaper; Symphony orchestra; Television station. 381 registered organizations, 42 honor societies, 30 religious organizations, 31 fraternities, 24 sororities, on campus. **Athletics (Intercollegiate):** *Men:* basketball, cross-country, football, golf, track/field (outdoor), track/field (indoor). *Women:* basketball, cross-country, diving, golf, softball, swimming, tennis, track/field (outdoor), track/field (indoor), volleyball, water polo. **On-Campus Highlights:** Lory Student Center. **Environmental**

Initiatives: Several renewable energy sources went live in the year 2010 including: a second phase of a large solar array that now totals 5,300 kilowatts on the Foothills Campus, an 18.9 kW solar array on the roof of the Engineering building, and a 12.6 kW solar array at the Academic Village residence hall, 133 kW solar array on the roof of the Lake Street Parking Garage, a 15.8 kW on the Behavioral Sciences Building and a 54 kW solar array at the Research Innovation Center. The five smaller arrays are owned and operated by the University, the larger array is owned by a third party and Colorado State serves as a site host and purchases the power produced by the panels. In addition to solar power, CSU's Foothills Campus is also home to a biomass heating plant on the Foothills Campus. This plant burns wood chips to produce hot water for building heat and displaces natural gas use.

ADMISSIONS

Freshman Academic Profile: Average high school GPA 3.7. 21% in top 10% of high school class, 48% in top 25% of high school class, 83% in top 50% of high school class. **Test scores:** SAT Math middle 50% range 530–640. SAT EBRW middle 50% range 540–650. ACT middle 50% range 23–29. **Basis for Candidate Selection:** *Very important factors include:* rigor of secondary school record, academic GPA. *Important factors include:* class rank, application essay, standardized test scores, recommendation(s). *Other factors include:* extracurricular activities, talent/ability, character/personal qualities, first generation, alumni/ae relation, geographical residence, volunteer work, work experience. **Freshman Admission Requirements:** High school diploma is required and GED is accepted. *Academic units required:* 4 English, 4 math, 3 science, 2 science labs, 1 foreign language, 3 social studies, 1 history, 2 academic electives. *Academic units recommended:* 4 English, 4 math, 3 science, 2 science labs, 2 foreign language, 3 social studies, 1 history, 2 academic electives. **Freshman Admission Statistics:** 28,319 applied, 81% admitted, 23% enrolled. **Transfer Admission Requirements:** college transcript(s), essay or personal statement, Minimum college GPA of 2.0 required. Lowest grade transferable C-. **General Admission Information:** Application fee $50. Priority deadline 2/1. Regular application deadline 7/1. Non-fall registration accepted. Admission may be deferred for a maximum of 12 months.

COSTS AND FINANCIAL AID

Annual in-state tuition $9,426. Annual out-of-state tuition $28,147. Room and board $12,430. Required fees $2,475. Average book and supplies expense $1,200. **Required Forms and Deadlines:** FAFSA; Institution's own financial aid form. **Notification of Awards:** Applicants will be notified of awards on a rolling basis beginning 3/1. **Types of Aid:** *Need-based scholarships/grants:* College/university scholarship or grant aid from institutional funds; Federal Pell; Private scholarships; SEOG; State scholarships/grants. *Loans:* Direct PLUS loans; Direct Subsidized Stafford Loans; Direct Unsubsidized Stafford Loans. **Student Employment:** Federal Work-Study Program available. Institutional employment available. **Financial Aid Statistics:** 73% needy freshmen, 68% needy undergrads receive need-based scholarship or grant aid. 43% freshmen, 29% undergrads receive non-need-based scholarship or grant aid. 62% freshmen, 68% undergrads receive need-based self-help aid. 0% freshmen, 1% undergrads receive athletic scholarships. 77.8% freshmen, 72.26% undergrads receive any aid. 53% undergrads borrow to pay for school. Average cumulative indebtedness $27,142. **Criteria awarding aid:** *Need-based:* Academics *Non-Need-based:* Academics, Alumni affiliation, Art, Athletics, Leadership, Music/drama, State/district residency.

COLORADO STATE UNIVERSITY—PUEBLO

Admissions, Pueblo, CO 81001
Phone: 719-549-2461 **Financial Aid Phone:** 719-549-2178
E-mail: info@colostate-pueblo.edu **CEEB Code:** 4611
Fax: 719-549-2419 **Website:** www.colostate-pueblo.edu **ACT Code:** 524

This public school was founded in 1933. It has a 275 acre campus.

RATINGS

Admissions Selectivity Rating: 73   **Fire Safety Rating:** 79   **Green Rating:** 60*

STUDENTS AND FACULTY

Enrollment: 3,947. **Student Body:** 57% female, 43% male, 7% out-of-state, 2% international (27 countries represented). Asian 3%, African American 6%, Caucasian 55%, Hispanic 25%, Native American 2%, Race unknown 6%.
Retention and Graduation: 63% freshmen return for sophomore year.
Faculty: Student/faculty ratio 17:1. 155 full-time faculty, 0% hold PhDs, 17%

are members of minority groups, 47% are women. 0% of classes are taught by teaching assistants.

ACADEMICS

Degrees: Bachelor's; Master's. **Classes:** Most classes have 10–19 students. Most lab/discussion sessions have 10–19 students. **Most popular majors:** Biology/Biological Sciences, General; Liberal Arts and Sciences/Liberal Studies. **Special Study Options:** Accelerated program; Cooperative education program; Distance learning; Double major; Dual enrollment; English as a Second Language (ESL); External degree program; Independent study; Internships; Liberal arts/career combination; Study abroad; Teacher certification program; Weekend college. **Honors programs:** We do not have an Honor Program, however, we offer several undergraduate honor courses. **Disability Services offered:** Note-taking services; Reader services; Tape recorders; Tutors.

FACILITIES

Housing: Apartments for single students; Coed dorms; Special housing for disabled students; 100% of campus accessible to physically disabled. **Special Academic Facilities/Equipment:** Recital hall, public television and radio station. **Campus Network:** 100% of classrooms, 100% of dorms, 100% of student union, 100% of libraries, 100% of dining areas, 75% of common outdoor areas, have wireless network access.

CAMPUS LIFE

Environment: City. **Activities:** Choral groups; Concert band; Dance; Jazz band; Literary magazine; Music ensembles; Pep band; Student government; Student newspaper; Symphony orchestra; Television station. 24 registered organizations, 6 honor societies, 4 religious organizations, 2 fraternities, 1 sororities, on campus. **Athletics (Intercollegiate):** *Men:* baseball, basketball, golf, soccer, tennis. *Women:* basketball, cross-country, golf, soccer, softball, tennis, volleyball. **On-Campus Highlights:** University Library.

ADMISSIONS

Freshman Academic Profile: Average high school GPA 3.1. 2% in top 10% of high school class, 8% in top 25% of high school class, 36% in top 50% of high school class. 85% from public high schools. **Test scores:** SAT Math middle 50% range 420–550. SAT EBRW middle 50% range 420–530. ACT middle 50% range 18–22. **Basis for Candidate Selection:** *Very important factors include:* rigor of secondary school record, academic GPA, standardized test scores. *Important factors include:* class rank. *Other factors include:* application essay, recommendation(s), interview, talent/ability, character/personal qualities, volunteer work, work experience, level of applicant's interest. **Freshman Admission Requirements:** High school diploma is required and GED is accepted. *Academic units required:* 4 English, 3 math, 3 science, 2 science labs, 2 foreign language, 2 social studies, 1 history. *Academic units recommended:* 4 English, 3 math, 3 science, 2 science labs, 2 foreign language, 2 social studies, 1 history. **Freshman Admission Statistics:** 1,698 applied, 96% admitted, 39% enrolled. **Transfer Admission Requirements:** college transcript(s), Minimum college GPA of 2.3 required. Lowest grade transferable C-. **General Admission Information:** Application fee $25. Regular application deadline 8/1. Non-fall registration accepted. Admission may be deferred for a maximum of 1 semester.

COSTS AND FINANCIAL AID

Annual in-state tuition $3,422. Annual out-of-state tuition $13,543. Room and board $6,300. Required fees $996. Average book and supplies expense $1,698. **Required Forms and Deadlines:** FAFSA; Institution's own financial aid form. **Notification of Awards:** Applicants will be notified of awards on a rolling basis beginning 3/15. **Types of Aid:** *Need-based scholarships/grants:* College/university scholarship or grant aid from institutional funds; Federal Pell; Private scholarships; SEOG; State scholarships/grants. **Financial Aid Statistics:** 81% needy freshmen, 80% needy undergrads receive need-based scholarship or grant aid. 7% freshmen, 4% undergrads receive non-need-based scholarship or grant aid. 78% freshmen, 86% undergrads receive need-based self-help aid. 3% freshmen, 4% undergrads receive athletic scholarships. 81% freshmen, 86% undergrads receive any aid. **Criteria awarding aid:** *Need-based:* Academics, Alumni affiliation, Minority status. *Non-Need-based:* Academics, Alumni affiliation, Art, Athletics, Leadership, Minority status, Music/drama, State/district residency.

COLORADO TECHNICAL UNIVERSITY

4435 North Chestnut Street, Colorado Springs, CO 80907-3740
Phone: 719-598-0200
E-mail: cosadmissions@coloradotech.edu
Website: http://www.coloradotech.edu/

This is a proprietary school.

RATINGS
Admissions Selectivity Rating: 60*   **Fire Safety Rating:** 60*   **Green Rating:** 60*

STUDENTS AND FACULTY

Student Body: 1% international. Asian 4%, African American 8%, Caucasian 73%, Hispanic 6%, Native American <1%, Race unknown 9%.
Faculty: Student/faculty ratio 25:1. 31 full-time faculty, 52% hold PhDs, 13% are members of minority groups, 35% are women.

ACADEMICS

Degrees: Associate; Bachelor's; Certificate; Master's; Transfer Associate. **Classes:** Most classes have 10–19 students. **Special Study Options:** Accelerated program; Double major; Independent study; Internships; Weekend college.

CAMPUS LIFE

Activities: Student government.

ADMISSIONS

Basis for Candidate Selection: *Other factors include:* rigor of secondary school record, class rank, standardized test scores, recommendation(s), interview, character/personal qualities, alumni/ae relation, work experience. **Freshman Admission Requirements:** *Academic units required:* 1 English, 1 math, 1 science, 1 science labs. *Academic units recommended:* 2 English, 2 math, 2 science, 1 science labs. **Transfer Admission Requirements:** college transcript(s), statement of good standing from prior institution(s). Lowest grade transferable C. **General Admission Information:** Application fee $50. Regular application deadline 10/2. Non-fall registration accepted.

COSTS AND FINANCIAL AID

Average book and supplies expense $1,000. **Required Forms and Deadlines:** FAFSA; Institution's own financial aid form; State aid form. **Notification of Awards:** Applicants will be notified of awards on a rolling basis beginning 2/1.

COLUMBIA COLLEGE CHICAGO (IL)

600 South Michigan Avenue, Chicago, IL 60605-1996
Phone: 1-312-369-7130 **Financial Aid Phone:** 312-369-7831
E-mail: admissions@colum.edu **CEEB Code:** 1135
Fax: 312-369-8024 **Website:** www.colum.edu **ACT Code:** 1002

This private school was founded in 1890.

RATINGS
Admissions Selectivity Rating: 76   **Fire Safety Rating:** 81   **Green Rating:** 60*

STUDENTS AND FACULTY

Enrollment: 8,929. **Student Body:** 56% female, 44% male, 40% out-of-state, 3% international (48 countries represented). Asian 3%, African American 16%, Caucasian 57%, Hispanic 10%, Native American <1%, Pacific Islander <1%, Two or more races 5%, Race unknown 6%.
Retention and Graduation: 71% freshmen return for sophomore year. 9% grads go on to further study within 1 year. 10% grads pursue arts and sciences degrees. **Faculty:** Student/faculty ratio 11:1. 374 full-time faculty, 51% hold PhDs, 17% are members of minority groups, 47% are women. 0% of classes are taught by teaching assistants.

ACADEMICS

Degrees: Bachelor's; Master's. **Classes:** Most classes have 10–19 students. **Most popular majors:** Photography; Cinematography and Film/Video Production; Drama and Dramatics/Theatre Arts, General. **Special Study Options:** Cooperative education program; Distance learning; Double major; English as a Second Language (ESL); Exchange student program (domestic); Honors program; Independent study; Internships; Liberal arts/career combination; Student-designed major; Study abroad; Teacher certification program. **Disability Services offered:** Note-taking services; Reader services; Tape recorders; Tutors. **Career services:** Alumni network; Alumni services; Internships.

FACILITIES

Housing: Apartments for single students; Coed dorms 90% of campus accessible to physically disabled. **Special Academic Facilities/Equipment:** Art galleries, center for black music research, contemporary photography museum, dance center. **Campus Network:** 100% of classrooms, 100% of dorms, 100% of student union, 100% of libraries, 100% of dining areas, 10% of common outdoor areas, have wireless network access.

CAMPUS LIFE

Environment: Metropolis. **Activities:** Campus Ministries; Choral groups; Concert band; Dance; Drama/theater; International Student Organization; Jazz band; Literary magazine; Music ensembles; Musical theater; Radio station; Student government; Student newspaper; Student-run film society; Television station. 64 registered organizations, on campus. **On-Campus Highlights:** Museum of Contemporary Photography **Environmental Initiatives:** Campus-wide recycling of paper, plastic, glass, technology.

ADMISSIONS

Freshman Academic Profile: Average high school GPA 3.3. 8% in top 10% of high school class, 29% in top 25% of high school class, 63% in top 50% of high school class. **Test scores:** SAT Math middle 50% range 440–570. SAT EBRW middle 50% range 485–605. ACT middle 50% range 19–25. **Basis for Candidate Selection:** *Very important factors include:* application essay. *Important factors include:* academic GPA, recommendation(s), character/personal qualities, level of applicant's interest. *Other factors include:* rigor of secondary school record, class rank, standardized test scores, extracurricular activities, talent/ability, volunteer work, work experience. **Freshman Admission Requirements:** High school diploma is required and GED is accepted. **Freshman Admission Statistics:** 8,953 applied, 82% admitted, 25% enrolled. **Transfer Admission Requirements:** High school transcript, college transcript(s), essay or personal statement, Lowest grade transferable C. **General Admission Information:** Application fee $35. Priority deadline 5/1. Non-fall registration accepted. Admission may be deferred for a maximum of 1 year.

COSTS AND FINANCIAL AID

Annual tuition $22,884. Room and board $12,450. Required fees $660. Average book and supplies expense $1,708. **Required Forms and Deadlines:** FAFSA; Institution's own financial aid form. **Types of Aid:** *Need-based scholarships/grants:* College/university scholarship or grant aid from institutional funds; Federal Pell; Private scholarships; SEOG; State scholarships/grants. *Loans:* Direct PLUS loans; Direct Subsidized Stafford Loans; Direct Unsubsidized Stafford Loans. **Student Employment:** Federal Work-Study Program available. **Financial Aid Statistics:** 90% needy freshmen, 82% needy undergrads receive need-based scholarship or grant aid. 0% freshmen, 0% undergrads receive non-need-based scholarship or grant aid. 0% freshmen, 1% undergrads receive need-based self-help aid. 0% freshmen, 0% undergrads receive athletic scholarships. 72.8% freshmen, 71.3% undergrads receive any aid. **Criteria awarding aid:** *Need-based:* Academics, Art, Leadership, Music/drama *Non-Need-based:* Academics, Art, Leadership, Music/drama, State/district residency.

COLUMBIA COLLEGE (MO)

1001 Rogers St., Columbia, MO 65211
Phone: 573-875-7352 **Financial Aid Phone:** 573-875-7390
E-mail: admissions@ccis.edu **CEEB Code:** 6095
Fax: 573-875-7506 **Website:** http://www.ccis.edu **ACT Code:** 2276

This private school, affiliated with the Disciples of Christ Church, was founded in 1851. It has a 33 acre campus.

RATINGS

Admissions Selectivity Rating: 87   **Fire Safety Rating:** 90   **Green Rating:** 66

STUDENTS AND FACULTY

Enrollment: 941. **Student Body:** 61% female, 39% male, 13% out-of-state, 7% international (36 countries represented). Asian 2%, African American 4%, Caucasian 76%, Hispanic 4%, Native American <1%, Pacific Islander <1%, Two or more races 5%, Race unknown 3%.

Retention and Graduation: 70% freshmen return for sophomore year. 53% freshmen graduate within 4 years. 59% freshmen graduate within 6 years. 21% grads go on to further study within 1 year. 2% grads pursue arts and sciences degrees. 26% grads pursue law degrees. 2% grads pursue business degrees. 2% grads pursue medical degrees. **Faculty:** Student/faculty ratio 10:1. 72 full-time faculty, 76% hold PhDs, 14% are members of minority groups, 53% are women. 0% of classes are taught by teaching assistants.

ACADEMICS

Degrees: Associate; Bachelor's; Certificate; Master's. **Classes:** Most classes have fewer than 10 students. Most lab/discussion sessions have fewer than 10 students. **Most popular majors:** Criminal Justice/Law Enforcement Administration; Business Administration and Management, General; Psychology, General. **Special Study Options:** Cooperative education program; Cross-registration; Distance learning; Double major; Dual enrollment; English as a Second Language (ESL); Exchange student program (domestic); Honors program; Independent study; Internships; Liberal arts/career combination; Student-designed major; Study abroad; Teacher certification program. **Honors programs:** The Honors Program is designed for high achieving students who are philosophers in the literal sense, i.e., lovers of wisdom. The goal of the program is to promote genuine inquiry and collaborative learning, emphasizing the dialogic nature of academic work and intellectual discovery. **Disability Services offered:** Note-taking services; Reader services; Tape recorders. **Career services:** Alumni network; Alumni services; Career assessment; Career/job search classes; Internships; Regional alumni.

FACILITIES

Housing: Apartments for single students; Coed dorms; Special housing for disabled students; Theme housing; Women's dorms 100% of campus accessible to physically disabled. **Special Academic Facilities/Equipment:** Most classrooms are multimedia with SmartBoards, arts center, Larson Gallery, Jane Froman Archive, Music practice Hall, Kirkman house for Graduate Studies.

CAMPUS LIFE

Environment: City. **Activities:** Campus Ministries; Choral groups; Drama/theater; International Student Organization; Model UN; Musical theater; Pep band; Student government. 54 registered organizations, 18 honor societies, 4 religious organizations, on campus. **Athletics (Intercollegiate):** *Men:* basketball, soccer. *Women:* basketball, softball, volleyball. **Environmental Initiatives:** 77% of campus building square footage is on highly efficient ground source water heat pump system.

ADMISSIONS

Freshman Academic Profile: Average high school GPA 3.6. 24% in top 10% of high school class, 46% in top 25% of high school class, 81% in top 50% of high school class. **Test scores:** SAT Math middle 50% range 490–608. SAT EBRW middle 50% range 470–595. ACT middle 50% range 20–26. **Basis for Candidate Selection:** *Very important factors include:* academic GPA, standardized test scores. *Other factors include:* rigor of secondary school record, class rank. **Freshman Admission Requirements:** High school diploma is required and GED is accepted. *Academic units recommended:* 4 English, 3 math, 3 science, 2 social studies. **Freshman Admission Statistics:** 2,390 applied, 44% admitted, 13% enrolled. **Transfer Admission Requirements:** college transcript(s), statement of good standing from prior institution(s). Minimum college GPA of 2.0 required. Lowest grade transferable 2. **General Admission Information:** Non-fall registration accepted.

COSTS AND FINANCIAL AID

Annual tuition $24,320. **Required Forms and Deadlines:** FAFSA. **Types of Aid:** *Need-based scholarships/grants:* College/university scholarship or grant aid from institutional funds; Federal Pell; Private scholarships; SEOG; State scholarships/grants. *Loans:* Direct PLUS loans; Direct Subsidized Stafford Loans; Direct Unsubsidized Stafford Loans. **Student Employment:** Federal Work-Study Program available. Institutional employment available. **Financial Aid Statistics:** 65% needy freshmen, 72% needy undergrads receive need-based scholarship or grant aid. 97% freshmen, 85% undergrads receive non-need-based scholarship or grant aid. 54% freshmen, 65% undergrads receive need-based self-help aid. 39% freshmen, 29% undergrads receive athletic scholarships. 62% freshmen, 56% undergrads receive any aid. 59% undergrads borrow to pay for school. Average cumulative indebtedness $23,979. **Criteria awarding aid:** *Need-based:* Academics, Art *Non-Need-based:* Academics, Alumni affiliation, Art, Athletics, Job skills, Leadership, Minority status, Music/drama, Religious affiliation, State/district residency.

COLUMBIA COLLEGE (SC)

1301 Columbia College Drive, Columbia, SC 29203
Phone: 803-786-3871 **Financial Aid Phone:** 803-786-3612
E-mail: admissions@columbiasc.edu **CEEB Code:** 5117
Fax: 803-786-3674 **Website:** www.columbiacollegesc.edu **ACT Code:** 3850

This private school, affiliated with the Methodist Church, was founded in 1854. It has a 33 acre campus.

RATINGS
Admissions Selectivity Rating: 75   **Fire Safety Rating:** 86   **Green Rating:** 60*

STUDENTS AND FACULTY
Enrollment: 1,552. **Student Body:** 78% female, 22% male, 7% out-of-state, international (14 countries represented).
Retention and Graduation: 62% freshmen return for sophomore year.
Faculty: Student/faculty ratio 3:1. 79 full-time faculty, 77% hold PhDs, 18% are members of minority groups, 68% are women. 0% of classes are taught by teaching assistants.

ACADEMICS
Degrees: Bachelor's; Master's; Post-bachelor's certificate. **Classes:** Most classes have 10–19 students. **Most popular majors:** Business Administration and Management, General; Elementary Education and Teaching; Human Development, Family Studies, and Related Services, Other. **Special Study Options:** Distance learning; Double major; Dual enrollment; Honors program; Independent study; Internships; Student-designed major; Study abroad; Teacher certification program. **Honors programs:** The Columbia College Honors Program provides enriched academic and co-curricular experiences for outstanding, motivated students committed to excellence. Offering a variety of opportunities for superior, engaged learning both within and outside the classroom, honors challenges students to reach their highest potential as scholars, individual thinkers, and leaders by emphasizing rigorous intellectual standards, risk, creativity, integrity, and dedication to service and leadership. The program is deeply active in the National Collegiate Honors Council and its regional association, regularly sponsoring numerous faculty and students at annual conferences and in executive leadership positions; honors has also earned special recognition through national and regional awards for honors faculty and students. To complete honors, students take 24 semester hours across disciplines in honors courses, including the 3 hour interdisciplinary senior seminar and the 3–4 hour mentored independent project. Students must maintain at least a 3.4 cumulative GPA to remain in honors. **Career services:** Career assessment; Career/job search classes; Internships.

FACILITIES
Housing:; Women's dorms 75% of campus accessible to physically disabled.
Special Academic Facilities/Equipment: Language lab, Alumnae Hall, Barbara Bush Center for Science and Technology, Breed Leadership Center for Women.
Campus Network: 100% of classrooms, 100% of dorms, 100% of student union, 100% of libraries, 100% of dining areas, 90% of common outdoor areas, have wireless network access.

CAMPUS LIFE
Environment: Metropolis. **Activities:** Campus Ministries; Choral groups; Concert band; Dance; Drama/theater; International Student Organization; Literary magazine; Music ensembles; Musical theater; Opera; Student government; Student newspaper; Yearbook. 53 registered organizations, 10 honor societies, 7 religious organizations, on campus. **Athletics (Intercollegiate):** *Women:* basketball, soccer, softball, tennis, volleyball. **On-Campus Highlights:** Leadership Center **Environmental Initiatives:** Student-sponsored and initiated recycling program.

ADMISSIONS
Freshman Academic Profile: Average high school GPA 3.7. 15% in top 10% of high school class, 47% in top 25% of high school class, 78% in top 50% of high school class. **Test scores:** SAT Math middle 50% range 410–520. SAT EBRW middle 50% range 430–550. ACT middle 50% range 18–24. **Basis for Candidate Selection:** *Very important factors include:* rigor of secondary school record, standardized test scores, recommendation(s). *Important factors include:* class rank, character/personal qualities. *Other factors include:* application essay, extracurricular activities, talent/ability, alumni/ae relation, volunteer work. **Freshman Admission Requirements:** High school diploma is required and GED is accepted. *Academic units recommended:* 4 English, 3 math, 2 science, 2 science labs, 2 foreign language, 2 social studies, 1 history, 2 academic electives. **Freshman Admission Statistics:** 506 applied, 89% admitted, 41%

enrolled. **Transfer Admission Requirements:** High school transcript, college transcript(s), standardized test scores, statement of good standing from prior institution(s). Minimum college GPA of 2.0 required. Lowest grade transferable C. **General Admission Information:** Application fee $25. Regular application deadline 8/1. Non-fall registration accepted. Admission may be deferred for a maximum of 1 year.

COSTS AND FINANCIAL AID
Annual tuition $28,100. Room and board $7,400. Average book and supplies expense $850. **Required Forms and Deadlines:** FAFSA. **Notification of Awards:** Applicants will be notified of awards on a rolling basis beginning 3/1. **Types of Aid:** *Need-based scholarships/grants:* College/university scholarship or grant aid from institutional funds; Federal Pell; Private scholarships; SEOG; State scholarships/grants; United Negro College Fund. **Student Employment:** Federal Work-Study Program available. Institutional employment available. **Financial Aid Statistics:** 82% needy freshmen, 94% needy undergrads receive need-based scholarship or grant aid. 18% freshmen, 15% undergrads receive non-need-based scholarship or grant aid. 76% freshmen, 77% undergrads receive need-based self-help aid. 6% freshmen, 5% undergrads receive athletic scholarships. 99% freshmen, 92% undergrads receive any aid. 90% undergrads borrow to pay for school. Average cumulative indebtedness $29,407. **Criteria awarding aid:** *Need-based:* Academics, Alumni affiliation, Religious affiliation. *Non-Need-based:* Academics, Alumni affiliation, Art, Athletics, Leadership, Music/drama.

COLUMBIA INTERNATIONAL UNIVERSITY

PO Box 3122, Columbia, SC 29230-3122
Phone: 803-754-4100
E-mail: yesciu@ciu.edu
Fax: 803-786-4041 **Website:** www.ciu.edu **ACT Code:** 5016

This private school was founded in 1923. It has a 400 acre campus.

RATINGS
Admissions Selectivity Rating: 75   **Fire Safety Rating:** 60*   **Green Rating:** 60*

STUDENTS AND FACULTY
Enrollment: 568. **Student Body:** 54% female, 46% male, 56% out-of-state, 0% international. Asian 0%, African American 0%, Caucasian 0%, Hispanic 0%, Native American 0%, Race unknown 0%.
Retention and Graduation: 77% freshmen return for sophomore year.
Faculty: Student/faculty ratio 19:1. 19 full-time faculty, 58% hold PhDs, 11% are members of minority groups, 21% are women.

ACADEMICS
Degrees: Associate; Bachelor's; Certificate; Doctoral degree—professional practice; Master's; Post-bachelor's certificate; Terminal Associate; Transfer Associate. **Special Study Options:** Cross-registration; Distance learning; Double major; Dual enrollment; English as a Second Language (ESL); Independent study; Internships; Liberal arts/career combination; Study abroad. **Disability Services offered:** Note-taking services; Reader services; Tape recorders; Tutors. **Career services:** Alumni services.

FACILITIES
Housing: Apartments for single students; Men's dorms; Women's dorms **Campus Network:** 100% of classrooms, 100% of dorms, 100% of student union, 100% of libraries, 100% of dining areas, 100% of common outdoor areas, have wireless network access.

CAMPUS LIFE
Environment: Village. **Activities:** Choral groups; Concert band; Drama/theater; Music ensembles; Student government; Symphony orchestra; Yearbook. 4 religious organizations, on campus.

ADMISSIONS
Freshman Academic Profile: Average high school GPA 3.9. 27% in top 10% of high school class, 47% in top 25% of high school class, 75% in top 50% of high school class. **Test scores:** SAT Math middle 50% range 490–580. SAT EBRW middle 50% range 530–630. ACT middle 50% range 20–26. **Basis for Candidate Selection:** *Very important factors include:* academic GPA, application essay, standardized test scores, recommendation(s), character/ personal qualities, religious affiliation/commitment. *Important factors include:* class rank, extracurricular activities, volunteer work. *Other factors include:* rigor of secondary school record, interview, talent/ability, alumni/ae relation, work

experience. **Freshman Admission Requirements:** High school diploma is required and GED is accepted. *Academic units recommended:* 4 English, 2 math, 1 science, 2 foreign language, 2 history. **Freshman Admission Statistics:** 163 applied, 99% admitted, 52% enrolled. **Transfer Admission Requirements:** college transcript(s), essay or personal statement, statement of good standing from prior institution(s). Minimum college GPA of 2.0 required. Lowest grade transferable C. **General Admission Information:** Application fee $45. Priority deadline 2/28. Regular application deadline 8/1. Non-fall registration accepted. Admission may be deferred for a maximum of 1 year.

COSTS AND FINANCIAL AID

Annual tuition $8,980. Room and board $4,520. Average book and supplies expense $800. **Required Forms and Deadlines:** FAFSA. **Types of Aid:** *Need-based scholarships/grants:* College/university scholarship or grant aid from institutional funds; Federal Pell; Private scholarships; SEOG; State scholarships/grants. **Student Employment:** Federal Work-Study Program available. **Financial Aid Statistics:** 75% needy freshmen, 78% needy undergrads receive need-based scholarship or grant aid. 18% freshmen, 23% undergrads receive non-need-based scholarship or grant aid. 99% freshmen, 97% undergrads receive need-based self-help aid. 0% freshmen, 0% undergrads receive athletic scholarships. **Criteria awarding aid:** *Need-based:* Academics, Leadership, Minority status, Music/drama.

COLUMBIA UNIVERSITY

212 Hamilton Hall MC 2807, New York, NY 10027
Phone: 212-854-2522 **Financial Aid Phone:** 212-854-3711
CEEB Code: 2116
Fax: 212-854-1209 **Website:** www.columbia.edu **ACT Code:** 2717

This private school was founded in 1754. It has a 36 acre campus.

RATINGS

Admissions Selectivity Rating: 99   **Fire Safety Rating:** 86   **Green Rating:** 96

STUDENTS AND FACULTY

Enrollment: 6,298. **Student Body:** 50% female, 50% male, 79% out-of-state, 17% international (115 countries represented). Asian 21%, African American 9%, Caucasian 33%, Hispanic 13%, Native American 1%, Pacific Islander <1%, Two or more races 3%, Race unknown 2%.
Retention and Graduation: 99% freshmen return for sophomore year. 87% freshmen graduate within 4 years. 96% freshmen graduate within 6 years.
Faculty: Student/faculty ratio 6:1. 1,476 full-time faculty, 100% hold PhDs, 24% are members of minority groups, 34% are women.

ACADEMICS

Degrees: Bachelor's; Doctoral degree—other; Doctoral degree—professional practice; Doctoral degree research/scholarship; Master's. **Classes:** Most classes have 10–19 students. **Most popular majors:** Computer Science; Political Science and Government, General; Economics, General. **Special Study Options:** Accelerated program; Cooperative education program; Cross-registration; Double major; Dual enrollment; English as a Second Language (ESL); Exchange student program (domestic); Independent study; Internships; Liberal arts/career combination; Student-designed major; Study abroad; Teacher certification program. **Combined degree programs:** BA/JD. **Disability Services offered:** Note-taking services; Reader services; Tape recorders; Tutors. **Career services:** Alumni network; Alumni services; Career assessment; Career/job search classes; Internships.

FACILITIES

Housing: Coed dorms; Cooperative housing; Fraternity/sorority housing; Special housing for disabled students; Theme housing; Wellness housing.
Special Academic Facilities/Equipment: Art and Architecture Galleries, Theatres, Cinema, Observatory, Makerspace, Clean Room.

CAMPUS LIFE

Environment: Metropolis. **Activities:** Campus Ministries; Choral groups; Concert band; Dance; Drama/theater; International Student Organization; Jazz band; Literary magazine; Marching band; Model UN; Music ensembles; Musical theater; Opera; Pep band; Radio station; Student government;

Student newspaper; Student-run film society; Symphony orchestra; Television station; Yearbook. 500 registered organizations, 30 religious organizations, 17 fraternities, 11 sororities, on campus. **Athletics (Intercollegiate):** *Men:* baseball, basketball, crew/rowing, cross-country, diving, fencing, football, golf, soccer, swimming, tennis, track/field (outdoor), track/field (indoor), wrestling. *Women:* archery, basketball, crew/rowing, cross-country, diving, fencing, field hockey, golf, lacrosse, soccer, softball, swimming, tennis, track/field (outdoor), track/field (indoor), volleyball. **On-Campus Highlights:** Low Library and Plaza **Environmental Initiatives:** Greenhouse gas reduction program targeted to meet a 30% reduction by 2017 and clean heat initiative to improve air quality and asthma rates by phasing out the use of heavy heating oils to cleaner fuels like natural gas and low-sulfur #2 oil. Columbia has also converted its entire 14 car public safety fleet to hybrid vehicles. As part of our energy efficiency initiatives, 45% of all food purchased is local and/ororganic. All honey and apples are purchased through vendors at the on-campus green market from NY farmers. Annually Dining Services contracts with a local NY farmer and canner to make all the salsa and strawberry jam for the year. In addition all milk is local and hormone free. Liquid eggs are certified humane. All coffee is roasted locally and is fair-trade, organic, shade grown and bird friendly. Tomatoes are also fair trade. All bakery items and grab and go sandwiches are purchased from local vendors. 50% of daily meals served in the dining halls are vegetarian and Meatless Mondays are run every Monday.

ADMISSIONS

Freshman Academic Profile: 96% in top 10% of high school class, 99% in top 25% of high school class, 100% in top 50% of high school class. 56% from public high schools. **Test scores:** SAT Math middle 50% range 740–800. SAT EBRW middle 50% range 710–770. ACT middle 50% range 33–35. **Basis for Candidate Selection:** *Very important factors include:* rigor of secondary school record, class rank, academic GPA, application essay, standardized test scores, recommendation(s), extracurricular activities, character/personal qualities. *Important factors include:* talent/ability. *Other factors include:* interview, first generation, alumni/ae relation, geographical residence, racial/ethnic status, volunteer work, work experience. **Freshman Admission Requirements:** High school diploma is required and GED is accepted. *Academic units required:* 4 English, 3 math, 3 science, 3 science labs, 3 foreign language, 3 history, 3 academic electives. *Academic units recommended:* 4 English, 4 math, 4 science, 4 science labs, 4 foreign language, 4 history, 4 academic electives. **Freshman Admission Statistics:** 42,569 applied, 5% admitted, 62% enrolled. **Transfer Admission Requirements:** High school transcript, college transcript(s), essay or personal statement, standardized test scores, statement of good standing from prior institution(s). Lowest grade transferable C. **General Admission Information:** Application fee $85. Regular application deadline 1/1. Admission may be deferred for a maximum of 2 years.

COSTS AND FINANCIAL AID

Annual tuition $58,920. Room and board $14,490. Required fees $3,510. Average book and supplies expense $1,294. **Required Forms and Deadlines:** CSS/Financial Aid PROFILE; FAFSA; Noncustodial PROFILE;. **Notification of Awards:** Applicants will be notified of awards on or about 4/1. **Types of Aid:** *Need-based scholarships/grants:* College/university scholarship or grant aid from institutional funds; Federal Pell; Private scholarships; SEOG; State scholarships/grants. *Loans:* Direct PLUS loans; Direct Subsidized Stafford Loans; Direct Unsubsidized Stafford Loans. **Student Employment:** Federal Work-Study Program available. Institutional employment available. **Financial Aid Statistics:** 99% needy freshmen, 99% needy undergrads receive need-based scholarship or grant aid. 7% freshmen, 5% undergrads receive non-need-based scholarship or grant aid. 72% freshmen, 78% undergrads receive need-based self-help aid. 0% freshmen, 0% undergrads receive athletic scholarships. 53% freshmen, 50% undergrads receive any aid. 21% undergrads borrow to pay for school. Average cumulative indebtedness $27,595.

COLUMBIA UNIVERSITY SCHOOL OF GENERAL STUDIES

408 Lewisohn Hall, Mail Code 4101, New York, NY 10027
Phone: (212) 854-2772 **Financial Aid Phone:** (212) 854-5410
E-mail: gsdegree@columbia.edu **CEEB Code:** 2095
Fax: (212) 854-6316 **Website:** www.gs.columbia.edu **ACT Code:** 2716

This private school was founded in 1947. It has a 36 acre campus.

RATINGS
Admissions Selectivity Rating: 95 **Fire Safety Rating:** 88 **Green Rating:** 60*

STUDENTS AND FACULTY
Enrollment: 2,005. **Student Body:** 41% female, 59% male, 56% out-of-state, 18% international (62 countries represented). Asian 8%, African American 5%, Caucasian 49%, Hispanic 10%, Native American <1%, Pacific Islander <1%, Two or more races <1%, Race unknown 9%.

ACADEMICS
Degrees: Bachelor's; Post-bachelor's certificate. **Most popular majors:** English Language and Literature, General; Economics, General; Political Science and Government, General. **Special Study Options:** Accelerated program; Cross-registration; Double major; Dual enrollment; Exchange student program (domestic); Honors program; Independent study; Internships; Student-designed major; Study abroad; Teacher certification program. **Honors programs:** Honor Society of School of General Studies. **Combined degree programs:** BA/DDS; BA/JD; BA/MA; BA/MEng. **Disability Services offered:** Note-taking services; Reader services; Tape recorders; Tutors. **Career services:** Alumni network; Alumni services; Career assessment; Career/job search classes; Internships; Regional alumni.

FACILITIES
Housing: Apartments for married students; Apartments for single students; Coed dorms; Cooperative housing; Fraternity/sorority housing; Special housing for international students; Theme housing 100% of campus accessible to physically disabled. **Special Academic Facilities/Equipment:** Earth Institute, Lamont-Doherty Earth Observatory University Art Collection Miller Theatre Low Memorial Library Rotunda LeRoy Neiman Center for Print Studies Music at St. Paul's Postcrypt Coffeehouse Miriam and Ira D. Wallach Art Gallery Language Houses.

CAMPUS LIFE
Environment: Metropolis. **Activities:** Campus Ministries; Choral groups; Concert band; Dance; Drama/theater; International Student Organization; Jazz band; Literary magazine; Marching band; Model UN; Music ensembles; Musical theater; Opera; Radio station; Student government; Student newspaper; Student-run film society; Television station; Yearbook. 500 registered organizations, 33 religious organizations, 17 fraternities, 11 sororities, on campus. **Athletics (Intercollegiate):** *Men:* baseball, basketball, crew/rowing, cross-country, diving, fencing, football, golf, soccer, swimming, track/field (outdoor), track/field (indoor). *Women:* archery, basketball, crew/rowing, cross-country, diving, fencing, field hockey, golf, lacrosse, soccer, softball, swimming, track/field (outdoor), track/field (indoor), volleyball. **On-Campus Highlights:** Low Memorial Library. **Environmental Initiatives:** Greenhouse gas reduction program targeted to meet a 30% reduction by 2017 and clean heat initiative to improve air quality and asthma rates by phasing out the use of heavy heating oils to cleaner fuels like natural gas and low-sulfur #2 oil. Columbia has also converted its entire 14 car public safety fleet to hybrid vehicles. As part of our energy efficiency initiatives, 45% of all food purchased is local and/ororganic. All honey and apples are purchased through vendors at the on-campus green market from NY farmers. Annually Dining Services contracts with a local NY farmer and canner to make all the salsa and strawberry jam for the year. In addition all milk is local and hormone free. Liquid eggs are certified humane. All coffee is roasted locally and is fair-trade, organic, shade grown and bird friendly. Tomatoes are also fair trade. All bakery items and grab and go sandwiches are purchased from local vendors. 50% of daily meals served in the dining halls are vegetarian and Meatless Mondays are run every Monday.

ADMISSIONS
Freshman Academic Profile: Average high school GPA 3.7. % in top 10% of high school class, % in top 25% of high school class, % in top 50% of high school class. **Test scores:** SAT Math middle 50% range 630–740. SAT EBRW middle 50% range 630–750. ACT middle 50% range 29–32. **Basis for Candidate Selection:** *Very important factors include:* rigor of secondary school record, academic GPA, application essay, standardized test scores,

interview, character/personal qualities, first generation, work experience, level of applicant's interest. *Important factors include:* class rank, recommendation(s), extracurricular activities, talent/ability. *Other factors include:* alumni/ae relation, geographical residence, state residency, volunteer work. **Freshman Admission Requirements:** High school diploma is required and GED is accepted. **Freshman Admission Statistics:** 661 applied, 33% admitted, 59% enrolled. **Transfer Admission Requirements:** High school transcript, college transcript(s), Lowest grade transferable C. **General Admission Information:** Application fee $80. Priority deadline 3/1. Regular application deadline 6/1. Non-fall registration accepted. Admission may be deferred for a maximum of 2 semesters.

COSTS AND FINANCIAL AID
Annual tuition $48,900. Room and board $10,356. Required fees $2,585. Average book and supplies expense $1,400. **Required Forms and Deadlines:** FAFSA; Institution's own financial aid form. **Types of Aid:** *Need-based scholarships/grants:* College/university scholarship or grant aid from institutional funds; Federal Pell; Private scholarships; SEOG; State scholarships/grants. *Loans:* Direct PLUS loans; Direct Subsidized Stafford Loans; Direct Unsubsidized Stafford Loans. **Student Employment:** Federal Work-Study Program available. Institutional employment available. **Financial Aid Statistics:** 93% needy freshmen, 98% needy undergrads receive need-based scholarship or grant aid. 0% freshmen, 2% undergrads receive non-need-based scholarship or grant aid. 82% freshmen, 87% undergrads receive need-based self-help aid. 0% freshmen, 0% undergrads receive athletic scholarships. % freshmen, 70% undergrads receive any aid. **Criteria awarding aid:** *Need-based:* Academics. *Non-Need-based:* Academics.

COLUMBUS COLLEGE OF ART AND DESIGN

Admissions, Columbus, OH 43215-3875
Phone: 614-222-3261 **Financial Aid Phone:** 614.222.3295
E-mail: admissions@ccad.edu **CEEB Code:** 1085
Fax: 614-232-8344 **Website:** www.ccad.edu **ACT Code:** 3281

This private school was founded in 1879. It has a 9 acre campus.

RATINGS
Admissions Selectivity Rating: 76 **Fire Safety Rating:** 91 **Green Rating:** 60*

STUDENTS AND FACULTY
Enrollment: 1,261. **Student Body:** 62% female, 38% male, 27% out-of-state, 8% international (35 countries represented). Asian 3%, African American 8%, Caucasian 68%, Hispanic 5%, Native American <1%, Pacific Islander 0%, Two or more races 4%, Race unknown 3%.
Retention and Graduation: 78% freshmen return for sophomore year. 8% grads go on to further study within 1 year. 7% grads pursue arts and sciences degrees. 1% grads pursue medical degrees. **Faculty:** Student/faculty ratio 11:1. 72 full-time faculty, 69% hold PhDs, 7% are members of minority groups, 38% are women. 0% of classes are taught by teaching assistants.

ACADEMICS
Degrees: Bachelor's; Master's. **Classes:** Most classes have 10–19 students. **Most popular majors:** Illustration; Graphic Design. **Special Study Options:** Accelerated program; Cooperative education program; Cross-registration; Distance learning; Double major; English as a Second Language (ESL); Exchange student program (domestic); Honors program; Independent study; Internships; Study abroad. **Honors programs:** The CCAD Honors Program centers around seminar courses offered each semester and the creation of individualized learning contracts, culminating in a thesis/capstone project. The program activities are designed to assist students in integrating various community and academic projects with their individual creative interests within the CCAD curriculum. Benefits include honors designation on transcripts, recognition at commencement, and the opportunity to propose and implement projects that move students toward their personal, academic, and career goals. Participants in the CCAD Honors Program must maintain a cumulative GPA of at least 3.5, participate in four seminar courses during their time at CCAD, and complete a Senior Honors Thesis or Capstone Project. **Disability Services offered:** Note-taking services; Reader services; Tutors. **Career services:** Alumni services; Career assessment; Career/job search classes; Internships.

FACILITIES
Housing: Apartments for married students; Apartments for single students; Coed dorms; Special housing for disabled students; Special housing for

international students. **Special Academic Facilities/Equipment:** Multiple art galleries, auditorium, recreation center, library, specialized studios and fabrication labs. **Campus Network:** 90% of classrooms, 100% of dorms, 0% of student union, 100% of libraries, 100% of dining areas, 75% of common outdoor areas, have wireless network access.

CAMPUS LIFE

Environment: Metropolis. **Activities:** International Student Organization; Literary magazine; Student government; Student-run film society. 27 registered organizations, on campus. **On-Campus Highlights:** Joseph V. Canzani Center.

ADMISSIONS

Freshman Academic Profile: Average high school GPA 3.2. 6% in top 10% of high school class, 18% in top 25% of high school class, 59% in top 50% of high school class. **Test scores:** SAT Math middle 50% range 450–570. SAT EBRW middle 50% range 470–610. ACT middle 50% range 19–25. **Basis for Candidate Selection:** *Very important factors include:* academic GPA, application essay, standardized test scores, recommendation(s), talent/ability. *Other factors include:* rigor of secondary school record, interview, extracurricular activities, character/personal qualities, first generation, alumni/ae relation, geographical residence, state residency, volunteer work, work experience. **Freshman Admission Requirements:** High school diploma is required and GED is accepted. *Academic units recommended:* 4 English, 2 math, 2 science, 2 foreign language. **Freshman Admission Statistics:** 666 applied, 87% admitted, 40% enrolled. **Transfer Admission Requirements:** High school transcript, college transcript(s), essay or personal statement, Minimum college GPA of 2.0 required. Lowest grade transferable C. **General Admission Information:** Application fee $40. Priority deadline 2/15. Regular application deadline 8/22. Non-fall registration accepted.

COSTS AND FINANCIAL AID

Annual tuition $28,872. Room and board $7,740. Average book and supplies expense $4,000. **Required Forms and Deadlines:** FAFSA. **Notification of Awards:** Applicants will be notified of awards on a rolling basis beginning 3/15. **Types of Aid:** *Need-based scholarships/grants:* College/university scholarship or grant aid from institutional funds; Federal Pell; SEOG; State scholarships/grants. *Loans:* Direct PLUS loans; Direct Subsidized Stafford Loans; Direct Unsubsidized Stafford Loans. **Student Employment:** Federal Work-Study Program available. Institutional employment available. **Financial Aid Statistics:** 100% needy freshmen, 98% needy undergrads receive need-based scholarship or grant aid. 4% freshmen, 3% undergrads receive non-need-based scholarship or grant aid. 84% freshmen, 83% undergrads receive need-based self-help aid. 0% freshmen, 0% undergrads receive athletic scholarships. 74% freshmen, 81% undergrads receive any aid. **Criteria awarding aid:** *Non-Need-based:* Academics, Art.

COLUMBUS STATE UNIVERSITY

4225 University Avenue, Columbus, GA 31907-5645
Phone: 706-568-2035 **Financial Aid Phone:** 706-507-8800
E-mail: admissions@colstate.edu
Fax: 706-568-5091 **Website:** www.columbusstate.edu

This public school was founded in 1958. It has a 150 acre campus.

RATINGS

Admissions Selectivity Rating: 86   **Fire Safety Rating:** 87   **Green Rating:** 60*

STUDENTS AND FACULTY

Enrollment: 6,890. **Student Body:** 60% female, 40% male, 14% out-of-state, 1% international (67 countries represented). Asian 2%, African American 35%, Caucasian 55%, Hispanic 4%, Native American 1%, Pacific Islander <1%, Two or more races 2%, Race unknown 0%.
Retention and Graduation: 69% freshmen return for sophomore year.
Faculty: Student/faculty ratio 18:1. 279 full-time faculty, 78% hold PhDs, 23% are members of minority groups, 43% are women. 0% of classes are taught by teaching assistants.

ACADEMICS

Degrees: Bachelor's; Certificate; Doctoral degree research/scholarship; Master's; Post-master's certificate; Terminal Associate; Transfer Associate. **Classes:** Most classes have 20–29 students. Most lab/discussion sessions have 20–29 students. **Most popular majors:** Business/Commerce, General; Early Childhood Education and Teaching; Nursing/Registered Nurse (Rn, Asn, Bsn, Msn).

Special Study Options: Accelerated program; Cooperative education program; Distance learning; Double major; Dual enrollment; English as a Second Language (ESL); Honors program; Independent study; Internships; Liberal arts/career combination; Study abroad; Teacher certification program. **Honors programs:** Honors Program Servant Leadership Program. **Disability Services offered:** Note-taking services; Reader services; Tape recorders; Tutors. **Career services:** Alumni network; Alumni services; Career assessment; Career/job search classes; Internships; Regional alumni.

FACILITIES

Housing: Apartments for married students; Apartments for single students; Fraternity/sorority housing; Special housing for disabled students; Special housing for international students; Theme housing 100% of campus accessible to physically disabled. **Campus Network:** 100% of classrooms, 100% of dorms, 100% of student union, 100% of libraries, 100% of dining areas, 80% of common outdoor areas, have wireless network access.

CAMPUS LIFE

Environment: City. **Activities:** Campus Ministries; Choral groups; Concert band; Dance; Drama/theater; International Student Organization; Jazz band; Literary magazine; Model UN; Music ensembles; Musical theater; Pep band; Student government; Student newspaper; Symphony orchestra. 90 registered organizations, 22 honor societies, 10 religious organizations, 7 fraternities, 6 sororities, on campus. **Athletics (Intercollegiate):** *Men:* baseball, basketball, cheerleading, cross-country, golf, riflery, tennis. *Women:* basketball, cheerleading, cross-country, golf, riflery, soccer, softball, tennis. **On-Campus Highlights:** Einstein Bos. Bagels. **Environmental Initiatives:** Green Seal Cleaning Products.

ADMISSIONS

Freshman Academic Profile: Average high school GPA 3.0. **Test scores:** SAT Math middle 50% range 420–540. SAT EBRW middle 50% range 430–550. ACT middle 50% range 17–22. **Basis for Candidate Selection:** *Very important factors include:* rigor of secondary school record. *Important factors include:* academic GPA, standardized test scores. *Other factors include:* interview, extracurricular activities, talent/ability, geographical residence. **Freshman Admission Requirements:** High school diploma is required and GED is not accepted. *Academic units required:* 4 English, 4 math, 3 science, 2 science labs, 2 foreign language, 3 social studies. **Freshman Admission Statistics:** 3,454 applied, 60% admitted, 60% enrolled. **Transfer Admission Requirements:** college transcript(s), statement of good standing from prior institution(s). Minimum college GPA of 2.00 required. Lowest grade transferable D. **General Admission Information:** Application fee $30. Priority deadline 5/15. Regular application deadline 6/30. Non-fall registration accepted. Admission may be deferred for a maximum of one year.

COSTS AND FINANCIAL AID

Annual in-state tuition $4,596. Annual out-of-state tuition $16,572. Room and board $7,280. Required fees $1,300. Average book and supplies expense $1,072. **Required Forms and Deadlines:** FAFSA. **Notification of Awards:** Applicants will be notified of awards on a rolling basis beginning 5/15. **Types of Aid:** *Need-based scholarships/grants:* College/university scholarship or grant aid from institutional funds; Federal Pell; Private scholarships; SEOG; State scholarships/grants. *Loans:* Direct PLUS loans; Direct Subsidized Stafford Loans; Direct Unsubsidized Stafford Loans. **Student Employment:** Federal Work-Study Program available. Institutional employment available. **Financial Aid Statistics:** 71% needy freshmen, 72% needy undergrads receive need-based scholarship or grant aid. 50% freshmen, 33% undergrads receive non-need-based scholarship or grant aid. 66% freshmen, 72% undergrads receive need-based self-help aid. 4% freshmen, 4% undergrads receive athletic scholarships. 87% freshmen, 78% undergrads receive any aid. **Criteria awarding aid:** *Need-based:* Academics, Alumni affiliation, Art, Athletics, Job skills, Leadership, Minority status, Music/drama *Non-Need-based:* Academics, Alumni affiliation, Art, Athletics, Job skills, Leadership, Minority status, Music/drama.

CONCORDIA COLLEGE (MOORHEAD, MN)

901 8th Street South, Moorhead, MN 56562
Phone: 218-299-3004 **Financial Aid Phone:** 218.299.3010
E-mail: admissions@cord.edu **CEEB Code:** 6113
Fax: 218-299-4720 **Website:** https://www.concordiacollege.edu **ACT Code:** 2104

This private school, affiliated with the Lutheran Church, was founded in 1891. It has a 120 acre campus.

RATINGS

Admissions Selectivity Rating: 83   **Fire Safety Rating:** 85   **Green Rating:** 83

STUDENTS AND FACULTY

Enrollment: 1,967. **Student Body:** 58% female, 42% male, 29% out-of-state, 5% international (28 countries represented). Asian 2%, African American 2%, Caucasian 83%, Hispanic 2%, Native American 1%, Pacific Islander <1%, Two or more races 2%, Race unknown 4%.
Retention and Graduation: 82% freshmen return for sophomore year. 70% freshmen graduate within 4 years. 74% freshmen graduate within 6 years. 24% grads go on to further study within 1 year. 5% grads pursue arts and sciences degrees. 4% grads pursue law degrees. 3% grads pursue business degrees. 4% grads pursue medical degrees. **Faculty:** Student/faculty ratio 11:1. 166 full-time faculty, 83% hold PhDs, 7% are members of minority groups, 48% are women. 0% of classes are taught by teaching assistants.

ACADEMICS

Degrees: Bachelor's; Master's. **Classes:** Most classes have 10–19 students. Most lab/discussion sessions have 10–19 students. **Most popular majors:** Education, General; Biology/Biological Sciences, General; Business Administration and Management, General. **Special Study Options:** Accelerated program; Cooperative education program; Cross-registration; Distance learning; Double major; Dual enrollment; English as a Second Language (ESL); Exchange student program (domestic); Honors program; Independent study; Internships; Liberal arts/career combination; Student-designed major; Study abroad; Teacher certification program. **Disability Services offered:** Note-taking services; Reader services; Tape recorders; Tutors. **Career services:** Alumni network; Alumni services; Career assessment; Career/job search classes; Internships.

FACILITIES

Housing: Apartments for single students; Coed dorms; Theme housing 95% of campus accessible to physically disabled. **Special Academic Facilities/Equipment:** Cyrus M. Running Gallery. **Campus Network:** 90% of classrooms, 100% of dorms, 100% of student union, 100% of libraries, 100% of dining areas, 100% of common outdoor areas, have wireless network access.

CAMPUS LIFE

Environment: City. **Activities:** Campus Ministries; Choral groups; Concert band; Dance; Drama/theater; International Student Organization; Jazz band; Literary magazine; Music ensembles; Musical theater; Pep band; Radio station; Student government; Student newspaper; Symphony orchestra; Television station. 100 registered organizations, 22 honor societies, 12 religious organizations, 1 fraternities, 1 sororities, on campus. **Athletics (Intercollegiate):** *Men:* baseball, basketball, cross-country, football, golf, ice hockey, soccer, tennis, track/field (outdoor), track/field (indoor), wrestling. *Women:* basketball, cross-country, diving, golf, ice hockey, soccer, softball, swimming, tennis, track/field (outdoor), track/field (indoor), volleyball. **On-Campus Highlights:** Knutson Campus Center.

ADMISSIONS

Freshman Academic Profile: Average high school GPA 3.6. 27% in top 10% of high school class, 55% in top 25% of high school class, 85% in top 50% of high school class. ACT middle 50% range 22–28. **Basis for Candidate Selection:** *Very important factors include:* rigor of secondary school record. *Important factors include:* academic GPA, standardized test scores. *Other factors include:* class rank, application essay, recommendation(s), interview, extracurricular activities, talent/ability, character/personal qualities, first generation, alumni/ae relation, racial/ethnic status, volunteer work, work experience, level of applicant's interest. **Freshman Admission Requirements:** High school diploma is required and GED is accepted. *Academic units recommended:* 4 English, 3 math, 3 science, 2 foreign language, 3 social studies, 1 computer science, 1 visual/performing arts. **Freshman Admission Statistics:** 4,539 applied, 61% admitted, 20% enrolled. **Transfer Admission Requirements:** college transcript(s), Minimum college GPA of 2.0 required. Lowest grade transferable C-. **General Admission Information:** Regular

application deadline 9/10. Non-fall registration accepted. Admission may be deferred for a maximum of 1 year.

COSTS AND FINANCIAL AID

Annual tuition $39,650. Room and board $8,230. Required fees $228. Average book and supplies expense $1,000. **Required Forms and Deadlines:** FAFSA. **Notification of Awards:** Applicants will be notified of awards on a rolling basis beginning 12/1. *Types of Aid: Need-based scholarships/grants:* Federal Pell; Private scholarships; SEOG; State scholarships/grants. *Loans:* Direct PLUS loans; Direct Subsidized Stafford Loans; Direct Unsubsidized Stafford Loans. **Student Employment:** Federal Work-Study Program available. Institutional employment available. **Financial Aid Statistics:** 98% needy freshmen, 98% needy undergrads receive need-based scholarship or grant aid. 21% freshmen, 16% undergrads receive non-need-based scholarship or grant aid. 79% freshmen, 83% undergrads receive need-based self-help aid. 0% freshmen, 0% undergrads receive athletic scholarships. 100% freshmen, 96% undergrads receive any aid. 77% undergrads borrow to pay for school. Average cumulative indebtedness $39,803. **Criteria awarding aid:** *Need-based:* Academics, Minority status. *Non-Need-based:* Academics, Art, Leadership, Minority status, Music/drama.

CONCORDIA COLLEGE (NY)

171 White Plains Road, Bronxville, NY 10708
Phone: 914-337-9300
E-mail: admission@concordia-ny.edu **CEEB Code:** 2096
Fax: 914-395-4636 **Website:** www.concordia-ny.edu **ACT Code:** 2722

This private school, affiliated with the Lutheran Church, was founded in 1881. It has a 33 acre campus.

RATINGS

Admissions Selectivity Rating: 70   **Fire Safety Rating:** 60*   **Green Rating:** 60*

STUDENTS AND FACULTY

Enrollment: 887. **Student Body:** female, male, 27% out-of-state, international (36 countries represented).
Retention and Graduation: 69% freshmen return for sophomore year. 40% grads go on to further study within 1 year. 30% grads pursue arts and sciences degrees. 2% grads pursue law degrees. 30% grads pursue business degrees. 10% grads pursue medical degrees. **Faculty:** Student/faculty ratio 12:1. 54 full-time faculty, 0% hold PhDs, 0% are members of minority groups, 0% are women. 0% of classes are taught by teaching assistants.

ACADEMICS

Degrees: Associate; Bachelor's; Master's. **Most popular majors:** Education, General; Business/Commerce, General; Social Sciences, General. **Special Study Options:** Accelerated program; Cooperative education program; Cross-registration; Double major; English as a Second Language (ESL); Exchange student program (domestic); Honors program; Independent study; Internships; Liberal arts/career combination; Student-designed major; Study abroad; Teacher certification program. **Disability Services offered:** Reader services; Tutors. **Career services:** Career assessment; Career/job search classes; Internships.

FACILITIES

Housing: Men's dorms; Women's dorms 50% of campus accessible to physically disabled. **Special Academic Facilities/Equipment:** Art gallery, center for worship and performing arts, English language center, distance learning classroom. **Campus Network:** 100% of classrooms, 100% of dorms, 100% of student union, 100% of libraries, 100% of dining areas, 100% of common outdoor areas, have wireless network access.

CAMPUS LIFE

Environment: Village. **Activities:** Choral groups; Concert band; Dance; Drama/theater; International Student Organization; Jazz band; Literary magazine; Music ensembles; Musical theater; Student government; Student newspaper; Yearbook. 35 registered organizations, 1 honor societies, 3 religious organizations, on campus. **Athletics (Intercollegiate):** *Men:* baseball, basketball, soccer, tennis, volleyball. *Women:* basketball, soccer, softball, tennis, volleyball.

ADMISSIONS

Freshman Academic Profile: Average high school GPA 2.7. 60% from public high schools. **Test scores:** SAT Math middle 50% range 415–505. SAT EBRW middle 50% range 420–500. ACT middle 50% range 16–20. **Basis for Candidate Selection:** *Very important factors include:* rigor of secondary school record. *Important factors include:* class rank, standardized test scores, interview, character/personal qualities. *Other factors include:* application essay, recommendation(s), extracurricular activities, talent/ability, alumni/ae relation, religious affiliation/commitment, volunteer work, work experience. **Freshman Admission Requirements:** High school diploma is required and GED is accepted. **Freshman Admission Statistics:** applied, admitted, enrolled. **Transfer Admission Requirements:** High school transcript, college transcript(s), statement of good standing from prior institution(s). Minimum college GPA of 2.0 required. Lowest grade transferable C. **General Admission Information:** Application fee $50. Priority deadline 3/15. Regular application deadline 3/15. Non-fall registration accepted.

COSTS AND FINANCIAL AID

Annual tuition $27,740. Room and board $10,265. Required fees $1,030. Average book and supplies expense $1,000. **Student Employment:** Federal Work-Study Program available. Institutional employment available.

CONCORDIA UNIVERSITY (CA)

1530 Concordia West, Irvine, CA 92612-3299
Phone: 949-854-8002 **Financial Aid Phone:** 949-854-8002
E-mail: admission@cui.edu
Fax: 949-854-6894 **Website:** www.cui.edu **ACT Code:** 227

This private school, affiliated with the Lutheran Church, was founded in 1976. It has a 70 acre campus.

RATINGS
Admissions Selectivity Rating: 84 **Fire Safety Rating:** 90 **Green Rating:** 60*

STUDENTS AND FACULTY
Enrollment: 1,203. **Student Body:** 61% female, 39% male, 17% out-of-state, 2% international (18 countries represented). Asian 4%, African American 4%, Caucasian 68%, Hispanic 13%, Native American 1%, Race unknown 7%. **Retention and Graduation:** 73% freshmen return for sophomore year. **Faculty:** Student/faculty ratio 14:1. 91 full-time faculty, 67% hold PhDs, 0% are members of minority groups, 37% are women. 0% of classes are taught by teaching assistants.

ACADEMICS
Degrees: Associate; Bachelor's; Master's; Post-bachelor's certificate. **Classes:** Most classes have 10–19 students. **Most popular majors:** Business/Commerce, General; Liberal Arts and Sciences/Liberal Studies; Psychology, General. **Special Study Options:** Accelerated program; Cross-registration; Distance learning; Double major; Dual enrollment; English as a Second Language (ESL); Exchange student program (domestic); Honors program; Independent study; Internships; Liberal arts/career combination; Student-designed major; Study abroad; Teacher certification program. **Honors programs:** General Education Honor Programs. **Combined degree programs:** BA/MA. **Disability Services offered:** Tutors.

FACILITIES
Housing: Men's dorms; Special housing for disabled studentss; Women's dorms 75% of campus accessible to physically disabled. **Special Academic Facilities/Equipment:** A hi-tech Educational/Business/Technology building, which was recently completed, houses also an art gallery. **Campus Network:** 100% of classrooms, 100% of dorms, 100% of student union, 100% of libraries, 100% of dining areas, 70% of common outdoor areas, have wireless network access.

CAMPUS LIFE
Environment: City. **Activities:** Campus Ministries; Choral groups; Concert band; Dance; Drama/theater; Literary magazine; Music ensembles; Musical theater; Pep band; Radio station; Student government; Student newspaper; Student-run film society; Yearbook. 18 registered organizations, 5 honor societies, 8 religious organizations, on campus. **Athletics (Intercollegiate):** *Men:* baseball, basketball, cross-country, golf, soccer, swimming, tennis, track/field (outdoor), water polo. *Women:* basketball, cross-country, golf, soccer, softball, swimming, tennis, track/field (outdoor), volleyball, water polo. **On-Campus Highlights:** The Gym.

ADMISSIONS
Freshman Academic Profile: Average high school GPA 3.5. 20% in top 10% of high school class, 54% in top 25% of high school class, 84% in top 50% of high school class. **Test scores:** SAT Math middle 50% range 450–570. SAT

EBRW middle 50% range 450–570. ACT middle 50% range 20–24. **Basis for Candidate Selection:** *Very important factors include:* rigor of secondary school record, class rank, academic GPA, standardized test scores, character/personal qualities. *Important factors include:* recommendation(s), religious affiliation/commitment. *Other factors include:* application essay, interview, extracurricular activities, talent/ability, alumni/ae relation, racial/ethnic status, volunteer work, work experience, level of applicant's interest. **Freshman Admission Requirements:** High school diploma is required and GED is accepted. *Academic units required:* 4 English, 3 math, 3 science, 2 foreign language, 2 social studies. **Freshman Admission Statistics:** 897 applied, 66% admitted, 39% enrolled. **Transfer Admission Requirements:** High school transcript, college transcript(s), statement of good standing from prior institution(s). Minimum college GPA of 2.3 required. Lowest grade transferable D. **General Admission Information:** Application fee $50. Priority deadline 3/2. Non-fall registration accepted. Admission may be deferred for a maximum of 12 months.

COSTS AND FINANCIAL AID
Annual tuition $23,400. Room and board $7,650. Required fees $300. **Required Forms and Deadlines:** FAFSA; Institution's own financial aid form; State aid form. **Notification of Awards:** Applicants will be notified of awards on a rolling basis beginning 2/1. **Types of Aid:** *Need-based scholarships/grants:* College/university scholarship or grant aid from institutional funds; Federal Pell; Private scholarships; SEOG; State scholarships/grants. **Financial Aid Statistics:** 95% needy freshmen, 92% needy undergrads receive need-based scholarship or grant aid. 18% freshmen, 13% undergrads receive non-need-based scholarship or grant aid. 71% freshmen, 76% undergrads receive need-based self-help aid. 10% freshmen, 7% undergrads receive athletic scholarships. 74.09% freshmen, 71.46% undergrads receive any aid. **Criteria awarding aid:** *Need-based:* Job skills *Non-Need-based:* Academics, Art, Athletics, Leadership, Music/drama, Religious affiliation.

CONCORDIA UNIVERSITY (NE)

800 North Columbia Avenue, Seward, NE 68434-1556
Phone: 800-535-5494 **Financial Aid Phone:** 800 535-5494
E-mail: admiss@cune.edu **CEEB Code:** 6116
Fax: 402-643-4073 **Website:** www.cune.edu **ACT Code:** 2442

This private school, affiliated with the Lutheran Church, was founded in 1894. It has a 120 acre campus.

RATINGS
Admissions Selectivity Rating: 77 **Fire Safety Rating:** 89 **Green Rating:** 60*

STUDENTS AND FACULTY
Enrollment: 1,233. **Student Body:** 52% female, 48% male, 52% out-of-state, 2% international (9 countries represented). Asian 1%, African American 4%, Caucasian 78%, Hispanic 6%, Native American <1%, Pacific Islander <1%, Two or more races 1%, Race unknown 9%. **Retention and Graduation:** 74% freshmen return for sophomore year. 50% freshmen graduate within 4 years. 67% freshmen graduate within 6 years. 17% grads go on to further study within 1 year. 7% grads pursue arts and sciences degrees. <1% grads pursue law degrees. <1% grads pursue business degrees. 6% grads pursue medical degrees. **Faculty:** Student/faculty ratio 14:1. 61 full-time faculty, 77% hold PhDs, 3% are members of minority groups, 34% are women. 0% of classes are taught by teaching assistants.

ACADEMICS
Degrees: Bachelor's; Master's. **Classes:** Most classes have 20–29 students. Most lab/discussion sessions have 10–19 students. **Most popular majors:** Business/Commerce, General; Biology/Biological Sciences, General; Elementary Education and Teaching. **Special Study Options:** Accelerated program; Distance learning; Double major; Exchange student program (domestic); Independent study; Internships; Study abroad; Teacher certification program. **Disability Services offered:** Note-taking services; Reader services; Tape recorders; Tutors. **Career services:** Alumni network; Alumni services; Career assessment; Career/job search classes; Internships; Regional alumni.

FACILITIES
Housing: Apartments for married students; Apartments for single students; Men's dorms; Special housing for disabled studentss; Wellness housing; Women's dorms 75% of campus accessible to physically disabled. **Special Academic Facilities/Equipment:** Marxhausen Gallery of Art, Bartels Rock Museum, Osten Observatory, arboretum.

CAMPUS LIFE

Environment: Village. **Activities:** Campus Ministries; Choral groups; Concert band; Dance; Drama/theater; International Student Organization; Jazz band; Literary magazine; Music ensembles; Musical theater; Pep band; Student government; Student newspaper; Symphony orchestra; Yearbook. 30 registered organizations, 4 honor societies, 8 religious organizations, on campus. **Athletics (Intercollegiate):** *Men:* baseball, basketball, cross-country, football, golf, soccer, tennis, track/field (outdoor), track/field (indoor), wrestling. *Women:* basketball, cross-country, golf, soccer, softball, tennis, track/field (outdoor), track/field (indoor), volleyball. **On-Campus Highlights:** Student Center / Game Room. **Environmental Initiatives:** The committee is charged with outlining short-term and long-term plans that will render the university carbon neutral as soon as is feasible and to report progress periodically. Specific plans have not yet been formulated.

ADMISSIONS

Freshman Academic Profile: Average high school GPA 3.5. 18% in top 10% of high school class, 43% in top 25% of high school class, 72% in top 50% of high school class. **Test scores:** SAT Math middle 50% range 440–550. SAT EBRW middle 50% range 480–550. ACT middle 50% range 21–26. **Basis for Candidate Selection:** *Very important factors include:* academic GPA, standardized test scores. *Important factors include:* rigor of secondary school record, class rank, character/personal qualities. *Other factors include:* application essay, recommendation(s), interview, extracurricular activities, alumni/ae relation, religious affiliation/commitment. **Freshman Admission Requirements:** High school diploma is required and GED is accepted. *Academic units recommended:* 4 English, 3 math, 2 science, 1 foreign language, 3 social studies. **Freshman Admission Statistics:** 1,537 applied, 75% admitted, 30% enrolled. **Transfer Admission Requirements:** High school transcript, college transcript(s), Minimum college GPA of 2.0 required. Lowest grade transferable D. **General Admission Information:** Priority deadline 7/1. Regular application deadline 8/1. Non-fall registration accepted. Admission may be deferred for a maximum of 1 year.

COSTS AND FINANCIAL AID

Annual tuition $31,620. Room and board $8,470. Required fees $600. Average book and supplies expense $1,000. **Required Forms and Deadlines:** FAFSA. **Notification of Awards:** Applicants will be notified of awards on a rolling basis beginning 3/1. **Types of Aid:** *Need-based scholarships/grants:* College/university scholarship or grant aid from institutional funds; Federal Pell; Private scholarships; SEOG; State scholarships/grants. *Loans:* Direct PLUS loans; Direct Subsidized Stafford Loans; Direct Unsubsidized Stafford Loans. **Student Employment:** Federal Work-Study Program available. Institutional employment available. **Financial Aid Statistics:** 100% needy freshmen, 100% needy undergrads receive need-based scholarship or grant aid. 23% freshmen, 19% undergrads receive non-need-based scholarship or grant aid. 69% freshmen, 68% undergrads receive need-based self-help aid. 15% freshmen, 13% undergrads receive athletic scholarships. 100% freshmen, 99% undergrads receive any aid. 65% undergrads borrow to pay for school. Average cumulative indebtedness $27,722. **Criteria awarding aid:** *Need-based:* Minority status. *Non-Need-based:* Academics, Alumni affiliation, Art, Athletics, Leadership, Music/drama, Religious affiliation.

CONCORDIA UNIVERSITY (ST. PAUL, MN)

1282 Concordia Avenue, St. Paul, MN 55104-5494
Phone: 651-641-8230 **Financial Aid Phone:** 651-603-6300
E-mail: admission@csp.edu **CEEB Code:** 6114
Fax: 651-603-6320 **Website:** www.csp.edu **ACT Code:** 2106

This private school, affiliated with the Lutheran Church, was founded in 1893. It has a 37 acre campus.

RATINGS

Admissions Selectivity Rating: 71   **Fire Safety Rating:** 92   **Green Rating:** 60*

STUDENTS AND FACULTY

Enrollment: 2,747. **Student Body:** 61% female, 39% male, 21% out-of-state, 4% international (15 countries represented). Asian 10%, African American 12%, Caucasian 59%, Hispanic 7%, Native American <1%, Pacific Islander <1%, Two or more races 4%, Race unknown 3%.

Retention and Graduation: 64% freshmen return for sophomore year. 41% freshmen graduate within 4 years. 52% freshmen graduate within 6 years. 10% grads go on to further study within 1 year. **Faculty:** Student/faculty ratio 18:1. 100 full-time faculty, 73% hold PhDs, 6% are members of minority groups, 63% are women. 0% of classes are taught by teaching assistants.

ACADEMICS

Degrees: Associate; Bachelor's; Certificate; Doctoral degree—professional practice; Doctoral degree research/scholarship; Master's; Post-bachelor's certificate; Post-master's certificate. **Classes:** Most classes have fewer than 10 students. **Most popular majors:** Education, Other; Exercise Science and Kinesiology; Business/Commerce, General. **Special Study Options:** Accelerated program; Cross-registration; Distance learning; Double major; Dual enrollment; Independent study; Internships; Student-designed major; Study abroad; Teacher certification program. **Combined degree programs:** BA/MA. **Disability Services offered:** Note-taking services; Reader services; Tape recorders; Tutors. **Career services:** Career assessment; Career/job search classes; Internships.

FACILITIES

Housing: Apartments for married students; Apartments for single students; Coed dorms; Men's dorms; Women's dorms 90% of campus accessible to physically disabled. **Campus Network:** 100% of classrooms, 100% of dorms, 100% of student union, 100% of libraries, 100% of dining areas, 100% of common outdoor areas, have wireless network access.

CAMPUS LIFE

Environment: Metropolis. **Activities:** Campus Ministries; Choral groups; Concert band; Dance; Drama/theater; International Student Organization; Jazz band; Music ensembles; Musical theater; Pep band; Student government; Student newspaper. 40 registered organizations, 1 religious organizations, on campus. **Athletics (Intercollegiate):** *Men:* baseball, basketball, cross-country, football, golf, track/field (outdoor), track/field (indoor). *Women:* basketball, cross-country, golf, soccer, softball, track/field (outdoor), track/field (indoor), volleyball. **On-Campus Highlights:** Residence Life Center.

ADMISSIONS

Freshman Academic Profile: Average high school GPA 3.2. 92% from public high schools. ACT middle 50% range 17–24. **Basis for Candidate Selection:** *Very important factors include:* academic GPA. *Important factors include:* rigor of secondary school record. *Other factors include:* class rank, application essay, standardized test scores, recommendation(s), extracurricular activities, talent/ability, volunteer work, work experience, level of applicant's interest. **Freshman Admission Requirements:** High school diploma is required and GED is accepted. *Academic units required:* 4 English, 2 math, 2 science, 2 social studies, 1 history, 2 visual/performing arts, 1 unit from above areas or other academic areas. *Academic units recommended:* 4 English, 3 math, 3 science, 2 social studies, 2 history, 2 visual/performing arts. **Freshman Admission Statistics:** 1,323 applied, 98% admitted, 27% enrolled. **Transfer Admission Requirements:** college transcript(s), statement of good standing from prior institution(s). Minimum college GPA of 2.0 required. Lowest grade transferable D. **General Admission Information:** Priority deadline 12/1. Regular application deadline 8/1. Non-fall registration accepted. Admission may be deferred for a maximum of 1 year.

COSTS AND FINANCIAL AID

Annual tuition $23,400. Room and board $9,600. Average book and supplies expense $2,000. **Required Forms and Deadlines:** FAFSA; State aid form. **Notification of Awards:** Applicants will be notified of awards on a rolling basis beginning 12/1. **Types of Aid:** *Need-based scholarships/grants:* College/university scholarship or grant aid from institutional funds; Federal Pell; Private scholarships; SEOG; State scholarships/grants. *Loans:* Direct PLUS loans; Direct Subsidized Stafford Loans; Direct Unsubsidized Stafford Loans. **Student Employment:** Federal Work-Study Program available. Institutional employment available. **Financial Aid Statistics:** 100% needy freshmen, 94% needy undergrads receive need-based scholarship or grant aid. 7% freshmen, 6% undergrads receive non-need-based scholarship or grant aid. 90% freshmen, 82% undergrads receive need-based self-help aid. 7% freshmen, 6% undergrads receive athletic scholarships. 97% freshmen, 88% undergrads receive any aid. 75% undergrads borrow to pay for school. Average cumulative indebtedness $32,815. **Criteria awarding aid:** *Need-based:* Academics, Art, Athletics, Leadership, Music/drama, Religious affiliation. *Non-Need-based:* Academics, Art, Athletics, Music/drama, Religious affiliation.

CONCORDIA UNIVERSITY (WI)

12800 North Lake Shore Drive, Mequon, WI 53097-2418
Phone: 262-243-5700 **Financial Aid Phone:** (262) 243-4392
E-mail: admissions@cuw.edu **CEEB Code:** 1139
Fax: (262) 243-4545 **Website:** www.cuw.edu **ACT Code:** 4574

This private school, affiliated with the Lutheran Church, was founded in 1881. It has a 192 acre campus.

RATINGS

Admissions Selectivity Rating: 80   **Fire Safety Rating:** 60*   **Green Rating:** 60*

STUDENTS AND FACULTY

Enrollment: 4,326. **Student Body:** 65% female, 35% male, 20% out-of-state, 1% international (23 countries represented). Asian 2%, African American 18%, Caucasian 67%, Hispanic 2%, Native American 1%, Pacific Islander <1%, Two or more races 2%, Race unknown 6%.
Retention and Graduation: 74% freshmen return for sophomore year. 28% grads go on to further study within 1 year. **Faculty:** Student/faculty ratio 14:1. 162 full-time faculty, 77% hold PhDs, 6% are members of minority groups, 49% are women. 0% of classes are taught by teaching assistants.

ACADEMICS

Degrees: Associate; Bachelor's; Certificate; Doctoral degree—professional practice; Master's; Post-master's certificate. **Classes:** Most classes have 20–29 students. Most lab/discussion sessions have 20–29 students. **Most popular majors:** Education, General; Business/Commerce, General; Health Professions And Related Programs. **Special Study Options:** Accelerated program; Cross-registration; Distance learning; Double major; Dual enrollment; English as a Second Language (ESL); Exchange student program (domestic); Independent study; Internships; Liberal arts/career combination; Student-designed major; Study abroad; Teacher certification program. **Disability Services offered:** Note-taking services; Reader services; Tape recorders; Tutors. **Career services:** Alumni network; Alumni services; Career assessment; Career/job search classes; Internships; Regional alumni.

FACILITIES

Housing: Men's dorms; Women's dorms **Campus Network:** 25% of classrooms, 0% of dorms, 100% of student union, 75% of libraries, 100% of dining areas, 50% of common outdoor areas, have wireless network access.

CAMPUS LIFE

Environment: Village. **Activities:** Campus Ministries; Choral groups; Concert band; Dance; Drama/theater; International Student Organization; Jazz band; Music ensembles; Musical theater; Pep band; Radio station; Student government; Student newspaper. **Athletics (Intercollegiate):** *Men:* baseball, basketball, cross-country, football, ice hockey, soccer, tennis, track/field (outdoor), volleyball, wrestling. *Women:* basketball, cross-country, ice hockey, soccer, softball, tennis, track/field (outdoor), volleyball. **On-Campus Highlights:** Coberg Residence Hall—new **Environmental Initiatives:** Construction of environmental education center with LEED status.

ADMISSIONS

Freshman Academic Profile: Average high school GPA 3.3. 16% in top 10% of high school class, 40% in top 25% of high school class, 75% in top 50% of high school class. **Test scores:** SAT Math middle 50% range 453–600. SAT EBRW middle 50% range 450–530. ACT middle 50% range 20–25. **Basis for Candidate Selection:** *Very important factors include:* rigor of secondary school record, academic GPA, application essay. *Important factors include:* standardized test scores, character/personal qualities. *Other factors include:* class rank, recommendation(s), interview, extracurricular activities, talent/ability, alumni/ae relation, state residency, religious affiliation/commitment, racial/ethnic status, volunteer work. **Freshman Admission Requirements:** High school diploma is required and GED is accepted. *Academic units required:* 3 English, 2 math, 2 science, 2 social studies, 5 academic electives. *Academic units recommended:* 4 English, 3 math, 2 foreign language, 5 academic electives. **Freshman Admission Statistics:** 2,517 applied, 70% admitted, 35% enrolled. **Transfer Admission Requirements:** college transcript(s), statement of good standing from prior institution(s). Minimum college GPA of 2.0 required. Lowest grade transferable C. **General Admission Information:** Application fee $35. Regular application deadline 8/15.

COSTS AND FINANCIAL AID

Required Forms and Deadlines: FAFSA. **Notification of Awards:** Applicants will be notified of awards on a rolling basis beginning 2/1. **Types of Aid:**

Need-based scholarships/grants: College/university scholarship or grant aid from institutional funds; Federal Pell; Private scholarships; SEOG; State scholarships/grants. *Loans:* Direct PLUS loans; Direct Subsidized Stafford Loans; Direct Unsubsidized Stafford Loans. **Financial Aid Statistics:** 97% needy freshmen, 93% needy undergrads receive need-based scholarship or grant aid. 22% freshmen, 16% undergrads receive non-need-based scholarship or grant aid. 82% freshmen, 83% undergrads receive need-based self-help aid. 0% freshmen, 0% undergrads receive athletic scholarships. 95% freshmen receive any aid. **Criteria awarding aid:** *Need-based:* Academics. *Non-Need-based:* Academics, Art, Minority status, Music/drama.

CONCORD UNIVERSITY

1000 Vermillion Street, Athens, WV 24712
Phone: 304-384-5248 **Financial Aid Phone:** 304-384-6069
E-mail: admissions@concord.edu **CEEB Code:** 5120
Fax: 304-384-9044 **Website:** www.concord.edu **ACT Code:** 003810

This public school was founded in 1872. It has a 123 acre campus.

RATINGS

Admissions Selectivity Rating: 84   **Fire Safety Rating:** 91   **Green Rating:** 60*

STUDENTS AND FACULTY

Enrollment: 2,611. **Student Body:** 55% female, 45% male, 18% out-of-state, 0% international (16 countries represented). Asian 2%, African American 6%, Caucasian 91%, Hispanic 1%, Native American <1%, Pacific Islander 0%, Two or more races 0%, Race unknown 0%.
Retention and Graduation: 65% freshmen return for sophomore year. 33% grads go on to further study within 1 year. 8% grads pursue arts and sciences degrees. 2% grads pursue law degrees. 10% grads pursue business degrees. 3% grads pursue medical degrees. **Faculty:** Student/faculty ratio 23:1. 121 full-time faculty, 64% hold PhDs, 3% are members of minority groups, 41% are women.

ACADEMICS

Degrees: Associate; Bachelor's; Master's; Terminal Associate. **Classes:** Most classes have 10–19 students. **Most popular majors:** Education, General; Business Administration and Management, General; Social Sciences, General. **Special Study Options:** Cooperative education program; Double major; Dual enrollment; English as a Second Language (ESL); Honors program; Independent study; Student-designed major; Teacher certification program. **Career services:** Alumni services; Career assessment; Career/job search classes; Internships.

FACILITIES

Housing: Apartments for married students; Coed dorms; Men's dorms; Special housing for disabled studentss; Special housing for international students; Women's dorms 100% of campus accessible to physically disabled. **Campus Network:** 100% of classrooms, 100% of dorms, 100% of student union, 100% of libraries, 100% of dining areas, 100% of common outdoor areas, have wireless network access.

CAMPUS LIFE

Environment: Rural. **Activities:** Campus Ministries; Choral groups; Concert band; Drama/theater; International Student Organization; Jazz band; Marching band; Pep band; Radio station; Student government; Student newspaper; Student-run film society; Television station; Yearbook. 57 registered organizations, 1 honor societies, 2 religious organizations, 6 fraternities, 4 sororities, on campus. **Athletics (Intercollegiate):** *Men:* baseball, basketball, cheerleading, cross-country, football, golf, soccer, tennis, track/field (outdoor). *Women:* basketball, cheerleading, cross-country, golf, soccer, softball, tennis, track/field (outdoor), volleyball. **On-Campus Highlights:** Rahall Technology Ctr.

ADMISSIONS

Freshman Academic Profile: Average high school GPA 3.2. 18% in top 10% of high school class, 45% in top 25% of high school class, 73% in top 50% of high school class. 95% from public high schools. **Test scores:** SAT Math middle 50% range 420–520. SAT EBRW middle 50% range 420–540. ACT middle 50% range 17–25. **Basis for Candidate Selection:** *Very important factors include:* rigor of secondary school record. *Important factors include:* class rank, standardized test scores, extracurricular activities. *Other factors include:* application essay, recommendation(s), interview, talent/ability, character/personal qualities, alumni/ae relation, geographical residence, racial/ethnic status, volunteer work, work experience. **Freshman Admission Requirements:** High school diploma is required and GED is accepted. *Academic units required:* 4 English, 4 math, 3 science, 3 science labs, 2 foreign language, 2 social studies, 1 history, 1 visual/performing arts. **Freshman Admission Statistics:** 2,290 applied, 61% admitted, 41% enrolled. **Transfer Admission Requirements:** college transcript(s), Lowest grade transferable D. **General Admission Information:** Non-fall registration accepted. Admission may be deferred for a maximum of 1 year.

COSTS AND FINANCIAL AID

Annual in-state tuition $4,974. Annual out-of-state tuition $11,050. Room and board $6,962. Required fees $85. Average book and supplies expense $1,100. **Required Forms and Deadlines:** FAFSA; Institution's own financial aid form;. **Notification of Awards:** Applicants will be notified of awards on a rolling basis beginning 4/15. **Types of Aid:** *Need-based scholarships/grants:* College/university scholarship or grant aid from institutional funds; Federal Pell; Private scholarships; SEOG; State scholarships/grants. *Loans:* Direct PLUS loans; Direct Subsidized Stafford Loans; Direct Unsubsidized Stafford Loans. **Student Employment:** Federal Work-Study Program available. Institutional employment available. **Financial Aid Statistics:** 84% needy freshmen, 83% needy undergrads receive need-based scholarship or grant aid. 52% freshmen, 36% undergrads receive non-need-based scholarship or grant aid. 73% freshmen, 74% undergrads receive need-based self-help aid. 5% freshmen, 4% undergrads receive athletic scholarships. 90% freshmen, 77% undergrads receive any aid. **Criteria awarding aid:** *Non-Need-based:* Academics, Alumni affiliation, Art, Athletics, Job skills, Leadership, Minority status, Music/drama, State/district residency.

CONNECTICUT COLLEGE

Best Colleges

270 Mohegan Avenue, New London, CT 06320
Phone: 860-439-2200 **Financial Aid Phone:** 860-439-2058
E-mail: admission@conncoll.edu **CEEB Code:** 3284
Fax: 860-439-4301 **Website:** www.conncoll.edu **ACT Code:** 0556

This private school was founded in 1911. It has a 750 acre campus.

RATINGS
Admissions Selectivity Rating: 93   **Fire Safety Rating:** 62   **Green Rating:** 91

STUDENTS AND FACULTY
Enrollment: 1,798. **Student Body:** 62% female, 38% male, 81% out-of-state, 7% international (42 countries represented). Asian 5%, African American 4%, Caucasian 70%, Hispanic 9%, Native American <1%, Pacific Islander <1%, Two or more races 4%, Race unknown 2%.
Retention and Graduation: 91% freshmen return for sophomore year. 80% freshmen graduate within 4 years. 85% freshmen graduate within 6 years. 12% grads go on to further study within 1 year. **Faculty:** Student/faculty ratio 9:1. 172 full-time faculty, 94% hold PhDs, 20% are members of minority groups, 53% are women. 0% of classes are taught by teaching assistants.

ACADEMICS
Degrees: Bachelor's. **Classes:** Most classes have 10–19 students. Most lab/discussion sessions have 10–19 students. **Most popular majors:** Psychology, General; English Language and Literature, General; Economics, General. **Special Study Options:** Accelerated program; Cross-registration; Double major; Exchange student program (domestic); Independent study; Internships; Student-designed major; Study abroad; Teacher certification program. **Disability Services offered:** Note-taking services; Reader services; Tape recorders; Tutors. **Career services:** Alumni network; Alumni services; Career assessment; Career/job search classes; Internships; Regional alumni.

FACILITIES
Housing: Apartments for single students; Coed dorms; Theme housing; Wellness housing **Special Academic Facilities/Equipment:** Fully renovated life sciences building and main college library, Children's Program used as "lab school" for human development program, language lab, 750-acre arboretum, botanical garden, greenhouse, environment control labs, transmission and scanning electron microscope, ion accelerator, GIS lab, refracting telescope, observatory. **Campus Network:** 100% of classrooms, 100% of dorms, 100%

of student union, 100% of libraries, 100% of dining areas, 100% of common outdoor areas, have wireless network access.

CAMPUS LIFE
Environment: Town. **Activities:** Campus Ministries; Choral groups; Concert band; Dance; Drama/theater; International Student Organization; Jazz band; Literary magazine; Music ensembles; Musical theater; Radio station; Student government; Student newspaper; Student-run film society; Symphony orchestra. 80 registered organizations, 8 honor societies, on campus. **Athletics (Intercollegiate):** *Men:* basketball, crew/rowing, cross-country, diving, ice hockey, lacrosse, sailing, soccer, squash, swimming, tennis, track/field (outdoor), track/field (indoor), water polo. *Women:* basketball, crew/rowing, cross-country, diving, field hockey, ice hockey, lacrosse, sailing, soccer, squash, swimming, tennis, track/field (outdoor), track/field (indoor), volleyball, water polo. **On-Campus Highlights:** College Center (Crozier-Williams).

ADMISSIONS
Freshman Academic Profile: 49% in top 10% of high school class, 80% in top 25% of high school class, 98% in top 50% of high school class. 50% from public high schools. **Test scores:** SAT Math middle 50% range 640–720. SAT EBRW middle 50% range 650–710. ACT middle 50% range 30–32. **Basis for Candidate Selection:** *Very important factors include:* rigor of secondary school record, class rank, academic GPA, character/personal qualities. *Important factors include:* application essay, recommendation(s), interview, extracurricular activities, talent/ability. *Other factors include:* standardized test scores, first generation, alumni/ae relation, geographical residence, state residency, religious affiliation/commitment, level of applicant's interest. **Freshman Admission Requirements:** High school diploma is required and GED is accepted. **Freshman Admission Statistics:** 6,433 applied, 38% admitted, 21% enrolled. **Transfer Admission Requirements:** High school transcript, college transcript(s), essay or personal statement, statement of good standing from prior institution(s). Lowest grade transferable C. **General Admission Information:** Regular application deadline 1/1. Non-fall registration accepted. Admission may be deferred for a maximum of 1 year.

COSTS AND FINANCIAL AID
Annual tuition $56,540. Room and board $15,700. Required fees $350. Average book and supplies expense $1,000. **Required Forms and Deadlines:** CSS/Financial Aid PROFILE; FAFSA; Noncustodial PROFILE. **Notification of Awards:** Applicants will be notified of awards on or about 4/1. **Types of Aid:** *Need-based scholarships/grants:* College/university scholarship or grant aid from institutional funds; Federal Pell; SEOG; State scholarships/grants. *Loans:* Direct PLUS loans; Direct Subsidized Stafford Loans; Direct Unsubsidized Stafford Loans. **Student Employment:** Federal Work-Study Program available. Institutional employment available. **Financial Aid Statistics:** 97% needy freshmen, 95% needy undergrads receive need-based scholarship or grant aid. 13% freshmen, 9% undergrads receive non-need-based scholarship or grant aid. 82% freshmen, 87% undergrads receive need-based self-help aid. 0% freshmen, 0% undergrads receive athletic scholarships. 93% freshmen receive any aid. 45% undergrads borrow to pay for school. Average cumulative indebtedness $33,608. **Criteria awarding aid:** *Need-based:* Academics, Alumni affiliation, Art, Athletics, Job skills, Leadership, Minority status, Music/drama, Religious affiliation.

CONVERSE COLLEGE

580 East Main Street, Spartanburg, SC 29302
Phone: 864-596-9040 **Financial Aid Phone:** 864-596-9019
E-mail: admissions@converse.edu **CEEB Code:** 5121
Fax: 864-596-9225 **Website:** www.converse.edu **ACT Code:** 3852

This private school was founded in 1889. It has a 70 acre campus.

RATINGS
Admissions Selectivity Rating: 86   **Fire Safety Rating:** 79   **Green Rating:** 60*

STUDENTS AND FACULTY
Enrollment: 687. **Student Body:** 100% female, 0% male, 23% out-of-state, 1% international. Asian 1%, African American 8%, Caucasian 46%, Hispanic 3%, Native American <1%, Pacific Islander <1%, Two or more races 3%, Race unknown 39%.
Retention and Graduation: 76% freshmen return for sophomore year. 37% grads go on to further study within 1 year. **Faculty:** Student/faculty ratio 11:1.

76 full-time faculty, 91% hold PhDs, 7% are members of minority groups, 59% are women. 0% of classes are taught by teaching assistants.

ACADEMICS

Degrees: Bachelor's; Master's; Post-master's certificate. **Classes:** Most classes have fewer than 10 students. Most lab/discussion sessions have fewer than 10 students. **Most popular majors:** Education, General; Biology, General; Psychology, General. **Special Study Options:** Cross-registration; Double major; English as a Second Language (ESL); Honors program; Independent study; Internships; Liberal arts/career combination; Student-designed major; Study abroad; Teacher certification program. **Honors programs:** Nisbet Honors Program. **Disability Services offered:** Note-taking services; Tape recorders; Tutors. **Career services:** Alumni network; Alumni services; Career assessment; Career/job search classes; Internships; Regional alumni.

FACILITIES

Housing: Apartments for single students; Wellness housing; Women's dorms. **Special Academic Facilities/Equipment:** Phifer Science Building, Blackman Auditorium (Music), DNA sequencer and lab. Twitchel Auditorium (Performing Arts).

CAMPUS LIFE

Environment: City. **Activities:** Campus Ministries; Choral groups; Concert band; Dance; Drama/theater; International Student Organization; Literary magazine; Model UN; Music ensembles; Musical theater; Opera; Student government; Student newspaper; Symphony orchestra; Yearbook. 55 registered organizations, 16 honor societies, 7 religious organizations, on campus. **Athletics (Intercollegiate):** *Women:* basketball, cross-country, lacrosse, soccer, swimming, tennis, volleyball. **On-Campus Highlights:** Montgomery Student Life Center. **Environmental Initiatives:** LEED Certified new construction.

ADMISSIONS

Freshman Academic Profile: 18% in top 10% of high school class, 43% in top 25% of high school class, 80% in top 50% of high school class. 80% from public high schools. **Test scores:** SAT Math middle 50% range 460–570. SAT EBRW middle 50% range 470–600. ACT middle 50% range 20–26. **Basis for Candidate Selection:** *Very important factors include:* academic GPA, standardized test scores. *Important factors include:* rigor of secondary school record, class rank. *Other factors include:* application essay, recommendation(s), talent/ability, alumni/ae relation. **Freshman Admission Requirements:** High school diploma is required and GED is accepted. *Academic units recommended:* 4 English, 3 math, 3 science, 1 science labs, 2 foreign language, 2 social studies, 2 history, 8 academic electives. **Freshman Admission Statistics:** 1,383 applied, 51% admitted, 26% enrolled. **Transfer Admission Requirements:** college transcript(s), statement of good standing from prior institution(s). Minimum college GPA of 2.0 required. Lowest grade transferable C. **General Admission Information:** Priority deadline 3/1. Non-fall registration accepted. Admission may be deferred for a maximum of 1 year.

COSTS AND FINANCIAL AID

Annual tuition $27,276. Room and board $8,854. Required fees $1,000. Average book and supplies expense $1,000. **Required Forms and Deadlines:** FAFSA. **Notification of Awards:** Applicants will be notified of awards on a rolling basis beginning 3/1. *Types of Aid: Need-based scholarships/grants:* College/university scholarship or grant aid from institutional funds; Federal Pell; Private scholarships; SEOG; State scholarships/grants. *Loans:* Direct PLUS loans; Direct Subsidized Stafford Loans; Direct Unsubsidized Stafford Loans. **Student Employment:** Federal Work-Study Program available. Institutional employment available. **Financial Aid Statistics:** 100% needy freshmen, 98% needy undergrads receive need-based scholarship or grant aid. 18% freshmen, 17% undergrads receive non-need-based scholarship or grant aid. 79% freshmen, 76% undergrads receive need-based self-help aid. 14% freshmen, 8% undergrads receive athletic scholarships. 95% freshmen, 93% undergrads receive any aid. **Criteria awarding aid:** *Need-based:* Academics, Art, Athletics, Music/drama *Non-Need-based:* Academics, Art, Athletics, Music/drama.

THE COOPER UNION FOR THE ADVANCEMENT OF SCIENCE AND ART

30 Cooper Square, 3rd Floor, New York, NY 10003
Phone: 212-353-4120 **Financial Aid Phone:** 212-353-4113
E-mail: admissions@cooper.edu **CEEB Code:** 2097
Fax: 212-353-4342 **Website:** www.cooper.edu **ACT Code:** 2724

This private school was founded in 1859.

RATINGS
Admissions Selectivity Rating: 97   **Fire Safety Rating:** 97   **Green Rating:** 60*

STUDENTS AND FACULTY
Enrollment: 844. **Student Body:** 41% female, 59% male, 44% out-of-state, 16% international. Asian 24%, African American 5%, Caucasian 32%, Hispanic 12%, Native American 0%, Pacific Islander 0%, Two or more races 4%, Race unknown 8%.
Retention and Graduation: 93% freshmen return for sophomore year. 69% freshmen graduate within 4 years. 91% freshmen graduate within 6 years. 30% grads go on to further study within 1 year. **Faculty:** Student/faculty ratio 8:1. 54 full-time faculty, 94% hold PhDs, 19% are members of minority groups, 31% are women. 0% of classes are taught by teaching assistants.

ACADEMICS
Degrees: Bachelor's; Master's. **Classes:** Most classes have 10–19 students. Most lab/discussion sessions have 10–19 students. **Most popular majors:** Electrical and Electronics Engineering; Mechanical Engineering. **Special Study Options:** Independent study; Study abroad. **Honors programs:** Cooper Union is in essence an all-honors college. **Combined degree programs:** BA/MEng. **Disability Services offered:** Tape recorders; Tutors. **Career services:** Alumni network; Alumni services; Career assessment; Career/job search classes; Internships; Regional alumni.

FACILITIES
Housing: Coed dorms. **Special Academic Facilities/Equipment:** The Great Hall; Houghton Gallery; Institute for Sustainable Design; Center for Innovation and Applied Technology; SEA²M³; S*PROCOM²; Center for Urban Infrastructure; Institute for Urban Security; Maurice Kanbar Center for Biomedical Engineering.

CAMPUS LIFE
Environment: Metropolis. **Activities:** Student government; Student newspaper. 72 registered organizations, 18 honor societies, 8 religious organizations, 1 fraternity, on campus. **Athletics (Intercollegiate):** *Men:* baseball, basketball, cross-country, soccer, tennis, volleyball. *Women:* basketball, cross-country, soccer, tennis, volleyball. **On-Campus Highlights:** Great Hall. **Environmental Initiatives:** 41 Cooper Square Building is LEED Certified (see cooper.edu); Faculty research Hosted Climate Week.

ADMISSIONS
Freshman Academic Profile: Average high school GPA 3.8. **Test scores:** SAT Math middle 50% range 655–790. SAT EBRW middle 50% range 650–740. ACT middle 50% range 30–35. **Basis for Candidate Selection:** *Very important factors include:* academic GPA, standardized test scores, talent/ability. *Important factors include:* rigor of secondary school record, application essay, recommendation(s), interview, character/personal qualities. *Other factors include:* class rank, extracurricular activities, first generation, alumni/ae relation, racial/ethnic status, volunteer work, work experience, level of applicant's interest. **Freshman Admission Requirements:** High school diploma is required and GED is accepted. *Academic units required:* 4 English, 1 math, 1 science, 1 social studies, 1 history, 8 academic electives. *Academic units recommended:* 4 English, 4 math, 4 science, 3 science labs, 2 foreign language, 4 social studies. **Freshman Admission Statistics:** 2,326 applied, 16% admitted, 50% enrolled. **Transfer Admission Requirements:** High school transcript, college transcript(s), essay or personal statement, standardized test scores, statement of good standing from prior institution(s). Minimum college GPA of 3.0 required. Lowest grade transferable B. **General Admission Information:** Application fee $75. Regular application deadline 1/6.

COSTS AND FINANCIAL AID

Annual tuition $44,550. Required fees $2,270. Average book and supplies expense $1,800. **Required Forms and Deadlines:** FAFSA. **Notification of Awards:** Applicants will be notified of awards on a rolling basis beginning 12/20. **Types of Aid:** *Need-based scholarships/grants:* College/university scholarship or grant aid from institutional funds; Federal Pell; Private scholarships; SEOG; State scholarships/grants. *Loans:* Direct PLUS loans; Direct Subsidized Stafford Loans; Direct Unsubsidized Stafford Loans. **Student Employment:** Federal Work-Study Program available. Institutional employment available. **Financial Aid Statistics:** 100% needy freshmen, 100% needy undergrads receive need-based scholarship or grant aid. 100% freshmen, 100% undergrads receive non-need-based scholarship or grant aid. 23% freshmen, 25% undergrads receive need-based self-help aid. 0% freshmen, 0% undergrads receive athletic scholarships. 100% freshmen, 100% undergrads receive any aid. 53% undergrads borrow to pay for school. Average cumulative indebtedness $10,742. **Criteria awarding aid:** *Need-based:* Academics. *Non-Need-based:* Academics.

CORBAN UNIVERSITY

5000 Deer Park Drive SE, Salem, OR 97317
Phone: 503-375-7005 **Financial Aid Phone:** 503-375-7030
E-mail: admissions@corban.edu
Fax: 503-585-4316 **Website:** www.corban.edu **ACT Code:** 477

This private school, affiliated with the Evangelical Church, was founded in 1935. It has a 145 acre campus.

RATINGS

Admissions Selectivity Rating: 88   **Fire Safety Rating:** 85   **Green Rating:** 60*

STUDENTS AND FACULTY

Enrollment: 933. **Student Body:** 60% female, 40% male, 50% out-of-state, 2% international (7 countries represented). Asian 3%, African American 1%, Caucasian 78%, Hispanic 3%, Native American 1%, Pacific Islander 1%, Two or more races 6%, Race unknown 6%.
Retention and Graduation: 77% freshmen return for sophomore year.
Faculty: Student/faculty ratio 14:1. 49 full-time faculty, 73% hold PhDs, 0% are members of minority groups, 22% are women. 0% of classes are taught by teaching assistants.

ACADEMICS

Degrees: Associate; Bachelor's; Doctoral degree—other; Master's. **Classes:** Most classes have 10–19 students. Most lab/discussion sessions have 10–19 students. **Most popular majors:** Education, General; Pre-Medicine/Pre-Medical Studies; Business Administration and Management, General. **Special Study Options:** Accelerated program; Cross-registration; Distance learning; Double major; Dual enrollment; Honors program; Independent study; Internships; Liberal arts/career combination; Study abroad; Teacher certification program. **Honors programs:** In keeping with the broad educational mission of Corban University, the Honors Program is rooted in the notion that we may glorify God through our intellectual endeavors. The program provides highly motivated students with academic enrichment above and beyond the regular undergraduate curriculum, encouraging a more proficient understanding of and appreciation for the Christian worldview through the lens of classical studies, especially history, literature, philosophy, and the arts. Honors students are given the opportunity to interact with distinguished scholars at special events and to participate in at least three Honors courses while at Corban. They also may choose to work with a faculty member on a senior project. **Combined degree programs:** BA/MA. **Disability Services offered:** Note-taking services; Reader services; Tape recorders; Tutors. **Career services:** Career assessment; Career/job search classes; Internships.

FACILITIES

Housing: Apartments for single students; Men's dorms; Women's dorms 80% of campus accessible to physically disabled. **Special Academic Facilities/ Equipment:** Prewitt-Allen Archeological Museum Psalms Performing Arts Center.

CAMPUS LIFE

Environment: City. **Activities:** Campus Ministries; Choral groups; Concert band; Drama/theater; Jazz band; Literary magazine; Music ensembles; Musical theater; Radio station; Student government; Student newspaper; Student-run film society; Symphony orchestra; Yearbook. 21 registered organizations, 1 honor societies, on campus. **Athletics (Intercollegiate):** *Men:* baseball, basketball, cross-country, golf, soccer, track/field (outdoor). *Women:* basketball, cross-country, golf, soccer, softball, track/field (outdoor), volleyball. **On-Campus Highlights:** Common Grounds Coffee Shop.

ADMISSIONS

Freshman Academic Profile: Average high school GPA 3.6. 26% in top 10% of high school class, 58% in top 25% of high school class, 88% in top 50% of high school class. 60% from public high schools. **Test scores:** SAT Math middle 50% range 440–560. SAT EBRW middle 50% range 455–580. ACT middle 50% range 18–25. **Basis for Candidate Selection:** *Very important factors include:* academic GPA, application essay, recommendation(s), religious affiliation/commitment. *Important factors include:* rigor of secondary school record, standardized test scores, character/personal qualities. *Other factors include:* class rank, interview, extracurricular activities, alumni/ae relation. **Freshman Admission Requirements:** High school diploma is required and GED is accepted. *Academic units recommended:* 4 English, 3 math, 2 science, 2 foreign language, 3 social studies. **Freshman Admission Statistics:** 2,678 applied, 37% admitted, 22% enrolled. **Transfer Admission Requirements:** High school transcript, college transcript(s), essay or personal statement, Minimum college GPA of 2.00 required. Lowest grade transferable C-. **General Admission Information:** Application fee $40. Priority deadline 3/1. Regular application deadline 8/1. Non-fall registration accepted.

COSTS AND FINANCIAL AID

Annual tuition $28,980. Room and board $9,240. Required fees $660. Average book and supplies expense $900. **Required Forms and Deadlines:** FAFSA. **Notification of Awards:** Applicants will be notified of awards on a rolling basis beginning 3/1. **Types of Aid:** *Need-based scholarships/grants:* College/university scholarship or grant aid from institutional funds; Federal Pell; Private scholarships; SEOG; State scholarships/grants. *Loans:* Direct PLUS loans; Direct Subsidized Stafford Loans; Direct Unsubsidized Stafford Loans. **Student Employment:** Federal Work-Study Program available. Institutional employment available. **Financial Aid Statistics:** needy freshmen, needy undergrads receive need-based scholarship or grant aid. 13% freshmen, 12% undergrads receive non-need-based scholarship or grant aid. 76% freshmen, 74% undergrads receive need-based self-help aid. 10% freshmen, 10% undergrads receive athletic scholarships. 97% freshmen, 97% undergrads receive any aid. **Criteria awarding aid:** *Need-based:* Academics, Alumni affiliation, Athletics, Leadership.

CORCORAN COLLEGE OF ART AND DESIGN

500 17th Street NW, Washington, DC 20006-4804
Phone: 202-639-1814 **Financial Aid Phone:** (202) 639-1851
E-mail: admissions@corcoran.org
Fax: 202-639-1830 **Website:** www.corcoran.edu

This private school was founded in 1890.

RATINGS

Admissions Selectivity Rating: 60*   **Fire Safety Rating:** 67   **Green Rating:** 60*

STUDENTS AND FACULTY

Enrollment: 600.
Faculty: Student/faculty ratio 15:1. 0% of classes are taught by teaching assistants.

ACADEMICS

Degrees: Associate; Bachelor's; Certificate; Master's. **Most popular majors:** Photography; Graphic Design; Fine/Studio Arts, General. **Career services:** Alumni network; Alumni services; Career/job search classes; Internships.

FACILITIES

Special Academic Facilities/Equipment: Art gallery. Student exhibition spaces. **Campus Network:** 100% of classrooms, 100% of dorms, 100% of student union, 100% of libraries, 100% of dining areas, 100% of common outdoor areas, have wireless network access.

CAMPUS LIFE

Environment: Metropolis. **On-Campus Highlights:** Corcoran Gallery.

ADMISSIONS

Freshman Admission Requirements: High school diploma is required and GED is accepted. **Freshman Admission Statistics:** applied, admitted, enrolled. **Transfer Admission Requirements:** High school transcript, college transcript(s), Minimum college GPA of 2.5 required. Lowest grade transferable C. **General Admission Information:** Application fee $45.

COSTS AND FINANCIAL AID

Annual tuition $30,930.

CORNELL COLLEGE

600 First Street South West, Mount Vernon, IA 52314-1098
Phone: 319-895-4215 **Financial Aid Phone:** 319-895-4216
E-mail: admission@cornellcollege.edu **CEEB Code:** 6119
Fax: 319-895-4451 **Website:** www.cornellcollege.edu **ACT Code:** 1296

This private school, affiliated with the Methodist Church, was founded in 1853. It has a 129 acre campus.

RATINGS

Admissions Selectivity Rating: 86   **Fire Safety Rating:** 83   **Green Rating:** 60*

STUDENTS AND FACULTY

Enrollment: 1,015. **Student Body:** 48% female, 52% male, 76% out-of-state, 7% international (19 countries represented). Asian 4%, African American 6%, Caucasian 68%, Hispanic 8%, Native American 2%, Pacific Islander <1%, Two or more races 1%, Race unknown 4%.
Retention and Graduation: 82% freshmen return for sophomore year. 65% freshmen graduate within 4 years. 68% freshmen graduate within 6 years. 17% grads go on to further study within 1 year. 16% grads pursue arts and sciences degrees. 5% grads pursue law degrees. 1% grads pursue business degrees. 3% grads pursue medical degrees. **Faculty:** Student/faculty ratio 12:1. 74 full-time faculty, 97% hold PhDs, 8% are members of minority groups, 51% are women. 0% of classes are taught by teaching assistants.

ACADEMICS

Degrees: Bachelor's. **Classes:** Most classes have 10–19 students. **Most popular majors:** Psychology, General; Economics, General. **Special Study Options:** Double major; Dual enrollment; Independent study; Internships; Student-designed major; Study abroad; Teacher certification program. **Combined degree programs:** BA/JD; BA/MA. **Disability Services offered:** Note-taking services; Reader services; Tape recorders; Tutors. **Career services:** Alumni network; Alumni services; Career assessment; Career/job search classes; Internships; Regional alumni.

FACILITIES

Housing: Apartments for single students; Coed dorms; Theme housing; Women's dorms 51% of campus accessible to physically disabled. **Special Academic Facilities/Equipment:** Geology center and museum, MNR machine in West Sc. Building, Luce Art Gallery. **Campus Network:** 100% of classrooms, 100% of dorms, 100% of student union, 100% of libraries, 100% of dining areas, 100% of common outdoor areas, have wireless network access.

CAMPUS LIFE

Environment: Rural. **Activities:** Campus Ministries; Choral groups; Concert band; Dance; Drama/theater; International Student Organization; Jazz band; Literary magazine; Music ensembles; Musical theater; Radio station; Student government; Student newspaper; Symphony orchestra; Yearbook. 63 registered organizations, 16 honor societies, 6 religious organizations, 8 fraternities, 7 sororities, on campus. **Athletics (Intercollegiate):** *Men:* baseball, basketball, cross-country, football, golf, soccer, tennis, track/field (outdoor), track/field (indoor), wrestling. *Women:* basketball, cross-country, golf, soccer, softball, tennis, track/field (outdoor), track/field (indoor), volleyball. **On-Campus Highlights:** Thomas Commons—Orange Carpet—student center **Environmental Initiatives:** Engineering study on costs of replacing current campus-side steam heat network, including specific costs and energy savings payback times for each building. Implementation of plan in two building remodels and designed into two upcoming remodel projects.

ADMISSIONS

Freshman Academic Profile: Average high school GPA 3.5. 25% in top 10% of high school class, 50% in top 25% of high school class, 83% in top 50% of high school class. 85% from public high schools. **Test scores:** SAT Math middle 50% range 540–650. SAT EBRW middle 50% range 540–670. ACT middle 50% range 23–30. **Basis for Candidate Selection:** *Very important factors include:* academic GPA. *Important factors include:* application essay, standardized test scores. *Other factors include:* rigor of secondary school record, class rank, recommendation(s), interview, extracurricular activities, character/personal qualities, first generation, alumni/ae relation, geographical residence, state residency, racial/ethnic status, volunteer work, work experience, level of applicant's interest. **Freshman Admission Requirements:** High school diploma is required and GED is accepted. *Academic units recommended:* 4 English, 3 math, 3 science, 1 science labs, 2 foreign language, 3 social studies. **Freshman Admission Statistics:** 2,532 applied, 61% admitted, 19% enrolled. **Transfer Admission Requirements:** College transcript(s), essay or personal statement, statement of good standing from prior institution(s). Lowest grade transferable C. **General Admission Information:** Admission may be deferred for a maximum of 2 years.

COSTS AND FINANCIAL AID

Annual tuition $43,550. Room and board $9,760. Required fees $426. Average book and supplies expense $1,200. **Required Forms and Deadlines:** FAFSA. **Notification of Awards:** Applicants will be notified of awards on a rolling basis beginning 3/1. **Types of Aid:** *Need-based scholarships/grants:* College/university scholarship or grant aid from institutional funds; Federal Pell; SEOG; State scholarships/grants. *Loans:* Direct PLUS loans; Direct Subsidized Stafford Loans; Direct Unsubsidized Stafford Loans. **Student Employment:** Federal Work-Study Program available. Institutional employment available. **Financial Aid Statistics:** 100% needy freshmen, 100% needy undergrads receive need-based scholarship or grant aid. 23% freshmen, 16% undergrads receive non-need-based scholarship or grant aid. 71% freshmen, 78% undergrads receive need-based self-help aid. 0% freshmen, 0% undergrads receive athletic scholarships. 100% freshmen, 99% undergrads receive any aid. 73% undergrads borrow to pay for school. Average cumulative indebtedness $31,142. **Criteria awarding aid:** *Non-Need-based:* Academics, Alumni affiliation, Art, Leadership, Music/drama, Religious affiliation, State/district residency.

CORNELL UNIVERSITY

410 Thurston Ave, Ithaca, NY 14850
Phone: 607-255-5241 **Financial Aid Phone:** 607-255-5145
E-mail: admissions@cornell.edu **CEEB Code:** 2098
Fax: 607-255-0659 **Website:** www.cornell.edu **ACT Code:** 2726

This private school was founded in 1865. It has a 745 acre campus.

RATINGS

Admissions Selectivity Rating: 99   **Fire Safety Rating:** 96   **Green Rating:** 99

STUDENTS AND FACULTY

Enrollment: 14,976. **Student Body:** 54% female, 46% male, 10% international (90 countries represented). Asian 20%, African American 7%, Caucasian 36%, Hispanic 14%, Native American <1%, Pacific Islander <1%, Two or more races 5%, Race unknown 8%.
Retention and Graduation: 97% freshmen return for sophomore year. 87% freshmen graduate within 4 years. 95% freshmen graduate within 6 years.
Faculty: Student/faculty ratio 9:1. 1,817 full-time faculty, 93% hold PhDs, 19% are members of minority groups, 37% are women.

ACADEMICS

Degrees: Bachelor's; Doctoral degree—professional practice; Doctoral degree research/scholarship; Master's. **Classes:** Most classes have 10–19 students. Most lab/discussion sessions have 10–19 students. **Most popular majors:** Biology/Biological Sciences, General. **Special Study Options:** Accelerated program; Cooperative education program; Cross-registration; Distance learning; Double major; English as a Second Language (ESL); Exchange student program (domestic); Honors program; Independent study; Internships; Liberal arts/career combination; Student-designed major; Study abroad. **Disability Services**

For more free content, visit PrincetonReview.com

offered: Note-taking services; Reader services; Tape recorders; Tutors. **Career services:** Alumni network; Alumni services; Career assessment; Career/job search classes; Internships; Regional alumni.

FACILITIES

Housing: Apartments for single students; Coed dorms; Cooperative housing; Fraternity/sorority housing; Special housing for disabled students; Special housing for international students; Theme housing; Women's dorms **Special Academic Facilities/Equipment:** Institute of Biotechnology, performing arts center, veterinary medical center, a woods sanctuary, 4 designated national resource centers, 2 local optical observatories, Africana studies and research center, arboretum, botanical garden, particle accelerator, supercomputer, national research centers, art museum, lab of ornithology, vertebrates museum, living and learning communities, campus orchard, dairy pilot plant, mineralogical museum, animal teaching hospital, 2 agricultural experiment stations, and marine laboratory.

CAMPUS LIFE

Environment: Town. **Activities:** Campus Ministries; Choral groups; Concert band; Dance; Drama/theater; International Student Organization; Jazz band; Literary magazine; Marching band; Model UN; Music ensembles; Musical theater; Pep band; Radio station; Student government; Student newspaper; Student-run film society; Symphony orchestra; Television station; Yearbook. 1275 registered organizations, 15 honor societies, 26 religious organizations, 37 fraternities, 19 sororities, on campus. **Athletics (Intercollegiate):** *Men:* baseball, basketball, crew/rowing, cross-country, diving, football, golf, ice hockey, lacrosse, polo, soccer, squash, swimming, tennis, track/field (outdoor), track/field (indoor), wrestling. *Women:* basketball, crew/rowing, cross-country, diving, equestrian sports, fencing, field hockey, gymnastics, ice hockey, lacrosse, polo, soccer, softball, squash, swimming, tennis, track/field (outdoor), track/field (indoor), volleyball. **On-Campus Highlights:** Lynah Rink **Environmental Initiatives:** The Sustainable Cornell Council (SCC, formed in 2019) is an interdisciplinary, cross-campus team responsible for directing and coordinating Cornell's role in addressing climate change and sustainability, advancing meaningful progress in our operations, and advancing active engagement from the campus community. The Council includes three steering committees, a leadership team, and working groups. Steering Committees identify working priorities and lead short-term groups each year with broad membership from the campus to advance sustainability projects, initiatives, and campus research. The Campus Sustainability Office helps coordinate the SCC, and hosted several Orientations/Trainings/Coaching sessions for its members. The SCC provides outreach and engagement opportunities to the entire campus community, including annual Sustainability Leadership Summits, university-wide educational outreach and communications, and opportunities for the campus community to propose and collaborate on initiatives. Members of the SCC lead conversations within their teams and units focused on enacting our Climate Action Plan, advancing sustainable change in their areas, etc—and bring back ideas back to the SCC for consideration. The SCC has members from our university assemblies, and engages in assembly meetings as part of its outreach activities.

ADMISSIONS

Freshman Academic Profile: 83% in top 10% of high school class, 96% in top 25% of high school class, 99% in top 50% of high school class. **Test scores:** SAT Math middle 50% range 720–800. SAT EBRW middle 50% range 680–760. ACT middle 50% range 32–35. **Basis for Candidate Selection:** *Very important factors include:* rigor of secondary school record, academic GPA, application essay, standardized test scores, recommendation(s), extracurricular activities, talent/ability, character/personal qualities. *Important factors include:* class rank. *Other factors include:* interview, first generation, alumni/ae relation, geographical residence, state residency, racial/ethnic status, volunteer work, work experience. **Freshman Admission Requirements:** High school diploma or equivalent is not required **Freshman Admission Statistics:** 49,114 applied, 11% admitted, 60% enrolled. **Transfer Admission Requirements:** High school transcript, college transcript(s), essay or personal statement, statement of good standing from prior institution(s). Lowest grade transferable C. **General Admission Information:** Application fee $80. Regular application deadline 1/2. Non-fall registration accepted.

COSTS AND FINANCIAL AID

Annual tuition $56,550. Room and board $14,816. Required fees $604. Average book and supplies expense $970. **Required Forms and Deadlines:** CSS/Financial Aid PROFILE; FAFSA; Noncustodial PROFILE. **Notification of Awards:** Applicants will be notified of awards on or about 4/1. **Types of Aid:** *Need-based scholarships/grants:* College/university scholarship or grant aid from institutional funds; Federal Pell; Private scholarships; SEOG; State scholarships/grants. *Loans:* Direct PLUS loans; Direct Subsidized Stafford Loans; Direct

Unsubsidized Stafford Loans. **Student Employment:** Federal Work-Study Program available. Institutional employment available. **Financial Aid Statistics:** 97% needy freshmen, 96% needy undergrads receive need-based scholarship or grant aid. 0% freshmen, 0% undergrads receive non-need-based scholarship or grant aid. 86% freshmen, 91% undergrads receive need-based self-help aid. 0% freshmen, 0% undergrads receive athletic scholarships. 47% freshmen, 47% undergrads receive any aid. 40% undergrads borrow to pay for school. Average cumulative indebtedness $27,094. **Criteria awarding aid:** *Need-based:* Leadership.

CORNERSTONE UNIVERSITY

1001 East Beltline Avenue, NE, Grand Rapids, MI 49525-5897
Phone: 616-222-1418 **Financial Aid Phone:** 616-949-5300
E-mail: admissions@cornerstone.edu
Fax: 616-222-1418 **Website:** www.cornerstone.edu **ACT Code:** 2002

This private school, affiliated with the Christian (Nondenominational) Church, was founded in 1941. It has a 130 acre campus.

RATINGS

Admissions Selectivity Rating: 77 · **Fire Safety Rating:** 96 · **Green Rating:** 60*

STUDENTS AND FACULTY

Enrollment: 1,741. **Student Body:** 59% female, 41% male, 16% out-of-state, 1% international (15 countries represented). Asian 1%, African American 11%, Caucasian 83%, Hispanic 4%, Native American <1%, Race unknown 0%. **Retention and Graduation:** 69% freshmen return for sophomore year. 15% grads go on to further study within 1 year. 10% grads pursue arts and sciences degrees. 1% grads pursue law degrees. 3% grads pursue business degrees. 1% grads pursue medical degrees. **Faculty:** Student/faculty ratio 13:1. 62 full-time faculty, 50% hold PhDs, 5% are members of minority groups, 32% are women. 0% of classes are taught by teaching assistants.

ACADEMICS

Degrees: Associate; Bachelor's; Certificate; Diploma; Master's; Terminal Associate. **Classes:** Most classes have 10–19 students. **Most popular majors:** Youth Ministry; Elementary Education and Teaching; Mass Communication/Media Studies. **Special Study Options:** Accelerated program; Distance learning; Double major; Dual enrollment; English as a Second Language (ESL); Honors program; Independent study; Internships; Liberal arts/career combination; Study abroad; Teacher certification program; Weekend college. **Honors programs:** Honors Program based on a "great books" curriculum. **Disability Services offered:** Note-taking services; Reader services; Tape recorders; Tutors. **Career services:** Career assessment; Career/job search classes; Internships.

FACILITIES

Housing: Apartments for married students; Apartments for single students; Men's dorms; Special housing for disabled students; Theme housing; Women's dorms 100% of campus accessible to physically disabled.

CAMPUS LIFE

Environment: City. **Activities:** Campus Ministries; Choral groups; Concert band; Dance; Drama/theater; International Student Organization; Jazz band; Literary magazine; Music ensembles; Musical theater; Opera; Pep band; Radio station; Student government; Student newspaper; Student-run film society. 11 registered organizations, 2 honor societies, 1 religious organizations, on campus. **Athletics (Intercollegiate):** *Men:* basketball, cross-country, golf, soccer, track/field (outdoor), track/field (indoor). *Women:* basketball, cross-country, golf, soccer, softball, track/field (outdoor), track/field (indoor), volleyball. **On-Campus Highlights:** Corum Student Union. **Environmental Initiatives:** On campus dialogue and focus on sustainability issues.

ADMISSIONS

Freshman Academic Profile: Average high school GPA 3.3. % in top 10% of high school class, % in top 25% of high school class, % in top 50% of high school class. 60% from public high schools. **Test scores:** SAT Math middle 50% range 440–540. SAT EBRW middle 50% range 360–580. ACT middle 50% range 20–25. **Basis for Candidate Selection:** *Very important factors include:* academic GPA, application essay, standardized test scores, recommendation(s), character/personal qualities, religious affiliation/commitment. *Important factors include:* rigor of secondary school record, class rank. *Other factors include:* level of applicant's interest. **Freshman Admission Requirements:** High school diploma is required and GED is accepted. *Academic units recommended:* 4

English, 3 math, 2 science, 1 science labs, 2 foreign language, 3 social studies, 2 history, 4 academic electives. **Freshman Admission Statistics:** 1,109 applied, 73% admitted, 27% enrolled. **Transfer Admission Requirements:** High school transcript, college transcript(s), essay or personal statement, Minimum college GPA of 2.0 required. Lowest grade transferable C-. **General Admission Information:** Application fee $25. Priority deadline 7/1. Non-fall registration accepted.

COSTS AND FINANCIAL AID

Annual tuition $19,190. Room and board $6,500. Required fees $340. Average book and supplies expense $1,000. **Required Forms and Deadlines:** FAFSA. **Notification of Awards:** Applicants will be notified of awards on a rolling basis beginning 2/15. **Types of Aid:** *Need-based scholarships/grants:* College/university scholarship or grant aid from institutional funds; Federal Pell; Private scholarships; SEOG; State scholarships/grants. **Student Employment:** Federal Work-Study Program available. **Financial Aid Statistics:** 100% needy freshmen, 99% needy undergrads receive need-based scholarship or grant aid. 100% freshmen, 94% undergrads receive non-need-based scholarship or grant aid. 81% freshmen, 79% undergrads receive need-based self-help aid. 23% freshmen, 15% undergrads receive athletic scholarships. 100% freshmen, 98% undergrads receive any aid. **Criteria awarding aid:** *Need-based:* Academics, Alumni affiliation, Minority status. *Non-Need-based:* Academics, Athletics, Leadership, Music/drama, State/district residency.

CORNISH COLLEGE OF THE ARTS

1000 Lenora Street, Seattle, WA 98121
Phone: 206-726-5016 **Financial Aid Phone:** 206-726-5013
E-mail: admissions@cornish.edu **CEEB Code:** 58
Fax: 206-720-1011 **Website:** www.cornish.edu **ACT Code:** 4801

This private school was founded in 1914. It has a 4 acre campus.

RATINGS

Admissions Selectivity Rating: 64   **Fire Safety Rating:** 60*   **Green Rating:** 60*

STUDENTS AND FACULTY

Enrollment: 765. **Student Body:** 64% female, 36% male, 52% out-of-state, 4% international (25 countries represented). Asian 6%, African American 4%, Caucasian 63%, Hispanic 9%, Native American 1%, Pacific Islander <1%, Two or more races 7%, Race unknown 6%.
Retention and Graduation: 12% grads go on to further study within 1 year. 5% grads pursue arts and sciences degrees. **Faculty:** Student/faculty ratio 8:1.

ACADEMICS

Degrees: Bachelor's; Post-bachelor's certificate. **Classes:** Most classes have 10–19 students. **Most popular majors:** Music Performance, General; Drama and Dramatics/Theatre Arts, General; Design and Visual Communications, General. **Special Study Options:** Exchange student program (domestic); Independent study; Internships; Study abroad. **Disability Services offered:** Note-taking services; Tape recorders. **Career services:** Internships.

FACILITIES

Housing: Coed dorms 50% of campus accessible to physically disabled. **Special Academic Facilities/Equipment:** Art galleries, extensive art studio space, theatres, electronic music studio, dance studio, concert hall.

CAMPUS LIFE

Environment: Metropolis. **Activities:** Choral groups; Concert band; Dance; Drama/theater; Jazz band; Literary magazine; Music ensembles; Musical theater; Opera; Radio station; Student government; Student-run film society. 18 registered organizations, 6 honor societies, 1 religious organizations, on campus. **On-Campus Highlights:** Raisbeck Performance Hall.

ADMISSIONS

Freshman Academic Profile: Average high school GPA 3.2. 75% from public high schools. **Basis for Candidate Selection:** *Very important factors include:* talent/ability. *Important factors include:* rigor of secondary school record, application essay, *Other factors include:* academic GPA, standardized test scores, recommendation(s), interview, extracurricular activities. **Freshman Admission Requirements:** High school diploma is required and GED is accepted. *Academic units required:* 4 English, 2 math, 2 science, 1 science labs, 3 social studies. *Academic units recommended:* 4 math, 4 science, 2 foreign language. **Freshman Admission Statistics:** 1,134 applied, 86% admitted, 17% enrolled. **Transfer Admission Requirements:** High school transcript, college

transcript(s), essay or personal statement, interview, Minimum college GPA of 2.0 required. Lowest grade transferable C. **General Admission Information:** Application fee $40. Priority deadline 2/1. Regular application deadline 8/15. Admission may be deferred for a maximum of 12 months.

COSTS AND FINANCIAL AID

Annual tuition $31,980. **Required Forms and Deadlines:** FAFSA; Institution's own financial aid form. **Notification of Awards:** Applicants will be notified of awards on or about 5/15. **Types of Aid:** *Need-based scholarships/grants:* Federal Pell; SEOG; State scholarships/grants. **Student Employment:** Federal Work-Study Program available. **Financial Aid Statistics:** needy freshmen, 84% needy undergrads receive need-based scholarship or grant aid. freshmen, 100% undergrads receive non-need-based scholarship or grant aid. freshmen, 84% undergrads receive need-based self-help aid. freshmen, 0% undergrads receive athletic scholarships. **Criteria awarding aid:** *Need-based:* Academics, Art, Music/drama. *Non-Need-based:* Academics, Art, Music/drama.

COVENANT COLLEGE

Admissions Office 14049 Scenic Highway, Lookout Mountain, GA 30750
Phone: 706-820-2398 **Financial Aid Phone:** 706-419-1126
E-mail: admissions@covenant.edu **CEEB Code:** 6124
Fax: 706-820-0893 **Website:** www.covenant.edu **ACT Code:** 3951

This private school, affiliated with the Presbyterian Church in America, was founded in 1955. It has a 350 acre campus.

RATINGS

Admissions Selectivity Rating: 77   **Fire Safety Rating:** 88   **Green Rating:** 60*

STUDENTS AND FACULTY

Enrollment: 904. **Student Body:** 53% female, 47% male, 71% out-of-state, 3% international (21 countries represented). Asian 1%, African American 3%, Caucasian 84%, Hispanic 1%, Native American 1%, Pacific Islander <1%, Two or more races 5%, Race unknown 1%.
Retention and Graduation: 84% freshmen return for sophomore year. 59% freshmen graduate within 4 years. 65% freshmen graduate within 6 years. 28% grads go on to further study within 1 year. 10% grads pursue arts and sciences degrees. 1% grads pursue law degrees. 2% grads pursue business degrees. 1% grads pursue medical degrees. **Faculty:** Student/faculty ratio 12:1. 62 full-time faculty, 89% hold PhDs, 10% are members of minority groups, 24% are women. 0% of classes are taught by teaching assistants.

ACADEMICS

Degrees: Bachelor's; Master's. **Classes:** Most classes have 10–19 students. Most lab/discussion sessions have 10–19 students. **Most popular majors:** English Language and Literature, General; Elementary Education and Teaching; Sociology, General. **Special Study Options:** Double major; Dual enrollment; English as a Second Language (ESL); Exchange student program (domestic); Independent study; Internships; Student-designed major; Study abroad; Teacher certification program. **Disability Services offered:** Note-taking services; Tape recorders; Tutors. **Career services:** Alumni network; Alumni services; Career assessment; Internships.

FACILITIES

Housing: Apartments for single students; Coed dorms 95% of campus accessible to physically disabled. **Campus Network:** 100% of classrooms, 100% of dorms, 100% of student union, 100% of libraries, 100% of dining areas, 10% of common outdoor areas, have wireless network access.

CAMPUS LIFE

Environment: City. **Activities:** Campus Ministries; Choral groups; Concert band; Dance; Drama/theater; International Student Organization; Jazz band; Literary magazine; Model UN; Music ensembles; Musical theater; Radio station; Student government; Student newspaper; Student-run film society; Symphony orchestra; Yearbook. 40 registered organizations, 4 honor societies, 1 religious organizations, on campus. **Athletics (Intercollegiate):** *Men:* baseball, basketball, cross-country, golf, soccer, tennis. *Women:* basketball, cross-country, golf, soccer, softball, tennis, volleyball. **On-Campus Highlights:** Probasco Visitor's Center.

ADMISSIONS

Freshman Academic Profile: Average high school GPA 3.7. 33% in top 10% of high school class, 50% in top 25% of high school class, 71% in top 50%

of high school class. 55% from public high schools. **Test scores**: SAT Math middle 50% range 530–650. SAT EBRW middle 50% range 570–680. ACT middle 50% range 23–29. **Basis for Candidate Selection**: *Very important factors include:* rigor of secondary school record, academic GPA, application essay, standardized test scores, recommendation(s), character/personal qualities, religious affiliation/commitment. *Important factors include:* interview. *Other factors include:* class rank, extracurricular activities, first generation, alumni/ae relation, racial/ethnic status, volunteer work, level of applicant's interest. **Freshman Admission Requirements:** High school diploma is required and GED is accepted. *Academic units required:* 4 English, 3 math, 2 science, 2 social studies, 3 academic electives. *Academic units recommended:* 4 English, 3 math, 2 science, 2 foreign language, 2 social studies, 3 academic electives. **Freshman Admission Statistics:** 561 applied, 98% admitted, 40% enrolled. **Transfer Admission Requirements:** High school transcript, college transcript(s), essay or personal statement, interview, standardized test scores, statement of good standing from prior institution(s). Minimum college GPA of 2.0 required. Lowest grade transferable C-. **General Admission Information:** Application fee $35. Regular application deadline 2/1. Non-fall registration accepted.

COSTS AND FINANCIAL AID

Annual tuition $35,670. Room and board $10,970. Required fees $1,040. Average book and supplies expense $1,170. **Required Forms and Deadlines:** FAFSA; State aid form. **Notification of Awards:** Applicants will be notified of awards on or about 3/15. **Types of Aid:** *Need-based scholarships/grants:* College/university scholarship or grant aid from institutional funds; Federal Pell; Private scholarships; SEOG; State scholarships/grants. **Student Employment:** Federal Work-Study Program available. Institutional employment available. **Financial Aid Statistics:** 99% needy freshmen, 100% needy undergrads receive need-based scholarship or grant aid. 29% freshmen, 21% undergrads receive non-need-based scholarship or grant aid. 83% freshmen, 86% undergrads receive need-based self-help aid. 0% freshmen, 0% undergrads receive athletic scholarships. 100% freshmen, 98.8% undergrads receive any aid. 58% undergrads borrow to pay for school. Average cumulative indebtedness $23,723. **Criteria awarding aid:** *Need-based:* Academics, Alumni affiliation, Art, Job skills, Leadership, Minority status, Music/drama *Non-Need-based:* Academics, Alumni affiliation, Art, Job skills, Leadership, Minority status, Music/drama, Religious affiliation, State/district residency.

CREIGHTON UNIVERSITY

Best Colleges

2500 California Plaza, Omaha, NE 68178
Phone: 402-280-2703 **Financial Aid Phone:** 402-280-2731
E-mail: admissions@creighton.edu **CEEB Code:** 6121
Fax: 402-280-2685 **Website:** www.creighton.edu **ACT Code:** 2444

This private school, affiliated with the Roman Catholic Church, was founded in 1878. It has a 139 acre campus.

RATINGS

Admissions Selectivity Rating: 86   Fire Safety Rating: 96   Green Rating: 86

STUDENTS AND FACULTY

Enrollment: 4,431. **Student Body:** 58% female, 42% male, 78% out-of-state, 2% international (27 countries represented). Asian 9%, African American 2%, Caucasian 72%, Hispanic 8%, Native American <1%, Pacific Islander <1%, Two or more races 5%, Race unknown 1%.
Retention and Graduation: 90% freshmen return for sophomore year. 73% freshmen graduate within 4 years. 81% freshmen graduate within 6 years. **Faculty:** Student/faculty ratio 11:1. 592 full-time faculty, 83% hold PhDs, 15% are members of minority groups, 48% are women. 0% of classes are taught by teaching assistants.

ACADEMICS

Degrees: Associate; Bachelor's; Certificate; Doctoral degree—professional practice; Doctoral degree research/scholarship; Master's; Post-bachelor's certificate; Post-master's certificate. **Classes:** Most classes have 10–19 students. Most lab/discussion sessions have 10–19 students. **Most popular majors:** Registered Nursing/Registered Nurse; Biology/Biological Sciences, General; Psychology, General. **Special Study Options:** Accelerated program; Cross-registration; Distance learning; Double major; Dual enrollment; English as a

Second Language (ESL); Honors program; Independent study; Internships; Liberal arts/career combination; Study abroad; Teacher certification program. **Honors programs:** Designed for talented, imaginative students desirous of participation in small, discussion-oriented classes and in courses on interdisciplinary and topical issues. For more information, visit http://www.creighton.edu/ccas/honorsprogram/. **Combined degree programs:** BA/JD. **Disability Services offered:** Note-taking services; Reader services; Tape recorders; Tutors. **Career services:** Alumni network; Alumni services; Career assessment; Career/job search classes; Internships; Regional alumni.

FACILITIES

Housing: Apartments for married students; Apartments for single students; Coed dorms; Special housing for disabled students; Theme housing 87% of campus accessible to physically disabled. **Special Academic Facilities/Equipment:** St John's Church is at the center of the Creighton University campus and serves the Omaha community as well. The Lied Art Gallery is open seven days a week and is free to the public. The University is home to a wind energy collection system and the state's largest solar array that acts as an outdoor classroom for students in the energy technology program. iJAY, an Apple Authorized Campus Store, uniquely blends commercial and educational interests by doubling as a learning center, giving students the opportunity to gain hands-on experience running a retail store as part of a practicum course. The Heider Securities Investment and Analysis Center in the business college is a state-of-the-art trading room complete with a real-time stock ticker, interactive market boards and 11 Bloomberg terminals.

CAMPUS LIFE

Environment: Metropolis. **Activities:** Campus Ministries; Choral groups; Dance; Drama/theater; International Student Organization; Model UN; Music ensembles; Musical theater; Pep band; Student government; Student newspaper; Symphony orchestra. 219 registered organizations, 15 honor societies, 18 religious organizations, 6 fraternities, 8 sororities, on campus. **Athletics (Intercollegiate):** *Men:* baseball, basketball, cross-country, golf, soccer, tennis. *Women:* basketball, crew/rowing, cross-country, golf, soccer, softball, tennis, volleyball. **On-Campus Highlights:** Heider College of Business/Harper Center. **Environmental Initiatives:** Stewardship of the environment has become central to the mission of Creighton University and the wider Jesuit community. The Energy Technology Program has allowed the university to become more sustainable, with 120 kW of renewable energy generated on site, including the largest solar photovoltaic array in Nebraska. Not only have these technologies reduced Creighton's environmental footprint, but they have also become the foundation for a hands-on educational platform, allowing students to work and conduct research on professional systems. The University has continued to expand renewable energy sources including solar photovoltaic and solar thermal panels, four wind turbines designed for urban environments, geothermal hearing, low voltage lighting, solar hot water, and a ground source heat pump. The presence of these technologies at Creighton exposes everyone in the community to them and concretely conveys Creighton's commitment to environmental responsibility. The Energy Technology academic program regularly connects with the community for their projects. For instance, student teams engaged with several local schools to develop a renewable energy plan for the school plus a level one energy audit for their facility. The project included a formal report and presentation to the school boards as well as teaching classes in sustainable energy related topics. Other projects have included developing a plan for solar power on a local homeless shelter and working with a hospital in Nigeria.

ADMISSIONS

Freshman Academic Profile: Average high school GPA 3.8. 35% in top 10% of high school class, 66% in top 25% of high school class, 91% in top 50% of high school class. 51% from public high schools. **Test scores:** SAT Math middle 50% range 580–680. SAT EBRW middle 50% range 590–670. ACT middle 50% range 23–29. **Basis for Candidate Selection:** *Very important factors include:* rigor of secondary school record, academic GPA. *Important factors include:* application essay, standardized test scores. *Other factors include:* class rank, recommendation(s), extracurricular activities, talent/ability, character/personal qualities, first generation, racial/ethnic status, volunteer work, level of applicant's interest. **Freshman Admission Requirements:** High school diploma is required and GED is accepted. *Academic units required:* 4 English, 3 math, 2 science, 1 science labs, 2 foreign language, 2 social studies, 3 academic electives. *Academic units recommended:* 4 English, 4 math, 3 science, 2 science labs, 3 foreign language, 4 social studies, 3 academic electives. **Freshman Admission Statistics:** 9,381 applied, 74% admitted, 16% enrolled. **Transfer Admission Requirements:** High school transcript, college transcript(s), statement of good standing from prior institution(s). Minimum college GPA of 2.50 required. Lowest grade transferable C. **General Admission Information:** Application fee $40. Priority deadline 12/1. Non-fall registration accepted.

COSTS AND FINANCIAL AID

Annual tuition $41,176. Room and board $11,600. Required fees $1,842. Average book and supplies expense $1,200. **Required Forms and Deadlines:** FAFSA; Institution's own financial aid form. **Notification of Awards:** Applicants will be notified of awards on a rolling basis beginning 2/15. **Types of Aid:** *Need-based scholarships/grants:* College/university scholarship or grant aid from institutional funds; Federal Pell; Private scholarships; SEOG; State scholarships/grants. *Loans:* Direct PLUS loans; Direct Subsidized Stafford Loans; Direct Unsubsidized Stafford Loans. **Student Employment:** Federal Work-Study Program available. Institutional employment available. **Financial Aid Statistics:** 99% needy freshmen, 94% needy undergrads receive need-based scholarship or grant aid. 30% freshmen, 22% undergrads receive non-need-based scholarship or grant aid. 72% freshmen, 78% undergrads receive need-based self-help aid. 4% freshmen, 4% undergrads receive athletic scholarships. 99.7% freshmen, 96.6% undergrads receive any aid. 59% undergrads borrow to pay for school. Average cumulative indebtedness $38,042. **Criteria awarding aid:** *Need-based:* Academics, Leadership *Non-Need-based:* Academics, Alumni affiliation, Art, Athletics, Leadership, Minority status, Music/drama.

CROWN COLLEGE

8700 College View Drive, St. Bonifacius, MN 55375-9001
Phone: 952-446-4142 **Financial Aid Phone:** (952) 446-4175
E-mail: info@crown.edu
Fax: 952-446-4149 **Website:** www.crown.edu **ACT Code:** 2152

This private school, affiliated with the Christian & Missionary Alliance Church, was founded in 1916. It has a 215 acre campus.

RATINGS

Admissions Selectivity Rating: 80   Fire Safety Rating: 74   Green Rating: 60*

STUDENTS AND FACULTY

Enrollment: 1,017. **Student Body:** 57% female, 43% male, 31% out-of-state, 1% international (21 countries represented). Asian 7%, African American 4%, Caucasian 78%, Hispanic 2%, Native American 1%, Pacific Islander <1%, Two or more races 1%, Race unknown 7%.
Retention and Graduation: 63% freshmen return for sophomore year.
Faculty: Student/faculty ratio 14:1. 34 full-time faculty, 47% hold PhDs, 6% are members of minority groups, 26% are women. 0% of classes are taught by teaching assistants.

ACADEMICS

Degrees: Associate; Bachelor's; Certificate; Master's; Post-bachelor's certificate. **Classes:** Most classes have 10–19 students. Most lab/discussion sessions have 10–19 students. **Most popular majors:** Business Administration and Management, General; Theology and Religious Vocations, Other; Elementary Education and Teaching. **Special Study Options:** Distance learning; Double major; Exchange student program (domestic); Honors program; Independent study; Internships; Study abroad; Teacher certification program. **Honors programs:** The Honors Program. **Disability Services offered:** Note-taking services; Reader services; Tape recorders; Tutors. **Career services:** Alumni services; Career assessment; Career/job search classes; Internships.

FACILITIES

Housing: Apartments for married students; Apartments for single students; Men's dorms; Special housing for disabled students; Women's dorms 95% of campus accessible to physically disabled. **Special Academic Facilities/ Equipment:** Peter Watne Memorial Library.

CAMPUS LIFE

Environment: Rural. **Activities:** Campus Ministries; Choral groups; Dance; Drama/theater; International Student Organization; Jazz band; Literary magazine; Music ensembles; Musical theater; Pep band; Radio station; Student government; Student newspaper; Student-run film society; Symphony orchestra; Yearbook. 19 registered organizations, 1 honor societies, 6 religious organizations, on campus. **Athletics (Intercollegiate):** *Men:* baseball, basketball, cross-country, football, golf, soccer. *Women:* basketball, cross-country, golf, soccer, softball, volleyball. **On-Campus Highlights:** Storm Cafe/Student Union **Environmental Initiatives:** The College recycles all cardboard and provides co-mingled recycling containers in all common areas, each classroom, and in each office. We post recycling program notes on our website from time to time and also posters throughout the building quarterly. Large amounts of metals, plastics, light bulbs, electronics, etc. are recycled each month by facilities mgmt.

ADMISSIONS

Freshman Academic Profile: Average high school GPA 3.4. 13% in top 10% of high school class, 38% in top 25% of high school class, 79% in top 50% of high school class. **Test scores:** SAT Math middle 50% range 475–598. SAT EBRW middle 50% range 508–600. ACT middle 50% range 21–25. **Basis for Candidate Selection:** *Very important factors include:* academic GPA, application essay, standardized test scores, religious affiliation/commitment. *Other factors include:* rigor of secondary school record, recommendation(s). **Freshman Admission Requirements:** High school diploma is required and GED is accepted. *Academic units recommended:* 4 English, 3 math, 3 science, 2 foreign language, 3 social studies. **Freshman Admission Statistics:** 453 applied, 78% admitted, 42% enrolled. **Transfer Admission Requirements:** High school transcript, college transcript(s), essay or personal statement, Minimum college GPA of 2.0 required. Lowest grade transferable C. **General Admission Information:** Application fee $20. Regular application deadline 8/20. Non-fall registration accepted. Admission may be deferred for a maximum of 1 year.

COSTS AND FINANCIAL AID

Annual tuition $22,100. Room and board $7,480. Average book and supplies expense $1,140. **Required Forms and Deadlines:** FAFSA; Institution's own financial aid form. **Notification of Awards:** Applicants will be notified of awards on a rolling basis beginning 3/1. **Types of Aid:** *Need-based scholarships/ grants:* College/university scholarship or grant aid from institutional funds; Federal Pell; Private scholarships; SEOG; State scholarships/grants. *Loans:* Direct PLUS loans; Direct Subsidized Stafford Loans; Direct Unsubsidized Stafford Loans. **Student Employment:** Federal Work-Study Program available. **Financial Aid Statistics:** needy freshmen, needy undergrads receive need-based scholarship or grant aid. freshmen, undergrads receive non-need-based scholarship or grant aid. freshmen, undergrads receive need-based self-help aid. freshmen, undergrads receive athletic scholarships. 84% freshmen, 83% undergrads receive any aid. **Criteria awarding aid:** *Need-based:* Academics. *Non-Need-based:* Academics, Alumni affiliation, Leadership, Minority status, Music/drama, Religious affiliation.

THE CULINARY INSTITUTE OF AMERICA

1946 Campus Drive, Hyde Park, NY 12538
Phone: 8454529430 **Financial Aid Phone:** 845-451-1500
E-mail: admissions@culinary.edu **CEEB Code:** 3301
Fax: 8454511068 **Website:** www.ciachef.edu **ACT Code:** 2728

This private school was founded in 1946. It has a 170 acre campus.

RATINGS

Admissions Selectivity Rating: 75   Fire Safety Rating: 98   Green Rating: 60*

STUDENTS AND FACULTY

Enrollment: 2,956. **Student Body:** 51% female, 49% male, 66% out-of-state, 15% international (46 countries represented). Asian 7%, African American 7%, Caucasian 47%, Hispanic 16%, Native American 1%, Pacific Islander <1%, Two or more races 5%, Race unknown 5%.
Retention and Graduation: 76% freshmen return for sophomore year.
Faculty: Student/faculty ratio 18:1. 146 full-time faculty, 0% hold PhDs, 9% are members of minority groups, 31% are women. 0% of classes are taught by teaching assistants.

ACADEMICS

Degrees: Associate; Bachelor's; Certificate; Master's; Post-bachelor's certificate. **Classes:** Most classes have 10–19 students. **Most popular majors:** Multi-/ Interdisciplinary Studies, Other; Restaurant/Food Services Management; Culinary Science/Culinology. **Special Study Options:** Double major; Internships; Study abroad. **Disability Services offered:** Note-taking services; Reader services; Tape recorders; Tutors. **Career services:** Alumni network; Career assessment; Career/job search classes; Internships.

FACILITIES

Housing: Coed dorms.

CAMPUS LIFE

Environment: Village. **Activities:** International Student Organization; Student government; Student newspaper. 27 registered organizations, 1 honor societies, 3 religious organizations, on campus. **On-Campus Highlights:** Library Learning Commons.

ADMISSIONS

Freshman Academic Profile: Average high school GPA 3.2. **Test scores:** SAT Math middle 50% range 510–610. SAT EBRW middle 50% range 510–610. ACT middle 50% range 20–25. **Basis for Candidate Selection:** *Important factors include:* rigor of secondary school record, academic GPA. *Other factors include:* class rank, application essay, standardized test scores, recommendation(s), extracurricular activities, talent/ability, character/personal qualities, alumni/ae relation, volunteer work, work experience, level of applicant's interest. **Freshman Admission Requirements:** High school diploma is required and GED is accepted. *Academic units required:* 4 English, 3 math, 3 science, 4 social studies. *Academic units recommended:* 4 English, 3 math, 3 science, 2 foreign language, 4 social studies. **Freshman Admission Statistics:** 1,035 applied, 98% admitted, 47% enrolled. **General Admission Information:** Application fee $50. Non-fall registration accepted. Admission may be deferred for a maximum of 1 year.

COSTS AND FINANCIAL AID

Required Forms and Deadlines: FAFSA; State aid form. **Notification of Awards:** Applicants will be notified of awards on a rolling basis beginning 3/5. **Types of Aid:** *Need-based scholarships/grants:* College/university scholarship or grant aid from institutional funds; Federal Pell; Private scholarships; SEOG; State scholarships/grants. *Loans:* Direct PLUS loans; Direct Subsidized Stafford Loans; Direct Unsubsidized Stafford Loans. **Student Employment:** Federal Work-Study Program available. Institutional employment available. 94% freshmen, 83% undergrads receive any aid. **Criteria awarding aid:** *Non-Need-based:* Academics, Alumni affiliation, Job skills, Leadership.

CULVER-STOCKTON COLLEGE

One College Hill, Canton, MO 63435
Phone: 573-288-6331 **Financial Aid Phone:** 573-288-6307
E-mail: admission@culver.edu **CEEB Code:** 6123
Fax: 573-288-6618 **ACT Code:** 2290

This private school, affiliated with the Disciples of Christ Church, was founded in 1853. It has a 139 acre campus.

RATINGS

Admissions Selectivity Rating: 86 **Fire Safety Rating:** 75 **Green Rating:** 60*

STUDENTS AND FACULTY

Enrollment: 975. **Student Body:** 49% female, 51% male, 45% out-of-state, 5% international (20 countries represented). Asian <1%, African American 13%, Caucasian 73%, Hispanic 5%, Native American <1%, Pacific Islander <1%, Two or more races 3%, Race unknown <1%.
Retention and Graduation: 67% freshmen return for sophomore year. 40% freshmen graduate within 4 years. % freshmen graduate within 6 years. 15% grads go on to further study within 1 year. 9% grads pursue arts and sciences degrees. 2% grads pursue law degrees. 4% grads pursue business degrees. **Faculty:** Student/faculty ratio 14:1. 54 full-time faculty, 63% hold PhDs, 7% are members of minority groups, 44% are women. 0% of classes are taught by teaching assistants.

ACADEMICS

Degrees: Bachelor's; Master's. **Classes:** Most classes have 10–19 students. Most lab/discussion sessions have fewer than 10 students. **Most popular majors:** Criminal Justice/Law Enforcement Administration; Business Administration and Management, General; Psychology, General. **Special Study Options:** Accelerated program; Cross-registration; Distance learning; Double major; Dual enrollment; Honors program; Independent study; Internships; Student-designed major; Study abroad; Teacher certification program. **Honors programs:** Honors Scholars are expected to complete both an academic and enrichment requirement. **Disability Services offered:** Note-taking services; Reader services; Tape recorders; Tutors. **Career services:** Alumni network; Alumni services; Career assessment; Career/job search classes; Internships; Regional alumni.

FACILITIES

Housing: Coed dorms; Fraternity/sorority housing; Wellness housing 50% of campus accessible to physically disabled. **Special Academic Facilities/Equipment:** Phage genomics research facility with DNA sequencer, astronomy observation deck, biological research station, collegiate teaching greenhouse, fine arts multi-media editing suite and recording studio, art gallery, radio broadcasting and television studio, mock trial courtroom and legal research library. **Campus Network:** 100% of classrooms, 100% of dorms, 100% of student union, 100% of libraries, 100% of dining areas, have wireless network access.

CAMPUS LIFE

Environment: Rural. **Activities:** Campus Ministries; Choral groups; Concert band; Dance; Drama/theater; International Student Organization; Jazz band; Literary magazine; Music ensembles; Musical theater; Radio station; Student government; Student newspaper; Television station. 50 registered organizations, 11 honor societies, 5 religious organizations, 7 fraternities, 3 sororities, on campus. **Athletics (Intercollegiate):** *Men:* baseball, basketball, cheerleading, cross-country, football, golf, soccer, track/field (outdoor), track/field (indoor). *Women:* basketball, cheerleading, cross-country, golf, soccer, softball, track/field (outdoor), track/field (indoor), volleyball. **On-Campus Highlights:** The Lab Coffee House. **Environmental Initiatives:** Thermostat control.

ADMISSIONS

Freshman Academic Profile: Average high school GPA 3.3. 9% in top 10% of high school class, 28% in top 25% of high school class, 64% in top 50% of high school class. 95% from public high schools. **Test scores:** SAT Math middle 50% range 470–570. SAT EBRW middle 50% range 480–570. ACT middle 50% range 18–23. **Basis for Candidate Selection:** *Very important factors include:* academic GPA, standardized test scores. *Important factors include:* rigor of secondary school record. *Other factors include:* class rank, application essay, recommendation(s), interview. **Freshman Admission Requirements:** High school diploma is required and GED is accepted. *Academic units recommended:* 4 English, 2 math, 2 science, 1 foreign language, 3 social studies, 3 history. **Freshman Admission Statistics:** 4,784 applied, 46% admitted, 13% enrolled. **Transfer Admission Requirements:** college transcript(s), Minimum college GPA of 2.0 required. Lowest grade transferable C-. **General Admission Information:** Regular application deadline 8/15. Non-fall registration accepted. Admission may be deferred for a maximum of 1 year.

COSTS AND FINANCIAL AID

Annual tuition $26,255. Room and board $8,520. Required fees $425. Average book and supplies expense $1,100. **Required Forms and Deadlines:** FAFSA; Institution's own financial aid form. **Notification of Awards:** Applicants will be notified of awards on a rolling basis beginning 11/15. **Types of Aid:** *Need-based scholarships/grants:* College/university scholarship or grant aid from institutional funds; Federal Pell; Private scholarships; SEOG; State scholarships/grants. *Loans:* Direct PLUS loans; Direct Subsidized Stafford Loans; Direct Unsubsidized Stafford Loans. **Student Employment:** Federal Work-Study Program available. Institutional employment available. **Financial Aid Statistics:** 100% needy freshmen, 100% needy undergrads receive need-based scholarship or grant aid. 12% freshmen, 13% undergrads receive non-need-based scholarship or grant aid. 86% freshmen, 87% undergrads receive need-based self-help aid. 20% freshmen, 18% undergrads receive athletic scholarships. 99% freshmen, 98.6% undergrads receive any aid. 82% undergrads borrow to pay for school. Average cumulative indebtedness $27,434. **Criteria awarding aid:** *Need-based:* Academics, Art, Athletics, Music/drama, Religious affiliation. *Non-Need-based:* Academics, Alumni affiliation, Art, Athletics, Leadership, Music/drama, Religious affiliation.

CURRY COLLEGE

1071 Blue Hill Avenue, Milton, MA 02186
Phone: 617-333-2210
E-mail: curryadm@curry.edu **CEEB Code:** 3285
Fax: 617-333-2114 **Website:** www.curry.edu **ACT Code:** 1814

This private school was founded in 1879. It has a 137 acre campus.

RATINGS

Admissions Selectivity Rating: 73 **Fire Safety Rating:** 60* **Green Rating:** 60*

STUDENTS AND FACULTY

Enrollment: 2,843. **Student Body:** 63% female, 37% male, 22% out-of-state, 1% international (20 countries represented). Asian 2%, African American 9%, Caucasian 69%, Hispanic 5%, Native American <1%, Pacific Islander 0%, Two or more races 2%, Race unknown 12%.

Retention and Graduation: 71% freshmen return for sophomore year. 17% grads go on to further study within 1 year. 10% grads pursue arts and sciences degrees. 1% grads pursue law degrees. 2% grads pursue business degrees. **Faculty:** Student/faculty ratio 11:1. 122 full-time faculty, 81% hold PhDs, 7% are members of minority groups, 67% are women. 0% of classes are taught by teaching assistants.

ACADEMICS

Degrees: Bachelor's; Master's. **Classes:** Most classes have 10–19 students. Most lab/discussion sessions have fewer than 10 students. **Special Study Options:** Accelerated program; Cross-registration; Double major; English as a Second Language (ESL); Honors program; Independent study; Internships; Liberal arts/career combination; Student-designed major; Study abroad; Teacher certification program. **Disability Services offered:** Tape recorders; Tutors.

FACILITIES

Housing: Coed dorms; Men's dorms; Special housing for disabled students; Theme housing; Women's dorms. **Special Academic Facilities/Equipment:** On-campus preschool, nursing lab, psychology lab.

CAMPUS LIFE

Environment: Village. **Activities:** Campus Ministries; Choral groups; Dance; Drama/theater; International Student Organization; Literary magazine; Music ensembles; Radio station; Student government; Student newspaper; Student-run film society; Television station; Yearbook. 1 honor societies, 2 religious organizations, on campus. **Athletics (Intercollegiate):** *Men:* baseball, basketball, cheerleading, football, ice hockey, lacrosse, soccer, tennis. *Women:* basketball, cheerleading, cross-country, lacrosse, soccer, softball, tennis. **On-Campus Highlights:** Drapkin Student Center.

ADMISSIONS

Freshman Academic Profile: Average high school GPA 2.8. 5% in top 10% of high school class, 18% in top 25% of high school class, 53% in top 50% of high school class. 76% from public high schools. **Test scores:** SAT Math middle 50% range 430–520. SAT EBRW middle 50% range 420–520. ACT middle 50% range 18–21. **Basis for Candidate Selection:** *Very important factors include:* rigor of secondary school record. *Important factors include:* academic GPA, application essay, standardized test scores, recommendation(s), interview, extracurricular activities, character/personal qualities. *Other factors include:* class rank, talent/ability, alumni/ae relation, volunteer work, work experience, level of applicant's interest. **Freshman Admission Requirements:** High school diploma is required and GED is accepted. *Academic units required:* 4 English, 3 math. *Academic units recommended:* 2 science, 1 science labs, 2 foreign language, 2 social studies, 2 history. **Freshman Admission Statistics:** 5,448 applied, 87% admitted, 14% enrolled. **Transfer Admission Requirements:** college transcript(s), essay or personal statement, Minimum college GPA of 2.0 required. Lowest grade transferable C-. **General Admission Information:** Application fee $50. Priority deadline 4/1. Non-fall registration accepted.

COSTS AND FINANCIAL AID

Annual tuition $34,730. Room and board $13,900. Required fees $2,035. Average book and supplies expense $1,150. **Required Forms and Deadlines:** FAFSA. **Notification of Awards:** Applicants will be notified of awards on a rolling basis beginning 3/1. **Types of Aid:** *Need-based scholarships/grants:* College/university scholarship or grant aid from institutional funds; Federal Pell; Private scholarships; SEOG; State scholarships/grants. *Loans:* Direct PLUS loans; Direct Subsidized Stafford Loans; Direct Unsubsidized Stafford Loans. **Financial Aid Statistics:** 79% needy freshmen, 85% needy undergrads receive need-based scholarship or grant aid. 8% freshmen, 6% undergrads receive non-need-based scholarship or grant aid. 86% freshmen, 89% undergrads receive need-based self-help aid. 0% freshmen, 0% undergrads receive athletic scholarships. **Criteria awarding aid:** *Non-Need-based:* Academics, Alumni affiliation, Leadership.

DAEMEN COLLEGE

4380 Main Street, Amherst, NY 14226-3592
Phone: 716-839-8225 **Financial Aid Phone:** 716-839-8254
E-mail: admissions@daemen.edu **CEEB Code:** 2762
Fax: 716-839-8229 **Website:** www.daemen.edu **ACT Code:** 2874

This private school was founded in 1947. It has a 35 acre campus.

RATINGS

Admissions Selectivity Rating: 85   **Fire Safety Rating:** 96   **Green Rating:** 60*

STUDENTS AND FACULTY

Enrollment: 1,884. **Student Body:** 70% female, 30% male, 5% out-of-state, 1% international (21 countries represented). Asian 2%, African American 11%, Caucasian 74%, Hispanic 7%, Native American <1%, Pacific Islander <1%, Two or more races 1%, Race unknown 2%. **Retention and Graduation:** 79% freshmen return for sophomore year. **Faculty:** Student/faculty ratio 16:1. 122 full-time faculty, 76% hold PhDs, 6% are members of minority groups, 59% are women. 0% of classes are taught by teaching assistants.

ACADEMICS

Degrees: Bachelor's; Certificate; Doctoral degree—professional practice; Master's; Post-bachelor's certificate; Post-master's certificate. **Classes:** Most classes have 10–19 students. **Most popular majors:** Physician Assistant; Physical Therapy/Therapist; Registered Nursing/Registered Nurse. **Special Study Options:** Accelerated program; Cross-registration; Distance learning; Double major; Dual enrollment; Exchange student program (domestic); Honors program; Independent study; Internships; Liberal arts/career combination; Student-designed major; Study abroad; Teacher certification program; Weekend college. **Honors programs:** The Honors Program provides an enriched curriculum relying upon multiple perspectives and using primary sources rather than textbooks. Honors program students enjoy special residential accommodations, priority registration by class rank, opportunities for domestic and international travel, and unique offerings such as field trips, access to campus speakers, and research and publication opportunities. **Disability Services offered:** Note-taking services; Tape recorders; Tutors. **Career services:** Alumni network; Alumni services; Career assessment; Career/job search classes; Internships; Regional alumni.

FACILITIES

Housing: Apartments for single students; Coed dorms; Women's dorms 99% of campus accessible to physically disabled. **Special Academic Facilities/Equipment:** Research & Information Commons (RIC); Tower Gallery, Haberman Gacioch Arts Center; Natural and Health Sciences Research Center **Campus Network:** 100% of classrooms, 100% of dorms, 100% of student union, 100% of libraries, 100% of dining areas, 80% of common outdoor areas, have wireless network access.

CAMPUS LIFE

Environment: City. **Activities:** Choral groups; Dance; Drama/theater; Literary magazine; Musical theater; Radio station; Student government; Student newspaper. 72 registered organizations, 7 honor societies, 1 religious organizations, 1 fraternities, 3 sororities, on campus. **Athletics (Intercollegiate):** *Men:* basketball, cross-country, golf, soccer. *Women:* basketball, cross-country, soccer, volleyball. **On-Campus Highlights:** Research and Information Commons. **Environmental Initiatives:** College has hosted conferences and symposia on campus: Annual Environmental Summit; Green Jobs Workshop; World on Your Plate Symposium, Focus the Nation Teach-In.

ADMISSIONS

Freshman Academic Profile: Average high school GPA 3.6. 28% in top 10% of high school class, 58% in top 25% of high school class, 89% in top 50% of high school class. **Test scores:** SAT Math middle 50% range 470–590. SAT EBRW middle 50% range 450–570. ACT middle 50% range 21–27. **Basis for Candidate Selection:** *Very important factors include:* rigor of secondary school record, academic GPA, application essay, standardized test scores. *Important factors include:* recommendation(s). *Other factors include:* class rank, interview, talent/ability, character/personal qualities, alumni/ae relation, volunteer work, work experience, level of applicant's interest. **Freshman Admission Requirements:** High school diploma is required and GED is accepted. *Academic units recommended:* 4 English, 4 math, 4 science, 1 science labs, 4 social studies. **Freshman Admission Statistics:** 3,249 applied, 54% admitted, 19% enrolled. **Transfer Admission Requirements:** college transcript(s), statement of good standing from prior institution(s). Minimum college GPA of

2.0 required. Lowest grade transferable C. **General Admission Information:** Application fee $25. Non-fall registration accepted. Admission may be deferred for a maximum of 12 months.

COSTS AND FINANCIAL AID
Annual tuition $21,800. Room and board $10,840. Required fees $510. Average book and supplies expense $800. **Required Forms and Deadlines:** FAFSA; State aid form. **Notification of Awards:** Applicants will be notified of awards on a rolling basis beginning 2/15. **Types of Aid:** *Need-based scholarships/ grants:* College/university scholarship or grant aid from institutional funds; Federal Pell; Private scholarships; SEOG; State scholarships/grants. *Loans:* Direct PLUS loans; Direct Subsidized Stafford Loans; Direct Unsubsidized Stafford Loans. **Student Employment:** Federal Work-Study Program available. Institutional employment available. **Financial Aid Statistics:** 92% needy freshmen, 94% needy undergrads receive need-based scholarship or grant aid. 96% freshmen, 96% undergrads receive non-need-based scholarship or grant aid. 91% freshmen, 92% undergrads receive need-based self-help aid. 5% freshmen, 5% undergrads receive athletic scholarships. 99% freshmen, 84% undergrads receive any aid. **Criteria awarding aid:** *Need-based:* Academics. *Non-Need-based:* Academics, Art, Athletics, Leadership.

DAKOTA STATE UNIVERSITY

820 North Washington Ave., Madison, SD 57042
Phone: 605-256-5139 **Financial Aid Phone:** (605) 256-5152
E-mail: admissions@dsu.edu **CEEB Code:** 6247
Fax: 605-256-5020 **Website:** www.dsu.edu **ACT Code:** 3910

This public school was founded in 1881. It has a 62 acre campus.

RATINGS
Admissions Selectivity Rating: 84   Fire Safety Rating: 87   Green Rating: 61

STUDENTS AND FACULTY
Enrollment: 2,067. **Student Body:** 32% female, 68% male, 40% out-of-state, 2% international (31 countries represented). Asian 2%, African American 3%, Caucasian 82%, Hispanic 4%, Native American 1%, Pacific Islander <1%, Two or more races 4%, Race unknown 1%.
Retention and Graduation: 66% freshmen return for sophomore year. 29% freshmen graduate within 4 years. 44% freshmen graduate within 6 years.
Faculty: Student/faculty ratio 16:1. 105 full-time faculty, 75% hold PhDs, 8% are members of minority groups, 31% are women. 1% of classes are taught by teaching assistants.

ACADEMICS
Degrees: Associate; Bachelor's; Certificate; Doctoral degree research/ scholarship; Master's; Post-bachelor's certificate. **Classes:** Most classes have 10–19 students. Most lab/discussion sessions have fewer than 10 students. **Most popular majors:** Computer and Information Sciences, General; System, Networking, and Lan/Wan Management/Manager; Computer and Information Systems Security/Auditing/Information Assurance. **Special Study Options:** Cooperative education program; Cross-registration; Distance learning; Double major; Dual enrollment; Exchange student program (domestic); Honors program; Independent study; Internships; Study abroad; Teacher certification program. **Honors programs:** Center of Excellence(CEX), General Beadle Honors Program. **Disability Services offered:** Note-taking services; Reader services; Tutors. **Career services:** Alumni network; Alumni services; Career assessment; Career/job search classes; Internships; Regional alumni.

FACILITIES
Housing: Apartments for single students; Coed dorms; Men's dorms 90% of campus accessible to physically disabled. **Special Academic Facilities/ Equipment:** Smith Zimmerman Museum, Beacom Institute of Technology, The Community Center.

CAMPUS LIFE
Environment: Village. **Activities:** Choral groups; Drama/theater; International Student Organization; Literary magazine; Model UN; Music ensembles; Musical theater; Radio station; Student government; Student newspaper; Student-run film society. 50 registered organizations, 5 honor societies, 3 religious organizations, on campus. **Athletics (Intercollegiate):** *Men:* baseball, basketball, cheerleading, cross-country, football, track/field (outdoor), track/ field (indoor). *Women:* basketball, cheerleading, cross-country, softball, track/ field (outdoor), track/field (indoor), volleyball. **On-Campus Highlights:**

Beacom Institute of Technology. **Environmental Initiatives:** 2-LEED Silver projects Completed and Certified (1 LEED Silver project in review and 1 Green Globes project in design).

ADMISSIONS
Freshman Academic Profile: Average high school GPA 3.7. 8% in top 10% of high school class, 23% in top 25% of high school class, 56% in top 50% of high school class. **Test scores:** SAT Math middle 50% range 505–630. SAT EBRW middle 50% range 500–640. ACT middle 50% range 19–25. **Basis for Candidate Selection:** *Important factors include:* class rank, academic GPA, standardized test scores. **Freshman Admission Requirements:** High school diploma is required and GED is accepted. *Academic units recommended:* 4 English, 3 math, 3 science, 3 science labs, 3 social studies, 1 visual/performing arts. **Freshman Admission Statistics:** 978 applied, 77% admitted, 56% enrolled. **Transfer Admission Requirements:** High school transcript, college transcript(s), Minimum college GPA of 2.0 required. Lowest grade transferable D. **General Admission Information:** Application fee $20. Non-fall registration accepted. Admission may be deferred for a maximum of 1 semester.

COSTS AND FINANCIAL AID
Annual in-state tuition $7,541. Annual out-of-state tuition $10,611. Room and board $7,033. Required fees $1,995. Average book and supplies expense $1,200. **Required Forms and Deadlines:** FAFSA;. **Notification of Awards:** Applicants will be notified of awards on a rolling basis beginning 4/1. **Types of Aid:** *Need-based scholarships/grants:* College/university scholarship or grant aid from institutional funds; Federal Pell; Private scholarships; SEOG; State scholarships/grants. *Loans:* Direct PLUS loans; Direct Subsidized Stafford Loans; Direct Unsubsidized Stafford Loans. **Student Employment:** Federal Work-Study Program available. Institutional employment available. **Financial Aid Statistics:** 54% needy freshmen, 57% needy undergrads receive need-based scholarship or grant aid. 75% freshmen, 52% undergrads receive non-need-based scholarship or grant aid. 87% freshmen, 88% undergrads receive need-based self-help aid. 32% freshmen, 17% undergrads receive athletic scholarships. 74% freshmen, 74% undergrads receive any aid. 77% undergrads borrow to pay for school. Average cumulative indebtedness $27,928. **Criteria awarding aid:** *Need-based:* Academics, Athletics, Minority status. *Non-Need-based:* Academics, Alumni affiliation, Art, Athletics, Leadership, Minority status, Music/drama, State/district residency.

DALLAS BAPTIST UNIVERSITY

3000 Mountain Creek Parkway, Dallas, TX 75211-9299
Phone: 214-333-5360 **Financial Aid Phone:** 214-333-5363
E-mail: admiss@dbu.edu **CEEB Code:** 6159
Fax: 214-333-5447 **Website:** http://www.dbu.edu/ **ACT Code:** 4080

This private school, affiliated with the Baptist Church, was founded in 1898. It has a 292 acre campus.

RATINGS
Admissions Selectivity Rating: 75   Fire Safety Rating: 91   Green Rating: 60*

STUDENTS AND FACULTY
Enrollment: 2,761. **Student Body:** 59% female, 41% male, 8% out-of-state, 7% international (43 countries represented). Asian 2%, African American 10%, Caucasian 61%, Hispanic 19%, Native American <1%, Pacific Islander <1%, Two or more races 2%, Race unknown 0%.
Retention and Graduation: 72% freshmen return for sophomore year. 44% freshmen graduate within 4 years. 58% freshmen graduate within 6 years.
Faculty: Student/faculty ratio 13:1. 134 full-time faculty, 82% hold PhDs, 13% are members of minority groups, 40% are women. 0% of classes are taught by teaching assistants.

ACADEMICS
Degrees: Associate; Bachelor's; Certificate; Doctoral degree research/scholarship; Master's; Post-bachelor's certificate; Post-master's certificate; Transfer Associate. **Classes:** Most classes have 10–19 students. Most lab/discussion sessions have 10–19 students. **Most popular majors:** Psychology, General; Business Administration and Management, General; Biology/Biological Sciences, General. **Special Study Options:** Accelerated program; Cross-registration; Distance learning; Double major; Dual enrollment; English as a Second Language (ESL); Exchange student program (domestic); Honors program; Independent study; Internships; Study abroad; Teacher certification program; Weekend college. **Honors programs:** The University Honors Program exists to help some of our brightest and most gifted

students discover the extent of their own abilities and callings. Our program with its interdisciplinary core is designed to help students make connections across their classes and to encourage a high level of critical thinking. Additional information can be found at https://www.dbu.edu/honors. **Combined degree programs:** BA/MA. **Disability Services offered:** Note-taking services; Reader services; Tape recorders; Tutors. **Career services:** Alumni services; Career assessment; Career/job search classes; Internships; Regional alumni.

FACILITIES

Housing: Apartments for single students; Men's dorms; Special housing for disabled students; Special housing for international students; Theme housing; Wellness housing; Women's dorms 90% of campus accessible to physically disabled. **Special Academic Facilities/Equipment:** Music Recording Studio; Corrie ten Boom Collection; Special University Library Collections and Archives; Decatur Collection; Lord Braine of Wheatley Archives. **Campus Network:** 100% of classrooms, 100% of dorms, 100% of student union, 100% of libraries, 100% of dining areas, 100% of common outdoor areas, have wireless network access.

CAMPUS LIFE

Environment: Metropolis. **Activities:** Campus Ministries; Choral groups; Dance; Drama/theater; International Student Organization; Music ensembles; Musical theater; Opera; Pep band; Student government; Yearbook. 52 registered organizations, 12 honor societies, 13 religious organizations, 4 fraternities, 7 sororities, on campus. **Athletics (Intercollegiate):** *Men:* baseball, cross-country, golf, soccer, tennis, track/field (outdoor). *Women:* cross-country, golf, soccer, tennis, track/field (outdoor), volleyball. **On-Campus Highlights:** Residence Halls.

ADMISSIONS

Freshman Academic Profile: Average high school GPA 3.8. 24% in top 10% of high school class, 55% in top 25% of high school class, 83% in top 50% of high school class. 78% from public high schools. **Test scores:** SAT Math middle 50% range 510–620. SAT EBRW middle 50% range 520–630. ACT middle 50% range 21–26. **Basis for Candidate Selection:** *Very important factors include:* rigor of secondary school record, class rank, academic GPA, standardized test scores, talent/ability, character/personal qualities, religious affiliation/commitment. *Important factors include:* interview, extracurricular activities. *Other factors include:* recommendation(s), alumni/ae relation, volunteer work, work experience, level of applicant's interest. **Freshman Admission Requirements:** High school diploma is required and GED is accepted. *Academic units recommended:* 4 English, 3 math, 2 science, 1 science labs, 2 foreign language, 4 social studies, 3 history. **Freshman Admission Statistics:** 3,241 applied, 90% admitted, 20% enrolled. **Transfer Admission Requirements:** college transcript(s), essay or personal statement, Minimum college GPA of 2.5 required. Lowest grade transferable C. **General Admission Information:** Priority deadline 11/1. Non-fall registration accepted. Admission may be deferred for a maximum of 1 year.

COSTS AND FINANCIAL AID

Annual tuition $30,690. Room and board $8,568. Required fees $1,250. Average book and supplies expense $1,320. **Required Forms and Deadlines:** FAFSA; Institution's own financial aid form. **Notification of Awards:** Applicants will be notified of awards on a rolling basis beginning 2/1. **Types of Aid:** *Need-based scholarships/grants:* College/university scholarship or grant aid from institutional funds; Federal Pell; Private scholarships; SEOG; State scholarships/grants. *Loans:* Direct PLUS loans; Direct Subsidized Stafford Loans; Direct Unsubsidized Stafford Loans. **Student Employment:** Federal Work-Study Program available. Institutional employment available. **Financial Aid Statistics:** 64% needy freshmen, 59% needy undergrads receive need-based scholarship or grant aid. 97% freshmen, 93% undergrads receive non-need-based scholarship or grant aid. 92% freshmen, 83% undergrads receive need-based self-help aid. 7% freshmen, 6% undergrads receive athletic scholarships. 98.9% freshmen, 91.4% undergrads receive any aid. 78% undergrads borrow to pay for school. Average cumulative indebtedness $27,248. **Criteria awarding aid:** *Non-Need-based:* Academics, Athletics, Job skills, Leadership, Music/drama, Religious affiliation.

DARTMOUTH COLLEGE

6016 McNutt Hall, Hanover, NH 03755
Phone: 603-646-2875 **Financial Aid Phone:** (800) 443-3605
E-mail: admissions.office@dartmouth.edu **CEEB Code:** 3351
Fax: 603-646-1216 **Website:** www.dartmouth.edu **ACT Code:** 2508

This private school was founded in 1769. It has a 265 acre campus.

RATINGS

Admissions Selectivity Rating: 99 **Fire Safety Rating:** 89 **Green Rating:** 91

STUDENTS AND FACULTY

Enrollment: 4,340. **Student Body:** 49% female, 51% male, 97% out-of-state, 9% international (70 countries represented). Asian 15%, African American 7%, Caucasian 50%, Hispanic 10%, Native American 2%, Pacific Islander <1%, Two or more races 5%, Race unknown 2%.
Retention and Graduation: 97% freshmen return for sophomore year. 88% freshmen graduate within 4 years. 96% freshmen graduate within 6 years.
Faculty: Student/faculty ratio 7:1. 610 full-time faculty, 95% hold PhDs, 19% are members of minority groups, 37% are women. 1% of classes are taught by teaching assistants.

ACADEMICS

Degrees: Bachelor's; Doctoral degree—professional practice; Doctoral degree research/scholarship; Master's. **Classes:** Most classes have 10–19 students. **Most popular majors:** Economics, General; Political Science and Government, General; Psychology, General. **Special Study Options:** Double major; Exchange student program (domestic); Honors program; Independent study; Internships; Student-designed major; Study abroad; Teacher certification program. **Honors programs:** Presidential Scholarship Research Program; Senior Honors Thesis; Senior Fellowship. **Disability Services offered:** Note-taking services; Reader services; Tape recorders; Tutors. **Career services:** Alumni network; Alumni services; Career assessment; Career/job search classes; Internships; Regional alumni.

FACILITIES

Housing: Apartments for married students; Coed dorms; Cooperative housing; Fraternity/sorority housing; Special housing for international students; Theme housing; Wellness housing 75% of campus accessible to physically disabled. **Special Academic Facilities/Equipment:** Hood Museum of Art, Hopkins Center for Performing Arts, Tucker Foundation for volunteer services, observatory, centers for humanities, social science, and science. **Campus Network:** 100% of classrooms, 100% of dorms, 100% of student union, 100% of libraries, 100% of dining areas, 100% of common outdoor areas, have wireless network access.

CAMPUS LIFE

Environment: Village. **Activities:** Campus Ministries; Choral groups; Concert band; Dance; Drama/theater; International Student Organization; Jazz band; Literary magazine; Marching band; Model UN; Music ensembles; Musical theater; Opera; Pep band; Radio station; Student government; Student newspaper; Student-run film society; Symphony orchestra; Television station; Yearbook. 350 registered organizations, 4 honor societies, 24 religious organizations, 17 fraternities, 11 sororities, on campus. **Athletics (Intercollegiate):** *Men:* baseball, basketball, crew/rowing, cross-country, diving, equestrian sports, fencing, football, golf, ice hockey, lacrosse, sailing, skiing (downhill/Alpine), skiing (Nordic/cross-country), soccer, squash, swimming, tennis, track/field (outdoor), track/field (indoor). *Women:* basketball, crew/rowing, cross-country, diving, equestrian sports, fencing, field hockey, golf, ice hockey, lacrosse, sailing, skiing (downhill/Alpine), skiing (Nordic/cross-country), soccer, softball, squash, swimming, tennis, track/field (outdoor), track/field (indoor), volleyball. **On-Campus Highlights:** Hopkins Center for Creative and Performing Arts **Environmental Initiatives:** As part of our commitment to reduce greenhouse gas emissions, Dartmouth commissioned an energy audit for the buildings that collectively use 75% of the energy on campus. Based on the results of this audit, the Trustees invested $12.5 million in 250 energy conservation and efficiency projects in existing buildings, which are now underway.

ADMISSIONS

Freshman Academic Profile: 93% in top 10% of high school class, 98% in top 25% of high school class, 99% in top 50% of high school class. 55% from public high schools. **Test score**s: SAT Math middle 50% range 720–790. SAT EBRW middle 50% range 710–770. ACT middle 50% range 30–34. **Basis for Candidate Selection:** *Very important factors include:* rigor of secondary school record, class rank, academic GPA, application essay, standardized test scores, recommendation(s), extracurricular activities, character/personal qualities. *Important factors include:* talent/ability, volunteer work. *Other factors include:* interview, first generation, alumni/ae relation, geographical residence, racial/ethnic status. **Freshman Admission Requirements:** High school diploma or equivalent is not required *Academic units recommended:* 4 English, 4 math, 4 science, 4 foreign language, 4 social studies. **Freshman Admission Statistics:** 20,035 applied, 10% admitted, 58% enrolled. **Transfer Admission Requirements:** High school transcript, college transcript(s), essay or personal statement, standardized test scores, statement of good standing from prior institution(s). Lowest grade transferable B. **General Admission Information:** Application fee $80. Regular application deadline 1/1.

COSTS AND FINANCIAL AID

Annual tuition $55,605. Room and board $16,374. Required fees $2,017. Average book and supplies expense $1,100. **Required Forms and Deadlines:** Business/Farm Supplement; CSS/Financial Aid PROFILE; FAFSA; Noncustodial PROFILE;. **Notification of Awards:** Applicants will be notified of awards on or about 4/2. *Types of Aid:* *Need-based scholarships/grants:* College/university scholarship or grant aid from institutional funds; Federal Pell; Private scholarships; SEOG; State scholarships/grants. *Loans:* Direct PLUS loans; Direct Subsidized Stafford Loans; Direct Unsubsidized Stafford Loans. **Student Employment:** Federal Work-Study Program available. Institutional employment available. **Financial Aid Statistics:** 94% needy freshmen, 95% needy undergrads receive need-based scholarship or grant aid. 0% freshmen, 0% undergrads receive non-need-based scholarship or grant aid. 90% freshmen, 92% undergrads receive need-based self-help aid. 0% freshmen, 0% undergrads receive athletic scholarships. 58.3% freshmen, 53.9% undergrads receive any aid. 49% undergrads borrow to pay for school. Average cumulative indebtedness $18,903.

DAVIDSON COLLEGE

PO Box 7156, Davidson, NC 28035-7156
Phone: 704-894-2230
E-mail: admission@davidson.edu **CEEB Code:** 5150
Fax: 704-894-2016 **Website:** www.davidson.edu **ACT Code:** 3086

This private school, affiliated with the Presbyterian Church, was founded in 1837. It has a 665 acre campus.

RATINGS

Admissions Selectivity Rating: 97   **Fire Safety Rating:** 60*   **Green Rating:** 63

STUDENTS AND FACULTY

Enrollment: 1,800. **Student Body:** 49% female, 51% male, 77% out-of-state, 7% international (42 countries represented). Asian 6%, African American 7%, Caucasian 67%, Hispanic 8%, Native American <1%, Pacific Islander <1%, Two or more races 5%, Race unknown 1%.
Retention and Graduation: 95% freshmen return for sophomore year. 21% grads go on to further study within 1 year. **Faculty:** Student/faculty ratio 9:1. 191 full-time faculty, 97% hold PhDs, 23% are members of minority groups, 45% are women. 0% of classes are taught by teaching assistants.

ACADEMICS

Degrees: Bachelor's. **Classes:** Most classes have 10–19 students. Most lab/discussion sessions have 10–19 students. **Most popular majors:** Biology/Biological Sciences, General; Political Science and Government, General; Psychology, General. **Special Study Options:** Cross-registration; Double major; Exchange student program (domestic); Independent study; Internships; Student-designed major; Study abroad. **Disability Services offered:** Note-taking services; Reader services; Tape recorders; Tutors. **Career services:** Alumni network; Alumni services; Career assessment; Career/job search classes; Internships.

FACILITIES

Housing: Apartments for single students; Coed dorms; Cooperative housing; Theme housing; Wellness housing 90% of campus accessible to physically disabled. **Special Academic Facilities/Equipment:** Art gallery, scanning electron microscopes, UV-visible spectrometer, laser systems, Baker sports complex, Visual Arts building.

CAMPUS LIFE

Environment: Village. **Activities:** Campus Ministries; Choral groups; Dance; Drama/theater; International Student Organization; Jazz band; Literary magazine; Music ensembles; Musical theater; Pep band; Radio station; Student government; Student newspaper; Symphony orchestra; Yearbook. 168 registered organizations, 15 honor societies, 16 religious organizations, 8 fraternities, 6 sororities, on campus. **Athletics (Intercollegiate):** *Men:* baseball, basketball, cross-country, diving, football, golf, soccer, swimming, tennis, track/field (outdoor), wrestling. *Women:* basketball, cross-country, diving, field hockey, lacrosse, soccer, swimming, tennis, track/field (outdoor), volleyball. **On-Campus Highlights:** Belk Visual Arts Center. **Environmental Initiatives:** Solar PV and solar thermal array on Baker Sports Complex.

ADMISSIONS

Freshman Academic Profile: Average high school GPA 3.9. 76% in top 10% of high school class, 95% in top 25% of high school class, 99% in top 50% of high school class. 47% from public high schools. **Test score**s: SAT Math middle 50% range 650–730. SAT EBRW middle 50% range 660–740. ACT middle 50% range 30–33. **Basis for Candidate Selection:** *Very important factors include:* rigor of secondary school record, recommendation(s), character/personal qualities, volunteer work. *Important factors include:* application essay, standardized test scores, extracurricular activities, talent/ability. *Other factors include:* class rank, academic GPA, alumni/ae relation. **Freshman Admission Requirements:** High school diploma is required and GED is not accepted. *Academic units required:* 4 English, 3 math, 2 science, 2 foreign language, 2 unit from above areas or other academic areas. *Academic units recommended:* 4 math, 4 science, 4 foreign language. **Freshman Admission Statistics:** 5,673 applied, 20% admitted, 45% enrolled. **Transfer Admission Requirements:** High school transcript, college transcript(s), essay or personal statement, standardized test scores, statement of good standing from prior institution(s). Minimum college GPA of 3.0 required. Lowest grade transferable C. **General Admission Information:** Application fee $50. Regular application deadline 1/2. Non-fall registration accepted. Admission may be deferred for a maximum of 1 year.

COSTS AND FINANCIAL AID

Annual tuition $52,524. Room and board $14,803. Required fees $525. Average book and supplies expense $1,000. **Required Forms and Deadlines:** Business/Farm Supplement; CSS/Financial Aid PROFILE; FAFSA; Noncustodial PROFILE;. **Notification of Awards:** Applicants will be notified of awards on or about 4/1. *Types of Aid:* *Need-based scholarships/grants:* College/university scholarship or grant aid from institutional funds; Federal Pell; Private scholarships; SEOG; State scholarships/grants. *Loans:* Direct PLUS loans; Direct Subsidized Stafford Loans; Direct Unsubsidized Stafford Loans. **Student Employment:** Federal Work-Study Program available. Institutional employment available. **Financial Aid Statistics:** 100% needy freshmen, 100% needy undergrads receive need-based scholarship or grant aid. 38% freshmen, 28% undergrads receive non-need-based scholarship or grant aid. 55% freshmen, 64% undergrads receive need-based self-help aid. 8% freshmen, 8% undergrads receive athletic scholarships. 52% freshmen, 52% undergrads receive any aid. 29% undergrads borrow to pay for school. Average cumulative indebtedness $22,599. **Criteria awarding aid:** *Non-Need-based:* Academics, Alumni affiliation, Art, Athletics, Leadership, Minority status, Music/drama.

DEEP SPRINGS COLLEGE

Applications Committee, Dyer, NV 89010
Phone: 760-872-2000 **Financial Aid Phone:** 760 872 2000
E-mail: apcom@deepsprings.edu **CEEB Code:** 4281
Fax: 760-872-4466 **Website:** www.deepsprings.edu **ACT Code:** 0252

This private school was founded in 1917. It has a 30000 acre campus.

RATINGS
Admissions Selectivity Rating: 99   **Fire Safety Rating:** 88   **Green Rating:** 60*

STUDENTS AND FACULTY
Enrollment: 30. **Student Body:** 33% female, 67% male, 82% out-of-state, 14% international (5 countries represented). Asian 14%, African American 0%, Caucasian 64%, Hispanic 4%, Native American 0%, Pacific Islander 0%, Two or more races 4%, Race unknown 0%.
Retention and Graduation: 92% freshmen return for sophomore year.
Faculty: Student/faculty ratio 4:1. 3 full-time faculty, 100% hold PhDs, 0% are members of minority groups, 67% are women. 0% of classes are taught by teaching assistants.

ACADEMICS
Degrees: Associate. **Classes:** Most classes have 10–19 students. **Most popular majors:** Liberal Arts and Sciences, General Studies and Humanities, Other. **Special Study Options:** Independent study; Internships.

FACILITIES
Housing: Cooperative housing; Men's dorms; Special housing for disabled students; Theme housing; Wellness housing 100% of campus accessible to physically disabled. **Special Academic Facilities/Equipment:** Ranch- 300 cattle, 20 horses, organic farm growing hay and produce; thousands of acres of wilderness surround the college.

CAMPUS LIFE
Environment: Rural. **Activities:** Campus Ministries; Choral groups; Concert band; Dance; Drama/theater; International Student Organization; Literary magazine; Music ensembles; Musical theater; Radio station; Student government; Student newspaper; Student-run film society. **On-Campus Highlights:** Boarding House.

ADMISSIONS
Freshman Academic Profile: 100% in top 10% of high school class, 100% in top 25% of high school class, 100% in top 50% of high school class. 67% from public high schools. **Test scores:** SAT Math middle 50% range 670–740. SAT EBRW middle 50% range 740–800. **Basis for Candidate Selection:** *Very important factors include:* application essay, interview, character/personal qualities, level of applicant's interest. *Important factors include:* rigor of secondary school record, academic GPA, extracurricular activities, volunteer work, work experience. *Other factors include:* class rank, standardized test scores, recommendation(s), talent/ability, first generation, racial/ethnic status. **Freshman Admission Requirements:** High school diploma or equivalent is not required. **Freshman Admission Statistics:** 200 applied, 10% admitted, 84% enrolled. **Transfer Admission Requirements:** High school transcript, college transcript(s), essay or personal statement, interview, standardized test scores. **General Admission Information:** Regular application deadline 11/7.

COSTS AND FINANCIAL AID
Average book and supplies expense $1,200. **Financial Aid Statistics:** 0% freshmen, 0% undergrads receive athletic scholarships. 100% freshmen, 100% undergrads receive any aid. **Criteria awarding aid:** *Non-Need-based:* Academics, Art, Job skills, Leadership.

DEFIANCE COLLEGE

701 North Clinton Street, Defiance, OH 43512-1695
Phone: 419-783-2359 **Financial Aid Phone:** 419-783-2458
E-mail: http://www.defiance.edu/admissions/index.html **CEEB Code:** 1162
Fax: 419-783-2468 **Website:** www.defiance.edu **ACT Code:** 3264

This private school, affiliated with the United Church of Christ, was founded in 1850. It has a 150 acre campus.

RATINGS
Admissions Selectivity Rating: 79   **Fire Safety Rating:** 90   **Green Rating:** 64

STUDENTS AND FACULTY
Enrollment: 195. **Student Body:** 42% female, 58% male, 28% out-of-state, 2% international (2 countries represented). Asian 1%, African American 13%, Caucasian 74%, Hispanic 7%, Native American <1%, Pacific Islander 0%, Two or more races 3%, Race unknown 1%.
Retention and Graduation: 61% freshmen return for sophomore year.
Faculty: Student/faculty ratio 11:1. 36 full-time faculty, 61% hold PhDs, 17% are members of minority groups, 42% are women. 0% of classes are taught by teaching assistants.

ACADEMICS
Degrees: Associate; Bachelor's; Certificate; Master's. **Classes:** Most classes have fewer than 10 students. Most lab/discussion sessions have fewer than 10 students. **Most popular majors:** Education, General; Criminal Justice and Corrections. **Special Study Options:** Distance learning; Double major; Dual enrollment; Honors program; Independent study; Internships; Student-designed major; Study abroad; Teacher certification program. **Disability Services offered:** Note-taking services; Reader services; Tape recorders; Tutors. **Career services:** Alumni network; Alumni services; Career assessment; Career/job search classes; Internships; Regional alumni.

FACILITIES
Housing: Apartments for single students; Coed dorms; Theme housing; Wellness housing 100% of campus accessible to physically disabled. **Special Academic Facilities/Equipment:** Art gallery, media center, Eisenhower archives room, curriculum resource center, Cultural Arts Center, Indian wars collection. **Campus Network:** 100% of classrooms, 100% of dorms, 100% of student union, 100% of libraries, 100% of dining areas, have wireless network access.

CAMPUS LIFE
Environment: Village. **Activities:** Campus Ministries; Choral groups; Concert band; Dance; Drama/theater; Jazz band; Literary magazine; Marching band; Music ensembles; Musical theater; Pep band; Student government; Student newspaper. 36 registered organizations, 3 honor societies, 2 religious organizations, 1 fraternities, 1 sororities, on campus. **Athletics (Intercollegiate):** *Men:* baseball, basketball, cross-country, football, golf, soccer, tennis, track/field (outdoor), track/field (indoor). *Women:* basketball, cross-country, golf, soccer, softball, tennis, track/field (outdoor), track/field (indoor), volleyball. **On-Campus Highlights:** George M. Smart Athletic Center. **Environmental Initiatives:** Lowering Electrical, Gas, and Water Usage.

ADMISSIONS
Freshman Academic Profile: Average high school GPA 3.1. 12% in top 10% of high school class, 29% in top 25% of high school class, 57% in top 50% of high school class. 97% from public high schools. **Test scores:** SAT Math middle 50% range 340–470. SAT EBRW middle 50% range 360–490. ACT middle 50% range 18–22. **Basis for Candidate Selection:** *Very important factors include:* rigor of secondary school record, academic GPA, standardized test scores. *Other factors include:* class rank, application essay, recommendation(s), interview, extracurricular activities, character/personal qualities, volunteer work, work experience. **Freshman Admission Requirements:** High school diploma is required and GED is accepted. *Academic units recommended:* 4 English, 3 math, 3 science, 2 science labs, 2 foreign language, 2 social studies, 2 visual/performing arts. **Freshman Admission Statistics:** 1,257 applied, 56% admitted, 21% enrolled. **Transfer Admission Requirements:** High school transcript, college transcript(s), essay or personal statement, statement of good standing from prior institution(s). Minimum college GPA of 2.0 required. Lowest grade transferable C. **General Admission Information:** Application fee $25. Non-fall registration accepted. Admission may be deferred for a maximum of one year.

COSTS AND FINANCIAL AID
Annual tuition $31,990. Room and board $10,220. Required fees $740. Average book and supplies expense $1,400. **Required Forms and Deadlines:** FAFSA. **Notification of Awards:** Applicants will be notified of awards on a rolling basis beginning 2/1. **Types of Aid:** *Need-based scholarships/grants:* College/university scholarship or grant aid from institutional funds; Federal Pell; Private scholarships; SEOG; State scholarships/grants. *Loans:* Direct PLUS loans; Direct Subsidized Stafford Loans; Direct Unsubsidized Stafford Loans. **Student Employment:** Federal Work-Study Program available. Institutional employment available. **Financial Aid Statistics:** 86% needy freshmen, 83% needy undergrads receive need-based scholarship or grant aid. 100% freshmen, 97% undergrads receive non-need-based scholarship or grant aid. 93% freshmen, 92% undergrads receive need-based self-help aid. 0% freshmen, 0% undergrads receive athletic scholarships. 100% freshmen, 99% undergrads receive any aid. **Criteria awarding aid:** *Need-based:* Alumni affiliation, Religious affiliation. *Non-Need-based:* Academics, Leadership, Minority status, Music/drama.

DELAWARE VALLEY UNIVERSITY

700 East Butler Avenue, Doylestown, PA 18901
Phone: 215-489-2211 **Financial Aid Phone:** 215-489-2975
E-mail: ADMITME@delval.edu **CEEB Code:** 2510
Fax: 215-230-2968 **Website:** www.delval.edu **ACT Code:** 3551

This private school was founded in 1896. It has a 571 acre campus.

RATINGS
Admissions Selectivity Rating: 74   **Fire Safety Rating:** 82   **Green Rating:** 61

STUDENTS AND FACULTY
Enrollment: 1,757. **Student Body:** 60% female, 40% male, 38% out-of-state, <1% international (4 countries represented). Asian 1%, African American 9%, Caucasian 68%, Hispanic 8%, Native American <1%, Pacific Islander <1%, Two or more races 2%, Race unknown 11%.
Retention and Graduation: 72% freshmen return for sophomore year. 55% freshmen graduate within 4 years. 61% freshmen graduate within 6 years. **Faculty:** Student/faculty ratio 13:1. 90 full-time faculty, 70% hold PhDs, 11% are members of minority groups, 46% are women. 0% of classes are taught by teaching assistants.

ACADEMICS
Degrees: Associate; Bachelor's; Certificate; Doctoral degree research/scholarship; Master's; Post-bachelor's certificate. **Classes:** Most classes have 10–19 students. Most lab/discussion sessions have 10–19 students. **Most popular majors:** Animal Sciences, General; Biology/Biological Sciences, General; Business Administration and Management, General. **Special Study Options:** Distance learning; Double major; Dual enrollment; Honors program; Independent study; Internships; Student-designed major; Study abroad; Teacher certification program. **Honors programs:** The Honors Program at DelVal is an educational enrichment program for students with exceptional promise. This four-year sequence of courses offers superior students intellectual opportunities beyond the scope of most collegiate programs: smaller discussion-based classes, direct contact with top faculty members, opportunities for international study and the freedom to pursue individualized programs with a cross-disciplinary flavor. During alternate years, the Honors Program sponsors special foreign study colloquia, which allow students the opportunity to augment their investigation of a major international city with travel to that city over spring break. Led by faculty with expertise in that particular region, these courses allow students the opportunity to explore the world around them and provide a forum for meaningful discussion of history and culture. **Combined degree programs:** BA/MA. **Disability Services offered:** Note-taking services; Reader services; Tape recorders. **Career services:** Alumni network; Alumni services; Career assessment; Career/job search classes; Internships.

FACILITIES
Housing: Coed dorms.

CAMPUS LIFE
Environment: Village. **Activities:** Choral groups; Jazz band; Literary magazine; Student government. 73 registered organizations, 5 honor societies, 4 religious organizations, 2 fraternities, 3 sororities, on campus. **Athletics (Intercollegiate):** *Men:* baseball, basketball, cross-country, football, golf, soccer, track/field (outdoor), track/field (indoor), wrestling. *Women:* basketball,

cheerleading, cross-country, field hockey, soccer, softball, track/field (outdoor), track/field (indoor), volleyball. **On-Campus Highlights:** Life Sciences Building.

ADMISSIONS
Freshman Academic Profile: Average high school GPA 3.3. 15% in top 10% of high school class, 35% in top 25% of high school class, 66% in top 50% of high school class. 98% from public high schools. **Test scores:** SAT Math middle 50% range 480–570. SAT EBRW middle 50% range 490–600. ACT middle 50% range 18–27. **Basis for Candidate Selection:** *Very important factors include:* academic GPA, standardized test scores. *Important factors include:* rigor of secondary school record, interview. *Other factors include:* class rank, application essay, recommendation(s), extracurricular activities, talent/ability, character/personal qualities, alumni/ae relation, volunteer work, work experience, level of applicant's interest. **Freshman Admission Requirements:** High school diploma is required and GED is accepted. *Academic units required:* 3 English, 2 math, 2 science, 1 science labs, 2 social studies, 6 academic electives. **Freshman Admission Statistics:** 1,676 applied, 93% admitted, 24% enrolled. **Transfer Admission Requirements:** High school transcript, college transcript(s), statement of good standing from prior institution(s). Minimum college GPA of 2.0 required. Lowest grade transferable C. **General Admission Information:** Application fee $50. Priority deadline 5/1. Non-fall registration accepted. Admission may be deferred for a maximum of 12 months.

COSTS AND FINANCIAL AID
Annual tuition $38,070. Room and board $14,620. Required fees $2,550. Average book and supplies expense $1,000. **Required Forms and Deadlines:** FAFSA; State aid form. **Types of Aid:** *Need-based scholarships/grants:* College/university scholarship or grant aid from institutional funds; Federal Pell; Private scholarships; SEOG; State scholarships/grants. *Loans:* Direct PLUS loans; Direct Subsidized Stafford Loans; Direct Unsubsidized Stafford Loans. **Student Employment:** Federal Work-Study Program available. Institutional employment available. **Financial Aid Statistics:** 99% needy freshmen, 100% needy undergrads receive need-based scholarship or grant aid. 98% freshmen, 99% undergrads receive non-need-based scholarship or grant aid. 84% freshmen, 86% undergrads receive need-based self-help aid. 0% freshmen, 0% undergrads receive athletic scholarships. 99% freshmen, 98% undergrads receive any aid. 79% undergrads borrow to pay for school. Average cumulative indebtedness $48,278. **Criteria awarding aid:** *Non-Need-based:* Academics, Alumni affiliation, Music/drama, State/district residency.

DENISON UNIVERSITY

100 West College Street, Granville, OH 43023
Phone: 740-587-6276 **Financial Aid Phone:** 740-587-6279
E-mail: admissions@denison.edu **CEEB Code:** 1164
Fax: 740-587-6306 **Website:** denison.edu **ACT Code:** 3266

This private school was founded in 1831. It has a 930 acre campus.

RATINGS
Admissions Selectivity Rating: 93   **Fire Safety Rating:** 96   **Green Rating:** 96

STUDENTS AND FACULTY
Enrollment: 2,368. **Student Body:** 54% female, 46% male, 74% out-of-state, 12% international (37 countries represented). Asian 4%, African American 6%, Caucasian 63%, Hispanic 9%, Native American 0%, Pacific Islander <1%, Two or more races 3%, Race unknown 2%.
Retention and Graduation: 89% freshmen return for sophomore year. 84% freshmen graduate within 4 years. 87% freshmen graduate within 6 years. 16% grads go on to further study within 1 year. 9% grads pursue arts and sciences degrees. 2% grads pursue law degrees. 2% grads pursue business degrees. 2% grads pursue medical degrees. **Faculty:** Student/faculty ratio 10:1. 226 full-time faculty, 99% hold PhDs, 22% are members of minority groups, 44% are women. 0% of classes are taught by teaching assistants.

ACADEMICS
Degrees: Bachelor's. **Classes:** Most classes have 10–19 students. **Most popular majors:** Economics, General; Biology, General; Psychology, General. **Special Study Options:** Double major; Independent study; Internships; Student-designed major; Study abroad. **Disability Services offered:** Note-taking

services; Reader services; Tape recorders; Tutors. **Career services:** Alumni network; Alumni services; Career assessment; Career/job search classes; Internships; Regional alumni.

FACILITIES

Housing: Apartments for single students; Coed dorms; Cooperative housing; Men's dorms; Theme housing; Wellness housing; Women's dorms 75% of campus accessible to physically disabled. **Special Academic Facilities/ Equipment:** Burmese art collection in the Dension Museum, language lab, research station in 350-acre biological reserve, observatory, high resolution spectrometer lab, nuclear magnetic resonance spectrometer, planetarium, economics computer laboratories. **Campus Network:** 90% of classrooms, 0% of dorms, 100% of student union, 100% of libraries, 100% of dining areas, 5% of common outdoor areas, have wireless network access.

CAMPUS LIFE

Environment: Village. **Activities:** Campus Ministries; Choral groups; Dance; Drama/theater; International Student Organization; Jazz band; Literary magazine; Music ensembles; Musical theater; Radio station; Student government; Student newspaper; Student-run film society; Television station; Yearbook. 175 registered organizations, 8 honor societies, 10 religious organizations, 9 fraternities, 9 sororities, on campus. **Athletics (Intercollegiate):** *Men:* baseball, basketball, cross-country, diving, football, golf, lacrosse, soccer, swimming, tennis, track/field (outdoor), track/field (indoor). *Women:* basketball, cross-country, diving, field hockey, golf, lacrosse, soccer, softball, swimming, tennis, track/field (outdoor), track/field (indoor), volleyball. **On-Campus Highlights:** Samson Talbot Hall of Biological Science. **Environmental Initiatives:** The signing of the ACUPCC and the development of a standing Campus Sustainability Committee as part of the campus governance system.

ADMISSIONS

Freshman Academic Profile: 64% in top 10% of high school class, 85% in top 25% of high school class, 100% in top 50% of high school class. 67% from public high schools. **Test scores:** SAT Math middle 50% range 610–710. SAT EBRW middle 50% range 600–670. ACT middle 50% range 28–31. **Basis for Candidate Selection:** *Very important factors include:* rigor of secondary school record, academic GPA, application essay, recommendation(s). *Important factors include:* interview, extracurricular activities, talent/ability. *Other factors include:* class rank, standardized test scores, character/personal qualities, first generation, alumni/ae relation, geographical residence, state residency, racial/ethnic status, volunteer work, work experience, level of applicant's interest. **Freshman Admission Requirements:** High school diploma is required and GED is accepted. *Academic units recommended:* 4 English, 4 math, 4 science, 4 foreign language, 4 social studies. **Freshman Admission Statistics:** 8,042 applied, 34% admitted, 24% enrolled. **Transfer Admission Requirements:** High school transcript, college transcript(s), essay or personal statement, statement of good standing from prior institution(s). Minimum college GPA of 3.0 required. Lowest grade transferable C–. **General Admission Information:** Priority deadline 1/15. Regular application deadline 1/15. Admission may be deferred for a maximum of 1 year.

COSTS AND FINANCIAL AID

Annual tuition $52,620. Room and board $13,050. Required fees $1,210. Average book and supplies expense $1,000. **Required Forms and Deadlines:** CSS/Financial Aid PROFILE; FAFSA; Noncustodial PROFILE. **Notification of Awards:** Applicants will be notified of awards on or about 3/15. **Types of Aid:** *Need-based scholarships/grants:* College/university scholarship or grant aid from institutional funds; Federal Pell; Private scholarships; SEOG; State scholarships/grants. *Loans:* Direct PLUS loans; Direct Subsidized Stafford Loans; Direct Unsubsidized Stafford Loans. **Student Employment:** Federal Work-Study Program available. Institutional employment available. **Financial Aid Statistics:** 100% needy freshmen, 100% needy undergrads receive need-based scholarship or grant aid. 17% freshmen, 15% undergrads receive non-need-based scholarship or grant aid. 80% freshmen, 84% undergrads receive need-based self-help aid. 0% freshmen, 0% undergrads receive athletic scholarships. 93% freshmen, 95% undergrads receive any aid. 53% undergrads borrow to pay for school. Average cumulative indebtedness $31,551. **Criteria awarding aid:** *Need-based:* Academics, Alumni affiliation, Art, Leadership, Minority status, Music/drama *Non-Need-based:* Academics, Alumni affiliation, Art, Leadership, Minority status, Music/drama, State/district residency.

DEPAUL UNIVERSITY

Best Colleges

1 East Jackson Boulevard, Chicago, IL 60604-2287
Phone: 312-362-8300 **Financial Aid Phone:** 312-362-8610
E-mail: admission@depaul.edu **CEEB Code:** 1165
Fax: 312-362-5749 **Website:** www.depaul.edu **ACT Code:** 1012

This private school, affiliated with the Roman Catholic Church, was founded in 1898. It has a 38 acre campus.

RATINGS

Admissions Selectivity Rating: 81   **Fire Safety Rating:** 99   **Green Rating:** 60*

STUDENTS AND FACULTY

Enrollment: 14,009. **Student Body:** 53% female, 47% male, 25% out-of-state, 3% international (114 countries represented). Asian 11%, African American 8%, Caucasian 52%, Hispanic 20%, Native American <1%, Pacific Islander <1%, Two or more races 4%, Race unknown 2%.
Retention and Graduation: 85% freshmen return for sophomore year. 61% freshmen graduate within 4 years. 74% freshmen graduate within 6 years. 16% grads go on to further study within 1 year. **Faculty:** Student/faculty ratio 16:1. 870 full-time faculty, 81% hold PhDs, 19% are members of minority groups, 46% are women.

ACADEMICS

Degrees: Bachelor's; Certificate; Doctoral degree—professional practice; Doctoral degree research/scholarship; Master's; Post-bachelor's certificate; Post-master's certificate. **Classes:** Most classes have 20–29 students. Most lab/discussion sessions have 20–29 students. **Most popular majors:** Public Relations, Advertising, and Applied Communication, Other; Accounting; Finance, General. **Special Study Options:** Accelerated program; Distance learning; Double major; English as a Second Language (ESL); Honors program; Independent study; Internships; Liberal arts/career combination; Study abroad; Teacher certification program; Weekend college. **Honors programs:** DePaul's honors program offers small classes organized in a seminar format and taught by faculty committed to academic excellence and the attainment of lifelong learning strategies. Benefits of our scholarly community include academic advising, an Honors Lounge, a student government, peer mentoring, student-faculty dinners, newsletters, cultural outings, service activities, a designated Honors floor in a residence hall, and many other experiences that enrich the Honors community while extending the Honors experience beyond the classroom. **Combined degree programs:** BA/JD; BA/MA. **Disability Services offered:** Note-taking services; Reader services; Tape recorders. **Career services:** Alumni network; Alumni services; Career assessment; Career/job search classes; Internships; Regional alumni.

FACILITIES

Housing: Apartments for single students; Coed dorms; Special housing for disabled students; Special housing for international students; Theme housing; Wellness housing 97% of campus accessible to physically disabled. **Special Academic Facilities/Equipment:** LEED-certified environmental science & chemistry building with greenhouse & green roof, digital cinema laboratory with motion-capture system, green-screen studio, converged newsroom, 10 specialized computer research labs including artificial intelligence, biomedics informatics & mobile e-commerce, 1,300-seat theatre, art museum, fitness & a recreational center with pool. **Campus Network:** 100% of classrooms, 100% of dorms, 100% of student union, 100% of libraries, 100% of dining areas, 100% of common outdoor areas, have wireless network access.

CAMPUS LIFE

Environment: Metropolis. **Activities:** Campus Ministries; Choral groups; Concert band; Dance; Drama/theater; International Student Organization; Jazz band; Literary magazine; Model UN; Music ensembles; Musical theater; Opera; Pep band; Radio station; Student government; Student newspaper; Student-run film society; Symphony orchestra. 282 registered organizations, 24 honor societies, 18 religious organizations, 12 fraternities, 16 sororities, on campus. **Athletics (Intercollegiate):** *Men:* basketball, cross-country, golf, soccer, tennis, track/field (outdoor), track/field (indoor). *Women:* basketball, cross-country, soccer, softball, tennis, track/field (outdoor), track/field (indoor), volleyball. **On-Campus Highlights:** Student Center, Lincoln Park Campus.

ADMISSIONS

Freshman Academic Profile: Average high school GPA 3.7. 81% from public high schools. **Test scores:** SAT Math middle 50% range 530–640. SAT EBRW middle 50% range 540–650. **Basis for Candidate Selection:** *Very important factors include:* rigor of secondary school record, academic GPA, standardized test scores. *Important factors include:* class rank, recommendation(s), extracurricular activities, talent/ability, character/personal qualities. *Other factors include:* application essay, interview, first generation, alumni/ae relation, geographical residence, state residency, religious affiliation/commitment, racial/ethnic status. **Freshman Admission Requirements:** High school diploma is required and GED is accepted. *Academic units required:* 4 English, 3 math, 3 science, 2 science labs, 2 unit from above areas or other academic areas. *Academic units recommended:* 4 English, 3 math, 3 science, 2 science labs, 2 foreign language. **Freshman Admission Statistics:** 26,895 applied, 68% admitted, 14% enrolled. **Transfer Admission Requirements:** college transcript(s), Minimum college GPA of 2.0 required. Lowest grade transferable D. **General Admission Information:** Priority deadline 11/15. Regular application deadline 2/1. Non-fall registration accepted. Admission may be deferred for a maximum of 1 year.

COSTS AND FINANCIAL AID

Annual tuition $40,551. Room and board $14,736. Required fees $651. Average book and supplies expense $1,104. **Required Forms and Deadlines:** FAFSA. **Notification of Awards:** Applicants will be notified of awards on a rolling basis beginning 12/15. *Types of Aid: Need-based scholarships/grants:* College/university scholarship or grant aid from institutional funds; Federal Pell; Private scholarships; SEOG; State scholarships/grants. *Loans:* Direct PLUS loans; Direct Subsidized Stafford Loans; Direct Unsubsidized Stafford Loans. **Student Employment:** Federal Work-Study Program available. Institutional employment available. **Financial Aid Statistics:** 99% needy freshmen, 96% needy undergrads receive need-based scholarship or grant aid. 11% freshmen, 7% undergrads receive non-need-based scholarship or grant aid. 67% freshmen, 74% undergrads receive need-based self-help aid. 1% freshmen, 1% undergrads receive athletic scholarships. 97% freshmen, 86% undergrads receive any aid. 64% undergrads borrow to pay for school. Average cumulative indebtedness $29,621. **Criteria awarding aid:** *Non-Need-based:* Academics, Art, Athletics, Leadership, Music/drama, State/district residency.

DEPAUW UNIVERSITY

204 E. Seminary Street, Greencastle, IN 46135
Phone: 765-658-4006 **Financial Aid Phone:** 765-658-4030
E-mail: admission@depauw.edu **CEEB Code:** 1166
Fax: 765-658-4007 **Website:** www.depauw.edu **ACT Code:** 1184

This private school, affiliated with the Methodist Church, was founded in 1837. It has a 1100 acre campus.

RATINGS

Admissions Selectivity Rating: 86   **Fire Safety Rating:** 73   **Green Rating:** 60*

STUDENTS AND FACULTY

Enrollment: 2,137. **Student Body:** 52% female, 48% male, 61% out-of-state, 10% international (38 countries represented). Asian 4%, African American 5%, Caucasian 66%, Hispanic 7%, Native American <1%, Pacific Islander 0%, Two or more races 5%, Race unknown 2%.
Retention and Graduation: 89% freshmen return for sophomore year. 78% freshmen graduate within 4 years. 85% freshmen graduate within 6 years. 23% grads go on to further study within 1 year. 15% grads pursue arts and sciences degrees. 5% grads pursue law degrees. 1% grads pursue business degrees. 2% grads pursue medical degrees. **Faculty:** Student/faculty ratio 9:1. 228 full-time faculty, 98% hold PhDs, 21% are members of minority groups, 43% are women. 0% of classes are taught by teaching assistants.

ACADEMICS

Degrees: Bachelor's. **Classes:** Most classes have 10–19 students. Most lab/discussion sessions have 10–19 students. **Most popular majors:** Economics, General; Speech Communication and Rhetoric. **Special Study Options:** Double major; Dual enrollment; Exchange student program (domestic); Honors program;

Independent study; Internships; Student-designed major; Study abroad. **Honors programs:** Please visit the following website for information about DePauw's honors programs: http://www.depauw.edu/honors/index.asp. **Disability Services offered:** Note-taking services; Reader services; Tape recorders; Tutors. **Career services:** Alumni network; Alumni services; Career assessment; Career/job search classes; Internships; Regional alumni.

FACILITIES

Housing: Apartments for single students; Coed dorms; Fraternity/sorority housing; Special housing for disabled students; Special housing for international students 85% of campus accessible to physically disabled. **Special Academic Facilities/Equipment:** Recently opened Peeler Art Center housing gallery and studio space; Center for Contemporary Media; Performing Arts Center; Anthropology Museum; Shidzuo Iikudo Museum. **Campus Network:** 100% of classrooms, 0% of dorms, 100% of student union, 100% of libraries, 100% of dining areas, 0% of common outdoor areas, have wireless network access.

CAMPUS LIFE

Environment: Village. **Activities:** Campus Ministries; Choral groups; Concert band; Dance; Drama/theater; International Student Organization; Jazz band; Literary magazine; Music ensembles; Musical theater; Opera; Pep band; Radio station; Student government; Student newspaper; Student-run film society; Symphony orchestra; Television station. 119 registered organizations, 13 honor societies, 10 religious organizations, 13 fraternities, 11 sororities, on campus. **Athletics (Intercollegiate):** *Men:* baseball, basketball, cross-country, diving, football, golf, soccer, swimming, tennis, track/field (outdoor), track/field (indoor). *Women:* basketball, cross-country, diving, field hockey, golf, soccer, softball, swimming, tennis, track/field (outdoor), track/field (indoor), volleyball. **On-Campus Highlights:** DePauw University School of Music. **Environmental Initiatives:** LEED certified construction of the Janet Prindle Institute for Ethics.

ADMISSIONS

Freshman Academic Profile: Average high school GPA 3.8. 40% in top 10% of high school class, 70% in top 25% of high school class, 95% in top 50% of high school class. 83% from public high schools. **Test scores:** SAT Math middle 50% range 550–680. SAT EBRW middle 50% range 560–650. ACT middle 50% range 24–29. **Basis for Candidate Selection:** *Very important factors include:* rigor of secondary school record, academic GPA, standardized test scores. *Important factors include:* class rank, application essay, recommendation(s). *Other factors include:* interview, extracurricular activities, talent/ability, character/personal qualities, first generation, alumni/ae relation, geographical residence, state residency, volunteer work, work experience, level of applicant's interest. **Freshman Admission Requirements:** High school diploma is required and GED is accepted. *Academic units recommended:* 4 English, 4 math, 3 science, 2 science labs, 2 foreign language, 2 social studies. **Freshman Admission Statistics:** 5,173 applied, 67% admitted, 17% enrolled. **Transfer Admission Requirements:** High school transcript, college transcript(s), essay or personal statement, statement of good standing from prior institution(s). Minimum college GPA of 3.0 required. Lowest grade transferable C. **General Admission Information:** Regular application deadline 2/1. Non-fall registration accepted. Admission may be deferred for a maximum of 1 year.

COSTS AND FINANCIAL AID

Annual tuition $50,278. Room and board $13,400. Required fees $868. Average book and supplies expense $1,000. **Required Forms and Deadlines:** FAFSA; Institution's own financial aid form. **Notification of Awards:** Applicants will be notified of awards on a rolling basis beginning 2/1. **Types of Aid:** *Need-based scholarships/grants:* College/university scholarship or grant aid from institutional funds; Federal Pell; Private scholarships; SEOG; State scholarships/grants. *Loans:* Direct Subsidized Stafford Loans; Direct Unsubsidized Stafford Loans. **Student Employment:** Federal Work-Study Program available. Institutional employment available. **Financial Aid Statistics:** 100% needy freshmen, 100% needy undergrads receive need-based scholarship or grant aid. 18% freshmen, 17% undergrads receive non-need-based scholarship or grant aid. 79% freshmen, 81% undergrads receive need-based self-help aid. 0% freshmen, 0% undergrads receive athletic scholarships. 80% undergrads borrow to pay for school. Average cumulative indebtedness $25,813. **Criteria awarding aid:** *Non-Need-based:* Academics, Leadership, Music/drama.

DESALES UNIVERSITY

2755 Station Ave., Center Valley, PA 18034
Phone: 610-282-4443 **Financial Aid Phone:** 610-282-4443
E-mail: admiss@desales.edu **CEEB Code:** 2021
Fax: 610-282-0131 **Website:** www.desales.edu **ACT Code:** 3525

This private school, affiliated with the Roman Catholic Church, was founded in 1964. It has a 500 acre campus.

RATINGS
Admissions Selectivity Rating: 78   **Fire Safety Rating:** 88   **Green Rating:** 61

STUDENTS AND FACULTY
Enrollment: 2,295. **Student Body:** 61% female, 39% male, 24% out-of-state, <1% international (5 countries represented). Asian 3%, African American 4%, Caucasian 72%, Hispanic 13%, Native American 0%, Pacific Islander <1%, Two or more races 3%, Race unknown 5%.
Retention and Graduation: 81% freshmen return for sophomore year. 59% freshmen graduate within 4 years. 67% freshmen graduate within 6 years. **Faculty:** Student/faculty ratio 12:1. 126 full-time faculty, 83% hold PhDs, 5% are members of minority groups, 52% are women. 0% of classes are taught by teaching assistants.

ACADEMICS
Degrees: Bachelor's; Certificate; Doctoral degree—professional practice; Master's; Post-bachelor's certificate; Post-master's certificate. **Classes:** Most classes have 10–19 students. Most lab/discussion sessions have fewer than 10 students. **Most popular majors:** Drama and Dramatics/Theatre Arts, General; Registered Nursing/Registered Nurse; Health Professions and Related Clinical Sciences, Other. **Special Study Options:** Accelerated program; Cross-registration; Distance learning; Double major; Dual enrollment; Exchange student program (domestic); External degree program; Honors program; Independent study; Internships; Liberal arts/career combination; Student-designed major; Study abroad; Teacher certification program; Weekend college. **Honors programs:** Student participation in the Faith & Reason Honors Program is competitive, usually limited to a maximum of fifteen (15) students in each academic class. The aim of this program is to provide scholarship-level students with a unique opportunity to explore the "big questions" in life, in a small cohort of students, guided by senior-level faculty at DeSales University. Each semester, students in the Honors Program enjoy "priority pre-registration" for all their classes. Students who complete all components of the program have their participation noted on their university transcripts and receive recognition of their accomplishment at the University's commencement ceremonies. **Disability Services offered:** Note-taking services; Reader services; Tape recorders; Tutors. **Career services:** Alumni network; Alumni services; Career assessment; Career/job search classes; Internships.

FACILITIES
Housing: Coed dorms; Cooperative housing; Men's dorms; Special housing for disabled students; Theme housing; Women's dorms 99% of campus accessible to physically disabled. **Special Academic Facilities/Equipment:** The Gambet Center for Business and Health Care includes a replica commodities trading center and the only human gross anatomy laboratory in the region in addition to simulation labs.

CAMPUS LIFE
Environment: Town. **Activities:** Campus Ministries; Choral groups; Dance; Drama/theater; International Student Organization; Jazz band; Literary magazine; Marching band; Model UN; Music ensembles; Musical theater; Pep band; Radio station; Student government; Student newspaper; Student-run film society; Television station; Yearbook. 60 registered organizations, 12 honor societies, 1 religious organizations, on campus. **Athletics (Intercollegiate):** *Men:* baseball, basketball, cross-country, golf, lacrosse, soccer, tennis, track/field (outdoor), track/field (indoor). *Women:* basketball, cross-country, field hockey, soccer, softball, tennis, track/field (outdoor), track/field (indoor), volleyball. **On-Campus Highlights:** Billera Athletics and Recreation Center.

ADMISSIONS
Freshman Academic Profile: Average high school GPA 3.3. 34% in top 10% of high school class, 52% in top 25% of high school class, 79% in top 50% of high school class. 62% from public high schools. **Test scores:** SAT Math middle 50% range 500–610. SAT EBRW middle 50% range 510–618. ACT middle 50% range 23–27. **Basis for Candidate Selection:** *Very important factors include:* rigor of secondary school record, academic GPA, character/personal

qualities. *Important factors include:* class rank, application essay, standardized test scores, recommendation(s), interview, level of applicant's interest. *Other factors include:* extracurricular activities, talent/ability, first generation, volunteer work, work experience. **Freshman Admission Requirements:** High school diploma is required and GED is accepted. *Academic units required:* 4 English, 3 math, 2 science, 2 science labs, 2 foreign language, 3 social studies. *Academic units recommended:* 4 English, 4 math, 3 science, 3 science labs, 4 foreign language, 3 social studies. **Freshman Admission Statistics:** 2,979 applied, 73% admitted, 19% enrolled. **Transfer Admission Requirements:** High school transcript, college transcript(s), statement of good standing from prior institution(s). Minimum college GPA of 2.00 required. Lowest grade transferable 2. **General Admission Information:** Priority deadline 3/1. Regular application deadline 8/1. Non-fall registration accepted.

COSTS AND FINANCIAL AID
Required Forms and Deadlines: FAFSA;. **Notification of Awards:** Applicants will be notified of awards on a rolling basis beginning 12/1. **Types of Aid:** *Need-based scholarships/grants:* College/university scholarship or grant aid from institutional funds; Federal Pell; Private scholarships; SEOG; State scholarships/grants. *Loans:* Direct PLUS loans; Direct Subsidized Stafford Loans; Direct Unsubsidized Stafford Loans. **Student Employment:** Federal Work-Study Program available. Institutional employment available. **Financial Aid Statistics:** 100% needy freshmen, 94% needy undergrads receive need-based scholarship or grant aid. 94% freshmen, 82% undergrads receive non-need-based scholarship or grant aid. 79% freshmen, 82% undergrads receive need-based self-help aid. 0% freshmen, 0% undergrads receive athletic scholarships. 99% freshmen, 82% undergrads receive any aid. 79% undergrads borrow to pay for school. Average cumulative indebtedness $42,536. **Criteria awarding aid:** *Need-based:* Academics, Alumni affiliation. *Non-Need-based:* Academics, Alumni affiliation, Art, Leadership, Music/drama, Religious affiliation.

DICKINSON COLLEGE

P.O. Box 1773, Carlisle, PA 17013-2896
Phone: 717-245-1231 **Financial Aid Phone:** 717-245-1308
E-mail: admissions@dickinson.edu **CEEB Code:** 2186
Fax: 717-245-1442 **Website:** www.dickinson.edu/ **ACT Code:** 3550

This private school was founded in 1783. It has a 144 acre campus.

RATINGS
Admissions Selectivity Rating: 91   **Fire Safety Rating:** 92   **Green Rating:** 99

STUDENTS AND FACULTY
Enrollment: 2,098. **Student Body:** 57% female, 43% male, 75% out-of-state, 13% international (46 countries represented). Asian 4%, African American 5%, Caucasian 64%, Hispanic 9%, Native American <1%, Pacific Islander <1%, Two or more races 4%, Race unknown 1%.
Retention and Graduation: 87% freshmen return for sophomore year. 80% freshmen graduate within 4 years. 83 15% grads go on to further study within 1 year. 71% grads pursue arts and sciences degrees. 14% grads pursue law degrees. 4% grads pursue business degrees. 5% grads pursue medical degrees. **Faculty:** Student/faculty ratio 8:1. 218 full-time faculty, 94% hold PhDs, 17% are members of minority groups, 52% are women. 0% of classes are taught by teaching assistants.

ACADEMICS
Degrees: Bachelor's. **Classes:** Most classes have 10–19 students. **Most popular majors:** International Business/Trade/Commerce; Political Science and Government, General; International Relations and Affairs. **Special Study Options:** Accelerated program; Cross-registration; Double major; Dual enrollment; English as a Second Language (ESL); Exchange student program (domestic); Independent study; Internships; Liberal arts/career combination; Student-designed major; Study abroad. **Combined degree programs:** BA/JD; BA/MEng. **Disability Services offered:** Note-taking services; Reader services; Tape recorders; Tutors. **Career services:** Alumni network; Alumni services; Career assessment; Career/job search classes; Internships; Regional alumni.

FACILITIES

Housing: Apartments for single students; Coed dorms; Fraternity/sorority housing; Special housing for disabled students; Special housing for international students; Theme housing; Wellness housing 72% of campus accessible to physically disabled. **Special Academic Facilities/Equipment:** Old West; Rector Science Complex; Greenhouse & Center for Sustainable living; Trout Gallery; Weiss Center for the Arts; Goodyear Art Studios; planetarium; observatory; scanning electron microscope; Keck Archaeology Lab, Dog House, biogas facility, College Farm, the Hive (apiary). **Campus Network:** 70% of classrooms, 100% of dorms, 100% of student union, 100% of libraries, 100% of dining areas, 20% of common outdoor areas, have wireless network access.

CAMPUS LIFE

Environment: Town. **Activities:** Choral groups; Concert band; Dance; Drama/theater; International Student Organization; Jazz band; Literary magazine; Model UN; Music ensembles; Musical theater; Radio station; Student government; Student newspaper; Student-run film society; Symphony orchestra; Yearbook. 153 registered organizations, 15 honor societies, 5 religious organizations, 3 fraternities, 6 sororities, on campus. **Athletics (Intercollegiate):** *Men:* baseball, basketball, cross-country, football, golf, lacrosse, soccer, swimming, tennis, track/field (outdoor), track/field (indoor). *Women:* basketball, cross-country, field hockey, golf, lacrosse, soccer, softball, swimming, tennis, track/field (outdoor), track/field (indoor), volleyball. **On-Campus Highlights:** Old West, designed by Benjamin Latrobe. **Environmental Initiatives:** Integrating sustainability throughout the curriculum, supported by the Center for Sustainability Education.

ADMISSIONS

Freshman Academic Profile: 43% in top 10% of high school class, 73% in top 25% of high school class, 96% in top 50% of high school class. 55% from public high schools. **Test scores:** SAT Math middle 50% range 590–700. SAT EBRW middle 50% range 600–690. ACT middle 50% range 26–32. **Basis for Candidate Selection:** *Very important factors include:* rigor of secondary school record, academic GPA, application essay, recommendation(s), extracurricular activities, talent/ability, character/personal qualities, volunteer work, level of applicant's interest. *Important factors include:* class rank, standardized test scores, interview, alumni/ae relation, geographical residence, state residency, racial/ethnic status. *Other factors include:* first generation. **Freshman Admission Requirements:** High school diploma is required and GED is accepted. *Academic units required:* 4 English, 3 math, 3 science, 2 science labs, 2 foreign language, 2 social studies, 2 academic electives. *Academic units recommended:* 3 foreign language. **Freshman Admission Statistics:** 6,426 applied, 40% admitted, 18% enrolled. **Transfer Admission Requirements:** High school transcript, college transcript(s), essay or personal statement, statement of good standing from prior institution(s). Minimum college GPA of 2 required. Lowest grade transferable C. **General Admission Information:** Application fee $65. Regular application deadline 1/15. Admission may be deferred for a maximum of 2 years.

COSTS AND FINANCIAL AID

Average book and supplies expense $1,290. **Required Forms and Deadlines:** CSS/Financial Aid PROFILE; FAFSA; Noncustodial PROFILE; State aid form. **Types of Aid:** *Need-based scholarships/grants:* College/university scholarship or grant aid from institutional funds; Federal Pell; Private scholarships; SEOG; State scholarships/grants. *Loans:* Direct PLUS loans; Direct Subsidized Stafford Loans; Direct Unsubsidized Stafford Loans. **Student Employment:** Federal Work-Study Program available. Institutional employment available. **Financial Aid Statistics:** 97% needy freshmen, 98% needy undergrads receive need-based scholarship or grant aid. 7% freshmen, 7% undergrads receive non-need-based scholarship or grant aid. 91% freshmen, 90% undergrads receive need-based self-help aid. 0% freshmen, 0% undergrads receive athletic scholarships. 85% freshmen, 82% undergrads receive any aid. 55% undergrads borrow to pay for school. Average cumulative indebtedness $27,030. **Criteria awarding aid:** *Need-based:* Music/drama *Non-Need-based:* Academics, Leadership, Music/drama.

DICKINSON STATE UNIVERSITY

Office of Enrollment Services, Dickinson, ND 58601-4896
Phone: 701-483-2175 **Financial Aid Phone:** 701-483-2371
E-mail: dsu.hawks@dsu.nodak.edu
Fax: 701-483-2409 **Website:** www.dickinsonstate.com **ACT Code:** 3210

This public school was founded in 1918. It has a 137 acre campus.

RATINGS

Admissions Selectivity Rating: 76   **Fire Safety Rating:** 60*   **Green Rating:** 60*

STUDENTS AND FACULTY

Enrollment: 2,669. **Student Body:** 59% female, 41% male, 34% out-of-state, 12% international (30 countries represented). Asian <1%, African American 1%, Caucasian 71%, Hispanic 1%, Native American 2%, Race unknown 12%. **Retention and Graduation:** 60% freshmen return for sophomore year. **Faculty:** Student/faculty ratio 19:1. 86 full-time faculty, 52% hold PhDs, 6% are members of minority groups, 43% are women.

ACADEMICS

Degrees: Associate; Bachelor's; Certificate; Terminal Associate; Transfer Associate. **Classes:** Most classes have 10–19 students. **Most popular majors:** Business/Commerce, General; Teacher Education, Multiple Levels; Nursing/Registered Nurse (Rn, Asn, Bsn, Msn). **Special Study Options:** Accelerated program; Distance learning; Double major; Dual enrollment; Honors program; Independent study; Internships; Liberal arts/career combination; Student-designed major; Study abroad; Teacher certification program. **Career services:** Alumni network; Alumni services; Career assessment; Career/job search classes; Internships.

FACILITIES

Housing: Apartments for married students; Apartments for single students; Coed dorms; Men's dorms; Special housing for disabled students; Women's dorms. **Special Academic Facilities/Equipment:** Art gallery, smart classrooms.

CAMPUS LIFE

Environment: Rural. **Activities:** Choral groups; Concert band; Dance; Drama/theater; International Student Organization; Jazz band; Literary magazine; Marching band; Music ensembles; Musical theater; Pep band; Student government; Student newspaper; Student-run film society; Yearbook. 51 registered organizations, 7 honor societies, 6 religious organizations, on campus. **Athletics (Intercollegiate):** *Men:* baseball, basketball, cheerleading, cross-country, football, golf, rodeo, track/field (outdoor), track/field (indoor), wrestling. *Women:* basketball, cheerleading, cross-country, golf, rodeo, softball, track/field (outdoor), track/field (indoor), volleyball. **On-Campus Highlights:** Murphy Hall.

ADMISSIONS

Freshman Academic Profile: Average high school GPA 3.2. 6% in top 10% of high school class, 19% in top 25% of high school class, 53% in top 50% of high school class. 98% from public high schools. **Test scores:** SAT Math middle 50% range 470–590. SAT EBRW middle 50% range 430–530. ACT middle 50% range 18–23. **Basis for Candidate Selection: Freshman Admission Requirements:** High school diploma is required and GED is accepted. *Academic units required:* 4 English, 3 math, 3 science, 3 unit from above areas or other academic areas. **Freshman Admission Statistics:** 527 applied, 96% admitted, 75% enrolled. **Transfer Admission Requirements:** college transcript(s), Minimum college GPA of 2.0 required. Lowest grade transferable D. **General Admission Information:** Application fee $35. Non-fall registration accepted.

COSTS AND FINANCIAL AID

Annual in-state tuition $3,828. Annual out-of-state tuition $10,222. Room and board $4,076. Average book and supplies expense $900. **Required Forms and Deadlines:** FAFSA. **Notification of Awards:** Applicants will be notified of awards on a rolling basis beginning 4/30. **Types of Aid:** *Need-based scholarships/grants:* College/university scholarship or grant aid from institutional funds; Federal Pell; Private scholarships; SEOG; State scholarships/grants. **Student Employment:** Federal Work-Study Program available. Institutional employment available. **Criteria awarding aid:** *Need-based:* Academics, Job skills, Minority status. *Non-Need-based:* Academics, Alumni affiliation, Art, Athletics, Job skills, Leadership, Minority status, Music/drama, State/district residency.

DIGIPEN INSTITUTE OF TECHNOLOGY

9931 Willows Road NE, Redmond, WA 98052
Phone: 425-629-5001 **Financial Aid Phone:** 425-629-5002
E-mail: admissions@digipen.edu **CEEB Code:** 37243
Fax: 425-558-0378 **Website:** https://www.digipen.edu **ACT Code:** 6659

This proprietary school was founded in 1988. It has a 2 acre campus.

RATINGS
Admissions Selectivity Rating: 92   **Fire Safety Rating:** 87   **Green Rating:** 60*

STUDENTS AND FACULTY
Enrollment: 1,069. **Student Body:** 25% female, 75% male.
Retention and Graduation: 82% freshmen return for sophomore year.
Faculty: Student/faculty ratio 10:1. 82 full-time faculty, 35% hold PhDs, 0% are members of minority groups, 22% are women. 0% of classes are taught by teaching assistants.

ACADEMICS
Degrees: Bachelor's; Master's. **Classes:** Most classes have 10–19 students. Most lab/discussion sessions have fewer than 10 students. **Most popular majors:** Modeling, Virtual Environments and Simulation; Game and Interactive Media Design; Animation, Interactive Technology, Video Graphics and Special Effects. **Special Study Options:** Accelerated program; English as a Second Language (ESL); Independent study; Internships; Study abroad. **Disability Services offered:** Note-taking services; Reader services; Tape recorders; Tutors. **Career services:** Alumni network; Alumni services; Career/job search classes; Internships.

FACILITIES
Housing: Men's dorms; Special housing for international students; Women's dorms 100% of campus accessible to physically disabled. **Special Academic Facilities/Equipment:** DIT's campus was designed to meet the needs of our students and create an environment that would stimulate collaboration and creativity. The campus is located in Redmond, WA, over 350 game and game-related companies, granting students greater access to internships, jobs, and networking opportunities. DIT's close proximity to companies allows industry leaders to lecture and serve on DIT's program advisory committees.

CAMPUS LIFE
Environment: City. **Activities:** Choral groups; International Student Organization; Jazz band; Music ensembles; Student government. 46 registered organizations, on campus. **On-Campus Highlights:** Edison Production Lab.

ADMISSIONS
Freshman Academic Profile: Test scores: SAT Math middle 50% range 568–700. SAT EBRW middle 50% range 560–700. ACT middle 50% range 25–30. **Basis for Candidate Selection:** *Important factors include:* rigor of secondary school record, academic GPA, application essay, standardized test scores, talent/ability, level of applicant's interest. *Other factors include:* recommendation(s), extracurricular activities, character/personal qualities, work experience. **Freshman Admission Requirements:** High school diploma is required and GED is accepted. *Academic units recommended:* 4 English, 4 math, 4 science, 1 computer science, 1 visual/performing arts. **Freshman Admission Statistics:** 997 applied, 34% admitted, 56% enrolled. **General Admission Information:** Application fee $60. Admission may be deferred for a maximum of 1 year.

COSTS AND FINANCIAL AID
Annual tuition $33,700. Required fees $200. **Required Forms and Deadlines:** FAFSA. **Notification of Awards:** Applicants will be notified of awards on a rolling basis beginning 12/1. **Types of Aid:** *Need-based scholarships/grants:* College/university scholarship or grant aid from institutional funds; Federal Pell; Private scholarships; SEOG; State scholarships/grants. *Loans:* Direct PLUS loans; Direct Subsidized Stafford Loans; Direct Unsubsidized Stafford Loans. **Student Employment:** Institutional employment available. **Financial Aid Statistics:** 55% needy freshmen, 57% needy undergrads receive need-based scholarship or grant aid. 24% freshmen, 19% undergrads receive non-need-based scholarship or grant aid. 43% freshmen, 48% undergrads receive need-based self-help aid. 0% freshmen, 0% undergrads receive athletic scholarships. 52% undergrads borrow to pay for school. Average cumulative indebtedness $37,380.

DIVINE WORD COLLEGE

Office of Admissions, Epworth, IA 52045
Phone: 563-876-3332
E-mail: svdvocations@dwci.edu **CEEB Code:** 6174
Fax: 563-876-5515

This private school, affiliated with the Roman Catholic Church, was founded in 1964. It has a 30 acre campus.

RATINGS
Admissions Selectivity Rating: 68   **Fire Safety Rating:** 60*   **Green Rating:** 60*

STUDENTS AND FACULTY
Enrollment: 65. **Student Body:** female, male, 100% out-of-state, international (12 countries represented).
Faculty: Student/faculty ratio 3:1. 16 full-time faculty, 56% hold PhDs, 25% are members of minority groups, 56% are women. 0% of classes are taught by teaching assistants.

ACADEMICS
Degrees: Associate; Bachelor's. **Special Study Options:** Double major; English as a Second Language (ESL); Independent study; Liberal arts/career combination.

FACILITIES
Housing: Men's dorms. **Campus Network:** 100% of classrooms, 100% of dorms, 100% of student union, 100% of libraries, 100% of dining areas, 100% of common outdoor areas, have wireless network access.

CAMPUS LIFE
Environment: Rural. **Activities:** Campus Ministries; Choral groups; International Student Organization; Student government; Yearbook. **Athletics (Intercollegiate):** *Men:* soccer.

ADMISSIONS
Basis for Candidate Selection: *Very important factors include:* interview, character/personal qualities, religious affiliation/commitment, level of applicant's interest. *Important factors include:* academic GPA, application essay, recommendation(s). *Other factors include:* rigor of secondary school record, class rank, standardized test scores, extracurricular activities, talent/ability, geographical residence, volunteer work, work experience. **Freshman Admission Requirements:** High school diploma is required and GED is accepted. **Freshman Admission Statistics:** 3 applied, 67% admitted, enrolled. **Transfer Admission Requirements:** High school transcript, college transcript(s), essay or personal statement, interview, statement of good standing from prior institution(s). **General Admission Information:** Application fee $25. Non-fall registration accepted. Admission may be deferred for a maximum of one semester.

COSTS AND FINANCIAL AID
Annual tuition $10,400. Room and board $2,700. Required fees $120. Average book and supplies expense $500. **Types of Aid:** *Need-based scholarships/grants:* College/university scholarship or grant aid from institutional funds; Federal Pell; Private scholarships; SEOG; State scholarships/grants. *Loans:* Direct Subsidized Stafford Loans; Direct Unsubsidized Stafford Loans. **Student Employment:** Federal Work-Study Program available. **Criteria awarding aid:** *Need-based:* Academics, Leadership.

DOANE UNIVERSITY

1014 Boswell Avenue, Crete, NE 68333
Phone: 402-826-8222 **Financial Aid Phone:** 402-826-8260
E-mail: admissions@doane.edu **CEEB Code:** 6165
Fax: 402-826-8600 **Website:** www.doane.edu **ACT Code:** 2448

This private school, affiliated with the United Church of Christ, was founded in 1872. It has a 300 acre campus.

RATINGS
Admissions Selectivity Rating: 76   Fire Safety Rating: 91   Green Rating: 60*

STUDENTS AND FACULTY
Enrollment: 1,308. **Student Body:** 51% female, 49% male, 23% out-of-state, 2% international (8 countries represented). Asian 2%, African American 3%, Caucasian 78%, Hispanic 9%, Native American <1%, Pacific Islander <1%, Two or more races 4%, Race unknown 1%. **Retention and Graduation:** 71% freshmen return for sophomore year. 44% freshmen graduate within 4 years. 54% freshmen graduate within 6 years. 32% grads go on to further study within 1 year. 16% grads pursue arts and sciences degrees. 1% grads pursue law degrees. 1% grads pursue business degrees. 5% grads pursue medical degrees. **Faculty:** Student/faculty ratio 11:1. 88 full-time faculty, 86% hold PhDs, 2% are members of minority groups, 45% are women. 0% of classes are taught by teaching assistants.

ACADEMICS
Degrees: Bachelor's; Doctoral degree research/scholarship; Master's; Post-master's certificate. **Classes:** Most classes have 10–19 students. Most lab/discussion sessions have fewer than 10 students. **Most popular majors:** Business Administration and Management, General; Elementary Education and Teaching; Biological and Physical Sciences. **Special Study Options:** Double major; English as a Second Language (ESL); Honors program; Independent study; Internships; Student-designed major; Study abroad; Teacher certification program. **Honors programs:** The Honors Program is designed to enrich, in a variety of ways, the educational experience of selected Doane students. Specialized, interdisciplinary, one-credit honors seminars form the intellectual core of the program. Another component is the study abroad experience undertaken during the junior or senior year. The culminating experience is a collaborative research project. **Combined degree programs:** BA/MEng. **Disability Services offered:** Tutors. **Career services:** Alumni network; Career assessment; Internships.

FACILITIES
Housing: Coed dorms; Theme housing 60% of campus accessible to physically disabled. **Special Academic Facilities/Equipment:** Art gallery, language lab, communication studies facilities, electron microscope, observatory, outdoor challenge course. **Campus Network:** 100% of classrooms, 60% of dorms, 100% of student union, 100% of libraries, 100% of dining areas, 30% of common outdoor areas, have wireless network access.

CAMPUS LIFE
Environment: Rural. **Activities:** Campus Ministries; Choral groups; Concert band; Dance; Drama/theater; Jazz band; Literary magazine; Marching band; Music ensembles; Musical theater; Pep band; Radio station; Student government; Student newspaper; Television station; Yearbook. 50 registered organizations, 8 honor societies, 2 religious organizations, 5 fraternities, 4 sororities, on campus. **Athletics (Intercollegiate):** *Men:* baseball, basketball, cross-country, football, golf, soccer, tennis, track/field (outdoor), track/field (indoor). *Women:* basketball, cheerleading, cross-country, golf, soccer, softball, tennis, track/field (outdoor), track/field (indoor), volleyball. **On-Campus Highlights:** Tiger Inn. **Environmental Initiatives:** Recycling.

ADMISSIONS
Freshman Academic Profile: Average high school GPA 3.5. 13% in top 10% of high school class, 39% in top 25% of high school class, 73% in top 50% of high school class. 90% from public high schools. **Test scores:** ACT middle 50% range 20–25. **Basis for Candidate Selection:** *Very important factors include:* academic GPA. *Important factors include:* rigor of secondary school record, character/personal qualities, alumni/ae relation. *Other factors include:* class rank, standardized test scores, recommendation(s), interview, extracurricular activities, talent/ability, racial/ethnic status, volunteer work, work experience. **Freshman Admission Requirements:** High school diploma is required and GED is accepted. *Academic units recommended:* 4 English, 3 math, 3 science, 2 foreign language, 3 social studies. **Freshman Admission Statistics:** 2,116 applied,

71% admitted, 21% enrolled. **Transfer Admission Requirements:** High school transcript, college transcript(s), statement of good standing from prior institution(s). Minimum college GPA of 2.0 required. Lowest grade transferable C-. **General Admission Information:** Non-fall registration accepted. Admission may be deferred for a maximum of one year.

COSTS AND FINANCIAL AID
Annual tuition $34,500. Room and board $9,800. Required fees $800. Average book and supplies expense $1,000. **Required Forms and Deadlines:** FAFSA. **Notification of Awards:** Applicants will be notified of awards on a rolling basis beginning 3/15. **Types of Aid:** *Need-based scholarships/grants:* College/university scholarship or grant aid from institutional funds; Federal Pell; SEOG; State scholarships/grants. *Loans:* Direct PLUS loans; Direct Subsidized Stafford Loans; Direct Unsubsidized Stafford Loans. **Student Employment:** Federal Work-Study Program available. Institutional employment available. **Financial Aid Statistics:** 100% needy freshmen, 100% needy undergrads receive need-based scholarship or grant aid. 22% freshmen, 22% undergrads receive non-need-based scholarship or grant aid. 69% freshmen, 75% undergrads receive need-based self-help aid. 12% freshmen, 18% undergrads receive athletic scholarships. 100% freshmen, 96% undergrads receive any aid. 84% undergrads borrow to pay for school. Average cumulative indebtedness $28,490. **Criteria awarding aid:** *Non-Need-based:* Academics, Alumni affiliation, Athletics, Leadership, Music/drama, Religious affiliation.

DOMINICAN COLLEGE

470 Western Highway, Orangeburg, NY 10962-1210
Phone: 845-848-7901 **Financial Aid Phone:** 845-848-7818
E-mail: admissions@dc.edu **CEEB Code:** 2190
Fax: 845-365-3150 **Website:** http://www.dc.edu **ACT Code:** 2730

This private school was founded in 1952. It has a 70 acre campus.

RATINGS
Admissions Selectivity Rating: 67   Fire Safety Rating: 93   Green Rating: 60*

STUDENTS AND FACULTY
Enrollment: 1,552. **Student Body:** 66% female, 34% male, 25% out-of-state, 1% international (15 countries represented). Asian 7%, African American 17%, Caucasian 32%, Hispanic 29%, Native American 0%, Pacific Islander <1%, Two or more races 3%, Race unknown 11%. **Retention and Graduation:** 71% freshmen return for sophomore year. **Faculty:** Student/faculty ratio 16:1. 73 full-time faculty, 68% hold PhDs, 15% are members of minority groups, 70% are women. 0% of classes are taught by teaching assistants.

ACADEMICS
Degrees: Associate; Bachelor's; Master's. **Classes:** Most classes have 10–19 students. **Most popular majors:** Business/Commerce, General; Social Sciences, General. **Special Study Options:** Accelerated program; Cooperative education program; Distance learning; Dual enrollment; Honors program; Independent study; Internships; Liberal arts/career combination; Study abroad; Teacher certification program; Weekend college. **Disability Services offered:** Note-taking services; Reader services; Tutors. **Career services:** Career assessment; Career/job search classes; Internships; Regional alumni.

FACILITIES
Housing: Coed dorms; Wellness housing 100% of campus accessible to physically disabled. **Special Academic Facilities/Equipment:** New State of the Art Prusmack Center for Health Care Programs and Science Education.

CAMPUS LIFE
Environment: Village. **Activities:** Campus Ministries; Choral groups; Dance; Drama/theater; Literary magazine; Model UN; Musical theater; Radio station; Student government; Student newspaper; Yearbook. 26 registered organizations, 12 honor societies, 1 religious organizations, on campus. **Athletics (Intercollegiate):** *Men:* baseball, basketball, golf, lacrosse, soccer. *Women:* basketball, cross-country, lacrosse, soccer, softball, track/field (outdoor), volleyball. **On-Campus Highlights:** Prusmack Center for Health and Science Education. **Environmental Initiatives:** Geothermal HVAC system installed in most recently constructed academic building.

ADMISSIONS

Freshman Academic Profile: Average high school GPA 3.0. 69% from public high schools. **Basis for Candidate Selection:** *Important factors include:* academic GPA, standardized test scores, recommendation(s). *Other factors include:* rigor of secondary school record, application essay, interview, extracurricular activities, talent/ability, character/personal qualities, volunteer work, work experience, level of applicant's interest. **Freshman Admission Requirements:** High school diploma is required and GED is accepted. *Academic units required:* 4 English, 3 math, 3 science, 1 science labs, 1 foreign language, 3 social studies, 3 history, 2 academic electives. *Academic units recommended:* 4 English, 3 math, 3 science, 1 science labs, 2 foreign language, 4 social studies, 4 history, 2 academic electives. **Freshman Admission Statistics:** 1,959 applied, 71% admitted, 26% enrolled. **Transfer Admission Requirements:** college transcript(s), Minimum college GPA of 2.0 required. Lowest grade transferable C. **General Admission Information:** Application fee $35. Non-fall registration accepted. Admission may be deferred for a maximum of 1 year.

COSTS AND FINANCIAL AID

Annual tuition $26,578. Room and board $12,420. Required fees $860. Average book and supplies expense $1,350. **Required Forms and Deadlines:** FAFSA; State aid form. **Notification of Awards:** Applicants will be notified of awards on a rolling basis beginning 2/1. **Types of Aid:** *Need-based scholarships/grants:* College/university scholarship or grant aid from institutional funds; Federal Pell; Private scholarships; SEOG; State scholarships/grants. *Loans:* Direct PLUS loans; Direct Subsidized Stafford Loans; Direct Unsubsidized Stafford Loans. **Student Employment:** Federal Work-Study Program available. Institutional employment available. **Financial Aid Statistics:** 97% needy freshmen, 95% needy undergrads receive need-based scholarship or grant aid. 9% freshmen, 8% undergrads receive non-need-based scholarship or grant aid. 84% freshmen, 84% undergrads receive need-based self-help aid. 8% freshmen, 5% undergrads receive athletic scholarships. 98% freshmen, 97% undergrads receive any aid. **Criteria awarding aid:** *Need-based:* Academics, Athletics *Non-Need-based:* Academics, Athletics.

DOMINICAN SCHOOL OF PHILOSOPHY AND THEOLOGY

2301 Vine Street, Berkeley, CA 94708
Phone: 510-883-2073
E-mail: admissions@dspt.edu
Fax: 510-849-1372 **Website:** www.dspt.edu

This private school, affiliated with the Roman Catholic Church, was founded in 1932. It has a 1 acre campus.

RATINGS

Admissions Selectivity Rating: 60*   **Fire Safety Rating:** 60*   **Green Rating:** 60*

STUDENTS AND FACULTY

Enrollment: 5. **Student Body:** 40% female, 60% male, 0% international (6 countries represented). Asian 40%, African American 0%, Caucasian 20%, Hispanic 40%, Native American 0%, Race unknown 0%.
Retention and Graduation: 100% freshmen return for sophomore year. 50% grads go on to further study within 1 year. 60% grads pursue arts and sciences degrees. 10% grads pursue law degrees. 0% grads pursue business degrees. 50% grads pursue medical degrees. **Faculty:** Student/faculty ratio 4:1. 12 full-time faculty, 100% hold PhDs, 0% are members of minority groups, 17% are women. 10% of classes are taught by teaching assistants.

ACADEMICS

Degrees: Bachelor's; Certificate; Master's. **Classes:** Most classes have 10–19 students. **Special Study Options:** Cross-registration; Independent study; Study abroad.

FACILITIES

Housing: Apartments for married students; Apartments for single students; Men's dorms; Women's dorms 50% of campus accessible to physically disabled. **Campus Network:** 100% of classrooms, 100% of dorms, 100% of student union, 100% of libraries, 100% of dining areas, 95% of common outdoor areas, have wireless network access.

CAMPUS LIFE

Environment: City. **Activities:** Choral groups; Concert band; Music ensembles; Student government; Yearbook.

ADMISSIONS

Freshman Admission Requirements: High school diploma is required and GED is accepted. **Freshman Admission Statistics:** applied, admitted, enrolled. **Transfer Admission Requirements:** college transcript(s), essay or personal statement, Minimum college GPA of 2.3 required. Lowest grade transferable C. **General Admission Information:** Application fee $40. Priority deadline 3/15. Admission may be deferred for a maximum of 1 year.

COSTS AND FINANCIAL AID

Annual tuition $11,880. Average book and supplies expense $1,113.

DOMINICAN UNIVERSITY

7900 West Division, River Forest, IL 60305
Phone: 708-524-6800 **Financial Aid Phone:** 708-524-6950
E-mail: domadmis@dom.edu **CEEB Code:** 1667
Fax: 708-524-6864 **Website:** www.dom.edu **ACT Code:** 1126

This private school, affiliated with the Roman Catholic Church, was founded in 1901. It has a 37 acre campus.

RATINGS

Admissions Selectivity Rating: 80   **Fire Safety Rating:** 96   **Green Rating:** 73

STUDENTS AND FACULTY

Enrollment: 2,098. **Student Body:** 68% female, 32% male, 7% out-of-state, 2% international (10 countries represented). Asian 3%, African American 6%, Caucasian 30%, Hispanic 56%, Native American <1%, Pacific Islander <1%, Two or more races 1%, Race unknown 2%.
Retention and Graduation: 83% freshmen return for sophomore year. 47% freshmen graduate within 4 years. 62% freshmen graduate within 6 years. 24% grads go on to further study within 1 year. **Faculty:** Student/faculty ratio 10:1. 158 full-time faculty, 85% hold PhDs, 27% are members of minority groups, 60% are women. 0% of classes are taught by teaching assistants.

ACADEMICS

Degrees: Bachelor's; Doctoral degree research/scholarship; Master's; Post-bachelor's certificate; Post-master's certificate. **Classes:** Most classes have 10–19 students. Most lab/discussion sessions have 10–19 students. **Most popular majors:** Business/Commerce, General; Psychology, General; Sociology, General. **Special Study Options:** Accelerated program; Cross-registration; Distance learning; Double major; Dual enrollment; English as a Second Language (ESL); Honors program; Independent study; Internships; Liberal arts/career combination; Study abroad; Teacher certification program. **Honors programs:** Honors seminars for high ability students; Honors Program. **Combined degree programs:** BA/MA. **Disability Services offered:** Note-taking services; Reader services; Tape recorders; Tutors. **Career services:** Alumni network; Alumni services; Career assessment; Career/job search classes; Internships; Regional alumni.

FACILITIES

Housing: Apartments for married students; Apartments for single students; Coed dorms; Special housing for disabled students; Wellness housing; Women's dorms 100% of campus accessible to physically disabled. **Special Academic Facilities/Equipment:** Art Gallery, clinical simulation lab for nursing, Butler Children's Literature Center, cadaver lab.

CAMPUS LIFE

Environment: Metropolis. **Activities:** Campus Ministries; Choral groups; Concert band; Dance; Drama/theater; International Student Organization; Literary magazine; Model UN; Musical theater; Student government; Student newspaper. 35 registered organizations, 12 honor societies, 2 religious organizations, on campus. **Athletics (Intercollegiate):** *Men:* baseball, basketball, cross-country, soccer, tennis. *Women:* basketball, cross-country, soccer, softball, tennis, volleyball. **On-Campus Highlights:** Cybercafe. **Environmental Initiatives:** Over half the surface parking lots have permeable pavers.

ADMISSIONS

Freshman Academic Profile: Average high school GPA 3.7. 22% in top 10% of high school class, 52% in top 25% of high school class, 86% in top 50% of high school class. 80% from public high schools. **Test scores:** SAT Math middle 50% range 470–560. SAT EBRW middle 50% range 480–570. ACT middle 50% range 19–24. **Basis for Candidate Selection:** *Very important factors include:* rigor of secondary school record, class rank, academic GPA, standardized test scores. *Other factors include:* application essay, recommendation(s), interview, extracurricular activities, talent/ability, character/personal qualities, first generation, alumni/ae relation. **Freshman Admission Requirements:** High school diploma is required and GED is accepted. **Freshman Admission Statistics:** 4,813 applied, 64% admitted, 15% enrolled. **Transfer Admission Requirements:** college transcript(s), essay or personal statement, Minimum college GPA of 2.5 required. Lowest grade transferable C-. **General Admission Information:** Application fee $25. Regular application deadline 8/26. Non-fall registration accepted. Admission may be deferred for a maximum of 1 semester.

COSTS AND FINANCIAL AID

Annual tuition $32,964. Room and board $10,241. Required fees $470. Average book and supplies expense $1,200. **Required Forms and Deadlines:** FAFSA. **Notification of Awards:** Applicants will be notified of awards on a rolling basis beginning 2/15. **Types of Aid:** *Need-based scholarships/grants:* College/university scholarship or grant aid from institutional funds; Federal Pell; Private scholarships; SEOG; State scholarships/grants. *Loans:* Direct PLUS loans; Direct Subsidized Stafford Loans; Direct Unsubsidized Stafford Loans. **Student Employment:** Federal Work-Study Program available. Institutional employment available. **Financial Aid Statistics:** 100% needy freshmen, 98% needy undergrads receive need-based scholarship or grant aid. 9% freshmen, 6% undergrads receive non-need-based scholarship or grant aid. 90% freshmen, 91% undergrads receive need-based self-help aid. 0% freshmen, 0% undergrads receive athletic scholarships. 100% freshmen, 90% undergrads receive any aid. 87% undergrads borrow to pay for school. Average cumulative indebtedness $28,387. **Criteria awarding aid:** *Need-based:* Academics, Alumni affiliation, Art, Minority status, Religious affiliation. *Non-Need-based:* Academics, Alumni affiliation, Art, Minority status, Religious affiliation.

DOMINICAN UNIVERSITY OF CALIFORNIA

Admissions, San Rafael, CA 94901-2298
Phone: 415-485-3204 **Financial Aid Phone:** 415-257-1302
E-mail: enroll@dominican.edu **CEEB Code:** 4284
Website: www.dominican.edu **ACT Code:** 0256

This private school, affiliated with the Roman Catholic Heritage, was founded in 1890. It has a 80 acre campus.

RATINGS
Admissions Selectivity Rating: 77   Fire Safety Rating: 95   Green Rating: 60*

STUDENTS AND FACULTY
Enrollment: 1,284. **Student Body:** 74% female, 26% male, 9% out-of-state, 1% international (17 countries represented). Asian 26%, African American 5%, Caucasian 32%, Hispanic 21%, Native American 1%, Pacific Islander 1%, Two or more races 8%, Race unknown 6%.
Retention and Graduation: 86% freshmen return for sophomore year. 56% freshmen graduate within 4 years. 71% freshmen graduate within 6 years.
Faculty: Student/faculty ratio 9:1. 106 full-time faculty, 70% hold PhDs, 15% are members of minority groups, 54% are women. 0% of classes are taught by teaching assistants.

ACADEMICS
Degrees: Bachelor's; Master's; Post-bachelor's certificate. **Classes:** Most classes have 10–19 students. Most lab/discussion sessions have fewer than 10 students. **Most popular majors:** Psychology, General; Nursing/Registered Nurse (Rn, Asn, Bsn, Msn); Business Administration and Management, General. **Special Study Options:** Accelerated program; Cross-registration; Distance learning; Double major; Dual enrollment; Exchange student program (domestic); Honors program; Independent study; Internships; Student-designed major; Study abroad; Teacher certification program; Weekend college. **Honors programs:** Honors Program Scholar in the World. **Disability Services offered:** Note-taking services; Reader services; Tape recorders; Tutors. **Career services:** Alumni network; Alumni services; Career assessment; Career/job search classes; Internships; Regional alumni.

FACILITIES
Housing: Coed dorms 65% of campus accessible to physically disabled. **Special Academic Facilities/Equipment:** Art Gallery, Science Lab, Computer Labs, Nursing Skills Lab.

CAMPUS LIFE
Environment: Town. **Activities:** Campus Ministries; Choral groups; Dance; Drama/theater; International Student Organization; Jazz band; Literary magazine; Music ensembles; Radio station; Student government; Student newspaper. 19 registered organizations, 7 honor societies, 4 religious organizations, on campus. **Athletics (Intercollegiate):** *Men:* basketball, golf, lacrosse, soccer. *Women:* basketball, golf, soccer, softball, tennis, volleyball. **On-Campus Highlights:** Conlan Recreation Center. **Environmental Initiatives:** We established the Dominican Center for Sustainability. The Center serves as ground central for Dominican University's numerous green activities, including educational programs, scholarships, community outreach, and national and international partnerships. We created the Center to tap the wealth of intellectual capital in place at Dominican in order to support existing and emerging "green" programs. The Center identifies and promotes economically viable green business practices and serves as a think-tank for ongoing green projects on a community, regional, and global level.

ADMISSIONS
Freshman Academic Profile: Average high school GPA 3.7. 20% in top 10% of high school class, 57% in top 25% of high school class, 89% in top 50% of high school class. **Test scores:** SAT Math middle 50% range 510–595. SAT EBRW middle 50% range 530–620. ACT middle 50% range 20–25. **Basis for Candidate Selection:** *Very important factors include:* rigor of secondary school record, academic GPA, application essay, standardized test scores, recommendation(s), character/personal qualities. *Important factors include:* class rank, interview, extracurricular activities, talent/ability, volunteer work. *Other factors include:* alumni/ae relation. **Freshman Admission Requirements:** High school diploma is required and GED is accepted. *Academic units required:* 4 English, 2 math, 1 science, 1 science labs, 2 foreign language, 1 history. *Academic units recommended:* 3 math, 2 science, 2 history. **Freshman Admission Statistics:** 1,867 applied, 76% admitted, 17% enrolled. **Transfer Admission Requirements:** college transcript(s), essay or personal statement, Minimum college GPA of 2.0 required. Lowest grade transferable C. **General Admission Information:** Priority deadline 2/1. Non-fall registration accepted. Admission may be deferred for a maximum of one term.

COSTS AND FINANCIAL AID
Annual tuition $44,240. Room and board $14,650. Required fees $450. Average book and supplies expense $1,854. **Required Forms and Deadlines:** FAFSA; Institution's own financial aid form. **Notification of Awards:** Applicants will be notified of awards on a rolling basis beginning 3/15. **Types of Aid:** *Need-based scholarships/grants:* College/university scholarship or grant aid from institutional funds; Federal Pell; Private scholarships; SEOG; State scholarships/grants. *Loans:* Direct PLUS loans; Direct Subsidized Stafford Loans; Direct Unsubsidized Stafford Loans. **Student Employment:** Federal Work-Study Program available. Institutional employment available. **Financial Aid Statistics:** 100% needy freshmen, 99% needy undergrads receive need-based scholarship or grant aid. 17% freshmen, 13% undergrads receive non-need-based scholarship or grant aid. 72% freshmen, 80% undergrads receive need-based self-help aid. 3% freshmen, 3% undergrads receive athletic scholarships. 98% freshmen, 95% undergrads receive any aid. 82% undergrads borrow to pay for school. Average cumulative indebtedness $35,369. **Criteria awarding aid:** *Need-based:* Academics, Athletics, Leadership, Minority status, Music/drama. *Non-Need-based:* Academics, Alumni affiliation, Athletics, Leadership, Minority status, Music/drama.

DORDT COLLEGE

498 4th Avenue Northeast, Sioux Center, IA 51250
Phone: 712-722-6080 **Financial Aid Phone:** 712-722-6087
E-mail: admissions@dordt.edu **CEEB Code:** 6171
Fax: 712-722-6035 **Website:** www.dordt.edu **ACT Code:** 1301

This private school, affiliated with the Christian Reformed Church, was founded in 1955. It has a 150 acre campus.

RATINGS
Admissions Selectivity Rating: 81   Fire Safety Rating: 89   Green Rating: 60*

STUDENTS AND FACULTY
Enrollment: 1,331. **Student Body:** 45% female, 55% male, 57% out-of-state, 8% international (21 countries represented). Asian 1%, African American 1%, Caucasian 85%, Hispanic 1%, Native American <1%, Pacific Islander 0%, Two or more races 0%, Race unknown 4%.

Retention and Graduation: 80% freshmen return for sophomore year. 15% grads go on to further study within 1 year. 9% grads pursue arts and sciences degrees. 1% grads pursue law degrees. 3% grads pursue business degrees. 2% grads pursue medical degrees. **Faculty:** Student/faculty ratio 12:1. 81 full-time faculty, 68% hold PhDs, 1% are members of minority groups, 15% are women. 0% of classes are taught by teaching assistants.

ACADEMICS

Degrees: Associate; Bachelor's; Master's; Terminal Associate. **Classes:** Most classes have 10–19 students. Most lab/discussion sessions have 10–19 students. **Most popular majors:** Business/Commerce, General; Education, General; Engineering, General. **Special Study Options:** Double major; English as a Second Language (ESL); Exchange student program (domestic); Honors program; Independent study; Internships; Student-designed major; Study abroad; Teacher certification program. **Disability Services offered:** Note-taking services; Reader services; Tape recorders; Tutors. **Career services:** Alumni network; Alumni services; Career assessment; Career/job search classes; Internships; Regional alumni.

FACILITIES

Housing: Apartments for married students; Apartments for single students; Men's dorms; Special housing for disabled students; Women's dorms 100% of campus accessible to physically disabled. **Special Academic Facilities/Equipment:** observatories 160 acre research farm for Ag program, modern recreation facilities which include indoor track, swimming and ice arena.

CAMPUS LIFE

Environment: Village. **Activities:** Campus Ministries; Choral groups; Concert band; Dance; Drama/theater; International Student Organization; Jazz band; Literary magazine; Music ensembles; Musical theater; Opera; Pep band; Radio station; Student government; Student newspaper; Student-run film society; Symphony orchestra; Yearbook. 40 registered organizations, 4 honor societies, 6 religious organizations, on campus. **Athletics (Intercollegiate):** *Men:* baseball, basketball, cross-country, football, golf, ice hockey, soccer, tennis, track/field (outdoor), track/field (indoor). *Women:* basketball, cross-country, soccer, softball, tennis, track/field (outdoor), track/field (indoor), volleyball. **On-Campus Highlights:** Campus Center.

ADMISSIONS

Freshman Academic Profile: Average high school GPA 3.5. 21% in top 10% of high school class, 44% in top 25% of high school class, 73% in top 50% of high school class. 30% from public high schools. **Test scores:** SAT Math middle 50% range 500–630. SAT EBRW middle 50% range 450–610. ACT middle 50% range 21–28. **Basis for Candidate Selection:** *Very important factors include:* rigor of secondary school record, academic GPA, standardized test scores, religious affiliation/commitment. *Other factors include:* class rank, recommendation(s), extracurricular activities, talent/ability, character/personal qualities, first generation, alumni/ae relation, level of applicant's interest. **Freshman Admission Requirements:** High school diploma is required and GED is accepted. *Academic units required:* 3 English, 2 math, 2 science, 2 foreign language, 2 history, 6 academic electives. *Academic units recommended:* 4 English, 3 math, 4 science, 3 foreign language, 1 social studies. **Freshman Admission Statistics:** 1,356 applied, 75% admitted, 37% enrolled. **Transfer Admission Requirements:** High school transcript, college transcript(s), standardized test scores, Minimum college GPA of 2.0 required. Lowest grade transferable C. **General Admission Information:** Priority deadline 7/1. Regular application deadline 8/1. Non-fall registration accepted. Admission may be deferred for a maximum of 1 year.

COSTS AND FINANCIAL AID

Annual tuition $26,100. Room and board $7,620. Required fees $440. Average book and supplies expense $910. **Required Forms and Deadlines:** FAFSA; Institution's own financial aid form. **Notification of Awards:** Applicants will be notified of awards on a rolling basis beginning 3/1. **Types of Aid:** *Need-based scholarships/grants:* College/university scholarship or grant aid from institutional funds; Federal Pell; Private scholarships; SEOG; State scholarships/grants. *Loans:* Direct PLUS loans; Direct Subsidized Stafford Loans; Direct Unsubsidized Stafford Loans. **Financial Aid Statistics:** 100% needy freshmen, 100% needy undergrads receive need-based scholarship or grant aid. 14% freshmen, 14% undergrads receive non-need-based scholarship or grant aid. 99% freshmen, 100% undergrads receive need-based self-help aid. 8% freshmen, 7% undergrads receive athletic scholarships. 98% freshmen, 98% undergrads receive any aid. **Criteria awarding aid:** *Need-based:* Academics, Alumni affiliation, Art, Athletics, Job skills, Leadership, Minority status, Music/drama, Religious affiliation. *Non-Need-based:* Academics, Alumni affiliation, Art, Athletics, Job skills, Leadership, Minority status, Music/drama, Religious affiliation, State/district residency.

DRAKE UNIVERSITY

2507 University Avenue, Des Moines, IA 50311-4505
Phone: 515-271-3181 **Financial Aid Phone:** 515-271-2905
E-mail: admission@drake.edu **CEEB Code:** 6168
Fax: 515-271-2831 **Website:** www.drake.edu **ACT Code:** 1302

This private school was founded in 1881. It has a 150 acre campus.

RATINGS

Admissions Selectivity Rating: 86   **Fire Safety Rating:** 98   **Green Rating:** 60*

STUDENTS AND FACULTY

Enrollment: 2,952. **Student Body:** 58% female, 42% male, 65% out-of-state, 4% international (43 countries represented). Asian 4%, African American 5%, Caucasian 77%, Hispanic 6%, Native American <1%, Pacific Islander 0%, Two or more races 3%, Race unknown <1%.
Retention and Graduation: 89% freshmen return for sophomore year. 73% freshmen graduate within 4 years. 79% freshmen graduate within 6 years. 22% grads go on to further study within 1 year. 9% grads pursue arts and sciences degrees. 4% grads pursue law degrees. 3% grads pursue business degrees. 4% grads pursue medical degrees. **Faculty:** Student/faculty ratio 10:1. 305 full-time faculty, 95% hold PhDs, 13% are members of minority groups, 48% are women. 0% of classes are taught by teaching assistants.

ACADEMICS

Degrees: Bachelor's; Doctoral degree—other; Doctoral degree—professional practice; Doctoral degree research/scholarship; Master's; Post-bachelor's certificate; Post-master's certificate. **Classes:** Most classes have 10–19 students. Most lab/discussion sessions have 10–19 students. **Most popular majors:** Pharmacy; Actuarial Science; Psychology, General. **Special Study Options:** Accelerated program; Cooperative education program; Distance learning; Double major; Dual enrollment; English as a Second Language (ESL); Honors program; Independent study; Internships; Liberal arts/career combination; Student-designed major; Study abroad; Teacher certification program. **Honors programs:** The Honors Program is designed for motivated students who want to participate in challenging, discussion-based courses on interdisciplinary and topical issues. The program provides a unique opportunity for intellectual enrichment both in and out of the classroom. **Combined degree programs:** BA/JD. **Disability Services offered:** Note-taking services; Reader services; Tape recorders; Tutors. **Career services:** Alumni network; Alumni services; Career assessment; Career/job search classes; Internships; Regional alumni.

FACILITIES

Housing: Apartments for single students; Coed dorms; Fraternity/sorority housing; Theme housing 93% of campus accessible to physically disabled. **Special Academic Facilities/Equipment:** Language lab, observatory, media service center, Anderson art gallery, Oreon E. Scott Chapel. **Campus Network:** 100% of classrooms, 85% of dorms, 100% of student union, 100% of libraries, 100% of dining areas, 100% of common outdoor areas, have wireless network access.

CAMPUS LIFE

Environment: Metropolis. **Activities:** Choral groups; Concert band; Dance; Drama/theater; International Student Organization; Jazz band; Literary magazine; Marching band; Model UN; Music ensembles; Musical theater; Pep band; Radio station; Student government; Student newspaper; Symphony orchestra. 160 registered organizations, 24 honor societies, 10 religious organizations, 9 fraternities, 5 sororities, on campus. **Athletics (Intercollegiate):** *Men:* basketball, cheerleading, cross-country, football, golf, soccer, tennis, track/field (outdoor), track/field (indoor). *Women:* basketball, cheerleading, crew/rowing, cross-country, golf, soccer, softball, tennis, track/field (outdoor), track/field (indoor), volleyball. **On-Campus Highlights:** Athletic Facilities. **Environmental Initiatives:** Sustainable building practices.

ADMISSIONS

Freshman Academic Profile: Average high school GPA 3.7. 39% in top 10% of high school class, 68% in top 25% of high school class, 92% in top 50% of high school class. **Test scores:** SAT Math middle 50% range 560–680. SAT EBRW middle 50% range 580–680. ACT middle 50% range 24–30. **Basis for Candidate Selection:** *Very important factors include:* rigor of secondary school record, academic GPA. *Important factors include:* standardized test scores, interview. *Other factors include:* class rank, application essay, recommendation(s), extracurricular activities, talent/ability, character/personal qualities, alumni/ae relation, racial/ethnic status, volunteer work, work experience, level of applicant's interest. **Freshman Admission Requirements:** High school diploma is required and GED is accepted. *Academic units recommended:* 4 English, 3 math, 2 science, 1 science labs, 2 foreign language, 4 social studies. **Freshman Admission Statistics:** 6,886 applied, 68% admitted, 16% enrolled. **Transfer Admission Requirements:** college transcript(s), Minimum college GPA of 2.0 required. Lowest grade transferable C. **General Admission Information:** Priority deadline 3/1. Non-fall registration accepted. Admission may be deferred for a maximum of 12 months.

COSTS AND FINANCIAL AID

Annual tuition $42,694. Room and board $10,848. Required fees $146. Average book and supplies expense $1,100. **Required Forms and Deadlines:** FAFSA. **Notification of Awards:** Applicants will be notified of awards on a rolling basis beginning 1/1. **Types of Aid:** *Need-based scholarships/grants:* College/university scholarship or grant aid from institutional funds; Federal Pell; Private scholarships; SEOG; State scholarships/grants. *Loans:* Direct PLUS loans; Direct Subsidized Stafford Loans; Direct Unsubsidized Stafford Loans. **Student Employment:** Federal Work-Study Program available. Institutional employment available. **Financial Aid Statistics:** 97% needy freshmen, 97% needy undergrads receive need-based scholarship or grant aid. 21% freshmen, 20% undergrads receive non-need-based scholarship or grant aid. 81% freshmen, 82% undergrads receive need-based self-help aid. 3% freshmen, 4% undergrads receive athletic scholarships. 99% freshmen, 97% undergrads receive any aid. 58% undergrads borrow to pay for school. Average cumulative indebtedness $34,391. **Criteria awarding aid:** *Need-based:* Academics. *Non-Need-based:* Academics, Alumni affiliation, Art, Athletics, Music/drama, State/district residency.

DREW UNIVERSITY

Best Colleges

Office of Undergraduate Admissions, Madison, NJ 07940-1493
Phone: 973-408-3739 **Financial Aid Phone:** 973-408-3112
E-mail: cadm@drew.edu **CEEB Code:** 2193
Fax: 973-408-3068 **Website:** www.drew.edu **ACT Code:** 2550

This private school, affiliated with the Methodist Church, was founded in 1868. It has a 186 acre campus.

RATINGS

Admissions Selectivity Rating: 81   **Fire Safety Rating:** 92   **Green Rating:** 77

STUDENTS AND FACULTY

Enrollment: 1,577. **Student Body:** 60% female, 40% male, 33% out-of-state, 12% international (52 countries represented). Asian 5%, African American 8%, Caucasian 50%, Hispanic 17%, Native American <1%, Pacific Islander 0%, Two or more races 3%, Race unknown 4%.
Retention and Graduation: 85% freshmen return for sophomore year. 66% freshmen graduate within 4 years. 69% freshmen graduate within 6 years. 31% grads go on to further study within 1 year. 19% grads pursue arts and sciences degrees. 2% grads pursue law degrees. 1% grads pursue business degrees. 3% grads pursue medical degrees. **Faculty:** Student/faculty ratio 12:1. 139 full-time faculty, 99% hold PhDs, 23% are members of minority groups, 47% are women. 0% of classes are taught by teaching assistants.

ACADEMICS

Degrees: Bachelor's; Doctoral degree—other; Doctoral degree—professional practice; Doctoral degree research/scholarship; Master's; Post-bachelor's certificate; Post-master's certificate. **Classes:** Most classes have 10–19 students. Most lab/discussion sessions have 10–19 students. **Most popular majors:** Biology/Biological Sciences, General; Business Administration and Management, General; Psychology, General. **Special Study Options:** Accelerated program; Cross-registration; Double major; Dual enrollment; English as a Second Language (ESL); Exchange student program (domestic); Honors program; Independent study; Internships; Liberal arts/career combination; Student-designed major; Study abroad; Teacher certification program. **Honors programs:** Baldwin Honors Scholars are Drew's highest-achieving students, chosen for their strong academic record and exceptional leadership to pursue opportunities for independent learning, engagement and research beyond the regular undergraduate curriculum. Baldwin Scholars

complete an advanced curriculum that includes honors colloquia, participation in a community initiative, and the completion of a capstone honors thesis or project. Scholars also take part in unique learning and leadership opportunities and have access to distinguished campus visitors, cultural events, and research grants. **Combined degree programs:** BA/JD; BA/MA; BA/MD. **Disability Services offered:** Note-taking services; Tape recorders; Tutors. **Career services:** Alumni network; Alumni services; Career assessment; Career/job search classes; Internships; Regional alumni.

FACILITIES

Housing: Coed dorms; Special housing for disabled students; Special housing for international students; Theme housing; Wellness housing **Special Academic Facilities/Equipment:** The Dorothy Young Center for the Arts houses the Korn Art Gallery and a 400-seat performance hall. Drew is also home to the Zuck Arboretum, the Drew Observatory, and the New Jersey Shakespeare Festival.

CAMPUS LIFE

Environment: Village. **Activities:** Campus Ministries; Choral groups; Dance; Drama/theater; International Student Organization; Jazz band; Literary magazine; Model UN; Music ensembles; Musical theater; Pep band; Radio station; Student government; Student newspaper; Student-run film society; Symphony orchestra; Yearbook. 133 registered organizations, 17 honor societies, 8 religious organizations, on campus. **Athletics (Intercollegiate):** *Men:* baseball, basketball, cross-country, fencing, lacrosse, soccer, swimming, tennis. *Women:* basketball, cross-country, fencing, field hockey, lacrosse, soccer, softball, swimming, tennis. **On-Campus Highlights:** The Commons. **Environmental Initiatives:** Newly renovated student center, Ehinger Student Center, meets USGBC Leadership in Energy and Environmental Design (LEED) Silver certification.

ADMISSIONS

Freshman Academic Profile: Average high school GPA 3.5. 23% in top 10% of high school class, 49% in top 25% of high school class, 86% in top 50% of high school class. 63% from public high schools. **Test scores:** SAT Math middle 50% range 535–650. SAT EBRW middle 50% range 570–650. ACT middle 50% range 23–29. **Basis for Candidate Selection:** *Very important factors include:* rigor of secondary school record, academic GPA, interview. *Important factors include:* application essay, recommendation(s), extracurricular activities, talent/ability, character/personal qualities. *Other factors include:* class rank, standardized test scores, first generation, alumni/ae relation, racial/ethnic status, volunteer work, work experience, level of applicant's interest. **Freshman Admission Requirements:** High school diploma is required and GED is accepted. *Academic units recommended:* 4 English, 3 math, 2 science, 2 foreign language, 2 social studies, 2 history, 3 academic electives. **Freshman Admission Statistics:** 3,928 applied, 71% admitted, 14% enrolled. **Transfer Admission Requirements:** High school transcript, college transcript(s), essay or personal statement, statement of good standing from prior institution(s). Lowest grade transferable C. **General Admission Information:** Application fee $40. Priority deadline 11/15. Regular application deadline 2/1. Non-fall registration accepted. Admission may be deferred for a maximum of 1 year.

COSTS AND FINANCIAL AID

Annual tuition $39,828. Room and board $14,672. Required fees $1,132. Average book and supplies expense $1,200. **Required Forms and Deadlines:** FAFSA. **Notification of Awards:** Applicants will be notified of awards on or about 3/25. **Types of Aid:** *Need-based scholarships/grants:* College/university scholarship or grant aid from institutional funds; Federal Pell; Private scholarships; SEOG; State scholarships/grants. *Loans:* Direct PLUS loans; Direct Subsidized Stafford Loans; Direct Unsubsidized Stafford Loans. **Student Employment:** Federal Work-Study Program available. Institutional employment available. **Financial Aid Statistics:** 100% needy freshmen, 100% needy undergrads receive need-based scholarship or grant aid. 9% freshmen, 8% undergrads receive non-need-based scholarship or grant aid. 82% freshmen, 82% undergrads receive need-based self-help aid. 0% freshmen, 0% undergrads receive athletic scholarships. 99% freshmen, 96% undergrads receive any aid. 62% undergrads borrow to pay for school. Average cumulative indebtedness $25,049. **Criteria awarding aid:** *Need-based:* Academics. *Non-Need-based:* Academics, Art, Leadership, Minority status, Music/drama.

DREXEL UNIVERSITY

Best Colleges

3141 Chestnut Street, Main Building,, Philadelphia, PA 19104
Phone: 215-895-2400 **Financial Aid Phone:** 215-895-2537
E-mail: enroll@drexel.edu **CEEB Code:** 2194
Fax: 215-895-1285 **Website:** www.drexel.edu **ACT Code:** 3556

This private school was founded in 1891. It has a 96 acre campus.

RATINGS

Admissions Selectivity Rating: 83   Fire Safety Rating: 97   Green Rating: 88

STUDENTS AND FACULTY

Enrollment: 15,500. **Student Body:** 48% female, 52% male, 49% out-of-state, 11% international (115 countries represented). Asian 18%, African American 7%, Caucasian 52%, Hispanic 7%, Native American <1%, Pacific Islander <1%, Two or more races 4%, Race unknown 2%.
Retention and Graduation: 89% freshmen return for sophomore year. 71% freshmen graduate within 6 years. 13% grads go on to further study within 1 year. **Faculty:** Student/faculty ratio 11:1. 1,099 full-time faculty, 86% hold PhDs, 19% are members of minority groups, 46% are women.

ACADEMICS

Degrees: Bachelor's; Certificate; Doctoral degree—professional practice; Doctoral degree research/scholarship; Master's; Post-bachelor's certificate; Post-master's certificate. **Classes:** Most classes have 10–19 students. **Most popular majors:** Business/Commerce, General; Registered Nursing/Registered Nurse; Mechanical Engineering. **Special Study Options:** Accelerated program; Cooperative education program; Distance learning; Double major; Dual enrollment; English as a Second Language (ESL); Honors program; Independent study; Internships; Student-designed major; Study abroad; Teacher certification program; Weekend college. **Honors programs:** The Pennoni Honors College enriches the University experience for students from all majors with demonstrated academic achievement and broad intellectual interests. Established in 1991 with 33 students, the Honors Program has grown exponentially. Today, Honors Students represent nearly every major and college offered at Drexel University; Honors freshmen fill the Honors Residence Hall, and hundreds of students graduate with Honors Distinction each June. **Combined degree programs:** BA/MA; BA/MD; BA/MEng. **Disability Services offered:** Note-taking services; Reader services; Tape recorders; Tutors. **Career services:** Alumni services; Career assessment; Career/job search classes; Internships.

FACILITIES

Housing: Apartments for single students; Coed dorms; Fraternity/sorority housing; Special housing for disabled students; Special housing for international students 98% of campus accessible to physically disabled. **Special Academic Facilities/Equipment:** Art museum, theatre, TV studio, recreational center, center for automation technology. **Campus Network:** 100% of classrooms, 100% of dorms, 100% of student union, 100% of libraries, 100% of dining areas, 100% of common outdoor areas, have wireless network access.

CAMPUS LIFE

Environment: Metropolis. **Activities:** Campus Ministries; Choral groups; Concert band; Dance; Drama/theater; Jazz band; Literary magazine; Model UN; Music ensembles; Musical theater; Pep band; Radio station; Student government; Student newspaper; Student-run film society; Symphony orchestra; Television station; Yearbook. 367 registered organizations, 9 honor societies, 19 religious organizations, 20 fraternities, 11 sororities, on campus. **Athletics (Intercollegiate):** *Men:* basketball, cheerleading, crew/rowing, diving, golf, lacrosse, soccer, swimming, tennis, wrestling. *Women:* basketball, cheerleading, crew/rowing, diving, field hockey, lacrosse, soccer, softball, swimming, tennis, volleyball. **On-Campus Highlights:** Drexel Recreation Center. **Environmental Initiatives:** Green Power: In 2002, Drexel became one of the first universities to purchase wind generated energy. In 2006, Drexel entered into a contract with PECO Wind, to purchase wind energy directly linked to the Exelon-Community Energy Wind Farms located in the PJM Interconnection, supplying Drexel with 4,000.8 MWH per year, which translated into approximately 7.92% of Drexel's total annual electric use. In 2008, Drexel entered into a contract with Community Energy, Inc. to purchase energy linked to the PJM Interconnection, which translated into 12.9% of Drexel's total

annual use; the University increased its purchase to 30% of its total annual electric usage the following year. In 2010, Drexel entered into a new agreement with Community Energy to purchase Renewable Energy Certificates equal to 100% of the University's total energy use (84,268 MWH) starting in January 2011, making Drexel one of the top 50 purchasers of wind energy in the nation according to the EPA Green Power Partnership Rankings. In 2013, Drexel expanded its leadership with a renewed commitment to purchase 100% wind and solar energy from Community Energy.

ADMISSIONS

Freshman Academic Profile: Average high school GPA 3.7. 33% in top 10% of high school class, 64% in top 25% of high school class, 90% in top 50% of high school class. **Test scores:** SAT Math middle 50% range 590–710. SAT EBRW middle 50% range 580–670. ACT middle 50% range 25–30. **Basis for Candidate Selection:** *Very important factors include:* rigor of secondary school record, class rank, academic GPA, standardized test scores. *Important factors include:* application essay, recommendation(s), character/personal qualities. *Other factors include:* interview, extracurricular activities, talent/ability, first generation, alumni/ae relation, volunteer work, work experience, level of applicant's interest. **Freshman Admission Requirements:** High school diploma is required and GED is accepted. *Academic units required:* 3 math, 1 science, 1 science labs. *Academic units recommended:* 1 foreign language. **Freshman Admission Statistics:** 30,242 applied, 77% admitted, 14% enrolled. **Transfer Admission Requirements:** college transcript(s), Minimum college GPA of 2.5 required. Lowest grade transferable C. **General Admission Information:** Application fee $50. Regular application deadline 1/15. Non-fall registration accepted.

COSTS AND FINANCIAL AID

Annual tuition $52,146. Room and board $14,241. Required fees $2,370. Average book and supplies expense $1,200. **Required Forms and Deadlines:** CSS/Financial Aid PROFILE; FAFSA. **Notification of Awards:** Applicants will be notified of awards on or about 4/1. **Types of Aid:** *Need-based scholarships/grants:* College/university scholarship or grant aid from institutional funds; Federal Pell; Private scholarships; SEOG; State scholarships/grants. *Loans:* Direct PLUS loans; Direct Subsidized Stafford Loans; Direct Unsubsidized Stafford Loans. **Student Employment:** Federal Work-Study Program available. Institutional employment available. **Financial Aid Statistics:** 100% needy freshmen, 96% needy undergrads receive need-based scholarship or grant aid. 15% freshmen, 11% undergrads receive non-need-based scholarship or grant aid. 66% freshmen, 73% undergrads receive need-based self-help aid. 1% freshmen, 1% undergrads receive athletic scholarships. 99.8% freshmen, 94.2% undergrads receive any aid. **Criteria awarding aid:** *Need-based:* Academics, Art, Athletics, Music/drama *Non-Need-based:* Academics, Art, Athletics, Music/drama, State/district residency.

DRURY UNIVERSITY

Best Colleges

900 North Benton Avenue, Springfield, MO 65802-3712
Phone: 417-873-7205 **Financial Aid Phone:** 417-873-7312
E-mail: druryad@drury.edu **CEEB Code:** 6169
Fax: 417-866-3873 **Website:** www.drury.edu **ACT Code:** 2292

This private school, affiliated with the Christian Church (Disciples of Christ), UCC, was founded in 1873. It has a 84 acre campus.

RATINGS

Admissions Selectivity Rating: 85   Fire Safety Rating: 81   Green Rating: 67

STUDENTS AND FACULTY

Enrollment: 1,477. **Student Body:** 58% female, 42% male, 20% out-of-state, 6% international (53 countries represented). Asian 1%, African American 3%, Caucasian 81%, Hispanic 2%, Native American 1%, Pacific Islander <1%, Two or more races 3%, Race unknown 2%.
Retention and Graduation: 79% freshmen return for sophomore year. 39% freshmen graduate within 4 years. 57 19% grads go on to further study within 1 year. 50% grads pursue arts and sciences degrees. 10% grads pursue law degrees. 15% grads pursue business degrees. 23% grads pursue medical degrees. **Faculty:** Student/faculty ratio 13:1. 111 full-time faculty, 94% hold PhDs, 10% are

members of minority groups, 46% are women. 0% of classes are taught by teaching assistants.

ACADEMICS

Degrees: Bachelor's; Master's; Post-bachelor's certificate. **Classes:** Most classes have 10–19 students. Most lab/discussion sessions have 10–19 students. **Most popular majors:** Architectural and Building Sciences/Technology; Biology/Biological Sciences, General; Business Administration and Management, General. **Special Study Options:** Double major; Dual enrollment; English as a Second Language (ESL); Exchange student program (domestic); Honors program; Independent study; Internships; Liberal arts/career combination; Student-designed major; Study abroad; Teacher certification program. **Honors programs:** Drury's Honors Program features small liberal arts reading seminars and student research opportunities. All honors students complete three seminars on classical debates or contemporary issues, participate in student-led reading groups, and complete two honors research projects. Students in the program present their research at the Drury Honors Symposium and at academic conferences in their major. All honors students complete community service hour and attend cultural events on campus and in the community. **Combined degree programs:** BA/MEng. **Disability Services offered:** Note-taking services; Reader services; Tape recorders; Tutors. **Career services:** Alumni network; Alumni services; Career assessment; Career/job search classes; Internships; Regional alumni.

FACILITIES

Housing: Apartments for married students; Apartments for single students; Coed dorms; Fraternity/sorority housing; Theme housing 97% of campus accessible to physically disabled. **Special Academic Facilities/Equipment:** Science center with greenhouse and astronomical observation station, visual art center with two galleries, TV studio, radio station, teleconference facility, language lab, electronic music lab, laser lab. **Campus Network:** 100% of classrooms, 100% of dorms, 100% of student union, 100% of libraries, 100% of dining areas, 75% of common outdoor areas, have wireless network access.

CAMPUS LIFE

Environment: Metropolis. **Activities:** Campus Ministries; Choral groups; Concert band; Dance; Drama/theater; International Student Organization; Jazz band; Model UN; Music ensembles; Musical theater; Pep band; Radio station; Student government; Student newspaper; Symphony orchestra; Television station. 74 registered organizations, 9 honor societies, 5 religious organizations, 4 fraternities, 4 sororities, on campus. **Athletics (Intercollegiate):** *Men:* baseball, basketball, cheerleading, cross-country, diving, golf, soccer, softball, swimming, tennis. *Women:* basketball, cheerleading, cross-country, diving, golf, soccer, softball, swimming, tennis, volleyball. **On-Campus Highlights:** O'Reilly Family Event Center.

ADMISSIONS

Freshman Academic Profile: Average high school GPA 3.8. 29% in top 10% of high school class, 60% in top 25% of high school class, 87% in top 50% of high school class. 88% from public high schools. **Test scores:** SAT Math middle 50% range 525–605. SAT EBRW middle 50% range 520–620. ACT middle 50% range 22–28. **Basis for Candidate Selection:** *Very important factors include:* academic GPA, standardized test scores. *Important factors include:* rigor of secondary school record, talent/ability. *Other factors include:* application essay, recommendation(s), interview, extracurricular activities, character/personal qualities, first generation, alumni/ae relation, religious affiliation/commitment, racial/ethnic status, volunteer work, work experience, level of applicant's interest. **Freshman Admission Requirements:** High school diploma is required and GED is accepted. *Academic units required:* 3 math. *Academic units recommended:* 4 English, 3 math, 3 science, 2 foreign language, 3 social studies. **Freshman Admission Statistics:** 1,664 applied, 64% admitted, 32% enrolled. **Transfer Admission Requirements:** High school transcript, college transcript(s), essay or personal statement, Minimum college GPA of 2.0 required. Lowest grade transferable C. **General Admission Information:** Regular application deadline 8/30. Non-fall registration accepted. Admission may be deferred for a maximum of 1 year.

COSTS AND FINANCIAL AID

Annual tuition $29,900. Room and board $9,236. Required fees $1,315. Average book and supplies expense $1,200. **Notification of Awards:** Applicants will be notified of awards on a rolling basis beginning 2/15. **Types of Aid:** *Need-based scholarships/grants:* College/university scholarship or grant aid from institutional funds; Federal Pell; Private scholarships; SEOG; State scholarships/grants. *Loans:* Direct PLUS loans; Direct Subsidized Stafford Loans; Direct Unsubsidized Stafford Loans. **Student Employment:** Federal Work-Study Program available. Institutional employment available. **Financial Aid Statistics:** 100% needy freshmen, 100% needy undergrads receive need-based scholarship

or grant aid. 18% freshmen, 20% undergrads receive non-need-based scholarship or grant aid. 66% freshmen, 66% undergrads receive need-based self-help aid. 15% freshmen, 16% undergrads receive athletic scholarships. 100% freshmen, 98% undergrads receive any aid. 62% undergrads borrow to pay for school. Average cumulative indebtedness $37,144. **Criteria awarding aid:** *Need-based:* Alumni affiliation, Job skills. *Non-Need-based:* Academics, Alumni affiliation, Art, Athletics, Job skills, Leadership, Minority status, Music/drama, Religious affiliation.

DUKE UNIVERSITY

Best Colleges

2138 Campus Drive, Durham, NC 27708
Phone: 919-684-3214
E-mail: undergrad-admissions@duke.edu **CEEB Code:** 5156
Fax: 919-668-1661 **Website:** www.duke.edu **ACT Code:** 3088

This private school, affiliated with the Methodist Church, was founded in 1838. It has a 8500 acre campus.

RATINGS

Admissions Selectivity Rating: 99   **Fire Safety Rating:** 60*   **Green Rating:** 60*

STUDENTS AND FACULTY

Enrollment: 6,596. **Student Body:** 50% female, 50% male, 85% out-of-state, 10% international (89 countries represented). Asian 22%, African American 10%, Caucasian 42%, Hispanic 9%, Native American 1%, Pacific Islander <1%, Two or more races 2%, Race unknown 4%.
Retention and Graduation: 98% freshmen return for sophomore year. 87% freshmen graduate within 4 years. 96% freshmen graduate within 6 years. 38% grads go on to further study within 1 year. 14% grads pursue arts and sciences degrees. 11% grads pursue law degrees. 1% grads pursue business degrees. 12% grads pursue medical degrees. **Faculty:** Student/faculty ratio 6:1. 1,481 full-time faculty, 96% hold PhDs, 22% are members of minority groups, 40% are women. 4% of classes are taught by teaching assistants.

ACADEMICS

Degrees: Bachelor's; Doctoral degree—professional practice; Doctoral degree research/scholarship; Master's; Post-bachelor's certificate; Post-master's certificate. **Classes:** Most classes have 10–19 students. Most lab/discussion sessions have 10–19 students. **Most popular majors:** Public Policy Analysis, General; Economics, General; Psychology, General. **Special Study Options:** Cross-registration; Double major; Exchange student program (domestic); Independent study; Internships; Student-designed major; Study abroad; Teacher certification program. **Combined degree programs:** BA/MA; BA/MEng. **Disability Services offered:** Note-taking services; Reader services; Tape recorders; Tutors. **Career services:** Alumni services; Career assessment; Career/job search classes; Internships.

FACILITIES

Housing: Apartments for single students; Coed dorms; Men's dorms; Theme housing; Wellness housing; Women's dorms **Special Academic Facilities/Equipment:** Art museum, language lab, university forest, primate center, phytotron, electron laser, nuclear magnetic resonance machine, nuclear lab. **Campus Network:** 100% of classrooms, 100% of dorms, 80% of libraries, 100% of dining areas, 50% of common outdoor areas, have wireless network access.

CAMPUS LIFE

Environment: Metropolis. **Activities:** Campus Ministries; Choral groups; Concert band; Dance; Drama/theater; International Student Organization; Jazz band; Literary magazine; Marching band; Model UN; Music ensembles; Musical theater; Opera; Pep band; Radio station; Student government; Student newspaper; Student-run film society; Symphony orchestra; Television station. 200 registered organizations, 10 honor societies, 25 religious organizations, 21 fraternities, 14 sororities, on campus. **Athletics (Intercollegiate):** *Men:* baseball, basketball, cross-country, diving, fencing, football, golf, lacrosse, soccer, swimming, tennis, track/field (outdoor), track/field (indoor), volleyball, wrestling. *Women:* basketball, crew/rowing, cross-country, diving, fencing, field hockey, golf, lacrosse, soccer, swimming, tennis, track/field (outdoor), track/field (indoor), volleyball. **On-Campus Highlights:** Duke Chapel.

Environmental Initiatives: Duke has signed the ACUPCC and made a commitment to make Duke a climate neutral institution.

ADMISSIONS

Freshman Academic Profile: 95% in top 10% of high school class, 98% in top 25% of high school class, 100% in top 50% of high school class. 65% from public high schools. **Test scores:** SAT Math middle 50% range 740–800. SAT EBRW middle 50% range 710–770. ACT middle 50% range 33–35. **Basis for Candidate Selection:** *Very important factors include:* rigor of secondary school record, academic GPA, application essay, standardized test scores, recommendation(s), extracurricular activities, talent/ability, character/personal qualities. *Other factors include:* interview, first generation, alumni/ae relation, geographical residence, state residency, religious affiliation/commitment, racial/ethnic status, volunteer work, work experience, level of applicant's interest. **Freshman Admission Requirements:** High school diploma is required and GED is not accepted. *Academic units recommended:* 4 English, 3 math, 3 science, 3 foreign language, 3 social studies. **Freshman Admission Statistics:** 35,767 applied, 9% admitted, 55% enrolled. **Transfer Admission Requirements:** High school transcript, college transcript(s), essay or personal statement, standardized test scores, Lowest grade transferable C. **General Admission Information:** Application fee $85. Priority deadline 12/20. Regular application deadline 1/3. Admission may be deferred for a maximum of 1 year.

COSTS AND FINANCIAL AID

Annual tuition $55,880. Room and board $15,588. Required fees $2,051. Average book and supplies expense $1,434. **Required Forms and Deadlines:** Business/Farm Supplement; CSS/Financial Aid PROFILE; FAFSA; Noncustodial PROFILE. **Types of Aid:** *Need-based scholarships/grants:* College/university scholarship or grant aid from institutional funds; Federal Pell; Private scholarships; SEOG; State scholarships/grants. *Loans:* Direct PLUS loans; Direct Subsidized Stafford Loans; Direct Unsubsidized Stafford Loans. **Student Employment:** Federal Work-Study Program available. Institutional employment available. **Financial Aid Statistics:** 94% needy freshmen, 95% needy undergrads receive need-based scholarship or grant aid. 16% freshmen, 10% undergrads receive non-need-based scholarship or grant aid. 73% freshmen, 81% undergrads receive need-based self-help aid. 7% freshmen, 6% undergrads receive athletic scholarships. 32% undergrads borrow to pay for school. Average cumulative indebtedness $21,525. **Criteria awarding aid:** *Need-based:* Academics, Alumni affiliation, Leadership, Minority status, Music/drama, Religious affiliation. *Non-Need-based:* Academics, Alumni affiliation, Athletics, Leadership, Minority status, Music/drama, Religious affiliation, State/district residency.

DUQUESNE UNIVERSITY

600 Forbes Avenue, Pittsburgh, PA 15282
Phone: 412-396-6222 **Financial Aid Phone:** 412-396-6607
E-mail: admissions@duq.edu
Fax: 412-396-6223 **Website:** www.duq.edu

This private school, affiliated with the Roman Catholic Church, was founded in 1878. It has a 49.5 acre campus.

RATINGS

Admissions Selectivity Rating: 82   **Fire Safety Rating:** 98   **Green Rating:** 86

STUDENTS AND FACULTY

Enrollment: 5,837. **Student Body:** 64% female, 36% male, 28% out-of-state, 2% international (42 countries represented). Asian 3%, African American 5%, Caucasian 81%, Hispanic 4%, Native American <1%, Pacific Islander <1%, Two or more races 3%, Race unknown 1%.
Retention and Graduation: 85% freshmen return for sophomore year. 71% freshmen graduate within 4 years. 80% freshmen graduate within 6 years. 31% grads go on to further study within 1 year. 23% grads pursue arts and sciences degrees. 2% grads pursue law degrees. 3% grads pursue business degrees. 2% grads pursue medical degrees. **Faculty:** Student/faculty ratio 14:1. 494 full-time faculty, 94% hold PhDs, 9% are members of minority groups, 51% are women.

ACADEMICS

Degrees: Bachelor's; Doctoral degree—professional practice; Doctoral degree research/scholarship; Master's; Post-bachelor's certificate; Post-master's certificate. **Classes:** Most classes have 20–29 students. Most lab/discussion sessions have 20–29 students. **Most popular majors:** Biology/Biological Sciences, General; Pharmacy; Nursing Science. **Special Study Options:** Accelerated program; Cross-registration; Distance learning; Double major; Dual enrollment; English as a Second Language (ESL); Exchange student program (domestic); External degree program; Honors program; Independent study; Internships; Liberal arts/career combination; Student-designed major; Study abroad; Teacher certification program; Weekend college. **Honors programs:** Duquesne University offers its most qualified and outstanding freshmen the opportunity to participate in the Honors College. The Honors College works within the student's own course of study while providing enhanced opportunities for creative and critical thinking, leadership and service, education in the humanities, and global perspectives. The foundation of Duquesne's Honors College is its enhanced track of the liberal arts-based University Core Curriculum. Special honors sections of the core courses feature some of the University's most distinguished faculty and maintain small class sections, allowing close interaction and encouraging individual initiative as well as collaborative learning. Students who have completed their Honors College Core requirements may apply to Duquesne University's Honors Fellows Program, which allows students to design and implement a research project based on their academic major and personal interests. Students are also invited to apply for an Endowed Fellowship to receive funding for travel and equipment that will contribute to the success of their Honors Fellows Project. **Combined degree programs:** BA/JD; BA/MA. **Disability Services offered:** Reader services; Tape recorders; Tutors. **Career services:** Alumni network; Alumni services; Career assessment; Career/job search classes; Internships; Regional alumni.

FACILITIES

Housing: Apartments for single students; Coed dorms; Fraternity/sorority housing; Men's dorms; Special housing for disabled students; Women's dorms. **Special Academic Facilities/Equipment:** Art Gallery, Nursing Simulation Center, Genesius Theater, Science and Pharmacy Labs. **Campus Network:** 100% of classrooms, 100% of dorms, 100% of student union, 100% of libraries, 100% of dining areas, 100% of common outdoor areas, have wireless network access.

CAMPUS LIFE

Environment: Metropolis. **Activities:** Campus Ministries; Choral groups; Concert band; Dance; Drama/theater; International Student Organization; Jazz band; Literary magazine; Model UN; Music ensembles; Musical theater; Opera; Pep band; Radio station; Student government; Student newspaper; Student-run film society; Symphony orchestra; Television station; Yearbook. 260 registered organizations, 21 honor societies, 12 religious organizations, 9 fraternities, 11 sororities, on campus. **Athletics (Intercollegiate):** *Men:* basketball, cross-country, football, soccer, tennis, track/field (outdoor). *Women:* basketball, crew/rowing, cross-country, lacrosse, soccer, swimming, tennis, track/field (outdoor), track/field (indoor), volleyball. **On-Campus Highlights:** Gumberg Library. **Environmental Initiatives:** Duquesne University relies 100 percent on clean energy. For over 20 years, the University has produced the bulk of its own electricity with a clean-burning natural gas turbine located at the heart of campus. This cogeneration plant produces approximately 85 percent of the power used to light, heat and cool the campus with overall efficiency greater than 70 percent. It is Pennsylvania's first approved generation system for creating Alternative Energy Credits. Sustainable initiatives reached an exceptional level with the purchase of more than 14 million kilowatt hours of renewable energy credits. This combination of energy generation and renewable energy purchase led Duquesne University to rely 100 percent on clean energy.

ADMISSIONS

Freshman Academic Profile: Average high school GPA 3.7. 25% in top 10% of high school class, 55% in top 25% of high school class, 85% in top 50% of high school class. **Test scores:** SAT Math middle 50% range 560–650. SAT EBRW middle 50% range 570–650. ACT middle 50% range 23–28. **Basis for Candidate Selection:** *Very important factors include:* rigor of secondary school record, academic GPA. *Important factors include:* standardized test scores. *Other factors include:* class rank, application essay, recommendation(s), interview, extracurricular activities, talent/ability, character/personal qualities, first generation, alumni/ae relation, racial/ethnic status, volunteer work, work experience, level of applicant's interest. **Freshman Admission Requirements:** High school diploma is required and GED is accepted. *Academic units recommended:* 4 English, 2 math, 2 science, 2 foreign language, 2 social studies, 4 academic electives. **Freshman Admission Statistics:** 7,231 applied, 74%

admitted, 24% enrolled. **Transfer Admission Requirements:** High school transcript, college transcript(s), essay or personal statement, statement of good standing from prior institution(s). Minimum college GPA of 2.5 required. Lowest grade transferable C. **General Admission Information:** Priority deadline 11/1. Regular application deadline 7/1. Non-fall registration accepted. Admission may be deferred for a maximum of one academic year.

COSTS AND FINANCIAL AID

Annual tuition $41,892. Room and board $13,612. Average book and supplies expense $1,400. **Required Forms and Deadlines:** FAFSA; Institution's own financial aid form. **Notification of Awards:** Applicants will be notified of awards on a rolling basis beginning 1/31. **Types of Aid:** *Need-based scholarships/ grants:* College/university scholarship or grant aid from institutional funds; Federal Pell; Private scholarships; SEOG; State scholarships/grants; United Negro College Fund. *Loans:* Direct PLUS loans; Direct Subsidized Stafford Loans; Direct Unsubsidized Stafford Loans. **Student Employment:** Federal Work-Study Program available. Institutional employment available. **Financial Aid Statistics:** 100% needy freshmen, 98% needy undergrads receive need-based scholarship or grant aid. 100% freshmen, 97% undergrads receive non-need-based scholarship or grant aid. 81% freshmen, 85% undergrads receive need-based self-help aid. 6% freshmen, 6% undergrads receive athletic scholarships. 99% freshmen, 99% undergrads receive any aid. 58% undergrads borrow to pay for school. Average cumulative indebtedness $44,243. **Criteria awarding aid:** *Need-based:* Academics, Athletics, Minority status. *Non-Need-based:* Academics, Athletics, Music/drama.

D'YOUVILLE COLLEGE

320 Porter Avenue, Buffalo, NY 14201
Phone: 716-829-7600 **Financial Aid Phone:** 716-829-7500
E-mail: admissions@dyc.edu **CEEB Code:** 2197
Fax: 716-829-7790 **Website:** www.dyc.edu **ACT Code:** 2732

This private school was founded in 1908. It has a 7 acre campus.

RATINGS

Admissions Selectivity Rating: 77   Fire Safety Rating: 82   Green Rating: 60*

STUDENTS AND FACULTY

Enrollment: 1,982. **Student Body:** 73% female, 27% male, 4% out-of-state, 7% international (55 countries represented). Asian 3%, African American 10%, Caucasian 70%, Hispanic 4%, Native American 1%, Pacific Islander 0%, Two or more races 1%, Race unknown 4%.
Retention and Graduation: 72% freshmen return for sophomore year.
Faculty: Student/faculty ratio 8:1. 180 full-time faculty, 76% hold PhDs, 8% are members of minority groups, 61% are women. 0% of classes are taught by teaching assistants.

ACADEMICS

Degrees: Bachelor's; Doctoral degree—professional practice; Doctoral degree research/scholarship; Master's; Post-bachelor's certificate; Post-master's certificate. **Classes:** Most classes have 10–19 students. Most lab/discussion sessions have 10–19 students. **Most popular majors:** Education, General; Business/Commerce, General; Nursing/Registered Nurse (Rn, Asn, Bsn, Msn). **Special Study Options:** Accelerated program; Cooperative education program; Cross-registration; Distance learning; Double major; Dual enrollment; Honors program; Independent study; Internships; Study abroad; Teacher certification program; Weekend college. **Disability Services offered:** Note-taking services; Reader services; Tape recorders; Tutors.

FACILITIES

Housing: Apartments for single students; Coed dorms; Special housing for disabled students 100% of campus accessible to physically disabled. **Special Academic Facilities/Equipment:** Kavinoky Theatre (professional theatre).

CAMPUS LIFE

Environment: City. **Activities:** Campus Ministries; Choral groups; Drama/ theater; Literary magazine; Student government; Student newspaper; Yearbook. 25 registered organizations, 3 honor societies, 1 religious organizations, on campus. **Athletics (Intercollegiate):** *Men:* baseball, basketball, golf, soccer, volleyball. *Women:* basketball, crew/rowing, golf, soccer, softball, volleyball. **On-Campus Highlights:** New Academic Center.

ADMISSIONS

Freshman Academic Profile: 18% in top 10% of high school class, 52% in top 25% of high school class, 87% in top 50% of high school class. 75% from public high schools. **Test scores:** SAT Math middle 50% range 490–580. SAT EBRW middle 50% range 470–550. ACT middle 50% range 21–25. **Basis for Candidate Selection:** *Very important factors include:* rigor of secondary school record, academic GPA, standardized test scores. *Important factors include:* class rank. *Other factors include:* recommendation(s), interview, extracurricular activities, talent/ability, character/personal qualities, alumni/ae relation, volunteer work, work experience. **Freshman Admission Requirements:** High school diploma is required and GED is accepted. *Academic units recommended:* 4 English, 3 math, 3 science, 3 foreign language, 3 social studies. **Freshman Admission Statistics:** 1,023 applied, 80% admitted, 29% enrolled. **Transfer Admission Requirements:** High school transcript, college transcript(s), Minimum college GPA of 2.0 required. Lowest grade transferable C. **General Admission Information:** Application fee $25. Non-fall registration accepted. Admission may be deferred for a maximum of 12 months.

COSTS AND FINANCIAL AID

Annual tuition $21,930. Room and board $10,250. Required fees $310. Average book and supplies expense $1,200. **Required Forms and Deadlines:** FAFSA; State aid form. **Notification of Awards:** Applicants will be notified of awards on a rolling basis beginning 4/15. **Types of Aid:** *Need-based scholarships/ grants:* College/university scholarship or grant aid from institutional funds; Federal Pell; Private scholarships; SEOG; State scholarships/grants. *Loans:* Direct PLUS loans; Direct Subsidized Stafford Loans; Direct Unsubsidized Stafford Loans. **Student Employment:** Federal Work-Study Program available. Institutional employment available. **Financial Aid Statistics:** 10% freshmen, 5% undergrads receive non-need-based scholarship or grant aid. 88% freshmen, 92% undergrads receive need-based self-help aid. 0% freshmen, 0% undergrads receive athletic scholarships. **Criteria awarding aid:** *Need-based:* Academics, Alumni affiliation *Non-Need-based:* Academics, Leadership, Religious affiliation.

EARLHAM COLLEGE

801 National Road West, Richmond, IN 47374-4095
Phone: 765-983-1600 **Financial Aid Phone:** 765-983-1217
E-mail: admissions@earlham.edu **CEEB Code:** 1195
Fax: 765-983-1560 **Website:** www.earlham.edu **ACT Code:** 1186

This private school, affiliated with the Quaker Church, was founded in 1847. It has a 800 acre campus.

RATINGS

Admissions Selectivity Rating: 87   Fire Safety Rating: 94   Green Rating: 83

STUDENTS AND FACULTY

Enrollment: 927. **Student Body:** 57% female, 43% male, 90% out-of-state, 23% international (63 countries represented). Asian 4%, African American 7%, Caucasian 51%, Hispanic 8%, Native American 0%, Pacific Islander 0%, Two or more races 5%, Race unknown 2%.
Retention and Graduation: 80% freshmen return for sophomore year. 56% freshmen graduate within 4 years. 1% freshmen graduate within 6 years. 20% grads go on to further study within 1 year. 7% grads pursue arts and sciences degrees. 0% grads pursue law degrees. 2% grads pursue business degrees. 1% grads pursue medical degrees. **Faculty:** Student/faculty ratio 10:1. 95 full-time faculty, 97% hold PhDs, 29% are members of minority groups, 47% are women. 0% of classes are taught by teaching assistants.

ACADEMICS

Degrees: Bachelor's; Master's; Post-bachelor's certificate. **Classes:** Most classes have 10–19 students. Most lab/discussion sessions have 10–19 students. **Special Study Options:** Cross-registration; Double major; Dual enrollment; English as a Second Language (ESL); Honors program; Independent study; Internships; Student-designed major; Study abroad; Teacher certification program. **Honors programs:** Honors students are a specific cohort (like international students or first-generation students) who share a specific set of needs. Their own definitions of what it means to succeed in College, or what it means to have a satisfying experience in College, are often different from those of other students.

In order to attract high-achieving and highly-motivated students, and in order to retain them, we need a clear, structured pathway for these students to achieve the kinds of success they value. These aren't limited to, but certainly include, post-baccalaureate fellowships like the Fulbright, Rhodes, Marshall, Watson, and Mitchell, as well as undergraduate prizes like the Hult. For that reason, our Honors Program overtly prepares students to demonstrate their success according to four criteria that broadly reflect the priorities of the fellowships and prizes for which we prepare Honors students to apply. These are: 1. Using their talents to the full, 2. Demonstrating their abilities as leaders and collaborators, 3. Achieving academic and technical excellence, and 4. Improving the conditions of their fellow human beings. **Combined degree programs:** BA/MA. **Disability Services offered:** Note-taking services; Reader services; Tape recorders; Tutors. **Career services:** Alumni network; Alumni services; Career assessment; Career/job search classes; Internships; Regional alumni.

FACILITIES

Housing: Apartments for single students; Coed dorms; Cooperative housing; Men's dorms; Special housing for disabled students; Theme housing; Wellness housing; Women's dorms 80% of campus accessible to physically disabled. **Special Academic Facilities/Equipment:** Earlham has recently invested in a new Center for Science and Technology (CST) and a Center for the Visual and Performing Arts. Other notable facilities include the Landrum Bolling Center, which features the Center for Career and Community Engagement and the Center for Global Education, the CoLab (dedicated to collaborative learning), theme residential houses, an observatory, herbarium, and a greenhouse.

CAMPUS LIFE

Environment: Town. **Activities:** Campus Ministries; Choral groups; Dance; Drama/theater; International Student Organization; Literary magazine; Music ensembles; Radio station; Student government; Student newspaper; Symphony orchestra. 60 registered organizations, 1 honor societies, 8 religious organizations, on campus. **Athletics (Intercollegiate):** *Men:* baseball, basketball, cross-country, football, soccer, tennis, track/field (outdoor), track/field (indoor). *Women:* basketball, cross-country, field hockey, soccer, tennis, track/field (outdoor), track/field (indoor), volleyball. **On-Campus Highlights:** Center for the Visual and Performing Arts.

ADMISSIONS

Freshman Academic Profile: Average high school GPA 3.6. 42% in top 10% of high school class, 71% in top 25% of high school class, 93% in top 50% of high school class. 60% from public high schools. **Test scores:** SAT Math middle 50% range 550–690. SAT EBRW middle 50% range 550–680. ACT middle 50% range 23–30. **Basis for Candidate Selection:** *Very important factors include:* rigor of secondary school record, academic GPA. *Important factors include:* application essay, extracurricular activities, character/personal qualities. *Other factors include:* class rank, standardized test scores, recommendation(s), interview, talent/ability, racial/ethnic status, volunteer work, work experience. **Freshman Admission Requirements:** High school diploma is required and GED is accepted. *Academic units required:* 4 English, 3 math, 3 science, 2 science labs, 2 foreign language, 2 social studies, 2 history. *Academic units recommended:* 4 English, 4 math, 4 science, 2 science labs, 2 foreign language, 2 social studies, 2 history. **Freshman Admission Statistics:** 2,070 applied, 63% admitted, 13% enrolled. **Transfer Admission Requirements:** High school transcript, college transcript(s), essay or personal statement, standardized test scores, statement of good standing from prior institution(s). Minimum college GPA of 2.7 required. Lowest grade transferable C. **General Admission Information:** Priority deadline 12/1. Regular application deadline 2/1. Non-fall registration accepted. Admission may be deferred for a maximum of 1 year.

COSTS AND FINANCIAL AID

Annual tuition $47,106. Room and board $11,347. Required fees $985. Average book and supplies expense $1,050. **Required Forms and Deadlines:** FAFSA. **Notification of Awards:** Applicants will be notified of awards on or about 3/15. **Types of Aid:** *Need-based scholarships/grants:* College/university scholarship or grant aid from institutional funds; Federal Pell; Private scholarships; SEOG; State scholarships/grants. *Loans:* Direct PLUS loans; Direct Subsidized Stafford Loans; Direct Unsubsidized Stafford Loans. **Student Employment:** Federal Work-Study Program available. Institutional employment available. **Financial Aid Statistics:** 100% needy freshmen, 100% needy undergrads receive need-based scholarship or grant aid. 18% freshmen, 21% undergrads receive non-need-based scholarship or grant aid. 90% freshmen, 96% undergrads receive need-based self-help aid. 0% freshmen, 0% undergrads receive athletic scholarships. 92% freshmen, 93% undergrads receive any aid. 44% undergrads borrow to pay for school. Average cumulative indebtedness $26,103. **Criteria awarding aid:** *Non-Need-based:* Academics, Leadership, Minority status, Religious affiliation.

EAST CAROLINA UNIVERSITY

Office of Undergraduate Admissions, Greenville, NC 27858-4353
Phone: 252-328-6640 **Financial Aid Phone:** 252-328-4347
E-mail: admis@ecu.edu **CEEB Code:** 5180
Fax: 252-328-6945 **Website:** www.ecu.edu **ACT Code:** 3094

This public school was founded in 1907. It has a 1600 acre campus.

RATINGS

Admissions Selectivity Rating: 77   **Fire Safety Rating:** 97   **Green Rating:** 88

STUDENTS AND FACULTY

Enrollment: 22,330. **Student Body:** 56% female, 44% male, 10% out-of-state, <1% international (52 countries represented). Asian 3%, African American 16%, Caucasian 67%, Hispanic 7%, Native American 1%, Pacific Islander <1%, Two or more races 4%, Race unknown 3%.
Retention and Graduation: 81% freshmen return for sophomore year. 36% freshmen graduate within 4 years. 61% freshmen graduate within 6 years.
Faculty: Student/faculty ratio 18:1. 1,215 full-time faculty, 82% hold PhDs, 16% are members of minority groups, 51% are women.

ACADEMICS

Degrees: Bachelor's; Doctoral degree—professional practice; Doctoral degree research/scholarship; Master's; Post-bachelor's certificate; Post-master's certificate. **Classes:** Most classes have 20–29 students. Most lab/discussion sessions have 20–29 students. **Most popular majors:** Business Administration and Management, General; Registered Nursing/Registered Nurse; Biology/Biological Sciences, General. **Special Study Options:** Accelerated program; Cooperative education program; Cross-registration; Distance learning; Double major; Dual enrollment; English as a Second Language (ESL); Exchange student program (domestic); Honors program; Independent study; Internships; Student-designed major; Study abroad; Teacher certification program. **Honors programs:** The Honors College at East Carolina University is a diverse intellectual community for academically talented students of strong character. Our students engage in stimulating coursework that spans disciplines across campus, providing for a challenging and innovative curricular and co-curricular model. Honors students are provided with the opportunity to engage in immersive service-learning, undergraduate research, and pre-professional experiences throughout their undergraduate years. Students will leave the Honors College with a foundation of skills and experiences designed to make them competitive for graduate programs, scholarships, and careers following graduation. **Disability Services offered:** Note-taking services; Reader services; Tape recorders; Tutors. **Career services:** Alumni network; Alumni services; Career assessment; Career/job search classes; Internships; Regional alumni.

FACILITIES

Housing: Coed dorms; Fraternity/sorority housing; Special housing for disabled students; Theme housing; Wellness housing; Women's dorms 95% of campus accessible to physically disabled. **Special Academic Facilities/Equipment:** Wellington B. Gray Gallery, Ledonia Wright Cultural Center, A.J. Fletcher Recital Hall, Hendrix Theatre, Jenkins Fine Arts Center, McGinnis Theatre, and Mendenhall Student Center.

CAMPUS LIFE

Environment: City. **Activities:** Campus Ministries; Choral groups; Concert band; Dance; Drama/theater; International Student Organization; Jazz band; Literary magazine; Marching band; Model UN; Music ensembles; Musical theater; Opera; Pep band; Radio station; Student government; Student newspaper; Student-run film society; Symphony orchestra; Television station; Yearbook. 425 registered organizations, 21 honor societies, 28 religious organizations, 23 fraternities, 14 sororities, on campus. **Athletics (Intercollegiate):** *Men:* baseball, basketball, cheerleading, cross-country, diving, football, golf, swimming, tennis, track/field (outdoor). *Women:* basketball, cheerleading, cross-country, diving, golf, soccer, softball, swimming, tennis, track/field (outdoor), volleyball. **On-Campus Highlights:** Main Student Center. **Environmental Initiatives:** Water conservation.

ADMISSIONS

Freshman Academic Profile: Average high school GPA 3.8. 13% in top 10% of high school class, 38% in top 25% of high school class, 76% in top 50%

of high school class. **Test scores**: SAT Math middle 50% range 510–590. SAT EBRW middle 50% range 520–590. ACT middle 50% range 19–24. **Basis for Candidate Selection**: *Very important factors include:* rigor of secondary school record, academic GPA, standardized test scores, state residency. *Important factors include:* class rank. *Other factors include:* application essay, extracurricular activities, talent/ability, character/personal qualities, first generation, alumni/ae relation, volunteer work, work experience, level of applicant's interest. **Freshman Admission Requirements:** High school diploma is required and GED is accepted. *Academic units required:* 4 English, 4 math, 3 science, 1 science labs, 2 foreign language, 1 social studies, 1 history. *Academic units recommended:* 4 English, 4 math, 3 science, 1 science labs, 2 foreign language, 2 social studies, 1 history, 1 visual/performing arts. **Freshman Admission Statistics:** 17,551 applied, 82% admitted, 29% enrolled. **Transfer Admission Requirements:** High school transcript, college transcript(s), Minimum college GPA of 2.0 required. Lowest grade transferable C. **General Admission Information:** Application fee $75. Regular application deadline 3/1. Non-fall registration accepted. Admission may be deferred for a maximum of 1 semester.

COSTS AND FINANCIAL AID
Annual in-state tuition $4,452. Annual out-of-state tuition $20,729. Room and board $10,354. Required fees $2,736. Average book and supplies expense $1,432. **Required Forms and Deadlines:** FAFSA. **Notification of Awards:** Applicants will be notified of awards on a rolling basis beginning 4/1. **Types of Aid:** *Need-based scholarships/grants:* College/university scholarship or grant aid from institutional funds; Federal Nursing Scholarships; Federal Pell; Private scholarships; SEOG; State scholarships/grants. *Loans:* Direct PLUS loans; Direct Subsidized Stafford Loans; Direct Unsubsidized Stafford Loans. **Student Employment:** Federal Work-Study Program available. Institutional employment available. **Financial Aid Statistics:** 71% needy freshmen, 74% needy undergrads receive need-based scholarship or grant aid. 23% freshmen, 17% undergrads receive non-need-based scholarship or grant aid. 83% freshmen, 84% undergrads receive need-based self-help aid. 2% freshmen, 2% undergrads receive athletic scholarships. 70% freshmen, 66% undergrads receive any aid. 69% undergrads borrow to pay for school. Average cumulative indebtedness $29,646. **Criteria awarding aid:** *Need-based:* Academics. *Non-Need-based:* Academics, Alumni affiliation, Art, Athletics, Music/drama.

EASTERN CONNECTICUT STATE UNIVERSITY

83 Windham Street, Willimantic, CT 06226
Phone: 860-465-5286 **Financial Aid Phone:** 860-365-5205
E-mail: admissions@easternct.edu **CEEB Code:** 3966
Fax: 860-465-5286 **Website:** www.easternct.edu

This public school was founded in 1889. It has a 182 acre campus.

RATINGS
Admissions Selectivity Rating: 85   **Fire Safety Rating:** 96   **Green Rating:** 89

STUDENTS AND FACULTY
Enrollment: 5,035. **Student Body:** 53% female, 47% male, 7% out-of-state, 1% international (44 countries represented). Asian 2%, African American 7%, Caucasian 79%, Hispanic 7%, Native American <1%, Pacific Islander <1%, Two or more races 2%, Race unknown 2%.
Retention and Graduation: 77% freshmen return for sophomore year. 30% grads go on to further study within 1 year. **Faculty:** Student/faculty ratio 16:1. 198 full-time faculty, 96% hold PhDs, 22% are members of minority groups, 44% are women. 0% of classes are taught by teaching assistants.

ACADEMICS
Degrees: Associate; Bachelor's; Master's. **Classes:** Most classes have 20–29 students. Most lab/discussion sessions have 10–19 students. **Most popular majors:** Business/Commerce, General; Communication and Media Studies, Other; Psychology, General. **Special Study Options:** Accelerated program; Cooperative education program; Cross-registration; Distance learning; Double major; Dual enrollment; Exchange student program (domestic); Honors program; Independent study; Internships; Student-designed major; Study abroad; Teacher certification program; Weekend college. **Honors programs:** University Honor Scholars Program offers interdisciplinary and independent study opportunities. **Disability Services offered:** Note-taking services; Reader services; Tape recorders; Tutors. **Career services:** Alumni network; Alumni services; Career assessment; Career/job search classes; Internships; Regional alumni.

FACILITIES
Housing: Apartments for single students; Coed dorms 95% of campus accessible to physically disabled. **Special Academic Facilities/Equipment:** Art Gallery, Arboretum, Church Farm, Family/Child Development Center (2007), Green science bldg/labs (2008), electron microscope, planetarium, Media center with TV and radio station, Sports/Fitness Center and Studios, Center for Connecticut studies. **Campus Network:** 100% of classrooms, 100% of dorms, 100% of student union, 100% of libraries, 100% of dining areas, 100% of common outdoor areas, have wireless network access.

CAMPUS LIFE
Environment: Village. **Activities:** Choral groups; Concert band; Dance; Drama/theater; International Student Organization; Jazz band; Literary magazine; Music ensembles; Musical theater; Radio station; Student government; Student newspaper; Television station; Yearbook. 68 registered organizations, 17 honor societies, 3 religious organizations, on campus. **Athletics (Intercollegiate):** *Men:* baseball, basketball, cross-country, golf, lacrosse, soccer, track/field (outdoor), track/field (indoor). *Women:* basketball, cross-country, diving, field hockey, lacrosse, soccer, softball, swimming, track/field (outdoor), track/field (indoor), volleyball. **On-Campus Highlights:** Library. **Environmental Initiatives:** Education Project http://www.ctenergyeducation.com/

ADMISSIONS
Freshman Academic Profile: Average high school GPA 3.0. 7% in top 10% of high school class, 25% in top 25% of high school class, 70% in top 50% of high school class. **Test scores:** SAT Math middle 50% range 480–580. SAT EBRW middle 50% range 470–570. **Basis for Candidate Selection:** *Very important factors include:* class rank, standardized test scores, talent/ability. *Important factors include:* rigor of secondary school record, academic GPA, recommendation(s), level of applicant's interest. *Other factors include:* application essay, interview, extracurricular activities, character/personal qualities, volunteer work, work experience. **Freshman Admission Requirements:** High school diploma is required and GED is accepted. *Academic units required:* 4 English, 3 math, 2 science, 1 science labs, 2 foreign language, 2 social studies, 3 history. *Academic units recommended:* 4 math, 3 social studies. **Freshman Admission Statistics:** 3,493 applied, 65% admitted, 41% enrolled. **Transfer Admission Requirements:** High school transcript, college transcript(s), Minimum college GPA of 2.0 required. Lowest grade transferable C-. **General Admission Information:** Application fee $50. Priority deadline 5/1. Non-fall registration accepted.

COSTS AND FINANCIAL AID
Annual in-state tuition $4,510. Annual out-of-state tuition $14,594. Room and board $11,168. Average book and supplies expense $1,554. **Required Forms and Deadlines:** FAFSA. **Types of Aid:** *Need-based scholarships/grants:* College/university scholarship or grant aid from institutional funds; Federal Pell; Private scholarships; SEOG; State scholarships/grants. **Student Employment:** Federal Work-Study Program available. Institutional employment available. **Financial Aid Statistics:** 68% needy freshmen, 66% needy undergrads receive need-based scholarship or grant aid. 4% freshmen, 1% undergrads receive non-need-based scholarship or grant aid. 90% freshmen, 90% undergrads receive need-based self-help aid. 0% freshmen, 0% undergrads receive athletic scholarships. 69% freshmen, 75% undergrads receive any aid. **Criteria awarding aid:** *Need-based:* Academics. *Non-Need-based:* Academics.

EASTERN ILLINOIS UNIVERSITY

600 Lincoln Avenue, Charleston, IL 61920
Phone: 217-581-2223 **Financial Aid Phone:** 217-581-6405
E-mail: admissions@eiu.edu **CEEB Code:** 1199
Fax: 217-581-7060 **Website:** https://www.eiu.edu/ **ACT Code:** 1016

This public school was founded in 1895. It has a 320 acre campus.

RATINGS
Admissions Selectivity Rating: 84   **Fire Safety Rating:** 97   **Green Rating:** 71

STUDENTS AND FACULTY
Enrollment: 4,631. **Student Body:** 59% female, 41% male, 7% out-of-state, 2% international (46 countries represented). Asian 1%, African American 21%, Caucasian 61%, Hispanic 8%, Native American <1%, Pacific Islander <1%, Two or more races 3%, Race unknown 2%.

Retention and Graduation: 70% freshmen return for sophomore year. 38% freshmen graduate within 4 years. % freshmen graduate within 6 years. **Faculty:** Student/faculty ratio 13:1. 381 full-time faculty, 70% hold PhDs, 15% are members of minority groups, 49% are women.

ACADEMICS

Degrees: Bachelor's; Master's; Post-bachelor's certificate; Post-master's certificate. **Classes:** Most classes have 10–19 students. **Most popular majors:** Liberal Arts and Sciences/Liberal Studies; Psychology, General; Biology/Biological Sciences, General. **Special Study Options:** Accelerated program; Distance learning; Double major; Dual enrollment; English as a Second Language (ESL); Exchange student program (domestic); Honors program; Independent study; Internships; Study abroad; Teacher certification program. **Honors programs:** Pine Honors College. **Disability Services offered:** Note-taking services; Reader services; Tape recorders; Tutors. **Career services:** Alumni network; Alumni services; Career assessment; Career/job search classes; Internships; Regional alumni.

FACILITIES

Housing: Apartments for married students; Apartments for single students; Coed dorms; Fraternity/sorority housing; Men's dorms; Women's dorms 80% of campus accessible to physically disabled. **Special Academic Facilities/Equipment:** Tarble Arts Center, Scanning Electron Microscope, Observatory, Thut Greenhouse, Laboratory School Exhibit, Center for Clean Energy Research and Education, Doudna Fine Arts Center. **Campus Network:** 90% of classrooms, 100% of dorms, 100% of student union, 100% of libraries, 100% of dining areas, 75% of common outdoor areas, have wireless network access.

CAMPUS LIFE

Environment: Village. **Activities:** Campus Ministries; Choral groups; Concert band; Dance; Drama/theater; International Student Organization; Jazz band; Literary magazine; Marching band; Music ensembles; Musical theater; Pep band; Radio station; Student government; Student newspaper; Symphony orchestra; Television station; Yearbook. 214 registered organizations, 20 honor societies, 16 religious organizations, 11 fraternities, 12 sororities, on campus. **Athletics (Intercollegiate):** *Men:* baseball, basketball, cross-country, football, golf, soccer, swimming, tennis, track/field (outdoor), track/field (indoor). *Women:* basketball, cross-country, golf, rugby, soccer, softball, swimming, tennis, track/field (outdoor), track/field (indoor), volleyball. **On-Campus Highlights:** Doudna Fine Arts Center.

ADMISSIONS

Freshman Academic Profile: Average high school GPA 3.2. 11% in top 10% of high school class, 34% in top 25% of high school class, 71% in top 50% of high school class. **Test scores:** SAT Math middle 50% range 450–540. SAT EBRW middle 50% range 470–570. ACT middle 50% range 18–22. **Basis for Candidate Selection:** *Very important factors include:* rigor of secondary school record, academic GPA, standardized test scores. *Other factors include:* class rank, application essay, recommendation(s), talent/ability, character/personal qualities. **Freshman Admission Requirements:** High school diploma is required and GED is accepted. *Academic units required:* 4 English, 3 math, 3 science, 3 science labs, 3 social studies, 2 academic electives. *Academic units recommended:* 2 foreign language. **Freshman Admission Statistics:** 8,580 applied, 55% admitted, 17% enrolled. **Transfer Admission Requirements:** High school transcript, college transcript(s), standardized test scores, Minimum college GPA of 2.0 required. **General Admission Information:** Application fee $30. Regular application deadline 8/15. Non-fall registration accepted. Admission may be deferred for a maximum of 1 year.

COSTS AND FINANCIAL AID

Annual in-state tuition $8,880. Annual out-of-state tuition $11,100. Room and board $9,882. Required fees $2,923. Average book and supplies expense $150. **Required Forms and Deadlines:** FAFSA. **Notification of Awards:** Applicants will be notified of awards on a rolling basis beginning 3/1. **Types of Aid:** *Need-based scholarships/grants:* College/university scholarship or grant aid from institutional funds; Federal Pell; Private scholarships; SEOG; State scholarships/grants. *Loans:* Direct PLUS loans; Direct Subsidized Stafford Loans; Direct Unsubsidized Stafford Loans. **Student Employment:** Federal Work-Study Program available. Institutional employment available. **Financial Aid Statistics:** 80% needy freshmen, 78% needy undergrads receive need-based scholarship or grant aid. 60% freshmen, 53% undergrads receive non-need-based scholarship or grant aid. 81% freshmen, 76% undergrads receive need-based self-help aid. 5% freshmen, 4% undergrads receive athletic scholarships. 80% freshmen, 69% undergrads receive any aid. 60% undergrads borrow to pay for school. Average cumulative indebtedness $28,213. **Criteria awarding aid:** *Need-based:* Minority status. *Non-Need-based:* Academics, Art, Athletics, Leadership, Music/drama.

EASTERN KENTUCKY UNIVERSITY

SSB CPO 54, Richmond, KY 40475
Phone: 859-622-2106 **Financial Aid Phone:** 859-622-2361
E-mail: admissions@eku.edu **CEEB Code:** 1200
Fax: 859-622-8024 **Website:** www.eku.edu **ACT Code:** 1512

This public school was founded in 1906. It has a 675 acre campus.

RATINGS

Admissions Selectivity Rating: 77   **Fire Safety Rating:** 90   **Green Rating:** 80

STUDENTS AND FACULTY

Enrollment: 13,333. **Student Body:** 56% female, 44% male, 13% out-of-state, international (36 countries represented).
Retention and Graduation: 68% freshmen return for sophomore year. **Faculty:** Student/faculty ratio 16:1. 697 full-time faculty, 68% hold PhDs, 10% are members of minority groups, 52% are women. 0% of classes are taught by teaching assistants.

ACADEMICS

Degrees: Associate; Bachelor's; Certificate; Doctoral degree—professional practice; Master's; Post-bachelor's certificate. **Classes:** Most classes have 10–19 students. **Most popular majors:** Criminal Justice/Law Enforcement Administration; Elementary Education and Teaching; Nursing/Registered Nurse (Rn, Asn, Bsn, Msn). **Special Study Options:** Cooperative education program; Distance learning; Double major; Dual enrollment; English as a Second Language (ESL); Honors program; Independent study; Internships; Student-designed major; Study abroad; Teacher certification program. **Honors programs:** Honors Program: www.honors.eku.edu. **Disability Services offered:** Note-taking services; Reader services; Tape recorders; Tutors. **Career services:** Alumni network; Alumni services; Career assessment; Career/job search classes; Internships; Regional alumni.

FACILITIES

Housing: Apartments for married students; Apartments for single students; Coed dorms; Fraternity/sorority housing; Men's dorms; Special housing for disabled students; Special housing for international students; Theme housing; Wellness housing; Women's dorms 90% of campus accessible to physically disabled. **Special Academic Facilities/Equipment:** Hummel Planetarium, Giles Gallery.

CAMPUS LIFE

Environment: Town. **Activities:** Campus Ministries; Choral groups; Concert band; Dance; Drama/theater; International Student Organization; Jazz band; Literary magazine; Marching band; Music ensembles; Musical theater; Pep band; Radio station; Student government; Student newspaper; Student-run film society; Symphony orchestra; Yearbook. 178 registered organizations, 30 honor societies, 11 religious organizations, 16 fraternities, 13 sororities, on campus. **Athletics (Intercollegiate):** *Men:* baseball, basketball, cheerleading, cross-country, football, golf, tennis, track/field (outdoor), track/field (indoor). *Women:* basketball, cheerleading, cross-country, golf, soccer, softball, tennis, track/field (outdoor), track/field (indoor), volleyball. **On-Campus Highlights:** Student Wellness Center (New).

ADMISSIONS

Freshman Academic Profile: Average high school GPA 3.2. 13% in top 10% of high school class, 34% in top 25% of high school class, 66% in top 50% of high school class. **Test scores:** ACT middle 50% range 19–24. **Basis for Candidate Selection:** *Very important factors include:* rigor of secondary school record, academic GPA, standardized test scores. **Freshman Admission Requirements:** High school diploma is required and GED is accepted. *Academic units required:* 4 English, 3 math, 3 science, 1 science labs, 2 foreign language, 3 social studies, 7 academic electives, 2 unit from above areas or other academic areas. **Freshman Admission Statistics:** 9,776 applied, 74% admitted, 38% enrolled. **Transfer Admission Requirements:** college transcript(s), Minimum college GPA of 2.0 required. Lowest grade transferable D. **General Admission Information:** Application fee $35. Regular application deadline 8/1. Non-fall registration accepted. Admission may be deferred for a maximum of 1 semester.

COSTS AND FINANCIAL AID

Annual in-state tuition $8,150. Annual out-of-state tuition $17,640. Room and board $8,188. Average book and supplies expense $1,000. **Required Forms and Deadlines:** FAFSA. **Notification of Awards:** Applicants will be notified of awards on a rolling basis beginning 4/1. **Types of Aid:** *Need-based scholarships/*

grants: College/university scholarship or grant aid from institutional funds; Federal Pell; Private scholarships; SEOG; State scholarships/grants. *Loans:* Direct PLUS loans; Direct Subsidized Stafford Loans; Direct Unsubsidized Stafford Loans. **Student Employment:** Federal Work-Study Program available. Institutional employment available. **Financial Aid Statistics:** 66% needy freshmen, 66% needy undergrads receive need-based scholarship or grant aid. 91% freshmen, 60% undergrads receive non-need-based scholarship or grant aid. 81% freshmen, 82% undergrads receive need-based self-help aid. 2% freshmen, 3% undergrads receive athletic scholarships. 94% freshmen, 86% undergrads receive any aid. 71% undergrads borrow to pay for school. Average cumulative indebtedness $27,438. **Criteria awarding aid:** *Non-Need-based:* Academics, Alumni affiliation, Athletics, Leadership, Minority status, Music/drama.

EASTERN MICHIGAN UNIVERSITY

Eastern Michigan University, Ypsilanti, MI 48197
Phone: 734-487-3060 **Financial Aid Phone:** (734) 487-0455
E-mail: admissions@emich.edu **CEEB Code:** 1201
Fax: 734-487-1484 **Website:** www.emich.edu **ACT Code:** 1990

This public school was founded in 1849. It has a 460 acre campus.

RATINGS
Admissions Selectivity Rating: 77   **Fire Safety Rating:** 86   **Green Rating:** 60*

STUDENTS AND FACULTY
Enrollment: 17,256. **Student Body:** 59% female, 41% male, 10% out-of-state, 2% international (80 countries represented). Asian 2%, African American 20%, Caucasian 65%, Hispanic 5%, Native American <1%, Pacific Islander <1%, Two or more races 4%, Race unknown 2%.
Retention and Graduation: 74% freshmen return for sophomore year.
Faculty: Student/faculty ratio 17:1. 766 full-time faculty, 81% hold PhDs, 20% are members of minority groups, 51% are women. 3% of classes are taught by teaching assistants.

ACADEMICS
Degrees: Bachelor's; Doctoral degree research/scholarship; Master's; Post-bachelor's certificate; Post-master's certificate. **Classes:** Most classes have 20–29 students. Most lab/discussion sessions have 10–19 students. **Most popular majors:** Social Work; Registered Nursing/Registered Nurse; Psychology, General. **Special Study Options:** Accelerated program; Cooperative education program; Distance learning; Double major; Dual enrollment; English as a Second Language (ESL); External degree program; Honors program; Independent study; Internships; Student-designed major; Study abroad; Teacher certification program; Weekend college. **Combined degree programs:** BA/MA. **Disability Services offered:** Note-taking services; Reader services; Tape recorders; Tutors. **Career services:** Alumni network; Alumni services; Career assessment; Career/job search classes; Internships.

FACILITIES
Housing: Apartments for married students; Apartments for single students; Coed dorms; Cooperative housing; Fraternity/sorority housing; Special housing for disabled students; Special housing for international students; Theme housing; Wellness housing 80% of campus accessible to physically disabled. **Special Academic Facilities/Equipment:** Intermedia art gallery, paint research center, Sherzer observatory, Bruce T. Halle Library, Terrestial and Aquatics Ecology Research Facility, Coatings Research Institute, the John W. Porter Building housing the College of Education and the Marshall Building housing the College of Health and Human Services.

CAMPUS LIFE
Environment: City. **Activities:** Campus Ministries; Choral groups; Concert band; Dance; Drama/theater; International Student Organization; Jazz band; Literary magazine; Marching band; Model UN; Music ensembles; Musical theater; Opera; Pep band; Radio station; Student government; Student newspaper; Student-run film society; Symphony orchestra; Television station. 300 registered organizations, 14 honor societies, 24 religious organizations, 11 fraternities, 13 sororities, on campus. **Athletics (Intercollegiate):** *Men:* basketball, diving, football, golf, swimming, track/field (outdoor), track/field (indoor), wrestling. *Women:* basketball, crew/rowing, diving, golf, gymnastics, soccer, softball, swimming, tennis, track/field (outdoor), track/field (indoor), volleyball. **On-Campus Highlights:** New Student Center. **Environmental Initiatives:** Energy performance contract.

ADMISSIONS
Freshman Academic Profile: Average high school GPA 3.3. 13% in top 10% of high school class, 39% in top 25% of high school class, 75% in top 50% of high school class. 85% from public high schools. **Test scores:** SAT Math middle 50% range 450–570. SAT EBRW middle 50% range 460–550. ACT middle 50% range 19–25. **Basis for Candidate Selection:** *Very important factors include:* academic GPA, standardized test scores. *Important factors include:* rigor of secondary school record. *Other factors include:* application essay, recommendation(s). **Freshman Admission Requirements:** High school diploma is required and GED is accepted. *Academic units recommended:* 4 English, 4 math, 4 science, 1 science labs, 2 foreign language, 2 social studies, 1 history, 4 academic electives. **Freshman Admission Statistics:** 14,736 applied, 73% admitted, 26% enrolled. **Transfer Admission Requirements:** college transcript(s), Minimum college GPA of 2.0 required. Lowest grade transferable C. **General Admission Information:** Application fee $35. Non-fall registration accepted. Admission may be deferred for a maximum of 1 year.

COSTS AND FINANCIAL AID
Annual in-state tuition $12,120. Annual out-of-state tuition $12,120. Room and board $9,344. Required fees $1,529. Average book and supplies expense $1,000. **Required Forms and Deadlines:** FAFSA. **Notification of Awards:** Applicants will be notified of awards on a rolling basis beginning 12/12. **Types of Aid:** *Need-based scholarships/grants:* College/university scholarship or grant aid from institutional funds; Federal Nursing Scholarships; Federal Pell; Private scholarships; SEOG; State scholarships/grants. **Student Employment:** Federal Work-Study Program available. Institutional employment available. **Financial Aid Statistics:** 68% needy freshmen, 72% needy undergrads receive need-based scholarship or grant aid. 75% freshmen, 47% undergrads receive non-need-based scholarship or grant aid. 67% freshmen, 76% undergrads receive need-based self-help aid. 4% freshmen, 3% undergrads receive athletic scholarships. 98% freshmen receive any aid. 68% undergrads borrow to pay for school. Average cumulative indebtedness $30,588. **Criteria awarding aid:** *Non-Need-based:* Academics, Alumni affiliation, Art, Athletics, Leadership, Music/drama.

EASTERN NEW MEXICO UNIVERSITY

Station #7, Portales, NM 88130
Phone: 575-562-2178 **Financial Aid Phone:** 575-562-2194
E-mail: admissions@enmu.edu **CEEB Code:** 4299
Fax: 575-562-2118 **ACT Code:** 2636

This public school was founded in 1934. It has a 400 acre campus.

RATINGS
Admissions Selectivity Rating: 85   **Fire Safety Rating:** 92   **Green Rating:** 60*

STUDENTS AND FACULTY
Enrollment: 3,618. **Student Body:** 57% female, 43% male, 23% out-of-state, 3% international (23 countries represented). Asian 1%, African American 5%, Caucasian 54%, Hispanic 33%, Native American 3%, Pacific Islander <1%, Two or more races 2%, Race unknown 1%.
Retention and Graduation: 62% freshmen return for sophomore year.
Faculty: Student/faculty ratio 17:1. 146 full-time faculty, 76% hold PhDs, 14% are members of minority groups, 47% are women. 3% of classes are taught by teaching assistants.

ACADEMICS
Degrees: Associate; Bachelor's; Master's; Terminal Associate; Transfer Associate. **Classes:** Most classes have 10–19 students. Most lab/discussion sessions have fewer than 10 students. **Most popular majors:** Business Administration and Management, General; Elementary Education and Teaching; General Studies. **Special Study Options:** Accelerated program; Distance learning; Double major; Dual enrollment; English as a Second Language (ESL); Independent study; Internships; Student-designed major; Teacher certification program. **Disability Services offered:** Note-taking services; Reader services; Tape recorders; Tutors. **Career services:** Alumni network; Career assessment; Internships.

FACILITIES
Housing: Apartments for married students; Apartments for single students; Coed dorms; Fraternity/sorority housing; Special housing for disabled students; Women's dorms 100% of campus accessible to physically disabled. **Special Academic Facilities/Equipment:** Natural history, mineral, and anthropology museums, performance theatre, child development center, audiovisual center, scanning electron microscope (SEM), gas chromatograph/mass spectrometer

(GC/MS), nuclear magnetic resonance spectrometer (NMR), infrared spectrometer (FT/IR), UV/visible spectrometer, X-ray diffraction (XRD), X-ray fluorescence (XRF), KNEW Broadcast Center.

CAMPUS LIFE

Environment: Village. **Activities:** Campus Ministries; Choral groups; Concert band; Dance; Drama/theater; International Student Organization; Jazz band; Literary magazine; Marching band; Music ensembles; Musical theater; Radio station; Student government; Student newspaper; Student-run film society; Television station; Yearbook. 55 registered organizations, 2 honor societies, 4 religious organizations, 4 fraternities, 2 sororities, on campus. **Athletics (Intercollegiate):** *Men:* baseball, basketball, cross-country, football, rodeo, soccer, track/field (outdoor). *Women:* basketball, cross-country, rodeo, soccer, softball, track/field (outdoor), volleyball. **On-Campus Highlights:** New Art/ Anthropology builiding. **Environmental Initiatives:** Water savings project.

ADMISSIONS

Freshman Academic Profile: Average high school GPA 3.2. 11% in top 10% of high school class, 34% in top 25% of high school class, 68% in top 50% of high school class. 98% from public high schools. **Test scores:** SAT Math middle 50% range 430–530. SAT EBRW middle 50% range 420–525. ACT middle 50% range 17–23. **Basis for Candidate Selection:** *Very important factors include:* academic GPA, standardized test scores. **Freshman Admission Requirements:** High school diploma is required and GED is accepted. *Academic units recommended:* 4 English, 4 math, 2 science, 2 social studies. **Freshman Admission Statistics:** 2,164 applied, 60% admitted, 48% enrolled. **Transfer Admission Requirements:** college transcript(s), statement of good standing from prior institution(s). Minimum college GPA of 2.0 required. Lowest grade transferable D. **General Admission Information:** Priority deadline 8/1. Non-fall registration accepted. Admission may be deferred for a maximum of 1 semester.

COSTS AND FINANCIAL AID

Annual in-state tuition $2,688. Annual out-of-state tuition $8,220. Room and board $5,612. Required fees $1,212. Average book and supplies expense $500. **Required Forms and Deadlines:** FAFSA. **Notification of Awards:** Applicants will be notified of awards on a rolling basis beginning 5/1. **Types of Aid:** *Need-based scholarships/grants:* College/university scholarship or grant aid from institutional funds; Federal Pell; SEOG; State scholarships/grants. *Loans:* Direct PLUS loans; Direct Subsidized Stafford Loans; Direct Unsubsidized Stafford Loans. **Student Employment:** Federal Work-Study Program available. Institutional employment available. **Financial Aid Statistics:** 97% needy freshmen, 97% needy undergrads receive need-based scholarship or grant aid. 88% freshmen, 56% undergrads receive non-need-based scholarship or grant aid. 25% freshmen, 27% undergrads receive need-based self-help aid. 10% freshmen, 8% undergrads receive athletic scholarships. 98.87% freshmen, 90.79% undergrads receive any aid. **Criteria awarding aid:** *Non-Need-based:* Academics, Alumni affiliation, Art, Athletics, Leadership, Music/drama, State/ district residency.

EASTERN OREGON UNIVERSITY

One University Blvd, La Grande, OR 97850
Phone: 1-541-962-3393 **Financial Aid Phone:** 1 (800) 452-8639
E-mail: admissions@eou.edu **CEEB Code:** 4300
Fax: 541-962-3418 **Website:** www.eou.edu **ACT Code:** 3460

This public school was founded in 1929. It has a 121 acre campus.

RATINGS

Admissions Selectivity Rating: 80   **Fire Safety Rating:** 89   **Green Rating:** 60*

STUDENTS AND FACULTY

Enrollment: 2,997. **Student Body:** 63% female, 37% male, 28% out-of-state, 2% international (20 countries represented). Asian 2%, African American 3%, Caucasian 76%, Hispanic 6%, Native American 3%, Pacific Islander 1%, Two or more races 2%, Race unknown 6%.
Retention and Graduation: 58% freshmen return for sophomore year.
Faculty: Student/faculty ratio 22:1. 106 full-time faculty, 75% hold PhDs, 8% are members of minority groups, 42% are women.

ACADEMICS

Degrees: Associate; Bachelor's; Certificate; Master's. **Classes:** Most classes have 10–19 students. Most lab/discussion sessions have 10–19 students. **Most**

popular majors: Business Administration, Management and Operations, Other; Education, Other; Liberal Arts and Sciences/Liberal Studies. **Special Study Options:** Cooperative education program; Cross-registration; Distance learning; Double major; Dual enrollment; Exchange student program (domestic); External degree program; Honors program; Independent study; Internships; Liberal arts/career combination; Student-designed major; Study abroad; Teacher certification program; Weekend college. **Honors programs:** Eastern Oregon University is committed to encouraging and recognizing student excellence. To this end, the Honors Program Committee is currently developing an Honors Degree. https://www.eou.edu/honors/. **Disability Services offered:** Note-taking services; Reader services; Tape recorders; Tutors. **Career services:** Alumni services; Career assessment; Career/job search classes; Internships.

FACILITIES

Housing: Apartments for married students; Coed dorms; Special housing for disabled students 95% of campus accessible to physically disabled. **Special Academic Facilities/Equipment:** Art gallery, archaeological museum.

CAMPUS LIFE

Environment: Village. **Activities:** Choral groups; Concert band; Dance; Drama/theater; International Student Organization; Jazz band; Literary magazine; Music ensembles; Musical theater; Radio station; Student government; Student newspaper; Symphony orchestra. 57 registered organizations, 2 honor societies, 4 religious organizations, on campus. **Athletics (Intercollegiate):** *Men:* basketball, cross-country, football, track/field (outdoor), track/field (indoor). *Women:* basketball, cross-country, soccer, softball, track/ field (outdoor), track/field (indoor), volleyball. **On-Campus Highlights:** Loso Hall.

ADMISSIONS

Freshman Academic Profile: Average high school GPA 3.2. 9% in top 10% of high school class, 36% in top 25% of high school class, 74% in top 50% of high school class. **Test scores:** SAT Math middle 50% range 410–520. SAT EBRW middle 50% range 410–530. ACT middle 50% range 18–24. **Basis for Candidate Selection:** *Very important factors include:* rigor of secondary school record, academic GPA. *Important factors include:* recommendation(s), talent/ability. *Other factors include:* class rank, application essay, standardized test scores, extracurricular activities, first generation, geographical residence, volunteer work, work experience, level of applicant's interest. **Freshman Admission Requirements:** High school diploma is required and GED is accepted. *Academic units required:* 4 English, 3 math, 3 science, 2 foreign language, 3 social studies. *Academic units recommended:* 1 science labs. **Freshman Admission Statistics:** 1,530 applied, 64% admitted, 32% enrolled. **Transfer Admission Requirements:** college transcript(s), Minimum college GPA of 2.2 required. Lowest grade transferable D-. **General Admission Information:** Priority deadline 2/1. Regular application deadline 9/1. Non-fall registration accepted. Admission may be deferred for a maximum of 1 year.

COSTS AND FINANCIAL AID

Annual in-state tuition $6,030. Annual out-of-state tuition $16,110. Room and board $9,642. Required fees $1,410. Average book and supplies expense $1,425. **Required Forms and Deadlines:** FAFSA. **Notification of Awards:** Applicants will be notified of awards on a rolling basis beginning 4/1. **Types of Aid:** *Need-based scholarships/grants:* College/university scholarship or grant aid from institutional funds; Federal Pell; Private scholarships; SEOG; State scholarships/grants. *Loans:* Direct PLUS loans; Direct Subsidized Stafford Loans; Direct Unsubsidized Stafford Loans. **Student Employment:** Federal Work-Study Program available. Institutional employment available. **Financial Aid Statistics:** 69% needy freshmen, 75% needy undergrads receive need-based scholarship or grant aid. 10% freshmen, 7% undergrads receive non-need-based scholarship or grant aid. 86% freshmen, 90% undergrads receive need-based self-help aid. 13% freshmen, 9% undergrads receive athletic scholarships. **Criteria awarding aid:** *Need-based:* Academics. *Non-Need-based:* Academics, Art, Leadership, Minority status, Music/drama, State/district residency.

EASTERN WASHINGTON UNIVERSITY

304 Sutton Hall, Cheney, WA 99004
Phone: 509-359-6692 **Financial Aid Phone:** 509-359-2314
E-mail: admissions@ewu.edu **CEEB Code:** 4301
Fax: 509-359-6692 **Website:** www.ewu.edu **ACT Code:** 4454

This public school was founded in 1882. It has a 335 acre campus.

RATINGS
Admissions Selectivity Rating: 73   **Fire Safety Rating:** 88   **Green Rating:** 84

STUDENTS AND FACULTY
Enrollment: 10,500. **Student Body:** 53% female, 47% male, 5% out-of-state, 5% international (38 countries represented). Asian 3%, African American 3%, Caucasian 63%, Hispanic 16%, Native American 1%, Pacific Islander <1%, Two or more races 7%, Race unknown 2%.
Retention and Graduation: 76% freshmen return for sophomore year. 21% freshmen graduate within 4 years. 46% freshmen graduate within 6 years. 44% grads go on to further study within 1 year. **Faculty:** Student/faculty ratio 21:1. 483 full-time faculty, 77% hold PhDs, 18% are members of minority groups, 48% are women. 1% of classes are taught by teaching assistants.

ACADEMICS
Degrees: Bachelor's; Certificate; Doctoral degree—other; Master's; Post-bachelor's certificate. **Classes:** Most classes have 10–19 students. Most lab/discussion sessions have fewer than 10 students. **Most popular majors:** Biology/Biological Sciences, General; Business Administration and Management, General; Psychology, General. **Special Study Options:** Distance learning; Double major; Dual enrollment; English as a Second Language (ESL); Honors program; Independent study; Internships; Student-designed major; Study abroad; Teacher certification program. **Honors programs:** Honors at Eastern Washington University seeks to cultivate excellence in undergraduate education by providing enhanced educational opportunities to superior students and special teaching opportunities to outstanding faculty. Honors courses and Honors activities seek to develop thorough knowledge and appreciation of the liberal arts and sciences; cultivate excellent writing, calculation and critical thinking skills; and inspire an attitude of self-responsibility, lifelong intellectual development, and service to the world. Admission to Honors at Eastern is based entirely on demonstrated and potential intellectual and academic qualifications. **Combined degree programs:** BA/MA. **Disability Services offered:** Note-taking services; Reader services; Tape recorders. **Career services:** Alumni network; Alumni services; Career assessment; Career/job search classes; Internships; Regional alumni.

FACILITIES
Housing: Apartments for married students; Coed dorms; Fraternity/sorority housing; Special housing for disabled students; Theme housing; Wellness housing 77% of campus accessible to physically disabled. **Special Academic Facilities/Equipment:** Anthropology museum, education lab, marine biology lab, ecological studies lab, wildlife refuge, planetarium, Map Library, Crime Lab, State of Washington Digital Archives **Campus Network:** 100% of classrooms, 100% of dorms, 100% of student union, 100% of libraries, 100% of dining areas, 50% of common outdoor areas, have wireless network access.

CAMPUS LIFE
Environment: Town. **Activities:** Campus Ministries; Choral groups; Concert band; Dance; Drama/theater; International Student Organization; Jazz band; Literary magazine; Marching band; Model UN; Music ensembles; Musical theater; Pep band; Radio station; Student government; Student newspaper; Student-run film society; Symphony orchestra. 99 registered organizations, 9 honor societies, 12 religious organizations, 9 fraternities, 11 sororities, on campus. **Athletics (Intercollegiate):** *Men:* basketball, cross-country, football, golf, tennis, track/field (outdoor), track/field (indoor). *Women:* basketball, cross-country, golf, soccer, tennis, track/field (outdoor), track/field (indoor), volleyball. **On-Campus Highlights:** Roos Stadium: "The Inferno" red turf. **Environmental Initiatives:** Facilities Maintenance Energy Management Program: Limiting the greenhouse gas emission.

ADMISSIONS
Freshman Academic Profile: Average high school GPA 3.2. 95% from public high schools. **Test scores:** SAT Math middle 50% range 430–560. SAT EBRW middle 50% range 440–530. ACT middle 50% range 17–24. **Basis for Candidate Selection:** *Very important factors include:* academic GPA, standardized test scores. *Important factors include:* rigor of secondary school record, application essay, *Other factors include:* recommendation(s), extracurricular activities, talent/ability, character/personal qualities, volunteer work, work experience. **Freshman Admission Requirements:** High school diploma or equivalent is not required *Academic units required:* 4 English, 3 math, 2 science, 2 science labs, 2 foreign language, 3 social studies, 1 visual/performing arts, 1 unit from above areas or other academic areas. **Freshman Admission Statistics:** 4,444 applied, 96% admitted, 39% enrolled. **Transfer Admission Requirements:** college transcript(s), essay or personal statement, Minimum college GPA of 2.0 required. Lowest grade transferable D-. **General Admission Information:** Application fee $50. Priority deadline 2/15. Regular application deadline 5/15. Non-fall registration accepted. Admission may be deferred for a maximum of 1 year.

COSTS AND FINANCIAL AID
Student Employment: Federal Work-Study Program available. Institutional employment available. **Financial Aid Statistics:** needy freshmen, needy undergrads receive need-based scholarship or grant aid. freshmen, undergrads receive non-need-based scholarship or grant aid. freshmen, undergrads receive need-based self-help aid. freshmen, undergrads receive athletic scholarships. 72% freshmen, 75% undergrads receive any aid. **Criteria awarding aid:** *Need-based:* Academics, Alumni affiliation, Art, Athletics, Job skills, Music/drama *Non-Need-based:* Academics, Alumni affiliation, Art, Athletics, Job skills, Music/drama, State/district residency.

EAST STROUDSBURG UNIVERSITY OF PENNSYLVANIA

East Stroudsburg University, East Stroudsburg, PA 18301-2999
Phone: 570-422-3542 **Financial Aid Phone:** 570-422-2800
E-mail: undergrads@po-box.esu.edu **CEEB Code:** 2650
Fax: 570-422-3933 **Website:** www4.esu.edu **ACT Code:** 3700

This public school was founded in 1893. It has a 213 acre campus.

RATINGS
Admissions Selectivity Rating: 81   **Fire Safety Rating:** 98   **Green Rating:** 60*

STUDENTS AND FACULTY
Enrollment: 6,274. **Student Body:** 55% female, 45% male, 25% out-of-state, 1% international (24 countries represented). Asian 1%, African American 7%, Caucasian 76%, Hispanic 7%, Native American <1%, Pacific Islander <1%, Two or more races <1%, Race unknown 8%.
Retention and Graduation: 78% freshmen return for sophomore year. **Faculty:** Student/faculty ratio 17:1. 330 full-time faculty, 74% hold PhDs, 16% are members of minority groups, 51% are women. 0% of classes are taught by teaching assistants.

ACADEMICS
Degrees: Associate; Bachelor's; Master's. **Classes:** Most classes have 20–29 students. Most lab/discussion sessions have 20–29 students. **Most popular majors:** Physical Education Teaching and Coaching; Business Administration and Management, General; Elementary Education and Teaching. **Special Study Options:** Accelerated program; Cross-registration; Distance learning; Double major; Dual enrollment; Exchange student program (domestic); Honors program; Independent study; Internships; Student-designed major; Study abroad; Teacher certification program. **Honors programs:** The Honors Program at ESU offers academically superior students an opportunity to challenge themselves intellectually both within and beyond the classroom setting. The focus of the Program was, and is, located in the area of the liberal arts general education curriculum. The goal of the program is to foster in the students an appreciation of the liberal arts perspective and a commitment to lifelong learning. **Disability Services offered:** Note-taking services; Reader services; Tape recorders; Tutors. **Career services:** Career assessment.

FACILITIES
Housing: Coed dorms 95% of campus accessible to physically disabled. **Special Academic Facilities/Equipment:** Natural history museum, human performance lab, TV production studios, 119-acre student-owned/operated recreation area and wildlife sanctuary, observatory, electron microscopes.

CAMPUS LIFE
Environment: Village. **Activities:** Campus Ministries; Choral groups; Concert band; Dance; Drama/theater; International Student Organization; Jazz band; Literary magazine; Marching band; Music ensembles; Musical theater; Pep band; Radio station; Student government; Student newspaper;

Symphony orchestra. 110 registered organizations, 28 honor societies, 3 religious organizations, 5 fraternities, 5 sororities, on campus. **Athletics (Intercollegiate):** *Men:* baseball, basketball, cross-country, football, soccer, tennis, track/field (outdoor), track/field (indoor), wrestling. *Women:* basketball, cross-country, field hockey, golf, lacrosse, soccer, softball, swimming, tennis, track/field (outdoor), track/field (indoor), volleyball. **On-Campus Highlights:** Recreation Center.

ADMISSIONS

Freshman Academic Profile: 7% in top 10% of high school class, 30% in top 25% of high school class, 72% in top 50% of high school class. 90% from public high schools. **Test scores:** SAT Math middle 50% range 460–550. SAT EBRW middle 50% range 440–530. **Basis for Candidate Selection:** *Very important factors include:* rigor of secondary school record, class rank, academic GPA, standardized test scores. **Freshman Admission Requirements:** High school diploma is required and GED is accepted. *Academic units recommended:* 4 English, 4 math, 3 science, 2 science labs, 2 foreign language, 3 social studies. **Freshman Admission Statistics:** 7,258 applied, 63% admitted, 26% enrolled. **Transfer Admission Requirements:** college transcript(s), Minimum college GPA of 2.0 required. Lowest grade transferable C. **General Admission Information:** Application fee $35. Regular application deadline 4/1. Non-fall registration accepted.

COSTS AND FINANCIAL AID

Annual in-state tuition $5,804. Annual out-of-state tuition $14,510. Room and board $6,658. Required fees $1,974. Average book and supplies expense $1,200. **Required Forms and Deadlines:** FAFSA. **Notification of Awards:** Applicants will be notified of awards on or about 4/1. **Types of Aid:** *Need-based scholarships/grants:* College/university scholarship or grant aid from institutional funds; Federal Pell; Private scholarships; SEOG; State scholarships/grants. *Loans:* Direct PLUS loans; Direct Subsidized Stafford Loans; Direct Unsubsidized Stafford Loans. **Student Employment:** Federal Work-Study Program available. Institutional employment available. **Financial Aid Statistics:** 55% needy freshmen, 56% needy undergrads receive need-based scholarship or grant aid. 5% freshmen, 4% undergrads receive non-need-based scholarship or grant aid. 76% freshmen, 73% undergrads receive need-based self-help aid. 6% freshmen, 4% undergrads receive athletic scholarships. 75% freshmen, 84% undergrads receive any aid. **Criteria awarding aid:** *Need-based:* Academics. *Non-Need-based:* Academics, Alumni affiliation, Art, Athletics, Leadership, Minority status, Music/drama, Religious affiliation, State/district residency.

EAST TENNESSEE STATE UNIVERSITY

ETSU Box 70731, Johnson City, TN 37614
Phone: 423-439-4213 **Financial Aid Phone:** (423) 439-4300
E-mail: go2etsu@etsu.edu **CEEB Code:** 1198
Fax: 423-439-4630 **Website:** www.etsu.edu **ACT Code:** 3958

This public school was founded in 1911. It has a 366 acre campus.

RATINGS

Admissions Selectivity Rating: 76 **Fire Safety Rating:** 60* **Green Rating:** 60*

STUDENTS AND FACULTY

Enrollment: 10,960. **Student Body:** 56% female, 44% male, 14% out-of-state, 3% international (57 countries represented). Asian 1%, African American 7%, Caucasian 82%, Hispanic 2%, Native American <1%, Pacific Islander <1%, Two or more races 3%, Race unknown 1%.
Retention and Graduation: 71% freshmen return for sophomore year.
Faculty: Student/faculty ratio 17:1. 575 full-time faculty, 0% hold PhDs, 11% are members of minority groups, 47% are women.

ACADEMICS

Degrees: Bachelor's; Certificate; Doctoral degree—professional practice; Doctoral degree research/scholarship; Master's; Post-bachelor's certificate; Post-master's certificate. **Classes:** Most classes have 20–29 students. Most lab/discussion sessions have 20–29 students. **Most popular majors:** Business Administration and Management, General. **Special Study Options:** Cooperative education program; Distance learning; Double major; Dual enrollment; English as a Second Language (ESL); Exchange student program (domestic); External degree program; Honors program; Independent study; Internships; Student-designed major; Study abroad; Teacher certification program. **Honors programs:** University Honors Program Honors-in-Discipline Programs. **Disability Services offered:** Note-taking services; Reader services;

Tape recorders; Tutors. **Career services:** Alumni network; Alumni services; Career assessment; Career/job search classes; Internships; Regional alumni.

FACILITIES

Housing: Apartments for married students; Apartments for single students; Coed dorms; Fraternity/sorority housing; Men's dorms; Special housing for disabled students; Wellness housing; Women's dorms 75% of campus accessible to physically disabled. **Special Academic Facilities/Equipment:** Regional history museum, art gallery, archives of Appalachia, planetarium.

CAMPUS LIFE

Environment: Town. **Activities:** Campus Ministries; Choral groups; Concert band; Drama/theater; International Student Organization; Jazz band; Literary magazine; Marching band; Music ensembles; Pep band; Radio station; Student government; Student newspaper; Television station. 200 registered organizations, 19 honor societies, 13 religious organizations, 9 fraternities, 7 sororities, on campus. **Athletics (Intercollegiate):** *Men:* baseball, basketball, cheerleading, cross-country, golf, soccer, tennis, track/field (outdoor), track/field (indoor). *Women:* basketball, cheerleading, cross-country, golf, soccer, softball, tennis, track/field (outdoor), track/field (indoor), volleyball. **On-Campus Highlights:** Memorial Center.

ADMISSIONS

Freshman Academic Profile: Average high school GPA 3.4. 20% in top 10% of high school class, 47% in top 25% of high school class, 75% in top 50% of high school class. 90% from public high schools. **Test scores:** SAT Math middle 50% range 420–590. SAT EBRW middle 50% range 420–540. ACT middle 50% range 20–26. **Basis for Candidate Selection:** *Very important factors include:* rigor of secondary school record, academic GPA. *Important factors include:* standardized test scores. **Freshman Admission Requirements:** High school diploma is required and GED is accepted. *Academic units required:* 4 English, 3 math, 2 science, 1 science labs, 2 foreign language, 1 social studies, 1 history, 1 visual/performing arts. *Academic units recommended:* 4 English, 4 math, 3 science, 1 science labs, 2 foreign language, 1 social studies, 1 history, 1 visual/performing arts. **Freshman Admission Statistics:** 8,253 applied, 79% admitted, 31% enrolled. **Transfer Admission Requirements:** High school transcript, college transcript(s), Minimum college GPA of 2.0 required. Lowest grade transferable D. **General Admission Information:** Application fee $25. Priority deadline 2/1. Regular application deadline 8/15. Non-fall registration accepted.

COSTS AND FINANCIAL AID

Annual in-state tuition $7,002. Annual out-of-state tuition $25,098. Room and board $7,952. Required fees $1,669. Average book and supplies expense $1,090. **Required Forms and Deadlines:** FAFSA. **Notification of Awards:** Applicants will be notified of awards on a rolling basis beginning 3/15. **Types of Aid:** *Need-based scholarships/grants:* College/university scholarship or grant aid from institutional funds; Federal Nursing Scholarships; Federal Pell; Private scholarships; SEOG; State scholarships/grants. *Loans:* Direct PLUS loans; Direct Subsidized Stafford Loans; Direct Unsubsidized Stafford Loans. **Student Employment:** Federal Work-Study Program available. Institutional employment available. **Financial Aid Statistics:** 0% freshmen, 0% undergrads receive athletic scholarships. **Criteria awarding aid:** *Need-based:* Academics, Alumni affiliation, Art, Athletics, Job skills, Leadership, Minority status, Music/drama, Religious affiliation. *Non-Need-based:* Academics, Alumni affiliation, Art, Athletics, Leadership, Minority status, Music/drama, Religious affiliation, State/district residency.

EAST TEXAS BAPTIST UNIVERSITY

One Tiger Drive, Marshall, TX 75670-1498
Phone: 903-923-2000 **Financial Aid Phone:** (903) 923-2137
E-mail: admissions@etbu.edu **CEEB Code:** 6187
Fax: 903-923-2001 **Website:** https://www.etbu.edu **ACT Code:** 4086

This private school, affiliated with the Baptist Church, was founded in 1912. It has a 250 acre campus.

RATINGS

Admissions Selectivity Rating: 85 **Fire Safety Rating:** 82 **Green Rating:** 60*

STUDENTS AND FACULTY

Enrollment: 1,333. **Student Body:** 56% female, 44% male, 12% out-of-state, 1% international (6 countries represented). Asian 1%, African American 17%, Caucasian 64%, Hispanic 13%, Native American 1%, Pacific Islander <1%, Two or more races 4%, Race unknown <1%.

Retention and Graduation: 62% freshmen return for sophomore year. 37% freshmen graduate within 4 years. 44% freshmen graduate within 6 years. 28% grads go on to further study within 1 year. **Faculty:** Student/faculty ratio 14:1. 73 full-time faculty, 84% hold PhDs, 10% are members of minority groups, 37% are women. 0% of classes are taught by teaching assistants.

ACADEMICS
Degrees: Bachelor's; Certificate; Master's. **Classes:** Most classes have 10–19 students. Most lab/discussion sessions have 10–19 students. **Most popular majors:** Elementary Education and Teaching; Multi-/Interdisciplinary Studies, Other; Registered Nursing/Registered Nurse. **Special Study Options:** Accelerated program; Distance learning; Double major; Dual enrollment; English as a Second Language (ESL); Honors program; Independent study; Internships; Student-designed major; Teacher certification program. **Honors programs:** The mission of the ETBU Honors Program is to provide a tight-knit community of scholars in pursuit of the Christian intellectual life through the pairing of academic rigor with informed reflection for thoughtful engagement with the world. We accomplish our mission with an academic minor complementary to any major field of study offered at the university. The Honors Program curriculum provides an intellectual backdrop to students' chosen fields of study; gives students needed context for study at the graduate level; and equips students with critical thinking, reading, writing, and discussion skills that will prove invaluable in the workforce. Students in the Honors Program see that intellectual pursuits are not reserved for those in the academy but have a productive, positive bearing in all vocations. For more information, please visit: https://www.etbu.edu/admissions/apply/honors-program. **Combined degree programs:** BA/MA. **Disability Services offered:** Tutors. **Career services:** Alumni services; Career assessment; Career/job search classes; Internships.

FACILITIES
Housing: Apartments for married students; Apartments for single students; Men's dorms; Wellness housing; Women's dorms 95% of campus accessible to physically disabled.

CAMPUS LIFE
Environment: Town. **Activities:** Campus Ministries; Choral groups; Concert band; Dance; Drama/theater; Jazz band; Literary magazine; Marching band; Model UN; Music ensembles; Musical theater; Opera; Pep band; Student government; Symphony orchestra. 21 registered organizations, 9 honor societies, 3 religious organizations, 1 sororities, on campus. **Athletics (Intercollegiate):** *Men:* baseball, basketball, cross-country, football, soccer. *Women:* basketball, cross-country, soccer, softball, volleyball. **On-Campus Highlights:** Ornelas Student Center.

ADMISSIONS
Freshman Academic Profile: Average high school GPA 3.4. 15% in top 10% of high school class, 41% in top 25% of high school class, 71% in top 50% of high school class. **Test scores:** SAT Math middle 50% range 460–560. SAT EBRW middle 50% range 460–560. ACT middle 50% range 17–22. **Basis for Candidate Selection:** *Very important factors include:* class rank, academic GPA, standardized test scores. *Important factors include:* rigor of secondary school record, religious affiliation/commitment. *Other factors include:* recommendation(s), extracurricular activities, talent/ability, character/personal qualities, alumni/ae relation, level of applicant's interest. **Freshman Admission Requirements:** High school diploma is required and GED is accepted. **Freshman Admission Statistics:** 1,777 applied, 59% admitted, 33% enrolled. **Transfer Admission Requirements:** college transcript(s), statement of good standing from prior institution(s). Minimum college GPA of 2.00 required. Lowest grade transferable D. **General Admission Information:** Application fee $25. Regular application deadline 8/25. Non-fall registration accepted. Admission may be deferred for a maximum of 1 year.

COSTS AND FINANCIAL AID
Required Forms and Deadlines: FAFSA; Institution's own financial aid form. **Notification of Awards:** Applicants will be notified of awards on a rolling basis beginning 1/1. **Types of Aid:** *Need-based scholarships/grants:* College/university scholarship or grant aid from institutional funds; Federal Pell; Private scholarships; SEOG; State scholarships/grants. *Loans:* Direct PLUS loans; Direct Subsidized Stafford Loans; Direct Unsubsidized Stafford Loans. **Student Employment:** Federal Work-Study Program available. Institutional employment available. **Financial Aid Statistics:** 72% needy freshmen, 72% needy undergrads receive need-based scholarship or grant aid. 99% freshmen, 97% undergrads receive non-need-based scholarship or grant aid. 69% freshmen, 74% undergrads receive need-based self-help aid. 0% freshmen, 0% undergrads receive athletic scholarships. 99% freshmen, 98% undergrads

receive any aid. 77% undergrads borrow to pay for school. Average cumulative indebtedness $30,351. **Criteria awarding aid:** *Non-Need-based:* Academics, Alumni affiliation, Leadership, Music/drama, Religious affiliation, State/district residency.

ECKERD COLLEGE

4200 54th Avenue South, St.Petersburg, FL 33711
Phone: 727-864-8331 **Financial Aid Phone:** 727-864-8854
E-mail: admissions@eckerd.edu
Fax: 727-866-2304 **Website:** www.eckerd.edu **ACT Code:** 0731

This private school, affiliated with the Presbyterian Church, was founded in 1958. It has a 188 acre campus.

RATINGS
Admissions Selectivity Rating: 83   **Fire Safety Rating:** 91   **Green Rating:** 82

STUDENTS AND FACULTY
Enrollment: 1,989. **Student Body:** 67% female, 33% male, 79% out-of-state, 3% international (36 countries represented). Asian 3%, African American 3%, Caucasian 78%, Hispanic 9%, Native American 1%, Pacific Islander <1%, Two or more races 4%, Race unknown <1%.
Retention and Graduation: 81% freshmen return for sophomore year. 60% freshmen graduate within 4 years. 66% freshmen graduate within 6 years. **Faculty:** Student/faculty ratio 12:1. 155 full-time faculty, 87% hold PhDs, 14% are members of minority groups, 52% are women. 0% of classes are taught by teaching assistants.

ACADEMICS
Degrees: Bachelor's. **Classes:** Most classes have 20–29 students. Most lab/discussion sessions have 20–29 students. **Most popular majors:** Environmental Studies; Biology/Biological Sciences, General; Psychology, General. **Special Study Options:** Accelerated program; Double major; English as a Second Language (ESL); Honors program; Independent study; Internships; Liberal arts/career combination; Student-designed major; Study abroad. **Honors programs:** Ford Scholar program: Each year up to twenty rising Juniors are given the opportunity to participate in a two year course of study designed to prepare them for graduate school and to pursue a career in college or university teaching. Faculty select and sponsor the participants on the basis of academic achievement, intellectual promise, and a willingness to explore college teaching as career. The program involves special coursework, summer research in collaboration with a faculty sponsor, a major project during the Senior year, and supervised teaching experience. Honors program: The Honors Program at Eckerd College provides enhanced opportunities for students of outstanding ability to interact and learn from each other through class discussions and group activities. Selected students are brought together for close interaction and advanced work, such studies receiving permanent recognition on the students' transcripts. **Combined degree programs:** BA/JD. **Disability Services offered:** Note-taking services; Reader services; Tape recorders. **Career services:** Alumni network; Alumni services; Career assessment; Career/job search classes; Internships.

FACILITIES
Housing: Apartments for single students; Coed dorms; Special housing for disabled students; Theme housing; Wellness housing; Women's dorms 90% of campus accessible to physically disabled. **Special Academic Facilities/Equipment:** Theatre, galleries, chapel, writing center, oral communication center, marine science lab. **Campus Network:** 95% of classrooms, 100% of student union, 100% of libraries, 100% of dining areas, have wireless network access.

CAMPUS LIFE
Environment: City. **Activities:** Campus Ministries; Choral groups; Concert band; Dance; Drama/theater; International Student Organization; Literary magazine; Music ensembles; Radio station; Student government; Student newspaper. 117 registered organizations, 8 honor societies, 5 religious organizations, on campus. **Athletics (Intercollegiate):** *Men:* baseball, basketball, golf, sailing, soccer, tennis. *Women:* basketball, golf, sailing, soccer, softball, tennis, volleyball. **On-Campus Highlights:** the James Center for Molecular and

Life Sciences. **Environmental Initiatives:** The yellow bike has in recent years become a new symbol of Eckerd College. The Yellow Bike Program started in the spring of 2004, and since then it has gained national recognition. Students, faculty, staff, and even the College President can be spotted riding them. The goal of the program is to have less vehicle traffic which decreases greenhouse gas emissions and reduces our harm to the environment. The bikes on campus will help lead to a mostly walking campus, and an eco-friendly campus. The Yellow Bike Program was recognized in 2005 by the National Wildlife Federation, and it has gained local and national news attention.

ADMISSIONS

Freshman Academic Profile: Average high school GPA 3.5. **Test scores:** SAT Math middle 50% range 530–630. SAT EBRW middle 50% range 560–650. ACT middle 50% range 23–29. **Basis for Candidate Selection:** *Very important factors include:* rigor of secondary school record, academic GPA. *Important factors include:* application essay, standardized test scores, recommendation(s), interview, extracurricular activities, talent/ability, character/personal qualities, volunteer work. *Other factors include:* class rank, first generation, alumni/ae relation. **Freshman Admission Requirements:** High school diploma is required and GED is accepted. *Academic units recommended:* 4 English, 3 math, 3 science, 2 science labs, 2 foreign language, 2 social studies, 1 history, 3 academic electives. **Freshman Admission Statistics:** 4,644 applied, 67% admitted, 17% enrolled. **Transfer Admission Requirements:** college transcript(s), essay or personal statement, statement of good standing from prior institution(s). Minimum college GPA of 2.5 required. Lowest grade transferable C. **General Admission Information:** Application fee $40. Non-fall registration accepted.

COSTS AND FINANCIAL AID

Annual tuition $45,452. Room and board $13,026. Required fees $644. Average book and supplies expense $1,350. **Required Forms and Deadlines:** FAFSA. **Types of Aid:** *Need-based scholarships/grants:* College/university scholarship or grant aid from institutional funds; Federal Pell; SEOG; State scholarships/grants. *Loans:* Direct PLUS loans; Direct Subsidized Stafford Loans; Direct Unsubsidized Stafford Loans. **Student Employment:** Federal Work-Study Program available. Institutional employment available. **Financial Aid Statistics:** 99% needy freshmen, 100% needy undergrads receive need-based scholarship or grant aid. 0% freshmen, 0% undergrads receive non-need-based scholarship or grant aid. 87% freshmen, 86% undergrads receive need-based self-help aid. 2% freshmen, 3% undergrads receive athletic scholarships. 99% freshmen, 86% undergrads receive any aid. 58% undergrads borrow to pay for school. Average cumulative indebtedness $33,661. **Criteria awarding aid:** *Need-based:* Religious affiliation. *Non-Need-based:* Academics, Art, Athletics, Music/drama, State/district residency.

EDGEWOOD COLLEGE

1000 Edgewood College Drive, Madison, WI 53711-1997
Phone: 608-663-2294 **Financial Aid Phone:** 608-663-4300
E-mail: admissions@edgewood.edu **CEEB Code:** 1202
Fax: 608-663-2214 **Website:** www.edgewood.edu **ACT Code:** 4582

This private school, affiliated with the Roman Catholic Church, was founded in 1927. It has a 55 acre campus.

RATINGS

Admissions Selectivity Rating: 80   **Fire Safety Rating:** 94   **Green Rating:** 73

STUDENTS AND FACULTY

Enrollment: 1,330. **Student Body:** 73% female, 27% male, 9% out-of-state, 3% international (16 countries represented). Asian 2%, African American 4%, Caucasian 76%, Hispanic 9%, Native American <1%, Pacific Islander <1%, Two or more races 4%, Race unknown 2%.
Retention and Graduation: 79% freshmen return for sophomore year. 41% freshmen graduate within 4 years. 64% freshmen graduate within 6 years. 12% grads go on to further study within 1 year. **Faculty:** Student/faculty ratio 10:1. 144 full-time faculty, 76% hold PhDs, 15% are members of minority groups, 65% are women. 0% of classes are taught by teaching assistants.

ACADEMICS

Degrees: Bachelor's; Certificate; Doctoral degree—professional practice; Doctoral degree research/scholarship; Master's; Post-bachelor's certificate.
Classes: Most classes have 10–19 students. **Most popular majors:** Communication and Media Studies; Registered Nursing/Registered Nurse; Business/Commerce, General. **Special Study Options:** Accelerated program;

Cooperative education program; Distance learning; Double major; Dual enrollment; Honors program; Independent study; Internships; Liberal arts/career combination; Student-designed major; Study abroad; Teacher certification program. **Honors programs:** We have an Honors Program for undergraduates. **Disability Services offered:** Note-taking services; Reader services; Tape recorders; Tutors. **Career services:** Alumni network; Alumni services; Career assessment; Career/job search classes; Internships; Regional alumni.

FACILITIES

Housing: Apartments for single students; Coed dorms; Cooperative housing; Special housing for disabled students; Theme housing 90% of campus accessible to physically disabled. **Special Academic Facilities/Equipment:** The Stream, and Science Exploration Center.

CAMPUS LIFE

Environment: City. **Activities:** Campus Ministries; Drama/theater; International Student Organization; Music ensembles; Musical theater; Student government; Student newspaper; Symphony orchestra. 48 registered organizations, 4 honor societies, 1 religious organizations, on campus. **Athletics (Intercollegiate):** *Men:* baseball, basketball, cross-country, golf, soccer, tennis, track/field (outdoor), track/field (indoor). *Women:* basketball, cross-country, golf, soccer, softball, tennis, track/field (outdoor), track/field (indoor), volleyball. **On-Campus Highlights:** Wingra Cafe, Commons. **Environmental Initiatives:** The Campus Sustainability Coordinating Team has completed a Campus Sustainability Plan, components of which are incorporated into the College's Master Plan.

ADMISSIONS

Freshman Academic Profile: Average high school GPA 3.5. 16% in top 10% of high school class, 50% in top 25% of high school class, 83% in top 50% of high school class. 94% from public high schools. **Test scores:** SAT Math middle 50% range 490–600. SAT EBRW middle 50% range 460–610. ACT middle 50% range 20–25. **Basis for Candidate Selection:** *Very important factors include:* class rank, academic GPA, standardized test scores. *Other factors include:* application essay, recommendation(s). **Freshman Admission Requirements:** High school diploma is required and GED is accepted. *Academic units required:* 4 English, 2 math, 2 science, 1 science labs, 2 foreign language, 2 social studies, 1 history. *Academic units recommended:* 4 English, 2 math, 2 science, 1 science labs, 2 foreign language, 2 social studies, 1 history. **Freshman Admission Statistics:** 1,397 applied, 72% admitted, 24% enrolled. **Transfer Admission Requirements:** High school transcript, college transcript(s), Minimum college GPA of 2.0 required. Lowest grade transferable C-. **General Admission Information:** Application fee $30. Priority deadline 3/1. Regular application deadline 8/1. Non-fall registration accepted. Admission may be deferred for a maximum of 12 months.

COSTS AND FINANCIAL AID

Annual tuition $30,600. Room and board $11,350. Average book and supplies expense $800. **Required Forms and Deadlines:** FAFSA. **Notification of Awards:** Applicants will be notified of awards on a rolling basis beginning 12/15. **Types of Aid:** *Need-based scholarships/grants:* College/university scholarship or grant aid from institutional funds; Federal Pell; Private scholarships; SEOG; State scholarships/grants. *Loans:* Direct PLUS loans; Direct Subsidized Stafford Loans; Direct Unsubsidized Stafford Loans. **Student Employment:** Federal Work-Study Program available. Institutional employment available. **Financial Aid Statistics:** 100% needy freshmen, 98% needy undergrads receive need-based scholarship or grant aid. 7% freshmen, 8% undergrads receive non-need-based scholarship or grant aid. 88% freshmen, 86% undergrads receive need-based self-help aid. 0% freshmen, 0% undergrads receive athletic scholarships. 100% freshmen, 87% undergrads receive any aid. 77% undergrads borrow to pay for school. Average cumulative indebtedness $37,332. **Criteria awarding aid:** *Need-based:* Academics, Alumni affiliation, Religious affiliation. *Non-Need-based:* Academics, Alumni affiliation, Art, Leadership, Music/drama, Religious affiliation.

EDINBORO UNIVERSITY OF PENNSYLVANIA

200 East Normal Street, Edinboro, PA 16444
Phone: 814-732-2761 **Financial Aid Phone:** 814-732-3500
E-mail: eup_admissions@edinboro.edu **CEEB Code:** 2651
Fax: 814-732-2420 **Website:** http://www.edinboro.edu/ **ACT Code:** 3702

This public school was founded in 1857. It has a 585 acre campus.

RATINGS
Admissions Selectivity Rating: 77   **Fire Safety Rating:** 97   **Green Rating:** 64

STUDENTS AND FACULTY
Enrollment: 6,301. **Student Body:** 56% female, 44% male, 11% out-of-state, 1% international (31 countries represented). Asian 1%, African American 9%, Caucasian 86%, Hispanic 2%, Native American <1%, Race unknown 1%. **Retention and Graduation:** 75% freshmen return for sophomore year. **Faculty:** 346 full-time faculty, 0% hold PhDs, 7% are members of minority groups, 46% are women. 0% of classes are taught by teaching assistants.

ACADEMICS
Degrees: Associate; Bachelor's; Master's; Post-bachelor's certificate; Post-master's certificate. **Classes:** Most classes have 20–29 students. **Most popular majors:** Criminal Justice/Safety Studies; Fine/Studio Arts, General; Business Administration and Management, General. **Special Study Options:** Cooperative education program; Cross-registration; Distance learning; Double major; Dual enrollment; Honors program; Independent study; Internships; Liberal arts/career combination; Student-designed major; Study abroad; Teacher certification program. **Honors programs:** Admission to the Upper Division Honors Program, may be made by any full time EUP student who has completed 63 credit hours with an overall GPA of 3.4 or higher. They must also provide letters of support from two faculty members, secure approval of their academic advisor, and complete a proposal for the Senior Project in consultation with the Honors Director, Academic Advisor and and Faculty Member who will supervise the Senior Project. **Combined degree programs:** BA/MEng. **Disability Services offered:** Note-taking services; Reader services; Tape recorders; Tutors. **Career services:** Alumni services; Career assessment; Career/job search classes; Internships.

FACILITIES
Housing: Coed dorms; Special housing for disabled students 98% of campus accessible to physically disabled. **Special Academic Facilities/Equipment:** Planetarium, Solar Observatory, Bates Art Gallery, Bruce Gallery. **Campus Network:** 100% of classrooms, 100% of dorms, 100% of student union, 100% of libraries, 100% of dining areas, 95% of common outdoor areas, have wireless network access.

CAMPUS LIFE
Environment: Rural. **Activities:** Campus Ministries; Choral groups; Dance; Drama/theater; International Student Organization; Jazz band; Literary magazine; Marching band; Music ensembles; Opera; Radio station; Student government; Student newspaper; Student-run film society; Television station. 175 registered organizations, 13 honor societies, 8 religious organizations, 7 fraternities, 7 sororities, on campus. **Athletics (Intercollegiate):** *Men:* basketball, cross-country, football, swimming, track/field (outdoor), track/field (indoor), wheel-chair basketball, wrestling. *Women:* basketball, cross-country, lacrosse, soccer, softball, swimming, track/field (outdoor), track/field (indoor), volleyball. **On-Campus Highlights:** Tilles Center for the Performing Arts.

ADMISSIONS
Freshman Academic Profile: Average high school GPA 3.2. 5% in top 10% of high school class, 20% in top 25% of high school class, 51% in top 50% of high school class. **Test scores:** SAT Math middle 50% range 410–520. SAT EBRW middle 50% range 415–520. ACT middle 50% range 17–23. **Basis for Candidate Selection:** *Very important factors include:* rigor of secondary school record, class rank, academic GPA, standardized test scores. *Other factors include:* application essay, recommendation(s), interview, extracurricular activities, talent/ability, character/personal qualities, volunteer work, work experience. **Freshman Admission Requirements:** High school diploma is required and GED is accepted. *Academic units recommended:* 4 English, 3 math, 3 science, 2 foreign language, 4 social studies, 1 computer science. **Freshman Admission Statistics:** 4,411 applied, 73% admitted, 44% enrolled. **Transfer Admission Requirements:** High school transcript, college transcript(s), statement of good standing from prior institution(s). Minimum college GPA of 2.0 required. Lowest grade transferable C-. **General Admission Information:** Application fee

$30. Non-fall registration accepted. Admission may be deferred for a maximum of 1 year.

COSTS AND FINANCIAL AID
Annual in-state tuition $5,554. Annual out-of-state tuition $8,332. Room and board $7,130. Required fees $1,762. Average book and supplies expense $900. **Required Forms and Deadlines:** FAFSA. **Notification of Awards:** Applicants will be notified of awards on a rolling basis beginning 3/22. **Types of Aid:** *Need-based scholarships/grants:* College/university scholarship or grant aid from institutional funds; Federal Pell; Private scholarships; SEOG; State scholarships/grants. *Loans:* Direct Subsidized Stafford Loans; Direct Unsubsidized Stafford Loans. **Student Employment:** Federal Work-Study Program available. Institutional employment available. **Financial Aid Statistics:** 90% needy freshmen, 92% needy undergrads receive need-based scholarship or grant aid. 94% freshmen, 94% undergrads receive non-need-based scholarship or grant aid. 82% freshmen, 86% undergrads receive need-based self-help aid. 3% freshmen, 2% undergrads receive athletic scholarships. 91% freshmen, 88% undergrads receive any aid. **Criteria awarding aid:** *Need-based:* Academics, Alumni affiliation, Art, Athletics, Job skills, Leadership, Minority status, Music/drama, Religious affiliation. *Non-Need-based:* Academics, Alumni affiliation, Art, Athletics, Job skills, Leadership, Minority status, Music/drama, Religious affiliation, State/district residency.

ELIZABETHTOWN COLLEGE

Leffler House, Elizabethtown, PA 17022-2298
Phone: 717-361-1400 **Financial Aid Phone:** 717-361-1404
E-mail: admissions@etown.edu **CEEB Code:** 2225
Fax: 717-361-1365 **Website:** www.etown.edu **ACT Code:** 3568

This private school, affiliated with the Church of Brethren, was founded in 1899. It has a 193 acre campus.

RATINGS
Admissions Selectivity Rating: 77   **Fire Safety Rating:** 62   **Green Rating:** 60*

STUDENTS AND FACULTY
Enrollment: 1,687. **Student Body:** 61% female, 39% male, 28% out-of-state, 1% international (17 countries represented). Asian 3%, African American 4%, Caucasian 86%, Hispanic 4%, Native American <1%, Pacific Islander <1%, Two or more races 2%, Race unknown 1%. **Retention and Graduation:** 87% freshmen return for sophomore year. 65% freshmen graduate within 4 years. 69% freshmen graduate within 6 years. 20% grads go on to further study within 1 year. **Faculty:** Student/faculty ratio 11:1. 123 full-time faculty, 94% hold PhDs, 8% are members of minority groups, 52% are women. 0% of classes are taught by teaching assistants.

ACADEMICS
Degrees: Associate; Bachelor's; Certificate; Doctoral degree—professional practice; Master's; Post-bachelor's certificate. **Classes:** Most classes have 10–19 students. Most lab/discussion sessions have 10–19 students. **Most popular majors:** Business/Commerce, General. **Special Study Options:** Accelerated program; Distance learning; Double major; Dual enrollment; English as a Second Language (ESL); Exchange student program (domestic); Honors program; Independent study; Internships; Student-designed major; Study abroad; Teacher certification program. **Combined degree programs:** BA/MA; BA/MD. **Disability Services offered:** Tape recorders; Tutors.

FACILITIES
Housing: Apartments for single students; Coed dorms; Cooperative housing; Special housing for disabled students; Special housing for international students; Theme housing; Wellness housing 75% of campus accessible to physically disabled. **Special Academic Facilities/Equipment:** Art gallery, Mineral gallery, Meetinghouse/center for Anabaptist and Pietist studies, chapel/performance center, Fourier transform multinuclear NMR spectrometer, blood gas analyzer, scanning densitometer, PCR machine, radiometer/data logger, automated ion analyzer, computerized language lab.

CAMPUS LIFE
Environment: Village. **Activities:** Campus Ministries; Choral groups; Concert band; Dance; Drama/theater; International Student Organization; Jazz band; Literary magazine; Model UN; Music ensembles; Musical theater; Radio station; Student government; Student newspaper; Symphony orchestra; Television station; Yearbook. 80 registered organizations, 22 honor societies, 6

religious organizations, on campus. **Athletics (Intercollegiate):** *Men:* baseball, basketball, cross-country, diving, golf, lacrosse, soccer, swimming, tennis, track/field (outdoor), track/field (indoor), wrestling. *Women:* basketball, cross-country, diving, field hockey, lacrosse, soccer, softball, swimming, tennis, track/field (outdoor), track/field (indoor), volleyball. **On-Campus Highlights:** Brossman Commons Students Center.

ADMISSIONS

Freshman Academic Profile: 29% in top 10% of high school class, 61% in top 25% of high school class, 86% in top 50% of high school class. 80% from public high schools. **Test scores:** SAT Math middle 50% range 530–650. SAT EBRW middle 50% range 550–640. ACT middle 50% range 21–28. **Basis for Candidate Selection:** *Very important factors include:* rigor of secondary school record. *Important factors include:* class rank, academic GPA, application essay, standardized test scores, recommendation(s), interview. *Other factors include:* extracurricular activities, talent/ability, character/personal qualities, first generation, alumni/ae relation, geographical residence, state residency, religious affiliation/commitment, racial/ethnic status, volunteer work, work experience, level of applicant's interest. **Freshman Admission Requirements:** High school diploma is required and GED is accepted. *Academic units required:* 4 English, 3 math, 2 science, 2 science labs, 2 foreign language, 2 social studies, 2 history. *Academic units recommended:* 4 English, 4 math, 4 science, 3 science labs, 2 foreign language, 2 social studies, 2 history. **Freshman Admission Statistics:** 1,893 applied, 81% admitted, 25% enrolled. **Transfer Admission Requirements:** High school transcript, college transcript(s), essay or personal statement, standardized test scores, statement of good standing from prior institution(s). Minimum college GPA of 2.5 required. Lowest grade transferable C. **General Admission Information:** Priority deadline 4/1. Non-fall registration accepted. Admission may be deferred for a maximum of 1 year.

COSTS AND FINANCIAL AID

Annual tuition $32,960. Room and board $12,060. Average book and supplies expense $1,100. **Required Forms and Deadlines:** FAFSA. **Notification of Awards:** Applicants will be notified of awards on a rolling basis beginning 12/3. **Types of Aid:** *Need-based scholarships/grants:* College/university scholarship or grant aid from institutional funds; Federal Pell; Private scholarships; SEOG; State scholarships/grants. *Loans:* Direct PLUS loans; Direct Subsidized Stafford Loans; Direct Unsubsidized Stafford Loans. **Financial Aid Statistics:** 100% needy freshmen, 100% needy undergrads receive need-based scholarship or grant aid. 16% freshmen, 13% undergrads receive non-need-based scholarship or grant aid. 79% freshmen, 82% undergrads receive need-based self-help aid. 0% freshmen, 0% undergrads receive athletic scholarships. 96% freshmen, 94% undergrads receive any aid. 79% undergrads borrow to pay for school. Average cumulative indebtedness $42,548. **Criteria awarding aid:** *Need-based:* Academics, Alumni affiliation, Art, Minority status, Music/drama, Religious affiliation. *Non-Need-based:* Academics, Alumni affiliation, Art, Music/drama, Religious affiliation.

ELMHURST COLLEGE

190 S Prospect Avenue, Elmhurst, IL 60126
Phone: 630-617-3400 **Financial Aid Phone:** 630-617-3075
E-mail: admit@elmhurst.edu **CEEB Code:** 1204
Fax: 630-617-5501 **Website:** www.elmhurst.edu **ACT Code:** 1020

This private school, affiliated with the United Church of Christ, was founded in 1871. It has a 38 acre campus.

RATINGS

Admissions Selectivity Rating: 81 **Fire Safety Rating:** 89 **Green Rating:** 60*

STUDENTS AND FACULTY

Enrollment: 2,807. **Student Body:** 62% female, 38% male, 9% out-of-state, 1% international (25 countries represented). Asian 6%, African American 5%, Caucasian 58%, Hispanic 25%, Native American <1%, Pacific Islander <1%, Two or more races 3%, Race unknown 2%.
Retention and Graduation: 82% freshmen return for sophomore year. 57% freshmen graduate within 4 years. 70% freshmen graduate within 6 years. 17% grads go on to further study within 1 year. 0% grads pursue arts and sciences degrees. 1% grads pursue law degrees. 8% grads pursue business degrees. 2% grads pursue medical degrees. **Faculty:** Student/faculty ratio 14:1. 152 full-time faculty, 82% hold PhDs, 12% are members of minority groups, 63% are women. 0% of classes are taught by teaching assistants.

ACADEMICS

Degrees: Bachelor's; Master's; Post-bachelor's certificate. **Classes:** Most classes have 20–29 students. **Most popular majors:** Business Administration and Management, General; Psychology, General; Health Professions And Related Programs. **Special Study Options:** Accelerated program; Distance learning; Double major; Dual enrollment; Honors program; Independent study; Internships; Liberal arts/career combination; Student-designed major; Study abroad; Teacher certification program. **Honors programs:** The Elmhurst College Honors program provides a challenging set of educational experiences for the most academically students featuring small, stimulating seminar courses where class discussions are lively and engaging; opportunities to conduct and present professional-level research; private receptions with distinguished guest speakers; trips to theatre and dance performances, social events, and more. **Combined degree programs:** BA/JD; BA/MEng. **Disability Services offered:** Note-taking services; Reader services; Tape recorders; Tutors. **Career services:** Alumni network; Career assessment; Career/job search classes; Internships.

FACILITIES

Housing: Apartments for single students; Coed dorms 95% of campus accessible to physically disabled. **Special Academic Facilities/Equipment:** Accelerator/art space, language lab, recording studio, computer science/technology center, four electron microscopes.

CAMPUS LIFE

Environment: Town. **Activities:** Campus Ministries; Choral groups; Concert band; Dance; Drama/theater; International Student Organization; Jazz band; Literary magazine; Model UN; Music ensembles; Musical theater; Radio station; Student government; Student newspaper; Symphony orchestra; Yearbook. 106 registered organizations, 15 honor societies, 6 religious organizations, 3 fraternities, 6 sororities, on campus. **Athletics (Intercollegiate):** *Men:* baseball, basketball, cross-country, football, golf, soccer, tennis, track/field (outdoor), wrestling. *Women:* basketball, bowling, cross-country, golf, soccer, softball, tennis, track/field (outdoor), volleyball. **On-Campus Highlights:** Alumni Circle. **Environmental Initiatives:** Development and execution of our Sustainability Plan. It is a living document that continues to expand as goals are achieved.

ADMISSIONS

Freshman Academic Profile: Average high school GPA 3.6. 92% from public high schools. **Test scores:** SAT Math middle 50% range 500–600. SAT EBRW middle 50% range 490–610. ACT middle 50% range 20–26. **Basis for Candidate Selection:** *Very important factors include:* rigor of secondary school record, academic GPA, standardized test scores. *Important factors include:* application essay, recommendation(s), interview. *Other factors include:* extracurricular activities, talent/ability, character/personal qualities, alumni/ae relation. **Freshman Admission Requirements:** High school diploma is required and GED is accepted. *Academic units required:* 4 English, 2 math, 2 science, 2 science labs, 1 foreign language, 2 social studies, 1 history, 4 academic electives. *Academic units recommended:* 4 English, 3 math, 3 science, 3 science labs, 2 foreign language, 3 social studies, 2 history. **Freshman Admission Statistics:** 4,175 applied, 68% admitted, 19% enrolled. **Transfer Admission Requirements:** High school transcript, college transcript(s), statement of good standing from prior institution(s). Minimum college GPA of 2.6 required. Lowest grade transferable C. **General Admission Information:** Non-fall registration accepted. Admission may be deferred for a maximum of 2 years.

COSTS AND FINANCIAL AID

Annual tuition $37,464. Room and board $10,710. Required fees $300. Average book and supplies expense $1,200. **Required Forms and Deadlines:** FAFSA. **Notification of Awards:** Applicants will be notified of awards on a rolling basis beginning 12/1. **Types of Aid:** *Need-based scholarships/grants:* College/university scholarship or grant aid from institutional funds; Federal Pell; Private scholarships; SEOG; State scholarships/grants. *Loans:* Direct PLUS loans; Direct Subsidized Stafford Loans; Direct Unsubsidized Stafford Loans. **Student Employment:** Federal Work-Study Program available. Institutional employment available. **Financial Aid Statistics:** 100% needy freshmen, 100% needy undergrads receive need-based scholarship or grant aid. 19% freshmen, 7% undergrads receive non-need-based scholarship or grant aid. 87% freshmen, 90% undergrads receive need-based self-help aid. 0% freshmen, 0% undergrads receive athletic scholarships. 95% freshmen, 87% undergrads receive any aid. 69% undergrads borrow to pay for school. Average cumulative indebtedness $29,432. **Criteria awarding aid:** *Need-based:* Academics, Music/drama, Religious affiliation. *Non-Need-based:* Academics, Alumni affiliation, Art, Minority status, Music/drama, Religious affiliation, State/district residency.

ELMIRA COLLEGE

One Park Place, Elmira, NY 14901
Phone: 607-735-1724 **Financial Aid Phone:** 607-735-1728
E-mail: admissions@elmira.edu **CEEB Code:** 2226
Fax: 607-735-1718 **Website:** www.elmira.edu **ACT Code:** 2736

This private school was founded in 1855. It has a 55 acre campus.

RATINGS
Admissions Selectivity Rating: 75   **Fire Safety Rating:** 88   **Green Rating:** 60*

STUDENTS AND FACULTY
Enrollment: 787. **Student Body:** 68% female, 32% male, 34% out-of-state, 4% international (12 countries represented). Asian 2%, African American 5%, Caucasian 76%, Hispanic 5%, Native American 1%, Pacific Islander <1%, Two or more races 2%, Race unknown 5%.
Retention and Graduation: 78% freshmen return for sophomore year. 57% freshmen graduate within 4 years. 60% freshmen graduate within 6 years.
Faculty: Student/faculty ratio 10:1. 66 full-time faculty, 83% hold PhDs, 12% are members of minority groups, 55% are women. 0% of classes are taught by teaching assistants.

ACADEMICS
Degrees: Associate; Bachelor's; Master's; Post-bachelor's certificate. **Classes:** Most classes have 10–19 students. Most lab/discussion sessions have 10–19 students. **Most popular majors:** Education, General; Business Administration and Management, General; Psychology, General. **Special Study Options:** Accelerated program; Double major; Honors program; Independent study; Internships; Liberal arts/career combination; Student-designed major; Study abroad; Teacher certification program. **Career services:** Alumni network; Alumni services; Career assessment; Internships.

FACILITIES
Housing: Apartments for single students; Coed dorms; Special housing for disabled students; Wellness housing; Women's dorms 25% of campus accessible to physically disabled. **Special Academic Facilities/Equipment:** Center for Mark Twain Studies; Cowles Hall, Health Sciences building with state-of-the-art simulation labs. **Campus Network:** 100% of classrooms, 100% of dorms, 100% of student union, 100% of libraries, 100% of dining areas, 0% of common outdoor areas, have wireless network access.

CAMPUS LIFE
Environment: Town. **Activities:** Campus Ministries; Choral groups; Concert band; Dance; Drama/theater; International Student Organization; Literary magazine; Model UN; Music ensembles; Musical theater; Radio station; Student government; Student newspaper; Yearbook. 80 registered organizations, 19 honor societies, 3 religious organizations, on campus. **Athletics (Intercollegiate):** *Men:* basketball, cheerleading, golf, ice hockey, lacrosse, soccer, tennis. *Women:* basketball, cheerleading, field hockey, golf, ice hockey, lacrosse, soccer, softball, tennis, volleyball. **On-Campus Highlights:** Starbucks at the 1855 Room.

ADMISSIONS
Freshman Academic Profile: Average high school GPA 3.3. **Test scores:** SAT Math middle 50% range 540–610. SAT EBRW middle 50% range 530–600. ACT middle 50% range 22–26. **Basis for Candidate Selection:** *Very important factors include:* rigor of secondary school record, academic GPA, application essay, character/personal qualities. *Important factors include:* class rank, recommendation(s), interview, extracurricular activities. *Other factors include:* standardized test scores, talent/ability, alumni/ae relation, geographical residence, state residency, racial/ethnic status, volunteer work, work experience. **Freshman Admission Requirements:** High school diploma is required and GED is not accepted. *Academic units required:* 4 English, 3 math, 3 science, 2 science labs, 3 social studies, 1 history, 2 academic electives. *Academic units recommended:* 2 foreign language. **Freshman Admission Statistics:** 2,110 applied, 84% admitted, 12% enrolled. **Transfer Admission Requirements:** college transcript(s), essay or personal statement, statement of good standing from prior institution(s). Minimum college GPA of 2.0 required. Lowest grade transferable C-. **General Admission Information:** Priority deadline 2/15. Non-fall registration accepted. Admission may be deferred for a maximum of 1 year.

COSTS AND FINANCIAL AID
Annual tuition $33,900. Room and board $12,500. Required fees $1,500. Average book and supplies expense $600. **Required Forms and Deadlines:** FAFSA; State aid form. **Notification of Awards:** Applicants will be notified of awards on a rolling basis beginning 12/1. **Types of Aid:** *Need-based scholarships/grants:* College/university scholarship or grant aid from institutional funds; Federal Pell; Private scholarships; SEOG; State scholarships/grants. *Loans:* Direct PLUS loans; Direct Subsidized Stafford Loans; Direct Unsubsidized Stafford Loans. **Student Employment:** Federal Work-Study Program available. Institutional employment available. **Financial Aid Statistics:** 100% needy freshmen, 100% needy undergrads receive need-based scholarship or grant aid. 20% freshmen, 16% undergrads receive non-need-based scholarship or grant aid. 77% freshmen, 80% undergrads receive need-based self-help aid. 0% freshmen, 0% undergrads receive athletic scholarships. % freshmen, 99% undergrads receive any aid. 82% undergrads borrow to pay for school. Average cumulative indebtedness $30,084. **Criteria awarding aid:** *Need-based:* Academics. *Non-Need-based:* Academics, Leadership, State/district residency.

ELON UNIVERSITY

50 Campus Drive, Elon, NC 27244-2010
Phone: 336-278-3566 **Financial Aid Phone:** 336-278-7640
E-mail: admissions@elon.edu **CEEB Code:** 5183
Fax: 336-278-7699 **Website:** www.elon.edu **ACT Code:** 3096

This private school was founded in 1889. It has a 636 acre campus.

RATINGS
Admissions Selectivity Rating: 84   **Fire Safety Rating:** 90   **Green Rating:** 90

STUDENTS AND FACULTY
Enrollment: 6,277. **Student Body:** 60% female, 40% male, 81% out-of-state, 2% international (47 countries represented). Asian 2%, African American 5%, Caucasian 80%, Hispanic 7%, Native American <1%, Pacific Islander <1%, Two or more races 3%, Race unknown <1%.
Retention and Graduation: 91% freshmen return for sophomore year. 82% freshmen graduate within 4 years. 85% freshmen graduate within 6 years. 26% grads go on to further study within 1 year. 7% grads pursue arts and sciences degrees. 2% grads pursue law degrees. 3% grads pursue business degrees. 5% grads pursue medical degrees. **Faculty:** Student/faculty ratio 12:1. 446 full-time faculty, 86% hold PhDs, 17% are members of minority groups, 50% are women. 0% of classes are taught by teaching assistants.

ACADEMICS
Degrees: Bachelor's; Doctoral degree—professional practice; Master's. **Classes:** Most classes have 10–19 students. **Most popular majors:** Communication and Media Studies; Psychology, General; Business Administration and Management, General. **Special Study Options:** Accelerated program; Cross-registration; Distance learning; Double major; Dual enrollment; English as a Second Language (ESL); Exchange student program (domestic); Honors program; Independent study; Internships; Liberal arts/career combination; Student-designed major; Study abroad; Teacher certification program. **Honors programs:** Forty first-year students are selected for the Honors Fellows program, which has benefits of specialized courses, $13,500 scholarship renewable annually based on academic performance and participation in the program, $1,000 study abroad grant, development and presentation of their honors thesis, and housing options such as a living-learning community for Fellows. **Disability Services offered:** Note-taking services; Reader services; Tape recorders; Tutors. **Career services:** Alumni network; Alumni services; Career assessment; Career/job search classes; Internships; Regional alumni.

FACILITIES
Housing: Apartments for single students; Coed dorms; Fraternity/sorority housing; Men's dorms; Special housing for international students; Theme housing; Wellness housing; Women's dorms 85% of campus accessible to physically disabled. **Special Academic Facilities/Equipment:** Writing resource center, multi-faith center, fine arts center with recital hall, theatre, television studios, music rooms, campus center, athletic center, art gallery.

CAMPUS LIFE

Environment: Town. **Activities:** Campus Ministries; Choral groups; Concert band; Dance; Drama/theater; International Student Organization; Jazz band; Literary magazine; Marching band; Model UN; Music ensembles; Musical theater; Pep band; Radio station; Student government; Student newspaper; Student-run film society; Symphony orchestra; Television station; Yearbook. 284 registered organizations, 27 honor societies, 27 religious organizations, 13 fraternities, 13 sororities, on campus. **Athletics (Intercollegiate):** *Men:* baseball, basketball, cheerleading, cross-country, football, golf, soccer, tennis. *Women:* basketball, cheerleading, cross-country, golf, soccer, softball, tennis, track/field (outdoor), track/field (indoor), volleyball. **On-Campus Highlights:** Belk Library. **Environmental Initiatives:** Reducing greenhouse gas emissions toward carbon neutrality by 2037.

ADMISSIONS

Freshman Academic Profile: Average high school GPA 4.0. 25% in top 10% of high school class, 56% in top 25% of high school class, 84% in top 50% of high school class. 60% from public high schools. **Test scores:** SAT Math middle 50% range 570–660. SAT EBRW middle 50% range 590–660. ACT middle 50% range 25–30. **Basis for Candidate Selection:** *Very important factors include:* rigor of secondary school record, academic GPA, application essay, standardized test scores, recommendation(s). *Important factors include:* extracurricular activities, talent/ability, alumni/ae relation. *Other factors include:* class rank, character/personal qualities, first generation, geographical residence, state residency, racial/ethnic status, level of applicant's interest. **Freshman Admission Requirements:** High school diploma is required and GED is accepted. *Academic units required:* 4 English, 3 math, 3 science, 1 science labs, 2 foreign language, 2 social studies, 1 history. *Academic units recommended:* 4 English, 4 math, 3 science, 1 science labs, 3 foreign language, 2 social studies, 1 history. **Freshman Admission Statistics:** 10,500 applied, 78% admitted, 20% enrolled. **Transfer Admission Requirements:** High school transcript, college transcript(s), standardized test scores, statement of good standing from prior institution(s). Minimum college GPA of 2.7 required. Lowest grade transferable C-. **General Admission Information:** Application fee $60. Priority deadline 11/1. Regular application deadline 1/10. Non-fall registration accepted. Admission may be deferred for a maximum of 1 year.

COSTS AND FINANCIAL AID

Annual tuition $36,082. Room and board $12,685. Required fees $489. Average book and supplies expense $900. **Required Forms and Deadlines:** CSS/Financial Aid PROFILE; FAFSA. **Notification of Awards:** Applicants will be notified of awards on a rolling basis beginning 1/31. **Types of Aid:** *Need-based scholarships/grants:* College/university scholarship or grant aid from institutional funds; Federal Pell; Private scholarships; SEOG; State scholarships/grants; United Negro College Fund. *Loans:* Direct PLUS loans; Direct Subsidized Stafford Loans; Direct Unsubsidized Stafford Loans. **Student Employment:** Federal Work-Study Program available. Institutional employment available. **Financial Aid Statistics:** 88% needy freshmen, 90% needy undergrads receive need-based scholarship or grant aid. 63% freshmen, 55% undergrads receive non-need-based scholarship or grant aid. 81% freshmen, 80% undergrads receive need-based self-help aid. 4% freshmen, 5% undergrads receive athletic scholarships. 69% freshmen, 66% undergrads receive any aid. 34% undergrads borrow to pay for school. Average cumulative indebtedness $32,028. **Criteria awarding aid:** *Need-based:* Religious affiliation. *Non-Need-based:* Academics, Alumni affiliation, Art, Athletics, Leadership, Music/drama, Religious affiliation.

EMBRY RIDDLE AERONAUTICAL UNIVERSITY (AZ)

3700 Willow Creek, Prescott, AZ 86301
Phone: (928) 777-6600 **Financial Aid Phone:** 928-777-3765
E-mail: prescott@erau.edu **CEEB Code:** 4305
Fax: (928) 777-6606 **Website:** www.prescott.erau.edu **ACT Code:** 725

This private school was founded in 1926. It has a 539 acre campus.

RATINGS

Admissions Selectivity Rating: 85 **Fire Safety Rating:** 76 **Green Rating:** 60*

STUDENTS AND FACULTY

Enrollment: 2,598. **Student Body:** 24% female, 76% male, 77% out-of-state, 7% international (31 countries represented). Asian 6%, African American 2%, Caucasian 62%, Hispanic 6%, Native American <1%, Pacific Islander 1%, Two or more races 10%, Race unknown 7%.

Retention and Graduation: 87% freshmen return for sophomore year. 32% freshmen graduate within 4 years. % freshmen graduate within 6 years. 21% grads go on to further study within 1 year. 3% grads pursue arts and sciences degrees. 3% grads pursue business degrees. **Faculty:** Student/faculty ratio 17:1. 120 full-time faculty, 78% hold PhDs, 13% are members of minority groups, 24% are women. 0% of classes are taught by teaching assistants.

ACADEMICS

Degrees: Bachelor's; Master's. **Classes:** Most classes have 20–29 students. Most lab/discussion sessions have 10–19 students. **Most popular majors:** Aerospace, Aeronautical, and Astronautical/Space Engineering, General; International Relations and Affairs; Airline/Commercial/Professional Pilot and Flight Crew. **Special Study Options:** Cooperative education program; Double major; Dual enrollment; English as a Second Language (ESL); Honors program; Internships; Study abroad. **Honors programs:** The Honors Program at Embry-Riddle, Prescott is highly selective, offering students an enriched educational experience focused on leadership, research, and ethics, while also giving them opportunities to enhance campus and community life for others. Honors Program students enroll in three Honors Seminars, complete Honors directed research, and participate in the Honors Student Association service, community, and professional development events. Graduates of the Honors Program are models of academic excellence and student leadership. **Disability Services offered:** Reader services; Tape recorders. **Career services:** Alumni network; Alumni services; Career assessment; Career/job search classes; Internships; Regional alumni.

FACILITIES

Housing: Coed dorms 80% of campus accessible to physically disabled.

CAMPUS LIFE

Environment: Town. **Activities:** Campus Ministries; Choral groups; International Student Organization; Model UN; Music ensembles; Radio station; Student government; Student newspaper; Student-run film society. 100 registered organizations, 2 honor societies, 6 religious organizations, 6 fraternities, 3 sororities, on campus. **Athletics (Intercollegiate):** *Men:* wrestling. **On-Campus Highlights:** Flight Line Facilities.

ADMISSIONS

Freshman Academic Profile: Average high school GPA 3.7. 25% in top 10% of high school class, 55% in top 25% of high school class, 82% in top 50% of high school class. **Test scores:** SAT Math middle 50% range 570–680. SAT EBRW middle 50% range 560–670. ACT middle 50% range 23–29. **Basis for Candidate Selection:** *Very important factors include:* standardized test scores. *Important factors include:* rigor of secondary school record, class rank, academic GPA, application essay, recommendation(s). *Other factors include:* interview, extracurricular activities, alumni/ae relation, work experience. **Freshman Admission Requirements:** High school diploma is required and GED is accepted. *Academic units required:* 4 English, 3 math, 2 science, 1 science labs, 2 social studies. *Academic units recommended:* 4 English, 4 math, 3 science, 1 science labs, 2 social studies. **Freshman Admission Statistics:** 2,168 applied, 77% admitted, 41% enrolled. **Transfer Admission Requirements:** college transcript(s). **General Admission Information:** Application fee $50. Priority deadline 3/1. Non-fall registration accepted. Admission may be deferred for a maximum of 1 year.

COSTS AND FINANCIAL AID

Annual tuition $34,392. Room and board $11,394. Required fees $1,433. Average book and supplies expense $1,400. **Required Forms and Deadlines:** FAFSA. **Types of Aid:** *Need-based scholarships/grants:* College/university scholarship or grant aid from institutional funds; Federal Pell; Private scholarships; SEOG; State scholarships/grants. *Loans:* Direct PLUS loans; Direct Subsidized Stafford Loans; Direct Unsubsidized Stafford Loans. **Student Employment:** Federal Work-Study Program available. Institutional employment available. **Criteria awarding aid:** *Need-based:* Academics, Athletics, Leadership.

EMBRY RIDDLE AERONAUTICAL UNIVERSITY (FL)

600 South Clyde Morris Boulevard, Daytona Beach, FL 32114-3900
Phone: 386-226-6100 **Financial Aid Phone:** 800-226-6307
E-mail: dbadmit@erau.edu **CEEB Code:** 5190
Fax: 386-226-7070 **Website:** https://daytonabeach.erau.edu **ACT Code:** 725

This private school was founded in 1926. It has a 185 acre campus.

RATINGS
Admissions Selectivity Rating: 85   **Fire Safety Rating:** 94   **Green Rating:** 60*

STUDENTS AND FACULTY
Enrollment: 5,689. **Student Body:** 22% female, 78% male, 64% out-of-state, 12% international (100 countries represented). Asian 5%, African American 5%, Caucasian 56%, Hispanic 7%, Native American <1%, Pacific Islander <1%, Two or more races 7%, Race unknown 7%.
Retention and Graduation: 80% freshmen return for sophomore year. 29% freshmen graduate within 4 years. % freshmen graduate within 6 years. 28% grads go on to further study within 1 year. <1% grads pursue arts and sciences degrees. 5% grads pursue business degrees. **Faculty:** Student/faculty ratio 15:1. 324 full-time faculty, 76% hold PhDs, 14% are members of minority groups, 26% are women. 0% of classes are taught by teaching assistants.

ACADEMICS
Degrees: Associate; Bachelor's; Doctoral degree research/scholarship; Master's. **Classes:** Most classes have 20–29 students. Most lab/discussion sessions have 10–19 students. **Most popular majors:** Aerospace, Aeronautical, and Astronautical/Space Engineering, General; Airline/Commercial/Professional Pilot and Flight Crew; Mechanical Engineering. **Special Study Options:** Accelerated program; Cooperative education program; Double major; Dual enrollment; English as a Second Language (ESL); Exchange student program (domestic); Honors program; Internships; Student-designed major; Study abroad. **Honors programs:** The Embry-Riddle Honors Program is highly selective, offering its student members enriched educational experiences. Emphasizing Honors course work in General Education and in the majors, the Program involves selected faculty who develop innovative courses and establish mentoring relationships with students. The Program is designed to attract and retain top students and to develop their communicative, analytical, critical, and research skills, nurturing a love of life-long learning, leadership, and service. **Disability Services offered:** Reader services; Tape recorders. **Career services:** Alumni network; Alumni services; Career assessment; Career/job search classes; Internships.

FACILITIES
Housing: Coed dorms 95% of campus accessible to physically disabled. **Special Academic Facilities/Equipment:** Advanced Flight Simulation Center; Fleet Maintenance Hangar; Flight Operations Center; Next Gen Test Bed facility; Advanced Vehicles Green Garage; Eagle Flight Research Center; Wind Tunnel Laboratory; Eagle Fitness Center, Swimming Pool, ICI Center & Outdoor Sports Facilities. **Campus Network:** 100% of classrooms, 100% of dorms, 100% of student union, 100% of libraries, 100% of dining areas, 90% of common outdoor areas, have wireless network access.

CAMPUS LIFE
Environment: Town. **Activities:** Campus Ministries; Choral groups; International Student Organization; Model UN; Pep band; Radio station; Student government; Student newspaper; Student-run film society. 151 registered organizations, 14 honor societies, 7 religious organizations, 10 fraternities, 5 sororities, on campus. **Athletics (Intercollegiate):** *Men:* baseball, basketball, cheerleading, cross-country, golf, soccer, softball, tennis, track/field (outdoor), volleyball. *Women:* basketball, cheerleading, cross-country, golf, soccer, softball, tennis, track/field (outdoor), volleyball. **On-Campus Highlights:** Hagedorn Aviation Complex **Environmental Initiatives:** Embry-Riddle Opens 'Green Garage' Doors: EcoCAR Project Advances University's Environmental Commitment Daytona Beach, Fla., Dec. 10, 2009—Embry-Riddle Aeronautical University has opened the doors of a new "green garage," where engineering students are using aerospace techniques to develop the car of tomorrow. The garage includes a rotary vehicle lift, dedicated high-voltage room, and integrated hardware-in-the-loop laboratory donated by National Instruments. It also showcases an environmental focus at Embry-Riddle's College of Engineering. Every component in the lab was chosen to reduce environmental impact, including the floor covering, which is made from recycled tires. Interior design students from Daytona State College assisted in designing the new facility. http://givingto.erau.edu/givingnews/09releases/ecocar.html

ADMISSIONS
Freshman Academic Profile: Average high school GPA 3.7. 23% in top 10% of high school class, 50% in top 25% of high school class, 83% in top 50% of high school class. **Test scores:** SAT Math middle 50% range 540–670. SAT EBRW middle 50% range 540–650. ACT middle 50% range 22–28. **Basis for Candidate Selection:** *Very important factors include:* standardized test scores. *Important factors include:* rigor of secondary school record, class rank, academic GPA, application essay, recommendation(s). *Other factors include:* interview, extracurricular activities, alumni/ae relation, work experience. **Freshman Admission Requirements:** High school diploma is required and GED is accepted. *Academic units required:* 4 English, 3 math, 2 science, 1 science labs, 3 social studies. *Academic units recommended:* 4 English, 4 math, 3 science, 1 science labs, 3 social studies. **Freshman Admission Statistics:** 4,564 applied, 75% admitted, 40% enrolled. **Transfer Admission Requirements:** college transcript(s), Minimum college GPA of 2.0 required. Lowest grade transferable C. **General Admission Information:** Application fee $50. Priority deadline 3/1. Non-fall registration accepted. Admission may be deferred for a maximum of 1 year.

COSTS AND FINANCIAL AID
Annual tuition $34,292. Room and board $10,826. Required fees $1,422. Average book and supplies expense $1,400. **Required Forms and Deadlines:** FAFSA. **Types of Aid:** *Need-based scholarships/grants:* College/university scholarship or grant aid from institutional funds; Federal Pell; Private scholarships; SEOG; State scholarships/grants. *Loans:* Direct PLUS loans; Direct Subsidized Stafford Loans; Direct Unsubsidized Stafford Loans. **Student Employment:** Federal Work-Study Program available. Institutional employment available. **Criteria awarding aid:** *Need-based:* Academics, Alumni affiliation, Athletics, Leadership.

EMBRY RIDDLE AERONAUTICAL UNIVERSITY—WORLDWIDE

600 S. Clyde Morris Blvd., Daytona Beach, FL 32114
E-mail: worldwide@erau.edu
Website: https://worldwide.erau.edu

This is a private school.

RATINGS
Admissions Selectivity Rating: 71   **Fire Safety Rating:** 60*   **Green Rating:** 60*

STUDENTS AND FACULTY
Enrollment: 11,433. **Student Body:** 12% female, 88% male, 3% international. Asian 4%, African American 8%, Caucasian 55%, Hispanic 9%, Native American 1%, Pacific Islander 1%, Two or more races 6%, Race unknown 14%.
Retention and Graduation: 20% freshmen graduate within 4 years. % freshmen graduate within 6 years. **Faculty:** Student/faculty ratio 13:1. 113 full-time faculty, 78% hold PhDs, 10% are members of minority groups, 36% are women.

ACADEMICS
Degrees: Associate; Bachelor's; Certificate; Doctoral degree research/scholarship; Master's. **Special Study Options:** Accelerated program; Cooperative education program; Distance learning; Independent study; Study abroad; Weekend college.

ADMISSIONS
Basis for Candidate Selection: *Important factors include:* class rank, academic GPA. *Other factors include:* rigor of secondary school record, application essay, standardized test scores, recommendation(s), alumni/ae relation, work experience. **Freshman Admission Requirements:** High school diploma is required and GED is accepted. *Academic units required:* 4 English, 3 math, 2 science, 1 science labs, 2 history. **Freshman Admission Statistics:** 1,225 applied, 65% admitted, 75% enrolled. **General Admission Information:** Application fee $50. Non-fall registration accepted. Admission may be deferred for a maximum of 1 year.

COSTS AND FINANCIAL AID

Annual tuition $9,360. Average book and supplies expense $1,160. **Required Forms and Deadlines:** FAFSA. **Types of Aid:** *Need-based scholarships/grants:* College/university scholarship or grant aid from institutional funds; Federal Pell; Private scholarships; SEOG; State scholarships/grants. *Loans:* Direct PLUS loans; Direct Subsidized Stafford Loans; Direct Unsubsidized Stafford Loans. **Financial Aid Statistics:** 81% needy freshmen, 83% needy undergrads receive need-based scholarship or grant aid. 22% freshmen, 38% undergrads receive non-need-based scholarship or grant aid. 54% freshmen, 50% undergrads receive need-based self-help aid. 0% freshmen, 0% undergrads receive athletic scholarships.

EMERSON COLLEGE

Best Colleges

120 Boylston Street, Boston, MA 02116-4624
Phone: 617-824-8600 **Financial Aid Phone:** 617-824-8655
E-mail: admission@emerson.edu **CEEB Code:** 3367
Fax: 617-824-8609 **Website:** www.emerson.edu **ACT Code:** 1820

This private school was founded in 1880. It has a 10 acre campus.

RATINGS

Admissions Selectivity Rating: 92 **Fire Safety Rating:** 94 **Green Rating:** 99

STUDENTS AND FACULTY

Enrollment: 3,871. **Student Body:** 61% female, 39% male, 13% international (60 countries represented). Asian 5%, African American 4%, Caucasian 59%, Hispanic 13%, Native American <1%, Pacific Islander <1%, Two or more races 4%, Race unknown 2%.
Retention and Graduation: 89% freshmen return for sophomore year. 79% freshmen graduate within 4 years. 82% freshmen graduate within 6 years.
Faculty: Student/faculty ratio 13:1. 212 full-time faculty, 69% hold PhDs, 21% are members of minority groups, 47% are women.

ACADEMICS

Degrees: Bachelor's; Master's; Post-bachelor's certificate. **Classes:** Most classes have 10–19 students. Most lab/discussion sessions have 10–19 students. **Most popular majors:** Theatre/Theater; Cinematography and Film/Video Production; Journalism. **Special Study Options:** Cross-registration; Double major; Honors program; Independent study; Internships; Liberal arts/career combination; Student-designed major; Study abroad; Teacher certification program. **Combined degree programs:** BA/MA. **Disability Services offered:** Note-taking services; Reader services; Tape recorders; Tutors. **Career services:** Alumni network; Alumni services; Career assessment; Career/job search classes; Internships; Regional alumni.

FACILITIES

Housing: Coed dorms; Theme housing; Wellness housing 90% of campus accessible to physically disabled. **Campus Network:** 100% of classrooms, 100% of dorms, 100% of student union, 100% of libraries, 75% of dining areas, 25% of common outdoor areas, have wireless network access.

CAMPUS LIFE

Environment: Metropolis. **Activities:** Campus Ministries; Choral groups; Dance; Drama/theater; International Student Organization; Literary magazine; Model UN; Music ensembles; Musical theater; Radio station; Student government; Student newspaper; Student-run film society; Television station; Yearbook. 80 registered organizations, on campus. **Athletics (Intercollegiate):** *Men:* baseball, basketball, cross-country, golf, lacrosse, soccer, tennis, track/field (indoor), volleyball. *Women:* basketball, cross-country, golf, lacrosse, soccer, softball, tennis, track/field (indoor), volleyball. **Environmental Initiatives:** 3 LEED certified buildings (Colonial Building, Piano Row, and Emerson Los Angeles).

ADMISSIONS

Freshman Academic Profile: Average high school GPA 3.7. 27% in top 10% of high school class, 65% in top 25% of high school class, 93% in top 50% of high school class. **Test scores:** SAT Math middle 50% range 590–710. SAT EBRW middle 50% range 610–700. ACT middle 50% range 27–31. **Basis for**

Candidate Selection: *Very important factors include:* academic GPA, application essay. *Important factors include:* rigor of secondary school record, class rank, recommendation(s), extracurricular activities, talent/ability, character/personal qualities. *Other factors include:* standardized test scores, first generation, alumni/ae relation, geographical residence, racial/ethnic status, volunteer work, work experience. **Freshman Admission Requirements:** High school diploma is required and GED is accepted. *Academic units required:* 4 English, 3 math, 3 science, 3 foreign language, 3 social studies. *Academic units recommended:* 4 English, 3 math, 3 science, 3 foreign language, 3 social studies, 4 academic electives. **Freshman Admission Statistics:** 15,353 applied, 33% admitted, 18% enrolled. **Transfer Admission Requirements:** High school transcript, college transcript(s), essay or personal statement, statement of good standing from prior institution(s). Minimum college GPA of 3.0 required. Lowest grade transferable C. **General Admission Information:** Application fee $65. Regular application deadline 1/15. Non-fall registration accepted. Admission may be deferred for a maximum of 1 year.

COSTS AND FINANCIAL AID

Annual tuition $48,560. Room and board $18,400. Required fees $872. Average book and supplies expense $1,150. **Required Forms and Deadlines:** Business/Farm Supplement; CSS/Financial Aid PROFILE; FAFSA; Noncustodial PROFILE. **Notification of Awards:** Applicants will be notified of awards on or about 4/1. **Types of Aid:** *Need-based scholarships/grants:* College/university scholarship or grant aid from institutional funds; Federal Pell; Private scholarships; SEOG; State scholarships/grants. *Loans:* Direct PLUS loans; Direct Subsidized Stafford Loans; Direct Unsubsidized Stafford Loans. **Student Employment:** Federal Work-Study Program available. Institutional employment available. **Financial Aid Statistics:** 94% needy freshmen, 90% needy undergrads receive need-based scholarship or grant aid. 13% freshmen, 6% undergrads receive non-need-based scholarship or grant aid. 89% freshmen, 88% undergrads receive need-based self-help aid. 0% freshmen, 0% undergrads receive athletic scholarships. 61% undergrads borrow to pay for school. Average cumulative indebtedness $24,193. **Criteria awarding aid:** *Need-based:* Academics, Music/drama *Non-Need-based:* Academics, Leadership, Music/drama, State/district residency.

EMILY CARR UNIVERSITY OF ART + DESIGN

1399 Johnston Street, Vancouver, BC V6H 3R9
Phone: 604-844-3897 **Financial Aid Phone:** 1-604-844-3844
E-mail: admissions@ecuad.ca
Fax: 604-844-3089 **Website:** www.ecuad.ca

This public school was founded in 1925.

RATINGS

Admissions Selectivity Rating: 72 **Fire Safety Rating:** 60* **Green Rating:** 60*

STUDENTS AND FACULTY

Enrollment: 2,000. **Student Body:** female, male, 32% out-of-state, international (53 countries represented).
Retention and Graduation: 85% freshmen return for sophomore year.
Faculty: 0% of classes are taught by teaching assistants.

ACADEMICS

Degrees: Bachelor's; Master's. **Most popular majors:** Fine and Studio Arts; Industrial and Product Design; Design and Visual Communications, General. **Special Study Options:** Cooperative education program; Cross-registration; Distance learning; Exchange student program (domestic); External degree program; Independent study; Internships; Liberal arts/career combination; Student-designed major; Study abroad. **Disability Services offered:** Note-taking services; Reader services; Tape recorders; Tutors. **Career services:** Alumni network; Alumni services; Career assessment; Career/job search classes; Internships; Regional alumni.

FACILITIES

Housing: 100% of campus accessible to physically disabled. **Special Academic Facilities/Equipment:** Two Galleries A Centre for Art and Technology.

CAMPUS LIFE

Environment: Metropolis. **Activities:** International Student Organization; Student government; Student newspaper; Student-run film society; Yearbook.

ADMISSIONS

Freshman Academic Profile: 85% from public high schools. **Basis for Candidate Selection:** *Very important factors include:* talent/ability, character/personal qualities, level of applicant's interest. *Important factors include:* rigor of secondary school record, academic GPA. *Other factors include:* extracurricular activities, volunteer work, work experience. **Freshman Admission Requirements:** High school diploma is required and GED is not accepted. *Academic units required:* 3 English, 6 academic electives, 6 visual/performing arts. **Freshman Admission Statistics:** 1,112 applied, 57% admitted, 65% enrolled. **Transfer Admission Requirements:** college transcript(s), essay or personal statement, statement of good standing from prior institution(s). Minimum college GPA of 2.0 required. Lowest grade transferable C. **General Admission Information:** Application fee $70. Regular application deadline 2/1. Non-fall registration accepted. Admission may be deferred for a maximum of one year.

COSTS AND FINANCIAL AID

Annual in-state tuition $3,788. Average book and supplies expense $3,000. **Student Employment:** Institutional employment available.

EMMANUEL COLLEGE

400 The Fenway, Boston, MA 02115
Phone: 617-735-9715 **Financial Aid Phone:** 617-735-9938
E-mail: enroll@emmanuel.edu **CEEB Code:** 3368
Fax: 617-735-9801 **Website:** www.emmanuel.edu **ACT Code:** 1822

This private school, affiliated with the Roman Catholic Church, was founded in 1919. It has a 17 acre campus.

RATINGS

Admissions Selectivity Rating: 79   **Fire Safety Rating:** 99   **Green Rating:** 71

STUDENTS AND FACULTY

Enrollment: 1,976. **Student Body:** 75% female, 25% male, 40% out-of-state, 2% international (52 countries represented). Asian 5%, African American 7%, Caucasian 69%, Hispanic 12%, Native American <1%, Pacific Islander <1%, Two or more races 3%, Race unknown 3%.
Retention and Graduation: 78% freshmen return for sophomore year. 58% freshmen graduate within 4 years. 66% freshmen graduate within 6 years. 13% grads go on to further study within 1 year. **Faculty:** Student/faculty ratio 13:1. 94 full-time faculty, 84% hold PhDs, 18% are members of minority groups, 62% are women. 0% of classes are taught by teaching assistants.

ACADEMICS

Degrees: Bachelor's; Master's; Post-bachelor's certificate; Post-master's certificate. **Classes:** Most classes have 10–19 students. Most lab/discussion sessions have 10–19 students. **Most popular majors:** Counseling Psychology; Business Administration and Management, General; Biology/Biological Sciences, General. **Special Study Options:** Accelerated program; Cross-registration; Distance learning; Double major; Honors program; Independent study; Internships; Liberal arts/career combination; Student-designed major; Study abroad; Teacher certification program. **Disability Services offered:** Note-taking services; Reader services; Tape recorders; Tutors. **Career services:** Alumni network; Alumni services; Career assessment; Career/job search classes; Internships.

FACILITIES

Housing: Apartments for single students; Coed dorms; Theme housing 100% of campus accessible to physically disabled. **Campus Network:** 100% of classrooms, 100% of dorms, 100% of student union, 100% of libraries, 100% of dining areas, 80% of common outdoor areas, have wireless network access.

CAMPUS LIFE

Environment: Metropolis. **Activities:** Campus Ministries; Choral groups; Dance; Drama/theater; Jazz band; Literary magazine; Model UN; Music ensembles; Musical theater; Pep band; Radio station; Student government; Student newspaper; Student-run film society; Symphony orchestra. 69 registered organizations, 17 honor societies, on campus. **Athletics (Intercollegiate):** *Men:* basketball, cross-country, golf, soccer, track/field (outdoor), track/field (indoor), volleyball. *Women:* basketball, cross-country, lacrosse, soccer, softball, tennis, track/field (outdoor), track/field (indoor), volleyball. **On-Campus Highlights:** New Residence Hall. **Environmental**

Initiatives: Significant reduction of the College's solid waste stream through introduction of single-stream recycling and composting programs.

ADMISSIONS

Freshman Academic Profile: Average high school GPA 3.7. 16% in top 10% of high school class, 27% in top 25% of high school class, 77% in top 50% of high school class. 79% from public high schools. **Test scores:** SAT Math middle 50% range 540–630. SAT EBRW middle 50% range 560–650. ACT middle 50% range 24–27. **Basis for Candidate Selection:** *Very important factors include:* rigor of secondary school record, academic GPA, application essay, recommendation(s). *Important factors include:* extracurricular activities, character/personal qualities, volunteer work. *Other factors include:* class rank, standardized test scores, interview, talent/ability, first generation, alumni/ae relation, geographical residence, religious affiliation/commitment, work experience. **Freshman Admission Requirements:** High school diploma is required and GED is accepted. *Academic units required:* 4 English, 3 math, 3 science, 2 science labs, 3 foreign language, 3 social studies. **Freshman Admission Statistics:** 5,770 applied, 77% admitted, 13% enrolled. **Transfer Admission Requirements:** High school transcript, college transcript(s), essay or personal statement, standardized test scores, statement of good standing from prior institution(s). Minimum college GPA of n/a required. Lowest grade transferable C. **General Admission Information:** Application fee $60. Priority deadline 11/1. Regular application deadline 2/15. Non-fall registration accepted. Admission may be deferred for a maximum of one year.

COSTS AND FINANCIAL AID

Annual tuition $39,544. Room and board $14,994. Required fees $610. Average book and supplies expense $880. **Required Forms and Deadlines:** FAFSA. **Notification of Awards:** Applicants will be notified of awards on a rolling basis beginning 2/1. **Types of Aid:** *Need-based scholarships/grants:* College/university scholarship or grant aid from institutional funds; Federal Pell; Private scholarships; SEOG; State scholarships/grants. *Loans:* Direct PLUS loans; Direct Subsidized Stafford Loans; Direct Unsubsidized Stafford Loans. **Student Employment:** Federal Work-Study Program available. Institutional employment available. **Financial Aid Statistics:** 86% needy freshmen, 91% needy undergrads receive need-based scholarship or grant aid. 100% freshmen, 99% undergrads receive non-need-based scholarship or grant aid. 100% freshmen, 91% undergrads receive need-based self-help aid. 0% freshmen, 0% undergrads receive athletic scholarships. 99% freshmen, 97% undergrads receive any aid. **Criteria awarding aid:** *Non-Need-based:* Academics, Alumni affiliation, Leadership.

EMORY AND HENRY COLLEGE

PO Box 10, Emory, VA 24327
Phone: 276-944-6133 **Financial Aid Phone:** 866-794-0010
E-mail: ehadmiss@ehc.edu **CEEB Code:** 5185
Fax: 276-944-6935 **Website:** http://www.ehc.edu **ACT Code:** 4350

This private school, affiliated with the Methodist Church, was founded in 1836. It has a 331 acre campus.

RATINGS

Admissions Selectivity Rating: 77   **Fire Safety Rating:** 60*   **Green Rating:** 60*

STUDENTS AND FACULTY

Enrollment: 900. **Student Body:** 47% female, 53% male, 36% out-of-state, 1% international (5 countries represented). Asian <1%, African American 10%, Caucasian 80%, Hispanic 2%, Native American <1%, Pacific Islander 0%, Two or more races 2%, Race unknown 4%.
Retention and Graduation: 74% freshmen return for sophomore year. 37% grads go on to further study within 1 year. 24% grads pursue arts and sciences degrees. 31% grads pursue law degrees. 23% grads pursue business degrees. 12% grads pursue medical degrees. **Faculty:** Student/faculty ratio 10:1. 72 full-time faculty, 82% hold PhDs, 10% are members of minority groups, 49% are women. 0% of classes are taught by teaching assistants.

ACADEMICS

Degrees: Bachelor's; Master's. **Classes:** Most classes have 10–19 students. **Most popular majors:** Education, General; Pre-Medicine/Pre-Medical Studies; Business Administration and Management, General. **Special Study Options:** Accelerated program; Double major; External degree program; Honors program; Independent study; Liberal arts/career combination; Student-designed major; Study abroad; Teacher certification program. **Combined degree programs:** BA/MA. **Disability Services offered:** Reader services; Tape recorders; Tutors. **Career services:** Career assessment; Career/job search classes; Internships.

FACILITIES

Housing: Coed dorms; Men's dorms; Special housing for disabled students; Theme housing; Wellness housing; Women's dorms. **Special Academic Facilities/Equipment:** Language lab, capillary gas chromatograph, DNA vertical slab gel electrophoretic equipment, infrared spectrophotometer. Theatre Studio, Art gallery. **Campus Network:** 100% of classrooms, 100% of dorms, 100% of student union, 100% of libraries, 100% of dining areas, 100% of common outdoor areas, have wireless network access.

CAMPUS LIFE

Environment: Rural. **Activities:** Campus Ministries; Choral groups; Concert band; Dance; Drama/theater; International Student Organization; Literary magazine; Music ensembles; Musical theater; Opera; Pep band; Radio station; Student government; Student newspaper; Television station; Yearbook. 53 registered organizations, 7 honor societies, 4 religious organizations, 7 fraternities, 6 sororities, on campus. **Athletics (Intercollegiate):** *Men:* baseball, basketball, cross-country, football, golf, soccer, tennis. *Women:* basketball, cross-country, soccer, softball, swimming, tennis, volleyball. **On-Campus Highlights:** McGlothlin-Street Hall (new science building), Memorial Chapel, Byars Hall (Arts, Music, and Theater), King Athletic Center, Emory Mercantile (campus bookstore). **Environmental Initiatives:** Recycling is now in full swing, with a widespread distribution of recycling bins for paper, cardboard, aluminum, plastics and steel. There are thirty bins specially made for the college from sustainably-harvested local poplar. We have already reduced our trash volume significantly. We are a participant in the national Recyclemania competition, in the waste minimization category.

ADMISSIONS

Freshman Academic Profile: Average high school GPA 3.5. 20% in top 10% of high school class, 45% in top 25% of high school class, 80% in top 50% of high school class. 92% from public high schools. **Test scores:** SAT Math middle 50% range 445–560. SAT EBRW middle 50% range 430–555. ACT middle 50% range 19–26. **Basis for Candidate Selection:** *Very important factors include:* rigor of secondary school record, academic GPA, recommendation(s), character/personal qualities, level of applicant's interest. *Important factors include:* application essay, standardized test scores, interview, extracurricular activities, talent/ability, geographical residence, state residency, volunteer work. *Other factors include:* class rank, first generation, alumni/ae relation, religious affiliation/commitment, racial/ethnic status, work experience. **Freshman Admission Requirements:** High school diploma is required and GED is accepted. *Academic units required:* 4 English, 3 math, 2 science, 2 science labs, 2 foreign language, 2 social studies. *Academic units recommended:* 1 visual/performing arts. **Freshman Admission Statistics:** 1,217 applied, 72% admitted, 28% enrolled. **Transfer Admission Requirements:** High school transcript, college transcript(s), statement of good standing from prior institution(s). Minimum college GPA of 2.5 required. Lowest grade transferable C. **General Admission Information:** Non-fall registration accepted. Admission may be deferred for a maximum of 1 year.

COSTS AND FINANCIAL AID

Annual tuition $23,860. Room and board $7,980. Average book and supplies expense $800. **Required Forms and Deadlines:** FAFSA; State aid form. **Notification of Awards:** Applicants will be notified of awards on a rolling basis beginning 3/1. **Types of Aid:** *Need-based scholarships/grants:* College/university scholarship or grant aid from institutional funds; Federal Pell; Private scholarships; SEOG; State scholarships/grants. **Financial Aid Statistics:** 80% needy freshmen, 87% needy undergrads receive need-based scholarship or grant aid. 20% freshmen, 13% undergrads receive non-need-based scholarship or grant aid. 70% freshmen, 0% undergrads receive need-based self-help aid. 0% freshmen, 0% undergrads receive athletic scholarships. **Criteria awarding aid:** *Non-Need-based:* Academics, Art, Music/drama, Religious affiliation, State/district residency.

EMORY UNIVERSITY

Emory University, Boiseuillet Jones Center, Atlanta, GA 30322
Phone: 404-727-6036 **Financial Aid Phone:** 404-727-6039
E-mail: admiss@emory.edu **CEEB Code:** 5186
Fax: 404-727-4303 **Website:** www.emory.edu **ACT Code:** 851

This private school, affiliated with the Methodist Church, was founded in 1836. It has a 630 acre campus.

RATINGS
Admissions Selectivity Rating: 98   **Fire Safety Rating:** 65   **Green Rating:** 95

STUDENTS AND FACULTY
Enrollment: 7,023. **Student Body:** 60% female, 40% male, 80% out-of-state, 15% international. Asian 22%, African American 8%, Caucasian 39%, Hispanic 11%, Native American <1%, Pacific Islander <1%, Two or more races 4%, Race unknown 1%.
Retention and Graduation: 95% freshmen return for sophomore year. 82% freshmen graduate within 4 years. 90% freshmen graduate within 6 years. **Faculty:** Student/faculty ratio 9:1. 1,102 full-time faculty, 96% hold PhDs, 25% are members of minority groups, 43% are women.

ACADEMICS
Degrees: Bachelor's; Doctoral degree—professional practice; Doctoral degree research/scholarship; Master's; Post-bachelor's certificate; Post-master's certificate. **Classes:** Most classes have 10–19 students. Most lab/discussion sessions have 10–19 students. **Most popular majors:** Registered Nursing/Registered Nurse; Biology/Biological Sciences, General; Business Administration and Management, General. **Special Study Options:** Accelerated program; Cross-registration; Distance learning; Double major; Dual enrollment; English as a Second Language (ESL); Honors program; Independent study; Internships; Liberal arts/career combination; Study abroad. **Combined degree programs:** BA/MA. **Disability Services offered:** Note-taking services; Reader services; Tape recorders; Tutors. **Career services:** Alumni network; Alumni services; Career assessment; Career/job search classes; Internships; Regional alumni.

FACILITIES
Housing: Apartments for single students; Coed dorms; Fraternity/sorority housing; Theme housing.

CAMPUS LIFE
Environment: City. **Activities:** Campus Ministries; Choral groups; Concert band; Dance; Drama/theater; International Student Organization; Jazz band; Literary magazine; Model UN; Music ensembles; Musical theater; Opera; Radio station; Student government; Student newspaper; Student-run film society; Symphony orchestra; Television station. 161 registered organizations, 28 honor societies, 26 religious organizations, 17 fraternities, 12 sororities, on campus. **Athletics (Intercollegiate):** *Men:* baseball, basketball, cross-country, diving, golf, soccer, swimming, tennis, track/field (outdoor). *Women:* basketball, cross-country, diving, soccer, softball, swimming, tennis, track/field (outdoor), volleyball. **On-Campus Highlights:** Michael C. Carlos Museum. **Environmental Initiatives:** Emory has among the highest number of square feet of LEED-certified space of any campus in America. Emory constructed the first LEED-certified building in the Southeast in the 1990's, the first Good LEED-EB in the U.S., and since 2001 all new and future construction must be LEED (with Silver currently the minimum). We also are auditing and retrofitting exisiting buildings—roughly 1 million square feet are currently underway with additional 1 million in planning phase.

ADMISSIONS
Freshman Academic Profile: Average high school GPA 3.8. 84% in top 10% of high school class, 97% in top 25% of high school class, 100% in top 50% of high school class. **Test scores:** SAT Math middle 50% range 690–790. SAT EBRW middle 50% range 670–740. ACT middle 50% range 31–34. **Basis for Candidate Selection:** *Very important factors include:* rigor of secondary school record, academic GPA, recommendation(s), extracurricular activities, talent/ability, character/personal qualities. *Important factors include:* application essay, standardized test scores. *Other factors include:* class rank, interview, first generation, alumni/ae relation, geographical residence, state residency,

racial/ethnic status, work experience. **Freshman Admission Requirements:** High school diploma is required and GED is not accepted. *Academic units recommended:* 4 English, 4 math, 4 science, 2 science labs, 4 foreign language, 2 social studies, 2 history, 1 computer science, 1 visual/performing arts. **Freshman Admission Statistics:** 30,017 applied, 16% admitted, 29% enrolled. **Transfer Admission Requirements:** High school transcript, college transcript(s), essay or personal statement, standardized test scores, statement of good standing from prior institution(s). Minimum college GPA of 3.00 required. Lowest grade transferable C. **General Admission Information:** Application fee $75. Regular application deadline 1/1. Admission may be deferred for a maximum of 2 years.

COSTS AND FINANCIAL AID
Annual tuition $53,070. Room and board $14,972. Required fees $734. Average book and supplies expense $1,224. **Required Forms and Deadlines:** CSS/Financial Aid PROFILE; FAFSA; Noncustodial PROFILE. **Notification of Awards:** Applicants will be notified of awards on or about 4/1. **Types of Aid:** *Need-based scholarships/grants:* College/university scholarship or grant aid from institutional funds; Federal Pell; Private scholarships; SEOG; State scholarships/grants. *Loans:* Direct PLUS loans; Direct Subsidized Stafford Loans; Direct Unsubsidized Stafford Loans. **Student Employment:** Federal Work-Study Program available. Institutional employment available. **Financial Aid Statistics:** 94% needy freshmen, 96% needy undergrads receive need-based scholarship or grant aid. 34% freshmen, 22% undergrads receive non-need-based scholarship or grant aid. 89% freshmen, 90% undergrads receive need-based self-help aid. 0% freshmen, 0% undergrads receive athletic scholarships. 35% undergrads borrow to pay for school. Average cumulative indebtedness $24,889. **Criteria awarding aid:** *Need-based:* Religious affiliation. *Non-Need-based:* Academics, Art, Leadership, Music/drama, Religious affiliation, State/district residency.

EMPORIA STATE UNIVERSITY

1 Kellogg Circle, Emporia, KS 66801-5087
Phone: 620-341-5465 **Financial Aid Phone:** 620-341-5457
E-mail: go2esu@emporia.edu **CEEB Code:** 6335
Fax: 620-341-5599 **Website:** www.emporia.edu **ACT Code:** 1430

This public school was founded in 1863. It has a 212 acre campus.

RATINGS
Admissions Selectivity Rating: 76   **Fire Safety Rating:** 77   **Green Rating:** 60*

STUDENTS AND FACULTY
Enrollment: 3,258. **Student Body:** 63% female, 37% male, 9% out-of-state, 5% international (38 countries represented). Asian 1%, African American 5%, Caucasian 70%, Hispanic 7%, Native American <1%, Pacific Islander <1%, Two or more races 10%, Race unknown 2%.
Retention and Graduation: 77% freshmen return for sophomore year. 29% freshmen graduate within 4 years. 50% freshmen graduate within 6 years. 20% grads go on to further study within 1 year. **Faculty:** Student/faculty ratio 17:1. 249 full-time faculty, 81% hold PhDs, 17% are members of minority groups, 52% are women. 8% of classes are taught by teaching assistants.

ACADEMICS
Degrees: Bachelor's; Doctoral degree research/scholarship; Master's; Post-bachelor's certificate; Post-master's certificate. **Classes:** Most classes have 10–19 students. Most lab/discussion sessions have greater than 100 students. **Most popular majors:** Business/Commerce, General; Elementary Education and Teaching; Nursing/Registered Nurse (Rn, Asn, Bsn, Msn). **Special Study Options:** Distance learning; Double major; Dual enrollment; Honors program; Independent study; Internships; Liberal arts/career combination; Student-designed major; Study abroad; Teacher certification program. **Honors programs:** Honors Programs. **Disability Services offered:** Note-taking services; Reader services; Tape recorders; Tutors. **Career services:** Alumni network; Alumni services; Career assessment; Internships.

FACILITIES
Housing: Coed dorms; Cooperative housing; Fraternity/sorority housing; Special housing for disabled students; Special housing for international students; Theme housing; Wellness housing 100% of campus accessible to physically disabled. **Special Academic Facilities/Equipment:** Art gallery, geology and natural history museums, Great Plains study center, planetarium. **Campus Network:** 100% of classrooms, 100% of dorms, 100% of student union, 100% of libraries, 100% of dining areas, 70% of common outdoor areas, have wireless network access.

CAMPUS LIFE
Environment: Town. **Activities:** Campus Ministries; Choral groups; Concert band; Dance; Drama/theater; International Student Organization; Jazz band; Literary magazine; Marching band; Music ensembles; Musical theater; Opera; Pep band; Student government; Student newspaper; Student-run film society; Symphony orchestra; Yearbook. 141 registered organizations, 15 honor societies, 11 religious organizations, 6 fraternities, 4 sororities, on campus. **Athletics (Intercollegiate):** *Men:* baseball, basketball, cheerleading, cross-country, football, tennis, track/field (outdoor), track/field (indoor). *Women:* basketball, cheerleading, cross-country, soccer, softball, tennis, track/field (outdoor), track/field (indoor), volleyball. **On-Campus Highlights:** Student Recreation Center.

ADMISSIONS
Freshman Academic Profile: Average high school GPA 3.4. 15% in top 10% of high school class, 38% in top 25% of high school class, 73% in top 50% of high school class. 96% from public high schools. **Test scores:** SAT Math middle 50% range 470–540. SAT EBRW middle 50% range 480–515. ACT middle 50% range 19–25. **Basis for Candidate Selection:** *Very important factors include:* class rank, academic GPA, standardized test scores. *Important factors include:* talent/ability. *Other factors include:* application essay, extracurricular activities. **Freshman Admission Requirements:** High school diploma is required and GED is accepted. *Academic units required:* 4 English, 3 math, 3 science, 3 social studies, 1 computer science. *Academic units recommended:* 4 English, 3 math, 3 science, 3 social studies, 1 computer science. **Freshman Admission Statistics:** 1,670 applied, 85% admitted, 48% enrolled. **Transfer Admission Requirements:** college transcript(s), Minimum college GPA of 2.0 required. Lowest grade transferable D. **General Admission Information:** Application fee $30. Non-fall registration accepted. Admission may be deferred for a maximum of 1 year.

COSTS AND FINANCIAL AID
Annual in-state tuition $5,154. Annual out-of-state tuition $19,071. Room and board $9,412. Required fees $1,806. Average book and supplies expense $1,000. **Required Forms and Deadlines:** FAFSA; State aid form. **Notification of Awards:** Applicants will be notified of awards on a rolling basis beginning 2/2. **Types of Aid:** *Need-based scholarships/grants:* College/university scholarship or grant aid from institutional funds; Federal Pell; Private scholarships; SEOG; State scholarships/grants. *Loans:* Direct PLUS loans; Direct Subsidized Stafford Loans; Direct Unsubsidized Stafford Loans. **Student Employment:** Federal Work-Study Program available. Institutional employment available. **Financial Aid Statistics:** 100% needy freshmen, 100% needy undergrads receive need-based scholarship or grant aid. 11% freshmen, 6% undergrads receive non-need-based scholarship or grant aid. 80% freshmen, 85% undergrads receive need-based self-help aid. 6% freshmen, 6% undergrads receive athletic scholarships. 97% freshmen, 88% undergrads receive any aid. 65% undergrads borrow to pay for school. Average cumulative indebtedness $22,692. **Criteria awarding aid:** *Need-based:* Job skills, Minority status. *Non-Need-based:* Academics, Alumni affiliation, Art, Athletics, Job skills, Leadership, Minority status, Music/drama, Religious affiliation, State/district residency.

ENDICOTT COLLEGE

376 Hale Street, Beverly, MA 01915
Phone: 978-921-1000 **Financial Aid Phone:** 978-232-2060
E-mail: admissio@endicott.edu **CEEB Code:** 3369
Fax: 978-232-2520 **Website:** www.endicott.edu **ACT Code:** 1824

This private school was founded in 1939. It has a 235 acre campus.

RATINGS
Admissions Selectivity Rating: 83   **Fire Safety Rating:** 97   **Green Rating:** 88

STUDENTS AND FACULTY
Enrollment: 3,191. **Student Body:** 63% female, 37% male, 48% out-of-state, 2% international (41 countries represented). Asian 2%, African American 2%, Caucasian 81%, Hispanic 4%, Native American <1%, Pacific Islander <1%, Two or more races 3%, Race unknown 7%.
Retention and Graduation: 86% freshmen return for sophomore year. 70% freshmen graduate within 4 years. 74% freshmen graduate within 6 years. 32% grads go on to further study within 1 year. **Faculty:** Student/faculty ratio 13:1. 112 full-time faculty, 75% hold PhDs, 15% are members of minority groups, 61% are women. 0% of classes are taught by teaching assistants.

ACADEMICS

Degrees: Associate; Bachelor's; Certificate; Doctoral degree—professional practice; Doctoral degree research/scholarship; Master's; Post-bachelor's certificate; Post-master's certificate; Terminal Associate. **Classes:** Most classes have 10–19 students. Most lab/discussion sessions have 10–19 students. **Most popular majors:** Sport and Fitness Administration/Management; Registered Nursing/Registered Nurse; Business Administration and Management, General. **Special Study Options:** Accelerated program; Cross-registration; Distance learning; Double major; Dual enrollment; English as a Second Language (ESL); Exchange student program (domestic); Honors program; Independent study; Internships; Liberal arts/career combination; Student-designed major; Study abroad; Teacher certification program. **Honors programs:** Alpha Phi Sigma (Criminal Justice), Eta Sigma Delta (Hospitality), Iota Gamma Chi (Liberal Studies), Kappa Delta Pi (Education), Lambda Pi Eta (Communication), Mortar Board (Community Service), Phi Alpha Theta (History), Phi Epsilon Kappa (Physical education), Phi Sigma (Biological Sciences), Phi Signma Alpha (Political Science), Psi Chi (Psychology), Sigma Beta Delta (Business/Technology), Sigma Iota Rho (International Studies), Sigma Tau Delta (English), Sigma Theta Tau (Nursing), Sigma Xi (research), Endicott College Honors Program, National Honor Society for students in Senior Year. **Disability Services offered:** Note-taking services; Reader services; Tape recorders; Tutors. **Career services:** Alumni network; Alumni services; Career assessment; Career/job search classes; Internships; Regional alumni.

FACILITIES

Housing: Apartments for single students; Coed dorms; Special housing for disabled students; Special housing for international students; Theme housing; Wellness housing; Women's dorms 90% of campus accessible to physically disabled. **Special Academic Facilities/Equipment:** DNA Sequencing lab, Incubator, Biotech labs, Center for the Arts (galleries, theaters, specialty studios and labs); State-of-the-art television/radio station. https://www.endicott.edu/student-life/activities-events/endicott-tv-radio; Specialized Nursing lab; La Chanterelle, a student-run restaurant https://www.endicott.edu/academics/schools/hospitality-management/la-chanterelle-restaurant, https://www.endicott.edu/academics/academic-resources-support/halle-library/endicott-archives **Campus Network:** 100% of classrooms, 50% of dorms, 100% of student union, 100% of libraries, 100% of dining areas, 100% of common outdoor areas, have wireless network access.

CAMPUS LIFE

Environment: Town. **Activities:** Campus Ministries; Choral groups; Dance; Drama/theater; International Student Organization; Jazz band; Literary magazine; Model UN; Music ensembles; Musical theater; Pep band; Radio station; Student government; Student newspaper; Television station; Yearbook. 62 registered organizations, 16 honor societies, 2 religious organizations, on campus. **Athletics (Intercollegiate):** *Men:* baseball, basketball, cross-country, equestrian sports, football, golf, lacrosse, soccer, tennis, volleyball. *Women:* basketball, cross-country, equestrian sports, field hockey, lacrosse, soccer, softball, tennis, volleyball. **On-Campus Highlights:** Center for Life Science and Business.

ADMISSIONS

Freshman Academic Profile: Average high school GPA 3.5. 20% in top 10% of high school class, 45% in top 25% of high school class, 81% in top 50% of high school class. 79% from public high schools. **Test scores:** SAT Math middle 50% range 540–610. SAT EBRW middle 50% range 550–630. ACT middle 50% range 22–27. **Basis for Candidate Selection:** *Very important factors include:* rigor of secondary school record, academic GPA, character/personal qualities. *Important factors include:* class rank, application essay, standardized test scores, extracurricular activities, talent/ability, alumni/ae relation, geographical residence. *Other factors include:* recommendation(s), interview, first generation, state residency, racial/ethnic status, level of applicant's interest. **Freshman Admission Requirements:** High school diploma is required and GED is accepted. *Academic units recommended:* 4 English, 3 math, 2 science, 2 social studies, 1 history, 4 academic electives. **Freshman Admission Statistics:** 5,031 applied, 69% admitted, 24% enrolled. **Transfer Admission Requirements:** High school transcript, college transcript(s), essay or personal statement, standardized test scores, statement of good standing from prior institution(s). Minimum college GPA of 2.5 required. Lowest grade transferable C. **General Admission Information:** Application fee $50. Priority deadline 2/15. Regular application deadline 2/15. Non-fall registration accepted. Admission may be deferred for a maximum of 1 year.

COSTS AND FINANCIAL AID

Annual tuition $34,470. Room and board $16,130. Required fees $850. Average book and supplies expense $1,218. **Required Forms and Deadlines:** FAFSA; Institution's own financial aid form. **Notification of Awards:** Applicants will be notified of awards on a rolling basis beginning 1/15. **Types of Aid:** *Need-based scholarships/grants:* College/university scholarship or grant aid from institutional funds; Federal Pell; Private scholarships; SEOG; State scholarships/grants. *Loans:* Direct PLUS loans; Direct Subsidized Stafford Loans; Direct Unsubsidized Stafford Loans. **Student Employment:** Federal Work-Study Program available. Institutional employment available. **Financial Aid Statistics:** 99% needy freshmen, 98% needy undergrads receive need-based scholarship or grant aid. 98% freshmen, 95% undergrads receive non-need-based scholarship or grant aid. 90% freshmen, 87% undergrads receive need-based self-help aid. 0% freshmen, 0% undergrads receive athletic scholarships. 96% freshmen, 93% undergrads receive any aid. 77% undergrads borrow to pay for school. Average cumulative indebtedness $44,178. **Criteria awarding aid:** *Need-based:* Academics, Art, Leadership *Non-Need-based:* Academics, Alumni affiliation, Art, Job skills, Leadership, Music/drama, Religious affiliation, State/district residency.

ERSKINE COLLEGE

Erskine College, Due West, SC 29639
Phone: 864-379-8838 **Financial Aid Phone:** 864-379-8832
E-mail: admissions@erskine.edu
Fax: 864-379-2172 **Website:** www.erskine.edu

This private school, affiliated with the Presbyterian Church, was founded in 1839. It has a 90 acre campus.

RATINGS

Admissions Selectivity Rating: 80 **Fire Safety Rating:** 68 **Green Rating:** 60*

STUDENTS AND FACULTY

Enrollment: 548. **Student Body:** 53% female, 47% male, 24% out-of-state, 4% international (10 countries represented). Asian 1%, African American 8%, Caucasian 70%, Hispanic 1%, Native American 0%, Pacific Islander 0%, Two or more races 1%, Race unknown 16%.
Retention and Graduation: 77% freshmen return for sophomore year. **Faculty:** Student/faculty ratio 11:1. 41 full-time faculty, 85% hold PhDs, 7% are members of minority groups, 39% are women. 0% of classes are taught by teaching assistants.

ACADEMICS

Degrees: Bachelor's; Certificate; Doctoral degree research/scholarship; Master's. **Classes:** Most classes have 10–19 students. Most lab/discussion sessions have 10–19 students. **Most popular majors:** Business/Commerce, General; Biology/Biological Sciences, General; Elementary Education and Teaching. **Special Study Options:** Double major; Independent study; Internships; Study abroad; Teacher certification program. **Disability Services offered:** Tutors. **Career services:** Career/job search classes.

FACILITIES

Housing: Men's dorms; Women's dorms 75% of campus accessible to physically disabled. **Special Academic Facilities/Equipment:** Bowie Arts Center.

CAMPUS LIFE

Environment: Rural. **Activities:** Campus Ministries; Choral groups; Concert band; Dance; Drama/theater; Jazz band; Literary magazine; Music ensembles; Musical theater; Radio station; Student government; Student newspaper; Yearbook. 51 registered organizations, on campus. **Athletics (Intercollegiate):** *Men:* baseball, basketball, cross-country, golf, soccer, tennis. *Women:* basketball, cross-country, golf, lacrosse, soccer, softball, tennis, volleyball. **On-Campus Highlights:** Java City.

ADMISSIONS

Freshman Academic Profile: 39% in top 10% of high school class, 65% in top 25% of high school class, 87% in top 50% of high school class. 85% from public high schools. **Test scores:** SAT Math middle 50% range 480–605. SAT EBRW middle 50% range 460–590. ACT middle 50% range 21–26. **Basis for Candidate Selection:** *Very important factors include:* rigor of secondary school record, academic GPA, application essay, standardized test scores, recommendation(s), alumni/ae relation. *Important factors include:* extracurricular activities, talent/ability, character/personal qualities. *Other factors include:* class rank, interview, first generation, geographical residence, state residency, religious affiliation/commitment, racial/ethnic status, volunteer work, work experience, level of applicant's interest. **Freshman Admission Requirements:** High school diploma is required and GED is accepted. *Academic units required:* 4 English, 2 math, 2 science, 2 science labs. **Freshman Admission Statistics:** 500 applied, 75% admitted, 39% enrolled. **Transfer Admission Requirements:** college transcript(s), essay or personal statement, statement of good standing from prior institution(s). Minimum college GPA of 2.0 required. Lowest grade transferable C. **General Admission Information:** Application fee $25. Non-fall registration accepted.

COSTS AND FINANCIAL AID

Required Forms and Deadlines: FAFSA; Institution's own financial aid form; State aid form. **Notification of Awards:** Applicants will be notified of awards on a rolling basis beginning 11/1. **Types of Aid:** *Need-based scholarships/grants:* College/university scholarship or grant aid from institutional funds; Federal Pell; Private scholarships; SEOG; State scholarships/grants. *Loans:* Direct PLUS loans; Direct Subsidized Stafford Loans; Direct Unsubsidized Stafford Loans. **Student Employment:** Federal Work-Study Program available. Institutional employment available. **Financial Aid Statistics:** 100% needy freshmen, 100% needy undergrads receive need-based scholarship or grant aid. 100% freshmen, 100% undergrads receive non-need-based scholarship or grant aid. 95% freshmen, 99% undergrads receive need-based self-help aid. 49% freshmen, 42% undergrads receive athletic scholarships. **Criteria awarding aid:** *Need-based:* Academics, Alumni affiliation, Athletics, Leadership, Minority status, Religious affiliation. *Non-Need-based:* Academics, Alumni affiliation, Athletics, Leadership, Minority status, Music/drama, Religious affiliation, State/district residency.

EUGENE LANG COLLEGE OF LIBERAL ARTS AT THE NEW SCHOOL

79 5th Avenue, Floor 5, New York, NY 10003
Phone: 212-229-5150 **Financial Aid Phone:** 212 229 8930
E-mail: lang@newschool.edu **CEEB Code:** 2521
Fax: 212.229.3040 **Website:** www.newschool.edu/ **ACT Code:** 2828

This private school was founded in 1972.

RATINGS

Admissions Selectivity Rating: 78   **Fire Safety Rating:** 89   **Green Rating:** 90

STUDENTS AND FACULTY

Enrollment: 1,880. **Student Body:** 80% female, 20% male, 78% out-of-state, 8% international (52 countries represented). Asian 7%, African American 6%, Caucasian 50%, Hispanic 17%, Native American <1%, Pacific Islander <1%, Two or more races 6%, Race unknown 5%. **Retention and Graduation:** 69% freshmen return for sophomore year. 46% freshmen graduate within 4 years. 55% freshmen graduate within 6 years. **Faculty:** Student/faculty ratio 11:1. 119 full-time faculty, 20% hold PhDs, 24% are members of minority groups, 55% are women. 0% of classes are taught by teaching assistants.

ACADEMICS

Degrees: Bachelor's. **Classes:** Most classes have 10–19 students. Most lab/discussion sessions have 10–19 students. **Most popular majors:** Mass Communication/Media Studies; General Literature; Liberal Arts and Sciences/Liberal Studies. **Special Study Options:** Cross-registration; Double major; Exchange student program (domestic); Independent study; Internships; Student-designed major; Study abroad. **Combined degree programs:** BA/MA. **Disability Services offered:** Note-taking services; Reader services; Tape recorders. **Career services:** Alumni services; Career assessment; Career/job search classes; Internships.

FACILITIES

Housing: Coed dorms; Special housing for disabled students 99% of campus accessible to physically disabled. **Special Academic Facilities/Equipment:** Art gallery, photography gallery, extensive collections of contemporary art, concert hall, public lectures, conferences, cultural and intellectual events.

CAMPUS LIFE

Environment: Metropolis. **Activities:** Campus Ministries; Dance; Drama/theater; International Student Organization; Literary magazine; Music ensembles; Radio station; Student government; Student newspaper; Student-run film society; Symphony orchestra. 42 registered organizations, 4 religious organizations, on campus. **On-Campus Highlights:** Lang Cafe **Environmental Initiatives:** Lighting Retrofits: 2W 13th St. and 66 5th Ave are in the midst of an ongoing replacement of all non-LED fixtures. The majority of the building's T8 fluorescent bulbs are being replaced with LED, stairwells are being replaced with dimming-occupancy based bi-level fixtures, and all rooms will be equiped with vacancy sensors. The main lobby and gallery spaces will also recieve significant upgrades as well. These same upgrades are being applied to 2 other large buildings, with a goal of completing the entire campus by early 2017.

ADMISSIONS

Freshman Academic Profile: Average high school GPA 3.5. 17% in top 10% of high school class, 45% in top 25% of high school class, 84% in top 50% of high school class. 50% from public high schools. **Test scores:** SAT Math middle 50% range 530–630. SAT EBRW middle 50% range 590–680. ACT middle 50% range 25–30. **Basis for Candidate Selection:** *Very important factors include:* academic GPA, application essay, extracurricular activities. *Important factors include:* rigor of secondary school record, recommendation(s), character/personal qualities. *Other factors include:* class rank, standardized test scores, interview, talent/ability, volunteer work, work experience, level of applicant's interest. **Freshman Admission Requirements:** High school diploma is required and GED is accepted. *Academic units required:* 4 English. *Academic units recommended:* 4 math, 4 science, 4 foreign language, 4 social studies, 4 history. **Freshman Admission Statistics:** 2,939 applied, 80% admitted, 18% enrolled. **Transfer Admission Requirements:** High school transcript, college transcript(s), essay or personal statement, standardized test scores, Minimum college GPA of 3.0 required. Lowest grade transferable C. **General Admission Information:** Application fee $50. Priority deadline 1/15. Regular application deadline 8/1. Non-fall registration accepted. Admission may be deferred for a maximum of 1 year.

COSTS AND FINANCIAL AID

Annual tuition $48,760. Room and board $17,600. Required fees $1,216. Average book and supplies expense $2,050. **Required Forms and Deadlines:** FAFSA. **Notification of Awards:** Applicants will be notified of awards on a rolling basis beginning 4/1. **Types of Aid:** *Need-based scholarships/grants:* College/university scholarship or grant aid from institutional funds; Federal Pell; Private scholarships; SEOG; State scholarships/grants; United Negro College Fund. *Loans:* Direct PLUS loans; Direct Subsidized Stafford Loans; Direct Unsubsidized Stafford Loans. **Student Employment:** Federal Work-Study Program available. Institutional employment available. **Financial Aid Statistics:** 74% needy freshmen, 81% needy undergrads receive need-based scholarship or grant aid. 80% freshmen, 77% undergrads receive non-need-based scholarship or grant aid. 17% freshmen, 15% undergrads receive need-based self-help aid. 0% freshmen, 0% undergrads receive athletic scholarships. 62% freshmen, 54% undergrads receive any aid. 61% undergrads borrow to pay for school. Average cumulative indebtedness $32,153. **Criteria awarding aid:** *Need-based:* Academics, Art, Leadership, Minority status, Music/drama *Non-Need-based:* Academics, Art, Leadership, Minority status, Music/drama, State/district residency.

THE EVERGREEN STATE COLLEGE

2700 Evergreen Pkwy NW, Olympia, WA 98505
Phone: 360-867-6170 **Financial Aid Phone:** 360-867-6205
E-mail: admissions@evergreen.edu **CEEB Code:** 4292
Fax: 360-867-5114 **Website:** www.evergreen.edu **ACT Code:** 4457

This public school was founded in 1967. It has a 1000 acre campus.

RATINGS
Admissions Selectivity Rating: 73   **Fire Safety Rating:** 90   **Green Rating:** 60*

STUDENTS AND FACULTY
Enrollment: 2,527. **Student Body:** 59% female, 41% male, 16% out-of-state, <1% international (13 countries represented). Asian 3%, African American 5%, Caucasian 63%, Hispanic 13%, Native American 4%, Pacific Islander <1%, Two or more races 6%, Race unknown 5%.
Retention and Graduation: 65% freshmen return for sophomore year. 37% freshmen graduate within 4 years. 50% freshmen graduate within 6 years. 21% grads go on to further study within 1 year. 15% grads pursue arts and sciences degrees. 1% grads pursue law degrees. 0% grads pursue business degrees. 1% grads pursue medical degrees. **Faculty:** Student/faculty ratio 21:1. 134 full-time faculty, 94% hold PhDs, 25% are members of minority groups, 59% are women. 0% of classes are taught by teaching assistants.

ACADEMICS
Degrees: Bachelor's; Master's. **Classes:** Most classes have 20–29 students. **Most popular majors:** Liberal Arts and Sciences/Liberal Studies; Natural Sciences; Social Sciences, Other. **Special Study Options:** Accelerated program; Double major; Exchange student program (domestic); Independent study; Internships; Student-designed major; Study abroad; Teacher certification program; Weekend college. **Disability Services offered:** Note-taking services; Tape recorders; Tutors. **Career services:** Alumni network; Alumni services; Career assessment; Career/job search classes; Internships; Regional alumni.

FACILITIES
Housing: Apartments for married students; Apartments for single students; Coed dorms; Special housing for disabled students; Special housing for international students; Theme housing; Wellness housing 85% of campus accessible to physically disabled.

CAMPUS LIFE
Environment: City. **Activities:** Campus Ministries; Choral groups; Dance; Drama/theater; Jazz band; Literary magazine; Music ensembles; Radio station; Student government; Student newspaper; Student-run film society; Television station. **Athletics (Intercollegiate):** *Men:* basketball, cross-country, soccer, track/field (outdoor), track/field (indoor). *Women:* basketball, cross-country, soccer, track/field (outdoor), track/field (indoor), volleyball. **On-Campus Highlights:** College Activities Building.

ADMISSIONS
Freshman Academic Profile: Average high school GPA 3.1. 19% in top 10% of high school class, 24% in top 25% of high school class, 60% in top 50% of high school class. **Test scores:** SAT Math middle 50% range 470–580. SAT EBRW middle 50% range 530–640. ACT middle 50% range 20–27. **Basis for Candidate Selection:** *Very important factors include:* rigor of secondary school record, academic GPA. *Important factors include:* standardized test scores, level of applicant's interest. *Other factors include:* application essay, recommendation(s), interview, extracurricular activities, volunteer work, work experience. **Freshman Admission Requirements:** High school diploma is required and GED is accepted. *Academic units required:* 4 English, 3 math, 2 science, 2 science labs, 2 foreign language, 3 social studies, 1 academic electives, 1 unit from above areas or other academic areas. **Freshman Admission Statistics:** 1,303 applied, 98% admitted, 20% enrolled. **Transfer Admission Requirements:** college transcript(s), Minimum college GPA of 2 required. Lowest grade transferable 2. **General Admission Information:** Application fee $50. Priority deadline 2/1. Non-fall registration accepted. Admission may be deferred for a maximum of one quarter.

COSTS AND FINANCIAL AID
Annual in-state tuition $7,005. Annual out-of-state tuition $26,325. Room and board $12,363. Required fees $1,203. Average book and supplies expense $900. **Required Forms and Deadlines:** FAFSA. **Notification of Awards:** Applicants will be notified of awards on a rolling basis beginning 4/1. **Types of Aid:** *Need-based scholarships/grants:* College/university scholarship or grant aid from institutional funds; Federal Pell; Private scholarships; SEOG; State scholarships/grants. *Loans:* Direct PLUS loans; Direct Subsidized Stafford Loans; Direct Unsubsidized Stafford Loans. **Student Employment:** Federal Work-Study Program available. Institutional employment available. **Financial Aid Statistics:** 92% needy freshmen, 87% needy undergrads receive need-based scholarship or grant aid. 3% freshmen, 1% undergrads receive non-need-based scholarship or grant aid. 69% freshmen, 73% undergrads receive need-based self-help aid. 1% freshmen, 1% undergrads receive athletic scholarships. 67% freshmen, 67% undergrads receive any aid. 58% undergrads borrow to pay for school. Average cumulative indebtedness $20,488. **Criteria awarding aid:** *Non-Need-based:* Academics, Art, Athletics, Leadership, State/district residency.

EXCELSIOR COLLEGE

7 Columbia Circle, Albany, NY 12203-5159
Phone: 518-464-8500 **Financial Aid Phone:** 518-464-8500
E-mail: admissions@excelsior.edu **CEEB Code:** 759
Fax: 518-464-8777 **Website:** https://www.excelsior.edu/ **ACT Code:** 20214

This private school was founded in 1970.

RATINGS
Admissions Selectivity Rating: 62   **Fire Safety Rating:** 60*   **Green Rating:** 60*

STUDENTS AND FACULTY
Enrollment: 32,133. **Student Body:** 58% female, 42% male, 90% out-of-state, <1% international (56 countries represented). Asian 4%, African American 17%, Caucasian 58%, Hispanic 5%, Native American 1%, Race unknown 14%.

ACADEMICS
Degrees: Associate; Bachelor's; Master's; Post-bachelor's certificate; Post-master's certificate. **Classes:** Most classes have 10–19 students. **Most popular majors:** Business Administration and Management, General; Liberal Arts and Sciences/Liberal Studies; Nursing/Registered Nurse (Rn, Asn, Bsn, Msn). **Special Study Options:** Accelerated program; Distance learning; External degree program; Honors program; Independent study. **Career services:** Alumni network; Alumni services; Career assessment.

FACILITIES
Campus Network: 100% of classrooms, 100% of dorms, 100% of student union, 100% of libraries, 100% of dining areas, 95% of common outdoor areas, have wireless network access.

CAMPUS LIFE
Environment: City. 1 honor societies, on campus. **Environmental Initiatives:** EC has a staff created and led committee that looks for opportunites to create a more 'green' environment.

ADMISSIONS
Freshman Admission Requirements: High school diploma is required and GED is accepted. **Freshman Admission Statistics:** Lowest grade transferable C. **General Admission Information:** Application fee $75. Non-fall registration accepted.

COSTS AND FINANCIAL AID
Required Forms and Deadlines: FAFSA; Institution's own financial aid form. **Notification of Awards:** Applicants will be notified of awards on a rolling basis beginning 8/1. **Types of Aid:** *Need-based scholarships/grants:* College/university scholarship or grant aid from institutional funds; Federal Pell; Private scholarships; State scholarships/grants. *Loans:* Direct PLUS loans; Direct Subsidized Stafford Loans; Direct Unsubsidized Stafford Loans. **Financial Aid Statistics:** 3% undergrads receive any aid.

FAIRFIELD UNIVERSITY

1073 North Benson Road, Fairfield, CT 06824
Phone: 203-254-4100 **Financial Aid Phone:** 203-254-4125
E-mail: admis@fairfield.edu **CEEB Code:** 3390
Fax: 203-254-4199 **Website:** www.fairfield.edu **ACT Code:** 560

This private school, affiliated with the Roman Catholic-Jesuit Church, was founded in 1942. It has a 200 acre campus.

RATINGS
Admissions Selectivity Rating: 89   **Fire Safety Rating:** 98   **Green Rating:** 77

STUDENTS AND FACULTY
Enrollment: 4,250. **Student Body:** 59% female, 41% male, 73% out-of-state, 4% international (49 countries represented). Asian 3%, African American 2%, Caucasian 77%, Hispanic 7%, Native American <1%, Pacific Islander <1%, Two or more races 2%, Race unknown 6%.
Retention and Graduation: 90% freshmen return for sophomore year. 80% freshmen graduate within 4 years. 83% freshmen graduate within 6 years. 27% grads go on to further study within 1 year. 15% grads pursue arts and sciences degrees. 10% grads pursue law degrees. 47% grads pursue business degrees. 1% grads pursue medical degrees. **Faculty:** Student/faculty ratio 12:1. 300 full-time faculty, 91% hold PhDs, 14% are members of minority groups, 56% are women. 0% of classes are taught by teaching assistants.

ACADEMICS
Degrees: Bachelor's; Doctoral degree—professional practice; Master's; Post-bachelor's certificate; Post-master's certificate. **Classes:** Most classes have 20–29 students. Most lab/discussion sessions have fewer than 10 students. **Most popular majors:** Registered Nursing/Registered Nurse; Finance, General; Marketing/Marketing Management, General. **Special Study Options:** Accelerated program; Cross-registration; Distance learning; Double major; Exchange student program (domestic); Honors program; Independent study; Internships; Liberal arts/career combination; Student-designed major; Study abroad; Teacher certification program. **Honors programs:** Brennan Fund for Global Immersion CAS Faculty/Student Research Corrigan Research Scholars (research based) Dr. Robert and Patricia Femia Science Endowment Four Year Honors Program Hardiman Research Scholars (research based) Hulseman Fund for Global Programs Ignatian Scholars Kathleen McGuinness Mentorship Program Lawrence Research Scholars (research based) Loyola Scholars Magis Scholars Mancini Family Student Research Fund Risica Family Faculty/Student CAS History Research Fund Student Faculty Collaborative Research Xavier Scholars. **Combined degree programs:** BA/MA; BA/MEng. **Disability Services offered:** Note-taking services; Reader services; Tape recorders; Tutors. **Career services:** Alumni network; Alumni services; Career assessment; Career/job search classes; Internships.

FACILITIES
Housing: Apartments for single students; Coed dorms; Special housing for disabled students; Theme housing; Wellness housing 97% of campus accessible to physically disabled. **Special Academic Facilities/Equipment:** Fairfield University is home to a multi-media production facility, a 750-seat concert hall/theater, a black box 150-seat theater, a business ideation/innovation space, a financial trading simulation classroom, an information security computer lab, a MALDI-TOF mass spectrometer, a 3D anatomy visualization system, a simulated hospital floor and human patient simulators in the nursing facility, an art gallery and an art museum, a museum classroom and a museum educator, mobile-friendly active learning classrooms, and a resource center for core science. **Campus Network:** 100% of classrooms, 100% of dorms, 100% of student union, 100% of libraries, 100% of dining areas, 50% of common outdoor areas, have wireless network access.

CAMPUS LIFE
Environment: Town. **Activities:** Campus Ministries; Choral groups; Concert band; Dance; Drama/theater; International Student Organization; Jazz band; Literary magazine; Model UN; Music ensembles; Musical theater; Pep band; Radio station; Student government; Student newspaper; Student-run film society; Symphony orchestra; Television station; Yearbook. 112 registered organizations, 21 honor societies, 24 religious organizations, on campus. **Athletics (Intercollegiate):** *Men:* baseball, basketball, crew/rowing, cross-country, diving, golf, lacrosse, soccer, swimming, tennis. *Women:* basketball, crew/rowing, cross-country, diving, field hockey, golf, lacrosse, soccer, softball, swimming, tennis, volleyball. **On-Campus Highlights:** Barone Campus Center **Environmental Initiatives:** Built a Co-generation facility providing 90% of campus electricity; 60% campus heating.

ADMISSIONS
Freshman Academic Profile: Average high school GPA 3.6. 41% in top 10% of high school class, 73% in top 25% of high school class, 97% in top 50% of high school class. 60% from public high schools. **Test scores:** SAT Math middle 50% range 600–680. SAT EBRW middle 50% range 610–670. ACT middle 50% range 26–30. **Basis for Candidate Selection:** *Very important factors include:* rigor of secondary school record, academic GPA, application essay, recommendation(s). *Important factors include:* interview, extracurricular activities, talent/ability, character/personal qualities, first generation, volunteer work. *Other factors include:* class rank, standardized test scores, alumni/ae relation, geographical residence, racial/ethnic status. **Freshman Admission Requirements:** High school diploma is required and GED is accepted. *Academic units required:* 4 English, 3 math, 3 science, 2 science labs, 2 foreign language, 2 social studies, 2 history. *Academic units recommended:* 4 English, 4 math, 4 science, 4 foreign language, 2 social studies, 2 history. **Freshman Admission Statistics:** 12,315 applied, 57% admitted, 17% enrolled. **Transfer Admission Requirements:** High school transcript, college transcript(s), essay or personal statement, statement of good standing from prior institution(s). Minimum college GPA of .03 required. Lowest grade transferable C. **General Admission Information:** Application fee $60. Regular application deadline 1/15. Non-fall registration accepted. Admission may be deferred for a maximum of 1 year.

COSTS AND FINANCIAL AID
Annual tuition $49,080. Room and board $15,150. Required fees $750. Average book and supplies expense $1,150. **Required Forms and Deadlines:** Business/Farm Supplement; CSS/Financial Aid PROFILE; FAFSA; Noncustodial PROFILE. **Notification of Awards:** Applicants will be notified of awards on or about 4/1. **Types of Aid:** *Need-based scholarships/grants:* College/university scholarship or grant aid from institutional funds; Federal Pell; Private scholarships; SEOG; State scholarships/grants. *Loans:* Direct PLUS loans; Direct Subsidized Stafford Loans; Direct Unsubsidized Stafford Loans. **Student Employment:** Federal Work-Study Program available. Institutional employment available. **Financial Aid Statistics:** 75% needy freshmen, 81% needy undergrads receive need-based scholarship or grant aid. 93% freshmen, 90% undergrads receive non-need-based scholarship or grant aid. 74% freshmen, 78% undergrads receive need-based self-help aid. 7% freshmen, 7% undergrads receive athletic scholarships. 97% freshmen, 90% undergrads receive any aid. 61% undergrads borrow to pay for school. Average cumulative indebtedness $39,214. **Criteria awarding aid:** *Need-based:* Academics. *Non-Need-based:* Academics, Alumni affiliation, Art, Athletics, Leadership, Music/drama.

FAIRLEIGH DICKINSON UNIVERSITY, COLLEGE AT FLORHAM

285 Madison Ave, Madison, NJ 07940
Phone: 800-338-8803
E-mail: globaleducation@fdu.edu **CEEB Code:** 226241
Fax: 973-443-8088 **Website:** www.fdu.edu **ACT Code:** 2554

This private school was founded in 1942. It has a 178 acre campus.

RATINGS
Admissions Selectivity Rating: 76   **Fire Safety Rating:** 91   **Green Rating:** 60*

STUDENTS AND FACULTY
Enrollment: 2,356. **Student Body:** 55% female, 45% male, 16% out-of-state, 1% international (25 countries represented). Asian 4%, African American 11%, Caucasian 62%, Hispanic 13%, Native American 1%, Pacific Islander 0%, Two or more races 1%, Race unknown 8%.
Retention and Graduation: 76% freshmen return for sophomore year.
Faculty: Student/faculty ratio 12:1. 141 full-time faculty, 0% hold PhDs, 0% are members of minority groups, 45% are women.

ACADEMICS
Degrees: Bachelor's; Doctoral degree—professional practice; Master's; Post-bachelor's certificate; Post-master's certificate. **Most popular majors:** Business Administration and Management, General; Psychology, General; Speech Communication and Rhetoric. **Special Study Options:** Accelerated program; Cooperative education program; Cross-registration; Distance learning; Double major; Dual enrollment; External degree program; Honors program; Independent study; Internships; Liberal arts/career combination; Student-designed major; Study abroad; Teacher certification program; Weekend college. **Combined degree programs:** BA/DDS; BA/MA; BA/MD. **Disability Services offered:** Note-taking services; Reader services; Tape recorders; Tutors. **Career services:** Alumni network; Alumni services; Career assessment; Career/job search classes; Internships.

FACILITIES
Housing: Coed dorms; Special housing for disabled students; Theme housing 34% of campus accessible to physically disabled. **Campus Network:** 100% of classrooms, 100% of dorms, 100% of student union, 100% of libraries, 100% of dining areas, 100% of common outdoor areas, have wireless network access.

CAMPUS LIFE
Environment: Village. **Activities:** Campus Ministries; Choral groups; Dance; Drama/theater; International Student Organization; Literary magazine; Musical theater; Radio station; Student government; Student newspaper; Student-run film society. 43 registered organizations, 9 honor societies, 3 religious organizations, 7 fraternities, 5 sororities, on campus. **Athletics (Intercollegiate):** *Men:* baseball, basketball, cross-country, football, golf, lacrosse, soccer, swimming, tennis. *Women:* basketball, cross-country, field hockey, lacrosse, soccer, softball, swimming, tennis, volleyball. **On-Campus Highlights:** Recreation Center. **Environmental Initiatives:** Recyclemania, Recycling Bins.

ADMISSIONS
Freshman Academic Profile: Average high school GPA 3.1. 14% in top 10% of high school class, 36% in top 25% of high school class, 75% in top 50% of high school class. **Test scores:** SAT Math middle 50% range 460–570. SAT EBRW middle 50% range 450–560. **Basis for Candidate Selection:** *Very important factors include:* academic GPA, standardized test scores. *Important factors include:* rigor of secondary school record, recommendation(s). *Other factors include:* class rank, application essay, interview, extracurricular activities, talent/ability, character/personal qualities, alumni/ae relation, volunteer work, level of applicant's interest. **Freshman Admission Requirements:** High school diploma is required and GED is accepted. *Academic units required:* 4 English, 3 math, 2 science, 2 science labs, 2 history, 3 academic electives. *Academic units recommended:* 4 English, 3 math, 3 science, 2 science labs, 2 foreign language, 2 history, 4 academic electives. **Freshman Admission Statistics:** 3,647 applied, 78% admitted, 21% enrolled. **Transfer Admission Requirements:** college transcript(s), Minimum college GPA of 2.0 required. Lowest grade transferable C. **General Admission Information:** Application fee $40. Priority deadline 1/15. Non-fall registration accepted.

COSTS AND FINANCIAL AID
Annual tuition $36,386. Room and board $12,294. Required fees $958.
Student Employment: Federal Work-Study Program available. Institutional employment available.

FAIRLEIGH DICKINSON UNIVERSITY, METROPOLITAN CAMPUS

1000 River Road, Teaneck, NJ 07666-1966
Phone: 201-692-2553
E-mail: globaleducation@fdu.edu **CEEB Code:** 226341
Fax: 201-692-7319 **Website:** www.fdu.edu **ACT Code:** 2552

This private school was founded in 1942. It has a 68 acre campus.

RATINGS
Admissions Selectivity Rating: 76   **Fire Safety Rating:** 91   **Green Rating:** 60*

STUDENTS AND FACULTY
Enrollment: 4,101. **Student Body:** 57% female, 43% male, 14% out-of-state, 7% international (83 countries represented). Asian 5%, African American 14%, Caucasian 29%, Hispanic 34%, Native American <1%, Pacific Islander <1%, Two or more races 1%, Race unknown 11%.
Retention and Graduation: 70% freshmen return for sophomore year.
Faculty: Student/faculty ratio 15:1. 190 full-time faculty, 0% hold PhDs, 0% are members of minority groups, 46% are women.

ACADEMICS
Degrees: Associate; Bachelor's; Certificate; Doctoral degree—professional practice; Doctoral degree research/scholarship; Master's; Post-bachelor's certificate; Post-master's certificate. **Most popular majors:** Criminal Justice/Law Enforcement Administration; Registered Nursing/Registered Nurse; Psychology, General. **Special Study Options:** Accelerated program; Cooperative education program; Cross-registration; Distance learning; Double major; English as a Second Language (ESL); Exchange student program (domestic); Honors program; Independent study; Internships; Liberal arts/career combination; Student-designed major; Study abroad; Teacher certification program; Weekend college. **Combined degree programs:** BA/DDS; BA/MA; BA/MD. **Disability Services offered:** Note-taking services; Reader services; Tape recorders; Tutors. **Career services:** Alumni network; Alumni services; Career assessment; Career/job search classes; Internships.

FACILITIES
Housing: Coed dorms; Men's dorms; Theme housing; Women's dorms 41% of campus accessible to physically disabled. **Campus Network:** 100% of classrooms, 100% of dorms, 100% of student union, 100% of libraries, 100% of dining areas, have wireless network access.

CAMPUS LIFE
Environment: Town. **Activities:** Campus Ministries; Choral groups; Dance; Drama/theater; International Student Organization; Literary magazine; Music ensembles; Musical theater; Radio station; Student government; Student newspaper; Student-run film society. 79 registered organizations, 10 honor societies, 4 religious organizations, 5 fraternities, 7 sororities, on campus. **Athletics (Intercollegiate):** *Men:* baseball, basketball, cross-country, golf, soccer, tennis, track/field (indoor). *Women:* basketball, bowling, cross-country, fencing, golf, soccer, softball, tennis, track/field (indoor), volleyball. **On-Campus Highlights:** Weiner Library. **Environmental Initiatives:** Recyclemania, Recycling Bins.

ADMISSIONS
Freshman Academic Profile: Average high school GPA 3.2. 18% in top 10% of high school class, 45% in top 25% of high school class, 83% in top 50% of high school class. **Test scores:** SAT Math middle 50% range 450–550. SAT EBRW middle 50% range 440–530. **Basis for Candidate Selection:** *Very important factors include:* academic GPA, standardized test scores. *Important factors include:* rigor of secondary school record, recommendation(s). *Other factors include:* class rank, application essay, interview, extracurricular activities, talent/ability, character/personal qualities, alumni/ae relation, volunteer work,

level of applicant's interest. **Freshman Admission Requirements:** High school diploma is required and GED is accepted. *Academic units required:* 4 English, 3 math, 2 science, 2 science labs, 2 history, 3 academic electives. *Academic units recommended:* 4 English, 3 math, 3 science, 2 science labs, 2 foreign language, 2 history, 4 academic electives. **Freshman Admission Statistics:** 5,193 applied, 73% admitted, 20% enrolled. **Transfer Admission Requirements:** college transcript(s), Minimum college GPA of 2.0 required. Lowest grade transferable C. **General Admission Information:** Application fee $40. Priority deadline 1/15. Non-fall registration accepted.

COSTS AND FINANCIAL AID
Annual tuition $33,920. Room and board $12,742. Required fees $958. **Student Employment:** Federal Work-Study Program available.

FAITH BAPTIST BIBLE COLLEGE AND THEOLOGICAL SEMINARY

1900 NW 4th Street, Ankeny, IA 50023
Phone: 1.888.faith.4.u **Financial Aid Phone:** 515-964-0601
E-mail: admissions@faith.edu **CEEB Code:** 6214
Fax: 515-964-1638 **Website:** http://www.faith.edu/ **ACT Code:** 1315

This private school, affiliated with the Baptist Church, was founded in 1921. It has a 52 acre campus.

RATINGS
Admissions Selectivity Rating: 87   **Fire Safety Rating:** 97   **Green Rating:** 60*

STUDENTS AND FACULTY
Enrollment: 232. **Student Body:** 55% female, 45% male, 56% out-of-state, 0% international. Asian <1%, African American 2%, Caucasian 92%, Hispanic 1%, Native American 1%, Pacific Islander 1%, Two or more races 1%, Race unknown <1%.
Retention and Graduation: 65% freshmen return for sophomore year. 23% grads go on to further study within 1 year. **Faculty:** Student/faculty ratio 13:1. 17 full-time faculty, 65% hold PhDs, 0% are members of minority groups, 12% are women. 0% of classes are taught by teaching assistants.

ACADEMICS
Degrees: Associate; Bachelor's; Master's. **Classes:** Most classes have fewer than 10 students. **Most popular majors:** Bible/Biblical Studies; Religious Education; Elementary Education and Teaching. **Special Study Options:** Distance learning; Double major; Dual enrollment; Independent study; Internships; Study abroad; Teacher certification program. **Career services:** Alumni services; Internships.

FACILITIES
Housing: Apartments for married students; Apartments for single students; Men's dorms; Special housing for disabled students; Women's dorms **Special Academic Facilities/Equipment:** 0 **Campus Network:** 100% of classrooms, 100% of dorms, 100% of student union, 100% of libraries, 100% of dining areas, 5% of common outdoor areas, have wireless network access.

CAMPUS LIFE
Environment: Town. **Activities:** Campus Ministries; Choral groups; Concert band; Drama/theater; Music ensembles; Student government; Symphony orchestra. 1 registered organizations, 1 religious organizations, on campus. **Athletics (Intercollegiate):** *Men:* basketball, soccer. *Women:* basketball, soccer, volleyball. **On-Campus Highlights:** Convocation Building.

ADMISSIONS
Freshman Academic Profile: Average high school GPA 3.5. 9% in top 10% of high school class, 40% in top 25% of high school class, 60% in top 50% of high school class. 33% from public high schools. **Test scores:** SAT Math middle 50% range 390–560. SAT EBRW middle 50% range 410–550. ACT middle 50% range 19–24. **Basis for Candidate Selection:** *Very important factors include:* religious affiliation/commitment. *Important factors include:* application essay, *Other factors include:* class rank, academic GPA, standardized test scores, recommendation(s), interview, extracurricular activities, talent/ability, character/personal qualities, volunteer work, level of applicant's interest. **Freshman Admission Requirements:** High school diploma is required and GED is accepted. *Academic units recommended:* 4 English, 4 math, 2 science, 2 social studies, 2 history. **Freshman Admission Statistics:** 150 applied, 67% admitted, 87% enrolled. **Transfer Admission Requirements:** college transcript(s), essay

or personal statement, statement of good standing from prior institution(s). Minimum college GPA of 2.0 required. Lowest grade transferable C. **General Admission Information:** Application fee $45. Non-fall registration accepted. Admission may be deferred for a maximum of 1 year.

COSTS AND FINANCIAL AID
Required Forms and Deadlines: FAFSA. **Types of Aid:** *Need-based scholarships/grants:* College/university scholarship or grant aid from institutional funds; Federal Pell; Private scholarships; State scholarships/grants. **Student Employment:** Institutional employment available. **Financial Aid Statistics:** 70% freshmen, 95% undergrads receive any aid. **Criteria awarding aid:** *Need-based:* Academics, Leadership, Music/drama. *Non-Need-based:* Academics, Leadership, Music/drama, State/district residency.

FASHION INSTITUTE OF TECHNOLOGY

227 West 27th Street, New York, NY 10001-5992
Phone: 212-217-3760 **Financial Aid Phone:** 212-217-3560
E-mail: fitinfo@fitsuny.edu **CEEB Code:** 2257
Fax: 212-217-3761 **Website:** fitnyc.edu **ACT Code:** 2744

This public school was founded in 1944.

RATINGS
Admissions Selectivity Rating: 60*   **Fire Safety Rating:** 91   **Green Rating:** 60*

STUDENTS AND FACULTY
Enrollment: 8,229. **Student Body:** 86% female, 14% male, 14% international (70 countries represented). Asian 10%, African American 9%, Caucasian 47%, Hispanic 17%, Native American <1%, Pacific Islander <1%, Two or more races 4%, Race unknown <1%.
Faculty: Student/faculty ratio 17:1.

ACADEMICS
Degrees: Associate; Bachelor's; Certificate; Master's. **Special Study Options:** Distance learning; English as a Second Language (ESL); Exchange student program (domestic); Honors program; Independent study; Internships; Liberal arts/career combination; Study abroad. **Disability Services offered:** Note-taking services; Tutors. **Career services:** Alumni services; Career assessment; Career/job search classes; Internships.

FACILITIES
Housing: Apartments for single students; Coed dorms; Special housing for disabled students; Wellness housing; Women's dorms **Special Academic Facilities/Equipment:** The Museum at FIT.

CAMPUS LIFE
Environment: Metropolis. **Activities:** Campus Ministries; Choral groups; Dance; Drama/theater; International Student Organization; Literary magazine; Musical theater; Radio station; Student government; Student newspaper; Television station; Yearbook. 65 registered organizations, 7 honor societies, 3 religious organizations, on campus. **On-Campus Highlights:** The Museum at FIT.

ADMISSIONS
Basis for Candidate Selection: *Very important factors include:* rigor of secondary school record, academic GPA, application essay, talent/ability. *Other factors include:* class rank, extracurricular activities, character/personal qualities, first generation, alumni/ae relation, volunteer work, work experience, level of applicant's interest. **Freshman Admission Requirements:** High school diploma is required and GED is accepted. **General Admission Information:** Application fee $50. Regular application deadline 1/1. Non-fall registration accepted.

COSTS AND FINANCIAL AID
Required Forms and Deadlines: FAFSA; State aid form. **Notification of Awards:** Applicants will be notified of awards on a rolling basis beginning 4/1. **Types of Aid:** *Need-based scholarships/grants:* College/university scholarship or grant aid from institutional funds; Federal Pell; Private scholarships; SEOG; State scholarships/grants. *Loans:* Direct PLUS loans; Direct Subsidized Stafford Loans; Direct Unsubsidized Stafford Loans. **Student Employment:** Federal Work-Study Program available.

FAULKNER UNIVERSITY

5345 Atlanta Highway, Montgomery, AL 36109-3398
Phone: 334-386-7200 **Financial Aid Phone:** 334-386-7195
E-mail: admissions@faulkner.edu **CEEB Code:** 1034
Fax: 334-386-7137 **Website:** www.faulkner.edu **ACT Code:** 3

This private school, affiliated with the Church of Christ, was founded in 1942. It has a 78 acre campus.

RATINGS
Admissions Selectivity Rating: 83   **Fire Safety Rating:** 79   **Green Rating:** 60*

STUDENTS AND FACULTY
Enrollment: 2,282. **Student Body:** 61% female, 39% male, 14% out-of-state, 2% international (15 countries represented). Asian <1%, African American 51%, Caucasian 40%, Hispanic 2%, Native American 1%, Pacific Islander <1%, Two or more races 2%, Race unknown 2%.
Retention and Graduation: 57% freshmen return for sophomore year. 80% grads go on to further study within 1 year. 35% grads pursue arts and sciences degrees. 12% grads pursue law degrees. 32% grads pursue business degrees. 19% grads pursue medical degrees. **Faculty:** Student/faculty ratio 15:1. 120 full-time faculty, 66% hold PhDs, 10% are members of minority groups, 40% are women. 0% of classes are taught by teaching assistants.

ACADEMICS
Degrees: Associate; Bachelor's; Doctoral degree—professional practice; Doctoral degree research/scholarship; Master's. **Classes:** Most classes have 10–19 students. Most lab/discussion sessions have 10–19 students. **Most popular majors:** Business/Commerce, General; Management Information Systems, General. **Special Study Options:** Cross-registration; Distance learning; Double major; Dual enrollment; Honors program; Independent study; Internships; Study abroad; Teacher certification program; Weekend college. **Honors programs:** Great Books Honors College. **Disability Services offered:** Note-taking services; Reader services; Tape recorders; Tutors. **Career services:** Alumni services; Career assessment; Career/job search classes; Internships.

FACILITIES
Housing: Men's dorms; Special housing for disabled students; Women's dorms 75% of campus accessible to physically disabled.

CAMPUS LIFE
Environment: City. **Activities:** Choral groups; Concert band; Drama/theater; International Student Organization; Literary magazine; Marching band; Music ensembles; Musical theater; Pep band; Student government; Student newspaper; Yearbook. 12 registered organizations, 5 honor societies, 3 religious organizations, 5 fraternities, 5 sororities, on campus. **Athletics (Intercollegiate):** *Men:* baseball, basketball, cheerleading, fishing, football, golf, soccer. *Women:* cheerleading, fishing, soccer, softball, volleyball. **On-Campus Highlights:** Cafe Sienna.

ADMISSIONS
Freshman Academic Profile: Average high school GPA 3.3. % in top 10% of high school class, % in top 25% of high school class, % in top 50% of high school class. 75% from public high schools. **Test scores:** SAT Math middle 50% range 440–510. SAT EBRW middle 50% range 430–520. ACT middle 50% range 18–24. **Basis for Candidate Selection:** *Very important factors include:* academic GPA, standardized test scores. *Important factors include:* rigor of secondary school record, class rank, recommendation(s), interview, character/personal qualities, religious affiliation/commitment, level of applicant's interest. *Other factors include:* application essay, extracurricular activities, talent/ability, first generation, alumni/ae relation, volunteer work, work experience.
Freshman Admission Requirements: High school diploma is required and GED is accepted. *Academic units required:* 3 English, 3 math, 3 science, 3 history. *Academic units recommended:* 4 English, 4 math, 4 science, 1 science labs, 1 foreign language, 2 social studies, 2 history. **Freshman Admission Statistics:** 1,712 applied, 57% admitted, 30% enrolled. **Transfer Admission Requirements:** High school transcript, college transcript(s), standardized test scores, statement of good standing from prior institution(s). Minimum college GPA of 2.0 required. Lowest grade transferable C. **General Admission Information:** Regular application deadline 8/1. Non-fall registration accepted.

COSTS AND FINANCIAL AID
Annual tuition $17,500. Room and board $7,130. Required fees $1,780. Average book and supplies expense $1,800. **Required Forms and Deadlines:** FAFSA; Institution's own financial aid form; State aid form. **Notification of**

Awards: Applicants will be notified of awards on or about 5/1. **Types of Aid:** *Need-based scholarships/grants:* College/university scholarship or grant aid from institutional funds; Federal Pell; Private scholarships; SEOG; State scholarships/grants. *Loans:* Direct PLUS loans; Direct Subsidized Stafford Loans; Direct Unsubsidized Stafford Loans. **Student Employment:** Federal Work-Study Program available. Institutional employment available. **Financial Aid Statistics:** 100% needy freshmen, 96% needy undergrads receive need-based scholarship or grant aid. 7% freshmen, 7% undergrads receive non-need-based scholarship or grant aid. 84% freshmen, 55% undergrads receive need-based self-help aid. 10% freshmen, 9% undergrads receive athletic scholarships. 95% freshmen, 93% undergrads receive any aid. **Criteria awarding aid:** *Need-based:* Academics, Alumni affiliation, Art, Athletics, Leadership, Music/drama, Religious affiliation.

FERRIS STATE UNIVERSITY

1201 South State Street, Big Rapids, MI 49307
Phone: 231-591-2100 **Financial Aid Phone:** 231-591-2115
E-mail: admissions@ferris.edu **CEEB Code:** 1222
Fax: 231-591-3944 **Website:** www.ferris.edu **ACT Code:** 1994

This public school was founded in 1884. It has a 935 acre campus.

RATINGS
Admissions Selectivity Rating: 75   **Fire Safety Rating:** 96   **Green Rating:** 76

STUDENTS AND FACULTY
Enrollment: 10,398. **Student Body:** 52% female, 48% male, 5% out-of-state, 1% international (43 countries represented). Asian 1%, African American 8%, Caucasian 77%, Hispanic 6%, Native American <1%, Pacific Islander <1%, Two or more races 4%, Race unknown 1%.
Retention and Graduation: 76% freshmen return for sophomore year. 30% freshmen graduate within 4 years. 53% freshmen graduate within 6 years. **Faculty:** Student/faculty ratio 16:1. 570 full-time faculty, 48% hold PhDs, 9% are members of minority groups, 46% are women. 0% of classes are taught by teaching assistants.

ACADEMICS
Degrees: Associate; Bachelor's; Certificate; Doctoral degree—other; Doctoral degree—professional practice; Master's; Post-bachelor's certificate; Terminal Associate; Transfer Associate. **Classes:** Most classes have 10–19 students. Most lab/discussion sessions have 10–19 students. **Most popular majors:** Criminal Justice/Law Enforcement Administration; Pharmacy; Registered Nursing/Registered Nurse. **Special Study Options:** Accelerated program; Cooperative education program; Double major; Dual enrollment; English as a Second Language (ESL); Exchange student program (domestic); External degree program; Honors program; Independent study; Internships; Liberal arts/career combination; Student-designed major; Study abroad; Teacher certification program; Weekend college. **Honors programs:** Honors/Bachelor in Business Administration in three years. Earn MBA as a fourth year option. **Combined degree programs:** BA/MA. **Disability Services offered:** Note-taking services; Reader services; Tape recorders; Tutors. **Career services:** Career assessment; Career/job search classes; Internships.

FACILITIES
Housing: Apartments for married students; Apartments for single students; Coed dorms; Special housing for disabled students; Special housing for international students; Theme housing 98% of campus accessible to physically disabled. **Special Academic Facilities/Equipment:** Rankin Art Gallery, Student Recreation Center, Card Wildlife Museum, Jim Crowe Museum, Elastomer Center, FLITE. **Campus Network:** 100% of classrooms, 20% of dorms, 90% of student union, 100% of libraries, 50% of dining areas, 25% of common outdoor areas, have wireless network access.

CAMPUS LIFE
Environment: Village. **Activities:** Campus Ministries; Choral groups; Concert band; Dance; Drama/theater; International Student Organization; Jazz band; Music ensembles; Musical theater; Opera; Pep band; Radio station; Student government; Student newspaper; Student-run film society; Symphony orchestra; Television station. 240 registered organizations, 19 honor societies, 10 religious organizations, 5 fraternities, 3 sororities, on campus. **Athletics (Intercollegiate):** *Men:* basketball, cheerleading, cross-country, football, golf, ice hockey, tennis, track/field (outdoor). *Women:* basketball, cheerleading,

cross-country, golf, soccer, softball, tennis, track/field (outdoor), volleyball. **On-Campus Highlights:** University Center.

ADMISSIONS

Freshman Academic Profile: Average high school GPA 3.3. **Test scores:** SAT Math middle 50% range 460–580. SAT EBRW middle 50% range 470–590. ACT middle 50% range 18–25. **Basis for Candidate Selection:** *Very important factors include:* rigor of secondary school record. *Important factors include:* academic GPA, standardized test scores, character/personal qualities. *Other factors include:* class rank, first generation, alumni/ae relation, geographical residence, volunteer work, work experience. **Freshman Admission Requirements:** High school diploma is required and GED is accepted. *Academic units recommended:* 4 English, 4 math, 3 science, 2 foreign language, 3 social studies, 1 academic electives, 1 visual/performing arts. **Freshman Admission Statistics:** 9,175 applied, 87% admitted, 24% enrolled. **Transfer Admission Requirements:** college transcript(s), statement of good standing from prior institution(s). Minimum college GPA of 2.0 required. Lowest grade transferable C. **General Admission Information:** Regular application deadline 8/1. Non-fall registration accepted. Admission may be deferred for a maximum of 1 year.

COSTS AND FINANCIAL AID

Annual in-state tuition $12,930. Annual out-of-state tuition $12,930. Room and board $10,340. Average book and supplies expense $859. **Required Forms and Deadlines:** FAFSA. **Notification of Awards:** Applicants will be notified of awards on a rolling basis beginning 12/14. **Types of Aid:** *Need-based scholarships/grants:* College/university scholarship or grant aid from institutional funds; Federal Pell; Private scholarships; SEOG; State scholarships/grants. *Loans:* Direct PLUS loans; Direct Subsidized Stafford Loans; Direct Unsubsidized Stafford Loans. **Student Employment:** Federal Work-Study Program available. Institutional employment available. **Financial Aid Statistics:** 84% needy freshmen, 82% needy undergrads receive need-based scholarship or grant aid. 83% freshmen, 68% undergrads receive non-need-based scholarship or grant aid. 70% freshmen, 72% undergrads receive need-based self-help aid. 4% freshmen, 3% undergrads receive athletic scholarships. 93% freshmen, 79% undergrads receive any aid. 74% undergrads borrow to pay for school. Average cumulative indebtedness $34,590. **Criteria awarding aid:** *Need-based:* Academics, Athletics, Job skills, Leadership, Minority status. *Non-Need-based:* Academics, Alumni affiliation, Art, Athletics, Job skills, Leadership, Minority status, Music/drama, State/district residency.

FISK UNIVERSITY

1000 17th Ave N, Nasville, TN
Phone: 1-800-443-3475
Website: www.fisk.edu

This is a private school.

RATINGS

Admissions Selectivity Rating: 89   **Fire Safety Rating:** 60*   **Green Rating:** 60*

STUDENTS AND FACULTY

Enrollment: 853.

ACADEMICS

Special Study Options: Cross-registration; Double major; Exchange student program (domestic); Honors program; Independent study; Internships; Student-designed major; Study abroad; Teacher certification program.

FACILITIES

Campus Network: 100% of classrooms, 100% of dorms, 100% of student union, 100% of libraries, 100% of dining areas, 100% of common outdoor areas, have wireless network access.

ADMISSIONS

Freshman Academic Profile: Average high school GPA 3.3. 10% in top 10% of high school class, 30% in top 25% of high school class, 75% in top 50% of high school class. 92% from public high schools. **Test scores:** SAT Math middle 50% range 455–540. SAT EBRW middle 50% range 467–546. ACT middle 50% range 18–23. **Basis for Candidate Selection:** *Very important factors include:* rigor of secondary school record. *Important factors include:* class rank, academic GPA, application essay, standardized

test scores, interview, extracurricular activities, character/personal qualities. *Other factors include:* recommendation(s), talent/ability, alumni/ae relation, geographical residence, volunteer work, level of applicant's interest. **Freshman Admission Requirements:** High school diploma is required and GED is accepted. *Academic units required:* 4 English, 3 math, 3 science, 2 science labs, 1 foreign language, 1 history. *Academic units recommended:* 4 English, 4 math, 3 science, 2 science labs, 2 foreign language, 1 history. **Freshman Admission Statistics:** 2,700 applied, 45% admitted, 51% enrolled. **Transfer Admission Requirements:** college transcript(s), essay or personal statement, statement of good standing from prior institution(s). Minimum college GPA of 2.5 required. Lowest grade transferable C. **General Admission Information:** Application fee $50. Priority deadline 3/1. Regular application deadline 3/1. Admission may be deferred for a maximum of 1 year.

COSTS AND FINANCIAL AID

Annual tuition $15,140. Room and board $7,730. Required fees $1,100. Average book and supplies expense $1,500.

FITCHBURG STATE COLLEGE

160 Pearl Street, Fitchburg, MA 01420-2697
Phone: 978-665-3144 **Financial Aid Phone:** (978) 665-3156
E-mail: admissions@fitchburgstate.edu **CEEB Code:** 3518
Fax: 978-665-4540 **Website:** www.fitchburgstate.edu **ACT Code:** 1902

This public school was founded in 1894. It has a 78 acre campus.

RATINGS

Admissions Selectivity Rating: 80   **Fire Safety Rating:** 95   **Green Rating:** 60*

STUDENTS AND FACULTY

Enrollment: 3,958. **Student Body:** 54% female, 46% male, 8% out-of-state, <1% international (6 countries represented). Asian 2%, African American 4%, Caucasian 81%, Hispanic 6%, Native American <1%, Pacific Islander <1%, Two or more races 2%, Race unknown 5%.
Retention and Graduation: 73% freshmen return for sophomore year. 10% grads go on to further study within 1 year. **Faculty:** Student/faculty ratio 16:1. 184 full-time faculty, 91% hold PhDs, 11% are members of minority groups, 46% are women. 0% of classes are taught by teaching assistants.

ACADEMICS

Degrees: Bachelor's; Certificate; Master's; Post-bachelor's certificate; Post-master's certificate. **Classes:** Most classes have 20–29 students. Most lab/discussion sessions have 10–19 students. **Most popular majors:** Education, General; Business Administration and Management, General; Speech Communication and Rhetoric. **Special Study Options:** Cross-registration; Distance learning; Double major; Dual enrollment; Honors program; Independent study; Internships; Liberal arts/career combination; Student-designed major; Study abroad; Teacher certification program. **Honors programs:** Leadership Academy Honors Program. **Disability Services offered:** Note-taking services; Reader services; Tape recorders; Tutors. **Career services:** Alumni network; Alumni services; Career assessment; Career/job search classes; Internships.

FACILITIES

Housing: Apartments for single students; Coed dorms; Special housing for disabled students 90% of campus accessible to physically disabled. **Special Academic Facilities/Equipment:** Art gallery, on-campus teacher education school, 120-acre conservation area.

CAMPUS LIFE

Environment: Town. **Activities:** Choral groups; Concert band; Dance; Drama/theater; Jazz band; Literary magazine; Model UN; Radio station; Student government; Student newspaper; Student-run film society. 60 registered organizations, 12 honor societies, 1 religious organizations, 2 fraternities, 3 sororities, on campus. **Athletics (Intercollegiate):** *Men:* baseball, basketball, cross-country, football, ice hockey, soccer, track/field (outdoor), track/field (indoor). *Women:* basketball, cross-country, field hockey, lacrosse, soccer, softball, track/field (outdoor), track/field (indoor). **On-Campus Highlights:** Campus Recreation Center. **Environmental Initiatives:** Single stream recycling program.

ADMISSIONS

Freshman Academic Profile: Average high school GPA 3.1. 90% from public high schools. **Test scores:** SAT Math middle 50% range 460–560. SAT EBRW middle 50% range 450–560. ACT middle 50% range 19–23. **Basis for Candidate Selection:** *Very important factors include:* rigor of secondary school record. *Important factors include:* academic GPA, application essay, standardized test scores. *Other factors include:* recommendation(s), extracurricular activities, talent/ability, character/personal qualities, alumni/ae relation, volunteer work, work experience, level of applicant's interest. **Freshman Admission Requirements:** High school diploma is required and GED is accepted. *Academic units required:* 4 English, 3 math, 3 science, 2 science labs, 2 foreign language, 1 social studies, 1 history, 2 academic electives. **Freshman Admission Statistics:** 3,104 applied, 70% admitted, 32% enrolled. **Transfer Admission Requirements:** college transcript(s), essay or personal statement, Minimum college GPA of 2.0 required. Lowest grade transferable C. **General Admission Information:** Application fee $25. Non-fall registration accepted. Admission may be deferred for a maximum of 1 year.

COSTS AND FINANCIAL AID

Annual in-state tuition $970. Annual out-of-state tuition $7,050. Room and board $8,256. Required fees $7,330. Average book and supplies expense $800. **Required Forms and Deadlines:** FAFSA. **Notification of Awards:** Applicants will be notified of awards on a rolling basis beginning 3/15. **Types of Aid:** *Need-based scholarships/grants:* College/university scholarship or grant aid from institutional funds; Federal Pell; Private scholarships; SEOG; State scholarships/grants. *Loans:* Direct PLUS loans; Direct Subsidized Stafford Loans; Direct Unsubsidized Stafford Loans. **Student Employment:** Federal Work-Study Program available. Institutional employment available. **Criteria awarding aid:** *Need-based:* Academics, Alumni affiliation, Job skills. *Non-Need-based:* Academics, Alumni affiliation, Job skills, Leadership.

FIVE TOWNS COLLEGE

Five Towns College, Dix Hills, NY 11746
Phone: 631-656-2110 **Financial Aid Phone:** 631-656-2164
E-mail: admissions@ftc.edu **CEEB Code:** 3142
Fax: 631-656-2172 **Website:** http://www.ftc.edu/

This proprietary school was founded in 1972. It has a 35 acre campus.

RATINGS

Admissions Selectivity Rating: 83   Fire Safety Rating: 99   Green Rating: 60*

STUDENTS AND FACULTY

Enrollment: 630. **Student Body:** 32% female, 68% male, 8% out-of-state, 0% international (4 countries represented). Asian 4%, African American 20%, Caucasian 50%, Hispanic 15%, Native American 1%, Pacific Islander <1%, Two or more races 4%, Race unknown 5%.
Retention and Graduation: 74% freshmen return for sophomore year.
Faculty: Student/faculty ratio 15:1. 22 full-time faculty, 45% hold PhDs, 14% are members of minority groups, 36% are women. 0% of classes are taught by teaching assistants.

ACADEMICS

Degrees: Associate; Bachelor's; Master's. **Classes:** Most classes have fewer than 10 students. **Most popular majors:** Music; Film/Cinema/Media Studies; Recording Arts Technology/Technician. **Special Study Options:** Distance learning; Independent study; Internships; Liberal arts/career combination; Teacher certification program. **Disability Services offered:** Note-taking services; Reader services; Tape recorders; Tutors. **Career services:** Career assessment; Career/job search classes; Internships.

FACILITIES

Housing: Coed dorms 100% of campus accessible to physically disabled. **Campus Network:** 100% of classrooms, 95% of dorms, 80% of student union, 100% of libraries, 100% of dining areas, 100% of common outdoor areas, have wireless network access.

CAMPUS LIFE

Environment: Town. **Activities:** Choral groups; Concert band; Dance; Drama/theater; Jazz band; Music ensembles; Musical theater; Radio station; Student government; Student newspaper; Student-run film society; Yearbook. 16 registered organizations, 1 honor societies, on campus. **On-Campus Highlights:** Dorms.

ADMISSIONS

Freshman Academic Profile: 91% from public high schools. **Test scores:** SAT Math middle 50% range 380–490. SAT EBRW middle 50% range 390–490. ACT middle 50% range 16–24. **Basis for Candidate Selection:** *Very important factors include:* rigor of secondary school record, academic GPA, application essay, recommendation(s), talent/ability, character/personal qualities. *Important factors include:* class rank, interview, extracurricular activities, level of applicant's interest. *Other factors include:* standardized test scores, volunteer work, work experience. **Freshman Admission Requirements:** High school diploma is required and GED is accepted. *Academic units required:* 4 English, 3 math, 3 science, 2 science labs, 2 foreign language, 4 social studies, 4 academic electives. *Academic units recommended:* 4 English, 3 math, 3 science, 2 science labs, 2 foreign language, 4 social studies, 4 academic electives. **Freshman Admission Statistics:** 379 applied, 63% admitted, 50% enrolled. **Transfer Admission Requirements:** High school transcript, college transcript(s), essay or personal statement, statement of good standing from prior institution(s). Minimum college GPA of 2.5 required. Lowest grade transferable C. **General Admission Information:** Application fee $35. Non-fall registration accepted. Admission may be deferred for a maximum of 1 year.

COSTS AND FINANCIAL AID

Annual tuition $21,000. Room and board $12,270. Required fees $700. Average book and supplies expense $1,400. **Required Forms and Deadlines:** FAFSA; State aid form. **Notification of Awards:** Applicants will be notified of awards on a rolling basis beginning 4/30. **Types of Aid:** *Need-based scholarships/grants:* College/university scholarship or grant aid from institutional funds; Federal Pell; Private scholarships; SEOG; State scholarships/grants. *Loans:* Direct PLUS loans; Direct Subsidized Stafford Loans; Direct Unsubsidized Stafford Loans. **Student Employment:** Federal Work-Study Program available. Institutional employment available. **Financial Aid Statistics:** 73% needy freshmen, 73% needy undergrads receive need-based scholarship or grant aid. 91% freshmen, 81% undergrads receive non-need-based scholarship or grant aid. 78% freshmen, 80% undergrads receive need-based self-help aid. 0% freshmen, 0% undergrads receive athletic scholarships. 78% freshmen, 75% undergrads receive any aid. 88% undergrads borrow to pay for school. Average cumulative indebtedness $35,340. **Criteria awarding aid:** *Need-based:* Academics, Art, Music/drama. *Non-Need-based:* Academics, Art, Leadership, Music/drama.

FLAGLER COLLEGE

Best
Colleges

74 King Street, St. Augustine, FL 32085-1027
Phone: 904-819-6220 **Financial Aid Phone:** 904-819-6225
E-mail: admissions@flagler.edu **CEEB Code:** 5235
Fax: 904-819-6466 **Website:** www.flagler.edu **ACT Code:** 772

This private school was founded in 1968. It has a 49 acre campus.

RATINGS

Admissions Selectivity Rating: 84   Fire Safety Rating: 88   Green Rating: 70

STUDENTS AND FACULTY

Enrollment: 2,862. **Student Body:** 68% female, 32% male, 59% out-of-state, 3% international (52 countries represented). Asian 1%, African American 5%, Caucasian 74%, Hispanic 10%, Native American <1%, Pacific Islander <1%, Two or more races 3%, Race unknown 4%.
Retention and Graduation: 72% freshmen return for sophomore year. 41% freshmen graduate within 4 years. 53% freshmen graduate within 6 years.
Faculty: Student/faculty ratio 16:1. 131 full-time faculty, 15% are members of minority groups, 57% are women. 0% of classes are taught by teaching assistants.

ACADEMICS

Degrees: Bachelor's; Master's. **Classes:** Most classes have 10–19 students. **Most popular majors:** Psychology, General; Business Administration and Management, General; Environmental Science. **Special Study Options:** Distance learning; Double major; Exchange student program (domestic); Honors program; Independent study; Internships; Study abroad; Teacher certification program. **Honors programs:** Only a small percentage of students (around 5% of each class of incoming freshmen) are invited to join the Honors Program each year, and other students may join the program through a faculty recommendation during their freshman or sophomore years. From first-year courses that are specially designed for each incoming class to the senior capstone project, the program offers coursework and extracurricular activities that are designed to challenge you, while also elevating your educational experience. Students successfully completing all elements of the Honors Program will be recognized at graduation and will have an Honors designation placed on their official academic transcripts. **Disability Services offered:** Note-taking services; Reader services; Tape recorders; Tutors. **Career services:** Alumni network; Alumni services; Career assessment; Career/job search classes; Internships; Regional alumni.

FACILITIES

Housing: Coed dorms; Men's dorms; Women's dorms 95% of campus accessible to physically disabled. **Special Academic Facilities/Equipment:** Northeast Florida Archeological Association, Crisp-Ellert Art Museum, Ponce Hall and Kenan building are on the National Register of Historic Places. **Campus Network:** 100% of classrooms, 100% of dorms, 100% of student union, 100% of libraries, 100% of dining areas, 50% of common outdoor areas, have wireless network access.

CAMPUS LIFE

Environment: Village. **Activities:** Campus Ministries; Choral groups; Dance; Drama/theater; International Student Organization; Literary magazine; Model UN; Musical theater; Radio station; Student government; Student newspaper; Student-run film society. 49 registered organizations, 13 honor societies, 7 religious organizations, on campus. **Athletics (Intercollegiate):** *Men:* baseball, basketball, cross-country, golf, soccer, tennis. *Women:* basketball, cross-country, golf, soccer, softball, tennis, volleyball. **On-Campus Highlights:** Ringhaver Student Center. **Environmental Initiatives:** Chiller upgrades.

ADMISSIONS

Freshman Academic Profile: Average high school GPA 3.5. **Test scores:** SAT Math middle 50% range 500–580. SAT EBRW middle 50% range 530–630. ACT middle 50% range 21–26. **Basis for Candidate Selection:** *Very important factors include:* academic GPA, standardized test scores. *Important factors include:* rigor of secondary school record, application essay, recommendation(s), first generation, geographical residence. *Other factors include:* extracurricular activities, character/personal qualities, alumni/ae relation, volunteer work, work experience, level of applicant's interest. **Freshman Admission Requirements:** High school diploma is required and GED is accepted. *Academic units recommended:* 4 English, 4 math, 3 science, 1 science labs, 2 foreign language, 1 social studies, 3 history. **Freshman Admission Statistics:** 4,569 applied, 65% admitted, 22% enrolled. **Transfer Admission Requirements:** college transcript(s), essay or personal statement, Minimum college GPA of 2.0 required. Lowest grade transferable C. **General Admission Information:** Application fee $50. Regular application deadline 3/1. Non-fall registration accepted. Admission may be deferred for a maximum of 1 year.

COSTS AND FINANCIAL AID

Annual tuition $19,940. Room and board $12,540. Required fees $100. Average book and supplies expense $1,100. **Required Forms and Deadlines:** FAFSA; State aid form. **Notification of Awards:** Applicants will be notified of awards on a rolling basis beginning 11/1. **Types of Aid:** *Need-based scholarships/grants:* College/university scholarship or grant aid from institutional funds; Federal Pell; Private scholarships; SEOG; State scholarships/grants. *Loans:* Direct PLUS loans; Direct Subsidized Stafford Loans; Direct Unsubsidized Stafford Loans. **Student Employment:** Federal Work-Study Program available. Institutional employment available. **Financial Aid Statistics:** 98% needy freshmen, 97% needy undergrads receive need-based scholarship or grant aid. 8% freshmen, 8% undergrads receive non-need-based scholarship or grant aid. 76% freshmen, 76% undergrads receive need-based self-help aid. 3% freshmen, 4% undergrads receive athletic scholarships. 94% freshmen, 91% undergrads receive any aid. 67% undergrads borrow to pay for school. Average cumulative indebtedness $29,837. **Criteria awarding aid:** *Need-based:* Academics, Art, Athletics, Job skills, Leadership, Minority status, Music/drama. *Non-Need-based:* Academics, Art, Athletics, Job skills, Leadership, Minority status, Music/drama, Religious affiliation, State/district residency.

FLORIDA A&M UNIVERSITY

Room 204, Tallahassee, FL 32307-3200
Phone: 850-599-3796 **Financial Aid Phone:** 850-599-3730
E-mail: ugrdadmissions@famu.edu **CEEB Code:** 5215
Fax: 850-599-3069 **Website:** www.famu.edu **ACT Code:** 0726

This public school was founded in 1887. It has a 419 acre campus.

RATINGS

Admissions Selectivity Rating: 91   **Fire Safety Rating:** 99   **Green Rating:** 60*

STUDENTS AND FACULTY

Enrollment: 7,365. **Student Body:** 65% female, 35% male, 13% out-of-state, 1% international (43 countries represented). Asian 1%, African American 90%, Caucasian 3%, Hispanic 2%, Native American <1%, Pacific Islander <1%, Two or more races 3%, Race unknown 0%. **Retention and Graduation:** 83% freshmen return for sophomore year. 27% grads go on to further study within 1 year. 14% grads pursue arts and sciences degrees. <1% grads pursue law degrees. 3% grads pursue business degrees. 2% grads pursue medical degrees. **Faculty:** Student/faculty ratio 15:1. 544 full-time faculty, 74% hold PhDs, 81% are members of minority groups, 46% are women. 0% of classes are taught by teaching assistants.

ACADEMICS

Degrees: Associate; Bachelor's; Doctoral degree—professional practice; Doctoral degree research/scholarship; Master's; Post-master's certificate. **Classes:** Most classes have 20–29 students. Most lab/discussion sessions have 20–29 students. **Most popular majors:** Criminal Justice/Safety Studies; Biology/Biological Sciences, General; Business Administration and Management, General. **Special Study Options:** Accelerated program; Cooperative education program; Cross-registration; Distance learning; Double major; Dual enrollment; Honors program; Independent study; Internships; Study abroad; Teacher certification program; Weekend college. **Honors programs:** Honors Program Mission The mission of the Florida Agricultural and Mechanical University Honors Program is to provide a series of challenging courses and academic enhancement experiences for undergraduate students who excel. Enhancement of academic performance should lead to consummate intellectual engagement and strong research orientation as a launch to both graduate and professional schools, as well as career paths. The program stresses four major areas of concentration: academic achievement, development of leadership potential, community service and cultural enrichment. Honors Program Objectives 1. To create an environment where academically talented students can develop and thrive. 2. To provide mentoring, nurturing and academic support to assist students in achieving their full potential. 3. To promote students' interest in international education. 4. To provide opportunities for internships and service learning involvement. **Disability Services offered:** Note-taking services; Reader services; Tape recorders; Tutors. **Career services:** Alumni network; Alumni services; Career assessment; Career/job search classes; Internships; Regional alumni.

FACILITIES

Housing: Apartments for married students; Apartments for single students; Coed dorms; Men's dorms; Special housing for disabled students; Theme housing; Women's dorms 90% of campus accessible to physically disabled. **Special Academic Facilities/Equipment:** Black Archives and Resource Ctr. Coleman Memorial Library Foster Tanner Music/Art Bldg.

CAMPUS LIFE

Environment: City. **Activities:** Campus Ministries; Choral groups; Concert band; Dance; Drama/theater; International Student Organization; Jazz band; Literary magazine; Marching band; Music ensembles; Musical theater; Pep band; Radio station; Student government; Student newspaper; Symphony orchestra; Television station; Yearbook. 169 registered organizations, 9 honor societies, 5 religious organizations, 5 fraternities, 3 sororities, on campus. **Athletics (Intercollegiate):** *Men:* baseball, basketball, cheerleading, cross-country, football, golf, swimming, tennis, track/field (outdoor), track/field (indoor). *Women:* basketball, bowling, cheerleading, cross-country, golf, softball, swimming, tennis, track/field (outdoor), track/field (indoor), volleyball. **On-Campus Highlights:** The Black Archives. **Environmental Initiatives:** Establishment of an advisory body—the Environment & Sustainability Council to design and oversee the implementation of a sustainability strategic plan which informs and guides the various operatives on campus of the principles of sustainability as they apply specifically to the respective facets of the University—Administrative, Academic, Operations and Community.

ADMISSIONS

Freshman Academic Profile: Average high school GPA 3.5. 16% in top 10% of high school class, 48% in top 25% of high school class, 85% in top 50% of high school class. 87% from public high schools. **Test scores:** SAT Math middle 50% range 440–530. SAT EBRW middle 50% range 460–550. ACT middle 50% range 19–24. **Basis for Candidate Selection:** *Very important factors include:* rigor of secondary school record, academic GPA, application essay, standardized test scores, recommendation(s), first generation. *Important factors include:* extracurricular activities, talent/ability, character/personal qualities, state residency. *Other factors include:* alumni/ae relation, volunteer work, work experience. **Freshman Admission Requirements:** High school diploma is required and GED is accepted. *Academic units required:* 4 English, 4 math, 3 science, 2 science labs, 2 foreign language, 3 social studies, 2 academic electives. **Freshman Admission Statistics:** 6,988 applied, 31% admitted, 50% enrolled. **Transfer Admission Requirements:** college transcript(s), Minimum college GPA of 2.0 required. Lowest grade transferable C. **General Admission Information:** Application fee $30. Regular application deadline 5/15. Non-fall registration accepted.

COSTS AND FINANCIAL AID

Annual in-state tuition $5,645. Annual out-of-state tuition $17,585. Room and board $10,058. Required fees $140. Average book and supplies expense $1,138. **Required Forms and Deadlines:** FAFSA. **Notification of Awards:** Applicants will be notified of awards on a rolling basis beginning 4/15. **Types of Aid:** *Need-based scholarships/grants:* College/university scholarship or grant aid from institutional funds; Federal Pell; Private scholarships; SEOG; State scholarships/grants; United Negro College Fund. *Loans:* Direct PLUS loans; Direct Subsidized Stafford Loans; Direct Unsubsidized Stafford Loans. **Student Employment:** Federal Work-Study Program available. Institutional employment available. **Financial Aid Statistics:** 88% needy freshmen, 86% needy undergrads receive need-based scholarship or grant aid. 50% freshmen, 39% undergrads receive non-need-based scholarship or grant aid. 75% freshmen, 75% undergrads receive need-based self-help aid. 3% freshmen, 3% undergrads receive athletic scholarships. 95.73% freshmen receive any aid. 86% undergrads borrow to pay for school. Average cumulative indebtedness $33,568. **Criteria awarding aid:** *Need-based:* Academics, Art, Leadership. *Non-Need-based:* Academics, Art, Athletics, Leadership, Music/drama.

FLORIDA ATLANTIC UNIVERSITY

777 Glades Road, Boca Raton, FL 33431-0991
Phone: 561-297-3040 **Financial Aid Phone:** 561-297-3530
E-mail: admissions@fau.edu **CEEB Code:** 5229
Fax: 561-297-2758 **Website:** www.fau.edu **ACT Code:** 729

This public school was founded in 1961. It has a 860 acre campus.

RATINGS

Admissions Selectivity Rating: 89   **Fire Safety Rating:** 98   **Green Rating:** 60*

STUDENTS AND FACULTY

Enrollment: 24,228. **Student Body:** 57% female, 43% male, 5% out-of-state, 2% international. Asian 4%, African American 20%, Caucasian 45%, Hispanic 25%, Native American <1%, Pacific Islander <1%, Two or more races 3%, Race unknown 1%.
Faculty: Student/faculty ratio 20:1. 730 full-time faculty, 87% hold PhDs, 26% are members of minority groups, 42% are women. 15% of classes are taught by teaching assistants.

ACADEMICS

Degrees: Associate; Bachelor's; Certificate; Doctoral degree—professional practice; Doctoral degree research/scholarship; Master's; Post-master's certificate; Transfer Associate. **Classes:** Most classes have 20–29 students. Most lab/discussion sessions have 20–29 students. **Most popular majors:** Education, General; Biology/Biological Sciences, General; Psychology, General. **Special Study Options:** Accelerated program; Cooperative education program; Cross-registration; Distance learning; Double major; Dual enrollment; English as a Second Language (ESL); Exchange student program (domestic); External degree program; Honors program; Independent study; Internships; Liberal arts/career combination; Student-designed major; Study abroad; Teacher certification program; Weekend college. **Honors programs:** The Harriet L. Wilkes Honors College of Florida Atlantic University, which opened in the Fall of 1999, is the first public honors institution to be built from the ground up in the United

States. The University Honors Program is available to those students who prefer to attend the Boca Raton campus. **Combined degree programs:** BA/MEng. **Disability Services offered:** Note-taking services; Reader services; Tape recorders; Tutors. **Career services:** Alumni network; Alumni services; Career assessment; Career/job search classes; Internships; Regional alumni.

FACILITIES

Housing: Apartments for single students; Coed dorms; Theme housing 100% of campus accessible to physically disabled. **Special Academic Facilities/Equipment:** Art gallery, on-campus elementary school, robotics lab, marine research facilities. **Campus Network:** 100% of classrooms, 100% of dorms, 100% of student union, 100% of libraries, 100% of dining areas, 100% of common outdoor areas, have wireless network access.

CAMPUS LIFE

Environment: City. **Activities:** Campus Ministries; Choral groups; Concert band; Dance; Drama/theater; International Student Organization; Jazz band; Literary magazine; Marching band; Model UN; Music ensembles; Musical theater; Opera; Pep band; Radio station; Student government; Student newspaper; Student-run film society; Symphony orchestra; Television station. 300 registered organizations, 11 honor societies, 6 religious organizations, 16 fraternities, 12 sororities, on campus. **Athletics (Intercollegiate):** *Men:* baseball, basketball, cheerleading, cross-country, diving, football, golf, soccer, swimming, tennis. *Women:* basketball, cheerleading, cross-country, diving, golf, soccer, softball, swimming, tennis, track/field (outdoor), volleyball. **On-Campus Highlights:** Student Services Building. **Environmental Initiatives:** All new construction is designed and built to a minimum LEED silver certification level. This has been surpassed on every project to date, FAU currently has 1 platinum, 5 gold, and 2 pending gold certified buildings.

ADMISSIONS

Freshman Academic Profile: Average high school GPA 3.5. 11% in top 10% of high school class, 35% in top 25% of high school class, 78% in top 50% of high school class. **Test scores:** SAT Math middle 50% range 490–580. SAT EBRW middle 50% range 480–570. ACT middle 50% range 21–25. **Basis for Candidate Selection:** *Very important factors include:* academic GPA, standardized test scores. *Important factors include:* rigor of secondary school record, class rank. *Other factors include:* application essay, recommendation(s), extracurricular activities, talent/ability, character/personal qualities, first generation, alumni/ae relation, volunteer work, level of applicant's interest. **Freshman Admission Requirements:** High school diploma is required and GED is accepted. *Academic units required:* 4 English, 4 math, 3 science, 2 science labs, 2 foreign language, 3 social studies, 3 academic electives. *Academic units recommended:* 4 English, 4 math, 3 science, 2 science labs, 2 foreign language, 3 social studies, 3 academic electives. **Freshman Admission Statistics:** 27,888 applied, 39% admitted, 30% enrolled. **Transfer Admission Requirements:** college transcript(s), Minimum college GPA of 3.0 required. Lowest grade transferable D-. **General Admission Information:** Application fee $30. Priority deadline 2/15. Regular application deadline 5/1. Non-fall registration accepted. Admission may be deferred for a maximum of 3 semesters.

COSTS AND FINANCIAL AID

Annual in-state tuition $5,986. Annual out-of-state tuition $21,543. Room and board $11,353. Average book and supplies expense $1,203. **Required Forms and Deadlines:** FAFSA. **Notification of Awards:** Applicants will be notified of awards on a rolling basis beginning 5/1. **Types of Aid:** *Need-based scholarships/grants:* College/university scholarship or grant aid from institutional funds; Federal Nursing Scholarships; Federal Pell; Private scholarships; SEOG; State scholarships/grants. **Student Employment:** Federal Work-Study Program available. Institutional employment available. **Financial Aid Statistics:** 91% needy freshmen, 86% needy undergrads receive need-based scholarship or grant aid. 7% freshmen, 4% undergrads receive non-need-based scholarship or grant aid. 71% freshmen, 73% undergrads receive need-based self-help aid. 1% freshmen, 1% undergrads receive athletic scholarships. **Criteria awarding aid:** *Need-based:* Academics. *Non-Need-based:* Academics, Athletics, Music/drama, State/district residency.

FLORIDA COLLEGE

Admissions Office, Temple Terrace, FL 33617-5578
Phone: 813-988-5131 **Financial Aid Phone:** (813) 988-5131
E-mail: Admissions@FloridaCollege.edu **CEEB Code:** 1562
Fax: 813-899-6722 **Website:** www.floridacollege.edu **ACT Code:** 1482

This private school was founded in 1946.

RATINGS
Admissions Selectivity Rating: 83   **Fire Safety Rating:** 97   **Green Rating:** 60*

STUDENTS AND FACULTY
Enrollment: 533. **Student Body:** 51% female, 49% male, 63% out-of-state, 4% international (9 countries represented). Asian <1%, African American 6%, Caucasian 77%, Hispanic 7%, Native American 1%, Pacific Islander 0%, Two or more races 5%, Race unknown 1%.
Faculty: Student/faculty ratio 13:1. 34 full-time faculty, 44% hold PhDs, 9% are members of minority groups, 21% are women. 0% of classes are taught by teaching assistants.

ACADEMICS
Degrees: Associate; Bachelor's; Transfer Associate. **Classes:** Most classes have fewer than 10 students. Most lab/discussion sessions have fewer than 10 students. **Most popular majors:** Business Administration and Management, General; Liberal Arts and Sciences/Liberal Studies; Elementary Education and Teaching. **Special Study Options:** Cross-registration; Distance learning; Double major; Independent study; Teacher certification program. **Disability Services offered:** Tape recorders; Tutors.

FACILITIES
Housing: Men's dorms; Special housing for disabled students; Women's dorms.

CAMPUS LIFE
Environment: Town. **Activities:** Choral groups; Concert band; Drama/theater; Jazz band; Music ensembles; Musical theater; Pep band; Student government; Yearbook. 2 honor societies, 2 religious organizations, on campus. **Athletics (Intercollegiate):** *Men:* basketball, cross-country, soccer. *Women:* cheerleading, cross-country, soccer, volleyball. **On-Campus Highlights:** Riverwalk.

ADMISSIONS
Test scores: SAT Math middle 50% range 460–580. SAT EBRW middle 50% range 460–630. ACT middle 50% range 20–26. **Basis for Candidate Selection:** *Very important factors include:* academic GPA, standardized test scores, recommendation(s), character/personal qualities, religious affiliation/commitment. *Important factors include:* rigor of secondary school record, class rank. **Freshman Admission Requirements:** High school diploma is required and GED is accepted. *Academic units required:* 4 English, 3 math, 2 science, 2 science labs, 2 social studies. *Academic units recommended:* 2 foreign language, 3 social studies. **Freshman Admission Statistics:** 284 applied, 79% admitted, 71% enrolled. **Transfer Admission Requirements:** High school transcript, college transcript(s), standardized test scores, statement of good standing from prior institution(s). Minimum college GPA of 2.0 required. Lowest grade transferable C. **General Admission Information:** Application fee $40. Regular application deadline 8/25. Non-fall registration accepted.

COSTS AND FINANCIAL AID
Annual tuition $15,670. Room and board $8,230. Required fees $880. Average book and supplies expense $1,300. **Required Forms and Deadlines:** FAFSA; State aid form. **Notification of Awards:** Applicants will be notified of awards on a rolling basis beginning 11/1. **Types of Aid:** *Need-based scholarships/grants:* College/university scholarship or grant aid from institutional funds; Federal Pell; Private scholarships; SEOG; State scholarships/grants. **Financial Aid Statistics:** 85% needy freshmen, 86% needy undergrads receive need-based scholarship or grant aid. 94% freshmen, 92% undergrads receive non-need-based scholarship or grant aid. 76% freshmen, 77% undergrads receive need-based self-help aid. 3% freshmen, 13% undergrads receive athletic scholarships. **Criteria awarding aid:** *Need-based:* Academics, Athletics, Music/drama. *Non-Need-based:* Academics, Athletics, Music/drama, State/district residency.

FLORIDA GULF COAST UNIVERSITY

10501 FGCU Blvd. South, Fort Myers, FL 33965-6565
Phone: 239-590-7878 **Financial Aid Phone:** 239-590-7920
E-mail: admissions@fgcu.edu **CEEB Code:** 5221
Fax: 239-590-7894 **ACT Code:** 733

This public school was founded in 1991. It has a 760 acre campus.

RATINGS
Admissions Selectivity Rating: 85   **Fire Safety Rating:** 95   **Green Rating:** 96

STUDENTS AND FACULTY
Enrollment: 13,648. **Student Body:** 56% female, 44% male, 8% out-of-state, 2% international (89 countries represented). Asian 2%, African American 7%, Caucasian 63%, Hispanic 21%, Native American <1%, Pacific Islander <1%, Two or more races 3%, Race unknown 1%.
Retention and Graduation: 78% freshmen return for sophomore year. 22% freshmen graduate within 4 years. 48% freshmen graduate within 6 years.
Faculty: Student/faculty ratio 22:1. 477 full-time faculty, 72% hold PhDs, 20% are members of minority groups, 46% are women. 0% of classes are taught by teaching assistants.

ACADEMICS
Degrees: Associate; Bachelor's; Certificate; Doctoral degree—professional practice; Doctoral degree research/scholarship; Master's; Transfer Associate. **Classes:** Most classes have fewer than 10 students. **Most popular majors:** Business/Commerce, General; Liberal Arts and Sciences/Liberal Studies; Elementary Education and Teaching. **Special Study Options:** Accelerated program; Cross-registration; Distance learning; Double major; Dual enrollment; Honors program; Independent study; Internships; Study abroad; Teacher certification program. **Honors programs:** The University Honors Program at Florida Gulf Coast University offers special opportunities for superior students to pursue academic work that challenges their interests and abilities. The program is university-wide, which gives students full access to the faculty and the entire range of programs at FGCU. Since the honors program at Florida Gulf Coast University is exclusive, we have the ability to design a unique program for each individual student. Scholarship opportunities and special programs that support the honors student's educational, intellectual, and personal goals will be designed individually with the student and his or her faculty mentor. **Disability Services offered:** Note-taking services; Reader services; Tape recorders; Tutors. **Career services:** Alumni network; Alumni services; Career assessment; Career/job search classes; Internships.

FACILITIES
Housing: Apartments for single students; Coed dorms; Theme housing 100% of campus accessible to physically disabled. **Special Academic Facilities/Equipment:** Art Gallery, Observatory. **Campus Network:** 75% of classrooms, 100% of dorms, 100% of student union, 100% of libraries, 100% of dining areas, 50% of common outdoor areas, have wireless network access.

CAMPUS LIFE
Environment: City. **Activities:** Campus Ministries; Choral groups; Dance; Drama/theater; International Student Organization; Literary magazine; Model UN; Radio station; Student government; Student newspaper. 105 registered organizations, 7 honor societies, 8 religious organizations, 4 fraternities, 4 sororities, on campus. **Athletics (Intercollegiate):** *Men:* baseball, basketball, cross-country, golf, soccer, tennis. *Women:* basketball, cross-country, diving, golf, soccer, softball, swimming, tennis, volleyball. **On-Campus Highlights:** Alico Arena.

ADMISSIONS
Freshman Academic Profile: Average high school GPA 3.9. 14% in top 10% of high school class, 39% in top 25% of high school class, 74% in top 50% of high school class. **Test scores:** SAT Math middle 50% range 520–590. SAT EBRW middle 50% range 540–620. ACT middle 50% range 21–25. **Basis for Candidate Selection:** *Very important factors include:* rigor of secondary school record, academic GPA, standardized test scores. *Important factors include:* class rank, level of applicant's interest. *Other factors include:* extracurricular activities, talent/ability, volunteer work. **Freshman Admission Requirements:** High school diploma is required and GED is accepted. *Academic units required:* 4 English, 4 math, 3 science, 2 science labs, 2 foreign language, 3 social studies, 2 academic electives. *Academic units recommended:* 4 English, 4 math, 3 science, 2 science labs, 2 foreign language, 3 social studies, 1 history, 2 academic

electives. **Freshman Admission Statistics:** 14,702 applied, 65% admitted, 30% enrolled. **Transfer Admission Requirements:** college transcript(s), Minimum college GPA of 2.0 required. Lowest grade transferable D. **General Admission Information:** Application fee $30. Priority deadline 2/15. Regular application deadline 7/1. Non-fall registration accepted. Admission may be deferred for a maximum of 2 semesters.

COSTS AND FINANCIAL AID

Annual in-state tuition $4,191. Required fees $1,979. Average book and supplies expense $1,200. **Required Forms and Deadlines:** FAFSA; Institution's own financial aid form; State aid form. **Types of Aid:** *Need-based scholarships/grants:* College/university scholarship or grant aid from institutional funds; Federal Pell; Private scholarships; SEOG; State scholarships/grants. *Loans:* Direct PLUS loans; Direct Subsidized Stafford Loans; Direct Unsubsidized Stafford Loans. **Financial Aid Statistics:** 66% needy freshmen, 72% needy undergrads receive need-based scholarship or grant aid. 45% freshmen, 31% undergrads receive non-need-based scholarship or grant aid. 57% freshmen, 63% undergrads receive need-based self-help aid. 1% freshmen, 1% undergrads receive athletic scholarships. 88% freshmen, 35% undergrads receive any aid. 50% undergrads borrow to pay for school. Average cumulative indebtedness $26,488. **Criteria awarding aid:** *Need-based:* Academics, Athletics, Leadership, Minority status, Religious affiliation. *Non-Need-based:* Academics, Alumni affiliation, Athletics, Leadership, Minority status, Music/drama, Religious affiliation, State/district residency.

FLORIDA INSTITUTE OF TECHNOLOGY

150 West University Boulevard, Melbourne, FL 32901-6975
Phone: 321-674-8030 **Financial Aid Phone:** 800-666-4348
E-mail: admission@fit.edu **CEEB Code:** 5080
Fax: 321-674-8004 **Website:** www.fit.edu **ACT Code:** 716

This private school was founded in 1958. It has a 130 acre campus.

RATINGS

Admissions Selectivity Rating: 84   **Fire Safety Rating:** 93   **Green Rating:** 83

STUDENTS AND FACULTY

Enrollment: 3,293. **Student Body:** 29% female, 71% male, 46% out-of-state, 24% international (102 countries represented). Asian 2%, African American 6%, Caucasian 52%, Hispanic 10%, Native American <1%, Pacific Islander <1%, Two or more races 3%, Race unknown 2%.
Retention and Graduation: 79% freshmen return for sophomore year. 44% freshmen graduate within 4 years. 59% freshmen graduate within 6 years. 31% grads go on to further study within 1 year. 10% grads pursue arts and sciences degrees. 0% grads pursue law degrees. 5% grads pursue business degrees. 1% grads pursue medical degrees. **Faculty:** Student/faculty ratio 14:1. 292 full-time faculty, 91% hold PhDs, 25% are members of minority groups, 26% are women. 0% of classes are taught by teaching assistants.

ACADEMICS

Degrees: Associate; Bachelor's; Certificate; Doctoral degree—other; Doctoral degree—professional practice; Doctoral degree research/scholarship; Master's; Post-master's certificate. **Classes:** Most classes have 20–29 students. Most lab/discussion sessions have 10–19 students. **Most popular majors:** Computer Science; Aerospace, Aeronautical, and Astronautical/Space Engineering, General; Mechanical Engineering. **Special Study Options:** Accelerated program; Cooperative education program; Cross-registration; Distance learning; Double major; Dual enrollment; English as a Second Language (ESL); Honors program; Independent study; Internships; Student-designed major; Study abroad; Teacher certification program. **Honors programs:** Florida Tech's Honors College recognizes the talents and initiative of high-performing students in the College of Aeronautics, Nathan M. Bisk College of Business, College of Engineering and Science, and College of Psychology and Liberal Arts. Students in the Honors College have the opportunity to enroll in interdisciplinary seminars, advance study in their disciplines, work with faculty members on independent research projects, and participate in social and cultural activities that foster a global mindset, civic engagement, and professional and personal development. Honors College students take an interdisciplinary Honors Seminar and a range of Honors courses that satisfy the General Education Core and program requirements. Honors courses are often smaller sections to facilitate a discussion-based format and encourage in-depth explorations of topics. Students are able to work with faculty members offering Honors options to non-Honors courses, expanding their skills in directed

research, and on independent research projects. Beyond the classroom, Honors College students are part of a community of scholars with shared and diverse interests. Programmatic activities are a cornerstone of the Honors experience at Florida Tech, guiding the development of Honors students and the Honors College. Students will have the opportunity to expand their studies through lectures, panel discussions and colloquia with faculty members, alumni and guest speakers. Mentorship and leadership opportunities promote personal and professional development in addition to extra-curricular activities that also inspire students to become involved within local and global communities. The Honors experience at Florida Tech provides a range of opportunities that can be customized to suit students across majors. **Disability Services offered:** Note-taking services; Reader services; Tape recorders; Tutors. **Career services:** Alumni services; Career/job search classes; Internships; Regional alumni.

FACILITIES

Housing: Apartments for single students; Coed dorms; Fraternity/sorority housing; Theme housing 99% of campus accessible to physically disabled. **Special Academic Facilities/Equipment:** While hands-on learning is at the heart of all things Florida Tech, the Panther experience is about more than education. Outside of the classroom, students can choose from more than 100 clubs and organizations—academic, athletic, philanthropic, cultural, social and more. Athletics are also a big part of Panther life, whether by playing on one of our 20 men's and women's varsity sports teams, participating in club sports, or cheering from the stands. Students can embrace the arts at various museums like the Ruth Funk Center for Textile Arts and the Foosaner Art Museum or at the Gleason Performing Arts Center, and in just a short drive from campus, they can check out Melbourne's beautiful beaches and bustling downtown area.

CAMPUS LIFE

Environment: City. **Activities:** Campus Ministries; Choral groups; Concert band; Dance; Drama/theater; International Student Organization; Jazz band; Literary magazine; Music ensembles; Musical theater; Pep band; Radio station; Student government; Student newspaper; Student-run film society; Television station. 134 registered organizations, 9 honor societies, 4 religious organizations, 9 fraternities, 3 sororities, on campus. **Athletics (Intercollegiate):** *Men:* baseball, basketball, cross-country, golf, soccer, tennis. *Women:* basketball, crew/rowing, cross-country, golf, soccer, softball, tennis, volleyball. **On-Campus Highlights:** Clemente Center for Sports & Recreation **Environmental Initiatives:** Year 10 of Sustainability Academics and Student Breakthroughs for Local Cities: Fall 2019 was the beginning of the tenth year of the Florida Tech Sustainability program with 150 graduates of the Bachelor of Science degree or the Sustainability Minor. Student sustainability research projects this year included 4 students funded by local cities or NGOs on research projects that are bringing SUS actions to 3 new City Sustainability Boards, including the building of first ever City Sustainability Plans in coastal east Florida.

ADMISSIONS

Freshman Academic Profile: Average high school GPA 3.7. 26% in top 10% of high school class, 58% in top 25% of high school class, 85% in top 50% of high school class. **Test scores:** SAT Math middle 50% range 580–690. SAT EBRW middle 50% range 570–670. ACT middle 50% range 24–30. **Basis for Candidate Selection:** *Very important factors include:* rigor of secondary school record, academic GPA, standardized test scores. *Other factors include:* class rank, application essay, recommendation(s), interview, extracurricular activities, character/personal qualities, alumni/ae relation, work experience. **Freshman Admission Requirements:** High school diploma is required and GED is accepted. *Academic units required:* 4 English, 3 math, 3 science, 3 science labs, 2 social studies, 2 history, 2 academic electives. *Academic units recommended:* 4 English, 4 math, 4 science, 3 science labs, 2 foreign language, 2 social studies, 2 history, 2 academic electives, 2 computer science. **Freshman Admission Statistics:** 9,743 applied, 66% admitted, 10% enrolled. **Transfer Admission Requirements:** college transcript(s), Minimum college GPA of 2.5 required. Lowest grade transferable C. **General Admission Information:** Non-fall registration accepted. Admission may be deferred for a maximum of 1 year.

COSTS AND FINANCIAL AID

Annual tuition $41,100. Room and board $12,880. Required fees $750. Average book and supplies expense $1,200. **Required Forms and Deadlines:** FAFSA; State aid form. **Notification of Awards:** Applicants will be notified of awards on a rolling basis beginning 12/15. **Types of Aid:** *Need-based scholarships/grants:* College/university scholarship or grant aid from institutional funds; Federal Pell; Private scholarships; SEOG; State scholarships/grants. *Loans:* Direct PLUS loans; Direct Subsidized Stafford Loans; Direct Unsubsidized Stafford Loans. **Student Employment:** Federal Work-Study Program available. Institutional employment available. **Financial Aid Statistics:** 100% needy freshmen, 99% needy undergrads receive need-based scholarship or grant aid. 98% freshmen, 92% undergrads receive non-need-based scholarship or grant aid. 64% freshmen, 64% undergrads receive need-based self-help aid. 2% freshmen, 4% undergrads receive athletic scholarships. 88% freshmen, 90% undergrads receive any aid. 50% undergrads borrow to pay for school. Average cumulative indebtedness $38,943. **Criteria awarding aid:** *Need-based:* Academics, Minority status. *Non-Need-based:* Academics, Alumni affiliation, Athletics, Music/drama, State/district residency.

FLORIDA INTERNATIONAL UNIVERSITY

Modesto Maidique Campus, Miami, FL 33199
Phone: 305-348-2363 **Financial Aid Phone:** 305-348-7272
E-mail: admiss@fiu.edu **CEEB Code:** 5206
Fax: 305-348-3648 **Website:** www.fiu.edu **ACT Code:** 776

This public school was founded in 1965. It has a 576 acre campus.

RATINGS
Admissions Selectivity Rating: 88   **Fire Safety Rating:** 95   **Green Rating:** 92

STUDENTS AND FACULTY
Enrollment: 41,865. **Student Body:** 56% female, 44% male, 4% out-of-state, 7% international (168 countries represented). Asian 2%, African American 12%, Caucasian 9%, Hispanic 67%, Native American <1%, Pacific Islander <1%, Two or more races 2%, Race unknown <1%.
Retention and Graduation: 89% freshmen return for sophomore year. 33% freshmen graduate within 4 years. 61% freshmen graduate within 6 years.
Faculty: Student/faculty ratio 25:1. 1,275 full-time faculty, 84% hold PhDs, 41% are members of minority groups, 43% are women.

ACADEMICS
Degrees: Associate; Bachelor's; Doctoral degree—professional practice; Doctoral degree research/scholarship; Master's; Post-bachelor's certificate. **Classes:** Most classes have 20–29 students. Most lab/discussion sessions have 20–29 students. **Most popular majors:** Biology/Biological Sciences, General; Business Administration and Management, General; Psychology, General. **Special Study Options:** Accelerated program; Cooperative education program; Distance learning; Double major; Dual enrollment; Exchange student program (domestic); Honors program; Independent study; Internships; Study abroad; Teacher certification program; Weekend college. **Honors programs:** Please visit the honors college website at http://honors.fiu.edu/. **Combined degree programs:** BA/JD; BA/MA; BA/MEng. **Disability Services offered:** Note-taking services; Reader services; Tape recorders; Tutors. **Career services:** Alumni services; Career assessment; Career/job search classes; Internships; Regional alumni.

FACILITIES
Housing: Apartments for married students; Apartments for single students; Coed dorms; Fraternity/sorority housing 100% of campus accessible to physically disabled. **Special Academic Facilities/Equipment:** The Frost Art Museum, The Wolfsonian Art Museum, Natural Preserve, Biscayne Bay Preserve.

CAMPUS LIFE
Environment: Metropolis. **Activities:** Campus Ministries; Choral groups; Drama/theater; International Student Organization; Jazz band; Marching band; Model UN; Music ensembles; Opera; Radio station; Student government; Student newspaper; Symphony orchestra; Yearbook. 374 registered organizations, 15 honor societies, 7 religious organizations, 29 fraternities, 15 sororities, on campus. **Athletics (Intercollegiate):** *Men:* baseball, basketball, cross-country, football, soccer, track/field (outdoor), track/field (indoor). *Women:* basketball, cross-country, diving, golf, soccer, softball, swimming, tennis, track/field (outdoor), track/field (indoor), volleyball. **On-Campus Highlights:** The Frost Museum. **Environmental Initiatives:** FIU has been a smoking-free campus since 2011, which helps to provide clean and smoke-free air to the community.

ADMISSIONS
Freshman Academic Profile: Average high school GPA 4.0. 35% in top 10% of high school class, 63% in top 25% of high school class, 91% in top 50% of high school class. **Test scores:** SAT Math middle 50% range 540–630. SAT EBRW middle 50% range 570–650. ACT middle 50% range 23–28. **Basis for Candidate Selection:** *Very important factors include:* rigor of secondary school record, class rank, academic GPA, standardized test scores. *Other factors include:* application essay, recommendation(s), extracurricular activities, talent/ability,

character/personal qualities, first generation, alumni/ae relation, geographical residence, state residency, volunteer work, work experience, level of applicant's interest. **Freshman Admission Requirements:** High school diploma is required and GED is accepted. *Academic units required:* 4 English, 4 math, 3 science, 2 science labs, 2 foreign language, 3 social studies, 2 academic electives. **Freshman Admission Statistics:** 18,492 applied, 58% admitted, 38% enrolled. **Transfer Admission Requirements:** college transcript(s), statement of good standing from prior institution(s). Minimum college GPA of 2.0 required. Lowest grade transferable D. **General Admission Information:** Application fee $30. Regular application deadline 5/1. Non-fall registration accepted. Admission may be deferred for a maximum of 1 year.

COSTS AND FINANCIAL AID
Annual in-state tuition $6,168. Annual out-of-state tuition $18,566. Room and board $11,136. Required fees $398. Average book and supplies expense $1,350. **Required Forms and Deadlines:** FAFSA. **Notification of Awards:** Applicants will be notified of awards on a rolling basis beginning 2/1. **Types of Aid:** *Need-based scholarships/grants:* College/university scholarship or grant aid from institutional funds; Federal Pell; Private scholarships; SEOG; State scholarships/grants. *Loans:* Direct PLUS loans; Direct Subsidized Stafford Loans; Direct Unsubsidized Stafford Loans. **Student Employment:** Federal Work-Study Program available. Institutional employment available. **Financial Aid Statistics:** 67% needy freshmen, 83% needy undergrads receive need-based scholarship or grant aid. 72% freshmen, 35% undergrads receive non-need-based scholarship or grant aid. 20% freshmen, 39% undergrads receive need-based self-help aid. 2% freshmen, 1% undergrads receive athletic scholarships. 87% freshmen, 63% undergrads receive any aid. 45% undergrads borrow to pay for school. Average cumulative indebtedness $19,705. **Criteria awarding aid:** *Need-based:* Academics. *Non-Need-based:* Academics, Art, Athletics, Minority status, Music/drama, State/district residency.

FLORIDA SOUTHERN COLLEGE

Best Colleges

111 Lake Hollingworth Drive, Lakeland, FL 33801
Phone: 863-680-4131 **Financial Aid Phone:** 863-680-4140
E-mail: fscadm@flsouthern.edu **CEEB Code:** 5218
Fax: 863-680-4120 **Website:** www.flsouthern.edu **ACT Code:** 732

This private school, affiliated with the Methodist Church, was founded in 1883. It has a 113 acre campus.

RATINGS
Admissions Selectivity Rating: 83   **Fire Safety Rating:** 90   **Green Rating:** 65

STUDENTS AND FACULTY
Enrollment: 2,665. **Student Body:** 63% female, 37% male, 32% out-of-state, 3% international (37 countries represented). Asian 3%, African American 7%, Caucasian 71%, Hispanic 13%, Native American 1%, Pacific Islander <1%, Two or more races <1%, Race unknown 1%.
Retention and Graduation: 82% freshmen return for sophomore year. 57% freshmen graduate within 4 years. % freshmen graduate within 6 years. 16% grads go on to further study within 1 year. 4% grads pursue arts and sciences degrees. 1% grads pursue law degrees. 3% grads pursue business degrees. <1% grads pursue medical degrees. **Faculty:** Student/faculty ratio 14:1. 158 full-time faculty, 89% hold PhDs, 15% are members of minority groups, 49% are women. 0% of classes are taught by teaching assistants.

ACADEMICS
Degrees: Bachelor's; Doctoral degree—professional practice; Doctoral degree research/scholarship; Master's. **Classes:** Most classes have 10–19 students. Most lab/discussion sessions have 10–19 students. **Most popular majors:** Biology/Biological Sciences, General; Registered Nursing/Registered Nurse; Business Administration and Management, General. **Special Study Options:** Accelerated program; Distance learning; Double major; Dual enrollment; External degree program; Honors program; Independent study; Internships; Student-designed major; Study abroad; Teacher certification program. **Honors programs:** The Honors Program at Florida Southern College offers special academic options to students who seek independent and inter-disciplinary learning opportunities. Honors students enjoy collaborative courses with exceptional faculty, a series of "supper seminars" that host expert speakers, and specially designated facilities—including classrooms, the Honors Lounge, and special housing—that foster

an enriching living-learning environment. All honors students receive priority registration and are able to take course overloads without paying additional fees. Three-year and four-year undergraduate tracks are available. **Combined degree programs:** BA/MA; BA/MEng. **Career services:** Alumni network; Alumni services; Career assessment; Career/job search classes; Internships; Regional alumni.

FACILITIES

Housing: Apartments for single students; Coed dorms; Fraternity/sorority housing; Men's dorms; Special housing for disabled students; Theme housing; Women's dorms 85% of campus accessible to physically disabled. **Special Academic Facilities/Equipment:** The Rinker Technology Center; numerous computer labs across campus, and the popular TuTu's Cyber Cafe provide free computer access for all, in addition to the campus' free WiFi. The Christoverson Humanities Building features a film studies theater and modern language lab, and the Chatlos Communications Building offers a newly renovated television studio. The state-of-the-art, recently expanded Blanton Nursing Building houses high-tech classrooms and a clinical learning lab with a full complement of patient simulators and the latest patient information technology used in Florida hospitals. Science majors enjoy an on-site planetarium, world-class heritage rose garden, greenhouse, a citrus grove, ecological wetlands research station. The McKay Archives Center houses the College's original Frank Lloyd Wright drawings and documents, the Florida Citrus Hall of Fame, and the Center for Florida History. The Davis Performing Arts Center features the nationally renowned Branscomb Auditorium; the modern Buckner Theatre; the Melvin Art Gallery; and newly constructed facilities to house the Imperial Symphony Orchestra, a regional professional orchestra with which Florida Southern collaborates. This partnership gives FSC students the opportunity to perform with world-renowned ISO guest artists. Other special facilities for the arts include the Wynee Warden Dance Studio, opened in fall 2014, a professional-quality dance studio that features a soaring glass half-rotunda with amazing views of Lake Hollingsworth and plenty of sunshine to illuminate the rehearsal floor. For education majors, the campus is home to an on-site Preschool Learning Lab, the Roberts Center for Learning and Literacy and The Roberts Academy, a transitional school for gifted elementary-age students with dyslexia. Exciting news for business majors: the new, cutting-edge Bill '65 and Mary Ann Becker Business Building includes a simulated trading floor, high-tech classrooms, and a state-of-the-art market observation room. Finally, the new Sharp Family Tourism and Education Center celebrates the campus' architectural significance as the largest single-site collection of Frank Lloyd Wright architecture in the world, educating visitors through a film, museum, and tours. **Campus Network:** 100% of classrooms, 100% of dorms, 100% of student union, 100% of libraries, 100% of dining areas, 100% of common outdoor areas, have wireless network access.

CAMPUS LIFE

Environment: City. **Activities:** Campus Ministries; Choral groups; Concert band; Dance; Drama/theater; International Student Organization; Jazz band; Literary magazine; Model UN; Music ensembles; Musical theater; Opera; Pep band; Student government; Student newspaper; Symphony orchestra; Television station. 122 registered organizations, 13 honor societies, 8 religious organizations, 7 fraternities, 7 sororities, on campus. **Athletics (Intercollegiate):** *Men:* baseball, basketball, cross-country, golf, lacrosse, soccer, swimming, tennis, track/field (outdoor). *Women:* basketball, cross-country, golf, soccer, softball, swimming, tennis, track/field (outdoor), volleyball. **On-Campus Highlights:** TuTu's Cyber Cafe. **Environmental Initiatives:** Florida Southern College has installed filtered water bottle stations throughout campus that provide users with an opportunity to fill and refill reusable bottles rather than purchasing new filtered water bottles. Additionally, FSC's Student Government Association distributes refillable water bottles to each new class at Orientation, encouraging new students to make use of the stations and to be environmentally minded from the start.

ADMISSIONS

Freshman Academic Profile: Average high school GPA 3.7. 25% in top 10% of high school class, 58% in top 25% of high school class, 87% in top 50% of high school class. 75% from public high schools. **Test scores:** SAT Math middle 50% range 550–620. SAT EBRW middle 50% range 570–645. ACT middle 50% range 24–29. **Basis for Candidate Selection:** *Very important factors include:* rigor of secondary school record, academic GPA. *Important factors include:* application essay, standardized test scores, recommendation(s), extracurricular activities, talent/ability, character/personal qualities. *Other factors include:* class rank, interview, first generation, alumni/ae relation, religious affiliation/commitment, racial/ethnic status, volunteer work, work experience. **Freshman Admission Requirements:** High school diploma is required and GED is accepted. *Academic units required:* 4 English, 3 math, 2

science, 2 science labs, 3 social studies, 3 history, 1 academic electives. *Academic units recommended:* 4 English, 3 math, 2 science, 2 science labs, 2 foreign language, 3 social studies, 3 history, 1 academic electives. **Freshman Admission Statistics:** 5,914 applied, 71% admitted, 16% enrolled. **Transfer Admission Requirements:** college transcript(s), essay or personal statement, statement of good standing from prior institution(s). Minimum college GPA of 2.0 required. Lowest grade transferable C. **General Admission Information:** Priority deadline 3/1. Regular application deadline 5/1. Non-fall registration accepted. Admission may be deferred for a maximum of 1 year.

COSTS AND FINANCIAL AID

Annual tuition $36,860. Room and board $11,880. Required fees $780. Average book and supplies expense $1,250. **Required Forms and Deadlines:** FAFSA; Institution's own financial aid form. **Notification of Awards:** Applicants will be notified of awards on a rolling basis beginning 3/1. **Types of Aid:** *Need-based scholarships/grants:* College/university scholarship or grant aid from institutional funds; Federal Nursing Scholarships; Federal Pell; Private scholarships; SEOG; State scholarships/grants. *Loans:* Direct PLUS loans; Direct Subsidized Stafford Loans; Direct Unsubsidized Stafford Loans. **Student Employment:** Federal Work-Study Program available. Institutional employment available. **Financial Aid Statistics:** 100% needy freshmen, 99% needy undergrads receive need-based scholarship or grant aid. 68% freshmen, 72% undergrads receive non-need-based scholarship or grant aid. 1% freshmen, 6% undergrads receive need-based self-help aid. 3% freshmen, 6% undergrads receive athletic scholarships. 100% freshmen, 92.31% undergrads receive any aid. 89% undergrads borrow to pay for school. Average cumulative indebtedness $25,576. **Criteria awarding aid:** *Need-based:* Academics, Alumni affiliation, Art, Athletics, Job skills, Leadership, Minority status, Music/drama, Religious affiliation. *Non-Need-based:* Academics, Alumni affiliation, Art, Athletics, Job skills, Leadership, Minority status, Music/drama, Religious affiliation, State/district residency.

FLORIDA STATE UNIVERSITY

PO Box 3062400, Tallahassee, FL 32306-2400
Phone: 850-644-6200 **Financial Aid Phone:** 850-644-5716
E-mail: admissions@fsu.edu **CEEB Code:** 5219
Fax: 850-644-0197 **Website:** www.fsu.edu **ACT Code:** 734

This public school was founded in 1851. It has a 474.5 acre campus.

RATINGS

Admissions Selectivity Rating: 93   **Fire Safety Rating:** 90   **Green Rating:** 96

STUDENTS AND FACULTY

Enrollment: 32,649. **Student Body:** 57% female, 43% male, 11% out-of-state, 2% international (107 countries represented). Asian 3%, African American 9%, Caucasian 60%, Hispanic 22%, Native American <1%, Pacific Islander <1%, Two or more races 4%, Race unknown 1%.
Retention and Graduation: 93% freshmen return for sophomore year. 68% freshmen graduate within 4 years. 83% freshmen graduate within 6 years. 26% grads go on to further study within 1 year. 10% grads pursue arts and sciences degrees. 6% grads pursue law degrees. 8% grads pursue business degrees. 9% grads pursue medical degrees. **Faculty:** Student/faculty ratio 21:1. 1,601 full-time faculty, 95% hold PhDs, 23% are members of minority groups, 42% are women. 28% of classes are taught by teaching assistants.

ACADEMICS

Degrees: Associate; Bachelor's; Certificate; Doctoral degree—professional practice; Doctoral degree research/scholarship; Master's; Post-bachelor's certificate; Post-master's certificate; Transfer Associate. **Classes:** Most classes have 10–19 students. Most lab/discussion sessions have 20–29 students. **Most popular majors:** Psychology, General; Criminal Justice/Safety Studies; Finance, General. **Special Study Options:** Accelerated program; Cooperative education program; Cross-registration; Distance learning; Double major; Dual enrollment; English as a Second Language (ESL); Honors program; Independent study; Internships; Study abroad; Teacher certification program. **Honors programs:** The Florida State University Honors Program provides an enriched curriculum and special opportunities for exceptional, high-achieving students who are entering college for the first time. Each fall, freshmen who are admitted into this program attend the University Honors Colloquium, a weekly forum that features stimulating lectures by distinguished faculty as well as informative presentations from directors of academic programs. As they work to meet their liberal study requirements, University Honors students then have the chance to take small, honors-only courses and special topic seminars with some of the university's best researchers and teachers. With its emphasis on small classes taught by top faculty, this program provides the atmosphere of a small liberal arts college within a large research university. **Combined degree programs:** BA/MA. **Disability Services offered:** Note-taking services; Reader services; Tape recorders; Tutors. **Career services:** Alumni network; Alumni services; Career assessment; Career/job search classes; Internships; Regional alumni.

FACILITIES

Housing: Apartments for single students; Coed dorms; Fraternity/sorority housing; Special housing for disabled students; Theme housing 99% of campus accessible to physically disabled. **Special Academic Facilities/Equipment:** Art gallery, museum, developmental research school, marine lab, oceanographic institute, tandem Van de Graaff accelerator, national high magnetic field lab.

CAMPUS LIFE

Environment: City. **Activities:** Campus Ministries; Choral groups; Concert band; Dance; Drama/theater; International Student Organization; Jazz band; Literary magazine; Marching band; Model UN; Music ensembles; Musical theater; Opera; Pep band; Radio station; Student government; Student newspaper; Student-run film society; Symphony orchestra; Television station; Yearbook. 763 registered organizations, 63 honor societies, 56 religious organizations, 23 fraternities, 24 sororities, on campus. **Athletics (Intercollegiate):** *Men:* baseball, basketball, cheerleading, cross-country, diving, football, golf, swimming, tennis, track/field (outdoor), track/field (indoor). *Women:* basketball, cheerleading, cross-country, diving, golf, soccer, softball, swimming, tennis, track/field (outdoor), track/field (indoor), volleyball. **On-Campus Highlights:** Suwannee Dining Hall. **Environmental Initiatives:** Creation of the FSU Office of Sustainability and the hiring of a full-time Director of Campus Sustainability to help build a comprehensive sustainable campus program.

ADMISSIONS

Freshman Academic Profile: Average high school GPA 4.1. 47% in top 10% of high school class, 73% in top 25% of high school class, 95% in top 50% of high school class. 79% from public high schools. **Test scores:** SAT Math middle 50% range 590–670. SAT EBRW middle 50% range 610–670. ACT middle 50% range 26–30. **Basis for Candidate Selection:** *Very important factors include:* rigor of secondary school record. *Important factors include:* academic GPA, standardized test scores, talent/ability, state residency. *Other factors include:* class rank, application essay, extracurricular activities, character/personal qualities, first generation, geographical residence, volunteer work, work experience. **Freshman Admission Requirements:** High school diploma is required and GED is accepted. *Academic units required:* 4 English, 4 math, 3 science, 2 science labs, 2 foreign language, 1 social studies, 2 history, 3 academic electives. *Academic units recommended:* 4 English, 4 math, 4 science, 2 science labs, 4 foreign language, 2 social studies, 2 history, 3 academic electives. **Freshman Admission Statistics:** 58,936 applied, 36% admitted, 34% enrolled. **Transfer Admission Requirements:** college transcript(s), Minimum college GPA of 3.0 required. Lowest grade transferable D-. **General Admission Information:** Application fee $30. Priority deadline 11/1. Regular application deadline 3/1. Non-fall registration accepted.

COSTS AND FINANCIAL AID

Annual in-state tuition $4,640. Annual out-of-state tuition $19,806. Room and board $10,666. Required fees $1,877. Average book and supplies expense $1,000. **Required Forms and Deadlines:** FAFSA; State aid form. **Notification of Awards:** Applicants will be notified of awards on a rolling basis beginning 4/5. **Types of Aid:** *Need-based scholarships/grants:* College/university scholarship or grant aid from institutional funds; Federal Pell; Private scholarships; SEOG; State scholarships/grants; United Negro College Fund. *Loans:* Direct PLUS loans; Direct Subsidized Stafford Loans; Direct Unsubsidized Stafford Loans. **Student Employment:** Federal Work-Study Program available. Institutional employment available. **Financial Aid Statistics:** 93% needy freshmen, 87% needy undergrads receive need-based scholarship or grant aid. 85% freshmen, 63% undergrads receive non-need-based scholarship or grant aid. 35% freshmen, 50% undergrads receive need-based self-help aid. 2% freshmen, 1% undergrads receive athletic scholarships. 97% freshmen, 89% undergrads receive any aid. 42% undergrads borrow to pay for school. Average cumulative indebtedness $25,013. **Criteria awarding aid:** *Non-Need-based:* Academics; Art, Athletics, Leadership, Music/drama.

FONTBONNE UNIVERSITY

6800 Wydown Boulevard, Saint Louis, MO 63105
Phone: 314-889-1400 **Financial Aid Phone:** 314-889-1414
E-mail: fcadmis@fontbonne.edu **CEEB Code:** 6216
Fax: 314-889-1451 **Website:** www.fontbonne.edu **ACT Code:** 2298

This private school, affiliated with the Roman Catholic Church, was founded in 1917. It has a 13 acre campus.

RATINGS
Admissions Selectivity Rating: 82   **Fire Safety Rating:** 90   **Green Rating:** 60*

STUDENTS AND FACULTY
Enrollment: 1,993. **Student Body:** 72% female, 28% male, 12% out-of-state, 1% international (23 countries represented). Asian 1%, African American 34%, Caucasian 62%, Hispanic 1%, Native American <1%, Race unknown 1%. **Retention and Graduation:** 58% freshmen return for sophomore year. 25% grads go on to further study within 1 year. **Faculty:** Student/faculty ratio 16:1. 73 full-time faculty, 71% hold PhDs, 10% are members of minority groups, 68% are women. 0% of classes are taught by teaching assistants.

ACADEMICS
Degrees: Bachelor's; Certificate; Master's; Post-bachelor's certificate. **Classes:** Most classes have 10–19 students. Most lab/discussion sessions have 10–19 students. **Most popular majors:** Special Education and Teaching, General; Business Administration and Management, General; Elementary Education and Teaching. **Special Study Options:** Accelerated program; Cooperative education program; Cross-registration; Distance learning; Double major; English as a Second Language (ESL); Exchange student program (domestic); Honors program; Independent study; Internships; Liberal arts/career combination; Student-designed major; Study abroad; Teacher certification program; Weekend college. **Combined degree programs:** BA/MEng. **Disability Services offered:** Note-taking services; Reader services; Tape recorders; Tutors. **Career services:** Alumni services; Career assessment; Career/job search classes; Internships.

FACILITIES
Housing: Apartments for single students; Coed dorms; Special housing for international students 85% of campus accessible to physically disabled. **Special Academic Facilities/Equipment:** Art gallery.

CAMPUS LIFE
Environment: Metropolis. **Activities:** Campus Ministries; Choral groups; Dance; Drama/theater; Literary magazine; Music ensembles; Radio station; Student government; Student newspaper. 34 registered organizations, 7 honor societies, 4 religious organizations, on campus. **Athletics (Intercollegiate):** *Men:* baseball, basketball, cross-country, field hockey, golf, lacrosse, soccer, tennis. *Women:* basketball, bowling, cross-country, field hockey, golf, lacrosse, soccer, softball, tennis, volleyball. **On-Campus Highlights:** Ryan Hall.

ADMISSIONS
Freshman Academic Profile: Average high school GPA 3.1. 7% in top 10% of high school class, 28% in top 25% of high school class, 61% in top 50% of high school class. 56% from public high schools. **Test scores:** SAT Math middle 50% range 470–625. SAT EBRW middle 50% range 500–625. ACT middle 50% range 18–24. **Basis for Candidate Selection:** *Very important factors include:* rigor of secondary school record, class rank, academic GPA, standardized test scores, character/personal qualities. *Other factors include:* application essay, recommendation(s), interview, extracurricular activities, talent/ability, first generation, alumni/ae relation, volunteer work, work experience, level of applicant's interest. **Freshman Admission Requirements:** High school diploma is required and GED is accepted. *Academic units required:* 4 English, 3 math, 3 science, 1 science labs, 3 social studies, 3 academic electives. **Freshman Admission Statistics:** 588 applied, 76% admitted, 43% enrolled. **Transfer Admission Requirements:** college transcript(s), essay or personal statement, Minimum college GPA of 2.0 required. Lowest grade transferable D. **General Admission Information:** Application fee $25. Priority deadline 1/15. Regular application deadline 8/1. Non-fall registration accepted. Admission may be deferred for a maximum of 1 year.

COSTS AND FINANCIAL AID
Annual tuition $20,860. Room and board $8,319. Required fees $440. Average book and supplies expense $650. **Required Forms and Deadlines:** FAFSA; Institution's own financial aid form. **Types of Aid:** *Need-based scholarships/grants:* College/university scholarship or grant aid from institutional funds; Federal Pell; Private scholarships; SEOG; State scholarships/grants. **Student**

Employment: Federal Work-Study Program available. **Financial Aid Statistics:** 96% needy freshmen, 98% needy undergrads receive need-based scholarship or grant aid. 99% freshmen, 67% undergrads receive non-need-based scholarship or grant aid. 93% freshmen, 90% undergrads receive need-based self-help aid. 0% freshmen, 0% undergrads receive athletic scholarships. **Criteria awarding aid:** *Need-based:* Job skills *Non-Need-based:* Academics, Alumni affiliation, Art, Job skills, Leadership, Minority status, Religious affiliation.

FORDHAM UNIVERSITY

441 East Fordham Road, Bronx, NY 10458
Phone: 718-817-4000 **Financial Aid Phone:** 718-817-3800
E-mail: enroll@fordham.edu **CEEB Code:** 2259
Fax: 718-817-0549 **Website:** www.fordham.edu **ACT Code:** 2748

This private school, affiliated with the Roman Catholic Church, was founded in 1841. It has a 93 acre campus.

RATINGS

Admissions Selectivity Rating: 91   Fire Safety Rating: 96   Green Rating: 64

STUDENTS AND FACULTY

Enrollment: 9,422. **Student Body:** 57% female, 43% male, 58% out-of-state, 8% international (81 countries represented). Asian 11%, African American 4%, Caucasian 56%, Hispanic 16%, Native American <1%, Pacific Islander <1%, Two or more races 4%, Race unknown 1%.
Retention and Graduation: 91% freshmen return for sophomore year. 78% freshmen graduate within 4 years. 83% freshmen graduate within 6 years. 20% grads go on to further study within 1 year. 8% grads pursue arts and sciences degrees. 4% grads pursue law degrees. 4% grads pursue business degrees. 1% grads pursue medical degrees. **Faculty:** Student/faculty ratio 14:1. 742 full-time faculty, 92% hold PhDs, 28% are members of minority groups, 43% are women.

ACADEMICS

Degrees: Bachelor's; Doctoral degree—professional practice; Doctoral degree research/scholarship; Master's; Post-bachelor's certificate; Post-master's certificate. **Classes:** Most classes have 10–19 students. Most lab/discussion sessions have 10–19 students. **Most popular majors:** Business Administration and Management, General; Finance, General; Psychology, General. **Special Study Options:** Accelerated program; Cross-registration; Distance learning; Double major; English as a Second Language (ESL); Exchange student program (domestic); Honors program; Independent study; Internships; Liberal arts/career combination; Student-designed major; Study abroad; Teacher certification program; Weekend college. **Honors programs:** Each undergraduate college has its own Honors Program. Each program offers enriched academic opportunity for qualified and interested students. Students are automatically considered for Honors programs as part of the application review process. **Combined degree programs:** BA/JD; BA/MA. **Disability Services offered:** Note-taking services; Reader services; Tape recorders; Tutors. **Career services:** Alumni network; Alumni services; Career assessment; Career/job search classes; Internships; Regional alumni.

FACILITIES

Housing: Apartments for single students; Coed dorms; 90% of campus accessible to physically disabled. **Special Academic Facilities/Equipment:** WFUV: NPR affiliate on campus, television station, white and black box theatres, media and visual arts labs Greek and Etruscan art gallery, seismic station, 113 acre biological field station The Louis Calder Center in Armonk, NY. **Campus Network:** 85% of classrooms, 100% of dorms, 100% of student union, 100% of libraries, 100% of dining areas, 50% of common outdoor areas, have wireless network access.

CAMPUS LIFE

Environment: Metropolis. **Activities:** Campus Ministries; Choral groups; Concert band; Dance; Drama/theater; International Student Organization; Jazz band; Literary magazine; Marching band; Music ensembles; Musical theater; Pep band; Radio station; Student government; Student newspaper; Student-run film society; Symphony orchestra; Television station; Yearbook. 233 registered organizations, 13 honor societies, on campus. **Athletics (Intercollegiate):** *Men:* baseball, basketball, cross-country, diving, football, golf, soccer, squash, swimming, tennis, track/field (outdoor), track/field (indoor), water polo. *Women:* basketball, cheerleading, crew/rowing, cross-country, diving, soccer, softball, swimming, tennis, track/field (outdoor), track/field (indoor), volleyball. **On-Campus Highlights:** McKeon Hall—Lincoln Center.

ADMISSIONS

Freshman Academic Profile: Average high school GPA 3.6. 46% in top 10% of high school class, 80% in top 25% of high school class, 97% in top 50% of high school class. 63% from public high schools. **Test scores:** SAT Math middle 50% range 620–740. SAT EBRW middle 50% range 620–710. ACT middle 50% range 28–32. **Basis for Candidate Selection:** *Very important factors include:* rigor of secondary school record, academic GPA, standardized test scores. *Important factors include:* application essay, recommendation(s), extracurricular activities, talent/ability, character/personal qualities, volunteer work. *Other factors include:* class rank, first generation, alumni/ae relation, geographical residence, racial/ethnic status, work experience, level of applicant's interest. **Freshman Admission Requirements:** High school diploma is required and GED is accepted. *Academic units required:* 4 English, 3 math, 3 science, 2 foreign language, 3 social studies. *Academic units recommended:* 4 English, 4 math, 4 science, 4 foreign language, 4 social studies. **Freshman Admission Statistics:** 47,930 applied, 46% admitted, 10% enrolled. **Transfer Admission Requirements:** High school transcript, college transcript(s), essay or personal statement, statement of good standing from prior institution(s). Minimum college GPA of 3.0 required. Lowest grade transferable C. **General Admission Information:** Application fee $70. Priority deadline 11/1. Regular application deadline 1/1. Non-fall registration accepted. Admission may be deferred for a maximum of 1 year.

COSTS AND FINANCIAL AID

Annual tuition $52,980. Room and board $18,510. Required fees $1,413. Average book and supplies expense $1,039. **Required Forms and Deadlines:** Business/Farm Supplement; CSS/Financial Aid PROFILE; FAFSA; Noncustodial PROFILE; State aid form. **Notification of Awards:** Applicants will be notified of awards on or about 4/1. **Types of Aid:** *Need-based scholarships/grants:* College/university scholarship or grant aid from institutional funds; Federal Pell; Private scholarships; SEOG; State scholarships/grants. **Loans:** Direct PLUS loans; Direct Subsidized Stafford Loans; Direct Unsubsidized Stafford Loans. **Student Employment:** Federal Work-Study Program available. Institutional employment available. **Financial Aid Statistics:** 95% needy freshmen, 96% needy undergrads receive need-based scholarship or grant aid. 62% freshmen, 22% undergrads receive non-need-based scholarship or grant aid. 69% freshmen, 71% undergrads receive need-based self-help aid. 1% freshmen, 2% undergrads receive athletic scholarships. 91% freshmen, 85.5% undergrads receive any aid. 62% undergrads borrow to pay for school. Average cumulative indebtedness $37,429. **Criteria awarding aid:** *Need-based:* Academics, Athletics *Non-Need-based:* Academics, Athletics.

FORT HAYS STATE UNIVERSITY

600 Park Street, Hays, KS 67601-4099
Phone: 785.628.3478 **Financial Aid Phone:** 785-628-4408
E-mail: tigers@fhsu.edu **CEEB Code:** 6218
Fax: 800.432.0248 **Website:** www.fhsu.edu **ACT Code:** 1408

This public school was founded in 1902. It has a 4160 acre campus.

RATINGS

Admissions Selectivity Rating: 74   Fire Safety Rating: 84   Green Rating: 60*

STUDENTS AND FACULTY

Enrollment: 11,503. **Student Body:** 61% female, 39% male, 31% out-of-state, 29% international. Asian 1%, African American 4%, Caucasian 57%, Hispanic 7%, Native American <1%, Pacific Islander <1%, Two or more races 2%, Race unknown 1%.
Retention and Graduation: 69% freshmen return for sophomore year. 20% grads go on to further study within 1 year. **Faculty:** Student/faculty ratio 16:1. 315 full-time faculty, 61% hold PhDs, 10% are members of minority groups, 45% are women. 1% of classes are taught by teaching assistants.

ACADEMICS

Degrees: Associate; Bachelor's; Certificate; Master's; Post-master's certificate. **Classes:** Most classes have 20–29 students. Most lab/discussion sessions have 10–19 students. **Most popular majors:** Business/Commerce, General; Elementary Education and Teaching; Sports, Kinesiology, and Physical Education/Fitness, General. **Special Study Options:** Distance learning; Double major; Dual enrollment; English as a Second Language (ESL); Exchange student program (domestic); External degree program; Honors program; Independent study; Internships; Liberal arts/career combination; Student-designed major; Study abroad; Teacher certification program; Weekend college. **Combined degree programs:** BA/MEng. **Disability Services offered:** Note-taking services; Reader services; Tutors. **Career services:** Alumni network; Alumni services; Career assessment; Career/job search classes; Internships.

FACILITIES

Housing: Apartments for married students; Apartments for single students; Coed dorms; Fraternity/sorority housing; Men's dorms; Women's dorms 100% of campus accessible to physically disabled. **Special Academic Facilities/Equipment:** Paleontology; natural history, visual arts and media center, farm, NMR gas analyzer, telescope (HG).

CAMPUS LIFE

Environment: Village. **Activities:** Campus Ministries; Choral groups; Concert band; Dance; Drama/theater; Jazz band; Literary magazine; Marching band; Model UN; Music ensembles; Musical theater; Opera; Pep band; Radio station; Student government; Student newspaper; Symphony orchestra; Television station. 103 registered organizations, 20 honor societies, 2 religious organizations, 3 fraternities, 3 sororities, on campus. **Athletics (Intercollegiate):** *Men:* baseball, basketball, cheerleading, cross-country, football, golf, track/field (outdoor), track/field (indoor), wrestling. *Women:* basketball, cheerleading, cross-country, golf, softball, tennis, track/field (outdoor), track/field (indoor), volleyball. **On-Campus Highlights:** www.tigersportszone.com. **Environmental Initiatives:** Clean up of Big Creek.

ADMISSIONS

Freshman Academic Profile: Average high school GPA 3.4. 13% in top 10% of high school class, 32% in top 25% of high school class, 64% in top 50% of high school class. 95% from public high schools. **Test scores:** ACT middle 50% range 18–24. **Basis for Candidate Selection:** *Other factors include:* rigor of secondary school record, class rank, academic GPA, standardized test scores. **Freshman Admission Requirements:** High school diploma is required and GED is accepted. *Academic units recommended:* 4 English, 3 math, 3 science, 2 social studies, 1 history, 1 computer science. **Freshman Admission Statistics:** 2,337 applied, 86% admitted, 24% enrolled. **Transfer Admission Requirements:** college transcript(s), Minimum college GPA of 2.0 required. Lowest grade transferable D. **General Admission Information:** Application fee $30. Non-fall registration accepted. Admission may be deferred for a maximum of 1 year.

COSTS AND FINANCIAL AID

Required Forms and Deadlines: FAFSA; Institution's own financial aid form. **Notification of Awards:** Applicants will be notified of awards on a rolling basis beginning 3/15. **Types of Aid:** *Need-based scholarships/grants:* College/university scholarship or grant aid from institutional funds; Federal Pell; Private scholarships; SEOG; State scholarships/grants. *Loans:* Direct PLUS loans; Direct Subsidized Stafford Loans; Direct Unsubsidized Stafford Loans. **Student Employment:** Federal Work-Study Program available. **Financial Aid Statistics:** 82% needy freshmen, 80% needy undergrads receive need-based scholarship or grant aid. 3% freshmen, 3% undergrads receive non-need-based scholarship or grant aid. 82% freshmen, 10% undergrads receive need-based self-help aid. 4% freshmen, 3% undergrads receive athletic scholarships. 70% undergrads borrow to pay for school. Average cumulative indebtedness $27,462. **Criteria awarding aid:** *Non-Need-based:* Academics, Alumni affiliation, Art, Athletics, Job skills, Leadership, Minority status, Music/drama, State/district residency.

FORT LEWIS COLLEGE

1000 Rim Drive, Durango, CO 81301
Financial Aid Phone: 970-247-7142
E-mail: admisson@fortlewis.edu **CEEB Code:** 4310
Fax: 970-247-7179 **Website:** www.fortlewis.edu **ACT Code:** 510

This public school was founded in 1911. It has a 362 acre campus.

RATINGS

Admissions Selectivity Rating: 74 **Fire Safety Rating:** 92 **Green Rating:** 96

STUDENTS AND FACULTY

Enrollment: 3,089. **Student Body:** 53% female, 47% male, 58% out-of-state, 1% international (15 countries represented). Asian 1%, African American 1%, Caucasian 46%, Hispanic 12%, Native American 29%, Pacific Islander <1%, Two or more races 10%, Race unknown 2%.
Retention and Graduation: 62% freshmen return for sophomore year. 28% freshmen graduate within 4 years. 41% freshmen graduate within 6 years. 14% grads go on to further study within 1 year. **Faculty:** Student/faculty ratio 15:1. 183 full-time faculty, 89% hold PhDs, 13% are members of minority groups, 52% are women. 0% of classes are taught by teaching assistants.

ACADEMICS

Degrees: Bachelor's; Certificate; Master's; Post-bachelor's certificate. **Classes:** Most classes have 10–19 students. Most lab/discussion sessions have 20–29 students. **Most popular majors:** Biology/Biological Sciences, General; Business Administration and Management, General; Psychology, General. **Special Study Options:** Accelerated program; Cooperative education program; Distance learning; Double major; Dual enrollment; English as a Second Language (ESL); Exchange student program (domestic); Honors program; Independent study; Internships; Liberal arts/career combination; Study abroad; Teacher certification program. **Honors programs:** Reed Honors is an interdisciplinary program that plugs students into a dynamic community who are hungry for intellectual challenge, creative expression, cultural enrichment, professional development, and personal growth experiences. Offering both curricular and extra-curricular activities, Reed Honors students explore, discover, and engage with the community with the guidance of FLC's top professors. Upon completion of the Reed Honors Program, you will graduate with a Minor in Honors, prepared to excel at whatever you put your mind to and to also make a positive impact on the world around you. The minor is designated on your transcript and signifies to prospective employers and graduate schools that you have completed a rigorous course of study, one steeped in critical thinking activities and place-based learning experiences. **Combined degree programs:** BA/MA. **Disability Services offered:** Note-taking services; Reader services; Tape recorders; Tutors. **Career services:** Alumni network; Alumni services; Career assessment; Career/job search classes; Internships; Regional alumni.

FACILITIES

Housing: Apartments for married students; Apartments for single students; Coed dorms; Special housing for disabled students; Theme housing 100% of campus accessible to physically disabled. **Special Academic Facilities/Equipment:** Center for Southwest Studies; Thermal Hydraulics Lab; Health & Human Performance Lab.

CAMPUS LIFE

Environment: Village. **Activities:** Campus Ministries; Choral groups; Concert band; Dance; Drama/theater; Jazz band; Literary magazine; Music ensembles; Musical theater; Pep band; Radio station; Student government; Student newspaper. 70 registered organizations, 6 honor societies, 6 religious organizations, on campus. **Athletics (Intercollegiate):** *Men:* basketball, cross-country, football, golf, soccer. *Women:* basketball, cross-country, lacrosse, soccer, softball, volleyball. **On-Campus Highlights:** Student Union. **Environmental Initiatives:** All new construction or renovation follow at minimum LEED Silver standards.

ADMISSIONS

Freshman Academic Profile: Average high school GPA 3.3. 13% in top 10% of high school class, 20% in top 25% of high school class, 67% in top 50% of high school class. **Test scores:** SAT Math middle 50% range 480–590. SAT EBRW middle 50% range 500–610. ACT middle 50% range 17–23. **Basis for Candidate Selection:** *Very important factors include:* rigor of secondary school record, class rank, academic GPA, standardized test scores. *Other factors* *include:* recommendation(s). **Freshman Admission Requirements:** High school diploma is required and GED is accepted. *Academic units required:* 4 English, 4 math, 3 science, 2 science labs, 1 foreign language, 2 social studies, 1 history, 3 academic electives. **Freshman Admission Statistics:** 3,757 applied, 91% admitted, 22% enrolled. **Transfer Admission Requirements:** college transcript(s), Minimum college GPA of 2.40 required. Lowest grade transferable C-. **General Admission Information:** Application fee $40. Regular application deadline 8/1. Non-fall registration accepted. Admission may be deferred for a maximum of 1 year.

COSTS AND FINANCIAL AID

Annual in-state tuition $7,056. Annual out-of-state tuition $17,712. Room and board $10,076. Required fees $1,816. Average book and supplies expense $1,240. **Required Forms and Deadlines:** FAFSA. **Notification of Awards:** Applicants will be notified of awards on a rolling basis beginning 3/1. **Types of Aid:** *Need-based scholarships/grants:* College/university scholarship or grant aid from institutional funds; Federal Pell; Private scholarships; SEOG; State scholarships/grants. *Loans:* Direct PLUS loans; Direct Subsidized Stafford Loans; Direct Unsubsidized Stafford Loans. **Student Employment:** Federal Work-Study Program available. Institutional employment available. **Financial Aid Statistics:** 90% needy freshmen, 89% needy undergrads receive need-based scholarship or grant aid. 8% freshmen, 7% undergrads receive non-need-based scholarship or grant aid. 60% freshmen, 67% undergrads receive need-based self-help aid. 12% freshmen, 1% undergrads receive athletic scholarships. 89% freshmen, 86% undergrads receive any aid. 58% undergrads borrow to pay for school. Average cumulative indebtedness $19,429. **Criteria awarding aid:** *Need-based:* Academics, Alumni affiliation, Art, Athletics, Leadership, Music/drama. *Non-Need-based:* Academics, Alumni affiliation, Art, Athletics, Leadership, Music/drama, State/district residency.

FRAMINGHAM STATE UNIVERSITY

100 State Street, Framingham, MA 01701-9101
Phone: 508-626-4500 **Financial Aid Phone:** 508-626-4534
E-mail: admissions@framingham.edu **CEEB Code:** 3519
Fax: 508-626-4017 **Website:** www.framingham.edu **ACT Code:** 1904

This public school was founded in 1839. It has a 143 acre campus.

RATINGS

Admissions Selectivity Rating: 77   **Fire Safety Rating:** 98   **Green Rating:** 90

STUDENTS AND FACULTY

Enrollment: 3,745. **Student Body:** 57% female, 43% male, 5% out-of-state, <1% international (12 countries represented). Asian 3%, African American 14%, Caucasian 61%, Hispanic 17%, Native American <1%, Pacific Islander 0%, Two or more races 4%, Race unknown 1%.
Retention and Graduation: 74% freshmen return for sophomore year. 48% freshmen graduate within 4 years. 61% freshmen graduate within 6 years. 26% grads go on to further study within 1 year. **Faculty:** Student/faculty ratio 13:1. 198 full-time faculty, 90% hold PhDs, 19% are members of minority groups, 57% are women. 0% of classes are taught by teaching assistants.

ACADEMICS

Degrees: Bachelor's; Master's; Post-bachelor's certificate. **Classes:** Most classes have 10–19 students. Most lab/discussion sessions have 10–19 students. **Most popular majors:** Business/Commerce, General; Psychology, General; Criminology. **Special Study Options:** Cooperative education program; Cross-registration; Distance learning; Double major; Dual enrollment; English as a Second Language (ESL); Honors program; Independent study; Internships; Liberal arts/career combination; Student-designed major; Study abroad; Teacher certification program. **Honors programs:** The Commonwealth Honors Program at Framingham State University offers challenging courses and extracurricular activities for qualified students, and sponsors events which contribute to the intellectual life of the College community. **Combined degree programs:** BA/JD; BA/MA. **Disability Services offered:** Note-taking services; Reader services; Tape recorders; Tutors. **Career services:** Alumni network; Alumni services; Career assessment; Career/job search classes; Internships.

FACILITIES

Housing: Coed dorms; Special housing for disabled students; Special housing for international students; Theme housing; Wellness housing; Women's dorms 95% of campus accessible to physically disabled. **Special Academic Facilities/Equipment:** Mazmanian Art Gallery, McAuliffe Challenger Learning Center,

Greenhouse, Early Childhood Development Lab, Education Curriculum Library, Planetarium. **Campus Network:** 95% of classrooms, 10% of dorms, 100% of student union, 100% of libraries, 100% of dining areas, 0% of common outdoor areas, have wireless network access.

CAMPUS LIFE

Environment: City. **Activities:** Campus Ministries; Choral groups; Concert band; Dance; Drama/theater; Literary magazine; Musical theater; Radio station; Student government; Student newspaper; Student-run film society. 50 registered organizations, 10 honor societies, 1 religious organizations, on campus. **Athletics (Intercollegiate):** *Men:* baseball, basketball, cross-country, football, ice hockey, soccer. *Women:* basketball, cross-country, field hockey, lacrosse, soccer, softball, volleyball. **On-Campus Highlights:** Residence Halls **Environmental Initiatives:** Conversion of our power plant from #6 oil to natural gas, decreasing our carbon footprint from the plant by 30%.

ADMISSIONS

Freshman Academic Profile: Average high school GPA 3.1. **Test scores:** SAT Math middle 50% range 480–560. SAT EBRW middle 50% range 480–570. ACT middle 50% range 19–25. **Basis for Candidate Selection:** *Very important factors include:* rigor of secondary school record, academic GPA, standardized test scores. *Important factors include:* extracurricular activities, talent/ability, character/personal qualities. *Other factors include:* class rank, application essay, recommendation(s), interview, first generation, volunteer work, work experience, level of applicant's interest. **Freshman Admission Requirements:** High school diploma is required and GED is accepted. *Academic units required:* 4 English, 4 math, 3 science, 3 science labs, 2 foreign language, 1 social studies, 1 history, 2 academic electives. *Academic units recommended:* 4 English, 4 math, 4 science, 4 foreign language, 2 social studies, 2 history. **Freshman Admission Statistics:** 5,942 applied, 74% admitted, 18% enrolled. **Transfer Admission Requirements:** High school transcript, college transcript(s), essay or personal statement, Minimum college GPA of 2.5 required. Lowest grade transferable C-. **General Admission Information:** Application fee $50. Priority deadline 3/1. Non-fall registration accepted. Admission may be deferred for a maximum of 12 months.

COSTS AND FINANCIAL AID

Annual in-state tuition $970. Annual out-of-state tuition $7,050. Room and board $11,820. Required fees $8,950. Average book and supplies expense $1,000. **Required Forms and Deadlines:** FAFSA. **Notification of Awards:** Applicants will be notified of awards on a rolling basis beginning 3/15. **Types of Aid:** *Need-based scholarships/grants:* College/university scholarship or grant aid from institutional funds; Federal Pell; Private scholarships; SEOG; State scholarships/grants. *Loans:* Direct PLUS loans; Direct Subsidized Stafford Loans; Direct Unsubsidized Stafford Loans. **Student Employment:** Federal Work-Study Program available. Institutional employment available. **Financial Aid Statistics:** 85% needy freshmen, 81% needy undergrads receive need-based scholarship or grant aid. 13% freshmen, 4% undergrads receive non-need-based scholarship or grant aid. 84% freshmen, 81% undergrads receive need-based self-help aid. 0% freshmen, 0% undergrads receive athletic scholarships. 87% freshmen, 69% undergrads receive any aid. 83% undergrads borrow to pay for school. Average cumulative indebtedness $30,781. **Criteria awarding aid:** *Need-based:* Academics. *Non-Need-based:* Academics, State/district residency.

FRANCISCAN UNIVERSITY OF STEUBENVILLE

1235 University Boulevard., Steubenville, OH 43952-1763
Phone: 740-283-6226 **Financial Aid Phone:** (740) 284-5216
E-mail: admissions@franciscan.edu **CEEB Code:** 1133
Fax: 740-284-5456 **Website:** www.franciscan.edu **ACT Code:** 3258

This private school, affiliated with the Roman Catholic Church, was founded in 1946. It has a 235 acre campus.

RATINGS

Admissions Selectivity Rating: 80   **Fire Safety Rating:** 84   **Green Rating:** 60*

STUDENTS AND FACULTY

Enrollment: 2,038. **Student Body:** 61% female, 39% male, 80% out-of-state, 1% international (10 countries represented). Asian 2%, African American 1%, Caucasian 82%, Hispanic 11%, Native American <1%, Pacific Islander <1%, Two or more races 2%, Race unknown 2%.
Retention and Graduation: 84% freshmen return for sophomore year. 20% grads go on to further study within 1 year. 17% grads pursue arts and sciences

degrees. 1% grads pursue law degrees. 1% grads pursue business degrees. 1% grads pursue medical degrees. **Faculty:** Student/faculty ratio 14:1. 127 full-time faculty, 82% hold PhDs, 2% are members of minority groups, 24% are women. 0% of classes are taught by teaching assistants.

ACADEMICS

Degrees: Associate; Bachelor's; Master's. **Classes:** Most classes have 10–19 students. Most lab/discussion sessions have 10–19 students. **Most popular majors:** Registered Nursing/Registered Nurse; Business Administration, Management and Operations; Theology/Theological Studies. **Special Study Options:** Accelerated program; Distance learning; Double major; Dual enrollment; Honors program; Independent study; Internships; Study abroad; Teacher certification program. **Honors programs:** Our Great Books program is limited to 40 students in each year and prepares them for graduate school and careers in all fields. **Combined degree programs:** BA/MA. **Disability Services offered:** Note-taking services; Reader services; Tape recorders; Tutors. **Career services:** Career assessment; Career/job search classes; Internships.

FACILITIES

Housing: Apartments for single students; Men's dorms; Women's dorms 75% of campus accessible to physically disabled. **Special Academic Facilities/Equipment:** Art Gallery. **Campus Network:** 100% of classrooms, 100% of dorms, 100% of student union, 100% of libraries, 100% of dining areas, 100% of common outdoor areas, have wireless network access.

CAMPUS LIFE

Environment: Village. **Activities:** Campus Ministries; Choral groups; Drama/theater; International Student Organization; Literary magazine; Music ensembles; Radio station; Student government; Student newspaper; Yearbook. 34 registered organizations, 6 honor societies, 6 religious organizations, on campus. **On-Campus Highlights:** JC Williams Student Center.

ADMISSIONS

Freshman Academic Profile: Average high school GPA 3.6. 25% in top 10% of high school class, 50% in top 25% of high school class, 81% in top 50% of high school class. 37% from public high schools. **Test scores:** SAT Math middle 50% range 500–630. SAT EBRW middle 50% range 540–670. ACT middle 50% range 22–28. **Basis for Candidate Selection:** *Very important factors include:* rigor of secondary school record, academic GPA, standardized test scores, interview, character/personal qualities. *Important factors include:* extracurricular activities, talent/ability. *Other factors include:* recommendation(s). **Freshman Admission Requirements:** High school diploma is required and GED is accepted. *Academic units recommended:* 4 English, 3 math, 3 science, 3 science labs, 2 foreign language, 2 social studies, 1 history. **Freshman Admission Statistics:** 1,760 applied, 79% admitted, 33% enrolled. **Transfer Admission Requirements:** High school transcript, college transcript(s), essay or personal statement, Minimum college GPA of 2.2 required. Lowest grade transferable C. **General Admission Information:** Application fee $20. Non-fall registration accepted. Admission may be deferred for a maximum of one year.

COSTS AND FINANCIAL AID

Required Forms and Deadlines: FAFSA. **Notification of Awards:** Applicants will be notified of awards on a rolling basis beginning 2/15. **Types of Aid:** *Need-based scholarships/grants:* College/university scholarship or grant aid from institutional funds; Federal Pell; Private scholarships; SEOG; State scholarships/grants. *Loans:* Direct PLUS loans; Direct Subsidized Stafford Loans; Direct Unsubsidized Stafford Loans. **Student Employment:** Federal Work-Study Program available. Institutional employment available. **Financial Aid Statistics:** 99% needy freshmen, 99% needy undergrads receive need-based scholarship or grant aid. 10% freshmen, 9% undergrads receive non-need-based scholarship or grant aid. 89% freshmen, 90% undergrads receive need-based self-help aid. 0% freshmen, 0% undergrads receive athletic scholarships. 98% freshmen, 64% undergrads receive any aid. **Criteria awarding aid:** *Need-based:* Leadership, Religious affiliation. *Non-Need-based:* Academics, Alumni affiliation, Leadership, Religious affiliation.

FRANCIS MARION UNIVERSITY

Office of Admissions, Florence, SC 29502-0547
Phone: 843-661-1231 **Financial Aid Phone:** 843-661-1190
E-mail: admissions@fmarion.edu **CEEB Code:** 5442
Fax: 843-661-4635 **Website:** www.fmarion.edu **ACT Code:** 3856

This public school was founded in 1970. It has a 400 acre campus.

RATINGS

Admissions Selectivity Rating: 83   **Fire Safety Rating:** 84   **Green Rating:** 61

STUDENTS AND FACULTY

Enrollment: 3,380. **Student Body:** 68% female, 32% male, 3% out-of-state, 1% international (19 countries represented). Asian 1%, African American 50%, Caucasian 45%, Hispanic 1%, Native American <1%, Pacific Islander <1%, Two or more races <1%, Race unknown 1%.
Retention and Graduation: 67% freshmen return for sophomore year. **Faculty:** Student/faculty ratio 15:1. 204 full-time faculty, 79% hold PhDs, 11% are members of minority groups, 49% are women. 0% of classes are taught by teaching assistants.

ACADEMICS

Degrees: Bachelor's; Master's; Post-master's certificate. **Classes:** Most classes have 20–29 students. Most lab/discussion sessions have 20–29 students. **Most popular majors:** Registered Nursing/Registered Nurse; Biology/Biological Sciences, General; Psychology, General. **Special Study Options:** Accelerated program; Cooperative education program; Distance learning; Double major; Dual enrollment; Honors program; Independent study; Internships; Study abroad; Teacher certification program. **Honors programs:** Link to the Honors Program web page: http://www.fmarion.edu/academics/programdescription. **Disability Services offered:** Note-taking services; Reader services; Tape recorders; Tutors. **Career services:** Alumni network; Career assessment; Career/job search classes; Internships; Regional alumni.

FACILITIES

Housing: Apartments for married students; Apartments for single students; Men's dorms; Special housing for disabled students; Women's dorms 100% of campus accessible to physically disabled. **Special Academic Facilities/Equipment:** Media center, planetarium, observatory. **Campus Network:** 100% of classrooms, 100% of dorms, 100% of student union, 100% of libraries, 100% of dining areas, 90% of common outdoor areas, have wireless network access.

CAMPUS LIFE

Environment: Rural. **Activities:** Campus Ministries; Choral groups; Dance; Drama/theater; International Student Organization; Jazz band; Literary magazine; Model UN; Music ensembles; Student government; Student newspaper; Symphony orchestra. 46 registered organizations, 14 honor societies, 7 religious organizations, 4 fraternities, 7 sororities, on campus. **Athletics (Intercollegiate):** *Men:* baseball, basketball, cross-country, golf, soccer, tennis; track/field (outdoor). *Women:* basketball, cross-country, soccer, softball, tennis, track/field (outdoor), volleyball. **On-Campus Highlights:** The Cottage.

ADMISSIONS

Freshman Academic Profile: Average high school GPA 3.6. 15% in top 10% of high school class, 15% in top 25% of high school class, 81% in top 50% of high school class. 91% from public high schools. **Test scores:** SAT Math middle 50% range 420–530. SAT EBRW middle 50% range 410–530. ACT middle 50% range 17–22. **Basis for Candidate Selection:** *Very important factors include:* rigor of secondary school record, academic GPA, standardized test scores. *Important factors include:* class rank. *Other factors include:* recommendation(s). **Freshman Admission Requirements:** High school diploma is required and GED is accepted. *Academic units required:* 4 English, 4 math, 3 science, 3 science labs, 2 foreign language, 2 social studies, 1 history, 1 academic electives, 1 visual/performing arts, 1 unit from above areas or other academic areas. **Freshman Admission Statistics:** 3,952 applied, 57% admitted, 33% enrolled. **Transfer Admission Requirements:** High school transcript, college transcript(s), statement of good standing from prior institution(s). Minimum college GPA of 2.0 required. Lowest grade transferable C. **General Admission Information:** Application fee $33. Priority deadline 7/1. Regular application deadline 8/15. Non-fall registration accepted. Admission may be deferred for a maximum of 1 year.

COSTS AND FINANCIAL AID

Annual in-state tuition $9,266. Annual out-of-state tuition $18,532. Room and board $7,256. Required fees $472. Average book and supplies expense $999. **Required Forms and Deadlines:** FAFSA. **Notification of Awards:** Applicants will be notified of awards on a rolling basis beginning 1/30. **Types of Aid:** *Need-based scholarships/grants:* College/university scholarship or grant aid from institutional funds; Federal Pell; Private scholarships; SEOG; State scholarships/grants. *Loans:* Direct PLUS loans; Direct Subsidized Stafford Loans; Direct Unsubsidized Stafford Loans. **Student Employment:** Federal Work-Study Program available. Institutional employment available. **Financial Aid Statistics:** 99% needy freshmen, 76% needy undergrads receive need-based scholarship or grant aid. 7% freshmen, 4% undergrads receive non-need-based scholarship or grant aid. 75% freshmen, 88% undergrads receive need-based self-help aid. 0% freshmen, 0% undergrads receive athletic scholarships. 88% freshmen, 82% undergrads receive any aid. **Criteria awarding aid:** *Non-Need-based:* Academics, Alumni affiliation, Art, Athletics, Job skills, Leadership, Minority status, Music/drama, Religious affiliation, State/district residency.

FRANKLIN & MARSHALL COLLEGE

Best Colleges

P.O. Box 3003, Lancaster, PA 17604-3003
Phone: 717-358-3953 **Financial Aid Phone:** 717-358-3991
E-mail: admission@fandm.edu **CEEB Code:** 2261
Fax: 717-358-4389 **Website:** www.fandm.edu **ACT Code:** 3574

This private school was founded in 1787. It has a 220 acre campus.

RATINGS

Admissions Selectivity Rating: 94   **Fire Safety Rating:** 97   **Green Rating:** 95

STUDENTS AND FACULTY

Enrollment: 2,298. **Student Body:** 55% female, 45% male, 72% out-of-state, 18% international (52 countries represented). Asian 5%, African American 6%, Caucasian 56%, Hispanic 10%, Native American <1%, Pacific Islander <1%, Two or more races 2%, Race unknown 3%.
Retention and Graduation: 92% freshmen return for sophomore year. 80% freshmen graduate within 4 years. 85% freshmen graduate within 6 years.
Faculty: Student/faculty ratio 9:1. 242 full-time faculty, 95% hold PhDs, 13% are members of minority groups, 49% are women. 0% of classes are taught by teaching assistants.

ACADEMICS

Degrees: Bachelor's. **Classes:** Most classes have 10–19 students. Most lab/discussion sessions have 10–19 students. **Most popular majors:** Psychology, General; Political Science and Government, General; Business Administration, Management and Operations. **Special Study Options:** Double major; Independent study; Internships; Student-designed major; Study abroad; Teacher certification program. **Disability Services offered:** Note-taking services; Reader services; Tape recorders; Tutors. **Career services:** Alumni network; Alumni services; Career assessment; Career/job search classes; Internships; Regional alumni.

FACILITIES

Housing: Apartments for single students; Coed dorms; Fraternity/sorority housing; Special housing for disabled students; Special housing for international students; Theme housing; Wellness housing 80% of campus accessible to physically disabled. **Special Academic Facilities/Equipment:** Art gallery, associated with natural history museums, bronze casting foundry, retail sales complex, psychology and language labs, TV and radio station, observatory/planetarium, Writers House.

CAMPUS LIFE

Environment: Town. **Activities:** Campus Ministries; Choral groups; Concert band; Dance; Drama/theater; International Student Organization; Jazz band; Literary magazine; Model UN; Music ensembles; Musical theater; Pep band; Radio station; Student government; Student newspaper; Symphony orchestra; Yearbook. 90 registered organizations, 13 honor societies, 8 religious organizations, 7 fraternities, 4 sororities, on campus. **Athletics (Intercollegiate):** *Men:* baseball, basketball, crew/rowing, cross-country,

football, golf, lacrosse, soccer, squash, swimming, tennis, track/field (outdoor), track/field (indoor), wrestling. *Women:* basketball, crew/rowing, cross-country, field hockey, golf, lacrosse, soccer, softball, squash, swimming, tennis, track/field (outdoor), track/field (indoor), volleyball. **On-Campus Highlights:** Alumni Sport and Fitness Center. **Environmental Initiatives:** We have established The Center for the Sustainable Environment, including a Director, student staff member, and partnership with the Millport Conservancy.

ADMISSIONS

Freshman Academic Profile: 59% in top 10% of high school class, 84% in top 25% of high school class, 97% in top 50% of high school class. 60% from public high schools. **Test scores:** SAT Math middle 50% range 640–750. SAT EBRW middle 50% range 620–690. ACT middle 50% range 28–32. **Basis for Candidate Selection:** *Very important factors include:* rigor of secondary school record, class rank, academic GPA, character/personal qualities. *Important factors include:* application essay, standardized test scores, recommendation(s), interview, extracurricular activities, talent/ability, volunteer work. *Other factors include:* alumni/ae relation, geographical residence, racial/ethnic status, work experience, level of applicant's interest. **Freshman Admission Requirements:** High school diploma is required and GED is accepted. *Academic units required:* 4 English, 3 math, 2 science, 2 science labs, 2 foreign language, 1 social studies, 2 history, 1 visual/performing arts. *Academic units recommended:* 4 math, 3 science, 3 science labs, 4 foreign language, 3 social studies, 3 history. **Freshman Admission Statistics:** 6,557 applied, 35% admitted, 26% enrolled. **Transfer Admission Requirements:** High school transcript, college transcript(s), essay or personal statement, interview, standardized test scores, statement of good standing from prior institution(s). Lowest grade transferable C-. **General Admission Information:** Application fee $60. Regular application deadline 1/15. Non-fall registration accepted. Admission may be deferred for a maximum of one year.

COSTS AND FINANCIAL AID

Annual tuition $58,615. Room and board $14,450. Required fees $385. Average book and supplies expense $1,200. **Required Forms and Deadlines:** CSS/Financial Aid PROFILE; FAFSA; Noncustodial PROFILE. **Notification of Awards:** Applicants will be notified of awards on or about 4/1. **Types of Aid:** *Need-based scholarships/grants:* College/university scholarship or grant aid from institutional funds; Federal Pell; Private scholarships; SEOG; State scholarships/grants. *Loans:* Direct PLUS loans; Direct Subsidized Stafford Loans; Direct Unsubsidized Stafford Loans. **Student Employment:** Federal Work-Study Program available. **Financial Aid Statistics:** 100% needy freshmen, 100% needy undergrads receive need-based scholarship or grant aid. 24% freshmen, 20% undergrads receive non-need-based scholarship or grant aid. 90% freshmen, 94% undergrads receive need-based self-help aid. 0% freshmen, 0% undergrads receive athletic scholarships. 54% freshmen, 56% undergrads receive any aid. 54% undergrads borrow to pay for school. Average cumulative indebtedness $27,149. **Criteria awarding aid:** *Need-based:* Academics, Religious affiliation. *Non-Need-based:* Music/drama.

FRANKLIN COLLEGE

101 Branigin Blvd, Franklin, IN 46131-2623
Phone: 317-738-8075 **Financial Aid Phone:** 317-738-8075
E-mail: admissions@franklincollege.edu **CEEB Code:** 1228
Fax: 317-738-8274 **Website:** www.franklincollege.edu **ACT Code:** 1194

This private school, affiliated with the American Baptist Church, was founded in 1834. It has a 207 acre campus.

RATINGS

Admissions Selectivity Rating: 75   **Fire Safety Rating:** 85   **Green Rating:** 60*

STUDENTS AND FACULTY

Enrollment: 977. **Student Body:** 51% female, 49% male, 8% out-of-state, 1% international (9 countries represented). Asian 1%, African American 5%, Caucasian 84%, Hispanic 3%, Native American <1%, Pacific Islander 0%, Two or more races 4%, Race unknown 2%.
Retention and Graduation: 74% freshmen return for sophomore year. 20% grads go on to further study within 1 year. 14% grads pursue arts and sciences degrees. 2% grads pursue law degrees. 1% grads pursue business degrees. 3% grads pursue medical degrees. **Faculty:** Student/faculty ratio 11:1. 78 full-time faculty, 88% hold PhDs, 13% are members of minority groups, 42% are women. 0% of classes are taught by teaching assistants.

ACADEMICS

Degrees: Bachelor's; Master's. **Classes:** Most classes have 10–19 students. Most lab/discussion sessions have 10–19 students. **Most popular majors:** Business/Commerce, General; Biology/Biological Sciences, General; Elementary Education and Teaching. **Special Study Options:** Cross-registration; Double major; Exchange student program (domestic); Independent study; Internships; Liberal arts/career combination; Student-designed major; Study abroad; Teacher certification program. **Honors programs:** The intercultural Honors Experience is a freshman-year program designed to attract and retain superior students and faculty to FC while internationalizing the FC community. The program is designed to help students build a solid intercultural foundation, introduce them to interdisciplinary learning, and provide them with opportunities and incentives to study abroad. Faculty development is an integral part of the project. **Combined degree programs:** BA/MA. **Disability Services offered:** Note-taking services; Reader services; Tape recorders; Tutors. **Career services:** Alumni services; Career assessment; Career/job search classes.

FACILITIES

Housing: Coed dorms; Fraternity/sorority housing; Men's dorms; Special housing for disabled students; Theme housing; Women's dorms 100% of campus accessible to physically disabled. **Special Academic Facilities/Equipment:** Pulliam School of Journalism, Dietz Center for Professional Development, Leadership Center. **Campus Network:** 100% of classrooms, 100% of dorms, 100% of student union, 100% of libraries, 100% of dining areas, 100% of common outdoor areas, have wireless network access.

CAMPUS LIFE

Environment: Village. **Activities:** Campus Ministries; Choral groups; Concert band; Dance; Drama/theater; International Student Organization; Literary magazine; Model UN; Music ensembles; Pep band; Radio station; Student government; Student newspaper. 51 registered organizations, 13 honor societies, 2 religious organizations, 5 fraternities, 3 sororities, on campus. **Athletics (Intercollegiate):** *Men:* baseball, basketball, cross-country, diving, football, golf, soccer, swimming, tennis, track/field (outdoor). *Women:* basketball, cheerleading, cross-country, diving, golf, soccer, softball, swimming, tennis, track/field (outdoor), volleyball. **On-Campus Highlights:** Napolitan Student Center. **Environmental Initiatives:** Completing green house car emissions inventory.

ADMISSIONS

Freshman Academic Profile: Average high school GPA 3.5. 26% in top 10% of high school class, 54% in top 25% of high school class, 85% in top 50% of high school class. 90% from public high schools. **Test scores:** SAT Math middle 50% range 430–550. SAT EBRW middle 50% range 420–530. ACT middle 50% range 19–25. **Basis for Candidate Selection:** *Very important factors include:* rigor of secondary school record, class rank, academic GPA, standardized test scores. *Important factors include:* application essay, extracurricular activities, alumni/ae relation. *Other factors include:* recommendation(s), interview, talent/ability, first generation, geographical residence, state residency, religious affiliation/commitment, racial/ethnic status, volunteer work, work experience, level of applicant's interest. **Freshman Admission Requirements:** High school diploma is required and GED is accepted. *Academic units required:* 4 English, 4 math, 2 science, 3 social studies. *Academic units recommended:* 2 foreign language. **Freshman Admission Statistics:** 1,479 applied, 78% admitted, 21% enrolled. **Transfer Admission Requirements:** High school transcript, college transcript(s), essay or personal statement, statement of good standing from prior institution(s). Minimum college GPA of 2.0 required. Lowest grade transferable C-. **General Admission Information:** Priority deadline 12/1. Non-fall registration accepted. Admission may be deferred for a maximum of 1 year.

COSTS AND FINANCIAL AID

Annual tuition $29,840. Room and board $9,355. Required fees $185. Average book and supplies expense $1,200. **Required Forms and Deadlines:** FAFSA; Institution's own financial aid form. **Notification of Awards:** Applicants will be notified of awards on a rolling basis beginning 11/1. **Types of Aid:** *Need-based scholarships/grants:* College/university scholarship or grant aid from institutional funds; Federal Pell; Private scholarships; SEOG; State scholarships/grants. *Loans:* Direct PLUS loans; Direct Subsidized Stafford Loans; Direct Unsubsidized Stafford Loans. **Student Employment:** Federal Work-Study Program available. Institutional employment available. **Financial Aid Statistics:** 100% needy freshmen, 100% needy undergrads receive need-based scholarship or grant aid. 17% freshmen, 14% undergrads receive non-need-based scholarship or grant aid. 83% freshmen, 85% undergrads receive need-based self-help aid. 0% freshmen, 0% undergrads receive athletic scholarships. 100% freshmen, 98% undergrads receive any aid. 86% undergrads borrow to pay for school. Average cumulative indebtedness $34,884. **Criteria awarding aid:**

Need-based: Minority status, Religious affiliation. *Non-Need-based:* Academics, Alumni affiliation, Art, Minority status, Music/drama, Religious affiliation, State/district residency.

FRANKLIN PIERCE UNIVERSITY

Admissions Office, Rindge, NH 03461
Phone: 603-899-4050 **Financial Aid Phone:** 603-899-4180
E-mail: admissions@franklinpierce.edu **CEEB Code:** 3395
Fax: 603-889-4394 **Website:** www.franklinpierce.edu **ACT Code:** 2509

This private school was founded in 1962. It has a 1200 acre campus.

RATINGS

Admissions Selectivity Rating: 64   **Fire Safety Rating:** 94   **Green Rating:** 60*

STUDENTS AND FACULTY

Enrollment: 1,474. **Student Body:** 52% female, 48% male.
Retention and Graduation: 26% grads go on to further study within 1 year. 5% grads pursue arts and sciences degrees. 3% grads pursue law degrees. 7% grads pursue business degrees. 1% grads pursue medical degrees. **Faculty:** Student/faculty ratio 18:1. 100 full-time faculty, 68% hold PhDs, 1% are members of minority groups, 45% are women. 0% of classes are taught by teaching assistants.

ACADEMICS

Degrees: Associate; Bachelor's; Certificate; Master's; Post-master's certificate. **Classes:** Most classes have 10–19 students. Most lab/discussion sessions have fewer than 10 students. **Most popular majors:** Education, General; Criminal Justice/Safety Studies; Accounting and Business/Management. **Special Study Options:** Accelerated program; Double major; Dual enrollment; English as a Second Language (ESL); Honors program; Independent study; Internships; Liberal arts/career combination; Student-designed major; Study abroad; Teacher certification program. **Honors programs:** Honors Program. **Disability Services offered:** Note-taking services; Reader services; Tape recorders; Tutors. **Career services:** Alumni network; Alumni services; Career assessment; Career/job search classes; Internships; Regional alumni.

FACILITIES

Housing: Apartments for single students; Coed dorms; Special housing for disabled students; Wellness housing 67% of campus accessible to physically disabled. **Special Academic Facilities/Equipment:** Thoreau Art Gallery; Flynt Center; Fitzwater Communications Center; Dance Studio; Pottery Kiln; Glass Blowing Studio; TV Station; Radio Station; Grimshaw-Gudewicz Activities Center: Lakeside Activity Center. **Campus Network:** 100% of classrooms, 100% of dorms, 100% of student union, 100% of libraries, 100% of dining areas, 100% of common outdoor areas, have wireless network access.

CAMPUS LIFE

Environment: Rural. **Activities:** Campus Ministries; Choral groups; Dance; Drama/theater; Literary magazine; Music ensembles; Musical theater; Radio station; Student government; Student newspaper; Television station. 35 registered organizations, 8 honor societies, 3 religious organizations, on campus. **Athletics (Intercollegiate):** *Men:* baseball, basketball, crew/rowing, golf, ice hockey, rugby, soccer, tennis. *Women:* basketball, crew/rowing, cross-country, field hockey, lacrosse, soccer, softball, volleyball. **On-Campus Highlights:** Peterson Hall. **Environmental Initiatives:** Development of on enhanced on-campus recycling program.

ADMISSIONS

Freshman Academic Profile: Average high school GPA 2.8. 89% from public high schools. **Basis for Candidate Selection:** *Very important factors include:* academic GPA, recommendation(s), character/personal qualities. *Important factors include:* rigor of secondary school record, application essay, *Other factors include:* class rank, standardized test scores, interview, extracurricular activities, talent/ability, volunteer work, work experience. **Freshman Admission Requirements:** High school diploma is required and GED is accepted. *Academic units required:* 4 English, 3 math, 2 science, 2 science labs, 3 social studies, 4 academic electives, 4 unit from above areas or other academic areas. **Freshman Admission Statistics:** 3,740 applied, 80% admitted, 16% enrolled. **Transfer Admission Requirements:** college transcript(s), essay or personal statement, Minimum college GPA of 2.0 required. Lowest grade transferable C-. **General Admission Information:** Non-fall registration accepted. Admission may be deferred for a maximum of 1 year.

COSTS AND FINANCIAL AID

Annual tuition $30,870. Room and board $12,546. Required fees $2,450. Average book and supplies expense $1,000. **Required Forms and Deadlines:** FAFSA. **Notification of Awards:** Applicants will be notified of awards on a rolling basis beginning 2/1. **Types of Aid:** *Need-based scholarships/ grants:* College/university scholarship or grant aid from institutional funds; Federal Pell; Private scholarships; SEOG; State scholarships/grants. **Student Employment:** Federal Work-Study Program available. Institutional employment available. **Financial Aid Statistics:** 99% needy freshmen, 99% needy undergrads receive need-based scholarship or grant aid. 9% freshmen, 9% undergrads receive non-need-based scholarship or grant aid. 90% freshmen, 90% undergrads receive need-based self-help aid. 4% freshmen, 5% undergrads receive athletic scholarships. 99% freshmen, 87% undergrads receive any aid. **Criteria awarding aid:** *Need-based:* Academics, Athletics *Non-Need-based:* Academics, Alumni affiliation, Athletics, Leadership, Minority status, Music/ drama.

FRANKLIN UNIVERSITY

201 S Grant Ave, Columbus, OH 43215
Phone: 614-797-4700
E-mail: info@franklin.edu **CEEB Code:** 1229
Fax: 614-224-8027 **ACT Code:** 3275

This private school was founded in 1902. It has a 14 acre campus.

RATINGS

Admissions Selectivity Rating: 63   **Fire Safety Rating:** 60*   **Green Rating:** 60*

STUDENTS AND FACULTY

Enrollment: 5,682. **Student Body:** 55% female, 45% male, 26% out-of-state, 6% international. Asian 3%, African American 21%, Caucasian 73%, Hispanic 2%, Native American <1%, Race unknown 5%.
Retention and Graduation: 72% freshmen return for sophomore year.
Faculty: Student/faculty ratio 19:1. 36 full-time faculty, 64% hold PhDs, 6% are members of minority groups, 44% are women.

ACADEMICS

Degrees: Associate; Bachelor's; Master's. **Classes:** Most classes have 10–19 students. **Most popular majors:** Business/Commerce, General; Accounting; Computer And Information Sciences And Support Services. **Special Study Options:** Accelerated program; Cooperative education program; Cross-registration; Distance learning; Double major; Dual enrollment; English as a Second Language (ESL); Independent study; Internships; Study abroad; Weekend college. **Disability Services offered:** Note-taking services; Reader services; Tape recorders; Tutors. **Career services:** Alumni network; Alumni services; Internships.

FACILITIES

100% of campus accessible to physically disabled.

CAMPUS LIFE

6 registered organizations, on campus.

ADMISSIONS

Freshman Admission Requirements: High school diploma is required and GED is accepted. *Academic units recommended:* 3 math. **Freshman Admission Statistics:** 262 applied, 100% admitted, 47% enrolled. **Transfer Admission Requirements:** college transcript(s), Lowest grade transferable C-. **General Admission Information:** Non-fall registration accepted. Admission may be deferred for a maximum of indefinite.

COSTS AND FINANCIAL AID

Annual tuition $6,990. **Required Forms and Deadlines:** FAFSA. **Types of Aid:** *Need-based scholarships/grants:* College/university scholarship or grant aid from institutional funds; Federal Pell; Private scholarships; SEOG; State scholarships/grants. **Student Employment:** Federal Work-Study Program available. Institutional employment available. **Financial Aid Statistics:** 72% needy freshmen, 64% needy undergrads receive need-based scholarship or grant aid. 85% freshmen, 82% undergrads receive non-need-based scholarship or grant aid. 92% freshmen, 94% undergrads receive need-based self-help aid. 0% freshmen, 0% undergrads receive athletic scholarships. **Criteria awarding aid:** *Need-based:* Academics. *Non-Need-based:* Academics, Leadership, Minority status.

FRANKLIN W. OLIN COLLEGE OF ENGINEERING

1000 Olin Way, Needham, MA 02492-1200
Phone: 781-292-2222 **Financial Aid Phone:** 781-292-2215
E-mail: info@olin.edu **CEEB Code:** 2824
Website: www.olin.edu **ACT Code:** 1883

This private school was founded in 1997. It has a 75 acre campus.

RATINGS

Admissions Selectivity Rating: 98   **Fire Safety Rating:** 99   **Green Rating:** 64

STUDENTS AND FACULTY

Enrollment: 347. **Student Body:** 51% female, 49% male, 88% out-of-state, 8% international (10 countries represented). Asian 16%, African American 3%, Caucasian 47%, Hispanic 12%, Native American 0%, Pacific Islander 0%, Two or more races 9%, Race unknown 6%.
Retention and Graduation: 99% freshmen return for sophomore year. 80% freshmen graduate within 4 years. 96% freshmen graduate within 6 years. 10% grads go on to further study within 1 year. 10% grads pursue arts and sciences degrees. 0% grads pursue law degrees. 0% grads pursue business degrees. 0% grads pursue medical degrees. **Faculty:** Student/faculty ratio 8:1. 42 full-time faculty, 98% hold PhDs, 17% are members of minority groups, 50% are women. 0% of classes are taught by teaching assistants.

ACADEMICS

Degrees: Bachelor's. **Classes:** Most classes have 20–29 students. **Most popular majors:** Engineering, General; Electrical and Electronics Engineering; Mechanical Engineering. **Special Study Options:** Cross-registration; Exchange student program (domestic); Independent study; Internships; Student-designed major; Study abroad. **Disability Services offered:** Note-taking services; Reader services; Tape recorders; Tutors. **Career services:** Alumni network; Alumni services; Career/job search classes; Internships; Regional alumni.

FACILITIES

Housing: Coed dorms; Special housing for disabled students; 100% of campus accessible to physically disabled.

CAMPUS LIFE

Environment: Town. **Activities:** Campus Ministries; Choral groups; Drama/ theater; International Student Organization; Music ensembles; Student government; Student newspaper. 57 registered organizations, on campus.
Environmental Initiatives: Replacing site-wide external lighting with LEDs.

ADMISSIONS

Freshman Academic Profile: Average high school GPA 3.9. **Test scores:** SAT Math middle 50% range 760–800. SAT EBRW middle 50% range 700–760. ACT middle 50% range 34–35. **Basis for Candidate Selection:** *Very important factors include:* rigor of secondary school record, academic GPA, application essay, recommendation(s), interview, extracurricular activities, talent/ability, character/personal qualities, level of applicant's interest. *Important factors include:* class rank, standardized test scores. *Other factors include:* first generation, alumni/ae relation, geographical residence, state residency. **Freshman Admission Requirements:** High school diploma is required and GED is accepted. *Academic units recommended:* 4 English, 4 math, 4 science, 3 science labs, 2 foreign language, 2 social studies, 2 history. **Freshman Admission Statistics:** 905 applied, 16% admitted, 60% enrolled. **Transfer Admission Requirements:** college transcript(s), Minimum college GPA of 2.0 required. Lowest grade transferable C. **General Admission Information:** Application fee $85. Regular application deadline 1/1. Admission may be deferred for a maximum of 2 years.

COSTS AND FINANCIAL AID

Annual tuition $52,164. Room and board $16,872. Required fees $3,336. Average book and supplies expense $200. **Required Forms and Deadlines:** FAFSA. **Notification of Awards:** Applicants will be notified of awards on or about 4/1. **Types of Aid:** *Need-based scholarships/grants:* College/university scholarship or grant aid from institutional funds; Federal Pell; SEOG. *Loans:* Direct PLUS loans; Direct Subsidized Stafford Loans; Direct Unsubsidized Stafford Loans. **Student Employment:** Institutional employment available. **Financial Aid Statistics:** 100% needy freshmen, 100% needy undergrads receive need-based scholarship or grant aid. 100% freshmen, 99% undergrads receive non-need-based scholarship or grant aid. 63% freshmen, 63% undergrads receive need-based self-help aid. 0% freshmen, 0% undergrads receive athletic scholarships. 100% freshmen, 100% undergrads receive any aid. 28% undergrads borrow to pay for school. Average cumulative indebtedness $13,480. **Criteria awarding aid:** *Non-Need-based:* Academics, Leadership.

FREED-HARDEMAN UNIVERSITY

158 East Main Street, Henderson, TN 38340
Phone: 731-989-6651 **Financial Aid Phone:** 731-989-6662
E-mail: jathoms1@yahoo.com **CEEB Code:** 1230
Fax: 731-989-6047 **Website:** web.fhu.edu **ACT Code:** 3962

This private school, affiliated with the Church of Christ, was founded in 1869. It has a 122 acre campus.

RATINGS
Admissions Selectivity Rating: 88   **Fire Safety Rating:** 66   **Green Rating:** 60*

STUDENTS AND FACULTY
Enrollment: 1,428. **Student Body:** 55% female, 45% male, 50% out-of-state, 3% international (26 countries represented). Asian <1%, African American 4%, Caucasian 91%, Hispanic 1%, Native American <1%, Race unknown <1%. **Retention and Graduation:** 74% freshmen return for sophomore year. 40% grads go on to further study within 1 year. **Faculty:** Student/faculty ratio 14:1. 108 full-time faculty, 69% hold PhDs, 5% are members of minority groups, 31% are women. 0% of classes are taught by teaching assistants.

ACADEMICS
Degrees: Bachelor's; Master's; Post-bachelor's certificate; Post-master's certificate. **Classes:** Most classes have 10–19 students. Most lab/discussion sessions have 10–19 students. **Most popular majors:** Liberal Arts and Sciences, General Studies and Humanities, Other; Bible/Biblical Studies; Biology/Biological Sciences, General. **Special Study Options:** Accelerated program; Cooperative education program; Cross-registration; Distance learning; Double major; Dual enrollment; Honors program; Independent study; Internships; Liberal arts/career combination; Student-designed major; Study abroad; Teacher certification program. **Honors programs:** Exceptional students may be admitted to the Honors College, where he or she may graduate as an Honors College Scholar, or as an Honors College Scholar with University Honors. **Disability Services offered:** Note-taking services; Reader services; Tutors. **Career services:** Alumni network; Career assessment; Internships.

FACILITIES
Housing: Apartments for single students; Men's dorms; Women's dorms 70% of campus accessible to physically disabled. **Special Academic Facilities/Equipment:** Child development lab, nursery school.

CAMPUS LIFE
Environment: Rural. **Activities:** Choral groups; Concert band; Drama/theater; Jazz band; Music ensembles; Musical theater; Pep band; Radio station; Student government; Student newspaper; Television station; Yearbook. 52 registered organizations, 4 honor societies, 5 religious organizations, 6 fraternities, 6 sororities, on campus. **Athletics (Intercollegiate):** *Men:* baseball, basketball, cheerleading, soccer. *Women:* basketball, cheerleading, soccer, softball, volleyball. **On-Campus Highlights:** The Commons.

ADMISSIONS
Freshman Academic Profile: Average high school GPA 3.4. 25% in top 10% of high school class, 51% in top 25% of high school class, 79% in top 50% of high school class. **Test scores:** SAT Math middle 50% range 480–600. SAT EBRW middle 50% range 480–640. ACT middle 50% range 20–26. **Basis for Candidate Selection:** *Very important factors include:* rigor of secondary school record, academic GPA, standardized test scores. *Other factors include:* recommendation(s), extracurricular activities, character/personal qualities, alumni/ae relation, religious affiliation/commitment, racial/ethnic status, volunteer work, work experience. **Freshman Admission Requirements:** High school diploma is required and GED is accepted. *Academic units recommended:* 4 English, 2 math, 2 science, 2 social studies, 10 academic electives. **Freshman Admission Statistics:** 1,326 applied, 55% admitted, 53% enrolled. **Transfer Admission Requirements:** college transcript(s), statement of good standing from prior institution(s). Lowest grade transferable D. **General Admission Information:** Non-fall registration accepted. Admission may be deferred for a maximum of 2 years.

COSTS AND FINANCIAL AID
Annual tuition $13,192. Room and board $6,560. Average book and supplies expense $1,710. **Required Forms and Deadlines:** FAFSA. **Notification of Awards:** Applicants will be notified of awards on a rolling basis beginning 3/1. **Types of Aid:** *Need-based scholarships/grants:* College/university scholarship or grant aid from institutional funds; Federal Pell; Private scholarships; SEOG; State scholarships/grants. **Student Employment:** Federal Work-Study Program available. Institutional employment available. **Financial Aid Statistics:** 97% needy freshmen, 91% needy undergrads receive need-based scholarship or grant aid. 19% freshmen, 17% undergrads receive non-need-based scholarship or grant aid. 73% freshmen, 78% undergrads receive need-based self-help aid. 4% freshmen, 4% undergrads receive athletic scholarships. 86% freshmen receive any aid. **Criteria awarding aid:** *Non-Need-based:* Academics, Art, Athletics, Leadership, Minority status, Music/drama, State/district residency.

FRESNO PACIFIC UNIVERSITY

1717 S. Chestnut Ave, Fresno, CA 93702
Phone: 559-453-2039 **Financial Aid Phone:** 559-453-2041
E-mail: ugadmis@fresno.edu
Fax: 559-453-2007 **Website:** http://www.fresno.edu/

This private school, affiliated with the Mennonite Church, was founded in 1944. It has a 42 acre campus.

RATINGS
Admissions Selectivity Rating: 60*   **Fire Safety Rating:** 60*   **Green Rating:** 60*

STUDENTS AND FACULTY
Enrollment: 1,459. **Student Body:** 68% female, 32% male, 2% international. Asian 4%, African American 4%, Caucasian 53%, Hispanic 26%, Native American 1%, Pacific Islander 0%, Two or more races 0%, Race unknown 10%. **Retention and Graduation:** 70% freshmen return for sophomore year.

ACADEMICS
Degrees: Associate; Bachelor's; Certificate; Master's; Post-bachelor's certificate. **Most popular majors:** Education, General; Bible/Biblical Studies; Business/Commerce, General. **Special Study Options:** Accelerated program; Cooperative education program; Cross-registration; Distance learning; Double major; English as a Second Language (ESL); Independent study; Internships; Liberal arts/career combination; Student-designed major; Study abroad; Teacher certification program. **Disability Services offered:** Note-taking services; Reader services; Tutors. **Career services:** Alumni services; Career assessment; Career/job search classes; Internships.

FACILITIES
Housing: Apartments for single students; Men's dorms; Special housing for disabled students; Women's dorms 100% of campus accessible to physically disabled. **Special Academic Facilities/Equipment:** English Language Training Institute **Campus Network:** 100% of classrooms, 0% of dorms, 100% of student union, 100% of libraries, 100% of dining areas, 100% of common outdoor areas, have wireless network access.

CAMPUS LIFE
Environment: Metropolis. **Activities:** Campus Ministries; Choral groups; Concert band; Dance; Drama/theater; International Student Organization; Jazz band; Music ensembles; Musical theater; Pep band; Student government; Student newspaper; Yearbook. 36 registered organizations, 1 honor societies, 11 religious organizations, on campus. **Athletics (Intercollegiate):** *Men:* baseball, basketball, cross-country, soccer, tennis, track/field (outdoor). *Women:* basketball, cross-country, soccer, tennis, track/field (outdoor), volleyball. **On-Campus Highlights:** Special Events Center (Gym).

ADMISSIONS
Basis for Candidate Selection: *Very important factors include:* rigor of secondary school record, standardized test scores. *Important factors include:* class rank, academic GPA, application essay, recommendation(s), religious affiliation/commitment. *Other factors include:* character/personal qualities. **Freshman Admission Requirements:** High school diploma is required and GED is accepted. *Academic units required:* 4 English, 3 math, 1 science, 1 science labs, 2 foreign language, 2 social studies. **Transfer Admission Requirements:** High school transcript, college transcript(s), essay or personal statement, Minimum college GPA of 2.4 required. Lowest grade transferable C. **General Admission**

Information: Application fee $40. Priority deadline 12/1. Regular application deadline 7/31. Non-fall registration accepted.

COSTS AND FINANCIAL AID
Annual tuition $24,960. Required fees $276. Average book and supplies expense $1,665. **Required Forms and Deadlines:** FAFSA. **Notification of Awards:** Applicants will be notified of awards on a rolling basis beginning 2/21. **Types of Aid:** *Need-based scholarships/grants:* College/university scholarship or grant aid from institutional funds; Federal Pell; Private scholarships; SEOG; State scholarships/grants. *Loans:* Direct PLUS loans; Direct Subsidized Stafford Loans; Direct Unsubsidized Stafford Loans. **Student Employment:** Federal Work-Study Program available. Institutional employment available. **Financial Aid Statistics:** 81% needy freshmen, 81% needy undergrads receive need-based scholarship or grant aid. 98% freshmen, 51% undergrads receive non-need-based scholarship or grant aid. 74% freshmen, 79% undergrads receive need-based self-help aid. 14% freshmen, 9% undergrads receive athletic scholarships. **Criteria awarding aid:** *Non-Need-based:* Academics, Alumni affiliation, Art, Athletics, Leadership, Minority status, Music/drama, Religious affiliation.

FRIENDS UNIVERSITY

2100 University Avenue, Wichita, KS 67213
Phone: 316-295-5100 **Financial Aid Phone:** 316-295-5200
E-mail: learn@friends.edu **CEEB Code:** 6224
Fax: 316-295-5101 **Website:** www.friends.edu **ACT Code:** 1918

This private school was founded in 1898. It has a 54 acre campus.

RATINGS
Admissions Selectivity Rating: 85   Fire Safety Rating: 89   Green Rating: 60*

STUDENTS AND FACULTY
Enrollment: 1,737. **Student Body:** 56% female, 44% male, 19% out-of-state, 0% international (13 countries represented). Asian 3%, African American 11%, Caucasian 71%, Hispanic 4%, Native American 2%, Pacific Islander <1%, Two or more races 5%, Race unknown 4%.
Retention and Graduation: 60% freshmen return for sophomore year.
Faculty: Student/faculty ratio 11:1. 75 full-time faculty, 71% hold PhDs, 5% are members of minority groups, 41% are women. 0% of classes are taught by teaching assistants.

ACADEMICS
Degrees: Associate; Bachelor's; Master's; Post-bachelor's certificate. **Classes:** Most classes have fewer than 10 students. Most lab/discussion sessions have 10–19 students. **Most popular majors:** Business Administration and Management, General; Wildlife Biology; Psychology, General. **Special Study Options:** Accelerated program; Cross-registration; Distance learning; Double major; Dual enrollment; Exchange student program (domestic); Honors program; Independent study; Internships; Student-designed major; Study abroad; Teacher certification program. **Honors programs:** The Friends University Honors Program is designed to enrich the educational experience of selected students through a process involving group interchange of ideas and independent research projects. Participating students are challenged by their peers and by faculty members to reflect upon significant contemporary issues in a number of different fields and to attempt to respond to and integrate the ideas encountered with their own personal values and faith. The experience is intended to develop powers of analysis and evaluation in an environment where encouragement is given to pursue excellence. It is also intended to deepen the appreciation of those involved for the entire range of the liberal arts. **Disability Services offered:** Note-taking services; Reader services; Tape recorders; Tutors. **Career services:** Alumni network; Alumni services; Career assessment; Career/job search classes; Internships; Regional alumni.

FACILITIES
Housing: Apartments for single students; Coed dorms; 95% of campus accessible to physically disabled. **Special Academic Facilities/Equipment:** Davis Administration Buidling built in the 1800's and is the National Registry of Historic Places.

CAMPUS LIFE
Environment: Metropolis. **Activities:** Campus Ministries; Choral groups; Concert band; Dance; Drama/theater; International Student Organization; Jazz band; Literary magazine; Model UN; Music ensembles; Musical theater; Opera; Pep band; Student government; Student newspaper; Symphony orchestra; Yearbook. 24 registered organizations, 6 honor societies, 2 religious organizations, on campus. **Athletics (Intercollegiate):** *Men:* baseball, basketball, cheerleading, cross-country, football, golf, soccer, tennis, track/field (outdoor). *Women:* basketball, cheerleading, cross-country, soccer, softball, tennis, track/field (outdoor), volleyball. **On-Campus Highlights:** Casado Campus Center.

ADMISSIONS
Freshman Academic Profile: Average high school GPA 3.4. 20% in top 10% of high school class, 36% in top 25% of high school class, 68% in top 50% of high school class. 84% from public high schools. **Test scores:** SAT Math middle 50% range 400–510. SAT EBRW middle 50% range 390–515. ACT middle 50% range 18–26. **Basis for Candidate Selection:** *Very important factors include:* academic GPA, standardized test scores. *Important factors include:* rigor of secondary school record, class rank, extracurricular activities, talent/ability, character/personal qualities, alumni/ae relation. *Other factors include:* interview. **Freshman Admission Requirements:** High school diploma is required and GED is accepted. *Academic units required:* 2 foreign language, 2 social studies, 2 history. *Academic units recommended:* 3 English, 3 math, 1 science, 1 science labs, 2 foreign language, 2 social studies, 2 history, 1 computer science. **Freshman Admission Statistics:** 786 applied, 58% admitted, 43% enrolled. **Transfer Admission Requirements:** college transcript(s), statement of good standing from prior institution(s). Minimum college GPA of 2.0 required. Lowest grade transferable C. **General Admission Information:** Application fee $35. Regular application deadline 8/28. Non-fall registration accepted.

COSTS AND FINANCIAL AID
Annual tuition $23,250. Room and board $6,800. Required fees $180. Average book and supplies expense $1,500. **Required Forms and Deadlines:** FAFSA. **Notification of Awards:** Applicants will be notified of awards on a rolling basis beginning 3/1. **Types of Aid:** *Need-based scholarships/grants:* College/university scholarship or grant aid from institutional funds; Federal Pell; Private scholarships; SEOG; State scholarships/grants. *Loans:* Direct PLUS loans; Direct Subsidized Stafford Loans; Direct Unsubsidized Stafford Loans. **Student Employment:** Federal Work-Study Program available. Institutional employment available. **Financial Aid Statistics:** 100% needy freshmen, 84% needy undergrads receive need-based scholarship or grant aid. 24% freshmen, 13% undergrads receive non-need-based scholarship or grant aid. 78% freshmen, 89% undergrads receive need-based self-help aid. 21% freshmen, 3% undergrads receive athletic scholarships. 87% freshmen, 77% undergrads receive any aid. **Criteria awarding aid:** *Non-Need-based:* Academics, Alumni affiliation, Art, Athletics, Leadership, Music/drama, Religious affiliation.

FROSTBURG STATE UNIVERSITY

FSU, 101 Braddock Road, Frostburg, MD 21532
Phone: 301-687-4201 **Financial Aid Phone:** 301-687-4301
E-mail: fsuadmissions@frostburg.edu **CEEB Code:** 5402
Fax: 301-687-7074 **Website:** www.frostburg.edu **ACT Code:** 1714

This public school was founded in 1898. It has a 260 acre campus.

RATINGS
Admissions Selectivity Rating: 78   Fire Safety Rating: 87   Green Rating: 60*

STUDENTS AND FACULTY
Enrollment: 4,486. **Student Body:** 52% female, 48% male, 7% out-of-state, 1% international (25 countries represented). Asian 2%, African American 33%, Caucasian 52%, Hispanic 6%, Native American <1%, Pacific Islander <1%, Two or more races 4%, Race unknown 1%.
Retention and Graduation: 74% freshmen return for sophomore year. 28% freshmen graduate within 4 years. 49% freshmen graduate within 6 years.
Faculty: Student/faculty ratio 15:1. 249 full-time faculty, 78% hold PhDs, 13% are members of minority groups, 44% are women.

ACADEMICS

Degrees: Bachelor's; Doctoral degree research/scholarship; Master's. **Classes:** Most classes have 10–19 students. Most lab/discussion sessions have 10–19 students. **Most popular majors:** Business/Commerce, General; Elementary Education and Teaching; Psychology, General. **Special Study Options:** Distance learning; Double major; Dual enrollment; Honors program; Independent study; Internships; Study abroad; Teacher certification program. **Disability Services offered:** Note-taking services; Reader services; Tape recorders; Tutors. **Career services:** Alumni network; Alumni services; Career assessment; Career/job search classes; Internships; Regional alumni.

FACILITIES

Housing: Coed dorms; Men's dorms; Theme housing; Wellness housing; Women's dorms 100% of campus accessible to physically disabled. **Special Academic Facilities/Equipment:** State-of-the-art science center, planetarium, science discovery center, art gallery. **Campus Network:** 100% of classrooms, 100% of dorms, 100% of student union, 100% of libraries, 100% of dining areas, 100% of common outdoor areas, have wireless network access.

CAMPUS LIFE

Environment: Village. **Activities:** Campus Ministries; Choral groups; Dance; Drama/theater; International Student Organization; Jazz band; Literary magazine; Marching band; Model UN; Music ensembles; Pep band; Radio station; Student government; Student newspaper; Television station; Yearbook. 95 registered organizations, 18 honor societies, 6 religious organizations, 9 fraternities, 6 sororities, on campus. **Athletics (Intercollegiate):** *Men:* baseball, basketball, cross-country, diving, football, golf, soccer, swimming, tennis, track/field (outdoor), track/field (indoor). *Women:* basketball, cross-country, diving, field hockey, lacrosse, soccer, softball, swimming, tennis, track/field (outdoor), track/field (indoor), volleyball. **On-Campus Highlights:** Lane University Center. **Environmental Initiatives:** Adopted an energy-efficient appliance purchasing policy requiring purchase of ENERGY STAR-certified products in all areas for which such ratings exist.

ADMISSIONS

Freshman Academic Profile: Average high school GPA 3.2. 11% in top 10% of high school class, 31% in top 25% of high school class, 66% in top 50% of high school class. **Test scores:** SAT Math middle 50% range 450–550. SAT EBRW middle 50% range 470–560. ACT middle 50% range 17–23. **Basis for Candidate Selection:** *Very important factors include:* rigor of secondary school record, academic GPA, standardized test scores. *Important factors include:* recommendation(s), interview. *Other factors include:* extracurricular activities, talent/ability, character/personal qualities, alumni/ae relation. **Freshman Admission Requirements:** High school diploma is required and GED is accepted. *Academic units required:* 4 English, 3 math, 3 science, 2 science labs, 2 foreign language, 3 history. **Freshman Admission Statistics:** 3,436 applied, 72% admitted, 31% enrolled. **Transfer Admission Requirements:** college transcript(s), Minimum college GPA of 2.0 required. Lowest grade transferable C. **General Admission Information:** Application fee $45. Priority deadline 6/1. Non-fall registration accepted.

COSTS AND FINANCIAL AID

Annual in-state tuition $6,468. Annual out-of-state tuition $19,816. Room and board $9,210. Required fees $2,446. Average book and supplies expense $1,400. **Required Forms and Deadlines:** FAFSA. **Notification of Awards:** Applicants will be notified of awards on a rolling basis beginning 3/15. **Types of Aid:** *Need-based scholarships/grants:* College/university scholarship or grant aid from institutional funds; Federal Pell; Private scholarships; SEOG; State scholarships/grants. *Loans:* Direct PLUS loans; Direct Subsidized Stafford Loans; Direct Unsubsidized Stafford Loans. **Student Employment:** Federal Work-Study Program available. Institutional employment available. **Financial Aid Statistics:** 72% needy freshmen, 72% needy undergrads receive need-based scholarship or grant aid. 24% freshmen, 30% undergrads receive non-need-based scholarship or grant aid. 78% freshmen, 78% undergrads receive need-based self-help aid. 0% freshmen, 0% undergrads receive athletic scholarships. 72% freshmen, 65% undergrads receive any aid. 75% undergrads borrow to pay for school. Average cumulative indebtedness $24,827. **Criteria awarding aid:** *Need-based:* Academics. *Non-Need-based:* Academics, Alumni affiliation, Art, Leadership, Music/drama, State/district residency.

FULL SAIL UNIVERSITY

3300 University Blvd, Winter Park, FL 32792
Phone: 800-226-7625
E-mail: admissions@fullsail.com
Website: http://www.fullsail.edu/

This proprietary school was founded in 1979. It has a 91 acre campus.

RATINGS
Admissions Selectivity Rating: 60*   **Fire Safety Rating:** 60*   **Green Rating:** 60*

STUDENTS AND FACULTY
Enrollment: 4,628.

ACADEMICS
Degrees: Associate; Bachelor's; Master's; Terminal Associate. **Most popular majors:** Cinematography and Film/Video Production; Animation, Interactive Technology, Video Graphics and Special Effects; Recording Arts Technology/Technician. **Special Study Options:** Accelerated program.

CAMPUS LIFE
Environment: Metropolis.

ADMISSIONS
Freshman Admission Requirements: High school diploma is required and GED is accepted. **Freshman Admission Statistics:** applied, admitted, enrolled. **Transfer Admission Requirements:** college transcript(s), essay or personal statement, statement of good standing from prior institution(s). Minimum college GPA of 2.6 required. Lowest grade transferable C.

COSTS AND FINANCIAL AID
Financial Aid Statistics: needy freshmen, needy undergrads receive need-based scholarship or grant aid. freshmen, undergrads receive non-need-based scholarship or grant aid. freshmen, undergrads receive need-based self-help aid. freshmen, undergrads receive athletic scholarships.

FURMAN UNIVERSITY

3300 Poinsett Highway, Greenville, SC 29613
Phone: 864-294-2034 **Financial Aid Phone:** 864.294.2030
E-mail: admissions@furman.edu **CEEB Code:** 5222
Fax: 864-294-2018 **Website:** www.furman.edu **ACT Code:** 3858

This private school was founded in 1826. It has a 800 acre campus.

RATINGS
Admissions Selectivity Rating: 90   **Fire Safety Rating:** 93   **Green Rating:** 87

STUDENTS AND FACULTY
Enrollment: 2,678. **Student Body:** 61% female, 39% male, 70% out-of-state, 3% international (49 countries represented). Asian 3%, African American 6%, Caucasian 79%, Hispanic 5%, Native American <1%, Pacific Islander <1%, Two or more races 3%, Race unknown 1%.
Retention and Graduation: 90% freshmen return for sophomore year. 78% freshmen graduate within 4 years. 83% freshmen graduate within 6 years. 38% grads go on to further study within 1 year. 28% grads pursue arts and sciences degrees. 3% grads pursue law degrees. 2% grads pursue business degrees. 4% grads pursue medical degrees. **Faculty:** Student/faculty ratio 10:1. 243 full-time faculty, 97% hold PhDs, 16% are members of minority groups, 42% are women. 0% of classes are taught by teaching assistants.

ACADEMICS
Degrees: Bachelor's; Certificate; Master's; Post-bachelor's certificate. **Classes:** Most classes have 20–29 students. **Most popular majors:** Business/Commerce, General; Health Professions and Related Clinical Sciences, Other; Political Science and Government, General. **Special Study Options:** Double major; English as a Second Language (ESL); Independent study; Internships; Liberal arts/career combination; Student-designed major; Study abroad; Teacher

certification program. **Combined degree programs:** BA/MA. **Disability Services offered:** Note-taking services; Reader services; Tape recorders; Tutors. **Career services:** Alumni network; Alumni services; Career assessment; Career/job search classes; Internships.

FACILITIES

Housing: Apartments for single students; Coed dorms; Men's dorms; Special housing for disabled students; Special housing for international students; Theme housing; Wellness housing; Women's dorms 98% of campus accessible to physically disabled. **Special Academic Facilities/Equipment:** Visual arts gallery and teaching facility, language lab. Astronomical lab; Center for Engaged Learning; and Center for Collaborative Learning and Communication.

CAMPUS LIFE

Environment: City. **Activities:** Campus Ministries; Choral groups; Concert band; Dance; Drama/theater; International Student Organization; Jazz band; Literary magazine; Marching band; Model UN; Music ensembles; Musical theater; Opera; Pep band; Radio station; Student government; Student newspaper; Student-run film society; Symphony orchestra; Television station; Yearbook. 165 registered organizations, 29 honor societies, 24 religious organizations, 6 fraternities, 7 sororities, on campus. **Athletics (Intercollegiate):** *Men:* baseball, basketball, cheerleading, cross-country, football, golf, soccer, tennis, track/field (outdoor), track/field (indoor). *Women:* basketball, cheerleading, cross-country, golf, soccer, softball, tennis, track/field (outdoor), track/field (indoor), volleyball. **On-Campus Highlights:** Daniel Dining Hall **Environmental Initiatives:** Sustainable Furman: The approval of Sustainable Furman, the university's comprehensive sustainability master plan. The plan covers all aspects of the university; the 8 goals of Sustainable Furman address sustainability in the curriculum, co-curricular activities, campus culture, renewable energy, efficiency in operations and maintenance, transportation, sustainability service, and continuing national leadership in the sustainability arena. In addition, the plan sets out a path for the university to reach carbon neutrality by 2026.

ADMISSIONS

Freshman Academic Profile: Average high school GPA 3.6. 55% in top 10% of high school class, 75% in top 25% of high school class, 96% in top 50% of high school class. 54% from public high schools. **Test scores:** SAT Math middle 50% range 610–710. SAT EBRW middle 50% range 630–710. ACT middle 50% range 28–32. **Basis for Candidate Selection:** *Very important factors include:* rigor of secondary school record. *Important factors include:* class rank, academic GPA, application essay, extracurricular activities, character/personal qualities. *Other factors include:* standardized test scores, recommendation(s), interview, talent/ability, first generation, alumni/ae relation, racial/ethnic status, volunteer work, work experience, level of applicant's interest. **Freshman Admission Requirements:** High school diploma is required and GED is accepted. *Academic units required:* 4 English, 3 math, 2 science, 2 science labs, 2 foreign language, 3 social studies. *Academic units recommended:* 4 English, 4 math, 3 science, 2 science labs, 3 foreign language, 4 social studies. **Freshman Admission Statistics:** 5,258 applied, 57% admitted, 22% enrolled. **Transfer Admission Requirements:** High school transcript, college transcript(s), essay or personal statement, standardized test scores, statement of good standing from prior institution(s). Minimum college GPA of 3.0 required. Lowest grade transferable C. **General Admission Information:** Application fee $50. Priority deadline 1/15. Regular application deadline 1/15. Admission may be deferred for a maximum of 1 year.

COSTS AND FINANCIAL AID

Average book and supplies expense $810. **Required Forms and Deadlines:** Business/Farm Supplement; CSS/Financial Aid PROFILE; FAFSA; Noncustodial PROFILE. **Notification of Awards:** Applicants will be notified of awards on or about 4/1. **Types of Aid:** *Need-based scholarships/grants:* College/university scholarship or grant aid from institutional funds; Federal Pell; Private scholarships; SEOG; State scholarships/grants. *Loans:* Direct PLUS loans; Direct Subsidized Stafford Loans; Direct Unsubsidized Stafford Loans. **Student Employment:** Federal Work-Study Program available. Institutional employment available. **Financial Aid Statistics:** 100% needy freshmen, 100% needy undergrads receive need-based scholarship or grant aid. 43% freshmen, 51% undergrads receive non-need-based scholarship or grant aid. 63% freshmen, 63% undergrads receive need-based self-help aid. 6% freshmen, 7% undergrads receive athletic scholarships. 41% undergrads borrow to pay for school. Average cumulative indebtedness $30,388. **Criteria awarding aid:** *Need-based:* Academics, Alumni affiliation, Art, Athletics, Leadership, Music/drama, Religious affiliation. *Non-Need-based:* Academics, Alumni affiliation, Art, Athletics, Leadership, Music/drama, Religious affiliation, State/district residency.

GALLAUDET UNIVERSITY

800 Florida Avenue, NE, Washington, DC 20002
Phone: 202-651-5750 **Financial Aid Phone:** 202-651-5290
E-mail: admissions.office@gallaudet.edu **CEEB Code:** 5240
Fax: 202-651-5744 **Website:** http://www.gallaudet.edu/ **ACT Code:** 662

This private school was founded in 1864. It has a 99 acre campus.

RATINGS
Admissions Selectivity Rating: 87   **Fire Safety Rating:** 92   **Green Rating:** 75

STUDENTS AND FACULTY

Enrollment: 1,112. **Student Body:** 54% female, 46% male, 98% out-of-state, 4% international (20 countries represented). Asian 4%, African American 16%, Caucasian 51%, Hispanic 12%, Native American 1%, Pacific Islander 1%, Two or more races 4%, Race unknown 8%.
Retention and Graduation: 72% freshmen return for sophomore year. 26% freshmen graduate within 4 years. 47% freshmen graduate within 6 years.
Faculty: Student/faculty ratio 6:1. 188 full-time faculty, 76% hold PhDs, 30% are members of minority groups, 62% are women.

ACADEMICS

Degrees: Bachelor's; Certificate; Doctoral degree—other; Doctoral degree research/scholarship; Master's; Post-bachelor's certificate; Post-master's certificate. **Classes:** Most classes have 10–19 students. Most lab/discussion sessions have 10–19 students. **Most popular majors:** Sign Language Interpretation and Translation; Social Work, Other; Business Administration and Management, General. **Special Study Options:** Cross-registration; Distance learning; Double major; Dual enrollment; English as a Second Language (ESL); Honors program; Independent study; Internships; Student-designed major; Study abroad; Teacher certification program. **Honors programs:** The Gallaudet Honors Program is a Learning Community for the most academically capable and motivated students. The overall goal is to foster skills, work habits, and attitudes conducive to future achievement and lifelong learning. To this end, the Program focuses on linking rigorous, challenging, and innovative curricular offerings with co-curricular activities. It also serves as a leader in and test laboratory of curricular, co-curricular, and extracurricular innovations; successes may then be replicated for all students. **Disability Services offered:** Tutors. **Career services:** Alumni network; Alumni services; Career assessment; Career/job search classes; Internships.

FACILITIES

Housing: Apartments for married students; Coed dorms; Special housing for disabled students 100% of campus accessible to physically disabled. **Special Academic Facilities/Equipment:** Kendall Demonstration Elementary School and Model Secondary School for the Deaf. **Campus Network:** 100% of classrooms, 100% of dorms, 100% of student union, 100% of libraries, 100% of dining areas, have wireless network access.

CAMPUS LIFE

Environment: Metropolis. **Activities:** Campus Ministries; Dance; Drama/theater; International Student Organization; Literary magazine; Student government; Student newspaper; Student-run film society; Television station; Yearbook. 28 registered organizations, 1 honor societies, 4 fraternities, 3 sororities, on campus. **Athletics (Intercollegiate):** *Men:* baseball, basketball, cross-country, diving, football, soccer, swimming, tennis, track/field (outdoor), wrestling. *Women:* basketball, cross-country, diving, soccer, softball, swimming, tennis, track/field (outdoor), volleyball. **On-Campus Highlights:** Rathskellar.

ADMISSIONS

Freshman Academic Profile: Average high school GPA 3.2. **Test scores:** SAT Math middle 50% range 402–530. SAT EBRW middle 50% range 390–547. ACT middle 50% range 15–20. **Basis for Candidate Selection:** *Very important factors include:* rigor of secondary school record, academic GPA, application essay, standardized test scores, recommendation(s). *Other factors include:* class rank, interview, extracurricular activities, talent/ability, character/personal qualities, first generation, volunteer work, work experience, level of applicant's interest. **Freshman Admission Requirements:** High school diploma is required and GED is accepted. *Academic units recommended:* 4 English, 3 math, 2 science, 2 foreign language, 2 social studies, 1 visual/performing arts. **Freshman Admission Statistics:** 496 applied, 57% admitted, 71% enrolled. **Transfer Admission Requirements:** college transcript(s), essay or personal statement, Lowest grade transferable C-. **General Admission Information:** Application fee $50. Non-fall registration accepted. Admission may be deferred for a maximum of 2 years.

COSTS AND FINANCIAL AID

Annual tuition $16,512. Room and board $14,100. Required fees $526. Average book and supplies expense $1,600. **Required Forms and Deadlines:** FAFSA. **Notification of Awards:** Applicants will be notified of awards on a rolling basis beginning 3/1. **Types of Aid:** *Need-based scholarships/grants:* College/university scholarship or grant aid from institutional funds; Federal Pell; Private scholarships; SEOG; State scholarships/grants. *Loans:* Direct PLUS loans; Direct Subsidized Stafford Loans; Direct Unsubsidized Stafford Loans. **Student Employment:** Federal Work-Study Program available. Institutional employment available. **Financial Aid Statistics:** 99% needy freshmen, 98% needy undergrads receive need-based scholarship or grant aid. 24% freshmen, 19% undergrads receive non-need-based scholarship or grant aid. 34% freshmen, 45% undergrads receive need-based self-help aid. 0% freshmen, 0% undergrads receive athletic scholarships.**Criteria awarding aid:** *Need-based:* Academics. *Non-Need-based:* Academics.

GANNON UNIVERSITY

109 University Square, Erie, PA 16541
Phone: 814-871-7407 **Financial Aid Phone:** 814-871-7337
E-mail: admissions@gannon.edu **CEEB Code:** 2270
Fax: 814-871-5826 **Website:** www.gannon.edu **ACT Code:** 3576

This private school, affiliated with the Roman Catholic Church, was founded in 1925. It has a 52 acre campus.

RATINGS
Admissions Selectivity Rating: 80   **Fire Safety Rating:** 97   **Green Rating:** 70

STUDENTS AND FACULTY
Enrollment: 2,866. **Student Body:** 61% female, 39% male, 28% out-of-state, 9% international (39 countries represented). Asian 2%, African American 5%, Caucasian 70%, Hispanic 4%, Native American <1%, Pacific Islander <1%, Two or more races 3%, Race unknown 6%.
Retention and Graduation: 82% freshmen return for sophomore year. 52% freshmen graduate within 4 years. % freshmen graduate within 6 years. 47% grads go on to further study within 1 year. 4% grads pursue law degrees. 4% grads pursue business degrees. 6% grads pursue medical degrees. **Faculty:** Student/faculty ratio 13:1. 234 full-time faculty, 76% hold PhDs, 13% are members of minority groups, 52% are women. 1% of classes are taught by teaching assistants.

ACADEMICS
Degrees: Associate; Bachelor's; Certificate; Doctoral degree—professional practice; Doctoral degree research/scholarship; Master's; Post-bachelor's certificate; Post-master's certificate; Terminal Associate. **Classes:** Most classes have 20–29 students. Most lab/discussion sessions have 10–19 students. **Most popular majors:** Health Professions and Related Clinical Sciences, Other; Registered Nursing/Registered Nurse; Exercise Science and Kinesiology. **Special Study Options:** Accelerated program; Cooperative education program; Distance learning; Double major; Dual enrollment; English as a Second Language (ESL); Exchange student program (domestic); Honors program; Independent study; Internships; Liberal arts/career combination; Study abroad; Teacher certification program. **Honors programs:** The Gannon honors program challenges and nurtures students as ethical, global leaders. Our small class sizes, reading and writing intensive courses, opportunities for travel, and service-learning engage our highly motivated students. **Combined degree programs:** BA/JD; BA/MA; BA/MD. **Disability Services offered:** Note-taking services; Reader services; Tape recorders. **Career services:** Alumni network; Alumni services; Career assessment; Career/job search classes; Internships; Regional alumni.

FACILITIES
Housing: Apartments for single students; Coed dorms; Fraternity/sorority housing; Theme housing; 70% of campus accessible to physically disabled. **Special Academic Facilities/Equipment:** Patient Simulation Center, Environaut research vessel, computer-integrated manufacturing facilities, atomic force microscope, Schuster Art Gallery, Schuster Theatres, Erie Technology Incubator.

CAMPUS LIFE
Environment: City. **Activities:** Campus Ministries; Choral groups; Concert band; Dance; Drama/theater; International Student Organization; Literary magazine; Model UN; Pep band; Radio station; Student government;

Student newspaper. 91 registered organizations, 16 honor societies, 5 religious organizations, 7 fraternities, 5 sororities, on campus. **Athletics (Intercollegiate):** *Men:* baseball, basketball, cheerleading, cross-country, football, golf, soccer, swimming, water polo, wrestling. *Women:* basketball, cheerleading, cross-country, golf, lacrosse, soccer, softball, swimming, volleyball, water polo. **On-Campus Highlights:** Waldron Campus Center. **Environmental Initiatives:** Switching out all campus light bulbs to compact flourescent.

ADMISSIONS
Freshman Academic Profile: Average high school GPA 3.6. 31% in top 10% of high school class, 63% in top 25% of high school class, 93% in top 50% of high school class. 83% from public high schools. **Test scores:** SAT Math middle 50% range 510–620. SAT EBRW middle 50% range 520–620. ACT middle 50% range 19–26. **Basis for Candidate Selection:** *Very important factors include:* rigor of secondary school record, academic GPA, standardized test scores. *Other factors include:* class rank, application essay, recommendation(s), interview, extracurricular activities, character/personal qualities, alumni/ae relation, work experience. **Freshman Admission Requirements:** High school diploma is required and GED is accepted. *Academic units required:* 4 English, 2 math, 2 science, 2 science labs, 2 social studies, 1 history, 3 academic electives. *Academic units recommended:* 4 English, 4 math, 4 science, 3 science labs, 2 foreign language, 2 social studies, 1 history, 3 academic electives, 1 computer science, 1 visual/performing arts. **Freshman Admission Statistics:** 4,727 applied, 76% admitted, 21% enrolled. **Transfer Admission Requirements:** college transcript(s), statement of good standing from prior institution(s). Minimum college GPA of 2.0 required. Lowest grade transferable C. **General Admission Information:** Application fee $25. Non-fall registration accepted.

COSTS AND FINANCIAL AID
Required Forms and Deadlines: FAFSA. **Notification of Awards:** Applicants will be notified of awards on a rolling basis beginning 11/1. **Types of Aid:** *Need-based scholarships/grants:* College/university scholarship or grant aid from institutional funds; Federal Nursing Scholarships; Federal Pell; Private scholarships; SEOG; State scholarships/grants. *Loans:* Direct PLUS loans; Direct Subsidized Stafford Loans; Direct Unsubsidized Stafford Loans. **Student Employment:** Federal Work-Study Program available. Institutional employment available. **Financial Aid Statistics:** 99% needy freshmen, 99% needy undergrads receive need-based scholarship or grant aid. 17% freshmen, 14% undergrads receive non-need-based scholarship or grant aid. 73% freshmen, 81% undergrads receive need-based self-help aid. 4% freshmen, 5% undergrads receive athletic scholarships. 98% freshmen, 95% undergrads receive any aid. **Criteria awarding aid:** *Non-Need-based:* Academics, Athletics, Leadership, Music/drama, Religious affiliation.

GARDNER-WEBB UNIVERSITY

PO Box 817, Boiling Springs, NC 28017
Phone: 704-406-4498 **Financial Aid Phone:** 704-406-4243
E-mail: admissions@gardner-webb.edu **CEEB Code:** 5242
Fax: 704-406-4488 **Website:** www.gardner-webb.edu **ACT Code:** 3102

This private school, affiliated with the Baptist Church, was founded in 1905. It has a 250 acre campus.

RATINGS
Admissions Selectivity Rating: 80   **Fire Safety Rating:** 98   **Green Rating:** 60*

STUDENTS AND FACULTY
Enrollment: 2,640. **Student Body:** 65% female, 35% male, 21% out-of-state, <1% international (22 countries represented). Asian <1%, African American 19%, Caucasian 72%, Hispanic 2%, Native American 1%, Race unknown 6%. **Retention and Graduation:** 74% freshmen return for sophomore year. **Faculty:** Student/faculty ratio 13:1. 140 full-time faculty, 80% hold PhDs, 4% are members of minority groups, 46% are women. 0% of classes are taught by teaching assistants.

ACADEMICS
Degrees: Associate; Bachelor's; Master's. **Classes:** Most classes have 10–19 students. **Most popular majors:** Social Sciences, Other; Business/Commerce, General; Religion/Religious Studies. **Special Study Options:** Accelerated program; Distance learning; Double major; Dual enrollment; English as a Second Language (ESL); Honors program; Independent study; Internships; Liberal arts/career combination; Study abroad; Teacher certification program.

Honors programs: Alpha Chi Honors Program Beta Beta Beta Delta Mu Delta Sigma Delta Pi Sigma Tau Delta Theta Alpha Kappa Pi Delta Phi Psi Chi Sigma Zeta Sigma Theta Tau Who's Who. **Disability Services offered:** Note-taking services; Reader services; Tape recorders; Tutors. **Career services:** Alumni network; Career assessment; Career/job search classes; Internships.

FACILITIES

Housing: Apartments for single students; Men's dorms; Special housing for disabled students; Wellness housing; Women's dorms 100% of campus accessible to physically disabled. **Special Academic Facilities/Equipment:** Williams Observatory, Millennium Playhouse, Broyhill Adventure Course, Lake Hollifield Complex and Carillon.

CAMPUS LIFE

Environment: Rural. **Activities:** Campus Ministries; Choral groups; Concert band; Dance; Drama/theater; International Student Organization; Jazz band; Literary magazine; Marching band; Music ensembles; Musical theater; Opera; Pep band; Radio station; Student government; Student newspaper; Symphony orchestra; Yearbook. 65 registered organizations, 12 honor societies, 11 religious organizations, on campus. **Athletics (Intercollegiate):** *Men:* baseball, basketball, cheerleading, cross-country, football, golf, soccer, swimming, tennis, track/field (outdoor), track/field (indoor), wrestling. *Women:* basketball, cheerleading, cross-country, golf, soccer, softball, swimming, tennis, track/field (outdoor), track/field (indoor), volleyball. **On-Campus Highlights:** Dover Campus Center **Environmental Initiatives:** recycling programs.

ADMISSIONS

Freshman Academic Profile: Average high school GPA 3.5. 32% in top 10% of high school class, 49% in top 25% of high school class, 72% in top 50% of high school class. 84% from public high schools. **Test scores:** SAT Math middle 50% range 420–550. SAT EBRW middle 50% range 440–560. ACT middle 50% range 18–23. **Basis for Candidate Selection:** *Very important factors include:* rigor of secondary school record, academic GPA, standardized test scores, level of applicant's interest. *Important factors include:* class rank, recommendation(s), extracurricular activities, character/personal qualities. *Other factors include:* application essay, interview, talent/ability, volunteer work. **Freshman Admission Requirements:** High school diploma is required and GED is accepted. *Academic units recommended:* 4 English, 3 math, 3 science, 2 science labs, 2 foreign language, 1 social studies, 1 history. **Freshman Admission Statistics:** 3,277 applied, 62% admitted, 22% enrolled. **Transfer Admission Requirements:** college transcript(s), statement of good standing from prior institution(s). Minimum college GPA of 2.25 required. Lowest grade transferable C. **General Admission Information:** Application fee $40. Non-fall registration accepted. Admission may be deferred for a maximum of 2 semesters.

COSTS AND FINANCIAL AID

Annual tuition $22,050. Room and board $7,195. Required fees $465. Average book and supplies expense $1,000. **Required Forms and Deadlines:** FAFSA; State aid form. **Notification of Awards:** Applicants will be notified of awards on a rolling basis beginning 3/1. **Types of Aid:** *Need-based scholarships/grants:* College/university scholarship or grant aid from institutional funds; Federal Pell; Private scholarships; SEOG; State scholarships/grants. **Student Employment:** Federal Work-Study Program available. Institutional employment available. **Financial Aid Statistics:** 96% needy freshmen, 34% needy undergrads receive need-based scholarship or grant aid. 77% freshmen, 70% undergrads receive non-need-based scholarship or grant aid. 66% freshmen, 75% undergrads receive need-based self-help aid. freshmen, undergrads receive athletic scholarships. 100% freshmen receive any aid. **Criteria awarding aid:** *Need-based:* Academics, Leadership, Minority status, Music/drama, Religious affiliation. *Non-Need-based:* Academics, Athletics, Leadership, Music/drama, State/district residency.

GEORGE FOX UNIVERSITY

414 N. Meridian St., Newberg, OR 97132
Phone: 503-554-2240 **Financial Aid Phone:** 503-554-2300
E-mail: admissions@georgefox.edu **CEEB Code:** 4325
Fax: 503-554-3110 **Website:** www.georgefox.edu **ACT Code:** 3462

This private school, affiliated with the Evangelical Friends Church, was founded in 1891. It has a 108 acre campus.

RATINGS

Admissions Selectivity Rating: 80   **Fire Safety Rating:** 88   **Green Rating:** 60*

STUDENTS AND FACULTY

Enrollment: 2,358. **Student Body:** 57% female, 43% male, 35% out-of-state, 6% international (43 countries represented). Asian 4%, African American 2%, Caucasian 70%, Hispanic 7%, Native American <1%, Pacific Islander <1%, Two or more races 5%, Race unknown 4%.
Retention and Graduation: 82% freshmen return for sophomore year. 11% grads go on to further study within 1 year. 6% grads pursue arts and sciences degrees. 0% grads pursue law degrees. 2% grads pursue business degrees. 2% grads pursue medical degrees. **Faculty:** Student/faculty ratio 14:1. 168 full-time faculty, 76% hold PhDs, 14% are members of minority groups, 40% are women. 0% of classes are taught by teaching assistants.

ACADEMICS

Degrees: Bachelor's; Doctoral degree—professional practice; Master's; Post-bachelor's certificate; Post-master's certificate. **Classes:** Most classes have 10–19 students. Most lab/discussion sessions have 10–19 students. **Most popular majors:** Registered Nursing/Registered Nurse; Business Administration and Management, General; Elementary Education and Teaching. **Special Study Options:** Accelerated program; Cross-registration; Distance learning; Double major; Dual enrollment; English as a Second Language (ESL); Exchange student program (domestic); Honors program; Independent study; Internships; Student-designed major; Study abroad; Teacher certification program. **Honors programs:** Richter Scholars, Advance Leadership Development Program. The William Penn Honors Program is an alternative liberal arts general education program for undergraduate students. Modeled on the Socratic tutorial style, the program is designed to hone students' critical thinking skills by exposing them to classical texts and using discussion as the primary mode of instruction. Graduates of the program will be prepared to engage their culture meaningfully at the deepest levels—and they will be able to do so in a humble and gracious manner from an orthodox Christian perspective. **Disability Services offered:** Note-taking services; Reader services; Tape recorders; Tutors. **Career services:** Alumni network; Alumni services; Career assessment; Career/job search classes; Internships; Regional alumni.

FACILITIES

Housing: Apartments for single students; Men's dorms; Special housing for disabled students; Theme housing; Wellness housing; Women's dorms 98% of campus accessible to physically disabled. **Special Academic Facilities/Equipment:** Nuclear magnetic resonance spectrometer, Providence Nursing Learning Lab, language lab, electron microscope. **Campus Network:** 100% of classrooms, 100% of dorms, 100% of student union, 100% of libraries, 100% of dining areas, 100% of common outdoor areas, have wireless network access.

CAMPUS LIFE

Environment: Village. **Activities:** Campus Ministries; Choral groups; Concert band; Drama/theater; International Student Organization; Jazz band; Literary magazine; Music ensembles; Musical theater; Pep band; Radio station; Student government; Student newspaper; Symphony orchestra; Yearbook. 20 registered organizations, 3 honor societies, 3 religious organizations, on campus. **Athletics (Intercollegiate):** *Men:* baseball, basketball, cross-country, golf, soccer, tennis, track/field (outdoor). *Women:* basketball, cross-country, golf, soccer, softball, tennis, track/field (outdoor), volleyball. **On-Campus Highlights:** Bruin Den-Cafe in the Student Union Bldg. **Environmental Initiatives:** LEED-certified residence hall.

ADMISSIONS

Freshman Academic Profile: Average high school GPA 3.6. 27% in top 10% of high school class, 57% in top 25% of high school class, 85% in top 50% of high school class. 73% from public high schools. **Test scores:** SAT Math middle 50% range 470–600. SAT EBRW middle 50% range 470–600. ACT middle 50% range 20–26. **Basis for Candidate Selection:** *Very important factors include:* rigor of secondary school record, academic GPA, application essay, standardized test scores, recommendation(s). *Important factors include:* character/personal qualities. *Other factors include:* class rank, interview, extracurricular activities, talent/ability, religious affiliation/commitment, volunteer work, work experience. **Freshman Admission Requirements:** High school diploma is required and GED is accepted. *Academic units recommended:* 4 English, 2 math, 2 science, 2 science labs, 2 foreign language, 3 social studies, 2 history. **Freshman Admission Statistics:** 2,431 applied, 75% admitted, 34% enrolled. **Transfer Admission Requirements:** college transcript(s), essay or personal statement, statement of good standing from prior institution(s). Minimum college GPA of 2.6 required. Lowest grade transferable C-. **General Admission Information:** Application fee $40. Priority deadline 2/1. Non-fall registration accepted. Admission may be deferred for a maximum of 1 year.

COSTS AND FINANCIAL AID
Annual tuition $33,370. Room and board $10,528. Required fees $360. Average book and supplies expense $950. **Required Forms and Deadlines:** FAFSA; State aid form. **Notification of Awards:** Applicants will be notified of awards on a rolling basis beginning 3/1. **Types of Aid:** *Need-based scholarships/ grants:* College/university scholarship or grant aid from institutional funds; Federal Pell; Private scholarships; SEOG; State scholarships/grants. *Loans:* Direct PLUS loans; Direct Subsidized Stafford Loans; Direct Unsubsidized Stafford Loans. **Student Employment:** Federal Work-Study Program available. Institutional employment available. **Financial Aid Statistics:** 98% needy freshmen, 96% needy undergrads receive need-based scholarship or grant aid. 7% freshmen, 6% undergrads receive non-need-based scholarship or grant aid. 87% freshmen, 88% undergrads receive need-based self-help aid. 0% freshmen, 0% undergrads receive athletic scholarships. 99.5% freshmen, 96.1% undergrads receive any aid. 79% undergrads borrow to pay for school. Average cumulative indebtedness $22,996. **Criteria awarding aid:** *Need-based:* Minority status, Religious affiliation. *Non-Need-based:* Academics, Alumni affiliation, Art, Job skills, Leadership, Minority status, Music/drama, Religious affiliation.

GEORGE MASON UNIVERSITY

4400 University Drive, Fairfax, VA 22030-4444
Phone: 703-993-2400 **Financial Aid Phone:** 703-993-2353
E-mail: admissions@gmu.edu **CEEB Code:** 5827
Fax: 703-993-4622 **Website:** https://www2.gmu.edu **ACT Code:** 4357

This public school was founded in 1972. It has a 817 acre campus.

RATINGS
Admissions Selectivity Rating: 76   **Fire Safety Rating:** 98   **Green Rating:** 93

STUDENTS AND FACULTY
Enrollment: 26,013. **Student Body:** 49% female, 51% male, 10% out-of-state, 6% international (108 countries represented). Asian 21%, African American 11%, Caucasian 38%, Hispanic 16%, Native American <1%, Pacific Islander <1%, Two or more races 5%, Race unknown 3%.
Retention and Graduation: 86% freshmen return for sophomore year. 50% freshmen graduate within 4 years. 71% freshmen graduate within 6 years. **Faculty:** Student/faculty ratio 17:1. 1,385 full-time faculty, 91% hold PhDs, 23% are members of minority groups, 44% are women. 6% of classes are taught by teaching assistants.

ACADEMICS
Degrees: Bachelor's; Doctoral degree—professional practice; Doctoral degree research/scholarship; Master's; Post-bachelor's certificate; Post-master's certificate. **Classes:** Most classes have 20–29 students. Most lab/discussion sessions have 20–29 students. **Most popular majors:** Information Technology; Computer Science; Biology/Biological Sciences, General. **Special Study Options:** Accelerated program; Cooperative education program; Cross-registration; Distance learning; Double major; Dual enrollment; English as a Second Language (ESL); Exchange student program (domestic); Honors program; Independent study; Internships; Liberal arts/career combination; Student-designed major; Study abroad; Teacher certification program. **Honors programs:** The Mission of the Honors College is to recruit the most highly motivated undergraduates from every background and in every field of study; to foster their capabilities to listen to, learn from, and work with people whose

perspectives differ from their own; and to engage them in transformational learning experiences that prepare them to meet the challenges facing our community, our nation, and our world. Through the resources of the Honors College, the university provides students the support to excel academically and to pursue life-long goals. Included in these resources is the Honors College curriculum, which offers challenging courses that fulfill core academic requirements at Mason. Senior faculty, including Mason's Robinson Professors, teach small classes of students taking the curriculum. A select group of entering students is invited to become part of the University Scholars, a community of learners and leaders who receive Mason's most competitive merit-based scholarships. All Honors College students have direct access to the Office of Fellowships, which provides guidance and support to high-achieving Mason undergraduates and recent alumni about the application process for nationally competitive fellowships. The benefits of being part of the Honors College include participating in a diverse living-learning community. Community programs include special lectures, events, and excursions on and off campus, as well as opportunities to take advantage of internships and cultural programs in Washington, D.C. All students in the Honors College receive individualized academic advising, priority registration, and opportunities for close interaction with faculty for one-on-one mentoring and graduate and professional advising. **Combined degree programs:** BA/MA. **Disability Services offered:** Note-taking services; Reader services; Tape recorders. **Career services:** Alumni network; Alumni services; Career assessment; Career/job search classes; Internships; Regional alumni.

FACILITIES
Housing: Apartments for single students; Coed dorms; Special housing for disabled students; Special housing for international students; Theme housing 95% of campus accessible to physically disabled. **Special Academic Facilities/ Equipment:** Smithsonian-Mason School of Conservation George Mason University Observatory Point of View International Retreat and Conference Center EagleBank Arena Mason Enterprise Center/Virginia Small Business Development Center Mason Innovation Exchange Mason Trails Carty House (mock crime scene house for forensic science program) Potomac Science Center Center for the Arts Hylton Performing Arts Center Presidents Park Greenhouse Sports Medicine Assessment Research and Testing (SMART) laboratory The EDGE: Mason Center for Team and Organizational Learning. **Campus Network:** 100% of classrooms, 100% of dorms, 100% of student union, 100% of libraries, 100% of dining areas, 100% of common outdoor areas, have wireless network access.

CAMPUS LIFE
Environment: City. **Activities:** Campus Ministries; Choral groups; Concert band; Dance; Drama/theater; International Student Organization; Jazz band; Literary magazine; Model UN; Music ensembles; Musical theater; Opera; Pep band; Radio station; Student government; Student newspaper; Student-run film society; Symphony orchestra; Television station; Yearbook. 464 registered organizations, 15 honor societies, 46 religious organizations, 24 fraternities, 19 sororities, on campus. **Athletics (Intercollegiate):** *Men:* baseball, basketball, cheerleading, cross-country, diving, golf, soccer, swimming, tennis, track/ field (outdoor), track/field (indoor), volleyball, wrestling. *Women:* basketball, cheerleading, crew/rowing, cross-country, diving, lacrosse, soccer, softball, swimming, tennis, track/field (outdoor), track/field (indoor), volleyball. **On-Campus Highlights:** Johnson Center.

ADMISSIONS
Freshman Academic Profile: Average high school GPA 3.7. 15% in top 10% of high school class, 44% in top 25% of high school class, 81% in top 50% of high school class. 72% from public high schools. **Test scores:** SAT Math middle 50% range 550–660. SAT EBRW middle 50% range 560–660. ACT middle 50% range 24–30. **Basis for Candidate Selection:** *Very important factors include:* rigor of secondary school record, academic GPA. *Important factors include:* standardized test scores, talent/ability. *Other factors include:* class rank, application essay, recommendation(s), extracurricular activities, character/ personal qualities, first generation, geographical residence, state residency, volunteer work, work experience, level of applicant's interest. **Freshman Admission Requirements:** High school diploma is required and GED is accepted. *Academic units required:* 4 English, 3 math, 2 science, 2 science labs, 2 foreign language, 3 social studies, 3 academic electives. *Academic units recommended:* 4 English, 4 math, 3 science, 3 science labs, 3 foreign language, 4 social studies, 5 academic electives. **Freshman Admission Statistics:** 19,554 applied, 87% admitted, 22% enrolled. **Transfer Admission Requirements:** college transcript(s), Minimum college GPA of 2.0 required. Lowest grade transferable C. **General Admission Information:** Application fee $70. Priority deadline 11/1. Regular application deadline 1/15. Non-fall registration accepted. Admission may be deferred for a maximum of 1 year.

COSTS AND FINANCIAL AID

Annual in-state tuition $9,060. Annual out-of-state tuition $32,520. Room and board $11,705. Required fees $3,504. Average book and supplies expense $1,278. **Required Forms and Deadlines:** FAFSA. **Notification of Awards:** Applicants will be notified of awards on a rolling basis beginning 4/1. **Types of Aid:** *Need-based scholarships/grants:* College/university scholarship or grant aid from institutional funds; Federal Pell; Private scholarships; SEOG; State scholarships/grants. *Loans:* Direct PLUS loans; Direct Subsidized Stafford Loans; Direct Unsubsidized Stafford Loans. **Student Employment:** Federal Work-Study Program available. Institutional employment available. **Financial Aid Statistics:** 84% needy freshmen, 85% needy undergrads receive need-based scholarship or grant aid. 39% freshmen, 21% undergrads receive non-need-based scholarship or grant aid. 75% freshmen, 72% undergrads receive need-based self-help aid. 2% freshmen, 1% undergrads receive athletic scholarships. 74% freshmen, 65% undergrads receive any aid. 58% undergrads borrow to pay for school. Average cumulative indebtedness $33,362. **Criteria awarding aid:** *Non-Need-based:* Academics, Athletics, Minority status, Music/drama.

GEORGETOWN COLLEGE

400 East College Street, Georgetown, KY 40324
Phone: 502-863-8009 **Financial Aid Phone:** 502-863-8027
E-mail: admissions@georgetowncollege.edu **CEEB Code:** 1249
Fax: 502-868-7733 **Website:** www.georgetowncollege.edu **ACT Code:** 1514

This private school was founded in 1829. It has a 104 acre campus.

RATINGS

Admissions Selectivity Rating: 79   **Fire Safety Rating:** 82   **Green Rating:** 63

STUDENTS AND FACULTY

Enrollment: 942. **Student Body:** 53% female, 47% male, 23% out-of-state, 1% international (12 countries represented). Asian 1%, African American 9%, Caucasian 79%, Hispanic 1%, Native American <1%, Pacific Islander 0%, Two or more races 4%, Race unknown 5%.
Retention and Graduation: 71% freshmen return for sophomore year.
Faculty: Student/faculty ratio 11:1. 77 full-time faculty, 95% hold PhDs, 6% are members of minority groups, 47% are women. 0% of classes are taught by teaching assistants.

ACADEMICS

Degrees: Bachelor's; Master's; Post-master's certificate. **Classes:** Most classes have 10–19 students. **Most popular majors:** Biology/Biological Sciences, General; Psychology, General; Athletic Training/Trainer. **Special Study Options:** Accelerated program; Cooperative education program; Distance learning; Double major; Dual enrollment; English as a Second Language (ESL); Honors program; Independent study; Internships; Liberal arts/career combination; Student-designed major; Study abroad; Teacher certification program. **Honors programs:** Academic Honors Program, Spanish Immersion Program, Equine Scholars Program. **Disability Services offered:** Note-taking services; Reader services; Tape recorders; Tutors. **Career services:** Alumni network; Alumni services; Career assessment; Career/job search classes; Internships; Regional alumni.

FACILITIES

Housing: Apartments for married students; Apartments for single students; Fraternity/sorority housing; Men's dorms; Women's dorms. **Special Academic Facilities/Equipment:** The Anna Ashcraft Ensor Learning Resource Center, an arboretum, three antebellum buildings, the Asher Science Center, the Anne Wright Wilson Fine Arts Building, and the Wilson Laboratory Theatre.

CAMPUS LIFE

Environment: Town. **Activities:** Campus Ministries; Choral groups; Concert band; Dance; Drama/theater; Literary magazine; Model UN; Music ensembles; Musical theater; Pep band; Radio station; Student government; Student newspaper. 100 registered organizations, 20 honor societies, 8 religious organizations, 5 fraternities, 5 sororities, on campus. **Athletics (Intercollegiate):** *Men:* baseball, basketball, cross-country, football, golf, soccer, tennis, track/field (outdoor), track/field (indoor). *Women:* basketball, cheerleading, cross-country, golf, soccer, softball, tennis, track/field (outdoor), track/field (indoor), volleyball. **On-Campus Highlights:** The Ensor Learning Resource Center. **Environmental Initiatives:** Recycling with Pepsi Co.

ADMISSIONS

Freshman Academic Profile: 80% from public high schools. **Test scores:** SAT Math middle 50% range 420–530. SAT EBRW middle 50% range 450–530. ACT middle 50% range 20–26. **Basis for Candidate Selection:** *Very important factors include:* academic GPA. *Important factors include:* rigor of secondary school record, standardized test scores. *Other factors include:* class rank, application essay, recommendation(s), interview, extracurricular activities, talent/ability, character/personal qualities, volunteer work, work experience. **Freshman Admission Requirements:** High school diploma is required and GED is accepted. *Academic units recommended:* 4 English, 3 math, 3 science, 2 foreign language, 2 social studies. **Freshman Admission Statistics:** 2,127 applied, 66% admitted, 21% enrolled. **Transfer Admission Requirements:** High school transcript, college transcript(s), statement of good standing from prior institution(s). Minimum college GPA of 2.5 required. Lowest grade transferable C. **General Admission Information:** Application fee $30. Priority deadline 5/1. Regular application deadline 8/15. Non-fall registration accepted. Admission may be deferred for a maximum of 1 year.

COSTS AND FINANCIAL AID

Annual tuition $35,650. Room and board $9,050. Average book and supplies expense $1,250. **Required Forms and Deadlines:** FAFSA. **Notification of Awards:** Applicants will be notified of awards on a rolling basis beginning 3/1. **Types of Aid:** *Need-based scholarships/grants:* College/university scholarship or grant aid from institutional funds; Federal Pell; Private scholarships; SEOG; State scholarships/grants. *Loans:* Direct PLUS loans; Direct Subsidized Stafford Loans; Direct Unsubsidized Stafford Loans. **Student Employment:** Federal Work-Study Program available. Institutional employment available. **Financial Aid Statistics:** 100% needy freshmen, 100% needy undergrads receive need-based scholarship or grant aid. 89% freshmen, 86% undergrads receive non-need-based scholarship or grant aid. 78% freshmen, 80% undergrads receive need-based self-help aid. 3% freshmen, 3% undergrads receive athletic scholarships. 100% freshmen, 96% undergrads receive any aid. 76% undergrads borrow to pay for school. Average cumulative indebtedness $31,267. **Criteria awarding aid:** *Need-based:* Academics, Alumni affiliation, Athletics, Leadership, Music/drama, Religious affiliation. *Non-Need-based:* Academics, Alumni affiliation, Art, Athletics, Leadership, Music/drama, Religious affiliation, State/district residency.

GEORGETOWN UNIVERSITY

Room 103 White Gravenor Hall, Washington, DC 20057
Phone: 202-687-3600 **Financial Aid Phone:** 202-687-4547
E-mail: guadmiss@georgetown.edu **CEEB Code:** 5244
Fax: 202-687-5084 **Website:** www.georgetown.edu **ACT Code:** 668

This private school, affiliated with the Roman Catholic Church, was founded in 1789. It has a 104 acre campus.

RATINGS

Admissions Selectivity Rating: 98   **Fire Safety Rating:** 88   **Green Rating:** 60*

STUDENTS AND FACULTY

Enrollment: 7,083. **Student Body:** 56% female, 44% male, 98% out-of-state, 14% international (138 countries represented). Asian 10%, African American 7%, Caucasian 52%, Hispanic 10%, Native American <1%, Pacific Islander <1%, Two or more races 5%, Race unknown 2%.
Retention and Graduation: 96% freshmen return for sophomore year. 90% freshmen graduate within 4 years. 95% freshmen graduate within 6 years.
Faculty: Student/faculty ratio 11:1. 8% of classes are taught by teaching assistants.

ACADEMICS

Degrees: Bachelor's; Certificate; Doctoral degree—professional practice; Doctoral degree research/scholarship; Master's; Post-bachelor's certificate; Post-master's certificate. **Classes:** Most classes have 10–19 students. Most lab/discussion sessions have 10–19 students. **Most popular majors:** English Language and Literature, General; International Relations and Affairs; Political Science and Government, General. **Special Study Options:** Cross-registration; Distance learning; Double major; English as a Second Language

For more free content, visit PrincetonReview.com

(ESL); Honors program; Independent study; Internships; Student-designed major; Study abroad. **Honors programs:** The John Carroll Programs guide and support a highly selective group of academically talented and ambitious students from around the world. The Programs seek individuals who desire to make a lasting difference in the fields and communities they touch. For these young men and women, the Programs provide models and skills to help them make the most effective use of their undergraduate years, and to assists them in moving from the undergraduate experience to their post-graduate academic and professional lives. The Programs invite students to take as their own the Carroll motto, mentis vita pro vita mundi: the life of the mind for the life of the world. **Combined degree programs:** BA/MA. **Disability Services offered:** Note-taking services; Reader services; Tape recorders; Tutors. **Career services:** Alumni network; Alumni services; Career assessment; Career/job search classes; Internships; Regional alumni.

FACILITIES

Housing: Apartments for single students; Coed dorms; Special housing for disabled students; Wellness housing; 92% of campus accessible to physically disabled. **Special Academic Facilities/Equipment:** Language lab, seismological observatory.

CAMPUS LIFE

Environment: Metropolis. **Activities:** Campus Ministries; Choral groups; Concert band; Dance; Drama/theater; International Student Organization; Jazz band; Literary magazine; Model UN; Music ensembles; Musical theater; Pep band; Radio station; Student government; Student newspaper; Student-run film society; Symphony orchestra; Television station; Yearbook. 139 registered organizations, 14 honor societies, 20 religious organizations, on campus. **Athletics (Intercollegiate):** *Men:* baseball, basketball, crew/rowing, cross-country, diving, football, golf, lacrosse, sailing, soccer, swimming, tennis, track/field (outdoor), track/field (indoor). *Women:* basketball, crew/rowing, cross-country, diving, field hockey, golf, lacrosse, sailing, soccer, softball, swimming, tennis, track/field (outdoor), track/field (indoor), volleyball. **On-Campus Highlights:** White-Gravenor. **Environmental Initiatives:** Set LEED certification as the standard for new constructions & major renovations.

ADMISSIONS

Freshman Academic Profile: Average high school GPA 3.9. 89% in top 10% of high school class, 97% in top 25% of high school class, 99% in top 50% of high school class. 49% from public high schools. **Test scores:** SAT Math middle 50% range 690–780. SAT EBRW middle 50% range 680–750. ACT middle 50% range 31–34. **Basis for Candidate Selection:** *Very important factors include:* rigor of secondary school record, class rank, academic GPA, application essay, standardized test scores, recommendation(s), talent/ability, character/personal qualities, first generation. *Important factors include:* interview, extracurricular activities. *Other factors include:* alumni/ae relation, geographical residence, state residency, racial/ethnic status, work experience. **Freshman Admission Requirements:** High school diploma is required and GED is accepted. *Academic units required:* 4 English, 2 math, 1 science, 2 foreign language, 2 social studies, 2 history. **Freshman Admission Statistics:** 22,872 applied, 15% admitted, 49% enrolled. **Transfer Admission Requirements:** High school transcript, college transcript(s), essay or personal statement, standardized test scores, statement of good standing from prior institution(s). Minimum college GPA of 3.0 required. Lowest grade transferable C. **General Admission Information:** Application fee $75. Regular application deadline 1/10.

COSTS AND FINANCIAL AID

Annual tuition $55,440. Room and board $18,218. Required fees $618. **Required Forms and Deadlines:** Business/Farm Supplement; CSS/Financial Aid PROFILE; FAFSA. **Types of Aid:** *Need-based scholarships/grants:* Federal Pell; Private scholarships; SEOG; State scholarships/grants. *Loans:* Direct PLUS loans; Direct Subsidized Stafford Loans; Direct Unsubsidized Stafford Loans. **Student Employment:** Federal Work-Study Program available. Institutional employment available. **Financial Aid Statistics:** 93% needy freshmen, 93% needy undergrads receive need-based scholarship or grant aid. 34% freshmen, 30% undergrads receive non-need-based scholarship or grant aid. 83% freshmen, 83% undergrads receive need-based self-help aid. 6% freshmen, 5% undergrads receive athletic scholarships. 37% undergrads borrow to pay for school. Average cumulative indebtedness $25,726. **Criteria awarding aid:** *Non-Need-based:* Athletics.

800 21st St NW Suite 100, Washington, DC 20052
Phone: 202-994-6040
E-mail: gwadm@gwu.edu **CEEB Code:** 5246
Fax: 202-994-0325 **Website:** www.gwu.edu **ACT Code:** 664

This private school was founded in 1821. It has a 45 acre campus.

RATINGS

Admissions Selectivity Rating: 93   **Fire Safety Rating:** 60*   **Green Rating:** 92

STUDENTS AND FACULTY

Enrollment: 12,161. **Student Body:** 61% female, 39% male, 96% out-of-state, 11% international (122 countries represented). Asian 11%, African American 7%, Caucasian 51%, Hispanic 10%, Native American <1%, Pacific Islander <1%, Two or more races 4%, Race unknown 6%.
Retention and Graduation: 93% freshmen return for sophomore year. 73% freshmen graduate within 4 years. 81% freshmen graduate within 6 years. 22% grads go on to further study within 1 year. 48% grads pursue arts and sciences degrees. 31% grads pursue law degrees. 2% grads pursue business degrees. 18% grads pursue medical degrees. **Faculty:** Student/faculty ratio 13:1. 1,101 full-time faculty, 24% are members of minority groups, 45% are women. 3% of classes are taught by teaching assistants.

ACADEMICS

Degrees: Associate; Bachelor's; Certificate; Doctoral degree—professional practice; Doctoral degree research/scholarship; Master's; Post-bachelor's certificate; Post-master's certificate; Terminal Associate. **Classes:** Most classes have 10–19 students. Most lab/discussion sessions have 20–29 students. **Most popular majors:** International Relations and Affairs; Business Administration and Management, General; Psychology, General. **Special Study Options:** Accelerated program; Cooperative education program; Cross-registration; Distance learning; Double major; Dual enrollment; Exchange student program (domestic); Honors program; Independent study; Internships; Liberal arts/career combination; Student-designed major; Study abroad. **Combined degree programs:** BA/JD; BA/MA; BA/MD. **Disability Services offered:** Note-taking services; Reader services; Tape recorders; Tutors. **Career services:** Alumni network; Alumni services; Career assessment; Career/job search classes; Internships; Regional alumni.

FACILITIES

Housing: Apartments for single students; Coed dorms; Fraternity/sorority housing; Theme housing; Women's dorms; 95% of campus accessible to physically disabled. **Special Academic Facilities/Equipment:** Art gallery, language lab, word processing center. **Campus Network:** 100% of classrooms, 100% of dorms, 100% of student union, 100% of libraries, 100% of dining areas, 25% of common outdoor areas, have wireless network access.

CAMPUS LIFE

Environment: Metropolis. **Activities:** Choral groups; Concert band; Dance; Drama/theater; International Student Organization; Jazz band; Literary magazine; Marching band; Model UN; Music ensembles; Musical theater; Pep band; Radio station; Student government; Student newspaper; Student-run film society; Symphony orchestra; Television station; Yearbook. 220 registered organizations, 3 honor societies, 5 religious organizations, 12 fraternities, 9 sororities, on campus. **Athletics (Intercollegiate):** *Men:* baseball, basketball, crew/rowing, cross-country, diving, fencing, golf, rugby, soccer, squash, swimming, tennis, water polo. *Women:* basketball, crew/rowing, cross-country, fencing, gymnastics, soccer, swimming, tennis, volleyball. **On-Campus Highlights:** The Smith Center. **Environmental Initiatives:** 1. GW's mission is to be the premier university on policy and governance for sustainable systems through practice, teaching, research, and outreach. The University is deploying a pan-university approach that bridges traditional disciplines. As of 2012, GW offers an interdisciplinary Minor in Sustainability to all undergraduate students. The minor is a pan-university offering that provides students with inter-disciplinary teaching (with a team-taught course taught by faculty representing several schools) and experiential learning (which challenges students to apply knowledge, theory and methods learned in the classroom to analyze a real-world sustainability issue and/or practice).

ADMISSIONS

Freshman Academic Profile: 61% in top 10% of high school class, 88% in top 25% of high school class, 99% in top 50% of high school class. 70% from public high schools. **Test scores:** SAT Math middle 50% range 640–740. SAT EBRW middle 50% range 640–720. ACT middle 50% range 29–32. **Basis for Candidate Selection:** *Very important factors include:* rigor of secondary school record, academic GPA. *Important factors include:* application essay, recommendation(s), extracurricular activities, talent/ability, volunteer work. *Other factors include:* standardized test scores, character/personal qualities, first generation, alumni/ae relation, geographical residence, racial/ethnic status, work experience, level of applicant's interest. **Freshman Admission Requirements:** High school diploma is required and GED is accepted. *Academic units required:* 4 English, 2 math, 2 science, 1 science labs, 2 foreign language, 2 social studies. *Academic units recommended:* 4 English, 4 math, 4 science, 4 foreign language, 4 social studies. **Freshman Admission Statistics:** 26,510 applied, 42% admitted, 26% enrolled. **Transfer Admission Requirements:** High school transcript, college transcript(s), essay or personal statement, standardized test scores, Lowest grade transferable C. **General Admission Information:** Application fee $75. Priority deadline 11/1. Regular application deadline 1/5. Non-fall registration accepted.

COSTS AND FINANCIAL AID

Annual tuition $56,845. Room and board $18,000. Required fees $90. Average book and supplies expense $1,400. **Required Forms and Deadlines:** CSS/Financial Aid PROFILE; FAFSA; Noncustodial PROFILE. **Notification of Awards:** Applicants will be notified of awards on a rolling basis beginning 3/24. **Types of Aid:** *Need-based scholarships/grants:* College/university scholarship or grant aid from institutional funds; Federal Pell; SEOG; State scholarships/grants. *Loans:* Direct PLUS loans; Direct Subsidized Stafford Loans; Direct Unsubsidized Stafford Loans. **Student Employment:** Federal Work-Study Program available. Institutional employment available. **Financial Aid Statistics:** 97% needy freshmen, 91% needy undergrads receive need-based scholarship or grant aid. 76% freshmen, 59% undergrads receive non-need-based scholarship or grant aid. 75% freshmen, 77% undergrads receive need-based self-help aid. 1% freshmen, 1% undergrads receive athletic scholarships. 49% undergrads borrow to pay for school. Average cumulative indebtedness $32,482. **Criteria awarding aid:** *Need-based:* Minority status. *Non-Need-based:* Academics, Art, Athletics, Music/drama.

GEORGIA COLLEGE & STATE UNIVERSITY

Campus Box 23, Milledgeville, GA 31061
Phone: 478-445-1283 **Financial Aid Phone:** 478-445-5149
E-mail: admissions@gcsu.edu **CEEB Code:** 5252
Fax: 478-445-1914 **Website:** www.gcsu.edu **ACT Code:** 828

This public school was founded in 1889. It has a 601.8 acre campus.

RATINGS

Admissions Selectivity Rating: 83   Fire Safety Rating: 99   Green Rating: 75

STUDENTS AND FACULTY

Enrollment: 5,857. **Student Body:** 62% female, 38% male, 1% out-of-state, <1% international (33 countries represented). Asian 2%, African American 5%, Caucasian 84%, Hispanic 5%, Native American <1%, Pacific Islander <1%, Two or more races 3%, Race unknown <1%.
Retention and Graduation: 85% freshmen return for sophomore year. 42% freshmen graduate within 4 years. 59% freshmen graduate within 6 years.
Faculty: Student/faculty ratio 17:1. 330 full-time faculty, 82% hold PhDs, 20% are members of minority groups, 56% are women.

ACADEMICS

Degrees: Bachelor's; Doctoral degree—professional practice; Master's; Post-master's certificate. **Classes:** Most classes have 20–29 students. Most lab/discussion sessions have 20–29 students. **Most popular majors:** Health Teacher Education; Registered Nursing/Registered Nurse; Business Administration and Management, General. **Special Study Options:** Accelerated program; Distance learning; Double major; English as a Second Language (ESL); Honors program; Independent study; Internships; Student-designed major; Study abroad; Teacher certification program. **Honors programs:** Honors Program. **Disability Services offered:** Note-taking services; Reader services; Tape recorders; Tutors. **Career services:** Alumni network; Career assessment; Career/job search classes; Internships.

FACILITIES

Housing: Apartments for single students; Coed dorms; Special housing for disabled students; Special housing for international students; Theme housing 90% of campus accessible to physically disabled. **Special Academic Facilities/Equipment:** Education archives museum, old governor's mansion, Museum of Fine Arts, Natural History Museum and Planetarium.

CAMPUS LIFE

Environment: Town. **Activities:** Campus Ministries; Choral groups; Concert band; Dance; Drama/theater; International Student Organization; Jazz band; Literary magazine; Music ensembles; Musical theater; Pep band; Radio station; Student government; Student newspaper; Television station. 206 registered organizations, 10 fraternities, 12 sororities, on campus. **Athletics (Intercollegiate):** *Men:* baseball, basketball, cross-country, golf, tennis. *Women:* basketball, cross-country, softball, speed skating, tennis. **On-Campus Highlights:** The Wellness and Recreation Center. **Environmental Initiatives:** recycling program.

ADMISSIONS

Freshman Academic Profile: Average high school GPA 3.5. **Test scores:** SAT Math middle 50% range 540–620. SAT EBRW middle 50% range 560–640. ACT middle 50% range 23–27. **Basis for Candidate Selection:** *Very important factors include:* rigor of secondary school record, academic GPA, application essay, standardized test scores, recommendation(s), first generation, level of applicant's interest. *Important factors include:* class rank, extracurricular activities, talent/ability, character/personal qualities, state residency. *Other factors include:* interview, alumni/ae relation, geographical residence, volunteer work, work experience. **Freshman Admission Requirements:** High school diploma is required and GED is accepted. *Academic units required:* 4 English, 4 math, 4 science, 2 science labs, 2 foreign language, 3 social studies. **Freshman Admission Statistics:** 4,089 applied, 79% admitted, 45% enrolled. **Transfer Admission Requirements:** college transcript(s), statement of good standing from prior institution(s). Minimum college GPA of 2.0 required. **General Admission Information:** Application fee $40. Regular application deadline 4/1. Non-fall registration accepted. Admission may be deferred for a maximum of 1 year.

COSTS AND FINANCIAL AID

Annual in-state tuition $7,180. Annual out-of-state tuition $25,528. Room and board $11,946. Required fees $2,022. Average book and supplies expense $1,500. **Required Forms and Deadlines:** FAFSA. **Notification of Awards:** Applicants will be notified of awards on a rolling basis beginning 3/1. **Types of Aid:** *Need-based scholarships/grants:* College/university scholarship or grant aid from institutional funds; Federal Pell; Private scholarships; SEOG; State scholarships/grants. *Loans:* Direct PLUS loans; Direct Subsidized Stafford Loans; Direct Unsubsidized Stafford Loans. **Student Employment:** Federal Work-Study Program available. Institutional employment available. **Criteria awarding aid:** *Non-Need-based:* Academics, Alumni affiliation, Art, Athletics, Leadership, Music/drama, State/district residency.

GEORGIA INSTITUTE OF TECHNOLOGY

Office of Undergraduate Admissions, Atlanta, GA 30332-0320
Phone: 404-894-4154 **Financial Aid Phone:** 404-894-4160
E-mail: admission@gatech.edu **CEEB Code:** 5248
Fax: 404-894-9511 **Website:** www.gatech.edu **ACT Code:** 0818

This public school was founded in 1885. It has a 400 acre campus.

RATINGS

Admissions Selectivity Rating: 97   Fire Safety Rating: 96   Green Rating: 96

STUDENTS AND FACULTY

Enrollment: 15,212. **Student Body:** 38% female, 62% male, 34% out-of-state, 8% international (113 countries represented). Asian 22%, African American 7%, Caucasian 48%, Hispanic 7%, Native American <1%, Pacific Islander <1%, Two or more races 4%, Race unknown 4%.
Retention and Graduation: 97% freshmen return for sophomore year. 39% freshmen graduate within 4 years. 85% freshmen graduate within 6 years. 18% grads go on to further study within 1 year. 4% grads pursue arts and sciences

degrees. <1% grads pursue law degrees. <1% grads pursue business degrees. 2% grads pursue medical degrees. **Faculty:** Student/faculty ratio 21:1. 1,128 full-time faculty, 90% hold PhDs, 34% are members of minority groups, 26% are women.

ACADEMICS

Degrees: Bachelor's; Doctoral degree research/scholarship; Master's. **Classes:** Most classes have 20–29 students. Most lab/discussion sessions have 10–19 students. **Most popular majors:** Computer and Information Sciences, General; Mechanical Engineering; Industrial Engineering. **Special Study Options:** Accelerated program; Cooperative education program; Cross-registration; Distance learning; Double major; Dual enrollment; English as a Second Language (ESL); Honors program; Independent study; Internships; Liberal arts/career combination; Student-designed major; Study abroad; Teacher certification program; Weekend college. **Honors programs:** Mission Statement: The Georgia Tech Honors Program fosters curiosity, creativity, and connection—to the Honors Program, Georgia Tech, and communities beyond. Honors Program students are encouraged to pursue their curiosity, creativity, and connection across disciplinary boundaries and the boundary between theory and practice. In advancing its mission, the Honors Program enhances the capacity of our highly motivated students and future alumni to advance the Georgia Tech mission of "Progress and Service." Living-Learning Community: Georgia Tech Honors Program students consistently rate the opportunity to live together as one of the best features of the Honors Program. Honors Program students are diverse in many ways—including majors, interests, career aspirations, backgrounds, experiences—generating many opportunities to learn from and collaborate with one another. And those opportunities are easy to find and pursue, thanks to the ways in which Honors Programs students are alike: highly motivated, curious, creative, connected to community, and willing and able to cross disciplinary boundaries and move from theory to practice. Classes: The Honors Program specially arranges a menu of Honors Program classes offered each fall (about 25 classes) and spring (about 15 classes), and one or two Honors Program classes are offered each summer in the Georgia Tech Oxford Summer Study Abroad Program. Classes are typically small, with high levels of student and faculty engagement, and incorporate one or more active-learning elements: seminar-style class discussions, class presentations, team problem-solving, team projects, or service-learning opportunities on the Georgia Tech campus or in the Atlanta community. Many Honors Program classes, including some "core" classes (English, lab science), are interdisciplinary in scope. Honors Program classes are designed for students who are highly motivated to pursue their curiosity, creativity, and connection with communities, often crossing disciplinary boundaries and proceeding from theory to practical application. Honors Program students are eager for an active learning environment, curious about important questions, open to the experiences of others and willing to share their ideas with faculty and other students from a variety of backgrounds. The Honors Program student body is composed of representatives from all majors, making for a highly interdisciplinary living/learning experience. **Disability Services offered:** Note-taking services; Reader services; Tape recorders. **Career services:** Career assessment; Career/job search classes; Internships.

FACILITIES

Housing: Apartments for married students; Apartments for single students; Coed dorms; Fraternity/sorority housing; Men's dorms; Special housing for disabled students; Special housing for international students; Theme housing; Women's dorms; 75% of campus accessible to physically disabled. **Special Academic Facilities/Equipment:** Clough Undergraduate Learning Commons, Nuclear Magnetic Resonance Spectroscopy Center, Georgia Tech Research Institute, Paper Museum, Mechanical Properties Research Laboratory with scanning electron microscope, Virtual Factory Laboratory, Ferris-Goldsmith Trading Floor, Klaus Advanced Computing Building, Electron Microscope, Marcus Nanotechnology Research Center, Solar Decathlon House at College of Architecture, Wind Tunnel, GT Smart House. **Campus Network:** 100% of classrooms, 100% of dorms, 100% of student union, 100% of libraries, 100% of dining areas, 100% of common outdoor areas, have wireless network access.

CAMPUS LIFE

Environment: Metropolis. **Activities:** Campus Ministries; Choral groups; Concert band; Dance; Drama/theater; International Student Organization; Jazz band; Literary magazine; Marching band; Model UN; Music ensembles; Musical theater; Pep band; Radio station; Student government; Student newspaper; Student-run film society; Symphony orchestra; Television station; Yearbook. 533 registered organizations, 16 honor societies, 36 religious organizations, 40 fraternities, 15 sororities, on campus. **Athletics (Intercollegiate):** *Men:* baseball, basketball, cheerleading, cross-country, diving, football, golf, swimming, tennis, track/field (outdoor), track/field (indoor).

Women: basketball, cheerleading, cross-country, diving, softball, swimming, tennis, track/field (outdoor), track/field (indoor), volleyball. **On-Campus Highlights:** Tech Square—Bookstore/Hotel/College of, Olympic Aquatic Center/Campus Recreation, The Hill/Tech Tower, Student Center Commons and the Library, Ferst Center for the Arts. **Environmental Initiatives:** Education: Over 200 courses are offered across all of the colleges with the goal that every student who graduates has taken at least one sustainability course. Many degree programs at the undergraduate and graduate levels, and many continuing education and certificate programs focus on sustainability and major areas of sustainability. Sustainability has been included in the Institute Mission Statement and Strategic Plan since 1994. Our office updated the Sutainability Strategie Plan in 2010, and we are in the final states of finalizing and sharing the Institute Strategic Plan for Sustainable Practice in 2018. The Institute's Serve*Learn*Sustain has incorporated the UN's "Grand Challenges" in the Strategic Plan to align with, "Improving the Human Condition and a Sustainable Global Economy."

ADMISSIONS

Freshman Academic Profile: Average high school GPA 3.8. 89% in top 10% of high school class, 97% in top 25% of high school class, 99% in top 50% of high school class. **Test scores:** SAT Math middle 50% range 690–790. SAT EBRW middle 50% range 640–730. ACT middle 50% range 30–34. **Basis for Candidate Selection:** *Very important factors include:* rigor of secondary school record, academic GPA, extracurricular activities. *Important factors include:* application essay, standardized test scores, talent/ability, character/personal qualities, geographical residence, state residency, volunteer work. *Other factors include:* recommendation(s), first generation, alumni/ae relation, racial/ethnic status, level of applicant's interest. **Freshman Admission Requirements:** High school diploma is required and GED is not accepted. *Academic units required:* 4 English, 4 math, 4 science, 2 science labs, 2 foreign language, 3 social studies. **Freshman Admission Statistics:** 35,611 applied, 23% admitted, 39% enrolled. **Transfer Admission Requirements:** college transcript(s), statement of good standing from prior institution(s). Minimum college GPA of 2.7 required. Lowest grade transferable C. **General Admission Information:** Application fee $75. Priority deadline 10/15. Regular application deadline 1/1. Non-fall registration accepted. Admission may be deferred for a maximum of 1 year.

COSTS AND FINANCIAL AID

Annual in-state tuition $10,258. Annual out-of-state tuition $31,370. Room and board $12,090. Required fees $2,424. Average book and supplies expense $800. **Required Forms and Deadlines:** CSS/Financial Aid PROFILE; FAFSA; Institution's own financial aid form. **Notification of Awards:** Applicants will be notified of awards on or about 4/1. **Types of Aid:** *Need-based scholarships/grants:* College/university scholarship or grant aid from institutional funds; Federal Pell; Private scholarships; SEOG; State scholarships/grants; United Negro College Fund. *Loans:* Direct PLUS loans; Direct Subsidized Stafford Loans; Direct Unsubsidized Stafford Loans. **Student Employment:** Federal Work-Study Program available. Institutional employment available. **Financial Aid Statistics:** 90% needy freshmen, 88% needy undergrads receive need-based scholarship or grant aid. 68% freshmen, 42% undergrads receive non-need-based scholarship or grant aid. 46% freshmen, 54% undergrads receive need-based self-help aid. 2% freshmen, 1% undergrads receive athletic scholarships. 46% freshmen, 45% undergrads receive any aid. 36% undergrads borrow to pay for school. Average cumulative indebtedness $32,760. **Criteria awarding aid:** *Need-based:* Academics, Leadership, Minority status. *Non-Need-based:* Academics, Athletics, Leadership, Music/drama, State/district residency.

GEORGIAN COURT UNIVERSITY

900 Lakewood Avenue, Lakewood, NJ 08701-2697
Phone: 732-987-2700 **Financial Aid Phone:** 732-987-2254
E-mail: admissions@georgian.edu **CEEB Code:** 2274
Fax: 732-987-2000 **Website:** georgian.edu **ACT Code:** 2562

This private school, affiliated with the Roman Catholic Church, was founded in 1908. It has a 156 acre campus.

RATINGS

Admissions Selectivity Rating: 77   **Fire Safety Rating:** 98   **Green Rating:** 60*

STUDENTS AND FACULTY

Enrollment: 1,550. **Student Body:** 75% female, 25% male, 7% out-of-state, 2% international (21 countries represented). Asian 3%, African American 10%,

Caucasian 63%, Hispanic 15%, Native American 1%, Pacific Islander <1%, Two or more races 1%, Race unknown 5%.
Retention and Graduation: 79% freshmen return for sophomore year. 39% freshmen graduate within 4 years. 54% freshmen graduate within 6 years.
Faculty: Student/faculty ratio 12:1. 91 full-time faculty, 97% hold PhDs, 24% are members of minority groups, 66% are women. 0% of classes are taught by teaching assistants.

ACADEMICS

Degrees: Bachelor's; Certificate; Doctoral degree—professional practice; Master's; Post-bachelor's certificate; Post-master's certificate. **Classes:** Most classes have 10–19 students. **Most popular majors:** Psychology, General; Registered Nursing/Registered Nurse. **Special Study Options:** Accelerated program; Distance learning; Double major; Dual enrollment; English as a Second Language (ESL); Honors program; Independent study; Internships; Liberal arts/career combination; Study abroad; Teacher certification program; Weekend college. **Honors programs:** Members of the University Honors Program receive an enriched academic curriculum featuring: * Faculty chosen for their excellence as teaching-scholars * Challenging interactive classroom format * Emphasis on primary texts and sources * Rigorous scholarly writing assignments and oral presentations * Close faculty mentoring * Preference in academic advisement and course registration * A strong sense of belonging to a community of scholars * Sponsorship in funding presentations at regional and national conferences * Special advisement by faculty regarding graduate and professional school applications and prestigious fellowship opportunities * Special recognition at commencement ceremonies. **Disability Services offered:** Note-taking services; Reader services; Tape recorders; Tutors. **Career services:** Alumni network; Alumni services; Career assessment; Career/job search classes; Internships.

FACILITIES

Housing: Coed dorms; Special housing for disabled students 90% of campus accessible to physically disabled. **Special Academic Facilities/Equipment:** Art gallery, arboretum, Wellness Center, NASA ERC.

CAMPUS LIFE

Environment: Town. **Activities:** Campus Ministries; Choral groups; Concert band; Dance; Drama/theater; International Student Organization; Jazz band; Literary magazine; Model UN; Music ensembles; Student government; Student newspaper. 40 registered organizations, 19 honor societies, 2 religious organizations, on campus. **Athletics (Intercollegiate):** *Women:* basketball, cross-country, lacrosse, soccer, softball, tennis, track/field (outdoor), volleyball. **On-Campus Highlights:** Arboretum. **Environmental Initiatives:** We have included a sustainability commitment in our strategic plan.

ADMISSIONS

Freshman Academic Profile: Average high school GPA 3.5. 15% in top 10% of high school class, 33% in top 25% of high school class, 81% in top 50% of high school class. **Test scores:** SAT Math middle 50% range 478–580. SAT EBRW middle 50% range 480–580. ACT middle 50% range 19–25. **Basis for Candidate Selection:** *Very important factors include:* rigor of secondary school record, academic GPA. *Important factors include:* standardized test scores. *Other factors include:* class rank, application essay, recommendation(s), interview, extracurricular activities, talent/ability, character/personal qualities, first generation, religious affiliation/commitment, volunteer work, work experience, level of applicant's interest. **Freshman Admission Requirements:** High school diploma is required and GED is accepted. *Academic units required:* 4 English, 2 math, 1 science, 1 science labs, 2 foreign language, 1 history, 6 academic electives. **Freshman Admission Statistics:** 1,934 applied, 71% admitted, 14% enrolled. **Transfer Admission Requirements:** college transcript(s), Minimum college GPA of 2.0 required. Lowest grade transferable C. **General Admission Information:** Application fee $40. Regular application deadline 8/1. Non-fall registration accepted. Admission may be deferred for a maximum of 1 year.

COSTS AND FINANCIAL AID

Annual tuition $32,050. Room and board $11,200. Required fees $1,560. Average book and supplies expense $1,350. **Required Forms and Deadlines: FAFSA. **Notification of Awards:** Applicants will be notified of awards on a rolling basis beginning 12/1. **Types of Aid:** *Need-based scholarships/grants:* College/university scholarship or grant aid from institutional funds; Federal Pell; Private scholarships; SEOG; State scholarships/grants. **Loans:** Direct PLUS loans; Direct Subsidized Stafford Loans; Direct Unsubsidized Stafford Loans. **Student Employment:** Federal Work-Study Program available. Institutional employment available. **Financial Aid Statistics:** 99% needy freshmen, 99% needy undergrads receive need-based scholarship or grant aid. 11% freshmen, 11% undergrads receive non-need-based scholarship or grant aid. 70% freshmen, 75% undergrads receive need-based self-help aid. 6% freshmen,

4% undergrads receive athletic scholarships. 83% undergrads borrow to pay for school. Average cumulative indebtedness $38,183. **Criteria awarding aid:** *Need-based:* Academics, Alumni affiliation, Art, Athletics, Leadership, Religious affiliation. *Non-Need-based:* Academics, Alumni affiliation, Art, Athletics, Leadership, Religious affiliation, State/district residency.

GEORGIA SOUTHERN UNIVERSITY

P.O. Box 8024, Statesboro, GA 30460
Phone: 912-478-5391 **Financial Aid Phone:** 912-478-5413
E-mail: admissions@georgiasouthern.edu **CEEB Code:** 5253
Fax: 912-478-7240 **Website:** http://www.georgiasouthern.edu/ **ACT Code:** 830

This public school was founded in 1906. It has a 900 acre campus.

RATINGS

Admissions Selectivity Rating: 86   **Fire Safety Rating:** 97   **Green Rating:** 83

STUDENTS AND FACULTY

Enrollment: 22,242. **Student Body:** 54% female, 46% male, 6% out-of-state, 1% international (73 countries represented). Asian 2%, African American 25%, Caucasian 59%, Hispanic 7%, Native American <1%, Pacific Islander <1%, Two or more races 4%, Race unknown 1%.
Retention and Graduation: 80% freshmen return for sophomore year. 25% freshmen graduate within 4 years. % freshmen graduate within 6 years. 8% grads go on to further study within 1 year. **Faculty:** Student/faculty ratio 21:1. 811 full-time faculty, 84% hold PhDs, 26% are members of minority groups, 48% are women. 3% of classes are taught by teaching assistants.

ACADEMICS

Degrees: Associate; Bachelor's; Certificate; Doctoral degree—professional practice; Doctoral degree research/scholarship; Master's; Post-bachelor's certificate; Post-master's certificate. **Classes:** Most classes have 20–29 students. Most lab/discussion sessions have 20–29 students. **Most popular majors:** Mechanical Engineering; Biology/Biological Sciences, General; Exercise Science and Kinesiology. **Special Study Options:** Accelerated program; Cooperative education program; Distance learning; Double major; Dual enrollment; English as a Second Language (ESL); Honors program; Independent study; Internships; Student-designed major; Study abroad; Teacher certification program. **Honors programs:** The University Honors Program seeks scholars interested in research, change agents interested in engaging local and global communities, and individuals seeking to explore their curiosity and express their creativity. Honors Program students in both Statesboro and Savannah take advantage of honors sections of core courses that are seminar-based and differently designed to foster inquiry and research. During junior and senior years, students develop an honors thesis to further deepen their knowledge of their major field. Additionally, honors students engage in at least one experiential learning project each year and include study abroad, alternative break trips, research outside of coursework, leadership, and intensive volunteer experiences. **Disability Services offered:** Note-taking services; Reader services; Tape recorders; Tutors. **Career services:** Alumni network; Alumni services; Career assessment; Career/job search classes; Internships.

FACILITIES

Housing: Apartments for single students; Coed dorms; Special housing for disabled students; Special housing for international students; Theme housing 97% of campus accessible to physically disabled. **Special Academic Facilities/Equipment:** Bureau of business research and economic development, center for addiction recovery, center for bio-statistics and survey, center for entrepreneurial learning and leadership, center for forensic studies in accounting, center for international studies, center for Irish studies, center for retail studies, center for sustainability, center for wildlife education, child development center, graduate academic services center (GASC), institute for coastal plain science, coastlands AHEC, national youth-at-risk center (NYAR), small business development center, black box theatre, performing arts center, and botanic garden. **Campus Network:** 100% of classrooms, 100% of dorms, 100% of student union, 100% of libraries, 100% of dining areas, 100% of common outdoor areas, have wireless network access.

CAMPUS LIFE

Environment: Town. **Activities:** Campus Ministries; Choral groups; Concert band; Dance; Drama/theater; International Student Organization; Jazz band; Literary magazine; Marching band; Music ensembles; Musical theater; Opera; Radio station; Student government; Student newspaper; Student-run film society; Symphony orchestra. 280 registered organizations, 17 honor societies, 24 religious organizations, 48 fraternities, 12 sororities, on campus. **Athletics (Intercollegiate):** *Men:* baseball, basketball, cheerleading, football, golf, soccer, tennis. *Women:* basketball, cheerleading, cross-country, diving, soccer, softball, swimming, tennis, track/field (outdoor), volleyball. **On-Campus Highlights:** Russell Union. **Environmental Initiatives:** Georgia Southern's Student Sustainability Fee Committee has allocated > $1,000,000 in funding for 68 sustainability projects at Georgia Southern University since FY2015. The grant winners display their funded projects in a Sustainability Showcase Exhibit in the university library, viewed by thousands in the campus community during a two weeks period towards the end of each fiscal year.

ADMISSIONS

Freshman Academic Profile: Average high school GPA 3.4. 18% in top 10% of high school class, 44% in top 25% of high school class, 77% in top 50% of high school class. 86% from public high schools. **Test scores:** SAT Math middle 50% range 520–590. SAT EBRW middle 50% range 540–610. ACT middle 50% range 21–25. **Basis for Candidate Selection:** *Very important factors include:* rigor of secondary school record, academic GPA, standardized test scores. *Other factors include:* class rank. **Freshman Admission Requirements:** High school diploma is required and GED is not accepted. *Academic units required:* 4 English, 4 math, 4 science, 2 science labs, 2 foreign language, 3 social studies. **Freshman Admission Statistics:** 11,522 applied, 68% admitted, 56% enrolled. **Transfer Admission Requirements:** college transcript(s), statement of good standing from prior institution(s). Minimum college GPA of 2.0 required. Lowest grade transferable D. **General Admission Information:** Application fee $30. Priority deadline 4/1. Regular application deadline 5/1. Non-fall registration accepted. Admission may be deferred for a maximum of circumstantial.

COSTS AND FINANCIAL AID

Annual in-state tuition $5,330. Annual out-of-state tuition $18,812. Room and board $10,070. Required fees $2,092. Average book and supplies expense $1,200. **Required Forms and Deadlines:** FAFSA. **Notification of Awards:** Applicants will be notified of awards on a rolling basis beginning 4/20. **Types of Aid:** *Need-based scholarships/grants:* College/university scholarship or grant aid from institutional funds; Federal Pell; Private scholarships; SEOG; State scholarships/grants. *Loans:* Direct PLUS loans; Direct Subsidized Stafford Loans; Direct Unsubsidized Stafford Loans. **Student Employment:** Federal Work-Study Program available. Institutional employment available. **Financial Aid Statistics:** 90% needy freshmen, 82% needy undergrads receive need-based scholarship or grant aid. 4% freshmen, 2% undergrads receive non-need-based scholarship or grant aid. 68% freshmen, 75% undergrads receive need-based self-help aid. 1% freshmen, 1% undergrads receive athletic scholarships. 92% freshmen, 88% undergrads receive any aid. 69% undergrads borrow to pay for school. Average cumulative indebtedness $29,030. **Criteria awarding aid:** *Non-Need-based:* Academics, Alumni affiliation, Art, Athletics, Leadership, Minority status, Music/drama, State/district residency.

GEORGIA SOUTHWESTERN STATE UNIVERSITY

800 Georgia Southwestern State University Dr., Americus, GA 31709-4693
Phone: 229-928-1273 **Financial Aid Phone:** 229-928-1378
E-mail: admissions@gsw.edu **CEEB Code:** 5250
Fax: 229-931-2983 **Website:** www.gsw.edu **ACT Code:** 824

This public school was founded in 1906. It has a 325 acre campus.

RATINGS

Admissions Selectivity Rating: 82   **Fire Safety Rating:** 94   **Green Rating:** 60*

STUDENTS AND FACULTY

Enrollment: 2,413. **Student Body:** 62% female, 38% male, 4% out-of-state, 2% international (29 countries represented). Asian 1%, African American 27%, Caucasian 63%, Hispanic 4%, Native American <1%, Pacific Islander <1%, Two or more races 2%, Race unknown <1%.
Retention and Graduation: 70% freshmen return for sophomore year.
Faculty: Student/faculty ratio 18:1. 112 full-time faculty, 73% hold PhDs, 14%

are members of minority groups, 51% are women. 0% of classes are taught by teaching assistants.

ACADEMICS

Degrees: Bachelor's; Master's; Post-bachelor's certificate; Post-master's certificate. **Classes:** Most classes have 20–29 students. **Most popular majors:** Accounting; Registered Nursing/Registered Nurse; Business Administration and Management, General. **Special Study Options:** Accelerated program; Distance learning; Double major; English as a Second Language (ESL); Honors program; Internships; Study abroad; Teacher certification program. **Disability Services offered:** Note-taking services; Reader services; Tape recorders; Tutors.

FACILITIES

Housing: Coed dorms; 99% of campus accessible to physically disabled. **Special Academic Facilities/Equipment:** Observatory, Glass-blowing studio, Golf Course. **Campus Network:** 100% of classrooms, 0% of dorms, 100% of student union, 100% of libraries, 100% of dining areas, have wireless network access.

CAMPUS LIFE

Environment: Village. **Activities:** Campus Ministries; Choral groups; Concert band; Drama/theater; International Student Organization; Jazz band; Literary magazine; Student government; Student newspaper; Television station. 58 registered organizations, 3 honor societies, 4 religious organizations, 5 fraternities, 6 sororities, on campus. **Athletics (Intercollegiate):** *Men:* baseball, basketball, golf, soccer, tennis. *Women:* basketball, cross-country, soccer, softball, tennis. **On-Campus Highlights:** Student Success Center.

ADMISSIONS

Freshman Academic Profile: Average high school GPA 3.3. 15% in top 10% of high school class, 42% in top 25% of high school class, 75% in top 50% of high school class. 82% from public high schools. **Test scores:** SAT Math middle 50% range 430–520. SAT EBRW middle 50% range 440–540. ACT middle 50% range 19–23. **Basis for Candidate Selection:** *Very important factors include:* rigor of secondary school record, academic GPA, standardized test scores. *Important factors include:* class rank. *Other factors include:* application essay, recommendation(s), interview, extracurricular activities, talent/ability. **Freshman Admission Requirements:** High school diploma is required and GED is not accepted. *Academic units required:* 4 English, 4 math, 4 science, 2 science labs, 2 foreign language, 3 unit from above areas or other academic areas. *Academic units recommended:* 2 academic electives. **Freshman Admission Statistics:** 1,389 applied, 68% admitted, 51% enrolled. **Transfer Admission Requirements:** college transcript(s), Minimum college GPA of 2.0 required. Lowest grade transferable D. **General Admission Information:** Application fee $25. Regular application deadline 7/21. Non-fall registration accepted. Admission may be deferred for a maximum of 12 months.

COSTS AND FINANCIAL AID

Annual in-state tuition $4,858. Annual out-of-state tuition $17,678. Room and board $8,952. Required fees $1,340. Average book and supplies expense $1,400. **Required Forms and Deadlines:** FAFSA; Institution's own financial aid form; State aid form. **Notification of Awards:** Applicants will be notified of awards on a rolling basis beginning 5/1. **Types of Aid:** *Need-based scholarships/grants:* College/university scholarship or grant aid from institutional funds; Federal Pell; Private scholarships; SEOG; State scholarships/grants. *Loans:* Direct PLUS loans; Direct Subsidized Stafford Loans; Direct Unsubsidized Stafford Loans. **Student Employment:** Federal Work-Study Program available. Institutional employment available. **Financial Aid Statistics:** 65% needy freshmen, 67% needy undergrads receive need-based scholarship or grant aid. 69% freshmen, 46% undergrads receive non-need-based scholarship or grant aid. 86% freshmen, 85% undergrads receive need-based self-help aid. 2% freshmen, 3% undergrads receive athletic scholarships. 76% undergrads borrow to pay for school. Average cumulative indebtedness $27,939. **Criteria awarding aid:** *Non-Need-based:* Academics, Alumni affiliation, Art, Athletics, Leadership, Music/drama, State/district residency.

GEORGIA STATE UNIVERSITY

PO Box 4009, Atlanta, GA 30302-4009
Phone: 404-413-2500 **Financial Aid Phone:** 404-413-2600
E-mail: admissions@gsu.edu **CEEB Code:** 5251
Fax: 404-413-2002 **Website:** www.gsu.edu **ACT Code:** 826

This public school was founded in 1913. It has a 71.5 acre campus.

RATINGS

Admissions Selectivity Rating: 87   **Fire Safety Rating:** 88   **Green Rating:** 60*

STUDENTS AND FACULTY

Enrollment: 27,296. **Student Body:** 59% female, 41% male, 5% out-of-state, 3% international (160 countries represented). Asian 15%, African American 41%, Caucasian 22%, Hispanic 12%, Native American <1%, Pacific Islander <1%, Two or more races 6%, Race unknown 1%.
Retention and Graduation: 80% freshmen return for sophomore year. 28% freshmen graduate within 4 years. 55% freshmen graduate within 6 years. **Faculty:** Student/faculty ratio 26:1. 1,178 full-time faculty, 91% hold PhDs, 30% are members of minority groups, 46% are women.

ACADEMICS

Degrees: Associate; Bachelor's; Certificate; Doctoral degree—professional practice; Doctoral degree research/scholarship; Master's; Post-bachelor's certificate; Post-master's certificate. **Classes:** Most classes have 20–29 students. **Most popular majors:** Biology/Biological Sciences, General; Psychology, General; Finance, General. **Special Study Options:** Cooperative education program; Cross-registration; Distance learning; Double major; Dual enrollment; English as a Second Language (ESL); Honors program; Independent study; Internships; Study abroad; Teacher certification program. **Honors programs:** The Honors College provides the advantages of a small, highly selective college with breadth of programs and opportunities of a large research university. It is open to incoming freshmen, transfer students, and currently enrolled students who meet eligibility requirements. Honors students take small, seminar-based classes and develop close contact with outstanding faculty members. Honors sections of a number of regular courses, many of which meet core curriculum requirements, are offered throughout the academic year. In addition, students in the Honors College can enroll in special interdisciplinary courses, help design a colloquium on a topic of their choice, and, at the upper division, research and write an honors thesis. Students in the college may earn honors recognitions, which are noted on their diplomas and transcripts, and they may pursue additional opportunities to enrich the quality of their education and enhance their chances of future success. Honors students may also take advantage of dedicated facilities, priority registration, merit scholarships, graduate and professional school counseling, special travel and study abroad opportunities, and honors housing in the University Commons. **Combined degree programs:** BA/JD; BA/MA. **Disability Services offered:** Note-taking services; Reader services; Tape recorders; Tutors. **Career services:** Alumni network; Alumni services; Career assessment; Career/job search classes; Internships.

FACILITIES

Housing: Apartments for married students; Apartments for single students; Coed dorms; Fraternity/sorority housing; Special housing for disabled students; Special housing for international students; Theme housing 100% of campus accessible to physically disabled. **Special Academic Facilities/Equipment:** Cartography Production Laboratory,Commuter Student Services,Cooperative Learning Laboratory,Economic Forecasting Center,Ernest G. Welch School of Art and Design Gallery, Instructional Technology Center, James M. Cox, Jr. Multi-Media Instructional Lab and Satellite Downlink Facility,Kopleff Recital Hall,Lanette L. Suttles Child Development Center,Language Acquisition and Resource Center, Mathematics Assistance Complex, Mathematics Interactive Learning Environment, Music Media Center, Rialto Center for the Performing Arts, Small Business Development Center, Visual Resource Center, Writing Studio. Digital Aquarium. **Campus Network:** 100% of classrooms, 100% of dorms, 100% of student union, 100% of libraries, 100% of dining areas, 100% of common outdoor areas, have wireless network access.

CAMPUS LIFE

Environment: Metropolis. **Activities:** Campus Ministries; Choral groups; Concert band; Dance; Drama/theater; International Student Organization; Jazz band; Literary magazine; Marching band; Model UN; Music ensembles; Musical theater; Opera; Pep band; Radio station; Student government; Student newspaper; Student-run film society; Symphony orchestra; Television station. 520 registered organizations, 43 honor societies, 37 religious organizations, 17 fraternities, 17 sororities, on campus. **Athletics (Intercollegiate):** *Men:* baseball, basketball, cross-country, golf, soccer, tennis, track/field (outdoor), volleyball. *Women:* basketball, cross-country, golf, soccer, softball, tennis, track/field (outdoor), volleyball. **On-Campus Highlights:** Recreation Center.

ADMISSIONS

Freshman Academic Profile: Average high school GPA 3.5. **Test scores:** SAT Math middle 50% range 500–590. SAT EBRW middle 50% range 970–1150. ACT middle 50% range 20–26. **Basis for Candidate Selection:** *Very important factors include:* rigor of secondary school record, academic GPA, standardized test scores. *Other factors include:* application essay, recommendation(s), talent/ability. **Freshman Admission Requirements:** High school diploma is required and GED is not accepted. *Academic units required:* 4 English, 4 math, 4 science, 2 science labs, 2 foreign language, 3 social studies. *Academic units recommended:* 4 English, 4 math, 4 science, 2 science labs, 2 foreign language, 3 social studies. **Freshman Admission Statistics:** 20,949 applied, 57% admitted, 42% enrolled. **Transfer Admission Requirements:** college transcript(s), Minimum college GPA of 2.5 required. Lowest grade transferable D. **General Admission Information:** Application fee $60. Priority deadline 3/1. Regular application deadline 6/1. Non-fall registration accepted. Admission may be deferred for a maximum of 2 terms.

COSTS AND FINANCIAL AID

Annual in-state tuition $8,948. Annual out-of-state tuition $27,986. Room and board $14,908. Required fees $2,128. Average book and supplies expense $2,000. **Required Forms and Deadlines:** FAFSA. **Notification of Awards:** Applicants will be notified of awards on a rolling basis beginning 3/1. **Types of Aid:** *Need-based scholarships/grants:* College/university scholarship or grant aid from institutional funds; Federal Pell; Private scholarships; SEOG; State scholarships/grants; United Negro College Fund. *Loans:* Direct PLUS loans; Direct Subsidized Stafford Loans; Direct Unsubsidized Stafford Loans. **Student Employment:** Federal Work-Study Program available. Institutional employment available. **Financial Aid Statistics:** 67% needy freshmen, 75% needy undergrads receive need-based scholarship or grant aid. 88% freshmen, 93% undergrads receive non-need-based scholarship or grant aid. 55% freshmen, 59% undergrads receive need-based self-help aid. 0% freshmen, 0% undergrads receive athletic scholarships. 67% undergrads borrow to pay for school. Average cumulative indebtedness $28,864. **Criteria awarding aid:** *Non-Need-based:* Academics, Alumni affiliation, Art, Athletics, Job skills, Leadership, Minority status, Music/drama, Religious affiliation, State/district residency.

GETTYSBURG COLLEGE

Admissions Office, Gettysburg, PA 17325-1484
Phone: 717-337-6100 **Financial Aid Phone:** 717-337-6611
E-mail: admiss@gettysburg.edu **CEEB Code:** 2275
Fax: 717-337-6145 **Website:** www.gettysburg.edu **ACT Code:** 3580

This private school, affiliated with the Lutheran Church, was founded in 1832. It has a 200 acre campus.

RATINGS

Admissions Selectivity Rating: 92   **Fire Safety Rating:** 98   **Green Rating:** 86

STUDENTS AND FACULTY

Enrollment: 2,370. **Student Body:** 52% female, 48% male, 72% out-of-state, 6% international (33 countries represented). Asian 2%, African American 4%, Caucasian 74%, Hispanic 9%, Native American <1%, Pacific Islander 0%, Two or more races 3%, Race unknown 2%.
Retention and Graduation: 91% freshmen return for sophomore year. 77% freshmen graduate within 4 years. 81% freshmen graduate within 6 years. 20% grads go on to further study within 1 year. **Faculty:** Student/faculty ratio 9:1. 229 full-time faculty, 98% hold PhDs, 20% are members of minority groups, 44% are women. 0% of classes are taught by teaching assistants.

ACADEMICS

Degrees: Bachelor's. **Classes:** Most classes have 10–19 students. **Most popular majors:** Psychology, General; Political Science and Government, General; Business/Commerce, General. **Special Study Options:** Cross-registration; Double major; Independent study; Internships; Student-designed major; Study

For more free content, visit PrincetonReview.com

abroad; Teacher certification program. **Career services:** Alumni network; Alumni services; Career assessment; Career/job search classes; Internships; Regional alumni.

FACILITIES
Housing: Apartments for single students; Coed dorms; Fraternity/sorority housing; Theme housing; Women's dorms. **Special Academic Facilities/Equipment:** 86,000 square-foot Science Center; state-of-the-art science facilities including Anatomage virtual dissection tables, a proton accelerator, two electron microscopes (transmission and scanning units), an atomic force microscope, Fourier Transform Infrared and NMR Spectrometers, an optics laboratory, greenhouse, planetarium, observatory, and a plasma physics laboratory; an Innovation and Creativity Lab to explore and use a variety of 3-D Printers, CNC, CO_2 Laser Cutting, Laser Engraving, Virtual Reality (VR) hardware and more; 18 public computer labs with over 350 computers; high-speed internet access from all campus buildings along with wireless connections throughout campus; extensive facilities for fine arts, music, and drama including the Sunderman Conservatory, Majestic Theater, and Schmucker Art Gallery.

CAMPUS LIFE
Environment: Village. **Activities:** Campus Ministries; Choral groups; Concert band; Dance; Drama/theater; International Student Organization; Jazz band; Literary magazine; Marching band; Model UN; Music ensembles; Musical theater; Radio station; Student government; Student newspaper; Student-run film society; Symphony orchestra; Television station; Yearbook. 120 registered organizations, 18 honor societies, 6 religious organizations, 9 fraternities, 7 sororities, on campus. **Athletics (Intercollegiate):** *Men:* baseball, basketball, cheerleading, cross-country, football, golf, lacrosse, soccer, swimming, tennis, track/field (outdoor), track/field (indoor), wrestling. *Women:* basketball, cheerleading, cross-country, field hockey, golf, lacrosse, soccer, softball, swimming, tennis, track/field (outdoor), track/field (indoor), volleyball. **On-Campus Highlights:** Beautiful 225-acre campus. **Environmental Initiatives:** The Center for Athletics, Recreation, and Fitness has received LEED Gold certification.

ADMISSIONS
Freshman Academic Profile: 62% in top 10% of high school class, 83% in top 25% of high school class, 99% in top 50% of high school class. **Test scores:** SAT Math middle 50% range 635–710. SAT EBRW middle 50% range 635–710. ACT middle 50% range 26–30. **Basis for Candidate Selection:** *Very important factors include:* rigor of secondary school record, academic GPA, application essay, recommendation(s). *Important factors include:* class rank, standardized test scores, interview, extracurricular activities, talent/ability, character/personal qualities, volunteer work. *Other factors include:* first generation, alumni/ae relation, geographical residence, racial/ethnic status, work experience, level of applicant's interest. **Freshman Admission Requirements:** High school diploma is required and GED is accepted. *Academic units required:* 4 English, 3 math, 3 science, 3 science labs, 3 foreign language, 3 social studies, 3 history. *Academic units recommended:* 4 English, 4 math, 4 science, 4 science labs, 4 foreign language, 4 social studies, 4 history. **Freshman Admission Statistics:** 6,269 applied, 45% admitted, 26% enrolled. **Transfer Admission Requirements:** High school transcript, college transcript(s), essay or personal statement, standardized test scores, statement of good standing from prior institution(s). Minimum college GPA of 2.5 required. Lowest grade transferable C. **General Admission Information:** Application fee $60. Priority deadline 1/15. Regular application deadline 1/15. Admission may be deferred for a maximum of 1 year.

COSTS AND FINANCIAL AID
Annual tuition $56,390. Room and board $13,460. Average book and supplies expense $1,000. **Required Forms and Deadlines:** CSS/Financial Aid PROFILE; FAFSA. **Notification of Awards:** Applicants will be notified of awards on or about 3/18. **Types of Aid:** *Need-based scholarships/grants:* College/university scholarship or grant aid from institutional funds; Federal Pell; Private scholarships; SEOG; State scholarships/grants. *Loans:* Direct PLUS loans; Direct Subsidized Stafford Loans; Direct Unsubsidized Stafford Loans. **Student Employment:** Federal Work-Study Program available. Institutional employment available. **Financial Aid Statistics:** 98% needy freshmen, 98% needy undergrads receive need-based scholarship or grant aid. 62% freshmen, 58% undergrads receive non-need-based scholarship or grant aid. 85% freshmen, 83% undergrads receive need-based self-help aid. 0% freshmen, 0% undergrads receive athletic scholarships. 67% freshmen, 61% undergrads receive any aid. 60% undergrads borrow to pay for school. Average cumulative indebtedness $34,630. **Criteria awarding aid:** *Need-based:* Academics, Leadership, Minority status, Music/drama *Non-Need-based:* Academics, Music/drama.

GODDARD COLLEGE

123 Pitkin Road, Plainfield, VT 05667
Phone: 802-454-8311
E-mail: admissions@goddard.edu
Fax: 802-454-1029 **Website:** www.goddard.edu

This is a private school.

RATINGS
Admissions Selectivity Rating: 67   **Fire Safety Rating:** 60*   **Green Rating:** 88

STUDENTS AND FACULTY
Enrollment: 186. **Student Body:** 70% female, 30% male, 0% out-of-state, 0% international. Asian 0%, African American 1%, Caucasian 68%, Hispanic 2%, Native American 3%, Pacific Islander 0%, Two or more races 5%, Race unknown 17%.
Faculty: 16 full-time faculty, 0% hold PhDs, 0% are members of minority groups, 69% are women.

ACADEMICS
Degrees: Bachelor's; Master's. **Special Study Options:** Accelerated program; Distance learning; Dual enrollment; Independent study; Liberal arts/career combination; Student-designed major; Teacher certification program. **Combined degree programs:** BA/MA.

FACILITIES
Housing: Coed dorms; Special housing for disabled students.

CAMPUS LIFE
Activities: Literary magazine; Radio station; Student government. **On-Campus Highlights:** Haybarn Theatre **Environmental Initiatives:** Reducing emissions by 30% since 2007.

ADMISSIONS
Basis for Candidate Selection: *Very important factors include:* application essay, interview, character/personal qualities, level of applicant's interest. *Important factors include:* recommendation(s), talent/ability, volunteer work. *Other factors include:* rigor of secondary school record, academic GPA, extracurricular activities, first generation, alumni/ae relation, racial/ethnic status, work experience. **Freshman Admission Requirements:** High school diploma is required and GED is accepted. *Academic units recommended:* 4 English, 4 math, 4 science, 3 science labs, 2 foreign language, 4 social studies. **Freshman Admission Statistics:** 5 applied, 80% admitted, 50% enrolled. **General Admission Information:** Application fee $40. Priority deadline 6/15. Regular application deadline 7/15. Non-fall registration accepted. Admission may be deferred for a maximum of 2 semesters.

COSTS AND FINANCIAL AID
Annual tuition $15,786. Average book and supplies expense $600. **Required Forms and Deadlines:** FAFSA. **Types of Aid:** *Need-based scholarships/grants:* College/university scholarship or grant aid from institutional funds; Federal Pell; Private scholarships; SEOG; State scholarships/grants. **Financial Aid Statistics:** 100% needy freshmen, 82% needy undergrads receive need-based scholarship or grant aid. 0% freshmen, 0% undergrads receive non-need-based scholarship or grant aid. 100% freshmen, 86% undergrads receive need-based self-help aid. 0% freshmen, 0% undergrads receive athletic scholarships.

GOLDEN GATE UNIVERSITY

536 Mission Street, San Francisco, CA 94105
Phone: 415-442-7800
E-mail: info@ggu.edu **CEEB Code:** 4329
Fax: 415-442-7807 **Website:** www.ggu.edu **ACT Code:** 278

This private school was founded in 1901.

RATINGS
Admissions Selectivity Rating: 60*   **Fire Safety Rating:** 60*   **Green Rating:** 60*

STUDENTS AND FACULTY
Enrollment: 421. **Student Body:** female, male, 5% out-of-state, international (61 countries represented).

Retention and Graduation: 15% grads go on to further study within 1 year. 0% grads pursue arts and sciences degrees. 30% grads pursue business degrees. 0% grads pursue medical degrees. **Faculty:** Student/faculty ratio 13:1. 81 full-time faculty, 0% hold PhDs, 0% are members of minority groups, 0% are women. 0% of classes are taught by teaching assistants.

ACADEMICS

Degrees: Bachelor's; Certificate; Doctoral degree—professional practice; Doctoral degree research/scholarship; Master's; Post-bachelor's certificate; Post-master's certificate. **Classes:** Most classes have 10–19 students. **Special Study Options:** Accelerated program; Cooperative education program; Distance learning; Dual enrollment; English as a Second Language (ESL); Independent study; Internships; Weekend college. **Disability Services offered:** Tape recorders. **Career services:** Alumni network; Alumni services; Career assessment; Career/job search classes; Internships.

FACILITIES

100% of campus accessible to physically disabled. **Campus Network:** 100% of classrooms, 100% of dorms, 100% of student union, 100% of libraries, 100% of dining areas, 85% of common outdoor areas, have wireless network access.

CAMPUS LIFE

Activities: Student government; Student newspaper. 16 registered organizations, 5 honor societies, on campus.

ADMISSIONS

Freshman Academic Profile: Average high school GPA 2.7. **Basis for Candidate Selection:** *Very important factors include:* rigor of secondary school record. *Other factors include:* class rank, application essay, standardized test scores, recommendation(s). **Freshman Admission Requirements:** High school diploma is required and GED is accepted. *Academic units recommended:* 4 English, 3 math, 2 science, 1 science labs, 2 foreign language, 1 social studies, 1 history. **Freshman Admission Statistics:** applied, admitted, enrolled. **Transfer Admission Requirements:** college transcript(s), Minimum college GPA of 2.0 required. Lowest grade transferable C-. **General Admission Information:** Application fee $55. Priority deadline 7/1. Non-fall registration accepted. Admission may be deferred for a maximum of 12 months.

COSTS AND FINANCIAL AID

Annual tuition $18,000. Average book and supplies expense $1,920. **Required Forms and Deadlines:** FAFSA; Institution's own financial aid form. **Notification of Awards:** Applicants will be notified of awards on a rolling basis beginning 7/15. **Types of Aid:** *Need-based scholarships/grants:* College/university scholarship or grant aid from institutional funds; Federal Pell; Private scholarships; SEOG; State scholarships/grants. *Loans:* Direct Subsidized Stafford Loans; Direct Unsubsidized Stafford Loans. **Student Employment:** Federal Work-Study Program available. Institutional employment available. **Financial Aid Statistics:** needy freshmen, 20% needy undergrads receive need-based scholarship or grant aid. freshmen, 24% undergrads receive non-need-based scholarship or grant aid. freshmen, 100% undergrads receive need-based self-help aid. freshmen, 0% undergrads receive athletic scholarships. **Criteria awarding aid:** *Need-based:* Academics, Alumni affiliation, Leadership, Minority status. *Non-Need-based:* Academics, Alumni affiliation, Leadership.

GONZAGA UNIVERSITY

502 E. Boone Avenue, Spokane, WA 99258
Phone: 509-313-6572 **Financial Aid Phone:** 509-313-6582
E-mail: admissions@gonzaga.edu **CEEB Code:** 4330
Fax: 509-313-5780 **Website:** www.gonzaga.edu **ACT Code:** 4458

This private school, affiliated with the Roman Catholic Church, was founded in 1887. It has a 152 acre campus.

RATINGS

Admissions Selectivity Rating: 88   **Fire Safety Rating:** 96   **Green Rating:** 93

STUDENTS AND FACULTY

Enrollment: 5,146. **Student Body:** 53% female, 47% male, 52% out-of-state, 1% international (63 countries represented). Asian 6%, African American 1%, Caucasian 71%, Hispanic 11%, Native American <1%, Pacific Islander <1%, Two or more races 7%, Race unknown 2%.

Retention and Graduation: 94% freshmen return for sophomore year. 75% freshmen graduate within 4 years. 85% freshmen graduate within 6 years. 17% grads go on to further study within 1 year. 2% grads pursue law degrees. 2% grads pursue business degrees. 2% grads pursue medical degrees. **Faculty:** Student/faculty ratio 11:1. 454 full-time faculty, 87% hold PhDs, 16% are members of minority groups, 44% are women. 0% of classes are taught by teaching assistants.

ACADEMICS

Degrees: Bachelor's; Doctoral degree—professional practice; Doctoral degree research/scholarship; Master's. **Classes:** Most classes have 20–29 students. Most lab/discussion sessions have 10–19 students. **Special Study Options:** Cross-registration; Distance learning; Double major; Dual enrollment; English as a Second Language (ESL); Exchange student program (domestic); Honors program; Independent study; Internships; Liberal arts/career combination; Study abroad; Teacher certification program. **Honors programs:** Hogan Entrepreneurial Leadership Program—The mission of the Hogan Entrepreneurial Leadership Program is to create the leaders the world needs most—individuals who seek out opportunities to create change by combining their passions and the power of entrepreneurship. The three-year, cross-curricular, honors-model approach identifies students who have a passion for exploring new ideas and provides them with the perspective to see the world in a new way. By connecting entrepreneurial education with service, leadership, and ethics, we prepare students to leverage their passions and abilities to create a positive difference in the Jesuit tradition. Unique features include: a three-year immersion in entrepreneurial contexts, a minor along with any major(s), hands-on experience, networking, $1,000/yr scholarship, and a rigorous personalized learning environment. Comprehensive Leadership Program (CLP)—CLP develops future leaders—women and men capable of crafting a vision for a better world. Through academic coursework leading to a Minor in Leadership Studies, reflective self-study, and co-curricular activities, this interdisciplinary, undergraduate leadership program will prepare you to be a great leaders on campus, in your community, and in your profession. **Combined degree programs:** BA/MA. **Disability Services offered:** Note-taking services; Reader services; Tape recorders. **Career services:** Alumni network; Alumni services; Career assessment; Career/job search classes; Internships; Regional alumni.

FACILITIES

Housing: Apartments for married students; Apartments for single students; Coed dorms; Men's dorms; Special housing for disabled students; Special housing for international students; Theme housing; Wellness housing; Women's dorms 90% of campus accessible to physically disabled. **Special Academic Facilities/Equipment:** Art center, art museum, Bing Crosby House, language lab, finance lab, TV production center, radio station, student educational center, two electron microscopes.

CAMPUS LIFE

Environment: Metropolis. **Activities:** Campus Ministries; Choral groups; Concert band; Dance; Drama/theater; International Student Organization; Jazz band; Literary magazine; Model UN; Music ensembles; Musical theater; Pep band; Radio station; Student government; Student newspaper; Symphony orchestra; Television station; Yearbook. 202 registered organizations, 16 honor societies, 5 religious organizations, on campus. **Athletics (Intercollegiate):** *Men:* baseball, basketball, crew/rowing, cross-country, golf, soccer, tennis, track/field (outdoor). *Women:* basketball, crew/rowing, cross-country, golf, soccer, tennis, track/field (outdoor), volleyball. **On-Campus Highlights:** St Aloysius Cathedral. **Environmental Initiatives:** Updating the Gonzaga University Climate Action Plan so that the strategies are measurable and actionable with clear costs and savings, prioritized in a decision matrix.

ADMISSIONS

Freshman Academic Profile: Average high school GPA 3.8. 40% in top 10% of high school class, 75% in top 25% of high school class, 95% in top 50% of high school class. 68% from public high schools. **Test scores:** SAT Math middle 50% range 600–690. SAT EBRW middle 50% range 600–670. ACT middle 50% range 25–30. **Basis for Candidate Selection:** *Very important factors include:* rigor of secondary school record, academic GPA, character/personal qualities, first generation. *Important factors include:* application essay, standardized test scores, recommendation(s), extracurricular activities, talent/ability. *Other factors include:* interview, alumni/ae relation, racial/ethnic status, volunteer work, work experience, level of applicant's interest. **Freshman Admission Requirements:** High school diploma is required and GED is not accepted. *Academic units required:* 4 English, 3 math, 3 science, 3 science labs, 2 foreign language, 2 social studies, 2 history, 2 academic electives. *Academic units recommended:* 4 English, 4 math, 4 science, 4 science labs, 3 foreign language, 3 social studies, 3 history, 3 academic electives. **Freshman Admission Statistics:** 9,279 applied, 62% admitted, 22% enrolled. **Transfer Admission Requirements:** college transcript(s), essay or personal statement, statement of good standing from prior institution(s). Minimum college GPA of 2.7 required. Lowest grade transferable C. **General Admission Information:** Application fee $50. Priority deadline 12/1. Regular application deadline 2/1. Non-fall registration accepted. Admission may be deferred for a maximum of 1 year.

COSTS AND FINANCIAL AID
Annual tuition $46,060. Room and board $12,951. Required fees $860. Average book and supplies expense $1,196. **Required Forms and Deadlines:** FAFSA. **Notification of Awards:** Applicants will be notified of awards on a rolling basis beginning 3/1. **Types of Aid:** *Need-based scholarships/grants:* College/university scholarship or grant aid from institutional funds; Federal Pell; Private scholarships; SEOG; State scholarships/grants. *Loans:* Direct PLUS loans; Direct Subsidized Stafford Loans; Direct Unsubsidized Stafford Loans. **Student Employment:** Federal Work-Study Program available. Institutional employment available. **Financial Aid Statistics:** 94% needy freshmen, 93% needy undergrads receive need-based scholarship or grant aid. 99% freshmen, 98% undergrads receive non-need-based scholarship or grant aid. 70% freshmen, 70% undergrads receive need-based self-help aid. 2% freshmen, 2% undergrads receive athletic scholarships. 99% freshmen, 98% undergrads receive any aid. 54% undergrads borrow to pay for school. Average cumulative indebtedness $29,685. **Criteria awarding aid:** *Need-based:* Academics, Leadership, Minority status. *Non-Need-based:* Academics, Alumni affiliation, Athletics, Leadership, Minority status, Music/drama.

GORDON COLLEGE

Best Colleges

255 Grapevine Road, Wenham, MA 01984-1899
Phone: 978-867-4218 **Financial Aid Phone:** 978-867-4246
E-mail: admissions@gordon.edu **CEEB Code:** 3417
Fax: 978-867-4682 **Website:** www.gordon.edu **ACT Code:** 1838

This private school, affiliated with the Multidenominational - Evangelical Church, was founded in 1889. It has a 485 acre campus.

RATINGS
Admissions Selectivity Rating: 81   **Fire Safety Rating:** 97   **Green Rating:** 85

STUDENTS AND FACULTY
Enrollment: 1,478. **Student Body:** 61% female, 39% male, 66% out-of-state, 10% international (52 countries represented). Asian 4%, African American 4%, Caucasian 68%, Hispanic 10%, Native American 0%, Pacific Islander <1%, Two or more races 3%, Race unknown 1%.
Retention and Graduation: 83% freshmen return for sophomore year. 60% freshmen graduate within 4 years. 69% freshmen graduate within 6 years. 24% grads go on to further study within 1 year. 0% grads pursue arts and sciences degrees. 0% grads pursue law degrees. 0% grads pursue business degrees. 14% grads pursue medical degrees. **Faculty:** Student/faculty ratio 10:1. 85 full-time faculty, 88% hold PhDs, 19% are members of minority groups, 40% are women. 0% of classes are taught by teaching assistants.

ACADEMICS
Degrees: Bachelor's; Master's. **Classes:** Most classes have 10–19 students. Most lab/discussion sessions have 10–19 students. **Most popular majors:** Speech Communication and Rhetoric; Psychology, General; Business Administration, Management and Operations. **Special Study Options:** Cooperative education program; Cross-registration; Double major; Dual enrollment; Exchange student program (domestic); Honors program; Independent study; Internships; Liberal arts/career combination; Student-designed major; Study abroad; Teacher certification program. **Honors programs:** The Gordon Global Honors Institute is home to three unique four-year honors scholarship programs (Global Honors Scholars, A.J. Gordon Scholars, and Clarendon Scholars) and additional honors offerings for students beyond their first year. Each of the four-year scholarship programs is built on the cohort model of learning and provides significant financial aid. All initiatives in the Global Honors Institute are designed with the unique goals of each program in mind and include some combination of advanced learning opportunities, co-curricular events, travel, internships,

personal mentoring and service opportunities. **Disability Services offered:** Note-taking services; Reader services; Tape recorders; Tutors. **Career services:** Alumni network; Alumni services; Career assessment; Career/job search classes; Internships.

FACILITIES
Housing: Apartments for single students; Coed dorms; Men's dorms; Special housing for disabled students; Theme housing; Women's dorms 86% of campus accessible to physically disabled. **Special Academic Facilities/Equipment:** The Barrington Center for the Arts features gallery space and theaters. Ken Olsen Science Center is equipped with an electron microscope and gene sequencing machine; human anatomy and physiology cadaver lab; and a pre-fabrication lab. The Phillips Music center includes recital space. (include Ken O Archive). The Biomechanics Laboratory contains a 6-camera Vicon Motion Capture System and two AMTI force plates embedded into the floor of the data capture space. **Campus Network:** 100% of classrooms, 93% of dorms, 100% of student union, 100% of libraries, 100% of dining areas, 0% of common outdoor areas, have wireless network access.

CAMPUS LIFE
Environment: Village. **Activities:** Campus Ministries; Choral groups; Concert band; Dance; Drama/theater; International Student Organization; Jazz band; Literary magazine; Model UN; Music ensembles; Musical theater; Radio station; Student government; Student newspaper; Student-run film society; Symphony orchestra; Yearbook. 120 registered organizations, 8 honor societies, 65 religious organizations, on campus. **Athletics (Intercollegiate):** *Men:* baseball, basketball, cross-country, lacrosse, soccer, swimming, tennis, track/field (outdoor), track/field (indoor). *Women:* basketball, cross-country, field hockey, lacrosse, soccer, softball, swimming, tennis, track/field (outdoor), track/field (indoor), volleyball. **On-Campus Highlights:** Gillies Lounge/Claymore Cafe **Environmental Initiatives:** Campus wide LED installations.

ADMISSIONS
Freshman Academic Profile: Average high school GPA 3.6. 25% in top 10% of high school class, 51% in top 25% of high school class, 80% in top 50% of high school class. 53% from public high schools. **Test scores:** SAT Math middle 50% range 520–650. SAT EBRW middle 50% range 540–660. ACT middle 50% range 21–30. **Basis for Candidate Selection:** *Very important factors include:* rigor of secondary school record, academic GPA, application essay, standardized test scores, recommendation(s), interview, talent/ability, character/ personal qualities, religious affiliation/commitment. *Important factors include:* class rank, extracurricular activities, volunteer work. *Other factors include:* alumni/ae relation, racial/ethnic status. **Freshman Admission Requirements:** High school diploma is required and GED is accepted. *Academic units required:* 4 English, 2 math, 2 science, 1 science labs, 2 foreign language, 2 social studies, 5 academic electives. *Academic units recommended:* 4 English, 3 math, 3 science, 1 science labs, 4 foreign language, 2 social studies, 5 academic electives. **Freshman Admission Statistics:** 2,624 applied, 74% admitted, 18% enrolled. **Transfer Admission Requirements:** college transcript(s), essay or personal statement, interview, statement of good standing from prior institution(s). Minimum college GPA of 2.0 required. Lowest grade transferable C. **General Admission Information:** Application fee $50. Priority deadline 12/1. Regular application deadline 8/1. Non-fall registration accepted. Admission may be deferred for a maximum of 2 semesters.

COSTS AND FINANCIAL AID
Annual tuition $37,560. Room and board $11,420. Required fees $1,670. Average book and supplies expense $950. **Required Forms and Deadlines:** FAFSA. **Notification of Awards:** Applicants will be notified of awards on a rolling basis beginning 1/15. **Types of Aid:** *Need-based scholarships/grants:* College/university scholarship or grant aid from institutional funds; Federal Pell; Private scholarships; SEOG; State scholarships/grants. *Loans:* Direct PLUS loans; Direct Subsidized Stafford Loans; Direct Unsubsidized Stafford Loans. **Student Employment:** Federal Work-Study Program available. Institutional employment available. **Financial Aid Statistics:** 100% needy freshmen, 100% needy undergrads receive need-based scholarship or grant aid. 18% freshmen, 15% undergrads receive non-need-based scholarship or grant aid. 80% freshmen, 81% undergrads receive need-based self-help aid. 0% freshmen, 0% undergrads receive athletic scholarships. 99% freshmen, 98% undergrads receive any aid. 66% undergrads borrow to pay for school. Average cumulative indebtedness $35,210. **Criteria awarding aid:** *Need-based:* Academics, Alumni affiliation, Art, Leadership, Minority status, Music/drama, Religious affiliation. *Non-Need-based:* Academics, Alumni affiliation, Art, Leadership, Minority status, Music/drama, State/district residency.

GOSHEN COLLEGE

1700 South Main Street, Goshen, IN 46526-4794
Phone: 574-535-7535 **Financial Aid Phone:** 574-535-7525
E-mail: admission@goshen.edu **CEEB Code:** 1251
Fax: 574-535-7609 **Website:** www.goshen.edu **ACT Code:** 1196

This private school, affiliated with the Mennonite Church, was founded in 1894. It has a 135 acre campus.

RATINGS
Admissions Selectivity Rating: 87   **Fire Safety Rating:** 97   **Green Rating:** 84

STUDENTS AND FACULTY
Enrollment: 750. **Student Body:** 58% female, 42% male, 48% out-of-state, 9% international (25 countries represented). Asian 2%, African American 4%, Caucasian 68%, Hispanic 13%, Native American 0%, Pacific Islander 0%, Two or more races 3%, Race unknown 1%.
Retention and Graduation: 77% freshmen return for sophomore year. 15% grads go on to further study within 1 year. 13% grads pursue arts and sciences degrees. 3% grads pursue law degrees. 1% grads pursue business degrees. 3% grads pursue medical degrees. **Faculty:** Student/faculty ratio 10:1. 65 full-time faculty, 66% hold PhDs, 9% are members of minority groups, 49% are women. 0% of classes are taught by teaching assistants.

ACADEMICS
Degrees: Bachelor's; Master's. **Classes:** Most classes have 10–19 students. Most lab/discussion sessions have 10–19 students. **Most popular majors:** Music; Registered Nursing/Registered Nurse; Biology/Biological Sciences, General. **Special Study Options:** Cross-registration; Double major; Dual enrollment; Independent study; Internships; Liberal arts/career combination; Student-designed major; Study abroad; Teacher certification program. **Disability Services offered:** Note-taking services; Reader services; Tape recorders; Tutors. **Career services:** Alumni network; Career/job search classes; Internships; Regional alumni.

FACILITIES
Housing: Apartments for married students; Apartments for single students; Coed dorms; Men's dorms; Special housing for disabled students; Wellness housing; Women's dorms 90% of campus accessible to physically disabled. **Special Academic Facilities/Equipment:** X-ray precision lab, lab kindergarten, Mennonite Historical Library. **Campus Network:** 100% of classrooms, 100% of dorms, 100% of student union, 100% of libraries, 100% of dining areas, have wireless network access.

CAMPUS LIFE
Environment: Town. **Activities:** Campus Ministries; Choral groups; Concert band; Drama/theater; International Student Organization; Jazz band; Music ensembles; Musical theater; Opera; Pep band; Radio station; Student government; Student newspaper; Student-run film society; Symphony orchestra; Television station; Yearbook. 24 registered organizations, 4 religious organizations, on campus. **Athletics (Intercollegiate):** *Men:* baseball, basketball, cross-country, golf, soccer, tennis, track/field (outdoor), track/field (indoor). *Women:* basketball, cross-country, soccer, softball, tennis, track/field (outdoor), track/field (indoor), volleyball. **On-Campus Highlights:** Music Center **Environmental Initiatives:** Built the first Platinum LEED Certified facility in Indiana at our Merry Lea Environmental Center. www.goshen.edu/merrylea

ADMISSIONS
Freshman Academic Profile: Average high school GPA 3.5. 38% in top 10% of high school class, 63% in top 25% of high school class, 85% in top 50% of high school class. 90% from public high schools. **Test scores:** SAT Math middle 50% range 500–635. SAT EBRW middle 50% range 475–620. ACT middle 50% range 21–28. **Basis for Candidate Selection:** *Very important factors include:* academic GPA, standardized test scores. *Important factors include:* rigor of secondary school record, class rank. *Other factors include:* application essay, recommendation(s), extracurricular activities, talent/ability, character/personal qualities, first generation, alumni/ae relation, volunteer work, work experience, level of applicant's interest. **Freshman Admission Requirements:** High school diploma is required and GED is accepted. *Academic units recommended:* 4

English, 4 math, 3 science, 4 foreign language, 3 history. **Freshman Admission Statistics:** 900 applied, 54% admitted, 33% enrolled. **Transfer Admission Requirements:** college transcript(s), essay or personal statement, statement of good standing from prior institution(s). Lowest grade transferable C. **General Admission Information:** Application fee $25. Regular application deadline 8/15. Non-fall registration accepted. Admission may be deferred for a maximum of 1 year.

COSTS AND FINANCIAL AID
Annual tuition $29,700. Room and board $9,700. Average book and supplies expense $900. **Required Forms and Deadlines:** FAFSA. **Notification of Awards:** Applicants will be notified of awards on a rolling basis beginning 2/1. **Types of Aid:** *Need-based scholarships/grants:* College/university scholarship or grant aid from institutional funds; Federal Pell; Private scholarships; SEOG; State scholarships/grants. *Loans:* Direct PLUS loans; Direct Subsidized Stafford Loans; Direct Unsubsidized Stafford Loans. **Student Employment:** Federal Work-Study Program available. Institutional employment available. **Financial Aid Statistics:** 100% needy freshmen, 98% needy undergrads receive need-based scholarship or grant aid. 20% freshmen, 16% undergrads receive non-need-based scholarship or grant aid. 77% freshmen, 81% undergrads receive need-based self-help aid. 5% freshmen, 9% undergrads receive athletic scholarships. 100% freshmen, 99% undergrads receive any aid. **Criteria awarding aid:** *Need-based:* Academics, Minority status, Religious affiliation. *Non-Need-based:* Academics, Art, Athletics, Leadership, Minority status, Music/drama.

GOUCHER COLLEGE

Admissions Office, 2021 Dulaney Valley Road, Baltimore, MD 21204-2794
Phone: 410-337-6100 **Financial Aid Phone:** 410-337-6141
E-mail: admissions@goucher.edu **CEEB Code:** 5257
Fax: 410-337-6354 **Website:** www.goucher.edu **ACT Code:** 1696

This private school was founded in 1885. It has a 287 acre campus.

RATINGS
Admissions Selectivity Rating: 77   **Fire Safety Rating:** 95   **Green Rating:** 93

STUDENTS AND FACULTY
Enrollment: 1,444. **Student Body:** 69% female, 31% male, 65% out-of-state, 3% international (27 countries represented). Asian 4%, African American 14%, Caucasian 59%, Hispanic 9%, Native American 0%, Pacific Islander <1%, Two or more races 5%, Race unknown 4%.
Retention and Graduation: 53% freshmen graduate within 4 years. 62% freshmen graduate within 6 years. 27% grads go on to further study within 1 year. 20% grads pursue arts and sciences degrees. 0% grads pursue law degrees. 1% grads pursue business degrees. 1% grads pursue medical degrees. **Faculty:** Student/faculty ratio 10:1. 133 full-time faculty, 92% hold PhDs, 17% are members of minority groups, 60% are women. 0% of classes are taught by teaching assistants.

ACADEMICS
Degrees: Bachelor's; Master's; Post-bachelor's certificate. **Classes:** Most classes have 10–19 students. **Most popular majors:** English Language and Literature, General; Business Administration and Management, General; Psychology, General. **Special Study Options:** Cross-registration; Distance learning; Double major; Dual enrollment; Independent study; Internships; Student-designed major; Study abroad; Teacher certification program. **Career services:** Alumni network; Alumni services; Career assessment; Internships.

FACILITIES
Housing: Apartments for single students; Coed dorms; Men's dorms; Special housing for disabled students; Theme housing; Wellness housing; Women's dorms 100% of campus accessible to physically disabled. **Special Academic Facilities/Equipment:** The Athenaeum is the flagship building of campus,

weaving together the various threads of life at Goucher under one roof. The 103,000 square foot building, open 24 hours a day during the semester, features a technologically superior library; a forum for public events; classrooms; a café; an art gallery; a center for community service programming; and spaces for exercise, conversation, and relaxation. The recently renovated 62,000-square-foot Academic Center at Julia Rogers is a place where science, humanities, and social science disciplines merge into one academic whole. The facility boasts technology-enhanced classrooms and state-of-the-art research and teaching labs, an international commons to facilitate cultural exchange, and the Welch Center for Graduate and Professional Studies. The Academic Center for Excellence offers study-skills workshops, peer-led supplemental instruction, and yoga, meditation, and Reiki sessions. Goucher also has a TV studio, three multi-purpose performance spaces ranging in size from a few hundred to 1,000 seats, a robotics lab, a rooftop observatory providing public observing, advanced teaching labs for physics and computer science, research labs for math, physics, and psychology, a technology/learning center, international technology and media center, and centers for writing, math, and politics. Also located on Goucher's campus are equestrian stables and riding areas, a community garden, and nature trails.

CAMPUS LIFE

Environment: City. **Activities:** Campus Ministries; Choral groups; Concert band; Dance; Drama/theater; International Student Organization; Jazz band; Literary magazine; Model UN; Music ensembles; Musical theater; Opera; Pep band; Radio station; Student government; Student newspaper; Student-run film society; Yearbook. 60 registered organizations, 1 honor societies, 5 religious organizations, on campus. **Athletics (Intercollegiate):** *Men:* basketball, cross-country, lacrosse, soccer, swimming, tennis, track/field (outdoor), track/field (indoor). *Women:* basketball, cross-country, equestrian sports, field hockey, lacrosse, soccer, swimming, tennis, track/field (outdoor), track/field (indoor), volleyball. **On-Campus Highlights:** The Library at the Athenaeum **Environmental Initiatives:** Goucher ensures that every student fulfills a sustainability learning requirement regardless of their course of study.

ADMISSIONS

Freshman Academic Profile: Average high school GPA 3.1. 28% in top 10% of high school class, 54% in top 25% of high school class, 78% in top 50% of high school class. 62% from public high schools. **Test scores:** SAT Math middle 50% range 500–600. SAT EBRW middle 50% range 550–660. ACT middle 50% range 23–29. **Basis for Candidate Selection:** *Very important factors include:* rigor of secondary school record, academic GPA. *Important factors include:* application essay, recommendation(s), extracurricular activities, talent/ability. *Other factors include:* class rank, standardized test scores, interview, character/personal qualities, first generation, alumni/ae relation, geographical residence, state residency, racial/ethnic status, work experience, level of applicant's interest. **Freshman Admission Requirements:** High school diploma is required and GED is accepted. *Academic units required:* 4 English, 3 math, 2 science, 2 science labs, 2 foreign language, 3 social studies, 2 academic electives. *Academic units recommended:* 4 English, 4 math, 3 science, 3 science labs, 4 foreign language, 3 social studies, 2 academic electives. **Freshman Admission Statistics:** 3,474 applied, 79% admitted, 15% enrolled. **Transfer Admission Requirements:** college transcript(s), essay or personal statement, Lowest grade transferable C.

COSTS AND FINANCIAL AID

Annual tuition $43,412. Room and board $14,506. Required fees $888. Average book and supplies expense $1,200. **Required Forms and Deadlines:** FAFSA. **Notification of Awards:** Applicants will be notified of awards on a rolling basis beginning 12/15. **Types of Aid:** *Need-based scholarships/grants:* College/university scholarship or grant aid from institutional funds; Federal Pell; Private scholarships; SEOG; State scholarships/grants. *Loans:* Direct PLUS loans; Direct Subsidized Stafford Loans; Direct Unsubsidized Stafford Loans. **Student Employment:** Federal Work-Study Program available. Institutional employment available. **Financial Aid Statistics:** 100% needy freshmen, 100% needy undergrads receive need-based scholarship or grant aid. 16% freshmen, 13% undergrads receive non-need-based scholarship or grant aid. 82% freshmen, 86% undergrads receive need-based self-help aid. 0% freshmen, 0% undergrads receive athletic scholarships. 100% freshmen, 95% undergrads receive any aid. 59% undergrads borrow to pay for school. Average cumulative indebtedness $28,321. **Criteria awarding aid:** *Non-Need-based:* Academics, Art, Leadership, Music/drama.

GOVERNORS STATE UNIVERSITY

1 University Parkway, University Park, IL 60484
Phone: 708-534-4490 **Financial Aid Phone:** 708-534-4480
E-mail: gsunow@govst.edu
Fax: 708-534-1640 **Website:** www.govst.edu

This public school was founded in 1969. It has a 720 acre campus.

RATINGS
Admissions Selectivity Rating: 60*   **Fire Safety Rating:** 60*   **Green Rating:** 60*

STUDENTS AND FACULTY
Enrollment: 3,103. **Student Body:** 68% female, 32% male, 3% out-of-state, <1% international (17 countries represented). Asian 2%, African American 37%, Caucasian 44%, Hispanic 10%, Native American <1%, Pacific Islander <1%, Two or more races 1%, Race unknown 7%.
Retention and Graduation: 34% grads go on to further study within 1 year. 17% grads pursue arts and sciences degrees. 1% grads pursue law degrees. 16% grads pursue business degrees. 0% grads pursue medical degrees. **Faculty:** Student/faculty ratio 11:1. 211 full-time faculty, 59% hold PhDs, 37% are members of minority groups, 59% are women. 0% of classes are taught by teaching assistants.

ACADEMICS
Degrees: Bachelor's; Doctoral degree—other; Doctoral degree—professional practice; Master's; Post-master's certificate. **Classes:** Most classes have 10–19 students. Most lab/discussion sessions have 10–19 students. **Most popular majors:** Business/Commerce, General; Elementary Education and Teaching. **Special Study Options:** Cross-registration; Distance learning; Dual enrollment; External degree program; Honors program; Independent study; Internships; Student-designed major; Study abroad; Teacher certification program. **Disability Services offered:** Note-taking services; Reader services; Tape recorders; Tutors. **Career services:** Alumni network; Alumni services; Career assessment; Career/job search classes; Internships.

FACILITIES
99% of campus accessible to physically disabled. **Special Academic Facilities/Equipment:** Manilow Sculpture Park

CAMPUS LIFE
Environment: Village. **Activities:** Drama/theater; Literary magazine; Student government; Student newspaper; Student-run film society. 7 honor societies, on campus.

ADMISSIONS
Freshman Admission Statistics: applied, admitted, enrolled. **Transfer Admission Requirements:** college transcript(s), statement of good standing from prior institution(s). Minimum college GPA of 2.0 required. Lowest grade transferable C.

COSTS AND FINANCIAL AID
Types of Aid: *Need-based scholarships/grants:* College/university scholarship or grant aid from institutional funds; Federal Nursing Scholarships; Federal Pell; Private scholarships; SEOG; State scholarships/grants. *Loans:* Direct Subsidized Stafford Loans. **Student Employment:** Federal Work-Study Program available. Institutional employment available. **Criteria awarding aid:** *Need-based:* Academics. *Non-Need-based:* Academics.

GRACE COLLEGE AND SEMINARY

200 Seminary Drive, Winona Lake, IN 46590
Phone: 800-544-7223 **Financial Aid Phone:** 574-372-5100
E-mail: enroll@grace.edu **CEEB Code:** 1252
Fax: 574-372-5120 **Website:** www.grace.edu **ACT Code:** 1198

This private school, affiliated with the Fellowship of Grace Brethren Churches, was founded in 1948. It has a 150 acre campus.

RATINGS
Admissions Selectivity Rating: 76 **Fire Safety Rating:** 83 **Green Rating:** 60*

STUDENTS AND FACULTY
Enrollment: 1,813. **Student Body:** 58% female, 42% male, 33% out-of-state, 1% international (9 countries represented). Asian 1%, African American 3%, Caucasian 83%, Hispanic 7%, Native American <1%, Pacific Islander <1%, Two or more races 2%, Race unknown 2%.
Retention and Graduation: 81% freshmen return for sophomore year. 66% freshmen graduate within 4 years. % freshmen graduate within 6 years. **Faculty:** Student/faculty ratio 19:1. 50 full-time faculty, 78% hold PhDs, 4% are members of minority groups, 38% are women. 0% of classes are taught by teaching assistants.

ACADEMICS
Degrees: Associate; Bachelor's; Certificate; Diploma; Doctoral degree—other; Master's; Post-bachelor's certificate. **Classes:** Most classes have 20–29 students. Most lab/discussion sessions have 10–19 students. **Most popular majors:** Business/Commerce, General; Elementary Education and Teaching; Psychology, General. **Special Study Options:** Cooperative education program; Cross-registration; Distance learning; Double major; Dual enrollment; Exchange student program (domestic); Honors program; Independent study; Internships; Liberal arts/career combination; Study abroad; Teacher certification program. **Disability Services offered:** Note-taking services; Reader services; Tape recorders; Tutors. **Career services:** Career assessment.

FACILITIES
Housing: Apartments for single students; Men's dorms; Women's dorms 85% of campus accessible to physically disabled. **Special Academic Facilities/Equipment:** Reneker Museum of Winona History **Campus Network:** 98% of classrooms, 100% of dorms, 100% of student union, 100% of libraries, 100% of dining areas, 25% of common outdoor areas, have wireless network access.

CAMPUS LIFE
Environment: Village. **Activities:** Campus Ministries; Choral groups; Concert band; Drama/theater; Literary magazine; Music ensembles; Musical theater; Pep band; Student government; Student newspaper; Symphony orchestra; Yearbook. 9 registered organizations, 1 honor societies, 8 religious organizations, on campus. **Athletics (Intercollegiate):** *Men:* baseball, basketball, cheerleading, cross-country, golf, soccer, tennis, track/field (outdoor). *Women:* basketball, cheerleading, cross-country, soccer, softball, tennis, track/field (outdoor), volleyball. **On-Campus Highlights:** Gordon Recreation Center.

ADMISSIONS
Freshman Academic Profile: Average high school GPA 3.6. 22% in top 10% of high school class, 51% in top 25% of high school class, 81% in top 50% of high school class. 71% from public high schools. **Test scores:** SAT Math middle 50% range 510–610. SAT EBRW middle 50% range 510–640. ACT middle 50% range 20–27. **Basis for Candidate Selection:** *Very important factors include:* rigor of secondary school record, application essay, standardized test scores, recommendation(s), religious affiliation/commitment. *Important factors include:* academic GPA, character/personal qualities. *Other factors include:* class rank, interview, extracurricular activities, talent/ability, alumni/ae relation. **Freshman Admission Requirements:** High school diploma is required and GED is accepted. *Academic units recommended:* 4 English, 2 math, 2 science, 1 science labs, 2 foreign language, 2 social studies, 1 history. **Freshman Admission Statistics:** 3,753 applied, 81% admitted, 11% enrolled. **Transfer Admission Requirements:** college transcript(s), essay or personal statement, standardized test scores, Minimum college GPA of 2.0 required. Lowest grade transferable C-. **General Admission Information:** Application fee $30. Priority deadline 6/1. Regular application deadline 8/15. Non-fall registration accepted. Admission may be deferred for a maximum of 1 semester.

COSTS AND FINANCIAL AID
Annual tuition $25,512. Room and board $9,316. Required fees $750. Average book and supplies expense $1,000. **Required Forms and Deadlines:** FAFSA. **Notification of Awards:** Applicants will be notified of awards on a rolling basis beginning 3/1. **Types of Aid:** *Need-based scholarships/grants:* College/university scholarship or grant aid from institutional funds; Federal Pell; Private scholarships; SEOG; State scholarships/grants. **Student Employment:** Federal Work-Study Program available. Institutional employment available. **Criteria awarding aid:** *Need-based:* Minority status, Religious affiliation. *Non-Need-based:* Academics, Art, Athletics, Leadership, Music/drama.

GRACELAND UNIVERSITY

1 University Place, Lamoni, IA 50140
Phone: 641-784-5196 **Financial Aid Phone:** 641 784 5051
E-mail: admissions@graceland.edu **CEEB Code:** 6249
Fax: 641-784-5480 **Website:** www.graceland.edu **ACT Code:** 1314

This private school, affiliated with the Community of Christ Church, was founded in 1895. It has a 170 acre campus.

RATINGS
Admissions Selectivity Rating: 83 **Fire Safety Rating:** 88 **Green Rating:** 74

STUDENTS AND FACULTY
Enrollment: 972. **Student Body:** 58% female, 42% male, 72% out-of-state, 6% international (26 countries represented). Asian 1%, African American 9%, Caucasian 60%, Hispanic 10%, Native American <1%, Pacific Islander 2%, Two or more races 4%, Race unknown 8%.
Retention and Graduation: 66% freshmen return for sophomore year. 32% freshmen graduate within 4 years. 45% freshmen graduate within 6 years. **Faculty:** Student/faculty ratio 14:1. 74 full-time faculty, 74% hold PhDs, 9% are members of minority groups, 53% are women. 0% of classes are taught by teaching assistants.

ACADEMICS
Degrees: Bachelor's; Certificate; Doctoral degree—other; Master's; Post-master's certificate. **Classes:** Most classes have 10–19 students. Most lab/discussion sessions have fewer than 10 students. **Most popular majors:** Elementary Education and Teaching; Business Administration and Management, General; Registered Nursing/Registered Nurse. **Special Study Options:** Accelerated program; Distance learning; Double major; Dual enrollment; Honors program; Independent study; Internships; Liberal arts/career combination; Student-designed major; Study abroad; Teacher certification program. **Honors programs:** The Graceland University Honors Program includes courses in Honors Discourse I & II, Honors Humanities, Jr. and Sr. Honors Seminar, and Honors Contracts to be created with instructors in any academic course the students choose. Completion of the Honors Program requires 21 hours of honors credit, completion of the Jr. and Sr. Honors Seminars, and a minimum 3.5 gpa overall and in their honors work. Honors Students with a 3.75 gpa or higher are eligible for an Honors Scholarship. Incoming students with a 3.75 gpa and an ACT of 27 or higher may apply for full tuition Prestigious Honors Scholarship, which are available on a competitive basis, and require an interview. Graceland University offers an Excellent Education in a caring community. So we believe the best reason to participate in the Honors Program is the people in it, and to participate in the Honors community. **Disability Services offered:** Note-taking services; Reader services; Tape recorders. **Career services:** Alumni network; Alumni services; Career/job search classes; Internships; Regional alumni.

FACILITIES
Housing: Apartments for single students; Men's dorms; Special housing for disabled students; Theme housing; Women's dorms 95% of campus accessible to physically disabled. **Special Academic Facilities/Equipment:** Shaw Center for the Performing Arts which includes a recital facility, outdoor amphitheatre, 500-seat auditorium, and a black box theatre.

CAMPUS LIFE
Environment: Rural. **Activities:** Campus Ministries; Choral groups; Concert band; Dance; Drama/theater; International Student Organization; Jazz band; Literary magazine; Marching band; Music ensembles; Musical theater; Pep band; Radio station; Student government; Student newspaper; Symphony orchestra; Yearbook. 34 registered organizations, 1 honor societies, 3 religious

organizations, on campus. **Athletics (Intercollegiate):** *Men:* baseball, basketball, cross-country, football, golf, soccer, tennis, track/field (outdoor), track/field (indoor), volleyball. *Women:* basketball, cross-country, golf, soccer, softball, tennis, track/field (outdoor), track/field (indoor), volleyball. **On-Campus Highlights:** Shaw Center. **Environmental Initiatives:** Installation of Hoop House garden to produce vegetables for campus dining services.

ADMISSIONS

Freshman Academic Profile: Average high school GPA 3.4. 12% in top 10% of high school class, 34% in top 25% of high school class, 70% in top 50% of high school class. **Test scores:** SAT Math middle 50% range 450–550. SAT EBRW middle 50% range 470–570. ACT middle 50% range 18–24. **Basis for Candidate Selection:** *Very important factors include:* academic GPA, standardized test scores. *Important factors include:* rigor of secondary school record, class rank. *Other factors include:* application essay, recommendation(s), interview, talent/ability. **Freshman Admission Requirements:** High school diploma is required and GED is accepted. *Academic units recommended:* 4 English, 3 math, 2 science, 1 foreign language, 3 social studies. **Freshman Admission Statistics:** 2,514 applied, 58% admitted, 13% enrolled. **Transfer Admission Requirements:** college transcript(s), Minimum college GPA of 2.0 required. Lowest grade transferable D. **General Admission Information:** Non-fall registration accepted.

COSTS AND FINANCIAL AID

Annual tuition $30,650. Room and board $9,440. Required fees $670. Average book and supplies expense $1,320. **Required Forms and Deadlines:** FAFSA. **Notification of Awards:** Applicants will be notified of awards on a rolling basis beginning 2/1. **Types of Aid:** *Need-based scholarships/grants:* College/university scholarship or grant aid from institutional funds; Federal Pell; Private scholarships; SEOG; State scholarships/grants. *Loans:* Direct PLUS loans; Direct Subsidized Stafford Loans; Direct Unsubsidized Stafford Loans. **Student Employment:** Federal Work-Study Program available. Institutional employment available. **Financial Aid Statistics:** 100% needy freshmen, 98% needy undergrads receive need-based scholarship or grant aid. 38% freshmen, 31% undergrads receive non-need-based scholarship or grant aid. 86% freshmen, 85% undergrads receive need-based self-help aid. 16% freshmen, 16% undergrads receive athletic scholarships. 89% undergrads borrow to pay for school. Average cumulative indebtedness $44,984. **Criteria awarding aid:** *Need-based:* Job skills, Minority status. *Non-Need-based:* Academics, Alumni affiliation, Art, Athletics, Job skills, Leadership, Music/drama, Religious affiliation.

GRAND RAPIDS THEOLOGICAL SEMINARY

1001 E Beltline Ave. NE, Grand Rapids, MI 49525
Phone: 1-800-697-1133 **Financial Aid Phone:** 616-949-5300
E-mail: grts@cornerstone.edu
Fax: 616-254-1623 **Website:** http://grts.cornerstone.edu

This is a private school.

RATINGS
Admissions Selectivity Rating: 60*   **Fire Safety Rating:** 96   **Green Rating:** 60*

STUDENTS AND FACULTY
Enrollment: 3,000.
Retention and Graduation: 15% grads go on to further study within 1 year. 10% grads pursue arts and sciences degrees. 1% grads pursue law degrees. 3% grads pursue business degrees. 1% grads pursue medical degrees. **Faculty:** Student/faculty ratio 17:1. 9 full-time faculty, 0% of classes are taught by teaching assistants.

ACADEMICS
Degrees: Certificate; Master's. **Most popular majors:** Education, General; Business/Commerce, General; Psychology, General. **Special Study Options:** Distance learning; Double major; Dual enrollment; Honors program; Independent study; Internships; Study abroad. **Honors programs:** Honors Program based on a "great books" curriculum. **Disability Services offered:** Note-taking services; Reader services; Tape recorders; Tutors. **Career services:** Career assessment; Career/job search classes; Internships.

FACILITIES
Housing: Apartments for married students; Apartments for single students; Men's dorms; Special housing for disabled students; Women's dorms 100% of campus accessible to physically disabled.

CAMPUS LIFE
Activities: Campus Ministries; International Student Organization; Student government. 11 registered organizations, 2 honor societies, 1 religious organizations, on campus. **Athletics (Intercollegiate):** *Men:* basketball, cross-country, golf, soccer, track/field (outdoor), track/field (indoor). *Women:* basketball, cross-country, golf, soccer, softball, track/field (outdoor), track/field (indoor), volleyball. **On-Campus Highlights:** Corum Student Union **Environmental Initiatives:** On campus dialogue and focus on sustainability issues.

ADMISSIONS
Freshman Academic Profile: 60% from public high schools. **Basis for Candidate Selection:** *Very important factors include:* academic GPA, application essay, recommendation(s), religious affiliation/commitment. *Important factors include:* standardized test scores, extracurricular activities, character/personal qualities, volunteer work, level of applicant's interest. *Other factors include:* rigor of secondary school record, talent/ability, work experience. **Freshman Admission Requirements:** High school diploma is required and GED is accepted. **Transfer Admission Requirements:** college transcript(s), essay or personal statement, Minimum college GPA of 2.5 required. Lowest grade transferable C.

COSTS AND FINANCIAL AID
Types of Aid: *Need-based scholarships/grants:* College/university scholarship or grant aid from institutional funds; Private scholarships; State scholarships/grants. *Loans:* Direct Subsidized Stafford Loans; Direct Unsubsidized Stafford Loans. **Student Employment:** Federal Work-Study Program available. **Financial Aid Statistics:** needy freshmen, needy undergrads receive need-based scholarship or grant aid. freshmen, undergrads receive non-need-based scholarship or grant aid. freshmen, undergrads receive need-based self-help aid. freshmen, undergrads receive athletic scholarships. 100% freshmen, 98% undergrads receive any aid. **Criteria awarding aid:** *Need-based:* Academics, Job skills, Leadership, Minority status, Religious affiliation. *Non-Need-based:* Academics, Job skills, Leadership, Minority status, Religious affiliation.

GRAND VALLEY STATE UNIVERSITY

1 Campus Drive, Allendale, MI 49401
Phone: 616-331-2025 **Financial Aid Phone:** 616-331-3234
E-mail: admissions@gvsu.edu **CEEB Code:** 1258
Fax: 616-331-2000 **Website:** www.gvsu.edu **ACT Code:** 2005

This public school was founded in 1960. It has a 1391 acre campus.

RATINGS
Admissions Selectivity Rating: 77   **Fire Safety Rating:** 90   **Green Rating:** 97

STUDENTS AND FACULTY
Enrollment: 21,568. **Student Body:** 59% female, 41% male, 8% out-of-state, 1% international (68 countries represented). Asian 2%, African American 5%, Caucasian 82%, Hispanic 6%, Native American <1%, Pacific Islander <1%, Two or more races 4%, Race unknown <1%.
Retention and Graduation: 85% freshmen return for sophomore year. 36% freshmen graduate within 4 years. 65% freshmen graduate within 6 years. **Faculty:** Student/faculty ratio 16:1. 1,188 full-time faculty, 76% hold PhDs, 17% are members of minority groups, 50% are women. 0% of classes are taught by teaching assistants.

ACADEMICS
Degrees: Bachelor's; Certificate; Doctoral degree—professional practice; Master's; Post-bachelor's certificate; Post-master's certificate. **Classes:** Most classes have 20–29 students. Most lab/discussion sessions have 20–29 students. **Most popular majors:** Education, General; Registered Nursing/Registered Nurse; Business/Commerce, General. **Special Study Options:** Distance learning; Double major; Dual enrollment; English as a Second Language (ESL); Honors program; Independent study; Internships; Student-designed major; Study abroad; Teacher certification program. **Honors programs:** Honor's College. **Combined degree programs:** BA/JD; BA/MEng. **Disability**

Services offered: Reader services; Tape recorders; Tutors. **Career services:** Alumni network; Alumni services; Career assessment; Career/job search classes; Internships; Regional alumni.

FACILITIES

Housing: Apartments for married students; Apartments for single students; Coed dorms; Fraternity/sorority housing; Theme housing 99% of campus accessible to physically disabled. **Special Academic Facilities/Equipment:** two Great Lakes research vessels, audio-visual center, performance/recital hall, pipe organ, physical therapy/human performance lab. **Campus Network:** 100% of classrooms, 100% of dorms, 100% of student union, 100% of libraries, 100% of dining areas, 50% of common outdoor areas, have wireless network access.

CAMPUS LIFE

Environment: City. **Activities:** Campus Ministries; Choral groups; Concert band; Dance; Drama/theater; International Student Organization; Jazz band; Literary magazine; Marching band; Music ensembles; Musical theater; Pep band; Radio station; Student government; Student newspaper; Symphony orchestra; Television station. 407 registered organizations, 20 honor societies, 16 religious organizations, 14 fraternities, 14 sororities, on campus. **Athletics (Intercollegiate):** *Men:* baseball, basketball, cross-country, diving, football, golf, swimming, tennis, track/field (outdoor), track/field (indoor). *Women:* basketball, cross-country, diving, golf, soccer, softball, swimming, tennis, track/field (outdoor), track/field (indoor), volleyball. **On-Campus Highlights:** Living Centers. **Environmental Initiatives:** Climate Mitigation: GVSU is a signatory to American College and University Presidents Climate Commitment and has recently completed its Climate Action Plan and set a goal of climate neutrality by 2037. The climate action plan is available online. Currently there are over 650 colleges and universities that have signed on to this agreement. LEED construction projects and bus transportation are both important climate mitigation strategies. GVSU has completed and certified 10 LEED projects with 2 more LEED projects under construction. These 12 LEED projects represent over 925,000 square feet and ~19% of total square footage. Annual bus ridership is over ~ 2MM bus rides per year for faculty and students and saves millions of dollars in annual fuel purchases and vehicle maintenance costs while reducing our carbon footprint.

ADMISSIONS

Freshman Academic Profile: Average high school GPA 3.6. 20% in top 10% of high school class, 47% in top 25% of high school class, 83% in top 50% of high school class. 78% from public high schools. **Test scores:** SAT Math middle 50% range 520–610. SAT EBRW middle 50% range 530–630. ACT middle 50% range 21–27. **Basis for Candidate Selection:** *Very important factors include:* rigor of secondary school record, academic GPA. *Important factors include:* standardized test scores. *Other factors include:* class rank, application essay, recommendation(s), extracurricular activities, talent/ability, first generation, alumni/ae relation, volunteer work, work experience. **Freshman Admission Requirements:** High school diploma is required and GED is accepted. *Academic units required:* 4 English, 3 math, 3 science, 2 science labs, 2 foreign language, 3 social studies. **Freshman Admission Statistics:** 17,509 applied, 81% admitted, 29% enrolled. **Transfer Admission Requirements:** college transcript(s), statement of good standing from prior institution(s). Minimum college GPA of 2.5 required. Lowest grade transferable D. **General Admission Information:** Application fee $30. Priority deadline 5/1. Non-fall registration accepted.

COSTS AND FINANCIAL AID

Annual in-state tuition $12,484. Annual out-of-state tuition $17,762. Room and board $8,690. Average book and supplies expense $700. **Required Forms and Deadlines:** FAFSA. **Notification of Awards:** Applicants will be notified of awards on a rolling basis beginning 1/16. **Types of Aid:** *Need-based scholarships/grants:* College/university scholarship or grant aid from institutional funds; Federal Pell; Private scholarships; SEOG; State scholarships/grants. *Loans:* Direct PLUS loans; Direct Subsidized Stafford Loans; Direct Unsubsidized Stafford Loans. **Student Employment:** Federal Work-Study Program available. Institutional employment available. **Financial Aid Statistics:** 86% needy freshmen, 83% needy undergrads receive need-based scholarship or grant aid. 9% freshmen, 5% undergrads receive non-need-based scholarship or grant aid. 79% freshmen, 85% undergrads receive need-based self-help aid. 1% freshmen, 1% undergrads receive athletic scholarships. 85.7% freshmen, 82.7% undergrads receive any aid. 71% undergrads borrow to pay for school. Average cumulative indebtedness $28,415. **Criteria awarding aid:** *Non-Need-based:* Academics, Alumni affiliation, Art, Athletics, Music/drama, State/district residency.

GRAND VIEW UNIVERSITY

1200 Grandview Avenue, Des Moines, IA 50316-1599
Phone: 515-263-2810 **Financial Aid Phone:** 515-263-2963
E-mail: admissions@GrandView.edu **CEEB Code:** 6251
Fax: 515-263-2974 **Website:** www.admissions.grandview.edu **ACT Code:** 1316

This private school, affiliated with the Lutheran Church, was founded in 1896. It has a 35 acre campus.

RATINGS

Admissions Selectivity Rating: 73   **Fire Safety Rating:** 60*   **Green Rating:** 60*

STUDENTS AND FACULTY

Enrollment: 2,079. **Student Body:** 58% female, 42% male, 13% out-of-state, 2% international (16 countries represented). Asian 3%, African American 8%, Caucasian 74%, Hispanic 3%, Native American <1%, Pacific Islander <1%, Two or more races 3%, Race unknown 7%.
Retention and Graduation: 69% freshmen return for sophomore year. **Faculty:** Student/faculty ratio 13:1. 95 full-time faculty, 68% hold PhDs, 7% are members of minority groups, 56% are women. 0% of classes are taught by teaching assistants.

ACADEMICS

Degrees: Bachelor's; Certificate; Master's; Post-bachelor's certificate. **Classes:** Most classes have 10–19 students. Most lab/discussion sessions have 10–19 students. **Most popular majors:** Education, General; Business/Commerce, General; Nursing/Registered Nurse (Rn, Asn, Bsn, Msn). **Special Study Options:** Accelerated program; Cooperative education program; Cross-registration; Distance learning; Double major; Dual enrollment; Exchange student program (domestic); Honors program; Independent study; Internships; Liberal arts/career combination; Student-designed major; Study abroad; Teacher certification program; Weekend college. **Honors programs:** Logos Honors Program.

FACILITIES

Housing: Apartments for single students; Coed dorms. **Special Academic Facilities/Equipment:** Danish American Archives.

CAMPUS LIFE

Activities: Campus Ministries; Choral groups; Concert band; Dance; Drama/theater; International Student Organization; Jazz band; Literary magazine; Music ensembles; Pep band; Radio station; Student government; Student newspaper; Television station. 28 registered organizations, 1 religious organizations, on campus. **Athletics (Intercollegiate):** *Men:* baseball, basketball, cross-country, golf, soccer. *Women:* basketball, cross-country, golf, soccer, softball, volleyball.

ADMISSIONS

Freshman Academic Profile: Average high school GPA 3.2. 15% in top 10% of high school class, 33% in top 25% of high school class, 64% in top 50% of high school class. **Test scores:** SAT Math middle 50% range 400–480. SAT EBRW middle 50% range 380–450. ACT middle 50% range 19–23. **Basis for Candidate Selection:** *Very important factors include:* rigor of secondary school record, class rank, academic GPA, character/personal qualities. *Important factors include:* standardized test scores. *Other factors include:* extracurricular activities, talent/ability, alumni/ae relation, volunteer work, work experience. **Freshman Admission Requirements:** High school diploma is required and GED is accepted. *Academic units recommended:* 4 English, 3 math, 3 science, 2 foreign language, 3 social studies. **Freshman Admission Statistics:** 805 applied, 96% admitted, 39% enrolled. **Transfer Admission Requirements:** college transcript(s), Minimum college GPA of 2.0 required. Lowest grade transferable D. **General Admission Information:** Regular application deadline 8/15. Non-fall registration accepted. Admission may be deferred for a maximum of 1 semester.

COSTS AND FINANCIAL AID

Annual tuition $22,986. Room and board $7,554. Required fees $530. Average book and supplies expense $880. **Required Forms and Deadlines:** FAFSA. **Notification of Awards:** Applicants will be notified of awards on a rolling basis beginning 3/1. **Types of Aid:** *Need-based scholarships/grants:* College/university scholarship or grant aid from institutional funds; Federal Pell; Private scholarships; SEOG; State scholarships/grants. **Student Employment:** Federal Work-Study Program available. Institutional employment available. **Financial Aid Statistics:** 88% needy freshmen, 92% needy undergrads receive need-based scholarship or grant aid. 20% freshmen, 11% undergrads receive non-need-based scholarship or grant aid. 80% freshmen, 88% undergrads receive need-based self-help aid. 63% freshmen, 10% undergrads receive athletic scholarships. 97% freshmen, 99% undergrads receive any aid. **Criteria awarding aid:** *Need-based:* Academics, Leadership *Non-Need-based:* Academics, Alumni affiliation, Art, Athletics, Leadership, Music/drama.

GRANTHAM UNIVERSITY

7200 NW 86th Street, Kansas City, MO 64153
E-mail: admissions@grantham.edu
Fax: 816-595-5757 **Website:** http://www.grantham.edu/

This is a proprietary school.

RATINGS
Admissions Selectivity Rating: 60*   **Fire Safety Rating:** 60*   **Green Rating:** 60*

STUDENTS AND FACULTY
Enrollment: 9,500.

ACADEMICS
Degrees: Associate; Bachelor's; Master's. **Special Study Options:** Accelerated program; Distance learning; External degree program; Independent study.

ADMISSIONS
Freshman Admission Requirements: High school diploma is required and GED is accepted. **Transfer Admission Requirements:** High school transcript, college transcript(s), Minimum college GPA of 2.0 required. Lowest grade transferable C. **General Admission Information:** Non-fall registration accepted.

COSTS AND FINANCIAL AID
Annual tuition $7,500.

GREENVILLE COLLEGE

315 East College Avenue, Greenville, IL 62246
Phone: 618-664-7100 **Financial Aid Phone:** 618-664-7108
E-mail: admissions@greenville.edu **CEEB Code:** 1256
Fax: 618-664-9841 **Website:** www.greenville.edu **ACT Code:** 1032

This private school, affiliated with the Free Methodist Church, was founded in 1892. It has a 40 acre campus.

RATINGS
Admissions Selectivity Rating: 86   **Fire Safety Rating:** 97   **Green Rating:** 60*

STUDENTS AND FACULTY
Enrollment: 938. **Student Body:** 47% female, 53% male, 30% out-of-state, 5% international (14 countries represented). Asian <1%, African American 15%, Caucasian 66%, Hispanic 6%, Native American 0%, Pacific Islander 0%, Two or more races 2%, Race unknown 4%.
Retention and Graduation: 70% freshmen return for sophomore year. 36% freshmen graduate within 4 years. 43% freshmen graduate within 6 years.
Faculty: Student/faculty ratio 13:1. 0% of classes are taught by teaching assistants.

ACADEMICS
Degrees: Bachelor's; Master's. **Classes:** Most classes have 10–19 students. **Most popular majors:** Music Management; Biology/Biological Sciences, General; Elementary Education and Teaching. **Special Study Options:** Accelerated program; Cooperative education program; Cross-registration; Double major; External degree program; Honors program; Independent study; Internships; Liberal arts/career combination; Student-designed major; Study abroad; Teacher certification program. **Honors programs:** Greenville University's McAllaster Scholars Program is an academic program that was established in 1995 to provide a "value-added" dimension to the excellent, Christ-centered education students regularly receive at Greenville University. The Honors Program consists of a blend of enriched sections of several general education classes, special honors seminars, and experiential learning opportunities offered in an enhanced educational environment that strives for small class sizes to encourage total student participation, facilitate spirited discussions and promote greater student-faculty interaction. Outside the classroom, the Honors Programs offers a co-curricular program consisting of diversified cultural, social and educationally-oriented activities and events developed especially for program members. The Honors Program encourages its members to be persons with multi-dimensional interests who participate in a wide range of university sponsored events, activities, and organizations. Students admitted to The Honors Program automatically become members of The Honors Society, the student organization within the program which elects officers who assist with the planning and implementation of the aforementioned activities and other community building opportunities. The Greenville College Honors Program strives to emulate the guidelines, "Basic Characteristics of a Fully-Developed Honors Program," developed by the National Collegiate Honors Council. It, also, cooperates with member institutions of the Council of Christian Colleges and Universities by encouraging GC students to participate in one of the nearly twenty semester-long academic programs coordinated and promoted by CCCU that are offered at off-campus sites, both domestic and abroad. Locally, The Honors Program is administered by a director who is assisted by an Honors Council composed of faculty and students. To graduate with Honors Program recognition, students must fulfill the requirements of their academic major, earn a minimum of 25 credit hours of honors work, maintain a cumulative grade point average of 3.50 and complete a Departmental Honors Thesis under the supervision of a three-person faculty thesis committee. Graduates of the Honors Program are awarded a special medallion and receive special recognition at commencement. **Disability Services offered:** Tutors. **Career services:** Career/job search classes.

FACILITIES
Housing: Apartments for single students; Coed dorms; Men's dorms; Special housing for international students; Women's dorms 40% of campus accessible to physically disabled. **Special Academic Facilities/Equipment:** Sculpture museum, sports training facility.

CAMPUS LIFE
Environment: Village. **Activities:** Campus Ministries; Choral groups; Concert band; Drama/theater; Jazz band; Marching band; Music ensembles; Musical theater; Pep band; Radio station; Student government; Student newspaper. 25 registered organizations, 6 honor societies, 2 religious organizations, on campus. **Athletics (Intercollegiate):** *Men:* baseball, basketball, cross-country, football, soccer, tennis, track/field (outdoor), track/field (indoor). *Women:* basketball, cross-country, soccer, softball, tennis, track/field (outdoor), track/field (indoor), volleyball. **On-Campus Highlights:** Jo's Java.

ADMISSIONS
Test scores: ACT middle 50% range 17–27. **Basis for Candidate Selection:** *Very important factors include:* academic GPA, application essay, standardized test scores. *Important factors include:* character/personal qualities, religious affiliation/commitment. *Other factors include:* volunteer work. **Freshman Admission Requirements:** High school diploma is required and GED is accepted. *Academic units recommended:* 4 English, 2 math, 3 science, 1 science labs, 2 foreign language, 2 social studies, 1 history. **Freshman Admission Statistics:** 2,245 applied, 48% admitted, 21% enrolled. **Transfer Admission Requirements:** High school transcript, college transcript(s), essay or personal statement, Minimum college GPA of 2.0 required. Lowest grade transferable C. **General Admission Information:** Priority deadline 5/1. Regular application deadline 8/15. Non-fall registration accepted. Admission may be deferred for a maximum of one year.

COSTS AND FINANCIAL AID
Annual tuition $27,580. Room and board $9,348. Required fees $374. Average book and supplies expense $950. **Required Forms and Deadlines:** FAFSA. **Notification of Awards:** Applicants will be notified of awards on a rolling basis beginning 11/1. **Types of Aid:** *Need-based scholarships/grants:* College/university scholarship or grant aid from institutional funds; Federal Pell; Private scholarships; SEOG; State scholarships/grants. *Loans:* Direct PLUS loans; Direct Subsidized Stafford Loans; Direct Unsubsidized Stafford Loans. **Student Employment:** Federal Work-Study Program available. Institutional employment available. **Financial Aid Statistics:** 100% needy freshmen, 100% needy undergrads receive need-based scholarship or grant aid. 10% freshmen, 10% undergrads receive non-need-based scholarship or grant aid. 84% freshmen, 85% undergrads receive need-based self-help aid. 0% freshmen, 0% undergrads receive athletic scholarships. 94% freshmen, 92% undergrads receive any aid. 74% undergrads borrow to pay for school. Average cumulative indebtedness $32,956. **Criteria awarding aid:** *Need-based:* Academics, Alumni affiliation, Leadership, Music/drama, Religious affiliation. *Non-Need-based:* Academics, Alumni affiliation, Leadership, Music/drama, Religious affiliation.

GRINNELL COLLEGE

Best Colleges

1227 Park Street, Grinnell, IA 50112-1690
Phone: 641-269-3600 **Financial Aid Phone:** 641-269-3250
E-mail: admission@grinnell.edu **CEEB Code:** 6252
Fax: 641-269-4800 **Website:** www.grinnell.edu **ACT Code:** 1318

This private school was founded in 1846. It has a 120 acre campus.

RATINGS

Admissions Selectivity Rating: 96   Fire Safety Rating: 93   Green Rating: 78

STUDENTS AND FACULTY

Enrollment: 1,697. **Student Body:** 53% female, 47% male, 91% out-of-state, 20% international (45 countries represented). Asian 8%, African American 5%, Caucasian 51%, Hispanic 8%, Native American 0%, Pacific Islander 0%, Two or more races 4%, Race unknown 4%.
Retention and Graduation: 94% freshmen return for sophomore year. 85% freshmen graduate within 4 years. 89% freshmen graduate within 6 years. 22% grads go on to further study within 1 year. **Faculty:** Student/faculty ratio 9:1. 175 full-time faculty, 99% hold PhDs, 23% are members of minority groups, 46% are women. 0% of classes are taught by teaching assistants.

ACADEMICS

Degrees: Bachelor's. **Classes:** Most classes have 10–19 students. Most lab/discussion sessions have fewer than 10 students. **Most popular majors:** Computer Science; Biology/Biological Sciences, General. **Special Study Options:** Accelerated program; Double major; Dual enrollment; Independent study; Internships; Liberal arts/career combination; Student-designed major; Study abroad; Teacher certification program. **Disability Services offered:** Note-taking services; Reader services; Tape recorders; Tutors. **Career services:** Alumni network; Alumni services; Career assessment; Internships; Regional alumni.

FACILITIES

Housing: Coed dorms; Cooperative housing; Special housing for disabled students; Theme housing; Wellness housing 85% of campus accessible to physically disabled. **Special Academic Facilities/Equipment:** Art galleries, language lab, Data Analysis and Social Inquiry Lab, nuclear magnetic resonance spectrometer, electron microscope, 3D printer, 24-inch reflecting telescope, 365-acre environmental research area.

CAMPUS LIFE

Environment: Village. **Activities:** Campus Ministries; Choral groups; Concert band; Dance; Drama/theater; International Student Organization; Jazz band; Literary magazine; Model UN; Music ensembles; Musical theater; Pep band; Radio station; Student government; Student newspaper; Student-run film society; Symphony orchestra; Yearbook. 110 registered organizations, 2 honor societies, 5 religious organizations, on campus. **Athletics (Intercollegiate):** *Men:* baseball, basketball, cross-country, diving, football, golf, soccer, swimming, tennis, track/field (outdoor), track/field (indoor). *Women:* basketball, cross-country, diving, golf, soccer, softball, swimming, tennis, track/field (outdoor), track/field (indoor), volleyball. **On-Campus Highlights:** Humanities and Social Studies Center (HSSC). **Environmental Initiatives:** All new buildings are LEED Silver equivalent.

ADMISSIONS

Freshman Academic Profile: 62% in top 10% of high school class, 87% in top 25% of high school class, 98% in top 50% of high school class. **Test scores:** SAT Math middle 50% range 700–790. SAT EBRW middle 50% range 670–740. ACT middle 50% range 31–34. **Basis for Candidate Selection:** *Very important factors include:* rigor of secondary school record, class rank, academic GPA, recommendation(s). *Important factors include:* application essay, standardized test scores, extracurricular activities, talent/ability. *Other factors include:* interview, character/personal qualities, first generation, alumni/ae relation, geographical residence, state residency, racial/ethnic status, volunteer work, work experience, level of applicant's interest. **Freshman Admission Requirements:** High school diploma is required and GED is accepted. *Academic units recommended:* 4 English, 4 math, 3 science, 3 science labs, 3 foreign language, 3 social studies, 3 history.

Freshman Admission Statistics: 8,004 applied, 23% admitted, 25% enrolled. **Transfer Admission Requirements:** High school transcript, college transcript(s), essay or personal statement, standardized test scores, statement of good standing from prior institution(s). Lowest grade transferable C. **General Admission Information:** Regular application deadline 1/15. Admission may be deferred for a maximum of 1 year.

COSTS AND FINANCIAL AID

Annual tuition $56,188. Room and board $13,864. Required fees $492. Average book and supplies expense $900. **Required Forms and Deadlines:** CSS/Financial Aid PROFILE; FAFSA; Noncustodial PROFILE. **Notification of Awards:** Applicants will be notified of awards on or about 4/1. **Types of Aid:** *Need-based scholarships/grants:* College/university scholarship or grant aid from institutional funds; Federal Pell; Private scholarships; SEOG; State scholarships/grants. *Loans:* Direct PLUS loans; Direct Subsidized Stafford Loans; Direct Unsubsidized Stafford Loans. **Student Employment:** Federal Work-Study Program available. Institutional employment available. **Financial Aid Statistics:** 100% needy freshmen, 100% needy undergrads receive need-based scholarship or grant aid. 17% freshmen, 14% undergrads receive non-need-based scholarship or grant aid. 83% freshmen, 86% undergrads receive need-based self-help aid. 0% freshmen, 0% undergrads receive athletic scholarships. 86% freshmen, 86% undergrads receive any aid. 61% undergrads borrow to pay for school. Average cumulative indebtedness $20,093. **Criteria awarding aid:** *Non-Need-based:* Academics, State/district residency.

GROVE CITY COLLEGE

Best Colleges

100 Campus Drive, Grove City, PA 16127-2104
Phone: 724-458-2100 **Financial Aid Phone:** 724-458-3300
E-mail: admissions@gcc.edu **CEEB Code:** 2277
Fax: 724-458-3395 **Website:** www.gcc.edu **ACT Code:** 3582

This private school was founded in 1876. It has a 180 acre campus.

RATINGS

Admissions Selectivity Rating: 86   Fire Safety Rating: 94   Green Rating: 63

STUDENTS AND FACULTY

Enrollment: 2,186. **Student Body:** 47% female, 53% male, 44% out-of-state, 1% international (11 countries represented). Asian 2%, African American 1%, Caucasian 92%, Hispanic 1%, Native American <1%, Pacific Islander <1%, Two or more races 3%, Race unknown <1%.
Retention and Graduation: 90% freshmen return for sophomore year. 82% freshmen graduate within 4 years. 1% freshmen graduate within 6 years. 16% grads go on to further study within 1 year. 10% grads pursue arts and sciences degrees. 2% grads pursue law degrees. 0% grads pursue business degrees. 2% grads pursue medical degrees. **Faculty:** Student/faculty ratio 13:1. 155 full-time faculty, 85% hold PhDs, 5% are members of minority groups, 34% are women. 0% of classes are taught by teaching assistants.

ACADEMICS

Degrees: Bachelor's. **Classes:** Most classes have 10–19 students. Most lab/discussion sessions have 10–19 students. **Most popular majors:** Computer Science; Mechanical Engineering; Accounting. **Special Study Options:** Accelerated program; Distance learning; Double major; Dual enrollment; Independent study; Internships; Study abroad; Teacher certification program. **Disability Services offered:** Note-taking services; Reader services; Tutors. **Career services:** Alumni network; Alumni services; Career assessment; Career/job search classes; Internships; Regional alumni.

FACILITIES

Housing: Apartments for single students; Men's dorms; Wellness housing; Women's dorms 10% of campus accessible to physically disabled. **Special Academic Facilities/Equipment:** Fine arts center, on-campus preschool, technological learning center. **Campus Network:** 100% of classrooms, 100% of dorms, 100% of student union, 100% of libraries, 100% of dining areas, 100% of common outdoor areas, have wireless network access.

CAMPUS LIFE

Environment: Village. **Activities:** Campus Ministries; Choral groups; Concert band; Dance; Drama/theater; International Student Organization; Jazz band; Literary magazine; Marching band; Music ensembles; Musical theater; Opera; Pep band; Radio station; Student government; Student newspaper; Symphony orchestra; Television station; Yearbook. 145 registered organizations, 25 honor societies, 22 religious organizations, 10 fraternities, 8 sororities, on campus. **Athletics (Intercollegiate):** *Men:* baseball, basketball, cross-country, diving, football, golf, soccer, swimming, tennis, track/field (outdoor). *Women:* basketball, cheerleading, cross-country, diving, golf, soccer, softball, swimming, tennis, track/field (outdoor), volleyball, water polo. **On-Campus Highlights:** Student Union. **Environmental Initiatives:** Use of high-efficiency condensing boilers in newer construction or existing retrofits.

ADMISSIONS

Freshman Academic Profile: Average high school GPA 3.7. 39% in top 10% of high school class, 84% in top 25% of high school class, 93% in top 50% of high school class. 60% from public high schools. **Test scores:** SAT Math middle 50% range 554–693. SAT EBRW middle 50% range 576–691. ACT middle 50% range 23–30. **Basis for Candidate Selection:** *Very important factors include:* rigor of secondary school record, academic GPA, application essay, standardized test scores, interview, character/personal qualities, level of applicant's interest. *Important factors include:* recommendation(s), extracurricular activities. *Other factors include:* class rank, talent/ability, first generation, alumni/ae relation, geographical residence, state residency, religious affiliation/commitment, racial/ethnic status, volunteer work, work experience. **Freshman Admission Requirements:** High school diploma is required and GED is accepted. *Academic units required:* 4 English, 3 math, 3 science, 2 history. *Academic units recommended:* 4 English, 3 math, 3 science, 2 science labs, 2 foreign language, 3 social studies, 2 history. **Freshman Admission Statistics:** 1,697 applied, 79% admitted, 36% enrolled. **Transfer Admission Requirements:** High school transcript, college transcript(s), essay or personal statement, standardized test scores, statement of good standing from prior institution(s). Minimum college GPA of 2.0 required. Lowest grade transferable C. **General Admission Information:** Application fee $50. Regular application deadline 3/20. Non-fall registration accepted. Admission may be deferred for a maximum of 1 year.

COSTS AND FINANCIAL AID

Average book and supplies expense $1,000. **Required Forms and Deadlines:** Institution's own financial aid form. **Notification of Awards:** Applicants will be notified of awards on a rolling basis beginning 3/1. **Types of Aid:** *Need-based scholarships/grants:* College/university scholarship or grant aid from institutional funds; Private scholarships; State scholarships/grants. **Student Employment:** Institutional employment available. **Financial Aid Statistics:** 100% needy freshmen, 100% needy undergrads receive need-based scholarship or grant aid. 14% freshmen, 7% undergrads receive non-need-based scholarship or grant aid. 60% freshmen, 63% undergrads receive need-based self-help aid. 0% freshmen, 0% undergrads receive athletic scholarships. 79% freshmen, 80% undergrads receive any aid. 57% undergrads borrow to pay for school. Average cumulative indebtedness $41,690. **Criteria awarding aid:** *Need-based:* Academics, Art, Leadership, Minority status, Music/drama, Religious affiliation. *Non-Need-based:* Academics, Leadership, Music/drama.

GUILFORD COLLEGE

Best Colleges

5800 West Friendly Avenue, Greensboro, NC 27410
Phone: 336-316-2100 **Financial Aid Phone:** 336-316-2410
E-mail: admission@guilford.edu **CEEB Code:** 5261
Fax: 336-316-2954 **Website:** https://www.guilford.edu **ACT Code:** 3106

This private school, affiliated with the Quaker Church, was founded in 1837. It has a 340 acre campus.

RATINGS

Admissions Selectivity Rating: 73   Fire Safety Rating: 94   Green Rating: 95

STUDENTS AND FACULTY

Enrollment: 1,493. **Student Body:** 54% female, 46% male, 29% out-of-state, 1% international (10 countries represented). Asian 3%, African American 25%, Caucasian 56%, Hispanic 9%, Native American 1%, Pacific Islander <1%, Two or more races 4%, Race unknown 1%.
Retention and Graduation: 66% freshmen return for sophomore year. 47% freshmen graduate within 4 years. 61% freshmen graduate within 6 years. 12% grads go on to further study within 1 year. 50% grads pursue arts and sciences degrees. 18% grads pursue law degrees. 5% grads pursue business degrees. 0% grads pursue medical degrees. **Faculty:** Student/faculty ratio 12:1. 101 full-time faculty, 85% hold PhDs, 12% are members of minority groups, 52% are women. 0% of classes are taught by teaching assistants.

ACADEMICS

Degrees: Bachelor's; Master's; Post-bachelor's certificate. **Classes:** Most classes have 10–19 students. Most lab/discussion sessions have 10–19 students. **Special Study Options:** Cross-registration; Double major; Dual enrollment; Honors program; Independent study; Internships; Student-designed major; Study abroad; Teacher certification program. **Honors programs:** * The Honors Program at Guilford College provides a supportive community for students who are committed to achieving academic excellence and have demonstrated the ability to excel. The Guilford Honors Program provides a sequence of classes and research opportunities for students designed to reward, intellectually challenge students, and empower students. Honors classes are small and usually taught as discussion-style seminars. Students complete a senior thesis or project under the supervision of a faculty advisor. Students also attend professional and undergraduate research conferences where they have the opportunity to present papers. * Guilford College is a participating member of the National Collegiate Honors Council. Membership in the NCHC means that students in the Guilford College Honors Program can participate in the NCHC Honors Semesters. These semester programs are regularly offered in different sites around the world and enable Honors students from across the country to meet and learn in unique settings. * In recent years, Guilford College students have participated in the Study Abroad programs sponsored by Honors Programs at other colleges and universities. The University of North Carolina at Wilmington offers an Honors Semester Program at the University of Wales Swansea. For more information visit the following site: www.swan.ac.uk. Eastern Illinois University offers an Honors Summer Program at the Universite Catholique de Louvain in Belgium that features archaeological study of historic sites. For more information, one can visit: www.eiu.edu/-honprog/abroad.htm. Both these programs offer college credit courses that are transferable. **Disability Services offered:** Note-taking services; Reader services; Tape recorders; Tutors. **Career services:** Alumni network; Alumni services; Career assessment; Career/job search classes; Internships; Regional alumni.

FACILITIES

Housing: Coed dorms; Theme housing; Women's dorms 97% of campus accessible to physically disabled. **Special Academic Facilities/Equipment:** Cline Observatory.

CAMPUS LIFE

Environment: City. **Activities:** Campus Ministries; Choral groups; Drama/theater; International Student Organization; Jazz band; Music ensembles; Pep band; Radio station; Student government; Student newspaper; Student-run film society; Yearbook. 54 registered organizations, 1 honor societies, 5 religious organizations, on campus. **Athletics (Intercollegiate):** *Men:* baseball, basketball, cross-country, football, golf, lacrosse, rugby, soccer, tennis. *Women:* basketball, cross-country, lacrosse, rugby, soccer, softball, swimming, tennis, volleyball. **On-Campus Highlights:** Hege Library and Art Gallery. **Environmental Initiatives:** Purchasing policy that only allows Energy Star rated appliances.

ADMISSIONS

Freshman Academic Profile: Average high school GPA 3.2. 13% in top 10% of high school class, 32% in top 25% of high school class, 66% in top 50% of high school class. 75% from public high schools. **Test scores:** SAT Math middle 50% range 463–558. SAT EBRW middle 50% range 440–585. ACT middle 50% range 19–25. **Basis for Candidate Selection:** *Important factors include:* rigor of secondary school record, class rank, academic GPA, application essay, standardized test scores, character/personal qualities. *Other factors include:* recommendation(s), interview, extracurricular activities, talent/ability, first generation, alumni/ae relation, geographical residence, state residency, religious affiliation/commitment, racial/ethnic status, work experience. **Freshman Admission Requirements:** High school diploma is required and GED is accepted. *Academic units recommended:* 4 English, 3 math, 3 science, 2 foreign language, 3 social studies. **Freshman Admission Statistics:** 1,865 applied, 91% admitted, 20% enrolled. **Transfer Admission Requirements:** High school transcript, college transcript(s), essay or personal statement, standardized test scores, statement of good standing from prior institution(s). Minimum college GPA of 2.5 required. Lowest grade transferable C. **General Admission**

Information: Priority deadline 11/15. Non-fall registration accepted. Admission may be deferred for a maximum of 1 year.

COSTS AND FINANCIAL AID

Annual tuition $37,920. Room and board $11,800. Required fees $830. Average book and supplies expense $1,650. **Required Forms and Deadlines:** FAFSA; Institution's own financial aid form. **Notification of Awards:** Applicants will be notified of awards on a rolling basis beginning 3/1. **Types of Aid:** *Need-based scholarships/grants:* College/university scholarship or grant aid from institutional funds; Federal Pell; Private scholarships; SEOG; State scholarships/grants. *Loans:* Direct PLUS loans; Direct Subsidized Stafford Loans; Direct Unsubsidized Stafford Loans. **Student Employment:** Federal Work-Study Program available. Institutional employment available. **Financial Aid Statistics:** 100% needy freshmen, 97% needy undergrads receive need-based scholarship or grant aid. 100% freshmen, 83% undergrads receive non-need-based scholarship or grant aid. 95% freshmen, 94% undergrads receive need-based self-help aid. 0% freshmen, 0% undergrads receive athletic scholarships. 98% freshmen, 86% undergrads receive any aid. 70% undergrads borrow to pay for school. Average cumulative indebtedness $39,658. **Criteria awarding aid:** *Need-based:* Academics. *Non-Need-based:* Academics.

GUSTAVUS ADOLPHUS COLLEGE

800 College Avenue, Saint Peter, MN 56082
Phone: 507-933-7676 **Financial Aid Phone:** 507-933-7527
E-mail: admission@gustavus.edu **CEEB Code:** 6253
Fax: 507-933-7474 **Website:** www.gustavus.edu **ACT Code:** 2112

This private school, affiliated with the Lutheran Church, was founded in 1862. It has a 340 acre campus.

RATINGS

Admissions Selectivity Rating: 83 **Fire Safety Rating:** 96 **Green Rating:** 60*

STUDENTS AND FACULTY

Enrollment: 2,190. **Student Body:** 56% female, 44% male, 17% out-of-state, 5% international (26 countries represented). Asian 5%, African American 2%, Caucasian 78%, Hispanic 5%, Native American <1%, Pacific Islander <1%, Two or more races 4%, Race unknown 1%.
Retention and Graduation: 88% freshmen return for sophomore year. 79% freshmen graduate within 4 years. 80% freshmen graduate within 6 years. 36% grads go on to further study within 1 year. 11% grads pursue arts and sciences degrees. 4% grads pursue law degrees. 3% grads pursue business degrees. 5% grads pursue medical degrees. **Faculty:** Student/faculty ratio 11:1. 184 full-time faculty, 91% hold PhDs, 14% are members of minority groups, 52% are women. 0% of classes are taught by teaching assistants.

ACADEMICS

Degrees: Bachelor's. **Classes:** Most classes have 10–19 students. Most lab/discussion sessions have 10–19 students. **Most popular majors:** Business/Commerce, General; Biology/Biological Sciences, General; Psychology, General. **Special Study Options:** Cross-registration; Double major; Dual enrollment; Exchange student program (domestic); Honors program; Independent study; Internships; Liberal arts/career combination; Student-designed major; Study abroad; Teacher certification program. **Honors programs:** 3 Crowns Curriculum—Gustavus is unusual in having two general education choices. Both general education programs introduce students to a variety of ways of knowing. Curriculum I students choose from a list of courses to fulfill area requirements. Curriculum II, which is limited to sixty students, is an integrated sequence of courses focused on the development of the Western tradition with comparisons to non-Western cultures, the examination of values, and the theme of the individual and community. Retreats and trips to the Twin Cities for cultural events also foster a sense of community within the group. Although CII attracts some of the college's best students, it is not an honors program. We welcome all students who are intellectually curious and interested in interdisciplinary learning, the examination of values, and good discussion. If you are interested in how things connect—the past to the present, knowledge to your life—if you are interested in the big questions—How did our society come to be this way? What do I value and why? What makes for a good life?—CII may be for you!. **Disability Services offered:** Note-taking services; Reader services; Tape recorders; Tutors. **Career services:** Alumni network; Alumni services; Career assessment; Internships; Regional alumni.

FACILITIES

Housing: Apartments for single students; Coed dorms; Special housing for disabled students; Special housing for international students; Theme housing; Wellness housing 100% of campus accessible to physically disabled. **Special Academic Facilities/Equipment:** Art gallery, mineral museum, electron microscopes, arboretum, 14-inch computer-guided Celestron telescope, artificial intelligence laboratory, materials science laboratory, 300-MHz NMR spectrometer, five-section greenhouse. **Campus Network:** 100% of classrooms, 100% of dorms, 100% of student union, 100% of libraries, 100% of dining areas, 100% of common outdoor areas, have wireless network access.

CAMPUS LIFE

Environment: Village. **Activities:** Campus Ministries; Choral groups; Concert band; Dance; Drama/theater; International Student Organization; Jazz band; Literary magazine; Music ensembles; Musical theater; Pep band; Radio station; Student government; Student newspaper; Symphony orchestra; Yearbook. 134 registered organizations, 8 honor societies, 7 religious organizations, 5 fraternities, 5 sororities, on campus. **Athletics (Intercollegiate):** *Men:* baseball, basketball, cross-country, diving, football, golf, ice hockey, skiing (Nordic/cross-country), soccer, swimming, tennis, track/field (outdoor), track/field (indoor). *Women:* basketball, cross-country, diving, golf, gymnastics, ice hockey, skiing (Nordic/cross-country), soccer, softball, swimming, tennis, track/field (outdoor), track/field (indoor), volleyball. **On-Campus Highlights:** Campus Center. **Environmental Initiatives:** Seeking to acquire 5 MW of wind generator capacity.

ADMISSIONS

Freshman Academic Profile: Average high school GPA 3.6. 33% in top 10% of high school class, 65% in top 25% of high school class, 93% in top 50% of high school class. 94% from public high schools. **Test scores:** ACT middle 50% range 24–30. **Basis for Candidate Selection:** *Very important factors include:* rigor of secondary school record, academic GPA. *Important factors include:* class rank, application essay, recommendation(s), interview. *Other factors include:* standardized test scores, extracurricular activities, talent/ability, character/personal qualities, first generation, alumni/ae relation, geographical residence, state residency, religious affiliation/commitment, racial/ethnic status, volunteer work, work experience. **Freshman Admission Requirements:** High school diploma is required and GED is accepted. *Academic units required:* 4 English, 3 math, 2 science, 2 science labs, 2 foreign language, 2 social studies, 2 history. *Academic units recommended:* 4 math, 3 science, 3 science labs, 3 foreign language, 2 academic electives. **Freshman Admission Statistics:** 4,834 applied, 68% admitted, 18% enrolled. **Transfer Admission Requirements:** High school transcript, college transcript(s), essay or personal statement, standardized test scores, statement of good standing from prior institution(s). Minimum college GPA of 2.4 required. Lowest grade transferable 2. **General Admission Information:** Regular application deadline 4/1. Non-fall registration accepted. Admission may be deferred for a maximum of 1 year.

COSTS AND FINANCIAL AID

Annual tuition $46,520. Room and board $10,150. Required fees $520. Average book and supplies expense $900. **Required Forms and Deadlines:** FAFSA. **Notification of Awards:** Applicants will be notified of awards on a rolling basis beginning 12/15. **Types of Aid:** *Need-based scholarships/grants:* College/university scholarship or grant aid from institutional funds; Federal Pell; Private scholarships; SEOG; State scholarships/grants. *Loans:* Direct PLUS loans; Direct Subsidized Stafford Loans; Direct Unsubsidized Stafford Loans. **Student Employment:** Federal Work-Study Program available. Institutional employment available. **Financial Aid Statistics:** 100% needy freshmen, 100% needy undergrads receive need-based scholarship or grant aid. 17% freshmen, 12% undergrads receive non-need-based scholarship or grant aid. 100% freshmen, 99% undergrads receive need-based self-help aid. 0% freshmen, 0% undergrads receive athletic scholarships. 95% freshmen, 95% undergrads receive any aid. 71% undergrads borrow to pay for school. Average cumulative indebtedness $38,968. **Criteria awarding aid:** *Need-based:* Minority status, Religious affiliation. *Non-Need-based:* Academics, Alumni affiliation, Art, Minority status, Music/drama, Religious affiliation.

GWYNEDD MERCY UNIVERSITY

1325 Sumneytown Pike, Gwynedd Valley, PA 19437-0901
Phone: 215-641-5510 **Financial Aid Phone:** 215-646-7300
E-mail: admissions@gmercyu.edu **CEEB Code:** 2278
Fax: 215-641-5556 **Website:** www.gmercyu.edu **ACT Code:** 3583

This private school, affiliated with the Roman Catholic Church, was founded in 1948. It has a 160 acre campus.

RATINGS
Admissions Selectivity Rating: 73   Fire Safety Rating: 82   Green Rating: 60*

STUDENTS AND FACULTY
Enrollment: 1,944. **Student Body:** 76% female, 24% male, 13% out-of-state, <1% international (32 countries represented). Asian 5%, African American 20%, Caucasian 50%, Hispanic 4%, Native American <1%, Pacific Islander 0%, Two or more races 0%, Race unknown 21%.
Retention and Graduation: 84% freshmen return for sophomore year. 60% grads go on to further study within 1 year. **Faculty:** Student/faculty ratio 11:1. 80 full-time faculty, 45% hold PhDs, 5% are members of minority groups, 71% are women. 0% of classes are taught by teaching assistants.

ACADEMICS
Degrees: Associate; Bachelor's; Certificate; Doctoral degree—professional practice; Master's; Post-bachelor's certificate; Post-master's certificate. **Classes:** Most classes have 10–19 students. Most lab/discussion sessions have 10–19 students. **Most popular majors:** Education, General; Registered Nursing, Nursing Administration, Nursing Research and Clinical Nursing; Business Administration and Management, General. **Special Study Options:** Accelerated program; Cross-registration; Distance learning; Double major; Dual enrollment; Honors program; Independent study; Internships; Liberal arts/career combination; Study abroad; Teacher certification program; Weekend college. **Honors programs:** The Honors Program in Liberal Studies consists of six interdisciplinary, team-taught courses developing the theme of "The Quest for Community and Freedom: The Individual and Society." **Disability Services offered:** Reader services; Tutors. **Career services:** Alumni services; Career assessment; Internships.

FACILITIES
Housing: Coed dorms 95% of campus accessible to physically disabled. **Special Academic Facilities/Equipment:** Keiss Hall (Health and Science Center), television production room and small theater, computer labs.

CAMPUS LIFE
Environment: Metropolis. **Activities:** Campus Ministries; Choral groups; Dance; Literary magazine; Student government; Student newspaper. 22 registered organizations, 10 honor societies, 1 religious organizations, on campus. **Athletics (Intercollegiate):** *Men:* baseball, basketball, cross-country, golf, soccer, tennis, track/field (outdoor), track/field (indoor). *Women:* basketball, cross-country, field hockey, lacrosse, soccer, softball, tennis, track/field (outdoor), track/field (indoor), volleyball. **On-Campus Highlights:** Assumption Hall.

ADMISSIONS
Freshman Academic Profile: Average high school GPA 3.3. 7% in top 10% of high school class, 20% in top 25% of high school class, 57% in top 50% of high school class. 57% from public high schools. **Test scores:** SAT Math middle 50% range 420–520. SAT EBRW middle 50% range 420–510. ACT middle 50% range 16–23. **Basis for Candidate Selection:** *Very important factors include:* rigor of secondary school record. *Important factors include:* class rank, academic GPA, standardized test scores, recommendation(s), extracurricular activities. *Other factors include:* application essay, interview, character/personal qualities, alumni/ae relation, volunteer work, work experience. **Freshman Admission Requirements:** High school diploma is required and GED is accepted. *Academic units required:* 4 English, 3 math, 3 science, 1 history, 3 academic electives. **Freshman Admission Statistics:** 904 applied, 91% admitted, 27% enrolled. **Transfer Admission Requirements:** High school transcript, college transcript(s), Minimum college GPA of 2.0 required. Lowest grade transferable C. **General Admission Information:** Priority deadline 4/1. Regular application deadline 8/20. Non-fall registration accepted. Admission may be deferred for a maximum of 12 months.

COSTS AND FINANCIAL AID
Annual tuition $25,160. Room and board $9,760. Required fees $450. Average book and supplies expense $600. **Required Forms and Deadlines:** FAFSA; Institution's own financial aid form;. **Notification of Awards:** Applicants will be notified of awards on a rolling basis beginning 2/15. **Types of Aid:** *Need-based scholarships/grants:* College/university scholarship or grant aid from institutional funds; Federal Pell; Private scholarships; SEOG; State scholarships/grants. *Loans:* Direct PLUS loans; Direct Subsidized Stafford Loans; Direct Unsubsidized Stafford Loans. **Student Employment:** Federal Work-Study Program available. **Financial Aid Statistics:** 100% needy freshmen, 88% needy undergrads receive need-based scholarship or grant aid. 8% freshmen, 8% undergrads receive non-need-based scholarship or grant aid. 91% freshmen, 87% undergrads receive need-based self-help aid. 0% freshmen, 0% undergrads receive athletic scholarships. 97% freshmen, 92% undergrads receive any aid. 88% undergrads borrow to pay for school. Average cumulative indebtedness $43,789. **Criteria awarding aid:** *Need-based:* Alumni affiliation. *Non-Need-based:* Academics, Leadership.

HAMILTON COLLEGE

Office of Admission, Clinton, NY 13323
Phone: 315-859-4421 **Financial Aid Phone:** 800-859-4413
E-mail: admission@hamilton.edu **CEEB Code:** 2286
Fax: 315-859-4457 **Website:** www.hamilton.edu **ACT Code:** 2754

This private school was founded in 1812. It has a 1300 acre campus.

RATINGS
Admissions Selectivity Rating: 97   Fire Safety Rating: 92   Green Rating: 60*

STUDENTS AND FACULTY
Enrollment: 1,914. **Student Body:** 53% female, 47% male, 72% out-of-state, 7% international (46 countries represented). Asian 7%, African American 4%, Caucasian 64%, Hispanic 9%, Native American <1%, Pacific Islander 0%, Two or more races 5%, Race unknown 4%.
Retention and Graduation: 95% freshmen return for sophomore year. 89% freshmen graduate within 4 years. 93% freshmen graduate within 6 years. 10% grads go on to further study within 1 year. **Faculty:** Student/faculty ratio 9:1. 194 full-time faculty, 96% hold PhDs, 22% are members of minority groups, 50% are women. 0% of classes are taught by teaching assistants.

ACADEMICS
Degrees: Bachelor's. **Classes:** Most classes have 10–19 students. Most lab/discussion sessions have 10–19 students. **Most popular majors:** Mathematics, General; Economics, General; Political Science and Government, General. **Special Study Options:** Accelerated program; Cross-registration; Double major; English as a Second Language (ESL); Independent study; Internships; Student-designed major; Study abroad. **Combined degree programs:** BA/JD. **Disability Services offered:** Note-taking services; Reader services; Tape recorders; Tutors. **Career services:** Alumni network; Alumni services; Career assessment; Career/job search classes; Internships; Regional alumni.

FACILITIES
Housing: Apartments for married students; Apartments for single students; Coed dorms; Cooperative housing; Special housing for disabled students; Wellness housing. **Special Academic Facilities/Equipment:** Wellin Museum of Art, language lab, cultural center, observatory, two electron microscopes. Arthur Levitt Public Affairs Center, Nesbitt-Johnston Writing Center, Jazz Archive. **Campus Network:** 100% of classrooms, 100% of dorms, 100% of student union, 100% of libraries, 100% of dining areas, 100% of common outdoor areas, have wireless network access.

CAMPUS LIFE
Environment: Rural. **Activities:** Campus Ministries; Choral groups; Dance; Drama/theater; International Student Organization; Jazz band; Literary magazine; Model UN; Music ensembles; Musical theater; Radio station; Student government; Student newspaper; Student-run film society; Symphony orchestra; Television station; Yearbook. 218 registered organizations, 8 honor societies, 8 religious organizations, 8 fraternities, 4 sororities, on campus. **Athletics (Intercollegiate):** *Men:* baseball, basketball, crew/rowing, cross-country, diving, football, golf, ice hockey, lacrosse, soccer, squash, swimming, tennis, track/field (outdoor), track/field (indoor). *Women:* basketball, crew/rowing, cross-country, diving, field hockey, ice hockey, lacrosse, soccer, softball,

squash, swimming, tennis, track/field (outdoor), track/field (indoor), volleyball. **On-Campus Highlights:** Kennedy Center for Theatre and the Studio Arts (2014).

ADMISSIONS

Freshman Academic Profile: 83% in top 10% of high school class, 96% in top 25% of high school class, 100% in top 50% of high school class. 60% from public high schools. **Test scores:** SAT Math middle 50% range 700–780. SAT EBRW middle 50% range 670–740. ACT middle 50% range 32–34. **Basis for Candidate Selection:** *Very important factors include:* rigor of secondary school record, class rank, academic GPA. *Important factors include:* application essay, standardized test scores, recommendation(s), interview, character/personal qualities. *Other factors include:* extracurricular activities, talent/ability, first generation, alumni/ae relation, geographical residence, state residency, racial/ethnic status, volunteer work, work experience, level of applicant's interest. **Freshman Admission Requirements:** High school diploma is required and GED is accepted. *Academic units recommended:* 4 English, 3 math, 3 science, 3 foreign language, 3 social studies. **Freshman Admission Statistics:** 8,339 applied, 16% admitted, 35% enrolled. **Transfer Admission Requirements:** High school transcript, college transcript(s), essay or personal statement, standardized test scores, statement of good standing from prior institution(s). Lowest grade transferable C. **General Admission Information:** Application fee $60. Regular application deadline 1/1. Non-fall registration accepted.

COSTS AND FINANCIAL AID

Average book and supplies expense $1,000. **Required Forms and Deadlines:** Business/Farm Supplement; CSS/Financial Aid PROFILE; FAFSA; Institution's own financial aid form; Noncustodial PROFILE. **Notification of Awards:** Applicants will be notified of awards on or about 4/1. **Types of Aid:** *Need-based scholarships/grants:* College/university scholarship or grant aid from institutional funds; Federal Pell; Private scholarships; SEOG; State scholarships/grants. *Loans:* Direct PLUS loans; Direct Subsidized Stafford Loans; Direct Unsubsidized Stafford Loans. **Student Employment:** Federal Work-Study Program available. Institutional employment available. **Financial Aid Statistics:** 100% needy freshmen, 100% needy undergrads receive need-based scholarship or grant aid. 0% freshmen, 0% undergrads receive non-need-based scholarship or grant aid. 89% freshmen, 80% undergrads receive need-based self-help aid. 0% freshmen, 0% undergrads receive athletic scholarships. 55% freshmen, 52% undergrads receive any aid. 44% undergrads borrow to pay for school. Average cumulative indebtedness $17,292.

HAMLINE UNIVERSITY

1536 Hewitt Ave, Saint Paul, MN 55104
Phone: 651-523-2207 **Financial Aid Phone:** 651-523-3000
E-mail: CLA-admis@hamline.edu **CEEB Code:** 6265
Fax: 651-523-2458 **Website:** www.hamline.edu **ACT Code:** 2114

This private school, affiliated with the Methodist Church, was founded in 1854. It has a 77 acre campus.

RATINGS

Admissions Selectivity Rating: 80   **Fire Safety Rating:** 89   **Green Rating:** 60*

STUDENTS AND FACULTY

Enrollment: 1,986. **Student Body:** 58% female, 42% male, 15% out-of-state, 3% international (53 countries represented). Asian 6%, African American 5%, Caucasian 75%, Hispanic 2%, Native American 1%, Race unknown 9%. **Retention and Graduation:** 82% freshmen return for sophomore year. 27% grads go on to further study within 1 year. 17% grads pursue arts and sciences degrees. 4% grads pursue law degrees. 2% grads pursue business degrees. 1% grads pursue medical degrees. **Faculty:** Student/faculty ratio 14:1. 173 full-time faculty, 87% hold PhDs, 11% are members of minority groups, 49% are women. 0% of classes are taught by teaching assistants.

ACADEMICS

Degrees: Bachelor's; Master's; Post-bachelor's certificate. **Classes:** Most classes have 10–19 students. Most lab/discussion sessions have 10–19 students. **Most popular majors:** Business/Commerce, General; Criminal Justice/Police Science; Psychology, General. **Special Study Options:** Cross-registration; Double major; Dual enrollment; English as a Second Language (ESL); Exchange student program (domestic); Honors program; Independent study; Internships;

Student-designed major; Study abroad; Teacher certification program. **Combined degree programs:** BA/JD; BA/MEng. **Disability Services offered:** Note-taking services; Reader services; Tape recorders; Tutors. **Career services:** Alumni network; Alumni services; Career assessment; Career/job search classes; Internships; Regional alumni.

FACILITIES

Housing: Apartments for married students; Apartments for single students; Coed dorms; Cooperative housing; Fraternity/sorority housing; 80% of campus accessible to physically disabled. **Special Academic Facilities/Equipment:** theatre, music hall, art gallery, science center.

CAMPUS LIFE

Environment: Metropolis. **Activities:** Campus Ministries; Choral groups; Concert band; Dance; Drama/theater; International Student Organization; Jazz band; Literary magazine; Model UN; Music ensembles; Musical theater; Pep band; Radio station; Student government; Student newspaper; Symphony orchestra; Television station; Yearbook. 77 registered organizations, 11 honor societies, 9 religious organizations, 1 fraternities, 2 sororities, on campus. **Athletics (Intercollegiate):** *Men:* baseball, basketball, cross-country, diving, football, ice hockey, soccer, swimming, tennis, track/field (outdoor), track/field (indoor). *Women:* basketball, cross-country, diving, gymnastics, ice hockey, soccer, softball, swimming, tennis, track/field (outdoor), track/field (indoor), volleyball. **On-Campus Highlights:** Klas Center (stadium and food service). **Environmental Initiatives:** Recycling program.

ADMISSIONS

Freshman Academic Profile: Average high school GPA 3.4. 20% in top 10% of high school class, 49% in top 25% of high school class, 79% in top 50% of high school class. 90% from public high schools. **Test scores:** SAT Math middle 50% range 540–640. SAT EBRW middle 50% range 513–645. ACT middle 50% range 21–27. **Basis for Candidate Selection:** *Very important factors include:* rigor of secondary school record, class rank. *Important factors include:* academic GPA, application essay, standardized test scores, recommendation(s), interview, extracurricular activities, talent/ability. *Other factors include:* character/personal qualities, first generation, alumni/ae relation, racial/ethnic status, volunteer work, work experience. **Freshman Admission Requirements:** High school diploma is required and GED is accepted. *Academic units recommended:* 4 English, 3 math, 3 science, 3 science labs, 2 foreign language, 4 social studies, 4 academic electives. **Freshman Admission Statistics:** 2,018 applied, 78% admitted, 29% enrolled. **Transfer Admission Requirements:** college transcript(s), essay or personal statement, Minimum college GPA of 2.0 required. Lowest grade transferable C-. **General Admission Information:** Priority deadline 5/1. Non-fall registration accepted. Admission may be deferred for a maximum of 2 years.

COSTS AND FINANCIAL AID

Annual tuition $36,888. Room and board $9,736. Required fees $998. **Required Forms and Deadlines:** FAFSA. **Notification of Awards:** Applicants will be notified of awards on a rolling basis beginning 3/15. **Types of Aid:** *Need-based scholarships/grants:* College/university scholarship or grant aid from institutional funds; Federal Pell; Private scholarships; SEOG; State scholarships/grants. *Loans:* Direct PLUS loans; Direct Subsidized Stafford Loans; Direct Unsubsidized Stafford Loans. **Student Employment:** Federal Work-Study Program available. Institutional employment available. **Financial Aid Statistics:** 100% needy freshmen, 99% needy undergrads receive need-based scholarship or grant aid. 15% freshmen, 10% undergrads receive non-need-based scholarship or grant aid. 87% freshmen, 91% undergrads receive need-based self-help aid. 0% freshmen, 0% undergrads receive athletic scholarships. 98% freshmen, 95% undergrads receive any aid. **Criteria awarding aid:** *Need-based:* Academics, Alumni affiliation, Art, Minority status, Music/drama, Religious affiliation. *Non-Need-based:* Academics, Alumni affiliation, Art, Leadership, Minority status, Music/drama, Religious affiliation.

HAMPDEN-SYDNEY COLLEGE

PO Box 667, Hampden-Sydney, VA 23943-0667
Phone: 434-223-6120 **Financial Aid Phone:** 434-223-6119
E-mail: hsapp@hsc.edu **CEEB Code:** 5291
Fax: 434-223-6346 **Website:** www.hsc.edu **ACT Code:** 4356

This private school, affiliated with the Presbyterian Church, was founded in 1775. It has a 1343 acre campus.

RATINGS
Admissions Selectivity Rating: 85   **Fire Safety Rating:** 88   **Green Rating:** 69

STUDENTS AND FACULTY
Enrollment: 1,072. **Student Body:** 0% female, 100% male, 30% out-of-state, <1% international (5 countries represented). Asian 1%, African American 5%, Caucasian 86%, Hispanic 4%, Native American <1%, Pacific Islander <1%, Two or more races 3%, Race unknown 1%.
Retention and Graduation: 81% freshmen return for sophomore year. 61% freshmen graduate within 4 years. 63% freshmen graduate within 6 years. 29% grads go on to further study within 1 year. 12% grads pursue arts and sciences degrees. 8% grads pursue law degrees. 2% grads pursue business degrees. 6% grads pursue medical degrees. **Faculty:** Student/faculty ratio 11:1. 96 full-time faculty, 91% hold PhDs, 7% are members of minority groups, 31% are women. 0% of classes are taught by teaching assistants.

ACADEMICS
Degrees: Bachelor's. **Classes:** Most classes have 10–19 students. **Most popular majors:** Economics, General; History, General; Business/Managerial Economics. **Special Study Options:** Cooperative education program; Cross-registration; Double major; Dual enrollment; Exchange student program (domestic); Honors program; Independent study; Internships; Study abroad. **Honors programs:** Student Summer Research programs, Departmental Honors, Senior Fellowship. **Disability Services offered:** Note-taking services; Reader services; Tutors. **Career services:** Alumni network; Alumni services; Career assessment; Internships; Regional alumni.

FACILITIES
Housing: Apartments for married students; Apartments for single students; Fraternity/sorority housing; Men's dorms; Special housing for international students; Theme housing; Wellness housing 75% of campus accessible to physically disabled. **Special Academic Facilities/Equipment:** History museum, language lab, international communications center, observatory, Energy Research Lab. **Campus Network:** 0% of dorms, 100% of student union, 100% of libraries, 100% of dining areas, 100% of common outdoor areas, have wireless network access.

CAMPUS LIFE
Environment: Rural. **Activities:** Campus Ministries; Choral groups; Drama/theater; International Student Organization; Literary magazine; Music ensembles; Radio station; Student government; Student newspaper. 96 registered organizations, 14 honor societies, 9 religious organizations, 10 fraternities, on campus. **Athletics (Intercollegiate):** *Men:* baseball, basketball, cross-country, football, golf, lacrosse, soccer, tennis. **On-Campus Highlights:** Bortz Library **Environmental Initiatives:** Electrical energy conservation.

ADMISSIONS
Freshman Academic Profile: Average high school GPA 3.5. 11% in top 10% of high school class, 22% in top 25% of high school class, 64% in top 50% of high school class. 64% from public high schools. **Test scores:** SAT Math middle 50% range 520–620. SAT EBRW middle 50% range 530–630. ACT middle 50% range 21–27. **Basis for Candidate Selection:** *Very important factors include:* rigor of secondary school record, academic GPA, application essay, standardized test scores, recommendation(s), character/personal qualities. *Important factors include:* class rank, extracurricular activities. *Other factors include:* interview, talent/ability, first generation, alumni/ae relation, volunteer work, work experience, level of applicant's interest. **Freshman Admission Requirements:** High school diploma is required and GED is accepted. *Academic units required:* 4 English, 3 math, 2 science, 1 science labs, 2 foreign language, 1 social studies, 1 history, 3 academic electives. *Academic units recommended:* 4 math, 3 science, 3 foreign language. **Freshman Admission**

Statistics: 3,240 applied, 59% admitted, 18% enrolled. **Transfer Admission Requirements:** High school transcript, college transcript(s), essay or personal statement, standardized test scores, statement of good standing from prior institution(s). Minimum college GPA of 2.5 required. Lowest grade transferable C. **General Admission Information:** Application fee $30. Regular application deadline 3/1. Non-fall registration accepted.

COSTS AND FINANCIAL AID
Annual tuition $44,532. Room and board $13,712. Required fees $2,358. Average book and supplies expense $1,000. **Required Forms and Deadlines:** FAFSA; State aid form. **Notification of Awards:** Applicants will be notified of awards on a rolling basis beginning 12/15. **Types of Aid:** *Need-based scholarships/grants:* College/university scholarship or grant aid from institutional funds; Federal Pell; Private scholarships; SEOG; State scholarships/grants. *Loans:* Direct PLUS loans; Direct Subsidized Stafford Loans; Direct Unsubsidized Stafford Loans. **Student Employment:** Federal Work-Study Program available. Institutional employment available. **Financial Aid Statistics:** 100% needy freshmen, 100% needy undergrads receive need-based scholarship or grant aid. 24% freshmen, 20% undergrads receive non-need-based scholarship or grant aid. 75% freshmen, 74% undergrads receive need-based self-help aid. 0% freshmen, 0% undergrads receive athletic scholarships. 99.4% freshmen, 99.6% undergrads receive any aid. 67% undergrads borrow to pay for school. Average cumulative indebtedness $33,777. **Criteria awarding aid:** *Need-based:* Academics, Leadership, Minority status, Music/drama *Non-Need-based:* Academics, Leadership, Minority status, Music/drama, State/district residency.

HAMPSHIRE COLLEGE

Admissions Office (AD), Amherst, MA 01002
Phone: 413-559-5471 **Financial Aid Phone:** 413-559-5725
E-mail: admissions@hampshire.edu **CEEB Code:** 3447
Fax: 413-559-4631 **Website:** https://www.hampshire.edu/ **ACT Code:** 1842

This private school was founded in 1965. It has a 850 acre campus.

RATINGS
Admissions Selectivity Rating: 64   **Fire Safety Rating:** 75   **Green Rating:** 85

STUDENTS AND FACULTY
Enrollment: 745. **Student Body:** 61% female, 39% male, 78% out-of-state, 6% international (12 countries represented). Asian 3%, African American 8%, Caucasian 60%, Hispanic 12%, Native American <1%, Pacific Islander 0%, Two or more races 5%, Race unknown 6%.
Retention and Graduation: 67% freshmen return for sophomore year. 51% freshmen graduate within 4 years. 63% freshmen graduate within 6 years. 10% grads go on to further study within 1 year. 8% grads pursue arts and sciences degrees. 1% grads pursue law degrees. 0% grads pursue business degrees. 1% grads pursue medical degrees. **Faculty:** Student/faculty ratio 13:1. 42 full-time faculty, 0% hold PhDs, 31% are members of minority groups, 45% are women. 0% of classes are taught by teaching assistants.

ACADEMICS
Degrees: Bachelor's. **Classes:** Most classes have 10–19 students. Most lab/discussion sessions have 10–19 students. **Most popular majors:** Cultural Studies/Critical Theory and Analysis; Creative Writing; Film/Video and Photographic Arts, Other. **Special Study Options:** Cross-registration; Exchange student program (domestic); Independent study; Internships; Liberal arts/career combination; Student-designed major; Study abroad; Teacher certification program. **Disability Services offered:** Note-taking services; Reader services. **Career services:** Alumni network; Alumni services; Career assessment; Career/job search classes; Internships; Regional alumni.

FACILITIES
Housing: Apartments for single students; Coed dorms; Cooperative housing; Men's dorms; Special housing for disabled students; Theme housing; Wellness housing; Women's dorms 50% of campus accessible to physically disabled.
Special Academic Facilities/Equipment: Performing and visual arts center, bioshelter (integrated greenhouse/aquaculture facility), farm center, electronic music and TV production studios, extensive film and photography facilities, multimedia center. **Campus Network:** 100% of classrooms, 100% of dorms, 100% of student union, 100% of libraries, 100% of dining areas, 20% of common outdoor areas, have wireless network access.

CAMPUS LIFE

Environment: Town. **Activities:** Campus Ministries; Choral groups; Dance; Drama/theater; International Student Organization; Literary magazine; Model UN; Music ensembles; Radio station; Student government; Student newspaper; Student-run film society. 145 registered organizations, 3 religious organizations, on campus. **On-Campus Highlights:** R. W. Kern Center.

ADMISSIONS

Basis for Candidate Selection: *Very important factors include:* application essay, character/personal qualities. *Important factors include:* rigor of secondary school record, academic GPA, recommendation(s), extracurricular activities, talent/ability. *Other factors include:* class rank, standardized test scores, interview, first generation, alumni/ae relation, geographical residence, racial/ethnic status, volunteer work, work experience, level of applicant's interest. **Freshman Admission Requirements:** High school diploma is required and GED is accepted. *Academic units required:* 4 English, 3 math, 3 science, 2 science labs, 3 foreign language, 3 history. *Academic units recommended:* 4 English, 4 math, 4 science, 2 science labs, 4 foreign language, 4 history. **Freshman Admission Statistics:** 2,485 applied, 2% admitted, 41% enrolled. **Transfer Admission Requirements:** High school transcript, college transcript(s), essay or personal statement, Lowest grade transferable C. **General Admission Information:** Priority deadline 1/15. Regular application deadline 1/15. Non-fall registration accepted. Admission may be deferred for a maximum of 1 year.

COSTS AND FINANCIAL AID

Annual tuition $50,030. Room and board $14,120. Required fees $2,398. Average book and supplies expense $850. **Required Forms and Deadlines:** CSS/Financial Aid PROFILE; FAFSA; Noncustodial PROFILE. **Notification of Awards:** Applicants will be notified of awards on or about 4/1. **Types of Aid:** *Need-based scholarships/grants:* College/university scholarship or grant aid from institutional funds; Federal Pell; Private scholarships; SEOG; State scholarships/grants. *Loans:* Direct PLUS loans; Direct Subsidized Stafford Loans; Direct Unsubsidized Stafford Loans. **Student Employment:** Federal Work-Study Program available. **Financial Aid Statistics:** 100% needy freshmen, 100% needy undergrads receive need-based scholarship or grant aid. 0% freshmen, 5% undergrads receive non-need-based scholarship or grant aid. 100% freshmen, 94% undergrads receive need-based self-help aid. 0% freshmen, 0% undergrads receive athletic scholarships. 70% undergrads borrow to pay for school. Average cumulative indebtedness $29,499. **Criteria awarding aid:** *Non-Need-based:* Academics, Art, Leadership, Music/drama.

HAMPTON UNIVERSITY

Office of Admissions, Hampton, VA 23668
Phone: 757-727-5328 **Financial Aid Phone:** 757-727-5332
E-mail: admit@hamptonu.edu **CEEB Code:** 5292
Fax: 757-727-5095 **Website:** www.hamptonu.edu **ACT Code:** 4358

This private school was founded in 1868. It has a 314 acre campus.

RATINGS

Admissions Selectivity Rating: 90   **Fire Safety Rating:** 72   **Green Rating:** 60*

STUDENTS AND FACULTY

Enrollment: 3,672. **Student Body:** 66% female, 34% male, 83% out-of-state, 1% international (22 countries represented). Asian <1%, African American 96%, Caucasian 1%, Hispanic 1%, Native American <1%, Pacific Islander <1%, Two or more races 0%, Race unknown <1%.
Retention and Graduation: 74% freshmen return for sophomore year. 38% freshmen graduate within 4 years. 55% freshmen graduate within 6 years. 37% grads go on to further study within 1 year. 13% grads pursue arts and sciences degrees. 4% grads pursue law degrees. 6% grads pursue business degrees. 2% grads pursue medical degrees. **Faculty:** Student/faculty ratio 14:1. 281 full-time faculty, 72% hold PhDs, 76% are members of minority groups, 47% are women. 0% of classes are taught by teaching assistants.

ACADEMICS

Degrees: Associate; Bachelor's; Certificate; Doctoral degree—professional practice; Doctoral degree research/scholarship; Master's; Post-master's certificate. **Classes:** Most classes have 50–99 students. Most lab/discussion sessions have

10–19 students. **Most popular majors:** Biology, General; Psychology, General; Business Administration, Management and Operations, Other. **Special Study Options:** Accelerated program; Cooperative education program; Cross-registration; Distance learning; Double major; Dual enrollment; English as a Second Language (ESL); Honors program; Independent study; Internships; Study abroad; Teacher certification program. **Honors programs:** Honors College-Designed to augment, enhance and extend the undergraduate academic experience through community, exposure and expectations. Leadership Institute—Offers the undergraduate student a curricular option that enhances the university experience. **Disability Services offered:** Note-taking services; Reader services; Tape recorders; Tutors. **Career services:** Alumni network; Alumni services; Career assessment; Career/job search classes; Internships.

FACILITIES

Housing: Apartments for single students; Coed dorms; Men's dorms; Special housing for disabled students; Special housing for international students; Wellness housing; Women's dorms 90% of campus accessible to physically disabled. **Special Academic Facilities/Equipment:** African, Native American, and Oceanic museums, and gallery. New Student Center. **Campus Network:** 100% of classrooms, 100% of dorms, 100% of libraries, 100% of dining areas, have wireless network access.

CAMPUS LIFE

Environment: City. **Activities:** Campus Ministries; Choral groups; Concert band; Dance; Drama/theater; International Student Organization; Jazz band; Literary magazine; Marching band; Music ensembles; Musical theater; Opera; Pep band; Radio station; Student government; Student newspaper; Symphony orchestra; Television station; Yearbook. 85 registered organizations, 16 honor societies, 3 religious organizations, 5 fraternities, 4 sororities, on campus. **Athletics (Intercollegiate):** *Men:* basketball, cross-country, football, golf, sailing, tennis, track/field (outdoor), track/field (indoor). *Women:* basketball, bowling, cross-country, golf, sailing, softball, tennis, track/field (outdoor), track/field (indoor), volleyball. **On-Campus Highlights:** Emancipation Oak.

ADMISSIONS

Freshman Academic Profile: Average high school GPA 3.3. 13% in top 10% of high school class, 22% in top 25% of high school class, 61% in top 50% of high school class. 90% from public high schools. **Test scores:** SAT Math middle 50% range 510–640. SAT EBRW middle 50% range 530–670. ACT middle 50% range 19–24. **Basis for Candidate Selection:** *Very important factors include:* rigor of secondary school record, academic GPA, application essay, character/personal qualities. *Important factors include:* class rank, recommendation(s). *Other factors include:* interview, extracurricular activities, talent/ability, volunteer work, work experience, level of applicant's interest. **Freshman Admission Requirements:** High school diploma is required and GED is accepted. *Academic units required:* 4 English, 3 math, 2 science, 2 science labs, 2 social studies, 6 academic electives. *Academic units recommended:* 2 foreign language. **Freshman Admission Statistics:** 13,028 applied, 36% admitted, 20% enrolled. **Transfer Admission Requirements:** college transcript(s), essay or personal statement, statement of good standing from prior institution(s). Minimum college GPA of 2.3 required. Lowest grade transferable C. **General Admission Information:** Application fee $35. Priority deadline 3/1. Non-fall registration accepted. Admission may be deferred for a maximum of 1 year.

COSTS AND FINANCIAL AID

Annual tuition $23,762. Room and board $11,778. Required fees $2,940. Average book and supplies expense $1,100. **Required Forms and Deadlines:** FAFSA;. **Notification of Awards:** Applicants will be notified of awards on a rolling basis beginning 2/1. **Types of Aid:** *Need-based scholarships/grants:* College/university scholarship or grant aid from institutional funds; Federal Nursing Scholarships; Federal Pell; Private scholarships; SEOG; State scholarships/grants. *Loans:* Direct PLUS loans; Direct Subsidized Stafford Loans; Direct Unsubsidized Stafford Loans. **Student Employment:** Federal Work-Study Program available. **Financial Aid Statistics:** 96% needy freshmen, 96% needy undergrads receive need-based scholarship or grant aid. 80% freshmen, 69% undergrads receive non-need-based scholarship or grant aid. 79% freshmen, 83% undergrads receive need-based self-help aid. 6% freshmen, 2% undergrads receive athletic scholarships. 42.5% freshmen, 44% undergrads receive any aid. 80% undergrads borrow to pay for school. Average cumulative indebtedness $33,095. **Criteria awarding aid:** *Non-Need-based:* Academics, Athletics, Job skills, Leadership, Music/drama.

HANNIBAL-LAGRANGE UNIVERSITY

2800 Palmyra Road, Hannibal, MO 63401
Phone: 573-221-3113 **Financial Aid Phone:** 573-629-3280
E-mail: admissio@hlg.edu
Fax: 573-221-6594 **Website:** http://www.hlg.edu/ **ACT Code:** 2320

This private school, affiliated with the Southern Baptist Church, was founded in 1858. It has a 110 acre campus.

RATINGS
Admissions Selectivity Rating: 71   **Fire Safety Rating:** 78   **Green Rating:** 60*

STUDENTS AND FACULTY
Enrollment: 911. **Student Body:** female, male, 23% out-of-state, international (11 countries represented).
Retention and Graduation: 58% freshmen return for sophomore year.
Faculty: Student/faculty ratio 11:1. 60 full-time faculty, 28% hold PhDs, 2% are members of minority groups, 52% are women. 0% of classes are taught by teaching assistants.

ACADEMICS
Degrees: Associate; Bachelor's; Certificate; Master's. **Classes:** Most classes have 10–19 students. Most lab/discussion sessions have fewer than 10 students. **Most popular majors:** Elementary Education and Teaching; Secondary Education and Teaching; Non-Profit/Public/Organizational Management. **Special Study Options:** Accelerated program; Distance learning; Dual enrollment; Honors program; Independent study; Internships; Liberal arts/career combination; Student-designed major; Study abroad; Teacher certification program. **Honors programs:** Honors Program qualifies a student for a semester of study at Harlaxton College, Grantham, England. **Disability Services offered:** Tape recorders; Tutors. **Career services:** Career assessment; Internships.

FACILITIES
Housing: Apartments for single students; Men's dorms; Special housing for disabled students; Women's dorms 98% of campus accessible to physically disabled. **Special Academic Facilities/Equipment:** Roland Fine Arts Center, Carroll Mission Center, Nature Trail, Mabee Sport Complex.

CAMPUS LIFE
Environment: Village. **Activities:** Campus Ministries; Choral groups; Concert band; Drama/theater; International Student Organization; Jazz band; Music ensembles; Musical theater; Student government; Student newspaper; Yearbook. 22 registered organizations, 1 honor societies, 3 religious organizations, 1 fraternities, 1 sororities, on campus. **Athletics (Intercollegiate):** *Men:* baseball, basketball, cross-country, golf, soccer, swimming, track/field (outdoor), volleyball, wrestling. *Women:* basketball, cheerleading, cross-country, golf, soccer, softball, swimming, track/field (outdoor), volleyball. **On-Campus Highlights:** Fireside Cafe.

ADMISSIONS
Freshman Academic Profile: 21% in top 10% of high school class, 37% in top 25% of high school class, 52% in top 50% of high school class. **Test scores:** SAT Math middle 50% range 440–480. SAT EBRW middle 50% range 260–490. ACT middle 50% range 19–24. **Basis for Candidate Selection:** *Very important factors include:* academic GPA, standardized test scores. *Important factors include:* rigor of secondary school record. *Other factors include:* class rank, recommendation(s), extracurricular activities, talent/ability, character/personal qualities, religious affiliation/commitment, level of applicant's interest. **Freshman Admission Requirements:** High school diploma is required and GED is accepted. *Academic units recommended:* 4 English, 3 math, 2 science, 1 science labs, 3 history. **Freshman Admission Statistics:** applied, admitted, enrolled. **Transfer Admission Requirements:** college transcript(s), Minimum college GPA of 2.0 required. Lowest grade transferable 1. **General Admission Information:** Application fee $25. Non-fall registration accepted. Admission may be deferred for a maximum of 1 semester.

COSTS AND FINANCIAL AID
Annual tuition $21,450. Room and board $8,108. Average book and supplies expense $1,070. **Required Forms and Deadlines:** FAFSA; Institution's own financial aid form. **Types of Aid:** *Need-based scholarships/grants:* College/university scholarship or grant aid from institutional funds; Federal Pell; Private scholarships; SEOG; State scholarships/grants. *Loans:* Direct Subsidized Stafford Loans; Direct Unsubsidized Stafford Loans. **Student Employment:** Federal Work-Study Program available. Institutional employment available. **Criteria awarding aid:** *Non-Need-based:* Academics, Art, Athletics, Music/drama, Religious affiliation.

HANOVER COLLEGE

Best Colleges

P.O. Box 108, Hanover, IN 47243-0108
Phone: 800-213-2178 **Financial Aid Phone:** 812-866-7029
E-mail: admission@hanover.edu **CEEB Code:** 1290
Fax: 812-866-7098 **Website:** www.hanover.edu **ACT Code:** 1200

This private school, affiliated with the Presbyterian Church, was founded in 1827. It has a 650 acre campus.

RATINGS
Admissions Selectivity Rating: 77   **Fire Safety Rating:** 95   **Green Rating:** 81

STUDENTS AND FACULTY
Enrollment: 1,082. **Student Body:** 54% female, 46% male, 33% out-of-state, 2% international (17 countries represented). Asian 1%, African American 5%, Caucasian 76%, Hispanic 3%, Native American 1%, Pacific Islander <1%, Two or more races 2%, Race unknown 9%.
Retention and Graduation: 79% freshmen return for sophomore year. 67% freshmen graduate within 4 years. 71% freshmen graduate within 6 years. 22% grads go on to further study within 1 year. 16% grads pursue arts and sciences degrees. 2% grads pursue law degrees. 2% grads pursue business degrees. 1% grads pursue medical degrees. **Faculty:** Student/faculty ratio 13:1. 84 full-time faculty, 93% hold PhDs, 6% are members of minority groups, 42% are women. 0% of classes are taught by teaching assistants.

ACADEMICS
Degrees: Bachelor's. **Classes:** Most classes have 10–19 students. **Most popular majors:** Economics, General; Psychology, General; Speech Communication and Rhetoric. **Special Study Options:** Double major; Dual enrollment; Independent study; Internships; Student-designed major; Study abroad; Teacher certification program. **Disability Services offered:** Note-taking services; Tutors. **Career services:** Alumni network; Alumni services; Career assessment; Career/job search classes; Internships; Regional alumni.

FACILITIES
Housing: Apartments for single students; Coed dorms; Fraternity/sorority housing; Men's dorms; Theme housing; Wellness housing; Women's dorms 50% of campus accessible to physically disabled. **Special Academic Facilities/Equipment:** cadaver lab, geological museum, electronic language lab, observatory.

CAMPUS LIFE
Environment: Rural. **Activities:** Campus Ministries; Choral groups; Concert band; Dance; Drama/theater; International Student Organization; Jazz band; Literary magazine; Music ensembles; Musical theater; Pep band; Radio station; Student government; Student newspaper; Student-run film society; Symphony orchestra; Television station; Yearbook. 60 registered organizations, 8 honor societies, 4 religious organizations, 4 fraternities, 4 sororities, on campus. **Athletics (Intercollegiate):** *Men:* baseball, basketball, cross-country, football, golf, lacrosse, soccer, tennis, track/field (outdoor). *Women:* basketball, cross-country, golf, soccer, softball, tennis, track/field (outdoor), volleyball. **On-Campus Highlights:** Science Center. **Environmental Initiatives:** The College is currently developing a new strategic plan and re-evaluating our green initiatives and sustainability program as an integral component of the plan.

ADMISSIONS
Freshman Academic Profile: Average high school GPA 3.6. 32% in top 10% of high school class, 60% in top 25% of high school class, 90% in top 50% of high school class. 85% from public high schools. **Test scores:** SAT Math middle 50% range 530–620. SAT EBRW middle 50% range 540–640. ACT middle 50% range 22–27. **Basis for Candidate Selection:** *Very important factors include:* rigor of secondary school record, class rank, academic GPA. *Important factors include:* standardized test scores, talent/ability, character/personal qualities. *Other factors include:* application essay, recommendation(s), interview,

extracurricular activities, first generation, alumni/ae relation, geographical residence, state residency, racial/ethnic status, volunteer work, work experience, level of applicant's interest. **Freshman Admission Requirements:** High school diploma is required and GED is not accepted. *Academic units required:* 4 English, 3 math, 3 science, 2 science labs, 2 foreign language, 2 social studies, 2 history, 2 academic electives. *Academic units recommended:* 4 English, 4 math, 4 science, 3 science labs, 4 foreign language, 3 social studies, 3 history, 3 academic electives, 1 visual/performing arts. **Freshman Admission Statistics:** 2,757 applied, 84% admitted, 15% enrolled. **Transfer Admission Requirements:** High school transcript, college transcript(s), essay or personal statement, standardized test scores, statement of good standing from prior institution(s). Minimum college GPA of 2.0 required. Lowest grade transferable C-. **General Admission Information:** Non-fall registration accepted. Admission may be deferred for a maximum of 1 year.

COSTS AND FINANCIAL AID

Annual tuition $36,900. Room and board $11,580. Required fees $770. Average book and supplies expense $1,200. **Required Forms and Deadlines:** FAFSA. **Notification of Awards:** Applicants will be notified of awards on or about 3/1. **Types of Aid:** *Need-based scholarships/grants:* College/university scholarship or grant aid from institutional funds; Federal Pell; Private scholarships; SEOG; State scholarships/grants. *Loans:* Direct PLUS loans; Direct Subsidized Stafford Loans; Direct Unsubsidized Stafford Loans. **Student Employment:** Federal Work-Study Program available. Institutional employment available. **Financial Aid Statistics:** 100% needy freshmen, 100% needy undergrads receive need-based scholarship or grant aid. 31% freshmen, 20% undergrads receive non-need-based scholarship or grant aid. 66% freshmen, 78% undergrads receive need-based self-help aid. 0% freshmen, 0% undergrads receive athletic scholarships. 100% freshmen, 100% undergrads receive any aid. 72% undergrads borrow to pay for school. Average cumulative indebtedness $30,835. **Criteria awarding aid:** *Need-based:* Academics, Alumni affiliation, Art, Leadership, Minority status, Music/drama, Religious affiliation. *Non-Need-based:* Academics, Alumni affiliation, Art, Leadership, Minority status, Music/drama, Religious affiliation, State/district residency.

HARDING UNIVERSITY

Box 12255, Searcy, AR 72149
Phone: 501-279-4407 **Financial Aid Phone:** 501-279-4257
E-mail: admissions@harding.edu **CEEB Code:** 10311
Fax: 501-279-4129 **Website:** www.harding.edu **ACT Code:** 0124

This private school, affiliated with the Church of Christ, was founded in 1924. It has a 350 acre campus.

RATINGS

Admissions Selectivity Rating: 88 **Fire Safety Rating:** 91 **Green Rating:** 60*

STUDENTS AND FACULTY

Enrollment: 3,953. **Student Body:** 54% female, 46% male, 70% out-of-state, 6% international (54 countries represented). Asian 1%, African American 4%, Caucasian 81%, Hispanic 4%, Native American <1%, Pacific Islander <1%, Two or more races 3%, Race unknown <1%.
Retention and Graduation: 85% freshmen return for sophomore year. 46% freshmen graduate within 4 years. 67% freshmen graduate within 6 years.
Faculty: Student/faculty ratio 14:1. 305 full-time faculty, 74% hold PhDs, 5% are members of minority groups, 35% are women. 0% of classes are taught by teaching assistants.

ACADEMICS

Degrees: Bachelor's; Doctoral degree—professional practice; Doctoral degree research/scholarship; Master's; Post-master's certificate. **Classes:** Most classes have 10–19 students. **Most popular majors:** Accounting; Business Administration and Management, General; Early Childhood Education and Teaching. **Special Study Options:** Accelerated program; Cooperative education program; Distance learning; Double major; Dual enrollment; English as a Second Language (ESL); Honors program; Independent study; Internships; Liberal arts/career combination; Student-designed major; Study abroad; Teacher certification program. **Disability Services offered:** Note-taking services; Reader services; Tape recorders; Tutors. **Career services:** Alumni network; Alumni services; Career assessment; Career/job search classes; Internships.

FACILITIES

Housing: Apartments for married students; Apartments for single students; Men's dorms; Special housing for disabled students; Women's dorms 95% of campus accessible to physically disabled. **Special Academic Facilities/Equipment:** On-campus academy (prep school grades PreK-12). **Campus Network:** 100% of classrooms, 100% of dorms, 100% of student union, 100% of libraries, 100% of dining areas, 85% of common outdoor areas, have wireless network access.

CAMPUS LIFE

Environment: Village. **Activities:** Campus Ministries; Choral groups; Concert band; Drama/theater; International Student Organization; Jazz band; Literary magazine; Marching band; Music ensembles; Musical theater; Pep band; Radio station; Student government; Student newspaper; Student-run film society; Symphony orchestra; Television station; Yearbook. 101 registered organizations, 12 honor societies, 10 religious organizations, on campus. **Athletics (Intercollegiate):** *Men:* baseball, basketball, cross-country, football, golf, soccer, tennis, track/field (outdoor). *Women:* basketball, cheerleading, cross-country, golf, soccer, tennis, track/field (outdoor), volleyball. **On-Campus Highlights:** Rhodes Memorial Field House. **Environmental Initiatives:** Recycling.

ADMISSIONS

Freshman Academic Profile: Average high school GPA 3.7. 23% in top 10% of high school class, 50% in top 25% of high school class, 77% in top 50% of high school class. 66% from public high schools. **Test scores:** SAT Math middle 50% range 520–640. SAT EBRW middle 50% range 540–660. ACT middle 50% range 22–29. **Basis for Candidate Selection:** *Very important factors include:* rigor of secondary school record, standardized test scores, recommendation(s), interview, character/personal qualities. *Important factors include:* class rank, academic GPA, talent/ability. *Other factors include:* application essay, extracurricular activities, first generation, alumni/ae relation, geographical residence, state residency, volunteer work, work experience, level of applicant's interest. **Freshman Admission Requirements:** High school diploma is required and GED is accepted. *Academic units required:* 4 English, 3 math, 2 science, 3 social studies, 3 academic electives. *Academic units recommended:* 4 English, 4 math, 4 science, 2 foreign language, 4 social studies, 2 academic electives. **Freshman Admission Statistics:** 1,927 applied, 68% admitted, 65% enrolled. **Transfer Admission Requirements:** college transcript(s), essay or personal statement, statement of good standing from prior institution(s). Minimum college GPA of 2 required. Lowest grade transferable C. **General Admission Information:** Application fee $50. Non-fall registration accepted. Admission may be deferred for a maximum of one year.

COSTS AND FINANCIAL AID

Annual tuition $20,010. Room and board $7,170. Required fees $725. Average book and supplies expense $1,200. **Required Forms and Deadlines:** FAFSA. **Notification of Awards:** Applicants will be notified of awards on a rolling basis beginning 2/15. **Types of Aid:** *Need-based scholarships/grants:* College/university scholarship or grant aid from institutional funds; Federal Pell; Private scholarships; SEOG; State scholarships/grants. *Loans:* Direct PLUS loans; Direct Subsidized Stafford Loans; Direct Unsubsidized Stafford Loans. **Student Employment:** Federal Work-Study Program available. Institutional employment available. **Financial Aid Statistics:** 98% needy freshmen, 93% needy undergrads receive need-based scholarship or grant aid. 16% freshmen, 80% undergrads receive non-need-based scholarship or grant aid. 76% freshmen, 80% undergrads receive need-based self-help aid. 3% freshmen, 3% undergrads receive athletic scholarships. 90% freshmen, 77% undergrads receive any aid. 65% undergrads borrow to pay for school. Average cumulative indebtedness $33,915. **Criteria awarding aid:** *Need-based:* Academics, Alumni affiliation, Job skills, Minority status. *Non-Need-based:* Academics, Alumni affiliation, Art, Athletics, Leadership, Music/drama, Religious affiliation, State/district residency.

HARDIN-SIMMONS UNIVERSITY

Box 16050, Abilene, TX 79698
Phone: 325-670-1206 **Financial Aid Phone:** 325-670-1217
E-mail: enroll@hsutx.edu **CEEB Code:** 6268
Fax: 325-671-2115 **Website:** www.hsutx.edu **ACT Code:** 4096

This private school, affiliated with the Baptist Church, was founded in 1891. It has a 220 acre campus.

RATINGS
Admissions Selectivity Rating: 77 **Fire Safety Rating:** 76 **Green Rating:** 63

STUDENTS AND FACULTY
Enrollment: 1,671. **Student Body:** 52% female, 48% male, 3% out-of-state, 2% international (27 countries represented). Asian 1%, African American 8%, Caucasian 64%, Hispanic 19%, Native American <1%, Pacific Islander <1%, Two or more races 5%, Race unknown 1%.
Retention and Graduation: 75% freshmen return for sophomore year. 37% freshmen graduate within 4 years. 52% freshmen graduate within 6 years. 45% grads go on to further study within 1 year. 17% grads pursue arts and sciences degrees. 3% grads pursue law degrees. 2% grads pursue business degrees. 7% grads pursue medical degrees. **Faculty:** Student/faculty ratio 12:1. 134 full-time faculty, 90% hold PhDs, 4% are members of minority groups, 38% are women. 0% of classes are taught by teaching assistants.

ACADEMICS
Degrees: Bachelor's; Doctoral degree—professional practice; Doctoral degree research/scholarship; Master's; Post-master's certificate. **Classes:** Most classes have 10–19 students. Most lab/discussion sessions have 10–19 students. **Most popular majors:** Education, General; Business, Management, Marketing, and Related Support Services, Other; Registered Nursing/Registered Nurse. **Special Study Options:** Accelerated program; Cross-registration; Distance learning; Double major; Dual enrollment; Honors program; Independent study; Internships; Study abroad; Teacher certification program. **Honors programs:** The Hardin-Simmons University Honors Program provides an enriched educational environment for undergraduate students of exceptional promise who have a wide variety of interests and seek an enhanced learning opportunity. The Honors Program promotes creative and critical thinking skills to equip individuals for success in today's world. The Program, which serves as an integral part of the academic community, includes courses taught by selected faculty members interested in working with highly motivated students. The Honors Program expects participants to strive for excellence and assume personal accountability for their intellectual growth. **Disability Services offered:** Note-taking services; Reader services; Tape recorders; Tutors. **Career services:** Alumni network; Alumni services; Career assessment; Career/job search classes; Internships; Regional alumni.

FACILITIES
Housing: Apartments for married students; Apartments for single students; Men's dorms; Special housing for disabled students; Women's dorms; 100% of campus accessible to physically disabled. **Special Academic Facilities/Equipment:** Art center, observatory with 14-inch telescope, rare and fine book room, SIX WHITE HORSE facility, Holland Health Science Medical High School. **Campus Network:** 100% of classrooms, 100% of dorms, 100% of libraries, 100% of dining areas, 100% of common outdoor areas, have wireless network access.

CAMPUS LIFE
Environment: City. **Activities:** Campus Ministries; Choral groups; Concert band; Dance; Drama/theater; International Student Organization; Jazz band; Literary magazine; Marching band; Model UN; Music ensembles; Musical theater; Opera; Student government; Student newspaper; Symphony orchestra; Yearbook. 49 registered organizations, 15 honor societies, 5 religious organizations, 5 fraternities, 4 sororities, on campus. **Athletics (Intercollegiate): Men:** baseball, basketball, cheerleading, cross-country, football, golf, soccer, tennis, track/field (outdoor). **Women:** basketball, cheerleading, cross-country, golf, soccer, softball, tennis, track/field (outdoor), volleyball. **On-Campus Highlights:** Moody Center (Student Center) **Environmental Initiatives:** Estabishing a recycling program.

ADMISSIONS
Freshman Academic Profile: Average high school GPA 3.6. 18% in top 10% of high school class, 44% in top 25% of high school class, 76% in top 50% of high school class. 91% from public high schools. **Test scores:** SAT Math

middle 50% range 500–580. SAT EBRW middle 50% range 500–590. ACT middle 50% range 18–24. **Basis for Candidate Selection:** *Important factors include:* standardized test scores. *Other factors include:* rigor of secondary school record, class rank, academic GPA, recommendation(s), extracurricular activities, character/personal qualities, first generation, volunteer work, work experience. **Freshman Admission Requirements:** High school diploma is required and GED is accepted. **Freshman Admission Statistics:** 1,673 applied, 82% admitted, 33% enrolled. **Transfer Admission Requirements:** college transcript(s), Minimum college GPA of 2.0 required. Lowest grade transferable C. **General Admission Information:** Non-fall registration accepted.

COSTS AND FINANCIAL AID
Annual tuition $27,290. Room and board $8,080. Required fees $1,700. Average book and supplies expense $800. **Notification of Awards:** Applicants will be notified of awards on a rolling basis beginning 12/1. **Types of Aid:** *Need-based scholarships/grants:* College/university scholarship or grant aid from institutional funds; Federal Pell; Private scholarships; SEOG; State scholarships/grants. *Loans:* Direct PLUS loans; Direct Subsidized Stafford Loans; Direct Unsubsidized Stafford Loans. **Student Employment:** Federal Work-Study Program available. Institutional employment available. **Financial Aid Statistics:** 79% needy freshmen, 78% needy undergrads receive need-based scholarship or grant aid. 100% freshmen, 98% undergrads receive non-need-based scholarship or grant aid. 91% freshmen, 91% undergrads receive need-based self-help aid. 0% freshmen, 0% undergrads receive athletic scholarships. 99% freshmen, 90% undergrads receive any aid. 68% undergrads borrow to pay for school. Average cumulative indebtedness $51,346. **Criteria awarding aid:** *Non-Need-based:* Academics, Alumni affiliation, Art, Leadership, Minority status, Music/drama, Religious affiliation.

HARRISBURG UNIVERSITY OF SCIENCE AND TECHNOLOGY

326 Market Street, Harrisburg, PA 17101
Phone: 717-901-5101 **Financial Aid Phone:** 717-901-5115
E-mail: admissions@HarrisburgU.edu **CEEB Code:** 4511
Fax: 717-901-3101 **Website:** www.HarrisburgU.edu **ACT Code:** 3637

This private school was founded in 2001. It has a 2 acre campus.

RATINGS
Admissions Selectivity Rating: 85 **Fire Safety Rating:** 60* **Green Rating:** 60*

STUDENTS AND FACULTY
Enrollment: 272. **Student Body:** 46% female, 54% male, 17% out-of-state, 1% international (3 countries represented). Asian 4%, African American 32%, Caucasian 49%, Hispanic 8%, Native American <1%, Pacific Islander 0%, Two or more races 3%, Race unknown 2%.
Retention and Graduation: 54% freshmen return for sophomore year. 10% grads go on to further study within 1 year. 10% grads pursue arts and sciences degrees. 0% grads pursue law degrees. 0% grads pursue business degrees. 0% grads pursue medical degrees. **Faculty:** Student/faculty ratio 11:1. 10 full-time faculty, 100% hold PhDs, 40% are members of minority groups, 50% are women. 0% of classes are taught by teaching assistants.

ACADEMICS
Degrees: Bachelor's; Master's. **Classes:** Most classes have 20–29 students. **Most popular majors:** Computer and Information Sciences, General; Biotechnology; Physical Sciences, General. **Special Study Options:** Dual enrollment; Internships; Student-designed major. **Career services:** Internships.

FACILITIES
Housing: Coed dorms; Special housing for disabled students; 100% of campus accessible to physically disabled.

CAMPUS LIFE
Environment: City. **On-Campus Highlights:** Conference Center.

ADMISSIONS
Freshman Academic Profile: 90% from public high schools. **Test scores:** SAT Math middle 50% range 420–550. SAT EBRW middle 50% range 440–530. ACT middle 50% range 20–24. **Basis for Candidate Selection:** *Very important factors include:* academic GPA, application essay. *Important factors include:* interview. *Other factors include:* standardized test scores, recommendation(s). **Freshman Admission Requirements:** High school diploma is required and GED is accepted. **Freshman Admission Statistics:** 1,827 applied,

47% admitted, 15% enrolled. **General Admission Information:** Non-fall registration accepted.

COSTS AND FINANCIAL AID
Annual tuition $23,800. Room and board $6,340. Average book and supplies expense $1,500. **Required Forms and Deadlines:** FAFSA. **Types of Aid:** *Need-based scholarships/grants:* College/university scholarship or grant aid from institutional funds; Federal Pell; Private scholarships; SEOG; State scholarships/grants. *Loans:* Direct PLUS loans; Direct Subsidized Stafford Loans; Direct Unsubsidized Stafford Loans. **Student Employment:** Federal Work-Study Program available. Institutional employment available. **Financial Aid Statistics:** 99% needy freshmen, 100% needy undergrads receive need-based scholarship or grant aid. 9% freshmen, 6% undergrads receive non-need-based scholarship or grant aid. 87% freshmen, 82% undergrads receive need-based self-help aid. 0% freshmen, 0% undergrads receive athletic scholarships. 98% freshmen, 94% undergrads receive any aid. **Criteria awarding aid:** *Non-Need-based:* Academics.

HARTWICK COLLEGE

PO Box 4022, Oneonta, NY 13820-4020
Phone: 607-431-4154 **Financial Aid Phone:** 607-431-4130
E-mail: admissions@hartwick.edu **CEEB Code:** 2288
Fax: 607-431-4102 **Website:** www.hartwick.edu/ **ACT Code:** 2756

This private school was founded in 1797. It has a 425 acre campus.

RATINGS
Admissions Selectivity Rating: 76   **Fire Safety Rating:** 93   **Green Rating:** 64

STUDENTS AND FACULTY
Enrollment: 1,181. **Student Body:** 56% female, 44% male, 21% out-of-state, 2% international (19 countries represented). Asian 3%, African American 10%, Caucasian 63%, Hispanic 7%, Native American 1%, Pacific Islander <1%, Two or more races 0%, Race unknown 15%.
Retention and Graduation: 74% freshmen return for sophomore year. 19% grads go on to further study within 1 year. 3% grads pursue arts and sciences degrees. 2% grads pursue law degrees. 2% grads pursue business degrees.
Faculty: Student/faculty ratio 9:1. 101 full-time faculty, 87% hold PhDs, 10% are members of minority groups, 50% are women. 0% of classes are taught by teaching assistants.

ACADEMICS
Degrees: Bachelor's. **Classes:** Most classes have 10–19 students. Most lab/discussion sessions have fewer than 10 students. **Most popular majors:** Psychology, General; Business Administration and Management, General. **Special Study Options:** Accelerated program; Distance learning; Double major; Honors program; Independent study; Internships; Student-designed major; Study abroad; Teacher certification program. **Honors programs:** Requirements for the Honors Program are: Challenges—4 must be completed by graduation; Divisions—3 must be represented in Challenges; Honors Forum—a presentation of a project; Academic Excellence—a 3.50 Grade Point Average. Also, students in the Honors program can choose to live on the Honors floor in a campus residence hall. **Combined degree programs:** BA/JD; BA/MEng. **Disability Services offered:** Note-taking services; Reader services; Tape recorders; Tutors. **Career services:** Alumni network; Career/job search classes; Internships.

FACILITIES
Housing: Apartments for single students; Coed dorms; Fraternity/sorority housing; Theme housing; 50% of campus accessible to physically disabled. **Special Academic Facilities/Equipment:** Art and history museums, Indian artifact collection, environmental center, observatory, tissue culture lab.

CAMPUS LIFE
Environment: Village. **Activities:** Choral groups; Concert band; Dance; Drama/theater; International Student Organization; Jazz band; Literary magazine; Model UN; Music ensembles; Radio station; Student government; Student newspaper. 70 registered organizations, 10 honor societies, 1 religious organizations, 4 fraternities, 3 sororities, on campus. **Athletics (Intercollegiate):** *Men:* basketball, cross-country, diving, football, lacrosse, soccer, swimming, tennis. *Women:* basketball, cheerleading, cross-country, diving, equestrian sports, field hockey, lacrosse, soccer, swimming, tennis, volleyball, water polo. **On-Campus Highlights:** Yager Museum. **Environmental Initiatives:** Hartwick is a signatory of the Talloires Declaration

and is a member of the Association for the Advancement of Sustainability in Higher Education. In 2005, the College received a Kresge Green Building Iniative planning grant to partially fund green design of its first LEED-certified building, Golisano Hall. In keeping with Hartwick's emphasis on hands-on learning, the project provided the basis for a course entitled "Sustainable Design", taught by Richard Rittelman, FAIA principal architect and Karl Seeley, PhD. of Hartwick's economics department. The LEED-certification process for Golisano Hall is currently underway. The process involves commissioning the building's systems, which are estimated to use 75% less energy than the average building on Hartwick's campus.

ADMISSIONS
Freshman Academic Profile: 86% from public high schools. **Test scores:** SAT Math middle 50% range 510–600. SAT EBRW middle 50% range 520–610. ACT middle 50% range 20–25. **Basis for Candidate Selection:** *Very important factors include:* rigor of secondary school record, academic GPA. *Important factors include:* extracurricular activities, character/personal qualities, alumni/ae relation, volunteer work. *Other factors include:* class rank, application essay, standardized test scores, recommendation(s), interview, talent/ability, level of applicant's interest. **Freshman Admission Requirements:** High school diploma is required and GED is accepted. *Academic units recommended:* 4 English, 3 math, 3 science, 2 science labs, 3 foreign language, 2 social studies, 2 history. **Freshman Admission Statistics:** 4,449 applied, 80% admitted, 11% enrolled. **Transfer Admission Requirements:** college transcript(s), essay or personal statement, statement of good standing from prior institution(s). Minimum college GPA of 2.0 required. Lowest grade transferable C-. **General Admission Information:** Non-fall registration accepted. Admission may be deferred for a maximum of 12 months.

COSTS AND FINANCIAL AID
Annual tuition $45,990. Room and board $12,834. Required fees $1,336. Average book and supplies expense $700. **Required Forms and Deadlines:** FAFSA. **Notification of Awards:** Applicants will be notified of awards on a rolling basis beginning 12/14. **Types of Aid:** *Need-based scholarships/grants:* College/university scholarship or grant aid from institutional funds; Federal Pell; Private scholarships; SEOG; State scholarships/grants. *Loans:* Direct PLUS loans; Direct Subsidized Stafford Loans; Direct Unsubsidized Stafford Loans. **Student Employment:** Federal Work-Study Program available. Institutional employment available. **Financial Aid Statistics:** 99% needy freshmen, 99% needy undergrads receive need-based scholarship or grant aid. 13% freshmen, 12% undergrads receive non-need-based scholarship or grant aid. 83% freshmen, 85% undergrads receive need-based self-help aid. 0% freshmen, 0% undergrads receive athletic scholarships. 87% freshmen, 83% undergrads receive any aid. **Criteria awarding aid:** *Need-based:* Music/drama. *Non-Need-based:* Academics, Alumni affiliation, Art, Athletics, Music/drama.

HARVARD COLLEGE

86 Brattle Street, Cambridge, MA 02138
Phone: 617-495-1551 **Financial Aid Phone:** 617-495-1581
E-mail: college@fas.harvard.edu **CEEB Code:** 3434
Fax: 617-495-8821 **Website:** www.college.harvard.edu **ACT Code:** 1840

This private school was founded in 1636. It has a 380 acre campus.

RATINGS
Admissions Selectivity Rating: 99   **Fire Safety Rating:** 60*   **Green Rating:** 60*

STUDENTS AND FACULTY
Enrollment: 6,695. **Student Body:** 49% female, 51% male, 84% out-of-state, 12% international (100 countries represented). Asian 21%, African American 9%, Caucasian 37%, Hispanic 11%, Native American <1%, Pacific Islander <1%, Two or more races 8%, Race unknown 1%.
Retention and Graduation: 97% freshmen return for sophomore year. 85% freshmen graduate within 4 years. 97% freshmen graduate within 6 years.
Faculty: Student/faculty ratio 6:1. 1,013 full-time faculty, 85% hold PhDs, 25% are members of minority groups, 37% are women. 0% of classes are taught by teaching assistants.

ACADEMICS

Degrees: Bachelor's; Doctoral degree research/scholarship; Master's. **Classes:** Most classes have fewer than 10 students. Most lab/discussion sessions have fewer than 10 students. **Most popular majors:** Social Sciences, General; Economics, General; Computer Science. **Special Study Options:** Accelerated program; Cross-registration; Double major; Exchange student program (domestic); Honors program; Independent study; Student-designed major; Study abroad; Teacher certification program. **Combined degree programs:** BA/MA; BA/MEng. **Disability Services offered:** Note-taking services; Reader services; Tape recorders; Tutors. **Career services:** Alumni network; Alumni services.

FACILITIES

Housing: Apartments for married students; Apartments for single students; Coed dorms; Cooperative housing; Special housing for disabled students. **Special Academic Facilities/Equipment:** Museums (University Arts Museums, Museums of Cultural History, many others), language labs, observatory, many science and research laboratories and facilities, new state-of-the-art computer science facility.

CAMPUS LIFE

Environment: City. **Activities:** Campus Ministries; Choral groups; Concert band; Dance; Drama/theater; International Student Organization; Jazz band; Literary magazine; Marching band; Model UN; Music ensembles; Musical theater; Opera; Pep band; Radio station; Student government; Student newspaper; Student-run film society; Symphony orchestra; Television station; Yearbook. 451 registered organizations, 1 honor societies, 25 religious organizations, on campus. **Athletics (Intercollegiate):** *Men:* baseball, basketball, crew/rowing, cross-country, diving, fencing, football, golf, ice hockey, lacrosse, sailing, skiing (downhill/Alpine), skiing (Nordic/cross-country), soccer, squash, swimming, tennis, track/field (outdoor), track/field (indoor), volleyball, water polo, wrestling. *Women:* basketball, crew/rowing, cross-country, diving, fencing, field hockey, golf, ice hockey, lacrosse, sailing, skiing (downhill/Alpine), skiing (Nordic/cross-country), soccer, softball, squash, swimming, tennis, track/field (outdoor), track/field (indoor), volleyball, water polo. **On-Campus Highlights:** Widener Library **Environmental Initiatives:** Campus-wide Sustainability Principles that provide a broad vision to guide University operations and planning (adopted in 2004) and an established University-wide Office for Sustainability (green.harvard.edu) that oversees implementation of Harvard's GHG reduction goal and sustainability commitments. The University has had a formal sustainability office for a decade initially created by a faculty and staff initiative with strong student involvement.

ADMISSIONS

Freshman Academic Profile: Average high school GPA 4.2. 93% in top 10% of high school class, 98% in top 25% of high school class, 100% in top 50% of high school class. 59% from public high schools. **Test scores:** SAT Math middle 50% range 750–800. SAT EBRW middle 50% range 710–770. ACT middle 50% range 33–35. **Basis for Candidate Selection:** *Other factors include:* rigor of secondary school record, academic GPA, application essay, standardized test scores, recommendation(s), interview, extracurricular activities, talent/ability, character/personal qualities, first generation, alumni/ae relation, geographical residence, racial/ethnic status, volunteer work, work experience. **Freshman Admission Requirements:** High school diploma or equivalent is not required *Academic units recommended:* 4 English, 4 math, 4 science, 4 foreign language, 3 social studies, 2 history. **Freshman Admission Statistics:** 43,330 applied, 5% admitted, 82% enrolled. **General Admission Information:** Application fee $75. Regular application deadline 1/1. Admission may be deferred for a maximum of 1 year.

COSTS AND FINANCIAL AID

Annual tuition $46,340. Room and board $17,160. Required fees $4,080. Average book and supplies expense $1,000. **Required Forms and Deadlines:** Business/Farm Supplement; CSS/Financial Aid PROFILE; FAFSA; Noncustodial PROFILE;. **Notification of Awards:** Applicants will be notified of awards on or about 4/1. **Types of Aid:** *Need-based scholarships/grants:* College/university scholarship or grant aid from institutional funds; Federal Pell; Private scholarships; SEOG; State scholarships/grants. *Loans:* Direct PLUS loans; Direct Subsidized Stafford Loans; Direct Unsubsidized Stafford Loans. **Student Employment:** Federal Work-Study Program available. Institutional employment available. **Financial Aid Statistics:** 99% needy freshmen, 100% needy undergrads receive need-based scholarship or grant aid. 0% freshmen, 0% undergrads receive non-need-based scholarship or grant aid. freshmen, undergrads receive need-based self-help aid. 0% freshmen, 0% undergrads receive athletic scholarships. 76% freshmen, 68% undergrads receive any aid. 7% undergrads borrow to pay for school. Average cumulative indebtedness $6,170.

HARVEY MUDD COLLEGE

301 Platt Boulevard, Claremont, CA 91711
Phone: 909-621-8011 **Financial Aid Phone:** 909-621-8055
E-mail: admission@hmc.edu **CEEB Code:** 4341
Fax: 909-607-7046 **Website:** https://www.hmc.edu/

This private school was founded in 1955. It has a 33 acre campus.

RATINGS

Admissions Selectivity Rating: 98   **Fire Safety Rating:** 84   **Green Rating:** 76

STUDENTS AND FACULTY

Enrollment: 893. **Student Body:** 50% female, 50% male, 54% out-of-state, 8% international (26 countries represented). Asian 20%, African American 4%, Caucasian 31%, Hispanic 20%, Native American <1%, Pacific Islander 1%, Two or more races 11%, Race unknown 6%.
Retention and Graduation: 97% freshmen return for sophomore year. 86% freshmen graduate within 4 years. 92% freshmen graduate within 6 years.
Faculty: Student/faculty ratio 8:1. 103 full-time faculty, 98% hold PhDs, 25% are members of minority groups, 36% are women. 0% of classes are taught by teaching assistants.

ACADEMICS

Degrees: Bachelor's. **Classes:** Most classes have 10–19 students. Most lab/discussion sessions have 10–19 students. **Most popular majors:** Engineering, General; Computer and Information Sciences, General; Mathematics, General. **Special Study Options:** Cross-registration; Double major; Dual enrollment; Independent study; Internships; Student-designed major; Study abroad. **Disability Services offered:** Note-taking services; Reader services; Tape recorders; Tutors. **Career services:** Alumni network; Alumni services; Career assessment; Internships.

FACILITIES

Housing: Apartments for married students; Apartments for single students; Coed dorms; 90% of campus accessible to physically disabled.

CAMPUS LIFE

Environment: Town. **Activities:** Campus Ministries; Choral groups; Concert band; Dance; Drama/theater; International Student Organization; Jazz band; Literary magazine; Music ensembles; Radio station; Student government; Student newspaper; Symphony orchestra; Yearbook. 123 registered organizations, 4 honor societies, 6 religious organizations, on campus. **Athletics (Intercollegiate):** *Men:* baseball, basketball, cross-country, diving, football, golf, soccer, swimming, tennis, track/field (outdoor), water polo. *Women:* basketball, cross-country, diving, golf, lacrosse, soccer, softball, swimming, tennis, track/field (outdoor), volleyball, water polo. **On-Campus Highlights:** Dorm Lounges **Environmental Initiatives:** In February 2008 Harvey Mudd College President Maria Klawe signed the American College & University Presidents Climate Commitment and Harvey Mudd College Board of Trustees adopted HMC Sustainability Policy Statement. Additionally, the Board of Trustees passed a resolution where the standard for new buildings will be at least U.S. Green Building Council LEED Silver standard or equivalent and premium rated or ENERGY STAR certified products are purchased for use on campus where possible.

ADMISSIONS

Freshman Academic Profile: 65% from public high schools. **Test scores:** SAT Math middle 50% range 780–800. SAT EBRW middle 50% range 710–770. ACT middle 50% range 33–35. **Basis for Candidate Selection:** *Very important factors include:* rigor of secondary school record, academic GPA, application essay, recommendation(s). *Important factors include:* standardized test scores, extracurricular activities, character/personal qualities. *Other factors include:* class rank, interview, talent/ability, first generation, alumni/ae relation, geographical residence, state residency, racial/ethnic status, volunteer work, work experience. **Freshman Admission Requirements:** High school diploma or equivalent is not required. *Academic units required:* 4 English, 4 math, 3 science, 1 history. *Academic units recommended:* 4 English, 4 math, 4 science, 2 science labs, 2 foreign language, 2 social studies, 2 history, 2 academic electives. **Freshman Admission Statistics:** 4,045 applied, 14% admitted, 41% enrolled. **Transfer Admission Requirements:** High school transcript, college transcript(s), essay or personal statement, statement of good standing from prior institution(s). Minimum college GPA of 3.0 required. Lowest grade transferable C. **General Admission Information:** Application fee $70. Regular application deadline 1/5.

COSTS AND FINANCIAL AID
Annual tuition $58,359. Room and board $18,679. Required fees $551. Average book and supplies expense $800. **Required Forms and Deadlines:** Business/Farm Supplement; CSS/Financial Aid PROFILE; FAFSA; Noncustodial PROFILE; State aid form. **Notification of Awards:** Applicants will be notified of awards on or about 4/1. **Types of Aid:** *Need-based scholarships/grants:* College/university scholarship or grant aid from institutional funds; Federal Pell; Private scholarships; SEOG; State scholarships/grants. *Loans:* Direct PLUS loans; Direct Subsidized Stafford Loans; Direct Unsubsidized Stafford Loans. **Student Employment:** Federal Work-Study Program available. Institutional employment available. **Financial Aid Statistics:** 97% needy freshmen, 97% needy undergrads receive need-based scholarship or grant aid. 37% freshmen, 43% undergrads receive non-need-based scholarship or grant aid. 61% freshmen, 66% undergrads receive need-based self-help aid. 0% freshmen, 0% undergrads receive athletic scholarships. 74% freshmen, 71% undergrads receive any aid. 47% undergrads borrow to pay for school. Average cumulative indebtedness $29,139. **Criteria awarding aid:** *Non-Need-based:* Academics.

HASTINGS COLLEGE

Hastings College, Hastings, NE 68901
Phone: 402-461-7403 **Financial Aid Phone:** 402-461-7431
E-mail: mmolliconi@hastings.edu **CEEB Code:** 6270
Fax: 402-461-7490 **Website:** www.hastings.edu **ACT Code:** 2456

This private school, affiliated with the Presbyterian Church, was founded in 1882. It has a 109 acre campus.

RATINGS
Admissions Selectivity Rating: 77   **Fire Safety Rating:** 79   **Green Rating:** 60*

STUDENTS AND FACULTY
Enrollment: 1,067. **Student Body:** 46% female, 54% male, 28% out-of-state, 1% international (7 countries represented). Asian 1%, African American 2%, Caucasian 92%, Hispanic 3%, Native American <1%, Race unknown 1%. **Retention and Graduation:** 76% freshmen return for sophomore year. 24% grads go on to further study within 1 year. 16% grads pursue arts and sciences degrees. 2% grads pursue law degrees. 1% grads pursue business degrees. 1% grads pursue medical degrees. **Faculty:** Student/faculty ratio 11:1. 87 full-time faculty, 71% hold PhDs, 1% are members of minority groups, 34% are women. 0% of classes are taught by teaching assistants.

ACADEMICS
Degrees: Bachelor's; Master's. **Classes:** Most classes have 10–19 students. Most lab/discussion sessions have fewer than 10 students. **Most popular majors:** Education, General; Business/Commerce, General; Psychology, General. **Special Study Options:** Double major; Exchange student program (domestic); Independent study; Internships; Student-designed major; Study abroad; Teacher certification program. **Disability Services offered:** Note-taking services; Reader services; Tape recorders; Tutors. **Career services:** Alumni network; Alumni services; Career assessment; Career/job search classes; Internships; Regional alumni.

FACILITIES
Housing: Apartments for single students; Coed dorms; Men's dorms; Women's dorms; 90% of campus accessible to physically disabled. **Special Academic Facilities/Equipment:** center for communication arts, glass-blowing studio, observatory, art gallery. **Campus Network:** 100% of classrooms, 100% of dorms, 100% of student union, 100% of libraries, 100% of dining areas, 60% of common outdoor areas, have wireless network access.

CAMPUS LIFE
Environment: Village. **Activities:** Campus Ministries; Choral groups; Concert band; Dance; Drama/theater; Jazz band; Literary magazine; Marching band; Music ensembles; Musical theater; Pep band; Radio station; Student government; Student newspaper; Symphony orchestra; Television station; Yearbook. 85 registered organizations, 13 honor societies, 10 religious organizations, 4 fraternities, 4 sororities, on campus. **Athletics**

(Intercollegiate): *Men:* baseball, basketball, cross-country, football, golf, soccer, tennis, track/field (outdoor), track/field (indoor), wrestling. *Women:* basketball, cheerleading, cross-country, golf, soccer, softball, tennis, track/field (outdoor), track/field (indoor), volleyball. **On-Campus Highlights:** Fleharty Educational Center and weight room.

ADMISSIONS
Freshman Academic Profile: Average high school GPA 3.2. 16% in top 10% of high school class, 40% in top 25% of high school class, 65% in top 50% of high school class. 88% from public high schools. **Test scores:** SAT Math middle 50% range 490–605. SAT EBRW middle 50% range 500–600. ACT middle 50% range 20–26. **Basis for Candidate Selection:** *Very important factors include:* rigor of secondary school record, class rank, academic GPA, standardized test scores, recommendation(s). *Important factors include:* extracurricular activities, talent/ability, character/personal qualities. *Other factors include:* application essay, interview, alumni/ae relation, racial/ethnic status, level of applicant's interest. **Freshman Admission Requirements:** High school diploma is required and GED is accepted. *Academic units required:* 3 English, 3 math, 3 science, 3 science labs, 4 social studies, 3 history. *Academic units recommended:* 4 English, 4 math, 4 science, 4 science labs, 2 foreign language, 4 social studies, 4 history. **Freshman Admission Statistics:** 1,210 applied, 81% admitted, 32% enrolled. **Transfer Admission Requirements:** High school transcript, college transcript(s), statement of good standing from prior institution(s). Minimum college GPA of 2.0 required. Lowest grade transferable C. **General Admission Information:** Application fee $20. Non-fall registration accepted.

COSTS AND FINANCIAL AID
Annual tuition $27,300. Room and board $8,080. Average book and supplies expense $730. **Required Forms and Deadlines:** FAFSA; Institution's own financial aid form. **Notification of Awards:** Applicants will be notified of awards on a rolling basis beginning 3/1. **Types of Aid:** *Need-based scholarships/grants:* College/university scholarship or grant aid from institutional funds; Federal Pell; Private scholarships; SEOG; State scholarships/grants. **Student Employment:** Federal Work-Study Program available. Institutional employment available. **Financial Aid Statistics:** 100% needy freshmen, 98% needy undergrads receive need-based scholarship or grant aid. 20% freshmen, 16% undergrads receive non-need-based scholarship or grant aid. 73% freshmen, 79% undergrads receive need-based self-help aid. 23% freshmen, 16% undergrads receive athletic scholarships. 97% freshmen, 98% undergrads receive any aid. **Criteria awarding aid:** *Need-based:* Academics, Art, Athletics, Leadership, Music/drama *Non-Need-based:* Academics, Art, Athletics, Leadership, Music/drama.

HAVERFORD COLLEGE

370 Lancaster Avenue, Haverford, PA 19041
Phone: 610-896-1350 **Financial Aid Phone:** (610)896-1350
E-mail: http://www.haverford.edu/admission/ **CEEB Code:** 2289
Fax: 610-896-1338 **Website:** www.haverford.edu **ACT Code:** 3409

This private school was founded in 1833. It has a 200 acre campus.

RATINGS
Admissions Selectivity Rating: 98   **Fire Safety Rating:** 89   **Green Rating:** 89

STUDENTS AND FACULTY
Enrollment: 1,305. **Student Body:** 51% female, 49% male, 86% out-of-state, 11% international (36 countries represented). Asian 13%, African American 7%, Caucasian 53%, Hispanic 10%, Native American <1%, Pacific Islander 0%, Two or more races 3%, Race unknown 3%. **Retention and Graduation:** 97% freshmen return for sophomore year. 87% freshmen graduate within 4 years. 93% freshmen graduate within 6 years. 20% grads go on to further study within 1 year. 13% grads pursue arts and sciences degrees. 1% grads pursue law degrees. 1% grads pursue business degrees. 3% grads pursue medical degrees. **Faculty:** Student/faculty ratio 9:1. 135 full-time faculty, 99% hold PhDs, 21% are members of minority groups, 51% are women. 0% of classes are taught by teaching assistants.

ACADEMICS

Degrees: Bachelor's. **Classes:** Most classes have 10–19 students. **Most popular majors:** English Language and Literature, General; Biology/Biological Sciences, General; Psychology, General. **Special Study Options:** Cross-registration; Double major; Exchange student program (domestic); External degree program; Independent study; Internships; Student-designed major; Study abroad; Teacher certification program. **Combined degree programs:** BA/MEng. **Disability Services offered:** Note-taking services; Tape recorders. **Career services:** Alumni network; Alumni services; Career assessment; Internships; Regional alumni.

FACILITIES

Housing: Apartments for single students; Coed dorms; Men's dorms; Special housing for disabled students; Theme housing; Women's dorms; 66% of campus accessible to physically disabled. **Special Academic Facilities/Equipment:** Art gallery, arboretum, observatory, foundry. **Campus Network:** 100% of classrooms, 100% of dorms, 100% of student union, 100% of libraries, 100% of dining areas, 50% of common outdoor areas, have wireless network access.

CAMPUS LIFE

Environment: Town. **Activities:** Campus Ministries; Choral groups; Dance; Drama/theater; International Student Organization; Literary magazine; Music ensembles; Musical theater; Student government; Student newspaper; Yearbook. 145 registered organizations, 1 honor societies, 14 religious organizations, on campus. **Athletics (Intercollegiate):** *Men:* baseball, basketball, cross-country, fencing, lacrosse, soccer, squash, tennis, track/field (outdoor), track/field (indoor). *Women:* basketball, cross-country, fencing, field hockey, lacrosse, soccer, softball, squash, tennis, track/field (outdoor), track/field (indoor), volleyball. **On-Campus Highlights:** Integrated Natural Sciences Center **Environmental Initiatives:** The athletic center is the 1st gold LEED certified recreation center in the United States (opened in 2005).

ADMISSIONS

Freshman Academic Profile: 95% in top 10% of high school class, 97% in top 25% of high school class, 100% in top 50% of high school class. 60% from public high schools. **Test scores:** SAT Math middle 50% range 690–780. SAT EBRW middle 50% range 680–750. ACT middle 50% range 32–34. **Basis for Candidate Selection:** *Very important factors include:* rigor of secondary school record, academic GPA, application essay, recommendation(s), extracurricular activities, character/personal qualities. *Important factors include:* class rank, standardized test scores, talent/ability, volunteer work. *Other factors include:* interview, first generation, alumni/ae relation, geographical residence, racial/ethnic status, level of applicant's interest. **Freshman Admission Requirements:** High school diploma is required and GED is accepted. *Academic units recommended:* 4 English, 3 math, 3 science, 3 science labs, 3 foreign language, 3 social studies. **Freshman Admission Statistics:** 4,672 applied, 19% admitted, 41% enrolled. **Transfer Admission Requirements:** college transcript(s), essay or personal statement, standardized test scores, statement of good standing from prior institution(s). Minimum college GPA of 3.0 required. Lowest grade transferable C. **General Admission Information:** Application fee $65. Regular application deadline 1/15. Admission may be deferred for a maximum of 1 year.

COSTS AND FINANCIAL AID

Annual tuition $54,100. Room and board $16,402. Required fees $738. Average book and supplies expense $1,194. **Required Forms and Deadlines:** Business/Farm Supplement; CSS/Financial Aid PROFILE; FAFSA; Noncustodial PROFILE. **Notification of Awards:** Applicants will be notified of awards on or about 3/25. **Types of Aid:** *Need-based scholarships/grants:* College/university scholarship or grant aid from institutional funds; Federal Pell; Private scholarships; SEOG; State scholarships/grants. *Loans:* Direct PLUS loans; Direct Subsidized Stafford Loans; Direct Unsubsidized Stafford Loans. **Student Employment:** Federal Work-Study Program available. Institutional employment available. **Financial Aid Statistics:** 100% needy freshmen, 100% needy undergrads receive need-based scholarship or grant aid. 0% freshmen, 0% undergrads receive non-need-based scholarship or grant aid. 92% freshmen, 93% undergrads receive need-based self-help aid. 0% freshmen, 0% undergrads receive athletic scholarships. 47% freshmen, 46% undergrads receive any aid. 36% undergrads borrow to pay for school. Average cumulative indebtedness $11,000.

HAWAI'I PACIFIC UNIVERSITY

1 Aloha Tower Drive, Honolulu, HI 96813
Phone: 808-544-0238 **Financial Aid Phone:** 808-544-0253
E-mail: admissions@hpu.edu **CEEB Code:** 4352
Fax: 808-544-1136 **Website:** www.hpu.edu **ACT Code:** 4352

This private school was founded in 1965. It has a 135 acre campus.

RATINGS

Admissions Selectivity Rating: 77   **Fire Safety Rating:** 92   **Green Rating:** 60*

STUDENTS AND FACULTY

Enrollment: 3,236. **Student Body:** 59% female, 41% male, 42% out-of-state, 11% international (62 countries represented). Asian 16%, African American 6%, Caucasian 27%, Hispanic 16%, Native American 1%, Pacific Islander 2%, Two or more races 17%, Race unknown 4%.
Retention and Graduation: 64% freshmen return for sophomore year.
Faculty: Student/faculty ratio 12:1. 140 full-time faculty, 74% hold PhDs, 30% are members of minority groups, 49% are women. 0% of classes are taught by teaching assistants.

ACADEMICS

Degrees: Associate; Bachelor's; Certificate; Doctoral degree—professional practice; Master's; Post-bachelor's certificate; Post-master's certificate. **Classes:** Most classes have 10–19 students. Most lab/discussion sessions have 10–19 students. **Special Study Options:** Accelerated program; Cooperative education program; Distance learning; Double major; Dual enrollment; English as a Second Language (ESL); Exchange student program (domestic); Honors program; Independent study; Internships; Liberal arts/career combination; Student-designed major; Study abroad; Teacher certification program. **Honors programs:** The Residential Honors Program at Hawai'i Pacific University is designed for exceptionally capable and motivated students to help get the most out of their college experience. Through a myriad of challenging coursework, meaningful research, creative endeavors, and an international study abroad experience, it gives students the tools and opportunities to excel intellectually and academically. For more information visit our website: https://hpu.edu/honorsprogram/index.html#howToApply. **Combined degree programs:** BA/MA.

FACILITIES

Housing: Apartments for married students; Apartments for single students; Coed dorms; Theme housing; Wellness housing. **Special Academic Facilities/Equipment:** Hawaii Pacific University Art Gallery, Hawaii Pacific University Theatre.

CAMPUS LIFE

Environment: Metropolis. **Activities:** Campus Ministries; Choral groups; Concert band; Dance; Drama/theater; International Student Organization; Jazz band; Literary magazine; Model UN; Music ensembles; Musical theater; Pep band; Student government; Student newspaper; Student-run film society; Symphony orchestra. 50 registered organizations, 3 religious organizations, on campus. **Athletics (Intercollegiate):** *Men:* baseball, basketball, cheerleading, cross-country, golf, tennis. *Women:* cheerleading, cross-country, golf, softball, tennis, volleyball.

ADMISSIONS

Freshman Academic Profile: Average high school GPA 3.4. **Test scores:** SAT Math middle 50% range 490–590. SAT EBRW middle 50% range 510–608. ACT middle 50% range 20–25. **Basis for Candidate Selection:** *Very important factors include:* rigor of secondary school record, academic GPA. *Important factors include:* application essay, standardized test scores, extracurricular activities. *Other factors include:* recommendation(s), interview, talent/ability, character/personal qualities, first generation, volunteer work, work experience. **Freshman Admission Requirements:** High school diploma is required and GED is accepted. *Academic units recommended:* 4 English, 3 math, 3 science, 1 science labs, 2 foreign language, 2 social studies, 2 history. **Freshman Admission Statistics:** 6,551 applied, 75% admitted, 10% enrolled. **Transfer Admission Requirements:** college transcript(s), Minimum college GPA of 2.0 required. Lowest grade transferable C. **General Admission Information:** Application fee $50. Non-fall registration accepted. Admission may be deferred for a maximum of 2 years.

COSTS AND FINANCIAL AID

Annual tuition $25,630. Room and board $17,616. Required fees $350. Average book and supplies expense $1,200. **Required Forms and Deadlines:** FAFSA. **Notification of Awards:** Applicants will be notified of awards on or about 3/15. **Types of Aid:** *Need-based scholarships/grants:* College/university scholarship or grant aid from institutional funds; Federal Nursing Scholarships; Federal Pell; Private scholarships; SEOG; State scholarships/grants. *Loans:* Direct PLUS loans; Direct Subsidized Stafford Loans; Direct Unsubsidized Stafford Loans. **Financial Aid Statistics:** 94% needy freshmen, 78% needy undergrads receive need-based scholarship or grant aid. 81% freshmen, 72% undergrads receive non-need-based scholarship or grant aid. 82% freshmen, 94% undergrads receive need-based self-help aid. 11% freshmen, 10% undergrads receive athletic scholarships. 59% undergrads borrow to pay for school. Average cumulative indebtedness $27,481. **Criteria awarding aid:** *Non-Need-based:* Academics, Alumni affiliation, Athletics, Job skills, Leadership, Music/drama, Religious affiliation.

HEIDELBERG UNIVERSITY

310 East Market Street, Tiffin, OH 44883
Phone: 419-448-2330 **Financial Aid Phone:** 419-448-2293
E-mail: admission@heidelberg.edu **CEEB Code:** 1292
Fax: 419-448-2334 **Website:** www.heidelberg.edu **ACT Code:** 3278

This private school, affiliated with the United Church of Christ, was founded in 1850. It has a 120 acre campus.

RATINGS
Admissions Selectivity Rating: 77   Fire Safety Rating: 63   Green Rating: 60*

STUDENTS AND FACULTY
Enrollment: 1,089. **Student Body:** 48% female, 52% male, 15% out-of-state, 1% international. Asian 1%, African American 7%, Caucasian 78%, Hispanic 2%, Native American <1%, Pacific Islander 0%, Two or more races 2%, Race unknown 9%.
Retention and Graduation: 61% freshmen return for sophomore year. 25% grads go on to further study within 1 year. 15% grads pursue arts and sciences degrees. 2% grads pursue law degrees. 5% grads pursue business degrees. 3% grads pursue medical degrees. **Faculty:** Student/faculty ratio 12:1. 50 full-time faculty, 86% hold PhDs, 6% are members of minority groups, 46% are women. 0% of classes are taught by teaching assistants.

ACADEMICS
Degrees: Bachelor's; Master's. **Classes:** Most classes have 10–19 students. Most lab/discussion sessions have 20–29 students. **Most popular majors:** Education, General; Business/Commerce, General; Biological and Physical Sciences. **Special Study Options:** Cross-registration; Double major; Dual enrollment; English as a Second Language (ESL); Exchange student program (domestic); Honors program; Independent study; Internships; Liberal arts/career combination; Student-designed major; Study abroad; Teacher certification program. **Honors programs:** The Honors Program, entitled "The Life of the Mind," integrates learning and life experiences, stems from the mission of the University. It features extensive contact with the fundamental values that underpin self-worth and integrity, free inquiry, and intellectual rigor, an understanding of other cultures and traditions, and a lifelong habit of commitment to the community and concern for social responsibility. **Disability Services offered:** Tutors. **Career services:** Alumni network; Career assessment; Internships.

FACILITIES
Housing: Apartments for married students; Apartments for single students; Coed dorms; Cooperative housing; Fraternity/sorority housing; Special housing for disabled students; Special housing for international students; Theme housing; Women's dorms; 65% of campus accessible to physically disabled. **Special Academic Facilities/Equipment:** Forest research lots, water quality lab, Center for Historic and Military Archaeology.

CAMPUS LIFE
Environment: Village. **Activities:** Campus Ministries; Choral groups; Concert band; Drama/theater; International Student Organization; Jazz band; Literary magazine; Marching band; Model UN; Music ensembles; Musical theater; Pep band; Radio station; Student government; Student newspaper; Television station; Yearbook. 75 registered organizations, 9 honor societies, 5 religious organizations, 5 fraternities, 5 sororities, on campus. **Athletics**

(Intercollegiate): *Men:* baseball, basketball, cheerleading, cross-country, football, golf, soccer, tennis, track/field (outdoor), track/field (indoor), wrestling. *Women:* basketball, cheerleading, cross-country, golf, soccer, softball, tennis, track/field (outdoor), track/field (indoor), volleyball. **On-Campus Highlights:** Gillmor Science Center.

ADMISSIONS
Freshman Academic Profile: Average high school GPA 3.2. 14% in top 10% of high school class, 33% in top 25% of high school class, 62% in top 50% of high school class. 61% from public high schools. **Test scores:** SAT Math middle 50% range 420–570. SAT EBRW middle 50% range 420–590. ACT middle 50% range 19–25. **Basis for Candidate Selection:** *Very important factors include:* rigor of secondary school record, academic GPA, standardized test scores, interview, talent/ability, character/personal qualities. *Important factors include:* class rank, application essay, extracurricular activities. *Other factors include:* recommendation(s), first generation, alumni/ae relation, geographical residence, volunteer work, work experience. **Freshman Admission Requirements:** High school diploma is required and GED is accepted. *Academic units recommended:* 4 English, 3 math, 3 science, 1 science labs, 2 foreign language, 3 social studies, 2 history, 3 academic electives. **Freshman Admission Statistics:** 1,726 applied, 71% admitted, 29% enrolled. **Transfer Admission Requirements:** High school transcript, college transcript(s), standardized test scores, statement of good standing from prior institution(s). Minimum college GPA of 2.0 required. Lowest grade transferable C-. **General Admission Information:** Application fee $25. Priority deadline 1/1. Regular application deadline 8/1. Non-fall registration accepted. Admission may be deferred for a maximum of 3 years.

COSTS AND FINANCIAL AID
Average book and supplies expense $1,500. **Required Forms and Deadlines:** FAFSA. **Notification of Awards:** Applicants will be notified of awards on a rolling basis beginning 3/1. **Types of Aid:** *Need-based scholarships/grants:* College/university scholarship or grant aid from institutional funds; Federal Pell; Private scholarships; SEOG; State scholarships/grants. *Loans:* Direct PLUS loans; Direct Subsidized Stafford Loans; Direct Unsubsidized Stafford Loans. **Student Employment:** Federal Work-Study Program available. Institutional employment available. **Financial Aid Statistics:** 100% needy freshmen, 100% needy undergrads receive need-based scholarship or grant aid. 89% freshmen, 70% undergrads receive non-need-based scholarship or grant aid. 89% freshmen, 89% undergrads receive need-based self-help aid. 0% freshmen, 0% undergrads receive athletic scholarships. 99% freshmen, 97% undergrads receive any aid. **Criteria awarding aid:** *Non-Need-based:* Academics, Music/drama, Religious affiliation, State/district residency.

HELLENIC COLLEGE

50 Goddard Avenue, Brookline, MA 02445
Phone: 617-850-1260 **Financial Aid Phone:** 617-850-1239
E-mail: admissions@hchc.edu
Fax: 617-850-1460 **Website:** www.hchc.edu **ACT Code:** 1843

This private school, affiliated with the Greek Orthodox Church, was founded in 1937. It has a 52 acre campus.

RATINGS
Admissions Selectivity Rating: 65   Fire Safety Rating: 99   Green Rating: 60*

STUDENTS AND FACULTY
Enrollment: 78. **Student Body:** 42% female, 58% male, 86% out-of-state, 5% international (9 countries represented). Asian 0%, African American 1%, Caucasian 75%, Hispanic 6%, Native American 1%, Pacific Islander 0%, Two or more races 1%, Race unknown 11%.
Retention and Graduation: 80% freshmen return for sophomore year. 24% grads go on to further study within 1 year. 24% grads pursue arts and sciences degrees. 2% grads pursue law degrees. 5% grads pursue business degrees. 0% grads pursue medical degrees. **Faculty:** Student/faculty ratio 8:1. 21 full-time faculty, 95% hold PhDs, 0% are members of minority groups, 29% are women.

ACADEMICS
Degrees: Bachelor's; Master's. **Classes:** Most classes have fewer than 10 students. Most lab/discussion sessions have fewer than 10 students. **Most popular majors:** Business/Commerce, General; Religion/Religious Studies; Psychology, General. **Special Study Options:** Accelerated program; Cross-registration; Exchange student program (domestic); Honors program;

Independent study; Internships; Liberal arts/career combination; Study abroad; Teacher certification program. **Honors programs:** Interdisciplinary Honors Program with rigorous Thesis direction. **Disability Services offered:** Tutors. **Career services:** Alumni network; Alumni services; Career assessment; Career/job search classes; Internships; Regional alumni.

FACILITIES

Housing: Apartments for married students; Apartments for single students; Men's dorms; Women's dorms; 20% of campus accessible to physically disabled. **Campus Network:** 100% of classrooms, 100% of dorms, 100% of student union, 100% of libraries, 100% of dining areas, 100% of common outdoor areas, have wireless network access.

CAMPUS LIFE

Environment: City. **Activities:** Campus Ministries; Choral groups; Literary magazine; Student government; Student newspaper; Yearbook. **Athletics (Intercollegiate):** *Men:* basketball. *Women:* tennis.

ADMISSIONS

Freshman Academic Profile: Average high school GPA 3.3. 97% from public high schools. **Basis for Candidate Selection:** *Very important factors include:* academic GPA, application essay, recommendation(s). *Important factors include:* rigor of secondary school record, class rank, standardized test scores, interview, character/personal qualities. *Other factors include:* extracurricular activities, first generation, alumni/ae relation, religious affiliation/commitment, volunteer work, work experience, level of applicant's interest. **Freshman Admission Requirements:** High school diploma is required and GED is accepted. *Academic units required:* 4 English, 2 math, 2 science, 2 foreign language, 2 social studies, 2 history. **Freshman Admission Statistics:** 20 applied, 100% admitted, 45% enrolled. **Transfer Admission Requirements:** college transcript(s), essay or personal statement, interview, Minimum college GPA of 2.0 required. Lowest grade transferable C+. **General Admission Information:** Priority deadline 2/1. Regular application deadline 8/15. Non-fall registration accepted.

COSTS AND FINANCIAL AID

Annual tuition $21,940. Room and board $12,142. Average book and supplies expense $600. **Required Forms and Deadlines:** FAFSA; Institution's own financial aid form. **Notification of Awards:** Applicants will be notified of awards on a rolling basis beginning 4/1. *Types of Aid: Need-based scholarships/grants:* College/university scholarship or grant aid from institutional funds; Federal Pell; Private scholarships; SEOG; State scholarships/grants. *Loans:* Direct PLUS loans; Direct Subsidized Stafford Loans; Direct Unsubsidized Stafford Loans. **Student Employment:** Federal Work-Study Program available. Institutional employment available. **Financial Aid Statistics:** 100% needy freshmen, 100% needy undergrads receive need-based scholarship or grant aid. 0% freshmen, 0% undergrads receive non-need-based scholarship or grant aid. 100% freshmen, 100% undergrads receive need-based self-help aid. 0% freshmen, 0% undergrads receive athletic scholarships. 100% freshmen, 100% undergrads receive any aid. 100% undergrads borrow to pay for school. Average cumulative indebtedness $15,500. **Criteria awarding aid:** *Need-based:* Academics, Leadership, Religious affiliation. *Non-Need-based:* Academics, Alumni affiliation, Religious affiliation.

HENDERSON STATE UNIVERSITY

1100 Henderson Street, Arkadelphia, AR 71999-0001
Phone: 870-230-5028 **Financial Aid Phone:** 870-230-5148
E-mail: admissions@hsu.edu **CEEB Code:** 6272
Fax: 870-230-5066 **Website:** www.hsu.edu **ACT Code:** 126

This public school was founded in 1890. It has a 151 acre campus.

RATINGS

Admissions Selectivity Rating: 75   **Fire Safety Rating:** 64   **Green Rating:** 60*

STUDENTS AND FACULTY

Enrollment: 2,995. **Student Body:** 57% female, 43% male, 15% out-of-state, 1% international (26 countries represented). Asian 1%, African American 21%, Caucasian 66%, Hispanic 5%, Native American <1%, Pacific Islander <1%, Two or more races 4%, Race unknown 1%.
Retention and Graduation: 65% freshmen return for sophomore year.
Faculty: Student/faculty ratio 14:1. 181 full-time faculty, 72% hold PhDs, 19%

are members of minority groups, 49% are women. 0% of classes are taught by teaching assistants.

ACADEMICS

Degrees: Associate; Bachelor's; Certificate; Master's; Post-bachelor's certificate; Post-master's certificate. **Classes:** Most classes have 10–19 students. Most lab/discussion sessions have fewer than 10 students. **Most popular majors:** Elementary Education and Teaching; Biology/Biological Sciences, General; Business/Commerce, General. **Special Study Options:** Cross-registration; Distance learning; Dual enrollment; Honors program; Internships; Teacher certification program. **Honors programs:** The overarching purpose of the Honors College is summed up in the single ancient Greek word, areté (highest excellence), which the students and faculty of the College have taken as their motto. In working to achieve this purpose, the Honors College shares the university's goal "to excel in undergraduate education, always striving to enrich the quality of learning and teaching." The program is directly involved in "actively recruiting, challenging, and supporting those students" who are among the most "highly motivated toward achieving academic success." **Disability Services offered:** Note-taking services; Tutors. **Career services:** Alumni services; Career assessment; Internships.

FACILITIES

Housing: Apartments for single students; Coed dorms; Men's dorms; Special housing for international students; Theme housing; Women's dorms; 95% of campus accessible to physically disabled. **Special Academic Facilities/Equipment:** closed-circuit TV studio, Planetarium.

CAMPUS LIFE

Environment: Rural. **Activities:** Choral groups; Concert band; Dance; Drama/theater; International Student Organization; Jazz band; Literary magazine; Marching band; Music ensembles; Pep band; Radio station; Student government; Student newspaper; Television station; Yearbook. 86 registered organizations, 16 honor societies, 7 religious organizations, 7 fraternities, 5 sororities, on campus. **Athletics (Intercollegiate):** *Men:* baseball, basketball, cross-country, football, golf, swimming. *Women:* basketball, cross-country, golf, softball, swimming, tennis, volleyball. **On-Campus Highlights:** HSU Planetarium **Environmental Initiatives:** Recycling paper, cans and bottles on campus.

ADMISSIONS

Freshman Academic Profile: Average high school GPA 3.4. 14% in top 10% of high school class, 22% in top 25% of high school class, 68% in top 50% of high school class. 92% from public high schools. **Test scores:** SAT Math middle 50% range 490–560. SAT EBRW middle 50% range 488–570. ACT middle 50% range 19–25. **Basis for Candidate Selection:** *Very important factors include:* rigor of secondary school record, academic GPA, standardized test scores. *Important factors include:* class rank. **Freshman Admission Requirements:** High school diploma is required and GED is accepted. *Academic units required:* 4 English, 4 math, 3 science, 2 social studies, 1 history, 8 unit from above areas or other academic areas. *Academic units recommended:* 4 English, 4 math, 4 science, 2 foreign language, 2 social studies, 2 history. **Freshman Admission Statistics:** 2,856 applied, 91% admitted, 33% enrolled. **Transfer Admission Requirements:** college transcript(s), Lowest grade transferable C. **General Admission Information:** Regular application deadline 8/1. Non-fall registration accepted.

COSTS AND FINANCIAL AID

Required Forms and Deadlines: FAFSA; Institution's own financial aid form. **Notification of Awards:** Applicants will be notified of awards on a rolling basis beginning 3/1. *Types of Aid: Need-based scholarships/grants:* College/university scholarship or grant aid from institutional funds; Federal Pell; Private scholarships; SEOG; State scholarships/grants. *Loans:* Direct PLUS loans; Direct Subsidized Stafford Loans; Direct Unsubsidized Stafford Loans. **Student Employment:** Federal Work-Study Program available. **Financial Aid Statistics:** 65% needy freshmen, 79% needy undergrads receive need-based scholarship or grant aid. 83% freshmen, 75% undergrads receive non-need-based scholarship or grant aid. 57% freshmen, 62% undergrads receive need-based self-help aid. 13% freshmen, 10% undergrads receive athletic scholarships. 72% undergrads borrow to pay for school. Average cumulative indebtedness $24,849. **Criteria awarding aid:** *Non-Need-based:* Academics, Alumni affiliation, Art, Athletics, Leadership, Minority status, Music/drama.

HENDRIX COLLEGE

1600 Washington Avenue, Conway, AR 72032
Phone: 501-450-1362 **Financial Aid Phone:** 501-450-1368
E-mail: adm@hendrix.edu **CEEB Code:** 6273
Fax: 501-450-3843 **Website:** www.hendrix.edu **ACT Code:** 128

This private school, affiliated with the Methodist Church, was founded in 1876. It has a 160 acre campus.

RATINGS
Admissions Selectivity Rating: 80 **Fire Safety Rating:** 81 **Green Rating:** 60*

STUDENTS AND FACULTY
Enrollment: 1,303. **Student Body:** 53% female, 47% male, 52% out-of-state, 3% international (13 countries represented). Asian 5%, African American 5%, Caucasian 78%, Hispanic 5%, Native American 1%, Pacific Islander <1%, Two or more races 3%, Race unknown 1%.
Retention and Graduation: 79% freshmen return for sophomore year. 63% grads go on to further study within 1 year. 43% grads pursue arts and sciences degrees. 10% grads pursue law degrees. 3% grads pursue business degrees. 6% grads pursue medical degrees. **Faculty:** Student/faculty ratio 11:1. 107 full-time faculty, 93% hold PhDs, 13% are members of minority groups, 44% are women. 0% of classes are taught by teaching assistants.

ACADEMICS
Degrees: Bachelor's; Master's. **Classes:** Most classes have 10–19 students. **Most popular majors:** Biology/Biological Sciences, General; Psychology, General. **Special Study Options:** Cooperative education program; Double major; English as a Second Language (ESL); Independent study; Internships; Student-designed major; Study abroad; Teacher certification program. **Combined degree programs:** BA/MEng. **Disability Services offered:** Note-taking services; Tape recorders. **Career services:** Alumni network; Alumni services; Career assessment; Career/job search classes; Internships.

FACILITIES
Housing: Apartments for married students; Apartments for single students; Coed dorms; Men's dorms; Special housing for disabled students; Special housing for international students; Theme housing; Wellness housing; Women's dorms; 49% of campus accessible to physically disabled. **Special Academic Facilities/Equipment:** Herbarium, Wilbur A. Mills Library.

CAMPUS LIFE
Environment: Town. **Activities:** Campus Ministries; Choral groups; Concert band; Dance; Drama/theater; International Student Organization; Jazz band; Literary magazine; Marching band; Model UN; Music ensembles; Musical theater; Radio station; Student government; Student newspaper; Student-run film society; Symphony orchestra; Yearbook. 80 registered organizations, 6 honor societies, 5 religious organizations, on campus. **Athletics (Intercollegiate):** *Men:* baseball, basketball, cross-country, diving, golf, lacrosse, soccer, swimming, tennis, track/field (outdoor). *Women:* basketball, cross-country, diving, field hockey, golf, soccer, softball, swimming, tennis, track/field (outdoor), volleyball. **On-Campus Highlights:** Student Life & Technology Center. **Environmental Initiatives:** Reduction in paper utilization.

ADMISSIONS
Freshman Academic Profile: Average high school GPA 3.9. 48% in top 10% of high school class, % in top 25% of high school class, 96% in top 50% of high school class. 77% from public high schools. **Test scores:** SAT Math middle 50% range 580–660. SAT EBRW middle 50% range 640–680. ACT middle 50% range 25–32. **Basis for Candidate Selection:** *Very important factors include:* rigor of secondary school record, academic GPA, application essay, standardized test scores. *Important factors include:* class rank, recommendation(s), interview, extracurricular activities. *Other factors include:* talent/ability, racial/ethnic status, volunteer work. **Freshman Admission Requirements:** High school diploma is required and GED is accepted. *Academic units recommended:* 4 English, 3 math, 2 science, 2 foreign language, 3 social studies. **Freshman Admission Statistics:** 1,656 applied, 83% admitted, 29% enrolled. **Transfer Admission Requirements:** college transcript(s), essay or personal statement, statement of good standing from prior institution(s). Minimum college GPA of 2.5 required. Lowest grade transferable C. **General Admission Information:** Application fee $40. Priority deadline 2/1. Regular application deadline 6/1. Non-fall registration accepted.

COSTS AND FINANCIAL AID
Required Forms and Deadlines: FAFSA;. **Notification of Awards:** Applicants will be notified of awards on a rolling basis beginning 3/1. **Types of Aid:** *Need-based scholarships/grants:* College/university scholarship or grant aid from institutional funds; Federal Pell; Private scholarships; SEOG; State scholarships/grants. *Loans:* Direct PLUS loans; Direct Subsidized Stafford Loans; Direct Unsubsidized Stafford Loans. **Student Employment:** Federal Work-Study Program available. Institutional employment available. **Financial Aid Statistics:** 100% needy freshmen, 100% needy undergrads receive need-based scholarship or grant aid. 31% freshmen, 34% undergrads receive non-need-based scholarship or grant aid. 69% freshmen, 65% undergrads receive need-based self-help aid. 0% freshmen, 0% undergrads receive athletic scholarships. 100% freshmen, 100% undergrads receive any aid. 47% undergrads borrow to pay for school. Average cumulative indebtedness $30,213. **Criteria awarding aid:** *Non-Need-based:* Academics, Art, Leadership, Music/drama, State/district residency.

HIGH POINT UNIVERSITY

One University Parkway, High Point, NC 27268
Phone: 336-841-9216 **Financial Aid Phone:** 336-841-9032
E-mail: admiss@highpoint.edu **CEEB Code:** 5293
Fax: 336-888-6382 **Website:** www.highpoint.edu **ACT Code:** 3108

This private school, affiliated with the Methodist Church, was founded in 1924. It has a 430 acre campus.

RATINGS
Admissions Selectivity Rating: 80 **Fire Safety Rating:** 90 **Green Rating:** 60*

STUDENTS AND FACULTY
Enrollment: 4,561. **Student Body:** 56% female, 44% male, 74% out-of-state, 2% international (30 countries represented). Asian 2%, African American 5%, Caucasian 78%, Hispanic 6%, Native American <1%, Pacific Islander <1%, Two or more races 5%, Race unknown 2%.
Retention and Graduation: 83% freshmen return for sophomore year. 61% freshmen graduate within 4 years. 65% freshmen graduate within 6 years. 21% grads go on to further study within 1 year. 11% grads pursue arts and sciences degrees. 2% grads pursue law degrees. 4% grads pursue business degrees. 1% grads pursue medical degrees. **Faculty:** Student/faculty ratio 15:1. 329 full-time faculty, 82% hold PhDs, 12% are members of minority groups, 49% are women. 0% of classes are taught by teaching assistants.

ACADEMICS
Degrees: Bachelor's; Doctoral degree—professional practice; Doctoral degree research/scholarship; Master's; Post-bachelor's certificate. **Classes:** Most classes have 10–19 students. Most lab/discussion sessions have 20–29 students. **Most popular majors:** Communication and Media Studies; Exercise Science and Kinesiology; Business Administration and Management, General. **Special Study Options:** Cross-registration; Distance learning; Double major; English as a Second Language (ESL); Honors program; Independent study; Internships; Student-designed major; Study abroad; Teacher certification program. **Honors programs:** Established in 1985, the Honors Scholar Program at High Point University is now home to 300+ student scholars dedicated to pursuing intellectual curiosity and educational excellence. Honors students engage in multidisciplinary, collaborative project-based learning experiences throughout their courses and co-curriculum, and they reside for their first two years in a living-learning community in Finch Hall, forging meaningful relationships with one another both inside and outside the classroom. **Combined degree programs:** BA/MA. **Disability Services offered:** Note-taking services; Reader services; Tape recorders; Tutors. **Career services:** Alumni network; Alumni services; Career assessment; Career/job search classes; Internships; Regional alumni.

FACILITIES
Housing: Apartments for single students; Coed dorms; Fraternity/sorority housing; Men's dorms; Special housing for disabled students; Theme housing; Wellness housing; Women's dorms; 98% of campus accessible to physically disabled. **Special Academic Facilities/Equipment:** planetarium, center for

student success, biomechanics lab, conservatory (under construction), arena (under construction), full-size TV studio, interactive media and game design lab, live stock ticker room **Campus Network:** 100% of classrooms, 100% of dorms, 100% of student union, 100% of libraries, 100% of dining areas, 75% of common outdoor areas, have wireless network access.

CAMPUS LIFE
Environment: City. **Activities:** Campus Ministries; Choral groups; Concert band; Dance; Drama/theater; International Student Organization; Jazz band; Literary magazine; Model UN; Music ensembles; Musical theater; Opera; Pep band; Radio station; Student government; Student newspaper; Student-run film society; Symphony orchestra; Television station; Yearbook. 139 registered organizations, 23 honor societies, 6 religious organizations, 6 fraternities, 10 sororities, on campus. **Athletics (Intercollegiate):** *Men:* baseball, basketball, cheerleading, cross-country, golf, soccer, tennis, track/field (outdoor), track/field (indoor). *Women:* basketball, cheerleading, cross-country, golf, soccer, tennis, track/field (outdoor), track/field (indoor), volleyball. **On-Campus Highlights:** Wanek University Center. **Environmental Initiatives:** Arboreatum and Tree Campus USA.

ADMISSIONS
Freshman Academic Profile: Average high school GPA 3.3. 17% in top 10% of high school class, 43% in top 25% of high school class, 73% in top 50% of high school class. 61% from public high schools. **Test scores:** SAT Math middle 50% range 540–630. SAT EBRW middle 50% range 550–630. ACT middle 50% range 22–28. **Basis for Candidate Selection:** *Very important factors include:* academic GPA. *Important factors include:* rigor of secondary school record, application essay, standardized test scores, recommendation(s), interview, extracurricular activities, talent/ability, character/personal qualities, volunteer work. *Other factors include:* class rank, first generation, alumni/ae relation. **Freshman Admission Requirements:** High school diploma is required and GED is accepted. *Academic units required:* 4 English, 3 math, 3 science, 1 science labs, 2 foreign language, 3 social studies. *Academic units recommended:* 4 English, 4 math, 3 science, 1 science labs, 3 foreign language, 3 social studies. **Freshman Admission Statistics:** 11,298 applied, 75% admitted, 17% enrolled. **Transfer Admission Requirements:** High school transcript, college transcript(s), standardized test scores, statement of good standing from prior institution(s). Minimum college GPA of 2.0 required. Lowest grade transferable C. **General Admission Information:** Application fee $50. Priority deadline 11/15. Regular application deadline 3/1. Non-fall registration accepted. Admission may be deferred for a maximum of 1 year.

COSTS AND FINANCIAL AID
Annual tuition $31,768. Room and board $14,702. Required fees $4,500. Average book and supplies expense $1,500. **Required Forms and Deadlines:** FAFSA; State aid form. **Notification of Awards:** Applicants will be notified of awards on a rolling basis beginning 4/1. **Types of Aid:** *Need-based scholarships/ grants:* College/university scholarship or grant aid from institutional funds; Federal Pell; Private scholarships; SEOG; State scholarships/grants. *Loans:* Direct PLUS loans; Direct Subsidized Stafford Loans; Direct Unsubsidized Stafford Loans. **Student Employment:** Federal Work-Study Program available. Institutional employment available. **Financial Aid Statistics:** 100% needy freshmen, 99% needy undergrads receive need-based scholarship or grant aid. 90% freshmen, 84% undergrads receive non-need-based scholarship or grant aid. 69% freshmen, 75% undergrads receive need-based self-help aid. 3% freshmen, 3% undergrads receive athletic scholarships. 89% freshmen, 84% undergrads receive any aid. 47% undergrads borrow to pay for school. Average cumulative indebtedness $34,079. **Criteria awarding aid:** *Non-Need-based:* Academics, Alumni affiliation, Art, Athletics, Leadership, Music/drama, Religious affiliation, State/district residency.

HILBERT COLLEGE

5200 South Park Avenue, Hamburg, NY 14075-1597
Phone: 716-649-7900 **Financial Aid Phone:** 716-649-7900
E-mail: admissions@hilbert.edu **CEEB Code:** 2334
Fax: 716-649-0702 **Website:** www.hilbert.edu **ACT Code:** 2759

This private school, affiliated with the Roman Catholic Church, was founded in 1957. It has a 40 acre campus.

RATINGS
Admissions Selectivity Rating: 74 **Fire Safety Rating:** 93 **Green Rating:** 60*

STUDENTS AND FACULTY
Enrollment: 998. **Student Body:** 60% female, 40% male, 10% out-of-state, <1% international (4 countries represented). Asian <1%, African American 6%, Caucasian 82%, Hispanic 2%, Native American 2%, Race unknown 7%. **Retention and Graduation:** 70% freshmen return for sophomore year. 15% grads go on to further study within 1 year. 4% grads pursue arts and sciences degrees. 4% grads pursue law degrees. 4% grads pursue business degrees. 0% grads pursue medical degrees. **Faculty:** Student/faculty ratio 13:1. 48 full-time faculty, 50% hold PhDs, 2% are members of minority groups, 48% are women. 0% of classes are taught by teaching assistants.

ACADEMICS
Degrees: Associate; Bachelor's; Certificate; Terminal Associate. **Classes:** Most classes have 10–19 students. Most lab/discussion sessions have fewer than 10 students. **Most popular majors:** Business/Commerce, General; Criminal Justice/Law Enforcement Administration. **Special Study Options:** Cross-registration; Distance learning; Dual enrollment; Honors program; Independent study; Internships; Study abroad. **Honors programs:** The Hilbert Honors Program will give you more from your college experience. You will enroll in regular classes and fulfill honors credit requirements by doing advanced work, or in lieu of projects. These special projects allow you to work one-on-one with Hilbert's outstanding honors faculty in your major and in other academic areas. As an honors student, you will also have a student mentor for your first semester and personal faculty advisement. **Disability Services offered:** Note-taking services; Reader services; Tape recorders; Tutors. **Career services:** Alumni network; Alumni services; Career assessment; Internships.

FACILITIES
Housing: Apartments for single students; Coed dorms 95% of campus accessible to physically disabled. **Special Academic Facilities/Equipment:** Honors Lounge, Institute for Law and Justice, Center for Creative Media, **Campus Network:** 100% of classrooms, 100% of dorms, 100% of student union, 100% of libraries, 100% of dining areas, 100% of common outdoor areas, have wireless network access.

CAMPUS LIFE
Environment: Village. **Activities:** Campus Ministries; Choral groups; Drama/theater; Literary magazine; Student government; Student newspaper. 20 registered organizations, 5 honor societies, 1 religious organizations, on campus. **Athletics (Intercollegiate):** *Men:* baseball, basketball, cross-country, golf, soccer, volleyball. *Women:* basketball, cross-country, golf, soccer, softball, volleyball. **On-Campus Highlights:** Hafner Recreation Center.

ADMISSIONS
Freshman Academic Profile: Average high school GPA 2.8. 2% in top 10% of high school class, 13% in top 25% of high school class, 40% in top 50% of high school class. 85% from public high schools. **Test scores:** SAT Math middle 50% range 400–510. SAT EBRW middle 50% range 400–510. ACT middle 50% range 17–22. **Basis for Candidate Selection:** *Very important factors include:* rigor of secondary school record, academic GPA. *Important factors include:* recommendation(s). *Other factors include:* application essay, interview, extracurricular activities, talent/ability, character/personal qualities, volunteer work, work experience. **Freshman Admission Requirements:** High school diploma is required and GED is accepted. *Academic units required:* 4 English, 2 math, 2 science, 1 science labs, 2 social studies, 2 history, 4 academic electives. *Academic units recommended:* 4 English, 3 math, 3 science, 1 foreign language, 3 social studies, 3 history, 3 academic electives. **Freshman Admission Statistics:** 726 applied, 85% admitted, 35% enrolled. **Transfer Admission Requirements:** High school transcript, college transcript(s), Minimum college GPA of 2.0 required. Lowest grade transferable C. **General Admission Information:** Application fee $20. Priority deadline 6/3. Regular application deadline 9/1. Non-fall registration accepted. Admission may be deferred for a maximum of 1 year.

COSTS AND FINANCIAL AID
Annual tuition $16,000. Room and board $6,600. Required fees $600. Average book and supplies expense $700. **Required Forms and Deadlines:** FAFSA; State aid form. **Notification of Awards:** Applicants will be notified of awards on a rolling basis beginning 3/1. **Types of Aid:** *Need-based scholarships/grants:* College/university scholarship or grant aid from institutional funds; Federal Pell; Private scholarships; SEOG; State scholarships/grants. **Student Employment:** Federal Work-Study Program available. Institutional employment available. **Financial Aid Statistics:** 99% needy freshmen, 98% needy undergrads receive need-based scholarship or grant aid. 4% freshmen, 5% undergrads receive non-need-based scholarship or grant aid. 90% freshmen, 88% undergrads receive need-based self-help aid. 0% freshmen, 0% undergrads receive athletic scholarships. 92% freshmen, 87% undergrads receive any aid. **Criteria awarding aid:** *Non-Need-based:* Academics, Leadership, Minority status.

HILLSDALE COLLEGE

33 East College Street, Hillsdale, MI 49242
Phone: 517-607-2327 **Financial Aid Phone:** 517-607-2350
E-mail: admissions@hillsdale.edu **CEEB Code:** 1295
Fax: 517-607-2223 **Website:** www.hillsdale.edu **ACT Code:** 2010

This private school, affiliated with the Christian (Nondenominational) Church, was founded in 1844. It has a 400 acre campus.

RATINGS
Admissions Selectivity Rating: 92   **Fire Safety Rating:** 91   **Green Rating:** 62

STUDENTS AND FACULTY
Enrollment: 1,454. **Student Body:** 49% female, 51% male, 69% out-of-state, 0% international (10 countries represented). Asian 0%, African American 0%, Caucasian 0%, Hispanic 0%, Native American 0%, Pacific Islander 0%, Two or more races 0%, Race unknown 100%.
Retention and Graduation: 96% freshmen return for sophomore year. 74% freshmen graduate within 4 years. 86% freshmen graduate within 6 years. 22% grads go on to further study within 1 year. 17% grads pursue arts and sciences degrees. 1% grads pursue law degrees. 3% grads pursue business degrees. 1% grads pursue medical degrees. **Faculty:** Student/faculty ratio 9:1. 146 full-time faculty, 92% hold PhDs, 0% are members of minority groups, 25% are women. 0% of classes are taught by teaching assistants.

ACADEMICS
Degrees: Bachelor's; Doctoral degree research/scholarship; Master's. **Classes:** Most classes have fewer than 10 students. Most lab/discussion sessions have 10–19 students. **Most popular majors:** Economics, General; History, General; English Language and Literature, General. **Special Study Options:** Double major; Dual enrollment; Honors program; Independent study; Internships; Student-designed major; Study abroad. **Honors programs:** The Collegiate Scholars program provides highly motivated students, who have demonstrated academic excellence at Hillsdale College, with an enhanced program of study that reinforces the highest ideals of the college's core curriculum. Students selected to be Collegiate Scholars benefit from small, interdisciplinary seminars giving close attention to the authors and works covered more generally in the core. These scholars serve the campus community by reaching beyond specialization to help bind the campus together within a common conversation about liberal arts education and the life of the mind. Foreign travel after the junior year widens the experience even further, and a senior thesis provides exceptional experience in crafting a well-researched, well-written argument defended before a faculty committee and a college audience. **Disability Services offered:** Tape recorders; Tutors. **Career services:** Alumni network; Alumni services; Career assessment; Internships; Regional alumni.

FACILITIES
Housing: Apartments for single students; Cooperative housing; Fraternity/sorority housing; Men's dorms; Women's dorms; 85% of campus accessible to physically disabled. **Special Academic Facilities/Equipment:** Greenhouse, Sage Center for the Arts, Howard Music Hall, media center, K-8 private academy, Slayton Arboretum, rare books library, shooting range, Herbert Henry Dow Science Building, Daniel M. Fisk Museum of Natural History, Strosaker Science Center, Mary Randall Preschool, Hayden Park, Golf simulator, JAM wieght room, Mauck Solarium. **Campus Network:** 100% of classrooms, 100% of dorms, 100% of student union, 100% of libraries, 100% of dining areas, 100% of common outdoor areas, have wireless network access.

CAMPUS LIFE
Environment: Village. **Activities:** Campus Ministries; Choral groups; Concert band; Dance; Drama/theater; International Student Organization; Jazz band; Literary magazine; Music ensembles; Musical theater; Opera; Pep band; Radio station; Student government; Student newspaper; Student-run film society; Symphony orchestra; Yearbook. 117 registered organizations, 24 honor societies, 9 religious organizations, 4 fraternities, 3 sororities, on campus. **Athletics (Intercollegiate):** *Men:* baseball, basketball, cheerleading, cross-country, football, track/field (outdoor), track/field (indoor). *Women:* basketball, cheerleading, cross-country, diving, equestrian sports, softball, swimming, track/field (outdoor), track/field (indoor), volleyball. **On-Campus Highlights:** Student Union.

ADMISSIONS
Freshman Academic Profile: Average high school GPA 3.9. 45% from public high schools. **Test scores:** SAT Math middle 50% range 640–730. SAT EBRW middle 50% range 660–740. ACT middle 50% range 29–33. **Basis for Candidate Selection:** *Very important factors include:* rigor of secondary school record, academic GPA, application essay, standardized test scores, interview, extracurricular activities, character/personal qualities, level of applicant's interest. *Important factors include:* recommendation(s), volunteer work. *Other factors include:* talent/ability, alumni/ae relation. **Freshman Admission Requirements:** High school diploma is required and GED is accepted. *Academic units required:* 4 English, 3 math, 3 science, 2 social studies, 3 history. *Academic units recommended:* 4 English, 4 math, 4 science, 2 science labs, 3 foreign language, 4 social studies, 4 history. **Freshman Admission Statistics:** 1,593 applied, 48% admitted, 45% enrolled. **Transfer Admission Requirements:** High school transcript, college transcript(s), essay or personal statement, standardized test scores, statement of good standing from prior institution(s). Minimum college GPA of 3.25 required. Lowest grade transferable C. **General Admission Information:** Application fee $35. Priority deadline 1/1. Regular application deadline 4/1. Non-fall registration accepted.

COSTS AND FINANCIAL AID
Annual tuition $27,090. Room and board $11,390. Required fees $1,278. Average book and supplies expense $1,200. **Required Forms and Deadlines:** Institution's own financial aid form. **Types of Aid:** *Need-based scholarships/grants:* College/university scholarship or grant aid from institutional funds; Private scholarships. **Student Employment:** Institutional employment available. **Financial Aid Statistics:** 59% needy freshmen, 66% needy undergrads receive need-based scholarship or grant aid. 86% freshmen, 83% undergrads receive non-need-based scholarship or grant aid. 55% freshmen, 65% undergrads receive need-based self-help aid. 19% freshmen, 17% undergrads receive athletic scholarships. 99% freshmen, 96% undergrads receive any aid. 45% undergrads borrow to pay for school. Average cumulative indebtedness $32,198. **Criteria awarding aid:** *Non-Need-based:* Academics, Alumni affiliation, Art, Athletics, Leadership, Music/drama.

HIRAM COLLEGE

PO Box 96, Hiram, OH 44234
Phone: 330-569-5169 **Financial Aid Phone:** (330) 569-5107
E-mail: admission@hiram.edu **CEEB Code:** 1297
Fax: 330-569-5944 **Website:** www.hiram.edu **ACT Code:** 3280

This private school, affiliated with the Disciples of Christ Church, was founded in 1850. It has a 110 acre campus.

RATINGS
Admissions Selectivity Rating: 81   **Fire Safety Rating:** 60*   **Green Rating:** 60*

STUDENTS AND FACULTY
Enrollment: 896. **Student Body:** 56% female, 44% male, 21% out-of-state, 1% international (11 countries represented). Asian 2%, African American 19%, Caucasian 58%, Hispanic 6%, Native American <1%, Pacific Islander <1%, Two or more races 4%, Race unknown 10%.
Retention and Graduation: 68% freshmen return for sophomore year. 45% freshmen graduate within 4 years. 54% freshmen graduate within 6 years.

Faculty: Student/faculty ratio 12:1. 64 full-time faculty, 89% hold PhDs, 9% are members of minority groups, 58% are women. 0% of classes are taught by teaching assistants.

ACADEMICS

Degrees: Bachelor's; Master's. **Classes:** Most classes have 10–19 students. Most lab/discussion sessions have fewer than 10 students. **Most popular majors:** Registered Nursing/Registered Nurse; Business Administration and Management, General; Accounting and Finance. **Special Study Options:** Accelerated program; Cross-registration; Distance learning; Double major; Dual enrollment; English as a Second Language (ESL); Exchange student program (domestic); Honors program; Independent study; Internships; Liberal arts/career combination; Student-designed major; Study abroad; Teacher certification program; Weekend college. **Honors programs:** The Hiram College Eclectic Scholars Program aims to serve committed, self-motivated, intellectually curious students with an enriched undergraduate liberal arts education. Toward this end, it provides opportunities for creative, interdisciplinary scholarship; intimate interactions with renowned scholars in Hiram's Centers of Distinction; and professional career development. **Disability Services offered:** Note-taking services; Tutors. **Career services:** Alumni network; Alumni services; Career assessment; Career/job search classes; Internships.

FACILITIES

Housing: Apartments for single students; Coed dorms; Special housing for disabled students; Special housing for international students; Theme housing; Women's dorms; 55% of campus accessible to physically disabled. **Special Academic Facilities/Equipment:** James H. Barrow Field Station, Northwoods Field Station, Stephens Memorial Observatory **Campus Network:** 100% of classrooms, 100% of dorms, 100% of student union, 100% of libraries, 100% of dining areas, 10% of common outdoor areas, have wireless network access.

CAMPUS LIFE

Environment: Rural. **Activities:** Campus Ministries; Choral groups; Concert band; Dance; Drama/theater; International Student Organization; Jazz band; Literary magazine; Model UN; Music ensembles; Musical theater; Opera; Pep band; Student government; Symphony orchestra. 40 registered organizations, 7 honor societies, 2 religious organizations, 3 sororities, on campus. **Athletics (Intercollegiate):** *Men:* baseball, basketball, cheerleading, cross-country, diving, football, golf, soccer, swimming, tennis, track/field (outdoor), track/field (indoor). *Women:* basketball, cheerleading, cross-country, diving, golf, soccer, softball, swimming, tennis, track/field (outdoor), track/field (indoor), volleyball. **On-Campus Highlights:** James H. Barrow Field Station.

ADMISSIONS

Freshman Academic Profile: Average high school GPA 3.3. 12% in top 10% of high school class, 27% in top 25% of high school class, 52% in top 50% of high school class. **Test scores:** SAT Math middle 50% range 430–573. SAT EBRW middle 50% range 430–580. ACT middle 50% range 18–25. **Basis for Candidate Selection:** *Very important factors include:* rigor of secondary school record, academic GPA, character/personal qualities, level of applicant's interest. *Important factors include:* application essay, interview, extracurricular activities, talent/ability. *Other factors include:* class rank, standardized test scores, recommendation(s), alumni/ae relation, volunteer work, work experience. **Freshman Admission Requirements:** High school diploma is required and GED is accepted. *Academic units required:* 4 English, 4 math, 3 science, 1 science labs, 1 foreign language, 1 social studies, 1 history, 1 academic electives. *Academic units recommended:* 4 English, 4 math, 3 science, 1 science labs, 2 foreign language, 1 social studies, 1 history, 2 academic electives. **Freshman Admission Statistics:** 2,834 applied, 60% admitted, 13% enrolled. **General Admission Information:** Non-fall registration accepted. Admission may be deferred for a maximum of 1 year.

COSTS AND FINANCIAL AID

Annual tuition $24,500. Room and board $10,290. Average book and supplies expense $800. **Required Forms and Deadlines:** FAFSA. **Types of Aid:** *Need-based scholarships/grants:* College/university scholarship or grant aid from institutional funds; Federal Pell; Private scholarships; SEOG; State scholarships/grants. *Loans:* Direct PLUS loans; Direct Subsidized Stafford Loans; Direct Unsubsidized Stafford Loans. **Student Employment:** Federal Work-Study Program available. Institutional employment available. **Financial Aid Statistics:** 100% needy freshmen, 99% needy undergrads receive need-based scholarship or grant aid. 4% freshmen, 5% undergrads receive non-need-based scholarship or grant aid. 92% freshmen, 90% undergrads receive need-based self-help aid. 0% freshmen, 0% undergrads receive athletic scholarships. 75% undergrads borrow to pay for school. Average cumulative indebtedness $37,771. **Criteria awarding aid:** *Non-Need-based:* Academics, Alumni affiliation, Art, Music/drama, Religious affiliation.

HOBART AND WILLIAM SMITH COLLEGES

629 South Main Street, Geneva, NY 14456
Phone: 315-781-3622 **Financial Aid Phone:** (315) 781-3315
E-mail: admissions@hws.edu **CEEB Code:** 2294
Fax: 315-781-3914 **Website:** www.hws.edu **ACT Code:** 2758

This private school was founded in 1822. It has a 320 acre campus.

RATINGS

Admissions Selectivity Rating: 86   **Fire Safety Rating:** 96   **Green Rating:** 91

STUDENTS AND FACULTY

Enrollment: 2,036. **Student Body:** 52% female, 48% male, 61% out-of-state, 5% international (34 countries represented). Asian 3%, African American 6%, Caucasian 73%, Hispanic 6%, Native American <1%, Pacific Islander <1%, Two or more races 2%, Race unknown 4%.
Retention and Graduation: 88% freshmen return for sophomore year. 73% freshmen graduate within 4 years. 77% freshmen graduate within 6 years.
Faculty: Student/faculty ratio 10:1. 203 full-time faculty, 98% hold PhDs, 20% are members of minority groups, 48% are women. 0% of classes are taught by teaching assistants.

ACADEMICS

Degrees: Bachelor's; Master's. **Classes:** Most classes have 10–19 students. Most lab/discussion sessions have fewer than 10 students. **Most popular majors:** Mass Communication/Media Studies; Biology/Biological Sciences, General; Economics, General. **Special Study Options:** Double major; English as a Second Language (ESL); Honors program; Independent study; Internships; Student-designed major; Study abroad; Teacher certification program. **Honors programs:** The Honors Program at Hobart and William Smith Colleges makes possible the most sustained and sophisticated work available for juniors and seniors in the HWS curriculum. It affords students the opportunity to pursue skills and interests at the advanced level and grow in self-knowledge as their project develops. It also can greatly assist students in pursuing their professional ambitions after graduation. **Combined degree programs:** BA/MA. **Disability Services offered:** Note-taking services; Reader services; Tape recorders; Tutors. **Career services:** Alumni network; Alumni services; Career assessment; Career/job search classes; Internships; Regional alumni.

FACILITIES

Housing: Apartments for married students; Apartments for single students; Coed dorms; Cooperative housing; Fraternity/sorority housing; Men's dorms; Special housing for disabled students; Special housing for international students; Theme housing; Wellness housing; Women's dorms; **Special Academic Facilities/Equipment:** The Gearan Center for the Performing Arts, Davis Gallery at Houghton House, William Scandling research vessel, Melly Academic Center, Rosenberg science center, Finger Lakes Institute, Centennial Center for Leadership, Richard S. Perkin Observatory (a teaching and outreach facility), 100 acre Hanley Nature Preserve, HWS solar farms and the HWS Fribolin Farm. **Campus Network:** 100% of classrooms, 100% of dorms, 100% of student union, 100% of libraries, 100% of dining areas, 10% of common outdoor areas, have wireless network access.

CAMPUS LIFE

Environment: Village. **Activities:** Campus Ministries; Choral groups; Concert band; Dance; Drama/theater; International Student Organization; Jazz band; Literary magazine; Music ensembles; Radio station; Student government; Student newspaper; Student-run film society. 112 registered organizations, 12 honor societies, 1 religious organizations, 6 fraternities, 1 sororities, on campus. **Athletics (Intercollegiate):** *Men:* basketball, crew/rowing, cross-country, football, golf, ice hockey, lacrosse, sailing, soccer, squash, tennis. *Women:* basketball, crew/rowing, cross-country, diving, field hockey, golf, lacrosse, sailing, soccer, squash, swimming, tennis. **On-Campus Highlights:** Scandling Campus Center. **Environmental Initiatives:** Integrating the Colleges' Sustainability "living laboratory" approach in the Climate Action Plan. The living laboratory approach is exemplified through student projects—class, independent study or service work that directly effect the Colleges' impact on the environment and culture of environmental sustainability. For example, The Finger Lakes Institute's renovation was directed by a first-year Energy class project that identified specific environmental parameters to be incorporated into the building. These students' vision and project qualified the Finger Lakes Institute for the Energy Star Small Business Award. This living laboratory, student-oriented learning approach is at the core of the Colleges' Sustainability Program and enhanced by the Colleges' Climate Action Plan.

ADMISSIONS

Freshman Academic Profile: Average high school GPA 3.5. 33% in top 10% of high school class, 63% in top 25% of high school class, 90% in top 50% of high school class. 65% from public high schools. **Test score**s: SAT Math middle 50% range 590–690. SAT EBRW middle 50% range 590–670. ACT middle 50% range 26–30. **Basis for Candidate Selection:** *Very important factors include:* rigor of secondary school record, academic GPA. *Important factors include:* application essay, recommendation(s), interview, extracurricular activities. *Other factors include:* class rank, character/personal qualities, alumni/ae relation, geographical residence, state residency, religious affiliation/commitment, racial/ethnic status, level of applicant's interest. **Freshman Admission Requirements:** High school diploma is required and GED is accepted. *Academic units required:* 4 English, 3 math, 3 science, 2 science labs, 2 foreign language, 2 social studies, 2 academic electives. *Academic units recommended:* 3 foreign language, 3 social studies, 4 academic electives. **Freshman Admission Statistics:** 3,439 applied, 66% admitted, 20% enrolled. **Transfer Admission Requirements:** High school transcript, college transcript(s), essay or personal statement, standardized test scores, Minimum college GPA of 2.5 required. Lowest grade transferable C. **General Admission Information:** Regular application deadline 2/1. Non-fall registration accepted.

COSTS AND FINANCIAL AID

Annual tuition $55,835. Room and board $14,570. Average book and supplies expense $1,300. **Required Forms and Deadlines:** CSS/Financial Aid PROFILE; FAFSA; Noncustodial PROFILE; State aid form. **Notification of Awards:** Applicants will be notified of awards on or about 4/1. **Types of Aid:** *Need-based scholarships/grants:* College/university scholarship or grant aid from institutional funds; Federal Pell; Private scholarships; SEOG; State scholarships/grants. *Loans:* Direct PLUS loans; Direct Subsidized Stafford Loans; Direct Unsubsidized Stafford Loans. **Student Employment:** Federal Work-Study Program available. Institutional employment available. **Financial Aid Statistics:** 100% needy freshmen, 100% needy undergrads receive need-based scholarship or grant aid. 19% freshmen, 18% undergrads receive non-need-based scholarship or grant aid. 79% freshmen, 80% undergrads receive need-based self-help aid. 0% freshmen, 0% undergrads receive athletic scholarships. 89% freshmen, 86.5% undergrads receive any aid. 72% undergrads borrow to pay for school. Average cumulative indebtedness $36,561. **Criteria awarding aid:** *Need-based:* Academics, Alumni affiliation, Art, Leadership, Music/drama, Religious affiliation. *Non-Need-based:* Academics, Alumni affiliation, Art, Leadership, Music/drama, Religious affiliation.

HODGES UNIVERSITY

2655 Northbrooke Drive, Naples, FL 34119
Phone: 239-513-1122 **Financial Aid Phone:** 239-513-1122
E-mail: admit@internationalcollege.edu **CEEB Code:** 7113
Fax: 239-598-6254 **Website:** www.hodges.edu **ACT Code:** 4775

This private school was founded in 1990.

RATINGS

Admissions Selectivity Rating: 70 **Fire Safety Rating:** 60* **Green Rating:** 60*

STUDENTS AND FACULTY

Enrollment: 1,475. **Student Body:** 68% female, 32% male, <1% out-of-state, <1% international (40 countries represented). Asian 2%, African American 16%, Caucasian 55%, Hispanic 24%, Native American <1%, Race unknown 2%.
Faculty: Student/faculty ratio 17:1. 61 full-time faculty, 66% hold PhDs, 8% are members of minority groups, 33% are women. 0% of classes are taught by teaching assistants.

ACADEMICS

Degrees: Associate; Bachelor's; Certificate; Master's. **Classes:** Most classes have 10–19 students. **Most popular majors:** Multi-/Interdisciplinary Studies, Other; Health Professions and Related Clinical Sciences, Other; Business, Management, Marketing, and Related Support Services, Other. **Special Study Options:** Accelerated program; Cooperative education program; Distance learning; Double major; English as a Second Language (ESL); Independent

study; Internships; Weekend college. **Career services:** Alumni services; Career assessment; Career/job search classes.

FACILITIES

Housing: Coed dorms 100% of campus accessible to physically disabled.
Campus Network: 0% of classrooms, 0% of dorms, 100% of student union, 50% of libraries, 100% of dining areas, 30% of common outdoor areas, have wireless network access.

CAMPUS LIFE

Environment: City. **Activities:** Dance; Drama/theater; International Student Organization; Model UN; Musical theater; Radio station; Student government; Student newspaper; Yearbook. 1 honor societies, on campus. **Environmental Initiatives:** Reduction in energy usage

ADMISSIONS

Basis for Candidate Selection: *Important factors include:* interview, level of applicant's interest. **Freshman Admission Requirements:** High school diploma is required and GED is accepted. **Freshman Admission Statistics:** 210 applied, 79% admitted, 94% enrolled. **Transfer Admission Requirements:** High school transcript, essay or personal statement, Lowest grade transferable C. **General Admission Information:** Application fee $20. Non-fall registration accepted. Admission may be deferred for a maximum of 1 year.

COSTS AND FINANCIAL AID

Required Forms and Deadlines: FAFSA. **Types of Aid:** *Need-based scholarships/grants:* College/university scholarship or grant aid from institutional funds; Federal Pell; Private scholarships; SEOG; State scholarships/grants. **Student Employment:** Federal Work-Study Program available. Institutional employment available. **Financial Aid Statistics:** 90% needy freshmen, 94% needy undergrads receive need-based scholarship or grant aid. 41% freshmen, 66% undergrads receive non-need-based scholarship or grant aid. 87% freshmen, 91% undergrads receive need-based self-help aid. 0% freshmen, 0% undergrads receive athletic scholarships. **Criteria awarding aid:** *Non-Need-based:* Academics, Leadership.

HOFSTRA UNIVERSITY

100 Hofstra University, Hempstead, NY 11549
Phone: 516-463-6700 **Financial Aid Phone:** 516-463-8000
E-mail: admission@hofstra.edu **CEEB Code:** 2295
Fax: 516-463-5100 **Website:** http://www.hofstra.edu **ACT Code:** 2760

This private school was founded in 1935. It has a 244 acre campus.

RATINGS

Admissions Selectivity Rating: 85 **Fire Safety Rating:** 98 **Green Rating:** 88

STUDENTS AND FACULTY

Enrollment: 6,400. **Student Body:** 55% female, 45% male, 37% out-of-state, 5% international (77 countries represented). Asian 12%, African American 9%, Caucasian 55%, Hispanic 13%, Native American <1%, Pacific Islander <1%, Two or more races 3%, Race unknown 2%.
Retention and Graduation: 83% freshmen return for sophomore year. 55% freshmen graduate within 4 years. 65% freshmen graduate within 6 years. 29% grads go on to further study within 1 year. 4% grads pursue arts and sciences degrees. 2% grads pursue law degrees. 5% grads pursue business degrees. 1% grads pursue medical degrees. **Faculty:** Student/faculty ratio 13:1. 485 full-time faculty, 92% hold PhDs, 21% are members of minority groups, 46% are women. 0% of classes are taught by teaching assistants.

ACADEMICS

Degrees: Bachelor's; Certificate; Doctoral degree—professional practice; Doctoral degree research/scholarship; Master's; Post-bachelor's certificate; Post-master's certificate. **Classes:** Most classes have 10–19 students. Most lab/discussion sessions have 10–19 students. **Most popular majors:** Psychology, General; Finance, General; Biology/Biological Sciences, General. **Special Study Options:** Accelerated program; Cooperative education program; Cross-registration; Distance learning; Double major; Dual enrollment; English as a Second Language (ESL); External degree program; Honors program; Independent study; Internships; Liberal arts/career combination;

Student-designed major; Study abroad; Teacher certification program. **Honors programs:** Hofstra University's Honors College (HUHC) is the leading edge of Hofstra's pursuit of academic excellence. We enrich the education of exceptional students both inside the classroom and beyond by promoting intellectual engagement, creativity, conversation, leadership, civic responsibility and global reach. In short, HUHC serves and challenges students in ways that radiate throughout their undergraduate careers and across the entire Hofstra community. HUHC's highly flexible curriculum maps onto all degree plans. As a result, HUHC students are diverse in personal backgrounds and in their intellectual interests, coming from every major and school at Hofstra. This flexibility allows students to tailor their honors work to fit their passions and interests. It includes a unique sequence of first year courses (called Culture and Expression), small, discussion-based honors seminars, and the opportunity to turn any regular course into an honors experience via our Honors Option Program. Beyond the classroom, HUHC faculty mentors sponsor a rich array of cultural and social experiences, including opportunities to enjoy regular trips to New York City to visit museums, Broadway shows, concerts, lectures, and major league sporting events. Many HUHC students opt to live in honors housing, where they enjoy an even greater sense of community and an exceptional level of support from professional staff and student leaders. HUHC students are student government leaders, newspaper editors, and champions of social and political causes. They are committed to the arts and to sports (including some 40 Division I athletes in a variety of sports) and can be found in leadership roles in just about every student club or program imaginable. They come from all across the United States, and increasingly, from abroad as well. Most of all, they are curious about one another and the wider world. HUHC students are regularly admitted to the most competitive law, medical, graduate and other professional schools. Several have won Fulbright and National Science fellowships. For the most recent graduating class, 79% of HUHC students undertake one or more internships before graduation, many of which lead directly into full-time positions after graduation. Among our 2017–2018 Honors College graduates who earned a Bachelor's degree, 95% of the respondent's report that within one year of graduation they were employed (83%) or attending/plan to attend graduate school (39%). Outcomes are based on the 88% of 2017–2018 Hofstra University Honors College undergraduate degree recipients who responded to a survey or for whom data was gathered from LinkedIn within one year of graduation. All students who qualify for admission to HUHC are also recipients of Hofstra's Merit-Based Presidential Scholarships of approximately $20,000 or more depending on their high school record. Students whose achievements place them among the top 5% of applicants may be named Trustee Scholars. Trustee Scholars receive full tuition and additional privileges. Outside of Honors College (HUHC), each academic department has a listing for a capstone course that allows a student with a minimum GPA of 3.5 in the major and 3.4 overall to pursue Departmental Honors through the completion of a supervised advanced research or creative project and its subsequent presentation (or 'defense') before the department of committee, which can then award departmental Honors or High Honors. The awarded designation is noted on the transcript and at commencement. This form of capstone project for Departmental Honors is central to the Undergraduate Research program at Hofstra, though it does not encompass all of undergraduate research, which might also be done in other discrete courses, with topical or research listings, or as an independent study. Further, individual disciplines support Hofstra chapters of national honor societies. These honor organizations sponsor events which include lectures, seminars, workshops, social events, open meetings, department activities, group discussions, field trips, exhibitions, and demonstrations. **Combined degree programs:** BA/JD; BA/MA; BA/MD. **Disability Services offered:** Note-taking services; Reader services; Tape recorders; Tutors. **Career services:** Alumni network; Alumni services; Career assessment; Career/job search classes; Internships; Regional alumni.

FACILITIES

Housing: Apartments for single students; Coed dorms; Special housing for disabled students; Special housing for international students; Theme housing; Wellness housing 100% of campus accessible to physically disabled. **Special Academic Facilities/Equipment:** New state of the art Zarb School of Business building with Center for Entrepreneurship (IdeaHUb & Incubator), a behavioral science in business lab, and Cybersecurity Innovation and Research Center. Engineering labs including: Cell and Tissue Engineering Lab, Civil/Environmental Engineering Lab, Applied Science Production Studio, Electrical and Signal Processing Lab, Engineering Computer Lab, Aerodynamics & Transport Phenomena Lab, First Year Engineering Lab/Technology & Public Policy Forensic Analysis Lab, Materials Analysis Lab, Robotics and Advanced Manufacturing Lab, Thermodynamics Lab, Advanced Manufacturing Lab, and Ultrasound Research Lab. School of Medicine Structural/Anatomy Lab

Occupational Therapy Lab Biology Collaboratorium The Martin B. Greenberg Trading Room — access and analyze a vast array of financial and economic data, apply analytical methods Center for Academic Excellence Student Learning Hub Center for Innovation 4K Ultra High Definition Cameras (School of Communication television studio) Professional Film Audio Editing/Mixing Suite Film Screening Room/Theater WRHU Radio Station facility Joan & Donald Schaeffer Black Box Theater Shakespearean Globe Theatre Stage located in the recently renovated and expanded Adams Playhouse Hofstra Museum. **Campus Network:** 100% of classrooms, 100% of dorms, 100% of student union, 100% of libraries, 100% of dining areas, 50% of common outdoor areas, have wireless network access.

CAMPUS LIFE

Environment: City. **Activities:** Campus Ministries; Choral groups; Concert band; Dance; Drama/theater; Jazz band; Literary magazine; Model UN; Music ensembles; Musical theater; Opera; Pep band; Radio station; Student government; Student newspaper; Student-run film society; Symphony orchestra; Television station. 223 registered organizations, 39 honor societies, 6 religious organizations, 10 fraternities, 10 sororities, on campus. **Athletics (Intercollegiate):** *Men:* baseball, basketball, cross-country, golf, lacrosse, soccer, tennis, wrestling. *Women:* basketball, cross-country, field hockey, golf, lacrosse, soccer, softball, tennis, volleyball. **On-Campus Highlights:** Mack Student Center: the focal point of campus community life and home to a newly renovated full-service Starbucks, a large game room/e-sports, bookstore, diverse dinning venues—including vegan, organic, kosher, halal, gluten free/food sensitivity and ethnic food and a late night pizza and salad station—and spacious lounges throughout where students meet for meals, socializing, club and organizational events. **Environmental Initiatives:** In 2019, the new School of Business Building achieved LEED Silver Certification. The approximate 52,500 sq. ft building opened in January 2019.

ADMISSIONS

Freshman Academic Profile: Average high school GPA 3.7. 32% in top 10% of high school class, 60% in top 25% of high school class, 91% in top 50% of high school class. **Test scores:** SAT Math middle 50% range 580–680. SAT EBRW middle 50% range 580–660. ACT middle 50% range 25–30. **Basis for Candidate Selection:** *Very important factors include:* rigor of secondary school record, class rank, academic GPA, application essay, recommendation(s). *Important factors include:* interview, extracurricular activities, talent/ability, character/personal qualities. *Other factors include:* standardized test scores, first generation, alumni/ae relation, geographical residence, racial/ethnic status, volunteer work, work experience, level of applicant's interest. **Freshman Admission Requirements:** High school diploma is required and GED is accepted. *Academic units required:* 4 English, 3 math, 3 science, 1 science labs, 2 foreign language, 3 social studies. *Academic units recommended:* 4 math, 4 science, 2 science labs, 3 foreign language, 4 social studies. **Freshman Admission Statistics:** 24,425 applied, 68% admitted, 9% enrolled. **Transfer Admission Requirements:** college transcript(s), statement of good standing from prior institution(s). Lowest grade transferable C-. **General Admission Information:** Application fee $70. Non-fall registration accepted. Admission may be deferred for a maximum of 1 year.

COSTS AND FINANCIAL AID

Annual tuition $46,450. Room and board $16,428. Required fees $1,060. Average book and supplies expense $1,000. **Required Forms and Deadlines:** FAFSA; State aid form. **Notification of Awards:** Applicants will be notified of awards on a rolling basis beginning 1/15. **Types of Aid:** *Need-based scholarships/grants:* College/university scholarship or grant aid from institutional funds; Federal Pell; Private scholarships; SEOG; State scholarships/grants; United Negro College Fund. *Loans:* Direct PLUS loans; Direct Subsidized Stafford Loans; Direct Unsubsidized Stafford Loans. **Student Employment:** Federal Work-Study Program available. Institutional employment available. **Financial Aid Statistics:** 99% needy freshmen, 96% needy undergrads receive need-based scholarship or grant aid. 21% freshmen, 17% undergrads receive non-need-based scholarship or grant aid. 79% freshmen, 72% undergrads receive need-based self-help aid. 2% freshmen, 2% undergrads receive athletic scholarships. 97% freshmen, 91% undergrads receive any aid. 60% undergrads borrow to pay for school. **Criteria awarding aid:** *Need-based:* Academics, Alumni affiliation, Art, Leadership, Music/drama *Non-Need-based:* Academics, Alumni affiliation, Art, Athletics, Leadership, Minority status, Music/drama, State/district residency.

HOLLINS UNIVERSITY

7916 Williamson Road, Box 9707, Roanoke, VA 24020-1707
Phone: 540-362-6401 **Financial Aid Phone:** 540-362-6332
E-mail: huadm@hollins.edu **CEEB Code:** 5294
Fax: 540-362-6218 **Website:** www.hollins.edu **ACT Code:** 4360

This private school was founded in 1842. It has a 475 acre campus.

RATINGS

Admissions Selectivity Rating: 83   Fire Safety Rating: 85   Green Rating: 78

STUDENTS AND FACULTY

Enrollment: 666. **Student Body:** 100% female, 0% male, 50% out-of-state, 7% international (20 countries represented). Asian 2%, African American 10%, Caucasian 64%, Hispanic 8%, Native American 1%, Pacific Islander <1%, Two or more races 7%, Race unknown 2%.
Retention and Graduation: 78% freshmen return for sophomore year. 52% freshmen graduate within 4 years. 56% freshmen graduate within 6 years. 21% grads go on to further study within 1 year. 17% grads pursue arts and sciences degrees. 0% grads pursue law degrees. 1% grads pursue business degrees. 3% grads pursue medical degrees. **Faculty:** Student/faculty ratio 10:1. 69 full-time faculty, 99% hold PhDs, 6% are members of minority groups, 57% are women. 1% of classes are taught by teaching assistants.

ACADEMICS

Degrees: Bachelor's; Master's; Post-master's certificate. **Classes:** Most classes have 10–19 students. Most lab/discussion sessions have 10–19 students. **Most popular majors:** English Language and Literature, General. **Special Study Options:** Accelerated program; Cross-registration; Double major; Dual enrollment; Exchange student program (domestic); Independent study; Internships; Student-designed major; Study abroad; Teacher certification program. **Honors programs:** A number of university departments offer honors programs. The specific nature of departmental honors varies from department to department. The programs, which are undertaken for at least the full senior year, may involve research, theses, oral or written examinations, seminars, reading programs, or any combination thereof. **Disability Services offered:** Reader services; Tape recorders. **Career services:** Alumni network; Alumni services; Career assessment; Career/job search classes; Internships; Regional alumni.

FACILITIES

Housing: Apartments for single students; Special housing for disabled students; Special housing for international students; Theme housing; Wellness housing; Women's dorms; 44% of campus accessible to physically disabled. **Special Academic Facilities/Equipment:** Athletic complex, a writing center, language labs, campus-wide computer network, scientific equipment and instrumentation, art museum, and a state-of-the-art library. **Campus Network:** 100% of classrooms, 100% of dorms, 100% of student union, 100% of libraries, 100% of dining areas, 100% of common outdoor areas, have wireless network access.

CAMPUS LIFE

Environment: City. **Activities:** Campus Ministries; Choral groups; Dance; Drama/theater; International Student Organization; Literary magazine; Model UN; Music ensembles; Musical theater; Student government; Student-run film society. 20 registered organizations, 17 honor societies, 1 religious organizations, on campus. **Athletics (Intercollegiate):** *Women:* basketball, equestrian sports, golf, lacrosse, soccer, swimming, tennis. **On-Campus Highlights:** Front Quadrangle. **Environmental Initiatives:** Signing the President's Climate Agreement.

ADMISSIONS

Freshman Academic Profile: Average high school GPA 3.7. 23% in top 10% of high school class, 55% in top 25% of high school class, 82% in top 50% of high school class. 80% from public high schools. **Test scores:** SAT Math middle 50% range 510–620. SAT EBRW middle 50% range 560–660. ACT middle 50% range 24–29. **Basis for Candidate Selection:** *Very important factors include:* academic GPA, standardized test scores. *Important factors include:* rigor of secondary school record, application essay, recommendation(s). *Other factors include:* class rank, interview, extracurricular activities, talent/ability, character/personal qualities, first generation, alumni/ae relation, volunteer work, work

experience, level of applicant's interest. **Freshman Admission Requirements:** High school diploma is required and GED is accepted. *Academic units required:* 4 English, 3 math, 3 science, 3 social studies. *Academic units recommended:* 3 foreign language. **Freshman Admission Statistics:** 3,667 applied, 64% admitted, 8% enrolled. **Transfer Admission Requirements:** High school transcript, college transcript(s), essay or personal statement, Minimum college GPA of 2.5 required. Lowest grade transferable C. **General Admission Information:** Priority deadline 2/1. Non-fall registration accepted. Admission may be deferred for a maximum of 1 year.

COSTS AND FINANCIAL AID

Annual tuition $39,360. Room and board $13,520. Required fees $635. Average book and supplies expense $800. **Required Forms and Deadlines:** FAFSA; State aid form. **Notification of Awards:** Applicants will be notified of awards on a rolling basis beginning 3/1. **Types of Aid:** *Need-based scholarships/ grants:* College/university scholarship or grant aid from institutional funds; Federal Pell; Private scholarships; SEOG; State scholarships/grants. *Loans:* Direct PLUS loans; Direct Subsidized Stafford Loans; Direct Unsubsidized Stafford Loans. **Student Employment:** Federal Work-Study Program available. Institutional employment available. **Financial Aid Statistics:** 100% needy freshmen, 100% needy undergrads receive need-based scholarship or grant aid. 100% freshmen, 100% undergrads receive non-need-based scholarship or grant aid. 69% freshmen, 74% undergrads receive need-based self-help aid. 0% freshmen, 0% undergrads receive athletic scholarships. 100% freshmen, 99% undergrads receive any aid. 77% undergrads borrow to pay for school. Average cumulative indebtedness $33,408. **Criteria awarding aid:** *Need-based:* Academics, Alumni affiliation, Art, Leadership, Minority status, Music/drama *Non-Need-based:* Academics, Alumni affiliation, Art, Leadership, Music/drama, State/district residency.

HOLY FAMILY UNIVERSITY

9801 Frankford Avenue, Philadelphia, PA 19114-2009
Phone: 215-637-7700 **Financial Aid Phone:** 267-341-3234
E-mail: admissions@holyfamily.edu gradstudy@holyfamily.edu **CEEB Code:** 2297
Fax: 215-281-1022 **Website:** www.holyfamily.edu **ACT Code:** 3592

This private school, affiliated with the Roman Catholic Church, was founded in 1954. It has a 46 acre campus.

RATINGS

Admissions Selectivity Rating: 77   Fire Safety Rating: 99   Green Rating: 61

STUDENTS AND FACULTY

Enrollment: 1,766. **Student Body:** 74% female, 26% male, 14% out-of-state, <1% international (8 countries represented). Asian 5%, African American 12%, Caucasian 62%, Hispanic 6%, Native American <1%, Pacific Islander <1%, Two or more races 0%, Race unknown 15%.
Retention and Graduation: 76% freshmen return for sophomore year.
Faculty: Student/faculty ratio 13:1. 76 full-time faculty, 82% hold PhDs, 13% are members of minority groups, 71% are women. 0% of classes are taught by teaching assistants.

ACADEMICS

Degrees: Associate; Bachelor's; Certificate; Master's; Post-bachelor's certificate; Post-master's certificate. **Classes:** Most classes have 10–19 students. Most lab/discussion sessions have fewer than 10 students. **Most popular majors:** Education, General; Registered Nursing/Registered Nurse; Business Administration and Management, General. **Special Study Options:** Accelerated program; Cooperative education program; Cross-registration; Distance learning; English as a Second Language (ESL); Honors program; Independent study; Internships; Liberal arts/career combination; Study abroad; Teacher certification program; Weekend college. **Honors programs:** Honor's Program. Honor's classes in the core curriculum. **Combined degree programs:** BA/ MA. **Disability Services offered:** Note-taking services; Reader services; Tape recorders; Tutors. **Career services:** Alumni services; Career assessment; Career/ job search classes; Internships.

FACILITIES

Housing: Apartments for single students; Coed dorms; Special housing for disabled students. **Special Academic Facilities/Equipment:** On-campus nursery school, art gallery. **Campus Network:** 100% of classrooms, 100% of dorms, 100% of student union, 100% of libraries, 100% of dining areas, 5% of common outdoor areas, have wireless network access.

CAMPUS LIFE

Environment: Metropolis. **Activities:** Campus Ministries; Choral groups; Dance; Drama/theater; International Student Organization; Literary magazine; Musical theater; Student government; Student newspaper; Television station; Yearbook. 23 registered organizations, 19 honor societies, 1 religious organizations, on campus. **Athletics (Intercollegiate):** *Men:* basketball, cross-country, golf, soccer, track/field (outdoor), track/field (indoor). *Women:* basketball, cross-country, lacrosse, soccer, softball, tennis, track/field (outdoor), track/field (indoor), volleyball. **On-Campus Highlights:** Campus Center.

ADMISSIONS

Freshman Academic Profile: Average high school GPA 3.1. 10% in top 10% of high school class, 25% in top 25% of high school class, 62% in top 50% of high school class. 60% from public high schools. **Test scores:** SAT Math middle 50% range 410–520. SAT EBRW middle 50% range 420–510. **Basis for Candidate Selection:** *Very important factors include:* academic GPA. *Important factors include:* standardized test scores. *Other factors include:* rigor of secondary school record, class rank, application essay, recommendation(s), interview, extracurricular activities, character/personal qualities, alumni/ae relation, volunteer work. **Freshman Admission Requirements:** High school diploma is required and GED is accepted. *Academic units required:* 4 English, 3 math, 2 science, 2 foreign language, 2 history, 3 academic electives. **Freshman Admission Statistics:** 1,441 applied, 68% admitted, 34% enrolled. **Transfer Admission Requirements:** High school transcript, college transcript(s), essay or personal statement, statement of good standing from prior institution(s). Minimum college GPA of 2.5 required. Lowest grade transferable C. **General Admission Information:** Application fee $25. Non-fall registration accepted. Admission may be deferred for a maximum of 1 year.

COSTS AND FINANCIAL AID

Annual tuition $29,338. Room and board $13,576. Required fees $1,008. Average book and supplies expense $1,090. **Required Forms and Deadlines:** FAFSA. **Notification of Awards:** Applicants will be notified of awards on a rolling basis beginning 3/15. **Types of Aid:** *Need-based scholarships/grants:* College/university scholarship or grant aid from institutional funds; Federal Pell; Private scholarships; SEOG; State scholarships/grants. *Loans:* Direct PLUS loans; Direct Subsidized Stafford Loans; Direct Unsubsidized Stafford Loans. **Student Employment:** Federal Work-Study Program available. **Financial Aid Statistics:** 99% needy freshmen, 94% needy undergrads receive need-based scholarship or grant aid. 99% freshmen, 91% undergrads receive non-need-based scholarship or grant aid. 96% freshmen, 92% undergrads receive need-based self-help aid. 14% freshmen, 9% undergrads receive athletic scholarships. 100% freshmen, 93% undergrads receive any aid. 86% undergrads borrow to pay for school. Average cumulative indebtedness $39,664. **Criteria awarding aid:** *Need-based:* Academics. *Non-Need-based:* Academics, Athletics, Leadership.

HOOD COLLEGE

401 Rosemont Avenue, Frederick, MD 21701
Phone: 301-696-3400 **Financial Aid Phone:** 301-696-3411
E-mail: admission@hood.edu **CEEB Code:** 5296
Fax: 301-696-3819 **Website:** www.hood.edu **ACT Code:** 1702

This private school, affiliated with the United Church of Christ, was founded in 1893. It has a 50 acre campus.

RATINGS

Admissions Selectivity Rating: 81   Fire Safety Rating: 98   Green Rating: 60*

STUDENTS AND FACULTY

Enrollment: 1,126. **Student Body:** 63% female, 37% male, 26% out-of-state, 2% international (14 countries represented). Asian 4%, African American 18%, Caucasian 58%, Hispanic 12%, Native American 0%, Pacific Islander <1%, Two or more races 6%, Race unknown 2%.
Retention and Graduation: 75% freshmen return for sophomore year. 55% freshmen graduate within 4 years. 65% freshmen graduate within 6 years. 36% grads go on to further study within 1 year. 18% grads pursue arts and sciences degrees. 5% grads pursue law degrees. 16% grads pursue business degrees. 0% grads pursue medical degrees. **Faculty:** Student/faculty ratio 10:1. 132 full-time faculty, 74% hold PhDs, 19% are members of minority groups, 48% are women. 0% of classes are taught by teaching assistants.

ACADEMICS

Degrees: Bachelor's; Certificate; Doctoral degree research/scholarship; Master's; Post-bachelor's certificate. **Classes:** Most classes have 10–19 students. Most lab/discussion sessions have 10–19 students. **Most popular majors:** Business Administration, Management and Operations; Biology/Biological Sciences, General; Psychology, General. **Special Study Options:** Distance learning; Double major; Dual enrollment; Honors program; Independent study; Internships; Liberal arts/career combination; Student-designed major; Study abroad; Teacher certification program. **Honors programs:** The honors program at Hood is highly selective, admitting a limited number of outstanding students across all majors each year. Students form a diverse, supportive learning community through a four-year series of seminars, co-curricular activities and social events based in the classroom and the Marx Center and supplemented by numerous off-campus excursions. Classes are seminar style, with an emphasis on discussion and critical thinking. Testing is de-emphasized in favor of writing and collaborative projects. **Combined degree programs:** BA/MA. **Disability Services offered:** Note-taking services; Reader services; Tape recorders; Tutors. **Career services:** Alumni network; Alumni services; Career assessment; Career/job search classes; Internships; Regional alumni.

FACILITIES

Housing: Coed dorms; Theme housing; 70% of campus accessible to physically disabled. **Special Academic Facilities/Equipment:** Art gallery, child development lab, language lab, observatory, science labs, nursing lab, Hood History Museum, Financial trading room, Mock trial courtroom. **Campus Network:** 100% of classrooms, 100% of dorms, 100% of student union, 100% of libraries, 100% of dining areas, 90% of common outdoor areas, have wireless network access.

CAMPUS LIFE

Environment: Town. **Activities:** Campus Ministries; Choral groups; Dance; Drama/theater; International Student Organization; Jazz band; Literary magazine; Model UN; Music ensembles; Musical theater; Radio station; Student government; Student newspaper; Television station. 50 registered organizations, 16 honor societies, 8 religious organizations, on campus. **Athletics (Intercollegiate):** *Men:* basketball, cross-country, golf, lacrosse, soccer, swimming, tennis, track/field (outdoor). *Women:* basketball, cross-country, field hockey, golf, lacrosse, soccer, softball, swimming, tennis, track/field (outdoor), volleyball. **On-Campus Highlights:** Whitaker Campus Center. **Environmental Initiatives:** Reduction of natural gas consumption through the use of new decentralized building heating boilers and software controls programming.

ADMISSIONS

Freshman Academic Profile: Average high school GPA 3.3. 10% in top 10% of high school class, 37% in top 25% of high school class, 77% in top 50% of high school class. 81% from public high schools. **Test scores:** SAT Math middle 50% range 490–600. SAT EBRW middle 50% range 510–610. ACT middle 50% range 19–24. **Basis for Candidate Selection:** *Very important factors include:* rigor of secondary school record, academic GPA. *Important factors include:* application essay, interview, extracurricular activities, character/personal qualities, alumni/ae relation. *Other factors include:* class rank, standardized test scores, recommendation(s), talent/ability, volunteer work, work experience, level of applicant's interest. **Freshman Admission Requirements:** High school diploma is required and GED is accepted. *Academic units required:* 4 English, 3 math, 3 science, 2 science labs, 2 foreign language, 3 social studies, 1 academic electives. *Academic units recommended:* 4 English, 4 math, 3 science, 2 science labs, 3 foreign language, 3 social studies, 2 academic electives. **Freshman Admission Statistics:** 3,515 applied, 65% admitted, 14% enrolled. **Transfer Admission Requirements:** college transcript(s), Minimum college GPA of 2.5 required. Lowest grade transferable C-. **General Admission Information:** Priority deadline 4/15. Non-fall registration accepted.

COSTS AND FINANCIAL AID

Annual tuition $41,680. Room and board $13,010. Required fees $620. Average book and supplies expense $1,270. **Required Forms and Deadlines:** FAFSA; State aid form. **Notification of Awards:** Applicants will be notified of awards on or about 3/1. **Types of Aid:** *Need-based scholarships/grants:* College/university scholarship or grant aid from institutional funds; Federal Pell; Private scholarships; SEOG; State scholarships/grants. *Loans:* Direct PLUS loans; Direct Subsidized Stafford Loans; Direct Unsubsidized Stafford Loans. **Student Employment:** Federal Work-Study Program available. Institutional employment available. **Financial Aid Statistics:** 100% needy freshmen, 99% needy undergrads receive need-based scholarship or grant aid. 15% freshmen, 14% undergrads receive non-need-based scholarship or grant aid. 75% freshmen, 77% undergrads receive need-based self-help aid. 0% freshmen, 0% undergrads receive athletic scholarships. 99.6% freshmen, 98.7% undergrads receive any aid. 74% undergrads borrow to pay for school.

Average cumulative indebtedness $33,024. **Criteria awarding aid:** *Need-based:* Leadership, Minority status, Music/drama, Religious affiliation. *Non-Need-based:* Academics, Alumni affiliation, Leadership, Minority status, Music/drama, Religious affiliation, State/district residency.

HOPE COLLEGE

69 East 10th, Holland, MI 49422-9000
Phone: 616-395-7850 **Financial Aid Phone:** 616-395-7765
E-mail: admissions@hope.edu **CEEB Code:** 1301
Fax: 616-395-7130 **Website:** www.hope.edu **ACT Code:** 2012

This private school, affiliated with the Reformed Church, was founded in 1862. It has a 120 acre campus.

RATINGS
Admissions Selectivity Rating: 80 **Fire Safety Rating:** 89 **Green Rating:** 94

STUDENTS AND FACULTY
Enrollment: 2,966. **Student Body:** 62% female, 38% male, 29% out-of-state, 2% international (35 countries represented). Asian 2%, African American 2%, Caucasian 82%, Hispanic 8%, Native American <1%, Pacific Islander 0%, Two or more races 3%, Race unknown <1%.
Retention and Graduation: 92% freshmen return for sophomore year. 72% freshmen graduate within 4 years. 81% freshmen graduate within 6 years. 20% grads go on to further study within 1 year. **Faculty:** Student/faculty ratio 11:1. 231 full-time faculty, 15% are members of minority groups, 48% are women. 0% of classes are taught by teaching assistants.

ACADEMICS
Degrees: Bachelor's. **Classes:** Most classes have 10–19 students. Most lab/discussion sessions have 10–19 students. **Special Study Options:** Double major; Dual enrollment; Exchange student program (domestic); Independent study; Internships; Student-designed major; Study abroad; Teacher certification program. **Disability Services offered:** Note-taking services; Reader services; Tape recorders; Tutors. **Career services:** Alumni network; Alumni services; Career assessment; Career/job search classes; Internships; Regional alumni.

FACILITIES
Housing: Apartments for married students; Coed dorms; Fraternity/sorority housing; Men's dorms; Special housing for disabled students; Special housing for international students; Theme housing; Women's dorms; 95% of campus accessible to physically disabled. **Special Academic Facilities/Equipment:** Art gallery, particle accelerator, computational chemistry lab, electron microscopes, spectrometers, ultracentrifuge, observatory, new $38M science building.

CAMPUS LIFE
Environment: Town. **Activities:** Campus Ministries; Choral groups; Concert band; Dance; Drama/theater; International Student Organization; Jazz band; Literary magazine; Music ensembles; Radio station; Student government; Student newspaper; Yearbook. 67 registered organizations, 22 honor societies, 6 religious organizations, 6 fraternities, 7 sororities, on campus. **Athletics (Intercollegiate):** *Men:* baseball, basketball, cheerleading, cross-country, diving, football, golf, soccer, swimming, tennis, track/field (outdoor), track/field (indoor). *Women:* basketball, cheerleading, cross-country, diving, golf, soccer, softball, swimming, tennis, track/field (outdoor), track/field (indoor), volleyball. **On-Campus Highlights:** Bultman Student Center. **Environmental Initiatives:** Electrical use reduction.

ADMISSIONS
Freshman Academic Profile: Average high school GPA 3.9. 37% in top 10% of high school class, 71% in top 25% of high school class, 94% in top 50% of high school class. 88% from public high schools. **Test scores:** SAT EBRW middle 50% range 560–670. ACT middle 50% range 22–28. **Basis for Candidate Selection:** *Important factors include:* rigor of secondary school record, academic GPA, standardized test scores. *Other factors include:* class rank, application essay, recommendation(s), extracurricular activities, talent/ability, alumni/ae relation, geographical residence. **Freshman Admission Requirements:** High school diploma is required and GED is accepted. *Academic units recommended:* 4 English, 4 math, 4 science, 2 science labs, 4 foreign language, 4 social studies, 4 history. **Freshman Admission Statistics:** 3,748 applied, 86% admitted, 21% enrolled. **Transfer Admission Requirements:** High school transcript, college transcript(s), essay or personal statement, standardized test scores, statement of good standing from prior

institution(s). Minimum college GPA of 2.5 required. Lowest grade transferable C. **General Admission Information:** Application fee $35. Priority deadline 11/1. Non-fall registration accepted.

COSTS AND FINANCIAL AID
Annual tuition $34,990. Room and board $10,690. Required fees $340. Average book and supplies expense $980. **Required Forms and Deadlines:** FAFSA. **Notification of Awards:** Applicants will be notified of awards on a rolling basis beginning 3/15. **Types of Aid:** *Need-based scholarships/grants:* College/university scholarship or grant aid from institutional funds; Federal Pell; Private scholarships; SEOG; State scholarships/grants. *Loans:* Direct PLUS loans; Direct Subsidized Stafford Loans; Direct Unsubsidized Stafford Loans. **Student Employment:** Federal Work-Study Program available. Institutional employment available. **Financial Aid Statistics:** 91% needy freshmen, 87% needy undergrads receive need-based scholarship or grant aid. 92% freshmen, 84% undergrads receive non-need-based scholarship or grant aid. 78% freshmen, 78% undergrads receive need-based self-help aid. 0% freshmen, 0% undergrads receive athletic scholarships. 96% freshmen, 95% undergrads receive any aid. 59% undergrads borrow to pay for school. Average cumulative indebtedness $35,856. **Criteria awarding aid:** *Need-based:* Academics, Minority status. *Non-Need-based:* Academics, Art, Minority status, Music/drama, Religious affiliation.

HOPE INTERNATIONAL UNIVERSITY

Undergraduate Admissions, Fullerton, CA 92831
Phone: 866-722-4673 **Financial Aid Phone:** (714)879-3901
E-mail: pccadmissions@hiu.edu
Fax: 714-681-7423 **Website:** www.hiu.edu **ACT Code:** 356

This private school, affiliated with the Church of Christ, was founded in 1928. It has a 18 acre campus.

RATINGS
Admissions Selectivity Rating: 87 **Fire Safety Rating:** 70 **Green Rating:** 60*

STUDENTS AND FACULTY
Enrollment: 521. **Student Body:** 60% female, 40% male, 24% out-of-state, 2% international. Asian 5%, African American 5%, Caucasian 63%, Hispanic 16%, Native American 1%, Race unknown 7%.
Retention and Graduation: 71% freshmen return for sophomore year. **Faculty:** Student/faculty ratio 15:1. 32 full-time faculty, 59% hold PhDs, 6% are members of minority groups, 25% are women. 0% of classes are taught by teaching assistants.

ACADEMICS
Degrees: Associate; Bachelor's; Certificate; Master's; Post-bachelor's certificate. **Classes:** Most classes have 10–19 students. Most lab/discussion sessions have fewer than 10 students. **Most popular majors:** Youth Ministry; Psychology, General; Teacher Education, Multiple Levels. **Special Study Options:** Accelerated program; Cross-registration; Distance learning; Double major; Dual enrollment; English as a Second Language (ESL); Independent study; Internships; Liberal arts/career combination; Student-designed major; Study abroad; Teacher certification program. **Disability Services offered:** Note-taking services; Tape recorders; Tutors.

FACILITIES
Housing: Men's dorms; Women's dorms; 95% of campus accessible to physically disabled.

CAMPUS LIFE
Environment: City. **Activities:** Choral groups; Drama/theater; Jazz band; Music ensembles; Musical theater; Student government; Student newspaper; Yearbook. **Athletics (Intercollegiate):** *Men:* basketball, soccer, tennis, volleyball. *Women:* basketball, soccer, softball, tennis, volleyball. **On-Campus Highlights:** Lawson-Fulton Student Center.

ADMISSIONS
Freshman Academic Profile: Average high school GPA 3.3. 20% in top 10% of high school class, 37% in top 25% of high school class, 77% in top 50% of high school class. 95% from public high schools. **Test scores:** SAT Math middle 50% range 420–530. SAT EBRW middle 50% range 440–540. ACT middle 50% range 18–21. **Basis for Candidate Selection:** *Very important factors include:* rigor of secondary school record, class rank, academic GPA, application essay, standardized test scores, recommendation(s). *Important factors include:*

level of applicant's interest. *Other factors include:* interview, extracurricular activities, talent/ability, character/personal qualities, religious affiliation/commitment, volunteer work. **Freshman Admission Requirements:** High school diploma is required and GED is accepted. *Academic units recommended:* 4 English, 2 math, 1 science, 1 science labs, 1 foreign language, 1 social studies, 1 history, 3 academic electives. **Freshman Admission Statistics:** 413 applied, 32% admitted. **Transfer Admission Requirements:** college transcript(s), essay or personal statement, statement of good standing from prior institution(s). Minimum college GPA of 2.5 required. Lowest grade transferable C. **General Admission Information:** Application fee $40. Non-fall registration accepted.

COSTS AND FINANCIAL AID

Annual tuition $21,560. Room and board $6,940. Average book and supplies expense $1,386. **Required Forms and Deadlines:** FAFSA; Institution's own financial aid form. **Notification of Awards:** Applicants will be notified of awards on a rolling basis beginning 3/15. **Types of Aid:** *Need-based scholarships/grants:* College/university scholarship or grant aid from institutional funds; Federal Pell; Private scholarships; SEOG; State scholarships/grants. *Loans:* Direct PLUS loans; Direct Subsidized Stafford Loans; Direct Unsubsidized Stafford Loans. **Student Employment:** Federal Work-Study Program available. Institutional employment available. **Financial Aid Statistics:** 98% needy freshmen, 96% needy undergrads receive need-based scholarship or grant aid. 19% freshmen, 14% undergrads receive non-need-based scholarship or grant aid. 74% freshmen, 77% undergrads receive need-based self-help aid. 0% freshmen, 0% undergrads receive athletic scholarships. 67% freshmen, 73% undergrads receive any aid. **Criteria awarding aid:** *Need-based:* Academics, Alumni affiliation, Athletics, Job skills, Leadership, Music/drama, Religious affiliation. *Non-Need-based:* Academics, Alumni affiliation, Athletics, Leadership, Music/drama, Religious affiliation.

HOUGHTON COLLEGE

PO Box 128, Houghton, NY 14744
Phone: 585-567-9353 **Financial Aid Phone:** 585-567-9328
E-mail: admission@houghton.edu **CEEB Code:** 2299
Fax: 716-567-9522 **Website:** www.houghton.edu **ACT Code:** 2766

This private school, affiliated with the Wesleyan Church, was founded in 1883. It has a 1300 acre campus.

RATINGS

Admissions Selectivity Rating: 76 **Fire Safety Rating:** 82 **Green Rating:** 72

STUDENTS AND FACULTY

Enrollment: 1,021. **Student Body:** 62% female, 38% male, 35% out-of-state, 10% international (31 countries represented). Asian 4%, African American 4%, Caucasian 73%, Hispanic 2%, Native American <1%, Pacific Islander <1%, Two or more races 5%, Race unknown 2%.
Retention and Graduation: 80% freshmen return for sophomore year. 67% freshmen graduate within 4 years. % freshmen graduate within 6 years. 18% grads go on to further study within 1 year. 11% grads pursue arts and sciences degrees. <1% grads pursue law degrees. 1% grads pursue business degrees. 1% grads pursue medical degrees. **Faculty:** Student/faculty ratio 12:1. 65 full-time faculty, 94% hold PhDs, 0% are members of minority groups, 38% are women. 0% of classes are taught by teaching assistants.

ACADEMICS

Degrees: Associate; Bachelor's; Master's. **Classes:** Most classes have fewer than 10 students. **Most popular majors:** Digital Communication and Media/Multimedia; Biology/Biological Sciences, General; Business Administration and Management, General. **Special Study Options:** Accelerated program; Cross-registration; Distance learning; Double major; Dual enrollment; Exchange student program (domestic); Honors program; Independent study; Internships; Liberal arts/career combination; Student-designed major; Study abroad; Teacher certification program. **Honors programs:** Three honors programs for first-year students: two programs involving studying abroad in London or Eastern Europe as well as a hands-on science honors program. **Disability Services offered:** Note-taking services; Reader services; Tape recorders; Tutors. **Career services:** Alumni network; Alumni services; Career assessment; Career/job search classes; Internships; Regional alumni.

FACILITIES

Housing: Apartments for married students; Apartments for single students; Cooperative housing; Men's dorms; Special housing for disabled students;

Women's dorms; 80% of campus accessible to physically disabled. **Special Academic Facilities/Equipment:** Electron microscope, Art Gallery, Greenhouse. **Campus Network:** 95% of classrooms, 100% of dorms, 95% of student union, 100% of libraries, 90% of dining areas, 5% of common outdoor areas, have wireless network access.

CAMPUS LIFE

Environment: Rural. **Activities:** Campus Ministries; Choral groups; Concert band; Dance; Drama/theater; International Student Organization; Jazz band; Literary magazine; Music ensembles; Musical theater; Opera; Pep band; Student government; Student newspaper; Symphony orchestra; Yearbook. 34 registered organizations, 2 honor societies, 12 religious organizations, on campus. **Athletics (Intercollegiate):** *Men:* basketball, cross-country, soccer, track/field (outdoor), track/field (indoor). *Women:* basketball, cross-country, field hockey, soccer, track/field (outdoor), track/field (indoor), volleyball. **On-Campus Highlights:** Campus Center. **Environmental Initiatives:** Achieving carbon neutrality by 2050.

ADMISSIONS

Freshman Academic Profile: Average high school GPA 3.5. 26% in top 10% of high school class, 54% in top 25% of high school class, 80% in top 50% of high school class. 66% from public high schools. **Test scores:** SAT Math middle 50% range 520–650. SAT EBRW middle 50% range 540–670. ACT middle 50% range 22–29. **Basis for Candidate Selection:** *Very important factors include:* class rank, academic GPA, religious affiliation/commitment. *Important factors include:* rigor of secondary school record, application essay, recommendation(s), character/personal qualities. *Other factors include:* standardized test scores, interview, extracurricular activities, talent/ability, first generation, alumni/ae relation, racial/ethnic status, volunteer work, work experience, level of applicant's interest. **Freshman Admission Requirements:** High school diploma is required and GED is accepted. *Academic units recommended:* 4 English, 3 math, 2 science, 2 science labs, 2 foreign language, 1 social studies, 3 history. **Freshman Admission Statistics:** 821 applied, 91% admitted, 29% enrolled. **Transfer Admission Requirements:** college transcript(s), essay or personal statement, Lowest grade transferable C-. **General Admission Information:** Application fee $40. Priority deadline 3/1. Non-fall registration accepted. Admission may be deferred for a maximum of 2 years.

COSTS AND FINANCIAL AID

Annual tuition $31,040. Room and board $9,018. Required fees $500. Average book and supplies expense $1,000. **Required Forms and Deadlines:** FAFSA; State aid form. **Notification of Awards:** Applicants will be notified of awards on a rolling basis beginning 3/1. **Types of Aid:** *Need-based scholarships/grants:* College/university scholarship or grant aid from institutional funds; Federal Pell; Private scholarships; SEOG; State scholarships/grants. *Loans:* Direct PLUS loans; Direct Subsidized Stafford Loans; Direct Unsubsidized Stafford Loans. **Student Employment:** Federal Work-Study Program available. Institutional employment available. **Financial Aid Statistics:** 90% needy freshmen, 88% needy undergrads receive need-based scholarship or grant aid. 76% freshmen, 76% undergrads receive non-need-based scholarship or grant aid. 90% freshmen, 89% undergrads receive need-based self-help aid. 0% freshmen, 5% undergrads receive athletic scholarships. 100% freshmen, 98% undergrads receive any aid. **Criteria awarding aid:** *Need-based:* Academics, Leadership, Minority status, Religious affiliation. *Non-Need-based:* Academics, Alumni affiliation, Art, Music/drama, Religious affiliation, State/district residency.

HOUSTON BAPTIST UNIVERSITY

7502 Fondren Road, Houston, TX 77074
Phone: 281-649-3211 **Financial Aid Phone:** 281-649-3749
E-mail: admissions@hbu.edu **CEEB Code:** 3576
Fax: 281-649-3217 **Website:** www.hbu.edu **ACT Code:** 4101

This private school, affiliated with the Southern Baptist Church, was founded in 1960. It has a 100 acre campus.

RATINGS

Admissions Selectivity Rating: 78 **Fire Safety Rating:** 60* **Green Rating:** 60*

STUDENTS AND FACULTY

Enrollment: 2,619. **Student Body:** 66% female, 34% male, 5% out-of-state, 4% international (37 countries represented). Asian 8%, African American 20%, Caucasian 23%, Hispanic 37%, Native American <1%, Pacific Islander <1%, Two or more races 3%, Race unknown 4%.

Retention and Graduation: 71% freshmen return for sophomore year. 30% freshmen graduate within 4 years. 44% freshmen graduate within 6 years. **Faculty:** Student/faculty ratio 14:1. 138 full-time faculty, 85% hold PhDs, 23% are members of minority groups, 42% are women. 0% of classes are taught by teaching assistants.

ACADEMICS

Degrees: Bachelor's; Doctoral degree research/scholarship; Master's. **Classes:** Most classes have 10–19 students. Most lab/discussion sessions have 10–19 students. **Most popular majors:** Biology/Biological Sciences, General; Psychology, General; Marketing/Marketing Management, General. **Special Study Options:** Accelerated program; Distance learning; Double major; Dual enrollment; Honors program; Independent study; Internships; Teacher certification program. **Honors programs:** The Honors College provides students with an interdisciplinary curriculum rooted in the Christian faith that cultivates knowledge, character, and wisdom by examining the great works of Western civilization and exploring timeless questions. **Disability Services offered:** Note-taking services; Tape recorders; Tutors. **Career services:** Alumni network; Career assessment; Career/job search classes; Internships.

FACILITIES

Housing: Apartments for married students; Apartments for single students; Coed dorms; Men's dorms; Special housing for disabled students; Theme housing; Women's dorms; **Special Academic Facilities/Equipment:** The Bible Museum, Lyceum, Academic Success Center, Lighthouse Lab.

CAMPUS LIFE

Environment: Metropolis. **Activities:** Campus Ministries; Choral groups; Dance; Drama/theater; International Student Organization; Marching band; Music ensembles; Student government; Student newspaper. 55 registered organizations, 11 honor societies, 7 religious organizations, 1 fraternities, 5 sororities, on campus. **Athletics (Intercollegiate):** *Men:* baseball, basketball, cheerleading. *Women:* basketball, cheerleading, softball, volleyball. **On-Campus Highlights:** MD Anderson Student Center.

ADMISSIONS

Freshman Academic Profile: Average high school GPA 3.4. 24% in top 10% of high school class, 57% in top 25% of high school class, 83% in top 50% of high school class. 88% from public high schools. **Test scores:** SAT Math middle 50% range 510–580. SAT EBRW middle 50% range 510–600. ACT middle 50% range 19–24. **Basis for Candidate Selection:** *Important factors include:* class rank, academic GPA, standardized test scores. *Other factors include:* rigor of secondary school record, recommendation(s), extracurricular activities, religious affiliation/commitment. **Freshman Admission Requirements:** High school diploma is required and GED is accepted. *Academic units required:* 4 English, 3 math, 3 science, 3 science labs, 3 social studies, 3 history, 1.5 academic electives, 1.5 computer science, 2 unit from above areas or other academic areas. *Academic units recommended:* 4 English, 4 math, 4 science, 4 science labs, 2 foreign language, 4 social studies, 3 history, 1.5 academic electives, 1.5 computer science, 1 visual/performing arts. **Freshman Admission Statistics:** 8,441 applied, 70% admitted, 12% enrolled. **Transfer Admission Requirements:** college transcript(s), essay or personal statement, statement of good standing from prior institution(s). Minimum college GPA of 2.0 required. Lowest grade transferable C. **General Admission Information:** Non-fall registration accepted. Admission may be deferred for a maximum of 6 months.

COSTS AND FINANCIAL AID

Annual tuition $32,350. Room and board $9,130. Average book and supplies expense $1,000. **Required Forms and Deadlines:** FAFSA. **Notification of Awards:** Applicants will be notified of awards on a rolling basis beginning 12/15. **Types of Aid:** *Need-based scholarships/grants:* College/university scholarship or grant aid from institutional funds; Federal Pell; Private scholarships; SEOG; State scholarships/grants. *Loans:* Direct PLUS loans; Direct Subsidized Stafford Loans; Direct Unsubsidized Stafford Loans. **Student Employment:** Federal Work-Study Program available. Institutional employment available. **Financial Aid Statistics:** 100% needy freshmen, 99% needy undergrads receive need-based scholarship or grant aid. 100% freshmen, 96% undergrads receive non-need-based scholarship or grant aid. 77% freshmen, 78% undergrads receive need-based self-help aid. 10% freshmen, 14% undergrads receive athletic scholarships. 100% freshmen, 95% undergrads receive any aid. 68% undergrads borrow to pay for school. Average cumulative indebtedness $32,538. **Criteria awarding aid:** *Need-based:* Religious affiliation. *Non-Need-based:* Academics, Alumni affiliation, Art, Athletics, Leadership, Music/drama.

HOWARD UNIVERSITY

2400 Sixth Street, NW, Suite 111, Washington, DC 20059
Phone: 202-806-2755 **Financial Aid Phone:** (202) 806-2840
E-mail: admission@howard.edu **CEEB Code:** 5297
Fax: (202) 806-4465 **Website:** www.howard.edu **ACT Code:** 0674

This private school was founded in 1867. It has a 258 acre campus.

RATINGS

Admissions Selectivity Rating: 92   **Fire Safety Rating:** 98   **Green Rating:** 60*

STUDENTS AND FACULTY

Enrollment: 6,158. **Student Body:** 69% female, 31% male, 97% out-of-state, 6% international (86 countries represented). Asian 1%, African American 89%, Caucasian 2%, Hispanic 1%, Native American <1%, Pacific Islander 1%, Two or more races 0%, Race unknown 0%.
Retention and Graduation: 85% freshmen return for sophomore year. 43% freshmen graduate within 4 years. 63% freshmen graduate within 6 years. 60% grads go on to further study within 1 year. 42% grads pursue arts and sciences degrees. 12% grads pursue law degrees. 15% grads pursue business degrees. 11% grads pursue medical degrees. **Faculty:** Student/faculty ratio 12:1. 630 full-time faculty, 85% hold PhDs, 70% are members of minority groups, 45% are women.

ACADEMICS

Degrees: Bachelor's; Certificate; Doctoral degree—professional practice; Doctoral degree research/scholarship; Master's; Post-bachelor's certificate; Post-master's certificate. **Classes:** Most classes have 10–19 students. Most lab/discussion sessions have 20–29 students. **Most popular majors:** Biology/Biological Sciences, General. **Special Study Options:** Accelerated program; Cooperative education program; Cross-registration; Distance learning; Double major; Honors program; Independent study; Internships; Study abroad; Teacher certification program. **Combined degree programs:** BA/DDS; BA/MD. **Disability Services offered:** Note-taking services; Reader services. **Career services:** Career assessment; Career/job search classes; Internships.

FACILITIES

Housing: Apartments for married students; Apartments for single students; Coed dorms; Men's dorms; Women's dorms; 100% of campus accessible to physically disabled. **Special Academic Facilities/Equipment:** Moorland-Spingarn Research Center; Ralph J Bunche Center; Afro-American Resource Center; Patent/TM Resource Center; Channing Pollock Theater Collection. **Campus Network:** 88% of classrooms, 0% of dorms, 100% of libraries, 100% of common outdoor areas, have wireless network access.

CAMPUS LIFE

Environment: Metropolis. **Activities:** Campus Ministries; Choral groups; Concert band; Dance; Drama/theater; International Student Organization; Jazz band; Marching band; Music ensembles; Musical theater; Opera; Pep band; Radio station; Student government; Student newspaper; Student-run film society; Symphony orchestra; Television station; Yearbook. 155 registered organizations, 20 honor societies, 3 religious organizations, 10 fraternities, 8 sororities, on campus. **Athletics (Intercollegiate):** *Men:* basketball, cheerleading, cross-country, diving, football, soccer, swimming, tennis, track/field (outdoor). *Women:* basketball, bowling, boxing, cheerleading, cross-country, diving, lacrosse, soccer, softball, swimming, tennis, track/field (outdoor), volleyball. **On-Campus Highlights:** Founders Library.

ADMISSIONS

Freshman Academic Profile: Average high school GPA 3.6. 27% in top 10% of high school class, 58% in top 25% of high school class, 89% in top 50% of high school class. 80% from public high schools. **Test scores:** SAT Math middle 50% range 550–635. SAT EBRW middle 50% range 590–650. ACT middle 50% range 22–27. **Basis for Candidate Selection:** *Very important factors include:* rigor of secondary school record, class rank, academic GPA, standardized test scores. *Other factors include:* application essay, recommendation(s), extracurricular activities, talent/ability, first generation, alumni/ae relation, volunteer work, work experience, level of applicant's interest. **Freshman Admission Requirements:** High school diploma is required and GED is accepted. *Academic units required:* 4 English, 3 math, 2 science, 2 science labs, 2 foreign language, 2 social studies, 4 academic electives. **Freshman Admission Statistics:** 20,946 applied, 32% admitted, 23% enrolled. **Transfer Admission Requirements:** college transcript(s), statement of good standing from prior institution(s). Minimum college GPA of 2.5 required. Lowest grade transferable C. **General Admission Information:** Application fee $45. Priority deadline 2/15. Regular application deadline 2/15. Non-fall registration accepted. Admission may be deferred for a maximum of 1 semester.

COSTS AND FINANCIAL AID

Annual tuition $24,966. Room and board $13,895. Required fees $1,790. Average book and supplies expense $1,500. **Required Forms and Deadlines:** FAFSA. **Notification of Awards:** Applicants will be notified of awards on a rolling basis beginning 4/1. **Types of Aid:** *Need-based scholarships/grants:* College/university scholarship or grant aid from institutional funds; Federal Nursing Scholarships; Federal Pell; Private scholarships; SEOG; State scholarships/grants; United Negro College Fund. *Loans:* Direct PLUS loans; Direct Subsidized Stafford Loans; Direct Unsubsidized Stafford Loans. **Student Employment:** Federal Work-Study Program available. Institutional employment available. **Financial Aid Statistics:** 61% needy freshmen, 63% needy undergrads receive need-based scholarship or grant aid. 41% freshmen, 41% undergrads receive non-need-based scholarship or grant aid. 64% freshmen, 72% undergrads receive need-based self-help aid. 3% freshmen, 4% undergrads receive athletic scholarships. 96% freshmen, 96% undergrads receive any aid. 78% undergrads borrow to pay for school. Average cumulative indebtedness $25,090. **Criteria awarding aid:** *Need-based:* Academics, Leadership, Music/drama *Non-Need-based:* Academics, Art, Athletics, Leadership, Music/drama.

HULT INTERNATIONAL BUSINESS SCHOOL

1 Education Street, Massachusetts, MA 02141
Phone: +1 617-746-1990 **Financial Aid Phone:** 617-619-2094
E-mail: bachelor@hult.edu **CEEB Code:** San Francisco: 7754 | London: 6385 | Boston: 7695
Website: http://www.hult.edu/ **ACT Code:** 1835

This private school was founded in 1964.

RATINGS
Admissions Selectivity Rating: 73   **Fire Safety Rating:** 96   **Green Rating:** 63

STUDENTS AND FACULTY
Enrollment: 1,636. **Student Body:** 38% female, 62% male, 94% international (211 countries represented). Asian 1%, African American 1%, Caucasian 2%, Hispanic 1%, Race unknown 1%.
Retention and Graduation: 81% freshmen return for sophomore year.
Faculty: Student/faculty ratio 28:1. 40 full-time faculty, 53% hold PhDs, 23% are women. 0% of classes are taught by teaching assistants.

ACADEMICS
Degrees: Bachelor's; Doctoral degree—professional practice; Master's.
Classes: Most classes have 50–99 students. **Most popular majors:** Business Administration and Management, General; Entrepreneurship/Entrepreneurial Studies; Marketing. **Special Study Options:** Accelerated program; English as a Second Language (ESL); Honors program; Independent study; Internships; Study abroad. **Honors programs:** Deans List Students who achieve a GPA of 3.60 or higher for a given semester are recognized on the Dean's List for the subsequent semester. To be eligible for the Dean's List a student must earn at least 12 credits during Fall or Spring Semester, and at least 6 credits during Summer 1 or Summer 2 terms. Qualifying participants receive notification from the Dean with appropriate recording in the student's permanent academic record. The Dean's List is published each semester, including the names of all qualifying students who consent to their name being published. Academic Excellence At Hult, the most academically talented students graduate with Distinction (final cumulative GPA of 3.60 or higher). Students who achieve a cumulative 3.60 GPA at Hult, having completed a minimum of 12 credits at Hult, are automatically added to the Academic Excellence Track. For as long as they maintain this level of academic excellence, students are entitled to the following privileges: •Accelerated degree progression. Students on the Academic Excellence Track are entitled to take one extra course in the Fall and Spring Semesters. (Note: Students, including those on Academic Excellence, who take more than 30 credits per year will be charged for additional credits on a pro rata basis.) •Exclusive elective classes. The School runs a number of elective classes to provide additional challenges for top undergraduate students. •Each campus

holds dedicated events for its Academic Excellence students, which may include speakers, networking events, and social activities. The privileges of Academic Excellence are awarded on a rolling basis to any student whose cumulative GPA is 3.60 or higher, and are awarded for a single semester to any student who is on the Dean's List that semester. **Disability Services offered:** Note-taking services; Reader services; Tutors. **Career services:** Alumni network; Alumni services; Career assessment; Career/job search classes; Internships; Regional alumni.

FACILITIES
Housing: Apartments for married students; Apartments for single students; Coed dorms; 92% of campus accessible to physically disabled.

CAMPUS LIFE
Environment: Metropolis. **Activities:** Dance; Drama/theater; International Student Organization; Model UN; Music ensembles; Student government; Student newspaper; Student-run film society; Yearbook. 92 registered organizations, on campus. **On-Campus Highlights:** Benugo Cafe & The Warehouse—Pizzeria & Bar in London; Little Lingo in Boston.

ADMISSIONS
Freshman Academic Profile: Average high school GPA 3.0. **Basis for Candidate Selection:** *Very important factors include:* academic GPA, application essay, recommendation(s), extracurricular activities, volunteer work, work experience. *Important factors include:* rigor of secondary school record, interview, talent/ability, character/personal qualities, level of applicant's interest. *Other factors include:* class rank, standardized test scores. **Freshman Admission Requirements:** High school diploma is required and GED is accepted. **Freshman Admission Statistics:** 3,904 applied, 38% admitted, 33% enrolled. **General Admission Information:** Application fee $75. Priority deadline 12/15. Non-fall registration accepted. Admission may be deferred for a maximum of 1 year.

COSTS AND FINANCIAL AID
Annual tuition $49,100. Room and board $14,000. Required fees $850. Average book and supplies expense $1,000. **Required Forms and Deadlines:** FAFSA; Institution's own financial aid form. **Types of Aid:** *Need-based scholarships/grants:* College/university scholarship or grant aid from institutional funds; Federal Pell; Private scholarships. *Loans:* Direct PLUS loans; Direct Subsidized Stafford Loans; Direct Unsubsidized Stafford Loans. **Student Employment:** Institutional employment available. **Criteria awarding aid:** *Need-based:* Academics, Leadership *Non-Need-based:* Academics, Leadership, State/district residency.

HUMBOLDT STATE UNIVERSITY

1 Harpst Street, Arcata, CA 95521-8299
Phone: 707-826-4402 **Financial Aid Phone:** 707-826-4321
E-mail: hsuinfo@humboldt.edu **CEEB Code:** 4345
Fax: 707-826-6190 **Website:** www.humboldt.edu **ACT Code:** 286

This public school was founded in 1913. It has a 161 acre campus.

RATINGS
Admissions Selectivity Rating: 73   **Fire Safety Rating:** 95   **Green Rating:** 94

STUDENTS AND FACULTY
Enrollment: 6,422. **Student Body:** 57% female, 43% male, 6% out-of-state, 1% international (33 countries represented). Asian 3%, African American 3%, Caucasian 44%, Hispanic 35%, Native American 1%, Pacific Islander <1%, Two or more races 7%, Race unknown 6%.
Retention and Graduation: 75% freshmen return for sophomore year. 17% freshmen graduate within 4 years. 49% freshmen graduate within 6 years.
Faculty: Student/faculty ratio 19:1. 243 full-time faculty, 100% hold PhDs, 19% are members of minority groups, 51% are women.

ACADEMICS
Degrees: Bachelor's; Master's; Post-bachelor's certificate. **Classes:** Most classes have 20–29 students. Most lab/discussion sessions have 20–29 students. **Most popular majors:** Biology/Biological Sciences, General; Psychology, General; Business Administration and Management, General. **Special Study Options:** Distance learning; Double major; English as a Second Language (ESL); Exchange student program (domestic); Independent study; Internships; Study abroad; Teacher certification program. **Disability Services offered:** Note-taking

services; Reader services; Tape recorders; Tutors. **Career services:** Alumni services; Career assessment; Career/job search classes; Internships; Regional alumni.

FACILITIES

Housing: Coed dorms; Theme housing; 85% of campus accessible to physically disabled. **Special Academic Facilities/Equipment:** Art and geology museums, marine research lab, fish hatchery, wildlife game pen, observatory, First Street Gallery.

CAMPUS LIFE

Environment: Village. **Activities:** Choral groups; Concert band; Dance; Drama/theater; International Student Organization; Jazz band; Literary magazine; Model UN; Music ensembles; Musical theater; Pep band; Radio station; Student government; Student newspaper; Student-run film society; Symphony orchestra. 187 registered organizations, 3 honor societies, 6 religious organizations, 2 fraternities, 4 sororities, on campus. **Athletics (Intercollegiate):** *Men:* basketball, cross-country, football, soccer, track/field (outdoor). *Women:* basketball, crew/rowing, cross-country, soccer, softball, track/field (outdoor), volleyball. **On-Campus Highlights:** Founders Hall. **Environmental Initiatives:** Campus Center for Appropriate Technology (CCAT): For 35 years, the Campus Center for Appropriate Technology's live-in demonstration home for sustainability annually exposes over 2,000 students, faculty, staff, and visitors through tours, student-taught courses, workshops, presentations and hands-on projects. The first of its kind, CCAT has been the inspiration for similar projects on college campuses across the nation. http://www.humboldt.edu/~ccat/

ADMISSIONS

Freshman Academic Profile: Average high school GPA 3.2. 5% in top 10% of high school class, 31% in top 25% of high school class, 71% in top 50% of high school class. 90% from public high schools. **Test scores:** SAT Math middle 50% range 480–590. SAT EBRW middle 50% range 490–610. ACT middle 50% range 17–25. **Basis for Candidate Selection:** *Very important factors include:* rigor of secondary school record, academic GPA. *Important factors include:* geographical residence, state residency. *Other factors include:* standardized test scores. **Freshman Admission Requirements:** High school diploma is required and GED is accepted. *Academic units required:* 4 English, 3 math, 2 science, 2 science labs, 2 foreign language, 1 social studies, 1 history, 1 academic electives, 1 visual/performing arts. **Freshman Admission Statistics:** 16,335 applied, 91% admitted, 6% enrolled. **Transfer Admission Requirements:** college transcript(s), statement of good standing from prior institution(s). Minimum college GPA of 2.00 required. Lowest grade transferable D-. **General Admission Information:** Application fee $70. Priority deadline 11/30. Regular application deadline 4/30. Non-fall registration accepted. Admission may be deferred for a maximum of 1 year.

COSTS AND FINANCIAL AID

Annual in-state tuition $5,738. Annual out-of-state tuition $17,618. Room and board $15,610. Required fees $2,120. Average book and supplies expense $1,010. **Required Forms and Deadlines:** FAFSA;. **Notification of Awards:** Applicants will be notified of awards on a rolling basis beginning 4/15. **Types of Aid:** *Need-based scholarships/grants:* College/university scholarship or grant aid from institutional funds; Federal Pell; Private scholarships; SEOG; State scholarships/grants. *Loans:* Direct PLUS loans; Direct Subsidized Stafford Loans; Direct Unsubsidized Stafford Loans. **Student Employment:** Federal Work-Study Program available. Institutional employment available. **Financial Aid Statistics:** 95% needy freshmen, 94% needy undergrads receive need-based scholarship or grant aid. 4% freshmen, 1% undergrads receive non-need-based scholarship or grant aid. 82% freshmen, 87% undergrads receive need-based self-help aid. 2% freshmen, 1% undergrads receive athletic scholarships. 74% undergrads borrow to pay for school. Average cumulative indebtedness $22,656. **Criteria awarding aid:** *Non-Need-based:* Academics, Alumni affiliation, Athletics, Leadership, Minority status, State/district residency.

HUMPHREYS COLLEGE

6650 Inglewood Avenue, Stockton, CA 95207
Phone: 209-478-0800 **Financial Aid Phone:** 209-478-0800
E-mail: slopez@humphreys.edu
Fax: 209-478-0800 **Website:** http://www.humphreys.edu/

This private school was founded in 1896. It has a 10 acre campus.

RATINGS

Admissions Selectivity Rating: 70   **Fire Safety Rating:** 60*   **Green Rating:** 60*

STUDENTS AND FACULTY

Enrollment: 692. **Student Body:** 85% female, 15% male, 0% out-of-state, <1% international. Asian 13%, African American 17%, Caucasian 29%, Hispanic 37%, Native American 1%, Race unknown 2%.
Retention and Graduation: 64% freshmen return for sophomore year. 54% grads go on to further study within 1 year. 20% grads pursue arts and sciences degrees. 30% grads pursue law degrees. 40% grads pursue business degrees. 1% grads pursue medical degrees. **Faculty:** Student/faculty ratio 18:1. 18 full-time faculty, 17% hold PhDs, 6% are members of minority groups, 67% are women. 0% of classes are taught by teaching assistants.

ACADEMICS

Degrees: Associate; Bachelor's; Certificate. **Classes:** Most classes have greater than 100 students. **Special Study Options:** Distance learning; Double major; Dual enrollment; Independent study; Internships. **Career services:** Alumni services; Internships.

FACILITIES

Housing: Apartments for single students; 100% of campus accessible to physically disabled. **Campus Network:** 0% of classrooms, 0% of dorms, 100% of student union, 100% of libraries, 100% of dining areas, 100% of common outdoor areas, have wireless network access.

CAMPUS LIFE

Environment: Village. **Activities:** Literary magazine; Student newspaper. 3 registered organizations, on campus.

ADMISSIONS

Freshman Academic Profile: Average high school GPA 3.0. 15% in top 50% of high school class. 95% from public high schools. **Basis for Candidate Selection:** *Very important factors include:* interview. *Important factors include:* character/personal qualities. *Other factors include:* level of applicant's interest. **Freshman Admission Requirements:** High school diploma is required and GED is accepted. **Freshman Admission Statistics:** 143 applied, 81% admitted, 100% enrolled. **Transfer Admission Requirements:** High school transcript, college transcript(s), interview, Minimum college GPA of 2.0 required. Lowest grade transferable C-. **General Admission Information:** Application fee $35. Non-fall registration accepted.

COSTS AND FINANCIAL AID

Required Forms and Deadlines: FAFSA. **Types of Aid:** *Need-based scholarships/grants:* Federal Pell; Private scholarships; SEOG; State scholarships/grants. **Financial Aid Statistics:** 100% needy freshmen, 100% needy undergrads receive need-based scholarship or grant aid. 0% freshmen, 0% undergrads receive non-need-based scholarship or grant aid. 23% freshmen, 7% undergrads receive need-based self-help aid. 0% freshmen, 0% undergrads receive athletic scholarships. 98% freshmen, 98% undergrads receive any aid. **Criteria awarding aid:** *Need-based:* Academics.

HUNTINGDON COLLEGE

1500 East Fairview Avenue, Montgomery, AL 36106-2148
Phone: 334-833-4497 **Financial Aid Phone:** 334-833-4428
E-mail: admiss@huntingdon.edu **CEEB Code:** 1303
Fax: 334-833-4347 **Website:** www.huntingdon.edu **ACT Code:** 0018

This private school, affiliated with the Methodist Church, was founded in 1854. It has a 71 acre campus.

RATINGS

Admissions Selectivity Rating: 86   **Fire Safety Rating:** 85   **Green Rating:** 60*

STUDENTS AND FACULTY

Enrollment: 1,099. **Student Body:** 52% female, 48% male, 30% out-of-state, <1% international (4 countries represented). Asian <1%, African American 21%, Caucasian 64%, Hispanic 6%, Native American 1%, Pacific Islander <1%, Two or more races 5%, Race unknown 3%.
Retention and Graduation: 65% freshmen return for sophomore year. 26% freshmen graduate within 4 years. 39% freshmen graduate within 6 years.
Faculty: Student/faculty ratio 15:1. 47 full-time faculty, 74% hold PhDs, 4% are members of minority groups, 47% are women. 0% of classes are taught by teaching assistants.

ACADEMICS

Degrees: Bachelor's. **Classes:** Most classes have fewer than 10 students. Most lab/discussion sessions have 10–19 students. **Most popular majors:** Sport and Fitness Administration/Management; Business/Commerce, General. **Special Study Options:** Cross-registration; Distance learning; Double major; Honors program; Independent study; Internships; Liberal arts/career combination; Student-designed major; Study abroad; Teacher certification program. **Honors programs:** The Joyce and Truman Hobbs Honors Program at Huntingdon College encourages students to embrace the social nature of knowledge through enriched classroom experiences and challenging civic service. Asked to commit to the high ideals of "faith, wisdom, and service," honors students will better understand their responsibility to humankind in Montgomery and around the world. Some specific advantages to the students participating in the Honors Program include classes designed specifically for Honors students, recognition at graduation and on the student's transcript, and enriching experiences outside the classroom (honors colloquia, etc.). Departmental Honors—An outstanding student in a particular major has the opportunity to create an individualized honors project within the major to meet a particular need and interest.
Disability Services offered: Reader services; Tape recorders; Tutors. **Career services:** Alumni network; Alumni services; Career assessment; Career/job search classes; Internships.

FACILITIES

Housing: Coed dorms; Fraternity/sorority housing; Men's dorms; Special housing for disabled students; Women's dorms; 85% of campus accessible to physically disabled. **Special Academic Facilities/Equipment:** The Bowman Ecological Center, a place where students collect and study samples of plants, trees, and aquatic life. Sybil Smith Hall, a fully equipped music facility with recital hall, reception hall, faculty offices and an extensive music collection. The Dr. Laurie Jean Weil Center for Human Performance, adjacent to the College's main training/fitness facility for athletes. The Methodist Archives Center, the central depository for the archival and historical records of the Alabama-West Florida Conference of the United Methodist Church and of Huntingdon College, located in Huntingdon College's Houghton Memorial Library. Leo J. Drum Jr. Theater, a theater with 246 retractable seats, theatrical lighting, glassed-in control room, and sound system, housed in the historic auditorium where treasured architectural details from the building's original Cloverdale construction have been preserved. Roland Band Hall, a new space recently renovated to include offices, instrument storage, lockers, and a work room, as well as a large rehearsal room. **Campus Network:** 98% of classrooms, 100% of dorms, 98% of student union, 100% of libraries, 95% of dining areas, 50% of common outdoor areas, have wireless network access.

CAMPUS LIFE

Environment: City. **Activities:** Campus Ministries; Choral groups; Concert band; Dance; Drama/theater; Jazz band; Literary magazine; Marching band; Music ensembles; Pep band; Student government. 40 registered organizations, 15 honor societies, 1 religious organizations, 3 fraternities, 4 sororities, on campus. **Athletics (Intercollegiate):** *Men:* baseball, basketball, cross-country, football, golf, soccer, tennis. *Women:* basketball, cross-country, golf, soccer, softball, tennis, volleyball. **On-Campus Highlights:** Roland Student Center (Hawk's Nest, Fitness Center, Massey Beach).

ADMISSIONS

Freshman Academic Profile: Average high school GPA 3.4. 13% in top 10% of high school class, 27% in top 25% of high school class, 69% in top 50% of high school class. 82% from public high schools. **Test scores:** SAT Math middle 50% range 500–580. SAT EBRW middle 50% range 490–595. ACT middle 50% range 19–24. **Basis for Candidate Selection:** *Very important factors include:* rigor of secondary school record, academic GPA, standardized test scores. *Other factors include:* class rank, application essay, recommendation(s), interview. **Freshman Admission Requirements:** High school diploma is required and GED is accepted. *Academic units recommended:* 4 English, 3 math, 2 science, 2 foreign language, 3 social studies, 3 history. **Freshman Admission Statistics:** 2,074 applied, 56% admitted, 25% enrolled. **Transfer Admission Requirements:** High school transcript, college transcript(s), statement of good standing from prior institution(s). Minimum college GPA of 2.25 required. Lowest grade transferable C. **General Admission Information:** Non-fall registration accepted. Admission may be deferred for a maximum of 1 semester.

COSTS AND FINANCIAL AID

Required Forms and Deadlines: FAFSA. **Notification of Awards:** Applicants will be notified of awards on a rolling basis beginning 3/1. **Types of Aid:** *Need-based scholarships/grants:* College/university scholarship or grant aid from institutional funds; Federal Pell; SEOG; State scholarships/grants. *Loans:* Direct PLUS loans; Direct Subsidized Stafford Loans; Direct Unsubsidized Stafford Loans. **Student Employment:** Federal Work-Study Program available. Institutional employment available. **Financial Aid Statistics:** 100% needy freshmen, 100% needy undergrads receive need-based scholarship or grant aid. 13% freshmen, 11% undergrads receive non-need-based scholarship or grant aid. 83% freshmen, 82% undergrads receive need-based self-help aid. 0% freshmen, 0% undergrads receive athletic scholarships. 100% freshmen, 100% undergrads receive any aid. 85% undergrads borrow to pay for school. Average cumulative indebtedness $32,201. **Criteria awarding aid:** *Need-based:* Art, Music/drama, Religious affiliation. *Non-Need-based:* Academics, Alumni affiliation, Leadership, Music/drama, Religious affiliation, State/district residency.

HUNTINGTON UNIVERSITY

2303 College Avenue, Huntington, IN 46750
Phone: (260) 359-4000 **Financial Aid Phone:** 800-642-6493
E-mail: admissions@huntington.edu **CEEB Code:** 1304
Fax: (260) 358-3699 **Website:** www.huntington.edu **ACT Code:** 1202

This private school, affiliated with the Protestant Church, was founded in 1897. It has a 170 acre campus.

RATINGS

Admissions Selectivity Rating: 74   **Fire Safety Rating:** 96   **Green Rating:** 60*

STUDENTS AND FACULTY

Enrollment: 968. **Student Body:** 57% female, 43% male, 35% out-of-state, 4% international (20 countries represented). Asian <1%, African American 2%, Caucasian 88%, Hispanic 3%, Native American <1%, Pacific Islander <1%, Two or more races 1%, Race unknown 0%.
Retention and Graduation: 79% freshmen return for sophomore year. 14% grads go on to further study within 1 year. 13% grads pursue arts and sciences degrees. 0% grads pursue law degrees. 0% grads pursue business degrees. 1% grads pursue medical degrees. **Faculty:** Student/faculty ratio 13:1. 55 full-time faculty, 87% hold PhDs, 2% are members of minority groups, 38% are women. 0% of classes are taught by teaching assistants.

ACADEMICS

Degrees: Associate; Bachelor's; Master's. **Classes:** Most classes have 10–19 students. Most lab/discussion sessions have 10–19 students. **Most popular majors:** Cinematography and Film/Video Production; Animation, Interactive Technology, Video Graphics and Special Effects; Practical Nursing, Vocational Nursing and Nursing Assistants, Other. **Special Study Options:** Accelerated program; Distance learning; Double major; Dual enrollment; Honors program; Independent study; Internships; Study abroad; Teacher certification program.
Honors programs: Our honors program pushing students beyond their typical academic classes. Students will work through the "Great Books" curriculum and have opportunities for seminars and field trips. Learn more at http://www.huntington.edu/honors/. **Disability Services offered:** Note-taking services; Reader services; Tutors. **Career services:** Alumni network; Alumni services; Career assessment; Career/job search classes; Internships; Regional alumni.

FACILITIES

Housing: Apartments for married students; Apartments for single students; Men's dorms; Special housing for disabled students; Theme housing; Women's dorms 61% of campus accessible to physically disabled. **Special Academic Facilities/Equipment:** Thornhill Nature Preserve, Herbarium, BOD POD, greenhouse **Campus Network:** 100% of classrooms, 100% of dorms, 100% of student union, 100% of libraries, 100% of dining areas, 100% of common outdoor areas, have wireless network access.

CAMPUS LIFE

Environment: Town. **Activities:** Campus Ministries; Choral groups; Concert band; Dance; Drama/theater; International Student Organization; Literary magazine; Music ensembles; Musical theater; Radio station; Student government; Student newspaper; Student-run film society; Television station. 35 registered organizations, 11 honor societies, 2 religious organizations, on campus. **Athletics (Intercollegiate):** *Men:* baseball, basketball, cheerleading, cross-country, golf, soccer, tennis, track/field (outdoor), track/field (indoor). *Women:* basketball, cheerleading, cross-country, golf, soccer, softball, tennis, track/field (outdoor), track/field (indoor), volleyball. **On-Campus Highlights:** Residence Halls-lounges. **Environmental Initiatives:** Campus recycling program.

ADMISSIONS

Freshman Academic Profile: Average high school GPA 3.5. 26% in top 10% of high school class, 53% in top 25% of high school class, 80% in top 50% of high school class. 81% from public high schools. **Test scores:** SAT Math middle 50% range 440–560. SAT EBRW middle 50% range 440–570. ACT middle 50% range 21–27. **Basis for Candidate Selection:** *Very important factors include:* academic GPA, standardized test scores. *Important factors include:* rigor of secondary school record, class rank, application essay, *Other factors include:* recommendation(s), interview, extracurricular activities, talent/ability, character/personal qualities, first generation, alumni/ae relation, geographical residence, state residency, religious affiliation/commitment, racial/ethnic status, volunteer work, work experience, level of applicant's interest. **Freshman Admission Requirements:** High school diploma is required and GED is accepted. *Academic units recommended:* 4 English, 2 math, 3 social studies. **Freshman Admission Statistics:** 780 applied, 97% admitted, 30% enrolled. **Transfer Admission Requirements:** college transcript(s), essay or personal statement, Minimum college GPA of 2.0 required. Lowest grade transferable C. **General Admission Information:** Application fee $20. Priority deadline 3/1. Regular application deadline 8/1. Non-fall registration accepted. Admission may be deferred for a maximum of 1 year.

COSTS AND FINANCIAL AID

Annual tuition $23,976. Room and board $8,306. Required fees $795. Average book and supplies expense $1,000. **Required Forms and Deadlines:** FAFSA. **Notification of Awards:** Applicants will be notified of awards on a rolling basis beginning 2/15. **Types of Aid:** *Need-based scholarships/grants:* College/university scholarship or grant aid from institutional funds; Federal Pell; Private scholarships; SEOG; State scholarships/grants. *Loans:* Direct PLUS loans; Direct Subsidized Stafford Loans; Direct Unsubsidized Stafford Loans. **Student Employment:** Federal Work-Study Program available. Institutional employment available. **Financial Aid Statistics:** 94% needy freshmen, 94% needy undergrads receive need-based scholarship or grant aid. 22% freshmen, 17% undergrads receive non-need-based scholarship or grant aid. 88% freshmen, 90% undergrads receive need-based self-help aid. 6% freshmen, 5% undergrads receive athletic scholarships. 98% freshmen, 94% undergrads receive any aid. **Criteria awarding aid:** *Need-based:* Minority status, Religious affiliation. *Non-Need-based:* Academics, Alumni affiliation, Art, Athletics, Leadership, Minority status, Music/drama, Religious affiliation.

HUSSON UNIVERSITY

1 College Circle, Bangor, ME 04401
Phone: 207-941-7100 **Financial Aid Phone:** 207-973-1090
E-mail: admit@husson.edu **CEEB Code:** 3440
Fax: 207-941-7935 **Website:** www.husson.edu **ACT Code:** 1646

This private school was founded in 1898. It has a 208 acre campus.

RATINGS

Admissions Selectivity Rating: 76   **Fire Safety Rating:** 99   **Green Rating:** 87

STUDENTS AND FACULTY

Enrollment: 2,724. **Student Body:** 54% female, 46% male, 22% out-of-state, 3% international (19 countries represented). Asian 1%, African American 4%, Caucasian 86%, Hispanic 2%, Native American 1%, Pacific Islander <1%, Two or more races 2%, Race unknown 2%.

Retention and Graduation: 76% freshmen return for sophomore year. 20% grads go on to further study within 1 year. 1% grads pursue arts and sciences degrees. 1% grads pursue law degrees. 10% grads pursue business degrees. 1% grads pursue medical degrees. **Faculty:** Student/faculty ratio 14:1. 147 full-time faculty, 64% hold PhDs, 6% are members of minority groups, 48% are women. 0% of classes are taught by teaching assistants.

ACADEMICS

Degrees: Associate; Bachelor's; Certificate; Doctoral degree—professional practice; Master's; Post-bachelor's certificate; Post-master's certificate; Transfer Associate. **Classes:** Most classes have 20–29 students. Most lab/discussion sessions have fewer than 10 students. **Most popular majors:** Business/Commerce, General; Criminal Justice/Law Enforcement Administration; Registered Nursing/Registered Nurse. **Special Study Options:** Accelerated program; Distance learning; Double major; Dual enrollment; English as a Second Language (ESL); Internships; Liberal arts/career combination; Student-designed major; Study abroad; Teacher certification program; Weekend college. **Disability Services offered:** Note-taking services; Tape recorders; Tutors. **Career services:** Alumni network; Alumni services; Career assessment; Career/job search classes; Internships; Regional alumni.

FACILITIES

Housing: Apartments for single students; Coed dorms; Special housing for disabled students; 100% of campus accessible to physically disabled. **Special Academic Facilities/Equipment:** White Art Gallery Dahl Anatomy Lab Kenduskeag Research Institute Gracie Theater. **Campus Network:** 100% of classrooms, 100% of dorms, 100% of student union, 100% of libraries, 100% of dining areas, 90% of common outdoor areas, have wireless network access.

CAMPUS LIFE

Environment: Town. **Activities:** Campus Ministries; Choral groups; Drama/theater; International Student Organization; Literary magazine; Pep band; Radio station; Student government; Yearbook. 60 registered organizations, 1 honor societies, 1 religious organizations, 2 fraternities, 3 sororities, on campus. **Athletics (Intercollegiate):** *Men:* baseball, basketball, football, golf, lacrosse, soccer. *Women:* basketball, field hockey, lacrosse, soccer, softball, swimming, tennis, volleyball. **On-Campus Highlights:** Swan Fitness Center. **Environmental Initiatives:** Green Cleaning Supplies.

ADMISSIONS

Freshman Academic Profile: Average high school GPA 3.3. 10% in top 10% of high school class, 39% in top 25% of high school class, 77% in top 50% of high school class. 90% from public high schools. **Test scores:** SAT Math middle 50% range 430–540. SAT EBRW middle 50% range 430–530. ACT middle 50% range 17–23. **Basis for Candidate Selection:** *Very important factors include:* rigor of secondary school record, academic GPA. *Important factors include:* class rank, application essay, standardized test scores, recommendation(s), interview, extracurricular activities, talent/ability, character/personal qualities. *Other factors include:* alumni/ae relation, volunteer work, work experience, level of applicant's interest. **Freshman Admission Requirements:** High school diploma is required and GED is accepted. *Academic units recommended:* 4 English, 3 math, 3 science, 2 science labs, 1 social studies, 1 history. **Freshman Admission Statistics:** 2,460 applied, 80% admitted, 32% enrolled. **Transfer Admission Requirements:** High school transcript, college transcript(s), essay or personal statement, Minimum college GPA of 2.0 required. Lowest grade transferable C. **General Admission Information:** Application fee $40. Priority deadline 3/1. Regular application deadline 8/15. Non-fall registration accepted. Admission may be deferred for a maximum of 1 year.

COSTS AND FINANCIAL AID

Annual tuition $17,081. Room and board $9,498. Required fees $480. Average book and supplies expense $1,150. **Required Forms and Deadlines:** FAFSA. **Notification of Awards:** Applicants will be notified of awards on a rolling basis beginning 12/1. **Types of Aid:** *Need-based scholarships/grants:* College/university scholarship or grant aid from institutional funds; Federal Pell; Private scholarships; SEOG; State scholarships/grants. *Loans:* Direct PLUS loans; Direct Subsidized Stafford Loans; Direct Unsubsidized Stafford Loans. **Student Employment:** Federal Work-Study Program available. **Financial Aid Statistics:** 89% needy freshmen, 84% needy undergrads receive need-based scholarship or grant aid. 98% freshmen, 79% undergrads receive non-need-based scholarship or grant aid. 93% freshmen, 93% undergrads receive need-based self-help aid. 0% freshmen, 0% undergrads receive athletic scholarships. 92% freshmen, 94% undergrads receive any aid. 88% undergrads borrow to pay for school. **Criteria awarding aid:** *Need-based:* Academics, Leadership *Non-Need-based:* Academics, Leadership.

HUSTON-TILLOTSON UNIVERSITY

900 Chicon Street, Austin, TX 78702
Phone: 512-505-3028 **Financial Aid Phone:** 512.505.3028
E-mail: admission@htu.edu **CEEB Code:** 6280
Fax: 512-505-3192 **Website:** www.htu.edu./ **ACT Code:** 4104

This private school was founded in 1875. It has a 23 acre campus.

RATINGS

Admissions Selectivity Rating: 72 **Fire Safety Rating:** 60* **Green Rating:** 60*

STUDENTS AND FACULTY

Enrollment: 889. **Student Body:** 51% female, 49% male, 3% out-of-state, 3% international (11 countries represented). Asian 0%, African American 72%, Caucasian 5%, Hispanic 19%, Native American 0%, Pacific Islander 0%, Two or more races <1%, Race unknown 0%.
Retention and Graduation: 50% freshmen return for sophomore year.
Faculty: Student/faculty ratio 15:1. 47 full-time faculty, 70% hold PhDs, 57% are members of minority groups, 53% are women. 0% of classes are taught by teaching assistants.

ACADEMICS

Degrees: Bachelor's; Post-bachelor's certificate. **Classes:** Most classes have 20–29 students. **Most popular majors:** Education, General; Business, Management, Marketing, And Related Support Services; Computer And Information Sciences And Support Services. **Special Study Options:** Cooperative education program; Cross-registration; Distance learning; Double major; Dual enrollment; External degree program; Honors program; Independent study; Internships; Liberal arts/career combination; Study abroad; Teacher certification program. **Honors programs:** W.E.B. DuBois Honors Program.

FACILITIES

Housing: Men's dorms; Wellness housing; Women's dorms. **Campus Network:** 100% of classrooms, 100% of dorms, 25% of student union, 100% of libraries, 100% of dining areas, 10% of common outdoor areas, have wireless network access.

CAMPUS LIFE

Environment: Metropolis. **Activities:** Campus Ministries; Choral groups; Dance; Drama/theater; International Student Organization; Jazz band; Literary magazine; Model UN; Music ensembles; Student government; Student-run film society. **Athletics (Intercollegiate):** *Men:* baseball, basketball, soccer, track/field (outdoor). *Women:* basketball, track/field (outdoor), volleyball.

ADMISSIONS

Freshman Academic Profile: Average high school GPA 2.8. 6% in top 10% of high school class, 12% in top 25% of high school class, 53% in top 50% of high school class. **Test scores:** SAT Math middle 50% range 360–460. SAT EBRW middle 50% range 350–460. ACT middle 50% range 14–19. **Basis for Candidate Selection:** *Very important factors include:* rigor of secondary school record, academic GPA. *Important factors include:* class rank, standardized test scores, interview. *Other factors include:* application essay, recommendation(s), extracurricular activities, talent/ability, first generation, alumni/ae relation, work experience. **Freshman Admission Requirements:** High school diploma is required and GED is accepted. *Academic units required:* 4 English, 3 math, 2

science, 3 social studies, 1 computer science, 2 unit from above areas or other academic areas. *Academic units recommended:* 2 foreign language. **Freshman Admission Statistics:** 652 applied, 96% admitted, 43% enrolled. **Transfer Admission Requirements:** college transcript(s), essay or personal statement, Minimum college GPA of 2.0 required. Lowest grade transferable C. **General Admission Information:** Application fee $25. Priority deadline 3/15. Regular application deadline 7/1. Non-fall registration accepted. Admission may be deferred for a maximum of 1 semester.

COSTS AND FINANCIAL AID

Annual tuition $10,396. Room and board $6,946. Required fees $2,034. Average book and supplies expense $600. **Required Forms and Deadlines:** FAFSA;. **Notification of Awards:** Applicants will be notified of awards on a rolling basis beginning 3/1. **Types of Aid:** *Need-based scholarships/grants:* College/university scholarship or grant aid from institutional funds; Federal Pell; Private scholarships; SEOG; State scholarships/grants; United Negro College Fund. *Loans:* Direct PLUS loans; Direct Subsidized Stafford Loans; Direct Unsubsidized Stafford Loans. **Student Employment:** Federal Work-Study Program available. **Financial Aid Statistics:** 25% needy freshmen, 33% needy undergrads receive need-based scholarship or grant aid. 33% freshmen, 35% undergrads receive non-need-based scholarship or grant aid. 100% freshmen, 100% undergrads receive need-based self-help aid. 15% freshmen, 14% undergrads receive athletic scholarships. 97% undergrads receive any aid. **Criteria awarding aid:** *Non-Need-based:* Academics, Alumni affiliation, Art, Athletics, Job skills, Leadership, Minority status, Music/drama, Religious affiliation, State/district residency.

IDAHO STATE UNIVERSITY

Museum of Natural History 319, Pocatello, ID 83209-8270
Phone: 208-282-2475 **Financial Aid Phone:** 208-282-2981
E-mail: admiss@isu.edu **CEEB Code:** 4355
Fax: 208-282-4511 **Website:** www.isu.edu **ACT Code:** 918

This public school was founded in 1901. It has a 1100 acre campus.

RATINGS

Admissions Selectivity Rating: 82 **Fire Safety Rating:** 73 **Green Rating:** 60*

STUDENTS AND FACULTY

Enrollment: 8,974. **Student Body:** 50% female, 50% male, 8% out-of-state, 14% international (63 countries represented). Asian 1%, African American 1%, Caucasian 67%, Hispanic 10%, Native American 1%, Pacific Islander <1%, Two or more races 3%, Race unknown 2%.
Retention and Graduation: 71% freshmen return for sophomore year.
Faculty: Student/faculty ratio 15:1. 585 full-time faculty, 51% hold PhDs, 9% are members of minority groups, 45% are women.

ACADEMICS

Degrees: Associate; Bachelor's; Certificate; Doctoral degree—professional practice; Doctoral degree research/scholarship; Master's; Post-bachelor's certificate; Post-master's certificate. **Classes:** Most classes have 10–19 students. Most lab/discussion sessions have 10–19 students. **Most popular majors:** Biology/Biological Sciences, General; Elementary Education and Teaching; Secondary Education and Teaching. **Special Study Options:** Accelerated program; Cooperative education program; Cross-registration; Distance learning; Double major; Dual enrollment; English as a Second Language (ESL); Exchange student program (domestic); Honors program; Independent study; Internships; Liberal arts/career combination; Student-designed major; Study abroad; Teacher certification program; Weekend college. **Honors programs:** Honors courses are offered in small classes and deal with interdisciplinary issues and confront some aspect of the human condition. Innovative teaching and assignments are encourages and interaction with faculty and class members is lively. **Disability Services offered:** Note-taking services; Reader services; Tape recorders; Tutors. **Career services:** Career assessment; Career/job search classes.

FACILITIES

Housing: Apartments for married students; Apartments for single students; Coed dorms; Men's dorms; Special housing for disabled students; Women's dorms; 100% of campus accessible to physically disabled. **Special Academic Facilities/Equipment:** Museum of Natural History, Idaho Accelerator Center, Rendezvous Center. **Campus Network:** 100% of classrooms, 100% of dorms, 100% of student union, 100% of libraries, 100% of dining areas, 25% of common outdoor areas, have wireless network access.

CAMPUS LIFE

Environment: Town. **Activities:** Campus Ministries; Choral groups; Concert band; Dance; Drama/theater; International Student Organization; Jazz band; Marching band; Music ensembles; Musical theater; Opera; Pep band; Radio station; Student government; Student newspaper; Symphony orchestra; Television station; Yearbook. 142 registered organizations, 8 honor societies, 7 religious organizations, 2 fraternities, 3 sororities, on campus. **Athletics (Intercollegiate):** *Men:* basketball, cheerleading, cross-country, football, golf, tennis, track/field (outdoor). *Women:* basketball, cheerleading, cross-country, golf, soccer, softball, tennis, track/field (outdoor), volleyball. **On-Campus Highlights:** Idaho Museum of Natural History.

ADMISSIONS

Freshman Academic Profile: Average high school GPA 3.2. 11% in top 10% of high school class, 30% in top 25% of high school class, 59% in top 50% of high school class. **Test scores:** SAT Math middle 50% range 420–530. SAT EBRW middle 50% range 420–540. ACT middle 50% range 19–25. **Basis for Candidate Selection:** *Other factors include:* academic GPA, standardized test scores. **Freshman Admission Requirements:** High school diploma is required and GED is accepted. *Academic units required:* 4 English, 3 math, 3 science, 1 science labs, 1 foreign language, 2.5 social studies, 1.5 unit from above areas or other academic areas. *Academic units recommended:* 4 math. **Freshman Admission Statistics:** 3,057 applied, 53% admitted, 90% enrolled. **Transfer Admission Requirements:** High school transcript, college transcript(s), standardized test scores, Minimum college GPA of 2.0 required. Lowest grade transferable D. **General Admission Information:** Application fee $50. Non-fall registration accepted. Admission may be deferred for a maximum of 3 years.

COSTS AND FINANCIAL AID

Annual in-state tuition $5,106. Annual out-of-state tuition $18,504. Room and board $6,338. Required fees $1,678. Average book and supplies expense $1,000. **Required Forms and Deadlines:** FAFSA. **Notification of Awards:** Applicants will be notified of awards on a rolling basis beginning 4/1. **Types of Aid:** *Need-based scholarships/grants:* College/university scholarship or grant aid from institutional funds; Federal Nursing Scholarships; Federal Pell; Private scholarships; SEOG; State scholarships/grants. *Loans:* Direct PLUS loans; Direct Subsidized Stafford Loans; Direct Unsubsidized Stafford Loans. **Student Employment:** Federal Work-Study Program available. Institutional employment available. **Financial Aid Statistics:** 77% needy freshmen, 77% needy undergrads receive need-based scholarship or grant aid. 55% freshmen, 30% undergrads receive non-need-based scholarship or grant aid. 70% freshmen, 78% undergrads receive need-based self-help aid. 3% freshmen, 3% undergrads receive athletic scholarships. 73% freshmen, 74.1% undergrads receive any aid. 69% undergrads borrow to pay for school. Average cumulative indebtedness $29,983. **Criteria awarding aid:** *Non-Need-based:* Academics, Alumni affiliation, Art, Athletics, Leadership, Minority status, Music/drama, State/district residency.

ILLINOIS COLLEGE

1101 West College Avenue, Jacksonville, IL 62650
Phone: 217-245-3030
E-mail: admissions@mail.ic.edu **CEEB Code:** 1315
Fax: 217-245-3034 **Website:** www.ic.edu **ACT Code:** 1034

This private school, affiliated with the Presbyterian Church, was founded in 1829. It has a 62 acre campus.

RATINGS

Admissions Selectivity Rating: 85   **Fire Safety Rating:** 60*   **Green Rating:** 60*

STUDENTS AND FACULTY

Enrollment: 947. **Student Body:** 51% female, 49% male, 14% out-of-state, 5% international. Asian 1%, African American 11%, Caucasian 71%, Hispanic 9%, Native American <1%, Pacific Islander <1%, Two or more races 3%, Race unknown 0%.
Retention and Graduation: 77% freshmen return for sophomore year. 59% freshmen graduate within 4 years. 68% freshmen graduate within 6 years. 22% grads go on to further study within 1 year. 13% grads pursue arts and sciences degrees. 5% grads pursue law degrees. 2% grads pursue business degrees. 4% grads pursue medical degrees. **Faculty:** Student/faculty ratio 12:1. 75 full-time faculty, 85% hold PhDs, 7% are members of minority groups, 37% are women.

ACADEMICS

Degrees: Bachelor's; Master's. **Classes:** Most classes have 10–19 students. Most lab/discussion sessions have 10–19 students. **Special Study Options:** Cross-registration; Double major; Dual enrollment; English as a Second Language (ESL); Honors program; Independent study; Internships; Liberal arts/career combination; Student-designed major; Study abroad; Teacher certification program. **Career services:** Career assessment; Career/job search classes; Internships.

FACILITIES

Housing: Apartments for single students; Coed dorms; Men's dorms; Theme housing; Women's dorms. **Special Academic Facilities/Equipment:** Art gallery, language lab.

CAMPUS LIFE

Environment: Rural. **Activities:** Campus Ministries; Choral groups; Concert band; Dance; Drama/theater; International Student Organization; Jazz band; Literary magazine; Model UN; Music ensembles; Pep band; Radio station; Student government; Student newspaper; Symphony orchestra; Yearbook. 72 registered organizations, 12 honor societies, 3 religious organizations, 4 fraternities, 3 sororities, on campus. **Athletics (Intercollegiate):** *Men:* baseball, basketball, cross-country, football, golf, soccer, tennis, track/field (outdoor), track/field (indoor), wrestling. *Women:* basketball, cheerleading, cross-country, golf, soccer, softball, tennis, track/field (outdoor), track/field (indoor), volleyball.

ADMISSIONS

Freshman Academic Profile: Average high school GPA 3.5. 14% in top 10% of high school class, 41% in top 25% of high school class, 80% in top 50% of high school class. 80% from public high schools. **Test scores:** SAT Math middle 50% range 510–620. SAT EBRW middle 50% range 470–610. ACT middle 50% range 19–25. **Basis for Candidate Selection:** *Very important factors include:* rigor of secondary school record, academic GPA, character/personal qualities. *Important factors include:* class rank, application essay, recommendation(s), interview, extracurricular activities, talent/ability. *Other factors include:* standardized test scores, first generation, alumni/ae relation, geographical residence, racial/ethnic status, volunteer work, work experience, level of applicant's interest. **Freshman Admission Requirements:** High school diploma is required and GED is accepted. *Academic units required:* 4 English, 3 math, 2 science, 2 science labs, 1 social studies, 1 history, 3 academic electives. *Academic units recommended:* 4 English, 3 math, 3 science, 3 science labs, 2 foreign language, 1 social studies, 1 history, 3 academic electives. **Freshman Admission Statistics:** 4,121 applied, 55% admitted, 11% enrolled. **Transfer Admission Requirements:** High school transcript, college transcript(s), Minimum college GPA of 2.50 required. Lowest grade transferable C. **General Admission Information:** Non-fall registration accepted. Admission may be deferred for a maximum of 1 year.

COSTS AND FINANCIAL AID

Annual tuition $33,190. Room and board $9,374. Required fees $550. **Required Forms and Deadlines:** FAFSA. **Notification of Awards:** Applicants will be notified of awards on a rolling basis beginning 12/15. **Types of Aid:** *Need-based scholarships/grants:* College/university scholarship or grant aid from institutional funds; Federal Pell; Private scholarships; SEOG; State scholarships/grants. *Loans:* Direct PLUS loans; Direct Subsidized Stafford Loans; Direct Unsubsidized Stafford Loans. **Student Employment:** Federal Work-Study Program available. Institutional employment available. **Financial Aid Statistics:** 100% needy freshmen, 100% needy undergrads receive need-based scholarship or grant aid. 16% freshmen, 15% undergrads receive non-need-based scholarship or grant aid. 83% freshmen, 87% undergrads receive need-based self-help aid. 0% freshmen, 0% undergrads receive athletic scholarships. 86% undergrads borrow to pay for school. Average cumulative indebtedness $32,740. **Criteria awarding aid:** *Non-Need-based:* Academics, Art, Music/drama.

ILLINOIS INSTITUTE OF TECHNOLOGY

10 West 33rd Street, Chicago, IL 60616
Phone: 312-567-3025 **Financial Aid Phone:** 312-567-7219
E-mail: admission@iit.edu **CEEB Code:** 1318
Fax: 312-567-6939 **Website:** http://www.iit.edu/ **ACT Code:** 1040

This private school was founded in 1892. It has a 120 acre campus.

RATINGS
Admissions Selectivity Rating: 88   **Fire Safety Rating:** 83   **Green Rating:** 78

STUDENTS AND FACULTY
Enrollment: 2,722. **Student Body:** 31% female, 69% male, 26% out-of-state, 21% international (94 countries represented). Asian 14%, African American 6%, Caucasian 33%, Hispanic 16%, Native American <1%, Pacific Islander <1%, Two or more races 3%, Race unknown 7%.
Retention and Graduation: 93% freshmen return for sophomore year. 36% freshmen graduate within 4 years. 71% freshmen graduate within 6 years. **Faculty:** Student/faculty ratio 12:1. 413 full-time faculty, 97% hold PhDs, 21% are members of minority groups, 27% are women. 0% of classes are taught by teaching assistants.

ACADEMICS
Degrees: Bachelor's; Doctoral degree—professional practice; Doctoral degree research/scholarship; Master's; Post-bachelor's certificate; Post-master's certificate. **Classes:** Most classes have 10–19 students. Most lab/discussion sessions have fewer than 10 students. **Most popular majors:** Architecture; Computer and Information Sciences, General; Mechanical Engineering. **Special Study Options:** Cooperative education program; Cross-registration; Distance learning; Double major; Dual enrollment; English as a Second Language (ESL); Independent study; Internships; Liberal arts/career combination; Study abroad; Teacher certification program. **Combined degree programs:** BA/JD; BA/MA. **Disability Services offered:** Note-taking services; Reader services; Tape recorders; Tutors. **Career services:** Alumni network; Alumni services; Career assessment; Career/job search classes; Internships; Regional alumni.

FACILITIES
Housing: Apartments for married students; Apartments for single students; Coed dorms; Fraternity/sorority housing; 90% of campus accessible to physically disabled. **Special Academic Facilities/Equipment:** The Center for Accelerator and Particle Physics (CAPP), The Center for Complex Systems and Dynamics (CCSD), The Center for Digital Design and Manufacturing (CDDM), The Center for Electrochemical Science and Engineering, The Center for Excellence in Polymer Science and Engineering, The Center for Integrative Neuroscience and Neuroengineering Research, The Center for the Management of Medical Technology (CMMT), The Center for Molecular Study of Soft Condensed Matter (CMS2), The Center for Strategic Competitiveness (CSC), The Center for the Study of Ethics in the Professions (CSEP), The Center for Synchrotron Radiation Research and Instrumentation, The Center for Work Zone Safety and Mobility (CWZSM), Electric Power and Power Electronics Center (EPPEC), Energy + Power Center, Energy and Sustainability Institute, The Engineering Center For Diabetes Research and Education (ECDRE), The Fluid Dynamics Research Center, The High Performance Computing Center (HPCC), IIT Research Institute (IITRI), The International Center for Sensor Science and Engineering (ICSSE), The International Center for Sustainable New Cities (ICSNC), The Medical Imaging Research Center (MIRC), The National Center for Food Safety and Technology (NCFST), The Particle Technology and Crystallization Center (PTCC), The Pritzker Institute of Biomedical Science and Engineering, The Thermal Processing Technology Center (TPTC), The Wireless Network and Communications Research Center (WiNCom), Main Campus design by Ludwig Mies van der Rohe, McCormick Tribune Campus Center (MTCC) design by Rem Koolhaas, residence hall designed by Helmut Jahn, IIT Research Institute (IITRI), University Technology Park At IIT (UTP), Kemper Room Art Gallery, Illinois Tech Model Railroad (ITMR).

CAMPUS LIFE
Environment: Metropolis. **Activities:** Campus Ministries; Choral groups; Concert band; Dance; Drama/theater; International Student Organization; Literary magazine; Music ensembles; Musical theater; Radio station; Student

government; Student newspaper; Student-run film society; Television station. 100 registered organizations, 4 honor societies, 10 religious organizations, 7 fraternities, 3 sororities, on campus. **Athletics (Intercollegiate):** *Men:* baseball, cross-country, diving, soccer, swimming. *Women:* cross-country, diving, soccer, swimming, volleyball. **On-Campus Highlights:** S.R. Crown Hall (Architecture Building). **Environmental Initiatives:** Creation of an Office of Campus Energy and Sustainability and the Wanger Institute of Sustainable Energy Research bringing students, faculty, staff, and alumni together to address complex sustainability issues.

ADMISSIONS
Freshman Academic Profile: 87% from public high schools. **Test score**s: SAT Math middle 50% range 650–730. SAT EBRW middle 50% range 580–680. ACT middle 50% range 25–31. **Basis for Candidate Selection:** *Very important factors include:* rigor of secondary school record, academic GPA, standardized test scores. *Important factors include:* class rank, recommendation(s). *Other factors include:* application essay, interview, extracurricular activities, talent/ability, character/personal qualities, first generation, alumni/ae relation, volunteer work, work experience, level of applicant's interest. **Freshman Admission Requirements:** High school diploma is required and GED is accepted. *Academic units required:* 4 English, 4 math, 3 science, 2 science labs, 2 foreign language, 2 social studies. *Academic units recommended:* 4 English, 4 math, 3 science, 2 science labs, 2 foreign language, 2 social studies, 2 history, 1 computer science, 1 visual/performing arts. **Freshman Admission Statistics:** 4,708 applied, 54% admitted, 19% enrolled. **Transfer Admission Requirements:** college transcript(s), essay or personal statement, statement of good standing from prior institution(s). Minimum college GPA of 3.0 required. Lowest grade transferable C. **General Admission Information:** Priority deadline 12/1. Regular application deadline 8/1. Non-fall registration accepted.

COSTS AND FINANCIAL AID
Annual tuition $45,872. Room and board $12,762. Required fees $1,774. Average book and supplies expense $1,250. **Required Forms and Deadlines:** FAFSA. **Notification of Awards:** Applicants will be notified of awards on a rolling basis beginning 2/15. **Types of Aid:** *Need-based scholarships/grants:* College/university scholarship or grant aid from institutional funds; Federal Pell; Private scholarships; SEOG; State scholarships/grants. *Loans:* Direct PLUS loans; Direct Subsidized Stafford Loans; Direct Unsubsidized Stafford Loans. **Student Employment:** Federal Work-Study Program available. Institutional employment available. **Financial Aid Statistics:** 99% needy freshmen, 100% needy undergrads receive need-based scholarship or grant aid. 20% freshmen, 12% undergrads receive non-need-based scholarship or grant aid. 65% freshmen, 71% undergrads receive need-based self-help aid. 0% freshmen, 0% undergrads receive athletic scholarships. 99% freshmen, 97% undergrads receive any aid. 54% undergrads borrow to pay for school. Average cumulative indebtedness $32,671. **Criteria awarding aid:** *Non-Need-based:* Academics, Alumni affiliation, Leadership.

ILLINOIS STATE UNIVERSITY

Office of Admissions, Normal, IL 61790-2200
Phone: 309-438-2181 **Financial Aid Phone:** 309-438-2231
E-mail: admissions@illinoisstate.edu **CEEB Code:** 1319
Fax: 309-438-3932 **Website:** https://illinoisstate.edu/ **ACT Code:** 1042

This public school was founded in 1857. It has a 1100 acre campus.

RATINGS
Admissions Selectivity Rating: 77   **Fire Safety Rating:** 71   **Green Rating:** 83

STUDENTS AND FACULTY
Enrollment: 18,199. **Student Body:** 55% female, 45% male, 2% out-of-state, 1% international (71 countries represented). Asian 2%, African American 9%, Caucasian 72%, Hispanic 12%, Native American <1%, Pacific Islander <1%, Two or more races 3%, Race unknown <1%.
Retention and Graduation: 79% freshmen return for sophomore year. 50% freshmen graduate within 4 years. 70% freshmen graduate within 6 years. **Faculty:** Student/faculty ratio 19:1. 911 full-time faculty, 82% hold PhDs, 15% are members of minority groups, 52% are women.

ACADEMICS
Degrees: Bachelor's; Doctoral degree—professional practice; Doctoral degree research/scholarship; Master's; Post-bachelor's certificate; Post-master's certificate. **Classes:** Most classes have 20–29 students. Most lab/discussion

sessions have 20–29 students. **Most popular majors:** Special Education and Teaching, General; Business Administration and Management, General; Elementary Education and Teaching. **Special Study Options:** Accelerated program; Cooperative education program; Distance learning; Double major; Dual enrollment; English as a Second Language (ESL); Exchange student program (domestic); Honors program; Independent study; Internships; Student-designed major; Study abroad; Teacher certification program. **Honors programs:** The Honors Program at Illinois State University promotes exceptional learning for exceptional learners by enriching students' learning experiences at Illinois State University. This is done by providing opportunities, resources, and support for Honors students to customize their learning in ways that are valuable to them in General Education and across all disciplines. **Combined degree programs:** BA/MA. **Disability Services offered:** Note-taking services; Reader services; Tape recorders; Tutors. **Career services:** Alumni services; Career assessment; Internships.

FACILITIES

Housing: Apartments for married students; Apartments for single students; Coed dorms; Fraternity/sorority housing; Special housing for disabled students; Special housing for international students; Theme housing; Wellness housing; Women's dorms; 100% of campus accessible to physically disabled. **Special Academic Facilities/Equipment:** Art gallery, cultural museums, on-campus elementary and secondary schools, greenhouse, farm, planetarium.

CAMPUS LIFE

Environment: City. **Activities:** Campus Ministries; Choral groups; Concert band; Dance; Drama/theater; International Student Organization; Jazz band; Literary magazine; Marching band; Model UN; Music ensembles; Musical theater; Opera; Pep band; Radio station; Student government; Student newspaper; Student-run film society; Symphony orchestra; Television station. 370 registered organizations, 24 honor societies, 20 fraternities, 19 sororities, on campus. **Athletics (Intercollegiate):** *Men:* baseball, basketball, cheerleading, cross-country, football, golf, tennis, track/field (outdoor), track/field (indoor). *Women:* basketball, cheerleading, cross-country, diving, golf, gymnastics, soccer, softball, swimming, tennis, track/field (outdoor), track/field (indoor), volleyball. **On-Campus Highlights:** Student Fitness Center. **Environmental Initiatives:** Establishing a formal Office of Sustainability with 2 full time staff, 1 graduate assistant and multiple interns.

ADMISSIONS

Freshman Academic Profile: Average high school GPA 3.5. 92% from public high schools. **Test scores:** SAT Math middle 50% range 510–610. SAT EBRW middle 50% range 510–610. ACT middle 50% range 20–26. **Basis for Candidate Selection:** *Very important factors include:* academic GPA, standardized test scores. *Other factors include:* application essay, talent/ability, first generation, geographical residence, state residency, racial/ethnic status. **Freshman Admission Requirements:** High school diploma is required and GED is accepted. *Academic units required:* 8 English, 6 math, 4 science, 4 science labs, 4 foreign language, 4 social studies, 4 history, 4 visual/performing arts. **Freshman Admission Statistics:** 16,151 applied, 82% admitted, 29% enrolled. **Transfer Admission Requirements:** college transcript(s), essay or personal statement, Minimum college GPA of 3.0 required. Lowest grade transferable D. **General Admission Information:** Application fee $50. Priority deadline 11/15. Regular application deadline 4/1. Non-fall registration accepted. Admission may be deferred for a maximum of 2 semesters.

COSTS AND FINANCIAL AID

Annual in-state tuition $11,524. Annual out-of-state tuition $23,048. Room and board $9,850. Required fees $3,308. Average book and supplies expense $802. **Required Forms and Deadlines:** FAFSA. **Notification of Awards:** Applicants will be notified of awards on a rolling basis beginning 4/1. **Types of Aid:** *Need-based scholarships/grants:* College/university scholarship or grant aid from institutional funds; Federal Nursing Scholarships; Federal Pell; Private scholarships; SEOG; State scholarships/grants. *Loans:* Direct PLUS loans; Direct Subsidized Stafford Loans; Direct Unsubsidized Stafford Loans. **Student Employment:** Federal Work-Study Program available. Institutional employment available. **Financial Aid Statistics:** 56% needy freshmen, 56% needy undergrads receive need-based scholarship or grant aid. 55% freshmen, 39% undergrads receive non-need-based scholarship or grant aid. 73% freshmen, 74% undergrads receive need-based self-help aid. 2% freshmen, 2% undergrads receive athletic scholarships. 68% undergrads borrow to pay for school. Average cumulative indebtedness $31,687. **Criteria awarding aid:** *Need-based:* Academics, Art, Music/drama *Non-Need-based:* Academics, Art, Athletics, Music/drama.

ILLINOIS WESLEYAN UNIVERSITY

P.O. Box 2900, Bloomington, IL 61702-2900
Phone: 309-556-3031 **Financial Aid Phone:** 309-556-3096
E-mail: iwuadmit@iwu.edu **CEEB Code:** 1320
Fax: 309-556-3820 **Website:** www.iwu.edu **ACT Code:** 1044

This private school was founded in 1850. It has a 82 acre campus.

RATINGS

Admissions Selectivity Rating: 86   **Fire Safety Rating:** 94   **Green Rating:** 64

STUDENTS AND FACULTY

Enrollment: 1,685. **Student Body:** 52% female, 48% male, 16% out-of-state, 6% international (23 countries represented). Asian 6%, African American 6%, Caucasian 70%, Hispanic 9%, Native American 0%, Pacific Islander 0%, Two or more races 3%, Race unknown 1%. **Retention and Graduation:** 91% freshmen return for sophomore year. 71% freshmen graduate within 4 years. 78% freshmen graduate within 6 years. 21% grads go on to further study within 1 year. **Faculty:** Student/faculty ratio 11:1. 130 full-time faculty, 95% hold PhDs, 5% are members of minority groups, 45% are women. 0% of classes are taught by teaching assistants.

ACADEMICS

Degrees: Bachelor's. **Classes:** Most classes have 10–19 students. Most lab/discussion sessions have 10–19 students. **Most popular majors:** Business/Commerce, General; Accounting; Registered Nursing/Registered Nurse. **Special Study Options:** Double major; Exchange student program (domestic); Honors program; Independent study; Internships; Student-designed major; Study abroad; Teacher certification program. **Honors programs:** IWU offers a research honors designation to eligible senior students who successfully complete and defend an intensive, advanced research or creative project under the direction of an interdisciplinary faculty committee. Performance Honors designations are also available in the Art, Music, and Theatre Arts. **Disability Services offered:** Note-taking services; Reader services; Tape recorders; Tutors. **Career services:** Alumni network; Alumni services; Career assessment; Career/job search classes; Internships; Regional alumni.

FACILITIES

Housing: Apartments for single students; Coed dorms; Fraternity/sorority housing; Special housing for disabled students; Special housing for international students; 80% of campus accessible to physically disabled. **Special Academic Facilities/Equipment:** observatory, computerized music lab, graphic design studio, Ames Library archives and special collections, visual anthropology lab, social science lab, maker space.

CAMPUS LIFE

Environment: City. **Activities:** Campus Ministries; Choral groups; Concert band; Dance; Drama/theater; International Student Organization; Jazz band; Literary magazine; Model UN; Music ensembles; Musical theater; Opera; Pep band; Radio station; Student government; Student newspaper; Student-run film society; Symphony orchestra; Television station; Yearbook. 200 registered organizations, 29 honor societies, 8 religious organizations, 5 fraternities, 4 sororities, on campus. **Athletics (Intercollegiate):** *Men:* baseball, basketball, cross-country, diving, football, golf, soccer, swimming, tennis, track/field (outdoor), track/field (indoor). *Women:* basketball, cross-country, diving, golf, soccer, softball, swimming, tennis, track/field (outdoor), track/field (indoor), volleyball. **On-Campus Highlights:** The Ames Library. **Environmental Initiatives:** IWU has a commitment to environmental sustainability in its mission statement.

ADMISSIONS

Freshman Academic Profile: Average high school GPA 3.8. 34% in top 10% of high school class, 63% in top 25% of high school class, 95% in top 50% of high school class. 85% from public high schools. **Test scores:** SAT Math middle 50% range 550–665. SAT EBRW middle 50% range 570–660. ACT middle 50% range 24–29. **Basis for Candidate Selection:** *Very important factors include:* rigor of secondary school record, academic GPA, interview. *Important factors include:* class rank, application essay, standardized test scores, extracurricular activities, talent/ability, character/personal qualities. *Other factors include:* recommendation(s), first generation, alumni/ae relation, geographical residence, state residency, racial/ethnic status, volunteer work, work experience, level of applicant's interest. **Freshman Admission Requirements:** High school diploma is required and GED is accepted. *Academic units recommended:* 4 English, 3 math, 3 science, 2 science labs, 3 foreign language, 2 social studies. **Freshman Admission Statistics:** 3,785 applied, 59% admitted, 22% enrolled. **Transfer Admission Requirements:** High school transcript, college transcript(s), essay or personal statement, standardized test scores, Minimum college GPA of 2.0 required. Lowest grade transferable C-. **General Admission Information:** Non-fall registration accepted. Admission may be deferred for a maximum of 1 year.

COSTS AND FINANCIAL AID

Annual tuition $49,284. Room and board $11,412. Required fees $204. Average book and supplies expense $800. **Required Forms and Deadlines:** FAFSA; Institution's own financial aid form. **Notification of Awards:** Applicants will be notified of awards on a rolling basis beginning 3/1. **Types of Aid:** *Need-based scholarships/grants:* College/university scholarship or grant aid from institutional funds; Federal Pell; Private scholarships; SEOG; State scholarships/grants. *Loans:* Direct PLUS loans; Direct Subsidized Stafford Loans; Direct Unsubsidized Stafford Loans. **Student Employment:** Federal Work-Study Program available. Institutional employment available. **Financial Aid Statistics:** 100% needy freshmen, 100% needy undergrads receive need-based scholarship or grant aid. 17% freshmen, 11% undergrads receive non-need-based scholarship or grant aid. 79% freshmen, 74% undergrads receive need-based self-help aid. 0% freshmen, 0% undergrads receive athletic scholarships. 100% freshmen, 99% undergrads receive any aid. 68% undergrads borrow to pay for school. Average cumulative indebtedness $35,077. **Criteria awarding aid:** *Need-based:* Academics, Art, Music/drama. *Non-Need-based:* Academics, Art, Music/drama.

IMMACULATA UNIVERSITY

1145 West King Road, Immaculata, PA 19345-0642
Phone: (610)647-4400 x3060 **Financial Aid Phone:** 610-647-4400
E-mail: admiss@immaculata.edu **CEEB Code:** 2320
Fax: 610-640-0836 **Website:** www.immaculata.edu **ACT Code:** 3596

This private school, affiliated with the Roman Catholic Church, was founded in 1920. It has a 373 acre campus.

RATINGS

Admissions Selectivity Rating: 76   **Fire Safety Rating:** 60*   **Green Rating:** 60*

STUDENTS AND FACULTY

Enrollment: 1,304. **Student Body:** 71% female, 29% male, 23% out-of-state, 2% international. Asian 2%, African American 16%, Caucasian 70%, Hispanic 7%, Native American 0%, Pacific Islander 0%, Two or more races 2%, Race unknown 1%.
Retention and Graduation: 86% freshmen return for sophomore year. 56% freshmen graduate within 4 years. 67% freshmen graduate within 6 years.
Faculty: Student/faculty ratio 9:1. 85 full-time faculty, 79% hold PhDs, 11% are members of minority groups, 68% are women. 0% of classes are taught by teaching assistants.

ACADEMICS

Degrees: Associate; Bachelor's; Certificate; Doctoral degree—professional practice; Doctoral degree research/scholarship; Master's; Post-bachelor's certificate; Post-master's certificate. **Classes:** Most classes have 10–19 students. Most lab/discussion sessions have 10–19 students. **Most popular majors:** Teacher Education and Professional Development, Specific Levels and Methods, Other; Exercise Science and Kinesiology; Registered Nursing/Registered Nurse. **Special Study Options:** Accelerated program; Cross-registration; Distance learning; Double major; Dual enrollment; Honors program; Independent study; Internships; Liberal arts/career combination; Study abroad; Teacher certification program. **Honors programs:** Please see website for a description of the honors program: https://www.immaculata.edu/academics/honors-program/. **Disability Services offered:** Note-taking services; Reader services; Tape recorders; Tutors. **Career services:** Alumni network; Alumni services; Career assessment; Career/job search classes; Internships.

FACILITIES

Housing: Apartments for single students; Coed dorms; Men's dorms; Women's dorms 100% of campus accessible to physically disabled. **Campus Network:** 100% of classrooms, 100% of dorms, 100% of student union, 100% of

libraries, 100% of dining areas, 90% of common outdoor areas, have wireless network access.

CAMPUS LIFE

Environment: Town. **Activities:** Campus Ministries; Choral groups; Concert band; Dance; Drama/theater; International Student Organization; Jazz band; Literary magazine; Music ensembles; Musical theater; Student government; Student newspaper; Symphony orchestra. 40 registered organizations, on campus. **Athletics (Intercollegiate):** *Men:* basketball, golf, soccer, tennis. *Women:* basketball, cross-country, field hockey, golf, lacrosse, soccer, softball, tennis, volleyball. **On-Campus Highlights:** Gabriele Library.

ADMISSIONS

Freshman Academic Profile: Average high school GPA 3.3. 7% in top 10% of high school class, 19% in top 25% of high school class, 57% in top 50% of high school class. **Test scores:** SAT Math middle 50% range 480–590. SAT EBRW middle 50% range 500–608. ACT middle 50% range 18–24. **Basis for Candidate Selection:** *Very important factors include:* rigor of secondary school record, academic GPA. *Important factors include:* class rank, application essay, recommendation(s), first generation. *Other factors include:* standardized test scores, interview, extracurricular activities, talent/ability, character/personal qualities, alumni/ae relation, religious affiliation/commitment, volunteer work, work experience, level of applicant's interest. **Freshman Admission Requirements:** High school diploma is required and GED is accepted. *Academic units required:* 4 English, 2 math, 2 science, 1 science labs, 2 foreign language, 2 social studies, 4 academic electives. **Freshman Admission Statistics:** 1,969 applied, 81% admitted, 16% enrolled. **Transfer Admission Requirements:** High school transcript, college transcript(s), Minimum college GPA of 2.0 required. Lowest grade transferable C. **General Admission Information:** Application fee $35. Non-fall registration accepted.

COSTS AND FINANCIAL AID

Annual tuition $26,900. Room and board $12,620. Required fees $1,200. Average book and supplies expense $2,166. **Required Forms and Deadlines:** FAFSA. **Notification of Awards:** Applicants will be notified of awards on a rolling basis beginning 10/1. **Types of Aid:** *Need-based scholarships/grants:* College/university scholarship or grant aid from institutional funds; Federal Pell; Private scholarships; SEOG; State scholarships/grants; United Negro College Fund. *Loans:* Direct PLUS loans; Direct Subsidized Stafford Loans; Direct Unsubsidized Stafford Loans. **Student Employment:** Federal Work-Study Program available. Institutional employment available. **Financial Aid Statistics:** 64% needy freshmen, 69% needy undergrads receive need-based scholarship or grant aid. 97% freshmen, 90% undergrads receive non-need-based scholarship or grant aid. 83% freshmen, 84% undergrads receive need-based self-help aid. 0% freshmen, 0% undergrads receive athletic scholarships. 100% freshmen receive any aid. 85% undergrads borrow to pay for school. Average cumulative indebtedness $55,126.

INDIANA STATE UNIVERSITY

Office of Admissions, 318 N 6th Street, Terre Haute, IN 47809-1902
Phone: 812-237-2121 **Financial Aid Phone:** 812-237-2215
E-mail: admissions@indstate.edu **CEEB Code:** 1322
Fax: 812-237-8023 **Website:** www.indstate.edu **ACT Code:** 1206

This public school was founded in 1865. It has a 435 acre campus.

RATINGS

Admissions Selectivity Rating: 74   **Fire Safety Rating:** 92   **Green Rating:** 87

STUDENTS AND FACULTY

Enrollment: 9,604. **Student Body:** 56% female, 44% male, 28% out-of-state, 2% international (52 countries represented). Asian 1%, African American 18%, Caucasian 67%, Hispanic 5%, Native American <1%, Pacific Islander <1%, Two or more races 4%, Race unknown 1%.
Retention and Graduation: 65% freshmen return for sophomore year. 29% freshmen graduate within 4 years. 41% freshmen graduate within 6 years. 13% grads go on to further study within 1 year. 6% grads pursue arts and sciences degrees. 1% grads pursue law degrees. 2% grads pursue business degrees. <1% grads pursue medical degrees. **Faculty:** Student/faculty ratio 18:1. 474 full-time faculty, 78% hold PhDs, 17% are members of minority groups, 47% are women. 3% of classes are taught by teaching assistants.

ACADEMICS

Degrees: Bachelor's; Certificate; Doctoral degree—professional practice; Doctoral degree research/scholarship; Master's; Post-bachelor's certificate; Post-master's certificate. **Classes:** Most classes have 20–29 students. **Most popular majors:** Registered Nursing/Registered Nurse; Business Administration and Management, General. **Special Study Options:** Accelerated program; Cooperative education program; Distance learning; Double major; Dual enrollment; English as a Second Language (ESL); Honors program; Independent study; Internships; Study abroad; Teacher certification program. **Honors programs:** University Honors Program. **Disability Services offered:** Note-taking services; Reader services; Tape recorders; Tutors. **Career services:** Alumni network; Alumni services; Career assessment; Career/job search classes; Internships; Regional alumni.

FACILITIES

Housing: Apartments for married students; Apartments for single students; Coed dorms; Fraternity/sorority housing; Special housing for disabled students; Theme housing; 98% of campus accessible to physically disabled. **Special Academic Facilities/Equipment:** Some of our special buildings/equipment on campus include music hall, art gallery, civic center, museum, flight simulator, audio-visual center, observatory, theaters, and a nursing training simulator. **Campus Network:** 100% of classrooms, 100% of dorms, 100% of student union, 100% of libraries, 100% of dining areas, 100% of common outdoor areas, have wireless network access.

CAMPUS LIFE

Environment: Town. **Activities:** Campus Ministries; Choral groups; Concert band; Dance; Drama/theater; International Student Organization; Jazz band; Literary magazine; Marching band; Music ensembles; Musical theater; Pep band; Radio station; Student government; Student newspaper; Student-run film society; Symphony orchestra; Yearbook. 261 registered organizations, 22 honor societies, 17 religious organizations, 14 fraternities, 14 sororities, on campus. **Athletics (Intercollegiate):** *Men:* baseball, basketball, cross-country, football, track/field (outdoor), track/field (indoor). *Women:* basketball, cross-country, golf, soccer, softball, track/field (outdoor), track/field (indoor), volleyball. **On-Campus Highlights:** Hulman Memorial Student Union. **Environmental Initiatives:** The signing of the American Colleges & Universities President's Climate Commitment that resulted in the development of a Climate Action Plan and three rounds of carbon footprint analyses.

ADMISSIONS

Freshman Academic Profile: Average high school GPA 3.2. 13% in top 10% of high school class, 33% in top 25% of high school class, 68% in top 50% of high school class. **Test scores:** SAT Math middle 50% range 450–560. SAT EBRW middle 50% range 460–580. ACT middle 50% range 16–23. **Basis for Candidate Selection:** *Very important factors include:* rigor of secondary school record, academic GPA. *Other factors include:* class rank, application essay, standardized test scores, recommendation(s), interview, extracurricular activities, talent/ability, character/personal qualities. **Freshman Admission Requirements:** High school diploma is required and GED is accepted. *Academic units recommended:* 4 English, 4 math, 3 science, 3 science labs, 1 foreign language, 2 social studies, 1 history, 2 academic electives, 2 unit from above areas or other academic areas. **Freshman Admission Statistics:** 10,008 applied, 90% admitted, 21% enrolled. **Transfer Admission Requirements:** college transcript(s), Minimum college GPA of 2.0 required. Lowest grade transferable C. **General Admission Information:** Application fee $25. Priority deadline 6/1. Regular application deadline 8/15. Non-fall registration accepted.

COSTS AND FINANCIAL AID

Annual in-state tuition $9,036. Annual out-of-state tuition $19,960. Room and board $10,800. Required fees $200. Average book and supplies expense $1,200. **Required Forms and Deadlines:** FAFSA. **Notification of Awards:** Applicants will be notified of awards on a rolling basis beginning 2/1. **Types of Aid:** *Need-based scholarships/grants:* College/university scholarship or grant aid from institutional funds; Federal Pell; SEOG; State scholarships/grants. *Loans:* Direct PLUS loans; Direct Subsidized Stafford Loans; Direct Unsubsidized Stafford Loans. **Student Employment:** Federal Work-Study Program available. Institutional employment available. **Financial Aid Statistics:** 62% needy freshmen, 61% needy undergrads receive need-based scholarship or grant aid. 62% freshmen, 51% undergrads receive non-need-based scholarship or grant aid. 70% freshmen, 71% undergrads receive need-based self-help aid. 4% freshmen, 4% undergrads receive athletic scholarships. 92% freshmen, 81% undergrads receive any aid. 69% undergrads borrow to pay for school. Average cumulative indebtedness $26,223. **Criteria awarding aid:** *Need-based:* Academics. *Non-Need-based:* Academics, Alumni affiliation, Art, Athletics, Minority status, Music/drama, State/district residency.

INDIANA UNIVERSITY—BLOOMINGTON

940 E. Seventh Street, Bloomington, IN 47405
Phone: 812-855-0661 **Financial Aid Phone:** 812-855-6500
E-mail: iuadmit@indiana.edu **CEEB Code:** 1324
Fax: 812-855-5102 **Website:** https://www.indiana.edu/ **ACT Code:** 1210

This public school was founded in 1820. It has a 1939 acre campus.

RATINGS

Admissions Selectivity Rating: 85   **Fire Safety Rating:** 94   **Green Rating:** 86

STUDENTS AND FACULTY

Enrollment: 32,794. **Student Body:** 49% female, 51% male, 36% out-of-state, 8% international (116 countries represented). Asian 6%, African American 5%, Caucasian 69%, Hispanic 7%, Native American <1%, Pacific Islander <1%, Two or more races 5%, Race unknown <1%.
Retention and Graduation: 90% freshmen return for sophomore year. 67% freshmen graduate within 4 years. 79% freshmen graduate within 6 years.
Faculty: Student/faculty ratio 16:1. 2,210 full-time faculty, 90% hold PhDs, 20% are members of minority groups, 40% are women.

ACADEMICS

Degrees: Associate; Bachelor's; Certificate; Diploma; Doctoral degree—professional practice; Doctoral degree research/scholarship; Master's; Post-bachelor's certificate; Post-master's certificate. **Classes:** Most classes have 20–29 students. Most lab/discussion sessions have 20–29 students. **Most popular majors:** Public Administration; Business/Commerce, General. **Special Study Options:** Accelerated program; Cooperative education program; Distance learning; Double major; Dual enrollment; English as a Second Language (ESL); External degree program; Honors program; Independent study; Internships; Liberal arts/career combination; Student-designed major; Study abroad; Teacher certification program. **Honors programs:** Hutton Honors College and Hudson & Holland Scholar Program. **Combined degree programs:** BA/MA. **Disability Services offered:** Note-taking services; Reader services; Tape recorders; Tutors. **Career services:** Alumni network; Alumni services; Career assessment; Career/job search classes; Internships; Regional alumni.

FACILITIES

Housing: Apartments for married students; Apartments for single students; Coed dorms; Cooperative housing; Fraternity/sorority housing; Men's dorms; Special housing for disabled students; Special housing for international students; Theme housing; Women's dorms; 95% of campus accessible to physically disabled. **Special Academic Facilities/Equipment:** Art Gallery, Art Museum, Mathers Museum of World Cultures, Kirkwood Observatory, Hilltop Garden and Nature Center, Student Recreational Sports and Aquatic Center, Musical Arts Center, Wildermuth Intramural Center, Lilly Library.

CAMPUS LIFE

Environment: City. **Activities:** Campus Ministries; Choral groups; Concert band; Dance; Drama/theater; International Student Organization; Jazz band; Literary magazine; Marching band; Model UN; Music ensembles; Musical theater; Opera; Pep band; Radio station; Student government; Student newspaper; Symphony orchestra; Television station; Yearbook. 830 registered organizations, 43 honor societies, 51 religious organizations, 35 fraternities, 33 sororities, on campus. **Athletics (Intercollegiate):** *Men:* baseball, basketball, cheerleading, cross-country, diving, football, golf, soccer, swimming, tennis, track/field (outdoor), wrestling. *Women:* basketball, cheerleading, cross-country, diving, field hockey, golf, soccer, softball, swimming, tennis, track/field (outdoor), volleyball, water polo. **On-Campus Highlights:** Indiana Memorial Union. **Environmental Initiatives:** The Bicentennial Strategic Plan (IU turns 200 in 2020) was adopted by the Board of Trustees in December establishing Core Value 7: "Sustainability, stewardship and accountability for the natural, human, and economic resources and relationships entrusted to IU." Bicentennial Priority 3: Support innovative campus "living laboratory" initiatives that provide opportunities to integrate campus operations, faculty and student research, education, student life, and community engagement to applied, solutions-oriented sustainability research. Bicentennial Priority

8: Building for Excellence—IU has also become a leader in high-quality environmentally conscious design, and leads the Big Ten in LEED-certified green buildings with twelve certified to date, including four at the gold level (platinum is the highest certification). This strategy pays dividends for the life of each building in terms of occupant health and productivity, resource efficiency, life cycle cost savings and retention of human capital. Bicentennial Action Item 3: IU will implement plans to solidify IU's Focus on efficient and environmentally conscious campus design and operation by: a. Completing and implementing pedestrian, transportation, and bicycle sub-master plans on each campus. b. Certifying all major new buildings with the LEED Green Building Certification System and elevate the minimum certification level to Gold. c. Continuing to explore and research a variety of energy and utility supply and delivery options that reflect changes in economies, demand, and climate variables. d. Achieving the goals for energy efficiency and emissions reductions called for in the Campus Master Plan and the Integrated Energy Master Plan for the IU Bloomington campus; expand that analysis to all campuses. e. Increasing energy and utility system efficiency while reducing demand and consumption. Continuing Priorities Give special emphasis on all campuses to improving traffic flow, making them more "pedestrian and bicycle friendly," and to improving parking and alternative modes of transportation for students, faculty, and staff. Expand efforts to make all IU campuses more energy efficient and sustainable.

ADMISSIONS

Freshman Academic Profile: Average high school GPA 3.7. 35% in top 10% of high school class, 69% in top 25% of high school class, 95% in top 50% of high school class. **Test scores:** SAT Math middle 50% range 570–690. SAT EBRW middle 50% range 580–670. ACT middle 50% range 24–31. **Basis for Candidate Selection:** *Very important factors include:* rigor of secondary school record, class rank, academic GPA, standardized test scores. *Important factors include:* application essay, *Other factors include:* recommendation(s), interview, extracurricular activities, talent/ability, character/personal qualities, first generation, alumni/ae relation, geographical residence, state residency, racial/ethnic status, volunteer work, work experience. **Freshman Admission Requirements:** High school diploma is required and GED is accepted. *Academic units required:* 4 English, 3.5 math, 3 science, 2 science labs, 2 foreign language, 3 social studies, 1.5 academic electives. **Freshman Admission Statistics:** 42,902 applied, 78% admitted, 25% enrolled. **Transfer Admission Requirements:** college transcript(s), Minimum college GPA of 2.0 required. Lowest grade transferable C. **General Admission Information:** Application fee $65. Priority deadline 2/1. Non-fall registration accepted. Admission may be deferred for a maximum of 1 year.

COSTS AND FINANCIAL AID

Annual in-state tuition $9,575. Annual out-of-state tuition $35,140. Room and board $10,830. Required fees $1,372. Average book and supplies expense $1,110. **Required Forms and Deadlines:** FAFSA. **Notification of Awards:** Applicants will be notified of awards on a rolling basis beginning 2/15. **Types of Aid:** *Need-based scholarships/grants:* College/university scholarship or grant aid from institutional funds; Federal Pell; Private scholarships; SEOG; State scholarships/grants. *Loans:* Direct PLUS loans; Direct Subsidized Stafford Loans; Direct Unsubsidized Stafford Loans. **Student Employment:** Federal Work-Study Program available. Institutional employment available. **Financial Aid Statistics:** 87% needy freshmen, 81% needy undergrads receive need-based scholarship or grant aid. 24% freshmen, 19% undergrads receive non-need-based scholarship or grant aid. 51% freshmen, 56% undergrads receive need-based self-help aid. 1% freshmen, 1% undergrads receive athletic scholarships. 84.7% freshmen, 74.6% undergrads receive any aid. 44% undergrads borrow to pay for school. Average cumulative indebtedness $27,555. **Criteria awarding aid:** *Need-based:* Academics, Alumni affiliation, Art, Athletics, Leadership, Minority status, Music/drama. *Non-Need-based:* Academics, Art, Athletics, Leadership, Minority status, Music/drama, Religious affiliation.

INDIANA UNIVERSITY EAST

2325 Chester Boulevard, Richmond, IN 47374-1289
Phone: 765-973-8208 **Financial Aid Phone:** 765-973-8206
E-mail: applynow@iue.edu **CEEB Code:** 1194
Fax: 765-973-8209 **Website:** https://www.iue.edu/ **ACT Code:** 1216

This public school was founded in 1971. It has a 182 acre campus.

RATINGS
Admissions Selectivity Rating: 85   **Fire Safety Rating:** 60*   **Green Rating:** 60*

STUDENTS AND FACULTY
Enrollment: 3,135. **Student Body:** 65% female, 35% male, 28% out-of-state, 2% international (44 countries represented). Asian 1%, African American 5%, Caucasian 76%, Hispanic 4%, Native American <1%, Pacific Islander <1%, Two or more races 4%, Race unknown 8%.
Retention and Graduation: 63% freshmen return for sophomore year. 30% freshmen graduate within 4 years. 40% freshmen graduate within 6 years.
Faculty: Student/faculty ratio 15:1. 111 full-time faculty, 80% hold PhDs, 14% are members of minority groups, 65% are women.

ACADEMICS
Degrees: Bachelor's; Certificate; Master's; Post-bachelor's certificate. **Classes:** Most classes have 10–19 students. **Most popular majors:** Psychology, General; Registered Nursing/Registered Nurse; Business Administration and Management, General. **Special Study Options:** Distance learning; Double major; Dual enrollment; External degree program; Honors program; Independent study; Internships; Study abroad; Teacher certification program. **Honors programs:** The Honors Program requirements include: the completion of at least 21 credit hours of relevant coursework, participation in extra-curricular activities and advising specific to the Honors Program, as well as the submission of a final portfolio. **Disability Services offered:** Note-taking services; Reader services; Tape recorders. **Career services:** Alumni network; Alumni services; Career assessment; Career/job search classes; Internships; Regional alumni.

CAMPUS LIFE
Environment: Town. **Activities:** Campus Ministries; Choral groups; Literary magazine; Music ensembles; Pep band; Student government; Television station. 35 registered organizations, 5 honor societies, 2 religious organizations, on campus. **Athletics (Intercollegiate):** *Men:* basketball, golf. *Women:* volleyball. **On-Campus Highlights:** Graf Recreation Center.

ADMISSIONS
Freshman Academic Profile: Average high school GPA 3.3. 12% in top 10% of high school class, 35% in top 25% of high school class, 69% in top 50% of high school class. **Test scores:** SAT Math middle 50% range 460–560. SAT EBRW middle 50% range 470–580. ACT middle 50% range 17–23. **Basis for Candidate Selection:** *Very important factors include:* rigor of secondary school record, class rank, standardized test scores. *Important factors include:* academic GPA. *Other factors include:* recommendation(s), geographical residence, state residency. **Freshman Admission Requirements:** High school diploma is required and GED is accepted. *Academic units required:* 4 English, 3 math, 3 science, 3 science labs, 3 social studies, 4 academic electives. **Freshman Admission Statistics:** 2,316 applied, 63% admitted, 31% enrolled. **Transfer Admission Requirements:** college transcript(s), Minimum college GPA of 2.0 required. Lowest grade transferable C. **General Admission Information:** Application fee $35. Priority deadline 5/1. Non-fall registration accepted.

COSTS AND FINANCIAL AID
Annual in-state tuition $6,895. Annual out-of-state tuition $19,346. Required fees $632. **Required Forms and Deadlines:** FAFSA; Institution's own financial aid form. **Notification of Awards:** Applicants will be notified of awards on a rolling basis beginning 5/1. **Types of Aid:** *Need-based scholarships/grants:* College/university scholarship or grant aid from institutional funds; Federal Pell; Private scholarships; SEOG; State scholarships/grants. *Loans:* Direct PLUS loans; Direct Subsidized Stafford Loans; Direct Unsubsidized Stafford Loans. **Student Employment:** Federal Work-Study Program available. Institutional employment available. **Financial Aid Statistics:** 94% needy freshmen, 83% needy undergrads receive need-based scholarship or grant aid. 13% freshmen, 10% undergrads receive non-need-based scholarship or grant aid. 45% freshmen, 55% undergrads receive need-based self-help aid. 5% freshmen, 6% undergrads receive athletic scholarships. 92.1% freshmen, 77.4% undergrads receive any aid. 71% undergrads borrow to pay for school. Average cumulative

indebtedness $22,513. **Criteria awarding aid:** *Need-based:* Academics, Alumni affiliation, Leadership. *Non-Need-based:* Academics, Alumni affiliation, Leadership.

INDIANA UNIVERSITY—KOKOMO

Kelley Student Center, Room 230, Kokomo, IN 46902-9003
Phone: 765-455-9217 **Financial Aid Phone:** (765) 455-9216
E-mail: iuadmis@iuk.edu **CEEB Code:** 1337
Fax: 765-455-9537 **Website:** http://www.iuk.edu/ **ACT Code:** 1219

This public school was founded in 1945. It has a 52 acre campus.

RATINGS

Admissions Selectivity Rating: 80   **Fire Safety Rating:** 60*   **Green Rating:** 60*

STUDENTS AND FACULTY

Enrollment: 2,752. **Student Body:** 66% female, 34% male, 3% out-of-state, 1% international (25 countries represented). Asian 1%, African American 4%, Caucasian 83%, Hispanic 6%, Native American <1%, Pacific Islander 0%, Two or more races 3%, Race unknown 1%.
Retention and Graduation: 64% freshmen return for sophomore year. 22% freshmen graduate within 4 years. 38% freshmen graduate within 6 years.
Faculty: Student/faculty ratio 15:1. 136 full-time faculty, 64% hold PhDs, 13% are members of minority groups, 64% are women.

ACADEMICS

Degrees: Associate; Bachelor's; Certificate; Master's; Post-bachelor's certificate.
Classes: Most classes have 20–29 students. Most lab/discussion sessions have fewer than 10 students. **Most popular majors:** Registered Nursing/Registered Nurse; Business/Commerce, General; Elementary Education and Teaching.
Special Study Options: Accelerated program; Distance learning; Double major; Dual enrollment; English as a Second Language (ESL); Honors program; Independent study; Internships; Liberal arts/career combination; Study abroad; Teacher certification program. **Honors programs:** The Indiana University Kokomo Honors Program offers unique educational and cultural opportunities for bright, highly motivated and creative students like you. Honors Courses and other activities are specially designed to cultivate academic excellence in different disciplines and challenge you to reach your full potential. The Honors Program is committed to guiding you in different disciplines, leading to self-improvement, and preparing you to make important contributions to society. **Disability Services offered:** Note-taking services; Reader services; Tape recorders. **Career services:** Alumni network; Alumni services; Career assessment; Career/job search classes; Internships; Regional alumni.

FACILITIES

Special Academic Facilities/Equipment: Observatory, Art Gallery **Campus Network:** 100% of classrooms, 100% of dorms, 100% of student union, 100% of libraries, 100% of dining areas, 100% of common outdoor areas, have wireless network access.

CAMPUS LIFE

Environment: Town. **Activities:** Campus Ministries; Choral groups; Concert band; Dance; Drama/theater; International Student Organization; Literary magazine; Model UN; Music ensembles; Musical theater; Opera; Student government; Student newspaper. 49 registered organizations, 7 honor societies, 5 religious organizations, 1 sororities, on campus. **On-Campus Highlights:** Kelley Student Center.

ADMISSIONS

Freshman Academic Profile: Average high school GPA 3.3. 8% in top 10% of high school class, 33% in top 25% of high school class, 70% in top 50% of high school class. **Test scores:** SAT Math middle 50% range 490–560. SAT EBRW middle 50% range 480–570. ACT middle 50% range 18–23. **Basis for Candidate Selection:** *Very important factors include:* rigor of secondary school record, class rank, standardized test scores. *Important factors include:* academic GPA. **Freshman Admission Requirements:** High school diploma is required and GED is accepted. *Academic units required:* 4 English, 3 math, 3 science, 3 science labs, 3 social studies, 4 academic electives. **Freshman Admission Statistics:** 2,333 applied, 74% admitted, 37% enrolled. **Transfer Admission Requirements:** college transcript(s), Minimum college GPA of 2.0 required. Lowest grade transferable C. **General Admission Information:** Application fee $35. Priority deadline 3/1. Non-fall registration accepted. Admission may be deferred for a maximum of 1 year.

COSTS AND FINANCIAL AID

Annual in-state tuition $6,895. Annual out-of-state tuition $19,346. Required fees $632. **Required Forms and Deadlines:** FAFSA. **Notification of Awards:** Applicants will be notified of awards on a rolling basis beginning 1/10. **Types of Aid:** *Need-based scholarships/grants:* College/university scholarship or grant aid from institutional funds; Federal Pell; Private scholarships; SEOG; State scholarships/grants. *Loans:* Direct PLUS loans; Direct Subsidized Stafford Loans; Direct Unsubsidized Stafford Loans. **Student Employment:** Federal Work-Study Program available. Institutional employment available. **Financial Aid Statistics:** 83% needy freshmen, 81% needy undergrads receive need-based scholarship or grant aid. 9% freshmen, 8% undergrads receive non-need-based scholarship or grant aid. 42% freshmen, 51% undergrads receive need-based self-help aid. 2% freshmen, 2% undergrads receive athletic scholarships. 87.7% freshmen, 82.3% undergrads receive any aid. 63% undergrads borrow to pay for school. Average cumulative indebtedness $23,518. **Criteria awarding aid:** *Need-based:* Academics, Athletics, Leadership. *Non-Need-based:* Academics, Athletics, Leadership.

INDIANA UNIVERSITY NORTHWEST

3400 Broadway, Gary, IN 46408
Phone: 219-980-6991 **Financial Aid Phone:** (219) 980-6539
E-mail: admit@iun.edu **CEEB Code:** 1338
Fax: 219-981-4219 **Website:** https://www.iun.edu/ **ACT Code:** 1218

This public school was founded in 1963. It has a 43 acre campus.

RATINGS

Admissions Selectivity Rating: 78   **Fire Safety Rating:** 60*   **Green Rating:** 60*

STUDENTS AND FACULTY

Enrollment: 3,286. **Student Body:** 72% female, 28% male, 4% out-of-state, 1% international (30 countries represented). Asian 3%, African American 15%, Caucasian 51%, Hispanic 25%, Native American <1%, Pacific Islander <1%, Two or more races 4%, Race unknown 1%.
Retention and Graduation: 64% freshmen return for sophomore year. 16% freshmen graduate within 4 years. 34% freshmen graduate within 6 years.
Faculty: Student/faculty ratio 14:1. 166 full-time faculty, 83% hold PhDs, 30% are members of minority groups, 53% are women.

ACADEMICS

Degrees: Associate; Bachelor's; Certificate; Master's; Post-bachelor's certificate.
Classes: Most classes have 10–19 students. Most lab/discussion sessions have 10–19 students. **Most popular majors:** Registered Nursing/Registered Nurse; Business/Commerce, General. **Special Study Options:** Accelerated program; Cross-registration; Distance learning; Double major; Dual enrollment; External degree program; Honors program; Independent study; Internships; Liberal arts/career combination; Student-designed major; Study abroad; Teacher certification program; Weekend college. **Disability Services offered:** Note-taking services; Reader services; Tape recorders. **Career services:** Alumni network; Alumni services; Career assessment; Career/job search classes; Internships; Regional alumni.

FACILITIES

Special Academic Facilities/Equipment: Gallery for Contemporary Art, IU Northwest Theatre at the Arts and Science Building.

CAMPUS LIFE

Environment: City. **Activities:** Campus Ministries; Drama/theater; Literary magazine; Musical theater; Radio station; Student government. 65 registered organizations, 12 honor societies, 7 religious organizations, 1 fraternities, 2 sororities, on campus. **Athletics (Intercollegiate):** *Men:* baseball, basketball, cheerleading, golf. *Women:* basketball, cheerleading, volleyball. **On-Campus Highlights:** The Savannah Center.

ADMISSIONS

Freshman Academic Profile: Average high school GPA 3.1. 11% in top 10% of high school class, 37% in top 25% of high school class, 70% in top 50% of high school class. **Test scores:** SAT Math middle 50% range 450–540. SAT EBRW middle 50% range 460–560. ACT middle 50% range 17–22. **Basis for Candidate Selection:** *Very important factors include:* rigor of secondary school record, academic GPA, standardized test scores. *Important factors include:* class rank. *Other factors include:* recommendation(s). **Freshman Admission Requirements:** High school diploma is required and GED is accepted.

Academic units required: 4 English, 3 math, 3 science, 3 science labs, 2 social studies, 1 history, 7 academic electives. *Academic units recommended:* 2 foreign language. **Freshman Admission Statistics:** 2,486 applied, 75% admitted, 37% enrolled. **Transfer Admission Requirements:** High school transcript, college transcript(s), Minimum college GPA of 2.0 required. Lowest grade transferable C. **General Admission Information:** Application fee $35. Priority deadline 7/1. Non-fall registration accepted. Admission may be deferred for a maximum of 1 years.

COSTS AND FINANCIAL AID
Annual in-state tuition $6,895. Annual out-of-state tuition $19,346. Required fees $632. **Required Forms and Deadlines:** FAFSA. **Notification of Awards:** Applicants will be notified of awards on a rolling basis beginning 4/15. **Types of Aid:** *Need-based scholarships/grants:* College/university scholarship or grant aid from institutional funds; Federal Nursing Scholarships; Federal Pell; Private scholarships; SEOG; State scholarships/grants; United Negro College Fund. *Loans:* Direct PLUS loans; Direct Subsidized Stafford Loans; Direct Unsubsidized Stafford Loans. **Student Employment:** Federal Work-Study Program available. Institutional employment available. **Financial Aid Statistics:** 81% needy freshmen, 81% needy undergrads receive need-based scholarship or grant aid. 8% freshmen, 8% undergrads receive non-need-based scholarship or grant aid. 38% freshmen, 50% undergrads receive need-based self-help aid. 1% freshmen, 1% undergrads receive athletic scholarships. 84% freshmen, 78.6% undergrads receive any aid. 66% undergrads borrow to pay for school. Average cumulative indebtedness $26,940. **Criteria awarding aid:** *Need-based:* Academics, Minority status. *Non-Need-based:* Academics, Athletics.

INDIANA UNIVERSITY OF PENNSYLVANIA

1011 South Drive, Indiana, PA 15705
Phone: 724-357-2230 **Financial Aid Phone:** 724-357-2218
E-mail: admissions-inquiry@iup.edu **CEEB Code:** 2652
Fax: 724-357-6281 **Website:** www.iup.edu **ACT Code:** 3704

This public school was founded in 1875. It has a 374 acre campus.

RATINGS
Admissions Selectivity Rating: 73   Fire Safety Rating: 97   Green Rating: 60*

STUDENTS AND FACULTY
Enrollment: 7,959. **Student Body:** 59% female, 41% male, 5% out-of-state, 2% international (30 countries represented). Asian 1%, African American 12%, Caucasian 74%, Hispanic 5%, Native American <1%, Pacific Islander <1%, Two or more races 5%, Race unknown 1%.
Retention and Graduation: 72% freshmen return for sophomore year. 40% freshmen graduate within 4 years. % freshmen graduate within 6 years. **Faculty:** Student/faculty ratio 15:1. 478 full-time faculty, 0% hold PhDs, 17% are members of minority groups, 50% are women. 0% of classes are taught by teaching assistants.

ACADEMICS
Degrees: Associate; Bachelor's; Certificate; Doctoral degree—professional practice; Doctoral degree research/scholarship; Master's; Post-bachelor's certificate; Post-master's certificate. **Classes:** Most classes have 30–39 students. Most lab/discussion sessions have 20–29 students. **Most popular majors:** Criminology; Registered Nursing/Registered Nurse; Marketing/Marketing Management, General. **Special Study Options:** Accelerated program; Cooperative education program; Cross-registration; Distance learning; Double major; Dual enrollment; English as a Second Language (ESL); Exchange student program (domestic); External degree program; Honors program; Independent study; Internships; Liberal arts/career combination; Student-designed major; Study abroad; Teacher certification program; Weekend college. **Honors programs:** Cook Honors College. **Combined degree programs:** BA/MA. **Disability Services offered:** Note-taking services; Reader services; Tape recorders. **Career services:** Alumni services; Career assessment; Career/job search classes; Internships.

FACILITIES
Housing: Coed dorms; Special housing for disabled students; Special housing for international students; Theme housing; Wellness housing; 99% of campus

accessible to physically disabled. **Special Academic Facilities/Equipment:** Art museum, lodge, farm, co-generation plant, ski slope, sailing base.

CAMPUS LIFE
Environment: Village. **Activities:** Campus Ministries; Choral groups; Concert band; Dance; Drama/theater; International Student Organization; Jazz band; Literary magazine; Marching band; Model UN; Music ensembles; Musical theater; Opera; Pep band; Radio station; Student government; Student newspaper; Student-run film society; Symphony orchestra; Television station. 278 registered organizations, 24 honor societies, 27 religious organizations, 18 fraternities, 15 sororities, on campus. **Athletics (Intercollegiate):** *Men:* baseball, basketball, cross-country, diving, football, golf, swimming, track/field (outdoor), track/field (indoor). *Women:* basketball, cross-country, diving, field hockey, lacrosse, soccer, softball, swimming, tennis, track/field (outdoor), track/field (indoor), volleyball. **On-Campus Highlights:** Housing.

ADMISSIONS
Freshman Academic Profile: Average high school GPA 3.3. 9% in top 10% of high school class, 27% in top 25% of high school class, 59% in top 50% of high school class. **Test scores:** SAT Math middle 50% range 450–550. SAT EBRW middle 50% range 460–570. ACT middle 50% range 16–23. **Basis for Candidate Selection:** *Very important factors include:* academic GPA. *Important factors include:* rigor of secondary school record, standardized test scores. *Other factors include:* class rank, application essay, recommendation(s), interview, extracurricular activities, talent/ability, character/personal qualities, first generation. **Freshman Admission Requirements:** High school diploma is required and GED is accepted. *Academic units required:* 4 English, 3 math, 3 science, 2 science labs. *Academic units recommended:* 2 foreign language, 3 social studies. **Freshman Admission Statistics:** 10,061 applied, 93% admitted, 19% enrolled. **Transfer Admission Requirements:** High school transcript, college transcript(s), statement of good standing from prior institution(s). Minimum college GPA of 2.0 required. Lowest grade transferable C-. **General Admission Information:** Non-fall registration accepted. Admission may be deferred for a maximum of 1 year.

COSTS AND FINANCIAL AID
Annual in-state tuition $9,570. Annual out-of-state tuition $13,890. Room and board $12,744. Required fees $3,784. Average book and supplies expense $1,100. **Required Forms and Deadlines:** FAFSA; State aid form. **Notification of Awards:** Applicants will be notified of awards on a rolling basis beginning 12/15. **Types of Aid:** *Need-based scholarships/grants:* College/university scholarship or grant aid from institutional funds; Federal Pell; Private scholarships; SEOG; State scholarships/grants; United Negro College Fund. *Loans:* Direct PLUS loans; Direct Subsidized Stafford Loans; Direct Unsubsidized Stafford Loans. **Student Employment:** Federal Work-Study Program available. Institutional employment available. **Financial Aid Statistics:** 68% needy freshmen, 66% needy undergrads receive need-based scholarship or grant aid. 57% freshmen, 61% undergrads receive non-need-based scholarship or grant aid. 93% freshmen, 90% undergrads receive need-based self-help aid. 2% freshmen, 2% undergrads receive athletic scholarships. 82% freshmen, 82% undergrads receive any aid. 84% undergrads borrow to pay for school. Average cumulative indebtedness $41,222. **Criteria awarding aid:** *Need-based:* Academics, Alumni affiliation, Art, Job skills, Leadership, Music/drama. *Non-Need-based:* Academics, Alumni affiliation, Art, Athletics, Job skills, Leadership, Music/drama, State/district residency.

INDIANA UNIVERSITY— PURDUE UNIVERSITY INDIANAPOLIS

425 University Boulevard, Indianapolis, IN 46202
Phone: 317-274-4591 **Financial Aid Phone:** (317) 274-4162
E-mail: apply@iupui.edu **CEEB Code:** 1325
Fax: 317-278-1862 **Website:** https://www.iupui.edu/ **ACT Code:** 1214

This public school was founded in 1969. It has a 534 acre campus.

RATINGS
Admissions Selectivity Rating: 77   Fire Safety Rating: 98   Green Rating: 98

STUDENTS AND FACULTY
Enrollment: 20,500. **Student Body:** 58% female, 42% male, 6% out-of-state, 4% international (123 countries represented). Asian 5%, African American 9%, Caucasian 67%, Hispanic 9%, Native American <1%, Pacific Islander <1%, Two or more races 5%, Race unknown <1%.

Retention and Graduation: 73% freshmen return for sophomore year. 28% freshmen graduate within 4 years. 51% freshmen graduate within 6 years. **Faculty:** Student/faculty ratio 15:1. 2,592 full-time faculty, 85% hold PhDs, 23% are members of minority groups, 45% are women.

ACADEMICS

Degrees: Associate; Bachelor's; Certificate; Doctoral degree—professional practice; Doctoral degree research/scholarship; Master's; Post-bachelor's certificate; Post-master's certificate. **Classes:** Most classes have 10–19 students. Most lab/discussion sessions have 10–19 students. **Most popular majors:** Liberal Arts and Sciences, General Studies and Humanities, Other; Registered Nursing/Registered Nurse; Business/Commerce, General. **Special Study Options:** Accelerated program; Cooperative education program; Cross-registration; Distance learning; Double major; Dual enrollment; English as a Second Language (ESL); Exchange student program (domestic); External degree program; Honors program; Independent study; Internships; Liberal arts/career combination; Student-designed major; Study abroad; Teacher certification program. **Honors programs:** The IUPUI Honors College offers a unique experience with housing, peer mentoring, student organizations, and more benefits that will make your time at IUPUI challenging, engaging, meaningful, and relevant. The IUPUI Honors College is comprised of high-achieving students from a variety of academic degree programs. Honors coursework, one-on-one advising, and opportunities for research, international study, service, and experiential learning allow you to build strong foundations inside and outside the classroom. **Combined degree programs:** BA/MA. **Disability Services offered:** Note-taking services; Reader services; Tape recorders. **Career services:** Alumni network; Alumni services; Career assessment; Career/job search classes; Internships; Regional alumni.

FACILITIES

Housing: Apartments for married students; Apartments for single students; Coed dorms; Special housing for disabled students; Special housing for international students; Theme housing; Wellness housing; 90% of campus accessible to physically disabled. **Special Academic Facilities/Equipment:** IU Natatorium, The Herron Gallery, The IUPUI Cultural Arts Gallery.

CAMPUS LIFE

Environment: Metropolis. **Activities:** Campus Ministries; Choral groups; Dance; Drama/theater; International Student Organization; Jazz band; Literary magazine; Model UN; Music ensembles; Pep band; Student government; Student newspaper; Student-run film society; Symphony orchestra. 566 registered organizations, 28 honor societies, 34 religious organizations, 14 fraternities, 16 sororities, on campus. **Athletics (Intercollegiate):** *Men:* basketball, cross-country, diving, golf, soccer, swimming, tennis. *Women:* basketball, cross-country, diving, golf, soccer, softball, swimming, tennis, volleyball. **On-Campus Highlights:** IUPUI Sport Complex.

ADMISSIONS

Freshman Academic Profile: Average high school GPA 3.5. 14% in top 10% of high school class, 42% in top 25% of high school class, 84% in top 50% of high school class. **Test scores:** SAT Math middle 50% range 500–600. SAT EBRW middle 50% range 500–600. ACT middle 50% range 19–25. **Basis for Candidate Selection:** *Very important factors include:* rigor of secondary school record, academic GPA, standardized test scores. *Other factors include:* class rank, application essay, character/personal qualities, first generation, volunteer work, work experience. **Freshman Admission Requirements:** High school diploma is required and GED is accepted. *Academic units required:* 4 English, 3 math, 3 science, 3 science labs, 3 social studies, 7 academic electives. **Freshman Admission Statistics:** 15,040 applied, 81% admitted, 35% enrolled. **Transfer Admission Requirements:** college transcript(s), Minimum college GPA of 2.0 required. Lowest grade transferable C. **General Admission Information:** Application fee $65. Priority deadline 5/1. Non-fall registration accepted.

COSTS AND FINANCIAL AID

Annual in-state tuition $8,580. Annual out-of-state tuition $29,589. Room and board $9,104. Required fees $1,121. Average book and supplies expense $1,110. **Required Forms and Deadlines:** FAFSA. **Notification of Awards:** Applicants will be notified of awards on a rolling basis beginning 12/25. **Types of Aid:** *Need-based scholarships/grants:* College/university scholarship or grant aid from institutional funds; Federal Pell; Private scholarships; SEOG; State scholarships/grants. *Loans:* Direct PLUS loans; Direct Subsidized Stafford Loans; Direct Unsubsidized Stafford Loans. **Student Employment:** Federal Work-Study Program available. Institutional employment available. **Financial Aid Statistics:** 85% needy freshmen, 82% needy undergrads receive need-based scholarship or grant aid. 14% freshmen, 11% undergrads receive non-need-based scholarship or grant aid. 46% freshmen, 54% undergrads receive need-based self-help aid. 1% freshmen, 1% undergrads receive athletic scholarships.

88.5% freshmen, 82.2% undergrads receive any aid. 65% undergrads borrow to pay for school. Average cumulative indebtedness $27,022. **Criteria awarding aid:** *Need-based:* Academics. *Non-Need-based:* Academics, Alumni affiliation, Art, Athletics, Leadership, State/district residency.

INDIANA UNIVERSITY SOUTH BEND

Administration Building 140, South Bend, IN 46634-7111
Phone: 574-520-4839 **Financial Aid Phone:** 574-520-4270
E-mail: admissions@iusb.edu **CEEB Code:** 1339
Fax: 574-520-4834 **Website:** https://www.iusb.edu/ **ACT Code:** 1225

This public school was founded in 1922. It has a 104 acre campus.

RATINGS

Admissions Selectivity Rating: 78   **Fire Safety Rating:** 99   **Green Rating:** 63

STUDENTS AND FACULTY

Enrollment: 4,432. **Student Body:** 64% female, 36% male, 5% out-of-state, 3% international (63 countries represented). Asian 2%, African American 8%, Caucasian 67%, Hispanic 14%, Native American <1%, Pacific Islander <1%, Two or more races 5%, Race unknown 1%.
Retention and Graduation: 68% freshmen return for sophomore year. 16% freshmen graduate within 4 years. 38% freshmen graduate within 6 years. **Faculty:** Student/faculty ratio 13:1. 259 full-time faculty, 77% hold PhDs, 18% are members of minority groups, 49% are women.

ACADEMICS

Degrees: Associate; Bachelor's; Certificate; Diploma; Master's; Post-bachelor's certificate. **Classes:** Most classes have 10–19 students. Most lab/discussion sessions have 10–19 students. **Most popular majors:** Registered Nursing/Registered Nurse; Business/Commerce, General. **Special Study Options:** Accelerated program; Cross-registration; Distance learning; Double major; Dual enrollment; English as a Second Language (ESL); External degree program; Honors program; Independent study; Internships; Liberal arts/career combination; Study abroad; Teacher certification program. **Honors programs:** The IU South Bend Honors Program offers motivated students the opportunity for an enriched and unique college experience. The Honors Program is a community of students who are given an extraordinary chance to reach their full academic potential. No matter what their professional or life goals may be, the Honors Program will work to make their college experience meaningful and one that constructs a strong foundation for the rest of their lives. The benefits of participation include: Honors Scholarships for all students, early registration privileges, enrollment in small discussion-based Honors Courses, research opportunities, interaction with a supportive group of Honors peers (membership in the Honors Club), participation in Honors social events and travel opportunities, the opportunity to live in the Honors Living Learning Community at River Crossing, and use of the Honors Lounge. Additionally, the Honors Diploma will help students gain a competitive edge in employment and in professional graduate student applications. **Disability Services offered:** Note-taking services; Reader services; Tape recorders. **Career services:** Alumni network; Alumni services; Career assessment; Career/job search classes; Internships; Regional alumni.

FACILITIES

Housing: Apartments for single students; Coed dorms; Special housing for international students. **Special Academic Facilities/Equipment:** Art Gallery.

CAMPUS LIFE

Environment: City. **Activities:** Campus Ministries; Choral groups; Dance; Drama/theater; International Student Organization; Jazz band; Literary magazine; Music ensembles; Musical theater; Student government; Student newspaper; Student-run film society. 112 registered organizations, 10 honor societies, 9 religious organizations, 3 fraternities, 2 sororities, on campus. **Athletics (Intercollegiate):** *Men:* basketball. *Women:* basketball. **On-Campus Highlights:** Student Activities Center.

ADMISSIONS

Freshman Academic Profile: Average high school GPA 3.2. 8% in top 10% of high school class, 30% in top 25% of high school class, 68% in top 50% of high school class. **Test scores:** SAT Math middle 50% range 480–560. SAT EBRW middle 50% range 470–570. ACT middle 50% range 17–23. **Basis for Candidate Selection:** *Very important factors include:* rigor of secondary school record. *Important factors include:* academic GPA, standardized test scores.

Other factors include: recommendation(s), interview, extracurricular activities, geographical residence, state residency. **Freshman Admission Requirements:** High school diploma is required and GED is accepted. *Academic units required:* 4 English, 3 math, 3 science, 3 science labs, 3 social studies, 7 academic electives. *Academic units recommended:* 2 foreign language. **Freshman Admission Statistics:** 2,959 applied, 78% admitted, 37% enrolled. **Transfer Admission Requirements:** college transcript(s), Minimum college GPA of 2.0 required. Lowest grade transferable C. **General Admission Information:** Application fee $35. Priority deadline 8/1. Non-fall registration accepted. Admission may be deferred for a maximum of 1 year.

COSTS AND FINANCIAL AID

Annual in-state tuition $6,895. Annual out-of-state tuition $19,346. Room and board $7,346. Required fees $632. Average book and supplies expense $1,110. **Required Forms and Deadlines:** FAFSA; Institution's own financial aid form. **Notification of Awards:** Applicants will be notified of awards on a rolling basis beginning 5/1. **Types of Aid:** *Need-based scholarships/grants:* College/university scholarship or grant aid from institutional funds; Federal Pell; Private scholarships; SEOG; State scholarships/grants. *Loans:* Direct PLUS loans; Direct Subsidized Stafford Loans; Direct Unsubsidized Stafford Loans. **Student Employment:** Federal Work-Study Program available. Institutional employment available. **Financial Aid Statistics:** 90% needy freshmen, 85% needy undergrads receive need-based scholarship or grant aid. 10% freshmen, 7% undergrads receive non-need-based scholarship or grant aid. 41% freshmen, 52% undergrads receive need-based self-help aid. 1% freshmen, 1% undergrads receive athletic scholarships. 91.1% freshmen, 80.8% undergrads receive any aid. 68% undergrads borrow to pay for school. Average cumulative indebtedness $24,879. **Criteria awarding aid:** *Need-based:* Academics, Alumni affiliation, Art, Athletics, Job skills, Leadership, Minority status. *Non-Need-based:* Academics, Athletics.

INDIANA UNIVERSITY SOUTHEAST

4201 Grant Line Road, New Albany, IN 47150-6405
Phone: 812-941-2212 **Financial Aid Phone:** (812) 941-2246
E-mail: admissions@ius.edu **CEEB Code:** 1314
Fax: 812-941-2595 **Website:** https://www.ius.edu/ **ACT Code:** 1229

This public school was founded in 1941. It has a 180 acre campus.

RATINGS

Admissions Selectivity Rating: 77   Fire Safety Rating: 99   Green Rating: 63

STUDENTS AND FACULTY

Enrollment: 4,316. **Student Body:** 61% female, 39% male, 29% out-of-state, 1% international (47 countries represented). Asian 2%, African American 7%, Caucasian 81%, Hispanic 5%, Native American <1%, Pacific Islander <1%, Two or more races 4%, Race unknown 1%.
Retention and Graduation: 62% freshmen return for sophomore year. 19% freshmen graduate within 4 years. 36% freshmen graduate within 6 years.
Faculty: Student/faculty ratio 13:1. 210 full-time faculty, 81% hold PhDs, 15% are members of minority groups, 56% are women.

ACADEMICS

Degrees: Associate; Bachelor's; Certificate; Master's; Post-bachelor's certificate. **Classes:** Most classes have 10–19 students. Most lab/discussion sessions have 10–19 students. **Most popular majors:** Registered Nursing/Registered Nurse; Business/Commerce, General. **Special Study Options:** Accelerated program; Cross-registration; Distance learning; Double major; Dual enrollment; External degree program; Honors program; Independent study; Internships; Student-designed major; Study abroad; Teacher certification program. **Honors programs:** The Honors Program invites applications from intellectually curious and motivated students. Our courses are designed to challenge, but not overwhelm, students with subjects and activities that derive from a variety of disciplines. The social, conference, and service activities of the Honors Program, like our courses, encourage students to develop their academic and personal strengths, while also venturing into things with which they might be less comfortable. Thus, students who thrive with applied learning opportunities are able to do so, without losing sight of the academic issues at stake. For their part, students who are comfortable writing long and thoughtful research projects

also learn how to work with other people on group projects, or in service efforts. **Disability Services offered:** Note-taking services; Reader services; Tape recorders; Tutors. **Career services:** Alumni network; Alumni services; Career assessment; Career/job search classes; Internships; Regional alumni.

FACILITIES

Housing: Apartments for single students; 95% of campus accessible to physically disabled. **Special Academic Facilities/Equipment:** The Ogle Center contains: four indoor theaters, an amphitheater, a concert hall, a recital hall, and an art gallery.

CAMPUS LIFE

Environment: Town. **Activities:** Campus Ministries; Choral groups; Concert band; Drama/theater; International Student Organization; Literary magazine; Marching band; Model UN; Music ensembles; Musical theater; Pep band; Radio station; Student government; Student newspaper; Student-run film society; Symphony orchestra. 113 registered organizations, 11 honor societies, 6 religious organizations, 3 fraternities, 3 sororities, on campus. **Athletics (Intercollegiate):** *Men:* baseball, basketball, cross-country, tennis. *Women:* basketball, cross-country, softball, tennis, volleyball. **On-Campus Highlights:** Paul W. Ogle Cultural & Community Center. **Environmental Initiatives:** Recycling IU Southeast has a single stream recycling program. Recycling bins are located in each building where all of these items can be thrown in the same container: Cardboard boxes (broken down); Magazines, newspapers, and inserts; All white, colored, and coated papers; Brochures and pamphlets; Correspondence papers (letterhead, mail, and adverting); Envelopes (even with plastic windows or labels); Folders (manila, coated, or colored); Manuals with glued bindings; Paper from legal pads, memo pads, note pads, scratch pads, and steno pads; Posters; Store receipts; Self-adhesive notes; Soft covered books; Cereal boxes; Frozen food boxes; Plastic containers #1 thru #7 (Examples: food and beverage bottles and containers); Stretch film; Aluminum beverage and food containers; Steel beverage and food containers.

ADMISSIONS

Freshman Academic Profile: Average high school GPA 3.2. 9% in top 10% of high school class, 30% in top 25% of high school class, 64% in top 50% of high school class. **Test scores:** SAT Math middle 50% range 460–560. SAT EBRW middle 50% range 470–580. ACT middle 50% range 17–23. **Basis for Candidate Selection:** *Very important factors include:* rigor of secondary school record, academic GPA. *Other factors include:* standardized test scores. **Freshman Admission Requirements:** High school diploma is required and GED is accepted. *Academic units required:* 4 English, 3 math, 3 science, 3 science labs, 3 social studies, 7 academic electives. *Academic units recommended:* 2 foreign language. **Freshman Admission Statistics:** 2,831 applied, 82% admitted, 41% enrolled. **Transfer Admission Requirements:** college transcript(s), Lowest grade transferable C. **General Admission Information:** Application fee $35. Non-fall registration accepted. Admission may be deferred for a maximum of 1 year.

COSTS AND FINANCIAL AID

Annual in-state tuition $6,895. Annual out-of-state tuition $19,346. Room and board $6,920. Required fees $632. Average book and supplies expense $1,110. **Required Forms and Deadlines:** FAFSA. **Notification of Awards:** Applicants will be notified of awards on a rolling basis beginning 2/10. **Types of Aid:** *Need-based scholarships/grants:* College/university scholarship or grant aid from institutional funds; Federal Pell; Private scholarships; SEOG; State scholarships/grants. *Loans:* Direct PLUS loans; Direct Subsidized Stafford Loans; Direct Unsubsidized Stafford Loans. **Student Employment:** Federal Work-Study Program available. Institutional employment available. **Financial Aid Statistics:** 84% needy freshmen, 82% needy undergrads receive need-based scholarship or grant aid. 6% freshmen, 6% undergrads receive non-need-based scholarship or grant aid. 42% freshmen, 50% undergrads receive need-based self-help aid. 1% freshmen, 1% undergrads receive athletic scholarships. 83% freshmen, 74.6% undergrads receive any aid. 60% undergrads borrow to pay for school. Average cumulative indebtedness $21,460. **Criteria awarding aid:** *Need-based:* Academics, Alumni affiliation, Art, Athletics, Leadership, Minority status. *Non-Need-based:* Academics, Art, Athletics, Leadership, Minority status, Music/drama.

INDIANA WESLEYAN UNIVERSITY

4201 South Washington Street, Marion, IN 46953
Phone: 765-677-2138 **Financial Aid Phone:** 765-677-2116
E-mail: admissions@indwes.edu **CEEB Code:** 1446
Fax: 765-677-2333 **Website:** www.indwes.edu **ACT Code:** 1226

This private school, affiliated with the Wesleyan Church, was founded in 1920. It has a 300 acre campus.

RATINGS

Admissions Selectivity Rating: 78 **Fire Safety Rating:** 96 **Green Rating:** 60*

STUDENTS AND FACULTY

Enrollment: 2,647. **Student Body:** 64% female, 36% male, 46% out-of-state, 2% international (21 countries represented). Asian 2%, African American 3%, Caucasian 84%, Hispanic 4%, Native American <1%, Pacific Islander <1%, Two or more races 4%, Race unknown 2%.
Retention and Graduation: 82% freshmen return for sophomore year.
Faculty: Student/faculty ratio 10:1. 175 full-time faculty, 73% hold PhDs, 12% are members of minority groups, 48% are women. 0% of classes are taught by teaching assistants.

ACADEMICS

Degrees: Associate; Bachelor's; Doctoral degree research/scholarship; Master's; Post-bachelor's certificate; Post-master's certificate. **Classes:** Most classes have 10–19 students. Most lab/discussion sessions have 10–19 students. **Most popular majors:** Registered Nursing/Registered Nurse; Business Administration and Management, General; Psychology, General. **Special Study Options:** Accelerated program; Cross-registration; Distance learning; Double major; Honors program; Independent study; Internships; Study abroad; Teacher certification program. **Honors programs:** John Wesley Honors College. **Disability Services offered:** Note-taking services; Reader services; Tape recorders; Tutors. **Career services:** Alumni network; Alumni services; Career assessment; Career/job search classes; Internships; Regional alumni.

FACILITIES

Housing: Apartments for married students; Apartments for single students; Men's dorms; Theme housing; Women's dorms; 99% of campus accessible to physically disabled. **Special Academic Facilities/Equipment:** Lee Howard art collection (European artists) Lewis Jackson Library (2003) Tom and Joanne Phillippe Performing Arts Center (1998) Bronze statues from Israel (1998–2002) Williams chapel—medieval replica (2001) Burns Hall of Science and Nursing (2000) Luckey Recreation and Wellness Center (2001) John Maxwell Business Center (1999).

CAMPUS LIFE

Environment: Town. **Activities:** Campus Ministries; Choral groups; Concert band; Dance; Drama/theater; International Student Organization; Jazz band; Literary magazine; Model UN; Music ensembles; Musical theater; Opera; Pep band; Radio station; Student government; Student newspaper; Student-run film society; Symphony orchestra; Television station. 35 registered organizations, 3 honor societies, 5 religious organizations, on campus. **Athletics (Intercollegiate):** *Men:* baseball, basketball, cheerleading, cross-country, golf, soccer, tennis, track/field (outdoor), track/field (indoor). *Women:* basketball, cheerleading, cross-country, soccer, softball, tennis, track/field (outdoor), track/field (indoor), volleyball. **On-Campus Highlights:** McConn Coffee Shop.
Environmental Initiatives: Creation of a multi-disciplinary Task Force for Campus Sustainabilty.

ADMISSIONS

Freshman Academic Profile: Average high school GPA 3.6. 22% in top 10% of high school class, 50% in top 25% of high school class, 83% in top 50% of high school class. **Test scores:** SAT Math middle 50% range 450–530. SAT EBRW middle 50% range 460–520. ACT middle 50% range 21–26. **Basis for Candidate Selection:** *Very important factors include:* academic GPA, standardized test scores. *Important factors include:* application essay, recommendation(s). *Other factors include:* rigor of secondary school record, class rank, extracurricular activities, talent/ability, character/personal qualities, first generation, alumni/ae relation, religious affiliation/commitment.
Freshman Admission Requirements: High school diploma is required and GED is accepted. *Academic units recommended:* 4 English, 3 math, 3 science, 2 foreign language, 3 social studies, 5 academic electives. **Freshman Admission Statistics:** 4,733 applied, 68% admitted, 24% enrolled. **Transfer Admission Requirements:** College transcript(s), statement of good standing from prior

institution(s). Minimum college GPA of 2.0 required. Lowest grade transferable C. **General Admission Information:** Non-fall registration accepted.

COSTS AND FINANCIAL AID

Annual tuition $27,296. Room and board $8,768. Required fees $188. Average book and supplies expense $1,386. **Required Forms and Deadlines:** FAFSA; Institution's own financial aid form. **Types of Aid:** *Need-based scholarships/grants:* College/university scholarship or grant aid from institutional funds; Federal Nursing Scholarships; Federal Pell; Private scholarships; SEOG; State scholarships/grants. *Loans:* Direct PLUS loans; Direct Subsidized Stafford Loans; Direct Unsubsidized Stafford Loans. **Student Employment:** Federal Work-Study Program available. Institutional employment available. **Financial Aid Statistics:** 78% needy freshmen, 81% needy undergrads receive need-based scholarship or grant aid. 100% freshmen, 93% undergrads receive non-need-based scholarship or grant aid. 86% freshmen, 88% undergrads receive need-based self-help aid. 12% freshmen, 9% undergrads receive athletic scholarships. 94% freshmen, 95% undergrads receive any aid. Average cumulative indebtedness $30,355. **Criteria awarding aid:** *Need-based:* Alumni affiliation, Minority status, Religious affiliation. *Non-Need-based:* Academics, Alumni affiliation, Art, Athletics, Music/drama, State/district residency.

IONA COLLEGE

715 North Avenue, New Rochelle, NY 10801
Phone: 914-633-2502 **Financial Aid Phone:** 914-633-2497
E-mail: admissions@iona.edu **CEEB Code:** 2324
Fax: 914-633-2182 **Website:** www.iona.edu **ACT Code:** 2770

This private school, affiliated with the Roman Catholic Church, was founded in 1940. It has a 45 acre campus.

RATINGS

Admissions Selectivity Rating: 75 **Fire Safety Rating:** 92 **Green Rating:** 64

STUDENTS AND FACULTY

Enrollment: 2,743. **Student Body:** 48% female, 52% male, 23% out-of-state, 3% international (37 countries represented). Asian 3%, African American 12%, Caucasian 51%, Hispanic 25%, Native American 1%, Pacific Islander <1%, Two or more races 2%, Race unknown 4%.
Retention and Graduation: 72% freshmen return for sophomore year. 59% freshmen graduate within 4 years. 64% freshmen graduate within 6 years.
Faculty: Student/faculty ratio 14:1. 169 full-time faculty, 94% hold PhDs, 23% are members of minority groups, 49% are women. 0% of classes are taught by teaching assistants.

ACADEMICS

Degrees: Bachelor's; Master's; Post-bachelor's certificate; Post-master's certificate. **Classes:** Most classes have 20–29 students. Most lab/discussion sessions have 10–19 students. **Most popular majors:** Mass Communication/Media Studies; Psychology, General; Finance, General. **Special Study Options:** Accelerated program; Distance learning; Double major; Dual enrollment; English as a Second Language (ESL); External degree program; Honors program; Independent study; Internships; Liberal arts/career combination; Student-designed major; Study abroad; Teacher certification program; Weekend college. **Honors programs:** The Iona College Honors program is designed to meet the educational needs of the most highly motivated students at Iona. Grounded in a challenging curriculum, the program offers gifted students the resources and opportunities to develop their talents and to perform at the peak of their capabilities. The course of study is designed to develop intellectual curiosity, analytic abilities and awareness of ethical and civic responsibilities. The program encourages the development of a small community of independent learners able to inspire each other academically. It fosters a sense of self-respect in students, encouraging them to stretch their abilities in pursuit of lifelong learning, independent thinking, and personal fulfillment. **Combined degree programs:** BA/MA. **Disability Services offered:** Note-taking services; Reader services; Tape recorders; Tutors. **Career services:** Alumni network; Alumni services; Career assessment; Career/job search classes; Internships; Regional alumni.

FACILITIES

Housing: Apartments for single students; Coed dorms; Special housing for disabled students; Special housing for international students; Theme housing; Wellness housing; 70% of campus accessible to physically disabled. **Special Academic Facilities/Equipment:** Iona College Arts Center, Br. Kenneth Chapman Gallery, Murphy Science and Technology Center, Advanced Computer Laboratory, TV Production Studio, LaPenta Student Union, Hynes Athletic Center, Rowing tank, Arrigoni Center, Blessed Edmund Ignatius Rice Chapel. **Campus Network:** 100% of classrooms, 100% of dorms, 100% of student union, 100% of libraries, 100% of dining areas, 85% of common outdoor areas have wireless network access.

CAMPUS LIFE

Environment: City. **Activities:** Campus Ministries; Choral groups; Concert band; Dance; Drama/theater; International Student Organization; Literary magazine; Model UN; Music ensembles; Musical theater; Pep band; Radio station; Student government; Student newspaper; Student-run film society; Television station; Yearbook. 80 registered organizations, 26 honor societies, 3 religious organizations, 3 fraternities, 5 sororities on campus. **Athletics (Intercollegiate): Men:** baseball, basketball, crew/rowing, cross-country, diving, golf, soccer, swimming, track/field (outdoor), track/field (indoor), water polo. *Women:* basketball, crew/rowing, cross-country, diving, lacrosse, soccer, softball, swimming, track/field (outdoor), track/field (indoor), volleyball, water polo. **On-Campus Highlights:** LaPenta Student Union.

ADMISSIONS

Freshman Academic Profile: Average high school GPA 3.0. 11% in top 10% of high school class, 35% in top 25% of high school class, 68% in top 50% of high school class. **Test Scores:** SAT Math middle 50% range 490–580. SAT EBRW middle 50% range 500–590. ACT middle 50% range 20–26. **Basis for Candidate Selection:** *Very important factors include:* rigor of secondary school record, academic GPA. *Important factors include:* character/personal qualities. *Other factors include:* class rank, application essay, standardized test scores, recommendation(s), interview, extracurricular activities, talent/ability, first generation, alumni/ae relation, geographical residence, volunteer work, work experience. **Freshman Admission Requirements:** High school diploma is required and GED is accepted. *Academic units required:* 4 English, 3 math, 3 science, 2 science labs, 2 foreign language, 2 social studies, 1 history, 1 academic elective. *Academic units recommended:* 4 math, 2 history, 3 academic electives. **Freshman Admission Statistics:** 9,965 applied, 84% admitted, 8% enrolled. **Transfer Admission Requirements:** High school transcript, college transcript(s), essay or personal statement. Minimum college GPA of 2.5 required. Lowest grade transferable C. **General Admission Information:** Regular application deadline 2/15. Non-fall registration accepted. Admission may be deferred for a maximum of 1 year.

COSTS AND FINANCIAL AID

Annual tuition $37,972. Room and board $15,736. Required fees $2,200. Average book and supplies expense $1,500. **Required Forms and Deadlines:** FAFSA; State aid form. **Notification of Awards:** Applicants will be notified of awards on a rolling basis beginning 2/1. **Types of Aid:** *Need-based scholarships/grants:* College/university scholarship or grant aid from institutional funds; Federal Pell; Private scholarships; SEOG; State scholarships/grants. *Loans:* Direct PLUS loans; Direct Subsidized Stafford Loans; Direct Unsubsidized Stafford Loans. **Student Employment:** Federal Work-Study Program available. Institutional employment available. **Financial Aid Statistics:** 40% needy freshmen, 41% needy undergrads receive need-based scholarship or grant aid. 100% freshmen, 99% undergrads receive non-need-based scholarship or grant aid. 72% freshmen, 71% undergrads receive need-based self-help aid. 8% freshmen, 9% undergrads receive athletic scholarships. 100% freshmen, 98% undergrads receive any aid. 74% undergrads borrow to pay for school. Average cumulative indebtedness $32,948. **Criteria awarding aid:** *Non-need-based:* Academics, Alumni affiliation, Athletics.

IOWA STATE UNIVERSITY

100 Enrollment Services Center, Ames, IA 50011-2011
Phone: 515-294-5836 **Financial Aid Phone:** 515-294-2223
E-mail: admissions@iastate.edu **CEEB Code:** 6306
Fax: 515-294-2592 **Website:** www.iastate.edu **ACT Code:** 1320

This public school was founded in 1858. It has a 1813 acre campus.

RATINGS
Admissions Selectivity Rating: 79   **Fire Safety Rating:** 89   **Green Rating:** 99

STUDENTS AND FACULTY
Enrollment: 27,936. **Student Body:** 43% female, 57% male, 37% out-of-state, 5% international (118 countries represented). Asian 4%, African American 3%, Caucasian 76%, Hispanic 6%, Native American <1%, Pacific Islander <1%, Two or more races 3%, Race unknown 4%.
Retention and Graduation: 87% freshmen return for sophomore year. 47% freshmen graduate within 4 years. 74% freshmen graduate within 6 years. 16% grads go on to further study within 1 year. **Faculty:** Student/faculty ratio 18:1. 1,581 full-time faculty, 93% hold PhDs, 23% are members of minority groups, 37% are women.

ACADEMICS
Degrees: Bachelor's; Doctoral degree—professional practice; Doctoral degree research/scholarship; Master's; Post-bachelor's certificate; Post-master's certificate. **Classes:** Most classes have 20–29 students. Most lab/discussion sessions have 20–29 students. **Special Study Options:** Accelerated program; Cooperative education program; Cross-registration; Distance learning; Double major; Dual enrollment; English as a Second Language (ESL); Exchange student program (domestic); External degree program; Honors program; Independent study; Internships; Student-designed major; Study abroad; Teacher certification program. **Honors programs:** ISU offers both a University Honors Program and a Freshman Honors Program. Each program promotes an enhanced academic environment for students of high ability and emphasizes the development of an enriched, individualized program study that meets each student's particular needs, interests and abilities. Honors gives students a supportive community in which to pursue their goals and stretch their horizons. Benefits include unique courses, small class sizes, research opportunities and funding, access to graduate-level courses, and priority registration. **Combined degree programs:** BA/MEng. **Disability Services offered:** Note-taking services; Reader services; Tape recorders; Tutors. **Career services:** Alumni network; Alumni services; Career assessment; Career/job search classes; Internships.

FACILITIES
Housing: Apartments for married students; Apartments for single students; Coed dorms; Fraternity/sorority housing; Men's dorms; Special housing for disabled students; Special housing for international students; Theme housing; Women's dorms; 96% of campus accessible to physically disabled. **Special Academic Facilities/Equipment:** Brunnier art museum, Farm House museum, observatory, numerous institutes, research centers, College of Design Gallery, Virtual Reality Application Center, Pappajohn Center for Entrepreneurship. **Campus Network:** 98% of classrooms, 99% of dorms, 100% of student union, 100% of libraries, 100% of dining areas have wireless network access.

CAMPUS LIFE
Environment: Town. **Activities:** Campus Ministries; Choral groups; Concert band; Dance; Drama/theater; International Student Organization; Jazz band; Literary magazine; Marching band; Model UN; Music ensembles; Musical theater; Pep band; Radio station; Student government; Student newspaper; Student-run film society; Symphony orchestra; Television station. 898 registered organizations, 28 honor societies, 39 religious organizations, 44 fraternities, 36 sororities on campus. **Athletics (Intercollegiate):** *Men:* basketball, cross-country, football, golf, track/field (outdoor), track/field (indoor), wrestling. *Women:* basketball, cross-country, diving, golf, gymnastics, soccer, softball, swimming, tennis, track/field (outdoor), track/field (indoor), volleyball. **On-Campus Highlights:** Union Drive Community Center (dining center).

ADMISSIONS
Freshman Academic Profile: Average high school GPA 3.7. 28% in top 10% of high school class, 62% in top 25% of high school class, 93% in top 50% of

high school class. **Test Scores:** SAT Math middle 50% range 560–690. SAT EBRW middle 50% range 540–650. ACT middle 50% range 22–28. **Basis for Candidate Selection:** *Very important factors include:* rigor of secondary school record, class rank, academic GPA, standardized test scores. *Other factors include:* application essay, recommendation(s), interview, extracurricular activities, talent/ability, character/personal qualities, geographical residence, state residency, volunteer work, work experience. **Freshman Admission Requirements:** High school diploma is required and GED is accepted. *Academic units required:* 4 English, 3 math, 3 science, 2 science labs, 2 foreign language, 2 social studies. *Academic units recommended:* 4 English, 4 math, 4 science, 3 science labs, 3 foreign language, 4 social studies. **Freshman Admission Statistics:** 18,246 applied, 92% admitted, 33% enrolled. **Transfer Admission Requirements:** College transcript(s), statement of good standing from prior institution(s). Minimum college GPA of 2.0 required. Lowest grade transferable D. **General Admission Information:** Application fee $40. Priority deadline 3/1. Non-fall registration accepted. Admission may be deferred for a maximum of 1 year.

COSTS AND FINANCIAL AID

Annual in-state tuition $8,042. Annual out-of-state tuition $23,230. Room and board $9,149. Required fees $1,278. Average book and supplies expense $1,041. **Required Forms and Deadlines:** FAFSA. **Notification of Awards:** Applicants will be notified of awards on a rolling basis beginning 1/30. **Types of Aid:** *Need-based scholarships/grants:* College/university scholarship or grant aid from institutional funds; Federal Pell; SEOG; State scholarships/grants. *Loans:* Direct PLUS loans; Direct Subsidized Stafford Loans; Direct Unsubsidized Stafford Loans. **Student Employment:** Federal Work-Study Program available. Institutional employment available. **Financial Aid Statistics:** 98% needy freshmen, 97% needy undergrads receive need-based scholarship or grant aid. 47% freshmen, 44% undergrads receive non-need-based scholarship or grant aid. 66% freshmen, 70% undergrads receive need-based self-help aid. 2% freshmen, 2% undergrads receive athletic scholarships. 90.6% freshmen, 81.6% undergrads receive any aid. 56% undergrads borrow to pay for school. Average cumulative indebtedness $28,097. **Criteria awarding aid:** *Need-based:* Academics, Minority status. *Non-need-based:* Academics, Alumni affiliation, Art, Athletics, Leadership, Minority status, Music/drama, State/district residency.

ITHACA COLLEGE

Ithaca College, Office of Admission, Ithaca, NY 14850-7002
Phone: (607) 274-3124 **Financial Aid Phone:** 607-274-3131
E-mail: admission@ithaca.edu **CEEB Code:** 2325
Fax: (607) 274-1900 **Website:** www.ithaca.edu **ACT Code:** 2772

This private school was founded in 1892. It has a 669 acre campus.

RATINGS

Admissions Selectivity Rating: 84   **Fire Safety Rating:** 93   **Green Rating:** 98

STUDENTS AND FACULTY

Enrollment: 6,072. **Student Body:** 57% female, 43% male, 55% out-of-state, 2% international (52 countries represented). Asian 4%, African American 6%, Caucasian 73%, Hispanic 9%, Native American <1%, Pacific Islander <1%, Two or more races 3%, Race unknown 3%.
Retention and Graduation: 85% freshmen return for sophomore year. 72% freshmen graduate within 4 years. 23% grads go on to further study within 1 year. 15% grads pursue arts and sciences degrees. 1% grads pursue law degrees. 1% grads pursue business degrees. 1% grads pursue medical degrees. **Faculty:** Student/faculty ratio 11:1. 519 full-time faculty, 81% hold PhDs, 13% are members of minority groups, 50% are women. 2% of classes are taught by teaching assistants.

ACADEMICS

Degrees: Bachelor's; Certificate; Doctoral degree—professional practice; Master's. **Classes:** Most classes have 10–19 students. **Most popular majors:** Radio and Television; Music, General; Business Administration, Management and Operations. **Special Study Options:** Accelerated program; Cross-registration; Distance learning; Double major; Dual enrollment; Honors program; Independent study; Internships; Liberal arts/career combination; Student-designed major; Study abroad; Teacher certification program. **Honors**

programs: The Ithaca College Honors Program provides students with a highly enhanced, integrated, and comprehensive liberal arts program that emphasizes critical thinking, intellectual curiosity, and lifelong learning. The Honors Program supports an innovative community of faculty and students and encourages a culture of intellectual engagement through curricular, co-curricular, and extracurricular opportunities. Honors seminars are unique to the Honors Program and the program offers a variety of three-credit and one-credit courses to feed student's curiosity, challenge their thinking, and expand their intellect. Often, professors and the program supplement classroom education with out-of-class activities such as trips or speakers. In order to graduate with Ithaca College honors, students must demonstrate by portfolio that they have experienced significant involvement in five important areas: academic challenge, global citizenship, cultural engagement, scholarly achievement, and civic engagement. To a greater extent than other students, honors students are held personally responsible for their learning and are expected to incorporate into the portfolio artifacts and reflections demonstrating their learning in each area. Honors is open to any qualified student in any school or department at Ithaca College. The Honors Program does not conflict with departmental honors programs; qualified students can complete both. **Disability Services offered:** Note-taking services; Reader services; Tape recorders. **Career services:** Alumni network; Alumni services; Career assessment; Career/job search classes; Internships; Regional alumni.

FACILITIES

Housing: Apartments for single students; Coed dorms; Fraternity/sorority housing; Special housing for disabled students; Theme housing. **Special Academic Facilities/Equipment:** The Dorothy D. and Roy H. Park Center for Business and Sustainable Enterprise, and the Peggy Ryan Williams Center are both Platinum LEED-certified buildings. In addition, the LINK Connector between Job Hall and Dillingham Center for the Performing Arts has been certified LEED Gold. The new Athletics and Events Center was certified LEED Gold. The Handwerker Gallery provides an outlet for creative work and intellectual discourse for students and faculty in diverse programs across campus. **Campus Network:** 100% of classrooms, 100% of libraries, 100% of dining areas, 100% of common outdoor areas have wireless network access.

CAMPUS LIFE

Environment: Town. **Activities:** Campus Ministries; Choral groups; Concert band; Dance; Drama/theater; International Student Organization; Jazz band; Literary magazine; Model UN; Music ensembles; Musical theater; Opera; Pep band; Radio station; Student government; Student newspaper; Student-run film society; Symphony orchestra; Television station. 219 registered organizations, 28 honor societies, 10 religious organizations, 3 fraternities on campus. **Athletics (Intercollegiate):** *Men:* baseball, basketball, crew/rowing, cross-country, diving, football, lacrosse, soccer, swimming, tennis, track/field (outdoor), wrestling. *Women:* basketball, crew/rowing, cross-country, diving, field hockey, golf, gymnastics, lacrosse, soccer, softball, swimming, tennis, track/field (outdoor), volleyball. **On-Campus Highlights:** IC Square and Food Court. **Environmental Initiatives:** Sustainability Initiative that spurs and chronicles progress in three separate but highly inter-related areas: development of curriculum to infuse considerations of sustainability and applied research opportunities to study and solve sustainability challenges; modification of campus operations to incorporate more sustainable decision-making; and campus in-reach and community outreach to share our experiences as a learning organization seeking to become more sustainable.

ADMISSIONS

Freshman Academic Profile: 24% in top 10% of high school class, 56% in top 25% of high school class, 91% in top 50% of high school class. 83% from public high schools. **Test Scores:** SAT Math middle 50% range 570–668. SAT EBRW middle 50% range 590–670. ACT middle 50% range 25–30. **Basis for Candidate Selection:** *Very important factors include:* rigor of secondary school record, academic GPA, level of applicant's interest. *Important factors include:* application essay, recommendation(s), extracurricular activities, talent/ability, character/personal qualities. *Other factors include:* class rank, standardized test scores, interview, first generation, alumni/ae relation, volunteer work, work experience. **Freshman Admission Requirements:** High school diploma is required and GED is accepted. *Academic units required:* 4 English, 3 math, 3 science, 2 foreign language, 3 social studies, 1 academic elective. *Academic units recommended:* 4 English, 4 math, 4 science, 3 foreign language, 4 social studies, 1 academic elective. **Freshman Admission Statistics:** 15,278 applied, 69% admitted, 16% enrolled. **Transfer Admission Requirements:** High school transcript, college transcript(s), essay or personal statement, statement of good standing from prior institution(s). Minimum college GPA of 2.75 required. Lowest grade transferable C-. **General Admission Information:** Application fee $60. Regular application deadline 2/1. Non-fall registration accepted. Admission may be deferred for a maximum of 1 year.

COSTS AND FINANCIAL AID

Annual tuition $45,274. Room and board $15,856. Average book and supplies expense $1,200. **Required Forms and Deadlines:** CSS/Financial Aid PROFILE; FAFSA. **Notification of Awards:** Applicants will be notified of awards on a rolling basis beginning 2/15. **Types of Aid:** *Need-based scholarships/grants:* College/university scholarship or grant aid from institutional funds; Federal Pell; Private scholarships; SEOG; State scholarships/grants. *Loans:* Direct PLUS loans; Direct Subsidized Stafford Loans; Direct Unsubsidized Stafford Loans. **Student Employment:** Federal Work-Study Program available. Institutional employment available. **Financial Aid Statistics:** 98% needy freshmen, 73% needy undergrads receive need-based scholarship or grant aid. 35% freshmen, 12% undergrads receive non-need-based scholarship or grant aid. 88% freshmen, 66% undergrads receive need-based self-help aid. 0% freshmen, 0% undergrads receive athletic scholarships. 95.7% freshmen, 92.6% undergrads receive any aid. 69% undergrads borrow to pay for school. Average cumulative indebtedness $39,913. **Criteria awarding aid:** *Need-based:* Academics, Minority status, Music/drama. *Non-need-based:* Academics, Alumni affiliation, Leadership, Minority status, Music/drama.

JACKSON STATE UNIVERSITY

1400 J. R. Lynch Street, Jackson, MS 39217
Phone: (601) 979-2100 **Financial Aid Phone:** 601-979-2227
E-mail: admappl@jsums.edu **CEEB Code:** 1341
Fax: 601-979-3445 **Website:** www.jsums.edu **ACT Code:** 2204

This public school was founded in 1877. It has a 175 acre campus.

RATINGS

Admissions Selectivity Rating: 74   **Fire Safety Rating:** 89   **Green Rating:** 60*

STUDENTS AND FACULTY

Enrollment: 6,844. **Student Body:** 62% female, 38% male, 17% out-of-state, 2% international (35 countries represented). Asian <1%, African American 93%, Caucasian 3%, Hispanic <1%, Native American <1%, Pacific Islander 0%, Two or more races 1%, Race unknown 0%.
Retention and Graduation: 78% freshmen return for sophomore year. **Faculty:** Student/faculty ratio 17:1. 378 full-time faculty, 81% hold PhDs, 81% are members of minority groups, 46% are women.

ACADEMICS

Degrees: Bachelor's; Master's; Post-master's certificate. **Classes:** Most classes have 20–29 students. Most lab/discussion sessions have 10–19 students. **Most popular majors:** Criminal Justice/Safety Studies; Biology/Biological Sciences, General; Elementary Education and Teaching. **Special Study Options:** Distance learning; Double major; Dual enrollment; English as a Second Language (ESL); Honors program; Independent study; Internships; Study abroad; Teacher certification program; Weekend college. **Honors programs:** Honors College. **Disability Services offered:** Note-taking services; Reader services; Tape recorders; Tutors. **Career services:** Career assessment; Career/job search classes; Internships.

FACILITIES

Housing: Men's dorms; Women's dorms; 100% of campus accessible to physically disabled. **Special Academic Facilities/Equipment:** Research center, science observatory, e-center.

CAMPUS LIFE

Environment: Metropolis. **Activities:** Campus Ministries; Choral groups; Concert band; Dance; Drama/theater; International Student Organization; Jazz band; Literary magazine; Marching band; Music ensembles; Opera; Radio station; Student government; Student newspaper; Student-run film society; Symphony orchestra; Television station; Yearbook. 130 registered organizations, 22 honor societies, 11 religious organizations, 5 fraternities, 4 sororities on campus. **Athletics (Intercollegiate):** *Men:* baseball, basketball, cross-country, football, golf, soccer, tennis, track/field (indoor), track/field (outdoor), volleyball. *Women:* basketball, cross-country, golf, soccer, softball, tennis, track/field (outdoor), track/field (indoor), volleyball. **On-Campus Highlights:** Student Center.

ADMISSIONS

Freshman Academic Profile: Average high school GPA 2.9. 85% from public high schools. **Test Scores:** ACT middle 50% range 17–20. **Basis for Candidate Selection:** *Very important factors include:* rigor of secondary school record, academic GPA, standardized test scores. *Important factors include:* level of applicant's interest. **Freshman Admission Requirements:** High school diploma

---

is required and GED is accepted. *Academic units required:* 4 English, 3 math, 3 science, 3 social studies, 2 academic electives, 0.5 computer science. **Freshman Admission Statistics:** 7,265 applied, 74% admitted, 19% enrolled. **Transfer Admission Requirements:** High school transcript, college transcript(s). Minimum college GPA of 2.0 required. Lowest grade transferable C. **General Admission Information:** Priority deadline 8/1. Regular application deadline 8/1. Non-fall registration accepted.

COSTS AND FINANCIAL AID

Annual in-state tuition $5,504. Annual out-of-state tuition $13,494. Room and board $6,494. Average book and supplies expense $800. **Required Forms and Deadlines:** FAFSA; Institution's own financial aid form; State aid form. **Notification of Awards:** Applicants will be notified of awards on a rolling basis beginning 2/15. **Types of Aid:** *Need-based scholarships/grants:* College/university scholarship or grant aid from institutional funds; Federal Pell; Private scholarships; SEOG; State scholarships/grants. **Student Employment:** Federal Work-Study Program available. Institutional employment available. **Criteria awarding aid:** *Need-based:* Academics.

JACKSONVILLE UNIVERSITY

Office of Admissions, Jacksonville, FL 32211
Phone: 904-256-7000 **Financial Aid Phone:** 800-558-3467
E-mail: admissions@ju.edu **CEEB Code:** 5331
Website: http://www.ju.edu/ **ACT Code:** 740

This private school was founded in 1934. It has a 198 acre campus.

RATINGS

Admissions Selectivity Rating: 87   **Fire Safety Rating:** 82   **Green Rating:** 60*

STUDENTS AND FACULTY

Enrollment: 3,122. **Student Body:** 59% female, 41% male, 29% out-of-state, 1% international (50 countries represented). Asian 4%, African American 19%, Caucasian 60%, Hispanic 7%, Native American 1%, Pacific Islander <1%, Two or more races 8%, Race unknown 0%.
Retention and Graduation: 60% freshmen return for sophomore year. 22% grads go on to further study within 1 year. **Faculty:** Student/faculty ratio 13:1. 180 full-time faculty, 79% hold PhDs, 9% are members of minority groups, 43% are women. 0% of classes are taught by teaching assistants.

ACADEMICS

Degrees: Bachelor's; Master's; Post-master's certificate. **Classes:** Most classes have 10–19 students. **Most popular majors:** Business/Commerce, General; Aviation/Airway Management and Operations; Nursing/Registered Nurse (Rn, Asn, Bsn, Msn). **Special Study Options:** Accelerated program; Cooperative education program; Distance learning; Double major; Dual enrollment; Honors program; Independent study; Internships; Liberal arts/career combination; Student-designed major; Study abroad; Teacher certification program. **Honors programs:** University Honors Program. **Disability Services offered:** Note-taking services; Reader services; Tutors.

FACILITIES

Housing: Apartments for single students; Coed dorms; Fraternity/sorority housing; Men's dorms; Special housing for disabled students; Wellness housing; Women's dorms. **Special Academic Facilities/Equipment:** Art museum, dance pavilion, concert hall, on-campus pre-school.

CAMPUS LIFE

Environment: Metropolis. **Activities:** Campus Ministries; Choral groups; Concert band; Dance; Drama/theater; International Student Organization; Jazz band; Literary magazine; Marching band; Music ensembles; Musical theater; Pep band; Radio station; Student government; Student newspaper; Symphony orchestra; Television station; Yearbook. 60 registered organizations, 16 honor societies, 9 fraternities, 6 sororities on campus. **Athletics (Intercollegiate):** *Men:* baseball, basketball, crew/rowing, cross-country, football, golf, soccer, tennis. *Women:* basketball, crew/rowing, cross-country, golf, soccer, softball, tennis, track/field (outdoor), track/field (indoor), volleyball. **On-Campus Highlights:** Alexander Brest Fine Arts Museum.

ADMISSIONS

Freshman Academic Profile: Average high school GPA 3.5. **Test Scores:** SAT Math middle 50% range 480–570. SAT EBRW middle 50% range 470–560. ACT middle 50% range 20–26. **Basis for Candidate Selection:** *Very important factors include:* academic GPA, standardized test scores. *Important factors include:* rigor of secondary school record, talent/ability. *Other factors include:* application essay, recommendation(s), interview, extracurricular activities, character/personal qualities, volunteer work, work experience. **Freshman Admission Requirements:** High school diploma is required and GED is accepted. *Academic units required:* 4 English, 3 math, 3 science, 2 science labs, 3 social studies. *Academic units recommended:* 4 English, 4 math, 3 science, 2 science labs, 2 foreign language, 3 social studies. **Freshman Admission Statistics:** 8,096 applied, 42% admitted, 16% enrolled. **Transfer Admission Requirements:** College transcript(s), essay or personal statement, statement of good standing from prior institution(s). Minimum college GPA of 2.0 required. Lowest grade transferable C. **General Admission Information:** Application fee $30. Priority deadline 3/1. Non-fall registration accepted.

COSTS AND FINANCIAL AID

Required Forms and Deadlines: FAFSA; Institution's own financial aid form; State aid form. **Notification of Awards:** Applicants will be notified of awards on a rolling basis beginning 2/15. **Types of Aid:** *Need-based scholarships/grants:* College/university scholarship or grant aid from institutional funds; Federal Pell; Private scholarships; SEOG; State scholarships/grants. **Financial Aid Statistics:** 98% needy freshmen, 99% needy undergrads receive need-based scholarship or grant aid. 1% freshmen, 1% undergrads receive non-need-based scholarship or grant aid. 62% freshmen, 69% undergrads receive need-based self-help aid. 2% freshmen, 4% undergrads receive athletic scholarships. 97% freshmen, 87% undergrads receive any aid. **Criteria awarding aid:** *Need-based:* Job skills, Leadership. *Non-need-based:* Academics, Art, Athletics, Job skills, Leadership, Music/drama, State/district residency.

JAMES MADISON UNIVERSITY

Sonner Hall, Harrisonburg, VA 22807
Phone: 540-568-5681 **Financial Aid Phone:** 540-568-7820
E-mail: admissions@jmu.edu **CEEB Code:** 5392
Fax: 540-568-3332 **Website:** www.jmu.edu **ACT Code:** 4370

This public school was founded in 1908. It has a 785 acre campus.

RATINGS

Admissions Selectivity Rating: 82   **Fire Safety Rating:** 85   **Green Rating:** 98

STUDENTS AND FACULTY

Enrollment: 19,666. **Student Body:** 59% female, 41% male, 23% out-of-state, 2% international (70 countries represented). Asian 5%, African American 5%, Caucasian 75%, Hispanic 7%, Native American <1%, Pacific Islander <1%, Two or more races 4%, Race unknown 3%.
Retention and Graduation: 90% freshmen return for sophomore year. 58% freshmen graduate within 4 years. 29% grads go on to further study within 1 year. 14% grads pursue arts and sciences degrees. 1% grads pursue law degrees. 2% grads pursue business degrees. 1% grads pursue medical degrees. **Faculty:** Student/faculty ratio 16:1. 1,044 full-time faculty, 78% hold PhDs, 13% are members of minority groups, 49% are women. 1% of classes are taught by teaching assistants.

ACADEMICS

Degrees: Bachelor's; Doctoral degree—professional practice; Doctoral degree research/scholarship; Master's. **Classes:** Most classes have 20–29 students. Most lab/discussion sessions have 20–29 students. **Most popular majors:** Community Health Services/Liaison/Counseling; Psychology, General; Speech Communication and Rhetoric. **Special Study Options:** Accelerated program; Distance learning; Double major; Dual enrollment; Honors program; Independent study; Internships; Study abroad; Teacher certification program. **Honors programs:** Academic honors program, honors scholars (3.25 or above), honors courses, and senior honors project (3.25). **Disability Services offered:** Note-taking services; Reader services; Tape recorders. **Career services:** Alumni network; Alumni services; Career assessment; Career/job search classes; Internships; Regional alumni.

FACILITIES

Housing: Apartments for single students; Coed dorms; Fraternity/sorority housing; Special housing for disabled students; Theme housing; Wellness housing; 90% of campus accessible to physically disabled. **Special Academic**

Facilities/Equipment: Language lab, music and fine arts buildings, herbarium, university farm, planetarium, arboretum, mineral museum, Science on a Sphere.

CAMPUS LIFE

Environment: Town. **Activities:** Campus Ministries; Choral groups; Concert band; Dance; Drama/theater; International Student Organization; Jazz band; Literary magazine; Marching band; Music ensembles; Musical theater; Opera; Pep band; Radio station; Student government; Student newspaper; Student-run film society; Symphony orchestra; Yearbook. 353 registered organizations, 22 honor societies, 32 religious organizations, 15 fraternities, 13 sororities on campus. **Athletics (Intercollegiate):** *Men:* baseball, basketball, cheerleading, football, golf, soccer, tennis. *Women:* basketball, cheerleading, cross-country, diving, field hockey, golf, lacrosse, soccer, softball, swimming, tennis, track/field (outdoor), volleyball. **On-Campus Highlights:** Quad. **Environmental Initiatives:** Development of student learning outcomes for environmental literacy and an assessment.

ADMISSIONS

Freshman Academic Profile: 16% in top 10% of high school class, 51% in top 25% of high school class, 94% in top 50% of high school class. 60% from public high schools. **Test Scores:** SAT Math middle 50% range 540–620. SAT EBRW middle 50% range 560–640. ACT middle 50% range 23–28. **Basis for Candidate Selection:** *Very important factors include:* rigor of secondary school record, academic GPA. *Other factors include:* application essay, standardized test scores, recommendation(s), extracurricular activities, talent/ability, character/personal qualities, first generation, alumni/ae relation, geographical residence, state residency, racial/ethnic status, volunteer work, work experience. **Freshman Admission Requirements:** High school diploma is required and GED is accepted. *Academic units required:* 4 English, 4 math, 3 science, 3 foreign language, 2 social studies, 3 history. *Academic units recommended:* 4 English, 4 math, 3 science, 3 foreign language, 2 social studies, 3 history. **Freshman Admission Statistics:** 21,099 applied, 75% admitted, 29% enrolled. **Transfer Admission Requirements:** High school transcript, college transcript(s). Minimum college GPA of 2.0 required. Lowest grade transferable C. **General Admission Information:** Application fee $70. Regular application deadline 1/15. Admission may be deferred for a maximum of 1 year.

COSTS AND FINANCIAL AID

Annual in-state tuition $7,250. Annual out-of-state tuition $24,100. Room and board $10,740. Required fees $4,956. Average book and supplies expense $1,038. **Required Forms and Deadlines:** FAFSA. **Notification of Awards:** Applicants will be notified of awards on a rolling basis beginning 4/1. **Types of Aid:** *Need-based scholarships/grants:* College/university scholarship or grant aid from institutional funds; Federal Pell; Private scholarships; SEOG; State scholarships/grants. *Loans:* Direct PLUS loans; Direct Subsidized Stafford Loans; Direct Unsubsidized Stafford Loans. **Student Employment:** Federal Work-Study Program available. Institutional employment available. **Financial Aid Statistics:** 56% needy freshmen, 55% needy undergrads receive need-based scholarship or grant aid. 7% freshmen, 7% undergrads receive non-need-based scholarship or grant aid. 72% freshmen, 65% undergrads receive need-based self-help aid. 2% freshmen, 2% undergrads receive athletic scholarships. 62% freshmen, 58% undergrads receive any aid. 51% undergrads borrow to pay for school. Average cumulative indebtedness $29,189. **Criteria awarding aid:** *Need-based:* Academics, Leadership, Minority status, Religious affiliation. *Non-need-based:* Academics, Alumni affiliation, Art, Athletics, Leadership, Minority status, Music/drama, State/district residency.

JARVIS CHRISTIAN COLLEGE

P.O. BOX 1470, Hawkins, TX 75765-1470
Phone: 903-769-5730 **Financial Aid Phone:** 903-769-5740
E-mail: felecia_tyiska@jarvis.edu
Fax: 903-769-1282 **Website:** http://www.jarvis.edu/ **ACT Code:** 4110

This private school, affiliated with the Disciples of Christ Church, was founded in 1912. It has a 243 acre campus.

RATINGS

Admissions Selectivity Rating: 63   **Fire Safety Rating:** 92   **Green Rating:** 60*

STUDENTS AND FACULTY

Enrollment: 547. **Student Body:** 60% female, 40% male, 15% out-of-state, <1% international (2 countries represented). Asian 0%, African American 95%, Caucasian 1%, Hispanic 3%, Native American <1%, Race unknown 0%.

Retention and Graduation: 41% freshmen return for sophomore year. 2% grads go on to further study within 1 year. 1% grads pursue business degrees. 0% grads pursue medical degrees. **Faculty:** Student/faculty ratio 13:1. 35 full-time faculty, 46% hold PhDs, 63% are members of minority groups, 49% are women. 0% of classes are taught by teaching assistants.

ACADEMICS
Degrees: Bachelor's. **Classes:** Most classes have fewer than 10 students. Most lab/discussion sessions have 10–19 students. **Most popular majors:** Criminal Justice/Law Enforcement Administration; Biology/Biological Sciences, General; Sports, Kinesiology, and Physical Education/Fitness, General. **Special Study Options:** Cross-registration; Distance learning; Double major; Dual enrollment; English as a Second Language (ESL); Honors program; Independent study; Internships; Liberal arts/career combination; Student-designed major; Teacher certification program. **Honors programs:** JETS Honors Program. **Disability Services offered:** Reader services; Tutors. **Career services:** Alumni network; Alumni services.

FACILITIES
Housing: Apartments for married students; Apartments for single students; Men's dorms; Special housing for disabled students; Women's dorms; 95% of campus accessible to physically disabled. **Special Academic Facilities/ Equipment:** Archives. **Campus Network:** 100% of classrooms, 100% of dorms, 100% of student union, 100% of libraries, 100% of dining areas, 50% of common outdoor areas have wireless network access.

CAMPUS LIFE
Environment: Rural. **Activities:** Choral groups; Drama/theater; International Student Organization; Music ensembles; Pep band; Student government. 33 registered organizations, 6 honor societies, 5 religious organizations, 4 fraternities, 4 sororities on campus. **Athletics (Intercollegiate):** *Men:* baseball, basketball. *Women:* basketball, volleyball. **On-Campus Highlights:** E. W. Rand Health, Physical Education, and Recreat.

ADMISSIONS
Freshman Academic Profile: Average high school GPA 2.6. 0% in top 10% of high school class, 6% in top 25% of high school class, 23% in top 50% of high school class. 99% from public high schools. **Basis for Candidate Selection:** *Other factors include:* rigor of secondary school record, class rank, academic GPA, standardized test scores, extracurricular activities, talent/ability, character/ personal qualities. **Freshman Admission Requirements:** High school diploma is required and GED is accepted. *Academic units required:* 3 English, 2 math, 1 science, 3 social studies, 7 academic electives. *Academic units recommended:* 3 English, 2 math, 1 science, 3 social studies, 7 academic electives. **Freshman Admission Statistics:** 525 applied, 92% admitted, 25% enrolled. **Transfer Admission Requirements:** High school transcript, college transcript(s), standardized test scores, Lowest grade transferable F. **General Admission Information:** Application fee $50. Priority deadline 5/1. Non-fall registration accepted. Admission may be deferred for a maximum of one year.

COSTS AND FINANCIAL AID
Annual tuition $8,528. Room and board $6,715. Required fees $1,080. Average book and supplies expense $1,000. **Required Forms and Deadlines:** FAFSA; Institution's own financial aid form; State aid form. **Notification of Awards:** Applicants will be notified of awards on a rolling basis beginning 5/1. **Types of Aid:** *Need-based scholarships/grants:* College/university scholarship or grant aid from institutional funds; Federal Pell; Private scholarships; SEOG; State scholarships/grants; United Negro College Fund. *Loans:* Direct PLUS loans; Direct Subsidized Stafford Loans; Direct Unsubsidized Stafford Loans. **Student Employment:** Federal Work-Study Program available. **Financial Aid Statistics:** 94% needy freshmen, 100% needy undergrads receive need-based scholarship or grant aid. 41% freshmen, 23% undergrads receive non-need-based scholarship or grant aid. 79% freshmen, 89% undergrads receive need-based self-help aid. 3% freshmen, 6% undergrads receive athletic scholarships. 98% freshmen, 98% undergrads receive any aid. **Criteria awarding aid:** *Non-need-based:* Academics, Athletics, Religious affiliation, State/district residency.

JEWISH THEOLOGICAL SEMINARY, ALBERT A. LIST COLLEGE

3080 Broadway, New York, NY 10027
Phone: 212-678-8832 **Financial Aid Phone:** 212-678-8007
E-mail: lcadmissions@jtsa.edu **CEEB Code:** 2339
Fax: 212-280-6022 **Website:** www.jtsa.edu **ACT Code:** 2776

This private school, affiliated with the Jewish Church, was founded in 1886. It has a 1 acre campus.

RATINGS
Admissions Selectivity Rating: 91 **Fire Safety Rating:** 60* **Green Rating:** 60*

STUDENTS AND FACULTY
Enrollment: 177. **Student Body:** 54% female, 46% male, 84% out-of-state, 3% international (10 countries represented). Asian 0%, African American 0%, Caucasian 94%, Hispanic 1%, Native American 0%, Race unknown 2%. **Retention and Graduation:** 89% freshmen return for sophomore year. 15% grads go on to further study within 1 year. 6% grads pursue arts and sciences degrees. 6% grads pursue law degrees. 0% grads pursue business degrees. 3% grads pursue medical degrees. **Faculty:** Student/faculty ratio 6:1. 52 full-time faculty, 0% of classes are taught by teaching assistants.

ACADEMICS
Degrees: Bachelor's; Doctoral degree—professional practice; Doctoral degree research/scholarship; Master's. **Classes:** Most classes have 10–19 students. **Most popular majors:** Bible/Biblical Studies; Jewish/Judaic Studies. **Special Study Options:** Cross-registration; Distance learning; Double major; Exchange student program (domestic); Honors program; Independent study; Internships; Liberal arts/career combination; Student-designed major; Study abroad. **Combined degree programs:** BA/MA. **Disability Services offered:** Tape recorders; Tutors. **Career services:** Alumni network; Alumni services; Career/ job search classes; Internships.

FACILITIES
Housing: Apartments for married students; Apartments for single students; Coed dorms. **Special Academic Facilities/Equipment:** The Jewish Museum and the Rare Book Room of the Library.

CAMPUS LIFE
Environment: Metropolis. **Activities:** Choral groups; Concert band; Dance; Drama/theater; Jazz band; Literary magazine; Music ensembles; Musical theater; Radio station; Student government; Student newspaper; Yearbook. 1 religious organization on campus. **Athletics (Intercollegiate):** *Men:* baseball, basketball, crew/rowing, soccer, tennis, track/field (outdoor), volleyball. *Women:* baseball, basketball, crew/rowing, soccer, tennis, track/field (outdoor), volleyball. **On-Campus Highlights:** The Library of the Jewish Theological Seminary. **Environmental Initiatives:** 4-Day work week to save on electricity.

ADMISSIONS
Freshman Academic Profile: Average high school GPA 3.7. **Test Scores:** SAT Math middle 50% range 620–660. SAT EBRW middle 50% range 640–700. ACT middle 50% range 30–32. **Basis for Candidate Selection:** *Very important factors include:* rigor of secondary school record, academic GPA, standardized test scores. *Important factors include:* class rank, application essay, recommendation(s), interview. *Other factors include:* extracurricular activities, talent/ability, character/ personal qualities, first generation, alumni/ae relation, religious affiliation/ commitment, volunteer work, level of applicant's interest. **Freshman Admission Requirements:** High school diploma is required and GED is not accepted. *Academic units recommended:* 4 English, 4 math, 4 science, 4 foreign language, 1 social studies, 3 history, 4 academic electives. **Freshman Admission Statistics:** 102 applied, 62% admitted, 65% enrolled. **Transfer Admission Requirements:** High school transcript, college transcript(s), essay or personal statement, standardized test scores, statement of good standing from prior institution(s). **General Admission Information:** Application fee $65. Priority deadline 1/15. Regular application deadline 2/15. Non-fall registration accepted.

COSTS AND FINANCIAL AID
Annual tuition $14,200. Room and board $9,200. Required fees $800. Average book and supplies expense $500. **Required Forms and Deadlines:** Business/ Farm Supplement; CSS/Financial Aid PROFILE; FAFSA; Institution's own financial aid form; Noncustodial PROFILE; State aid form. **Notification of Awards:** Applicants will be notified of awards on a rolling basis beginning 4/1. **Types of Aid:** *Need-based scholarships/grants:* College/university scholarship or

grant aid from institutional funds; Private scholarships. *Loans:* Direct Subsidized Stafford Loans; Direct Unsubsidized Stafford Loans. **Student Employment:** Federal Work-Study Program available. Institutional employment available. **Financial Aid Statistics:** 100% needy freshmen, 100% needy undergrads receive need-based scholarship or grant aid. 50% freshmen, 41% undergrads receive non-need-based scholarship or grant aid. 86% freshmen, 97% undergrads receive need-based self-help aid. 0% freshmen, 0% undergrads receive athletic scholarships. **Criteria awarding aid:** *Non-need-based:* Academics, Alumni affiliation, Leadership.

JOHN BROWN UNIVERSITY

2000 West University Street, Siloam Springs, AR 72761
Phone: 479-524-7454 **Financial Aid Phone:** 479-524-7424
E-mail: jbuinfo@jbu.edu **CEEB Code:** 6321
Fax: 479-524-4196 **Website:** www.jbu.edu **ACT Code:** 130

This private school was founded in 1919. It has a 200 acre campus.

RATINGS

Admissions Selectivity Rating: 84   **Fire Safety Rating:** 88   **Green Rating:** 75

STUDENTS AND FACULTY

Enrollment: 1,577. **Student Body:** 59% female, 41% male, 51% out-of-state, 6% international (40 countries represented). Asian 1%, African American 3%, Caucasian 73%, Hispanic 7%, Native American 2%, Pacific Islander <1%, Two or more races 4%, Race unknown 4%.
Retention and Graduation: 80% freshmen return for sophomore year. 59% freshmen graduate within 4 years. 73% freshmen graduate within 6 years. 18% grads go on to further study within 1 year. **Faculty:** Student/faculty ratio 13:1. 90 full-time faculty, 77% hold PhDs, 11% are members of minority groups, 31% are women. 0% of classes are taught by teaching assistants.

ACADEMICS

Degrees: Associate; Bachelor's; Master's; Post-master's certificate. **Classes:** Most classes have 10–19 students. Most lab/discussion sessions have 10–19 students. **Most popular majors:** Engineering, General; Registered Nursing/Registered Nurse; Graphic Design. **Special Study Options:** Accelerated program; Distance learning; Double major; Dual enrollment; English as a Second Language (ESL); Exchange student program (domestic); Honors program; Independent study; Internships; Liberal arts/career combination; Student-designed major; Study abroad; Teacher certification program. **Honors programs:** The Honors Scholars Program consists of enriched Core Curriculum courses developed especially for gifted and highly motivated students. Emphasizing the use of primary texts, instructors challenge students through individual research, critical reflection, incisive discussion, interactive projects, and professional presentations.
Disability Services offered: Note-taking services; Reader services; Tutors.
Career services: Alumni network; Career assessment; Career/job search classes.

FACILITIES

Housing: Apartments for married students; Apartments for single students; Coed dorms; Men's dorms; Special housing for disabled students; Women's dorms; 90% of campus accessible to physically disabled. **Special Academic Facilities/Equipment:** Art Gallery, Human Anatomy Lab, TV Studio, Radio Station, Outdoor Learning Center, Center for Relationship Enrichment, Soderquist Center for Business and Ethics.

CAMPUS LIFE

Environment: Village. **Activities:** Campus Ministries; Choral groups; Concert band; Dance; Drama/theater; International Student Organization; Jazz band; Literary magazine; Music ensembles; Musical theater; Pep band; Radio station; Student government; Student newspaper; Student-run film society; Television station; Yearbook. 20 registered organizations, 5 honor societies on campus.
Athletics (Intercollegiate): *Men:* basketball, golf, soccer, tennis. *Women:* basketball, soccer, swimming, tennis, volleyball. **On-Campus Highlights:** Walker Student Center.

ADMISSIONS

Freshman Academic Profile: Average high school GPA 3.8. 34% in top 10% of high school class, 58% in top 25% of high school class, 85% in top 50% of high school class. **Test Scores:** SAT Math middle 50% range 530–670. SAT EBRW middle 50% range 580–695. ACT middle 50% range 23–30.
Basis for Candidate Selection: *Very important factors include:* academic GPA, standardized test scores, recommendation(s). *Important factors include:* class rank, application essay, interview, character/personal qualities, religious

affiliation/commitment. *Other factors include:* rigor of secondary school record, extracurricular activities, talent/ability, first generation, alumni/ae relation, level of applicant's interest. **Freshman Admission Requirements:** High school diploma is required and GED is accepted. *Academic units recommended:* 4 English, 3 math, 2 science, 1 science lab, 2 foreign language, 2 social studies, 1 history. **Freshman Admission Statistics:** 1,094 applied, 77% admitted, 38% enrolled. **Transfer Admission Requirements:** High school transcript, college transcript(s), essay or personal statement. Minimum college GPA of 2.5 required. Lowest grade transferable C. **General Admission Information:** Application fee $25. Priority deadline 5/1. Non-fall registration accepted. Admission may be deferred for a maximum of 1 year.

COSTS AND FINANCIAL AID

Annual tuition $25,750. Room and board $9,224. Average book and supplies expense $800. **Required Forms and Deadlines:** FAFSA; Institution's own financial aid form; State aid form. **Notification of Awards:** Applicants will be notified of awards on a rolling basis beginning 3/1. **Types of Aid:** *Need-based scholarships/grants:* College/university scholarship or grant aid from institutional funds; Federal Pell; Private scholarships; SEOG; State scholarships/grants. *Loans:* Direct PLUS loans; Direct Subsidized Stafford Loans; Direct Unsubsidized Stafford Loans. **Student Employment:** Federal Work-Study Program available. Institutional employment available. **Financial Aid Statistics:** 93% needy freshmen, 90% needy undergrads receive need-based scholarship or grant aid. 95% freshmen, 77% undergrads receive non-need-based scholarship or grant aid. 83% freshmen, 79% undergrads receive need-based self-help aid. 6% freshmen, 5% undergrads receive athletic scholarships. 98% freshmen, 91% undergrads receive any aid. 56% undergrads borrow to pay for school. Average cumulative indebtedness $27,732. **Criteria awarding aid:** *Non-need-based:* Academics, Alumni affiliation, Art, Athletics, Leadership, Music/drama.

JOHN CARROLL UNIVERSITY

1 John Carroll Boulevard, University Heights, OH 44118-4581
Phone: 216-397-4294 **Financial Aid Phone:** 216-397-4248
E-mail: enrollment@jcu.edu **CEEB Code:** 1342
Fax: 216-397-4981 **Website:** http://sites.jcu.edu/ **ACT Code:** 3282

This private school, affiliated with the Roman Catholic Church, was founded in 1886. It has a 62 acre campus.

RATINGS

Admissions Selectivity Rating: 77   **Fire Safety Rating:** 87   **Green Rating:** 71

STUDENTS AND FACULTY

Enrollment: 3,013. **Student Body:** 47% female, 53% male, 34% out-of-state, 2% international (25 countries represented). Asian 2%, African American 4%, Caucasian 85%, Hispanic 4%, Native American <1%, Pacific Islander 0%, Two or more races 2%, Race unknown 1%.
Retention and Graduation: 84% freshmen return for sophomore year. 72% freshmen graduate within 4 years. 78% freshmen graduate within 6 years. 28% grads go on to further study within 1 year. **Faculty:** Student/faculty ratio 13:1. 179 full-time faculty, 95% hold PhDs, 15% are members of minority groups, 45% are women.

ACADEMICS

Degrees: Bachelor's; Master's; Post-master's certificate. **Classes:** Most classes have 10–19 students. Most lab/discussion sessions have 10–19 students. **Most popular majors:** Speech Communication and Rhetoric; Psychology, General; Marketing/Marketing Management, General. **Special Study Options:** Cross-registration; Double major; Dual enrollment; Exchange student program (domestic); Honors program; Independent study; Internships; Liberal arts/career combination; Student-designed major; Study abroad; Teacher certification program. **Honors programs:** JCU's Honors Program provides a framework of opportunities for academically outstanding students. Students have access to funds to attend one or more cultural events each semester. The program also includes opportunities to engage in faculty and student dialogue through academic seminars and social events. **Combined degree programs:** BA/MA. **Disability Services offered:** Note-taking services; Reader services; Tape recorders; Tutors. **Career services:** Alumni network; Alumni services; Career assessment; Career/job search classes; Internships; Regional alumni.

FACILITIES

Housing: Apartments for single students; Coed dorms; Fraternity/sorority housing; Special housing for disabled students; Theme housing; 94% of campus accessible to physically disabled. **Special Academic Facilities/Equipment:** The first known handwritten and illuminated Bible in more than 500 years is on permanent display in The Grasselli Library and Breen Learning Center at John Carroll University.

CAMPUS LIFE

Environment: Metropolis. **Activities:** Campus Ministries; Choral groups; Concert band; Dance; Drama/theater; International Student Organization; Jazz band; Literary magazine; Music ensembles; Musical theater; Pep band; Radio station; Student government; Student newspaper; Television station; Yearbook. 100 registered organizations, 5 religious organizations, 4 fraternities, 5 sororities on campus. **Athletics (Intercollegiate):** *Men:* baseball, basketball, cross-country, diving, football, golf, soccer, swimming, tennis, track/field (outdoor), track/field (indoor), wrestling. *Women:* basketball, cheerleading, cross-country, diving, golf, soccer, softball, swimming, tennis, track/field (outdoor), track/field (indoor), volleyball. **On-Campus Highlights:** St. Francis Chapel. **Environmental Initiatives:** Reuse building materials on campus or divert from landfills.

ADMISSIONS

Freshman Academic Profile: Average high school GPA 3.6. 24% in top 10% of high school class, 53% in top 25% of high school class, 87% in top 50% of high school class. 53% from public high schools. **Test Scores:** SAT Math middle 50% range 540–650. SAT EBRW middle 50% range 550–640. ACT middle 50% range 22–28. **Basis for Candidate Selection:** *Very important factors include:* rigor of secondary school record, academic GPA, extracurricular activities. *Important factors include:* application essay, standardized test scores, talent/ability, character/personal qualities, volunteer work. *Other factors include:* class rank, recommendation(s), interview, first generation, alumni/ae relation, geographical residence, level of applicant's interest. **Freshman Admission Requirements:** High school diploma is required and GED is accepted. *Academic units required:* 4 English, 3 math, 2 science, 2 science labs, 2 foreign language, 2 social studies, 3 academic electives. *Academic units recommended:* 4 English, 4 math, 3 science, 3 science labs, 3 foreign language, 4 social studies, 3 academic electives. **Freshman Admission Statistics:** 4,007 applied, 83% admitted, 25% enrolled. **Transfer Admission Requirements:** High school transcript, college transcript(s), essay or personal statement, standardized test scores, statement of good standing from prior institution(s). Lowest grade transferable 2. **General Admission Information:** Priority deadline 12/1. Non-fall registration accepted. Admission may be deferred for a maximum of 1 year.

COSTS AND FINANCIAL AID

Annual tuition $41,230. Room and board $12,232. Required fees $1,680. Average book and supplies expense $1,250. **Required Forms and Deadlines:** FAFSA. **Notification of Awards:** Applicants will be notified of awards on a rolling basis beginning 2/15. **Types of Aid:** *Need-based scholarships/grants:* College/university scholarship or grant aid from institutional funds; Federal Pell; Private scholarships; SEOG; State scholarships/grants. *Loans:* Direct PLUS loans; Direct Subsidized Stafford Loans; Direct Unsubsidized Stafford Loans. **Student Employment:** Federal Work-Study Program available. Institutional employment available. **Financial Aid Statistics:** 98% needy freshmen, 98% needy undergrads receive need-based scholarship or grant aid. 98% freshmen, 98% undergrads receive non-need-based scholarship or grant aid. 80% freshmen, 83% undergrads receive need-based self-help aid. 0% freshmen, 0% undergrads receive athletic scholarships. 99% freshmen, 94% undergrads receive any aid. 71% undergrads borrow to pay for school. Average cumulative indebtedness $33,508. **Criteria awarding aid:** *Non-need-based:* Academics, Leadership.

JOHNS HOPKINS UNIVERSITY

3400 North Charles Street, Baltimore, MD 21218
Phone: 410-516-8171 **Financial Aid Phone:** 410-516-8028
E-mail: gotojhu@jhu.edu **CEEB Code:** 5332
Fax: 410-516-6025 **Website:** www.jhu.edu

This private school was founded in 1876. It has a 140 acre campus.

RATINGS

Admissions Selectivity Rating: 99   **Fire Safety Rating:** 99   **Green Rating:** 94

STUDENTS AND FACULTY

Enrollment: 5,414. **Student Body:** 52% female, 48% male, 89% out-of-state, 11% international (65 countries represented). Asian 27%, African American

8%, Caucasian 28%, Hispanic 16%, Native American <1%, Pacific Islander <1%, Two or more races 6%, Race unknown 5%.
Retention and Graduation: 98% freshmen return for sophomore year. 88% freshmen graduate within 4 years. 94% freshmen graduate within 6 years. 35% grads go on to further study within 1 year. 17% grads pursue arts and sciences degrees. 2% grads pursue law degrees. 1% grads pursue business degrees. 4% grads pursue medical degrees. **Faculty:** Student/faculty ratio 7:1. 738 full-time faculty, 96% hold PhDs, 37% are women.

ACADEMICS

Degrees: Bachelor's; Certificate; Diploma; Doctoral degree research/scholarship; Master's; Post-bachelor's certificate. **Classes:** Most classes have 10–19 students. **Most popular majors:** Neuroscience; Public Health, General; Cell/Cellular and Molecular Biology. **Special Study Options:** Cross-registration; Double major; Independent study; Internships; Student-designed major; Study abroad. **Honors programs:** There are no honors programs but there are honor societies. **Combined degree programs:** BA/MA; BA/MEng. **Disability Services offered:** Note-taking services; Reader services; Tape recorders; Tutors. **Career services:** Alumni network; Alumni services; Career assessment; Career/job search classes; Internships; Regional alumni.

FACILITIES

Housing: Apartments for single students; Coed dorms; Special housing for disabled students; Wellness housing. **Special Academic Facilities/Equipment:** Baltimore Museum of Art, on-campus Digital Media Center, art gallery, electron microscope, Space Telescope Science Institute, four major research centers. **Campus Network:** 100% of classrooms, 100% of dorms, 100% of student union, 100% of libraries, 100% of dining areas, 40% of common outdoor areas have wireless network access.

CAMPUS LIFE

Environment: Metropolis. **Activities:** Campus Ministries; Choral groups; Concert band; Dance; Drama/theater; International Student Organization; Jazz band; Literary magazine; Model UN; Music ensembles; Musical theater; Opera; Pep band; Radio station; Student government; Student newspaper; Student-run film society; Symphony orchestra; Yearbook. 417 registered organizations, 13 honor societies, 14 religious organizations, 12 fraternities, 13 sororities on campus. **Athletics (Intercollegiate):** *Men:* baseball, basketball, cross-country, diving, fencing, football, lacrosse, soccer, swimming, tennis, track/field (outdoor), track/field (indoor), water polo, wrestling. *Women:* basketball, cross-country, diving, fencing, field hockey, lacrosse, soccer, swimming, tennis, track/field (outdoor), track/field (indoor), volleyball. **On-Campus Highlights:** Brody Learning Commons. **Environmental Initiatives:** Comprehensive climate commitment includes reaching a 51% reduction in GHG by 2025, investing over $73 million in GHG reduction projects, and seed grants for climate researchers.

ADMISSIONS

Freshman Academic Profile: Average high school GPA 3.9. 98% in top 10% of high school class, 99% in top 25% of high school class, 100% in top 50% of high school class. 56% from public high schools. **Test Scores:** SAT Math middle 50% range 760–800. SAT EBRW middle 50% range 710–770. ACT middle 50% range 33–35. **Basis for Candidate Selection:** *Very important factors include:* rigor of secondary school record, academic GPA, application essay, standardized test scores, recommendation(s), character/personal qualities. *Important factors include:* class rank, extracurricular activities, talent/ability. *Other factors include:* first generation, geographical residence, state residency, racial/ethnic status, volunteer work, work experience. **Freshman Admission Requirements:** High school diploma or equivalent is not required *Academic units recommended:* 4 English, 4 math, 4 science, 4 foreign language, 2 social studies, 2 history. **Freshman Admission Statistics:** 30,164 applied, 10% admitted, 46% enrolled. **Transfer Admission Requirements:** High school transcript, college transcript(s), essay or personal statement, statement of good standing from prior institution(s). Minimum college GPA of 3.0 required. Lowest grade transferable C. **General Admission Information:** Application fee $70. Regular application deadline 1/1.

COSTS AND FINANCIAL AID

Annual tuition $55,350. Room and board $16,310. Required fees $500. Average book and supplies expense $1,250. **Required Forms and Deadlines:** CSS/Financial Aid PROFILE; FAFSA; Noncustodial PROFILE. **Notification of Awards:** Applicants will be notified of awards on or about 4/1. **Types of Aid:** *Need-based scholarships/grants:* College/university scholarship or grant aid from institutional funds; Federal Pell; Private scholarships; SEOG; State scholarships/grants. *Loans:* Direct PLUS loans; Direct Subsidized Stafford Loans; Direct Unsubsidized Stafford Loans. **Student Employment:** Federal Work-Study Program available. Institutional employment available. **Financial Aid Statistics:**

100% needy freshmen, 98% needy undergrads receive need-based scholarship or grant aid. 16% freshmen, 14% undergrads receive non-need-based scholarship or grant aid. 83% freshmen, 87% undergrads receive need-based self-help aid. 1% freshmen, 1% undergrads receive athletic scholarships. 56% freshmen, 55% undergrads receive any aid. 46% undergrads borrow to pay for school. Average cumulative indebtedness $25,697. **Criteria awarding aid:** *Need-based:* Academics, Leadership. *Non-need-based:* Academics, Athletics, Leadership, State/district residency.

JOHNSON & WALES UNIVERSITY—CHARLOTTE

801 W Trade St., Charlotte, NC
Phone: 980-598-1100 **Financial Aid Phone:**
E-mail: clt@admissions.jwu.edu
Fax: 980-598-1111 **Website:** https://www1.jwu.edu/charlotte/

This is a private school.

RATINGS

Admissions Selectivity Rating: 68   **Fire Safety Rating:** 60*   **Green Rating:** 61

STUDENTS AND FACULTY

Enrollment: 2,218. **Student Body:** 66% female, 34% male, 62% out-of-state, 1% international. Asian 1%, African American 37%, Caucasian 43%, Hispanic 6%, Native American <1%, Pacific Islander 0%, Two or more races 7%, Race unknown 5%.
Retention and Graduation: 76% freshmen return for sophomore year.
Faculty: Student/faculty ratio 23:1. 83 full-time faculty, 0% hold PhDs, 0% are members of minority groups, 0% are women.

ACADEMICS

Degrees: Associate; Bachelor's. **Classes:** Most classes have 10–19 students. **Special Study Options:** Accelerated program; Cooperative education program; Dual enrollment; English as a Second Language (ESL); Exchange student program (domestic); Honors program; Independent study; Internships; Study abroad.

FACILITIES

Housing: Apartments for single students; Coed dorms; Special housing for disabled students; Wellness housing.

CAMPUS LIFE

Activities: Campus Ministries; Dance; International Student Organization; Student government; Student newspaper; Yearbook.

ADMISSIONS

Freshman Academic Profile: Average high school GPA 3.5. **Basis for Candidate Selection:** *Very important factors include:* rigor of secondary school record, class rank, academic GPA. *Important factors include:* application essay, interview, extracurricular activities. *Other factors include:* standardized test scores, recommendation(s), talent/ability, character/personal qualities, alumni/ae relation, volunteer work, work experience, level of applicant's interest.
Freshman Admission Requirements: High school diploma is required and GED is accepted. *Academic units required:* 4 English, 3 math, 3 science, 2 social studies. **Freshman Admission Statistics:** 4,537 applied, 72% admitted, 20% enrolled. **General Admission Information:** Non-fall registration accepted.

COSTS AND FINANCIAL AID

Annual tuition $30,396. Room and board $13,242. Required fees $350. Average book and supplies expense $1,500.

JOHNSON & WALES UNIVERSITY—NORTH MIAMI

1701 NE 127th Street, North Miami, FL 33181
Phone: 1-866-598-3567
E-mail: mia@admissions.jwu.edu
Fax: 305-892-7020 **Website:** http://admissions.jwu.edu

This is a private school.

RATINGS

Admissions Selectivity Rating: 66   **Fire Safety Rating:** 60*   **Green Rating:** 60*

STUDENTS AND FACULTY

Enrollment: 1,752. **Student Body:** 63% female, 37% male, 53% out-of-state, 10% international. Asian <1%, African American 31%, Caucasian 24%, Hispanic 23%, Native American <1%, Pacific Islander <1%, Two or more races 8%, Race unknown 5%.
Retention and Graduation: 69% freshmen return for sophomore year.
Faculty: Student/faculty ratio 25:1. 57 full-time faculty, 0% hold PhDs, 0% are members of minority groups, 0% are women.

ACADEMICS

Degrees: Associate; Bachelor's. **Classes:** Most classes have 10–19 students. Most lab/discussion sessions have 10–19 students. **Special Study Options:** Accelerated program; Cooperative education program; Dual enrollment; English as a Second Language (ESL); Exchange student program (domestic); Honors program; Independent study; Internships; Study abroad.

FACILITIES

Housing: Apartments for single students; Coed dorms; Theme housing; Wellness housing. **Campus Network:** 100% of classrooms, 100% of dorms, 100% of student union, 100% of libraries, 100% of dining areas, 100% of common outdoor areas have wireless network access.

CAMPUS LIFE

Activities: Campus Ministries; Dance; International Student Organization; Music ensembles; Pep band; Student government; Student newspaper.

ADMISSIONS

Freshman Academic Profile: Average high school GPA 3.2. **Basis for Candidate Selection:** *Very important factors include:* rigor of secondary school record, class rank, academic GPA. *Important factors include:* application essay, interview, extracurricular activities. *Other factors include:* standardized test scores, recommendation(s), talent/ability, character/personal qualities, alumni/ae relation, volunteer work, work experience, level of applicant's interest.
Freshman Admission Requirements: High school diploma is required and GED is accepted. *Academic units required:* 4 English, 3 math, 3 science, 2 social studies. **Freshman Admission Statistics:** 4,049 applied, 76% admitted, 14% enrolled. **Transfer Admission Requirements:** High school transcript, college transcript(s). Minimum college GPA of 2.0 required. Lowest grade transferable C. **General Admission Information:** Non-fall registration accepted. Admission may be deferred for a maximum of 1 year.

COSTS AND FINANCIAL AID

Annual tuition $30,396. Room and board $8,268. Required fees $350. Average book and supplies expense $1,500. **Required Forms and Deadlines:** FAFSA. **Notification of Awards:** Applicants will be notified of awards on a rolling basis beginning 3/1. **Types of Aid:** *Need-based scholarships/grants:* College/university scholarship or grant aid from institutional funds; Federal Pell; Private scholarships; SEOG; State scholarships/grants. **Financial Aid Statistics:** 71% freshmen, 63% undergrads receive non-need-based scholarship or grant aid. 98% freshmen, 97% undergrads receive need-based self-help aid. 0% freshmen, 0% undergrads receive athletic scholarships. **Criteria awarding aid:** *Need-based:* Academics. *Non-need-based:* Academics, Alumni affiliation, Job skills, Leadership, State/district residency.

JOHNSON AND WALES UNIVERSITY—DENVER

7150 Montview Boulevard, Denver, CO 80220
Phone: 303-256-9300
E-mail: den@admissions.jwu.edu
Fax: 303-256-9333 **Website:** http://www.jwu.edu/denver

This private school was founded in 1914.

RATINGS
Admissions Selectivity Rating: 66   **Fire Safety Rating:** 60*   **Green Rating:** 60*

STUDENTS AND FACULTY
Enrollment: 1,356. **Student Body:** 59% female, 41% male, 63% out-of-state, 1% international. Asian 2%, African American 9%, Caucasian 54%, Hispanic 19%, Native American <1%, Pacific Islander <1%, Two or more races 8%, Race unknown 6%.
Retention and Graduation: 75% freshmen return for sophomore year.
Faculty: Student/faculty ratio 16:1. 52 full-time faculty, 0% hold PhDs, 0% are members of minority groups, 0% are women.

ACADEMICS
Degrees: Associate; Bachelor's; Master's. **Classes:** Most classes have 10–19 students. **Most popular majors:** Business/Commerce, General; Restaurant/Food Services Management; Hotel/Motel Administration/Management. **Special Study Options:** Accelerated program; Cooperative education program; Dual enrollment; English as a Second Language (ESL); Exchange student program (domestic); Honors program; Independent study; Internships; Study abroad.

FACILITIES
Housing: Apartments for single students; Coed dorms; Special housing for disabled students; Wellness housing.

CAMPUS LIFE
Activities: Campus Ministries; Dance; International Student Organization; Student government; Student newspaper; Yearbook.

ADMISSIONS
Freshman Academic Profile: Average high school GPA 3.2. **Basis for Candidate Selection:** *Very important factors include:* rigor of secondary school record, class rank, academic GPA. *Important factors include:* application essay, interview, extracurricular activities. *Other factors include:* standardized test scores, recommendation(s), talent/ability, character/personal qualities, alumni/ae relation, volunteer work, work experience, level of applicant's interest.
Freshman Admission Requirements: High school diploma is required and GED is accepted. *Academic units required:* 4 English, 3 math, 3 science, 2 social studies. **Freshman Admission Statistics:** 2,319 applied, 81% admitted, 18% enrolled. **Transfer Admission Requirements:** High school transcript, college transcript(s). Minimum college GPA of 2.0 required. Lowest grade transferable C. **General Admission Information:** Non-fall registration accepted.

COSTS AND FINANCIAL AID
Annual tuition $30,396. Room and board $11,961. Required fees $350. Average book and supplies expense $1,500. **Required Forms and Deadlines:** FAFSA. **Notification of Awards:** Applicants will be notified of awards on a rolling basis beginning 3/1. **Types of Aid:** *Need-based scholarships/grants:* College/university scholarship or grant aid from institutional funds; Federal Pell; Private scholarships; SEOG; State scholarships/grants. **Financial Aid Statistics:** 91% needy freshmen, 84% needy undergrads receive need-based scholarship or grant aid. 85% freshmen, 74% undergrads receive non-need-based scholarship or grant aid. 90% freshmen, 94% undergrads receive need-based self-help aid. 0% freshmen, 0% undergrads receive athletic scholarships. **Criteria awarding aid:** *Need-based:* Academics. *Non-need-based:* Academics, Alumni affiliation, Job skills, Leadership, State/district residency.

JOHNSON AND WALES UNIVERSITY—PROVIDENCE CAMPUS

8 Abbott Park Pl, Providence, RI
Phone: 1-401-598-1000
E-mail: pvd@admissions.jwu.edu
Website: http://admissions.jwu.edu/ **ACT Code:** 3804

This private school was founded in 1914. It has a 50 acre campus.

RATINGS
Admissions Selectivity Rating: 66   **Fire Safety Rating:** 60*   **Green Rating:** 60*

STUDENTS AND FACULTY
Enrollment: 8,718. **Student Body:** 60% female, 40% male, 81% out-of-state, 9% international. Asian 1%, African American 11%, Caucasian 56%, Hispanic 11%, Native American <1%, Pacific Islander <1%, Two or more races 8%, Race unknown 4%.
Retention and Graduation: 78% freshmen return for sophomore year.
Faculty: Student/faculty ratio 20:1. 294 full-time faculty, 0% hold PhDs, 0% are members of minority groups, 0% are women.

ACADEMICS
Degrees: Associate; Bachelor's; Certificate; Diploma; Doctoral degree research/scholarship; Master's. **Classes:** Most classes have 10–19 students. Most lab/discussion sessions have fewer than 10 students. **Special Study Options:** Accelerated program; Cooperative education program; Dual enrollment; English as a Second Language (ESL); Exchange student program (domestic); Honors program; Independent study; Internships; Study abroad.

FACILITIES
Housing: Apartments for single students; Coed dorms; Special housing for disabled students; Wellness housing. **Special Academic Facilities/Equipment:** Culinary Archives and Museum.

CAMPUS LIFE
Environment: City. **Activities:** Campus Ministries; Dance; International Student Organization; Student government; Student newspaper; Yearbook. **Athletics (Intercollegiate):** *Men:* baseball, basketball, cheerleading, cross-country, equestrian sports, golf, ice hockey, soccer, tennis, volleyball, wrestling. *Women:* basketball, cheerleading, cross-country, equestrian sports, golf, ice hockey, soccer, softball, tennis, volleyball.

ADMISSIONS
Freshman Academic Profile: Average high school GPA 3.1. **Basis for Candidate Selection:** *Very important factors include:* rigor of secondary school record, class rank, academic GPA. *Important factors include:* application essay, interview, extracurricular activities. *Other factors include:* standardized test scores, recommendation(s), talent/ability, character/personal qualities, alumni/ae relation, volunteer work, work experience, level of applicant's interest.
Freshman Admission Requirements: High school diploma is required and GED is accepted. *Academic units required:* 4 English, 3 math, 3 science, 2 social studies. **Freshman Admission Statistics:** 11,971 applied, 82% admitted, 20% enrolled. **Transfer Admission Requirements:** High school transcript, college transcript(s). Minimum college GPA of 2.0 required. Lowest grade transferable C. **General Admission Information:** Non-fall registration accepted.

COSTS AND FINANCIAL AID
Annual tuition $30,396. Room and board $12,672. Required fees $350. Average book and supplies expense $1,500. **Required Forms and Deadlines:** FAFSA. **Notification of Awards:** Applicants will be notified of awards on a rolling basis beginning 3/1. **Types of Aid:** *Need-based scholarships/grants:* College/university scholarship or grant aid from institutional funds; Federal Pell; Private scholarships; SEOG; State scholarships/grants. **Financial Aid Statistics:** 90% needy freshmen, 84% needy undergrads receive need-based scholarship or grant aid. 71% freshmen, 59% undergrads receive non-need-based scholarship or grant aid. 93% freshmen, 95% undergrads receive need-based self-help aid. 0% freshmen, 0% undergrads receive athletic scholarships. **Criteria awarding aid:** *Need-based:* Academics. *Non-need-based:* Academics, Alumni affiliation, Job skills, Leadership, State/district residency.

JOHNSON UNIVERSITY

7900 Johnson Drive, Knoxville, TN 37998
Phone: 800-827-2122 **Financial Aid Phone:** 865-251-2303
E-mail: http://www.johnsonu.edu/ **CEEB Code:** 1345
Fax: 865-251-2336 **Website:** http://www.johnsonu.edu/ **ACT Code:** 3968

This private school, affiliated with the Christian (Nondenominational) Church, was founded in 1893. It has a 350 acre campus.

RATINGS
Admissions Selectivity Rating: 75   **Fire Safety Rating:** 81   **Green Rating:** 60*

STUDENTS AND FACULTY
Enrollment: 725. **Student Body:** 78% out-of-state, 2% international (12 countries represented). Asian 1%, African American 2%, Caucasian 90%, Hispanic 2%, Native American 1%, Pacific Islander 0%, Two or more races 2%, Race unknown 0%.
Retention and Graduation: 73% freshmen return for sophomore year.
Faculty: Student/faculty ratio 21:1. 30 full-time faculty, 63% hold PhDs, 0% are members of minority groups, 17% are women. 0% of classes are taught by teaching assistants.

ACADEMICS
Degrees: Associate; Bachelor's; Certificate; Master's. **Special Study Options:** Accelerated program; Cooperative education program; Distance learning; Double major; English as a Second Language (ESL); Honors program; Independent study; Internships; Teacher certification program. **Disability Services offered:** Reader services; Tape recorders.

FACILITIES
Housing: Apartments for married students; Men's dorms; Women's dorms. **Campus Network:** 100% of classrooms, 100% of dorms, 100% of student union, 100% of libraries, 100% of dining areas, 100% of common outdoor areas have wireless network access.

CAMPUS LIFE
Environment: Rural. **Activities:** Choral groups; Music ensembles; Musical theater; Radio station; Student government; Yearbook. 3 honor societies, 3 religious organizations on campus. **Athletics (Intercollegiate):** *Men:* baseball, basketball, cheerleading, soccer. *Women:* basketball, cheerleading, volleyball. **On-Campus Highlights:** Women's residence hall.

ADMISSIONS
Freshman Academic Profile: Average high school GPA 3.0. 21% in top 10% of high school class, 48% in top 25% of high school class, 78% in top 50% of high school class. **Test Scores:** SAT Math middle 50% range 470–560. SAT EBRW middle 50% range 480–612. ACT middle 50% range 20–26. **Basis for Candidate Selection:** *Very important factors include:* rigor of secondary school record, class rank, standardized test scores, recommendation(s), character/personal qualities, religious affiliation/commitment. *Important factors include:* application essay, interview. *Other factors include:* extracurricular activities, talent/ability, alumni/ae relation, volunteer work. **Freshman Admission Requirements:** High school diploma is required and GED is accepted. **Freshman Admission Statistics:** 296 applied, 95% admitted, 42% enrolled. **Transfer Admission Requirements:** High school transcript, college transcript(s), essay or personal statement, statement of good standing from prior institution(s). Lowest grade transferable C. **General Admission Information:** Application fee $35. Regular application deadline 7/1. Non-fall registration accepted. Admission may be deferred for a maximum of one year.

COSTS AND FINANCIAL AID
Annual tuition $7,000. Room and board $4,890. Average book and supplies expense $1,300. **Required Forms and Deadlines:** FAFSA; Institution's own financial aid form. **Notification of Awards:** Applicants will be notified of awards on or about 3/30. *Types of Aid: Need-based scholarships/grants:* College/university scholarship or grant aid from institutional funds; Federal Pell; Private scholarships; SEOG; State scholarships/grants. **Student Employment:** Federal Work-Study Program available. Institutional employment available. **Financial Aid Statistics:** 97% needy freshmen, 98% needy undergrads receive need-based scholarship or grant aid. 24% freshmen, 26% undergrads receive non-need-based scholarship or grant aid. 59% freshmen, 58% undergrads receive need-based self-help aid. 0% freshmen, 0% undergrads receive athletic scholarships. 97% undergrads receive any aid. *Criteria awarding aid: Non-need-based:* Academics, Minority status, Music/drama, Religious affiliation, State/district residency.

JONES INTERNATIONAL UNIVERSITY

9697 E. Mineral Avenue, Centennial, CO 80112
Phone: 800-811-5663
E-mail: admissions@international.edu
Fax: 303-799-0966 **Website:** www.jonesinternational.edu

This is a private school.

RATINGS
Admissions Selectivity Rating: 66   **Fire Safety Rating:** 60*   **Green Rating:** 60*

STUDENTS AND FACULTY
Enrollment: 22. **Student Body:** 50% female, 50% male.
Retention and Graduation: 97% freshmen return for sophomore year.

ACADEMICS
Degrees: Bachelor's; Certificate; Master's. **Special Study Options:** Accelerated program; Distance learning; External degree program.

ADMISSIONS
Freshman Admission Requirements: High school diploma is required and GED is accepted. **Freshman Admission Statistics:** 22 applied, 100% admitted, 86% enrolled. **Transfer Admission Requirements:** High school transcript, college transcript(s). Lowest grade transferable C. **General Admission Information:** Application fee $75. Non-fall registration accepted. Admission may be deferred for a maximum of 1 year.

COSTS AND FINANCIAL AID
Annual tuition $835. Average book and supplies expense $100.

JUDSON COLLEGE (AL)

302 Bibb Street, Marion, AL 36756
Phone: 334-683-5110 **Financial Aid Phone:** 334-683-5157
E-mail: admissions@judson.edu **CEEB Code:** 1349
Fax: 334-683-5282 **Website:** www.judson.edu **ACT Code:** 22

This private school, affiliated with the Baptist Church, was founded in 1838. It has a 80 acre campus.

RATINGS
Admissions Selectivity Rating: 77   **Fire Safety Rating:** 75   **Green Rating:** 60*

STUDENTS AND FACULTY
Enrollment: 315. **Student Body:** 97% female, 3% male, 29% out-of-state, 1% international (3 countries represented). Asian 0%, African American 12%, Caucasian 83%, Hispanic 1%, Native American 1%, Race unknown 1%.
Retention and Graduation: 61% freshmen return for sophomore year. 15% grads go on to further study within 1 year. 83% grads pursue arts and sciences degrees. 0% grads pursue law degrees. 0% grads pursue business degrees. 17% grads pursue medical degrees. **Faculty:** Student/faculty ratio 11:1. 18 full-time faculty, 83% hold PhDs, 0% are members of minority groups, 39% are women. 0% of classes are taught by teaching assistants.

ACADEMICS
Degrees: Bachelor's. **Classes:** Most classes have fewer than 10 students. Most lab/discussion sessions have fewer than 10 students. **Most popular majors:** Biology/Biological Sciences, General; Elementary Education and Teaching; Psychology, General. **Special Study Options:** Accelerated program; Cross-registration; Distance learning; Double major; Dual enrollment; Independent study; Internships; Student-designed major; Study abroad; Teacher certification program. **Disability Services offered:** Tutors. **Career services:** Alumni services; Career assessment; Internships.

FACILITIES
Housing: Women's dorms; 50% of campus accessible to physically disabled. **Special Academic Facilities/Equipment:** Alabama Women's Hall of Fame. **Campus Network:** 100% of classrooms, 100% of dorms, 50% of student union, 100% of libraries, 100% of dining areas, 20% of common outdoor areas have wireless network access.

CAMPUS LIFE

Environment: Rural. **Activities:** Campus Ministries; Choral groups; Drama/theater; Literary magazine; Marching band; Music ensembles; Student government; Student newspaper; Yearbook. 23 registered organizations, 8 honor societies, 1 religious organization on campus. **Athletics (Intercollegiate):** *Women:* basketball, equestrian sports, soccer, softball, volleyball. **On-Campus Highlights:** Residence Hall Lobbies.

ADMISSIONS

Freshman Academic Profile: Average high school GPA 3.4. 32% in top 10% of high school class, 22% in top 25% of high school class, 84% in top 50% of high school class. 78% from public high schools. **Test Scores:** SAT Math middle 50% range 470–590. SAT EBRW middle 50% range 540–590. ACT middle 50% range 19–26. **Basis for Candidate Selection:** *Very important factors include:* class rank, academic GPA, standardized test scores. *Other factors include:* rigor of secondary school record, recommendation(s), extracurricular activities, talent/ability, character/personal qualities, alumni/ae relation, level of applicant's interest. **Freshman Admission Requirements:** High school diploma is required and GED is accepted. *Academic units required:* 4 English, 2 math, 2 science, 3 social studies, 5 academic electives. *Academic units recommended:* 4 English, 4 math, 4 science, 2 foreign language, 4 social studies, 2 history. **Freshman Admission Statistics:** 306 applied, 84% admitted, 38% enrolled. **Transfer Admission Requirements:** College transcript(s). Minimum college GPA of 2.0 required. Lowest grade transferable C-. **General Admission Information:** Application fee $35. Non-fall registration accepted. Admission may be deferred for a maximum of 1 year.

COSTS AND FINANCIAL AID

Annual tuition $12,327. Room and board $7,969. Required fees $330. Average book and supplies expense $1,200. **Required Forms and Deadlines:** FAFSA; Institution's own financial aid form; State aid form. **Notification of Awards:** Applicants will be notified of awards on a rolling basis beginning 11/15. **Types of Aid:** *Need-based scholarships/grants:* College/university scholarship or grant aid from institutional funds; Federal Pell; Private scholarships; SEOG; State scholarships/grants. **Student Employment:** Federal Work-Study Program available. Institutional employment available. **Financial Aid Statistics:** 97% needy freshmen, 97% needy undergrads receive need-based scholarship or grant aid. 11% freshmen, 12% undergrads receive non-need-based scholarship or grant aid. 75% freshmen, 86% undergrads receive need-based self-help aid. 12% freshmen, 12% undergrads receive athletic scholarships. 99% freshmen, 96% undergrads receive any aid. **Criteria awarding aid:** *Need-based:* Academics, Alumni affiliation, Art, Athletics, Leadership, Music/drama. *Non-need-based:* Academics, Alumni affiliation, Art, Athletics, Music/drama, Religious affiliation, State/district residency.

THE JUILLIARD SCHOOL

60 Lincoln Center Plaza, New York, NY 10023-6588
Phone: 212-799-2000 ext.223 **Financial Aid Phone:** 212-799-5000
E-mail: admissions@juilliard.edu **CEEB Code:** 2340
Fax: 212-769-6420 **Website:** www.juilliard.edu

This private school was founded in 1905.

RATINGS

Admissions Selectivity Rating: 88   **Fire Safety Rating:** 69   **Green Rating:** 60*

STUDENTS AND FACULTY

Enrollment: 485. **Student Body:** 47% female, 53% male, 82% out-of-state, 28% international (40 countries represented). Asian 12%, African American 8%, Caucasian 35%, Hispanic 9%, Native American 0%, Pacific Islander <1%, Two or more races 7%, Race unknown <1%.
Retention and Graduation: 94% freshmen graduate within 4 years. 95% freshmen graduate within 6 years. **Faculty:** Student/faculty ratio 4:1. 128 full-time faculty, 0% hold PhDs, 13% are members of minority groups, 41% are women.

ACADEMICS

Degrees: Bachelor's; Diploma; Doctoral degree research/scholarship; Master's; Post-bachelor's certificate; Post-master's certificate. **Classes:** Most classes have 10–19 students. **Most popular majors:** Keyboard Instruments; Stringed Instruments; Voice and Opera. **Special Study Options:** Accelerated program; Double major; English as a Second Language (ESL); Honors program.

FACILITIES

Housing: Coed dorms. **Special Academic Facilities/Equipment:** 2 recital halls, 1 theater (seats 1,000 people), 1 drama theater (seats 200 people), 15 two-story studios, 35 private teaching studios, 106 practice rooms, organ studios, 200+ pianos, recording studio, The Peter Jay Sharp Special Collections Room.

CAMPUS LIFE

Environment: Metropolis. **Activities:** Dance; Drama/theater; International Student Organization; Jazz band; Music ensembles; Musical theater; Opera; Student government; Student newspaper; Symphony orchestra. 5 registered organizations, 2 religious organizations on campus. **On-Campus Highlights:** Lila Acheson Wallace Library.

ADMISSIONS

Basis for Candidate Selection: *Very important factors include:* talent/ability. *Important factors include:* interview. *Other factors include:* academic GPA, application essay, recommendation(s), extracurricular activities. **Freshman Admission Requirements:** High school diploma is required and GED is accepted. *Academic units recommended:* 4 visual/performing arts. **Freshman Admission Statistics:** 4,045 applied, 5% admitted, 60% enrolled. **Transfer Admission Requirements:** College transcript(s), essay or personal statement, interview, Lowest grade transferable C. **General Admission Information:** Application fee $110. Priority deadline 12/1. Regular application deadline 12/1.

COSTS AND FINANCIAL AID

Annual tuition $45,110. Room and board $15,990. Required fees $250. Average book and supplies expense $600. **Required Forms and Deadlines:** CSS/Financial Aid PROFILE; FAFSA. **Notification of Awards:** Applicants will be notified of awards on or about 4/1. **Types of Aid:** *Need-based scholarships/grants:* College/university scholarship or grant aid from institutional funds; Federal Pell; Private scholarships; SEOG; State scholarships/grants. *Loans:* Direct PLUS loans; Direct Subsidized Stafford Loans; Direct Unsubsidized Stafford Loans. **Financial Aid Statistics:** 100% needy freshmen, 98% needy undergrads receive need-based scholarship or grant aid. 9% freshmen, 2% undergrads receive non-need-based scholarship or grant aid. 100% freshmen, 100% undergrads receive need-based self-help aid. 0% freshmen, 0% undergrads receive athletic scholarships. 40% undergrads borrow to pay for school. Average cumulative indebtedness $24,702. **Criteria awarding aid:** *Need-based:* Music/drama. *Non-need-based:* Music/drama.

JUNIATA COLLEGE

1700 Moore Street, Huntingdon, PA 16652
Phone: 814-641-3420 **Financial Aid Phone:** 814-641-3144
E-mail: admissions@juniata.edu **CEEB Code:** 2341
Fax: 814-641-3100 **Website:** www.juniata.edu **ACT Code:** 3600

This private school was founded in 1876. It has a 800 acre campus.

RATINGS

Admissions Selectivity Rating: 85   **Fire Safety Rating:** 87   **Green Rating:** 60*

STUDENTS AND FACULTY

Enrollment: 1,304. **Student Body:** 56% female, 44% male, 30% out-of-state, 7% international (31 countries represented). Asian 3%, African American 3%, Caucasian 76%, Hispanic 5%, Native American <1%, Pacific Islander 0%, Two or more races 3%, Race unknown 2%.
Retention and Graduation: 84% freshmen return for sophomore year. 80% freshmen graduate within 4 years. 84% freshmen graduate within 6 years. 28% grads go on to further study within 1 year. 35% grads pursue arts and sciences degrees. 0% grads pursue law degrees. 6% grads pursue business degrees. 15% grads pursue medical degrees. **Faculty:** Student/faculty ratio 10:1. 124 full-time faculty, 85% hold PhDs, 7% are members of minority groups, 48% are women. 0% of classes are taught by teaching assistants.

ACADEMICS

Degrees: Bachelor's; Certificate; Master's. **Classes:** Most classes have 10–19 students. Most lab/discussion sessions have 10–19 students. **Most popular majors:** Biology/Biological Sciences, General; Business/Commerce, General. **Special Study Options:** Distance learning; Double major; Dual enrollment;

English as a Second Language (ESL); Exchange student program (domestic); Honors program; Independent study; Internships; Student-designed major; Study abroad; Teacher certification program. **Honors programs:** Entire college is considered to be an honors program. **Combined degree programs:** BA/DDS; BA/JD; BA/MA; BA/MD; BA/MEng. **Disability Services offered:** Reader services; Tape recorders; Tutors. **Career services:** Alumni network; Alumni services; Career assessment; Career/job search classes; Internships.

FACILITIES

Housing: Apartments for single students; Coed dorms; Special housing for international students; Theme housing; Women's dorms; 75% of campus accessible to physically disabled. **Special Academic Facilities/Equipment:** Environmental Studies Field Station, Juniata Museum of Art, Early Childhood Education Center, Ceramics studio and Anagama Kiln, Nature preserve and Peace Chapel, Observatory, Electron microscopes, Nuclear magnetic resonance spectrometers, Human Interaction Lab, three story/free form theater. **Campus Network:** 100% of classrooms, 100% of dorms, 100% of student union, 100% of libraries, 100% of dining areas, 100% of common outdoor areas have wireless network access.

CAMPUS LIFE

Environment: Village. **Activities:** Campus Ministries; Choral groups; Concert band; Dance; Drama/theater; International Student Organization; Jazz band; Literary magazine; Music ensembles; Musical theater; Radio station; Student government; Student-run film society; Symphony orchestra. 91 registered organizations, 16 honor societies, 6 religious organizations on campus. **On-Campus Highlights:** Von Liebig Science Center.

ADMISSIONS

Freshman Academic Profile: Average high school GPA 3.8. 31% in top 10% of high school class, 67% in top 25% of high school class, 93% in top 50% of high school class. 70% from public high schools. **Test Scores:** SAT Math middle 50% range 540–660. SAT EBRW middle 50% range 540–660. ACT middle 50% range 27–32. **Basis for Candidate Selection:** *Very important factors include:* rigor of secondary school record, academic GPA, application essay, recommendation(s), character/personal qualities. *Important factors include:* extracurricular activities, talent/ability, first generation. *Other factors include:* class rank, standardized test scores, interview, alumni/ae relation, geographical residence, state residency, racial/ethnic status, work experience, level of applicant's interest. **Freshman Admission Requirements:** High school diploma is required and GED is accepted. *Academic units required:* 4 English, 3 math, 3 science, 2 science labs, 1 social studies, 3 history. *Academic units recommended:* 4 English, 3 math, 3 science, 2 science labs, 2 foreign language, 1 social studies, 3 history. **Freshman Admission Statistics:** 2,437 applied, 70% admitted, 20% enrolled. **Transfer Admission Requirements:** High school transcript, college transcript(s), essay or personal statement. Minimum college GPA of 2.5 required. Lowest grade transferable C-. **General Admission Information:** Priority deadline 11/15. Regular application deadline 3/15. Non-fall registration accepted. Admission may be deferred for a maximum of 1 year.

COSTS AND FINANCIAL AID

Annual tuition $46,250. Room and board $12,800. Required fees $825. Average book and supplies expense $1,000. **Required Forms and Deadlines:** FAFSA. **Types of Aid:** *Need-based scholarships/grants:* College/university scholarship or grant aid from institutional funds; Federal Pell; Private scholarships; SEOG; State scholarships/grants. *Loans:* Direct PLUS loans; Direct Subsidized Stafford Loans; Direct Unsubsidized Stafford Loans. **Student Employment:** Federal Work-Study Program available. Institutional employment available. **Financial Aid Statistics:** 99% needy freshmen, 99% needy undergrads receive need-based scholarship or grant aid. 19% freshmen, 13% undergrads receive non-need-based scholarship or grant aid. 83% freshmen, 87% undergrads receive need-based self-help aid. 0% freshmen, 0% undergrads receive athletic scholarships. 99% freshmen, 98% undergrads receive any aid. 77% undergrads borrow to pay for school. Average cumulative indebtedness $31,156. **Criteria awarding aid:** *Need-based:* Academics, Minority status, Music/drama. *Non-need-based:* Academics, Alumni affiliation, Art, Minority status, Music/drama.

KALAMAZOO COLLEGE

1200 Academy Street, Kalamazoo, MI 49006
Phone: 269-337-7166 **Financial Aid Phone:** 269-337-7192
E-mail: admission@kzoo.edu **CEEB Code:** 1365
Fax: 269-552-5083 **Website:** www.kzoo.edu **ACT Code:** 2018

This private school was founded in 1833. It has a 60 acre campus.

RATINGS

Admissions Selectivity Rating: 87   **Fire Safety Rating:** 83   **Green Rating:** 60*

STUDENTS AND FACULTY

Enrollment: 1,446. **Student Body:** 57% female, 43% male, 33% out-of-state, 6% international (28 countries represented). Asian 7%, African American 8%, Caucasian 58%, Hispanic 14%, Native American <1%, Pacific Islander 0%, Two or more races 4%, Race unknown 3%.
Retention and Graduation: 91% freshmen return for sophomore year. 82% freshmen graduate within 4 years. 86% freshmen graduate within 6 years.
Faculty: Student/faculty ratio 13:1. 105 full-time faculty, 96% hold PhDs, 31% are members of minority groups, 51% are women. 0% of classes are taught by teaching assistants.

ACADEMICS

Degrees: Bachelor's. **Classes:** Most classes have 10–19 students. Most lab/discussion sessions have 10–19 students. **Most popular majors:** English Language and Literature, General; Economics, General; Psychology, General. **Special Study Options:** Accelerated program; Cross-registration; Double major; Dual enrollment; English as a Second Language (ESL); Exchange student program (domestic); Independent study; Internships; Student-designed major; Study abroad. **Disability Services offered:** Note-taking services; Tape recorders; Tutors. **Career services:** Alumni network; Alumni services; Career assessment; Career/job search classes; Internships; Regional alumni.

FACILITIES

Housing: Coed dorms; Theme housing; Wellness housing; 25% of campus accessible to physically disabled. **Special Academic Facilities/Equipment:** Science center, Rare book room. **Campus Network:** 100% of classrooms, 100% of dorms, 100% of student union, 100% of libraries, 100% of dining areas, 20% of common outdoor areas have wireless network access.

CAMPUS LIFE

Environment: City. **Activities:** Campus Ministries; Choral groups; Concert band; Dance; Drama/theater; International Student Organization; Jazz band; Literary magazine; Model UN; Music ensembles; Musical theater; Radio station; Student government; Student newspaper; Symphony orchestra; Television station; Yearbook. 50 registered organizations, 3 honor societies, 5 religious organizations on campus. **Athletics (Intercollegiate):** *Men:* baseball, basketball, cross-country, diving, football, golf, soccer, swimming, tennis. *Women:* basketball, cross-country, diving, golf, soccer, softball, swimming, tennis, volleyball. **On-Campus Highlights:** Upjohn Library Commons.

ADMISSIONS

Freshman Academic Profile: Average high school GPA 3.8. 54% in top 10% of high school class, 84% in top 25% of high school class, 99% in top 50% of high school class. 80% from public high schools. **Test Scores:** SAT Math middle 50% range 550–680. SAT EBRW middle 50% range 590–690. ACT middle 50% range 24–31. **Basis for Candidate Selection:** *Very important factors include:* rigor of secondary school record, academic GPA, extracurricular activities. *Important factors include:* application essay, recommendation(s). *Other factors include:* standardized test scores, interview, talent/ability, character/personal qualities, first generation, alumni/ae relation, geographical residence, state residency, racial/ethnic status, volunteer work, work experience, level of applicant's interest. **Freshman Admission Requirements:** High school diploma is required and GED is accepted. *Academic units required:* 4 English, 3 math, 3 science, 3 foreign language, 2 social studies, 2 history. *Academic units recommended:* 4 English, 4 math, 4 science, 4 foreign language, 2 social studies, 2 history. **Freshman Admission Statistics:** 3,371 applied, 73% admitted, 17% enrolled. **Transfer Admission Requirements:** High school transcript, college transcript(s), essay or personal statement, standardized test scores, statement of good standing from prior institution(s). Lowest grade transferable C. **General**

Admission Information: Priority deadline 11/15. Regular application deadline 1/15. Admission may be deferred for a maximum of 1 year.

COSTS AND FINANCIAL AID

Annual tuition $50,046. Room and board $10,134. Required fees $516. Average book and supplies expense $825. **Required Forms and Deadlines:** FAFSA. **Notification of Awards:** Applicants will be notified of awards on a rolling basis beginning 1/15. **Types of Aid:** *Need-based scholarships/grants:* College/university scholarship or grant aid from institutional funds; Federal Pell; Private scholarships; SEOG; State scholarships/grants. *Loans:* Direct PLUS loans; Direct Subsidized Stafford Loans; Direct Unsubsidized Stafford Loans. **Student Employment:** Federal Work-Study Program available. Institutional employment available. **Financial Aid Statistics:** 97% needy freshmen, 98% needy undergrads receive need-based scholarship or grant aid. 23% freshmen, 18% undergrads receive non-need-based scholarship or grant aid. 76% freshmen, 79% undergrads receive need-based self-help aid. 0% freshmen, 0% undergrads receive athletic scholarships. 98% freshmen, 97% undergrads receive any aid. 61% undergrads borrow to pay for school. Average cumulative indebtedness $32,226. **Criteria awarding aid:** *Need-based:* Academics. *Non-need-based:* Academics, Alumni affiliation, Art, Leadership, Music/drama.

KANSAS CITY ART INSTITUTE

4415 Warwick Boulevard, Kansas City, MO 64111
Phone: 800-522-5224 **Financial Aid Phone:** 816-802-3337
E-mail: admiss@kcai.edu **CEEB Code:** 6330
Fax: 816-802-3309 **Website:** www.kcai.edu **ACT Code:** 2277

This private school was founded in 1885. It has a 15 acre campus.

RATINGS

Admissions Selectivity Rating: 78   **Fire Safety Rating:** 71   **Green Rating:** 60*

STUDENTS AND FACULTY

Enrollment: 671. **Student Body:** 55% female, 45% male, 62% out-of-state, 1% international (6 countries represented). Asian 4%, African American 3%, Caucasian 80%, Hispanic 6%, Native American 1%, Race unknown 6%. **Retention and Graduation:** 78% freshmen return for sophomore year. 40% grads go on to further study within 1 year. **Faculty:** Student/faculty ratio 12:1. 51 full-time faculty, 84% hold PhDs, 2% are members of minority groups, 37% are women. 0% of classes are taught by teaching assistants.

ACADEMICS

Degrees: Bachelor's. **Classes:** Most classes have 20–29 students. **Most popular majors:** Film/Video and Photographic Arts, Other; Painting; Design and Visual Communications, General. **Special Study Options:** Cross-registration; Double major; Exchange student program (domestic); Independent study; Internships; Student-designed major; Study abroad. **Disability Services offered:** Tape recorders; Tutors. **Career services:** Alumni network; Alumni services; Career assessment; Career/job search classes; Internships; Regional alumni.

FACILITIES

Housing: Apartments for single students; Coed dorms. **Special Academic Facilities/Equipment:** H and R Block Art Space. **Campus Network:** 100% of classrooms, 100% of dorms, 100% of student union, 100% of libraries, 100% of dining areas, 99% of common outdoor areas have wireless network access.

CAMPUS LIFE

Environment: Metropolis. **Activities:** Student government. **On-Campus Highlights:** Dodge Painting Building.

ADMISSIONS

Freshman Academic Profile: Average high school GPA 3.2. 11% in top 10% of high school class, 39% in top 25% of high school class, 73% in top 50% of high school class. 80% from public high schools. **Test Scores:** SAT Math middle 50% range 430–590. SAT EBRW middle 50% range 430–580. ACT middle 50% range 20–25. **Basis for Candidate Selection:** *Very important factors include:* recommendation(s). *Important factors include:* rigor of secondary school record, academic GPA, application essay, standardized test scores. *Other factors include:* interview, extracurricular activities, talent/ability, character/personal qualities, first generation, volunteer work, work experience, level of applicant's interest. **Freshman Admission Requirements:** High school diploma is required and GED is accepted. *Academic units recommended:* 3 social studies, 3 academic electives, 4 unit from above areas or other academic areas. **Freshman Admission Statistics:** 603 applied, 72% admitted, 32% enrolled. **Transfer**

Admission Requirements: High school transcript, college transcript(s), essay or personal statement, statement of good standing from prior institution(s). Minimum college GPA of 2.5 required. Lowest grade transferable C. **General Admission Information:** Application fee $35. Priority deadline 1/15. Non-fall registration accepted.

COSTS AND FINANCIAL AID

Annual tuition $27,220. Room and board $8,294. Average book and supplies expense $1,500. **Required Forms and Deadlines:** FAFSA. **Notification of Awards:** Applicants will be notified of awards on a rolling basis beginning 4/1. **Types of Aid:** *Need-based scholarships/grants:* College/university scholarship or grant aid from institutional funds; Federal Pell; SEOG; State scholarships/grants. **Student Employment:** Federal Work-Study Program available. Institutional employment available. **Financial Aid Statistics:** 100% needy freshmen, 100% needy undergrads receive need-based scholarship or grant aid. 15% freshmen, 9% undergrads receive non-need-based scholarship or grant aid. 78% freshmen, 87% undergrads receive need-based self-help aid. 0% freshmen, 0% undergrads receive athletic scholarships. 99% freshmen, 95% undergrads receive any aid. **Criteria awarding aid:** *Need-based:* Academics, Art. *Non-need-based:* Academics, Art.

KANSAS STATE UNIVERSITY

119 Anderson Hall, Manhattan, KS 66506
Phone: 785-532-6250 **Financial Aid Phone:** 785-532-6420
E-mail: k-state@k-state.edu **CEEB Code:** 6334
Fax: 785-532-6393 **Website:** www.k-state.edu **ACT Code:** 1428

This public school was founded in 1863. It has a 668 acre campus.

RATINGS

Admissions Selectivity Rating: 75   **Fire Safety Rating:** 88   **Green Rating:** 64

STUDENTS AND FACULTY

Enrollment: 18,171. **Student Body:** 47% female, 53% male, 18% out-of-state, 5% international (107 countries represented). Asian 1%, African American 3%, Caucasian 78%, Hispanic 7%, Native American <1%, Pacific Islander <1%, Two or more races 4%, Race unknown 1%. **Retention and Graduation:** 84% freshmen return for sophomore year. 31% freshmen graduate within 4 years. 63% freshmen graduate within 6 years. 22% grads go on to further study within 1 year. **Faculty:** Student/faculty ratio 18:1. 1,092 full-time faculty, 85% hold PhDs, 17% are members of minority groups, 43% are women. 17% of classes are taught by teaching assistants.

ACADEMICS

Degrees: Associate; Bachelor's; Certificate; Doctoral degree—professional practice; Doctoral degree research/scholarship; Master's; Post-bachelor's certificate. **Classes:** Most classes have 10–19 students. **Most popular majors:** Business Administration and Management, General; Animal Sciences, General; Mechanical Engineering. **Special Study Options:** Cooperative education program; Distance learning; Double major; Dual enrollment; English as a Second Language (ESL); Exchange student program (domestic); Honors program; Independent study; Internships; Liberal arts/career combination; Study abroad; Teacher certification program. **Honors programs:** The University Honors Program is an opportunity for undergraduate students from all colleges to enhance their education with special classes and opportunities for personal growth. **Disability Services offered:** Note-taking services; Reader services; Tape recorders; Tutors. **Career services:** Alumni services; Career assessment; Career/job search classes.

FACILITIES

Housing: Apartments for married students; Apartments for single students; Coed dorms; Cooperative housing; Fraternity/sorority housing; Men's dorms; Special housing for international students; Women's dorms; 75% of campus accessible to physically disabled. **Special Academic Facilities/Equipment:** South Asian area study center, education communications center, center for cancer research, planetarium, nuclear reactor/accelerator, Beach Art museum.

CAMPUS LIFE

Environment: Town. **Activities:** Campus Ministries; Choral groups; Concert band; Dance; Drama/theater; International Student Organization; Jazz band; Marching band; Music ensembles; Musical theater; Pep band; Radio station; Student government; Student newspaper; Symphony orchestra; Television station; Yearbook. 594 registered organizations, 36 honor societies, 37 religious organizations, 28 fraternities, 16 sororities on campus. **Athletics (Intercollegiate):** *Men:* baseball, basketball, cheerleading, cross-country, football, golf, track/field (outdoor), track/field (indoor). *Women:* basketball, cheerleading, crew/rowing, cross-country, equestrian sports, golf, tennis, track/field (outdoor), track/field (indoor), volleyball. **On-Campus Highlights:** Peters Recreation Complex. **Environmental Initiatives:** A university-wide task force for long-term visioning and planning in all areas of the university, including campus operations, curriculum, research, and external relations/outreach.

ADMISSIONS

Freshman Academic Profile: Average high school GPA 3.5. 25% in top 10% of high school class, 51% in top 25% of high school class, 80% in top 50% of high school class. 80% from public high schools. **Test Scores:** ACT middle 50% range 22–28. **Basis for Candidate Selection:** *Very important factors include:* rigor of secondary school record, class rank, academic GPA, standardized test scores. *Important factors include:* level of applicant's interest. *Other factors include:* recommendation(s). **Freshman Admission Requirements:** High school diploma is required and GED is accepted. *Academic units required:* 4 English, 3 math, 3 science, 3 social studies, 3 academic electives. **Freshman Admission Statistics:** 8,310 applied, 95% admitted, 43% enrolled. **Transfer Admission Requirements:** College transcript(s). Minimum college GPA of 2.0 required. Lowest grade transferable C. **General Admission Information:** Application fee $40. Priority deadline 12/1. Non-fall registration accepted.

COSTS AND FINANCIAL AID

Required Forms and Deadlines: FAFSA. **Notification of Awards:** Applicants will be notified of awards on a rolling basis beginning 4/1. **Types of Aid:** *Need-based scholarships/grants:* College/university scholarship or grant aid from institutional funds; Federal Pell; Private scholarships; SEOG; State scholarships/grants. *Loans:* Direct PLUS loans; Direct Subsidized Stafford Loans; Direct Unsubsidized Stafford Loans. **Student Employment:** Federal Work-Study Program available. Institutional employment available. **Financial Aid Statistics:** 53% needy freshmen, 56% needy undergrads receive need-based scholarship or grant aid. 75% freshmen, 51% undergrads receive non-need-based scholarship or grant aid. 65% freshmen, 74% undergrads receive need-based self-help aid. 2% freshmen, 2% undergrads receive athletic scholarships. 70% freshmen, 59% undergrads receive any aid. 57% undergrads borrow to pay for school. Average cumulative indebtedness $27,198. **Criteria awarding aid:** *Non-need-based:* Academics, Alumni affiliation, Art, Athletics, Leadership, Music/drama, State/district residency.

KANSAS WESLEYAN UNIVERSITY

100 E. Claflin, Salina, KS 67401
Financial Aid Phone: 785-827-5541
Fax: 785-827-0927 **Website:** www.kwu.edu **ACT Code:** 1434

This private school, affiliated with the Methodist Church, was founded in 1886. It has a 28 acre campus.

RATINGS

Admissions Selectivity Rating: 85 **Fire Safety Rating:** 80 **Green Rating:** 60*

STUDENTS AND FACULTY

Enrollment: 742. **Student Body:** 57% female, 43% male, 29% out-of-state, 2% international (8 countries represented). Asian 1%, African American 9%, Caucasian 77%, Hispanic 9%, Native American 1%, Race unknown 0%. **Retention and Graduation:** 53% freshmen return for sophomore year. 30% grads go on to further study within 1 year. 24% grads pursue arts and sciences degrees. **Faculty:** Student/faculty ratio 15:1. 42 full-time faculty, 67% hold PhDs, 0% are members of minority groups, 38% are women. 0% of classes are taught by teaching assistants.

ACADEMICS

Degrees: Associate; Bachelor's; Master's. **Classes:** Most classes have 10–19 students. **Special Study Options:** Cross-registration; Double major; Honors program; Independent study; Internships; Student-designed major; Study abroad; Teacher certification program. **Honors programs:** Alpha Chi Beta; Beta

Beta Sigma; Pi Sigma Alpha; Psi Omega Phi; Alpha Theta. **Career services:** Alumni services; Career assessment; Internships; Regional alumni.

FACILITIES

Housing: Apartments for married students; Apartments for single students; Coed dorms; Men's dorms; Special housing for disabled students; Women's dorms; 95% of campus accessible to physically disabled.

CAMPUS LIFE

Environment: Town. **Activities:** Campus Ministries; Choral groups; Concert band; Dance; Drama/theater; International Student Organization; Jazz band; Literary magazine; Model UN; Music ensembles; Musical theater; Pep band; Student government; Student newspaper; Symphony orchestra; Yearbook. 20 registered organizations, 5 honor societies, 3 religious organizations on campus. **Athletics (Intercollegiate):** *Men:* baseball, basketball, cheerleading, cross-country, football, golf, racquetball, soccer, tennis, track/field (outdoor). *Women:* basketball, cheerleading, cross-country, golf, racquetball, soccer, softball, tennis, track/field (outdoor), volleyball. **On-Campus Highlights:** Student Center & Gym.

ADMISSIONS

Freshman Academic Profile: Average high school GPA 3.2. 9% in top 10% of high school class, 32% in top 25% of high school class, 62% in top 50% of high school class. **Test Scores:** SAT Math middle 50% range 500–590. SAT EBRW middle 50% range 420–520. ACT middle 50% range 22–. **Basis for Candidate Selection:** *Very important factors include:* academic GPA, standardized test scores. **Freshman Admission Requirements:** High school diploma is required and GED is accepted. **Freshman Admission Statistics:** 442 applied, 61% admitted, 43% enrolled. **Transfer Admission Requirements:** College transcript(s). Minimum college GPA of 2.0 required. Lowest grade transferable D. **General Admission Information:** Application fee $20. Non-fall registration accepted.

COSTS AND FINANCIAL AID

Annual tuition $18,200. Room and board $6,400. Average book and supplies expense $800. **Required Forms and Deadlines:** FAFSA. **Types of Aid:** *Need-based scholarships/grants:* College/university scholarship or grant aid from institutional funds; Federal Pell; Private scholarships; SEOG; State scholarships/grants. *Loans:* Direct PLUS loans; Direct Subsidized Stafford Loans; Direct Unsubsidized Stafford Loans. **Student Employment:** Federal Work-Study Program available. **Financial Aid Statistics:** 0% freshmen, 0% undergrads receive athletic scholarships. 75% undergrads receive any aid. **Criteria awarding aid:** *Need-based:* Academics, Alumni affiliation, Art, Athletics, Music/drama. *Non-need-based:* Academics, Alumni affiliation, Art, Athletics, Music/drama.

KEAN UNIVERSITY

Office of Admissions -Kean Hall, Union, NJ 07083-0411
Phone: 908-737-7100 **Financial Aid Phone:** 908-737-3190
E-mail: admitme@kean.edu **CEEB Code:** 2517
Fax: 908-737-7105 **Website:** www.kean.edu **ACT Code:** 2582

This public school was founded in 1855. It has a 185 acre campus.

RATINGS

Admissions Selectivity Rating: 79 **Fire Safety Rating:** 98 **Green Rating:** 71

STUDENTS AND FACULTY

Enrollment: 11,947. **Student Body:** 60% female, 40% male, 2% out-of-state, 4% international (49 countries represented). Asian 6%, African American 20%, Caucasian 30%, Hispanic 31%, Native American <1%, Pacific Islander <1%, Two or more races 2%, Race unknown 7%. **Retention and Graduation:** 74% freshmen return for sophomore year. 21% freshmen graduate within 4 years. 47% freshmen graduate within 6 years. **Faculty:** Student/faculty ratio 17:1. 358 full-time faculty, 75% hold PhDs, 33% are members of minority groups, 56% are women.

ACADEMICS

Degrees: Bachelor's; Doctoral degree—professional practice; Doctoral degree research/scholarship; Master's; Post-master's certificate. **Classes:** Most classes have 20–29 students. **Most popular majors:** Psychology, General; Speech Communication and Rhetoric; Business Administration and Management, General. **Special Study Options:** Accelerated program; Cooperative education program; Cross-registration; Distance learning; Double major; Dual enrollment;

English as a Second Language (ESL); Exchange student program (domestic); External degree program; Honors program; Independent study; Internships; Study abroad; Teacher certification program. **Honors programs:** Please see our online Undergraduate Catalog available at: www.kean.edu. **Disability Services offered:** Note-taking services; Tape recorders; Tutors. **Career services:** Alumni network; Alumni services; Career assessment; Career/job search classes; Internships.

FACILITIES

Housing: Apartments for single students; Coed dorms; Special housing for disabled students; Special housing for international students; Theme housing; 100% of campus accessible to physically disabled. **Special Academic Facilities/ Equipment:** Liberty Hall Museum; Holocaust Resource Center; Wynona Moore Lipman Ethnic Studies Center; Human Rights Institute; Maxine & Jack Lane Center for Academic Success; Harwood Arena, New Jersey Center for Science, Technology and Mathematics; CAS & Vaughn Eames Art Galleries; Enlow Recital Hall; Wilkins Theater, Planetarium.

CAMPUS LIFE

Environment: City. **Activities:** Campus Ministries; Choral groups; Concert band; Dance; Drama/theater; International Student Organization; Jazz band; Literary magazine; Model UN; Music ensembles; Musical theater; Pep band; Radio station; Student government; Student newspaper; Student-run film society; Symphony orchestra; Television station; Yearbook. 124 registered organizations, 30 honor societies, 8 religious organizations, 15 fraternities, 15 sororities on campus. **Athletics (Intercollegiate):** *Men:* baseball, basketball, football, lacrosse, soccer, track/field (outdoor). *Women:* basketball, field hockey, lacrosse, soccer, softball, tennis, track/field (outdoor), volleyball. **On-Campus Highlights:** University (Student) Center. **Environmental Initiatives:** Creation of a bachelor of science degree and minor in sustainability.

ADMISSIONS

Freshman Academic Profile: Average high school GPA 3.1. **Test Scores:** SAT Math middle 50% range 460–550. SAT EBRW middle 50% range 460–550. ACT middle 50% range 17–23. **Basis for Candidate Selection:** *Very important factors include:* rigor of secondary school record, academic GPA. *Important factors include:* standardized test scores. *Other factors include:* application essay, recommendation(s), interview, extracurricular activities, talent/ability, character/ personal qualities, alumni/ae relation, volunteer work, work experience. **Freshman Admission Requirements:** High school diploma is required and GED is accepted. *Academic units required:* 4 English, 3 math, 2 science, 2 science labs, 2 history, 5 academic electives. *Academic units recommended:* 4 English, 3 math, 2 science, 2 science labs, 2 foreign language, 2 social studies, 2 history, 5 academic electives. **Freshman Admission Statistics:** 9,540 applied, 69% admitted, 27% enrolled. **Transfer Admission Requirements:** College transcript(s), statement of good standing from prior institution(s). Minimum college GPA of 2.0 required. Lowest grade transferable C. **General Admission Information:** Application fee $75. Priority deadline 4/30. Regular application deadline 8/15. Non-fall registration accepted. Admission may be deferred for a maximum of 1 semester.

COSTS AND FINANCIAL AID

Required Forms and Deadlines: FAFSA; State aid form. **Notification of Awards:** Applicants will be notified of awards on a rolling basis beginning 12/1. **Types of Aid:** *Need-based scholarships/grants:* College/university scholarship or grant aid from institutional funds; Federal Pell; Private scholarships; SEOG; State scholarships/grants. *Loans:* Direct PLUS loans; Direct Subsidized Stafford Loans; Direct Unsubsidized Stafford Loans. **Student Employment:** Federal Work-Study Program available. Institutional employment available. **Financial Aid Statistics:** 75% needy freshmen, 74% needy undergrads receive need-based scholarship or grant aid. 31% freshmen, 22% undergrads receive non-need-based scholarship or grant aid. 96% freshmen, 95% undergrads receive need-based self-help aid. 0% freshmen, 0% undergrads receive athletic scholarships. 91.4% freshmen, 78.8% undergrads receive any aid. 77% undergrads borrow to pay for school. Average cumulative indebtedness $34,275. **Criteria awarding aid:** *Non-need-based:* Academics, Art, Leadership, Music/drama.

KEENE STATE COLLEGE

229 Main Street, Keene, NH 03435-2604
Phone: 603-358-2276 **Financial Aid Phone:** 603-358-2281
E-mail: admissions@keene.edu **CEEB Code:** 3472
Fax: 603-358-2767 **Website:** www.keene.edu **ACT Code:** 2510

This public school was founded in 1909. It has a 150 acre campus.

RATINGS

Admissions Selectivity Rating: 74   **Fire Safety Rating:** 95   **Green Rating:** 93

STUDENTS AND FACULTY

Enrollment: 3,340. **Student Body:** 54% female, 46% male, 55% out-of-state, <1% international (11 countries represented). Asian 1%, African American 2%, Caucasian 83%, Hispanic 4%, Native American <1%, Pacific Islander <1%, Two or more races 2%, Race unknown 6%.
Retention and Graduation: 72% freshmen return for sophomore year. 55% freshmen graduate within 4 years. 63% freshmen graduate within 6 years. **Faculty:** Student/faculty ratio 14:1. 188 full-time faculty, 87% hold PhDs, 11% are members of minority groups, 50% are women. 0% of classes are taught by teaching assistants.

ACADEMICS

Degrees: Bachelor's; Certificate; Master's; Post-bachelor's certificate; Post-master's certificate. **Classes:** Most classes have 10–19 students. Most lab/discussion sessions have fewer than 10 students. **Most popular majors:** Elementary Education and Teaching; Occupational Safety and Health Technology/Technician; Psychology, General. **Special Study Options:** Accelerated program; Cooperative education program; Distance learning; Double major; Exchange student program (domestic); Honors program; Independent study; Internships; Liberal arts/ career combination; Student-designed major; Study abroad; Teacher certification program. **Honors programs:** The Keene State College Honors Program provides exceptional students with intellectual stimulation and academically rich experiences for personal and professional growth. National Society of Collegiate Scholars. **Disability Services offered:** Note-taking services; Reader services; Tape recorders; Tutors. **Career services:** Alumni network; Alumni services; Career assessment; Career/job search classes; Internships.

FACILITIES

Housing: Apartments for single students; Coed dorms; Fraternity/sorority housing; Women's dorms; 98% of campus accessible to physically disabled. **Special Academic Facilities/Equipment:** Thorne-Sagendorph Art gallery, Redfern Arts Center, Recreational Center, Science Center, Mason Library, Media Arts Center, Cohen Center for Holocaust Studies, Center for Writing, Child Development Center, Alumni Center.

CAMPUS LIFE

Environment: Village. **Activities:** Campus Ministries; Choral groups; Concert band; Dance; Drama/theater; International Student Organization; Jazz band; Literary magazine; Music ensembles; Musical theater; Radio station; Student government; Student newspaper; Student-run film society; Television station; Yearbook. 96 registered organizations, 26 honor societies, 3 religious organizations, 5 fraternities, 3 sororities on campus. **Athletics (Intercollegiate):** *Men:* baseball, basketball, cheerleading, cross-country, diving, lacrosse, soccer, swimming, track/field (outdoor), track/field (indoor). *Women:* basketball, cheerleading, cross-country, diving, field hockey, lacrosse, soccer, softball, swimming, track/field (outdoor), track/field (indoor), volleyball. **On-Campus Highlights:** Technology, Design, and Safety Center. **Environmental Initiatives:** LEED Silver residence hall (awarded 2008).

ADMISSIONS

Freshman Academic Profile: Average high school GPA 3.1. 5% in top 10% of high school class, 20% in top 25% of high school class, 49% in top 50% of high school class. **Test Scores:** SAT Math middle 50% range 470–560. SAT EBRW middle 50% range 490–580. ACT middle 50% range 19–26. **Basis for Candidate Selection:** *Important factors include:* rigor of secondary school record, academic GPA, application essay, recommendation(s). *Other factors include:* class rank, standardized test scores, extracurricular activities, talent/ ability, character/personal qualities, first generation, alumni/ae relation, racial/ ethnic status, volunteer work, work experience, level of applicant's interest. **Freshman Admission Requirements:** High school diploma is required and GED is accepted. *Academic units required:* 4 English, 3 math, 3 science, 2 social studies, 2 academic electives. **Freshman Admission Statistics:** 4,978 applied, 89% admitted, 19% enrolled. **Transfer Admission Requirements:** High school transcript, college transcript(s), essay or personal statement, statement of good standing from prior institution(s). Minimum college GPA of 2.0 required. Lowest grade transferable C. **General Admission Information:** Application fee $50. Regular application deadline 4/1. Non-fall registration accepted. Admission may be deferred for a maximum of 1 year.

COSTS AND FINANCIAL AID
Annual in-state tuition $11,754. Annual out-of-state tuition $20,942. Room and board $11,560. Required fees $2,814. Average book and supplies expense $900. **Required Forms and Deadlines:** FAFSA. **Types of Aid:** *Need-based scholarships/grants:* College/university scholarship or grant aid from institutional funds; Federal Pell; Private scholarships; SEOG; State scholarships/grants. *Loans:* Direct PLUS loans; Direct Subsidized Stafford Loans; Direct Unsubsidized Stafford Loans. **Student Employment:** Federal Work-Study Program available. Institutional employment available. **Financial Aid Statistics:** 80% needy freshmen, 76% needy undergrads receive need-based scholarship or grant aid. 82% freshmen, 70% undergrads receive non-need-based scholarship or grant aid. 82% freshmen, 85% undergrads receive need-based self-help aid. 0% freshmen, 0% undergrads receive athletic scholarships. 97% freshmen, 94% undergrads receive any aid. 84% undergrads borrow to pay for school. Average cumulative indebtedness $40,125. **Criteria awarding aid:** *Need-based:* Alumni affiliation. *Non-need-based:* Academics, Alumni affiliation, Art, Music/drama.

KENDALL COLLEGE OF ART AND DESIGN OF FERRIS STATE UNIVERSITY

17 Fountain Street NW, Grand Rapids, MI 49503-3002
Phone: 616-451-2787 **Financial Aid Phone:** 616-451-2787
E-mail: brittons@ferris.edu **CEEB Code:** 1983
Fax: 616-831-9689 **Website:** www.kcad.edu **ACT Code:** 1983

This public school was founded in 1928. It has a 2 acre campus.

RATINGS
Admissions Selectivity Rating: 71   **Fire Safety Rating:** 60*   **Green Rating:** 60*

STUDENTS AND FACULTY
Enrollment: 1,141. **Student Body:** 13% out-of-state, 0% international (15 countries represented).
Retention and Graduation: 12% grads go on to further study within 1 year. 12% grads pursue arts and sciences degrees. **Faculty:** Student/faculty ratio 15:1. 50 full-time faculty, 6% hold PhDs, 4% are members of minority groups, 0% are women. 0% of classes are taught by teaching assistants.

ACADEMICS
Degrees: Bachelor's; Master's. **Most popular majors:** Illustration; Interior Design; Graphic Design. **Special Study Options:** Cooperative education program; Double major; Dual enrollment; Independent study; Internships; Liberal arts/career combination; Study abroad; Teacher certification program. **Disability Services offered:** Note-taking services; Reader services; Tape recorders; Tutors. **Career services:** Alumni network; Alumni services; Career/job search classes; Internships; Regional alumni.

FACILITIES
Housing: Apartments for married students; Apartments for single students; 100% of campus accessible to physically disabled.

CAMPUS LIFE
Environment: Metropolis. 12 registered organizations, 1 religious organization on campus. **On-Campus Highlights:** Studio Spaces.

ADMISSIONS
Freshman Academic Profile: Average high school GPA 3.1. 10% in top 10% of high school class, 20% in top 25% of high school class, 75% in top 50% of high school class. **Basis for Candidate Selection:** *Very important factors include:* rigor of secondary school record, academic GPA, application essay, standardized test scores, talent/ability. *Important factors include:* interview, character/personal qualities. *Other factors include:* class rank, recommendation(s), extracurricular activities. **Freshman Admission Requirements:** High school diploma is required and GED is accepted. **Freshman Admission Statistics:** 338 applied, 78% admitted, 91% enrolled. **Transfer Admission Requirements:** High school transcript, college transcript(s), essay or personal statement, Lowest grade transferable C. **General Admission Information:** Application fee $30.

Non-fall registration accepted. Admission may be deferred for a maximum of one semester.

COSTS AND FINANCIAL AID
Annual in-state tuition $12,674. Annual out-of-state tuition $19,220. Required fees $420. Average book and supplies expense $3,604. **Required Forms and Deadlines:** FAFSA. **Notification of Awards:** Applicants will be notified of awards on a rolling basis beginning 4/1. **Types of Aid:** *Need-based scholarships/grants:* College/university scholarship or grant aid from institutional funds; Federal Pell; Private scholarships; SEOG; State scholarships/grants. *Loans:* Direct PLUS loans; Direct Subsidized Stafford Loans; Direct Unsubsidized Stafford Loans. **Student Employment:** Federal Work-Study Program available. Institutional employment available. **Criteria awarding aid:** *Non-need-based:* Academics, Alumni affiliation, Art.

KENNESAW STATE UNIVERSITY

3391 Town Point Drive, Suite 1000, Kennesaw, GA 30144-5591
Phone: 770-423-6300 **Financial Aid Phone:** 770-423-6074
E-mail: ksuadmit@kennesaw.edu **CEEB Code:** 5359
Fax: 470-578-9169 **Website:** http://www.kennesaw.edu **ACT Code:** 833

This public school was founded in 1963. It has a 602 acre campus.

RATINGS
Admissions Selectivity Rating: 89   **Fire Safety Rating:** 92   **Green Rating:** 95

STUDENTS AND FACULTY
Enrollment: 31,514. **Student Body:** 47% female, 53% male, 13% out-of-state, 2% international (129 countries represented). Asian 5%, African American 21%, Caucasian 55%, Hispanic 10%, Native American <1%, Pacific Islander <1%, Two or more races 5%, Race unknown 2%.
Retention and Graduation: 79% freshmen return for sophomore year. 12% freshmen graduate within 4 years. 42% freshmen graduate within 6 years. **Faculty:** Student/faculty ratio 20:1. 1,182 full-time faculty, 78% hold PhDs, 27% are members of minority groups, 49% are women. 0% of classes are taught by teaching assistants.

ACADEMICS
Degrees: Bachelor's; Certificate; Doctoral degree research/scholarship; Master's; Post-bachelor's certificate; Post-master's certificate. **Classes:** Most classes have 20–29 students. Most lab/discussion sessions have 20–29 students. **Most popular majors:** Biology/Biological Sciences, General; Registered Nursing/Registered Nurse; Psychology, General. **Special Study Options:** Cooperative education program; Cross-registration; Distance learning; Double major; Dual enrollment; English as a Second Language (ESL); Exchange student program (domestic); Honors program; Internships; Study abroad; Teacher certification program; Weekend college. **Honors programs:** The Honors College offers a community within a university to academically talented,highly motivated students who enjoy lively discussion, creative expression, and intellectual challenge. We offer small honors sections of core courses and interdisciplinary honors seminars, where students focus on deep understanding within an innovative curriculum.We also provide opportunities for undergraduate research, domestic and international travel experiences, and community service activities. The Honors College houses the University Honors Program, including the President's Emerging Global Scholars cohort and the Great Books cohort, available to entering first-year students. The University Honors Program provides more challenging educational experiences for eligible students eager to broaden themselves intellectually, enhance the critical thinking skills essential to most careers, and join an intimate community of like-minded peers. The mission of the President's Emerging Global Scholars (PEGS) program is to accelerate the personal, professional, and academic development of exceptional Honors students. The objective of PEGS is to prepare our students to actively engage in their communities, develop global competencies, and grow as exceptional scholars. The Great Books program is a select cohort within the University Honors Program. The cohort is limited to no more than twenty-five (25) students who are chosen by the Great Books Steering Committee. **Disability Services offered:** Note-taking services; Reader services; Tape recorders; Tutors. **Career services:** Alumni network; Alumni services; Career assessment; Career/job search classes; Internships.

FACILITIES
Housing: Apartments for single students; Theme housing 100% of campus accessible to physically disabled. **Special Academic Facilities/Equipment:**

Museum of History and Holocaust Education, Zuckerman Museum of Art, 3D Center, Center for Advanced Materials Research and Education, The Center for African and African Diaspora Studies, Center for Applied Gaming and Media Arts, Center for Conflict Management, Center for Machine Vision and Security Research, Center for Professional Selling, Center for Student Leadership, Center for the Study of the Civil War Era, Center for Young Adult Addiction and Recovery, Cultural and Community Centers, The Cultural Awareness and Resource Center, ESL Center, Georgia Pavement and Traffic Research Center, The Intensive English Program, The Internal Audit Center, Shore Entrepreneurship Center, The Science and Math Academic Resource and Tutoring (SMART) Center, Student Recreation and Activities Center, The Talon One Service Center, Teacher Resource & Activity Corner, The Women's Resource Center, Writing Center. **Campus Network:** 100% of classrooms, 100% of student union, 100% of libraries have wireless network access.

CAMPUS LIFE

Environment: Town. **Activities:** Campus Ministries; Choral groups; Concert band; Dance; Drama/theater; International Student Organization; Jazz band; Literary magazine; Marching band; Music ensembles; Musical theater; Opera; Pep band; Radio station; Student government; Student newspaper; Symphony orchestra. 275 registered organizations, 18 honor societies, 35 religious organizations, 19 fraternities, 11 sororities on campus. **Athletics (Intercollegiate):** *Men:* baseball, basketball, cross-country, golf, tennis, track/field (outdoor), track/field (indoor). *Women:* basketball, cheerleading, cross-country, golf, soccer, softball, tennis, track/field (outdoor), track/field (indoor), volleyball. **On-Campus Highlights:** The Commons (Student Culinary Center). **Environmental Initiatives:** Commitment by former KSU President Daniel S. Papp to reduce the university's carbon footprint, in line with a national coalition of college and university presidents. He also established the President's Commission on Sustainability, which convenes monthly to advance campus sustainability initiatives.

ADMISSIONS

Freshman Academic Profile: Average high school GPA 3.4. 16% in top 10% of high school class, 45% in top 25% of high school class, 80% in top 50% of high school class. **Test Scores:** SAT Math middle 50% range 530–630. SAT EBRW middle 50% range 550–640. ACT middle 50% range 21–26. **Basis for Candidate Selection:** *Very important factors include:* academic GPA, standardized test scores. **Freshman Admission Requirements:** High school diploma is required and GED is not accepted. *Academic units required:* 4 English, 4 math, 4 science, 2 science labs, 2 foreign language, 1 social studies, 2 history. *Academic units recommended:* 4 English, 4 math, 4 science, 2 science labs, 2 foreign language, 1 social studies, 2 history. **Freshman Admission Statistics:** 13,427 applied, 58% admitted, 61% enrolled. **Transfer Admission Requirements:** College transcript(s). Minimum college GPA of 2.0 required. Lowest grade transferable D. **General Admission Information:** Application fee $40. Priority deadline 10/26. Regular application deadline 5/3. Non-fall registration accepted.

COSTS AND FINANCIAL AID

Annual in-state tuition $5,562. Annual out-of-state tuition $19,630. Room and board $11,467. Required fees $2,006. Average book and supplies expense $1,500. **Required Forms and Deadlines:** FAFSA. *Types of Aid: Need-based scholarships/grants:* College/university scholarship or grant aid from institutional funds; Federal Pell; Private scholarships; SEOG; State scholarships/grants; United Negro College Fund. *Loans:* Direct PLUS loans; Direct Subsidized Stafford Loans; Direct Unsubsidized Stafford Loans. **Student Employment:** Federal Work-Study Program available. Institutional employment available. **Financial Aid Statistics:** 44% needy freshmen, 52% needy undergrads receive need-based scholarship or grant aid. 84% freshmen, 61% undergrads receive non-need-based scholarship or grant aid. 87% freshmen, 89% undergrads receive need-based self-help aid. 0% freshmen, 0% undergrads receive athletic scholarships. 61% undergrads borrow to pay for school. Average cumulative indebtedness $25,525. **Criteria awarding aid:** *Need-based:* Academics, Art, Athletics, Job skills, Leadership, Minority status. *Non-need-based:* Academics, Alumni affiliation, Art, Athletics, Job skills, Leadership, Minority status, Music/drama, State/district residency.

KENT STATE UNIVERSITY—KENT CAMPUS

161 Schwartz Center, Kent, OH 44242-0001
Phone: 330-672-2444 **Financial Aid Phone:** 330-672-6000
E-mail: kentadm@kent.edu **CEEB Code:** 1367
Fax: 330-672-2499 **Website:** http://www.kent.edu **ACT Code:** 3284

This public school was founded in 1910. It has a 946 acre campus.

RATINGS

Admissions Selectivity Rating: 76 **Fire Safety Rating:** 92 **Green Rating:** 77

STUDENTS AND FACULTY

Enrollment: 21,431. **Student Body:** 62% female, 38% male, 16% out-of-state, 3% international (67 countries represented). Asian 2%, African American 9%, Caucasian 75%, Hispanic 4%, Native American <1%, Pacific Islander <1%, Two or more races 4%, Race unknown 3%.
Retention and Graduation: 81% freshmen return for sophomore year. 40% freshmen graduate within 4 years. 60% freshmen graduate within 6 years.
Faculty: Student/faculty ratio 19:1. 970 full-time faculty, 0% hold PhDs, 14% are members of minority groups, 53% are women. 6% of classes are taught by teaching assistants.

ACADEMICS

Degrees: Bachelor's; Certificate; Doctoral degree—professional practice; Doctoral degree research/scholarship; Master's; Post-bachelor's certificate; Post-master's certificate. **Classes:** Most classes have 10–19 students. **Most popular majors:** Fashion Merchandising; Registered Nursing/Registered Nurse; Psychology, General. **Special Study Options:** Accelerated program; Cooperative education program; Cross-registration; Distance learning; Double major; Dual enrollment; English as a Second Language (ESL); Exchange student program (domestic); Honors program; Independent study; Internships; Liberal arts/career combination; Student-designed major; Study abroad; Teacher certification program. **Honors programs:** The Kent State University Honors College is an institutional member of the National Collegiate Honors Council and the Mid-East Honors Association. The Honors College is open to all majors and provides talented and motivated undergraduate students a small liberal arts experience with the opportunities of a large public research university. This mission is carried out through the offering of smaller sections of courses, individualized interaction with faculty through research and other projects, the option of living in our learning community in the Stopher-Johnson complex, community service opportunities, personal advising, and several other educational opportunities and enhancements The Honors College is guided by two basic principles: the responsibility to provide academic work that offers intellectual challenge that demands the best efforts of students, and the belief that all students should be liberally educated, regardless of degree program. Our goal is to help students find the opportunities that will enrich their Kent State educations and empower them in directing their talents for a successful future. **Combined degree programs:** BA/MA; BA/MD. **Disability Services offered:** Note-taking services; Reader services; Tape recorders; Tutors. **Career services:** Alumni network; Alumni services; Career assessment; Career/job search classes; Internships; Regional alumni.

FACILITIES

Housing: Apartments for married students; Apartments for single students; Coed dorms; Cooperative housing; Fraternity/sorority housing; Men's dorms; Special housing for disabled students; Special housing for international students; Theme housing; Wellness housing; Women's dorms; 95% of campus accessible to physically disabled. **Special Academic Facilities/Equipment:** May 4th Visitors Center, KSU Museum: The Fashion School, The Tom S. and Miwako K. Cooperrider Herbarium, Glenn H. Brown Liquid Crystal Institute, Planetarium, KSU Airport. Kenneth W. Berger Hearing Aid Museum.

CAMPUS LIFE

Environment: Town. **Activities:** Campus Ministries; Choral groups; Concert band; Dance; Drama/theater; International Student Organization; Jazz band; Literary magazine; Marching band; Model UN; Music ensembles; Musical theater; Opera; Pep band; Radio station; Student government; Student newspaper; Symphony orchestra; Television station. 423 registered organizations, 7 honor societies, 21 religious organizations, 19 fraternities, 8 sororities on campus. **Athletics (Intercollegiate):** *Men:* baseball, basketball, cheerleading, cross-country, football, golf, track/field (outdoor), track/field (indoor), wrestling. *Women:* basketball, cheerleading, cross-country, field hockey, football, golf, gymnastics, soccer, softball, track/field (outdoor), track/field (indoor), volleyball. **On-Campus Highlights:** Student Recreation and

Wellness Center. **Environmental Initiatives:** Kent State's focus on energy includes ongoing energy efficiency retrofits which have reduced consumption by over 15% to date, a combined heat and power plant on campus which is about twice as efficient as a utility power plant, and a half-megawatt solar array installed in spring 2012 as part of our renewable energy master plan.

ADMISSIONS

Freshman Academic Profile: Average high school GPA 3.5. 17% in top 10% of high school class, 43% in top 25% of high school class, 77% in top 50% of high school class. **Test Scores:** SAT Math middle 50% range 510–610. SAT EBRW middle 50% range 530–620. ACT middle 50% range 20–26. **Basis for Candidate Selection:** *Very important factors include:* academic GPA, standardized test scores. *Important factors include:* rigor of secondary school record. *Other factors include:* application essay, recommendation(s), interview, talent/ability, level of applicant's interest. **Freshman Admission Requirements:** High school diploma is required and GED is accepted. *Academic units recommended:* 4 English, 4 math, 3 science, 2 science labs, 2 foreign language, 3 social studies, 1 visual/performing arts. **Freshman Admission Statistics:** 16,308 applied, 86% admitted, 31% enrolled. **Transfer Admission Requirements:** College transcript(s). Minimum college GPA of 2.0 required. Lowest grade transferable C. **General Admission Information:** Application fee $50. Priority deadline 3/1. Regular application deadline 5/1. Non-fall registration accepted.

COSTS AND FINANCIAL AID

Required Forms and Deadlines: FAFSA. **Notification of Awards:** Applicants will be notified of awards on a rolling basis beginning 1/15. **Types of Aid:** *Need-based scholarships/grants:* College/university scholarship or grant aid from institutional funds; Federal Pell; Private scholarships; SEOG; State scholarships/grants. *Loans:* Direct PLUS loans; Direct Subsidized Stafford Loans; Direct Unsubsidized Stafford Loans. **Student Employment:** Federal Work-Study Program available. Institutional employment available. **Financial Aid Statistics:** 96% needy freshmen, 90% needy undergrads receive need-based scholarship or grant aid. 12% freshmen, 9% undergrads receive non-need-based scholarship or grant aid. 76% freshmen, 80% undergrads receive need-based self-help aid. 1% freshmen, 1% undergrads receive athletic scholarships. 72% undergrads borrow to pay for school. Average cumulative indebtedness $31,113. **Criteria awarding aid:** *Need-based:* Academics, Alumni affiliation, Athletics, Leadership, Minority status. *Non-need-based:* Academics, Alumni affiliation, Art, Athletics, Leadership, Minority status, Music/drama, State/district residency.

KENTUCKY STATE UNIVERSITY

400 East Main Street, Frankfort, KY 40601
Phone: 502-597-6813 **Financial Aid Phone:** 502-597-5959
E-mail: admissions@kysu.edu **CEEB Code:** 1368
Fax: 502-597-5814 **Website:** www.kysu.edu **ACT Code:** 1516

This public school was founded in 1886. It has a 916.03 acre campus.

RATINGS

Admissions Selectivity Rating: 85   **Fire Safety Rating:** 97   **Green Rating:** 73

STUDENTS AND FACULTY

Enrollment: 1,349. **Student Body:** 58% female, 42% male, 31% out-of-state, 1% international (9 countries represented). Asian 1%, African American 63%, Caucasian 24%, Hispanic 3%, Native American 1%, Pacific Islander 0%, Two or more races 4%, Race unknown 5%.
Retention and Graduation: 59% freshmen return for sophomore year. 34% grads go on to further study within 1 year. 18% grads pursue arts and sciences degrees. 2% grads pursue law degrees. 2% grads pursue business degrees. 3% grads pursue medical degrees. **Faculty:** Student/faculty ratio 11:1. 106 full-time faculty, 69% hold PhDs, 43% are members of minority groups, 48% are women. 0% of classes are taught by teaching assistants.

ACADEMICS

Degrees: Associate; Bachelor's; Certificate; Doctoral degree—professional practice; Master's; Terminal Associate; Transfer Associate. **Classes:** Most classes have 10–19 students. **Most popular majors:** Criminal Justice/Safety Studies; Registered Nursing/Registered Nurse; Business Administration and Management, General. **Special Study Options:** Cooperative education program; Distance learning; Double major; Dual enrollment; Honors program; Independent study; Internships; Liberal arts/career combination; Student-designed major; Study abroad; Teacher certification program. **Honors programs:** The Honors Program is an integrated liberal arts program that

emphasizes student discussion of excellent books. Honors students can complete the core general studies requirements through the Honors Program and then go on to major in any field. Honors students may also major or minor in Liberal Studies. The Honors Program features small classes with fifteen or fewer students, a challenging interdisciplinary and multicultural curriculum, a faculty devoted to undergraduate education, and a community spirit among faculty and students. It also offers scholarships, opportunities for study abroad, internships, and participation in state, regional and national honors conferences. **Disability Services offered:** Note-taking services; Reader services; Tape recorders; Tutors. **Career services:** Alumni network; Alumni services; Career assessment; Career/job search classes; Internships; Regional alumni.

FACILITIES

Housing: Coed dorms; Men's dorms; Women's dorms; 100% of campus accessible to physically disabled. **Special Academic Facilities/Equipment:** Art gallery, nutrition lab, agriculture research building, research farm, fish hatchery, electron microscope.

CAMPUS LIFE

Environment: Town. **Activities:** Campus Ministries; Choral groups; Concert band; Dance; Drama/theater; International Student Organization; Jazz band; Marching band; Music ensembles; Musical theater; Pep band; Student government; Student newspaper. 40 registered organizations, 4 honor societies, 4 religious organizations, 7 fraternities, 5 sororities on campus. **Athletics (Intercollegiate):** *Men:* baseball, basketball, cross-country, football, golf, track/field (outdoor), track/field (indoor). *Women:* basketball, cross-country, softball, track/field (outdoor), track/field (indoor), volleyball. **On-Campus Highlights:** Jackson Hall. **Environmental Initiatives:** Energy efficient fixtures for Power & water.

ADMISSIONS

Freshman Academic Profile: Average high school GPA 2.8. **Test Scores:** SAT Math middle 50% range 400–510. SAT EBRW middle 50% range 418–500. ACT middle 50% range 16–21. **Basis for Candidate Selection:** *Very important factors include:* academic GPA, standardized test scores. *Important factors include:* rigor of secondary school record, class rank. *Other factors include:* application essay, recommendation(s), interview, extracurricular activities, talent/ability, character/personal qualities, first generation, alumni/ae relation, geographical residence, state residency, level of applicant's interest. **Freshman Admission Requirements:** High school diploma is required and GED is accepted. *Academic units required:* 4 English, 3 math, 3 science, 2 foreign language, 3 social studies, 3 history, 7 academic electives, 1 visual/performing arts, 0.5 unit from above areas or other academic areas. **Freshman Admission Statistics:** 2,078 applied, 45% admitted, 14% enrolled. **Transfer Admission Requirements:** College transcript(s). Minimum college GPA of 2.0 required. Lowest grade transferable C. **General Admission Information:** Application fee $30. Priority deadline 2/15. Regular application deadline 7/31. Non-fall registration accepted.

COSTS AND FINANCIAL AID

Annual in-state tuition $7,700. Annual out-of-state tuition $11,550. Room and board $5,570. Required fees $390. Average book and supplies expense $650. **Required Forms and Deadlines:** FAFSA. **Notification of Awards:** Applicants will be notified of awards on a rolling basis beginning 3/15. **Types of Aid:** *Need-based scholarships/grants:* College/university scholarship or grant aid from institutional funds; Federal Pell; Private scholarships; SEOG; State scholarships/grants; United Negro College Fund. *Loans:* Direct PLUS loans; Direct Subsidized Stafford Loans; Direct Unsubsidized Stafford Loans. **Student Employment:** Federal Work-Study Program available. Institutional employment available. **Financial Aid Statistics:** 100% needy freshmen, 100% needy undergrads receive need-based scholarship or grant aid. 6% freshmen, 6% undergrads receive non-need-based scholarship or grant aid. 70% freshmen, 74% undergrads receive need-based self-help aid. 3% freshmen, 2% undergrads receive athletic scholarships. 73% freshmen, 85% undergrads receive any aid. 73% undergrads borrow to pay for school. Average cumulative indebtedness $29,553. **Criteria awarding aid:** *Non-need-based:* Academics, Alumni affiliation, Art, Athletics, Leadership, Music/drama.

KENTUCKY WESLEYAN COLLEGE

3000 Frederica Street, Owensboro, KY 42301
Phone: 270-852-3120 **Financial Aid Phone:** 270-852-3130
E-mail: http://www.kwc.edu/page.php?page=353 **CEEB Code:** 1369
Fax: 270-852-3133 **Website:** www.kwc.edu **ACT Code:** 1518

*This private school, affiliated with the Methodist Church, was founded in 1858.
It has a 52 acre campus.*

RATINGS
Admissions Selectivity Rating: 78 **Fire Safety Rating:** 85 **Green Rating:** 60*

STUDENTS AND FACULTY
Enrollment: 657. **Student Body:** 48% female, 52% male, 28% out-of-state,
2% international (8 countries represented). Asian <1%, African American 12%,
Caucasian 74%, Hispanic 2%, Native American <1%, Pacific Islander 0%, Two
or more races 0%, Race unknown 10%.
Retention and Graduation: 54% freshmen return for sophomore year. 25%
grads go on to further study within 1 year. **Faculty:** Student/faculty ratio 12:1.
48 full-time faculty, 71% hold PhDs, 6% are members of minority groups,
48% are women. 0% of classes are taught by teaching assistants.

ACADEMICS
Degrees: Bachelor's. **Classes:** Most classes have fewer than 10 students. Most
lab/discussion sessions have 10–19 students. **Most popular majors:** Criminal
Justice/Safety Studies; Business/Commerce, General; Biology/Biological Sciences,
General. **Special Study Options:** Distance learning; Double major; Dual
enrollment; Independent study; Internships; Liberal arts/career combination;
Student-designed major; Study abroad; Teacher certification program. **Disability
Services offered:** Note-taking services; Reader services; Tape recorders; Tutors.
Career services: Alumni network; Alumni services; Career assessment; Career/job
search classes; Internships; Regional alumni.

FACILITIES
Housing: Apartments for married students; Apartments for single students;
Coed dorms; Fraternity/sorority housing; Men's dorms; Special housing for
disabled students; Women's dorms; 100% of campus accessible to physically
disabled. **Special Academic Facilities/Equipment:** President's Hall/Library
Learning Center; Ralph Center for Fine Arts; Woodward Health and Recreation
Center; Yu Hak Hahn Center for the Sciences. **Campus Network:** 100% of
classrooms, 100% of dorms, 100% of student union, 100% of libraries, 100%
of dining areas, 80% of common outdoor areas have wireless network access.

CAMPUS LIFE
Environment: City. **Activities:** Campus Ministries; Choral groups; Concert
band; Dance; Drama/theater; Literary magazine; Marching band; Music
ensembles; Musical theater; Pep band; Radio station; Student government;
Student newspaper; Yearbook. 42 registered organizations, 6 honor societies,
6 religious organizations, 3 fraternities, 2 sororities on campus. **Athletics
(Intercollegiate):** *Men:* baseball, basketball, cheerleading, cross-country,
football, golf, soccer. *Women:* basketball, cheerleading, cross-country, golf,
soccer, softball, tennis, volleyball. **On-Campus Highlights:** Winchester Center-
New Campus Center.

ADMISSIONS
Freshman Academic Profile: Average high school GPA 3.2. 20% in top 10%
of high school class, 44% in top 25% of high school class, 68% in top 50%
of high school class. 90% from public high schools. **Test Scores:** SAT Math
middle 50% range 410–555. SAT EBRW middle 50% range 410–540. ACT
middle 50% range 19–25. **Basis for Candidate Selection:** *Very important
factors include:* academic GPA, standardized test scores. *Important factors
include:* rigor of secondary school record, interview, extracurricular activities.
Other factors include: class rank, recommendation(s), talent/ability, character/
personal qualities, alumni/ae relation, volunteer work, work experience, level
of applicant's interest. **Freshman Admission Requirements:** High school
diploma is required and GED is accepted. *Academic units required:* 4 English,
3 math, 3 science, 3 social studies. *Academic units recommended:* 2 foreign
language. **Freshman Admission Statistics:** 1,006 applied, 67% admitted, 24%
enrolled. **Transfer Admission Requirements:** College transcript(s). Minimum
college GPA of 2.0 required. Lowest grade transferable C. **General Admission
Information:** Non-fall registration accepted. Admission may be deferred for a
maximum of 12 months.

COSTS AND FINANCIAL AID
Annual tuition $21,400. Room and board $7,800. Required fees $800. Average
book and supplies expense $1,400. **Required Forms and Deadlines:** FAFSA.
Notification of Awards: Applicants will be notified of awards on a rolling basis
beginning 2/15. **Types of Aid:** *Need-based scholarships/grants:* College/university
scholarship or grant aid from institutional funds; Federal Pell; Private scholarships;
SEOG; State scholarships/grants. *Loans:* Direct PLUS loans; Direct Subsidized
Stafford Loans; Direct Unsubsidized Stafford Loans. **Student Employment:**
Federal Work-Study Program available. Institutional employment available.
Financial Aid Statistics: 99% needy freshmen, 98% needy undergrads receive
need-based scholarship or grant aid. 7% freshmen, 11% undergrads receive
non-need-based scholarship or grant aid. 80% freshmen, 76% undergrads
receive need-based self-help aid. 0% freshmen, 0% undergrads receive athletic
scholarships. 99% freshmen, 85% undergrads receive any aid. **Criteria awarding
aid:** *Need-based:* Academics, Alumni affiliation, Art, Athletics, Leadership, Music/
drama, Religious affiliation. *Non-need-based:* Academics, Alumni affiliation, Art,
Athletics, Leadership, Music/drama, Religious affiliation, State/district residency.

KENYON COLLEGE

Kenyon College Admissions Office, Gambier, OH 43022-9623
Phone: 740-427-5776 **Financial Aid Phone:** 740-427-5240
E-mail: admissions@kenyon.edu **CEEB Code:** 1370
Fax: 740-427-5770 **Website:** www.kenyon.edu **ACT Code:** 3286

*This private school, affiliated with the Episcopal Church, was founded in 1824. It
has a 1000 acre campus.*

RATINGS
Admissions Selectivity Rating: 93 **Fire Safety Rating:** 89 **Green Rating:** 80

STUDENTS AND FACULTY
Enrollment: 1,719. **Student Body:** 55% female, 45% male, 87% out-of-state,
7% international (49 countries represented). Asian 4%, African American 4%,
Caucasian 70%, Hispanic 8%, Native American 0%, Pacific Islander 0%, Two
or more races 5%, Race unknown 3%.
Retention and Graduation: 91% freshmen return for sophomore year. 86%
freshmen graduate within 4 years. 91% freshmen graduate within 6 years. 19%
grads go on to further study within 1 year. **Faculty:** Student/faculty ratio 10:1.
156 full-time faculty, 88% hold PhDs, 28% are members of minority groups,
44% are women. 0% of classes are taught by teaching assistants.

ACADEMICS
Degrees: Bachelor's. **Classes:** Most classes have 10–19 students. **Most popular
majors:** English Language and Literature, General; Economics, General;
Psychology, General. **Special Study Options:** Double major; Honors program;
Independent study; Internships; Student-designed major; Study abroad. **Honors
programs:** Honors programs are offered by all departmental and interdepartmental
majors. **Disability Services offered:** Note-taking services; Reader services; Tape
recorders; Tutors. **Career services:** Alumni network; Alumni services; Career
assessment; Career/job search classes; Internships; Regional alumni.

FACILITIES
Housing: Apartments for single students; Coed dorms; Fraternity/sorority
housing; Special housing for disabled students; Special housing for international
students; Theme housing; Wellness housing; Women's dorms; 70% of campus
accessible to physically disabled. **Special Academic Facilities/Equipment:**
Gund Art Gallery; Bolton and Hill theaters; Rosse and Storer halls for music;
Science quadrangle; greenhouse; observatory; environmental center; new Lentz
House (English), $70-million fitness, recreation, and athletics facility; new
studio art building.

CAMPUS LIFE
Environment: Rural. **Activities:** Campus Ministries; Choral groups; Concert
band; Dance; Drama/theater; International Student Organization; Jazz band;
Literary magazine; Model UN; Music ensembles; Musical theater; Opera;
Radio station; Student government; Student newspaper; Student-run film
society; Symphony orchestra. 146 registered organizations, 5 honor societies,
7 religious organizations, 7 fraternities, 4 sororities on campus. **Athletics
(Intercollegiate):** *Men:* baseball, basketball, cross-country, diving, football, golf,
lacrosse, soccer, swimming, tennis, track/field (outdoor), track/field (indoor).

Women: basketball, cross-country, diving, field hockey, lacrosse, soccer, softball, swimming, tennis, track/field (outdoor), track/field (indoor), volleyball. **On-Campus Highlights:** Kenyon College Bookstore. **Environmental Initiatives:** 1 Food for Thought (purchase of local foods for dining hall and building a county-wide sustainable food system) http://rurallife.kenyon.edu.

ADMISSIONS

Freshman Academic Profile: Average high school GPA 3.9. 55% in top 10% of high school class, 79% in top 25% of high school class, 96% in top 50% of high school class. 50% from public high schools. **Test Scores:** SAT Math middle 50% range 640–740. SAT EBRW middle 50% range 640–730. ACT middle 50% range 29–33. **Basis for Candidate Selection:** *Very important factors include:* rigor of secondary school record, academic GPA, application essay, recommendation(s). *Important factors include:* class rank, standardized test scores, interview, extracurricular activities, talent/ability, character/personal qualities. *Other factors include:* first generation, alumni/ae relation, geographical residence, state residency, racial/ethnic status, volunteer work, work experience. **Freshman Admission Requirements:** High school diploma is required and GED is accepted. *Academic units required:* 4 English, 4 math, 3 science, 3 science labs, 3 foreign language, 3 social studies, 3 academic electives. *Academic units recommended:* 4 English, 4 math, 4 science, 3 science labs, 4 foreign language, 3 social studies, 3 academic electives. **Freshman Admission Statistics:** 6,152 applied, 36% admitted, 24% enrolled. **Transfer Admission Requirements:** High school transcript, college transcript(s), essay or personal statement, standardized test scores, statement of good standing from prior institution(s). Minimum college GPA of 3.0 required. Lowest grade transferable C. **General Admission Information:** Priority deadline 1/15. Regular application deadline 1/15. Admission may be deferred for a maximum of 1 year.

COSTS AND FINANCIAL AID

Annual tuition $56,430. Room and board $12,580. Average book and supplies expense $1,900. **Required Forms and Deadlines:** CSS/Financial Aid PROFILE; FAFSA; Noncustodial PROFILE. **Types of Aid:** *Need-based scholarships/grants:* College/university scholarship or grant aid from institutional funds; Federal Pell; Private scholarships; SEOG; State scholarships/grants. *Loans:* Direct PLUS loans; Direct Subsidized Stafford Loans; Direct Unsubsidized Stafford Loans. **Student Employment:** Federal Work-Study Program available. Institutional employment available. **Financial Aid Statistics:** 100% needy freshmen, 100% needy undergrads receive need-based scholarship or grant aid. 40% freshmen, 31% undergrads receive non-need-based scholarship or grant aid. 80% freshmen, 88% undergrads receive need-based self-help aid. 0% freshmen, 0% undergrads receive athletic scholarships. 42% freshmen, 42% undergrads receive any aid. 46% undergrads borrow to pay for school. Average cumulative indebtedness $26,271. **Criteria awarding aid:** *Non-need-based:* Academics, Art, Minority status, Music/drama.

KETTERING UNIVERSITY

1700 University Ave., Flint, MI 48504-6214
Phone: 810-762-9500 **Financial Aid Phone:** 810-762-7859
CEEB Code: 1246
Website: www.kettering.edu **ACT Code:** 1998

This private school was founded in 1919. It has a 85 acre campus.

RATINGS

Admissions Selectivity Rating: 86   **Fire Safety Rating:** 78   **Green Rating:** 60*

STUDENTS AND FACULTY

Enrollment: 1,850. **Student Body:** 19% female, 81% male, 15% out-of-state, 4% international (24 countries represented). Asian 4%, African American 3%, Caucasian 76%, Hispanic 5%, Native American <1%, Pacific Islander 0%, Two or more races 3%, Race unknown 5%.
Retention and Graduation: 93% freshmen return for sophomore year. 9% freshmen graduate within 4 years. 59% freshmen graduate within 6 years.
Faculty: Student/faculty ratio 15:1. 114 full-time faculty, 87% hold PhDs, 25% are members of minority groups, 29% are women. 0% of classes are taught by teaching assistants.

ACADEMICS

Degrees: Bachelor's; Master's; Post-bachelor's certificate. **Classes:** Most classes have 10–19 students. Most lab/discussion sessions have 10–19 students. **Most**

popular majors: Computer Science; Chemical Engineering. **Special Study Options:** Cooperative education program; Distance learning; Double major; Dual enrollment; English as a Second Language (ESL); Honors program; Independent study; Internships; Liberal arts/career combination; Study abroad. **Disability Services offered:** Note-taking services; Reader services; Tape recorders; Tutors.

FACILITIES

Housing: Coed dorms; Fraternity/sorority housing; Men's dorms; Special housing for disabled students; Theme housing; Women's dorms; 100% of campus accessible to physically disabled. **Special Academic Facilities/Equipment:** Humanities Art Museum Factory; 5 D Spaces; 1 TSpace. **Campus Network:** 100% of classrooms, 100% of dorms, 100% of student union, 100% of libraries, 100% of dining areas, 20% of common outdoor areas have wireless network access.

CAMPUS LIFE

Environment: City. **Activities:** Campus Ministries; Concert band; Dance; International Student Organization; Jazz band; Model UN; Radio station; Student government; Student newspaper. 42 registered organizations, 15 honor societies, 1 religious organization, 13 fraternities, 5 sororities on campus. **On-Campus Highlights:** CS Mott Engineering and Science Center.

ADMISSIONS

Freshman Academic Profile: Average high school GPA 3.7. 32% in top 10% of high school class, 60% in top 25% of high school class, 91% in top 50% of high school class. 82% from public high schools. **Test Scores:** SAT Math middle 50% range 610–690. SAT EBRW middle 50% range 580–660. ACT middle 50% range 24–29. **Basis for Candidate Selection:** *Very important factors include:* rigor of secondary school record, academic GPA, standardized test scores. *Important factors include:* extracurricular activities. *Other factors include:* class rank, application essay, recommendation(s), talent/ability, racial/ethnic status, volunteer work, work experience, level of applicant's interest. **Freshman Admission Requirements:** High school diploma is required and GED is accepted. *Academic units required:* 3 English, 3.5 math, 2 science, 2 science labs. *Academic units recommended:* 4 English, 4 math, 3 science, 3 science labs, 2 social studies, 2 history, 1 academic elective. **Freshman Admission Statistics:** 1,931 applied, 70% admitted, 27% enrolled. **Transfer Admission Requirements:** College transcript(s). Minimum college GPA of 3.0 required. Lowest grade transferable C. **General Admission Information:** Admission may be deferred for a maximum of 1 year.

COSTS AND FINANCIAL AID

Annual tuition $44,380. Room and board $8,410. Average book and supplies expense $1,100. **Required Forms and Deadlines:** FAFSA. **Notification of Awards:** Applicants will be notified of awards on or about 3/1. **Types of Aid:** *Need-based scholarships/grants:* College/university scholarship or grant aid from institutional funds; Federal Pell; Private scholarships; SEOG; State scholarships/grants; United Negro College Fund. *Loans:* Direct PLUS loans; Direct Subsidized Stafford Loans; Direct Unsubsidized Stafford Loans. **Student Employment:** Federal Work-Study Program available. Institutional employment available. **Financial Aid Statistics:** 99% needy freshmen, 99% needy undergrads receive need-based scholarship or grant aid. 36% freshmen, 29% undergrads receive non-need-based scholarship or grant aid. 71% freshmen, 75% undergrads receive need-based self-help aid. 0% freshmen, 0% undergrads receive athletic scholarships. 99% freshmen, 88% undergrads receive any aid. **Criteria awarding aid:** *Non-need-based:* Academics, Leadership.

KEUKA COLLEGE

Office of Admissions, Keuka Park, NY 14478-0098
Phone: 315-279-5254 **Financial Aid Phone:** 315-279-5646
E-mail: admissions@mail.keuka.edu **CEEB Code:** 2744
Fax: 315-536-5386 **Website:** www.keuka.edu **ACT Code:** 2782

This private school, affiliated with the American Baptist Church, was founded in 1890. It has a 203 acre campus.

RATINGS

Admissions Selectivity Rating: 74   **Fire Safety Rating:** 87   **Green Rating:** 60*

STUDENTS AND FACULTY

Enrollment: 1,738. **Student Body:** 76% female, 24% male, 6% out-of-state, 0% international (3 countries represented). Asian 1%, African American 8%, Caucasian 84%, Hispanic <1%, Native American 1%, Pacific Islander <1%, Two or more races 1%, Race unknown 6%.

Retention and Graduation: 72% freshmen return for sophomore year. 28% grads go on to further study within 1 year. **Faculty:** Student/faculty ratio 15:1. 90 full-time faculty, 70% hold PhDs, 18% are members of minority groups, 61% are women. 0% of classes are taught by teaching assistants.

ACADEMICS

Degrees: Bachelor's; Master's. **Classes:** Most classes have 20–29 students. Most lab/discussion sessions have 10–19 students. **Most popular majors:** Special Education and Teaching, General; Occupational Therapy/Therapist; Business Administration and Management, General. **Special Study Options:** Accelerated program; Cooperative education program; Cross-registration; Double major; Dual enrollment; Independent study; Internships; Student-designed major; Study abroad; Teacher certification program. **Disability Services offered:** Note-taking services; Reader services; Tape recorders; Tutors. **Career services:** Alumni network; Alumni services; Career assessment; Career/job search classes; Internships; Regional alumni.

FACILITIES

Housing: Coed dorms; Cooperative housing; Men's dorms; Special housing for disabled students; Women's dorms; 61% of campus accessible to physically disabled. **Special Academic Facilities/Equipment:** Bird Museum, Lightner Gallery. **Campus Network:** 100% of classrooms, 100% of dorms, 100% of student union, 100% of libraries, 100% of dining areas, 99% of common outdoor areas have wireless network access.

CAMPUS LIFE

Environment: Rural. **Activities:** Choral groups; Concert band; Dance; Drama/theater; Literary magazine; Musical theater; Radio station; Student government; Student newspaper; Student-run film society; Yearbook. 32 registered organizations, 7 honor societies, 2 religious organizations on campus. **Athletics (Intercollegiate):** *Men:* baseball, basketball, cross-country, golf, lacrosse, soccer, tennis. *Women:* basketball, cross-country, golf, lacrosse, soccer, softball, synchronized swimming, tennis, volleyball. **On-Campus Highlights:** The Weed Physical Arts Center (Gym, pool, fitness rooms, coaches offices).

ADMISSIONS

Freshman Academic Profile: Average high school GPA 3.1. 7% in top 10% of high school class, 27% in top 25% of high school class, 75% in top 50% of high school class. 96% from public high schools. **Test Scores:** SAT Math middle 50% range 430–530. SAT EBRW middle 50% range 430–520. ACT middle 50% range 18–23. **Basis for Candidate Selection:** *Very important factors include:* rigor of secondary school record, standardized test scores. *Important factors include:* class rank, academic GPA, application essay, recommendation(s), interview, extracurricular activities. *Other factors include:* talent/ability, alumni/ae relation, volunteer work, work experience, level of applicant's interest. **Freshman Admission Requirements:** High school diploma is required and GED is accepted. *Academic units recommended:* 4 English, 3 math, 3 science, 2 science labs, 3 foreign language, 3 social studies, 2 history. **Freshman Admission Statistics:** 1,371 applied, 83% admitted, 19% enrolled. **Transfer Admission Requirements:** College transcript(s), essay or personal statement. Minimum college GPA of 2.0 required. Lowest grade transferable C. **General Admission Information:** Application fee $50. Non-fall registration accepted.

COSTS AND FINANCIAL AID

Annual tuition $26,490. Room and board $10,590. Required fees $790. Average book and supplies expense $1,500. **Required Forms and Deadlines:** FAFSA. **Notification of Awards:** Applicants will be notified of awards on a rolling basis beginning 3/1. **Types of Aid:** *Need-based scholarships/grants:* College/university scholarship or grant aid from institutional funds; Federal Pell; SEOG; State scholarships/grants. *Loans:* Direct PLUS loans; Direct Subsidized Stafford Loans; Direct Unsubsidized Stafford Loans. **Financial Aid Statistics:** 91% needy freshmen, 80% needy undergrads receive need-based scholarship or grant aid. 83% freshmen, 57% undergrads receive non-need-based scholarship or grant aid. 97% freshmen, 91% undergrads receive need-based self-help aid. 0% freshmen, 0% undergrads receive athletic scholarships. 92% freshmen, 93% undergrads receive any aid. **Criteria awarding aid:** *Need-based:* Academics, Alumni affiliation, Leadership, Minority status, Religious affiliation. *Non-need-based:* Academics, Alumni affiliation, Leadership, Minority status, Religious affiliation.

KEYSTONE COLLEGE

One College Green, La Plume, PA 18440
Phone: 570-945-8111 **Financial Aid Phone:** 570-945-8132
E-mail: admissions@keystone.edu **CEEB Code:** 2351
Fax: 570-945-7916 **Website:** www.keystone.edu **ACT Code:** 2602

This private school was founded in 1868. It has a 270 acre campus.

RATINGS

Admissions Selectivity Rating: 75   Fire Safety Rating: 97   Green Rating: 60*

STUDENTS AND FACULTY

Enrollment: 1,191. **Student Body:** 56% female, 44% male, 20% out-of-state, <1% international (9 countries represented). Asian 1%, African American 13%, Caucasian 67%, Hispanic 8%, Native American 1%, Pacific Islander <1%, Two or more races 3%, Race unknown 7%.
Retention and Graduation: 58% freshmen return for sophomore year. 37% freshmen graduate within 4 years. 46% freshmen graduate within 6 years. 25% grads go on to further study within 1 year. 1% grads pursue arts and sciences degrees. 1% grads pursue law degrees. 1% grads pursue business degrees. 1% grads pursue medical degrees. **Faculty:** Student/faculty ratio 13:1. 45 full-time faculty, 51% hold PhDs, 0% are members of minority groups, 60% are women. 0% of classes are taught by teaching assistants.

ACADEMICS

Degrees: Associate; Bachelor's; Certificate; Master's; Terminal Associate; Transfer Associate. **Classes:** Most classes have 10–19 students. Most lab/discussion sessions have 10–19 students. **Most popular majors:** Education, General; Homeland Security, Law Enforcement, Firefighting and Related Protective Services, Other; Business Administration and Management, General. **Special Study Options:** Distance learning; Double major; Dual enrollment; Honors program; Independent study; Internships; Study abroad; Teacher certification program. **Honors programs:** Freshmen Honor's Program. **Disability Services offered:** Note-taking services; Reader services; Tutors. **Career services:** Alumni network; Alumni services; Career assessment; Career/job search classes; Internships; Regional alumni.

FACILITIES

Housing: Apartments for single students; Coed dorms; Special housing for disabled students; Theme housing; 80% of campus accessible to physically disabled. **Special Academic Facilities/Equipment:** Linder Art Gallery; Cupillari Astronomical Observatory; Willary Water Resource Center.

CAMPUS LIFE

Environment: Rural. **Activities:** Campus Ministries; Choral groups; Concert band; Drama/theater; International Student Organization; Jazz band; Literary magazine; Musical theater; Pep band; Radio station; Student government; Student newspaper; Symphony orchestra. 26 registered organizations, 1 honor society, 1 religious organization on campus. **Athletics (Intercollegiate):** *Men:* baseball, basketball, cross-country, golf, soccer, tennis, track/field (outdoor), track/field (indoor). *Women:* basketball, cross-country, field hockey, soccer, softball, tennis, track/field (outdoor), track/field (indoor), volleyball. **On-Campus Highlights:** Lindner Art Gallery in Miller Library. **Environmental Initiatives:** A recycling program.

ADMISSIONS

Freshman Academic Profile: Average high school GPA 3.0. **Test Scores:** SAT Math middle 50% range 400–510. SAT EBRW middle 50% range 480–560. ACT middle 50% range 14–22. **Basis for Candidate Selection:** *Very important factors include:* rigor of secondary school record, academic GPA. *Important factors include:* interview, talent/ability, character/personal qualities. *Other factors include:* class rank, application essay, standardized test scores, recommendation(s), extracurricular activities, first generation, alumni/ae relation, volunteer work, work experience, level of applicant's interest. **Freshman Admission Requirements:** High school diploma is required and GED is accepted. *Academic units required:* 4 English, 3 math, 2 science, 1 science lab, 2 social studies, 4 academic electives. *Academic units recommended:* 4 English, 3 math, 3 science, 1 science lab, 2 foreign language, 2 social studies, 2 history, 4 academic electives, 1 computer science, 1 visual/performing arts. **Freshman Admission Statistics:** 2,051 applied, 79% admitted, 22% enrolled. **Transfer Admission Requirements:** College transcript(s), essay or personal statement, standardized test scores, statement of good standing from prior institution(s). Minimum college GPA of 2 required. Lowest grade transferable

2. **General Admission Information:** Priority deadline 7/1. Non-fall registration accepted. Admission may be deferred for a maximum of 2 years.

COSTS AND FINANCIAL AID

Annual tuition $14,500. Room and board $11,900. Required fees $2,500. Average book and supplies expense $1,200. **Required Forms and Deadlines:** FAFSA; State aid form. **Notification of Awards:** Applicants will be notified of awards on or about 3/1. **Types of Aid:** *Need-based scholarships/grants:* College/university scholarship or grant aid from institutional funds; Federal Pell; Private scholarships; SEOG; State scholarships/grants. *Loans:* Direct PLUS loans; Direct Subsidized Stafford Loans; Direct Unsubsidized Stafford Loans. **Student Employment:** Federal Work-Study Program available. Institutional employment available. **Financial Aid Statistics:** 88% freshmen, 91% undergrads receive any aid. **Criteria awarding aid:** *Non-need-based:* Academics, Alumni affiliation, Art.

KING'S COLLEGE (PA)

133 North River Street, Wilkes-Barre, PA 18711
Phone: 570-208-5858 **Financial Aid Phone:** 570-208-5868
E-mail: admissions@kings.edu **CEEB Code:** 2353
Fax: 570-208-5971 **Website:** www.kings.edu **ACT Code:** 3604

This private school, affiliated with the Roman Catholic Church, was founded in 1946. It has a 48 acre campus.

RATINGS

Admissions Selectivity Rating: 76   Fire Safety Rating: 96   Green Rating: 62

STUDENTS AND FACULTY

Enrollment: 2,092. **Student Body:** 46% female, 54% male, 28% out-of-state, 9% international (9 countries represented). Asian 2%, African American 4%, Caucasian 69%, Hispanic 9%, Native American <1%, Pacific Islander <1%, Two or more races 3%, Race unknown 4%.
Retention and Graduation: 72% freshmen return for sophomore year. 57% freshmen graduate within 4 years. 64% freshmen graduate within 6 years. 28% grads go on to further study within 1 year. 19% grads pursue arts and sciences degrees. 2% grads pursue law degrees. 5% grads pursue business degrees. 1% grads pursue medical degrees. **Faculty:** Student/faculty ratio 13:1. 139 full-time faculty, 86% hold PhDs, 2% are members of minority groups, 53% are women. 0% of classes are taught by teaching assistants.

ACADEMICS

Degrees: Bachelor's; Master's; Post-bachelor's certificate. **Classes:** Most classes have 10–19 students. Most lab/discussion sessions have 10–19 students. **Most popular majors:** Physician Assistant; Accounting; Business Administration and Management, General. **Special Study Options:** Accelerated program; Cross-registration; Distance learning; Double major; Dual enrollment; English as a Second Language (ESL); Honors program; Independent study; Internships; Student-designed major; Study abroad; Teacher certification program; Weekend college. **Disability Services offered:** Note-taking services; Reader services; Tape recorders; Tutors. **Career services:** Alumni network; Alumni services; Career assessment; Career/job search classes; Internships; Regional alumni.

FACILITIES

Housing: Apartments for single students; Coed dorms; Men's dorms; Special housing for disabled students; Women's dorms; 99% of campus accessible to physically disabled. **Special Academic Facilities/Equipment:** Electron microscope, rooftop greenhouse, molecular biology lab, computer graphics lab.

CAMPUS LIFE

Environment: City. **Activities:** Campus Ministries; Choral groups; Dance; Drama/theater; International Student Organization; Literary magazine; Music ensembles; Pep band; Radio station; Student government; Student newspaper; Yearbook. 50 registered organizations, 22 honor societies, 2 religious organizations on campus. **Athletics (Intercollegiate):** *Men:* baseball, basketball, cheerleading, cross-country, football, golf, lacrosse, soccer, swimming, tennis, wrestling. *Women:* basketball, cheerleading, cross-country, field hockey, lacrosse, soccer, softball, swimming, tennis, volleyball. **On-Campus Highlights:** Sheehy-Farmer Campus Center.

ADMISSIONS

Freshman Academic Profile: Average high school GPA 3.4. 15% in top 10% of high school class, 35% in top 25% of high school class, 67% in top 50% of high school class. 83% from public high schools. **Test Scores:** SAT Math

middle 50% range 490–610. SAT EBRW middle 50% range 500–610. ACT middle 50% range 20–28. **Basis for Candidate Selection:** *Very important factors include:* rigor of secondary school record, class rank, academic GPA. *Important factors include:* application essay, standardized test scores, character/personal qualities. *Other factors include:* recommendation(s), interview, extracurricular activities, alumni/ae relation, volunteer work, work experience. **Freshman Admission Requirements:** High school diploma is required and GED is accepted. *Academic units required:* 4 English, 3 math, 3 science, 2 science labs, 2 foreign language, 3 social studies, 1 history. *Academic units recommended:* 4 English, 4 math, 4 science, 2 science labs, 4 foreign language, 3 social studies, 1 history, 2 academic electives, 2 computer science. **Freshman Admission Statistics:** 4,176 applied, 81% admitted, 17% enrolled. **Transfer Admission Requirements:** High school transcript, college transcript(s), essay or personal statement. Minimum college GPA of 2.0 required. Lowest grade transferable C. **General Admission Information:** Application fee $30. Non-fall registration accepted. Admission may be deferred for a maximum of 1 year.

COSTS AND FINANCIAL AID

Annual tuition $36,774. Room and board $13,464. Required fees $1,950. Average book and supplies expense $1,300. **Required Forms and Deadlines:** FAFSA. **Notification of Awards:** Applicants will be notified of awards on a rolling basis beginning 3/1. **Types of Aid:** *Need-based scholarships/grants:* College/university scholarship or grant aid from institutional funds; Federal Pell; Private scholarships; SEOG; State scholarships/grants. *Loans:* Direct PLUS loans; Direct Subsidized Stafford Loans; Direct Unsubsidized Stafford Loans. **Student Employment:** Federal Work-Study Program available. Institutional employment available. **Financial Aid Statistics:** 100% needy freshmen, 100% needy undergrads receive need-based scholarship or grant aid. 11% freshmen, 11% undergrads receive non-need-based scholarship or grant aid. 86% freshmen, 85% undergrads receive need-based self-help aid. 0% freshmen, 0% undergrads receive athletic scholarships. 97% freshmen, 92% undergrads receive any aid. 83% undergrads borrow to pay for school. Average cumulative indebtedness $40,818. **Criteria awarding aid:** *Non-need-based:* Academics, Leadership.

KING UNIVERSITY

1350 King College Road, Bristol, TN 37620-2699
Phone: 423-652-4861 **Financial Aid Phone:** 423-652-4728
E-mail: admissions@king.edu **CEEB Code:** 1371
Fax: 423-652-4727 **Website:** www.king.edu **ACT Code:** 3970

This private school, affiliated with the Presbyterian Church, was founded in 1867. It has a 135 acre campus.

RATINGS

Admissions Selectivity Rating: 83   Fire Safety Rating: 95   Green Rating: 60*

STUDENTS AND FACULTY

Enrollment: 1,561. **Student Body:** 65% female, 35% male, 41% out-of-state, 3% international (27 countries represented). Asian 1%, African American 6%, Caucasian 82%, Hispanic 2%, Native American 1%, Pacific Islander <1%, Two or more races 1%, Race unknown 4%.
Retention and Graduation: 67% freshmen return for sophomore year. 48% freshmen graduate within 4 years. 58% freshmen graduate within 6 years. 20% grads go on to further study within 1 year. 8% grads pursue arts and sciences degrees. 1% grads pursue law degrees. 6% grads pursue business degrees. 1% grads pursue medical degrees. **Faculty:** Student/faculty ratio 13:1. 88 full-time faculty, 70% hold PhDs, 0% are members of minority groups, 64% are women. 0% of classes are taught by teaching assistants.

ACADEMICS

Degrees: Associate; Bachelor's; Doctoral degree—professional practice; Master's; Post-master's certificate. **Classes:** Most classes have fewer than 10 students. Most lab/discussion sessions have 10–19 students. **Most popular majors:** Psychology; Health Professions And Related Programs; Business, Management, Marketing, And Related Support Services. **Special Study Options:** Distance learning; Double major; Dual enrollment; English as a Second Language (ESL); Honors program; Independent study; Internships; Liberal arts/career combination; Student-designed major; Study abroad; Teacher certification program. **Honors programs:** The Jack E. Snider Honors Center allows students to interact with other students and faculty of diverse interests. Participants take selected courses that stimulate thinking and allow for creative response while engaging in special opportunities such as meeting with faculty members and outside guests. Other courses may allow honors students, for extra credit, to develop more extensive research projects. The honors seminars also examine ideas from a variety of academic disciplines. Participants serve both the campus and the larger community by tutoring and mentoring and are encouraged to explore other perspectives through study abroad experiences. **Disability Services offered:** Note-taking services; Reader services; Tape recorders; Tutors. **Career services:** Career assessment; Career/job search classes; Internships.

FACILITIES

Housing: Men's dorms; Women's dorms; 53% of campus accessible to physically disabled. **Special Academic Facilities/Equipment:** Electron microscope; Burke Observatory; Sign of the George Press; Nuclear Physics Lab; One-Button Studio; Dark Room. **Campus Network:** 100% of classrooms, 100% of dorms, 100% of student union, 100% of libraries, 100% of dining areas, 100% of common outdoor areas have wireless network access.

CAMPUS LIFE

Environment: Town. **Activities:** Campus Ministries; Choral groups; Concert band; Dance; Drama/theater; International Student Organization; Jazz band; Literary magazine; Music ensembles; Musical theater; Student government; Student newspaper. 25 registered organizations, 5 honor societies, 1 religious organization on campus. **Athletics (Intercollegiate):** *Men:* baseball, basketball, bowling, cheerleading, cross-country, cycling, diving, golf, soccer, swimming, tennis, track/field (outdoor), track/field (indoor), wrestling. *Women:* basketball, bowling, cheerleading, cross-country, cycling, diving, golf, soccer, softball, swimming, tennis, track/field (outdoor), track/field (indoor), volleyball, wrestling. **On-Campus Highlights:** Student Center/Athletic Complex.

ADMISSIONS

Freshman Academic Profile: Average high school GPA 3.5. 19% in top 10% of high school class, 41% in top 25% of high school class, 75% in top 50% of high school class. 88% from public high schools. **Test Scores:** SAT Math middle 50% range 1010–1185. SAT EBRW middle 50% range 500–605. ACT middle 50% range 20–25. **Basis for Candidate Selection:** *Very important factors include:* academic GPA. *Important factors include:* rigor of secondary school record. *Other factors include:* application essay, recommendation(s). **Freshman Admission Requirements:** High school diploma is required and GED is accepted. *Academic units required:* 4 English, 3 math, 2 science, 2 science labs, 2 foreign language, 1 social studies, 1 history, 4 academic electives. *Academic units recommended:* 4 English, 4 math, 4 science, 4 science labs, 2 foreign language, 2 social studies, 2 history, 2 academic electives. **Freshman Admission Statistics:** 967 applied, 61% admitted, 35% enrolled. **Transfer Admission Requirements:** College transcript(s). Minimum college GPA of 2.0 required. Lowest grade transferable C-. **General Admission Information:** Non-fall registration accepted.

COSTS AND FINANCIAL AID

Annual tuition $30,106. Room and board $9,386. Required fees $1,734. Average book and supplies expense $1,560. **Required Forms and Deadlines:** FAFSA. **Notification of Awards:** Applicants will be notified of awards on a rolling basis beginning 12/15. *Types of Aid: Need-based scholarships/grants:* College/university scholarship or grant aid from institutional funds; Federal Pell; Private scholarships; SEOG; State scholarships/grants. *Loans:* Direct PLUS loans; Direct Subsidized Stafford Loans; Direct Unsubsidized Stafford Loans. **Student Employment:** Federal Work-Study Program available. Institutional employment available. **Financial Aid Statistics:** 99% needy freshmen, 85% needy undergrads receive need-based scholarship or grant aid. 14% freshmen, 8% undergrads receive non-need-based scholarship or grant aid. 77% freshmen, 78% undergrads receive need-based self-help aid. 14% freshmen, 9% undergrads receive athletic scholarships. 100% freshmen, 97% undergrads receive any aid. 68% undergrads borrow to pay for school. Average cumulative indebtedness $29,417. **Criteria awarding aid:** *Need-based:* Alumni affiliation. *Non-need-based:* Academics, Art, Athletics, Job skills, Music/drama, State/district residency.

KNOX COLLEGE

2 East South Street, Campus Box 148, Galesburg, IL 61401
Phone: 309-341-7100 **Financial Aid Phone:** 309-341-7149
E-mail: admission@knox.edu **CEEB Code:** 1372
Fax: 309-341-7070 **Website:** www.knox.edu **ACT Code:** 1052

This private school was founded in 1837. It has a 82 acre campus.

RATINGS

Admissions Selectivity Rating: 85   **Fire Safety Rating:** 96   **Green Rating:** 92

STUDENTS AND FACULTY

Enrollment: 1,229. **Student Body:** 57% female, 43% male, 46% out-of-state, 19% international (48 countries represented). Asian 5%, African American 8%, Caucasian 46%, Hispanic 14%, Native American <1%, Pacific Islander <1%, Two or more races 6%, Race unknown 2%.
Retention and Graduation: 81% freshmen return for sophomore year. 65% freshmen graduate within 4 years. 74% freshmen graduate within 6 years. 20% grads go on to further study within 1 year. **Faculty:** Student/faculty ratio 10:1. 108 full-time faculty, 93% hold PhDs, 14% are members of minority groups, 39% are women. 0% of classes are taught by teaching assistants.

ACADEMICS

Degrees: Bachelor's. **Classes:** Most classes have 10–19 students. Most lab/discussion sessions have 10–19 students. **Most popular majors:** Creative Writing; Biology/Biological Sciences, General; Research and Experimental Psychology, Other. **Special Study Options:** Cooperative education program; Double major; English as a Second Language (ESL); Honors program; Independent study; Internships; Liberal arts/career combination; Student-designed major; Study abroad; Teacher certification program. **Honors programs:** Specialized independent research, scholarship, and creative work are supported by our Honors Program, which may be undertaken as early as junior year, though most projects are conducted during the senior year. Candidates for Honors obtain the endorsement from their department and complete advanced study under the supervision and guidance of an interdisciplinary faculty committee. At the end of their year-long research projects, which comprise fully a third of the student's coursework during the year, students defend their thesis or creative project or have it critiqued before a qualified outside examiner, modeling the dissertation defense of many grad programs. Often, the Honors experience can jump-start a meaningful career or admission into a top-notch graduate program. **Disability Services offered:** Note-taking services; Reader services; Tape recorders; Tutors. **Career services:** Alumni network; Alumni services; Career assessment; Career/job search classes; Internships; Regional alumni.

FACILITIES

Housing: Apartments for single students; Coed dorms; Fraternity/sorority housing; Men's dorms; Special housing for disabled students; Special housing for international students; Theme housing; Women's dorms; 55% of campus accessible to physically disabled. **Special Academic Facilities/Equipment:** The Umbeck Science-Mathematics Center is home to an electron microscopy lab, a greenhouse, and a science makerspace that includes a 3D printer, laser cutter, and computer-controlled milling machine. The Ford Center for Fine Arts houses a black-box studio theatre, a large-scale production theatre that includes a revolving stage, a recital hall, and art gallery. The Whitcomb Art Center, Knox's new art and art history building, includes studios for painting, printmaking, design, sculpture, ceramics, drawing, and digital art, as well as metalworking and woodworking shops, a seminar room, and dedicated studio space for seniors working on capstone projects.

CAMPUS LIFE

Environment: Town. **Activities:** Choral groups; Dance; Drama/theater; International Student Organization; Jazz band; Literary magazine; Model UN; Music ensembles; Radio station; Student government; Student newspaper. 90 registered organizations, 13 honor societies, 5 religious organizations, 6 fraternities, 4 sororities on campus. **Athletics (Intercollegiate):** *Men:* baseball, basketball, cross-country, football, golf, soccer, swimming, tennis, track/field (outdoor), track/field (indoor), wrestling. *Women:* basketball, cross-country, golf, soccer, softball, swimming, tennis, track/field (outdoor), track/field (indoor), volleyball. **On-Campus Highlights:** Taylor Lounge & Games

Room. **Environmental Initiatives:** Knox continues to make great strides in waste recovery. This is exemplified by the sharing culture on Knox' campus. Initiatives include a car-share program, a student-run bike share, and the institutionalization of the campus Share Shop and Office Supply Share, a place to donate gently used clothes and goods for other students to be able to take without charge. These initiatives find a new home for items that might have been destined for the landfill and encourage alternative transportation options to students, faculty, and staff. Move out at Knox features the "There's No Away" campaign that collects donations from students as they are packing to leave for the summer. This past year we collected just under 6 tons of still-good items that were donated to local thrift stores, properly disposed of or recycled, or sorted into the campus Share Shop and Office Supply Share. Knox also finds ways to divert other items from the landfill. The non-traditional recycling program collects hard to recycle items, from batteries to toothbrushes, and has found places that collect them for recycling. Food waste is also combated. Last year the Knox chapter of the Food Recovery Network diverted and donated more than 9,000 pounds of food to local organizations. Also, the annual zero waste lunch at Commencement continues to be a success. In 2018 the event served 1,500 guests and created less than a pound of landfill-only waste.

ADMISSIONS

Freshman Academic Profile: 35% in top 10% of high school class, 69% in top 25% of high school class, 97% in top 50% of high school class. 70% from public high schools. **Test Scores:** SAT Math middle 50% range 540–680. SAT EBRW middle 50% range 550–670. ACT middle 50% range 24–31. **Basis for Candidate Selection:** *Very important factors include:* rigor of secondary school record, academic GPA. *Important factors include:* class rank, application essay, recommendation(s). *Other factors include:* standardized test scores, interview, extracurricular activities, talent/ability, character/personal qualities, first generation, alumni/ae relation, geographical residence, state residency, racial/ethnic status, volunteer work, work experience, level of applicant's interest. **Freshman Admission Requirements:** High school diploma is required and GED is accepted. *Academic units recommended:* 4 English, 4 math, 3 science, 2 science labs, 3 foreign language, 2 social studies, 1 history. **Freshman Admission Statistics:** 3,397 applied, 68% admitted, 14% enrolled. **Transfer Admission Requirements:** High school transcript, college transcript(s), essay or personal statement, statement of good standing from prior institution(s). Minimum college GPA of 3.0 required. Lowest grade transferable C. **General Admission Information:** Application fee $50. Priority deadline 11/1. Regular application deadline 1/15. Non-fall registration accepted. Admission may be deferred for a maximum of 1 year.

COSTS AND FINANCIAL AID

Annual tuition $49,815. Room and board $10,170. Required fees $789. Average book and supplies expense $900. **Required Forms and Deadlines:** FAFSA; Institution's own financial aid form. **Notification of Awards:** Applicants will be notified of awards on a rolling basis beginning 12/1. **Types of Aid:** *Need-based scholarships/grants:* College/university scholarship or grant aid from institutional funds; Federal Pell; Private scholarships; SEOG; State scholarships/grants. *Loans:* Direct PLUS loans; Direct Subsidized Stafford Loans; Direct Unsubsidized Stafford Loans. **Student Employment:** Federal Work-Study Program available. Institutional employment available. **Financial Aid Statistics:** 100% needy freshmen, 98% needy undergrads receive need-based scholarship or grant aid. 29% freshmen, 20% undergrads receive non-need-based scholarship or grant aid. 100% freshmen, 87% undergrads receive need-based self-help aid. 0% freshmen, 0% undergrads receive athletic scholarships. 99% freshmen, 98% undergrads receive any aid. 61% undergrads borrow to pay for school. Average cumulative indebtedness $29,988. **Criteria awarding aid:** *Non-need-based:* Academics, Art, Leadership, Music/drama.

KUTZTOWN UNIVERSITY OF PENNSYLVANIA

Admissions Office, Kutztown, PA 19530-0730
Phone: 610-683-4060 **Financial Aid Phone:** 610-683-4032
E-mail: admissions@kutztown.edu **CEEB Code:** 2653
Fax: 610-683-1375 **Website:** www.kutztown.edu **ACT Code:** 3706

This public school was founded in 1866. It has a 289 acre campus.

RATINGS

Admissions Selectivity Rating: 74   **Fire Safety Rating:** 98   **Green Rating:** 60*

STUDENTS AND FACULTY

Enrollment: 6,862. **Student Body:** 55% female, 45% male, 12% out-of-state, 1% international (32 countries represented). Asian 2%, African American 8%,

Caucasian 74%, Hispanic 9%, Native American <1%, Pacific Islander <1%, Two or more races 3%, Race unknown 3%.
Retention and Graduation: 74% freshmen return for sophomore year. 38% freshmen graduate within 4 years. 54% freshmen graduate within 6 years. 12% grads go on to further study within 1 year. **Faculty:** Student/faculty ratio 17:1. 376 full-time faculty, 87% hold PhDs, 20% are members of minority groups, 48% are women. 0% of classes are taught by teaching assistants.

ACADEMICS

Degrees: Bachelor's; Certificate; Doctoral degree research/scholarship; Master's; Post-bachelor's certificate; Post-master's certificate. **Classes:** Most classes have 20–29 students. Most lab/discussion sessions have 20–29 students. **Most popular majors:** Education; Business Administration and Management, General. **Special Study Options:** Cross-registration; Distance learning; Double major; Dual enrollment; Honors program; Independent study; Internships; Liberal arts/career combination; Student-designed major; Study abroad; Teacher certification program. **Honors programs:** 1) University Honors Program; 2) Various Honor Societies. **Disability Services offered:** Note-taking services; Reader services; Tape recorders; Tutors. **Career services:** Alumni network; Alumni services; Career assessment; Career/job search classes; Internships; Regional alumni.

FACILITIES

Housing: Apartments for married students; Apartments for single students; Coed dorms; Cooperative housing; Women's dorms; 90% of campus accessible to physically disabled. **Special Academic Facilities/Equipment:** Art Gallery, German Cultural Heritage Center, Early Childhood Learning Center, Cartography Lab, Observatory, Planetarium, Daycare Center. **Campus Network:** 90% of classrooms, 100% of dorms, 100% of student union, 100% of libraries, 100% of dining areas, 50% of common outdoor areas have wireless network access.

CAMPUS LIFE

Environment: Rural. **Activities:** Campus Ministries; Choral groups; Concert band; Dance; Drama/theater; International Student Organization; Jazz band; Literary magazine; Marching band; Model UN; Music ensembles; Musical theater; Radio station; Student government; Student newspaper; Student-run film society; Symphony orchestra; Television station; Yearbook. 239 registered organizations, 13 honor societies, 7 religious organizations, 10 fraternities, 6 sororities on campus. **Athletics (Intercollegiate):** *Men:* baseball, basketball, cross-country, football, tennis, track/field (outdoor), track/field (indoor), wrestling. *Women:* basketball, bowling, cross-country, field hockey, golf, lacrosse, soccer, softball, swimming, tennis, track/field (outdoor), track/field (indoor), volleyball. **On-Campus Highlights:** Taylor and Burnes Gourmet Coffee. **Environmental Initiatives:** Recycling program.

ADMISSIONS

Freshman Academic Profile: Average high school GPA 3.2. 8% in top 10% of high school class, 27% in top 25% of high school class, 60% in top 50% of high school class. 92% from public high schools. **Test Scores:** SAT Math middle 50% range 480–560. SAT EBRW middle 50% range 490–580. ACT middle 50% range 18–24. **Basis for Candidate Selection:** *Very important factors include:* rigor of secondary school record, class rank, standardized test scores. *Other factors include:* academic GPA, recommendation(s), talent/ability. **Freshman Admission Requirements:** High school diploma is required and GED is accepted. *Academic units required:* 4 English, 3 math, 3 science, 2 science labs, 3 social studies. **Freshman Admission Statistics:** 6,893 applied, 89% admitted, 23% enrolled. **Transfer Admission Requirements:** College transcript(s), statement of good standing from prior institution(s). Minimum college GPA of 2.0 required. Lowest grade transferable C-. **General Admission Information:** Application fee $35. Priority deadline 12/1. Non-fall registration accepted. Admission may be deferred for a maximum of 1 year.

COSTS AND FINANCIAL AID

Annual in-state tuition $7,716. Annual out-of-state tuition $11,574. Room and board $10,434. Required fees $3,547. Average book and supplies expense $1,440. **Required Forms and Deadlines:** FAFSA. **Notification of Awards:** Applicants will be notified of awards on a rolling basis beginning 3/30. **Types of Aid:** *Need-based scholarships/grants:* College/university scholarship or grant aid from institutional funds; Federal Pell; Private scholarships; SEOG; State scholarships/grants. *Loans:* Direct PLUS loans; Direct Subsidized Stafford Loans; Direct Unsubsidized Stafford Loans. **Student Employment:** Federal Work-Study Program available. Institutional employment available. **Financial Aid Statistics:** 62% needy freshmen, 62% needy undergrads receive need-based scholarship or grant aid. 72% freshmen, 46% undergrads receive non-need-based scholarship or grant aid. 83% freshmen, 85% undergrads receive need-based self-help aid. 4% freshmen, 4% undergrads receive athletic scholarships. 75% freshmen, 87% undergrads receive any aid. 84% undergrads borrow to pay for school. Average cumulative indebtedness $40,592. **Criteria awarding aid:** *Need-based:* Academics. *Non-need-based:* Academics, Art, Athletics, Leadership, Minority status, Music/drama.

LAFAYETTE COLLEGE

730 High Street, Easton, PA 18042
Phone: 610-330-5100 **Financial Aid Phone:** 610 330-5055
E-mail: admissions@lafayette.edu **CEEB Code:** 2361
Fax: 610-330-5355 **Website:** http://www.lafayette.edu/

This private school was founded in 1826. It has a 340 acre campus.

RATINGS
Admissions Selectivity Rating: 94   Fire Safety Rating: 91   Green Rating: 81

STUDENTS AND FACULTY
Enrollment: 2,616. **Student Body:** 52% female, 48% male, 81% out-of-state, 10% international (57 countries represented). Asian 4%, African American 5%, Caucasian 66%, Hispanic 7%, Native American 0%, Pacific Islander 0%, Two or more races 3%, Race unknown 5%.
Retention and Graduation: 93% freshmen return for sophomore year. 83% freshmen graduate within 4 years. 87% freshmen graduate within 6 years. 16% grads go on to further study within 1 year. 2% grads pursue law degrees. 2% grads pursue medical degrees. **Faculty:** Student/faculty ratio 10:1. 239 full-time faculty, 98% hold PhDs, 20% are members of minority groups, 42% are women. 0% of classes are taught by teaching assistants.

ACADEMICS
Degrees: Bachelor's. **Classes:** Most classes have 10–19 students. Most lab/discussion sessions have 10–19 students. **Most popular majors:** Social Sciences, Other; Biology/Biological Sciences, General; Engineering, General. **Special Study Options:** Cross-registration; Double major; Dual enrollment; Exchange student program (domestic); Honors program; Independent study; Internships; Student-designed major; Study abroad. **Disability Services offered:** Tutors. **Career services:** Alumni network; Alumni services; Career assessment; Career/job search classes; Internships; Regional alumni.

FACILITIES
Housing: Apartments for single students; Coed dorms; Fraternity/sorority housing; Men's dorms; Special housing for disabled students; Theme housing; Wellness housing; Women's dorms. **Special Academic Facilities/Equipment:** Art and geological museums, center for the arts, engineering labs, INSTRON materials testing machine, electron microscopes, transform nuclear magnetic resonance spectrometer, computerized gas chromatograph/mass spectrometer.

CAMPUS LIFE
Environment: City. **Activities:** Campus Ministries; Choral groups; Concert band; Dance; Drama/theater; International Student Organization; Jazz band; Literary magazine; Model UN; Music ensembles; Musical theater; Pep band; Radio station; Student government; Student newspaper; Student-run film society; Symphony orchestra; Yearbook. 250 registered organizations, 17 honor societies, 8 religious organizations, 3 fraternities, 6 sororities on campus. **Athletics (Intercollegiate):** *Men:* baseball, basketball, cheerleading, crew/rowing, cross-country, diving, equestrian sports, fencing, football, golf, gymnastics, ice hockey, lacrosse, soccer, softball, swimming, tennis, track/field (outdoor), track/field (indoor), volleyball, wrestling. *Women:* basketball, cheerleading, crew/rowing, cross-country, diving, equestrian sports, fencing, field hockey, golf, gymnastics, softball, swimming, tennis, track/field (outdoor), track/field (indoor), volleyball. **On-Campus Highlights:** Skillman and Kirby Libraries. **Environmental Initiatives:** In addition to signing American College and University Presidents Climate Commitment, three undertakings summarize the College's efforts towards responsible stewardship of the environment: Recycling, including composting; purchases of materials/goods made from recycled materials and/or virgin material that is recyclable and produced from renewable sources.

ADMISSIONS
Freshman Academic Profile: Average high school GPA 3.5. 52% in top 10% of high school class, 78% in top 25% of high school class, 96% in

top 50% of high school class. 53% from public high schools. **Test Scores:** SAT Math middle 50% range 630–735. SAT EBRW middle 50% range 620–700. ACT middle 50% range 27–32. **Basis for Candidate Selection:** *Very important factors include:* rigor of secondary school record, academic GPA. *Important factors include:* class rank, application essay, standardized test scores, recommendation(s), interview, extracurricular activities, talent/ability, character/personal qualities. *Other factors include:* first generation, alumni/ae relation, geographical residence, racial/ethnic status, volunteer work, work experience, level of applicant's interest. **Freshman Admission Requirements:** High school diploma or equivalent is not required *Academic units recommended:* 4 English, 3 math, 2 science, 2 science labs, 2 foreign language, 5 academic electives. **Freshman Admission Statistics:** 9,237 applied, 29% admitted, 27% enrolled. **Transfer Admission Requirements:** High school transcript, college transcript(s), essay or personal statement, statement of good standing from prior institution(s). Lowest grade transferable C. **General Admission Information:** Application fee $65. Regular application deadline 1/15. Admission may be deferred for a maximum of 1 year.

COSTS AND FINANCIAL AID
Annual tuition $54,512. Room and board $16,264. Required fees $1,240. Average book and supplies expense $1,000. **Required Forms and Deadlines:** CSS/Financial Aid PROFILE; FAFSA; Noncustodial PROFILE. **Notification of Awards:** Applicants will be notified of awards on or about 4/1. **Types of Aid:** *Need-based scholarships/grants:* College/university scholarship or grant aid from institutional funds; Federal Pell; Private scholarships; SEOG; State scholarships/grants. *Loans:* Direct PLUS loans; Direct Subsidized Stafford Loans; Direct Unsubsidized Stafford Loans. **Student Employment:** Federal Work-Study Program available. Institutional employment available. **Financial Aid Statistics:** 94% needy freshmen, 96% needy undergrads receive need-based scholarship or grant aid. 21% freshmen, 16% undergrads receive non-need-based scholarship or grant aid. 85% freshmen, 90% undergrads receive need-based self-help aid. 8% freshmen, 8% undergrads receive athletic scholarships. 59% freshmen, 57% undergrads receive any aid. 39% undergrads borrow to pay for school. Average cumulative indebtedness $26,341. **Criteria awarding aid:** *Need-based:* Academics, Athletics, Leadership. *Non-need-based:* Academics, Athletics, Leadership.

LAGRANGE COLLEGE

Office of Admission, LaGrange, GA 30240
Phone: 706-880-8005 **Financial Aid Phone:** 888-253-9918
E-mail: lgcadmis@lagrange.edu **CEEB Code:** 5362
Fax: 706-880-8010 **Website:** www.lagrange.edu **ACT Code:** 834

This private school, affiliated with the Methodist Church, was founded in 1831. It has a 120 acre campus.

RATINGS
Admissions Selectivity Rating: 83   Fire Safety Rating: 60*   Green Rating: 60*

STUDENTS AND FACULTY
Enrollment: 860. **Student Body:** 55% female, 45% male, 11% out-of-state, 2% international (10 countries represented). Asian 1%, African American 22%, Caucasian 72%, Hispanic 2%, Native American <1%, Race unknown 1%.
Retention and Graduation: 71% freshmen return for sophomore year.
Faculty: Student/faculty ratio 10:1. 65 full-time faculty, 83% hold PhDs, 0% are members of minority groups, 48% are women. 0% of classes are taught by teaching assistants.

ACADEMICS
Degrees: Associate; Bachelor's; Master's. **Classes:** Most classes have 10–19 students. Most lab/discussion sessions have 10–19 students. **Most popular majors:** Organizational Behavior Studies; Business Administration and Management, General; Teacher Education, Multiple Levels. **Special Study Options:** Double major; Dual enrollment; Independent study; Internships; Liberal arts/career combination; Study abroad; Teacher certification program. **Career services:** Alumni network; Alumni services; Career assessment; Career/job search classes; Internships.

FACILITIES
Housing: Apartments for single students; Coed dorms; Fraternity/sorority housing; Men's dorms; Theme housing; Women's dorms; 75% of campus accessible to physically disabled. **Special Academic Facilities/Equipment:** Lamar Dodd Art Center, Price Theater, Callaway Auditorium. **Campus**

Network: 50% of classrooms, 80% of dorms, 100% of student union, 100% of libraries, 33% of dining areas, 10% of common outdoor areas have wireless network access.

CAMPUS LIFE

Environment: Village. **Activities:** Campus Ministries; Choral groups; Drama/theater; International Student Organization; Literary magazine; Music ensembles; Musical theater; Pep band; Student government; Student newspaper; Symphony orchestra; Yearbook. 49 registered organizations, 11 honor societies, 8 religious organizations, 3 fraternities, 6 sororities on campus. **Athletics (Intercollegiate):** *Men:* baseball, basketball, cross-country, football, golf, soccer, swimming, tennis. *Women:* basketball, cheerleading, cross-country, soccer, softball, swimming, tennis, volleyball. **On-Campus Highlights:** Turner Student Center. **Environmental Initiatives:** Building a LEED library.

ADMISSIONS

Freshman Academic Profile: Average high school GPA 3.5. 25% in top 10% of high school class, 54% in top 25% of high school class, 92% in top 50% of high school class. **Test Scores:** SAT Math middle 50% range 460–570. SAT EBRW middle 50% range 460–570. ACT middle 50% range 20–25. **Basis for Candidate Selection:** *Very important factors include:* academic GPA, standardized test scores, character/personal qualities. *Important factors include:* class rank, recommendation(s), extracurricular activities. *Other factors include:* rigor of secondary school record, application essay, interview, talent/ability, alumni/ae relation, geographical residence, volunteer work. **Freshman Admission Requirements:** High school diploma is required and GED is accepted. *Academic units required:* 4 English, 4 math, 3 science, 3 social studies. *Academic units recommended:* 4 English, 4 math, 3 science, 2 foreign language, 3 social studies. **Freshman Admission Statistics:** 1,342 applied, 65% admitted, 27% enrolled. **Transfer Admission Requirements:** College transcript(s), statement of good standing from prior institution(s). Minimum college GPA of 2.0 required. Lowest grade transferable 1. **General Admission Information:** Application fee $30. Priority deadline 3/1. Non-fall registration accepted. Admission may be deferred for a maximum of one term.

COSTS AND FINANCIAL AID

Annual tuition $19,900. Room and board $8,168. **Required Forms and Deadlines:** FAFSA; State aid form. **Notification of Awards:** Applicants will be notified of awards on a rolling basis beginning 3/15. **Types of Aid:** *Need-based scholarships/grants:* College/university scholarship or grant aid from institutional funds; Federal Pell; Private scholarships; SEOG; State scholarships/grants. **Student Employment:** Federal Work-Study Program available. Institutional employment available. **Financial Aid Statistics:** 100% needy freshmen, 100% needy undergrads receive need-based scholarship or grant aid. 24% freshmen, 17% undergrads receive non-need-based scholarship or grant aid. 69% freshmen, 77% undergrads receive need-based self-help aid. 0% freshmen, 0% undergrads receive athletic scholarships. **Criteria awarding aid:** *Need-based:* Minority status, Religious affiliation. *Non-need-based:* Academics, Art, Leadership, Music/drama, Religious affiliation, State/district residency.

LAKE ERIE COLLEGE

391 West Washington Street, Painesville, OH 44077-3389
Phone: (440) 375-7050 **Financial Aid Phone:** 440-375-7100
E-mail: admissions@lec.edu **CEEB Code:** 1391
Fax: (440) 375-7005 **Website:** www.lec.edu **ACT Code:** 3288

This private school was founded in 1856. It has a 48 acre campus.

RATINGS

Admissions Selectivity Rating: 80   **Fire Safety Rating:** 93   **Green Rating:** 60*

STUDENTS AND FACULTY

Enrollment: 750. **Student Body:** 48% female, 52% male, 26% out-of-state, 4% international. Asian 1%, African American 14%, Caucasian 72%, Hispanic 2%, Native American 1%, Pacific Islander 0%, Two or more races 3%, Race unknown 3%.
Retention and Graduation: 70% freshmen return for sophomore year. 23% grads go on to further study within 1 year. **Faculty:** Student/faculty ratio 14:1. 42 full-time faculty, 74% hold PhDs, 0% are members of minority groups, 64% are women. 0% of classes are taught by teaching assistants.

ACADEMICS

Degrees: Bachelor's; Master's; Post-bachelor's certificate. **Classes:** Most classes have 10–19 students. **Most popular majors:** Biology/Biological Sciences, General; Business Administration and Management, General; Psychology, General. **Special Study Options:** Accelerated program; Cross-registration; Double major; Dual enrollment; Honors program; Independent study; Internships; Liberal arts/career combination; Student-designed major; Study abroad; Teacher certification program. **Honors programs:** Mortar Board. **Disability Services offered:** Tape recorders; Tutors. **Career services:** Alumni network; Alumni services; Career assessment; Career/job search classes; Internships.

FACILITIES

Housing: Apartments for married students; Apartments for single students; Coed dorms; Men's dorms; Women's dorms; 90% of campus accessible to physically disabled. **Special Academic Facilities/Equipment:** Pheasant Run Airport, Equestrian Facility. **Campus Network:** 100% of dorms, 100% of student union, 100% of libraries, 100% of dining areas have wireless network access.

CAMPUS LIFE

Environment: Town. **Activities:** Choral groups; Dance; Drama/theater; International Student Organization; Music ensembles; Student government. 31 registered organizations, 3 honor societies, 1 religious organization, 1 fraternity, 1 sorority on campus. **Athletics (Intercollegiate):** *Men:* baseball, basketball, cross-country, equestrian sports, football, golf, soccer. *Women:* basketball, cross-country, equestrian sports, soccer, softball, volleyball. **On-Campus Highlights:** College Hall. **Environmental Initiatives:** Recent initiation of Sustainability committee.

ADMISSIONS

Freshman Academic Profile: Average high school GPA 3.1. 91% from public high schools. **Test Scores:** SAT Math middle 50% range 420–510. SAT EBRW middle 50% range 420–510. ACT middle 50% range 18–22. **Basis for Candidate Selection:** *Very important factors include:* rigor of secondary school record, academic GPA, recommendation(s), interview, character/personal qualities. *Important factors include:* class rank, application essay, standardized test scores, extracurricular activities, talent/ability. *Other factors include:* alumni/ae relation, volunteer work, work experience, level of applicant's interest. **Freshman Admission Requirements:** High school diploma is required and GED is accepted. *Academic units required:* 4 English, 3 math, 3 science, 2 science labs, 2 foreign language, 3 social studies. *Academic units recommended:* 4 English, 3 math, 3 science, 2 science labs, 2 foreign language, 3 social studies. **Freshman Admission Statistics:** 1,485 applied, 63% admitted, 23% enrolled. **Transfer Admission Requirements:** High school transcript, college transcript(s), statement of good standing from prior institution(s). Minimum college GPA of 2.0 required. Lowest grade transferable C. **General Admission Information:** Application fee $30. Priority deadline 5/1. Regular application deadline 8/1. Non-fall registration accepted. Admission may be deferred for a maximum of 1 year.

COSTS AND FINANCIAL AID

Annual tuition $29,426. Room and board $9,132. Required fees $1,436. Average book and supplies expense $1,100. **Required Forms and Deadlines:** FAFSA. **Notification of Awards:** Applicants will be notified of awards on a rolling basis beginning 2/15. **Types of Aid:** *Need-based scholarships/grants:* College/university scholarship or grant aid from institutional funds; Federal Pell; Private scholarships; SEOG; State scholarships/grants. *Loans:* Direct PLUS loans; Direct Subsidized Stafford Loans; Direct Unsubsidized Stafford Loans. **Student Employment:** Federal Work-Study Program available. Institutional employment available. **Financial Aid Statistics:** 99% needy freshmen, 100% needy undergrads receive need-based scholarship or grant aid. 17% freshmen, 13% undergrads receive non-need-based scholarship or grant aid. 82% freshmen, 85% undergrads receive need-based self-help aid. 11% freshmen, 10% undergrads receive athletic scholarships. 99.5% freshmen, 98% undergrads receive any aid. 77% undergrads borrow to pay for school. Average cumulative indebtedness $38,234. **Criteria awarding aid:** *Need-based:* Academics, Athletics, Leadership. *Non-need-based:* Academics, Art, Athletics, Leadership, Music/drama, State/district residency.

LAKE FOREST COLLEGE

555 North Sheridan Road, Lake Forest, IL 60045
Phone: 847-735-5000 **Financial Aid Phone:** 847-725-5103
E-mail: admissions@lakeforest.edu **CEEB Code:** 1392
Fax: 847-735-6271 **Website:** www.lakeforest.edu **ACT Code:** 1054

This private school was founded in 1857. It has a 107 acre campus.

RATINGS

Admissions Selectivity Rating: 87   **Fire Safety Rating:** 89   **Green Rating:** 60*

STUDENTS AND FACULTY

Enrollment: 1,527. **Student Body:** 58% female, 42% male, 38% out-of-state, 11% international (85 countries represented). Asian 5%, African American 5%, Caucasian 55%, Hispanic 14%, Native American <1%, Pacific Islander <1%, Two or more races 4%, Race unknown 5%.
Retention and Graduation: 88% freshmen return for sophomore year. 71% freshmen graduate within 4 years. 76% freshmen graduate within 6 years. 16% grads go on to further study within 1 year. **Faculty:** Student/faculty ratio 12:1. 101 full-time faculty, 96% hold PhDs, 17% are members of minority groups, 48% are women. 0% of classes are taught by teaching assistants.

ACADEMICS

Degrees: Bachelor's; Master's. **Classes:** Most classes have 10–19 students. Most lab/discussion sessions have 10–19 students. **Most popular majors:** Research and Experimental Psychology, Other; Business/Commerce, General; Finance, General. **Special Study Options:** Accelerated program; Double major; Dual enrollment; Honors program; Independent study; Internships; Liberal arts/career combination; Student-designed major; Study abroad; Teacher certification program. **Honors programs:** The Richter Scholar Summer Research Program provides students, early in their academic careers, with the opportunity to conduct independent, individual research with Lake Forest College faculty. In the summer between their first and second year, each student in the Richter Program is employed for a ten week period and works one-on-one with a faculty member, doing independent research in a particular field. Rosalind Franklin University Summer Research Program allows 15–18 undergraduates, from first year to senior thesis students, to conduct 10–12 weeks of paid research every summer as summer fellows at Rosalind Franklin University of Medicine and Science (RFUMS). **Combined degree programs:** BA/JD; BA/MA. **Disability Services offered:** Note-taking services; Reader services; Tape recorders; Tutors. **Career services:** Alumni network; Alumni services; Career assessment; Career/job search classes; Internships; Regional alumni.

FACILITIES

Housing: Coed dorms; Theme housing; 80% of campus accessible to physically disabled. **Special Academic Facilities/Equipment:** Center for Chicago Programs, Virtual reality space, 3D printer, art galleries, language labs, technology resource center, speech and video production room, "smart" classrooms, music/recording studio with synthesizers, public access computer labs, electron microscope, computer molecular modeling equipment, high-resolution FT-IR, NMR spectrometer, neutron howitzer, digital storage oscilloscopes, flourescence microscope. **Campus Network:** 100% of classrooms, 100% of dorms, 100% of student union, 100% of libraries, 100% of dining areas, 100% of common outdoor areas have wireless network access.

CAMPUS LIFE

Environment: Village. **Activities:** Campus Ministries; Choral groups; Concert band; Dance; Drama/theater; International Student Organization; Jazz band; Literary magazine; Model UN; Music ensembles; Musical theater; Radio station; Student government; Student newspaper; Symphony orchestra. 84 registered organizations, 14 honor societies, 6 religious organizations, 4 fraternities, 5 sororities on campus. **Athletics (Intercollegiate):** *Men:* basketball, cross-country, diving, football, handball, ice hockey, soccer, swimming, tennis. *Women:* basketball, cross-country, diving, handball, ice hockey, soccer, softball, swimming, tennis, volleyball. **On-Campus Highlights:** Donnelley and Lee Library. **Environmental Initiatives:** The organic campus garden provides internship opportunities for students and it supplies the campus cafeteria with food during the summer and fall.

ADMISSIONS

Freshman Academic Profile: Average high school GPA 3.7. 40% in top 10% of high school class, 63% in top 25% of high school class, 87% in top 50% of high school class. **Test Scores:** SAT Math middle 50% range 540–640. SAT EBRW middle 50% range 540–640. ACT middle 50% range 23–29. **Basis for Candidate Selection:** *Very important factors include:* rigor of secondary school record, application essay, interview, extracurricular activities, talent/ability, character/personal qualities. *Important factors include:* academic GPA. *Other factors include:* class rank, standardized test scores, recommendation(s), first generation, alumni/ae relation, geographical residence, volunteer work, work experience, level of applicant's interest. **Freshman Admission Requirements:** High school diploma is required and GED is accepted. *Academic units required:* 4 English, 3 math, 3 science, 3 science labs, 2 foreign language, 2 social studies, 2 history, 3 academic electives. *Academic units recommended:* 4 English, 4 math, 4 science, 4 science labs, 4 foreign language, 2 social studies, 2 history, 3 academic electives. **Freshman Admission Statistics:** 4,739 applied, 55% admitted, 14% enrolled. **Transfer Admission Requirements:** High school transcript, college transcript(s), essay or personal statement. Minimum college GPA of 2.5 required. Lowest grade transferable C-. **General Admission Information:** Regular application deadline 2/15. Non-fall registration accepted. Admission may be deferred for a maximum of 1 year.

COSTS AND FINANCIAL AID

Annual tuition $48,920. Room and board $10,954. Average book and supplies expense $1,000. **Required Forms and Deadlines:** FAFSA. **Notification of Awards:** Applicants will be notified of awards on a rolling basis beginning 12/15. **Types of Aid:** *Need-based scholarships/grants:* College/university scholarship or grant aid from institutional funds; Federal Pell; Private scholarships; SEOG; State scholarships/grants. *Loans:* Direct PLUS loans; Direct Subsidized Stafford Loans; Direct Unsubsidized Stafford Loans. **Student Employment:** Federal Work-Study Program available. Institutional employment available. **Financial Aid Statistics:** 100% needy freshmen, 100% needy undergrads receive need-based scholarship or grant aid. 0% freshmen, 0% undergrads receive non-need-based scholarship or grant aid. 88% freshmen, 85% undergrads receive need-based self-help aid. 0% freshmen, 0% undergrads receive athletic scholarships. 98% freshmen, 95% undergrads receive any aid. 72% undergrads borrow to pay for school. Average cumulative indebtedness $33,440. **Criteria awarding aid:** *Non-need-based:* Academics, Alumni affiliation, Art, Leadership, Music/drama.

LAKEHEAD UNIVERSITY

955 Oliver Road, Thunder Bay, ON P7B 5E1
Phone: (807) 343-8500 **Financial Aid Phone:** (807) 343-8206
E-mail: admissions@lakeheadu.ca
Fax: (807) 766-7209 **Website:** www.lakeheadu.ca

This public school was founded in 1965. It has a 288 acre campus.

RATINGS

Admissions Selectivity Rating: 60*   **Fire Safety Rating:** 60*   **Green Rating:** 60*

STUDENTS AND FACULTY

Enrollment: 7,139.
Retention and Graduation: 85% freshmen return for sophomore year.
Faculty: Student/faculty ratio 24:1.

ACADEMICS

Degrees: Bachelor's; Certificate; Diploma; Master's. **Classes:** Most classes have 30–39 students. **Most popular majors:** Engineering, General; Forestry, General; Business Administration and Management, General.

FACILITIES

Housing: Apartments for single students; Coed dorms; Special housing for disabled students; Wellness housing.

CAMPUS LIFE

Environment: City. **Activities:** Campus Ministries; Choral groups; Concert band; Dance; Drama/theater; International Student Organization; Jazz band; Literary magazine; Model UN; Music ensembles; Musical theater; Radio station; Student government; Student newspaper. **Athletics (Intercollegiate):** *Men:* basketball, cross-country, ice hockey, skiing (Nordic/cross-country), track/field (outdoor), track/field (indoor), wrestling. *Women:* basketball, cross-country, skiing (Nordic/cross-country), track/field (outdoor), track/field (indoor), volleyball, wrestling.

ADMISSIONS

Freshman Admission Requirements: High school diploma is required and GED is accepted. **General Admission Information:** Application fee $105. Priority deadline 6/1. Regular application deadline 9/24. Non-fall registration accepted. Admission may be deferred for a maximum of one year.

COSTS AND FINANCIAL AID

Annual in-state tuition $4,670. Annual out-of-state tuition $4,670.

LAKE REGION STATE COLLEGE

1801 College Drive N, Devils Lake, ND 58301-1598
Phone: 701-662-1514 **Financial Aid Phone:** 701-662-1516
E-mail: lrsc.admissions@lrsc.edu
Fax: 701-662-1581 **Website:** www.lrsc.edu **ACT Code:** 3198

This public school was founded in 1941. It has a 120 acre campus.

RATINGS

Admissions Selectivity Rating: 76   **Fire Safety Rating:** 96   **Green Rating:** 60*

STUDENTS AND FACULTY

Enrollment: 696. **Student Body:** 53% female, 47% male, 12% out-of-state, 3% international (14 countries represented). Asian 2%, African American 4%, Caucasian 82%, Hispanic 2%, Native American 5%, Race unknown 3%. **Faculty:** Student/faculty ratio 13:1. 35 full-time faculty, 14% hold PhDs, 3% are members of minority groups, 51% are women. 0% of classes are taught by teaching assistants.

ACADEMICS

Degrees: Associate; Certificate; Diploma; Terminal Associate; Transfer Associate. **Classes:** Most classes have 10–19 students. **Most popular majors:** Criminal Justice/Police Science; Business Administration and Management, General; Liberal Arts and Sciences/Liberal Studies. **Special Study Options:** Cooperative education program; Cross-registration; Distance learning; Dual enrollment; English as a Second Language (ESL); Internships; Liberal arts/career combination. **Disability Services offered:** Note-taking services; Reader services; Tape recorders; Tutors. **Career services:** Career/job search classes; Internships.

FACILITIES

Housing: Apartments for married students; Apartments for single students; Men's dorms; Special housing for disabled students; Women's dorms; 100% of campus accessible to physically disabled. **Special Academic Facilities/Equipment:** Paul Hoghaug Library and Law Library.

CAMPUS LIFE

Environment: Village. **Activities:** Drama/theater; Literary magazine; Musical theater; Student government; Symphony orchestra. 12 registered organizations, 1 religious organization on campus. **Athletics (Intercollegiate):** *Men:* basketball. *Women:* basketball. **On-Campus Highlights:** Student Union.

ADMISSIONS

Freshman Academic Profile: 98% from public high schools. **Test Scores:** ACT middle 50% range 18–25. **Basis for Candidate Selection: Freshman Admission Requirements:** High school diploma is required and GED is accepted. *Academic units recommended:* 4 English, 3 math, 3 science, 2 science labs, 2 foreign language, 3 social studies. **Freshman Admission Statistics:** 233 applied, 99% admitted, 95% enrolled. **Transfer Admission Requirements:** High school transcript, college transcript(s), statement of good standing from prior institution(s). Minimum college GPA of 2.0 required. Lowest grade transferable D. **General Admission Information:** Application fee $35. Non-fall registration accepted. Admission may be deferred for a maximum of one semester.

COSTS AND FINANCIAL AID

Annual in-state tuition $3,065. Annual out-of-state tuition $3,065. Room and board $5,230. Required fees $843. Average book and supplies expense $900. **Required Forms and Deadlines:** FAFSA. **Notification of Awards:** Applicants will be notified of awards on a rolling basis beginning 5/15. **Types of Aid:** *Need-based scholarships/grants:* College/university scholarship or grant aid from institutional funds; Federal Pell; Private scholarships; SEOG; State scholarships/grants. **Student Employment:** Federal Work-Study Program available.

Institutional employment available. **Financial Aid Statistics:** 93% needy freshmen, 87% needy undergrads receive need-based scholarship or grant aid. 1% freshmen, 0% undergrads receive non-need-based scholarship or grant aid. 85% freshmen, 89% undergrads receive need-based self-help aid. 6% freshmen, 6% undergrads receive athletic scholarships. 80% undergrads receive any aid. **Criteria awarding aid:** *Need-based:* Academics, Athletics, Minority status. *Non-need-based:* Academics, Athletics, Leadership, Minority status, Music/drama.

LAKE SUPERIOR STATE UNIVERSITY

650 W. Easterday Avenue, Sault Ste. Marie, MI 49783-1699
Phone: 906-635-2231 **Financial Aid Phone:** 906-635-2678
E-mail: admissions@lssu.edu **CEEB Code:** 1421
Fax: 906-635-6669 **ACT Code:** 2031

This public school was founded in 1946. It has a 115 acre campus.

RATINGS

Admissions Selectivity Rating: 74   **Fire Safety Rating:** 60*   **Green Rating:** 60*

STUDENTS AND FACULTY

Enrollment: 2,440. **Student Body:** 50% female, 50% male, 5% out-of-state, 7% international. Asian 1%, African American 1%, Caucasian 79%, Hispanic 2%, Native American 8%, Pacific Islander 0%, Two or more races <1%, Race unknown 2%. **Retention and Graduation:** 70% freshmen return for sophomore year. **Faculty:** Student/faculty ratio 17:1. 114 full-time faculty, 53% hold PhDs, 5% are members of minority groups, 46% are women. 0% of classes are taught by teaching assistants.

ACADEMICS

Degrees: Associate; Bachelor's; Certificate; Master's. **Classes:** Most classes have 10–19 students. Most lab/discussion sessions have 10–19 students. **Special Study Options:** Cooperative education program; Distance learning; Double major; Dual enrollment; Honors program; Independent study; Internships; Student-designed major; Study abroad; Teacher certification program. **Disability Services offered:** Note-taking services; Reader services; Tape recorders; Tutors.

FACILITIES

Housing: Apartments for single students; Coed dorms; Men's dorms; Women's dorms; 90% of campus accessible to physically disabled. **Special Academic Facilities/Equipment:** Natural science, Michigan history, and Great Lakes shipping museums, planetarium, industrial robots, atomic absorption/flame emission spectrophotometer. **Campus Network:** 95% of classrooms, 95% of dorms, 100% of student union, 100% of libraries, 100% of dining areas, 80% of common outdoor areas have wireless network access.

CAMPUS LIFE

Environment: City. **Activities:** Campus Ministries; Choral groups; Dance; Drama/theater; International Student Organization; Literary magazine; Model UN; Pep band; Radio station; Student government; Student newspaper. 60 registered organizations, 4 fraternities, 4 sororities on campus. **Athletics (Intercollegiate):** *Men:* basketball, cross-country, ice hockey, tennis, track/field (outdoor), track/field (indoor). *Women:* basketball, cross-country, softball, tennis, track/field (outdoor), track/field (indoor), volleyball.

ADMISSIONS

Freshman Academic Profile: Average high school GPA 3.3. 14% in top 10% of high school class, 40% in top 25% of high school class, 75% in top 50% of high school class. **Test Scores:** ACT middle 50% range 20–25. **Basis for Candidate Selection:** *Very important factors include:* rigor of secondary school record, academic GPA, standardized test scores. *Other factors include:* class rank, recommendation(s), interview, geographical residence. **Freshman Admission Requirements:** High school diploma is required and GED is accepted. *Academic units recommended:* 4 English, 3 math, 3 science, 3 science labs, 2 foreign language, 2 social studies, 1 history. **Freshman Admission Statistics:** 1,425 applied, 90% admitted, 34% enrolled. **Transfer Admission Requirements:** College transcript(s). Minimum college GPA of 2.0 required. Lowest grade transferable C-. **General Admission Information:** Application fee $35. Priority deadline 3/1. Non-fall registration accepted. Admission may be deferred for a maximum of 1 year.

COSTS AND FINANCIAL AID

Annual in-state tuition $9,540. Annual out-of-state tuition $14,410. Room and board $8,481. Required fees $350. Average book and supplies expense $1,200. **Required Forms and Deadlines:** FAFSA. **Notification of Awards:** Applicants will be notified of awards on a rolling basis beginning 10/11. **Types of Aid:** *Need-based scholarships/grants:* College/university scholarship or grant aid from institutional funds; Federal Nursing Scholarships; Federal Pell; Private scholarships; SEOG; State scholarships/grants. *Loans:* Direct PLUS loans; Direct Subsidized Stafford Loans; Direct Unsubsidized Stafford Loans. **Financial Aid Statistics:** 75% needy freshmen, 75% needy undergrads receive need-based scholarship or grant aid. 61% freshmen, 40% undergrads receive non-need-based scholarship or grant aid. 82% freshmen, 90% undergrads receive need-based self-help aid. 10% freshmen, 9% undergrads receive athletic scholarships. 83% undergrads receive any aid. **Criteria awarding aid:** *Need-based:* Academics, Alumni affiliation, Athletics, Job skills, Leadership, Minority status. *Non-need-based:* Academics, Athletics, State/district residency.

LAMAR UNIVERSITY

P.O. Box 10009, Beaumont, TX 77710
Phone: 409-880-8888
E-mail: admissions@hal.lamar.edu **CEEB Code:** 6360
Fax: 409-880-8463 **Website:** www.lamar.edu **ACT Code:** 4114

This public school was founded in 1923. It has a 200 acre campus.

RATINGS
Admissions Selectivity Rating: 62 **Fire Safety Rating:** 60* **Green Rating:** 60*

STUDENTS AND FACULTY
Enrollment: 9,057. **Student Body:** 55% female, 45% male, 1% out-of-state, 1% international. Asian 3%, African American 21%, Caucasian 70%, Hispanic 4%, Native American 1%, Race unknown 0%.

ACADEMICS
Degrees: Bachelor's; Master's. **Special Study Options:** Cooperative education program; Distance learning; Double major; Dual enrollment; English as a Second Language (ESL); Honors program; Internships; Study abroad; Teacher certification program. **Disability Services offered:** Note-taking services; Reader services; Tape recorders; Tutors. **Career services:** Alumni services; Career assessment; Career/job search classes.

FACILITIES
Housing: Apartments for single students; Coed dorms; Fraternity/sorority housing; Men's dorms; Women's dorms. **Special Academic Facilities/Equipment:** Museum. **Campus Network:** 100% of classrooms, 100% of dorms, 100% of student union, 100% of libraries, 100% of dining areas, 100% of common outdoor areas have wireless network access.

CAMPUS LIFE
Environment: Village. **Activities:** Student government; Student newspaper. 145 registered organizations, 11 fraternities, 8 sororities on campus. **Athletics (Intercollegiate):** *Men:* baseball, basketball, cross-country, golf, tennis, track/field (outdoor). *Women:* basketball, cross-country, golf, tennis, track/field (outdoor), volleyball.

ADMISSIONS
Freshman Academic Profile: 10% in top 10% of high school class, 27% in top 25% of high school class, 90% in top 50% of high school class. 96% from public high schools. **Freshman Admission Requirements:** High school diploma is required and GED is accepted.; High school diploma is required and GED is not accepted. *Academic units recommended:* 4 English, 3 math, 2 science, 2 social studies, 2 academic electives. **Transfer Admission Requirements:** Minimum college GPA of 2.0 required. Lowest grade transferable D. **General Admission Information:** Regular application deadline 8/1. Non-fall registration accepted.

COSTS AND FINANCIAL AID
Annual in-state tuition $864. Annual out-of-state tuition $5,976. Room and board $3,040. Required fees $840. **Required Forms and Deadlines:** FAFSA; Institution's own financial aid form; State aid form. **Types of Aid:** *Need-based scholarships/grants:* **Student Employment:** Federal Work-Study Program available. Institutional employment available.

LAMBUTH UNIVERSITY

705 Lambuth Boulevard, Jackson, TN 38301-5296
Phone: 731-425-3223 **Financial Aid Phone:** 731-425-3332
E-mail: admit@lambuth.edu **CEEB Code:** 1394
Fax: 731-425-3496 **Website:** www.lambuth.edu **ACT Code:** 3974

This private school, affiliated with the Methodist Church, was founded in 1843. It has a 50 acre campus.

RATINGS
Admissions Selectivity Rating: 86 **Fire Safety Rating:** 87 **Green Rating:** 60*

STUDENTS AND FACULTY
Enrollment: 765. **Student Body:** 47% female, 53% male, 21% out-of-state, 9 countries represented.
Retention and Graduation: 60% freshmen return for sophomore year. 20% grads go on to further study within 1 year. 5% grads pursue arts and sciences degrees. 5% grads pursue law degrees. 5% grads pursue business degrees. 5% grads pursue medical degrees. **Faculty:** Student/faculty ratio 12:1. 51 full-time faculty, 78% hold PhDs, 2% are members of minority groups, 41% are women. 0% of classes are taught by teaching assistants.

ACADEMICS
Degrees: Bachelor's. **Classes:** Most classes have 10–19 students. Most lab/discussion sessions have 20–29 students. **Most popular majors:** Business/Commerce, General; Sports, Kinesiology, and Physical Education/Fitness, General; Psychology, General. **Special Study Options:** Cross-registration; Double major; Honors program; Independent study; Internships; Student-designed major; Study abroad; Teacher certification program. **Honors programs:** University Honors is a 3-semester sequence of courses designed to offer more in-depth study of classic literature and themes. Various topics are considered including art, psychology, ecology, history, ethics, politics, science, sociology, business, religion, and literature. Honors study is available in most disciplines and consists of an 8-hour sequence of research over the last 3 semesters of study in a particular discipline. **Disability Services offered:** Tape recorders; Tutors. **Career services:** Alumni network; Alumni services; Career assessment; Career/job search classes; Internships; Regional alumni.

FACILITIES
Housing: Apartments for single students; Coed dorms; Fraternity/sorority housing; Men's dorms; Special housing for disabled students; Women's dorms; 80% of campus accessible to physically disabled. **Special Academic Facilities/Equipment:** Academic Support Center, Interior Design lab, M.D. Anderson Planetarium, Oxley Biological Field Station.

CAMPUS LIFE
Environment: City. **Activities:** Campus Ministries; Choral groups; Concert band; Dance; Drama/theater; International Student Organization; Jazz band; Literary magazine; Model UN; Music ensembles; Musical theater; Student government; Student newspaper; Yearbook. 41 registered organizations, 6 honor societies, 3 religious organizations, 3 fraternities, 3 sororities on campus. **Athletics (Intercollegiate):** *Men:* baseball, basketball, football, golf, soccer, tennis. *Women:* basketball, golf, soccer, softball, tennis. **On-Campus Highlights:** Eagle's Nest Bistro.

ADMISSIONS
Freshman Academic Profile: Average high school GPA 3.3. 21% in top 10% of high school class, 42% in top 25% of high school class, 71% in top 50% of high school class. 85% from public high schools. **Test Scores:** SAT Math middle 50% range 460–570. SAT EBRW middle 50% range 440–570. ACT middle 50% range 20–25. **Basis for Candidate Selection:** *Very important factors include:* rigor of secondary school record, academic GPA, standardized test scores. *Important factors include:* application essay, recommendation(s), interview, extracurricular activities. *Other factors include:* class rank, talent/ability, first generation, alumni/ae relation, geographical residence, state residency, religious affiliation/commitment, volunteer work, work experience. **Freshman Admission Requirements:** High school diploma is required and GED is accepted. *Academic units recommended:* 4 English, 3 math, 3 science, 1 foreign language, 2 social studies, 1 history. **Freshman Admission Statistics:** 1,042 applied, 53% admitted, 37% enrolled. **Transfer Admission Requirements:** College transcript(s), essay or personal statement, statement of good standing from prior institution(s). Minimum college GPA of 2.0 required. Lowest grade transferable D. **General Admission Information:** Application fee $25. Non-fall registration accepted. Admission may be deferred for a maximum of one year.

COSTS AND FINANCIAL AID

Annual tuition $17,000. Room and board $7,160. Required fees $400. Average book and supplies expense $1,200. **Required Forms and Deadlines:** FAFSA; Institution's own financial aid form. **Notification of Awards:** Applicants will be notified of awards on a rolling basis beginning 2/15. **Types of Aid:** *Need-based scholarships/grants:* College/university scholarship or grant aid from institutional funds; Federal Pell; Private scholarships; SEOG; State scholarships/grants. **Student Employment:** Federal Work-Study Program available. Institutional employment available. **Financial Aid Statistics:** 98% needy freshmen, 97% needy undergrads receive need-based scholarship or grant aid. 23% freshmen, 22% undergrads receive non-need-based scholarship or grant aid. 66% freshmen, 68% undergrads receive need-based self-help aid. 9% freshmen, 9% undergrads receive athletic scholarships. 99% freshmen, 99% undergrads receive any aid. **Criteria awarding aid:** *Need-based:* Academics, Alumni affiliation, Art, Athletics, Job skills, Leadership, Music/drama, Religious affiliation. *Non-need-based:* Academics, Alumni affiliation, Art, Athletics, Job skills, Leadership, Music/drama, Religious affiliation.

LANCASTER BIBLE COLLEGE

901 Eden Rd, Lancaster, PA 17601-5036
Phone: 717-560-8271 **Financial Aid Phone:** 717-560-8254
E-mail: admissions@lbc.edu **CEEB Code:** 2388
Fax: 717-560-8213 **Website:** www.lbc.edu **ACT Code:** 3707

This private school was founded in 1933. It has a 100 acre campus.

RATINGS

Admissions Selectivity Rating: 64   **Fire Safety Rating:** 77   **Green Rating:** 60*

STUDENTS AND FACULTY

Enrollment: 702. **Student Body:** 47% female, 53% male, 26% out-of-state, 1% international. Asian 1%, African American 3%, Caucasian 73%, Hispanic 1%, Native American <1%, Race unknown 20%.
Retention and Graduation: 77% freshmen return for sophomore year.
Faculty: Student/faculty ratio 10:1. 48 full-time faculty, 52% hold PhDs, 2% are members of minority groups, 25% are women. 0% of classes are taught by teaching assistants.

ACADEMICS

Degrees: Associate; Bachelor's; Certificate; Master's; Post-bachelor's certificate. **Classes:** Most classes have 10–19 students. Most lab/discussion sessions have 10–19 students. **Most popular majors:** Bible/Biblical Studies; Theology and Religious Vocations, Other; Elementary Education and Teaching. **Special Study Options:** Accelerated program; Double major; Independent study; Internships; Study abroad; Teacher certification program. **Disability Services offered:** Note-taking services; Reader services; Tape recorders; Tutors. **Career services:** Alumni network; Internships.

FACILITIES

Housing: Men's dorms; Women's dorms; 80% of campus accessible to physically disabled.

CAMPUS LIFE

Environment: Village. **Activities:** Choral groups; Concert band; Drama/theater; Music ensembles; Musical theater; Student government; Student newspaper; Yearbook. 20 registered organizations on campus. **Athletics (Intercollegiate):** *Men:* baseball, basketball, cheerleading, soccer, volleyball. *Women:* basketball, cheerleading, lacrosse, soccer, volleyball.

ADMISSIONS

Freshman Academic Profile: 60% from public high schools. **Basis for Candidate Selection:** *Very important factors include:* rigor of secondary school record, application essay, standardized test scores, recommendation(s), character/personal qualities, religious affiliation/commitment. *Important factors include:* extracurricular activities. *Other factors include:* interview, talent/ability, volunteer work. **Freshman Admission Requirements:** High school diploma is required and GED is accepted. **Freshman Admission Statistics:** 314 applied, 97% admitted, 44% enrolled. **Transfer Admission Requirements:** High school transcript, college transcript(s), essay or personal statement, standardized test scores, statement of good standing from prior institution(s). Minimum college GPA of 2.0 required. Lowest grade transferable C. **General Admission Information:** Application fee $25. Priority deadline 8/1. Non-fall registration accepted. Admission may be deferred for a maximum of 1 year.

COSTS AND FINANCIAL AID

Annual tuition $15,930. Room and board $7,110. Required fees $630. Average book and supplies expense $1,000. **Required Forms and Deadlines:** FAFSA; State aid form. **Notification of Awards:** Applicants will be notified of awards on a rolling basis beginning 3/1. **Types of Aid:** *Need-based scholarships/grants:* College/university scholarship or grant aid from institutional funds; Federal Pell; Private scholarships; SEOG; State scholarships/grants. **Student Employment:** Federal Work-Study Program available. Institutional employment available. **Financial Aid Statistics:** 98% needy freshmen, 94% needy undergrads receive need-based scholarship or grant aid. 96% freshmen, 79% undergrads receive non-need-based scholarship or grant aid. 82% freshmen, 88% undergrads receive need-based self-help aid. 0% freshmen, 0% undergrads receive athletic scholarships. **Criteria awarding aid:** *Non-need-based:* Academics, Alumni affiliation, Leadership, Music/drama.

LANDMARK COLLEGE

19 River Road South, Putney, VT 05346-0820
Phone: 802-387-6718 **Financial Aid Phone:** 802-387-7179
E-mail: admissions@landmark.edu
Fax: Website: http://www.landmark.edu/ **ACT Code:** 4317

This private school was founded in 1984. It has a 128 acre campus.

RATINGS

Admissions Selectivity Rating: 74   **Fire Safety Rating:** 84   **Green Rating:** 60*

STUDENTS AND FACULTY

Enrollment: 393. **Student Body:** 31% female, 69% male, 95% out-of-state, 1% international (14 countries represented). Asian 4%, African American 3%, Caucasian 66%, Hispanic 6%, Native American 1%, Pacific Islander 0%, Two or more races 2%, Race unknown 17%.
Retention and Graduation: 47% freshmen return for sophomore year. 0% grads pursue law degrees. 0% grads pursue medical degrees. **Faculty:** Student/faculty ratio 6:1. 86 full-time faculty, 0% hold PhDs, 1% are members of minority groups, 64% are women. 0% of classes are taught by teaching assistants.

ACADEMICS

Degrees: Associate; Bachelor's; Post-bachelor's certificate; Terminal Associate; Transfer Associate. **Classes:** Most classes have 10–19 students. **Special Study Options:** Cross-registration; Distance learning; Double major; Dual enrollment; Independent study; Internships; Liberal arts/career combination; Student-designed major; Study abroad. **Honors programs:** Phi Theta Kappa.

FACILITIES

Housing: Coed dorms; Theme housing; Wellness housing; 65% of campus accessible to physically disabled.

CAMPUS LIFE

Environment: Rural. **Activities:** Choral groups; Drama/theater; International Student Organization; Literary magazine; Music ensembles; Radio station; Student government; Student newspaper.

ADMISSIONS

Freshman Academic Profile: 68% from public high schools. **Basis for Candidate Selection:** *Very important factors include:* interview. *Important factors include:* rigor of secondary school record, recommendation(s), character/personal qualities. *Other factors include:* academic GPA, application essay, standardized test scores, extracurricular activities, talent/ability, alumni/ae relation, volunteer work, work experience. **Freshman Admission Requirements:** High school diploma is required and GED is accepted. *Academic units recommended:* 4 English, 3 math, 3 science, 3 science labs, 3 social studies, 3 history, 1 academic elective, 1 visual/performing arts. **Freshman Admission Statistics:** 395 applied, 54% admitted, 54% enrolled. **Transfer Admission Requirements:** High school transcript, college transcript(s), essay or personal statement, interview, Lowest grade transferable C-. **General Admission Information:** Application fee $75. Priority deadline 5/1. Non-fall registration accepted. Admission may be deferred for a maximum of 1 calendar year.

COSTS AND FINANCIAL AID

Annual tuition $56,800. Room and board $11,840. Average book and supplies expense $1,400. **Required Forms and Deadlines:** FAFSA; State aid form. **Notification of Awards:** Applicants will be notified of awards on a rolling basis beginning 3/15. **Types of Aid:** *Need-based scholarships/grants:* College/ university scholarship or grant aid from institutional funds; Federal Pell; Private scholarships; SEOG; State scholarships/grants. *Loans:* Direct PLUS loans; Direct Subsidized Stafford Loans; Direct Unsubsidized Stafford Loans. **Student Employment:** Federal Work-Study Program available. Institutional employment available. **Financial Aid Statistics:** 100% needy freshmen, 97% needy undergrads receive need-based scholarship or grant aid. 100% freshmen, 100% undergrads receive non-need-based scholarship or grant aid. 98% freshmen, 98% undergrads receive need-based self-help aid. 0% freshmen, 0% undergrads receive athletic scholarships. 35% freshmen, 42% undergrads receive any aid. 67% undergrads borrow to pay for school. Average cumulative indebtedness $33,683. **Criteria awarding aid:** *Non-need-based:* Academics, Art, Athletics, Leadership, Minority status, Music/drama.

LANE COLLEGE

545 Lane Avenue, Jackson, TN 38301
Phone: 731-426-7533 **Financial Aid Phone:** (731) 426-7536
E-mail: admissions@lanecollege.edu
Fax: 731-426-7559 **Website:** www.lanecollege.edu **ACT Code:** 3976

This private school, affiliated with the Methodist Church, was founded in 1882. It has a 25 acre campus.

RATINGS
Admissions Selectivity Rating: 76   **Fire Safety Rating:** 95   **Green Rating:** 60*

STUDENTS AND FACULTY
Enrollment: 1,427. **Student Body:** 47% female, 53% male, 40% out-of-state, <1% international (1 countries represented). Asian <1%, African American 90%, Caucasian <1%, Hispanic <1%, Native American <1%, Pacific Islander 0%, Two or more races 1%, Race unknown 8%.
Retention and Graduation: 62% freshmen return for sophomore year. 35% grads go on to further study within 1 year. 37% grads pursue arts and sciences degrees. 6% grads pursue law degrees. 10% grads pursue business degrees. 7% grads pursue medical degrees. **Faculty:** Student/faculty ratio 19:1. 65 full-time faculty, 65% hold PhDs, 57% are members of minority groups, 38% are women. 0% of classes are taught by teaching assistants.

ACADEMICS
Degrees: Associate; Bachelor's. **Classes:** Most classes have 20–29 students. **Most popular majors:** Business/Commerce, General; Criminal Justice/Law Enforcement Administration; Biology/Biological Sciences, General. **Special Study Options:** Dual enrollment; Honors program; Independent study; Internships; Study abroad. **Disability Services offered:** Tutors. **Career services:** Alumni services; Career assessment; Career/job search classes; Internships.

FACILITIES
Housing: Coed dorms; Men's dorms; Women's dorms; 98% of campus accessible to physically disabled. **Special Academic Facilities/Equipment:** The Grand Student Center; The Cyber Café.

CAMPUS LIFE
Environment: Town. **Activities:** Campus Ministries; Choral groups; Concert band; Dance; Drama/theater; Jazz band; Marching band; Music ensembles; Pep band; Radio station; Student government; Student newspaper; Student-run film society. 21 registered organizations, 6 honor societies, 4 religious organizations, 4 fraternities, 4 sororities on campus. **Athletics (Intercollegiate): Men:** baseball, basketball, cross-country, football, tennis, track/field (outdoor). *Women:* basketball, cheerleading, cross-country, softball, tennis, track/field (outdoor), volleyball. **On-Campus Highlights:** Pond at the Plain.

ADMISSIONS
Freshman Academic Profile: Average high school GPA 2.6. 5% in top 10% of high school class, 17% in top 25% of high school class, 52% in top 50% of high school class. 96% from public high schools. **Test Scores:** ACT middle 50% range 14–16. **Basis for Candidate Selection:** *Very important factors include:* rigor of secondary school record, recommendation(s), first generation. *Important factors include:* academic GPA, standardized test scores. *Other factors include:* class rank, interview, extracurricular activities, character/personal qualities, alumni/ae relation, religious affiliation/commitment, level of applicant's interest. **Freshman Admission Requirements:** High school diploma is required and GED is accepted. *Academic units recommended:* 4 English, 2 math, 2 science, 2 foreign language, 2 social studies. **Freshman Admission**

Statistics: 5,311 applied, 50% admitted, 15% enrolled. **Transfer Admission Requirements:** College transcript(s), standardized test scores, statement of good standing from prior institution(s). Lowest grade transferable C. **General Admission Information:** Non-fall registration accepted. Admission may be deferred for a maximum of 2 semesters.

COSTS AND FINANCIAL AID
Annual tuition $9,000. Room and board $7,270. Required fees $1,690. Average book and supplies expense $1,300. **Required Forms and Deadlines:** FAFSA. **Notification of Awards:** Applicants will be notified of awards on a rolling basis beginning 3/1. **Types of Aid:** *Need-based scholarships/grants:* College/ university scholarship or grant aid from institutional funds; Federal Pell; Private scholarships; SEOG; State scholarships/grants; United Negro College Fund. *Loans:* Direct PLUS loans; Direct Subsidized Stafford Loans; Direct Unsubsidized Stafford Loans. **Student Employment:** Federal Work-Study Program available. Institutional employment available. **Financial Aid Statistics:** 98% needy freshmen, 94% needy undergrads receive need-based scholarship or grant aid. 85% freshmen, 81% undergrads receive non-need-based scholarship or grant aid. 94% freshmen, 87% undergrads receive need-based self-help aid. 12% freshmen, 10% undergrads receive athletic scholarships. 96% freshmen, 98% undergrads receive any aid. **Criteria awarding aid:** *Need-based:* Academics, Athletics, Religious affiliation. *Non-need-based:* Academics, Athletics, Religious affiliation.

LA ROCHE UNIVERSITY

9000 Babcock Boulevard, Pittsburgh, PA 15237
Phone: 412-536-1271 **Financial Aid Phone:** 412-536-1120
E-mail: admissions@laroche.edu **CEEB Code:** 2379
Fax: 412-847-1820 **Website:** www.laroche.edu **ACT Code:** 3607

This private school, affiliated with the Roman Catholic Church, was founded in 1963. It has a 43 acre campus.

RATINGS
Admissions Selectivity Rating: 72   **Fire Safety Rating:** 93   **Green Rating:** 60*

STUDENTS AND FACULTY
Enrollment: 1,220. **Student Body:** 56% female, 44% male, 11% out-of-state, 15% international (27 countries represented). Asian 1%, African American 10%, Caucasian 61%, Hispanic 5%, Native American <1%, Pacific Islander <1%, Two or more races 3%, Race unknown 5%.
Retention and Graduation: 73% freshmen return for sophomore year. 40% freshmen graduate within 4 years. 55% freshmen graduate within 6 years. 6% grads go on to further study within 1 year. **Faculty:** Student/faculty ratio 12:1. 61 full-time faculty, 85% hold PhDs, 10% are members of minority groups, 57% are women. 0% of classes are taught by teaching assistants.

ACADEMICS
Degrees: Associate; Bachelor's; Certificate; Doctoral degree—professional practice; Master's; Post-bachelor's certificate; Terminal Associate. **Classes:** Most classes have 10–19 students. Most lab/discussion sessions have fewer than 10 students. **Most popular majors:** Psychology, General; Criminal Justice/Safety Studies; Accounting. **Special Study Options:** Accelerated program; Cross-registration; Distance learning; Double major; Dual enrollment; English as a Second Language (ESL); Honors program; Independent study; Internships; Student-designed major; Study abroad. **Honors programs:** The Honors Institute at La Roche University is designed to recognize and promote academic excellence and focuses on those academically gifted students who are searching for a challenge. With a program designed specifically for honors-level students executed by fine scholars in their field and coupled with exclusive co-curricular activities, housing and study areas specifically for Honors Institute students, the program is tailored to exemplary students who are looking for an outstanding educational opportunity that will serve as the pathway for a successful future. **Combined degree programs:** BA/MA. **Disability Services offered:** Note-taking services; Reader services; Tutors. **Career services:** Career assessment; Career/job search classes; Internships; Regional alumni.

FACILITIES
Housing: Coed dorms; 100% of campus accessible to physically disabled. **Special Academic Facilities/Equipment:** Cantellopes Art Gallery; Huber Academic Center has state of the art smart classrooms.

CAMPUS LIFE

Environment: City. **Activities:** Campus Ministries; Dance; International Student Organization; Literary magazine; Radio station; Student government; Student newspaper; Student-run film society. 51 registered organizations, 4 honor societies, 2 religious organizations on campus. **Athletics (Intercollegiate):** *Men:* baseball, basketball, cross-country, golf, lacrosse, soccer. *Women:* basketball, cheerleading, cross-country, soccer, softball, tennis, volleyball. **On-Campus Highlights:** Sports and Fitness Center.

ADMISSIONS

Freshman Academic Profile: Average high school GPA 3.2. 8% in top 10% of high school class, 26% in top 25% of high school class, 63% in top 50% of high school class. 80% from public high schools. **Test Scores:** SAT Math middle 50% range 420–550. SAT EBRW middle 50% range 450–590. ACT middle 50% range 17–21. **Basis for Candidate Selection:** *Very important factors include:* rigor of secondary school record, academic GPA. *Important factors include:* standardized test scores. *Other factors include:* class rank, application essay, recommendation(s), interview, extracurricular activities, talent/ability, character/personal qualities, first generation, alumni/ae relation, volunteer work, work experience, level of applicant's interest. **Freshman Admission Requirements:** High school diploma is required and GED is accepted. *Academic units required:* 4 English, 2 math, 3 science, 2 science labs, 2 social studies, 2 history, 2 academic electives. *Academic units recommended:* 4 English, 3 math, 4 science, 3 science labs, 2 foreign language, 2 social studies, 2 history, 3 academic electives, 1 computer science. **Freshman Admission Statistics:** 1,220 applied, 99% admitted, 17% enrolled. **Transfer Admission Requirements:** College transcript(s), essay or personal statement. Minimum college GPA of 2.0 required. Lowest grade transferable C. **General Admission Information:** Application fee $50. Non-fall registration accepted. Admission may be deferred for a maximum of 1 year.

COSTS AND FINANCIAL AID

Annual tuition $29,470. Room and board $12,270. Required fees $850. Average book and supplies expense $1,200. **Required Forms and Deadlines:** FAFSA. **Notification of Awards:** Applicants will be notified of awards on a rolling basis beginning 11/1. **Types of Aid:** *Need-based scholarships/grants:* College/university scholarship or grant aid from institutional funds; Federal Pell; Private scholarships; SEOG; State scholarships/grants. *Loans:* Direct PLUS loans; Direct Subsidized Stafford Loans; Direct Unsubsidized Stafford Loans. **Student Employment:** Federal Work-Study Program available. **Financial Aid Statistics:** 54% needy freshmen, 71% needy undergrads receive need-based scholarship or grant aid. 79% freshmen, 100% undergrads receive non-need-based scholarship or grant aid. 66% freshmen, 83% undergrads receive need-based self-help aid. 0% freshmen, 0% undergrads receive athletic scholarships. 93% freshmen, 93% undergrads receive any aid. 68% undergrads borrow to pay for school. Average cumulative indebtedness $33,433. **Criteria awarding aid:** *Non-need-based:* Academics, Religious affiliation.

LASALLE COLLEGE VANCOUVER

2665 Renfrew Street, Vancouver, BC V5M0A7
Phone: 604-683-2006
E-mail: admissions@lasallecollegevancouver.com
Fax: 604-684-8839 **Website:** http://lasallecollegevancouver.com

This is a proprietary school.

RATINGS

Admissions Selectivity Rating: 60*　　**Fire Safety Rating:** 60*　　**Green Rating:** 60*

STUDENTS AND FACULTY

Enrollment: 300. **Student Body:** 64% female, 36% male.
Faculty: Student/faculty ratio 10:1.

ACADEMICS

Degrees: Bachelor's; Certificate; Diploma. **Special Study Options:** Cooperative education program; Distance learning; Independent study; Internships; Liberal arts/career combination; Study abroad; Weekend college.

CAMPUS LIFE

Activities: Dance; Music ensembles; Student government; Student-run film society.

ADMISSIONS

Freshman Academic Profile: Basis for Candidate Selection: *Very important factors include:* application essay, interview, level of applicant's interest. *Other factors include:* rigor of secondary school record, class rank, academic GPA, standardized test scores, recommendation(s), extracurricular activities, talent/ability, character/personal qualities, volunteer work, work experience. **Freshman Admission Requirements:** High school diploma is required and GED is accepted. **General Admission Information:** Application fee $150. Regular application deadline 10/1. Non-fall registration accepted.

LA SALLE UNIVERSITY

1900 West Olney Avenue, Philadelphia, PA 19141-1199
Phone: 215-951-1500 **Financial Aid Phone:** 215-951-1070
E-mail: admiss@lasalle.edu **CEEB Code:** 2363
Fax: 215-951-1656 **Website:** http://www.lasalle.edu **ACT Code:** 3608

This private school, affiliated with the Roman Catholic Church, was founded in 1863. It has a 133 acre campus.

RATINGS

Admissions Selectivity Rating: 75　　**Fire Safety Rating:** 87　　**Green Rating:** 63

STUDENTS AND FACULTY

Enrollment: 3,761. **Student Body:** 62% female, 38% male, 31% out-of-state, 2% international (45 countries represented). Asian 5%, African American 20%, Caucasian 48%, Hispanic 20%, Native American <1%, Pacific Islander <1%, Two or more races 3%, Race unknown 2%. **Retention and Graduation:** 74% freshmen return for sophomore year. 61% freshmen graduate within 4 years. 18% grads go on to further study within 1 year. **Faculty:** Student/faculty ratio 12:1. 219 full-time faculty, 79% hold PhDs, 12% are members of minority groups, 59% are women. 0% of classes are taught by teaching assistants.

ACADEMICS

Degrees: Associate; Bachelor's; Doctoral degree—professional practice; Master's; Post-bachelor's certificate; Post-master's certificate. **Classes:** Most classes have 10–19 students. Most lab/discussion sessions have fewer than 10 students. **Most popular majors:** Communication and Media Studies; Registered Nursing/Registered Nurse; Marketing/Marketing Management, General. **Special Study Options:** Accelerated program; Cooperative education program; Cross-registration; Distance learning; Double major; Dual enrollment; English as a Second Language (ESL); Exchange student program (domestic); Honors program; Independent study; Internships; Student-designed major; Study abroad; Teacher certification program. **Honors programs:** Business Scholars Co-op Program, graduate in 4-years with two full-time co-op work experiences; La Salle University Honors Program, similarly-talented peers, meeting in small seminar settings with faculty dedicated to undergraduate teaching is but one of the hallmarks of the La Salle Honors community. You will be participating in a Program which has as its specific objective the challenge of educating the superior student. **Combined degree programs:** BA/MA. **Disability Services offered:** Note-taking services; Reader services; Tape recorders; Tutors. **Career services:** Alumni network; Alumni services; Career assessment; Career/job search classes; Internships; Regional alumni.

FACILITIES

Housing: Apartments for single students; Coed dorms; Special housing for disabled students; Theme housing; Wellness housing; 95% of campus accessible to physically disabled. **Special Academic Facilities/Equipment:** Hugh and Nancy Devlin Science and Technology Center, West Campus School of Nursing and Health Science (formally Germantown Hospital), Art Museum, Japanese tea house, language lab, and child development center. **Campus Network:** 100% of classrooms, 100% of dorms, 100% of student union, 100% of libraries, 100% of dining areas, 100% of common outdoor areas have wireless network access.

CAMPUS LIFE

Environment: Metropolis. **Activities:** Campus Ministries; Choral groups; Dance; Drama/theater; International Student Organization; Jazz band; Literary magazine; Music ensembles; Musical theater; Pep band; Radio station; Student government; Student newspaper; Student-run film society; Television station; Yearbook. 110 registered organizations, 17 honor societies, 5 religious organizations, 6 fraternities, 5 sororities on campus. **Athletics (Intercollegiate):** *Men:* baseball, basketball, cheerleading, crew/rowing, cross-country, diving, football, golf, soccer, swimming, tennis, track/field (outdoor), wrestling.

Women: basketball, cheerleading, crew/rowing, cross-country, diving, field hockey, golf, lacrosse, soccer, softball, swimming, tennis, track/field (outdoor), volleyball. **On-Campus Highlights:** Hayman Center (sports facility).

ADMISSIONS
Freshman Academic Profile: Average high school GPA 3.4. 11% in top 10% of high school class, 30% in top 25% of high school class, 67% in top 50% of high school class. 55% from public high schools. **Test Scores:** SAT Math middle 50% range 480–570. SAT EBRW middle 50% range 490–590. ACT middle 50% range 17–23. **Basis for Candidate Selection:** *Very important factors include:* rigor of secondary school record, academic GPA. *Important factors include:* extracurricular activities. *Other factors include:* application essay, standardized test scores, recommendation(s), interview, talent/ability, character/ personal qualities, alumni/ae relation, volunteer work, work experience. **Freshman Admission Requirements:** High school diploma is required and GED is accepted. *Academic units required:* 4 English, 3 math, 1 science, 1 science lab, 2 foreign language, 1 history, 5 academic electives. **Freshman Admission Statistics:** 6,642 applied, 81% admitted, 19% enrolled. **Transfer Admission Requirements:** High school transcript, college transcript(s), essay or personal statement, standardized test scores, statement of good standing from prior institution(s). Minimum college GPA of 2.5 required. Lowest grade transferable C. **General Admission Information:** Non-fall registration accepted. Admission may be deferred for a maximum of 1 year.

COSTS AND FINANCIAL AID
Annual tuition $29,810. Room and board $15,080. Required fees $900. Average book and supplies expense $1,000. **Required Forms and Deadlines:** FAFSA. **Notification of Awards:** Applicants will be notified of awards on a rolling basis beginning 2/1. **Types of Aid:** *Need-based scholarships/grants:* College/university scholarship or grant aid from institutional funds; Federal Nursing Scholarships; Federal Pell; Private scholarships; SEOG; State scholarships/grants. *Loans:* Direct PLUS loans; Direct Subsidized Stafford Loans; Direct Unsubsidized Stafford Loans. **Student Employment:** Federal Work-Study Program available. Institutional employment available. **Financial Aid Statistics:** 99% needy freshmen, 98% needy undergrads receive need-based scholarship or grant aid. 7% freshmen, 5% undergrads receive non-need-based scholarship or grant aid. 81% freshmen, 82% undergrads receive need-based self-help aid. 5% freshmen, 6% undergrads receive athletic scholarships. 97% freshmen, 94% undergrads receive any aid. 77% undergrads borrow to pay for school. Average cumulative indebtedness $36,095. **Criteria awarding aid:** *Need-based:* Academics. *Non-need-based:* Academics, Athletics.

LASELL COLLEGE

Office of Undergraduate Admissions, Newton, MA 02466
Phone: 617-243-2225 **Financial Aid Phone:** 617-243-2227
E-mail: info@lasell.edu **CEEB Code:** 3481
Fax: 617-243-2380 **Website:** www.lasell.edu **ACT Code:** 1848

This private school was founded in 1851. It has a 55 acre campus.

RATINGS
Admissions Selectivity Rating: 76 . **Fire Safety Rating:** 78 **Green Rating:** 60*

STUDENTS AND FACULTY
Enrollment: 1,650. **Student Body:** 64% female, 36% male, 40% out-of-state, 6% international (22 countries represented). Asian 2%, African American 8%, Caucasian 67%, Hispanic 10%, Native American <1%, Pacific Islander <1%, Two or more races 2%, Race unknown 5%.
Retention and Graduation: 68% freshmen return for sophomore year. 50% freshmen graduate within 4 years. 54% freshmen graduate within 6 years.
Faculty: Student/faculty ratio 14:1. 85 full-time faculty, 82% hold PhDs, 20% are members of minority groups, 64% are women. 0% of classes are taught by teaching assistants.

ACADEMICS
Degrees: Bachelor's; Master's. **Classes:** Most classes have 10–19 students. Most lab/discussion sessions have 10–19 students. **Most popular majors:** Sport and Fitness Administration/Management; Communication and Media Studies; Fashion Merchandising. **Special Study Options:** Accelerated program; Cross-registration; Distance learning; Double major; Dual enrollment; English as a Second Language (ESL); Exchange student program (domestic); Honors program; Independent study; Internships; Liberal arts/career combination; Student-designed major; Study abroad; Teacher certification program. **Honors**

programs: Lasell College Honor's Program. **Disability Services offered:** Note-taking services; Reader services; Tape recorders; Tutors. **Career services:** Alumni services; Career assessment; Career/job search classes; Internships.

FACILITIES
Housing: Coed dorms; Theme housing; Wellness housing; Women's dorms. **Special Academic Facilities/Equipment:** Center for Public Service—Yamawaki Art/Cultural Center. **Campus Network:** 100% of classrooms, 100% of dorms, 100% of student union, 100% of libraries, 100% of dining areas, 25% of common outdoor areas have wireless network access.

CAMPUS LIFE
Environment: City. **Activities:** Choral groups; Dance; Drama/theater; International Student Organization; Jazz band; Literary magazine; Music ensembles; Musical theater; Radio station; Student government; Student newspaper; Yearbook. 71 registered organizations, 4 honor societies, 1 religious organization on campus. **Athletics (Intercollegiate):** *Men:* basketball, cross-country, lacrosse, soccer, volleyball. *Women:* basketball, cross-country, field hockey, lacrosse, soccer, softball, volleyball. **On-Campus Highlights:** Science and Technology Center.

ADMISSIONS
Freshman Academic Profile: Average high school GPA 3.0. 10% in top 10% of high school class, 30% in top 25% of high school class, 67% in top 50% of high school class. 80% from public high schools. **Test Scores:** SAT Math middle 50% range 490–580. SAT EBRW middle 50% range 490–590. ACT middle 50% range 16–25. **Basis for Candidate Selection:** *Very important factors include:* rigor of secondary school record, academic GPA, interview. *Important factors include:* application essay, recommendation(s), extracurricular activities, volunteer work. *Other factors include:* standardized test scores, talent/ ability, character/personal qualities, alumni/ae relation, level of applicant's interest. **Freshman Admission Requirements:** High school diploma is required and GED is accepted. *Academic units required:* 4 English, 3 math, 2 science, 2 science labs, 1 social studies, 1 history. *Academic units recommended:* 4 English, 4 math, 3 science, 3 science labs, 2 foreign language, 2 social studies, 2 history. **Freshman Admission Statistics:** 3,180 applied, 80% admitted, 15% enrolled. **Transfer Admission Requirements:** College transcript(s), standardized test scores, statement of good standing from prior institution(s). Minimum college GPA of 2.3 required. Lowest grade transferable C. **General Admission Information:** Application fee $40. Priority deadline 11/15. Admission may be deferred for a maximum of 1 year.

COSTS AND FINANCIAL AID
Annual tuition $35,700. Room and board $16,000. Required fees $1,300. Average book and supplies expense $1,000. **Required Forms and Deadlines:** FAFSA. **Notification of Awards:** Applicants will be notified of awards on a rolling basis beginning 12/1. **Types of Aid:** *Need-based scholarships/grants:* College/university scholarship or grant aid from institutional funds; Federal Pell; Private scholarships; SEOG; State scholarships/grants. *Loans:* Direct PLUS loans; Direct Subsidized Stafford Loans; Direct Unsubsidized Stafford Loans. **Student Employment:** Federal Work-Study Program available. Institutional employment available. **Financial Aid Statistics:** 100% needy freshmen, 100% needy undergrads receive need-based scholarship or grant aid. 0% freshmen, 0% undergrads receive non-need-based scholarship or grant aid. 99% freshmen, 89% undergrads receive need-based self-help aid. 0% freshmen, 0% undergrads receive athletic scholarships. 82% undergrads borrow to pay for school. Average cumulative indebtedness $41,476. **Criteria awarding aid:** *Need-based:* Academics, Alumni affiliation, Leadership. *Non-need-based:* Academics, Alumni affiliation, Leadership.

LA SIERRA UNIVERSITY

4500 Riverwalk Parkway, Riverside, CA 92515
Phone: 951-785-2176
E-mail: admissions@lasierra.edu
Fax: 9517852477 **Website:** www.lasierra.edu **ACT Code:** 0294

This private school, affiliated with the Seventh Day Adventist Church, was founded in 1922. It has a 100 acre campus.

RATINGS
Admissions Selectivity Rating: 86 **Fire Safety Rating:** 60* **Green Rating:** 60*

STUDENTS AND FACULTY
Enrollment: 2,060. **Student Body:** 58% female, 42% male, 6% out-of-state, 12% international. Asian 16%, African American 7%, Caucasian 16%,

Hispanic 42%, Native American <1%, Pacific Islander 2%, Two or more races 4%, Race unknown <1%.

Retention and Graduation: 76% freshmen return for sophomore year. **Faculty:** Student/faculty ratio 14:1. 103 full-time faculty, 95% hold PhDs, 32% are members of minority groups, 44% are women.

ACADEMICS

Degrees: Bachelor's; Certificate; Doctoral degree research/scholarship; Master's; Post-bachelor's certificate; Post-master's certificate. **Classes:** Most classes have 10–19 students. Most lab/discussion sessions have fewer than 10 students. **Special Study Options:** Cross-registration; Distance learning; Double major; Dual enrollment; English as a Second Language (ESL); Honors program; Independent study; Internships; Student-designed major; Study abroad; Teacher certification program.

FACILITIES

Housing: Apartments for married students; Apartments for single students; Men's dorms; Special housing for international students; Wellness housing; Women's dorms.

CAMPUS LIFE

Environment: City. **Activities:** Campus Ministries; Choral groups; Concert band; Drama/theater; International Student Organization; Jazz band; Literary magazine; Music ensembles; Student government; Student newspaper; Symphony orchestra; Yearbook.

ADMISSIONS

Freshman Academic Profile: Average high school GPA 3.3. 10% in top 10% of high school class, 41% in top 25% of high school class, 63% in top 50% of high school class. **Test Scores:** SAT Math middle 50% range 410–530. SAT EBRW middle 50% range 400–510. ACT middle 50% range 17–22. **Basis for Candidate Selection:** *Very important factors include:* rigor of secondary school record, academic GPA, standardized test scores, character/personal qualities. *Important factors include:* application essay, recommendation(s), religious affiliation/commitment, level of applicant's interest. **Freshman Admission Requirements:** High school diploma is required and GED is accepted. *Academic units required:* 4 English, 3 math, 2 science, 2 science labs, 2 foreign language, 2 social studies, 1 visual/performing arts, 1 unit from above areas or other academic areas. *Academic units recommended:* 4 math, 3 science, 3 science labs, 3 foreign language. **Freshman Admission Statistics:** 3,479 applied, 47% admitted, 29% enrolled. **General Admission Information:** Application fee $30. Regular application deadline 8/15. Non-fall registration accepted.

COSTS AND FINANCIAL AID

Annual tuition $27,972. Room and board $7,500. Required fees $1,131. Average book and supplies expense $1,710.

LAWRENCE TECHNOLOGICAL UNIVERSITY

Best Colleges

21000 West Ten Mile Rd., Southfield, MI 48075-1058
Phone: 248-204-3160 **Financial Aid Phone:** 248-204-2280
E-mail: admissions@ltu.edu **CEEB Code:** 1399
Fax: 248-204-3188 **Website:** www.ltu.edu **ACT Code:** 2020

This private school was founded in 1932. It has a 107 acre campus.

RATINGS

Admissions Selectivity Rating: 86   **Fire Safety Rating:** 95   **Green Rating:** 75

STUDENTS AND FACULTY

Enrollment: 1,978. **Student Body:** 26% female, 74% male, 8% out-of-state, 15% international (49 countries represented). Asian 3%, African American 6%, Caucasian 65%, Hispanic 3%, Native American <1%, Pacific Islander 0%, Two or more races 2%, Race unknown 6%.
Retention and Graduation: 82% freshmen return for sophomore year. 43% freshmen graduate within 4 years. 53% freshmen graduate within 6 years. 10% grads go on to further study within 1 year. **Faculty:** Student/faculty ratio 11:1. 127 full-time faculty, 0% hold PhDs, 25% are members of minority groups, 31% are women. 0% of classes are taught by teaching assistants.

ACADEMICS

Degrees: Associate; Bachelor's; Certificate; Doctoral degree research/scholarship; Master's; Post-bachelor's certificate. **Classes:** Most classes have 10–19 students. Most lab/discussion sessions have 10–19 students. **Most popular majors:** Mechanical Engineering; Business Administration and Management, General; Architecture. **Special Study Options:** Cooperative education program; Cross-registration; Distance learning; English as a Second Language (ESL); Honors program; Independent study; Internships; Study abroad. **Honors programs:** The LTU Honors Program is designed for highly qualified students who want an educational experience that will take full advantage of the challenging curricula offered at Lawrence Tech. **Combined degree programs:** BA/MEng. **Disability Services offered:** Note-taking services; Reader services; Tape recorders; Tutors. **Career services:** Alumni services; Career assessment; Internships.

FACILITIES

Housing: Apartments for married students; Apartments for single students; Special housing for disabled students; 97% of campus accessible to physically disabled. **Special Academic Facilities/Equipment:** Albert Kahn Library Center for Innovative Materials Research; Applied Research Center; Environmental Scanning Electron Microscope; Confocal Microscope; Center for Innovative Materials Research; Robotics Lab.

CAMPUS LIFE

Environment: City. **Activities:** Drama/theater; Literary magazine; Music ensembles; Student government; Student newspaper. 54 registered organizations, 4 honor societies, 1 religious organization, 6 fraternities, 4 sororities on campus. **On-Campus Highlights:** Atrium. **Environmental Initiatives:** Reuss Hall and Taubman Complex were both designed to environmental management without consideration of submittal and LEED recognition.

ADMISSIONS

Freshman Academic Profile: Average high school GPA 3.5. 38% in top 10% of high school class, 54% in top 25% of high school class, 100% in top 50% of high school class. **Test Scores:** SAT Math middle 50% range 530–660. SAT EBRW middle 50% range 530–620. ACT middle 50% range 21–28. **Basis for Candidate Selection:** *Very important factors include:* rigor of secondary school record, academic GPA, standardized test scores. *Other factors include:* application essay, recommendation(s). **Freshman Admission Requirements:** High school diploma is required and GED is accepted. *Academic units required:* 4 English, 3 math, 2 science, 3 social studies. *Academic units recommended:* 4 English, 4 math, 4 science, 2 science labs, 2 history. **Freshman Admission Statistics:** 2,173 applied, 60% admitted, 29% enrolled. **Transfer Admission Requirements:** High school transcript, college transcript(s). Minimum college GPA of 2.2 required. Lowest grade transferable C. **General Admission Information:** Application fee $30. Non-fall registration accepted. Admission may be deferred for a maximum of 3 years.

COSTS AND FINANCIAL AID

Annual tuition $34,080. Room and board $9,950. Required fees $1,200. Average book and supplies expense $1,536. **Required Forms and Deadlines:** FAFSA. **Notification of Awards:** Applicants will be notified of awards on a rolling basis beginning 4/1. **Types of Aid:** *Need-based scholarships/grants:* College/university scholarship or grant aid from institutional funds; Federal Pell; Private scholarships; SEOG; State scholarships/grants. *Loans:* Direct PLUS loans; Direct Subsidized Stafford Loans; Direct Unsubsidized Stafford Loans. **Student Employment:** Federal Work-Study Program available. Institutional employment available. **Financial Aid Statistics:** 97% needy freshmen, 93% needy undergrads receive need-based scholarship or grant aid. 91% freshmen, 79% undergrads receive non-need-based scholarship or grant aid. 75% freshmen, 81% undergrads receive need-based self-help aid. 27% freshmen, 16% undergrads receive athletic scholarships. 97% freshmen, 73% undergrads receive any aid. 67% undergrads borrow to pay for school. Average cumulative indebtedness $36,049. **Criteria awarding aid:** *Non-need-based:* Academics, Alumni affiliation, Athletics, Leadership, Minority status, State/district residency.

LAWRENCE UNIVERSITY

711 East Boldt Way, Appleton, WI 54911-5699
Phone: 920-832-6500 **Financial Aid Phone:** 920-832-6584
E-mail: admissions@lawrence.edu **CEEB Code:** 1398
Fax: 920-832-6782 **Website:** www.lawrence.edu **ACT Code:** 4596

This private school was founded in 1847. It has a 84 acre campus.

RATINGS
Admissions Selectivity Rating: 87   **Fire Safety Rating:** 88   **Green Rating:** 86

STUDENTS AND FACULTY
Enrollment: 1,441. **Student Body:** 54% female, 46% male, 71% out-of-state, 12% international (62 countries represented). Asian 5%, African American 5%, Caucasian 65%, Hispanic 9%, Native American <1%, Pacific Islander <1%, Two or more races 4%, Race unknown 1%.
Retention and Graduation: 88% freshmen return for sophomore year. 64% freshmen graduate within 4 years. 79% freshmen graduate within 6 years. 24% grads go on to further study within 1 year. 51% grads pursue arts and sciences degrees. 7% grads pursue law degrees. 7% grads pursue business degrees. 0% grads pursue medical degrees. **Faculty:** Student/faculty ratio 8:1. 174 full-time faculty, 91% hold PhDs, 16% are members of minority groups, 44% are women. 0% of classes are taught by teaching assistants.

ACADEMICS
Degrees: Bachelor's. **Classes:** Most classes have 10–19 students. **Most popular majors:** Psychology, General; Economics; Music Performance, General. **Special Study Options:** Double major; Independent study; Internships; Student-designed major; Study abroad; Teacher certification program. **Disability Services offered:** Note-taking services; Reader services; Tape recorders; Tutors. **Career services:** Alumni network; Alumni services; Career assessment; Career/job search classes; Internships; Regional alumni.

FACILITIES
Housing: Apartments for married students; Apartments for single students; Coed dorms; Cooperative housing; Fraternity/sorority housing; Men's dorms; Special housing for disabled students; Theme housing; Wellness housing; Women's dorms. **Special Academic Facilities/Equipment:** Film production studio, sound stage, editing rooms, screening rooms, cinema; music studios; baroque instrument collection; art galleries, anthropology collection, 425-acre estate on Lake Michigan hosting retreats and seminars for students, electron microscope, laser physics lab, physics/computational graphics lab, nuclear magnetic resonance spectrometer, Wriston Art Center, Mudd Gallery, Teekwood Room, The Maker Space with 3D Printer, Chapel-Organ. **Campus Network:** 95% of classrooms, 100% of dorms, 100% of student union, 100% of libraries, 100% of dining areas, 50% of common outdoor areas have wireless network access.

CAMPUS LIFE
Environment: City. **Activities:** Campus Ministries; Choral groups; Concert band; Dance; Drama/theater; International Student Organization; Jazz band; Literary magazine; Model UN; Music ensembles; Musical theater; Opera; Pep band; Radio station; Student government; Student newspaper; Student-run film society; Symphony orchestra. 101 registered organizations, 2 honor societies, 3 religious organizations, 4 fraternities, 4 sororities on campus. **Athletics (Intercollegiate):** *Men:* baseball, basketball, cross-country, diving, fencing, football, golf, ice hockey, soccer, swimming, tennis, track/field (outdoor), track/field (indoor), wrestling. *Women:* basketball, cross-country, diving, fencing, soccer, softball, swimming, tennis, track/field (outdoor), track/field (indoor), volleyball. **On-Campus Highlights:** Warch Campus Center. **Environmental Initiatives:** Construction of LEED certified Student Center—Gold.

ADMISSIONS
Freshman Academic Profile: Average high school GPA 3.5. 38% in top 10% of high school class, 68% in top 25% of high school class, 94% in top 50% of high school class. **Test Scores:** SAT Math middle 50% range 600–730. SAT EBRW middle 50% range 620–730. ACT middle 50% range 25–32. **Basis for Candidate Selection:** *Very important factors include:* rigor of secondary school record, class rank, academic GPA, talent/ability, character/personal qualities. *Important factors include:* application essay, recommendation(s), interview, extracurricular activities. *Other factors include:* standardized test scores, first

generation, alumni/ae relation, geographical residence, racial/ethnic status, volunteer work, work experience, level of applicant's interest. **Freshman Admission Requirements:** High school diploma is required and GED is accepted. *Academic units recommended:* 4 English, 3 math, 3 science, 2 foreign language, 2 social studies, 2 history. **Freshman Admission Statistics:** 3,612 applied, 61% admitted, 16% enrolled. **Transfer Admission Requirements:** High school transcript, college transcript(s), essay or personal statement. Minimum college GPA of 2.75 required. Lowest grade transferable C-. **General Admission Information:** Regular application deadline 1/15. Non-fall registration accepted. Admission may be deferred for a maximum of 1 year.

COSTS AND FINANCIAL AID
Annual tuition $47,175. Room and board $10,341. Required fees $300. Average book and supplies expense $900. **Required Forms and Deadlines:** CSS/Financial Aid PROFILE; FAFSA; Noncustodial PROFILE. **Notification of Awards:** Applicants will be notified of awards on or about 1/15. **Types of Aid:** *Need-based scholarships/grants:* College/university scholarship or grant aid from institutional funds; Federal Pell; Private scholarships; SEOG; State scholarships/grants. *Loans:* Direct PLUS loans; Direct Subsidized Stafford Loans; Direct Unsubsidized Stafford Loans. **Student Employment:** Federal Work-Study Program available. Institutional employment available. **Financial Aid Statistics:** 98% needy freshmen, 98% needy undergrads receive need-based scholarship or grant aid. 0% freshmen, 0% undergrads receive non-need-based scholarship or grant aid. 79% freshmen, 82% undergrads receive need-based self-help aid. 0% freshmen, 0% undergrads receive athletic scholarships. 100% freshmen, 99% undergrads receive any aid. 60% undergrads borrow to pay for school. Average cumulative indebtedness $32,488. **Criteria awarding aid:** *Need-based:* Academics, Music/drama. *Non-need-based:* Academics, Alumni affiliation, Leadership, Minority status, Music/drama.

LEBANON VALLEY COLLEGE

101 North College Avenue, Annville, PA 17003-1400
Phone: 717-867-6181 **Financial Aid Phone:** 717-867-6126
E-mail: admission@lvc.edu **CEEB Code:** 2364
Fax: 717-867-6026 **Website:** www.lvc.edu **ACT Code:** 3610

This private school, affiliated with the Methodist Church, was founded in 1866. It has a 357 acre campus.

RATINGS
Admissions Selectivity Rating: 82   **Fire Safety Rating:** 94   **Green Rating:** 79

STUDENTS AND FACULTY
Enrollment: 1,658. **Student Body:** 55% female, 45% male, 20% out-of-state, 1% international (12 countries represented). Asian 2%, African American 3%, Caucasian 83%, Hispanic 6%, Native American <1%, Pacific Islander <1%, Two or more races 3%, Race unknown 2%.
Retention and Graduation: 81% freshmen return for sophomore year. 69% freshmen graduate within 4 years. 73% freshmen graduate within 6 years. 42% grads go on to further study within 1 year. 19% grads pursue arts and sciences degrees. 1% grads pursue law degrees. 1% grads pursue business degrees. 2% grads pursue medical degrees. **Faculty:** Student/faculty ratio 10:1. 118 full-time faculty, 90% hold PhDs, 10% are members of minority groups, 42% are women. 0% of classes are taught by teaching assistants.

ACADEMICS
Degrees: Bachelor's; Doctoral degree—professional practice; Master's; Post-bachelor's certificate. **Classes:** Most classes have 10–19 students. Most lab/discussion sessions have 10–19 students. **Most popular majors:** Early Childhood Education and Teaching; Exercise Science and Kinesiology; International Business/Trade/Commerce. **Special Study Options:** Accelerated program; Cooperative education program; Distance learning; Double major; Dual enrollment; English as a Second Language (ESL); Independent study; Internships; Liberal arts/career combination; Student-designed major; Study abroad; Teacher certification program. **Disability Services offered:** Note-taking services; Reader services; Tape recorders; Tutors. **Career services:** Alumni network; Alumni services; Internships.

FACILITIES
Housing: Apartments for single students; Coed dorms; Special housing for disabled students; Theme housing; Wellness housing; 80% of campus accessible to physically disabled. **Special Academic Facilities/Equipment:** Major-specific computer labs and resource libraries; animal behaviors labs;

genetic testing equipment; psychology tests for personality and intelligence; bio-feedback equipment; technology, equipment, and materials for gene isolation, amplification, quantitation, mutation, including a Real-Time PCR machine; technology, equipment, and materials for recombinant protein production, purification, and analysis; mass spectrometers such as the MALDI-TOF MS and an ESI-Triple quad LC-MS; UV, visible, and fluorescent spectrophotometers, including a SpectraMax Plus 384 Absorbance UV/Vis Microplate Reader for use in biochemical and immunological assays such as ELISAs; tissue culture facility; animal facility; analytical and preparative liquid chromatography and electrophoresis systems for biomolecules; 20 acres of woodland dedicated to field studies in ecology, animal behavior, and plant science; game cameras to remotely sample wildlife populations; two greenhouses for botanical collection and experimentation; oversized Morris water maze, video camera, and Smart Maze software for behavioral studies; scanning electron microscope; transmission electron microscope; Thermo Scientific cryostat; biotechnology suite with a new RT-PCR instrument; sound recording studios; optics, atomic/nuclear, electronics, advanced physics, atomic force microscopy, and computational physics laboratories; physical therapy wellness pool and center; and more. **Campus Network:** 100% of classrooms, 100% of dorms, 100% of student union, 100% of libraries, 100% of dining areas, 75% of common outdoor areas have wireless network access.

CAMPUS LIFE

Environment: Rural. **Activities:** Campus Ministries; Choral groups; Concert band; Dance; Drama/theater; Jazz band; Literary magazine; Marching band; Music ensembles; Musical theater; Student government; Student newspaper; Symphony orchestra. 95 registered organizations, 19 honor societies, 14 religious organizations, 4 fraternities, 4 sororities on campus. **Athletics (Intercollegiate):** *Men:* baseball, basketball, cross-country, football, golf, ice hockey, lacrosse, soccer, swimming, tennis, track/field (outdoor), track/field (indoor). *Women:* basketball, cross-country, field hockey, lacrosse, soccer, softball, swimming, tennis, track/field (outdoor), track/field (indoor), volleyball. **On-Campus Highlights:** Peace Garden. **Environmental Initiatives:** Energy conservation.

ADMISSIONS

Freshman Academic Profile: Average high school GPA 3.7. 28% in top 10% of high school class, 55% in top 25% of high school class, 85% in top 50% of high school class. **Test Scores:** SAT Math middle 50% range 530–630. SAT EBRW middle 50% range 533–620. ACT middle 50% range 22–26. **Basis for Candidate Selection:** *Very important factors include:* rigor of secondary school record, class rank, academic GPA. *Important factors include:* interview, extracurricular activities, talent/ability, character/personal qualities. *Other factors include:* application essay, standardized test scores, recommendation(s), first generation, alumni/ae relation, geographical residence, state residency, racial/ethnic status, volunteer work, work experience. **Freshman Admission Requirements:** High school diploma is required and GED is accepted. *Academic units required:* 4 English, 3 math, 3 science, 2 foreign language, 3 social studies, 1 unit from above areas or other academic areas. *Academic units recommended:* 2 science labs, 3 foreign language, 2 history. **Freshman Admission Statistics:** 2,833 applied, 73% admitted, 23% enrolled. **Transfer Admission Requirements:** High school transcript, college transcript(s), essay or personal statement, statement of good standing from prior institution(s). Minimum college GPA of 2.0 required. Lowest grade transferable C-. **General Admission Information:** Regular application deadline 2/15. Non-fall registration accepted.

COSTS AND FINANCIAL AID

Annual tuition $42,420. Room and board $11,860. Required fees $1,230. Average book and supplies expense $1,200. **Required Forms and Deadlines:** FAFSA. **Notification of Awards:** Applicants will be notified of awards on a rolling basis beginning 12/5. **Types of Aid:** *Need-based scholarships/grants:* College/university scholarship or grant aid from institutional funds; Federal Pell; Private scholarships; SEOG; State scholarships/grants. *Loans:* Direct PLUS loans; Direct Subsidized Stafford Loans; Direct Unsubsidized Stafford Loans. **Student Employment:** Federal Work-Study Program available. Institutional employment available. **Financial Aid Statistics:** 100% needy freshmen, 99% needy undergrads receive need-based scholarship or grant aid. 9% freshmen, 11% undergrads receive non-need-based scholarship or grant aid. 90% freshmen, 85% undergrads receive need-based self-help aid. 0% freshmen, 0% undergrads receive athletic scholarships. 99% freshmen, 99% undergrads receive any aid. 80% undergrads borrow to pay for school. Average cumulative indebtedness $43,588. **Criteria awarding aid:** *Need-based:* Academics, Minority status. *Non-need-based:* Academics, Alumni affiliation, Music/drama.

LEE UNIVERSITY

P.O. Box 3450, Cleveland, TN 37320-3450
Phone: 423-614-8500 **Financial Aid Phone:** 423-614-8300
E-mail: admissions@leeuniversity.edu **CEEB Code:** 1401
Fax: 423-614-8533 **Website:** www.leeuniversity.edu **ACT Code:** 3978

This private school, affiliated with the Church of God, was founded in 1918. It has a 120 acre campus.

RATINGS

Admissions Selectivity Rating: 77   **Fire Safety Rating:** 93   **Green Rating:** 60*

STUDENTS AND FACULTY

Enrollment: 4,077. **Student Body:** 61% female, 39% male, 52% out-of-state, 3% international (50 countries represented). Asian 1%, African American 5%, Caucasian 83%, Hispanic 2%, Native American <1%, Pacific Islander <1%, Two or more races 4%, Race unknown 3%.
Retention and Graduation: 78% freshmen return for sophomore year. 41% freshmen graduate within 4 years. 59% freshmen graduate within 6 years. 19% grads go on to further study within 1 year. 6% grads pursue arts and sciences degrees. 1% grads pursue law degrees. 4% grads pursue business degrees. 1% grads pursue medical degrees. **Faculty:** Student/faculty ratio 15:1. 188 full-time faculty, 76% hold PhDs, 11% are members of minority groups, 42% are women. 0% of classes are taught by teaching assistants.

ACADEMICS

Degrees: Bachelor's; Doctoral degree—professional practice; Doctoral degree research/scholarship; Master's; Post-master's certificate. **Classes:** Most classes have 10–19 students. Most lab/discussion sessions have 10–19 students.
Most popular majors: Business Administration and Management, General; Psychology, General; Pastoral Studies/Counseling. **Special Study Options:** Distance learning; Double major; Dual enrollment; English as a Second Language (ESL); External degree program; Honors program; Independent study; Internships; Student-designed major; Study abroad; Teacher certification program. **Honors programs:** The Kairos Scholars Honors Program. Also, several academic subject honors societies like Psychology, Business, Music and Pre-Med. **Disability Services offered:** Note-taking services; Reader services; Tutors. **Career services:** Alumni network; Alumni services; Career assessment; Internships.

FACILITIES

Housing: Apartments for married students; Apartments for single students; Men's dorms; Women's dorms; 77% of campus accessible to physically disabled. **Special Academic Facilities/Equipment:** Curriculum Library in the College of Education. **Campus Network:** 100% of classrooms, 100% of dorms, 100% of student union, 100% of libraries, 100% of dining areas, 100% of common outdoor areas have wireless network access.

CAMPUS LIFE

Environment: Town. **Activities:** Campus Ministries; Choral groups; Concert band; Drama/theater; International Student Organization; Jazz band; Literary magazine; Model UN; Music ensembles; Musical theater; Opera; Pep band; Student government; Student newspaper; Symphony orchestra; Yearbook. 100 registered organizations, 17 honor societies, 15 religious organizations, 5 fraternities, 4 sororities on campus. **Athletics (Intercollegiate):** *Men:* baseball, basketball, cheerleading, cross-country, golf, soccer, tennis. *Women:* basketball, cheerleading, cross-country, soccer, softball, tennis, volleyball. **On-Campus Highlights:** Paul Conn Student Union-Bookstore; Chick-Fil-A.

ADMISSIONS

Freshman Academic Profile: Average high school GPA 3.7. 28% in top 10% of high school class, 49% in top 25% of high school class, 74% in top 50% of high school class. **Test Scores:** SAT Math middle 50% range 450–610. SAT EBRW middle 50% range 460–620. ACT middle 50% range 21–28. **Basis for Candidate Selection:** *Very important factors include:* rigor of secondary school record, academic GPA, standardized test scores. *Important factors include:* class rank, character/personal qualities. *Other factors include:* application essay, recommendation(s), interview, extracurricular activities, talent/ability, first generation, alumni/ae relation. **Freshman Admission Requirements:** High school diploma is required and GED is accepted. *Academic units required:* 4 English, 3 math, 2 science, 1 foreign language, 2 social studies, 1 history. *Academic units recommended:* 4 English, 3 math, 2 science, 1 foreign language, 2 social studies, 1 history, 1 computer science. **Freshman Admission Statistics:** 2,416 applied, 82% admitted, 40% enrolled. **Transfer Admission**

Requirements: College transcript(s). Minimum college GPA of 2.0 required. Lowest grade transferable D. **General Admission Information:** Application fee $25. Priority deadline 4/15. Non-fall registration accepted. Admission may be deferred for a maximum of 1 semester.

COSTS AND FINANCIAL AID
Annual tuition $18,840. Room and board $8,260. Required fees $700. Average book and supplies expense $1,600. **Required Forms and Deadlines:** FAFSA. **Notification of Awards:** Applicants will be notified of awards on a rolling basis beginning 2/1. **Types of Aid:** *Need-based scholarships/grants:* College/university scholarship or grant aid from institutional funds; Federal Pell; Private scholarships; SEOG; State scholarships/grants. *Loans:* Direct PLUS loans; Direct Subsidized Stafford Loans; Direct Unsubsidized Stafford Loans. **Student Employment:** Federal Work-Study Program available. Institutional employment available. **Financial Aid Statistics:** 96% needy freshmen, 92% needy undergrads receive need-based scholarship or grant aid. 21% freshmen, 13% undergrads receive non-need-based scholarship or grant aid. 59% freshmen, 70% undergrads receive need-based self-help aid. 5% freshmen, 4% undergrads receive athletic scholarships. 97% freshmen, 89% undergrads receive any aid. 61% undergrads borrow to pay for school. Average cumulative indebtedness $30,846. **Criteria awarding aid:** *Non-need-based:* Academics, Alumni affiliation, Athletics, Leadership, Minority status, Music/drama, Religious affiliation, State/district residency.

LEHIGH UNIVERSITY

27 Memorial Drive West, Bethlehem, PA 18015
Phone: 610-758-3100 **Financial Aid Phone:** 610-758-3181
E-mail: admissions@lehigh.edu **CEEB Code:** 2365
Fax: 610-758-4361 **Website:** www.lehigh.edu **ACT Code:** 3612

This private school was founded in 1865. It has a 2355 acre campus.

RATINGS
Admissions Selectivity Rating: 94   **Fire Safety Rating:** 97   **Green Rating:** 96

STUDENTS AND FACULTY
Enrollment: 5,164. **Student Body:** 46% female, 54% male, 73% out-of-state, 9% international (70 countries represented). Asian 8%, African American 4%, Caucasian 62%, Hispanic 9%, Native American <1%, Pacific Islander <1%, Two or more races 4%, Race unknown 4%.
Retention and Graduation: 93% freshmen return for sophomore year. 72% freshmen graduate within 4 years. 87% freshmen graduate within 6 years. 21% grads go on to further study within 1 year. 29% grads pursue arts and sciences degrees. 4% grads pursue law degrees. 22% grads pursue business degrees. 7% grads pursue medical degrees. **Faculty:** Student/faculty ratio 9:1. 548 full-time faculty, 95% hold PhDs, 21% are members of minority groups, 35% are women.

ACADEMICS
Degrees: Bachelor's; Doctoral degree research/scholarship; Master's; Post-bachelor's certificate; Post-master's certificate. **Classes:** Most classes have 10–19 students. Most lab/discussion sessions have 10–19 students. **Most popular majors:** Mechanical Engineering; Accounting; Finance, General. **Special Study Options:** Accelerated program; Cooperative education program; Cross-registration; Distance learning; Double major; English as a Second Language (ESL); Exchange student program (domestic); External degree program; Honors program; Independent study; Internships; Liberal arts/career combination; Study abroad. **Honors programs:** Integrated Business and Engineering (IBE) Honors Program, program description available at https://ibe.lehigh.edu. **Disability Services offered:** Note-taking services; Reader services; Tape recorders. **Career services:** Alumni network; Alumni services; Career assessment; Career/job search classes; Internships; Regional alumni.

FACILITIES
Housing: Apartments for married students; Apartments for single students; Coed dorms; Fraternity/sorority housing; Special housing for disabled students; Special housing for international students; Theme housing; Wellness housing. **Special Academic Facilities/Equipment:** Zoellner Arts Center; Art Gallery; Electron optical labs; Wilbur Powerhouse.

CAMPUS LIFE
Environment: City. **Activities:** Campus Ministries; Choral groups; Concert band; Dance; Drama/theater; International Student Organization; Jazz band; Literary magazine; Marching band; Model UN; Music ensembles; Musical theater; Pep band; Radio station; Student government; Student newspaper; Student-run film society; Symphony orchestra; Yearbook. 150 registered organizations, 18 honor societies, 14 religious organizations, 14 fraternities, 10 sororities on campus. **Athletics (Intercollegiate):** *Men:* baseball, basketball, cross-country, diving, football, golf, lacrosse, soccer, swimming, tennis, track/field (outdoor), track/field (indoor), wrestling. *Women:* basketball, crew/rowing, cross-country, diving, field hockey, golf, lacrosse, soccer, softball, swimming, tennis, track/field (outdoor), track/field (indoor), volleyball. **On-Campus Highlights:** Linderman Library.

ADMISSIONS
Freshman Academic Profile: 58% in top 10% of high school class, 85% in top 25% of high school class, 97% in top 50% of high school class. **Test Scores:** SAT Math middle 50% range 660–760. SAT EBRW middle 50% range 620–690. ACT middle 50% range 29–33. **Basis for Candidate Selection:** *Very important factors include:* rigor of secondary school record, class rank, academic GPA, standardized test scores, talent/ability, character/personal qualities. *Important factors include:* application essay, recommendation(s), extracurricular activities, first generation, geographical residence, racial/ethnic status, volunteer work. *Other factors include:* interview, alumni/ae relation, work experience. **Freshman Admission Requirements:** High school diploma is required and GED is accepted. *Academic units required:* 4 English, 3 math, 2 science, 2 science labs, 2 foreign language, 2 social studies, 2 history, 2 academic electives. *Academic units recommended:* 4 English, 4 math, 4 science, 3 science labs, 3 foreign language, 3 social studies, 2 history, 2 academic electives, 1 computer science, 1 visual/performing arts. **Freshman Admission Statistics:** 15,649 applied, 32% admitted, 28% enrolled. **Transfer Admission Requirements:** High school transcript, college transcript(s), essay or personal statement, statement of good standing from prior institution(s). Minimum college GPA of 3.25 required. **General Admission Information:** Application fee $70. Regular application deadline 1/1. Non-fall registration accepted. Admission may be deferred for a maximum of 1 year.

COSTS AND FINANCIAL AID
Required Forms and Deadlines: CSS/Financial Aid PROFILE; FAFSA; Noncustodial PROFILE. **Notification of Awards:** Applicants will be notified of awards on or about 3/30. **Types of Aid:** *Need-based scholarships/grants:* College/university scholarship or grant aid from institutional funds; Federal Pell; Private scholarships; State scholarships/grants. *Loans:* Direct PLUS loans; Direct Subsidized Stafford Loans; Direct Unsubsidized Stafford Loans. **Student Employment:** Federal Work-Study Program available. Institutional employment available. **Financial Aid Statistics:** 99% needy freshmen, 99% needy undergrads receive need-based scholarship or grant aid. 15% freshmen, 18% undergrads receive non-need-based scholarship or grant aid. 96% freshmen, 95% undergrads receive need-based self-help aid. 5% freshmen, 6% undergrads receive athletic scholarships. 57.5% freshmen, 57.7% undergrads receive any aid. 50% undergrads borrow to pay for school. Average cumulative indebtedness $39,609. **Criteria awarding aid:** *Need-based:* Academics, Athletics, Minority status, Religious affiliation. *Non-need-based:* Academics, Art, Athletics, Leadership, Music/drama.

LE MOYNE COLLEGE

1419 Salt Springs Rd., Syracuse, NY 13214-1301
Phone: 315-445-4300 **Financial Aid Phone:** 315-445-4400
E-mail: admission@lemoyne.edu **CEEB Code:** 2366
Fax: 315-445-4711 **Website:** www.lemoyne.edu **ACT Code:** 2790

This private school, affiliated with the Roman Catholic Church, was founded in 1946. It has a 161 acre campus.

RATINGS
Admissions Selectivity Rating: 78   **Fire Safety Rating:** 90   **Green Rating:** 84

STUDENTS AND FACULTY
Enrollment: 2,642. **Student Body:** 60% female, 40% male, 7% out-of-state, 1% international (49 countries represented). Asian 3%, African American 6%,

Caucasian 76%, Hispanic 7%, Native American <1%, Pacific Islander <1%, Two or more races 3%, Race unknown 2%.
Retention and Graduation: 87% freshmen return for sophomore year. 65% freshmen graduate within 4 years. 74% freshmen graduate within 6 years. 16% grads go on to further study within 1 year. 7% grads pursue arts and sciences degrees. 2% grads pursue law degrees. 1% grads pursue business degrees. 5% grads pursue medical degrees. **Faculty:** Student/faculty ratio 12:1. 177 full-time faculty, 89% hold PhDs, 18% are members of minority groups, 45% are women. 0% of classes are taught by teaching assistants.

ACADEMICS
Degrees: Bachelor's; Doctoral degree research/scholarship; Master's; Post-bachelor's certificate; Post-master's certificate. **Classes:** Most classes have 10–19 students. Most lab/discussion sessions have 10–19 students. **Most popular majors:** Biology/Biological Sciences, General; Psychology, General; Registered Nursing/Registered Nurse. **Special Study Options:** Accelerated program; Cross-registration; Distance learning; Double major; Dual enrollment; Honors program; Independent study; Internships; Study abroad; Teacher certification program. **Honors programs:** Students in the program complete a 21-hour sequence of interdisciplinary humanities courses that replaces the standard core requirements in English, history, philosophy, and religious studies. Seniors complete an honors project working in close collaboration with a faculty advisor. **Combined degree programs:** BA/DDS; BA/JD; BA/MA; BA/MD; BA/MEng. **Disability Services offered:** Note-taking services; Reader services; Tape recorders; Tutors. **Career services:** Alumni network; Alumni services; Career assessment; Career/job search classes; Internships; Regional alumni.

FACILITIES
Housing: Apartments for single students; Coed dorms; Special housing for disabled students; Theme housing; Wellness housing; 98% of campus accessible to physically disabled. **Special Academic Facilities/Equipment:** W. Carroll Coyne Center for the Performing Arts, Panasci Family Chapel, Wilson Art Gallery, Audio Visual Center, electron microscopes, Le Moyne College Archives, Media Center, NMR Room, Student Wellness Center, Writing Center, Student Success Center, and Quantitative Reasoning Center.

CAMPUS LIFE
Environment: City. **Activities:** Campus Ministries; Choral groups; Concert band; Dance; Drama/theater; International Student Organization; Jazz band; Literary magazine; Model UN; Music ensembles; Musical theater; Radio station; Student government; Student newspaper; Student-run film society; Symphony orchestra; Television station; Yearbook. 108 registered organizations, 21 honor societies, 9 religious organizations on campus. **Athletics (Intercollegiate):** *Men:* baseball, basketball, cross-country, diving, golf, lacrosse, soccer, swimming, tennis. *Women:* basketball, cross-country, diving, golf, lacrosse, soccer, softball, swimming, tennis, volleyball. **On-Campus Highlights:** The Thomas J. Niland Athletic Complex. **Environmental Initiatives:** LEED GOLD certification on new science building.

ADMISSIONS
Freshman Academic Profile: Average high school GPA 3.5. 21% in top 10% of high school class, 53% in top 25% of high school class, 87% in top 50% of high school class. 83% from public high schools. **Test Scores:** SAT Math middle 50% range 540–640. SAT EBRW middle 50% range 533–640. ACT middle 50% range 22–28. **Basis for Candidate Selection:** *Very important factors include:* rigor of secondary school record, academic GPA. *Important factors include:* class rank, application essay, recommendation(s), interview, extracurricular activities, talent/ability. *Other factors include:* standardized test scores, character/personal qualities, alumni/ae relation, geographical residence, state residency, volunteer work, level of applicant's interest. **Freshman Admission Requirements:** High school diploma is required and GED is accepted. *Academic units required:* 4 English, 3 math, 3 science, 3 foreign language, 4 social studies. *Academic units recommended:* 4 math, 4 science, 3 science labs. **Freshman Admission Statistics:** 7,323 applied, 74% admitted, 12% enrolled. **Transfer Admission Requirements:** College transcript(s), essay or personal statement. Minimum college GPA of 2.6 required. Lowest grade transferable C-. **General Admission Information:** Priority deadline 2/1. Non-fall registration accepted. Admission may be deferred for a maximum of 12 months.

COSTS AND FINANCIAL AID
Annual tuition $34,230. Room and board $14,120. Required fees $1,000. Average book and supplies expense $1,300. **Required Forms and Deadlines:** FAFSA; State aid form. **Notification of Awards:** Applicants will be notified of awards on or about 2/15. **Types of Aid:** *Need-based scholarships/grants:* College/university scholarship or grant aid from institutional funds; Federal Pell; Private scholarships; SEOG; State scholarships/grants. *Loans:* Direct PLUS

loans; Direct Subsidized Stafford Loans; Direct Unsubsidized Stafford Loans. **Student Employment:** Federal Work-Study Program available. Institutional employment available. **Financial Aid Statistics:** 100% needy freshmen, 100% needy undergrads receive need-based scholarship or grant aid. 21% freshmen, 19% undergrads receive non-need-based scholarship or grant aid. 76% freshmen, 76% undergrads receive need-based self-help aid. 6% freshmen, 7% undergrads receive athletic scholarships. 89% freshmen, 91% undergrads receive any aid. 88% undergrads borrow to pay for school. Average cumulative indebtedness $40,522. **Criteria awarding aid:** *Non-need-based:* Academics, Alumni affiliation, Athletics, Leadership, Minority status.

LENOIR-RHYNE UNIVERSITY

524 7th Ave NE, Hickory, NC 28603
Phone: 828.328.7300 **Financial Aid Phone:** (828) 328-7182
E-mail: admission@lr.edu **CEEB Code:** 5365
Fax: Website: www.lr.edu **ACT Code:** 2941

This private school, affiliated with the Lutheran Church, was founded in 1891. It has a 100 acre campus.

RATINGS
Admissions Selectivity Rating: 82   **Fire Safety Rating:** 87   **Green Rating:** 67

STUDENTS AND FACULTY
Enrollment: 1,699. **Student Body:** 60% female, 40% male, 16% out-of-state, 3% international (19 countries represented). Asian 2%, African American 11%, Caucasian 68%, Hispanic 8%, Native American 1%, Pacific Islander <1%, Two or more races 4%, Race unknown 3%.
Retention and Graduation: 68% freshmen return for sophomore year. 32% freshmen graduate within 4 years. 43% freshmen graduate within 6 years. 24% grads go on to further study within 1 year. **Faculty:** Student/faculty ratio 13:1. 130 full-time faculty, 88% hold PhDs, 8% are members of minority groups, 55% are women. 0% of classes are taught by teaching assistants.

ACADEMICS
Degrees: Bachelor's; Doctoral degree—other; Master's; Post-bachelor's certificate. **Classes:** Most classes have 20–29 students. Most lab/discussion sessions have 10–19 students. **Most popular majors:** Registered Nursing/Registered Nurse; Exercise Science and Kinesiology; Psychology, General. **Special Study Options:** Accelerated program; Cross-registration; Distance learning; Double major; Dual enrollment; Honors program; Independent study; Internships; Study abroad; Teacher certification program. **Combined degree programs:** BA/MEng. **Disability Services offered:** Note-taking services; Reader services; Tape recorders; Tutors. **Career services:** Alumni network; Alumni services; Career assessment; Career/job search classes; Internships; Regional alumni.

FACILITIES
Housing: Coed dorms; Fraternity/sorority housing; Special housing for international students; Theme housing; 75% of campus accessible to physically disabled. **Campus Network:** 100% of classrooms, 100% of dorms, 100% of student union, 100% of libraries, 100% of dining areas, 90% of common outdoor areas have wireless network access.

CAMPUS LIFE
Environment: Town. **Activities:** Campus Ministries; Choral groups; Concert band; Dance; Drama/theater; International Student Organization; Jazz band; Literary magazine; Marching band; Model UN; Music ensembles; Musical theater; Pep band; Radio station; Student government; Student newspaper; Student-run film society; Symphony orchestra; Yearbook. 57 registered organizations, 12 honor societies, 7 religious organizations, 4 fraternities, 5 sororities on campus. **Athletics (Intercollegiate):** *Men:* baseball, basketball, cheerleading, cross-country, football, golf, soccer. *Women:* basketball, cheerleading, cross-country, golf, soccer, softball, volleyball. **On-Campus Highlights:** McCrorie Center. **Environmental Initiatives:** Environmental Stewardship Committee; Reese Institute for Conservation of Natural Resources; MS in Sustainability Studies.

ADMISSIONS
Freshman Academic Profile: Average high school GPA 3.4. 87% from public high schools. **Test Scores:** SAT Math middle 50% range 480–590. SAT EBRW middle 50% range 480–590. **Basis for Candidate Selection:** *Very important factors include:* academic GPA, standardized test scores. *Important*

factors include: rigor of secondary school record, class rank, application essay, recommendation(s), extracurricular activities, character/personal qualities, volunteer work, work experience. **Freshman Admission Requirements:** High school diploma is required and GED is accepted. *Academic units required:* 4 English, 3 math, 1 science, 1 science lab, 2 foreign language, 1 history. *Academic units recommended:* 4 English, 4 math, 2 science, 1 science lab, 3 foreign language, 2 history. **Freshman Admission Statistics:** 5,087 applied, 65% admitted, 16% enrolled. **Transfer Admission Requirements:** College transcript(s), statement of good standing from prior institution(s). Minimum college GPA of 2.5 required. Lowest grade transferable C. **General Admission Information:** Application fee $35. Priority deadline 10/17. Non-fall registration accepted. Admission may be deferred for a maximum of 1 year.

COSTS AND FINANCIAL AID

Annual tuition $36,400. Room and board $12,510. Average book and supplies expense $1,160. **Required Forms and Deadlines:** FAFSA. **Types of Aid:** *Need-based scholarships/grants:* College/university scholarship or grant aid from institutional funds; Federal Pell; Private scholarships; SEOG; State scholarships/grants. *Loans:* Direct PLUS loans; Direct Subsidized Stafford Loans; Direct Unsubsidized Stafford Loans. **Student Employment:** Federal Work-Study Program available. Institutional employment available. **Financial Aid Statistics:** 100% needy freshmen, 99% needy undergrads receive need-based scholarship or grant aid. 13% freshmen, 11% undergrads receive non-need-based scholarship or grant aid. 82% freshmen, 85% undergrads receive need-based self-help aid. 12% freshmen, 12% undergrads receive athletic scholarships. 100% freshmen, 88% undergrads receive any aid. 88% undergrads borrow to pay for school. Average cumulative indebtedness $30,156. **Criteria awarding aid:** *Need-based:* Academics, Alumni affiliation, Athletics, Leadership, Minority status, Music/drama, Religious affiliation. *Non-need-based:* Academics, Alumni affiliation, Athletics, Leadership, Religious affiliation.

LESLEY UNIVERSITY

Lesley University Undergraduate Admissio, Cambridge, MA 02140
Phone: 617-349-8800 **Financial Aid Phone:** 617-349-8710
E-mail: admissions@lesley.edu **CEEB Code:** 3483
Fax: 617-349-8810 **Website:** www.lesley.edu **ACT Code:** 1850

This private school was founded in 1909. It has a 1 acre campus.

RATINGS

Admissions Selectivity Rating: 77   **Fire Safety Rating:** 91   **Green Rating:** 60*

STUDENTS AND FACULTY

Enrollment: 1,418. **Student Body:** 75% female, 25% male, 57% out-of-state, 2% international (30 countries represented). Asian 4%, African American 4%, Caucasian 71%, Hispanic 10%, Native American <1%, Pacific Islander <1%, Two or more races 4%, Race unknown 5%.
Retention and Graduation: 78% freshmen return for sophomore year.
Faculty: Student/faculty ratio 9:1. 80 full-time faculty, 80% hold PhDs, 16% are members of minority groups, 50% are women. 0% of classes are taught by teaching assistants.

ACADEMICS

Degrees: Associate; Bachelor's; Certificate; Doctoral degree research/scholarship; Master's; Post-bachelor's certificate; Post-master's certificate.
Classes: Most classes have 10–19 students. **Most popular majors:** Counseling Psychology; Marketing/Marketing Management, General; Elementary Education and Teaching. **Special Study Options:** Accelerated program; Cross-registration; Distance learning; Double major; Dual enrollment; Exchange student program (domestic); Honors program; Independent study; Internships; Liberal arts/career combination; Student-designed major; Study abroad; Teacher certification program. **Combined degree programs:** BA/MA. **Disability Services offered:** Note-taking services; Reader services; Tape recorders; Tutors. **Career services:** Alumni network; Alumni services; Career assessment; Career/job search classes; Internships; Regional alumni.

FACILITIES

Housing: Coed dorms; Theme housing; Wellness housing; Women's dorms; 85% of campus accessible to physically disabled. **Special Academic Facilities/Equipment:** Kresge Center for Teaching Resources and Educational Software Collection, Marran Art Gallery, Porter Exchange Gallery, AIB Main Gallery.

CAMPUS LIFE

Environment: Metropolis. **Activities:** Campus Ministries; Choral groups; Dance; Drama/theater; International Student Organization; Literary magazine; Musical theater; Student government; Student newspaper. 25 registered organizations, 2 honor societies, 2 religious organizations on campus.
Athletics (Intercollegiate): *Men:* basketball, cross-country, soccer, tennis, volleyball. *Women:* basketball, crew/rowing, cross-country, soccer, softball, tennis, volleyball. **On-Campus Highlights:** Student Center. **Environmental Initiatives:** The continual enhancement of recycling, waste management, and composting programs on campus.

ADMISSIONS

Freshman Academic Profile: Average high school GPA 3.3. 15% in top 10% of high school class, 44% in top 25% of high school class, 80% in top 50% of high school class. 83% from public high schools. **Test Scores:** SAT Math middle 50% range 460–570. SAT EBRW middle 50% range 490–600. ACT middle 50% range 21–25. **Basis for Candidate Selection:** *Very important factors include:* rigor of secondary school record, academic GPA, interview. *Important factors include:* class rank, application essay, standardized test scores, recommendation(s), extracurricular activities, talent/ability, character/personal qualities, volunteer work. *Other factors include:* first generation, alumni/ae relation, racial/ethnic status, work experience. **Freshman Admission Requirements:** High school diploma is required and GED is accepted. *Academic units required:* 4 English, 3 math, 3 science, 2 science labs, 1 social studies, 1 history, 4 academic electives. *Academic units recommended:* 4 English, 4 math, 4 science, 2 science labs, 2 foreign language, 2 social studies, 2 history. **Freshman Admission Statistics:** 3,115 applied, 69% admitted, 18% enrolled. **Transfer Admission Requirements:** High school transcript, college transcript(s), essay or personal statement, statement of good standing from prior institution(s). Minimum college GPA of 2.5 required. Lowest grade transferable C. **General Admission Information:** Priority deadline 2/15. Non-fall registration accepted. Admission may be deferred for a maximum of 1 year.

COSTS AND FINANCIAL AID

Annual tuition $25,500. Room and board $15,300. Required fees $2,508. **Required Forms and Deadlines:** FAFSA. **Notification of Awards:** Applicants will be notified of awards on a rolling basis beginning 2/1. **Types of Aid:** *Need-based scholarships/grants:* College/university scholarship or grant aid from institutional funds; Federal Pell; Private scholarships; SEOG; State scholarships/grants. *Loans:* Direct PLUS loans; Direct Subsidized Stafford Loans; Direct Unsubsidized Stafford Loans. **Student Employment:** Federal Work-Study Program available. Institutional employment available. **Financial Aid Statistics:** 96% needy freshmen, 97% needy undergrads receive need-based scholarship or grant aid. 7% freshmen, 5% undergrads receive non-need-based scholarship or grant aid. 86% freshmen, 91% undergrads receive need-based self-help aid. 0% freshmen, 0% undergrads receive athletic scholarships. 70% freshmen, 70% undergrads receive any aid. 75% undergrads borrow to pay for school. Average cumulative indebtedness $2,300.

LETOURNEAU UNIVERSITY

PO Box 7001, Longview, TX 75607
Phone: 903-233-4300 **Financial Aid Phone:**
E-mail: admissions@letu.edu **CEEB Code:** 6365
Fax: 903-233-4301 **Website:** www.letu.edu **ACT Code:** 4120

This private school, affiliated with the Nondenominational Christian Church, was founded in 1946. It has a 162 acre campus.

RATINGS

Admissions Selectivity Rating: 90   **Fire Safety Rating:** 60*   **Green Rating:** 60*

STUDENTS AND FACULTY

Enrollment: 1,776. **Student Body:** 41% female, 59% male, 30% out-of-state, 5% international (40 countries represented). Asian 1%, African American 10%, Caucasian 64%, Hispanic 6%, Native American 1%, Pacific Islander <1%, Two or more races 6%, Race unknown 6%.
Retention and Graduation: 76% freshmen return for sophomore year. 47% freshmen graduate within 4 years. **Faculty:** Student/faculty ratio 13:1. 94 full-time faculty, 74% hold PhDs, 14% are members of minority groups, 18% are women.

ACADEMICS

Degrees: Associate; Bachelor's; Certificate; Master's. **Classes:** Most classes have 10–19 students. Most lab/discussion sessions have 10–19 students. **Special Study Options:** Accelerated program; Cooperative education program; Cross-registration; Distance learning; Double major; Dual enrollment; English as a Second Language (ESL); Exchange student program (domestic); Honors program; Independent study; Internships; Study abroad; Teacher certification program. **Honors programs:** The Honors College at LeTourneau University seeks to provide enriched educational experiences. Through offering experiences that are intellectual, formational, and practical, the Honors College seeks to form students in understanding their call or vocation, growing in character and wisdom, and seeking the good of their community. The Honors College program offers unique classroom experiences and curriculum, intentional communal living in the Honors Dorm, and additional educational and social experiences. It is a place to be further formed into the image of God. **Disability Services offered:** Tutors. **Career services:** Alumni network; Alumni services; Career assessment; Career/job search classes; Internships.

FACILITIES

Housing: Apartments for married students; Apartments for single students; Fraternity/sorority housing; Men's dorms; Special housing for disabled students; Special housing for international students; Theme housing; Women's dorms.

CAMPUS LIFE

Environment: City. **Activities:** Campus Ministries; Choral groups; Concert band; Dance; Drama/theater; International Student Organization; Jazz band; Music ensembles; Student government. **Athletics (Intercollegiate):** *Men:* baseball, basketball, cross-country, golf, soccer, tennis. *Women:* basketball, cross-country, golf, soccer, softball, tennis, volleyball.

ADMISSIONS

Freshman Academic Profile: Average high school GPA 3.6. 26% in top 10% of high school class, 53% in top 25% of high school class, 83% in top 50% of high school class. **Test Scores:** SAT Math middle 50% range 540–660. SAT EBRW middle 50% range 550–650. ACT middle 50% range 22–29. **Basis for Candidate Selection:** *Very important factors include:* rigor of secondary school record, academic GPA, standardized test scores, character/personal qualities. *Important factors include:* religious affiliation/commitment. *Other factors include:* class rank, interview, extracurricular activities, talent/ability, first generation, alumni/ae relation, volunteer work, work experience, level of applicant's interest. **Freshman Admission Requirements:** High school diploma is required and GED is accepted. **Freshman Admission Statistics:** 2,314 applied, 45% admitted, 35% enrolled. **Transfer Admission Requirements:** College transcript(s), essay or personal statement. Minimum college GPA of 2.0 required. Lowest grade transferable C. **General Admission Information:** Non-fall registration accepted. Admission may be deferred for a maximum of 2 semesters.

COSTS AND FINANCIAL AID

Annual tuition $31,740. Room and board $10,070. Required fees $750. Average book and supplies expense $1,612. **Required Forms and Deadlines:** FAFSA. **Notification of Awards:** Applicants will be notified of awards on a rolling basis beginning 11/30. **Types of Aid:** *Need-based scholarships/grants:* College/university scholarship or grant aid from institutional funds; Federal Pell; Private scholarships; SEOG; State scholarships/grants. *Loans:* Direct PLUS loans; Direct Subsidized Stafford Loans; Direct Unsubsidized Stafford Loans. **Student Employment:** Federal Work-Study Program available. Institutional employment available. **Financial Aid Statistics:** 100% needy freshmen, 97% needy undergrads receive need-based scholarship or grant aid. 16% freshmen, 10% undergrads receive non-need-based scholarship or grant aid. 84% freshmen, 86% undergrads receive need-based self-help aid. 0% freshmen, 0% undergrads receive athletic scholarships. 70% undergrads borrow to pay for school. Average cumulative indebtedness $36,103. **Criteria awarding aid:** *Need-based:* Academics, Alumni affiliation, Leadership, Minority status, Religious affiliation. *Non-need-based:* Academics, Alumni affiliation, Leadership, Minority status, Religious affiliation, State/district residency.

LEWIS & CLARK COLLEGE

0615 SW Palatine Hill Road, Portland, OR 97219-7899
Phone: 503-768-7040 **Financial Aid Phone:** 503-768-7090
E-mail: admissions@lclark.edu **CEEB Code:** 4384
Fax: 503-768-7055 **Website:** www.lclark.edu **ACT Code:** 3464

This private school was founded in 1867. It has a 137 acre campus.

RATINGS

Admissions Selectivity Rating: 83   **Fire Safety Rating:** 87   **Green Rating:** 92

STUDENTS AND FACULTY

Enrollment: 2,011. **Student Body:** 61% female, 39% male, 80% out-of-state, 5% international (55 countries represented). Asian 5%, African American 3%, Caucasian 63%, Hispanic 12%, Native American 1%, Pacific Islander <1%, Two or more races 7%, Race unknown 3%.
Retention and Graduation: 82% freshmen return for sophomore year. 75% freshmen graduate within 4 years. 80% freshmen graduate within 6 years.
Faculty: Student/faculty ratio 12:1. 213 full-time faculty, 93% hold PhDs, 20% are members of minority groups, 54% are women. 0% of classes are taught by teaching assistants.

ACADEMICS

Degrees: Bachelor's; Doctoral degree—professional practice; Master's; Post-master's certificate. **Classes:** Most classes have 20–29 students. Most lab/discussion sessions have 10–19 students. **Most popular majors:** Psychology, General; Sociology and Anthropology. **Special Study Options:** Cross-registration; Double major; Dual enrollment; English as a Second Language (ESL); Honors program; Independent study; Internships; Student-designed major; Study abroad. **Honors programs:** Honors are designated by each department. **Disability Services offered:** Note-taking services; Reader services; Tape recorders; Tutors. **Career services:** Alumni network; Alumni services; Career assessment; Career/job search classes; Internships; Regional alumni.

FACILITIES

Housing: Apartments for single students; Coed dorms; Theme housing; Wellness housing; Women's dorms; 85% of campus accessible to physically disabled. **Special Academic Facilities/Equipment:** Art gallery, observatory, world music room, 85 Rank Casavant organ, renovated greenhouse. **Campus Network:** 100% of classrooms, 100% of libraries, 100% of dining areas have wireless network access.

CAMPUS LIFE

Environment: Metropolis. **Activities:** Campus Ministries; Choral groups; Concert band; Dance; Drama/theater; International Student Organization; Jazz band; Literary magazine; Model UN; Music ensembles; Musical theater; Pep band; Radio station; Student government; Student newspaper; Symphony orchestra. 167 registered organizations, 2 honor societies, 7 religious organizations on campus. **Athletics (Intercollegiate):** *Men:* baseball, basketball, crew/rowing, cross-country, football, golf, swimming, tennis, track/field (outdoor). *Women:* basketball, crew/rowing, cross-country, golf, soccer, softball, swimming, tennis, track/field (outdoor), volleyball. **On-Campus Highlights:** Aubrey Watzek Library. **Environmental Initiatives:** Our undergraduate students voluntary contribute to the purchase of renewable energy and greenhouse gas offsets to account for 100% of our carbon footprint.

ADMISSIONS

Freshman Academic Profile: Average high school GPA 3.9. 77% from public high schools. **Test Scores:** SAT Math middle 50% range 590–680. SAT EBRW middle 50% range 640–710. ACT middle 50% range 27–31. **Basis for Candidate Selection:** *Very important factors include:* rigor of secondary school record, academic GPA. *Important factors include:* application essay, standardized test scores, recommendation(s), extracurricular activities, talent/ability, character/personal qualities, volunteer work. *Other factors include:* class rank, interview, first generation, alumni/ae relation, geographical residence, racial/ethnic status, level of applicant's interest. **Freshman Admission Requirements:** High school diploma is required and GED is accepted. *Academic units recommended:* 4 English, 4 math, 3 science, 2 science labs, 2 foreign language, 3 social studies, 1 visual/performing arts. **Freshman Admission Statistics:** 6,139 applied, 74% admitted, 12% enrolled. **Transfer Admission Requirements:** High school transcript, college transcript(s), essay or personal statement,

statement of good standing from prior institution(s). Minimum college GPA of 2.0 required. Lowest grade transferable C. **General Admission Information:** Priority deadline 1/15. Regular application deadline 1/15. Non-fall registration accepted. Admission may be deferred for a maximum of one year.

COSTS AND FINANCIAL AID
Annual tuition $50,574. Room and board $12,490. Required fees $360. Average book and supplies expense $1,050. **Required Forms and Deadlines:** CSS/Financial Aid PROFILE; FAFSA. **Notification of Awards:** Applicants will be notified of awards on a rolling basis beginning 1/30. **Types of Aid:** *Need-based scholarships/grants:* College/university scholarship or grant aid from institutional funds; Federal Pell; Private scholarships; SEOG; State scholarships/ grants. *Loans:* Direct PLUS loans; Direct Subsidized Stafford Loans; Direct Unsubsidized Stafford Loans. **Student Employment:** Federal Work-Study Program available. Institutional employment available. **Financial Aid Statistics:** 99% needy freshmen, 99% needy undergrads receive need-based scholarship or grant aid. 19% freshmen, 11% undergrads receive non-need-based scholarship or grant aid. 89% freshmen, 90% undergrads receive need-based self-help aid. 0% freshmen, 0% undergrads receive athletic scholarships. 94% freshmen, 93% undergrads receive any aid. 59% undergrads borrow to pay for school. Average cumulative indebtedness $32,379. **Criteria awarding aid:** *Need-based:* Academics. *Non-need-based:* Academics, Leadership, Music/drama.

LEWIS-CLARK STATE COLLEGE

500 Eighth Avenue, Lewiston, ID 83501
Phone: 208-792-2210 **Financial Aid Phone:** 208-792-2224
E-mail: admissions@lcsc.edu **CEEB Code:** 4385
Fax: 208-792-2876 **Website:** www.lcsc.edu **ACT Code:** 920

This public school was founded in 1893. It has a 44 acre campus.

RATINGS
Admissions Selectivity Rating: 74 **Fire Safety Rating:** 78 **Green Rating:** 60*

STUDENTS AND FACULTY
Enrollment: 3,172. **Student Body:** 61% female, 39% male, 20% out-of-state, 4% international (32 countries represented). Asian 1%, African American 1%, Caucasian 82%, Hispanic 6%, Native American 2%, Pacific Islander <1%, Two or more races 3%, Race unknown 2%.
Retention and Graduation: 61% freshmen return for sophomore year. 7% grads go on to further study within 1 year. **Faculty:** Student/faculty ratio 18:1. 159 full-time faculty, 47% hold PhDs, 4% are members of minority groups, 53% are women. 0% of classes are taught by teaching assistants.

ACADEMICS
Degrees: Associate; Bachelor's; Certificate; Terminal Associate; Transfer Associate. **Classes:** Most classes have 10–19 students. Most lab/discussion sessions have fewer than 10 students. **Most popular majors:** Business/ Commerce, General; Elementary Education and Teaching; Nursing/Registered Nurse (Rn, Asn, Bsn, Msn). **Special Study Options:** Accelerated program; Cooperative education program; Distance learning; Double major; Dual enrollment; Independent study; Internships; Liberal arts/career combination; Student-designed major; Study abroad; Teacher certification program. **Disability Services offered:** Note-taking services; Reader services; Tape recorders; Tutors.

FACILITIES
Housing: Apartments for married students; Apartments for single students; Coed dorms; Special housing for international students; Theme housing; 95% of campus accessible to physically disabled. **Special Academic Facilities/ Equipment:** Museum/art gallery, Media Services.

CAMPUS LIFE
Environment: Town. **Activities:** Campus Ministries; Drama/theater; International Student Organization; Jazz band; Literary magazine; Radio station; Student government; Student newspaper. 52 registered organizations, 1 honor society, 3 religious organizations on campus. **Athletics (Intercollegiate):** *Men:* baseball, basketball, cross-country, golf, tennis. *Women:* basketball, cross-country, golf, tennis, volleyball. **On-Campus Highlights:** Information Commons in the Library.

ADMISSIONS
Freshman Academic Profile: Average high school GPA 3.1. 5% in top 10% of high school class, 18% in top 25% of high school class, 46% in top 50%

of high school class. 99% from public high schools. **Test Scores:** SAT Math middle 50% range 400–520. SAT EBRW middle 50% range 410–510. ACT middle 50% range 17–22. **Basis for Candidate Selection:** *Other factors include:* academic GPA, standardized test scores. **Freshman Admission Requirements:** High school diploma is required and GED is accepted. *Academic units required:* 4 English, 3 math, 3 science, 1 science lab, 2.5 social studies, 1.5 academic electives, 1 unit from above areas or other academic areas. **Freshman Admission Statistics:** 852 applied, 99% admitted, 61% enrolled. **Transfer Admission Requirements:** College transcript(s). Minimum college GPA of 2.0 required. Lowest grade transferable D. **General Admission Information:** Regular application deadline 8/8. Non-fall registration accepted. Admission may be deferred for a maximum of 1 year.

COSTS AND FINANCIAL AID
Annual in-state tuition $9,132. Room and board $6,194. Required fees $2,724. **Required Forms and Deadlines:** FAFSA. **Notification of Awards:** Applicants will be notified of awards on a rolling basis beginning 4/15. **Types of Aid:** *Need-based scholarships/grants:* College/university scholarship or grant aid from institutional funds; Federal Pell; Private scholarships; SEOG; State scholarships/grants. **Student Employment:** Federal Work-Study Program available. Institutional employment available. **Financial Aid Statistics:** 58% needy freshmen, 66% needy undergrads receive need-based scholarship or grant aid. 52% freshmen, 24% undergrads receive non-need-based scholarship or grant aid. 73% freshmen, 81% undergrads receive need-based self-help aid. 5% freshmen, 8% undergrads receive athletic scholarships. 85% freshmen, 76% undergrads receive any aid. **Criteria awarding aid:** *Need-based:* Academics, Alumni affiliation, Minority status. *Non-need-based:* Academics, Alumni affiliation, Art, Athletics, Leadership, Minority status, Music/drama.

LEWIS UNIVERSITY

1 University Parkway, Romeoville, IL 60446
Phone: (815) 836-5250 **Financial Aid Phone:** (815) 836-5263
E-mail: admissions@lewisu.edu **CEEB Code:** 1404
Fax: (815) 836-5002 **Website:** www.lewisu.edu **ACT Code:** 1058

This private school, affiliated with the Roman Catholic Church, was founded in 1932. It has a 410 acre campus.

RATINGS
Admissions Selectivity Rating: 81 **Fire Safety Rating:** 97 **Green Rating:** 80

STUDENTS AND FACULTY
Enrollment: 4,125. **Student Body:** 51% female, 49% male, 8% out-of-state, 2% international (39 countries represented). Asian 5%, African American 6%, Caucasian 59%, Hispanic 22%, Native American <1%, Pacific Islander <1%, Two or more races 2%, Race unknown 3%.
Retention and Graduation: 84% freshmen return for sophomore year. 51% freshmen graduate within 4 years. 67% freshmen graduate within 6 years. **Faculty:** Student/faculty ratio 13:1. 237 full-time faculty, 81% hold PhDs, 14% are members of minority groups, 53% are women. 0% of classes are taught by teaching assistants.

ACADEMICS
Degrees: Associate; Bachelor's; Certificate; Doctoral degree—other; Doctoral degree research/scholarship; Master's; Post-bachelor's certificate; Post-master's certificate. **Classes:** Most classes have 10–19 students. Most lab/discussion sessions have 10–19 students. **Most popular majors:** Aviation/Airway Management and Operations; Registered Nursing/Registered Nurse; Computer Science. **Special Study Options:** Accelerated program; Distance learning; Double major; Dual enrollment; English as a Second Language (ESL); Honors program; Independent study; Internships; Liberal arts/career combination; Student-designed major; Study abroad; Teacher certification program. **Honors programs:** Lewis' Honors Program provides exclusive intellectual opportunities for academically gifted undergraduate students guided by four pillars—Inquiry, Integration, Dialogue, and Service. For information on our Scholars Academy use the following url: http://www.lewisu.edu/academics/scholars/index.htm. **Combined degree programs:** BA/MA. **Disability Services offered:** Note-taking services; Tape recorders; Tutors. **Career services:** Alumni network; Alumni services; Career assessment; Career/job search classes; Internships; Regional alumni.

FACILITIES

Housing: Coed dorms; Special housing for disabled students; Theme housing; Wellness housing; 90% of campus accessible to physically disabled. **Special Academic Facilities/Equipment:** 1) The Lewis University aviation program continues to provide hard-working students with top-of-the-line equipment and state-of-the-art facilities. Lewis' aviation facilities include: An airplane hangar and machine shops includes a Snap-on Tools partnership, Flight simulators, a Boeing 737 for maintenance training, Seven Cessna 152's, 13 Cessna 172's, four Cessna 182's and one Piper Seminole and the Harold E. White Aviation Center. Located adjacent to the main campus is the Lewis University Airport which serves as a reliever airport for O'Hare International. 2) The Oremus Fine Arts Center is one of the most highly-used buildings on campus and home of the Philip Lynch Theatre, Lewis' largest auditorium and meeting space, the Oremus Fine Arts Center hosts hundreds of student performances, concerts, community events, and lectures each year and is visited by more than 28,000 patrons from surrounding communities. 3) JFK Student Recreation and Fitness Center houses: an aerobics studio with a suspended floor where you can take classes such as Pilates and spinning, a fitness center with weights and cardiovascular machines, a 25 yard, 8-lane collegiate size swimming pool, a field house that features four playing courts used primarily for basketball, volleyball, tennis, and floor hockey, Surrounded by a 200-meter track and the Neil Carey Arena where indoor varsity athletics are played. 4) The Andrew Center for Electronic Media, Lewis' state-of-the-art multimedia facility, provides students with the tools, technology and environment to assemble an impressive portfolio of work. Another multimedia lab features the latest Macs, equipped for animation, desktop publishing, podcasting, web design, video-editing and more.

CAMPUS LIFE

Environment: City. **Activities:** Campus Ministries; Choral groups; Dance; Drama/theater; International Student Organization; Jazz band; Literary magazine; Model UN; Music ensembles; Musical theater; Pep band; Radio station; Student government; Student newspaper; Symphony orchestra; Television station. 120 registered organizations, 15 honor societies, 4 religious organizations, 6 fraternities, 4 sororities on campus. **Athletics (Intercollegiate):** *Men:* baseball, basketball, cheerleading, cross-country, golf, soccer, swimming, tennis, track/field (outdoor), track/field (indoor), volleyball. *Women:* basketball, cheerleading, cross-country, golf, soccer, softball, swimming, tennis, track/field (outdoor), track/field (indoor), volleyball. **On-Campus Highlights:** Brother James Gaffney, FSC Student Center. **Environmental Initiatives:** The Lewis University Environment and Energy Conservation Council sponsors annual events such as an Earth Day event in spring where we clear out Buckthorn (an invasive plant species) from the nature trail here on campus, the Arbor Day Initiative in which we plant an assortment of native trees back into the University nature trail, and the America Recycles Day each fall.

ADMISSIONS

Freshman Academic Profile: Average high school GPA 3.5. 18% in top 10% of high school class, 46% in top 25% of high school class, 84% in top 50% of high school class. **Test Scores:** SAT Math middle 50% range 510–600. SAT EBRW middle 50% range 500–600. ACT middle 50% range 21–27. **Basis for Candidate Selection:** *Very important factors include:* rigor of secondary school record, academic GPA. *Important factors include:* application essay, standardized test scores. *Other factors include:* class rank, recommendation(s), interview, extracurricular activities, talent/ability, character/personal qualities, first generation, alumni/ae relation, geographical residence, racial/ethnic status, volunteer work, work experience, level of applicant's interest. **Freshman Admission Requirements:** High school diploma is required and GED is accepted. *Academic units required:* 3 English, 2 math, 2 science, 1 science lab, 2 social studies, 1 history, 8 academic electives. *Academic units recommended:* 4 English, 3 math, 2 science, 1 science lab, 2 foreign language, 2 social studies, 1 history, 8 academic electives. **Freshman Admission Statistics:** 6,674 applied, 64% admitted, 15% enrolled. **Transfer Admission Requirements:** College transcript(s). Minimum college GPA of 2.0 required. Lowest grade transferable D. **General Admission Information:** Application fee $40. Priority deadline 4/15. Non-fall registration accepted. Admission may be deferred for a maximum of 1 year.

COSTS AND FINANCIAL AID

Annual tuition $34,268. Room and board $11,050. Required fees $210. Average book and supplies expense $1,500. **Required Forms and Deadlines:** FAFSA. **Notification of Awards:** Applicants will be notified of awards on a rolling basis beginning 11/1. **Types of Aid:** *Need-based scholarships/ grants:* College/university scholarship or grant aid from institutional funds; Federal Nursing Scholarships; Federal Pell; Private scholarships; SEOG; State scholarships/grants. *Loans:* Direct PLUS loans; Direct Subsidized Stafford Loans; Direct Unsubsidized Stafford Loans. **Student Employment:** Federal

Work-Study Program available. Institutional employment available. **Financial Aid Statistics:** 100% needy freshmen, 96% needy undergrads receive need-based scholarship or grant aid. 21% freshmen, 18% undergrads receive non-need-based scholarship or grant aid. 82% freshmen, 89% undergrads receive need-based self-help aid. 5% freshmen, 4% undergrads receive athletic scholarships. 100% freshmen, 95% undergrads receive any aid. 81% undergrads borrow to pay for school. Average cumulative indebtedness $36,653. **Criteria awarding aid:** *Non-need-based:* Academics, Alumni affiliation, Art, Athletics, Music/drama, Religious affiliation.

LIBERTY UNIVERSITY

1971 University Blvd, Lynchburg, VA 24515
Phone: 434-582-2000 **Financial Aid Phone:** 434-582-2270
E-mail: admissions@liberty.edu **CEEB Code:** 5385
Fax: 800-628-7977 **Website:** https://www.liberty.edu/ **ACT Code:** 4364

This private school, affiliated with the Baptist Church, was founded in 1971. It has a 4400 acre campus.

RATINGS

Admissions Selectivity Rating: 90   **Fire Safety Rating:** 65   **Green Rating:** 60*

STUDENTS AND FACULTY

Enrollment: 12,984. **Student Body:** 55% female, 45% male, 60% out-of-state, 4% international (125 countries represented). Asian 2%, African American 4%, Caucasian 72%, Hispanic 5%, Native American <1%, Pacific Islander <1%, Two or more races 3%, Race unknown 9%.
Retention and Graduation: 85% freshmen return for sophomore year. 37% freshmen graduate within 4 years. 59% freshmen graduate within 6 years.
Faculty: 0% of classes are taught by teaching assistants.

ACADEMICS

Degrees: Associate; Bachelor's; Certificate; Doctoral degree—professional practice; Doctoral degree research/scholarship; Master's; Post-bachelor's certificate; Post-master's certificate; Terminal Associate. **Classes:** Most classes have 20–29 students. Most lab/discussion sessions have 20–29 students. **Most popular majors:** Business/Commerce, General; Religion/Religious Studies; Psychology, General. **Special Study Options:** Accelerated program; Cooperative education program; Distance learning; Double major; Dual enrollment; External degree program; Honors program; Independent study; Internships; Student-designed major; Study abroad; Teacher certification program. **Honors programs:** An early class registration period, smaller class size (15:1) for general education Honors seminars, and a generous scholarship based on grade point average are just a few of the benefits enjoyed by our Honors students. Once Honors students reach Junior status, they petition one Honors course per semester in their desired major field of study. **Disability Services offered:** Note-taking services; Tutors. **Career services:** Career assessment; Internships.

FACILITIES

Housing: Apartments for single students; Men's dorms; Special housing for disabled students; Women's dorms; 98% of campus accessible to physically disabled. **Special Academic Facilities/Equipment:** Displays from the Museum of Life and Earth History are located in the Library. The Jerry Falwell Museum located in the main lobby of DeMoss Hall. **Campus Network:** 95% of classrooms, 100% of dorms, 95% of libraries have wireless network access.

CAMPUS LIFE

Environment: Town. **Activities:** Campus Ministries; Choral groups; Concert band; Drama/theater; Literary magazine; Marching band; Music ensembles; Musical theater; Pep band; Radio station; Student government; Student newspaper; Symphony orchestra; Television station; Yearbook. 25 registered organizations, 8 honor societies, 10 religious organizations on campus. **Athletics (Intercollegiate):** *Men:* baseball, basketball, cheerleading, cross-country, football, golf, soccer, tennis, track/field (outdoor), track/field (indoor), wrestling. *Women:* basketball, cheerleading, cross-country, soccer, softball, tennis, track/field (outdoor), track/field (indoor), volleyball. **On-Campus Highlights:** LaHaye Student Center.

ADMISSIONS

Freshman Academic Profile: Average high school GPA 3.5. 44% in top 10% of high school class, 67% in top 25% of high school class, 89% in top 50% of high school class. **Test Scores:** SAT Math middle 50% range 510–620. SAT EBRW middle 50% range 530–640. ACT middle 50% range 21–28. **Basis**

for Candidate Selection: *Very important factors include:* rigor of secondary school record, academic GPA. *Important factors include:* standardized test scores, character/personal qualities. *Other factors include:* class rank, application essay, recommendation(s), extracurricular activities, talent/ability, level of applicant's interest. **Freshman Admission Requirements:** High school diploma is required and GED is accepted. *Academic units recommended:* 4 English, 3 math, 2 science, 2 science labs, 2 foreign language, 2 social studies, 4 academic electives. **Freshman Admission Statistics:** 20,183 applied, 35% admitted, 47% enrolled. **Transfer Admission Requirements:** High school transcript, college transcript(s), essay or personal statement, statement of good standing from prior institution(s). Minimum college GPA of 2.0 required. Lowest grade transferable C. **General Admission Information:** Application fee $50. Priority deadline 1/31. Non-fall registration accepted. Admission may be deferred for a maximum of 12 months.

COSTS AND FINANCIAL AID
Annual tuition $23,800. Room and board $10,478. Required fees $1,476. Average book and supplies expense $1,414. **Required Forms and Deadlines:** FAFSA; State aid form. **Notification of Awards:** Applicants will be notified of awards on a rolling basis beginning 3/15. **Types of Aid:** *Need-based scholarships/grants:* College/university scholarship or grant aid from institutional funds; Federal Pell; Private scholarships; SEOG; State scholarships/grants. *Loans:* Direct PLUS loans; Direct Subsidized Stafford Loans; Direct Unsubsidized Stafford Loans. **Financial Aid Statistics:** 99% needy freshmen, 99% needy undergrads receive need-based scholarship or grant aid. 18% freshmen, 18% undergrads receive non-need-based scholarship or grant aid. 69% freshmen, 72% undergrads receive need-based self-help aid. 1% freshmen, 1% undergrads receive athletic scholarships. 61% undergrads borrow to pay for school. Average cumulative indebtedness $21,875. **Criteria awarding aid:** *Non-need-based:* Academics, Alumni affiliation, Athletics, Leadership, Music/drama, Religious affiliation, State/district residency.

LIFE UNIVERSITY

1269 Barclay Circle, Marietta, GA 30060
Phone: 770.426.2884 **Financial Aid Phone:** 770.426.2667
E-mail: admissions@life.edu
Website: http://www.life.edu/

This private school was founded in 1974. It has a 104 acre campus.

RATINGS
Admissions Selectivity Rating: 68 **Fire Safety Rating:** 60* **Green Rating:** 60*

STUDENTS AND FACULTY
Enrollment: 811. **Student Body:** 48% female, 52% male, 31 countries represented. Asian 3%, African American 25%, Caucasian 34%, Hispanic 8%, Native American 1%, Pacific Islander 0%, Two or more races 0%, Race unknown 29%.
Faculty: Student/faculty ratio 17:1. 124 full-time faculty, 86% hold PhDs, 0% are members of minority groups, 44% are women.

ACADEMICS
Degrees: Associate; Bachelor's; Certificate; Master's. **Special Study Options:** Accelerated program; Double major; English as a Second Language (ESL); Independent study; Internships; Study abroad. **Career services:** Alumni network; Internships; Regional alumni.

FACILITIES
Housing: Apartments for married students; Apartments for single students; Coed dorms.

CAMPUS LIFE
Environment: Metropolis. **Activities:** International Student Organization; Student government; Student newspaper. 1 honor society on campus. **On-Campus Highlights:** Socrates Café.

ADMISSIONS
Basis for Candidate Selection: *Important factors include:* academic GPA, extracurricular activities, talent/ability, alumni/ae relation. *Other factors include:* rigor of secondary school record, class rank, character/personal qualities, work experience. **Freshman Admission Requirements:** High school diploma is required and GED is accepted. **Freshman Admission Statistics:** 259 applied, 68% admitted, 43% enrolled. **General Admission Information:** Application fee $50. Regular application deadline 9/1. Non-fall registration accepted.

COSTS AND FINANCIAL AID
Annual tuition $9,874. Room and board $12,480. Required fees $747. **Required Forms and Deadlines:** FAFSA. **Types of Aid:** *Need-based scholarships/grants:* Federal Pell; SEOG. *Loans:* Direct PLUS loans; Direct Subsidized Stafford Loans; Direct Unsubsidized Stafford Loans. **Financial Aid Statistics:** 74% needy freshmen, 66% needy undergrads receive need-based scholarship or grant aid. 85% freshmen, 67% undergrads receive non-need-based scholarship or grant aid. 91% freshmen, 87% undergrads receive need-based self-help aid. 32% freshmen, 16% undergrads receive athletic scholarships. **Criteria awarding aid:** *Non-need-based:* Academics, Alumni affiliation, Athletics, Leadership, State/district residency.

LIM COLLEGE

12 East 53rd Street, New York, NY 10022
Phone: 212-310-0639 **Financial Aid Phone:** (212) 310-0689
E-mail: admissions@limcollege.edu **CEEB Code:** 2380
Website: www.limcollege.edu **ACT Code:** 4807

This proprietary school was founded in 1939.

RATINGS
Admissions Selectivity Rating: 75 **Fire Safety Rating:** 81 **Green Rating:** 60*

STUDENTS AND FACULTY
Enrollment: 1,503. **Student Body:** 89% female, 11% male, 61% out-of-state, 1% international (28 countries represented). Asian 11%, African American 19%, Caucasian 46%, Hispanic 12%, Native American 1%, Pacific Islander 1%, Two or more races <1%, Race unknown 8%.
Retention and Graduation: 75% freshmen return for sophomore year. 34% freshmen graduate within 4 years. 47% freshmen graduate within 6 years.
Faculty: Student/faculty ratio 9:1. 31 full-time faculty, 0% hold PhDs, 0% are members of minority groups, 0% are women. 0% of classes are taught by teaching assistants.

ACADEMICS
Degrees: Associate; Bachelor's; Certificate; Master's; Post-bachelor's certificate. **Classes:** Most classes have 20–29 students. **Most popular majors:** Marketing/Marketing Management, General; Fashion Merchandising. **Special Study Options:** Distance learning; Honors program; Internships; Study abroad. **Disability Services offered:** Tape recorders; Tutors. **Career services:** Alumni network; Alumni services; Career assessment; Career/job search classes; Internships.

FACILITIES
Housing: Coed dorms; 100% of campus accessible to physically disabled.

CAMPUS LIFE
Environment: Metropolis. **Activities:** Dance; International Student Organization; Literary magazine; Student government. 18 registered organizations, 1 honor society on campus.

ADMISSIONS
Freshman Academic Profile: Average high school GPA 3.0. **Test Scores:** SAT Math middle 50% range 480–570. SAT EBRW middle 50% range 490–580. ACT middle 50% range 18–23. **Basis for Candidate Selection:** *Very important factors include:* rigor of secondary school record, academic GPA. *Important factors include:* application essay, recommendation(s). *Other factors include:* class rank, interview, extracurricular activities, talent/ability, character/personal qualities, alumni/ae relation, volunteer work, work experience. **Freshman Admission Requirements:** High school diploma is required and GED is accepted. **Freshman Admission Statistics:** 1,348 applied, 83% admitted, 26% enrolled. **Transfer Admission Requirements:** High school transcript, college transcript(s), essay or personal statement. Minimum college GPA of 2.0 required. Lowest grade transferable D-. **General Admission Information:** Application fee $40. Non-fall registration accepted. Admission may be deferred for a maximum of 1 semester.

COSTS AND FINANCIAL AID
Annual tuition $27,936. Room and board $17,346. Required fees $820. Average book and supplies expense $900. **Required Forms and Deadlines:** FAFSA; Institution's own financial aid form. **Types of Aid:** *Need-based scholarships/grants:* College/university scholarship or grant aid from institutional funds; Federal Pell; Private scholarships; SEOG; State scholarships/grants. *Loans:* Direct PLUS loans; Direct Subsidized Stafford Loans; Direct

Unsubsidized Stafford Loans. **Student Employment:** Federal Work-Study Program available. Institutional employment available. **Financial Aid Statistics:** 87% needy freshmen receive need-based scholarship or grant aid. 88% freshmen receive non-need-based scholarship or grant aid. 67% freshmen receive need-based self-help aid. 0% freshmen receive athletic scholarships. 72% undergrads borrow to pay for school. Average cumulative indebtedness $40,085. **Criteria awarding aid:** *Need-based:* Academics, Alumni affiliation, Minority status. *Non-need-based:* Academics, Leadership, State/district residency.

LIMESTONE COLLEGE

1115 College Drive, Gaffney, SC 29340-3799
Phone: 864-488-4549 **Financial Aid Phone:** 864-488-8800
E-mail: admiss@limestone.edu **CEEB Code:** 5366
Fax: 864-487-8706 **Website:** www.limestone.edu **ACT Code:** 3862

This private school was founded in 1845. It has a 119 acre campus.

RATINGS

Admissions Selectivity Rating: 86   **Fire Safety Rating:** 81   **Green Rating:** 60*

STUDENTS AND FACULTY

Enrollment: 1,052. **Student Body:** 38% female, 62% male, 42% out-of-state, 9% international. Asian <1%, African American 29%, Caucasian 54%, Hispanic 4%, Native American <1%, Pacific Islander 0%, Two or more races 2%, Race unknown 1%.
Retention and Graduation: 57% freshmen return for sophomore year.
Faculty: Student/faculty ratio 13:1. 75 full-time faculty, 80% hold PhDs, 5% are members of minority groups, 51% are women. 0% of classes are taught by teaching assistants.

ACADEMICS

Degrees: Bachelor's; Master's; Transfer Associate. **Classes:** Most classes have 10–19 students. Most lab/discussion sessions have fewer than 10 students. **Most popular majors:** Sports, Kinesiology, and Physical Education/Fitness, Other; Business/Managerial Economics; Elementary Education and Teaching. **Special Study Options:** Accelerated program; Distance learning; Double major; Dual enrollment; Honors program; Independent study; Internships; Liberal arts/career combination; Student-designed major; Teacher certification program. **Honors programs:** The Honors Program was established at Limestone College in 1983 to create a challenging academic environment for gifted and special ability students. **Disability Services offered:** Note-taking services; Tape recorders; Tutors. **Career services:** Alumni services; Career assessment.

FACILITIES

Housing: Apartments for single students; Men's dorms; Women's dorms; 90% of campus accessible to physically disabled. **Special Academic Facilities/Equipment:** Computer graphic arts lab; Museum of Limestone College History in Winnie Davis Hall. **Campus Network:** 100% of classrooms, 100% of dorms, 100% of student union, 100% of libraries, 100% of dining areas, 100% of common outdoor areas have wireless network access.

CAMPUS LIFE

Environment: Town. **Activities:** Campus Ministries; Choral groups; Concert band; Drama/theater; Jazz band; Literary magazine; Marching band; Music ensembles; Musical theater; Pep band; Student government; Yearbook. 22 registered organizations, 5 honor societies, 3 religious organizations, 1 fraternity on campus. **Athletics (Intercollegiate):** *Men:* baseball, basketball, cross-country, golf, lacrosse, soccer, swimming, tennis, track/field (outdoor), volleyball, wrestling. *Women:* basketball, cross-country, field hockey, golf, lacrosse, soccer, softball, swimming, tennis, track/field (outdoor), volleyball. **On-Campus Highlights:** Dixie Lodge Student Center. **Environmental Initiatives:** Community Garden.

ADMISSIONS

Freshman Academic Profile: Average high school GPA 3.2. 3% in top 10% of high school class, 19% in top 25% of high school class, 51% in top 50% of high school class. 90% from public high schools. **Test Scores:** SAT Math middle 50% range 480–560. SAT EBRW middle 50% range 450–530. **Basis for Candidate Selection:** *Very important factors include:* rigor of secondary school record, academic GPA, standardized test scores. *Important factors include:* class rank. *Other factors include:* recommendation(s), interview. **Freshman Admission Requirements:** High school diploma is required and GED is accepted. *Academic units required:* 4 English, 3 math, 2 science, 2 science labs, 3

social studies. **Freshman Admission Statistics:** 2,318 applied, 54% admitted, 33% enrolled. **Transfer Admission Requirements:** College transcript(s), statement of good standing from prior institution(s). Minimum college GPA of 2.0 required. Lowest grade transferable C. **General Admission Information:** Application fee $25. Priority deadline 6/1. Regular application deadline 8/25. Non-fall registration accepted. Admission may be deferred for a maximum of 18 months.

COSTS AND FINANCIAL AID

Annual tuition $23,000. Room and board $7,800. Average book and supplies expense $2,304. **Required Forms and Deadlines:** FAFSA. **Notification of Awards:** Applicants will be notified of awards on a rolling basis beginning 1/15. **Types of Aid:** *Need-based scholarships/grants:* College/university scholarship or grant aid from institutional funds; Federal Pell; Private scholarships; SEOG; State scholarships/grants. *Loans:* Direct PLUS loans; Direct Subsidized Stafford Loans; Direct Unsubsidized Stafford Loans. **Student Employment:** Federal Work-Study Program available. Institutional employment available. **Financial Aid Statistics:** 100% needy freshmen, 100% needy undergrads receive need-based scholarship or grant aid. 8% freshmen, 10% undergrads receive non-need-based scholarship or grant aid. 86% freshmen, 85% undergrads receive need-based self-help aid. 12% freshmen, 16% undergrads receive athletic scholarships. 98% freshmen, 98% undergrads receive any aid. **Criteria awarding aid:** *Need-based:* Academics, Art, Athletics, Leadership, Music/drama. *Non-need-based:* Academics, Art, Athletics, Leadership, Music/drama, State/district residency.

LINCOLN CHRISTIAN COLLEGE AND SEMINARY

100 Campus View Dr, Lincoln, IL 62656-2167
Phone: 2177323168 x:2251 **Financial Aid Phone:** (217) 732-3168
E-mail: coladmis@lccs.edu
Fax: 2177324199 **Website:** www.lccs.edu **ACT Code:** 1060

This private school, affiliated with the Church of Christ, was founded in 1944. It has a 100 acre campus.

RATINGS

Admissions Selectivity Rating: 77   **Fire Safety Rating:** 84   **Green Rating:** 60*

STUDENTS AND FACULTY

Enrollment: 601. **Student Body:** 51% female, 49% male, 40% out-of-state, 0% international (19 countries represented). Asian <1%, African American 5%, Caucasian 91%, Hispanic 2%, Native American <1%, Race unknown 1%.
Retention and Graduation: 66% freshmen return for sophomore year. 17% grads go on to further study within 1 year. **Faculty:** Student/faculty ratio 15:1. 44 full-time faculty, 45% hold PhDs, 5% are members of minority groups, 18% are women. 0% of classes are taught by teaching assistants.

ACADEMICS

Degrees: Associate; Bachelor's; Certificate; Master's. **Special Study Options:** Distance learning; Double major; Honors program; Independent study; Internships; Study abroad; Teacher certification program; Weekend college. **Honors programs:** Students with at least sophomore standing and a cumulative grade average of 3.5 or higher may apply for acceptance into an honors degree program. The honors degree requires 5 additional semester hours of study under a mentoring professor and the completion of a capstone project. The additional work may be completed in the area of the student's ministry specialization or in an area of interest outside the specialization. Since the program is funded by memorial gifts, honors degree students do not pay tuition for the additional 5 hours. For students who complete the honors degree requirements, special recognition will be given at the Commencement service, and an honors designation will be included on the academic transcript. **Disability Services offered:** Reader services; Tape recorders; Tutors.

FACILITIES

Housing: Apartments for married students; Men's dorms; Women's dorms; 80% of campus accessible to physically disabled. **Campus Network:** 100% of classrooms, 100% of dorms, 100% of student union, 100% of libraries, 100% of dining areas, 60% of common outdoor areas have wireless network access.

CAMPUS LIFE

Environment: Village. **Activities:** Campus Ministries; Choral groups; Drama/theater; International Student Organization; Music ensembles; Musical theater; Student government; Student newspaper. 7 registered organizations on campus. **Athletics (Intercollegiate):** *Men:* baseball, basketball, soccer. *Women:* basketball, softball, volleyball. **On-Campus Highlights:** The Warehouse.

ADMISSIONS
Freshman Academic Profile: 19% in top 10% of high school class, 45% in top 25% of high school class, 76% in top 50% of high school class. **Test Scores:** ACT middle 50% range 19–25. **Basis for Candidate Selection:** *Very important factors include:* rigor of secondary school record, application essay, standardized test scores, state residency, religious affiliation/commitment, level of applicant's interest. *Important factors include:* class rank, academic GPA, extracurricular activities, character/personal qualities, alumni/ae relation, geographical residence, racial/ethnic status, volunteer work. *Other factors include:* recommendation(s), interview, talent/ability, work experience. **Freshman Admission Requirements:** High school diploma is required and GED is accepted. *Academic units recommended:* 4 English, 3 math, 2 science, 2 foreign language, 3 social studies, 3 history. **Freshman Admission Statistics:** 195 applied, 84% admitted, 65% enrolled. **Transfer Admission Requirements:** High school transcript, college transcript(s), essay or personal statement. Minimum college GPA of 2.0 required. Lowest grade transferable 2. **General Admission Information:** Application fee $25. Non-fall registration accepted. Admission may be deferred for a maximum of 1 semester.

COSTS AND FINANCIAL AID
Annual tuition $11,790. Room and board $5,355. **Required Forms and Deadlines:** FAFSA. **Notification of Awards:** Applicants will be notified of awards on a rolling basis beginning 3/1. **Types of Aid:** *Need-based scholarships/grants:* Federal Pell; SEOG; State scholarships/grants. **Student Employment:** Federal Work-Study Program available. Institutional employment available. **Financial Aid Statistics:** 55% needy freshmen, 64% needy undergrads receive need-based scholarship or grant aid. 84% freshmen, 78% undergrads receive non-need-based scholarship or grant aid. 66% freshmen, 71% undergrads receive need-based self-help aid. 0% freshmen, 0% undergrads receive athletic scholarships. 80% freshmen, 80% undergrads receive any aid. **Criteria awarding aid:** *Non-need-based:* Academics.

LINCOLN MEMORIAL UNIVERSITY

6965 Cumberland Gap Parkway, Harrogate, TN 37752
Phone: 423-869-6281 **Financial Aid Phone:** 423.869.6336
E-mail: admissions@lmunet.edu **CEEB Code:** 1408
Fax: 423-869-6444 **Website:** https://www.lmunet.edu/index.php **ACT Code:** 3982

This private school was founded in 1897. It has a 1000 acre campus.

RATINGS
Admissions Selectivity Rating: 88   **Fire Safety Rating:** 93   **Green Rating:** 61

STUDENTS AND FACULTY
Enrollment: 1,911. **Student Body:** 71% female, 29% male, 37% out-of-state, 4% international (34 countries represented). Asian 1%, African American 6%, Caucasian 85%, Hispanic <1%, Native American 1%, Pacific Islander 0%, Two or more races 0%, Race unknown 3%.
Retention and Graduation: 77% freshmen return for sophomore year. 45% freshmen graduate within 4 years. 56% freshmen graduate within 6 years.
Faculty: Student/faculty ratio 16:1. 240 full-time faculty, 84% hold PhDs, 5% are members of minority groups, 59% are women. 0% of classes are taught by teaching assistants.

ACADEMICS
Degrees: Associate; Bachelor's; Doctoral degree—professional practice; Doctoral degree research/scholarship; Master's; Post-master's certificate. **Classes:** Most classes have 10–19 students. Most lab/discussion sessions have 10–19 students. **Special Study Options:** Distance learning; Double major; Dual enrollment; English as a Second Language (ESL); Honors program; Independent study; Internships; Study abroad; Teacher certification program. **Disability Services offered:** Note-taking services; Reader services; Tape recorders; Tutors. **Career services:** Career assessment; Career/job search classes.

FACILITIES
Housing: Apartments for married students; Apartments for single students; Coed dorms; Fraternity/sorority housing; Men's dorms; Special housing for disabled students; Women's dorms; 93.89% of campus accessible to physically disabled. **Special Academic Facilities/Equipment:** Abraham Lincoln Library and Museum, including memorabilia collection of over 6,000 books, paintings, and manuscripts. **Campus Network:** 100% of classrooms, 100% of dorms,

100% of student union, 100% of libraries, 100% of dining areas, 100% of common outdoor areas have wireless network access.

CAMPUS LIFE
Environment: Village. **Activities:** Campus Ministries; Choral groups; Concert band; Drama/theater; International Student Organization; Music ensembles; Musical theater; Pep band; Student government; Yearbook. 51 registered organizations, 4 honor societies, 3 religious organizations, 3 fraternities, 3 sororities on campus. **Athletics (Intercollegiate):** *Men:* baseball, basketball, cross-country, golf, soccer, tennis. *Women:* basketball, cross-country, golf, soccer, softball, tennis, volleyball. **On-Campus Highlights:** College of Osteopathic Medicine.

ADMISSIONS
Freshman Academic Profile: Average high school GPA 3.5. 22% in top 10% of high school class, 47% in top 25% of high school class, 77% in top 50% of high school class. **Test Scores:** SAT Math middle 50% range 490–590. SAT EBRW middle 50% range 500–620. ACT middle 50% range 19–25. **Basis for Candidate Selection:** *Very important factors include:* academic GPA, standardized test scores. **Freshman Admission Requirements:** High school diploma is required and GED is accepted. *Academic units required:* 4 English, 3 math, 2 science, 2 foreign language, 1 social studies, 1 history, 1 visual/performing arts. *Academic units recommended:* 1 math, 1 visual/performing arts. **Freshman Admission Statistics:** 1,549 applied, 42% admitted, 44% enrolled. **Transfer Admission Requirements:** High school transcript, college transcript(s), standardized test scores. Minimum college GPA of 2.0 required. Lowest grade transferable C. **General Admission Information:** Non-fall registration accepted. Admission may be deferred for a maximum of 1 semester.

COSTS AND FINANCIAL AID
Annual tuition $22,200. Room and board $10,500. Required fees $600. Average book and supplies expense $1,400. **Required Forms and Deadlines:** FAFSA. **Notification of Awards:** Applicants will be notified of awards on a rolling basis beginning 3/1. **Types of Aid:** *Need-based scholarships/grants:* College/university scholarship or grant aid from institutional funds; Federal Pell; Private scholarships; SEOG; State scholarships/grants. *Loans:* Direct PLUS loans; Direct Subsidized Stafford Loans; Direct Unsubsidized Stafford Loans. **Student Employment:** Federal Work-Study Program available. Institutional employment available. **Financial Aid Statistics:** 99% needy freshmen, 79% needy undergrads receive need-based scholarship or grant aid. 31% freshmen, 21% undergrads receive non-need-based scholarship or grant aid. 60% freshmen, 53% undergrads receive need-based self-help aid. 10% freshmen, 5% undergrads receive athletic scholarships. 97% freshmen, 98% undergrads receive any aid. **Criteria awarding aid:** *Non-need-based:* Academics, Alumni affiliation, Athletics, Leadership, Music/drama.

LINCOLN UNIVERSITY (CA)

401 15th Street, Oakland, CA 94612
Phone: 510-628-8010 **Financial Aid Phone:** 510-628-8023
E-mail: admissions@lincolnuca.edu
Fax: 510-628-8012 **Website:** www.lincolnuca.edu

This private school was founded in 1919.

RATINGS
Admissions Selectivity Rating: 66   **Fire Safety Rating:** 60*   **Green Rating:** 60*

STUDENTS AND FACULTY
Enrollment: 91. **Student Body:** 57% female, 43% male.
Faculty: 11 full-time faculty, 82% hold PhDs, 0% are members of minority groups, 9% are women.

ACADEMICS
Degrees: Bachelor's; Certificate; Master's. **Most popular majors:** Education, General; Bible/Biblical Studies; Youth Ministry. **Special Study Options:** Cross-registration; Double major; English as a Second Language (ESL); Internships; Student-designed major. **Career services:** Alumni network; Internships.

FACILITIES
Housing: Campus Network: 100% of classrooms, 100% of dorms, 100% of student union, 100% of libraries, 100% of dining areas have wireless network access.

CAMPUS LIFE

Environment: Metropolis. **Activities:** Student government.

ADMISSIONS

Basis for Candidate Selection: *Very important factors include:* rigor of secondary school record. *Important factors include:* academic GPA. *Other factors include:* class rank, standardized test scores. **Freshman Admission Requirements:** High school diploma is required and GED is accepted. **Freshman Admission Statistics:** 130 applied, 82% admitted, 40% enrolled. **Transfer Admission Requirements:** College transcript(s). Minimum college GPA of 2.0 required. Lowest grade transferable C. **General Admission Information:** Application fee $75. Non-fall registration accepted.

COSTS AND FINANCIAL AID

Annual tuition $9,600. Average book and supplies expense $400. **Types of Aid:** *Need-based scholarships/grants:* Federal Pell.

LINCOLN UNIVERSITY (MO)

820 Chestnut Street, Jefferson City, MO 65101
Phone: 573-681-5102 **Financial Aid Phone:** 573-681-6156
E-mail: admissions@lincolnu.edu
Fax: 573-681-5889 **Website:** www.lincolnu.edu **ACT Code:** 2322

This public school was founded in 1866. It has a 174 acre campus.

RATINGS

Admissions Selectivity Rating: 80   **Fire Safety Rating:** 91   **Green Rating:** 73

STUDENTS AND FACULTY

Enrollment: 1,733. **Student Body:** 64% female, 36% male, 30% out-of-state, 3% international (14 countries represented). Asian 1%, African American 57%, Caucasian 29%, Hispanic 2%, Native American <1%, Pacific Islander <1%, Two or more races 3%, Race unknown 5%.
Retention and Graduation: 54% freshmen return for sophomore year. 8% freshmen graduate within 4 years. 26% freshmen graduate within 6 years. **Faculty:** Student/faculty ratio 15:1. 106 full-time faculty, 65% hold PhDs, 32% are members of minority groups, 46% are women. 0% of classes are taught by teaching assistants.

ACADEMICS

Degrees: Associate; Bachelor's; Master's; Post-bachelor's certificate; Post-master's certificate. **Classes:** Most classes have 20–29 students. Most lab/discussion sessions have 10–19 students. **Most popular majors:** Criminal Justice/Law Enforcement Administration; Registered Nursing/Registered Nurse; Business Administration and Management, General. **Special Study Options:** Accelerated program; Cooperative education program; Cross-registration; Distance learning; Double major; Dual enrollment; Exchange student program (domestic); Honors program; Independent study; Internships; Study abroad; Teacher certification program. **Honors programs:** Lincoln University offers a 18-credit-hour Honors Program which features small classes, unique academic challenges, individual attention from Honors faculty, and association with other like-minded students. An Honors student has opportunities to compete for summer mentorships, work closely with a faculty member on a research or creative project; to do sustained research or creative work leading to a thesis in the student's major; and to present his/her work at regional, national, and international conferences. These students also qualify for Honors housing, certain restricted courses, and other activities. **Disability Services offered:** Note-taking services; Reader services; Tape recorders; Tutors. **Career services:** Alumni network; Alumni services; Career assessment; Career/job search classes; Internships.

FACILITIES

Housing: Coed dorms; Men's dorms; Women's dorms; 100% of campus accessible to physically disabled. **Special Academic Facilities/Equipment:** University Archives/Ethnic Studies Center; Media Center; Academic Support Services; Agriculture and Extension Information Center; Education Curriculum Library.

CAMPUS LIFE

Environment: Town. **Activities:** Campus Ministries; Choral groups; Concert band; Dance; International Student Organization; Jazz band; Literary magazine; Marching band; Model UN; Music ensembles; Pep band; Radio station; Student government; Student newspaper; Television station. 23 registered organizations, 7 honor societies, 1 religious organization, 5 fraternities, 4 sororities on campus. **Athletics (Intercollegiate):** *Men:* baseball, basketball,

football, golf, track/field (outdoor). *Women:* basketball, cheerleading, cross-country, golf, softball, tennis, track/field (outdoor). **On-Campus Highlights:** Clifford G. Scruggs University Center (SUC). **Environmental Initiatives:** Environmental Health & Safety Management provides resources and services to ensure the proper management and disposal of hazardous materials around campus.

ADMISSIONS

Freshman Academic Profile: Average high school GPA 2.7. 5% in top 10% of high school class, 13% in top 25% of high school class, 43% in top 50% of high school class. **Test Scores:** SAT Math middle 50% range 370–460. SAT EBRW middle 50% range 390–453. ACT middle 50% range 14–19. **Basis for Candidate Selection:** *Other factors include:* rigor of secondary school record, academic GPA, standardized test scores, state residency. **Freshman Admission Requirements:** High school diploma is required and GED is accepted. *Academic units required:* 4 English, 3 math, 3 science, 1 science lab, 3 social studies, 3 academic electives, 1 visual/performing arts. *Academic units recommended:* 4 English, 3 math, 3 science, 1 science lab, 2 foreign language, 3 social studies, 3 academic electives, 1 visual/performing arts. **Freshman Admission Statistics:** 4,295 applied, 53% admitted, 17% enrolled. **Transfer Admission Requirements:** College transcript(s). Minimum college GPA of 2.0 required. Lowest grade transferable C. **General Admission Information:** Non-fall registration accepted. Admission may be deferred for a maximum of 1 semester.

COSTS AND FINANCIAL AID

Required Forms and Deadlines: FAFSA; Institution's own financial aid form. **Notification of Awards:** Applicants will be notified of awards on a rolling basis beginning 1/15. **Types of Aid:** *Need-based scholarships/grants:* Federal Pell; SEOG. *Loans:* Direct PLUS loans; Direct Subsidized Stafford Loans; Direct Unsubsidized Stafford Loans. **Student Employment:** Federal Work-Study Program available. Institutional employment available. **Financial Aid Statistics:** 91% needy freshmen, 96% needy undergrads receive need-based scholarship or grant aid. 48% freshmen, 41% undergrads receive non-need-based scholarship or grant aid. 87% freshmen, 80% undergrads receive need-based self-help aid. 1% freshmen, 1% undergrads receive athletic scholarships. 83.12% freshmen, 85.21% undergrads receive any aid. 81% undergrads borrow to pay for school. Average cumulative indebtedness $30,439. **Criteria awarding aid:** *Need-based:* Alumni affiliation. *Non-need-based:* Academics, Art, Athletics, Job skills, Leadership, Minority status, Music/drama, State/district residency.

THE LINCOLN UNIVERSITY (PA)

1570 Baltimore Pike, Lincoln University, PA 19352
Phone: 484-365-8000 **Financial Aid Phone:** (800) 561-2606
E-mail: admissions@lincoln.edu **CEEB Code:** 2367
Fax: 484 365-8109 **Website:** www.lincoln.edu **ACT Code:** 3614

This public school was founded in 1854. It has a 422 acre campus.

RATINGS

Admissions Selectivity Rating: 74   **Fire Safety Rating:** 92   **Green Rating:** 64

STUDENTS AND FACULTY

Enrollment: 2,032. **Student Body:** 66% female, 34% male, 50% out-of-state, 3% international (12 countries represented). Asian <1%, African American 85%, Caucasian 1%, Hispanic 5%, Native American <1%, Pacific Islander 0%, Two or more races 3%, Race unknown 4%.
Retention and Graduation: 71% freshmen return for sophomore year. 31% freshmen graduate within 4 years. 47% freshmen graduate within 6 years. 28% grads go on to further study within 1 year. 13% grads pursue arts and sciences degrees. 1% grads pursue law degrees. 6% grads pursue business degrees. 0% grads pursue medical degrees. **Faculty:** Student/faculty ratio 15:1. 100 full-time faculty, 83% hold PhDs, 66% are members of minority groups, 46% are women. 0% of classes are taught by teaching assistants.

ACADEMICS

Degrees: Bachelor's; Master's. **Classes:** Most classes have 20–29 students. Most lab/discussion sessions have 10–19 students. **Most popular majors:** Public Administration And Social Service Professions; Criminal Justice/Safety Studies; Health Professions And Related Programs. **Special Study Options:** Double major; Honors program; Independent study; Internships; Study abroad; Teacher certification program; Weekend college. **Honors programs:** The Horace Mann Bond Honors Program is designed to encourage academically talented students to become problem solvers and more responsive to the needs of the human community. It does so by combining excellence in Liberal Arts education with traditional virtues of adult accountability: reason, respect, reverence, reciprocity, restraint, reliability, and responsibility. **Disability Services offered:** Note-taking services; Reader services; Tape recorders; Tutors. **Career services:** Alumni services; Career assessment; Career/job search classes; Internships.

FACILITIES

Housing: Apartments for single students; Coed dorms; Men's dorms; Special housing for disabled students; Special housing for international students; Women's dorms. **Special Academic Facilities/Equipment:** The Student Union Building (SUB): houses two television studios, and a radio studio. Danjuma African Art Center: houses select installations of the university's extensive collection of African art and artifacts. International Cultural Center: houses a 1,049-seat theater, conference facility and art gallery. Wright Hall: houses the Learning Resource Center and planetarium. Langston Hughes Memorial Library: contains areas for microforms, periodicals, computer labs, reading lounges, individual and group study rooms, special collections, and the University archives. Ware Fine Arts Center: houses a ceramic studio, 2D/3D design studio, printmaking studio, graphic arts studio, painting/drawing studio, clavinova labs and an auditorium, fully equipped for digital recording and transmission.

CAMPUS LIFE

Environment: Village. **Activities:** Campus Ministries; Choral groups; Concert band; Dance; Drama/theater; International Student Organization; Jazz band; Marching band; Music ensembles; Musical theater; Opera; Pep band; Radio station; Student government; Student newspaper; Television station; Yearbook. 53 registered organizations, 8 honor societies, 12 religious organizations, 5 fraternities, 4 sororities on campus. **Athletics (Intercollegiate):** *Men:* baseball, basketball, cross-country, soccer, tennis, track/field (outdoor), track/field (indoor). *Women:* basketball, cross-country, soccer, tennis, track/field (outdoor), track/field (indoor), volleyball. **On-Campus Highlights:** Langston Hughes Memorial Library.

ADMISSIONS

Freshman Academic Profile: Average high school GPA 3.0. 7% in top 10% of high school class, 16% in top 25% of high school class, 53% in top 50% of high school class. **Test Scores:** SAT Math middle 50% range 430–500. SAT EBRW middle 50% range 440–510. ACT middle 50% range 16–18. **Basis for Candidate Selection:** *Very important factors include:* academic GPA, standardized test scores, level of applicant's interest. *Other factors include:* rigor of secondary school record, class rank, interview, talent/ability, character/personal qualities, geographical residence, state residency. **Freshman Admission Requirements:** High school diploma is required and GED is accepted. *Academic units required:* 4 English, 3 math, 3 science, 3 social studies, 5 academic electives, 2 visual/performing arts, 1 unit from above areas or other academic areas. *Academic units recommended:* 4 English, 4 math, 3 science, 3 social studies, 5 academic electives, 2 visual/performing arts. **Freshman Admission Statistics:** 4,429 applied, 83% admitted, 12% enrolled. **Transfer Admission Requirements:** College transcript(s), essay or personal statement, statement of good standing from prior institution(s). Minimum college GPA of 2.0 required. Lowest grade transferable C. **General Admission Information:** Priority deadline 3/1. Regular application deadline 5/1. Non-fall registration accepted. Admission may be deferred for a maximum of 1 year.

COSTS AND FINANCIAL AID

Required Forms and Deadlines: FAFSA. **Notification of Awards:** Applicants will be notified of awards on a rolling basis beginning 2/20. **Types of Aid:** *Need-based scholarships/grants:* College/university scholarship or grant aid from institutional funds; Federal Pell; Private scholarships; SEOG; State scholarships/grants. *Loans:* Direct PLUS loans; Direct Subsidized Stafford Loans; Direct Unsubsidized Stafford Loans. **Student Employment:** Federal Work-Study Program available. Institutional employment available. **Financial Aid Statistics:** 79% needy freshmen, 80% needy undergrads receive need-based scholarship or grant aid. 41% freshmen, 51% undergrads receive non-need-based scholarship or grant aid. 90% freshmen, 87% undergrads receive need-based self-help aid. 6% freshmen, 7% undergrads receive athletic scholarships. 97% freshmen, 95% undergrads receive any aid. 91% undergrads borrow to pay for school. Average cumulative indebtedness $36,567. **Criteria awarding aid:** *Need-based:* Academics, Leadership. *Non-need-based:* Academics, Alumni affiliation, Leadership, Music/drama.

LINDENWOOD UNIVERSITY

209 South Kingshighway, Saint Charles, MO 63301-1695
Phone: 314-949-4949 **Financial Aid Phone:** 636-949-4106
E-mail: admissions@lindenwood.edu **CEEB Code:** 6367
Fax: 314-949-4989 **Website:** www.lindenwood.edu **ACT Code:** 2324

This private school, affiliated with the Presbyterian Church, was founded in 1827. It has a 550 acre campus.

RATINGS

Admissions Selectivity Rating: 75   **Fire Safety Rating:** 73   **Green Rating:** 60*

STUDENTS AND FACULTY

Enrollment: 5,521. **Student Body:** 55% female, 45% male, 37% out-of-state, 11% international (99 countries represented). Asian 1%, African American 13%, Caucasian 58%, Hispanic 5%, Native American <1%, Pacific Islander 1%, Two or more races 3%, Race unknown 9%. **Retention and Graduation:** 68% freshmen return for sophomore year. 32% freshmen graduate within 4 years. 50% freshmen graduate within 6 years. **Faculty:** Student/faculty ratio 12:1. 258 full-time faculty, 84% hold PhDs, 11% are members of minority groups, 51% are women. 0% of classes are taught by teaching assistants.

ACADEMICS

Degrees: Bachelor's; Certificate; Doctoral degree research/scholarship; Master's; Post-bachelor's certificate; Post-master's certificate. **Classes:** Most classes have 10–19 students. Most lab/discussion sessions have 20–29 students. **Most popular majors:** Education, Other; Criminology. **Special Study Options:** Accelerated program; Cross-registration; Distance learning; Double major; Dual enrollment; English as a Second Language (ESL); Exchange student program (domestic); External degree program; Honors program; Independent study; Internships; Student-designed major; Study abroad; Teacher certification program. **Honors programs:** Honors College. **Disability Services offered:** Reader services; Tutors. **Career services:** Alumni services; Career assessment; Career/job search classes; Internships.

FACILITIES

Housing: Apartments for single students; Coed dorms; Fraternity/sorority housing; Men's dorms; Special housing for disabled students; Women's dorms. **Special Academic Facilities/Equipment:** University archives. **Campus Network:** 100% of classrooms, 100% of dorms, 100% of student union, 100% of libraries, 100% of dining areas, 50% of common outdoor areas have wireless network access.

CAMPUS LIFE

Environment: Town. **Activities:** Campus Ministries; Choral groups; Concert band; Dance; Drama/theater; International Student Organization; Jazz band; Literary magazine; Marching band; Music ensembles; Musical theater; Pep band; Radio station; Student government; Student newspaper; Student-run film society; Symphony orchestra; Television station. 78 registered organizations, 20 honor societies, 10 religious organizations, 2 fraternities, 2 sororities on campus. **Athletics (Intercollegiate):** *Men:* baseball, basketball, cheerleading, cross-country, diving, football, golf, ice hockey, lacrosse, riflery, soccer, swimming, tennis, track/field (outdoor), track/field (indoor), volleyball, water polo, wrestling. *Women:* basketball, cheerleading, cross-country, diving, field hockey, golf, ice hockey, lacrosse, riflery, soccer, softball, swimming, tennis, track/field (outdoor), track/field (indoor), volleyball, water polo. **On-Campus Highlights:** J. Scheidegger Center. **Environmental Initiatives:** Paper recycling.

ADMISSIONS

Freshman Academic Profile: Average high school GPA 3.4. **Test Scores:** SAT Math middle 50% range 490–590. SAT EBRW middle 50% range 490–580. ACT middle 50% range 20–25. **Basis for Candidate Selection:** *Very important factors include:* academic GPA. *Important factors include:* rigor of secondary school record. *Other factors include:* class rank, application essay, standardized test scores, recommendation(s), extracurricular activities, talent/ability, character/personal qualities, first generation, alumni/ae relation, volunteer work, work experience. **Freshman Admission Requirements:** High school diploma is required and GED is accepted. *Academic units recommended:* 4 English, 3 math, 3 science, 1 science lab, 2 foreign language, 3 social studies, 1 history, 1 visual/performing arts. **Freshman Admission Statistics:** 3,899 applied, 88% admitted, 22% enrolled. **Transfer Admission Requirements:** College transcript(s). Minimum college GPA of 2.0 required. Lowest grade transferable D. **General Admission Information:** Non-fall registration accepted. Admission may be deferred for a maximum of 1 year.

COSTS AND FINANCIAL AID

Annual tuition $18,500. Room and board $9,300. Required fees $100. Average book and supplies expense $1,300. **Required Forms and Deadlines:** FAFSA. **Types of Aid:** *Need-based scholarships/grants:* College/university scholarship or grant aid from institutional funds; Federal Pell; Private scholarships; SEOG; State scholarships/grants. *Loans:* Direct PLUS loans; Direct Subsidized Stafford Loans; Direct Unsubsidized Stafford Loans. **Student Employment:** Federal Work-Study Program available. Institutional employment available. **Financial Aid Statistics:** 99% needy freshmen, 93% needy undergrads receive need-based scholarship or grant aid. 30% freshmen, 18% undergrads receive non-need-based scholarship or grant aid. 92% freshmen, 93% undergrads receive need-based self-help aid. 9% freshmen, 3% undergrads receive athletic scholarships. 63% undergrads borrow to pay for school. Average cumulative indebtedness $33,365. **Criteria awarding aid:** *Non-need-based:* Academics, Art, Athletics, Leadership, Minority status, Music/drama, Religious affiliation, State/district residency.

LINFIELD COLLEGE

900 South East Baker Street, McMinnville, OR 97128-6894
Phone: 503-883-2213 **Financial Aid Phone:** 503-883-2269
E-mail: admission@linfield.edu **CEEB Code:** 4387
Fax: 503-883-2472 **Website:** www.linfield.edu **ACT Code:** 3466

This private school, affiliated with the American Baptist Church, was founded in 1858. It has a 189 acre campus.

RATINGS

Admissions Selectivity Rating: 77 **Fire Safety Rating:** 97 **Green Rating:** 83

STUDENTS AND FACULTY

Enrollment: 1,383. **Student Body:** 62% female, 38% male, 40% out-of-state, 2% international (20 countries represented). Asian 5%, African American 1%, Caucasian 62%, Hispanic 19%, Native American 1%, Pacific Islander 1%, Two or more races 7%, Race unknown 2%.
Retention and Graduation: 84% freshmen return for sophomore year. 63% freshmen graduate within 4 years. 74% freshmen graduate within 6 years. 14% grads go on to further study within 1 year. 4% grads pursue arts and sciences degrees. 1% grads pursue law degrees. 1% grads pursue business degrees. 1% grads pursue medical degrees. **Faculty:** Student/faculty ratio 11:1. 105 full-time faculty, 95% hold PhDs, 15% are members of minority groups, 55% are women. 0% of classes are taught by teaching assistants.

ACADEMICS

Degrees: Bachelor's. **Classes:** Most classes have 10–19 students. Most lab/discussion sessions have 10–19 students. **Most popular majors:** Elementary Education and Teaching; Registered Nursing/Registered Nurse; Business Administration and Management, General. **Special Study Options:** Cross-registration; Distance learning; Double major; Dual enrollment; English as a Second Language (ESL); External degree program; Independent study; Internships; Liberal arts/career combination; Student-designed major; Study abroad; Teacher certification program. **Disability Services offered:** Note-taking services; Reader services; Tape recorders; Tutors. **Career services:** Alumni network; Alumni services; Career assessment; Career/job search classes; Internships; Regional alumni.

FACILITIES

Housing: Apartments for single students; Coed dorms; Fraternity/sorority housing; Men's dorms; Special housing for disabled students; Wellness housing; Women's dorms; 80% of campus accessible to physically disabled. **Special Academic Facilities/Equipment:** Student-run garden, pristine concert hall, Steinway concert grand piano, student-run radio station, anthropology museum, cadaver lab, music technology lab, field house for spring training, student-run bicycle rental and repair shop.

CAMPUS LIFE

Environment: Town. **Activities:** Campus Ministries; Choral groups; Concert band; Dance; Drama/theater; International Student Organization; Jazz band; Literary magazine; Marching band; Model UN; Music ensembles; Musical theater; Opera; Pep band; Radio station; Student government; Student newspaper; Symphony orchestra. 40 registered organizations, 19 honor societies, 5 religious organizations, 3 fraternities, 4 sororities on campus. **Athletics (Intercollegiate):** *Men:* baseball, basketball, cross-country, football, golf, soccer, swimming, tennis, track/field (outdoor). *Women:* basketball, cross-

country, golf, lacrosse, soccer, softball, swimming, tennis, track/field (outdoor), volleyball. **On-Campus Highlights:** Nicholson Library.

ADMISSIONS

Freshman Academic Profile: Average high school GPA 3.7. 90% from public high schools. **Test Scores:** SAT Math middle 50% range 520–610. SAT EBRW middle 50% range 520–620. ACT middle 50% range 20–26. **Basis for Candidate Selection:** *Very important factors include:* rigor of secondary school record. *Important factors include:* academic GPA, application essay, recommendation(s). *Other factors include:* standardized test scores, extracurricular activities, talent/ability, character/personal qualities, first generation, alumni/ae relation, geographical residence, racial/ethnic status, volunteer work, work experience, level of applicant's interest. **Freshman Admission Requirements:** High school diploma is required and GED is accepted. *Academic units recommended:* 4 English, 4 math, 4 science, 4 foreign language, 4 social studies. **Freshman Admission Statistics:** 2,390 applied, 82% admitted, 24% enrolled. **Transfer Admission Requirements:** College transcript(s), essay or personal statement, Lowest grade transferable C. **General Admission Information:** Priority deadline 2/1. Non-fall registration accepted. Admission may be deferred for a maximum of 1 year.

COSTS AND FINANCIAL AID

Annual tuition $43,560. Room and board $12,670. Required fees $502. Average book and supplies expense $900. **Required Forms and Deadlines:** FAFSA. **Notification of Awards:** Applicants will be notified of awards on a rolling basis beginning 4/15. **Types of Aid:** *Need-based scholarships/grants:* College/university scholarship or grant aid from institutional funds; Federal Pell; Private scholarships; SEOG; State scholarships/grants. *Loans:* Direct PLUS loans; Direct Subsidized Stafford Loans; Direct Unsubsidized Stafford Loans. **Student Employment:** Federal Work-Study Program available. Institutional employment available. **Financial Aid Statistics:** 78% needy freshmen, 80% needy undergrads receive need-based scholarship or grant aid. 97% freshmen, 96% undergrads receive non-need-based scholarship or grant aid. 80% freshmen, 79% undergrads receive need-based self-help aid. 0% freshmen, 0% undergrads receive athletic scholarships. 99% freshmen, 98% undergrads receive any aid. 74% undergrads borrow to pay for school. Average cumulative indebtedness $36,082. **Criteria awarding aid:** *Need-based:* Academics, Minority status, Music/drama. *Non-need-based:* Academics, Leadership, Minority status, Music/drama.

LIPSCOMB UNIVERSITY

One University Park Dr., Nashville, TN 37204-3951
Phone: 615-966-1776 **Financial Aid Phone:** 615-966-1791
E-mail: admissions@lipscomb.edu **CEEB Code:** 1161
Fax: 615-966-1804 **Website:** http://www.lipscomb.edu **ACT Code:** 3956

This private school, affiliated with the Church of Christ, was founded in 1891. It has a 88.5 acre campus.

RATINGS

Admissions Selectivity Rating: 87 **Fire Safety Rating:** 94 **Green Rating:** 77

STUDENTS AND FACULTY

Enrollment: 2,973. **Student Body:** 61% female, 39% male, 34% out-of-state, 3% international (45 countries represented). Asian 3%, African American 7%, Caucasian 76%, Hispanic 7%, Native American <1%, Pacific Islander <1%, Two or more races 3%, Race unknown 1%.
Retention and Graduation: 79% freshmen return for sophomore year. 48% freshmen graduate within 4 years. 58% freshmen graduate within 6 years. **Faculty:** Student/faculty ratio 14:1. 213 full-time faculty, 84% hold PhDs, 8% are members of minority groups, 40% are women. 0% of classes are taught by teaching assistants.

ACADEMICS

Degrees: Associate; Bachelor's; Certificate; Doctoral degree—professional practice; Doctoral degree research/scholarship; Master's; Post-bachelor's certificate. **Classes:** Most classes have 10–19 students. Most lab/discussion sessions have 10–19 students. **Most popular majors:** Biology/Biological Sciences, General; Registered Nursing/Registered Nurse; Human Resources Management/Personnel Administration, General. **Special Study Options:** Accelerated program; Cross-registration; Distance learning; Double major; Dual enrollment; English as a Second Language (ESL); Honors program; Independent study; Internships; Student-designed major; Study abroad; Teacher certification program. **Honors programs:** The Honors College at Lipscomb University seeks to provide students with a significant enhancement to their university education through a challenging academic program, through cultural and entertainment opportunities, and through planning and mentoring for the future. Courses within the program offer more student participation, a deeper exploration of key ideas, and an opportunity for students to develop critical thinking, problem-solving, and project management skills. In addition to a strong academic challenge, students in The Honors College explore different cultural ideas and events by attending Broadway plays which come to Nashville, foreign films, and ethnic dining experiences. We sponsor a Masquerade Ball each year and have several other social functions designed to strengthen the friendships established in classes with other honors students. Finally all students receive mentoring in planning their careers at Lipscomb University and beyond, including information and advice on major national competitive scholarships like the U. S. Fulbright Scholar, the Goldwater Scholarship, and the Truman Scholarship and on appropriate study abroad and internship possibilities. The program seeks students who have a lot of ambition, who are creative, and who are willing to take some risks to create an outstanding educational experience at Lipscomb University. **Disability Services offered:** Note-taking services; Reader services; Tape recorders; Tutors. **Career services:** Alumni network; Alumni services; Career assessment; Career/job search classes; Internships.

FACILITIES

Housing: Apartments for single students; Men's dorms; Women's dorms; 100% of campus accessible to physically disabled. **Special Academic Facilities/Equipment:** On-campus elementary, middle, and secondary schools. **Campus Network:** 100% of classrooms, 100% of dorms, 100% of student union, 100% of libraries, 100% of dining areas, 10% of common outdoor areas have wireless network access.

CAMPUS LIFE

Environment: Metropolis. **Activities:** Campus Ministries; Choral groups; Concert band; Dance; Drama/theater; International Student Organization; Jazz band; Music ensembles; Musical theater; Pep band; Radio station; Student government; Student newspaper; Yearbook. 50 registered organizations, 5 honor societies, 6 religious organizations, 5 fraternities, 8 sororities on campus. **Athletics (Intercollegiate):** *Men:* baseball, basketball, cross-country, golf, soccer, tennis, track/field (outdoor). *Women:* basketball, cheerleading, cross-country, soccer, softball, tennis, track/field (outdoor), track/field (indoor), volleyball. **On-Campus Highlights:** Bennett Campus Center. **Environmental Initiatives:** First and only comprehensive sustainability academic program in the SE US.

ADMISSIONS

Freshman Academic Profile: Average high school GPA 3.6. 29% in top 10% of high school class, 54% in top 25% of high school class, 80% in top 50% of high school class. 50% from public high schools. **Test Scores:** SAT Math middle 50% range 520–660. SAT EBRW middle 50% range 540–670. ACT middle 50% range 23–29. **Basis for Candidate Selection:** *Very important factors include:* class rank, standardized test scores. *Important factors include:* rigor of secondary school record, academic GPA, recommendation(s). *Other factors include:* application essay, extracurricular activities, talent/ability, character/personal qualities, first generation, volunteer work, work experience. **Freshman Admission Requirements:** High school diploma is required and GED is accepted. **Freshman Admission Statistics:** 3,581 applied, 60% admitted, 30% enrolled. **Transfer Admission Requirements:** College transcript(s), interview, statement of good standing from prior institution(s). Minimum college GPA of 2.0 required. Lowest grade transferable C. **General Admission Information:** Application fee $50. Non-fall registration accepted. Admission may be deferred for a maximum of 1 year.

COSTS AND FINANCIAL AID

Annual tuition $29,676. Room and board $12,652. Required fees $2,468. Average book and supplies expense $1,500. **Required Forms and Deadlines:** FAFSA. **Notification of Awards:** Applicants will be notified of awards on a rolling basis beginning 3/1. **Types of Aid:** *Need-based scholarships/grants:* College/university scholarship or grant aid from institutional funds; Federal Pell; Private scholarships; SEOG; State scholarships/grants. *Loans:* Direct PLUS loans; Direct Subsidized Stafford Loans; Direct Unsubsidized Stafford Loans. **Student Employment:** Federal Work-Study Program available. Institutional employment available. **Financial Aid Statistics:** 100% needy freshmen, 98% needy undergrads receive need-based scholarship or grant aid. 99% freshmen, 85% undergrads receive non-need-based scholarship or grant aid. 75% freshmen, 77% undergrads receive need-based self-help aid. 3% freshmen, 3% undergrads receive athletic scholarships. 98% freshmen, 0.77% undergrads receive any aid. 59% undergrads borrow to pay for school. Average cumulative indebtedness $29,673. **Criteria awarding aid:** *Need-based:* Leadership. *Non-*

need-based: Academics, Art, Athletics, Job skills, Leadership, Minority status, Music/drama, Religious affiliation, State/district residency.

LOCK HAVEN UNIVERSITY OF PENNSYLVANIA

LHU Office of Admissions, Lock Haven, PA 17745
Phone: 570-484-2027
E-mail: admissions@lhup.edu **CEEB Code:** 2654
Fax: 570-484-2201 **Website:** www.lhup.edu **ACT Code:** 3708

This public school was founded in 1870. It has a 175 acre campus.

RATINGS

Admissions Selectivity Rating: 74   **Fire Safety Rating:** 62   **Green Rating:** 60*

STUDENTS AND FACULTY

Enrollment: 3,425. **Student Body:** 58% female, 42% male, 5% out-of-state, 1% international (39 countries represented). Asian 1%, African American 10%, Caucasian 81%, Hispanic 2%, Native American 1%, Pacific Islander <1%, Two or more races 1%, Race unknown 4%.
Retention and Graduation: 70% freshmen return for sophomore year. 32% freshmen graduate within 4 years. 48% freshmen graduate within 6 years.
Faculty: Student/faculty ratio 17:1. 203 full-time faculty, 88% hold PhDs, 15% are members of minority groups, 49% are women. 0% of classes are taught by teaching assistants.

ACADEMICS

Degrees: Associate; Bachelor's; Master's. **Classes:** Most classes have 10–19 students. Most lab/discussion sessions have 10–19 students. **Most popular majors:** Sports, Kinesiology, and Physical Education/Fitness, Other; Health Professions and Related Clinical Sciences, Other; Elementary Education and Teaching. **Special Study Options:** Accelerated program; Cross-registration; Distance learning; Double major; Dual enrollment; Honors program; Independent study; Internships; Student-designed major; Study abroad; Teacher certification program. **Honors programs:** The University Honors Program provides students and faculty opportunities for creative intellectual engagement through a mix of special curricular and co-curricular opportunities. Students may apply for entry as a first-year freshman or after completing 1–4 semesters of college-level work. Entry as a first-year freshman may be either directly into the University Honors or through the First Year Excellence Program. Students successfully completing the First Year Excellence Program receive certificate recognition. Students completing the University Honors Program receive recognition on their transcript, on their diploma and at commencement. Students in both the First Year Excellence and University Honors programs must participate in co-curricular activities and community service in addition to their curriculum. Engaging activity groups and Speaker Series allow students in the Honors Program to bond together and learn from each other, creating a community of both friends and scholars. **Disability Services offered:** Note-taking services; Reader services; Tape recorders; Tutors. **Career services:** Alumni network; Alumni services; Career assessment; Career/job search classes; Internships; Regional alumni.

FACILITIES

Housing: Apartments for single students; Coed dorms; 98% of campus accessible to physically disabled. **Special Academic Facilities/Equipment:** Planetarium, Sloan Art Gallery, Library Archives. **Campus Network:** 100% of classrooms, 100% of dorms, 100% of student union, 100% of libraries, 100% of dining areas have wireless network access.

CAMPUS LIFE

Environment: Village. **Activities:** Campus Ministries; Choral groups; Concert band; Dance; Drama/theater; International Student Organization; Jazz band; Literary magazine; Marching band; Music ensembles; Musical theater; Pep band; Radio station; Student government; Student newspaper; Symphony orchestra; Television station; Yearbook. 96 registered organizations, 10 honor societies, 7 religious organizations, 6 fraternities, 4 sororities on campus. **Athletics (Intercollegiate):** *Men:* baseball, basketball, football, soccer, track/field (outdoor), track/field (indoor), wrestling. *Women:* basketball, field hockey, lacrosse, soccer, softball, swimming, track/field (outdoor), track/field (indoor), volleyball. **On-Campus Highlights:** Student Recreation Center.

ADMISSIONS

Freshman Academic Profile: Average high school GPA 3.3. 8% in top 10% of high school class, 27% in top 25% of high school class, 58% in top 50% of

high school class. **Test Scores:** SAT Math middle 50% range 450–550. SAT EBRW middle 50% range 460–560. ACT middle 50% range 16–22. **Basis for Candidate Selection:** *Very important factors include:* rigor of secondary school record, class rank, academic GPA, talent/ability, character/personal qualities. *Important factors include:* standardized test scores, racial/ethnic status. *Other factors include:* application essay, recommendation(s), interview, extracurricular activities, first generation, volunteer work, work experience, level of applicant's interest. **Freshman Admission Requirements:** High school diploma is required and GED is accepted. *Academic units required:* 4 English, 3 math, 3 science, 2 science labs, 2 social studies, 2 history. *Academic units recommended:* 4 English, 4 math, 4 science, 3 science labs, 2 foreign language, 2 social studies, 2 history. **Freshman Admission Statistics:** 3,020 applied, 89% admitted, 29% enrolled. **Transfer Admission Requirements:** College transcript(s), statement of good standing from prior institution(s). Minimum college GPA of 2.0 required. Lowest grade transferable C. **General Admission Information:** Application fee $25. Non-fall registration accepted. Admission may be deferred for a maximum of 1 year.

COSTS AND FINANCIAL AID

Annual in-state tuition $7,492. Annual out-of-state tuition $16,730. Room and board $9,968. Required fees $3,084. Average book and supplies expense $1,700. **Required Forms and Deadlines:** FAFSA; State aid form. **Notification of Awards:** Applicants will be notified of awards on a rolling basis beginning 4/10. **Types of Aid:** *Need-based scholarships/grants:* College/university scholarship or grant aid from institutional funds; Federal Pell; Private scholarships; SEOG; State scholarships/grants. *Loans:* Direct PLUS loans; Direct Subsidized Stafford Loans; Direct Unsubsidized Stafford Loans. **Student Employment:** Federal Work-Study Program available. Institutional employment available. **Financial Aid Statistics:** 70% needy freshmen, 68% needy undergrads receive need-based scholarship or grant aid. 20% freshmen, 10% undergrads receive non-need-based scholarship or grant aid. 94% freshmen, 90% undergrads receive need-based self-help aid. 7% freshmen, 5% undergrads receive athletic scholarships. 95% undergrads borrow to pay for school. Average cumulative indebtedness $34,863. **Criteria awarding aid:** *Need-based:* Academics, Athletics, Leadership. *Non-need-based:* Academics, Art, Athletics, Leadership, Minority status, Music/drama, State/district residency.

LONG ISLAND UNIVERSITY

720 Northern Blvd., Brookville, NY 11548
Phone: 516-299-2900 **Financial Aid Phone:** 516-299-2553
E-mail: enroll@liu.edu **CEEB Code:** 2070
Fax: 516-299-2137 **Website:** www.liu.edu **ACT Code:** 2687

This private school was founded in 1954. It has a 308 acre campus.

RATINGS

Admissions Selectivity Rating: 77   **Fire Safety Rating:** 98   **Green Rating:** 60*

STUDENTS AND FACULTY

Enrollment: 6,164. **Student Body:** 67% female, 33% male, 12% out-of-state, 4% international (48 countries represented). Asian 11%, African American 14%, Caucasian 38%, Hispanic 14%, Native American <1%, Pacific Islander <1%, Two or more races 2%, Race unknown 16%.
Retention and Graduation: 75% freshmen return for sophomore year. 27% freshmen graduate within 4 years. 46% freshmen graduate within 6 years. 24% grads go on to further study within 1 year. 31% grads pursue arts and sciences degrees. 4% grads pursue law degrees. 9% grads pursue business degrees. 16% grads pursue medical degrees. **Faculty:** Student/faculty ratio 12:1. 502 full-time faculty, 83% hold PhDs, 28% are members of minority groups, 52% are women.

ACADEMICS

Degrees: Associate; Bachelor's; Certificate; Doctoral degree—professional practice; Doctoral degree research/scholarship; Master's; Post-bachelor's certificate; Post-master's certificate; Terminal Associate. **Classes:** Most classes have 10–19 students. **Most popular majors:** Health Professions And Related Programs. **Special Study Options:** Accelerated program; Cooperative education program; Distance learning; Double major; Dual enrollment; English as a Second Language (ESL); Exchange student program (domestic); Honors program; Independent study; Internships; Liberal arts/career combination; Student-designed major; Study abroad; Teacher certification program. **Honors programs:** Honors College. **Combined degree programs:** BA/JD; BA/MA. **Disability Services offered:** Note-taking services; Reader services; Tape

recorders; Tutors. **Career services:** Alumni network; Alumni services; Career assessment; Career/job search classes; Internships; Regional alumni.

FACILITIES

Housing: Apartments for single students; Coed dorms; Fraternity/sorority housing; Special housing for disabled students; Special housing for international students; Theme housing; 80% of campus accessible to physically disabled.
Special Academic Facilities/Equipment: Tilles Center for the Performing Arts, a concert hall that features a wide range of dance, music, and theater events, where students in the School of Visual and Performing Arts are able to perform alongside world-renowned performers and engage in live stage productions. Student-Run Businesses: These fully functional business operations afford students unique experiential learning opportunities as they make executive-level decisions. They include Browse, a high-tech, Apple-licensed technology store, with "Genius Bar" inspired customer service that employs students; Post Marketing and PR Agency, a full-service agency managed by students; The Student Body Boutique, a trendy clothing boutique that sells the latest fashions at an affordable price; Eateries that include, Hutton & Post, which offers traditional snacks in addition to healthy options; End Zone, a lounge that offers a full menu and HD televisions for watching sports and other entertainment; and Time Out Smoothie Bar, a juice bar that sells nutritious offerings for students on the go. Wall Street Trading Floor: Featuring Bloomberg terminals and other business technology, this simulated trading floor empowers students to utilize the latest financial tools and learn in a real-time trading environment; home to the University's student-run LIU-iF. Investment Fund Student Innovation Incubator: a physical and virtual workspace for students to launch startup businesses and collaborate with successful entrepreneurs. Equestrian Stables: North Shore Equestrian Center houses the LIU Post Equine Studies program, offering a large indoor arena and two spacious outdoor rings. On-campus nursery school, Psychobiology Lab, marine station and fleet of research vessels, Silicon Graphics Computer Lab. **Campus Network:** 100% of classrooms, 100% of dorms, 100% of student union, 100% of libraries, 100% of dining areas, 50% of common outdoor areas have wireless network access.

CAMPUS LIFE

Environment: Metropolis. **Activities:** Campus Ministries; Choral groups; Concert band; Dance; Drama/theater; International Student Organization; Jazz band; Literary magazine; Marching band; Model UN; Music ensembles; Musical theater; Pep band; Radio station; Student government; Student newspaper; Student-run film society; Symphony orchestra; Television station; Yearbook. 68 registered organizations, 20 honor societies, 3 religious organizations, 5 fraternities, 4 sororities on campus. **Athletics (Intercollegiate):** *Men:* baseball, basketball, cross-country, football, soccer, tennis, track/field (outdoor), track/field (indoor), volleyball. *Women:* basketball, cross-country, field hockey, soccer, softball, swimming, tennis, track/field (outdoor), track/field (indoor), volleyball. **On-Campus Highlights:** Tilles Center for the Performing Arts.

ADMISSIONS

Freshman Academic Profile: Average high school GPA 3.4. 27% in top 10% of high school class, 55% in top 25% of high school class, 73% in top 50% of high school class. 79% from public high schools. **Test Scores:** SAT Math middle 50% range 540–650. SAT EBRW middle 50% range 540–640. ACT middle 50% range 22–28. **Basis for Candidate Selection:** *Very important factors include:* rigor of secondary school record, class rank, academic GPA, standardized test scores, talent/ability, character/personal qualities. *Important factors include:* application essay, interview, extracurricular activities, volunteer work. *Other factors include:* recommendation(s), first generation, alumni/ae relation, work experience. **Freshman Admission Requirements:** High school diploma is required and GED is accepted. *Academic units recommended:* 4 English, 3 math, 3 science, 3 science labs, 2 foreign language, 4 social studies. **Freshman Admission Statistics:** 13,328 applied, 80% admitted, 12% enrolled. **General Admission Information:** Application fee $50. Priority deadline 12/15. Non-fall registration accepted. Admission may be deferred for a maximum of one year.

COSTS AND FINANCIAL AID

Annual tuition $36,452. Room and board $14,350. Required fees $1,916. Average book and supplies expense $2,000. **Required Forms and Deadlines:** FAFSA; State aid form. **Notification of Awards:** Applicants will be notified of awards on a rolling basis beginning 12/20. **Types of Aid:** *Need-based scholarships/grants:* College/university scholarship or grant aid from institutional funds; Federal Pell; Private scholarships; SEOG; State scholarships/grants; United Negro College Fund. *Loans:* Direct PLUS loans; Direct Subsidized Stafford Loans; Direct Unsubsidized Stafford Loans. **Student Employment:** Federal Work-Study Program available. Institutional employment available. **Financial Aid Statistics:** 57% needy freshmen, 64% needy undergrads receive need-based scholarship or grant aid. 89% freshmen, 69% undergrads receive non-need-based scholarship or grant aid. 61% freshmen, 73% undergrads receive need-based self-help aid. 11% freshmen, 8% undergrads receive athletic scholarships. 92% freshmen, 66% undergrads receive any aid. 71% undergrads borrow to pay for school. Average cumulative indebtedness $45,218.

LONGWOOD UNIVERSITY

Admissions Office, Farmville, VA 23909
Phone: 434-395-2060 **Financial Aid Phone:** 800-281-4677
E-mail: admissions@longwood.edu **CEEB Code:** 5368
Fax: 434-395-2332 **Website:** www.whylongwood.com **ACT Code:** 4366

This public school was founded in 1839. It has a 160 acre campus.

RATINGS
Admissions Selectivity Rating: 77   **Fire Safety Rating:** 97   **Green Rating:** 60*

STUDENTS AND FACULTY
Enrollment: 4,185. **Student Body:** 66% female, 34% male, 3% out-of-state, 1% international (46 countries represented). Asian 1%, African American 7%, Caucasian 81%, Hispanic 4%, Native American <1%, Pacific Islander <1%, Two or more races 3%, Race unknown 3%.
Retention and Graduation: 79% freshmen return for sophomore year.
Faculty: Student/faculty ratio 18:1. 222 full-time faculty, 85% hold PhDs, 8% are members of minority groups, 48% are women. 0% of classes are taught by teaching assistants.

ACADEMICS
Degrees: Bachelor's; Master's; Post-bachelor's certificate; Post-master's certificate. **Classes:** Most classes have 20–29 students. Most lab/discussion sessions have 20–29 students. **Most popular majors:** Business/Commerce, General; Elementary Education and Teaching; Psychology, General. **Special Study Options:** Accelerated program; Cross-registration; Distance learning; Double major; Dual enrollment; Honors program; Independent study; Internships; Study abroad; Teacher certification program. **Honors programs:** The Cormier Honors College at Longwood University is designed to meet the needs of academically gifted and talented undergraduate students. Challenging courses with high academic standards enable students to expand their intellectual and creative horizons. The Honors Program focuses on the exchange of ideas and the enrichment of students' educational and cultural experiences. Learning takes place not only in the classroom, but also through cultural events, conferences, field trips, and study abroad. In keeping with the University's mission, the Longwood Honors Program strives to develop citizens who are committed to using their learning to provide service to their local communities as well as to the larger national and global communities. The concept of linking learning with the practice of citizenship is the distinctive feature of our Program. **Combined degree programs:** BA/MA. **Disability Services offered:** Note-taking services; Reader services; Tape recorders; Tutors. **Career services:** Alumni network; Career assessment; Career/job search classes; Internships.

FACILITIES
Housing: Apartments for single students; Coed dorms; Fraternity/sorority housing; Special housing for disabled students; Women's dorms; 100% of campus accessible to physically disabled. **Special Academic Facilities/Equipment:** Longwood Center for the Visual Arts. **Campus Network:** 100% of classrooms, 100% of student union, 100% of libraries, 80% of dining areas, 50% of common outdoor areas have wireless network access.

CAMPUS LIFE
Environment: Village. **Activities:** Campus Ministries; Choral groups; Concert band; Dance; Drama/theater; Jazz band; Music ensembles; Pep band; Radio station; Student government; Student newspaper. 175 registered organizations, 16 honor societies, 11 religious organizations, 10 fraternities, 12 sororities on campus. **Athletics (Intercollegiate):** *Men:* baseball, basketball, cheerleading, cross-country, golf, soccer, tennis. *Women:* basketball, cheerleading, cross-country, field hockey, golf, lacrosse, soccer, softball, tennis. **On-Campus Highlights:** Brock Commons.

ADMISSIONS
Freshman Academic Profile: Average high school GPA 3.4. 12% in top 10% of high school class, 39% in top 25% of high school class, 79% in top 50% of high school class. 92% from public high schools. **Test Scores:** SAT Math middle 50% range 470–560. SAT EBRW middle 50% range 480–570. ACT

middle 50% range 20–24. **Basis for Candidate Selection:** *Very important factors include:* rigor of secondary school record, academic GPA, application essay, standardized test scores. *Important factors include:* class rank, extracurricular activities, talent/ability, character/personal qualities, first generation, alumni/ae relation, geographical residence. *Other factors include:* recommendation(s), state residency. **Freshman Admission Requirements:** High school diploma is required and GED is accepted. *Academic units required:* 4 English, 3 math, 3 science, 2 science labs, 2 foreign language, 2 social studies, 2 history, 1 visual/performing arts, 2 unit from above areas or other academic areas. *Academic units recommended:* 4 English, 4 math, 4 science, 3 science labs, 4 foreign language, 2 social studies, 2 history, 1 visual/performing arts. **Freshman Admission Statistics:** 4,166 applied, 78% admitted, 32% enrolled. **Transfer Admission Requirements:** High school transcript, college transcript(s), essay or personal statement. Minimum college GPA of 2.50 required. Lowest grade transferable C-. **General Admission Information:** Application fee $50. Priority deadline 3/1. Non-fall registration accepted. Admission may be deferred for a maximum of 1 year.

COSTS AND FINANCIAL AID
Annual in-state tuition $11,340. Annual out-of-state tuition $24,210. Room and board $9,584. Required fees $4,890. Average book and supplies expense $1,000. **Required Forms and Deadlines:** FAFSA. **Notification of Awards:** Applicants will be notified of awards on a rolling basis beginning 2/4. **Types of Aid:** *Need-based scholarships/grants:* College/university scholarship or grant aid from institutional funds; Federal Pell; Private scholarships; SEOG; State scholarships/grants. *Loans:* Direct PLUS loans; Direct Subsidized Stafford Loans; Direct Unsubsidized Stafford Loans. **Student Employment:** Federal Work-Study Program available. Institutional employment available. **Financial Aid Statistics:** 85% needy freshmen, 79% needy undergrads receive need-based scholarship or grant aid. 2% freshmen, 2% undergrads receive non-need-based scholarship or grant aid. 85% freshmen, 84% undergrads receive need-based self-help aid. 3% freshmen, 3% undergrads receive athletic scholarships. 60% freshmen receive any aid. **Criteria awarding aid:** *Non-need-based:* Academics, Alumni affiliation, Art, Athletics, Leadership, Music/drama, State/district residency.

LORAS COLLEGE

1450 Alta Vista, Dubuque, IA 52001
Phone: 563-588-7236 **Financial Aid Phone:** 563-588-7136
E-mail: admission@loras.edu **CEEB Code:** 6370
Fax: 563-588-7119 **Website:** www.loras.edu **ACT Code:** 1328

This private school, affiliated with the Roman Catholic Church, was founded in 1839. It has a 64 acre campus.

RATINGS
Admissions Selectivity Rating: 77   **Fire Safety Rating:** 96   **Green Rating:** 60*

STUDENTS AND FACULTY
Enrollment: 1,293. **Student Body:** 44% female, 56% male, 59% out-of-state, 2% international (9 countries represented). Asian 1%, African American 4%, Caucasian 79%, Hispanic 9%, Native American 0%, Pacific Islander <1%, Two or more races 2%, Race unknown 3%.
Retention and Graduation: 76% freshmen return for sophomore year. 58% freshmen graduate within 4 years. 66% freshmen graduate within 6 years. 23% grads go on to further study within 1 year. 6% grads pursue arts and sciences degrees. 1% grads pursue law degrees. 1% grads pursue business degrees. 1% grads pursue medical degrees. **Faculty:** Student/faculty ratio 12:1. 104 full-time faculty, 86% hold PhDs, 4% are members of minority groups, 43% are women. 0% of classes are taught by teaching assistants.

ACADEMICS
Degrees: Bachelor's; Master's; Post-bachelor's certificate. **Classes:** Most classes have 20–29 students. Most lab/discussion sessions have 10–19 students. **Most popular majors:** Elementary Education and Teaching; Psychology, General; Business Administration and Management, General. **Special Study Options:** Accelerated program; Cross-registration; Distance learning; Double major; Dual enrollment; Honors program; Independent study; Internships; Student-designed major; Study abroad; Teacher certification program. **Honors programs:** The Loras College Honors Program offers academically challenging, experiential, and interdisciplinary courses taken with a peer group of active learners. We encourage students to employ analytical and creative thinking

as they explore the various disciplines that comprise the liberal arts. A key component of the Honors Program is a long-term, interdisciplinary group project that emphasizes community engagement and research in collaboration with a faculty mentor. The Honors Program curriculum focuses on real-world problem solving and cultivates essential skills for professional success, graduate education, and meaningful contributions to the community. **Disability Services offered:** Note-taking services; Reader services; Tape recorders; Tutors. **Career services:** Alumni network; Alumni services; Career assessment; Career/job search classes; Internships.

FACILITIES

Housing: Apartments for single students; Coed dorms; 63% of campus accessible to physically disabled. **Special Academic Facilities/Equipment:** Planetarium, observatory, regional history archive, residential arts complex, television studio.

CAMPUS LIFE

Environment: Town. **Activities:** Campus Ministries; Choral groups; Concert band; Dance; Drama/theater; International Student Organization; Jazz band; Literary magazine; Music ensembles; Pep band; Radio station; Student government; Student newspaper; Television station; Yearbook. 58 registered organizations, 3 honor societies, 7 religious organizations, 1 fraternity, 1 sorority on campus. **Athletics (Intercollegiate):** *Men:* baseball, basketball, cross-country, diving, football, golf, soccer, swimming, tennis, track/field (outdoor), track/field (indoor), wrestling. *Women:* basketball, cross-country, diving, golf, soccer, softball, swimming, tennis, track/field (outdoor), track/field (indoor), volleyball. **On-Campus Highlights:** Academic Resource Center.

ADMISSIONS

Freshman Academic Profile: Average high school GPA 3.5. 72% from public high schools. **Test Scores:** SAT Math middle 50% range 485–570. SAT EBRW middle 50% range 480–575. ACT middle 50% range 20–25. **Basis for Candidate Selection:** *Very important factors include:* rigor of secondary school record, academic GPA, standardized test scores. *Other factors include:* class rank, application essay, recommendation(s), interview, extracurricular activities, character/personal qualities, racial/ethnic status, volunteer work, work experience, level of applicant's interest. **Freshman Admission Requirements:** High school diploma is required and GED is accepted. *Academic units recommended:* 4 English, 4 math, 3 science, 2 science labs, 3 social studies, 2 academic electives. **Freshman Admission Statistics:** 1,491 applied, 75% admitted, 29% enrolled. **Transfer Admission Requirements:** High school transcript, college transcript(s), standardized test scores. Minimum college GPA of 2.0 required. Lowest grade transferable C. **General Admission Information:** Non-fall registration accepted. Admission may be deferred for a maximum of 1 year.

COSTS AND FINANCIAL AID

Annual tuition $33,500. Room and board $8,600. Required fees $1,718. Average book and supplies expense $1,100. **Required Forms and Deadlines:** FAFSA. **Types of Aid:** *Need-based scholarships/grants:* College/university scholarship or grant aid from institutional funds; Federal Pell; Private scholarships; SEOG; State scholarships/grants. *Loans:* Direct PLUS loans; Direct Subsidized Stafford Loans; Direct Unsubsidized Stafford Loans. **Student Employment:** Federal Work-Study Program available. Institutional employment available. **Financial Aid Statistics:** 100% needy freshmen, 100% needy undergrads receive need-based scholarship or grant aid. 16% freshmen, 18% undergrads receive non-need-based scholarship or grant aid. 81% freshmen, 76% undergrads receive need-based self-help aid. 0% freshmen, 0% undergrads receive athletic scholarships. 100% freshmen, 100% undergrads receive any aid. 75% undergrads borrow to pay for school. Average cumulative indebtedness $28,964. **Criteria awarding aid:** *Non-need-based:* Academics, Art.

LOUISIANA COLLEGE

1140 College Drive, Pineville, LA 71359-0566
Phone: 318-487-7259 **Financial Aid Phone:** 318-487-7387
E-mail: admissions@lacollege.edu **CEEB Code:** 6371
Website: www.lacollege.edu **ACT Code:** 1586

This private school, affiliated with the Southern Baptist Church, was founded in 1906. It has a 81 acre campus.

RATINGS

Admissions Selectivity Rating: 80   **Fire Safety Rating:** 86   **Green Rating:** 60*

STUDENTS AND FACULTY

Enrollment: 936. **Student Body:** 48% female, 52% male, 12% out-of-state, 1% international (12 countries represented). Asian 1%, African American 25%, Caucasian 67%, Hispanic 3%, Native American 1%, Pacific Islander 0%, Two or more races 3%, Race unknown <1%.
Retention and Graduation: 65% freshmen return for sophomore year. 20% freshmen graduate within 4 years. 37% freshmen graduate within 6 years.
Faculty: Student/faculty ratio 10:1. 74 full-time faculty, 77% hold PhDs, 12% are members of minority groups, 59% are women. 0% of classes are taught by teaching assistants.

ACADEMICS

Degrees: Associate; Bachelor's; Certificate; Master's. **Classes:** Most classes have 10–19 students. Most lab/discussion sessions have fewer than 10 students. **Most popular majors:** Sports, Kinesiology, and Physical Education/Fitness, General; Business/Managerial Economics; Elementary Education and Teaching. **Special Study Options:** Accelerated program; Distance learning; Double major; Dual enrollment; English as a Second Language (ESL); Honors program; Independent study; Internships; Liberal arts/career combination; Student-designed major; Study abroad; Teacher certification program. **Honors programs:** The C. S. Lewis Honors Program at Louisiana College is an interdisciplinary program that caters to students who perform at the highest academic standards. Its small, seminar-style courses focus on integrating faith and learning through writing, discussion, service learning, and travel. Students enter during their freshman year and complete the honors curriculum as a cohort. **Disability Services offered:** Note-taking services; Reader services; Tutors. **Career services:** Career assessment; Career/job search classes; Internships.

FACILITIES

Housing: Apartments for married students; Apartments for single students; Men's dorms; Wellness housing; Women's dorms; 95% of campus accessible to physically disabled. **Special Academic Facilities/Equipment:** Art gallery, radio station, performing arts center, theater. **Campus Network:** 100% of classrooms, 100% of dorms, 100% of student union, 100% of libraries, 100% of dining areas, 100% of common outdoor areas have wireless network access.

CAMPUS LIFE

Environment: Town. **Activities:** Campus Ministries; Choral groups; Concert band; Drama/theater; Jazz band; Marching band; Music ensembles; Musical theater; Opera; Pep band; Radio station; Student government; Symphony orchestra. 12 registered organizations, 13 honor societies, 6 religious organizations on campus. **On-Campus Highlights:** Healthplex/Wellness Center.

ADMISSIONS

Freshman Academic Profile: Average high school GPA 3.3. 76% from public high schools. **Test Scores:** SAT Math middle 50% range 450–520. SAT EBRW middle 50% range 460–540. ACT middle 50% range 18–23. **Basis for Candidate Selection:** *Very important factors include:* academic GPA, standardized test scores. *Other factors include:* rigor of secondary school record. **Freshman Admission Requirements:** High school diploma is required and GED is accepted. *Academic units required:* 4 English, 4 math, 3 science, 2 science labs, 3 social studies, 8 unit from above areas or other academic areas. **Freshman Admission Statistics:** 1,018 applied, 69% admitted, 36% enrolled. **General Admission Information:** Application fee $25. Regular application deadline 8/15. Non-fall registration accepted. Admission may be deferred for a maximum of 1 semester.

COSTS AND FINANCIAL AID

Annual tuition $17,500. Room and board $5,646. Average book and supplies expense $1,220. **Required Forms and Deadlines:** FAFSA; Institution's own financial aid form. **Notification of Awards:** Applicants will be notified of awards on a rolling basis beginning 1/1. **Types of Aid:** *Need-based scholarships/ grants:* College/university scholarship or grant aid from institutional funds; Federal Pell; Private scholarships; SEOG; State scholarships/grants. *Loans:* Direct PLUS loans; Direct Subsidized Stafford Loans; Direct Unsubsidized Stafford Loans. **Student Employment:** Federal Work-Study Program available. Institutional employment available. **Financial Aid Statistics:** 100% needy freshmen, 96% needy undergrads receive need-based scholarship or grant aid. 18% freshmen, 19% undergrads receive non-need-based scholarship or grant aid. 79% freshmen, 74% undergrads receive need-based self-help aid. 0% freshmen, 0% undergrads receive athletic scholarships. 94.5% freshmen, 90.04% undergrads receive any aid. 77% undergrads borrow to pay for school. Average cumulative indebtedness $23,938.

LOUISIANA STATE UNIVERSITY—BATON ROUGE

Pleasant Hall, Baton Rouge, LA 70803
Phone: 225-578-1175 **Financial Aid Phone:** 225-578-3103
E-mail: admissions@lsu.edu **CEEB Code:** 6373
Fax: 225-578-4433 **Website:** www.lsu.edu **ACT Code:** 1590

This public school was founded in 1860. It has a 2000 acre campus.

RATINGS
Admissions Selectivity Rating: 83   **Fire Safety Rating:** 98   **Green Rating:** 88

STUDENTS AND FACULTY
Enrollment: 23,596. **Student Body:** 52% female, 48% male, 17% out-of-state, 2% international (71 countries represented). Asian 4%, African American 13%, Caucasian 71%, Hispanic 7%, Native American <1%, Pacific Islander <1%, Two or more races 2%, Race unknown 1%.
Retention and Graduation: 84% freshmen return for sophomore year. 40% freshmen graduate within 4 years. 67% freshmen graduate within 6 years. 17% grads go on to further study within 1 year. 14% grads pursue arts and sciences degrees. 8% grads pursue law degrees. 9% grads pursue business degrees. 13% grads pursue medical degrees. **Faculty:** Student/faculty ratio 20:1. 1,329 full-time faculty, 86% hold PhDs, 19% are members of minority groups, 37% are women. 7% of classes are taught by teaching assistants.

ACADEMICS
Degrees: Bachelor's; Certificate; Doctoral degree—professional practice; Doctoral degree research/scholarship; Master's; Post-bachelor's certificate; Post-master's certificate. **Classes:** Most classes have 10–19 students. Most lab/ discussion sessions have 10–19 students. **Most popular majors:** Physical Education Teaching and Coaching; Biology/Biological Sciences, General; Mass Communication/Media Studies. **Special Study Options:** Accelerated program; Cooperative education program; Cross-registration; Distance learning; Double major; Dual enrollment; English as a Second Language (ESL); Exchange student program (domestic); Honors program; Independent study; Internships; Student-designed major; Study abroad; Teacher certification program. **Honors programs:** Admissions to the Honors College. **Disability Services offered:** Note-taking services; Reader services; Tape recorders. **Career services:** Alumni services; Career assessment; Career/job search classes; Internships; Regional alumni.

FACILITIES
Housing: Apartments for married students; Apartments for single students; Coed dorms; Fraternity/sorority housing; Men's dorms; Special housing for disabled students; Theme housing; Women's dorms; 75% of campus accessible to physically disabled. **Special Academic Facilities/Equipment:** Art Museum, Natural Science Museum, Rural Life Museum, Lichen/Bryophyte Mycological and Vascular Plant herbariums on campus K-12 schools, geoscience and mycological museums, electron microscope, nuclear science center and civil war center. **Campus Network:** 100% of classrooms, 100% of dorms, 100% of student union, 100% of libraries, 100% of dining areas, 100% of common outdoor areas have wireless network access.

CAMPUS LIFE
Environment: City. **Activities:** Campus Ministries; Choral groups; Concert band; Dance; Drama/theater; International Student Organization; Jazz band; Literary magazine; Marching band; Music ensembles; Musical theater; Opera;

Pep band; Radio station; Student government; Student newspaper; Student-run film society; Symphony orchestra; Television station; Yearbook. 572 registered organizations, 27 honor societies, 44 religious organizations, 22 fraternities, 14 sororities on campus. **Athletics (Intercollegiate):** *Men:* baseball, basketball, cheerleading, cross-country, diving, football, golf, swimming, tennis, track/ field (outdoor), track/field (indoor). *Women:* basketball, cheerleading, cross-country, diving, golf, gymnastics, soccer, softball, swimming, tennis, track/ field (outdoor), track/field (indoor), volleyball. **On-Campus Highlights:** LSU Student Union. **Environmental Initiatives:** Goal to increase recycling rate to 50%.

ADMISSIONS
Freshman Academic Profile: Average high school GPA 3.4. 23% in top 10% of high school class, 48% in top 25% of high school class, 77% in top 50% of high school class. 64% from public high schools. **Test Scores:** SAT Math middle 50% range 530–640. SAT EBRW middle 50% range 530–640. ACT middle 50% range 23–28. **Basis for Candidate Selection:** *Very important factors include:* rigor of secondary school record, academic GPA, standardized test scores. *Important factors include:* talent/ability. *Other factors include:* class rank, application essay, recommendation(s), interview, extracurricular activities, first generation, alumni/ae relation, level of applicant's interest. **Freshman Admission Requirements:** High school diploma is required and GED is accepted. *Academic units required:* 4 English, 4 math, 4 science, 2 foreign language, 3 social studies, 1 history, 1 visual/performing arts. **Freshman Admission Statistics:** 24,280 applied, 74% admitted, 32% enrolled. **Transfer Admission Requirements:** College transcript(s). Minimum college GPA of 2.5 required. Lowest grade transferable D. **General Admission Information:** Application fee $50. Priority deadline 11/15. Regular application deadline 4/15. Non-fall registration accepted. Admission may be deferred for a maximum of 1 academic year.

COSTS AND FINANCIAL AID
Annual in-state tuition $8,038. Annual out-of-state tuition $24,715. Room and board $12,276. Required fees $3,924. Average book and supplies expense $1,038. **Required Forms and Deadlines:** FAFSA; Institution's own financial aid form. **Notification of Awards:** Applicants will be notified of awards on a rolling basis beginning 11/15. **Types of Aid:** *Need-based scholarships/grants:* College/university scholarship or grant aid from institutional funds; Federal Pell; Private scholarships; SEOG; State scholarships/grants. *Loans:* Direct PLUS loans; Direct Subsidized Stafford Loans; Direct Unsubsidized Stafford Loans. **Student Employment:** Federal Work-Study Program available. Institutional employment available. **Financial Aid Statistics:** 97% needy freshmen, 89% needy undergrads receive need-based scholarship or grant aid. 6% freshmen, 3% undergrads receive non-need-based scholarship or grant aid. 54% freshmen, 65% undergrads receive need-based self-help aid. 2% freshmen, 2% undergrads receive athletic scholarships. 96% freshmen, 77.9% undergrads receive any aid. 42% undergrads borrow to pay for school. Average cumulative indebtedness $26,821. **Criteria awarding aid:** *Need-based:* Academics. *Non-need-based:* Academics, Athletics, Music/drama.

LOUISIANA TECH UNIVERSITY

P. O. Box 3178, Ruston, LA 71272
Phone: 318-257-3036
E-mail: bulldog@latech.edu
Fax: 318-257-2499 **Website:** www.latech.edu

This is a public school.

RATINGS
Admissions Selectivity Rating: 85   **Fire Safety Rating:** 60*   **Green Rating:** 60*

STUDENTS AND FACULTY
Enrollment: 7,047. **Student Body:** 43% female, 57% male, 10% out-of-state, 4% international. Asian 1%, African American 15%, Caucasian 68%, Hispanic 1%, Native American <1%, Pacific Islander <1%, Two or more races 1%, Race unknown 8%.
Retention and Graduation: 79% freshmen return for sophomore year. **Faculty:** Student/faculty ratio 23:1. 352 full-time faculty, 79% hold PhDs, 0% are members of minority groups, 39% are women.

ACADEMICS
Degrees: Associate; Bachelor's; Doctoral degree—professional practice; Doctoral degree research/scholarship; Master's; Post-bachelor's certificate; Post-

master's certificate. **Classes:** Most classes have fewer than 10 students. **Special Study Options:** Distance learning; Double major; Dual enrollment; Honors program; Independent study; Internships; Study abroad; Teacher certification program. **Career services:** Alumni network; Alumni services; Career assessment; Career/job search classes; Internships; Regional alumni.

FACILITIES

Housing: Apartments for married students; Apartments for single students; Men's dorms; Special housing for disabled students; Theme housing; Women's dorms. **Campus Network:** 100% of classrooms, 100% of dorms, 100% of student union, 100% of libraries, 100% of dining areas, 100% of common outdoor areas have wireless network access.

CAMPUS LIFE

Activities: Campus Ministries; Choral groups; Concert band; Dance; Drama/theater; International Student Organization; Jazz band; Marching band; Music ensembles; Musical theater; Pep band; Radio station; Student government; Student newspaper; Student-run film society; Television station; Yearbook.

ADMISSIONS

Freshman Academic Profile: Average high school GPA 3.4. 24% in top 10% of high school class, 51% in top 25% of high school class, 80% in top 50% of high school class. 77% from public high schools. **Test Scores:** SAT Math middle 50% range 490–600. SAT EBRW middle 50% range 450–590. ACT middle 50% range 21–26. **Basis for Candidate Selection:** *Very important factors include:* rigor of secondary school record, class rank, academic GPA, standardized test scores. *Important factors include:* talent/ability. *Other factors include:* recommendation(s), extracurricular activities, first generation, alumni/ae relation. **Freshman Admission Requirements:** High school diploma is required and GED is not accepted. *Academic units required:* 4 English, 4 math, 4 science, 2 foreign language, 4 social studies, 1 visual/performing arts. **Freshman Admission Statistics:** 5,077 applied, 67% admitted, 45% enrolled. **General Admission Information:** Application fee $20. Non-fall registration accepted.

COSTS AND FINANCIAL AID

Required Forms and Deadlines: FAFSA; Institution's own financial aid form. **Notification of Awards:** Applicants will be notified of awards on a rolling basis beginning 4/1. **Types of Aid:** *Need-based scholarships/grants:* College/university scholarship or grant aid from institutional funds; Federal Pell; Private scholarships; SEOG; State scholarships/grants. *Loans:* Direct PLUS loans; Direct Subsidized Stafford Loans; Direct Unsubsidized Stafford Loans. **Financial Aid Statistics:** 94% needy freshmen, 89% needy undergrads receive need-based scholarship or grant aid. 17% freshmen, 15% undergrads receive non-need-based scholarship or grant aid. 49% freshmen, 60% undergrads receive need-based self-help aid. 1% freshmen, 2% undergrads receive athletic scholarships. **Criteria awarding aid:** *Non-need-based:* Academics, Alumni affiliation, Art, Athletics, Job skills, Leadership, Music/drama, State/district residency.

LOURDES UNIVERSITY

6832 Convent Road, Sylvania, OH 43560-2898
Phone: 419-885-5291 **Financial Aid Phone:** 419-824-3732
E-mail: AdmissionsLCAdmits@lourdes.edu **CEEB Code:** 1427
Fax: 419-824-3916 **Website:** www.lourdes.edu **ACT Code:** 3598

This private school, affiliated with the Roman Catholic Church, was founded in 1958. It has a 113 acre campus.

RATINGS
Admissions Selectivity Rating: 77   **Fire Safety Rating:** 85   **Green Rating:** 60*

STUDENTS AND FACULTY

Enrollment: 1,666. **Student Body:** 71% female, 29% male, 14% out-of-state, <1% international. Asian 1%, African American 18%, Caucasian 72%, Hispanic 6%, Native American <1%, Pacific Islander 0%, Two or more races 2%, Race unknown 2%.
Retention and Graduation: 63% freshmen return for sophomore year.
Faculty: Student/faculty ratio 10:1. 100 full-time faculty, 59% hold PhDs, 10% are members of minority groups, 67% are women. 2% of classes are taught by teaching assistants.

ACADEMICS

Degrees: Associate; Bachelor's; Certificate; Master's; Post-bachelor's certificate; Post-master's certificate. **Classes:** Most classes have 10–19 students. Most lab/

discussion sessions have fewer than 10 students. **Most popular majors:** Social Work; Registered Nursing/Registered Nurse; Business Administration and Management, General. **Special Study Options:** Distance learning; Double major; Dual enrollment; Independent study; Internships; Liberal arts/career combination; Student-designed major; Study abroad; Teacher certification program. **Disability Services offered:** Note-taking services; Reader services; Tape recorders; Tutors. **Career services:** Career assessment; Career/job search classes.

FACILITIES

Housing: Apartments for single students; Coed dorms. **Special Academic Facilities/Equipment:** Planetarium. **Campus Network:** 100% of classrooms, 0% of dorms, 100% of student union, 100% of libraries, 100% of dining areas, 20% of common outdoor areas have wireless network access.

CAMPUS LIFE

Environment: Village. **Activities:** Campus Ministries; Choral groups; Drama/theater; Literary magazine; Student government. 17 registered organizations, 8 honor societies on campus. **Athletics (Intercollegiate):** *Men:* basketball, golf. *Women:* golf, volleyball. **On-Campus Highlights:** Delp Hall.

ADMISSIONS

Freshman Academic Profile: Average high school GPA 3.0. 8% in top 10% of high school class, 27% in top 25% of high school class, 59% in top 50% of high school class. **Test Scores:** SAT Math middle 50% range 350–500. SAT EBRW middle 50% range 410–540. ACT middle 50% range 17–22. **Basis for Candidate Selection:** *Very important factors include:* academic GPA, standardized test scores. *Other factors include:* interview. **Freshman Admission Requirements:** High school diploma is required and GED is accepted. *Academic units recommended:* 4 English, 3 math, 3 science, 2 foreign language, 3 social studies, 1 visual/performing arts, 1 unit from above areas or other academic areas. **Freshman Admission Statistics:** 1,296 applied, 68% admitted, 29% enrolled. **Transfer Admission Requirements:** College transcript(s). Minimum college GPA of 2.0 required. Lowest grade transferable C. **General Admission Information:** Application fee $25. Non-fall registration accepted. Admission may be deferred for a maximum of 4 years.

COSTS AND FINANCIAL AID

Annual tuition $17,455. Room and board $8,400. Required fees $200. Average book and supplies expense $1,275. **Required Forms and Deadlines:** FAFSA. **Notification of Awards:** Applicants will be notified of awards on a rolling basis beginning 3/1. **Types of Aid:** *Need-based scholarships/grants:* College/university scholarship or grant aid from institutional funds; Federal Pell; Private scholarships; SEOG; State scholarships/grants. *Loans:* Direct PLUS loans; Direct Subsidized Stafford Loans; Direct Unsubsidized Stafford Loans. **Student Employment:** Federal Work-Study Program available. Institutional employment available. **Financial Aid Statistics:** 88% needy freshmen, 82% needy undergrads receive need-based scholarship or grant aid. 89% freshmen, 63% undergrads receive non-need-based scholarship or grant aid. 92% freshmen, 91% undergrads receive need-based self-help aid. 28% freshmen, 18% undergrads receive athletic scholarships. 96% freshmen, 84% undergrads receive any aid. **Criteria awarding aid:** *Need-based:* Academics, Alumni affiliation, Art, Leadership, Minority status, Religious affiliation. *Non-need-based:* Academics, Art, Athletics, Minority status, Music/drama, Religious affiliation, State/district residency.

LOYOLA MARYMOUNT UNIVERSITY

1 LMU Drive, Los Angeles, CA 90045-2659
Phone: 310-338-2750 **Financial Aid Phone:** 310-338-2753
E-mail: admissions@lmu.edu **CEEB Code:** 4403
Website: www.lmu.edu **ACT Code:** 326

This private school, affiliated with the Roman Catholic Church, was founded in 1911. It has a 142 acre campus.

RATINGS
Admissions Selectivity Rating: 91   **Fire Safety Rating:** 89   **Green Rating:** 99

STUDENTS AND FACULTY
Enrollment: 6,638. **Student Body:** 55% female, 45% male. 33% out-of-state, 11% international (89 countries represented), Asian 10%, African American

7%, Caucasian 43%, Hispanic 23%, Native American <1%, Pacific Islander <1%, Two or more races 7%, Race unknown 0%.
Retention and Graduation: 89% freshmen return for sophomore year. 73% freshmen graduate within 4 years. 80 15% grads go on to further study within 1 year. **Faculty:** 1% of classes are taught by teaching assistants.

ACADEMICS
Degrees: Bachelor's; Doctoral degree—professional practice; Doctoral degree research/scholarship; Master's; Postbachelor's certificate; Post-master's certificate. **Classes:** Most classes have 10–19 students. Most lab/discussion sessions have 10–19 students. **Most popular majors:** Speech Communication and Rhetoric; Psychology, General; Marketing/Marketing Management, General. **Special Study Options:** Accelerated program; Cross-registration ; Distance learning; Double major; Dual enrollment; Exchange student program (domestic); Honors program ; Independent study ; Internships ; Liberal arts/career combination; Student-designed major ; Study abroad ; Teacher certification program; Weekend college. **Honors programs:** University Honors Program. **Combined degree programs:** BA/MA; BA/MEng. **Disability Services offered:** Note-taking services; Reader services; Tape recorders; Tutors. **Career services:** Alumni network; Alumni services; Career assessment; Career/job search classes; Internships; Regional alumni.

FACILITIES
Housing: Apartments for single students; Coed dorms; Men's dorms; Special housing for disabled students; Special housing for international students; Theme housing; Women's dorms; 95% of campus accessible to physically disabled. **Special Academic Facilities/Equipment:** Fine arts complex with recital hall and recording arts facilities, marine station, new life sciences building with green roof that is a "living laboratory" for research. Laband Art Gallery, TV production labs, computer graphics labs, ROAR studios and KXLU radio station.

CAMPUS LIFE
Environment: Town. **Activities:** Campus Ministries; Choral groups; Dance ; Drama/theater; International Student Organization; Literary magazine; Model UN; Music ensembles; Opera; Radio station ; Student government; Student newspaper; Student-run film society; Television station; Yearbook. 185 registered organizations, 23 honor societies, 9 religious organizations, 11 fraternities, 12 sororities on campus. **Athletics (Intercollegiate):** *Men:* baseball, basketball, crew/rowing, cross-country, golf, soccer, tennis, water polo. *Women:* basketball, crew/rowing, cross-country, soccer, softball, swimming, tennis, volleyball, water polo. **On-Campus Highlights:** Wm. H. Hannon Library. **Environmental Initiatives:** LEED Building Program: LMU's new LEED Gold Life Science Building is a 120,000-GSF building is designed with state-of-the-art laboratory technologies, collaborative research space, and energy efficiency features, complementing our 5 other LEED-certified campus buildings and signifying LMU's commitment to continued leadership in environmental stewardship. The building will also act as a 'living lab' for students studying with a 200,000 kwh Solar Array and a green roof with research functionality. The building also houses 9,000 SF of faculty research lab space, 24 teaching labs, lab support spaces, vivarium, faculty offices, classrooms, shared public spaces, conference rooms, and a 292-fixed seat auditorium.

ADMISSIONS
Freshman Academic Profile: Average high school GPA 3.9. 47% in top 10% of high school class, 79% in top 25% of high school class, 98% in top 50% of high school class. 50% from public high schools. **Test scores:** SAT Math middle 50% range 610–710. SAT EBRW middle 50% range 620–700. ACT middle 50% range 27–31. **Basis for Candidate Selection:** *Very important factors include:* academic GPA. *Important factors include:* rigor of secondary school record, application essay, standardized test scores, talent/ability, character/personal qualities. *Other factors include:* class rank, recommendation(s), extracurricular activities, first generation, alumni/ae relation, volunteer work, work experience. **Freshman Admission Requirements:** High school diploma is required and GED is accepted *Academic units recommended:* 4 English, 3 math, 2 science, 2 science labs, 3 foreign language, 3 social studies, 1 academic electives. **Freshman Admission Statistics:** 18,592 applied, 44% admitted, 18% enrolled. **Transfer Admission Requirements:** College transcript(s), essay or personal statement, statement of good standing from prior institution(s). Minimum college GPA of 2.8 required. Lowest grade transferable C. **General Admission Information:** Application fee $60. Regular application deadline 1/15. Nonfall registration accepted. Admission may be deferred for a maximum of 1 year.

COSTS AND FINANCIAL AID
Required Forms and Deadlines: FAFSA. **Types of Aid:** *Need-based scholarships/grants:* College/university scholarship or grant aid from institutional funds;

Federal Pell; Private scholarships; SEOG; State scholarships/grants. *Loans:* Direct PLUS loans; Direct Subsidized Stafford Loans; Direct Unsubsidized Stafford Loans. **Student Employment:** Federal Work-Study Program available. Institutional employment available. **Financial Aid Statistics:** 97% needy freshmen, 96% needy undergrads receive need-based scholarship or grant aid. 19% freshmen, 17% undergrads receive non-need-based scholarship or grant aid. 66% freshmen, 71% undergrads receive need-based self-help aid. 2% freshmen, 3% undergrads receive athletic scholarships. 92% freshmen, 85% undergrads receive any aid. 49% undergrads borrow to pay for school. Average cumulative indebtedness $33,742. **Criteria awarding aid:** *Need-based:* Academics, Leadership, Minority status, Religious affiliation. *Non-need-based:* Academics, Alumni affiliation, Art, Athletics, Music/drama, Religious affiliation.

LOYOLA UNIVERSITY MARYLAND

4501 North Charles Street, Baltimore, MD 21212
Phone: 410-617-5012 **Financial Aid Phone:** 410-617-2576
E-mail: admissions@loyola.edu **CEEB Code:** 5370
Fax: 410-617-2176 **Website:** www.loyola.edu

This private school, affiliated with the Roman Catholic Church, was founded in 1852. It has a 89 acre campus.

RATINGS
Admissions Selectivity Rating: 80 **Fire Safety Rating:** 94 **Green Rating:** 70

STUDENTS AND FACULTY
Enrollment: 3,860. **Student Body:** 58% female, 42% male, 80% out-of-state, 1% international (53 countries represented). Asian 4%, African American 6%, Caucasian 76%, Hispanic 10%, Native American <1%, Pacific Islander <1%, Two or more races 3%, Race unknown <1%.
Retention and Graduation: 88% freshmen return for sophomore year. 77% freshmen graduate within 4 years. 81% freshmen graduate within 6 years. 21% grads go on to further study within 1 year. 53% grads pursue arts and sciences degrees. 10% grads pursue law degrees. 4% grads pursue business degrees. 7% grads pursue medical degrees. **Faculty:** Student/faculty ratio 12:1. 359 full-time faculty, 84% hold PhDs, 19% are members of minority groups, 53% are women. 0% of classes are taught by teaching assistants.

ACADEMICS
Degrees: Bachelor's; Doctoral degree—professional practice; Doctoral degree research/scholarship; Master's; Post-bachelor's certificate; Post-master's certificate. **Classes:** Most classes have 20–29 students. Most lab/discussion sessions have 20–29 students. **Most popular majors:** Social Sciences, Other; Communication and Media Studies; Communication and Media Studies. **Special Study Options:** Cross-registration; Double major; Exchange student program (domestic); Honors program; Independent study; Internships; Liberal arts/career combination; Study abroad; Teacher certification program. **Honors programs:** http://www.loyola.edu/academic/honorsprogram. **Disability Services offered:** Note-taking services; Reader services; Tape recorders; Tutors. **Career services:** Alumni network; Alumni services; Career assessment; Career/job search classes; Internships; Regional alumni.

FACILITIES
Housing: Coed dorms; Theme housing; Wellness housing 100% of campus accessible to physically disabled. **Special Academic Facilities/Equipment:** Art gallery, advanced biology lab, humanities building, speech pathology lab and audiology center, black box theater

CAMPUS LIFE
Environment: Metropolis. **Activities:** Campus Ministries; Choral groups; Dance; Drama/theater; International Student Organization; Jazz band; Literary magazine; Music ensembles; Musical theater; Radio station; Student government; Student newspaper; Student-run film society; Television station; Yearbook. 144 registered organizations, 34 honor societies, 10 religious organizations on campus. **Athletics (Intercollegiate):** *Men:* basketball, crew/rowing, cross-country, diving, golf, lacrosse, soccer, swimming, tennis. *Women:* basketball, crew/rowing, cross-country, diving, lacrosse, soccer, swimming, tennis, track/field (outdoor), track/field (indoor), volleyball. **On-Campus Highlights:** Reverend Harold Ridley, S.J., Athletic Complex. **Environmental**

Initiatives: Our commitment to responsible building can be seen in our 100,000-sq. ft. green residential hall that was built in 2007. In 2010, we completed construction of an athletic facility that was built on a landfill and is considered an example of smart growth.

ADMISSIONS

Freshman Academic Profile: Average high school GPA 3.5. 28% in top 10% of high school class, 61% in top 25% of high school class, 90% in top 50% of high school class. **Test Scores:** SAT Math middle 50% range 560–650. SAT EBRW middle 50% range 580–660. ACT middle 50% range 25–30. **Basis for Candidate Selection:** *Very important factors include:* rigor of secondary school record, academic GPA, application essay, recommendation(s), character/personal qualities. *Important factors include:* extracurricular activities, talent/ability, volunteer work. *Other factors include:* class rank, standardized test scores, first generation, alumni/ae relation, geographical residence, racial/ethnic status, work experience, level of applicant's interest. **Freshman Admission Requirements:** High school diploma is required and GED is accepted. *Academic units required:* 4 English, 3 math, 3 science, 3 foreign language, 2 social studies, 2 history. *Academic units recommended:* 4 English, 4 math, 4 science, 4 foreign language, 3 social studies, 3 history, 1 computer science, 1 visual/performing arts. **Freshman Admission Statistics:** 10,251 applied, 85% admitted, 12% enrolled. **Transfer Admission Requirements:** High school transcript, college transcript(s), essay or personal statement, statement of good standing from prior institution(s). Minimum college GPA of 2.7 required. Lowest grade transferable C. **General Admission Information:** Application fee $60. Priority deadline 11/15. Regular application deadline 1/15. Non-fall registration accepted. Admission may be deferred for a maximum of 1 year.

COSTS AND FINANCIAL AID

Annual tuition $48,700. Room and board $16,040. Required fees $1,565. Average book and supplies expense $1,250. **Student Employment:** Federal Work-Study Program available. Institutional employment available. **Financial Aid Statistics:** 60% needy freshmen, 69% needy undergrads receive need-based scholarship or grant aid. 74% freshmen, 65% undergrads receive non-need-based scholarship or grant aid. 81% freshmen, 88% undergrads receive need-based self-help aid. 4% freshmen, 4% undergrads receive athletic scholarships. 74.9% freshmen, 70.1% undergrads receive any aid. **Criteria awarding aid:** *Non-need-based:* Academics, Athletics.

LOYOLA UNIVERSITY NEW ORLEANS

6363 St. Charles Avenue, New Orleans, LA 70118-6195
Phone: 504-865-3240 **Financial Aid Phone:** 504-865-3231
E-mail: admit@loyno.edu **CEEB Code:** 6374
Fax: 504-865-3383 **Website:** www.loyno.edu **ACT Code:** 1592

This private school, affiliated with the Roman Catholic-Jesuit Church, was founded in 1912. It has a 26 acre campus.

RATINGS

Admissions Selectivity Rating: 75   Fire Safety Rating: 98   Green Rating: 86

STUDENTS AND FACULTY

Enrollment: 2,868. **Student Body:** 63% female, 37% male, 57% out-of-state, 2% international (37 countries represented). Asian 3%, African American 17%, Caucasian 47%, Hispanic 18%, Native American <1%, Pacific Islander <1%, Two or more races 4%, Race unknown 8%.
Retention and Graduation: 85% freshmen return for sophomore year. 47% freshmen graduate within 4 years. 56% freshmen graduate within 6 years. 14% grads go on to further study within 1 year. **Faculty:** Student/faculty ratio 12:1. 234 full-time faculty, 91% hold PhDs, 18% are members of minority groups, 44% are women. 0% of classes are taught by teaching assistants.

ACADEMICS

Degrees: Bachelor's; Doctoral degree—other; Doctoral degree—professional practice; Master's; Post-bachelor's certificate; Post-master's certificate. **Classes:** Most classes have 10–19 students. Most lab/discussion sessions have 10–19 students. **Most popular majors:** Psychology, General; Music Management; Business Administration and Management, General. **Special Study Options:** Accelerated program; Cross-registration; Distance learning; Double major;

Dual enrollment; English as a Second Language (ESL); Exchange student program (domestic); External degree program; Honors program; Independent study; Internships; Liberal arts/career combination; Student-designed major; Study abroad; Teacher certification program. **Honors programs:** The Loyola University Honors Program offers the opportunity for academically superior, highly motivated students to take challenging Honors courses and to participate in special cultural and intellectual enrichment activities. The University Honors Program is open to qualified students of all undergraduate colleges and majors. The Honors courses replace other required courses, and therefore do not add to the number of requirements for graduation. **Disability Services offered:** Note-taking services; Reader services; Tape recorders; Tutors. **Career services:** Alumni network; Alumni services; Career assessment; Career/job search classes; Internships; Regional alumni.

FACILITIES

Housing: Apartments for single students; Coed dorms; Theme housing; Wellness housing; 95% of campus accessible to physically disabled. **Special Academic Facilities/Equipment:** Monroe Hall, complete with a 3D printing machine, state-of-the-art 3,000-square-foot greenhouse, specialized science labs and exhibit spaces; multimedia classrooms throughout campus; The Maroon newsroom, complete with in-house TV studio and digital communications laboratory; Carlos F. Ayala Stock Trading Room in the College of Business; Collins C. Diboll Art Gallery; The Brand Lab in the School of Mass Communication; Shawn M. Donnelley Center for Nonprofit Communications; audio recording/video editing studio; Center for International Education; University Sports Complex with suspended pool; Career Development Center; Jesuit Social Research Institute; Business Portfolio Program; Office of Service Learning; the Pan-American Life Student Success Center; Louis J. Roussel Hall and Nunemaker Auditorium used for performances. **Campus Network:** 100% of classrooms, 100% of dorms, 100% of student union, 100% of libraries, 100% of dining areas, 50% of common outdoor areas have wireless network access.

CAMPUS LIFE

Environment: Metropolis. **Activities:** Campus Ministries; Choral groups; Concert band; Dance; Drama/theater; International Student Organization; Jazz band; Literary magazine; Music ensembles; Musical theater; Opera; Pep band; Student government; Student newspaper; Student-run film society; Symphony orchestra. 126 registered organizations, 8 honor societies, 6 religious organizations, 5 fraternities, 7 sororities on campus. **Athletics (Intercollegiate):** *Men:* baseball, basketball, cross-country, track/field (outdoor), track/field (indoor). *Women:* basketball, cross-country, track/field (outdoor), track/field (indoor), volleyball. **On-Campus Highlights:** J. Edgar and Louise S. Monroe Library. **Environmental Initiatives:** Formation of a committee that has representatives from important units on campus, including SGA and other student organizations. Full support of the Administration, starting with the President and Provost.

ADMISSIONS

Freshman Academic Profile: Average high school GPA 3.5. 25% in top 10% of high school class, 51% in top 25% of high school class, 76% in top 50% of high school class. 58% from public high schools. **Test Scores:** SAT Math middle 50% range 510–600. SAT EBRW middle 50% range 550–640. ACT middle 50% range 22–28. **Basis for Candidate Selection:** *Very important factors include:* rigor of secondary school record, academic GPA, standardized test scores. *Important factors include:* application essay, recommendation(s), extracurricular activities, talent/ability. *Other factors include:* class rank, interview, character/personal qualities, alumni/ae relation, geographical residence, volunteer work, work experience, level of applicant's interest. **Freshman Admission Requirements:** High school diploma is required and GED is accepted. *Academic units required:* 4 English, 2 math, 2 science, 2 social studies. *Academic units recommended:* 4 English, 3 math, 3 science, 1 science lab, 2 foreign language, 2 social studies, 2 history. **Freshman Admission Statistics:** 4,514 applied, 94% admitted, 19% enrolled. **Transfer Admission Requirements:** College transcript(s), essay or personal statement, statement of good standing from prior institution(s). Minimum college GPA of 2.25 required. Lowest grade transferable C. **General Admission Information:** Priority deadline 11/15. Non-fall registration accepted. Admission may be deferred for a maximum of 1 year restr.

COSTS AND FINANCIAL AID

Annual tuition $38,926. Room and board $13,548. Required fees $1,916. Average book and supplies expense $1,276. **Required Forms and Deadlines:** FAFSA. **Notification of Awards:** Applicants will be notified of awards on a rolling basis beginning 3/1. **Types of Aid:** *Need-based scholarships/grants:* College/university scholarship or grant aid from institutional funds; Federal Pell; Private scholarships; SEOG; State scholarships/grants; United Negro

College Fund. *Loans:* Direct PLUS loans; Direct Subsidized Stafford Loans; Direct Unsubsidized Stafford Loans. **Student Employment:** Federal Work-Study Program available. Institutional employment available. **Financial Aid Statistics:** 100% needy freshmen, 99% needy undergrads receive need-based scholarship or grant aid. 12% freshmen, 12% undergrads receive non-need-based scholarship or grant aid. 85% freshmen, 84% undergrads receive need-based self-help aid. 3% freshmen, 3% undergrads receive athletic scholarships. 87.8% freshmen, 88.4% undergrads receive any aid. 72% undergrads borrow to pay for school. Average cumulative indebtedness $31,341. **Criteria awarding aid:** *Need-based:* Academics, Alumni affiliation. *Non-need-based:* Academics, Alumni affiliation, Art, Athletics, Music/drama.

LOYOLA UNIVERSITY OF CHICAGO

Best Colleges

820 North Michigan Avenue, Chicago, IL 60611
Phone: 312-915-6500 **Financial Aid Phone:** 773-508-7704
E-mail: admission@luc.edu **CEEB Code:** 1412
Fax: 312-915-7216 **Website:** www.luc.edu/.

This private school, affiliated with the Roman Catholic-Jesuit Church, was founded in 1870. It has a 105 acre campus.

RATINGS
Admissions Selectivity Rating: 86 **Fire Safety Rating:** 97 **Green Rating:** 99

STUDENTS AND FACULTY
Enrollment: 12,104. **Student Body:** 67% female, 33% male, 39% out-of-state, 4% international (102 countries represented). Asian 12%, African American 5%, Caucasian 56%, Hispanic 17%, Native American <1%, Pacific Islander <1%, Two or more races 4%, Race unknown 1%.
Retention and Graduation: 86% freshmen return for sophomore year. 66% freshmen graduate within 4 years. 74% freshmen graduate within 6 years. **Faculty:** Student/faculty ratio 14:1. 838 full-time faculty, 92% hold PhDs, 17% are members of minority groups, 49% are women. 0% of classes are taught by teaching assistants.

ACADEMICS
Degrees: Associate; Bachelor's; Certificate; Doctoral degree—professional practice; Doctoral degree research/scholarship; Master's; Post-bachelor's certificate; Post-master's certificate. **Classes:** Most classes have 10–19 students. Most lab/discussion sessions have fewer than 10 students. **Most popular majors:** Biology/Biological Sciences, General; Psychology, General; Registered Nursing/Registered Nurse. **Special Study Options:** Accelerated program; Distance learning; Double major; Dual enrollment; English as a Second Language (ESL); Exchange student program (domestic); External degree program; Honors program; Independent study; Internships; Liberal arts/career combination; Study abroad; Teacher certification program. **Honors programs:** Loyola University Chicago offers an Interdisciplinary Honors Program that integrates a challenging academic program with service-learning opportunities. Taking a series of team-taught, interdisciplinary courses, students learn to perceive unexpected convergences among discrete facts, to synthesize information from many sources, and to use their knowledge to benefit society. **Combined degree programs:** BA/MA. **Disability Services offered:** Note-taking services; Reader services; Tape recorders. **Career services:** Alumni network; Alumni services; Career assessment; Career/job search classes; Internships; Regional alumni.

FACILITIES
Housing: Apartments for single students; Coed dorms; Special housing for disabled students; 90% of campus accessible to physically disabled. **Special Academic Facilities/Equipment:** Theaters, art museums, digital media labs, convergence media studio, language learning resource center, neuroscience labs, clean energy lab, mock trial room, performance and specialized fine arts rooms, clinical simulation nursing laboratory, histology lab, geothermal system, ecodome greenhouse, aquaponics system showcase, artificial stream research facility, retreat and ecology campus.

CAMPUS LIFE
Environment: Metropolis. **Activities:** Campus Ministries; Choral groups; Concert band; Dance; Drama/theater; International Student Organization; Jazz band; Literary magazine; Model UN; Music ensembles; Musical theater;

Opera; Pep band; Radio station; Student government; Student newspaper; Student-run film society; Symphony orchestra; Television station. 230 registered organizations, 9 honor societies, 7 religious organizations, 9 fraternities, 10 sororities on campus. **Athletics (Intercollegiate):** *Men:* basketball, cheerleading, cross-country, golf, soccer, track/field (outdoor), track/field (indoor), volleyball. *Women:* basketball, cheerleading, cross-country, golf, soccer, softball, track/field (outdoor), track/field (indoor), volleyball. **On-Campus Highlights:** Damen Student center. **Environmental Initiatives:** Carbon Neutral by 2025—Climate Acton Plan sets out goals for energy and conservation, clean energy, and green transportation: Adopt green building design standards for all new construction. 30% reduction in greenhouse gas emissions since 2008. Lighting, heating/cooling retrofits, largest geothermal installation in Chicago. Biodiesel production from dining hall's waster vegetable oil used in campus shuttles (www.luc.edu/biodiesel). Transportation—walk-to-work program, bicycle program, electric vehicles, public transit passes for students, car sharing program.

ADMISSIONS
Freshman Academic Profile: Average high school GPA 3.7. 35% in top 10% of high school class, 68% in top 25% of high school class, 93% in top 50% of high school class. 67% from public high schools. **Test Scores:** SAT Math middle 50% range 560–660. SAT EBRW middle 50% range 570–660. ACT middle 50% range 25–30. **Basis for Candidate Selection:** *Very important factors include:* rigor of secondary school record, academic GPA, standardized test scores. *Important factors include:* application essay, recommendation(s), extracurricular activities, character/personal qualities. *Other factors include:* class rank, interview, talent/ability, first generation, alumni/ae relation, geographical residence, state residency. **Freshman Admission Requirements:** High school diploma is required and GED is accepted. *Academic units required:* 4 English, 3 math, 3 science, 2 foreign language, 2 social studies, 1 history. *Academic units recommended:* 4 English, 4 math, 3 science, 2 foreign language, 2 social studies, 2 history, 3 academic electives. **Freshman Admission Statistics:** 25,583 applied, 67% admitted, 15% enrolled. **Transfer Admission Requirements:** college transcript(s). Minimum college GPA of 2.0 required. Lowest grade transferable C. **General Admission Information:** Priority deadline 12/1. Non-fall registration accepted.

COSTS AND FINANCIAL AID
Annual tuition $45,500. Room and board $15,020. Required fees $1,398. Average book and supplies expense $1,200. **Required Forms and Deadlines:** FAFSA. **Notification of Awards:** Applicants will be notified of awards on a rolling basis beginning 2/15. **Types of Aid:** *Need-based scholarships/grants:* College/university scholarship or grant aid from institutional funds; Federal Pell; Private scholarships; SEOG; State scholarships/grants. *Loans:* Direct PLUS loans; Direct Subsidized Stafford Loans; Direct Unsubsidized Stafford Loans. **Student Employment:** Institutional employment available. **Financial Aid Statistics:** 99% needy freshmen, 95% needy undergrads receive need-based scholarship or grant aid. 15% freshmen, 11% undergrads receive non-need-based scholarship or grant aid. 80% freshmen, 80% undergrads receive need-based self-help aid. 1% freshmen, 1% undergrads receive athletic scholarships. 99.5% freshmen, 91.2% undergrads receive any aid. 65% undergrads borrow to pay for school. Average cumulative indebtedness $35,509. **Criteria awarding aid:** *Non-need-based:* Academics, Art, Athletics, Leadership, Music/drama, Religious affiliation.

LUBBOCK CHRISTIAN UNIVERSITY

5601 19th Street, Lubbock, TX 79407
Phone: 800-720-7151 **Financial Aid Phone:** 806-720-7176
E-mail: admissions@lcu.edu **CEEB Code:** 6378
Fax: 806-720-7162 **Website:** www.lcu.edu **ACT Code:** 4123

This private school, affiliated with the Church of Christ, was founded in 1957. It has a 120 acre campus.

RATINGS
Admissions Selectivity Rating: 73 **Fire Safety Rating:** 72 **Green Rating:** 60*

STUDENTS AND FACULTY
Enrollment: 1,496. **Student Body:** 59% female, 41% male, 9% out-of-state, 2% international (21 countries represented). Asian 1%, African American 5%, Caucasian 66%, Hispanic 25%, Native American 1%, Pacific Islander <1%, Two or more races 0%, Race unknown 0%.

Retention and Graduation: 73% freshmen return for sophomore year. 16% grads go on to further study within 1 year. 0% grads pursue arts and sciences degrees. 14% grads pursue law degrees. 7% grads pursue business degrees. 0% grads pursue medical degrees. **Faculty:** Student/faculty ratio 13:1. 99 full-time faculty, 73% hold PhDs, 4% are members of minority groups, 43% are women. 0% of classes are taught by teaching assistants.

ACADEMICS

Degrees: Associate; Bachelor's; Master's. **Classes:** Most classes have 10–19 students. Most lab/discussion sessions have fewer than 10 students. **Special Study Options:** Distance learning; Double major; Dual enrollment; Honors program; Internships; Liberal arts/career combination; Study abroad; Teacher certification program. **Honors programs:** Honors program available to all majors. **Disability Services offered:** Tape recorders; Tutors. **Career services:** Alumni services; Career assessment; Career/job search classes; Internships.

FACILITIES

Housing: Apartments for married students; Apartments for single students; Men's dorms; Women's dorms; 78% of campus accessible to physically disabled. **Special Academic Facilities/Equipment:** Pioneer Gallery, Rhodes Perrin Rec Center.

CAMPUS LIFE

Environment: City. **Activities:** Campus Ministries; Choral groups; Concert band; Drama/theater; International Student Organization; Jazz band; Music ensembles; Musical theater; Pep band; Radio station; Student government; Student newspaper; Yearbook. 24 registered organizations, 3 honor societies, 4 fraternities, 4 sororities on campus. **Athletics (Intercollegiate):** *Men:* baseball, basketball, cheerleading, golf. *Women:* basketball, cheerleading, golf, volleyball. **On-Campus Highlights:** Student Union Building.

ADMISSIONS

Freshman Academic Profile: Average high school GPA 3.5. 19% in top 10% of high school class, 43% in top 25% of high school class, 74% in top 50% of high school class. 83% from public high schools. **Test Scores:** SAT Math middle 50% range 430–555. SAT EBRW middle 50% range 440–550. ACT middle 50% range 19–25. **Basis for Candidate Selection:** *Very important factors include:* standardized test scores. *Other factors include:* rigor of secondary school record, class rank, academic GPA, recommendation(s), extracurricular activities, talent/ability, character/personal qualities, first generation, alumni/ae relation, volunteer work, work experience, level of applicant's interest. **Freshman Admission Requirements:** High school diploma is required and GED is accepted. *Academic units recommended:* 4 English, 3 math, 3 science, 2 science labs, 2 foreign language, 1 social studies, 2 history, 2 academic electives, 1 computer science, 1 visual/performing arts. **Freshman Admission Statistics:** 867 applied, 96% admitted, 33% enrolled. **Transfer Admission Requirements:** College transcript(s), statement of good standing from prior institution(s). Lowest grade transferable C. **General Admission Information:** Application fee $25. Regular application deadline 6/1. Non-fall registration accepted.

COSTS AND FINANCIAL AID

Annual tuition $20,360. Room and board $6,070. Average book and supplies expense $1,100. **Required Forms and Deadlines:** FAFSA; Institution's own financial aid form. **Notification of Awards:** Applicants will be notified of awards on a rolling basis beginning 3/1. **Types of Aid:** *Need-based scholarships/grants:* Federal Pell; SEOG; State scholarships/grants. *Loans:* Direct PLUS loans; Direct Subsidized Stafford Loans; Direct Unsubsidized Stafford Loans. **Student Employment:** Federal Work-Study Program available. **Financial Aid Statistics:** 99% needy freshmen, 97% needy undergrads receive need-based scholarship or grant aid. 9% freshmen, 10% undergrads receive non-need-based scholarship or grant aid. 90% freshmen, 89% undergrads receive need-based self-help aid. 8% freshmen, 6% undergrads receive athletic scholarships. 98% freshmen, 83% undergrads receive any aid. **Criteria awarding aid:** *Non-need-based:* Academics, Athletics, Leadership, Music/drama, Religious affiliation.

LUTHER COLLEGE

700 College Drive, Decorah, IA 52101-1042
Phone: 563-387-1287 **Financial Aid Phone:** (563) 387-1018
E-mail: admissions@luther.edu **CEEB Code:** 6375
Fax: 563-387-2159 **Website:** www.luther.edu **ACT Code:** 1330

This private school, affiliated with the Lutheran Church, was founded in 1861. It has a 200 acre campus.

RATINGS

Admissions Selectivity Rating: 85 **Fire Safety Rating:** 74 **Green Rating:** 96

STUDENTS AND FACULTY

Enrollment: 2,008. **Student Body:** 55% female, 45% male, 71% out-of-state, 8% international (73 countries represented). Asian 1%, African American 2%, Caucasian 81%, Hispanic 5%, Native American <1%, Pacific Islander <1%, Two or more races 2%, Race unknown 0%.
Retention and Graduation: 83% freshmen return for sophomore year. 72% freshmen graduate within 4 years. 79% freshmen graduate within 6 years. 16% grads go on to further study within 1 year. 10% grads pursue arts and sciences degrees. 5% grads pursue law degrees. 2% grads pursue business degrees. 16% grads pursue medical degrees. **Faculty:** Student/faculty ratio 11:1. 168 full-time faculty, 95% hold PhDs, 11% are members of minority groups, 48% are women. 0% of classes are taught by teaching assistants.

ACADEMICS

Degrees: Bachelor's. **Classes:** Most classes have 10–19 students. Most lab/discussion sessions have 10–19 students. **Most popular majors:** Biology/Biological Sciences, General; Psychology, General. **Special Study Options:** Double major; Dual enrollment; Honors program; Independent study; Internships; Student-designed major; Study abroad; Teacher certification program. **Honors programs:** The Scholars Program at Luther has the following goals: to challenge intellectually talented students to excel academically, to encourage them to develop a wide-ranging interest in the conversation of ideas and to engage in independent and self-motivated learning, to offer them opportunities to enrich the cultural life of the community, to enable them to become attractive candidates for graduate and professional school and professional employment, and to prepare them for exceptional achievement and service. **Disability Services offered:** Note-taking services; Reader services; Tutors. **Career services:** Alumni network; Career assessment; Career/job search classes; Internships; Regional alumni.

FACILITIES

Housing: Apartments for married students; Apartments for single students; Coed dorms; Special housing for disabled students; Wellness housing; 95% of campus accessible to physically disabled. **Special Academic Facilities/Equipment:** Natural history museum, Norwegian-American museum, five art galleries, planetarium, live animal center, archaeological research center, computer music lab, two electron microscopes, wind turbine.

CAMPUS LIFE

Environment: Village. **Activities:** Campus Ministries; Choral groups; Concert band; Dance; Drama/theater; International Student Organization; Jazz band; Literary magazine; Model UN; Music ensembles; Musical theater; Opera; Pep band; Radio station; Student government; Student newspaper; Symphony orchestra. 104 registered organizations, 13 honor societies, 8 religious organizations, 1 fraternity, 3 sororities on campus. **Athletics (Intercollegiate):** *Men:* baseball, basketball, cross-country, diving, football, golf, soccer, swimming, tennis, track/field (outdoor), track/field (indoor), wrestling. *Women:* basketball, cross-country, diving, golf, soccer, softball, swimming, tennis, track/field (outdoor), track/field (indoor), volleyball. **On-Campus Highlights:** Marty's Cyber Café. **Environmental Initiatives:** Energy audit and efficiency upgrades totaling $1.5 million and has reduced campus carbon footprint by 15%.

ADMISSIONS

Freshman Academic Profile: Average high school GPA 3.7. 26% in top 10% of high school class, 54% in top 25% of high school class, 86% in top 50% of high school class. 90% from public high schools. **Test Scores:** SAT Math middle 50% range 520–665. SAT EBRW middle 50% range 503–640. ACT middle 50% range 23–28. **Basis for Candidate Selection:** *Very important factors include:* rigor of secondary school record, class rank, academic GPA, standardized test scores, recommendation(s). *Important factors include:* extracurricular activities, talent/ability, character/personal qualities. *Other* *factors include:* application essay, interview, first generation, alumni/ae relation, racial/ethnic status, volunteer work, level of applicant's interest. **Freshman Admission Requirements:** High school diploma is required and GED is accepted. *Academic units recommended:* 4 English, 3 math, 2 science, 1 science lab, 2 foreign language, 3 social studies. **Freshman Admission Statistics:** 4,288 applied, 65% admitted, 19% enrolled. **Transfer Admission Requirements:** High school transcript, college transcript(s), essay or personal statement, standardized test scores. Minimum college GPA of 2.50 required. Lowest grade transferable C. **General Admission Information:** Non-fall registration accepted. Admission may be deferred for a maximum of 1 year.

COSTS AND FINANCIAL AID

Annual tuition $41,950. Room and board $9,460. Required fees $340. Average book and supplies expense $1,040. **Required Forms and Deadlines:** FAFSA; Institution's own financial aid form. **Notification of Awards:** Applicants will be notified of awards on a rolling basis beginning 3/15. **Types of Aid:** *Need-based scholarships/grants:* College/university scholarship or grant aid from institutional funds; Federal Pell; Private scholarships; SEOG; State scholarships/grants. *Loans:* Direct PLUS loans; Direct Subsidized Stafford Loans; Direct Unsubsidized Stafford Loans. **Student Employment:** Federal Work-Study Program available. Institutional employment available. **Financial Aid Statistics:** 100% needy freshmen, 100% needy undergrads receive need-based scholarship or grant aid. 20% freshmen, 17% undergrads receive non-need-based scholarship or grant aid. 79% freshmen, 81% undergrads receive need-based self-help aid. 0% freshmen, 0% undergrads receive athletic scholarships. 100% freshmen, 98% undergrads receive any aid. 71% undergrads borrow to pay for school. Average cumulative indebtedness $36,685. **Criteria awarding aid:** *Non-need-based:* Academics, Alumni affiliation, Art, Minority status, Music/drama.

LYCOMING COLLEGE

700 College Place, Williamsport, PA 17701
Phone: 570-321-4026 **Financial Aid Phone:** 570-321-4040
E-mail: admissions@lycoming.edu **CEEB Code:** 2372
Fax: 570-321-4317 **Website:** www.lycoming.edu **ACT Code:** 3622

This private school, affiliated with the Methodist Church, was founded in 1812. It has a 39 acre campus.

RATINGS

Admissions Selectivity Rating: 83   **Fire Safety Rating:** 87   **Green Rating:** 82

STUDENTS AND FACULTY

Enrollment: 1,131. **Student Body:** 53% female, 47% male, 41% out-of-state, 6% international (18 countries represented). Asian 1%, African American 13%, Caucasian 60%, Hispanic 12%, Native American <1%, Pacific Islander <1%, Two or more races 3%, Race unknown 5%.
Retention and Graduation: 75% freshmen return for sophomore year. 59% freshmen graduate within 4 years. 67% freshmen graduate within 6 years. **Faculty:** Student/faculty ratio 12:1. 88 full-time faculty, 97% hold PhDs, 5% are members of minority groups, 43% are women. 0% of classes are taught by teaching assistants.

ACADEMICS

Degrees: Bachelor's. **Classes:** Most classes have 10–19 students. Most lab/discussion sessions have fewer than 10 students. **Most popular majors:** Biology/Biological Sciences, General; Psychology, General; Business Administration and Management, General. **Special Study Options:** Accelerated program; Cooperative education program; Cross-registration; Double major; Dual enrollment; Exchange student program (domestic); Honors program; Independent study; Internships; Student-designed major; Study abroad; Teacher certification program. **Honors programs:** Scholars Program offered to students through admissions process; each major also provides an Honors major option for students who wish to graduate with honors within their field of study. **Disability Services offered:** Note-taking services; Reader services; Tutors. **Career services:** Alumni network; Alumni services; Career assessment; Career/job search classes; Internships; Regional alumni.

FACILITIES

Housing: Apartments for single students; Coed dorms; Fraternity/sorority housing; Special housing for disabled students; Theme housing; Wellness housing; Women's dorms. **Special Academic Facilities/Equipment:** Krapf Gateway Center, Lynn Science Center and Detwiler Planetarium, Center for Enhanced Academic Experiences, Clean Water Institute, 120+ acre Biology Field Station, Chemistry Research Lab, Greenhouse, Center for Energy and the Future, Office of Spiritual Life and Community Service, Center for the Study of Community and Economy, State-of-the-art Digital Graphics Lab, Downtown/community Art Gallery, Outdoor Leadership and Education, Partnership with the Community Arts Center in downtown Williamsport, Institute for Management Studies, Archaeological Field School in Cyprus, Archaeology Lab, Hope Preschool and Early Learning Program, Language Laboratory, Music Library, 204-seat Mary L. Welch Theatre, Sustainability Office, Neuroscience lab facilities.

CAMPUS LIFE

Environment: Town. **Activities:** Campus Ministries; Choral groups; Concert band; Dance; Drama/theater; International Student Organization; Jazz band; Literary magazine; Music ensembles; Musical theater; Pep band; Radio station; Student government; Student newspaper; Student-run film society; Symphony orchestra; Yearbook. 60 registered organizations, 22 honor societies, 3 religious organizations, 3 fraternities, 5 sororities on campus. **Athletics (Intercollegiate):** *Men:* basketball, cross-country, football, golf, lacrosse, soccer, swimming, tennis, wrestling. *Women:* basketball, cross-country, golf, lacrosse, soccer, softball, swimming, tennis, volleyball. **On-Campus Highlights:** Lynn Science Center. **Environmental Initiatives:** The College has a Sustainability Committee that is comprised of faculty, administrators and students. Several initiatives have emerged from this group including using the grease waste from campus dining and converting it into biodiesel.

ADMISSIONS

Freshman Academic Profile: Average high school GPA 3.5. 21% in top 10% of high school class, 46% in top 25% of high school class, 79% in top 50% of high school class. 90% from public high schools. **Test Scores:** SAT Math middle 50% range 500–598. SAT EBRW middle 50% range 510–600. ACT middle 50% range 19–24. **Basis for Candidate Selection:** *Very important factors include:* rigor of secondary school record, recommendation(s). *Important factors include:* class rank, academic GPA, application essay, standardized test scores, interview. *Other factors include:* extracurricular activities, talent/ability, character/personal qualities, first generation, alumni/ae relation, geographical residence, state residency, racial/ethnic status, volunteer work, work experience, level of applicant's interest. **Freshman Admission Requirements:** High school diploma is required and GED is accepted. *Academic units required:* 4 English, 3 math, 3 science, 2 foreign language, 3 social studies, 2 academic electives. *Academic units recommended:* 4 English, 4 math, 3 science, 3 foreign language, 4 social studies, 3 academic electives. **Freshman Admission Statistics:** 2,433 applied, 66% admitted, 20% enrolled. **Transfer Admission Requirements:** College transcript(s), statement of good standing from prior institution(s). Minimum college GPA of 2.0 required. Lowest grade transferable C-. **General Admission Information:** Priority deadline 12/1. Non-fall registration accepted. Admission may be deferred for a maximum of 1 year.

COSTS AND FINANCIAL AID

Annual tuition $39,360. Room and board $12,568. Required fees $955. Average book and supplies expense $1,200. **Required Forms and Deadlines:** FAFSA. **Notification of Awards:** Applicants will be notified of awards on a rolling basis beginning 2/1. **Types of Aid:** *Need-based scholarships/grants:* College/university scholarship or grant aid from institutional funds; Federal Pell; Private scholarships; SEOG; State scholarships/grants; United Negro College Fund. *Loans:* Direct PLUS loans; Direct Subsidized Stafford Loans; Direct Unsubsidized Stafford Loans. **Student Employment:** Federal Work-Study Program available. Institutional employment available. **Financial Aid Statistics:** 100% needy freshmen, 100% needy undergrads receive need-based scholarship or grant aid. 9% freshmen, 11% undergrads receive non-need-based scholarship or grant aid. 75% freshmen, 88% undergrads receive need-based self-help aid. 0% freshmen, 0% undergrads receive athletic scholarships. 100% freshmen, 100% undergrads receive any aid. **Criteria awarding aid:** *Need-based:* Academics, Minority status. *Non-need-based:* Academics, Art, Minority status, Music/drama.

LYME ACADEMY COLLEGE OF FINE ARTS

84 Lyme St, Old Lyme, CT 06371
Phone: 860-434-3571 x118 **Financial Aid Phone:** 860-434-5232
E-mail: admissions@lymeacademy.edu **CEEB Code:** 1971
Fax: 860-434-8725 **Website:** http://www.lymeacademy.edu/

This private school was founded in 1976. It has a 47 acre campus.

RATINGS
Admissions Selectivity Rating: 82   **Fire Safety Rating:** 60*   **Green Rating:** 60*

STUDENTS AND FACULTY
Enrollment: 92. **Student Body:** 63% female, 37% male, 47% out-of-state, 0% international. Asian 1%, African American 4%, Caucasian 88%, Hispanic 1%, Native American 3%, Pacific Islander 1%, Two or more races 3%, Race unknown 0%.
Retention and Graduation: 89% freshmen return for sophomore year. 10% grads go on to further study within 1 year. **Faculty:** Student/faculty ratio 14:1. 8 full-time faculty, 75% hold PhDs, 0% are members of minority groups, 38% are women. 0% of classes are taught by teaching assistants.

ACADEMICS
Degrees: Bachelor's; Certificate; Post-bachelor's certificate. **Classes:** Most classes have 10–19 students. **Most popular majors:** Illustration; Painting; Sculpture. **Special Study Options:** Independent study.

FACILITIES
Housing: 95% of campus accessible to physically disabled. **Special Academic Facilities/Equipment:** Sill House Gallery, Chauncey Stillman Gallery, Academy Wood Shop, Sculpture Casting rooms.

CAMPUS LIFE
Environment: Village. **Activities:** Literary magazine; Student government; Student-run film society. **On-Campus Highlights:** Chauncey Stillman Art Gallery.

ADMISSIONS
Freshman Academic Profile: Average high school GPA 3.2. 85% from public high schools. **Test Scores:** SAT Math middle 50% range 395–555. SAT EBRW middle 50% range 440–650. **Basis for Candidate Selection:** *Very important factors include:* academic GPA, interview, talent/ability, character/personal qualities, level of applicant's interest. *Important factors include:* rigor of secondary school record, application essay, recommendation(s). *Other factors include:* standardized test scores, racial/ethnic status. **Freshman Admission Requirements:** High school diploma is required and GED is accepted. **Freshman Admission Statistics:** 82 applied, 68% admitted, 41% enrolled. **Transfer Admission Requirements:** College transcript(s), essay or personal statement, interview. Minimum college GPA of 2.0 required. Lowest grade transferable C. **General Admission Information:** Application fee $55. Non-fall registration accepted. Admission may be deferred for a maximum of 1 year.

COSTS AND FINANCIAL AID
Annual tuition $25,248. Required fees $1,536. Average book and supplies expense $1,500. **Required Forms and Deadlines:** FAFSA. **Notification of Awards:** Applicants will be notified of awards on a rolling basis beginning 3/1. **Types of Aid:** *Need-based scholarships/grants:* College/university scholarship or grant aid from institutional funds; Federal Pell; Private scholarships; SEOG; State scholarships/grants. *Loans:* Direct PLUS loans; Direct Subsidized Stafford Loans; Direct Unsubsidized Stafford Loans. **Student Employment:** Federal Work-Study Program available. Institutional employment available. **Financial Aid Statistics:** 0% freshmen, 0% undergrads receive athletic scholarships. 88% freshmen, 84% undergrads receive any aid. **Criteria awarding aid:** *Need-based:* Alumni affiliation, Art, Job skills, Minority status. *Non-need-based:* Academics, Art, Leadership.

LYNN UNIVERSITY

3601 North Military Trail, Boca Raton, FL 33431-5598
Phone: 561-237-7900 **Financial Aid Phone:** (561) 237-7973
E-mail: admission@lynn.edu **CEEB Code:** 5437
Fax: 561-237-7100 **Website:** www.lynn.edu **ACT Code:** 0706

This private school was founded in 1962. It has a 123 acre campus.

RATINGS
Admissions Selectivity Rating: 76   **Fire Safety Rating:** 98   **Green Rating:** 95

STUDENTS AND FACULTY
Enrollment: 2,401. **Student Body:** 50% female, 50% male, 45% out-of-state, 16% international (91 countries represented). Asian 1%, African American 10%, Caucasian 46%, Hispanic 18%, Native American <1%, Pacific Islander <1%, Two or more races 2%, Race unknown 5%.
Retention and Graduation: 71% freshmen return for sophomore year. 51% freshmen graduate within 4 years. 51% freshmen graduate within 6 years. **Faculty:** Student/faculty ratio 18:1. 130 full-time faculty, 56% hold PhDs, 12% are members of minority groups, 42% are women. 0% of classes are taught by teaching assistants.

ACADEMICS
Degrees: Associate; Bachelor's; Certificate; Doctoral degree—other; Master's; Post-bachelor's certificate; Post-master's certificate. **Classes:** Most classes have 20–29 students. Most lab/discussion sessions have 10–19 students. **Special Study Options:** Accelerated program; Distance learning; Double major; Dual enrollment; English as a Second Language (ESL); Independent study; Internships; Student-designed major; Study abroad; Teacher certification program. **Combined degree programs:** BA/JD. **Disability Services offered:** Note-taking services; Reader services; Tape recorders; Tutors. **Career services:** Alumni network; Alumni services; Career assessment; Career/job search classes; Internships; Regional alumni.

FACILITIES
Housing: Coed dorms; Special housing for disabled students; 99% of campus accessible to physically disabled. **Special Academic Facilities/Equipment:** 3D Printer, IBC, Lynn Library. **Campus Network:** 100% of classrooms, 100% of dorms, 100% of student union, 100% of libraries, 100% of dining areas, 100% of common outdoor areas have wireless network access.

CAMPUS LIFE
Environment: City. **Activities:** Campus Ministries; Dance; Drama/theater; International Student Organization; Literary magazine; Model UN; Music ensembles; Musical theater; Radio station; Student government; Student newspaper; Student-run film society; Symphony orchestra; Television station. 33 registered organizations, 2 honor societies, 3 religious organizations, 3 fraternities, 2 sororities on campus. **Athletics (Intercollegiate):** *Men:* baseball, basketball, golf, soccer, tennis. *Women:* basketball, golf, soccer, softball, tennis, volleyball. **On-Campus Highlights:** Christine E. Lynn University Center.

ADMISSIONS
Freshman Academic Profile: Average high school GPA 3.2. 57% from public high schools. **Test Scores:** SAT Math middle 50% range 428–494. SAT EBRW middle 50% range 462–516. ACT middle 50% range 19–21. **Basis for Candidate Selection:** *Very important factors include:* rigor of secondary school record, academic GPA, application essay. *Important factors include:* class rank, standardized test scores, recommendation(s), interview, extracurricular activities, character/personal qualities, volunteer work, work experience. *Other factors include:* level of applicant's interest. **Freshman Admission Requirements:** High school diploma is required and GED is accepted. *Academic units recommended:* 4 English, 4 math, 4 science, 2 social studies, 2 history. **Freshman Admission Statistics:** 7,577 applied, 70% admitted, 14% enrolled. **Transfer Admission Requirements:** College transcript(s), essay or personal statement, statement of good standing from prior institution(s). Minimum college GPA of 2.0 required. Lowest grade transferable C. **General Admission Information:** Priority deadline 3/1. Regular application deadline 8/1. Non-fall registration accepted. Admission may be deferred for a maximum of 1 year.

COSTS AND FINANCIAL AID
Annual tuition $37,600. Room and board $12,470. Required fees $2,250. Average book and supplies expense $800. **Required Forms and Deadlines:** FAFSA. **Notification of Awards:** Applicants will be notified of awards on a rolling basis beginning 11/1. **Types of Aid:** *Need-based scholarships/grants:* College/university scholarship or grant aid from institutional funds; Federal

Pell; Private scholarships; SEOG; State scholarships/grants. *Loans:* Direct PLUS loans; Direct Subsidized Stafford Loans; Direct Unsubsidized Stafford Loans. **Student Employment:** Federal Work-Study Program available. Institutional employment available. **Financial Aid Statistics:** 82% needy freshmen, 86% needy undergrads receive need-based scholarship or grant aid. 98% freshmen, 91% undergrads receive non-need-based scholarship or grant aid. 81% freshmen, 79% undergrads receive need-based self-help aid. 12% freshmen, 18% undergrads receive athletic scholarships. 99.3% freshmen, 94.4% undergrads receive any aid. 42% undergrads borrow to pay for school. Average cumulative indebtedness $3,451. **Criteria awarding aid:** *Need-based:* Leadership. *Non-need-based:* Academics, Alumni affiliation, Athletics, Leadership, Music/drama.

LYON COLLEGE

P.O. Box 2317, Batesville, AR 72503-2317
Phone: 870-307-7250 **Financial Aid Phone:** 870-307-7257
E-mail: admissions@lyon.edu **CEEB Code:** 1088
Website: www.lyon.edu **ACT Code:** 112

This private school, affiliated with the Presbyterian Church, was founded in 1872. It has a 136 acre campus.

RATINGS
Admissions Selectivity Rating: 83 **Fire Safety Rating:** 83 **Green Rating:** 60*

STUDENTS AND FACULTY
Enrollment: 664. **Student Body:** 45% female, 55% male, 32% out-of-state, 4% international (12 countries represented). Asian 3%, African American 7%, Caucasian 70%, Hispanic 8%, Native American 2%, Pacific Islander 0%, Two or more races 0%, Race unknown 6%.
Retention and Graduation: 62% freshmen return for sophomore year. 32% freshmen graduate within 4 years. 39% freshmen graduate within 6 years. 26% grads go on to further study within 1 year. **Faculty:** Student/faculty ratio 14:1. 43 full-time faculty, 98% hold PhDs, 5% are members of minority groups, 33% are women. 0% of classes are taught by teaching assistants.

ACADEMICS
Degrees: Bachelor's. **Classes:** Most classes have 10–19 students. Most lab/discussion sessions have 10–19 students. **Most popular majors:** English Language and Literature, General; Biology/Biological Sciences, General; Psychology, General. **Special Study Options:** Double major; Dual enrollment; English as a Second Language (ESL); Honors program; Independent study; Internships; Student-designed major; Study abroad; Teacher certification program. **Combined degree programs:** BA/MEng. **Disability Services offered:** Tape recorders. **Career services:** Alumni network; Alumni services; Career assessment; Career/job search classes; Internships; Regional alumni.

FACILITIES
Housing: Apartments for married students; Apartments for single students; Coed dorms; Theme housing; 80% of campus accessible to physically disabled. **Special Academic Facilities/Equipment:** Ozark Regional Studies Center.

CAMPUS LIFE
Environment: Village. **Activities:** Campus Ministries; Choral groups; Dance; Drama/theater; International Student Organization; Jazz band; Marching band; Model UN; Pep band; Student government; Student newspaper; Student-run film society. 45 registered organizations, 9 honor societies, 7 religious organizations, 3 fraternities, 2 sororities on campus. **Athletics (Intercollegiate):** *Men:* baseball, basketball, cheerleading, cross-country, golf, soccer. *Women:* basketball, cheerleading, cross-country, golf, soccer, softball, volleyball. **On-Campus Highlights:** Derby Center for Science and Mathematics.

ADMISSIONS
Freshman Academic Profile: Average high school GPA 3.6. 27% in top 10% of high school class, 49% in top 25% of high school class, 82% in top 50% of high school class. **Test Scores:** SAT Math middle 50% range 520–633. SAT EBRW middle 50% range 510–603. ACT middle 50% range 22–28. **Basis for Candidate Selection:** *Very important factors include:* academic GPA, standardized test scores. **Freshman Admission Requirements:** High school diploma is required and GED is accepted. **Freshman Admission Statistics:** 1,652 applied, 64% admitted, 18% enrolled. **Transfer Admission Requirements:** College transcript(s), statement of good standing from prior institution(s). Minimum college GPA of 2.75 required. Lowest grade

transferable C. **General Admission Information:** Non-fall registration accepted. Admission may be deferred for a maximum of 1 Fall term.

COSTS AND FINANCIAL AID
Annual tuition $28,200. Room and board $9,130. Required fees $590. Average book and supplies expense $1,500. **Required Forms and Deadlines:** FAFSA; State aid form. **Notification of Awards:** Applicants will be notified of awards on a rolling basis beginning 12/1. **Types of Aid:** *Need-based scholarships/grants:* College/university scholarship or grant aid from institutional funds; Federal Pell; Private scholarships; SEOG; State scholarships/grants. *Loans:* Direct PLUS loans; Direct Subsidized Stafford Loans; Direct Unsubsidized Stafford Loans. **Student Employment:** Federal Work-Study Program available. Institutional employment available. **Financial Aid Statistics:** 99% needy freshmen, 100% needy undergrads receive need-based scholarship or grant aid. 22% freshmen, 21% undergrads receive non-need-based scholarship or grant aid. 65% freshmen, 67% undergrads receive need-based self-help aid. 15% freshmen, 15% undergrads receive athletic scholarships. 100% freshmen, 99% undergrads receive any aid. 74% undergrads borrow to pay for school. Average cumulative indebtedness $26,353. **Criteria awarding aid:** *Non-need-based:* Academics, Alumni affiliation, Art, Athletics, Music/drama, Religious affiliation, State/district residency.

MACALESTER COLLEGE

1600 Grand Avenue, St. Paul, MN 55105
Phone: 651-696-6357 **Financial Aid Phone:** 651-696-6214
E-mail: admissions@macalester.edu **CEEB Code:** 6390
Fax: 651-696-6724 **Website:** www.macalester.edu **ACT Code:** 2122

This private school was founded in 1874. It has a 53 acre campus.

RATINGS
Admissions Selectivity Rating: 94 **Fire Safety Rating:** 98 **Green Rating:** 95

STUDENTS AND FACULTY
Enrollment: 2,160. **Student Body:** 59% female, 41% male, 82% out-of-state, 16% international (96 countries represented). Asian 8%, African American 3%, Caucasian 58%, Hispanic 8%, Native American <1%, Pacific Islander <1%, Two or more races 6%, Race unknown <1%.
Retention and Graduation: 96% freshmen return for sophomore year. 85% freshmen graduate within 4 years. 87% freshmen graduate within 6 years. 12% grads go on to further study within 1 year. 8% grads pursue arts and sciences degrees. 1% grads pursue law degrees. 0% grads pursue business degrees. 1% grads pursue medical degrees. **Faculty:** Student/faculty ratio 10:1. 188 full-time faculty, 94% hold PhDs, 26% are members of minority groups, 54% are women. 0% of classes are taught by teaching assistants.

ACADEMICS
Degrees: Bachelor's. **Classes:** Most classes have 10–19 students. Most lab/discussion sessions have 10–19 students. **Most popular majors:** Mathematics, General; Political Science and Government, General; Econometrics and Quantitative Economics. **Special Study Options:** Cross-registration; Double major; Honors program; Independent study; Internships; Student-designed major; Study abroad. **Honors programs:** The Honors Program is designed to enable seniors with demonstrated ability to undertake substantial independent work that culminates in a project of exceptionally high quality. **Disability Services offered:** Note-taking services; Reader services; Tape recorders. **Career services:** Alumni network; Alumni services; Career assessment; Internships; Regional alumni.

FACILITIES
Housing: Apartments for single students; Coed dorms; Cooperative housing; Special housing for disabled students; Theme housing; Wellness housing; 90% of campus accessible to physically disabled. **Special Academic Facilities/Equipment:** Digital Resource Center, econometrics lab, cartography lab, 250-acre nature preserve, observatory and planetarium, two electron microscopes, nuclear magnetic resonance spectrometer, laser spectroscopy lab, X-ray diffractometer, Center for Study Away, Center for Scholarship and Teaching, Ethnographic lab, GIS lab, state-of-the-art science labs, fine arts gallery. **Campus Network:** 100% of classrooms, 100% of dorms, 100% of student

union, 100% of libraries, 100% of dining areas, 100% of common outdoor areas have wireless network access.

CAMPUS LIFE

Environment: Metropolis. **Activities:** Campus Ministries; Choral groups; Concert band; Dance; Drama/theater; International Student Organization; Jazz band; Literary magazine; Model UN; Music ensembles; Musical theater; Radio station; Student government; Student newspaper; Symphony orchestra. 106 registered organizations, 17 honor societies, 8 religious organizations on campus. **Athletics (Intercollegiate):** *Men:* baseball, basketball, cross-country, diving, football, golf, soccer, swimming, tennis, track/field (outdoor), track/field (indoor). *Women:* basketball, cross-country, diving, golf, soccer, softball, swimming, tennis, track/field (outdoor), track/field (indoor), volleyball, water polo. **On-Campus Highlights:** Ruth Stricker Dayton Campus Center. **Environmental Initiatives:** Developed a comprehensive sustainability plan.

ADMISSIONS

Freshman Academic Profile: 63% in top 10% of high school class, 91% in top 25% of high school class, 99% in top 50% of high school class. 67% from public high schools. **Test Scores:** SAT Math middle 50% range 660–770. SAT EBRW middle 50% range 650–730. ACT middle 50% range 29–33. **Basis for Candidate Selection:** *Very important factors include:* rigor of secondary school record, academic GPA. *Important factors include:* application essay, standardized test scores, recommendation(s), extracurricular activities, character/personal qualities. *Other factors include:* class rank, interview, talent/ability, first generation, alumni/ae relation, racial/ethnic status, volunteer work, work experience. **Freshman Admission Requirements:** High school diploma or equivalent is not required *Academic units recommended:* 4 English, 3 math, 3 science, 3 science labs, 3 foreign language, 3 social studies. **Freshman Admission Statistics:** 5,985 applied, 41% admitted, 25% enrolled. **Transfer Admission Requirements:** High school transcript, college transcript(s), essay or personal statement, standardized test scores, statement of good standing from prior institution(s). Lowest grade transferable C–. **General Admission Information:** Application fee $40. Regular application deadline 1/15. Admission may be deferred for a maximum of 1 year.

COSTS AND FINANCIAL AID

Annual tuition $54,114. Room and board $12,156. Required fees $230. Average book and supplies expense $1,168. **Required Forms and Deadlines:** CSS/Financial Aid PROFILE; FAFSA; Noncustodial PROFILE. **Notification of Awards:** Applicants will be notified of awards on or about 4/1. **Types of Aid:** *Need-based scholarships/grants:* College/university scholarship or grant aid from institutional funds; Federal Pell; Private scholarships; SEOG; State scholarships/grants. *Loans:* Direct PLUS loans; Direct Subsidized Stafford Loans; Direct Unsubsidized Stafford Loans. **Student Employment:** Federal Work-Study Program available. Institutional employment available. **Financial Aid Statistics:** 100% needy freshmen, 100% needy undergrads receive need-based scholarship or grant aid. 11% freshmen, 6% undergrads receive non-need-based scholarship or grant aid. 87% freshmen, 91% undergrads receive need-based self-help aid. 0% freshmen, 0% undergrads receive athletic scholarships. 79% freshmen, 80% undergrads receive any aid. 66% undergrads borrow to pay for school. Average cumulative indebtedness $24,880. **Criteria awarding aid:** *Non-need-based:* Academics, Minority status.

MACMURRAY COLLEGE

447 East College, Jacksonville, IL 62650
Phone: 217-479-7056 **Financial Aid Phone:** 217-479-7041
E-mail: admissions@mac.edu **CEEB Code:** 1435
Fax: 217-291-0702 **Website:** www.mac.edu **ACT Code:** 1068

This private school, affiliated with the Methodist Church, was founded in 1846. It has a 60 acre campus.

RATINGS

Admissions Selectivity Rating: 80 **Fire Safety Rating:** 72 **Green Rating:** 60*

STUDENTS AND FACULTY

Enrollment: 581. **Student Body:** 66% female, 34% male, 11% out-of-state, <1% international (2 countries represented). Asian 1%, African American 13%, Caucasian 73%, Hispanic 3%, Native American 0%, Race unknown 10%. **Retention and Graduation:** 72% freshmen return for sophomore year. 25% grads go on to further study within 1 year. 9% grads pursue arts and sciences degrees. 1% grads pursue law degrees. 12% grads pursue business degrees. 1%

grads pursue medical degrees. **Faculty:** Student/faculty ratio 14:1. 35 full-time faculty, 63% hold PhDs, 3% are members of minority groups, 74% are women. 0% of classes are taught by teaching assistants.

ACADEMICS

Degrees: Associate; Bachelor's. **Classes:** Most classes have 10–19 students. Most lab/discussion sessions have 10–19 students. **Most popular majors:** Business, Management, Marketing, And Related Support Services; Special Education and Teaching, General; Nursing/Registered Nurse (Rn, Asn, Bsn, Msn). **Special Study Options:** Cooperative education program; Double major; Dual enrollment; Independent study; Internships; Liberal arts/career combination; Student-designed major; Study abroad; Teacher certification program. **Combined degree programs:** BA/MEng. **Disability Services offered:** Note-taking services; Reader services; Tape recorders; Tutors. **Career services:** Alumni network; Alumni services; Career assessment; Career/job search classes; Internships; Regional alumni.

FACILITIES

Housing: Coed dorms; Special housing for disabled students; Women's dorms; 50% of campus accessible to physically disabled. **Special Academic Facilities/Equipment:** Art gallery, language lab, music hall, nursing labs.

CAMPUS LIFE

Environment: Village. **Activities:** Campus Ministries; Choral groups; Dance; Drama/theater; Literary magazine; Student government; Yearbook. 37 registered organizations, 2 honor societies, 2 religious organizations, 2 fraternities, 1 sorority on campus. **Athletics (Intercollegiate):** *Men:* baseball, basketball, football, golf, soccer, wrestling. *Women:* basketball, golf, soccer, softball, volleyball. **On-Campus Highlights:** Gamble Campus.

ADMISSIONS

Freshman Academic Profile: Average high school GPA 2.8. 4% in top 10% of high school class, 28% in top 25% of high school class, 55% in top 50% of high school class. 75% from public high schools. **Test Scores:** SAT Math middle 50% range 430–500. SAT EBRW middle 50% range 370–470. ACT middle 50% range 17–23. **Basis for Candidate Selection:** *Very important factors include:* rigor of secondary school record, academic GPA, standardized test scores. *Important factors include:* class rank, extracurricular activities, character/personal qualities. *Other factors include:* application essay, recommendation(s), interview, volunteer work, work experience. **Freshman Admission Requirements:** High school diploma is required and GED is accepted. *Academic units recommended:* 4 English, 3 math, 3 science, 2 science labs, 2 foreign language, 2 social studies, 3 history. **Freshman Admission Statistics:** 1,004 applied, 56% admitted, 16% enrolled. **Transfer Admission Requirements:** College transcript(s). Minimum college GPA of 2.0 required. Lowest grade transferable C. **General Admission Information:** Application fee $25. Priority deadline 5/1. Non-fall registration accepted.

COSTS AND FINANCIAL AID

Annual tuition $15,500. Room and board $5,998. Required fees $250. Average book and supplies expense $775. **Required Forms and Deadlines:** FAFSA. **Notification of Awards:** Applicants will be notified of awards on a rolling basis beginning 2/1. **Types of Aid:** *Need-based scholarships/grants:* College/university scholarship or grant aid from institutional funds; Federal Nursing Scholarships; Federal Pell; Private scholarships; SEOG; State scholarships/grants. **Student Employment:** Federal Work-Study Program available. Institutional employment available. **Financial Aid Statistics:** 100% needy freshmen, 100% needy undergrads receive need-based scholarship or grant aid. 9% freshmen, 7% undergrads receive non-need-based scholarship or grant aid. 79% freshmen, 86% undergrads receive need-based self-help aid. 0% freshmen, 0% undergrads receive athletic scholarships. 95% freshmen, 97% undergrads receive any aid. **Criteria awarding aid:** *Need-based:* Academics, Alumni affiliation, Art, Music/drama. *Non-need-based:* Academics, Alumni affiliation, Art, Leadership, Music/drama, Religious affiliation.

MAHARISHI UNIVERSITY OF MANAGEMENT

1000 North Fourth Street, Fairfield, IA 52557
Phone: 641-472-1110 **Financial Aid Phone:** 641-472-1156
E-mail: admissions@mum.edu
Fax: 641-472-1179 **Website:** www.mum.edu **ACT Code:** 1317

This private school was founded in 1971. It has a 242 acre campus.

RATINGS
Admissions Selectivity Rating: 65   **Fire Safety Rating:** 60*   **Green Rating:** 60*

STUDENTS AND FACULTY
Enrollment: 320. **Student Body:** 56% female, 44% male, 76% out-of-state, 6% international. Asian 3%, African American 7%, Caucasian 34%, Hispanic 8%, Native American 1%, Pacific Islander 1%, Two or more races 4%, Race unknown 37%.
Retention and Graduation: 70% freshmen return for sophomore year. 84% grads go on to further study within 1 year. **Faculty:** 107 full-time faculty, 32% hold PhDs, 29% are members of minority groups, 26% are women. 0% of classes are taught by teaching assistants.

ACADEMICS
Degrees: Bachelor's; Certificate; Master's; Post-bachelor's certificate. **Classes:** Most classes have 10–19 students. Most lab/discussion sessions have 10–19 students. **Most popular majors:** Business/Commerce, General; Environmental Studies; Fine/Studio Arts, General. **Special Study Options:** Distance learning; Double major; English as a Second Language (ESL); Independent study; Internships; Student-designed major; Study abroad.

FACILITIES
Housing: Apartments for married students; Men's dorms; Special housing for disabled students; Women's dorms; 80% of campus accessible to physically disabled. **Special Academic Facilities/Equipment:** Art gallery; scanning electron microscope; real-time cell-imaging computer system; DNA synthesizer; rock-climbing wall.

CAMPUS LIFE
Environment: Village. **Activities:** Choral groups; International Student Organization; Radio station; Student government; Student newspaper; Student-run film society; Yearbook. 25 registered organizations, 3 honor societies, 1 religious organization on campus. **Athletics (Intercollegiate):** *Men:* golf. *Women:* golf. **On-Campus Highlights:** Sustainable Living Center. **Environmental Initiatives:** Four-year bachelors of Science degree offered in Sustainable Living.

ADMISSIONS
Freshman Academic Profile: Average high school GPA 3.6. 0% in top 10% of high school class, 0% in top 25% of high school class, 80% in top 50% of high school class. **Basis for Candidate Selection:** *Very important factors include:* application essay, recommendation(s), interview, level of applicant's interest. *Important factors include:* rigor of secondary school record, academic GPA, talent/ability, character/personal qualities. *Other factors include:* standardized test scores, extracurricular activities, alumni/ae relation, volunteer work, work experience. **Freshman Admission Requirements:** High school diploma is required and GED is accepted. *Academic units recommended:* 4 English, 3 math, 2 science, 1 science lab, 1 social studies, 1 computer science. **Freshman Admission Statistics:** 83 applied, 89% admitted, 31% enrolled. **Transfer Admission Requirements:** High school transcript, college transcript(s), essay or personal statement, interview. Minimum college GPA of 2.5 required. Lowest grade transferable 2. **General Admission Information:** Application fee $20. Non-fall registration accepted. Admission may be deferred for a maximum of one semester.

COSTS AND FINANCIAL AID
Annual tuition $27,000. Room and board $7,400. Required fees $530. Average book and supplies expense $800. **Required Forms and Deadlines:** FAFSA. **Notification of Awards:** Applicants will be notified of awards on a rolling basis beginning 3/1. **Types of Aid:** *Need-based scholarships/grants:* College/university scholarship or grant aid from institutional funds; Federal Pell; Private scholarships; SEOG; State scholarships/grants. **Student Employment:** Federal Work-Study Program available. **Financial Aid Statistics:** 100% needy freshmen, 100% needy undergrads receive need-based scholarship or grant aid. 0% freshmen, 7% undergrads receive non-need-based scholarship or grant aid. 100% freshmen, 100% undergrads receive need-based self-help aid. 0% freshmen, 0% undergrads receive athletic scholarships. 93% freshmen, 98%

undergrads receive any aid. **Criteria awarding aid:** *Need-based:* Academics, Minority status, Music/drama. *Non-need-based:* Academics, Alumni affiliation, Music/drama, State/district residency.

MALONE UNIVERSITY

2600 Cleveland Avenue NW, Canton, OH 44709
Phone: 330-471-8145 **Financial Aid Phone:** 330-471-8161
E-mail: admissions@malone.edu **CEEB Code:** 1439
Fax: 330-471-8149 **Website:** www.malone.edu **ACT Code:** 3289

This private school, affiliated with the Evangelical Friends Church - Eastern Region, was founded in 1892. It has a 96 acre campus.

RATINGS
Admissions Selectivity Rating: 78   **Fire Safety Rating:** 86   **Green Rating:** 60*

STUDENTS AND FACULTY
Enrollment: 1,496. **Student Body:** 58% female, 42% male, 14% out-of-state, 1% international (17 countries represented). Asian 1%, African American 8%, Caucasian 84%, Hispanic 2%, Native American <1%, Pacific Islander <1%, Two or more races 2%, Race unknown <1%.
Retention and Graduation: 70% freshmen return for sophomore year. **Faculty:** Student/faculty ratio 12:1. 95 full-time faculty, 78% hold PhDs, 4% are members of minority groups, 52% are women. 0% of classes are taught by teaching assistants.

ACADEMICS
Degrees: Bachelor's; Master's; Post-master's certificate. **Classes:** Most classes have 10–19 students. Most lab/discussion sessions have fewer than 10 students. **Most popular majors:** Business/Commerce, General; Registered Nursing, Nursing Administration, Nursing Research and Clinical Nursing; Early Childhood Education and Teaching. **Special Study Options:** Accelerated program; Cross-registration; Distance learning; Double major; Dual enrollment; Exchange student program (domestic); Honors program; Independent study; Internships; Student-designed major; Study abroad; Teacher certification program. **Honors programs:** The purpose of the Malone University Honors Program is to support the university's intellectually gifted and highly motivated students, to create a community of students and faculty engaged in serious, substantive, and sustained critical inquiry, and to underscore the university's commitment to academic excellence. The Honors Program fulfills this purpose through pursuit of the following goals: 1. Challenging students to fulfill their intellectual and personal potential through enriching and stimulating experiences in and out of the classroom. 2. Cultivating an esprit de corps, committed to an earnest, cooperative, free, and open pursuit of truth. 3. Developing students' understanding of the unity of knowledge and the interrelationship of the academic disciplines. 4. Providing students the occasion for mentoring relationships with faculty. 5. Preparing students for the pursuit of original and advanced research, scholarship, and performance. 6. Equipping students for outstanding leadership in service to God, their communities, and the world. **Disability Services offered:** Note-taking services; Reader services; Tape recorders; Tutors. **Career services:** Alumni network; Alumni services; Career assessment; Career/job search classes; Internships.

FACILITIES
Housing: Men's dorms; Special housing for disabled students; Theme housing; Women's dorms.

CAMPUS LIFE
Environment: City. **Activities:** Campus Ministries; Choral groups; Concert band; Drama/theater; International Student Organization; Jazz band; Literary magazine; Marching band; Music ensembles; Musical theater; Opera; Radio station; Student government; Student newspaper; Student-run film society; Television station. 50 registered organizations, 10 honor societies, 7 religious organizations on campus. **Athletics (Intercollegiate):** *Men:* baseball, basketball, cheerleading, cross-country, diving, football, golf, soccer, swimming, tennis, track/field (outdoor), track/field (indoor). *Women:* basketball, cheerleading, cross-country, diving, golf, soccer, softball, swimming, tennis, track/field (outdoor), track/field (indoor), volleyball. **On-Campus Highlights:** Hoover Dining Commons—Brehme Centennial Center. **Environmental Initiatives:** Recycling.

ADMISSIONS

Freshman Academic Profile: Average high school GPA 3.3. 18% in top 10% of high school class, 44% in top 25% of high school class, 76% in top 50% of high school class. 80% from public high schools. **Test Scores:** SAT Math middle 50% range 473–570. SAT EBRW middle 50% range 430–570. ACT middle 50% range 20–25. **Basis for Candidate Selection:** *Very important factors include:* rigor of secondary school record, academic GPA, standardized test scores, character/personal qualities. *Important factors include:* class rank, talent/ability, religious affiliation/commitment. *Other factors include:* application essay, recommendation(s), interview, extracurricular activities, alumni/ae relation, racial/ethnic status, volunteer work, level of applicant's interest. **Freshman Admission Requirements:** High school diploma is required and GED is accepted. *Academic units required:* 4 English, 3 math, 3 science, 1 science lab, 2 foreign language, 2 social studies, 1 history, 2 academic electives, 1 visual/performing arts. **Freshman Admission Statistics:** 1,327 applied, 72% admitted, 33% enrolled. **Transfer Admission Requirements:** High school transcript, college transcript(s), statement of good standing from prior institution(s). Minimum college GPA of 2.0 required. **General Admission Information:** Application fee $20. Non-fall registration accepted. Admission may be deferred for a maximum of 2 years.

COSTS AND FINANCIAL AID

Annual tuition $26,456. Room and board $9,266. Required fees $984. Average book and supplies expense $1,200. **Required Forms and Deadlines:** FAFSA. **Notification of Awards:** Applicants will be notified of awards on a rolling basis beginning 3/1. **Types of Aid:** *Need-based scholarships/grants:* College/university scholarship or grant aid from institutional funds; Federal Pell; Private scholarships; SEOG; State scholarships/grants. *Loans:* Direct PLUS loans; Direct Subsidized Stafford Loans; Direct Unsubsidized Stafford Loans. **Student Employment:** Federal Work-Study Program available. Institutional employment available. **Financial Aid Statistics:** 100% needy freshmen, 98% needy undergrads receive need-based scholarship or grant aid. 13% freshmen, 13% undergrads receive non-need-based scholarship or grant aid. 82% freshmen, 81% undergrads receive need-based self-help aid. 12% freshmen, 10% undergrads receive athletic scholarships. 99.7% freshmen, 95% undergrads receive any aid. **Criteria awarding aid:** *Need-based:* Academics, Athletics, Leadership, Music/drama, Religious affiliation. *Non-need-based:* Academics, Athletics, Leadership, Music/drama, Religious affiliation.

MANCHESTER UNIVERSITY

604 E. College Avenue, North Manchester, IN 46962
Phone: 260-982-5055 **Financial Aid Phone:** 260-982-5066
E-mail: admitinfo@manchester.edu **CEEB Code:** 1440
Fax: 260-982-5239 **Website:** www.manchester.edu **ACT Code:** 1222

This private school, affiliated with the Church of Brethren, was founded in 1889. It has a 125 acre campus.

RATINGS

Admissions Selectivity Rating: 72   Fire Safety Rating: 87   Green Rating: 60*

STUDENTS AND FACULTY

Enrollment: 1,071. **Student Body:** 54% female, 46% male, 18% out-of-state, 3% international (18 countries represented). Asian 1%, African American 9%, Caucasian 70%, Hispanic 8%, Native American <1%, Pacific Islander 0%, Two or more races 5%, Race unknown 3%.
Retention and Graduation: 67% freshmen return for sophomore year. 46% freshmen graduate within 4 years. 54% freshmen graduate within 6 years.
Faculty: Student/faculty ratio 12:1. 74 full-time faculty, 95% hold PhDs, 14% are members of minority groups, 48% are women. 0% of classes are taught by teaching assistants.

ACADEMICS

Degrees: Associate; Bachelor's; Doctoral degree—professional practice; Master's. **Classes:** Most classes have 10–19 students. Most lab/discussion sessions have 10–19 students. **Most popular majors:** Education, General; Health Professions And Related Programs; Health Professions And Related Programs. **Special Study Options:** Accelerated program; Distance learning; Double major; Dual enrollment; Exchange student program (domestic); Honors program; Independent study; Internships; Liberal arts/career combination; Student-designed major; Study abroad; Teacher certification program. **Honors programs:** The MU Honors Program provides: an interdisciplinary educational program; unique learning opportunities that engage and challenge students; the opportunity to develop close mentoring relationships with faculty across disciplines. **Disability Services offered:** Reader services; Tape recorders; Tutors. **Career services:** Alumni network; Alumni services; Career assessment; Career/job search classes; Internships; Regional alumni.

FACILITIES

Housing: Coed dorms; Special housing for disabled students. **Special Academic Facilities/Equipment:** Observatory, environmental center and labs.

CAMPUS LIFE

Environment: Rural. **Activities:** Campus Ministries; Choral groups; Concert band; Dance; Drama/theater; International Student Organization; Jazz band; Literary magazine; Model UN; Music ensembles; Opera; Pep band; Radio station; Student government; Student newspaper; Symphony orchestra; Yearbook. 61 registered organizations, 5 honor societies, 4 religious organizations on campus. **Athletics (Intercollegiate):** *Men:* baseball, basketball, cheerleading, cross-country, football, golf, soccer, tennis, track/field (outdoor), wrestling. *Women:* basketball, cheerleading, cross-country, golf, soccer, softball, tennis, track/field (outdoor), volleyball. **On-Campus Highlights:** Jean Childs Young Intercultural Center. **Environmental Initiatives:** Over 25 years of active recyling on campus.

ADMISSIONS

Freshman Academic Profile: Average high school GPA 3.4. 15% in top 10% of high school class, 40% in top 25% of high school class, 77% in top 50% of high school class. **Basis for Candidate Selection:** *Very important factors include:* rigor of secondary school record, class rank, academic GPA, recommendation(s). *Important factors include:* extracurricular activities, talent/ability, character/personal qualities. *Other factors include:* standardized test scores, interview, alumni/ae relation, volunteer work, work experience, level of applicant's interest. **Freshman Admission Requirements:** High school diploma is required and GED is accepted. *Academic units required:* 4 English, 2 math, 2 science, 2 science labs, 1 social studies, 1 history, 2 academic electives. *Academic units recommended:* 4 English, 3 math, 3 science, 2 science labs, 2 foreign language, 2 social studies, 2 history, 2 academic electives, 1 computer science, 1 visual/performing arts. **Freshman Admission Statistics:** 4,707 applied, 56% admitted, 13% enrolled. **Transfer Admission Requirements:** High school transcript, college transcript(s), statement of good standing from prior institution(s). Minimum college GPA of 2.0 required. **General Admission Information:** Non-fall registration accepted. Admission may be deferred for a maximum of 2 years.

COSTS AND FINANCIAL AID

Annual tuition $33,178. Room and board $10,122. Required fees $1,258. Average book and supplies expense $1,000. **Required Forms and Deadlines:** FAFSA. **Notification of Awards:** Applicants will be notified of awards on a rolling basis beginning 12/15. **Types of Aid:** *Need-based scholarships/grants:* College/university scholarship or grant aid from institutional funds; Federal Pell; Private scholarships; SEOG; State scholarships/grants. *Loans:* Direct PLUS loans; Direct Subsidized Stafford Loans; Direct Unsubsidized Stafford Loans. **Student Employment:** Federal Work-Study Program available. Institutional employment available. **Financial Aid Statistics:** 100% needy freshmen, 100% needy undergrads receive need-based scholarship or grant aid. 22% freshmen, 15% undergrads receive non-need-based scholarship or grant aid. 84% freshmen, 85% undergrads receive need-based self-help aid. freshmen, undergrads receive athletic scholarships. 100% freshmen, 99% undergrads receive any aid. 82% undergrads borrow to pay for school. Average cumulative indebtedness $33,061. **Criteria awarding aid:** *Non-need-based:* Academics, Alumni affiliation, Leadership, Minority status, Music/drama, Religious affiliation.

MANHATTAN COLLEGE

Manhattan College Parkway, Riverdale, NY 10471
Phone: 718-862-7200 **Financial Aid Phone:** 718-862-7100
E-mail: admit@manhattan.edu **CEEB Code:** 2395
Fax: 718-862-8019 **Website:** www.manhattan.edu

This private school, affiliated with the Roman Catholic Church, was founded in 1853. It has a 22 acre campus.

RATINGS
Admissions Selectivity Rating: 79   **Fire Safety Rating:** 83   **Green Rating:** 65

STUDENTS AND FACULTY
Enrollment: 3,654. **Student Body:** 45% female, 55% male, 31% out-of-state, 3% international (46 countries represented). Asian 5%, African American 6%, Caucasian 55%, Hispanic 23%, Native American <1%, Pacific Islander <1%, Two or more races 2%, Race unknown 6%.
Retention and Graduation: 82% freshmen return for sophomore year. 58% freshmen graduate within 4 years. 75% freshmen graduate within 6 years. 28% grads go on to further study within 1 year. 1% grads pursue law degrees. 2% grads pursue business degrees. 1% grads pursue medical degrees. **Faculty:** Student/faculty ratio 13:1. 242 full-time faculty, 19% are members of minority groups, 47% are women. 0% of classes are taught by teaching assistants.

ACADEMICS
Degrees: Associate; Bachelor's; Master's; Post-master's certificate. **Classes:** Most classes have 20–29 students. Most lab/discussion sessions have 20–29 students. **Most popular majors:** Marketing/Marketing Management, General; Special Education and Teaching, Other; Civil Engineering, General. **Special Study Options:** Distance learning; Double major; English as a Second Language (ESL); Independent study; Internships; Study abroad; Teacher certification program. **Honors programs:** Honors Enrichment Program. **Combined degree programs:** BA/MA; BA/MEng. **Disability Services offered:** Note-taking services; Reader services; Tape recorders; Tutors. **Career services:** Alumni network; Alumni services; Career assessment; Career/job search classes; Internships.

FACILITIES
Housing: Apartments for married students; Apartments for single students; Coed dorms; Special housing for disabled students; Special housing for international students; Theme housing; 100% of campus accessible to physically disabled. **Special Academic Facilities/Equipment:** Research and learning center; 24-hour Internet café; Holocaust, Genocide and Interfaith Education Center, Center for Academic Success.

CAMPUS LIFE
Environment: Metropolis. **Activities:** Campus Ministries; Choral groups; Concert band; Dance; Drama/theater; International Student Organization; Jazz band; Literary magazine; Model UN; Music ensembles; Musical theater; Pep band; Radio station; Student government; Student newspaper; Student-run film society; Symphony orchestra; Television station; Yearbook. 64 registered organizations, 22 honor societies, 2 religious organizations, 2 fraternities, 2 sororities on campus. **Athletics (Intercollegiate):** *Men:* baseball, basketball, cross-country, golf, lacrosse, soccer, tennis, track/field (outdoor), track/field (indoor). *Women:* basketball, cross-country, lacrosse, soccer, softball, swimming, tennis, track/field (outdoor), track/field (indoor), volleyball. **On-Campus Highlights:** Quadrangle.

ADMISSIONS
Freshman Academic Profile: 23% in top 10% of high school class, 54% in top 25% of high school class, 79% in top 50% of high school class. 57% from public high schools. **Test Scores:** SAT Math middle 50% range 530–630. SAT EBRW middle 50% range 540–630. ACT middle 50% range 23–28. **Basis for Candidate Selection:** *Very important factors include:* rigor of secondary school record, class rank, academic GPA, standardized test scores. *Important factors include:* application essay, recommendation(s). *Other factors include:* talent/ability, character/personal qualities, first generation, alumni/ae relation, geographical residence, volunteer work, work experience, level of applicant's interest. **Freshman Admission Requirements:** High school diploma is required and GED is accepted. *Academic units required:* 4 English, 3 math, 2 science, 2 science labs, 2 foreign language, 3 social studies, 2 academic electives. *Academic*

units recommended: 4 English, 4 math, 4 science, 4 science labs, 3 foreign language, 4 social studies. **Freshman Admission Statistics:** 7,882 applied, 75% admitted, 13% enrolled. **Transfer Admission Requirements:** High school transcript, college transcript(s), standardized test scores, statement of good standing from prior institution(s). Minimum college GPA of 2.5 required. Lowest grade transferable C. **General Admission Information:** Application fee $75. Priority deadline 3/1. Non-fall registration accepted. Admission may be deferred for a maximum of 1 year.

COSTS AND FINANCIAL AID
Annual tuition $40,400. Room and board $16,870. Required fees $1,964. Average book and supplies expense $1,200. **Required Forms and Deadlines:** FAFSA. **Notification of Awards:** Applicants will be notified of awards on a rolling basis beginning 2/15. **Types of Aid:** *Need-based scholarships/grants:* College/university scholarship or grant aid from institutional funds; Federal Pell; Private scholarships; SEOG; State scholarships/grants. *Loans:* Direct PLUS loans; Direct Subsidized Stafford Loans; Direct Unsubsidized Stafford Loans. **Student Employment:** Federal Work-Study Program available. Institutional employment available. **Financial Aid Statistics:** 12% freshmen, 14% undergrads receive non-need-based scholarship or grant aid. 64% freshmen, 59% undergrads receive need-based self-help aid. 1% freshmen, 2% undergrads receive athletic scholarships. 88% freshmen, 86% undergrads receive any aid. 97% undergrads borrow to pay for school. Average cumulative indebtedness $46,498. **Criteria awarding aid:** *Need-based:* Academics, Music/drama. *Non-need-based:* Academics, Athletics, State/district residency.

MANHATTANVILLE COLLEGE

2900 Purchase Street, Purchase, NY 10577
Phone: 914-323-5464 **Financial Aid Phone:** 914-323-5357
E-mail: admissions@mville.edu **CEEB Code:** 2397
Fax: 914-694-1732 **Website:** www.mville.edu **ACT Code:** 2800

This private school was founded in 1841. It has a 100 acre campus.

RATINGS
Admissions Selectivity Rating: 74   **Fire Safety Rating:** 98   **Green Rating:** 79

STUDENTS AND FACULTY
Enrollment: 1,504. **Student Body:** 58% female, 42% male, 25% out-of-state, 5% international (36 countries represented). Asian 2%, African American 10%, Caucasian 48%, Hispanic 29%, Native American <1%, Pacific Islander <1%, Two or more races 3%, Race unknown 3%.
Retention and Graduation: 70% freshmen return for sophomore year. 54% freshmen graduate within 4 years. 60% freshmen graduate within 6 years. 23% grads go on to further study within 1 year. 25% grads pursue arts and sciences degrees. 0% grads pursue law degrees. 17% grads pursue business degrees. 1% grads pursue medical degrees. **Faculty:** Student/faculty ratio 11:1. 113 full-time faculty, 83% hold PhDs, 14% are members of minority groups, 50% are women. 0% of classes are taught by teaching assistants.

ACADEMICS
Degrees: Bachelor's; Doctoral degree research/scholarship; Master's; Post-bachelor's certificate; Post-master's certificate. **Classes:** Most classes have 10–19 students. Most lab/discussion sessions have 10–19 students. **Most popular majors:** Communication and Media Studies; Psychology, General; Business/Commerce, General. **Special Study Options:** Accelerated program; Cross-registration; Double major; Dual enrollment; Exchange student program (domestic); Honors program; Independent study; Internships; Liberal arts/career combination; Student-designed major; Study abroad; Teacher certification program; Weekend college. **Honors programs:** The Castle Scholars Honors Program offers students of exceptional ability a broader and more intensive program of study than the usual college curriculum. It provides motivated students in any major field with challenging, cross-disciplinary courses that encourage their academic and personal growth. Participation in the Castle Scholars Program encourages intellectual exchange among students and faculty and fosters independent initiative in academic and creative realms. Castle Scholars are well prepared for success in graduate and professional schools, as well as in the professional world. Castle Scholars build relationships with each other and with the college's faculty in specially-designed Honors

Seminars and other unique academic opportunities, as well as in a host of social events throughout the year. Through their studies, research, and service, the Scholars contribute to the intellectual and social life of the college. Studies are augmented by participation in the wider New York City community. Privileges accorded to Castle Scholars include priority registration, the ability to register for 21 credits per semester without a financial penalty (after the first year), and access to research or travel funds in their junior and senior year. To remain in good standing, Castle Scholars must maintain a GPA of 3.6. The Castle Scholars Honors Program complements a student's chosen major and is distinct from honors options within the major. Castle Scholars are recognized annually at college-wide awards receptions, and honors courses are noted on student academic transcripts. Successful completion of the program will be noted on the final transcript as well as on printed graduation materials. **Combined degree programs:** BA/MA. **Disability Services offered:** Note-taking services; Reader services; Tutors. **Career services:** Alumni network; Alumni services; Career assessment; Career/job search classes; Internships; Regional alumni.

FACILITIES

Housing: Coed dorms; Special housing for disabled students; Wellness housing; 90% of campus accessible to physically disabled. **Special Academic Facilities/ Equipment:** Berman Student Center contains art gallery and theater, Center for Design Thinking, Founder's Hall contains the Center for Inclusion, the Sister Mary T. Clark, RSCJ Center For Religion and Social Justice, and the Connie Hogarth Center for Social Action, Library, and Music Building, which contains Pius X Theater, Ohnell Environmental Center, and Rose Institute for Literacy and Learning.

CAMPUS LIFE

Environment: Town. **Activities:** Campus Ministries; Choral groups; Concert band; Dance; Drama/theater; International Student Organization; Jazz band; Literary magazine; Model UN; Music ensembles; Musical theater; Opera; Radio station; Student government; Student newspaper; Student-run film society. 50 registered organizations, 3 honor societies, 4 religious organizations on campus. **Athletics (Intercollegiate):** *Men:* baseball, basketball, golf, ice hockey, lacrosse, soccer, tennis. *Women:* basketball, cheerleading, field hockey, ice hockey, lacrosse, soccer, softball, tennis, volleyball. **On-Campus Highlights:** Center for Design Thinking. **Environmental Initiatives:** The LEED Gold-Rated Berman Student Center.

ADMISSIONS

Freshman Academic Profile: Average high school GPA 3.2. 14% in top 10% of high school class, 19% in top 25% of high school class, 75% in top 50% of high school class. 87% from public high schools. **Test Scores:** SAT Math middle 50% range 490–590. SAT EBRW middle 50% range 490–580. ACT middle 50% range 19–27. **Basis for Candidate Selection:** *Very important factors include:* rigor of secondary school record, academic GPA, application essay, recommendation(s), extracurricular activities, talent/ability, character/personal qualities, alumni/ae relation, level of applicant's interest. *Important factors include:* geographical residence. *Other factors include:* class rank, standardized test scores, interview, first generation, state residency, work experience. **Freshman Admission Requirements:** High school diploma is required and GED is accepted. *Academic units required:* 4 English, 3 math, 2 science, 2 social studies, 5 academic electives. **Freshman Admission Statistics:** 3,435 applied, 90% admitted, 13% enrolled. **Transfer Admission Requirements:** College transcript(s), statement of good standing from prior institution(s). Minimum college GPA of 2.5 required. Lowest grade transferable C. **General Admission Information:** Application fee $50. Priority deadline 3/1. Non-fall registration accepted. Admission may be deferred for a maximum of 1 year.

COSTS AND FINANCIAL AID

Annual tuition $38,880. Room and board $14,810. Required fees $1,450. Average book and supplies expense $800. **Required Forms and Deadlines:** FAFSA; State aid form. **Notification of Awards:** Applicants will be notified of awards on a rolling basis beginning 11/15. *Types of Aid: Need-based scholarships/grants:* College/university scholarship or grant aid from institutional funds; Federal Pell; Private scholarships; SEOG; State scholarships/grants; United Negro College Fund. *Loans:* Direct PLUS loans; Direct Subsidized Stafford Loans; Direct Unsubsidized Stafford Loans. **Student Employment:** Federal Work-Study Program available. Institutional employment available. **Financial Aid Statistics:** 81% needy freshmen, 84% needy undergrads receive need-based scholarship or grant aid. 99% freshmen, 95% undergrads receive non-need-based scholarship or grant aid. 100% freshmen, 84% undergrads receive need-based self-help aid. 0% freshmen, 0% undergrads receive athletic scholarships. 98.21% freshmen, 94.23% undergrads receive any aid. 68% undergrads borrow to pay for school. Average cumulative indebtedness $35,092. **Criteria awarding aid:** *Non-need-based:* Academics, Alumni affiliation, Art, Leadership, Music/drama.

MANSFIELD UNIVERSITY OF PENNSYLVANIA

71 Academy Street, Mansfield, PA 16933
Phone: 570-662-4243 **Financial Aid Phone:** 570-664-4129
E-mail: admissions@mansfield.edu **CEEB Code:** 2655
Fax: 570-662-4121 **Website:** mansfield.edu **ACT Code:** 3710

This public school was founded in 1857. It has a 174 acre campus.

RATINGS

Admissions Selectivity Rating: 80   **Fire Safety Rating:** 79   **Green Rating:** 60*

STUDENTS AND FACULTY

Enrollment: 1,771. **Student Body:** 59% female, 41% male, 17% out-of-state, 1% international (15 countries represented). Asian 1%, African American 10%, Caucasian 81%, Hispanic 4%, Native American <1%, Pacific Islander <1%, Two or more races 2%, Race unknown 2%.
Retention and Graduation: 71% freshmen return for sophomore year. 33% freshmen graduate within 4 years. 55% freshmen graduate within 6 years. 23% grads go on to further study within 1 year. **Faculty:** Student/faculty ratio 15:1. 100 full-time faculty, 85% hold PhDs, 52% are members of minority groups, 48% are women. 0% of classes are taught by teaching assistants.

ACADEMICS

Degrees: Associate; Bachelor's; Master's; Post-bachelor's certificate. **Classes:** Most classes have 10–19 students. Most lab/discussion sessions have 10–19 students. **Most popular majors:** Criminal Justice/Law Enforcement Administration; Psychology, General; Music Teacher Education. **Special Study Options:** Cross-registration; Distance learning; Double major; Dual enrollment; English as a Second Language (ESL); Exchange student program (domestic); Honors program; Independent study; Internships; Liberal arts/career combination; Student-designed major; Study abroad; Teacher certification program. **Honors programs:** The program includes a 22-credit curriculum that fits within most General Education and Degree program requirements. These courses include the following core principles of an Honors Education: Discussion-based instruction and small class sizes; critical thinking through speaking and writing; experiential learning and interdisciplinary integration. The curriculum culminates in a Senior Honors Project, in which students choose a topic of interest and work individually with a faculty mentor to complete their project. These projects are presented to the community at large, and students are encouraged to apply their findings to create real-world solutions within the university, local, or regional communities. In addition to the curriculum, the Honors Program also includes extracurricular events, both educational and social. The majority of extracurricular activities are created, programmed, and executed by our Honors students, primarily through the Honors Association (a student government group) and the MOHBs (Mansfield Outstanding Honors Buddy system). All first-year students are assigned a MOHB, led by an upper-class Honors student (the MOHB Boss), which meets 8–10 times a semester. The MOHBs create social events, provide study skills workshops, registration advice, workshop student papers, and carry out service projects. **Disability Services offered:** Note-taking services; Reader services; Tape recorders; Tutors. **Career services:** Career assessment; Career/job search classes; Internships.

FACILITIES

Housing: Coed dorms; Fraternity/sorority housing; 90% of campus accessible to physically disabled. **Special Academic Facilities/Equipment:** Science museum, two art galleries, animal collection, planetarium, solar collector.

CAMPUS LIFE

Environment: Rural. **Activities:** Campus Ministries; Choral groups; Concert band; Dance; Drama/theater; International Student Organization; Jazz band; Literary magazine; Marching band; Music ensembles; Musical theater; Pep band; Radio station; Student government; Student newspaper; Student-run film society; Symphony orchestra; Television station; Yearbook. 93 registered organizations, 10 honor societies, 4 religious organizations, 6 fraternities, 4 sororities on campus. **Athletics (Intercollegiate):** *Men:* baseball, basketball, cross-country, football, track/field (outdoor), track/field (indoor). *Women:* basketball, cheerleading, cross-country, diving, field hockey, soccer, softball, swimming, track/field (outdoor), track/field (indoor). **On-Campus Highlights:** North Hall Library.

ADMISSIONS

Freshman Academic Profile: Average high school GPA 3.4. 8% in top 10% of high school class, 29% in top 25% of high school class, 70% in top 50% of high school class. **Test Scores:** SAT Math middle 50% range 470–560.

SAT EBRW middle 50% range 480–570. **Basis for Candidate Selection:** *Very important factors include:* rigor of secondary school record, class rank, academic GPA, standardized test scores. *Other factors include:* application essay, recommendation(s), interview, extracurricular activities, talent/ability, character/ personal qualities, first generation, alumni/ae relation, geographical residence, volunteer work, work experience, level of applicant's interest. **Freshman Admission Requirements:** High school diploma is required and GED is accepted. *Academic units required:* 4 English, 3 math, 2 science, 2 science labs, 2 foreign language, 4 history, 6 academic electives. *Academic units recommended:* 4 English, 4 math, 3 science, 3 science labs, 4 foreign language. **Freshman Admission Statistics:** 2,501 applied, 68% admitted, 22% enrolled. **Transfer Admission Requirements:** College transcript(s). Minimum college GPA of 2.0 required. Lowest grade transferable D. **General Admission Information:** Application fee $25. Priority deadline 11/30.

COSTS AND FINANCIAL AID
Annual in-state tuition $9,450. Annual out-of-state tuition $18,900. Room and board $11,928. Required fees $2,866. Average book and supplies expense $2,000. **Required Forms and Deadlines:** FAFSA; State aid form. **Types of Aid:** *Need-based scholarships/grants:* College/university scholarship or grant aid from institutional funds; Federal Pell; Private scholarships; SEOG; State scholarships/ grants. *Loans:* Direct PLUS loans; Direct Subsidized Stafford Loans; Direct Unsubsidized Stafford Loans. **Student Employment:** Federal Work-Study Program available. Institutional employment available. **Financial Aid Statistics:** 74% needy freshmen, 78% needy undergrads receive need-based scholarship or grant aid. 59% freshmen, 38% undergrads receive non-need-based scholarship or grant aid. 93% freshmen, 93% undergrads receive need-based self-help aid. 4% freshmen, 3% undergrads receive athletic scholarships. 90% freshmen, 90% undergrads receive any aid. 85% undergrads borrow to pay for school. Average cumulative indebtedness $36,624. **Criteria awarding aid:** *Need-based:* Academics. *Non-need-based:* Academics, Alumni affiliation, Art, Athletics, Job skills, Leadership, Minority status, Music/drama, Religious affiliation, State/ district residency.

MARIAN UNIVERSITY (IN)

3200 Cold Spring Rd., Indianapolis, IN 46222-1997
Phone: 317-955-6300 **Financial Aid Phone:** (800) 834-5494
E-mail: admissions@marian.edu **CEEB Code:** 1442
Fax: 317-955-6401 **Website:** www.marian.edu **ACT Code:** 1224

This private school, affiliated with the Roman Catholic Church, was founded in 1851. It has a 114 acre campus.

RATINGS
Admissions Selectivity Rating: 84   **Fire Safety Rating:** 83   **Green Rating:** 62

STUDENTS AND FACULTY
Enrollment: 2,237. **Student Body:** 63% female, 37% male, 18% out-of-state, 2% international (27 countries represented). Asian 3%, African American 12%, Caucasian 70%, Hispanic 7%, Native American <1%, Pacific Islander <1%, Two or more races 4%, Race unknown 2%.
Retention and Graduation: 83% freshmen return for sophomore year. 43% freshmen graduate within 4 years. 62% freshmen graduate within 6 years. 8% grads go on to further study within 1 year. 33% grads pursue arts and sciences degrees. 0% grads pursue law degrees. 20% grads pursue business degrees. 13% grads pursue medical degrees. **Faculty:** Student/faculty ratio 13:1. 143 full-time faculty, 59% hold PhDs, 16% are members of minority groups, 59% are women. 0% of classes are taught by teaching assistants.

ACADEMICS
Degrees: Associate; Bachelor's; Doctoral degree—professional practice; Master's. **Classes:** Most classes have 10–19 students. Most lab/discussion sessions have 10–19 students. **Most popular majors:** Registered Nursing/Registered Nurse; Business Administration and Management, General; Biology/Biological Sciences, General. **Special Study Options:** Accelerated program; Cooperative education program; Cross-registration; Distance learning; Double major; Dual enrollment; Honors program; Independent study; Internships; Liberal arts/ career combination; Study abroad; Teacher certification program. **Combined degree programs:** BA/MA. **Disability Services offered:** Note-taking services; Reader services; Tape recorders; Tutors. **Career services:** Alumni network; Alumni services; Career assessment; Career/job search classes; Internships; Regional alumni.

FACILITIES
Housing: Apartments for married students; Apartments for single students; Coed dorms; Cooperative housing; Special housing for disabled students; Theme housing; Wellness housing. **Special Academic Facilities/Equipment:** Art Gallery.

CAMPUS LIFE
Environment: Metropolis. **Activities:** Campus Ministries; Choral groups; Concert band; Dance; Drama/theater; International Student Organization; Jazz band; Literary magazine; Marching band; Model UN; Music ensembles; Musical theater; Pep band; Student government; Student newspaper; Yearbook. 35 registered organizations, 11 honor societies, 10 religious organizations, 1 fraternity, 1 sorority on campus. **Athletics (Intercollegiate):** *Men:* baseball, basketball, cheerleading, cross-country, cycling, football, golf, tennis, track/ field (outdoor), track/field (indoor). *Women:* basketball, cheerleading, cross-country, cycling, golf, softball, tennis, track/field (outdoor), track/field (indoor), volleyball. **On-Campus Highlights:** Micheal A. Evans Center for Health Sciences. **Environmental Initiatives:** Recycling.

ADMISSIONS
Freshman Academic Profile: Average high school GPA 3.6. 25% in top 10% of high school class, 51% in top 25% of high school class, 79% in top 50% of high school class. **Test Scores:** SAT Math middle 50% range 480–590. SAT EBRW middle 50% range 490–590. ACT middle 50% range 18–25. **Basis for Candidate Selection:** *Very important factors include:* academic GPA, standardized test scores. *Important factors include:* rigor of secondary school record, class rank, recommendation(s). *Other factors include:* application essay, interview, extracurricular activities, talent/ability, character/personal qualities, alumni/ae relation, volunteer work, level of applicant's interest. **Freshman Admission Requirements:** High school diploma is required and GED is accepted. *Academic units required:* 4 English, 2 math, 2 science, 2 science labs, 1 social studies, 1 history, 9 academic electives. *Academic units recommended:* 4 English, 3 math, 3 science, 2 science labs, 2 foreign language, 1 social studies, 1 history, 8 academic electives. **Freshman Admission Statistics:** 2,525 applied, 62% admitted, 25% enrolled. **Transfer Admission Requirements:** College transcript(s). Minimum college GPA of 2 required. Lowest grade transferable C-. **General Admission Information:** Priority deadline 3/1. Regular application deadline 8/1. Non-fall registration accepted. Admission may be deferred for a maximum of 1 year.

COSTS AND FINANCIAL AID
Annual tuition $36,000. Room and board $11,320. Average book and supplies expense $1,200. **Required Forms and Deadlines:** FAFSA. **Notification of Awards:** Applicants will be notified of awards on a rolling basis beginning 12/15. **Types of Aid:** *Need-based scholarships/grants:* College/university scholarship or grant aid from institutional funds; Federal Pell; Private scholarships; SEOG; State scholarships/grants. *Loans:* Direct PLUS loans; Direct Subsidized Stafford Loans; Direct Unsubsidized Stafford Loans. **Student Employment:** Federal Work-Study Program available. Institutional employment available. **Financial Aid Statistics:** 100% needy freshmen, 100% needy undergrads receive need-based scholarship or grant aid. 75% freshmen, 81% undergrads receive non-need-based scholarship or grant aid. 76% freshmen, 77% undergrads receive need-based self-help aid. 40% freshmen, 35% undergrads receive athletic scholarships. 99% freshmen receive any aid. 78% undergrads borrow to pay for school. Average cumulative indebtedness $34,435. **Criteria awarding aid:** *Need-based:* Minority status. *Non-need-based:* Academics, Alumni affiliation, Art, Athletics, Leadership, Music/ drama, Religious affiliation.

MARIAN UNIVERSITY (WI)

45 South National Avenue, Fond du Lac, WI 54935
Phone: 920-923-7650 **Financial Aid Phone:** 920-923-7614
E-mail: admissions@marianuniversity.edu **CEEB Code:** 1443
Fax: 920-923-8755 **Website:** www.marianuniversity.edu **ACT Code:** 4606

This private school, affiliated with the Roman Catholic Church, was founded in 1936. It has a 100 acre campus.

RATINGS
Admissions Selectivity Rating: 75   **Fire Safety Rating:** 66   **Green Rating:** 60*

STUDENTS AND FACULTY
Enrollment: 1,903. **Student Body:** 75% female, 25% male, 7% out-of-state, 1% international (13 countries represented). Asian 1%, African American 5%, Caucasian 88%, Hispanic 2%, Native American 1%, Race unknown 1%.

Retention and Graduation: 71% freshmen return for sophomore year. 16% grads go on to further study within 1 year. **Faculty:** Student/faculty ratio 12:1. 83 full-time faculty, 60% hold PhDs, 6% are members of minority groups, 55% are women. 0% of classes are taught by teaching assistants.

ACADEMICS

Degrees: Bachelor's; Master's. **Classes:** Most classes have 10–19 students. Most lab/discussion sessions have 10–19 students. **Most popular majors:** Business/Commerce, General; Teacher Education and Professional Development, Specific Levels and Methods, Other; Nursing/Registered Nurse (Rn, Asn, Bsn, Msn). **Special Study Options:** Accelerated program; Cooperative education program; Distance learning; Double major; Dual enrollment; Honors program; Independent study; Internships; Liberal arts/career combination; Student-designed major; Study abroad; Teacher certification program. **Disability Services offered:** Note-taking services; Reader services; Tape recorders; Tutors. **Career services:** Career assessment; Career/job search classes; Internships.

FACILITIES

Housing: Apartments for single students; Coed dorms; Fraternity/sorority housing; Special housing for disabled students; 95% of campus accessible to physically disabled. **Special Academic Facilities/Equipment:** On-campus child-care center, electron microscope.

CAMPUS LIFE

Environment: Town. **Activities:** Campus Ministries; Choral groups; Concert band; Dance; Drama/theater; Jazz band; Literary magazine; Model UN; Music ensembles; Pep band; Student government; Student newspaper; Symphony orchestra. 40 registered organizations, 6 honor societies, 1 religious organization, 1 fraternity, 2 sororities on campus. **Athletics (Intercollegiate):** *Men:* baseball, basketball, cross-country, golf, ice hockey, soccer, tennis. *Women:* basketball, cross-country, golf, ice hockey, soccer, softball, tennis, volleyball.

ADMISSIONS

Freshman Academic Profile: Average high school GPA 3.0. 9% in top 10% of high school class, 30% in top 25% of high school class, 66% in top 50% of high school class. 87% from public high schools. **Test Scores:** ACT middle 50% range 18–22. **Basis for Candidate Selection:** *Very important factors include:* rigor of secondary school record, class rank, academic GPA, standardized test scores. *Important factors include:* interview, character/personal qualities. *Other factors include:* application essay, recommendation(s), extracurricular activities, talent/ability, alumni/ae relation, volunteer work, work experience. **Freshman Admission Requirements:** High school diploma is required and GED is accepted. *Academic units required:* 4 English, 2 math, 1 science, 1 science lab, 1 history. *Academic units recommended:* 3 math, 2 science, 2 foreign language. **Freshman Admission Statistics:** 754 applied, 85% admitted, 45% enrolled. **Transfer Admission Requirements:** High school transcript, college transcript(s). Minimum college GPA of 2.0 required. Lowest grade transferable C. **General Admission Information:** Application fee $20. Priority deadline 4/1. Non-fall registration accepted. Admission may be deferred for a maximum of case by case.

COSTS AND FINANCIAL AID

Annual tuition $19,590. Room and board $5,380. Required fees $350. Average book and supplies expense $700. **Required Forms and Deadlines:** FAFSA; Institution's own financial aid form. **Notification of Awards:** Applicants will be notified of awards on a rolling basis beginning 3/1. **Types of Aid:** *Need-based scholarships/grants:* College/university scholarship or grant aid from institutional funds; Federal Pell; Private scholarships; SEOG; State scholarships/grants. **Student Employment:** Federal Work-Study Program available. Institutional employment available. **Financial Aid Statistics:** 100% needy freshmen, 97% needy undergrads receive need-based scholarship or grant aid. 91% freshmen, 85% undergrads receive non-need-based scholarship or grant aid. 89% freshmen, 91% undergrads receive need-based self-help aid. 0% freshmen, 0% undergrads receive athletic scholarships. 99% freshmen, 94% undergrads receive any aid. **Criteria awarding aid:** *Need-based:* Academics, Alumni affiliation, Art, Leadership, Music/drama, Religious affiliation. *Non-need-based:* Academics, State/district residency.

MARIETTA COLLEGE

215 Fifth Street, Marietta, OH 45750
Phone: 740-376-4600 **Financial Aid Phone:** 740-376-4712
E-mail: admit@marietta.edu **CEEB Code:** 1444
Fax: 740-376-8888 **Website:** www.marietta.edu **ACT Code:** 3290

This private school was founded in 1835. It has a 90 acre campus.

RATINGS

Admissions Selectivity Rating: 80   **Fire Safety Rating:** 88   **Green Rating:** 63

STUDENTS AND FACULTY

Enrollment: 1,470. **Student Body:** 43% female, 57% male, 36% out-of-state, 12% international (15 countries represented). Asian 1%, African American 6%, Caucasian 71%, Hispanic 2%, Native American <1%, Pacific Islander 0%, Two or more races 1%, Race unknown 6%.
Retention and Graduation: 75% freshmen return for sophomore year. 20% grads go on to further study within 1 year. 9% grads pursue arts and sciences degrees. 3% grads pursue law degrees. 2% grads pursue business degrees. 2% grads pursue medical degrees. **Faculty:** Student/faculty ratio 12:1. 110 full-time faculty, 89% hold PhDs, 7% are members of minority groups, 45% are women. 0% of classes are taught by teaching assistants.

ACADEMICS

Degrees: Associate; Bachelor's; Certificate; Master's. **Classes:** Most classes have 10–19 students. **Most popular majors:** Education, General; Petroleum Engineering; Athletic Training/Trainer. **Special Study Options:** Double major; Dual enrollment; English as a Second Language (ESL); Exchange student program (domestic); Honors program; Independent study; Internships; Liberal arts/career combination; Student-designed major; Study abroad; Teacher certification program. **Honors programs:** Four Year Program for Top Scholarship Winners. **Combined degree programs:** BA/MA. **Disability Services offered:** Note-taking services; Reader services; Tape recorders; Tutors. **Career services:** Alumni network; Alumni services; Career assessment; Career/job search classes; Internships; Regional alumni.

FACILITIES

Housing: Apartments for single students; Coed dorms; Fraternity/sorority housing; Men's dorms; Special housing for disabled students; Theme housing; Wellness housing; Women's dorms; 90% of campus accessible to physically disabled. **Special Academic Facilities/Equipment:** Mass media building, fine arts center, natural science field camp, observatory, special collections in library. **Campus Network:** 100% of classrooms, 100% of dorms, 100% of student union, 100% of libraries, 100% of dining areas, 0% of common outdoor areas have wireless network access.

CAMPUS LIFE

Environment: Town. **Activities:** Campus Ministries; Choral groups; Concert band; Dance; Drama/theater; International Student Organization; Jazz band; Literary magazine; Model UN; Music ensembles; Musical theater; Radio station; Student government; Student newspaper; Television station; Yearbook. 80 registered organizations, 23 honor societies, 2 religious organizations, 3 fraternities, 4 sororities on campus. **Athletics (Intercollegiate):** *Men:* baseball, basketball, crew/rowing, cross-country, football, soccer, tennis, track/field (outdoor), track/field (indoor). *Women:* basketball, crew/rowing, cross-country, soccer, softball, tennis, track/field (outdoor), track/field (indoor), volleyball. **On-Campus Highlights:** Gathering Place. **Environmental Initiatives:** Added Sustainable Energy Minor under the Petroleum Engineering Program.

ADMISSIONS

Freshman Academic Profile: Average high school GPA 3.5. 30% in top 10% of high school class, 56% in top 25% of high school class, 84% in top 50% of high school class. 89% from public high schools. **Test Scores:** SAT Math middle 50% range 490–610. SAT EBRW middle 50% range 480–610. ACT middle 50% range 21–26. **Basis for Candidate Selection:** *Very important factors include:* rigor of secondary school record, class rank, academic GPA, standardized test scores. *Important factors include:* application essay, recommendation(s), interview, character/personal qualities. *Other factors include:* extracurricular activities, talent/ability, first generation, alumni/ae relation, geographical residence, state residency, racial/ethnic status, volunteer work, work experience, level of applicant's interest. **Freshman Admission Requirements:** High school diploma is required and GED is accepted. *Academic units required:* 4 English, 3 math, 3 science, 2 science labs, 2 foreign language, 2 social studies, 2 history. **Freshman Admission Statistics:** 4,157 applied, 68% admitted, 14% enrolled. **Transfer Admission Requirements:** College transcript(s), essay or personal statement, statement of good standing from prior institution(s). Minimum college GPA of 2.3 required. Lowest grade transferable C. **General Admission Information:** Application fee $25. Priority deadline 3/1. Non-fall registration accepted. Admission may be deferred for a maximum of 12 months.

COSTS AND FINANCIAL AID
Annual tuition $30,090. Room and board $9,560. Required fees $850. Average book and supplies expense $1,136. **Required Forms and Deadlines:** FAFSA. **Notification of Awards:** Applicants will be notified of awards on a rolling basis beginning 3/15. **Types of Aid:** *Need-based scholarships/grants:* College/university scholarship or grant aid from institutional funds; Federal Pell; Private scholarships; SEOG; State scholarships/grants. *Loans:* Direct PLUS loans; Direct Subsidized Stafford Loans; Direct Unsubsidized Stafford Loans. **Student Employment:** Federal Work-Study Program available. Institutional employment available. **Financial Aid Statistics:** 98% needy freshmen, 97% needy undergrads receive need-based scholarship or grant aid. 71% freshmen, 85% undergrads receive non-need-based scholarship or grant aid. 86% freshmen, 86% undergrads receive need-based self-help aid. 0% freshmen, 0% undergrads receive athletic scholarships. 98% freshmen, 94% undergrads receive any aid. **Criteria awarding aid:** *Need-based:* Academics, Leadership. *Non-need-based:* Academics, Alumni affiliation, Art, Leadership, Minority status, Music/drama, State/district residency.

MARIST COLLEGE

3399 North Road, Poughkeepsie, NY 12601-1387
Phone: 845-575-3226 **Financial Aid Phone:** 845-575-3230
E-mail: Admission@Marist.edu **CEEB Code:** 2400
Fax: 845-575-3215 **Website:** http://www.Marist.edu/ **ACT Code:** 2804

This private school was founded in 1929. It has a 210 acre campus.

RATINGS
Admissions Selectivity Rating: 89   **Fire Safety Rating:** 65   **Green Rating:** 84

STUDENTS AND FACULTY
Enrollment: 5,460. **Student Body:** 58% female, 42% male, 48% out-of-state, 3% international (50 countries represented). Asian 3%, African American 4%, Caucasian 74%, Hispanic 12%, Native American <1%, Pacific Islander <1%, Two or more races 3%, Race unknown 1%.
Retention and Graduation: 88% freshmen return for sophomore year. 77% freshmen graduate within 4 years. 84% freshmen graduate within 6 years. 22% grads go on to further study within 1 year. **Faculty:** Student/faculty ratio 16:1. 253 full-time faculty, 81% hold PhDs, 21% are members of minority groups, 53% are women. 0% of classes are taught by teaching assistants.

ACADEMICS
Degrees: Bachelor's; Certificate; Doctoral degree—professional practice; Master's; Post-bachelor's certificate. **Classes:** Most classes have 20–29 students. Most lab/discussion sessions have 10–19 students. **Most popular majors:** Communication and Media Studies; Psychology, General; Business Administration and Management, General. **Special Study Options:** Accelerated program; Cross-registration; Distance learning; Double major; Dual enrollment; English as a Second Language (ESL); Honors program; Independent study; Internships; Liberal arts/career combination; Study abroad; Teacher certification program; Weekend college. **Honors programs:** The Marist College Honors Program brings together talented students with some of the College's best faculty in honors-enriched classes that often coordinate with co-curricular activities such as field trips and lectures. The Program encourages undergraduate research, civic engagement, and ethical leadership. The Program encourages students to move beyond standard curricula and engage in a broader range of ideas and experiences consonant with their interests. **Combined degree programs:** BA/MA. **Disability Services offered:** Note-taking services; Reader services; Tape recorders; Tutors. **Career services:** Alumni network; Alumni services; Career assessment; Career/job search classes; Internships; Regional alumni.

FACILITIES
Housing: Apartments for single students; Coed dorms; Special housing for disabled students; Theme housing; 95% of campus accessible to physically disabled. **Special Academic Facilities/Equipment:** Art gallery, language lab, estuarine and environmental studies lab, public opinion institute, audiovisual/TV center, communications center, high tech classroom, digital state of the art library.

CAMPUS LIFE
Environment: Town. **Activities:** Campus Ministries; Choral groups; Concert band; Dance; Drama/theater; International Student Organization; Jazz band; Literary magazine; Marching band; Model UN; Music ensembles; Musical theater; Pep band; Radio station; Student government; Student newspaper; Symphony orchestra; Television station. 81 registered organizations, 20 honor societies, 5 religious organizations, 3 fraternities, 4 sororities on campus. **Athletics (Intercollegiate):** *Men:* baseball, basketball, crew/rowing, cross-country, diving, football, lacrosse, soccer, swimming, tennis, track/field (outdoor). *Women:* basketball, crew/rowing, cross-country, diving, lacrosse, soccer, softball, swimming, tennis, track/field (outdoor), volleyball, water polo. **On-Campus Highlights:** James A Cannavino Library. **Environmental Initiatives:** Sustainable food purchases.

ADMISSIONS
Freshman Academic Profile: Average high school GPA 3.3. 24% in top 10% of high school class, 51% in top 25% of high school class, 84% in top 50% of high school class. **Test Scores:** SAT Math middle 50% range 580–670. SAT EBRW middle 50% range 580–660. ACT middle 50% range 25–30. **Basis for Candidate Selection:** *Very important factors include:* rigor of secondary school record, academic GPA. *Important factors include:* class rank, application essay, recommendation(s), extracurricular activities, talent/ability, character/personal qualities, geographical residence, state residency, volunteer work. *Other factors include:* standardized test scores, first generation, alumni/ae relation, racial/ethnic status, level of applicant's interest. **Freshman Admission Requirements:** High school diploma is required and GED is accepted. *Academic units required:* 4 English, 3 math, 3 science, 2 science labs, 2 foreign language, 2 social studies, 1 history, 2 academic electives. *Academic units recommended:* 4 math, 4 science, 3 science labs, 3 foreign language. **Freshman Admission Statistics:** 11,260 applied, 49% admitted, 24% enrolled. **Transfer Admission Requirements:** High school transcript, college transcript(s), essay or personal statement. Minimum college GPA of 2.8 required. Lowest grade transferable 2. **General Admission Information:** Application fee $50. Regular application deadline 2/1. Non-fall registration accepted. Admission may be deferred for a maximum of 1 year.

COSTS AND FINANCIAL AID
Annual tuition $44,800. Room and board $18,530. Required fees $730. Average book and supplies expense $1,125. **Required Forms and Deadlines:** FAFSA. **Notification of Awards:** Applicants will be notified of awards on or about 3/31. **Types of Aid:** *Need-based scholarships/grants:* College/university scholarship or grant aid from institutional funds; Federal Pell; Private scholarships; SEOG; State scholarships/grants. *Loans:* Direct PLUS loans; Direct Subsidized Stafford Loans; Direct Unsubsidized Stafford Loans. **Student Employment:** Federal Work-Study Program available. Institutional employment available. **Financial Aid Statistics:** 98% needy freshmen, 96% needy undergrads receive need-based scholarship or grant aid. 14% freshmen, 11% undergrads receive non-need-based scholarship or grant aid. 83% freshmen, 84% undergrads receive need-based self-help aid. 4% freshmen, 4% undergrads receive athletic scholarships. 65% undergrads borrow to pay for school. Average cumulative indebtedness $40,007. **Criteria awarding aid:** *Need-based:* Academics, Alumni affiliation, Art, Leadership, Minority status, Music/drama. *Non-need-based:* Academics, Athletics, Music/drama, State/district residency.

MARLBORO COLLEGE

PO Box A, Marlboro, VT 05344-0300
Phone: 802-258-9236 **Financial Aid Phone:** 802-258-9312
E-mail: admissions@marlboro.edu **CEEB Code:** 3509
Fax: 802-451-7555 **Website:** www.marlboro.edu **ACT Code:** 4304

This private school was founded in 1946. It has a 350 acre campus.

RATINGS
Admissions Selectivity Rating: 75   **Fire Safety Rating:** 82   **Green Rating:** 60*

STUDENTS AND FACULTY
Enrollment: 174. **Student Body:** 53% female, 47% male, 11% out-of-state, 2% international (4 countries represented). Asian 1%, African American 4%, Caucasian 78%, Hispanic 3%, Native American 1%, Pacific Islander 0%, Two or more races 5%, Race unknown 7%.
Retention and Graduation: 85% freshmen return for sophomore year. 24% grads go on to further study within 1 year. **Faculty:** Student/faculty ratio 5:1. 32 full-time faculty, 91% hold PhDs, 6% are members of minority groups, 53% are women. 0% of classes are taught by teaching assistants.

ACADEMICS
Degrees: Bachelor's; Certificate; Master's; Post-bachelor's certificate. **Classes:** Most classes have 10–19 students. **Most popular majors:** English Language and Literature, General; Social Sciences, General; Visual and Performing Arts, Other. **Special Study Options:** Cross-registration; Double major; Dual enrollment; English as a Second Language (ESL); Exchange student program (domestic); Independent study; Internships; Student-designed major; Study abroad. **Combined degree programs:** BA/MA. **Disability Services offered:** Note-taking services; Reader services; Tape recorders; Tutors. **Career services:** Alumni network; Alumni services; Career assessment; Career/job search classes; Internships; Regional alumni.

FACILITIES
Housing: Apartments for married students; Apartments for single students; Coed dorms; Cooperative housing; Special housing for disabled students; Theme housing; Wellness housing; Women's dorms; 80% of campus accessible to physically disabled. **Special Academic Facilities/Equipment:** Serkin Center for the Performing Arts, Drury art gallery, theater, dance studio, observatory, darkroom, art studios, music practice and performance spaces.

CAMPUS LIFE
Environment: Rural. **Activities:** Choral groups; Dance; Drama/theater; Jazz band; Literary magazine; Music ensembles; Radio station; Student government; Student newspaper; Student-run film society. 22 registered organizations on campus. **On-Campus Highlights:** The Rice-Aron Library. **Environmental Initiatives:** Energy audits of all campus buildings in preparation for efficiency upgrades.

ADMISSIONS
Freshman Academic Profile: Average high school GPA 3.1. 0% in top 10% of high school class, 0% in top 25% of high school class, 0% in top 50% of high school class. 66% from public high schools. **Test Scores:** SAT Math middle 50% range 550–630. SAT EBRW middle 50% range 600–710. ACT middle 50% range 24–32. **Basis for Candidate Selection:** *Very important factors include:* application essay, interview. *Important factors include:* rigor of secondary school record, academic GPA, recommendation(s), extracurricular activities, talent/ability, character/personal qualities, level of applicant's interest. *Other factors include:* standardized test scores, volunteer work, work experience. **Freshman Admission Requirements:** High school diploma is required and GED is accepted. *Academic units recommended:* 4 English, 3 math, 3 science, 2 foreign language, 2 social studies, 2 history. **Freshman Admission Statistics:** 120 applied, 97% admitted, 24% enrolled. **Transfer Admission Requirements:** High school transcript, college transcript(s), essay or personal statement, interview. Minimum college GPA of 2.0 required. Lowest grade transferable C-. **General Admission Information:** Application fee $50. Priority deadline 3/1. Non-fall registration accepted. Admission may be deferred for a maximum of 2 semesters.

COSTS AND FINANCIAL AID
Annual tuition $39,870. Room and board $12,385. Required fees $970. Average book and supplies expense $1,200. **Required Forms and Deadlines:** FAFSA. **Notification of Awards:** Applicants will be notified of awards on a rolling basis beginning 3/1. **Types of Aid:** *Need-based scholarships/grants:* College/university scholarship or grant aid from institutional funds; Federal Pell; Private scholarships; SEOG; State scholarships/grants. *Loans:* Direct PLUS loans; Direct Subsidized Stafford Loans; Direct Unsubsidized Stafford Loans. **Student Employment:** Federal Work-Study Program available. Institutional employment available. **Financial Aid Statistics:** 100% needy freshmen, 100% needy undergrads receive need-based scholarship or grant aid. 29% freshmen, 19% undergrads receive non-need-based scholarship or grant aid. 100% freshmen, 94% undergrads receive need-based self-help aid. 0% freshmen, 0% undergrads receive athletic scholarships. 100% freshmen, 98.94% undergrads receive any aid. **Criteria awarding aid:** *Non-need-based:* Academics, Art, Leadership, Music/drama.

MARQUETTE UNIVERSITY

PO Box 1881, Milwaukee, WI 53201-1881
Phone: 414-288-7302 **Financial Aid Phone:** 414-288-7390
E-mail: admissions@Marquette.edu **CEEB Code:** 1448
Fax: 414-288-3764 **Website:** www.marquette.edu **ACT Code:** 4610

This private school, affiliated with the Roman Catholic-Jesuit Church, was founded in 1881. It has a 107 acre campus.

RATINGS
Admissions Selectivity Rating: 80   **Fire Safety Rating:** 98   **Green Rating:** 73

STUDENTS AND FACULTY
Enrollment: 8,352. **Student Body:** 54% female, 46% male, 70% out-of-state, 2% international (43 countries represented). Asian 7%, African American 4%, Caucasian 69%, Hispanic 14%, Native American <1%, Pacific Islander <1%, Two or more races 3%, Race unknown 1%.
Retention and Graduation: 90% freshmen return for sophomore year. 64% freshmen graduate within 4 years. 82% freshmen graduate within 6 years. **Faculty:** Student/faculty ratio 14:1. 696 full-time faculty, 88% hold PhDs, 18% are members of minority groups, 46% are women.

ACADEMICS
Degrees: Bachelor's; Doctoral degree—professional practice; Doctoral degree research/scholarship; Master's; Post-bachelor's certificate; Post-master's certificate. **Classes:** Most classes have 10–19 students. Most lab/discussion sessions have 10–19 students. **Most popular majors:** Mechanical Engineering; Biomedical Sciences, General; Registered Nursing/Registered Nurse. **Special Study Options:** Accelerated program; Cooperative education program; Cross-registration; Distance learning; Double major; English as a Second Language (ESL); External degree program; Honors program; Independent study; Internships; Student-designed major; Study abroad; Teacher certification program; Weekend college. **Honors programs:** Pre-Dental Scholars Program Pre-Law Scholars Program. **Combined degree programs:** BA/DDS; BA/JD; BA/MA. **Disability Services offered:** Note-taking services; Reader services; Tape recorders; Tutors. **Career services:** Alumni network; Alumni services; Career assessment; Career/job search classes; Internships; Regional alumni.

FACILITIES
Housing: Apartments for married students; Apartments for single students; Coed dorms; Cooperative housing; Fraternity/sorority housing; Men's dorms; Special housing for disabled students; Special housing for international students; Theme housing; Wellness housing; Women's dorms; 95% of campus accessible to physically disabled. **Special Academic Facilities/Equipment:** Haggerty Museum of Art, Helfaer Theatre, Al McGuire Center Broadcast Facilities, Dental School/Clinic.

CAMPUS LIFE
Environment: Metropolis. **Activities:** Campus Ministries; Choral groups; Concert band; Dance; Drama/theater; International Student Organization; Jazz band; Literary magazine; Model UN; Music ensembles; Musical theater; Pep band; Radio station; Student government; Student newspaper; Symphony

For more free content, visit PrincetonReview.com

orchestra; Television station; Yearbook. 300 registered organizations, 16 honor societies, 14 religious organizations, 10 fraternities, 13 sororities on campus. **Athletics (Intercollegiate):** *Men:* basketball, cheerleading, cross-country, golf, soccer, tennis, track/field (outdoor), track/field (indoor). *Women:* basketball, cheerleading, cross-country, soccer, tennis, track/field (outdoor), track/field (indoor), volleyball. **On-Campus Highlights:** Saint Joan of Arc Chapel. **Environmental Initiatives:** President Lovell signed the St. Francis Pledge in April 2015. "Taking the St. Francis Pledge commits you or your organization to respond to the moral call for action on climate change. By pledging, you commit to praying, acting, and advocating to solve climate change."

ADMISSIONS

Freshman Academic Profile: 33% in top 10% of high school class, 63% in top 25% of high school class, 94% in top 50% of high school class. 61% from public high schools. **Test Scores:** SAT Math middle 50% range 560–670. SAT EBRW middle 50% range 560–650. ACT middle 50% range 24–29. **Basis for Candidate Selection:** *Very important factors include:* rigor of secondary school record, academic GPA. *Important factors include:* application essay, standardized test scores, extracurricular activities, volunteer work. *Other factors include:* class rank, recommendation(s), talent/ability, character/personal qualities, first generation, alumni/ae relation, racial/ethnic status, work experience. **Freshman Admission Requirements:** High school diploma is required and GED is accepted. *Academic units required:* 4 English, 2 math, 2 science, 2 science labs, 2 social studies, 2 academic electives. *Academic units recommended:* 4 English, 4 math, 4 science, 3 science labs, 2 foreign language, 3 social studies, 2 history, 5 academic electives. **Freshman Admission Statistics:** 15,078 applied, 83% admitted, 16% enrolled. **Transfer Admission Requirements:** High school transcript, college transcript(s), essay or personal statement, Lowest grade transferable C. **General Admission Information:** Priority deadline 12/1. Regular application deadline 12/1. Non-fall registration accepted.

COSTS AND FINANCIAL AID

Annual tuition $44,970. Room and board $13,656. Required fees $696. Average book and supplies expense $816. **Required Forms and Deadlines:** FAFSA. **Notification of Awards:** Applicants will be notified of awards on a rolling basis beginning 1/9. **Types of Aid:** *Need-based scholarships/grants:* College/university scholarship or grant aid from institutional funds; Federal Pell; Private scholarships; SEOG; State scholarships/grants. *Loans:* Direct PLUS loans; Direct Subsidized Stafford Loans; Direct Unsubsidized Stafford Loans. **Student Employment:** Federal Work-Study Program available. Institutional employment available. **Financial Aid Statistics:** 99% needy freshmen, 98% needy undergrads receive need-based scholarship or grant aid. 10% freshmen, 10% undergrads receive non-need-based scholarship or grant aid. 81% freshmen, 82% undergrads receive need-based self-help aid. 2% freshmen, 2% undergrads receive athletic scholarships. 59% undergrads borrow to pay for school. Average cumulative indebtedness $38,173. **Criteria awarding aid:** *Need-based:* Minority status. *Non-need-based:* Academics, Athletics, Leadership, Music/drama.

MARSHALL UNIVERSITY

One John Marshall Drive, Huntington, WV 25755
Phone: 304-696-3160 **Financial Aid Phone:** (304) 696-3162
E-mail: admissions@marshall.edu **CEEB Code:** 5396
Fax: 304-696-3135 **Website:** www.marshall.edu **ACT Code:** 4526

This public school was founded in 1837. It has a 70 acre campus.

RATINGS

Admissions Selectivity Rating: 74   Fire Safety Rating: 67   Green Rating: 60*

STUDENTS AND FACULTY

Enrollment: 8,086. **Student Body:** 57% female, 43% male, 18% out-of-state, 2% international. Asian 1%, African American 6%, Caucasian 84%, Hispanic 2%, Native American <1%, Pacific Islander <1%, Two or more races 3%, Race unknown 1%.
Retention and Graduation: 72% freshmen return for sophomore year. 29% freshmen graduate within 4 years. 49% freshmen graduate within 6 years. 27% grads go on to further study within 1 year. **Faculty:** Student/faculty ratio 18:1. 484 full-time faculty, 80% hold PhDs, 17% are members of minority groups, 47% are women.

ACADEMICS

Degrees: Associate; Bachelor's; Certificate; Doctoral degree—professional practice; Doctoral degree research/scholarship; Master's; Post-bachelor's certificate; Post-master's certificate. **Classes:** Most classes have 20–29 students. **Most popular majors:** Business/Commerce, General; Elementary Education and Teaching; Psychology, General. **Special Study Options:** Accelerated program; Cooperative education program; Cross-registration; Distance learning; Double major; Dual enrollment; English as a Second Language (ESL); Exchange student program (domestic); Honors program; Independent study; Internships; Study abroad; Teacher certification program. **Honors programs:** John Marshall Scholars, Society of Yeager Scholars. **Disability Services offered:** Note-taking services; Reader services; Tutors. **Career services:** Alumni network; Alumni services; Career assessment; Career/job search classes; Internships; Regional alumni.

FACILITIES

Housing: Coed dorms; Special housing for disabled students; Theme housing; Women's dorms; 100% of campus accessible to physically disabled. **Special Academic Facilities/Equipment:** Art gallery, audiovisual center, language lab, superconducting nuclear magnetic resonance spectrometer.

CAMPUS LIFE

Environment: Town. **Activities:** Campus Ministries; Choral groups; Concert band; Dance; Drama/theater; International Student Organization; Jazz band; Literary magazine; Marching band; Model UN; Music ensembles; Musical theater; Opera; Pep band; Radio station; Student government; Student newspaper; Symphony orchestra; Television station. 100 registered organizations, 11 honor societies, 10 religious organizations, 12 fraternities, 7 sororities on campus. **Athletics (Intercollegiate):** *Men:* baseball, basketball, cross-country, football, golf, soccer, track/field (outdoor). *Women:* basketball, cross-country, golf, soccer, softball, swimming, tennis, track/field (outdoor), volleyball. **On-Campus Highlights:** Memorial Student Center Plaza.

ADMISSIONS

Freshman Academic Profile: Average high school GPA 3.5. **Test Scores:** SAT Math middle 50% range 440–550. SAT EBRW middle 50% range 470–580. ACT middle 50% range 19–25. **Basis for Candidate Selection:** *Very important factors include:* academic GPA, standardized test scores. *Other factors include:* rigor of secondary school record, recommendation(s). **Freshman Admission Requirements:** High school diploma is required and GED is accepted. *Academic units recommended:* 4 English, 4 math, 3 science, 3 science labs, 2 foreign language, 3 social studies, 1 visual/performing arts. **Freshman Admission Statistics:** 4,987 applied, 91% admitted, 37% enrolled. **Transfer Admission Requirements:** College transcript(s). **General Admission Information:** Application fee $40. Non-fall registration accepted.

COSTS AND FINANCIAL AID

Annual in-state tuition $7,006. Annual out-of-state tuition $17,492. Room and board $10,450. Required fees $1,122. Average book and supplies expense $1,100. **Required Forms and Deadlines:** FAFSA; State aid form. **Notification of Awards:** Applicants will be notified of awards on a rolling basis beginning 4/1. **Types of Aid:** *Need-based scholarships/grants:* College/university scholarship or grant aid from institutional funds; Federal Nursing Scholarships; Federal Pell; Private scholarships; SEOG; State scholarships/grants. *Loans:* Direct PLUS loans; Direct Subsidized Stafford Loans; Direct Unsubsidized Stafford Loans. **Financial Aid Statistics:** 84% needy freshmen, 78% needy undergrads receive need-based scholarship or grant aid. 66% freshmen, 51% undergrads receive non-need-based scholarship or grant aid. 63% freshmen, 70% undergrads receive need-based self-help aid. 5% freshmen, 5% undergrads receive athletic scholarships. 66% undergrads borrow to pay for school. Average cumulative indebtedness $27,420. **Criteria awarding aid:** *Non-need-based:* Academics, Alumni affiliation, Art, Athletics, Minority status, Music/drama, State/district residency.

MARY BALDWIN UNIVERSITY

Undergraduate Admissions, Staunton, VA 24401
Phone: 540-887-7019 **Financial Aid Phone:** 540-887-7022
E-mail: admit@marybaldwin.edu **CEEB Code:** 5397
Fax: 540-887-7292 **Website:** www.marybaldwin.edu **ACT Code:** 4374

This private school, affiliated with the Presbyterian Church, was founded in 1842. It has a 58.5 acre campus.

RATINGS
Admissions Selectivity Rating: 71   Fire Safety Rating: 88   Green Rating: 60*

STUDENTS AND FACULTY
Enrollment: 1,243. **Student Body:** 88% female, 12% male, 27% out-of-state, 1% international (6 countries represented). Asian 1%, African American 24%, Caucasian 53%, Hispanic 9%, Native American 1%, Pacific Islander <1%, Two or more races 5%, Race unknown 5%.
Retention and Graduation: 75% freshmen return for sophomore year. 43% freshmen graduate within 4 years. 24% grads go on to further study within 1 year. **Faculty:** Student/faculty ratio 10:1. 104 full-time faculty, 87% hold PhDs, 13% are members of minority groups, 74% are women.

ACADEMICS
Degrees: Bachelor's; Certificate; Doctoral degree—professional practice; Master's; Post-bachelor's certificate. **Classes:** Most classes have 10–19 students. Most lab/discussion sessions have 10–19 students. **Most popular majors:** Liberal Arts and Sciences/Liberal Studies; Psychology, General; Business Administration and Management, General. **Special Study Options:** Accelerated program; Distance learning; Double major; Dual enrollment; Exchange student program (domestic); Honors program; Independent study; Internships; Student-designed major; Study abroad; Teacher certification program. **Combined degree programs:** BA/MEng. **Disability Services offered:** Note-taking services; Reader services; Tape recorders; Tutors. **Career services:** Alumni services; Career assessment; Career/job search classes; Internships.

FACILITIES
Housing: Coed dorms; Special housing for international students; Women's dorms; 75% of campus accessible to physically disabled. **Special Academic Facilities/Equipment:** Audiovisual center, TV studio, communications lab, electron microscope, gas chromatoscope, greenhouse.

CAMPUS LIFE
Environment: Town. **Activities:** Choral groups; Dance; Drama/theater; International Student Organization; Literary magazine; Marching band; Music ensembles; Musical theater; Student government; Yearbook. 48 registered organizations, 18 honor societies, 4 religious organizations on campus. **Athletics (Intercollegiate):** *Women:* basketball, field hockey, soccer, softball, swimming, tennis, volleyball. **On-Campus Highlights:** Spencer Center for Civic and Global Engagement.

ADMISSIONS
Freshman Academic Profile: Average high school GPA 3.4. 11% in top 10% of high school class, 34% in top 25% of high school class, 63% in top 50% of high school class. **Test Scores:** SAT Math middle 50% range 460–540. SAT EBRW middle 50% range 490–590. ACT middle 50% range 18–24. **Basis for Candidate Selection:** *Very important factors include:* rigor of secondary school record, academic GPA. *Important factors include:* standardized test scores, character/personal qualities. *Other factors include:* class rank, application essay, recommendation(s), interview, extracurricular activities, talent/ability, first generation, alumni/ae relation, volunteer work, work experience, level of applicant's interest. **Freshman Admission Requirements:** High school diploma is required and GED is accepted. *Academic units required:* 4 English, 3 math, 2 science, 2 science labs, 2 foreign language, 1 social studies, 2 history. *Academic units recommended:* 4 English, 3 math, 2 science, 2 science labs, 2 foreign language, 1 social studies, 2 history, 2 academic electives. **Freshman Admission Statistics:** 6,371 applied, 100% admitted, 6% enrolled. **Transfer Admission Requirements:** High school transcript, college transcript(s), statement of good standing from prior institution(s). Minimum college GPA of 2.0 required. Lowest grade transferable C-. **General Admission Information:** Non-fall registration accepted. Admission may be deferred for a maximum of 1 year.

COSTS AND FINANCIAL AID
Annual tuition $30,690. Room and board $9,410. Required fees $395. Average book and supplies expense $900. **Required Forms and Deadlines:** FAFSA; State aid form. **Notification of Awards:** Applicants will be notified of awards on a rolling basis beginning 3/15. **Types of Aid:** *Need-based scholarships/grants:* College/university scholarship or grant aid from institutional funds; Federal Pell; Private scholarships; SEOG; State scholarships/grants. *Loans:* Direct PLUS loans; Direct Subsidized Stafford Loans; Direct Unsubsidized Stafford Loans. **Student Employment:** Federal Work-Study Program available. Institutional employment available. **Financial Aid Statistics:** 100% needy freshmen, 100% needy undergrads receive need-based scholarship or grant aid. 0% freshmen, 0% undergrads receive non-need-based scholarship or grant aid. 26% freshmen, 66% undergrads receive need-based self-help aid. 0% freshmen, 0% undergrads receive athletic scholarships. 100% freshmen, 81% undergrads receive any aid. 86% undergrads borrow to pay for school. Average cumulative indebtedness $37,097. **Criteria awarding aid:** *Need-based:* Academics, Leadership. *Non-need-based:* Academics, Leadership, State/district residency.

MARYLAND INSTITUTE COLLEGE OF ART

1300 West Mount Royal Avenue, Baltimore, MD 21217
Phone: 410-225-2222 **Financial Aid Phone:** 410-225-2285
E-mail: admissions@mica.edu **CEEB Code:** 5399
Fax: 410-225-2337 **Website:** www.mica.edu **ACT Code:** 1710

This private school was founded in 1826. It has a 16 acre campus.

RATINGS
Admissions Selectivity Rating: 84   Fire Safety Rating: 93   Green Rating: 65

STUDENTS AND FACULTY
Enrollment: 1,701. **Student Body:** 75% female, 25% male, 74% out-of-state, 27% international (62 countries represented). Asian 11%, African American 8%, Caucasian 37%, Hispanic 3%, Native American 0%, Pacific Islander <1%, Two or more races 13%, Race unknown 2%.
Retention and Graduation: 88% freshmen return for sophomore year. 67% freshmen graduate within 4 years. 72% freshmen graduate within 6 years. **Faculty:** Student/faculty ratio 9:1. 157 full-time faculty, 0% hold PhDs, 0% are members of minority groups, 0% are women. 0% of classes are taught by teaching assistants.

ACADEMICS
Degrees: Bachelor's; Master's; Post-bachelor's certificate. **Classes:** Most classes have 20–29 students. **Most popular majors:** Illustration; Graphic Design; Painting. **Special Study Options:** Accelerated program; Cross-registration; Distance learning; Double major; Exchange student program (domestic); Independent study; Internships; Liberal arts/career combination; Study abroad; Teacher certification program. **Combined degree programs:** BA/MA. **Disability Services offered:** Note-taking services; Tape recorders; Tutors. **Career services:** Alumni network; Alumni services; Career assessment; Career/job search classes; Internships; Regional alumni.

FACILITIES
Housing: Apartments for single students; Coed dorms; Special housing for disabled students; Special housing for international students; Theme housing; Wellness housing; 85% of campus accessible to physically disabled. **Special Academic Facilities/Equipment:** There are seven art galleries open to the public year-round featuring work by MICA faculty, students, and nationally/internationally known artists; a nature library; and an extensive slide library containing over 215,000 slides. **Campus Network:** 20% of classrooms, 100% of student union, 100% of libraries, 100% of dining areas, 40% of common outdoor areas have wireless network access.

CAMPUS LIFE
Environment: Metropolis. **Activities:** Campus Ministries; Choral groups; Dance; Drama/theater; International Student Organization; Literary magazine; Music ensembles; Musical theater; Radio station; Student government; Student-run film society. 63 registered organizations, 6 religious organizations on campus. **On-Campus Highlights:** Founders Green, our new dormitory. **Environmental Initiatives:** Single-Stream recycling of recyclable waste.

ADMISSIONS
Freshman Academic Profile: Average high school GPA 3.5. 70% from public high schools. **Test Scores:** SAT Math middle 50% range 530–660. SAT EBRW middle 50% range 500–630. ACT middle 50% range 22–29. **Basis for Candidate Selection:** *Very important factors include:* rigor of secondary school record, academic GPA, talent/ability, level of applicant's interest. *Important factors include:* class rank, application essay, standardized test scores, interview,

extracurricular activities. *Other factors include:* recommendation(s), character/personal qualities, alumni/ae relation, racial/ethnic status, volunteer work. **Freshman Admission Requirements:** High school diploma is required and GED is accepted. *Academic units required:* 4 English, 2 math, 2 science, 1 science lab, 4 social studies, 3 history, 6 academic electives, 2 unit from above areas or other academic areas. *Academic units recommended:* 4 English, 3 math, 3 science, 4 social studies, 4 history. **Freshman Admission Statistics:** 3,702 applied, 64% admitted, 18% enrolled. **Transfer Admission Requirements:** High school transcript, college transcript(s), essay or personal statement. Minimum college GPA of 2.8 required. Lowest grade transferable C. **General Admission Information:** Application fee $70. Regular application deadline 2/1. Non-fall registration accepted. Admission may be deferred for a maximum of 1 year.

COSTS AND FINANCIAL AID
Annual tuition $48,510. Room and board $13,720. Required fees $1,820. Average book and supplies expense $1,500. **Required Forms and Deadlines:** FAFSA; Institution's own financial aid form. **Notification of Awards:** Applicants will be notified of awards on or about 4/1. **Types of Aid:** *Need-based scholarships/grants:* College/university scholarship or grant aid from institutional funds; Federal Pell; Private scholarships; SEOG; State scholarships/grants. *Loans:* Direct PLUS loans; Direct Subsidized Stafford Loans; Direct Unsubsidized Stafford Loans. **Student Employment:** Federal Work-Study Program available. Institutional employment available. **Criteria awarding aid:** *Need-based:* Academics, Art. *Non-need-based:* Academics, Art.

MARYMOUNT CALIFORNIA UNIVERSITY

Marymount California University, Rancho Palos Verdes, CA 90275
Phone: 310-377-5501 **Financial Aid Phone:** (310) 303-7311
E-mail: admissions@marymountcalifornia.edu **CEEB Code:** 4515
Fax: 310-265-0962 **Website:** http://www.marymountcalifornia.edu/ **ACT Code:** 0316

This private school, affiliated with the Roman Catholic Church, was founded in 1932. It has a 22 acre campus.

RATINGS
Admissions Selectivity Rating: 82   **Fire Safety Rating:** 93   **Green Rating:** 60*

STUDENTS AND FACULTY
Enrollment: 1,034. **Student Body:** 55% female, 45% male, 5% out-of-state, 14% international (42 countries represented). Asian 5%, African American 8%, Caucasian 25%, Hispanic 36%, Native American <1%, Pacific Islander 1%, Two or more races 4%, Race unknown 6%.
Retention and Graduation: 68% freshmen return for sophomore year.
Faculty: Student/faculty ratio 17:1. 28 full-time faculty, 68% hold PhDs, 18% are members of minority groups, 43% are women. 0% of classes are taught by teaching assistants.

ACADEMICS
Degrees: Associate; Bachelor's; Master's. **Classes:** Most classes have 10–19 students. **Most popular majors:** Liberal Arts and Sciences, General Studies and Humanities, Other; Business, Management, Marketing, and Related Support Services, Other; Psychology, Other. **Special Study Options:** Distance learning; Double major; Dual enrollment; English as a Second Language (ESL); Honors program; Internships; Liberal arts/career combination; Study abroad. **Honors programs:** Marymount Honors Program; Phi Theta Kappa; Delta Epsilon Sigma. **Combined degree programs:** BA/MA. **Disability Services offered:** Note-taking services; Reader services; Tape recorders; Tutors. **Career services:** Alumni network; Alumni services; Career assessment; Internships; Regional alumni.

FACILITIES
Housing: Apartments for single students; Coed dorms; Special housing for disabled students; 100% of campus accessible to physically disabled.

CAMPUS LIFE
Environment: Town. **Activities:** Campus Ministries; Choral groups; Dance; Drama/theater; International Student Organization; Jazz band; Literary magazine; Musical theater; Student government; Student-run film society. 28 registered organizations, 3 honor societies, 3 religious organizations on campus. **Athletics (Intercollegiate):** *Men:* soccer. *Women:* soccer.

ADMISSIONS
Freshman Academic Profile: Average high school GPA 3.0. 30% from public high schools. **Test Scores:** SAT Math middle 50% range 390–520. SAT

EBRW middle 50% range 410–520. ACT middle 50% range 16–22. **Basis for Candidate Selection:** *Very important factors include:* rigor of secondary school record, academic GPA. *Other factors include:* class rank, application essay, standardized test scores, recommendation(s), interview, extracurricular activities, talent/ability, character/personal qualities, alumni/ae relation, volunteer work, level of applicant's interest. **Freshman Admission Requirements:** High school diploma is required and GED is accepted. *Academic units recommended:* 4 English, 3 math, 2 science, 2 foreign language, 2 social studies, 2 history, 1 academic elective. **Freshman Admission Statistics:** 1,612 applied, 59% admitted, 30% enrolled. **Transfer Admission Requirements:** High school transcript, college transcript(s). Lowest grade transferable C-. **General Admission Information:** Application fee $50. Priority deadline 3/1. Non-fall registration accepted. Admission may be deferred for a maximum of 1 year.

COSTS AND FINANCIAL AID
Required Forms and Deadlines: FAFSA. **Notification of Awards:** Applicants will be notified of awards on or about 3/1. **Types of Aid:** *Need-based scholarships/grants:* College/university scholarship or grant aid from institutional funds; Federal Pell; Private scholarships; SEOG; State scholarships/grants. *Loans:* Direct PLUS loans; Direct Subsidized Stafford Loans; Direct Unsubsidized Stafford Loans. **Student Employment:** Federal Work-Study Program available. Institutional employment available. **Financial Aid Statistics:** 100% needy freshmen, 100% needy undergrads receive need-based scholarship or grant aid. 86% freshmen, 88% undergrads receive non-need-based scholarship or grant aid. 1% freshmen, 6% undergrads receive need-based self-help aid. 5% freshmen, 5% undergrads receive athletic scholarships. 84% freshmen, 74% undergrads receive any aid. **Criteria awarding aid:** *Need-based:* Academics. *Non-need-based:* Academics, Art, Athletics.

MARYMOUNT MANHATTAN COLLEGE

221 East 71 Street, New York, NY 10021
Phone: 212-517-0430 **Financial Aid Phone:** 212-517-0500
E-mail: admissions@mmm.edu **CEEB Code:** 2405
Fax: 212-517-0448 **Website:** www.mmm.edu **ACT Code:** 2810

This private school was founded in 1936. It has a 1 acre campus.

RATINGS
Admissions Selectivity Rating: 74   **Fire Safety Rating:** 60*   **Green Rating:** 60*

STUDENTS AND FACULTY
Enrollment: 1,875. **Student Body:** 77% female, 23% male, 59% out-of-state, 5% international (66 countries represented). Asian 4%, African American 10%, Caucasian 57%, Hispanic 18%, Native American 1%, Pacific Islander <1%, Two or more races 1%, Race unknown 5%.
Retention and Graduation: 74% freshmen return for sophomore year.
Faculty: Student/faculty ratio 11:1. 94 full-time faculty, 95% hold PhDs, 10% are members of minority groups, 62% are women. 0% of classes are taught by teaching assistants.

ACADEMICS
Degrees: Associate; Bachelor's. **Classes:** Most classes have 10–19 students. Most lab/discussion sessions have 10–19 students. **Most popular majors:** Visual and Performing Arts, General; Communication and Media Studies, Other; Psychology, General. **Special Study Options:** Accelerated program; Cross-registration; Distance learning; Double major; Exchange student program (domestic); Honors program; Independent study; Internships; Liberal arts/career combination; Student-designed major; Study abroad. **Honors programs:** The College Honors Program described in detail at http://www.mmm.edu/academics/college-honors-program.php. **Disability Services offered:** Note-taking services; Reader services; Tape recorders; Tutors. **Career services:** Alumni network; Alumni services; Career assessment; Career/job search classes; Internships; Regional alumni.

FACILITIES
Housing: Coed dorms. **Special Academic Facilities/Equipment:** Gallery, communications and learning center, theatre, media center, college skills center, mathematics lab, Samuel Freeman science center, Comm Arts multimedia suite.

CAMPUS LIFE
Environment: Metropolis. **Activities:** Campus Ministries; Choral groups; Dance; Drama/theater; International Student Organization; Musical theater; Radio station; Student government; Student newspaper; Yearbook. 3 religious

organizations on campus. **On-Campus Highlights:** Theresa Lang Theatre. **Environmental Initiatives:** Purchase of renewable energy.

ADMISSIONS

Freshman Academic Profile: Average high school GPA 3.3. **Test Scores:** SAT Math middle 50% range 440–550. SAT EBRW middle 50% range 470–590. ACT middle 50% range 20–26. **Basis for Candidate Selection:** *Very important factors include:* rigor of secondary school record, academic GPA, standardized test scores. *Important factors include:* application essay, recommendation(s), talent/ability, character/personal qualities. *Other factors include:* interview, extracurricular activities, first generation, alumni/ae relation, geographical residence, state residency, volunteer work, work experience. **Freshman Admission Requirements:** High school diploma is required and GED is accepted. *Academic units required:* 4 English, 3 math, 3 science, 3 social studies, 4 academic electives. *Academic units recommended:* 2 science labs, 2 foreign language. **Freshman Admission Statistics:** 4,459 applied, 84% admitted, 14% enrolled. **Transfer Admission Requirements:** High school transcript, college transcript(s), essay or personal statement, statement of good standing from prior institution(s). Minimum college GPA of 2.5 required. Lowest grade transferable C-. **General Admission Information:** Application fee $60. Priority deadline 8/1. Non-fall registration accepted. Admission may be deferred for a maximum of FA-SP only.

COSTS AND FINANCIAL AID

Annual tuition $28,870. Room and board $15,990. Required fees $1,420. Average book and supplies expense $1,000. **Required Forms and Deadlines:** FAFSA; State aid form. **Notification of Awards:** Applicants will be notified of awards on a rolling basis beginning 3/15. **Types of Aid:** *Need-based scholarships/ grants:* College/university scholarship or grant aid from institutional funds; Federal Pell; Private scholarships; SEOG; State scholarships/grants. *Loans:* Direct PLUS loans; Direct Subsidized Stafford Loans; Direct Unsubsidized Stafford Loans. **Student Employment:** Federal Work-Study Program available. Institutional employment available. **Financial Aid Statistics:** 99% needy freshmen, 99% needy undergrads receive need-based scholarship or grant aid. 0% freshmen, 0% undergrads receive non-need-based scholarship or grant aid. 72% freshmen, 79% undergrads receive need-based self-help aid. 0% freshmen, 0% undergrads receive athletic scholarships. 66% undergrads borrow to pay for school. Average cumulative indebtedness $30,159. **Criteria awarding aid:** *Need-based:* Academics. *Non-need-based:* Academics, Art, Leadership, Music/ drama, State/district residency.

MARYMOUNT UNIVERSITY

2807 North Glebe Road, Arlington, VA 22207
Phone: 703-284-1500 **Financial Aid Phone:** 703-284-1530
E-mail: admissions@marymount.edu **CEEB Code:** 5405
Fax: 703-522-0349 **Website:** http://www.marymount.edu **ACT Code:** 4378

This private school, affiliated with the Roman Catholic Church, was founded in 1950. It has a 21 acre campus.

RATINGS

Admissions Selectivity Rating: 75   **Fire Safety Rating:** 86   **Green Rating:** 60*

STUDENTS AND FACULTY

Enrollment: 2,199. **Student Body:** 75% female, 25% male, 42% out-of-state, 6% international (70 countries represented). Asian 8%, African American 15%, Caucasian 46%, Hispanic 12%, Native American 1%, Pacific Islander 0%, Two or more races 0%, Race unknown 13%.
Retention and Graduation: 71% freshmen return for sophomore year.
Faculty: Student/faculty ratio 14:1. 138 full-time faculty, 89% hold PhDs, 5% are members of minority groups, 74% are women. 0% of classes are taught by teaching assistants.

ACADEMICS

Degrees: Bachelor's; Certificate; Master's; Post-bachelor's certificate; Post-master's certificate. **Classes:** Most classes have 10–19 students. **Most popular majors:** Biology/Biological Sciences, General; Fashion/Apparel Design; Business Administration and Management, General. **Special Study Options:** Accelerated program; Cross-registration; Distance learning; Double major; English as a Second Language (ESL); Honors program; Independent study; Internships; Student-designed major; Study abroad; Teacher certification program. **Honors programs:** The Honors Program at Marymount University. **Disability Services offered:** Note-taking services; Reader services; Tape recorders; Tutors. **Career services:** Alumni network; Career/job search classes; Internships.

FACILITIES

Housing: Coed dorms; Men's dorms; Women's dorms; 75% of campus accessible to physically disabled. **Special Academic Facilities/Equipment:** Art gallery, learning resource center, audiovisual center, studio, and computer labs **Campus Network:** 85% of classrooms, 95% of dorms, 100% of libraries, 100% of dining areas, 0% of common outdoor areas have wireless network access.

CAMPUS LIFE

Environment: City. **Activities:** Campus Ministries; Choral groups; Dance; Drama/theater; International Student Organization; Literary magazine; Student government; Student newspaper; Yearbook. 42 registered organizations, 11 honor societies, 2 religious organizations on campus. **Athletics (Intercollegiate):** *Men:* basketball, cross-country, golf, lacrosse, soccer, swimming. *Women:* basketball, cross-country, lacrosse, soccer, swimming, volleyball. **On-Campus Highlights:** Student Center. **Environmental Initiatives:** Recycling program.

ADMISSIONS

Freshman Academic Profile: Average high school GPA 3.1. 15% in top 10% of high school class, 41% in top 25% of high school class, 81% in top 50% of high school class. 68% from public high schools. **Test Scores:** SAT Math middle 50% range 450–550. SAT EBRW middle 50% range 450–560. ACT middle 50% range 18–24. **Basis for Candidate Selection:** *Very important factors include:* rigor of secondary school record, academic GPA, standardized test scores. *Important factors include:* class rank, recommendation(s), interview, talent/ability. *Other factors include:* application essay, extracurricular activities, character/personal qualities, first generation, alumni/ae relation, volunteer work, work experience, level of applicant's interest. **Freshman Admission Requirements:** High school diploma is required and GED is accepted. *Academic units recommended:* 4 English, 3 math, 2 science, 3 foreign language, 3 social studies. **Freshman Admission Statistics:** 1,904 applied, 81% admitted, 26% enrolled. **Transfer Admission Requirements:** College transcript(s), statement of good standing from prior institution(s). Minimum college GPA of 2.0 required. Lowest grade transferable C. **General Admission Information:** Application fee $40. Priority deadline 5/1. Non-fall registration accepted. Admission may be deferred for a maximum of 1 year.

COSTS AND FINANCIAL AID

Annual tuition $23,700. Room and board $8,705. Required fees $220. Average book and supplies expense $800. **Required Forms and Deadlines:** FAFSA. **Notification of Awards:** Applicants will be notified of awards on a rolling basis beginning 3/15. **Types of Aid:** *Need-based scholarships/grants:* College/ university scholarship or grant aid from institutional funds; Federal Pell; Private scholarships; SEOG; State scholarships/grants. *Loans:* Direct Subsidized Stafford Loans; Direct Unsubsidized Stafford Loans. **Student Employment:** Federal Work-Study Program available. Institutional employment available. **Financial Aid Statistics:** 83% needy freshmen, 74% needy undergrads receive need-based scholarship or grant aid. 79% freshmen, 73% undergrads receive non-need-based scholarship or grant aid. 77% freshmen, 82% undergrads receive need-based self-help aid. 0% freshmen, 0% undergrads receive athletic scholarships. 92% freshmen, 84% undergrads receive any aid. **Criteria awarding aid:** *Need-based:* Academics, Religious affiliation. *Non-need-based:* Academics, Alumni affiliation, Leadership, State/district residency.

MARYVILLE COLLEGE

502 East Lamar Alexander Parkway, Maryville, TN 37804-5907
Phone: 865-981-8092 **Financial Aid Phone:** 865-981-8100
E-mail: admissions@maryvillecollege.edu **CEEB Code:** 1454
Fax: 865-981-8005 **Website:** www.maryvillecollege.edu **ACT Code:** 3988

This private school, affiliated with the Presbyterian Church, was founded in 1819. It has a 370 acre campus.

RATINGS

Admissions Selectivity Rating: 79   **Fire Safety Rating:** 92   **Green Rating:** 60*

STUDENTS AND FACULTY

Enrollment: 1,114. **Student Body:** 55% female, 45% male, 24% out-of-state, 4% international (20 countries represented). Asian 1%, African American 5%, Caucasian 86%, Hispanic 2%, Native American <1%, Race unknown 2%.
Retention and Graduation: 67% freshmen return for sophomore year. 28% grads go on to further study within 1 year. **Faculty:** Student/faculty ratio 12:1.

79 full-time faculty, 76% hold PhDs, 4% are members of minority groups, 54% are women. 0% of classes are taught by teaching assistants.

ACADEMICS

Degrees: Bachelor's. **Classes:** Most classes have 10–19 students. Most lab/discussion sessions have 10–19 students. **Most popular majors:** Education, General; Business/Commerce, General; Biology/Biological Sciences, General. **Special Study Options:** Double major; English as a Second Language (ESL); Honors program; Independent study; Internships; Liberal arts/career combination; Student-designed major; Study abroad; Teacher certification program. **Honors programs:** Presidential and Deans scholars participate in honors courses and honors tutorial practicum. Most courses may be taken with "honors" status. **Disability Services offered:** Note-taking services; Reader services; Tape recorders; Tutors. **Career services:** Alumni network; Alumni services; Career assessment; Career/job search classes; Internships; Regional alumni.

FACILITIES

Housing: Apartments for single students; Coed dorms; Men's dorms; Special housing for disabled students; Women's dorms; 90% of campus accessible to physically disabled. **Special Academic Facilities/Equipment:** Art gallery, theatre, greenhouse, College Woods. **Campus Network:** 100% of classrooms, 100% of dorms, 100% of student union, 100% of libraries, 100% of dining areas, 70% of common outdoor areas have wireless network access.

CAMPUS LIFE

Environment: Town. **Activities:** Campus Ministries; Choral groups; Concert band; Dance; Drama/theater; Jazz band; Literary magazine; Music ensembles; Musical theater; Student government; Student newspaper; Symphony orchestra; Yearbook. 63 registered organizations, 15 honor societies, 5 religious organizations on campus. **Athletics (Intercollegiate):** *Men:* baseball, basketball, cross-country, equestrian sports, football, soccer, tennis. *Women:* basketball, cross-country, equestrian sports, soccer, softball, tennis, volleyball. **On-Campus Highlights:** Isaacs Student Center. **Environmental Initiatives:** Steam plant boiler is fueled by recycled wood products.

ADMISSIONS

Freshman Academic Profile: Average high school GPA 3.6. 34% in top 10% of high school class, 65% in top 25% of high school class, 89% in top 50% of high school class. 91% from public high schools. **Test Scores:** SAT Math middle 50% range 480–610. SAT EBRW middle 50% range 470–630. ACT middle 50% range 21–28. **Basis for Candidate Selection:** *Very important factors include:* rigor of secondary school record, class rank, standardized test scores. *Important factors include:* academic GPA, recommendation(s), interview, extracurricular activities. *Other factors include:* application essay, talent/ability, character/personal qualities, first generation, alumni/ae relation, volunteer work, level of applicant's interest. **Freshman Admission Requirements:** High school diploma is required and GED is accepted. *Academic units required:* 4 English, 3 math, 2 science, 1 science lab, 2 foreign language, 2 social studies, 1 academic elective. *Academic units recommended:* 1 history. **Freshman Admission Statistics:** 1,291 applied, 78% admitted, 30% enrolled. **Transfer Admission Requirements:** College transcript(s), statement of good standing from prior institution(s). Minimum college GPA of 2.0 required. Lowest grade transferable C. **General Admission Information:** Priority deadline 1/15. Non-fall registration accepted. Admission may be deferred for a maximum of 1 year.

COSTS AND FINANCIAL AID

Annual tuition $26,272. Room and board $8,240. Required fees $675. Average book and supplies expense $880. **Required Forms and Deadlines:** FAFSA. **Types of Aid:** *Need-based scholarships/grants:* College/university scholarship or grant aid from institutional funds; Federal Pell; Private scholarships; SEOG; State scholarships/grants. *Loans:* Direct PLUS loans; Direct Subsidized Stafford Loans; Direct Unsubsidized Stafford Loans. **Student Employment:** Federal Work-Study Program available. **Financial Aid Statistics:** 75% needy freshmen, 98% needy undergrads receive need-based scholarship or grant aid. 31% freshmen, 25% undergrads receive non-need-based scholarship or grant aid. 78% freshmen, 61% undergrads receive need-based self-help aid. 0% freshmen, 0% undergrads receive athletic scholarships. 100% freshmen, 98% undergrads receive any aid. **Criteria awarding aid:** *Need-based:* Academics, Art, Leadership, Minority status, Music/drama, Religious affiliation. *Non-need-based:* Academics, Art, Leadership, Minority status, Music/drama, Religious affiliation, State/district residency.

MARYVILLE UNIVERSITY OF SAINT LOUIS

650 Maryville University Drive, St. Louis, MO 63141-7299
Phone: 314-529-9350 **Financial Aid Phone:** 314-529-9360
E-mail: admissions@maryville.edu **CEEB Code:** 6399
Fax: 314-529-9927 **Website:** www.maryville.edu **ACT Code:** 2326

This private school was founded in 1872. It has a 130 acre campus.

RATINGS

Admissions Selectivity Rating: 77   **Fire Safety Rating:** 93   **Green Rating:** 67

STUDENTS AND FACULTY

Enrollment: 4,373. **Student Body:** 66% female, 34% male, 38% out-of-state, 4% international (42 countries represented). Asian 3%, African American 12%, Caucasian 68%, Hispanic 6%, Native American <1%, Pacific Islander 0%, Two or more races 4%, Race unknown 4%.
Retention and Graduation: 83% freshmen return for sophomore year. 58% freshmen graduate within 4 years. 71% freshmen graduate within 6 years. **Faculty:** Student/faculty ratio 14:1. 166 full-time faculty, 79% hold PhDs, 18% are members of minority groups, 61% are women. 0% of classes are taught by teaching assistants.

ACADEMICS

Degrees: Bachelor's; Certificate; Doctoral degree research/scholarship; Master's; Post-bachelor's certificate; Post-master's certificate. **Classes:** Most classes have 10–19 students. Most lab/discussion sessions have 10–19 students. **Most popular majors:** Business/Commerce, General; Physical Therapy/Therapist; Registered Nursing/Registered Nurse. **Special Study Options:** Accelerated program; Cooperative education program; Cross-registration; Distance learning; Double major; Dual enrollment; Exchange student program (domestic); External degree program; Honors program; Independent study; Internships; Liberal arts/career combination; Student-designed major; Study abroad; Teacher certification program; Weekend college. **Honors programs:** Bascom Honors Program. **Disability Services offered:** Note-taking services; Reader services; Tape recorders; Tutors. **Career services:** Alumni services; Career assessment; Career/job search classes; Internships.

FACILITIES

Housing: Apartments for single students; Coed dorms; Wellness housing; 100% of campus accessible to physically disabled. **Special Academic Facilities/Equipment:** University Center, art galleries, auditorium, chapel, observatory, teaching lab, clinical labs, art and design labs, Apple Distinguished University.

CAMPUS LIFE

Environment: Metropolis. **Activities:** Campus Ministries; Choral groups; Dance; Drama/theater; International Student Organization; Literary magazine; Music ensembles; Pep band; Student government; Student newspaper; Symphony orchestra. 100 registered organizations, 3 honor societies, 8 religious organizations on campus. **Athletics (Intercollegiate):** *Men:* baseball, basketball, cheerleading, cross-country, golf, soccer, tennis. *Women:* basketball, cheerleading, cross-country, golf, soccer, softball, tennis, volleyball. **On-Campus Highlights:** Gander Dining Hall.

ADMISSIONS

Freshman Academic Profile: Average high school GPA 3.6. 25% in top 10% of high school class, 55% in top 25% of high school class, 85% in top 50% of high school class. 77% from public high schools. **Test Scores:** SAT Math middle 50% range 530–620. SAT EBRW middle 50% range 510–630. ACT middle 50% range 20–25. **Basis for Candidate Selection:** *Very important factors include:* academic GPA, standardized test scores. *Important factors include:* rigor of secondary school record, extracurricular activities. *Other factors include:* class rank, application essay, recommendation(s), interview, talent/ability, character/personal qualities. **Freshman Admission Requirements:** High school diploma is required and GED is accepted. *Academic units required:* 4 English, 3 math, 2 science, 2 social studies, 3 unit from above areas or other academic areas. **Freshman Admission Statistics:** 2,897 applied, 83% admitted, 28% enrolled. **Transfer Admission Requirements:** College transcript(s). Minimum college GPA of 2.0 required. Lowest grade transferable C-. **General Admission Information:** Priority deadline 12/15. Regular application deadline 8/15. Non-fall registration accepted. Admission may be deferred for a maximum of 1 year.

COSTS AND FINANCIAL AID

Annual tuition $26,070. Room and board $10,088. Required fees $2,400. **Required Forms and Deadlines:** FAFSA. **Notification of Awards:** Applicants will be notified of awards on or about 12/1. **Types of Aid:** *Need-based scholarships/grants:* College/university scholarship or grant aid from institutional funds; Federal Pell; Private scholarships; SEOG; State scholarships/grants; United Negro College Fund. *Loans:* Direct PLUS loans; Direct Subsidized Stafford Loans; Direct Unsubsidized Stafford Loans. **Student Employment:** Federal Work-Study Program available. Institutional employment available. **Financial Aid Statistics:** 100% needy freshmen, 100% needy undergrads receive need-based scholarship or grant aid. 17% freshmen, 13% undergrads receive non-need-based scholarship or grant aid. 72% freshmen, 64% undergrads receive need-based self-help aid. 4% freshmen, 5% undergrads receive athletic scholarships. 78% freshmen, 74% undergrads receive any aid. 70% undergrads borrow to pay for school. Average cumulative indebtedness $30,657. **Criteria awarding aid:** *Need-based:* Academics, Art, Minority status, Music/drama. *Non-need-based:* Academics, Art, Athletics, Job skills, Leadership, Minority status, Music/drama, State/district residency.

MARYWOOD UNIVERSITY

Office of University Admissions, Scranton, PA 18509
Phone: 570-348-6234 **Financial Aid Phone:** 866-279-9663
E-mail: yourfuture@marywood.edu **CEEB Code:** 2407
Fax: 570-961-4763 **Website:** www.marywood.edu **ACT Code:** 3626

This private school, affiliated with the Roman Catholic Church, was founded in 1915. It has a 122.7 acre campus.

RATINGS
Admissions Selectivity Rating: 78   **Fire Safety Rating:** 95   **Green Rating:** 60*

STUDENTS AND FACULTY
Enrollment: 1,817. **Student Body:** 68% female, 32% male, 30% out-of-state, 1% international (8 countries represented). Asian 2%, African American 2%, Caucasian 79%, Hispanic 6%, Native American <1%, Pacific Islander <1%, Two or more races 2%, Race unknown 8%.
Retention and Graduation: 83% freshmen return for sophomore year. 40% grads go on to further study within 1 year. 6% grads pursue arts and sciences degrees. <1% grads pursue law degrees. 1% grads pursue business degrees. 1% grads pursue medical degrees. **Faculty:** Student/faculty ratio 11:1. 160 full-time faculty, 91% hold PhDs, 14% are members of minority groups, 56% are women. 0% of classes are taught by teaching assistants.

ACADEMICS
Degrees: Bachelor's; Certificate; Doctoral degree—professional practice; Doctoral degree research/scholarship; Master's; Post-bachelor's certificate; Post-master's certificate. **Classes:** Most classes have 10–19 students. Most lab/discussion sessions have 10–19 students. **Most popular majors:** Audiology/Audiologist and Speech-Language Pathology/Pathologist; Registered Nursing/Registered Nurse; Psychology, General. **Special Study Options:** Cross-registration; Distance learning; Double major; Dual enrollment; English as a Second Language (ESL); Honors program; Independent study; Internships; Student-designed major; Study abroad; Teacher certification program; Weekend college. **Honors programs:** Open Honors program focused on both scholarship and research. **Combined degree programs:** BA/MA. **Disability Services offered:** Note-taking services; Reader services; Tape recorders; Tutors. **Career services:** Alumni network; Alumni services; Career assessment; Career/job search classes; Internships; Regional alumni.

FACILITIES
Housing: Apartments for single students; Coed dorms; Special housing for disabled students; Women's dorms; 98% of campus accessible to physically disabled. **Special Academic Facilities/Equipment:** Academic excellence center; student counseling center; human physiology lab; human development (counseling, psychology) laboratories; biotechnology lab; communication sciences and disorders clinic; nutrition and dietetics lab; assistive technology center; outpatient mental health clinic; multiple "smart" classrooms; multiple computer labs; full-service library; television studio and editing suites; radio station and studio; 60,000-square-foot studio art center (including ceramic, painting, drawing/foundation, sculpture, glass, metal, clay, wood, photography, fabric, jewelry, and printmaking studios); 15,000-square foot visual arts center (including graphic design and interior architecture computer labs, two art exhibit galleries; Maslow Collection of Contemporary Art; and Maslow Study Gallery); 1,100-seat performance theater; black box theater; 1,500-seat athletics arena (2,500 seats for events); 5,000-square-foot fitness center; NCAA

regulation pool and Aquatics Center; additional basketball courts; exterior tennis courts; 1,200-square foot dance/aerobic studio; hydro-therapy room, separate team and student locker facilities; Center for Architectural Studies studios, arboretum.

CAMPUS LIFE
Environment: Town. **Activities:** Campus Ministries; Choral groups; Concert band; Dance; Drama/theater; International Student Organization; Jazz band; Literary magazine; Music ensembles; Musical theater; Opera; Radio station; Student government; Student newspaper; Symphony orchestra; Television station. 60 registered organizations, 31 honor societies, 4 religious organizations, 2 sororities on campus. **Athletics (Intercollegiate):** *Men:* baseball, basketball, cross-country, diving, lacrosse, soccer, swimming, tennis. *Women:* basketball, cross-country, diving, field hockey, lacrosse, soccer, softball, swimming, tennis, volleyball. **On-Campus Highlights:** Center for Athletics and Wellness. **Environmental Initiatives:** Purchase of renewable fuel sources; wind and solar power $28,800 annually.

ADMISSIONS
Freshman Academic Profile: Average high school GPA 3.5. 13% in top 10% of high school class, 48% in top 25% of high school class, 80% in top 50% of high school class. 89% from public high schools. **Test Scores:** SAT Math middle 50% range 470–560. SAT EBRW middle 50% range 460–560. **Basis for Candidate Selection:** *Very important factors include:* rigor of secondary school record, class rank, academic GPA, standardized test scores, interview, character/personal qualities. *Important factors include:* application essay, recommendation(s), extracurricular activities, talent/ability. *Other factors include:* volunteer work, work experience, level of applicant's interest. **Freshman Admission Requirements:** High school diploma is required and GED is accepted. *Academic units required:* 4 English, 2 math, 1 science, 1 science lab, 3 social studies, 6 academic electives. **Freshman Admission Statistics:** 2,273 applied, 71% admitted, 23% enrolled. **Transfer Admission Requirements:** High school transcript, college transcript(s). Minimum college GPA of 2.25 required. Lowest grade transferable C. **General Admission Information:** Application fee $35. Non-fall registration accepted. Admission may be deferred for a maximum of 1 year.

COSTS AND FINANCIAL AID
Annual tuition $30,942. Room and board $13,900. Required fees $1,750. Average book and supplies expense $1,000. **Required Forms and Deadlines:** FAFSA; State aid form. **Notification of Awards:** Applicants will be notified of awards on a rolling basis beginning 3/15. **Types of Aid:** *Need-based scholarships/grants:* College/university scholarship or grant aid from institutional funds; Federal Pell; Private scholarships; SEOG; State scholarships/grants. *Loans:* Direct PLUS loans; Direct Subsidized Stafford Loans; Direct Unsubsidized Stafford Loans. **Student Employment:** Federal Work-Study Program available. **Financial Aid Statistics:** 100% needy freshmen, 99% needy undergrads receive need-based scholarship or grant aid. 16% freshmen, 12% undergrads receive non-need-based scholarship or grant aid. 79% freshmen, 83% undergrads receive need-based self-help aid. 0% freshmen, 0% undergrads receive athletic scholarships. 99% freshmen, 99% undergrads receive any aid. 83% undergrads borrow to pay for school. Average cumulative indebtedness $29,064. **Criteria awarding aid:** *Need-based:* Academics, Art, Leadership, Music/drama. *Non-need-based:* Academics, Alumni affiliation, Art, Leadership, Music/drama.

MASSACHUSETTS COLLEGE OF ART AND DESIGN

621 Huntington Avenue, Boston, MA 02115
Phone: 617-879-7222 **Financial Aid Phone:** 617.879.7850
E-mail: admissions@massart.edu **CEEB Code:** 3516
Fax: 617-879-7250 **ACT Code:** 1846

This public school was founded in 1873. It has a 5 acre campus.

RATINGS
Admissions Selectivity Rating: 66   **Fire Safety Rating:** 90   **Green Rating:** 60*

STUDENTS AND FACULTY
Enrollment: 1,813. **Student Body:** 71% female, 29% male, 32% out-of-state, 4% international. Asian 9%, African American 5%, Caucasian 65%, Hispanic 11%, Native American <1%, Pacific Islander <1%, Two or more races 2%, Race unknown 4%.
Retention and Graduation: 87% freshmen return for sophomore year. 55% freshmen graduate within 4 years. 72% freshmen graduate within 6 years.

Faculty: Student/faculty ratio 9:1. 111 full-time faculty, 82% hold PhDs, 14% are members of minority groups, 51% are women. 0% of classes are taught by teaching assistants.

ACADEMICS

Degrees: Bachelor's; Certificate; Master's; Post-bachelor's certificate. **Classes:** Most classes have 10–19 students. **Most popular majors:** Illustration; Graphic Design; Painting. **Special Study Options:** Cross-registration; Double major; Exchange student program (domestic); Independent study; Internships; Liberal arts/career combination; Student-designed major; Study abroad; Teacher certification program. **Disability Services offered:** Note-taking services; Reader services; Tutors. **Career services:** Alumni network; Alumni services; Career assessment; Career/job search classes; Internships.

FACILITIES

Housing: Apartments for single students; Coed dorms; 95% of campus accessible to physically disabled. **Special Academic Facilities/Equipment:** Ten art galleries, foundry, glass furnaces, ceramic kilns, video and film studios, performance spaces, Polaroid 20x24 camera, individual studio spaces, design research unit, printmaking facilities, video and photography equipment and facilities, specialized computer labs, specialized equipment and facilities for all art and design programs and levels.

CAMPUS LIFE

Environment: Metropolis. **Activities:** Dance; Drama/theater; Music ensembles; Radio station; Student government; Student newspaper; Student-run film society; Television station; Yearbook. 30 registered organizations, 1 honor society on campus. **Athletics (Intercollegiate):** *Men:* baseball, basketball, cross-country, golf, lacrosse, soccer, softball, tennis, volleyball. *Women:* basketball, cross-country, golf, lacrosse, soccer, softball, tennis, volleyball. **On-Campus Highlights:** 10 art galleries. **Environmental Initiatives:** http://inside.massart.edu/Administration/Administration_and_Finance/Facilities/Sustainability.html.

ADMISSIONS

Freshman Academic Profile: Average high school GPA 3.5. **Basis for Candidate Selection:** *Very important factors include:* rigor of secondary school record, academic GPA, application essay, talent/ability. *Important factors include:* state residency. *Other factors include:* recommendation(s), extracurricular activities, character/personal qualities, geographical residence, volunteer work, work experience. **Freshman Admission Requirements:** High school diploma is required and GED is accepted. *Academic units required:* 4 English, 2 math, 2 science, 2 science labs, 2 foreign language, 2 social studies, 2 academic electives, 2 unit from above areas or other academic areas. *Academic units recommended:* 1 history. **Freshman Admission Statistics:** 2,082 applied, 81% admitted, 25% enrolled. **Transfer Admission Requirements:** College transcript(s), essay or personal statement, statement of good standing from prior institution(s). Minimum college GPA of 2.5 required. Lowest grade transferable C. **General Admission Information:** Application fee $70. Regular application deadline 2/1. Admission may be deferred for a maximum of 12 months.

COSTS AND FINANCIAL AID

Annual in-state tuition $12,700. Annual out-of-state tuition $34,400. Room and board $13,500. Average book and supplies expense $2,100. **Required Forms and Deadlines:** FAFSA. **Types of Aid:** *Need-based scholarships/grants:* College/university scholarship or grant aid from institutional funds; Federal Pell; Private scholarships; SEOG; State scholarships/grants. *Loans:* Direct PLUS loans; Direct Subsidized Stafford Loans; Direct Unsubsidized Stafford Loans. **Student Employment:** Federal Work-Study Program available. Institutional employment available. **Financial Aid Statistics:** 85% needy freshmen, 74% needy undergrads receive need-based scholarship or grant aid. 27% freshmen, 21% undergrads receive non-need-based scholarship or grant aid. 89% freshmen, 91% undergrads receive need-based self-help aid. 0% freshmen, 0% undergrads receive athletic scholarships. **Criteria awarding aid:** *Need-based:* Academics, Leadership. *Non-need-based:* Academics, Art, Leadership, State/district residency.

MASSACHUSETTS COLLEGE OF PHARMACY AND HEALTH SCIENCES

Office of Admissions, Boston, MA 02115
Phone: 617-732-2850 **Financial Aid Phone:** 617-732-2864
E-mail: admissions@mcphs.edu **CEEB Code:** 3512
Fax: 617-732-2118 **Website:** www.mcphs.edu **ACT Code:** 1860

This private school was founded in 1823. It has a 3 acre campus.

RATINGS

Admissions Selectivity Rating: 75   **Fire Safety Rating:** 97   **Green Rating:** 60*

STUDENTS AND FACULTY

Enrollment: 3,791. **Student Body:** 71% female, 29% male, 42% out-of-state, 13% international (32 countries represented). Asian 23%, African American 7%, Caucasian 41%, Hispanic 6%, Native American <1%, Pacific Islander <1%, Two or more races 2%, Race unknown 7%.
Retention and Graduation: 85% freshmen return for sophomore year.
Faculty: 309 full-time faculty, 91% hold PhDs, 0% are members of minority groups, 0% are women. 0% of classes are taught by teaching assistants.

ACADEMICS

Degrees: Bachelor's; Certificate; Doctoral degree—professional practice; Doctoral degree research/scholarship; Master's; Post-bachelor's certificate; Post-master's certificate. **Most popular majors:** Pre-Medicine/Pre-Medical Studies; Pharmacy; Nursing/Registered Nurse (Rn, Asn, Bsn, Msn). **Special Study Options:** Accelerated program; Cross-registration; Distance learning; Double major; Study abroad. **Disability Services offered:** Note-taking services; Reader services; Tape recorders; Tutors. **Career services:** Alumni network; Alumni services; Regional alumni.

FACILITIES

Housing: Apartments for single students; Coed dorms; Special housing for disabled students; Theme housing; Wellness housing; 100% of campus accessible to physically disabled. **Special Academic Facilities/Equipment:** Museum of Fine Arts and Isabella Stewart Gardner museum next door.

CAMPUS LIFE

Environment: Metropolis. **Activities:** Campus Ministries; Choral groups; Dance; Drama/theater; International Student Organization; Jazz band; Student government; Student newspaper. 66 registered organizations, 5 honor societies, 2 religious organizations on campus. **On-Campus Highlights:** New Building, residence hall, labs.

ADMISSIONS

Freshman Academic Profile: Average high school GPA 3.5. **Test Scores:** SAT Math middle 50% range 490–620. SAT EBRW middle 50% range 460–560. ACT middle 50% range 21–27. **Basis for Candidate Selection:** *Very important factors include:* rigor of secondary school record, academic GPA, standardized test scores. *Other factors include:* class rank, application essay, recommendation(s), interview, extracurricular activities, talent/ability, character/personal qualities, first generation, alumni/ae relation, volunteer work, work experience, level of applicant's interest. **Freshman Admission Requirements:** High school diploma is required and GED is accepted. *Academic units required:* 4 English, 3 math, 2 science, 2 science labs, 1 social studies, 1 history, 5 academic electives. **Freshman Admission Statistics:** 5,530 applied, 84% admitted, 17% enrolled. **Transfer Admission Requirements:** College transcript(s), essay or personal statement. Minimum college GPA of 2.5 required. Lowest grade transferable C. **General Admission Information:** Non-fall registration accepted.

COSTS AND FINANCIAL AID

Annual tuition $30,600. Room and board $15,834. Required fees $1,070. Average book and supplies expense $1,028. **Required Forms and Deadlines:** FAFSA. **Notification of Awards:** Applicants will be notified of awards on a rolling basis beginning 2/15. **Types of Aid:** *Need-based scholarships/grants:* College/university scholarship or grant aid from institutional funds; Federal Pell; SEOG; State scholarships/grants. *Loans:* Direct PLUS loans; Direct Subsidized Stafford Loans; Direct Unsubsidized Stafford Loans. **Student Employment:** Federal Work-Study Program available. **Financial Aid Statistics:** 100% needy freshmen, 93% needy undergrads receive need-based scholarship or grant aid. 0% freshmen, 0% undergrads receive non-need-based scholarship or grant aid. 89% freshmen, 90% undergrads receive need-based self-help aid. 0% freshmen, 0% undergrads receive athletic scholarships. 90% freshmen, 90% undergrads receive any aid. **Criteria awarding aid:** *Non-need-based:* Academics.

MASSACHUSETTS INSTITUTE OF TECHNOLOGY

77 Massachusetts Avenue, Cambridge, MA 02139
Phone: 617-253-3400 **Financial Aid Phone:** 617-258-8600
E-mail: admissions@mit.edu **CEEB Code:** 3514
Fax: 617-258-8304 **Website:** web.mit.edu **ACT Code:** 1858

This private school was founded in 1861. It has a 168 acre campus.

RATINGS
Admissions Selectivity Rating: 99   **Fire Safety Rating:** 91   **Green Rating:** 93

STUDENTS AND FACULTY
Enrollment: 4,550. **Student Body:** 47% female, 53% male, 91% out-of-state, 10% international (103 countries represented). Asian 28%, African American 6%, Caucasian 32%, Hispanic 15%, Native American <1%, Pacific Islander <1%, Two or more races 7%, Race unknown 2%.
Retention and Graduation: 98% freshmen return for sophomore year. 85% freshmen graduate within 4 years. 94% freshmen graduate within 6 years. 37% grads go on to further study within 1 year. 26% grads pursue arts and sciences degrees. 2% grads pursue law degrees. 0% grads pursue business degrees. 7% grads pursue medical degrees. **Faculty:** Student/faculty ratio 3:1. 1,312 full-time faculty, 92% hold PhDs, 18% are members of minority groups, 27% are women.

ACADEMICS
Degrees: Bachelor's; Doctoral degree research/scholarship; Master's. **Classes:** Most classes have 10–19 students. Most lab/discussion sessions have 10–19 students. **Most popular majors:** Computer Science; Mechanical Engineering; Mathematics, General. **Special Study Options:** Cooperative education program; Cross-registration; Double major; Internships; Study abroad; Teacher certification program. **Disability Services offered:** Note-taking services; Reader services; Tape recorders. **Career services:** Alumni network; Alumni services; Career assessment; Career/job search classes; Internships; Regional alumni.

FACILITIES
Housing: Apartments for married students; Apartments for single students; Coed dorms; Cooperative housing; Fraternity/sorority housing; Special housing for disabled students; Theme housing; Women's dorms. **Special Academic Facilities/Equipment:** List Visual Arts Center; MIT Museum; Ray and Maria Stata Center for Computer, Information, and Intelligence Sciences; numerous labs and centers.

CAMPUS LIFE
Environment: City. **Activities:** Campus Ministries; Choral groups; Concert band; Dance; Drama/theater; International Student Organization; Jazz band; Literary magazine; Marching band; Model UN; Music ensembles; Musical theater; Radio station; Student government; Student newspaper; Student-run film society; Symphony orchestra; Television station; Yearbook. 500 registered organizations, 9 honor societies, 24 religious organizations, 28 fraternities, 10 sororities on campus. **Athletics (Intercollegiate):** *Men:* baseball, basketball, crew/rowing, cross-country, diving, fencing, football, golf, gymnastics, lacrosse, pistol, riflery, sailing, skiing (downhill/Alpine), skiing (Nordic/cross-country), soccer, squash, swimming, tennis, track/field (outdoor), track/field (indoor), volleyball, water polo, wrestling. *Women:* basketball, crew/rowing, cross-country, diving, fencing, field hockey, gymnastics, ice hockey, lacrosse, pistol, riflery, sailing, skiing (downhill/Alpine), skiing (Nordic/cross-country), soccer, softball, swimming, tennis, track/field (outdoor), track/field (indoor), volleyball.
On-Campus Highlights: Ray and Maria Stata Center. **Environmental Initiatives:** In 2013, MIT created a new Office of Sustainability reporting directly to our Executive Vice President, which is the highest administrative for operations office. This creates an office at the highest level with a new director to scale up MIT's already robust sustainability programs. MIT has also launched a Sustainability Executive Committee (comprised of the Provost, Directors of MIT's top sustainability research programs, Chancellor, and Vice President for Research) and a Campus Sustainability Task Force (comprised of respresentatives of all 5 schools, and key operational areas and students) to coordinate implementation of MIT's sustainability plans.

ADMISSIONS
Freshman Academic Profile: 97% in top 10% of high school class, 100% in top 25% of high school class, 100% in top 50% of high school class. 70%

from public high schools. **Test Scores:** SAT Math middle 50% range 780–800. SAT EBRW middle 50% range 720–770. ACT middle 50% range 34–36.
Basis for Candidate Selection: *Very important factors include:* character/personal qualities. *Important factors include:* rigor of secondary school record, academic GPA, application essay, standardized test scores, recommendation(s), interview, extracurricular activities, talent/ability. *Other factors include:* class rank, first generation, geographical residence, racial/ethnic status, volunteer work, work experience. **Freshman Admission Requirements:** High school diploma or equivalent is not required *Academic units recommended:* 4 English, 4 math, 4 science, 2 foreign language, 2 social studies. **Freshman Admission Statistics:** 21,706 applied, 7% admitted, 76% enrolled. **Transfer Admission Requirements:** High school transcript, college transcript(s), essay or personal statement, standardized test scores, statement of good standing from prior institution(s). Lowest grade transferable B. **General Admission Information:** Application fee $75. Regular application deadline 1/1. Admission may be deferred for a maximum of 2 years.

COSTS AND FINANCIAL AID
Annual tuition $53,450. Room and board $16,390. Required fees $340. Average book and supplies expense $820. **Required Forms and Deadlines:** CSS/Financial Aid PROFILE; FAFSA; Noncustodial PROFILE. **Notification of Awards:** Applicants will be notified of awards on or about 3/15. **Types of Aid:** *Need-based scholarships/grants:* College/university scholarship or grant aid from institutional funds; Federal Pell; Private scholarships; SEOG; State scholarships/grants; United Negro College Fund. *Loans:* Direct PLUS loans; Direct Subsidized Stafford Loans; Direct Unsubsidized Stafford Loans. **Student Employment:** Federal Work-Study Program available. Institutional employment available. **Financial Aid Statistics:** 98% needy freshmen, 98% needy undergrads receive need-based scholarship or grant aid. 3% freshmen, 3% undergrads receive non-need-based scholarship or grant aid. 63% freshmen, 70% undergrads receive need-based self-help aid. 0% freshmen, 0% undergrads receive athletic scholarships. 83% freshmen, 70% undergrads receive any aid. 29% undergrads borrow to pay for school. Average cumulative indebtedness $22,696.

MASSACHUSETTS MARITIME ACADEMY

101 Academy Drive, Buzzards Bay, MA 02532
Phone: 800-544-3411 **Financial Aid Phone:** 508-830-5087
E-mail: admissions@maritime.edu **CEEB Code:** 3515
Fax: 508-830-5077 **Website:** https://www.maritime.edu

This public school was founded in 1891. It has a 54 acre campus.

RATINGS
Admissions Selectivity Rating: 77   **Fire Safety Rating:** 60*   **Green Rating:** 60*

STUDENTS AND FACULTY
Enrollment: 1,654. **Student Body:** 12% female, 88% male, 20% out-of-state, 1% international. Asian 1%, African American 1%, Caucasian 85%, Hispanic 4%, Native American <1%, Pacific Islander 0%, Two or more races 3%, Race unknown 5%.
Retention and Graduation: 87% freshmen return for sophomore year. 63% freshmen graduate within 4 years. 76% freshmen graduate within 6 years. **Faculty:** Student/faculty ratio 15:1. 88 full-time faculty, 63% hold PhDs, 15% are members of minority groups, 34% are women. 0% of classes are taught by teaching assistants.

ACADEMICS
Degrees: Bachelor's; Master's. **Classes:** Most classes have 20–29 students. **Most popular majors:** Naval Architecture and Marine Engineering; Marine Science/Merchant Marine Officer. **Special Study Options:** Cooperative education program; Double major; Dual enrollment; Independent study; Internships; Study abroad. **Disability Services offered:** Note-taking services; Tape recorders; Tutors. **Career services:** Alumni network; Alumni services; Career/job search classes; Internships.

FACILITIES
Housing: Coed dorms; Wellness housing.

CAMPUS LIFE
Environment: Rural. **Activities:** Concert band; Drama/theater; International Student Organization; Jazz band; Literary magazine; Marching band; Music ensembles; Pep band; Student government; Yearbook.

ADMISSIONS

Test Scores: SAT Math middle 50% range 510–590. SAT EBRW middle 50% range 510–590. ACT middle 50% range 19–24. **Basis for Candidate Selection:** *Very important factors include:* rigor of secondary school record, academic GPA, application essay, standardized test scores, recommendation(s). *Important factors include:* interview, extracurricular activities. *Other factors include:* class rank, talent/ability, character/personal qualities, first generation, alumni/ae relation, racial/ethnic status, volunteer work, work experience. **Freshman Admission Requirements:** High school diploma is required and GED is accepted. *Academic units required:* 4 English, 4 math, 3 science, 3 science labs, 2 foreign language, 1 social studies, 1 history, 2 academic electives. *Academic units recommended:* 4 English, 4 math, 4 science, 3 science labs, 2 foreign language, 1 social studies, 1 history, 2 academic electives. **Freshman Admission Statistics:** 774 applied, 91% admitted, 57% enrolled. **General Admission Information:** Application fee $50. Regular application deadline 4/15. Admission may be deferred for a maximum of 1 year.

COSTS AND FINANCIAL AID

Average book and supplies expense $1,500. **Required Forms and Deadlines:** FAFSA. **Notification of Awards:** Applicants will be notified of awards on a rolling basis beginning 2/1. **Types of Aid:** *Need-based scholarships/grants:* College/university scholarship or grant aid from institutional funds; Federal Pell; Private scholarships; SEOG; State scholarships/grants. *Loans:* Direct PLUS loans; Direct Subsidized Stafford Loans; Direct Unsubsidized Stafford Loans. **Student Employment:** Federal Work-Study Program available. Institutional employment available. **Financial Aid Statistics:** 53% needy freshmen, 55% needy undergrads receive need-based scholarship or grant aid. 27% freshmen, 19% undergrads receive non-need-based scholarship or grant aid. 95% freshmen, 97% undergrads receive need-based self-help aid. 0% freshmen, 0% undergrads receive athletic scholarships. 77% undergrads borrow to pay for school. Average cumulative indebtedness $38,437.

THE MASTER'S UNIVERSITY AND SEMINARY

21726 Placerita Canyon Road, Santa Clarita, CA 91321
Phone: (661) 362-2363 **Financial Aid Phone:** 661-362-2293
E-mail: admissions@masters.edu **CEEB Code:** 4411
Fax: (661) 362-2718 **Website:** www.masters.edu **ACT Code:** 0303

This private school, affiliated with the Nondenominational Christian, was founded in 1927. It has a 110 acre campus.

RATINGS

Admissions Selectivity Rating: 81 **Fire Safety Rating:** 85 **Green Rating:** 60*

STUDENTS AND FACULTY

Enrollment: 1,186. **Student Body:** 46% female, 54% male, 33% out-of-state, 2% international (25 countries represented). Asian 3%, African American 2%, Caucasian 64%, Hispanic 8%, Native American <1%, Pacific Islander <1%, Two or more races 8%, Race unknown 14%.
Retention and Graduation: 83% freshmen return for sophomore year. 47% freshmen graduate within 4 years. 55% freshmen graduate within 6 years.
Faculty: Student/faculty ratio 10:1. 51 full-time faculty, 61% hold PhDs, 8% are members of minority groups, 20% are women. 0% of classes are taught by teaching assistants.

ACADEMICS

Degrees: Bachelor's; Diploma; Doctoral degree—other; Doctoral degree—professional practice; Doctoral degree research/scholarship; Master's. **Classes:** Most classes have 10–19 students. Most lab/discussion sessions have 10–19 students. **Most popular majors:** Bible/Biblical Studies; Business/Commerce, General; Communication and Media Studies. **Special Study Options:** Accelerated program; Distance learning; Double major; Dual enrollment; Independent study; Internships; Liberal arts/career combination; Study abroad; Teacher certification program. **Disability Services offered:** Note-taking services; Reader services; Tape recorders; Tutors. **Career services:** Alumni services; Career assessment; Career/job search classes; Internships.

FACILITIES

Housing: Apartments for married students; Apartments for single students; Men's dorms; Women's dorms; 95% of campus accessible to physically disabled.

CAMPUS LIFE

Environment: City. **Activities:** Campus Ministries; Choral groups; Concert band; Drama/theater; International Student Organization; Music ensembles; Musical theater; Opera; Pep band; Student government; Student newspaper; Symphony orchestra. 10 registered organizations, 1 honor society, 10 religious organizations on campus. **Athletics (Intercollegiate):** *Men:* baseball, basketball, cross-country, golf, soccer, track/field (outdoor). *Women:* basketball, cross-country, soccer, tennis, track/field (outdoor), volleyball. **On-Campus Highlights:** MacArthur Center (chapel and gym).

ADMISSIONS

Freshman Academic Profile: Average high school GPA 3.7. 27% in top 10% of high school class, 48% in top 25% of high school class, 85% in top 50% of high school class. 40% from public high schools. **Test Scores:** SAT Math middle 50% range 490–600. ACT middle 50% range 21–27. **Basis for Candidate Selection:** *Very important factors include:* academic GPA, application essay, standardized test scores, recommendation(s), character/personal qualities, religious affiliation/commitment. *Important factors include:* rigor of secondary school record. *Other factors include:* extracurricular activities, talent/ability, alumni/ae relation, level of applicant's interest. **Freshman Admission Requirements:** High school diploma is required and GED is accepted. *Academic units required:* 4 English, 3 math, 2 science, 2 history. *Academic units recommended:* 3 academic electives. **Freshman Admission Statistics:** 718 applied, 77% admitted, 49% enrolled. **Transfer Admission Requirements:** High school transcript, college transcript(s), essay or personal statement, interview, statement of good standing from prior institution(s). Minimum college GPA of 2.5 required. Lowest grade transferable C. **General Admission Information:** Application fee $40. Priority deadline 3/2. Non-fall registration accepted. Admission may be deferred for a maximum of 2 semesters.

COSTS AND FINANCIAL AID

Annual tuition $24,950. Room and board $11,200. Required fees $440. Average book and supplies expense $1,918. **Required Forms and Deadlines:** FAFSA; Institution's own financial aid form. **Notification of Awards:** Applicants will be notified of awards on a rolling basis beginning 2/18. **Types of Aid:** *Need-based scholarships/grants:* College/university scholarship or grant aid from institutional funds; Federal Pell; Private scholarships; SEOG; State scholarships/grants. *Loans:* Direct PLUS loans; Direct Subsidized Stafford Loans; Direct Unsubsidized Stafford Loans. **Student Employment:** Federal Work-Study Program available. Institutional employment available. **Financial Aid Statistics:** 99% needy freshmen, 99% needy undergrads receive need-based scholarship or grant aid. 11% freshmen, 10% undergrads receive non-need-based scholarship or grant aid. 86% freshmen, 87% undergrads receive need-based self-help aid. 4% freshmen, 4% undergrads receive athletic scholarships. 95% freshmen, 90% undergrads receive any aid. 72% undergrads borrow to pay for school. Average cumulative indebtedness $28,117. **Criteria awarding aid:** *Need-based:* Job skills. *Non-need-based:* Academics, Alumni affiliation, Art, Athletics, Music/drama.

MAYNOOTH UNIVERSITY

International Office Maynooth University, Co Kildare, IR Co Kildare
Phone: +353 1 708 3868
E-mail: international.office@nuim.ie
Fax: 353 1 628 9063 **Website:** www.maynoothuniversity.ie **ACT Code:** 5483

This public school was founded in 1997. It has a 100 acre campus.

RATINGS

Admissions Selectivity Rating: 85 **Fire Safety Rating:** 93 **Green Rating:** 60*

STUDENTS AND FACULTY

Enrollment: 9,144. **Student Body:** 55% female, 45% male, 90 countries represented.
Retention and Graduation: 88% freshmen return for sophomore year.
Faculty: Student/faculty ratio 28:1. 381 full-time faculty, 0% hold PhDs, 0% are members of minority groups, 0% are women. 0% of classes are taught by teaching assistants.

ACADEMICS

Degrees: Bachelor's; Diploma; Doctoral degree—other; Doctoral degree—professional practice; Doctoral degree research/scholarship; Master's; Post-bachelor's certificate; Post-master's certificate. **Classes:** Most classes have greater than 100 students. **Most popular majors:** Business/Commerce,

General; Liberal Arts and Sciences, General Studies and Humanities; Multi/Interdisciplinary Studies. **Special Study Options:** Distance learning; Double major; Dual enrollment; English as a Second Language (ESL); Exchange student program (domestic); Honors program; Independent study; Internships; Liberal arts/career combination; Study abroad; Teacher certification program. **Honors programs:** Geography; International Development; Anthropology; Music (performance is particularly strong); Electronic Engineering; Media Studies; Law. **Disability Services offered:** Note-taking services; Reader services; Tape recorders. **Career services:** Alumni network; Career/job search classes; Internships; Regional alumni.

FACILITIES

Housing: Coed dorms; Special housing for disabled students; Special housing for international students; 75% of campus accessible to physically disabled. **Special Academic Facilities/Equipment:** The National Science Museum of Ireland is located on the South Campus. We offer two libraries: Our main library has access to 16 types of study spaces and over 45,000 materials and our Rare books and Manuscripts library contains materials from the 11th century on. The South Campus is home to several medieval buildings dating from the 1800s, including some designed by the famous architect Augustus Pugin, and the chapel on the south campus is a beautiful building. The Science facilities include laboratories for Biology, Chemistry, Pharmacy, and Physics and are all only 15 years old, so are home to very modern facilities. Eight Research Institutes are housed on campus: Hamilton Institute, Institute of Immunology, Callan Institute, National Centre for Geocomputation, Innovation Value Institute, National Institute for Regional and Spatial Analysis, An Foras Feasa, and Edward M Kennedy Centre for Conflict Resolution and Mediation.

CAMPUS LIFE

Environment: Village. **Activities:** Campus Ministries; Choral groups; Concert band; Dance; Drama/theater; International Student Organization; Jazz band; Literary magazine; Music ensembles; Musical theater; Radio station; Student government; Student newspaper; Student-run film society; Symphony orchestra. 100 registered organizations on campus. **On-Campus Highlights:** St Joseph's Square and Chapel (19th century). **Environmental Initiatives:** To provide and coordinate the travel strategy at Maynooth University to enable a lasting and maintained shift to sustainable travel in line with the University's vision of becoming a sustainable campus by providing the best range of travel options to staff, students, and visitors.

ADMISSIONS

Freshman Academic Profile: Average high school GPA 3.2. **Basis for Candidate Selection:** *Very important factors include:* rigor of secondary school record, academic GPA, standardized test scores. *Important factors include:* class rank. *Other factors include:* talent/ability, character/personal qualities, level of applicant's interest. **Freshman Admission Requirements:** High school diploma is required and GED is not accepted. **Freshman Admission Statistics:** 14,112 applied, 23% admitted, 90% enrolled. **General Admission Information:** Regular application deadline 7/31. Admission may be deferred for a maximum of 1 year.

COSTS AND FINANCIAL AID

Room and board $8,500. Required fees $15,300. Average book and supplies expense $600. **Required Forms and Deadlines:** FAFSA. **Notification of Awards:** Applicants will be notified of awards on a rolling basis beginning 3/1. **Types of Aid:** *Need-based scholarships/grants:* Federal Pell. *Loans:* Direct PLUS loans; Direct Subsidized Stafford Loans; Direct Unsubsidized Stafford Loans. **Criteria awarding aid:** *Need-based:* Academics. *Non-need-based:* Academics.

MAYVILLE STATE UNIVERSITY

330 Third Street Northeast, Mayville, ND 58257-1299
Phone: 701-788-4842 **Financial Aid Phone:** 701-788-4767
E-mail: MaSU.admissions@mayvillestate.edu **CEEB Code:** 6478
Fax: 701-788-4656 **Website:** www.mayvillestate.edu **ACT Code:** 3212

This public school was founded in 1889. It has a 55 acre campus.

RATINGS

Admissions Selectivity Rating: 87   **Fire Safety Rating:** 81   **Green Rating:** 60*

STUDENTS AND FACULTY

Enrollment: 819. **Student Body:** 56% female, 44% male, 43% out-of-state, 3% international (7 countries represented). Asian <1%, African American 8%,

Caucasian 78%, Hispanic 5%, Native American 1%, Pacific Islander 1%, Two or more races 3%, Race unknown 1%.
Retention and Graduation: 49% freshmen return for sophomore year. 12% grads go on to further study within 1 year. 1% grads pursue arts and sciences degrees. 0% grads pursue law degrees. 4% grads pursue business degrees. 0% grads pursue medical degrees. **Faculty:** Student/faculty ratio 13:1. 49 full-time faculty, 41% hold PhDs, 2% are members of minority groups, 49% are women. 0% of classes are taught by teaching assistants.

ACADEMICS

Degrees: Bachelor's; Transfer Associate. **Classes:** Most classes have 10–19 students. **Most popular majors:** Business/Commerce, General; Physical Education Teaching and Coaching; Elementary Education and Teaching. **Special Study Options:** Accelerated program; Cooperative education program; Distance learning; Double major; Dual enrollment; Independent study; Internships; Student-designed major; Teacher certification program. **Disability Services offered:** Note-taking services; Tape recorders; Tutors. **Career services:** Alumni network; Alumni services; Career assessment; Career/job search classes; Internships; Regional alumni.

FACILITIES

Housing: Apartments for married students; Apartments for single students; Coed dorms; Men's dorms; Women's dorms; 80% of campus accessible to physically disabled. **Campus Network:** 100% of classrooms, 100% of libraries, 100% of dining areas, 100% of common outdoor areas have wireless network access.

CAMPUS LIFE

Environment: Rural. **Activities:** Choral groups; Concert band; Drama/theater; International Student Organization; Jazz band; Music ensembles; Musical theater; Radio station; Student government; Student newspaper. 22 registered organizations, 1 honor society, 3 religious organizations on campus. **Athletics (Intercollegiate):** *Men:* baseball, basketball, football. *Women:* basketball, softball, volleyball. **On-Campus Highlights:** Lewy Lee Fieldhouse.

ADMISSIONS

Freshman Academic Profile: Average high school GPA 3.0. 95% from public high schools. **Test Scores:** ACT middle 50% range 17–22. **Basis for Candidate Selection:** *Very important factors include:* rigor of secondary school record, academic GPA. *Important factors include:* standardized test scores. *Other factors include:* interview, character/personal qualities. **Freshman Admission Requirements:** High school diploma is required and GED is accepted. *Academic units required:* 4 English, 3 math, 3 science, 3 science labs, 3 social studies. *Academic units recommended:* 2 foreign language. **Freshman Admission Statistics:** 336 applied, 54% admitted, 76% enrolled. **Transfer Admission Requirements:** College transcript(s), statement of good standing from prior institution(s). Minimum college GPA of 2.0 required. Lowest grade transferable D. **General Admission Information:** Application fee $35. Non-fall registration accepted.

COSTS AND FINANCIAL AID

Annual in-state tuition $4,930. Annual out-of-state tuition $7,395. Room and board $5,904. Required fees $1,450. Average book and supplies expense $1,000. **Required Forms and Deadlines:** FAFSA. **Notification of Awards:** Applicants will be notified of awards on a rolling basis beginning 5/1. **Types of Aid:** *Need-based scholarships/grants:* College/university scholarship or grant aid from institutional funds; Federal Pell; Private scholarships; SEOG; State scholarships/grants. *Loans:* Direct PLUS loans; Direct Subsidized Stafford Loans; Direct Unsubsidized Stafford Loans. **Student Employment:** Federal Work-Study Program available. Institutional employment available. **Financial Aid Statistics:** 94% needy freshmen, 88% needy undergrads receive need-based scholarship or grant aid. 9% freshmen, 6% undergrads receive non-need-based scholarship or grant aid. 79% freshmen, 81% undergrads receive need-based self-help aid. 8% freshmen, 8% undergrads receive athletic scholarships. 83% freshmen, 78% undergrads receive any aid. 71% undergrads borrow to pay for school. Average cumulative indebtedness $32,424. **Criteria awarding aid:** *Need-based:* Academics, Athletics, Leadership, Minority status, Music/drama. *Non-need-based:* Academics, Athletics, Leadership, Minority status, Music/drama, State/district residency.

MCDANIEL COLLEGE

2 College Hill, Westminster, MD 21157
Phone: 410-857-2230 **Financial Aid Phone:** 410-857-2233
E-mail: admissions@mcdaniel.edu **CEEB Code:** 5898
Website: www.mcdaniel.edu **ACT Code:** 1756

This private school was founded in 1867. It has a 160 acre campus.

RATINGS
Admissions Selectivity Rating: 75   **Fire Safety Rating:** 88   **Green Rating:** 60*

STUDENTS AND FACULTY
Enrollment: 1,669. **Student Body:** 52% female, 48% male, 32% out-of-state, 3% international (30 countries represented). Asian 2%, African American 21%, Caucasian 57%, Hispanic 6%, Native American <1%, Pacific Islander 0%, Two or more races 3%, Race unknown 7%.
Retention and Graduation: 77% freshmen return for sophomore year. 60% freshmen graduate within 4 years. 68% freshmen graduate within 6 years.
Faculty: Student/faculty ratio 12:1. 130 full-time faculty, 91% hold PhDs, 13% are members of minority groups, 54% are women. 0% of classes are taught by teaching assistants.

ACADEMICS
Degrees: Bachelor's; Master's; Post-bachelor's certificate. **Classes:** Most classes have 10–19 students. **Special Study Options:** Accelerated program; Cooperative education program; Distance learning; Double major; Dual enrollment; Exchange student program (domestic); Honors program; Independent study; Internships; Student-designed major; Study abroad; Teacher certification program. **Honors programs:** Honors Program allows students to be a part of a community of scholars who are dedicated to academic rigor and the pursuit of liberal arts in the classroom and beyond. McDaniel is also one of only 280 U.S. colleges and universities with a Phi Beta Kappa chapter. Additionally, there are numerous other honorary societies on campus. Three societies oriented toward general accomplishment are Omicron Delta Kappa, a national society recognizing leadership qualities; Alpha Lambda Delta, a national honor society for first-year students; and the Trumpeters, a local society honoring senior students dedicated to service. National and international honor societies which recognize academic accomplishment in specific fields are Beta Beta Beta (Biology), Gamma Sigma Epsilon (Chemistry), Lambda Pi Eta (Communication), Omicron Delta Epsilon (Economics), Kappa Delta Pi (Education), Phi Alpha Theta (History), Lambda Iota Tau (Literature), Phi Sigma Iota (Foreign Languages), Kappa Mu Epsilon (Mathematics), Omicron Psi (Nontraditional Students), Phi Sigma Tau (Philosophy), Sigma Pi Sigma (Physics), Pi Sigma Alpha (Political Science), Psi Chi (Psychology), Pi Gamma Mu (Social Sciences), Phi Alpha (Social Work), and Alpha Psi Omega (Theatre Arts). **Disability Services offered:** Note-taking services; Reader services; Tape recorders; Tutors. **Career services:** Alumni network; Alumni services; Career assessment; Career/job search classes; Internships; Regional alumni.

FACILITIES
Housing: Apartments for single students; Coed dorms; Fraternity/sorority housing; Special housing for disabled students; Theme housing; 85% of campus accessible to physically disabled. **Special Academic Facilities/Equipment:** Rice Art Gallery, Human Performance Lab, Merritt Fitness Center, video production lab, Writing Center, 9-hole golf course, photo studio, graphics lab, observatory, student research science labs, radio station, TV station.

CAMPUS LIFE
Environment: Town. **Activities:** Campus Ministries; Choral groups; Concert band; Dance; Drama/theater; International Student Organization; Jazz band; Literary magazine; Model UN; Music ensembles; Musical theater; Pep band; Radio station; Student government; Student newspaper; Student-run film society; Television station; Yearbook. 90 registered organizations, 28 honor societies, 3 religious organizations, 5 fraternities, 6 sororities on campus. **Athletics (Intercollegiate):** *Men:* baseball, basketball, cross-country, football, golf, lacrosse, soccer, swimming, tennis, track/field (outdoor), track/field (indoor), volleyball, wrestling. *Women:* basketball, cross-country, field hockey, golf, lacrosse, soccer, softball, swimming, tennis, track/field (outdoor), track/field (indoor), volleyball. **On-Campus Highlights:** The Hoover Library & Caseys' Corner.

ADMISSIONS
Freshman Academic Profile: Average high school GPA 3.5. 20% in top 10% of high school class, 44% in top 25% of high school class, 75% in top 50% of high school class. **Test Scores:** SAT Math middle 50% range 488–590. SAT EBRW middle 50% range 500–600. ACT middle 50% range 19–25. **Basis for Candidate Selection:** *Very important factors include:* rigor of secondary school record, academic GPA. *Important factors include:* application essay, recommendation(s). *Other factors include:* class rank, interview, extracurricular activities, talent/ability, character/personal qualities, first generation, alumni/ae relation, volunteer work, work experience. **Freshman Admission Requirements:** High school diploma is required and GED is accepted. *Academic units required:* 4 English, 3 math, 3 science, 3 science labs, 3 foreign language, 3 social studies. *Academic units recommended:* 4 English, 4 math, 4 science, 4 foreign language, 3 social studies. **Freshman Admission Statistics:** 3,761 applied, 92% admitted, 17% enrolled. **General Admission Information:** Priority deadline 2/1. Non-fall registration accepted. Admission may be deferred for a maximum of 1 year.

COSTS AND FINANCIAL AID
Annual tuition $44,540. Room and board $11,772. Average book and supplies expense $1,200. **Required Forms and Deadlines:** FAFSA. **Notification of Awards:** Applicants will be notified of awards on a rolling basis beginning 12/15. **Types of Aid:** *Need-based scholarships/grants:* College/university scholarship or grant aid from institutional funds; Federal Pell; Private scholarships; SEOG; State scholarships/grants. *Loans:* Direct PLUS loans; Direct Subsidized Stafford Loans; Direct Unsubsidized Stafford Loans. **Student Employment:** Federal Work-Study Program available. Institutional employment available. **Financial Aid Statistics:** 100% needy freshmen, 100% needy undergrads receive need-based scholarship or grant aid. 13% freshmen, 22% undergrads receive non-need-based scholarship or grant aid. 77% freshmen, 70% undergrads receive need-based self-help aid. 0% freshmen, 0% undergrads receive athletic scholarships. 67% undergrads borrow to pay for school. Average cumulative indebtedness $16,622. **Criteria awarding aid:** *Non-need-based:* Academics, State/district residency.

MCGILL UNIVERSITY

3415 McTavish St., Montreal, QC H3A 0C8
Phone: 514-398-7878 **Financial Aid Phone:** 514-398-6013
CEEB Code: 935
Fax: 514-398-5544 **Website:** http://www.mcgill.ca/admissions/ **ACT Code:** 5231

This public school was founded in 1821. It has a 80 acre campus.

RATINGS
Admissions Selectivity Rating: 87   **Fire Safety Rating:** 79   **Green Rating:** 60*

STUDENTS AND FACULTY
Enrollment: 25,081. **Student Body:** 37% out-of-state, 136 countries represented.
Faculty: Student/faculty ratio 16:1.

ACADEMICS
Degrees: Bachelor's; Certificate; Diploma; Master's; Post-bachelor's certificate. **Classes:** Most classes have 10–19 students. Most lab/discussion sessions have 20–29 students. **Most popular majors:** Business/Commerce, General; Political Science and Government, General; Psychology, General. **Special Study Options:** Accelerated program; Cooperative education program; Cross-registration; Distance learning; Double major; English as a Second Language (ESL); Exchange student program (domestic); Honors program; Independent study; Internships; Study abroad; Teacher certification program. **Honors programs:** McGill's Faculties of Arts, Science, and Engineering, the Desautels Faculty of Management, and the McGill School of Environment offer many outstanding honours and joint honours programs. Honours programs offer specialization and research in one academic discipline while joint honours programs offer specialization and research in a combination of disciplines. **Disability Services offered:** Note-taking services; Reader services; Tape recorders; Tutors. **Career services:** Career assessment; Career/job search classes.

FACILITIES

Housing: Apartments for single students; Coed dorms; Special housing for disabled students; Women's dorms; 90% of campus accessible to physically disabled. **Special Academic Facilities/Equipment:** McCord Museum of Canadian History, Redpath Museum of Natural History, Lyman Entomological Museum and Research Laboratory, Ecomuseum, Rutherford Museum, Lawrence Lande Collection of Canadiana, Canadian Architecture Collection, Morgan Arboretum, Gault Nature Reserve, Herbarium, McGill Archives (Canadian History), Islamic Studies Library, Bellairs Research Institute, McConnell Brain Imaging Centre, McConnell Winter Arena, McGill Sports Centre Gymnasiums, Percival Molson Stadium, Memorial Pool, Richard Tomlinson Fieldhouse, Outdoor Tennis Courts, McGill Arctic Research Station, McGill Subarctic Research Station, Phytotron, Schulich School of Music (world-class sound stage, recording studio), McGill Centre for Interdisciplinary Research in Music, Media and Technology, Research Greenhouse, J. S. Marshall Weather Radar Observatory, Mountain and Glen Campuses (McGill University Health Centre Teaching Hospitals), McGill Medical Simulation Centre, McGill Reproductive Centre, McGill University and Genome Quebec Innovation Centre.

CAMPUS LIFE

Environment: Metropolis. **Activities:** Choral groups; Concert band; Dance; Drama/theater; International Student Organization; Jazz band; Literary magazine; Marching band; Music ensembles; Musical theater; Opera; Pep band; Radio station; Student government; Student newspaper; Student-run film society; Symphony orchestra; Television station; Yearbook. 250 registered organizations, 2 honor societies, 10 religious organizations, 8 fraternities, 4 sororities on campus. **Athletics (Intercollegiate):** *Men:* badminton, baseball, basketball, cheerleading, crew/rowing, cross-country, curling, cycling, fencing, football, golf, ice hockey, lacrosse, rugby, sailing, skiing (downhill/Alpine), skiing (Nordic/cross-country), soccer, squash, swimming, tennis, track/field (indoor), ultimate frisbee, volleyball, wrestling. *Women:* badminton, basketball, cheerleading, crew/rowing, cross-country, curling, cycling, fencing, field hockey, golf, ice hockey, lacrosse, rugby, sailing, skiing (downhill/Alpine), skiing (Nordic/cross-country), soccer, squash, swimming, synchronized swimming, tennis, track/field (indoor), ultimate frisbee, volleyball, wrestling. **On-Campus Highlights:** Arts Building. **Environmental Initiatives:** Excellence in environmental research and teaching (e.g. School of Environment, GEC3, Brace, VERT, etc.).

ADMISSIONS

Freshman Academic Profile: Test Scores: SAT Math middle 50% range 650–720. SAT EBRW middle 50% range 640–740. ACT middle 50% range 29–32. **Basis for Candidate Selection:** *Very important factors include:* rigor of secondary school record, academic GPA, standardized test scores. *Important factors include:* class rank. *Other factors include:* recommendation(s). **Freshman Admission Requirements:** High school diploma is required and GED is not accepted. *Academic units recommended:* 4 English, 4 math, 3 science, 3 science labs, 3 foreign language, 2 social studies, 2 history. **Freshman Admission Statistics:** 24,901 applied, 56% admitted, enrolled. **Transfer Admission Requirements:** High school transcript, college transcript(s). Minimum college GPA of 3.00 required. Lowest grade transferable C. **General Admission Information:** Application fee $102.2. Regular application deadline 1/15. Non-fall registration accepted. Admission may be deferred for a maximum of 1 year.

COSTS AND FINANCIAL AID

Annual in-state tuition $2,294. Annual out-of-state tuition $7,031. Required fees $2,552. Average book and supplies expense $1,000. **Required Forms and Deadlines:** Institution's own financial aid form. **Notification of Awards:** Applicants will be notified of awards on a rolling basis beginning 3/1. **Types of Aid:** *Need-based scholarships/grants:* College/university scholarship or grant aid from institutional funds; Private scholarships. **Student Employment:** Institutional employment available. **Financial Aid Statistics:** 63% needy undergrads receive need-based scholarship or grant aid. 31% undergrads receive non-need-based scholarship or grant aid. 89% undergrads receive need-based self-help aid. 0% undergrads receive athletic scholarships. 28% undergrads receive any aid. **Criteria awarding aid:** *Need-based:* Academics, Alumni affiliation, Leadership, Minority status. *Non-need-based:* Academics, Art, Athletics, Leadership, Music/drama, State/district residency.

MCMURRY UNIVERSITY

1 McMurry University, #278, Abilene, TX 79697
Phone: 325-793-4700 **Financial Aid Phone:** 325-793-4713
E-mail: admissions@mcm.edu **CEEB Code:** 3591
Fax: 325-793-4701 **Website:** ww2.mcm.edu **ACT Code:** 4130

This private school, affiliated with the United Methodist Church, was founded in 1923. It has a 52 acre campus.

RATINGS

Admissions Selectivity Rating: 88   **Fire Safety Rating:** 87   **Green Rating:** 60*

STUDENTS AND FACULTY

Enrollment: 1,080. **Student Body:** 50% female, 50% male, 3% out-of-state, 5% international (11 countries represented). Asian 1%, African American 13%, Caucasian 49%, Hispanic 26%, Native American 1%, Pacific Islander <1%, Two or more races 3%, Race unknown 2%.
Retention and Graduation: 62% freshmen return for sophomore year. 28% freshmen graduate within 4 years. 36% freshmen graduate within 6 years. 32% grads go on to further study within 1 year. 24% grads pursue arts and sciences degrees. 2% grads pursue law degrees. 3% grads pursue business degrees. 3% grads pursue medical degrees. **Faculty:** Student/faculty ratio 11:1. 79 full-time faculty, 80% hold PhDs, 0% are members of minority groups, 41% are women. 0% of classes are taught by teaching assistants.

ACADEMICS

Degrees: Bachelor's; Master's. **Classes:** Most classes have 10–19 students. Most lab/discussion sessions have fewer than 10 students. **Most popular majors:** Psychology, General; Sociology, General; Business/Commerce, General. **Special Study Options:** Accelerated program; Cross-registration; Distance learning; Double major; Dual enrollment; English as a Second Language (ESL); Honors program; Internships; Liberal arts/career combination; Student-designed major; Study abroad; Teacher certification program. **Honors programs:** The McMurry University Honors Program is a four-year honors track designed to enrich the academic experience of our most outstanding students. More information is available at https://academics.mcm.edu/Honors/index.html. **Combined degree programs:** BA/DDS. **Disability Services offered:** Note-taking services; Tutors. **Career services:** Alumni services; Career assessment; Internships.

FACILITIES

Housing: Apartments for single students; Coed dorms; Men's dorms; Special housing for disabled students; Wellness housing; Women's dorms; 85% of campus accessible to physically disabled. **Special Academic Facilities/ Equipment:** Academic Enrichment Center in the Jay Rollins Library (which is a member of the Abilene Library Consortium along with three other local university libraries and the Abilene Public Library).

CAMPUS LIFE

Environment: City. **Activities:** Campus Ministries; Choral groups; Concert band; Drama/theater; Jazz band; Literary magazine; Marching band; Model UN; Music ensembles; Musical theater; Student government; Student newspaper; Yearbook. 40 registered organizations, 14 honor societies, 3 religious organizations, 4 fraternities, 6 sororities on campus. **On-Campus Highlights:** Garrison Campus Center. **Environmental Initiatives:** Effluent water—The University uses effluent water for all landscape irrigation.

ADMISSIONS

Freshman Academic Profile: Average high school GPA 3.5. 12% in top 10% of high school class, 40% in top 25% of high school class, 72% in top 50% of high school class. 98% from public high schools. **Test Scores:** SAT Math middle 50% range 470–570. SAT EBRW middle 50% range 480–580. ACT middle 50% range 18–23. **Basis for Candidate Selection:** *Very important factors include:* rigor of secondary school record, class rank, academic GPA, standardized test scores. *Important factors include:* application essay, interview, extracurricular activities, talent/ability, character/personal qualities. *Other factors include:* recommendation(s), first generation, alumni/ae relation, geographical residence, state residency, religious affiliation/commitment, work experience, level of applicant's interest. **Freshman Admission Requirements:** High school diploma is required and GED is accepted. *Academic units recommended:* 4 English, 4 math, 4 science, 2 foreign language, 4 social studies. **Freshman Admission Statistics:** 1,826 applied, 41% admitted, 29% enrolled. **General Admission Information:** Application fee $25. Priority deadline 3/1. Regular application deadline 8/15. Non-fall registration accepted. Admission may be deferred for a maximum of 1 year.

COSTS AND FINANCIAL AID

Annual tuition $27,154. Room and board $8,602. Required fees $265. Average book and supplies expense $1,200. **Required Forms and Deadlines:** FAFSA; Institution's own financial aid form. **Notification of Awards:** Applicants will be notified of awards on a rolling basis beginning 11/1. **Types of Aid:** *Need-based scholarships/grants:* College/university scholarship or grant aid from institutional funds; Federal Nursing Scholarships; Federal Pell; Private scholarships; SEOG; State scholarships/grants. *Loans:* Direct PLUS loans; Direct Subsidized Stafford Loans; Direct Unsubsidized Stafford Loans. **Student Employment:** Federal Work-Study Program available. Institutional employment available. **Financial Aid Statistics:** 100% needy freshmen, 100% needy undergrads receive need-based scholarship or grant aid. 8% freshmen, 9% undergrads receive non-need-based scholarship or grant aid. 91% freshmen, 90% undergrads receive need-based self-help aid. 0% freshmen, 0% undergrads receive athletic scholarships. 98% freshmen, 90% undergrads receive any aid. 87% undergrads borrow to pay for school. Average cumulative indebtedness $36,323. **Criteria awarding aid:** *Need-based:* Minority status, Religious affiliation. *Non-need-based:* Academics, Art, Athletics, Job skills, Leadership, Music/drama, Religious affiliation.

MCNEESE STATE UNIVERSITY

Box 91740, Lake Charles, LA 70609
Phone: 337-475-5504 **Financial Aid Phone:** 337 475-5065
E-mail: admissions@mcneese.edu
Fax: 337-475-5151 **Website:** www.mcneese.edu **ACT Code:** 1594

This public school was founded in 1939.

RATINGS

Admissions Selectivity Rating: 78   **Fire Safety Rating:** 60*   **Green Rating:** 60*

STUDENTS AND FACULTY

Enrollment: 6,598. **Student Body:** 60% female, 40% male, 8% out-of-state, 7% international (53 countries represented). Asian 2%, African American 18%, Caucasian 68%, Hispanic 3%, Native American 1%, Pacific Islander <1%, Two or more races 2%, Race unknown <1%.
Retention and Graduation: 67% freshmen return for sophomore year.
Faculty: Student/faculty ratio 20:1. 256 full-time faculty, 65% hold PhDs, 0% are members of minority groups, 47% are women.

ACADEMICS

Degrees: Associate; Bachelor's; Master's; Post-bachelor's certificate; Post-master's certificate.

FACILITIES

Campus Network: 100% of classrooms, 50% of dorms, 100% of student union, 100% of libraries, 100% of dining areas, 50% of common outdoor areas have wireless network access.

CAMPUS LIFE

Environment: City. **Activities:** Campus Ministries; Choral groups; Concert band; Drama/theater; International Student Organization; Jazz band; Marching band; Musical theater; Pep band; Student government; Student newspaper; Yearbook.

ADMISSIONS

Freshman Academic Profile: 18% in top 10% of high school class, 41% in top 25% of high school class, 73% in top 50% of high school class. **Test Scores:** SAT Math middle 50% range 470–580. SAT EBRW middle 50% range 440–530. ACT middle 50% range 20–24. **Freshman Admission Statistics:** 3,002 applied, 82% admitted, 58% enrolled. **Transfer Admission Requirements:** College transcript(s), statement of good standing from prior institution(s). Minimum college GPA of 2.00 required. Lowest grade transferable C.

MCPHERSON COLLEGE

P.O. Box 1402, McPherson, KS 67460
Phone: 620-241-0731 **Financial Aid Phone:** 800-365-7402
E-mail: admiss@mcpherson.edu **CEEB Code:** 6404
Fax: 620-241-8443 **ACT Code:** 1440

This private school, affiliated with the Church of Brethren, was founded in 1887. It has a 23 acre campus.

RATINGS

Admissions Selectivity Rating: 76   **Fire Safety Rating:** 60*   **Green Rating:** 60*

STUDENTS AND FACULTY

Enrollment: 573. **Student Body:** 43% female, 57% male, 5% out-of-state, 1% international. Asian 2%, African American 10%, Caucasian 77%, Hispanic 7%, Native American 3%, Race unknown 0%.
Retention and Graduation: 67% freshmen return for sophomore year. 9% grads go on to further study within 1 year. 9% grads pursue medical degrees.
Faculty: Student/faculty ratio 15:1. 34 full-time faculty, 82% hold PhDs, 12% are members of minority groups, 32% are women. 0% of classes are taught by teaching assistants.

ACADEMICS

Degrees: Bachelor's. **Classes:** Most classes have 10–19 students. Most lab/discussion sessions have 10–19 students. **Special Study Options:** Cross-registration; Double major; Dual enrollment; English as a Second Language (ESL); Independent study; Internships; Student-designed major; Study abroad; Teacher certification program.

FACILITIES

Housing: Coed dorms; Men's dorms; Special housing for disabled students; Women's dorms. **Special Academic Facilities/Equipment:** Natural history museum. **Campus Network:** 100% of classrooms, 100% of dorms, 100% of student union, 100% of libraries, 100% of dining areas, 95% of common outdoor areas have wireless network access.

CAMPUS LIFE

Environment: Village. **Activities:** Campus Ministries; Choral groups; Concert band; Dance; Drama/theater; Jazz band; Music ensembles; Musical theater; Pep band; Student government; Student newspaper; Yearbook. **Athletics (Intercollegiate):** *Men:* baseball, basketball, cross-country, football, soccer, tennis, track/field (outdoor). *Women:* basketball, cross-country, golf, tennis, track/field (outdoor), volleyball.

ADMISSIONS

Freshman Academic Profile: Average high school GPA 3.2. 9% in top 10% of high school class, 25% in top 25% of high school class, 60% in top 50% of high school class. 99% from public high schools. **Test Scores:** SAT Math middle 50% range 450–563. SAT EBRW middle 50% range 448–560. ACT middle 50% range 19–24. **Basis for Candidate Selection:** *Very important factors include:* rigor of secondary school record, academic GPA, standardized test scores. *Other factors include:* class rank, recommendation(s), interview, extracurricular activities, talent/ability, character/personal qualities, first generation, volunteer work, work experience, level of applicant's interest. **Freshman Admission Requirements:** High school diploma is required and GED is accepted. **Freshman Admission Statistics:** 474 applied, 87% admitted, 54% enrolled. **Transfer Admission Requirements:** High school transcript, college transcript(s), statement of good standing from prior institution(s). Minimum college GPA of 2.0 required. Lowest grade transferable C. **General Admission Information:** Application fee $25. Priority deadline 3/1. Non-fall registration accepted. Admission may be deferred for a maximum of 1 year.

COSTS AND FINANCIAL AID

Annual tuition $17,900. Room and board $6,910. Required fees $500. Average book and supplies expense $1,170. **Required Forms and Deadlines:** FAFSA; State aid form. **Notification of Awards:** Applicants will be notified of awards on a rolling basis beginning 3/1. **Types of Aid:** *Need-based scholarships/grants:* College/university scholarship or grant aid from institutional funds; Federal Pell; Private scholarships; SEOG; State scholarships/grants; United Negro College Fund. **Student Employment:** Federal Work-Study Program available. Institutional employment available. **Financial Aid Statistics:** 85% needy freshmen, 85% needy undergrads receive need-based scholarship or grant aid. 95% freshmen, 98% undergrads receive non-need-based scholarship or grant aid. 86% freshmen, 88% undergrads receive need-based self-help aid. 66% freshmen, 38% undergrads receive athletic scholarships. **Criteria awarding aid:** *Non-need-based:* Academics, Alumni affiliation, Art, Athletics, Music/drama, Religious affiliation, State/district residency.

MEDCENTER ONE COLLEGE OF NURSING

512 North 7th Street, Bismarck, ND 58501
Phone: 701-323-6271 **Financial Aid Phone:** 701-323-6270
E-mail: msmith@mohs.org
Fax: 701-323-6289 **Website:** www.medcenterone.com/collegeofnursing **ACT Code:** 3197

This private school was founded in 1988.

RATINGS
Admissions Selectivity Rating: 60*   **Fire Safety Rating:** 60*   **Green Rating:** 60*

STUDENTS AND FACULTY
Enrollment: 91. **Student Body:** 91% female, 9% male, 6% out-of-state, 0% international. Asian 1%, African American 4%, Caucasian 90%, Hispanic 1%, Native American 0%, Pacific Islander 0%, Two or more races 3%, Race unknown 0%.
Faculty: Student/faculty ratio 8:1. 10 full-time faculty, 10% hold PhDs, 0% are members of minority groups, 100% are women. 0% of classes are taught by teaching assistants.

ACADEMICS
Degrees: Bachelor's. **Classes:** Most classes have 40–49 students. Most lab/discussion sessions have fewer than 10 students. **Most popular majors:** Nursing/Registered Nurse (Rn, Asn, Bsn, Msn). **Special Study Options:** Independent study; Internships.

FACILITIES
Special Academic Facilities/Equipment: Alumni Corner. **Campus Network:** 100% of classrooms, 100% of dorms, 100% of student union, 100% of libraries, 100% of dining areas, 25% of common outdoor areas have wireless network access.

CAMPUS LIFE
Environment: Rural. **Activities:** Student government. 2 registered organizations, 1 honor society on campus. **On-Campus Highlights:** Simulation Lab.

ADMISSIONS
Freshman Admission Requirements: High school diploma is required and GED is accepted. **Transfer Admission Requirements:** High school transcript, college transcript(s), essay or personal statement, interview. Minimum college GPA of 2.5 required. Lowest grade transferable C. **General Admission Information:** Application fee $40. Priority deadline 11/1.

COSTS AND FINANCIAL AID
Annual tuition $9,720. Average book and supplies expense $1,169. **Notification of Awards:** Applicants will be notified of awards on a rolling basis beginning 6/1. **Types of Aid:** *Need-based scholarships/grants:* College/university scholarship or grant aid from institutional funds; Federal Pell; Private scholarships; SEOG; State scholarships/grants. **Student Employment:** Federal Work-Study Program available. **Financial Aid Statistics:** 78% needy undergrads receive need-based scholarship or grant aid. 29% undergrads receive non-need-based scholarship or grant aid. 77% undergrads receive need-based self-help aid. 0% undergrads receive athletic scholarships. **Criteria awarding aid:** *Need-based:* Academics, Alumni affiliation, Leadership. *Non-need-based:* Academics, Alumni affiliation, Leadership.

MEDICAL UNIVERSITY OF SOUTH CAROLINA

41 Bee Street, Charleston, SC 29425-0203
Phone: 843-792-3281.**Financial Aid Phone:** (843)792-2536
E-mail: oesadmis@musc.edu
Fax: 843-792-6615 **Website:** www.musc.edu **ACT Code:** 6440

This public school was founded in 1824. It has a 82 acre campus.

RATINGS
Admissions Selectivity Rating: 60*   **Fire Safety Rating:** 60*   **Green Rating:** 60*

STUDENTS AND FACULTY
Enrollment: 198. **Student Body:** 79% female, 21% male, 12% out-of-state, 0% international (26 countries represented). Asian 3%, African American 11%, Caucasian 73%, Hispanic 6%, Native American 1%, Pacific Islander 0%, Two or more races 1%, Race unknown 5%.
Faculty: Student/faculty ratio 2:1. 153 full-time faculty, 92% hold PhDs, 10% are members of minority groups, 56% are women. 0% of classes are taught by teaching assistants.

ACADEMICS
Degrees: Bachelor's; Doctoral degree—professional practice; Doctoral degree research/scholarship; Master's; Post-bachelor's certificate; Post-master's certificate. **Classes:** Most classes have 50–99 students. **Most popular majors:** Registered Nursing/Registered Nurse. **Special Study Options:** Cross-registration; Distance learning. **Disability Services offered:** Note-taking services; Reader services; Tape recorders; Tutors. **Career services:** Internships.

FACILITIES
Housing: 97% of campus accessible to physically disabled. **Special Academic Facilities/Equipment:** Dental Museum, Medical Museum, Pharmacy Museum, and Waring Historical Library. **Campus Network:** 100% of classrooms, 100% of dorms, 100% of student union, 100% of libraries, 50% of dining areas, 74% of common outdoor areas have wireless network access.

CAMPUS LIFE
Environment: City. **Activities:** Campus Ministries; Choral groups; International Student Organization; Literary magazine; Music ensembles; Student government. 77 registered organizations, 4 honor societies on campus. **On-Campus Highlights:** Student Activity and Fitness Center. **Environmental Initiatives:** Installed ground source heat pump as first renewable energy project.

ADMISSIONS
Freshman Admission Requirements: High school diploma is required and GED is accepted. **General Admission Information:** Application fee $95. Regular application deadline 6/30.

COSTS AND FINANCIAL AID
Annual in-state tuition $14,018. Annual out-of-state tuition $23,824. **Required Forms and Deadlines:** FAFSA; Institution's own financial aid form. **Types of Aid:** *Need-based scholarships/grants:* College/university scholarship or grant aid from institutional funds; Federal Nursing Scholarships; Federal Pell; Private scholarships; SEOG; State scholarships/grants. **Student Employment:** Federal Work-Study Program available. **Financial Aid Statistics:** 49% needy undergrads receive need-based scholarship or grant aid. 23% undergrads receive non-need-based scholarship or grant aid. 98% undergrads receive need-based self-help aid. 0% undergrads receive athletic scholarships. 75% undergrads receive any aid. **Criteria awarding aid:** *Need-based:* Academics, Alumni affiliation, Minority status. *Non-need-based:* Academics, Alumni affiliation, Minority status, State/district residency.

MENLO COLLEGE

1000 El Camino Real, Atherton, CA 94027
Phone: 650-543-3753 **Financial Aid Phone:** 650-543-3880
E-mail: admissions@menlo.edu **CEEB Code:** 1236
Fax: 650-543-4103 **Website:** www.menlo.edu **ACT Code:** 0330

This private school was founded in 1927. It has a 45 acre campus.

RATINGS
Admissions Selectivity Rating: 72   **Fire Safety Rating:** 78   **Green Rating:** 60*

STUDENTS AND FACULTY
Enrollment: 774. **Student Body:** 45% female, 55% male, 19% out-of-state, 14% international (35 countries represented). Asian 10%, African American 6%, Caucasian 26%, Hispanic 23%, Native American 1%, Pacific Islander 2%, Two or more races 9%, Race unknown 10%.
Retention and Graduation: 77% freshmen return for sophomore year.
Faculty: Student/faculty ratio 14:1. 30 full-time faculty, 87% hold PhDs, 33% are members of minority groups, 53% are women. 0% of classes are taught by teaching assistants.

ACADEMICS
Degrees: Bachelor's. **Classes:** Most classes have 20–29 students. Most lab/discussion sessions have 20–29 students. **Most popular majors:** Accounting; Marketing/Marketing Management, General; Sport and Fitness Administration/Management. **Special Study Options:** Accelerated program; Double major; English as a Second Language (ESL); Independent study; Internships; Student-designed major; Study abroad. **Disability Services offered:** Note-taking services; Reader services; Tape recorders; Tutors. **Career services:** Alumni network; Alumni services; Career assessment; Career/job search classes; Internships; Regional alumni.

FACILITIES
Housing: Coed dorms; Men's dorms; Special housing for disabled students; Women's dorms; 95% of campus accessible to physically disabled.

CAMPUS LIFE
Environment: Town. **Activities:** Dance; International Student Organization; Student government; Student newspaper; Student-run film society. 38 registered organizations, 3 honor societies on campus. **Athletics (Intercollegiate):** *Men:* baseball, basketball, cross-country, football, golf, soccer, wrestling. *Women:* basketball, cross-country, soccer, softball, volleyball, wrestling. **On-Campus Highlights:** Brawner Hall **Environmental Initiatives:** Plastic bottle and styrofoam cups free campus.

ADMISSIONS
Freshman Academic Profile: Average high school GPA 3.2. 80% from public high schools. **Basis for Candidate Selection:** *Very important factors include:* rigor of secondary school record, academic GPA, standardized test scores. *Important factors include:* class rank, application essay, recommendation(s), character/personal qualities, volunteer work. *Other factors include:* interview, alumni/ae relation, work experience, level of applicant's interest. **Freshman Admission Requirements:** High school diploma is required and GED is accepted. *Academic units recommended:* 4 English, 3 math, 3 science, 2 foreign language, 3 social studies. **Freshman Admission Statistics:** 2,195 applied, 41% admitted, 18% enrolled. **Transfer Admission Requirements:** College transcript(s), essay or personal statement, statement of good standing from prior institution(s). Minimum college GPA of 2.0 required. Lowest grade transferable C-. **General Admission Information:** Application fee $40. Priority deadline 2/1. Regular application deadline 4/1. Non-fall registration accepted. Admission may be deferred for a maximum of 2 semesters.

COSTS AND FINANCIAL AID
Annual tuition $40,625. Room and board $13,680. Required fees $725. Average book and supplies expense $550. **Required Forms and Deadlines:** FAFSA; State aid form. **Notification of Awards:** Applicants will be notified of awards on a rolling basis beginning 12/15. **Types of Aid:** *Need-based scholarships/grants:* College/university scholarship or grant aid from institutional funds; Federal Pell; SEOG; State scholarships/grants. *Loans:* Direct PLUS loans; Direct Subsidized Stafford Loans; Direct Unsubsidized Stafford Loans. **Student Employment:** Federal Work-Study Program available. Institutional employment available. **Financial Aid Statistics:** 100% needy freshmen, 100% needy undergrads receive need-based scholarship or grant aid. 14% freshmen, 9% undergrads receive non-need-based scholarship or grant aid. 83% freshmen, 88% undergrads receive need-based self-help aid. 12% freshmen,

16% undergrads receive athletic scholarships. 97% freshmen, 96% undergrads receive any aid. 65% undergrads borrow to pay for school. Average cumulative indebtedness $30,145. **Criteria awarding aid:** *Need-based:* Academics, Athletics. *Non-need-based:* Academics, Athletics.

MERCER UNIVERSITY

1501 Mercer University Drive, Macon, GA 31207-0001
Phone: 478-301-2650 **Financial Aid Phone:** 478-301-2670
E-mail: admissions@mercer.edu **CEEB Code:** 5409
Fax: 478-301-2828 **Website:** www.mercer.edu **ACT Code:** 838

This private school was founded in 1833. It has a 150 acre campus.

RATINGS
Admissions Selectivity Rating: 85   **Fire Safety Rating:** 63   **Green Rating:** 60*

STUDENTS AND FACULTY
Enrollment: 3,385. **Student Body:** 54% female, 46% male, 16% out-of-state, 2% international (34 countries represented). Asian 10%, African American 20%, Caucasian 54%, Hispanic 7%, Native American <1%, Pacific Islander <1%, Two or more races 4%, Race unknown 3%.
Retention and Graduation: 86% freshmen return for sophomore year. 52% freshmen graduate within 4 years. 66% freshmen graduate within 6 years. 38% grads go on to further study within 1 year. **Faculty:** Student/faculty ratio 13:1. 402 full-time faculty, 93% hold PhDs, 26% are members of minority groups, 51% are women. 0% of classes are taught by teaching assistants.

ACADEMICS
Degrees: Bachelor's; Certificate; Doctoral degree—other; Doctoral degree—professional practice; Doctoral degree research/scholarship; Master's; Post-bachelor's certificate; Post-master's certificate. **Classes:** Most classes have 10–19 students. Most lab/discussion sessions have 20–29 students. **Most popular majors:** Engineering, General; Biology/Biological Sciences, General; Business/Commerce, General. **Special Study Options:** Accelerated program; Cross-registration; Distance learning; Double major; Dual enrollment; English as a Second Language (ESL); Honors program; Independent study; Internships; Liberal arts/career combination; Student-designed major; Study abroad; Teacher certification program. **Honors programs:** The University Honors Program provides academically advanced students with the supportive environment needed to pursue their intellectual interests through engaged-learning coursework and experiences. The University Honors Program consists of several distinct programs. For more information please see the Mercer Catalog. **Combined degree programs:** BA/MD; BA/MEng. **Disability Services offered:** Note-taking services; Reader services; Tape recorders; Tutors. **Career services:** Alumni network; Alumni services; Career assessment; Career/job search classes; Internships; Regional alumni.

FACILITIES
Housing: Apartments for single students; Coed dorms; Fraternity/sorority housing; Men's dorms; Special housing for international students; Women's dorms; 85% of campus accessible to physically disabled. **Special Academic Facilities/Equipment:** McCorkle Music Building; Spearman C. Godsey Science Building.

CAMPUS LIFE
Environment: City. **Activities:** Campus Ministries; Choral groups; Concert band; Drama/theater; International Student Organization; Jazz band; Literary magazine; Marching band; Model UN; Music ensembles; Musical theater; Opera; Pep band; Radio station; Student government; Student newspaper; Student-run film society; Symphony orchestra. 150 registered organizations, 18 honor societies, 12 religious organizations, 11 fraternities, 7 sororities on campus. **Athletics (Intercollegiate):** *Men:* baseball, basketball, cross-country, golf, riflery, soccer, tennis. *Women:* basketball, cross-country, golf, soccer, softball, tennis, volleyball. **On-Campus Highlights:** University Center. **Environmental Initiatives:** We have long-standing community partnerships to improve and rehabilitate housing and commerical stock in Macon proper, which has significant positive impact on the sustability of the community.

ADMISSIONS

Freshman Academic Profile: Average high school GPA 3.9. 36% in top 10% of high school class, 68% in top 25% of high school class, 92% in top 50% of high school class. **Test Scores:** SAT Math middle 50% range 580–670. SAT EBRW middle 50% range 590–670. ACT middle 50% range 25–30. **Basis for Candidate Selection:** *Very important factors include:* rigor of secondary school record, academic GPA, standardized test scores, level of applicant's interest. *Important factors include:* application essay, recommendation(s), extracurricular activities, talent/ability, character/personal qualities, volunteer work. *Other factors include:* class rank, interview, work experience. **Freshman Admission Requirements:** High school diploma is required and GED is accepted. *Academic units required:* 4 English, 4 math, 4 science, 3 science labs, 2 foreign language, 1 social studies, 2 history. **Freshman Admission Statistics:** 5,034 applied, 74% admitted, 24% enrolled. **Transfer Admission Requirements:** College transcript(s), statement of good standing from prior institution(s). Minimum college GPA of 2.5 required. Lowest grade transferable C. **General Admission Information:** Application fee $50. Priority deadline 2/1. Regular application deadline 7/1. Non-fall registration accepted. Admission may be deferred for a maximum of 1 year.

COSTS AND FINANCIAL AID

Annual tuition $37,508. Room and board $12,968. Required fees $300. Average book and supplies expense $1,200. **Required Forms and Deadlines:** FAFSA. **Notification of Awards:** Applicants will be notified of awards on a rolling basis beginning 1/15. **Types of Aid:** *Need-based scholarships/grants:* College/university scholarship or grant aid from institutional funds; Federal Pell; Private scholarships; SEOG; State scholarships/grants. *Loans:* Direct PLUS loans; Direct Subsidized Stafford Loans; Direct Unsubsidized Stafford Loans. **Student Employment:** Federal Work-Study Program available. **Financial Aid Statistics:** 99% needy freshmen, 99% needy undergrads receive need-based scholarship or grant aid. 27% freshmen, 26% undergrads receive non-need-based scholarship or grant aid. 60% freshmen, 63% undergrads receive need-based self-help aid. 5% freshmen, 5% undergrads receive athletic scholarships. 99% freshmen, 98% undergrads receive any aid. 59% undergrads borrow to pay for school. Average cumulative indebtedness $27,949. **Criteria awarding aid:** *Need-based:* Job skills. *Non-need-based:* Academics, Art, Athletics, Job skills, Leadership, Music/drama, State/district residency.

MERCY COLLEGE

555 Broadway, Dobbs Ferry, NY 10522
Phone: (877) 637-2946 **Financial Aid Phone:** 1-877-MERCY-GO
E-mail: admissions@mercy.edu **CEEB Code:** 2409
Fax: 914-674-7382 **Website:** https://www.mercy.edu/ **ACT Code:** 2814

This private school was founded in 1950. It has a 66 acre campus.

RATINGS

Admissions Selectivity Rating: 75   Fire Safety Rating: 96   Green Rating: 64

STUDENTS AND FACULTY

Enrollment: 7,213. **Student Body:** 70% female, 30% male, 7% out-of-state, 1% international (37 countries represented). Asian 4%, African American 27%, Caucasian 17%, Hispanic 40%, Native American <1%, Pacific Islander <1%, Two or more races 1%, Race unknown 9%. **Retention and Graduation:** 77% freshmen return for sophomore year. 28% freshmen graduate within 4 years. 44% freshmen graduate within 6 years. **Faculty:** Student/faculty ratio 17:1. 247 full-time faculty, 81% hold PhDs, 28% are members of minority groups, 62% are women. 0% of classes are taught by teaching assistants.

ACADEMICS

Degrees: Associate; Bachelor's; Certificate; Doctoral degree—professional practice; Master's; Post-bachelor's certificate; Post-master's certificate. **Classes:** Most classes have 10–19 students. Most lab/discussion sessions have fewer than 10 students. **Most popular majors:** Business Administration and Management, General; Psychology, General; Social Sciences, General. **Special Study Options:** Accelerated program; Cooperative education program; Distance learning; Double major; Honors program; Independent study; Internships; Study abroad; Teacher certification program; Weekend college. **Honors programs:** The Mercy College Honors Program is a scholarly community of highly motivated full-time undergraduate students and dedicated faculty who share a passion for integrated learning, service, and leadership and who seek a challenging

and self-directed intellectual environment. Advantages of participating in the Honors Program include, but are not limited to: Enrollment in small, engaging, seminar-style classes that allow for close interaction with hand-picked Honors faculty as well as other highly motivated students; Priority registration; Opportunity to participate in unique learning experiences and established High Impact Practices, including Living Learning Communities, Study Abroad and Alternative Spring Break, common reads, community-based learning, self-directed research, and attendance or presentation at undergraduate conferences; Opportunities to participate in a variety of special extracurricular activities and events, including receptions, invited speakers, and trips to local cultural and historical attractions; Mentorship from students and faculty in the Honors Program; Official recognition at Commencement. **Combined degree programs:** BA/MA. **Disability Services offered:** Note-taking services; Reader services; Tape recorders; Tutors. **Career services:** Alumni network; Alumni services; Career assessment; Career/job search classes; Internships; Regional alumni.

FACILITIES

Housing: Coed dorms; 75% of campus accessible to physically disabled. **Special Academic Facilities/Equipment:** Students, faculty and the community are further enriched by a number of centers including our Business Program Trading Room, Center for Global Engagement, Cybersecurity Education Center, Speech and Hearing Center, and Centers of Excellence within the Business School including the Strategic Consulting Institute, Center for Entrepreneurship, and Women's Leadership Institute.

CAMPUS LIFE

Environment: Town. **Activities:** Campus Ministries; Choral groups; Dance; Drama/theater; International Student Organization; Jazz band; Model UN; Musical theater; Student government; Student newspaper. 48 registered organizations, 18 honor societies, 1 religious organization on campus. **Athletics (Intercollegiate):** *Men:* baseball, basketball, cross-country, lacrosse, soccer, tennis, track/field (outdoor). *Women:* basketball, cross-country, lacrosse, soccer, softball, track/field (outdoor), volleyball. **On-Campus Highlights:** Waterfront campus on the Hudson River. **Environmental Initiatives:** Updated Central Heating Plant.

ADMISSIONS

Freshman Academic Profile: Average high school GPA 3.2. **Test Scores:** SAT Math middle 50% range 440–540. SAT EBRW middle 50% range 450–540. ACT middle 50% range 17–24. **Basis for Candidate Selection:** *Very important factors include:* academic GPA. *Other factors include:* rigor of secondary school record, class rank, application essay, standardized test scores, recommendation(s), interview, extracurricular activities, talent/ability, character/personal qualities, alumni/ae relation, volunteer work, work experience, level of applicant's interest. **Freshman Admission Requirements:** High school diploma is required and GED is accepted. *Academic units required:* 4 English, 4 math, 3 science, 1 science lab, 3 foreign language, 2 social studies, 2 history, 3 academic electives. *Academic units recommended:* 4 English, 4 math, 3 science, 1 science lab, 3 foreign language, 2 social studies, 2 history, 3 academic electives. **Freshman Admission Statistics:** 6,720 applied, 82% admitted, 18% enrolled. **Transfer Admission Requirements:** College transcript(s). Minimum college GPA of 2.0 required. Lowest grade transferable C. **General Admission Information:** Application fee $40. Non-fall registration accepted. Admission may be deferred for a maximum of 1 year.

COSTS AND FINANCIAL AID

Annual tuition $18,934. Room and board $14,400. Required fees $660. Average book and supplies expense $1,620. **Required Forms and Deadlines:** FAFSA; State aid form. **Notification of Awards:** Applicants will be notified of awards on a rolling basis beginning 2/15. **Types of Aid:** *Need-based scholarships/grants:* College/university scholarship or grant aid from institutional funds; Federal Pell; Private scholarships; SEOG; State scholarships/grants. *Loans:* Direct PLUS loans; Direct Subsidized Stafford Loans; Direct Unsubsidized Stafford Loans. **Student Employment:** Federal Work-Study Program available. Institutional employment available. **Financial Aid Statistics:** 90% needy freshmen, 89% needy undergrads receive need-based scholarship or grant aid. 82% freshmen, 52% undergrads receive non-need-based scholarship or grant aid. 52% freshmen, 68% undergrads receive need-based self-help aid. 6% freshmen, 3% undergrads receive athletic scholarships. 94.7% freshmen, 88.6% undergrads receive any aid. 78% undergrads borrow to pay for school. Average cumulative indebtedness $23,942. **Criteria awarding aid:** *Non-need-based:* Academics, Athletics.

MERCYHURST UNIVERSITY

Admissions, Erie, PA 16546
Phone: 814-824-2202 **Financial Aid Phone:** 814 824 2288
E-mail: admissions@mercyhurst.edu **CEEB Code:** 2410
Fax: 814-824-2071 **Website:** www.mercyhurst.edu **ACT Code:** 3629

This private school, affiliated with the Roman Catholic Church, was founded in 1926. It has a 75 acre campus.

RATINGS
Admissions Selectivity Rating: 77   Fire Safety Rating: 91   Green Rating: 95

STUDENTS AND FACULTY
Enrollment: 2,680. **Student Body:** 56% female, 44% male, 48% out-of-state, 8% international. Asian 1%, African American 4%, Caucasian 77%, Hispanic 2%, Native American <1%, Pacific Islander 0%, Two or more races 0%, Race unknown 7%. **Retention and Graduation:** 79% freshmen return for sophomore year. **Faculty:** Student/faculty ratio 14:1. 164 full-time faculty, 68% hold PhDs, 9% are members of minority groups, 44% are women. 0% of classes are taught by teaching assistants.

ACADEMICS
Degrees: Bachelor's; Master's; Post-bachelor's certificate. **Classes:** Most classes have 20–29 students. Most lab/discussion sessions have 10–19 students. **Most popular majors:** International/Globalization Studies; Business Administration and Management, General; Elementary Education and Teaching. **Special Study Options:** Cross-registration; Distance learning; Double major; Honors program; Independent study; Internships; Liberal arts/career combination; Student-designed major; Study abroad; Teacher certification program. **Disability Services offered:** Note-taking services; Reader services; Tape recorders; Tutors. **Career services:** Alumni network; Alumni services; Career assessment; Career/job search classes; Internships.

FACILITIES
Housing: Apartments for single students; Coed dorms; Men's dorms; Theme housing; Women's dorms. **Special Academic Facilities/Equipment:** Art gallery, college-owned restaurant for hotel/restaurant management department, observatory, archaeology lab.

CAMPUS LIFE
Environment: City. **Activities:** Campus Ministries; Choral groups; Dance; Drama/theater; International Student Organization; Jazz band; Literary magazine; Model UN; Music ensembles; Musical theater; Pep band; Radio station; Student government; Student newspaper; Television station; Yearbook. 80 registered organizations, 9 honor societies, 2 religious organizations on campus. **Athletics (Intercollegiate):** *Men:* baseball, basketball, cheerleading, crew/rowing, cross-country, football, golf, ice hockey, lacrosse, soccer, tennis, volleyball, water polo, wrestling. *Women:* basketball, cheerleading, crew/rowing, cross-country, field hockey, golf, ice hockey, lacrosse, soccer, softball, tennis, volleyball, water polo. **On-Campus Highlights:** Performing Arts Center. **Environmental Initiatives:** Sustainability Studies academic program.

ADMISSIONS
Freshman Academic Profile: Average high school GPA 3.4. 21% in top 10% of high school class, 29% in top 25% of high school class, 87% in top 50% of high school class. 55% from public high schools. **Test Scores:** SAT Math middle 50% range 470–570. SAT EBRW middle 50% range 470–580. ACT middle 50% range 21–26. **Basis for Candidate Selection:** *Very important factors include:* rigor of secondary school record, class rank, academic GPA, standardized test scores. *Important factors include:* application essay, recommendation(s), interview, extracurricular activities, talent/ability, character/personal qualities. *Other factors include:* alumni/ae relation, geographical residence, state residency, religious affiliation/commitment, racial/ethnic status, volunteer work, work experience, level of applicant's interest. **Freshman Admission Requirements:** High school diploma is required and GED is accepted. *Academic units required:* 4 English, 3 math, 2 science, 1 science lab, 2 foreign language, 5 social studies. *Academic units recommended:* 4 English, 3 math, 3 science, 2 science labs, 2 foreign language, 5 social studies. **Freshman Admission Statistics:** 2,938 applied, 75% admitted, 27% enrolled. **Transfer Admission Requirements:** High school transcript, college transcript(s), standardized test scores. Minimum college GPA of 2.0 required. Lowest grade transferable C. **General Admission Information:** Application fee $30. Priority deadline 5/1. Non-fall registration accepted. Admission may be deferred for a maximum of 1 year.

COSTS AND FINANCIAL AID
Annual tuition $29,600. Room and board $10,800. Required fees $1,885. Average book and supplies expense $1,000. **Notification of Awards:** Applicants will be notified of awards on a rolling basis beginning 2/15. **Types of Aid:** *Need-based scholarships/grants:* College/university scholarship or grant aid from institutional funds; Federal Pell; Private scholarships; SEOG; State scholarships/grants. *Loans:* Direct PLUS loans; Direct Subsidized Stafford Loans; Direct Unsubsidized Stafford Loans. **Student Employment:** Federal Work-Study Program available. Institutional employment available. **Financial Aid Statistics:** 95% needy freshmen, 94% needy undergrads receive need-based scholarship or grant aid. 75% freshmen, 66% undergrads receive non-need-based scholarship or grant aid. 82% freshmen, 87% undergrads receive need-based self-help aid. 5% freshmen, 5% undergrads receive athletic scholarships. 93% freshmen receive any aid. **Criteria awarding aid:** *Need-based:* Academics, Alumni affiliation, Art, Athletics, Leadership, Music/drama, Religious affiliation. *Non-need-based:* Academics, Alumni affiliation, Art, Athletics, Leadership, Music/drama, Religious affiliation.

MEREDITH COLLEGE

3800 Hillsborough St., Raleigh, NC
Financial Aid Phone: 919-760-8565
CEEB Code: 5410
Website: www.meredith.edu **ACT Code:** 3126

This private school was founded in 1891. It has a 225 acre campus.

RATINGS
Admissions Selectivity Rating: 85 · Fire Safety Rating: 71   Green Rating: 64

STUDENTS AND FACULTY
Enrollment: 1,563. **Student Body:** 100% female, 0% male, 15% out-of-state, 1% international (24 countries represented). Asian 3%, African American 8%, Caucasian 69%, Hispanic 9%, Native American 1%, Pacific Islander <1%, Two or more races 3%, Race unknown 6%. **Retention and Graduation:** 80% freshmen return for sophomore year. 53% freshmen graduate within 4 years. 63% freshmen graduate within 6 years. **Faculty:** Student/faculty ratio 11:1. 134 full-time faculty, 90% hold PhDs, 8% are members of minority groups, 69% are women. 0% of classes are taught by teaching assistants.

ACADEMICS
Degrees: Bachelor's; Master's; Post-bachelor's certificate. **Classes:** Most classes have 10–19 students. Most lab/discussion sessions have 10–19 students. **Most popular majors:** Business/Commerce, General; Biology/Biological Sciences, General; Psychology, General. **Special Study Options:** Accelerated program; Cooperative education program; Cross-registration; Double major; Dual enrollment; Honors program; Independent study; Internships; Student-designed major; Study abroad; Teacher certification program. **Honors programs:** Meredith offers an enriched academic and co-curricular Honors Program that spans the four years and involves honors courses in general education, in the major field, and a thesis or equivalent project. Interdisciplinary honors courses and weekend trips/programs enrich the experience, and a Focus on Excellence series offers a variety of outings to cultural/intellectual/entertainment venues. Scholarships are provided for Honors Program participants. **Disability Services offered:** Note-taking services; Reader services; Tape recorders; Tutors. **Career services:** Alumni network; Alumni services; Career assessment; Career/job search classes; Internships.

FACILITIES
Housing: Apartments for single students; Women's dorms; 80% of campus accessible to physically disabled. **Special Academic Facilities/Equipment:** Art gallery, amphitheatre, child-care lab, learning center and fitness center. Experimental and clinical psychology labs including an autism lab. A new Science and Mathematics Building provides a rooftop telescope platform for astronomy observations, an electron microscope suite, greenhouse, and 15 student/faculty research labs.

CAMPUS LIFE
Environment: Metropolis. **Activities:** Campus Ministries; Choral groups; Dance; Drama/theater; International Student Organization; Literary magazine; Model UN; Music ensembles; Musical theater; Student government; Student newspaper; Symphony orchestra; Yearbook. 100 registered organizations, 28 honor societies, 8 religious organizations on campus. **Athletics**

(Intercollegiate): *Women:* basketball, cross-country, soccer, softball, tennis, volleyball. **On-Campus Highlights:** Science and Math Building.

ADMISSIONS

Freshman Academic Profile: Average high school GPA 3.4. 17% in top 10% of high school class, 48% in top 25% of high school class, 79% in top 50% of high school class. **Test Scores:** SAT Math middle 50% range 490–590. SAT EBRW middle 50% range 510–610. ACT middle 50% range 19–26. **Basis for Candidate Selection:** *Very important factors include:* academic GPA, application essay, recommendation(s), character/personal qualities. *Important factors include:* rigor of secondary school record, class rank, standardized test scores, interview, extracurricular activities, talent/ability, volunteer work. *Other factors include:* first generation, alumni/ae relation. **Freshman Admission Requirements:** High school diploma is required and GED is accepted.; High school diploma is required and GED is not accepted. *Academic units required:* 4 English, 3 math, 3 science, 2 foreign language, 1 academic elective. **Freshman Admission Statistics:** 1,897 applied, 63% admitted, 34% enrolled. **Transfer Admission Requirements:** High school transcript, college transcript(s), statement of good standing from prior institution(s). Minimum college GPA of 2.0 required. Lowest grade transferable C. **General Admission Information:** Application fee $40. Priority deadline 2/15. Regular application deadline 2/15. Non-fall registration accepted.

COSTS AND FINANCIAL AID

Annual tuition $38,520. Room and board $11,360. Required fees $100. Average book and supplies expense $850. **Required Forms and Deadlines:** FAFSA. **Notification of Awards:** Applicants will be notified of awards on a rolling basis beginning 12/10. **Types of Aid:** *Need-based scholarships/ grants:* College/university scholarship or grant aid from institutional funds; Federal Pell; Private scholarships; SEOG; State scholarships/grants. *Loans:* Direct PLUS loans; Direct Subsidized Stafford Loans; Direct Unsubsidized Stafford Loans. **Financial Aid Statistics:** 100% needy freshmen, 100% needy undergrads receive need-based scholarship or grant aid. 0% freshmen, 0% undergrads receive non-need-based scholarship or grant aid. 89% freshmen, 91% undergrads receive need-based self-help aid. 0% freshmen, 0% undergrads receive athletic scholarships. 71% undergrads borrow to pay for school. Average cumulative indebtedness $34,993. **Criteria awarding aid:** *Need-based:* Academics, Art, Leadership, Minority status, Music/drama, Religious affiliation. *Non-need-based:* Academics, Art, Leadership, Minority status, Music/drama, Religious affiliation, State/district residency.

MERRIMACK COLLEGE

Office of Admission, North Andover, MA 01845
Phone: 978-837-5100 **Financial Aid Phone:** 978-837-5186
E-mail: admission@merrimack.edu **CEEB Code:** 3525
Fax: 978-837-5133 **Website:** www.merrimack.edu

This private school, affiliated with the Roman Catholic Church, was founded in 1947. It has a 220 acre campus.

RATINGS

Admissions Selectivity Rating: 65 · **Fire Safety Rating:** 98 · **Green Rating:** 63

STUDENTS AND FACULTY

Enrollment: 3,664. **Student Body:** 51% female, 49% male, 29% out-of-state, 2% international (28 countries represented). Asian 2%, African American 3%, Caucasian 77%, Hispanic 7%, Native American 0%, Pacific Islander <1%, Two or more races 2%, Race unknown 0%.
Retention and Graduation: 85% freshmen return for sophomore year. 63% freshmen graduate within 4 years. 68% freshmen graduate within 6 years.
Faculty: Student/faculty ratio 14:1. 197 full-time faculty, 88% hold PhDs, 15% are members of minority groups, 54% are women. 0% of classes are taught by teaching assistants.

ACADEMICS

Degrees: Bachelor's; Master's; Post-master's certificate. **Classes:** Most classes have 20–29 students. **Most popular majors:** Human Development and Family Studies, General; Marketing; Health Professions and Related Clinical Sciences, Other. **Special Study Options:** Accelerated program; Cooperative education program; Cross-registration; Distance learning; Double major; Dual enrollment; Honors program; Independent study; Internships; Liberal arts/career combination; Student-designed major; Study abroad; Teacher certification program. **Honors programs:** The Honors Program offers students

with strong academic credentials, class standing, and leadership qualities the opportunity to study with other exceptional students in smaller and more challenging classes. It is an innovative and exciting approach to fulfilling the college's general education requirements and includes a variety of social and co-curricular activities. **Disability Services offered:** Note-taking services; Reader services; Tape recorders; Tutors. **Career services:** Alumni network; Alumni services; Career assessment; Career/job search classes; Internships; Regional alumni.

FACILITIES

Housing: Apartments for single students; Coed dorms; Special housing for disabled students; Theme housing; 95% of campus accessible to physically disabled. **Special Academic Facilities/Equipment:** The Writers House, The Markets Lab, Financial Capability Center, Astronomy Dome and Telescope, Rogers Center for the Arts, Diversity Education Center, Center for Campus Ministry, Center for the Study of Jewish-Christian-Muslim Relations, Center for Engaged Democracy, RFID (Radio Frequency Identification) Technology Lab, Center for Campus Ministry, Center for Excellence in Teaching & Learning, Service Learning Center, Memory & Sleep Lab, Center for Sustainability and the Environment, Interdisciplinary Institute, Merrimack Institute for New Teacher Support.

CAMPUS LIFE

Environment: Town. **Activities:** Campus Ministries; Choral groups; Dance; Drama/theater; International Student Organization; Jazz band; Model UN; Music ensembles; Musical theater; Pep band; Radio station; Student government; Student newspaper; Student-run film society; Television station; Yearbook. 59 registered organizations, 2 religious organizations, 1 fraternity, 2 sororities on campus. **Athletics (Intercollegiate):** *Men:* baseball, basketball, cross-country, football, ice hockey, lacrosse, soccer, tennis. *Women:* basketball, cross-country, field hockey, lacrosse, soccer, softball, tennis, volleyball. **On-Campus Highlights:** The Sanctuary Coffeehouse.

ADMISSIONS

Freshman Academic Profile: Average high school GPA 3.2. 76% from public high schools. **Basis for Candidate Selection:** *Very important factors include:* rigor of secondary school record, academic GPA, application essay. *Important factors include:* class rank, recommendation(s), interview, extracurricular activities, talent/ability, character/personal qualities, volunteer work. *Other factors include:* standardized test scores, first generation, alumni/ae relation, geographical residence, religious affiliation/commitment, racial/ethnic status. **Freshman Admission Requirements:** High school diploma is required and GED is accepted. *Academic units required:* 4 English, 3 math, 2 science, 2 foreign language, 2 history. **Freshman Admission Statistics:** 8,668 applied, 83% admitted, 16% enrolled. **Transfer Admission Requirements:** College transcript(s), essay or personal statement. Minimum college GPA of 2.5 required. Lowest grade transferable C. **General Admission Information:** Regular application deadline 2/15. Non-fall registration accepted. Admission may be deferred for a maximum of 1 year.

COSTS AND FINANCIAL AID

Annual tuition $39,390. Room and board $15,845. Required fees $2,370. Average book and supplies expense $1,000. **Required Forms and Deadlines:** FAFSA. **Notification of Awards:** Applicants will be notified of awards on a rolling basis beginning 3/15. **Types of Aid:** *Need-based scholarships/grants:* College/university scholarship or grant aid from institutional funds; Federal Pell; Private scholarships; SEOG; State scholarships/grants. *Loans:* Direct PLUS loans; Direct Subsidized Stafford Loans; Direct Unsubsidized Stafford Loans. **Student Employment:** Federal Work-Study Program available. Institutional employment available. **Financial Aid Statistics:** 100% needy freshmen, 99% needy undergrads receive need-based scholarship or grant aid. 14% freshmen, 12% undergrads receive non-need-based scholarship or grant aid. 80% freshmen, 83% undergrads receive need-based self-help aid. 7% freshmen, 7% undergrads receive athletic scholarships. **Criteria awarding aid:** *Need-based:* Athletics. *Non-need-based:* Academics, Alumni affiliation, Athletics, Leadership, Music/drama, Religious affiliation.

MESSIAH COLLEGE

One College Avenue, Mechanicsburg, PA 17055
Phone: (717) 691-6000 **Financial Aid Phone:** (717) 691-6007
E-mail: admissions@messiah.edu **CEEB Code:** 2411
Fax: 717-691-2307 **Website:** www.messiah.edu **ACT Code:** 3630

This private school, affiliated with the Interdenominational Christian, was founded in 1909. It has a 471 acre campus.

RATINGS
Admissions Selectivity Rating: 85 **Fire Safety Rating:** 86 **Green Rating:** 79

STUDENTS AND FACULTY
Enrollment: 2,579. **Student Body:** 60% female, 40% male, 35% out-of-state, 4% international (28 countries represented). Asian 2%, African American 3%, Caucasian 81%, Hispanic 6%, Native American <1%, Pacific Islander 0%, Two or more races 4%, Race unknown <1%.
Retention and Graduation: 89% freshmen return for sophomore year. 75% freshmen graduate within 4 years. 79% freshmen graduate within 6 years. 17% grads go on to further study within 1 year. 42% grads pursue arts and sciences degrees. 2% grads pursue law degrees. 6% grads pursue business degrees. 13% grads pursue medical degrees. **Faculty:** Student/faculty ratio 12:1. 201 full-time faculty, 85% hold PhDs, 11% are members of minority groups, 42% are women. 0% of classes are taught by teaching assistants.

ACADEMICS
Degrees: Bachelor's; Certificate; Doctoral degree—professional practice; Master's; Post-bachelor's certificate; Post-master's certificate. **Classes:** Most classes have 10–19 students. Most lab/discussion sessions have 10–19 students. **Most popular majors:** Engineering, General; Health Professions And Related Programs; Registered Nursing/Registered Nurse. **Special Study Options:** Accelerated program; Double major; Dual enrollment; English as a Second Language (ESL); Exchange student program (domestic); Honors program; Independent study; Internships; Student-designed major; Study abroad; Teacher certification program. **Honors programs:** The College Honors Program is designed for students who demonstrate high scholarly ability early in their academic career. The program provides a series of interdisciplinary honors courses which satisfy selected general education requirements. Participation in the program culminates in an honors research project, typically during the senior year. In addition, various campus activities are designed each semester for participants in the College Honors Program. Admission to the program is highly competitive and students selected for the College Honors Program receive either full tuition or partial tuition scholarships. **Disability Services offered:** Note-taking services; Reader services; Tape recorders; Tutors. **Career services:** Alumni network; Alumni services; Career assessment; Internships; Regional alumni.

FACILITIES
Housing: Apartments for single students; Coed dorms; Men's dorms; Special housing for disabled students; Special housing for international students; Theme housing; Women's dorms; 80% of campus accessible to physically disabled. **Special Academic Facilities/Equipment:** Ernest L. Boyer Center; Brethren in Christ Historical Society and Archives; Oakes Museum of Natural History.

CAMPUS LIFE
Environment: Village. **Activities:** Campus Ministries; Choral groups; Concert band; Dance; Drama/theater; International Student Organization; Jazz band; Literary magazine; Music ensembles; Musical theater; Pep band; Radio station; Student government; Student newspaper; Student-run film society; Symphony orchestra; Television station; Yearbook. 75 registered organizations, 4 honor societies, 8 religious organizations on campus. **Athletics (Intercollegiate):** *Men:* baseball, basketball, cross-country, golf, lacrosse, soccer, swimming, tennis, track/field (outdoor), track/field (indoor), ultimate frisbee, wrestling. *Women:* basketball, cross-country, field hockey, lacrosse, soccer, softball, swimming, tennis, track/field (outdoor), track/field (indoor), volleyball. **On-Campus Highlights:** Boyer Hall (Schools of Humanities, Ed. and Soc. Sci.

ADMISSIONS
Freshman Academic Profile: Average high school GPA 3.8. 34% in top 10% of high school class, 64% in top 25% of high school class, 91% in top 50% of high school class. 71% from public high schools. **Test Scores:** SAT Math middle 50% range 530–650. SAT EBRW middle 50% range 560–660. ACT middle 50% range 23–30. **Basis for Candidate Selection:** *Very important factors include:* rigor of secondary school record, class rank, academic GPA, standardized test scores, extracurricular activities, talent/ability, character/

personal qualities, religious affiliation/commitment. *Important factors include:* application essay, volunteer work. *Other factors include:* recommendation(s), alumni/ae relation, racial/ethnic status, work experience, level of applicant's interest. **Freshman Admission Requirements:** High school diploma is required and GED is accepted. *Academic units required:* 4 English, 2 math, 2 science, 2 science labs, 2 foreign language, 2 social studies, 4 academic electives. *Academic units recommended:* 4 English, 3 math, 3 science, 3 science labs, 2 foreign language, 2 social studies, 2 history, 4 academic electives. **Freshman Admission Statistics:** 2,640 applied, 76% admitted, 30% enrolled. **Transfer Admission Requirements:** College transcript(s), essay or personal statement, statement of good standing from prior institution(s). Minimum college GPA of 2.5 required. Lowest grade transferable C. **General Admission Information:** Application fee $50. Non-fall registration accepted.

COSTS AND FINANCIAL AID
Required Forms and Deadlines: FAFSA. **Notification of Awards:** Applicants will be notified of awards on a rolling basis beginning 12/1. **Types of Aid:** *Need-based scholarships/grants:* College/university scholarship or grant aid from institutional funds; Federal Nursing Scholarships; Federal Pell; Private scholarships; SEOG; State scholarships/grants. *Loans:* Direct PLUS loans; Direct Subsidized Stafford Loans; Direct Unsubsidized Stafford Loans. **Student Employment:** Federal Work-Study Program available. Institutional employment available. **Financial Aid Statistics:** 100% needy freshmen, 99% needy undergrads receive need-based scholarship or grant aid. 14% freshmen, 13% undergrads receive non-need-based scholarship or grant aid. 80% freshmen, 79% undergrads receive need-based self-help aid. 0% freshmen, 0% undergrads receive athletic scholarships. 100% freshmen, 92% undergrads receive any aid. 73% undergrads borrow to pay for school. Average cumulative indebtedness $41,859. **Criteria awarding aid:** *Need-based:* Academics. *Non-need-based:* Academics, Art, Leadership, Music/drama, Religious affiliation.

METHODIST UNIVERSITY

5400 Ramsey Street, Fayetteville, NC 28311
Phone: 910-630-7027 **Financial Aid Phone:** 910-630-7192
E-mail: admissions@methodist.edu **CEEB Code:** 5426
Fax: 910-630-7285 **Website:** www.methodist.edu **ACT Code:** 3127

This private school, affiliated with the Methodist Church, was founded in 1956. It has a 620 acre campus.

RATINGS
Admissions Selectivity Rating: 82 **Fire Safety Rating:** 79 **Green Rating:** 60*

STUDENTS AND FACULTY
Enrollment: 2,226. **Student Body:** 48% female, 52% male, 30% out-of-state, 5% international (53 countries represented). Asian 1%, African American 24%, Caucasian 48%, Hispanic 6%, Native American 1%, Pacific Islander <1%, Two or more races 5%, Race unknown 10%.
Retention and Graduation: 62% freshmen return for sophomore year. 38% grads go on to further study within 1 year. 8% grads pursue arts and sciences degrees. 1% grads pursue law degrees. 12% grads pursue business degrees. 7% grads pursue medical degrees. **Faculty:** Student/faculty ratio 13:1. 142 full-time faculty, 69% hold PhDs, 13% are members of minority groups, 49% are women. 0% of classes are taught by teaching assistants.

ACADEMICS
Degrees: Associate; Bachelor's; Master's; Terminal Associate. **Classes:** Most classes have 10–19 students. Most lab/discussion sessions have 20–29 students. **Most popular majors:** Business/Commerce, General; Cell/Cellular and Molecular Biology; Secondary Education and Teaching. **Special Study Options:** Cooperative education program; Distance learning; Double major; Dual enrollment; English as a Second Language (ESL); Honors program; Independent study; Internships; Liberal arts/career combination; Student-designed major; Study abroad; Teacher certification program; Weekend college. **Honors programs:** The Methodist College Honors Program is based on the "Great Books" and is an outstanding opportunity for high acheiving students. **Disability Services offered:** Note-taking services; Reader services; Tape recorders; Tutors. **Career services:** Career assessment; Career/job search classes; Internships.

FACILITIES
Housing: Apartments for single students; Fraternity/sorority housing; Men's dorms; Wellness housing; Women's dorms; 80% of campus accessible to

physically disabled. **Special Academic Facilities/Equipment:** Art gallery, Nature Trail, 18-hole golf course with practice facilities for PGM students, Academic Developement Center.

CAMPUS LIFE

Environment: City. **Activities:** Campus Ministries; Choral groups; Concert band; Dance; Drama/theater; International Student Organization; Jazz band; Literary magazine; Marching band; Model UN; Music ensembles; Musical theater; Opera; Pep band; Radio station; Student government; Student newspaper; Symphony orchestra; Yearbook. 104 registered organizations, 15 honor societies, 8 religious organizations, 3 fraternities, 2 sororities on campus. **Athletics (Intercollegiate):** *Men:* baseball, basketball, cheerleading, cross-country, football, golf, soccer, tennis, track/field (outdoor). *Women:* basketball, cheerleading, cross-country, golf, lacrosse, soccer, softball, tennis, track/field (outdoor), volleyball.

ADMISSIONS

Freshman Academic Profile: Average high school GPA 3.3. 9% in top 10% of high school class, 34% in top 25% of high school class, 73% in top 50% of high school class. 86% from public high schools. **Test Scores:** SAT Math middle 50% range 450–550, SAT EBRW middle 50% range 430–520. ACT middle 50% range 17–23. **Basis for Candidate Selection:** *Very important factors include:* rigor of secondary school record, academic GPA. *Important factors include:* class rank, standardized test scores, interview. *Other factors include:* application essay, recommendation(s), extracurricular activities, talent/ability, character/personal qualities, first generation, alumni/ae relation. **Freshman Admission Requirements:** High school diploma is required and GED is accepted. *Academic units required:* 4 English, 3 math, 3 science, 1 science lab, 1 social studies, 2 history, 4 academic electives. *Academic units recommended:* 4 English, 4 math, 4 science, 1 science lab, 2 foreign language, 2 social studies, 2 history. **Freshman Admission Statistics:** 3,823 applied, 61% admitted, 21% enrolled. **Transfer Admission Requirements:** High school transcript, college transcript(s), statement of good standing from prior institution(s). Minimum college GPA of 2.0 required. Lowest grade transferable C. **General Admission Information:** Application fee $25. Non-fall registration accepted. Admission may be deferred for a maximum of 1 academic year.

COSTS AND FINANCIAL AID

Annual tuition $25,160. Room and board $9,521. Required fees $465. Average book and supplies expense $1,200. **Required Forms and Deadlines:** FAFSA. **Notification of Awards:** Applicants will be notified of awards on a rolling basis beginning 3/1. **Types of Aid:** *Need-based scholarships/grants:* College/university scholarship or grant aid from institutional funds; Federal Pell; Private scholarships; SEOG; State scholarships/grants. **Student Employment:** Federal Work-Study Program available. **Financial Aid Statistics:** 96% needy freshmen, 90% needy undergrads receive need-based scholarship or grant aid. 71% freshmen, 79% undergrads receive non-need-based scholarship or grant aid. 92% freshmen, 87% undergrads receive need-based self-help aid. 0% freshmen, 0% undergrads receive athletic scholarships. 90% freshmen, 86% undergrads receive any aid. **Criteria awarding aid:** *Need-based:* Academics, Alumni affiliation, Leadership, Music/drama, Religious affiliation. *Non-need-based:* Academics, Alumni affiliation, Leadership, Music/drama, Religious affiliation, State/district residency.

METROPOLITAN STATE UNIVERSITY

700 E 7th St., St. Paul,
Website: Http://www.metrostate.edu

This public school was founded in 1971.

RATINGS

Admissions Selectivity Rating: 60*   **Fire Safety Rating:** 60*   **Green Rating:** 60*

STUDENTS AND FACULTY
Enrollment: 8,943.

ACADEMICS
Degrees: Bachelor's; Certificate; Master's.

CAMPUS LIFE
Environment: City. **Activities:** Student government; Student newspaper.

ADMISSIONS

Freshman Admission Requirements: High school diploma is required and GED is accepted. **Transfer Admission Requirements:** High school transcript, college transcript(s), essay or personal statement, standardized test scores. Lowest grade transferable C. **General Admission Information:** Application fee $20.

COSTS AND FINANCIAL AID

Annual in-state tuition $2,918. Annual out-of-state tuition $5,670.

MIAMI UNIVERSITY

301 S. Campus Ave., Oxford, OH 45056
Phone: 513-529-2531 **Financial Aid Phone:** 513-529-0001
E-mail: admission@miamioh.edu **CEEB Code:** 1463
Fax: 513-529-1550 **Website:** http://www.miamioh.edu/ **ACT Code:** 3294

This public school was founded in 1809. It has a 2100 acre campus.

RATINGS
Admissions Selectivity Rating: 84   **Fire Safety Rating:** 95   **Green Rating:** 92

STUDENTS AND FACULTY

Enrollment: 17,038. **Student Body:** 50% female, 50% male, 35% out-of-state, 14% international (74 countries represented). Asian 2%, African American 3%, Caucasian 71%, Hispanic 5%, Native American <1%, Pacific Islander <1%, Two or more races 4%, Race unknown <1%.
Retention and Graduation: 92% freshmen return for sophomore year. 67% freshmen graduate within 4 years. 79% freshmen graduate within 6 years.
Faculty: Student/faculty ratio 17:1. 994 full-time faculty, 86% hold PhDs, 19% are members of minority groups, 44% are women. 5% of classes are taught by teaching assistants.

ACADEMICS

Degrees: Associate; Bachelor's; Certificate; Doctoral degree research/scholarship; Master's; Post-master's certificate. **Classes:** Most classes have 20–29 students. Most lab/discussion sessions have 10–19 students. **Most popular majors:** Finance, General; Marketing/Marketing Management, General; Psychology, General. **Special Study Options:** Cooperative education program; Cross-registration; Distance learning; Double major; Dual enrollment; English as a Second Language (ESL); Exchange student program (domestic); Honors program; Independent study; Internships; Liberal arts/career combination; Student-designed major; Study abroad; Teacher certification program. **Honors programs:** Miami has a University Honors Program. Students selected to participate receive a renewable scholarship, priority registration, and other special opportunities. **Combined degree programs:** BA/MA. **Disability Services offered:** Note-taking services; Reader services; Tape recorders; Tutors. **Career services:** Alumni network; Alumni services; Career assessment; Career/job search classes; Internships; Regional alumni.

FACILITIES

Housing: Apartments for married students; Apartments for single students; Coed dorms; Cooperative housing; Fraternity/sorority housing; Men's dorms; Special housing for disabled students; Special housing for international students; Theme housing; Wellness housing; Women's dorms; 100% of campus accessible to physically disabled. **Special Academic Facilities/Equipment:** Geology, art, anthropology, and zoology museums, performing arts center, herbarium, ecology research center, 400-acre nature preserve, electron microscope center.

CAMPUS LIFE

Environment: Village. **Activities:** Campus Ministries; Choral groups; Concert band; Dance; Drama/theater; International Student Organization; Jazz band; Literary magazine; Marching band; Model UN; Music ensembles; Musical theater; Opera; Pep band; Radio station; Student government; Student newspaper; Student-run film society; Symphony orchestra; Television station; Yearbook. 735 registered organizations, 27 honor societies, 25 religious organizations, 25 fraternities, 20 sororities on campus. **Athletics (Intercollegiate):** *Men:* baseball, basketball, cross-country, diving, football, golf, ice hockey, swimming, track/field (outdoor). *Women:* basketball, cross-country, diving, field hockey, soccer, softball, swimming, tennis, track/field (outdoor), volleyball. **On-Campus Highlights:** Farmer School of Business.

ADMISSIONS

Freshman Academic Profile: Average high school GPA 3.8. 34% in top 10% of high school class, 66% in top 25% of high school class, 92% in top 50% of high school class. 70% from public high schools. **Test Scores:** SAT Math middle 50% range 610–710. SAT EBRW middle 50% range 590–670. ACT middle 50% range 25–30. **Basis for Candidate Selection:** *Very important factors include:* rigor of secondary school record, class rank, academic GPA, application essay, standardized test scores, recommendation(s), talent/ability, character/personal qualities. *Other factors include:* extracurricular activities, first generation, alumni/ae relation, geographical residence, state residency, volunteer work, work experience. **Freshman Admission Requirements:** High school diploma is required and GED is accepted. *Academic units recommended:* 4 English, 4 math, 3 science, 2 foreign language, 2 social studies, 1 history, 1 visual/performing arts. **Freshman Admission Statistics:** 30,126 applied, 75% admitted, 18% enrolled. **Transfer Admission Requirements:** High school transcript, college transcript(s), essay or personal statement, statement of good standing from prior institution(s). Minimum college GPA of 2.0 required. Lowest grade transferable C. **General Admission Information:** Application fee $50. Regular application deadline 2/1. Non-fall registration accepted.

COSTS AND FINANCIAL AID

Annual in-state tuition $14,315. Annual out-of-state tuition $33,832. Room and board $13,860. Required fees $1,063. Average book and supplies expense $1,234. **Required Forms and Deadlines:** FAFSA. **Notification of Awards:** Applicants will be notified of awards on a rolling basis beginning 3/20. **Types of Aid:** *Need-based scholarships/grants:* College/university scholarship or grant aid from institutional funds; Federal Pell; Private scholarships; SEOG; State scholarships/grants. *Loans:* Direct PLUS loans; Direct Subsidized Stafford Loans; Direct Unsubsidized Stafford Loans. **Student Employment:** Federal Work-Study Program available. Institutional employment available. **Financial Aid Statistics:** 85% needy freshmen, 86% needy undergrads receive need-based scholarship or grant aid. 21% freshmen, 16% undergrads receive non-need-based scholarship or grant aid. 72% freshmen, 78% undergrads receive need-based self-help aid. 2% freshmen, 2% undergrads receive athletic scholarships. 49% undergrads borrow to pay for school. Average cumulative indebtedness $29,434. **Criteria awarding aid:** *Need-based:* Academics, Art, Athletics, Leadership, Minority status, Music/drama. *Non-need-based:* Academics, Art, Athletics, Leadership, Minority status, Music/drama, State/district residency.

MICHIGAN STATE UNIVERSITY

250 Administration Building, East Lansing, MI 48824
Phone: 517-355-8332 **Financial Aid Phone:** 517-353-5940
E-mail: admis@msu.edu **CEEB Code:** 1465
Fax: 517-353-1647 **Website:** www.msu.edu **ACT Code:** 2032

This public school was founded in 1855. It has a 5200 acre campus.

RATINGS

Admissions Selectivity Rating: 84   **Fire Safety Rating:** 60*   **Green Rating:** 98

STUDENTS AND FACULTY

Enrollment: 38,950. **Student Body:** 51% female, 49% male, 14% out-of-state, 9% international (107 countries represented). Asian 6%, African American 7%, Caucasian 68%, Hispanic 5%, Native American <1%, Pacific Islander <1%, Two or more races 3%, Race unknown 1%.
Retention and Graduation: 92% freshmen return for sophomore year. 56% freshmen graduate within 4 years. 81% freshmen graduate within 6 years. 25% grads go on to further study within 1 year. 6% grads pursue law degrees. 1% grads pursue business degrees. **Faculty:** Student/faculty ratio 16:1. 2,551 full-time faculty, 90% hold PhDs, 24% are members of minority groups, 43% are women.

ACADEMICS

Degrees: Bachelor's; Certificate; Doctoral degree—professional practice; Doctoral degree research/scholarship; Master's; Post-bachelor's certificate; Post-master's certificate. **Classes:** Most classes have 20–29 students. Most lab/discussion sessions have 20–29 students. **Special Study Options:** Accelerated program; Cooperative education program; Distance learning; Double major; Dual enrollment; English as a Second Language (ESL); Exchange student program (domestic); Honors program; Independent study; Internships; Liberal arts/career combination; Student-designed major; Study abroad; Teacher certification program; Weekend college. **Honors programs:** MSU's Honors College embodies MSU's long-standing commitment to provide programs of study that attract and challenge unusually talented undergraduates utilizing carefully planned, highly individualized programs of study that will meet the needs of academically talented students. **Combined degree programs:** BA/MA. **Disability Services offered:** Note-taking services; Reader services; Tape recorders; Tutors. **Career services:** Alumni network; Alumni services; Career assessment; Career/job search classes; Internships; Regional alumni.

FACILITIES

Housing: Apartments for married students; Apartments for single students; Coed dorms; Cooperative housing; Fraternity/sorority housing; Special housing for disabled students; Special housing for international students; Theme housing; Women's dorms. **Special Academic Facilities/Equipment:** Eli & Edythe Broad Art Museum, natural history, Michigan history, anthropology museums, art center, on-campus preschool and elementary school, biological station, experimental farms, botanical garden, planetarium, two superconducting cyclotrons, observatory. **Campus Network:** 100% of classrooms, 100% of dorms, 100% of student union, 100% of libraries, 100% of dining areas, 90% of common outdoor areas have wireless network access.

CAMPUS LIFE

Environment: City. **Activities:** Campus Ministries; Choral groups; Concert band; Dance; Drama/theater; International Student Organization; Jazz band; Literary magazine; Marching band; Model UN; Music ensembles; Musical theater; Opera; Pep band; Radio station; Student government; Student newspaper; Student-run film society; Symphony orchestra; Television station; Yearbook. 700 registered organizations, 47 honor societies, 50 religious organizations, 38 fraternities, 23 sororities on campus. **Athletics (Intercollegiate):** *Men:* baseball, basketball, cheerleading, cross-country, diving, football, golf, ice hockey, soccer, swimming, tennis, track/field (outdoor), track/field (indoor), wrestling. *Women:* basketball, cheerleading, crew/rowing, cross-country, diving, field hockey, golf, gymnastics, soccer, softball, swimming, tennis, track/field (outdoor), track/field (indoor), volleyball. **On-Campus Highlights:** MSU Student Union. **Environmental Initiatives:** Chicago Climate Exchange.

ADMISSIONS

Freshman Academic Profile: Average high school GPA 3.8. 28% in top 10% of high school class, 65% in top 25% of high school class, 93% in top 50% of high school class. **Test Scores:** SAT Math middle 50% range 550–670. SAT EBRW middle 50% range 550–650. ACT middle 50% range 23–29. **Basis for Candidate Selection:** *Very important factors include:* academic GPA, application essay, standardized test scores. *Important factors include:* rigor of secondary school record. *Other factors include:* class rank, recommendation(s), interview, extracurricular activities, talent/ability, character/personal qualities, first generation, alumni/ae relation, geographical residence, state residency, volunteer work, work experience, level of applicant's interest. **Freshman Admission Requirements:** High school diploma is required and GED is accepted. *Academic units required:* 4 English, 3 math, 3 science, 1 science lab, 2 foreign language, 3 social studies. *Academic units recommended:* 4 English, 3 math, 3 science, 2 foreign language, 3 social studies. **Freshman Admission Statistics:** 44,322 applied, 71% admitted, 28% enrolled. **Transfer Admission Requirements:** College transcript(s), essay or personal statement, statement of good standing from prior institution(s). Minimum college GPA of 2.0 required. Lowest grade transferable C. **General Admission Information:** Application fee $65. Priority deadline 11/1. Non-fall registration accepted.

COSTS AND FINANCIAL AID

Annual in-state tuition $16,650. Annual out-of-state tuition $41,002. Room and board $10,522. Average book and supplies expense $1,134. **Required Forms and Deadlines:** FAFSA. **Notification of Awards:** Applicants will be notified of awards on a rolling basis beginning 1/1. **Types of Aid:** *Need-based scholarships/grants:* College/university scholarship or grant aid from institutional funds; Federal Pell; Private scholarships; SEOG; State scholarships/grants; United Negro College Fund. *Loans:* Direct PLUS loans; Direct Subsidized Stafford Loans; Direct Unsubsidized Stafford Loans. **Student Employment:** Federal Work-Study Program available. Institutional employment available. **Financial Aid Statistics:** 72% needy freshmen, 74% needy undergrads receive need-based scholarship or grant aid. 48% freshmen, 37% undergrads receive non-need-based scholarship or grant aid. 69% freshmen, 73% undergrads receive need-based self-help aid. 1% freshmen, 2% undergrads receive athletic scholarships. 69% freshmen, 65% undergrads receive any aid. 51% undergrads borrow to pay for school. Average cumulative indebtedness $31,393. **Criteria awarding aid:** *Need-based:* Academics. *Non-need-based:* Academics, Alumni affiliation, Art, Athletics, Leadership, Music/drama, State/district residency.

MICHIGAN TECHNOLOGICAL UNIVERSITY

1400 Townsend Drive, Houghton, MI 49931
Phone: 906-487-2335 **Financial Aid Phone:** 906-487-2622
E-mail: mtu4u@mtu.edu **CEEB Code:** 1464
Fax: 906-487-2125 **Website:** www.mtu.edu **ACT Code:** 2030

This public school was founded in 1885. It has a 925 acre campus.

RATINGS
Admissions Selectivity Rating: 85 Fire Safety Rating: 96 Green Rating: 79

STUDENTS AND FACULTY
Enrollment: 5,688. **Student Body:** 28% female, 72% male, 22% out-of-state, 2% international (30 countries represented). Asian 2%, African American 1%, Caucasian 88%, Hispanic 2%, Native American <1%, Pacific Islander <1%, Two or more races 4%, Race unknown 1%.
Retention and Graduation: 84% freshmen return for sophomore year. 30% freshmen graduate within 4 years. 70% freshmen graduate within 6 years.
Faculty: Student/faculty ratio 12:1. 409 full-time faculty, 87% hold PhDs, 21% are members of minority groups, 31% are women. 6% of classes are taught by teaching assistants.

ACADEMICS
Degrees: Associate; Bachelor's; Certificate; Doctoral degree research/scholarship; Master's; Post-bachelor's certificate; Terminal Associate. **Classes:** Most classes have 10–19 students. Most lab/discussion sessions have 10–19 students. **Most popular majors:** Chemical Engineering; Electrical and Electronics Engineering; Mechanical Engineering. **Special Study Options:** Accelerated program; Cooperative education program; Distance learning; Double major; Dual enrollment; English as a Second Language (ESL); Honors program; Independent study; Internships; Study abroad. **Honors programs:** The Pavlis Honors College at Michigan Technological University is a vibrant community of scholars and leaders committed to education in and out of the classroom. Our mission is to serve all of Michigan Tech's highly motivated students, regardless of GPA, by providing countless (and unexpected) ways to enhance the college experience. Learn more at www.mtu.edu/honors. **Disability Services offered:** Note-taking services; Reader services; Tape recorders; Tutors. **Career services:** Alumni network; Alumni services; Career assessment; Career/job search classes; Internships; Regional alumni.

FACILITIES
Housing: Apartments for married students; Apartments for single students; Coed dorms; Fraternity/sorority housing; Special housing for disabled students; Theme housing; Wellness housing; 80% of campus accessible to physically disabled. **Special Academic Facilities/Equipment:** A. E. Seaman Mineral Museum, which is the official mineral museum of Michigan; Rozsa Center for the Performing Arts, 1,100-seat, state-of-the-art theater; Ford Center with 4,000-acre Ford Forest; newly renovated MacInnes Student Ice Arena with suites; Cosmic Ray Observatory; X-ray Fluorescence Spectrometer; Unit Operations Lab and Process Simulation and Control Center; Earth, Planetary and Space Sciences Institute; Computer-aided Engineering Lab; Microfabrication Facility; and the Great Lakes Research Center.

CAMPUS LIFE
Environment: Village. **Activities:** Campus Ministries; Choral groups; Concert band; Dance; Drama/theater; International Student Organization; Jazz band; Literary magazine; Music ensembles; Musical theater; Pep band; Radio station; Student government; Student newspaper; Student-run film society; Symphony orchestra. 244 registered organizations, 15 honor societies, 7 religious organizations, 12 fraternities, 7 sororities on campus. **Athletics (Intercollegiate):** *Men:* basketball, cross-country, football, ice hockey, skiing (Nordic/cross-country), tennis, track/field (outdoor). *Women:* basketball, cross-country, skiing (Nordic/cross-country), tennis, track/field (outdoor), volleyball. **On-Campus Highlights:** Student Development Complex. **Environmental Initiatives:** Emphasis on multidisciplinary sustainability research (http://www.sfi.mtu.edu/research.php/), education (http://www.sfi.mtu.edu/education.php) and outreach, such as Sustainable Futures Institute, Center for Water and Society, Environmentally Responsible Design and Manufacturing Research Group, National Institute for Climatic Change Research (Midwestern Region), Advanced Power Systems Research Center, Materials in Sustainable Transportation Infrastructure, Power and Energy Research Center, International Sustainable Engineering Initiative, IGERT for Sustainable Futures, Graduate Certificate in Sustainability, D80 Center, Peace Corps Masters International Program, International Sustainable Development Engineering Certificate, International Senior Design Programs, Sustainability Research Experience for Undergraduates, Wood-to-Wheels Graduate Enterprise, sustainability-based undergraduate Enterprise Programs (Challenge X, Clean Snowmobile, Alternative Fuels Group, Aqua Terra Tech, Efficiency Through Engineering and Construction), Undergraduate and Graduate Colloquium in Sustainability, Sustainable Futures 1 and 2 courses.

ADMISSIONS
Freshman Academic Profile: Average high school GPA 3.8. 31% in top 10% of high school class, 65% in top 25% of high school class, 91% in top 50% of high school class. **Test Scores:** SAT Math middle 50% range 590–690. SAT EBRW middle 50% range 580–680. ACT middle 50% range 25–30. **Basis for Candidate Selection:** *Very important factors include:* academic GPA, standardized test scores. *Important factors include:* rigor of secondary school record. *Other factors include:* application essay, recommendation(s), extracurricular activities, talent/ability, character/personal qualities. **Freshman Admission Requirements:** High school diploma is required and GED is accepted. *Academic units required:* 3 English, 3 math, 2 science. *Academic units recommended:* 4 English, 4 math, 3 science, 2 foreign language, 3 social studies, 2 academic electives, 1 computer science. **Freshman Admission Statistics:** 5,978 applied, 74% admitted, 29% enrolled. **Transfer Admission Requirements:** College transcript(s), statement of good standing from prior institution(s). Minimum college GPA of 2.75 required. Lowest grade transferable C. **General Admission Information:** Priority deadline 1/15. Non-fall registration accepted. Admission may be deffered for up to 1 year.

COSTS AND FINANCIAL AID
Required Forms and Deadlines: FAFSA. **Notification of Awards:** Applicants will be notified of awards on a rolling basis beginning 1/1. **Types of Aid:** *Need-based scholarships/grants:* College/university scholarship or grant aid from institutional funds; Federal Pell; Private scholarships; SEOG; State scholarships/grants. *Loans:* Direct PLUS loans; Direct Subsidized Stafford Loans; Direct Unsubsidized Stafford Loans. **Student Employment:** Federal Work-Study Program available. Institutional employment available. **Financial Aid Statistics:** 86% needy freshmen, 77% needy undergrads receive need-based scholarship or grant aid. 93% freshmen, 85% undergrads receive non-need-based scholarship or grant aid. 74% freshmen, 82% undergrads receive need-based self-help aid. 6% freshmen, 5% undergrads receive athletic scholarships. 99% freshmen, 92% undergrads receive any aid. 70% undergrads borrow to pay for school. Average cumulative indebtedness $37,903. **Criteria awarding aid:** *Need-based:* Academics. *Non-need-based:* Academics, Alumni affiliation, Athletics, Job skills, Leadership, State/district residency.

MIDAMERICA NAZARENE UNIVERSITY

2030 College Way, Olathe, KS 66062
Phone: 913-791-3380 **Financial Aid Phone:** 913-971-3298
E-mail: admissions@mnu.edu **CEEB Code:** 6437
Fax: 913-791-3481 **Website:** www.mnu.edu **ACT Code:** 1445

This private school, affiliated with the Nazarene Church, was founded in 1966. It has a 105 acre campus.

RATINGS
Admissions Selectivity Rating: 85 Fire Safety Rating: 81 Green Rating: 60*

STUDENTS AND FACULTY
Enrollment: 1,224. **Student Body:** 58% female, 42% male, 42% out-of-state, 0% international (12 countries represented). Asian 2%, African American 12%, Caucasian 74%, Hispanic 2%, Native American 1%, Pacific Islander <1%, Two or more races 1%, Race unknown 8%.
Retention and Graduation: 68% freshmen return for sophomore year.
Faculty: Student/faculty ratio 17:1. 81 full-time faculty, 64% hold PhDs, 0% are members of minority groups, 47% are women. 0% of classes are taught by teaching assistants.

ACADEMICS
Degrees: Associate; Bachelor's; Master's; Post-bachelor's certificate; Post-master's certificate; Terminal Associate. **Classes:** Most classes have 10–19 students. Most lab/discussion sessions have 10–19 students. **Most popular majors:** Business/

Commerce, General; Elementary Education and Teaching. **Special Study Options:** Accelerated program; Cross-registration; Distance learning; Double major; Dual enrollment; Exchange student program (domestic); Honors program; Independent study; Internships; Student-designed major; Study abroad; Teacher certification program; Weekend college. **Disability Services offered:** Note-taking services; Reader services; Tape recorders; Tutors.

FACILITIES
Housing: Apartments for single students; Men's dorms; Special housing for disabled students; Wellness housing; Women's dorms; 90% of campus accessible to physically disabled. **Campus Network:** 100% of classrooms, 100% of dorms, 100% of student union, 100% of libraries, 100% of dining areas, 100% of common outdoor areas have wireless network access.

CAMPUS LIFE
Environment: City. **Activities:** Campus Ministries; Choral groups; Concert band; Drama/theater; International Student Organization; Jazz band; Literary magazine; Music ensembles; Musical theater; Pep band; Radio station; Student government; Student newspaper; Symphony orchestra; Television station; Yearbook. 43 registered organizations, 6 honor societies, 4 religious organizations on campus. **Athletics (Intercollegiate):** *Men:* baseball, basketball, cheerleading, cross-country, football, soccer, track/field (outdoor), track/field (indoor). *Women:* basketball, cheerleading, cross-country, soccer, softball, track/field (outdoor), track/field (indoor), volleyball. **On-Campus Highlights:** Cook Center.

ADMISSIONS
Freshman Academic Profile: Average high school GPA 3.2. 88% from public high schools. **Test Scores:** ACT middle 50% range 18–25. **Basis for Candidate Selection:** *Important factors include:* character/personal qualities. *Other factors include:* rigor of secondary school record, class rank, academic GPA, standardized test scores, recommendation(s), interview, extracurricular activities, talent/ability, alumni/ae relation, religious affiliation/commitment, volunteer work, level of applicant's interest. **Freshman Admission Requirements:** High school diploma is required and GED is accepted. *Academic units recommended:* 4 English, 3 math, 3 science, 1 foreign language, 3 social studies. **Freshman Admission Statistics:** 1,077 applied, 52% admitted, 32% enrolled. **Transfer Admission Requirements:** College transcript(s). Minimum college GPA of 2.0 required. Lowest grade transferable D. **General Admission Information:** Priority deadline 3/1. Regular application deadline 8/1. Non-fall registration accepted.

COSTS AND FINANCIAL AID
Annual tuition $29,170. Required fees $500. Average book and supplies expense $1,490. **Required Forms and Deadlines:** FAFSA. **Notification of Awards:** Applicants will be notified of awards on a rolling basis beginning 2/1. **Types of Aid:** *Need-based scholarships/grants:* College/university scholarship or grant aid from institutional funds; Federal Pell; Private scholarships; SEOG; State scholarships/grants. *Loans:* Direct Subsidized Stafford Loans; Direct Unsubsidized Stafford Loans. **Student Employment:** Federal Work-Study Program available. Institutional employment available. **Financial Aid Statistics:** 98% undergrads receive any aid. **Criteria awarding aid:** *Need-based:* Athletics, Job skills, Leadership, Minority status, Music/drama, Religious affiliation. *Non-need-based:* Academics, Athletics, Leadership, Minority status, Music/drama, Religious affiliation, State/district residency.

MID-ATLANTIC CHRISTIAN UNIVERSITY

715 N. Poindexter St., Elizabeth City, NC 27909-4054
Phone: 252-334-2028 **Financial Aid Phone:** 252-334-2020
E-mail: admissions@roanokebible.edu
Fax: 252-334-2064 **ACT Code:** 3153

This private school, affiliated with the Christian Church/Churches of Christ, was founded in 1948. It has a 20 acre campus.

RATINGS
Admissions Selectivity Rating: 87 **Fire Safety Rating:** 76 **Green Rating:** 60*

STUDENTS AND FACULTY
Enrollment: 166.
Retention and Graduation: 53% freshmen return for sophomore year.
Faculty: Student/faculty ratio 10:1. 9 full-time faculty, 56% hold PhDs, 0% are members of minority groups, 33% are women. 0% of classes are taught by teaching assistants.

ACADEMICS
Degrees: Associate; Bachelor's; Certificate. **Classes:** Most classes have fewer than 10 students. Most lab/discussion sessions have 10–19 students. **Most popular majors:** Bible/Biblical Studies. **Special Study Options:** Distance learning; Double major; Dual enrollment; Internships;. **Disability Services offered:** Tape recorders; Tutors.

FACILITIES
Housing: Apartments for married students; Apartments for single students; Men's dorms; Special housing for disabled students; Women's dorms; 90% of campus accessible to physically disabled. **Campus Network:** 100% of classrooms, 100% of dorms, 100% of student union, 100% of libraries, 100% of dining areas, 100% of common outdoor areas have wireless network access.

CAMPUS LIFE
Environment: Village. **Activities:** Choral groups; Drama/theater; Music ensembles; Musical theater; Student government; Yearbook. 1 honor society on campus. **Athletics (Intercollegiate):** *Men:* basketball. *Women:* basketball, volleyball. **On-Campus Highlights:** On the Pasquotank River. **Environmental Initiatives:** Geothermal heating & cooling.

ADMISSIONS
Freshman Academic Profile: Average high school GPA 2.8. 2% in top 10% of high school class, 14% in top 25% of high school class, 37% in top 50% of high school class. 87% from public high schools. **Test Scores:** SAT Math middle 50% range 420–590. SAT EBRW middle 50% range 410–565. **Basis for Candidate Selection:** *Very important factors include:* class rank, academic GPA, standardized test scores, recommendation(s), character/personal qualities, religious affiliation/commitment. *Important factors include:* rigor of secondary school record, application essay. *Other factors include:* interview, extracurricular activities, talent/ability, volunteer work, work experience, level of applicant's interest. **Freshman Admission Requirements:** High school diploma is required and GED is accepted. *Academic units required:* 4 English, 3 math, 3 science, 2 science labs, 2 social studies, 2 history, 4 academic electives. *Academic units recommended:* 6 foreign language, 1 computer science. **Freshman Admission Statistics:** 127 applied, 56% admitted, 58% enrolled. **Transfer Admission Requirements:** College transcript(s), essay or personal statement, statement of good standing from prior institution(s). Minimum college GPA of 2.0 required. Lowest grade transferable C. **General Admission Information:** Application fee $50. Non-fall registration accepted. Admission may be deferred for a maximum of 1 semester.

COSTS AND FINANCIAL AID
Required Forms and Deadlines: FAFSA; Institution's own financial aid form. **Notification of Awards:** Applicants will be notified of awards on a rolling basis beginning 5/1. **Types of Aid:** *Need-based scholarships/grants:* College/university scholarship or grant aid from institutional funds; Federal Pell; Private scholarships; SEOG; State scholarships/grants. **Student Employment:** Federal Work-Study Program available. Institutional employment available. **Financial Aid Statistics:** 100% needy freshmen, 100% needy undergrads receive need-based scholarship or grant aid. 29% freshmen, 23% undergrads receive non-need-based scholarship or grant aid. 68% freshmen, 82% undergrads receive need-based self-help aid. 0% freshmen, 0% undergrads receive athletic scholarships. 88% freshmen, 90% undergrads receive any aid. **Criteria awarding aid:** *Non-need-based:* Academics, Alumni affiliation, Art, Athletics, Leadership, Music/drama, Religious affiliation.

MIDDLEBURY COLLEGE

The Emma Willard House, Middlebury, VT 05753-6002
Phone: 802-443-3000 **Financial Aid Phone:** 802-443-5158
E-mail: admissions@middlebury.edu **CEEB Code:** 3526
Fax: 802-443-2056 **Website:** www.middlebury.edu **ACT Code:** 4306

This private school was founded in 1800. It has a 350 acre campus.

RATINGS

Admissions Selectivity Rating: 97   **Fire Safety Rating:** 65   **Green Rating:** 99

STUDENTS AND FACULTY

Enrollment: 2,555. **Student Body:** 53% female, 47% male, 95% out-of-state, 10% international (74 countries represented). Asian 7%, African American 4%, Caucasian 62%, Hispanic 10%, Native American <1%, Two or more races 5%, Race unknown 1%.
Retention and Graduation: 94% freshmen return for sophomore year. 85% freshmen graduate within 4 years. 93% freshmen graduate within 6 years. 12% grads go on to further study within 1 year. **Faculty:** Student/faculty ratio 8:1. 294 full-time faculty, 0% of classes are taught by teaching assistants.

ACADEMICS

Degrees: Bachelor's; Doctoral degree research/scholarship; Master's. **Classes:** Most classes have 10–19 students. **Most popular majors:** Economics, General; Psychology, General; Environmental Studies. **Special Study Options:** Accelerated program; Double major; Exchange student program (domestic); Honors program; Independent study; Internships; Student-designed major; Study abroad; Teacher certification program. **Honors programs:** http://www.middlebury.edu/about/handbook/academics/Grades_and_Records. **Disability Services offered:** Note-taking services; Reader services; Tape recorders; Tutors. **Career services:** Alumni network; Alumni services; Career assessment; Career/job search classes; Internships; Regional alumni.

FACILITIES

Housing: Apartments for single students; Coed dorms; Special housing for disabled students; Theme housing; 65% of campus accessible to physically disabled. **Special Academic Facilities/Equipment:** Art museum, theaters, language lab, observatory, electron microscope, mountain campus, downhill and cross-country ski areas, golf course, Franklin Environmental Center, organic garden.

CAMPUS LIFE

Environment: Village. **Activities:** Campus Ministries; Choral groups; Dance; Drama/theater; International Student Organization; Jazz band; Literary magazine; Model UN; Music ensembles; Musical theater; Pep band; Radio station; Student government; Student newspaper; Student-run film society; Symphony orchestra; Yearbook. 200 registered organizations on campus. **Athletics (Intercollegiate):** *Men:* baseball, basketball, cross-country, diving, football, golf, ice hockey, lacrosse, skiing (downhill/Alpine), skiing (Nordic/cross-country), soccer, swimming, tennis, track/field (outdoor), track/field (indoor). *Women:* basketball, cross-country, diving, field hockey, golf, ice hockey, lacrosse, skiing (downhill/Alpine), skiing (Nordic/cross-country), soccer, softball, squash, swimming, tennis, track/field (outdoor), track/field (indoor), volleyball. **On-Campus Highlights:** Science—Bicentennial Hall. **Environmental Initiatives:** Student initiated effort that led to Trustees resolution in 2007 charging the entire college community to work together to achieve carbon neutrality by 2016. A similar effort modeled on this one is also in progress with regard to divesting the college endowment from fossil fuel-related companies. Thus far, it has led to new proxy voting policies in support of open and transparent governance and environmental and social responsibility, a student member of the Advisory Committee on Socially Responsible Investing has been appointed to the Investment Committee of the Board, and the question of divesting from fossil fuels is currently being given full and open consideration by the Trustees with significant community involvement in the discussion.

ADMISSIONS

Freshman Academic Profile: Test Scores: SAT Math middle 50% range 690–780. SAT EBRW middle 50% range 670–750. ACT middle 50% range 32–34. **Basis for Candidate Selection:** *Very important factors include:* rigor of secondary school record, class rank, academic GPA, extracurricular activities, talent/ability, character/personal qualities. *Important factors include:* application essay, standardized test scores, recommendation(s), racial/ethnic status. *Other factors include:* interview, first generation, alumni/ae relation, geographical residence, volunteer work, work experience, level of applicant's interest.
Freshman Admission Requirements: High school diploma or equivalent is not required *Academic units recommended:* 4 English, 4 math, 3 science, 3 science labs, 4 foreign language, 3 social studies. **Freshman Admission Statistics:** 9,754 applied, 15% admitted, 40% enrolled. **Transfer Admission Requirements:** High school transcript, college transcript(s), essay or personal statement, statement of good standing from prior institution(s). Minimum college GPA of 3.0 required. Lowest grade transferable C-. **General Admission Information:** Application fee $65. Regular application deadline 1/1. Non-fall registration accepted.

COSTS AND FINANCIAL AID

Annual tuition $55,790. Room and board $16,032. Average book and supplies expense $1,000. **Required Forms and Deadlines:** CSS/Financial Aid PROFILE; FAFSA; Institution's own financial aid form; Noncustodial PROFILE. **Notification of Awards:** Applicants will be notified of awards on or about 4/1. **Types of Aid:** *Need-based scholarships/grants:* College/university scholarship or grant aid from institutional funds; Federal Pell; Private scholarships; SEOG; State scholarships/grants. *Loans:* Direct PLUS loans; Direct Subsidized Stafford Loans; Direct Unsubsidized Stafford Loans. **Student Employment:** Federal Work-Study Program available. Institutional employment available. **Financial Aid Statistics:** 98% needy freshmen, 96% needy undergrads receive need-based scholarship or grant aid. 0% freshmen, 0% undergrads receive non-need-based scholarship or grant aid. 89% freshmen, 89% undergrads receive need-based self-help aid. 0% freshmen, 0% undergrads receive athletic scholarships. 42% freshmen, 45% undergrads receive any aid. 50% undergrads borrow to pay for school. Average cumulative indebtedness $19,838.

MIDDLE TENNESSEE STATE UNIVERSITY

1301 East Main Street, Murfreesboro, TN 37132
Phone: 615-898-2111 **Financial Aid Phone:** 615-898-2111
E-mail: admissions@mtsu.edu **CEEB Code:** 1466
Fax: 615-898-5478 **Website:** www.mtsu.edu **ACT Code:** 3994

This public school was founded in 1911. It has a 500 acre campus.

RATINGS

Admissions Selectivity Rating: 75   **Fire Safety Rating:** 95   **Green Rating:** 60*

STUDENTS AND FACULTY

Enrollment: 18,093. **Student Body:** 53% female, 47% male, 7% out-of-state, 3% international (55 countries represented). Asian 4%, African American 19%, Caucasian 63%, Hispanic 7%, Native American <1%, Pacific Islander <1%, Two or more races 4%, Race unknown <1%.
Retention and Graduation: 75% freshmen return for sophomore year. 25% freshmen graduate within 4 years. 47% freshmen graduate within 6 years. **Faculty:** Student/faculty ratio 17:1. 964 full-time faculty, 81% hold PhDs, 19% are members of minority groups, 49% are women.

ACADEMICS

Degrees: Bachelor's; Certificate; Doctoral degree research/scholarship; Master's; Post-bachelor's certificate; Post-master's certificate. **Classes:** Most classes have 10–19 students. Most lab/discussion sessions have 20–29 students. **Most popular majors:** Biology/Biological Sciences, General; Psychology, General; Aeronautics/Aviation/Aerospace Science and Technology, General. **Special Study Options:** Accelerated program; Cooperative education program; Cross-registration; Distance learning; Double major; Dual enrollment; Exchange student program (domestic); Honors program; Independent study; Internships; Student-designed major; Study abroad; Teacher certification program. **Honors programs:** Honors College. **Combined degree programs:** BA/MA. **Disability Services offered:** Note-taking services; Reader services; Tape recorders; Tutors. **Career services:** Alumni network; Alumni services; Career assessment; Career/job search classes; Internships.

FACILITIES

Housing: Apartments for married students; Apartments for single students; Coed dorms; Cooperative housing; Fraternity/sorority housing; Men's dorms; Special housing for disabled students; Special housing for international students; Theme housing; Wellness housing; Women's dorms. **Campus Network:** 100% of classrooms, 100% of dorms, 100% of student union, 100% of libraries, 100% of dining areas, 10% of common outdoor areas have wireless network access.

CAMPUS LIFE

Environment: City. **Activities:** Campus Ministries; Choral groups; Concert band; Dance; Drama/theater; International Student Organization; Jazz band; Literary magazine; Marching band; Model UN; Music ensembles; Musical theater; Opera; Pep band; Radio station; Student government; Student newspaper; Student-run film society; Symphony orchestra; Television station. **On-Campus Highlights:** Student Union.

ADMISSIONS

Freshman Academic Profile: Average high school GPA 3.5. **Test Scores:** SAT Math middle 50% range 500–620. SAT EBRW middle 50% range 510–640. ACT middle 50% range 20–26. **Basis for Candidate Selection:** *Very important factors include:* academic GPA, standardized test scores. *Other factors include:* rigor of secondary school record, application essay, recommendation(s), extracurricular activities, talent/ability, character/personal qualities, volunteer work, work experience, level of applicant's interest. **Freshman Admission Requirements:** High school diploma is required and GED is accepted. *Academic units required:* 4 English, 4 math, 3 science, 1 science lab, 2 foreign language, 1 social studies, 1 history, 1 visual/performing arts. **Freshman Admission Statistics:** 8,973 applied, 94% admitted, 39% enrolled. **Transfer Admission Requirements:** College transcript(s). Minimum college GPA of 2.0 required. Lowest grade transferable D. **General Admission Information:** Application fee $25. Non-fall registration accepted.

COSTS AND FINANCIAL AID

Annual in-state tuition $7,554. Annual out-of-state tuition $27,168. Room and board $9,772. **Required Forms and Deadlines:** FAFSA. **Notification of Awards:** Applicants will be notified of awards on a rolling basis beginning 2/15. **Types of Aid:** *Need-based scholarships/grants:* College/university scholarship or grant aid from institutional funds; Federal Pell; Private scholarships; SEOG; State scholarships/grants. *Loans:* Direct PLUS loans; Direct Subsidized Stafford Loans; Direct Unsubsidized Stafford Loans. **Student Employment:** Federal Work-Study Program available. Institutional employment available. **Financial Aid Statistics:** 65% needy freshmen, 63% needy undergrads receive need-based scholarship or grant aid. 88% freshmen, 64% undergrads receive non-need-based scholarship or grant aid. 50% freshmen, 59% undergrads receive need-based self-help aid. 1% freshmen, 2% undergrads receive athletic scholarships. 59% undergrads borrow to pay for school. Average cumulative indebtedness $25,328. **Criteria awarding aid:** *Need-based:* Academics, Athletics. *Non-need-based:* Academics, Leadership, Minority status, Music/drama.

MIDWAY COLLEGE

512 East Stephen Street., Midway, KY 40347-1120
Phone: 859-846-5347 **Financial Aid Phone:** 859-846-5410
E-mail: admissions@midway.edu **CEEB Code:** 1975
Fax: 859-846-5787 **Website:** www.midway.edu **ACT Code:** 1528

This private school, affiliated with the Disciples of Christ Church, was founded in 1847. It has a 105 acre campus.

RATINGS

Admissions Selectivity Rating: 81   **Fire Safety Rating:** 66   **Green Rating:** 60*

STUDENTS AND FACULTY

Enrollment: 1,395. **Student Body:** 91% female, 9% male, 9% out-of-state, <1% international (1 countries represented). Asian 1%, African American 9%, Caucasian 85%, Hispanic 2%, Native American 1%, Race unknown 3%. **Retention and Graduation:** 76% freshmen return for sophomore year. **Faculty:** Student/faculty ratio 15:1. 41 full-time faculty, 46% hold PhDs, 0% are members of minority groups, 39% are women. 0% of classes are taught by teaching assistants.

ACADEMICS

Degrees: Associate; Bachelor's; Master's. **Classes:** Most classes have 10–19 students. Most lab/discussion sessions have 10–19 students. **Most popular majors:** Elementary Education and Teaching; Nursing/Registered Nurse (Rn, Asn, Bsn, Msn). **Special Study Options:** Accelerated program; Distance learning; Double major; Dual enrollment; Honors program; Study abroad; Teacher certification program; Weekend college. **Honors programs:** Ruth Slack Roach Leadership, President's Ambassadors, Gamma Beta Phi, Tri Beta. **Disability Services offered:** Note-taking services; Reader services; Tape recorders; Tutors.

FACILITIES

Housing: Women's dorms; 75% of campus accessible to physically disabled. **Campus Network:** 100% of classrooms, 100% of dorms, 100% of student union, 100% of libraries, 100% of dining areas, 95% of common outdoor areas have wireless network access.

CAMPUS LIFE

Environment: Rural. **Activities:** Choral groups; Music ensembles; Student government; Student newspaper; Yearbook. **Athletics (Intercollegiate):** *Women:* basketball, cross-country, equestrian sports, soccer, softball, tennis, volleyball. **On-Campus Highlights:** Anne Hart Raymond Center.

ADMISSIONS

Freshman Academic Profile: Average high school GPA 3.2. 12% in top 10% of high school class, 25% in top 25% of high school class, 64% in top 50% of high school class. **Test Scores:** SAT Math middle 50% range 400–560. SAT EBRW middle 50% range 420–560. ACT middle 50% range 18–22. **Basis for Candidate Selection:** *Very important factors include:* rigor of secondary school record, standardized test scores. *Important factors include:* alumni/ae relation. *Other factors include:* class rank, application essay, recommendation(s), interview, extracurricular activities, talent/ability, character/personal qualities, volunteer work, work experience. **Freshman Admission Requirements:** High school diploma is required and GED is accepted. *Academic units required:* 4 English. *Academic units recommended:* 3 math, 2 science, 1 foreign language, 1 social studies. **Freshman Admission Statistics:** 399 applied, 77% admitted, 66% enrolled. **Transfer Admission Requirements:** High school transcript, college transcript(s). Minimum college GPA of 2.0 required. Lowest grade transferable C. **General Admission Information:** Application fee $25. Priority deadline 4/1. Non-fall registration accepted.

COSTS AND FINANCIAL AID

Annual tuition $15,750. Room and board $6,000. Required fees $150. Average book and supplies expense $1,200. **Required Forms and Deadlines:** FAFSA; Institution's own financial aid form. **Types of Aid:** *Need-based scholarships/grants:* College/university scholarship or grant aid from institutional funds; Federal Pell; Private scholarships; SEOG; State scholarships/grants. **Student Employment:** Federal Work-Study Program available. Institutional employment available. **Financial Aid Statistics:** 100% needy freshmen, 93% needy undergrads receive need-based scholarship or grant aid. 8% freshmen, 8% undergrads receive non-need-based scholarship or grant aid. 81% freshmen, 88% undergrads receive need-based self-help aid. 1% freshmen, 1% undergrads receive athletic scholarships. 85% freshmen, 81% undergrads receive any aid. **Criteria awarding aid:** *Need-based:* Academics, Alumni affiliation, Athletics. *Non-need-based:* Academics, Alumni affiliation, Athletics, Leadership, Religious affiliation.

MILLERSVILLE UNIVERSITY OF PENNSYLVANIA

P.O. Box 1002, Millersville, PA 17551-0302
Phone: 717-871-4625 **Financial Aid Phone:** 717-871-5100
E-mail: admissions@millersville.edu **CEEB Code:** 2656
Fax: 717-871-7973 **Website:** www.millersville.edu **ACT Code:** 3712

This public school was founded in 1855. It has a 250 acre campus.

RATINGS

Admissions Selectivity Rating: 77   **Fire Safety Rating:** 95   **Green Rating:** 86

STUDENTS AND FACULTY

Enrollment: 6,615. **Student Body:** 58% female, 42% male, 8% out-of-state, 1% international (56 countries represented). Asian 3%, African American 9%, Caucasian 73%, Hispanic 11%, Native American <1%, Pacific Islander <1%, Two or more races 1%, Race unknown 1%.

Retention and Graduation: 77% freshmen return for sophomore year. 37% freshmen graduate within 4 years. 57% freshmen graduate within 6 years. **Faculty:** Student/faculty ratio 19:1. 274 full-time faculty, 99% hold PhDs, 20% are members of minority groups, 49% are women. 0% of classes are taught by teaching assistants.

ACADEMICS

Degrees: Associate; Bachelor's; Certificate; Doctoral degree—professional practice; Master's; Post-bachelor's certificate; Post-master's certificate. **Classes:** Most classes have 20–29 students. Most lab/discussion sessions have 20–29 students. **Most popular majors:** Biology/Biological Sciences, General; Business Administration and Management, General; Psychology, General. **Special Study Options:** Accelerated program; Cooperative education program; Cross-registration; Distance learning; Double major; Dual enrollment; English as a Second Language (ESL); Exchange student program (domestic); Honors program; Independent study; Internships; Student-designed major; Study abroad; Teacher certification program. **Honors programs:** Honors College. **Disability Services offered:** Note-taking services; Reader services; Tape recorders; Tutors. **Career services:** Alumni network; Alumni services; Career assessment; Career/job search classes; Internships.

FACILITIES

Housing: Apartments for single students; Coed dorms; Special housing for disabled students; Special housing for international students; Theme housing; Wellness housing; 85% of campus accessible to physically disabled. **Special Academic Facilities/Equipment:** Art galleries, Radio station, TV station, Recording studio, Teleconferencing center, Weather information center, Foreign language lab, Two performing arts centers—Winter and Ware, Atmospheric Research and Aerostat Facility, Center for Disaster Research & Education, Foucault Pendulum, Chincoteague Bay Field Station at the Marine Science Consortium, Servicemembers Opportunity Colleges Consortium (SOCC), Aircraft flight simulators, Safety engineering and training modules.

CAMPUS LIFE

Environment: Village. **Activities:** Campus Ministries; Choral groups; Concert band; Dance; Drama/theater; International Student Organization; Jazz band; Literary magazine; Marching band; Music ensembles; Musical theater; Radio station; Student government; Student newspaper; Student-run film society; Symphony orchestra; Television station. 208 registered organizations, 15 honor societies, 10 religious organizations, 9 fraternities, 8 sororities on campus. **Athletics (Intercollegiate):** *Men:* baseball, basketball, cross-country, football, golf, soccer, tennis, track/field (outdoor), track/field (indoor), wrestling. *Women:* basketball, cheerleading, cross-country, field hockey, lacrosse, soccer, softball, swimming, tennis, track/field (outdoor), track/field (indoor), volleyball. **On-Campus Highlights:** Student Memorial Center. **Environmental Initiatives:** First building in PA to be certified as zero energy by the International Living Future Institute.

ADMISSIONS

Freshman Academic Profile: Average high school GPA 3.4. 8% in top 10% of high school class, 29% in top 25% of high school class, 66% in top 50% of high school class. **Test Scores:** SAT Math middle 50% range 490–570. SAT EBRW middle 50% range 490–600. ACT middle 50% range 19–25. **Basis for Candidate Selection:** *Very important factors include:* rigor of secondary school record, class rank, academic GPA. *Important factors include:* application essay, standardized test scores, talent/ability, character/personal qualities. *Other factors include:* recommendation(s), extracurricular activities, first generation, racial/ethnic status, volunteer work, work experience, level of applicant's interest. **Freshman Admission Requirements:** High school diploma is required and GED is accepted. *Academic units required:* 4 English, 3 math, 3 science, 2 science labs, 3 social studies, 2 history. *Academic units recommended:* 4 English, 3 math, 3 science, 2 science labs, 2 foreign language, 3 social studies, 2 history, 4 academic electives. **Freshman Admission Statistics:** 6,560 applied, 76% admitted, 27% enrolled. **Transfer Admission Requirements:** High school transcript, college transcript(s), statement of good standing from prior institution(s). Minimum college GPA of 2.0 required. Lowest grade transferable C. **General Admission Information:** Application fee $50. Non-fall registration accepted. Admission may be deferred for a maximum of 1 year.

COSTS AND FINANCIAL AID

Annual in-state tuition $9,570. Annual out-of-state tuition $19,290. Room and board $12,980. Required fees $2,680. Average book and supplies expense $1,000. **Required Forms and Deadlines:** FAFSA. **Notification of Awards:** Applicants will be notified of awards on a rolling basis beginning 3/19. **Types of Aid:** *Need-based scholarships/grants:* College/university scholarship or grant aid from institutional funds; Federal Pell; Private scholarships; SEOG; State scholarships/grants. *Loans:* Direct PLUS loans; Direct Subsidized Stafford

Loans; Direct Unsubsidized Stafford Loans. **Student Employment:** Federal Work-Study Program available. Institutional employment available. **Financial Aid Statistics:** 73% needy freshmen, 71% needy undergrads receive need-based scholarship or grant aid. 24% freshmen, 12% undergrads receive non-need-based scholarship or grant aid. 82% freshmen, 85% undergrads receive need-based self-help aid. 2% freshmen, 2% undergrads receive athletic scholarships. 88% freshmen, 79% undergrads receive any aid. 73% undergrads borrow to pay for school. Average cumulative indebtedness $32,815. **Criteria awarding aid:** *Need-based:* Academics, Art, Minority status. *Non-need-based:* Academics, Athletics, Minority status.

MILLIGAN COLLEGE

P.O. Box 210, Milligan College, TN 37682
Phone: 423-461-8730 **Financial Aid Phone:** 423-461-8968
E-mail: admissions@milligan.edu **CEEB Code:** 1469
Fax: 423-461-8982 **Website:** http://www.milligan.edu/ **ACT Code:** 3996

This private school, affiliated with the Christian Churches/Churches of Christ (independent, was founded in 1866. It has a 181 acre campus.

RATINGS

Admissions Selectivity Rating: 75   **Fire Safety Rating:** 88   **Green Rating:** 68

STUDENTS AND FACULTY

Enrollment: 796. **Student Body:** 54% female, 46% male, 34% out-of-state, 7% international (17 countries represented). Asian 1%, African American 4%, Caucasian 82%, Hispanic 4%, Native American 0%, Pacific Islander <1%, Two or more races 2%, Race unknown <1%.
Retention and Graduation: 74% freshmen return for sophomore year. 59% freshmen graduate within 4 years. 63% freshmen graduate within 6 years. 13% grads go on to further study within 1 year. 4% grads pursue arts and sciences degrees. 1% grads pursue law degrees. 1% grads pursue business degrees. 11% grads pursue medical degrees. **Faculty:** Student/faculty ratio 9:1. 95 full-time faculty, 78% hold PhDs, 8% are members of minority groups, 45% are women. 0% of classes are taught by teaching assistants.

ACADEMICS

Degrees: Bachelor's; Certificate; Doctoral degree research/scholarship; Master's; Post-bachelor's certificate. **Classes:** Most classes have 10–19 students. **Most popular majors:** Sports, Kinesiology, and Physical Education/Fitness, General; Registered Nursing/Registered Nurse; Business Administration and Management, General. **Special Study Options:** Accelerated program; Cooperative education program; Distance learning; Double major; Dual enrollment; Honors program; Independent study; Internships; Student-designed major; Study abroad; Teacher certification program. **Honors programs:** Interdisciplinary Studies Major. **Disability Services offered:** Note-taking services; Tape recorders; Tutors. **Career services:** Alumni services; Career assessment; Career/job search classes; Internships; Regional alumni.

FACILITIES

Housing: Apartments for married students; Apartments for single students; Men's dorms; Women's dorms; 80% of campus accessible to physically disabled. **Special Academic Facilities/Equipment:** Gregory Liberal Arts Center, Seeger Chapel. **Campus Network:** 100% of classrooms have wireless network access.

CAMPUS LIFE

Environment: Town. **Activities:** Campus Ministries; Choral groups; Dance; Drama/theater; International Student Organization; Model UN; Music ensembles; Musical theater; Radio station; Student government; Student newspaper; Symphony orchestra; Television station. 45 registered organizations, 5 honor societies, 8 religious organizations on campus. **Athletics (Intercollegiate):** *Men:* baseball, basketball, cross-country, golf, mountain biking, soccer, swimming, tennis, track/field (outdoor), track/field (indoor). *Women:* basketball, cross-country, soccer, softball, swimming, tennis, track/field (outdoor), track/field (indoor), volleyball. **On-Campus Highlights:** The Gregory Center. **Environmental Initiatives:** Campus-wide recycling program including paper, plastic, cardboard, and aluminum.

ADMISSIONS

Freshman Academic Profile: Average high school GPA 3.8. 80% from public high schools. **Test Scores:** SAT Math middle 50% range 545–650. SAT EBRW middle 50% range 533–630. ACT middle 50% range 22–28. **Basis for Candidate Selection:** *Very important factors include:* rigor of secondary school record, academic GPA, standardized test scores. *Important factors include:* application essay, recommendation(s), character/personal qualities. *Other factors include:* class rank, interview, extracurricular activities, talent/ability, first generation, alumni/ae relation, volunteer work, work experience, level of applicant's interest. **Freshman Admission Requirements:** High school diploma is required and GED is accepted. *Academic units recommended:* 4 English, 4 math, 3 science, 3 science labs, 2 foreign language, 3 social studies, 3 academic electives, 1 visual/performing arts. **Freshman Admission Statistics:** 548 applied, 99% admitted, 37% enrolled. **Transfer Admission Requirements:** College transcript(s), essay or personal statement. Minimum college GPA of 2.0 required. Lowest grade transferable C-. **General Admission Information:** Application fee $30. Regular application deadline 8/28. Non-fall registration accepted. Admission may be deferred for a maximum of 1 year.

COSTS AND FINANCIAL AID
Annual tuition $34,150. Room and board $7,400. Required fees $1,450. Average book and supplies expense $1,300. **Required Forms and Deadlines:** FAFSA. **Notification of Awards:** Applicants will be notified of awards on a rolling basis beginning 12/1. **Types of Aid:** *Need-based scholarships/grants:* College/university scholarship or grant aid from institutional funds; Federal Pell; Private scholarships; SEOG; State scholarships/grants. *Loans:* Direct PLUS loans; Direct Subsidized Stafford Loans; Direct Unsubsidized Stafford Loans. **Student Employment:** Federal Work-Study Program available. Institutional employment available. **Financial Aid Statistics:** 100% needy freshmen, 99% needy undergrads receive need-based scholarship or grant aid. 24% freshmen, 26% undergrads receive non-need-based scholarship or grant aid. 58% freshmen, 62% undergrads receive need-based self-help aid. 30% freshmen, 25% undergrads receive athletic scholarships. 100% freshmen, 94% undergrads receive any aid. 69% undergrads borrow to pay for school. Average cumulative indebtedness $28,864. **Criteria awarding aid:** *Need-based:* Alumni affiliation. *Non-need-based:* Academics, Athletics, Job skills, Leadership, Minority status, Music/drama, Religious affiliation, State/district residency.

MILLIKIN UNIVERSITY

1184 West Main Street, Decatur, IL 62522-2084
Phone: 217-424-6210 **Financial Aid Phone:** 217-424-6317
E-mail: admis@millikin.edu **CEEB Code:** 1470
Fax: 217-425-4669 **Website:** millikin.edu **ACT Code:** 1080

This private school, affiliated with the Presbyterian Church, was founded in 1901. It has a 75 acre campus.

RATINGS
Admissions Selectivity Rating: 78   **Fire Safety Rating:** 98   **Green Rating:** 63

STUDENTS AND FACULTY
Enrollment: 1,928. **Student Body:** 55% female, 45% male, 22% out-of-state, 4% international (33 countries represented). Asian 2%, African American 14%, Caucasian 68%, Hispanic 5%, Native American <1%, Pacific Islander <1%, Two or more races 4%, Race unknown 3%.
Retention and Graduation: 75% freshmen return for sophomore year. 51% freshmen graduate within 4 years. 59% freshmen graduate within 6 years. 23% grads go on to further study within 1 year. 6% grads pursue arts and sciences degrees. 1% grads pursue law degrees. 5% grads pursue business degrees. 1% grads pursue medical degrees. **Faculty:** Student/faculty ratio 10:1. 153 full-time faculty, 78% hold PhDs, 9% are members of minority groups, 52% are women. 0% of classes are taught by teaching assistants.

ACADEMICS
Degrees: Bachelor's; Certificate; Doctoral degree—professional practice; Master's; Post-bachelor's certificate. **Classes:** Most classes have 10–19 students. Most lab/discussion sessions have 10–19 students. **Most popular majors:** Drama and Dramatics/Theatre Arts, General; Registered Nursing/Registered Nurse; Business Administration and Management, General. **Special Study Options:** Accelerated program; Distance learning; Double major; Dual enrollment; English as a Second Language (ESL); Exchange student program (domestic); Honors program; Independent study; Internships; Student-designed major; Study abroad; Teacher certification program; Weekend college. **Honors programs:** Millikin's honors programs are described at https://millikin.edu/scholars. **Disability Services offered:** Note-taking services; Reader services; Tape recorders; Tutors. **Career services:** Alumni network; Alumni services; Career assessment; Career/job search classes; Internships.

FACILITIES
Housing: Apartments for married students; Apartments for single students; Coed dorms; Fraternity/sorority housing; Special housing for disabled students; Special housing for international students; Theme housing; 66% of campus accessible to physically disabled. **Special Academic Facilities/Equipment:** Art galleries, fitness/wellness center, 32-channel recording studio, indoor sports center, greenhouse, observatory, 1900-seat performance center, multiple auditoriums, non-denominational chapel, artificial turf fields (baseball, football, softball), various student-run small business ventures. **Campus Network:** 100% of classrooms, 100% of dorms, 100% of student union, 100% of libraries have wireless network access.

CAMPUS LIFE
Environment: City. **Activities:** Choral groups; Concert band; Dance; Drama/theater; International Student Organization; Jazz band; Literary magazine; Model UN; Music ensembles; Musical theater; Opera; Radio station; Student government; Student newspaper; Symphony orchestra. 100 registered organizations, 15 honor societies, 5 religious organizations, 6 fraternities, 6 sororities on campus. **Athletics (Intercollegiate):** *Men:* baseball, basketball, cheerleading, cross-country, football, golf, soccer, swimming, track/field (outdoor), track/field (indoor). *Women:* basketball, cheerleading, cross-country, golf, soccer, softball, swimming, tennis, track/field (outdoor), track/field (indoor), volleyball. **On-Campus Highlights:** University Commons.

ADMISSIONS
Freshman Academic Profile: Average high school GPA 3.5. 20% in top 10% of high school class, 43% in top 25% of high school class, 68% in top 50% of high school class. 91% from public high schools. **Test Scores:** SAT Math middle 50% range 460–590. SAT EBRW middle 50% range 490–610. ACT middle 50% range 19–27. **Basis for Candidate Selection:** *Very important factors include:* rigor of secondary school record. *Important factors include:* class rank, academic GPA, standardized test scores, recommendation(s), interview. *Other factors include:* extracurricular activities, talent/ability, character/personal qualities, alumni/ae relation, volunteer work, work experience, level of applicant's interest. **Freshman Admission Requirements:** High school diploma is required and GED is accepted. *Academic units recommended:* 4 English, 3 math, 3 science, 2 foreign language, 2 social studies, 2 history. **Freshman Admission Statistics:** 3,531 applied, 71% admitted, 19% enrolled. **Transfer Admission Requirements:** High school transcript, college transcript(s). Minimum college GPA of 2.0 required. Lowest grade transferable C-. **General Admission Information:** Priority deadline 5/1. Non-fall registration accepted. Admission may be deferred for a maximum of 1 year.

COSTS AND FINANCIAL AID
Annual tuition $36,262. Room and board $11,818. Required fees $892. Average book and supplies expense $1,000. **Required Forms and Deadlines:** FAFSA. **Notification of Awards:** Applicants will be notified of awards on a rolling basis beginning 1/15. **Types of Aid:** *Need-based scholarships/grants:* College/university scholarship or grant aid from institutional funds; Federal Pell; Private scholarships; SEOG; State scholarships/grants. *Loans:* Direct PLUS loans; Direct Subsidized Stafford Loans; Direct Unsubsidized Stafford Loans. **Student Employment:** Federal Work-Study Program available. Institutional employment available. **Financial Aid Statistics:** 82% needy freshmen, 83% needy undergrads receive need-based scholarship or grant aid. 97% freshmen, 94% undergrads receive non-need-based scholarship or grant aid. 76% freshmen, 78% undergrads receive need-based self-help aid. 0% freshmen, 0% undergrads receive athletic scholarships. 100% freshmen, 100% undergrads receive any aid. 79% undergrads borrow to pay for school. Average cumulative indebtedness $35,596. **Criteria awarding aid:** *Need-based:* Academics. *Non-need-based:* Academics, Alumni affiliation, Art, Leadership, Minority status, Music/drama.

MILLSAPS COLLEGE

1701 North State Street, Jackson, MS 39210
Phone: 601-974-1050 **Financial Aid Phone:** 800-352-1050
E-mail: admissions@millsaps.edu **CEEB Code:** 1471
Fax: 601-974-1059 **Website:** www.millsaps.edu **ACT Code:** 2212

This private school, affiliated with the Methodist Church, was founded in 1890. It has a 100 acre campus.

RATINGS
Admissions Selectivity Rating: 85   **Fire Safety Rating:** 90   **Green Rating:** 68

STUDENTS AND FACULTY
Enrollment: 793. **Student Body:** 52% female, 48% male, 55% out-of-state, 5% international (31 countries represented). Asian 4%, African American 20%, Caucasian 63%, Hispanic 5%, Native American 1%, Pacific Islander 0%, Two or more races 0%, Race unknown 2%.
Retention and Graduation: 79% freshmen return for sophomore year. 62% freshmen graduate within 4 years. 67% freshmen graduate within 6 years. 44% grads go on to further study within 1 year. 15% grads pursue arts and sciences degrees. 6% grads pursue law degrees. 9% grads pursue business degrees. 5% grads pursue medical degrees. **Faculty:** Student/faculty ratio 9:1. 82 full-time faculty, 96% hold PhDs, 11% are members of minority groups, 50% are women. 0% of classes are taught by teaching assistants.

ACADEMICS
Degrees: Bachelor's; Master's. **Classes:** Most classes have 10–19 students. Most lab/discussion sessions have fewer than 10 students. **Most popular majors:** Business Administration, Management and Operations; Biology/Biological Sciences, General; Psychology, General. **Special Study Options:** Accelerated program; Double major; Honors program; Independent study; Internships; Liberal arts/career combination; Student-designed major; Study abroad; Teacher certification program; Weekend college. **Honors programs:** The Honors Program, Ford Teaching Fellows program (research and internships for students interested in college teaching), Weiner Pre-Medical Fellows Program (summer research), Lilly Fellows Faith and Work Initiative (connecting individual passions with learning, meaning, service, and career). **Disability Services offered:** Note-taking services; Reader services; Tutors. **Career services:** Alumni network; Alumni services; Career assessment; Internships; Regional alumni.

FACILITIES
Housing: Coed dorms; Fraternity/sorority housing; Men's dorms; Special housing for disabled students; Theme housing; Women's dorms; 90% of campus accessible to physically disabled. **Special Academic Facilities/Equipment:** Millsaps' W.M. Keck Center for Instrumental and Biochemical Comparative Archaeology is the only undergraduate facility of its kind in the world. The new multi-disciplinary research laboratory provides undergraduate students with the opportunity to explore complex archeological questions using advanced bioanalytical and biochemical techniques. 4–6 Keck Fellows assist each year in gathering the artifacts studied in the lab from the College's archaeological field programs in Mexico and northern Albania. The lab houses an inductively-coupled plasma spectrometer with laser ablation, a gas-chromotography spectrometer, a liquid-chromotography spectrometer, and a portable X-ray fluorescence spectrometer. In addition, the college's other labs include a unique array of spectrometers for measuring atomic absorption, infrared transitional modes, nuclear magnetic resonance, and other forms of energy. **Campus Network:** 100% of classrooms, 0% of dorms, 100% of student union, 100% of libraries, 0% of dining areas, 100% of common outdoor areas have wireless network access.

CAMPUS LIFE
Environment: Metropolis. **Activities:** Campus Ministries; Choral groups; Dance; Drama/theater; International Student Organization; Literary magazine; Model UN; Music ensembles; Musical theater; Student government; Student newspaper; Yearbook. 85 registered organizations, 28 honor societies, 8 religious organizations, 6 fraternities, 6 sororities on campus. **Athletics (Intercollegiate):** *Men:* baseball, basketball, cross-country, football, golf, lacrosse, soccer, tennis, track/field (outdoor). *Women:* basketball, cross-country, golf, lacrosse, soccer, softball, tennis, track/field (outdoor), volleyball. **On-Campus Highlights:** Hall Activities Center (fitness/athletic facility). **Environmental Initiatives:**

The College supports the Center for Research and Learning at the H. Moyers Biocultural Reserve operated by Kaxil Kiuic, Yucatán, Mexico. The Center is an off-the-grid facility built using sustainable design and technology. Applied Ecological Design, taught by Millsaps faculty at the Center, focuses on topics critical to planning, designing, and creating a sustainable home including sustainable construction, solar power, energy efficiency, water supply, waste and wastewater management, and agriculture/ permaculture; coursework includes on-site project experimentation, design, and construction.

ADMISSIONS
Freshman Academic Profile: Average high school GPA 3.7. 0% in top 10% of high school class, 100% in top 25% of high school class, 100% in top 50% of high school class. 55% from public high schools. **Test Scores:** SAT Math middle 50% range 530–630. SAT EBRW middle 50% range 550–630. ACT middle 50% range 22–28. **Basis for Candidate Selection:** *Very important factors include:* rigor of secondary school record, academic GPA, standardized test scores, character/personal qualities. *Important factors include:* class rank, application essay, recommendation(s), extracurricular activities, talent/ability. *Other factors include:* interview, volunteer work, work experience. **Freshman Admission Requirements:** High school diploma is required and GED is accepted. *Academic units required:* 4 English, 3 math, 3 science, 2 science labs, 1 foreign language, 2 social studies, 2 history, 1 academic elective. *Academic units recommended:* 4 English, 4 math, 4 science, 2 science labs, 2 foreign language, 2 social studies, 2 history, 2 academic electives. **Freshman Admission Statistics:** 4,161 applied, 59% admitted, 10% enrolled. **Transfer Admission Requirements:** College transcript(s), essay or personal statement, standardized test scores, statement of good standing from prior institution(s). Minimum college GPA of 2.75 required. Lowest grade transferable C. **General Admission Information:** Priority deadline 2/1. Regular application deadline 7/1. Non-fall registration accepted. Admission may be deferred for a maximum of 1 year.

COSTS AND FINANCIAL AID
Annual tuition $38,600. Room and board $14,210. Required fees $2,714. Average book and supplies expense $1,200. **Required Forms and Deadlines:** FAFSA. **Notification of Awards:** Applicants will be notified of awards on a rolling basis beginning 3/15. **Types of Aid:** *Need-based scholarships/grants:* College/university scholarship or grant aid from institutional funds; Federal Pell; Private scholarships; SEOG; State scholarships/grants. *Loans:* Direct PLUS loans; Direct Subsidized Stafford Loans; Direct Unsubsidized Stafford Loans. **Student Employment:** Federal Work-Study Program available. Institutional employment available. **Financial Aid Statistics:** 99% needy freshmen, 99% needy undergrads receive need-based scholarship or grant aid. 25% freshmen, 18% undergrads receive non-need-based scholarship or grant aid. 72% freshmen, 78% undergrads receive need-based self-help aid. 0% freshmen, 0% undergrads receive athletic scholarships. 100% freshmen, 98% undergrads receive any aid. 65% undergrads borrow to pay for school. Average cumulative indebtedness $34,619. **Criteria awarding aid:** *Need-based:* Minority status, Religious affiliation. *Non-need-based:* Academics, Art, Leadership, Music/drama, Religious affiliation.

MILLS COLLEGE

5000 MacArthur Boulevard, Oakland, CA 94613
Phone: 510-430-2135 **Financial Aid Phone:** (510) 430-2039
E-mail: admission@mills.edu **CEEB Code:** 4485
Fax: 510-430-3314 **Website:** www.mills.edu **ACT Code:** 4485

This private school was founded in 1852. It has a 135 acre campus.

RATINGS
Admissions Selectivity Rating: 75   **Fire Safety Rating:** 78   **Green Rating:** 88

STUDENTS AND FACULTY
Enrollment: 699. **Student Body:** 100% female, 0% male, 20% out-of-state, <1% international (4 countries represented). Asian 8%, African American 10%, Caucasian 37%, Hispanic 33%, Native American 1%, Pacific Islander 0%, Two or more races 11%, Race unknown 1%.
Retention and Graduation: 76% freshmen return for sophomore year. 47% freshmen graduate within 4 years. 56% freshmen graduate within 6 years. 29%

grads go on to further study within 1 year. 22% grads pursue arts and sciences degrees. 1% grads pursue law degrees. 2% grads pursue business degrees. 2% grads pursue medical degrees. **Faculty:** Student/faculty ratio 11:1. 77 full-time faculty, 86% hold PhDs, 39% are members of minority groups, 75% are women. 0% of classes are taught by teaching assistants.

ACADEMICS

Degrees: Bachelor's; Certificate; Doctoral degree—professional practice; Master's; Post-bachelor's certificate. **Classes:** Most classes have 10–19 students. Most lab/discussion sessions have 10–19 students. **Most popular majors:** English Language and Literature, General; Biology/Biological Sciences, General; Psychology, General. **Special Study Options:** Accelerated program; Cooperative education program; Cross-registration; Double major; Exchange student program (domestic); Independent study; Internships; Student-designed major; Study abroad; Teacher certification program. **Combined degree programs:** BA/MA; BA/MEng. **Disability Services offered:** Note-taking services; Reader services; Tape recorders; Tutors. **Career services:** Alumni network; Alumni services; Career assessment; Career/job search classes; Internships; Regional alumni.

FACILITIES

Housing: Apartments for married students; Apartments for single students; Coed dorms; Cooperative housing; Men's dorms; Special housing for disabled students; Theme housing; Wellness housing; Women's dorms; 75% of campus accessible to physically disabled. **Special Academic Facilities/Equipment:** Art Museum, Center for Contemporary Music, Campus Farm, Mills Elementary School (Laboratory School), Botanical Gardens, LEED-rated Natural Sciences Building and Lorry I. Lokey Graduate School of Business. **Campus Network:** 100% of classrooms, 100% of dorms, 100% of student union, 100% of libraries, 100% of dining areas, 42% of common outdoor areas have wireless network access.

CAMPUS LIFE

Environment: Metropolis. **Activities:** Campus Ministries; Choral groups; Dance; Drama/theater; International Student Organization; Literary magazine; Model UN; Music ensembles; Student government; Student newspaper; Yearbook. 55 registered organizations, 2 honor societies, 2 religious organizations on campus. **Athletics (Intercollegiate):** *Women:* crew/rowing, cross-country, soccer, swimming, tennis, track/field (outdoor), volleyball. **On-Campus Highlights:** The Mills College Art Museum. **Environmental Initiatives:** Mills recycles, composts, and reuses all consumer materials to the greatest extent possible. www.mills.edu/green/recycling Mills students, staff and faculty participate in Recycle Mania.

ADMISSIONS

Freshman Academic Profile: Average high school GPA 3.6. 81% from public high schools. **Test Scores:** SAT Math middle 50% range 495–600. SAT EBRW middle 50% range 513–640. ACT middle 50% range 21–29. **Basis for Candidate Selection:** *Very important factors include:* rigor of secondary school record. *Important factors include:* class rank, academic GPA, application essay, recommendation(s), extracurricular activities, character/personal qualities. *Other factors include:* interview, talent/ability, first generation, alumni/ae relation, geographical residence, state residency, racial/ethnic status, volunteer work, work experience. **Freshman Admission Requirements:** High school diploma is required and GED is accepted. *Academic units required:* 4 English, 3 math, 2 science, 2 science labs, 2 foreign language, 2 social studies, 2 history. *Academic units recommended:* 4 English, 4 math, 4 science, 2 science labs, 4 foreign language, 4 social studies, 4 history, 2 visual/performing arts. **Freshman Admission Statistics:** 1,003 applied, 86% admitted, 19% enrolled. **Transfer Admission Requirements:** High school transcript, college transcript(s), essay or personal statement, Lowest grade transferable C-. **General Admission Information:** Application fee $50. Priority deadline 1/15. Non-fall registration accepted. Admission may be deferred for a maximum of 1 semester.

COSTS AND FINANCIAL AID

Annual tuition $28,765. Room and board $13,448. Required fees $1,492. Average book and supplies expense $1,611. **Required Forms and Deadlines:** FAFSA; Noncustodial PROFILE. **Notification of Awards:** Applicants will be notified of awards on a rolling basis beginning 2/15. **Types of Aid:** *Need-based scholarships/grants:* College/university scholarship or grant aid from institutional funds; Federal Pell; Private scholarships; SEOG; State scholarships/grants. *Loans:* Direct PLUS loans; Direct Subsidized Stafford Loans; Direct Unsubsidized Stafford Loans. **Student Employment:** Federal Work-Study Program available. Institutional employment available. **Financial Aid Statistics:** 95% needy freshmen, 96% needy undergrads receive need-based scholarship or grant aid. 99% freshmen, 91% undergrads receive non-need-based scholarship or grant aid. 70% freshmen, 75% undergrads receive need-based self-help aid.

0% freshmen, 0% undergrads receive athletic scholarships. 100% freshmen, 99% undergrads receive any aid. 85% undergrads borrow to pay for school. Average cumulative indebtedness $29,693. **Criteria awarding aid:** *Non-need-based:* Academics, Leadership, Music/drama.

MILWAUKEE SCHOOL OF ENGINEERING

1025 North Broadway, Milwaukee, WI 53202-3109
Phone: 414-277-6763 **Financial Aid Phone:** 800-778-7223
E-mail: explore@msoe.edu **CEEB Code:** 1476
Fax: 414-277-7475 **Website:** www.msoe.edu **ACT Code:** 4616

This private school was founded in 1903. It has a 22 acre campus.

RATINGS

Admissions Selectivity Rating: 87   **Fire Safety Rating:** 98   **Green Rating:** 70

STUDENTS AND FACULTY

Enrollment: 2,605. **Student Body:** 27% female, 73% male, 34% out-of-state, 10% international (29 countries represented). Asian 4%, African American 2%, Caucasian 67%, Hispanic 6%, Native American <1%, Pacific Islander <1%, Two or more races 3%, Race unknown 8%.
Retention and Graduation: 85% freshmen return for sophomore year. 44% freshmen graduate within 4 years. 64% freshmen graduate within 6 years. 8% grads go on to further study within 1 year. 0% grads pursue arts and sciences degrees. 1% grads pursue law degrees. 3% grads pursue business degrees. 1% grads pursue medical degrees. **Faculty:** Student/faculty ratio 16:1. 139 full-time faculty, 83% hold PhDs, 10% are members of minority groups, 32% are women. 0% of classes are taught by teaching assistants.

ACADEMICS

Degrees: Bachelor's; Master's. **Classes:** Most classes have 20–29 students. Most lab/discussion sessions have 10–19 students. **Most popular majors:** Architectural Engineering; Electrical and Electronics Engineering; Mechanical Engineering. **Special Study Options:** Accelerated program; Double major; Dual enrollment; English as a Second Language (ESL); Honors program; Independent study; Internships; Study abroad. **Honors programs:** The University Scholars program encourages independent, collaborative, and cooperative learning. The benefits of participating in the USP include having classes with like-minded students; having greater opportunities to pursue individual interests; experiencing an enriched academic environment; the integration of diverse topics into the classroom, with more in-depth preparation for graduate school; the ability to hone your leadership skills through project work, professional presentations and interaction with regional leaders in various fields. **Combined degree programs:** BA/MEng. **Disability Services offered:** Note-taking services; Reader services; Tape recorders; Tutors. **Career services:** Alumni network; Alumni services; Career assessment; Career/job search classes; Internships; Regional alumni.

FACILITIES

Housing: Apartments for married students; Apartments for single students; Coed dorms; Fraternity/sorority housing; Special housing for disabled students; Wellness housing; 95% of campus accessible to physically disabled. **Special Academic Facilities/Equipment:** Grohmann Museum, Kern Center Health, Wellness, Fitness and Recreation Facility, Rader School of Business, Johnson Controls Software Engineering Lab, Fluid Power Institute, Rapid Prototyping Center, Applied Technology Center, Center for BioMolecular Modeling, Ruehlow Nursing Complex, Harley Davidson Design Lab, Johnson Controls Environmental Systems Lab. **Campus Network:** 100% of classrooms, 100% of dorms, 100% of student union, 100% of libraries, 100% of dining areas, 10% of common outdoor areas have wireless network access.

CAMPUS LIFE

Environment: Metropolis. **Activities:** Campus Ministries; Choral groups; Concert band; Dance; Drama/theater; International Student Organization; Jazz band; Literary magazine; Pep band; Radio station; Student government; Student-run film society; Symphony orchestra. 70 registered organizations, 5 honor societies, 4 religious organizations, 4 fraternities, 4 sororities on campus. **Athletics (Intercollegiate):** *Men:* baseball, basketball, cheerleading, crew/rowing, cross-country, golf, ice hockey, lacrosse, soccer, tennis, track/field (outdoor), track/field (indoor), volleyball, wrestling. *Women:* basketball, cheerleading, cross-country, golf, soccer, softball, tennis, track/field (outdoor), track/field (indoor), volleyball. **On-Campus Highlights:** Kern Center and Viets Field.

ADMISSIONS

Freshman Academic Profile: Average high school GPA 3.7. 92% from public high schools. **Test Scores:** SAT Math middle 50% range 603–710. SAT EBRW middle 50% range 550–650. ACT middle 50% range 25–30. **Basis for Candidate Selection:** *Very important factors include:* academic GPA, standardized test scores. *Important factors include:* rigor of secondary school record, extracurricular activities, talent/ability. *Other factors include:* character/personal qualities, alumni/ae relation. **Freshman Admission Requirements:** High school diploma is required and GED is accepted. *Academic units required:* 4 English, 4 math, 4 science. *Academic units recommended:* 3 science labs. **Freshman Admission Statistics:** 2,893 applied, 63% admitted, 29% enrolled. **Transfer Admission Requirements:** College transcript(s). Minimum college GPA of 2.5 required. Lowest grade transferable C. **General Admission Information:** Priority deadline 1/1. Regular application deadline 9/1. Non-fall registration accepted. Admission may be deferred for a maximum of 2 years.

COSTS AND FINANCIAL AID

Annual tuition $39,040. Required fees $1,710. Average book and supplies expense $1,000. **Required Forms and Deadlines:** FAFSA. **Notification of Awards:** Applicants will be notified of awards on a rolling basis beginning 1/15. **Types of Aid:** *Need-based scholarships/grants:* College/university scholarship or grant aid from institutional funds; Federal Pell; Private scholarships; SEOG; State scholarships/grants. *Loans:* Direct PLUS loans; Direct Subsidized Stafford Loans; Direct Unsubsidized Stafford Loans. **Student Employment:** Federal Work-Study Program available. Institutional employment available. **Financial Aid Statistics:** 100% needy freshmen, 100% needy undergrads receive need-based scholarship or grant aid. 15% freshmen, 16% undergrads receive non-need-based scholarship or grant aid. 82% freshmen, 82% undergrads receive need-based self-help aid. 0% freshmen, 0% undergrads receive athletic scholarships. 76% undergrads borrow to pay for school. Average cumulative indebtedness $38,421. **Criteria awarding aid:** *Non-need-based:* Academics.

MINERVA SCHOOLS AT KGI

1145 Market Street, San Francisco, CA 94103
Phone: 4156497658
E-mail: admissions@minerva.kgi.edu
Fax: 415.520.0517 **Website:** www.minerva.kgi.edu

This is a private school.

RATINGS

Admissions Selectivity Rating: 60*　**Fire Safety Rating:** 72　**Green Rating:** 60*

STUDENTS AND FACULTY

Enrollment: 111. **Student Body:** 48% female, 52% male, 78% international. **Retention and Graduation:** 90% freshmen return for sophomore year. **Faculty:** Student/faculty ratio 10:1. 12 full-time faculty, 100% hold PhDs, 17% are members of minority groups, 50% are women. 0% of classes are taught by teaching assistants.

ACADEMICS

Degrees: Bachelor's; Master's. **Classes:** Most classes have 10–19 students. **Special Study Options:** Distance learning; Double major; Independent study; Internships; Study abroad. **Career services:** Career assessment; Career/job search classes; Internships.

FACILITIES

Housing: Apartments for single students; Coed dorms.

CAMPUS LIFE

Environment: Metropolis. **Activities:** Drama/theater; International Student Organization; Music ensembles; Student government; Student newspaper; Student-run film society.

ADMISSIONS

Basis for Candidate Selection: *Very important factors include:* rigor of secondary school record, class rank, academic GPA, interview, extracurricular activities, talent/ability, character/personal qualities. *Important factors include:* volunteer work, work experience. **Freshman Admission Statistics:** 9,032 applied, 2% admitted, 53% enrolled. **General Admission Information:** Regular application deadline 1/17.

COSTS AND FINANCIAL AID

Annual tuition $10,000. Room and board $10,500. Required fees $1,450. Average book and supplies expense $1,000. **Required Forms and Deadlines:** CSS/Financial Aid PROFILE; Noncustodial PROFILE. **Notification of Awards:** Applicants will be notified of awards on or about 3/25. **Types of Aid:** *Need-based scholarships/grants:* College/university scholarship or grant aid from institutional funds. **Student Employment:** Institutional employment available. **Financial Aid Statistics:** 100% needy undergrads receive need-based scholarship or grant aid. 0% undergrads receive non-need-based scholarship or grant aid. 11% undergrads receive need-based self-help aid. 0% undergrads receive athletic scholarships. 89.2% freshmen, 89.2% undergrads receive any aid.

MINNEAPOLIS COLLEGE OF ART AND DESIGN

2501 Stevens Avenue, Minneapolis, MN 55404
Phone: 612-874-3760 **Financial Aid Phone:** 612-874-3782
E-mail: admissions@mcad.edu **CEEB Code:** 6411
Fax: 612-874-3701 **Website:** www.mcad.edu **ACT Code:** 2130

This private school was founded in 1886. It has a 3 acre campus.

RATINGS

Admissions Selectivity Rating: 86　**Fire Safety Rating:** 61　**Green Rating:** 60*

STUDENTS AND FACULTY

Enrollment: 717. **Student Body:** 69% female, 31% male, 43% out-of-state, 2% international (10 countries represented). Asian 9%, African American 6%, Caucasian 66%, Hispanic 8%, Native American 3%, Pacific Islander 1%, Two or more races 1%, Race unknown 4%. **Retention and Graduation:** 86% freshmen return for sophomore year. 49% freshmen graduate within 4 years. 59% freshmen graduate within 6 years. 10% grads go on to further study within 1 year. 10% grads pursue arts and sciences degrees. **Faculty:** Student/faculty ratio 11:1. 36 full-time faculty, 58% hold PhDs, 3% are members of minority groups, 47% are women. 0% of classes are taught by teaching assistants.

ACADEMICS

Degrees: Bachelor's; Master's; Post-bachelor's certificate. **Classes:** Most classes have 10–19 students. **Special Study Options:** Cross-registration; Distance learning; Dual enrollment; Exchange student program (domestic); Independent study; Internships; Study abroad. **Disability Services offered:** Note-taking services; Reader services; Tape recorders; Tutors. **Career services:** Alumni services; Career assessment; Internships.

FACILITIES

Housing: Apartments for single students; Coed dorms; Special housing for disabled students; Special housing for international students; 95% of campus accessible to physically disabled. **Special Academic Facilities/Equipment:** Art gallery.

CAMPUS LIFE

Environment: Metropolis. **Activities:** Student government. **On-Campus Highlights:** Main Gallery.

ADMISSIONS

Freshman Academic Profile: Average high school GPA 3.3. 89% from public high schools. **Test Scores:** SAT Math middle 50% range 490–570. SAT EBRW middle 50% range 540–650. ACT middle 50% range 19–26. **Basis for Candidate Selection:** *Very important factors include:* rigor of secondary school record, academic GPA, application essay, standardized test scores, talent/ability. *Important factors include:* recommendation(s), interview. *Other factors include:* extracurricular activities, character/personal qualities, volunteer work, work experience, level of applicant's interest. **Freshman Admission Requirements:** High school diploma is required and GED is accepted. *Academic units recommended:* 4 English, 4 social studies, 4 history, 6 visual/performing arts. **Freshman Admission Statistics:** 653 applied, 63% admitted, 43% enrolled. **Transfer Admission Requirements:** High school transcript, college transcript(s), essay or personal statement, standardized test scores. Minimum college GPA of 2.5 required. Lowest grade transferable C-. **General Admission Information:** Application fee $50. Priority deadline 2/15. Regular application deadline 4/1. Non-fall registration accepted.

COSTS AND FINANCIAL AID
Annual tuition $39,946. Room and board $5,780. Required fees $450. Average book and supplies expense $3,060. **Required Forms and Deadlines:** FAFSA. **Notification of Awards:** Applicants will be notified of awards on a rolling basis beginning 12/15. **Types of Aid:** *Need-based scholarships/grants:* College/university scholarship or grant aid from institutional funds; Federal Pell; Private scholarships; SEOG; State scholarships/grants. *Loans:* Direct PLUS loans; Direct Subsidized Stafford Loans; Direct Unsubsidized Stafford Loans. **Student Employment:** Federal Work-Study Program available. Institutional employment available. **Financial Aid Statistics:** 100% needy freshmen, 100% needy undergrads receive need-based scholarship or grant aid. 8% freshmen, 5% undergrads receive non-need-based scholarship or grant aid. 92% freshmen, 94% undergrads receive need-based self-help aid. 0% freshmen, 0% undergrads receive athletic scholarships. 84% freshmen, 82% undergrads receive any aid. 88% undergrads borrow to pay for school. Average cumulative indebtedness $38,989. **Criteria awarding aid:** *Need-based:* Academics, Art, Leadership, Minority status. *Non-need-based:* Academics, Alumni affiliation, Art, Leadership.

MINNESOTA STATE UNIVERSITY, MANKATO

122 Taylor Center, Mankato, MN 56001
Phone: 507-389-1822 **Financial Aid Phone:** 507-389-5124
E-mail: admissions@mnsu.edu **CEEB Code:** 6677
Fax: 507-389-1511 **Website:** www.mnsu.edu **ACT Code:** 2126

This public school was founded in 1868. It has a 354 acre campus.

RATINGS
Admissions Selectivity Rating: 82   Fire Safety Rating: 73   Green Rating: 60*

STUDENTS AND FACULTY
Enrollment: 11,528. **Student Body:** 52% female, 48% male, 17% out-of-state, 9% international (81 countries represented). Asian 4%, African American 5%, Caucasian 73%, Hispanic 5%, Native American <1%, Pacific Islander <1%, Two or more races 4%, Race unknown 1%.
Retention and Graduation: 74% freshmen return for sophomore year. 26% freshmen graduate within 4 years. 50% freshmen graduate within 6 years.
Faculty: Student/faculty ratio 22:1. 488 full-time faculty, 91% hold PhDs, 19% are members of minority groups, 48% are women.

ACADEMICS
Degrees: Associate; Bachelor's; Certificate; Doctoral degree research/scholarship; Master's; Post-bachelor's certificate; Post-master's certificate.
Classes: Most classes have 20–29 students. Most lab/discussion sessions have 20–29 students. **Most popular majors:** Registered Nursing/Registered Nurse; Business Administration and Management, General; Biology/Biological Sciences, General. **Special Study Options:** Cross-registration; Distance learning; Double major; Dual enrollment; English as a Second Language (ESL); Exchange student program (domestic); Honors program; Independent study; Internships; Study abroad; Teacher certification program. **Disability Services offered:** Note-taking services; Reader services; Tape recorders. **Career services:** Alumni network; Alumni services; Career assessment; Career/job search classes; Internships; Regional alumni.

FACILITIES
Housing: Apartments for single students; Coed dorms; Special housing for disabled students; 90% of campus accessible to physically disabled. **Special Academic Facilities/Equipment:** Two art galleries, day care facility, two astronomy observatories, main stage and studio theatres.

CAMPUS LIFE
Environment: Town. **Activities:** Campus Ministries; Choral groups; Concert band; Dance; Drama/theater; International Student Organization; Jazz band; Marching band; Music ensembles; Musical theater; Pep band; Radio station; Student government; Student newspaper; Student-run film society; Symphony orchestra. 205 registered organizations, 16 honor societies, 18 religious organizations, 7 fraternities, 4 sororities on campus. **Athletics (Intercollegiate):** *Men:* baseball, basketball, cross-country, diving, football, golf, ice hockey, swimming, tennis, track/field (outdoor), track/field (indoor), wrestling. *Women:* basketball, bowling, cross-country, diving, golf, ice hockey, soccer, softball, swimming, tennis, track/field (outdoor), track/field (indoor), volleyball. **On-Campus Highlights:** Student Union. **Environmental Initiatives:** Energy retrofit of building for lighting and motors.

ADMISSIONS
Freshman Academic Profile: Average high school GPA 3.3. 8% in top 10% of high school class, 26% in top 25% of high school class, 65% in top 50% of high school class. **Test Scores:** ACT middle 50% range 19–24. **Basis for Candidate Selection:** *Very important factors include:* academic GPA. *Important factors include:* class rank, standardized test scores. **Freshman Admission Requirements:** High school diploma is required and GED is accepted. *Academic units required:* 4 English, 3 math, 3 science, 3 science labs, 2 foreign language, 3 social studies, 1 unit from above areas or other academic areas. **Freshman Admission Statistics:** 10,349 applied, 63% admitted, 35% enrolled. **Transfer Admission Requirements:** College transcript(s), statement of good standing from prior institution(s). Minimum college GPA of 2.0 required. Lowest grade transferable D. **General Admission Information:** Application fee $20. Non-fall registration accepted. Admission may be deferred for a maximum of No set time frame.

COSTS AND FINANCIAL AID
Annual in-state tuition $7,394. Annual out-of-state tuition $15,686. Room and board $9,854. Required fees $1,044. Average book and supplies expense $1,042. **Required Forms and Deadlines:** FAFSA. **Notification of Awards:** Applicants will be notified of awards on a rolling basis beginning 3/30. **Types of Aid:** *Need-based scholarships/grants:* College/university scholarship or grant aid from institutional funds; Federal Pell; Private scholarships; SEOG; State scholarships/grants. *Loans:* Direct PLUS loans; Direct Subsidized Stafford Loans; Direct Unsubsidized Stafford Loans. **Student Employment:** Federal Work-Study Program available. Institutional employment available. **Financial Aid Statistics:** 82% needy freshmen, 80% needy undergrads receive need-based scholarship or grant aid. 6% freshmen, 6% undergrads receive non-need-based scholarship or grant aid. 95% freshmen, 95% undergrads receive need-based self-help aid. 2% freshmen, 2% undergrads receive athletic scholarships. 92% freshmen, 82% undergrads receive any aid. 75% undergrads borrow to pay for school. Average cumulative indebtedness $31,804. **Criteria awarding aid:** *Need-based:* Academics, Minority status. *Non-need-based:* Academics, Art, Athletics, Leadership, Minority status, Music/drama.

MINNESOTA STATE UNIVERSITY, MOORHEAD

1104 Seventh Avenue South, Moorhead, MN 56563
Phone: 218-477-2161 **Financial Aid Phone:** 218-477-2251
E-mail: admissions@mnstate.edu **CEEB Code:** 6678
Fax: 218-477-4374 **Website:** www.mnstate.edu **ACT Code:** 2134

This public school was founded in 1887. It has a 140 acre campus.

RATINGS
Admissions Selectivity Rating: 76   Fire Safety Rating: 60*   Green Rating: 60*

STUDENTS AND FACULTY
Enrollment: 5,025. **Student Body:** 60% female, 40% male, 33% out-of-state, 7% international (56 countries represented). Asian 1%, African American 3%, Caucasian 78%, Hispanic 3%, Native American 1%, Pacific Islander <1%, Two or more races 3%, Race unknown 5%.
Retention and Graduation: 73% freshmen return for sophomore year.
Faculty: Student/faculty ratio 17:1. 274 full-time faculty, 62% hold PhDs, 9% are members of minority groups, 49% are women.

ACADEMICS
Degrees: Associate; Bachelor's; Certificate; Master's; Post-bachelor's certificate; Post-master's certificate. **Classes:** Most classes have 20–29 students. Most lab/discussion sessions have 10–19 students. **Most popular majors:** Business Administration and Management, General; Elementary Education and Teaching; Mass Communication/Media Studies. **Special Study Options:** Cross-registration; Distance learning; Double major; Dual enrollment; Exchange student program (domestic); Honors program; Independent study; Internships; Student-designed major; Study abroad; Teacher certification program. **Honors programs:** Honors Program to reward and encourage superior academic achievement. **Disability Services offered:** Note-taking services; Reader services; Tape recorders; Tutors. **Career services:** Career assessment; Career/job search classes; Internships.

FACILITIES
Housing: Apartments for married students; Apartments for single students; Coed dorms; Men's dorms; Theme housing; Women's dorms; 95% of campus accessible to physically disabled. **Special Academic Facilities/Equipment:** Art

and biology museums on-campus, planetarium, regional science center, Center for Business, new Science Building, Center for Business, new Wellness Center.

CAMPUS LIFE
Environment: City. **Activities:** Campus Ministries; Choral groups; Concert band; Dance; Drama/theater; International Student Organization; Jazz band; Literary magazine; Model UN; Music ensembles; Musical theater; Pep band; Radio station; Student government; Student newspaper; Student-run film society; Television station. 130 registered organizations, 7 honor societies, 11 religious organizations, 2 sororities on campus. **Athletics (Intercollegiate):** *Men:* basketball, cross-country, football, track/field (outdoor), track/field (indoor), wrestling. *Women:* basketball, cross-country, soccer, softball, swimming, tennis, track/field (outdoor), track/field (indoor), volleyball. **On-Campus Highlights:** Underground Night Club.

ADMISSIONS
Freshman Academic Profile: 10% in top 10% of high school class, 35% in top 25% of high school class, 74% in top 50% of high school class. **Test Scores:** SAT Math middle 50% range 480–570. SAT EBRW middle 50% range 445–520. ACT middle 50% range 20–25. **Basis for Candidate Selection:** *Very important factors include:* class rank, academic GPA, standardized test scores. *Other factors include:* rigor of secondary school record, application essay, recommendation(s). **Freshman Admission Requirements:** High school diploma is required and GED is accepted. *Academic units required:* 4 English, 3 math, 3 science, 1 science lab, 2 foreign language, 3 social studies, 1 unit from above areas or other academic areas. **Freshman Admission Statistics:** 2,610 applied, 82% admitted, 34% enrolled. **Transfer Admission Requirements:** College transcript(s), statement of good standing from prior institution(s). Minimum college GPA of 2.0 required. Lowest grade transferable D. **General Admission Information:** Application fee $20. Regular application deadline 6/15. Non-fall registration accepted. Admission may be deferred for a maximum of one semester.

COSTS AND FINANCIAL AID
Annual in-state tuition $6,898. Annual out-of-state tuition $13,796. Room and board $7,798. Average book and supplies expense $800. **Required Forms and Deadlines:** FAFSA; State aid form. **Types of Aid:** *Need-based scholarships/grants:* College/university scholarship or grant aid from institutional funds; Private scholarships; State scholarships/grants. *Loans:* Direct PLUS loans; Direct Subsidized Stafford Loans; Direct Unsubsidized Stafford Loans. **Student Employment:** Federal Work-Study Program available. Institutional employment available. **Financial Aid Statistics:** 66% needy freshmen, 67% needy undergrads receive need-based scholarship or grant aid. 57% freshmen, 30% undergrads receive non-need-based scholarship or grant aid. 91% freshmen, 93% undergrads receive need-based self-help aid. 0% freshmen, 0% undergrads receive athletic scholarships. 75% freshmen, 58% undergrads receive any aid. **Criteria awarding aid:** *Non-need-based:* Academics, Athletics.

MISERICORDIA UNIVERSITY

301 Lake Street, Dallas, PA 18612
Phone: 570-674-6264 **Financial Aid Phone:** 570-674-6222
E-mail: admiss@misericordia.edu **CEEB Code:** 2087
Fax: 570-675-2441 **Website:** www.misericordia.edu **ACT Code:** 3539

This private school, affiliated with the Roman Catholic Church, was founded in 1924. It has a 123 acre campus.

RATINGS
Admissions Selectivity Rating: 76   **Fire Safety Rating:** 96   **Green Rating:** 60*

STUDENTS AND FACULTY
Enrollment: 1,942. **Student Body:** 68% female, 32% male, 28% out-of-state, <1% international (4 countries represented). Asian 1%, African American 3%, Caucasian 85%, Hispanic 3%, Native American <1%, Pacific Islander <1%, Two or more races 4%, Race unknown 3%.
Retention and Graduation: 82% freshmen return for sophomore year. 61% freshmen graduate within 4 years. 68% freshmen graduate within 6 years. 33% grads go on to further study within 1 year. 25% grads pursue arts and sciences degrees. 0% grads pursue law degrees. 8% grads pursue business degrees. 0% grads pursue medical degrees. **Faculty:** Student/faculty ratio 10:1. 144 full-time faculty, 81% hold PhDs, 10% are members of minority groups, 60% are women. 0% of classes are taught by teaching assistants.

ACADEMICS
Degrees: Bachelor's; Certificate; Doctoral degree—professional practice; Master's; Post-bachelor's certificate; Post-master's certificate. **Classes:** Most classes have 10–19 students. Most lab/discussion sessions have 10–19 students. **Most popular majors:** Registered Nursing/Registered Nurse; Business Administration and Management, General; Health/Health Care Administration/Management. **Special Study Options:** Accelerated program; Cross-registration; Distance learning; Double major; Dual enrollment; Honors program; Independent study; Internships; Student-designed major; Study abroad; Teacher certification program; Weekend college. **Honors programs:** The Honors Program is an interdisciplinary learning community based in a common sequence of enriched and intensified core curriculum courses which honors students take in place of the regular core offerings. Honors courses emphasize discussion over lecture, use writing as an integrative feature of learning, are highly interdisciplinary, and provide a very interactive relationship between student and faculty. Honors courses are not intended to be more difficult, but do approach topics in different ways than traditional core courses. **Disability Services offered:** Tape recorders; Tutors. **Career services:** Alumni network; Alumni services; Career assessment; Career/job search classes; Internships; Regional alumni.

FACILITIES
Housing: Coed dorms; 100% of campus accessible to physically disabled.

CAMPUS LIFE
Environment: Town. **Activities:** Campus Ministries; Choral groups; Dance; Drama/theater; Jazz band; Literary magazine; Music ensembles; Radio station; Student government; Student newspaper; Television station; Yearbook. 40 registered organizations, 15 honor societies, 1 religious organization on campus. **Athletics (Intercollegiate):** *Men:* baseball, basketball, cross-country, golf, lacrosse, soccer, swimming, tennis, track/field (outdoor). *Women:* basketball, cheerleading, cross-country, field hockey, lacrosse, soccer, softball, swimming, tennis, track/field (outdoor), volleyball. **On-Campus Highlights:** Anderson Sports and Health Center.

ADMISSIONS
Freshman Academic Profile: Average high school GPA 3.4. 18% in top 10% of high school class, 49% in top 25% of high school class, 80% in top 50% of high school class. 82% from public high schools. **Test Scores:** SAT Math middle 50% range 530–610. SAT EBRW middle 50% range 520–610. ACT middle 50% range 22–27. **Basis for Candidate Selection:** *Very important factors include:* rigor of secondary school record, academic GPA, standardized test scores. *Important factors include:* class rank, extracurricular activities, character/personal qualities, volunteer work. *Other factors include:* application essay, recommendation(s), interview, first generation, alumni/ae relation, geographical residence, work experience, level of applicant's interest. **Freshman Admission Requirements:** High school diploma is required and GED is accepted. *Academic units required:* 4 English, 4 math, 4 science, 4 social studies. **Freshman Admission Statistics:** 1,547 applied, 86% admitted, 31% enrolled. **Transfer Admission Requirements:** College transcript(s). Minimum college GPA of 2.0 required. Lowest grade transferable C. **General Admission Information:** Application fee $35. Non-fall registration accepted. Admission may be deferred for a maximum of 12 months.

COSTS AND FINANCIAL AID
Annual tuition $34,100. Room and board $14,520. Required fees $1,840. Average book and supplies expense $1,250. **Required Forms and Deadlines:** FAFSA. **Notification of Awards:** Applicants will be notified of awards on a rolling basis beginning 12/1. **Types of Aid:** *Need-based scholarships/grants:* College/university scholarship or grant aid from institutional funds; Federal Pell; Private scholarships; SEOG; State scholarships/grants. *Loans:* Direct PLUS loans; Direct Subsidized Stafford Loans; Direct Unsubsidized Stafford Loans. **Student Employment:** Federal Work-Study Program available. Institutional employment available. **Financial Aid Statistics:** 100% needy freshmen, 100% needy undergrads receive need-based scholarship or grant aid. 20% freshmen, 20% undergrads receive non-need-based scholarship or grant aid. 75% freshmen, 75% undergrads receive need-based self-help aid. 0% freshmen, 0% undergrads receive athletic scholarships. 99% freshmen, 99% undergrads receive any aid. 84% undergrads borrow to pay for school. Average cumulative indebtedness $46,756. **Criteria awarding aid:** *Need-based:* Minority status. *Non-need-based:* Academics, Alumni affiliation, Leadership, Minority status, State/district residency.

MISSISSIPPI COLLEGE

Box 4026, Clinton, MS 39058-0001
Phone: 601-925-3800 **Financial Aid Phone:** (601) 925-3212
E-mail: enrollment-services@mc.edu **CEEB Code:** 1477
Fax: 601-925-3950 **Website:** http://www.mc.edu **ACT Code:** 2214

This private school, affiliated with the Southern Baptist Church, was founded in 1826. It has a 474 acre campus.

RATINGS

Admissions Selectivity Rating: 86   **Fire Safety Rating:** 96   **Green Rating:** 60*

STUDENTS AND FACULTY

Enrollment: 3,030. **Student Body:** 61% female, 39% male, 24% out-of-state, 3% international (21 countries represented). Asian 1%, African American 24%, Caucasian 67%, Hispanic 2%, Native American 1%, Pacific Islander 0%, Two or more races 1%, Race unknown 2%.
Retention and Graduation: 73% freshmen return for sophomore year.
Faculty: Student/faculty ratio 15:1. 205 full-time faculty, 78% hold PhDs, 9% are members of minority groups, 48% are women. 0% of classes are taught by teaching assistants.

ACADEMICS

Degrees: Bachelor's; Doctoral degree—professional practice; Doctoral degree research/scholarship; Master's; Post-bachelor's certificate; Post-master's certificate. **Classes:** Most classes have 10–19 students. Most lab/discussion sessions have 10–19 students. **Most popular majors:** Biomedical Sciences, General; Business Administration and Management, General; Elementary Education and Teaching. **Special Study Options:** Accelerated program; Distance learning; Double major; Dual enrollment; English as a Second Language (ESL); Honors program; Independent study; Internships; Study abroad; Teacher certification program. **Honors programs:** Honors programs open to freshmen, sophomores, juniors, and seniors and administered by the Honors Council. Freshmen who have a high ACT score (established each year) are invited to participate in a program of study called Freshman Honors Seminar (IDS161), it is an interdisciplinary study dealing with contemporary issues and interests. Upperclassmen who maintain a high GPA may also participate in Sophomore and Senior Honors Seminars (IDS 261, 461). Successful completion of the Junior-Senior Honors Program leads to a degree "With Honors" or "With High Honors." **Combined degree programs:** BA/JD. **Disability Services offered:** Note-taking services; Reader services; Tape recorders; Tutors. **Career services:** Alumni services; Career assessment; Career/job search classes; Internships.

FACILITIES

Housing: Apartments for single students; Men's dorms; Special housing for disabled students; Wellness housing; Women's dorms; 100% of campus accessible to physically disabled. **Special Academic Facilities/Equipment:** Samuel Marshall Gore Art Gallery; Science Building with Cadaver Lab; Healthplex. **Campus Network:** 100% of classrooms, 100% of dorms, 100% of student union, 100% of libraries, 100% of dining areas, 80% of common outdoor areas have wireless network access.

CAMPUS LIFE

Environment: City. **Activities:** Campus Ministries; Choral groups; Concert band; Dance; Drama/theater; International Student Organization; Jazz band; Literary magazine; Marching band; Music ensembles; Musical theater; Opera; Radio station; Student government; Student newspaper; Yearbook. 74 registered organizations, 18 honor societies, 4 religious organizations, 4 fraternities, 4 sororities on campus. **Athletics (Intercollegiate):** *Men:* baseball, basketball, cross-country, football, golf, soccer, tennis, track/field (outdoor). *Women:* basketball, cheerleading, cross-country, equestrian sports, soccer, softball, tennis, track/field (outdoor), volleyball. **On-Campus Highlights:** Samuel Marshall Gore Art Gallery.

ADMISSIONS

Freshman Academic Profile: Average high school GPA 3.4. 33% in top 10% of high school class, 57% in top 25% of high school class, 74% in top 50% of high school class. **Test Scores:** SAT Math middle 50% range 470–580. SAT EBRW middle 50% range 470–613. ACT middle 50% range 20–27. **Basis for Candidate Selection:** *Very important factors include:* standardized test scores. *Important factors include:* rigor of secondary school record, extracurricular activities, character/personal qualities. *Other factors include:* class rank, academic GPA, recommendation(s), interview, talent/ability, alumni/ae relation, volunteer

work, work experience. **Freshman Admission Requirements:** High school diploma is required and GED is accepted. *Academic units recommended:* 4 English, 4 math, 4 science, 2 science labs, 1 foreign language, 2 social studies, 2 history, 3.5 academic electives, 0.5 computer science, 1 visual/performing arts. **Freshman Admission Statistics:** 2,178 applied, 58% admitted, 38% enrolled. **Transfer Admission Requirements:** College transcript(s), essay or personal statement, statement of good standing from prior institution(s). Minimum college GPA of 2.0 required. Lowest grade transferable C. **General Admission Information:** Application fee $25. Priority deadline 5/1. Non-fall registration accepted. Admission may be deferred for a maximum of 1 year.

COSTS AND FINANCIAL AID

Annual tuition $14,120. Room and board $7,150. Required fees $748. Average book and supplies expense $1,100. **Required Forms and Deadlines:** FAFSA; State aid form. **Notification of Awards:** Applicants will be notified of awards on a rolling basis beginning 3/1. **Types of Aid:** *Need-based scholarships/grants:* College/university scholarship or grant aid from institutional funds; Federal Pell; Private scholarships; SEOG; State scholarships/grants. *Loans:* Direct PLUS loans; Direct Subsidized Stafford Loans; Direct Unsubsidized Stafford Loans. **Student Employment:** Federal Work-Study Program available. Institutional employment available. **Financial Aid Statistics:** 89% needy freshmen, 86% needy undergrads receive need-based scholarship or grant aid. 96% freshmen, 86% undergrads receive non-need-based scholarship or grant aid. 81% freshmen, 84% undergrads receive need-based self-help aid. 0% freshmen, 0% undergrads receive athletic scholarships. 98% freshmen, 94% undergrads receive any aid. **Criteria awarding aid:** *Non-need-based:* Academics, Alumni affiliation, Art, Leadership, Music/drama, Religious affiliation.

MISSISSIPPI STATE UNIVERSITY

P. O. Box 6334, Mississippi State, MS 39762
Phone: 662-325-2224 **Financial Aid Phone:** 662-325-2450
E-mail: admit@msstate.edu **CEEB Code:** 1480
Fax: 662-325-1MSU **Website:** www.msstate.edu **ACT Code:** 2220

This public school was founded in 1878. It has a 4200 acre campus.

RATINGS

Admissions Selectivity Rating: 85   **Fire Safety Rating:** 91   **Green Rating:** 60*

STUDENTS AND FACULTY

Enrollment: 18,388. **Student Body:** 50% female, 50% male, 32% out-of-state, 1% international (60 countries represented). Asian 1%, African American 18%, Caucasian 73%, Hispanic 3%, Native American 1%, Pacific Islander <1%, Two or more races 2%, Race unknown <1%.
Retention and Graduation: 81% freshmen return for sophomore year. 31% freshmen graduate within 4 years. **Faculty:** Student/faculty ratio 17:1. 1,043 full-time faculty, 82% hold PhDs, 19% are members of minority groups, 42% are women.

ACADEMICS

Degrees: Bachelor's; Doctoral degree—professional practice; Doctoral degree research/scholarship; Master's; Post-master's certificate. **Classes:** Most classes have 10–19 students. Most lab/discussion sessions have 10–19 students. **Most popular majors:** Geology/Earth Science, General; Physical Education Teaching and Coaching; Business Administration and Management, General. **Special Study Options:** Cooperative education program; Cross-registration; Distance learning; Double major; Dual enrollment; English as a Second Language (ESL); Exchange student program (domestic); Honors program; Independent study; Internships; Liberal arts/career combination; Student-designed major; Study abroad; Teacher certification program. **Honors programs:** University Honors Program and the Montgomery Leadership Program. **Disability Services offered:** Note-taking services; Reader services; Tape recorders; Tutors. **Career services:** Alumni network; Alumni services; Career assessment; Career/job search classes; Internships; Regional alumni.

FACILITIES

Housing: Apartments for married students; Coed dorms; Fraternity/sorority housing; Men's dorms; Theme housing; Women's dorms; 95% of campus accessible to physically disabled. **Special Academic Facilities/Equipment:** Geology, archaeology, music, entomological museums; art gallery; flight research lab. **Campus Network:** 100% of classrooms, 90% of dorms, 100% of student union, 100% of libraries, 100% of dining areas, 50% of common outdoor areas have wireless network access.

CAMPUS LIFE

Environment: Town. **Activities:** Campus Ministries; Choral groups; Concert band; Dance; Drama/theater; International Student Organization; Jazz band; Literary magazine; Marching band; Model UN; Music ensembles; Musical theater; Pep band; Radio station; Student government; Student newspaper; Student-run film society; Symphony orchestra; Television station. 373 registered organizations, 21 honor societies, 21 religious organizations, 19 fraternities, 12 sororities on campus. **Athletics (Intercollegiate):** *Men:* baseball, basketball, cheerleading, cross-country, football, golf, tennis, track/field (outdoor). *Women:* basketball, cheerleading, cross-country, golf, soccer, softball, tennis, track/field (outdoor), volleyball. **On-Campus Highlights:** Scott Field Stadium. **Environmental Initiatives:** Recycling.

ADMISSIONS

Freshman Academic Profile: Average high school GPA 3.5. 30% in top 10% of high school class, 57% in top 25% of high school class, 85% in top 50% of high school class. **Test Scores:** SAT Math middle 50% range 530–650. SAT EBRW middle 50% range 540–630. ACT middle 50% range 22–30. **Basis for Candidate Selection:** *Very important factors include:* academic GPA, standardized test scores. *Important factors include:* class rank. *Other factors include:* rigor of secondary school record, state residency. **Freshman Admission Requirements:** High school diploma is required and GED is accepted. *Academic units required:* 4 English, 3 math, 3 science, 2 science labs, 1 foreign language, 1 social studies, 2 history, 1 academic elective, 0.5 computer science, 1 visual/performing arts. *Academic units recommended:* 4 English, 4 math, 4 science, 2 science labs, 1 foreign language, 2 social studies, 2 history, 1 academic elective, 0.5 computer science, 1 visual/performing arts. **Freshman Admission Statistics:** 18,269 applied, 66% admitted, 29% enrolled. **Transfer Admission Requirements:** College transcript(s), statement of good standing from prior institution(s). Minimum college GPA of 2.0 required. Lowest grade transferable D. **General Admission Information:** Application fee $40. Non-fall registration accepted.

COSTS AND FINANCIAL AID

Annual in-state tuition $8,880. Annual out-of-state tuition $23,840. Room and board $10,141. Average book and supplies expense $1,200. **Required Forms and Deadlines:** FAFSA; State aid form. **Notification of Awards:** Applicants will be notified of awards on a rolling basis beginning 12/1. **Types of Aid:** *Need-based scholarships/grants:* College/university scholarship or grant aid from institutional funds; Federal Pell; Private scholarships; SEOG; State scholarships/grants; United Negro College Fund. *Loans:* Direct PLUS loans; Direct Subsidized Stafford Loans; Direct Unsubsidized Stafford Loans. **Student Employment:** Federal Work-Study Program available. Institutional employment available. **Financial Aid Statistics:** 95% needy freshmen, 89% needy undergrads receive need-based scholarship or grant aid. 16% freshmen, 8% undergrads receive non-need-based scholarship or grant aid. 59% freshmen, 68% undergrads receive need-based self-help aid. 2% freshmen, 3% undergrads receive athletic scholarships. 71% freshmen, 64% undergrads receive any aid. 55% undergrads borrow to pay for school. Average cumulative indebtedness $31,060. **Criteria awarding aid:** *Need-based:* Academics, Alumni affiliation, Leadership, Minority status, Music/drama. *Non-need-based:* Academics, Alumni affiliation, Art, Athletics, Job skills, Leadership, Minority status, Music/drama, State/district residency.

MISSISSIPPI VALLEY STATE UNIVERSITY

14000 Highway 82 West, Itta Bena, MS 38941-1400
Phone: 662-254-3344 **Financial Aid Phone:** 662-254-3338
E-mail: nbtaylor@mvsu.edu **CEEB Code:** 1482
Fax: 662-254-3759 **Website:** www.mvsu.edu **ACT Code:** 2224

This public school was founded in 1950. It has a 250 acre campus.

RATINGS

Admissions Selectivity Rating: 86   **Fire Safety Rating:** 84   **Green Rating:** 60*

STUDENTS AND FACULTY

Enrollment: 2,357. **Student Body:** 62% female, 38% male, 11% out-of-state, 2 countries represented. Asian <1%, African American 93%, Caucasian 4%, Hispanic 1%, Native American <1%, Race unknown 2%.
Retention and Graduation: 55% freshmen return for sophomore year.
Faculty: Student/faculty ratio 21:1. 133 full-time faculty, 58% hold PhDs, 30%

are members of minority groups, 46% are women. 0% of classes are taught by teaching assistants.

ACADEMICS

Degrees: Bachelor's; Master's. **Classes:** Most classes have 20–29 students. Most lab/discussion sessions have 20–29 students. **Most popular majors:** Social Work; Business, Management, Marketing, and Related Support Services, Other; Kindergarten/Preschool Education and Teaching. **Special Study Options:** Cooperative education program; Distance learning; Double major; Honors program; Internships; Teacher certification program; Weekend college. **Disability Services offered:** Tape recorders; Tutors. **Career services:** Alumni services.

FACILITIES

Housing: Apartments for married students; Apartments for single students; Men's dorms; Women's dorms. **Campus Network:** 100% of classrooms, 100% of student union, 100% of libraries, 100% of dining areas have wireless network access.

CAMPUS LIFE

Environment: Rural. **Activities:** Choral groups; Concert band; Drama/theater; Marching band; Radio station; Student government; Student newspaper; Yearbook. 35 registered organizations, 19 honor societies, 4 religious organizations, 4 fraternities, 2 sororities on campus. **Athletics (Intercollegiate):** *Men:* baseball, basketball, cross-country, football, golf, tennis, track/field (outdoor). *Women:* basketball, cross-country, golf, soccer, softball, tennis, track/field (outdoor), volleyball. **On-Campus Highlights:** Student Union.

ADMISSIONS

Freshman Academic Profile: Average high school GPA 2.6. 96% from public high schools. **Test Scores:** ACT middle 50% range 15–19. **Basis for Candidate Selection:** *Very important factors include:* rigor of secondary school record, class rank, standardized test scores, state residency. *Other factors include:* recommendation(s), interview, extracurricular activities, talent/ability. **Freshman Admission Requirements:** High school diploma is required and GED is accepted. *Academic units required:* 4 English, 3 math, 3 science, 2 science labs, 1 foreign language, 3 social studies, 2 academic electives, 1 unit from above areas or other academic areas. *Academic units recommended:* 1 foreign language. **Freshman Admission Statistics:** 6,086 applied, 30% admitted, 23% enrolled. **Transfer Admission Requirements:** College transcript(s). Minimum college GPA of 2.0 required. Lowest grade transferable C. **General Admission Information:** Non-fall registration accepted.

COSTS AND FINANCIAL AID

Annual in-state tuition $4,575. Annual out-of-state tuition $11,410. Room and board $5,081. Average book and supplies expense $1,400. **Required Forms and Deadlines:** FAFSA; Institution's own financial aid form. **Notification of Awards:** Applicants will be notified of awards on or about 7/15. **Types of Aid:** *Need-based scholarships/grants:* College/university scholarship or grant aid from institutional funds; Federal Pell; Private scholarships; SEOG; State scholarships/grants. *Loans:* Direct PLUS loans; Direct Unsubsidized Stafford Loans. **Student Employment:** Federal Work-Study Program available. **Financial Aid Statistics:** 95% freshmen, 95% undergrads receive any aid.

MISSOURI UNIVERSITY OF SCIENCE AND TECHNOLOGY

106 Parker Hall; 300 W. 13th Street, Rolla, MO 65409-1060
Phone: 573-341-4165 **Financial Aid Phone:** 573-341-4282
E-mail: admissions@mst.edu **CEEB Code:** 6876
Fax: 573-341-4082 **Website:** www.mst.edu **ACT Code:** 2398

This public school was founded in 1870. It has a 284 acre campus.

RATINGS

Admissions Selectivity Rating: 83   **Fire Safety Rating:** 88   **Green Rating:** 87

STUDENTS AND FACULTY

Enrollment: 6,872. **Student Body:** 24% female, 76% male, 17% out-of-state, 3% international (60 countries represented). Asian 4%, African American 3%, Caucasian 81%, Hispanic 4%, Native American <1%, Pacific Islander <1%, Two or more races 3%, Race unknown 2%.

Retention and Graduation: 81% freshmen return for sophomore year. 22% freshmen graduate within 4 years. 64% freshmen graduate within 6 years. **Faculty:** Student/faculty ratio 19:1. 375 full-time faculty, 92% hold PhDs, 36% are members of minority groups, 27% are women. 15% of classes are taught by teaching assistants.

ACADEMICS
Degrees: Bachelor's; Certificate; Doctoral degree research/scholarship; Master's; Post-bachelor's certificate. **Classes:** Most classes have 20–29 students. Most lab/discussion sessions have 10–19 students. **Most popular majors:** Civil Engineering, General; Electrical and Electronics Engineering; Mechanical Engineering. **Special Study Options:** Accelerated program; Cooperative education program; Distance learning; Double major; Dual enrollment; English as a Second Language (ESL); Honors program; Independent study; Internships; Study abroad; Teacher certification program. **Honors programs:** Honors Academy and Master Student Fellowship Programs- http://academicsupport.mst.edu/. **Combined degree programs:** BA/MEng. **Disability Services offered:** Note-taking services; Reader services; Tape recorders; Tutors. **Career services:** Alumni network; Alumni services; Career assessment; Career/job search classes; Internships; Regional alumni.

FACILITIES
Housing: Apartments for married students; Apartments for single students; Coed dorms; Fraternity/sorority housing; Special housing for disabled students; Theme housing; Wellness housing; 95% of campus accessible to physically disabled. **Special Academic Facilities/Equipment:** Writing Center, Student Design Center, Nuclear Reactor, Observatory, Explosives Testing Lab, Underground Mine, Museum of Rocks, Minerals, and Gemstones, Centers for Environmental Research, Water Resources, Industrial Research, and Rock Mechanics Research, Geophysical Observatory, Computerized Manufacturing System, Millennium Arch, and Stonehenge.

CAMPUS LIFE
Environment: Village. **Activities:** Campus Ministries; Choral groups; Concert band; Dance; Drama/theater; International Student Organization; Jazz band; Literary magazine; Marching band; Model UN; Music ensembles; Musical theater; Pep band; Radio station; Student government; Student newspaper; Student-run film society; Symphony orchestra; Yearbook. 287 registered organizations, 17 honor societies, 15 religious organizations, 20 fraternities, 6 sororities on campus. **Athletics (Intercollegiate):** *Men:* baseball, basketball, cross-country, football, soccer, swimming, track/field (outdoor), track/field (indoor). *Women:* basketball, cross-country, soccer, softball, track/field (outdoor), track/field (indoor), volleyball. **On-Campus Highlights:** Havener Student Center. **Environmental Initiatives:** Reducing amount of paper being consumed.

ADMISSIONS
Freshman Academic Profile: Average high school GPA 3.6. 39% in top 10% of high school class, 72% in top 25% of high school class, 94% in top 50% of high school class. 85% from public high schools. **Test Scores:** SAT Math middle 50% range 580–700. SAT EBRW middle 50% range 520–640. ACT middle 50% range 25–31. **Basis for Candidate Selection:** *Very important factors include:* rigor of secondary school record, class rank, academic GPA, standardized test scores. *Important factors include:* recommendation(s). *Other factors include:* application essay, interview, extracurricular activities, talent/ability, character/personal qualities, volunteer work, work experience, level of applicant's interest. **Freshman Admission Requirements:** High school diploma is required and GED is accepted. *Academic units required:* 4 English, 4 math, 3 science, 1 science lab, 2 foreign language, 3 social studies, 1 visual/performing arts. **Freshman Admission Statistics:** 3,876 applied, 84% admitted, 44% enrolled. **Transfer Admission Requirements:** College transcript(s). Minimum college GPA of 2.5 required. **General Admission Information:** Application fee $50. Priority deadline 12/1. Regular application deadline 7/1.

COSTS AND FINANCIAL AID
Required Forms and Deadlines: FAFSA. **Notification of Awards:** Applicants will be notified of awards on a rolling basis beginning 4/1. **Types of Aid:** *Need-based scholarships/grants:* College/university scholarship or grant aid from institutional funds; Federal Pell; Private scholarships; SEOG; State scholarships/grants. **Student Employment:** Federal Work-Study Program available. Institutional employment available. **Financial Aid Statistics:** 94% needy freshmen, 91% needy undergrads receive need-based scholarship or grant aid. 30% freshmen, 40% undergrads receive non-need-based scholarship or grant aid. 100% freshmen, 100% undergrads receive need-based self-help aid. 5% freshmen, 4% undergrads receive athletic scholarships. 95% freshmen, 88% undergrads receive any aid. 66% undergrads borrow to pay for school. Average cumulative indebtedness $27,500. **Criteria awarding aid:** *Need-based:* Job

skills, Minority status. *Non-need-based:* Academics, Alumni affiliation, Athletics, Job skills, Leadership, Minority status, Music/drama, Religious affiliation, State/district residency.

MISSOURI VALLEY COLLEGE

500 East College Street, Marshall, MO 65340
Phone: 660-831-4114
E-mail: admissions@moval.edu
Fax: 660-831-4233 **Website:** www.moval.edu **ACT Code:** 2330

This private school, affiliated with the Presbyterian Church, was founded in 1889. It has a 150 acre campus.

RATINGS
Admissions Selectivity Rating: 72   **Fire Safety Rating:** 62   **Green Rating:** 60*

STUDENTS AND FACULTY
Enrollment: 1,329. **Student Body:** 39% female, 61% male, 53% out-of-state, 16% international (43 countries represented). Asian 1%, African American 20%, Caucasian 46%, Hispanic 10%, Native American 1%, Pacific Islander 1%, Two or more races 4%, Race unknown 2%.
Retention and Graduation: 45% freshmen return for sophomore year. 15% freshmen graduate within 4 years. 27% freshmen graduate within 6 years. 20% grads go on to further study within 1 year. **Faculty:** Student/faculty ratio 14:1. 87 full-time faculty, 38% hold PhDs, 3% are members of minority groups, 47% are women. 0% of classes are taught by teaching assistants.

ACADEMICS
Degrees: Associate; Bachelor's; Master's. **Classes:** Most classes have 10–19 students. **Most popular majors:** Business/Commerce, General; Criminal Justice/Law Enforcement Administration; Elementary Education and Teaching. **Special Study Options:** Distance learning; Double major; Dual enrollment; English as a Second Language (ESL); Honors program; Independent study; Internships; Liberal arts/career combination; Student-designed major; Study abroad; Teacher certification program. **Disability Services offered:** Reader services; Tutors. **Career services:** Internships.

FACILITIES
Housing: Apartments for single students; Fraternity/sorority housing; Men's dorms; Women's dorms.

CAMPUS LIFE
Environment: Village. **Activities:** Campus Ministries; Dance; Drama/theater; International Student Organization; Jazz band; Musical theater; Radio station; Student government; Student newspaper; Television station. 28 registered organizations, 8 honor societies, 7 religious organizations, 4 fraternities, 2 sororities on campus. **Athletics (Intercollegiate):** *Men:* baseball, basketball, cheerleading, cross-country, football, golf, rodeo, soccer, tennis, track/field (outdoor), track/field (indoor), volleyball, wrestling. *Women:* basketball, cheerleading, cross-country, golf, rodeo, soccer, softball, tennis, track/field (outdoor), track/field (indoor), volleyball, wrestling. **On-Campus Highlights:** Burns Gym.

ADMISSIONS
Freshman Academic Profile: Average high school GPA 2.9. 3% in top 10% of high school class, 16% in top 25% of high school class, 31% in top 50% of high school class. **Basis for Candidate Selection:** *Very important factors include:* academic GPA, standardized test scores. *Important factors include:* class rank. *Other factors include:* rigor of secondary school record, recommendation(s), talent/ability, character/personal qualities, first generation, alumni/ae relation. **Freshman Admission Requirements:** High school diploma is required and GED is accepted. **Freshman Admission Statistics:** 2,300 applied, 54% admitted, 32% enrolled. **Transfer Admission Requirements:** High school transcript, college transcript(s), standardized test scores. Minimum college GPA of 2.0 required. Lowest grade transferable C. **General Admission Information:** Regular application deadline 9/1. Non-fall registration accepted.

COSTS AND FINANCIAL AID
Annual tuition $19,300. Room and board $9,150. Required fees $1,300. Average book and supplies expense $2,890. **Required Forms and Deadlines:** FAFSA. **Notification of Awards:** Applicants will be notified of awards on a rolling basis beginning 10/30. **Types of Aid:** *Need-based scholarships/grants:* College/university scholarship or grant aid from institutional funds; Federal Pell; Private scholarships; SEOG; State scholarships/grants. *Loans:* Direct PLUS

loans; Direct Subsidized Stafford Loans; Direct Unsubsidized Stafford Loans. **Student Employment:** Federal Work-Study Program available. Institutional employment available. **Financial Aid Statistics:** 100% needy freshmen, 100% needy undergrads receive need-based scholarship or grant aid. 14% freshmen, 19% undergrads receive non-need-based scholarship or grant aid. 100% freshmen, 100% undergrads receive need-based self-help aid. 4% freshmen, 7% undergrads receive athletic scholarships. 98% freshmen, 92% undergrads receive any aid. 74% undergrads borrow to pay for school. Average cumulative indebtedness $31,508.

MITCHELL COLLEGE

437 Pequot Avenue, New London, CT 06320
Phone: 860-701-5011 **Financial Aid Phone:** 800-443-2811
E-mail: admissions@mitchell.edu **CEEB Code:** 3528
Fax: 860-444-1209 **Website:** http://www.mitchell.edu/ **ACT Code:** 572

This private school was founded in 1938. It has a 68 acre campus.

RATINGS
Admissions Selectivity Rating: 69   **Fire Safety Rating:** 72   **Green Rating:** 60*

STUDENTS AND FACULTY
Enrollment: 785. **Student Body:** 47% female, 53% male, 42% out-of-state, <1% international. Asian 2%, African American 11%, Caucasian 68%, Hispanic 13%, Native American 1%, Pacific Islander 0%, Two or more races 4%, Race unknown 2%.
Retention and Graduation: 57% freshmen return for sophomore year.
Faculty: Student/faculty ratio 14:1. 35 full-time faculty, 74% hold PhDs, 0% are members of minority groups, 51% are women. 0% of classes are taught by teaching assistants.

ACADEMICS
Degrees: Associate; Bachelor's. **Classes:** Most classes have 10–19 students. **Special Study Options:** Independent study; Internships; Liberal arts/career combination; Student-designed major; Teacher certification program. **Disability Services offered:** Note-taking services; Reader services; Tape recorders; Tutors. **Career services:** Career assessment.

FACILITIES
Housing: Apartments for single students; Coed dorms; Special housing for disabled students; Theme housing; 50% of campus accessible to physically disabled.

CAMPUS LIFE
Environment: Town. **Activities:** Dance; Drama/theater; Radio station; Student government. 30 registered organizations, 8 honor societies on campus. **Athletics (Intercollegiate):** *Men:* baseball, basketball, cross-country, golf, lacrosse, soccer, tennis. *Women:* basketball, cross-country, golf, soccer, softball, tennis, volleyball.

ADMISSIONS
Freshman Academic Profile: Average high school GPA 2.7. **Basis for Candidate Selection:** *Very important factors include:* academic GPA, interview. *Important factors include:* rigor of secondary school record, application essay, recommendation(s), extracurricular activities, character/personal qualities, volunteer work. *Other factors include:* standardized test scores, talent/ability, alumni/ae relation, work experience. **Freshman Admission Requirements:** High school diploma is required and GED is accepted. *Academic units recommended:* 4 English, 3 math, 3 science, 2 social studies, 2 history, 2 academic electives. **Freshman Admission Statistics:** 1,041 applied, 60% admitted, 24% enrolled. **Transfer Admission Requirements:** High school transcript, college transcript(s), essay or personal statement, standardized test scores. Minimum college GPA of 2.0 required. Lowest grade transferable C-. **General Admission Information:** Application fee $30. Priority deadline 4/1. Non-fall registration accepted. Admission may be deferred for a maximum of 1 year.

COSTS AND FINANCIAL AID
Annual tuition $26,774. Room and board $12,492. Required fees $1,720. Average book and supplies expense $1,500. **Required Forms and Deadlines:** FAFSA. **Notification of Awards:** Applicants will be notified of awards on a rolling basis beginning 3/1. **Types of Aid:** *Need-based scholarships/grants:* College/university scholarship or grant aid from institutional funds; Federal Pell; Private scholarships; SEOG; State scholarships/grants. *Loans:* Direct PLUS

loans; Direct Subsidized Stafford Loans; Direct Unsubsidized Stafford Loans. **Student Employment:** Federal Work-Study Program available. Institutional employment available. **Financial Aid Statistics:** 100% needy freshmen, 99% needy undergrads receive need-based scholarship or grant aid. 93% freshmen, 87% undergrads receive non-need-based scholarship or grant aid. 93% freshmen, 95% undergrads receive need-based self-help aid. 0% freshmen, 0% undergrads receive athletic scholarships. **Criteria awarding aid:** *Non-need-based:* Academics, Alumni affiliation, Art, Leadership.

MOLLOY COLLEGE

1000 Hempstead Avenue, Rockville Centre, NY 11570
Phone: 516-323-4000 **Financial Aid Phone:** 516.323.4209
E-mail: admissions@molloy.edu **CEEB Code:** 2415
Website: http://www.molloy.edu/ **ACT Code:** 2820

This private school was founded in 1955. It has a 35 acre campus.

RATINGS
Admissions Selectivity Rating: 77   **Fire Safety Rating:** 91   **Green Rating:** 60*

STUDENTS AND FACULTY
Enrollment: 3,426. **Student Body:** 73% female, 27% male, 5% out-of-state, 1% international (18 countries represented). Asian 8%, African American 9%, Caucasian 60%, Hispanic 19%, Native American <1%, Pacific Islander <1%, Two or more races 2%, Race unknown 2%.
Retention and Graduation: 84% freshmen return for sophomore year. 48% freshmen graduate within 4 years. 74% freshmen graduate within 6 years.
Faculty: Student/faculty ratio 10:1. 192 full-time faculty, 83% hold PhDs, 21% are members of minority groups, 71% are women. 0% of classes are taught by teaching assistants.

ACADEMICS
Degrees: Associate; Bachelor's; Doctoral degree research/scholarship; Master's; Post-bachelor's certificate; Post-master's certificate. **Classes:** Most classes have 10–19 students. Most lab/discussion sessions have 10–19 students. **Most popular majors:** Psychology, General; Registered Nursing/Registered Nurse; Business Administration and Management, General. **Special Study Options:** Distance learning; Double major; English as a Second Language (ESL); Honors program; Independent study; Internships; Liberal arts/career combination; Student-designed major; Study abroad; Teacher certification program. **Disability Services offered:** Note-taking services; Reader services; Tape recorders; Tutors. **Career services:** Alumni network; Alumni services; Internships; Regional alumni.

FACILITIES
Housing: Coed dorms; 100% of campus accessible to physically disabled. **Special Academic Facilities/Equipment:** Dance studio, Institute for Interfaith Dialogue, Institute of Gerontology, television studio.

CAMPUS LIFE
Environment: Village. **Activities:** Campus Ministries; Choral groups; Dance; Drama/theater; Jazz band; Literary magazine; Music ensembles; Student government; Student newspaper; Yearbook. 64 registered organizations, 21 honor societies, 3 religious organizations on campus. **Athletics (Intercollegiate):** *Men:* baseball, basketball, cross-country, lacrosse, soccer, track/field (outdoor), track/field (indoor). *Women:* basketball, cross-country, lacrosse, soccer, softball, tennis, track/field (outdoor), track/field (indoor), volleyball. **On-Campus Highlights:** Hagan Center for Nursing. **Environmental Initiatives:** The Sustainability Institute at Molloy College http://www.molloy.edu/si/index.asp.

ADMISSIONS
Freshman Academic Profile: Average high school GPA 3.0. 19% in top 10% of high school class, 56% in top 25% of high school class, 85% in top 50% of high school class. 64% from public high schools. **Test Scores:** SAT Math middle 50% range 520–620. SAT EBRW middle 50% range 530–620. ACT middle 50% range 22–28. **Basis for Candidate Selection:** *Very important factors include:* rigor of secondary school record, academic GPA, standardized test scores. *Other factors include:* class rank, application essay, recommendation(s), interview, extracurricular activities, talent/ability, volunteer work, work experience. **Freshman Admission Requirements:** High school diploma is required and GED is accepted. *Academic units required:* 4 English, 3 math, 3

science, 3 foreign language, 4 social studies, 3.5 academic electives. *Academic units recommended:* 4 English, 4 math, 4 science, 3 foreign language, 4 social studies, 1.5 academic electives. **Freshman Admission Statistics:** 4,624 applied, 78% admitted, 16% enrolled. **Transfer Admission Requirements:** College transcript(s). Minimum college GPA of 2.0 required. Lowest grade transferable C. **General Admission Information:** Application fee $40. Non-fall registration accepted. Admission may be deferred for a maximum of 1 year.

COSTS AND FINANCIAL AID

Annual tuition $31,330. Room and board $15,560. Required fees $1,270. Average book and supplies expense $1,470. **Required Forms and Deadlines:** FAFSA; State aid form. **Notification of Awards:** Applicants will be notified of awards on a rolling basis beginning 1/20. **Types of Aid:** *Need-based scholarships/ grants:* College/university scholarship or grant aid from institutional funds; Federal Nursing Scholarships; Federal Pell; Private scholarships; SEOG; State scholarships/grants. *Loans:* Direct PLUS loans; Direct Subsidized Stafford Loans; Direct Unsubsidized Stafford Loans. **Student Employment:** Federal Work-Study Program available. **Financial Aid Statistics:** 99% needy freshmen, 95% needy undergrads receive need-based scholarship or grant aid. 13% freshmen, 9% undergrads receive non-need-based scholarship or grant aid. 80% freshmen, 82% undergrads receive need-based self-help aid. 3% freshmen, 2% undergrads receive athletic scholarships. 75% undergrads borrow to pay for school. Average cumulative indebtedness $34,553. **Criteria awarding aid:** *Non-need-based:* Academics, Alumni affiliation, Art, Athletics, Leadership, Music/drama, Religious affiliation.

MONMOUTH COLLEGE

700 East Broadway, Monmouth, IL 61462
Phone: 309-457-2131 **Financial Aid Phone:** 309-457-2129
E-mail: admissions@monmouthcollege.edu **CEEB Code:** 1484
Fax: 309-457-2141 **Website:** www.monmouthcollege.edu **ACT Code:** 1084

This private school, affiliated with the Presbyterian Church, was founded in 1853. It has a 112 acre campus.

RATINGS

Admissions Selectivity Rating: 80   **Fire Safety Rating:** 92   **Green Rating:** 81

STUDENTS AND FACULTY

Enrollment: 1,174. **Student Body:** 52% female, 48% male, 9% out-of-state, 6% international (35 countries represented). Asian 2%, African American 10%, Caucasian 63%, Hispanic 12%, Native American 1%, Pacific Islander 0%, Two or more races 2%, Race unknown 5%.
Retention and Graduation: 74% freshmen return for sophomore year. 15% grads go on to further study within 1 year. 10% grads pursue arts and sciences degrees. 1% grads pursue law degrees. 0% grads pursue business degrees. 1% grads pursue medical degrees. **Faculty:** Student/faculty ratio 11:1. 92 full-time faculty, 88% hold PhDs, 5% are members of minority groups, 42% are women. 0% of classes are taught by teaching assistants.

ACADEMICS

Degrees: Bachelor's. **Classes:** Most classes have 10–19 students. Most lab/discussion sessions have 10–19 students. **Most popular majors:** Business Administration and Management, General; Psychology, General; Speech Communication and Rhetoric. **Special Study Options:** Double major; English as a Second Language (ESL); Exchange student program (domestic); Honors program; Independent study; Internships; Student-designed major; Study abroad; Teacher certification program. **Honors programs:** The Monmouth College Honors Program is intended for a select group of academically well-prepared and intellectually ambitious students. Acceptance into the program is determined competitively, normally occurring at the end of the first semester of the freshman year. The program consists of three levels: exploration of the history of the liberal arts as a field of inquiry, in-depth seminars upon historically significant persons, events, movements and ideas, and a senior capstone course. **Disability Services offered:** Note-taking services; Reader services; Tape recorders; Tutors. **Career services:** Alumni network; Alumni services; Career assessment; Career/job search classes; Internships; Regional alumni.

FACILITIES

Housing: Apartments for single students; Coed dorms; Fraternity/sorority housing; Men's dorms; Special housing for disabled students; Special housing for international students; Theme housing; Women's dorms; 98% of campus accessible to physically disabled. **Special Academic Facilities/Equipment:** Shields Art & Antiquities Collection, Wackerle Career & Leadership Center, the Teaching & Learning Center, MC-TV (student-run television station), WMCR (student-run radio station), Adolphson Observatory, LeSuer Nature Preserve.

CAMPUS LIFE

Environment: Village. **Activities:** Campus Ministries; Choral groups; Concert band; Dance; Drama/theater; International Student Organization; Jazz band; Literary magazine; Marching band; Music ensembles; Musical theater; Radio station; Student government; Student newspaper; Student-run film society; Symphony orchestra; Television station. 120 registered organizations, 18 honor societies, 4 religious organizations, 4 fraternities, 3 sororities on campus. **Athletics (Intercollegiate):** *Men:* baseball, basketball, cross-country, diving, football, golf, soccer, swimming, tennis, track/field (outdoor), track/field (indoor). *Women:* basketball, cross-country, diving, golf, soccer, softball, swimming, tennis, track/field (outdoor), track/field (indoor), volleyball. **On-Campus Highlights:** The Mellinger Commons in the Center for Science and Business. **Environmental Initiatives:** The College has a comprehensive recycling and waste diversion program. Recycling receptacles are provided for paper, glass, plastic, and aluminum in every office and every bedroom in all academic buildings and residence halls, with a recycling center for electronics, flourescent lights and cell phones in the Stockdale Center (the student center). All cardboard generated at the dining service is recycled. A fleet of 5 hybrid cars is used by Monmouth faculty and staff for college purposes.

ADMISSIONS

Freshman Academic Profile: Average high school GPA 3.3. 13% in top 10% of high school class, 36% in top 25% of high school class, 70% in top 50% of high school class. 80% from public high schools. **Test Scores:** ACT middle 50% range 20–26. **Basis for Candidate Selection:** *Very important factors include:* rigor of secondary school record. *Important factors include:* class rank, academic GPA, standardized test scores. *Other factors include:* application essay, recommendation(s), interview, extracurricular activities, talent/ability, character/personal qualities, alumni/ae relation, volunteer work, level of applicant's interest. **Freshman Admission Requirements:** High school diploma is required and GED is accepted. *Academic units required:* 4 English, 2 math, 2 science, 1 science lab, 1 social studies, 1 history. *Academic units recommended:* 4 English, 4 math, 3 science, 2 science labs, 2 foreign language, 1 social studies, 2 history, 2 academic electives, 2 visual/performing arts. **Freshman Admission Statistics:** 2,657 applied, 62% admitted, 16% enrolled. **Transfer Admission Requirements:** College transcript(s). Minimum college GPA of 2.5 required. Lowest grade transferable C-. **General Admission Information:** Non-fall registration accepted. Admission may be deferred for a maximum of 1 year.

COSTS AND FINANCIAL AID

Annual tuition $35,300. Room and board $8,300. Required fees $190. Average book and supplies expense $1,200. **Required Forms and Deadlines:** FAFSA. **Notification of Awards:** Applicants will be notified of awards on a rolling basis beginning 2/15. **Types of Aid:** *Need-based scholarships/grants:* College/university scholarship or grant aid from institutional funds; Federal Pell; Private scholarships; SEOG; State scholarships/grants. *Loans:* Direct PLUS loans; Direct Subsidized Stafford Loans; Direct Unsubsidized Stafford Loans. **Student Employment:** Federal Work-Study Program available. Institutional employment available. **Financial Aid Statistics:** 100% needy freshmen, 100% needy undergrads receive need-based scholarship or grant aid. 14% freshmen, 13% undergrads receive non-need-based scholarship or grant aid. 83% freshmen, 80% undergrads receive need-based self-help aid. 0% freshmen, 0% undergrads receive athletic scholarships. 99% freshmen, 99% undergrads receive any aid. 83% undergrads borrow to pay for school. Average cumulative indebtedness $33,646. **Criteria awarding aid:** *Need-based:* Academics. *Non-need-based:* Academics, Art, Leadership, Music/drama, Religious affiliation.

MONMOUTH UNIVERSITY (NJ)

Admission, Monmouth University, West Long Branch, NJ 07764-1898
Phone: 732-571-3456 **Financial Aid Phone:** 732-571-3463
E-mail: admission@monmouth.edu **CEEB Code:** 2416
Fax: 732-263-5166 **Website:** www.monmouth.edu **ACT Code:** 2571

This private school was founded in 1933. It has a 158.6 acre campus.

RATINGS
Admissions Selectivity Rating: 77   **Fire Safety Rating:** 99   **Green Rating:** 77

STUDENTS AND FACULTY
Enrollment: 4,594. **Student Body:** 58% female, 42% male, 17% out-of-state, 1% international (23 countries represented). Asian 3%, African American 5%, Caucasian 71%, Hispanic 14%, Native American <1%, Pacific Islander 0%, Two or more races 3%, Race unknown 4%.
Retention and Graduation: 81% freshmen return for sophomore year. 56% freshmen graduate within 4 years. 32% grads go on to further study within 1 year. **Faculty:** Student/faculty ratio 13:1. 312 full-time faculty, 79% hold PhDs, 17% are members of minority groups, 56% are women. 0% of classes are taught by teaching assistants.

ACADEMICS
Degrees: Associate; Bachelor's; Certificate; Doctoral degree—professional practice; Master's; Post-bachelor's certificate; Post-master's certificate. **Classes:** Most classes have 20–29 students. Most lab/discussion sessions have 10–19 students. **Most popular majors:** Speech Communication and Rhetoric; Business Administration and Management, General; Health Professions And Related Programs. **Special Study Options:** Accelerated program; Cooperative education program; Cross-registration; Distance learning; Double major; Dual enrollment; Honors program; Independent study; Internships; Liberal arts/career combination; Student-designed major; Study abroad; Teacher certification program. **Honors programs:** The Honors School is committed to providing motivated students with a unique learning environment in a community of scholars. By supporting both disciplinary and interdisciplinary approaches to education, the Honors School seeks to help students develop not only depth within their intended field of study, but also an appreciation for how that knowledge is embedded within a broader context of intellectual inquiry. The Honors School also is dedicated to raising students' level of cultural, ethical, and societal awareness as its participants develop into well-rounded scholars and citizens within a global community. **Combined degree programs:** BA/MA; BA/MD. **Disability Services offered:** Note-taking services; Reader services; Tape recorders; Tutors. **Career services:** Alumni network; Alumni services; Career assessment; Career/job search classes; Internships; Regional alumni.

FACILITIES
Housing: Apartments for single students; Coed dorms; Theme housing; 95% of campus accessible to physically disabled. **Special Academic Facilities/ Equipment:** Art galleries, instructional media center with TV and Radio stations, theatre, greenhouse, Financial Markets lab, community garden.

CAMPUS LIFE
Environment: Village. **Activities:** Campus Ministries; Choral groups; Concert band; Dance; Drama/theater; International Student Organization; Jazz band; Literary magazine; Model UN; Music ensembles; Musical theater; Pep band; Radio station; Student government; Student newspaper; Television station; Yearbook. 117 registered organizations, 26 honor societies, 6 religious organizations, 7 fraternities, 9 sororities on campus. **Athletics (Intercollegiate):** *Men:* baseball, basketball, cross-country, football, golf, soccer, tennis, track/field (outdoor), track/field (indoor). *Women:* basketball, cross-country, field hockey, golf, lacrosse, soccer, softball, tennis, track/field (outdoor), track/field (indoor). **On-Campus Highlights:** Rebecca Stafford Student Center. **Environmental Initiatives:** Monmouth University was the first private institution of higher education in New Jersey to enter into a voluntary Memorandum of Understanding (MOU) with the US Environmental Protection Agency (EPA). The MOU documents Monmouth's commitment as an environmental steward that has pledged to reduce its carbon footprint and to contribute to a better living environment. Monmouth University uses the EPA's environmental stewardship programs to develop policies, practices and specifications for environmental efficiency standards; to increase its stewardship awareness;

to remain current with EPA regulations and guidelines; and to increase the involvement and recognition of Monmouth's stakeholders in environmental sustainability programs. Monmouth University has pledged to partner with local government on environmental initiatives and addressing environmental concerns swiftly. Monmouth recognizes EPA's program requirements for outreach and involvement, data collecting and reporting, and strives to become a recognized leader and a candidate for EPA environmental stewardship awards.

ADMISSIONS
Freshman Academic Profile: Average high school GPA 3.4. 20% in top 10% of high school class, 42% in top 25% of high school class, 77% in top 50% of high school class. 85% from public high schools. **Test Scores:** SAT Math middle 50% range 520–590. SAT EBRW middle 50% range 520–600. ACT middle 50% range 19–25. **Basis for Candidate Selection:** *Very important factors include:* rigor of secondary school record, academic GPA, standardized test scores. *Important factors include:* application essay, recommendation(s), extracurricular activities, volunteer work. *Other factors include:* character/ personal qualities, alumni/ae relation. **Freshman Admission Requirements:** High school diploma is required and GED is accepted. *Academic units required:* 4 English, 3 math, 2 science, 1 science lab, 2 history, 5 academic electives. *Academic units recommended:* 4 English, 3 math, 2 science, 1 science lab, 2 foreign language, 2 social studies, 2 history, 5 academic electives. **Freshman Admission Statistics:** 9,226 applied, 77% admitted, 15% enrolled. **Transfer Admission Requirements:** College transcript(s), statement of good standing from prior institution(s). Minimum college GPA of 2.25 required. Lowest grade transferable C. **General Admission Information:** Application fee $50. Priority deadline 12/1. Regular application deadline 3/1. Non-fall registration accepted. Admission may be deferred for a maximum of 2 semesters.

COSTS AND FINANCIAL AID
Annual tuition $38,880. Room and board $14,534. Required fees $712. Average book and supplies expense $996. **Required Forms and Deadlines:** FAFSA. **Notification of Awards:** Applicants will be notified of awards on a rolling basis beginning 2/1. **Types of Aid:** *Need-based scholarships/grants:* College/university scholarship or grant aid from institutional funds; Federal Pell; Private scholarships; SEOG; State scholarships/grants. *Loans:* Direct PLUS loans; Direct Subsidized Stafford Loans; Direct Unsubsidized Stafford Loans. **Student Employment:** Federal Work-Study Program available. Institutional employment available. **Financial Aid Statistics:** 73% needy freshmen, 66% needy undergrads receive need-based scholarship or grant aid. 97% freshmen, 96% undergrads receive non-need-based scholarship or grant aid. 84% freshmen, 85% undergrads receive need-based self-help aid. 9% freshmen, 9% undergrads receive athletic scholarships. 99% freshmen, 97% undergrads receive any aid. 76% undergrads borrow to pay for school. Average cumulative indebtedness $24,767. **Criteria awarding aid:** *Non-need-based:* Academics, Alumni affiliation, Art, Athletics, State/district residency.

MONROE COLLEGE

2468 Jerome Avenue, Bronx, NY 10468
Phone: 718-933-6700
E-mail: cpatrick@monroecollege.edu
Fax: 718-364-3552 **Website:** http://www.monroecollege.edu/

This is a proprietary school.

RATINGS
Admissions Selectivity Rating: 72   **Fire Safety Rating:** 60*   **Green Rating:** 60*

STUDENTS AND FACULTY
Enrollment: 6,713. **Student Body:** 64% female, 36% male, 2% out-of-state, 5% international. Asian 1%, African American 46%, Caucasian 2%, Hispanic 42%, Native American <1%, Pacific Islander 0%, Two or more races 0%, Race unknown 5%.
Retention and Graduation: 75% freshmen return for sophomore year.
Faculty: Student/faculty ratio 21:1. 70 full-time faculty, 40% hold PhDs, 57% are members of minority groups, 44% are women.

ACADEMICS
Degrees: Associate; Bachelor's; Certificate; Master's. **Classes:** Most classes have 20–29 students. **Special Study Options:** Distance learning; Honors program; Independent study; Internships; Weekend college.

FACILITIES
Housing: Coed dorms.

CAMPUS LIFE

Activities: Literary magazine.

ADMISSIONS

Basis for Candidate Selection: *Very important factors include:* interview. *Important factors include:* application essay, *Other factors include:* rigor of secondary school record, class rank, standardized test scores, recommendation(s), extracurricular activities, talent/ability, character/personal qualities, alumni/ae relation, geographical residence, state residency, religious affiliation/commitment, racial/ethnic status, volunteer work, work experience. **Freshman Admission Requirements:** High school diploma or equivalent is not required. **Freshman Admission Statistics:** 2,108 applied, 67% admitted, 95% enrolled. **General Admission Information:** Application fee $35. Non-fall registration accepted.

COSTS AND FINANCIAL AID

Annual tuition $11,744. Room and board $11,660. Average book and supplies expense $900. **Required Forms and Deadlines:** FAFSA. **Notification of Awards:** Applicants will be notified of awards on or about 7/1. **Types of Aid:** *Need-based scholarships/grants:* College/university scholarship or grant aid from institutional funds; Federal Pell. *Loans:* Direct PLUS loans; Direct Subsidized Stafford Loans; Direct Unsubsidized Stafford Loans. **Financial Aid Statistics:** 97% needy freshmen, 100% needy undergrads receive need-based scholarship or grant aid. 1% freshmen, 1% undergrads receive non-need-based scholarship or grant aid. 41% freshmen, 43% undergrads receive need-based self-help aid. 1% freshmen, 0% undergrads receive athletic scholarships. **Criteria awarding aid:** *Need-based:* Academics.

MONTANA STATE UNIVERSITY

PO Box 172190, 201 Strand Union Bldg, Bozeman, MT 59717-2190
Phone: 406-994-2452 **Financial Aid Phone:** 406-994-2845
E-mail: admissions@montana.edu **CEEB Code:** 4488
Fax: 406-994-1923 **Website:** http://www.montana.edu **ACT Code:** 2420

This public school was founded in 1893. It has a 1850 acre campus.

RATINGS

Admissions Selectivity Rating: 77   **Fire Safety Rating:** 95   **Green Rating:** 96

STUDENTS AND FACULTY

Enrollment: 14,456. **Student Body:** 46% female, 54% male, 39% out-of-state, 2% international (55 countries represented). Asian 1%, African American <1%, Caucasian 85%, Hispanic 5%, Native American 1%, Pacific Islander <1%, Two or more races 5%, Race unknown 1%.
Retention and Graduation: 77% freshmen return for sophomore year. 27% freshmen graduate within 4 years. 56% freshmen graduate within 6 years. 31% grads go on to further study within 1 year. 20% grads pursue business degrees. 9% grads pursue medical degrees. **Faculty:** Student/faculty ratio 18:1. 634 full-time faculty, 77% hold PhDs, 10% are members of minority groups, 45% are women. 6% of classes are taught by teaching assistants.

ACADEMICS

Degrees: Associate; Bachelor's; Certificate; Doctoral degree—professional practice; Doctoral degree research/scholarship; Master's; Post-bachelor's certificate. **Classes:** Most classes have 10–19 students. Most lab/discussion sessions have 20–29 students. **Most popular majors:** Marketing/Marketing Management, General; Registered Nursing/Registered Nurse; Liberal Arts and Sciences/Liberal Studies. **Special Study Options:** Cooperative education program; Cross-registration; Distance learning; Double major; Dual enrollment; English as a Second Language (ESL); Exchange student program (domestic); Honors program; Independent study; Internships; Student-designed major; Study abroad; Teacher certification program. **Honors programs:** http://www.montana.edu/honors/. **Combined degree programs:** BA/MEng. **Disability Services offered:** Note-taking services; Reader services; Tape recorders; Tutors. **Career services:** Alumni network; Alumni services; Career assessment; Career/job search classes; Internships.

FACILITIES

Housing: Apartments for married students; Apartments for single students; Coed dorms; Cooperative housing; Fraternity/sorority housing; Men's dorms; Special housing for disabled students; Special housing for international students; Theme housing; Wellness housing; Women's dorms; 90% of campus accessible to physically disabled. **Special Academic Facilities/Equipment:** 1. Blackstone

Business Launchpad: http://montana.thelaunchpad.org/; 2. Museum of the Rockies: http://www.museumoftherockies.org/; 3. Jake Jabs College of Business and Entrepreneurship Center for Entrepreneurship: http://www.montana.edu/us/pdc/projects/allPrjs/JabsHall/; 4. Nursing Simulation Laboratory with 3G Mannequin: http://www.montana.edu/nursing/undergraduate/sim.html; 5. Space Science Engineering Lab (Physics & Engineering): https://www.ssel.montana.edu/; 6. Subzero Science and Engineering Research Facility: http://www.coe.montana.edu/ce/subzero/; 7. Optical Technology Center (OpTeC): http://www.optics.montana.edu/.

CAMPUS LIFE

Environment: Town. **Activities:** Campus Ministries; Choral groups; Concert band; Dance; Drama/theater; International Student Organization; Jazz band; Literary magazine; Marching band; Model UN; Music ensembles; Musical theater; Opera; Pep band; Radio station; Student government; Student newspaper; Student-run film society; Symphony orchestra; Television station. 140 registered organizations, 18 honor societies, 12 religious organizations, 9 fraternities, 4 sororities on campus. **Athletics (Intercollegiate):** *Men:* basketball, cheerleading, cross-country, football, rodeo, skiing (downhill/Alpine), skiing (Nordic/cross-country), tennis, track/field (outdoor), track/field (indoor). *Women:* basketball, cheerleading, cross-country, golf, rodeo, skiing (downhill/Alpine), skiing (Nordic/cross-country), tennis, track/field (outdoor), track/field (indoor), volleyball. **On-Campus Highlights:** Museum of the Rockies. **Environmental Initiatives:** Building Lighting Retrofit projects.

ADMISSIONS

Freshman Academic Profile: Average high school GPA 3.5. 21% in top 10% of high school class, 46% in top 25% of high school class, 75% in top 50% of high school class. **Test Scores:** SAT Math middle 50% range 540–660. SAT EBRW middle 50% range 550–650. ACT middle 50% range 21–27. **Basis for Candidate Selection:** *Very important factors include:* rigor of secondary school record, class rank, academic GPA, standardized test scores. **Freshman Admission Requirements:** High school diploma is required and GED is accepted. *Academic units required:* 4 English, 3 math, 2 science, 2 science labs, 3 social studies. **Freshman Admission Statistics:** 19,142 applied, 82% admitted, 21% enrolled. **Transfer Admission Requirements:** College transcript(s), standardized test scores, statement of good standing from prior institution(s). Minimum college GPA of 2.0 required. Lowest grade transferable D-. **General Admission Information:** Application fee $38. Non-fall registration accepted. Admission may be deferred for a maximum of one year.

COSTS AND FINANCIAL AID

Annual in-state tuition $5,654. Annual out-of-state tuition $23,890. Room and board $10,300. Required fees $1,818. Average book and supplies expense $1,450. **Required Forms and Deadlines:** FAFSA. **Notification of Awards:** Applicants will be notified of awards on a rolling basis beginning 4/1. **Types of Aid:** *Need-based scholarships/grants:* Federal Nursing Scholarships; Federal Pell; Private scholarships; SEOG; State scholarships/grants. *Loans:* Direct PLUS loans; Direct Subsidized Stafford Loans; Direct Unsubsidized Stafford Loans. **Student Employment:** Institutional employment available. **Financial Aid Statistics:** 73% needy freshmen, 69% needy undergrads receive need-based scholarship or grant aid. 6% freshmen, 3% undergrads receive non-need-based scholarship or grant aid. 75% freshmen, 77% undergrads receive need-based self-help aid. 1% freshmen, 1% undergrads receive athletic scholarships. 76% freshmen, 75% undergrads receive any aid. 52% undergrads borrow to pay for school. Average cumulative indebtedness $28,158. **Criteria awarding aid:** *Need-based:* Academics, Art, Job skills, Minority status. *Non-need-based:* Academics, Alumni affiliation, Art, Athletics, Job skills, Leadership, Minority status, Music/drama, State/district residency.

MONTANA STATE UNIVERSITY—BILLINGS

1500 University Drive, Billings, MT 59101
Phone: 406-657-2158 **Financial Aid Phone:** 406-657-1617
CEEB Code: 4298
Fax: 406-657-2302 **Website:** www.msubillings.edu **ACT Code:** 2416

This public school was founded in 1927. It has a 92 acre campus.

RATINGS

Admissions Selectivity Rating: 73   **Fire Safety Rating:** 82   **Green Rating:** 60*

STUDENTS AND FACULTY

Enrollment: 3,570. **Student Body:** 61% female, 39% male, 9% out-of-state, 2% international (21 countries represented). Asian 1%, African American 1%,

Caucasian 81%, Hispanic 6%, Native American 4%, Pacific Islander <1%, Two or more races 3%, Race unknown 1%.
Retention and Graduation: 55% freshmen return for sophomore year. 10% grads go on to further study within 1 year. 70% grads pursue arts and sciences degrees. 14% grads pursue business degrees. 1% grads pursue medical degrees. **Faculty:** Student/faculty ratio 17:1. 174 full-time faculty, 59% hold PhDs, 7% are members of minority groups, 44% are women. 0% of classes are taught by teaching assistants.

ACADEMICS

Degrees: Associate; Bachelor's; Certificate; Master's. **Classes:** Most classes have 10–19 students. Most lab/discussion sessions have 10–19 students. **Most popular majors:** Business/Commerce, General; Liberal Arts and Sciences/ Liberal Studies; Elementary Education and Teaching. **Special Study Options:** Accelerated program; Cooperative education program; Cross-registration; Distance learning; Double major; Dual enrollment; English as a Second Language (ESL); External degree program; Honors program; Independent study; Internships; Liberal arts/career combination; Student-designed major; Study abroad; Teacher certification program. **Honors programs:** The MSU-Billings University Honors Program is designed for curious students who are eager to participate actively in their education. Classes in the University Honors Program tend to be smaller than other classes and emphasize class discussion. Often these classes are interdisciplinary in nature; this helps students study issues from several perspectives. Some classes are team-taught, which also enriches the discussion. **Disability Services offered:** Note-taking services; Reader services; Tape recorders; Tutors. **Career services:** Career assessment; Career/job search classes; Internships.

FACILITIES

Housing: Apartments for married students; Coed dorms; Special housing for disabled students; 99% of campus accessible to physically disabled. **Special Academic Facilities/Equipment:** Montana Center for Disabilities, Business Enterprise, Small Business Institute, Urban Institute, Public Radio, Applied Economic Research, Biological Station, Northern Plains Studies Center, Montana Business Connections, Information Commons, Academic Support Center, Advising Center, TRIO Programs, SOS Programs, Northcutt Steele Gallery, Cisel Recital Hall, Petro Theatre, MSU-Billings Downtown.

CAMPUS LIFE

Environment: City. **Activities:** Campus Ministries; Choral groups; Concert band; Drama/theater; International Student Organization; Jazz band; Literary magazine; Music ensembles; Musical theater; Pep band; Radio station; Student newspaper; Symphony orchestra. 53 registered organizations, 10 honor societies, 38 religious organizations on campus. **Athletics (Intercollegiate): Men:** baseball, basketball, cross-country, golf, soccer, tennis, track/field (outdoor), track/field (indoor). **Women:** basketball, cross-country, golf, soccer, softball, tennis, track/field (outdoor), track/field (indoor), volleyball. **On-Campus Highlights:** Alterowitz Gym.

ADMISSIONS

Freshman Academic Profile: Average high school GPA 3.1. 10% in top 10% of high school class, 27% in top 25% of high school class, 63% in top 50% of high school class. 96% from public high schools. **Test Scores:** SAT Math middle 50% range 420–500. SAT EBRW middle 50% range 430–520. ACT middle 50% range 18–22. **Basis for Candidate Selection:** *Very important factors include:* rigor of secondary school record, class rank, academic GPA, standardized test scores. *Other factors include:* character/personal qualities, work experience. **Freshman Admission Requirements:** High school diploma is required and GED is accepted. *Academic units required:* 4 English, 3 math, 2 science, 2 science labs, 3 social studies, 2 unit from above areas or other academic areas. **Freshman Admission Statistics:** 1,478 applied, 100% admitted, 45% enrolled. **Transfer Admission Requirements:** College transcript(s), statement of good standing from prior institution(s). Minimum college GPA of 2.0 required. Lowest grade transferable C-. **General Admission Information:** Application fee $30. Priority deadline 3/1. Non-fall registration accepted.

COSTS AND FINANCIAL AID

Annual in-state tuition $4,397. Annual out-of-state tuition $16,662. Room and board $7,510. Required fees $1,429. Average book and supplies expense $1,460. **Required Forms and Deadlines:** FAFSA. **Notification of Awards:** Applicants will be notified of awards on a rolling basis beginning 3/1. **Types of Aid:** *Need-based scholarships/grants:* College/university scholarship or grant aid from institutional funds; Federal Pell; Private scholarships; SEOG; State scholarships/grants. *Loans:* Direct PLUS loans; Direct Subsidized Stafford Loans; Direct Unsubsidized Stafford Loans. **Student Employment:** Federal Work-Study Program available. Institutional employment available. **Financial**

Aid Statistics: 83% needy freshmen, 80% needy undergrads receive need-based scholarship or grant aid. 5% freshmen, 2% undergrads receive non-need-based scholarship or grant aid. 78% freshmen, 82% undergrads receive need-based self-help aid. 5% freshmen, 5% undergrads receive athletic scholarships. 65% undergrads borrow to pay for school. Average cumulative indebtedness $28,337. **Criteria awarding aid:** *Need-based:* Academics, Alumni affiliation, Art, Job skills, Leadership, Minority status, Music/. *Non-need-based:* Academics, Alumni affiliation, Art, Athletics, Job skills, Leadership, Minority status, Music/drama, State/district residency.

MONTANA TECH OF THE UNIVERSITY OF MONTANA

1300 West Park Street, Butte, MT 59701
Phone: 406-496-4256 **Financial Aid Phone:** 406-496-4213
E-mail: enrollment@mtech.edu **CEEB Code:** 4487
Fax: 406-496-4710 **Website:** www.mtech.edu **ACT Code:** 24180

This public school was founded in 1893. It has a 176 acre campus.

RATINGS

Admissions Selectivity Rating: 77   **Fire Safety Rating:** 98   **Green Rating:** 60*

STUDENTS AND FACULTY

Enrollment: 2,096. **Student Body:** 36% female, 64% male, 14% out-of-state, 10% international (10 countries represented). Asian 1%, African American 1%, Caucasian 78%, Hispanic 2%, Native American 2%, Pacific Islander 0%, Two or more races <1%, Race unknown 6%.
Retention and Graduation: 77% freshmen return for sophomore year. 46% freshmen graduate within 6 years. 15% grads go on to further study within 1 year. 5% grads pursue arts and sciences degrees. 0% grads pursue law degrees. 0% grads pursue business degrees. 1% grads pursue medical degrees. **Faculty:** Student/faculty ratio 13:1. 150 full-time faculty, 59% hold PhDs, 7% are members of minority groups, 35% are women.

ACADEMICS

Degrees: Associate; Bachelor's; Certificate; Master's; Post-bachelor's certificate. **Classes:** Most classes have 10–19 students. Most lab/discussion sessions have fewer than 10 students. **Most popular majors:** Engineering, General; Petroleum Engineering. **Special Study Options:** Cooperative education program; Cross-registration; Distance learning; Double major; Dual enrollment; External degree program; Honors program; Independent study; Internships; Teacher certification program. **Honors programs:** In order to fulfill requirements for the Montana Tech Honors program, students will complete the following by her or his graduation: 1. Six Semesters of Honors Seminar—Fall and Spring Semesters, 1 credits each; 2. Undergraduate Research—1–6 credits (A higher minimum number of credits may be established by accrediting agency for a particular degree program.); 3. Thesis—1 credit (Topic to be agreed upon by student, department head from student's major and the Honor's Committee. These could be a co-requirement with a particular department; however, the student could not receive credit twice for the same thesis.); 4. Twelve Credits of Honors Courses—Students may choose established honors courses, augment current non-honors courses, or create new honors courses in cooperation with faculty. **Combined degree programs:** BA/MA. **Disability Services offered:** Note-taking services; Reader services; Tape recorders; Tutors. **Career services:** Alumni network; Alumni services; Career assessment; Career/job search classes; Internships; Regional alumni.

FACILITIES

Housing: Apartments for married students; Apartments for single students; Coed dorms; Special housing for disabled students; 75% of campus accessible to physically disabled. **Special Academic Facilities/Equipment:** Mineral Museum World Museum of Mining.

CAMPUS LIFE

Environment: Town. **Activities:** Campus Ministries; Choral groups; International Student Organization; Pep band; Radio station; Student government; Student newspaper. 50 registered organizations, 3 honor societies on campus. **Athletics (Intercollegiate): Men:** basketball, football, golf. **Women:** basketball, golf, volleyball. **On-Campus Highlights:** Mineral Museum.

ADMISSIONS

Freshman Academic Profile: Average high school GPA 3.6. 25% in top 10% of high school class, 56% in top 25% of high school class, 87% in top 50% of high school class. **Test Scores:** SAT Math middle 50% range 575–670. SAT EBRW middle 50% range 540–630. ACT middle 50% range 22–27. **Basis for Candidate Selection:** *Very important factors include:* class rank, academic GPA, standardized test scores. **Freshman Admission Requirements:** High school diploma is required and GED is accepted. *Academic units required:* 4 English, 3 math, 2 science, 2 science labs, 3 social studies, 2 unit from above areas or other academic areas. *Academic units recommended:* 4 math. **Freshman Admission Statistics:** 981 applied, 92% admitted, 43% enrolled. **Transfer Admission Requirements:** College transcript(s). Minimum college GPA of 2.0 required. Lowest grade transferable C. **General Admission Information:** Application fee $30. Non-fall registration accepted. Admission may be deferred for a maximum of 1 semester.

COSTS AND FINANCIAL AID

Annual in-state tuition $7,431. Annual out-of-state tuition $22,595. Room and board $9,996. Average book and supplies expense $1,350. **Required Forms and Deadlines:** FAFSA. **Notification of Awards:** Applicants will be notified of awards on a rolling basis beginning 2/15. **Types of Aid:** *Need-based scholarships/grants:* College/university scholarship or grant aid from institutional funds; Federal Pell; Private scholarships; SEOG; State scholarships/grants. *Loans:* Direct PLUS loans; Direct Subsidized Stafford Loans; Direct Unsubsidized Stafford Loans. **Student Employment:** Federal Work-Study Program available. Institutional employment available. **Financial Aid Statistics:** 87% needy freshmen, 83% needy undergrads receive need-based scholarship or grant aid. 15% freshmen, 7% undergrads receive non-need-based scholarship or grant aid. 58% freshmen, 73% undergrads receive need-based self-help aid. 6% freshmen, 4% undergrads receive athletic scholarships. 87% freshmen, 62% undergrads receive any aid. 54% undergrads borrow to pay for school. Average cumulative indebtedness $27,926. **Criteria awarding aid:** *Need-based:* Academics, Athletics, Leadership, Minority status. *Non-need-based:* Academics, Alumni affiliation, Athletics, Leadership, Minority status, Music/drama, Religious affiliation, State/district residency.

MONTCLAIR STATE UNIVERSITY

One Normal Avenue, Montclair, NJ 07043-1624
Phone: 973-655-4444 **Financial Aid Phone:** 973-655-4461
E-mail: undergraduate.admissions@montclair.edu **CEEB Code:** 2520
Fax: 973-655-7700 **Website:** www.montclair.edu/ **ACT Code:** 2572

This public school was founded in 1908. It has a 275 acre campus.

RATINGS

Admissions Selectivity Rating: 81   **Fire Safety Rating:** 98   **Green Rating:** 98

STUDENTS AND FACULTY

Enrollment: 16,673. **Student Body:** 61% female, 39% male, 3% out-of-state, 1% international (106 countries represented). Asian 6%, African American 13%, Caucasian 41%, Hispanic 28%, Native American <1%, Pacific Islander <1%, Two or more races 3%, Race unknown 7%.
Retention and Graduation: 81% freshmen return for sophomore year. 39% freshmen graduate within 4 years. 65% freshmen graduate within 6 years. 21% grads go on to further study within 1 year. **Faculty:** Student/faculty ratio 17:1. 636 full-time faculty, 89% hold PhDs, 25% are members of minority groups, 50% are women.

ACADEMICS

Degrees: Bachelor's; Certificate; Doctoral degree—professional practice; Doctoral degree research/scholarship; Master's; Post-bachelor's certificate. **Classes:** Most classes have 20–29 students. **Special Study Options:** Cooperative education program; Double major; English as a Second Language (ESL); Honors program; Independent study; Internships; Study abroad; Teacher certification program. **Combined degree programs:** BA/MA. **Disability Services offered:** Note-taking services; Reader services; Tape recorders; Tutors. **Career services:** Alumni network; Alumni services; Career assessment; Internships; Regional alumni.

FACILITIES

Housing: Apartments for married students; Apartments for single students; Coed dorms; Special housing for disabled students; Special housing for international students; Theme housing; Women's dorms; 90% of campus

accessible to physically disabled. **Special Academic Facilities/Equipment:** The Dumont Television Center, Yogi Berra Museum and Stadium, Floyd Hall Arena, Cali School of Music, Kasser Theater, George Segal Gallery.

CAMPUS LIFE

Environment: Town. **Activities:** Campus Ministries; Choral groups; Concert band; Dance; Drama/theater; International Student Organization; Jazz band; Literary magazine; Marching band; Music ensembles; Musical theater; Opera; Pep band; Radio station; Student government; Student newspaper; Student-run film society; Symphony orchestra; Television station; Yearbook. 160 registered organizations, 4 honor societies, 8 religious organizations, 19 fraternities, 17 sororities on campus. **Athletics (Intercollegiate):** *Men:* baseball, basketball, diving, football, lacrosse, soccer, swimming, track/field (outdoor). *Women:* basketball, diving, field hockey, lacrosse, soccer, softball, swimming, track/field (outdoor), volleyball. **On-Campus Highlights:** Living Communities.

ADMISSIONS

Freshman Academic Profile: Average high school GPA 3.2. 10% in top 10% of high school class, 34% in top 25% of high school class, 76% in top 50% of high school class. **Test Scores:** SAT Math middle 50% range 490–570. SAT EBRW middle 50% range 500–580. **Basis for Candidate Selection:** *Very important factors include:* rigor of secondary school record, academic GPA, recommendation(s). *Important factors include:* application essay, *Other factors include:* class rank, standardized test scores, extracurricular activities, talent/ability, character/personal qualities, religious affiliation/commitment, work experience. **Freshman Admission Requirements:** High school diploma is required and GED is accepted. *Academic units required:* 4 English, 3 math, 2 science, 2 science labs, 2 foreign language, 2 social studies, 3 academic electives. **Freshman Admission Statistics:** 13,384 applied, 71% admitted, 32% enrolled. **Transfer Admission Requirements:** College transcript(s), statement of good standing from prior institution(s). Minimum college GPA of 2.0 required. Lowest grade transferable C-. **General Admission Information:** Application fee $65. Priority deadline 12/15. Regular application deadline 3/1. Non-fall registration accepted. Admission may be deferred for a maximum of 1 semester.

COSTS AND FINANCIAL AID

Annual in-state tuition $10,808. Annual out-of-state tuition $18,920. Room and board $13,466. Required fees $1,647. Average book and supplies expense $1,300. **Required Forms and Deadlines:** FAFSA; State aid form. **Notification of Awards:** Applicants will be notified of awards on a rolling basis beginning 2/15. **Types of Aid:** *Need-based scholarships/grants:* College/university scholarship or grant aid from institutional funds; Federal Pell; Private scholarships; SEOG; State scholarships/grants. *Loans:* Direct PLUS loans; Direct Subsidized Stafford Loans; Direct Unsubsidized Stafford Loans. **Student Employment:** Federal Work-Study Program available. Institutional employment available. **Financial Aid Statistics:** 63% needy freshmen, 64% needy undergrads receive need-based scholarship or grant aid. 5% freshmen, 4% undergrads receive non-need-based scholarship or grant aid. 89% freshmen, 91% undergrads receive need-based self-help aid. 0% freshmen, 0% undergrads receive athletic scholarships. 71% freshmen, 61% undergrads receive any aid. **Criteria awarding aid:** *Need-based:* Leadership. *Non-need-based:* Academics, Alumni affiliation, Art, Leadership, Minority status, Music/drama, Religious affiliation, State/district residency.

MOORE COLLEGE OF ART AND DESIGN

20th Street and The Parkway, Philadelphia, PA 19103-1179
Phone: 215-965-4017 **Financial Aid Phone:** 215-965-4042
E-mail: enroll@moore.edu **CEEB Code:** 2417
Fax: 215-568-3547 **Website:** www.moore.edu **ACT Code:** 2417

This private school was founded in 1848.

RATINGS

Admissions Selectivity Rating: 85   **Fire Safety Rating:** 97   **Green Rating:** 60*

STUDENTS AND FACULTY

Enrollment: 482. **Student Body:** 100% female, 0% male, 42% out-of-state, 3% international (15 countries represented). Asian 4%, African American 16%, Caucasian 65%, Hispanic 5%, Native American 1%, Pacific Islander 1%, Two or more races 5%, Race unknown 1%.
Retention and Graduation: 73% freshmen return for sophomore year.
Faculty: Student/faculty ratio 9:1. 24 full-time faculty, 50% hold PhDs, 8%

are members of minority groups, 67% are women. 0% of classes are taught by teaching assistants.

ACADEMICS

Degrees: Bachelor's; Master's; Post-bachelor's certificate. **Classes:** Most classes have 10–19 students. **Most popular majors:** Illustration; Fashion/Apparel Design; Fine/Studio Arts, General. **Special Study Options:** Double major; Exchange student program (domestic); Independent study; Internships; Study abroad; Teacher certification program. **Disability Services offered:** Tape recorders; Tutors. **Career services:** Alumni services; Internships; Regional alumni.

FACILITIES

Housing: Women's dorms. **Special Academic Facilities/Equipment:** Paley, Graham and Levy Galleries.

CAMPUS LIFE

Environment: Metropolis. **Activities:** Student government; Yearbook. 9 registered organizations on campus. **On-Campus Highlights:** Three art galleries.

ADMISSIONS

Freshman Academic Profile: Average high school GPA 3.2. **Test Scores:** SAT Math middle 50% range 420–520. SAT EBRW middle 50% range 450–560. ACT middle 50% range 17–22. **Basis for Candidate Selection:** *Very important factors include:* rigor of secondary school record, academic GPA, standardized test scores, interview, talent/ability, character/personal qualities, level of applicant's interest. *Important factors include:* application essay, recommendation(s), extracurricular activities. *Other factors include:* class rank, volunteer work, work experience. **Freshman Admission Requirements:** High school diploma is required and GED is accepted. *Academic units recommended:* 4 English, 2 math, 2 science, 2 foreign language, 4 social studies, 3 visual/performing arts. **Freshman Admission Statistics:** 607 applied, 54% admitted, 33% enrolled. **Transfer Admission Requirements:** High school transcript, college transcript(s), essay or personal statement, statement of good standing from prior institution(s). Minimum college GPA of 2.5 required. Lowest grade transferable C. **General Admission Information:** Application fee $40. Priority deadline 3/1. Regular application deadline 8/15. Non-fall registration accepted. Admission may be deferred for a maximum of 1 year.

COSTS AND FINANCIAL AID

Annual tuition $31,654. Room and board $12,298. Required fees $1,084. Average book and supplies expense $2,000. **Required Forms and Deadlines:** FAFSA. **Notification of Awards:** Applicants will be notified of awards on a rolling basis beginning 2/15. **Types of Aid:** *Need-based scholarships/grants:* College/university scholarship or grant aid from institutional funds; Federal Pell; Private scholarships; SEOG; State scholarships/grants. **Student Employment:** Federal Work-Study Program available. **Financial Aid Statistics:** 97% undergrads receive any aid. **Criteria awarding aid:** *Need-based:* Academics, Art, Leadership, Minority status. *Non-need-based:* Academics, Art, Leadership.

MORAVIAN COLLEGE

1200 Main Street, Bethlehem, PA 18018
Phone: 610-861-1320 **Financial Aid Phone:** (610) 861-1330
E-mail: admission@moravian.edu **CEEB Code:** 3301
Fax: 610-625-7930 **Website:** www.moravian.edu **ACT Code:** 3634

This private school, affiliated with the Moravian Church, was founded in 1742. It has a 85 acre campus.

RATINGS

Admissions Selectivity Rating: 81   **Fire Safety Rating:** 92   **Green Rating:** 75

STUDENTS AND FACULTY

Enrollment: 2,061. **Student Body:** 61% female, 39% male, 27% out-of-state, 4% international (12 countries represented). Asian 2%, African American 3%, Caucasian 72%, Hispanic 11%, Native American <1%, Pacific Islander <1%, Two or more races 2%, Race unknown 5%.

Retention and Graduation: 81% freshmen return for sophomore year. 59% freshmen graduate within 4 years. 63% freshmen graduate within 6 years. 18% grads go on to further study within 1 year. 5% grads pursue arts and sciences degrees. 3% grads pursue law degrees. 1% grads pursue business degrees. 2% grads pursue medical degrees. **Faculty:** Student/faculty ratio 11:1. 146 full-time faculty, 92% hold PhDs, 12% are members of minority groups, 60% are women. 0% of classes are taught by teaching assistants.

ACADEMICS

Degrees: Bachelor's; Doctoral degree—professional practice; Master's; Post-bachelor's certificate; Post-master's certificate. **Classes:** Most classes have 10–19 students. Most lab/discussion sessions have 10–19 students. **Most popular majors:** Registered Nursing/Registered Nurse; Sociology, General; Business Administration and Management, General. **Special Study Options:** Accelerated program; Cooperative education program; Cross-registration; Distance learning; Double major; Dual enrollment; Exchange student program (domestic); Honors program; Independent study; Internships; Student-designed major; Study abroad; Teacher certification program. **Honors programs:** Students can do honors projects within their selected major. **Disability Services offered:** Note-taking services; Reader services; Tape recorders; Tutors. **Career services:** Alumni network; Alumni services; Career assessment; Career/job search classes; Internships; Regional alumni.

FACILITIES

Housing: Apartments for single students; Coed dorms; Fraternity/sorority housing; Men's dorms; Special housing for international students; Theme housing; Women's dorms. **Special Academic Facilities/Equipment:** Payne [art] Gallery, Deputy Field Center for Environmental and Biological Sciences, Foy [concert] Hall, student art studios, observation room for psychology classes, Center for Leadership and Service, Sally Breidegam Miksiewicz Center for Health Sciences.

CAMPUS LIFE

Environment: City. **Activities:** Campus Ministries; Choral groups; Concert band; Dance; Drama/theater; International Student Organization; Jazz band; Literary magazine; Marching band; Model UN; Music ensembles; Opera; Pep band; Radio station; Student government; Student newspaper; Symphony orchestra; Yearbook. 84 registered organizations, 21 honor societies, 4 religious organizations, 4 fraternities, 4 sororities on campus. **Athletics (Intercollegiate):** *Men:* baseball, basketball, cross-country, football, golf, lacrosse, soccer, tennis, track/field (outdoor), track/field (indoor). *Women:* basketball, cross-country, field hockey, lacrosse, soccer, softball, tennis, track/field (outdoor), track/field (indoor), volleyball. **On-Campus Highlights:** Haupert Union Building. **Environmental Initiatives:** The Moravian College Green Hounds Fund (GHF) is a sustainability revolving loan fund established in 2017 to provide a formalized method for funding campus-based projects that advance operational efficiency and reduce the College's environmental impact.

ADMISSIONS

Freshman Academic Profile: Average high school GPA 3.5. 17% in top 10% of high school class, 48% in top 25% of high school class, 85% in top 50% of high school class. 88% from public high schools. **Test Scores:** SAT Math middle 50% range 520–590. SAT EBRW middle 50% range 530–610. ACT middle 50% range 21–25. **Basis for Candidate Selection:** *Very important factors include:* rigor of secondary school record, extracurricular activities, character/personal qualities. *Important factors include:* class rank, academic GPA, application essay, standardized test scores, recommendation(s), talent/ability, volunteer work. *Other factors include:* interview, first generation, alumni/ae relation, work experience. **Freshman Admission Requirements:** High school diploma is required and GED is accepted. *Academic units required:* 4 English, 3 math, 3 science, 2 science labs, 2 foreign language, 4 social studies. **Freshman Admission Statistics:** 2,443 applied, 73% admitted, 25% enrolled. **Transfer Admission Requirements:** High school transcript, college transcript(s), essay or personal statement, statement of good standing from prior institution(s). Minimum college GPA of 3.0 required. Lowest grade transferable C. **General Admission Information:** Priority deadline 3/1. Regular application deadline 3/1. Non-fall registration accepted. Admission may be deferred for a maximum of 1 year.

COSTS AND FINANCIAL AID

Annual tuition $43,581. Room and board $13,914. Required fees $1,731. Average book and supplies expense $1,200. **Required Forms and Deadlines:** FAFSA. **Notification of Awards:** Applicants will be notified of awards on a rolling basis beginning 11/30. **Types of Aid:** *Need-based scholarships/grants:* College/university scholarship or grant aid from institutional funds; Federal Nursing Scholarships; Federal Pell; Private scholarships; SEOG; State scholarships/grants; United Negro College Fund. *Loans:* Direct PLUS loans; Direct Subsidized Stafford Loans; Direct Unsubsidized Stafford Loans. **Student Employment:** Federal Work-Study Program available. Institutional employment available. **Financial Aid Statistics:** 100% needy freshmen, 97% needy undergrads receive need-based scholarship or grant aid. 14% freshmen, 10% undergrads receive non-need-based scholarship or grant aid. 72% freshmen, 90% undergrads receive need-based self-help aid. 0% freshmen, 0% undergrads receive athletic scholarships. 99% freshmen, 98% undergrads receive any aid. 81% undergrads borrow to pay for school. Average cumulative indebtedness $35,521. **Criteria awarding aid:** *Need-based:* Academics. *Non-need-based:* Academics, Alumni affiliation, Art, Leadership, Music/drama, Religious affiliation, State/district residency.

MOREHEAD STATE UNIVERSITY

Admissions Center, Morehead, KY 40351
Phone: 606-783-2000 **Financial Aid Phone:** 606-783-2011
E-mail: admissions@moreheadstate.edu
Fax: 606-783-5038 **Website:** http://www.moreheadstate.edu/ **ACT Code:** 1530

This public school was founded in 1922. It has a 1016 acre campus.

RATINGS
Admissions Selectivity Rating: 76   **Fire Safety Rating:** 88   **Green Rating:** 60*

STUDENTS AND FACULTY
Enrollment: 7,212. **Student Body:** 60% female, 40% male, 14% out-of-state, 1% international (35 countries represented). Asian <1%, African American 4%, Caucasian 90%, Hispanic 1%, Native American <1%, Pacific Islander <1%, Two or more races 1%, Race unknown 1%.
Retention and Graduation: 69% freshmen return for sophomore year.
Faculty: Student/faculty ratio 18:1. 359 full-time faculty, 0% hold PhDs, 7% are members of minority groups, 48% are women.

ACADEMICS
Degrees: Associate; Bachelor's; Certificate; Doctoral degree—other; Master's; Post-bachelor's certificate; Post-master's certificate. **Classes:** Most classes have fewer than 10 students. Most lab/discussion sessions have 10–19 students. **Most popular majors:** Elementary Education and Teaching; General Studies; Nursing/Registered Nurse (Rn, Asn, Bsn, Msn). **Special Study Options:** Accelerated program; Cooperative education program; Cross-registration; Distance learning; Double major; Dual enrollment; English as a Second Language (ESL); Exchange student program (domestic); Honors program; Independent study; Internships; Student-designed major; Study abroad; Teacher certification program; Weekend college. **Disability Services offered:** Note-taking services; Reader services; Tutors. **Career services:** Alumni network; Alumni services; Career assessment; Career/job search classes; Internships.

FACILITIES
Housing: Apartments for single students; Coed dorms; Fraternity/sorority housing; Special housing for disabled students; Special housing for international students 90% of campus accessible to physically disabled. **Special Academic Facilities/Equipment:** Ky. Folk Art Center, 320-acre agricultural complex, Space Science Center, Ky. Center for Traditional Music. **Campus Network:** 10% of classrooms, 5% of dorms, 100% of student union, 100% of libraries, 100% of dining areas, 20% of common outdoor areas have wireless network access.

CAMPUS LIFE
Environment: Village. **Activities:** Campus Ministries; Choral groups; Concert band; Dance; Drama/theater; International Student Organization; Jazz band; Literary magazine; Marching band; Music ensembles; Musical theater; Opera; Pep band; Radio station; Student government; Student newspaper; Symphony orchestra; Television station. 101 registered organizations, 11 honor societies, 7 religious organizations, 10 fraternities, 9 sororities on campus. **Athletics (Intercollegiate):** *Men:* baseball, basketball, cheerleading, cross-country, football, golf, riflery, tennis, track/field (outdoor). *Women:* basketball, cheerleading, cross-country, golf, riflery, soccer, softball, tennis, track/field (outdoor), track/field (indoor), volleyball. **On-Campus Highlights:** Adron Doran University Center. **Environmental Initiatives:** Environmental Education Center: Organizes educational workshops, Earth Day Activities, and community outreach.

ADMISSIONS
Freshman Academic Profile: Average high school GPA 3.3. 17% in top 10% of high school class, 42% in top 25% of high school class, 76% in top 50% of high school class. **Test Scores:** SAT Math middle 50% range 450–560. SAT EBRW middle 50% range 450–535. ACT middle 50% range 19–25. **Basis for Candidate Selection:** *Very important factors include:* rigor of secondary school record, academic GPA, standardized test scores. *Other factors include:* recommendation(s). **Freshman Admission Requirements:** High school diploma is required and GED is accepted. *Academic units required:* 4 English, 3 math, 3 science, 1 science lab, 2 foreign language, 3 social studies, 5 academic electives, 1 visual/performing arts, 1 unit from above areas or other academic areas. *Academic units recommended:* 1 computer science. **Freshman Admission Statistics:** 5,236 applied, 84% admitted, 34% enrolled. **Transfer Admission Requirements:** College transcript(s), statement of good standing from prior institution(s). Minimum college GPA of 2.0 required. Lowest grade transferable C. **General Admission Information:** Application fee $30. Non-fall registration accepted. Admission may be deferred for a maximum of one semester.

COSTS AND FINANCIAL AID
Average book and supplies expense $1,200. **Required Forms and Deadlines:** FAFSA; Institution's own financial aid form. **Types of Aid:** *Need-based scholarships/grants:* College/university scholarship or grant aid from institutional funds; Federal Pell; Private scholarships; SEOG; State scholarships/grants. *Loans:* Direct PLUS loans; Direct Subsidized Stafford Loans; Direct Unsubsidized Stafford Loans. **Student Employment:** Federal Work-Study Program available. Institutional employment available. **Financial Aid Statistics:** 67% needy freshmen, 69% needy undergrads receive need-based scholarship or grant aid. 45% freshmen, 62% undergrads receive non-need-based scholarship or grant aid. 65% freshmen, 73% undergrads receive need-based self-help aid. 6% freshmen, 5% undergrads receive athletic scholarships. **Criteria awarding aid:** *Non-need-based:* Academics, Alumni affiliation, Art, Athletics, Leadership, Minority status, Music/drama, State/district residency.

MOREHOUSE COLLEGE

830 Westview Drive, SW, Atlanta, GA 30314
Phone: 470-639-0391 **Financial Aid Phone:** (844) 512-6672
E-mail: admissions@morehouse.edu **CEEB Code:** 5415
Website: www.morehouse.edu **ACT Code:** 792

This private school was founded in 1867. It has a 61 acre campus.

RATINGS
Admissions Selectivity Rating: 86   **Fire Safety Rating:** 60*   **Green Rating:** 60*

STUDENTS AND FACULTY
Enrollment: 2,205. **Student Body:** 0% female, 100% male, 72% out-of-state, 1% international (19 countries represented). Asian 0%, African American 94%, Caucasian <1%, Hispanic <1%, Native American <1%, Pacific Islander 0%, Two or more races 3%, Race unknown 1%.
Retention and Graduation: 75% freshmen return for sophomore year. 43% freshmen graduate within 4 years. 54% freshmen graduate within 6 years.
Faculty: Student/faculty ratio 14:1. 154 full-time faculty, 50% are members of minority groups, 38% are women.

ACADEMICS
Degrees: Bachelor's. **Classes:** Most classes have 20–29 students. Most lab/discussion sessions have 10–19 students. **Most popular majors:** Business Administration and Management, General. **Special Study Options:** Cooperative education program; Cross-registration; Double major; Dual enrollment; Exchange student program (domestic); Honors program; Independent study; Internships; Study abroad; Teacher certification program. **Honors programs:** The Morehouse College Honors Program is a four-year comprehensive program providing special learning opportunities for students of outstanding intellectual ability, high motivation, and broad interests. The Program has majors from 14 of the College's 16 academic departments and emphasizes leadership and social outreach systematically in classes and in co-curricular activities from freshman year to graduation. The Program has established a record of actively supporting the College's internationalization focus by introducing its students at the freshman level, in classes and in external meetings—to active interest and participation in global studies and study-abroad commitments to balance the students' academic pursuits. **Combined degree programs:** BA/MEng. **Disability Services offered:** Reader services;

Tape recorders; Tutors. **Career services:** Career assessment; Career/job search classes; Internships.

FACILITIES

Housing: Apartments for single students; Men's dorms; Special housing for international students. **Campus Network:** 100% of classrooms, 100% of dorms, 100% of student union, 100% of libraries, 100% of dining areas, 50% of common outdoor areas have wireless network access.

CAMPUS LIFE

Activities: Campus Ministries; Choral groups; Concert band; Dance; Drama/theater; International Student Organization; Jazz band; Literary magazine; Marching band; Model UN; Music ensembles; Pep band; Student government; Student newspaper; Student-run film society; Symphony orchestra; Yearbook. **On-Campus Highlights:** Forbes Arena.

ADMISSIONS

Freshman Academic Profile: Average high school GPA 3.3. 18% in top 10% of high school class, 41% in top 25% of high school class, 71% in top 50% of high school class. **Test Scores:** SAT Math middle 50% range 500–600. SAT EBRW middle 50% range 510–610. ACT middle 50% range 20–25. **Basis for Candidate Selection:** *Very important factors include:* rigor of secondary school record, academic GPA, application essay, standardized test scores, interview, volunteer work, level of applicant's interest. *Important factors include:* class rank, recommendation(s), extracurricular activities, character/personal qualities. *Other factors include:* talent/ability, first generation, alumni/ae relation, work experience. **Freshman Admission Requirements:** High school diploma is required and GED is accepted. *Academic units required:* 4 English, 3 math, 2 science, 2 social studies. *Academic units recommended:* 4 English, 3 math, 2 science, 2 foreign language, 2 social studies, 3 academic electives. **Freshman Admission Statistics:** 3,554 applied, 58% admitted, 29% enrolled. **General Admission Information:** Application fee $50. Priority deadline 11/1. Regular application deadline 2/15. Non-fall registration accepted. Admission may be deferred for a maximum of 1 year.

COSTS AND FINANCIAL AID

Annual tuition $26,508. Room and board $14,041. Required fees $2,339. Average book and supplies expense $2,053. **Required Forms and Deadlines:** CSS/Financial Aid PROFILE; FAFSA; Institution's own financial aid form; State aid form. **Notification of Awards:** Applicants will be notified of awards on a rolling basis beginning 3/1. *Types of Aid: Need-based scholarships/grants:* College/university scholarship or grant aid from institutional funds; Federal Pell; Private scholarships; SEOG; State scholarships/grants; United Negro College Fund. *Loans:* Direct PLUS loans; Direct Subsidized Stafford Loans; Direct Unsubsidized Stafford Loans. **Student Employment:** Federal Work-Study Program available. Institutional employment available.

MORGAN STATE UNIVERSITY

1700 East Cold Spring Lane, Baltimore, MD
Phone: 800-332-6674
E-mail: tjenness@moac.morgan.edu **CEEB Code:** 5416
Fax: 410-319-3684 **Website:** www.morgan.edu **ACT Code:** 1722

This public school was founded in 1867. It has a 122 acre campus.

RATINGS

Admissions Selectivity Rating: 65   **Fire Safety Rating:** 60*   **Green Rating:** 60*

STUDENTS AND FACULTY

Enrollment: 5,397. **Student Body:** 40% out-of-state, 2% international. Asian 2%, African American 92%, Caucasian 2%, Hispanic 1%, Native American 1%, Race unknown 0%.
Retention and Graduation: 76% freshmen return for sophomore year.

ACADEMICS

Degrees: Bachelor's; Master's. **Special Study Options:** Cooperative education program. **Disability Services offered:** Tutors. **Career services:** Career assessment; Career/job search classes; Internships.

FACILITIES

Housing: Apartments for single students; Coed dorms; Men's dorms; Women's dorms. **Special Academic Facilities/Equipment:** African-American collection, new science complex and school of engineering. **Campus Network:** 100% of

classrooms, 100% of dorms, 100% of student union, 100% of libraries, 100% of dining areas, 100% of common outdoor areas have wireless network access.

CAMPUS LIFE

Activities: Radio station; Student government; Student newspaper; Television station; Yearbook. 250 registered organizations, 1 religious organization, 4 fraternities, 4 sororities on campus. **Athletics (Intercollegiate):** *Men:* basketball, cross-country, football, tennis, track/field (outdoor), volleyball. *Women:* basketball, cross-country, tennis, track/field (outdoor), volleyball. **On-Campus Highlights:** Fine Arts Center.

ADMISSIONS

Freshman Academic Profile: 10% in top 10% of high school class, 80% in top 25% of high school class, 96% in top 50% of high school class. 77% from public high schools. **Basis for Candidate Selection: Freshman Admission Requirements:** High school diploma is required and GED is accepted.; High school diploma is required and GED is not accepted. *Academic units recommended:* 4 English, 3 math, 3 science, 2 foreign language, 3 social studies, 2 history. **Transfer Admission Requirements:** Lowest grade transferable C. **General Admission Information:** Regular application deadline 4/15. Non-fall registration accepted.

COSTS AND FINANCIAL AID

Annual in-state tuition $1,853. Annual out-of-state tuition $4,405. Room and board $5,296. Required fees $762. Average book and supplies expense $1,500. **Required Forms and Deadlines:** FAFSA; Institution's own financial aid form; State aid form. **Types of Aid:** *Need-based scholarships/grants:* State scholarships/grants; United Negro College Fund. **Student Employment:** Federal Work-Study Program available. Institutional employment available.

MORNINGSIDE COLLEGE

1501 Morningside Avenue, Sioux City, IA 51106-1751
Phone: 712-274-5511 **Financial Aid Phone:** 712-274-5159
E-mail: mscadm@morningside.edu **CEEB Code:** 6415
Fax: 712-274-5101 **Website:** www.morningside.edu **ACT Code:** 1338

This private school, affiliated with the Methodist Church, was founded in 1894. It has a 68 acre campus.

RATINGS

Admissions Selectivity Rating: 74   **Fire Safety Rating:** 70   **Green Rating:** 60*

STUDENTS AND FACULTY

Enrollment: 1,180. **Student Body:** 54% female, 46% male, 32% out-of-state, 1% international (4 countries represented). Asian 2%, African American 1%, Caucasian 84%, Hispanic 3%, Native American 1%, Race unknown 9%.
Retention and Graduation: 70% freshmen return for sophomore year. 11% grads go on to further study within 1 year. 48% grads pursue arts and sciences degrees. 10% grads pursue law degrees. 0% grads pursue business degrees. 0% grads pursue medical degrees. **Faculty:** Student/faculty ratio 17:1. 69 full-time faculty, 77% hold PhDs, 3% are members of minority groups, 45% are women. 0% of classes are taught by teaching assistants.

ACADEMICS

Degrees: Bachelor's; Master's. **Classes:** Most classes have 10–19 students. Most lab/discussion sessions have 10–19 students. **Most popular majors:** Biology/Biological Sciences, General; Business Administration and Management, General; Elementary Education and Teaching. **Special Study Options:** Distance learning; Double major; Dual enrollment; English as a Second Language (ESL); Honors program; Independent study; Internships; Liberal arts/career combination; Student-designed major; Study abroad; Teacher certification program. **Combined degree programs:** BA/MA. **Disability Services offered:** Note-taking services; Reader services; Tape recorders; Tutors. **Career services:** Alumni network; Alumni services; Career assessment; Career/job search classes; Internships; Regional alumni.

FACILITIES

Housing: Apartments for married students; Apartments for single students; Coed dorms; Fraternity/sorority housing; 50% of campus accessible to physically disabled. **Special Academic Facilities/Equipment:** Media-enhanced "smart classroom," high-speed campus Internet connection, art gallery, theatre, totally renovated science facility. **Campus Network:** 95% of classrooms, 100% of dorms, 100% of student union, 100% of libraries, 100% of dining areas, 10% of common outdoor areas have wireless network access.

CAMPUS LIFE

Environment: City. **Activities:** Campus Ministries; Choral groups; Concert band; Dance; Drama/theater; International Student Organization; Jazz band; Literary magazine; Marching band; Music ensembles; Musical theater; Pep band; Radio station; Student government; Student newspaper; Television station; Yearbook. 40 registered organizations, 15 honor societies, 10 religious organizations, 2 fraternities, 1 sorority on campus. **Athletics (Intercollegiate):** *Men:* baseball, basketball, cheerleading, cross-country, football, golf, soccer, swimming, tennis, track/field (outdoor), track/field (indoor), wrestling. *Women:* basketball, cheerleading, cross-country, golf, soccer, softball, swimming, tennis, track/field (outdoor), track/field (indoor), volleyball.

ADMISSIONS

Freshman Academic Profile: Average high school GPA 3.4. 15% in top 10% of high school class, 42% in top 25% of high school class, 78% in top 50% of high school class. 94% from public high schools. **Test Scores:** ACT middle 50% range 20–25. **Basis for Candidate Selection:** *Very important factors include:* rigor of secondary school record, class rank, academic GPA, standardized test scores, recommendation(s). *Important factors include:* interview, extracurricular activities, talent/ability. *Other factors include:* application essay. **Freshman Admission Requirements:** High school diploma is required and GED is accepted. *Academic units recommended:* 3 English, 2 math, 2 science, 3 social studies. **Freshman Admission Statistics:** 1,240 applied, 90% admitted, 27% enrolled. **Transfer Admission Requirements:** High school transcript, college transcript(s), statement of good standing from prior institution(s). Minimum college GPA of 2.25 required. Lowest grade transferable C-. **General Admission Information:** Application fee $25. Priority deadline 8/15. Non-fall registration accepted. Admission may be deferred for a maximum of no limit.

COSTS AND FINANCIAL AID

Annual tuition $21,116. Room and board $6,729. Required fees $1,130. Average book and supplies expense $800. **Required Forms and Deadlines:** FAFSA. **Notification of Awards:** Applicants will be notified of awards on a rolling basis beginning 3/31. **Types of Aid:** *Need-based scholarships/ grants:* College/university scholarship or grant aid from institutional funds; Federal Pell; Private scholarships; SEOG; State scholarships/grants. **Student Employment:** Federal Work-Study Program available. Institutional employment available. **Financial Aid Statistics:** 73% needy freshmen, 76% needy undergrads receive need-based scholarship or grant aid. 0% freshmen, 0% undergrads receive non-need-based scholarship or grant aid. 83% freshmen, 86% undergrads receive need-based self-help aid. 56% freshmen, 45% undergrads receive athletic scholarships. 100% freshmen, 100% undergrads receive any aid. **Criteria awarding aid:** *Need-based:* Job skills. *Non-need-based:* Academics, Alumni affiliation, Art, Athletics, Job skills, Leadership, Music/ drama, Religious affiliation, State/district residency.

MORRIS COLLEGE

100 West College Street, Sumter, SC 29150
Phone: 803-934-3225 **Financial Aid Phone:** (803)934-3238
E-mail: gscriven@morris.edu **CEEB Code:** 5418
Fax: 803-773-8241 **Website:** http://www.morris.edu/ **ACT Code:** 3868

This private school, affiliated with the Baptist Church, was founded in 1908. It has a 41 acre campus.

RATINGS

Admissions Selectivity Rating: 64   **Fire Safety Rating:** 85   **Green Rating:** 60*

STUDENTS AND FACULTY

Enrollment: 595. **Student Body:** 59% female, 41% male, 13% out-of-state, 0% international (0 countries represented). Asian 0%, African American 93%, Caucasian 1%, Hispanic 1%, Native American <1%, Pacific Islander 0%, Two or more races 1%, Race unknown 4%.
Retention and Graduation: 49% freshmen return for sophomore year. 14% grads go on to further study within 1 year. 6% grads pursue arts and sciences degrees. 0% grads pursue law degrees. 6% grads pursue business degrees. 0% grads pursue medical degrees. **Faculty:** Student/faculty ratio 14:1. 36 full-time faculty, 61% hold PhDs, 72% are members of minority groups, 50% are women.

ACADEMICS

Degrees: Bachelor's. **Classes:** Most classes have 10–19 students. Most lab/ discussion sessions have 10–19 students. **Most popular majors:** Criminal

Justice/Law Enforcement Administration; Business Administration, Management and Operations, Other. **Special Study Options:** Accelerated program; Cooperative education program; Double major; Honors program; Internships; Study abroad; Teacher certification program. **Career services:** Alumni network; Alumni services; Career assessment; Career/job search classes; Internships.

FACILITIES

Housing: Men's dorms; Women's dorms; 90% of campus accessible to physically disabled. **Special Academic Facilities/Equipment:** WMMC-640AM Student Radio Station Forensics Center (Forensics-laboratories for ballistics, DNA, arson, and fingerprint).

CAMPUS LIFE

Environment: Town. **Activities:** Campus Ministries; Choral groups; Dance; Drama/theater; Radio station; Student government; Student newspaper; Yearbook. 58 registered organizations, 7 honor societies, 2 religious organizations, 4 fraternities, 4 sororities on campus. **Athletics (Intercollegiate):** *Men:* baseball, basketball, cheerleading, cross-country, golf, tennis, track/field (outdoor). *Women:* basketball, cheerleading, cross-country, softball, tennis, track/field (outdoor), volleyball. **On-Campus Highlights:** Student Center.

ADMISSIONS

Freshman Academic Profile: Average high school GPA 2.5. 0% in top 10% of high school class, 0% in top 25% of high school class, 19% in top 50% of high school class. 98% from public high schools. **Basis for Candidate Selection:** *Very important factors include:* academic GPA. *Important factors include:* class rank, standardized test scores. **Freshman Admission Requirements:** High school diploma is required and GED is accepted. *Academic units required:* 4 English, 4 math, 3 science, 1 foreign language, 1 social studies, 1 history, 7 academic electives, 1 computer science, 2 unit from above areas or other academic areas. *Academic units recommended:* 2 foreign language. **Freshman Admission Statistics:** 3,743 applied, 76% admitted, 7% enrolled. **Transfer Admission Requirements:** High school transcript, college transcript(s), standardized test scores, statement of good standing from prior institution(s). Minimum college GPA of 2.0 required. Lowest grade transferable C. **General Admission Information:** Application fee $20. Priority deadline 7/1. Non-fall registration accepted. Admission may be deferred for a maximum of 1 semester.

COSTS AND FINANCIAL AID

Annual tuition $12,965. Room and board $6,344. Average book and supplies expense $3,000. **Required Forms and Deadlines:** FAFSA; Institution's own financial aid form. **Notification of Awards:** Applicants will be notified of awards on a rolling basis beginning 4/30. **Types of Aid:** *Need-based scholarships/ grants:* College/university scholarship or grant aid from institutional funds; Federal Pell; Private scholarships; SEOG; State scholarships/grants; United Negro College Fund. *Loans:* Direct PLUS loans; Direct Subsidized Stafford Loans; Direct Unsubsidized Stafford Loans. **Student Employment:** Federal Work-Study Program available. **Financial Aid Statistics:** 99% needy freshmen, 99% needy undergrads receive need-based scholarship or grant aid. 18% freshmen, 5% undergrads receive non-need-based scholarship or grant aid. 96% freshmen, 97% undergrads receive need-based self-help aid. 17% freshmen, 6% undergrads receive athletic scholarships. 99% freshmen, 98% undergrads receive any aid. 98% undergrads borrow to pay for school. Average cumulative indebtedness $31,650. **Criteria awarding aid:** *Non-need-based:* Academics, Athletics, State/district residency.

MOUNT ALLISON UNIVERSITY

65 York Street, Sackville, NB E4L1E4
Phone: 506-364-2269 **Financial Aid Phone:** 506 364 2258
E-mail: admissions@mta.ca
Fax: 506-364-2272 **Website:** www.mta.ca

This public school was founded in 1839. It has a 25 acre campus.

RATINGS

Admissions Selectivity Rating: 67   **Fire Safety Rating:** 93   **Green Rating:** 60*

STUDENTS AND FACULTY

Enrollment: 2,521. **Student Body:** 58% female, 42% male, 43% out-of-state, 40 countries represented.
Retention and Graduation: 82% freshmen return for sophomore year. 30% grads go on to further study within 1 year. 10% grads pursue arts and sciences degrees. 3% grads pursue law degrees. 5% grads pursue business degrees. 12%

grads pursue medical degrees. **Faculty:** Student/faculty ratio 15:1. 132 full-time faculty, 92% hold PhDs, 0% are members of minority groups, 43% are women. 0% of classes are taught by teaching assistants.

ACADEMICS

Degrees: Bachelor's; Master's. **Classes:** Most classes have 20–29 students. **Most popular majors:** Business/Commerce, General; Geography; Chemistry, General. **Special Study Options:** Distance learning; Double major; English as a Second Language (ESL); Exchange student program (domestic); Honors program; Independent study; Internships; Student-designed major; Study abroad. **Disability Services offered:** Reader services; Tutors. **Career services:** Career/job search classes.

FACILITIES

Housing: Coed dorms; Cooperative housing; Special housing for disabled students; Special housing for international students; Wellness housing; Women's dorms; 80% of campus accessible to physically disabled. **Special Academic Facilities/Equipment:** Art gallery.

CAMPUS LIFE

Environment: Rural. **Activities:** Campus Ministries; Choral groups; Concert band; Dance; Drama/theater; International Student Organization; Jazz band; Music ensembles; Musical theater; Radio station; Student government; Student newspaper; Symphony orchestra; Yearbook. 106 registered organizations on campus. **Athletics (Intercollegiate):** *Men:* badminton, basketball, football, rugby, soccer, swimming. *Women:* badminton, basketball, rugby, soccer, swimming, volleyball. **On-Campus Highlights:** Ownes Art Gallery. **Environmental Initiatives:** Residence Climate Change Challenge expanded this year to include academic and administrative buildings—buildings reduced their consumption of utilities during the month of February from 10 to 25%.

ADMISSIONS

Freshman Academic Profile: 99% from public high schools. **Basis for Candidate Selection:** *Very important factors include:* rigor of secondary school record, academic GPA, interview, extracurricular activities, talent/ability. *Important factors include:* recommendation(s), character/personal qualities, volunteer work. *Other factors include:* class rank, application essay, standardized test scores, work experience. **Freshman Admission Requirements:** High school diploma is required and GED is accepted. **Freshman Admission Statistics:** 1,789 applied, 85% admitted, 49% enrolled. **Transfer Admission Requirements:** High school transcript, college transcript(s), essay or personal statement, statement of good standing from prior institution(s), Lowest grade transferable C-. **General Admission Information:** Application fee $50. Priority deadline 3/15. Non-fall registration accepted.

COSTS AND FINANCIAL AID

Annual in-state tuition $7,465. Annual out-of-state tuition $7,465. Room and board $9,595. Average book and supplies expense $1,200. **Required Forms and Deadlines:** FAFSA; Institution's own financial aid form. **Types of Aid:** *Need-based scholarships/grants:* College/university scholarship or grant aid from institutional funds; Private scholarships. **Financial Aid Statistics:** 100% needy freshmen, 100% needy undergrads receive need-based scholarship or grant aid. **Criteria awarding aid:** *Need-based:* Academics, Alumni affiliation, Art, Athletics, Job skills, Leadership, Minority status, Music/drama, Religious affiliation. *Non-need-based:* Academics, Alumni affiliation, Art, Athletics, Job skills, Leadership, Minority status, Music/drama, State/district residency.

MOUNT ALOYSIUS COLLEGE

7373 Admiral Peary Highway, Cresson, PA 16630
Phone: 814-886-6383 **Financial Aid Phone:** 814-886-6463
E-mail: admissions@mtaloy.edu **CEEB Code:** 2420
Fax: 814-886-6441 **Website:** www.mtaloy.edu **ACT Code:** 3635

This private school, affiliated with the Roman Catholic Church, was founded in 1853. It has a 193 acre campus.

RATINGS

Admissions Selectivity Rating: 83   **Fire Safety Rating:** 60*   **Green Rating:** 60*

STUDENTS AND FACULTY

Enrollment: 1,185. **Student Body:** 71% female, 29% male, 6% out-of-state, 6% international. Asian 1%, African American 3%, Caucasian 77%, Hispanic 1%, Native American <1%, Pacific Islander 0%, Two or more races 0%, Race unknown 12%.

Faculty: Student/faculty ratio 11:1. 71 full-time faculty, 0% hold PhDs, 3% are members of minority groups, 75% are women. 0% of classes are taught by teaching assistants.

ACADEMICS

Degrees: Associate; Bachelor's; Certificate; Master's; Terminal Associate. **Classes:** Most classes have 10–19 students. Most lab/discussion sessions have fewer than 10 students. **Most popular majors:** Medical Radiologic Technology/Science—Radiation Therapist; Registered Nursing/Registered Nurse; Business Administration and Management, General. **Special Study Options:** Accelerated program; Distance learning; Double major; Dual enrollment; Honors program; Independent study; Internships; Student-designed major; Study abroad; Teacher certification program. **Career services:** Alumni services; Career assessment; Career/job search classes; Internships.

FACILITIES

Housing: Coed dorms. **Campus Network:** 100% of classrooms, 100% of dorms, 100% of libraries, 100% of dining areas have wireless network access.

CAMPUS LIFE

Environment: Rural. **Activities:** Campus Ministries; Choral groups; Dance; Drama/theater; International Student Organization; Student government; Student newspaper. **Athletics (Intercollegiate):** *Men:* basketball, golf, soccer. *Women:* basketball, soccer, volleyball.

ADMISSIONS

Freshman Academic Profile: Average high school GPA 3.4. **Test Scores:** SAT Math middle 50% range 470–560. SAT EBRW middle 50% range 470–560. ACT middle 50% range 18–22. **Basis for Candidate Selection:** *Very important factors include:* rigor of secondary school record, academic GPA, interview, extracurricular activities, talent/ability, character/personal qualities, first generation, volunteer work. *Important factors include:* class rank, standardized test scores, recommendation(s), level of applicant's interest. *Other factors include:* application essay. **Freshman Admission Requirements:** High school diploma is required and GED is accepted. *Academic units required:* 4 English, 3 math, 3 science, 3 social studies, 3 academic electives. *Academic units recommended:* 2 foreign language, 3 history. **Freshman Admission Statistics:** 1,748 applied, 61% admitted, 25% enrolled. **Transfer Admission Requirements:** High school transcript, college transcript(s). Minimum college GPA of 2.0 required. Lowest grade transferable C. **General Admission Information:** Application fee $30. Non-fall registration accepted.

COSTS AND FINANCIAL AID

Required Forms and Deadlines: FAFSA. **Notification of Awards:** Applicants will be notified of awards on a rolling basis beginning 2/15. **Types of Aid:** *Need-based scholarships/grants:* Federal Pell; Private scholarships; SEOG; State scholarships/grants. *Loans:* Direct PLUS loans; Direct Subsidized Stafford Loans; Direct Unsubsidized Stafford Loans. **Student Employment:** Federal Work-Study Program available. Institutional employment available. **Financial Aid Statistics:** 100% needy freshmen, 100% needy undergrads receive need-based scholarship or grant aid. 24% freshmen, 28% undergrads receive non-need-based scholarship or grant aid. 100% freshmen, 100% undergrads receive need-based self-help aid. 0% freshmen, 0% undergrads receive athletic scholarships. **Criteria awarding aid:** *Non-need-based:* Academics, Art, Leadership, Music/drama, Religious affiliation.

MOUNT HOLYOKE COLLEGE

Newhall Center, South Hadley, MA 01075
Phone: 413-538-2023 **Financial Aid Phone:** 413-538-2291
E-mail: admission@mtholyoke.edu **CEEB Code:** 3529
Fax: 413-538-2409 **Website:** www.mtholyoke.edu **ACT Code:** 1866

This private school was founded in 1837. It has a 800 acre campus.

RATINGS

Admissions Selectivity Rating: 94   **Fire Safety Rating:** 85   **Green Rating:** 91

STUDENTS AND FACULTY

Enrollment: 2,175. **Student Body:** 100% female, 0% male, 81% out-of-state, 27% international (76 countries represented). Asian 8%, African American 5%,

Caucasian 47%, Hispanic 7%, Native American <1%, Pacific Islander <1%, Two or more races 4%, Race unknown 2%.
Retention and Graduation: 93% freshmen return for sophomore year. 79% freshmen graduate within 4 years. 83% freshmen graduate within 6 years. 23% grads go on to further study within 1 year. 18% grads pursue arts and sciences degrees. 2% grads pursue law degrees. 1% grads pursue business degrees. 2% grads pursue medical degrees. **Faculty:** Student/faculty ratio 9:1. 215 full-time faculty, 96% hold PhDs, 25% are members of minority groups, 59% are women. 0% of classes are taught by teaching assistants.

ACADEMICS

Degrees: Bachelor's; Master's. **Classes:** Most classes have 10–19 students. Most lab/discussion sessions have 10–19 students. **Most popular majors:** Biology/ Biological Sciences, General; Psychology, General. **Special Study Options:** Cross-registration; Distance learning; Double major; Exchange student program (domestic); Independent study; Internships; Liberal arts/career combination; Student-designed major; Study abroad; Teacher certification program. **Disability Services offered:** Note-taking services; Reader services; Tape recorders; Tutors. **Career services:** Alumni network; Alumni services; Career assessment; Career/job search classes; Internships; Regional alumni.

FACILITIES

Housing: Apartments for single students; Special housing for disabled students; Theme housing; Wellness housing; Women's dorms. **Special Academic Facilities/Equipment:** Art and historical museums, Fimbel Maker & Innovation Lab, bronze-casting foundry, child study center, audio-visual center, language learning center, greenhouse, Japanese meditation garden, equestrian center, observatory, linear accelerator, electron microscope, refracting telescope, nuclear magnetic resonance equipment, McCulloch Center for Global Initiatives, Weissman Center for Leadership and the Liberal Arts, Miller Worley Center for the Environment, Blanchard Community Center.

CAMPUS LIFE

Environment: Town. **Activities:** Campus Ministries; Choral groups; Dance; Drama/theater; International Student Organization; Jazz band; Literary magazine; Model UN; Music ensembles; Radio station; Student government; Student newspaper; Student-run film society; Symphony orchestra. 125 registered organizations, 5 honor societies, 19 religious organizations on campus. **Athletics (Intercollegiate):** *Women:* basketball, crew/rowing, cross-country, diving, equestrian sports, field hockey, golf, horseback riding, lacrosse, soccer, squash, swimming, tennis, track/field (outdoor), track/field (indoor), volleyball. **On-Campus Highlights:** Blanchard Community Center. **Environmental Initiatives:** The College's recently completed strategic Plan, The Plan for Mount Holyoke 2021, directs the community to amplify and promote environmental efforts to fulfill our responsibility to the future of our campus and the planet. Toward that end, the President has appointed a task force with broad representation to develop a sustainability plan to identify opportunities to pursue more aggressive action related to campus sustainability and the environmental curriculum.

ADMISSIONS

Freshman Academic Profile: Average high school GPA 3.8. 52% in top 10% of high school class, 82% in top 25% of high school class, 97% in top 50% of high school class. 62% from public high schools. **Test Scores:** SAT Math middle 50% range 640–770. SAT EBRW middle 50% range 630–720. ACT middle 50% range 27–32. **Basis for Candidate Selection:** *Very important factors include:* rigor of secondary school record, academic GPA, application essay, recommendation(s). *Important factors include:* class rank, interview, extracurricular activities, talent/ability, character/personal qualities, volunteer work. *Other factors include:* standardized test scores, first generation, alumni/ae relation, geographical residence, racial/ethnic status, level of applicant's interest. **Freshman Admission Requirements:** High school diploma is required and GED is accepted. *Academic units recommended:* 4 English, 3 math, 3 science, 3 science labs, 3 foreign language, 3 history, 1 academic elective. **Freshman Admission Statistics:** 3,908 applied, 38% admitted, 33% enrolled. **Transfer Admission Requirements:** High school transcript, college transcript(s), essay or personal statement, statement of good standing from prior institution(s). Minimum college GPA of 3.0 required. Lowest grade transferable C-. **General Admission Information:** Application fee $60. Regular application deadline 1/15. Non-fall registration accepted. Admission may be deferred for a maximum of 2 semesters.

COSTS AND FINANCIAL AID

Annual tuition $52,040. Room and board $15,320. Required fees $218. Average book and supplies expense $2,000. **Required Forms and Deadlines:** CSS/Financial Aid PROFILE; FAFSA; Noncustodial PROFILE. **Notification of Awards:** Applicants will be notified of awards on or about 4/1. **Types of Aid:**

Need-based scholarships/grants: College/university scholarship or grant aid from institutional funds; Federal Pell; Private scholarships; SEOG; State scholarships/ grants. *Loans:* Direct PLUS loans; Direct Subsidized Stafford Loans; Direct Unsubsidized Stafford Loans. **Student Employment:** Federal Work-Study Program available. Institutional employment available. **Financial Aid Statistics:** 98% needy freshmen, 100% needy undergrads receive need-based scholarship or grant aid. 16% freshmen, 15% undergrads receive non-need-based scholarship or grant aid. 84% freshmen, 87% undergrads receive need-based self-help aid. 0% freshmen, 0% undergrads receive athletic scholarships. 67% undergrads borrow to pay for school. Average cumulative indebtedness $25,811. **Criteria awarding aid:** *Non-need-based:* Academics, Leadership.

MOUNT MARY UNIVERSITY

2900 North Menomonee River Parkway, Milwaukee, WI 53222-4597
Phone: 414-930-3024 **Financial Aid Phone:** 414-930-3163
E-mail: mmu-admiss@mtmary.edu **CEEB Code:** 1490
Fax: 414-930-3708 **Website:** http://www.mtmary.edu/ **ACT Code:** 4620

This private school, affiliated with the Roman Catholic Church, was founded in 1913. It has a 80 acre campus.

RATINGS

Admissions Selectivity Rating: 82	Fire Safety Rating: 86	Green Rating: 66

STUDENTS AND FACULTY

Enrollment: 789. **Student Body:** 100% female, 0% male, 7% out-of-state, 2% international (15 countries represented). Asian 8%, African American 17%, Caucasian 52%, Hispanic 16%, Native American <1%, Pacific Islander 0%, Two or more races 4%, Race unknown <1%.
Retention and Graduation: 77% freshmen return for sophomore year.
Faculty: Student/faculty ratio 12:1. 61 full-time faculty, 79% hold PhDs, 0% are members of minority groups, 85% are women. 0% of classes are taught by teaching assistants.

ACADEMICS

Degrees: Bachelor's; Doctoral degree—professional practice; Master's; Post-bachelor's certificate; Post-master's certificate. **Classes:** Most classes have 10–19 students. Most lab/discussion sessions have 10–19 students. **Most popular majors:** Occupational Therapy/Therapist; Fashion Merchandising; Fashion/ Apparel Design. **Special Study Options:** Accelerated program; Double major; Honors program; Independent study; Internships; Liberal arts/career combination; Student-designed major; Study abroad; Teacher certification program. **Honors programs:** The purpose of the Mount Mary University Honors Program is to reward superior scholarly achievement and to provide special challenges to serious students who wish to achieve maximum benefit from their college education. Students completing the program receive the diploma citation, "Graduation in the Honors Program." **Disability Services offered:** Note-taking services; Reader services; Tape recorders; Tutors. **Career services:** Career assessment; Career/job search classes; Internships.

FACILITIES

Housing: Women's dorms; 90% of campus accessible to physically disabled. **Special Academic Facilities/Equipment:** Haggerty Library, Marian Art Gallery, Walter and Olive Steimke Memorial Hall and Conference Center.

CAMPUS LIFE

Environment: Metropolis. **Activities:** Campus Ministries; Choral groups; Dance; International Student Organization; Model UN; Music ensembles; Student government; Student newspaper. 25 registered organizations, 15 honor societies, 1 religious organization on campus. **Athletics (Intercollegiate):** *Women:* basketball, cross-country, soccer, softball, tennis, volleyball. **On-Campus Highlights:** Cyber Café. **Environmental Initiatives:** The university collaborates with our food service provider, FSI, to compost all food preparation materials, plant waste and coffee grounds. The efforts, which began in 2009, produce eight, 18 gallon totes of compost each week during the school year.

ADMISSIONS

Freshman Academic Profile: Average high school GPA 3.2. 23% in top 10% of high school class, 51% in top 25% of high school class, 84% in top 50% of high school class. **Test Scores:** ACT middle 50% range 18–23. **Basis for Candidate Selection:** *Very important factors include:* rigor of secondary school record, academic GPA. *Important factors include:* standardized test scores, talent/ ability, character/personal qualities. *Other factors include:* class rank, application essay, recommendation(s), extracurricular activities, volunteer work, work experience. **Freshman Admission Requirements:** High school diploma is required and GED is accepted. *Academic units required:* 4 English, 2 math, 4 science, 2 science labs, 2 social studies, 2 history, 2 academic electives. *Academic units recommended:* 4 English, 3 math, 5 science, 2 science labs, 2 foreign language, 2 social studies, 2 history, 2 academic electives. **Freshman Admission Statistics:** 689 applied, 56% admitted, 30% enrolled. **Transfer Admission Requirements:** High school transcript, college transcript(s). Minimum college GPA of 2.0 required. Lowest grade transferable C. **General Admission Information:** Non-fall registration accepted. Admission may be deferred for a maximum of 1 year.

COSTS AND FINANCIAL AID
Annual tuition $28,940. Room and board $8,530. Average book and supplies expense $1,400. **Required Forms and Deadlines:** FAFSA. **Notification of Awards:** Applicants will be notified of awards on a rolling basis beginning 3/1. **Types of Aid:** *Need-based scholarships/grants:* College/university scholarship or grant aid from institutional funds; Federal Pell; Private scholarships; SEOG; State scholarships/grants. *Loans:* Direct PLUS loans; Direct Subsidized Stafford Loans; Direct Unsubsidized Stafford Loans. **Student Employment:** Federal Work-Study Program available. Institutional employment available. **Financial Aid Statistics:** 100% needy freshmen, 100% needy undergrads receive need-based scholarship or grant aid. 8% freshmen, 7% undergrads receive non-need-based scholarship or grant aid. 86% freshmen, 91% undergrads receive need-based self-help aid. 0% freshmen, 0% undergrads receive athletic scholarships. 100% freshmen, 83% undergrads receive any aid. 88% undergrads borrow to pay for school. Average cumulative indebtedness $26,237. **Criteria awarding aid:** *Non-need-based:* Academics, Alumni affiliation, Art, Leadership, Music/drama.

MOUNT MERCY UNIVERSITY

1330 Elmhurst Drive Northeast, Cedar Rapids, IA 52402-4797
Phone: 319-368-6460 **Financial Aid Phone:** (319) 363-8213
E-mail: admission@mtmercy.edu
Fax: 319-363-5270 **Website:** www.mtmercy.edu **ACT Code:** 1340

This private school, affiliated with the Reformed Church, was founded in 1928. It has a 40 acre campus.

RATINGS
Admissions Selectivity Rating: 85   **Fire Safety Rating:** 60*   **Green Rating:** 60*

STUDENTS AND FACULTY
Enrollment: 1,417. **Student Body:** 71% female, 29% male, 6% out-of-state, 3% international (27 countries represented). Asian 1%, African American 4%, Caucasian 84%, Hispanic 2%, Native American <1%, Pacific Islander <1%, Two or more races 2%, Race unknown 4%.
Retention and Graduation: 81% freshmen return for sophomore year. 17% grads go on to further study within 1 year. **Faculty:** Student/faculty ratio 14:1. 84 full-time faculty, 54% hold PhDs, 10% are members of minority groups, 65% are women. 0% of classes are taught by teaching assistants.

ACADEMICS
Degrees: Bachelor's; Master's. **Classes:** Most classes have 10–19 students. Most lab/discussion sessions have fewer than 10 students. **Most popular majors:** Education, General; Business/Commerce, General; Registered Nursing/ Registered Nurse. **Special Study Options:** Accelerated program; Cooperative education program; Cross-registration; Double major; Dual enrollment; Honors program; Independent study; Internships; Liberal arts/career combination; Student-designed major; Study abroad; Teacher certification program; Weekend college. **Disability Services offered:** Note-taking services; Reader services; Tape recorders; Tutors. **Career services:** Alumni network; Alumni services; Career assessment; Career/job search classes; Internships; Regional alumni.

FACILITIES
Housing: Apartments for single students; Coed dorms; Theme housing; 95% of campus accessible to physically disabled. **Campus Network:** 70% of classrooms, 100% of dorms, 100% of student union, 100% of libraries have wireless network access.

CAMPUS LIFE
Environment: City. **Activities:** Choral groups; Drama/theater; Literary magazine; Pep band; Student government; Student newspaper. 30 registered organizations, 3 honor societies, 4 religious organizations on campus. **Athletics (Intercollegiate):** *Men:* baseball, basketball, cross-country, golf, soccer, track/ field (outdoor). *Women:* basketball, cross-country, golf, soccer, softball, track/ field (outdoor), volleyball. **On-Campus Highlights:** Lundy Commons: Game Room, TV Room, Convenience Store, Bookstore, Lounges.

ADMISSIONS
Freshman Academic Profile: Average high school GPA 3.4. 10% in top 10% of high school class, 38% in top 25% of high school class, 72% in top 50% of high school class. 83% from public high schools. **Test Scores:** ACT middle 50% range 19–25. **Basis for Candidate Selection:** *Very important factors include:* rigor of secondary school record, class rank, standardized test scores. *Important factors include:* application essay, recommendation(s), extracurricular activities. *Other factors include:* interview, talent/ability, character/personal qualities, volunteer work. **Freshman Admission Requirements:** High school diploma is required and GED is accepted. *Academic units recommended:* 4 English, 4 math, 3 science, 2 foreign language, 2 social studies, 2 history. **Freshman Admission Statistics:** 695 applied, 57% admitted, 42% enrolled. **Transfer Admission Requirements:** College transcript(s), statement of good standing from prior institution(s). Minimum college GPA of 2.5 required. Lowest grade transferable D. **General Admission Information:** Application fee $20. Regular application deadline 8/30. Non-fall registration accepted. Admission may be deferred for a maximum of 1 year.

COSTS AND FINANCIAL AID
Annual tuition $28,226. Room and board $8,600. Average book and supplies expense $1,200. **Required Forms and Deadlines:** FAFSA. **Notification of Awards:** Applicants will be notified of awards on a rolling basis beginning 3/15. **Types of Aid:** *Need-based scholarships/grants:* College/university scholarship or grant aid from institutional funds; Federal Pell; SEOG; State scholarships/ grants. *Loans:* Direct PLUS loans; Direct Subsidized Stafford Loans; Direct Unsubsidized Stafford Loans. **Student Employment:** Federal Work-Study Program available. Institutional employment available. **Financial Aid Statistics:** 100% needy freshmen, 99% needy undergrads receive need-based scholarship or grant aid. 14% freshmen, 11% undergrads receive non-need-based scholarship or grant aid. 82% freshmen, 84% undergrads receive need-based self-help aid. 16% freshmen, 9% undergrads receive athletic scholarships. 100% freshmen receive any aid. **Criteria awarding aid:** *Non-need-based:* Academics, Art, Leadership, Music/drama.

MOUNT OLIVE COLLEGE

634 Henderson Street, Mount Olive, NC 28365
Phone: 919-658-2502
E-mail: admissions@moc.edu **CEEB Code:** 5435
Fax: 919-658-9816 **Website:** www.moc.edu **ACT Code:** 3131

This private school, affiliated with the Baptist Church, was founded in 1951. It has a 138 acre campus.

RATINGS
Admissions Selectivity Rating: 86   **Fire Safety Rating:** 60*   **Green Rating:** 60*

STUDENTS AND FACULTY
Enrollment: 3,305. **Student Body:** 68% female, 32% male, 4% out-of-state, 0% international. Asian 1%, African American 36%, Caucasian 52%, Hispanic 3%, Native American <1%, Race unknown 7%.
Retention and Graduation: 68% freshmen return for sophomore year. 20% grads go on to further study within 1 year. **Faculty:** Student/faculty ratio 26:1. 80 full-time faculty, 96% hold PhDs, 15% are members of minority groups, 35% are women.

ACADEMICS
Degrees: Associate; Bachelor's; Terminal Associate; Transfer Associate. **Classes:** Most classes have 10–19 students. Most lab/discussion sessions have fewer than 10 students. **Special Study Options:** Accelerated program; Cooperative education program; Distance learning; Double major; Dual enrollment; External degree program; Honors program; Independent study; Internships; Liberal arts/career combination; Teacher certification program. **Disability Services offered:** Tutors. **Career services:** Alumni services; Career assessment; Career/job search classes; Internships.

FACILITIES

Housing: Apartments for single students; Men's dorms; Women's dorms; 95% of campus accessible to physically disabled. **Campus Network:** 90% of classrooms, 100% of dorms, 100% of student union, 100% of libraries, 100% of dining areas, 40% of common outdoor areas have wireless network access.

CAMPUS LIFE

Environment: Rural. **Activities:** Campus Ministries; Choral groups; Concert band; International Student Organization; Music ensembles; Musical theater; Student government. 33 registered organizations, 4 honor societies, 6 religious organizations on campus. **Athletics (Intercollegiate):** *Men:* baseball, basketball, cross-country, golf, soccer, tennis. *Women:* basketball, cross-country, soccer, softball, tennis, volleyball.

ADMISSIONS

Freshman Academic Profile: Average high school GPA 3.1. 9% in top 10% of high school class, 26% in top 25% of high school class, 59% in top 50% of high school class. **Test Scores:** SAT Math middle 50% range 420–520. SAT EBRW middle 50% range 410–490. ACT middle 50% range 15–20. **Basis for Candidate Selection:** *Very important factors include:* rigor of secondary school record, academic GPA, character/personal qualities. *Important factors include:* class rank, standardized test scores, interview, extracurricular activities, talent/ability. *Other factors include:* recommendation(s), alumni/ae relation, geographical residence. **Freshman Admission Requirements:** High school diploma is required and GED is accepted. *Academic units required:* 4 English, 3 math, 3 science, 1 science lab, 3 social studies, 3 academic electives. **Freshman Admission Statistics:** 1,838 applied, 50% admitted, 37% enrolled. **Transfer Admission Requirements:** High school transcript, college transcript(s). Minimum college GPA of 2.0 required. **General Admission Information:** Application fee $20. Regular application deadline 8/18. Non-fall registration accepted. Admission may be deferred for a maximum of 1 year.

COSTS AND FINANCIAL AID

Annual tuition $7,223. Room and board $2,775. Average book and supplies expense $656. **Required Forms and Deadlines:** FAFSA; State aid form. **Notification of Awards:** Applicants will be notified of awards on a rolling basis beginning 2/14. **Types of Aid:** *Need-based scholarships/grants:* College/ university scholarship or grant aid from institutional funds; Federal Pell; Private scholarships; SEOG; State scholarships/grants. *Loans:* Direct PLUS loans; Direct Subsidized Stafford Loans; Direct Unsubsidized Stafford Loans. **Student Employment:** Federal Work-Study Program available. **Financial Aid Statistics:** 97% needy freshmen, 93% needy undergrads receive need-based scholarship or grant aid. 5% freshmen, 4% undergrads receive non-need-based scholarship or grant aid. 82% freshmen, 84% undergrads receive need-based self-help aid. 7% freshmen, 2% undergrads receive athletic scholarships. **Criteria awarding aid:** *Need-based:* Art, Athletics, Music/drama, Religious affiliation. *Non-need-based:* Academics, Art, Athletics, Leadership, Music/drama, Religious affiliation.

MOUNT ST. JOSEPH UNIVERSITY

5701 Delhi Road, Cincinnati, OH 45233
Phone: 513-244-4531 **Financial Aid Phone:** 513-244-4418
E-mail: admissions@msj.edu **CEEB Code:** 1129
Fax: 513-244-4629 **Website:** www.msj.edu **ACT Code:** 3254

This private school, affiliated with the Roman Catholic Church, was founded in 1920. It has a 92 acre campus.

RATINGS

Admissions Selectivity Rating: 85　　**Fire Safety Rating:** 99　　**Green Rating:** 60*

STUDENTS AND FACULTY

Enrollment: 1,185. **Student Body:** 56% female, 44% male, 18% out-of-state, <1% international (3 countries represented). Asian 1%, African American 12%, Caucasian 79%, Hispanic 3%, Native American <1%, Pacific Islander <1%, Two or more races 4%, Race unknown 1%.
Retention and Graduation: 73% freshmen return for sophomore year. 44% freshmen graduate within 4 years. 52% freshmen graduate within 6 years.
Faculty: Student/faculty ratio 11:1. 99 full-time faculty, 27% hold PhDs, 4% are members of minority groups, 64% are women. 0% of classes are taught by teaching assistants.

ACADEMICS

Degrees: Associate; Bachelor's; Certificate; Doctoral degree—professional practice; Master's; Post-bachelor's certificate. **Classes:** Most classes have 10–19 students. Most lab/discussion sessions have fewer than 10 students. **Most popular majors:** Sport and Fitness Administration/Management; Registered Nursing, Nursing Administration, Nursing Research and Clinical Nursing; Business Administration and Management, General. **Special Study Options:** Accelerated program; Cooperative education program; Cross-registration; Distance learning; Double major; Dual enrollment; Honors program; Independent study; Internships; Liberal arts/career combination; Student-designed major; Study abroad; Teacher certification program. **Honors programs:** Honors program—designed to meet the interests of highly motivated students who are able to take responsibility for their own learning under the guidance of experienced faculty members. **Disability Services offered:** Note-taking services; Reader services; Tape recorders; Tutors. **Career services:** Alumni services; Career assessment; Career/job search classes; Internships.

FACILITIES

Housing: Coed dorms; Fraternity/sorority housing; Men's dorms; Theme housing; Women's dorms; 95% of campus accessible to physically disabled. **Special Academic Facilities/Equipment:** Art studio/gallery, Student Scholar Center, Computer Labs, Theatre.

CAMPUS LIFE

Environment: Metropolis. **Activities:** Campus Ministries; Choral groups; Concert band; Dance; Drama/theater; Jazz band; Literary magazine; Marching band; Musical theater; Pep band; Student government; Student newspaper. 44 registered organizations, 13 honor societies, 1 religious organization, 1 fraternity on campus. **Athletics (Intercollegiate):** *Men:* baseball, basketball, cross-country, football, golf, lacrosse, soccer, tennis, track/field (outdoor), track/field (indoor), volleyball, wrestling. *Women:* basketball, cheerleading, cross-country, golf, lacrosse, soccer, softball, tennis, track/field (outdoor), track/field (indoor), volleyball. **On-Campus Highlights:** Harrington Student Center/ Sports Complex.

ADMISSIONS

Freshman Academic Profile: Average high school GPA 3.5. 11% in top 10% of high school class, 33% in top 25% of high school class, 72% in top 50% of high school class. 72% from public high schools. **Test Scores:** SAT Math middle 50% range 490–570. SAT EBRW middle 50% range 500–570. ACT middle 50% range 20–25. **Basis for Candidate Selection:** *Very important factors include:* rigor of secondary school record, academic GPA, standardized test scores. *Important factors include:* extracurricular activities, volunteer work, work experience, level of applicant's interest. *Other factors include:* class rank, application essay, recommendation(s), interview, talent/ability, character/ personal qualities. **Freshman Admission Requirements:** High school diploma is required and GED is accepted. *Academic units required:* 4 English, 3 math, 2 science, 2 science labs, 2 foreign language, 1 visual/performing arts. *Academic units recommended:* 3 social studies, 3 history. **Freshman Admission Statistics:** 1,832 applied, 60% admitted, 29% enrolled. **Transfer Admission Requirements:** College transcript(s). Minimum college GPA of 2.0 required. Lowest grade transferable C. **General Admission Information:** Application fee $25. Priority deadline 3/3. Regular application deadline 8/17. Non-fall registration accepted. Admission may be deferred for a maximum of 12 months.

COSTS AND FINANCIAL AID

Annual tuition $29,100. Room and board $9,442. Average book and supplies expense $1,200. **Required Forms and Deadlines:** FAFSA. **Types of Aid:** *Need-based scholarships/grants:* College/university scholarship or grant aid from institutional funds; Federal Pell; Private scholarships; SEOG; State scholarships/ grants. *Loans:* Direct PLUS loans; Direct Subsidized Stafford Loans; Direct Unsubsidized Stafford Loans. **Student Employment:** Federal Work-Study Program available. Institutional employment available. **Financial Aid Statistics:** 100% needy freshmen, 99% needy undergrads receive need-based scholarship or grant aid. 12% freshmen, 11% undergrads receive non-need-based scholarship or grant aid. 82% freshmen, 80% undergrads receive need-based self-help aid. 0% freshmen, 0% undergrads receive athletic scholarships. 83.5% freshmen, 77.7% undergrads receive any aid. **Criteria awarding aid:** *Need-based:* Academics. *Non-need-based:* Academics, Alumni affiliation, Art, Leadership, Music/drama, State/district residency.

MOUNT SAINT MARY COLLEGE

330 Powell Avenue, Newburgh, NY 12550
Phone: 845-569-3488 **Financial Aid Phone:** 845-569-3194
E-mail: admissions@msmc.edu **CEEB Code:** 2423
Fax: 845-569-3438 **Website:** www.msmc.edu **ACT Code:** 2819

This private school, affiliated with the Roman Catholic Church, was founded in 1959. It has a 86 acre campus.

RATINGS

Admissions Selectivity Rating: 73   **Fire Safety Rating:** 97   **Green Rating:** 60*

STUDENTS AND FACULTY

Enrollment: 1,870. **Student Body:** 73% female, 27% male, 12% out-of-state, <1% international (7 countries represented). Asian 2%, African American 8%, Caucasian 57%, Hispanic 18%, Native American <1%, Pacific Islander 0%, Two or more races 1%, Race unknown 14%.
Retention and Graduation: 80% freshmen return for sophomore year. 49% freshmen graduate within 4 years. 63% freshmen graduate within 6 years. 34% grads go on to further study within 1 year. 21% grads pursue arts and sciences degrees. 0% grads pursue law degrees. 7% grads pursue business degrees. 0% grads pursue medical degrees. **Faculty:** Student/faculty ratio 13:1. 85 full-time faculty, 82% hold PhDs, 12% are members of minority groups, 54% are women. 0% of classes are taught by teaching assistants.

ACADEMICS

Degrees: Bachelor's; Certificate; Master's; Post-master's certificate. **Classes:** Most classes have 10–19 students. Most lab/discussion sessions have fewer than 10 students. **Most popular majors:** Registered Nursing/Registered Nurse; Business Administration and Management, General; Teacher Education and Professional Development, Specific Levels and Methods, Other. **Special Study Options:** Accelerated program; Cooperative education program; Cross-registration; Distance learning; Double major; Dual enrollment; Exchange student program (domestic); Honors program; Independent study; Internships; Liberal arts/career combination; Student-designed major; Study abroad; Teacher certification program. **Honors programs:** The Honors Program comprises academic, cultural, and social activities, each of which complements and reinforces the others. **Combined degree programs:** BA/MA. **Disability Services offered:** Tape recorders; Tutors. **Career services:** Alumni network; Alumni services; Career assessment; Career/job search classes; Internships.

FACILITIES

Housing: Coed dorms; Men's dorms; Special housing for disabled students; Women's dorms; 95% of campus accessible to physically disabled. **Special Academic Facilities/Equipment:** On-campus elementary school, television studio, and radio station. Multi-media lab.

CAMPUS LIFE

Environment: Town. **Activities:** Campus Ministries; Choral groups; Concert band; Dance; Drama/theater; Literary magazine; Music ensembles; Musical theater; Radio station; Student government; Student newspaper; Student-run film society; Yearbook. 33 registered organizations, 15 honor societies, 1 religious organization on campus. **Athletics (Intercollegiate): Men:** baseball, basketball, cross-country, lacrosse, soccer, swimming, tennis. **Women:** basketball, cross-country, lacrosse, soccer, softball, swimming, tennis, volleyball. **On-Campus Highlights:** Athletic Center with indoor pool, cardio/weight room. **Environmental Initiatives:** Use of high efficiency boilers.

ADMISSIONS

Freshman Academic Profile: 8% in top 10% of high school class, 28% in top 25% of high school class, 66% in top 50% of high school class. 76% from public high schools. **Test Scores:** SAT Math middle 50% range 480–580. SAT EBRW middle 50% range 490–580. ACT middle 50% range 19–24. **Basis for Candidate Selection:** *Very important factors include:* rigor of secondary school record, academic GPA. *Important factors include:* class rank, application essay, standardized test scores, recommendation(s), interview, talent/ability, character/personal qualities. *Other factors include:* extracurricular activities, first generation, alumni/ae relation, volunteer work, work experience, level of applicant's interest. **Freshman Admission Requirements:** High school diploma is required and GED is accepted. *Academic units recommended:* 4 English, 3 math, 3 science, 3 foreign language, 4 social studies, 3.5 academic electives. **Freshman Admission Statistics:** 3,249 applied, 94% admitted, 11% enrolled. **Transfer Admission Requirements:** High school transcript, college transcript(s), standardized test scores, statement of good standing from prior

institution(s). Minimum college GPA of 2.0 required. Lowest grade transferable C. **General Admission Information:** Application fee $45. Regular application deadline 8/15. Non-fall registration accepted. Admission may be deferred for a maximum of 1 year.

COSTS AND FINANCIAL AID

Annual tuition $33,126. Room and board $16,658. Required fees $1,286. Average book and supplies expense $1,300. **Required Forms and Deadlines:** FAFSA. **Notification of Awards:** Applicants will be notified of awards on a rolling basis beginning 3/1. **Types of Aid:** *Need-based scholarships/grants:* College/university scholarship or grant aid from institutional funds; Federal Nursing Scholarships; Federal Pell; Private scholarships; SEOG; State scholarships/grants. *Loans:* Direct PLUS loans; Direct Subsidized Stafford Loans; Direct Unsubsidized Stafford Loans. **Student Employment:** Federal Work-Study Program available. Institutional employment available. **Financial Aid Statistics:** 99% needy freshmen, 96% needy undergrads receive need-based scholarship or grant aid. 15% freshmen, 11% undergrads receive non-need-based scholarship or grant aid. 89% freshmen, 87% undergrads receive need-based self-help aid. 0% freshmen, 0% undergrads receive athletic scholarships. 99% freshmen, 91% undergrads receive any aid. 84% undergrads borrow to pay for school. Average cumulative indebtedness $28,313. **Criteria awarding aid:** *Non-need-based:* Academics, Alumni affiliation, Leadership, State/district residency.

MOUNT SAINT MARY'S UNIVERSITY (CA)

12001 Chalon Road, Los Angeles, CA 90049-1597
Financial Aid Phone: 310-954-4190
E-mail: admissions@msmu.edu **CEEB Code:** 4493
Fax: 310-954-4259 **Website:** www.msmu.edu **ACT Code:** 338

This private school, affiliated with the Roman Catholic Church, was founded in 1925. It has a 72 acre campus.

RATINGS

Admissions Selectivity Rating: 74   **Fire Safety Rating:** 99   **Green Rating:** 62

STUDENTS AND FACULTY

Enrollment: 2,227. **Student Body:** 93% female, 7% male, 3% out-of-state, <1% international (11 countries represented). Asian 15%, African American 7%, Caucasian 8%, Hispanic 59%, Native American <1%, Pacific Islander 1%, Two or more races 2%, Race unknown 8%.
Retention and Graduation: 72% freshmen return for sophomore year. **Faculty:** Student/faculty ratio 7:1. 134 full-time faculty, 66% hold PhDs, 28% are members of minority groups, 69% are women. 0% of classes are taught by teaching assistants.

ACADEMICS

Degrees: Associate; Bachelor's; Doctoral degree—professional practice; Master's; Post-bachelor's certificate; Post-master's certificate. **Classes:** Most classes have 10–19 students. Most lab/discussion sessions have fewer than 10 students. **Most popular majors:** Registered Nursing/Registered Nurse; Business Administration and Management, General; Sociology, General. **Special Study Options:** Accelerated program; Cooperative education program; Cross-registration; Distance learning; Double major; Exchange student program (domestic); Honors program; Independent study; Internships; Student-designed major; Study abroad; Teacher certification program; Weekend college. **Honors programs:** Honors program is available to qualifying incoming freshmen and college students meeting eligibility requirements. **Disability Services offered:** Note-taking services; Reader services; Tape recorders; Tutors. **Career services:** Alumni services; Career assessment; Career/job search classes; Internships.

FACILITIES

Housing: Coed dorms; Men's dorms; Theme housing; Women's dorms; 100% of campus accessible to physically disabled. **Special Academic Facilities/Equipment:** Drudis-Biada Art Gallery. **Campus Network:** 100% of classrooms, 100% of dorms, 100% of student union, 100% of libraries, 100% of dining areas, 50% of common outdoor areas have wireless network access.

CAMPUS LIFE

Environment: Metropolis. **Activities:** Campus Ministries; Choral groups; Dance; Literary magazine; Music ensembles; Student government; Student-run film society; Symphony orchestra; Yearbook. 31 registered organizations, 10 honor societies, 1 sorority on campus. **On-Campus Highlights:** Starbucks

Coffee. **Environmental Initiatives:** Water Conservation: Bottled water deliveries virtually canceled on both campuses. Activated Carbon Water filters added to bottle-free water dispensers on both campuses.

ADMISSIONS

Freshman Academic Profile: Average high school GPA 3.3. 20% in top 10% of high school class, 49% in top 25% of high school class, 81% in top 50% of high school class. 56% from public high schools. **Test Scores:** SAT Math middle 50% range 450–580. SAT EBRW middle 50% range 470–590. ACT middle 50% range 17–22. **Basis for Candidate Selection:** *Very important factors include:* rigor of secondary school record, academic GPA, application essay, standardized test scores, recommendation(s). *Other factors include:* interview, extracurricular activities, talent/ability, character/personal qualities, first generation, alumni/ae relation, volunteer work, work experience, level of applicant's interest. **Freshman Admission Requirements:** High school diploma is required and GED is accepted. *Academic units recommended:* 4 English, 3 math, 2 science, 1 science lab, 2 foreign language, 3 social studies, 2 history, 1 academic elective. **Freshman Admission Statistics:** 2,165 applied, 90% admitted, 21% enrolled. **Transfer Admission Requirements:** College transcript(s), essay or personal statement, statement of good standing from prior institution(s). Minimum college GPA of 2.4 required. Lowest grade transferable D. **General Admission Information:** Application fee $50. Priority deadline 12/1. Regular application deadline 8/1. Non-fall registration accepted.

COSTS AND FINANCIAL AID

Required Forms and Deadlines: FAFSA. **Notification of Awards:** Applicants will be notified of awards on a rolling basis beginning 3/1. **Types of Aid:** *Need-based scholarships/grants:* College/university scholarship or grant aid from institutional funds; Federal Pell; Private scholarships; SEOG; State scholarships/grants. *Loans:* Direct PLUS loans; Direct Subsidized Stafford Loans; Direct Unsubsidized Stafford Loans. **Student Employment:** Federal Work-Study Program available. Institutional employment available. **Financial Aid Statistics:** 99% needy freshmen, 84% needy undergrads receive need-based scholarship or grant aid. 0% freshmen, 3% undergrads receive non-need-based scholarship or grant aid. 74% freshmen, 86% undergrads receive need-based self-help aid. 0% freshmen, 0% undergrads receive athletic scholarships. 94% freshmen, 91% undergrads receive any aid. 78% undergrads borrow to pay for school. Average cumulative indebtedness $29,482. **Criteria awarding aid:** *Non-need-based:* Academics, Alumni affiliation, Music/drama.

MOUNT ST. MARY'S UNIVERSITY (MD)

16300 Old Emmitsburg Road, Emmitsburg, MD 21727
Phone: 301-447-5214 **Financial Aid Phone:** 301-447-5207
E-mail: admissions@msmary.edu **CEEB Code:** 5421
Fax: 301-447-5860 **Website:** https://msmary.edu **ACT Code:** 1726

This private school, affiliated with the Roman Catholic Church, was founded in 1808. It has a 1500 acre campus.

RATINGS

Admissions Selectivity Rating: 77   **Fire Safety Rating:** 99   **Green Rating:** 75

STUDENTS AND FACULTY

Enrollment: 1,831. **Student Body:** 50% female, 50% male, 42% out-of-state, 1% international (37 countries represented). Asian 3%, African American 17%, Caucasian 58%, Hispanic 13%, Native American <1%, Pacific Islander 1%, Two or more races 5%, Race unknown 1%.
Retention and Graduation: 79% freshmen return for sophomore year. 62% freshmen graduate within 4 years. 69% freshmen graduate within 6 years.
Faculty: Student/faculty ratio 12:1. 131 full-time faculty, 90% hold PhDs, 9% are members of minority groups, 39% are women.

ACADEMICS

Degrees: Bachelor's; Master's; Post-bachelor's certificate; Post-master's certificate. **Classes:** Most classes have 10–19 students. Most lab/discussion sessions have 10–19 students. **Most popular majors:** Business/Commerce, General; Accounting; Criminology. **Special Study Options:** Accelerated program; Cross-registration; Double major; Dual enrollment; Honors program; Independent study; Internships; Liberal arts/career combination; Student-designed major; Study abroad; Teacher certification program; Weekend college. **Honors programs:** The Honors Program offers talented and motivated students an educational experience that integrates curricular, co-curricular, and extra-curricular learning in both interdisciplinary and major areas of study. **Disability Services offered:** Note-taking services; Reader services; Tape recorders; Tutors.

Career services: Alumni network; Alumni services; Career assessment; Career/job search classes; Internships.

FACILITIES

Housing: Apartments for single students; Coed dorms; Special housing for disabled students; Theme housing; Wellness housing. **Special Academic Facilities/Equipment:** Historical art collection reflecting Catholic history in America and Marylandia. **Campus Network:** 0% of classrooms, 100% of dorms, 0% of student union, 100% of libraries, 100% of dining areas, 0% of common outdoor areas have wireless network access.

CAMPUS LIFE

Environment: Rural. **Activities:** Campus Ministries; Choral groups; Concert band; Dance; Drama/theater; International Student Organization; Jazz band; Literary magazine; Music ensembles; Musical theater; Pep band; Radio station; Student government; Student newspaper. 70 registered organizations, 15 honor societies, 9 religious organizations on campus. **Athletics (Intercollegiate):** *Men:* baseball, basketball, cross-country, golf, lacrosse, soccer, tennis, track/field (outdoor), track/field (indoor). *Women:* basketball, cross-country, golf, lacrosse, soccer, softball, swimming, tennis, track/field (outdoor), track/field (indoor). **On-Campus Highlights:** McGowan Student Center—Patriot Hall. **Environmental Initiatives:** We have 1.6 MW photovoltaic panels installed that provide a substantial fraction of electricity needs.

ADMISSIONS

Freshman Academic Profile: Average high school GPA 3.5. **Test Scores:** SAT Math middle 50% range 490–590. SAT EBRW middle 50% range 500–610. ACT middle 50% range 19–25. **Basis for Candidate Selection:** *Very important factors include:* academic GPA. *Important factors include:* rigor of secondary school record, application essay, standardized test scores, recommendation(s), extracurricular activities, talent/ability, character/personal qualities, level of applicant's interest. *Other factors include:* class rank, interview, volunteer work, work experience. **Freshman Admission Requirements:** High school diploma is required and GED is accepted. *Academic units required:* 4 English, 3 math, 3 science, 2 science labs, 2 foreign language, 3 social studies, 1 history. **Freshman Admission Statistics:** 4,716 applied, 75% admitted, 15% enrolled. **Transfer Admission Requirements:** College transcript(s), statement of good standing from prior institution(s). Minimum college GPA of 2.0 required. Lowest grade transferable C. **General Admission Information:** Application fee $45. Priority deadline 12/1. Regular application deadline 3/1. Non-fall registration accepted. Admission may be deferred for a maximum of 1 year.

COSTS AND FINANCIAL AID

Annual tuition $42,200. Room and board $13,630. Required fees $1,450. Average book and supplies expense $1,300. **Required Forms and Deadlines:** FAFSA. **Notification of Awards:** Applicants will be notified of awards on a rolling basis beginning 1/15. **Types of Aid:** *Need-based scholarships/grants:* College/university scholarship or grant aid from institutional funds; Federal Pell; Private scholarships; SEOG; State scholarships/grants. *Loans:* Direct PLUS loans; Direct Subsidized Stafford Loans; Direct Unsubsidized Stafford Loans. **Student Employment:** Federal Work-Study Program available. Institutional employment available. **Financial Aid Statistics:** 100% needy freshmen, 100% needy undergrads receive need-based scholarship or grant aid. 22% freshmen, 19% undergrads receive non-need-based scholarship or grant aid. 78% freshmen, 81% undergrads receive need-based self-help aid. 8% freshmen, 9% undergrads receive athletic scholarships. 73% undergrads borrow to pay for school. Average cumulative indebtedness $40,355. **Criteria awarding aid:** *Need-based:* Job skills. *Non-need-based:* Academics, Art, Athletics, Leadership.

MOUNT VERNON NAZARENE UNIVERSITY

800 Martinsburg Road, Mount Vernon, OH 43050
Phone: 740-392-6868 **Financial Aid Phone:** 866-686-8243
E-mail: admissions@mvnu.edu **CEEB Code:** 1531
Fax: 740-393-0511 **Website:** https://www.mvnu.edu/ **ACT Code:** 3372

This private school, affiliated with the Nazarene Church, was founded in 1964. It has a 332 acre campus.

RATINGS

Admissions Selectivity Rating: 80   **Fire Safety Rating:** 74   **Green Rating:** 61

STUDENTS AND FACULTY

Enrollment: 1,781. **Student Body:** 61% female, 39% male, 11% out-of-state, 1% international (12 countries represented). Asian <1%, African American 3%,

Caucasian 86%, Hispanic 3%, Native American <1%, Pacific Islander <1%, Two or more races 3%, Race unknown 3%. **Retention and Graduation:** 79% freshmen return for sophomore year. 57% freshmen graduate within 4 years. 68% freshmen graduate within 6 years. 17% grads go on to further study within 1 year. 1% grads pursue law degrees. 3% grads pursue business degrees. 2% grads pursue medical degrees. **Faculty:** Student/faculty ratio 16:1. 68 full-time faculty, 72% hold PhDs, 13% are members of minority groups, 40% are women. 0% of classes are taught by teaching assistants.

ACADEMICS

Degrees: Associate; Bachelor's; Master's. **Classes:** Most classes have 10–19 students. **Most popular majors:** Biology/Biological Sciences, General; Registered Nursing/Registered Nurse; Business Administration and Management, General. **Special Study Options:** Cross-registration; Distance learning; Double major; Dual enrollment; Honors program; Independent study; Internships; Liberal arts/career combination; Study abroad; Teacher certification program. **Honors programs:** The MVNU Honors Program is not about having gifted students simply do more work; instead, the program exists to enrich the academic and cultural experience for gifted students by offering unique and challenging courses, special extracurricular opportunities, and a supportive environment in which students can excel. The Honors Program adds depth to students' academic development and allows them to have input in designing their own curriculum by proposing study topics for Honors courses and by developing independent projects. Students will work closely with a faculty mentor to complete an Honors Project in their major. There are also opportunities for off-campus cultural enrichment and entertainment, as well as travel-study and experiential learning seminars. **Disability Services offered:** Note-taking services; Reader services; Tape recorders; Tutors. **Career services:** Alumni services; Career assessment; Career/job search classes.

FACILITIES

Housing: Apartments for married students; Apartments for single students; Men's dorms; Special housing for disabled students; Women's dorms; 95% of campus accessible to physically disabled. **Special Academic Facilities/Equipment:** Maker space, Buchwald Art Center, nature reserve.

CAMPUS LIFE

Environment: Village. **Activities:** Campus Ministries; Choral groups; Concert band; Drama/theater; International Student Organization; Jazz band; Literary magazine; Music ensembles; Musical theater; Pep band; Radio station; Student government; Student newspaper. 25 registered organizations, 6 honor societies, 14 religious organizations on campus. **Athletics (Intercollegiate):** *Men:* baseball, basketball, cross-country, golf, soccer. *Women:* basketball, cross-country, soccer, softball, volleyball. **On-Campus Highlights:** Ariel Arena. **Environmental Initiatives:** Campus-wide recycling program.

ADMISSIONS

Freshman Academic Profile: Average high school GPA 3.6. 22% in top 10% of high school class, 48% in top 25% of high school class, 82% in top 50% of high school class. 56% from public high schools. **Test Scores:** SAT Math middle 50% range 480–620. SAT EBRW middle 50% range 500–600. ACT middle 50% range 20–25. **Basis for Candidate Selection:** *Very important factors include:* academic GPA, standardized test scores. *Other factors include:* rigor of secondary school record, class rank, application essay, recommendation(s). **Freshman Admission Requirements:** High school diploma is required and GED is accepted. *Academic units required:* 2 foreign language. *Academic units recommended:* 4 English, 4 math, 3 science, 3 science labs, 3 foreign language, 3 social studies, 2 academic electives, 1 visual/performing arts. **Freshman Admission Statistics:** 1,305 applied, 73% admitted, 34% enrolled. **Transfer Admission Requirements:** High school transcript, college transcript(s), essay or personal statement, statement of good standing from prior institution(s). Minimum college GPA of 2.0 required. Lowest grade transferable C-. **General Admission Information:** Application fee $25. Priority deadline 4/15. Regular application deadline 7/15. Non-fall registration accepted. Admission may be deferred for a maximum of 1 year.

COSTS AND FINANCIAL AID

Annual tuition $31,360. Room and board $8,890. Required fees $250. Average book and supplies expense $1,400. **Required Forms and Deadlines:** FAFSA. **Notification of Awards:** Applicants will be notified of awards on a rolling basis beginning 11/15. **Types of Aid:** *Need-based scholarships/grants:* College/university scholarship or grant aid from institutional funds; Federal Pell; Private scholarships; SEOG; State scholarships/grants. *Loans:* Direct PLUS loans; Direct Subsidized Stafford Loans; Direct Unsubsidized Stafford Loans. **Student Employment:** Federal Work-Study Program available. Institutional employment available. **Financial Aid Statistics:** 100% needy freshmen, 97%

needy undergrads receive need-based scholarship or grant aid. 67% freshmen, 80% undergrads receive non-need-based scholarship or grant aid. 86% freshmen, 84% undergrads receive need-based self-help aid. 21% freshmen, 4% undergrads receive athletic scholarships. 100% freshmen, 87% undergrads receive any aid. **Criteria awarding aid:** *Need-based:* Academics. *Non-need-based:* Academics, Art, Athletics, Minority status, Music/drama, Religious affiliation, State/district residency.

MUHLENBERG COLLEGE

2400 West Chew Street, Allentown, PA 18104-5596
Phone: 484-664-3200 **Financial Aid Phone:** 484-664-3175
E-mail: admissions@muhlenberg.edu **CEEB Code:** 2424
Fax: 484-664-3032 **Website:** www.muhlenberg.edu **ACT Code:** 3640

This private school, affiliated with the Lutheran Church, was founded in 1848. It has a 81 acre campus.

RATINGS

Admissions Selectivity Rating: 86   **Fire Safety Rating:** 97   **Green Rating:** 95

STUDENTS AND FACULTY

Enrollment: 2,190. **Student Body:** 61% female, 39% male, 73% out-of-state, 3% international (20 countries represented). Asian 3%, African American 4%, Caucasian 74%, Hispanic 9%, Native American <1%, Pacific Islander 0%, Two or more races 2%, Race unknown 4%. **Retention and Graduation:** 88% freshmen return for sophomore year. 81% freshmen graduate within 4 years. 85% freshmen graduate within 6 years. 19% grads go on to further study within 1 year. 1% grads pursue law degrees. **Faculty:** Student/faculty ratio 9:1. 197 full-time faculty, 87% hold PhDs, 14% are members of minority groups, 48% are women. 0% of classes are taught by teaching assistants.

ACADEMICS

Degrees: Associate; Bachelor's; Certificate. **Classes:** Most classes have 10–19 students. Most lab/discussion sessions have 10–19 students. **Most popular majors:** Psychology, General; Drama and Dramatics/Theatre Arts, General; Business/Commerce, General. **Special Study Options:** Accelerated program; Cross-registration; Distance learning; Double major; Exchange student program (domestic); Honors program; Independent study; Internships; Student-designed major; Study abroad; Teacher certification program. **Honors programs:** Muhlenberg Scholar, Dana Associate, R.J. Fellow. **Combined degree programs:** BA/DDS; BA/MD. **Disability Services offered:** Note-taking services; Tutors. **Career services:** Alumni network; Alumni services; Career assessment; Career/job search classes; Internships; Regional alumni.

FACILITIES

Housing: Apartments for single students; Coed dorms; Fraternity/sorority housing; Special housing for disabled students; Special housing for international students; Women's dorms; 95% of campus accessible to physically disabled. **Special Academic Facilities/Equipment:** Martin art gallery, biology museum, Graver arboretum, greenhouse, mainstage theatre, recital hall, 20-foot boat for marine studies, 40-acre Raker environmental field station, two electron microscopes, dance studios, experimental theatres, proscenium theatres.

CAMPUS LIFE

Environment: City. **Activities:** Campus Ministries; Choral groups; Concert band; Dance; Drama/theater; International Student Organization; Jazz band; Literary magazine; Music ensembles; Musical theater; Opera; Pep band; Radio station; Student government; Student newspaper; Student-run film society; Symphony orchestra; Yearbook. 123 registered organizations, 12 honor societies, 7 religious organizations, 3 fraternities, 5 sororities on campus. **Athletics (Intercollegiate):** *Men:* baseball, basketball, cheerleading, cross-country, football, golf, lacrosse, soccer, tennis, track/field (outdoor), track/field (indoor), wrestling. *Women:* basketball, cheerleading, cross-country, field hockey, golf, lacrosse, soccer, softball, tennis, track/field (outdoor), track/field (indoor), volleyball. **On-Campus Highlights:** Seegers Union by fireplace & Java Joe's.

ADMISSIONS

Freshman Academic Profile: Average high school GPA 3.4. 35% in top 10% of high school class, 72% in top 25% of high school class, 95% in top 50% of high school class. 69% from public high schools. **Test Scores:** SAT Math middle 50% range 570–660. SAT EBRW middle 50% range 580–680. ACT middle 50% range 26–31. **Basis for Candidate Selection:** *Very important factors include:* rigor of secondary school record, academic GPA, character/personal qualities. *Important factors include:* application essay, standardized test scores, recommendation(s), interview, extracurricular activities, talent/ability, volunteer work. *Other factors include:* class rank, first generation, alumni/ae relation, geographical residence, racial/ethnic status, level of applicant's interest. **Freshman Admission Requirements:** High school diploma is required and GED is accepted. *Academic units required:* 4 English, 3 math, 2 science, 2 science labs, 2 foreign language, 2 history, 1 academic elective. *Academic units recommended:* 4 English, 4 math, 3 science, 3 science labs, 4 foreign language, 2 social studies, 2 history, 1 academic elective. **Freshman Admission Statistics:** 4,224 applied, 66% admitted, 19% enrolled. **Transfer Admission Requirements:** High school transcript, college transcript(s), essay or personal statement, interview, standardized test scores, statement of good standing from prior institution(s). Minimum college GPA of 2.5 required. Lowest grade transferable C. **General Admission Information:** Application fee $50. Regular application deadline 2/1. Non-fall registration accepted. Admission may be deferred for a maximum of 1 year.

COSTS AND FINANCIAL AID

Annual tuition $53,865. Room and board $12,165. Required fees $735. Average book and supplies expense $1,400. **Required Forms and Deadlines:** CSS/Financial Aid PROFILE; FAFSA; Institution's own financial aid form; Noncustodial PROFILE. **Notification of Awards:** Applicants will be notified of awards on or about 3/15. **Types of Aid:** *Need-based scholarships/grants:* College/university scholarship or grant aid from institutional funds; Federal Pell; Private scholarships; SEOG; State scholarships/grants; United Negro College Fund. *Loans:* Direct PLUS loans; Direct Subsidized Stafford Loans; Direct Unsubsidized Stafford Loans. **Student Employment:** Federal Work-Study Program available. Institutional employment available. **Financial Aid Statistics:** 98% needy freshmen, 96% needy undergrads receive need-based scholarship or grant aid. 17% freshmen, 16% undergrads receive non-need-based scholarship or grant aid. 76% freshmen, 73% undergrads receive need-based self-help aid. 0% freshmen, 0% undergrads receive athletic scholarships. 90% freshmen, 90% undergrads receive any aid. 60% undergrads borrow to pay for school. Average cumulative indebtedness $32,963. **Criteria awarding aid:** *Non-need-based:* Academics, Art, Leadership, Religious affiliation.

MULTNOMAH UNIVERSITY

8435 NE Glisan Street, Portland, OR 97220-5898
Phone: 503-251-6485 **Financial Aid Phone:** 503-251-5337
E-mail: admiss@multnomah.edu
Fax: 503-254-1268 **Website:** http://www.multnomah.edu/ **ACT Code:** 3476

This private school, affiliated with the Christian (Nondenominational) Church, was founded in 1936. It has a 25 acre campus.

RATINGS

Admissions Selectivity Rating: 88   **Fire Safety Rating:** 63   **Green Rating:** 61

STUDENTS AND FACULTY

Enrollment: 362. **Student Body:** 49% female, 51% male, 57% out-of-state, <1% international (2 countries represented). Asian 3%, African American 4%, Caucasian 68%, Hispanic 16%, Native American 1%, Pacific Islander 1%, Two or more races 5%, Race unknown 2%.
Retention and Graduation: 47% freshmen return for sophomore year. 50% grads go on to further study within 1 year. **Faculty:** Student/faculty ratio 10:1. 26 full-time faculty, 81% hold PhDs, 8% are members of minority groups, 31% are women. 0% of classes are taught by teaching assistants.

ACADEMICS

Degrees: Bachelor's; Doctoral degree—other; Master's; Post-bachelor's certificate. **Classes:** Most classes have fewer than 10 students. **Most popular majors:** Psychology, General; Business Administration and Management, General. **Special Study Options:** Double major; Study abroad. **Disability Services offered:** Note-taking services; Reader services; Tape recorders; Tutors.

Career services: Alumni services; Career assessment; Career/job search classes; Internships.

FACILITIES

Housing: Apartments for single students; Men's dorms; Special housing for disabled students; Women's dorms; 90% of campus accessible to physically disabled. **Campus Network:** 100% of classrooms, 100% of dorms, 100% of student union, 100% of libraries, 100% of dining areas, 60% of common outdoor areas have wireless network access.

CAMPUS LIFE

Environment: Metropolis. **Activities:** Choral groups; Student government. 5 registered organizations on campus. **Athletics (Intercollegiate):** *Men:* basketball. *Women:* volleyball. **On-Campus Highlights:** Roger's Café.

ADMISSIONS

Freshman Academic Profile: Average high school GPA 3.3. 20% in top 10% of high school class, 40% in top 25% of high school class, 62% in top 50% of high school class. 55% from public high schools. **Test Scores:** SAT Math middle 50% range 500–610. SAT EBRW middle 50% range 520–610. **Basis for Candidate Selection:** *Very important factors include:* academic GPA, application essay, recommendation(s), character/personal qualities, religious affiliation/commitment. *Important factors include:* rigor of secondary school record. *Other factors include:* class rank, standardized test scores, interview, extracurricular activities, talent/ability, first generation, alumni/ae relation, volunteer work, work experience. **Freshman Admission Requirements:** High school diploma is required and GED is accepted. *Academic units required:* 2 English. *Academic units recommended:* 4 English, 3 math, 2 science, 1 science lab, 3 social studies, 2 academic electives. **Freshman Admission Statistics:** 282 applied, 54% admitted, 42% enrolled. **Transfer Admission Requirements:** College transcript(s), essay or personal statement, statement of good standing from prior institution(s). Minimum college GPA of 2.0 required. Lowest grade transferable C-. **General Admission Information:** Application fee $40. Regular application deadline 8/1. Non-fall registration accepted.

COSTS AND FINANCIAL AID

Annual tuition $28,030. Room and board $9,870. Required fees $650. Average book and supplies expense $1,680. **Required Forms and Deadlines:** FAFSA. **Notification of Awards:** Applicants will be notified of awards on a rolling basis beginning 3/1. **Types of Aid:** *Need-based scholarships/grants:* College/university scholarship or grant aid from institutional funds; Federal Pell; Private scholarships; SEOG; State scholarships/grants. *Loans:* Direct PLUS loans; Direct Subsidized Stafford Loans; Direct Unsubsidized Stafford Loans. **Student Employment:** Federal Work-Study Program available. Institutional employment available. **Financial Aid Statistics:** 98% needy freshmen, 96% needy undergrads receive need-based scholarship or grant aid. 8% freshmen, 7% undergrads receive non-need-based scholarship or grant aid. 85% freshmen, 77% undergrads receive need-based self-help aid. 17% freshmen, 12% undergrads receive athletic scholarships. 97% freshmen, 85% undergrads receive any aid. 69% undergrads borrow to pay for school. Average cumulative indebtedness $16,057. **Criteria awarding aid:** *Need-based:* Minority status. *Non-need-based:* Academics, Alumni affiliation, Athletics.

MURRAY STATE UNIVERSITY

102 Curris Center, Murray, KY 42071-0009
Phone: 270-809-3741 **Financial Aid Phone:** (270) 809-2546
E-mail: msu.admissions@murraystate.edu **CEEB Code:** 1494
Fax: 270-809-3780 **Website:** www.murraystate.edu **ACT Code:** 1532

This public school was founded in 1922. It has a 253 acre campus.

RATINGS

Admissions Selectivity Rating: 75   **Fire Safety Rating:** 94   **Green Rating:** 69

STUDENTS AND FACULTY

Enrollment: 7,290. **Student Body:** 58% female, 42% male, 33% out-of-state, 3% international (43 countries represented). Asian 1%, African American 6%, Caucasian 82%, Hispanic 2%, Native American <1%, Pacific Islander <1%, Two or more races 3%, Race unknown 2%.
Retention and Graduation: 75% freshmen return for sophomore year. 25% freshmen graduate within 4 years. 49% freshmen graduate within 6 years. **Faculty:** Student/faculty ratio 15:1. 455 full-time faculty, 75% hold PhDs, 17% are members of minority groups, 47% are women.

ACADEMICS

Degrees: Associate; Bachelor's; Certificate; Doctoral degree—other; Doctoral degree—professional practice; Master's; Post-bachelor's certificate; Post-master's certificate. **Classes:** Most classes have 10–19 students. **Most popular majors:** Occupational Safety and Health Technology/Technician; Registered Nursing/Registered Nurse. **Special Study Options:** Accelerated program; Cooperative education program; Cross-registration; Distance learning; Double major; Dual enrollment; English as a Second Language (ESL); Exchange student program (domestic); External degree program; Honors program; Independent study; Internships; Liberal arts/career combination; Student-designed major; Study abroad; Teacher certification program; Weekend college. **Honors programs:** Our undergraduate honors college has been designed to provide future social and professional leaders with exceptional thinking and communication skills, an appropriate breadth and depth of knowledge, and a sense of cultural and social responsibility. The Honors Sequence is a curriculum that includes dedicated Honors seminars, competency courses (language, math, and science), study abroad, and the Honors thesis. **Disability Services offered:** Note-taking services; Reader services; Tape recorders; Tutors. **Career services:** Alumni network; Alumni services; Career assessment; Career/job search classes; Internships; Regional alumni.

FACILITIES

Housing: Apartments for married students; Apartments for single students; Coed dorms; Special housing for disabled students; Women's dorms. **Special Academic Facilities/Equipment:** Arboretum, Biological Research Station, Watershed Studies Institute, Mid-America Remote Sensing Center, Wrather Museum (museum and cultural events center), Lovett Auditorium and CFSB Center (used for musical and theater productions, concerts, and lectures), Price Doyle Fine Arts Center (for performances and exhibitions), State Farm Financial Services Center (applied learning for students in Finance and Economics), 4 agricultural research farms, Breathitt Veterinary Center (veterinary research center), Cherry Agricultural Exposition Center, use of federal Land Between the Lakes for research and field work, state center of excellence for telecommunications systems management.

CAMPUS LIFE

Environment: Village. **Activities:** Campus Ministries; Choral groups; Concert band; Dance; Drama/theater; International Student Organization; Jazz band; Literary magazine; Marching band; Model UN; Music ensembles; Musical theater; Opera; Pep band; Radio station; Student government; Student newspaper; Student-run film society; Symphony orchestra; Television station. 162 registered organizations, 16 honor societies, 12 religious organizations, 12 fraternities, 11 sororities on campus. **Athletics (Intercollegiate):** *Men:* baseball, basketball, bowling, cheerleading, cross-country, equestrian sports, football, golf, horseback riding, riflery, rodeo, tennis. *Women:* basketball, cheerleading, cross-country, equestrian sports, golf, horseback riding, riflery, rodeo, soccer, softball, tennis, track/field (outdoor), volleyball. **On-Campus Highlights:** Susan E. Bauernfeind Student Recreation and Wellness Center.

ADMISSIONS

Freshman Academic Profile: Average high school GPA 3.6. 25% in top 10% of high school class, 52% in top 25% of high school class, 80% in top 50% of high school class. **Test Scores:** SAT Math middle 50% range 518–593. SAT EBRW middle 50% range 478–560. ACT middle 50% range 21–27. **Basis for Candidate Selection:** *Very important factors include:* rigor of secondary school record, class rank, academic GPA, standardized test scores. **Freshman Admission Requirements:** High school diploma is required and GED is accepted. *Academic units required:* 4 English, 3 math, 3 science, 1 science lab, 2 foreign language, 3 social studies, 3 history, 5 academic electives, 1 unit from above areas or other academic areas. *Academic units recommended:* 4 math, 4 science, 1 computer science. **Freshman Admission Statistics:** 6,899 applied, 87% admitted, 24% enrolled. **Transfer Admission Requirements:** College transcript(s), statement of good standing from prior institution(s). Minimum college GPA of 2.0 required. Lowest grade transferable D. **General Admission Information:** Application fee $40. Non-fall registration accepted. Admission may be deferred for a maximum of 1 year.

COSTS AND FINANCIAL AID

Average book and supplies expense $1,265. **Required Forms and Deadlines:** FAFSA. **Notification of Awards:** Applicants will be notified of awards on a rolling basis beginning 12/15. **Types of Aid:** *Need-based scholarships/grants:* College/university scholarship or grant aid from institutional funds; Federal Pell; Private scholarships; SEOG; State scholarships/grants. *Loans:* Direct PLUS loans; Direct Subsidized Stafford Loans; Direct Unsubsidized Stafford Loans. **Student Employment:** Federal Work-Study Program available. Institutional employment available. **Financial Aid Statistics:** 94% needy freshmen, 86% needy undergrads receive need-based scholarship or grant aid. 14% freshmen,

10% undergrads receive non-need-based scholarship or grant aid. 61% freshmen, 69% undergrads receive need-based self-help aid. 3% freshmen, 3% undergrads receive athletic scholarships. 95.76% freshmen, 84.26% undergrads receive any aid. **Criteria awarding aid:** *Need-based:* Academics, Alumni affiliation, Job skills, Minority status, Music/drama. *Non-need-based:* Academics, Alumni affiliation, Art, Athletics, Job skills, Leadership, Minority status, Music/drama, State/district residency.

MUSKINGUM UNIVERSITY

163 Stormont Street, New Concord, OH 43762
Phone: 740-826-8137 **Financial Aid Phone:** 740-826-8137
E-mail: ssoba@muskingum.edu **CEEB Code:** 1496
Fax: 614-826-8100 **ACT Code:** 3305

This private school, affiliated with the Presbyterian Church, was founded in 1837. It has a 245 acre campus.

RATINGS
Admissions Selectivity Rating: 77   **Fire Safety Rating:** 60*   **Green Rating:** 60*

STUDENTS AND FACULTY
Enrollment: 1,524. **Student Body:** 56% female, 44% male, 8% out-of-state, 4% international (9 countries represented). Asian 1%, African American 5%, Caucasian 79%, Hispanic 3%, Native American <1%, Pacific Islander 0%, Two or more races 4%, Race unknown 5%.
Retention and Graduation: 74% freshmen return for sophomore year. 38% freshmen graduate within 4 years. 54% freshmen graduate within 6 years. 25% grads go on to further study within 1 year. 5% grads pursue arts and sciences degrees. 3% grads pursue law degrees. 4% grads pursue business degrees. 2% grads pursue medical degrees. **Faculty:** Student/faculty ratio 14:1. 95 full-time faculty, 93% hold PhDs, 12% are members of minority groups, 47% are women. 0% of classes are taught by teaching assistants.

ACADEMICS
Degrees: Bachelor's; Master's. **Classes:** Most classes have 10–19 students. Most lab/discussion sessions have 10–19 students. **Most popular majors:** Registered Nursing/Registered Nurse; Business Administration and Management, General; Early Childhood Education and Teaching. **Special Study Options:** Accelerated program; Distance learning; Double major; Dual enrollment; English as a Second Language (ESL); Exchange student program (domestic); Independent study; Internships; Liberal arts/career combination; Student-designed major; Study abroad; Teacher certification program; Weekend college. **Combined degree programs:** BA/MEng. **Disability Services offered:** Note-taking services; Reader services; Tape recorders; Tutors. **Career services:** Alumni network; Alumni services; Career assessment; Internships; Regional alumni.

FACILITIES
Housing: Apartments for single students; Coed dorms; Fraternity/sorority housing; Men's dorms; Theme housing; Women's dorms; 50% of campus accessible to physically disabled. **Special Academic Facilities/Equipment:** Art gallery, on-campus nursery school, electron microscope, 57-acre biology field station and mobile biology lab.

CAMPUS LIFE
Environment: Rural. **Activities:** Campus Ministries; Choral groups; Concert band; Dance; Drama/theater; International Student Organization; Jazz band; Literary magazine; Marching band; Model UN; Music ensembles; Musical theater; Pep band; Radio station; Student government; Student newspaper; Symphony orchestra; Television station. 96 registered organizations, 26 honor societies, 5 religious organizations, 6 fraternities, 6 sororities on campus.
Athletics (Intercollegiate): *Men:* baseball, basketball, cheerleading, cross-country, football, golf, soccer, tennis, track/field (outdoor), track/field (indoor), wrestling. *Women:* basketball, cheerleading, cross-country, golf, soccer, softball, tennis, track/field (outdoor), track/field (indoor), volleyball. **On-Campus Highlights:** Philip and Betsey Caldwell Hall.

ADMISSIONS
Freshman Academic Profile: Average high school GPA 3.2. 20% in top 10% of high school class, 40% in top 25% of high school class, 70% in top 50% of high school class. 92% from public high schools. **Test Scores:** SAT Math middle 50% range 460–530. SAT EBRW middle 50% range 463–578. ACT middle 50% range 18–24. **Basis for Candidate Selection:** *Very important factors include:* rigor of secondary school record, academic GPA. *Important factors*

include: class rank, standardized test scores. *Other factors include:* application essay, recommendation(s), interview, extracurricular activities, talent/ability, character/personal qualities, alumni/ae relation, geographical residence, racial/ethnic status, work experience. **Freshman Admission Requirements:** High school diploma is required and GED is accepted. *Academic units required:* 4 English, 2 math, 2 science, 1 science lab, 2 foreign language, 2 social studies. *Academic units recommended:* 4 English, 3 math, 3 science, 2 science labs, 2 foreign language, 3 social studies. **Freshman Admission Statistics:** 1,850 applied, 74% admitted, 28% enrolled. **Transfer Admission Requirements:** High school transcript, college transcript(s). Minimum college GPA of 2.0 required. Lowest grade transferable C. **General Admission Information:** Priority deadline 3/1. Regular application deadline 8/1. Non-fall registration accepted. Admission may be deferred for a maximum of 1 year.

COSTS AND FINANCIAL AID

Annual tuition $26,900. Room and board $11,040. Required fees $1,162. Average book and supplies expense $1,100. **Required Forms and Deadlines:** FAFSA. **Notification of Awards:** Applicants will be notified of awards on a rolling basis beginning 12/15. **Types of Aid:** *Need-based scholarships/grants:* College/university scholarship or grant aid from institutional funds; Federal Pell; Private scholarships; SEOG; State scholarships/grants. *Loans:* Direct PLUS loans; Direct Subsidized Stafford Loans; Direct Unsubsidized Stafford Loans. **Student Employment:** Federal Work-Study Program available. Institutional employment available. **Financial Aid Statistics:** 89% needy freshmen, 100% needy undergrads receive need-based scholarship or grant aid. 8% freshmen, 10% undergrads receive non-need-based scholarship or grant aid. 90% freshmen, 88% undergrads receive need-based self-help aid. 0% freshmen, 0% undergrads receive athletic scholarships. 98% freshmen, 98% undergrads receive any aid. 79% undergrads borrow to pay for school. Average cumulative indebtedness $4,717. **Criteria awarding aid:** *Need-based:* Academics, Leadership, Minority status. *Non-need-based:* Academics, Alumni affiliation, Art, Leadership, Minority status, Music/drama, Religious affiliation, State/district residency.

NAROPA UNIVERSITY

2130 Araphahoe Avenue, Boulder, CO 80302
Phone: 303-546-3572 **Financial Aid Phone:** (303) 546-3534
E-mail: admissions@naropa.edu **CEEB Code:** 908
Fax: 303-546-3583 **Website:** www.naropa.edu/ **ACT Code:** 4853

This private school was founded in 1974. It has a 12 acre campus.

RATINGS
Admissions Selectivity Rating: 66   **Fire Safety Rating:** 61   **Green Rating:** 60*

STUDENTS AND FACULTY
Enrollment: 464. **Student Body:** 61% female, 39% male, 74% out-of-state, 3% international (24 countries represented). Asian 3%, African American 2%, Caucasian 75%, Hispanic 4%, Native American 3%, Race unknown 11%. **Retention and Graduation:** 64% freshmen return for sophomore year. **Faculty:** Student/faculty ratio 9:1. 51 full-time faculty, 51% hold PhDs, 12% are members of minority groups, 57% are women. 0% of classes are taught by teaching assistants.

ACADEMICS
Degrees: Bachelor's; Certificate; Master's. **Classes:** Most classes have 10–19 students. **Most popular majors:** English Language and Literature, General; Visual and Performing Arts, General; Psychology, General. **Special Study Options:** Double major; Independent study; Internships; Student-designed major; Study abroad. **Disability Services offered:** Note-taking services; Reader services; Tape recorders; Tutors.

FACILITIES
Housing: Apartments for married students; Apartments for single students; 85% of campus accessible to physically disabled. **Special Academic Facilities/Equipment:** Maitri Rooms, meditation halls, Allen Ginsberg library and a preschool. **Campus Network:** 100% of classrooms, 100% of dorms, 100% of student union, 100% of libraries, 100% of dining areas, 65% of common outdoor areas have wireless network access.

CAMPUS LIFE
Environment: City. **Activities:** Choral groups; Dance; Drama/theater; Jazz band; Literary magazine; Music ensembles; Student government. 20 registered

---

organizations, 2 religious organizations on campus. **On-Campus Highlights:** Lincoln Building. **Environmental Initiatives:** We compost all of our paper towels in public restrooms diverting 25% of our landfill waste into compost.

ADMISSIONS
Freshman Academic Profile: Average high school GPA 3.0. **Basis for Candidate Selection:** *Very important factors include:* rigor of secondary school record, academic GPA, application essay, recommendation(s), interview. *Important factors include:* extracurricular activities, talent/ability, character/personal qualities, volunteer work. *Other factors include:* first generation, alumni/ae relation, racial/ethnic status, work experience. **Freshman Admission Requirements:** High school diploma is required and GED is accepted. *Academic units recommended:* 4 English, 3 math, 3 science, 2 science labs, 3 foreign language, 3 social studies, 3 history, 2 academic electives, 2 unit from above areas or other academic areas. **Freshman Admission Statistics:** 139 applied, 93% admitted, 53% enrolled. **Transfer Admission Requirements:** College transcript(s), essay or personal statement, interview, Lowest grade transferable C. **General Admission Information:** Application fee $50. Priority deadline 1/15. Non-fall registration accepted. Admission may be deferred for a maximum of 1 year.

COSTS AND FINANCIAL AID
Annual tuition $23,420. Room and board $8,478. Required fees $100. Average book and supplies expense $1,200. **Required Forms and Deadlines:** FAFSA. **Notification of Awards:** Applicants will be notified of awards on a rolling basis beginning 3/1. **Types of Aid:** *Need-based scholarships/grants:* College/university scholarship or grant aid from institutional funds; Federal Pell; Private scholarships; SEOG. **Student Employment:** Federal Work-Study Program available. **Financial Aid Statistics:** 87% needy freshmen, 88% needy undergrads receive need-based scholarship or grant aid. 0% freshmen, 0% undergrads receive non-need-based scholarship or grant aid. 94% freshmen, 91% undergrads receive need-based self-help aid. 0% freshmen, 0% undergrads receive athletic scholarships. 71% freshmen, 71% undergrads receive any aid. **Criteria awarding aid:** *Need-based:* Academics, Job skills, Leadership, Minority status, Music/drama, Religious affiliation.

NATIONAL UNIVERSITY OF HEALTH SCIENCES

200 E. Roosevelt Road, Lombard, IL 60148
Phone: 630-889-6566 **Financial Aid Phone:** 630-889-6700
E-mail: admissions@nuhs.edu
Fax: 630-889-6554 **Website:** www.nuhs.edu

This private school was founded in 1906. It has a 32 acre campus.

RATINGS
Admissions Selectivity Rating: 61   **Fire Safety Rating:** 60*   **Green Rating:** 60*

STUDENTS AND FACULTY
Enrollment: 74. **Student Body:** 16% female, 84% male, 70% out-of-state, 4% international (9 countries represented). Asian 5%, African American 16%, Caucasian 63%, Hispanic 5%, Native American 0%, Race unknown 7%. **Retention and Graduation:** 90% freshmen return for sophomore year. **Faculty:** Student/faculty ratio 6:1. 46 full-time faculty, 93% hold PhDs, 0% are members of minority groups, 17% are women.

ACADEMICS
Degrees: Bachelor's; Certificate; Doctoral degree—professional practice; Master's. **Classes:** Most classes have 40–49 students. Most lab/discussion sessions have 20–29 students. **Most popular majors:** Biomedical Sciences, General; Massage Therapy/Therapeutic Massage. **Special Study Options:** Internships.

FACILITIES
Housing: Apartments for married students; Apartments for single students; Coed dorms; Men's dorms; Women's dorms. **Special Academic Facilities/Equipment:** Museum; Fitness Center; Learning Resource Center; Health Care Clinic.

CAMPUS LIFE
Environment: Town. **Activities:** Student government; Student newspaper; Yearbook. 24 registered organizations, 1 religious organization, 2 fraternities, 1 sorority on campus. **On-Campus Highlights:** Janse Hall.

ADMISSIONS

Freshman Admission Requirements: High school diploma is required and GED is accepted. **Transfer Admission Requirements:** College transcript(s), statement of good standing from prior institution(s). Minimum college GPA of 2.5 required. Lowest grade transferable C. **General Admission Information:** Application fee $55. Non-fall registration accepted.

COSTS AND FINANCIAL AID

Types of Aid: *Need-based scholarships/grants:* College/university scholarship or grant aid from institutional funds; Federal Pell; Private scholarships; SEOG; State scholarships/grants. **Student Employment:** Federal Work-Study Program available. Institutional employment available. **Financial Aid Statistics:** 62% needy undergrads receive need-based scholarship or grant aid. 10% undergrads receive non-need-based scholarship or grant aid. 62% undergrads receive need-based self-help aid.

NAZARETH COLLEGE

Best Colleges

4245 East Avenue, Rochester, NY 14618-3790
Phone: 585-389-2860 **Financial Aid Phone:** 585-389-2310
E-mail: admissions@naz.edu **CEEB Code:** 2511
Fax: 585-389-2826 **Website:** www.naz.edu **ACT Code:** 2826

This private school was founded in 1924. It has a 150 acre campus.

RATINGS

Admissions Selectivity Rating: 85   **Fire Safety Rating:** 93   **Green Rating:** 71

STUDENTS AND FACULTY

Enrollment: 2,252. **Student Body:** 74% female, 26% male, 11% out-of-state, 1% international (34 countries represented). Asian 3%, African American 5%, Caucasian 78%, Hispanic 6%, Native American <1%, Pacific Islander <1%, Two or more races 2%, Race unknown 4%.
Retention and Graduation: 85% freshmen return for sophomore year. 56% freshmen graduate within 4 years. 66% freshmen graduate within 6 years.
Faculty: Student/faculty ratio 9:1. 181 full-time faculty, 77% hold PhDs, 15% are members of minority groups, 64% are women. 0% of classes are taught by teaching assistants.

ACADEMICS

Degrees: Bachelor's; Doctoral degree—professional practice; Master's. **Classes:** Most classes have 10–19 students. Most lab/discussion sessions have 10–19 students. **Most popular majors:** Education, General; Physical Therapy/Therapist; Business Administration, Management and Operations, Other. **Special Study Options:** Cross-registration; Distance learning; Double major; Dual enrollment; English as a Second Language (ESL); Exchange student program (domestic); Honors program; Independent study; Internships; Liberal arts/career combination; Study abroad; Teacher certification program. **Disability Services offered:** Note-taking services; Reader services; Tape recorders; Tutors. **Career services:** Alumni network; Alumni services; Career assessment; Career/job search classes; Internships; Regional alumni.

FACILITIES

Housing: Apartments for single students; Coed dorms; 80% of campus accessible to physically disabled. **Special Academic Facilities/Equipment:** Arts Center, speech/hearing/language clinics, reading clinic, psychology center, Center for Civic Engagement, Center for Service Learning, Center for Teaching Excellence, Center for Spirituality, and Center for International Education.

CAMPUS LIFE

Environment: Village. **Activities:** Campus Ministries; Choral groups; Concert band; Dance; Drama/theater; International Student Organization; Jazz band; Literary magazine; Music ensembles; Musical theater; Opera; Pep band; Radio station; Student government; Student newspaper; Symphony orchestra; Yearbook. 50 registered organizations, 21 honor societies, 5 religious organizations on campus. **Athletics (Intercollegiate):** *Men:* basketball, cross-country, diving, equestrian sports, golf, lacrosse, soccer, swimming, tennis, track/field (outdoor), track/field (indoor), volleyball. *Women:* basketball, cross-country, diving, equestrian sports, field hockey, golf, lacrosse, soccer, softball,

swimming, tennis, track/field (outdoor), track/field (indoor), volleyball. **On-Campus Highlights:** Golisano Training Center.

ADMISSIONS

Freshman Academic Profile: 25% in top 10% of high school class, 58% in top 25% of high school class, 88% in top 50% of high school class. 90% from public high schools. **Test Scores:** SAT Math middle 50% range 540–640. SAT EBRW middle 50% range 550–630. ACT middle 50% range 23–28. **Basis for Candidate Selection:** *Very important factors include:* rigor of secondary school record, class rank, academic GPA, application essay, recommendation(s). *Important factors include:* interview, extracurricular activities, talent/ability, character/personal qualities, geographical residence, state residency, racial/ethnic status, volunteer work. *Other factors include:* standardized test scores, first generation, alumni/ae relation. **Freshman Admission Requirements:** High school diploma is required and GED is accepted. *Academic units required:* 3 English, 3 math, 3 science, 3 foreign language, 3 social studies. *Academic units recommended:* 4 English, 4 math, 4 science, 4 foreign language, 4 social studies. **Freshman Admission Statistics:** 4,273 applied, 64% admitted, 20% enrolled. **Transfer Admission Requirements:** College transcript(s), essay or personal statement. Minimum college GPA of 2.5 required. Lowest grade transferable C. **General Admission Information:** Application fee $45. Priority deadline 12/1. Regular application deadline 2/1. Non-fall registration accepted. Admission may be deferred for a maximum of 1 year.

COSTS AND FINANCIAL AID

Annual tuition $33,836. Required fees $1,805. Average book and supplies expense $1,000. **Required Forms and Deadlines:** FAFSA; State aid form. **Notification of Awards:** Applicants will be notified of awards on a rolling basis beginning 2/1. **Types of Aid:** *Need-based scholarships/grants:* College/university scholarship or grant aid from institutional funds; Federal Pell; Private scholarships; SEOG; State scholarships/grants. *Loans:* Direct PLUS loans; Direct Subsidized Stafford Loans; Direct Unsubsidized Stafford Loans. **Student Employment:** Federal Work-Study Program available. Institutional employment available. **Financial Aid Statistics:** 100% needy freshmen, 100% needy undergrads receive need-based scholarship or grant aid. 51% freshmen, 38% undergrads receive non-need-based scholarship or grant aid. 92% freshmen, 93% undergrads receive need-based self-help aid. 0% freshmen, 0% undergrads receive athletic scholarships. 98% freshmen, 96% undergrads receive any aid. 86% undergrads borrow to pay for school. Average cumulative indebtedness $42,412. **Criteria awarding aid:** *Need-based:* Alumni affiliation. *Non-need-based:* Academics, Art, Minority status, Music/drama.

NEBRASKA METHODIST COLLEGE

720 North 87th Street, Omaha, NE 68114
Phone: 402-354-7200 **Financial Aid Phone:** 402-354-7225
E-mail: admissions@methodistcollege.edu **CEEB Code:** 6510
Fax: 402-354-7020 **ACT Code:** 2465

This private school, affiliated with the Methodist Church, was founded in 1891. It has a 6 acre campus.

RATINGS

Admissions Selectivity Rating: 76   **Fire Safety Rating:** 68   **Green Rating:** 60*

STUDENTS AND FACULTY

Enrollment: 504. **Student Body:** 92% female, 8% male, 35% out-of-state, 0% international (3 countries represented). Asian 3%, African American 3%, Caucasian 87%, Hispanic 1%, Native American 1%, Race unknown 5%.
Retention and Graduation: 81% freshmen return for sophomore year. 10% grads go on to further study within 1 year. 10% grads pursue arts and sciences degrees. **Faculty:** Student/faculty ratio 10:1. 43 full-time faculty, 28% hold PhDs, 7% are members of minority groups, 91% are women. 0% of classes are taught by teaching assistants.

ACADEMICS

Degrees: Associate; Bachelor's; Certificate; Master's; Post-master's certificate. **Classes:** Most classes have 10–19 students. Most lab/discussion sessions have 10–19 students. **Most popular majors:** Radiologic Technology/Science—Radiographer; Diagnostic Medical Sonography/Sonographer and Ultrasound Technician; Nursing/Registered Nurse (Rn, Asn, Bsn, Msn). **Special Study Options:** Accelerated program; Distance learning; Independent study. **Disability Services offered:** Note-taking services; Reader services; Tape

For more free content, visit PrincetonReview.com

recorders; Tutors. **Career services:** Alumni network; Alumni services; Career/job search classes.

FACILITIES
Housing: Apartments for single students; 90% of campus accessible to physically disabled.

CAMPUS LIFE
Environment: City. **Activities:** Student government. 11 registered organizations, 2 honor societies on campus. **On-Campus Highlights:** Student Center.

ADMISSIONS
Freshman Academic Profile: Average high school GPA 3.3. 11% in top 10% of high school class, 11% in top 25% of high school class, 50% in top 50% of high school class. 90% from public high schools. **Test Scores:** ACT middle 50% range 19–23. **Basis for Candidate Selection:** *Very important factors include:* rigor of secondary school record, academic GPA, standardized test scores. *Important factors include:* class rank, application essay, recommendation(s), interview, character/personal qualities. *Other factors include:* first generation, alumni/ae relation, geographical residence, state residency, racial/ethnic status, volunteer work, work experience, level of applicant's interest. **Freshman Admission Requirements:** High school diploma is required and GED is accepted. *Academic units required:* 4 English, 3 math, 2 science, 2 science labs, 2 social studies. **Freshman Admission Statistics:** 64 applied, 61% admitted, enrolled. **Transfer Admission Requirements:** High school transcript, college transcript(s), essay or personal statement, interview, statement of good standing from prior institution(s). Minimum college GPA of 2.5 required. Lowest grade transferable C. **General Admission Information:** Application fee $25. Priority deadline 1/1. Regular application deadline 3/1. Non-fall registration accepted. Admission may be deferred for a maximum of 12 months.

COSTS AND FINANCIAL AID
Annual tuition $12,840. Room and board $2,625. Required fees $600. Average book and supplies expense $1,300. **Required Forms and Deadlines:** FAFSA; Institution's own financial aid form. **Notification of Awards:** Applicants will be notified of awards on a rolling basis beginning 3/1. **Types of Aid:** *Need-based scholarships/grants:* College/university scholarship or grant aid from institutional funds; Federal Pell; Private scholarships; SEOG; State scholarships/grants. **Student Employment:** Federal Work-Study Program available. Institutional employment available. **Financial Aid Statistics:** 38% needy freshmen, 51% needy undergrads receive need-based scholarship or grant aid. 3% freshmen, 4% undergrads receive non-need-based scholarship or grant aid. 34% freshmen, 56% undergrads receive need-based self-help aid. 0% freshmen, 0% undergrads receive athletic scholarships. 85% freshmen, 69% undergrads receive any aid. **Criteria awarding aid:** *Need-based:* Minority status. *Non-need-based:* Academics, Minority status, Religious affiliation.

NEBRASKA WESLEYAN UNIVERSITY

5000 Saint Paul Ave., Lincoln, NE 68504
Phone: 402-465-2218 **Financial Aid Phone:** 402-465-2212
E-mail: admissions@nebrwesleyan.edu **CEEB Code:** 6470
Fax: 402-465-2177 **Website:** http://www.nebrwesleyan.edu **ACT Code:** 2474

This private school, affiliated with the Methodist Church, was founded in 1887. It has a 50 acre campus.

RATINGS
Admissions Selectivity Rating: 77　　**Fire Safety Rating:** 83　　**Green Rating:** 60*

STUDENTS AND FACULTY
Enrollment: 1,788. **Student Body:** 61% female, 39% male, 13% out-of-state, 1% international (20 countries represented). Asian 2%, African American 2%, Caucasian 84%, Hispanic 5%, Native American <1%, Pacific Islander <1%, Two or more races 2%, Race unknown 3%.
Retention and Graduation: 79% freshmen return for sophomore year.
Faculty: Student/faculty ratio 12:1. 106 full-time faculty, 92% hold PhDs, 2% are members of minority groups, 54% are women. 0% of classes are taught by teaching assistants.

ACADEMICS
Degrees: Bachelor's; Certificate; Master's; Post-bachelor's certificate; Post-master's certificate. **Classes:** Most classes have 10–19 students. Most lab/discussion sessions have 10–19 students. **Most popular majors:** Biology/Biological Sciences, General; Business Administration and Management, General; Psychology, General. **Special Study Options:** Double major; Dual enrollment; Independent study; Internships; Liberal arts/career combination; Student-designed major; Study abroad; Teacher certification program; Weekend college. **Disability Services offered:** Note-taking services; Reader services; Tape recorders; Tutors. **Career services:** Alumni network; Alumni services; Career assessment; Career/job search classes; Internships; Regional alumni.

FACILITIES
Housing: Apartments for single students; Coed dorms; Fraternity/sorority housing; Special housing for disabled students; Theme housing; Women's dorms. **Special Academic Facilities/Equipment:** Art galleries, observatory and planetarium, green house, laboratory theatre, herbarium, nuclear magnetic resonance laboratory. **Campus Network:** 100% of classrooms, 75% of dorms, 100% of student union, 100% of libraries, 100% of dining areas, 100% of common outdoor areas have wireless network access.

CAMPUS LIFE
Environment: City. **Activities:** Campus Ministries; Choral groups; Concert band; Dance; Drama/theater; International Student Organization; Jazz band; Literary magazine; Marching band; Model UN; Music ensembles; Musical theater; Opera; Pep band; Radio station; Student government; Student newspaper; Symphony orchestra. 80 registered organizations, 24 honor societies, 5 religious organizations, 3 fraternities, 3 sororities on campus. **Athletics (Intercollegiate):** *Men:* baseball, basketball, cross-country, football, golf, soccer, tennis, track/field (outdoor), track/field (indoor). *Women:* basketball, cross-country, golf, soccer, softball, tennis, track/field (outdoor), track/field (indoor), volleyball. **On-Campus Highlights:** Weary Center for Health and Fitness. **Environmental Initiatives:** Completed light inventory; retrofitted 80% of all lights.

ADMISSIONS
Freshman Academic Profile: Average high school GPA 3.6. 18% in top 10% of high school class, 50% in top 25% of high school class, 84% in top 50% of high school class. **Test Scores:** SAT Math middle 50% range 510–600. SAT EBRW middle 50% range 430–590. ACT middle 50% range 22–27. **Basis for Candidate Selection:** *Very important factors include:* academic GPA, standardized test scores. *Important factors include:* rigor of secondary school record, class rank, extracurricular activities, talent/ability, character/personal qualities. *Other factors include:* application essay, recommendation(s), interview, first generation, alumni/ae relation, geographical residence, state residency, racial/ethnic status, volunteer work, level of applicant's interest. **Freshman Admission Requirements:** High school diploma is required and GED is accepted. *Academic units recommended:* 4 English, 4 math, 3 science, 3 science labs, 3 foreign language, 3 social studies. **Freshman Admission Statistics:** 1,689 applied, 79% admitted, 33% enrolled. **Transfer Admission Requirements:** College transcript(s), statement of good standing from prior institution(s). Minimum college GPA of 2.0 required. Lowest grade transferable C-. **General Admission Information:** Priority deadline 5/1. Regular application deadline 8/15. Non-fall registration accepted. Admission may be deferred for a maximum of 1 year.

COSTS AND FINANCIAL AID
Annual tuition $29,200. Room and board $8,340. Required fees $600. Average book and supplies expense $1,000. **Required Forms and Deadlines:** FAFSA. **Notification of Awards:** Applicants will be notified of awards on a rolling basis beginning 2/1. **Types of Aid:** *Need-based scholarships/grants:* College/university scholarship or grant aid from institutional funds; Federal Pell; Private scholarships; SEOG; State scholarships/grants. *Loans:* Direct PLUS loans; Direct Subsidized Stafford Loans; Direct Unsubsidized Stafford Loans. **Student Employment:** Federal Work-Study Program available. Institutional employment available. **Financial Aid Statistics:** 99% needy freshmen, 98% needy undergrads receive need-based scholarship or grant aid. 19% freshmen, 12% undergrads receive non-need-based scholarship or grant aid. 76% freshmen, 82% undergrads receive need-based self-help aid. 0% freshmen, 0% undergrads receive athletic scholarships. 99% freshmen, 96% undergrads receive any aid. 78% undergrads borrow to pay for school. Average cumulative indebtedness $29,136. **Criteria awarding aid:** *Need-based:* Academics, Leadership, Minority status, Religious affiliation. *Non-need-based:* Academics, Alumni affiliation, Art, Leadership, Music/drama.

NEUMANN UNIVERSITY

Office of Admissions, Aston, PA 19014-1298
Phone: 610-558-5616 **Financial Aid Phone:** 610-558-5521
E-mail: neumann@neumann.edu **CEEB Code:** 2628
Fax: 610-361-2548 **Website:** www.neumann.edu **ACT Code:** 3649

This private school, affiliated with the Roman Catholic Church, was founded in 1965. It has a 68 acre campus.

RATINGS

Admissions Selectivity Rating: 81   **Fire Safety Rating:** 94   **Green Rating:** 63

STUDENTS AND FACULTY

Enrollment: 1,793. **Student Body:** 68% female, 32% male, 32% out-of-state, 1% international (8 countries represented). Asian 2%, African American 28%, Caucasian 56%, Hispanic 6%, Native American <1%, Pacific Islander <1%, Two or more races 3%, Race unknown 5%.
Retention and Graduation: 76% freshmen return for sophomore year. 36% freshmen graduate within 4 years. 52% freshmen graduate within 6 years. 6% grads go on to further study within 1 year. 3% grads pursue arts and sciences degrees. 0% grads pursue law degrees. 0% grads pursue business degrees. 0% grads pursue medical degrees. **Faculty:** Student/faculty ratio 14:1. 97 full-time faculty, 79% hold PhDs, 0% are members of minority groups, 59% are women. 0% of classes are taught by teaching assistants.

ACADEMICS

Degrees: Associate; Bachelor's; Doctoral degree—professional practice; Doctoral degree research/scholarship; Master's; Post-bachelor's certificate; Post-master's certificate. **Classes:** Most classes have 10–19 students. Most lab/discussion sessions have 10–19 students. **Most popular majors:** Liberal Arts and Sciences/Liberal Studies; Registered Nursing, Nursing Administration, Nursing Research and Clinical Nursing, Other; Business Administration and Management, General. **Special Study Options:** Accelerated program; Cooperative education program; Cross-registration; Distance learning; Double major; Dual enrollment; Honors program; Independent study; Internships; Liberal arts/career combination; Study abroad; Teacher certification program. **Honors programs:** The Neumann University Honors Program is based upon the belief that students who have demonstrated the motivation for learning, a desire to excel, and the capability for leadership should have the opportunity to further develop these abilities. The Honors Program is a two-tiered program consisting of a Freshman Honors Program and a University Honors Program for sophomores, juniors, and seniors. Students who complete the University Honors Program will receive a Certificate of Completion and medallion at the Academic Awards Convocation, and recognition in the Commencement Program. **Disability Services offered:** Note-taking services; Reader services; Tape recorders; Tutors. **Career services:** Alumni services; Career assessment; Internships.

FACILITIES

Housing: Apartments for single students; Coed dorms; Special housing for disabled students; 100% of campus accessible to physically disabled. **Special Academic Facilities/Equipment:** The Mirenda Center for Sport, Spirituality and Character Development; the Neumann Institute for Franciscan Studies; The Institute for Sport, Spirituality and Character Development; and the John J. Mullen Communication Center.

CAMPUS LIFE

Environment: Town. **Activities:** Campus Ministries; Choral groups; Dance; Drama/theater; Jazz band; Literary magazine; Music ensembles; Musical theater; Pep band; Radio station; Student government; Student newspaper; Symphony orchestra; Television station. 29 registered organizations, 15 honor societies on campus. **Athletics (Intercollegiate):** *Men:* baseball, basketball, cross-country, golf, ice hockey, lacrosse, soccer, tennis. *Women:* basketball, cross-country, field hockey, ice hockey, lacrosse, soccer, softball, tennis, volleyball. **On-Campus Highlights:** Knight's Café.

ADMISSIONS

Freshman Academic Profile: Average high school GPA 3.2. 76% from public high schools. **Test Scores:** SAT Math middle 50% range 460–540. SAT EBRW middle 50% range 460–550. ACT middle 50% range 16–20. **Basis for Candidate Selection:** *Very important factors include:* rigor of secondary school record, academic GPA, standardized test scores. *Important factors include:* application essay, recommendation(s), interview. *Other factors include:* extracurricular activities, talent/ability, character/personal qualities,

first generation, alumni/ae relation, volunteer work, work experience, level of applicant's interest. **Freshman Admission Requirements:** High school diploma is required and GED is accepted. *Academic units required:* 4 English, 2 math, 2 science, 1 science lab, 2 foreign language, 2 social studies, 4 academic electives. *Academic units recommended:* 4 English, 2 math, 3 science, 2 science labs, 2 foreign language, 2 social studies, 4 academic electives. **Freshman Admission Statistics:** 3,641 applied, 62% admitted, 18% enrolled. **Transfer Admission Requirements:** College transcript(s). Minimum college GPA of 2.0 required. Lowest grade transferable C. **General Admission Information:** Regular application deadline 8/30. Non-fall registration accepted. Admission may be deferred for a maximum of 2 semesters.

COSTS AND FINANCIAL AID

Annual tuition $31,500. Room and board $13,680. Required fees $1,460. Average book and supplies expense $1,488. **Required Forms and Deadlines:** FAFSA. **Notification of Awards:** Applicants will be notified of awards on a rolling basis beginning 3/1. **Types of Aid:** *Need-based scholarships/grants:* College/university scholarship or grant aid from institutional funds; Federal Pell; Private scholarships; SEOG; State scholarships/grants. *Loans:* Direct PLUS loans; Direct Subsidized Stafford Loans; Direct Unsubsidized Stafford Loans. **Student Employment:** Federal Work-Study Program available. **Financial Aid Statistics:** 100% needy freshmen, 99% needy undergrads receive need-based scholarship or grant aid. 0% freshmen, 0% undergrads receive non-need-based scholarship or grant aid. 88% freshmen, 88% undergrads receive need-based self-help aid. 0% freshmen, 0% undergrads receive athletic scholarships. 99% freshmen, 98% undergrads receive any aid. 88% undergrads borrow to pay for school. Average cumulative indebtedness $45,952. **Criteria awarding aid:** *Need-based:* Academics. *Non-need-based:* Academics.

NEUMONT COLLEGE

143 South Main Street, Salt Lake City, UT 84111
Phone: 888-638-6668 **Financial Aid Phone:** 801 302 2873
E-mail: admissions@neumont.edu
Fax: 801-302-2811 **Website:** www.neumont.edu

This proprietary school was founded in 2003.

RATINGS

Admissions Selectivity Rating: 76   **Fire Safety Rating:** 60*   **Green Rating:** 60*

STUDENTS AND FACULTY

Enrollment: 429. **Student Body:** 10% female, 90% male, 88% out-of-state, 0% international. Asian 3%, African American 5%, Caucasian 49%, Hispanic 10%, Native American 1%, Pacific Islander <1%, Two or more races 6%, Race unknown 25%.
Retention and Graduation: 85% freshmen return for sophomore year.
Faculty: Student/faculty ratio 21:1. 15 full-time faculty, 13% hold PhDs, 7% are members of minority groups, 0% are women.

ACADEMICS

Degrees: Bachelor's; Master's. **Special Study Options:** Accelerated program; Cooperative education program; Internships. **Disability Services offered:** Note-taking services; Reader services; Tape recorders; Tutors. **Career services:** Alumni network; Career assessment; Career/job search classes; Internships.

FACILITIES

Housing: Apartments for single students; Men's dorms; Women's dorms; 100% of campus accessible to physically disabled.

CAMPUS LIFE

Environment: Metropolis. **Activities:** Student government. 13 registered organizations on campus.

ADMISSIONS

Freshman Academic Profile: Average high school GPA 3.2. **Test Scores:** SAT Math middle 50% range 455–640. SAT EBRW middle 50% range 445–615. ACT middle 50% range 20–29. **Basis for Candidate Selection:** *Very important factors include:* academic GPA, application essay, standardized test scores. *Important factors include:* interview, extracurricular activities, talent/ability, character/personal qualities, volunteer work, work experience, level of applicant's interest. *Other factors include:* rigor of secondary school record, class rank, recommendation(s). **Freshman Admission Requirements:** High school diploma is required and GED is accepted. **Freshman Admission Statistics:**

727 applied, 83% admitted, 28% enrolled. **General Admission Information:** Application fee $35. Non-fall registration accepted. Admission may be deferred for a maximum of 1 year.

COSTS AND FINANCIAL AID

Annual tuition $22,950. Room and board $5,670. Required fees $1,500. Average book and supplies expense $1,200. **Required Forms and Deadlines:** FAFSA; Institution's own financial aid form. **Notification of Awards:** Applicants will be notified of awards on a rolling basis beginning 11/23. **Types of Aid:** *Need-based scholarships/grants:* College/university scholarship or grant aid from institutional funds; Federal Pell; Private scholarships; SEOG. *Loans:* Direct PLUS loans; Direct Subsidized Stafford Loans; Direct Unsubsidized Stafford Loans. **Financial Aid Statistics:** 96% needy freshmen, 88% needy undergrads receive need-based scholarship or grant aid. 79% freshmen, 57% undergrads receive non-need-based scholarship or grant aid. 0% freshmen, 0% undergrads receive need-based self-help aid. 0% freshmen, 0% undergrads receive athletic scholarships. 91% undergrads borrow to pay for school. Average cumulative indebtedness $39,623. **Criteria awarding aid:** *Need-based:* Academics. *Non-need-based:* Academics, Job skills, Leadership, State/district residency.

NEW COLLEGE OF FLORIDA

5800 Bay Shore Rd, Sarasota, FL 34243-2109
Phone: 941-487-5000 **Financial Aid Phone:** 941-487-5000
E-mail: admissions@ncf.edu **CEEB Code:** 39574
Fax: 941-487-5001 **Website:** www.ncf.edu **ACT Code:** 0750

This public school was founded in 1960. It has a 118.6 acre campus.

RATINGS

Admissions Selectivity Rating: 83   **Fire Safety Rating:** 87   **Green Rating:** 71

STUDENTS AND FACULTY

Enrollment: 702. **Student Body:** 63% female, 37% male, 17% out-of-state, 2% international (14 countries represented). Asian 3%, African American 3%, Caucasian 69%, Hispanic 18%, Native American 0%, Pacific Islander 0%, Two or more races 4%, Race unknown 1%.
Retention and Graduation: 86% freshmen return for sophomore year. 54% freshmen graduate within 4 years. 64% freshmen graduate within 6 years. 34% grads go on to further study within 1 year. 29% grads pursue arts and sciences degrees. 0% grads pursue law degrees. 0% grads pursue business degrees. 0% grads pursue medical degrees. **Faculty:** Student/faculty ratio 7:1. 98 full-time faculty, 98% hold PhDs, 19% are members of minority groups, 53% are women. 0% of classes are taught by teaching assistants.

ACADEMICS

Degrees: Bachelor's; Master's. **Classes:** Most classes have 10–19 students. **Most popular majors:** Psychology; Computer Science; Political Science and Government. **Special Study Options:** Accelerated program; Cross-registration; Double major; Exchange student program (domestic); Honors program; Independent study; Internships; Student-designed major; Study abroad. **Honors programs:** New College of Florida is the state's officially-designated "honors college for the liberal arts." **Disability Services offered:** Note-taking services; Reader services; Tape recorders. **Career services:** Alumni network; Alumni services; Career assessment; Career/job search classes; Internships; Regional alumni.

FACILITIES

Housing: Apartments for single students; Coed dorms; Special housing for disabled students; Special housing for international students; Theme housing; Wellness housing; 80% of campus accessible to physically disabled. **Special Academic Facilities/Equipment:** Anthropology and psychology labs. Electronic music lab. Individual studio space for senior art students. Marine biology research center with Living Ecosystem Teaching and Research Aquarium, wet lab, and seawater on tap. NMR, scanning electron microscope, inert atmosphere glovebox, transparent fume hoods, greenhouse.

CAMPUS LIFE

Environment: Town. **Activities:** Campus Ministries; Choral groups; Dance; Drama/theater; International Student Organization; Jazz band;

Literary magazine; Music ensembles; Musical theater; Radio station; Student government; Student newspaper; Student-run film society. 53 registered organizations, 1 honor society, 3 religious organizations on campus. **Athletics (Intercollegiate):** *Men:* sailing. *Women:* sailing. **On-Campus Highlights:** Pritzker Marine Biology Research Center. **Environmental Initiatives:** We've had an environmental studies program since 1972.

ADMISSIONS

Freshman Academic Profile: Average high school GPA 3.9. 22% in top 10% of high school class, 50% in top 25% of high school class, 88% in top 50% of high school class. 75% from public high schools. **Test Scores:** SAT Math middle 50% range 560–660. SAT EBRW middle 50% range 620–700. ACT middle 50% range 25–31. **Basis for Candidate Selection:** *Very important factors include:* rigor of secondary school record, academic GPA, application essay. *Important factors include:* class rank, standardized test scores, recommendation(s), extracurricular activities, character/personal qualities. *Other factors include:* talent/ability, first generation, alumni/ae relation, geographical residence, state residency. **Freshman Admission Requirements:** High school diploma is required and GED is accepted. *Academic units required:* 4 English, 4 math, 3 science, 2 science labs, 2 foreign language, 3 social studies, 2 academic electives. *Academic units recommended:* 4 English, 4 math, 4 science, 2 science labs, 4 foreign language, 4 social studies, 4 academic electives. **Freshman Admission Statistics:** 1,226 applied, 73% admitted, 16% enrolled. **Transfer Admission Requirements:** College transcript(s), essay or personal statement. Minimum college GPA of 2.0 required. Lowest grade transferable C. **General Admission Information:** Application fee $30. Priority deadline 11/1. Regular application deadline 4/15. Admission may be deferred for a maximum of 1 year.

COSTS AND FINANCIAL AID

Annual in-state tuition $6,916. Annual out-of-state tuition $29,944. Room and board $9,529. Average book and supplies expense $1,200. **Required Forms and Deadlines:** FAFSA. **Notification of Awards:** Applicants will be notified of awards on a rolling basis beginning 2/1. **Types of Aid:** *Need-based scholarships/grants:* College/university scholarship or grant aid from institutional funds; Federal Pell; Private scholarships; SEOG; State scholarships/grants. *Loans:* Direct PLUS loans; Direct Subsidized Stafford Loans; Direct Unsubsidized Stafford Loans. **Student Employment:** Federal Work-Study Program available. Institutional employment available. **Financial Aid Statistics:** 96% needy freshmen, 94% needy undergrads receive need-based scholarship or grant aid. 14% freshmen, 16% undergrads receive non-need-based scholarship or grant aid. 80% freshmen, 73% undergrads receive need-based self-help aid. 0% freshmen, 0% undergrads receive athletic scholarships. 99% freshmen, 96% undergrads receive any aid. 42% undergrads borrow to pay for school. Average cumulative indebtedness $18,953. **Criteria awarding aid:** *Need-based:* Academics. *Non-need-based:* Academics, State/district residency.

NEW ENGLAND COLLEGE

102 Bridge Street, Henniker, NH 03242
Phone: 603-428-2223 **Financial Aid Phone:** 603-428-2226
E-mail: admission@nec.edu **CEEB Code:** 3657
Fax: 603-428-3155 **Website:** www.nec.edu **ACT Code:** 2513

This private school was founded in 1946. It has a 225 acre campus.

RATINGS

Admissions Selectivity Rating: 71   **Fire Safety Rating:** 98   **Green Rating:** 72

STUDENTS AND FACULTY

Enrollment: 1,835. **Student Body:** 58% female, 42% male, 82% out-of-state, 4% international. Asian 2%, African American 24%, Caucasian 51%, Hispanic 8%, Native American 1%, Pacific Islander <1%, Two or more races 4%, Race unknown 6%.
Retention and Graduation: 56% freshmen return for sophomore year. 27% freshmen graduate within 4 years. 36% freshmen graduate within 6 years. 18% grads go on to further study within 1 year. 6% grads pursue arts and sciences degrees. 0% grads pursue law degrees. 6% grads pursue business degrees. 0% grads pursue medical degrees. **Faculty:** Student/faculty ratio 13:1. 39 full-time faculty, 64% hold PhDs, 8% are members of minority groups, 56% are women. 0% of classes are taught by teaching assistants.

ACADEMICS

Degrees: Associate; Bachelor's; Master's; Post-master's certificate. **Classes:** Most classes have 10–19 students. Most lab/discussion sessions have 10–19 students.

Most popular majors: Elementary Education and Teaching; Sport and Fitness Administration/Management; Business/Commerce, General. **Special Study Options:** Accelerated program; Cross-registration; Distance learning; Double major; English as a Second Language (ESL); External degree program; Honors program; Independent study; Internships; Liberal arts/career combination; Student-designed major; Study abroad; Teacher certification program. **Honors programs:** Honors Program. **Disability Services offered:** Note-taking services; Tape recorders; Tutors. **Career services:** Alumni network; Career assessment; Career/job search classes; Internships; Regional alumni.

FACILITIES

Housing: Apartments for single students; Coed dorms; Theme housing; Wellness housing; 75% of campus accessible to physically disabled. **Special Academic Facilities/Equipment:** New England Art Gallery; Graphic Design and Imaging Lab; Center for Educational Innovation; High Tech Building; John Lyons Center (Business); The Putnam Fine Arts Center.

CAMPUS LIFE

Environment: Rural. **Activities:** Drama/theater; International Student Organization; Literary magazine; Radio station; Student government; Student newspaper. 26 registered organizations, 3 honor societies, 1 religious organization, 1 sorority on campus. **Athletics (Intercollegiate):** *Men:* baseball, basketball, cross-country, ice hockey, lacrosse, soccer. *Women:* basketball, cheerleading, cross-country, field hockey, ice hockey, lacrosse, soccer, softball. **On-Campus Highlights:** Simon Center (Student Center). **Environmental Initiatives:** Addition of sustainability to the mission statement. A complete overhaul of lighting at the College for energy efficiency. Completion of a campus wide facilities plan.

ADMISSIONS

Freshman Academic Profile: Average high school GPA 2.9. 10% in top 10% of high school class, 34% in top 25% of high school class, 58% in top 50% of high school class. 89% from public high schools. **Test Scores:** SAT Math middle 50% range 420–530. SAT EBRW middle 50% range 430–550. **Basis for Candidate Selection:** *Very important factors include:* academic GPA. *Important factors include:* volunteer work. *Other factors include:* rigor of secondary school record, class rank, application essay, recommendation(s), extracurricular activities, talent/ability, character/personal qualities, alumni/ae relation. **Freshman Admission Requirements:** High school diploma is required and GED is accepted. *Academic units recommended:* 4 English, 3 math, 3 science, 1 science lab, 3 social studies. **Freshman Admission Statistics:** 8,616 applied, 100% admitted, 5% enrolled. **Transfer Admission Requirements:** High school transcript, college transcript(s), essay or personal statement, statement of good standing from prior institution(s). Lowest grade transferable C-. **General Admission Information:** Non-fall registration accepted. Admission may be deferred for a maximum of 1 year.

COSTS AND FINANCIAL AID

Annual tuition $36,754. Room and board $15,250. Required fees $1,160. Average book and supplies expense $1,000. **Required Forms and Deadlines:** CSS/Financial Aid PROFILE; FAFSA. **Notification of Awards:** Applicants will be notified of awards on a rolling basis beginning 2/1. **Types of Aid:** *Need-based scholarships/grants:* College/university scholarship or grant aid from institutional funds; Federal Pell; Private scholarships; SEOG; State scholarships/grants. *Loans:* Direct PLUS loans; Direct Subsidized Stafford Loans; Direct Unsubsidized Stafford Loans. **Student Employment:** Federal Work-Study Program available. Institutional employment available. **Financial Aid Statistics:** 98% needy freshmen, 91% needy undergrads receive need-based scholarship or grant aid. 5% freshmen, 4% undergrads receive non-need-based scholarship or grant aid. 90% freshmen, 91% undergrads receive need-based self-help aid. 0% freshmen, 0% undergrads receive athletic scholarships. 97% freshmen, 89% undergrads receive any aid. 85% undergrads borrow to pay for school. Average cumulative indebtedness $37,450. **Criteria awarding aid:** *Need-based:* Academics, Alumni affiliation, Art, Job skills, Leadership, Music/drama. *Non-need-based:* Academics, Alumni affiliation, Art, Job skills, Leadership, Music/drama.

NEW ENGLAND INSTITUTE OF TECHNOLOGY

One New England Tech Blvd., East Greenwich, RI 02818
Phone: 401-467-7744 **Financial Aid Phone:** 401-739-5000
E-mail: NEITAdmissions@neit.edu
Fax: 401-886-0868 **Website:** www.neit.edu **ACT Code:** 3803

This private school was founded in 1940. It has a 225 acre campus.

RATINGS

Admissions Selectivity Rating: 61   **Fire Safety Rating:** 60*   **Green Rating:** 66

STUDENTS AND FACULTY

Enrollment: 2,853. **Student Body:** 33% female, 67% male, 53% out-of-state, 3% international (19 countries represented). Asian 2%, African American 5%, Caucasian 62%, Hispanic 12%, Native American 1%, Pacific Islander <1%, Two or more races 2%, Race unknown 12%.
Faculty: Student/faculty ratio 13:1. 140 full-time faculty, 21% hold PhDs, 0% are members of minority groups, 0% are women. 0% of classes are taught by teaching assistants.

ACADEMICS

Degrees: Associate; Bachelor's; Master's. **Special Study Options:** Accelerated program; Distance learning; Double major; Dual enrollment; English as a Second Language (ESL); Internships; Student-designed major; Weekend college. **Career services:** Alumni services; Career assessment; Career/job search classes; Internships.

FACILITIES

Housing: 100% of campus accessible to physically disabled.

CAMPUS LIFE

Environment: Town. 20 registered organizations, 2 honor societies on campus. **On-Campus Highlights:** New Residence Hall. **Environmental Initiatives:** Recycling.

ADMISSIONS

Basis for Candidate Selection: *Very important factors include:* interview, level of applicant's interest. **Freshman Admission Requirements:** High school diploma is required and GED is accepted. **General Admission Information:** Application fee $25. Non-fall registration accepted.

COSTS AND FINANCIAL AID

Annual tuition $27,000. Required fees $1,740. **Required Forms and Deadlines:** FAFSA. **Types of Aid:** *Need-based scholarships/grants:* College/university scholarship or grant aid from institutional funds; Federal Pell; Private scholarships; SEOG; State scholarships/grants. *Loans:* Direct PLUS loans; Direct Subsidized Stafford Loans; Direct Unsubsidized Stafford Loans. **Student Employment:** Federal Work-Study Program available. **Financial Aid Statistics:** 95% freshmen, 69% undergrads receive any aid.

NEW HOPE CHRISTIAN COLLEGE

2155 Bailey Hill Road, Eugene, OR 97405-1194
Phone: 800-322-2638 **Financial Aid Phone:** 800-322-2638
E-mail: admissions@newhope.edu **CEEB Code:** 4274
Fax: 541-343-5801 **Website:** http://www.newhope.edu **ACT Code:** 3468

This private school was founded in 1925. It has a 33 acre campus.

RATINGS

Admissions Selectivity Rating: 61   **Fire Safety Rating:** 83   **Green Rating:** 60*

STUDENTS AND FACULTY

Enrollment: 162. **Student Body:** 49% female, 51% male, 54% out-of-state, 2% international (5 countries represented). Asian 4%, African American 4%, Caucasian 61%, Hispanic 9%, Native American 1%, Pacific Islander 4%, Two or more races 9%, Race unknown 6%.
Retention and Graduation: 100% freshmen return for sophomore year. 35% grads go on to further study within 1 year. **Faculty:** Student/faculty ratio 10:1. 10 full-time faculty, 30% hold PhDs, 20% are members of minority groups, 40% are women. 0% of classes are taught by teaching assistants.

ACADEMICS

Degrees: Associate; Bachelor's; Certificate; Master's. **Classes:** Most classes have 10–19 students. Most lab/discussion sessions have 10–19 students. **Most popular majors:** Bible/Biblical Studies; Pastoral Studies/Counseling; Youth Ministry. **Special Study Options:** Cooperative education program; Distance learning; Double major; Dual enrollment; Independent study; Internships; Liberal arts/career combination.

FACILITIES

Housing: Apartments for married students; Apartments for single students; Men's dorms; Women's dorms; 75% of campus accessible to physically disabled. **Special Academic Facilities/Equipment:** Music lab, computer lab. **Campus Network:** 100% of classrooms, 100% of dorms, 100% of student union, 100% of libraries, 100% of dining areas, 100% of common outdoor areas have wireless network access.

CAMPUS LIFE

Environment: City. **Activities:** Choral groups; Drama/theater; Music ensembles; Student government; Yearbook. **Athletics (Intercollegiate):** *Men:* basketball, soccer. *Women:* soccer, volleyball. **On-Campus Highlights:** Student Center.

ADMISSIONS

Freshman Academic Profile: 90% from public high schools. **Basis for Candidate Selection:** *Very important factors include:* application essay, recommendation(s), character/personal qualities, religious affiliation/commitment. *Important factors include:* rigor of secondary school record, academic GPA. *Other factors include:* class rank, standardized test scores, extracurricular activities, talent/ability, volunteer work, work experience, level of applicant's interest. **Freshman Admission Requirements:** High school diploma is required and GED is accepted. **Freshman Admission Statistics:** 92 applied, 100% admitted, enrolled. **Transfer Admission Requirements:** College transcript(s), essay or personal statement. Minimum college GPA of 2.0 required. Lowest grade transferable C. **General Admission Information:** Application fee $50. Regular application deadline 9/1. Non-fall registration accepted. Admission may be deferred for a maximum of 24 months.

COSTS AND FINANCIAL AID

Annual tuition $16,500. Room and board $6,100. Required fees $801. Average book and supplies expense $800. **Required Forms and Deadlines:** FAFSA. **Notification of Awards:** Applicants will be notified of awards on a rolling basis beginning 7/15. **Types of Aid:** *Need-based scholarships/grants:* College/university scholarship or grant aid from institutional funds; Federal Pell; SEOG. *Loans:* Direct PLUS loans; Direct Subsidized Stafford Loans; Direct Unsubsidized Stafford Loans. **Financial Aid Statistics:** 100% needy freshmen, 100% needy undergrads receive need-based scholarship or grant aid. 16% freshmen, 13% undergrads receive non-need-based scholarship or grant aid. 100% freshmen, 100% undergrads receive need-based self-help aid. 36% freshmen, 49% undergrads receive athletic scholarships. **Criteria awarding aid:** *Need-based:* Academics, Leadership, Music/drama, Religious affiliation. *Non-need-based:* Academics, Alumni affiliation, Athletics, Leadership, Music/drama.

NEW JERSEY CITY UNIVERSITY

2039 Kennedy Boulevard, Jersey City, NJ 07305
Financial Aid Phone: 201-200-3378
CEEB Code: 2316
Website: www.njcu.edu

This public school was founded in 1927. It has a 17 acre campus.

RATINGS

Admissions Selectivity Rating: 73   **Fire Safety Rating:** 85   **Green Rating:** 61

STUDENTS AND FACULTY

Enrollment: 5,962. **Student Body:** 58% female, 42% male, 1% out-of-state, 1% international (15 countries represented). Asian 8%, African American 24%, Caucasian 19%, Hispanic 39%, Native American <1%, Pacific Islander <1%, Two or more races 3%, Race unknown 5%.
Retention and Graduation: 73% freshmen return for sophomore year. 13% freshmen graduate within 4 years. 41% freshmen graduate within 6 years.
Faculty: Student/faculty ratio 14:1. 249 full-time faculty, 76% hold PhDs, 39% are members of minority groups, 48% are women. 0% of classes are taught by teaching assistants.

ACADEMICS

Degrees: Bachelor's; Certificate; Diploma; Doctoral degree—other; Master's; Post-bachelor's certificate; Post-master's certificate. **Classes:** Most classes have 20–29 students. **Most popular majors:** Registered Nursing/Registered Nurse; Corrections and Criminal Justice, Other; Psychology, General. **Special Study Options:** Distance learning; Double major; English as a Second Language (ESL); Honors program; Independent study; Internships; Study abroad; Teacher certification program. **Combined degree programs:** BA/MA. **Disability Services offered:** Note-taking services; Reader services; Tape recorders; Tutors. **Career services:** Career assessment; Internships.

FACILITIES

Housing: Coed dorms; 90% of campus accessible to physically disabled. **Special Academic Facilities/Equipment:** NJCU is located on a 51.46-acre site in Jersey City. The University's 27 buildings house a total of 180 classrooms, including 46 labs, 19 studios, three performance art spaces, three art galleries, two athletic training facilities, a 25-meter swimming pool, two dance studios, a media arts facility, two auditoriums, The Peter G. Mangin Real Estate Institute, and Margaret Williams Theatre. NJCU also maintains the A. Harry Moore School for Special Education and the University Academy Charter High School.

CAMPUS LIFE

Environment: City. **Activities:** Concert band; Drama/theater; Jazz band; Student government; Symphony orchestra; Yearbook. 23 registered organizations on campus. **Athletics (Intercollegiate):** *Men:* baseball, basketball, cross-country, soccer, track/field (outdoor), track/field (indoor), volleyball. *Women:* basketball, bowling, cross-country, soccer, softball, track/field (outdoor), track/field (indoor), volleyball. **On-Campus Highlights:** Student Union Building.

ADMISSIONS

Freshman Academic Profile: Average high school GPA 3.0. 15% in top 10% of high school class, 37% in top 25% of high school class, 63% in top 50% of high school class. **Test Scores:** SAT Math middle 50% range 430–540. SAT EBRW middle 50% range 430–540. **Basis for Candidate Selection:** *Very important factors include:* rigor of secondary school record, class rank, academic GPA. *Important factors include:* extracurricular activities. **Freshman Admission Requirements:** High school diploma is required and GED is accepted. *Academic units required:* 4 English, 4 math, 4 science, 2 science labs, 4 social studies. *Academic units recommended:* 4 English, 4 math, 4 science, 3 science labs, 2 foreign language, 4 social studies. **Freshman Admission Statistics:** 4,867 applied, 95% admitted, 22% enrolled. **Transfer Admission Requirements:** College transcript(s). Minimum college GPA of 2.0 required. Lowest grade transferable C. **General Admission Information:** Application fee $55. Non-fall registration accepted.

COSTS AND FINANCIAL AID

Annual in-state tuition $12,413. Annual out-of-state tuition $22,221. Room and board $14,574. Required fees $165. Average book and supplies expense $1,200. **Required Forms and Deadlines:** FAFSA. **Notification of Awards:** Applicants will be notified of awards on or about 5/15. **Types of Aid:** *Need-based scholarships/grants:* College/university scholarship or grant aid from institutional funds; Federal Pell. *Loans:* Direct PLUS loans; Direct Subsidized Stafford Loans; Direct Unsubsidized Stafford Loans. **Student Employment:** Federal Work-Study Program available. Institutional employment available. **Financial Aid Statistics:** 84% needy freshmen, 81% needy undergrads receive need-based scholarship or grant aid. 57% freshmen, 29% undergrads receive non-need-based scholarship or grant aid. 42% freshmen, 52% undergrads receive need-based self-help aid. 0% freshmen, 0% undergrads receive athletic scholarships. 80% undergrads receive any aid. 63% undergrads borrow to pay for school. Average cumulative indebtedness $25,463. **Criteria awarding aid:** *Need-based:* Academics. *Non-need-based:* Academics.

NEW JERSEY INSTITUTE OF TECHNOLOGY

Office of University Admissions, Newark, NJ 07102
Phone: 973-596-3300 **Financial Aid Phone:** 973-596-3479
E-mail: admissions@njit.edu **CEEB Code:** 2580
Fax: 973-596-3300 **Website:** www.njit.edu **ACT Code:** 2513

This public school was founded in 1881. It has a 48 acre campus.

RATINGS

Admissions Selectivity Rating: 85   **Fire Safety Rating:** 99   **Green Rating:** 79

STUDENTS AND FACULTY

Enrollment: 8,126. **Student Body:** 24% female, 76% male, 4% out-of-state, 6% international (93 countries represented). Asian 23%, African American 9%, Caucasian 34%, Hispanic 22%, Native American <1%, Pacific Islander <1%, Two or more races 3%, Race unknown 3%.
Retention and Graduation: 88% freshmen return for sophomore year. 37% freshmen graduate within 4 years. 67% freshmen graduate within 6 years.
Faculty: Student/faculty ratio 16:1. 462 full-time faculty, 93% hold PhDs, 33% are members of minority groups, 23% are women. 0% of classes are taught by teaching assistants.

ACADEMICS

Degrees: Bachelor's; Doctoral degree research/scholarship; Master's; Post-bachelor's certificate. **Classes:** Most classes have 20–29 students. **Most popular majors:** Computer and Information Sciences, General; Computer Engineering, General; ENGINEERING/ENGINEERING-RELATED TECHNOLOGIES/TECHNICIANS. **Special Study Options:** Accelerated program; Cooperative education program; Cross-registration; Distance learning; Double major; Dual enrollment; English as a Second Language (ESL); Honors program; Independent study; Internships; Study abroad; Teacher certification program; Weekend college. **Honors programs:** The Albert Dorman Honors College at the New Jersey Institute of Technology (NJIT) enrolls over 500 exceptional students who excel in the fields of engineering, architecture, computing sciences, management, and the sciences. **Combined degree programs:** BA/MA; BA/MD. **Disability Services offered:** Note-taking services; Reader services; Tape recorders; Tutors. **Career services:** Alumni network; Alumni services; Career assessment; Career/job search classes; Internships; Regional alumni.

FACILITIES

Housing: Coed dorms; Fraternity/sorority housing; 100% of campus accessible to physically disabled. **Special Academic Facilities/Equipment:** New Jersey Literary Hall of Fame and more than 50 research centers and sponsored research laboratories, including computer chip manufacturing center, manufacturing systems center, and many others.

CAMPUS LIFE

Environment: Metropolis. **Activities:** Choral groups; Concert band; Dance; Drama/theater; International Student Organization; Jazz band; Marching band; Music ensembles; Musical theater; Pep band; Radio station; Student government; Student newspaper; Student-run film society; Symphony orchestra; Yearbook. 91 registered organizations, 9 honor societies, 8 religious organizations, 18 fraternities, 6 sororities on campus. **Athletics (Intercollegiate): Men:** baseball, basketball, cheerleading, cross-country, fencing, soccer, swimming, tennis, track/field (outdoor), track/field (indoor), volleyball. *Women:* basketball, cheerleading, cross-country, fencing, soccer, swimming, tennis, track/field (outdoor), track/field (indoor), volleyball. **On-Campus Highlights:** Campus Center. **Environmental Initiatives:** Recycling.

ADMISSIONS

Freshman Academic Profile: Average high school GPA 3.6. 31% in top 10% of high school class, 57% in top 25% of high school class, 85% in top 50% of high school class. 89% from public high schools. **Test Scores:** SAT Math middle 50% range 610–710. SAT EBRW middle 50% range 580–670. ACT middle 50% range 24–31. **Basis for Candidate Selection:** *Very important factors include:* rigor of secondary school record, class rank, standardized test scores. *Important factors include:* academic GPA. *Other factors include:* application essay, recommendation(s), interview, extracurricular activities, talent/ability, character/personal qualities, alumni/ae relation, geographical residence, state residency, racial/ethnic status, volunteer work, work experience, level of applicant's

interest. **Freshman Admission Requirements:** High school diploma is required and GED is accepted. *Academic units required:* 4 English, 4 math, 2 science, 2 science labs. *Academic units recommended:* 2 foreign language, 1 social studies, 1 history, 2 academic electives. **Freshman Admission Statistics:** 8,201 applied, 73% admitted, 23% enrolled. **Transfer Admission Requirements:** College transcript(s). Minimum college GPA of 2.0 required. Lowest grade transferable C. **General Admission Information:** Application fee $75. Priority deadline 12/15. Regular application deadline 3/1. Admission may be deferred for a maximum of one semester.

COSTS AND FINANCIAL AID

Annual in-state tuition $14,448. Annual out-of-state tuition $30,160. Room and board $13,900. Required fees $3,226. Average book and supplies expense $2,900. **Required Forms and Deadlines:** FAFSA; State aid form. **Notification of Awards:** Applicants will be notified of awards on a rolling basis beginning 11/15. **Types of Aid:** *Need-based scholarships/grants:* College/university scholarship or grant aid from institutional funds; Federal Pell; Private scholarships; SEOG; State scholarships/grants. *Loans:* Direct PLUS loans; Direct Subsidized Stafford Loans; Direct Unsubsidized Stafford Loans. **Student Employment:** Federal Work-Study Program available. Institutional employment available. **Financial Aid Statistics:** 95% needy freshmen, 96% needy undergrads receive need-based scholarship or grant aid. 10% freshmen, 4% undergrads receive non-need-based scholarship or grant aid. 53% freshmen, 69% undergrads receive need-based self-help aid. 2% freshmen, 2% undergrads receive athletic scholarships. 82% freshmen, 63% undergrads receive any aid. 58% undergrads borrow to pay for school. Average cumulative indebtedness $38,718. **Criteria awarding aid:** *Need-based:* Academics, Alumni affiliation, Art, Athletics, Job skills, Leadership, Minority status, Music/drama, Religious affiliation. *Non-need-based:* Academics, Alumni affiliation, Art, Athletics, Job skills, Leadership, Minority status, Music/drama, Religious affiliation, State/district residency.

NEW MEXICO INSTITUTE OF MINING AND TECHNOLOGY

Campus Station, Socorro, NM 87801
Phone: 575-835-5424 **Financial Aid Phone:** 575-835-5333
E-mail: admission@nmt.edu **CEEB Code:** 4533
Fax: 575-835-5989 **Website:** www.nmt.edu **ACT Code:** 2642

This public school was founded in 1889. It has a 320 acre campus.

RATINGS

Admissions Selectivity Rating: 97   **Fire Safety Rating:** 60*   **Green Rating:** 60*

STUDENTS AND FACULTY

Enrollment: 1,333. **Student Body:** 28% female, 72% male, 10% out-of-state, 2% international. Asian 3%, African American 2%, Caucasian 52%, Hispanic 32%, Native American 4%, Pacific Islander <1%, Two or more races 4%, Race unknown 1%.
Retention and Graduation: 75% freshmen return for sophomore year. 20% freshmen graduate within 4 years. 47% freshmen graduate within 6 years.
Faculty: Student/faculty ratio 11:1. 129 full-time faculty, 0% hold PhDs, 29% are members of minority groups, 22% are women.

ACADEMICS

Degrees: Bachelor's; Doctoral degree research/scholarship; Master's; Post-bachelor's certificate; Terminal Associate. **Classes:** Most classes have 10–19 students. Most lab/discussion sessions have 10–19 students. **Most popular majors:** Computer and Information Sciences, General; Electrical and Electronics Engineering; Mechanical Engineering. **Special Study Options:** Accelerated program; Cooperative education program; Distance learning; Double major; Dual enrollment; Exchange student program (domestic); Independent study; Internships; Student-designed major; Teacher certification program. **Disability Services offered:** Note-taking services; Reader services; Tape recorders; Tutors. **Career services:** Career assessment; Career/job search classes; Internships.

FACILITIES

Housing: Apartments for married students; Apartments for single students; Coed dorms; Men's dorms; Women's dorms. **Special Academic Facilities/Equipment:** Mineral museum, observatory, radio telescope, seismic observatory and library, explosives labs.

CAMPUS LIFE

Environment: Village. **Activities:** Choral groups; Concert band; Dance; Drama/theater; International Student Organization; Jazz band; Music ensembles; Musical theater; Radio station; Student government; Student newspaper. 60 registered organizations, 7 honor societies, 3 religious organizations on campus. **On-Campus Highlights:** Fidel Student Center.

ADMISSIONS

Freshman Academic Profile: Average high school GPA 3.8. 40% in top 10% of high school class, 59% in top 25% of high school class, 92% in top 50% of high school class. 80% from public high schools. **Test Scores:** SAT Math middle 50% range 620–710. SAT EBRW middle 50% range 590–690. ACT middle 50% range 23–29. **Basis for Candidate Selection:** *Very important factors include:* rigor of secondary school record, academic GPA, standardized test scores. *Other factors include:* class rank, extracurricular activities, talent/ability. **Freshman Admission Requirements:** High school diploma is required and GED is accepted. *Academic units required:* 4 English, 3 math, 2 science, 2 science labs, 2 social studies, 1 history, 3 academic electives. *Academic units recommended:* 4 English, 4 math, 4 science, 3 science labs, 2 foreign language, 3 social studies, 1 history. **Freshman Admission Statistics:** 1,740 applied, 23% admitted, 75% enrolled. **Transfer Admission Requirements:** High school transcript, college transcript(s), statement of good standing from prior institution(s). Minimum college GPA of 2.0 required. Lowest grade transferable D. **General Admission Information:** Application fee $15. Priority deadline 3/1. Regular application deadline 8/1. Non-fall registration accepted. Admission may be deferred for a maximum of 1 year.

COSTS AND FINANCIAL AID

Annual in-state tuition $6,826. Annual out-of-state tuition $22,194. Room and board $8,624. Required fees $1,330. Average book and supplies expense $1,150. **Required Forms and Deadlines:** FAFSA. **Notification of Awards:** Applicants will be notified of awards on a rolling basis beginning 5/1. **Types of Aid:** *Need-based scholarships/grants:* College/university scholarship or grant aid from institutional funds; Federal Pell; Private scholarships; SEOG; State scholarships/grants. *Loans:* Direct PLUS loans; Direct Subsidized Stafford Loans; Direct Unsubsidized Stafford Loans. **Student Employment:** Federal Work-Study Program available. Institutional employment available. **Financial Aid Statistics:** 54% needy freshmen, 62% needy undergrads receive need-based scholarship or grant aid. 94% freshmen, 72% undergrads receive non-need-based scholarship or grant aid. 56% freshmen, 61% undergrads receive need-based self-help aid. 0% freshmen, 0% undergrads receive athletic scholarships. 49% undergrads borrow to pay for school. Average cumulative indebtedness $24,969. **Criteria awarding aid:** *Need-based:* Minority status. *Non-need-based:* Academics, Alumni affiliation, Minority status, State/district residency.

NEW MEXICO STATE UNIVERSITY

PO Box 30001, Las Cruces, NM 88003-8001
Phone: 575-646-3121 **Financial Aid Phone:** 575-646-4105
E-mail: admissions@nmsu.edu **CEEB Code:** 4531
Fax: 575-646-6330 **Website:** www.nmsu.edu **ACT Code:** 2638

This public school was founded in 1888. It has a 900 acre campus.

RATINGS

Admissions Selectivity Rating: 86   **Fire Safety Rating:** 65   **Green Rating:** 60*

STUDENTS AND FACULTY

Enrollment: 11,153. **Student Body:** 56% female, 44% male, 26% out-of-state, 3% international (45 countries represented). Asian 1%, African American 2%, Caucasian 25%, Hispanic 63%, Native American 2%, Pacific Islander <1%, Two or more races 2%, Race unknown 1%.
Retention and Graduation: 75% freshmen return for sophomore year. 22% freshmen graduate within 4 years. 48% freshmen graduate within 6 years.
Faculty: Student/faculty ratio 16:1. 628 full-time faculty, 88% hold PhDs, 37% are members of minority groups, 44% are women.

ACADEMICS

Degrees: Associate; Bachelor's; Doctoral degree—professional practice; Doctoral degree research/scholarship; Master's; Post-bachelor's certificate; Post-master's certificate. **Classes:** Most classes have 10–19 students. Most lab/discussion sessions have 20–29 students. **Most popular majors:** Animal Sciences, General; Biology/Biological Sciences, General; Criminal Justice/Safety Studies. **Special Study Options:** Cooperative education program; Distance

learning; Double major; Dual enrollment; English as a Second Language (ESL); Exchange student program (domestic); Honors program; Independent study; Internships; Student-designed major; Study abroad; Teacher certification program. **Combined degree programs:** BA/MA. **Disability Services offered:** Note-taking services; Reader services; Tutors. **Career services:** Alumni services; Career assessment; Career/job search classes; Internships.

FACILITIES

Housing: Apartments for married students; Apartments for single students; Coed dorms; Fraternity/sorority housing; Special housing for international students; 95% of campus accessible to physically disabled. **Special Academic Facilities/Equipment:** University and art department museums, theatre, horse farm, sports medicine training clinic, observatory, electron microscope, CRAY supercomputer.

CAMPUS LIFE

Environment: City. **Activities:** Campus Ministries; Choral groups; Concert band; Dance; Drama/theater; International Student Organization; Jazz band; Literary magazine; Marching band; Model UN; Music ensembles; Musical theater; Opera; Pep band; Radio station; Student government; Student newspaper; Symphony orchestra; Television station. 327 registered organizations, 23 honor societies, 17 religious organizations, 10 fraternities, 5 sororities on campus. **Athletics (Intercollegiate):** *Men:* baseball, basketball, cross-country, football, golf, tennis. *Women:* basketball, cross-country, golf, softball, swimming, tennis, track/field (outdoor), volleyball. **On-Campus Highlights:** Corbett Center Student Union.

ADMISSIONS

Freshman Academic Profile: Average high school GPA 3.5. 22% in top 10% of high school class, 52% in top 25% of high school class, 84% in top 50% of high school class. **Test Scores:** SAT Math middle 50% range 470–570. SAT EBRW middle 50% range 480–580. ACT middle 50% range 18–23. **Basis for Candidate Selection:** *Very important factors include:* academic GPA, standardized test scores. *Other factors include:* rigor of secondary school record, class rank. **Freshman Admission Requirements:** High school diploma is required and GED is accepted. *Academic units required:* 4 English, 4 math, 2 science, 2 science labs, 1 foreign language. **Freshman Admission Statistics:** 11,903 applied, 55% admitted, 34% enrolled. **Transfer Admission Requirements:** College transcript(s). Minimum college GPA of 2.0 required. Lowest grade transferable C. **General Admission Information:** Application fee $20. Non-fall registration accepted.

COSTS AND FINANCIAL AID

Required Forms and Deadlines: FAFSA. **Notification of Awards:** Applicants will be notified of awards on a rolling basis beginning 1/1. **Types of Aid:** *Need-based scholarships/grants:* College/university scholarship or grant aid from institutional funds; Federal Pell; Private scholarships; SEOG; State scholarships/grants. *Loans:* Direct PLUS loans; Direct Subsidized Stafford Loans; Direct Unsubsidized Stafford Loans. **Student Employment:** Federal Work-Study Program available. Institutional employment available. **Financial Aid Statistics:** 100% needy freshmen, 96% needy undergrads receive need-based scholarship or grant aid. 11% freshmen, 8% undergrads receive non-need-based scholarship or grant aid. 43% freshmen, 54% undergrads receive need-based self-help aid. 1% freshmen, 2% undergrads receive athletic scholarships. 78% freshmen, 68% undergrads receive any aid. 47% undergrads borrow to pay for school. Average cumulative indebtedness $21,124. **Criteria awarding aid:** *Need-based:* Academics, Athletics, Minority status, Music/drama. *Non-need-based:* Academics, Alumni affiliation, Athletics, Leadership, Minority status, Music/drama, State/district residency.

NEW YORK INSTITUTE OF TECHNOLOGY

PO Box 8000, Old Westbury, NY 11568
Phone: 516-686-7520 **Financial Aid Phone:** 516.686.7680
E-mail: admissions@nyit.edu **CEEB Code:** 2561
Website: www.nyit.edu **ACT Code:** 2832

This is a private school.

RATINGS

Admissions Selectivity Rating: 82   **Fire Safety Rating:** 60*   **Green Rating:** 60*

STUDENTS AND FACULTY

Enrollment: 3,652. **Student Body:** 39% female, 61% male, 14% out-of-state, 15% international. Asian 19%, African American 10%, Caucasian 26%,

Hispanic 19%, Native American <1%, Pacific Islander <1%, Two or more races 5%, Race unknown 6%.

Retention and Graduation: 72% freshmen return for sophomore year. 30% freshmen graduate within 4 years. 53% freshmen graduate within 6 years. 19% grads go on to further study within 1 year. 12% grads pursue arts and sciences degrees. 2% grads pursue law degrees. 15% grads pursue business degrees. 9% grads pursue medical degrees. **Faculty:** Student/faculty ratio 12:1. 325 full-time faculty, 94% hold PhDs, 26% are members of minority groups, 41% are women.

ACADEMICS

Degrees: Associate; Bachelor's; Certificate; Doctoral degree—professional practice; Doctoral degree research/scholarship; Master's; Post-bachelor's certificate; Post-master's certificate; Terminal Associate. **Classes:** Most classes have 10–19 students. **Special Study Options:** Accelerated program; Cooperative education program; Cross-registration; Distance learning; Double major; Dual enrollment; English as a Second Language (ESL); Honors program; Independent study; Internships; Liberal arts/career combination; Study abroad; Teacher certification program; Weekend college. **Honors programs:** Dean of Engineering Honors Program. **Disability Services offered:** Note-taking services; Reader services; Tape recorders; Tutors. **Career services:** Alumni network; Alumni services; Career assessment; Career/job search classes; Internships; Regional alumni.

FACILITIES

Housing: Coed dorms; Special housing for disabled students; Theme housing; 100% of campus accessible to physically disabled. **Special Academic Facilities/Equipment:** Simulated trading floor; motion capture lab; Entrepreneurship and Technology Innovation Center; NYITCOM Health Care Center; Parkinson's Disease Treatment Center; Gallery 61; NYIT Auditorium on Broadway; Cybersecurity Lab; Center of Excellence in Data Visualization, Entertainment, and Education Engineering.

CAMPUS LIFE

Environment: Village. **Activities:** Dance; International Student Organization; Radio station; Student government; Student newspaper; Television station. 50 registered organizations, 15 honor societies, 8 fraternities, 5 sororities on campus.

ADMISSIONS

Freshman Academic Profile: Average high school GPA 3.5. 0% in top 10% of high school class, 0% in top 25% of high school class, 0% in top 50% of high school class. **Test Scores:** SAT Math middle 50% range 540–665. SAT EBRW middle 50% range 530–630. ACT middle 50% range 22–29. **Basis for Candidate Selection:** *Very important factors include:* rigor of secondary school record, academic GPA, standardized test scores. *Important factors include:* application essay, *Other factors include:* recommendation(s), extracurricular activities, talent/ability, character/personal qualities, alumni/ae relation, volunteer work, work experience. **Freshman Admission Requirements:** High school diploma is required and GED is accepted. *Academic units required:* 4 English, 3 math, 3 science, 1 science lab, 3 social studies, 7 academic electives. *Academic units recommended:* 4 English, 3 math, 3 science, 1 science lab, 4 social studies, 7 academic electives. **Freshman Admission Statistics:** 11,848 applied, 68% admitted, 11% enrolled. **General Admission Information:** Application fee $50. Non-fall registration accepted. Admission may be deferred for a maximum of one year.

COSTS AND FINANCIAL AID

Annual tuition $38,060. Room and board $14,920. Required fees $2,400. Average book and supplies expense $1,104. **Required Forms and Deadlines:** FAFSA. **Types of Aid:** *Need-based scholarships/grants:* College/university scholarship or grant aid from institutional funds; Federal Pell; Private scholarships; SEOG; State scholarships/grants. *Loans:* Direct PLUS loans; Direct Subsidized Stafford Loans; Direct Unsubsidized Stafford Loans. **Student Employment:** Federal Work-Study Program available. Institutional employment available. **Financial Aid Statistics:** 73% needy freshmen, 80% needy undergrads receive need-based scholarship or grant aid. 98% freshmen, 89% undergrads receive non-need-based scholarship or grant aid. 66% freshmen, 70% undergrads receive need-based self-help aid. 7% freshmen, 6% undergrads receive athletic scholarships. 99% freshmen receive any aid.

NEW YORK SCHOOL OF INTERIOR DESIGN

170 East 70th Street, New York, NY 10021
Phone: 212-472-1500 **Financial Aid Phone:** 212-472-1500 x212
E-mail: admissions@nysid.edu **CEEB Code:** 333
Fax: 212-472-1867 **ACT Code:** 2829

This private school was founded in 1916.

RATINGS

Admissions Selectivity Rating: 71   **Fire Safety Rating:** 60*   **Green Rating:** 60*

STUDENTS AND FACULTY

Enrollment: 353. **Student Body:** 87% female, 13% male, 15% international. Asian 6%, African American 3%, Caucasian 48%, Hispanic 9%, Native American 0%, Pacific Islander 0%, Two or more races 2%, Race unknown 16%.
Faculty: 8 full-time faculty, 88% hold PhDs, 0% are members of minority groups, 50% are women. 0% of classes are taught by teaching assistants.

ACADEMICS

Degrees: Associate; Bachelor's; Certificate; Master's; Transfer Associate. **Classes:** Most classes have 10–19 students. **Most popular majors:** Interior Design. **Special Study Options:** Independent study; Internships; Study abroad. **Disability Services offered:** Tutors. **Career services:** Alumni network; Alumni services; Internships.

FACILITIES

100% of campus accessible to physically disabled. **Special Academic Facilities/Equipment:** Three galleries, lighting laboratory, student atelier. **Campus Network:** 90% of classrooms, 15% of dorms, 95% of student union, 90% of libraries, 20% of dining areas, 85% of common outdoor areas have wireless network access.

CAMPUS LIFE

Environment: Metropolis. 1 registered organizations on campus.

ADMISSIONS

Freshman Academic Profile: Basis for Candidate Selection: *Very important factors include:* rigor of secondary school record, application essay, talent/ability. *Important factors include:* academic GPA, recommendation(s). *Other factors include:* class rank, standardized test scores, interview, extracurricular activities, character/personal qualities, alumni/ae relation, work experience. **Freshman Admission Requirements:** High school diploma is required and GED is accepted. *Academic units recommended:* 4 English, 2 math, 2 science, 2 foreign language, 2 social studies, 2 history. **Freshman Admission Statistics:** 178 applied, 46% admitted, 19% enrolled. **Transfer Admission Requirements:** High school transcript, college transcript(s), essay or personal statement. Minimum college GPA of 3.0 required. Lowest grade transferable C. **General Admission Information:** Application fee $60. Priority deadline 2/1. Non-fall registration accepted. Admission may be deferred for a maximum of 1 year.

COSTS AND FINANCIAL AID

Annual tuition $30,195. Required fees $570. Average book and supplies expense $1,000. **Required Forms and Deadlines:** FAFSA; Institution's own financial aid form; State aid form. **Notification of Awards:** Applicants will be notified of awards on a rolling basis beginning 2/1. **Types of Aid:** *Need-based scholarships/grants:* College/university scholarship or grant aid from institutional funds; Federal Pell; SEOG; State scholarships/grants. **Student Employment:** Federal Work-Study Program available. **Criteria awarding aid:** *Need-based:* Academics, Art.

NEW YORK UNIVERSITY

383 Lafayette St, New York, NY 10012
Phone: 212-998-4500 **Financial Aid Phone:** 212-998-4444
E-mail: admissions@nyu.edu **CEEB Code:** 2562
Fax: 212-995-4902 **Website:** www.nyu.edu **ACT Code:** 2838

This private school was founded in 1831.

RATINGS
Admissions Selectivity Rating: 97   **Fire Safety Rating:** 98   **Green Rating:** 96

STUDENTS AND FACULTY
Enrollment: 26,612. **Student Body:** 58% female, 42% male, 67% out-of-state, 22% international (110 countries represented). Asian 19%, African American 8%, Caucasian 25%, Hispanic 16%, Native American <1%, Pacific Islander <1%, Two or more races 4%, Race unknown 5%.
Retention and Graduation: 77% freshmen graduate within 4 years. 85% freshmen graduate within 6 years. 13% grads go on to further study within 1 year. 31% grads pursue arts and sciences degrees. 14% grads pursue law degrees. 10% grads pursue business degrees. 14% grads pursue medical degrees. **Faculty:** Student/faculty ratio 9:1. 3,010 full-time faculty, 94% hold PhDs, 22% are members of minority groups, 44% are women.

ACADEMICS
Degrees: Associate; Bachelor's; Certificate; Diploma; Doctoral degree—other; Doctoral degree—professional practice; Doctoral degree research/scholarship; Master's; Post-bachelor's certificate; Post-master's certificate; Terminal Associate; Transfer Associate. **Classes:** Most classes have 10–19 students. Most lab/discussion sessions have 10–19 students. **Most popular majors:** Business/Commerce, General; Liberal Arts and Sciences/Liberal Studies; Drama and Dramatics/Theatre Arts, General. **Special Study Options:** Accelerated program; Cooperative education program; Cross-registration; Distance learning; Double major; English as a Second Language (ESL); Exchange student program (domestic); External degree program; Honors program; Independent study; Internships; Liberal arts/career combination; Student-designed major; Study abroad; Teacher certification program. **Honors programs:** There are various honors programs in the different Schools and Colleges. **Combined degree programs:** BA/DDS. **Disability Services offered:** Note-taking services; Reader services; Tape recorders. **Career services:** Alumni network; Alumni services; Career assessment; Career/job search classes; Internships; Regional alumni.

FACILITIES
Housing: Apartments for single students; Coed dorms; Cooperative housing; Fraternity/sorority housing; Special housing for disabled students; Special housing for international students; Theme housing; Wellness housing; 90% of campus accessible to physically disabled. **Special Academic Facilities/Equipment:** Bobst Library and study center; Grey Art Gallery and study center; Special academic facilities for arts, business, culture, education, international relations, language, law, media, music, public service, research, and social policy, and Skirball Center for Performing Arts.

CAMPUS LIFE
Environment: Metropolis. **Activities:** Campus Ministries; Choral groups; Concert band; Dance; Drama/theater; International Student Organization; Jazz band; Literary magazine; Model UN; Music ensembles; Musical theater; Opera; Pep band; Radio station; Student government; Student newspaper; Student-run film society; Symphony orchestra; Television station; Yearbook. 609 registered organizations, 14 honor societies, 41 religious organizations, 23 fraternities, 14 sororities on campus. **Athletics (Intercollegiate):** *Men:* basketball, cross-country, diving, fencing, golf, soccer, swimming, tennis, track/field (outdoor), track/field (indoor), volleyball, wrestling. *Women:* basketball, cross-country, diving, fencing, golf, soccer, swimming, tennis, track/field (outdoor), track/field (indoor), volleyball. **On-Campus Highlights:** Kimmel Center for Student Life. **Environmental Initiatives:** NYU's largest undertaking is to achieve a 50% emissions reduction by 2025 and ultimately carbon neutrality by 2040. To achieve this, we are systematically renovating buildings to be both ultra-low energy consumers as well as healthier and more comfortable. We are also focusing on electrifying buildings in order to take advantage of an eventually greener grid.

ADMISSIONS
Freshman Academic Profile: Average high school GPA 3.7. **Test Scores:** SAT Math middle 50% range 690–790. SAT EBRW middle 50% range 660–740. ACT middle 50% range 30–34. **Basis for Candidate Selection:** *Very important factors include:* rigor of secondary school record, class rank, academic GPA, standardized test scores, talent/ability. *Important factors include:* application essay, recommendation(s), extracurricular activities, character/personal qualities. *Other factors include:* interview, first generation, alumni/ae relation, geographical residence, racial/ethnic status, volunteer work, work experience, level of applicant's interest. **Freshman Admission Requirements:** High school diploma is required and GED is accepted. *Academic units required:* 4 English, 3 math, 3 science, 3 science labs, 3 foreign language, 3 social studies, 3 history. *Academic units recommended:* 4 English, 4 math, 4 science, 4 science labs, 4 foreign language, 4 social studies, 4 history. **Freshman Admission Statistics:** 79,462 applied, 16% admitted, 45% enrolled. **Transfer Admission Requirements:** High school transcript, college transcript(s), essay or personal statement, statement of good standing from prior institution(s). Lowest grade transferable C. **General Admission Information:** Application fee $80. Regular application deadline 1/1. Non-fall registration accepted. Admission may be deferred for a maximum of 2 years.

COSTS AND FINANCIAL AID
Annual tuition $50,684. Room and board $18,684. Required fees $2,624. Average book and supplies expense $752. **Required Forms and Deadlines:** CSS/Financial Aid PROFILE; FAFSA; Noncustodial PROFILE. **Notification of Awards:** Applicants will be notified of awards on or about 4/1. **Types of Aid:** *Need-based scholarships/grants:* College/university scholarship or grant aid from institutional funds; Federal Nursing Scholarships; Federal Pell; Private scholarships; SEOG; State scholarships/grants. *Loans:* Direct PLUS loans; Direct Subsidized Stafford Loans; Direct Unsubsidized Stafford Loans. **Student Employment:** Federal Work-Study Program available. Institutional employment available. **Financial Aid Statistics:** 97% needy freshmen, 94% needy undergrads receive need-based scholarship or grant aid. 5% freshmen, 6% undergrads receive non-need-based scholarship or grant aid. 78% freshmen, 72% undergrads receive need-based self-help aid. 0% freshmen, 0% undergrads receive athletic scholarships. **Criteria awarding aid:** *Need-based:* Academics, Art, Leadership, Music/drama. *Non-need-based:* Music/drama.

NIAGARA UNIVERSITY

Gacioch Family Center, Niagara University, NY 14109
Phone: 716-286-8700 **Financial Aid Phone:** 716-286-8669
E-mail: admissions@niagara.edu **CEEB Code:** 2558
Fax: 716-286-8710 **Website:** www.niagara.edu **ACT Code:** 2842

This private school, affiliated with the Roman Catholic Church, was founded in 1856. It has a 160 acre campus.

RATINGS
Admissions Selectivity Rating: 75   **Fire Safety Rating:** 82   **Green Rating:** 90

STUDENTS AND FACULTY
Enrollment: 2,748. **Student Body:** 64% female, 36% male, 10% out-of-state, 17% international (42 countries represented). Asian 1%, African American 5%, Caucasian 66%, Hispanic 5%, Native American 1%, Pacific Islander <1%, Two or more races 3%, Race unknown 3%.
Retention and Graduation: 87% freshmen return for sophomore year. 66% freshmen graduate within 4 years. 73% freshmen graduate within 6 years. 28% grads go on to further study within 1 year. 5% grads pursue arts and sciences degrees. 1% grads pursue law degrees. 12% grads pursue business degrees. 1% grads pursue medical degrees. **Faculty:** Student/faculty ratio 11:1. 156 full-time faculty, 93% hold PhDs, 13% are members of minority groups, 0% of classes are taught by teaching assistants.

ACADEMICS
Degrees: Associate; Bachelor's; Doctoral degree research/scholarship; Master's; Post-bachelor's certificate; Post-master's certificate. **Classes:** Most classes have 10–19 students. Most lab/discussion sessions have 10–19 students. **Most popular majors:** Teacher Education, Multiple Levels; Business/Commerce, General; Registered Nursing/Registered Nurse. **Special Study Options:** Accelerated program; Cooperative education program; Cross-registration; Distance learning; Double major; Dual enrollment; English as a Second Language (ESL); Exchange student program (domestic); Honors program;

Independent study; Internships; Liberal arts/career combination; Study abroad; Teacher certification program. **Disability Services offered:** Note-taking services; Reader services; Tape recorders; Tutors. **Career services:** Alumni network; Alumni services; Career assessment; Career/job search classes; Internships; Regional alumni.

FACILITIES

Housing: Apartments for single students; Coed dorms; Special housing for disabled students; Special housing for international students; Theme housing; 75% of campus accessible to physically disabled. **Special Academic Facilities/Equipment:** Castellani Art Museum; B. Thomas Golisano Center for Integrated Sciences.

CAMPUS LIFE

Environment: Town. **Activities:** Campus Ministries; Choral groups; Dance; Drama/theater; International Student Organization; Literary magazine; Model UN; Musical theater; Radio station; Student government; Student newspaper. 92 registered organizations, 22 honor societies, 6 religious organizations, 1 fraternity, 2 sororities on campus. **Athletics (Intercollegiate):** *Men:* baseball, basketball, cross-country, diving, golf, ice hockey, soccer, swimming, tennis. *Women:* basketball, cross-country, diving, golf, ice hockey, lacrosse, soccer, softball, swimming, tennis, volleyball. **On-Campus Highlights:** Gallagher Center. **Environmental Initiatives:** 50,000-sq. ft. science complex opened in Fall 2013 earned LEED Gold Certification. Installed 4 electric car charging stations on campus for students, employees and visitors.

ADMISSIONS

Freshman Academic Profile: Average high school GPA 3.4. 16% in top 10% of high school class, 40% in top 25% of high school class, 74% in top 50% of high school class. **Test Scores:** SAT Math middle 50% range 510–620. SAT EBRW middle 50% range 510–610. ACT middle 50% range 20–27. **Basis for Candidate Selection:** *Very important factors include:* rigor of secondary school record, class rank, academic GPA. *Important factors include:* recommendation(s), interview. *Other factors include:* application essay, standardized test scores, extracurricular activities, talent/ability, character/personal qualities, alumni/ae relation, volunteer work, work experience, level of applicant's interest. **Freshman Admission Requirements:** High school diploma is required and GED is accepted. *Academic units required:* 4 English, 2 math, 2 science, 2 foreign language, 2 social studies, 4 academic electives. **Freshman Admission Statistics:** 3,660 applied, 89% admitted, 19% enrolled. **Transfer Admission Requirements:** High school transcript, college transcript(s). Minimum college GPA of 2.0 required. Lowest grade transferable C. **General Admission Information:** Regular application deadline 8/30. Non-fall registration accepted. Admission may be deferred for a maximum of 1 year.

COSTS AND FINANCIAL AID

Annual tuition $33,000. Room and board $11,700. Required fees $1,510. Average book and supplies expense $1,250. **Required Forms and Deadlines:** FAFSA; State aid form. **Notification of Awards:** Applicants will be notified of awards on a rolling basis beginning 1/15. **Types of Aid:** *Need-based scholarships/grants:* College/university scholarship or grant aid from institutional funds; Federal Pell; Private scholarships; SEOG; State scholarships/grants. *Loans:* Direct PLUS loans; Direct Subsidized Stafford Loans; Direct Unsubsidized Stafford Loans. **Student Employment:** Federal Work-Study Program available. Institutional employment available. **Financial Aid Statistics:** 98% needy freshmen, 98% needy undergrads receive need-based scholarship or grant aid. 78% freshmen, 73% undergrads receive non-need-based scholarship or grant aid. 80% freshmen, 76% undergrads receive need-based self-help aid. 4% freshmen, 5% undergrads receive athletic scholarships. 100% freshmen, 90% undergrads receive any aid. 76% undergrads borrow to pay for school. Average cumulative indebtedness $34,046. **Criteria awarding aid:** *Need-based:* Academics, Athletics, Music/drama. *Non-need-based:* Academics, Athletics, Music/drama.

NICHOLLS STATE UNIVERSITY

P.O. Box 2004, Thibodaux, LA 70310
Phone: 985-448-4507 **Financial Aid Phone:** (985) 448-4048
E-mail: nicholls@nicholls.edu **CEEB Code:** 6221
Fax: 985-448-4929 **Website:** www.nicholls.edu **ACT Code:** 1580

This public school was founded in 1948. It has a 210 acre campus.

RATINGS

Admissions Selectivity Rating: 77   **Fire Safety Rating:** 85   **Green Rating:** 60*

STUDENTS AND FACULTY

Enrollment: 6,246. **Student Body:** 61% female, 39% male, 4% out-of-state, 2% international (40 countries represented). Asian 1%, African American 18%, Caucasian 73%, Hispanic 1%, Native American 2%, Race unknown 2%. **Retention and Graduation:** 66% freshmen return for sophomore year. **Faculty:** Student/faculty ratio 20:1. 295 full-time faculty, 54% hold PhDs, 11% are members of minority groups, 51% are women. 1% of classes are taught by teaching assistants.

ACADEMICS

Degrees: Associate; Bachelor's; Certificate; Master's; Post-master's certificate. **Classes:** Most classes have 20–29 students. **Most popular majors:** Business Administration and Management, General; General Studies; Nursing/Registered Nurse (Rn, Asn, Bsn, Msn). **Special Study Options:** Cooperative education program; Cross-registration; Distance learning; Dual enrollment; Honors program; Independent study; Internships; Study abroad; Teacher certification program. **Honors programs:** You can learn advanced material in small classes taught by outstanding professors. You can enrich your college experience through intellectually stimulating courses that allow you to reach your potential. The Honors Program invites all academically talented and intellectually curious students to participate. By joining the program you can become a select member of the campus community and associate with students who share similar goals and interests. The Program is designed to meet students' needs and interests. Therefore, students in the program determine their degree of involvement. You may take as many honors courses as you choose or simply successfully complete one three-hour honors course each year. And because honors classes fit degree requirements for all majors, participants graduate on time. **Combined degree programs:** BA/MA. **Disability Services offered:** Note-taking services; Reader services; Tape recorders; Tutors. **Career services:** Alumni network; Alumni services; Career assessment; Career/job search classes; Internships.

FACILITIES

Housing: Apartments for married students; Apartments for single students; Men's dorms; Special housing for disabled students; Special housing for international students; Wellness housing; Women's dorms. **Special Academic Facilities/Equipment:** Ameen Art Gallery.

CAMPUS LIFE

Environment: Village. **Activities:** Choral groups; Concert band; Dance; Drama/theater; Jazz band; Literary magazine; Marching band; Music ensembles; Musical theater; Radio station; Student government; Student newspaper; Student-run film society; Television station; Yearbook. 121 registered organizations, 24 honor societies, 6 religious organizations, 10 fraternities, 5 sororities on campus. **Athletics (Intercollegiate):** *Men:* baseball, basketball, cross-country, football, golf, tennis. *Women:* basketball, cross-country, golf, soccer, softball, tennis, track/field (outdoor), track/field (indoor), volleyball. **On-Campus Highlights:** Admissions Office.

ADMISSIONS

Freshman Academic Profile: Average high school GPA 3.2. 18% in top 10% of high school class, 43% in top 25% of high school class, 73% in top 50% of high school class. 68% from public high schools. **Test Scores:** ACT middle 50% range 24–20. **Basis for Candidate Selection:** *Very important factors include:* rigor of secondary school record. *Important factors include:* standardized test scores. *Other factors include:* class rank, academic GPA, talent/ability. **Freshman Admission Requirements:** High school diploma is required and GED is accepted. *Academic units required:* 4 English, 3 math, 3 science, 2 foreign language, 1 social studies, 2 history, 2 academic electives. **Freshman Admission Statistics:** 2,075 applied, 87% admitted, 70% enrolled. **Transfer Admission Requirements:** College transcript(s). Minimum college GPA of 2.0 required. Lowest grade transferable D. **General Admission Information:** Application fee $20. Priority deadline 8/15. Non-fall registration accepted. Admission may be deferred for a maximum of 1 semester.

COSTS AND FINANCIAL AID

Annual in-state tuition $2,231. Annual out-of-state tuition $7,679. Room and board $4,556. Required fees $1,364. Average book and supplies expense $1,200. **Required Forms and Deadlines:** FAFSA; Institution's own financial aid form; Noncustodial PROFILE; State aid form. **Types of Aid:** *Need-based scholarships/grants:* College/university scholarship or grant aid from institutional funds; Federal Pell; Private scholarships; SEOG; State scholarships/grants. **Student Employment:** Federal Work-Study Program available. Institutional employment available. **Financial Aid Statistics:** 93% needy freshmen, 86% needy undergrads receive need-based scholarship or grant aid. 68% freshmen, 32% undergrads receive non-need-based scholarship or grant aid. 50% freshmen, 69% undergrads receive need-based self-help aid. 3% freshmen, 3% undergrads receive athletic scholarships. 77% freshmen, 74% undergrads receive any aid. **Criteria awarding aid:** *Need-based:* Academics. *Non-need-based:* Academics, Athletics, State/district residency.

NICHOLS COLLEGE

PO Box 5000, Dudley, MA 01571-5000
Phone: 508-213-2203 **Financial Aid Phone:** 508-213-2340
E-mail: admissions@nichols.edu **CEEB Code:** 3666
Fax: 508-943-9885 **Website:** www.nichols.edu **ACT Code:** 1878

This private school was founded in 1815. It has a 200 acre campus.

RATINGS

Admissions Selectivity Rating: 75 **Fire Safety Rating:** 97 **Green Rating:** 64

STUDENTS AND FACULTY

Enrollment: 1,321. **Student Body:** 38% female, 62% male, 40% out-of-state, 2% international (12 countries represented). Asian 1%, African American 7%, Caucasian 77%, Hispanic 8%, Native American <1%, Pacific Islander <1%, Two or more races 3%, Race unknown <1%.
Retention and Graduation: 75% freshmen return for sophomore year. 48% freshmen graduate within 4 years. 51% freshmen graduate within 6 years. 9% grads go on to further study within 1 year. 2% grads pursue business degrees. **Faculty:** Student/faculty ratio 17:1. 51 full-time faculty, 51% hold PhDs, 10% are members of minority groups, 47% are women. 0% of classes are taught by teaching assistants.

ACADEMICS

Degrees: Associate; Bachelor's; Master's; Post-master's certificate. **Classes:** Most classes have 20–29 students. **Most popular majors:** Business/Commerce, General; Criminal Justice/Law Enforcement Administration; Sport and Fitness Administration/Management. **Special Study Options:** Accelerated program; Distance learning; Double major; Dual enrollment; Honors program; Independent study; Internships; Study abroad. **Honors programs:** Students with high academic promise should declare Honors Scholar candidacy during summer orientations for new students or during the Add/Drop periods at the beginning of the first, second, or at the latest, third semester of study. Throughout the program experience, all Honors candidates are required to maintain high standards of academic work and personal integrity as well as to meet all academic performance requirements. **Disability Services offered:** Note-taking services; Reader services; Tape recorders; Tutors. **Career services:** Alumni network; Alumni services; Career assessment; Career/job search classes; Internships.

FACILITIES

Housing: Apartments for single students; Coed dorms; Men's dorms; Special housing for disabled students; Wellness housing; Women's dorms; 80% of campus accessible to physically disabled.

CAMPUS LIFE

Environment: Village. **Activities:** Campus Ministries; Dance; International Student Organization; Literary magazine; Model UN; Radio station; Student government; Yearbook. 34 registered organizations, 6 honor societies, 2 religious organizations on campus. **Athletics (Intercollegiate):** *Men:* baseball, basketball, football, golf, ice hockey, lacrosse, soccer, tennis. *Women:* basketball, field hockey, golf, ice hockey, lacrosse, soccer, softball, tennis. **On-Campus Highlights:** Athletic and Recreation Complex.

ADMISSIONS

Freshman Academic Profile: Average high school GPA 3.0. 85% from public high schools. **Test Scores:** SAT Math middle 50% range 470–570. SAT EBRW middle 50% range 470–570. ACT middle 50% range 19–24.

Basis for Candidate Selection: *Very important factors include:* academic GPA. *Important factors include:* rigor of secondary school record, application essay, standardized test scores, recommendation(s), interview, extracurricular activities, character/personal qualities. *Other factors include:* class rank, alumni/ae relation, volunteer work, work experience, level of applicant's interest. **Freshman Admission Requirements:** High school diploma is required and GED is accepted. *Academic units required:* 4 English, 3 math, 3 science, 2 social studies, 1 history. **Freshman Admission Statistics:** 2,435 applied, 82% admitted, 18% enrolled. **Transfer Admission Requirements:** High school transcript, college transcript(s), essay or personal statement. Minimum college GPA of 2.0 required. Lowest grade transferable C. **General Admission Information:** Non-fall registration accepted. Admission may be deferred for a maximum of 1 year.

COSTS AND FINANCIAL AID

Annual tuition $33,800. Room and board $13,950. Required fees $1,000. Average book and supplies expense $1,400. **Required Forms and Deadlines:** FAFSA. **Notification of Awards:** Applicants will be notified of awards on a rolling basis beginning 12/1. **Types of Aid:** *Need-based scholarships/grants:* College/university scholarship or grant aid from institutional funds; Federal Pell; Private scholarships; SEOG; State scholarships/grants. *Loans:* Direct PLUS loans; Direct Subsidized Stafford Loans; Direct Unsubsidized Stafford Loans. **Student Employment:** Federal Work-Study Program available. Institutional employment available. **Financial Aid Statistics:** 100% needy freshmen, 100% needy undergrads receive need-based scholarship or grant aid. 5% freshmen, 18% undergrads receive non-need-based scholarship or grant aid. 97% freshmen, 97% undergrads receive need-based self-help aid. 0% freshmen, 0% undergrads receive athletic scholarships. 100% freshmen, 99% undergrads receive any aid. 84% undergrads borrow to pay for school. Average cumulative indebtedness $34,873. **Criteria awarding aid:** *Need-based:* Academics. *Non-need-based:* Academics.

NORTH CAROLINA A&T STATE UNIVERSITY

1601 East Market Street, Greensboro, NC 27411
Phone: 336-334-7946
E-mail: uadmit@ncat.edu
Fax: 336-334-7478 **Website:** www.ncat.edu

This is a public school.

RATINGS

Admissions Selectivity Rating: 80 **Fire Safety Rating:** 60* **Green Rating:** 60*

STUDENTS AND FACULTY

Enrollment: 8,921. **Student Body:** 54% female, 46% male, 16% out-of-state, 1% international. Asian 1%, African American 89%, Caucasian 4%, Hispanic 2%, Native American <1%, Pacific Islander <1%, Two or more races <1%, Race unknown 3%.
Retention and Graduation: 74% freshmen return for sophomore year. **Faculty:** 532 full-time faculty, 77% hold PhDs, 73% are members of minority groups, 44% are women.

ACADEMICS

Degrees: Bachelor's; Doctoral degree research/scholarship; Master's. **Classes:** Most classes have 20–29 students. Most lab/discussion sessions have 20–29 students. **Special Study Options:** Accelerated program; Cooperative education program; Cross-registration; Distance learning; Double major; Dual enrollment; Honors program; Internships; Liberal arts/career combination; Study abroad; Teacher certification program.

FACILITIES

Housing: Coed dorms; Men's dorms; Women's dorms. **Campus Network:** 100% of classrooms, 100% of dorms, 100% of student union, 100% of libraries, 100% of dining areas, 50% of common outdoor areas have wireless network access.

CAMPUS LIFE

Activities: Campus Ministries; Choral groups; Concert band; Dance; Drama/theater; International Student Organization; Jazz band; Marching band; Music ensembles; Pep band; Radio station; Student government; Student newspaper; Television station; Yearbook.

ADMISSIONS

Freshman Academic Profile: Average high school GPA 3.1. 0% in top 10% of high school class, 6% in top 25% of high school class, 34% in top 50% of high school class. 77% from public high schools. **Test Scores:** SAT Math middle

50% range 410–500. SAT EBRW middle 50% range 390–480. ACT middle 50% range 17–21. **Basis for Candidate Selection:** *Very important factors include:* rigor of secondary school record, academic GPA. *Important factors include:* class rank, standardized test scores. *Other factors include:* extracurricular activities, talent/ability, character/personal qualities, geographical residence, state residency, volunteer work, work experience, level of applicant's interest. **Freshman Admission Requirements:** High school diploma is required and GED is accepted. *Academic units required:* 4 English, 4 math, 3 science, 1 science lab, 2 foreign language, 1 social studies, 1 history, 4 academic electives. **Freshman Admission Statistics:** 6,692 applied, 66% admitted, 42% enrolled. **Transfer Admission Requirements:** High school transcript. Minimum college GPA of 2.0 required. Lowest grade transferable C. **General Admission Information:** Application fee $45. Priority deadline 2/15. Non-fall registration accepted. Admission may be deferred for a maximum of 1 year.

COSTS AND FINANCIAL AID

Annual in-state tuition $2,791. Annual out-of-state tuition $12,425. Room and board $7,225. Required fees $1,877. Average book and supplies expense $1,400. **Required Forms and Deadlines:** FAFSA. **Notification of Awards:** Applicants will be notified of awards on or about 4/15. **Types of Aid:** *Need-based scholarships/grants:* College/university scholarship or grant aid from institutional funds; Federal Pell; Private scholarships; SEOG; State scholarships/grants. *Loans:* Direct PLUS loans; Direct Subsidized Stafford Loans; Direct Unsubsidized Stafford Loans. **Financial Aid Statistics:** 78% needy freshmen, 75% needy undergrads receive need-based scholarship or grant aid. 92% freshmen, 84% undergrads receive non-need-based scholarship or grant aid. 84% freshmen, 84% undergrads receive need-based self-help aid. 3% freshmen, 2% undergrads receive athletic scholarships. **Criteria awarding aid:** *Non-need-based:* Academics.

NORTH CAROLINA STATE UNIVERSITY

Box 7103, Raleigh, NC 27695
Phone: 919-515-2434 **Financial Aid Phone:** 919-515-2421
E-mail: undergrad-admissions@ncsu.edu **CEEB Code:** 5496
Fax: 919-515-5039 **Website:** http://www.ncsu.edu/ **ACT Code:** 3164

This public school was founded in 1887. It has a 2100 acre campus.

RATINGS

Admissions Selectivity Rating: 92 **Fire Safety Rating:** 93 **Green Rating:** 98

STUDENTS AND FACULTY

Enrollment: 24,238. **Student Body:** 47% female, 53% male, 9% out-of-state, 4% international (106 countries represented). Asian 8%, African American 6%, Caucasian 68%, Hispanic 6%, Native American <1%, Pacific Islander <1%, Two or more races 4%, Race unknown 4%. **Retention and Graduation:** 94% freshmen return for sophomore year. 57% freshmen graduate within 4 years. 83% freshmen graduate within 6 years. 17% grads go on to further study within 1 year. 7% grads pursue arts and sciences degrees. 2% grads pursue law degrees. 2% grads pursue business degrees. 5% grads pursue medical degrees. **Faculty:** Student/faculty ratio 14:1. 1,769 full-time faculty, 91% hold PhDs, 21% are members of minority groups, 39% are women. 11% of classes are taught by teaching assistants.

ACADEMICS

Degrees: Bachelor's; Certificate; Doctoral degree—professional practice; Doctoral degree research/scholarship; Master's; Post-bachelor's certificate; Post-master's certificate; Terminal Associate. **Classes:** Most classes have 20–29 students. Most lab/discussion sessions have 20–29 students. **Most popular majors:** Engineering, General; Biology/Biological Sciences, General; Business Administration and Management, General. **Special Study Options:** Accelerated program; Cooperative education program; Cross-registration; Distance learning; Double major; Dual enrollment; English as a Second Language (ESL); Exchange student program (domestic); Honors program; Independent study; Internships; Liberal arts/career combination; Student-designed major; Study abroad; Teacher certification program. **Honors programs:** The University Honors Program recruits and provides programmatic support for a diverse group of nationally outstanding students, ensuring that they benefit fully

from the resources of a major land-grant, research university and the Research Triangle by emphasizing inquiry-, creativity-, and discovery-based learning. The program offers interdisciplinary seminars and a variety of credit-earning opportunites for out-of-classroom experiences. The program emphasizes participation in research by students from all disciplines. Entering students may instead choose to participate in the University Scholars program, which emphasizes enrichment activities and leadership development. There are over 30 honors programs located in the colleges or departments that invite students in their sophomore or junior years. These programs include honors sections of courses, honors seminars, and honors research. Some programs require a senior honor thesis. **Combined degree programs:** BA/MA. **Disability Services offered:** Note-taking services; Reader services; Tape recorders. **Career services:** Alumni services; Career assessment; Career/job search classes; Internships.

FACILITIES

Housing: Apartments for married students; Apartments for single students; Coed dorms; Cooperative housing; Fraternity/sorority housing; Men's dorms; Special housing for disabled students; Special housing for international students; Theme housing; Wellness housing; Women's dorms; 81% of campus accessible to physically disabled. **Special Academic Facilities/Equipment:** Art museum, arts/crafts center, innovation "sandbox," world-renowned technology library, research farms and forests, Phytotron with controlled atmosphere growth chambers, pulp/paper and wood products labs, processing equipment for fiber, fabric, and garment manufacture, electron microscopes, nuclear reactor, stable isotope lab, Clean Technology Center (Formerly the solar center), Cellular and Molecular Imaging Facility, Genomic Science Laboratory, Nanofabrication Facility, Analytical Instrumentation Facility, and a Molecular Education, Technology and Research Innovation Center. **Campus Network:** 100% of student union, 100% of libraries, 100% of dining areas have wireless network access.

CAMPUS LIFE

Environment: Metropolis. **Activities:** Campus Ministries; Choral groups; Concert band; Dance; Drama/theater; International Student Organization; Jazz band; Literary magazine; Marching band; Model UN; Music ensembles; Musical theater; Pep band; Radio station; Student government; Student newspaper; Student-run film society; Symphony orchestra; Yearbook. 646 registered organizations, 20 honor societies, 63 religious organizations, 29 fraternities, 20 sororities on campus. **Athletics (Intercollegiate):** *Men:* baseball, basketball, cheerleading, cross-country, diving, football, golf, riflery, soccer, swimming, tennis, track/field (outdoor), track/field (indoor), wrestling. *Women:* basketball, cheerleading, cross-country, diving, golf, gymnastics, riflery, soccer, softball, swimming, tennis, track/field (outdoor), track/field (indoor), volleyball. **On-Campus Highlights:** Hunt Library. **Environmental Initiatives:** NC State's 5-year Sustainability Strategic Plan (2017–2022) is a five-year roadmap that builds upon the university's strengths, momentum, and decades of sustainability progress. The campus-wide Sustainability Council is focused on making progress on the following five goals: Student Leadership; Academics and Research; Community and Culture; Operations, Planning and Design; and Communications.

ADMISSIONS

Freshman Academic Profile: Average high school GPA 3.8. 50% in top 10% of high school class, 86% in top 25% of high school class, 99% in top 50% of high school class. 83% from public high schools. **Test Scores:** SAT Math middle 50% range 630–730. SAT EBRW middle 50% range 620–690. ACT middle 50% range 27–32. **Basis for Candidate Selection:** *Very important factors include:* rigor of secondary school record, class rank, academic GPA, standardized test scores. *Other factors include:* application essay, recommendation(s), extracurricular activities, talent/ability, character/personal qualities, first generation, alumni/ae relation, geographical residence, state residency, racial/ethnic status, volunteer work, work experience, level of applicant's interest. **Freshman Admission Requirements:** High school diploma is required and GED is accepted. *Academic units required:* 4 English, 4 math, 3 science, 1 science lab, 2 foreign language, 1 social studies, 1 history. *Academic units recommended:* 4 English, 4 math, 3 science, 1 science lab, 2 foreign language, 1 social studies, 1 history. **Freshman Admission Statistics:** 30,995 applied, 45% admitted, 34% enrolled. **Transfer Admission Requirements:** College transcript(s). Minimum college GPA of 2.0 required. Lowest grade transferable C-. **General Admission Information:** Application fee $85. Priority deadline 11/1. Regular application deadline 1/15. Non-fall registration accepted. Admission may be deferred for a maximum of 1 year.

COSTS AND FINANCIAL AID

Annual in-state tuition $6,535. Annual out-of-state tuition $26,654. Room and board $11,601. Required fees $2,566. Average book and supplies expense $1,082. **Required Forms and Deadlines:** FAFSA. **Notification of Awards:**

Applicants will be notified of awards on a rolling basis beginning 4/1. **Types of Aid:** *Need-based scholarships/grants:* College/university scholarship or grant aid from institutional funds; Federal Pell; Private scholarships; SEOG; State scholarships/grants; United Negro College Fund. *Loans:* Direct PLUS loans; Direct Subsidized Stafford Loans; Direct Unsubsidized Stafford Loans. **Student Employment:** Federal Work-Study Program available. Institutional employment available. **Financial Aid Statistics:** 94% needy freshmen, 92% needy undergrads receive need-based scholarship or grant aid. 18% freshmen, 13% undergrads receive non-need-based scholarship or grant aid. 69% freshmen, 69% undergrads receive need-based self-help aid. 1% freshmen, 1% undergrads receive athletic scholarships. 84% freshmen, 75% undergrads receive any aid. 50% undergrads borrow to pay for school. Average cumulative indebtedness $15,651. **Criteria awarding aid:** *Need-based:* Academics, Alumni affiliation, Leadership. *Non-need-based:* Academics, Alumni affiliation, Athletics, Leadership, State/district residency.

NORTH CENTRAL COLLEGE

Office of Admissions, Naperville, IL 60566-7063
Phone: 630-637-5800 **Financial Aid Phone:** 630-637-5600
E-mail: admissions@noctrl.edu **CEEB Code:** 1555
Fax: 630-637-5819 **Website:** www.northcentralcollege.edu **ACT Code:** 1096

This private school, affiliated with the Methodist Church, was founded in 1861. It has a 63.5 acre campus.

RATINGS

Admissions Selectivity Rating: 86   **Fire Safety Rating:** 95   **Green Rating:** 79

STUDENTS AND FACULTY

Enrollment: 2,579. **Student Body:** 53% female, 47% male, 10% out-of-state, 3% international (42 countries represented). Asian 3%, African American 4%, Caucasian 66%, Hispanic 16%, Native American <1%, Pacific Islander <1%, Two or more races 3%, Race unknown 4%.
Retention and Graduation: 78% freshmen return for sophomore year. 61% freshmen graduate within 4 years. 69% freshmen graduate within 6 years. 18% grads go on to further study within 1 year. **Faculty:** Student/faculty ratio 14:1. 158 full-time faculty, 93% hold PhDs, 17% are members of minority groups, 55% are women. 0% of classes are taught by teaching assistants.

ACADEMICS

Degrees: Bachelor's; Master's; Post-bachelor's certificate. **Classes:** Most classes have 10–19 students. Most lab/discussion sessions have 20–29 students. **Most popular majors:** Psychology, General; Business Administration, Management and Operations, Other; Marketing/Marketing Management, General. **Special Study Options:** Accelerated program; Cross-registration; Double major; Dual enrollment; English as a Second Language (ESL); Exchange student program (domestic); Honors program; Independent study; Internships; Liberal arts/career combination; Student-designed major; Study abroad; Teacher certification program. **Honors programs:** The College Scholars is a comprehensive four year integrative program culminating in a senior honors thesis. The program is open to students from all academic disciplines. **Combined degree programs:** BA/MA. **Disability Services offered:** Note-taking services; Reader services; Tape recorders; Tutors. **Career services:** Alumni network; Alumni services; Career assessment; Career/job search classes; Internships; Regional alumni.

FACILITIES

Housing: Apartments for single students; Coed dorms; Special housing for disabled students; Wellness housing; Women's dorms; 95% of campus accessible to physically disabled. **Campus Network:** 100% of classrooms, 100% of dorms, 100% of student union, 100% of libraries, 100% of dining areas, 100% of common outdoor areas have wireless network access.

CAMPUS LIFE

Environment: City. **Activities:** Campus Ministries; Choral groups; Concert band; Dance; Drama/theater; International Student Organization; Jazz band; Literary magazine; Marching band; Model UN; Music ensembles; Musical theater; Opera; Pep band; Radio station; Student government; Student newspaper. 75 registered organizations, 24 honor societies, 5 religious organizations on campus. **Athletics (Intercollegiate):** *Men:* baseball, basketball, cross-country, football, golf, soccer, swimming, tennis, track/field (outdoor), track/field (indoor), wrestling. *Women:* basketball, cheerleading, cross-country, golf, lacrosse, soccer, softball, swimming, tennis, track/field (outdoor), track/

field (indoor), volleyball. **On-Campus Highlights:** Old Main—historic home of North Central College. **Environmental Initiatives:** The College created a green revolving fund, the Cardinal Sustainability Fund, committing a portion of the unrestricted endowment for sustainability initiatives.

ADMISSIONS

Freshman Academic Profile: Average high school GPA 3.7. 29% in top 10% of high school class, 55% in top 25% of high school class, 88% in top 50% of high school class. 90% from public high schools. **Test Scores:** SAT Math middle 50% range 520–630. SAT EBRW middle 50% range 510–630. ACT middle 50% range 21–27. **Basis for Candidate Selection:** *Very important factors include:* rigor of secondary school record, academic GPA, standardized test scores, character/personal qualities, volunteer work. *Important factors include:* extracurricular activities, talent/ability. *Other factors include:* application essay, recommendation(s), interview, first generation, alumni/ae relation, work experience, level of applicant's interest. **Freshman Admission Requirements:** High school diploma is required and GED is accepted. *Academic units required:* 4 English, 3 math, 3 science, 2 science labs, 2 social studies, 1 history, 3 academic electives. *Academic units recommended:* 3 science labs, 3 foreign language. **Freshman Admission Statistics:** 6,847 applied, 54% admitted, 15% enrolled. **Transfer Admission Requirements:** College transcript(s). Minimum college GPA of 2.25 required. Lowest grade transferable D. **General Admission Information:** Application fee $25. Priority deadline 4/15. Non-fall registration accepted. Admission may be deferred for a maximum of 1 year.

COSTS AND FINANCIAL AID

Annual tuition $39,860. Room and board $11,062. Required fees $180. Average book and supplies expense $1,200. **Required Forms and Deadlines:** FAFSA. **Notification of Awards:** Applicants will be notified of awards on a rolling basis beginning 12/1. **Types of Aid:** *Need-based scholarships/grants:* College/university scholarship or grant aid from institutional funds; Federal Pell; Private scholarships; SEOG; State scholarships/grants. *Loans:* Direct PLUS loans; Direct Subsidized Stafford Loans; Direct Unsubsidized Stafford Loans. **Student Employment:** Federal Work-Study Program available. Institutional employment available. **Financial Aid Statistics:** 100% needy freshmen, 100% needy undergrads receive need-based scholarship or grant aid. 22% freshmen, 17% undergrads receive non-need-based scholarship or grant aid. 77% freshmen, 80% undergrads receive need-based self-help aid. 0% freshmen, 0% undergrads receive athletic scholarships. 99% freshmen, 96% undergrads receive any aid. 76% undergrads borrow to pay for school. Average cumulative indebtedness $37,396. **Criteria awarding aid:** *Need-based:* Academics, Religious affiliation. *Non-need-based:* Academics, Art, Leadership, Minority status, Music/drama, Religious affiliation, State/district residency.

NORTH DAKOTA STATE UNIVERSITY

PO Box 6050 Dept 2832, Fargo, ND 58108
Phone: 701-231-8643 **Financial Aid Phone:** 800-726-3188
E-mail: ndsu.admission@ndsu.edu **CEEB Code:** 6474
Fax: 701-231-8802 **Website:** www.ndsu.edu **ACT Code:** 3202

This public school was founded in 1890. It has a 2100 acre campus.

RATINGS

Admissions Selectivity Rating: 76   **Fire Safety Rating:** 81   **Green Rating:** 60*

STUDENTS AND FACULTY

Enrollment: 11,609. **Student Body:** 45% female, 55% male, 57% out-of-state, 2% international (38 countries represented). Asian 1%, African American 3%, Caucasian 87%, Hispanic 2%, Native American 1%, Pacific Islander <1%, Two or more races 2%, Race unknown 2%.
Retention and Graduation: 78% freshmen return for sophomore year.
Faculty: Student/faculty ratio 17:1. 712 full-time faculty, 86% hold PhDs, 17% are members of minority groups, 40% are women.

ACADEMICS

Degrees: Bachelor's; Certificate; Doctoral degree—professional practice; Master's; Post-bachelor's certificate; Post-master's certificate. **Classes:** Most classes have 20–29 students. Most lab/discussion sessions have 20–29 students. **Most popular majors:** Civil Engineering, General; Business, Management, Marketing, and Related Support Services, Other; Mechanical Engineering. **Special Study Options:** Accelerated program; Cooperative education program; Cross-registration; Distance learning; Double major; Dual enrollment; English as a Second Language (ESL); Exchange student program (domestic); Honors program; Independent study; Internships; Student-designed major; Study abroad; Teacher certification program. **Honors programs:** Scholars Program. **Disability Services offered:** Note-taking services; Reader services; Tape recorders; Tutors. **Career services:** Career/job search classes; Internships.

FACILITIES

Housing: Apartments for married students; Apartments for single students; Coed dorms; Men's dorms; Special housing for disabled students; Special housing for international students; Wellness housing; Women's dorms.

CAMPUS LIFE

Environment: City. **Activities:** Campus Ministries; Choral groups; Concert band; Dance; Drama/theater; International Student Organization; Jazz band; Marching band; Model UN; Music ensembles; Musical theater; Opera; Pep band; Radio station; Student government; Student newspaper; Symphony orchestra; Television station. 300 registered organizations, 23 honor societies, 22 religious organizations, 12 fraternities, 3 sororities on campus. **Athletics (Intercollegiate):** *Men:* baseball, basketball, cross-country, football, golf, track/field (outdoor), track/field (indoor), wrestling. *Women:* basketball, cross-country, golf, soccer, softball, track/field (outdoor), track/field (indoor), volleyball. **On-Campus Highlights:** Wellness Center.

ADMISSIONS

Freshman Academic Profile: Average high school GPA 3.4. 15% in top 10% of high school class, 41% in top 25% of high school class, 71% in top 50% of high school class. **Test Scores:** SAT Math middle 50% range 500–630. SAT EBRW middle 50% range 480–630. ACT middle 50% range 21–26. **Basis for Candidate Selection:** *Very important factors include:* academic GPA, standardized test scores. **Freshman Admission Requirements:** High school diploma is required and GED is accepted. *Academic units required:* 4 English, 3 math, 3 science, 3 science labs, 3 social studies. **Freshman Admission Statistics:** 5,311 applied, 94% admitted, 51% enrolled. **Transfer Admission Requirements:** College transcript(s). Minimum college GPA of 2.0 required. Lowest grade transferable D. **General Admission Information:** Application fee $35. Regular application deadline 8/1. Non-fall registration accepted. Admission may be deferred for a maximum of 3 years.

COSTS AND FINANCIAL AID

Annual in-state tuition $6,762. Annual out-of-state tuition $18,056. Room and board $7,502. Required fees $1,216. Average book and supplies expense $1,100. **Required Forms and Deadlines:** FAFSA. **Notification of Awards:** Applicants will be notified of awards on a rolling basis beginning 4/1. **Types of Aid:** *Need-based scholarships/grants:* College/university scholarship or grant aid from institutional funds; Federal Pell; Private scholarships; SEOG; State scholarships/grants. *Loans:* Direct PLUS loans; Direct Subsidized Stafford Loans; Direct Unsubsidized Stafford Loans. **Student Employment:** Federal Work-Study Program available. Institutional employment available. **Financial Aid Statistics:** 77% needy freshmen, 71% needy undergrads receive need-based scholarship or grant aid. 8% freshmen, 5% undergrads receive non-need-based scholarship or grant aid. 79% freshmen, 80% undergrads receive need-based self-help aid. 2% freshmen, 1% undergrads receive athletic scholarships. 69% undergrads borrow to pay for school. Average cumulative indebtedness $30,740. **Criteria awarding aid:** *Need-based:* Academics, Alumni affiliation, Art, Athletics, Leadership, Minority status, Music/drama. *Non-need-based:* Academics, Alumni affiliation, Art, Athletics, Leadership, Minority status, Music/drama, State/district residency.

NORTHEASTERN ILLINOIS UNIVERSITY

5500 North St. Louis Avenue, Chicago, IL 60625-4699
Phone: 773-442-4000 **Financial Aid Phone:** 773-442-5009
E-mail: admrec@neiu.edu **CEEB Code:** 1090
Fax: 773-442-4020 **Website:** www.neiu.edu **ACT Code:** 993

This public school was founded in 1867. It has a 67 acre campus.

RATINGS

Admissions Selectivity Rating: 75   **Fire Safety Rating:** 60*   **Green Rating:** 74

STUDENTS AND FACULTY

Enrollment: 7,979. **Student Body:** 56% female, 44% male, 1% out-of-state, 4% international (91 countries represented). Asian 9%, African American 10%, Caucasian 33%, Hispanic 37%, Native American <1%, Pacific Islander <1%, Two or more races 2%, Race unknown 3%.

Retention and Graduation: 61% freshmen return for sophomore year. **Faculty:** Student/faculty ratio 14:1. 374 full-time faculty, 82% hold PhDs, 30% are members of minority groups, 53% are women.

ACADEMICS

Degrees: Bachelor's; Certificate; Master's. **Classes:** Most classes have 20–29 students. **Most popular majors:** Social Work; Biology/Biological Sciences, General; Psychology, General. **Special Study Options:** Distance learning; Double major; Dual enrollment; English as a Second Language (ESL); Honors program; Independent study; Internships; Liberal arts/career combination; Student-designed major; Study abroad; Teacher certification program; Weekend college. **Honors programs:** The University Honors Program is a four-year university wide program providing a challenging educational experience to qualified students. The program serves as a laboratory for academic innovation that will improve undergraduate education, and provide a place for students to discover the best in themselves. Through small classes emphasizing writing and critical thinking skills and close, continual academic advisement, the Honors Program seeks to provide access to excellent education for its students. **Disability Services offered:** Note-taking services; Reader services; Tape recorders; Tutors. **Career services:** Alumni network; Alumni services; Career assessment; Career/job search classes; Internships.

FACILITIES

98% of campus accessible to physically disabled. **Special Academic Facilities/ Equipment:** Art gallery, learning center with audiovisual, TV, multimedia, film, photography, graphic arts, and electronic instructional equipment, listening room.

CAMPUS LIFE

Environment: Metropolis. **Activities:** Campus Ministries; Choral groups; Concert band; Dance; Drama/theater; International Student Organization; Jazz band; Literary magazine; Model UN; Music ensembles; Musical theater; Opera; Radio station; Student government; Student newspaper; Student-run film society; Symphony orchestra. 90 registered organizations, 12 honor societies, 3 religious organizations, 7 fraternities, 9 sororities on campus. **On-Campus Highlights:** Angelina Pedroso Center. **Environmental Initiatives:** Recycling.

ADMISSIONS

Freshman Academic Profile: Average high school GPA 2.8. 3% in top 10% of high school class, 13% in top 25% of high school class, 44% in top 50% of high school class. 87% from public high schools. **Test Scores:** ACT middle 50% range 16–20. **Basis for Candidate Selection:** *Very important factors include:* class rank, academic GPA, standardized test scores. **Freshman Admission Requirements:** High school diploma is required and GED is accepted. *Academic units required:* 4 English, 3 math, 3 science, 3 social studies, 2 visual/performing arts. *Academic units recommended:* 4 English, 3 math, 3 science, 3 social studies, 2 visual/performing arts. **Freshman Admission Statistics:** 4,499 applied, 67% admitted, 25% enrolled. **Transfer Admission Requirements:** College transcript(s), statement of good standing from prior institution(s). Minimum college GPA of 2.0 required. Lowest grade transferable D. **General Admission Information:** Application fee $30. Regular application deadline 7/1. Non-fall registration accepted.

COSTS AND FINANCIAL AID

Annual in-state tuition $8,376. Annual out-of-state tuition $16,776. Room and board $11,100. Required fees $3,322. **Required Forms and Deadlines:** FAFSA. **Notification of Awards:** Applicants will be notified of awards on a rolling basis beginning 3/15. **Types of Aid:** *Need-based scholarships/grants:* College/university scholarship or grant aid from institutional funds; Federal Pell; Private scholarships; SEOG; State scholarships/grants. *Loans:* Direct PLUS loans; Direct Subsidized Stafford Loans; Direct Unsubsidized Stafford Loans. **Student Employment:** Federal Work-Study Program available. Institutional employment available. **Financial Aid Statistics:** 84% needy freshmen, 78% needy undergrads receive need-based scholarship or grant aid. 7% freshmen, 15% undergrads receive non-need-based scholarship or grant aid. 15% freshmen, 37% undergrads receive need-based self-help aid. 0% freshmen, 0% undergrads receive athletic scholarships. 59% freshmen, 55% undergrads receive any aid. 48% undergrads borrow to pay for school. Average cumulative indebtedness $15,713. **Criteria awarding aid:** *Non-need-based:* Academics, Art, Leadership, Music/drama.

NORTHEASTERN STATE UNIVERSITY

Office of Admissions and Recruitment, Tahlequah, OK 74464-2399
Phone: 918-444-2200 **Financial Aid Phone:** 918-444-3456
E-mail: nsuinfo@nsuok.edu **CEEB Code:** 6485
Fax: 918-458-2342 **ACT Code:** 3408

This public school was founded in 1846. It has a 200 acre campus.

RATINGS
Admissions Selectivity Rating: 75   **Fire Safety Rating:** 60*   **Green Rating:** 60*

STUDENTS AND FACULTY
Enrollment: 7,036. **Student Body:** 61% female, 39% male, 6% out-of-state, 2% international (41 countries represented). Asian 2%, African American 4%, Caucasian 49%, Hispanic 5%, Native American 20%, Pacific Islander <1%, Two or more races 17%, Race unknown 2%.
Retention and Graduation: 62% freshmen return for sophomore year.
Faculty: Student/faculty ratio 17:1. 306 full-time faculty, 77% hold PhDs, 21% are members of minority groups, 51% are women.

ACADEMICS
Degrees: Bachelor's; Master's; Post-bachelor's certificate; Post-master's certificate. **Classes:** Most classes have 20–29 students. Most lab/discussion sessions have fewer than 10 students. **Most popular majors:** Accounting; Elementary Education and Teaching; Psychology, General. **Special Study Options:** Distance learning; Double major; Dual enrollment; English as a Second Language (ESL); Honors program; Independent study; Internships; Student-designed major; Study abroad; Teacher certification program; Weekend college. **Honors programs:** NSU Honors Program: The Honors Program at Northeastern State University is a challenging educational option for academically talented students who enjoy learning. Honor students work with distinguished faculty members and peers in enhanced courses, pursue independent research, and participate in co-curricular cultural experiences. NSU President's Leadership Class: The President's Leadership Class is a unique leadership/scholarship program designed to cultivate outstanding potential in proven student leaders. Applicants for the PLC should display outstanding leadership capabilities, and must have an exceptionally strong academic record. **Disability Services offered:** Note-taking services; Reader services; Tape recorders; Tutors. **Career services:** Alumni services; Career assessment; Career/job search classes.

FACILITIES
Housing: Apartments for married students; Apartments for single students; Coed dorms; Fraternity/sorority housing; Special housing for disabled students; Theme housing; Women's dorms. **Campus Network:** 80% of classrooms, 100% of dorms, 100% of student union, 100% of libraries, 100% of dining areas, 90% of common outdoor areas have wireless network access.

CAMPUS LIFE
Environment: Village. **Activities:** Campus Ministries; Choral groups; Concert band; Dance; Drama/theater; International Student Organization; Jazz band; Marching band; Model UN; Music ensembles; Pep band; Student government; Student newspaper; Symphony orchestra; Television station. 88 registered organizations, 7 honor societies, 6 religious organizations, 6 fraternities, 5 sororities on campus. **Athletics (Intercollegiate):** *Men:* baseball, basketball, football, golf, soccer. *Women:* basketball, golf, soccer, softball, tennis. **On-Campus Highlights:** Seminary Hall.

ADMISSIONS
Freshman Academic Profile: Average high school GPA 3.4. 20% in top 10% of high school class, 47% in top 25% of high school class, 83% in top 50% of high school class. 95% from public high schools. **Test Scores:** ACT middle 50% range 19–23. **Basis for Candidate Selection:** *Very important factors include:* rigor of secondary school record, class rank, academic GPA, standardized test scores. *Other factors include:* interview, extracurricular activities, first generation, geographical residence, state residency, level of applicant's interest. **Freshman Admission Requirements:** High school diploma is required and GED is accepted. *Academic units required:* 4 English, 3 math, 3 science, 3 science labs, 2 social studies, 1 history, 2 unit from above areas or other academic areas. **Freshman Admission Statistics:** 1,512 applied, 92% admitted, 58% enrolled. **Transfer Admission Requirements:** College transcript(s). Minimum college GPA of 2.0 required. Lowest grade transferable D. **General Admission Information:** Application fee $25. Non-fall registration accepted.

COSTS AND FINANCIAL AID
Annual in-state tuition $4,425. Annual out-of-state tuition $11,775. Room and board $6,490. Required fees $1,122. Average book and supplies expense $1,200. **Required Forms and Deadlines:** FAFSA. **Notification of Awards:** Applicants will be notified of awards on a rolling basis beginning 3/1. **Types of Aid:** *Need-based scholarships/grants:* College/university scholarship or grant aid from institutional funds; Federal Pell; Private scholarships; SEOG; State scholarships/grants. *Loans:* Direct PLUS loans; Direct Subsidized Stafford Loans; Direct Unsubsidized Stafford Loans. **Student Employment:** Federal Work-Study Program available. Institutional employment available. **Financial Aid Statistics:** 94% needy freshmen, 86% needy undergrads receive need-based scholarship or grant aid. 31% freshmen, 15% undergrads receive non-need-based scholarship or grant aid. 80% freshmen, 88% undergrads receive need-based self-help aid. 4% freshmen, 3% undergrads receive athletic scholarships. 63% freshmen, 62% undergrads receive any aid. 62% undergrads borrow to pay for school. Average cumulative indebtedness $21,055. **Criteria awarding aid:** *Non-need-based:* Academics, Alumni affiliation, Art, Athletics, Leadership, Minority status, Music/drama, Religious affiliation, State/district residency.

NORTHEASTERN UNIVERSITY

360 Huntington Avenue, Boston, MA 02115
Phone: 617-373-2200 **Financial Aid Phone:** 617-373-3190
E-mail: admissions@northeastern.edu **CEEB Code:** 3667
Fax: 617-373-8780 **Website:** www.northeastern.edu **ACT Code:** 1880

This private school was founded in 1898. It has a 73 acre campus.

RATINGS
Admissions Selectivity Rating: 97   **Fire Safety Rating:** 94   **Green Rating:** 97

STUDENTS AND FACULTY
Enrollment: 18,191. **Student Body:** 51% female, 49% male, 73% out-of-state, 17% international (124 countries represented). Asian 14%, African American 4%, Caucasian 45%, Hispanic 8%, Native American <1%, Pacific Islander <1%, Two or more races 5%, Race unknown 6%.
Retention and Graduation: 96% freshmen return for sophomore year. 90% freshmen graduate within 6 years. **Faculty:** Student/faculty ratio 14:1. 1,371 full-time faculty, 94% hold PhDs, 19% are members of minority groups, 43% are women.

ACADEMICS
Degrees: Bachelor's; Doctoral degree—professional practice; Doctoral degree research/scholarship; Master's; Post-master's certificate. **Classes:** Most classes have 10–19 students. Most lab/discussion sessions have 10–19 students. **Most popular majors:** Engineering, General; Health Professions And Related Programs; Business Administration, Management and Operations. **Special Study Options:** Accelerated program; Cooperative education program; Cross-registration; Distance learning; Double major; English as a Second Language (ESL); Exchange student program (domestic); Honors program; Independent study; Internships; Liberal arts/career combination; Student-designed major; Study abroad; Teacher certification program. **Honors programs:** The University Honors Program at Northeastern offers exceptionally motivated students an opportunity to elevate their educational experience through deeper academic exploration, a higher level of engagement with faculty, and special options for service and leadership. Honors Program students are invited to choose one of several Living and Learning Communities (LLCs) proposed by the students each year. **Combined degree programs:** BA/JD; BA/MA; BA/MEng. **Disability Services offered:** Note-taking services; Reader services; Tape recorders. **Career services:** Alumni network; Alumni services; Career assessment; Career/job search classes; Internships; Regional alumni.

FACILITIES
Housing: Apartments for single students; Coed dorms; Theme housing; Wellness housing; 95% of campus accessible to physically disabled. **Special Academic Facilities/Equipment:** 'Gallery 360,' state-of-the-art homeland security research facility; complex network research, drug recovery, high-rate non-manufacturing, subsurface sensing and imaging systems, and urban and regional policy centers; chemical and biological analysis, information

assurance, urban health research, African-American, race and justice, and global innovation institutes. John D. O'Bryant African-American Institute, Egan Science/Engineering Center, Behrakis Health Sciences Center, Marine Science Center, Center for Subsurfacing Sensing and Imaging Systems (CenSSIS), Barnett Institute of Chemical and Biological Analysis, Research Vessel MYSIS, Badger-Rosen Squashbusters Center. **Campus Network:** 100% of classrooms, 100% of dorms, 100% of student union, 100% of libraries, 100% of dining areas, 100% of common outdoor areas have wireless network access.

CAMPUS LIFE

Environment: Metropolis. **Activities:** Choral groups; Concert band; Dance; Drama/theater; International Student Organization; Jazz band; Literary magazine; Model UN; Music ensembles; Musical theater; Pep band; Radio station; Student government; Student newspaper; Student-run film society; Symphony orchestra; Television station; Yearbook. 400 registered organizations, 22 religious organizations on campus. **Athletics (Intercollegiate):** *Men:* baseball, basketball, crew/rowing, cross-country, ice hockey, soccer, track/field (outdoor), track/field (indoor). *Women:* basketball, crew/rowing, cross-country, diving, field hockey, ice hockey, soccer, swimming, track/field (outdoor), track/field (indoor), volleyball. **On-Campus Highlights:** Curry Student. Center **Environmental Initiatives:** ACUPCC Presidents Climate Committee.

ADMISSIONS

Freshman Academic Profile: 75% in top 10% of high school class, 93% in top 25% of high school class, 99% in top 50% of high school class. **Test Scores:** SAT Math middle 50% range 710–790. SAT EBRW middle 50% range 680–750. ACT middle 50% range 32–35. **Basis for Candidate Selection:** *Very important factors include:* rigor of secondary school record, academic GPA, application essay, standardized test scores, recommendation(s). *Important factors include:* extracurricular activities, talent/ability, character/personal qualities, volunteer work. *Other factors include:* class rank, first generation, geographical residence, racial/ethnic status, level of applicant's interest. **Freshman Admission Requirements:** High school diploma is required and GED is accepted. *Academic units required:* 4 English, 3 math, 3 science, 2 science labs, 2 foreign language, 3 social studies, 2 history. *Academic units recommended:* 4 math, 4 science. **Freshman Admission Statistics:** 62,263 applied, 18% admitted, 27% enrolled. **Transfer Admission Requirements:** College transcript(s), essay or personal statement, statement of good standing from prior institution(s). Minimum college GPA of 2.0 required. Lowest grade transferable C. **General Admission Information:** Application fee $75. Regular application deadline 1/1. Non-fall registration accepted.

COSTS AND FINANCIAL AID

Annual tuition $52,420. Room and board $16,930. Required fees $1,086. Average book and supplies expense $1,000. **Required Forms and Deadlines:** Business/Farm Supplement; CSS/Financial Aid PROFILE; FAFSA; Noncustodial PROFILE. **Notification of Awards:** Applicants will be notified of awards on or about 4/1. **Types of Aid:** *Need-based scholarships/grants:* College/university scholarship or grant aid from institutional funds; Federal Pell; Private scholarships; SEOG; State scholarships/grants. *Loans:* Direct PLUS loans; Direct Subsidized Stafford Loans; Direct Unsubsidized Stafford Loans. **Student Employment:** Federal Work-Study Program available. Institutional employment available. **Financial Aid Statistics:** 99% needy freshmen, 94% needy undergrads receive need-based scholarship or grant aid. 47% freshmen, 48% undergrads receive non-need-based scholarship or grant aid. 87% freshmen, 84% undergrads receive need-based self-help aid. 2% freshmen, 2% undergrads receive athletic scholarships. **Criteria awarding aid:** *Non-need-based:* Academics, Athletics, Leadership.

NORTHERN ARIZONA UNIVERSITY

PO Box 4084, Flagstaff, AZ 86011-4084
Phone: 928-523-5511 **Financial Aid Phone:** 855.628.6333
E-mail: admissions@nau.edu **CEEB Code:** 4006
Fax: 928-523-6023 **Website:** https://www.nau.edu **ACT Code:** 0086

This public school was founded in 1899. It has a 683 acre campus.

RATINGS

Admissions Selectivity Rating: 76   **Fire Safety Rating:** 91   **Green Rating:** 94

STUDENTS AND FACULTY

Enrollment: 26,135. **Student Body:** 62% female, 38% male, 31% out-of-state, 4% international (57 countries represented). Asian 2%, African American 3%,

Caucasian 55%, Hispanic 25%, Native American 3%, Pacific Islander <1%, Two or more races 6%, Race unknown 2%.
Retention and Graduation: 78% freshmen return for sophomore year. 41% freshmen graduate within 4 years. 57% freshmen graduate within 6 years. 23% grads go on to further study within 1 year. **Faculty:** Student/faculty ratio 19:1. 1,151 full-time faculty, 78% hold PhDs, 17% are members of minority groups, 52% are women.

ACADEMICS

Degrees: Bachelor's; Certificate; Doctoral degree—professional practice; Doctoral degree research/scholarship; Master's; Post-bachelor's certificate; Post-master's certificate. **Classes:** Most classes have 20–29 students. Most lab/discussion sessions have 20–29 students. **Most popular majors:** Biomedical Sciences, General; Registered Nursing/Registered Nurse; Criminology. **Special Study Options:** Accelerated program; Cooperative education program; Distance learning; Double major; English as a Second Language (ESL); Exchange student program (domestic); Honors program; Independent study; Internships; Liberal arts/career combination; Student-designed major; Study abroad; Teacher certification program. **Honors programs:** Our rigorous, personalized program of study with honors-distinguished coursework challenges students' intellect and stimulates their love of learning. Upon graduation students will receive the honors distinction on their transcripts and diploma, helping graduates gain a competitive edge early in their chosen career. **Combined degree programs:** BA/JD; BA/MA; BA/MEng. **Disability Services offered:** Note-taking services; Reader services; Tape recorders; Tutors. **Career services:** Alumni services; Career assessment; Career/job search classes; Internships.

FACILITIES

Housing: Apartments for married students; Apartments for single students; Coed dorms; Fraternity/sorority housing; Special housing for disabled students; Special housing for international students; Theme housing; 98% of campus accessible to physically disabled. **Special Academic Facilities/Equipment:** Old Main, the first building on campus, is home to the NAU Art Museum and Weiss Gallery, a leading cultural institution in Northern Arizona, offering contemporary art, special exhibitions, and outreach efforts throughout Northern Arizona. Cline Library with its Special Collections and Archives holds NAU's historical records from the last 120 years. NAU's Atmospheric Research Observatory houses the research-grade Lutz Telescope. The J. Lawrence Walkup Skydome, NAU's multi-purpose facility, is the largest laminated wood beam structure of its kind in the world. **Campus Network:** 100% of dorms, 100% of libraries have wireless network access.

CAMPUS LIFE

Environment: Town. **Activities:** Campus Ministries; Choral groups; Concert band; Dance; Drama/theater; International Student Organization; Jazz band; Literary magazine; Marching band; Model UN; Music ensembles; Musical theater; Opera; Pep band; Radio station; Student government; Student newspaper; Student-run film society; Symphony orchestra; Television station. 386 registered organizations, 23 honor societies, 23 religious organizations, 16 fraternities, 15 sororities on campus. **Athletics (Intercollegiate):** *Men:* basketball, cheerleading, cross-country, football, tennis, track/field (outdoor). *Women:* basketball, cheerleading, cross-country, diving, golf, soccer, swimming, tennis, track/field (outdoor), volleyball. **On-Campus Highlights:** University Union. **Environmental Initiatives:** Sustainable Dining: Vegan options at dining locations, O_2GO reusable to-go containers, removing plastic straws from campus, and the Food Recovery Network that donates thousands of pounds of leftover food to the local Flagstaff Family Food Center.

ADMISSIONS

Freshman Academic Profile: Average high school GPA 3.6. 21% in top 10% of high school class, 51% in top 25% of high school class, 84% in top 50% of high school class. **Test Scores:** SAT Math middle 50% range 520–610. SAT EBRW middle 50% range 520–620. ACT middle 50% range 19–25. **Basis for Candidate Selection:** *Very important factors include:* academic GPA. *Important factors include:* rigor of secondary school record, standardized test scores. *Other factors include:* class rank. **Freshman Admission Requirements:** High school diploma is required and GED is accepted. *Academic units required:* 4 English, 4 math, 3 science, 3 science labs, 2 foreign language, 1 social studies, 1 history, 1 unit from above areas or other academic areas. **Freshman Admission Statistics:** 36,855 applied, 85% admitted, 17% enrolled. Minimum college GPA of 2.0 required. Lowest grade transferable C. **General Admission Information:** Application fee $25. Regular application deadline 8/1. Non-fall registration accepted.

COSTS AND FINANCIAL AID

Annual in-state tuition $10,650. Annual out-of-state tuition $25,270. Room and board $10,534. Required fees $1,246. Average book and supplies expense $1,000. **Required Forms and Deadlines:** FAFSA. **Notification of Awards:** Applicants will be notified of awards on a rolling basis beginning 2/1. **Types of Aid:** *Need-based scholarships/grants:* College/university scholarship or grant aid from institutional funds; Federal Nursing Scholarships; Federal Pell; Private scholarships; SEOG; State scholarships/grants. *Loans:* Direct PLUS loans; Direct Subsidized Stafford Loans; Direct Unsubsidized Stafford Loans. **Student Employment:** Federal Work-Study Program available. Institutional employment available. **Financial Aid Statistics:** 70% needy freshmen, 69% needy undergrads receive need-based scholarship or grant aid. 91% freshmen, 71% undergrads receive non-need-based scholarship or grant aid. 51% freshmen, 57% undergrads receive need-based self-help aid. 1% freshmen, 1% undergrads receive athletic scholarships. 95% freshmen, 80% undergrads receive any aid. 58% undergrads borrow to pay for school. Average cumulative indebtedness $23,560. **Criteria awarding aid:** *Need-based:* Academics, Art, Leadership, Minority status, Music/drama. *Non-need-based:* Academics, Alumni affiliation, Art, Athletics, Leadership, Minority status, Music/drama, State/district residency.

NORTHERN ILLINOIS UNIVERSITY

1425 Lincoln Hwy, DeKalb, IL
Financial Aid Phone: 815-753-1395
CEEB Code: 1559
ACT Code: 1102

This public school was founded in 1895. It has a 546 acre campus.

RATINGS
Admissions Selectivity Rating: 85   **Fire Safety Rating:** 60*   **Green Rating:** 60*

STUDENTS AND FACULTY
Enrollment: 14,036. **Student Body:** 49% female, 51% male, 3% out-of-state, 2% international. Asian 5%, African American 16%, Caucasian 56%, Hispanic 17%, Native American <1%, Pacific Islander <1%, Two or more races 4%, Race unknown 1%.
Retention and Graduation: 73% freshmen return for sophomore year. 16% grads pursue arts and sciences degrees. 3% grads pursue law degrees. 51% grads pursue business degrees. 1% grads pursue medical degrees. **Faculty:** Student/faculty ratio 15:1. 832 full-time faculty, 82% hold PhDs, 14% are members of minority groups, 46% are women.

ACADEMICS
Classes: Most classes have 20–29 students. Most lab/discussion sessions have fewer than 10 students. **Special Study Options:** Cooperative education program; Distance learning; Double major; Dual enrollment; External degree program; Honors program; Independent study; Internships; Student-designed major; Study abroad; Teacher certification program. **Combined degree programs:** BA/JD. **Disability Services offered:** Note-taking services; Reader services; Tape recorders. **Career services:** Alumni network; Alumni services; Career/job search classes; Internships; Regional alumni.

FACILITIES
Housing: Apartments for married students; Coed dorms; Fraternity/sorority housing; Men's dorms; Special housing for disabled students; Special housing for international students; Women's dorms; 90% of campus accessible to physically disabled. **Special Academic Facilities/Equipment:** Art and anthropology museums, plant molecular biology center.

CAMPUS LIFE
Environment: Village. **Activities:** Campus Ministries; Choral groups; Concert band; Dance; Drama/theater; International Student Organization; Jazz band; Marching band; Model UN; Music ensembles; Musical theater; Opera; Pep band; Radio station; Student government; Student newspaper; Student-run film society; Symphony orchestra; Television station. 355 registered organizations, 23 religious organizations, 27 fraternities, 19 sororities on campus. **Athletics (Intercollegiate):** *Men:* baseball, basketball, diving, football, golf, soccer, swimming, tennis, wrestling. *Women:* basketball, cross-country, golf, gymnastics, soccer, softball, swimming, tennis, volleyball. **On-Campus Highlights:** Barsema Hall.

ADMISSIONS
Freshman Academic Profile: 12% in top 10% of high school class, 36% in top 25% of high school class, 71% in top 50% of high school class. **Test Scores:** ACT middle 50% range 19–25. **Basis for Candidate Selection:** *Very important factors include:* rigor of secondary school record, class rank, standardized test scores. *Other factors include:* application essay, recommendation(s), interview, extracurricular activities, talent/ability, racial/ethnic status. **Freshman Admission Requirements:** High school diploma is required and GED is accepted. *Academic units required:* 4 English, 2 math, 2 science, 1 science lab, 1 foreign language, 2 social studies, 1 history. *Academic units recommended:* 4 math, 4 science, 2 science labs, 2 foreign language, 3 social studies. **Freshman Admission Statistics:** 14,980 applied, 52% admitted, 23% enrolled. **Transfer Admission Requirements:** College transcript(s). Minimum college GPA of 2.0 required. Lowest grade transferable C. **General Admission Information:** Application fee $40. Priority deadline 3/1. Regular application deadline 8/1. Non-fall registration accepted.

COSTS AND FINANCIAL AID
Annual in-state tuition $9,466. Annual out-of-state tuition $18,931. Room and board $9,670. Average book and supplies expense $1,400. **Required Forms and Deadlines:** FAFSA; Institution's own financial aid form; Noncustodial PROFILE. **Notification of Awards:** Applicants will be notified of awards on a rolling basis beginning 3/1. **Types of Aid:** *Need-based scholarships/grants:* College/university scholarship or grant aid from institutional funds; Federal Nursing Scholarships; Federal Pell; Private scholarships; SEOG; State scholarships/grants. **Student Employment:** Federal Work-Study Program available. Institutional employment available. **Financial Aid Statistics:** 97% needy freshmen, 83% needy undergrads receive need-based scholarship or grant aid. 6% freshmen, 3% undergrads receive non-need-based scholarship or grant aid. 87% freshmen, 91% undergrads receive need-based self-help aid. 2% freshmen, 2% undergrads receive athletic scholarships. 77% freshmen, 70% undergrads receive any aid. 78% undergrads borrow to pay for school. Average cumulative indebtedness $34,713. **Criteria awarding aid:** *Need-based:* Academics. *Non-need-based:* Academics, Alumni affiliation, Art, Athletics, Leadership, Music/drama.

NORTHERN KENTUCKY UNIVERSITY

Administrative Center 400, Highland Heights, KY 41099
Phone: 859-572-5220 **Financial Aid Phone:** 859-572-5143
E-mail: beanorse@nku.edu **CEEB Code:** 1574
Fax: 859-572-6665 **Website:** www.nku.edu **ACT Code:** 1566

This public school was founded in 1968. It has a 400 acre campus.

RATINGS
Admissions Selectivity Rating: 76   **Fire Safety Rating:** 86   **Green Rating:** 69

STUDENTS AND FACULTY
Enrollment: 10,220. **Student Body:** 57% female, 43% male, 30% out-of-state, 3% international (61 countries represented). Asian 1%, African American 7%, Caucasian 81%, Hispanic 3%, Native American <1%, Pacific Islander <1%, Two or more races 3%, Race unknown 1%.
Retention and Graduation: 67% freshmen return for sophomore year. 16% freshmen graduate within 4 years. 40% freshmen graduate within 6 years. **Faculty:** Student/faculty ratio 19:1. 559 full-time faculty, 71% hold PhDs, 13% are members of minority groups, 53% are women. 0% of classes are taught by teaching assistants.

ACADEMICS
Degrees: Associate; Bachelor's; Certificate; Doctoral degree—other; Doctoral degree—professional practice; Master's; Post-bachelor's certificate; Post-master's certificate. **Classes:** Most classes have 20–29 students. Most lab/discussion sessions have 10–19 students. **Most popular majors:** Social Work; Registered Nursing/Registered Nurse; Organizational Behavior Studies. **Special Study Options:** Accelerated program; Cooperative education program; Cross-registration; Distance learning; Double major; Dual enrollment; English as a Second Language (ESL); Honors program; Independent study; Internships; Liberal arts/career combination; Student-designed major; Study abroad; Teacher certification program. **Honors programs:** The Honors College prepares students for a lifetime of success by building such critical skills as understanding diverse points-of-view, communication and collaboration, information evaluation, and innovative thinking so they can spearhead the next

generation of achievement. **Combined degree programs:** BA/JD. **Disability Services offered:** Note-taking services; Reader services; Tape recorders; Tutors. **Career services:** Alumni services; Career assessment; Career/job search classes; Internships.

FACILITIES

Housing: Apartments for single students; Coed dorms; Fraternity/sorority housing; Special housing for disabled students; Special housing for international students; Theme housing; 100% of campus accessible to physically disabled. **Special Academic Facilities/Equipment:** Art gallery, The Museum of Anthropology, US Bank/Ralph V. Haile Planetarium, George and Ellen Rieveschl Digitorium.

CAMPUS LIFE

Environment: Village. **Activities:** Campus Ministries; Choral groups; Dance; Drama/theater; International Student Organization; Literary magazine; Model UN; Music ensembles; Musical theater; Opera; Pep band; Radio station; Student government; Student newspaper; Student-run film society; Television station. 245 registered organizations, 16 honor societies, 18 religious organizations, 13 fraternities, 9 sororities on campus. **Athletics (Intercollegiate):** *Men:* baseball, basketball, cheerleading, cross-country, golf, soccer, tennis. *Women:* basketball, cheerleading, cross-country, golf, soccer, softball, tennis, volleyball. **On-Campus Highlights:** Student Union. **Environmental Initiatives:** In an effort to reduce greenhouse gas emissions from commuting, NKU is committed to providing alternative transportation options to the campus community. Students, faculty, and staff can take advantage of the University's free bike share program, free access to all TANK buses, and the ZipCar car-sharing service.

ADMISSIONS

Test Scores: SAT Math middle 50% range 480–620. SAT EBRW middle 50% range 510–610. ACT middle 50% range 20–26. **Basis for Candidate Selection:** *Very important factors include:* rigor of secondary school record, academic GPA, standardized test scores. *Important factors include:* class rank. *Other factors include:* talent/ability. **Freshman Admission Requirements:** High school diploma is required and GED is accepted. *Academic units required:* 4 English, 3 math, 3 science, 1 science lab, 2 foreign language, 3 social studies. *Academic units recommended:* 1 history, 5 academic electives, 1 computer science, 1 visual/performing arts. **Freshman Admission Statistics:** 5,995 applied, 89% admitted, 37% enrolled. **Transfer Admission Requirements:** College transcript(s). Minimum college GPA of 2.0 required. Lowest grade transferable D. **General Admission Information:** Application fee $40. Priority deadline 5/1. Regular application deadline 8/15. Non-fall registration accepted. Admission may be deferred for a maximum of 1 year.

COSTS AND FINANCIAL AID

Annual in-state tuition $9,648. Annual out-of-state tuition $19,296. Room and board $10,022. Average book and supplies expense $800. **Required Forms and Deadlines:** FAFSA. **Notification of Awards:** Applicants will be notified of awards on a rolling basis beginning 3/15. **Types of Aid:** *Need-based scholarships/grants:* College/university scholarship or grant aid from institutional funds; Federal Pell; Private scholarships; SEOG; State scholarships/grants. *Loans:* Direct PLUS loans; Direct Subsidized Stafford Loans; Direct Unsubsidized Stafford Loans. **Student Employment:** Federal Work-Study Program available. Institutional employment available. **Financial Aid Statistics:** 53% needy freshmen, 56% needy undergrads receive need-based scholarship or grant aid. 95% freshmen, 70% undergrads receive non-need-based scholarship or grant aid. 83% freshmen, 85% undergrads receive need-based self-help aid. 2% freshmen, 2% undergrads receive athletic scholarships. 87% freshmen, 77% undergrads receive any aid. 65% undergrads borrow to pay for school. Average cumulative indebtedness $26,502. **Criteria awarding aid:** *Non-need-based:* Academics, Alumni affiliation, Art, Athletics, Leadership, Music/drama, State/district residency.

NORTHERN MICHIGAN UNIVERSITY

1401 Presque Isle Avenue, Marquette, MI 49855
Phone: 906-227-2650 **Financial Aid Phone:** 800-682-9797
E-mail: admissions@nmu.edu **CEEB Code:** 1560
Fax: 906-227-1747 **Website:** www.nmu.edu **ACT Code:** 2038

This public school was founded in 1899. It has a 350 acre campus.

RATINGS

Admissions Selectivity Rating: 78   **Fire Safety Rating:** 75   **Green Rating:** 86

STUDENTS AND FACULTY

Enrollment: 6,618. **Student Body:** 54% female, 46% male, 19% out-of-state, 1% international (30 countries represented). Asian 1%, African American 2%, Caucasian 86%, Hispanic 3%, Native American 1%, Pacific Islander <1%, Two or more races 5%, Race unknown 1%.
Retention and Graduation: 78% freshmen return for sophomore year. 25% freshmen graduate within 4 years. 50% freshmen graduate within 6 years. **Faculty:** Student/faculty ratio 20:1. 288 full-time faculty, 65% hold PhDs, 11% are members of minority groups, 45% are women.

ACADEMICS

Degrees: Associate; Bachelor's; Certificate; Doctoral degree—professional practice; Master's; Post-bachelor's certificate; Post-master's certificate; Terminal Associate; Transfer Associate. **Classes:** Most classes have 20–29 students. **Most popular majors:** Criminal Justice/Safety Studies; Nursing Science; Art/Art Studies, General. **Special Study Options:** Accelerated program; Distance learning; Double major; Dual enrollment; English as a Second Language (ESL); Honors program; Independent study; Internships; Student-designed major; Study abroad; Teacher certification program. **Honors programs:** Honors Program for eligible freshmen and transfer students. **Disability Services offered:** Note-taking services; Reader services; Tape recorders; Tutors. **Career services:** Alumni network; Career/job search classes; Internships.

FACILITIES

Housing: Apartments for married students; Apartments for single students; Coed dorms; Men's dorms; Special housing for disabled students; Women's dorms; 100% of campus accessible to physically disabled. **Special Academic Facilities/Equipment:** Seaborg Science Center, New Science facility, new and remodeled Music and Art and Design instructional rooms, DeVos Art Gallery.

CAMPUS LIFE

Environment: Village. **Activities:** Campus Ministries; Choral groups; Concert band; Dance; Drama/theater; International Student Organization; Jazz band; Literary magazine; Marching band; Model UN; Music ensembles; Musical theater; Opera; Pep band; Radio station; Student government; Student newspaper; Student-run film society; Symphony orchestra; Television station. 300 registered organizations, 8 honor societies, 20 religious organizations, 2 fraternities, 4 sororities on campus. **Athletics (Intercollegiate):** *Men:* basketball, football, golf, ice hockey, skiing (Nordic/cross-country). *Women:* basketball, cross-country, diving, skiing (Nordic/cross-country), soccer, swimming, track/field (outdoor), track/field (indoor), volleyball. **On-Campus Highlights:** Hedgcock Student Service Center. **Environmental Initiatives:** Northern is a member of the Association for the Advancement of Sustainability in Higher Education and USGBC.

ADMISSIONS

Freshman Academic Profile: Average high school GPA 3.2. **Test Scores:** SAT Math middle 50% range 460–560. SAT EBRW middle 50% range 480–590. ACT middle 50% range 20–26. **Basis for Candidate Selection:** *Very important factors include:* academic GPA, standardized test scores. **Freshman Admission Requirements:** High school diploma is required and GED is accepted. *Academic units recommended:* 4 English, 4 math, 4 science, 2 foreign language, 4 social studies. **Freshman Admission Statistics:** 6,173 applied, 74% admitted, 33% enrolled. **Transfer Admission Requirements:** College transcript(s), statement of good standing from prior institution(s). Minimum college GPA of 2.0 required. Lowest grade transferable C-. **General Admission Information:** Application fee $35. Non-fall registration accepted. Admission may be deferred for a maximum of 1 year.

COSTS AND FINANCIAL AID

Annual in-state tuition $9,528. Annual out-of-state tuition $15,024. Room and board $10,328. Required fees $962. Average book and supplies expense $800. **Required Forms and Deadlines:** FAFSA. **Notification of Awards:** Applicants will be notified of awards on a rolling basis beginning 12/15. **Types of Aid:**

Need-based scholarships/grants: College/university scholarship or grant aid from institutional funds; Federal Pell; Private scholarships; SEOG; State scholarships/grants. *Loans:* Direct PLUS loans; Direct Subsidized Stafford Loans; Direct Unsubsidized Stafford Loans. **Student Employment:** Federal Work-Study Program available. Institutional employment available. **Financial Aid Statistics:** 70% needy freshmen, 69% needy undergrads receive need-based scholarship or grant aid. 80% freshmen, 65% undergrads receive non-need-based scholarship or grant aid. 76% freshmen, 80% undergrads receive need-based self-help aid. 1% freshmen, 1% undergrads receive athletic scholarships. 74% undergrads borrow to pay for school. Average cumulative indebtedness $31,075. **Criteria awarding aid:** *Non-need-based:* Academics, Art, Athletics, Leadership, Minority status, Music/drama, Religious affiliation, State/district residency.

NORTHERN STATE UNIVERSITY

1200 South Jay Street, Aberdeen, SD 57401-7198
Phone: 605-626-2544 **Financial Aid Phone:** 605-626-2640
E-mail: admission2@northern.edu **CEEB Code:** 6487
Fax: 605-626-2531 **Website:** www.northern.edu **ACT Code:** 3916

This public school was founded in 1901. It has a 72 acre campus.

RATINGS
Admissions Selectivity Rating: 75   Fire Safety Rating: 79   Green Rating: 60*

STUDENTS AND FACULTY
Enrollment: 1,693. **Student Body:** 57% female, 43% male, 18% out-of-state, 4% international (35 countries represented). Asian 1%, African American 2%, Caucasian 84%, Hispanic 3%, Native American 2%, Pacific Islander <1%, Two or more races 2%, Race unknown <1%.
Retention and Graduation: 67% freshmen return for sophomore year. 33% grads go on to further study within 1 year. **Faculty:** Student/faculty ratio 21:1. 90 full-time faculty, 86% hold PhDs, 8% are members of minority groups, 37% are women. 0% of classes are taught by teaching assistants.

ACADEMICS
Degrees: Associate; Bachelor's; Certificate; Master's; Post-bachelor's certificate. **Classes:** Most classes have 20–29 students. **Most popular majors:** Business/Commerce, General; Elementary Education and Teaching; Sociology, General. **Special Study Options:** Accelerated program; Cooperative education program; Cross-registration; Distance learning; Double major; Dual enrollment; English as a Second Language (ESL); Exchange student program (domestic); Honors program; Independent study; Internships; Liberal arts/career combination; Student-designed major; Study abroad; Teacher certification program. **Honors programs:** Honors Program. **Disability Services offered:** Note-taking services; Reader services; Tape recorders; Tutors. **Career services:** Alumni network; Alumni services; Career assessment; Career/job search classes; Internships; Regional alumni.

FACILITIES
Housing: Apartments for married students; Apartments for single students; Coed dorms; Special housing for disabled students; Special housing for international students; 90% of campus accessible to physically disabled. **Special Academic Facilities/Equipment:** State-Wide E-Learning Center; Art galleries. **Campus Network:** 100% of classrooms, 100% of dorms, 100% of student union, 100% of libraries, 100% of dining areas, 100% of common outdoor areas have wireless network access.

CAMPUS LIFE
Environment: Town. **Activities:** Campus Ministries; Choral groups; Concert band; Dance; Drama/theater; International Student Organization; Jazz band; Literary magazine; Marching band; Music ensembles; Musical theater; Pep band; Student government; Student newspaper; Symphony orchestra; Television station. 100 registered organizations, 5 honor societies, 6 religious organizations on campus. **Athletics (Intercollegiate):** *Men:* baseball, basketball, cheerleading, cross-country, football, golf, track/field (outdoor), track/field (indoor), wrestling. *Women:* basketball, cheerleading, cross-country, golf, soccer, softball, swimming, tennis, track/field (outdoor), track/field (indoor), volleyball. **On-Campus Highlights:** NSU Student Center.

ADMISSIONS
Freshman Academic Profile: Average high school GPA 3.3. 7% in top 10% of high school class, 20% in top 25% of high school class, 60% in top 50% of high school class. **Test Scores:** SAT Math middle 50% range 370–580. SAT

EBRW middle 50% range 420–540. ACT middle 50% range 19–25. **Basis for Candidate Selection:** *Very important factors include:* rigor of secondary school record, class rank, standardized test scores. *Other factors include:* recommendation(s), interview, extracurricular activities, talent/ability, character/personal qualities. **Freshman Admission Requirements:** High school diploma is required and GED is accepted. *Academic units required:* 4 English, 3 math, 3 science, 3 science labs, 3 social studies. **Freshman Admission Statistics:** 1,379 applied, 83% admitted, 32% enrolled. **Transfer Admission Requirements:** High school transcript, college transcript(s), statement of good standing from prior institution(s). Minimum college GPA of 2.0 required. Lowest grade transferable C. **General Admission Information:** Application fee $20. Non-fall registration accepted.

COSTS AND FINANCIAL AID
Annual in-state tuition $3,993. Annual out-of-state tuition $5,992. Room and board $6,942. Required fees $3,570. Average book and supplies expense $1,200. **Required Forms and Deadlines:** FAFSA. **Notification of Awards:** Applicants will be notified of awards on a rolling basis beginning 4/15. **Types of Aid:** *Need-based scholarships/grants:* Federal Pell; SEOG; State scholarships/grants. *Loans:* Direct PLUS loans; Direct Subsidized Stafford Loans; Direct Unsubsidized Stafford Loans. **Student Employment:** Federal Work-Study Program available. Institutional employment available. **Financial Aid Statistics:** 92% needy freshmen, 83% needy undergrads receive need-based scholarship or grant aid. 8% freshmen, 6% undergrads receive non-need-based scholarship or grant aid. 86% freshmen, 88% undergrads receive need-based self-help aid. 12% freshmen, 9% undergrads receive athletic scholarships. **Criteria awarding aid:** *Need-based:* Minority status. *Non-need-based:* Academics, Art, Athletics, Leadership, Minority status, Music/drama.

NORTHLAND COLLEGE

1411 Ellis Avenue, Ashland, WI 54806-3999
Phone: 715-682-1224 **Financial Aid Phone:** 715-682-1255
E-mail: admit@northland.edu **CEEB Code:** 1561
Fax: 715-682-1258 **Website:** www.northland.edu **ACT Code:** 4624

This private school, affiliated with the United Church of Christ, was founded in 1892. It has a 130 acre campus.

RATINGS
Admissions Selectivity Rating: 82   Fire Safety Rating: 80   Green Rating: 96

STUDENTS AND FACULTY
Enrollment: 563. **Student Body:** 54% female, 46% male, 51% out-of-state, 5% international (5 countries represented). Asian 1%, African American 3%, Caucasian 74%, Hispanic 4%, Native American 4%, Pacific Islander 0%, Two or more races 3%, Race unknown 6%.
Retention and Graduation: 64% freshmen return for sophomore year. 51% freshmen graduate within 4 years. **Faculty:** Student/faculty ratio 11:1. 49 full-time faculty, 88% hold PhDs, 4% are members of minority groups, 41% are women. 0% of classes are taught by teaching assistants.

ACADEMICS
Degrees: Bachelor's. **Classes:** Most classes have 10–19 students. Most lab/discussion sessions have 20–29 students. **Special Study Options:** Cross-registration; Double major; Dual enrollment; Exchange student program (domestic); Independent study; Internships; Student-designed major; Study abroad; Teacher certification program. **Disability Services offered:** Note-taking services; Reader services; Tape recorders; Tutors.

FACILITIES
Housing: Apartments for single students; Coed dorms; Men's dorms; Special housing for disabled students; Theme housing; Women's dorms. **Special Academic Facilities/Equipment:** Sigurd Olson Environmental Institute, Mary Griggs Burke Center for Freshwater Innovation, Center for Rural Communities, Indigenous Cultures Center, Hulings Rice Food Center, Forest Lodge Educational Campus.

CAMPUS LIFE
Environment: Village. **Activities:** Campus Ministries; Choral groups; Concert band; Dance; Drama/theater; International Student Organization; Jazz band; Literary magazine; Music ensembles; Student government; Student newspaper; Symphony orchestra; Yearbook. **Athletics (Intercollegiate):** *Men:* baseball, basketball, cross-country, ice hockey, skiing (Nordic/cross-country), soccer.

Women: basketball, cross-country, skiing (Nordic/cross-country), soccer, softball, volleyball. **On-Campus Highlights:** Campus Center. **Environmental Initiatives:** Extensive local food systems work including an 80% local food purchasing goal; a new Food Systems Facility began operations on July 15, 2017 that is used to process and store local fruits and vegetables to help meet this 80% goal, provide work experience to students and community in food processing, and bolster sustainable food networks for rural communities; and the creation of a sophisticated new composting infrastructure as part of the Food Systems Facility to advance our ability to process up to a ton of compost a day from a variety of community and institutional sources.

ADMISSIONS

Freshman Academic Profile: Average high school GPA 3.2. 9% in top 10% of high school class, 30% in top 25% of high school class, 73% in top 50% of high school class. **Test Scores:** ACT middle 50% range 18–25. **Basis for Candidate Selection:** *Very important factors include:* class rank, academic GPA. *Important factors include:* rigor of secondary school record, standardized test scores, character/personal qualities, first generation. *Other factors include:* interview, extracurricular activities, volunteer work, work experience. **Freshman Admission Requirements:** High school diploma is required and GED is accepted. *Academic units required:* 4 English, 3 math, 3 science, 1 science lab, 3 social studies, 3 academic electives. **Freshman Admission Statistics:** 2,506 applied, 51% admitted, 11% enrolled. **Transfer Admission Requirements:** High school transcript, college transcript(s), essay or personal statement, statement of good standing from prior institution(s). Minimum college GPA of 2.0 required. Lowest grade transferable C-. **General Admission Information:** Application fee $50. Non-fall registration accepted.

COSTS AND FINANCIAL AID

Annual tuition $35,998. Room and board $9,406. Required fees $1,518. Average book and supplies expense $800. **Required Forms and Deadlines:** FAFSA. **Notification of Awards:** Applicants will be notified of awards on a rolling basis beginning 12/15. **Types of Aid:** *Need-based scholarships/grants:* College/university scholarship or grant aid from institutional funds; Federal Pell; Private scholarships; SEOG; State scholarships/grants. *Loans:* Direct PLUS loans; Direct Subsidized Stafford Loans; Direct Unsubsidized Stafford Loans. **Student Employment:** Federal Work-Study Program available. Institutional employment available. **Financial Aid Statistics:** 99% needy freshmen, 97% needy undergrads receive need-based scholarship or grant aid. 18% freshmen, 13% undergrads receive non-need-based scholarship or grant aid. 80% freshmen, 75% undergrads receive need-based self-help aid. 0% freshmen, 0% undergrads receive athletic scholarships. 99% freshmen, 97% undergrads receive any aid. 85% undergrads borrow to pay for school. Average cumulative indebtedness $31,106. **Criteria awarding aid:** *Need-based:* Academics, Job skills, Minority status, Music/drama. *Non-need-based:* Academics, Alumni affiliation, Art, Job skills, Leadership, Minority status, Music/drama, Religious affiliation, State/district residency.

NORTH PARK UNIVERSITY

3225 West Foster Avenue, Chicago, IL 60625-4895
Phone: 773-244-5500 **Financial Aid Phone:** 773-244-5506
E-mail: admission@northpark.edu **CEEB Code:** 1556
Fax: 773-244-5243 **Website:** www.northpark.edu **ACT Code:** 1098

This private school, affiliated with the Evangelical Covenant Church, was founded in 1891. It has a 30 acre campus.

RATINGS

Admissions Selectivity Rating: 83 **Fire Safety Rating:** 75 **Green Rating:** 60*

STUDENTS AND FACULTY

Enrollment: 2,188. **Student Body:** 63% female, 37% male, 31% out-of-state, 4% international (31 countries represented). Asian 7%, African American 9%, Caucasian 60%, Hispanic 10%, Native American <1%, Race unknown 10%. **Retention and Graduation:** 71% freshmen return for sophomore year. 15% grads go on to further study within 1 year. 15% grads pursue arts and sciences degrees. 2% grads pursue law degrees. 10% grads pursue business degrees. 3% grads pursue medical degrees. **Faculty:** Student/faculty ratio 14:1. 125 full-time faculty, 88% hold PhDs, 17% are members of minority groups, 50% are women. 0% of classes are taught by teaching assistants.

ACADEMICS

Degrees: Bachelor's; Master's; Post-bachelor's certificate. **Classes:** Most classes have 10–19 students. Most lab/discussion sessions have 20–29 students. **Most popular majors:** Education, General; Biology/Biological Sciences, General; Business Administration and Management, General. **Special Study Options:** Accelerated program; Distance learning; Double major; English as a Second Language (ESL); Honors program; Independent study; Internships; Liberal arts/career combination; Student-designed major; Study abroad; Teacher certification program. **Honors programs:** The North Park University Honors Congress brings together students of high academic ability with faculty in a learning community designed to promote academic excellence, rigorous intellectual development, community involvement, service to others, and vocational direction. As Honors Congress Scholars, students of promise are provided opportunities to excel during their first two years of undergraduate study. Honors courses during the second two years are offered in individual departments. We strive to take the words of Jesus, "To whom much is given, much is required," and give them special consideration in the Honors Congress. Our philosophy is simply this: The Honors Congress gives students of high intellectual ability an array of learning experiences from which to choose, places them side-by-side with faculty mentors who care, and offers them guidance and encouragement along the way. **Disability Services offered:** Note-taking services; Reader services; Tape recorders; Tutors. **Career services:** Alumni network; Career assessment; Career/job search classes; Internships.

FACILITIES

Housing: Apartments for single students; Men's dorms; Special housing for disabled students; Women's dorms. **Special Academic Facilities/Equipment:** Art gallery, language lab, Swedish Historical Society Archives.

CAMPUS LIFE

Environment: Metropolis. **Activities:** Campus Ministries; Choral groups; Concert band; Drama/theater; International Student Organization; Jazz band; Literary magazine; Music ensembles; Musical theater; Opera; Pep band; Student government; Student newspaper; Symphony orchestra; Yearbook. 4 honor societies, 1 religious organization on campus. **Athletics (Intercollegiate):** *Men:* baseball, basketball, cross-country, football, golf, soccer, track/field (outdoor), track/field (indoor). *Women:* basketball, crew/rowing, cross-country, golf, soccer, softball, track/field (outdoor), track/field (indoor), volleyball. **On-Campus Highlights:** Helwig Recreation Center.

ADMISSIONS

Freshman Academic Profile: Average high school GPA 3.1. 11% in top 10% of high school class, 35% in top 25% of high school class, 66% in top 50% of high school class. 80% from public high schools. **Test Scores:** SAT Math middle 50% range 460–590. SAT EBRW middle 50% range 470–580. ACT middle 50% range 19–24. **Basis for Candidate Selection:** *Very important factors include:* rigor of secondary school record, class rank, academic GPA, application essay, standardized test scores, recommendation(s), talent/ability, character/personal qualities. *Important factors include:* interview, extracurricular activities, first generation, racial/ethnic status, volunteer work. *Other factors include:* alumni/ae relation, geographical residence, work experience, level of applicant's interest. **Freshman Admission Requirements:** High school diploma is required and GED is accepted. *Academic units recommended:* 4 English, 3 math, 3 science, 2 foreign language, 1 social studies, 1 history. **Freshman Admission Statistics:** 1,304 applied, 70% admitted, 46% enrolled. **Transfer Admission Requirements:** College transcript(s), essay or personal statement, statement of good standing from prior institution(s). Minimum college GPA of 2.0 required. Lowest grade transferable D. **General Admission Information:** Application fee $40. Priority deadline 4/1. Regular application deadline 7/1. Non-fall registration accepted. Admission may be deferred for a maximum of 1 year.

COSTS AND FINANCIAL AID

Annual tuition $23,290. Room and board $8,600. Average book and supplies expense $1,000. **Required Forms and Deadlines:** FAFSA. **Notification of Awards:** Applicants will be notified of awards on a rolling basis beginning 3/15. **Types of Aid:** *Need-based scholarships/grants:* College/university scholarship or grant aid from institutional funds; Federal Nursing Scholarships; Federal Pell; Private scholarships; SEOG; State scholarships/grants. *Loans:* Direct PLUS loans; Direct Subsidized Stafford Loans; Direct Unsubsidized Stafford Loans. **Student Employment:** Federal Work-Study Program available. Institutional employment available. **Financial Aid Statistics:** 70% needy freshmen receive need-based scholarship or grant aid. 42% freshmen receive non-need-based scholarship or grant aid. 64% freshmen receive need-based self-help aid. 0% freshmen, 0% undergrads receive athletic scholarships. 90% freshmen, 90% undergrads receive any aid. **Criteria awarding aid:** *Non-need-based:* Academics, Art, Music/drama, Religious affiliation, State/district residency.

NORTHWESTERN COLLEGE (IA)

101 7th St SW, Orange City, IA 51041
Phone: 712-707-7130 Financial Aid Phone: 712-707-7131
E-mail: admissions@nwciowa.edu CEEB Code: 6490
Fax: 712-707-7164 Website: www.nwciowa.edu ACT Code: 1346

This private school, affiliated with the Reformed Church, was founded in 1882. It has a 100 acre campus.

RATINGS
Admissions Selectivity Rating: 83   Fire Safety Rating: 96   Green Rating: 60*

STUDENTS AND FACULTY
Enrollment: 1,038. **Student Body:** 55% female, 45% male, 45% out-of-state, 3% international (16 countries represented). Asian 1%, African American 2%, Caucasian 83%, Hispanic 5%, Native American <1%, Pacific Islander 0%, Two or more races 2%, Race unknown 4%.
Retention and Graduation: 76% freshmen return for sophomore year. 62% freshmen graduate within 4 years. 68% freshmen graduate within 6 years. 12% grads go on to further study within 1 year. 5% grads pursue arts and sciences degrees. 1% grads pursue law degrees. 1% grads pursue business degrees. 6% grads pursue medical degrees. **Faculty:** Student/faculty ratio 10:1. 78 full-time faculty, 74% hold PhDs, 9% are members of minority groups, 44% are women. 0% of classes are taught by teaching assistants.

ACADEMICS
Degrees: Bachelor's; Master's; Post-bachelor's certificate. **Classes:** Most classes have 10–19 students. Most lab/discussion sessions have 10–19 students. **Most popular majors:** Education, General; Registered Nursing/Registered Nurse; Business/Commerce, General. **Special Study Options:** Distance learning; Double major; Dual enrollment; English as a Second Language (ESL); Honors program; Independent study; Internships; Liberal arts/career combination; Student-designed major; Study abroad; Teacher certification program. **Honors programs:** Honors Program: Affords students an interdisciplinary approach to understanding perennial and contemporary issues, such as technology, war and peace, gender roles, work and calling, and humor. Affords students the opportunity to delve more deeply into a topic of their choice, working with selected faculty members to complete a project that goes beyond the normal upper-division work at the college. Encourages graduate education by sponsoring trips to regional graduate schools and financially supporting graduate school applications. **Disability Services offered:** Note-taking services; Reader services; Tape recorders; Tutors. **Career services:** Alumni network; Alumni services; Career assessment; Career/job search classes; Internships.

FACILITIES
Housing: Apartments for single students; Men's dorms; Special housing for disabled students; Theme housing; Women's dorms; 90% of campus accessible to physically disabled. **Special Academic Facilities/Equipment:** DeWitt Learning Commons and Library, Christ Chapel and DeWitt Music Hall, DeWitt Theatre Arts Center, Korver Visual Arts Center, Te Paske Art Gallery, Ramaker Center. **Campus Network:** 100% of classrooms, 100% of dorms, 100% of student union, 100% of libraries, 100% of dining areas, 50% of common outdoor areas have wireless network access.

CAMPUS LIFE
Environment: Rural. **Activities:** Campus Ministries; Choral groups; Concert band; Dance; Drama/theater; International Student Organization; Jazz band; Literary magazine; Music ensembles; Musical theater; Student government; Student newspaper; Symphony orchestra; Television station; Yearbook. 52 registered organizations, 2 honor societies, 8 religious organizations on campus. **Athletics (Intercollegiate):** *Men:* baseball, basketball, cheerleading, cross-country, football, golf, soccer, track/field (outdoor), track/field (indoor), wrestling. *Women:* basketball, cheerleading, cross-country, golf, soccer, softball, track/field (outdoor), track/field (indoor), volleyball. **On-Campus Highlights:** DeWitt Learning Commons.

ADMISSIONS
Freshman Academic Profile: Average high school GPA 3.6. 23% in top 10% of high school class, 49% in top 25% of high school class, 75% in top 50% of high school class. 74% from public high schools. **Test Scores:** SAT Math middle 50% range 520–620. SAT EBRW middle 50% range 510–620. ACT middle 50% range 21–27. **Basis for Candidate Selection:** *Very important factors include:* rigor of secondary school record, standardized test scores. *Important factors include:* class rank, academic GPA, recommendation(s), talent/ability. *Other factors include:* application essay, interview, extracurricular activities, character/personal qualities, religious affiliation/commitment, level of applicant's interest. **Freshman Admission Requirements:** High school diploma is required and GED is accepted. *Academic units recommended:* 4 English, 3 math, 3 science, 3 foreign language, 3 social studies. **Freshman Admission Statistics:** 1,371 applied, 69% admitted, 31% enrolled. **Transfer Admission Requirements:** College transcript(s). Minimum college GPA of 2.2 required. Lowest grade transferable C. **General Admission Information:** Priority deadline 6/1. Non-fall registration accepted. Admission may be deferred for a maximum of 4 years.

COSTS AND FINANCIAL AID
Annual tuition $32,700. Room and board $9,800. Required fees $220. Average book and supplies expense $1,200. **Notification of Awards:** Applicants will be notified of awards on a rolling basis beginning 12/1. **Types of Aid:** *Need-based scholarships/grants:* College/university scholarship or grant aid from institutional funds; Federal Pell; Private scholarships; SEOG; State scholarships/grants. *Loans:* Direct PLUS loans; Direct Subsidized Stafford Loans; Direct Unsubsidized Stafford Loans. **Student Employment:** Federal Work-Study Program available. Institutional employment available. **Financial Aid Statistics:** 100% needy freshmen, 100% needy undergrads receive need-based scholarship or grant aid. 37% freshmen, 33% undergrads receive non-need-based scholarship or grant aid. 46% freshmen, 55% undergrads receive need-based self-help aid. 17% freshmen, 15% undergrads receive athletic scholarships. 100% freshmen, 99% undergrads receive any aid. 65% undergrads borrow to pay for school. Average cumulative indebtedness $29,473. **Criteria awarding aid:** *Non-need-based:* Academics, Alumni affiliation, Art, Athletics, Music/drama, Religious affiliation.

NORTHWESTERN STATE UNIVERSITY

South Hall, Natchitoches, LA 71497
Phone: 318-357-4078 Financial Aid Phone: 800-823-3008
E-mail: applications@nsula.edu CEEB Code: 6492
Fax: 318-357-4660 Website: www.nsula.edu ACT Code: 1600

This public school was founded in 1884. It has a 916 acre campus.

RATINGS
Admissions Selectivity Rating: 76   Fire Safety Rating: 88   Green Rating: 60*

STUDENTS AND FACULTY
Enrollment: 7,333. **Student Body:** 68% female, 32% male, 9% out-of-state, 1% international (34 countries represented). Asian 1%, African American 30%, Caucasian 57%, Hispanic 3%, Native American 1%, Pacific Islander <1%, Two or more races 3%, Race unknown 4%.
Retention and Graduation: 71% freshmen return for sophomore year. **Faculty:** Student/faculty ratio 19:1. 291 full-time faculty, 60% hold PhDs, 8% are members of minority groups, 55% are women. 1% of classes are taught by teaching assistants.

ACADEMICS
Degrees: Associate; Bachelor's; Master's; Post-bachelor's certificate; Post-master's certificate. **Classes:** Most classes have 20–29 students. Most lab/discussion sessions have 10–19 students. **Most popular majors:** Business Administration and Management, General; General Studies; Nursing/Registered Nurse (Rn, Asn, Bsn, Msn). **Special Study Options:** Cooperative education program; Distance learning; Double major; Dual enrollment; Honors program; Independent study; Internships; Study abroad; Teacher certification program. **Honors programs:** The Louisiana Scholar's College is a special institution at Northwestern that enrolls students in a strong liberal arts program while simulataneously letting them take part in the other great areas of NSU. **Disability Services offered:** Note-taking services; Reader services; Tape recorders; Tutors. **Career services:** Alumni services; Career assessment; Career/job search classes; Internships.

FACILITIES
Housing: Apartments for married students; Apartments for single students; Coed dorms; Fraternity/sorority housing; Special housing for disabled students; Theme housing; 96% of campus accessible to physically disabled. **Special Academic Facilities/Equipment:** Cammie G. Henry Research Center; Louisiana Creole Heritage Center; Louisiana Folklife Center; Louisiana Regional Folklife Center; The Space Science Group; Williamson Museum.

CAMPUS LIFE

Environment: Village. **Activities:** Campus Ministries; Choral groups; Concert band; Dance; Drama/theater; International Student Organization; Jazz band; Literary magazine; Marching band; Music ensembles; Musical theater; Opera; Pep band; Radio station; Student government; Student newspaper; Symphony orchestra; Television station; Yearbook. 93 registered organizations, 9 honor societies, 7 religious organizations, 10 fraternities, 8 sororities on campus. **Athletics (Intercollegiate):** *Men:* baseball, basketball, cheerleading, cross-country, football, soccer, track/field (outdoor), track/field (indoor). *Women:* basketball, cheerleading, cross-country, soccer, softball, tennis, track/field (outdoor), track/field (indoor), volleyball. **On-Campus Highlights:** Wellness, Recreation, and Activity Center. **Environmental Initiatives:** NSU student groups and organizations participate in recycling, liter-abatement, campus beautification, and related 'Green' service (and service-learning) activities.

ADMISSIONS

Freshman Academic Profile: Average high school GPA 3.2. 16% in top 10% of high school class, 39% in top 25% of high school class, 72% in top 50% of high school class. **Test Scores:** SAT Math middle 50% range 435–555. SAT EBRW middle 50% range 435–550. ACT middle 50% range 19–23. **Basis for Candidate Selection:** *Very important factors include:* rigor of secondary school record, standardized test scores. *Important factors include:* class rank, academic GPA. *Other factors include:* extracurricular activities, talent/ability, alumni/ae relation, geographical residence, state residency. **Freshman Admission Requirements:** High school diploma is required and GED is accepted. *Academic units required:* 4 English, 3 math, 3 science, 3 science labs, 2 foreign language, 1 social studies, 2 history, 0.5 computer science, 1 visual/performing arts, 1 unit from above areas or other academic areas. **Freshman Admission Statistics:** 2,633 applied, 83% admitted, 51% enrolled. **Transfer Admission Requirements:** College transcript(s), statement of good standing from prior institution(s). Minimum college GPA of 2.0 required. Lowest grade transferable D. **General Admission Information:** Application fee $20. Regular application deadline 7/6. Non-fall registration accepted. Admission may be deferred for a maximum of 3 Semesters w/o Fee.

COSTS AND FINANCIAL AID

Required Forms and Deadlines: FAFSA; Institution's own financial aid form. **Notification of Awards:** Applicants will be notified of awards on a rolling basis beginning 5/1. **Types of Aid:** *Need-based scholarships/grants:* College/university scholarship or grant aid from institutional funds; Federal Nursing Scholarships; Federal Pell; Private scholarships; SEOG; State scholarships/grants; United Negro College Fund. *Loans:* Direct PLUS loans; Direct Subsidized Stafford Loans; Direct Unsubsidized Stafford Loans. **Student Employment:** Federal Work-Study Program available. Institutional employment available. **Financial Aid Statistics:** 64% needy freshmen, 65% needy undergrads receive need-based scholarship or grant aid. 67% freshmen, 45% undergrads receive non-need-based scholarship or grant aid. 56% freshmen, 64% undergrads receive need-based self-help aid. 6% freshmen, 5% undergrads receive athletic scholarships. 91% freshmen, 82% undergrads receive any aid. **Criteria awarding aid:** *Non-need-based:* Academics, Alumni affiliation, Art, Athletics, Job skills, Leadership, Minority status, Music/drama, Religious affiliation, State/district residency.

NORTHWESTERN UNIVERSITY

1801 Hinman Ave, Evanston, IL 60204
Phone: 847-491-7271 **Financial Aid Phone:** (847) 491-7400
E-mail: ug-admission@northwestern.edu **CEEB Code:** 1565
Website: www.northwestern.edu **ACT Code:** 1106

This private school was founded in 1851. It has a 240 acre campus.

RATINGS

Admissions Selectivity Rating: 99   **Fire Safety Rating:** 83   **Green Rating:** 94

STUDENTS AND FACULTY

Enrollment: 8,319. **Student Body:** 51% female, 49% male, 69% out-of-state, 10% international (77 countries represented). Asian 18%, African American 6%, Caucasian 44%, Hispanic 12%, Native American <1%, Pacific Islander <1%, Two or more races 6%, Race unknown 3%.

Retention and Graduation: 98% freshmen return for sophomore year. 84% freshmen graduate within 4 years. 94% freshmen graduate within 6 years. 23% grads go on to further study within 1 year. 7% grads pursue arts and sciences degrees. 3% grads pursue law degrees. 1% grads pursue business degrees. 7% grads pursue medical degrees. **Faculty:** Student/faculty ratio 6:1. 1,518 full-time faculty, 100% hold PhDs, 20% are members of minority groups, 39% are women.

ACADEMICS

Degrees: Bachelor's; Certificate; Doctoral degree—professional practice; Doctoral degree research/scholarship; Master's; Post-bachelor's certificate; Post-master's certificate. **Classes:** Most classes have 10–19 students. Most lab/discussion sessions have 10–19 students. **Most popular majors:** Engineering, General; Economics, General; Journalism. **Special Study Options:** Accelerated program; Cooperative education program; Double major; Honors program; Independent study; Internships; Liberal arts/career combination; Student-designed major; Study abroad; Teacher certification program. **Honors programs:** Honors Program in Medical Education (HPME), Integrated Science Program (ISP), MENU, MMSS. **Combined degree programs:** BA/MA; BA/MD. **Disability Services offered:** Note-taking services; Reader services; Tape recorders; Tutors. **Career services:** Alumni network; Alumni services; Career assessment; Career/job search classes; Internships; Regional alumni.

FACILITIES

Housing: Coed dorms; Fraternity/sorority housing; Theme housing; Women's dorms; 100% of campus accessible to physically disabled. **Special Academic Facilities/Equipment:** Art gallery, learning sciences institute, communicative disorders and materials and life sciences buildings, catalysis center, astronomical research center. Ford Motor Company Engineering Design Center for engineering students.

CAMPUS LIFE

Environment: City. **Activities:** Campus Ministries; Choral groups; Concert band; Dance; Drama/theater; International Student Organization; Jazz band; Literary magazine; Marching band; Model UN; Music ensembles; Musical theater; Opera; Pep band; Radio station; Student government; Student newspaper; Student-run film society; Symphony orchestra; Television station; Yearbook. 415 registered organizations, 23 honor societies, 29 religious organizations, 17 fraternities, 12 sororities on campus. **Athletics (Intercollegiate):** *Men:* baseball, basketball, cheerleading, diving, football, golf, soccer, swimming, tennis, wrestling. *Women:* basketball, cheerleading, cross-country, diving, fencing, field hockey, golf, lacrosse, soccer, softball, swimming, tennis, volleyball. **On-Campus Highlights:** Shakespeare Garden. **Environmental Initiatives:** The development of a Strategic Plan for sustainability that will detail the long-term sustainability vision and goals for Northwestern University as well as putting in place the governance and accountability for the implementation of that plan and communicating our progress to stakeholders at all levels.

ADMISSIONS

Freshman Academic Profile: 92% in top 10% of high school class, 100% in top 50% of high school class. 65% from public high schools. **Test Scores:** SAT Math middle 50% range 740–790. SAT EBRW middle 50% range 700–760. ACT middle 50% range 33–35. **Basis for Candidate Selection:** *Very important factors include:* rigor of secondary school record, class rank, academic GPA, standardized test scores. *Important factors include:* application essay, recommendation(s), extracurricular activities, talent/ability, character/personal qualities. *Other factors include:* interview, first generation, alumni/ae relation, racial/ethnic status, volunteer work, work experience, level of applicant's interest. **Freshman Admission Requirements:** High school diploma is required and GED is accepted. *Academic units recommended:* 4 English, 3 math, 2 science, 2 science labs, 2 foreign language, 2 social studies, 2 history, 1 academic elective. **Freshman Admission Statistics:** 40,585 applied, 9% admitted, 55% enrolled. **Transfer Admission Requirements:** High school transcript, college transcript(s), essay or personal statement, standardized test scores, statement of good standing from prior institution(s). Minimum college GPA of 3.0 required. Lowest grade transferable C. **General Admission Information:** Application fee $75. Regular application deadline 1/1. Non-fall registration accepted. Admission may be deferred for a maximum of 1 year.

COSTS AND FINANCIAL AID

Required Forms and Deadlines: CSS/Financial Aid PROFILE; FAFSA; Noncustodial PROFILE. **Notification of Awards:** Applicants will be notified of awards on or about 4/15. **Types of Aid:** *Need-based scholarships/grants:* College/university scholarship or grant aid from institutional funds; Federal Pell; SEOG; State scholarships/grants. *Loans:* Direct PLUS loans; Direct Subsidized Stafford Loans; Direct Unsubsidized Stafford Loans. **Student Employment:** Federal

Work-Study Program available. Institutional employment available. **Financial Aid Statistics:** 98% needy freshmen, 98% needy undergrads receive need-based scholarship or grant aid. 0% freshmen, 0% undergrads receive non-need-based scholarship or grant aid. 68% freshmen, 67% undergrads receive need-based self-help aid. 5% freshmen, 5% undergrads receive athletic scholarships. 34% undergrads borrow to pay for school. Average cumulative indebtedness $36,350. **Criteria awarding aid:** *Non-need-based:* Athletics, Music/drama.

NORTHWEST NAZARENE UNIVERSITY

623 S. University Blvd., Nampa, ID 83686
Phone: 208-467-8000 **Financial Aid Phone:** 208-467-8641
E-mail: admissions@nnu.edu **CEEB Code:** 4544
Fax: 208-467-8645 **Website:** www.nnu.edu **ACT Code:** 924

This private school, affiliated with the Nazarene Church, was founded in 1913. It has a 85 acre campus.

RATINGS
Admissions Selectivity Rating: 84   **Fire Safety Rating:** 70   **Green Rating:** 60*

STUDENTS AND FACULTY
Enrollment: 1,263. **Student Body:** 59% female, 41% male, 51% out-of-state, 2% international (20 countries represented). Asian 2%, African American 1%, Caucasian 75%, Hispanic 7%, Native American 1%, Pacific Islander <1%, Two or more races 1%, Race unknown 12%.
Faculty: Student/faculty ratio 14:1. 103 full-time faculty, 73% hold PhDs, 6% are members of minority groups, 45% are women. 0% of classes are taught by teaching assistants.

ACADEMICS
Degrees: Bachelor's; Doctoral degree—professional practice; Master's; Post-master's certificate. **Most popular majors:** Education, General; Business/Commerce, General; Nursing/Registered Nurse (Rn, Asn, Bsn, Msn). **Special Study Options:** Accelerated program; Cooperative education program; Cross-registration; Distance learning; Double major; Dual enrollment; English as a Second Language (ESL); Exchange student program (domestic); Honors program; Independent study; Internships; Liberal arts/career combination; Student-designed major; Study abroad; Teacher certification program. **Disability Services offered:** Reader services; Tape recorders; Tutors. **Career services:** Alumni network; Career/job search classes; Internships; Regional alumni.

FACILITIES
Housing: Apartments for married students; Apartments for single students; Coed dorms; Men's dorms; Women's dorms; 70% of campus accessible to physically disabled. **Campus Network:** 100% of classrooms, 100% of dorms, 100% of student union, 100% of libraries, 100% of dining areas, 100% of common outdoor areas have wireless network access.

CAMPUS LIFE
Environment: City. **Activities:** Campus Ministries; Choral groups; Concert band; Drama/theater; International Student Organization; Jazz band; Literary magazine; Music ensembles; Musical theater; Opera; Pep band; Student government; Student newspaper; Student-run film society; Symphony orchestra; Yearbook. 21 registered organizations, 6 honor societies, 8 religious organizations on campus. **Athletics (Intercollegiate):** *Men:* baseball, basketball, cross-country, golf, soccer, track/field (outdoor), track/field (indoor). *Women:* basketball, cross-country, soccer, softball, track/field (outdoor), track/field (indoor), volleyball. **On-Campus Highlights:** Helstrom Business Center.

ADMISSIONS
Freshman Academic Profile: Average high school GPA 3.5. 29% in top 10% of high school class, 52% in top 25% of high school class, 81% in top 50% of high school class. **Test Scores:** SAT Math middle 50% range 470–620. SAT EBRW middle 50% range 470–600. ACT middle 50% range 21–27. **Basis for Candidate Selection:** *Very important factors include:* class rank, academic GPA, standardized test scores, character/personal qualities. *Other factors include:* rigor of secondary school record, recommendation(s), extracurricular activities, talent/ability, alumni/ae relation, religious affiliation/commitment. **Freshman Admission Requirements:** High school diploma is required and GED is accepted. *Academic units recommended:* 4 English, 3 math, 3 science, 2 foreign language, 3 history. **Freshman Admission Statistics:** 984 applied, 69% admitted, 41% enrolled. **Transfer Admission Requirements:** College

transcript(s). Minimum college GPA of 2.0 required. Lowest grade transferable C-. **General Admission Information:** Application fee $25. Priority deadline 3/1. Regular application deadline 8/15. Non-fall registration accepted.

COSTS AND FINANCIAL AID
Annual tuition $26,150. Room and board $6,400. Required fees $400. Average book and supplies expense $1,160. **Required Forms and Deadlines:** FAFSA. **Notification of Awards:** Applicants will be notified of awards on a rolling basis beginning 4/1. **Types of Aid:** *Need-based scholarships/grants:* College/university scholarship or grant aid from institutional funds; Federal Pell; Private scholarships; SEOG; State scholarships/grants. *Loans:* Direct PLUS loans; Direct Subsidized Stafford Loans; Direct Unsubsidized Stafford Loans. **Student Employment:** Federal Work-Study Program available. Institutional employment available. **Financial Aid Statistics:** 100% needy freshmen, 95% needy undergrads receive need-based scholarship or grant aid. 14% freshmen, 8% undergrads receive non-need-based scholarship or grant aid. 72% freshmen, 79% undergrads receive need-based self-help aid. 9% freshmen, 9% undergrads receive athletic scholarships. **Criteria awarding aid:** *Need-based:* Athletics, Leadership, Religious affiliation. *Non-need-based:* Academics, Alumni affiliation, Art, Athletics, Leadership, Minority status, Music/drama, Religious affiliation.

NORTHWOOD UNIVERSITY

4000 Whiting Drive, Midland, MI 48640
Phone: 989-837-4273 **Financial Aid Phone:** 989-837-4320
E-mail: miadmit@northwood.edu **CEEB Code:** 1568
Fax: 989-837-4273 **Website:** www.northwood.edu **ACT Code:** 2041

This private school was founded in 1959. It has a 434 acre campus.

RATINGS
Admissions Selectivity Rating: 77   **Fire Safety Rating:** 77   **Green Rating:** 60*

STUDENTS AND FACULTY
Enrollment: 1,185. **Student Body:** 33% female, 67% male, 10% out-of-state, 6% international (23 countries represented). Asian 1%, African American 6%, Caucasian 72%, Hispanic 4%, Native American <1%, Pacific Islander <1%, Two or more races 3%, Race unknown 8%.
Retention and Graduation: 79% freshmen return for sophomore year. 55% freshmen graduate within 4 years. 68% freshmen graduate within 6 years.
Faculty: Student/faculty ratio 13:1. 49 full-time faculty, 41% hold PhDs, 12% are members of minority groups, 47% are women. 0% of classes are taught by teaching assistants.

ACADEMICS
Degrees: Associate; Bachelor's; Master's. **Classes:** Most classes have 20–29 students. **Most popular majors:** Sport and Fitness Administration/Management; Business Administration and Management, General; Finance, General. **Special Study Options:** Accelerated program; Distance learning; Double major; Dual enrollment; English as a Second Language (ESL); Exchange student program (domestic); Honors program; Independent study; Internships; Study abroad; Weekend college. **Honors programs:** The Honors Program began in Fall Term, 1991. In it, honors sections of eight critically important courses are offered. The best instructors and the most demanding material and expectations are used. **Disability Services offered:** Note-taking services; Reader services; Tutors. **Career services:** Alumni network; Alumni services; Career assessment; Career/job search classes; Internships.

FACILITIES
Housing: Apartments for single students; Coed dorms; Men's dorms; Special housing for disabled students; Women's dorms. **Special Academic Facilities/Equipment:** Hach Student Life Center, Gerstacker Student Union. **Campus Network:** 95% of classrooms, 100% of dorms, 100% of student union, 100% of libraries, 100% of dining areas, 100% of common outdoor areas have wireless network access.

CAMPUS LIFE
Environment: Town. **Activities:** Campus Ministries; Drama/theater; International Student Organization; Model UN; Student government; Television station. 60 registered organizations, 4 honor societies, 3 religious organizations, 7 fraternities, 3 sororities on campus. **Athletics (Intercollegiate):** *Men:* baseball, basketball, cheerleading, cross-country, football, golf, soccer, tennis, track/field (outdoor), track/field (indoor). *Women:* basketball, cheerleading, cross-country, golf, soccer, softball, tennis, track/field (outdoor),

track/field (indoor), volleyball. **On-Campus Highlights:** Hach Student Life Center.

ADMISSIONS

Freshman Academic Profile: Average high school GPA 3.4. 10% in top 10% of high school class, 26% in top 25% of high school class, 72% in top 50% of high school class. 70% from public high schools. **Test Scores:** SAT Math middle 50% range 510–600. SAT EBRW middle 50% range 490–590. ACT middle 50% range 18–25. **Basis for Candidate Selection:** *Very important factors include:* academic GPA, standardized test scores, level of applicant's interest. *Important factors include:* rigor of secondary school record, class rank, application essay, recommendation(s), interview, extracurricular activities, alumni/ae relation. *Other factors include:* talent/ability, volunteer work, work experience. **Freshman Admission Requirements:** High school diploma is required and GED is accepted. *Academic units recommended:* 4 English, 3 math, 3 science, 2 science labs, 1 foreign language, 3 social studies, 1 academic elective. **Freshman Admission Statistics:** 1,075 applied, 79% admitted, 33% enrolled. **Transfer Admission Requirements:** College transcript(s). Minimum college GPA of 2.0 required. Lowest grade transferable C. **General Admission Information:** Application fee $30. Non-fall registration accepted. Admission may be deferred for a maximum of 1 year.

COSTS AND FINANCIAL AID

Required Forms and Deadlines: FAFSA. **Notification of Awards:** Applicants will be notified of awards on a rolling basis beginning 1/1. **Types of Aid:** *Need-based scholarships/grants:* College/university scholarship or grant aid from institutional funds; Federal Pell; Private scholarships; SEOG; State scholarships/grants. *Loans:* Direct PLUS loans; Direct Subsidized Stafford Loans; Direct Unsubsidized Stafford Loans. **Student Employment:** Federal Work-Study Program available. Institutional employment available. **Financial Aid Statistics:** 82% needy freshmen, 85% needy undergrads receive need-based scholarship or grant aid. 45% freshmen, 43% undergrads receive non-need-based scholarship or grant aid. 78% freshmen, 83% undergrads receive need-based self-help aid. 10% freshmen, 11% undergrads receive athletic scholarships. 68% undergrads borrow to pay for school. Average cumulative indebtedness $32,254. **Criteria awarding aid:** *Non-need-based:* Academics, Alumni affiliation, Athletics, Leadership, Minority status, State/district residency.

NORTHWOOD UNIVERSITY, FLORIDA CAMPUS

2600 North Military Trail, West Palm Beach, FL 33409-2911
Phone: (561) 478-5500 **Financial Aid Phone:** 561-478-5590
E-mail: fladmit@northwood.edu **CEEB Code:** 4072
Fax: 561-681-7901 **Website:** northwood.edu **ACT Code:** 6736

This private school was founded in 1982. It has a 90 acre campus.

RATINGS

Admissions Selectivity Rating: 85   **Fire Safety Rating:** 85   **Green Rating:** 60*

STUDENTS AND FACULTY

Enrollment: 490. **Student Body:** 36% female, 64% male, 37% out-of-state, 39% international (40 countries represented). Asian 1%, African American 10%, Caucasian 25%, Hispanic 11%, Native American 1%, Pacific Islander 0%, Two or more races <1%, Race unknown 13%.
Retention and Graduation: 60% freshmen return for sophomore year.
Faculty: Student/faculty ratio 20:1. 16 full-time faculty, 38% hold PhDs, 0% are members of minority groups, 38% are women. 0% of classes are taught by teaching assistants.

ACADEMICS

Degrees: Associate; Bachelor's; Master's. **Classes:** Most classes have 10–19 students. **Most popular majors:** Marketing/Marketing Management, General; Banking and Financial Support Services. **Special Study Options:** Accelerated program; Distance learning; Double major; Dual enrollment; External degree program; Honors program; Internships; Study abroad; Weekend college. **Honors programs:** An Honors Program began in fall term 1991. In it, honors sections of a variety of critically important courses are offered. The best instructors and the most demanding material and expectations are used. Additionally, special one-credit-hour seminars, which include outside speakers, are offered to sophomores and juniors. Honor students having completed 17 credit hours in honors courses may apply for honors admission to Term in Europe, Term in Asia, or Term in Northern Europe and are eligible for a partial scholarship to support these travel abroad programs. This also provides

a powerful incentive for students to successfully compete in the Honors Program. **Disability Services offered:** Note-taking services. **Career services:** Alumni network; Alumni services; Career assessment; Career/job search classes; Internships.

FACILITIES

Housing: Coed dorms; Special housing for disabled students. **Special Academic Facilities/Equipment:** Art Gallery. **Campus Network:** 100% of classrooms, 100% of dorms, 100% of student union, 100% of libraries, 100% of dining areas, 20% of common outdoor areas have wireless network access.

CAMPUS LIFE

Environment: City. **Activities:** Dance; Drama/theater; Musical theater; Student government; Student-run film society. 23 registered organizations, 1 honor society on campus. **Athletics (Intercollegiate):** *Men:* baseball, basketball, golf, soccer, tennis. *Women:* basketball, golf, soccer, softball, tennis, volleyball. **On-Campus Highlights:** Countess de Hoernle Student Life Center. **Environmental Initiatives:** We keep use of paper to a minimum (e-mail attachments/files, Blackboard portal).

ADMISSIONS

Freshman Academic Profile: Average high school GPA 3.2. 13% in top 10% of high school class, 27% in top 25% of high school class, 57% in top 50% of high school class. 70% from public high schools. **Test Scores:** SAT Math middle 50% range 440–550. SAT EBRW middle 50% range 430–510. ACT middle 50% range 18–21. **Basis for Candidate Selection:** *Very important factors include:* rigor of secondary school record, class rank, academic GPA, application essay, standardized test scores, recommendation(s), interview, extracurricular activities, character/personal qualities, level of applicant's interest. *Important factors include:* talent/ability, volunteer work. *Other factors include:* first generation, alumni/ae relation. **Freshman Admission Requirements:** High school diploma is required and GED is accepted. **Freshman Admission Statistics:** 628 applied, 54% admitted, 31% enrolled. **Transfer Admission Requirements:** High school transcript, college transcript(s). Minimum college GPA of 2.0 required. Lowest grade transferable C. **General Admission Information:** Application fee $25. Regular application deadline 8/1. Non-fall registration accepted. Admission may be deferred for a maximum of 1 year.

COSTS AND FINANCIAL AID

Required Forms and Deadlines: FAFSA; State aid form. **Notification of Awards:** Applicants will be notified of awards on a rolling basis beginning 3/1. **Types of Aid:** *Need-based scholarships/grants:* College/university scholarship or grant aid from institutional funds; Federal Pell; Private scholarships; SEOG; State scholarships/grants. **Financial Aid Statistics:** 87% needy freshmen, 86% needy undergrads receive need-based scholarship or grant aid. 27% freshmen, 21% undergrads receive non-need-based scholarship or grant aid. 84% freshmen, 90% undergrads receive need-based self-help aid. 20% freshmen, 19% undergrads receive athletic scholarships. **Criteria awarding aid:** *Non-need-based:* Academics, Athletics, Leadership, Minority status.

NORTHWOOD UNIVERSITY, TEXAS CAMPUS

1114 West FM 1382, Cedar Hill, TX 75104-1204
Financial Aid Phone: 972-293-5430 **CEEB Code:** 6499
Website: northwood.edu **ACT Code:** 4135

This private school was founded in 1966. It has a 360 acre campus.

RATINGS

Admissions Selectivity Rating: 86   **Fire Safety Rating:** 71   **Green Rating:** 60*

STUDENTS AND FACULTY

Enrollment: 531. **Student Body:** 42% female, 58% male, 25% international (18 countries represented). Asian 2%, African American 14%, Caucasian 19%, Hispanic 24%, Native American <1%, Pacific Islander 0%, Two or more races <1%, Race unknown 15%.
Retention and Graduation: 58% freshmen return for sophomore year.
Faculty: Student/faculty ratio 19:1. 20 full-time faculty, 25% hold PhDs, 15% are members of minority groups, 45% are women. 0% of classes are taught by teaching assistants.

ACADEMICS

Degrees: Associate; Bachelor's; Master's. **Classes:** Most classes have 10–19 students. **Most popular majors:** Marketing/Marketing Management, General; International Business/Trade/Commerce; Entrepreneurship/Entrepreneurial

Studies. **Special Study Options:** Accelerated program; Distance learning; Double major; Dual enrollment; External degree program; Honors program; Internships; Study abroad; Weekend college. **Honors programs:** An Honors Program began in Fall Term, 1991. In it, honors sections of six critically important courses are offered. The best instructors and the most demanding material and expectations are used. Additionally, special one-credit hour seminars, which include outside speakers, are offered to sophomores and juniors. **Disability Services offered:** Tutors. **Career services:** Alumni network; Alumni services; Career assessment; Internships.

FACILITIES
Housing: Apartments for single students; Coed dorms; Men's dorms; Wellness housing. **Special Academic Facilities/Equipment:** Butler Gallery, Hopkins Display Cases, Hach Library.

CAMPUS LIFE
Environment: Village. **Activities:** Campus Ministries; Choral groups; Dance; Drama/theater; International Student Organization; Student newspaper. 17 registered organizations, 1 honor society, 2 religious organizations, 1 fraternity, 1 sorority on campus. **Athletics (Intercollegiate):** *Men:* baseball, cross-country, golf, soccer, track/field (outdoor), track/field (indoor). *Women:* cross-country, golf, soccer, softball, track/field (outdoor), track/field (indoor). **Environmental Initiatives:** Paper recycling. We have two large bins in one of the parking lots. The paper is collected twice a week from offices and common areas.

ADMISSIONS
Freshman Academic Profile: Average high school GPA 3.3. 8% in top 10% of high school class, 27% in top 25% of high school class, 65% in top 50% of high school class. 90% from public high schools. **Test Scores:** SAT Math middle 50% range 420–520. SAT EBRW middle 50% range 390–500. ACT middle 50% range 17–22. **Basis for Candidate Selection:** *Very important factors include:* rigor of secondary school record, academic GPA, standardized test scores, interview, extracurricular activities, character/personal qualities, level of applicant's interest. *Important factors include:* class rank, talent/ability, volunteer work. *Other factors include:* application essay, recommendation(s), first generation, alumni/ae relation. **Freshman Admission Requirements:** High school diploma is required and GED is accepted. *Academic units recommended:* 4 English, 3 math, 3 science, 2 science labs, 1 foreign language, 3 social studies, 1 computer science. **Freshman Admission Statistics:** 452 applied, 59% admitted, 65% enrolled. **Transfer Admission Requirements:** High school transcript, college transcript(s), essay or personal statement. Minimum college GPA of 2.0 required. Lowest grade transferable C. **General Admission Information:** Application fee $25. Regular application deadline 8/1. Non-fall registration accepted. Admission may be deferred for a maximum of 1 year.

COSTS AND FINANCIAL AID
Required Forms and Deadlines: FAFSA. **Notification of Awards:** Applicants will be notified of awards on a rolling basis beginning 3/1. **Types of Aid:** *Need-based scholarships/grants:* Federal Pell; Private scholarships; SEOG. **Financial Aid Statistics:** 92% needy freshmen, 89% needy undergrads receive need-based scholarship or grant aid. 24% freshmen, 22% undergrads receive non-need-based scholarship or grant aid. 90% freshmen, 91% undergrads receive need-based self-help aid. 11% freshmen, 12% undergrads receive athletic scholarships. **Criteria awarding aid:** *Non-need-based:* Academics, Alumni affiliation, Athletics, Leadership, Minority status.

NORWICH UNIVERSITY

Admissions Office, Northfield, VT 05663
Phone: 802-485-2001
E-mail: nuadm@norwich.edu
Fax: 802-485-2032 **Website:** www.norwich.edu

This private school was founded in 1819. It has a 1125 acre campus.

RATINGS
Admissions Selectivity Rating: 75   **Fire Safety Rating:** 60*   **Green Rating:** 60*

STUDENTS AND FACULTY
Enrollment: 2,201. **Student Body:** 26% female, 74% male, 84% out-of-state, 2% international. Asian 2%, African American 3%, Caucasian 72%, Hispanic 4%, Native American 1%, Pacific Islander <1%, Two or more races 2%, Race unknown 15%.

Retention and Graduation: 85% freshmen return for sophomore year. 10% grads go on to further study within 1 year. 2% grads pursue arts and sciences degrees. 2% grads pursue law degrees. 2% grads pursue business degrees. 1% grads pursue medical degrees. **Faculty:** Student/faculty ratio 14:1. 140 full-time faculty, 0% hold PhDs, 9% are members of minority groups, 36% are women. 0% of classes are taught by teaching assistants.

ACADEMICS
Degrees: Bachelor's; Master's; Post-bachelor's certificate. **Classes:** Most classes have 20–29 students. Most lab/discussion sessions have 10–19 students. **Most popular majors:** Criminal Justice/Law Enforcement Administration; Liberal Arts and Sciences/Liberal Studies. **Special Study Options:** Distance learning; Double major; Dual enrollment; English as a Second Language (ESL); Exchange student program (domestic); Honors program; Internships; Study abroad; Teacher certification program. **Disability Services offered:** Tutors. **Career services:** Career/job search classes.

FACILITIES
Housing: Coed dorms; 95% of campus accessible to physically disabled. **Special Academic Facilities/Equipment:** Museum, architecture and art building w/galery, new library. **Campus Network:** 40% of classrooms, 10% of dorms, 100% of student union, 100% of libraries, 100% of dining areas, 50% of common outdoor areas have wireless network access.

CAMPUS LIFE
Environment: Rural. **Activities:** Campus Ministries; Dance; Drama/theater; International Student Organization; Jazz band; Marching band; Model UN; Radio station; Student government; Student newspaper; Yearbook. 40 registered organizations, 8 honor societies, 4 religious organizations on campus. **Athletics (Intercollegiate):** *Men:* baseball, basketball, cross-country, diving, football, ice hockey, lacrosse, riflery, rugby, soccer, swimming, track/field (outdoor), volleyball, wrestling. *Women:* basketball, cross-country, diving, riflery, rugby, soccer, softball, swimming, track/field (outdoor), volleyball.

ADMISSIONS
Freshman Academic Profile: Average high school GPA 3.1. 11% in top 10% of high school class, 37% in top 25% of high school class, 74% in top 50% of high school class. **Test Scores:** SAT Math middle 50% range 500–640. SAT EBRW middle 50% range 480–580. ACT middle 50% range 21–26. **Basis for Candidate Selection:** *Very important factors include:* rigor of secondary school record, academic GPA, standardized test scores. *Other factors include:* class rank, application essay, recommendation(s), interview, extracurricular activities, talent/ability, character/personal qualities, alumni/ae relation, volunteer work, work experience. **Freshman Admission Requirements:** High school diploma is required and GED is accepted. *Academic units recommended:* 4 English, 4 math, 4 science, 3 science labs, 2 foreign language, 3 social studies, 3 history. **Freshman Admission Statistics:** 1,473 applied, 91% admitted, 37% enrolled. **Transfer Admission Requirements:** High school transcript, college transcript(s), Lowest grade transferable C-. **General Admission Information:** Application fee $35. Priority deadline 2/1. Non-fall registration accepted. Admission may be deferred for a maximum of 1 term.

COSTS AND FINANCIAL AID
Annual tuition $30,048. Room and board $10,976. Required fees $1,734. Average book and supplies expense $1,000. **Required Forms and Deadlines:** FAFSA. **Notification of Awards:** Applicants will be notified of awards on a rolling basis beginning 2/15. **Types of Aid:** *Need-based scholarships/grants:* College/university scholarship or grant aid from institutional funds; Federal Pell; Private scholarships; SEOG; State scholarships/grants. *Loans:* Direct PLUS loans; Direct Subsidized Stafford Loans; Direct Unsubsidized Stafford Loans. **Student Employment:** Federal Work-Study Program available. Institutional employment available. **Financial Aid Statistics:** 100% needy freshmen, 100% needy undergrads receive need-based scholarship or grant aid. 18% freshmen, 17% undergrads receive non-need-based scholarship or grant aid. 79% freshmen, 79% undergrads receive need-based self-help aid. 0% freshmen, 0% undergrads receive athletic scholarships. **Criteria awarding aid:** *Need-based:* Academics. *Non-need-based:* Academics.

NOVA SOUTHEASTERN UNIVERSITY

3301 College Avenue, Fort Lauderdale, FL 33314
Phone: 954-262-8000 Financial Aid Phone: 954-262-7456
E-mail: admissions@nova.edu CEEB Code: 5514
Fax: 954-262-3811 Website: www.nova.edu ACT Code: 6706

This private school was founded in 1964. It has a 300 acre campus.

RATINGS
Admissions Selectivity Rating: 86   Fire Safety Rating: 92   Green Rating: 60*

STUDENTS AND FACULTY
Enrollment: 6,246. **Student Body:** 71% female, 29% male, 16% out-of-state, 4% international. Asian 6%, African American 24%, Caucasian 28%, Hispanic 32%, Native American <1%, Pacific Islander <1%, Two or more races 1%, Race unknown 4%.
Retention and Graduation: 70% freshmen return for sophomore year.
Faculty: Student/faculty ratio 20:1. 814 full-time faculty, 88% hold PhDs, 30% are members of minority groups, 49% are women. 0% of classes are taught by teaching assistants.

ACADEMICS
Degrees: Associate; Bachelor's; Doctoral degree—other; Doctoral degree—professional practice; Doctoral degree research/scholarship; Master's; Post-bachelor's certificate; Post-master's certificate. **Classes:** Most classes have 10–19 students. **Most popular majors:** Biology/Biological Sciences, General; Business Administration and Management, General; Psychology, General. **Special Study Options:** Distance learning; Double major; Honors program; Independent study; Internships; Study abroad; Teacher certification program. **Honors programs:** For the academically motivated student, the NSU Honors program provides a value added experience. Students enjoy greater interaction with faculty through curricular and co-curricular activities, special invitations to events, and enhanced engagement in disciplinary inquiry. www.nova.edu/admissions/academics. **Combined degree programs:** BA/DDS; BA/JD; BA/MA. **Disability Services offered:** Note-taking services; Reader services; Tape recorders; Tutors. **Career services:** Alumni services; Career assessment; Internships; Regional alumni.

FACILITIES
Housing: Apartments for married students; Apartments for single students; Coed dorms; Special housing for disabled students; Theme housing. **Special Academic Facilities/Equipment:** Institute for Early Childhood Studies, University School for pre-kindergarten to grade 12, Oceanographic Center and Lab, Biofeedback and Learning Technology Labs, Audiology and Speech Language Pathology, and Psychology Clinics.

CAMPUS LIFE
Environment: City. **Activities:** Campus Ministries; Choral groups; Dance; Drama/theater; International Student Organization; Literary magazine; Radio station; Student government; Student newspaper; Television station. 70 registered organizations, 7 religious organizations, 5 fraternities, 6 sororities on campus. **Athletics (Intercollegiate):** *Men:* baseball, basketball, cross-country, golf, soccer, track/field (outdoor). *Women:* basketball, cheerleading, crew/rowing, cross-country, golf, soccer, softball, tennis, track/field (outdoor), volleyball. **On-Campus Highlights:** Don Taft Univeristy Center.

ADMISSIONS
Test Scores: SAT Math middle 50% range 470–590. SAT EBRW middle 50% range 460–570. ACT middle 50% range 20–25. **Basis for Candidate Selection:** *Very important factors include:* academic GPA, standardized test scores. *Important factors include:* rigor of secondary school record. *Other factors include:* application essay, recommendation(s), interview, extracurricular activities, talent/ability, character/personal qualities, volunteer work. **Freshman Admission Requirements:** High school diploma is required and GED is accepted. *Academic units recommended:* 4 English, 3 math, 3 science, 3 social studies. **Freshman Admission Statistics:** 3,780 applied, 58% admitted, 31% enrolled. **Transfer Admission Requirements:** College transcript(s), statement of good standing from prior institution(s). Minimum college GPA of 2.50 required. Lowest grade transferable D. **General Admission Information:** Application fee $50. Regular application deadline 8/1. Non-fall registration accepted. Admission may be deferred for a maximum of 1 year.

COSTS AND FINANCIAL AID
Annual tuition $21,600. Room and board $9,086. Required fees $550. Average book and supplies expense $1,500. **Required Forms and Deadlines:** FAFSA;

state aid form. **Notification of Awards:** Applicants will be notified of awards on a rolling basis beginning 3/15. **Types of Aid:** *Need-based scholarships/grants:* College/university scholarship or grant aid from institutional funds; Federal Pell; Private scholarships; SEOG; State scholarships/grants. *Loans:* Direct PLUS loans; Direct Subsidized Stafford Loans; Direct Unsubsidized Stafford Loans. **Student Employment:** Federal Work-Study Program available. Institutional employment available. **Financial Aid Statistics:** 97% needy freshmen, 96% needy undergrads receive need-based scholarship or grant aid. 99% freshmen, 99% undergrads receive non-need-based scholarship or grant aid. 83% freshmen, 87% undergrads receive need-based self-help aid. 12% freshmen, 7% undergrads receive athletic scholarships. 92% freshmen, 83% undergrads receive any aid. **Criteria awarding aid:** *Need-based:* Academics. *Non-need-based:* Academics, Athletics, Leadership, Music/drama.

OAK HILLS CHRISTIAN COLLEGE

1600 Oak Hills Rd SW, Bemidji, MN 56601
Phone: 218-751-8670 Financial Aid Phone: 218-751-8670
E-mail: admissions@oakhills.edu
Fax: 218-751-8825 Website: www.oakhills.edu ACT Code: 2167

This private school was founded in 1946. It has a 180 acre campus.

RATINGS
Admissions Selectivity Rating: 87   Fire Safety Rating: 71   Green Rating: 60*

STUDENTS AND FACULTY
Enrollment: 131. **Student Body:** 53% female, 47% male, 33% out-of-state, 1% international (1 countries represented). Asian 2%, African American 1%, Caucasian 95%, Hispanic 0%, Native American 1%, Pacific Islander 0%, Two or more races 0%, Race unknown 0%.
Retention and Graduation: 55% freshmen return for sophomore year.
Faculty: Student/faculty ratio 13:1. 6 full-time faculty, 67% hold PhDs, 0% are members of minority groups, 33% are women. 0% of classes are taught by teaching assistants.

ACADEMICS
Degrees: Associate; Bachelor's; Certificate. **Classes:** Most classes have 10–19 students. **Most popular majors:** Bible/Biblical Studies; Pastoral Studies/Counseling; Youth Ministry. **Special Study Options:** Cooperative education program; Double major; Independent study; Internships. **Disability Services offered:** Note-taking services; Reader services; Tape recorders; Tutors. **Career services:** Alumni network; Career assessment; Career/job search classes; Internships.

FACILITIES
Housing: Apartments for married students; Apartments for single students; Men's dorms; Special housing for disabled students; Women's dorms; 20% of campus accessible to physically disabled. **Special Academic Facilities/Equipment:** American Indian Resource Center. **Campus Network:** 100% of classrooms, 100% of dorms, 100% of student union, 100% of libraries, 100% of dining areas, 100% of common outdoor areas have wireless network access.

CAMPUS LIFE
Environment: Village. **Activities:** Campus Ministries; Choral groups; Music ensembles; Student government. **Athletics (Intercollegiate):** *Men:* basketball. *Women:* basketball, volleyball. **On-Campus Highlights:** The Fellowship Center Lounge.

ADMISSIONS
Freshman Academic Profile: 5% in top 10% of high school class, 5% in top 25% of high school class, 47% in top 50% of high school class. 79% from public high schools. **Test Scores:** ACT middle 50% range 16–21. **Basis for Candidate Selection:** *Important factors include:* rigor of secondary school record, class rank, academic GPA, application essay, recommendation(s), character/personal qualities. *Other factors include:* standardized test scores, interview, alumni/ae relation, religious affiliation/commitment. **Freshman Admission Requirements:** High school diploma is required and GED is accepted. **Freshman Admission Statistics:** 70 applied, 56% admitted, 79% enrolled. **Transfer Admission Requirements:** High school transcript, college transcript(s), essay or personal statement. Minimum college GPA of 2.0 required. Lowest grade transferable C. **General Admission Information:** Application fee $25. Non-fall registration accepted. Admission may be deferred for a maximum of 2 years.

COSTS AND FINANCIAL AID

Annual tuition $14,420. Room and board $5,180. Average book and supplies expense $990. **Required Forms and Deadlines:** FAFSA; Institution's own financial aid form. **Notification of Awards:** Applicants will be notified of awards on a rolling basis beginning 3/1. **Types of Aid:** *Need-based scholarships/grants:* College/university scholarship or grant aid from institutional funds; Federal Pell; Private scholarships; SEOG; State scholarships/grants. **Student Employment:** Federal Work-Study Program available. Institutional employment available. **Financial Aid Statistics:** 100% needy freshmen, 100% needy undergrads receive need-based scholarship or grant aid. 0% freshmen, 0% undergrads receive non-need-based scholarship or grant aid. 75% freshmen, 86% undergrads receive need-based self-help aid. 0% freshmen, 0% undergrads receive athletic scholarships. 100% freshmen, 100% undergrads receive any aid. **Criteria awarding aid:** *Non-need-based:* Academics, Alumni affiliation.

OAKLAND CITY UNIVERSITY

138 N. Lucretia Street, Oakland City, IN 47660
Phone: 812-749-1221
E-mail: ocuadmit@oak.edu
Fax: 812-749-1433 **Website:** http://www.oak.edu

This is a private school.

RATINGS

Admissions Selectivity Rating: 89   **Fire Safety Rating:** 60*   **Green Rating:** 60*

STUDENTS AND FACULTY

Enrollment: 1,492. **Student Body:** 53% female, 47% male, 17% out-of-state, 1% international. Asian 1%, African American 11%, Caucasian 84%, Hispanic <1%, Native American <1%, Race unknown 3%.
Retention and Graduation: 66% freshmen return for sophomore year.
Faculty: Student/faculty ratio 15:1. 58 full-time faculty, 0% hold PhDs, 0% are members of minority groups, 47% are women.

ACADEMICS

Degrees: Associate; Bachelor's; Certificate; Doctoral degree—professional practice; Master's. **Classes:** Most classes have 10–19 students. Most lab/discussion sessions have fewer than 10 students. **Special Study Options:** Distance learning; Double major; Dual enrollment; Independent study; Internships; Teacher certification program.

FACILITIES

Housing: Apartments for married students; Apartments for single students; Men's dorms; Women's dorms. **Campus Network:** 100% of classrooms, 100% of dorms, 100% of student union, 100% of libraries, 100% of dining areas have wireless network access.

CAMPUS LIFE

Activities: Campus Ministries; Choral groups; Drama/theater; Pep band; Student government; Student newspaper; Yearbook.

ADMISSIONS

Freshman Academic Profile: Average high school GPA 3.2. 9% in top 10% of high school class, 16% in top 25% of high school class, 41% in top 50% of high school class. **Test Scores:** SAT Math middle 50% range 420–530. SAT EBRW middle 50% range 400–510. ACT middle 50% range 17–23. **Basis for Candidate Selection:** *Very important factors include:* rigor of secondary school record, academic GPA, standardized test scores. *Other factors include:* class rank, interview, character/personal qualities, alumni/ae relation, level of applicant's interest. **Freshman Admission Requirements:** High school diploma is required and GED is accepted. *Academic units recommended:* 4 English, 3 math, 3 science, 2 social studies. **Freshman Admission Statistics:** 620 applied, 56% admitted, 100% enrolled. **Transfer Admission Requirements:** High school transcript, college transcript(s), standardized test scores. Minimum college GPA of 2.0 required. Lowest grade transferable C. **General Admission Information:** Application fee $35. Regular application deadline 9/5. Non-fall registration accepted.

COSTS AND FINANCIAL AID

Annual tuition $15,200. Room and board $6,000. Required fees $360. Average book and supplies expense $1,500. **Required Forms and Deadlines:** FAFSA. **Notification of Awards:** Applicants will be notified of awards on a rolling basis beginning 5/1. **Types of Aid:** *Need-based scholarships/grants:* College/university scholarship or grant aid from institutional funds; Federal Pell; Private

scholarships; SEOG; State scholarships/grants. **Financial Aid Statistics:** 0% freshmen, 0% undergrads receive athletic scholarships. **Criteria awarding aid:** *Non-need-based:* Academics, Alumni affiliation, Art, Athletics, Minority status, Music/drama, Religious affiliation.

OAKLAND UNIVERSITY

North Foundation Hall, Room 101, Rochester, MI 48309-4454
Phone: 248-370-3360 **Financial Aid Phone:** 248-370-2550
E-mail: visit@oakland.edu **CEEB Code:** 1497
Website: http://www.oakland.edu **ACT Code:** 2033

This public school was founded in 1957. It has a 1444 acre campus.

RATINGS

Admissions Selectivity Rating: 76   **Fire Safety Rating:** 89   **Green Rating:** 69

STUDENTS AND FACULTY

Enrollment: 15,864. **Student Body:** 56% female, 44% male, 1% out-of-state, 2% international (45 countries represented). Asian 5%, African American 7%, Caucasian 75%, Hispanic 4%, Native American <1%, Pacific Islander <1%, Two or more races 3%, Race unknown 4%.
Retention and Graduation: 77% freshmen return for sophomore year. 19% freshmen graduate within 4 years. 47% freshmen graduate within 6 years.
Faculty: Student/faculty ratio 21:1. 582 full-time faculty, 93% hold PhDs, 23% are members of minority groups, 47% are women. 1% of classes are taught by teaching assistants.

ACADEMICS

Degrees: Bachelor's; Doctoral degree—professional practice; Doctoral degree research/scholarship; Master's; Post-bachelor's certificate; Post-master's certificate. **Classes:** Most classes have 10–19 students. Most lab/discussion sessions have 10–19 students. **Most popular majors:** Biology/Biological Sciences, General; Mechanical Engineering; Registered Nursing/Registered Nurse. **Special Study Options:** Accelerated program; Cooperative education program; Cross-registration; Distance learning; Double major; Dual enrollment; English as a Second Language (ESL); Exchange student program (domestic); Honors program; Independent study; Internships; Liberal arts/career combination; Student-designed major; Study abroad; Teacher certification program. **Honors programs:** Honors College. **Disability Services offered:** Note-taking services; Reader services; Tape recorders; Tutors. **Career services:** Alumni network; Alumni services; Career assessment; Career/job search classes; Internships.

FACILITIES

Housing: Apartments for single students; Coed dorms; Fraternity/sorority housing; Special housing for disabled students; Special housing for international students; Theme housing; 90% of campus accessible to physically disabled. **Special Academic Facilities/Equipment:** Art gallery, robotics lab, Eye Research institute, Professional theater, Meadowbrook Hall, Meadowbrook Music Festival, two golf courses, Pawley Learning center, Lowry Early Childhood Education Center, Jack's Place for Autism at OU. **Campus Network:** 100% of classrooms, 100% of dorms, 100% of student union, 100% of libraries, 100% of dining areas, 100% of common outdoor areas have wireless network access.

CAMPUS LIFE

Environment: Town. **Activities:** Campus Ministries; Choral groups; Concert band; Dance; Drama/theater; International Student Organization; Jazz band; Literary magazine; Model UN; Music ensembles; Musical theater; Opera; Pep band; Radio station; Student government; Student newspaper; Student-run film society; Symphony orchestra; Television station. 308 registered organizations, 10 honor societies, 16 religious organizations, 9 fraternities, 11 sororities on campus. **Athletics (Intercollegiate):** *Men:* baseball, basketball, cross-country, diving, golf, soccer, swimming, track/field (outdoor). *Women:* basketball, cross-country, diving, golf, soccer, softball, swimming, tennis, track/field (outdoor), volleyball. **On-Campus Highlights:** Recreation Center **Environmental Initiatives:** $8 million Facility upgrade from 1998 to save on energy costs.

ADMISSIONS

Freshman Academic Profile: Average high school GPA 3.4. 20% in top 10% of high school class, 46% in top 25% of high school class, 79% in top 50% of high school class. 90% from public high schools. **Test Scores:** SAT Math middle 50% range 500–610. SAT EBRW middle 50% range 510–620. ACT middle 50% range 21–27. **Basis for Candidate Selection:** *Very important*

factors include: rigor of secondary school record, academic GPA. *Important factors include:* standardized test scores. *Other factors include:* class rank, application essay, recommendation(s), interview, extracurricular activities, talent/ability, character/personal qualities, volunteer work, work experience. **Freshman Admission Requirements:** High school diploma is required and GED is accepted. *Academic units required:* 4 English, 4 math, 3 science, 3 social studies. *Academic units recommended:* 2 foreign language. **Freshman Admission Statistics:** 10,362 applied, 84% admitted, 28% enrolled. **Transfer Admission Requirements:** College transcript(s), statement of good standing from prior institution(s). Minimum college GPA of 2.50 required. Lowest grade transferable C. **General Admission Information:** Regular application deadline 8/1. Non-fall registration accepted.

COSTS AND FINANCIAL AID
Annual in-state tuition $13,406. Annual out-of-state tuition $24,735. Room and board $9,910. Average book and supplies expense $764. **Required Forms and Deadlines:** FAFSA. **Types of Aid:** *Need-based scholarships/grants:* College/university scholarship or grant aid from institutional funds; Federal Pell; Private scholarships; SEOG; State scholarships/grants. *Loans:* Direct PLUS loans; Direct Subsidized Stafford Loans; Direct Unsubsidized Stafford Loans. **Student Employment:** Federal Work-Study Program available. Institutional employment available. **Financial Aid Statistics:** 78% needy freshmen, 70% needy undergrads receive need-based scholarship or grant aid. 48% freshmen, 55% undergrads receive non-need-based scholarship or grant aid. 62% freshmen, 71% undergrads receive need-based self-help aid. 2% freshmen, 2% undergrads receive athletic scholarships. 65% undergrads borrow to pay for school. Average cumulative indebtedness $27,669. **Criteria awarding aid:** *Need-based:* Academics. *Non-need-based:* Academics, Art, Athletics, Leadership, Music/drama, State/district residency.

OBERLIN COLLEGE

101 North Professor Street, Oberlin, OH 44074
Phone: 440-775-8411 **Financial Aid Phone:** 440-775-8142
E-mail: college.admissions@oberlin.edu **CEEB Code:** 1587
Fax: 440-775-6905 **Website:** www.oberlin.edu **ACT Code:** 3304

This private school was founded in 1833. It has a 452 acre campus.

RATINGS
Admissions Selectivity Rating: 94   Fire Safety Rating: 89   Green Rating: 99

STUDENTS AND FACULTY
Enrollment: 2,827. **Student Body:** 58% female, 42% male, 94% out-of-state, 10% international. Asian 4%, African American 5%, Caucasian 64%, Hispanic 8%, Native American <1%, Pacific Islander <1%, Two or more races 8%, Race unknown 1%.
Retention and Graduation: 91% freshmen return for sophomore year. 75% freshmen graduate within 4 years. % freshmen graduate within 6 years. 22% grads go on to further study within 1 year. **Faculty:** Student/faculty ratio 10:1. 331 full-time faculty, 0% hold PhDs, 0% are members of minority groups, 0% are women. 0% of classes are taught by teaching assistants.

ACADEMICS
Degrees: Bachelor's; Diploma; Master's; Post-bachelor's certificate. **Classes:** Most classes have 10–19 students. Most lab/discussion sessions have fewer than 10 students. **Most popular majors:** Environmental Studies; Political Science and Government; Economics. **Special Study Options:** Double major; English as a Second Language (ESL); Independent study; Student-designed major; Study abroad; Teacher certification program. **Honors programs:** Students with proven independence and high academic ability may achieve an Honors designation at graduation by completing an Honors project within their major during their senior year. Honors projects vary, but always involve independent work supervised by a faculty advisor. Projects may be completed in seminars or private readings, in research, or in the preparation of a thesis, exhibition, or performance. Every honors candidate must also pass an examination at the end of the senior year—oral, written, or both. **Disability Services offered:** Note-taking services; Reader services; Tape recorders; Tutors. **Career services:** Alumni network; Alumni services; Career assessment; Career/job search classes; Internships; Regional alumni.

FACILITIES
Housing: Apartments for single students; Coed dorms; Cooperative housing; Special housing for disabled students; Theme housing; Wellness housing; Women's dorms; 90% of campus accessible to physically disabled. **Special Academic Facilities/Equipment:** Allen Memorial Art museum (one of the top ranked in the U.S.), Theaters, music performance halls, observatory, environmental studies building that helped launch the green building movement, arboretum, high performance computer cluster. **Campus Network:** 95% of classrooms, 100% of dorms, 100% of student union, 95% of libraries, 95% of dining areas, 20% of common outdoor areas have wireless network access.

CAMPUS LIFE
Environment: Village. **Activities:** Campus Ministries; Choral groups; Concert band; Dance; Drama/theater; International Student Organization; Jazz band; Literary magazine; Marching band; Music ensembles; Musical theater; Opera; Pep band; Radio station; Student government; Student newspaper; Student-run film society; Symphony orchestra; Yearbook. 200 registered organizations, 3 honor societies, 12 religious organizations on campus. **Athletics (Intercollegiate):** *Men:* baseball, basketball, cross-country, diving, football, golf, lacrosse, soccer, swimming, tennis, track/field (outdoor), track/field (indoor). *Women:* basketball, cross-country, diving, field hockey, golf, lacrosse, soccer, softball, swimming, tennis, track/field (outdoor), track/field (indoor), volleyball. **On-Campus Highlights:** Allen Memorial Art Museum. **Environmental Initiatives:** Development of Campus Resource Monitoring System: oberlin.edu/dormenergy.

ADMISSIONS
Freshman Academic Profile: Average high school GPA 3.6. 58% in top 10% of high school class, 79% in top 25% of high school class, 97% in top 50% of high school class. 66% from public high schools. **Test Scores:** SAT Math middle 50% range 630–730. SAT EBRW middle 50% range 650–720. ACT middle 50% range 28–33. **Basis for Candidate Selection:** *Very important factors include:* rigor of secondary school record, class rank, academic GPA, standardized test scores. *Important factors include:* extracurricular activities, talent/ability, character/personal qualities, first generation. *Other factors include:* application essay, recommendation(s), interview, alumni/ae relation, racial/ethnic status, volunteer work, work experience, level of applicant's interest. **Freshman Admission Requirements:** High school diploma is required and GED is not accepted. *Academic units required:* 4 English, 3 math, 3 science, 3 foreign language, 3 social studies. *Academic units recommended:* 4 science. **Freshman Admission Statistics:** 7,762 applied, 34% admitted, 28% enrolled. **Transfer Admission Requirements:** High school transcript, college transcript(s), essay or personal statement, standardized test scores, statement of good standing from prior institution(s). Minimum college GPA of 3.0 required. Lowest grade transferable C-. **General Admission Information:** Priority deadline 1/15. Regular application deadline 1/15. Admission may be deferred for a maximum of 1 year.

COSTS AND FINANCIAL AID
Annual tuition $55,976. Room and board $16,826. Required fees $842. Average book and supplies expense $930. **Required Forms and Deadlines:** Business/Farm Supplement; CSS/Financial Aid PROFILE; FAFSA; Institution's own financial aid form; Noncustodial PROFILE. **Notification of Awards:** Applicants will be notified of awards on or about 4/1. **Types of Aid:** *Need-based scholarships/grants:* College/university scholarship or grant aid from institutional funds; Federal Pell; Private scholarships; SEOG; State scholarships/grants. *Loans:* Direct PLUS loans; Direct Subsidized Stafford Loans; Direct Unsubsidized Stafford Loans. **Student Employment:** Federal Work-Study Program available. Institutional employment available. **Financial Aid Statistics:** 95% needy freshmen, 85% needy undergrads receive need-based scholarship or grant aid. 82% freshmen, 80% undergrads receive non-need-based scholarship or grant aid. 88% freshmen, 89% undergrads receive need-based self-help aid. 0% freshmen, 0% undergrads receive athletic scholarships. 42% undergrads borrow to pay for school. Average cumulative indebtedness $29,781. **Criteria awarding aid:** *Non-need-based:* Academics, Music/drama.

OCAD UNIVERSITY

100 McCaul Street, Toronto, ON M5T 1W1
Phone: 416-977-6000 **Financial Aid Phone:** 416-977-6000 ext. 250
E-mail: admissions@ocadu.ca
Fax: 416-977-6006 **Website:** www.ocadu.ca

This public school was founded in 1876.

RATINGS
Admissions Selectivity Rating: 60*   **Fire Safety Rating:** 60*   **Green Rating:** 60*

STUDENTS AND FACULTY
Enrollment: 4,234. **Student Body:** 9% out-of-state.

ACADEMICS
Degrees: Bachelor's; Master's. **Special Study Options:** Exchange student program (domestic); Honors program; Independent study; Internships; Study abroad. **Career services:** Alumni network; Alumni services; Career assessment; Career/job search classes; Internships.

CAMPUS LIFE
Environment: Metropolis. **Activities:** International Student Organization; Student government; Student newspaper; Student-run film society. **On-Campus Highlights:** Sharp Centre for Design.

ADMISSIONS
Basis for Candidate Selection: *Very important factors include:* talent/ability, character/personal qualities. *Important factors include:* academic GPA, interview, level of applicant's interest. *Other factors include:* application essay. **Freshman Admission Requirements:** High school diploma is required and GED is not accepted. **General Admission Information:** Application fee $200. Regular application deadline 2/1.

COSTS AND FINANCIAL AID
Annual in-state tuition $6,340. Required fees $959. **Required Forms and Deadlines:** Institution's own financial aid form; State aid form.

OCCIDENTAL COLLEGE

1600 Campus Road, Los Angeles, CA 90041-3314
Phone: 800-825-5262 **Financial Aid Phone:** 323-259-2548
E-mail: admission@oxy.edu **CEEB Code:** 4581
Fax: 323-341-4875 **Website:** www.oxy.edu **ACT Code:** 0350

This private school was founded in 1887. It has a 120 acre campus.

RATINGS
Admissions Selectivity Rating: 93   **Fire Safety Rating:** 75   **Green Rating:** 78

STUDENTS AND FACULTY
Enrollment: 2,066. **Student Body:** 58% female, 42% male, 59% out-of-state, 6% international (26 countries represented). Asian 15%, African American 4%, Caucasian 49%, Hispanic 14%, Native American 0%, Pacific Islander <1%, Two or more races 9%, Race unknown 2%.
Retention and Graduation: 93% freshmen return for sophomore year. 80% freshmen graduate within 4 years. 86% freshmen graduate within 6 years. **Faculty:** Student/faculty ratio 10:1. 195 full-time faculty, 96% hold PhDs, 31% are members of minority groups, 50% are women. 0% of classes are taught by teaching assistants.

ACADEMICS
Degrees: Bachelor's; Master's. **Classes:** Most classes have 10–19 students. Most lab/discussion sessions have 10–19 students. **Most popular majors:** Biology/Biological Sciences, General; Economics, General; International Relations and Affairs. **Special Study Options:** Cross-registration; Double major; Exchange student program (domestic); Honors program; Independent study; Internships; Student-designed major; Study abroad. **Combined degree programs:** BA/JD. **Disability Services offered:** Note-taking services; Reader services; Tape recorders. **Career services:** Alumni network; Alumni services; Career/job search classes; Internships; Regional alumni.

FACILITIES
Housing: Coed dorms; Fraternity/sorority housing; Theme housing; Wellness housing; Women's dorms; 65% of campus accessible to physically disabled. **Special Academic Facilities/Equipment:** Keck Theater; Mullin Studio and Art Gallery; Moore Ornithology Collection; Cosman Shell Collection; Smiley Geological Collection; Morse Collection of Astronomical Instruments; superconducting magnet; paleomagnetic lab; vivarium. **Campus Network:** 100% of dorms, 100% of student union, 100% of libraries have wireless network access.

CAMPUS LIFE
Environment: Metropolis. **Activities:** Campus Ministries; Choral groups; Concert band; Dance; Drama/theater; International Student Organization; Jazz band; Literary magazine; Music ensembles; Musical theater; Radio station; Student government; Student newspaper; Student-run film society; Symphony orchestra; Yearbook. 117 registered organizations, 8 honor societies, 9 religious organizations, 2 fraternities, 4 sororities on campus. **Athletics (Intercollegiate):** *Men:* baseball, basketball, cross-country, diving, football, golf, soccer, swimming, tennis, track/field (outdoor), water polo. *Women:* basketball, cross-country, diving, golf, lacrosse, soccer, softball, swimming, tennis, track/field (outdoor), volleyball, water polo. **On-Campus Highlights:** Green Bean Coffee Lounge. **Environmental Initiatives:** In October 2014, the Board of Trustees approved the creation of a $3.5-million Green Revolving Fund within the endowment. The Green Revolving Fund, named the Occidental Sustainable Investment Fund (OSIF), will make loans across the campus community, enabling investments in energy and water efficiency upgrades, renewable energy, and other sustainability projects that generate utility cost savings and reduce the environmental impact of the College's operations. At the end of 2017, OSIF has funded an energy efficient streetlights project that would cut energy use close to 80% and save 95,804 kWh annually.

ADMISSIONS
Freshman Academic Profile: Average high school GPA 3.6. 53% in top 10% of high school class, 87% in top 25% of high school class, 97% in top 50% of high school class. **Test Scores:** SAT Math middle 50% range 650–750. SAT EBRW middle 50% range 650–730. ACT middle 50% range 28–32. **Basis for Candidate Selection:** *Very important factors include:* rigor of secondary school record, academic GPA, application essay. *Important factors include:* class rank, standardized test scores, recommendation(s), extracurricular activities, character/personal qualities, volunteer work. *Other factors include:* interview, talent/ability, first generation, alumni/ae relation, geographical residence, racial/ethnic status, level of applicant's interest. **Freshman Admission Requirements:** High school diploma is required and GED is accepted. *Academic units recommended:* 4 English, 4 math, 3 science, 3 foreign language, 3 social studies. **Freshman Admission Statistics:** 7,501 applied, 37% admitted, 20% enrolled. **Transfer Admission Requirements:** High school transcript, college transcript(s), essay or personal statement, statement of good standing from prior institution(s). Minimum college GPA of 3.0 required. Lowest grade transferable D. **General Admission Information:** Application fee $65. Regular application deadline 1/10. Admission may be deferred for a maximum of 1 year.

COSTS AND FINANCIAL AID
Annual tuition $55,980. Room and board $16,034. Required fees $596. Average book and supplies expense $1,240. **Required Forms and Deadlines:** CSS/Financial Aid PROFILE; FAFSA; Noncustodial PROFILE; State aid form. **Notification of Awards:** Applicants will be notified of awards on or about 3/25. **Types of Aid:** *Need-based scholarships/grants:* College/university scholarship or grant aid from institutional funds; Federal Pell; Private scholarships; SEOG; State scholarships/grants. *Loans:* Direct PLUS loans; Direct Subsidized Stafford Loans; Direct Unsubsidized Stafford Loans. **Student Employment:** Federal Work-Study Program available. Institutional employment available. **Financial Aid Statistics:** 98% needy freshmen, 99% needy undergrads receive need-based scholarship or grant aid. 54% freshmen, 45% undergrads receive non-need-based scholarship or grant aid. 82% freshmen, 87% undergrads receive need-based self-help aid. 0% freshmen, 0% undergrads receive athletic scholarships. 75% freshmen, 74% undergrads receive any aid. 59% undergrads borrow to pay for school. Average cumulative indebtedness $39,306. **Criteria awarding aid:** *Non-need-based:* Academics, Leadership, Music/drama, State/district residency.

OGLETHORPE UNIVERSITY

4484 Peachtree Road N.E., Atlanta, GA 30319
Phone: 404-364-8307 **Financial Aid Phone:** 404-364-8356
E-mail: admission@oglethorpe.edu **CEEB Code:** 5521
Fax: 404-364-8491 **Website:** www.oglethorpe.edu **ACT Code:** 850

This private school was founded in 1835. It has a 102 acre campus.

RATINGS

Admissions Selectivity Rating: 77 **Fire Safety Rating:** 83 **Green Rating:** 60*

STUDENTS AND FACULTY

Enrollment: 1,125. **Student Body:** 58% female, 42% male, 23% out-of-state, 7% international (24 countries represented). Asian 3%, African American 18%, Caucasian 33%, Hispanic 10%, Native American <1%, Pacific Islander <1%, Two or more races 3%, Race unknown 26%.
Retention and Graduation: 73% freshmen return for sophomore year. 40% grads go on to further study within 1 year. 19% grads pursue arts and sciences degrees. 9% grads pursue law degrees. 10% grads pursue business degrees. 2% grads pursue medical degrees. **Faculty:** Student/faculty ratio 15:1. 59 full-time faculty, 92% hold PhDs, 15% are members of minority groups, 39% are women. 0% of classes are taught by teaching assistants.

ACADEMICS

Degrees: Bachelor's. **Classes:** Most classes have 10–19 students. Most lab/discussion sessions have fewer than 10 students. **Most popular majors:** English Language and Literature, General; Business/Commerce, General; Psychology, General. **Special Study Options:** Accelerated program; Cooperative education program; Cross-registration; Double major; Dual enrollment; English as a Second Language (ESL); Exchange student program (domestic); Honors program; Independent study; Internships; Liberal arts/career combination; Student-designed major; Study abroad. **Disability Services offered:** Note-taking services; Tutors. **Career services:** Alumni services; Career assessment; Career/job search classes; Internships.

FACILITIES

Housing: Coed dorms; Fraternity/sorority housing; Theme housing 60% of campus accessible to physically disabled. **Special Academic Facilities/Equipment:** Art museum, scanning electron microscope. **Campus Network:** 100% of classrooms, 100% of dorms, 100% of student union, 100% of libraries, 100% of dining areas, 100% of common outdoor areas have wireless network access.

CAMPUS LIFE

Environment: Metropolis. **Activities:** Campus Ministries; Choral groups; Concert band; Dance; Drama/theater; International Student Organization; Literary magazine; Music ensembles; Musical theater; Pep band; Radio station; Student government; Student newspaper; Yearbook. 57 registered organizations, 10 honor societies, 5 religious organizations, 4 fraternities, 3 sororities on campus. **Athletics (Intercollegiate):** *Men:* baseball, basketball, cross-country, golf, lacrosse, soccer, tennis, track/field (outdoor). *Women:* basketball, cheerleading, cross-country, golf, lacrosse, soccer, tennis, track/field (outdoor), volleyball. **On-Campus Highlights:** Oglethorpe University Museum. **Environmental Initiatives:** New buildings are built according to LEED requirements.

ADMISSIONS

Freshman Academic Profile: Average high school GPA 3.5. 79% from public high schools. **Test Scores:** SAT Math middle 50% range 510–610. SAT EBRW middle 50% range 530–630. ACT middle 50% range 22–28. **Basis for Candidate Selection:** *Very important factors include:* rigor of secondary school record, academic GPA, standardized test scores. *Important factors include:* class rank, application essay, recommendation(s), interview, extracurricular activities, volunteer work. *Other factors include:* talent/ability, character/personal qualities, first generation, alumni/ae relation, work experience. **Freshman Admission Requirements:** High school diploma is required and GED is accepted. *Academic units required:* 4 English, 3 math, 2 science, 3 social studies. *Academic units recommended:* 2 foreign language. **Freshman Admission Statistics:** 2,768 applied, 78% admitted, 20% enrolled. **Transfer Admission Requirements:** College transcript(s), statement of good standing from prior institution(s). Minimum college GPA of 2.8 required. Lowest grade transferable C. **General Admission Information:** Application fee $50. Priority deadline 11/15. Non-fall registration accepted. Admission may be deferred for a maximum of 1 semester.

COSTS AND FINANCIAL AID

Annual tuition $35,000. Room and board $12,710. Required fees $425. Average book and supplies expense $1,100. **Required Forms and Deadlines:** FAFSA. **Notification of Awards:** Applicants will be notified of awards on a rolling basis beginning 3/1. **Types of Aid:** *Need-based scholarships/grants:* College/university scholarship or grant aid from institutional funds; Federal Pell; Private scholarships; SEOG; State scholarships/grants; United Negro College Fund. *Loans:* Direct Subsidized Stafford Loans; Direct Unsubsidized Stafford Loans. **Student Employment:** Federal Work-Study Program available. Institutional employment available. **Financial Aid Statistics:** 100% needy freshmen, 99% needy undergrads receive need-based scholarship or grant aid. 16% freshmen, 13% undergrads receive non-need-based scholarship or grant aid. 75% freshmen, 79% undergrads receive need-based self-help aid. 0% freshmen, 0% undergrads receive athletic scholarships. 95% freshmen, 95% undergrads receive any aid. 68% undergrads borrow to pay for school. Average cumulative indebtedness $23,212. **Criteria awarding aid:** *Need-based:* Academics, Leadership, Minority status, Music/drama. *Non-need-based:* Academics, Art, Leadership, Minority status, Music/drama, State/district residency.

OHIO DOMINICAN UNIVERSITY

1216 Sunbury Road, Columbus, OH 42319-2099
Phone: 614-251-4500 **Financial Aid Phone:** 614-251-4778
E-mail: admissions@ohiodominican.edu **CEEB Code:** 1131
Fax: 614-251-0156 **Website:** http://www.ohiodominican.edu **ACT Code:** 3256

This private school, affiliated with the Roman Catholic Church, was founded in 1911. It has a 75 acre campus.

RATINGS

Admissions Selectivity Rating: 77 **Fire Safety Rating:** 91 **Green Rating:** 66

STUDENTS AND FACULTY

Enrollment: 1,072. **Student Body:** 54% female, 46% male, 5% out-of-state, 2% international (8 countries represented). Asian 1%, African American 22%, Caucasian 56%, Hispanic 4%, Native American <1%, Pacific Islander 0%, Two or more races 5%, Race unknown 10%.
Retention and Graduation: 62% freshmen return for sophomore year. 29% freshmen graduate within 4 years. 37% freshmen graduate within 6 years. 17% grads go on to further study within 1 year. **Faculty:** Student/faculty ratio 14:1. 60 full-time faculty, 95% hold PhDs, 10% are members of minority groups, 47% are women. 0% of classes are taught by teaching assistants.

ACADEMICS

Degrees: Associate; Bachelor's; Certificate; Master's; Post-bachelor's certificate. **Classes:** Most classes have 20–29 students. **Most popular majors:** Biology/Biological Sciences, General; Exercise Science and Kinesiology; Business Administration and Management, General. **Special Study Options:** Accelerated program; Cross-registration; Distance learning; Double major; English as a Second Language (ESL); Honors program; Independent study; Internships; Liberal arts/career combination; Student-designed major; Study abroad; Teacher certification program. **Honors programs:** The Honors Program is designed for high-ability, motivated students. Honors-designed courses will be offered to specifically challenge and engage students in the program. **Combined degree programs:** BA/JD; BA/MA; BA/MEng. **Disability Services offered:** Note-taking services; Reader services; Tape recorders; Tutors. **Career services:** Alumni network; Alumni services; Career assessment; Career/job search classes; Internships; Regional alumni.

FACILITIES

Housing: Coed dorms; 98% of campus accessible to physically disabled. **Special Academic Facilities/Equipment:** Wehrle Art Gallery, Student Center (w/ eating facilities, bookstore, games, and TV), Athletic Facilities and Fitness Center.

CAMPUS LIFE

Environment: Metropolis. **Activities:** Campus Ministries; Choral groups; Concert band; Drama/theater; International Student Organization; Literary magazine; Marching band; Model UN; Music ensembles; Musical theater; Pep band; Radio station; Student government; Student newspaper. 35 registered organizations, 4 honor societies, 1 religious organization on campus. **Athletics (Intercollegiate):** *Men:* baseball, basketball, cross-country, football, golf, soccer, tennis. *Women:* basketball, cross-country, golf, soccer, softball, tennis, volleyball. **On-Campus Highlights:** Bishop James A. Griffin Student Center.

ADMISSIONS

Freshman Academic Profile: Average high school GPA 3.3. 15% in top 10% of high school class, 43% in top 25% of high school class, 76% in top 50% of high school class. **Test Scores:** SAT Math middle 50% range 510–610. SAT EBRW middle 50% range 460–600. ACT middle 50% range 19–24. **Basis for Candidate Selection:** *Very important factors include:* rigor of secondary school record, academic GPA, standardized test scores. *Other factors include:* class rank, application essay, recommendation(s), interview, extracurricular activities, talent/ability, character/personal qualities, volunteer work, work experience, level of applicant's interest. **Freshman Admission Requirements:** High school diploma is required and GED is accepted. *Academic units recommended:* 4 English, 4 math, 4 science, 3 foreign language, 3 social studies. **Freshman Admission Statistics:** 1,238 applied, 77% admitted, 26% enrolled. **Transfer Admission Requirements:** College transcript(s). Lowest grade transferable C. **General Admission Information:** Priority deadline 12/2. Non-fall registration accepted.

COSTS AND FINANCIAL AID

Annual tuition $30,500. Room and board $10,948. Required fees $580. Average book and supplies expense $1,100. **Student Employment:** Federal Work-Study Program available. Institutional employment available. **Financial Aid Statistics:** 0% freshmen, 0% undergrads receive athletic scholarships. 100% freshmen, 81% undergrads receive any aid. **Criteria awarding aid:** *Non-need-based:* Academics, Athletics, Music/drama.

OHIO NORTHERN UNIVERSITY

525 South Main Street, Ada, OH 45810
Phone: 419-772-2260 **Financial Aid Phone:** 419-772-2272
E-mail: admissions-ug@onu.edu **CEEB Code:** 1591
Fax: 419-772-2313 **Website:** www.onu.edu **ACT Code:** 3310

This private school, affiliated with the Methodist Church, was founded in 1871. It has a 342 acre campus.

RATINGS

Admissions Selectivity Rating: 83   **Fire Safety Rating:** 62   **Green Rating:** 60*

STUDENTS AND FACULTY

Enrollment: 2,116. **Student Body:** 44% female, 56% male, 17% out-of-state, 4% international (17 countries represented). Asian 1%, African American 3%, Caucasian 84%, Hispanic 1%, Native American <1%, Pacific Islander 0%, Two or more races 3%, Race unknown 3%.
Retention and Graduation: 86% freshmen return for sophomore year.
Faculty: Student/faculty ratio 11:1. 211 full-time faculty, 84% hold PhDs, 14% are members of minority groups, 41% are women. 0% of classes are taught by teaching assistants.

ACADEMICS

Degrees: Bachelor's; Certificate; Doctoral degree—professional practice; Master's; Post-bachelor's certificate. **Classes:** Most classes have 10–19 students. **Most popular majors:** Registered Nursing/Registered Nurse; Biology/Biological Sciences, General; Mechanical Engineering. **Special Study Options:** Cooperative education program; Distance learning; Double major; Dual enrollment; English as a Second Language (ESL); Exchange student program (domestic); Honors program; Independent study; Internships; Liberal arts/career combination; Study abroad; Teacher certification program. **Honors programs:** Honors Program consisits of a First-Year Honors Seminar and 3 additional Honors Seminars, 2 "contract" courses and a final Honors project under the quarter system. **Combined degree programs:** BA/JD. **Disability Services offered:** Note-taking services; Reader services; Tape recorders; Tutors. **Career services:** Alumni network; Alumni services; Career assessment; Career/job search classes; Internships.

FACILITIES

Housing: Apartments for married students; Apartments for single students; Coed dorms; Fraternity/sorority housing; Men's dorms; Special housing for disabled students; Theme housing; Women's dorms; 95% of campus accessible

to physically disabled. **Special Academic Facilities/Equipment:** Art gallery, performing arts center, language lab, sports center, pharmacy museum.

CAMPUS LIFE

Environment: Village. **Activities:** Campus Ministries; Choral groups; Concert band; Dance; Drama/theater; International Student Organization; Jazz band; Literary magazine; Marching band; Model UN; Music ensembles; Musical theater; Pep band; Radio station; Student government; Student newspaper; Symphony orchestra; Television station; Yearbook. 200 registered organizations, 43 honor societies, 25 religious organizations, 6 fraternities, 4 sororities on campus. **Athletics (Intercollegiate):** *Men:* baseball, basketball, cross-country, diving, football, golf, soccer, swimming, tennis, track/field (outdoor), track/field (indoor), wrestling. *Women:* basketball, cross-country, diving, golf, soccer, softball, swimming, tennis, track/field (outdoor), track/field (indoor), volleyball. **On-Campus Highlights:** ONU Sports Center.

ADMISSIONS

Freshman Academic Profile: Average high school GPA 3.6. 32% in top 10% of high school class, 60% in top 25% of high school class, 85% in top 50% of high school class. **Test Scores:** SAT Math middle 50% range 530–640. SAT EBRW middle 50% range 480–600. ACT middle 50% range 23–28. **Basis for Candidate Selection:** *Very important factors include:* rigor of secondary school record, academic GPA, standardized test scores. *Important factors include:* class rank, interview, extracurricular activities. *Other factors include:* application essay, recommendation(s), talent/ability, character/personal qualities, first generation, alumni/ae relation, volunteer work, level of applicant's interest. **Freshman Admission Requirements:** High school diploma is required and GED is accepted. *Academic units required:* 4 English, 2 math, 2 science, 2 science labs, 2 social studies, 2 history, 4 academic electives. *Academic units recommended:* 4 English, 4 math, 3 science, 2 science labs, 2 foreign language, 3 social studies, 2 history, 4 academic electives, 1 computer science, 1 visual/performing arts. **Freshman Admission Statistics:** 3,108 applied, 69% admitted, 27% enrolled. **Transfer Admission Requirements:** High school transcript, college transcript(s), statement of good standing from prior institution(s). Minimum college GPA of 2.0 required. Lowest grade transferable C. **General Admission Information:** Priority deadline 12/1. Regular application deadline 8/15. Non-fall registration accepted.

COSTS AND FINANCIAL AID

Annual tuition $32,500. Room and board $12,040. Required fees $940. Average book and supplies expense $1,800. **Required Forms and Deadlines:** FAFSA. **Notification of Awards:** Applicants will be notified of awards on a rolling basis beginning 12/1. **Types of Aid:** *Need-based scholarships/grants:* College/university scholarship or grant aid from institutional funds; Federal Pell; Private scholarships; SEOG; State scholarships/grants. *Loans:* Direct PLUS loans; Direct Subsidized Stafford Loans; Direct Unsubsidized Stafford Loans. **Student Employment:** Federal Work-Study Program available. Institutional employment available. **Financial Aid Statistics:** 100% needy freshmen, 100% needy undergrads receive need-based scholarship or grant aid. 0% freshmen, 0% undergrads receive non-need-based scholarship or grant aid. 67% freshmen, 72% undergrads receive need-based self-help aid. 0% freshmen, 0% undergrads receive athletic scholarships. 75% undergrads borrow to pay for school. Average cumulative indebtedness $39,221. **Criteria awarding aid:** *Non-need-based:* Academics, Alumni affiliation, Art, Leadership, Minority status, Music/drama, State/district residency.

THE OHIO STATE UNIVERSITY—COLUMBUS

Student Academic Services Building, Columbus, OH 43210
Phone: 614-292-3980 **Financial Aid Phone:** 614-292-0300
E-mail: askabuckeye@osu.edu **CEEB Code:** 1592
Fax: 614-292-3980 **Website:** www.osu.edu **ACT Code:** 3312

This public school was founded in 1870. It has a 1665 acre campus.

RATINGS

Admissions Selectivity Rating: 91   **Fire Safety Rating:** 87   **Green Rating:** 94

STUDENTS AND FACULTY

Enrollment: 45,657. **Student Body:** 49% female, 51% male, 19% out-of-state, 8% international (66 countries represented). Asian 8%, African American 7%,

Caucasian 66%, Hispanic 5%, Native American <1%, Pacific Islander <1%, Two or more races 4%, Race unknown 3%.

Retention and Graduation: 94% freshmen return for sophomore year. 62% freshmen graduate within 4 years. 86% freshmen graduate within 6 years. **Faculty:** Student/faculty ratio 19:1. 4,379 full-time faculty, 99% hold PhDs, 28% are members of minority groups, 43% are women. 12% of classes are taught by teaching assistants.

ACADEMICS

Degrees: Associate; Bachelor's; Certificate; Diploma; Doctoral degree—professional practice; Doctoral degree research/scholarship; Master's; Post-bachelor's certificate; Post-master's certificate. **Classes:** Most classes have 20–29 students. Most lab/discussion sessions have 20–29 students. **Most popular majors:** Psychology, General; Finance, General; Marketing/Marketing Management, General. **Special Study Options:** Accelerated program; Cooperative education program; Cross-registration; Distance learning; Double major; Dual enrollment; English as a Second Language (ESL); Exchange student program (domestic); Honors program; Independent study; Internships; Liberal arts/career combination; Student-designed major; Study abroad; Teacher certification program; Weekend college. **Honors programs:** The University Honors Program promotes intellectual and personal development of undergraduate students through an enriched academic experience and integration of curricular and co-curricular programming. The Ohio State Scholars Program offers students the chance to live and learn with other students who share similar interests through 17 specialized communities. Each of the Scholars programs is centered around a unique theme, ranging from academic and professional pursuits to critical issues and leadership development. **Combined degree programs:** BA/MA; BA/MEng. **Disability Services offered:** Note-taking services; Reader services; Tape recorders. **Career services:** Alumni network; Alumni services; Career assessment; Career/job search classes; Internships; Regional alumni.

FACILITIES

Housing: Apartments for married students; Apartments for single students; Coed dorms; Cooperative housing; Fraternity/sorority housing; Men's dorms; Special housing for disabled students; Special housing for international students; Theme housing; Wellness housing; Women's dorms. **Special Academic Facilities/Equipment:** Wexner Center for the Arts; Zoology Museum; Geology Museum Art and Photography Galleries; Nuclear Research Reactor; Electrosciences Lab; Biomedical Engineering Center; Cartoon Art Museum.

CAMPUS LIFE

Environment: Metropolis. **Activities:** Campus Ministries; Choral groups; Concert band; Dance; Drama/theater; International Student Organization; Jazz band; Literary magazine; Marching band; Model UN; Music ensembles; Musical theater; Opera; Pep band; Radio station; Student government; Student newspaper; Student-run film society; Symphony orchestra; Television station. 1449 registered organizations, 46 honor societies, 63 religious organizations, 38 fraternities, 26 sororities on campus. **Athletics (Intercollegiate):** *Men:* baseball, basketball, cheerleading, cross-country, diving, fencing, football, golf, gymnastics, ice hockey, lacrosse, pistol, riflery, soccer, swimming, tennis, track/field (outdoor), track/field (indoor), volleyball, wrestling. *Women:* baseball, basketball, cheerleading, crew/rowing, cross-country, diving, fencing, field hockey, golf, gymnastics, ice hockey, lacrosse, pistol, riflery, soccer, softball, swimming, synchronized swimming, tennis, track/field (outdoor), track/field (indoor), volleyball. **On-Campus Highlights:** Hale Cultural Center. **Environmental Initiatives:** Ohio State has developed an holistic approach to sustainability endeavors through the establishment of university-wide sustainability goals that encompass the university's mission and physical operations. These include goals for Teaching and Learning, Research and Innovation, Outreach and Engagement, and Resource Stewardship. The goals have been embedded throughout the university to ensure widespread participation and achievement towards the goals. The goals can be found here: https://si.osu.edu/sites/default/files/UniversitySustainabilityGoals.pdf.

ADMISSIONS

Freshman Academic Profile: 60% in top 10% of high school class, 93% in top 25% of high school class, 99% in top 50% of high school class. 84% from public high schools. **Test Scores:** SAT Math middle 50% range 650–770. SAT EBRW middle 50% range 600–690. ACT middle 50% range 28–32. **Basis for Candidate Selection:** *Very important factors include:* rigor of secondary school record, class rank, academic GPA, standardized test scores. *Important factors include:* application essay, extracurricular activities, talent/ability, first generation. *Other factors include:* recommendation(s), character/personal qualities, geographical residence, state residency, racial/ethnic status. **Freshman Admission Requirements:** High school diploma is required and GED is accepted. *Academic units required:* 4 English, 3 math, 3 science, 3 science labs,

2 foreign language, 2 social studies, 1 academic elective, 1 visual/performing arts. *Academic units recommended:* 4 English, 4 math, 3 science, 3 science labs, 3 foreign language, 3 social studies, 1 academic elective, 1 visual/performing arts. **Freshman Admission Statistics:** 47,703 applied, 54% admitted, 30% enrolled. **Transfer Admission Requirements:** College transcript(s). Minimum college GPA of 2.0 required. Lowest grade transferable C-. **General Admission Information:** Application fee $60. Regular application deadline 2/1. Non-fall registration accepted. Admission may be deferred for a maximum of 1 year.

COSTS AND FINANCIAL AID

Room and board $12,708. Average book and supplies expense $1,082. **Required Forms and Deadlines:** FAFSA. *Types of Aid: Need-based scholarships/ grants:* College/university scholarship or grant aid from institutional funds; Federal Pell; Private scholarships; SEOG; State scholarships/grants. *Loans:* Direct PLUS loans; Direct Subsidized Stafford Loans; Direct Unsubsidized Stafford Loans. **Student Employment:** Federal Work-Study Program available. Institutional employment available. **Financial Aid Statistics:** 92% needy freshmen, 86% needy undergrads receive need-based scholarship or grant aid. 8% freshmen, 5% undergrads receive non-need-based scholarship or grant aid. 70% freshmen, 79% undergrads receive need-based self-help aid. 1% freshmen, 1% undergrads receive athletic scholarships. 87% freshmen, 76% undergrads receive any aid. 50% undergrads borrow to pay for school. Average cumulative indebtedness $27,242. **Criteria awarding aid:** *Need-based:* Academics, Alumni affiliation, Art, Athletics, Job skills, Leadership, Minority status, Music/drama. *Non-need-based:* Academics, Alumni affiliation, Art, Athletics, Job skills, Leadership, Minority status, Music/drama, State/district residency.

THE OHIO STATE UNIVERSITY—LIMA

Student Academic Services Building, Columbus, OH 45804-3596
Phone: 614-292-3980 **Financial Aid Phone:** 567-242-7520
E-mail: askabuckeye@osu.edu **CEEB Code:** 1541
Fax: 614-292-3980 **Website:** http://www.osu.edu **ACT Code:** 3312

This public school was founded in 1960. It has a 562 acre campus.

RATINGS

Admissions Selectivity Rating: 74   **Fire Safety Rating:** 60*   **Green Rating:** 80

STUDENTS AND FACULTY

Enrollment: 927. **Student Body:** 56% female, 44% male, 1% out-of-state, <1% international (2 countries represented). Asian 2%, African American 5%, Caucasian 83%, Hispanic 4%, Native American 0%, Pacific Islander 0%, Two or more races 4%, Race unknown 3%.
Retention and Graduation: 65% freshmen return for sophomore year. 10% freshmen graduate within 4 years. 28% freshmen graduate within 6 years. **Faculty:** Student/faculty ratio 19:1. 32 full-time faculty, 0% hold PhDs, 9% are members of minority groups, 41% are women. 0% of classes are taught by teaching assistants.

ACADEMICS

Degrees: Associate; Bachelor's; Master's. **Classes:** Most classes have 20–29 students. Most lab/discussion sessions have 10–19 students. **Most popular majors:** Elementary Education and Teaching; Biology/Biological Sciences, General; Psychology, General. **Special Study Options:** Accelerated program; Cooperative education program; Cross-registration; Distance learning; Double major; Dual enrollment; English as a Second Language (ESL); Exchange student program (domestic); Honors program; Independent study; Internships; Liberal arts/career combination; Student-designed major; Study abroad; Teacher certification program; Weekend college. **Honors programs:** The Honors Program on Ohio State Lima campus enriches the academic and social experiences of motivated students. Through a variety of curricular offerings, cultural events, and social activities, the Honors Program promotes the intellectual and personal development of qualified undergraduate students. By joining the Honors Program, you gain access to the very best academic and cultural opportunities the campus can offer. **Disability Services offered:** Note-taking services; Reader services; Tape recorders; Tutors. **Career services:** Career assessment; Career/job search classes; Internships.

FACILITIES

Housing: Special housing for disabled students; 90% of campus accessible to physically disabled. **Special Academic Facilities/Equipment:** Geological Museum; Greenhouse; Nature trails. **Campus Network:** 100% of classrooms,

100% of dorms, 100% of student union, 100% of libraries, 100% of dining areas, 100% of common outdoor areas have wireless network access.

CAMPUS LIFE

Environment: Town. **Activities:** Campus Ministries; Choral groups; Dance; Drama/theater; Literary magazine; Music ensembles; Musical theater; Student government. 23 registered organizations, 1 religious organization on campus.

ADMISSIONS

Freshman Academic Profile: 8% in top 10% of high school class, 34% in top 25% of high school class, 73% in top 50% of high school class. 94% from public high schools. **Test Scores:** SAT Math middle 50% range 498–658. SAT EBRW middle 50% range 498–608. ACT middle 50% range 20–26. **Basis for Candidate Selection:** *Other factors include:* standardized test scores. **Freshman Admission Requirements:** High school diploma is required and GED is accepted. *Academic units required:* 4 English, 3 math, 3 science, 3 science labs, 2 foreign language, 2 social studies, 1 academic elective, 1 visual/performing arts. *Academic units recommended:* 4 English, 4 math, 3 science, 3 science labs, 3 foreign language, 3 social studies, 1 academic elective, 1 visual/performing arts. **Freshman Admission Statistics:** 1,294 applied, 99% admitted, 25% enrolled. **Transfer Admission Requirements:** College transcript(s). Minimum college GPA of 2.0 required. Lowest grade transferable C-. **General Admission Information:** Application fee $60. Regular application deadline 6/1. Non-fall registration accepted.

COSTS AND FINANCIAL AID

Annual in-state tuition $7,644. Annual out-of-state tuition $27,660. Average book and supplies expense $1,168. **Required Forms and Deadlines:** FAFSA. **Notification of Awards:** Applicants will be notified of awards on or about 3/15. **Types of Aid:** *Need-based scholarships/grants:* College/university scholarship or grant aid from institutional funds; Federal Pell; Private scholarships; SEOG; State scholarships/grants. *Loans:* Direct PLUS loans; Direct Subsidized Stafford Loans; Direct Unsubsidized Stafford Loans. **Student Employment:** Federal Work-Study Program available. Institutional employment available. **Financial Aid Statistics:** 98% needy freshmen, 92% needy undergrads receive need-based scholarship or grant aid. 1% freshmen, 1% undergrads receive non-need-based scholarship or grant aid. 83% freshmen, 85% undergrads receive need-based self-help aid. 0% freshmen, 0% undergrads receive athletic scholarships. 91% freshmen, 84% undergrads receive any aid. **Criteria awarding aid:** *Need-based:* Academics, Alumni affiliation, Art, Athletics, Job skills, Leadership, Minority status, Music/drama. *Non-need-based:* Academics, Alumni affiliation, Art, Athletics, Job skills, Leadership, Minority status, Music/drama, State/district residency.

THE OHIO STATE UNIVERSITY—MANSFIELD

Student Services Building, Columbus, OH 43210
Phone: 614-292-3980 **Financial Aid Phone:** (614) 292-0330
E-mail: askabuckeye@osu.edu **CEEB Code:** 744
Website: www.osu.edu **ACT Code:** 3312

This public school was founded in 1958. It has a 620 acre campus.

RATINGS

Admissions Selectivity Rating: 74   **Fire Safety Rating:** 64   **Green Rating:** 79

STUDENTS AND FACULTY

Enrollment: 962. **Student Body:** 51% female, 49% male, 1% out-of-state, <1% international (1 countries represented). Asian 2%, African American 9%, Caucasian 78%, Hispanic 4%, Native American <1%, Pacific Islander 0%, Two or more races 3%, Race unknown 3%.
Retention and Graduation: 68% freshmen return for sophomore year. 20% freshmen graduate within 4 years. 42% freshmen graduate within 6 years. **Faculty:** Student/faculty ratio 18:1. 37 full-time faculty, 0% hold PhDs, 8% are members of minority groups, 43% are women. 0% of classes are taught by teaching assistants.

ACADEMICS

Degrees: Associate; Bachelor's; Master's. **Classes:** Most classes have 20–29 students. Most lab/discussion sessions have 10–19 students. **Most popular majors:** Elementary Education and Teaching; Junior High/Intermediate/Middle School Education and Teaching; Psychology, General. **Special Study Options:** Accelerated program; Cooperative education program; Cross-registration; Distance learning; Double major; Dual enrollment; English as a Second Language (ESL); Exchange student program (domestic); Honors program;

Independent study; Internships; Liberal arts/career combination; Student-designed major; Study abroad; Teacher certification program; Weekend college. **Career services:** Alumni network; Alumni services; Career assessment; Career/job search classes; Internships; Regional alumni.

FACILITIES

Housing: Coed dorms. **Campus Network:** 100% of classrooms, 100% of dorms, 100% of student union, 100% of libraries, 100% of dining areas, 100% of common outdoor areas have wireless network access.

CAMPUS LIFE

Environment: Town. **Activities:** Campus Ministries; Choral groups; Drama/theater; Musical theater. 20 registered organizations, 2 honor societies, 2 religious organizations on campus. **Athletics (Intercollegiate):** *Men:* baseball, basketball, soccer. *Women:* basketball, cheerleading, volleyball.

ADMISSIONS

Freshman Academic Profile: 7% in top 10% of high school class, 29% in top 25% of high school class, 64% in top 50% of high school class. 93% from public high schools. **Test Scores:** SAT Math middle 50% range 468–630. SAT EBRW middle 50% range 500–633. ACT middle 50% range 20–25. **Basis for Candidate Selection:** *Other factors include:* standardized test scores. **Freshman Admission Requirements:** High school diploma is required and GED is accepted. *Academic units required:* 4 English, 3 math, 3 science, 3 science labs, 2 foreign language, 2 social studies, 1 academic elective, 1 visual/performing arts. *Academic units recommended:* 4 English, 4 math, 3 science, 3 science labs, 3 foreign language, 3 social studies, 1 academic elective, 1 visual/performing arts. **Freshman Admission Statistics:** 1,770 applied, 99% admitted, 25% enrolled. **Transfer Admission Requirements:** college transcript(s). Minimum college GPA of 2.0 required. Lowest grade transferable C-. **General Admission Information:** Application fee $60. Regular application deadline 6/1. Non-fall registration accepted.

COSTS AND FINANCIAL AID

Annual in-state tuition $7,644. Annual out-of-state tuition $27,660. Room and board $8,094. Average book and supplies expense $1,168. **Required Forms and Deadlines:** FAFSA. **Notification of Awards:** Applicants will be notified of awards on or about 3/15. **Types of Aid:** *Need-based scholarships/grants:* College/university scholarship or grant aid from institutional funds; Federal Pell; Private scholarships; SEOG; State scholarships/grants. *Loans:* Direct PLUS loans; Direct Subsidized Stafford Loans; Direct Unsubsidized Stafford Loans. **Student Employment:** Federal Work-Study Program available. Institutional employment available. **Financial Aid Statistics:** 99% needy freshmen, 95% needy undergrads receive need-based scholarship or grant aid. 1% freshmen, 1% undergrads receive non-need-based scholarship or grant aid. 87% freshmen, 88% undergrads receive need-based self-help aid. 0% freshmen, 0% undergrads receive athletic scholarships. 91% freshmen, 86% undergrads receive any aid. **Criteria awarding aid:** *Need-based:* Academics, Alumni affiliation, Art, Athletics, Job skills, Leadership, Minority status, Music/drama. *Non-need-based:* Academics, Alumni affiliation, Art, Athletics, Job skills, Leadership, Minority status, Music/drama, State/district residency.

THE OHIO STATE UNIVERSITY—MARION

Student Academic Services Building, Columbus, OH 43210
Phone: 614-292-3980 **Financial Aid Phone:** (614) 292-0300
E-mail: askabuckeye@osu.edu **CEEB Code:** 752
Fax: 614-292-3980 **Website:** http://osu.edu/ **ACT Code:** 3312

This public school was founded in 1957. It has a 188 acre campus.

RATINGS

Admissions Selectivity Rating: 75   **Fire Safety Rating:** 60*   **Green Rating:** 86

STUDENTS AND FACULTY

Enrollment: 1,097. **Student Body:** 52% female, 48% male, 1% out-of-state, <1% international (1 countries represented). Asian 4%, African American 4%, Caucasian 81%, Hispanic 4%, Native American 1%, Pacific Islander <1%, Two or more races 3%, Race unknown 3%.
Retention and Graduation: 70% freshmen return for sophomore year. 15% freshmen graduate within 4 years. 38% freshmen graduate within 6 years. **Faculty:** Student/faculty ratio 19:1. 36 full-time faculty, 0% hold PhDs, 14% are members of minority groups, 50% are women. 0% of classes are taught by teaching assistants.

ACADEMICS

Degrees: Associate; Bachelor's. **Classes:** Most classes have 10–19 students. Most lab/discussion sessions have 20–29 students. **Most popular majors:** Elementary Education and Teaching; Junior High/Intermediate/Middle School Education and Teaching; English Language and Literature, General. **Special Study Options:** Accelerated program; Cooperative education program; Cross-registration; Distance learning; Double major; Dual enrollment; English as a Second Language (ESL); Exchange student program (domestic); Honors program; Independent study; Internships; Liberal arts/career combination; Student-designed major; Study abroad; Teacher certification program; Weekend college. **Honors programs:** The Honors & Scholars program at Ohio State University promotes the intellectual and personal development of high-ability undergraduate students both inside and outside the classroom. It provides students an opportunity to dive deeper into the topics of their courses and major. **Disability Services offered:** Note-taking services; Reader services; Tape recorders; Tutors. **Career services:** Alumni network; Alumni services; Career assessment; Career/job search classes; Internships; Regional alumni.

FACILITIES

90% of campus accessible to physically disabled. **Special Academic Facilities/Equipment:** Kuhn Art Gallery. **Campus Network:** 100% of classrooms, 100% of dorms, 100% of student union, 100% of libraries, 100% of dining areas have wireless network access.

CAMPUS LIFE

Environment: Town. **Activities:** Campus Ministries; Choral groups; Drama/theater; International Student Organization; Marching band; Musical theater; Student government. 24 registered organizations, 1 honor society, 1 religious organization on campus. **Athletics (Intercollegiate):** *Men:* basketball, gymnastics, volleyball. *Women:* gymnastics. **On-Campus Highlights:** Kuhn Fine Arts Gallery.

ADMISSIONS

Freshman Academic Profile: 8% in top 10% of high school class, 30% in top 25% of high school class, 73% in top 50% of high school class. 98% from public high schools. **Test Scores:** SAT Math middle 50% range 515–640. SAT EBRW middle 50% range 535–625. ACT middle 50% range 19–25. **Basis for Candidate Selection:** *Other factors include:* standardized test scores. **Freshman Admission Requirements:** High school diploma is required and GED is accepted. *Academic units required:* 4 English, 3 math, 3 science, 3 science labs, 2 foreign language, 2 social studies, 1 academic elective, 1 visual/performing arts. *Academic units recommended:* 4 English, 4 math, 3 science, 3 science labs, 3 foreign language, 3 social studies, 1 academic elective, 1 visual/performing arts. **Freshman Admission Statistics:** 1,025 applied, 99% admitted, 43% enrolled. **Transfer Admission Requirements:** College transcript(s). Minimum college GPA of 2.0 required. Lowest grade transferable C-. **General Admission Information:** Application fee $60. Regular application deadline 6/1. Non-fall registration accepted.

COSTS AND FINANCIAL AID

Annual in-state tuition $7,644. Annual out-of-state tuition $27,660. Average book and supplies expense $1,168. **Required Forms and Deadlines:** FAFSA. **Notification of Awards:** Applicants will be notified of awards on or about 3/15. **Types of Aid:** *Need-based scholarships/grants:* College/university scholarship or grant aid from institutional funds; Federal Pell; Private scholarships; SEOG; State scholarships/grants. *Loans:* Direct PLUS loans; Direct Subsidized Stafford Loans; Direct Unsubsidized Stafford Loans. **Student Employment:** Federal Work-Study Program available. Institutional employment available. **Financial Aid Statistics:** 99% needy freshmen, 95% needy undergrads receive need-based scholarship or grant aid. 2% freshmen, 1% undergrads receive non-need-based scholarship or grant aid. 82% freshmen, 83% undergrads receive need-based self-help aid. 0% freshmen, 0% undergrads receive athletic scholarships. 90% freshmen, 87% undergrads receive any aid. **Criteria awarding aid:** *Need-based:* Academics, Alumni affiliation, Art, Athletics, Job skills, Leadership, Minority status, Music/drama. *Non-need-based:* Academics, Alumni affiliation, Art, Athletics, Job skills, Leadership, Minority status, Music/drama, State/district residency.

THE OHIO STATE UNIVERSITY—NEWARK

Student Academic Services Building, Columbus, OH 43210
Phone: 614-292-39890 **Financial Aid Phone:** 614-292-0300
E-mail: askabuckeye@osu.edu **CEEB Code:** 824
Fax: 740-364-9645 **Website:** http://www.osu.edu **ACT Code:** 3312

This public school was founded in 1957. It has a 111 acre campus.

RATINGS

Admissions Selectivity Rating: 74   **Fire Safety Rating:** 82   **Green Rating:** 77

STUDENTS AND FACULTY

Enrollment: 2,518. **Student Body:** 51% female, 49% male, 1% out-of-state, <1% international (1 countries represented). Asian 4%, African American 15%, Caucasian 69%, Hispanic 3%, Native American <1%, Pacific Islander <1%, Two or more races 4%, Race unknown 4%.
Retention and Graduation: 68% freshmen return for sophomore year. 14% freshmen graduate within 4 years. 35% freshmen graduate within 6 years. **Faculty:** Student/faculty ratio 28:1. 47 full-time faculty, 0% hold PhDs, 21% are members of minority groups, 36% are women. 0% of classes are taught by teaching assistants.

ACADEMICS

Degrees: Associate; Bachelor's; Master's. **Classes:** Most classes have 20–29 students. Most lab/discussion sessions have 20–29 students. **Most popular majors:** Elementary Education and Teaching; Junior High/Intermediate/Middle School Education and Teaching; English Language and Literature, General. **Special Study Options:** Accelerated program; Cooperative education program; Cross-registration; Distance learning; Double major; Dual enrollment; English as a Second Language (ESL); Exchange student program (domestic); Honors program; Independent study; Internships; Liberal arts/career combination; Student-designed major; Study abroad; Teacher certification program; Weekend college. **Honors programs:** The Honors program promotes the intellectual and personal development of high-ability undergraduate students both inside and outside the classroom. Along with admission to Honors classes and the opportunity to graduate with Honors distinction, Honors students receive priority scheduling, access to free printing in the Honors lounge, and invitations to special outings through the Laurel Collegiate Society, the social club for high-achieving students (with 3.4 GPA and above). Honors students are given first priority in study abroad courses and many are recognized at the Ohio State Newark Salute to Undergraduate Achievement dinner every spring. **Disability Services offered:** Note-taking services; Reader services; Tape recorders; Tutors. **Career services:** Alumni services; Career assessment; Career/job search classes; Internships; Regional alumni.

FACILITIES

Housing: Apartments for single students; Coed dorms; Special housing for disabled students; 100% of campus accessible to physically disabled. **Campus Network:** 25% of classrooms, 100% of dorms, 100% of student union, 100% of libraries, 100% of dining areas, 0% of common outdoor areas have wireless network access.

CAMPUS LIFE

Environment: Town. **Activities:** Campus Ministries; Choral groups; Drama/theater; International Student Organization; Literary magazine; Student government. 30 registered organizations, 2 honor societies, 2 religious organizations on campus. **Athletics (Intercollegiate):** *Men:* basketball, golf, soccer. *Women:* basketball, soccer, softball, volleyball. **On-Campus Highlights:** Adena Recreation Center.

ADMISSIONS

Freshman Academic Profile: 4% in top 10% of high school class, 27% in top 25% of high school class, 63% in top 50% of high school class. 91% from public high schools. **Test Scores:** SAT Math middle 50% range 520–600. SAT EBRW middle 50% range 510–610. ACT middle 50% range 20–25. **Basis for Candidate Selection:** *Other factors include:* standardized test scores. **Freshman Admission Requirements:** High school diploma is required and GED is accepted. *Academic units required:* 4 English, 3 math, 3 science, 3 science labs, 2 foreign language, 2 social studies, 1 academic elective, 1 visual/performing arts. *Academic units recommended:* 4 English, 4 math, 3 science, 3 science labs, 3 foreign language, 3 social studies, 1 academic elective, 1 visual/performing arts. **Freshman Admission Statistics:** 3,665 applied, 99% admitted, 38% enrolled. **Transfer Admission Requirements:** college transcript(s). Minimum college GPA of 2.0 required. Lowest grade transferable C-. **General Admission**

Information: Application fee $60. Regular application deadline 6/1. Non-fall registration accepted.

COSTS AND FINANCIAL AID

Annual in-state tuition $7,912. Annual out-of-state tuition $28,889. Room and board $10,626. Average book and supplies expense $1,168. **Required Forms and Deadlines:** FAFSA. **Notification of Awards:** Applicants will be notified of awards on or about 3/15. **Types of Aid:** *Need-based scholarships/grants:* College/university scholarship or grant aid from institutional funds; Federal Pell; Private scholarships; SEOG; State scholarships/grants. *Loans:* Direct PLUS loans; Direct Subsidized Stafford Loans; Direct Unsubsidized Stafford Loans. **Student Employment:** Federal Work-Study Program available. Institutional employment available. **Financial Aid Statistics:** 84% needy freshmen, 86% needy undergrads receive need-based scholarship or grant aid. 1% freshmen, 1% undergrads receive non-need-based scholarship or grant aid. 88% freshmen, 86% undergrads receive need-based self-help aid. freshmen, undergrads receive athletic scholarships. 85% freshmen, 81% undergrads receive any aid. **Criteria awarding aid:** *Need-based:* Academics, Alumni affiliation, Art, Athletics, Job skills, Leadership, Minority status, Music/drama. *Non-need-based:* Academics, Alumni affiliation, Art, Athletics, Job skills, Leadership, Minority status, Music/drama, State/district residency.

OHIO UNIVERSITY—ATHENS

120 Chubb Hall, Athens, OH 45701
Phone: 740-593-4100 **Financial Aid Phone:** 740-593-4141
E-mail: admissions@ohio.edu **CEEB Code:** 1593
Fax: 740-593-0560 **Website:** www.ohio.edu **ACT Code:** 3314

This public school was founded in 1804. It has a 1774 acre campus.

RATINGS

Admissions Selectivity Rating: 77   Fire Safety Rating: 90   Green Rating: 60*

STUDENTS AND FACULTY

Enrollment: 20,406. **Student Body:** 60% female, 40% male, 12% out-of-state, 1% international (70 countries represented). Asian 1%, African American 6%, Caucasian 82%, Hispanic 3%, Native American <1%, Pacific Islander <1%, Two or more races 4%, Race unknown 2%.
Retention and Graduation: 82% freshmen return for sophomore year. 45% freshmen graduate within 4 years. 16% grads go on to further study within 1 year. 1% grads pursue arts and sciences degrees. 1% grads pursue law degrees. 1% grads pursue business degrees. 1% grads pursue medical degrees. **Faculty:** Student/faculty ratio 16:1. 1,015 full-time faculty, 77% hold PhDs, 17% are members of minority groups, 43% are women. 10% of classes are taught by teaching assistants.

ACADEMICS

Degrees: Associate; Bachelor's; Certificate; Doctoral degree—professional practice; Doctoral degree research/scholarship; Master's; Post-bachelor's certificate. **Classes:** Most classes have 10–19 students. Most lab/discussion sessions have 10–19 students. **Most popular majors:** Registered Nursing/Registered Nurse; Business Administration and Management, General; Speech Communication and Rhetoric. **Special Study Options:** Accelerated program; Cooperative education program; Cross-registration; Distance learning; Double major; Dual enrollment; English as a Second Language (ESL); External degree program; Honors program; Independent study; Internships; Liberal arts/career combination; Student-designed major; Study abroad; Teacher certification program. **Honors programs:** OHIO Honors Program: This university-wide honors program is committed to experiential learning. Students in the program are required to complete a blend of honors-level coursework and in-depth, carefully chosen out-of-class experiences. OHIO Honors Program advisors work closely with students to select classes and co-curricular experiences that collectively form a cohesive education in which hands-on learning complements instruction firmly grounded in theory. Facilitated reflection processes encourage students to make deep connections across their experiences. Unlike many honors programs at other institutions, honors-level coursework is carefully crafted by faculty and curated instead of having to be proposed and pitched to instructors by honors students. Open to students in any undergraduate major,

the recently created program currently includes approximately 350 students. First-year classes of 300–400 students are anticipated in the coming years. OHIO Honors-designated programs for which students are selected from within the OHIO Honors Program include the Copeland Scholars Program, Connavino Honors Program, Scripps Innovation Scholars, Cutler Scholars Program, and Office of Multicultural Student Access and Retention Programs. The Cutler Scholars Program offers generous merit scholarships for students driven to make a positive impact in their communities. Honors Tutorial College: The most selective of Ohio University's 10 undergraduate colleges, the Honor's Tutorial College is the oldest, largest, and most academically diverse degree-granting tutorial college in the country. Based on Oxbridge systems of tutorial education developed in England, it offers highly motivated, talented students the opportunity to receive a substantial part of their education through tutorials (one-on-one classes or small seminars). There are approximately 300 students in the Honors Tutorial College spread over 36 programs of study. To preserve the tutorial experience, HTC enrolls about 80 new students each year, and admission is highly competitive. **Disability Services offered:** Note-taking services; Reader services; Tape recorders; Tutors. **Career services:** Alumni network; Alumni services; Career assessment; Career/job search classes; Internships; Regional alumni.

FACILITIES

Housing: Coed dorms; Special housing for disabled students; Special housing for international students; Theme housing; Wellness housing; Women's dorms; 89% of campus accessible to physically disabled. **Special Academic Facilities/Equipment:** Museum of American Art, Innovation Center, Nuclear Accelerator, Electron Microscope, Biotech Center, Kennedy Museum of Art, Trisolini Gallery, Art Gallery in Multicultural Programs, Voinovich Center, Academic & Research Center, Greenhouse, Ridges Land Lab, Cartography & Meteorology Centers, Contemporary History Institute, Maker Space and 3d Printer.
Campus Network: 100% of classrooms, 100% of dorms, 100% of student union, 100% of libraries, 100% of dining areas, 100% of common outdoor areas have wireless network access.

CAMPUS LIFE

Environment: Town. **Activities:** Campus Ministries; Choral groups; Concert band; Dance; Drama/theater; International Student Organization; Jazz band; Literary magazine; Marching band; Music ensembles; Musical theater; Opera; Pep band; Radio station; Student government; Student newspaper; Student-run film society; Symphony orchestra; Television station; Yearbook. 639 registered organizations, 24 honor societies, 28 religious organizations, 18 fraternities, 13 sororities on campus. **Athletics (Intercollegiate):** *Men:* baseball, basketball, cheerleading, cross-country, football, golf, wrestling. *Women:* basketball, cheerleading, cross-country, diving, field hockey, golf, soccer, softball, swimming, track/field (outdoor), volleyball. **On-Campus Highlights:** Charles J. Ping Recreation Center. **Environmental Initiatives:** Ohio University has a long and storied responsible waste management history. The national RecycleMania competition was founded by the former Ohio University and Miami University recycling managers. Ohio University often wins national waste management competitions such as this month's win in the Diversion division of the GameDay Recycling Challenge. Ohio University also owns and operates the largest in-vessel composter (6 tons/day) of any college or university in the United States and provides annual reuse opportunities such as the Earth Day Reuse and Repair Fair, the Move Out event and the ReBike Sale.

ADMISSIONS

Freshman Academic Profile: Average high school GPA 3.6. 20% in top 10% of high school class, 47% in top 25% of high school class, 82% in top 50% of high school class. 80% from public high schools. **Test Scores:** SAT Math middle 50% range 520–620. SAT EBRW middle 50% range 530–640. ACT middle 50% range 21–26. **Basis for Candidate Selection:** *Very important factors include:* rigor of secondary school record, academic GPA, standardized test scores. *Important factors include:* class rank, application essay, first generation. *Other factors include:* recommendation(s), interview, extracurricular activities, talent/ability, character/personal qualities, alumni/ae relation, geographical residence, state residency, volunteer work, work experience. **Freshman Admission Requirements:** High school diploma is required and GED is accepted. *Academic units required:* 4 English, 4 math, 3 science, 2 foreign language, 3 social studies, 4 academic electives, 1 unit from above areas or other academic areas. *Academic units recommended:* 1 visual/performing arts. **Freshman Admission Statistics:** 24,179 applied, 82% admitted, 19% enrolled. **Transfer Admission Requirements:** College transcript(s). Minimum college GPA of 2.0 required. Lowest grade transferable C-. **General Admission Information:** Application fee $50. Priority deadline 12/1. Regular application deadline 2/1. Non-fall registration accepted. Admission may be deferred for a maximum of 12 months.

COSTS AND FINANCIAL AID

Annual in-state tuition $12,612. Annual out-of-state tuition $22,406. Room and board $12,172. Average book and supplies expense $962. **Required Forms and Deadlines:** FAFSA. **Notification of Awards:** Applicants will be notified of awards on or about 2/1. **Types of Aid:** *Need-based scholarships/grants:* College/university scholarship or grant aid from institutional funds; Federal Pell; Private scholarships; SEOG; State scholarships/grants. *Loans:* Direct PLUS loans; Direct Subsidized Stafford Loans; Direct Unsubsidized Stafford Loans. **Student Employment:** Federal Work-Study Program available. Institutional employment available. **Financial Aid Statistics:** 93% needy freshmen, 80% needy undergrads receive need-based scholarship or grant aid. 9% freshmen, 6% undergrads receive non-need-based scholarship or grant aid. 80% freshmen, 82% undergrads receive need-based self-help aid. 1% freshmen, 1% undergrads receive athletic scholarships. 94% freshmen, 88% undergrads receive any aid. 66% undergrads borrow to pay for school. Average cumulative indebtedness $28,856. **Criteria awarding aid:** *Non-need-based:* Academics, Art, Athletics, Minority status, Music/drama, Religious affiliation.

OHIO WESLEYAN UNIVERSITY

61 South Sandusky Street, Delaware, OH 43015
Phone: 740-368-3020 **Financial Aid Phone:** (740) 368-3050
E-mail: owuadmit@owu.edu **CEEB Code:** 1594
Fax: 740-368-3314 **Website:** www.owu.edu **ACT Code:** 3316

This private school, affiliated with the Methodist Church, was founded in 1842. It has a 200 acre campus.

RATINGS

Admissions Selectivity Rating: 81   **Fire Safety Rating:** 86   **Green Rating:** 60*

STUDENTS AND FACULTY

Enrollment: 1,554. **Student Body:** 54% female, 46% male, 43% out-of-state, 6% international (41 countries represented). Asian 3%, African American 9%, Caucasian 68%, Hispanic 6%, Native American , Pacific Islander <1%, Two or more races 5%, Race unknown 2%.

Retention and Graduation: 77% freshmen return for sophomore year. 61% freshmen graduate within 4 years. % freshmen graduate within 6 years. **Faculty:** Student/faculty ratio 9:1. 133 full-time faculty, 100% hold PhDs, 6% are members of minority groups, 41% are women. 0% of classes are taught by teaching assistants.

ACADEMICS

Degrees: Bachelor's. **Classes:** Most classes have 10–19 students. Most lab/discussion sessions have 10–19 students. **Most popular majors:** Zoology/Animal Biology; Economics, General; Psychology, General. **Special Study Options:** Distance learning; Double major; Dual enrollment; English as a Second Language (ESL); Exchange student program (domestic); Honors program; Independent study; Internships; Student-designed major; Study abroad; Teacher certification program. **Honors programs:** The Leland F. and Helen Schubert Honors Program recognizes the most talented students among Ohio Wesleyan's community of scholars and challenges them through Honors Tutorials, Honors Seminars, and Honors Scholarships. **Combined degree programs:** BA/MEng. **Disability Services offered:** Note-taking services; Tape recorders; Tutors. **Career services:** Alumni network; Alumni services; Career assessment.

FACILITIES

Housing: Apartments for single students; Coed dorms; Fraternity/sorority housing; Special housing for international students; Theme housing; Women's dorms; 60% of campus accessible to physically disabled. **Special Academic Facilities/Equipment:** Perkins and Student Observatories; Woltemade Center for Economics, Business and Entrepreneurship; Ross Art Museum; Schimmel/Conrades Science Center, 150,000 square foot science center with state-of-the art classrooms and equipment, including a new Scanning transmission electron microscope for undergraduate studies; Wireless campus. **Campus Network:** 100% of classrooms, 100% of dorms, 100% of student union, 100% of libraries, 100% of dining areas have wireless network access.

CAMPUS LIFE

Environment: Town. **Activities:** Campus Ministries; Choral groups; Dance; Drama/theater; International Student Organization; Jazz band; Literary magazine; Marching band; Model UN; Music ensembles; Musical theater; Opera; Pep band; Radio station; Student government; Student newspaper; Symphony orchestra; Yearbook. **Athletics (Intercollegiate):** *Men:* baseball, basketball, cross-country, diving, football, golf, lacrosse, sailing, soccer, swimming, tennis, track/field (outdoor), track/field (indoor). *Women:* basketball, cross-country, diving, field hockey, lacrosse, sailing, soccer, softball, swimming, tennis, track/field (outdoor), track/field (indoor), volleyball. **On-Campus Highlights:** Schimmel/Conrades Science Center. **Environmental Initiatives:** Waste reduction.

ADMISSIONS

Freshman Academic Profile: Average high school GPA 3.6. 25% in top 10% of high school class, 53% in top 25% of high school class, 81% in top 50% of high school class. 77% from public high schools. **Test Scores:** SAT Math middle 50% range 530–645. SAT EBRW middle 50% range 530–650. ACT middle 50% range 22–28. **Basis for Candidate Selection:** *Very important factors include:* rigor of secondary school record, academic GPA, application essay, recommendation(s), interview, character/personal qualities. *Important factors include:* class rank, standardized test scores, extracurricular activities, talent/ability. *Other factors include:* first generation, alumni/ae relation, geographical residence, volunteer work, work experience, level of applicant's interest. **Freshman Admission Requirements:** High school diploma is required and GED is accepted. *Academic units required:* 4 English, 3 math, 3 science, 2 foreign language, 3 social studies. *Academic units recommended:* 4 English, 4 math, 4 science, 3 foreign language, 4 social studies. **Freshman Admission Statistics:** 4,705 applied, 69% admitted, 14% enrolled. **Transfer Admission Requirements:** High school transcript, college transcript(s), essay or personal statement, statement of good standing from prior institution(s). Minimum college GPA of 2.5 required. Lowest grade transferable C-. **General Admission Information:** Priority deadline 1/15. Regular application deadline 3/1. Non-fall registration accepted.

COSTS AND FINANCIAL AID

Annual tuition $46,870. Room and board $12,800. Required fees $260. Average book and supplies expense $1,500. **Required Forms and Deadlines:** FAFSA. **Types of Aid:** *Need-based scholarships/grants:* College/university scholarship or grant aid from institutional funds; Federal Pell; Private scholarships; SEOG; State scholarships/grants. *Loans:* Direct PLUS loans; Direct Subsidized Stafford Loans; Direct Unsubsidized Stafford Loans. **Student Employment:** Federal Work-Study Program available. Institutional employment available. **Financial Aid Statistics:** 100% needy freshmen, 100% needy undergrads receive need-based scholarship or grant aid. 14% freshmen, 15% undergrads receive non-need-based scholarship or grant aid. 87% freshmen, 85% undergrads receive need-based self-help aid. 0% freshmen, 0% undergrads receive athletic scholarships. 69% undergrads borrow to pay for school. Average cumulative indebtedness $33,814. **Criteria awarding aid:** *Non-need-based:* Academics, Alumni affiliation, Art, Minority status, Music/drama, Religious affiliation, State/district residency.

OKLAHOMA BAPTIST UNIVERSITY

500 West University, Shawnee, OK 74804
Phone: 405-585-5000 **Financial Aid Phone:** 405-878-2016
E-mail: admissions@okbu.edu **CEEB Code:** 6541
Fax: 405-585-5017 **Website:** www.okbu.edu **ACT Code:** 3414

This private school, affiliated with the Southern Baptist Church, was founded in 1910. It has a 200 acre campus.

RATINGS

Admissions Selectivity Rating: 79   **Fire Safety Rating:** 83   **Green Rating:** 60*

STUDENTS AND FACULTY

Enrollment: 1,808. **Student Body:** 60% female, 40% male, 49% out-of-state, 4% international (35 countries represented). Asian 1%, African American 5%, Caucasian 67%, Hispanic 2%, Native American 5%, Pacific Islander <1%, Two or more races 12%, Race unknown 4%.

Retention and Graduation: 68% freshmen return for sophomore year. 14% grads go on to further study within 1 year. 8% grads pursue arts and sciences degrees. 1% grads pursue law degrees. 3% grads pursue medical degrees.

Faculty: Student/faculty ratio 15:1. 127 full-time faculty, 69% hold PhDs, 12% are members of minority groups, 0% are women. 0% of classes are taught by teaching assistants.

ACADEMICS

Degrees: Associate; Bachelor's; Certificate; Master's. **Classes:** Most classes have 10–19 students. Most lab/discussion sessions have 10–19 students. **Most popular majors:** Bible/Biblical Studies; Education, General; Health Professions And Related Programs. **Special Study Options:** Accelerated program; Cooperative education program; Double major; Dual enrollment; English as a Second Language (ESL); Exchange student program (domestic); Honors program; Independent study; Internships; Liberal arts/career combination; Student-designed major; Study abroad; Teacher certification program. **Honors programs:** The OBU Honors Program is a curricular program designed to enhance the undergraduate study experience for certain exceptionally well-qualified students. Students completing all of the requirements for gradulation in the Honors Program earn the designation "with Honors" on their OBU diplomas. **Combined degree programs:** BA/MA. **Disability Services offered:** Note-taking services; Reader services; Tape recorders; Tutors. **Career services:** Alumni network; Alumni services; Career assessment; Career/job search classes; Internships.

FACILITIES

Housing: Apartments for married students; Apartments for single students; Men's dorms; Wellness housing; Women's dorms; 100% of campus accessible to physically disabled. **Special Academic Facilities/Equipment:** Planetarium, Baptist Historical Society Archives, Avery T. Willis Center for Global Outreach.

CAMPUS LIFE

Environment: Town. **Activities:** Campus Ministries; Choral groups; Concert band; Dance; Drama/theater; International Student Organization; Jazz band; Literary magazine; Marching band; Model UN; Music ensembles; Musical theater; Opera; Pep band; Student government; Student newspaper; Symphony orchestra; Television station; Yearbook. 42 registered organizations, 8 honor societies, 16 religious organizations, 3 fraternities, 4 sororities on campus. **Athletics (Intercollegiate):** *Men:* baseball, basketball, cheerleading, cross-country, golf, soccer, tennis, track/field (outdoor), track/field (indoor). *Women:* basketball, cheerleading, cross-country, golf, soccer, softball, tennis, track/field (outdoor), track/field (indoor), volleyball. **On-Campus Highlights:** Geiger Center (Student Building).

ADMISSIONS

Freshman Academic Profile: Average high school GPA 3.7. 22% in top 10% of high school class, 49% in top 25% of high school class, 80% in top 50% of high school class. 79% from public high schools. **Test Scores:** SAT Math middle 50% range 490–580. SAT EBRW middle 50% range 500–620. ACT middle 50% range 20–26. **Basis for Candidate Selection:** *Very important factors include:* class rank, academic GPA, application essay. *Important factors include:* rigor of secondary school record, extracurricular activities. *Other factors include:* standardized test scores, interview, talent/ability, character/personal qualities, first generation, alumni/ae relation, religious affiliation/commitment, volunteer work, work experience. **Freshman Admission Requirements:** High school diploma is required and GED is accepted. *Academic units recommended:* 4 English, 3 math, 3 science, 2 science labs, 2 foreign language, 2 social studies, 1 history, 2 academic electives, 2 visual/performing arts. **Freshman Admission Statistics:** 4,119 applied, 87% admitted, 15% enrolled. **Transfer Admission Requirements:** College transcript(s). Minimum college GPA of 2.5 required. Lowest grade transferable D. **General Admission Information:** Priority deadline 4/1. Regular application deadline 8/1. Non-fall registration accepted.

COSTS AND FINANCIAL AID

Annual tuition $26,584. Room and board $7,490. Required fees $3,280. Average book and supplies expense $1,300. **Required Forms and Deadlines:** FAFSA. **Notification of Awards:** Applicants will be notified of awards on a rolling basis beginning 2/1. **Types of Aid:** *Need-based scholarships/grants:* College/university scholarship or grant aid from institutional funds; Federal Nursing Scholarships; Federal Pell; Private scholarships; SEOG; State scholarships/grants. *Loans:* Direct PLUS loans; Direct Subsidized Stafford Loans; Direct Unsubsidized Stafford Loans. **Student Employment:** Federal Work-Study Program available. Institutional employment available. **Financial Aid Statistics:** 75% needy freshmen, 74% needy undergrads receive need-based scholarship or grant aid. 100% freshmen, 95% undergrads receive non-need-based scholarship or grant aid. 76% freshmen, 76% undergrads receive need-based self-help aid. 16% freshmen, 18% undergrads receive athletic scholarships. 100% freshmen, 98% undergrads receive any aid. 63% undergrads borrow to pay for school. Average cumulative indebtedness $25,262. **Criteria awarding aid:** *Need-based:* Academics, Leadership, Minority status. *Non-need-based:* Academics, Art, Athletics, Leadership, Minority status, Music/drama, Religious affiliation.

OKLAHOMA CHRISTIAN UNIVERSITY

P.O. Box 11000, Oklahoma City, OK 73136-1100
Phone: 405-425-5050 **Financial Aid Phone:** 405-425-5190
E-mail: info@oc.edu
Fax: 405-425-5069 **Website:** www.oc.edu **ACT Code:** 3415

This private school, affiliated with the Church of Christ, was founded in 1950. It has a 240 acre campus.

RATINGS

Admissions Selectivity Rating: 89   Fire Safety Rating: 82   Green Rating: 60*

STUDENTS AND FACULTY

Enrollment: 1,910. **Student Body:** 49% female, 51% male, 63% out-of-state, 11% international (38 countries represented). Asian 1%, African American 3%, Caucasian 63%, Hispanic 3%, Native American 4%, Pacific Islander 0%, Two or more races 0%, Race unknown 14%.
Retention and Graduation: 73% freshmen return for sophomore year.
Faculty: Student/faculty ratio 13:1. 116 full-time faculty, 73% hold PhDs, 0% are members of minority groups, 30% are women. 0% of classes are taught by teaching assistants.

ACADEMICS

Degrees: Bachelor's; Master's. **Classes:** Most classes have 10–19 students. Most lab/discussion sessions have 10–19 students. **Most popular majors:** Registered Nursing/Registered Nurse; Liberal Arts and Sciences/Liberal Studies; Elementary Education and Teaching. **Special Study Options:** Cross-registration; Distance learning; Double major; English as a Second Language (ESL); Honors program; Independent study; Internships; Student-designed major; Study abroad; Teacher certification program. **Honors programs:** The Honors Program is designed for good thinkers who value knowledge for its intrinsic worth and its enabling power. Honors students have had strong academic experiences in high school. Honors students accept intellectual challenges to understand and perform at the highest possible level. Honors students are majoring in many disciplines, bringing their diverse insights to their work with other honors students. A detailed description of the OC Honors Program, and contact information, can be found at www.oc.edu/academics/honors. **Career services:** Alumni network; Alumni services; Career assessment; Career/job search classes; Internships.

FACILITIES

Housing: Apartments for married students; Apartments for single students; Men's dorms; Special housing for disabled students; Women's dorms. **Special Academic Facilities/Equipment:** Art Museum; Art Gallery.

CAMPUS LIFE

Environment: Metropolis. **Activities:** Campus Ministries; Choral groups; Concert band; Drama/theater; International Student Organization; Jazz band; Literary magazine; Music ensembles; Musical theater; Opera; Pep band; Student government; Student newspaper; Symphony orchestra; Television station; Yearbook. 20 registered organizations, 5 honor societies, 2 religious organizations, 6 fraternities, 6 sororities on campus. **Athletics (Intercollegiate):** *Men:* baseball, basketball, cross-country, golf, soccer, tennis, track/field (outdoor). *Women:* basketball, cheerleading, cross-country, soccer, softball, tennis, track/field (outdoor). **On-Campus Highlights:** Gaylord University Center. **Environmental Initiatives:** Trayless Cafeteria.

ADMISSIONS

Freshman Academic Profile: Average high school GPA 3.6. 30% in top 10% of high school class, 54% in top 25% of high school class, 80% in top 50% of high school class. **Test Scores:** SAT Math middle 50% range 470–640. SAT EBRW middle 50% range 440–620. ACT middle 50% range 21–28. **Basis for Candidate Selection:** *Very important factors include:* character/personal qualities. *Important factors include:* academic GPA, standardized test scores. *Other factors include:* rigor of secondary school record, class rank, recommendation(s), interview, extracurricular activities, talent/ability, religious affiliation/commitment, volunteer work, work experience, level of applicant's interest. **Freshman Admission Requirements:** High school diploma is required and GED is accepted. *Academic units required:* 4 English, 4 math, 4 science. *Academic units recommended:* 3 science labs, 2 foreign language, 3 social studies. **Freshman Admission Statistics:** 2,156 applied, 45% admitted, 47% enrolled. **Transfer Admission Requirements:** High school transcript, college transcript(s), standardized test scores, statement of good standing from prior institution(s). Lowest grade transferable D. **General Admission Information:** Application fee $25. Priority deadline 5/1. Non-fall registration accepted. Admission may be deferred for a maximum of 1 year.

COSTS AND FINANCIAL AID
Annual tuition $18,800. Room and board $6,775. Average book and supplies expense $1,000. **Required Forms and Deadlines:** FAFSA. **Notification of Awards:** Applicants will be notified of awards on a rolling basis beginning 2/15. **Types of Aid:** *Need-based scholarships/grants:* College/university scholarship or grant aid from institutional funds; Federal Pell; Private scholarships; SEOG; State scholarships/grants. *Loans:* Direct PLUS loans; Direct Subsidized Stafford Loans; Direct Unsubsidized Stafford Loans. **Student Employment:** Federal Work-Study Program available. Institutional employment available. **Financial Aid Statistics:** 58% needy freshmen, 58% needy undergrads receive need-based scholarship or grant aid. 82% freshmen, 77% undergrads receive non-need-based scholarship or grant aid. 60% freshmen, 42% undergrads receive need-based self-help aid. 9% freshmen, 9% undergrads receive athletic scholarships. 99.8% freshmen, 98% undergrads receive any aid. **Criteria awarding aid:** *Need-based:* Academics, Art, Athletics, Music/drama. *Non-need-based:* Religious affiliation.

OKLAHOMA CITY UNIVERSITY

2501 North Blackwelder, Oklahoma City, OK 73106
Phone: 405-208-5055 **Financial Aid Phone:** 405-208-5848
E-mail: uadmissions@okcu.edu **CEEB Code:** 6543
Fax: 405-208-5916 **Website:** www.okcu.edu **ACT Code:** 3416

This private school, affiliated with the Methodist Church, was founded in 1904. It has a 104 acre campus.

RATINGS
Admissions Selectivity Rating: 80   **Fire Safety Rating:** 95   **Green Rating:** 60*

STUDENTS AND FACULTY
Enrollment: 1,604. **Student Body:** 68% female, 32% male, 51% out-of-state, 6% international (35 countries represented). Asian 2%, African American 5%, Caucasian 65%, Hispanic 11%, Native American 2%, Pacific Islander 0%, Two or more races 9%, Race unknown <1%.
Retention and Graduation: 81% freshmen return for sophomore year. 46% freshmen graduate within 4 years. 59% freshmen graduate within 6 years. 10% grads go on to further study within 1 year. **Faculty:** Student/faculty ratio 10:1. 202 full-time faculty, 64% hold PhDs, 16% are members of minority groups, 51% are women. 0% of classes are taught by teaching assistants.

ACADEMICS
Degrees: Bachelor's; Doctoral degree—professional practice; Doctoral degree research/scholarship; Master's. **Classes:** Most classes have 10–19 students. Most lab/discussion sessions have 10–19 students. **Most popular majors:** Business/Commerce, General; Nursing Practice; Dance, General. **Special Study Options:** Accelerated program; Cooperative education program; Distance learning; Double major; Dual enrollment; English as a Second Language (ESL); Exchange student program (domestic); External degree program; Honors program; Independent study; Internships; Student-designed major; Study abroad; Teacher certification program. **Honors programs:** The mission of the University Honors program is to provide an enhanced learning environment for academically gifted undergraduate students. Each new class of Honors students at OCU will be a spcial community of scholars. Students will have the opportunity to become acquainted with one another and the Honors program in the Honors Colloquium, a course required for all new honors students during their first semester in the program. Honors students will have the opportunities to meet with visiting scholars and participate in special events. As part of a network of honors programs through the National Collegiate Honors Council and the Great Plains Honors Council, students may present research at national and regional honors conferences and participate in exciting summer and semester programs. **Combined degree programs:** BA/JD; BA/MA. **Disability Services offered:** Reader services; Tutors. **Career services:** Alumni network; Alumni services; Career assessment; Career/job search classes; Internships; Regional alumni.

FACILITIES
Housing: Apartments for married students; Apartments for single students; Coed dorms; Fraternity/sorority housing; Men's dorms; Special housing for disabled students; Special housing for international students; Theme housing; Women's dorms; 95% of campus accessible to physically disabled. **Special Academic Facilities/Equipment:** Art museum, audiovisual center, language lab.

CAMPUS LIFE
Environment: Metropolis. **Activities:** Campus Ministries; Choral groups; Concert band; Dance; Drama/theater; International Student Organization; Jazz band; Literary magazine; Music ensembles; Musical theater; Opera; Pep band; Student government; Student newspaper; Symphony orchestra; Television station; Yearbook. 64 registered organizations, 14 honor societies, 5 religious organizations, 3 fraternities, 4 sororities on campus. **Athletics (Intercollegiate):** *Men:* baseball, basketball, cheerleading, crew/rowing, golf, soccer, track/field (outdoor), wrestling. *Women:* basketball, cheerleading, crew/rowing, golf, soccer, softball, track/field (outdoor), volleyball, wrestling. **On-Campus Highlights:** Tom and Brenda McDaniel Univ Center. **Environmental Initiatives:** Computer recycling program, community garden.

ADMISSIONS
Freshman Academic Profile: Average high school GPA 3.8. 31% in top 10% of high school class, 56% in top 25% of high school class, 87% in top 50% of high school class. 88% from public high schools. **Test Scores:** SAT Math middle 50% range 540–620. SAT EBRW middle 50% range 550–660. ACT middle 50% range 23–29. **Basis for Candidate Selection:** *Very important factors include:* rigor of secondary school record, talent/ability. *Important factors include:* academic GPA, application essay, standardized test scores, character/personal qualities. *Other factors include:* class rank, recommendation(s), interview, extracurricular activities, volunteer work, work experience, level of applicant's interest. **Freshman Admission Requirements:** High school diploma is required and GED is accepted. *Academic units required:* 4 English, 3 math, 3 science, 2 science labs, 2 foreign language, 2 social studies, 2 history, 3 academic electives. *Academic units recommended:* 4 English, 4 math, 4 science, 3 science labs, 2 foreign language, 3 social studies, 1 history, 3 academic electives. **Freshman Admission Statistics:** 1,751 applied, 76% admitted, 28% enrolled. **Transfer Admission Requirements:** College transcript(s), essay or personal statement, statement of good standing from prior institution(s). Minimum college GPA of 2.0 required. Lowest grade transferable C-. **General Admission Information:** Application fee $55. Priority deadline 3/1. Non-fall registration accepted. Admission may be deferred for a maximum of 1 year.

COSTS AND FINANCIAL AID
Annual tuition $27,276. Room and board $10,796. Required fees $3,750. Average book and supplies expense $1,500. **Required Forms and Deadlines:** FAFSA. **Notification of Awards:** Applicants will be notified of awards on a rolling basis beginning 3/1. **Types of Aid:** *Need-based scholarships/grants:* College/university scholarship or grant aid from institutional funds; Federal Pell; Private scholarships; SEOG; State scholarships/grants. *Loans:* Direct PLUS loans; Direct Subsidized Stafford Loans; Direct Unsubsidized Stafford Loans. **Student Employment:** Federal Work-Study Program available. Institutional employment available. **Financial Aid Statistics:** 89% needy freshmen, 86% needy undergrads receive need-based scholarship or grant aid. 12% freshmen, 10% undergrads receive non-need-based scholarship or grant aid. 64% freshmen, 66% undergrads receive need-based self-help aid. 2% freshmen, 2% undergrads receive athletic scholarships. 96% freshmen, 85% undergrads receive any aid. 56% undergrads borrow to pay for school. Average cumulative indebtedness $27,209. **Criteria awarding aid:** *Non-need-based:* Academics, Art, Athletics, Leadership, Music/drama, Religious affiliation.

OKLAHOMA STATE UNIVERSITY

219 Student Union, Stillwater, OK 74078
Phone: 405-744-5358 **Financial Aid Phone:** 405-744-6604
E-mail: admissions@okstate.edu **CEEB Code:** 6546
Fax: 405-744-7092 **Website:** http://www.okstate.edu **ACT Code:** 3424

This public school was founded in 1890. It has a 840 acre campus.

RATINGS
Admissions Selectivity Rating: 85   **Fire Safety Rating:** 93   **Green Rating:** 84

STUDENTS AND FACULTY
Enrollment: 19,766. **Student Body:** 50% female, 50% male, 27% out-of-state, 3% international (64 countries represented). Asian 2%, African American 4%,

Caucasian 68%, Hispanic 8%, Native American 4%, Pacific Islander <1%, Two or more races 10%, Race unknown <1%. **Retention and Graduation:** 83% freshmen return for sophomore year. 41% freshmen graduate within 4 years. 65% freshmen graduate within 6 years. **Faculty:** Student/faculty ratio 18:1. 1,075 full-time faculty, 92% hold PhDs, 20% are members of minority groups, 39% are women. 24% of classes are taught by teaching assistants.

ACADEMICS
Degrees: Bachelor's; Doctoral degree—professional practice; Doctoral degree research/scholarship; Master's; Post-bachelor's certificate; Post-master's certificate. **Classes:** Most classes have 10–19 students. Most lab/discussion sessions have 10–19 students. **Most popular majors:** Animal Sciences, General; Mechanical Engineering; Business Administration and Management, General. **Special Study Options:** Accelerated program; Cross-registration; Distance learning; Double major; Dual enrollment; English as a Second Language (ESL); Exchange student program (domestic); Honors program; Independent study; Internships; Student-designed major; Study abroad; Teacher certification program. **Honors programs:** OSU has an Honors College that students across undergraduate disciplines can be a part of. For more information see https://honors.okstate.edu/. **Combined degree programs:** BA/MA. **Disability Services offered:** Note-taking services; Reader services; Tape recorders; Tutors. **Career services:** Alumni network; Alumni services; Career assessment; Career/job search classes; Internships; Regional alumni.

FACILITIES
Housing: Apartments for married students; Apartments for single students; Coed dorms; Fraternity/sorority housing; Men's dorms; Special housing for disabled students; Theme housing; Wellness housing; Women's dorms; 97% of campus accessible to physically disabled. **Special Academic Facilities/Equipment:** OSU Museum of Art, Gardiner Art Gallery, Seretean Wellness Center, Colvin Recreation Center, laser research center, Henry Bellmon Research Center, ENDEAVOR Lab, McKnight Center for the Performing Arts, Watson Trading Floor, OSU Botanic Garden.

CAMPUS LIFE
Environment: Town. **Activities:** Campus Ministries; Choral groups; Concert band; Dance; Drama/theater; International Student Organization; Jazz band; Literary magazine; Marching band; Model UN; Music ensembles; Musical theater; Opera; Pep band; Radio station; Student government; Student newspaper; Student-run film society; Symphony orchestra; Television station. 518 registered organizations, 36 honor societies, 25 religious organizations, 27 fraternities, 18 sororities on campus. **Athletics (Intercollegiate):** *Men:* baseball, basketball, cross-country, football, golf, tennis, track/field (outdoor), wrestling. *Women:* basketball, cross-country, equestrian sports, golf, soccer, softball, tennis, track/field (outdoor). **On-Campus Highlights:** Colvin Recreational Center. **Environmental Initiatives:** The OSU Energy Management program focuses on behavior change to conserve energy across campus. This program has saved nearly $38 million for the OSU Stillwater campus since 2007.

ADMISSIONS
Freshman Academic Profile: Average high school GPA 3.6. 27% in top 10% of high school class, 54% in top 25% of high school class, 84% in top 50% of high school class. **Test Scores:** SAT Math middle 50% range 510–630. SAT EBRW middle 50% range 530–635. ACT middle 50% range 21–28. **Basis for Candidate Selection:** *Very important factors include:* class rank, academic GPA, standardized test scores. *Important factors include:* application essay, *Other factors include:* recommendation(s). **Freshman Admission Requirements:** High school diploma is required and GED is accepted. *Academic units required:* 4 English, 3 math, 3 science, 3 science labs, 2 social studies, 1 history. **Freshman Admission Statistics:** 15,277 applied, 70% admitted, 39% enrolled. **Transfer Admission Requirements:** College transcript(s). Minimum college GPA of 2.25 required. Lowest grade transferable D. **General Admission Information:** Application fee $40. Non-fall registration accepted.

COSTS AND FINANCIAL AID
Annual in-state tuition $5,357. Annual out-of-state tuition $20,877. Room and board $9,106. Required fees $3,662. Average book and supplies expense $1,120. **Required Forms and Deadlines:** FAFSA;. **Notification of Awards:** Applicants will be notified of awards on a rolling basis beginning 12/1. **Types of Aid:** *Need-based scholarships/grants:* College/university scholarship or grant aid from institutional funds; Federal Pell; Private scholarships; SEOG; State scholarships/grants. *Loans:* Direct PLUS loans; Direct Subsidized Stafford Loans; Direct Unsubsidized Stafford Loans. **Student Employment:** Federal Work-Study Program available. Institutional employment available. **Financial Aid Statistics:** 77% needy freshmen, 74% needy undergrads receive need-based scholarship or grant aid. 9% freshmen, 5% undergrads receive non-need-based scholarship or grant aid. 53% freshmen, 63% undergrads receive need-based

self-help aid. 2% freshmen, 2% undergrads receive athletic scholarships. 87.73% freshmen, 82.19% undergrads receive any aid. 50% undergrads borrow to pay for school. Average cumulative indebtedness $25,185. **Criteria awarding aid:** *Need-based:* Academics, Minority status. *Non-need-based:* Academics, Alumni affiliation, Art, Athletics, Leadership, Minority status, Music/drama, State/district residency.

OLD DOMINION UNIVERSITY

108 Rollins Hall, Norfolk, VA 23529-0050
Phone: 757-683-3685 **Financial Aid Phone:** 757-683-3683
E-mail: admissions@odu.edu **CEEB Code:** 5126
Fax: 757-683-3255 **Website:** www.odu.edu

This public school was founded in 1930. It has a 251 acre campus.

RATINGS
Admissions Selectivity Rating: 75   **Fire Safety Rating:** 89   **Green Rating:** 60*

STUDENTS AND FACULTY
Enrollment: 18,965. **Student Body:** 55% female, 45% male, 8% out-of-state, 1% international (93 countries represented). Asian 5%, African American 32%, Caucasian 44%, Hispanic 9%, Native American <1%, Pacific Islander <1%, Two or more races 7%, Race unknown 2%.
Retention and Graduation: 80% freshmen return for sophomore year. 29% freshmen graduate within 4 years. 53% freshmen graduate within 6 years. 17% grads go on to further study within 1 year. 8% grads pursue arts and sciences degrees. 1% grads pursue law degrees. 2% grads pursue business degrees. 1% grads pursue medical degrees. **Faculty:** Student/faculty ratio 17:1. 868 full-time faculty, 81% hold PhDs, 25% are members of minority groups, 46% are women.

ACADEMICS
Degrees: Bachelor's; Certificate; Doctoral degree—professional practice; Doctoral degree research/scholarship; Master's; Post-bachelor's certificate; Post-master's certificate. **Classes:** Most classes have 10–19 students. Most lab/discussion sessions have 20–29 students. **Most popular majors:** Biology/Biological Sciences, General; Psychology, General; Criminology. **Special Study Options:** Accelerated program; Cooperative education program; Cross-registration; Distance learning; Double major; Dual enrollment; English as a Second Language (ESL); Exchange student program (domestic); Honors program; Independent study; Internships; Liberal arts/career combination; Student-designed major; Study abroad; Teacher certification program. **Honors programs:** The Honors College was established to further the University's commitment to excellence in education. With an emphasis on teaching, innovation, and small classes, the college offers the experience of a small liberal arts college within the framework of the large university. The four-year experience offers specially designed, low-enrollment courses to honors students and selected juniors and seniors. Several out-of-class and off-campus experiences are often part of these courses—at no extra cost to students. A one credit honors tutorial is required in the junior year, and a senior honors colloquium is taken in the final year of study. All Honors College students are awarded an annual honors stipend. **Combined degree programs:** BA/MA; BA/MEng. **Disability Services offered:** Note-taking services; Reader services; Tape recorders; Tutors. **Career services:** Alumni network; Alumni services; Career assessment; Career/job search classes; Internships; Regional alumni.

FACILITIES
Housing: Apartments for single students; Coed dorms; Special housing for disabled students; Special housing for international students; Theme housing; Women's dorms; 100% of campus accessible to physically disabled. **Special Academic Facilities/Equipment:** Student art gallery, laser optics lab, robotics lab, sub-/super-sonic wind tunnels, centers for urban research/service, economic education, and child study, planetarium, marine science research vessel, random wave pool. **Campus Network:** 100% of classrooms, 100% of dorms, 100% of student union, 100% of libraries, 100% of dining areas, 100% of common outdoor areas have wireless network access.

CAMPUS LIFE
Environment: Metropolis. **Activities:** Campus Ministries; Choral groups; Concert band; Dance; Drama/theater; International Student Organization; Jazz band; Literary magazine; Marching band; Model UN; Music ensembles; Musical theater; Pep band; Radio station; Student government; Student newspaper; Student-run film society; Symphony orchestra. 341 registered organizations, 18 honor societies, 25 religious organizations, 18 fraternities,

8 sororities on campus. **Athletics (Intercollegiate):** *Men:* baseball, basketball, diving, football, golf, sailing, soccer, tennis, wrestling. *Women:* basketball, crew/rowing, diving, field hockey, golf, lacrosse, sailing, soccer, tennis. **On-Campus Highlights:** Webb Student Center.

ADMISSIONS

Freshman Academic Profile: Average high school GPA 3.3. 10% in top 10% of high school class, 28% in top 25% of high school class, 67% in top 50% of high school class. **Test Scores:** SAT Math middle 50% range 480–580. SAT EBRW middle 50% range 500–600. ACT middle 50% range 18–24. **Basis for Candidate Selection:** *Very important factors include:* rigor of secondary school record, academic GPA, standardized test scores. *Important factors include:* application essay, recommendation(s), extracurricular activities, volunteer work. *Other factors include:* class rank, talent/ability, character/personal qualities, first generation, alumni/ae relation, level of applicant's interest. **Freshman Admission Requirements:** High school diploma is required and GED is accepted. *Academic units required:* 4 English, 3 math, 3 science, 3 foreign language, 3 social studies. *Academic units recommended:* 4 English, 4 math, 3 science, 3 foreign language, 3 social studies. **Freshman Admission Statistics:** 13,761 applied, 89% admitted, 26% enrolled. **Transfer Admission Requirements:** College transcript(s). Minimum college GPA of 2.2 required. Lowest grade transferable C. **General Admission Information:** Application fee $50. Priority deadline 12/1. Regular application deadline 2/1. Non-fall registration accepted. Admission may be deferred for a maximum of 12 months.

COSTS AND FINANCIAL AID

Annual in-state tuition $11,020. Annual out-of-state tuition $31,180. Room and board $12,836. Required fees $340. Average book and supplies expense $1,300. **Required Forms and Deadlines:** FAFSA. **Notification of Awards:** Applicants will be notified of awards on a rolling basis beginning 3/1. **Types of Aid:** *Need-based scholarships/grants:* College/university scholarship or grant aid from institutional funds; Federal Nursing Scholarships; Federal Pell; Private scholarships; SEOG; State scholarships/grants; United Negro College Fund. *Loans:* Direct PLUS loans; Direct Subsidized Stafford Loans; Direct Unsubsidized Stafford Loans. **Student Employment:** Federal Work-Study Program available. Institutional employment available. **Financial Aid Statistics:** 75% needy freshmen, 77% needy undergrads receive need-based scholarship or grant aid. 37% freshmen, 22% undergrads receive non-need-based scholarship or grant aid. 74% freshmen, 76% undergrads receive need-based self-help aid. 2% freshmen, 2% undergrads receive athletic scholarships. 73% freshmen, 66% undergrads receive any aid. 73% undergrads borrow to pay for school. Average cumulative indebtedness $31,142. **Criteria awarding aid:** *Non-need-based:* Academics, Alumni affiliation, Art, Athletics, Leadership, Music/drama, State/district residency.

ORAL ROBERTS UNIVERSITY

7777 S. Lewis Avenue, Tulsa, OK 74171
Phone: 918-495-6518 **Financial Aid Phone:** (918) 495-6510
E-mail: admissions@oru.edu **CEEB Code:** 6552
Fax: 918-495-6222 **Website:** www.oru.edu **ACT Code:** 3427

This private school, affiliated with the Interdenominational, was founded in 1963. It has a 263 acre campus.

RATINGS

Admissions Selectivity Rating: 82   **Fire Safety Rating:** 98   **Green Rating:** 60*

STUDENTS AND FACULTY

Enrollment: 3,035. **Student Body:** 58% female, 42% male, 57% out-of-state, 14% international (100 countries represented). Asian 2%, African American 15%, Caucasian 44%, Hispanic 13%, Native American 3%, Pacific Islander 0%, Two or more races 5%, Race unknown 5%.
Retention and Graduation: 80% freshmen return for sophomore year. 43% freshmen graduate within 4 years. 51% freshmen graduate within 6 years. 16% grads go on to further study within 1 year. 18% grads pursue arts and sciences degrees. 2% grads pursue law degrees. 27% grads pursue business degrees. 9% grads pursue medical degrees. **Faculty:** Student/faculty ratio 17:1. 154 full-time faculty, 72% hold PhDs, 19% are members of minority groups, 47% are women. 0% of classes are taught by teaching assistants.

ACADEMICS

Degrees: Bachelor's; Certificate; Diploma; Doctoral degree—professional practice; Doctoral degree research/scholarship; Master's. **Classes:** Most classes have 10–19 students. Most lab/discussion sessions have 10–19 students. **Most popular majors:** Theology/Theological Studies; Marketing/Marketing Management, General; Visual And Performing Arts. **Special Study Options:** Accelerated program; Distance learning; Double major; Dual enrollment; English as a Second Language (ESL); Exchange student program (domestic); Honors program; Independent study; Internships; Student-designed major; Study abroad; Teacher certification program. **Honors programs:** ORU Honors Program includes "Scholars" and "Fellows," which are highly selective and include Beta Gamma Phi and other Honor Societies. **Disability Services offered:** Note-taking services; Reader services; Tape recorders; Tutors. **Career services:** Alumni network; Alumni services; Career assessment; Career/job search classes; Internships; Regional alumni.

FACILITIES

Housing: Men's dorms; Special housing for disabled students; Women's dorms; 100% of campus accessible to physically disabled. **Special Academic Facilities/Equipment:** Elsing Museum, Global Learning Center.

CAMPUS LIFE

Environment: Metropolis. **Activities:** Campus Ministries; Choral groups; Concert band; Dance; Drama/theater; International Student Organization; Jazz band; Literary magazine; Model UN; Music ensembles; Musical theater; Opera; Pep band; Radio station; Student government; Student newspaper; Symphony orchestra; Television station; Yearbook. 35 registered organizations on campus. **Athletics (Intercollegiate):** *Men:* baseball, basketball, cheerleading, cross-country, soccer, swimming, tennis, track/field (outdoor). *Women:* basketball, cheerleading, cross-country, soccer, swimming, tennis, track/field (outdoor), volleyball. **On-Campus Highlights:** Hammer Student Center.

ADMISSIONS

Freshman Academic Profile: Average high school GPA 3.6. 18% in top 10% of high school class, 43% in top 25% of high school class, 74% in top 50% of high school class. 75% from public high schools. **Test Scores:** SAT Math middle 50% range 490–610. SAT EBRW middle 50% range 498–630. ACT middle 50% range 18–25. **Basis for Candidate Selection:** *Very important factors include:* academic GPA, standardized test scores. **Freshman Admission Requirements:** High school diploma is required and GED is accepted. *Academic units recommended:* 4 English, 3 math, 3 science, 1 science lab, 2 foreign language, 2 social studies, 3 history, 8 academic electives. **Freshman Admission Statistics:** 3,437 applied, 68% admitted, 24% enrolled. **Transfer Admission Requirements:** High school transcript, college transcript(s), essay or personal statement. Minimum college GPA of 2.0 required. Lowest grade transferable 2. **General Admission Information:** Application fee $35. Non-fall registration accepted. Admission may be deferred for a maximum of 1 year.

COSTS AND FINANCIAL AID

Annual tuition $29,700. Room and board $8,650. Required fees $1,230. Average book and supplies expense $1,920. **Required Forms and Deadlines:** FAFSA. **Notification of Awards:** Applicants will be notified of awards on a rolling basis beginning 12/1. **Types of Aid:** *Need-based scholarships/grants:* College/university scholarship or grant aid from institutional funds; Federal Pell; Private scholarships; SEOG; State scholarships/grants. *Loans:* Direct PLUS loans; Direct Subsidized Stafford Loans; Direct Unsubsidized Stafford Loans. **Student Employment:** Federal Work-Study Program available. Institutional employment available. **Financial Aid Statistics:** 100% needy freshmen, 99% needy undergrads receive need-based scholarship or grant aid. 33% freshmen, 43% undergrads receive non-need-based scholarship or grant aid. 92% freshmen, 92% undergrads receive need-based self-help aid. 2% freshmen, 4% undergrads receive athletic scholarships. 95% freshmen, 87% undergrads receive any aid. Average cumulative indebtedness $35,230. **Criteria awarding aid:** *Non-need-based:* Academics, Alumni affiliation, Art, Athletics, Job skills, Leadership, Music/drama.

OREGON HEALTH & SCIENCE UNIVERSITY

3181 SW Sam Jackson Park Rd, Portland, OR 97239
Phone: 503-494-2998 **Financial Aid Phone:** (503) 494-7800
E-mail: proginfo@ohsu.edu **CEEB Code:** 4900
Fax: 503-494-3400 **Website:** www.ohsu.edu

This public school was founded in 1867. It has a 120 acre campus.

RATINGS
Admissions Selectivity Rating: 60*   **Fire Safety Rating:** 60*   **Green Rating:** 60*

STUDENTS AND FACULTY
Enrollment: 591. **Student Body:** 84% female, 16% male, 10% out-of-state, 1% international. Asian 5%, African American 1%, Caucasian 79%, Hispanic 5%, Native American 2%, Race unknown 6%.
Faculty: 1,290 full-time faculty, 0% hold PhDs, 0% are members of minority groups, 0% are women.

ACADEMICS
Degrees: Associate; Bachelor's; Master's; Post-bachelor's certificate; Post-master's certificate. **Most popular majors:** Emergency Medical Technology/Technician (Emt Paramedic); Clinical Laboratory Science/Medical Technology/Technologist; Nursing/Registered Nurse (Rn, Asn, Bsn, Msn). **Special Study Options:** Accelerated program; Distance learning.

FACILITIES
Campus Network: 100% of classrooms, 100% of dorms, 100% of student union, 100% of libraries, 100% of dining areas, 15% of common outdoor areas have wireless network access.

CAMPUS LIFE
Environment: Metropolis. **Activities:** Student government; Student newspaper; Yearbook. **On-Campus Highlights:** Portland Aerial Tram.

ADMISSIONS
Freshman Admission Requirements: High school diploma is required and GED is accepted. **Transfer Admission Requirements:** College transcript(s), essay or personal statement, standardized test scores, statement of good standing from prior institution(s). Lowest grade transferable C. **General Admission Information:** Application fee $120. Regular application deadline 1/15.

COSTS AND FINANCIAL AID
Annual out-of-state tuition $20,176. **Types of Aid:** *Need-based scholarships/grants:* College/university scholarship or grant aid from institutional funds; Federal Pell; Private scholarships; SEOG; State scholarships/grants. *Loans:* Direct PLUS loans; Direct Subsidized Stafford Loans; Direct Unsubsidized Stafford Loans. **Student Employment:** Federal Work-Study Program available. Institutional employment available. **Financial Aid Statistics:** 49% needy undergrads receive need-based scholarship or grant aid. 1% undergrads receive non-need-based scholarship or grant aid. 99% undergrads receive need-based self-help aid. 0% undergrads receive athletic scholarships. 70% undergrads receive any aid. **Criteria awarding aid:** *Need-based:* Academics, Minority status. *Non-need-based:* Academics, Minority status, State/district residency.

OREGON STATE UNIVERSITY

104 Kerr Administration Building, Corvallis, OR 97331-2106
Phone: 541-737-4411 **Financial Aid Phone:** 541-737-2241
E-mail: osuadmit@oregonstate.edu **CEEB Code:** 3210
Fax: 541-737-2482 **Website:** http://oregonstate.edu/ **ACT Code:** 3482

This public school was founded in 1868. It has a 421 acre campus.

RATINGS
Admissions Selectivity Rating: 80   **Fire Safety Rating:** 92   **Green Rating:** 94

STUDENTS AND FACULTY
Enrollment: 25,298. **Student Body:** 47% female, 53% male, 34% out-of-state, 7% international (81 countries represented). Asian 8%, African American 1%, Caucasian 64%, Hispanic 10%, Native American 1%, Pacific Islander <1%, Two or more races 7%, Race unknown 2%.
Retention and Graduation: 84% freshmen return for sophomore year. 37% freshmen graduate within 4 years. % freshmen graduate within 6 years. 19% grads go on to further study within 1 year. **Faculty:** Student/faculty ratio 17:1. 1,230 full-time faculty, 86% hold PhDs, 18% are members of minority groups, 40% are women. 8% of classes are taught by teaching assistants.

ACADEMICS
Degrees: Bachelor's; Certificate; Doctoral degree—professional practice; Doctoral degree research/scholarship; Master's; Post-bachelor's certificate.
Classes: Most classes have 20–29 students. Most lab/discussion sessions have 20–29 students. **Most popular majors:** Computer Science; Mechanical Engineering; Business Administration and Management, General. **Special Study Options:** Accelerated program; Cooperative education program; Cross-registration; Distance learning; Double major; Dual enrollment; English as a Second Language (ESL); Exchange student program (domestic); Honors program; Independent study; Internships; Liberal arts/career combination; Study abroad; Teacher certification program. **Honors programs:** As a small degree-granting college within Oregon State University, the UHC offers OSU's most prestigious degree, the Honors Baccalaureate Degree in any undergraduate major. The UHC Features: Challenging and creative curricula for students of all majors; Unique honors classes, typically limited to 12 or 20 students; Courses that complement, not complicate, other course work; OSU's finest professors, often hand-picked by UHC students; One-on-one mentoring by faculty members while preparing the Honors Thesis. **Disability Services offered:** Note-taking services; Reader services; Tape recorders; Tutors. **Career services:** Alumni network; Alumni services; Career assessment; Career/job search classes; Internships; Regional alumni.

FACILITIES
Housing: Apartments for married students; Apartments for single students; Coed dorms; Fraternity/sorority housing; Special housing for disabled students; Special housing for international students; Theme housing; Wellness housing 86% of campus accessible to physically disabled. **Special Academic Facilities/Equipment:** Museums, galleries, collections, exhibits of cultural and scientific materials, language lab. **Campus Network:** 100% of classrooms, 100% of dorms, 100% of student union, 100% of libraries, 100% of dining areas, 98% of common outdoor areas have wireless network access.

CAMPUS LIFE
Environment: Town. **Activities:** Campus Ministries; Choral groups; Concert band; Dance; Drama/theater; International Student Organization; Jazz band; Literary magazine; Marching band; Model UN; Music ensembles; Musical theater; Opera; Pep band; Radio station; Student government; Student newspaper; Student-run film society; Symphony orchestra; Television station; Yearbook. 400 registered organizations, 12 honor societies, 28 religious organizations, 27 fraternities, 22 sororities on campus. **Athletics (Intercollegiate):** *Men:* baseball, basketball, crew/rowing, football, golf, soccer, wrestling. *Women:* basketball, crew/rowing, cross-country, golf, gymnastics, soccer, softball, swimming, track/field (outdoor), volleyball. **On-Campus Highlights:** Memorial Union. **Environmental Initiatives:** OSU sustainability related research has impacts state- and nation-wide. Standout research occurs at the Oregon Climate Change Research Institute and within the colleges of Earth, Atmospheric and Oceanic Sciences, Agricultural Sciences and Engineering. More info at https://fa.oregonstate.edu/sustainability/research.

ADMISSIONS
Freshman Academic Profile: Average high school GPA 3.6. 28% in top 10% of high school class, 58% in top 25% of high school class, 89% in top 50% of high school class. **Test Scores:** SAT Math middle 50% range 540–660. SAT EBRW middle 50% range 540–650. ACT middle 50% range 22–28. **Basis for Candidate Selection:** *Very important factors include:* academic GPA. *Important factors include:* rigor of secondary school record, application essay, talent/ability, character/personal qualities, volunteer work, work experience. *Other factors include:* class rank, standardized test scores, recommendation(s), extracurricular activities, level of applicant's interest. **Freshman Admission Requirements:** High school diploma is required and GED is accepted. *Academic units required:* 4 English, 3 math, 3 science, 2 science labs, 2 foreign language, 3 social studies. *Academic units recommended:* 3 science labs. **Freshman Admission Statistics:** 14,890 applied, 81% admitted, 31% enrolled. **Transfer Admission Requirements:** College transcript(s), essay or personal statement, statement of good standing from prior institution(s). Minimum college GPA of 2.25 required. Lowest grade transferable D. **General Admission Information:** Application fee $65. Priority deadline 2/1. Regular application deadline 9/1. Non-fall registration accepted. Admission may be deferred for a maximum of 12 months.

COSTS AND FINANCIAL AID

Annual in-state tuition $9,390. Annual out-of-state tuition $28,365. Room and board $12,855. Average book and supplies expense $1,200. **Required Forms and Deadlines:** FAFSA. **Notification of Awards:** Applicants will be notified of awards on a rolling basis beginning 4/1. **Types of Aid:** *Need-based scholarships/ grants:* College/university scholarship or grant aid from institutional funds; Federal Pell; Private scholarships; SEOG; State scholarships/grants. *Loans:* Direct PLUS loans; Direct Subsidized Stafford Loans; Direct Unsubsidized Stafford Loans. **Student Employment:** Federal Work-Study Program available. Institutional employment available. **Financial Aid Statistics:** 83% needy freshmen, 77% needy undergrads receive need-based scholarship or grant aid. 3% freshmen, 2% undergrads receive non-need-based scholarship or grant aid. 96% freshmen, 96% undergrads receive need-based self-help aid. 1% freshmen, 1% undergrads receive athletic scholarships. 76.3% freshmen, 68.7% undergrads receive any aid. 56% undergrads borrow to pay for school. Average cumulative indebtedness $28,482. **Criteria awarding aid:** *Need-based:* Academics, Alumni affiliation, Athletics, Job skills, Leadership, Minority status. *Non-need-based:* Academics, Alumni affiliation, Athletics, Job skills, Leadership, Minority status, State/district residency.

OTIS COLLEGE OF ART AND DESIGN

9045 Lincoln Boulevard, Los Angeles, CA 90045
Phone: 310-665-6820 **Financial Aid Phone:** 310-665-6880
E-mail: admissions@otis.edu **CEEB Code:** 4394
Fax: 310-665-6821 **Website:** www.otis.edu **ACT Code:** 359

This private school was founded in 1918. It has a 5 acre campus.

RATINGS

Admissions Selectivity Rating: 76   **Fire Safety Rating:** 93   **Green Rating:** 60*

STUDENTS AND FACULTY

Enrollment: 1,125. **Student Body:** 69% female, 31% male, 37% out-of-state, 25% international. Asian 21%, African American 5%, Caucasian 23%, Hispanic 16%, Native American <1%, Pacific Islander 1%, Two or more races 6%, Race unknown 3%.
Faculty: Student/faculty ratio 8:1. 52 full-time faculty, 6% hold PhDs, 21% are members of minority groups, 54% are women. 0% of classes are taught by teaching assistants.

ACADEMICS

Degrees: Bachelor's; Master's. **Classes:** Most classes have 10–19 students. Most lab/discussion sessions have fewer than 10 students. **Most popular majors:** Fashion/Apparel Design; Design and Visual Communications, General; Digital Communication and Media/Multimedia. **Special Study Options:** Accelerated program; Cross-registration; Distance learning; Exchange student program (domestic); Honors program; Independent study; Internships; Study abroad; Teacher certification program. **Honors programs:** We have an honors program for qualified enrolled students. **Disability Services offered:** Note-taking services; Reader services; Tape recorders; Tutors. **Career services:** Alumni network; Alumni services; Career assessment; Career/job search classes; Internships; Regional alumni.

FACILITIES

Housing: Apartments for married students; Apartments for single students; Coed dorms; Special housing for disabled students; Theme housing; 100% of campus accessible to physically disabled. **Special Academic Facilities/ Equipment:** Art gallery, student gallery, Woodshop, Metal Shop, Photo lab, Digital Media lab, Printmaking lab, letterpress lab.

CAMPUS LIFE

Environment: Metropolis. **Activities:** Campus Ministries; Dance; International Student Organization; Literary magazine; Student government. 18 registered organizations, 1 religious organization on campus.

ADMISSIONS

Freshman Academic Profile: Average high school GPA 3.2. **Test Scores:** ACT middle 50% range 23–29. **Basis for Candidate Selection:** *Very important factors include:* rigor of secondary school record, academic GPA, talent/ability. *Other factors include:* application essay, recommendation(s), interview, extracurricular activities, character/personal qualities, first generation, alumni/ae relation, geographical residence, state residency, volunteer work, work experience, level of applicant's interest. **Freshman Admission Requirements:** High school diploma

is required and GED is accepted. *Academic units required:* 4 English, 3 math, 2 science, 1 science lab, 1 social studies, 2 history. *Academic units recommended:* 4 English, 4 math, 4 science, 4 science labs, 2 foreign language, 2 social studies, 3 history. **Freshman Admission Statistics:** 2,442 applied, 78% admitted, 14% enrolled. **Transfer Admission Requirements:** High school transcript, college transcript(s), essay or personal statement, statement of good standing from prior institution(s). Minimum college GPA of 2.5 required. Lowest grade transferable C. **General Admission Information:** Application fee $50. Non-fall registration accepted.

COSTS AND FINANCIAL AID

Annual tuition $45,200. Room and board $16,270. Required fees $3,180. Average book and supplies expense $840. **Required Forms and Deadlines:** FAFSA; State aid form. **Notification of Awards:** Applicants will be notified of awards on a rolling basis beginning 3/1. **Types of Aid:** *Need-based scholarships/ grants:* College/university scholarship or grant aid from institutional funds; Federal Pell; Private scholarships; SEOG; State scholarships/grants. *Loans:* Direct PLUS loans; Direct Subsidized Stafford Loans; Direct Unsubsidized Stafford Loans. **Student Employment:** Federal Work-Study Program available. Institutional employment available. **Financial Aid Statistics:** 35% needy freshmen, 44% needy undergrads receive need-based scholarship or grant aid. 100% freshmen, 99% undergrads receive non-need-based scholarship or grant aid. 70% freshmen, 74% undergrads receive need-based self-help aid. 0% freshmen, 0% undergrads receive athletic scholarships. 90% freshmen, 62% undergrads receive any aid. 54% undergrads borrow to pay for school. Average cumulative indebtedness $37,605. **Criteria awarding aid:** *Need-based:* Academics, Art, Leadership. *Non-need-based:* Academics, Art.

OTTERBEIN COLLEGE

Office of Admission, Westerville, OH 43081
Phone: 614-823-1500 **Financial Aid Phone:** 614-823-1502
E-mail: uotterb@otterbein.edu **CEEB Code:** 1597
Fax: 614-823-1200 **Website:** www.otterbein.edu **ACT Code:** 3318

This private school, affiliated with the Methodist Church, was founded in 1847. It has a 140 acre campus.

RATINGS

Admissions Selectivity Rating: 76   **Fire Safety Rating:** 60*   **Green Rating:** 60*

STUDENTS AND FACULTY

Enrollment: 2,746. **Student Body:** female, male, 10% out-of-state, 2% international (12 countries represented). Asian 1%, African American 6%, Caucasian 83%, Hispanic 1%, Native American <1%, Race unknown 5%.
Retention and Graduation: 92% freshmen return for sophomore year.
Faculty: Student/faculty ratio 12:1. 161 full-time faculty, 93% hold PhDs, 11% are members of minority groups, 55% are women. 0% of classes are taught by teaching assistants.

ACADEMICS

Degrees: Bachelor's; Master's. **Most popular majors:** Education, General; Business/Commerce, General; Nursing/Registered Nurse (Rn, Asn, Bsn, Msn). **Special Study Options:** Accelerated program; Cooperative education program; Cross-registration; Double major; Dual enrollment; Exchange student program (domestic); Honors program; Independent study; Internships; Liberal arts/career combination; Student-designed major; Study abroad; Teacher certification program; Weekend college. **Honors programs:** The Honors Program at Otterbein College is designed to provide intellectual stimulation and challenge for students with high academic ability and motivation. The four-year program provides the opportunity to participate in a community of students and faculty who have shared scholarly and creative interests. As part of that community students develop and complete their own Honors research and creative projects. Through the Honors seminars and Honors project, students develop advanced knowledge in their disciplinary fields and acquire the skills for independent work in their own areas of academic and professional interest. The Honors Program at Otterbein College is designed to provide intellectual stimulation and challenge for students with high academic ability and motivation. The four-year program provides the opportunity to participate in a community of students and faculty who have shared scholarly and creative interests. As part of that community, students develop and complete their own Honors research and creative projects. Through the Honors seminars and Honors project, students develop advanced knowledge in their disciplinary fields and acquire the skills for independent work in their own areas of academic and professional interest. **Disability Services offered:** Note-taking services; Reader services; Tape recorders; Tutors. **Career services:** Alumni network; Alumni services; Career assessment; Career/job search classes; Internships; Regional alumni.

FACILITIES

Housing: Apartments for single students; Coed dorms; Fraternity/sorority housing; Men's dorms; Women's dorms. **Special Academic Facilities/ Equipment:** Language lab, horse stable, observatory and planetarium, Celestron 8-inch and 14-inch telescopes, 3 art galleries. **Campus Network:** 50% of classrooms, 100% of dorms, 100% of student union, 100% of libraries, 100% of dining areas, 100% of common outdoor areas have wireless network access.

CAMPUS LIFE

Environment: Town. **Activities:** Choral groups; Concert band; Dance; Drama/ theater; International Student Organization; Jazz band; Literary magazine; Marching band; Music ensembles; Musical theater; Opera; Pep band; Radio station; Student government; Student newspaper; Symphony orchestra; Television station; Yearbook. 100 registered organizations, 7 fraternities, 6 sororities on campus. **Athletics (Intercollegiate):** *Men:* baseball, basketball, cheerleading, cross-country, equestrian sports, football, golf, soccer, tennis, track/field (outdoor), track/field (indoor). *Women:* basketball, cheerleading, cross-country, equestrian sports, golf, soccer, softball, tennis, track/field (outdoor), track/field (indoor), volleyball. **On-Campus Highlights:** Clements Recreation Center.

ADMISSIONS

Freshman Academic Profile: Average high school GPA 3.3. 24% in top 10% of high school class, 55% in top 25% of high school class, 85% in top 50% of high school class. **Test Scores:** SAT Math middle 50% range 480–590. SAT EBRW middle 50% range 470–600. ACT middle 50% range 20–25. **Basis for Candidate Selection:** *Important factors include:* rigor of secondary school record, class rank, standardized test scores. *Other factors include:* application essay, recommendation(s), interview, extracurricular activities, talent/ability, character/personal qualities, alumni/ae relation, racial/ethnic status, volunteer work, work experience. **Freshman Admission Requirements:** High school diploma is required and GED is accepted. *Academic units recommended:* 4 English, 3 math, 3 science, 2 foreign language, 3 social studies, 2 unit from above areas or other academic areas. **Freshman Admission Statistics:** 3,381 applied, 82% admitted, 24% enrolled. **Transfer Admission Requirements:** College transcript(s). Minimum college GPA of 2.5 required. Lowest grade transferable C-. **General Admission Information:** Application fee $25. Priority deadline 3/1. Non-fall registration accepted.

COSTS AND FINANCIAL AID

Annual tuition $26,319. Room and board $7,461. Average book and supplies expense $700. **Required Forms and Deadlines:** FAFSA. **Types of Aid:** *Need-based scholarships/grants:* College/university scholarship or grant aid from institutional funds; Federal Pell; Private scholarships; SEOG; State scholarships/ grants. *Loans:* Direct PLUS loans; Direct Subsidized Stafford Loans; Direct Unsubsidized Stafford Loans. **Student Employment:** Federal Work-Study Program available. Institutional employment available. **Criteria awarding aid:** *Non-need-based:* Academics, Alumni affiliation, Art, Leadership, Minority status, Music/drama, Religious affiliation.

OUACHITA BAPTIST UNIVERSITY

410 Ouachita St, Arkadelphia, AR 71998-0001
Phone: 870-245-5110 **Financial Aid Phone:** 870-245-5587
E-mail: admissions@alpha.obu.edu **CEEB Code:** 6549
Fax: 870-245-5500 **Website:** www.obu.edu **ACT Code:** 134

This private school, affiliated with the Arkansas Baptist State Convention Church, was founded in 1886. It has a 200 acre campus.

RATINGS

Admissions Selectivity Rating: 83   Fire Safety Rating: 94   Green Rating: 60*

STUDENTS AND FACULTY

Enrollment: 1,513. **Student Body:** 55% female, 45% male, 32% out-of-state, 2% international (36 countries represented). Asian <1%, African American 8%, Caucasian 82%, Hispanic 5%, Native American <1%, Pacific Islander <1%, Two or more races 2%, Race unknown 0%.

Retention and Graduation: 79% freshmen return for sophomore year. 59% freshmen graduate within 4 years. 70% freshmen graduate within 6 years. 44% grads go on to further study within 1 year. 22% grads pursue arts and sciences degrees. 2% grads pursue law degrees. 2% grads pursue business degrees. 13% grads pursue medical degrees. **Faculty:** Student/faculty ratio 12:1. 99 full-time faculty, 91% hold PhDs, 4% are members of minority groups, 36% are women. 0% of classes are taught by teaching assistants.

ACADEMICS

Degrees: Associate; Bachelor's. **Classes:** Most classes have 10–19 students. Most lab/discussion sessions have 10–19 students. **Most popular majors:** Biology/ Biological Sciences, General; Business Administration and Management, General; Mass Communication/Media Studies. **Special Study Options:** Cross-registration; Distance learning; Double major; English as a Second Language (ESL); Honors program; Independent study; Internships; Study abroad; Teacher certification program. **Honors programs:** The Carl Goodson Honors Program involves 7–8% of all students in ongoing writing and research activities. **Disability Services offered:** Note-taking services; Reader services; Tape recorders; Tutors. **Career services:** Alumni network; Alumni services; Career assessment; Career/job search classes; Internships.

FACILITIES

Housing: Apartments for married students; Apartments for single students; Men's dorms; Special housing for disabled students; Women's dorms 95% of campus accessible to physically disabled. **Special Academic Facilities/ Equipment:** Historical archives, Senator John McClellan collection, language lab, TV studio. **Campus Network:** 100% of classrooms, 100% of dorms, 100% of student union, 100% of libraries, 100% of dining areas, 100% of common outdoor areas have wireless network access.

CAMPUS LIFE

Environment: Village. **Activities:** Campus Ministries; Choral groups; Concert band; Dance; Drama/theater; International Student Organization; Jazz band; Literary magazine; Marching band; Model UN; Music ensembles; Musical theater; Opera; Pep band; Student government; Student newspaper; Television station; Yearbook. 60 registered organizations, 8 honor societies, 4 religious organizations, 5 fraternities, 5 sororities on campus. **Athletics (Intercollegiate):** *Men:* baseball, basketball, diving, football, golf, soccer, swimming, tennis, wrestling. *Women:* basketball, cross-country, diving, golf, soccer, softball, swimming, tennis, volleyball. **On-Campus Highlights:** Starbuck's. **Environmental Initiatives:** Employment of Energy Management Director.

ADMISSIONS

Freshman Academic Profile: Average high school GPA 3.6. 36% in top 10% of high school class, 64% in top 25% of high school class, 86% in top 50% of high school class. 86% from public high schools. **Test Scores:** SAT Math middle 50% range 480–620. SAT EBRW middle 50% range 540–640. ACT middle 50% range 21–28. **Basis for Candidate Selection:** *Very important factors include:* rigor of secondary school record, academic GPA, standardized test scores. *Other factors include:* talent/ability, character/personal qualities. **Freshman Admission Requirements:** High school diploma is required and GED is accepted. *Academic units required:* 4 English, 2 math, 2 science, 1 social studies, 2 history, 4 academic electives. *Academic units recommended:* 4 English, 3 math, 3 science, 2 foreign language, 1 social studies, 2 history, 4 academic electives. **Freshman Admission Statistics:** 1,786 applied, 71% admitted, 37% enrolled. **Transfer Admission Requirements:** College transcript(s), statement of good standing from prior institution(s). Minimum college GPA of 2.0 required. Lowest grade transferable C. **General Admission Information:** Priority deadline 12/1. Non-fall registration accepted. Admission may be deferred for a maximum of 1 year.

COSTS AND FINANCIAL AID

Annual tuition $26,200. Room and board $7,880. Required fees $590. Average book and supplies expense $1,100. **Required Forms and Deadlines:** FAFSA; State aid form. **Notification of Awards:** Applicants will be notified of awards on a rolling basis beginning 11/1. **Types of Aid:** *Need-based scholarships/grants:* College/university scholarship or grant aid from institutional funds; Federal Pell; Private scholarships; SEOG; State scholarships/grants. *Loans:* Direct PLUS loans; Direct Subsidized Stafford Loans; Direct Unsubsidized Stafford Loans. **Student Employment:** Federal Work-Study Program available. **Financial Aid Statistics:** 98% needy freshmen, 97% needy undergrads receive need-based scholarship or grant aid. 33% freshmen, 30% undergrads receive non-need-based scholarship or grant aid. 69% freshmen, 76% undergrads receive need-based self-help aid. 10% freshmen, 9% undergrads receive athletic scholarships. 98% freshmen, 96% undergrads receive any aid. 52% undergrads borrow to pay for school. Average cumulative indebtedness $28,406. **Criteria awarding aid:** *Non-need-based:* Academics, Alumni affiliation, Art, Athletics, Job skills, Leadership, Minority status, Music/drama, Religious affiliation, State/district residency.

OUR LADY OF THE LAKE UNIVERSITY (OLLU)

Admissions Office, San Antonio, TX 78207-4689
Phone: 210-431-3961 **Financial Aid Phone:** 800-324-4310
E-mail: webmaster@ollusa.edu **CEEB Code:** 6550
Fax: 210-431-4036 **Website:** www.ollusa.edu **ACT Code:** 4140

This private school, affiliated with the Roman Catholic Church, was founded in 1895. It has a 75 acre campus.

RATINGS
Admissions Selectivity Rating: 85   **Fire Safety Rating:** 64   **Green Rating:** 60*

STUDENTS AND FACULTY
Enrollment: 1,554. **Student Body:** 73% female, 27% male, 2% out-of-state, 1% international. Asian 1%, African American 8%, Caucasian 17%, Hispanic 63%, Native American 1%, Pacific Islander <1%, Two or more races 1%, Race unknown 8%.
Retention and Graduation: 60% freshmen return for sophomore year. 30% grads go on to further study within 1 year. **Faculty:** Student/faculty ratio 15:1. 101 full-time faculty, 80% hold PhDs, 35% are members of minority groups, 60% are women. 0% of classes are taught by teaching assistants.

ACADEMICS
Degrees: Bachelor's; Doctoral degree—professional practice; Doctoral degree research/scholarship; Master's; Post-bachelor's certificate; Post-master's certificate. **Classes:** Most classes have 10–19 students. **Most popular majors:** Biology/Biological Sciences, General; Business Administration and Management, General; Psychology, General. **Special Study Options:** Accelerated program; Cooperative education program; Cross-registration; Distance learning; Double major; Dual enrollment; Exchange student program (domestic); Honors program; Independent study; Internships; Study abroad; Teacher certification program; Weekend college. **Disability Services offered:** Note-taking services; Reader services; Tape recorders; Tutors. **Career services:** Alumni services; Career assessment; Internships.

FACILITIES
Housing: Coed dorms; Men's dorms; Theme housing; Women's dorms; 99% of campus accessible to physically disabled. **Special Academic Facilities/Equipment:** Lab school for children with language and learning disabilities, elementary demonstration school, intercultural institute for training and research, language lab. **Campus Network:** 50% of classrooms, 100% of dorms, 75% of student union, 75% of libraries, 100% of dining areas, 25% of common outdoor areas have wireless network access.

CAMPUS LIFE
Activities: Campus Ministries; Choral groups; Dance; Drama/theater; International Student Organization; Jazz band; Literary magazine; Music ensembles; Musical theater; Pep band; Student government; Student newspaper; Student-run film society; Symphony orchestra; Television station; Yearbook. **On-Campus Highlights:** Main Building.

ADMISSIONS
Freshman Academic Profile: Average high school GPA 3.3. 22% in top 10% of high school class, 49% in top 25% of high school class, 82% in top 50% of high school class. **Test Scores:** SAT Math middle 50% range 410–513. SAT EBRW middle 50% range 400–500. ACT middle 50% range 17–21. **Basis for Candidate Selection:** *Other factors include:* rigor of secondary school record, class rank, academic GPA, application essay, standardized test scores, recommendation(s), talent/ability, volunteer work, work experience. **Freshman Admission Requirements:** High school diploma is required and GED is accepted. *Academic units required:* 4 English, 3 math, 2 science, 3 social studies, 2 unit from above areas or other academic areas. **Freshman Admission Statistics:** 2,109 applied, 49% admitted, 29% enrolled. **Transfer Admission Requirements:** College transcript(s). Minimum college GPA of 2.0 required. Lowest grade transferable D. **General Admission Information:** Application fee $25. Non-fall registration accepted. Admission may be deferred for a maximum of 1 year.

COSTS AND FINANCIAL AID
Annual tuition $22,256. Room and board $7,327. Required fees $581. Average book and supplies expense $1,200. **Required Forms and Deadlines:** FAFSA; Institution's own financial aid form. **Notification of Awards:** Applicants will be notified of awards on a rolling basis beginning 3/31. **Types of Aid:** *Need-based scholarships/grants:* College/university scholarship or grant aid from institutional funds; Federal Pell; Private scholarships; SEOG; State scholarships/grants. *Loans:* Direct PLUS loans; Direct Subsidized Stafford Loans; Direct Unsubsidized Stafford Loans. **Student Employment:** Federal Work-Study Program available. Institutional employment available. **Financial Aid Statistics:** 99% needy freshmen, 96% needy undergrads receive need-based scholarship or grant aid. 3% freshmen, 6% undergrads receive non-need-based scholarship or grant aid. 71% freshmen, 83% undergrads receive need-based self-help aid. 5% freshmen, 7% undergrads receive athletic scholarships. 91% freshmen, 89% undergrads receive any aid. **Criteria awarding aid:** *Non-need-based:* Academics, Alumni affiliation, Art, Leadership, Music/drama.

PACE UNIVERSITY

1 Pace Plaza, New York, NY 10038
Phone: 212-346-1323 **Financial Aid Phone:** 212-346-1309
E-mail: undergradadmission@pace.edu **CEEB Code:** 2635, 2685
Fax: 212-346-1040 **Website:** www.pace.edu **ACT Code:** 2852, 2855

This private school was founded in 1906.

RATINGS
Admissions Selectivity Rating: 76   **Fire Safety Rating:** 91   **Green Rating:** 81

STUDENTS AND FACULTY
Enrollment: 8,238. **Student Body:** 62% female, 38% male, 46% out-of-state, 10% international (99 countries represented). Asian 8%, African American 10%, Caucasian 49%, Hispanic 14%, Native American <1%, Pacific Islander <1%, Two or more races 4%, Race unknown 5%.
Retention and Graduation: 78% freshmen return for sophomore year. 42% freshmen graduate within 4 years. 12% grads go on to further study within 1 year. 8% grads pursue arts and sciences degrees. 1% grads pursue law degrees. 1% grads pursue business degrees. **Faculty:** Student/faculty ratio 14:1. 519 full-time faculty, 85% hold PhDs, 23% are members of minority groups, 53% are women. 0% of classes are taught by teaching assistants.

ACADEMICS
Degrees: Associate; Bachelor's; Certificate; Doctoral degree—professional practice; Doctoral degree research/scholarship; Master's; Post-bachelor's certificate; Post-master's certificate. **Classes:** Most classes have 10–19 students. Most lab/discussion sessions have 10–19 students. **Most popular majors:** Registered Nursing/Registered Nurse; Accounting; Finance, General. **Special Study Options:** Accelerated program; Cooperative education program; Cross-registration; Distance learning; Double major; Dual enrollment; English as a Second Language (ESL); Honors program; Independent study; Internships; Study abroad; Teacher certification program. **Honors programs:** Pforzheimer Honors College for incoming freshmen. **Combined degree programs:** BA/JD; BA/MA. **Disability Services offered:** Note-taking services; Reader services; Tape recorders. **Career services:** Alumni network; Alumni services; Career assessment; Career/job search classes; Internships; Regional alumni.

FACILITIES
Housing: Apartments for single students; Coed dorms; Theme housing; Wellness housing; 80% of campus accessible to physically disabled. **Special Academic Facilities/Equipment:** Schimmel Center at Pace University, Laboratory Theatre, Communication Center, Language Center, Art Galleries, Environmental Center, English Language Institute.

CAMPUS LIFE
Environment: Metropolis. **Activities:** Choral groups; Dance; Drama/theater; International Student Organization; Literary magazine; Model UN; Musical theater; Radio station; Student government; Student newspaper; Student-run film society; Television station; Yearbook. 196 registered organizations, 34 honor societies, 3 religious organizations, 10 fraternities, 11 sororities on campus. **Athletics (Intercollegiate):** *Men:* baseball, basketball, cross-country, football, golf, lacrosse, swimming, tennis, track/field (outdoor), track/field (indoor). *Women:* basketball, cheerleading, cross-country, equestrian sports, soccer, softball, swimming, tennis, track/field (outdoor), track/field (indoor),

volleyball. **On-Campus Highlights:** Student Union. **Environmental Initiatives:** In September of 2017 Pace University partnered with Cenergistic, an energy consulting firm, to develop a behavior-based energy conservation program that required no initial capital investment. We are proud to announce that as of January of 2019 the program has realized over $1M in energy savings. The program targets the elimination of wasteful energy habits, especially focusing on periods when buildings are unoccupied.

ADMISSIONS

Freshman Academic Profile: 75% from public high schools. **Test Scores:** SAT Math middle 50% range 520–610. SAT EBRW middle 50% range 530–620. ACT middle 50% range 21–27. **Basis for Candidate Selection:** *Very important factors include:* rigor of secondary school record, application essay, standardized test scores. *Important factors include:* class rank, academic GPA, recommendation(s). *Other factors include:* interview, extracurricular activities, talent/ability, character/personal qualities, alumni/ae relation, volunteer work, work experience. **Freshman Admission Requirements:** High school diploma is required and GED is accepted. *Academic units required:* 4 English, 3 math, 2 science labs, 2 foreign language, 3 history, 2 academic electives. **Freshman Admission Statistics:** 22,411 applied, 79% admitted, 11% enrolled. **Transfer Admission Requirements:** College transcript(s), statement of good standing from prior institution(s). Minimum college GPA of 2.5 required. Lowest grade transferable C. **General Admission Information:** Application fee $50. Priority deadline 2/15. Non-fall registration accepted. Admission may be deferred for a maximum of 12 months.

COSTS AND FINANCIAL AID

Annual tuition $44,714. Room and board $20,018. Required fees $1,732. Average book and supplies expense $800. **Required Forms and Deadlines:** FAFSA. **Notification of Awards:** Applicants will be notified of awards on a rolling basis beginning 12/1. **Types of Aid:** *Need-based scholarships/grants:* College/university scholarship or grant aid from institutional funds; Federal Nursing Scholarships; Federal Pell; Private scholarships; SEOG; State scholarships/grants. *Loans:* Direct PLUS loans; Direct Subsidized Stafford Loans; Direct Unsubsidized Stafford Loans. **Student Employment:** Federal Work-Study Program available. Institutional employment available. **Financial Aid Statistics:** 100% needy freshmen, 99% needy undergrads receive need-based scholarship or grant aid. 15% freshmen, 13% undergrads receive non-need-based scholarship or grant aid. 75% freshmen, 76% undergrads receive need-based self-help aid. 1% freshmen, 1% undergrads receive athletic scholarships. 98% freshmen, 94% undergrads receive any aid. 64% undergrads borrow to pay for school. Average cumulative indebtedness $36,797. **Criteria awarding aid:** *Need-based:* Academics. *Non-need-based:* Academics, Alumni affiliation, Athletics, Music/drama.

PACIFIC LUTHERAN UNIVERSITY

Office of Admission, Tacoma, WA 98447
Phone: 253-535-7151 **Financial Aid Phone:** 253-535-8406
E-mail: admissions@plu.edu **CEEB Code:** 4597
Fax: 253-536-5136 **Website:** www.plu.edu **ACT Code:** 4597

This private school, affiliated with the Lutheran Church, was founded in 1890. It has a 156 acre campus.

RATINGS

Admissions Selectivity Rating: 80   **Fire Safety Rating:** 93   **Green Rating:** 60*

STUDENTS AND FACULTY

Enrollment: 2,676. **Student Body:** 63% female, 37% male, 22% out-of-state, 3% international (21 countries represented). Asian 10%, African American 3%, Caucasian 63%, Hispanic 9%, Native American 1%, Pacific Islander 1%, Two or more races 9%, Race unknown 1%.
Retention and Graduation: 83% freshmen return for sophomore year. 55% freshmen graduate within 4 years. 68% freshmen graduate within 6 years. 20% grads go on to further study within 1 year. **Faculty:** Student/faculty ratio 15:1. 184 full-time faculty, 95% hold PhDs, 14% are members of minority groups, 54% are women. 0% of classes are taught by teaching assistants.

ACADEMICS

Degrees: Bachelor's; Doctoral degree—professional practice; Master's; Post-bachelor's certificate; Post-master's certificate. **Classes:** Most classes have 10–19 students. Most lab/discussion sessions have 10–19 students. **Most popular majors:** Registered Nursing/Registered Nurse; Business Administration and Management, General; Social Sciences, General. **Special Study Options:** Cooperative education program; Cross-registration; Distance learning; Double major; Dual enrollment; English as a Second Language (ESL); Exchange student program (domestic); Honors program; Independent study; Internships; Liberal arts/career combination; Student-designed major; Study abroad; Teacher certification program. **Honors programs:** International Honors Program. **Combined degree programs:** BA/MEng. **Disability Services offered:** Note-taking services; Reader services; Tape recorders; Tutors. **Career services:** Alumni network; Alumni services; Career assessment; Career/job search classes; Internships; Regional alumni.

FACILITIES

Housing: Apartments for married students; Apartments for single students; Coed dorms; Special housing for disabled students; Special housing for international students; Theme housing; Women's dorms; 90% of campus accessible to physically disabled. **Special Academic Facilities/Equipment:** Mary Baker Russell Music Center; Wekell Art Gallery; Keck Observatory; Carol Sheffels Quigg Greenhouse; Rieke Science Center; Scandinavian Cultural Center; Morken Center for Learning and Technology; Karen Hille Phillips Center for the Performing Arts. **Campus Network:** 100% of classrooms, 100% of dorms, 100% of student union, 100% of libraries, 100% of dining areas, 10% of common outdoor areas have wireless network access.

CAMPUS LIFE

Environment: City. **Activities:** Campus Ministries; Choral groups; Concert band; Dance; Drama/theater; International Student Organization; Jazz band; Literary magazine; Model UN; Music ensembles; Musical theater; Opera; Pep band; Radio station; Student government; Student newspaper; Student-run film society; Symphony orchestra; Television station. 64 registered organizations, 17 honor societies, 9 religious organizations on campus. **Athletics (Intercollegiate):** *Men:* baseball, basketball, cheerleading, crew/rowing, cross-country, football, golf, soccer, swimming, tennis, track/field (outdoor), track/field (indoor). *Women:* basketball, cheerleading, crew/rowing, cross-country, golf, soccer, softball, swimming, tennis, track/field (outdoor), track/field (indoor), volleyball. **On-Campus Highlights:** Keck Observatory. **Environmental Initiatives:** Successfully building a community commitment to sustainability that encompasses students, faculty, and staff in part through sustainability fellowships.

ADMISSIONS

Freshman Academic Profile: Average high school GPA 3.7. **Test Scores:** SAT Math middle 50% range 520–630. SAT EBRW middle 50% range 520–640. ACT middle 50% range 21–27. **Basis for Candidate Selection:** *Very important factors include:* rigor of secondary school record, application essay. *Important factors include:* class rank, academic GPA, standardized test scores, recommendation(s), extracurricular activities, talent/ability, character/personal qualities. *Other factors include:* interview, first generation, alumni/ae relation, geographical residence, state residency, religious affiliation/commitment, racial/ethnic status, work experience. **Freshman Admission Requirements:** High school diploma is required and GED is accepted. *Academic units required:* 2 math, 2 foreign language. *Academic units recommended:* 4 English, 3 math, 2 science, 2 science labs, 2 foreign language, 2 social studies, 3 academic electives, 1 visual/performing arts. **Freshman Admission Statistics:** 3,629 applied, 75% admitted, 23% enrolled. **Transfer Admission Requirements:** High school transcript, college transcript(s), essay or personal statement, statement of good standing from prior institution(s). Minimum college GPA of 2.5 required. Lowest grade transferable C-. **General Admission Information:** Application fee $40. Priority deadline 2/1. Non-fall registration accepted. Admission may be deferred for a maximum of 2 years.

COSTS AND FINANCIAL AID

Annual tuition $41,696. Room and board $10,790. Required fees $370. Average book and supplies expense $870. **Required Forms and Deadlines:** FAFSA. **Notification of Awards:** Applicants will be notified of awards on a rolling basis beginning 12/16. **Types of Aid:** *Need-based scholarships/grants:* College/university scholarship or grant aid from institutional funds; Federal Nursing Scholarships; Federal Pell; Private scholarships; SEOG; State scholarships/grants. *Loans:* Direct PLUS loans; Direct Subsidized Stafford Loans; Direct Unsubsidized Stafford Loans. **Student Employment:** Federal Work-Study Program available. Institutional employment available. **Financial Aid Statistics:** 72% needy freshmen, 73% needy undergrads receive need-based scholarship or grant aid. 95% freshmen, 94% undergrads receive non-need-based scholarship or grant aid. 72% freshmen, 74% undergrads receive need-based self-help aid. 0% freshmen, 0% undergrads receive athletic scholarships. 99% freshmen, 97% undergrads receive any aid. 70% undergrads borrow to pay for school. Average cumulative indebtedness $26,379. **Criteria awarding aid:** *Need-based:* Academics. *Non-need-based:* Academics, Alumni affiliation, Art, Leadership, Music/drama, Religious affiliation, State/district residency.

PACIFIC STATES UNIVERSITY

3450 Wilshire blvd, 5th floor, Los Angeles, CA 90010
Phone: 323-731-2383 EXT:203
E-mail: admissions@psuca.edu
Fax: 323-731-7276 **Website:** www.psuca.edu

This private school was founded in 1928.

RATINGS
Admissions Selectivity Rating: 76   Fire Safety Rating: 60*   Green Rating: 60*

STUDENTS AND FACULTY
Enrollment: 14. **Student Body:** 29% female, 71% male, 5% out-of-state, 57% international. Asian 14%, African American 7%, Caucasian 7%, Hispanic 0%, Native American 0%, Pacific Islander 0%, Two or more races 0%, Race unknown 14%.
Retention and Graduation: 100% freshmen return for sophomore year.
Faculty: Student/faculty ratio 6:1. 7 full-time faculty, 43% hold PhDs, 0% are members of minority groups, 29% are women.

ACADEMICS
Degrees: Bachelor's; Doctoral degree research/scholarship; Master's; Post-bachelor's certificate. **Special Study Options:** Distance learning; Double major; English as a Second Language (ESL); Independent study.

FACILITIES
Housing: Coed dorms **Campus Network:** 75% of classrooms, 25% of dorms, 100% of student union, 100% of libraries, 100% of dining areas, 40% of common outdoor areas have wireless network access.

CAMPUS LIFE
Environment: Metropolis. **Activities:** International Student Organization; Television station; Yearbook.

ADMISSIONS
Basis for Candidate Selection: *Important factors include:* standardized test scores. *Other factors include:* rigor of secondary school record, academic GPA, application essay, level of applicant's interest. **Freshman Admission Requirements:** High school diploma is required and GED is accepted. **Freshman Admission Statistics:** 2 applied, 50% admitted, 100% enrolled. **Transfer Admission Requirements:** College transcript(s). Minimum college GPA of 2.5 required. Lowest grade transferable C. **General Admission Information:** Application fee $100. Non-fall registration accepted.

COSTS AND FINANCIAL AID
Annual tuition $14,055. Room and board $7,200. Required fees $540. Average book and supplies expense $1,800. **Required Forms and Deadlines:** FAFSA. **Types of Aid:** *Need-based scholarships/grants:* Federal Pell. *Loans:* Direct Subsidized Stafford Loans; Direct Unsubsidized Stafford Loans.

PACIFIC UNION COLLEGE

Enrollment Services, Angwin, CA 94508
Phone: 707-965-6336 **Financial Aid Phone:** 707-965-7200
E-mail: enroll@puc.edu **CEEB Code:** 4600
Fax: 707-965-6671 **Website:** www.puc.edu **ACT Code:** 362

This private school, affiliated with the Seventh Day Adventist Church, was founded in 1882. It has a 200 acre campus.

RATINGS
Admissions Selectivity Rating: 87   Fire Safety Rating: 89   Green Rating: 60*

STUDENTS AND FACULTY
Enrollment: 1,508. **Student Body:** 58% female, 42% male, 14% out-of-state, 3% international (21 countries represented). Asian 19%, African American 9%, Caucasian 26%, Hispanic 28%, Native American <1%, Pacific Islander 2%, Two or more races 7%, Race unknown 5%.
Retention and Graduation: 77% freshmen return for sophomore year.
Faculty: Student/faculty ratio 14:1. 94 full-time faculty, 52% hold PhDs, 26% are members of minority groups, 50% are women. 0% of classes are taught by teaching assistants.

ACADEMICS
Degrees: Associate; Bachelor's; Certificate; Master's; Terminal Associate; Transfer Associate. **Classes:** Most classes have 10–19 students. Most lab/discussion sessions have 20–29 students. **Most popular majors:** Business/Commerce, General; Registered Nursing/Registered Nurse; Biology/Biological Sciences, General. **Special Study Options:** Cooperative education program; Double major; Honors program; Independent study; Internships; Liberal arts/career combination; Study abroad; Teacher certification program. **Honors programs:** The Honors Program offers an alternative general-education program for academically motivated students. There are no other general education requirements. Students fulfilling the Honors Program graduate "With Honors." **Disability Services offered:** Note-taking services; Reader services; Tape recorders; Tutors. **Career services:** Alumni network; Career assessment; Career/job search classes; Internships.

FACILITIES
Housing: Apartments for married students; Men's dorms; Wellness housing; Women's dorms; 80% of campus accessible to physically disabled. **Special Academic Facilities/Equipment:** Flight training facility, observatory, art gallery, natural history collection, Pitcairn Island studies center, on-campus elementary and high schools, airport. **Campus Network:** 72% of classrooms, 100% of dorms, 100% of student union, 100% of libraries, 100% of dining areas, 0% of common outdoor areas have wireless network access.

CAMPUS LIFE
Environment: Rural. **Activities:** Campus Ministries; Choral groups; Concert band; Drama/theater; Jazz band; Literary magazine; Music ensembles; Student government; Student newspaper; Student-run film society; Symphony orchestra; Yearbook. 24 registered organizations, 8 honor societies, 10 religious organizations on campus. **Athletics (Intercollegiate):** *Men:* basketball, cross-country, volleyball. *Women:* basketball, cross-country, volleyball. **On-Campus Highlights:** Campus Center. **Environmental Initiatives:** Buy Locally (50%).

ADMISSIONS
Freshman Academic Profile: Average high school GPA 3.3. 31% from public high schools. **Test Scores:** SAT Math middle 50% range 430–570. SAT EBRW middle 50% range 420–560. ACT Middle 50% range 18–23. **Basis for Candidate Selection:** *Very important factors include:* academic GPA, recommendation(s). *Important factors include:* rigor of secondary school record, standardized test scores, character/personal qualities, level of applicant's interest. *Other factors include:* class rank, interview, extracurricular activities, talent/ability, religious affiliation/commitment. **Freshman Admission Requirements:** High school diploma is required and GED is accepted. *Academic units required:* 4 English, 2 math, 2 science, 2 history. *Academic units recommended:* 4 English, 3 math, 3 science, 2 foreign language, 2 history, 1 computer science. **Freshman Admission Statistics:** 2,041 applied, 45% admitted, 27% enrolled. **Transfer Admission Requirements:** High school transcript, college transcript(s). Minimum college GPA of 2.0 required. Lowest grade transferable C-. **General Admission Information:** Application fee $30. Non-fall registration accepted. Admission may be deferred for a maximum of 1 year.

COSTS AND FINANCIAL AID
Annual tuition $27,999. Room and board $7,695. Required fees $315. Average book and supplies expense $1,764. **Required Forms and Deadlines:** FAFSA; Institution's own financial aid form. **Notification of Awards:** Applicants will be notified of awards on a rolling basis beginning 4/1. **Types of Aid:** *Need-based scholarships/grants:* College/university scholarship or grant aid from institutional funds; Federal Pell; Private scholarships; SEOG; State scholarships/grants. *Loans:* Direct PLUS loans; Direct Subsidized Stafford Loans; Direct Unsubsidized Stafford Loans. **Student Employment:** Federal Work-Study Program available. Institutional employment available. **Financial Aid Statistics:** 100% needy freshmen, 100% needy undergrads receive need-based scholarship or grant aid. 39% freshmen, 31% undergrads receive non-need-based scholarship or grant aid. 95% freshmen, 97% undergrads receive need-based self-help aid. 2% freshmen, 0% undergrads receive athletic scholarships. 74% freshmen, 75% undergrads receive any aid. **Criteria awarding aid:** *Need-based:* Academics. *Non-need-based:* Academics, Art, Athletics, Leadership, Music/drama, Religious affiliation.

PACIFIC UNIVERSITY

2043 College Way, Forest Grove, OR 97116
Phone: 503-352-2218 **Financial Aid Phone:** (503) 352-2222
E-mail: admissions@pacificu.edu **CEEB Code:** 4601
Fax: 503-352-2975 **Website:** www.pacificu.edu

This private school was founded in 1849. It has a 60 acre campus.

RATINGS
Admissions Selectivity Rating: 76   **Fire Safety Rating:** 82   **Green Rating:** 90

STUDENTS AND FACULTY
Enrollment: 1,884. **Student Body:** 60% female, 40% male, 55% out-of-state, 2% international (32 countries represented). Asian 12%, African American 2%, Caucasian 52%, Hispanic 13%, Native American 1%, Pacific Islander 3%, Two or more races 12%, Race unknown 4%.
Retention and Graduation: 77% freshmen return for sophomore year. 24% grads go on to further study within 1 year. 11% grads pursue arts and sciences degrees. 4% grads pursue law degrees. 2% grads pursue business degrees. 2% grads pursue medical degrees. **Faculty:** Student/faculty ratio 10:1. 216 full-time faculty, 87% hold PhDs, 13% are members of minority groups, 51% are women. 0% of classes are taught by teaching assistants.

ACADEMICS
Degrees: Bachelor's; Doctoral degree—professional practice; Doctoral degree research/scholarship; Master's; Post-bachelor's certificate; Post-master's certificate. **Classes:** Most classes have 10–19 students. Most lab/discussion sessions have 20–29 students. **Most popular majors:** Biology/Biological Sciences, General; Business Administration and Management, General; Exercise Science and Kinesiology. **Special Study Options:** Accelerated program; Cross-registration; Distance learning; Double major; Dual enrollment; English as a Second Language (ESL); Independent study; Internships; Study abroad; Teacher certification program. **Disability Services offered:** Note-taking services; Reader services; Tape recorders; Tutors. **Career services:** Alumni network; Alumni services; Career assessment; Career/job search classes; Internships; Regional alumni.

FACILITIES
Housing: Apartments for single students; Coed dorms; Special housing for disabled students. **Special Academic Facilities/Equipment:** State history museum, performing arts center, media center, humanitarian center, Holocaust resource center, politics/law forum, Berglund Center for Internet Studies, electron microscopes.

CAMPUS LIFE
Environment: Village. **Activities:** Campus Ministries; Choral groups; Concert band; Dance; Drama/theater; International Student Organization; Jazz band; Literary magazine; Music ensembles; Pep band; Radio station; Student government; Student newspaper; Student-run film society; Symphony orchestra. 58 registered organizations, 2 honor societies, 4 religious organizations, 3 fraternities, 4 sororities on campus. **Athletics (Intercollegiate):** *Men:* baseball, basketball, cross-country, golf, soccer, swimming, tennis, track/field (outdoor), wrestling. *Women:* basketball, cross-country, golf, lacrosse, soccer, softball, swimming, tennis, track/field (outdoor), volleyball, wrestling. **On-Campus Highlights:** Pacific Athletic Center. **Environmental Initiatives:** Sustainability Committee.

ADMISSIONS
Freshman Academic Profile: Average high school GPA 3.6. 88% from public high schools. **Test Scores:** SAT Math middle 50% range 500–600. SAT EBRW middle 50% range 490–590. ACT middle 50% range 21–26. **Basis for Candidate Selection:** *Very important factors include:* rigor of secondary school record, academic GPA, standardized test scores, recommendation(s), extracurricular activities, character/personal qualities, volunteer work, level of applicant's interest. *Important factors include:* class rank, application essay, talent/ability. *Other factors include:* first generation, alumni/ae relation, work experience. **Freshman Admission Requirements:** High school diploma is required and GED is accepted. *Academic units recommended:* 4 English, 3 math, 3 science, 1 science lab, 2 foreign language, 3 social studies, 1 history, 4 academic electives. **Freshman Admission Statistics:** 3,004 applied, 79% admitted, 20% enrolled. **Transfer Admission Requirements:** College transcript(s), essay or personal statement, statement of good standing from prior institution(s). Minimum college GPA of 2.70 required. Lowest grade transferable C-. **General Admission Information:** Application fee $40.

Priority deadline 2/15. Regular application deadline 8/15. Non-fall registration accepted. Admission may be deferred for a maximum of 2 years.

COSTS AND FINANCIAL AID
Annual tuition $40,120. Room and board $11,822. Required fees $934. Average book and supplies expense $1,050. **Required Forms and Deadlines:** FAFSA. **Notification of Awards:** Applicants will be notified of awards on a rolling basis beginning 3/15. **Types of Aid:** *Need-based scholarships/grants:* College/university scholarship or grant aid from institutional funds; Federal Pell; Private scholarships; SEOG; State scholarships/grants. *Loans:* Direct PLUS loans; Direct Subsidized Stafford Loans; Direct Unsubsidized Stafford Loans. **Student Employment:** Federal Work-Study Program available. Institutional employment available. **Financial Aid Statistics:** 69% needy freshmen, 72% needy undergrads receive need-based scholarship or grant aid. 97% freshmen, 92% undergrads receive non-need-based scholarship or grant aid. 84% freshmen, 84% undergrads receive need-based self-help aid. 0% freshmen, 0% undergrads receive athletic scholarships. 93% freshmen, 93% undergrads receive any aid. 79% undergrads borrow to pay for school. Average cumulative indebtedness $30,081. **Criteria awarding aid:** *Need-based:* Academics, Leadership. *Non-need-based:* Academics, Alumni affiliation, Art, Music/drama.

PALM BEACH ATLANTIC UNIVERSITY

PO Box 24708, West Palm Beach, FL 33416-4708
Phone: 561-803-2100 **Financial Aid Phone:** 561-803-2126
E-mail: admit@pba.edu **CEEB Code:** 5553
Fax: 561-803-2115 **Website:** www.pba.edu **ACT Code:** 739

This private school, affiliated with the Christian (Nondenominational) Church, was founded in 1968. It has a 25 acre campus.

RATINGS
Admissions Selectivity Rating: 74   **Fire Safety Rating:** 60*   **Green Rating:** 60*

STUDENTS AND FACULTY
Enrollment: 2,376. **Student Body:** 65% female, 35% male, 35% out-of-state, 4% international (28 countries represented). Asian 2%, African American 10%, Caucasian 61%, Hispanic 15%, Native American <1%, Pacific Islander <1%, Two or more races 4%, Race unknown 5%.
Retention and Graduation: 76% freshmen return for sophomore year. 47% freshmen graduate within 4 years. 59% freshmen graduate within 6 years. **Faculty:** Student/faculty ratio 12:1. 178 full-time faculty, 86% hold PhDs, 15% are members of minority groups, 47% are women. 0% of classes are taught by teaching assistants.

ACADEMICS
Degrees: Bachelor's; Doctoral degree—professional practice; Master's. **Classes:** Most classes have 10–19 students. Most lab/discussion sessions have fewer than 10 students. **Most popular majors:** Education, General; Accounting and Business/Management; Psychology, General. **Special Study Options:** Accelerated program; Distance learning; Double major; Honors program; Independent study; Internships; Student-designed major; Study abroad; Teacher certification program. **Honors programs:** The Frederick M. Supper Honors Program exists to establish a community of scholars. The program encourages students to develop a thoughtful and insightful Christian worldview through enduring conversation to enable students to live the examined life and to facilitate character formation. **Career services:** Alumni network; Alumni services; Career assessment; Career/job search classes; Internships.

FACILITIES
Housing: Apartments for single students; Coed dorms; Men's dorms; Theme housing; Women's dorms. **Special Academic Facilities/Equipment:** DeSantis Family Chapel; Greene Sports Complex (Café); Helen K.Persson Recital Hall. **Campus Network:** 95% of classrooms, 100% of dorms, 100% of student union, 100% of libraries, 100% of dining areas, 85% of common outdoor areas have wireless network access.

CAMPUS LIFE
Environment: Metropolis. **Activities:** Campus Ministries; Choral groups; Concert band; Dance; Drama/theater; International Student Organization; Jazz band; Literary magazine; Music ensembles; Musical theater; Pep band; Student government; Student newspaper; Symphony orchestra. 67 registered organizations, 15 honor societies, 18 religious organizations on campus. **Athletics (Intercollegiate):** *Men:* baseball, basketball, cross-country, soccer, tennis. *Women:* basketball, cross-country, soccer, softball, tennis, volleyball. **On-Campus Highlights:** DeSantis Family Chapel.

ADMISSIONS

Test Scores: SAT Math middle 50% range 470–590. SAT EBRW middle 50% range 510–610. ACT middle 50% range 20–26. **Basis for Candidate Selection:** *Very important factors include:* academic GPA, application essay, standardized test scores, character/personal qualities, religious affiliation/commitment. *Important factors include:* rigor of secondary school record, recommendation(s), interview, extracurricular activities, talent/ability. *Other factors include:* class rank, alumni/ae relation, volunteer work, level of applicant's interest. **Freshman Admission Requirements:** High school diploma is required and GED is accepted. *Academic units required:* 4 English, 3 math, 3 science, 3 science labs, 5 academic electives. *Academic units recommended:* 4 English, 3 math, 3 science, 1 science lab, 2 foreign language. **Freshman Admission Statistics:** 1,534 applied, 95% admitted, 36% enrolled. **Transfer Admission Requirements:** college transcript(s), essay or personal statement. Minimum college GPA of 2.5 required. Lowest grade transferable C. **General Admission Information:** Application fee $50. Non-fall registration accepted. Admission may be deferred for a maximum of one year.

COSTS AND FINANCIAL AID

Annual tuition $32,880. Room and board $10,722. Required fees $595. Average book and supplies expense $1,104. **Required Forms and Deadlines:** FAFSA; State aid form. **Notification of Awards:** Applicants will be notified of awards on a rolling basis beginning 10/15. **Types of Aid:** *Need-based scholarships/grants:* College/university scholarship or grant aid from institutional funds; Federal Pell; Private scholarships; SEOG; State scholarships/grants; United Negro College Fund. *Loans:* Direct PLUS loans; Direct Subsidized Stafford Loans; Direct Unsubsidized Stafford Loans. **Student Employment:** Federal Work-Study Program available. Institutional employment available. **Financial Aid Statistics:** 100% needy freshmen, 99% needy undergrads receive need-based scholarship or grant aid. 13% freshmen, 12% undergrads receive non-need-based scholarship or grant aid. 62% freshmen, 67% undergrads receive need-based self-help aid. 6% freshmen, 5% undergrads receive athletic scholarships. 100% freshmen, 100% undergrads receive any aid. 60% undergrads borrow to pay for school. Average cumulative indebtedness $27,530. **Criteria awarding aid:** *Need-based:* Academics, Alumni affiliation *Non-need-based:* Academics, Alumni affiliation, Art, Athletics, Leadership, Music/drama, State/district residency.

PARK UNIVERSITY

8700 NW River Park Drive, Parkville, MO 64152
Phone: 816-584-6213 **Financial Aid Phone:** 816-548-6290
E-mail: admissions@mail.park.edu **CEEB Code:** 6574
Fax: 816-741-4462 **ACT Code:** 2340

This private school was founded in 1875. It has a 700 acre campus.

RATINGS

Admissions Selectivity Rating: 77   **Fire Safety Rating:** 75   **Green Rating:** 60*

STUDENTS AND FACULTY

Enrollment: 1,672. **Student Body:** 56% female, 44% male, 20% out-of-state, 19% international (93 countries represented). Asian <1%, African American 10%, Caucasian 61%, Hispanic 5%, Native American 1%, Pacific Islander <1%, Two or more races 3%, Race unknown 0%.
Retention and Graduation: 61% freshmen return for sophomore year. 7% grads go on to further study within 1 year. 6% grads pursue arts and sciences degrees. 1% grads pursue business degrees. **Faculty:** Student/faculty ratio 12:1. 82 full-time faculty, 66% hold PhDs, 4% are members of minority groups, 38% are women. 0% of classes are taught by teaching assistants.

ACADEMICS

Degrees: Associate; Bachelor's; Certificate; Master's; Post-bachelor's certificate. **Classes:** Most classes have 10–19 students. **Most popular majors:** Education, General; Computer and Information Sciences, General; Business Administration and Management, General. **Special Study Options:** Accelerated program; Cross-registration; Distance learning; Double major; Dual enrollment; English as a Second Language (ESL); Honors program; Independent study; Internships; Student-designed major; Study abroad; Teacher certification program; Weekend college. **Disability Services offered:** Note-taking services; Reader services; Tape recorders; Tutors.

FACILITIES

Housing: Apartments for married students; Coed dorms 90% of campus accessible to physically disabled.

CAMPUS LIFE

Environment: Town. **Activities:** Choral groups; Drama/theater; Literary magazine; Radio station; Student government; Student newspaper; Symphony orchestra; Yearbook. 15 registered organizations, 4 honor societies, 13 religious organizations on campus. **Athletics (Intercollegiate):** *Men:* baseball, basketball, cross-country, soccer, track/field (outdoor), track/field (indoor), volleyball. *Women:* basketball, cross-country, golf, soccer, softball, track/field (outdoor), track/field (indoor), volleyball. **On-Campus Highlights:** Gym.

ADMISSIONS

Freshman Academic Profile: Average high school GPA 3.3. 14% in top 10% of high school class, 37% in top 25% of high school class, 68% in top 50% of high school class. 80% from public high schools. **Test Scores:** ACT middle 50% range 17–23. **Basis for Candidate Selection:** *Very important factors include:* rigor of secondary school record, class rank, standardized test scores. *Other factors include:* application essay, recommendation(s). **Freshman Admission Requirements:** High school diploma is required and GED is accepted. *Academic units recommended:* 3 English, 2 math, 2 science, 1 science lab, 2 foreign language, 3 social studies, 1 history, 6 academic electives. **Freshman Admission Statistics:** 778 applied, 69% admitted, 39% enrolled. **Transfer Admission Requirements:** High school transcript, college transcript(s). Minimum college GPA of 2.0 required. Lowest grade transferable C. **General Admission Information:** Application fee $25. Priority deadline 4/15. Regular application deadline 7/1. Non-fall registration accepted. Admission may be deferred for a maximum of Maximum of 1 year.

COSTS AND FINANCIAL AID

Annual tuition $10,380. Required fees $100. Average book and supplies expense $1,800. **Required Forms and Deadlines:** FAFSA; Institution's own financial aid form. **Notification of Awards:** Applicants will be notified of awards on a rolling basis beginning 2/15. **Types of Aid:** *Need-based scholarships/grants:* Federal Pell; Private scholarships; SEOG; State scholarships/grants. *Loans:* Direct PLUS loans; Direct Subsidized Stafford Loans; Direct Unsubsidized Stafford Loans. **Student Employment:** Federal Work-Study Program available. Institutional employment available. **Financial Aid Statistics:** 78% needy freshmen, 73% needy undergrads receive need-based scholarship or grant aid. 75% freshmen, 52% undergrads receive non-need-based scholarship or grant aid. 56% freshmen, 70% undergrads receive need-based self-help aid. 17% freshmen, 11% undergrads receive athletic scholarships. 78% freshmen receive any aid. **Criteria awarding aid:** *Non-need-based:* Academics, Alumni affiliation, Art, Athletics, Job skills, State/district residency.

PARSONS SCHOOL OF DESIGN AT THE NEW SCHOOL

79 Fifth Avenue, New York, NY 10003
Phone: 212-229-5150 **Financial Aid Phone:** 212.229.8930
E-mail: thinkparsons@newschool.edu **CEEB Code:** 2638
Website: www.newschool.edu/parsons **ACT Code:** 2854

This private school was founded in 1896..

RATINGS

Admissions Selectivity Rating: 91   **Fire Safety Rating:** 89   **Green Rating:** 90

STUDENTS AND FACULTY

Enrollment: 4,381. **Student Body:** 79% female, 21% male, 78% out-of-state, 44% international (84 countries represented). Asian 14%, African American 3%, Caucasian 24%, Hispanic 10%, Native American <1%, Pacific Islander <1%, Two or more races 3%, Race unknown 3%.
Retention and Graduation: 90% freshmen return for sophomore year. 63% freshmen graduate within 4 years. 78% freshmen graduate within 6 years. **Faculty:** Student/faculty ratio 10:1. 170 full-time faculty, 65% hold PhDs, 25% are members of minority groups, 49% are women. 0% of classes are taught by teaching assistants.

ACADEMICS

Degrees: Associate; Bachelor's; Certificate; Master's. **Classes:** Most classes have 10–19 students. Most lab/discussion sessions have 20–29 students. **Most popular majors:** Fashion/Apparel Design; Graphic Design; Computer Software and Media Applications. **Special Study Options:** Accelerated program; Cross-registration; Distance learning; Double major; English as a Second Language (ESL); Exchange student program (domestic); Independent study; Internships; Liberal arts/career combination; Study abroad; Weekend college. **Disability Services offered:** Note-taking services; Reader services; Tape recorders. **Career services:** Alumni services; Career assessment; Career/job search classes; Internships.

FACILITIES

Housing: Coed dorms; Special housing for disabled students; 99% of campus accessible to physically disabled. **Special Academic Facilities/Equipment:** Art gallery, photography gallery, extensive collections of contemporary art, concert hall, public lectures, conferences, cultural and intellectual events.

CAMPUS LIFE

Environment: Metropolis. **Activities:** Campus Ministries; Dance; Drama/ theater; International Student Organization; Literary magazine; Music ensembles; Radio station; Student government; Student newspaper; Student-run film society; Symphony orchestra. 42 registered organizations, 4 religious organizations on campus. **On-Campus Highlights:** Sheila Johnson Design Center.

ADMISSIONS

Freshman Academic Profile: Average high school GPA 3.5. 22% in top 10% of high school class, 47% in top 25% of high school class, 77% in top 50% of high school class. 37% from public high schools. **Test Scores:** SAT Math middle 50% range 590–720. SAT EBRW middle 50% range 590–670. ACT middle 50% range 25–30. **Basis for Candidate Selection:** *Very important factors include:* academic GPA, application essay, extracurricular activities. *Important factors include:* rigor of secondary school record, recommendation(s), character/personal qualities. *Other factors include:* class rank, standardized test scores, interview, talent/ability, volunteer work, work experience, level of applicant's interest. **Freshman Admission Requirements:** High school diploma is required and GED is accepted. *Academic units required:* 4 English. *Academic units recommended:* 4 math, 4 science, 4 foreign language, 4 social studies, 4 history. **Freshman Admission Statistics:** 4,959 applied, 46% admitted, 39% enrolled. **Transfer Admission Requirements:** College transcript(s). Minimum college GPA of 2.0 required. Lowest grade transferable C. **General Admission Information:** Application fee $50. Priority deadline 1/15. Regular application deadline 8/1. Non-fall registration accepted. Admission may be deferred for a maximum of 1 year.

COSTS AND FINANCIAL AID

Annual tuition $50,460. Room and board $17,600. Required fees $1,216. Average book and supplies expense $2,050. **Required Forms and Deadlines:** FAFSA. **Notification of Awards:** Applicants will be notified of awards on a rolling basis beginning 4/1. **Types of Aid:** *Need-based scholarships/grants:* College/university scholarship or grant aid from institutional funds; Federal Pell; Private scholarships; SEOG; State scholarships/grants; United Negro College Fund. *Loans:* Direct PLUS loans; Direct Subsidized Stafford Loans; Direct Unsubsidized Stafford Loans. **Student Employment:** Federal Work-Study Program available. Institutional employment available. **Financial Aid Statistics:** 78% needy freshmen, 85% needy undergrads receive need-based scholarship or grant aid. 78% freshmen, 73% undergrads receive non-need-based scholarship or grant aid. 11% freshmen, 12% undergrads receive need-based self-help aid. 0% freshmen, 0% undergrads receive athletic scholarships. 85% freshmen, 94% undergrads receive any aid. 35% undergrads borrow to pay for school. Average cumulative indebtedness $32,624. **Criteria awarding aid:** *Need-based:* Academics, Art, Leadership, Minority status, Music/drama. *Non-need-based:* Academics, Art, Leadership, Minority status, Music/drama, State/district residency.

PATRICK HENRY COLLEGE

10 Patrick Henry Circle, Purcellville, VA 20132
Phone: 540-441-8110 **Financial Aid Phone:** 540-441-8142
E-mail: admissions@phc.edu **CEEB Code:** 2804
Fax: 540-441-8119 **Website:** www.phc.edu **ACT Code:** 4383

This private school, affiliated with the Christian (Nondenominational) Church, was founded in 2000. It has a 106 acre campus.

RATINGS

Admissions Selectivity Rating: 80   **Fire Safety Rating:** 90   **Green Rating:** 63

STUDENTS AND FACULTY

Enrollment: 288. **Student Body:** 45% female, 55% male, 81% out-of-state, 0% international. Asian 2%, African American 1%, Caucasian 77%, Hispanic 6%, Native American 0%, Pacific Islander 1%, Two or more races 0%, Race unknown 13%.
Retention and Graduation: 85% freshmen return for sophomore year. 57% freshmen graduate within 4 years. 67% freshmen graduate within 6 years. 35% grads go on to further study within 1 year. 23% grads pursue law degrees.
Faculty: Student/faculty ratio 10:1. 20 full-time faculty, 90% hold PhDs, 0% are members of minority groups, 15% are women. 0% of classes are taught by teaching assistants.

ACADEMICS

Degrees: Bachelor's. **Classes:** Most classes have 10–19 students. Most lab/ discussion sessions have 10–19 students. **Most popular majors:** Political Science and Government, General; Business/Managerial Economics; Strategic Intelligence. **Special Study Options:** Accelerated program; Cooperative education program; Cross-registration; Distance learning; Double major; Dual enrollment; Independent study; Internships; Liberal arts/career combination; Study abroad. **Disability Services offered:** Tutors. **Career services:** Alumni network; Alumni services; Career assessment; Career/job search classes; Internships.

FACILITIES

Housing: Men's dorms; Women's dorms; 99% of campus accessible to physically disabled.

CAMPUS LIFE

Environment: Village. **Activities:** Campus Ministries; Choral groups; Dance; Drama/theater; Literary magazine; Model UN; Music ensembles; Student government; Student newspaper; Symphony orchestra. 40 registered organizations, 40 religious organizations on campus. **Athletics (Intercollegiate):** *Men:* basketball, soccer. *Women:* basketball; soccer. **On-Campus Highlights:** Student Coffee Lounge. **Environmental Initiatives:** Water conservation.

ADMISSIONS

Freshman Academic Profile: Average high school GPA 3.9. 100% in top 25% of high school class, 100% in top 50% of high school class. 15% from public high schools. **Test Scores:** SAT Math middle 50% range 550–620. SAT EBRW middle 50% range 640–730. ACT middle 50% range 27–31. **Basis for Candidate Selection:** *Very important factors include:* character/ personal qualities, religious affiliation/commitment. *Important factors include:* rigor of secondary school record, application essay, standardized test scores, recommendation(s), interview, extracurricular activities, talent/ability, volunteer work, level of applicant's interest. *Other factors include:* academic GPA, work experience. **Freshman Admission Requirements:** High school diploma is required and GED is accepted. *Academic units required:* 4 English, 3 math, 2 science, 2 science labs, 1 foreign language, 2 history, 5 academic electives. *Academic units recommended:* 4 English, 3 math, 3 science, 3 science labs, 2 foreign language, 2 history, 5 academic electives. **Freshman Admission Statistics:** 174 applied, 98% admitted, 58% enrolled. **Transfer Admission Requirements:** High school transcript, college transcript(s), essay or personal statement, interview, standardized test scores, statement of good standing from prior institution(s). Lowest grade transferable C. **General Admission Information:** Application fee $40. Priority deadline 11/1. Regular application deadline 7/15. Non-fall registration accepted. Admission may be deferred for a maximum of one year.

COSTS AND FINANCIAL AID

Annual tuition $27,922. Room and board $10,728. Average book and supplies expense $750. **Required Forms and Deadlines:** CSS/Financial Aid PROFILE. **Notification of Awards:** Applicants will be notified of awards on a rolling basis beginning 3/1. **Types of Aid:** *Need-based scholarships/grants:* College/university scholarship or grant aid from institutional funds; Private scholarships. **Student Employment:** Institutional employment available. **Financial Aid Statistics:** 52% needy freshmen, 77% needy undergrads receive need-based scholarship or grant aid. 87% freshmen, 87% undergrads receive non-need-based scholarship or grant aid. 0% freshmen, 0% undergrads receive need-based self-help aid. 0% freshmen, 0% undergrads receive athletic scholarships. 94% freshmen, 94% undergrads receive any aid. 24% undergrads borrow to pay for school. Average cumulative indebtedness $78,345. **Criteria awarding aid:** *Non-need-based:* Academics, Leadership, Music/drama.

PENN STATE ABINGTON

106 Sutherland Building, Abington, PA 19001
Phone: 215-881-7600
E-mail: abingtonadmissions@psu.edu
Fax: 215-881-7655 **Website:** http://www.abington.psu.edu

This public school was founded in 1950. It has a 45 acre campus.

RATINGS

Admissions Selectivity Rating: 75   **Fire Safety Rating:** 60*   **Green Rating:** 60*

STUDENTS AND FACULTY

Enrollment: 3,490. **Student Body:** 51% female, 49% male, 7% out-of-state, 5% international. Asian 17%, African American 13%, Caucasian 50%, Hispanic 10%, Native American <1%, Pacific Islander <1%, Two or more races 2%, Race unknown 3%.
Retention and Graduation: 80% freshmen return for sophomore year.
Faculty: Student/faculty ratio 18:1. 136 full-time faculty, 65% hold PhDs, 17% are members of minority groups, 50% are women.

ACADEMICS

Degrees: Associate; Bachelor's; Certificate; Post-bachelor's certificate. **Classes:** Most classes have 20–29 students. Most lab/discussion sessions have 20–29 students. **Special Study Options:** Accelerated program; Cooperative education program; Distance learning; Double major; Dual enrollment; English as a Second Language (ESL); Exchange student program (domestic); External degree program; Honors program; Independent study; Internships; Liberal arts/career combination; Student-designed major; Study abroad; Teacher certification program; Weekend college.

FACILITIES

Campus Network: 100% of classrooms, 100% of dorms, 100% of student union, 100% of libraries, 100% of dining areas, 100% of common outdoor areas have wireless network access.

CAMPUS LIFE

Environment: Village. **Activities:** Campus Ministries; Choral groups; Dance; Drama/theater; International Student Organization; Jazz band; Literary magazine; Music ensembles; Student government; Student newspaper; Student-run film society. **Athletics (Intercollegiate):** *Men:* basketball, soccer, softball, tennis. *Women:* basketball, field hockey, softball, tennis, volleyball.

ADMISSIONS

Freshman Academic Profile: Average high school GPA 3.1. 8% in top 10% of high school class, 27% in top 25% of high school class, 64% in top 50% of high school class. **Test Scores:** SAT Math middle 50% range 430–570. SAT EBRW middle 50% range 420–520. ACT middle 50% range 19–25.
Basis for Candidate Selection: *Very important factors include:* academic GPA, standardized test scores. *Important factors include:* rigor of secondary school record. *Other factors include:* class rank, application essay, extracurricular activities, talent/ability, character/personal qualities, alumni/ae relation, geographical residence, state residency, volunteer work, work experience.
Freshman Admission Requirements: High school diploma is required and GED is accepted. *Academic units required:* 4 English, 3 math, 3 science, 2 foreign language, 3 social studies. *Academic units recommended:* 3 foreign language. **Freshman Admission Statistics:** 3,946 applied, 82% admitted, 27% enrolled. **Transfer Admission Requirements:** High school transcript, college transcript(s). Lowest grade transferable C. **General Admission Information:** Application fee $50. Priority deadline 11/30. Non-fall registration accepted. Admission may be deferred for a maximum of one year.

COSTS AND FINANCIAL AID

Annual in-state tuition $13,012. Annual out-of-state tuition $20,324. Required fees $942. **Required Forms and Deadlines:** FAFSA. **Types of Aid:** *Need-based scholarships/grants:* College/university scholarship or grant aid from institutional funds; Federal Pell; Private scholarships; SEOG; State scholarships/grants. *Loans:* Direct PLUS loans; Direct Subsidized Stafford Loans; Direct Unsubsidized Stafford Loans. **Financial Aid Statistics:** 77% needy freshmen, 80% needy undergrads receive need-based scholarship or grant aid. 35% freshmen, 28% undergrads receive non-need-based scholarship or grant aid. 69% freshmen, 80% undergrads receive need-based self-help aid. 0% freshmen, 0% undergrads receive athletic scholarships. 82% undergrads borrow to pay for school. Average cumulative indebtedness $35,013. **Criteria awarding aid:** *Need-based:* Academics, Alumni affiliation. *Non-need-based:* Academics, Alumni affiliation.

PENN STATE ALTOONA

E108 Smith Building, Altoona, PA 16601-3760
Phone: 814-949-5466
E-mail: aaadmit@psu.edu
Fax: 814-949-5564 **Website:** www.altoona.psu.edu

This public school was founded in 1929.

RATINGS

Admissions Selectivity Rating: 74   **Fire Safety Rating:** 60*   **Green Rating:** 60*

STUDENTS AND FACULTY

Enrollment: 3,772. **Student Body:** 44% female, 56% male, 17% out-of-state, 5% international. Asian 3%, African American 7%, Caucasian 77%, Hispanic 6%, Native American <1%, Pacific Islander <1%, Two or more races 2%, Race unknown 1%.
Retention and Graduation: 84% freshmen return for sophomore year.
Faculty: Student/faculty ratio 16:1. 203 full-time faculty, 67% hold PhDs, 12% are members of minority groups, 50% are women.

ACADEMICS

Degrees: Associate; Bachelor's; Certificate. **Classes:** Most classes have 20–29 students. Most lab/discussion sessions have 10–19 students. **Special Study Options:** Accelerated program; Cooperative education program; Cross-registration; Distance learning; Double major; Dual enrollment; English as a Second Language (ESL); Exchange student program (domestic); External degree program; Honors program; Independent study; Internships; Liberal arts/career combination; Student-designed major; Study abroad; Teacher certification program; Weekend college.

FACILITIES

Housing: Coed dorms; Special housing for disabled students; Theme housing; Wellness housing.

CAMPUS LIFE

Environment: Village. **Activities:** Campus Ministries; Choral groups; Dance; Drama/theater; International Student Organization; Jazz band; Literary magazine; Music ensembles; Musical theater; Pep band; Student government; Student newspaper; Student-run film society; Yearbook. **Athletics (Intercollegiate):** *Men:* basketball, diving, skiing (downhill/Alpine), soccer, swimming, tennis, volleyball. *Women:* basketball, diving, skiing (downhill/Alpine), swimming, tennis, volleyball.

ADMISSIONS

Freshman Academic Profile: Average high school GPA 3.1. 6% in top 10% of high school class, 24% in top 25% of high school class, 67% in top 50% of high school class. **Test Scores:** SAT Math middle 50% range 450–550. SAT EBRW middle 50% range 440–540. ACT middle 50% range 20–24.
Basis for Candidate Selection: *Very important factors include:* academic GPA, standardized test scores. *Important factors include:* rigor of secondary school record. *Other factors include:* class rank, application essay, extracurricular activities, talent/ability, character/personal qualities, alumni/ae relation, geographical residence, state residency, volunteer work, work experience.
Freshman Admission Requirements: High school diploma is required and GED is accepted. *Academic units required:* 4 English, 3 math, 3 science, 2 foreign language, 3 social studies. *Academic units recommended:* 3 foreign language. **Freshman Admission Statistics:** 5,738 applied, 89% admitted, 27% enrolled. **Transfer Admission Requirements:** High school transcript, college transcript(s). Lowest grade transferable C. **General Admission Information:** Application fee $50. Priority deadline 11/30. Non-fall registration accepted. Admission may be deferred for a maximum of one year.

COSTS AND FINANCIAL AID

Annual in-state tuition $13,658. Annual out-of-state tuition $21,392. Room and board $10,920. Required fees $952. Average book and supplies expense $1,840. **Required Forms and Deadlines:** FAFSA. **Types of Aid:** *Need-based scholarships/grants:* College/university scholarship or grant aid from institutional funds; Federal Pell; Private scholarships; SEOG; State scholarships/grants. *Loans:* Direct PLUS loans; Direct Subsidized Stafford Loans; Direct Unsubsidized Stafford Loans. **Financial Aid Statistics:** 58% needy freshmen, 62% needy undergrads receive need-based scholarship or grant aid. 49% freshmen, 44% undergrads receive non-need-based scholarship or grant aid. 79% freshmen, 83% undergrads receive need-based self-help aid. 0% freshmen, 0% undergrads receive athletic scholarships. 76% undergrads borrow to pay for school. Average cumulative indebtedness $39,091. **Criteria awarding aid:** *Need-based:* Academics, Alumni affiliation. *Non-need-based:* Academics, Alumni affiliation.

PENN STATE BEAVER

100 University Drive, 113 Student Union, Monaca, PA 15061-2799
Phone: (877) 564-6778
E-mail: br-admissions@psu.edu
Fax: (724)773-3769 **Website:** http://beaver.psu.edu

This is a public school.

RATINGS
Admissions Selectivity Rating: 74   **Fire Safety Rating:** 60*   **Green Rating:** 69

STUDENTS AND FACULTY
Enrollment: 639. **Student Body:** 39% female, 61% male, 9% out-of-state, 3% international. Asian 3%, African American 9%, Caucasian 75%, Hispanic 5%, Native American <1%, Pacific Islander <1%, Two or more races 2%, Race unknown 1%.
Retention and Graduation: 78% freshmen return for sophomore year.
Faculty: Student/faculty ratio 16:1. 32 full-time faculty, 66% hold PhDs, 22% are members of minority groups, 59% are women.

ACADEMICS
Degrees: Bachelor's; Certificate. **Classes:** Most classes have 10–19 students. Most lab/discussion sessions have 10–19 students. **Special Study Options:** Cross-registration; Distance learning; Double major; Dual enrollment; Honors program; Independent study; Internships; Study abroad.

FACILITIES
Housing: Coed dorms; Special housing for disabled students.

CAMPUS LIFE
Activities: Campus Ministries; Choral groups; Drama/theater; International Student Organization; Radio station; Student government; Student newspaper; Student-run film society.

ADMISSIONS
Freshman Academic Profile: Average high school GPA 3.1. 7% in top 10% of high school class, 31% in top 25% of high school class, 73% in top 50% of high school class. **Test Scores:** SAT Math middle 50% range 450–570. SAT EBRW middle 50% range 430–550. ACT middle 50% range 18–24.
Basis for Candidate Selection: *Very important factors include:* academic GPA, standardized test scores. *Important factors include:* rigor of secondary school record. *Other factors include:* class rank, application essay, extracurricular activities, talent/ability, character/personal qualities, alumni/ae relation, geographical residence, state residency, volunteer work, work experience.
Freshman Admission Requirements: High school diploma is required and GED is accepted. *Academic units required:* 4 English, 3 math, 3 science, 2 foreign language, 3 social studies. *Academic units recommended:* 3 foreign language. **Freshman Admission Statistics:** 653 applied, 95% admitted, 34% enrolled. **General Admission Information:** Application fee $50. Priority deadline 11/30. Non-fall registration accepted. Admission may be deferred for a maximum of one year.

COSTS AND FINANCIAL AID
Annual in-state tuition $12,718. Annual out-of-state tuition $19,404. Room and board $10,920. Required fees $942. Average book and supplies expense $1,840. **Required Forms and Deadlines:** FAFSA. **Types of Aid:** *Need-based scholarships/grants:* College/university scholarship or grant aid from institutional funds; Federal Pell; Private scholarships; SEOG; State scholarships/grants. *Loans:* Direct PLUS loans; Direct Subsidized Stafford Loans; Direct Unsubsidized Stafford Loans. **Financial Aid Statistics:** 72% needy freshmen, 75% needy undergrads receive need-based scholarship or grant aid. 69% freshmen, 56% undergrads receive non-need-based scholarship or grant aid. 85% freshmen, 86% undergrads receive need-based self-help aid. 0% freshmen, 0% undergrads receive athletic scholarships. 86% undergrads borrow to pay for school. Average cumulative indebtedness $37,485. **Criteria awarding aid:** *Need-based:* Academics, Alumni affiliation. *Non-need-based:* Academics, Alumni affiliation.

PENN STATE BERKS

Tulpehocken Road PO Box 7009, Reading, PA 19610-6009
Phone: 610-396-6060
E-mail: admissionsbk@psu.edu
Fax: 610-396-6077 **Website:** http://berks.psu.edu

This public school was founded in 1924. It has a 241 acre campus.

RATINGS
Admissions Selectivity Rating: 75   **Fire Safety Rating:** 60*   **Green Rating:** 60*

STUDENTS AND FACULTY
Enrollment: 2,778. **Student Body:** 43% female, 57% male, 8% out-of-state, 3% international. Asian 5%, African American 9%, Caucasian 68%, Hispanic 11%, Native American <1%, Pacific Islander <1%, Two or more races 2%, Race unknown 1%.
Retention and Graduation: 82% freshmen return for sophomore year.
Faculty: Student/faculty ratio 17:1. 136 full-time faculty, 70% hold PhDs, 15% are members of minority groups, 50% are women.

ACADEMICS
Degrees: Associate; Bachelor's; Certificate; Post-bachelor's certificate. **Classes:** Most classes have 20–29 students. Most lab/discussion sessions have 10–19 students. **Special Study Options:** Accelerated program; Cooperative education program; Cross-registration; Distance learning; Dual enrollment; English as a Second Language (ESL); Honors program; Independent study; Internships; Study abroad; Teacher certification program.

FACILITIES
Housing: Coed dorms; Special housing for disabled students.

CAMPUS LIFE
Environment: Village. **Activities:** Campus Ministries; Choral groups; Dance; Drama/theater; Literary magazine; Radio station; Student government; Student newspaper; Student-run film society. **Athletics (Intercollegiate):** *Men:* baseball, basketball, fencing, soccer, tennis, volleyball. *Women:* fencing, softball, tennis, volleyball.

ADMISSIONS
Freshman Academic Profile: Average high school GPA 3.1. 8% in top 10% of high school class, 29% in top 25% of high school class, 66% in top 50% of high school class. **Test Scores:** SAT Math middle 50% range 430–560. SAT EBRW middle 50% range 420–540. ACT middle 50% range 18–25.
Basis for Candidate Selection: *Very important factors include:* academic GPA, standardized test scores. *Important factors include:* rigor of secondary school record. *Other factors include:* class rank, application essay, extracurricular activities, talent/ability, character/personal qualities, alumni/ae relation, geographical residence, state residency, volunteer work, work experience.
Freshman Admission Requirements: High school diploma is required and GED is accepted. *Academic units required:* 4 English, 3 math, 3 science, 2 foreign language, 3 social studies. *Academic units recommended:* 3 foreign language. **Freshman Admission Statistics:** 2,413 applied, 85% admitted, 39% enrolled. **Transfer Admission Requirements:** High school transcript, college transcript(s). Lowest grade transferable C. **General Admission Information:** Application fee $50. Priority deadline 11/30. Non-fall registration accepted. Admission may be deferred for a maximum of one year.

COSTS AND FINANCIAL AID
Annual in-state tuition $13,658. Annual out-of-state tuition $21,392. Room and board $11,950. Required fees $952. Average book and supplies expense $1,840. **Required Forms and Deadlines:** FAFSA. **Types of Aid:** *Need-based scholarships/grants:* College/university scholarship or grant aid from institutional funds; Federal Pell; Private scholarships; SEOG; State scholarships/grants. *Loans:* Direct PLUS loans; Direct Subsidized Stafford Loans; Direct Unsubsidized Stafford Loans. **Financial Aid Statistics:** 66% needy freshmen, 70% needy undergrads receive need-based scholarship or grant aid. 37% freshmen, 33% undergrads receive non-need-based scholarship or grant aid. 82% freshmen, 85% undergrads receive need-based self-help aid. 0% freshmen, 0% undergrads receive athletic scholarships. 80% undergrads borrow to pay for school. Average cumulative indebtedness $35,853. **Criteria awarding aid:** *Need-based:* Academics, Alumni affiliation. *Non-need-based:* Academics, Alumni affiliation.

PENN STATE BRANDYWINE

25 Yearsley Mill Road, Media, PA 19063
Phone: (610)892-1200
E-mail: bwadmissions@psu.edu
Fax: (610)892-1320 **Website:** brandywine.psu.edu

This is a public school.

RATINGS

Admissions Selectivity Rating: 75   **Fire Safety Rating:** 60*   **Green Rating:** 60*

STUDENTS AND FACULTY

Enrollment: 1,291. **Student Body:** 44% female, 56% male, 5% out-of-state, 1% international. Asian 11%, African American 15%, Caucasian 63%, Hispanic 5%, Native American <1%, Pacific Islander <1%, Two or more races 2%, Race unknown 2%.
Retention and Graduation: 74% freshmen return for sophomore year.
Faculty: Student/faculty ratio 15:1. 68 full-time faculty, 71% hold PhDs, 15% are members of minority groups, 53% are women.

ACADEMICS

Degrees: Associate; Bachelor's; Certificate. **Classes:** Most classes have 10–19 students. Most lab/discussion sessions have 10–19 students. **Special Study Options:** Accelerated program; Distance learning; Double major; Dual enrollment; English as a Second Language (ESL); Honors program; Independent study; Internships; Study abroad.

CAMPUS LIFE

Activities: Literary magazine; Student government; Student newspaper.

ADMISSIONS

Freshman Academic Profile: Average high school GPA 3.0. 4% in top 10% of high school class, 18% in top 25% of high school class, 56% in top 50% of high school class. **Test Scores:** SAT Math middle 50% range 440–550. SAT EBRW middle 50% range 420–520. ACT middle 50% range 18–26.
Basis for Candidate Selection: *Very important factors include:* academic GPA, standardized test scores. *Important factors include:* rigor of secondary school record. *Other factors include:* class rank, application essay, extracurricular activities, talent/ability, character/personal qualities, alumni/ae relation, geographical residence, state residency, volunteer work, work experience.
Freshman Admission Requirements: High school diploma is required and GED is accepted. *Academic units required:* 4 English, 3 math, 3 science, 2 foreign language, 3 social studies. *Academic units recommended:* 3 foreign language. **Freshman Admission Statistics:** 1,265 applied, 83% admitted, 36% enrolled. **General Admission Information:** Application fee $50. Priority deadline 11/30. Non-fall registration accepted. Admission may be deferred for a maximum of one year.

COSTS AND FINANCIAL AID

Annual in-state tuition $13,012. Annual out-of-state tuition $20,206. Required fees $952. **Required Forms and Deadlines:** FAFSA. **Types of Aid:** *Need-based scholarships/grants:* College/university scholarship or grant aid from institutional funds; Federal Pell; Private scholarships; SEOG; State scholarships/grants. *Loans:* Direct PLUS loans; Direct Subsidized Stafford Loans; Direct Unsubsidized Stafford Loans. **Financial Aid Statistics:** 68% needy freshmen, 76% needy undergrads receive need-based scholarship or grant aid. 40% freshmen, 32% undergrads receive non-need-based scholarship or grant aid. 78% freshmen, 82% undergrads receive need-based self-help aid. 0% freshmen, 0% undergrads receive athletic scholarships. 78% undergrads borrow to pay for school. Average cumulative indebtedness $34,962. **Criteria awarding aid:** *Need-based:* Academics, Alumni affiliation. *Non-need-based:* Academics, Alumni affiliation.

PENN STATE DUBOIS

Hochrein House, 1 College Place, DuBois, PA 15801-3199
Phone: (814)375-4720
E-mail: duboisinfo@psu.edu
Fax: (814)375-4784 **Website:** http://dubois.psu.edu

This is a public school.

RATINGS

Admissions Selectivity Rating: 76   **Fire Safety Rating:** 60*   **Green Rating:** 60*

STUDENTS AND FACULTY

Enrollment: 512. **Student Body:** 44% female, 56% male, 3% out-of-state, <1% international. Asian 1%, African American 2%, Caucasian 94%, Hispanic 2%, Native American 0%, Pacific Islander <1%, Two or more races <1%, Race unknown 1%.
Retention and Graduation: 87% freshmen return for sophomore year.
Faculty: Student/faculty ratio 11:1. 42 full-time faculty, 57% hold PhDs, 19% are members of minority groups, 60% are women.

ACADEMICS

Degrees: Associate; Bachelor's; Certificate. **Classes:** Most classes have 10–19 students. Most lab/discussion sessions have 10–19 students. **Special Study Options:** Accelerated program; Cross-registration; Distance learning; Double major; Dual enrollment; Honors program; Independent study; Internships; Student-designed major; Study abroad.

CAMPUS LIFE

Activities: Campus Ministries; Choral groups; Student government; Student-run film society.

ADMISSIONS

Freshman Academic Profile: Average high school GPA 3.1. 9% in top 10% of high school class, 33% in top 25% of high school class, 68% in top 50% of high school class. **Test Scores:** SAT Math middle 50% range 420–560. SAT EBRW middle 50% range 420–530. ACT middle 50% range 21–25.
Basis for Candidate Selection: *Very important factors include:* academic GPA, standardized test scores. *Important factors include:* rigor of secondary school record. *Other factors include:* class rank, application essay, extracurricular activities, talent/ability, character/personal qualities, alumni/ae relation, geographical residence, state residency, volunteer work, work experience.
Freshman Admission Requirements: High school diploma is required and GED is accepted. *Academic units required:* 4 English, 3 math, 3 science, 2 foreign language, 3 social studies. *Academic units recommended:* 3 foreign language. **Freshman Admission Statistics:** 394 applied, 85% admitted, 49% enrolled. **General Admission Information:** Application fee $50. Priority deadline 11/30. Non-fall registration accepted. Admission may be deferred for a maximum of 1 year.

COSTS AND FINANCIAL AID

Annual in-state tuition $12,718. Annual out-of-state tuition $19,404. Required fees $828. **Required Forms and Deadlines:** FAFSA. **Types of Aid:** *Need-based scholarships/grants:* College/university scholarship or grant aid from institutional funds; Federal Pell; Private scholarships; SEOG; State scholarships/grants. *Loans:* Direct PLUS loans; Direct Subsidized Stafford Loans; Direct Unsubsidized Stafford Loans. **Financial Aid Statistics:** 87% needy freshmen, 89% needy undergrads receive need-based scholarship or grant aid. 48% freshmen, 37% undergrads receive non-need-based scholarship or grant aid. 80% freshmen, 86% undergrads receive need-based self-help aid. 0% freshmen, 0% undergrads receive athletic scholarships. 88% undergrads borrow to pay for school. Average cumulative indebtedness $43,504. **Criteria awarding aid:** *Need-based:* Academics, Alumni affiliation. *Non-need-based:* Academics, Alumni affiliation.

PENN STATE ERIE, THE BEHREND COLLEGE

Metzgar Admissions & Alumnia Ct, Erie, PA 16563-0105
Phone: 814-898-6100
E-mail: behrend.admissions@psu.edu
Fax: 814-898-6044 **Website:** http://psbehrend.psu.edu/ **ACT Code:** 3656

This public school was founded in 1948. It has a 732 acre campus.

RATINGS
Admissions Selectivity Rating: 75   **Fire Safety Rating:** 60*   **Green Rating:** 60*

STUDENTS AND FACULTY
Enrollment: 4,092. **Student Body:** 35% female, 65% male, 10% out-of-state, 9% international. Asian 3%, African American 4%, Caucasian 79%, Hispanic 2%, Native American <1%, Pacific Islander <1%, Two or more races 2%, Race unknown 1%.
Retention and Graduation: 85% freshmen return for sophomore year.
Faculty: Student/faculty ratio 15:1. 260 full-time faculty, 67% hold PhDs, 12% are members of minority groups, 37% are women. 0% of classes are taught by teaching assistants.

ACADEMICS
Degrees: Associate; Bachelor's; Certificate; Master's. **Classes:** Most classes have 20–29 students. Most lab/discussion sessions have 10–19 students. **Special Study Options:** Accelerated program; Cooperative education program; Distance learning; Double major; Dual enrollment; Honors program; Independent study; Internships; Liberal arts/career combination; Study abroad; Teacher certification program. **Disability Services offered:** Note-taking services; Reader services; Tape recorders; Tutors. **Career services:** Alumni services; Career assessment; Career/job search classes; Internships.

FACILITIES
Housing: Apartments for single students; Coed dorms; Men's dorms; Special housing for disabled students; Women's dorms. **Special Academic Facilities/Equipment:** Observatory, plastics lab.

CAMPUS LIFE
Environment: Village. **Activities:** Campus Ministries; Choral groups; Concert band; Dance; Drama/theater; International Student Organization; Jazz band; Literary magazine; Model UN; Music ensembles; Pep band; Radio station; Student government; Student newspaper; Student-run film society. 75 registered organizations, 46 honor societies, 26 religious organizations, 6 fraternities, 4 sororities on campus. **Athletics (Intercollegiate):** *Men:* baseball, basketball, cheerleading, cross-country, golf, soccer, swimming, tennis, track/field (outdoor), water polo, wrestling. *Women:* basketball, cheerleading, cross-country, golf, soccer, softball, swimming, tennis, track/field (outdoor), volleyball, water polo. **On-Campus Highlights:** Junker Athletic Center.

ADMISSIONS
Freshman Academic Profile: Average high school GPA 3.3. 13% in top 10% of high school class, 42% in top 25% of high school class, 80% in top 50% of high school class. **Test Scores:** SAT Math middle 50% range 480–610. SAT EBRW middle 50% range 460–560. ACT middle 50% range 20–25. **Basis for Candidate Selection:** *Very important factors include:* academic GPA, standardized test scores. *Important factors include:* rigor of secondary school record. *Other factors include:* class rank, application essay, extracurricular activities, talent/ability, character/personal qualities, alumni/ae relation, geographical residence, state residency, volunteer work, work experience. **Freshman Admission Requirements:** High school diploma is required and GED is accepted. *Academic units required:* 4 English, 3 math, 3 science, 2 foreign language, 3 social studies. *Academic units recommended:* 3 foreign language. **Freshman Admission Statistics:** 4,079 applied, 87% admitted, 33% enrolled. **Transfer Admission Requirements:** High school transcript, college transcript(s). Lowest grade transferable C. **General Admission Information:** Application fee $50. Priority deadline 11/30. Non-fall registration accepted. Admission may be deferred for a maximum of one year.

COSTS AND FINANCIAL AID
Annual in-state tuition $13,658. Annual out-of-state tuition $21,392. Room and board $10,920. Required fees $952. Average book and supplies expense $1,840. **Required Forms and Deadlines:** FAFSA. **Types of Aid:** *Need-based scholarships/grants:* College/university scholarship or grant aid from institutional funds; Federal Pell; Private scholarships; SEOG; State scholarships/grants. *Loans:* Direct PLUS loans; Direct Subsidized Stafford Loans; Direct Unsubsidized Stafford Loans. **Student Employment:** Federal Work-Study

Program available. Institutional employment available. **Financial Aid Statistics:** 63% needy freshmen, 64% needy undergrads receive need-based scholarship or grant aid. 45% freshmen, 39% undergrads receive non-need-based scholarship or grant aid. 85% freshmen, 87% undergrads receive need-based self-help aid. 0% freshmen, 0% undergrads receive athletic scholarships. 81% undergrads borrow to pay for school. Average cumulative indebtedness $39,346. **Criteria awarding aid:** *Need-based:* Academics, Alumni affiliation. *Non-need-based:* Academics, Alumni affiliation.

PENN STATE FAYETTE, THE EBERLY CAMPUS

110 Eberly Building, 2201 University Dri, Lemont Furnace, PA 15456
Phone: (724)430-4130
E-mail: feadm@psu.edu
Fax: (724)430-4175 **Website:** fe.psu.edu

This is a public school.

RATINGS
Admissions Selectivity Rating: 75   **Fire Safety Rating:** 60*   **Green Rating:** 60*

STUDENTS AND FACULTY
Enrollment: 671. **Student Body:** 59% female, 41% male, 5% out-of-state, 2% international. Asian <1%, African American 4%, Caucasian 89%, Hispanic 2%, Native American <1%, Pacific Islander 0%, Two or more races 3%, Race unknown 1%.
Retention and Graduation: 77% freshmen return for sophomore year.
Faculty: Student/faculty ratio 12:1. 44 full-time faculty, 48% hold PhDs, 2% are members of minority groups, 45% are women.

ACADEMICS
Degrees: Associate; Bachelor's; Certificate. **Classes:** Most classes have 10–19 students. Most lab/discussion sessions have fewer than 10 students. **Special Study Options:** Accelerated program; Cross-registration; Distance learning; Double major; Dual enrollment; Honors program; Independent study; Internships; Student-designed major; Study abroad.

CAMPUS LIFE
Activities: Campus Ministries; Choral groups; Drama/theater; Literary magazine; Musical theater; Student government; Student newspaper.

ADMISSIONS
Freshman Academic Profile: Average high school GPA 3.2. 10% in top 10% of high school class, 35% in top 25% of high school class, 73% in top 50% of high school class. **Test Scores:** SAT Math middle 50% range 410–520. SAT EBRW middle 50% range 390–510. ACT middle 50% range 17–22. **Basis for Candidate Selection:** *Very important factors include:* academic GPA, standardized test scores. *Important factors include:* rigor of secondary school record. *Other factors include:* class rank, application essay, extracurricular activities, talent/ability, character/personal qualities, alumni/ae relation, geographical residence, state residency, volunteer work, work experience. **Freshman Admission Requirements:** High school diploma is required and GED is accepted. *Academic units required:* 4 English, 3 math, 3 science, 2 foreign language, 3 social studies. *Academic units recommended:* 3 foreign language. **Freshman Admission Statistics:** 659 applied, 81% admitted, 36% enrolled. **General Admission Information:** Application fee $50. Priority deadline 11/30. Non-fall registration accepted. Admission may be deferred for a maximum of one year.

COSTS AND FINANCIAL AID
Annual in-state tuition $12,718. Annual out-of-state tuition $19,404. Required fees $890. **Required Forms and Deadlines:** FAFSA. **Types of Aid:** *Need-based scholarships/grants:* College/university scholarship or grant aid from institutional funds; Federal Pell; Private scholarships; SEOG; State scholarships/grants. *Loans:* Direct PLUS loans; Direct Subsidized Stafford Loans; Direct Unsubsidized Stafford Loans. **Financial Aid Statistics:** 80% needy freshmen, 82% needy undergrads receive need-based scholarship or grant aid. 54% freshmen, 44% undergrads receive non-need-based scholarship or grant aid. 73% freshmen, 80% undergrads receive need-based self-help aid. 0% freshmen, 0% undergrads receive athletic scholarships. 87% undergrads borrow to pay for school. Average cumulative indebtedness $37,338. **Criteria awarding aid:** *Need-based:* Academics, Alumni affiliation. *Non-need-based:* Academics, Alumni affiliation.

PENN STATE GREATER ALLEGHENY

123 Frable Bldg., 4000 University Drive, McKeesport, PA 15132-7698
Phone: (412)675-9010
E-mail: psuga@psu.edu
Fax: (412)675-9056 **Website:** http://ga.psu.edu

This is a public school.

RATINGS
Admissions Selectivity Rating: 76   **Fire Safety Rating:** 60*   **Green Rating:** 60*

STUDENTS AND FACULTY
Enrollment: 532. **Student Body:** 41% female, 59% male, 7% out-of-state, 4% international. Asian 5%, African American 19%, Caucasian 61%, Hispanic 7%, Native American 0%, Pacific Islander 0%, Two or more races 3%, Race unknown 1%.
Retention and Graduation: 80% freshmen return for sophomore year.
Faculty: Student/faculty ratio 11:1. 34 full-time faculty, 74% hold PhDs, 29% are members of minority groups, 59% are women.

ACADEMICS
Degrees: Associate; Bachelor's; Certificate; Master's. **Classes:** Most classes have 10–19 students. **Special Study Options:** Cross-registration; Distance learning; Double major; Dual enrollment; English as a Second Language (ESL); Honors program; Independent study; Internships; Liberal arts/career combination; Student-designed major; Study abroad.

FACILITIES
Housing: Special housing for disabled students; Wellness housing.

CAMPUS LIFE
Activities: Campus Ministries; Choral groups; Dance; Drama/theater; Literary magazine; Music ensembles; Radio station; Student government; Student newspaper; Television station.

ADMISSIONS
Freshman Academic Profile: Average high school GPA 3.1. 6% in top 10% of high school class, 22% in top 25% of high school class, 64% in top 50% of high school class. **Test Scores:** SAT Math middle 50% range 400–540. SAT EBRW middle 50% range 390–540. ACT middle 50% range 20–25.
Basis for Candidate Selection: *Very important factors include:* academic GPA, standardized test scores. *Important factors include:* rigor of secondary school record. *Other factors include:* class rank, application essay, extracurricular activities, talent/ability, character/personal qualities, alumni/ae relation, geographical residence, state residency, volunteer work, work experience.
Freshman Admission Requirements: High school diploma is required and GED is accepted. *Academic units required:* 4 English, 3 math, 3 science, 2 foreign language, 3 social studies. *Academic units recommended:* 3 foreign language. **Freshman Admission Statistics:** 594 applied, 79% admitted, 34% enrolled. **General Admission Information:** Application fee $50. Priority deadline 11/30. Non-fall registration accepted. Admission may be deferred for a maximum of one year.

COSTS AND FINANCIAL AID
Annual in-state tuition $12,718. Annual out-of-state tuition $19,404. Room and board $10,920. Required fees $942. Average book and supplies expense $1,840. **Required Forms and Deadlines:** FAFSA. **Types of Aid:** *Need-based scholarships/grants:* College/university scholarship or grant aid from institutional funds; Federal Pell; Private scholarships; SEOG; State scholarships/grants. *Loans:* Direct PLUS loans; Direct Subsidized Stafford Loans; Direct Unsubsidized Stafford Loans. **Financial Aid Statistics:** 86% needy freshmen, 84% needy undergrads receive need-based scholarship or grant aid. 71% freshmen, 52% undergrads receive non-need-based scholarship or grant aid. 77% freshmen, 84% undergrads receive need-based self-help aid. 0% freshmen, 0% undergrads receive athletic scholarships. 81% undergrads borrow to pay for school. Average cumulative indebtedness $38,931. **Criteria awarding aid:** *Need-based:* Academics, Alumni affiliation. *Non-need-based:* Academics, Alumni affiliation.

PENN STATE HARRISBURG

Swatara Bldg., Middletown, PA 17057-4898
Phone: 717-948-6250
E-mail: hbgadmit@psu.edu
Fax: 717-948-6325 **Website:** www.harrisburg.psu.edu

This public school was founded in 1966.

RATINGS
Admissions Selectivity Rating: 75   **Fire Safety Rating:** 60*   **Green Rating:** 60*

STUDENTS AND FACULTY
Enrollment: 3,740. **Student Body:** 39% female, 61% male, 16% out-of-state, 10% international. Asian 9%, African American 11%, Caucasian 59%, Hispanic 6%, Native American <1%, Pacific Islander <1%, Two or more races 3%, Race unknown 2%.
Retention and Graduation: 87% freshmen return for sophomore year.
Faculty: Student/faculty ratio 15:1. 229 full-time faculty, 85% hold PhDs, 20% are members of minority groups, 41% are women.

ACADEMICS
Degrees: Associate; Bachelor's; Certificate; Doctoral degree research/scholarship; Master's; Post-bachelor's certificate. **Classes:** Most classes have 20–29 students. Most lab/discussion sessions have 20–29 students. **Special Study Options:** Cooperative education program; Cross-registration; Distance learning; Double major; Dual enrollment; Honors program; Independent study; Internships; Student-designed major; Study abroad; Teacher certification program.

FACILITIES
Housing: Apartments for single students; Special housing for disabled students.

CAMPUS LIFE
Environment: Village. **Activities:** Choral groups; Dance; Drama/theater; Literary magazine; Music ensembles; Radio station; Student government; Student newspaper. 2 honor societies, 1 religious organization on campus.
Athletics (Intercollegiate): *Men:* basketball, skiing (downhill/Alpine), soccer, tennis, track/field (outdoor), volleyball. *Women:* skiing (downhill/Alpine), soccer, track/field (outdoor), volleyball.

ADMISSIONS
Freshman Academic Profile: Average high school GPA 3.1. 9% in top 10% of high school class, 33% in top 25% of high school class, 72% in top 50% of high school class. **Test Scores:** SAT Math middle 50% range 470–610. SAT EBRW middle 50% range 440–560. ACT middle 50% range 20–26.
Basis for Candidate Selection: *Very important factors include:* academic GPA, standardized test scores. *Important factors include:* rigor of secondary school record. *Other factors include:* class rank, application essay, extracurricular activities, talent/ability, character/personal qualities, alumni/ae relation, geographical residence, state residency, volunteer work, work experience.
Freshman Admission Requirements: High school diploma is required and GED is accepted. *Academic units required:* 4 English, 3 math, 3 science, 2 foreign language, 3 social studies. *Academic units recommended:* 3 foreign language. **Freshman Admission Statistics:** 3,938 applied, 85% admitted, 26% enrolled. **Transfer Admission Requirements:** High school transcript, college transcript(s). Lowest grade transferable C. **General Admission Information:** Application fee $50. Priority deadline 11/30. Non-fall registration accepted. Admission may be deferred for a maximum of one year.

COSTS AND FINANCIAL AID
Annual in-state tuition $13,658. Annual out-of-state tuition $21,392. Room and board $12,450. Required fees $952. Average book and supplies expense $1,840. **Required Forms and Deadlines:** FAFSA. **Types of Aid:** *Need-based scholarships/grants:* College/university scholarship or grant aid from institutional funds; Federal Pell; Private scholarships; SEOG; State scholarships/grants. *Loans:* Direct PLUS loans; Direct Subsidized Stafford Loans; Direct Unsubsidized Stafford Loans. **Financial Aid Statistics:** 62% needy freshmen, 66% needy undergrads receive need-based scholarship or grant aid. 67% freshmen, 45% undergrads receive non-need-based scholarship or grant aid. 74% freshmen, 81% undergrads receive need-based self-help aid. 0% freshmen, 0% undergrads receive athletic scholarships. 76% undergrads borrow to pay for school. Average cumulative indebtedness $40,639. **Criteria awarding aid:** *Need-based:* Academics, Alumni affiliation. *Non-need-based:* Academics, Alumni affiliation.

PENN STATE HAZLETON

110 Schiavo Hall, Hazleton, PA 18202-1291
Phone: (570)450-3142
E-mail: hn-admissions@psu.edu
Website: http://hazleton.psu.edu/

This is a public school.

RATINGS
Admissions Selectivity Rating: 75   **Fire Safety Rating:** 60*   **Green Rating:** 60*

STUDENTS AND FACULTY
Enrollment: 753. **Student Body:** 42% female, 58% male, 19% out-of-state, 2% international. Asian 3%, African American 12%, Caucasian 60%, Hispanic 19%, Native American <1%, Pacific Islander <1%, Two or more races 3%, Race unknown 1%.
Retention and Graduation: 79% freshmen return for sophomore year.
Faculty: Student/faculty ratio 13:1. 50 full-time faculty, 66% hold PhDs, 12% are members of minority groups, 38% are women.

ACADEMICS
Degrees: Associate; Bachelor's; Certificate; Post-bachelor's certificate. **Classes:** Most classes have 10–19 students. **Special Study Options:** Accelerated program; Cross-registration; Distance learning; Double major; Dual enrollment; English as a Second Language (ESL); Honors program; Independent study; Internships; Student-designed major; Study abroad.

FACILITIES
Housing: Coed dorms; Theme housing.

CAMPUS LIFE
Activities: Choral groups; Dance; Drama/theater; Literary magazine; Student government; Student newspaper.

ADMISSIONS
Freshman Academic Profile: Average high school GPA 3.1. 11% in top 10% of high school class, 36% in top 25% of high school class, 77% in top 50% of high school class. **Test Scores:** SAT Math middle 50% range 430–540. SAT EBRW middle 50% range 410–520. ACT middle 50% range 17–25.
Basis for Candidate Selection: *Very important factors include:* academic GPA, standardized test scores. *Important factors include:* rigor of secondary school record. *Other factors include:* class rank, application essay, extracurricular activities, talent/ability, character/personal qualities, alumni/ae relation, geographical residence, state residency, volunteer work, work experience.
Freshman Admission Requirements: High school diploma is required and GED is accepted. *Academic units required:* 4 English, 3 math, 3 science, 2 foreign language, 3 social studies. *Academic units recommended:* 3 foreign language. **Freshman Admission Statistics:** 763 applied, 84% admitted, 41% enrolled. **General Admission Information:** Application fee $50. Priority deadline 11/30. Non-fall registration accepted. Admission may be deferred for a maximum of one year.

COSTS AND FINANCIAL AID
Annual in-state tuition $13,012. Annual out-of-state tuition $20,206. Room and board $10,920. Required fees $890. Average book and supplies expense $1,840. **Required Forms and Deadlines:** FAFSA. **Types of Aid:** *Need-based scholarships/grants:* College/university scholarship or grant aid from institutional funds; Federal Pell; Private scholarships; SEOG; State scholarships/grants. *Loans:* Direct PLUS loans; Direct Subsidized Stafford Loans; Direct Unsubsidized Stafford Loans. **Financial Aid Statistics:** 74% needy freshmen, 76% needy undergrads receive need-based scholarship or grant aid. 59% freshmen, 49% undergrads receive non-need-based scholarship or grant aid. 80% freshmen, 85% undergrads receive need-based self-help aid. 0% freshmen, 0% undergrads receive athletic scholarships. 83% undergrads borrow to pay for school. Average cumulative indebtedness $45,582. **Criteria awarding aid:** *Need-based:* Academics, Alumni affiliation. *Non-need-based:* Academics, Alumni affiliation.

PENN STATE LEHIGH VALLEY

2809 Saucon Valley Road, Center Valley, PA 18034-8447
Phone: 610-285-5035
E-mail: admissions-lv@psu.edu
Fax: 610-285-5220 **Website:** www.lv.psu.edu

This public school was founded in 1912. It has a 42 acre campus.

RATINGS
Admissions Selectivity Rating: 75   **Fire Safety Rating:** 60*   **Green Rating:** 60*

STUDENTS AND FACULTY
Enrollment: 773. **Student Body:** 48% female, 52% male, 3% out-of-state, <1% international. Asian 10%, African American 6%, Caucasian 64%, Hispanic 16%, Native American 0%, Pacific Islander <1%, Two or more races 2%, Race unknown 1%.
Retention and Graduation: 78% freshmen return for sophomore year.
Faculty: Student/faculty ratio 14:1. 43 full-time faculty, 60% hold PhDs, 9% are members of minority groups, 65% are women.

ACADEMICS
Degrees: Associate; Bachelor's; Certificate; Post-bachelor's certificate. **Classes:** Most classes have 10–19 students. Most lab/discussion sessions have 10–19 students. **Special Study Options:** Cooperative education program; Cross-registration; Distance learning; Double major; Dual enrollment; Honors program; Independent study; Internships; Liberal arts/career combination; Study abroad; Teacher certification program.

CAMPUS LIFE
Activities: Choral groups; Dance; Drama/theater; Literary magazine; Student government; Student newspaper; Student-run film society. **Athletics (Intercollegiate):** *Men:* basketball, cross-country, golf, soccer, tennis, volleyball. *Women:* basketball, golf, tennis, volleyball.

ADMISSIONS
Freshman Academic Profile: Average high school GPA 3.0. 8% in top 10% of high school class, 33% in top 25% of high school class, 69% in top 50% of high school class. **Test Scores:** SAT Math middle 50% range 450–580. SAT EBRW middle 50% range 440–560. ACT middle 50% range 19–27.
Basis for Candidate Selection: *Very important factors include:* academic GPA, standardized test scores. *Important factors include:* rigor of secondary school record. *Other factors include:* class rank, application essay, extracurricular activities, talent/ability, character/personal qualities, alumni/ae relation, geographical residence, state residency, volunteer work, work experience.
Freshman Admission Requirements: High school diploma is required and GED is accepted. *Academic units required:* 4 English, 3 math, 3 science, 2 foreign language, 3 social studies. *Academic units recommended:* 3 foreign language. **Freshman Admission Statistics:** 843 applied, 86% admitted, 29% enrolled. **Transfer Admission Requirements:** High school transcript, college transcript(s). Lowest grade transferable C. **General Admission Information:** Application fee $50. Priority deadline 11/30. Non-fall registration accepted. Admission may be deferred for a maximum of 1 year.

COSTS AND FINANCIAL AID
Annual in-state tuition $13,012. Annual out-of-state tuition $20,206. Required fees $952. **Required Forms and Deadlines:** FAFSA. **Types of Aid:** *Need-based scholarships/grants:* College/university scholarship or grant aid from institutional funds; Federal Pell; Private scholarships; SEOG; State scholarships/grants. *Loans:* Direct PLUS loans; Direct Subsidized Stafford Loans; Direct Unsubsidized Stafford Loans. **Financial Aid Statistics:** 76% needy freshmen, 80% needy undergrads receive need-based scholarship or grant aid. 44% freshmen, 29% undergrads receive non-need-based scholarship or grant aid. 69% freshmen, 79% undergrads receive need-based self-help aid. 0% freshmen, 0% undergrads receive athletic scholarships. 79% undergrads borrow to pay for school. Average cumulative indebtedness $35,803. **Criteria awarding aid:** *Need-based:* Academics, Alumni affiliation. *Non-need-based:* Academics, Alumni affiliation.

PENN STATE MONT ALTO

1 Campus Drive, Mont Alto, PA 17237-9703
Phone: 717-749-6130
E-mail: psuma@psu.edu
Fax: 717-749-6132 **Website:** http://www.montalto.psu.edu

This public school was founded in 1929. It has a 62 acre campus.

RATINGS
Admissions Selectivity Rating: 77   **Fire Safety Rating:** 60*   **Green Rating:** 60*

STUDENTS AND FACULTY
Enrollment: 809. **Student Body:** 58% female, 42% male, 12% out-of-state, <1% international. Asian 2%, African American 8%, Caucasian 80%, Hispanic 5%, Native American 0%, Pacific Islander <1%, Two or more races 3%, Race unknown 1%.
Retention and Graduation: 77% freshmen return for sophomore year. 22% grads go on to further study within 1 year. **Faculty:** Student/faculty ratio 11:1. 56 full-time faculty, 46% hold PhDs, 11% are members of minority groups, 52% are women.

ACADEMICS
Degrees: Associate; Bachelor's; Certificate. **Classes:** Most classes have 10–19 students. Most lab/discussion sessions have 10–19 students. **Special Study Options:** Accelerated program; Cross-registration; Distance learning; Double major; Dual enrollment; Honors program; Independent study; Internships; Liberal arts/career combination; Student-designed major; Study abroad; Weekend college. **Honors programs:** The Schreyer Honors College is widely recognized as one of the best and most comprehensive undergraduate honors programs in the United States. http://www.scholars.psu.edu/index.cfm.
Combined degree programs: BA/MD; BA/MEng. **Disability Services offered:** Note-taking services; Reader services; Tape recorders; Tutors.

FACILITIES
Housing: Coed dorms; Special housing for disabled students; 99% of campus accessible to physically disabled.

CAMPUS LIFE
Environment: Village. **Activities:** Choral groups; Dance; Drama/theater; Jazz band; Student government; Student newspaper. **Athletics (Intercollegiate):** *Men:* basketball, soccer, tennis. *Women:* basketball, tennis.

ADMISSIONS
Freshman Academic Profile: Average high school GPA 3.1. 6% in top 10% of high school class, 36% in top 25% of high school class, 77% in top 50% of high school class. **Test Scores:** SAT Math middle 50% range 425–535. SAT EBRW middle 50% range 420–530. ACT middle 50% range 17–24. **Basis for Candidate Selection:** *Very important factors include:* academic GPA, standardized test scores. *Important factors include:* rigor of secondary school record. *Other factors include:* class rank, application essay, extracurricular activities, talent/ability, character/personal qualities, alumni/ae relation, geographical residence, state residency, volunteer work, work experience. **Freshman Admission Requirements:** High school diploma is required and GED is accepted. *Academic units required:* 4 English, 3 math, 3 science, 2 foreign language, 3 social studies. *Academic units recommended:* 3 foreign language. **Freshman Admission Statistics:** 688 applied, 79% admitted, 45% enrolled. **Transfer Admission Requirements:** High school transcript, college transcript(s). Lowest grade transferable C. **General Admission Information:** Application fee $50. Priority deadline 11/30. Non-fall registration accepted. Admission may be deferred for a maximum of one year.

COSTS AND FINANCIAL AID
Annual in-state tuition $12,718. Annual out-of-state tuition $19,404. Room and board $10,920. Required fees $952. Average book and supplies expense $1,840. **Required Forms and Deadlines:** FAFSA. **Types of Aid:** *Need-based scholarships/grants:* College/university scholarship or grant aid from institutional funds; Federal Pell; Private scholarships; SEOG; State scholarships/grants. *Loans:* Direct PLUS loans; Direct Subsidized Stafford Loans; Direct Unsubsidized Stafford Loans. **Financial Aid Statistics:** 76% needy freshmen, 75% needy undergrads receive need-based scholarship or grant aid. 56% freshmen, 47% undergrads receive non-need-based scholarship or grant aid. 81% freshmen, 85% undergrads receive need-based self-help aid. 0% freshmen, 0% undergrads receive athletic scholarships. 87% undergrads borrow to pay for school. Average cumulative indebtedness $46,030. **Criteria awarding aid:** *Need-based:* Academics, Alumni affiliation, Minority status. *Non-need-based:* Academics, Alumni affiliation, Minority status.

PENN STATE NEW KENSINGTON

Office of Admissions, 3550 7th Street Rd, New Kensington, PA 15068-1765
Phone: (724)334-5466
E-mail: nkadmissions@psu.edu
Fax: (724)334-6111 **Website:** http://nk.psu.edu

This is a public school.

RATINGS
Admissions Selectivity Rating: 77   **Fire Safety Rating:** 60*   **Green Rating:** 60*

STUDENTS AND FACULTY
Enrollment: 598. **Student Body:** 41% female, 59% male, 2% out-of-state, 2% international. Asian 2%, African American 5%, Caucasian 87%, Hispanic 2%, Native American <1%, Pacific Islander 0%, Two or more races 1%, Race unknown 1%.
Retention and Graduation: 67% freshmen return for sophomore year. **Faculty:** Student/faculty ratio 12:1. 35 full-time faculty, 63% hold PhDs, 20% are members of minority groups, 43% are women.

ACADEMICS
Degrees: Associate; Bachelor's; Certificate. **Classes:** Most classes have 10–19 students. Most lab/discussion sessions have 10–19 students. **Special Study Options:** Cross-registration; Distance learning; Double major; Dual enrollment; External degree program; Honors program; Independent study; Internships; Study abroad.

CAMPUS LIFE
Activities: Dance; Drama/theater; Jazz band; Literary magazine; Musical theater; Student government; Student newspaper.

ADMISSIONS
Freshman Academic Profile: Average high school GPA 3.1. 10% in top 10% of high school class, 29% in top 25% of high school class, 68% in top 50% of high school class. **Test Scores:** SAT Math middle 50% range 440–550. SAT EBRW middle 50% range 440–530. ACT middle 50% range 19–23. **Basis for Candidate Selection:** *Very important factors include:* academic GPA, standardized test scores. *Important factors include:* rigor of secondary school record. *Other factors include:* class rank, application essay, extracurricular activities, talent/ability, character/personal qualities, alumni/ae relation, geographical residence, state residency, volunteer work, work experience, level of applicant's interest. **Freshman Admission Requirements:** High school diploma is required and GED is accepted. *Academic units required:* 4 English, 3 math, 3 science, 2 foreign language, 3 social studies. *Academic units recommended:* 3 foreign language. **Freshman Admission Statistics:** 508 applied, 79% admitted, 44% enrolled. **General Admission Information:** Application fee $50. Priority deadline 11/30. Non-fall registration accepted. Admission may be deferred for a maximum of one year.

COSTS AND FINANCIAL AID
Annual in-state tuition $12,718. Annual out-of-state tuition $19,404. Required fees $890. **Required Forms and Deadlines:** FAFSA. **Types of Aid:** *Need-based scholarships/grants:* College/university scholarship or grant aid from institutional funds; Federal Pell; Private scholarships; SEOG; State scholarships/grants. *Loans:* Direct PLUS loans; Direct Subsidized Stafford Loans; Direct Unsubsidized Stafford Loans. **Financial Aid Statistics:** 81% needy freshmen, 77% needy undergrads receive need-based scholarship or grant aid. 62% freshmen, 40% undergrads receive non-need-based scholarship or grant aid. 65% freshmen, 80% undergrads receive need-based self-help aid. 0% freshmen, 0% undergrads receive athletic scholarships. 93% undergrads borrow to pay for school. Average cumulative indebtedness $33,237. **Criteria awarding aid:** *Need-based:* Academics, Alumni affiliation. *Non-need-based:* Academics, Alumni affiliation.

PENN STATE SCHUYLKILL

200 University Drive, Schuylkill Haven, PA 17972-2208
Phone: 570-385-6252
E-mail: sl-admissions@psu.edu
Fax: 570-385-3672 **Website:** http://www.sl.psu.edu

This public school was founded in 1934. It has a 42 acre campus.

RATINGS
Admissions Selectivity Rating: 77   **Fire Safety Rating:** 60*   **Green Rating:** 60*

STUDENTS AND FACULTY
Enrollment: 720. **Student Body:** 60% female, 40% male, 12% out-of-state, 1% international. Asian 1%, African American 18%, Caucasian 69%, Hispanic 7%, Native American <1%, Pacific Islander <1%, Two or more races 1%, Race unknown 2%.
Retention and Graduation: 76% freshmen return for sophomore year.
Faculty: Student/faculty ratio 13:1. 43 full-time faculty, 77% hold PhDs, 2% are members of minority groups, 40% are women.

ACADEMICS
Degrees: Associate; Bachelor's; Certificate. **Classes:** Most classes have 10–19 students. Most lab/discussion sessions have 10–19 students. **Special Study Options:** Accelerated program; Distance learning; Double major; Dual enrollment; English as a Second Language (ESL); Honors program; Independent study; Internships; Study abroad.

FACILITIES
Housing: Apartments for single students; Special housing for disabled students; Theme housing.

CAMPUS LIFE
Activities: Campus Ministries; Choral groups; Dance; Drama/theater; International Student Organization; Musical theater; Radio station; Student government. **Athletics (Intercollegiate):** *Men:* basketball, cross-country, softball, tennis, volleyball. *Women:* basketball, cross-country, softball, tennis, volleyball.

ADMISSIONS
Freshman Academic Profile: Average high school GPA 2.9. 5% in top 10% of high school class, 24% in top 25% of high school class, 51% in top 50% of high school class. **Test Scores:** SAT Math middle 50% range 420–510. SAT EBRW middle 50% range 410–520. ACT middle 50% range 16–19.
Basis for Candidate Selection: *Very important factors include:* academic GPA, standardized test scores. *Important factors include:* rigor of secondary school record. *Other factors include:* class rank, application essay, extracurricular activities, talent/ability, character/personal qualities, alumni/ae relation, geographical residence, state residency, volunteer work, work experience.
Freshman Admission Requirements: High school diploma is required and GED is accepted. *Academic units required:* 4 English, 3 math, 3 science, 2 foreign language, 3 social studies. *Academic units recommended:* 3 foreign language. **Freshman Admission Statistics:** 690 applied, 73% admitted, 44% enrolled. **Transfer Admission Requirements:** High school transcript, college transcript(s). Lowest grade transferable C. **General Admission Information:** Application fee $50. Priority deadline 11/30. Non-fall registration accepted. Admission may be deferred for a maximum of 1 year.

COSTS AND FINANCIAL AID
Annual in-state tuition $13,012. Annual out-of-state tuition $20,206. Room and board $10,060. Required fees $890. Average book and supplies expense $1,840. **Required Forms and Deadlines:** FAFSA. **Types of Aid:** *Need-based scholarships/grants:* College/university scholarship or grant aid from institutional funds; Federal Pell; Private scholarships; SEOG; State scholarships/grants. *Loans:* Direct PLUS loans; Direct Subsidized Stafford Loans; Direct Unsubsidized Stafford Loans. **Financial Aid Statistics:** 79% needy freshmen, 83% needy undergrads receive need-based scholarship or grant aid. 78% freshmen, 57% undergrads receive non-need-based scholarship or grant aid. 84% freshmen, 88% undergrads receive need-based self-help aid. 0% freshmen, 0% undergrads receive athletic scholarships. 92% undergrads borrow to pay for school. Average cumulative indebtedness $38,822. **Criteria awarding aid:** *Need-based:* Academics, Alumni affiliation. *Non-need-based:* Academics, Alumni affiliation.

PENN STATE SCRANTON

120 Ridge View Drive, Dawson Building, Dunmore, PA 18512-1602
Phone: (570)963-2500
E-mail: wsadmissions@psu.edu
Fax: (570)963-2524 **Website:** http://worthingtonscranton.psu.edu/

This is a public school.

RATINGS
Admissions Selectivity Rating: 76   **Fire Safety Rating:** 60*   **Green Rating:** 60*

STUDENTS AND FACULTY
Enrollment: 967. **Student Body:** 53% female, 47% male, 1% out-of-state, <1% international. Asian 5%, African American 3%, Caucasian 81%, Hispanic 6%, Native American 0%, Pacific Islander 0%, Two or more races 2%, Race unknown 2%.
Retention and Graduation: 75% freshmen return for sophomore year.
Faculty: Student/faculty ratio 14:1. 50 full-time faculty, 64% hold PhDs, 10% are members of minority groups, 52% are women.

ACADEMICS
Degrees: Associate; Bachelor's; Certificate. **Classes:** Most classes have 20–29 students. Most lab/discussion sessions have 10–19 students. **Special Study Options:** Accelerated program; Cooperative education program; Cross-registration; Distance learning; Double major; Dual enrollment; Honors program; Independent study; Internships; Liberal arts/career combination; Study abroad.

FACILITIES
Housing: Apartments for single students; Coed dorms.

CAMPUS LIFE
Activities: Choral groups; Drama/theater; Jazz band; Literary magazine; Music ensembles; Student government; Student newspaper.

ADMISSIONS
Freshman Academic Profile: Average high school GPA 3.0. 10% in top 10% of high school class, 30% in top 25% of high school class, 70% in top 50% of high school class. **Test Scores:** SAT Math middle 50% range 430–540. SAT EBRW middle 50% range 420–530. ACT middle 50% range 17–21.
Basis for Candidate Selection: *Very important factors include:* academic GPA, standardized test scores. *Important factors include:* rigor of secondary school record. *Other factors include:* class rank, application essay, extracurricular activities, talent/ability, character/personal qualities, alumni/ae relation, geographical residence, state residency, volunteer work, work experience.
Freshman Admission Requirements: High school diploma is required and GED is accepted. *Academic units required:* 4 English, 3 math, 3 science, 2 foreign language, 3 social studies. *Academic units recommended:* 3 foreign language. **Freshman Admission Statistics:** 733 applied, 81% admitted, 39% enrolled. **General Admission Information:** Application fee $50. Priority deadline 11/30. Non-fall registration accepted. Admission may be deferred for a maximum of one year.

COSTS AND FINANCIAL AID
Annual in-state tuition $13,012. Annual out-of-state tuition $20,206. Required fees $890. **Required Forms and Deadlines:** FAFSA. **Types of Aid:** *Need-based scholarships/grants:* College/university scholarship or grant aid from institutional funds; Federal Pell; Private scholarships; SEOG; State scholarships/grants. *Loans:* Direct PLUS loans; Direct Subsidized Stafford Loans; Direct Unsubsidized Stafford Loans. **Financial Aid Statistics:** 76% needy freshmen, 80% needy undergrads receive need-based scholarship or grant aid. 33% freshmen, 24% undergrads receive non-need-based scholarship or grant aid. 76% freshmen, 84% undergrads receive need-based self-help aid. 0% freshmen, 0% undergrads receive athletic scholarships. 76% undergrads borrow to pay for school. Average cumulative indebtedness $42,128. **Criteria awarding aid:** *Need-based:* Academics, Alumni affiliation. *Non-need-based:* Academics, Alumni affiliation.

PENN STATE SHENANGO

147 Shenango Ave., Sharon, PA 16146-1597
Phone: (724)983-2803
E-mail: psushenango@psu.edu
Fax: (724)983-2820 **Website:** http://shenango.psu.edu

This is a public school.

RATINGS
Admissions Selectivity Rating: 82   Fire Safety Rating: 60*   Green Rating: 60*

STUDENTS AND FACULTY
Enrollment: 436. **Student Body:** 73% female, 27% male, 22% out-of-state, 0% international. Asian 1%, African American 7%, Caucasian 85%, Hispanic 2%, Native American 0%, Pacific Islander 0%, Two or more races 3%, Race unknown 3%.
Retention and Graduation: 66% freshmen return for sophomore year.
Faculty: Student/faculty ratio 11:1. 28 full-time faculty, 50% hold PhDs, 7% are members of minority groups, 68% are women.

ACADEMICS
Degrees: Associate; Bachelor's; Certificate. **Classes:** Most classes have 10–19 students. Most lab/discussion sessions have 10–19 students. **Special Study Options:** Accelerated program; Cross-registration; Distance learning; Double major; Dual enrollment; Honors program; Independent study; Internships; Student-designed major; Study abroad.

CAMPUS LIFE
Activities: Choral groups; Drama/theater; Student government.

ADMISSIONS
Freshman Academic Profile: Average high school GPA 3.0. 1% in top 10% of high school class, 35% in top 25% of high school class, 72% in top 50% of high school class. **Test Scores:** SAT Math middle 50% range 410–520. SAT EBRW middle 50% range 410–530. ACT middle 50% range 19–22.
Basis for Candidate Selection: *Very important factors include:* academic GPA, standardized test scores. *Important factors include:* rigor of secondary school record. *Other factors include:* class rank, application essay, extracurricular activities, talent/ability, character/personal qualities, alumni/ae relation, geographical residence, state residency, volunteer work, work experience.
Freshman Admission Requirements: High school diploma is required and GED is accepted. *Academic units required:* 4 English, 3 math, 3 science, 2 foreign language, 3 social studies. *Academic units recommended:* 3 foreign language. **Freshman Admission Statistics:** 154 applied, 68% admitted, 54% enrolled. **General Admission Information:** Application fee $50. Priority deadline 11/30. Non-fall registration accepted. Admission may be deferred for a maximum of one year.

COSTS AND FINANCIAL AID
Annual in-state tuition $12,474. Annual out-of-state tuition $19,030. Required fees $880. **Required Forms and Deadlines:** FAFSA. **Types of Aid:** *Need-based scholarships/grants:* College/university scholarship or grant aid from institutional funds; Federal Pell; Private scholarships; SEOG; State scholarships/grants. *Loans:* Direct PLUS loans; Direct Subsidized Stafford Loans; Direct Unsubsidized Stafford Loans. **Financial Aid Statistics:** 75% needy freshmen, 85% needy undergrads receive need-based scholarship or grant aid. 66% freshmen, 54% undergrads receive non-need-based scholarship or grant aid. 75% freshmen, 87% undergrads receive need-based self-help aid. 0% freshmen, 0% undergrads receive athletic scholarships. 80% undergrads borrow to pay for school. Average cumulative indebtedness $35,187. **Criteria awarding aid:** *Need-based:* Academics, Alumni affiliation. *Non-need-based:* Academics, Alumni affiliation.

PENN STATE UNIVERSITY PARK

201 Shields Building, University Park, PA 16802
Phone: 814-865-5471 **Financial Aid Phone:** 814-865-6301
E-mail: admissions@psu.edu **CEEB Code:** 2660
Fax: 814-863-7590 **Website:** www.psu.edu **ACT Code:** 3656

This public school was founded in 1855. It has a 7958 acre campus.

RATINGS
Admissions Selectivity Rating: 89   Fire Safety Rating: 98   Green Rating: 92

STUDENTS AND FACULTY
Enrollment: 40,385. **Student Body:** 47% female, 53% male, 34% out-of-state, 12% international (105 countries represented). Asian 6%, African American 4%, Caucasian 65%, Hispanic 7%, Native American <1%, Pacific Islander <1%, Two or more races 3%, Race unknown 2%.
Retention and Graduation: 94% freshmen return for sophomore year. 68% freshmen graduate within 4 years. 86% freshmen graduate within 6 years. 16% grads go on to further study within 1 year. **Faculty:** Student/faculty ratio 14:1. 2,988 full-time faculty, 75% hold PhDs, 18% are members of minority groups, 41% are women.

ACADEMICS
Degrees: Associate; Bachelor's; Certificate; Doctoral degree—professional practice; Doctoral degree research/scholarship; Master's; Post-bachelor's certificate. **Classes:** Most classes have 20–29 students. Most lab/discussion sessions have 20–29 students. **Most popular majors:** Computer and Information Sciences, General; Engineering, General. **Special Study Options:** Accelerated program; Cooperative education program; Cross-registration; Distance learning; Double major; Dual enrollment; English as a Second Language (ESL); Exchange student program (domestic); External degree program; Honors program; Independent study; Internships; Liberal arts/career combination; Student-designed major; Study abroad; Teacher certification program; Weekend college. **Honors programs:** The Schreyer Honors College is widely recognized as one of the best and most comprehensive undergraduate honors program in the United States. http://shc.psu.edu/. **Combined degree programs:** BA/MA; BA/MD; BA/MEng. **Disability Services offered:** Note-taking services; Reader services; Tape recorders. **Career services:** Alumni network; Alumni services; Career assessment; Career/job search classes; Internships; Regional alumni.

FACILITIES
Housing: Apartments for married students; Apartments for single students; Coed dorms; Fraternity/sorority housing; Special housing for disabled students; Women's dorms; 95% of campus accessible to physically disabled. **Special Academic Facilities/Equipment:** The EMS Museum & Art Gallery, Frost Entomological Museum, Matson Museum of Anthropology, Palmer Museum of Art, Pasto Agricultural Museum, All-Sports Museum, Special Collections Library Exhibit Gallery, the Arboretum at Penn State, and Shaver's Creek Environmental Center. In addition, the campus features theaters, language labs, a weather station, and a nuclear reactor.

CAMPUS LIFE
Environment: Town. **Activities:** Campus Ministries; Choral groups; Concert band; Dance; Drama/theater; International Student Organization; Jazz band; Literary magazine; Marching band; Model UN; Music ensembles; Musical theater; Opera; Pep band; Radio station; Student government; Student newspaper; Student-run film society; Symphony orchestra; Television station; Yearbook. 1004 registered organizations, 36 honor societies, 57 religious organizations, 44 fraternities, 47 sororities on campus. **Athletics (Intercollegiate):** *Men:* baseball, basketball, cheerleading, cross-country, diving, fencing, football, golf, gymnastics, lacrosse, soccer, swimming, tennis, track/field (outdoor), track/field (indoor), volleyball, wrestling. *Women:* basketball, cheerleading, cross-country, diving, fencing, field hockey, golf, gymnastics, lacrosse, soccer, softball, swimming, tennis, track/field (outdoor), track/field (indoor), volleyball. **On-Campus Highlights:** Hetzel Union Building. **Environmental Initiatives:** In 2014, Penn State joined the U.S. Department of Energy's Better Buildings Challenge and pledged to reduce its energy use in 28 million square feet of building space by 20 percent over the next decade. In 2018–19, Penn State established a 2MW solar photovoltaic system at the edge of the University Park campus that will support

education and research, as well as supplying a portion of the campus's electricity needs. In February 2019 Penn State announced a project to install 70MW of large-scale solar energy in southern PA; the project will provide 25 percent of the University's statewide electricity needs over the next 25 years.

ADMISSIONS

Test Scores: SAT Math middle 50% range 580–700. SAT EBRW middle 50% range 580–670. ACT middle 50% range 25–30. **Basis for Candidate Selection:** *Very important factors include:* academic GPA, standardized test scores. *Important factors include:* rigor of secondary school record. *Other factors include:* class rank, application essay, extracurricular activities, talent/ability, character/personal qualities, alumni/ae relation, geographical residence, state residency, racial/ethnic status, volunteer work, work experience. **Freshman Admission Requirements:** High school diploma is required and GED is accepted. *Academic units required:* 4 English, 3 math, 3 science, 2 foreign language, 3 social studies. *Academic units recommended:* 3 foreign language. **Freshman Admission Statistics:** 71,903 applied, 49% admitted, 24% enrolled. **Transfer Admission Requirements:** High school transcript, college transcript(s). Lowest grade transferable C. **General Admission Information:** Application fee $65. Non-fall registration accepted. Admission may be deferred for a maximum of one year.

COSTS AND FINANCIAL AID

Annual in-state tuition $17,416. Annual out-of-state tuition $34,480. Room and board $11,884. Required fees $1,034. Average book and supplies expense $1,840. **Required Forms and Deadlines:** FAFSA. **Types of Aid:** *Need-based scholarships/grants:* College/university scholarship or grant aid from institutional funds; Federal Pell; Private scholarships; SEOG; State scholarships/grants; United Negro College Fund. *Loans:* Direct PLUS loans; Direct Subsidized Stafford Loans; Direct Unsubsidized Stafford Loans. **Student Employment:** Federal Work-Study Program available. Institutional employment available. **Financial Aid Statistics:** 34% needy freshmen, 45% needy undergrads receive need-based scholarship or grant aid. 55% freshmen, 55% undergrads receive non-need-based scholarship or grant aid. 71% freshmen, 76% undergrads receive need-based self-help aid. 2% freshmen, 2% undergrads receive athletic scholarships. 63% freshmen, 62% undergrads receive any aid. 52% undergrads borrow to pay for school. Average cumulative indebtedness $40,128. **Criteria awarding aid:** *Need-based:* Academics, Alumni affiliation, Athletics. *Non-need-based:* Academics, Alumni affiliation, Athletics.

PENN STATE WILKES-BARRE

Murphy Center 125, Lehman, PA 18627-0217
Phone: 570-675-9238
E-mail: wbadmissions@psu.edu
Fax: 570-675-9113 **Website:** http://www.wb.psu.edu

This is a public school.

RATINGS

Admissions Selectivity Rating: 75   Fire Safety Rating: 60*   Green Rating: 60*

STUDENTS AND FACULTY

Enrollment: 460. **Student Body:** 33% female, 67% male, 5% out-of-state, <1% international. Asian 1%, African American 3%, Caucasian 88%, Hispanic 5%, Native American <1%, Pacific Islander 0%, Two or more races 2%, Race unknown 1%.
Retention and Graduation: 84% freshmen return for sophomore year.
Faculty: Student/faculty ratio 13:1. 30 full-time faculty, 63% hold PhDs, 23% are members of minority groups, 33% are women.

ACADEMICS

Degrees: Associate; Bachelor's; Certificate; Post-bachelor's certificate. **Classes:** Most classes have 10–19 students. **Special Study Options:** Accelerated program; Cross-registration; Distance learning; Double major; Dual enrollment; Honors program; Independent study; Internships; Student-designed major; Study abroad.

CAMPUS LIFE

Activities: Dance; Radio station; Student government; Student newspaper.

ADMISSIONS

Freshman Academic Profile: Average high school GPA 3.1. 8% in top 10% of high school class, 30% in top 25% of high school class, 74% in top 50% of high school class. **Test Scores:** SAT Math middle 50% range 440–550.

SAT EBRW middle 50% range 430–540. ACT middle 50% range 18–26.
Basis for Candidate Selection: *Very important factors include:* academic GPA, standardized test scores. *Important factors include:* rigor of secondary school record. *Other factors include:* class rank, application essay, extracurricular activities, talent/ability, character/personal qualities, alumni/ae relation, geographical residence, state residency, volunteer work, work experience. **Freshman Admission Requirements:** High school diploma is required and GED is accepted. *Academic units required:* 4 English, 3 math, 3 science, 2 foreign language, 3 social studies. *Academic units recommended:* 3 foreign language. **Freshman Admission Statistics:** 411 applied, 88% admitted, 40% enrolled. **General Admission Information:** Application fee $50. Priority deadline 11/30. Non-fall registration accepted. Admission may be deferred for a maximum of 1 year.

COSTS AND FINANCIAL AID

Annual in-state tuition $12,718. Annual out-of-state tuition $19,404. Required fees $880. **Required Forms and Deadlines:** FAFSA. **Types of Aid:** *Need-based scholarships/grants:* College/university scholarship or grant aid from institutional funds; Federal Pell; Private scholarships; SEOG; State scholarships/grants. *Loans:* Direct PLUS loans; Direct Subsidized Stafford Loans; Direct Unsubsidized Stafford Loans. **Financial Aid Statistics:** 69% needy freshmen, 74% needy undergrads receive need-based scholarship or grant aid. 55% freshmen, 44% undergrads receive non-need-based scholarship or grant aid. 80% freshmen, 79% undergrads receive need-based self-help aid. 0% freshmen, 0% undergrads receive athletic scholarships. 85% undergrads borrow to pay for school. Average cumulative indebtedness $38,387. **Criteria awarding aid:** *Need-based:* Academics, Alumni affiliation. *Non-need-based:* Academics, Alumni affiliation.

PENN STATE YORK

1031 Edgecomb Ave, Main Classroom Bldg, York, PA 17403-3398
Phone: (717)771-4040
E-mail: ykadmission@psu.edu
Fax: (717)771-4005 **Website:** http://www.yk.psu.edu

This is a public school.

RATINGS

Admissions Selectivity Rating: 75   Fire Safety Rating: 60*   Green Rating: 60*

STUDENTS AND FACULTY

Enrollment: 935. **Student Body:** 43% female, 57% male, 9% out-of-state, 15% international. Asian 5%, African American 6%, Caucasian 63%, Hispanic 6%, Native American <1%, Pacific Islander <1%, Two or more races 3%, Race unknown 2%.
Retention and Graduation: 80% freshmen return for sophomore year.
Faculty: Student/faculty ratio 15:1. 50 full-time faculty, 72% hold PhDs, 16% are members of minority groups, 48% are women.

ACADEMICS

Degrees: Associate; Bachelor's; Certificate; Master's; Post-bachelor's certificate. **Classes:** Most classes have 10–19 students. Most lab/discussion sessions have fewer than 10 students. **Special Study Options:** Accelerated program; Cross-registration; Distance learning; Double major; Dual enrollment; English as a Second Language (ESL); Honors program; Independent study; Internships; Study abroad; Weekend college.

CAMPUS LIFE

Activities: International Student Organization; Literary magazine; Student government.

ADMISSIONS

Freshman Academic Profile: Average high school GPA 3.1. 8% in top 10% of high school class, 27% in top 25% of high school class, 64% in top 50% of high school class. **Test Scores:** SAT Math middle 50% range 470–630. SAT EBRW middle 50% range 430–560. ACT middle 50% range 21–26.
Basis for Candidate Selection: *Very important factors include:* academic GPA, standardized test scores. *Important factors include:* rigor of secondary school record. *Other factors include:* class rank, application essay, extracurricular activities, talent/ability, character/personal qualities, alumni/ae relation, geographical residence, state residency, volunteer work, work experience. **Freshman Admission Requirements:** High school diploma is required and GED is accepted. *Academic units required:* 4 English, 3 math, 3 science, 2

foreign language, 3 social studies. *Academic units recommended:* 3 foreign language. **Freshman Admission Statistics:** 1,397 applied, 86% admitted, 27% enrolled. **General Admission Information:** Application fee $50. Priority deadline 11/30. Non-fall registration accepted. Admission may be deferred for a maximum of one year.

COSTS AND FINANCIAL AID

Annual in-state tuition $13,012. Annual out-of-state tuition $20,206. Required fees $952. **Required Forms and Deadlines:** FAFSA. **Types of Aid:** *Need-based scholarships/grants:* College/university scholarship or grant aid from institutional funds; Federal Pell; Private scholarships; SEOG; State scholarships/grants. *Loans:* Direct PLUS loans; Direct Subsidized Stafford Loans; Direct Unsubsidized Stafford Loans. **Financial Aid Statistics:** 78% needy freshmen, 79% needy undergrads receive need-based scholarship or grant aid. 53% freshmen, 48% undergrads receive non-need-based scholarship or grant aid. 82% freshmen, 82% undergrads receive need-based self-help aid. 0% freshmen, 0% undergrads receive athletic scholarships. 75% undergrads borrow to pay for school. Average cumulative indebtedness $39,770. **Criteria awarding aid:** *Need-based:* Academics, Alumni affiliation. *Non-need-based:* Academics, Alumni affiliation.

THE PENNSYLVANIA ACADEMY OF THE FINE ARTS

128 North Broad Street, Philadelphia, PA 19102
Phone: 215-972-7625 **Financial Aid Phone:** 215-972-2019
E-mail: admissions@pafa.edu
Fax: 215-972-0839 **Website:** www.pafa.edu

This private school was founded in 1804.

RATINGS

Admissions Selectivity Rating: 60*   **Fire Safety Rating:** 60*   **Green Rating:** 60*

STUDENTS AND FACULTY

Enrollment: 169. **Student Body:** 66% female, 34% male, 25% out-of-state, 5% international (19 countries represented). Asian 6%, African American 7%, Caucasian 59%, Hispanic 7%, Native American 1%, Pacific Islander 0%, Two or more races 4%, Race unknown 12%.
Faculty: Student/faculty ratio 13:1. 0% of classes are taught by teaching assistants.

ACADEMICS

Degrees: Bachelor's; Certificate; Master's; Post-bachelor's certificate. **Most popular majors:** Fine/Studio Arts, General; Painting. **Special Study Options:** Dual enrollment; Exchange student program (domestic); Independent study; Internships.

FACILITIES

Special Academic Facilities/Equipment: PAFA's museum is the first art museum in the country, and one of the most important collections of American Art in the world.

CAMPUS LIFE

Environment: Metropolis. **Activities:** Student government; Student-run film society. **On-Campus Highlights:** Museum of American Art.

ADMISSIONS

Transfer Admission Requirements: High school transcript, essay or personal statement. Lowest grade transferable C. **General Admission Information:** Application fee $60. Priority deadline 12/1. Regular application deadline 2/15.

COSTS AND FINANCIAL AID

Annual tuition $32,960. Room and board $10,815. Required fees $1,450. Average book and supplies expense $1,511. **Required Forms and Deadlines:** FAFSA. **Notification of Awards:** Applicants will be notified of awards on a rolling basis beginning 3/1. **Types of Aid:** *Need-based scholarships/grants:* College/university scholarship or grant aid from institutional funds; Federal Pell; Private scholarships; SEOG; State scholarships/grants. *Loans:* Direct PLUS loans; Direct Subsidized Stafford Loans; Direct Unsubsidized Stafford Loans. **Student Employment:** Federal Work-Study Program available. Institutional employment available. **Financial Aid Statistics:** 80% freshmen, 80% undergrads receive any aid. **Criteria awarding aid:** *Non-need-based:* Academics, Art.

PENNSYLVANIA COLLEGE OF TECHNOLOGY

One College Avenue, Williamsport, PA 17701
Phone: (570) 327-4761 **Financial Aid Phone:** 570-327-4761
E-mail: admissions@pct.edu
Fax: (570) 321-5551 **Website:** www.pct.edu

This public school was founded in 1989. It has a 994 acre campus.

RATINGS

Admissions Selectivity Rating: 64   **Fire Safety Rating:** 60*   **Green Rating:** 60*

STUDENTS AND FACULTY

Enrollment: 5,416. **Student Body:** 36% female, 64% male, 10% out-of-state. **Retention and Graduation:** 75% freshmen return for sophomore year. **Faculty:** Student/faculty ratio 18:1. 293 full-time faculty, 0% hold PhDs, 5% are members of minority groups, 31% are women. 0% of classes are taught by teaching assistants.

ACADEMICS

Degrees: Associate; Bachelor's; Certificate. **Classes:** Most classes have 10–19 students. **Special Study Options:** Accelerated program; Cooperative education program; Cross-registration; Distance learning; Dual enrollment; English as a Second Language (ESL); Exchange student program (domestic); Honors program; Independent study; Internships; Student-designed major; Study abroad; Weekend college. **Disability Services offered:** Note-taking services; Reader services; Tape recorders; Tutors. **Career services:** Alumni services; Career assessment; Career/job search classes.

FACILITIES

Housing: Apartments for single students; Coed dorms; Wellness housing; 100% of campus accessible to physically disabled.

CAMPUS LIFE

Environment: Town. **Activities:** Campus Ministries; Dance; International Student Organization; Student government. 56 registered organizations, 3 fraternities on campus. **Athletics (Intercollegiate):** *Men:* archery, baseball, basketball, bowling, cross-country, golf, soccer, tennis, volleyball. *Women:* archery, basketball, bowling, cross-country, golf, soccer, softball, tennis, volleyball. **On-Campus Highlights:** Academic Facilities and Labs.

ADMISSIONS

Freshman Academic Profile: 4% in top 10% of high school class, 16% in top 25% of high school class, 48% in top 50% of high school class. **Freshman Admission Requirements:** High school diploma is required and GED is accepted. **Freshman Admission Statistics:** 3,144 applied, 85% admitted, enrolled. **Transfer Admission Requirements:** High school transcript, college transcript(s). Minimum college GPA of 2.5 required. Lowest grade transferable C. **General Admission Information:** Application fee $50. Regular application deadline 7/1. Non-fall registration accepted. Admission may be deferred for a maximum of 1 year.

COSTS AND FINANCIAL AID

Annual in-state tuition $13,320. Annual out-of-state tuition $19,980. Room and board $11,108. Required fees $2,490. Average book and supplies expense $1,400. **Required Forms and Deadlines:** FAFSA; Institution's own financial aid form. **Notification of Awards:** Applicants will be notified of awards on a rolling basis beginning 6/1. **Types of Aid:** *Need-based scholarships/grants:* Federal Pell; Private scholarships; SEOG; State scholarships/grants. **Student Employment:** Federal Work-Study Program available. Institutional employment available.

PEPPERDINE UNIVERSITY

24255 Pacific Coast Highway, Malibu, CA 90263
Phone: 310-506-4392 **Financial Aid Phone:** 310.506.4301
E-mail: admission-seaver@pepperdine.edu **CEEB Code:** 4630
Fax: 310-506-4861 **Website:** www.pepperdine.edu **ACT Code:** 373

This private school, affiliated with the Church of Christ, was founded in 1937. It has a 830 acre campus.

RATINGS

Admissions Selectivity Rating: 93 **Fire Safety Rating:** 60* **Green Rating:** 78

STUDENTS AND FACULTY

Enrollment: 3,581. **Student Body:** 58% female, 42% male, 45% out-of-state, 12% international (78 countries represented). Asian 11%, African American 5%, Caucasian 49%, Hispanic 14%, Native American <1%, Pacific Islander <1%, Two or more races 7%, Race unknown 2%.
Retention and Graduation: 91% freshmen return for sophomore year. 79% freshmen graduate within 4 years. 86% freshmen graduate within 6 years.
Faculty: Student/faculty ratio 13:1. 400 full-time faculty, 86% hold PhDs, 21% are members of minority groups, 45% are women.

ACADEMICS

Degrees: Bachelor's; Doctoral degree—professional practice; Doctoral degree research/scholarship; Master's; Post-bachelor's certificate. **Classes:** Most classes have 10–19 students. Most lab/discussion sessions have 10–19 students.
Most popular majors: Business Administration and Management, General; Psychology, General; Biology/Biological Sciences, General. **Special Study Options:** Distance learning; Double major; Honors program; Independent study; Internships; Student-designed major; Study abroad; Teacher certification program. **Disability Services offered:** Note-taking services; Reader services; Tape recorders; Tutors. **Career services:** Alumni network; Alumni services; Career assessment; Career/job search classes; Internships; Regional alumni.

FACILITIES

Housing: Apartments for single students; Men's dorms; Special housing for disabled students; Women's dorms. **Campus Network:** 100% of classrooms, 100% of dorms, 100% of student union, 100% of libraries, 100% of dining areas, 90% of common outdoor areas have wireless network access.

CAMPUS LIFE

Environment: City. **Activities:** Campus Ministries; Choral groups; Dance; Drama/theater; International Student Organization; Jazz band; Literary magazine; Model UN; Music ensembles; Musical theater; Opera; Pep band; Radio station; Student government; Student newspaper; Symphony orchestra; Television station. 87 registered organizations, 13 honor societies, 5 religious organizations, 5 fraternities, 8 sororities on campus. **Athletics (Intercollegiate):** *Men:* baseball, basketball, cross-country, golf, tennis, volleyball, water polo. *Women:* basketball, cheerleading, cross-country, golf, soccer, swimming, tennis, track/field (outdoor), volleyball. **On-Campus Highlights:** Weisman Art Museum. **Environmental Initiatives:** Pepperdine University has conserved billions of gallons of drinking water annually dating back to 1972. Pepperdine uses recycled water to irrigate over 99% of the University's managed grounds. The University carefully monitors irrigation practices and uses an automated irrigation program based upon historical trends and current climactic conditions to conserve water and reduce runoff.

ADMISSIONS

Freshman Academic Profile: Average high school GPA 3.7. 46% in top 10% of high school class, 77% in top 25% of high school class, 97% in top 50% of high school class. **Test Scores:** SAT Math middle 50% range 620–750. SAT EBRW middle 50% range 610–700. ACT middle 50% range 27–32. **Basis for Candidate Selection:** *Very important factors include:* rigor of secondary school record, academic GPA, application essay, extracurricular activities, talent/ability, character/personal qualities, religious affiliation/commitment. *Important factors include:* standardized test scores, recommendation(s), volunteer work. *Other factors include:* first generation, alumni/ae relation, racial/ethnic status, work experience. **Freshman Admission Requirements:** High school diploma is required and GED is accepted. **Freshman Admission Statistics:** 12,764

applied, 32% admitted, 18% enrolled. **Transfer Admission Requirements:** High school transcript, college transcript(s), essay or personal statement. Minimum college GPA of 3.00 required. Lowest grade transferable C. **General Admission Information:** Application fee $65. Regular application deadline 1/15. Non-fall registration accepted.

COSTS AND FINANCIAL AID

Required Forms and Deadlines: FAFSA. **Notification of Awards:** Applicants will be notified of awards on or about 4/5. **Types of Aid:** *Need-based scholarships/grants:* College/university scholarship or grant aid from institutional funds; Federal Pell; Private scholarships; SEOG; State scholarships/grants; United Negro College Fund. *Loans:* Direct PLUS loans; Direct Subsidized Stafford Loans; Direct Unsubsidized Stafford Loans. **Student Employment:** Federal Work-Study Program available. Institutional employment available. **Financial Aid Statistics:** 100% needy freshmen, 99% needy undergrads receive need-based scholarship or grant aid. 0% freshmen, 0% undergrads receive non-need-based scholarship or grant aid. 73% freshmen, 72% undergrads receive need-based self-help aid. 6% freshmen, 4% undergrads receive athletic scholarships. 91% freshmen, 88% undergrads receive any aid. 52% undergrads borrow to pay for school. Average cumulative indebtedness $34,711. **Criteria awarding aid:** *Need-based:* Alumni affiliation, Job skills, Minority status. *Non-need-based:* Academics, Art, Athletics, Leadership, Music/drama, Religious affiliation.

PIEDMONT COLLEGE

P.O. Box 10, Demorest, GA 30535
Phone: 706-776-0103 **Financial Aid Phone:** 706-778-3000
E-mail: ugrad@piedmont.edu **CEEB Code:** 5537
Fax: 706-776-6635 **Website:** www.piedmont.edu **ACT Code:** 853

This private school, affiliated with the National Association of Congregational Christian Churches and United Church of Christ, was founded in 1897. It has a 186 acre campus.

RATINGS

Admissions Selectivity Rating: 85 **Fire Safety Rating:** 60* **Green Rating:** 60*

STUDENTS AND FACULTY

Enrollment: 1,284. **Student Body:** 66% female, 34% male, 9% out-of-state, 1% international (4 countries represented). Asian 1%, African American 9%, Caucasian 71%, Hispanic 5%, Native American <1%, Pacific Islander <1%, Two or more races 2%, Race unknown 10%.
Retention and Graduation: 63% freshmen return for sophomore year.
Faculty: Student/faculty ratio 11:1. 128 full-time faculty, 74% hold PhDs, 0% are members of minority groups, 55% are women. 0% of classes are taught by teaching assistants.

ACADEMICS

Degrees: Bachelor's; Doctoral degree research/scholarship; Master's; Post-master's certificate. **Classes:** Most classes have fewer than 10 students. Most lab/discussion sessions have 10–19 students. **Most popular majors:** Business/Commerce, General; Nursing Practice; Elementary Education and Teaching. **Special Study Options:** Accelerated program; Distance learning; Double major; Dual enrollment; Honors program; Independent study; Internships; Student-designed major; Study abroad; Teacher certification program. **Career services:** Alumni network; Career assessment; Career/job search classes; Regional alumni.

FACILITIES

Housing: Apartments for single students; Coed dorms; Men's dorms; Special housing for disabled students; Women's dorms; 98% of campus accessible to physically disabled. **Special Academic Facilities/Equipment:** Art Gallery; Swanson Center, Johnny Mize Athletic Center, Student Commons. **Campus Network:** 100% of classrooms, 100% of dorms, 100% of student union, 100% of libraries, 100% of dining areas have wireless network access.

CAMPUS LIFE

Environment: Rural. **Activities:** Campus Ministries; Choral groups; Concert band; Drama/theater; Music ensembles; Musical theater; Opera; Pep band; Radio station; Student government; Student newspaper; Student-run film society; Television station; Yearbook. 40 registered organizations, 7 honor societies, 1 religious organization on campus. **Athletics (Intercollegiate):** *Men:* baseball, basketball, cross-country, golf, soccer, tennis. *Women:* basketball, cross-country, golf, soccer, softball, tennis, volleyball. **On-Campus Highlights:** Johnny Mize Athletic Center.

ADMISSIONS

Freshman Academic Profile: Average high school GPA 3.4. **Test Scores:** SAT Math middle 50% range 440–550. SAT EBRW middle 50% range 430–550. ACT middle 50% range 19–24. **Basis for Candidate Selection:** *Very important factors include:* rigor of secondary school record, academic GPA, standardized test scores. *Important factors include:* class rank, application essay, recommendation(s), interview, extracurricular activities, talent/ability, character/personal qualities, first generation. *Other factors include:* alumni/ae relation, geographical residence, state residency, volunteer work, work experience, level of applicant's interest. **Freshman Admission Requirements:** High school diploma is required and GED is accepted. *Academic units recommended:* 4 English, 4 math, 4 science, 2 foreign language, 1 social studies, 2 history. **Freshman Admission Statistics:** 1,135 applied, 57% admitted, 43% enrolled. **Transfer Admission Requirements:** College transcript(s), statement of good standing from prior institution(s). Minimum college GPA of 2.0 required. Lowest grade transferable C. **General Admission Information:** Regular application deadline 7/1. Non-fall registration accepted.

COSTS AND FINANCIAL AID

Annual tuition $21,990. Room and board $9,050. Average book and supplies expense $1,400. **Required Forms and Deadlines:** FAFSA; Institution's own financial aid form; State aid form. **Notification of Awards:** Applicants will be notified of awards on a rolling basis beginning 2/1. **Types of Aid:** *Need-based scholarships/grants:* College/university scholarship or grant aid from institutional funds; Federal Pell; Private scholarships; SEOG; State scholarships/grants. *Loans:* Direct PLUS loans; Direct Subsidized Stafford Loans; Direct Unsubsidized Stafford Loans. **Student Employment:** Federal Work-Study Program available. Institutional employment available. **Financial Aid Statistics:** 100% needy freshmen, 100% needy undergrads receive need-based scholarship or grant aid. 19% freshmen, 12% undergrads receive non-need-based scholarship or grant aid. 56% freshmen, 73% undergrads receive need-based self-help aid. 0% freshmen, 0% undergrads receive athletic scholarships. 99% freshmen, 99% undergrads receive any aid. 80% undergrads borrow to pay for school. Average cumulative indebtedness $29,289. **Criteria awarding aid:** *Need-based:* Academics, Leadership. *Non-need-based:* Academics, Alumni affiliation, Art, Leadership, Music/drama, Religious affiliation, State/district residency.

PITTSBURG STATE UNIVERSITY

1701 South Broadway, Pittsburg, KS 66762
Phone: 620-235-4251 **Financial Aid Phone:** 800-854-7488
CEEB Code: 6336
Fax: 620-235-6003 **Website:** www.pittstate.edu **ACT Code:** 1449

This public school was founded in 1903. It has a 630 acre campus.

RATINGS

Admissions Selectivity Rating: 75   **Fire Safety Rating:** 91   **Green Rating:** 60*

STUDENTS AND FACULTY

Enrollment: 5,067. **Student Body:** 48% female, 52% male, 29% out-of-state, 2% international (42 countries represented). Asian 1%, African American 4%, Caucasian 79%, Hispanic 6%, Native American 1%, Pacific Islander <1%, Two or more races 7%, Race unknown <1%.
Retention and Graduation: 75% freshmen return for sophomore year. 47% freshmen graduate within 6 years. **Faculty:** Student/faculty ratio 16:1. 308 full-time faculty, 10% are members of minority groups, 45% are women. 2% of classes are taught by teaching assistants.

ACADEMICS

Degrees: Associate; Bachelor's; Certificate; Doctoral degree—professional practice; Master's; Post-bachelor's certificate; Post-master's certificate. **Classes:** Most classes have 10–19 students. Most lab/discussion sessions have 10–19 students. **Most popular majors:** Education, General; Business Administration and Management, General; Engineering/Engineering-related Technologies/Technicians. **Special Study Options:** Accelerated program; Cooperative education program; Distance learning; Double major; Dual enrollment; Honors program; Independent study; Internships; Student-designed major; Study abroad; Teacher certification program. **Honors programs:** Honors College. **Disability Services offered:** Note-taking services; Reader services; Tape recorders; Tutors. **Career services:** Alumni services; Career assessment; Career/job search classes; Internships.

FACILITIES

Housing: Apartments for married students; Coed dorms; Special housing for disabled students; Theme housing; Wellness housing; 90% of campus accessible to physically disabled. **Special Academic Facilities/Equipment:** Planetarium, observatory, field biology reserve, nature reach, herbarium, technology center, mammal collection, greenhouse, art gallery, polymer research center, cadaver lab, Veterans Memorial Amphitheater, broadcasting lab, public radio station.

CAMPUS LIFE

Environment: Village. **Activities:** Campus Ministries; Choral groups; Dance; Drama/theater; International Student Organization; Literary magazine; Marching band; Music ensembles; Musical theater; Opera; Radio station; Student government; Student newspaper; Symphony orchestra; Television station; Yearbook. 150 registered organizations, 19 honor societies, 5 religious organizations, 7 fraternities, 3 sororities on campus. **Athletics (Intercollegiate):** *Men:* baseball, basketball, cheerleading, cross-country, football, golf, track/field (outdoor), track/field (indoor). *Women:* basketball, cheerleading, cross-country, softball, track/field (outdoor), track/field (indoor), volleyball. **On-Campus Highlights:** Planetarium. **Environmental Initiatives:** Addition of Sustainability as a goal in the university strategic plan.

ADMISSIONS

Freshman Academic Profile: Average high school GPA 3.4. 16% in top 10% of high school class, 21% in top 25% of high school class, 34% in top 50% of high school class. **Test Scores:** ACT middle 50% range 18–24. **Basis for Candidate Selection:** *Very important factors include:* rigor of secondary school record, class rank, academic GPA, standardized test scores. **Freshman Admission Requirements:** High school diploma is required and GED is accepted. *Academic units required:* 4 English, 4 math, 3 science, 3 social studies, 3 academic electives. **Freshman Admission Statistics:** 2,418 applied, 90% admitted, 44% enrolled. **Transfer Admission Requirements:** College transcript(s). Minimum college GPA of 2.0 required. Lowest grade transferable D. **General Admission Information:** Application fee $30. Non-fall registration accepted. Admission may be deferred for a maximum of 3 semesters.

COSTS AND FINANCIAL AID

Annual in-state tuition $5,694. Annual out-of-state tuition $17,038. Required fees $1,644. Average book and supplies expense $1,000. **Required Forms and Deadlines:** CSS/Financial Aid PROFILE; FAFSA. **Notification of Awards:** Applicants will be notified of awards on a rolling basis beginning 3/1. **Types of Aid:** *Need-based scholarships/grants:* College/university scholarship or grant aid from institutional funds; Federal Nursing Scholarships; Federal Pell; Private scholarships; SEOG; State scholarships/grants. *Loans:* Direct PLUS loans; Direct Subsidized Stafford Loans; Direct Unsubsidized Stafford Loans. **Student Employment:** Federal Work-Study Program available. Institutional employment available. **Financial Aid Statistics:** 0% freshmen, 0% undergrads receive athletic scholarships. 91% freshmen, 85% undergrads receive any aid. 64% undergrads borrow to pay for school. Average cumulative indebtedness $24,198. **Criteria awarding aid:** *Non-need-based:* Academics, Alumni affiliation, Art, Athletics, Leadership, Minority status, Music/drama.

PITZER COLLEGE

1050 North Mills Avenue, Claremont, CA 91711-6101
Phone: 909-621-8129 **Financial Aid Phone:** 909-621-8208
E-mail: admission@pitzer.edu **CEEB Code:** 4619
Fax: 909-621-8770 **Website:** www.pitzer.edu **ACT Code:** 363

This private school was founded in 1963. It has a 35 acre campus.

RATINGS

Admissions Selectivity Rating: 97   **Fire Safety Rating:** 60*   **Green Rating:** 99

STUDENTS AND FACULTY

Enrollment: 1,074. **Student Body:** 54% female, 46% male, 55% out-of-state, 9% international (33 countries represented). Asian 10%, African American 6%, Caucasian 47%, Hispanic 15%, Native American <1%, Pacific Islander <1%, Two or more races 7%, Race unknown 5%.
Retention and Graduation: 95% freshmen return for sophomore year. 76% freshmen graduate within 4 years. 83% freshmen graduate within 6 years.

Faculty: Student/faculty ratio 11:1. 82 full-time faculty, 100% hold PhDs, 46% are members of minority groups, 55% are women. 0% of classes are taught by teaching assistants.

ACADEMICS

Degrees: Bachelor's. **Classes:** Most classes have 10–19 students. **Most popular majors:** Political Science and Government, General; Biological and Physical Sciences; Psychology, General. **Special Study Options:** Cooperative education program; Cross-registration; Double major; English as a Second Language (ESL); Exchange student program (domestic); Honors program; Independent study; Internships; Liberal arts/career combination; Student-designed major; Study abroad. **Combined degree programs:** BA/MA. **Disability Services offered:** Note-taking services; Reader services; Tape recorders; Tutors. **Career services:** Alumni network; Career assessment; Career/job search classes; Internships.

FACILITIES

Housing: Coed dorms; Special housing for disabled students; 95% of campus accessible to physically disabled. **Special Academic Facilities/Equipment:** Theatre arts center; Black, Asian American and Chicano Study centers; film, TV, and videotape studios; arboretum; biological field station; student health services, Gold Student Center. **Campus Network:** 100% of classrooms, 100% of dorms, 100% of student union, 100% of libraries, 100% of dining areas have wireless network access.

CAMPUS LIFE

Environment: Town. **Activities:** Campus Ministries; Choral groups; Dance; Drama/theater; International Student Organization; Literary magazine; Model UN; Music ensembles; Musical theater; Radio station; Student government; Student newspaper; Student-run film society; Symphony orchestra. 120 registered organizations, 1 honor society on campus. **Athletics (Intercollegiate): Men:** baseball, basketball, cross-country, diving, football, golf, soccer, swimming, tennis, track/field (outdoor), water polo. **Women:** basketball, cross-country, diving, soccer, softball, swimming, tennis, track/field (outdoor), volleyball, water polo. **On-Campus Highlights:** Grove House. **Environmental Initiatives:** New 'Green' dorms.

ADMISSIONS

Freshman Academic Profile: Average high school GPA 3.9. 63% in top 10% of high school class, 88% in top 25% of high school class, 100% in top 50% of high school class. **Test Scores:** SAT Math middle 50% range 670–750. SAT EBRW middle 50% range 640–740. ACT middle 50% range 29–32. **Basis for Candidate Selection:** *Very important factors include:* rigor of secondary school record, academic GPA, application essay, character/personal qualities. *Important factors include:* recommendation(s), extracurricular activities, talent/ability. *Other factors include:* class rank, standardized test scores, interview, first generation, alumni/ae relation, geographical residence, state residency, racial/ethnic status, work experience, level of applicant's interest. **Freshman Admission Requirements:** High school diploma is required and GED is accepted. *Academic units recommended:* 4 English, 3 math, 3 science, 3 foreign language, 3 social studies. **Freshman Admission Statistics:** 3,753 applied, 16% admitted, 43% enrolled. **Transfer Admission Requirements:** College transcript(s), essay or personal statement, statement of good standing from prior institution(s). Minimum college GPA of 2.0 required. Lowest grade transferable C-. **General Admission Information:** Application fee $70. Regular application deadline 1/1. Admission may be deferred for a maximum of 1 year.

COSTS AND FINANCIAL AID

Annual tuition $55,734. Room and board $17,432. Required fees $284. Average book and supplies expense $1,000. **Required Forms and Deadlines:** Business/Farm Supplement; CSS/Financial Aid PROFILE; FAFSA; Institution's own financial aid form; Noncustodial PROFILE; State aid form. **Notification of Awards:** Applicants will be notified of awards on or about 3/15. **Types of Aid:** *Need-based scholarships/grants:* College/university scholarship or grant aid from institutional funds; Federal Pell; Private scholarships; SEOG; State scholarships/grants. *Loans:* Direct PLUS loans; Direct Subsidized Stafford Loans; Direct Unsubsidized Stafford Loans. **Student Employment:** Federal Work-Study Program available. Institutional employment available. **Financial Aid Statistics:** 97% needy freshmen, 98% needy undergrads receive need-based scholarship or grant aid. 2% freshmen, 1% undergrads receive non-need-based scholarship or grant aid. 92% freshmen, 88% undergrads receive need-based self-help aid. 0% freshmen, 0% undergrads receive athletic scholarships. 38.5% freshmen, 37% undergrads receive any aid. 40% undergrads borrow to pay for school. Average cumulative indebtedness $17,848. **Criteria awarding aid:** *Need-based:* Academics, Art, Leadership, Minority status, Music/drama. *Non-need-based:* Academics, Leadership.

PLYMOUTH STATE UNIVERSITY

17 High Street, Plymouth, NH 03264
Phone: 603-535-2237 **Financial Aid Phone:** 877-846-5755
E-mail: plymouthadmit@plymouth.edu **CEEB Code:** 3690
Fax: 603-535-2714 **Website:** www.plymouth.edu **ACT Code:** 2518

This public school was founded in 1871. It has a 170 acre campus.

RATINGS
Admissions Selectivity Rating: 75 **Fire Safety Rating:** 92 **Green Rating:** 60*

STUDENTS AND FACULTY
Enrollment: 4,135. **Student Body:** 50% female, 50% male, 53% out-of-state, 1% international (19 countries represented). Asian 2%, African American 2%, Caucasian 83%, Hispanic 3%, Native American <1%, Pacific Islander <1%, Two or more races 2%, Race unknown 6%.
Retention and Graduation: 70% freshmen return for sophomore year. 44% freshmen graduate within 4 years. 57% freshmen graduate within 6 years.
Faculty: Student/faculty ratio 17:1. 199 full-time faculty, 72% hold PhDs, 12% are members of minority groups, 52% are women. 0% of classes are taught by teaching assistants.

ACADEMICS
Degrees: Bachelor's; Certificate; Doctoral degree—professional practice; Doctoral degree research/scholarship; Master's; Post-bachelor's certificate; Post-master's certificate. **Classes:** Most classes have 10–19 students. Most lab/discussion sessions have 20–29 students. **Most popular majors:** Sports, Kinesiology, and Physical Education/Fitness, General; Health Professions And Related Programs. **Special Study Options:** Cross-registration; Distance learning; Double major; Exchange student program (domestic); Honors program; Independent study; Internships; Student-designed major; Study abroad; Teacher certification program. **Honors programs:** University Honors Program, Business Honors, Psychology Honors. **Disability Services offered:** Note-taking services; Reader services; Tape recorders; Tutors. **Career services:** Alumni network; Alumni services; Career assessment; Career/job search classes; Internships; Regional alumni.

FACILITIES
Housing: Apartments for married students; Apartments for single students; Coed dorms; Special housing for disabled students; Theme housing. **Special Academic Facilities/Equipment:** Karl Drerup Art gallery, Silver Cultural Arts Center, Sylvestre Planetarium, Child Development and Family Center (NAEYC-accredited lab school for children 2–6 years old), meteorology lab, Geographic Information System lab, psychology lab, graphic design computer lab, Museum of the White Mountains, Indoor track, Outdoor center, Ice Arena, AllWell Center.

CAMPUS LIFE
Environment: Village. **Activities:** Campus Ministries; Choral groups; Concert band; Dance; Drama/theater; International Student Organization; Jazz band; Literary magazine; Model UN; Music ensembles; Musical theater; Pep band; Radio station; Student government; Student newspaper; Student-run film society; Yearbook. 86 registered organizations, 15 honor societies, 4 religious organizations, 3 sororities on campus. **Athletics (Intercollegiate): Men:** baseball, basketball, football, ice hockey, lacrosse, skiing (downhill/Alpine), soccer, wrestling. **Women:** basketball, cheerleading, diving, field hockey, ice hockey, lacrosse, skiing (downhill/Alpine), soccer, softball, swimming, tennis, volleyball. **On-Campus Highlights:** Hartman Union Building. **Environmental Initiatives:** New degree program.

ADMISSIONS
Freshman Academic Profile: Average high school GPA 3.0. 4% in top 10% of high school class, 17% in top 25% of high school class, 47% in top 50% of high school class. 83% from public high schools. **Test Scores:** SAT Math middle 50% range 398–592. SAT EBRW middle 50% range 417–611. ACT middle 50% range 17–28. **Basis for Candidate Selection:** *Very important factors include:* rigor of secondary school record. *Important factors include:* academic GPA, extracurricular activities. *Other factors include:* application essay, recommendation(s), talent/ability, character/personal qualities, volunteer work, work experience. **Freshman Admission Requirements:** High school diploma is required and GED is accepted. *Academic units required:* 4 English, 3 math, 3 science, 1 science lab, 3 social studies. *Academic units recommended:* 2 foreign language. **Freshman Admission Statistics:** 6,646 applied, 82% admitted, 20% enrolled. **Transfer Admission Requirements:** High school transcript, college

transcript(s). Minimum college GPA of 2.0 required. Lowest grade transferable C. **General Admission Information:** Application fee $50. Priority deadline 4/1. Non-fall registration accepted. Admission may be deferred for a maximum of 1 year.

COSTS AND FINANCIAL AID
Annual in-state tuition $11,580. Annual out-of-state tuition $20,250. Room and board $11,100. Required fees $2,519. Average book and supplies expense $1,286. **Required Forms and Deadlines:** FAFSA. **Notification of Awards:** Applicants will be notified of awards on a rolling basis beginning 11/30. **Types of Aid:** *Need-based scholarships/grants:* College/university scholarship or grant aid from institutional funds; Federal Pell; Private scholarships; SEOG; State scholarships/grants. *Loans:* Direct PLUS loans; Direct Subsidized Stafford Loans; Direct Unsubsidized Stafford Loans. **Student Employment:** Federal Work-Study Program available. Institutional employment available. **Financial Aid Statistics:** 99% needy freshmen, 95% needy undergrads receive need-based scholarship or grant aid. 30% freshmen, 18% undergrads receive non-need-based scholarship or grant aid. 92% freshmen, 94% undergrads receive need-based self-help aid. 0% freshmen, 0% undergrads receive athletic scholarships. 99% freshmen, 95% undergrads receive any aid. 86% undergrads borrow to pay for school. Average cumulative indebtedness $36,932. **Criteria awarding aid:** *Non-need-based:* Academics, Alumni affiliation, Art, Leadership, Music/drama.

POINT LOMA NAZARENE UNIVERSITY

3900 Lomaland Drive, San Diego, CA 92106
Phone: 800-733-7779 **Financial Aid Phone:** 619-849-2538
E-mail: admissions@pointloma.edu **CEEB Code:** 4605
Fax: 619-849-2601 **ACT Code:** 370

This private school, affiliated with the Nazarene Church, was founded in 1902. It has a 90 acre campus.

RATINGS
Admissions Selectivity Rating: 85   Fire Safety Rating: 75   Green Rating: 60*

STUDENTS AND FACULTY
Enrollment: 3,184. **Student Body:** 65% female, 35% male, 17% out-of-state, 1% international (23 countries represented). Asian 7%, African American 2%, Caucasian 52%, Hispanic 27%, Native American <1%, Pacific Islander 1%, Two or more races 8%, Race unknown 2%.
Retention and Graduation: 85% freshmen return for sophomore year. 64% freshmen graduate within 4 years. 74% freshmen graduate within 6 years.
Faculty: Student/faculty ratio 14:1. 148 full-time faculty, 82% hold PhDs, 21% are members of minority groups, 47% are women. 0% of classes are taught by teaching assistants.

ACADEMICS
Degrees: Bachelor's; Doctoral degree—professional practice; Master's; Post-master's certificate. **Classes:** Most classes have 10–19 students. Most lab/discussion sessions have 20–29 students. **Special Study Options:** Accelerated program; Distance learning; Double major; External degree program; Honors program; Independent study; Internships; Study abroad; Teacher certification program. **Honors programs:** Honors Scholars Program. **Disability Services offered:** Note-taking services; Reader services; Tape recorders; Tutors. **Career services:** Alumni network; Alumni services; Career assessment; Career/job search classes; Internships; Regional alumni.

FACILITIES
Housing: Apartments for single students; Men's dorms; Special housing for disabled students; Women's dorms; 100% of campus accessible to physically disabled. **Special Academic Facilities/Equipment:** Language lab, on-campus preschool, electron microscope.

CAMPUS LIFE
Environment: Metropolis. **Activities:** Campus Ministries; Choral groups; Concert band; Drama/theater; International Student Organization; Jazz band; Literary magazine; Music ensembles; Musical theater; Opera; Radio station; Student government; Student newspaper; Student-run film society; Symphony orchestra; Television station; Yearbook. 30 registered organizations, 2 honor societies, 7 religious organizations on campus. **Athletics (Intercollegiate):** *Men:* baseball, basketball, cross-country, golf, soccer, tennis, track/field (outdoor). *Women:* basketball, cross-country, softball, tennis, track/field (outdoor), volleyball. **On-Campus Highlights:** ARC (student rec center).

ADMISSIONS
Freshman Academic Profile: Average high school GPA 3.9. 39% in top 10% of high school class, 70% in top 25% of high school class, 91% in top 50% of high school class. **Test Scores:** SAT Math middle 50% range 560–650. SAT EBRW middle 50% range 580–650. ACT middle 50% range 24–29. **Basis for Candidate Selection:** *Very important factors include:* rigor of secondary school record, academic GPA, standardized test scores, character/personal qualities, religious affiliation/commitment. *Important factors include:* application essay, recommendation(s), interview. *Other factors include:* extracurricular activities, talent/ability, first generation, alumni/ae relation, geographical residence, state residency, level of applicant's interest. **Freshman Admission Requirements:** High school diploma is required and GED is accepted. *Academic units recommended:* 4 English, 3 math, 3 science, 2 science labs, 2 foreign language, 2 social studies, 1 history. **Freshman Admission Statistics:** 3,473 applied, 69% admitted, 27% enrolled. **Transfer Admission Requirements:** College transcript(s), essay or personal statement, interview. Minimum college GPA of 2.0 required. Lowest grade transferable D. **General Admission Information:** Application fee $55. Priority deadline 2/15. Regular application deadline 2/15.

COSTS AND FINANCIAL AID
Annual tuition $35,100. Room and board $10,450. Required fees $600. Average book and supplies expense $1,918. **Required Forms and Deadlines:** FAFSA. **Notification of Awards:** Applicants will be notified of awards on a rolling basis beginning 12/15. **Types of Aid:** *Need-based scholarships/grants:* College/university scholarship or grant aid from institutional funds; Federal Nursing Scholarships; Federal Pell; Private scholarships; SEOG; State scholarships/grants. *Loans:* Direct PLUS loans; Direct Subsidized Stafford Loans; Direct Unsubsidized Stafford Loans. **Financial Aid Statistics:** 99% needy freshmen, 97% needy undergrads receive need-based scholarship or grant aid. 15% freshmen, 9% undergrads receive non-need-based scholarship or grant aid. 83% freshmen, 89% undergrads receive need-based self-help aid. 4% freshmen, 3% undergrads receive athletic scholarships. 69% undergrads borrow to pay for school. Average cumulative indebtedness $34,653. **Criteria awarding aid:** *Need-based:* Academics, Alumni affiliation, Leadership, Minority status, Religious affiliation. *Non-need-based:* Academics, Art, Athletics, Job skills, Music/drama, Religious affiliation.

POINT PARK UNIVERSITY

201 Wood Street, Pittsburgh, PA 15222
Phone: 412-392-3430 **Financial Aid Phone:** 412-392-3930
E-mail: enroll@pointpark.edu **CEEB Code:** 2676
Fax: 412-391-1980 **ACT Code:** 3530

This private school was founded in 1960.

RATINGS
Admissions Selectivity Rating: 76   Fire Safety Rating: 97   Green Rating: 60*

STUDENTS AND FACULTY
Enrollment: 3,167. **Student Body:** 58% female, 42% male, 21% out-of-state, 2% international (38 countries represented). Asian 1%, African American 17%, Caucasian 73%, Hispanic 3%, Native American <1%, Pacific Islander 0%, Two or more races 3%, Race unknown <1%.
Retention and Graduation: 74% freshmen return for sophomore year.
Faculty: Student/faculty ratio 13:1. 133 full-time faculty, 74% hold PhDs, 10% are members of minority groups, 38% are women. 0% of classes are taught by teaching assistants.

ACADEMICS
Degrees: Associate; Bachelor's; Certificate; Master's; Post-bachelor's certificate. **Classes:** Most classes have 10–19 students. **Most popular majors:** Teacher Education and Professional Development, Specific Subject Areas, Other; Drama and Dramatics/Theatre Arts, General; Dance, General. **Special Study Options:** Accelerated program; Cooperative education program; Cross-registration; Distance learning; Double major; Dual enrollment; English as a Second Language (ESL); Exchange student program (domestic); Honors program; Independent study; Internships; Liberal arts/career combination; Student-designed major; Study abroad; Teacher certification program; Weekend college. **Honors programs:** The Point Park Honors Program mission provides the foundation from which honors courses are developed. Honors courses will not be defined by more work but rather by a different kind of learning environment. Students will be introduced to the usual content and objectives of the course, but they will also develop in-depth understandings of topics.

Students will be expected to develop appropriate and higher-level research, writing and critical thinking skills, which should result in major documented papers or projects. Students will be encouraged to become adventurous, independent thinkers. Students should experience a variety of learning activities that may include collaborative learning, field experience, debates, documented projects, interviews, and presentations. Evaluation will be based on performance, creativity, imagination, critical thinking, and risk taking rather than on more assignments and tests. Honors students will be expected to participate in the quest for knowledge by being prepared and willing to contribute to all class activities. To earn an honors certificate, students need to complete 18 credits of honors classes. An honors thesis or project is optional, depending on students' career and graduate study goals. Honors students also may join our Honors Student Organization and participate in a variety of leadership and community service efforts and projects inside and outside the Point Park community. Students annually are offered the chance to travel for an alternative spring break, and they can present papers and research at national and regional honors conferences. Every effort is made to encourage all of them to assume leadership positions and propose their own activities and endeavors to complement their work in the classroom. As benefits, students register for classes each semester before other students and new students move in ahead of other resident students. Students who complete program requirements will be recognized in the program at graduation and will receive a separate certificate and notation on their transcript. **Disability Services offered:** Note-taking services; Reader services; Tape recorders; Tutors. **Career services:** Alumni network; Alumni services; Career assessment; Career/job search classes; Internships; Regional alumni.

FACILITIES

Housing: Apartments for single students; Coed dorms; Special housing for disabled students; Theme housing; Women's dorms; 95% of campus accessible to physically disabled. **Special Academic Facilities/Equipment:** Theater, engineering technology labs, television and radio studios, digital film editing suites, dance studios.

CAMPUS LIFE

Environment: Metropolis. **Activities:** Campus Ministries; Choral groups; Dance; Drama/theater; International Student Organization; Literary magazine; Musical theater; Radio station; Student government; Student newspaper; Student-run film society; Television station. 34 registered organizations, 3 honor societies, 1 religious organization on campus. **Athletics (Intercollegiate):** *Men:* baseball, basketball, cross-country, golf, soccer. *Women:* basketball, cross-country, golf, soccer, softball, volleyball. **On-Campus Highlights:** Point Café. **Environmental Initiatives:** Recycling.

ADMISSIONS

Freshman Academic Profile: Average high school GPA 3.2. 10% in top 10% of high school class, 30% in top 25% of high school class, 66% in top 50% of high school class. **Test Scores:** SAT Math middle 50% range 450–560. SAT EBRW middle 50% range 460–580. ACT middle 50% range 20–26. **Basis for Candidate Selection:** *Very important factors include:* standardized test scores, talent/ability. *Important factors include:* rigor of secondary school record. *Other factors include:* academic GPA, recommendation(s). **Freshman Admission Requirements:** High school diploma is required and GED is accepted. *Academic units recommended:* 4 English, 4 math, 3 science, 2 foreign language, 3 social studies, 3 history, 1 academic elective, 1 computer science, 1 visual/performing arts. **Freshman Admission Statistics:** 3,673 applied, 76% admitted, 19% enrolled. **Transfer Admission Requirements:** College transcript(s). Minimum college GPA of 2.0 required. Lowest grade transferable C. **General Admission Information:** Application fee $40. Non-fall registration accepted. Admission may be deferred for a maximum of 1 year.

COSTS AND FINANCIAL AID

Annual tuition $24,020. Room and board $9,920. Required fees $1,170. Average book and supplies expense $1,000. **Required Forms and Deadlines:** FAFSA. **Notification of Awards:** Applicants will be notified of awards on a rolling basis beginning 2/15. **Types of Aid:** *Need-based scholarships/grants:* College/university scholarship or grant aid from institutional funds; Federal Pell; Private scholarships; SEOG; State scholarships/grants. *Loans:* Direct PLUS loans; Direct Subsidized Stafford loans; Direct Unsubsidized Stafford loans. **Student Employment:** Federal Work-Study Program available. Institutional employment available. **Financial Aid Statistics:** 100% needy freshmen, 99% needy undergrads receive need-based scholarship or grant aid. 11% freshmen, 9% undergrads receive non-need-based scholarship or grant aid. 87% freshmen, 87% undergrads receive need-based self-help aid. 1% freshmen, 2% undergrads receive athletic scholarships. 99.6% freshmen, 93% undergrads receive any aid. **Criteria awarding aid:** *Non-need-based:* Academics, Athletics, Music/drama.

POINT UNIVERSITY

507 West 10th Street, West Point, GA 31833
Phone: 706-385-1202 **Financial Aid Phone:** 706-385-1045
E-mail: admissions@point.edu **CEEB Code:** 5029
Fax: 706-645-9473 **Website:** www.point.edu **ACT Code:** 0785

This private school, affiliated with the Christian (Nondenominational) Church, was founded in 1937.

RATINGS

Admissions Selectivity Rating: 86   **Fire Safety Rating:** 74   **Green Rating:** 60*

STUDENTS AND FACULTY

Enrollment: 1,358. **Student Body:** 50% female, 50% male, 37% out-of-state, 2% international (13 countries represented). Asian <1%, African American 34%, Caucasian 47%, Hispanic 6%, Native American <1%, Pacific Islander <1%, Two or more races 5%, Race unknown 5%.
Retention and Graduation: 68% freshmen return for sophomore year.
Faculty: Student/faculty ratio 18:1. 41 full-time faculty, 63% hold PhDs, 27% are members of minority groups, 59% are women. 0% of classes are taught by teaching assistants.

ACADEMICS

Degrees: Associate; Bachelor's; Certificate; Master's. **Classes:** Most classes have 10–19 students. **Most popular majors:** Bible/Biblical Studies; Business Administration and Management, General; Exercise Science and Kinesiology. **Special Study Options:** Accelerated program; Distance learning; Double major; Dual enrollment; Honors program; Independent study; Study abroad; Teacher certification program. **Honors programs:** Counseling Honor Program. **Disability Services offered:** Note-taking services; Reader services; Tape recorders; Tutors. **Career services:** Alumni network; Alumni services; Career/job search classes; Internships.

FACILITIES

Housing: Men's dorms; Theme housing; Women's dorms.

CAMPUS LIFE

Environment: Village. **Activities:** Campus Ministries; Choral groups; Concert band; Marching band; Student government. 8 registered organizations on campus. **Athletics (Intercollegiate):** *Men:* baseball, basketball, golf, soccer. *Women:* basketball, soccer, volleyball. **On-Campus Highlights:** John Smith Lanier Academic Center.

ADMISSIONS

Freshman Academic Profile: Average high school GPA 3.2. **Test Scores:** SAT Math middle 50% range 410–520. SAT EBRW middle 50% range 400–490. ACT middle 50% range 17–22. **Basis for Candidate Selection:** *Very important factors include:* academic GPA, character/personal qualities, religious affiliation/ commitment. *Important factors include:* rigor of secondary school record, class rank, standardized test scores, recommendation(s), extracurricular activities. *Other factors include:* application essay, interview, talent/ability, alumni/ ae relation, volunteer work, work experience, level of applicant's interest. **Freshman Admission Requirements:** High school diploma is required and GED is accepted. *Academic units recommended:* 4 English, 4 math, 4 science, 2 science labs, 2 foreign language, 3 social studies. **Freshman Admission Statistics:** 1,184 applied, 51% admitted, 53% enrolled. **Transfer Admission Requirements:** College transcript(s), statement of good standing from prior institution(s). Minimum college GPA of 2.0 required. Lowest grade transferable C. **General Admission Information:** Priority deadline 7/1. Regular application deadline 8/1. Non-fall registration accepted. Admission may be deferred for a maximum of 1 year.

COSTS AND FINANCIAL AID

Annual tuition $18,100. Room and board $7,700. Required fees $1,100. Average book and supplies expense $2,000. **Student Employment:** Federal Work-Study Program available. Institutional employment available. **Financial Aid Statistics:** 99% freshmen, 99% undergrads receive any aid.

POLYTECHNIC INSTITUTE OF NEW YORK UNIVERSITY— BROOKLYN

6 Metrotech Center, Brooklyn, NY 11201-2999
Phone: 718-260-5955 **Financial Aid Phone:** 718-260-3025
E-mail: uadmit@poly.edu **CEEB Code:** 2668
Fax: 718-260-3446 **Website:** www.poly.edu **ACT Code:** 2860

This private school was founded in 1854. It has a 3 acre campus.

RATINGS
Admissions Selectivity Rating: 86   **Fire Safety Rating:** 82   **Green Rating:** 60*

STUDENTS AND FACULTY
Enrollment: 2,000. **Student Body:** 20% female, 80% male, 19% out-of-state, 10% international (34 countries represented). Asian 35%, African American 6%, Caucasian 30%, Hispanic 10%, Native American <1%, Pacific Islander 0%, Two or more races 0%, Race unknown 9%.
Retention and Graduation: 84% freshmen return for sophomore year. 15% grads go on to further study within 1 year. **Faculty:** Student/faculty ratio 14:1. 157 full-time faculty, 91% hold PhDs, 29% are members of minority groups, 17% are women. 0% of classes are taught by teaching assistants.

ACADEMICS
Degrees: Bachelor's; Certificate; Doctoral degree research/scholarship; Master's; Post-bachelor's certificate. **Classes:** Most classes have 10–19 students. Most lab/discussion sessions have 10–19 students. **Most popular majors:** Civil Engineering, General; Electrical and Electronics Engineering; Mechanical Engineering. **Special Study Options:** Accelerated program; Cooperative education program; Distance learning; Double major; Dual enrollment; Honors program; Independent study; Internships; Study abroad. **Honors programs:** The Honors College serves as a magnet for attracting academically superior Undergraduates to the University. It accepts students of exceptional talent and promise from a variety of backgrounds. It offers outstanding Honors students the opportunity to earn a BS and possibly an MS degree in possibly as few as four years, including summers. Honors College students work one-on-one with faculty mentors, who, among other things, stress interdisciplinary research where appropriate, originality of thought, and active learning. Honors College students form a talented cadre of high-achievers who will become engineers, scientists, managers, and other professionals positioned for leadership roles in our emerging knowledge-based economy. They will also form a highly enthusiastic and supportive part of the University's alumni population and enhance the overall reputation of the University for delivering excellence in education. **Combined degree programs:** BA/MA; BA/MEng. **Disability Services offered:** Note-taking services; Tape recorders; Tutors. **Career services:** Alumni network; Alumni services; Career assessment; Career/job search classes; Internships.

FACILITIES
Housing: Coed dorms; Fraternity/sorority housing; 100% of campus accessible to physically disabled.

CAMPUS LIFE
Environment: Metropolis. **Activities:** Campus Ministries; Drama/theater; Literary magazine; Radio station; Student government; Student newspaper; Student-run film society; Yearbook. **Athletics (Intercollegiate):** *Men:* baseball, basketball, cross-country, soccer, tennis, track/field (outdoor), volleyball. *Women:* basketball, cross-country, softball, tennis, track/field (outdoor), volleyball. **On-Campus Highlights:** Recreation Center; Wunsch Student Center.

ADMISSIONS
Freshman Academic Profile: Average high school GPA 3.5. 46% in top 10% of high school class, 81% in top 25% of high school class, 95% in top 50% of high school class. 73% from public high schools. **Test Scores:** SAT Math middle 50% range 640–720. SAT EBRW middle 50% range 550–650. ACT middle 50% range 26–30. **Basis for Candidate Selection:** *Very important factors include:* rigor of secondary school record, standardized test scores. *Important factors include:* class rank. *Other factors include:* application essay, recommendation(s), interview. **Freshman Admission Requirements:** High school diploma is required and GED is accepted. *Academic units required:* 4 English, 4 math, 4 science, 3 social studies, 2 academic electives. *Academic units recommended:* 2 foreign language. **Freshman Admission Statistics:** 3,284 applied, 75% admitted, 20% enrolled. **Transfer Admission Requirements:**

College transcript(s). Minimum college GPA of 2.5 required. Lowest grade transferable C. **General Admission Information:** Application fee $65. Non-fall registration accepted.

COSTS AND FINANCIAL AID
Annual tuition $40,060. Room and board $13,500. Required fees $1,268. Average book and supplies expense $1,500. **Required Forms and Deadlines:** CSS/Financial Aid PROFILE; FAFSA; Institution's own financial aid form; State aid form. **Notification of Awards:** Applicants will be notified of awards on a rolling basis beginning 3/15. **Types of Aid:** *Need-based scholarships/grants:* College/university scholarship or grant aid from institutional funds; Federal Pell; Private scholarships; SEOG; State scholarships/grants; United Negro College Fund. *Loans:* Direct PLUS loans; Direct Subsidized Stafford Loans; Direct Unsubsidized Stafford Loans. **Student Employment:** Federal Work-Study Program available. Institutional employment available. **Financial Aid Statistics:** 93% needy freshmen, 93% needy undergrads receive need-based scholarship or grant aid. 88% freshmen, 59% undergrads receive non-need-based scholarship or grant aid. 85% freshmen, 86% undergrads receive need-based self-help aid. 0% freshmen, 0% undergrads receive athletic scholarships. 97% freshmen, 92% undergrads receive any aid. **Criteria awarding aid:** *Need-based:* Academics, Leadership, Minority status. *Non-need-based:* Academics, Minority status, State/district residency.

POLYTECHNIC UNIVERSITY OF PUERTO RICO

PO BOX 192017, San Juan, PR 00919-2017
Phone: 787.622.8000 **Financial Aid Phone:** 787.622.8000
CEEB Code: 614
Fax: 787.764.8712 **Website:** www.pupr.edu

This private school was founded in 1966. It has a 8 acre campus.

RATINGS
Admissions Selectivity Rating: 68   **Fire Safety Rating:** 68   **Green Rating:** 61

STUDENTS AND FACULTY
Enrollment: 3,334. **Student Body:** 20% female, 80% male, 0% international. Asian <1%, African American <1%, Caucasian <1%, Hispanic 100%, Native American 0%, Pacific Islander 0%, Two or more races 0%, Race unknown <1%.
Retention and Graduation: 77% freshmen return for sophomore year. 73% grads go on to further study within 1 year. 2% grads pursue arts and sciences degrees. 2% grads pursue law degrees. 12% grads pursue business degrees. 1% grads pursue medical degrees. **Faculty:** Student/faculty ratio 11:1. 131 full-time faculty, 37% hold PhDs, 0% are members of minority groups, 34% are women. 0% of classes are taught by teaching assistants.

ACADEMICS
Degrees: Associate; Bachelor's; Master's. **Classes:** Most classes have 10–19 students. **Most popular majors:** Civil Engineering, General; Electrical and Electronics Engineering; Mechanical Engineering. **Special Study Options:** Cooperative education program; Distance learning; Honors program. **Honors programs:** In a continuing effort to provide educational opportunities consistent with the ability of the individual student, the University invites a select group of students with a GPA of 3.25 or higher to enroll in and benefit from the Honor Program and corresponding Scholarship. The mission is to provide a dynamic intellectual environment for honors students through counseling and multiple activities. The program is designed to provide ample opportunities and high motivation to specially gifted students. This program consists of honors seminars, and special courses. The special courses enable students who excel to be challenged to their full intellectual capacity. The program is designed both to broaden and deepen the student's intellectual power. These specials courses involve topics at the forefront of current scientific interest. **Disability Services offered:** Note-taking services; Reader services; Tape recorders; Tutors. **Career services:** Career assessment; Career/job search classes; Internships.

FACILITIES
Housing: Special housing for international students. **Campus Network:** 100% of classrooms, 100% of dorms, 100% of student union, 100% of libraries, 100% of dining areas, 75% of common outdoor areas have wireless network access.

CAMPUS LIFE

Environment: Metropolis. **Activities:** Choral groups; Dance; Student government. 20 registered organizations, 1 honor society, 1 religious organization on campus. **Athletics (Intercollegiate):** *Men:* basketball, cross-country, martial arts, table tennis, tennis, track/field (outdoor), volleyball, wrestling. *Women:* cross-country, martial arts, table tennis, tennis, track/field (outdoor), volleyball. **On-Campus Highlights:** Coffee Shop—Cafeteria Mi Casa.

ADMISSIONS

Freshman Academic Profile: Average high school GPA 3.2. 39% from public high schools. **Basis for Candidate Selection:** *Very important factors include:* academic GPA. *Other factors include:* standardized test scores. **Freshman Admission Requirements:** High school diploma is required and GED is accepted. *Academic units required:* 3 English, 3 math, 3 science, 3 foreign language, 3 social studies. **Freshman Admission Statistics:** 611 applied, 85% admitted, 83% enrolled. **Transfer Admission Requirements:** College transcript(s), **General Admission Information:** Application fee $30. Non-fall registration accepted. Admission may be deferred for a maximum of 2 trimesters.

COSTS AND FINANCIAL AID

Annual tuition $7,488. Room and board $11,857. Required fees $840. Average book and supplies expense $2,342. **Required Forms and Deadlines:** FAFSA. **Student Employment:** Federal Work-Study Program available. **Financial Aid Statistics:** 97% needy freshmen, 97% needy undergrads receive need-based scholarship or grant aid. 51% freshmen, 32% undergrads receive non-need-based scholarship or grant aid. 12% freshmen, 19% undergrads receive need-based self-help aid. 66% freshmen, 41% undergrads receive athletic scholarships. 90.84% freshmen, 90.44% undergrads receive any aid.

POMONA COLLEGE

333 N College Way, Claremont, CA
Phone: 909-621-8134 **Financial Aid Phone:** 909-621-8205
E-mail: admissions@pomona.edu **CEEB Code:** 4607
Fax: 909-621-8952 **Website:** www.pomona.edu **ACT Code:** 372

This private school was founded in 1887. It has a 140 acre campus.

RATINGS

Admissions Selectivity Rating: 98   Fire Safety Rating: 97   Green Rating: 95

STUDENTS AND FACULTY

Enrollment: 1,688. **Student Body:** 53% female, 47% male, 11% international (41 countries represented). Asian 16%, African American 10%, Caucasian 34%, Hispanic 17%, Native American <1%, Pacific Islander <1%, Two or more races 7%, Race unknown 4%.
Retention and Graduation: 97% freshmen return for sophomore year. 89% freshmen graduate within 4 years. 93% freshmen graduate within 6 years. 20% grads go on to further study within 1 year. **Faculty:** Student/faculty ratio 8:1. 195 full-time faculty, 98% hold PhDs, 32% are members of minority groups, 46% are women. 0% of classes are taught by teaching assistants.

ACADEMICS

Degrees: Bachelor's. **Classes:** Most classes have 10–19 students. Most lab/discussion sessions have 10–19 students. **Most popular majors:** Mathematics; Neuroscience; Economics. **Special Study Options:** Cross-registration; Double major; Exchange student program (domestic); Independent study; Internships; Student-designed major; Study abroad. **Disability Services offered:** Note-taking services; Reader services; Tape recorders; Tutors. **Career services:** Alumni network; Alumni services; Career assessment; Career/job search classes; Internships; Regional alumni.

FACILITIES

Housing: Coed dorms; Theme housing; 85% of campus accessible to physically disabled. **Special Academic Facilities/Equipment:** Oldenborg Center for Foreign Languages, Museum of Art, Brackett Observatory. **Campus Network:** 100% of classrooms, 100% of dorms, 100% of student union, 100% of libraries, 100% of dining areas, 55% of common outdoor areas have wireless network access.

CAMPUS LIFE

Environment: Town. **Activities:** Campus Ministries; Choral groups; Concert band; Dance; Drama/theater; International Student Organization; Jazz band; Literary magazine; Model UN; Music ensembles; Musical theater; Pep band; Radio station; Student government; Student newspaper; Student-run film society; Symphony orchestra; Yearbook. 280 registered organizations, 8 honor societies, 5 religious organizations, 3 fraternities on campus. **Athletics (Intercollegiate):** *Men:* baseball, basketball, cross-country, diving, football, golf, soccer, swimming, tennis, track/field (outdoor), water polo. *Women:* basketball, cross-country, diving, golf, lacrosse, soccer, softball, swimming, tennis, track/field (outdoor), volleyball, water polo. **On-Campus Highlights:** Smith Campus Center. **Environmental Initiatives:** Pomona College is institutionally committed to a sustainable campus community. The SAVE strategic plan outlines measurable strategies that will lead the College to achieve ambitious sustainability goals and reach carbon neutrality by 2030. The seven key categories encompassed by the outlined goals are energy, water, waste, transportation, food, buildings and outdoor venues, and academic education.

ADMISSIONS

Freshman Academic Profile: 93% in top 10% of high school class, 100% in top 25% of high school class, 100% in top 50% of high school class. 68% from public high schools. **Test Scores:** SAT Math middle 50% range 700–790. SAT EBRW middle 50% range 690–750. ACT middle 50% range 32–35. **Basis for Candidate Selection:** *Very important factors include:* rigor of secondary school record, class rank, academic GPA, application essay, standardized test scores, recommendation(s), extracurricular activities, talent/ability, character/personal qualities. *Other factors include:* interview, first generation, geographical residence, racial/ethnic status, volunteer work, work experience. **Freshman Admission Requirements:** High school diploma or equivalent is not required *Academic units required:* 4 English, 3 math, 2 science, 2 science labs, 3 foreign language, 2 social studies. *Academic units recommended:* 4 English, 4 math, 4 science, 3 science labs, 4 foreign language, 4 social studies. **Freshman Admission Statistics:** 10,401 applied, 7% admitted, 54% enrolled. **Transfer Admission Requirements:** High school transcript, college transcript(s), essay or personal statement, standardized test scores, statement of good standing from prior institution(s). Lowest grade transferable C. **General Admission Information:** Application fee $70. Regular application deadline 1/1. Admission may be deferred for a maximum of 1 year.

COSTS AND FINANCIAL AID

Annual tuition $54,380. Room and board $17,218. Required fees $338. Average book and supplies expense $1,000. **Required Forms and Deadlines:** CSS/Financial Aid PROFILE; FAFSA; Noncustodial PROFILE; State aid form. **Notification of Awards:** Applicants will be notified of awards on or about 4/1. **Types of Aid:** *Need-based scholarships/grants:* College/university scholarship or grant aid from institutional funds; Federal Pell; Private scholarships; SEOG; State scholarships/grants. *Loans:* Direct PLUS loans; Direct Subsidized Stafford Loans; Direct Unsubsidized Stafford Loans. **Student Employment:** Federal Work-Study Program available. Institutional employment available. **Financial Aid Statistics:** 100% needy freshmen, 100% needy undergrads receive need-based scholarship or grant aid. 0% freshmen, 0% undergrads receive non-need-based scholarship or grant aid. 100% freshmen, 100% undergrads receive need-based self-help aid. 0% freshmen, 0% undergrads receive athletic scholarships. 58% freshmen, 54% undergrads receive any aid. 25% undergrads borrow to pay for school. Average cumulative indebtedness $18,829.

PONTIFICAL COLLEGE JOSEPHINUM

7625 North High Street, Columbus, OH 43235-1498
Phone: 614-885-5585 **Financial Aid Phone:** 614-885-5585
E-mail: admissions@pcj.edu
Fax: 614-885-2307

This private school, affiliated with the Roman Catholic Church, was founded in 1888. It has a 100 acre campus.

RATINGS

Admissions Selectivity Rating: 86   Fire Safety Rating: 60*   Green Rating: 60*

STUDENTS AND FACULTY

Enrollment: 78. **Student Body:** 0% female, 100% male, 64% out-of-state, 8% international (15 countries represented). Asian 1%, African American 0%, Caucasian 79%, Hispanic 10%, Native American 1%, Race unknown 0%.

Retention and Graduation: 92% freshmen return for sophomore year. 95% grads go on to further study within 1 year. 5% grads pursue arts and sciences degrees. **Faculty:** Student/faculty ratio 4:1. 17 full-time faculty, 76% hold PhDs, 0% are members of minority groups, 35% are women. 0% of classes are taught by teaching assistants.

ACADEMICS
Degrees: Bachelor's; Master's. **Classes:** Most classes have 10–19 students. **Special Study Options:** Cross-registration; Double major; Honors program; Independent study.

FACILITIES
Housing: Men's dorms. **Campus Network:** 100% of classrooms, 100% of dorms, 100% of student union, 100% of libraries, 100% of dining areas have wireless network access.

CAMPUS LIFE
Environment: Metropolis. **Activities:** Choral groups. 1 religious organization on campus.

ADMISSIONS
Freshman Academic Profile: 25% in top 10% of high school class, 35% in top 25% of high school class, 60% in top 50% of high school class. **Test Scores:** SAT Math middle 50% range 360–610. SAT EBRW middle 50% range 380–600. ACT middle 50% range 17–25. **Basis for Candidate Selection:** *Very important factors include:* rigor of secondary school record, standardized test scores, recommendation(s), religious affiliation/commitment. *Important factors include:* academic GPA, application essay, interview. *Other factors include:* class rank, extracurricular activities, talent/ability, character/personal qualities, volunteer work. **Freshman Admission Requirements:** High school diploma is required and GED is accepted. *Academic units required:* 4 English, 2 math, 1 science, 1 foreign language, 2 social studies. *Academic units recommended:* 4 math, 4 science, 2 foreign language, 4 social studies. **Freshman Admission Statistics:** 8 applied, 75% admitted, 100% enrolled. **Transfer Admission Requirements:** High school transcript, college transcript(s), essay or personal statement, interview, standardized test scores. Lowest grade transferable C. **General Admission Information:** Application fee $25. Priority deadline 7/31.

COSTS AND FINANCIAL AID
Annual tuition $16,701. Room and board $7,908. Required fees $720. Average book and supplies expense $1,100. **Required Forms and Deadlines:** FAFSA; Institution's own financial aid form. **Types of Aid:** *Need-based scholarships/grants:* College/university scholarship or grant aid from institutional funds; Federal Pell; Private scholarships; SEOG; State scholarships/grants. **Student Employment:** Federal Work-Study Program available. **Financial Aid Statistics:** 0% needy freshmen, 83% needy undergrads receive need-based scholarship or grant aid. 0% freshmen, 0% undergrads receive non-need-based scholarship or grant aid. 100% freshmen, 33% undergrads receive need-based self-help aid. 0% freshmen, 0% undergrads receive athletic scholarships. **Criteria awarding aid:** *Need-based:* Academics. *Non-need-based:* Academics.

PORTLAND STATE UNIVERSITY

Office of Admissions, Portland, OR 97207-0751
Phone: 503-725-3511 **Financial Aid Phone:** 800-547-8887
E-mail: admissions@pdx.edu **CEEB Code:** 4610
Fax: 503-725-5525 **Website:** http://www.pdx.edu/ **ACT Code:** 3492

This public school was founded in 1946. It has a 50 acre campus.

RATINGS
Admissions Selectivity Rating: 74   **Fire Safety Rating:** 88   **Green Rating:** 98

STUDENTS AND FACULTY
Enrollment: 17,827. **Student Body:** 54% female, 46% male, 16% out-of-state, 5% international (70 countries represented). Asian 10%, African American 4%, Caucasian 52%, Hispanic 17%, Native American 1%, Pacific Islander 1%, Two or more races 7%, Race unknown 4%.
Retention and Graduation: 73% freshmen return for sophomore year. 20% freshmen graduate within 4 years. 47% freshmen graduate within 6 years.
Faculty: Student/faculty ratio 19:1. 886 full-time faculty, 81% hold PhDs, 21%

are members of minority groups, 50% are women. 4% of classes are taught by teaching assistants.

ACADEMICS
Degrees: Bachelor's; Certificate; Doctoral degree research/scholarship; Master's; Post-bachelor's certificate; Post-master's certificate. **Classes:** Most classes have 10–19 students. Most lab/discussion sessions have 10–19 students. **Most popular majors:** Psychology, General; Business Administration and Management, General; Biology/Biological Sciences, General. **Special Study Options:** Accelerated program; Cooperative education program; Distance learning; Double major; Dual enrollment; English as a Second Language (ESL); Exchange student program (domestic); Honors program; Independent study; Internships; Liberal arts/career combination; Study abroad; Teacher certification program. **Honors programs:** University Honors Program. **Disability Services offered:** Note-taking services; Reader services; Tape recorders; Tutors. **Career services:** Alumni network; Alumni services; Career assessment; Career/job search classes; Internships.

FACILITIES
Housing: Apartments for married students; Apartments for single students; Coed dorms; Cooperative housing; Fraternity/sorority housing; Special housing for disabled students; Special housing for international students; 95% of campus accessible to physically disabled. **Special Academic Facilities/Equipment:** Art galleries, audiovisual resources, classroom multimedia computer systems, learning lab, child development center, native american center.

CAMPUS LIFE
Environment: Metropolis. **Activities:** Campus Ministries; Choral groups; Concert band; Dance; Drama/theater; International Student Organization; Jazz band; Literary magazine; Model UN; Music ensembles; Musical theater; Opera; Pep band; Radio station; Student government; Student newspaper; Student-run film society; Symphony orchestra; Television station. 160 registered organizations, 5 honor societies, 13 religious organizations, 4 fraternities, 6 sororities on campus. **Athletics (Intercollegiate):** *Men:* basketball, cross-country, football, tennis, track/field (outdoor), track/field (indoor). *Women:* basketball, cross-country, golf, soccer, softball, tennis, track/field (outdoor), track/field (indoor), volleyball. **On-Campus Highlights:** Park Blocks. **Environmental Initiatives:** Since 2002, PSU has focused on designing new buildings and retrofitting and renovating older campus buildings with sustainability in mind. Several PSU buildings serve as models of these kinds of innovative sustainable design and construction projects. These include the new Engineering Building, Broadway Housing Building, Stephen Epler Hall, and Native American Student and Community Center. In all but the latter, the U.S. Green Building Council's LEED certification program was used as the measuring stick and standard for sustainable design and construction.

ADMISSIONS
Freshman Academic Profile: Average high school GPA 3.5. 15% in top 10% of high school class, 43% in top 25% of high school class, 83% in top 50% of high school class. 85% from public high schools. **Test Scores:** SAT Math middle 50% range 500–590. SAT EBRW middle 50% range 500–630. ACT middle 50% range 18–24. **Basis for Candidate Selection:** *Very important factors include:* academic GPA. *Other factors include:* standardized test scores, recommendation(s). **Freshman Admission Requirements:** High school diploma is required and GED is accepted. *Academic units required:* 4 English, 3 math, 3 science, 2 foreign language, 3 social studies, 1 history. *Academic units recommended:* 1 science lab. **Freshman Admission Statistics:** 6,861 applied, 96% admitted, 30% enrolled. **Transfer Admission Requirements:** College transcript(s). Minimum college GPA of 2.25 required. Lowest grade transferable D-. **General Admission Information:** Application fee $50. Priority deadline 6/1. Non-fall registration accepted. Admission may be deferred for a maximum of one year.

COSTS AND FINANCIAL AID
Annual in-state tuition $8,078. Annual out-of-state tuition $26,910. Room and board $11,172. Required fees $1,500. Average book and supplies expense $1,263. **Required Forms and Deadlines:** FAFSA. **Notification of Awards:** Applicants will be notified of awards on a rolling basis beginning 2/27. **Types of Aid:** *Need-based scholarships/grants:* College/university scholarship or grant aid from institutional funds; Federal Pell; Private scholarships; SEOG; State scholarships/grants. *Loans:* Direct PLUS loans; Direct Subsidized Stafford Loans; Direct Unsubsidized Stafford Loans. **Student Employment:** Federal Work-Study Program available. Institutional employment available. **Financial Aid Statistics:** 79% needy freshmen, 92% needy undergrads receive need-based scholarship or grant aid. 50% freshmen, 61% undergrads receive non-need-based scholarship or grant aid. 65% freshmen, 65% undergrads receive need-based self-help aid.

1% freshmen, 1% undergrads receive athletic scholarships. 75% freshmen, 70% undergrads receive any aid. 55% undergrads borrow to pay for school. Average cumulative indebtedness $26,426. **Criteria awarding aid:** *Need-based:* Academics, Alumni affiliation, Art, Athletics, Leadership, Minority status, Music/drama. *Non-need-based:* Academics, Alumni affiliation, Art, Athletics, Leadership, Minority status, Music/drama, State/district residency.

PRAIRIE VIEW A&M UNIVERSITY

PO Box 519, Prairie View, TX 77446
Phone: 936-261-3500 **Financial Aid Phone:** 1-877-782-6830
CEEB Code: 6580
Website: www.pvamu.edu **ACT Code:** 4202

This public school was founded in 1876. It has a 1388 acre campus.

RATINGS
Admissions Selectivity Rating: 87   **Fire Safety Rating:** 82   **Green Rating:** 60*

STUDENTS AND FACULTY
Enrollment: 7,465. **Student Body:** 59% female, 41% male, 7% out-of-state, 2% international (40 countries represented). Asian 3%, African American 85%, Caucasian 2%, Hispanic 7%, Native American <1%, Pacific Islander <1%, Two or more races 1%, Race unknown <1%.
Retention and Graduation: 69% freshmen return for sophomore year.
Faculty: Student/faculty ratio 17:1. 394 full-time faculty, 67% hold PhDs, 80% are members of minority groups, 39% are women.

ACADEMICS
Degrees: Bachelor's; Master's. **Classes:** Most classes have 20–29 students. Most lab/discussion sessions have 20–29 students. **Most popular majors:** Multi-/Interdisciplinary Studies, Other; Business Administration and Management, General. **Special Study Options:** Accelerated program; Cooperative education program; Distance learning; Double major; Dual enrollment; English as a Second Language (ESL); Exchange student program (domestic); Honors program; Independent study; Internships; Liberal arts/career combination; Study abroad; Teacher certification program; Weekend college. **Disability Services offered:** Tape recorders; Tutors. **Career services:** Alumni network; Alumni services; Career assessment; Internships; Regional alumni.

FACILITIES
Housing: Apartments for single students; Coed dorms; Special housing for disabled students; 90% of campus accessible to physically disabled.

CAMPUS LIFE
Environment: Rural. **Activities:** Campus Ministries; Choral groups; Concert band; Dance; Drama/theater; International Student Organization; Jazz band; Marching band; Music ensembles; Radio station; Student government; Student newspaper; Symphony orchestra; Television station; Yearbook. 100 registered organizations, 15 honor societies, 6 religious organizations, 9 fraternities, 9 sororities on campus. **Athletics (Intercollegiate):** *Men:* baseball, basketball, cross-country, football, golf, tennis, track/field (outdoor), track/field (indoor). *Women:* basketball, cheerleading, cross-country, golf, soccer, softball, tennis, track/field (outdoor), track/field (indoor), volleyball. **On-Campus Highlights:** Purple Zone Student Sports Bar.

ADMISSIONS
Freshman Academic Profile: Average high school GPA 2.9. 5% in top 10% of high school class, 21% in top 25% of high school class, 56% in top 50% of high school class. **Test Scores:** SAT Math middle 50% range 380–440. SAT EBRW middle 50% range 370–450. ACT middle 50% range 15–19. **Basis for Candidate Selection:** *Very important factors include:* academic GPA, standardized test scores. *Important factors include:* rigor of secondary school record. *Other factors include:* extracurricular activities, character/personal qualities, first generation, volunteer work, work experience. **Freshman Admission Requirements:** High school diploma is required and GED is accepted. *Academic units required:* 4 English, 3 math, 2 science, 2.5 social studies, 1 computer science, 1 visual/performing arts, 0.5 unit from above areas or other academic areas. *Academic units recommended:* 4 English, 4 math, 4 science, 2 foreign language, 3.5 social studies, 1 computer science. **Freshman Admission Statistics:** 7,931 applied, 42% admitted, 52% enrolled. **Transfer Admission Requirements:** College transcript(s), statement of good standing from prior institution(s). Minimum college GPA of 2.0 required. Lowest grade

transferable C. **General Admission Information:** Application fee $25. Priority deadline 6/1. Regular application deadline 6/1. Non-fall registration accepted.

COSTS AND FINANCIAL AID
Annual in-state tuition $5,076. Annual out-of-state tuition $14,376. Room and board $7,064. Required fees $1,779. Average book and supplies expense $1,000. **Required Forms and Deadlines:** FAFSA; Institution's own financial aid form. **Notification of Awards:** Applicants will be notified of awards on or about 6/1. **Types of Aid:** *Need-based scholarships/grants:* College/university scholarship or grant aid from institutional funds; Federal Pell; Private scholarships; SEOG; State scholarships/grants; United Negro College Fund. *Loans:* Direct PLUS loans; Direct Subsidized Stafford Loans; Direct Unsubsidized Stafford Loans. **Student Employment:** Federal Work-Study Program available. Institutional employment available. **Financial Aid Statistics:** 69% needy freshmen, 63% needy undergrads receive need-based scholarship or grant aid. 26% freshmen, 13% undergrads receive non-need-based scholarship or grant aid. 69% freshmen, 63% undergrads receive need-based self-help aid. 1% freshmen, 4% undergrads receive athletic scholarships. 60.76% freshmen, 52.61% undergrads receive any aid. **Criteria awarding aid:** *Need-based:* Academics, Athletics. *Non-need-based:* Academics, Athletics, State/district residency.

PRATT INSTITUTE

200 Willoughby Avenue, Brooklyn, NY 11205
Phone: 718-636-3514 **Financial Aid Phone:** 718-636-3599
E-mail: admissions@pratt.edu **CEEB Code:** 2669
Fax: 718-636-3670 **Website:** http://www.pratt.edu **ACT Code:** 2862

This private school was founded in 1887. It has a 25 acre campus.

RATINGS
Admissions Selectivity Rating: 89   **Fire Safety Rating:** 84   **Green Rating:** 81

STUDENTS AND FACULTY
Enrollment: 3,444. **Student Body:** 71% female, 29% male, 74% out-of-state, 34% international (62 countries represented). Asian 13%, African American 3%, Caucasian 35%, Hispanic 9%, Native American <1%, Pacific Islander <1%, Two or more races 3%, Race unknown 1%.
Retention and Graduation: 89% freshmen return for sophomore year. 45% freshmen graduate within 4 years. 70 **Faculty:** Student/faculty ratio 9:1. 170 full-time faculty, 82% hold PhDs, 24% are members of minority groups, 52% are women. 0% of classes are taught by teaching assistants.

ACADEMICS
Degrees: Associate; Bachelor's; Master's; Post-master's certificate; Terminal Associate; Transfer Associate. **Classes:** Most classes have 10–19 students. **Most popular majors:** Architecture; Fine/Studio Arts, General; Design and Visual Communications, General. **Special Study Options:** English as a Second Language (ESL); Exchange student program (domestic); Independent study; Internships; Study abroad; Teacher certification program. **Combined degree programs:** BA/MA. **Disability Services offered:** Note-taking services; Reader services; Tutors. **Career services:** Alumni network; Alumni services; Career assessment; Career/job search classes; Internships; Regional alumni.

FACILITIES
Housing: Apartments for single students; Coed dorms; Special housing for disabled students; Theme housing; Wellness housing. **Special Academic Facilities/Equipment:** Five art galleries, fine arts center, printmaking center, digital arts lab.

CAMPUS LIFE
Environment: Metropolis. **Activities:** Campus Ministries; International Student Organization; Literary magazine; Music ensembles; Radio station; Student government; Student newspaper; Student-run film society; Television station. 50 registered organizations, 4 honor societies, 3 religious organizations, 3 fraternities, 1 sorority on campus. **Athletics (Intercollegiate):** *Men:* basketball, cross-country, soccer, tennis, track/field (outdoor), track/field (indoor). *Women:* basketball, cross-country, soccer, tennis, track/field (outdoor), volleyball. **On-Campus Highlights:** Studios. **Environmental Initiatives:** Givetake, which launched in 2016, is Pratt's art supply recycling initiative. Givetake opened as a free store in the basement of Steuben Hall on the Brooklyn campus on August 22, 2016. The Pratt givetake materials re-use initiative collects and offers used art supplies, free of charge, to students. Since

the initiative began in Aug 2016, we have collected and given over 19,000 lbs of materials back to students.

ADMISSIONS

Freshman Academic Profile: Average high school GPA 3.9. **Test Scores:** SAT Math middle 50% range 600–730. SAT EBRW middle 50% range 590–680. ACT middle 50% range 25–30. **Basis for Candidate Selection:** *Very important factors include:* rigor of secondary school record, academic GPA, standardized test scores, talent/ability. *Important factors include:* application essay, character/ personal qualities, alumni/ae relation. *Other factors include:* class rank, interview, extracurricular activities, volunteer work, work experience. **Freshman Admission Requirements:** High school diploma is required and GED is accepted. *Academic units recommended:* 4 English, 4 math, 2 science, 5 academic electives. **Freshman Admission Statistics:** 7,090 applied, 49% admitted, 19% enrolled. **Transfer Admission Requirements:** High school transcript, college transcript(s), essay or personal statement, statement of good standing from prior institution(s). Lowest grade transferable C. **General Admission Information:** Application fee $50. Regular application deadline 1/5. Non-fall registration accepted. Admission may be deferred for a maximum of 1 year for freshman only.

COSTS AND FINANCIAL AID

Annual tuition $53,570. Room and board $13,988. Required fees $2,060. Average book and supplies expense $1,750. **Required Forms and Deadlines:** FAFSA; State aid form. **Notification of Awards:** Applicants will be notified of awards on a rolling basis beginning 3/1. **Types of Aid:** *Need-based scholarships/ grants:* College/university scholarship or grant aid from institutional funds; Federal Pell; SEOG; State scholarships/grants. *Loans:* Direct PLUS loans; Direct Subsidized Stafford Loans; Direct Unsubsidized Stafford Loans. **Student Employment:** Federal Work-Study Program available. Institutional employment available. **Financial Aid Statistics:** 36% needy freshmen, 44% needy undergrads receive need-based scholarship or grant aid. 100% freshmen, 99% undergrads receive non-need-based scholarship or grant aid. 81% freshmen, 88% undergrads receive need-based self-help aid. 0% freshmen, 0% undergrads receive athletic scholarships. 60% undergrads borrow to pay for school. Average cumulative indebtedness $41,305. **Criteria awarding aid:** *Need-based:* Academics. *Non-need-based:* Academics.

PRESBYTERIAN COLLEGE

503 South Broad Street, Clinton, SC 29325
Phone: 864-833-8230 **Financial Aid Phone:** 864-833-8287
E-mail: admissions@presby.edu **CEEB Code:** 5540
Fax: 864-833-8195 **Website:** www.presby.edu **ACT Code:** 3874

This private school, affiliated with the Presbyterian Church, was founded in 1880. It has a 240 acre campus.

RATINGS

Admissions Selectivity Rating: 85   **Fire Safety Rating:** 97   **Green Rating:** 60*

STUDENTS AND FACULTY

Enrollment: 947. **Student Body:** 50% female, 50% male, 34% out-of-state, 5% international (23 countries represented). Asian 1%, African American 12%, Caucasian 75%, Hispanic 3%, Native American <1%, Pacific Islander 0%, Two or more races 3%, Race unknown 1%.
Retention and Graduation: 82% freshmen return for sophomore year. 62% freshmen graduate within 4 years. % freshmen graduate within 6 years. 28% grads go on to further study within 1 year. **Faculty:** Student/faculty ratio 13:1. 74 full-time faculty, 97% hold PhDs, 38% are women. 0% of classes are taught by teaching assistants.

ACADEMICS

Degrees: Bachelor's; Doctoral degree—professional practice. **Classes:** Most classes have 10–19 students. Most lab/discussion sessions have 20–29 students. **Most popular majors:** Biology/Biological Sciences, General; Psychology, General; Business Administration and Management, General. **Special Study Options:** Distance learning; Double major; Dual enrollment; English as a Second Language (ESL); Exchange student program (domestic); Honors program; Independent study; Internships; Study abroad; Teacher certification program. **Honors programs:** A variety of opportunities are available to highly motivated students with above average abilities through the normal programs of the College. These include research, internships, special projects, and directed studies. Presbyterian College also offers a special honors program for students

who are chosen on the basis of their demonstrated ability. Students with a 3.20 GPA in all courses and a 3.40 GPA in all courses in their major field may, with the approval of departmental faculty, undertake an honors research program during the junior and/or senior years. Oral and written presentations of the results of the project will be required. Students who successfully complete the departmental honors research program will graduate with honors in the major field. **Disability Services offered:** Tutors. **Career services:** Alumni network; Alumni services; Career assessment; Career/job search classes; Internships; Regional alumni.

FACILITIES

Housing: Apartments for single students; Coed dorms; Fraternity/sorority housing; Men's dorms; Special housing for international students; Women's dorms; 95% of campus accessible to physically disabled. **Special Academic Facilities/Equipment:** Art gallery, recital hall, media center, marine/ ecological center, scanning and transmission electron microscopes, visible spectrophotometer. **Campus Network:** 100% of classrooms, 100% of dorms, 100% of student union, 100% of libraries, 100% of dining areas, 100% of common outdoor areas have wireless network access.

CAMPUS LIFE

Environment: Village. **Activities:** Campus Ministries; Choral groups; Concert band; Dance; Drama/theater; International Student Organization; Jazz band; Literary magazine; Music ensembles; Pep band; Student government; Student newspaper; Symphony orchestra; Yearbook. 80 registered organizations, 11 honor societies, 6 religious organizations, 6 fraternities, 3 sororities on campus. **Athletics (Intercollegiate):** *Men:* baseball, basketball, cheerleading, cross-country, football, golf, lacrosse, soccer, tennis. *Women:* basketball, cheerleading, cross-country, golf, lacrosse, soccer, softball, tennis, volleyball. **On-Campus Highlights:** Neville Hall. **Environmental Initiatives:** Energy conservation.

ADMISSIONS

Freshman Academic Profile: Average high school GPA 3.3. 25% in top 10% of high school class, 62% in top 25% of high school class, 88% in top 50% of high school class. **Test Scores:** SAT Math middle 50% range 510–630. SAT EBRW middle 50% range 510–620. ACT middle 50% range 21–27. **Basis for Candidate Selection:** *Very important factors include:* rigor of secondary school record, class rank, academic GPA, application essay. *Important factors include:* recommendation(s), interview, extracurricular activities, talent/ability, character/personal qualities. *Other factors include:* standardized test scores, first generation, alumni/ae relation, volunteer work, work experience, level of applicant's interest. **Freshman Admission Requirements:** High school diploma is required and GED is accepted. *Academic units required:* 4 English, 4 math, 2 science, 2 science labs, 2 foreign language, 2 social studies, 2 history, 2 academic electives. *Academic units recommended:* 4 science, 3 foreign language. **Freshman Admission Statistics:** 2,277 applied, 63% admitted, 19% enrolled. **Transfer Admission Requirements:** High school transcript, college transcript(s), essay or personal statement, standardized test scores, statement of good standing from prior institution(s). Lowest grade transferable C. **General Admission Information:** Priority deadline 12/1. Regular application deadline 6/30. Non-fall registration accepted. Admission may be deferred for a maximum of 1 year.

COSTS AND FINANCIAL AID

Annual tuition $34,982. Room and board $9,750. Required fees $2,860. Average book and supplies expense $1,200. **Required Forms and Deadlines:** FAFSA. **Notification of Awards:** Applicants will be notified of awards on a rolling basis beginning 3/1. **Types of Aid:** *Need-based scholarships/grants:* College/university scholarship or grant aid from institutional funds; Federal Pell; Private scholarships; SEOG; State scholarships/grants. *Loans:* Direct PLUS loans; Direct Subsidized Stafford Loans; Direct Unsubsidized Stafford Loans. **Student Employment:** Federal Work-Study Program available. **Criteria awarding aid:** *Need-based:* Alumni affiliation, Art, Job skills, Leadership, Minority status, Music/drama, Religious affiliation. *Non-need-based:* Academics, Alumni affiliation, Athletics, Job skills, Leadership, Minority status, Music/ drama, Religious affiliation, State/district residency.

PRESCOTT COLLEGE

220 Grove Avenue, Prescott, AZ 86301
Phone: 928-350-2100 **Financial Aid Phone:** 928-350-1112
E-mail: admissions@prescott.edu **CEEB Code:** 9295
Fax: 928-776-5242 **Website:** www.prescott.edu **ACT Code:** 5022

This private school was founded in 1966. It has a 13 acre campus.

RATINGS
Admissions Selectivity Rating: 63   **Fire Safety Rating:** 78   **Green Rating:** 60*

STUDENTS AND FACULTY
Enrollment: 351. **Student Body:** 60% female, 40% male, 60% out-of-state,
1% international (11 countries represented). Asian <1%, African American 2%,
Caucasian 62%, Hispanic 7%, Native American 3%, Pacific Islander <1%, Two
or more races 11%, Race unknown 13%.
Retention and Graduation: 73% freshmen return for sophomore year. 16%
freshmen graduate within 4 years. 35% freshmen graduate within 6 years.
Faculty: Student/faculty ratio 8:1. 33 full-time faculty, 39% hold PhDs, 3%
are members of minority groups, 58% are women. 0% of classes are taught by
teaching assistants.

ACADEMICS
Degrees: Bachelor's; Doctoral degree research/scholarship; Master's; Post-
bachelor's certificate; Post-master's certificate. **Classes:** Most classes have 10–19
students. **Most popular majors:** Environmental Studies; Education, Other;
Elementary Education and Teaching. **Special Study Options:** Accelerated
program; Cross-registration; Distance learning; Double major; Dual enrollment;
Exchange student program (domestic); Independent study; Internships; Liberal
arts/career combination; Student-designed major; Teacher certification program.
Disability Services offered: Note-taking services; Tape recorders; Tutors.
Career services: Alumni network; Alumni services; Career assessment; Career/
job search classes; Regional alumni.

FACILITIES
Housing: Coed dorms; Special housing for disabled students; 90% of campus
accessible to physically disabled. **Special Academic Facilities/Equipment:**
Jenner Farm: An experimental agroecology farm; Centaur Leadership Services:
Equine Assisted Learning and Equine Assisted Mental Health programs; Kino
Bay Center, MX: A field station on the Gulf of CA; Prescott College Art
Gallery houses our visual arts center and Artist-in-Residence program; GIS
Lab (Geographic Information Systems); Several Computer Labs; Multi-Media
Center.

CAMPUS LIFE
Environment: Town. **Activities:** Literary magazine; Student government. 16
registered organizations on campus. **On-Campus Highlights:** Crossroads Café.
Environmental Initiatives: ACUPCC commitment and Climate Action Plan.

ADMISSIONS
Freshman Academic Profile: 78% from public high schools. **Basis for
Candidate Selection:** *Very important factors include:* rigor of secondary school
record, academic GPA, application essay, recommendation(s). *Important
factors include:* standardized test scores, extracurricular activities, character/
personal qualities. *Other factors include:* interview, talent/ability, first generation,
volunteer work, work experience. **Freshman Admission Requirements:**
High school diploma is required and GED is accepted. **Freshman Admission
Statistics:** 394 applied, 94% admitted, 17% enrolled. **Transfer Admission
Requirements:** College transcript(s), essay or personal statement. Lowest grade
transferable C. **General Admission Information:** Priority deadline 3/1. Regular
application deadline 8/15. Non-fall registration accepted. Admission may be
deferred for a maximum of 1 year.

COSTS AND FINANCIAL AID
Annual tuition $29,880. Room and board $7,700. Required fees $1,605.
Average book and supplies expense $982. **Required Forms and Deadlines:**
FAFSA. **Notification of Awards:** Applicants will be notified of awards on
a rolling basis beginning 1/15. **Types of Aid:** *Need-based scholarships/grants:*
College/university scholarship or grant aid from institutional funds; Federal
Pell; Private scholarships; SEOG; State scholarships/grants. *Loans:* Direct PLUS
loans; Direct Subsidized Stafford Loans; Direct Unsubsidized Stafford Loans.
Student Employment: Federal Work-Study Program available. Institutional
employment available. **Financial Aid Statistics:** 100% needy freshmen, 100%
needy undergrads receive need-based scholarship or grant aid. 9% freshmen,
4% undergrads receive non-need-based scholarship or grant aid. 89% freshmen,

95% undergrads receive need-based self-help aid. 0% freshmen, 0% undergrads
receive athletic scholarships. 93% freshmen, 88% undergrads receive any aid.
63% undergrads borrow to pay for school. Average cumulative indebtedness
$39,720. **Criteria awarding aid:** *Non-need-based:* Academics, Leadership.

PRINCETON UNIVERSITY

PO Box 430, Princeton, NJ 08544-0430
Phone: 609-258-3060 **Financial Aid Phone:** 609-258-3330
E-mail: uaoffice@princeton.edu **CEEB Code:** 2672
Fax: 609-258-6743 **Website:** www.princeton.edu **ACT Code:** 2588

This private school was founded in 1746. It has a 500 acre campus.

RATINGS
Admissions Selectivity Rating: 99   **Fire Safety Rating:** 94   **Green Rating:** 60*

STUDENTS AND FACULTY
Enrollment: 5,301. **Student Body:** 49% female, 51% male, 82% out-of-state,
12% international (99 countries represented). Asian 21%, African American
8%, Caucasian 42%, Hispanic 10%, Native American <1%, Pacific Islander
<1%, Two or more races 5%, Race unknown 1%.
Retention and Graduation: 98% freshmen return for sophomore year. 89%
freshmen graduate within 4 years. 97% freshmen graduate within 6 years. 19%
grads go on to further study within 1 year. <1% grads pursue arts and sciences
degrees. 2% grads pursue law degrees. <1% grads pursue business degrees. 2%
grads pursue medical degrees. **Faculty:** Student/faculty ratio 5:1. 985 full-time
faculty, 94% hold PhDs, 18% are members of minority groups, 35% are
women. 0% of classes are taught by teaching assistants.

ACADEMICS
Degrees: Bachelor's; Doctoral degree research/scholarship; Master's. **Classes:**
Most classes have 10–19 students. Most lab/discussion sessions have 10–19
students. **Most popular majors:** Computer Engineering, General; Public
Administration; Economics, General. **Special Study Options:** Cross-
registration; Exchange student program (domestic); Independent study;
Student-designed major; Study abroad; Teacher certification program.
Disability Services offered: Note-taking services; Reader services; Tape
recorders. **Career services:** Alumni network; Alumni services; Career
assessment; Career/job search classes; Internships; Regional alumni.

FACILITIES
Housing: Apartments for married students; Coed dorms; Cooperative housing;
Special housing for disabled students; Wellness housing. **Special Academic
Facilities/Equipment:** Art Museum, Natural history museum, energy and
environmental studies center, plasma physics lab, Center for Jewish Life, Center
for Human Values, Woodrow Wilson School of Public and International Affairs,
etc.

CAMPUS LIFE
Environment: Town. **Activities:** Campus Ministries; Choral groups; Concert
band; Dance; Drama/theater; International Student Organization; Jazz band;
Literary magazine; Marching band; Model UN; Music ensembles; Musical
theater; Opera; Pep band; Radio station; Student government; Student
newspaper; Student-run film society; Symphony orchestra; Television station;
Yearbook. 250 registered organizations, 30 honor societies, 28 religious
organizations on campus. **Athletics (Intercollegiate):** *Men:* baseball, basketball,
crew/rowing, cross-country, diving, fencing, football, golf, ice hockey, lacrosse,
light weight football, soccer, squash, swimming, tennis, track/field (outdoor),
track/field (indoor), volleyball, water polo, wrestling. *Women:* basketball, crew/
rowing, cross-country, diving, fencing, field hockey, golf, ice hockey, lacrosse,
soccer, softball, squash, swimming, tennis, track/field (outdoor), track/field
(indoor), volleyball, water polo. **On-Campus Highlights:** Nassau Hall.

ADMISSIONS
Freshman Academic Profile: Average high school GPA 3.9. 60% from public
high schools. **Test Scores:** SAT Math middle 50% range 730–800. SAT
EBRW middle 50% range 710–770. ACT middle 50% range 32–35. **Basis for
Candidate Selection:** *Very important factors include:* rigor of secondary school
record, class rank, academic GPA, application essay, standardized test scores,

recommendation(s), extracurricular activities, talent/ability, character/personal qualities. *Other factors include:* interview, first generation, alumni/ae relation, geographical residence, racial/ethnic status, volunteer work, work experience. **Freshman Admission Requirements:** High school diploma or equivalent is not required *Academic units recommended:* 4 English, 4 math, 4 science, 2 science labs, 4 foreign language, 2 social studies, 2 history, 1 visual/performing arts. **Freshman Admission Statistics:** 35,370 applied, 5% admitted, 69% enrolled. **General Admission Information:** Application fee $70. Regular application deadline 1/1. Admission may be deferred for a maximum of 1 year.

COSTS AND FINANCIAL AID

Annual tuition $49,450. Room and board $16,360. Required fees $890. Average book and supplies expense $1,050. **Required Forms and Deadlines:** FAFSA; Institution's own financial aid form. **Notification of Awards:** Applicants will be notified of awards on or about 4/1. **Types of Aid:** *Need-based scholarships/grants:* College/university scholarship or grant aid from institutional funds; Federal Pell; Private scholarships; SEOG; State scholarships/grants. *Loans:* Direct PLUS loans; Direct Subsidized Stafford Loans; Direct Unsubsidized Stafford Loans. **Student Employment:** Federal Work-Study Program available. Institutional employment available. **Financial Aid Statistics:** 100% needy freshmen, 100% needy undergrads receive need-based scholarship or grant aid. 0% freshmen, 0% undergrads receive non-need-based scholarship or grant aid. 100% freshmen, 100% undergrads receive need-based self-help aid. 0% freshmen, 0% undergrads receive athletic scholarships. 60% freshmen, 60% undergrads receive any aid. 18% undergrads borrow to pay for school. Average cumulative indebtedness $9,059.

PRINCIPIA COLLEGE

1 Maybeck Place, Elsah, IL 62028
Phone: 618-374-5181 **Financial Aid Phone:** 618-374-5187
E-mail: collegeadmissions@principia.edu **CEEB Code:** 1630
Fax: 618-374-4000 **Website:** www.principiacollege.edu **ACT Code:** 1118

This private school, affiliated with the Christian Science Church, was founded in 1898. It has a 2600 acre campus.

RATINGS

Admissions Selectivity Rating: 80 **Fire Safety Rating:** 92 **Green Rating:** 77

STUDENTS AND FACULTY

Enrollment: 402. **Student Body:** 49% female, 51% male, 86% out-of-state, 17% international (26 countries represented). Asian 3%, African American 2%, Caucasian 69%, Hispanic 5%, Native American 0%, Pacific Islander <1%, Two or more races 2%, Race unknown 1%.
Retention and Graduation: 94% freshmen return for sophomore year. 71% freshmen graduate within 4 years. 84% freshmen graduate within 6 years.
Faculty: Student/faculty ratio 5:1. 73 full-time faculty, 53% hold PhDs, 7% are members of minority groups, 52% are women. 0% of classes are taught by teaching assistants.

ACADEMICS

Degrees: Bachelor's. **Classes:** Most classes have 10–19 students. **Most popular majors:** Education, General; Business Administration and Management, General; Mass Communication/Media Studies. **Special Study Options:** Distance learning; Double major; Dual enrollment; Honors program; Independent study; Internships; Liberal arts/career combination; Student-designed major; Study abroad; Teacher certification program. **Career services:** Alumni network; Career assessment; Career/job search classes; Internships; Regional alumni.

FACILITIES

Housing: Coed dorms; Men's dorms; Women's dorms; 80% of campus accessible to physically disabled. **Special Academic Facilities/Equipment:** Science Center with indoor aviary, research greenhouse, and extensive curated collections; School of Nations Museum and Classrooms; Voney Art Studio; School of Government; Merrick-Davis building for Mass Communication and Theater; McVay Center for Performing Arts; Marshall Brooks Library.

CAMPUS LIFE

Environment: Rural. **Activities:** Choral groups; Concert band; Dance; Drama/theater; International Student Organization; Jazz band; Literary magazine; Model UN; Music ensembles; Musical theater; Radio station; Student government; Student newspaper; Student-run film society; Symphony orchestra; Television station; Yearbook. 29 registered organizations, 1 honor

society, 1 religious organization on campus. **Athletics (Intercollegiate):** *Men:* baseball, basketball, cross-country, diving, football, soccer, swimming, tennis, track/field (outdoor), track/field (indoor). *Women:* basketball, cross-country, diving, soccer, swimming, tennis, track/field (outdoor), track/field (indoor), volleyball. **On-Campus Highlights:** Piasa Pub. **Environmental Initiatives:** 100% renewable energy (electricity)—recognized as a Gold Partner by the U.S. Environmental Protection Agency's "Green Power Partnership."

ADMISSIONS

Freshman Academic Profile: Average high school GPA 3.5. 29% in top 10% of high school class, 57% in top 25% of high school class, 100% in top 50% of high school class. **Test Scores:** SAT Math middle 50% range 500–593. SAT EBRW middle 50% range 510–625. ACT middle 50% range 22–27. **Basis for Candidate Selection:** *Very important factors include:* academic GPA, application essay, standardized test scores, recommendation(s), character/personal qualities, religious affiliation/commitment. *Important factors include:* rigor of secondary school record, interview, extracurricular activities, level of applicant's interest. *Other factors include:* class rank, talent/ability. **Freshman Admission Requirements:** High school diploma is required and GED is accepted. *Academic units recommended:* 4 English, 4 math, 3 science, 1 science lab, 2 foreign language, 1 social studies, 2 history, 2 academic electives. **Freshman Admission Statistics:** 105 applied, 91% admitted, 69% enrolled. **Transfer Admission Requirements:** High school transcript, college transcript(s), essay or personal statement. Minimum college GPA of 2.0 required. Lowest grade transferable C-. **General Admission Information:** Priority deadline 5/1. Regular application deadline 7/1. Non-fall registration accepted. Admission may be deferred for a maximum of 1 year.

COSTS AND FINANCIAL AID

Annual tuition $29,970. Room and board $12,270. Required fees $750. Average book and supplies expense $1,000. **Required Forms and Deadlines:** Business/Farm Supplement; CSS/Financial Aid PROFILE; Institution's own financial aid form; Noncustodial PROFILE;. **Notification of Awards:** Applicants will be notified of awards on a rolling basis beginning 3/1. **Types of Aid:** *Need-based scholarships/grants:* College/university scholarship or grant aid from institutional funds; Private scholarships. **Student Employment:** Institutional employment available. **Financial Aid Statistics:** 100% needy freshmen, 100% needy undergrads receive need-based scholarship or grant aid. 48% freshmen, 40% undergrads receive non-need-based scholarship or grant aid. 64% freshmen, 64% undergrads receive need-based self-help aid. 0% freshmen, 0% undergrads receive athletic scholarships. 99% freshmen, 98% undergrads receive any aid. 66% undergrads borrow to pay for school. Average cumulative indebtedness $19,613. **Criteria awarding aid:** *Non-need-based:* Academics, Alumni affiliation, Leadership.

PROVIDENCE COLLEGE

Harkins Hall 103, Providence, RI 02918
Phone: 401-865-2535 **Financial Aid Phone:** 401-865-2286
E-mail: pcadmiss@providence.edu **CEEB Code:** 3693
Fax: 401-865-2826 **Website:** www.providence.edu **ACT Code:** 3806

This private school, affiliated with the Roman Catholic Church, was founded in 1917. It has a 105 acre campus.

RATINGS

Admissions Selectivity Rating: 88 **Fire Safety Rating:** 98 **Green Rating:** 60*

STUDENTS AND FACULTY

Enrollment: 4,233. **Student Body:** 55% female, 45% male, 91% out-of-state, 2% international (25 countries represented). Asian 1%, African American 4%, Caucasian 78%, Hispanic 9%, Native American <1%, Pacific Islander <1%, Two or more races 2%, Race unknown 4%.
Retention and Graduation: 92% freshmen return for sophomore year. 81% freshmen graduate within 4 years. 83% freshmen graduate within 6 years. 39% grads go on to further study within 1 year. 12% grads pursue arts and sciences degrees. 2% grads pursue law degrees. 8% grads pursue business degrees. 9% grads pursue medical degrees. **Faculty:** Student/faculty ratio 12:1. 298 full-time faculty, 88% hold PhDs, 13% are members of minority groups, 41% are women. 0% of classes are taught by teaching assistants.

ACADEMICS

Degrees: Associate; Bachelor's; Certificate; Master's; Post-bachelor's certificate. **Classes:** Most classes have 20–29 students. Most lab/discussion sessions have 10–19 students. **Most popular majors:** Biology/Biological Sciences, General; Finance, General; Marketing/Marketing Management, General. **Special Study Options:** Cross-registration; Distance learning; Double major; Dual enrollment; Exchange student program (domestic); Honors program; Independent study; Internships; Liberal arts/career combination; Student-designed major; Study abroad; Teacher certification program. **Honors programs:** Liberal Arts Honors Program. **Disability Services offered:** Note-taking services; Reader services; Tutors. **Career services:** Alumni network; Career assessment; Career/job search classes; Internships.

FACILITIES

Housing: Coed dorms; Men's dorms; Special housing for disabled students; Theme housing; Wellness housing; Women's dorms; 93% of campus accessible to physically disabled. **Special Academic Facilities/Equipment:** Hunt-Cavanagh Art Gallery, Blackfriar Theatre, Science Center Complex, Computer and Language Labs, Smith Center for the Arts.

CAMPUS LIFE

Environment: City. **Activities:** Campus Ministries; Choral groups; Concert band; Dance; Drama/theater; International Student Organization; Jazz band; Literary magazine; Music ensembles; Musical theater; Pep band; Radio station; Student government; Student newspaper; Student-run film society; Television station; Yearbook. 125 registered organizations, 22 honor societies, 1 religious organization on campus. **Athletics (Intercollegiate):** *Men:* basketball, cross-country, diving, ice hockey, lacrosse, soccer, swimming, track/field (outdoor), track/field (indoor). *Women:* basketball, cross-country, diving, field hockey, ice hockey, soccer, softball, swimming, tennis, track/field (outdoor), track/field (indoor), volleyball. **On-Campus Highlights:** Ryan Center for Business Studies. **Environmental Initiatives:** Solar Energy—One of the primary energy efficient elements of the addition to Slavin Center is the 1,850-sq. ft. Building Integrated Photovoltaic (BIPV) array located on the roof above the Slavin Center lobby entrance. Photovoltaic cells capture the sun's energy and convert it directly into electricity.

ADMISSIONS

Freshman Academic Profile: Average high school GPA 3.4. 36% in top 10% of high school class, 65% in top 25% of high school class, 92% in top 50% of high school class. 57% from public high schools. **Test Scores:** SAT Math middle 50% range 580–670. SAT EBRW middle 50% range 580–660. ACT middle 50% range 26–30. **Basis for Candidate Selection:** *Very important factors include:* rigor of secondary school record, academic GPA, application essay. *Important factors include:* recommendation(s), extracurricular activities, character/personal qualities. *Other factors include:* class rank, standardized test scores, talent/ability, first generation, alumni/ae relation, geographical residence, racial/ethnic status, volunteer work, work experience, level of applicant's interest. **Freshman Admission Requirements:** High school diploma is required and GED is not accepted. *Academic units required:* 4 English, 4 math, 3 science, 2 science labs, 3 foreign language, 2 social studies, 2 history. *Academic units recommended:* 4 English, 4 math, 4 science, 2 science labs, 4 foreign language, 2 social studies, 2 history. **Freshman Admission Statistics:** 11,251 applied, 52% admitted, 18% enrolled. **Transfer Admission Requirements:** High school transcript, college transcript(s), essay or personal statement, statement of good standing from prior institution(s). Minimum college GPA of 3.0 required. Lowest grade transferable C. **General Admission Information:** Application fee $65. Regular application deadline 1/15. Non-fall registration accepted. Admission may be deferred for a maximum of 1 year.

COSTS AND FINANCIAL AID

Required Forms and Deadlines: CSS/Financial Aid PROFILE; FAFSA. **Notification of Awards:** Applicants will be notified of awards on or about 3/15. **Types of Aid:** *Need-based scholarships/grants:* College/university scholarship or grant aid from institutional funds; Federal Pell; Private scholarships; SEOG; State scholarships/grants; United Negro College Fund. *Loans:* Direct PLUS loans; Direct Subsidized Stafford Loans; Direct Unsubsidized Stafford Loans. **Student Employment:** Federal Work-Study Program available. Institutional employment available. **Financial Aid Statistics:** 94% needy freshmen, 99% needy undergrads receive need-based scholarship or grant aid. 8% freshmen, 6% undergrads receive non-need-based scholarship or grant aid. 89% freshmen, 97% undergrads receive need-based self-help aid. 5% freshmen, 5% undergrads receive athletic scholarships. 79% freshmen, 75% undergrads receive any aid. 68% undergrads borrow to pay for school. Average cumulative indebtedness $41,383. **Criteria awarding aid:** *Need-based:* Minority status, Music/drama. *Non-need-based:* Academics, Athletics, Leadership, Minority status, Music/drama.

PURDUE UNIVERSITY—NORTHWEST

Office of Admissions, Hammond, IN 46323-2094
Phone: 219-989-2213 **Financial Aid Phone:** 219-989-2301
E-mail: adms@purduecal.edu **CEEB Code:** 1638
Fax: 219-989-2775 **Website:** http://www.purduecal.edu/ **ACT Code:** 1233

This public school was founded in 1946. It has a 194 acre campus.

RATINGS

Admissions Selectivity Rating: 77   **Fire Safety Rating:** 95   **Green Rating:** 60*

STUDENTS AND FACULTY

Enrollment: 8,403. **Student Body:** 55% female, 45% male, 11% out-of-state, 3% international (39 countries represented). Asian 1%, African American 19%, Caucasian 61%, Hispanic 15%, Native American <1%, Race unknown 0%. **Retention and Graduation:** 69% freshmen return for sophomore year. **Faculty:** Student/faculty ratio 21:1. 268 full-time faculty, 69% hold PhDs, 21% are members of minority groups, 48% are women.

ACADEMICS

Degrees: Associate; Bachelor's; Certificate; Master's; Post-bachelor's certificate. **Classes:** Most classes have 20–29 students. Most lab/discussion sessions have 20–29 students. **Most popular majors:** Marketing/Marketing Management, General; Engineering, General; Elementary Education and Teaching. **Special Study Options:** Accelerated program; Cooperative education program; Distance learning; Double major; Dual enrollment; English as a Second Language (ESL); Honors program; Independent study; Internships; Study abroad; Teacher certification program; Weekend college. **Honors programs:** Purdue Calumet Honors Program. **Disability Services offered:** Note-taking services; Reader services; Tape recorders; Tutors. **Career services:** Career assessment; Career/job search classes; Internships.

FACILITIES

Housing: Apartments for single students; 100% of campus accessible to physically disabled. **Special Academic Facilities/Equipment:** Audio-visual services, urban development institute.

CAMPUS LIFE

Environment: City. **Activities:** Campus Ministries; Choral groups; Dance; Drama/theater; International Student Organization; Radio station; Student government; Student newspaper. 56 registered organizations, 25 honor societies, 3 religious organizations, 2 fraternities, 3 sororities on campus. **Athletics (Intercollegiate):** *Men:* basketball. *Women:* basketball. **On-Campus Highlights:** Physical Education and Recreation Building. **Environmental Initiatives:** Campus-wide Recycling.

ADMISSIONS

Freshman Academic Profile: Average high school GPA 2.6. 10% in top 10% of high school class, 28% in top 25% of high school class, 58% in top 50% of high school class. **Test Scores:** SAT Math middle 50% range 410–520. SAT EBRW middle 50% range 410–510. ACT middle 50% range 17–23. **Basis for Candidate Selection:** *Important factors include:* rigor of secondary school record, class rank, academic GPA, standardized test scores. **Freshman Admission Requirements:** High school diploma is required and GED is accepted. *Academic units required:* 4 English, 2 math, 1 science, 1 science lab, 2 foreign language, 1 social studies, 1 history. *Academic units recommended:* 4 English, 2 math, 2 science, 2 science labs, 2 foreign language, 2 social studies, 1 history. **Freshman Admission Statistics:** 5,884 applied, 69% admitted, 33% enrolled. **Transfer Admission Requirements:** High school transcript. Minimum college GPA of 2.0 required. Lowest grade transferable C. **General Admission Information:** Non-fall registration accepted. Admission may be deferred for a maximum of 1 semester.

COSTS AND FINANCIAL AID

Average book and supplies expense $1,125. **Required Forms and Deadlines:** FAFSA. **Notification of Awards:** Applicants will be notified of awards on a rolling basis beginning 4/15. **Types of Aid:** *Need-based scholarships/grants:* College/university scholarship or grant aid from institutional funds; Federal Pell; SEOG; State scholarships/grants. *Loans:* Direct PLUS loans; Direct Subsidized Stafford Loans; Direct Unsubsidized Stafford Loans. **Student Employment:** Federal Work-Study Program available. **Financial Aid Statistics:** 61% needy freshmen, 65% needy undergrads receive need-based scholarship or grant aid. 25% freshmen, 15% undergrads receive non-need-based scholarship or grant aid. 61% freshmen, 72% undergrads receive need-based self-help aid. 1% freshmen, 0% undergrads receive athletic scholarships. **Criteria awarding** aid: *Need-based:* Academics, Minority status. *Non-need-based:* Academics, Athletics, Minority status, State/district residency.

PURDUE UNIVERSITY—WEST LAFAYETTE

475 Stadium Mall Drive, West Lafayette, IN 47907-2050
Phone: (765) 494-1776 **Financial Aid Phone:** (765) 494-0998
E-mail: admissions@purdue.edu **CEEB Code:** 1631
Fax: 765-494-0544 **Website:** www.purdue.edu **ACT Code:** 1230

This public school was founded in 1869. It has a 2602 acre campus.

RATINGS
Admissions Selectivity Rating: 88   **Fire Safety Rating:** 96   **Green Rating:** 60*

STUDENTS AND FACULTY
Enrollment: 30,831. **Student Body:** 43% female, 57% male, 36% out-of-state, 16% international (123 countries represented). Asian 8%, African American 3%, Caucasian 63%, Hispanic 5%, Native American <1%, Pacific Islander <1%, Two or more races 3%, Race unknown 2%.
Retention and Graduation: 92% freshmen return for sophomore year. 51% freshmen graduate within 4 years. 21% grads go on to further study within 1 year. **Faculty:** Student/faculty ratio 13:1. 2,287 full-time faculty, 98% hold PhDs, 26% are members of minority groups, 35% are women. 24% of classes are taught by teaching assistants.

ACADEMICS
Degrees: Bachelor's; Certificate; Doctoral degree—professional practice; Doctoral degree research/scholarship; Master's; Post-bachelor's certificate; Post-master's certificate; Terminal Associate. **Classes:** Most classes have 10–19 students. Most lab/discussion sessions have 20–29 students. **Most popular majors:** Mechanical/Mechanical Engineering Technology/Technician; Computer Science; Mechanical Engineering. **Special Study Options:** Accelerated program; Cooperative education program; Cross-registration; Distance learning; Double major; Dual enrollment; English as a Second Language (ESL); Honors program; Independent study; Internships; Liberal arts/career combination; Study abroad; Teacher certification program; Weekend college. **Honors programs:** University Honors Program. **Disability Services offered:** Note-taking services; Reader services; Tape recorders; Tutors. **Career services:** Alumni network; Alumni services; Career assessment; Career/job search classes; Internships; Regional alumni.

FACILITIES
Housing: Apartments for married students; Apartments for single students; Coed dorms; Cooperative housing; Fraternity/sorority housing; Men's dorms; Special housing for disabled students; Theme housing; Women's dorms. 93.4% of campus accessible to physically disabled. **Special Academic Facilities/Equipment:** Hall of music, child development lab, speech and hearing clinic, small animal veterinary clinic, horticulture park, linear accelerator, tornado simulator, nuclear accelerator. **Campus Network:** 100% of classrooms, 100% of dorms, 100% of libraries, 100% of dining areas, 100% of common outdoor areas have wireless network access.

CAMPUS LIFE
Environment: Town. **Activities:** Campus Ministries; Choral groups; Concert band; Dance; Drama/theater; International Student Organization; Jazz band; Literary magazine; Marching band; Model UN; Music ensembles; Pep band; Radio station; Student government; Student newspaper; Symphony orchestra; Television station. 919 registered organizations, 42 honor societies, 47 religious organizations, 30 fraternities, 25 sororities on campus. **Athletics (Intercollegiate):** *Men:* baseball, basketball, cross-country, diving, football, golf, swimming, tennis, track/field (outdoor), track/field (indoor), wrestling. *Women:* basketball, cross-country, diving, golf, soccer, softball, swimming, tennis, track/field (outdoor), track/field (indoor), volleyball. **On-Campus Highlights:** Purdue Memorial Union. **Environmental Initiatives:** Friday Night Lights (FNL) was launched as a collaborative partnership between the Student Sustainability Council, Office of University Sustainability, Building Services, Building Deputies, Purdue Police Department, and numerous student volunteers. Every Friday evening participants volunteer an hour of their time to turn off lights in classrooms of targeted academic buildings so they will not be left on over the weekend. Not only does this program reduce Purdue's energy use and carbon

footprint, it also increases social capital among those on campus and, ultimately, trims Purdue's bottom line.

ADMISSIONS
Freshman Academic Profile: Average high school GPA 3.8. 44% in top 10% of high school class, 78% in top 25% of high school class, 97% in top 50% of high school class. **Test Scores:** SAT Math middle 50% range 580–710. SAT EBRW middle 50% range 570–670. ACT middle 50% range 25–31. **Basis for Candidate Selection:** *Very important factors include:* rigor of secondary school record, academic GPA, standardized test scores. *Important factors include:* application essay, recommendation(s), extracurricular activities, character/personal qualities, first generation. *Other factors include:* class rank, talent/ability, alumni/ae relation, geographical residence, state residency, racial/ethnic status, volunteer work, work experience, level of applicant's interest. **Freshman Admission Requirements:** High school diploma is required and GED is accepted. *Academic units required:* 4 English, 3 math, 3 science, 2 science labs, 3 foreign language. **Freshman Admission Statistics:** 48,912 applied, 57% admitted, 27% enrolled. **Transfer Admission Requirements:** College transcript(s), essay or personal statement, statement of good standing from prior institution(s). Minimum college GPA of 2.5 required. Lowest grade transferable C. **General Admission Information:** Application fee $60. Priority deadline 2/1. Non-fall registration accepted.

COSTS AND FINANCIAL AID
Annual in-state tuition $9,208. Annual out-of-state tuition $28,010. Room and board $10,030. Required fees $784. Average book and supplies expense $1,160. **Required Forms and Deadlines:** FAFSA. **Notification of Awards:** Applicants will be notified of awards on or about 4/15. **Types of Aid:** *Need-based scholarships/grants:* College/university scholarship or grant aid from institutional funds; Federal Pell; Private scholarships; SEOG; State scholarships/grants. *Loans:* Direct PLUS loans; Direct Subsidized Stafford Loans; Direct Unsubsidized Stafford Loans. **Student Employment:** Federal Work-Study Program available. Institutional employment available. **Financial Aid Statistics:** 77% needy freshmen, 80% needy undergrads receive need-based scholarship or grant aid. 37% freshmen, 32% undergrads receive non-need-based scholarship or grant aid. 53% freshmen, 58% undergrads receive need-based self-help aid. 1% freshmen, 1% undergrads receive athletic scholarships. 74% freshmen, 77% undergrads receive any aid. 40% undergrads borrow to pay for school. Average cumulative indebtedness $28,440. **Criteria awarding aid:** *Non-need-based:* Academics, Athletics, Leadership, Music/drama, State/district residency.

QUEENS UNIVERSITY OF CHARLOTTE

1900 Selwyn Avenue, Charlotte, NC 28274
Phone: 704-337-2212 **Financial Aid Phone:** 704-337-2225
E-mail: admissions@queens.edu **CEEB Code:** 5560
Fax: 704-337-2403 **Website:** www.queens.edu **ACT Code:** 3148

This private school, affiliated with the Presbyterian Church, was founded in 1857. It has a 30 acre campus.

RATINGS
Admissions Selectivity Rating: 77   **Fire Safety Rating:** 70   **Green Rating:** 60*

STUDENTS AND FACULTY
Enrollment: 1,911. **Student Body:** 76% female, 24% male, 8% international. Asian 2%, African American 16%, Caucasian 55%, Hispanic 3%, Native American 1%, Pacific Islander 0%, Two or more races 2%, Race unknown 13%.
Retention and Graduation: 70% freshmen return for sophomore year.
Faculty: Student/faculty ratio 12:1. 123 full-time faculty, 72% hold PhDs, 7% are members of minority groups, 68% are women. 0% of classes are taught by teaching assistants.

ACADEMICS
Degrees: Bachelor's; Master's; Post-bachelor's certificate; Terminal Associate. **Classes:** Most classes have 10–19 students. Most lab/discussion sessions have 10–19 students. **Special Study Options:** Accelerated program; Distance learning; Double major; Honors program; Independent study; Internships; Liberal arts/career combination; Study abroad; Teacher certification program; Weekend college. **Disability Services offered:** Note-taking services; Reader services; Tape recorders; Tutors. **Career services:** Alumni network; Career/job search classes; Internships.

FACILITIES

Housing: Coed dorms; Special housing for disabled students; 63% of campus accessible to physically disabled. **Special Academic Facilities/Equipment:** Three art galleries, rare books museum.

CAMPUS LIFE

Environment: Metropolis. **Activities:** Campus Ministries; Choral groups; Concert band; Dance; Drama/theater; International Student Organization; Literary magazine; Model UN; Music ensembles; Musical theater; Student government; Student newspaper. 40 registered organizations, 12 honor societies, 6 religious organizations, 2 fraternities, 5 sororities on campus. **Athletics (Intercollegiate):** *Men:* basketball, cheerleading, cross-country, golf, lacrosse, soccer, tennis, track/field (outdoor). *Women:* basketball, cheerleading, cross-country, golf, lacrosse, soccer, softball, tennis, track/field (outdoor), volleyball. **On-Campus Highlights:** Levine Center.

ADMISSIONS

Freshman Academic Profile: Average high school GPA 3.5. 14% in top 10% of high school class, 39% in top 25% of high school class, 78% in top 50% of high school class. **Test Scores:** SAT Math middle 50% range 460–570. SAT EBRW middle 50% range 470–580. ACT middle 50% range 20–25. **Basis for Candidate Selection:** *Very important factors include:* rigor of secondary school record, academic GPA, standardized test scores, extracurricular activities, character/personal qualities. *Important factors include:* class rank, interview, volunteer work. *Other factors include:* application essay, recommendation(s), talent/ability, first generation, alumni/ae relation, work experience. **Freshman Admission Requirements:** High school diploma is required and GED is accepted. *Academic units required:* 4 English, 3 math, 2 science, 1 science lab, 2 foreign language, 2 social studies. **Freshman Admission Statistics:** 2,199 applied, 74% admitted, 22% enrolled. **Transfer Admission Requirements:** High school transcript, college transcript(s), essay or personal statement, statement of good standing from prior institution(s). Minimum college GPA of 2.0 required. Lowest grade transferable C. **General Admission Information:** Application fee $40. Non-fall registration accepted. Admission may be deferred for a maximum of 1 year.

COSTS AND FINANCIAL AID

Required Forms and Deadlines: FAFSA; State aid form. **Notification of Awards:** Applicants will be notified of awards on a rolling basis beginning 3/15. **Types of Aid:** *Need-based scholarships/grants:* College/university scholarship or grant aid from institutional funds; Federal Pell; Private scholarships; SEOG; State scholarships/grants. *Loans:* Direct PLUS loans; Direct Subsidized Stafford Loans; Direct Unsubsidized Stafford Loans. **Student Employment:** Federal Work-Study Program available. Institutional employment available. **Financial Aid Statistics:** 100% needy freshmen, 99% needy undergrads receive need-based scholarship or grant aid. 18% freshmen, 15% undergrads receive non-need-based scholarship or grant aid. 79% freshmen, 83% undergrads receive need-based self-help aid. 11% freshmen, 10% undergrads receive athletic scholarships. **Criteria awarding aid:** *Need-based:* Academics, Leadership, Minority status. *Non-need-based:* Academics, Art, Athletics, Leadership, Minority status, Music/drama, Religious affiliation.

QUINCY UNIVERSITY

1800 College Avenue, Quincy, IL 62301-2699
Phone: 217-228-5210 **Financial Aid Phone:** 217-228-5260
E-mail: admissions@quincy.edu **CEEB Code:** 1645
Fax: 217-228-5479 **Website:** www.quincy.edu **ACT Code:** 1120

This private school, affiliated with the Roman Catholic Church, was founded in 1860. It has a 70 acre campus.

RATINGS

Admissions Selectivity Rating: 74   **Fire Safety Rating:** 97   **Green Rating:** 60*

STUDENTS AND FACULTY

Enrollment: 1,075. **Student Body:** 56% female, 44% male, 28% out-of-state, 6 countries represented.
Retention and Graduation: 76% freshmen return for sophomore year. 22% grads go on to further study within 1 year. 11% grads pursue arts and sciences degrees. 2% grads pursue law degrees. 5% grads pursue business degrees. 2% grads pursue medical degrees. **Faculty:** Student/faculty ratio 14:1. 56 full-time faculty, 71% hold PhDs, 7% are members of minority groups, 39% are women. 0% of classes are taught by teaching assistants.

ACADEMICS

Degrees: Bachelor's; Master's; Transfer Associate. **Classes:** Most classes have 10–19 students. Most lab/discussion sessions have fewer than 10 students. **Most popular majors:** Registered Nursing/Registered Nurse; Management Science; Elementary Education and Teaching. **Special Study Options:** Accelerated program; Distance learning; Double major; Dual enrollment; Honors program; Independent study; Internships; Student-designed major; Study abroad; Teacher certification program. **Honors programs:** The Honors Program provides an academically challenging course of study which adds an interdisciplinary dimension to a student's major field. The program promotes academic excellence through critical thinking, original research, exceptional writing, and public presentation of scholarship. **Disability Services offered:** Note-taking services; Reader services; Tape recorders; Tutors. **Career services:** Alumni services; Career assessment; Career/job search classes; Internships.

FACILITIES

Housing: Apartments for single students; Coed dorms; Fraternity/sorority housing; Special housing for disabled students; Special housing for international students; Theme housing; 75% of campus accessible to physically disabled. **Special Academic Facilities/Equipment:** Reading center for student teachers, multimedia and graphic design labs, TV broadcast studio, art gallery, 200-seat theater, environmental studies institute, hospital simulation lab, aviation facility with flight simulator.

CAMPUS LIFE

Environment: Town. **Activities:** Campus Ministries; Choral groups; Concert band; Dance; Drama/theater; Jazz band; Literary magazine; Marching band; Music ensembles; Musical theater; Pep band; Student government; Student newspaper; Student-run film society; Symphony orchestra. 50 registered organizations, 8 honor societies, 4 religious organizations, 2 fraternities, 2 sororities on campus. **Athletics (Intercollegiate):** *Men:* baseball, basketball, cross-country, football, golf, soccer, tennis, volleyball. *Women:* basketball, cross-country, golf, soccer, softball, tennis, volleyball. **On-Campus Highlights:** Health and Fitness Center. **Environmental Initiatives:** Residence hall renovation: Helein Hall renovations included use of recycled furniture and the installation of an energy-efficient VRV hvac system.

ADMISSIONS

Freshman Academic Profile: 76% from public high schools. **Test Scores:** SAT Math middle 50% range 410–490. SAT EBRW middle 50% range 460–490. ACT middle 50% range 19–25. **Basis for Candidate Selection:** *Very important factors include:* rigor of secondary school record, academic GPA. *Important factors include:* class rank, application essay, standardized test scores, recommendation(s), extracurricular activities, character/personal qualities, volunteer work, work experience, level of applicant's interest. *Other factors include:* interview, talent/ability. **Freshman Admission Requirements:** High school diploma is required and GED is accepted. *Academic units recommended:* 4 English, 3 math, 3 science, 2 foreign language, 3 social studies. **Freshman Admission Statistics:** 903 applied, 89% admitted, 27% enrolled. **Transfer Admission Requirements:** College transcript(s), statement of good standing from prior institution(s). Minimum college GPA of 2.0 required. Lowest grade transferable D. **General Admission Information:** Application fee $25. Priority deadline 4/1. Non-fall registration accepted.

COSTS AND FINANCIAL AID

Annual tuition $25,598. Room and board $11,336. Required fees $974. Average book and supplies expense $1,250. **Required Forms and Deadlines:** FAFSA. **Notification of Awards:** Applicants will be notified of awards on a rolling basis beginning 3/1. **Types of Aid:** *Need-based scholarships/grants:* College/university scholarship or grant aid from institutional funds; Federal Pell; Private scholarships; SEOG; State scholarships/grants. *Loans:* Direct PLUS loans; Direct Subsidized Stafford Loans; Direct Unsubsidized Stafford Loans. **Student Employment:** Federal Work-Study Program available. Institutional employment available. **Financial Aid Statistics:** 98% needy freshmen, 92% needy undergrads receive need-based scholarship or grant aid. 23% freshmen, 16% undergrads receive non-need-based scholarship or grant aid. 69% freshmen, 72% undergrads receive need-based self-help aid. 8% freshmen, 4% undergrads receive athletic scholarships. 100% freshmen, 93% undergrads receive any aid. **Criteria awarding aid:** *Need-based:* Academics, Alumni affiliation, Art, Leadership, Minority status, Music/drama. *Non-need-based:* Academics, Alumni affiliation, Art, Athletics, Leadership, Music/drama.

QUINNIPIAC UNIVERSITY

275 Mount Carmel Avenue, Hamden, CT 06518
Phone: 203-582-8600 **Financial Aid Phone:** 203-582-8750
E-mail: admissions@qu.edu **CEEB Code:** 3712
Fax: 203-582-8906 **Website:** www.qu.edu **ACT Code:** 582

This private school was founded in 1929. It has a 600 acre campus.

RATINGS
Admissions Selectivity Rating: 80   **Fire Safety Rating:** 98   **Green Rating:** 60*

STUDENTS AND FACULTY
Enrollment: 7,371. **Student Body:** 61% female, 39% male, 2% international (45 countries represented). Asian 3%, African American 4%, Caucasian 77%, Hispanic 10%, Native American <1%, Pacific Islander <1%, Two or more races 2%, Race unknown 2%.
Retention and Graduation: 86% freshmen return for sophomore year. 70% freshmen graduate within 4 years. 77% freshmen graduate within 6 years. 43% grads go on to further study within 1 year. 19% grads pursue arts and sciences degrees. 2% grads pursue law degrees. 14% grads pursue business degrees. 2% grads pursue medical degrees. **Faculty:** Student/faculty ratio 14:1. 395 full-time faculty, 87% hold PhDs, 16% are members of minority groups, 56% are women. 0% of classes are taught by teaching assistants.

ACADEMICS
Degrees: Bachelor's; Doctoral degree—professional practice; Master's; Post-bachelor's certificate; Post-master's certificate. **Classes:** Most classes have 10–19 students. Most lab/discussion sessions have 10–19 students. **Most popular majors:** Psychology, General; Registered Nursing/Registered Nurse; Business/Commerce, General. **Special Study Options:** Accelerated program; Distance learning; Double major; Dual enrollment; Honors program; Independent study; Internships; Study abroad; Teacher certification program. **Honors programs:** The University Honors Program, limited to 80–85 freshmen who are selected following their acceptance, provides challenging coursework and opportunities for learning and service. **Combined degree programs:** BA/JD; BA/MA. **Career services:** Alumni network; Alumni services; Career assessment; Career/job search classes; Internships; Regional alumni.

FACILITIES
Housing: Coed dorms; Theme housing; Wellness housing; 100% of campus accessible to physically disabled. **Special Academic Facilities/Equipment:** Quinnipiac Polling Institute, Financial Technology Center, Motion Analysis Lab, Albert Schweitzer Institute, Critical Care Nursing Lab, Fully digital/high definition TV production studio, editing labs, news technology center, Irish Famine Museum "An Gorta Mor."

CAMPUS LIFE
Environment: Town. **Activities:** Campus Ministries; Choral groups; Dance; Drama/theater; International Student Organization; Jazz band; Literary magazine; Music ensembles; Musical theater; Pep band; Radio station; Student government; Student newspaper; Student-run film society; Television station; Yearbook. 145 registered organizations, 18 honor societies, 7 religious organizations, 8 fraternities, 10 sororities on campus. **Athletics (Intercollegiate):** *Men:* baseball, basketball, cross-country, ice hockey, lacrosse, soccer, tennis. *Women:* basketball, cheerleading, cross-country, field hockey, ice hockey, lacrosse, soccer, softball, tennis, track/field (outdoor), track/field (indoor), volleyball. **On-Campus Highlights:** Arnold Bernhard Library. **Environmental Initiatives:** 100% of Quinnipiac electricity requirements on all three of its campuses have been purchased from renewable energy credits.

ADMISSIONS
Freshman Academic Profile: Average high school GPA 3.4. 20% in top 10% of high school class, 58% in top 25% of high school class, 92% in top 50% of high school class. 77% from public high schools. **Test Scores:** SAT Math middle 50% range 540–630. SAT EBRW middle 50% range 550–630. ACT middle 50% range 23–28. **Basis for Candidate Selection:** *Very important factors include:* rigor of secondary school record, academic GPA, level of applicant's interest. *Important factors include:* class rank, application essay, standardized test scores, recommendation(s). *Other factors include:* interview, extracurricular activities, talent/ability, character/personal qualities, first generation, alumni/ae relation, state residency, racial/ethnic status, work

experience. **Freshman Admission Requirements:** High school diploma is required and GED ls accepted. *Academic units required:* 4 English, 3 math, 3 science, 2 foreign language, 2 social studies, 3 academic electives. **Freshman Admission Statistics:** 22,751 applied, 72% admitted, 12% enrolled. **Transfer Admission Requirements:** College transcript(s), essay or personal statement. Minimum college GPA of 2.5 required. Lowest grade transferable C. **General Admission Information:** Application fee $65. Non-fall registration accepted.

COSTS AND FINANCIAL AID
Annual tuition $46,790. Room and board $15,600. Required fees $2,490. Average book and supplies expense $800. **Required Forms and Deadlines:** FAFSA. **Notification of Awards:** Applicants will be notified of awards on a rolling basis beginning 1/15. **Types of Aid:** *Need-based scholarships/grants:* College/university scholarship or grant aid from institutional funds; Federal Pell; Private scholarships; SEOG; State scholarships/grants. *Loans:* Direct PLUS loans; Direct Subsidized Stafford Loans; Direct Unsubsidized Stafford Loans. **Student Employment:** Federal Work-Study Program available. Institutional employment available. **Financial Aid Statistics:** 98% needy freshmen, 98% needy undergrads receive need-based scholarship or grant aid. 93% freshmen, 78% undergrads receive non-need-based scholarship or grant aid. 75% freshmen, 80% undergrads receive need-based self-help aid. 5% freshmen, 5% undergrads receive athletic scholarships. 98% freshmen, 88% undergrads receive any aid. 70% undergrads borrow to pay for school. Average cumulative indebtedness $48,544. **Criteria awarding aid:** *Non-need-based:* Academics, Athletics.

RADFORD UNIVERSITY

PO Box 6903, Radford, VA 24142
Phone: 540-831-5371 **Financial Aid Phone:** 540-831-5408
E-mail: admissions@radford.edu **CEEB Code:** 5565
Fax: 540-831-5038 **Website:** www.radford.edu **ACT Code:** 4422

This public school was founded in 1910. It has a 204 acre campus.

RATINGS
Admissions Selectivity Rating: 76   **Fire Safety Rating:** 90   **Green Rating:** 87

STUDENTS AND FACULTY
Enrollment: 7,920. **Student Body:** 61% female, 39% male, 7% out-of-state, 1% international (54 countries represented). Asian 2%, African American 17%, Caucasian 64%, Hispanic 7%, Native American <1%, Pacific Islander <1%, Two or more races 6%, Race unknown 3%.
Retention and Graduation: 71% freshmen return for sophomore year. 40% freshmen graduate within 4 years. 55% freshmen graduate within 6 years. 18% grads go on to further study within 1 year. **Faculty:** Student/faculty ratio 15:1. 535 full-time faculty, 79% hold PhDs, 12% are members of minority groups, 56% are women. 2% of classes are taught by teaching assistants.

ACADEMICS
Degrees: Associate; Bachelor's; Certificate; Doctoral degree—other; Doctoral degree—professional practice; Doctoral degree research/scholarship; Master's; Post-bachelor's certificate; Post-master's certificate. **Classes:** Most classes have 10–19 students. Most lab/discussion sessions have 10–19 students. **Most popular majors:** Multi-/Interdisciplinary Studies, Other; Physical Education Teaching and Coaching; Registered Nursing/Registered Nurse. **Special Study Options:** Accelerated program; Distance learning; Double major; Dual enrollment; Honors program; Independent study; Internships; Student-designed major; Study abroad; Teacher certification program. **Honors programs:** A hallmark of a Radford education is faculty-student collaboration and nowhere is that more evident than in the university's Honors Academy. Honors courses fulfill requirements in the Core Curriculum and are taught by faculty in a highly interactive and engaging environment. In addition, Honors Academy students enjoy early registration, may elect to live in a designated residence hall, are supported financially to present results of their work at professional and undergraduate conferences, and receive an honors scholarship. The honors curriculum leads students to achieve the status of "Highlander Scholar" during their careers at RU. To graduate with this distinction, a student must complete 27 credit hours of honors coursework, present an honors capstone project in a public forum, and have a cumulative GPA of 3.5 at the time of graduation. Status as a Highlander Scholar is noted on the student's diploma and transcript. **Disability Services offered:** Note-taking services; Reader services; Tape recorders; Tutors. **Career services:** Alumni network;

Alumni services; Career assessment; Career/job search classes; Internships; Regional alumni.

FACILITIES

Housing: Apartments for single students; Coed dorms; Special housing for disabled students; Special housing for international students; Theme housing; Wellness housing; 98% of campus accessible to physically disabled. **Special Academic Facilities/Equipment:** College of Business and Economics; Covington Center for Visual and Performing Arts featuring international and national art exhibits; Museum of the Earth Sciences; 1,200-seat performance/lecture hall; also an observatory, planetarium, nature center, state-of-the-art motion analysis lab, clinical simulation center, cadaver lab, speech-language-hearing center and greenhouse. **Campus Network:** 100% of classrooms, 100% of dorms, 80% of student union, 100% of libraries, 100% of dining areas have wireless network access.

CAMPUS LIFE

Environment: Village. **Activities:** Campus Ministries; Choral groups; Concert band; Dance; Drama/theater; International Student Organization; Jazz band; Literary magazine; Model UN; Music ensembles; Musical theater; Opera; Pep band; Radio station; Student government; Student newspaper; Student-run film society; Yearbook. 295 registered organizations, 16 honor societies, 14 religious organizations, 12 fraternities, 10 sororities on campus. **Athletics (Intercollegiate):** *Men:* baseball, basketball, cheerleading, cross-country, golf, soccer, tennis, track/field (outdoor), track/field (indoor). *Women:* basketball, cheerleading, cross-country, diving, field hockey, golf, soccer, softball, swimming, tennis, track/field (outdoor), track/field (indoor), volleyball. **On-Campus Highlights:** Student Recreation & Wellness Center (opened fall 2014). **Environmental Initiatives:** Buildings: Per Commonwealth of Virginia Policy, RU constructs and completes major renovations to LEED Silver minimum standards. The University now has 11 LEED Certified buildings (10 Gold and 1 Silver). In addition, every building on campus is sub-metered, giving the university a clear and accurate way to monitor energy, water, and steam use, identify problem areas, and plan repairs or renovations.

ADMISSIONS

Freshman Academic Profile: Average high school GPA 3.3. 7% in top 10% of high school class, 28% in top 25% of high school class, 59% in top 50% of high school class. 95% from public high schools. **Test Scores:** SAT Math middle 50% range 460–540. SAT EBRW middle 50% range 480–570. ACT middle 50% range 17–23. **Basis for Candidate Selection:** *Very important factors include:* rigor of secondary school record. *Important factors include:* academic GPA. *Other factors include:* class rank, application essay, standardized test scores, recommendation(s), interview, extracurricular activities, talent/ability, character/personal qualities, first generation, alumni/ae relation, volunteer work, work experience, level of applicant's interest. **Freshman Admission Requirements:** High school diploma is required and GED is accepted. *Academic units recommended:* 4 English, 4 math, 4 science, 4 science labs, 4 foreign language, 2 social studies, 2 history. **Freshman Admission Statistics:** 16,013 applied, 75% admitted, 14% enrolled. **Transfer Admission Requirements:** College transcript(s). Minimum college GPA of 2.0 required. Lowest grade transferable C. **General Admission Information:** Priority deadline 2/1. Non-fall registration accepted. Admission may be deferred for a maximum of 1 year.

COSTS AND FINANCIAL AID

Annual in-state tuition $7,922. Annual out-of-state tuition $19,557. Room and board $9,637. Required fees $3,428. Average book and supplies expense $1,200. **Required Forms and Deadlines:** FAFSA. **Notification of Awards:** Applicants will be notified of awards on a rolling basis beginning 4/15. **Types of Aid:** *Need-based scholarships/grants:* College/university scholarship or grant aid from institutional funds; Federal Pell; Private scholarships; SEOG; State scholarships/grants. *Loans:* Direct PLUS loans; Direct Subsidized Stafford Loans; Direct Unsubsidized Stafford Loans. **Student Employment:** Federal Work-Study Program available. Institutional employment available. **Financial Aid Statistics:** 87% needy freshmen, 81% needy undergrads receive need-based scholarship or grant aid. 18% freshmen, 9% undergrads receive non-need-based scholarship or grant aid. 86% freshmen, 87% undergrads receive need-based self-help aid. 1% freshmen, 1% undergrads receive athletic scholarships. 91% freshmen, 81% undergrads receive any aid. 70% undergrads borrow to pay for school. Average cumulative indebtedness $32,261. **Criteria awarding aid:** *Need-based:* Academics. *Non-need-based:* Academics, Alumni affiliation, Art, Athletics, Leadership, Music/drama, State/district residency.

RAMAPO COLLEGE OF NEW JERSEY

505 Ramapo Valley Road-Admissions Office, Mahwah, NJ 07430-1680
Phone: 201-684-7300 **Financial Aid Phone:** 201-684-7550
E-mail: admissions@ramapo.edu **CEEB Code:** 2884
Fax: 201-684-7964 **Website:** www.ramapo.edu **ACT Code:** 2591

This public school was founded in 1971. It has a 300 acre campus.

RATINGS

Admissions Selectivity Rating: 86   **Fire Safety Rating:** 97   **Green Rating:** 60*

STUDENTS AND FACULTY

Enrollment: 5,314. **Student Body:** 55% female, 45% male, 6% out-of-state, 2% international (27 countries represented). Asian 8%, African American 5%, Caucasian 64%, Hispanic 16%, Native American 1%, Pacific Islander <1%, Two or more races 1%, Race unknown 5%.
Retention and Graduation: 86% freshmen return for sophomore year. 61% freshmen graduate within 4 years. 73% freshmen graduate within 6 years.
Faculty: Student/faculty ratio 18:1. 216 full-time faculty, 93% hold PhDs, 28% are members of minority groups, 51% are women. 0% of classes are taught by teaching assistants.

ACADEMICS

Degrees: Bachelor's; Certificate; Master's; Post-master's certificate. **Classes:** Most classes have 20–29 students. **Most popular majors:** Business Administration and Management, General; Psychology, General; Speech Communication and Rhetoric. **Special Study Options:** Accelerated program; Cooperative education program; Cross-registration; Distance learning; Double major; Dual enrollment; Exchange student program (domestic); External degree program; Honors program; Independent study; Internships; Liberal arts/career combination; Student-designed major; Study abroad; Teacher certification program; Weekend college. **Honors programs:** The Ramapo College Honors Program is designed for students who desire a scholarly environment and an opportunity to interact with challenging faculty members and like- minded students. The Honors Program provides expanded opportunities for learning and reflection. Other benefits of the College Honors Program include residence hall options, special seminars, and exciting trips. Graduation from the College Honors Program is one indicator of a highly motivated, highly skilled, self-initiating individual. Students may participate in the College Honors Program by completing three H-option courses and receiving an Honors Certificate or by completing three H-option courses and completing a senior project, in which case the student graduates with full college honors. Full college honors is indicated on the diploma. http://www.ramapo.edu/honors/. **Combined degree programs:** BA/DDS; BA/MA; BA/MD. **Disability Services offered:** Note-taking services; Reader services; Tape recorders; Tutors. **Career services:** Alumni network; Alumni services; Career assessment; Career/job search classes; Internships.

FACILITIES

Housing: Coed dorms; 100% of campus accessible to physically disabled. **Special Academic Facilities/Equipment:** Art museum, media center, international telecommunications center, electron microscope, astronomical observatory, Holocaust Studies Center, new sports/fitness complex.

CAMPUS LIFE

Environment: Town. **Activities:** Campus Ministries; Choral groups; Concert band; Dance; Drama/theater; International Student Organization; Jazz band; Literary magazine; Model UN; Music ensembles; Musical theater; Pep band; Radio station; Student government; Student newspaper; Television station; Yearbook. 80 registered organizations, 22 honor societies, 6 religious organizations, 14 fraternities, 12 sororities on campus. **Athletics (Intercollegiate):** *Men:* baseball, basketball, cross-country, soccer, swimming, tennis, track/field (outdoor), track/field (indoor), volleyball. *Women:* basketball, cross-country, field hockey, lacrosse, soccer, softball, swimming, tennis, track/field (outdoor), track/field (indoor), volleyball. **On-Campus Highlights:** Berrie Center for Performing and Visual Arts. **Environmental Initiatives:** Curriculum (and a new building for the Sustainability Education Center).

ADMISSIONS

Freshman Academic Profile: Average high school GPA 3.4. 16% in top 10% of high school class, 41% in top 25% of high school class, 79% in top 50% of high school class. **Test Scores:** SAT Math middle 50% range 520–610. SAT EBRW middle 50% range 530–620. ACT middle 50% range 21–26. **Basis for**

Candidate Selection: *Very important factors include:* rigor of secondary school record, academic GPA. *Important factors include:* application essay, standardized test scores, recommendation(s), extracurricular activities, talent/ability. *Other factors include:* class rank, character/personal qualities, first generation, alumni/ae relation, geographical residence, state residency, racial/ethnic status, volunteer work, work experience, level of applicant's interest. **Freshman Admission Requirements:** High school diploma is required and GED is accepted. *Academic units required:* 4 English, 3 math, 3 science, 2 science labs, 2 foreign language, 3 social studies, 3 academic electives. **Freshman Admission Statistics:** 6,695 applied, 57% admitted, 24% enrolled. **Transfer Admission Requirements:** College transcript(s), essay or personal statement. Minimum college GPA of 2.5 required. Lowest grade transferable C. **General Admission Information:** Application fee $65. Regular application deadline 3/1. Non-fall registration accepted. Admission may be deferred for a maximum of 1 year.

COSTS AND FINANCIAL AID

Annual in-state tuition $11,640. Annual out-of-state tuition $20,774. Room and board $12,180. Average book and supplies expense $1,569. **Required Forms and Deadlines:** FAFSA; State aid form. **Notification of Awards:** Applicants will be notified of awards on a rolling basis beginning 4/1. **Types of Aid:** *Need-based scholarships/grants:* College/university scholarship or grant aid from institutional funds; Federal Nursing Scholarships; Federal Pell; Private scholarships; SEOG; State scholarships/grants. *Loans:* Direct PLUS loans; Direct Subsidized Stafford Loans; Direct Unsubsidized Stafford Loans. **Student Employment:** Federal Work-Study Program available. Institutional employment available. **Financial Aid Statistics:** 47% needy freshmen, 52% needy undergrads receive need-based scholarship or grant aid. 24% freshmen, 20% undergrads receive non-need-based scholarship or grant aid. 76% freshmen, 82% undergrads receive need-based self-help aid. 0% freshmen, 0% undergrads receive athletic scholarships. 80% freshmen, 74% undergrads receive any aid. 49% undergrads borrow to pay for school. Average cumulative indebtedness $10,082. **Criteria awarding aid:** *Non-need-based:* Academics, Leadership, State/district residency.

RANDOLPH COLLEGE

2500 Rivermont Avenue, Lynchburg, VA 24503-1555
Phone: 434-947-8100 **Financial Aid Phone:** 434-947-8128
E-mail: admissions@randolphcollege.edu **CEEB Code:** 5567
Fax: 434-947-8996 **Website:** www.randolphcollege.com **ACT Code:** 4388

This private school, affiliated with the Methodist Church, was founded in 1891. It has a 100 acre campus.

RATINGS

Admissions Selectivity Rating: 74   **Fire Safety Rating:** 95   **Green Rating:** 99

STUDENTS AND FACULTY

Enrollment: 547. **Student Body:** 61% female, 39% male, 21% out-of-state, 3% international (23 countries represented). Asian 3%, African American 16%, Caucasian 60%, Hispanic 8%, Native American 1%, Pacific Islander 1%, Two or more races 7%, Race unknown 1%.
Retention and Graduation: 68% freshmen return for sophomore year. 44% freshmen graduate within 4 years. 51% freshmen graduate within 6 years.
Faculty: Student/faculty ratio 8:1. 69 full-time faculty, 96% hold PhDs, 14% are members of minority groups, 61% are women. 0% of classes are taught by teaching assistants.

ACADEMICS

Degrees: Bachelor's; Master's. **Classes:** Most classes have fewer than 10 students. **Most popular majors:** Biology/Biological Sciences, General; Psychology, General; Sports and Exercise. **Special Study Options:** Accelerated program; Cross-registration; Double major; Dual enrollment; Exchange student program (domestic); Honors program; Independent study; Internships; Liberal arts/career combination; Student-designed major; Study abroad; Teacher certification program. **Honors programs:** Juniors and seniors who have a cumulative 3.45 in all academic work and a 3.7 in the major are eligible to read for Honors in the Major. The Honors Program encourages students of exceptional ability to engage in independent and intensive study in their fields

of interest. **Combined degree programs:** BA/MA; BA/MEng. **Disability Services offered:** Note-taking services; Reader services; Tape recorders; Tutors. **Career services:** Alumni network; Alumni services; Career assessment; Internships; Regional alumni.

FACILITIES

Housing: Apartments for single students; Coed dorms; Theme housing; Wellness housing; 65% of campus accessible to physically disabled. **Special Academic Facilities/Equipment:** The Randolph College Art Collection (recognized as one of the most outstanding college collections in the nation), 100-acre equestrian center, language lab, science and math resource center, learning resources center, writing lab, nursery school, nature preserves, organic garden, observatory, electron microscope. **Campus Network:** 100% of classrooms, 100% of dorms, 100% of student union, 100% of libraries, 100% of dining areas, 100% of common outdoor areas have wireless network access.

CAMPUS LIFE

Environment: City. **Activities:** Choral groups; Dance; Drama/theater; International Student Organization; Literary magazine; Model UN; Music ensembles; Musical theater; Radio station; Student government; Student newspaper. 37 registered organizations, 18 honor societies, 6 religious organizations on campus. **Athletics (Intercollegiate):** *Men:* basketball, cross-country, equestrian sports, horseback riding, lacrosse, soccer, tennis. *Women:* basketball, cross-country, equestrian sports, horseback riding, lacrosse, soccer, softball, swimming, tennis, volleyball. **On-Campus Highlights:** The Maier Museum of Art.

ADMISSIONS

Freshman Academic Profile: Average high school GPA 3.6. 15% in top 10% of high school class, 49% in top 25% of high school class, 81% in top 50% of high school class. 83% from public high schools. **Test Scores:** SAT Math middle 50% range 480–580. SAT EBRW middle 50% range 490–600. ACT middle 50% range 19–25. **Basis for Candidate Selection:** *Very important factors include:* academic GPA. *Important factors include:* rigor of secondary school record, standardized test scores, extracurricular activities, alumni/ae relation. *Other factors include:* class rank, application essay, recommendation(s), interview, talent/ability, character/personal qualities, first generation, volunteer work, work experience. **Freshman Admission Requirements:** High school diploma is required and GED is accepted. *Academic units required:* 4 English, 3 math, 3 science, 2 science labs, 2 history, 1 academic elective. *Academic units recommended:* 4 math, 4 foreign language, 3 academic electives. **Freshman Admission Statistics:** 1,177 applied, 90% admitted, 14% enrolled. **Transfer Admission Requirements:** High school transcript, college transcript(s), essay or personal statement. Lowest grade transferable C-. **General Admission Information:** Non-fall registration accepted. Admission may be deferred for a maximum of 2 years.

COSTS AND FINANCIAL AID

Annual tuition $25,000. Room and board $11,000. Required fees $610. Average book and supplies expense $1,280. **Notification of Awards:** Applicants will be notified of awards on a rolling basis beginning 11/15. **Types of Aid:** *Need-based scholarships/grants:* College/university scholarship or grant aid from institutional funds; Federal Pell; Private scholarships; SEOG; State scholarships/grants; United Negro College Fund. *Loans:* Direct PLUS loans; Direct Subsidized Stafford Loans; Direct Unsubsidized Stafford Loans. **Student Employment:** Federal Work-Study Program available. Institutional employment available. **Financial Aid Statistics:** 100% needy freshmen, 100% needy undergrads receive need-based scholarship or grant aid. 23% freshmen, 18% undergrads receive non-need-based scholarship or grant aid. 68% freshmen, 73% undergrads receive need-based self-help aid. 0% freshmen, 0% undergrads receive athletic scholarships. 100% freshmen, 98% undergrads receive any aid. 78% undergrads borrow to pay for school. Average cumulative indebtedness $42,569. **Criteria awarding aid:** *Non-need-based:* Academics, Alumni affiliation, Art, Music/drama, Religious affiliation, State/district residency.

RANDOLPH-MACON COLLEGE

P. O. Box 5005, Ashland, VA 23005
Phone: 804-752-7305 **Financial Aid Phone:** (804) 752-7259
E-mail: admissions@rmc.edu **CEEB Code:** 5566
Fax: 804-752-4707 **Website:** www.rmc.edu **ACT Code:** 4386

This private school, affiliated with the Methodist Church, was founded in 1830. It has a 116 acre campus.

RATINGS

Admissions Selectivity Rating: 81   Fire Safety Rating: 93   Green Rating: 60*

STUDENTS AND FACULTY

Enrollment: 1,530. **Student Body:** 53% female, 47% male, 22% out-of-state, 2% international (26 countries represented). Asian 1%, African American 10%, Caucasian 77%, Hispanic 4%, Native American <1%, Pacific Islander <1%, Two or more races 5%, Race unknown 1%.
Retention and Graduation: 84% freshmen return for sophomore year. 63% freshmen graduate within 4 years. 68% freshmen graduate within 6 years.
Faculty: Student/faculty ratio 11:1. 113 full-time faculty, 94% hold PhDs, 8% are members of minority groups, 56% are women. 0% of classes are taught by teaching assistants.

ACADEMICS

Degrees: Bachelor's. **Classes:** Most classes have 10–19 students. **Most popular majors:** Communication and Media Studies; Biology/Biological Sciences, General; Business/Commerce, General. **Special Study Options:** Accelerated program; Cross-registration; Double major; Dual enrollment; Exchange student program (domestic); Honors program; Independent study; Internships; Liberal arts/career combination; Study abroad; Teacher certification program. **Honors programs:** The Honors Program offers qualified students the opportunity to take special honors classes, participate in unique programs and events for honors students, and an Honors House for recreation and socializing. **Combined degree programs:** BA/MA; BA/MD; BA/MEng. **Disability Services offered:** Note-taking services; Reader services; Tape recorders; Tutors. **Career services:** Alumni network; Alumni services; Career assessment; Career/job search classes; Internships; Regional alumni.

FACILITIES

Housing: Apartments for single students; Coed dorms; Fraternity/sorority housing; Men's dorms; Special housing for disabled students; Special housing for international students; Theme housing; Wellness housing; Women's dorms; 85% of campus accessible to physically disabled. **Special Academic Facilities/Equipment:** Language lab, learning center, media center, greenhouse, observatory with telescope, electron microscopes, nuclear magnetic resonator, art gallery, fine arts center. **Campus Network:** 90% of classrooms, 100% of dorms, 100% of student union, 100% of libraries, 100% of dining areas, 0% of common outdoor areas have wireless network access.

CAMPUS LIFE

Environment: Village. **Activities:** Campus Ministries; Choral groups; Concert band; Dance; Drama/theater; International Student Organization; Jazz band; Literary magazine; Music ensembles; Musical theater; Pep band; Student government; Student newspaper; Student-run film society; Yearbook. 85 registered organizations, 18 honor societies, 4 religious organizations, 7 fraternities, 4 sororities on campus. **Athletics (Intercollegiate):** *Men:* baseball, basketball, football, golf, lacrosse, soccer, tennis. *Women:* basketball, field hockey, lacrosse, soccer, softball, swimming, tennis, volleyball. **On-Campus Highlights:** Student Center at Brock Commons. **Environmental Initiatives:** Designing, Planning, Building and Operating a LEED-certified residence hall incorporating solar power, geothermal heat exchange, rainwater reclamation and other sustainable aspects.

ADMISSIONS

Freshman Academic Profile: Average high school GPA 3.7. 22% in top 10% of high school class, 50% in top 25% of high school class, 79% in top 50% of high school class. 77% from public high schools. **Test Scores:** SAT Math middle 50% range 510–610. SAT EBRW middle 50% range 540–630. ACT middle 50% range 20–26. **Basis for Candidate Selection:** *Very important factors include:* rigor of secondary school record, academic

GPA. *Important factors include:* class rank, application essay, standardized test scores, recommendation(s). *Other factors include:* interview, extracurricular activities, talent/ability, character/personal qualities, first generation, alumni/ae relation, racial/ethnic status, volunteer work, work experience, level of applicant's interest. **Freshman Admission Requirements:** High school diploma is required and GED is accepted. *Academic units required:* 4 English, 3 math, 2 science, 2 science labs, 2 foreign language, 2 social studies, 3 academic electives. *Academic units recommended:* 4 English, 4 math, 4 science, 4 science labs, 3 foreign language, 3 social studies, 4 academic electives. **Freshman Admission Statistics:** 2,460 applied, 71% admitted, 25% enrolled. **Transfer Admission Requirements:** High school transcript, college transcript(s), essay or personal statement, statement of good standing from prior institution(s). Minimum college GPA of 2.0 required. Lowest grade transferable C-. **General Admission Information:** Priority deadline 2/1. Regular application deadline 3/1. Non-fall registration accepted. Admission may be deferred for a maximum of 1 year.

COSTS AND FINANCIAL AID

Annual tuition $42,490. Room and board $12,680. Required fees $1,450. Average book and supplies expense $1,200. **Required Forms and Deadlines:** FAFSA; State aid form. **Notification of Awards:** Applicants will be notified of awards on or about 3/1. **Types of Aid:** *Need-based scholarships/grants:* College/university scholarship or grant aid from institutional funds; Federal Pell; Private scholarships; SEOG; State scholarships/grants. *Loans:* Direct PLUS loans; Direct Subsidized Stafford Loans; Direct Unsubsidized Stafford Loans. **Student Employment:** Federal Work-Study Program available. Institutional employment available. **Financial Aid Statistics:** 100% needy freshmen, 100% needy undergrads receive need-based scholarship or grant aid. 30% freshmen, 27% undergrads receive non-need-based scholarship or grant aid. 65% freshmen, 68% undergrads receive need-based self-help aid. 0% freshmen, 0% undergrads receive athletic scholarships. 100% freshmen, 99% undergrads receive any aid. 90% undergrads borrow to pay for school. Average cumulative indebtedness $22,206. **Criteria awarding aid:** *Need-based:* Academics, Religious affiliation. *Non-need-based:* Academics, Alumni affiliation, Minority status, Religious affiliation, State/district residency.

REED COLLEGE

3203 SE Woodstock Boulevard, Portland, OR 97202-8199
Phone: 503-777-7511 **Financial Aid Phone:** 503-777-7223
E-mail: admission@reed.edu **CEEB Code:** 4654
Fax: 503-777-7553 **Website:** www.reed.edu **ACT Code:** 3494

This private school was founded in 1908. It has a 116 acre campus.

RATINGS

Admissions Selectivity Rating: 94   Fire Safety Rating: 96   Green Rating: 60*

STUDENTS AND FACULTY

Enrollment: 1,456. **Student Body:** 54% female, 46% male, 93% out-of-state, 10% international (46 countries represented). Asian 7%, African American 2%, Caucasian 59%, Hispanic 10%, Native American <1%, Pacific Islander <1%, Two or more races 9%, Race unknown 3%.
Retention and Graduation: 88% freshmen return for sophomore year. 68% freshmen graduate within 4 years. 81% freshmen graduate within 6 years. 65% grads go on to further study within 1 year. 48% grads pursue arts and sciences degrees. 5% grads pursue law degrees. 3% grads pursue business degrees. 4% grads pursue medical degrees. **Faculty:** Student/faculty ratio 10:1. 152 full-time faculty, 95% hold PhDs, 16% are members of minority groups, 43% are women. 0% of classes are taught by teaching assistants.

ACADEMICS

Degrees: Bachelor's; Master's. **Classes:** Most classes have 10–19 students. Most lab/discussion sessions have 10–19 students. **Most popular majors:** English Language and Literature, General; Psychology, General; Anthropology, General. **Special Study Options:** Cross-registration; Double major; Dual enrollment; Exchange student program (domestic); Independent study; Internships; Liberal arts/career combination; Student-designed major; Study abroad. **Disability Services offered:** Note-taking services; Reader services; Tape recorders; Tutors. **Career services:** Alumni network; Alumni services; Career assessment; Career/job search classes; Internships; Regional alumni.

FACILITIES

Housing: Apartments for single students; Coed dorms; Cooperative housing; Special housing for disabled students; Theme housing; Wellness housing; Women's dorms; 85% of campus accessible to physically disabled. **Special Academic Facilities/Equipment:** Art gallery, studio art building, language labs, computerized music listening lab, nuclear research reactor, 20 music practice rooms and midi lab, 760-seat auditorium, academic support center (quantitative skills, writing, math support), educational technology center.

CAMPUS LIFE

Environment: Metropolis. **Activities:** Campus Ministries; Choral groups; Dance; Drama/theater; International Student Organization; Jazz band; Literary magazine; Model UN; Music ensembles; Musical theater; Radio station; Student government; Student newspaper; Student-run film society; Symphony orchestra; Yearbook. 130 registered organizations, 1 honor society, 5 religious organizations on campus. **On-Campus Highlights:** Thesis Tower. **Environmental Initiatives:** LEED construction.

ADMISSIONS

Freshman Academic Profile: 55% in top 10% of high school class, 78% in top 25% of high school class, 97% in top 50% of high school class. 59% from public high schools. **Test Scores:** SAT Math middle 50% range 640–770. SAT EBRW middle 50% range 670–750. ACT middle 50% range 30–33. **Basis for Candidate Selection:** *Very important factors include:* rigor of secondary school record, academic GPA, application essay. *Important factors include:* class rank, standardized test scores, recommendation(s), interview. *Other factors include:* extracurricular activities, talent/ability, character/personal qualities, first generation, alumni/ae relation, geographical residence, racial/ethnic status, volunteer work, work experience. **Freshman Admission Requirements:** High school diploma is required and GED is accepted. *Academic units recommended:* 4 English, 4 math, 3 science, 3 foreign language, 4 social studies. **Freshman Admission Statistics:** 5,957 applied, 35% admitted, 17% enrolled. **Transfer Admission Requirements:** High school transcript, college transcript(s), essay or personal statement, standardized test scores, statement of good standing from prior institution(s). Lowest grade transferable C-. **General Admission Information:** Regular application deadline 1/15.

COSTS AND FINANCIAL AID

Annual tuition $58,130. Room and board $14,620. Required fees $310. Average book and supplies expense $1,050. **Required Forms and Deadlines:** Business/Farm Supplement; CSS/Financial Aid PROFILE; FAFSA; Noncustodial PROFILE. **Notification of Awards:** Applicants will be notified of awards on or about 4/1. **Types of Aid:** *Need-based scholarships/grants:* College/university scholarship or grant aid from institutional funds; Federal Pell; Private scholarships; SEOG; State scholarships/grants. *Loans:* Direct PLUS loans; Direct Subsidized Stafford Loans; Direct Unsubsidized Stafford Loans. **Student Employment:** Federal Work-Study Program available. Institutional employment available. **Financial Aid Statistics:** 97% needy freshmen, 98% needy undergrads receive need-based scholarship or grant aid. 0% freshmen, 0% undergrads receive non-need-based scholarship or grant aid. 97% freshmen, 98% undergrads receive need-based self-help aid. 0% freshmen, 0% undergrads receive athletic scholarships. 53% freshmen, 54% undergrads receive any aid. 48% undergrads borrow to pay for school. Average cumulative indebtedness $21,697.

REGENT UNIVERSITY

1000 Regent University Drive, Virginia Beach, VA 23464
Phone: 800-373-5504 **Financial Aid Phone:** 757-352-4125
E-mail: admissions@regent.edu **CEEB Code:** 30913
Fax: 757-352-4381 **Website:** www.regent.edu **ACT Code:** 6738

This private school, affiliated with the Christian (Nondenominational) Church, was founded in 1978. It has a 70 acre campus.

RATINGS

Admissions Selectivity Rating: 75   Fire Safety Rating: 64   Green Rating: 60*

STUDENTS AND FACULTY

Enrollment: 4,125. **Student Body:** 61% female, 39% male, 59% out-of-state, <1% international (17 countries represented). Asian 2%, African American 27%, Caucasian 54%, Hispanic 9%, Native American <1%, Pacific Islander <1%, Two or more races 5%, Race unknown 2%.

Retention and Graduation: 78% freshmen return for sophomore year. 47% freshmen graduate within 4 years. 58% freshmen graduate within 6 years. **Faculty:** Student/faculty ratio 19:1. 138 full-time faculty, 89% hold PhDs, 16% are members of minority groups, 31% are women. 0% of classes are taught by teaching assistants.

ACADEMICS

Degrees: Associate; Bachelor's; Certificate; Doctoral degree—professional practice; Doctoral degree research/scholarship; Master's; Post-bachelor's certificate; Post-master's certificate. **Classes:** Most classes have 10–19 students. Most lab/discussion sessions have fewer than 10 students. **Most popular majors:** Business/Commerce, General; Religion/Religious Studies; Psychology, General. **Special Study Options:** Distance learning; Double major; Dual enrollment; Honors program; Independent study; Internships; Liberal arts/career combination; Study abroad; Teacher certification program. **Honors programs:** Being selected as an Honors College student is, well, an honor. During your four years at Regent, you'll participate in specialized classes that foster a sense of community and friendship. As an Honors College student, you'll also enjoy intellectual, spiritual and emotional transformation. We believe this has the potential to change relationships, families, households, companies, schools, and even governments and nations for the better. Your transformation, in effect, will help transform the world. **Combined degree programs:** BA/MA. **Disability Services offered:** Note-taking services; Reader services; Tape recorders; Tutors. **Career services:** Alumni network; Alumni services; Career assessment; Career/job search classes; Internships; Regional alumni.

FACILITIES

Housing: Apartments for married students; Apartments for single students; 100% of campus accessible to physically disabled. **Special Academic Facilities/Equipment:** The 31,000-square-foot Student Center on Regent's Virginia Beach Campus, opened in 2003, offers a central location for campus and student services. The building houses the university gift shop, student organizations and meeting rooms, a cafe/coffee shop, computer lab, student lounge, and offices for the Registrar, Admissions, and Financial Aid. The 135,000-square-foot Communication & Performing Arts Center, opened in 2002, includes film and animation studios, a state-of-the-art main theatre, screening rooms and editing suites in one of the most technologically advanced communication buildings on the east coast.

CAMPUS LIFE

Environment: City. **Activities:** Campus Ministries; Choral groups; Concert band; Dance; Drama/theater; International Student Organization; Music ensembles; Musical theater; Student government; Student-run film society. 55 registered organizations, 9 honor societies on campus. **On-Campus Highlights:** The Student Center. **Environmental Initiatives:** Our investment in "cool storage" systems since our beginning in 1978 allows us to shave peak demand when the power company desires. This helps reduce the size of the power plant needed to support this area. This results in a major decrease in greenhouse emissions for this area. This fact is recognized by VA Dominion Power, our supplier of electricity.

ADMISSIONS

Freshman Academic Profile: Average high school GPA 3.4. 10% in top 10% of high school class, 34% in top 25% of high school class, 65% in top 50% of high school class. **Test Scores:** SAT Math middle 50% range 470–590. SAT EBRW middle 50% range 520–630. ACT middle 50% range 19–25. **Basis for Candidate Selection:** *Very important factors include:* academic GPA, standardized test scores. *Important factors include:* application essay. *Other factors include:* rigor of secondary school record, recommendation(s), character/personal qualities. **Freshman Admission Requirements:** High school diploma is required and GED is accepted. *Academic units recommended:* 4 English, 3 math, 3 science, 3 foreign language, 3 social studies. **Freshman Admission Statistics:** 2,344 applied, 86% admitted, 19% enrolled. **Transfer Admission Requirements:** College transcript(s). Lowest grade transferable C. **General Admission Information:** Application fee $50. Priority deadline 8/1. Regular application deadline 8/1. Non-fall registration accepted. Admission may be deferred for a maximum of one year.

COSTS AND FINANCIAL AID

Annual tuition $18,720. Room and board $7,220. Required fees $1,400. Average book and supplies expense $1,000. **Required Forms and Deadlines:** FAFSA; Institution's own financial aid form; State aid form. **Notification of Awards:** Applicants will be notified of awards on a rolling basis beginning 12/1. **Types of Aid:** *Need-based scholarships/grants:* College/university scholarship or grant aid from institutional funds; Federal Pell; Private scholarships; State scholarships/grants. *Loans:* Direct PLUS loans; Direct Subsidized Stafford Loans; Direct Unsubsidized Stafford Loans. **Student Employment:**

Institutional employment available. **Financial Aid Statistics:** 98% needy freshmen, 92% needy undergrads receive need-based scholarship or grant aid. 21% freshmen, 8% undergrads receive non-need-based scholarship or grant aid. 85% freshmen, 93% undergrads receive need-based self-help aid. 0% freshmen, 2% undergrads receive athletic scholarships. 95% freshmen, 80% undergrads receive any aid. 75% undergrads borrow to pay for school. Average cumulative indebtedness $32,982. **Criteria awarding aid:** *Non-need-based:* Academics, Alumni affiliation, Leadership.

REGIS COLLEGE

235 Wellesley Street, Weston, MA 02493-1571
Phone: 781-768-7100 **Financial Aid Phone:** 781-768-7184
E-mail: admission@regiscollege.edu **CEEB Code:** 3723
Fax: 781-768-7071 **Website:** www.regiscollege.edu **ACT Code:** 1886

This private school, affiliated with the Roman Catholic Church, was founded in 1927. It has a 131 acre campus.

RATINGS

Admissions Selectivity Rating: 73   Fire Safety Rating: 89   Green Rating: 60*

STUDENTS AND FACULTY

Enrollment: 1,235. **Student Body:** 79% female, 21% male, 19% out-of-state, 2% international (17 countries represented). Asian 4%, African American 19%, Caucasian 49%, Hispanic 11%, Native American <1%, Pacific Islander <1%, Two or more races 1%, Race unknown 12%.
Retention and Graduation: 82% freshmen return for sophomore year. 28% grads go on to further study within 1 year. 16% grads pursue arts and sciences degrees. 1% grads pursue law degrees. 2% grads pursue business degrees. 2% grads pursue medical degrees. **Faculty:** Student/faculty ratio 11:1. 96 full-time faculty, 70% hold PhDs, 9% are members of minority groups, 76% are women. 0% of classes are taught by teaching assistants.

ACADEMICS

Degrees: Associate; Bachelor's; Doctoral degree—professional practice; Master's; Post-master's certificate; Transfer Associate. **Classes:** Most classes have 10–19 students. **Most popular majors:** Business/Commerce, General; Registered Nursing/Registered Nurse; Biology/Biological Sciences, General. **Special Study Options:** Accelerated program; Cross-registration; Double major; Dual enrollment; English as a Second Language (ESL); Exchange student program (domestic); Honors program; Independent study; Internships; Student-designed major; Study abroad; Teacher certification program. **Honors programs:** The Honors Program at Regis College offers qualified students a stimulating and challenging learning experience, and opportunities for distinguished scholarship. It prepares students to become leaders committed to the betterment of the human condition and our society, a goal that is central to the Regis College mission. **Disability Services offered:** Note-taking services; Tape recorders; Tutors. **Career services:** Alumni network; Alumni services; Career assessment; Career/job search classes; Internships.

FACILITIES

Housing: Coed dorms; Women's dorms; 85% of campus accessible to physically disabled. **Special Academic Facilities/Equipment:** Fine arts center, philatelic museum.

CAMPUS LIFE

Environment: Village. **Activities:** Campus Ministries; Choral groups; Dance; Drama/theater; Literary magazine; Model UN; Music ensembles; Musical theater; Radio station; Student government; Yearbook. 36 registered organizations, 9 honor societies, 2 religious organizations on campus. **Athletics (Intercollegiate):** *Men:* basketball, diving, soccer, swimming. *Women:* basketball, diving, field hockey, lacrosse, soccer, softball, swimming, tennis, track/field (outdoor), track/field (indoor), volleyball. **On-Campus Highlights:** College Hall. **Environmental Initiatives:** Replacement of steam boilers w/high efficiency designs.

ADMISSIONS

Freshman Academic Profile: Average high school GPA 3.1. 10% in top 10% of high school class, 35% in top 25% of high school class, 66% in top 50% of high school class. 75% from public high schools. **Test Scores:** SAT Math middle 50% range 420–540. SAT EBRW middle 50% range 420–520. ACT middle 50% range 19–23. **Basis for Candidate Selection:** *Very important factors include:* rigor of secondary school record, academic GPA, application

essay, recommendation(s), character/personal qualities. *Important factors include:* class rank, interview, extracurricular activities, talent/ability, volunteer work. *Other factors include:* standardized test scores, first generation, alumni/ae relation, geographical residence, level of applicant's interest. **Freshman Admission Requirements:** High school diploma is required and GED is accepted. *Academic units required:* 4 English, 3 math, 2 science, 1 science lab, 2 foreign language, 2 social studies, 3 academic electives. *Academic units recommended:* 4 math, 4 science, 3 foreign language, 4 social studies. **Freshman Admission Statistics:** 2,023 applied, 84% admitted, 16% enrolled. **Transfer Admission Requirements:** High school transcript, college transcript(s), essay or personal statement. Minimum college GPA of 2.0 required. Lowest grade transferable C. **General Admission Information:** Application fee $50. Priority deadline 2/15. Regular application deadline 6/1. Non-fall registration accepted. Admission may be deferred for a maximum of 1 year.

COSTS AND FINANCIAL AID

Annual tuition $37,540. Room and board $14,380. Average book and supplies expense $1,000. **Required Forms and Deadlines:** FAFSA. **Notification of Awards:** Applicants will be notified of awards on a rolling basis beginning 3/15. **Types of Aid:** *Need-based scholarships/grants:* College/university scholarship or grant aid from institutional funds; Federal Pell; Private scholarships; SEOG; State scholarships/grants. *Loans:* Direct PLUS loans; Direct Subsidized Stafford Loans; Direct Unsubsidized Stafford Loans. **Student Employment:** Federal Work-Study Program available. Institutional employment available. **Financial Aid Statistics:** 92% needy freshmen, 91% needy undergrads receive need-based scholarship or grant aid. 49% freshmen, 49% undergrads receive non-need-based scholarship or grant aid. 94% freshmen, 95% undergrads receive need-based self-help aid. 0% freshmen, 0% undergrads receive athletic scholarships. 91% freshmen, 84% undergrads receive any aid. 94% undergrads borrow to pay for school. Average cumulative indebtedness $49,217. **Criteria awarding aid:** *Need-based:* Leadership, Minority status, Religious affiliation. *Non-need-based:* Academics, Alumni affiliation, Religious affiliation.

REGIS UNIVERSITY

3333 Regis Boulevard, Denver, CO 80221-1099
Phone: 303-458-4900 **Financial Aid Phone:** 303-458-4126
E-mail: RUAdmissions@regis.edu **CEEB Code:** 4656
Fax: 303-964-5534 **Website:** www.regis.edu **ACT Code:** 526

This private school, affiliated with the Roman Catholic Church, was founded in 1877. It has a 90 acre campus.

RATINGS

Admissions Selectivity Rating: 84   Fire Safety Rating: 65   Green Rating: 66

STUDENTS AND FACULTY

Enrollment: 3,014. **Student Body:** 62% female, 38% male, 40% out-of-state, 1% international (8 countries represented). Asian 6%, African American 4%, Caucasian 54%, Hispanic 25%, Native American 1%, Pacific Islander <1%, Two or more races 5%, Race unknown 5%.
Retention and Graduation: 54% freshmen graduate within 4 years. 71% freshmen graduate within 6 years. **Faculty:** Student/faculty ratio 14:1. 311 full-time faculty, 79% hold PhDs, 14% are members of minority groups, 59% are women.

ACADEMICS

Degrees: Bachelor's; Certificate; Doctoral degree—professional practice; Master's; Post-bachelor's certificate; Post-master's certificate. **Classes:** Most classes have 10–19 students. Most lab/discussion sessions have 10–19 students. **Most popular majors:** Computer Science; Registered Nursing/Registered Nurse; Business Administration and Management, General. **Special Study Options:** Accelerated program; Distance learning; Double major; Dual enrollment; Honors program; Independent study; Internships; Liberal arts/career combination; Student-designed major; Study abroad; Teacher certification program; Weekend college. **Honors programs:** The Regis College Honors Program is available to self-motivated, conscientious Regis College students who wish to complete an alternate pathway through the core curriculum and be distinguished as an honors graduate. **Combined degree programs:** BA/MA. **Disability Services offered:** Note-taking services; Reader services; Tape recorders. **Career services:** Alumni services; Career assessment; Career/job search classes; Internships.

FACILITIES

Housing: Apartments for single students; Coed dorms; Special housing for disabled students; Theme housing; Wellness housing; 90% of campus accessible to physically disabled.

CAMPUS LIFE

Environment: Metropolis. **Activities:** Campus Ministries; Choral groups; Concert band; Dance; Drama/theater; International Student Organization; Jazz band; Literary magazine; Music ensembles; Musical theater; Radio station; Student government; Student newspaper; Yearbook. **Athletics (Intercollegiate):** *Men:* baseball, basketball, cross-country, golf, soccer. *Women:* basketball, cross-country, lacrosse, soccer, softball, volleyball. **On-Campus Highlights:** Residence Halls.

ADMISSIONS

Freshman Academic Profile: Average high school GPA 3.6. 25% in top 10% of high school class, 56% in top 25% of high school class, 86% in top 50% of high school class. **Test Scores:** SAT Math middle 50% range 520–610. SAT EBRW middle 50% range 530–620. ACT middle 50% range 21–27. **Basis for Candidate Selection:** *Very important factors include:* rigor of secondary school record, academic GPA, standardized test scores, character/personal qualities. *Important factors include:* application essay, *Other factors include:* class rank, recommendation(s), interview, extracurricular activities, talent/ability, first generation, alumni/ae relation, racial/ethnic status, volunteer work, work experience, level of applicant's interest. **Freshman Admission Requirements:** High school diploma is required and GED is accepted. *Academic units recommended:* 4 English, 3 math, 2 science, 1 science lab, 2 foreign language, 2 social studies, 1 academic elective. **Freshman Admission Statistics:** 7,282 applied, 60% admitted, 12% enrolled. **Transfer Admission Requirements:** College transcript(s), essay or personal statement. Minimum college GPA of 2.0 required. **General Admission Information:** Priority deadline 4/15. Regular application deadline 8/1. Non-fall registration accepted. Admission may be deferred for a maximum of 1 year.

COSTS AND FINANCIAL AID

Annual tuition $37,830. Room and board $12,460. Required fees $350. Average book and supplies expense $1,800. **Required Forms and Deadlines:** FAFSA. **Notification of Awards:** Applicants will be notified of awards on a rolling basis beginning 11/15. **Types of Aid:** *Need-based scholarships/grants:* College/university scholarship or grant aid from institutional funds; Federal Pell; Private scholarships; SEOG; State scholarships/grants. *Loans:* Direct PLUS loans; Direct Subsidized Stafford Loans; Direct Unsubsidized Stafford Loans. **Student Employment:** Federal Work-Study Program available. Institutional employment available. **Financial Aid Statistics:** 100% needy freshmen, 89% needy undergrads receive need-based scholarship or grant aid. 13% freshmen, 9% undergrads receive non-need-based scholarship or grant aid. 70% freshmen, 78% undergrads receive need-based self-help aid. 5% freshmen, 5% undergrads receive athletic scholarships. 77% freshmen, 62% undergrads receive any aid. 56% undergrads borrow to pay for school. Average cumulative indebtedness $24,531. **Criteria awarding aid:** *Need-based:* Academics, Athletics, Leadership, Music/drama, Religious affiliation. *Non-need-based:* Academics, Athletics, Leadership, Music/drama, Religious affiliation, State/district residency.

REINHARDT UNIVERSITY

7300 Reinhardt Circle, Waleska, GA 30183
Phone: 770-720-5526 **Financial Aid Phone:** (770) 720- 5667
Fax: 770-720-5899 **Website:** www.reinhardt.edu **ACT Code:** 856

This private school, affiliated with the Methodist Church, was founded in 1883. It has a 600 acre campus.

RATINGS

Admissions Selectivity Rating: 83 **Fire Safety Rating:** 97 **Green Rating:** 60*

STUDENTS AND FACULTY

Enrollment: 980. **Student Body:** 55% female, 45% male, 27% out-of-state, 0% international. Asian 1%, African American 13%, Caucasian 75%, Hispanic 4%, Native American 1%, Pacific Islander 0%, Two or more races 0%, Race unknown 6%.
Retention and Graduation: 56% freshmen return for sophomore year. 35% grads go on to further study within 1 year. 20% grads pursue arts and sciences degrees. 5% grads pursue law degrees. 45% grads pursue business degrees. 5% grads pursue medical degrees. **Faculty:** Student/faculty ratio 12:1. 62 full-time

faculty, 74% hold PhDs, 11% are members of minority groups, 48% are women. 0% of classes are taught by teaching assistants.

ACADEMICS

Degrees: Associate; Bachelor's; Master's; Transfer Associate. **Classes:** Most classes have 10–19 students. **Most popular majors:** Music; Business Administration and Management, General; Elementary Education and Teaching. **Special Study Options:** Accelerated program; Distance learning; Double major; Dual enrollment; External degree program; Honors program; Independent study; Student-designed major; Study abroad; Teacher certification program. **Honors programs:** The Honors Program is designed for students who are bright, curious, and enjoy being challenged. Entering freshmen with a high school GPA of at least 3.5 or a combined SAT of 1050 or higher, with verbal score of at least 580, will be invited to apply for admission to Reinhardt College's Honors Program. **Disability Services offered:** Note-taking services; Reader services; Tape recorders; Tutors. **Career services:** Alumni services; Career assessment; Career/job search classes; Internships; Regional alumni.

FACILITIES

Housing: Apartments for single students; Coed dorms; Men's dorms; Special housing for disabled students; Women's dorms; 99% of campus accessible to physically disabled. **Special Academic Facilities/Equipment:** Funk Heritage Center, Falany Performing Arts. **Campus Network:** 100% of classrooms, 100% of dorms, 100% of student union, 100% of libraries, 100% of dining areas, 70% of common outdoor areas have wireless network access.

CAMPUS LIFE

Environment: Rural. **Activities:** Campus Ministries; Choral groups; Concert band; Drama/theater; International Student Organization; Jazz band; Literary magazine; Music ensembles; Musical theater; Student government; Student newspaper; Student-run film society; Symphony orchestra; Television station; Yearbook. 40 registered organizations, 12 honor societies, 5 religious organizations on campus. **Athletics (Intercollegiate):** *Men:* baseball, basketball, cheerleading, cross-country, golf, soccer, tennis. *Women:* basketball, cheerleading, cross-country, golf, soccer, softball, tennis, volleyball. **On-Campus Highlights:** Falany Performing Arts Center. **Environmental Initiatives:** Recycle paper, RU Green.

ADMISSIONS

Freshman Academic Profile: Average high school GPA 3.0. 63% in top 50% of high school class. 98% from public high schools. **Test Scores:** SAT Math middle 50% range 430–530. SAT EBRW middle 50% range 410–540. ACT middle 50% range 17–22. **Basis for Candidate Selection:** *Very important factors include:* academic GPA, standardized test scores. *Important factors include:* rigor of secondary school record, class rank. **Freshman Admission Requirements:** High school diploma is required and GED is accepted. *Academic units required:* 4 English, 4 math, 3 science, 3 social studies. *Academic units recommended:* 2 foreign language. **Freshman Admission Statistics:** 1,310 applied, 59% admitted, 30% enrolled. **Transfer Admission Requirements:** College transcript(s), statement of good standing from prior institution(s). Minimum college GPA of 2.0 required. Lowest grade transferable C. **General Admission Information:** Application fee $25. Non-fall registration accepted.

COSTS AND FINANCIAL AID

Required Forms and Deadlines: FAFSA; State aid form. **Notification of Awards:** Applicants will be notified of awards on a rolling basis beginning 1/1. **Types of Aid:** *Need-based scholarships/grants:* College/university scholarship or grant aid from institutional funds; Federal Pell; Private scholarships; SEOG; State scholarships/grants. *Loans:* Direct PLUS loans; Direct Subsidized Stafford Loans; Direct Unsubsidized Stafford Loans. **Student Employment:** Federal Work-Study Program available. **Financial Aid Statistics:** 99% needy freshmen, 98% needy undergrads receive need-based scholarship or grant aid. 7% freshmen, 7% undergrads receive non-need-based scholarship or grant aid. 76% freshmen, 74% undergrads receive need-based self-help aid. 9% freshmen, 7% undergrads receive athletic scholarships. **Criteria awarding aid:** *Need-based:* Academics, Art, Athletics, Leadership, Music/drama, Religious affiliation. *Non-need-based:* Academics, Art, Athletics, Leadership, Music/drama, Religious affiliation, State/district residency.

RENSSELAER POLYTECHNIC INSTITUTE

110 Eighth Street, Troy, NY 12180-3590
Phone: 518-276-6216 **Financial Aid Phone:** 518-276-6813
E-mail: admissions@rpi.edu **CEEB Code:** 2757
Fax: 518-276-4072 **Website:** www.rpi.edu **ACT Code:** 2866

This private school was founded in 1824. It has a 284 acre campus.

RATINGS
Admissions Selectivity Rating: 93 **Fire Safety Rating:** 94 **Green Rating:** 60*

STUDENTS AND FACULTY
Enrollment: 6,203. **Student Body:** 32% female, 68% male, 66% out-of-state, 16% international (44 countries represented). Asian 15%, African American 4%, Caucasian 47%, Hispanic 10%, Native American <1%, Pacific Islander <1%, Two or more races 5%, Race unknown 3%.
Retention and Graduation: 92% freshmen return for sophomore year. 61% freshmen graduate within 4 years. 83% freshmen graduate within 6 years. 31% grads go on to further study within 1 year. 5% grads pursue arts and sciences degrees. 2% grads pursue business degrees. 2% grads pursue medical degrees.
Faculty: Student/faculty ratio 13:1. 483 full-time faculty, 94% hold PhDs, 30% are members of minority groups, 26% are women. 0% of classes are taught by teaching assistants.

ACADEMICS
Degrees: Bachelor's; Doctoral degree research/scholarship; Master's. **Classes:** Most classes have 10–19 students. **Most popular majors:** Business/Commerce, General; Computer Engineering, General; Electrical and Electronics Engineering. **Special Study Options:** Accelerated program; Cooperative education program; Cross-registration; Double major; Dual enrollment; Exchange student program (domestic); Honors program; Independent study; Internships; Liberal arts/career combination; Study abroad. **Honors programs:** The Rensselaer Medal Program, the Presidential Scholars Program. **Combined degree programs:** BA/MEng. **Disability Services offered:** Note-taking services; Reader services; Tape recorders; Tutors. **Career services:** Alumni network; Alumni services; Career assessment; Career/job search classes; Internships; Regional alumni.

FACILITIES
Housing: Apartments for married students; Apartments for single students; Coed dorms; Fraternity/sorority housing; Special housing for disabled students; Theme housing; 75% of campus accessible to physically disabled.
Special Academic Facilities/Equipment: Shelnutt Art Gallery in the Student Union; The George M. Low Gallery (museum); Center for Terahertz Research; Nanoscale Science and Engineering Centers (NSEC); Center for Biotechnology and Interdisciplinary Studies; Gaerttner Linear Accelerator (LINAC) Laboratory; Hirsch Observatory; RPIdeaLab and Incubator Program (supports student business ventures); Rensselaer Technology Park; Darrin Fresh Water Institute at Lake George; Experimental Media and Performing Arts Center (EMPAC—under construction); Lighting Research Center; Social and Behavioral Research Laboratory; O.T. Swanson Multidisciplinary Laboratory; and other research centers and laboratories as described at www.rpi.edu/research/research_centers.html, Computational Center for Nanotechnology Innovations (CCNI); Ecologic Environmental Library(EEC) (http://www.rpi.edu/dept/ess/greening/EECbooks.html).

CAMPUS LIFE
Environment: City. **Activities:** Campus Ministries; Choral groups; Concert band; Dance; Drama/theater; International Student Organization; Jazz band; Literary magazine; Music ensembles; Musical theater; Pep band; Radio station; Student government; Student newspaper; Student-run film society; Symphony orchestra; Television station; Yearbook. 229 registered organizations, 40 honor societies, 11 religious organizations, 29 fraternities, 5 sororities on campus. **Athletics (Intercollegiate):** *Men:* baseball, basketball, cross-country, diving, football, golf, ice hockey, lacrosse, soccer, swimming, tennis, track/field (outdoor), track/field (indoor). *Women:* basketball, cross-country, diving, field hockey, ice hockey, lacrosse, soccer, softball, swimming, tennis, track/field (outdoor), track/field (indoor). **On-Campus Highlights:** Rensselaer Union.
Environmental Initiatives: Student Sustainability Task Force.

ADMISSIONS
Freshman Academic Profile: Average high school GPA 3.9. 63% in top 10% of high school class, 92% in top 25% of high school class, 98% in top 50% of high school class. 70% from public high schools. **Test Scores:** SAT Math middle 50% range 670–780. SAT EBRW middle 50% range 620–710. ACT middle 50% range 28–34. **Basis for Candidate Selection:** *Very important factors include:* rigor of secondary school record, class rank, academic GPA, standardized test scores. *Important factors include:* application essay, recommendation(s), extracurricular activities, character/personal qualities. *Other factors include:* talent/ability, first generation, alumni/ae relation, racial/ethnic status, volunteer work, work experience, level of applicant's interest. **Freshman Admission Requirements:** High school diploma is required and GED is accepted. *Academic units required:* 4 English, 4 math, 3 science, 3 social studies. *Academic units recommended:* 4 science, 3 social studies. **Freshman Admission Statistics:** 18,635 applied, 47% admitted, 19% enrolled. **Transfer Admission Requirements:** College transcript(s), statement of good standing from prior institution(s). Minimum college GPA of 3.0 required. Lowest grade transferable C. **General Admission Information:** Application fee $70. Non-fall registration accepted. Admission may be deferred for a maximum of 1 year.

COSTS AND FINANCIAL AID
Annual tuition $54,000. Room and board $15,580. Required fees $1,375. Average book and supplies expense $2,858. **Required Forms and Deadlines:** CSS/Financial Aid PROFILE; FAFSA. **Notification of Awards:** Applicants will be notified of awards on or about 3/15. **Types of Aid:** *Need-based scholarships/grants:* College/university scholarship or grant aid from institutional funds; Federal Pell; Private scholarships; SEOG; State scholarships/grants. *Loans:* Direct PLUS loans; Direct Subsidized Stafford Loans; Direct Unsubsidized Stafford Loans. **Student Employment:** Federal Work-Study Program available. Institutional employment available. **Financial Aid Statistics:** 100% needy freshmen, 100% needy undergrads receive need-based scholarship or grant aid. 21% freshmen, 14% undergrads receive non-need-based scholarship or grant aid. 99% freshmen, 97% undergrads receive need-based self-help aid. 1% freshmen, 1% undergrads receive athletic scholarships. 83% freshmen, 86% undergrads receive any aid. 63% undergrads borrow to pay for school. **Criteria awarding aid:** *Need-based:* Academics, Alumni affiliation, Art, Leadership, Minority status, Music/drama. *Non-need-based:* Academics, Alumni affiliation, Art, Athletics, Leadership, Minority status, Music/drama.

RHODE ISLAND COLLEGE

600 Mount Pleasant Avenue, Providence, RI 02908
Phone: 401-456-8234 **Financial Aid Phone:** 401-456-8033
E-mail: admissions@ric.edu **CEEB Code:** 3407
Fax: 401-456-8817 **Website:** http://www.ric.edu **ACT Code:** 3810

This public school was founded in 1854. It has a 180 acre campus.

RATINGS
Admissions Selectivity Rating: 77 **Fire Safety Rating:** 60* **Green Rating:** 70

STUDENTS AND FACULTY
Enrollment: 6,903. **Student Body:** 69% female, 31% male, 14% out-of-state, <1% international. Asian 3%, African American 10%, Caucasian 58%, Hispanic 20%, Native American 1%, Pacific Islander <1%, Two or more races 2%, Race unknown 7%.
Retention and Graduation: 75% freshmen return for sophomore year. 19% freshmen graduate within 4 years. 47% freshmen graduate within 6 years.
Faculty: Student/faculty ratio 14:1. 335 full-time faculty, 90% hold PhDs, 17% are members of minority groups, 61% are women.

ACADEMICS
Degrees: Bachelor's; Certificate; Doctoral degree—professional practice; Doctoral degree research/scholarship; Master's; Post-bachelor's certificate; Post-master's certificate. **Classes:** Most classes have 20–29 students. Most lab/discussion sessions have 20–29 students. **Special Study Options:** Double major; Dual enrollment; English as a Second Language (ESL); Exchange student program (domestic); Honors program; Independent study; Internships; Student-designed major; Study abroad; Teacher certification program.

FACILITIES
Housing: Coed dorms; Special housing for disabled students.

CAMPUS LIFE

Environment: City. **Activities:** Choral groups; Concert band; Dance; Drama/ theater; International Student Organization; Jazz band; Literary magazine; Music ensembles; Musical theater; Radio station; Student government; Student newspaper; Student-run film society; Symphony orchestra; Television station. 80 registered organizations, 14 honor societies, 2 fraternities, 3 sororities on campus. **Environmental Initiatives:** The Sustainable Communities Initiative at RIC is an innovative pilot project which works to further inform RIC students and the general public on the local and global issues of sustainability, while providing a vehicle through which to take action for positive change. SCI has already exposed RIC students and community members to some of the region's and nation's most recognized sustainability thought leaders, trained nearly twenty SCI Community Leaders from twelve Rhode Island communities, established a nine person leadership committee and has begun to collaboratively work on the development of a participatory research tool that will empower community residents to evaluate and improve the sustainability performance of their own town and cities.

ADMISSIONS

Freshman Academic Profile: 12% in top 10% of high school class, 36% in top 25% of high school class, 73% in top 50% of high school class. 75% from public high schools. **Test Scores:** SAT Math middle 50% range 430–530. SAT EBRW middle 50% range 450–560. ACT middle 50% range 15–22. **Basis for Candidate Selection:** *Very important factors include:* rigor of secondary school record, class rank, academic GPA. *Important factors include:* application essay, standardized test scores, recommendation(s). *Other factors include:* interview, extracurricular activities, talent/ability, alumni/ae relation, volunteer work, work experience. **Freshman Admission Requirements:** High school diploma is required and GED is accepted. *Academic units required:* 4 English, 3 math, 2 science, 2 science labs, 2 foreign language, 2 social studies, 5 academic electives. **Freshman Admission Statistics:** 4,846 applied, 74% admitted, 29% enrolled. **General Admission Information:** Application fee $50. Regular application deadline 3/15. Non-fall registration accepted.

COSTS AND FINANCIAL AID

Annual in-state tuition $7,637. Annual out-of-state tuition $20,150. Room and board $11,335. Required fees $1,139. Average book and supplies expense $1,200. **Required Forms and Deadlines:** FAFSA; Institution's own financial aid form. **Notification of Awards:** Applicants will be notified of awards on a rolling basis beginning 2/15. **Types of Aid:** *Need-based scholarships/grants:* College/university scholarship or grant aid from institutional funds; Federal Pell; Private scholarships; SEOG; State scholarships/grants. *Loans:* Direct PLUS loans; Direct Subsidized Stafford Loans; Direct Unsubsidized Stafford Loans. **Student Employment:** Federal Work-Study Program available. Institutional employment available. **Financial Aid Statistics:** 86% needy freshmen, 84% needy undergrads receive need-based scholarship or grant aid. 2% freshmen, 2% undergrads receive non-need-based scholarship or grant aid. 82% freshmen, 79% undergrads receive need-based self-help aid. 0% freshmen, 0% undergrads receive athletic scholarships. 71% undergrads borrow to pay for school. Average cumulative indebtedness $25,791. **Criteria awarding aid:** *Need-based:* Academics. *Non-need-based:* Academics, Alumni affiliation, Art, Music/drama.

RHODE ISLAND SCHOOL OF DESIGN

2 College Street, Providence, RI 02903
Phone: 401-454-6300 **Financial Aid Phone:** 401-454-6661
E-mail: admissions@risd.edu **CEEB Code:** 3726
Fax: 401-454-6309 **Website:** www.risd.edu **ACT Code:** 3812

This private school was founded in 1877. It has a 19 acre campus.

RATINGS

Admissions Selectivity Rating: 96   **Fire Safety Rating:** 92   **Green Rating:** 77

STUDENTS AND FACULTY

Enrollment: 1,994. **Student Body:** 68% female, 32% male, 95% out-of-state, 30% international (46 countries represented). Asian 18%, African American 4%, Caucasian 30%, Hispanic 9%, Native American <1%, Pacific Islander 0%, Two or more races 5%, Race unknown 4%.
Retention and Graduation: 94% freshmen return for sophomore year. 66% freshmen graduate within 4 years. 91% freshmen graduate within 6 years.
Faculty: Student/faculty ratio 10:1. 161 full-time faculty, 81% hold PhDs, 14% are members of minority groups, 44% are women.

ACADEMICS

Degrees: Bachelor's; Master's. **Classes:** Most classes have 10–19 students. **Most popular majors:** Illustration; Graphic Design; Industrial and Product Design. **Special Study Options:** Cross-registration; Double major; Exchange student program (domestic); Honors program; Independent study; Internships; Study abroad; Teacher certification program. **Honors programs:** European Honors Program. See: http://www.risd.edu/Academics/International_Programs/ European_Honors_Program/. Brown/RISD Dual Degree. See: http://www. risd.edu/Policies/Academic/Brown_RISD_Dual_Degree/. **Disability Services offered:** Note-taking services; Reader services; Tape recorders; Tutors. **Career services:** Alumni network; Alumni services; Career assessment; Career/job search classes; Internships; Regional alumni.

FACILITIES

Housing: Apartments for married students; Apartments for single students; Coed dorms; Special housing for disabled students; 27% of campus accessible to physically disabled. **Special Academic Facilities/Equipment:** Art museum with over 45 galleries; extensive facilities for glassblowing, metalsmithing, lithography, sculpture, painting, and other art disciplines; Nature Lab; Library with extensive photograph, print and materials collections.

CAMPUS LIFE

Environment: City. **Activities:** Choral groups; Concert band; Dance; Drama/ theater; International Student Organization; Literary magazine; Musical theater; Radio station; Student government; Student newspaper; Student-run film society; Yearbook. 73 registered organizations, 4 religious organizations on campus. **On-Campus Highlights:** The RISD Museum.

ADMISSIONS

Test Scores: SAT Math middle 50% range 580–750. SAT EBRW middle 50% range 600–690. ACT middle 50% range 26–32. **Basis for Candidate Selection:** *Very important factors include:* rigor of secondary school record, academic GPA, talent/ability. *Important factors include:* application essay, standardized test scores. *Other factors include:* recommendation(s), extracurricular activities, character/personal qualities, first generation, alumni/ ae relation, geographical residence, racial/ethnic status, volunteer work, work experience. **Freshman Admission Requirements:** High school diploma is required and GED is accepted. **Freshman Admission Statistics:** 3,913 applied, 24% admitted, 51% enrolled. **Transfer Admission Requirements:** College transcript(s), essay or personal statement. Lowest grade transferable C. **General Admission Information:** Application fee $60. Regular application deadline 2/1. Admission may be deferred for a maximum of 1 year.

COSTS AND FINANCIAL AID

Annual tuition $49,900. Room and board $13,400. Average book and supplies expense $2,700. **Required Forms and Deadlines:** CSS/Financial Aid PROFILE; FAFSA. **Notification of Awards:** Applicants will be notified of awards on or about 4/1. **Types of Aid:** *Need-based scholarships/grants:* College/ university scholarship or grant aid from institutional funds; Federal Pell; Private scholarships; SEOG; State scholarships/grants. *Loans:* Direct PLUS loans; Direct Subsidized Stafford Loans; Direct Unsubsidized Stafford Loans. **Student Employment:** Federal Work-Study Program available. **Financial Aid Statistics:** 86% needy freshmen, 91% needy undergrads receive need-based scholarship or grant aid. 0% freshmen, 3% undergrads receive non-need-based scholarship or grant aid. 100% freshmen, 91% undergrads receive need-based self-help aid. 0% freshmen, 0% undergrads receive athletic scholarships. 39% freshmen, 37% undergrads receive any aid. 41% undergrads borrow to pay for school. Average cumulative indebtedness $31,037. **Criteria awarding aid:** *Need-based:* Academics, Art. *Non-need-based:* Academics, Art.

RHODES COLLEGE

2000 North Parkway, Memphis, TN 38112
Phone: 901-843-3700 **Financial Aid Phone:** 901-843-3810
E-mail: adminfo@rhodes.edu **CEEB Code:** 1730
Fax: 901-843-3631 **Website:** http://www.rhodes.edu **ACT Code:** 4008

This private school, affiliated with the Presbyterian Church, was founded in 1848. It has a 100 acre campus.

RATINGS
Admissions Selectivity Rating: 92   **Fire Safety Rating:** 90   **Green Rating:** 65

STUDENTS AND FACULTY
Enrollment: 1,941. **Student Body:** 58% female, 42% male, 71% out-of-state, 5% international (29 countries represented). Asian 6%, African American 10%, Caucasian 66%, Hispanic 7%, Native American <1%, Pacific Islander <1%, Two or more races 5%, Race unknown 1%.
Retention and Graduation: 92% freshmen return for sophomore year. 75% freshmen graduate within 4 years. 80% freshmen graduate within 6 years. 37% grads go on to further study within 1 year. 18% grads pursue arts and sciences degrees. 5% grads pursue law degrees. 5% grads pursue business degrees. 6% grads pursue medical degrees. **Faculty:** Student/faculty ratio 10:1. 182 full-time faculty, 98% hold PhDs, 21% are members of minority groups, 49% are women. 0% of classes are taught by teaching assistants.

ACADEMICS
Degrees: Bachelor's; Master's; Post-bachelor's certificate. **Classes:** Most classes have 10–19 students. Most lab/discussion sessions have 20–29 students.
Most popular majors: Business Administration and Management, General; Computer Science; Political Science and Government, General. **Special Study Options:** Cooperative education program; Cross-registration; Double major; Dual enrollment; English as a Second Language (ESL); Honors program; Independent study; Internships; Liberal arts/career combination; Student-designed major; Study abroad; Teacher certification program. **Honors programs:** The Honors program is a culminating experience in the major field, for seniors only. It is the principal means whereby a student may do more independent, intensive, and individual work than can be done in the regular degree programs. The Honors work offers an excellent introduction to graduate study as it employs the full resources of library and laboratory and encourages independent research and study. Honors is available in most majors. **Combined degree programs:** BA/MEng. **Disability Services offered:** Note-taking services; Reader services; Tape recorders; Tutors. **Career services:** Alumni network; Alumni services; Career assessment; Career/job search classes; Internships; Regional alumni.

FACILITIES
Housing: Apartments for single students; Coed dorms; Men's dorms; Theme housing; Women's dorms; 90% of campus accessible to physically disabled.
Special Academic Facilities/Equipment: 136,000 square foot library; Art gallery; archaeology lab; astronomy observation domes with 14 and 31.5 inch telescopes; machine and woodworking shops; scanning electron microscopes; cell culture lab; nuclear magnetic resonance instrument; gas chromatography systems; UV, X-ray, infrared, and atomic absorption spectrophotometers.

CAMPUS LIFE
Environment: Metropolis. **Activities:** Campus Ministries; Choral groups; Dance; Drama/theater; International Student Organization; Jazz band; Literary magazine; Model UN; Music ensembles; Musical theater; Pep band; Radio station; Student government; Student newspaper; Student-run film society; Symphony orchestra; Television station; Yearbook. 141 registered organizations, 15 honor societies, 7 religious organizations, 8 fraternities, 7 sororities on campus. **Athletics (Intercollegiate):** *Men:* baseball, basketball, cross-country, football, golf, soccer, swimming, tennis, track/field (outdoor). *Women:* basketball, cross-country, field hockey, golf, soccer, softball, swimming, tennis, track/field (outdoor), volleyball. **On-Campus Highlights:** Paul Barret, Jr. Library. **Environmental Initiatives:** $500,000 Andrew W. Mellon Foundation grant to expand Environmental Studies initiatives through community partnerships.

ADMISSIONS
Freshman Academic Profile: Average high school GPA 3.7. 52% in top 10% of high school class, 83% in top 25% of high school class, 99% in top 50% of high school class. 51% from public high schools. **Test Scores:** SAT Math middle 50% range 600–730. SAT EBRW middle 50% range 620–700. ACT middle 50% range 27–32. **Basis for Candidate Selection:** *Very important factors include:* rigor of secondary school record, class rank, academic GPA. *Important factors include:* application essay, standardized test scores, recommendation(s), character/personal qualities, alumni/ae relation. *Other factors include:* interview, extracurricular activities, talent/ability, first generation, geographical residence, state residency, volunteer work, work experience, level of applicant's interest. **Freshman Admission Requirements:** High school diploma is required and GED is accepted. *Academic units required:* 4 English, 3 math, 2 science, 2 science labs, 2 foreign language, 2 social studies, 3 academic electives. **Freshman Admission Statistics:** 5,207 applied, 45% admitted, 22% enrolled. **Transfer Admission Requirements:** High school transcript, college transcript(s), essay or personal statement, standardized test scores, statement of good standing from prior institution(s). Lowest grade transferable C-. **General Admission Information:** Non-fall registration accepted.

COSTS AND FINANCIAL AID
Annual tuition $48,888. Room and board $11,631. Required fees $310. Average book and supplies expense $1,125. **Required Forms and Deadlines:** CSS/Financial Aid PROFILE; FAFSA; Noncustodial PROFILE. **Types of Aid:** *Need-based scholarships/grants:* College/university scholarship or grant aid from institutional funds; Federal Pell; Private scholarships; SEOG; State scholarships/grants. *Loans:* Direct PLUS loans; Direct Subsidized Stafford Loans; Direct Unsubsidized Stafford Loans. **Student Employment:** Federal Work-Study Program available. Institutional employment available. **Financial Aid Statistics:** 99% needy freshmen, 99% needy undergrads receive need-based scholarship or grant aid. 43% freshmen, 36% undergrads receive non-need-based scholarship or grant aid. 53% freshmen, 59% undergrads receive need-based self-help aid. 0% freshmen, 0% undergrads receive athletic scholarships. 96% freshmen, 95% undergrads receive any aid. 46% undergrads borrow to pay for school. Average cumulative indebtedness $26,155. **Criteria awarding aid:** *Need-based:* Minority status. *Non-need-based:* Academics, Art, Minority status, Music/drama, Religious affiliation.

RICE UNIVERSITY

MS-17 PO Box 1892, Houston, TX 77251-1892
Phone: 713-348-7423 **Financial Aid Phone:** 713-348-4958
E-mail: admission@rice.edu **CEEB Code:** 6609
Website: www.rice.edu **ACT Code:** 4152

This private school was founded in 1912. It has a 300 acre campus.

RATINGS
Admissions Selectivity Rating: 98   **Fire Safety Rating:** 95   **Green Rating:** 91

STUDENTS AND FACULTY
Enrollment: 3,978. **Student Body:** 48% female, 52% male, 53% out-of-state, 12% international (55 countries represented). Asian 26%, African American 7%, Caucasian 32%, Hispanic 16%, Native American <1%, Pacific Islander <1%, Two or more races 5%, Race unknown 1%.
Retention and Graduation: 97% freshmen return for sophomore year. 84% freshmen graduate within 4 years. 93% freshmen graduate within 6 years.
Faculty: Student/faculty ratio 6:1. 694 full-time faculty, 97% hold PhDs, 22% are members of minority groups, 35% are women.

ACADEMICS
Degrees: Bachelor's; Doctoral degree research/scholarship; Master's. **Classes:** Most classes have 10–19 students. **Most popular majors:** Chemical Engineering; Computer Science; Biology/Biological Sciences, General. **Special Study Options:** Accelerated program; Cross-registration; Distance learning; Double major; Dual enrollment; English as a Second Language (ESL); Honors program; Independent study; Internships; Student-designed major; Study abroad; Teacher certification program; Weekend college. **Honors programs:** Honors programs through individual departments. **Combined degree programs:** BA/MD. **Disability Services offered:** Note-taking services; Reader

services; Tape recorders. **Career services:** Alumni network; Alumni services; Career assessment; Career/job search classes; Internships; Regional alumni.

FACILITIES

Housing: Coed dorms; Special housing for disabled students. **Special Academic Facilities/Equipment:** Art gallery, museum, media center, language labs, computer labs, civil engineering lab, observatory and NASA equipment for students in space physics courses.

CAMPUS LIFE

Environment: Metropolis. **Activities:** Campus Ministries; Choral groups; Concert band; Dance; Drama/theater; International Student Organization; Jazz band; Literary magazine; Marching band; Model UN; Music ensembles; Musical theater; Opera; Pep band; Radio station; Student government; Student newspaper; Student-run film society; Symphony orchestra; Yearbook. 284 registered organizations, 14 honor societies, 22 religious organizations on campus. **Athletics (Intercollegiate): Men:** baseball, basketball, cross-country, football, golf, tennis, track/field (outdoor), track/field (indoor). **Women:** basketball, cross-country, soccer, swimming, tennis, track/field (outdoor), track/field (indoor), volleyball. **On-Campus Highlights:** Rice Memorial Center. **Environmental Initiatives:** At present, we have roughly 1,000,000 square feet of facilities on campus that are under construction that will receive some level of LEED certification, including the student dormitory Duncan College which is targeted for LEED-Gold. In addition, an off-campus child care center is pursuing LEED certification. Also, an off-campus graduate student apartment complex has been designed to LEED standards although it will not be formally submitted for certification. With this complex, we anticipate savings in energy of about 30% and water savings of 20%. Further, the complex was constructed in an area with excellent pedestrian access, and it includes extensive bicycle storage along with shuttle bus service to campus and to major nearby grocery stores. Our campus standard for on-campus LEED certification for new buildings is LEED-Silver as a minimum. The University has also enjoyed significant successes with construction waste recycling, with many of our largest projects to date logging diversion rates of 85–90% to recycling.

ADMISSIONS

Freshman Academic Profile: 93% in top 10% of high school class, 99% in top 25% of high school class, 100% in top 50% of high school class. 72% from public high schools. **Test Scores:** SAT Math middle 50% range 750–800. SAT EBRW middle 50% range 720–770. ACT middle 50% range 33–35. **Basis for Candidate Selection:** *Very important factors include:* rigor of secondary school record, class rank, academic GPA, application essay, standardized test scores, recommendation(s), extracurricular activities, talent/ability, character/personal qualities. *Other factors include:* interview, first generation, alumni/ae relation, geographical residence, state residency, racial/ethnic status, volunteer work, work experience, level of applicant's interest. **Freshman Admission Requirements:** High school diploma or equivalent is not required *Academic units required:* 4 English, 3 math, 2 science, 2 science labs, 2 foreign language, 2 social studies, 3 academic electives. *Academic units recommended:* 4 English, 4 math, 4 science, 3 science labs, 4 foreign language, 3 social studies, 3 academic electives. **Freshman Admission Statistics:** 27,087 applied, 9% admitted, 41% enrolled. **Transfer Admission Requirements:** High school transcript, college transcript(s), essay or personal statement, standardized test scores, statement of good standing from prior institution(s). Minimum college GPA of 3.2 required. Lowest grade transferable C-. **General Admission Information:** Application fee $75. Regular application deadline 1/1. Admission may be deferred for a maximum of 2 years.

COSTS AND FINANCIAL AID

Annual tuition $48,330. Room and board $14,140. Required fees $782. Average book and supplies expense $1,200. **Required Forms and Deadlines:** CSS/Financial Aid PROFILE; FAFSA; Noncustodial PROFILE;. **Notification of Awards:** Applicants will be notified of awards on or about 4/1. **Types of Aid:** *Need-based scholarships/grants:* College/university scholarship or grant aid from institutional funds; Federal Pell; Private scholarships; SEOG; State scholarships/grants. *Loans:* Direct PLUS loans; Direct Subsidized Stafford Loans; Direct Unsubsidized Stafford Loans. **Student Employment:** Federal Work-Study Program available. Institutional employment available. **Financial Aid Statistics:** 97% needy freshmen, 98% needy undergrads receive need-based scholarship or grant aid. 11% freshmen, 8% undergrads receive non-need-based scholarship or grant aid. 36% freshmen, 40% undergrads receive need-based self-help aid. 6% freshmen, 6% undergrads receive athletic scholarships. 56% freshmen receive any aid. 25% undergrads borrow to pay for school. Average cumulative indebtedness $24,292. **Criteria awarding aid:** *Non-need-based:* Academics, Art, Athletics, Leadership, Minority status, Music/drama, State/district residency.

RICHMOND, THE AMERICAN INTERNATIONAL UNIVERSITY IN LONDON

Queen's Road, Richmond-upon-Thames, London, TW10 6JP
Phone: 617-450-5617 **Financial Aid Phone:** 011-44-20-8332-8244
E-mail: us_admissions@richmond.ac.uk **CEEB Code:** 823
Fax: 617-450-5601 **Website:** http://www.richmond.ac.uk/ **ACT Code:** 5244

This private school was founded in 1972. It has a 6 acre campus.

RATINGS

Admissions Selectivity Rating: 64   **Fire Safety Rating:** 72   **Green Rating:** 60*

STUDENTS AND FACULTY

Enrollment: 906. **Student Body:** 51% female, 49% male.
Retention and Graduation: 72% freshmen return for sophomore year. 35% grads go on to further study within 1 year. **Faculty:** Student/faculty ratio 17:1. 41 full-time faculty, 85% hold PhDs, 0% are members of minority groups, 39% are women. 0% of classes are taught by teaching assistants.

ACADEMICS

Degrees: Bachelor's; Master's. **Classes:** Most classes have 10–19 students. **Special Study Options:** English as a Second Language (ESL); Independent study; Internships; Liberal arts/career combination; Study abroad.

FACILITIES

Housing: Coed dorms; Men's dorms; Women's dorms.

CAMPUS LIFE

Environment: Metropolis. **Activities:** Choral groups; Dance; Drama/theater; Literary magazine; Music ensembles; Musical theater; Student government; Student newspaper; Yearbook. 1 honor society on campus. **Athletics (Intercollegiate): Men:** rugby, soccer. **Women:** rugby. **On-Campus Highlights:** Caffe del Mondo Gourmet Coffee Shop.

ADMISSIONS

Freshman Academic Profile: 29% in top 10% of high school class, 40% in top 25% of high school class, 94% in top 50% of high school class. 60% from public high schools. **Basis for Candidate Selection:** *Very important factors include:* rigor of secondary school record, academic GPA, application essay, recommendation(s). *Important factors include:* extracurricular activities. *Other factors include:* interview, talent/ability, character/personal qualities, alumni/ae relation. **Freshman Admission Requirements:** High school diploma is required and GED is accepted. *Academic units required:* 4 English, 3 math, 3 science. **Transfer Admission Requirements:** College transcript(s), essay or personal statement, statement of good standing from prior institution(s). Minimum college GPA of 2.5 required. Lowest grade transferable C. **General Admission Information:** Application fee $50. Regular application deadline 3/1. Non-fall registration accepted. Admission may be deferred for a maximum of 1 year.

COSTS AND FINANCIAL AID

Annual tuition $38,000. Room and board $12,900. Average book and supplies expense $1,000. **Required Forms and Deadlines:** FAFSA. **Types of Aid:** *Need-based scholarships/grants:* College/university scholarship or grant aid from institutional funds; Private scholarships. **Financial Aid Statistics:** 80% freshmen, 70% undergrads receive any aid. **Criteria awarding aid:** *Non-need-based:* Academics.

RIDER UNIVERSITY

2083 Lawrenceville Road, Lawrenceville, NJ 08648-3099
Phone: 609-896-5042 **Financial Aid Phone:** 609-896-5188
E-mail: admissions@rider.edu **CEEB Code:** 2758
Fax: 609-895-6645 **Website:** www.rider.edu **ACT Code:** 2590

This private school was founded in 1865. It has a 280 acre campus.

RATINGS

Admissions Selectivity Rating: 79   **Fire Safety Rating:** 85   **Green Rating:** 97

STUDENTS AND FACULTY

Enrollment: 3,898. **Student Body:** 58% female, 42% male, 23% out-of-state, 3% international (65 countries represented). Asian 5%, African American 13%, Caucasian 58%, Hispanic 16%, Native American <1%, Pacific Islander <1%, Two or more races 4%, Race unknown 4%.
Retention and Graduation: 78% freshmen return for sophomore year. 55% freshmen graduate within 4 years. 62% freshmen graduate within 6 years. 8% grads go on to further study within 1 year. 4% grads pursue arts and sciences degrees. 2% grads pursue law degrees. 4% grads pursue business degrees. 2% grads pursue medical degrees. **Faculty:** Student/faculty ratio 10:1. 234 full-time faculty, 97% hold PhDs, 16% are members of minority groups, 47% are women. 0% of classes are taught by teaching assistants.

ACADEMICS

Degrees: Associate; Bachelor's; Doctoral degree—professional practice; Master's; Post-master's certificate. **Classes:** Most classes have 10–19 students. Most lab/discussion sessions have 10–19 students. **Most popular majors:** Elementary Education and Teaching; Business Administration, Management and Operations, Other; Accounting. **Special Study Options:** Accelerated program; Cooperative education program; Cross-registration; Distance learning; Double major; Dual enrollment; Honors program; Independent study; Internships; Liberal arts/career combination; Study abroad; Teacher certification program; Weekend college. **Honors programs:** The Baccalaureate Honors Program is designed to enrich the educational opportunities for Rider students of proven intellectual capability who choose to become Baccalaureate Scholars. Through a series of team-taught seminars, small classes, personal contact with faculty, colloquia and symposia, as well as independent study opportunities, the scholars extend their ability to think critically, coherently, and systematically about the great themes, ideals, and movements of their human heritage. Students may apply, or be invited, as entering freshmen, currently enrolled freshmen or sophomores, or transfer freshmen or sophomores. **Combined degree programs:** BA/MA. **Disability Services offered:** Tape recorders; Tutors. **Career services:** Alumni network; Alumni services; Career assessment; Career/job search classes; Internships; Regional alumni.

FACILITIES

Housing: Apartments for single students; Coed dorms; Fraternity/sorority housing; Special housing for disabled students; Theme housing; Wellness housing; Women's dorms; 73% of campus accessible to physically disabled. **Special Academic Facilities/Equipment:** Art gallery, Holocaust/Genocide Resource Center, Joseph P. Vona Academic Annex, Bart Luedeke Center, Moore Library.

CAMPUS LIFE

Environment: Village. **Activities:** Campus Ministries; Choral groups; Concert band; Dance; Drama/theater; International Student Organization; Literary magazine; Model UN; Music ensembles; Musical theater; Opera; Pep band; Radio station; Student government; Student newspaper; Student-run film society; Symphony orchestra; Television station; Yearbook. 251 registered organizations, 15 honor societies, 5 religious organizations, 6 fraternities, 9 sororities on campus. **Athletics (Intercollegiate):** *Men:* baseball, basketball, cheerleading, cross-country, diving, golf, soccer, swimming, tennis, track/field (outdoor), wrestling. *Women:* basketball, cheerleading, cross-country, diving, field hockey, soccer, softball, swimming, tennis, track/field (outdoor), volleyball.
On-Campus Highlights: Student Recreation Center. **Environmental Initiatives:** Signed the American College & University Presidents Climate Commitment and formation of the Energy and Sustainability Steering Committee in 2007 to implement strategic plan establishing sustainability initiatives for the university. Signed the "We Are Still In Pledge" in summer 2017 to confirm our commitment.

ADMISSIONS

Freshman Academic Profile: Average high school GPA 3.4. 15% in top 10% of high school class, 38% in top 25% of high school class, 71% in top 50% of high school class. **Test Scores:** SAT Math middle 50% range 500–590. SAT EBRW middle 50% range 500–600. ACT middle 50% range 20–25. **Basis for Candidate Selection:** *Very important factors include:* rigor of secondary school record, academic GPA, application essay, recommendation(s). *Other factors include:* class rank, standardized test scores, interview, extracurricular activities, talent/ability, character/personal qualities, alumni/ae relation, geographical residence, state residency, volunteer work, work experience, level of applicant's interest. **Freshman Admission Requirements:** High school diploma is required and GED is accepted. *Academic units required:* 4 English, 3 math. *Academic units recommended:* 4 science, 4 science labs, 2 foreign language, 2 social studies, 2 history. **Freshman Admission Statistics:** 9,429 applied, 70% admitted, 14% enrolled. **Transfer Admission Requirements:** College transcript(s), essay or personal statement. Minimum college GPA of 2.5 required. Lowest grade transferable C. **General Admission Information:** Application fee $50. Priority deadline 1/15. Non-fall registration accepted. Admission may be deferred for a maximum of 1 year.

COSTS AND FINANCIAL AID

Annual tuition $42,120. Room and board $15,280. Required fees $740. Average book and supplies expense $1,500. **Required Forms and Deadlines:** FAFSA. **Notification of Awards:** Applicants will be notified of awards on a rolling basis beginning 2/1. **Types of Aid:** *Need-based scholarships/grants:* College/university scholarship or grant aid from institutional funds; Federal Pell; Private scholarships; SEOG; State scholarships/grants. *Loans:* Direct PLUS loans; Direct Subsidized Stafford Loans; Direct Unsubsidized Stafford Loans. **Student Employment:** Federal Work-Study Program available. Institutional employment available. **Financial Aid Statistics:** 100% needy freshmen, 99% needy undergrads receive need-based scholarship or grant aid. 13% freshmen, 15% undergrads receive non-need-based scholarship or grant aid. 81% freshmen, 82% undergrads receive need-based self-help aid. 8% freshmen, 7% undergrads receive athletic scholarships. 98% freshmen, 89% undergrads receive any aid. 77% undergrads borrow to pay for school. Average cumulative indebtedness $36,499. **Criteria awarding aid:** *Need-based:* Academics, Alumni affiliation, Athletics, Leadership, Music/drama. *Non-need-based:* Academics, Leadership.

RINGLING COLLEGE OF ART AND DESIGN

2700 N. Tamiami Trail, Sarasota, FL 34234-5895
Phone: 941-351-5100 **Financial Aid Phone:** 941-359-7532
E-mail: admissions@ringling.edu **CEEB Code:** 5573
Fax: 941-359-7517 **Website:** www.ringling.edu **ACT Code:** 6724

This private school was founded in 1931. It has a 49 acre campus.

RATINGS

Admissions Selectivity Rating: 69   **Fire Safety Rating:** 86   **Green Rating:** 60*

STUDENTS AND FACULTY

Enrollment: 1,561. **Student Body:** 69% female, 31% male, 56% out-of-state, 17% international (57 countries represented). Asian 9%, African American 3%, Caucasian 47%, Hispanic 16%, Native American <1%, Pacific Islander <1%, Two or more races 4%, Race unknown 3%.
Retention and Graduation: 81% freshmen return for sophomore year. 58% freshmen graduate within 4 years. 65% freshmen graduate within 6 years. 5% grads go on to further study within 1 year. **Faculty:** Student/faculty ratio 11:1. 116 full-time faculty, 55% hold PhDs, 4% are members of minority groups, 30% are women. 0% of classes are taught by teaching assistants.

ACADEMICS

Degrees: Bachelor's. **Classes:** Most classes have 10–19 students. **Most popular majors:** Game and Interactive Media Design; Illustration; Animation, Interactive Technology, Video Graphics and Special Effects. **Special Study Options:** Cross-registration; English as a Second Language (ESL); Exchange student program (domestic); Independent study; Internships; Study abroad. **Disability Services offered:** Note-taking services; Reader services; Tape recorders; Tutors. **Career services:** Alumni network; Alumni services; Career assessment; Career/job search classes; Internships; Regional alumni.

FACILITIES

Housing: Apartments for married students; Apartments for single students; Coed dorms; Men's dorms; Special housing for disabled students; Theme housing; Wellness housing; Women's dorms; 98% of campus accessible to physically disabled. **Special Academic Facilities/Equipment:** Selby Gallery; Richard & Barbara Basch Gallery; Crossley Gallery; Goldstein Gallery; Englewood Art Center and Galleries; Hammon Commons Gallery; Longboat Key Art Center and Galleries; Willis A. Smith Construction, Inc. Galleries; Diane Roskamp Exhibition Halls; Verman Kimbrough Memorial Library; Academic Building; College book and supply store; College-owned furnished apartments and residence halls; state-of-the-art studios; photography studios; Hammon Commons Dining Hall; The Brickman Café; Outtakes Café; Susan A. Palmer Recreation & Wellness Center; project rooms; labs; laundry facilities; mail room. **Campus Network:** 50% of classrooms, 100% of dorms, 100% of student union, 90% of libraries, 90% of dining areas, 0% of common outdoor areas have wireless network access.

CAMPUS LIFE

Environment: City. **Activities:** Campus Ministries; Choral groups; Dance; Drama/theater; International Student Organization; Student government; Television station. 29 registered organizations, 1 religious organization on campus. **On-Campus Highlights:** Ulla Searing Student Center and deck. **Environmental Initiatives:** The College has an active sustainability committee comprised of staff, faculty and student members. the charge of the committee is to review current and proposed sustainability practices, provide oversight in the implementation of these practices and to raise awareness of sustainability practices.

ADMISSIONS

Freshman Academic Profile: Average high school GPA 3.4. **Basis for Candidate Selection:** *Very important factors include:* rigor of secondary school record, academic GPA, recommendation(s), talent/ability. *Important factors include:* application essay, *Other factors include:* interview, extracurricular activities, alumni/ae relation, volunteer work, work experience, level of applicant's interest. **Freshman Admission Requirements:** High school diploma is required and GED is accepted. **Freshman Admission Statistics:** 2,306 applied, 67% admitted, 28% enrolled. **Transfer Admission Requirements:** High school transcript, college transcript(s), essay or personal statement. Minimum college GPA of 2.0 required. Lowest grade transferable C. **General Admission Information:** Application fee $70. Admission may be deferred for a maximum of 2 years.

COSTS AND FINANCIAL AID

Required Forms and Deadlines: FAFSA. **Notification of Awards:** Applicants will be notified of awards on a rolling basis beginning 10/1. **Types of Aid:** *Need-based scholarships/grants:* College/university scholarship or grant aid from institutional funds; Federal Pell; Private scholarships; SEOG; State scholarships/grants. *Loans:* Direct PLUS loans; Direct Subsidized Stafford Loans; Direct Unsubsidized Stafford Loans. **Student Employment:** Federal Work-Study Program available. Institutional employment available. **Financial Aid Statistics:** 100% needy freshmen, 100% needy undergrads receive need-based scholarship or grant aid. 5% freshmen, 4% undergrads receive non-need-based scholarship or grant aid. 91% freshmen, 94% undergrads receive need-based self-help aid. 0% freshmen, 0% undergrads receive athletic scholarships. 99% freshmen, 88% undergrads receive any aid. 68% undergrads borrow to pay for school. Average cumulative indebtedness $41,746. **Criteria awarding aid:** *Need-based:* Academics, Art. *Non-need-based:* Academics, Art.

RIPON COLLEGE

PO Box 248, Ripon, WI 54971
Phone: 920-748-8337 **Financial Aid Phone:** 920-748-8301
E-mail: adminfo@ripon.edu **CEEB Code:** 1664
Fax: 920-748-8335 **Website:** www.ripon.edu **ACT Code:** 4636

This private school was founded in 1851. It has a 250 acre campus.

RATINGS

Admissions Selectivity Rating: 79   **Fire Safety Rating:** 76   **Green Rating:** 65

STUDENTS AND FACULTY

Enrollment: 787. **Student Body:** 53% female, 47% male, 27% out-of-state, 3% international (12 countries represented). Asian 1%, African American 4%, Caucasian 79%, Hispanic 9%, Native American <1%, Pacific Islander <1%, Two or more races 3%, Race unknown <1%.

Retention and Graduation: 79% freshmen return for sophomore year. 61% freshmen graduate within 4 years. 68% freshmen graduate within 6 years. 24% grads go on to further study within 1 year. 17% grads pursue arts and sciences degrees. 3% grads pursue law degrees. 3% grads pursue medical degrees. **Faculty:** Student/faculty ratio 12:1. 60 full-time faculty, 98% hold PhDs, 7% are members of minority groups, 42% are women. 0% of classes are taught by teaching assistants.

ACADEMICS

Degrees: Bachelor's. **Classes:** Most classes have 10–19 students. Most lab/discussion sessions have 10–19 students. **Most popular majors:** Sports, Kinesiology, and Physical Education/Fitness, General; Business/Commerce, General; History, General. **Special Study Options:** Double major; Exchange student program (domestic); Independent study; Internships; Student-designed major; Study abroad; Teacher certification program. **Disability Services offered:** Tutors. **Career services:** Alumni network; Career assessment; Internships; Regional alumni.

FACILITIES

Housing: Apartments for single students; Coed dorms; Fraternity/sorority housing; Men's dorms; Special housing for disabled students; Theme housing; Women's dorms. **Special Academic Facilities/Equipment:** Caestecker Art Gallery, West Hall Museum, Farr Hall Greenhouse, Communicating Plus, Ceresco Prairie Conservancy, Lane Library Archives, language labs, WRPN college radio.

CAMPUS LIFE

Environment: Village. **Activities:** Campus Ministries; Choral groups; Concert band; Dance; Drama/theater; International Student Organization; Jazz band; Literary magazine; Music ensembles; Musical theater; Pep band; Radio station; Student government; Student newspaper; Student-run film society; Symphony orchestra; Television station; Yearbook. 45 registered organizations, 13 honor societies, 4 religious organizations, 5 fraternities, 3 sororities on campus. **Athletics (Intercollegiate):** *Men:* baseball, basketball, cross-country, cycling, football, golf, soccer, swimming, tennis, track/field (outdoor), track/field (indoor). *Women:* basketball, cross-country, cycling, golf, soccer, softball, swimming, tennis, track/field (outdoor), track/field (indoor), volleyball. **On-Campus Highlights:** Ceresco Prairie Conservancy.

ADMISSIONS

Freshman Academic Profile: Average high school GPA 3.4. 17% in top 10% of high school class, 38% in top 25% of high school class, 81% in top 50% of high school class. 75% from public high schools. **Test Scores:** SAT Math middle 50% range 500–600. SAT EBRW middle 50% range 500–610. ACT middle 50% range 20–27. **Basis for Candidate Selection:** *Very important factors include:* rigor of secondary school record, interview. *Important factors include:* class rank, academic GPA, extracurricular activities, character/personal qualities. *Other factors include:* application essay, standardized test scores, recommendation(s), talent/ability, volunteer work. **Freshman Admission Requirements:** High school diploma is required and GED is accepted. *Academic units required:* 4 English, 2 math, 2 science, 2 social studies. *Academic units recommended:* 4 math, 4 science, 2 foreign language, 4 social studies. **Freshman Admission Statistics:** 2,619 applied, 69% admitted, 15% enrolled. **Transfer Admission Requirements:** College transcript(s), essay or personal statement, statement of good standing from prior institution(s). Minimum college GPA of 2.0 required. Lowest grade transferable C. **General Admission Information:** Application fee $30. Priority deadline 3/15. Non-fall registration accepted. Admission may be deferred for a maximum of 1 year.

COSTS AND FINANCIAL AID

Annual tuition $44,813. Room and board $8,653. Required fees $300. Average book and supplies expense $750. **Required Forms and Deadlines:** FAFSA. **Notification of Awards:** Applicants will be notified of awards on a rolling basis beginning 3/1. **Types of Aid:** *Need-based scholarships/grants:* College/university scholarship or grant aid from institutional funds; Federal Pell; Private scholarships; SEOG; State scholarships/grants. *Loans:* Direct PLUS loans; Direct Subsidized Stafford Loans; Direct Unsubsidized Stafford Loans. **Student Employment:** Federal Work-Study Program available. Institutional employment available. **Financial Aid Statistics:** 100% needy freshmen, 100% needy undergrads receive need-based scholarship or grant aid. 15% freshmen, 13% undergrads receive non-need-based scholarship or grant aid. 82% freshmen, 84% undergrads receive need-based self-help aid. 0% freshmen, 0% undergrads receive athletic scholarships. 90% freshmen, 83% undergrads receive any aid. 84% undergrads borrow to pay for school. Average cumulative indebtedness $37,084. **Criteria awarding aid:** *Non-need-based:* Academics, Alumni affiliation, Art, Leadership, Minority status, Music/drama, Religious affiliation, State/district residency.

RIVIER UNIVERSITY

420 South Main Street, Nashua, NH 03060
Phone: 603-897-8219 **Financial Aid Phone:** 603-897-8810
E-mail: rivadmit@rivier.edu **CEEB Code:** 3728
Fax: 603-891-1799 **Website:** www.rivier.edu **ACT Code:** 2520

This private school, affiliated with the Roman Catholic Church, was founded in 1933. It has a 68 acre campus.

RATINGS
Admissions Selectivity Rating: 75 **Fire Safety Rating:** 89 **Green Rating:** 60*

STUDENTS AND FACULTY
Enrollment: 1,370. **Student Body:** 85% female, 15% male, 38% out-of-state, 0% international (12 countries represented). Asian 2%, African American 2%, Caucasian 75%, Hispanic 5%, Native American 1%, Pacific Islander 0%, Two or more races <1%, Race unknown 16%.
Retention and Graduation: 78% freshmen return for sophomore year.
Faculty: Student/faculty ratio 17:1. 68 full-time faculty, 75% hold PhDs, 0% are members of minority groups, 65% are women. 0% of classes are taught by teaching assistants.

ACADEMICS
Degrees: Associate; Bachelor's; Certificate; Master's; Post-bachelor's certificate; Post-master's certificate. **Classes:** Most classes have 10–19 students. Most lab/discussion sessions have 10–19 students. **Special Study Options:** Cross-registration; Distance learning; Double major; Dual enrollment; Independent study; Internships; Liberal arts/career combination; Student-designed major; Teacher certification program. **Disability Services offered:** Note-taking services; Reader services; Tape recorders; Tutors. **Career services:** Alumni services; Career assessment; Career/job search classes; Internships.

FACILITIES
Housing: Coed dorms; Wellness housing; 75% of campus accessible to physically disabled. **Special Academic Facilities/Equipment:** Art gallery, Early Childhood Center/Laboratory School, language lab, TV microscope, video/laser disk system, photospectrometer, high-performance liquid chromatograph, digital imaging lab, several art studios including a photography darkroom.

CAMPUS LIFE
Environment: City. **Activities:** Campus Ministries; Choral groups; Dance; Drama/theater; International Student Organization; Model UN; Music ensembles; Student government; Television station; Yearbook. 30 registered organizations, 2 honor societies, 2 religious organizations on campus. **Athletics (Intercollegiate):** *Men:* baseball, basketball, cross-country, soccer, volleyball. *Women:* basketball, cross-country, soccer, softball, volleyball. **On-Campus Highlights:** Regina Library.

ADMISSIONS
Freshman Academic Profile: Average high school GPA 3.0. 6% in top 10% of high school class, 27% in top 25% of high school class, 71% in top 50% of high school class. **Test Scores:** SAT Math middle 50% range 410–510. SAT EBRW middle 50% range 410–510. ACT middle 50% range 17–21. **Basis for Candidate Selection:** *Very important factors include:* rigor of secondary school record, academic GPA. *Important factors include:* class rank, application essay, standardized test scores, extracurricular activities, talent/ability, volunteer work, work experience. *Other factors include:* recommendation(s), interview, character/personal qualities. **Freshman Admission Requirements:** High school diploma is required and GED is accepted. *Academic units recommended:* 4 English, 3 math, 1 science, 1 science lab, 2 foreign language, 2 social studies, 1 history, 3 academic electives. **Freshman Admission Statistics:** 665 applied, 82% admitted, 36% enrolled. **Transfer Admission Requirements:** Essay or personal statement. Minimum college GPA of 2.0 required. Lowest grade transferable C. **General Admission Information:** Application fee $25. Admission may be deferred for a maximum of 1 year.

COSTS AND FINANCIAL AID
Annual tuition $25,410. Room and board $9,798. Required fees $600. Average book and supplies expense $1,200. **Required Forms and Deadlines:** FAFSA. **Notification of Awards:** Applicants will be notified of awards on a rolling basis beginning 3/1. **Types of Aid:** *Need-based scholarships/grants:* College/university scholarship or grant aid from institutional funds; Federal Pell; Private scholarships; SEOG; State scholarships/grants. *Loans:* Direct PLUS loans; Direct Subsidized Stafford Loans; Direct Unsubsidized Stafford Loans. **Student Employment:** Federal Work-Study Program available. Institutional employment available. **Financial Aid Statistics:** 100% needy freshmen, 91% needy undergrads receive need-based scholarship or grant aid. 4% freshmen, 4% undergrads receive non-need-based scholarship or grant aid. 91% freshmen, 86% undergrads receive need-based self-help aid. 0% freshmen, 0% undergrads receive athletic scholarships. 82% freshmen, 89% undergrads receive any aid. **Criteria awarding aid:** *Need-based:* Academics. *Non-need-based:* Academics, Alumni affiliation, Leadership.

ROANOKE COLLEGE

221 College Lane, Salem, VA 24153-3794
Phone: 540-375-2270 **Financial Aid Phone:** 540-375-2235
E-mail: admissions@roanoke.edu **CEEB Code:** 5571
Fax: 540-375-2267 **Website:** www.roanoke.edu **ACT Code:** 4392

This private school, affiliated with the Lutheran Church, was founded in 1842. It has a 80 acre campus.

RATINGS
Admissions Selectivity Rating: 79 **Fire Safety Rating:** 89 **Green Rating:** 69

STUDENTS AND FACULTY
Enrollment: 1,953. **Student Body:** 58% female, 42% male, 45% out-of-state, 2% international (32 countries represented). Asian 1%, African American 5%, Caucasian 81%, Hispanic 5%, Native American <1%, Pacific Islander <1%, Two or more races 4%, Race unknown 0%.
Retention and Graduation: 78% freshmen return for sophomore year. 63% freshmen graduate within 4 years. 70% freshmen graduate within 6 years. 20% grads go on to further study within 1 year. **Faculty:** Student/faculty ratio 11:1. 165 full-time faculty, 89% hold PhDs, 10% are members of minority groups, 55% are women. 0% of classes are taught by teaching assistants.

ACADEMICS
Degrees: Bachelor's. **Classes:** Most classes have 20–29 students. Most lab/discussion sessions have 10–19 students. **Most popular majors:** Psychology, General; Business Administration and Management, General; Biology/Biological Sciences, General. **Special Study Options:** Accelerated program; Cross-registration; Distance learning; Double major; Dual enrollment; English as a Second Language (ESL); Honors program; Independent study; Internships; Liberal arts/career combination; Study abroad; Teacher certification program. **Honors programs:** The Honors Program is designed for students with excellent academic performance, broad extracurricular interests, and leadership abilities. The Honors Program has a unique core curriculum as well as an Honors Portfolio of supplemental activities and service involvements. A special Distinction Project provides a uniquely integrated experience, leading to a distinct recognition on the diploma and transcript. Honors housing and a strong honors community are also key parts of the program. Roanoke also offers the Fellows Program which gives students practical experience. Projects in research, entrepreneurship, service leadership and Information Technology are among the current offerings. **Disability Services offered:** Note-taking services; Reader services; Tape recorders; Tutors. **Career services:** Alumni network; Alumni services; Career assessment; Career/job search classes; Internships; Regional alumni.

FACILITIES
Housing: Apartments for single students; Coed dorms; Fraternity/sorority housing; Special housing for disabled students; Special housing for international students; Theme housing; Women's dorms; 80% of campus accessible to physically disabled. **Special Academic Facilities/Equipment:** Fine arts center and gallery, community research center, language lab, Benne center for religion and society, center for leadership and entrepreneurial innovation, center for economic freedom. New athletic/health facility including indoor track and performance gymnasium. **Campus Network:** 100% of classrooms, 100% of dorms, 100% of student union, 100% of libraries, 100% of dining areas, 100% of common outdoor areas have wireless network access.

CAMPUS LIFE
Environment: City. **Activities:** Campus Ministries; Choral groups; Concert band; Dance; Drama/theater; International Student Organization; Jazz band; Literary magazine; Model UN; Music ensembles; Pep band; Radio

station; Student government; Student newspaper; Student-run film society. 100 registered organizations, 27 honor societies, 7 religious organizations, 5 fraternities, 4 sororities on campus. **Athletics (Intercollegiate):** *Men:* baseball, basketball, cross-country, golf, lacrosse, soccer, tennis, track/field (outdoor), track/field (indoor). *Women:* basketball, cross-country, field hockey, lacrosse, soccer, softball, tennis, track/field (outdoor), track/field (indoor), volleyball. **On-Campus Highlights:** Cregger Center & Belk Fitness Center. **Environmental Initiatives:** Lucas Hall was completely renovated and is LEED-Silver Certified. A new residence hall and a major new athletic center/campus community center were also built recently, to high efficiency environmental awareness standards, although the college is not seeking formal certification.

ADMISSIONS

Freshman Academic Profile: Average high school GPA 3.6. 17% in top 10% of high school class, 46% in top 25% of high school class, 82% in top 50% of high school class. 84% from public high schools. **Test Scores:** SAT Math middle 50% range 510–620. SAT EBRW middle 50% range 540–640. ACT middle 50% range 21–28. **Basis for Candidate Selection:** *Very important factors include:* rigor of secondary school record, academic GPA, character/ personal qualities. *Important factors include:* class rank, interview, extracurricular activities. *Other factors include:* application essay, standardized test scores, recommendation(s), talent/ability, alumni/ae relation, racial/ethnic status, volunteer work, work experience. **Freshman Admission Requirements:** High school diploma is required and GED is accepted. *Academic units required:* 4 English, 3 math, 2 science, 2 science labs, 2 foreign language, 2 social studies, 5 academic electives. *Academic units recommended:* 2 foreign language. **Freshman Admission Statistics:** 5,453 applied, 75% admitted, 14% enrolled. **Transfer Admission Requirements:** High school transcript, college transcript(s), statement of good standing from prior institution(s). Minimum college GPA of 2.2 required. Lowest grade transferable C-. **General Admission Information:** Application fee $30. Regular application deadline 3/15. Non-fall registration accepted. Admission may be deferred for a maximum of 2 years.

COSTS AND FINANCIAL AID

Annual tuition $45,200. Room and board $14,580. Required fees $1,820. Average book and supplies expense $1,000. **Required Forms and Deadlines:** FAFSA; State aid form. **Notification of Awards:** Applicants will be notified of awards on a rolling basis beginning 11/15. **Types of Aid:** *Need-based scholarships/grants:* College/university scholarship or grant aid from institutional funds; Federal Pell; Private scholarships; SEOG; State scholarships/ grants. *Loans:* Direct PLUS loans; Direct Subsidized Stafford Loans; Direct Unsubsidized Stafford Loans. **Student Employment:** Federal Work-Study Program available. Institutional employment available. **Financial Aid Statistics:** 97% needy freshmen, 98% needy undergrads receive need-based scholarship or grant aid. 97% freshmen, 97% undergrads receive non-need-based scholarship or grant aid. 78% freshmen, 78% undergrads receive need-based self-help aid. 0% freshmen, 0% undergrads receive athletic scholarships. 100% freshmen, 97% undergrads receive any aid. 71% undergrads borrow to pay for school. Average cumulative indebtedness $37,335. **Criteria awarding aid:** *Need-based:* Academics, Minority status, Religious affiliation. *Non-need-based:* Academics, Art, Minority status, Music/drama, Religious affiliation.

ROBERT MORRIS UNIVERSITY

6001 University Boulevard, Moon Township, PA 15108-1189
Phone: 412-397-5200 **Financial Aid Phone:** (412) 397-6250
E-mail: admissionsoffice@rmu.edu **CEEB Code:** 2769
Fax: 412-397-2425 **Website:** www.rmu.edu **ACT Code:** 3674

This private school was founded in 1921. It has a 230 acre campus.

RATINGS

Admissions Selectivity Rating: 75   **Fire Safety Rating:** 93   **Green Rating:** 60*

STUDENTS AND FACULTY

Enrollment: 3,734. **Student Body:** 44% female, 56% male, 14% out-of-state, 9% international (35 countries represented). Asian 1%, African American 7%, Caucasian 75%, Hispanic 3%, Native American <1%, Pacific Islander <1%, Two or more races 3%, Race unknown 2%.
Retention and Graduation: 83% freshmen return for sophomore year. 52% freshmen graduate within 4 years. 65% freshmen graduate within 6 years. 6% grads go on to further study within 1 year. **Faculty:** Student/faculty ratio 15:1.

197 full-time faculty, 94% hold PhDs, 22% are members of minority groups, 48% are women. 0% of classes are taught by teaching assistants.

ACADEMICS

Degrees: Bachelor's; Certificate; Doctoral degree—professional practice; Doctoral degree research/scholarship; Master's; Post-bachelor's certificate; Post-master's certificate. **Classes:** Most classes have 20–29 students. Most lab/ discussion sessions have 10–19 students. **Most popular majors:** Registered Nursing/Registered Nurse; Business Administration and Management, General; Accounting. **Special Study Options:** Accelerated program; Cross-registration; Distance learning; Double major; Honors program; Independent study; Internships; Study abroad; Teacher certification program. **Honors programs:** International Honors Program; Women's Leadership and Mentor Program. **Disability Services offered:** Note-taking services; Reader services; Tape recorders; Tutors. **Career services:** Alumni network; Alumni services; Career assessment; Career/job search classes; Internships; Regional alumni.

FACILITIES

Housing: Apartments for single students; Coed dorms; Fraternity/sorority housing; Men's dorms; Special housing for disabled students; Theme housing; Women's dorms; 80% of campus accessible to physically disabled.

CAMPUS LIFE

Environment: Metropolis. **Activities:** Campus Ministries; Choral groups; Concert band; Drama/theater; International Student Organization; Literary magazine; Marching band; Music ensembles; Musical theater; Pep band; Radio station; Student government; Student newspaper; Television station. 164 registered organizations, 21 honor societies, 5 religious organizations, 11 fraternities, 6 sororities on campus. **Athletics (Intercollegiate):** *Men:* basketball, football, golf, ice hockey, lacrosse, soccer, tennis, track/field (outdoor), track/ field (indoor). *Women:* basketball, crew/rowing, field hockey, golf, ice hockey, lacrosse, soccer, softball, tennis, track/field (outdoor), track/field (indoor), volleyball. **On-Campus Highlights:** Nicholson Student Center/Romo's Café. **Environmental Initiatives:** Recycling paper, cardboard, plastic, bottles and cans, and florescent bulbs.

ADMISSIONS

Freshman Academic Profile: Average high school GPA 3.6. 16% in top 10% of high school class, 42% in top 25% of high school class, 79% in top 50% of high school class. 89% from public high schools. **Test Scores:** SAT Math middle 50% range 510–600. SAT EBRW middle 50% range 510–600. ACT middle 50% range 21–27. **Basis for Candidate Selection:** *Very important factors include:* academic GPA, standardized test scores. *Important factors include:* rigor of secondary school record, class rank, interview, extracurricular activities, talent/ability, character/personal qualities. *Other factors include:* application essay, recommendation(s), alumni/ae relation, geographical residence, volunteer work, work experience. **Freshman Admission Requirements:** High school diploma is required and GED is accepted. *Academic units required:* 4 English, 3 math, 2 science, 4 social studies, 3 academic electives. *Academic units recommended:* 2 foreign language. **Freshman Admission Statistics:** 5,956 applied, 84% admitted, 14% enrolled. **Transfer Admission Requirements:** College transcript(s), statement of good standing from prior institution(s). Minimum college GPA of 2.0 required. Lowest grade transferable C. **General Admission Information:** Application fee $30. Non-fall registration accepted. Admission may be deferred for a maximum of 12 months.

COSTS AND FINANCIAL AID

Required Forms and Deadlines: FAFSA. **Notification of Awards:** Applicants will be notified of awards on a rolling basis beginning 11/15. **Types of Aid:** *Need-based scholarships/grants:* College/university scholarship or grant aid from institutional funds; Federal Pell; Private scholarships; SEOG; State scholarships/ grants. *Loans:* Direct PLUS loans; Direct Subsidized Stafford Loans; Direct Unsubsidized Stafford Loans. **Student Employment:** Federal Work-Study Program available. Institutional employment available. **Financial Aid Statistics:** 100% needy freshmen, 98% needy undergrads receive need-based scholarship or grant aid. 13% freshmen, 9% undergrads receive non-need-based scholarship or grant aid. 85% freshmen, 88% undergrads receive need-based self-help aid. 3% freshmen, 3% undergrads receive athletic scholarships. 81% freshmen, 72% undergrads receive any aid. **Criteria awarding aid:** *Non-need-based:* Academics, Athletics.

ROBERTS WESLEYAN COLLEGE

2301 Westside Drive, Rochester, NY 14624-1997
Phone: 585-594-6400 **Financial Aid Phone:** 585-594-6150
E-mail: admissions@roberts.edu **CEEB Code:** 2805
Fax: 585-594-6371 **Website:** www.roberts.edu **ACT Code:** 2868

This private school, affiliated with the Free Methodist Church, was founded in 1866. It has a 188 acre campus.

RATINGS
Admissions Selectivity Rating: 87   **Fire Safety Rating:** 73   **Green Rating:** 60*

STUDENTS AND FACULTY
Enrollment: 1,288. **Student Body:** 69% female, 31% male, 7% out-of-state, 3% international (33 countries represented). Asian 1%, African American 12%, Caucasian 75%, Hispanic 5%, Native American <1%, Pacific Islander <1%, Two or more races 2%, Race unknown 2%.
Retention and Graduation: 80% freshmen return for sophomore year. 24% grads go on to further study within 1 year. **Faculty:** 92 full-time faculty, 72% hold PhDs, 7% are members of minority groups, 52% are women. 0% of classes are taught by teaching assistants.

ACADEMICS
Degrees: Bachelor's; Master's. **Classes:** Most classes have 10–19 students. Most lab/discussion sessions have 10–19 students. **Most popular majors:** Elementary Education and Teaching; Music Teacher Education. **Special Study Options:** Accelerated program; Cross-registration; Distance learning; Double major; English as a Second Language (ESL); Honors program; Independent study; Internships; Liberal arts/career combination; Student-designed major; Study abroad; Teacher certification program. **Combined degree programs:** BA/MEng. **Disability Services offered:** Note-taking services; Reader services; Tape recorders; Tutors. **Career services:** Alumni network; Alumni services; Career assessment; Internships; Regional alumni.

FACILITIES
Housing: Apartments for married students; Apartments for single students; Coed dorms; Men's dorms; Special housing for disabled students; Women's dorms; 71% of campus accessible to physically disabled. **Special Academic Facilities/Equipment:** Davison Art Gallery.

CAMPUS LIFE
Environment: City. **Activities:** Campus Ministries; Choral groups; Concert band; Dance; Drama/theater; International Student Organization; Jazz band; Model UN; Music ensembles; Musical theater; Student government; Student newspaper; Symphony orchestra; Yearbook. 28 registered organizations, 11 religious organizations on campus. **Athletics (Intercollegiate):** *Men:* basketball, cross-country, golf, soccer, tennis, track/field (outdoor), track/field (indoor). *Women:* basketball, cross-country, soccer, tennis, track/field (outdoor), track/field (indoor), volleyball. **On-Campus Highlights:** Voller Athletic Center & Sports Complex.

ADMISSIONS
Freshman Academic Profile: Average high school GPA 3.4. 24% in top 10% of high school class, 49% in top 25% of high school class, 85% in top 50% of high school class. **Test Scores:** SAT Math middle 50% range 470–590. SAT EBRW middle 50% range 470–600. ACT middle 50% range 20–27. **Basis for Candidate Selection:** *Very important factors include:* rigor of secondary school record, academic GPA, standardized test scores, interview, character/personal qualities, religious affiliation/commitment. *Important factors include:* application essay, recommendation(s), extracurricular activities. *Other factors include:* class rank, talent/ability, alumni/ae relation, volunteer work, level of applicant's interest. **Freshman Admission Requirements:** High school diploma is required and GED is accepted. *Academic units required:* 4 English, 3 math, 3 science, 1 science lab, 3 social studies. *Academic units recommended:* 4 math, 4 science, 3 science labs, 3 foreign language. **Freshman Admission Statistics:** 1,928 applied, 47% admitted, 24% enrolled. **Transfer Admission Requirements:** College transcript(s), essay or personal statement. Minimum college GPA of 2.70 required. Lowest grade transferable C. **General Admission Information:** Application fee $35. Priority deadline 2/1. Non-fall registration accepted. Admission may be deferred for a maximum of 1 year.

COSTS AND FINANCIAL AID
Annual tuition $25,350. Room and board $9,264. Required fees $1,349. Average book and supplies expense $1,000. **Required Forms and Deadlines:** FAFSA; State aid form. **Notification of Awards:** Applicants will be notified of awards on a rolling basis beginning 3/1. **Types of Aid:** *Need-based scholarships/grants:* College/university scholarship or grant aid from institutional funds; Federal Pell; Private scholarships; SEOG; State scholarships/grants. *Loans:* Direct PLUS loans; Direct Subsidized Stafford Loans; Direct Unsubsidized Stafford Loans. **Student Employment:** Federal Work-Study Program available. Institutional employment available. **Financial Aid Statistics:** 100% needy freshmen, 98% needy undergrads receive need-based scholarship or grant aid. 12% freshmen, 7% undergrads receive non-need-based scholarship or grant aid. 86% freshmen, 89% undergrads receive need-based self-help aid. 6% freshmen, 3% undergrads receive athletic scholarships. 98% freshmen, 97% undergrads receive any aid. **Criteria awarding aid:** *Need-based:* Leadership. *Non-need-based:* Academics, Alumni affiliation, Art, Athletics, Music/drama, Religious affiliation.

ROCHESTER COLLEGE

800 West Avon Road, Rochester Hills, MI 48307
Phone: 248-218-2031
E-mail: admissions@rc.edu **CEEB Code:** 1516
Fax: 248-218-2035 **Website:** www.rc.edu **ACT Code:** 2072

This private school, affiliated with the Church of Christ, was founded in 1959. It has a 83 acre campus.

RATINGS
Admissions Selectivity Rating: 67   **Fire Safety Rating:** 60*   **Green Rating:** 60*

STUDENTS AND FACULTY
Enrollment: 927. **Student Body:** 39 % female, 61% male, 14% out-of-state, 3% international (10 countries represented). Asian 1%, African American 11%, Caucasian 83%, Hispanic 1%, Native American 1%, Race unknown 1%.
Retention and Graduation: 69% freshmen return for sophomore year. **Faculty:** Student/faculty ratio 15:1. 32 full-time faculty, 28% hold PhDs, 0% are members of minority groups, 34% are women. 0% of classes are taught by teaching assistants.

ACADEMICS
Degrees: Associate; Bachelor's; Master's; Transfer Associate. **Special Study Options:** Accelerated program; Cross-registration; Double major; Dual enrollment; Independent study; Internships; Liberal arts/career combination; Study abroad; Teacher certification program; Weekend college. **Disability Services offered:** Note-taking services; Reader services. **Career services:** Alumni network; Alumni services; Career assessment; Career/job search classes; Internships.

FACILITIES
Housing: Apartments for married students; Men's dorms; Special housing for disabled students; Women's dorms **Campus Network:** 100% of classrooms, 100% of dorms, 100% of student union, 100% of libraries, 100% of dining areas, 100% of common outdoor areas have wireless network access.

CAMPUS LIFE
Environment: Village. **Activities:** Choral groups; Drama/theater; Jazz band; Music ensembles; Student government; Student newspaper; Yearbook. 19 registered organizations, 3 honor societies, 1 religious organization on campus. **Athletics (Intercollegiate):** *Men:* baseball, basketball, cross-country, soccer, track/field (outdoor). *Women:* basketball, cross-country, softball, track/field (outdoor), volleyball.

ADMISSIONS
Basis for Candidate Selection: *Important factors include:* rigor of secondary school record, standardized test scores. *Other factors include:* interview. **Freshman Admission Requirements:** High school diploma is required and GED is accepted. **Freshman Admission Statistics:** 277 applied, 83% admitted, 65% enrolled. **Transfer Admission Requirements:** High school transcript, college transcript(s). Minimum college GPA of 2.0 required. Lowest grade transferable C. **General Admission Information:** Application fee $25. Non-fall registration accepted. Admission may be deferred for a maximum of 24 months.

COSTS AND FINANCIAL AID
Annual tuition $9,462. Room and board $5,342. Average book and supplies expense $600. **Required Forms and Deadlines:** FAFSA; Institution's own financial aid form. **Notification of Awards:** Applicants will be notified of awards on a rolling basis beginning 6/1. **Types of Aid:** *Need-based scholarships/grants:* College/university scholarship or grant aid from institutional funds; Federal Pell; Private scholarships; SEOG; State scholarships/grants. *Loans:*

Direct PLUS loans; Direct Subsidized Stafford Loans; Direct Unsubsidized Stafford Loans. **Student Employment:** Federal Work-Study Program available. Institutional employment available. **Financial Aid Statistics:** 87% needy freshmen receive need-based scholarship or grant aid. 79% freshmen receive non-need-based scholarship or grant aid. 84% freshmen receive need-based self-help aid. 29% freshmen receive athletic scholarships. **Criteria awarding aid:** *Non-need-based:* Academics, Alumni affiliation, Athletics, Leadership, Music/drama.

ROCHESTER INSTITUTE OF TECHNOLOGY

60 Lomb Memorial Drive, Rochester, NY 14623-5604
Phone: 585-475-6631 **Financial Aid Phone:** 585-475-2186
E-mail: admissions@rit.edu **CEEB Code:** 2760
Fax: 585-475-7424 **Website:** www.rit.edu **ACT Code:** 2870

This private school was founded in 1829. It has a 1300 acre campus.

RATINGS
Admissions Selectivity Rating: 86   **Fire Safety Rating:** 89   **Green Rating:** 96

STUDENTS AND FACULTY
Enrollment: 12,623. **Student Body:** 33% female, 67% male, 48% out-of-state, 6% international (71 countries represented). Asian 10%, African American 4%, Caucasian 65%, Hispanic 8%, Native American <1%, Pacific Islander <1%, Two or more races 4%, Race unknown 2%.
Retention and Graduation: 89% freshmen return for sophomore year. 25% freshmen graduate within 4 years. 69% freshmen graduate within 6 years. 14% grads go on to further study within 1 year. **Faculty:** Student/faculty ratio 13:1. 1,046 full-time faculty, 73% hold PhDs, 21% are members of minority groups, 37% are women. 1% of classes are taught by teaching assistants.

ACADEMICS
Degrees: Associate; Bachelor's; Certificate; Diploma; Doctoral degree research/scholarship; Master's; Post-bachelor's certificate. **Classes:** Most classes have 10–19 students. Most lab/discussion sessions have 10–19 students. **Most popular majors:** Modeling, Virtual Environments and Simulation; Computer Science; Mechanical Engineering. **Special Study Options:** Accelerated program; Cooperative education program; Cross-registration; Distance learning; Double major; English as a Second Language (ESL); Exchange student program (domestic); Honors program; Independent study; Internships; Liberal arts/career combination; Student-designed major; Study abroad; Weekend college. **Honors programs:** The RIT Honors Program provides a variety of curricular and extracurricular options and special Honors housing. **Combined degree programs:** BA/MEng. **Disability Services offered:** Note-taking services; Reader services; Tape recorders; Tutors. **Career services:** Alumni network; Alumni services; Career assessment; Career/job search classes; Internships; Regional alumni.

FACILITIES
Housing: Apartments for married students; Apartments for single students; Coed dorms; Fraternity/sorority housing; Special housing for disabled students; Special housing for international students; Theme housing; Wellness housing; 100% of campus accessible to physically disabled. **Special Academic Facilities/Equipment:** Art galleries, microelectronic engineering center, RIT Inn and Conference Center, observatory, student-managed restaurant, packaging testing facility, media resource center, Sunday 2000 printing press, Center for manufacturing studies, two OC3 connections to Internet and Internet2, laser optics laboratory, an observatory, an animal care facility, more than 100 color and black-and-white photography darkrooms, electronic prepress and publishing equipment, ceramic kilns, glass furnaces, a blacksmithing area, and computer graphics and robotic labs.

CAMPUS LIFE
Environment: City. **Activities:** Campus Ministries; Choral groups; Concert band; Dance; Drama/theater; International Student Organization; Jazz band; Literary magazine; Music ensembles; Musical theater; Pep band; Radio station; Student government; Student newspaper; Student-run film society; Symphony orchestra; Yearbook. 300 registered organizations, 9 honor societies, 10 religious organizations, 19 fraternities, 10 sororities on campus. **Athletics**

(Intercollegiate): *Men:* baseball, basketball, crew/rowing, cross-country, diving, ice hockey, lacrosse, soccer, swimming, tennis, track/field (outdoor), track/field (indoor), wrestling. *Women:* basketball, cheerleading, crew/rowing, cross-country, diving, ice hockey, lacrosse, soccer, softball, swimming, tennis, track/field (outdoor), track/field (indoor), volleyball. **On-Campus Highlights:** Java Wally's (Wallace Library coffee shop). **Environmental Initiatives:** RIT has signed the American College & University Presidents Climate Commitment (ACUPCC) and established 2030 as the target date for neutrality.

ADMISSIONS
Freshman Academic Profile: Average high school GPA 3.6. 40% in top 10% of high school class, 74% in top 25% of high school class, 95% in top 50% of high school class. 85% from public high schools. **Test Scores:** SAT Math middle 50% range 620–720. SAT EBRW middle 50% range 600–690. ACT middle 50% range 27–32. **Basis for Candidate Selection:** *Very important factors include:* rigor of secondary school record, academic GPA. *Important factors include:* class rank, standardized test scores. *Other factors include:* application essay, recommendation(s), interview, extracurricular activities, talent/ability, character/personal qualities, first generation, alumni/ae relation, geographical residence, racial/ethnic status, volunteer work, work experience, level of applicant's interest. **Freshman Admission Requirements:** High school diploma is required and GED is accepted. *Academic units required:* 4 English, 2 math, 2 science, 1 science lab, 4 social studies, 10 academic electives. *Academic units recommended:* 4 English, 3 math, 3 science, 2 science labs, 3 foreign language, 4 social studies, 5 academic electives. **Freshman Admission Statistics:** 19,744 applied, 71% admitted, 19% enrolled. **Transfer Admission Requirements:** College transcript(s), essay or personal statement. Minimum college GPA of 2.7 required. Lowest grade transferable C-. **General Admission Information:** Application fee $65. Priority deadline 1/15. Non-fall registration accepted. Admission may be deferred for a maximum of 12 months.

COSTS AND FINANCIAL AID
Annual tuition $45,244. Room and board $13,540. Required fees $646. Average book and supplies expense $1,082. **Required Forms and Deadlines:** FAFSA; State aid form. **Notification of Awards:** Applicants will be notified of awards on a rolling basis beginning 3/1. **Types of Aid:** *Need-based scholarships/grants:* College/university scholarship or grant aid from institutional funds; Federal Pell; Private scholarships; SEOG; State scholarships/grants. *Loans:* Direct PLUS loans; Direct Subsidized Stafford Loans; Direct Unsubsidized Stafford Loans. **Student Employment:** Federal Work-Study Program available. Institutional employment available. **Financial Aid Statistics:** 83% needy freshmen, 94% needy undergrads receive need-based scholarship or grant aid. 20% freshmen, 33% undergrads receive non-need-based scholarship or grant aid. 78% freshmen, 88% undergrads receive need-based self-help aid. 0% freshmen, 0% undergrads receive athletic scholarships. 77% freshmen, 77% undergrads receive any aid. 75% undergrads borrow to pay for school. Average cumulative indebtedness $41,202. **Criteria awarding aid:** *Need-based:* Academics. *Non-need-based:* Academics, Art, Leadership.

ROCKFORD UNIVERSITY

Admission, Rockford, IL 61108-2393
Phone: 815-226-4050 **Financial Aid Phone:** 815-226-4062
E-mail: RCAdmissions@rockford.edu **CEEB Code:** 1665
Fax: 815-226-2822 **Website:** www.rockford.edu **ACT Code:** 1122

This private school was founded in 1847. It has a 130 acre campus.

RATINGS
Admissions Selectivity Rating: 86   **Fire Safety Rating:** 82   **Green Rating:** 60*

STUDENTS AND FACULTY
Enrollment: 857. **Student Body:** 61% female, 39% male, 10% out-of-state, <1% international. Asian 2%, African American 8%, Caucasian 69%, Hispanic 6%, Native American 0%, Race unknown 14%.
Faculty: Student/faculty ratio 9:1. 69 full-time faculty, 68% hold PhDs, 3% are members of minority groups, 42% are women. 0% of classes are taught by teaching assistants.

ACADEMICS
Degrees: Bachelor's; Master's. **Classes:** Most classes have 10–19 students. Most lab/discussion sessions have fewer than 10 students. **Most popular majors:** Education, General; Business/Commerce, General; Nursing/Registered Nurse (Rn, Asn, Bsn, Msn). **Special Study Options:** Accelerated program; Distance

learning; Double major; English as a Second Language (ESL); Exchange student program (domestic); Honors program; Independent study; Internships; Study abroad; Teacher certification program. **Honors programs:** Honors program in Liberal Arts. **Disability Services offered:** Note-taking services; Reader services; Tutors. **Career services:** Career assessment; Internships.

FACILITIES

Housing: Coed dorms; Special housing for disabled students; Theme housing. **Special Academic Facilities/Equipment:** Language lab; Art Gallery; Sculpture Garden.

CAMPUS LIFE

Environment: City. **Activities:** Campus Ministries; Choral groups; Dance; Drama/theater; International Student Organization; Literary magazine; Model UN; Music ensembles; Musical theater; Opera; Pep band; Student government. 25 registered organizations, 6 honor societies, 1 religious organization on campus. **Athletics (Intercollegiate):** *Men:* baseball, basketball, cross-country, football, golf, soccer, tennis, track/field (outdoor), track/field (indoor). *Women:* basketball, cross-country, golf, soccer, softball, tennis, track/field (outdoor), track/field (indoor), volleyball. **On-Campus Highlights:** Residence Halls. **Environmental Initiatives:** Green Week.

ADMISSIONS

Freshman Academic Profile: Average high school GPA 3.1. 18% in top 10% of high school class, 33% in top 25% of high school class, 65% in top 50% of high school class. **Test Scores:** ACT middle 50% range 19–24. **Basis for Candidate Selection:** *Very important factors include:* academic GPA. *Important factors include:* rigor of secondary school record, application essay, standardized test scores. *Other factors include:* class rank, recommendation(s). **Freshman Admission Requirements:** High school diploma is required and GED is accepted. *Academic units required:* 4 English, 3 math, 3 science, 3 science labs, 3 social studies, 2 academic electives. *Academic units recommended:* 2 foreign language. **Freshman Admission Statistics:** 967 applied, 41% admitted, 23% enrolled. **Transfer Admission Requirements:** College transcript(s), statement of good standing from prior institution(s). Minimum college GPA of 2.3 required. Lowest grade transferable C. **General Admission Information:** Application fee $35. Non-fall registration accepted. Admission may be deferred for a maximum of 1 year.

COSTS AND FINANCIAL AID

Annual tuition $24,750. Room and board $6,950. Average book and supplies expense $1,200. **Required Forms and Deadlines:** FAFSA. **Notification of Awards:** Applicants will be notified of awards on a rolling basis beginning 3/1. **Types of Aid:** *Need-based scholarships/grants:* College/university scholarship or grant aid from institutional funds; Federal Pell; Private scholarships; SEOG; State scholarships/grants. **Student Employment:** Federal Work-Study Program available. Institutional employment available. **Financial Aid Statistics:** 98% needy freshmen, 95% needy undergrads receive need-based scholarship or grant aid. 12% freshmen, 16% undergrads receive non-need-based scholarship or grant aid. 94% freshmen, 98% undergrads receive need-based self-help aid. 0% freshmen, 0% undergrads receive athletic scholarships. 99% freshmen, 99% undergrads receive any aid. **Criteria awarding aid:** *Need-based:* Academics. *Non-need-based:* Academics, Alumni affiliation, Leadership, Minority status, Music/drama, State/district residency.

ROCKHURST UNIVERSITY

1100 Rockhurst Road, Kansas City, MO 64110
Phone: 816-501-4100 **Financial Aid Phone:** 816-501-4600
E-mail: admission@rockhurst.edu **CEEB Code:** 6611
Fax: 816-501-4241 **Website:** www.rockhurst.edu **ACT Code:** 2342

This private school, affiliated with the Roman Catholic Church, was founded in 1910. It has a 55 acre campus.

RATINGS

Admissions Selectivity Rating: 80   **Fire Safety Rating:** 80   **Green Rating:** 60*

STUDENTS AND FACULTY

Enrollment: 1,623. **Student Body:** 59% female, 41% male, 33% out-of-state, 1% international (17 countries represented). Asian 3%, African American 5%, Caucasian 72%, Hispanic 9%, Native American 1%, Pacific Islander 0%, Two or more races 3%, Race unknown 6%.

Retention and Graduation: 86% freshmen return for sophomore year. 63% freshmen graduate within 4 years. 72% freshmen graduate within 6 years. **Faculty:** Student/faculty ratio 13:1. 128 full-time faculty, 88% hold PhDs, 10% are members of minority groups, 55% are women. 0% of classes are taught by teaching assistants.

ACADEMICS

Degrees: Bachelor's; Certificate; Doctoral degree—professional practice; Master's; Post-bachelor's certificate. **Classes:** Most classes have 20–29 students. Most lab/discussion sessions have 10–19 students. **Most popular majors:** Biology/Biological Sciences, General; Psychology, General. **Special Study Options:** Accelerated program; Cooperative education program; Cross-registration; Distance learning; Double major; Dual enrollment; Exchange student program (domestic); Honors program; Independent study; Internships; Liberal arts/career combination; Study abroad; Teacher certification program. **Honors programs:** The Rockhurst University Honors Program is for motivated and talented students, regardless of major, who want to be active participants in designing their education. Students find honors courses to be more innovative, personal, and challenging than other courses. The Benefits Beginning in the first year, honors students have specially designed core courses that are usually small in enrollment and are taught by some of the University's most creative faculty. During the sophomore through senior years, honors students may earn honors credit through "honors options"—individually designed projects that allow students to explore areas of their own interest under the mentorship of a professor. An honors option is typically an offshoot of a regular course, but an option can also be arranged as an independent study course. It is through the honors option that honors students shape their curriculum. **Disability Services offered:** Note-taking services; Reader services; Tape recorders; Tutors. **Career services:** Alumni network; Alumni services; Career assessment; Career/job search classes; Internships; Regional alumni.

FACILITIES

Housing: Apartments for single students; Coed dorms; Special housing for disabled students; Theme housing; Women's dorms. **Special Academic Facilities/Equipment:** Greenlease Art Gallery, St. Ignatius Science Center. **Campus Network:** 100% of classrooms, 100% of dorms, 100% of student union, 100% of libraries, 100% of dining areas, 100% of common outdoor areas have wireless network access.

CAMPUS LIFE

Environment: Metropolis. **Activities:** Campus Ministries; Choral groups; Dance; Drama/theater; International Student Organization; Literary magazine; Model UN; Music ensembles; Musical theater; Student government; Student newspaper. 60 registered organizations, 18 honor societies, 4 religious organizations, 4 fraternities, 4 sororities on campus. **Athletics (Intercollegiate):** *Men:* baseball, basketball, golf, soccer, tennis. *Women:* basketball, golf, soccer, softball, tennis, volleyball. **On-Campus Highlights:** Rockhurst Bell Tower and Fountains.

ADMISSIONS

Freshman Academic Profile: Average high school GPA 3.6. 25% in top 10% of high school class, 56% in top 25% of high school class, 84% in top 50% of high school class. 51% from public high schools. **Test Scores:** SAT Math middle 50% range 540–640. SAT EBRW middle 50% range 510–590. ACT middle 50% range 22–27. **Basis for Candidate Selection:** *Very important factors include:* rigor of secondary school record, academic GPA. *Important factors include:* standardized test scores. *Other factors include:* recommendation(s), interview, extracurricular activities, talent/ability, character/personal qualities, alumni/ae relation, volunteer work. **Freshman Admission Requirements:** High school diploma is required and GED is accepted. *Academic units recommended:* 4 English, 3 math, 3 science, 3 science labs, 2 foreign language, 3 social studies, 2 history, 4 academic electives. **Freshman Admission Statistics:** 3,115 applied, 72% admitted, 19% enrolled. **Transfer Admission Requirements:** College transcript(s). Minimum college GPA of 2.5 required. Lowest grade transferable C-. **General Admission Information:** Non-fall registration accepted.

COSTS AND FINANCIAL AID

Annual tuition $35,800. Room and board $9,360. Required fees $790. Average book and supplies expense $1,530. **Required Forms and Deadlines:** FAFSA. **Notification of Awards:** Applicants will be notified of awards on a rolling basis beginning 1/1. **Types of Aid:** *Need-based scholarships/grants:* College/university scholarship or grant aid from institutional funds; Federal Pell; Private scholarships; SEOG; State scholarships/grants; United Negro College Fund. *Loans:* Direct PLUS loans; Direct Subsidized Stafford Loans; Direct Unsubsidized Stafford Loans. **Student Employment:** Federal Work-Study Program available. Institutional employment available. **Financial Aid Statistics:** 100% needy freshmen, 100% needy undergrads receive need-based scholarship or grant aid. 51% freshmen, 45% undergrads receive non-need-based scholarship or grant aid. 78% freshmen, 79% undergrads receive need-based self-help aid. 12% freshmen, 10% undergrads receive athletic scholarships. 100% freshmen, 93.97% undergrads receive any aid. 66% undergrads borrow to pay for school. Average cumulative indebtedness $32,157. **Criteria awarding aid:** *Need-based:* Minority status, Religious affiliation. *Non-need-based:* Academics, Alumni affiliation, Art, Athletics, Leadership, Music/drama.

ROCKY MOUNTAIN COLLEGE

1511 Poly Drive, Billings, MT 59102-1796
Phone: 406-657-1026 **Financial Aid Phone:** 406-657-1031
E-mail: admissions@rocky.edu **CEEB Code:** 4660
Fax: 406-657-1189 **Website:** www.rocky.edu **ACT Code:** 2426

This private school was founded in 1878. It has a 60 acre campus.

RATINGS
Admissions Selectivity Rating: 80   **Fire Safety Rating:** 87   **Green Rating:** 63

STUDENTS AND FACULTY
Enrollment: 984. **Student Body:** 49% female, 51% male, 44% out-of-state, 4% international (16 countries represented). Asian 1%, African American 3%, Caucasian 82%, Hispanic 4%, Native American 2%, Pacific Islander 1%, Two or more races 2%, Race unknown 2%.
Retention and Graduation: 67% freshmen return for sophomore year. 18% grads go on to further study within 1 year. 16% grads pursue arts and sciences degrees. 1% grads pursue law degrees. 1% grads pursue business degrees.
Faculty: Student/faculty ratio 12:1. 65 full-time faculty, 77% hold PhDs, 0% are members of minority groups, 40% are women. 0% of classes are taught by teaching assistants.

ACADEMICS
Degrees: Associate; Bachelor's; Master's. **Classes:** Most classes have 10–19 students. Most lab/discussion sessions have fewer than 10 students. **Most popular majors:** Biology/Biological Sciences, General; Business Administration and Management, General; Airline/Commercial/Professional Pilot and Flight Crew. **Special Study Options:** Accelerated program; Distance learning; Double major; Dual enrollment; English as a Second Language (ESL); Honors program; Independent study; Internships; Student-designed major; Study abroad; Teacher certification program. **Honors programs:** Successful honors students find that participation in this program not only brings them closer to professionals in their chosen fields, but also grants them a substantial credential in their applications to graduate schools or employment opportunities. **Disability Services offered:** Note-taking services; Reader services; Tape recorders; Tutors. **Career services:** Alumni network; Alumni services; Career assessment; Career/job search classes; Internships; Regional alumni.

FACILITIES
Housing: Apartments for married students; Apartments for single students; Coed dorms; Special housing for disabled students; 75% of campus accessible to physically disabled. **Special Academic Facilities/Equipment:** Billings Studio Theater, museum, studio, flight simulator/flight school, equestrian facilities, geology collection.

CAMPUS LIFE
Environment: City. **Activities:** Campus Ministries; Choral groups; Concert band; Drama/theater; International Student Organization; Jazz band; Music ensembles; Musical theater; Pep band; Student government; Student newspaper; Yearbook. 13 registered organizations, 1 honor society, 4 religious organizations on campus. **Athletics (Intercollegiate):** *Men:* basketball, cheerleading, football, golf, skiing (downhill/Alpine). *Women:* basketball, cheerleading, golf, skiing (downhill/Alpine), soccer, volleyball. **On-Campus Highlights:** Prescott Hall.

ADMISSIONS
Freshman Academic Profile: Average high school GPA 3.4. 10% in top 10% of high school class, 36% in top 25% of high school class, 70% in top 50% of high school class. **Test Scores:** SAT Math middle 50% range 450–550. SAT EBRW middle 50% range 440–540. ACT middle 50% range 20–25. **Basis for Candidate Selection:** *Very important factors include:* academic GPA, standardized test scores, level of applicant's interest. *Important factors include:* rigor of secondary school record, application essay, recommendation(s). *Other factors include:* class rank, interview, extracurricular activities, talent/ability, character/personal qualities, first generation, alumni/ae relation, work experience. **Freshman Admission Requirements:** High school diploma is

required and GED is accepted. *Academic units required:* 4 English, 4 math, 3 science, 3 social studies, 2 history, 3 academic electives. **Freshman Admission Statistics:** 1,347 applied, 64% admitted, 31% enrolled. **Transfer Admission Requirements:** College transcript(s). Minimum college GPA of 2.0 required. Lowest grade transferable C-. **General Admission Information:** Application fee $35. Priority deadline 3/1. Non-fall registration accepted. Admission may be deferred for a maximum of 1 year.

COSTS AND FINANCIAL AID
Annual tuition $22,442. Room and board $7,430. Required fees $450. Average book and supplies expense $1,300. **Required Forms and Deadlines:** FAFSA. **Notification of Awards:** Applicants will be notified of awards on a rolling basis beginning 2/15. **Types of Aid:** *Need-based scholarships/grants:* College/university scholarship or grant aid from institutional funds; Federal Pell; Private scholarships; SEOG; State scholarships/grants. *Loans:* Direct PLUS loans; Direct Subsidized Stafford Loans; Direct Unsubsidized Stafford Loans. **Student Employment:** Federal Work-Study Program available. Institutional employment available. **Financial Aid Statistics:** 98% needy freshmen, 97% needy undergrads receive need-based scholarship or grant aid. 96% freshmen, 94% undergrads receive non-need-based scholarship or grant aid. 84% freshmen, 84% undergrads receive need-based self-help aid. 26% freshmen, 27% undergrads receive athletic scholarships. 90% freshmen, 90% undergrads receive any aid. **Criteria awarding aid:** *Non-need-based:* Academics, Athletics.

ROCKY MOUNTAIN COLLEGE OF ART + DESIGN

1600 Pierce St, Denver, CO 80214
Phone: 303-753-6046 **Financial Aid Phone:** 303-753-6046
E-mail: admissions@rmcad.edu
Fax: 303-567-7281 **Website:** www.rmcad.edu **ACT Code:** 5359

This proprietary school was founded in 1963. It has a 23 acre campus.

RATINGS
Admissions Selectivity Rating: 61   **Fire Safety Rating:** 60*   **Green Rating:** 60*

STUDENTS AND FACULTY
Enrollment: 1,074. **Student Body:** 65% female, 35% male, 53% out-of-state, <1% international. Asian 2%, African American 9%, Caucasian 60%, Hispanic 9%, Native American 4%, Pacific Islander 0%, Two or more races 1%, Race unknown 15%.
Retention and Graduation: 52% freshmen return for sophomore year.
Faculty: Student/faculty ratio 9:1. 38 full-time faculty, 34% hold PhDs, 5% are members of minority groups, 55% are women.

ACADEMICS
Degrees: Bachelor's; Certificate; Master's. **Special Study Options:** Distance learning; Dual enrollment; Independent study; Internships. **Career services:** Alumni network; Alumni services; Career assessment; Career/job search classes; Internships.

FACILITIES
Special Academic Facilities/Equipment: Philip Steele Gallery; Fine Arts Exhibit Space; Drive Up Gallery.

CAMPUS LIFE
Environment: Metropolis. **Activities:** Campus Ministries; Student government.

ADMISSIONS
Basis for Candidate Selection: *Important factors include:* academic GPA, interview, extracurricular activities. **Freshman Admission Requirements:** High school diploma is required and GED is accepted. **Transfer Admission Requirements:** College transcript(s). Minimum college GPA of 2.0 required. **General Admission Information:** Application fee $50. Non-fall registration accepted. Admission may be deferred for a maximum of one semester.

COSTS AND FINANCIAL AID
Annual tuition $15,870. Room and board $8,640. Average book and supplies expense $1,045. **Required Forms and Deadlines:** FAFSA; Institution's own financial aid form. **Types of Aid:** *Need-based scholarships/grants:* College/university scholarship or grant aid from institutional funds; Federal Pell; Private scholarships; SEOG; State scholarships/grants. *Loans:* Direct PLUS loans; Direct Subsidized Stafford Loans; Direct Unsubsidized Stafford Loans. **Student Employment:** Federal Work-Study Program available. **Criteria awarding aid:** *Need-based:* Academics, Art. *Non-need-based:* Academics, Art.

ROGER WILLIAMS UNIVERSITY

One Old Ferry Road, Bristol, RI 02809-2921
Phone: 401-254-3500 **Financial Aid Phone:** 401-254-3100
E-mail: admit@rwu.edu **CEEB Code:** 3729
Website: www.rwu.edu **ACT Code:** 3814

This private school was founded in 1956. It has a 140 acre campus.

RATINGS
Admissions Selectivity Rating: 75   **Fire Safety Rating:** 97   **Green Rating:** 62

STUDENTS AND FACULTY
Enrollment: 4,292. **Student Body:** 51% female, 49% male, 78% out-of-state, 1% international (27 countries represented). Asian 2%, African American 2%, Caucasian 77%, Hispanic 8%, Native American <1%, Pacific Islander <1%, Two or more races 2%, Race unknown 7%.
Retention and Graduation: 85% freshmen return for sophomore year. 60% freshmen graduate within 4 years. 67% freshmen graduate within 6 years. 28% grads go on to further study within 1 year. 16% grads pursue arts and sciences degrees. 1% grads pursue law degrees. 2% grads pursue business degrees. <1% grads pursue medical degrees. **Faculty:** Student/faculty ratio 14:1. 209 full-time faculty, 93% hold PhDs, 16% are members of minority groups, 45% are women.

ACADEMICS
Degrees: Associate; Bachelor's; Certificate; Doctoral degree—professional practice; Master's; Post-bachelor's certificate. **Classes:** Most classes have 20–29 students. **Most popular majors:** Architecture; Psychology, General; Criminal Justice/Law Enforcement Administration. **Special Study Options:** Accelerated program; Cooperative education program; Distance learning; Double major; Dual enrollment; English as a Second Language (ESL); Exchange student program (domestic); Honors program; Independent study; Internships; Liberal arts/career combination; Student-designed major; Study abroad; Teacher certification program. **Honors programs:** The RWU Honors Program is an interdisciplinary program designed to enhance a student's undergraduate experience. Students enroll in special sections of their general education courses, participate in a community engagement project, and complete an Honors capstone project. **Combined degree programs:** BA/JD; BA/MA. **Disability Services offered:** Note-taking services; Reader services; Tape recorders. **Career services:** Alumni network; Alumni services; Career assessment; Career/job search classes; Internships.

FACILITIES
Housing: Apartments for single students; Coed dorms; Men's dorms; Special housing for disabled students; Theme housing; Wellness housing. **Special Academic Facilities/Equipment:** Marine and Natural Sciences Building with marine biology wetlab, School of Law and Law Library, Main Library, Architecture Building and Architecture Library, Performing Arts Center, Thomas J. Paolino Recreation Center, Global Heritage Hall, Sailing Center, Research Vessel.

CAMPUS LIFE
Environment: Town. **Activities:** Choral groups; Dance; Drama/theater; International Student Organization; Literary magazine; Model UN; Music ensembles; Radio station; Student government; Student newspaper; Student-run film society; Yearbook. 87 registered organizations, 17 honor societies, 2 religious organizations on campus. **Athletics (Intercollegiate):** *Men:* baseball, basketball, cross-country, diving, equestrian sports, lacrosse, sailing, soccer, swimming, tennis, track/field (outdoor), track/field (indoor), wrestling. *Women:* basketball, cross-country, diving, equestrian sports, lacrosse, sailing, soccer, softball, swimming, tennis, track/field (outdoor), track/field (indoor), volleyball. **On-Campus Highlights:** Recreation Center.

ADMISSIONS
Freshman Academic Profile: Average high school GPA 3.5. 12% in top 10% of high school class, 34% in top 25% of high school class, 66% in top 50% of high school class. **Test Scores:** SAT Math middle 50% range 530–610. SAT EBRW middle 50% range 535–630. ACT middle 50% range 22–27. **Basis for Candidate Selection:** *Very important factors include:* rigor of secondary school record, academic GPA, application essay, recommendation(s), character/personal qualities. *Important factors include:* extracurricular activities, volunteer work. *Other factors include:* class rank, standardized test scores, interview, talent/ability, first generation, alumni/ae relation. **Freshman Admission Requirements:** High school diploma is required and GED is accepted. *Academic units required:* 4 English, 3 math, 3 science, 2 science labs, 3 social studies, 2 history, 2 academic electives. *Academic units recommended:* 4 math, 4 science, 2 foreign language, 3 social studies, 3 history, 3 academic electives. **Freshman Admission Statistics:** 8,906 applied, 85% admitted, 15% enrolled. **Transfer Admission Requirements:** College transcript(s), essay or personal statement. Minimum college GPA of 2.5 required. Lowest grade transferable C. **General Admission Information:** Application fee $55. Priority deadline 2/1. Regular application deadline 2/1. Non-fall registration accepted. Admission may be deferred for a maximum of 1 year.

COSTS AND FINANCIAL AID
Annual tuition $36,648. Room and board $15,390. Required fees $330. Average book and supplies expense $900. **Required Forms and Deadlines:** FAFSA. **Types of Aid:** *Need-based scholarships/grants:* College/university scholarship or grant aid from institutional funds; Federal Pell; Private scholarships; SEOG; State scholarships/grants. *Loans:* Direct PLUS loans; Direct Subsidized Stafford Loans; Direct Unsubsidized Stafford Loans. **Student Employment:** Federal Work-Study Program available. Institutional employment available. **Financial Aid Statistics:** 73% needy freshmen, 58% needy undergrads receive need-based scholarship or grant aid. 98% freshmen, 94% undergrads receive non-need-based scholarship or grant aid. 86% freshmen, 73% undergrads receive need-based self-help aid. 0% freshmen, 0% undergrads receive athletic scholarships. 99% freshmen, 96% undergrads receive any aid. 64% undergrads borrow to pay for school. Average cumulative indebtedness $44,753. **Criteria awarding aid:** *Non-need-based:* Academics, Leadership.

ROLLINS COLLEGE

1000 Holt Avenue, Winter Park, FL 32789-4499
Phone: 407-646-2161 **Financial Aid Phone:** 407-646-2395
E-mail: admission@rollins.edu **CEEB Code:** 5572
Fax: 407-646-1502 **Website:** http://www.rollins.edu **ACT Code:** 0748

This private school was founded in 1885. It has a 80 acre campus.

RATINGS
Admissions Selectivity Rating: 86   **Fire Safety Rating:** 97   **Green Rating:** 87

STUDENTS AND FACULTY
Enrollment: 1,984. **Student Body:** 61% female, 39% male, 42% out-of-state, 10% international (57 countries represented). Asian 3%, African American 4%, Caucasian 60%, Hispanic 16%, Native American <1%, Pacific Islander 0%, Two or more races 4%, Race unknown 3%.
Retention and Graduation: 83% freshmen return for sophomore year. 67% freshmen graduate within 4 years. 73% freshmen graduate within 6 years. **Faculty:** Student/faculty ratio 10:1. 232 full-time faculty, 90% hold PhDs, 12% are members of minority groups, 50% are women. 0% of classes are taught by teaching assistants.

ACADEMICS
Degrees: Bachelor's; Doctoral degree research/scholarship; Master's. **Classes:** Most classes have 10–19 students. **Most popular majors:** Economics, General; International Business/Trade/Commerce; Communication and Media Studies, Other. **Special Study Options:** Accelerated program; Cross-registration; Double major; Dual enrollment; Exchange student program (domestic); Honors program; Independent study; Internships; Student-designed major; Study abroad; Teacher certification program. **Honors programs:** The academic excellence you will encounter at Rollins is reinforced every day through our acclaimed Honors Program. The Honors Program is designed for students who bring exceptional abilities and are looking for a heightened educational journey marked by a distinct core of interdisciplinary courses, team-taught honors seminars, significant independent research opportunities, and the chance to meet separately with distinguished visiting speakers and lecturers. The Honors Degree Program leads to a distinct and separate undergraduate degree Artium Baccalaureus Honoris, the Honors Bachelor of Arts Degree. **Disability Services offered:** Note-taking services; Reader services; Tape recorders; Tutors. **Career services:** Alumni network; Alumni services; Career assessment; Career/job search classes; Internships.

FACILITIES
Housing: Apartments for single students; Coed dorms; Fraternity/sorority housing; Special housing for disabled students; Theme housing; 80% of campus

accessible to physically disabled. **Special Academic Facilities/Equipment:** Fine arts museum, 2 theatres, child development center, high-tech classrooms, outdoor classroom.

CAMPUS LIFE

Environment: Town. **Activities:** Campus Ministries; Choral groups; Concert band; Dance; Drama/theater; International Student Organization; Jazz band; Literary magazine; Marching band; Model UN; Music ensembles; Musical theater; Opera; Pep band; Radio station; Student government; Student newspaper; Student-run film society; Symphony orchestra; Television station. 110 registered organizations, 9 honor societies, 3 religious organizations, 6 fraternities, 7 sororities on campus. **Athletics (Intercollegiate):** *Men:* baseball, basketball, crew/rowing, cross-country, golf, lacrosse, sailing, soccer, swimming, tennis, water skiing. *Women:* basketball, crew/rowing, cross-country, golf, lacrosse, sailing, soccer, softball, swimming, tennis, volleyball, water skiing. **On-Campus Highlights:** Cornell Campus Center. **Environmental Initiatives:** Reuse existing buildings, renovating and updating to conform to LEED principles, but limited to and bound by LEED criteria.

ADMISSIONS

Freshman Academic Profile: Average high school GPA 3.3. 36% in top 10% of high school class, 67% in top 25% of high school class, 88% in top 50% of high school class. 51% from public high schools. **Test Scores:** SAT Math middle 50% range 590–670. SAT EBRW middle 50% range 605–680. ACT middle 50% range 25–30. **Basis for Candidate Selection:** *Very important factors include:* rigor of secondary school record, academic GPA. *Important factors include:* application essay, standardized test scores, recommendation(s), extracurricular activities, talent/ability. *Other factors include:* class rank, character/personal qualities, first generation, alumni/ae relation, volunteer work, work experience, level of applicant's interest. **Freshman Admission Requirements:** High school diploma is required and GED is accepted. *Academic units required:* 4 English, 3 math, 2 science, 2 foreign language, 2 social studies, 2 history, 2 academic electives. *Academic units recommended:* 4 English, 4 math, 4 science, 3 foreign language, 3 social studies, 3 history, 3 academic electives. **Freshman Admission Statistics:** 5,297 applied, 64% admitted, 16% enrolled. **Transfer Admission Requirements:** High school transcript, college transcript(s), essay or personal statement, statement of good standing from prior institution(s). Lowest grade transferable C-. **General Admission Information:** Application fee $50. Regular application deadline 2/1. Non-fall registration accepted. Admission may be deferred for a maximum of one year.

COSTS AND FINANCIAL AID

Annual tuition $51,700. Room and board $15,034. Average book and supplies expense $716. **Required Forms and Deadlines:** FAFSA. **Notification of Awards:** Applicants will be notified of awards on a rolling basis beginning 3/1. **Types of Aid:** *Need-based scholarships/grants:* College/university scholarship or grant aid from institutional funds; Federal Pell; Private scholarships; SEOG; State scholarships/grants. *Loans:* Direct PLUS loans; Direct Subsidized Stafford Loans; Direct Unsubsidized Stafford Loans. **Student Employment:** Federal Work-Study Program available. Institutional employment available. **Financial Aid Statistics:** 94% needy freshmen, 93% needy undergrads receive need-based scholarship or grant aid. 23% freshmen, 17% undergrads receive non-need-based scholarship or grant aid. 61% freshmen, 68% undergrads receive need-based self-help aid. 3% freshmen, 5% undergrads receive athletic scholarships. 92.5% freshmen, 89.1% undergrads receive any aid. 45% undergrads borrow to pay for school. Average cumulative indebtedness $31,459. **Criteria awarding aid:** *Non-need-based:* Academics, Art, Athletics, Leadership, Music/drama, State/district residency.

ROOSEVELT UNIVERSITY

430 South Michigan Avenue, Chicago, IL 60605
Phone: 877-277-5978 **Financial Aid Phone:** (866) 421-0935
E-mail: admission@roosevelt.edu **CEEB Code:** 1666
Fax: 847-619-4216 **Website:** http://www.roosevelt.edu/Home.aspx **ACT Code:** 1124

This private school was founded in 1945. It has a 34 acre campus.

RATINGS

Admissions Selectivity Rating: 75   **Fire Safety Rating:** 95   **Green Rating:** 88

STUDENTS AND FACULTY

Enrollment: 2,710. **Student Body:** 64% female, 36% male, 15% out-of-state, 4% international (42 countries represented). Asian 5%, African American 18%, Caucasian 45%, Hispanic 24%, Native American <1%, Pacific Islander <1%, Two or more races 3%, Race unknown 1%.
Retention and Graduation: 65% freshmen return for sophomore year.
Faculty: Student/faculty ratio 11:1. 242 full-time faculty, 91% hold PhDs, 23% are members of minority groups, 43% are women. 0% of classes are taught by teaching assistants.

ACADEMICS

Degrees: Bachelor's; Doctoral degree—professional practice; Doctoral degree research/scholarship; Master's; Post-bachelor's certificate. **Classes:** Most classes have 10–19 students. Most lab/discussion sessions have 10–19 students. **Most popular majors:** Biology/Biological Sciences, General; Psychology, General; Musical Theatre. **Special Study Options:** Accelerated program; Distance learning; Double major; Dual enrollment; English as a Second Language (ESL); Exchange student program (domestic); Honors program; Independent study; Internships; Student-designed major; Study abroad; Teacher certification program. **Honors programs:** Roosevelt Honors program offers an enriched academic program combining the students' area of interest with an interdisciplinary approach that includes internships, and research opportunities. The Honors website is http://www.roosevelt.edu/honors. **Combined degree programs:** BA/JD; BA/MA. **Disability Services offered:** Note-taking services; Reader services; Tape recorders; Tutors. **Career services:** Alumni network; Alumni services; Career assessment; Career/job search classes; Internships; Regional alumni.

FACILITIES

Housing: Apartments for single students; Coed dorms; 90% of campus accessible to physically disabled. **Special Academic Facilities/Equipment:** The university's Gage Gallery features the work of artists that aligns with the social justice mission of Roosevelt. Within one mile of the Chicago Campus is the Field Museum of Natural History, Shedd Aquarium, Adler Planetarium and Art Institute of Chicago.

CAMPUS LIFE

Environment: Metropolis. **Activities:** Choral groups; Concert band; Dance; Drama/theater; International Student Organization; Jazz band; Literary magazine; Music ensembles; Musical theater; Opera; Pep band; Radio station; Student government; Student newspaper; Symphony orchestra. 60 registered organizations, 6 honor societies, 3 religious organizations, 2 fraternities, 5 sororities on campus. **On-Campus Highlights:** Vertical Campus: 32-story building downtown Chicago. **Environmental Initiatives:** Roosevelt has achieved LEED certification for both of its new campus buildings in the heart of downtown Chicago. LEED Gold for Wabash Building and LEED Silver for the Goodman Center. The university has also achieved SERF (Society of Environmentally Responsible Facilities) certification for the Wabash Building.

ADMISSIONS

Freshman Academic Profile: Average high school GPA 3.1. 8% in top 10% of high school class, 46% in top 25% of high school class, 62% in top 50% of high school class. 85% from public high schools. **Test Scores:** SAT Math middle 50% range 450–550. SAT EBRW middle 50% range 455–595. ACT middle 50% range 19–24. **Basis for Candidate Selection:** *Very important factors include:* academic GPA, standardized test scores. *Other factors include:* rigor of secondary school record, class rank, application essay, recommendation(s), interview, extracurricular activities, talent/ability, character/personal qualities, first generation, alumni/ae relation, level of applicant's interest. **Freshman Admission Requirements:** High school diploma is required and GED is accepted. *Academic units required:* 4 English, 3 math, 2 science, 2 science labs, 2 social studies. *Academic units recommended:* 4 English, 4 math, 3 science, 3 science labs, 2 foreign language, 3 social studies, 2 history, 2 academic electives. **Freshman Admission Statistics:** 5,996 applied, 73% admitted, 8% enrolled. **Transfer Admission Requirements:** College transcript(s), statement of good standing from prior institution(s). Minimum college GPA of 2.0 required. Lowest grade transferable D. **General Admission Information:** Application fee $25. Priority deadline 8/15. Non-fall registration accepted. Admission may be deferred for a maximum of 1 year.

COSTS AND FINANCIAL AID

Annual tuition $28,963. Average book and supplies expense $1,200. **Required Forms and Deadlines:** FAFSA; Institution's own financial aid form. **Notification of Awards:** Applicants will be notified of awards on a rolling basis beginning 2/1. **Types of Aid:** *Need-based scholarships/grants:* College/university scholarship or grant aid from institutional funds; Federal Pell; Private scholarships; SEOG; State scholarships/grants. *Loans:* Direct PLUS loans; Direct Subsidized Stafford Loans; Direct Unsubsidized Stafford Loans. **Student Employment:** Federal Work-Study Program available. Institutional employment available. **Financial Aid Statistics:** 93% needy freshmen, 91%

needy undergrads receive need-based scholarship or grant aid. 87% freshmen, 87% undergrads receive non-need-based scholarship or grant aid. 68% freshmen, 78% undergrads receive need-based self-help aid. 7% freshmen, 2% undergrads receive athletic scholarships. 98% freshmen, 90% undergrads receive any aid. **Criteria awarding aid:** *Need-based:* Minority status. *Non-need-based:* Academics, Alumni affiliation, Leadership, Minority status, Music/drama, State/district residency.

ROSE-HULMAN INSTITUTE OF TECHNOLOGY

5500 Wabash Avenue, Terre Haute, IN 47803-3999
Phone: 812-877-8213 **Financial Aid Phone:** 812-877-8259
E-mail: admissions@rose-hulman.edu **CEEB Code:** 1668
Fax: 812-877-8941 **Website:** www.rose-hulman.edu **ACT Code:** 1232

This private school was founded in 1874. It has a 200 acre campus.

RATINGS

Admissions Selectivity Rating: 91 Fire Safety Rating: 96 Green Rating: 78

STUDENTS AND FACULTY

Enrollment: 2,146. **Student Body:** 25% female, 75% male, 64% out-of-state, 15% international (11 countries represented). Asian 5%, African American 3%, Caucasian 68%, Hispanic 5%, Native American <1%, Pacific Islander <1%, Two or more races 5%, Race unknown 1%.
Retention and Graduation: 91% freshmen return for sophomore year. 67% freshmen graduate within 4 years. 18% grads go on to further study within 1 year. 16% grads pursue arts and sciences degrees. 0% grads pursue law degrees. 1% grads pursue business degrees. 1% grads pursue medical degrees. **Faculty:** Student/faculty ratio 11:1. 190 full-time faculty, 99% hold PhDs, 12% are members of minority groups, 24% are women. 0% of classes are taught by teaching assistants.

ACADEMICS

Degrees: Bachelor's; Master's. **Classes:** Most classes have 20–29 students. Most lab/discussion sessions have 20–29 students. **Most popular majors:** Chemical Engineering; Mechanical Engineering; Computer Science. **Special Study Options:** Accelerated program; Cooperative education program; Cross-registration; Double major; Dual enrollment; English as a Second Language (ESL); Exchange student program (domestic); Independent study; Study abroad. **Disability Services offered:** Note-taking services; Reader services; Tape recorders; Tutors. **Career services:** Alumni network; Alumni services; Career assessment; Career/job search classes; Internships.

FACILITIES

Housing: Apartments for single students; Coed dorms; Fraternity/sorority housing; Men's dorms; Theme housing; 95% of campus accessible to physically disabled. **Special Academic Facilities/Equipment:** Oakley Observatory.

CAMPUS LIFE

Environment: Town. **Activities:** Choral groups; Concert band; Dance; Drama/theater; International Student Organization; Jazz band; Music ensembles; Musical theater; Pep band; Radio station; Student government; Student newspaper; Symphony orchestra. 104 registered organizations, 7 honor societies, 2 religious organizations, 8 fraternities, 3 sororities on campus. **Athletics (Intercollegiate):** *Men:* baseball, basketball, cross-country, diving, football, golf, riflery, soccer, swimming, tennis, track/field (outdoor), track/field (indoor). *Women:* basketball, cross-country, diving, golf, riflery, soccer, softball, swimming, tennis, track/field (outdoor), track/field (indoor), volleyball. **On-Campus Highlights:** Sports and Recreation Center. **Environmental Initiatives:** Signing of the American College & University President's Climate Commitment.

ADMISSIONS

Freshman Academic Profile: Average high school GPA 4.0. 64% in top 10% of high school class, 91% in top 25% of high school class, 100% in top 50% of high school class. 63% from public high schools. **Test Scores:** SAT Math middle 50% range 650–760. SAT EBRW middle 50% range 610–690. ACT middle 50% range 27–32. **Basis for Candidate Selection:** *Very important factors include:* rigor of secondary school record, class rank, academic GPA. *Important*

factors include: standardized test scores, recommendation(s), extracurricular activities, character/personal qualities, volunteer work. *Other factors include:* application essay, talent/ability, alumni/ae relation, geographical residence, racial/ethnic status. **Freshman Admission Requirements:** High school diploma is required and GED is not accepted. *Academic units required:* 4 English, 4 math, 3 science, 3 science labs, 2 social studies, 4 academic electives. *Academic units recommended:* 5 math, 4 science. **Freshman Admission Statistics:** 4,473 applied, 61% admitted, 20% enrolled. **Transfer Admission Requirements:** College transcript(s), essay or personal statement, statement of good standing from prior institution(s). Minimum college GPA of 3.0 required. Lowest grade transferable C. **General Admission Information:** Application fee $50. Priority deadline 11/1. Regular application deadline 2/1. Admission may be deferred for a maximum of 12 months.

COSTS AND FINANCIAL AID

Annual tuition $46,641. Room and board $14,766. Required fees $930. Average book and supplies expense $1,500. **Required Forms and Deadlines:** FAFSA. **Notification of Awards:** Applicants will be notified of awards on or about 3/10. **Types of Aid:** *Need-based scholarships/grants:* College/university scholarship or grant aid from institutional funds; Federal Pell; SEOG; State scholarships/grants. *Loans:* Direct PLUS loans; Direct Subsidized Stafford Loans; Direct Unsubsidized Stafford Loans. **Student Employment:** Federal Work-Study Program available. Institutional employment available. **Financial Aid Statistics:** 99% needy freshmen, 99% needy undergrads receive need-based scholarship or grant aid. 45% freshmen, 90% undergrads receive non-need-based scholarship or grant aid. 69% freshmen, 73% undergrads receive need-based self-help aid. 0% freshmen, 0% undergrads receive athletic scholarships. 99% freshmen, 98% undergrads receive any aid. 58% undergrads borrow to pay for school. Average cumulative indebtedness $43,459. **Criteria awarding aid:** *Need-based:* Academics, Minority status. *Non-need-based:* Academics, Minority status.

ROSEMONT COLLEGE

1400 Montgomery Ave., Rosemont, PA 19010
Phone: 610-526-2966 **Financial Aid Phone:** 610 527 0200
E-mail: admissions@rosemont.edu **CEEB Code:** 2763
Fax: 610-520-4399 **Website:** www.rosemont.edu **ACT Code:** 3676

This private school, affiliated with the Roman Catholic Church, was founded in 1921. It has a 56 acre campus.

RATINGS

Admissions Selectivity Rating: 76 Fire Safety Rating: 83 Green Rating: 60*

STUDENTS AND FACULTY

Enrollment: 529. **Student Body:** 65% female, 35% male, 27% out-of-state, 2% international (11 countries represented). Asian 5%, African American 40%, Caucasian 38%, Hispanic 6%, Native American 0%, Pacific Islander 0%, Two or more races 4%, Race unknown 4%.
Retention and Graduation: 69% freshmen return for sophomore year. 36% grads go on to further study within 1 year. 35% grads pursue arts and sciences degrees. 2% grads pursue law degrees. 5% grads pursue business degrees. 9% grads pursue medical degrees. **Faculty:** Student/faculty ratio 10:1. 25 full-time faculty, 84% hold PhDs, 4% are members of minority groups, 48% are women. 0% of classes are taught by teaching assistants.

ACADEMICS

Degrees: Bachelor's; Master's; Post-bachelor's certificate. **Classes:** Most classes have 10–19 students. **Most popular majors:** Business/Commerce, General; Biology/Biological Sciences, General; Art/Art Studies, General. **Special Study Options:** Accelerated program; Cross-registration; Distance learning; Double major; Honors program; Independent study; Internships; Liberal arts/career combination; Student-designed major; Study abroad; Teacher certification program. **Honors programs:** The Honors Program provides intellectually challenging and stimulating honors courses for students interested in a broad educational experience. Honors courses are either disciplinary or interdisciplinary, and are distinguished from regular offerings with respect to depth of study and work expectations. The classes are small and emphasize discussion, providing students with a more enhanced encounter with the material and encouraging interaction with faculty mentors and other motivated and talented students. Students in the honors program have the opportunity to attend lectures, visit museums, attend musical performances, and other intellectual and artistic events. An important goal of the honors program is to foster a discriminative awareness of social responsibility and to encourage service for the public good. **Combined degree programs:** BA/MA. **Disability Services offered:** Note-taking services; Tape recorders; Tutors. **Career services:** Alumni services; Career assessment; Career/job search classes; Internships.

FACILITIES

Housing: Coed dorms; Theme housing; 45% of campus accessible to physically disabled. **Special Academic Facilities/Equipment:** Rotwitt Performing Arts Center.

CAMPUS LIFE

Environment: Village. **Activities:** Campus Ministries; Choral groups; Concert band; Dance; Drama/theater; Jazz band; Literary magazine; Marching band; Music ensembles; Musical theater; Opera; Pep band; Radio station; Student government; Student newspaper; Yearbook. 11 registered organizations, 6 honor societies, 3 religious organizations on campus. **Athletics (Intercollegiate):** *Men:* basketball, softball, tennis. *Women:* basketball, field hockey, lacrosse, softball, tennis, volleyball. **On-Campus Highlights:** Campus Grill. **Environmental Initiatives:** Energy Star Procurement Policy.

ADMISSIONS

Freshman Academic Profile: Average high school GPA 3.3. 70% from public high schools. **Test Scores:** SAT Math middle 50% range 380–505. SAT EBRW middle 50% range 400–520. ACT middle 50% range 15–20. **Basis for Candidate Selection:** *Very important factors include:* rigor of secondary school record, academic GPA, standardized test scores, interview, level of applicant's interest. *Important factors include:* class rank, application essay, extracurricular activities, talent/ability, volunteer work. *Other factors include:* recommendation(s), character/personal qualities, alumni/ae relation, work experience. **Freshman Admission Requirements:** High school diploma is required and GED is accepted. *Academic units required:* 4 English, 3 math, 3 science, 2 science labs, 1 social studies, 1 history, 7 academic electives. *Academic units recommended:* 4 English, 3 math, 3 science, 2 science labs, 2 foreign language, 2 social studies, 2 history, 4 academic electives. **Freshman Admission Statistics:** 875 applied, 71% admitted, 22% enrolled. **Transfer Admission Requirements:** College transcript(s). Minimum college GPA of 2.5 required. Lowest grade transferable C. **General Admission Information:** Priority deadline 8/1. Regular application deadline 8/1. Non-fall registration accepted. Admission may be deferred for a maximum of 1 year.

COSTS AND FINANCIAL AID

Annual tuition $18,500. Room and board $11,500. Required fees $980. Average book and supplies expense $1,500. **Required Forms and Deadlines:** FAFSA. **Notification of Awards:** Applicants will be notified of awards on a rolling basis beginning 3/1. **Types of Aid:** *Need-based scholarships/grants:* College/university scholarship or grant aid from institutional funds; Federal Pell; Private scholarships; SEOG; State scholarships/grants. **Student Employment:** Federal Work-Study Program available. Institutional employment available. **Financial Aid Statistics:** 99% needy freshmen, 99% needy undergrads receive need-based scholarship or grant aid. 10% freshmen, 12% undergrads receive non-need-based scholarship or grant aid. 95% freshmen, 99% undergrads receive need-based self-help aid. 0% freshmen, 0% undergrads receive athletic scholarships. 92% freshmen, 92% undergrads receive any aid. 90% undergrads borrow to pay for school. Average cumulative indebtedness $40,792. **Criteria awarding aid:** *Need-based:* Academics, Art, Leadership. *Non-need-based:* Academics, Alumni affiliation, Art, Leadership, Religious affiliation.

ROWAN UNIVERSITY

Savitz Hall 201 Mullica Hill Road, Glassboro, NJ 08028-1701
Phone: 856-256-4200 **Financial Aid Phone:** 856-256-4281
E-mail: admissions@rowan.edu **CEEB Code:** 2515
Fax: 856-256-4430 **Website:** www.rowan.edu **ACT Code:** 2560

This public school was founded in 1923. It has a 920 acre campus.

RATINGS

Admissions Selectivity Rating: 73 **Fire Safety Rating:** 97 **Green Rating:** 69

STUDENTS AND FACULTY

Enrollment: 15,752. **Student Body:** 46% female, 54% male, 7% out-of-state, 1% international (44 countries represented). Asian 5%, African American 10%, Caucasian 67%, Hispanic 11%, Native American <1%, Pacific Islander <1%, Two or more races 4%, Race unknown 1%.

Retention and Graduation: 93% freshmen return for sophomore year. 49% freshmen graduate within 4 years. 72% freshmen graduate within 6 years. **Faculty:** Student/faculty ratio 17:1. 489 full-time faculty, 66% hold PhDs, 19% are members of minority groups, 46% are women. 0% of classes are taught by teaching assistants.

ACADEMICS

Degrees: Bachelor's; Certificate; Doctoral degree—other; Doctoral degree—professional practice; Doctoral degree research/scholarship; Master's; Post-bachelor's certificate; Post-master's certificate. **Classes:** Most classes have 20–29 students. **Most popular majors:** Biology/Biological Sciences, General; Elementary Education and Teaching; Psychology, General. **Special Study Options:** Accelerated program; Cooperative education program; Cross-registration; Distance learning; Double major; Dual enrollment; English as a Second Language (ESL); Honors program; Independent study; Internships; Liberal arts/career combination; Study abroad; Teacher certification program; Weekend college. **Honors programs:** The Thomas N. Bantivoglio Honors Concentration offers qualified students access to a variety of academic, social, and cultural experiences including honors classes, the Honors Student Organization and events it sponsors, which include travel and cultural activities along the eastern seaboard. Students are guaranteed cluster housing and priority registration. **Combined degree programs:** BA/MA. **Disability Services offered:** Note-taking services; Reader services; Tape recorders; Tutors. **Career services:** Alumni network; Alumni services; Career assessment; Career/job search classes; Internships; Regional alumni.

FACILITIES

Housing: Apartments for single students; Coed dorms; Special housing for disabled students; Special housing for international students; Theme housing; 95% of campus accessible to physically disabled. **Special Academic Facilities/Equipment:** Concert hall; Cave Automated Virtual Environment (CAVE); two production studios; Exercise Science Research Laboratory; Rowan University Assessment and Learning Center; 130-seat screening theater; Planetarium; Rowan Radio 89.7 WGLS-FM–main studio; production studio; news studio; record room; Cooper Medical School of Rowan University; Bantivoglio Honors Program, containing offices, a lounge, and classroom space dedicated to honors students; glass collection; student recreation center; on-campus early childhood demonstration center; greenhouse for biological studies; observatory; art gallery; RCA museum in the library. **Campus Network:** 100% of classrooms, 100% of dorms, 100% of student union, 100% of libraries, 100% of dining areas, 100% of common outdoor areas have wireless network access.

CAMPUS LIFE

Environment: Town. **Activities:** Campus Ministries; Choral groups; Concert band; Dance; Drama/theater; Jazz band; Music ensembles; Musical theater; Opera; Pep band; Radio station; Student government; Student newspaper; Student-run film society; Symphony orchestra; Television station; Yearbook. 75 registered organizations, 10 honor societies, 7 religious organizations, 10 fraternities, 10 sororities on campus. **Athletics (Intercollegiate):** *Men:* baseball, basketball, cross-country, diving, football, soccer, swimming, track/field (outdoor), track/field (indoor). *Women:* basketball, cross-country, diving, field hockey, lacrosse, soccer, softball, swimming, track/field (outdoor), track/field (indoor), volleyball. **On-Campus Highlights:** Recreation Center.

ADMISSIONS

Freshman Academic Profile: Average high school GPA 3.6. **Test Scores:** SAT Math middle 50% range 470–580. SAT EBRW middle 50% range 520–620. ACT middle 50% range 21–27. **Basis for Candidate Selection:** *Very important factors include:* rigor of secondary school record. *Important factors include:* academic GPA, application essay, standardized test scores. *Other factors include:* class rank, recommendation(s), extracurricular activities, talent/ability, character/personal qualities, racial/ethnic status, volunteer work. **Freshman Admission Requirements:** High school diploma is required and GED is accepted. *Academic units required:* 4 English, 3 math, 2 science, 2 science labs, 2 history, 5 academic electives. *Academic units recommended:* 4 math, 3 science, 3 science labs, 2 foreign language, 2 social studies, 1 visual/performing arts. **Freshman Admission Statistics:** 10,676 applied, 100% admitted, 24% enrolled. **Transfer Admission Requirements:** College transcript(s). Minimum college GPA of 2.0 required. Lowest grade transferable D. **General Admission Information:** Application fee $65. Regular application deadline 3/1. Non-fall registration accepted. Admission may be deferred for a maximum of 1 year.

COSTS AND FINANCIAL AID

Annual in-state tuition $9,858. Annual out-of-state tuition $18,500. Room and board $14,854. Required fees $3,839. Average book and supplies expense $1,850. **Required Forms and Deadlines:** FAFSA. **Notification of Awards:** Applicants will be notified of awards on a rolling basis beginning 3/16. **Types** of Aid: *Need-based scholarships/grants:* Federal Pell; Private scholarships; SEOG; State scholarships/grants. *Loans:* Direct PLUS loans; Direct Subsidized Stafford Loans; Direct Unsubsidized Stafford Loans. **Student Employment:** Federal Work-Study Program available. Institutional employment available. **Financial Aid Statistics:** 50% needy freshmen, 54% needy undergrads receive need-based scholarship or grant aid. 43% freshmen, 27% undergrads receive non-need-based scholarship or grant aid. 74% freshmen, 78% undergrads receive need-based self-help aid. 0% freshmen, 0% undergrads receive athletic scholarships. 82.75% freshmen, 73.46% undergrads receive any aid. **Criteria awarding aid:** *Non-need-based:* Academics, Art, Music/drama.

RUSH UNIVERSITY

600 South Paulina, Chicago, IL 60612-3878
Phone: 312-942-7100 **Financial Aid Phone:** 312-942-6256
E-mail: Rush_Admissions@rush.edu
Fax: 312-942-2219 **Website:** www.rushu.rush.edu **ACT Code:** 1617

This private school was founded in 1972. It has a 35 acre campus.

RATINGS
Admissions Selectivity Rating: 60*   **Fire Safety Rating:** 79   **Green Rating:** 60*

STUDENTS AND FACULTY
Enrollment: 258. **Student Body:** 87% female, 13% male, 15% out-of-state, 2% international. Asian 18%, African American 7%, Caucasian 69%, Hispanic 3%, Native American <1%, Race unknown 2%.
Retention and Graduation: 25% grads go on to further study within 1 year. 5% grads pursue medical degrees. **Faculty:** Student/faculty ratio 8:1. 305 full-time faculty, 0% hold PhDs, 0% are members of minority groups, 65% are women. 0% of classes are taught by teaching assistants.

ACADEMICS
Degrees: Bachelor's; Master's. **Classes:** Most classes have 10–19 students. **Most popular majors:** Audiology/Audiologist and Speech-Language Pathology/Pathologist; Medicine; Nursing/Registered Nurse (Rn, Asn, Bsn, Msn). **Special Study Options:** Distance learning. **Disability Services offered:** Tape recorders; Tutors. **Career services:** Alumni network; Alumni services; Career assessment; Career/job search classes; Internships; Regional alumni.

FACILITIES
Housing: Apartments for married students; Apartments for single students; 85% of campus accessible to physically disabled. **Campus Network:** 100% of classrooms, 100% of dorms, 100% of student union, 100% of libraries, 100% of dining areas, 60% of common outdoor areas have wireless network access.

CAMPUS LIFE
Environment: Metropolis. **Activities:** Yearbook. 15 registered organizations, 2 honor societies, 1 religious organization on campus. **On-Campus Highlights:** Student Lounge. **Environmental Initiatives:** Launched new recycling commitment and awareness campaign on Earth Day 2008.

ADMISSIONS
Transfer Admission Requirements: College transcript(s), essay or personal statement. Minimum college GPA of 2.7 required. Lowest grade transferable C. **General Admission Information:**

COSTS AND FINANCIAL AID
Required Forms and Deadlines: Business/Farm Supplement; FAFSA; Institution's own financial aid form. **Types of Aid:** *Need-based scholarships/grants:* College/university scholarship or grant aid from institutional funds; Federal Pell; Private scholarships; SEOG; State scholarships/grants. **Student Employment:** Federal Work-Study Program available. Institutional employment available. **Financial Aid Statistics:** 74% needy undergrads receive need-based scholarship or grant aid. 13% undergrads receive non-need-based scholarship or grant aid. 84% undergrads receive need-based self-help aid. 0% undergrads receive athletic scholarships. 69% undergrads receive any aid. **Criteria awarding aid:** *Non-need-based:* Academics, Leadership, Minority status.

RUSSELL SAGE COLLEGE

Office of Admissions, Troy, NY 12180
Phone: 518-244-2217 **Financial Aid Phone:** (518)244-4525
E-mail: rscadm@sage.edu **CEEB Code:** 2764
Fax: 518-244-6880 **Website:** www.sage.edu **ACT Code:** 2876

This is a private school.

RATINGS
Admissions Selectivity Rating: 75   **Fire Safety Rating:** 71   **Green Rating:** 60*

STUDENTS AND FACULTY
Enrollment: 1,450. **Student Body:** 79% female, 21% male, 9% out-of-state, 1% international. Asian 4%, African American 11%, Caucasian 61%, Hispanic 10%, Native American <1%, Pacific Islander <1%, Two or more races 4%, Race unknown 9%.
Retention and Graduation: 78% freshmen return for sophomore year. 45% freshmen graduate within 4 years. 56% freshmen graduate within 6 years. 48% grads go on to further study within 1 year. 24% grads pursue arts and sciences degrees. 0% grads pursue law degrees. 5% grads pursue business degrees. 0% grads pursue medical degrees. **Faculty:** Student/faculty ratio 10:1. 122 full-time faculty, 79% hold PhDs, 14% are members of minority groups, 73% are women. 0% of classes are taught by teaching assistants.

ACADEMICS
Degrees: Bachelor's; Doctoral degree—professional practice; Doctoral degree research/scholarship; Master's; Post-bachelor's certificate; Post-master's certificate. **Classes:** Most classes have 10–19 students. Most lab/discussion sessions have 10–19 students. **Most popular majors:** Education, General; Psychology, General; Nursing, Other. **Special Study Options:** Accelerated program; Cross-registration; Distance learning; Double major; Dual enrollment; Exchange student program (domestic); Honors program; Independent study; Internships; Liberal arts/career combination; Student-designed major; Study abroad; Teacher certification program; Weekend college. **Combined degree programs:** BA/JD; BA/MEng. **Disability Services offered:** Tutors. **Career services:** Alumni services; Career assessment; Career/job search classes; Internships.

FACILITIES
Housing: Apartments for single students; Coed dorms; Cooperative housing; Theme housing; Wellness housing; Women's dorms; 70% of campus accessible to physically disabled. **Special Academic Facilities/Equipment:** Schacht fine arts center (home of NYS Theatre Institute); Robison Athletic and Recreational Ctr.; State of the Art lab and research facilities in biology; Historic 19th Century Brownstones.

CAMPUS LIFE
Environment: City. **Activities:** Campus Ministries; Choral groups; Dance; Drama/theater; International Student Organization; Literary magazine; Music ensembles; Musical theater; Student government; Student newspaper; Yearbook. 40 registered organizations, 14 honor societies, 4 religious organizations on campus. **On-Campus Highlights:** New York State Theatre Institute.

ADMISSIONS
Freshman Academic Profile: Average high school GPA 3.4. 30% in top 10% of high school class, 67% in top 25% of high school class, 95% in top 50% of high school class. **Test Scores:** SAT Math middle 50% range 470–570. SAT EBRW middle 50% range 470–570. ACT middle 50% range 17–22. **Basis for Candidate Selection:** *Very important factors include:* rigor of secondary school record, class rank, academic GPA, application essay, recommendation(s), level of applicant's interest. *Important factors include:* interview, extracurricular activities, talent/ability, first generation. *Other factors include:* standardized test scores, character/personal qualities, alumni/ae relation, volunteer work, work experience. **Freshman Admission Requirements:** High school diploma is required and GED is accepted. *Academic units required:* 4 English, 3 math, 3 science, 2 science labs, 2 foreign language, 4 social studies. *Academic units recommended:* 4 English, 4 math, 4 science, 3 science labs, 3 foreign language, 4 social studies. **Freshman Admission Statistics:** 2,389 applied, 93% admitted, 17% enrolled. **General Admission Information:** Application fee $30. Priority deadline 3/1. Non-fall registration accepted. Admission may be deferred for a maximum of 1 year.

COSTS AND FINANCIAL AID
Annual tuition $29,357. Room and board $12,618. Required fees $1,500. Average book and supplies expense $1,200. **Required Forms and Deadlines:**

FAFSA; State aid form. **Notification of Awards:** Applicants will be notified of awards on a rolling basis beginning 3/12. **Types of Aid:** *Need-based scholarships/ grants:* College/university scholarship or grant aid from institutional funds; Federal Pell; Private scholarships; SEOG; State scholarships/grants. *Loans:* Direct PLUS loans; Direct Subsidized Stafford Loans; Direct Unsubsidized Stafford Loans. **Financial Aid Statistics:** 25% needy freshmen, 36% needy undergrads receive need-based scholarship or grant aid. 24% freshmen, 34% undergrads receive non-need-based scholarship or grant aid. 38% freshmen, 59% undergrads receive need-based self-help aid. 0% freshmen, 0% undergrads receive athletic scholarships. 94% freshmen, 89% undergrads receive any aid.

RUST COLLEGE

150 Rust Avenue, Holly Springs, MS 38635
Phone: 662-252-8000 **Financial Aid Phone:** 662-252-8000, x4062
E-mail: jb_mcdonald@rustcollege.edu
Fax: 662-252-8895 **Website:** www.rustcollege.edu **ACT Code:** 2240

This private school, affiliated with the Methodist Church, was founded in 1866. It has a 126 acre campus.

RATINGS
Admissions Selectivity Rating: 81   Fire Safety Rating: 60*   Green Rating: 60*

STUDENTS AND FACULTY
Enrollment: 922. **Student Body:** 63% female, 37% male, 5% international. Asian <1%, African American 93%, Caucasian 1%, Hispanic 0%, Native American 0%, Pacific Islander 0%, Two or more races 0%, Race unknown 1%. **Retention and Graduation:** 53% freshmen return for sophomore year. **Faculty:** Student/faculty ratio 17:1. 48 full-time faculty, 0% hold PhDs, 90% are members of minority groups, 40% are women. 0% of classes are taught by teaching assistants.

ACADEMICS
Degrees: Associate; Bachelor's. **Classes:** Most classes have 10–19 students. Most lab/discussion sessions have 10–19 students. **Most popular majors:** Business/Commerce, General; Computer and Information Sciences, General; Biology/Biological Sciences, General. **Special Study Options:** Accelerated program; Distance learning; Double major; Dual enrollment; Honors program; Independent study; Internships; Liberal arts/career combination; Study abroad; Teacher certification program. **Disability Services offered:** Tutors.

FACILITIES
Housing: Men's dorms; Women's dorms. **Special Academic Facilities/ Equipment:** Dr. Ron Trojcak collection of African tribal art which includes fabrics, masks, and statues used for religious ceremonies, weddings, ritual dance, and funerals.

CAMPUS LIFE
Environment: Village. **Activities:** Campus Ministries; Choral groups; Concert band; Drama/theater; International Student Organization; Marching band; Music ensembles; Pep band; Radio station; Student government; Student newspaper; Television station; Yearbook. 35 registered organizations, 7 honor societies, 5 religious organizations, 3 fraternities, 4 sororities on campus. **Athletics (Intercollegiate):** *Men:* baseball, basketball, cheerleading, cross-country, soccer, tennis, track/field (outdoor). *Women:* basketball, cheerleading, cross-country, softball, tennis, track/field (outdoor), volleyball. **On-Campus Highlights:** Leontyne Price Library Exhibits.

ADMISSIONS
Freshman Academic Profile: 98% from public high schools. **Test Scores:** ACT middle 50% range 14–21. **Basis for Candidate Selection:** *Very important factors include:* first generation. *Important factors include:* rigor of secondary school record, class rank, academic GPA, application essay, standardized test scores, recommendation(s), character/personal qualities, alumni/ae relation. *Other factors include:* talent/ability, volunteer work. **Freshman Admission Requirements:** High school diploma is required and GED is accepted. *Academic units required:* 4 English, 3 math, 3 science, 3 social studies, 6 academic electives. **Freshman Admission Statistics:** 3,983 applied, 46% admitted, 15% enrolled. **Transfer Admission Requirements:** High school transcript, college transcript(s), statement of good standing from prior institution(s). Minimum college GPA of 2.0 required. Lowest grade transferable C. **General Admission Information:** Application fee $10. Priority deadline 7/15. Non-fall registration accepted. Admission may be deferred for a maximum of one year.

COSTS AND FINANCIAL AID
Annual tuition $8,100. Room and board $3,700. Average book and supplies expense $250. **Required Forms and Deadlines:** FAFSA; Institution's own financial aid form. **Notification of Awards:** Applicants will be notified of awards on a rolling basis beginning 4/1. **Types of Aid:** *Need-based scholarships/ grants:* Federal Pell; Private scholarships; SEOG; United Negro College Fund. **Financial Aid Statistics:** 86% needy freshmen, 87% needy undergrads receive need-based scholarship or grant aid. 43% freshmen, 29% undergrads receive non-need-based scholarship or grant aid. 87% freshmen, 89% undergrads receive need-based self-help aid. 0% freshmen, 0% undergrads receive athletic scholarships. **Criteria awarding aid:** *Non-need-based:* Academics, Leadership, Music/drama, Religious affiliation, State/district residency.

RUTGERS UNIVERSITY—CAMDEN

406 Penn Street, Camden, NJ 08102
Phone: 856-225-6104 **Financial Aid Phone:** 856-225-6039
E-mail: admissions@camden.rutgers.edu **CEEB Code:** 2092
Website: www.camden.rutgers.edu **ACT Code:** 2592

This public school was founded in 1926. It has a 29 acre campus.

RATINGS
Admissions Selectivity Rating: 76   Fire Safety Rating: 77   Green Rating: 60*

STUDENTS AND FACULTY
Enrollment: 5,626. **Student Body:** 62% female, 38% male, 4% out-of-state, 3% international (31 countries represented). Asian 11%, African American 18%, Caucasian 44%, Hispanic 17%, Native American <1%, Pacific Islander <1%, Two or more races 4%, Race unknown 2%. **Retention and Graduation:** 85% freshmen return for sophomore year. 34% freshmen graduate within 4 years. 65% freshmen graduate within 6 years.

ACADEMICS
Degrees: Bachelor's; Doctoral degree—professional practice; Doctoral degree research/scholarship; Master's; Post-bachelor's certificate; Post-master's certificate. **Most popular majors:** Health Professions And Related Programs; Registered Nursing/Registered Nurse; Business Administration and Management, General. **Special Study Options:** Accelerated program; Cooperative education program; Cross-registration; Distance learning; Double major; Dual enrollment; English as a Second Language (ESL); Exchange student program (domestic); Honors program; Independent study; Internships; Liberal arts/career combination; Student-designed major; Study abroad; Teacher certification program; Weekend college. **Honors programs:** Rutgers University-Camden Honors College. **Combined degree programs:** BA/JD; BA/MA. **Disability Services offered:** Note-taking services; Reader services; Tape recorders; Tutors. **Career services:** Alumni network; Alumni services; Career assessment; Career/job search classes; Internships; Regional alumni.

FACILITIES
Housing: Apartments for single students; Coed dorms; Special housing for disabled students; Theme housing. **Special Academic Facilities/Equipment:** Stedman Art Gallery, Rutgers-Camden Center for the Arts, Gordon Theater, Johnson Park.

CAMPUS LIFE
Environment: City. **Activities:** Choral groups; Concert band; Dance; Drama/ theater; International Student Organization; Jazz band; Literary magazine; Musical theater; Radio station; Student government; Student newspaper; Symphony orchestra. 150 registered organizations, 19 honor societies, 5 religious organizations, 5 fraternities, 7 sororities on campus. **Athletics (Intercollegiate):** *Men:* baseball, basketball, cross-country, golf, soccer, track/field (outdoor). *Women:* basketball, cross-country, soccer, softball, track/field (outdoor), volleyball. **On-Campus Highlights:** Stedman Art Gallery.

ADMISSIONS
Freshman Academic Profile: 19% in top 10% of high school class, 45% in top 25% of high school class, 81% in top 50% of high school class. **Test Scores:** SAT Math middle 50% range 490–580. SAT EBRW middle 50% range 490–590. ACT middle 50% range 18–22. **Basis for Candidate Selection:** *Very important factors include:* rigor of secondary school record, academic GPA. *Important factors include:* class rank, standardized test scores, extracurricular activities, talent/ability, level of applicant's interest. *Other factors include:* application essay, character/personal qualities, volunteer work, work experience.

Freshman Admission Requirements: High school diploma is required and GED is accepted. *Academic units required:* 4 English, 3 math, 2 science, 2 foreign language, 5 academic electives. **Freshman Admission Statistics:** 10,451 applied, 79% admitted, 9% enrolled. **Transfer Admission Requirements:** High school transcript, college transcript(s). **General Admission Information:** Application fee $70. Priority deadline 12/1. Non-fall registration accepted. Admission may be deferred for a maximum of Deferral is granted only for a full academic year, from one fall semester to the very next fall semester. A deferral is approved only when the student is officially notified in writing that the Office of Graduate and Undergraduate Admissions has granted the request.

COSTS AND FINANCIAL AID

Annual in-state tuition $12,230. Annual out-of-state tuition $28,466. Room and board $12,691. Required fees $3,034. Average book and supplies expense $1,350. **Required Forms and Deadlines:** FAFSA. **Notification of Awards:** Applicants will be notified of awards on a rolling basis beginning 2/15. **Types of Aid:** *Need-based scholarships/grants:* College/university scholarship or grant aid from institutional funds; Federal Nursing Scholarships; Federal Pell; SEOG; State scholarships/grants. *Loans:* Direct PLUS loans; Direct Subsidized Stafford Loans; Direct Unsubsidized Stafford Loans. **Student Employment:** Federal Work-Study Program available. Institutional employment available. **Criteria awarding aid:** *Need-based:* Academics, Alumni affiliation, Art, Leadership, Music/drama. *Non-need-based:* Academics, Alumni affiliation, Art, Athletics, Leadership, Music/drama, State/district residency.

RUTGERS UNIVERSITY—NEWARK

190 University Avenue, Newark, NJ 07102-1896
Phone: 973-353-5205 **Financial Aid Phone:** 973-353-5151
E-mail: newark@admissions.rutgers.edu **CEEB Code:** 8190
Website: www.newark.rutgers.edu **ACT Code:** 2592

This public school was founded in 1930. It has a 36 acre campus.

RATINGS

Admissions Selectivity Rating: 79   **Fire Safety Rating:** 77   **Green Rating:** 60*

STUDENTS AND FACULTY

Enrollment: 9,037. **Student Body:** 57% female, 43% male, 1% out-of-state, 9% international (65 countries represented). Asian 17%, African American 19%, Caucasian 20%, Hispanic 29%, Native American <1%, Pacific Islander <1%, Two or more races 3%, Race unknown 3%.
Retention and Graduation: 83% freshmen return for sophomore year. 40% freshmen graduate within 4 years. 69% freshmen graduate within 6 years.

ACADEMICS

Degrees: Bachelor's; Doctoral degree—professional practice; Doctoral degree research/scholarship; Master's; Post-bachelor's certificate; Post-master's certificate. **Most popular majors:** Criminal Justice/Safety Studies; Accounting; Finance, General. **Special Study Options:** Accelerated program; Cooperative education program; Cross-registration; Distance learning; Double major; Dual enrollment; English as a Second Language (ESL); Exchange student program (domestic); Honors program; Independent study; Internships; Liberal arts/career combination; Student-designed major; Study abroad; Teacher certification program; Weekend college. **Honors programs:** Honors College at Rutgers University–Newark. **Combined degree programs:** BA/JD; BA/MA; BA/MD; BA/MEng. **Disability Services offered:** Note-taking services; Reader services; Tape recorders; Tutors. **Career services:** Alumni network; Alumni services; Career assessment; Career/job search classes; Internships; Regional alumni.

FACILITIES

Housing: Apartments for single students; Coed dorms; Special housing for disabled students; Theme housing; Wellness housing. **Special Academic Facilities/Equipment:** Institute of Jazz Studies, TV/Radio media center, Institute of Animal Behavior, Center for Crime Prevention Studies, Center for Negotiation and Conflict Resolution, Center for Molecular and Behaviorial Neuroscience, Center for Nursing Research. **Campus Network:** 96% of classrooms, 100% of dorms, 100% of student union, 100% of libraries, 100% of dining areas, 10% of common outdoor areas have wireless network access.

CAMPUS LIFE

Environment: City. **Activities:** Campus Ministries; Choral groups; Dance; Drama/theater; International Student Organization; Jazz band; Literary

magazine; Music ensembles; Musical theater; Radio station; Student government; Student newspaper; Symphony orchestra. 200 registered organizations, 18 honor societies, 9 religious organizations, 12 fraternities, 11 sororities on campus. **Athletics (Intercollegiate):** *Men:* baseball, basketball, soccer, tennis, volleyball. *Women:* basketball, softball, tennis, volleyball. **On-Campus Highlights:** The Arts at Rutgers Newark.

ADMISSIONS

Freshman Academic Profile: 22% in top 10% of high school class, 51% in top 25% of high school class, 84% in top 50% of high school class. **Test Scores:** SAT Math middle 50% range 520–610. SAT EBRW middle 50% range 500–590. ACT middle 50% range 19–25. **Basis for Candidate Selection:** *Very important factors include:* rigor of secondary school record, class rank, academic GPA, standardized test scores. *Other factors include:* application essay, extracurricular activities, first generation, geographical residence, state residency, racial/ethnic status, volunteer work, work experience, level of applicant's interest. **Freshman Admission Requirements:** High school diploma is required and GED is accepted. *Academic units required:* 4 English, 3 math, 2 science, 2 foreign language, 5 academic electives. **Freshman Admission Statistics:** 13,732 applied, 72% admitted, 14% enrolled. **Transfer Admission Requirements:** High school transcript, college transcript(s). **General Admission Information:** Application fee $70. Priority deadline 12/1. Non-fall registration accepted. Deferral is granted only for a full academic year, from one fall semester to the very next fall semester. A deferral is official only when you are notified that the Office of University Undergraduate Admissions has granted your request.

COSTS AND FINANCIAL AID

Annual in-state tuition $12,230. Annual out-of-state tuition $29,012. Room and board $13,929. Required fees $2,596. Average book and supplies expense $1,350. **Required Forms and Deadlines:** FAFSA. **Notification of Awards:** Applicants will be notified of awards on a rolling basis beginning 2/15. **Types of Aid:** *Need-based scholarships/grants:* College/university scholarship or grant aid from institutional funds; Federal Pell; SEOG; State scholarships/grants. *Loans:* Direct PLUS loans; Direct Subsidized Stafford Loans; Direct Unsubsidized Stafford Loans. **Student Employment:** Federal Work-Study Program available. Institutional employment available. **Criteria awarding aid:** *Need-based:* Academics, Alumni affiliation, Art, Leadership, Music/drama. *Non-need-based:* Academics, Alumni affiliation, Art, Athletics, Leadership, Music/drama, State/district residency.

RUTGERS UNIVERSITY—NEW BRUNSWICK

Admissions Office, Piscataway, NJ 08854-8097
Phone: 732-932-4636 **Financial Aid Phone:** 848-932-7057
E-mail: admissions@ugadm.rutgers.edu **CEEB Code:** 2765
Fax: 732-445-8088 **Website:** www.newbrunswick.rutgers.edu **ACT Code:** 2592

This public school was founded in 1766. It has a 2695 acre campus.

RATINGS

Admissions Selectivity Rating: 88   **Fire Safety Rating:** 77   **Green Rating:** 60*

STUDENTS AND FACULTY

Enrollment: 35,760. **Student Body:** 50% female, 50% male, 6% out-of-state, 10% international (87 countries represented). Asian 29%, African American 6%, Caucasian 36%, Hispanic 13%, Native American <1%, Pacific Islander <1%, Two or more races 4%, Race unknown 2%.
Retention and Graduation: 93% freshmen return for sophomore year. 65% freshmen graduate within 4 years. 84% freshmen graduate within 6 years.

ACADEMICS

Degrees: Associate; Bachelor's; Certificate; Doctoral degree—professional practice; Doctoral degree research/scholarship; Master's; Post-bachelor's certificate; Post-master's certificate. **Most popular majors:** Computer and Information Sciences, General; Registered Nursing/Registered Nurse; Business Administration and Management, General. **Special Study Options:** Accelerated program; Cooperative education program; Cross-registration; Distance learning; Double major; Dual enrollment; English as a Second Language (ESL); Exchange student program (domestic); Honors program; Independent study;

Internships; Liberal arts/career combination; Student-designed major; Study abroad; Teacher certification program; Weekend college. **Honors programs:** Rutgers-New Brunswick Honors College. **Combined degree programs:** BA/DDS; BA/JD; BA/MA; BA/MD; BA/MEng. **Disability Services offered:** Note-taking services; Reader services; Tape recorders. **Career services:** Alumni network; Alumni services; Career assessment; Career/job search classes; Internships; Regional alumni.

FACILITIES

Housing: Apartments for married students; Apartments for single students; Coed dorms; Special housing for disabled students; Theme housing; Wellness housing; Women's dorms. **Special Academic Facilities/Equipment:** Zimmerli Art Museum, Mason Gross Galleries at Civic Square, Brodsky Center, Geology Museum, Robert A. Schommer Astronomical Observatory, Entomological Museum. **Campus Network:** 100% of classrooms, 100% of dorms, 100% of student union, 100% of libraries, 100% of dining areas, 80% of common outdoor areas have wireless network access.

CAMPUS LIFE

Environment: Town. **Activities:** Campus Ministries; Choral groups; Concert band; Dance; Drama/theater; International Student Organization; Jazz band; Literary magazine; Marching band; Model UN; Music ensembles; Musical theater; Opera; Pep band; Radio station; Student government; Student newspaper; Student-run film society; Symphony orchestra; Television station. 800 registered organizations, 35 honor societies, 50 religious organizations, 50 fraternities, 29 sororities on campus. **Athletics (Intercollegiate):** *Men:* baseball, basketball, cheerleading, cross-country, diving, football, golf, lacrosse, soccer, track/field (outdoor), track/field (indoor), wrestling. *Women:* basketball, cheerleading, crew/rowing, cross-country, diving, field hockey, golf, gymnastics, lacrosse, soccer, softball, swimming, tennis, track/field (outdoor), track/field (indoor), volleyball. **On-Campus Highlights:** Geology Museum.

ADMISSIONS

Freshman Academic Profile: 38% in top 10% of high school class, 73% in top 25% of high school class, 94% in top 50% of high school class. **Test Scores:** SAT Math middle 50% range 620–750. SAT EBRW middle 50% range 590–680. ACT middle 50% range 25–32. **Basis for Candidate Selection:** *Very important factors include:* rigor of secondary school record, academic GPA, standardized test scores. *Important factors include:* extracurricular activities. *Other factors include:* class rank, application essay, interview, talent/ability, character/personal qualities, first generation, geographical residence, state residency, racial/ethnic status, volunteer work, work experience. **Freshman Admission Requirements:** High school diploma is required and GED is accepted. *Academic units required:* 4 English, 3 math, 2 science, 2 foreign language, 5 academic electives. **Freshman Admission Statistics:** 41,286 applied, 61% admitted, 29% enrolled. **Transfer Admission Requirements:** High school transcript, college transcript(s). Lowest grade transferable C. **General Admission Information:** Application fee $70. Priority deadline 12/1. Non-fall registration accepted. Deferral is granted only for a full academic year, from one fall semester to the very next fall semester. A deferral is approved only when you are officially notified in writing that the Office of University Undergraduate Admissions has granted your request.

COSTS AND FINANCIAL AID

Annual in-state tuition $12,230. Annual out-of-state tuition $29,012. Room and board $13,075. Required fees $3,177. Average book and supplies expense $1,350. **Required Forms and Deadlines:** FAFSA. **Notification of Awards:** Applicants will be notified of awards on a rolling basis beginning 2/15. **Types of Aid:** *Need-based scholarships/grants:* College/university scholarship or grant aid from institutional funds; Federal Nursing Scholarships; Federal Pell; SEOG; State scholarships/grants. *Loans:* Direct PLUS loans; Direct Subsidized Stafford Loans; Direct Unsubsidized Stafford Loans. **Student Employment:** Federal Work-Study Program available. Institutional employment available. **Criteria awarding aid:** *Need-based:* Academics, Alumni affiliation, Art, Leadership, Music/drama. *Non-need-based:* Academics, Alumni affiliation, Art, Athletics, Leadership, Music/drama, State/district residency.

SACRED HEART UNIVERSITY

5151 Park Avenue, Fairfield, CT 06825
Phone: 203-371-7880 **Financial Aid Phone:** 203-371-7980
E-mail: enroll@sacredheart.edu **CEEB Code:** 3780
Fax: 203-365-7607 **Website:** www.sacredheart.edu **ACT Code:** 589

This private school, affiliated with the Roman Catholic Church, was founded in 1963. It has a 350 acre campus.

RATINGS
Admissions Selectivity Rating: 85   **Fire Safety Rating:** 96   **Green Rating:** 60*

STUDENTS AND FACULTY
Enrollment: 6,066. **Student Body:** 66% female, 34% male, 64% out-of-state, 1% international (30 countries represented). Asian 2%, African American 5%, Caucasian 73%, Hispanic 12%, Native American <1%, Pacific Islander <1%, Two or more races 2%, Race unknown 4%.
Retention and Graduation: 83% freshmen return for sophomore year. 68% freshmen graduate within 4 years. 73% freshmen graduate within 6 years. 35% grads go on to further study within 1 year. 40% grads pursue arts and sciences degrees. 26% grads pursue business degrees. **Faculty:** Student/faculty ratio 13:1. 329 full-time faculty, 81% hold PhDs, 11% are members of minority groups, 60% are women. 0% of classes are taught by teaching assistants.

ACADEMICS
Degrees: Associate; Bachelor's; Certificate; Doctoral degree—professional practice; Master's; Post-bachelor's certificate; Post-master's certificate. **Classes:** Most classes have 20–29 students. **Most popular majors:** Psychology, General; Registered Nursing/Registered Nurse; Marketing/Marketing Management, General. **Special Study Options:** Accelerated program; Distance learning; Double major; Dual enrollment; English as a Second Language (ESL); Honors program; Independent study; Internships; Study abroad; Teacher certification program; Weekend college. **Honors programs:** The Thomas More Honors Program includes workshops, discussions, unique courses, cultural events, trips, socials and service projects, while the Honors Living and Learning Community for residential students build a strong and dynamic community that engages with faculty in innovative learning experiences outside of the classroom. Honors students integrate a deep passion for learning within the greater context of their lives at the University. **Combined degree programs:** BA/MA. **Disability Services offered:** Note-taking services; Reader services; Tape recorders; Tutors. **Career services:** Alumni network; Alumni services; Career assessment; Career/job search classes; Internships; Regional alumni.

FACILITIES
Housing: Apartments for single students; Coed dorms; Special housing for disabled students; Theme housing; Wellness housing. **Special Academic Facilities/Equipment:** The Jack Welch College of Business & Technology at Sacred Heart University's West Campus features an active trading floor with work stations, Bloomberg terminals, wallboard ticker tapes and real time data from NASDAQ and NYSE; screening venues; smart classrooms with multi-media technology; interactive labs. It also includes an incubation space for student entrepreneurs to develop their businesses, an AI Lab and an IDEA Lab. The IDEA Lab is 10,000 square feet of the finest equipment and resources and a place for collaborative innovation, exploration, and learning. It features a metal and wood shop, electrical engineering room, drone room, materials characterization and manufacturing area, true 3D printing and modeling room, studio area, and more. The Center for Healthcare Education is where students studying nursing and the health professions attend classes. It includes a medical gym, audiology suite, motion analysis and human performance labs, an immersive acute care simulation lab with video and data capture capability, a simulated outpatient suite, high-fidelity manikins, a home-care suite, an expanded human anatomy lab and many more learning resources featuring the latest technology. The Frank and Marisa Martire Center for the Liberal Arts includes a motion capture lab, two large television studios for TV, video and film production. The campus also features art studios, a printing lab, a computer gaming lab, and more.

CAMPUS LIFE
Environment: Town. **Activities:** Campus Ministries; Choral groups; Concert band; Dance; Drama/theater; International Student Organization; Jazz band; Literary magazine; Marching band; Model UN; Music ensembles; Musical

theater; Pep band; Radio station; Student government; Student newspaper; Student-run film society; Symphony orchestra; Television station; Yearbook. 164 registered organizations, 21 honor societies, 3 religious organizations, 6 fraternities, 8 sororities on campus. **Athletics (Intercollegiate):** *Men:* baseball, basketball, cross-country, fencing, football, golf, ice hockey, lacrosse, soccer, tennis, track/field (outdoor), track/field (indoor), volleyball, wrestling. *Women:* basketball, bowling, crew/rowing, cross-country, diving, equestrian sports, fencing, field hockey, golf, ice hockey, lacrosse, soccer, softball, swimming, tennis, track/field (outdoor), track/field (indoor), volleyball. **On-Campus Highlights:** Bobby Valentine Health & Recreation Center.

ADMISSIONS

Freshman Academic Profile: Average high school GPA 3.6. 10% in top 10% of high school class, 35% in top 25% of high school class, 69% in top 50% of high school class. 66% from public high schools. **Test Scores:** SAT Math middle 50% range 550–630. SAT EBRW middle 50% range 570–630. ACT middle 50% range 23–28. **Basis for Candidate Selection:** *Very important factors include:* rigor of secondary school record, academic GPA, volunteer work, work experience, level of applicant's interest. *Important factors include:* class rank, application essay, recommendation(s), interview, extracurricular activities, talent/ability, character/personal qualities. *Other factors include:* standardized test scores, alumni/ae relation. **Freshman Admission Requirements:** High school diploma is required and GED is accepted. *Academic units required:* 4 English, 3 math, 3 science, 1 science lab, 2 foreign language, 3 social studies, 3 history, 3 academic electives. *Academic units recommended:* 4 English, 4 math, 4 science, 2 science labs, 4 foreign language, 4 social studies, 4 history, 4 academic electives. **Freshman Admission Statistics:** 11,748 applied, 64% admitted, 21% enrolled. **Transfer Admission Requirements:** High school transcript, college transcript(s), essay or personal statement. Minimum college GPA of 2.5 required. Lowest grade transferable C-. **General Admission Information:** Application fee $50. Priority deadline 2/15. Non-fall registration accepted. Admission may be deferred for a maximum of 1 year.

COSTS AND FINANCIAL AID

Annual tuition $42,800. Room and board $15,960. Required fees $270. Average book and supplies expense $1,200. **Required Forms and Deadlines:** CSS/Financial Aid PROFILE; FAFSA; Noncustodial PROFILE. **Notification of Awards:** Applicants will be notified of awards on a rolling basis beginning 3/1. **Types of Aid:** *Need-based scholarships/grants:* College/university scholarship or grant aid from institutional funds; Federal Pell; Private scholarships; SEOG; State scholarships/grants. *Loans:* Direct PLUS loans; Direct Subsidized Stafford Loans; Direct Unsubsidized Stafford Loans. **Student Employment:** Federal Work-Study Program available. Institutional employment available. **Financial Aid Statistics:** 100% needy freshmen, 99% needy undergrads receive need-based scholarship or grant aid. 18% freshmen, 15% undergrads receive non-need-based scholarship or grant aid. 77% freshmen, 80% undergrads receive need-based self-help aid. 5% freshmen, 5% undergrads receive athletic scholarships. 99.9% freshmen, 96.6% undergrads receive any aid. 72% undergrads borrow to pay for school. Average cumulative indebtedness $45,630. **Criteria awarding aid:** *Need-based:* Academics. *Non-need-based:* Academics, Alumni affiliation, Art, Athletics, Leadership, Music/drama, Religious affiliation, State/district residency.

SAGINAW VALLEY STATE UNIVERSITY

7400 Bay Road, University Center, MI 48710
Phone: 989-964-4200 **Financial Aid Phone:** 989-964-4103
E-mail: admissions@svsu.edu **CEEB Code:** 1766
Fax: 989-790-0180 **Website:** www.svsu.edu **ACT Code:** 2057

This public school was founded in 1963. It has a 782 acre campus.

RATINGS

Admissions Selectivity Rating: 79   **Fire Safety Rating:** 66   **Green Rating:** 60*

STUDENTS AND FACULTY

Enrollment: 7,209. **Student Body:** 61% female, 39% male, 2% out-of-state, 5% international (30 countries represented). Asian 1%, African American 8%, Caucasian 76%, Hispanic 5%, Native American <1%, Pacific Islander <1%, Two or more races 4%, Race unknown 2%.
Retention and Graduation: 74% freshmen return for sophomore year. 15% freshmen graduate within 4 years. 44% freshmen graduate within 6 years. 9% grads go on to further study within 1 year. **Faculty:** 286 full-time faculty, 91%

hold PhDs, 0% are members of minority groups, 48% are women. 0% of classes are taught by teaching assistants.

ACADEMICS

Degrees: Bachelor's; Doctoral degree—professional practice; Master's; Post-master's certificate. **Classes:** Most classes have 20–29 students. Most lab/discussion sessions have 10–19 students. **Most popular majors:** Criminal Justice/Safety Studies; Social Work; Registered Nursing/Registered Nurse. **Special Study Options:** Accelerated program; Cooperative education program; Distance learning; Double major; Dual enrollment; English as a Second Language (ESL); Honors program; Independent study; Internships; Study abroad; Teacher certification program. **Honors programs:** The University Honors Program allows students to pursue their major and minor degree work, while providing enriched academic experiences in Honors courses, seminars, research projects, and social activities. The Honors experience enables students to work more intensively with active teacher/scholars and to participate in interdisciplinary courses. Honors students will have ample opportunity to develop as critical thinkers, active learners, and problem solvers. **Disability Services offered:** Note-taking services; Reader services; Tutors. **Career services:** Alumni services; Career assessment; Internships.

FACILITIES

Housing: Apartments for single students; Coed dorms; Special housing for disabled students; Theme housing; 95% of campus accessible to physically disabled. **Special Academic Facilities/Equipment:** Sculpture gallery, fine arts center, center for health and physical education, independent testing lab, center for economic and business research, applied technology research center. **Campus Network:** 100% of classrooms, 100% of dorms, 100% of student union, 100% of libraries, 100% of dining areas, 100% of common outdoor areas have wireless network access.

CAMPUS LIFE

Environment: City. **Activities:** Campus Ministries; Choral groups; Concert band; Dance; Drama/theater; International Student Organization; Jazz band; Literary magazine; Marching band; Model UN; Music ensembles; Musical theater; Radio station; Student government; Student newspaper; Student-run film society. 159 registered organizations, 8 honor societies, 14 religious organizations, 6 fraternities, 5 sororities on campus. **Athletics (Intercollegiate):** *Men:* baseball, basketball, bowling, cheerleading, cross-country, football, golf, soccer, track/field (outdoor), track/field (indoor). *Women:* basketball, cheerleading, cross-country, soccer, softball, tennis, track/field (outdoor), track/field (indoor), volleyball. **On-Campus Highlights:** Student Center. **Environmental Initiatives:** Constructing facilities with energy savings in mind for many years.

ADMISSIONS

Freshman Academic Profile: Average high school GPA 3.4. 18% in top 10% of high school class, 44% in top 25% of high school class, 78% in top 50% of high school class. **Test Scores:** SAT Math middle 50% range 490–590. SAT EBRW middle 50% range 490–600. ACT middle 50% range 19–25. **Basis for Candidate Selection:** *Very important factors include:* academic GPA, standardized test scores, extracurricular activities. *Important factors include:* talent/ability. **Freshman Admission Requirements:** High school diploma is required and GED is accepted. *Academic units recommended:* 4 English, 3 math, 3 science, 2 foreign language, 3 social studies. **Freshman Admission Statistics:** 7,149 applied, 73% admitted, 28% enrolled. **Transfer Admission Requirements:** College transcript(s). Minimum college GPA of 2.0 required. Lowest grade transferable C-. **General Admission Information:** Application fee $30. Non-fall registration accepted. Admission may be deferred for a maximum of 1.5 years.

COSTS AND FINANCIAL AID

Required Forms and Deadlines: CSS/Financial Aid PROFILE; FAFSA; Institution's own financial aid form. **Notification of Awards:** Applicants will be notified of awards on a rolling basis beginning 3/1. **Types of Aid:** *Need-based scholarships/grants:* College/university scholarship or grant aid from institutional funds; Federal Pell; Private scholarships; SEOG; State scholarships/grants. *Loans:* Direct PLUS loans; Direct Subsidized Stafford Loans; Direct Unsubsidized Stafford Loans. **Student Employment:** Federal Work-Study Program available. Institutional employment available. **Financial Aid Statistics:** 100% needy freshmen, 88% needy undergrads receive need-based scholarship or grant aid. 12% freshmen, 7% undergrads receive non-need-based scholarship or grant aid. 59% freshmen, 73% undergrads receive need-based self-help aid. 3% freshmen, 3% undergrads receive athletic scholarships. 98% freshmen, 88% undergrads receive any aid. 73% undergrads borrow to pay for school. Average cumulative indebtedness $31,353. **Criteria awarding aid:** *Need-based:* Academics, Leadership, Minority status. *Non-need-based:* Academics, Art, Athletics, Leadership, Minority status, Music/drama.

ST. AMBROSE UNIVERSITY

310 West Locust Street, Davenport, IA 52803-2898
Phone: 563-333-6300 **Financial Aid Phone:** 563-333-5158
E-mail: admit@sau.edu **CEEB Code:** 6617
Fax: 563-333-6038 **Website:** www.sau.edu **ACT Code:** 1352

This private school, affiliated with the Roman Catholic Church, was founded in 1882. It has a 118 acre campus.

RATINGS
Admissions Selectivity Rating: 80   **Fire Safety Rating:** 60*   **Green Rating:** 60*

STUDENTS AND FACULTY
Enrollment: 2,248. **Student Body:** 55% female, 45% male, 66% out-of-state, 4% international (21 countries represented). Asian 1%, African American 5%, Caucasian 73%, Hispanic 9%, Native American <1%, Pacific Islander <1%, Two or more races 3%, Race unknown 4%.
Retention and Graduation: 76% freshmen return for sophomore year. 55% freshmen graduate within 4 years. 64% freshmen graduate within 6 years. 17% grads go on to further study within 1 year. **Faculty:** Student/faculty ratio 11:1. 201 full-time faculty, 89% hold PhDs, 12% are members of minority groups, 54% are women. 0% of classes are taught by teaching assistants.

ACADEMICS
Degrees: Bachelor's; Doctoral degree—professional practice; Doctoral degree research/scholarship; Master's; Post-master's certificate. **Classes:** Most classes have 10–19 students. Most lab/discussion sessions have 10–19 students. **Most popular majors:** Business/Commerce, General; Nursing Science; Psychology, General. **Special Study Options:** Accelerated program; Distance learning; Double major; English as a Second Language (ESL); Honors program; Independent study; Internships; Liberal arts/career combination; Student-designed major; Study abroad; Teacher certification program. **Honors programs:** Honors Program study is open to students who have been accepted to St. Ambrose University pursuing any major, as per the requirements described below. **Combined degree programs:** BA/MA. **Disability Services offered:** Note-taking services; Reader services; Tape recorders; Tutors. **Career services:** Alumni network; Alumni services; Career assessment; Career/job search classes; Internships; Regional alumni.

FACILITIES
Housing: Apartments for single students; Coed dorms; Men's dorms; Special housing for disabled students; Theme housing; Women's dorms; 95% of campus accessible to physically disabled. **Special Academic Facilities/Equipment:** Art gallery, observatory, language lab, and distance learning classrooms, Gottlieb Conference, Rogo.

CAMPUS LIFE
Environment: City. **Activities:** Campus Ministries; Choral groups; Concert band; Dance; Drama/theater; International Student Organization; Jazz band; Literary magazine; Marching band; Model UN; Music ensembles; Musical theater; Pep band; Radio station; Student government; Student newspaper; Television station. 84 registered organizations, 15 honor societies, 3 religious organizations on campus. **Athletics (Intercollegiate):** *Men:* baseball, basketball, bowling, cheerleading, cross-country, football, golf, soccer, tennis, track/field (outdoor), track/field (indoor), volleyball. *Women:* basketball, bowling, cheerleading, cross-country, golf, soccer, softball, tennis, track/field (outdoor), track/field (indoor), volleyball. **On-Campus Highlights:** Rogalski Center (Student Union).

ADMISSIONS
Freshman Academic Profile: Average high school GPA 3.4. 30% in top 10% of high school class, 57% in top 25% of high school class, 84% in top 50% of high school class. **Test Scores:** SAT Math middle 50% range 580–680. SAT EBRW middle 50% range 490–590. ACT middle 50% range 20–25. **Basis for Candidate Selection:** *Very important factors include:* rigor of secondary school record, class rank, academic GPA, standardized test scores. *Other factors include:* application essay, recommendation(s), interview, extracurricular activities, talent/ability, character/personal qualities, first generation, alumni/ae relation, racial/ethnic status, volunteer work. **Freshman Admission Requirements:** High school diploma is required and GED is accepted. *Academic units recommended:* 4 English, 3 math, 2 science, 2 science labs, 1 foreign language, 1 social studies, 1 history, 4 academic electives. **Freshman Admission Statistics:** 4,877 applied, 77% admitted, 13% enrolled. **Transfer Admission Requirements:** High school transcript, college transcript(s), standardized test scores, statement of good standing from prior institution(s). Minimum college GPA of 2.0 required.

Lowest grade transferable D. **General Admission Information:** Non-fall registration accepted.

COSTS AND FINANCIAL AID
Annual tuition $32,478. Room and board $11,354. Required fees $280. Average book and supplies expense $1,320. **Required Forms and Deadlines:** FAFSA. **Notification of Awards:** Applicants will be notified of awards on a rolling basis beginning 2/1. **Types of Aid:** *Need-based scholarships/grants:* College/university scholarship or grant aid from institutional funds; Federal Pell; Private scholarships; SEOG; State scholarships/grants. *Loans:* Direct PLUS loans; Direct Subsidized Stafford Loans; Direct Unsubsidized Stafford Loans. **Student Employment:** Federal Work-Study Program available. Institutional employment available. **Financial Aid Statistics:** 99% needy freshmen, 98% needy undergrads receive need-based scholarship or grant aid. 39% freshmen, 29% undergrads receive non-need-based scholarship or grant aid. 74% freshmen, 79% undergrads receive need-based self-help aid. 14% freshmen, 11% undergrads receive athletic scholarships. 100% freshmen, 94% undergrads receive any aid. 78% undergrads borrow to pay for school. Average cumulative indebtedness $38,149. **Criteria awarding aid:** *Need-based:* Academics, Minority status. *Non-need-based:* Academics, Alumni affiliation, Art, Athletics, Music/drama.

ST. ANDREWS UNIVERSITY

1700 Dogwood Mile, Laurinburg, NC 28352
Phone: 910-277-5555 **Financial Aid Phone:** 910-277-5560
E-mail: admissions@sapc.edu **CEEB Code:** 5214
Fax: 910-277-5020 **Website:** sapc.edu **ACT Code:** 3146

This private school, affiliated with the Presbyterian Church, was founded in 1958. It has a 600 acre campus.

RATINGS
Admissions Selectivity Rating: 74   **Fire Safety Rating:** 60*   **Green Rating:** 60*

STUDENTS AND FACULTY
Enrollment: 601. **Student Body:** 54% female, 46% male, 59% out-of-state, 12% international (8 countries represented). Asian 0%, African American 12%, Caucasian 61%, Hispanic 0%, Native American 0%, Pacific Islander 0%, Two or more races 2%, Race unknown 14%.
Retention and Graduation: 59% freshmen return for sophomore year. 40% grads go on to further study within 1 year. **Faculty:** Student/faculty ratio 15:1. 30 full-time faculty, 73% hold PhDs, 3% are members of minority groups, 47% are women. 0% of classes are taught by teaching assistants.

ACADEMICS
Degrees: Bachelor's; Diploma; Master's. **Classes:** Most classes have fewer than 10 students. **Most popular majors:** English Language and Literature, General; Business/Commerce, General; Elementary Education and Teaching. **Special Study Options:** Double major; English as a Second Language (ESL); Honors program; Independent study; Internships; Student-designed major; Study abroad; Teacher certification program. **Disability Services offered:** Note-taking services; Reader services; Tape recorders; Tutors. **Career services:** Alumni network; Alumni services; Career assessment; Career/job search classes; Internships; Regional alumni.

FACILITIES
Housing: Coed dorms; Men's dorms; Women's dorms; 90% of campus accessible to physically disabled. **Special Academic Facilities/Equipment:** Art gallery, anthropology museum, science lab, electron microscopy center with three electron microscopes, psychology lab, artronics graphics computer, Scottish Heritage Foundation. **Campus Network:** 80% of classrooms, 99% of student union, 99% of libraries, 99% of dining areas, 75% of common outdoor areas have wireless network access.

CAMPUS LIFE
Environment: Rural. **Activities:** 30 registered organizations, 3 honor societies, 1 religious organization on campus. **Athletics (Intercollegiate):** *Men:* baseball, basketball, cross-country, equestrian sports, golf, horseback riding, lacrosse, soccer, track/field (outdoor), wrestling. *Women:* basketball, cross-country, equestrian sports, horseback riding, lacrosse, soccer, softball, track/field (outdoor), volleyball, wrestling. **On-Campus Highlights:** Equesterian Center.

ADMISSIONS

Freshman Academic Profile: Average high school GPA 3.2. 7% in top 10% of high school class, 30% in top 25% of high school class, 66% in top 50% of high school class. **Test Scores:** SAT Math middle 50% range 355–605. **Basis for Candidate Selection:** *Important factors include:* academic GPA, standardized test scores, extracurricular activities, character/personal qualities. *Other factors include:* rigor of secondary school record, class rank, application essay, recommendation(s), interview, talent/ability, first generation, volunteer work, work experience. **Freshman Admission Requirements:** High school diploma is required and GED is accepted. *Academic units required:* 3 English, 3 math, 3 science, 1 foreign language, 3 social studies. **Freshman Admission Statistics:** 926 applied, 57% admitted, 29% enrolled. **Transfer Admission Requirements:** High school transcript, college transcript(s), statement of good standing from prior institution(s). Minimum college GPA of 2.5 required. Lowest grade transferable C-. **General Admission Information:** Application fee $35. Non-fall registration accepted.

COSTS AND FINANCIAL AID

Annual tuition $23,682. Average book and supplies expense $1,800. **Types of Aid:** *Need-based scholarships/grants:* College/university scholarship or grant aid from institutional funds; Federal Pell; Private scholarships; SEOG; State scholarships/grants. *Loans:* Direct PLUS loans; Direct Subsidized Stafford Loans; Direct Unsubsidized Stafford Loans. **Student Employment:** Federal Work-Study Program available. Institutional employment available. **Financial Aid Statistics:** 99% needy freshmen, 98% needy undergrads receive need-based scholarship or grant aid. 9% freshmen, 8% undergrads receive non-need-based scholarship or grant aid. 85% freshmen, 84% undergrads receive need-based self-help aid. 17% freshmen, 17% undergrads receive athletic scholarships. 99% freshmen, 98% undergrads receive any aid. **Criteria awarding aid:** *Non-need-based:* Academics, Alumni affiliation, Art, Athletics, Job skills, Leadership, Music/drama, Religious affiliation.

SAINT ANSELM COLLEGE

100 Saint Anselm Drive, Manchester, NH 03102-1310
Phone: 603-641-7500 **Financial Aid Phone:** 603-641-7110
E-mail: admission@anselm.edu **CEEB Code:** 3748
Fax: 603-641-7550 **Website:** www.anselm.edu **ACT Code:** 2522

This private school, affiliated with the Roman Catholic Church, was founded in 1889. It has a 380 acre campus.

RATINGS

Admissions Selectivity Rating: 81   **Fire Safety Rating:** 85   **Green Rating:** 63

STUDENTS AND FACULTY

Enrollment: 2,041. **Student Body:** 61% female, 39% male, 78% out-of-state, 1% international (9 countries represented). Asian 1%, African American 2%, Caucasian 87%, Hispanic 4%, Native American <1%, Pacific Islander <1%, Two or more races 2%, Race unknown 4%.
Retention and Graduation: 91% freshmen return for sophomore year. 78% freshmen graduate within 4 years. 80 16% grads go on to further study within 1 year. 11% grads pursue arts and sciences degrees. 3% grads pursue law degrees. 1% grads pursue business degrees. 2% grads pursue medical degrees. **Faculty:** Student/faculty ratio 9:1. 155 full-time faculty, 90% hold PhDs, 10% are members of minority groups, 55% are women. 0% of classes are taught by teaching assistants.

ACADEMICS

Degrees: Bachelor's. **Classes:** Most classes have 10–19 students. **Most popular majors:** Business Administration and Management, General; Nursing; Political Science and Government, General. **Special Study Options:** Cooperative education program; Cross-registration; Distance learning; Double major; English as a Second Language (ESL); External degree program; Honors program; Independent study; Internships; Liberal arts/career combination; Study abroad; Teacher certification program. **Honors programs:** Honors Program for Chancellor Scholars. **Disability Services offered:** Note-taking services; Reader services; Tape recorders; Tutors. **Career services:** Alumni network; Alumni services; Career assessment; Career/job search classes; Internships; Regional alumni.

FACILITIES

Housing: Apartments for single students; Coed dorms; Men's dorms; Women's dorms. **Special Academic Facilities/Equipment:** Alva de Mars Megan Chapel Art Center, New Hampshire Institute of Politics & Political Library, Izart Observatory, Koonz Theatre, Comiskey Studio (Fine Arts), Poisson Hall, Residential Living & Learning Community.

CAMPUS LIFE

Environment: City. **Activities:** Campus Ministries; Choral groups; Dance; Drama/theater; International Student Organization; Jazz band; Literary magazine; Model UN; Music ensembles; Musical theater; Student government; Student newspaper; Television station; Yearbook. 80 registered organizations, 11 honor societies, 7 religious organizations on campus. **Athletics (Intercollegiate):** *Men:* baseball, basketball, cross-country, football, golf, ice hockey, lacrosse, skiing (downhill/Alpine), soccer, tennis. *Women:* basketball, cross-country, field hockey, golf, ice hockey, lacrosse, skiing (downhill/Alpine), soccer, softball, tennis, volleyball. **On-Campus Highlights:** Residence Hall (Living and Learning Community).

ADMISSIONS

Freshman Academic Profile: Average high school GPA 3.3. 27% in top 10% of high school class, 55% in top 25% of high school class, 83% in top 50% of high school class. 65% from public high schools. **Test Scores:** SAT Math middle 50% range 550–650. SAT EBRW middle 50% range 570–660. ACT middle 50% range 24–29. **Basis for Candidate Selection:** *Very important factors include:* rigor of secondary school record, academic GPA. *Important factors include:* recommendation(s), extracurricular activities, character/personal qualities, volunteer work. *Other factors include:* class rank, application essay, standardized test scores, talent/ability, first generation, alumni/ae relation, geographical residence, racial/ethnic status, level of applicant's interest. **Freshman Admission Requirements:** High school diploma is required and GED is accepted. *Academic units required:* 4 English, 3 math, 3 science, 2 science labs, 2 foreign language, 2 social studies. *Academic units recommended:* 4 English, 4 math, 4 science, 2 science labs, 4 foreign language, 4 social studies. **Freshman Admission Statistics:** 3,896 applied, 77% admitted, 20% enrolled. **Transfer Admission Requirements:** High school transcript, college transcript(s), essay or personal statement, standardized test scores, statement of good standing from prior institution(s). Minimum college GPA of 2.5 required. Lowest grade transferable C. **General Admission Information:** Application fee $50. Regular application deadline 2/1. Non-fall registration accepted. Admission may be deferred for a maximum of 1 year.

COSTS AND FINANCIAL AID

Annual tuition $42,840. Room and board $15,120. Required fees $1,300. Average book and supplies expense $1,000. **Required Forms and Deadlines:** CSS/Financial Aid PROFILE; FAFSA; Noncustodial PROFILE;. **Types of Aid:** *Need-based scholarships/grants:* College/university scholarship or grant aid from institutional funds; Federal Pell; Private scholarships; SEOG; State scholarships/grants. *Loans:* Direct PLUS loans; Direct Subsidized Stafford Loans; Direct Unsubsidized Stafford Loans. **Student Employment:** Federal Work-Study Program available. Institutional employment available. **Financial Aid Statistics:** 100% needy freshmen, 100% needy undergrads receive need-based scholarship or grant aid. 26% freshmen, 19% undergrads receive non-need-based scholarship or grant aid. 77% freshmen, 81% undergrads receive need-based self-help aid. 4% freshmen, 5% undergrads receive athletic scholarships. 99% freshmen, 98% undergrads receive any aid. 80% undergrads borrow to pay for school. Average cumulative indebtedness $32,769. **Criteria awarding aid:** *Need-based:* Academics, Alumni affiliation, Athletics, Leadership, Minority status, Music/drama, Religious affiliation. *Non-need-based:* Academics, Alumni affiliation, Athletics, Leadership, Music/drama, State/district residency.

SAINT ANTHONY COLLEGE OF NURSING

5658 East State Street, Rockford, IL 61108-2468
Phone: 815-227-2141 **Financial Aid Phone:** 815-395-5089
E-mail: admissions@sacn.edu
Fax: 815-227-2730 **Website:** www.sacn.edu

This private school, affiliated with the Roman Catholic Church, was founded in 1915.

RATINGS
Admissions Selectivity Rating: 60*   **Fire Safety Rating:** 60*   **Green Rating:** 60*

STUDENTS AND FACULTY
Enrollment: 230. **Student Body:** 89% female, 11% male, 10% out-of-state, 0% international. Asian 5%, African American 2%, Caucasian 77%, Hispanic 13%, Native American 0%, Pacific Islander <1%, Two or more races 2%, Race unknown <1%.
Retention and Graduation: 100% freshmen return for sophomore year.
Faculty: Student/faculty ratio 7:1. 23 full-time faculty, 22% hold PhDs, 9% are members of minority groups, 91% are women. 0% of classes are taught by teaching assistants.

ACADEMICS
Degrees: Bachelor's; Doctoral degree—other; Master's; Post-master's certificate. **Classes:** Most classes have 20–29 students. Most lab/discussion sessions have 10–19 students. **Most popular majors:** Registered Nursing/Registered Nurse. **Special Study Options:** Independent study.

CAMPUS LIFE
Environment: City. **Activities:** Student government. 1 registered organizations on campus.

ADMISSIONS
Basis for Candidate Selection: *Very important factors include:* academic GPA. *Important factors include:* standardized test scores. *Other factors include:* level of applicant's interest. **Freshman Admission Requirements:** High school diploma is required and GED is accepted. *Academic units required:* 2.5 science. **Transfer Admission Requirements:** College transcript(s), essay or personal statement, interview. Minimum college GPA of 2.5 required. Lowest grade transferable C. **General Admission Information:** Application fee $75. Priority deadline 9/15. Regular application deadline 2/15. Non-fall registration accepted.

COSTS AND FINANCIAL AID
Annual tuition $22,144. **Types of Aid:** *Need-based scholarships/grants:* College/university scholarship or grant aid from institutional funds; Federal Pell; Private scholarships; State scholarships/grants. *Loans:* Direct PLUS loans; Direct Subsidized Stafford Loans; Direct Unsubsidized Stafford Loans. **Financial Aid Statistics:** 64% needy undergrads receive need-based scholarship or grant aid. 2% undergrads receive non-need-based scholarship or grant aid. 96% undergrads receive need-based self-help aid. 0% undergrads receive athletic scholarships. 86% undergrads receive any aid. **Criteria awarding aid:** *Need-based:* Academics, Leadership. *Non-need-based:* Academics.

ST. BONAVENTURE UNIVERSITY

3261 West State Road, St. Bonaventure, NY 14778
Phone: 716-375-2434 **Financial Aid Phone:** 716 375 7888
E-mail: admissions@sbu.edu **CEEB Code:** 2793
Fax: 716-375-4005 **Website:** www.sbu.edu **ACT Code:** 2882

This private school, affiliated with the Roman Catholic Church, was founded in 1858. It has a 500 acre campus.

RATINGS
Admissions Selectivity Rating: 79   **Fire Safety Rating:** 83   **Green Rating:** 95

STUDENTS AND FACULTY
Enrollment: 1,787. **Student Body:** 47% female, 53% male, 25% out-of-state, 3% international (24 countries represented). Asian 4%, African American 6%, Caucasian 74%, Hispanic 7%, Native American 1%, Pacific Islander <1%, Two or more races 2%, Race unknown 4%.
Retention and Graduation: 84% freshmen return for sophomore year. 69% freshmen graduate within 4 years. 74% freshmen graduate within 6 years.
Faculty: Student/faculty ratio 12:1. 142 full-time faculty, 82% hold PhDs, 6% are members of minority groups, 42% are women. 0% of classes are taught by teaching assistants.

ACADEMICS
Degrees: Bachelor's; Master's; Post-bachelor's certificate; Post-master's certificate. **Classes:** Most classes have 20–29 students. Most lab/discussion sessions have 20–29 students. **Most popular majors:** Biology/Biological Sciences, General; Business Administration and Management, General; Marketing/Marketing Management, General. **Special Study Options:** Accelerated program; Cross-registration; Double major; Exchange student program (domestic); Honors program; Independent study; Internships; Liberal arts/career combination; Student-designed major; Study abroad; Teacher certification program. **Honors programs:** The Honors Program brings highly motivated and academically qualified students into novel, stimulating, and productive interaction with faculty. **Disability Services offered:** Note-taking services; Reader services; Tape recorders; Tutors. **Career services:** Alumni network; Alumni services; Career assessment; Career/job search classes; Internships; Regional alumni.

FACILITIES
Housing: Apartments for single students; Coed dorms; Men's dorms; Special housing for disabled students; Theme housing; Wellness housing; Women's dorms; 70% of campus accessible to physically disabled. **Special Academic Facilities/Equipment:** Quick Center for the Arts, Digital Conferencing and Media Center, Franciscan Center for Social Concern, Franciscan Institute, Western New York Cybersecurity Research Center, Swan Business Center.

CAMPUS LIFE
Environment: Village. **Activities:** Campus Ministries; Choral groups; Concert band; Dance; Drama/theater; International Student Organization; Jazz band; Literary magazine; Model UN; Music ensembles; Pep band; Radio station; Student government; Student newspaper; Television station. 60 registered organizations, 15 honor societies, 4 religious organizations on campus. **Athletics (Intercollegiate):** *Men:* baseball, basketball, cross-country, diving, golf, soccer, swimming, tennis. *Women:* basketball, cross-country, diving, lacrosse, soccer, softball, swimming, tennis. **On-Campus Highlights:** Reilly Center. **Environmental Initiatives:** New campus construction: St. Bonaventure's William F. Walsh Science Center and the Friedsam Memorial Library Rare Books addition use underground water for cooling systems, reducing the release of carbon dioxide.

ADMISSIONS
Freshman Academic Profile: Average high school GPA 3.3. 16% in top 10% of high school class, 39% in top 25% of high school class, 73% in top 50% of high school class. 76% from public high schools. **Test Scores:** SAT Math middle 50% range 520–620. SAT EBRW middle 50% range 510–620. ACT middle 50% range 19–26. **Basis for Candidate Selection:** *Very important factors include:* rigor of secondary school record, academic GPA, recommendation(s), character/personal qualities. *Important factors include:* application essay, standardized test scores, extracurricular activities, talent/ability. *Other factors include:* class rank, interview, first generation, alumni/ae relation, geographical residence, state residency, work experience, level of applicant's interest. **Freshman Admission Requirements:** High school diploma is required and GED is accepted. *Academic units recommended:* 4 English, 3 math, 3 science, 3 science labs, 2 foreign language, 4 social studies. **Freshman Admission Statistics:** 3,058 applied, 75% admitted, 21% enrolled. **Transfer Admission Requirements:** High school transcript, college transcript(s), statement of good standing from prior institution(s). Minimum college GPA of 2.0 required. Lowest grade transferable C. **General Admission Information:** Priority deadline 2/15. Regular application deadline 7/30. Non-fall registration accepted. Admission may be deferred for a maximum of 1 year.

COSTS AND FINANCIAL AID
Annual tuition $34,366. Room and board $13,160. Required fees $1,065. Average book and supplies expense $800. **Required Forms and Deadlines:** FAFSA; State aid form. **Notification of Awards:** Applicants will be notified of awards on a rolling basis beginning 1/1. **Types of Aid:** *Need-based scholarships/grants:* College/university scholarship or grant aid from institutional funds; Federal Pell; Private scholarships; SEOG; State scholarships/grants. *Loans:* Direct PLUS loans; Direct Subsidized Stafford Loans; Direct Unsubsidized Stafford Loans. **Student Employment:** Federal Work-Study Program available. Institutional employment available. **Financial Aid Statistics:** 100% needy freshmen, 99% needy undergrads receive need-based scholarship or grant aid.

94% freshmen, 91% undergrads receive non-need-based scholarship or grant aid. 82% freshmen, 83% undergrads receive need-based self-help aid. 10% freshmen, 7% undergrads receive athletic scholarships. 98% freshmen, 94% undergrads receive any aid. Average cumulative indebtedness $34,877. **Criteria awarding aid:** *Need-based:* Job skills. *Non-need-based:* Academics, Athletics, Minority status, Music/drama, Religious affiliation, State/district residency.

ST. CATHERINE UNIVERSITY

2004 Randolph Avenue, Saint Paul, MN 55105
Financial Aid Phone: 651-690-6540
E-mail: admissions@stkate.edu **CEEB Code:** 6105
Fax: 651-690-8868 **Website:** www.stkate.edu **ACT Code:** 2096

This private school, affiliated with the Roman Catholic Church, was founded in 1905. It has a 110 acre campus.

RATINGS
Admissions Selectivity Rating: 83   Fire Safety Rating: 88   Green Rating: 60*

STUDENTS AND FACULTY
Enrollment: 3,100. **Student Body:** 97% female, 3% male, 12% out-of-state, 1% international (34 countries represented). Asian 11%, African American 10%, Caucasian 61%, Hispanic 9%, Native American <1%, Pacific Islander <1%, Two or more races 4%, Race unknown 3%.
Retention and Graduation: 81% freshmen return for sophomore year. 37% freshmen graduate within 4 years. 66% freshmen graduate within 6 years. 28% grads go on to further study within 1 year. 2% grads pursue arts and sciences degrees. 4% grads pursue law degrees. 10% grads pursue business degrees. 2% grads pursue medical degrees. **Faculty:** Student/faculty ratio 10:1. 292 full-time faculty, 59% hold PhDs, 12% are members of minority groups, 81% are women. 0% of classes are taught by teaching assistants.

ACADEMICS
Degrees: Associate; Bachelor's; Certificate; Doctoral degree—professional practice; Master's; Post-bachelor's certificate; Terminal Associate. **Classes:** Most classes have 10–19 students. Most lab/discussion sessions have 10–19 students. **Most popular majors:** Social Work; Registered Nursing, Nursing Administration, Nursing Research and Clinical Nursing; Elementary Education and Teaching. **Special Study Options:** Cross-registration; Distance learning; Double major; Dual enrollment; Exchange student program (domestic); Honors program; Independent study; Internships; Student-designed major; Study abroad; Teacher certification program. **Honors programs:** Antonian Scholars are students who exhibit exceptional academic performance in the University and who show promise as learners, researchers, writers, performers, campus or community leaders, and/or creative thinkers. Scholars possess both creativity and love of learning. Scholars are inquisitive and hard working. They love challenges. Scholars are also students who want to take an active role in "tailoring" their college experiences to their needs, interests, and passions. Scholars complete a five-component program that includes interdisciplinary seminars, as well as optional honors sections of TRW and/or GSJ, optional study abroad experiences, and a required Senior Honors Project. Scholars participate in at least two and up to four Honors seminars specifically designed for their learning needs and offered in an interdisciplinary format with two professors. All scholars as seniors are required to enroll in a four-credit independent study course in which they develop a senior project based on an interest, curiosity, or passion. Senior projects are completed with a faculty advisor and an interdisciplinary faculty committee who provide guidance and feedback on the project. Other privileges of membership in the Antonian Scholars Honors Program include priority registration for courses each semester, special diplomas and commencement recognition, and leadership opportunities in the Honors Program Student Organization. Scholars also have opportunities on a regular basis to socialize, network, and converse with others in the Honors Program. Scholars have access to the Honor's Hub in Coeur de Catherine. The Hub is a quiet place to study when you need one and also a place where Scholars may gather for special activities or conversation. **Disability Services offered:** Note-taking services; Reader services; Tape recorders; Tutors. **Career services:** Alumni network; Alumni services; Career assessment; Career/job search classes; Internships.

FACILITIES
Housing: Apartments for single students; Theme housing; Wellness housing; Women's dorms; 90% of campus accessible to physically disabled. **Special Academic Facilities/Equipment:** Art gallery, theatre, recital hall, experimental psychology lab, language lab, observatory. **Campus Network:** 100% of classrooms, 100% of dorms, 100% of student union, 100% of libraries, 100% of dining areas, 80% of common outdoor areas have wireless network access.

CAMPUS LIFE
Environment: Metropolis. **Activities:** Campus Ministries; Choral groups; Dance; Drama/theater; International Student Organization; Literary magazine; Music ensembles; Musical theater; Radio station; Student government; Student newspaper. 40 registered organizations, 24 honor societies, 4 religious organizations, 1 sorority on campus. **Athletics (Intercollegiate):** *Women:* basketball, cross-country, diving, ice hockey, soccer, softball, swimming, tennis, track/field (outdoor), track/field (indoor), volleyball. **On-Campus Highlights:** Coeur de Catherine. **Environmental Initiatives:** Retrofitted older building with green roof.

ADMISSIONS
Freshman Academic Profile: Average high school GPA 3.6. 24% in top 10% of high school class, 62% in top 25% of high school class, 94% in top 50% of high school class. 86% from public high schools. **Test Scores:** SAT Math middle 50% range 510–645. SAT EBRW middle 50% range 530–665. ACT middle 50% range 21–26. **Basis for Candidate Selection:** *Very important factors include:* rigor of secondary school record. *Important factors include:* class rank, academic GPA, application essay, standardized test scores, recommendation(s). *Other factors include:* interview, first generation, level of applicant's interest. **Freshman Admission Requirements:** High school diploma is required and GED is accepted. *Academic units recommended:* 4 English, 3 math, 2 science, 4 foreign language, 2 social studies. **Freshman Admission Statistics:** 2,682 applied, 70% admitted, 21% enrolled. **Transfer Admission Requirements:** High school transcript, college transcript(s), statement of good standing from prior institution(s). Minimum college GPA of 2.0 required. Lowest grade transferable C-. **General Admission Information:** Priority deadline 4/15. Non-fall registration accepted. Admission may be deferred for a maximum of 1 year.

COSTS AND FINANCIAL AID
Required Forms and Deadlines: FAFSA; Institution's own financial aid form. **Types of Aid:** *Need-based scholarships/grants:* College/university scholarship or grant aid from institutional funds; Federal Nursing Scholarships; Federal Pell; Private scholarships; SEOG; State scholarships/grants. *Loans:* Direct PLUS loans; Direct Subsidized Stafford Loans; Direct Unsubsidized Stafford Loans. **Student Employment:** Federal Work-Study Program available. Institutional employment available. **Financial Aid Statistics:** 85% needy freshmen, 76% needy undergrads receive need-based scholarship or grant aid. 100% freshmen, 98% undergrads receive non-need-based scholarship or grant aid. 73% freshmen, 77% undergrads receive need-based self-help aid. 0% freshmen, 0% undergrads receive athletic scholarships. 94% freshmen, 93% undergrads receive any aid. 84% undergrads borrow to pay for school. Average cumulative indebtedness $38,199. **Criteria awarding aid:** *Non-need-based:* Academics, Alumni affiliation, Leadership, State/district residency.

SAINT CHARLES BORROMEO SEMINARY

100 East Wynnewood Road, Wynnewood, PA 19096
Phone: 610-785-6291
Fax: 610-617-9267 **Website:** www.scs.edu

This is a private school.

RATINGS
Admissions Selectivity Rating: 82   Fire Safety Rating: 60*   Green Rating: 60*

STUDENTS AND FACULTY
Enrollment: 47. **Student Body:** 0% female, 100% male, 25% out-of-state, 0% international. Asian 2%, African American 0%, Caucasian 89%, Hispanic 9%, Native American 0%, Pacific Islander 0%, Two or more races 0%, Race unknown 0%.
Retention and Graduation: 77% freshmen return for sophomore year.
Faculty: Student/faculty ratio 6:1. 16 full-time faculty, 75% hold PhDs, 0% are members of minority groups, 13% are women.

ACADEMICS
Degrees: Bachelor's; Certificate; Master's. **Classes:** Most classes have 10–19 students. **Special Study Options:** Accelerated program; English as a Second Language (ESL); Independent study.

FACILITIES

Housing: Men's dorms; Wellness housing.

CAMPUS LIFE

Activities: Choral groups; Drama/theater; Music ensembles; Student government; Student newspaper.

ADMISSIONS

Freshman Academic Profile: 33% in top 25% of high school class, 67% in top 50% of high school class. **Test Scores:** SAT Math middle 50% range 530–640. SAT EBRW middle 50% range 550–690. **Basis for Candidate Selection:** *Very important factors include:* application essay, recommendation(s), interview, religious affiliation/commitment, level of applicant's interest. *Important factors include:* character/personal qualities. *Other factors include:* talent/ability. **Freshman Admission Requirements:** High school diploma is required and GED is accepted. *Academic units recommended:* 4 English, 3 math, 3 science, 3 foreign language, 3 social studies. **Freshman Admission Statistics:** 8 applied, 100% admitted, 88% enrolled. **General Admission Information:** Priority deadline 3/31. Regular application deadline 7/31. Non-fall registration accepted.

COSTS AND FINANCIAL AID

Annual tuition $17,600. Room and board $11,820. Required fees $1,175. Average book and supplies expense $1,100. **Required Forms and Deadlines:** FAFSA; Institution's own financial aid form. **Notification of Awards:** Applicants will be notified of awards on a rolling basis beginning 3/1. **Types of Aid:** *Need-based scholarships/grants:* College/university scholarship or grant aid from institutional funds; Federal Pell; SEOG; State scholarships/grants. *Loans:* Direct PLUS loans; Direct Subsidized Stafford Loans; Direct Unsubsidized Stafford Loans. **Financial Aid Statistics:** 57% needy freshmen, 48% needy undergrads receive need-based scholarship or grant aid. 100% freshmen, 100% undergrads receive non-need-based scholarship or grant aid. 100% freshmen, 64% undergrads receive need-based self-help aid. 0% freshmen, 0% undergrads receive athletic scholarships.

ST. EDWARD'S UNIVERSITY

3001 South Congress Avenue, Austin, TX 78704-6489
Phone: 512-448-8500 **Financial Aid Phone:** 512-448-8523
E-mail: seu.admit@stedwards.edu **CEEB Code:** 6619
Fax: 512-464-8877 **Website:** https://www.stedwards.edu **ACT Code:** 4156

This private school, affiliated with the Roman Catholic Church, was founded in 1885. It has a 160 acre campus.

RATINGS

Admissions Selectivity Rating: 76 **Fire Safety Rating:** 92 **Green Rating:** 90

STUDENTS AND FACULTY

Enrollment: 3,784. **Student Body:** 62% female, 38% male, 14% out-of-state, 8% international (57 countries represented). Asian 3%, African American 4%, Caucasian 36%, Hispanic 44%, Native American 1%, Pacific Islander <1%, Two or more races 3%, Race unknown 1%.
Retention and Graduation: 78% freshmen return for sophomore year. 52% freshmen graduate within 4 years. 64% freshmen graduate within 6 years. **Faculty:** Student/faculty ratio 15:1. 183 full-time faculty, 91% hold PhDs, 19% are members of minority groups, 53% are women. 0% of classes are taught by teaching assistants.

ACADEMICS

Degrees: Bachelor's; Master's; Post-bachelor's certificate. **Classes:** Most classes have 20–29 students. **Special Study Options:** Double major; Honors program; Internships; Study abroad; Teacher certification program. **Honors programs:** The Honors Program is designed for students in the traditional undergraduate program who are academically talented and passionate about learning. Students in the program take a minimum of seven Honors seminars and complete an Honors Senior Thesis project. They must maintain a minimum GPA in Honors courses of 3.50. Many Honors seminars may be substituted for General Education requirements. The Honors Program offers students small classes with other highly motivated students and distinguished professors. Classes require a high level of student participation and emphasize writing and critical thinking. **Disability Services offered:** Note-taking services; Reader services; Tape recorders; Tutors. **Career services:** Alumni network; Alumni services; Career assessment; Career/job search classes; Internships; Regional alumni.

FACILITIES

Housing: Apartments for single students; Coed dorms; Special housing for disabled students; Theme housing; 93% of campus accessible to physically disabled. **Special Academic Facilities/Equipment:** St. Edwards University's historic Main Building is a registered Texas Historic Landmark, and it, along with Holy Cross Hall, earned St. Edwards the distinction of National Historic Site on March 16, 1973. The Munday Library opened to students in fall 2013.

CAMPUS LIFE

Environment: Metropolis. **Activities:** Campus Ministries; Choral groups; Concert band; Dance; Drama/theater; International Student Organization; Jazz band; Literary magazine; Model UN; Music ensembles; Pep band; Radio station; Student government; Student newspaper; Student-run film society; Television station. 136 registered organizations, 13 honor societies, 4 religious organizations on campus. **Athletics (Intercollegiate):** *Men:* baseball, basketball, golf, soccer, tennis. *Women:* basketball, golf, soccer, softball, tennis, volleyball. **On-Campus Highlights:** Historic Main Building (view of Austin). **Environmental Initiatives:** The university supports a diverse energy portfolio including green energy. St. Edward's University partners with Austin Energy's GreenChoice Renewable Energy program as a Patron level member. St. Edward's University, and 20 other Patron level members from across the city of Austin, make a multiyear commitment to purchasing wind energy and help to make a huge impact. In 2017, Austin Energy supplied more than 708 million kWh of Texas wind to customers, like St. Edward's.

ADMISSIONS

Freshman Academic Profile: 62% from public high schools. **Test Scores:** SAT Math middle 50% range 530–620. SAT EBRW middle 50% range 550–650. ACT middle 50% range 22–27. **Basis for Candidate Selection:** *Very important factors include:* rigor of secondary school record, academic GPA, application essay, standardized test scores. *Important factors include:* class rank, recommendation(s), extracurricular activities. *Other factors include:* interview, talent/ability, character/personal qualities, first generation, alumni/ae relation, geographical residence, state residency, religious affiliation/commitment, racial/ethnic status, work experience, level of applicant's interest. **Freshman Admission Requirements:** High school diploma is required and GED is accepted. *Academic units required:* 4 English, 3 math, 2 science, 2 science labs, 2 foreign language, 1 social studies, 2 history. *Academic units recommended:* 4 English, 4 math, 3 science, 3 science labs, 3 foreign language, 1 social studies, 3 history, 1 academic elective, 1 computer science. **Freshman Admission Statistics:** 5,577 applied, 86% admitted, 17% enrolled. **Transfer Admission Requirements:** High school transcript, college transcript(s), essay or personal statement. Minimum college GPA of 2.50 required. Lowest grade transferable C. **General Admission Information:** Application fee $50. Priority deadline 2/1. Regular application deadline 5/1. Non-fall registration accepted. Admission may be deferred for a maximum of 1 year.

COSTS AND FINANCIAL AID

Annual tuition $46,690. Room and board $14,004. Required fees $750. Average book and supplies expense $1,200. **Required Forms and Deadlines:** FAFSA. **Notification of Awards:** Applicants will be notified of awards on a rolling basis beginning 11/1. **Types of Aid:** *Need-based scholarships/grants:* College/university scholarship or grant aid from institutional funds; Federal Pell; Private scholarships; SEOG; State scholarships/grants. *Loans:* Direct PLUS loans; Direct Subsidized Stafford Loans; Direct Unsubsidized Stafford Loans. **Student Employment:** Federal Work-Study Program available. Institutional employment available. **Financial Aid Statistics:** 90% needy freshmen, 92% needy undergrads receive need-based scholarship or grant aid. 72% freshmen, 69% undergrads receive non-need-based scholarship or grant aid. 72% freshmen, 74% undergrads receive need-based self-help aid. 4% freshmen, 5% undergrads receive athletic scholarships. 91% freshmen, 85% undergrads receive any aid. 63% undergrads borrow to pay for school. Average cumulative indebtedness $38,406. **Criteria awarding aid:** *Need-based:* Academics. *Non-need-based:* Academics, Athletics, Music/drama, State/district residency.

SAINT FRANCIS MEDICAL CENTER COLLEGE OF NURSING

511 NE. Greenleaf Street, Peoria, IL 61603
Phone: 309-624-8980 **Financial Aid Phone:** (309)655-4119
E-mail: janice.e.farquharson@osfhealthcare.org
Fax: 309-624-8973 **Website:** http://www.sfmccon.edu/

This private school, affiliated with the Roman Catholic Church, was founded in 1905.

RATINGS
Admissions Selectivity Rating: 60*   Fire Safety Rating: 98   Green Rating: 60*

STUDENTS AND FACULTY
Enrollment: 408. **Student Body:** 90% female, 10% male, 1% out-of-state, <1% international (2 countries represented). Asian 4%, African American 2%, Caucasian 91%, Hispanic 2%, Native American 0%, Pacific Islander 0%, Two or more races <1%, Race unknown 1%.
Faculty: Student/faculty ratio 10:1. 36 full-time faculty, 33% hold PhDs, 0% are members of minority groups, 97% are women. 0% of classes are taught by teaching assistants.

ACADEMICS
Degrees: Bachelor's; Master's; Post-master's certificate. **Classes:** Most classes have 10–19 students. Most lab/discussion sessions have 10–19 students. **Special Study Options:** Accelerated program; Distance learning; Independent study; Study abroad. **Disability Services offered:** Tutors.

FACILITIES
Housing: Coed dorms; 1% of campus accessible to physically disabled.

CAMPUS LIFE
Environment: City. **Activities:** Student government. 1 registered organizations on campus.

ADMISSIONS
Freshman Admission Requirements: High school diploma is required and GED is accepted. **Transfer Admission Requirements:** High school transcript, college transcript(s), essay or personal statement, statement of good standing from prior institution(s). Minimum college GPA of 2.50 required. Lowest grade transferable C. **General Admission Information:** Application fee $50. Priority deadline 9/15.

COSTS AND FINANCIAL AID
Annual tuition $19,140. Room and board $3,500. Average book and supplies expense $1,218. **Required Forms and Deadlines:** FAFSA; Institution's own financial aid form. **Notification of Awards:** Applicants will be notified of awards on a rolling basis beginning 5/15. **Types of Aid:** *Need-based scholarships/grants:* College/university scholarship or grant aid from institutional funds; Federal Pell; Private scholarships; State scholarships/grants. *Loans:* Direct PLUS loans; Direct Subsidized Stafford Loans; Direct Unsubsidized Stafford Loans. **Financial Aid Statistics:** 75% needy undergrads receive need-based scholarship or grant aid. 0% undergrads receive non-need-based scholarship or grant aid. 86% undergrads receive need-based self-help aid. 0% undergrads receive athletic scholarships. 81% undergrads receive any aid. **Criteria awarding aid:** *Non-need-based:* Academics, Alumni affiliation.

SAINT FRANCIS UNIVERSITY (PA)

PO Box 600, Loretto, PA 15940
Phone: 814-472-3000 **Financial Aid Phone:** 814-472-3010
E-mail: admissions@francis.edu **CEEB Code:** 2797
Fax: 814-472-3335 **ACT Code:** 3682

This private school, affiliated with the Roman Catholic Church, was founded in 1847. It has a 600 acre campus.

RATINGS
Admissions Selectivity Rating: 80   Fire Safety Rating: 84   Green Rating: 60*

STUDENTS AND FACULTY
Enrollment: 1,703. **Student Body:** 63% female, 37% male, 20% out-of-state, 5% international (25 countries represented). Asian 1%, African American 6%, Caucasian 79%, Hispanic 2%, Native American <1%, Pacific Islander <1%, Two or more races 1%, Race unknown 6%.
Retention and Graduation: 86% freshmen return for sophomore year. 29% grads go on to further study within 1 year. 5% grads pursue arts and sciences degrees. 3% grads pursue law degrees. 9% grads pursue business degrees. 3% grads pursue medical degrees. **Faculty:** Student/faculty ratio 14:1. 125 full-time faculty, 70% hold PhDs, 7% are members of minority groups, 56% are women. 0% of classes are taught by teaching assistants.

ACADEMICS
Degrees: Associate; Bachelor's; Doctoral degree—professional practice; Master's; Post-bachelor's certificate. **Classes:** Most classes have 10–19 students. Most lab/discussion sessions have 10–19 students. **Most popular majors:** Business/Commerce, General; Health Professions and Related Clinical Sciences, Other; Physician Assistant. **Special Study Options:** Cooperative education program; Distance learning; Double major; English as a Second Language (ESL); Honors program; Independent study; Internships; Liberal arts/career combination; Student-designed major; Study abroad; Teacher certification program. **Honors programs:** The Saint Francis University (SFU) Honors Program is designed to challenge highly motivated students by making them part of a community of learners, while at the same time affording them the opportunity to devise a personal program of study. Students are introduced to the Honors Program through a year-long learning community experience consisting of a four-course sequence with intense critical thinking, writing and speaking components. Successful completion of this sequence waives the university speech requirement for the Honors student. **Combined degree programs:** BA/DDS; BA/MD. **Disability Services offered:** Note-taking services; Tape recorders; Tutors. **Career services:** Alumni network; Career assessment; Career/job search classes; Internships.

FACILITIES
Housing: Apartments for single students; Coed dorms; Fraternity/sorority housing; Men's dorms; Women's dorms; 20% of campus accessible to physically disabled. **Special Academic Facilities/Equipment:** Art museum, elementary-level library for education majors, physician assistant practice facilities, cadaver lab, physical therapy lab, Center of Excellence for Remote and Medically Underserved Areas.

CAMPUS LIFE
Environment: Rural. **Activities:** Campus Ministries; Choral groups; Dance; Drama/theater; Jazz band; Marching band; Music ensembles; Pep band; Radio station; Student government; Student newspaper; Student-run film society; Television station; Yearbook. 70 registered organizations, 9 honor societies, 10 religious organizations, 6 fraternities, 5 sororities on campus. **Athletics (Intercollegiate):** *Men:* basketball, cross-country, football, golf, soccer, swimming, tennis, track/field (outdoor), track/field (indoor), volleyball. *Women:* basketball, cross-country, field hockey, golf, lacrosse, soccer, softball, swimming, tennis, track/field (outdoor), track/field (indoor), volleyball. **On-Campus Highlights:** DiSepio Institute.

ADMISSIONS
Freshman Academic Profile: 30% in top 10% of high school class, 50% in top 25% of high school class, 83% in top 50% of high school class. 79% from public high schools. **Test Scores:** SAT Math middle 50% range 470–590. SAT EBRW middle 50% range 460–570. ACT middle 50% range 21–26. **Basis for Candidate Selection:** *Very important factors include:* rigor of secondary school record, class rank, academic GPA, standardized test scores, extracurricular activities. *Important factors include:* application essay, recommendation(s), interview, talent/ability, character/personal qualities, volunteer work. *Other factors include:* alumni/ae relation, work experience. **Freshman Admission Requirements:** High school diploma is required and GED is accepted. *Academic units required:* 4 English, 2 math, 1 science, 2 social studies, 7 academic electives. *Academic units recommended:* 4 English, 4 math, 2 science, 1 science lab, 2 foreign language, 2 social studies, 7 academic electives. **Freshman Admission Statistics:** 2,045 applied, 70% admitted, 28% enrolled. **Transfer Admission Requirements:** High school transcript, college transcript(s), standardized test scores, statement of good standing from prior institution(s). Minimum college GPA of 2.0 required. Lowest grade transferable C. **General Admission Information:** Application fee $30. Priority deadline 4/1. Non-fall registration accepted.

COSTS AND FINANCIAL AID
Annual tuition $31,078. Room and board $11,190. Required fees $1,100. Average book and supplies expense $2,000. **Required Forms and Deadlines:** FAFSA. **Notification of Awards:** Applicants will be notified of awards on a rolling basis beginning 3/1. **Types of Aid:** *Need-based scholarships/grants:* College/university scholarship or grant aid from institutional funds; Federal Pell;

Private scholarships; SEOG; State scholarships/grants. **Student Employment:** Federal Work-Study Program available. Institutional employment available. **Financial Aid Statistics:** 55% needy freshmen, 59% needy undergrads receive need-based scholarship or grant aid. 100% freshmen, 94% undergrads receive non-need-based scholarship or grant aid. 72% freshmen, 77% undergrads receive need-based self-help aid. 33% freshmen, 27% undergrads receive athletic scholarships. 98% freshmen receive any aid. **Criteria awarding aid:** *Non-need-based:* Academics, Alumni affiliation, Athletics, Leadership, Music/drama, Religious affiliation.

ST. JOHN FISHER COLLEGE

3690 East Avenue, Rochester, NY 14618-3597
Phone: 585-385-8064 **Financial Aid Phone:** 585-385-8042
E-mail: admissions@sjfc.edu **CEEB Code:** 2798
Fax: 585-385-8386 **Website:** http://www.sjfc.edu/ **ACT Code:** 2798

This private school, affiliated with the Roman Catholic Church, was founded in 1948. It has a 154 acre campus.

RATINGS

Admissions Selectivity Rating: 85   Fire Safety Rating: 93   Green Rating: 76

STUDENTS AND FACULTY

Enrollment: 2,648. **Student Body:** 59% female, 41% male, 4% out-of-state, <1% international (4 countries represented). Asian 3%, African American 4%, Caucasian 84%, Hispanic 5%, Native American <1%, Pacific Islander 0%, Two or more races 2%, Race unknown 1%.
Retention and Graduation: 88% freshmen return for sophomore year. 67% freshmen graduate within 4 years. 75% freshmen graduate within 6 years. 3% grads pursue law degrees. 9% grads pursue business degrees. 3% grads pursue medical degrees. **Faculty:** Student/faculty ratio 11:1. 230 full-time faculty, 87% hold PhDs, 17% are members of minority groups, 58% are women. 0% of classes are taught by teaching assistants.

ACADEMICS

Degrees: Bachelor's; Certificate; Doctoral degree—professional practice; Doctoral degree research/scholarship; Master's; Post-bachelor's certificate; Post-master's certificate. **Classes:** Most classes have 20–29 students. Most lab/discussion sessions have 10–19 students. **Most popular majors:** Registered Nursing/Registered Nurse; Biology/Biological Sciences, General; Business Administration and Management, General. **Special Study Options:** Accelerated program; Cross-registration; Distance learning; Double major; Exchange student program (domestic); Honors program; Independent study; Internships; Liberal arts/career combination; Student-designed major; Study abroad; Teacher certification program; Weekend college. **Honors programs:** St John Fisher College Honors Program; Science Scholars Program. **Combined degree programs:** BA/JD. **Disability Services offered:** Note-taking services; Reader services; Tape recorders; Tutors. **Career services:** Alumni network; Career assessment; Career/job search classes; Internships; Regional alumni.

FACILITIES

Housing: Coed dorms; Special housing for disabled students; 100% of campus accessible to physically disabled. **Special Academic Facilities/Equipment:** Student Campus Center, State-of-the-Art Laboratories, Two Electron Microscopes, Multimedia Computer Lab, TV Studio Childcare Center (for observation and development), Cyber Café, Skalny Welcome Center Art Gallery.

CAMPUS LIFE

Environment: City. **Activities:** Campus Ministries; Choral groups; Dance; Drama/theater; Literary magazine; Musical theater; Pep band; Student government; Student newspaper; Television station; Yearbook. 79 registered organizations, 10 honor societies, 2 religious organizations on campus. **Athletics (Intercollegiate):** *Men:* baseball, basketball, football, golf, lacrosse, soccer, tennis. *Women:* basketball, golf, lacrosse, soccer, softball, tennis, volleyball. **On-Campus Highlights:** Upper Quad Dorm. **Environmental Initiatives:** Commitment to buying local, fresh, organic produce and foods—https://www.sjfc.edu/student-life/dining-services/.

ADMISSIONS

Freshman Academic Profile: Average high school GPA 3.6. 21% in top 10% of high school class, 55% in top 25% of high school class, 90% in top 50% of high school class. 92% from public high schools. **Test Scores:** SAT Math

middle 50% range 540–640. SAT EBRW middle 50% range 530–620. ACT middle 50% range 21–26. **Basis for Candidate Selection:** *Very important factors include:* rigor of secondary school record, academic GPA, recommendation(s), character/personal qualities, alumni/ae relation. *Important factors include:* class rank, application essay, standardized test scores, interview, extracurricular activities, talent/ability. *Other factors include:* first generation, geographical residence, state residency. **Freshman Admission Requirements:** High school diploma is required and GED is not accepted. *Academic units recommended:* 4 English, 4 math, 4 science, 3 foreign language, 4 social studies. **Freshman Admission Statistics:** 4,720 applied, 64% admitted, 20% enrolled. **Transfer Admission Requirements:** College transcript(s), statement of good standing from prior institution(s). Minimum college GPA of 2.0 required. Lowest grade transferable C. **General Admission Information:** Priority deadline 1/15. Admission may be deferred for a maximum of 2 semesters.

COSTS AND FINANCIAL AID

Annual tuition $34,340. Room and board $12,650. Required fees $810. Average book and supplies expense $1,100. **Required Forms and Deadlines:** FAFSA; State aid form. **Notification of Awards:** Applicants will be notified of awards on a rolling basis beginning 3/15. **Types of Aid:** *Need-based scholarships/grants:* College/university scholarship or grant aid from institutional funds; Federal Nursing Scholarships; Federal Pell; Private scholarships; SEOG; State scholarships/grants. *Loans:* Direct PLUS loans; Direct Subsidized Stafford Loans; Direct Unsubsidized Stafford Loans. **Student Employment:** Federal Work-Study Program available. Institutional employment available. **Financial Aid Statistics:** 100% needy freshmen, 100% needy undergrads receive need-based scholarship or grant aid. 83% freshmen, 81% undergrads receive non-need-based scholarship or grant aid. 90% freshmen, 93% undergrads receive need-based self-help aid. 0% freshmen, 0% undergrads receive athletic scholarships. 100% freshmen, 99% undergrads receive any aid. 80% undergrads borrow to pay for school. Average cumulative indebtedness $37,064. **Criteria awarding aid:** *Need-based:* Academics. *Non-need-based:* Academics, Leadership.

ST. JOHN'S COLLEGE (MD)

60 College Avenue, Annapolis, MD 21401
Phone: 410-626-2522 **Financial Aid Phone:** 410-626-2502
E-mail: Annapolis.Admissions@sjc.edu **CEEB Code:** 5598
Fax: 410-269-7916 **Website:** www.sjc.edu **ACT Code:** 1732

This private school was founded in 1696. It has a 36 acre campus.

RATINGS

Admissions Selectivity Rating: 89   Fire Safety Rating: 97   Green Rating: 60*

STUDENTS AND FACULTY

Enrollment: 458. **Student Body:** 47% female, 53% male, 62% out-of-state, 22% international (35 countries represented). Asian 4%, African American 2%, Caucasian 64%, Hispanic 6%, Native American 0%, Pacific Islander 0%, Two or more races 3%, Race unknown 0%.
Retention and Graduation: 87% freshmen return for sophomore year. 70% freshmen graduate within 4 years. 76% freshmen graduate within 6 years. 13% grads go on to further study within 1 year. 14% grads pursue arts and sciences degrees. 1% grads pursue law degrees. 0% grads pursue business degrees. 1% grads pursue medical degrees. **Faculty:** Student/faculty ratio 7:1. 65 full-time faculty, 88% hold PhDs, 9% are members of minority groups, 28% are women. 0% of classes are taught by teaching assistants.

ACADEMICS

Degrees: Bachelor's; Master's. **Classes:** Most classes have 10–19 students. **Most popular majors:** Liberal Arts and Sciences/Liberal Studies. **Special Study Options:** Exchange student program (domestic); Internships; Study abroad. **Disability Services offered:** Reader services; Tape recorders; Tutors. **Career services:** Alumni network; Alumni services; Career assessment; Career/job search classes; Internships; Regional alumni.

FACILITIES

Housing: Coed dorms; Wellness housing; 80% of campus accessible to physically disabled. **Special Academic Facilities/Equipment:** Art gallery, observatory, planetarium, pendulum, Ptolemy stone, Faraday cage, laboratories.

Campus Network: 100% of classrooms, 100% of dorms, 40% of student union, 100% of libraries, 100% of dining areas, 100% of common outdoor areas have wireless network access.

CAMPUS LIFE

Environment: Town. **Activities:** Campus Ministries; Choral groups; Concert band; Dance; Drama/theater; International Student Organization; Jazz band; Literary magazine; Music ensembles; Student government; Student newspaper; Student-run film society; Symphony orchestra; Yearbook. 40 registered organizations, 3 religious organizations on campus. **On-Campus Highlights:** McDowell Hall (classrooms, Great Hall, and coffee shop). **Environmental Initiatives:** Purchasing renewable energy credits for 100% of our electric consumption.

ADMISSIONS

Freshman Academic Profile: Average high school GPA 3.5. 36% in top 10% of high school class, 59% in top 25% of high school class, 87% in top 50% of high school class. 47% from public high schools. **Test Scores:** SAT Math middle 50% range 650–740. SAT EBRW middle 50% range 630–710. ACT middle 50% range 26–32. **Basis for Candidate Selection:** *Very important factors include:* application essay. *Important factors include:* rigor of secondary school record, recommendation(s), character/personal qualities. *Other factors include:* class rank, academic GPA, standardized test scores, interview, extracurricular activities, talent/ability, first generation, alumni/ae relation, geographical residence, volunteer work, work experience. **Freshman Admission Requirements:** High school diploma is required and GED is accepted. *Academic units required:* 3 math, 2 foreign language. *Academic units recommended:* 4 English, 4 math, 3 science, 3 science labs, 4 foreign language, 2 history. **Freshman Admission Statistics:** 753 applied, 55% admitted, 30% enrolled. **Transfer Admission Requirements:** High school transcript, college transcript(s), essay or personal statement. **General Admission Information:** Priority deadline 11/15. Non-fall registration accepted. Admission may be deferred for a maximum of 1 year.

COSTS AND FINANCIAL AID

Annual tuition $35,000. Room and board $13,635. Required fees $635. Average book and supplies expense $630. **Required Forms and Deadlines:** FAFSA; State aid form. **Notification of Awards:** Applicants will be notified of awards on a rolling basis beginning 12/15. **Types of Aid:** *Need-based scholarships/grants:* College/university scholarship or grant aid from institutional funds; Federal Pell; Private scholarships; SEOG; State scholarships/grants. *Loans:* Direct PLUS loans; Direct Subsidized Stafford Loans; Direct Unsubsidized Stafford Loans. **Student Employment:** Federal Work-Study Program available. Institutional employment available. **Financial Aid Statistics:** 98% needy freshmen, 99% needy undergrads receive need-based scholarship or grant aid. 16% freshmen, 19% undergrads receive non-need-based scholarship or grant aid. 89% freshmen, 87% undergrads receive need-based self-help aid. 0% freshmen, 0% undergrads receive athletic scholarships. 99% freshmen, 99% undergrads receive any aid. 74% undergrads borrow to pay for school. Average cumulative indebtedness $16,705. **Criteria awarding aid:** *Non-need-based:* Academics.

ST. JOHN'S COLLEGE (NM)

1160 Camino Cruz Blanca, Santa Fe, NM 87505
Phone: 505-984-6060 **Financial Aid Phone:** 505-984-6058
E-mail: SantaFe.Admissions@sjc.edu **CEEB Code:** 4737
Website: www.sjc.edu **ACT Code:** 2649

This private school was founded in 1696. It has a 250 acre campus.

RATINGS

Admissions Selectivity Rating: 87   **Fire Safety Rating:** 73   **Green Rating:** 71

STUDENTS AND FACULTY

Enrollment: 322. **Student Body:** 44% female, 56% male, 89% out-of-state, 26% international (28 countries represented). Asian 2%, African American 1%, Caucasian 55%, Hispanic 9%, Native American 0%, Pacific Islander 0%, Two or more races 6%, Race unknown 1%.

Retention and Graduation: 68% freshmen return for sophomore year. 42% freshmen graduate within 4 years. 48% freshmen graduate within 6 years. 14% grads go on to further study within 1 year. **Faculty:** Student/faculty ratio 8:1. 43 full-time faculty, 93% hold PhDs, 5% are members of minority groups, 26% are women. 0% of classes are taught by teaching assistants.

ACADEMICS

Degrees: Bachelor's; Master's. **Classes:** Most classes have 10–19 students. **Special Study Options:** Exchange student program (domestic); Internships; Study abroad. **Career services:** Alumni network; Alumni services; Career/job search classes; Internships; Regional alumni.

FACILITIES

Housing: Apartments for married students; Apartments for single students; Coed dorms; Men's dorms; Special housing for disabled students; Special housing for international students; Wellness housing; Women's dorms; 70% of campus accessible to physically disabled. **Special Academic Facilities/Equipment:** Art gallery, wood working studio, pottery studio, science labs **Campus Network:** 75% of classrooms, 100% of dorms, 100% of student union, 100% of libraries, 60% of dining areas, 35% of common outdoor areas have wireless network access.

CAMPUS LIFE

Environment: Town. **Activities:** Choral groups; Dance; Drama/theater; International Student Organization; Literary magazine; Music ensembles; Student government; Student newspaper. 15 registered organizations on campus. **On-Campus Highlights:** Student Activities Center. **Environmental Initiatives:** Paper, glass, plastic, cardboard recycling.

ADMISSIONS

Freshman Academic Profile: Average high school GPA 3.5. 37% in top 10% of high school class, 48% in top 25% of high school class, 74% in top 50% of high school class. 50% from public high schools. **Test Scores:** SAT Math middle 50% range 560–680. SAT EBRW middle 50% range 630–670. ACT middle 50% range 23–32. **Basis for Candidate Selection:** *Very important factors include:* application essay. *Important factors include:* rigor of secondary school record, recommendation(s), character/personal qualities. *Other factors include:* class rank, academic GPA, standardized test scores, interview, extracurricular activities, talent/ability, first generation, alumni/ae relation, geographical residence, volunteer work, work experience. **Freshman Admission Requirements:** High school diploma is required and GED is accepted. *Academic units required:* 3 math, 2 foreign language. *Academic units recommended:* 4 English, 4 math, 3 science, 3 science labs, 4 foreign language, 2 history. **Freshman Admission Statistics:** 342 applied, 63% admitted, 32% enrolled. **Transfer Admission Requirements:** High school transcript, college transcript(s), essay or personal statement. **General Admission Information:** Priority deadline 11/15. Non-fall registration accepted. Admission may be deferred for a maximum of 2 semesters.

COSTS AND FINANCIAL AID

Annual tuition $35,000. Room and board $12,860. Required fees $1,410. Average book and supplies expense $400. **Required Forms and Deadlines:** FAFSA. **Notification of Awards:** Applicants will be notified of awards on a rolling basis beginning 12/15. **Types of Aid:** *Need-based scholarships/grants:* College/university scholarship or grant aid from institutional funds; Federal Pell; Private scholarships; SEOG; State scholarships/grants. *Loans:* Direct PLUS loans; Direct Subsidized Stafford Loans; Direct Unsubsidized Stafford Loans. **Student Employment:** Federal Work-Study Program available. Institutional employment available. **Financial Aid Statistics:** 100% needy freshmen, 100% needy undergrads receive need-based scholarship or grant aid. 28% freshmen, 17% undergrads receive non-need-based scholarship or grant aid. 31% freshmen, 89% undergrads receive need-based self-help aid. 0% freshmen, 0% undergrads receive athletic scholarships. 97% freshmen, 84% undergrads receive any aid. 71% undergrads borrow to pay for school. Average cumulative indebtedness $18,434. **Criteria awarding aid:** *Need-based:* Academics. *Non-need-based:* Academics.

ST. JOHN'S UNIVERSITY (NY)

8000 Utopia Parkway, Queens, NY 11439
Phone: 718-990-2000 **Financial Aid Phone:** 718-990-2000
E-mail: admhelp@stjohns.edu **CEEB Code:** 2799
Fax: 718-990-2096 **Website:** www.stjohns.edu **ACT Code:** 2888

This private school, affiliated with the Roman Catholic Church, was founded in 1870. It has a 102 acre campus.

RATINGS

Admissions Selectivity Rating: 81   **Fire Safety Rating:** 94   **Green Rating:** 73

STUDENTS AND FACULTY

Enrollment: 11,691. **Student Body:** 56% female, 44% male, 22% out-of-state, 5% international (104 countries represented). Asian 16%, African American 14%, Caucasian 42%, Hispanic 15%, Native American <1%, Pacific Islander <1%, Two or more races 5%, Race unknown 3%.
Retention and Graduation: 82% freshmen return for sophomore year. 43% freshmen graduate within 4 years. 63% freshmen graduate within 6 years. 19% grads go on to further study within 1 year. 21% grads pursue arts and sciences degrees. 17% grads pursue law degrees. 29% grads pursue business degrees. 14% grads pursue medical degrees. **Faculty:** Student/faculty ratio 17:1. 663 full-time faculty, 94% hold PhDs, 30% are members of minority groups, 46% are women. 0% of classes are taught by teaching assistants.

ACADEMICS

Degrees: Associate; Bachelor's; Certificate; Doctoral degree—professional practice; Doctoral degree research/scholarship; Master's; Post-bachelor's certificate; Post-master's certificate. **Classes:** Most classes have 20–29 students. Most lab/discussion sessions have 20–29 students. **Most popular majors:** Biology/Biological Sciences, General; Pharmacy; Psychology, General.
Special Study Options: Accelerated program; Cross-registration; Distance learning; Double major; Dual enrollment; English as a Second Language (ESL); Honors program; Independent study; Internships; Liberal arts/career combination; Study abroad; Teacher certification program. **Honors programs:** The University Honors Program is available to qualified incoming freshmen. The program primarily comprises honors versions of the courses which are part of the core curriculum and may be completed in any of the colleges and schools of the University. Honors Program students must complete 30 credits of honors-designated courses to complete the program. Additional options for obtaining honors credits are also available through high school advanced placement courses as well as in the University's study abroad programs. The Honors Program also features a range of special activities and events including theatre and music events as well as visits to the major New York City museums and walking tours of New York City. **Combined degree programs:** BA/JD; BA/MA. **Disability Services offered:** Note-taking services; Reader services; Tape recorders. **Career services:** Alumni network; Alumni services; Career assessment; Career/job search classes; Internships.

FACILITIES

Housing: Apartments for single students; Coed dorms; Special housing for disabled students; Theme housing **Special Academic Facilities/Equipment:** University Gallery; Instructional Media Center; Institute of Asian Studies; Health Education Resource Center; Center for Psychological Services; Instructional Television and Radio Center; Speech and Hearing Center; Reading and Writing Education Center; Communication and Collaboration Commons; Computer Science Lab; Cyber Security Lab; Decision Lab; Homeland Security Lab; IDEA (Innovation and Design Enhancing the Arts); Innovation Labs; and MAD (Media Arts and Design) Lab.

CAMPUS LIFE

Environment: Metropolis. **Activities:** Campus Ministries; Choral groups; Dance; Drama/theater; International Student Organization; Jazz band; Literary magazine; Music ensembles; Musical theater; Pep band; Radio station; Student government; Student newspaper; Student-run film society; Television station; Yearbook. 140 registered organizations, 16 honor societies, 8 religious organizations, 13 fraternities, 16 sororities on campus. **Athletics (Intercollegiate):** *Men:* baseball, basketball, fencing, golf, lacrosse, soccer, softball, table tennis, tennis, volleyball, weight lifting. *Women:* basketball, cross-country, fencing, soccer, softball, table tennis, tennis, track/field (outdoor),

track/field (indoor), volleyball, weight lifting. **On-Campus Highlights:** The D'Angelo Center Living Room. **Environmental Initiatives:** Senior management signed the NYC Mayoral Challenge committing to 30% reduction in carbon emissions by the year 2017.

ADMISSIONS

Freshman Academic Profile: Average high school GPA 3.5. 21% in top 10% of high school class, 48% in top 25% of high school class, 79% in top 50% of high school class. **Test Scores:** SAT Math middle 50% range 540–660. SAT EBRW middle 50% range 540–640. ACT middle 50% range 23–29. **Basis for Candidate Selection:** *Very important factors include:* rigor of secondary school record, academic GPA. *Important factors include:* standardized test scores. *Other factors include:* class rank, application essay, recommendation(s), extracurricular activities, talent/ability, character/personal qualities, alumni/ae relation, volunteer work, work experience, level of applicant's interest. **Freshman Admission Requirements:** High school diploma is required and GED is accepted. *Academic units required:* 4 English, 2 math, 2 science, 1 history. *Academic units recommended:* 4 English, 3 math, 3 science, 2 foreign language, 2 social studies, 2 history. **Freshman Admission Statistics:** 29,059 applied, 72% admitted, 15% enrolled. **Transfer Admission Requirements:** College transcript(s). Lowest grade transferable C. **General Admission Information:** Priority deadline 2/1. Non-fall registration accepted. Admission may be deferred for a maximum of 1 year.

COSTS AND FINANCIAL AID

Annual tuition $41,900. Room and board $17,720. Required fees $1,100. Average book and supplies expense $656. **Required Forms and Deadlines:** FAFSA; State aid form. **Notification of Awards:** Applicants will be notified of awards on a rolling basis beginning 2/15. **Types of Aid:** *Need-based scholarships/grants:* College/university scholarship or grant aid from institutional funds; Federal Pell; Private scholarships; SEOG; State scholarships/grants. *Loans:* Direct PLUS loans; Direct Subsidized Stafford Loans; Direct Unsubsidized Stafford Loans. **Student Employment:** Federal Work-Study Program available. Institutional employment available. **Financial Aid Statistics:** 75% needy freshmen, 75% needy undergrads receive need-based scholarship or grant aid. 100% freshmen, 97% undergrads receive non-need-based scholarship or grant aid. 62% freshmen, 66% undergrads receive need-based self-help aid. 1% freshmen, 2% undergrads receive athletic scholarships. 99% freshmen, 98% undergrads receive any aid. 68% undergrads borrow to pay for school. Average cumulative indebtedness $28,264. **Criteria awarding aid:** *Non-need-based:* Academics, Alumni affiliation, Art, Athletics, Leadership, Music/drama, Religious affiliation.

ST. JOSEPH'S COLLEGE

245 Clinton Avenue, Brooklyn, NY 11205
Phone: 718-940-5800 **Financial Aid Phone:** 631-687-2611
E-mail: bkadmissions@sjcny.edu
Fax: 718-636-8303 **Website:** www.sjcny.edu **ACT Code:** 2890

This private school was founded in 1916. It has a 5 acre campus.

RATINGS

Admissions Selectivity Rating: 77   **Fire Safety Rating:** 60*   **Green Rating:** 60*

STUDENTS AND FACULTY

Enrollment: 953. **Student Body:** 65% female, 35% male, 9% out-of-state, 0% international (27 countries represented). Asian 7%, African American 18%, Caucasian 36%, Hispanic 26%, Native American <1%, Pacific Islander <1%, Two or more races 3%, Race unknown 9%.
Retention and Graduation: 81% freshmen return for sophomore year. 55% freshmen graduate within 4 years. 62% freshmen graduate within 6 years. **Faculty:** Student/faculty ratio 10:1. 58 full-time faculty, 78% hold PhDs, 21% are members of minority groups, 55% are women. 0% of classes are taught by teaching assistants.

ACADEMICS

Degrees: Bachelor's; Certificate; Master's; Post-bachelor's certificate; Post-master's certificate. **Classes:** Most classes have 10–19 students. **Most popular majors:** Special Education and Teaching, General; Business Administration and Management, General; Registered Nursing/Registered Nurse. **Special Study Options:** Accelerated program; Distance learning; Double major; Dual enrollment; Exchange student program (domestic); Honors program; Independent study; Internships; Liberal arts/career combination; Study abroad;

Teacher certification program. **Disability Services offered:** Note-taking services; Reader services; Tape recorders; Tutors. **Career services:** Alumni network; Alumni services; Career assessment; Career/job search classes; Internships; Regional alumni.

FACILITIES

Housing: Coed dorms; 40% of campus accessible to physically disabled. **Special Academic Facilities/Equipment:** Tuohy Student Lounge/Red Room; The Bear Cave Lounge; The Hill Center; MCE Cafeteria; The Center for Student Involvement & Leadership.

CAMPUS LIFE

Environment: Metropolis. **Activities:** Campus Ministries; Choral groups; Dance; Drama/theater; International Student Organization; Literary magazine; Music ensembles; Musical theater; Student government; Student newspaper. 31 registered organizations, 5 honor societies, 1 religious organization, 1 fraternity, 1 sorority on campus. **On-Campus Highlights:** Tuohy Student Lounge/Red Room.

ADMISSIONS

Freshman Academic Profile: Average high school GPA 3.2. 59% from public high schools. **Test Scores:** SAT Math middle 50% range 490–590. SAT EBRW middle 50% range 500–600. ACT middle 50% range 20–25. **Basis for Candidate Selection:** *Very important factors include:* rigor of secondary school record, academic GPA. *Important factors include:* class rank, application essay, standardized test scores, recommendation(s), character/personal qualities. *Other factors include:* interview, extracurricular activities, talent/ability, first generation, alumni/ae relation, volunteer work, work experience, level of applicant's interest. **Freshman Admission Requirements:** High school diploma is required and GED is accepted. *Academic units required:* 4 English, 3 math, 3 science, 2 foreign language, 4 social studies. **Freshman Admission Statistics:** 2,427 applied, 71% admitted, 12% enrolled. **Transfer Admission Requirements:** College transcript(s), interview, statement of good standing from prior institution(s). Minimum college GPA of 2.0 required. **General Admission Information:** Application fee $25. Priority deadline 3/15. Regular application deadline 8/31. Non-fall registration accepted. Admission may be deferred for a maximum of 1 year.

COSTS AND FINANCIAL AID

Annual tuition $28,590. Room and board $14,800. Required fees $600. Average book and supplies expense $1,000. **Required Forms and Deadlines:** FAFSA; State aid form. **Notification of Awards:** Applicants will be notified of awards on a rolling basis beginning 2/1. **Types of Aid:** *Need-based scholarships/grants:* College/university scholarship or grant aid from institutional funds; Federal Pell; Private scholarships; SEOG; State scholarships/grants. *Loans:* Direct PLUS loans; Direct Subsidized Stafford Loans; Direct Unsubsidized Stafford Loans. **Student Employment:** Federal Work-Study Program available. Institutional employment available. **Financial Aid Statistics:** 100% needy freshmen, 100% needy undergrads receive need-based scholarship or grant aid. 99% freshmen, 93% undergrads receive non-need-based scholarship or grant aid. 52% freshmen, 64% undergrads receive need-based self-help aid. 0% freshmen, 0% undergrads receive athletic scholarships. 68% freshmen, 63% undergrads receive any aid. 63% undergrads borrow to pay for school. Average cumulative indebtedness $27,278. **Criteria awarding aid:** *Non-need-based:* Academics, Alumni affiliation.

ST. JOSEPH'S COLLEGE, NEW YORK (PATCHOGUE)

155 West Roe Blvd, Patchogue, NY 11772
Phone: 631-687-4500 **Financial Aid Phone:** 631-687-2611
E-mail: liadmissions@sjcny.edu
Fax: 631-447-3601 **Website:** www.sjcny.edu

This private school was founded in 1916. It has a 56 acre campus.

RATINGS

Admissions Selectivity Rating: 83 **Fire Safety Rating:** 60* **Green Rating:** 60*

STUDENTS AND FACULTY

Enrollment: 2,996. **Student Body:** 69% female, 31% male, 1% out-of-state, 0% international (3 countries represented). Asian 2%, African American 5%, Caucasian 63%, Hispanic 17%, Native American <1%, Pacific Islander <1%, Two or more races 2%, Race unknown 11%.

Retention and Graduation: 82% freshmen return for sophomore year. 63% freshmen graduate within 4 years. 72% freshmen graduate within 6 years. **Faculty:** Student/faculty ratio 13:1. 102 full-time faculty, 75% hold PhDs, 8% are members of minority groups, 62% are women. 0% of classes are taught by teaching assistants.

ACADEMICS

Degrees: Bachelor's; Certificate; Master's; Post-bachelor's certificate; Post-master's certificate. **Classes:** Most classes have 10–19 students. **Most popular majors:** Special Education and Teaching, General; Registered Nursing/Registered Nurse; Business Administration and Management, General. **Special Study Options:** Accelerated program; Distance learning; Double major; English as a Second Language (ESL); Honors program; Independent study; Internships; Liberal arts/career combination; Study abroad; Teacher certification program; Weekend college. **Combined degree programs:** BA/MA. **Disability Services offered:** Note-taking services; Reader services; Tape recorders; Tutors. **Career services:** Alumni network; Alumni services; Career assessment; Career/job search classes; Internships.

FACILITIES

100% of campus accessible to physically disabled. **Special Academic Facilities/Equipment:** 3D Printer, Technology Building, Computer Labs, Clare Rose Playhouse.

CAMPUS LIFE

Environment: Town. **Activities:** Campus Ministries; Choral groups; Dance; Drama/theater; Literary magazine; Opera; Radio station; Student government; Student newspaper. 45 registered organizations, 16 honor societies, 2 religious organizations, 2 fraternities, 4 sororities on campus. **Athletics (Intercollegiate):** *Men:* baseball, basketball, cross-country, golf, soccer, tennis, track/field (outdoor). *Women:* basketball, cross-country, equestrian sports, soccer, softball, swimming, tennis, track/field (outdoor), volleyball. **On-Campus Highlights:** Cafeteria (Eagle's Nest) and Second Floor Lounge and Eagles Perch (Café).

ADMISSIONS

Freshman Academic Profile: Average high school GPA 3.5. 87% from public high schools. **Test Scores:** SAT Math middle 50% range 528–600. SAT EBRW middle 50% range 510–600. ACT middle 50% range 21–25. **Basis for Candidate Selection:** *Very important factors include:* rigor of secondary school record, class rank, academic GPA. *Important factors include:* application essay, standardized test scores, recommendation(s), interview, extracurricular activities, character/personal qualities. *Other factors include:* talent/ability, first generation, alumni/ae relation, volunteer work, work experience, level of applicant's interest. **Freshman Admission Requirements:** High school diploma is required and GED is accepted. *Academic units required:* 4 English, 3 math, 3 science, 3 science labs, 2 foreign language, 4 social studies, 3 academic electives, 2 visual/performing arts. *Academic units recommended:* 4 English, 4 math, 4 science, 4 science labs, 3 foreign language, 4 social studies, 4 academic electives, 2 visual/performing arts. **Freshman Admission Statistics:** 1,744 applied, 73% admitted, 34% enrolled. **Transfer Admission Requirements:** College transcript(s). Minimum college GPA of 2.0 required. **General Admission Information:** Application fee $25. Non-fall registration accepted. Admission may be deferred for a maximum of 1 year.

COSTS AND FINANCIAL AID

Annual tuition $28,590. Required fees $610. **Required Forms and Deadlines:** FAFSA; State aid form. **Notification of Awards:** Applicants will be notified of awards on a rolling basis beginning 2/1. **Types of Aid:** *Need-based scholarships/grants:* College/university scholarship or grant aid from institutional funds; Federal Pell; Private scholarships; SEOG; State scholarships/grants. *Loans:* Direct PLUS loans; Direct Subsidized Stafford Loans; Direct Unsubsidized Stafford Loans. **Student Employment:** Federal Work-Study Program available. Institutional employment available. **Financial Aid Statistics:** 100% needy freshmen, 97% needy undergrads receive need-based scholarship or grant aid. 98% freshmen, 88% undergrads receive non-need-based scholarship or grant aid. 53% freshmen, 65% undergrads receive need-based self-help aid. 0% freshmen, 0% undergrads receive athletic scholarships. 76% freshmen, 62% undergrads receive any aid. 69% undergrads borrow to pay for school. Average cumulative indebtedness $31,518. **Criteria awarding aid:** *Non-need-based:* Academics, Alumni affiliation.

SAINT JOSEPH SEMINARY COLLEGE

75376 River Road, St. Benedict, LA 70457
Phone: 985-867-2273 **Financial Aid Phone:** 985-867-2229
E-mail: registrar@sjasc.edu **CEEB Code:** 6689
Fax: 985-327-1085 **ACT Code:** 1604

This private school, affiliated with the Roman Catholic Church, was founded in 1891. It has a 1200 acre campus.

RATINGS
Admissions Selectivity Rating: 67 **Fire Safety Rating:** 60* **Green Rating:** 60*

STUDENTS AND FACULTY
Enrollment: 100. **Student Body:** 0% female, 100% male, 34% out-of-state, 0% international. Asian 5%, African American 0%, Caucasian 69%, Hispanic 26%, Native American 0%, Pacific Islander 0%, Two or more races 0%, Race unknown 0%.
Faculty: Student/faculty ratio 7:1. 16 full-time faculty, 31% hold PhDs, 0% are members of minority groups, 44% are women. 0% of classes are taught by teaching assistants.

ACADEMICS
Degrees: Bachelor's. **Classes:** Most classes have 10–19 students. **Special Study Options:** Distance learning; English as a Second Language (ESL); Independent study. **Disability Services offered:** Tape recorders; Tutors.

FACILITIES
Housing: Men's dorms; 100% of campus accessible to physically disabled.
Campus Network: 100% of classrooms, 100% of dorms, 100% of student union, 100% of libraries, 100% of dining areas, 30% of common outdoor areas have wireless network access.

CAMPUS LIFE
Environment: Rural. **Activities:** Choral groups; Drama/theater; Literary magazine; Student government; Student newspaper; Yearbook. 1 religious organization on campus.

ADMISSIONS
Basis for Candidate Selection: *Very important factors include:* rigor of secondary school record, character/personal qualities, religious affiliation/commitment. *Important factors include:* standardized test scores, recommendation(s). *Other factors include:* class rank, interview, extracurricular activities, volunteer work.
Freshman Admission Requirements: High school diploma is required and GED is accepted. *Academic units required:* 3 English, 2 math, 2 science, 2 foreign language, 1 history. *Academic units recommended:* 3 English, 2 math, 2 science, 2 foreign language, 1 history. **Freshman Admission Statistics:** 11 applied, 100% admitted, 100% enrolled. **Transfer Admission Requirements:** High school transcript, college transcript(s), standardized test scores. Lowest grade transferable C. **General Admission Information:** Non-fall registration accepted.

COSTS AND FINANCIAL AID
Annual tuition $13,500. Room and board $13,040. Average book and supplies expense $1,000. **Required Forms and Deadlines:** FAFSA; Institution's own financial aid form; State aid form. **Notification of Awards:** Applicants will be notified of awards on a rolling basis beginning 8/3. **Types of Aid:** *Need-based scholarships/grants:* College/university scholarship or grant aid from institutional funds; Federal Pell; Private scholarships; SEOG; State scholarships/grants. **Financial Aid Statistics:** 100% needy freshmen, 100% needy undergrads receive need-based scholarship or grant aid. 100% freshmen, 20% undergrads receive non-need-based scholarship or grant aid. 100% freshmen, 100% undergrads receive need-based self-help aid. 0% freshmen, 0% undergrads receive athletic scholarships.

SAINT JOSEPH'S UNIVERSITY (PA)

5600 City Avenue, Philadelphia, PA 19131
Phone: 888-BE-A-HAWK **Financial Aid Phone:** 610-660-1556
E-mail: admit@sju.edu **CEEB Code:** 2801
Fax: 610-660-1314 **Website:** www.sju.edu **ACT Code:** 3684

This private school, affiliated with the Roman Catholic-Jesuit Church, was founded in 1851. It has a 114 acre campus.

RATINGS
Admissions Selectivity Rating: 80 **Fire Safety Rating:** 90 **Green Rating:** 83

STUDENTS AND FACULTY
Enrollment: 4,678. **Student Body:** 54% female, 46% male, 54% out-of-state, 2% international (35 countries represented). Asian 3%, African American 6%, Caucasian 78%, Hispanic 8%, Native American <1%, Pacific Islander <1%, Two or more races 3%, Race unknown 1%.
Retention and Graduation: 88% freshmen return for sophomore year. 75% freshmen graduate within 4 years. 81% freshmen graduate within 6 years. 15% grads go on to further study within 1 year. 3% grads pursue arts and sciences degrees. 1% grads pursue law degrees. 3% grads pursue business degrees. 5% grads pursue medical degrees. **Faculty:** Student/faculty ratio 10:1. 294 full-time faculty, 89% hold PhDs, 17% are members of minority groups, 47% are women. 0% of classes are taught by teaching assistants.

ACADEMICS
Degrees: Associate; Bachelor's; Doctoral degree research/scholarship; Master's; Post-bachelor's certificate; Post-master's certificate. **Classes:** Most classes have 10–19 students. Most lab/discussion sessions have 10–19 students. **Most popular majors:** Finance, General; Marketing/Marketing Management, General; Accounting. **Special Study Options:** Accelerated program; Cooperative education program; Distance learning; Double major; Dual enrollment; English as a Second Language (ESL); Exchange student program (domestic); Honors program; Independent study; Internships; Student-designed major; Study abroad; Teacher certification program; Weekend college. **Honors programs:** There are distinctive benefits attached to belonging to the SJU Honors Program: Team-taught courses allow distinguished faculty members to share their knowledge and expertise with students in a challenging academic environment. Individual honors courses stress a detailed and thorough scholarly exploration of different fields of knowledge. Honors students register ahead of other students in their year. Honors suites in the residence halls allow like-minded students to live together, even as freshmen. Honors students are provided with free tickets and transportation to concerts and performances by world-renowned artists at some of Philadelphia's most revered centers of culture. Receptions, concerts, and lectures are regularly sponsored by the Honors Program for Honors Students. Students have access to Claver House, a quiet retreat where honors students can study, work with personal computers and attend receptions. Students have opportunities to present research and creative work at national conferences and seminars; they are also kept informed about scholarship and funding opportunities for graduate and professional work. **Disability Services offered:** Note-taking services; Reader services; Tape recorders; Tutors. **Career services:** Alumni network; Alumni services; Career assessment; Career/job search classes; Internships; Regional alumni.

FACILITIES
Housing: Apartments for single students; Coed dorms; Men's dorms; Special housing for international students; Theme housing; Women's dorms 85% of campus accessible to physically disabled. **Special Academic Facilities/Equipment:** Post Learning Commons Claver House—Honors Program; Mandeville Hall; Merion Hall; Moot Board Room; University Gallery; Wall Street Trading Room.

CAMPUS LIFE
Environment: Metropolis. **Activities:** Campus Ministries; Choral groups; Dance; Drama/theater; International Student Organization; Jazz band; Literary magazine; Music ensembles; Musical theater; Pep band; Radio station; Student government; Student newspaper; Student-run film society; Yearbook. 90 registered organizations, 23 honor societies, 4 fraternities, 5 sororities on campus. **Athletics (Intercollegiate):** *Men:* baseball, basketball, crew/rowing, cross-country, golf, lacrosse, soccer, tennis, track/field (outdoor), track/field

(indoor). *Women:* basketball, crew/rowing, cross-country, field hockey, lacrosse, soccer, softball, tennis, track/field (outdoor), track/field (indoor). **On-Campus Highlights:** Campion/The Perch. **Environmental Initiatives:** We have a full-time office of Health, Safety, and Environmental compliance.

ADMISSIONS

Freshman Academic Profile: Average high school GPA 3.7. 22% in top 10% of high school class, 52% in top 25% of high school class, 82% in top 50% of high school class. 50% from public high schools. **Test Scores:** SAT Math middle 50% range 550–650. SAT EBRW middle 50% range 570–650. ACT middle 50% range 23–29. **Basis for Candidate Selection:** *Very important factors include:* rigor of secondary school record, class rank, academic GPA. *Important factors include:* application essay, standardized test scores, recommendation(s). *Other factors include:* interview, extracurricular activities, talent/ability, character/personal qualities, first generation, alumni/ae relation, geographical residence, racial/ethnic status, volunteer work, work experience, level of applicant's interest. **Freshman Admission Requirements:** High school diploma is required and GED is accepted. *Academic units required:* 4 English, 3 math, 3 science, 2 foreign language, 3 social studies, 5 academic electives. **Freshman Admission Statistics:** 8,692 applied, 75% admitted, 17% enrolled. **Transfer Admission Requirements:** High school transcript, college transcript(s), statement of good standing from prior institution(s). Minimum college GPA of 2.5 required. Lowest grade transferable C. **General Admission Information:** Application fee $50. Regular application deadline 2/1. Non-fall registration accepted.

COSTS AND FINANCIAL AID

Annual tuition $46,350. Room and board $14,840. Required fees $200. Average book and supplies expense $893. **Required Forms and Deadlines:** FAFSA. **Notification of Awards:** Applicants will be notified of awards on a rolling basis beginning 3/31. **Types of Aid:** *Need-based scholarships/grants:* College/university scholarship or grant aid from institutional funds; Federal Pell; Private scholarships; SEOG; State scholarships/grants. *Loans:* Direct PLUS loans; Direct Subsidized Stafford Loans; Direct Unsubsidized Stafford Loans. **Student Employment:** Federal Work-Study Program available. Institutional employment available. **Financial Aid Statistics:** 99% needy freshmen, 98% needy undergrads receive need-based scholarship or grant aid. 16% freshmen, 17% undergrads receive non-need-based scholarship or grant aid. 75% freshmen, 74% undergrads receive need-based self-help aid. 5% freshmen, 5% undergrads receive athletic scholarships. 98% freshmen, 93% undergrads receive any aid. **Criteria awarding aid:** *Need-based:* Academics, Athletics, Minority status, Music/drama. *Non-need-based:* Academics, Alumni affiliation, Art, Athletics, Minority status, Music/drama.

ST. LAWRENCE UNIVERSITY

23 Romoda Drive, Canton, NY 13617
Phone: 315-229-5261 **Financial Aid Phone:** 315-229-5265
E-mail: admissions@stlawu.edu **CEEB Code:** 2805
Fax: 315-229-5818 **Website:** www.stlawu.edu **ACT Code:** 2896

This private school was founded in 1856. It has a 1000 acre campus.

RATINGS

Admissions Selectivity Rating: 89   **Fire Safety Rating:** 81   **Green Rating:** 94

STUDENTS AND FACULTY

Enrollment: 2,407. **Student Body:** 55% female, 45% male, 61% out-of-state, 9% international (62 countries represented). Asian 1%, African American 3%, Caucasian 78%, Hispanic 5%, Native American <1%, Pacific Islander 0%, Two or more races 2%, Race unknown 1%. **Retention and Graduation:** 89% freshmen return for sophomore year. 82% freshmen graduate within 4 years. 85% freshmen graduate within 6 years. 18% grads go on to further study within 1 year. 6% grads pursue arts and sciences degrees. 2% grads pursue law degrees. 1% grads pursue business degrees. 2% grads pursue medical degrees. **Faculty:** Student/faculty ratio 11:1. 171 full-time faculty, 99% hold PhDs, 12% are members of minority groups, 50% are women. 0% of classes are taught by teaching assistants.

ACADEMICS

Degrees: Bachelor's; Master's. **Classes:** Most classes have 10–19 students. Most lab/discussion sessions have 10–19 students. **Most popular majors:** Economics, General; Biology/Biological Sciences, General; Psychology, General. **Special Study Options:** Cross-registration; Double major; English as a Second Language (ESL); Exchange student program (domestic); Independent study; Internships; Student-designed major; Study abroad; Teacher certification program. **Honors programs:** The University Fellows program offers a stipend plus room for summer research on campus. This is a competitive program for students who wish to undertake a serious, independent academic project as their summer employment. **Disability Services offered:** Note-taking services; Reader services; Tape recorders; Tutors. **Career services:** Alumni network; Alumni services; Career assessment; Career/job search classes; Internships.

FACILITIES

Housing: Apartments for single students; Coed dorms; Fraternity/sorority housing; Special housing for disabled students; Special housing for international students; Theme housing; Wellness housing; Women's dorms; 60% of campus accessible to physically disabled. **Special Academic Facilities/Equipment:** Art gallery, arts technology center, language lab, center for international education, environmental research facility, 76-acre forest preserve, two electron microscopes, microscopy and sleep labs, Neuroscience lab, sustainability lab, environmental field study center.

CAMPUS LIFE

Environment: Village. **Activities:** Campus Ministries; Choral groups; Concert band; Dance; Drama/theater; International Student Organization; Jazz band; Literary magazine; Model UN; Music ensembles; Musical theater; Radio station; Student government; Student newspaper; Student-run film society; Yearbook. 117 registered organizations, 22 honor societies, 4 religious organizations, 2 fraternities, 4 sororities on campus. **Athletics (Intercollegiate):** *Men:* baseball, basketball, crew/rowing, cross-country, equestrian sports, football, golf, ice hockey, lacrosse, skiing (downhill/Alpine), skiing (Nordic/cross-country), soccer, squash, swimming, tennis, track/field (outdoor), track/field (indoor). *Women:* basketball, crew/rowing, cross-country, equestrian sports, field hockey, golf, ice hockey, lacrosse, skiing (downhill/Alpine), skiing (Nordic/cross-country), soccer, softball, squash, swimming, tennis, track/field (outdoor), track/field (indoor), volleyball. **On-Campus Highlights:** Newell Field House & Stafford Fitness Center. **Environmental Initiatives:** Pledge of climate neutrality.

ADMISSIONS

Freshman Academic Profile: Average high school GPA 3.6. 36% in top 10% of high school class, 73% in top 25% of high school class, 93% in top 50% of high school class. 67% from public high schools. **Test Scores:** SAT Math middle 50% range 590–680. SAT EBRW middle 50% range 590–670. ACT middle 50% range 26–30. **Basis for Candidate Selection:** *Very important factors include:* rigor of secondary school record, academic GPA, application essay, recommendation(s), character/personal qualities. *Important factors include:* class rank, interview, extracurricular activities. *Other factors include:* standardized test scores, talent/ability, first generation, alumni/ae relation, geographical residence, volunteer work, work experience, level of applicant's interest. **Freshman Admission Requirements:** High school diploma is required and GED is accepted. *Academic units recommended:* 4 English, 4 math, 4 science, 4 foreign language, 2 social studies, 2 history. **Freshman Admission Statistics:** 6,458 applied, 46% admitted, 22% enrolled. **Transfer Admission Requirements:** High school transcript, college transcript(s), essay or personal statement, statement of good standing from prior institution(s). Lowest grade transferable C. **General Admission Information:** Application fee $60. Regular application deadline 2/1. Non-fall registration accepted. Admission may be deferred for a maximum of 1 year.

COSTS AND FINANCIAL AID

Annual tuition $56,360. Room and board $14,628. Required fees $406. Average book and supplies expense $750. **Required Forms and Deadlines:** FAFSA. **Types of Aid:** *Need-based scholarships/grants:* College/university scholarship or grant aid from institutional funds; Federal Pell; Private scholarships; SEOG; State scholarships/grants. *Loans:* Direct PLUS loans; Direct Subsidized Stafford Loans; Direct Unsubsidized Stafford Loans. **Student Employment:** Federal Work-Study Program available. Institutional employment available. **Financial Aid Statistics:** 100% needy freshmen, 100% needy undergrads receive need-based scholarship or grant aid. 80% freshmen, 79% undergrads receive non-need-based scholarship or grant aid. 75% freshmen, 77% undergrads receive need-based self-help aid. 2% freshmen, 2% undergrads receive athletic scholarships. 98.8% freshmen, 96.9% undergrads receive any aid. 59% undergrads borrow to pay for school. Average cumulative indebtedness $36,067. **Criteria awarding aid:** *Need-based:* Academics, Minority status. *Non-need-based:* Academics, Alumni affiliation, Leadership, Minority status.

SAINT LEO UNIVERSITY

Office of Admission MC2008, Saint Leo, FL 33574-6665
Phone: (352)588-8283 **Financial Aid Phone:** 800-240-7658
E-mail: admissions@saintleo.edu **CEEB Code:** 5638
Fax: (352)588-8257 **Website:** www.saintleo.edu **ACT Code:** 755

This private school, affiliated with the Roman Catholic Church, was founded in 1889. It has a 297 acre campus.

RATINGS
Admissions Selectivity Rating: 80   **Fire Safety Rating:** 98   **Green Rating:** 60*

STUDENTS AND FACULTY
Enrollment: 2,280. **Student Body:** 58% female, 42% male, 26% out-of-state, 14% international (74 countries represented). Asian 1%, African American 14%, Caucasian 37%, Hispanic 21%, Native American <1%, Pacific Islander 0%, Two or more races 2%, Race unknown 10%.
Retention and Graduation: 69% freshmen return for sophomore year. 36% freshmen graduate within 4 years. 47% freshmen graduate within 6 years. 18% grads go on to further study within 1 year. 5% grads pursue business degrees.
Faculty: Student/faculty ratio 18:1. 100 full-time faculty, 84% hold PhDs, 12% are members of minority groups, 36% are women. 0% of classes are taught by teaching assistants.

ACADEMICS
Degrees: Associate; Bachelor's; Certificate; Doctoral degree—professional practice; Master's; Post-bachelor's certificate; Transfer Associate. **Classes:** Most classes have 20–29 students. Most lab/discussion sessions have 10–19 students. **Most popular majors:** Business Administration and Management, General; Political Science and Government, General; Psychology, General. **Special Study Options:** Accelerated program; Distance learning; Double major; Dual enrollment; English as a Second Language (ESL); Honors program; Independent study; Internships; Liberal arts/career combination; Study abroad; Teacher certification program; Weekend college. **Honors programs:** The Saint Leo University Honors Program consists of an integrated sequence of six interdisciplinary courses, spread over the first three years of college, and an extensive senior honors project carried out under the supervision of a distinguished faculty mentor. **Disability Services offered:** Note-taking services; Reader services; Tape recorders; Tutors. **Career services:** Alumni network; Alumni services; Career assessment; Career/job search classes; Internships; Regional alumni.

FACILITIES
Housing: Apartments for single students; Coed dorms; Men's dorms; Special housing for disabled students; Theme housing; Wellness housing; Women's dorms; 95% of campus accessible to physically disabled. **Campus Network:** 100% of classrooms, 100% of dorms, 100% of student union, 100% of libraries, 100% of dining areas, 100% of common outdoor areas have wireless network access.

CAMPUS LIFE
Environment: Rural. **Activities:** Campus Ministries; Choral groups; Dance; Drama/theater; International Student Organization; Literary magazine; Music ensembles; Musical theater; Radio station; Student government; Student newspaper; Yearbook. 66 registered organizations, 22 honor societies, 2 religious organizations, 7 fraternities, 7 sororities on campus. **Athletics (Intercollegiate):** *Men:* baseball, basketball, cross-country, golf, lacrosse, soccer, swimming, tennis. *Women:* basketball, cross-country, golf, soccer, softball, swimming, tennis, volleyball. **On-Campus Highlights:** School of Business.

ADMISSIONS
Freshman Academic Profile: Average high school GPA 3.1. 9% in top 10% of high school class, 27% in top 25% of high school class, 58% in top 50% of high school class. 76% from public high schools. **Test Scores:** SAT Math middle 50% range 510–590. SAT EBRW middle 50% range 530–600. ACT middle 50% range 22–27. **Basis for Candidate Selection:** *Very important factors include:* rigor of secondary school record, academic GPA. *Important factors include:* interview, character/personal qualities. *Other factors include:* class rank, application essay, standardized test scores, recommendation(s), extracurricular activities, talent/ability, first generation, alumni/ae relation, volunteer work, work experience, level of applicant's interest. **Freshman Admission Requirements:** High school diploma is required and GED is accepted. *Academic units recommended:* 4 English, 3 math, 2 science, 2 foreign language, 3 social studies, 2 academic electives. **Freshman Admission Statistics:** 5,195

applied, 72% admitted, 21% enrolled. **Transfer Admission Requirements:** College transcript(s), essay or personal statement, statement of good standing from prior institution(s). Minimum college GPA of 2.0 required. Lowest grade transferable D. **General Admission Information:** Priority deadline 1/15. Non-fall registration accepted. Admission may be deferred for a maximum of 1 year.

COSTS AND FINANCIAL AID
Annual tuition $23,900. Room and board $13,500. Required fees $960. Average book and supplies expense $1,116. **Required Forms and Deadlines:** FAFSA; State aid form. **Notification of Awards:** Applicants will be notified of awards on a rolling basis beginning 1/1. **Types of Aid:** *Need-based scholarships/grants:* College/university scholarship or grant aid from institutional funds; Federal Pell; Private scholarships; SEOG; State scholarships/grants; United Negro College Fund. *Loans:* Direct PLUS loans; Direct Subsidized Stafford Loans; Direct Unsubsidized Stafford Loans. **Student Employment:** Federal Work-Study Program available. Institutional employment available. **Financial Aid Statistics:** 100% needy freshmen, 100% needy undergrads receive need-based scholarship or grant aid. 8% freshmen, 9% undergrads receive non-need-based scholarship or grant aid. 90% freshmen, 86% undergrads receive need-based self-help aid. 4% freshmen, 7% undergrads receive athletic scholarships. 100% freshmen, 99% undergrads receive any aid. 69% undergrads borrow to pay for school. Average cumulative indebtedness $27,813. **Criteria awarding aid:** *Non-need-based:* Academics, Alumni affiliation, Athletics, Leadership, Minority status, Religious affiliation, State/district residency.

ST. LOUIS COLLEGE OF PHARMACY

4588 Parkview Place, Saint Louis, MO 63110
Phone: 314-367-8700
E-mail: connie.horrall@stlcop.edu **CEEB Code:** 6626
Fax: 314-446-8310 **Website:** www.stlcop.edu **ACT Code:** 2346

This private school was founded in 1864. It has a 7 acre campus.

RATINGS
Admissions Selectivity Rating: 90   **Fire Safety Rating:** 77   **Green Rating:** 60*

STUDENTS AND FACULTY
Enrollment: 723. **Student Body:** 60% female, 40% male, 53% out-of-state, 1% international. Asian 22%, African American 5%, Caucasian 66%, Hispanic 1%, Native American <1%, Pacific Islander <1%, Two or more races 1%, Race unknown 4%.
Retention and Graduation: 92% freshmen return for sophomore year.
Faculty: Student/faculty ratio 13:1. 91 full-time faculty, 100% hold PhDs, 9% are members of minority groups, 47% are women.

ACADEMICS
Degrees: Doctoral degree—professional practice. **Classes:** Most classes have 20–29 students. Most lab/discussion sessions have 20–29 students. **Career services:** Alumni services; Internships.

FACILITIES
Housing: Coed dorms.

CAMPUS LIFE
Activities: Campus Ministries; Choral groups; Concert band; Drama/theater; International Student Organization; Literary magazine; Musical theater; Student government; Student newspaper; Yearbook. 2 honor societies, 6 religious organizations, 5 fraternities on campus. **Athletics (Intercollegiate):** *Men:* basketball, cheerleading, cross-country. *Women:* cheerleading, cross-country, volleyball.

ADMISSIONS
Freshman Academic Profile: Average high school GPA 3.7. 50% in top 10% of high school class, 33% in top 25% of high school class, 17% in top 50% of high school class. **Test Scores:** SAT Math middle 50% range 640–730. SAT EBRW middle 50% range 570–660. ACT middle 50% range 25–29. **Basis for Candidate Selection:** *Very important factors include:* rigor of secondary school record, academic GPA, application essay, standardized test scores, recommendation(s), level of applicant's interest. *Other factors include:* class rank, extracurricular activities, character/personal qualities, alumni/ae relation, volunteer work, work experience. **Freshman Admission Requirements:** High school diploma is required and GED is accepted. *Academic units required:* 4 English, 4 math, 3 science, 2 science labs. *Academic units recommended:* 3 science. **Freshman Admission Statistics:** 555 applied, 63% admitted, 71%

enrolled. **Transfer Admission Requirements:** College transcript(s), essay or personal statement, standardized test scores. Minimum college GPA of 3.0 required. Lowest grade transferable C. **General Admission Information:** Application fee $50. Priority deadline 12/15. Regular application deadline 2/1.

COSTS AND FINANCIAL AID

Annual tuition $26,736. Room and board $9,555. Average book and supplies expense $1,500. **Required Forms and Deadlines:** FAFSA. **Notification of Awards:** Applicants will be notified of awards on a rolling basis beginning 2/19. **Types of Aid:** *Need-based scholarships/grants:* College/university scholarship or grant aid from institutional funds; Federal Pell; Private scholarships; SEOG; State scholarships/grants. *Loans:* Direct PLUS loans; Direct Subsidized Stafford Loans; Direct Unsubsidized Stafford Loans. **Student Employment:** Federal Work-Study Program available. Institutional employment available. **Financial Aid Statistics:** 99% needy freshmen, 90% needy undergrads receive need-based scholarship or grant aid. 9% freshmen, 5% undergrads receive non-need-based scholarship or grant aid. 82% freshmen, 89% undergrads receive need-based self-help aid. 4% freshmen, 2% undergrads receive athletic scholarships. **Criteria awarding aid:** *Need-based:* Academics, Athletics, Job skills, Minority status. *Non-need-based:* Academics, Athletics, Job skills, State/district residency.

SAINT LOUIS UNIVERSITY

Office of Admissions, DuBourg Hall, Saint Louis, MO 63103
Phone: (314) 977-2500 **Financial Aid Phone:** 314-977-2350
E-mail: admission@slu.edu **CEEB Code:** 6629
Fax: (314) 977-7136 **Website:** www.slu.edu **ACT Code:** 2352

This private school, affiliated with the Roman Catholic-Jesuit Church, was founded in 1818. It has a 281 acre campus.

RATINGS

Admissions Selectivity Rating: 88   Fire Safety Rating: 89   Green Rating: 81

STUDENTS AND FACULTY

Enrollment: 7,127. **Student Body:** 60% female, 40% male, 5% international. Asian 11%, African American 6%, Caucasian 67%, Hispanic 7%, Native American <1%, Pacific Islander <1%, Two or more races 4%, Race unknown 1%.
Retention and Graduation: 91% freshmen return for sophomore year. 71% freshmen graduate within 4 years. 79% freshmen graduate within 6 years.
Faculty: Student/faculty ratio 9:1. 695 full-time faculty, 88% hold PhDs, 16% are members of minority groups, 51% are women.

ACADEMICS

Degrees: Associate; Bachelor's; Certificate; Doctoral degree—professional practice; Doctoral degree research/scholarship; Master's; Post-bachelor's certificate; Post-master's certificate. **Classes:** Most classes have 20–29 students. Most lab/discussion sessions have 20–29 students. **Most popular majors:** Exercise Science and Kinesiology; Registered Nursing/Registered Nurse; Biology/Biological Sciences, General. **Special Study Options:** Accelerated program; Cooperative education program; Cross-registration; Distance learning; Double major; Dual enrollment; English as a Second Language (ESL); Exchange student program (domestic); Honors program; Independent study; Internships; Liberal arts/career combination; Student-designed major; Study abroad; Teacher certification program. **Honors programs:** www.slu.edu/honors/index.php. **Combined degree programs:** BA/JD; BA/MA. **Disability Services offered:** Note-taking services; Reader services; Tape recorders; Tutors. **Career services:** Alumni network; Alumni services; Career assessment; Career/job search classes; Internships; Regional alumni.

FACILITIES

Housing: Apartments for single students; Coed dorms; Fraternity/sorority housing; Special housing for disabled students; Special housing for international students; Theme housing. **Special Academic Facilities/Equipment:** Saint Louis University Museum of Art (SLUMA), Museum of Contemporary Religious Art (MOCRA), and The McNamee Gallery of Samuel Cupples House. **Campus Network:** 100% of classrooms, 100% of dorms, 100% of libraries, 100% of dining areas, 50% of common outdoor areas have wireless network access.

CAMPUS LIFE

Environment: Metropolis. **Activities:** Campus Ministries; Choral groups; Dance; Drama/theater; International Student Organization; Jazz band; Literary magazine; Model UN; Music ensembles; Musical theater; Pep band; Radio station; Student government; Student newspaper; Symphony orchestra; Television station. **Athletics (Intercollegiate):** *Men:* baseball, basketball, cross-country, diving, soccer, swimming, tennis, track/field (outdoor), track/field (indoor). *Women:* basketball, cross-country, diving, field hockey, soccer, softball, swimming, tennis, track/field (outdoor), track/field (indoor), volleyball. **On-Campus Highlights:** St. Francis Xavier Church.

ADMISSIONS

Freshman Academic Profile: Average high school GPA 3.9. 38% in top 10% of high school class, 72% in top 25% of high school class, 92% in top 50% of high school class. **Test Scores:** SAT Math middle 50% range 580–700. SAT EBRW middle 50% range 590–680. ACT middle 50% range 25–30. **Basis for Candidate Selection:** *Very important factors include:* academic GPA, standardized test scores. *Important factors include:* rigor of secondary school record, application essay, extracurricular activities, talent/ability, character/personal qualities, volunteer work. *Other factors include:* recommendation(s), interview, work experience. **Freshman Admission Requirements:** High school diploma is required and GED is accepted. *Academic units required:* 4 English, 4 math, 3 science, 3 foreign language, 3 social studies, 3 academic electives. *Academic units recommended:* 4 English, 4 math, 3 science, 3 foreign language, 3 social studies, 3 academic electives. **Freshman Admission Statistics:** 15,573 applied, 58% admitted, 21% enrolled. **Transfer Admission Requirements:** College transcript(s). Minimum college GPA of 2.0 required. Lowest grade transferable C. **General Admission Information:** Non-fall registration accepted. Admission may be deferred for a maximum of 1 year.

COSTS AND FINANCIAL AID

Required Forms and Deadlines: FAFSA. **Notification of Awards:** Applicants will be notified of awards on a rolling basis beginning 2/1. **Types of Aid:** *Need-based scholarships/grants:* College/university scholarship or grant aid from institutional funds; Federal Nursing Scholarships; Federal Pell; Private scholarships; SEOG; State scholarships/grants. *Loans:* Direct PLUS loans; Direct Subsidized Stafford Loans; Direct Unsubsidized Stafford Loans. **Student Employment:** Federal Work-Study Program available. Institutional employment available. **Criteria awarding aid:** *Non-need-based:* Academics, Art, Athletics, Leadership, Music/drama, Religious affiliation.

SAINT MARTIN'S UNIVERSITY

5000 Abbey Way SE, Lacey, WA 98503-7500
Phone: 360-438-4596 **Financial Aid Phone:** (360) 438-4397
E-mail: admissions@stmartin.edu **CEEB Code:** 4674
Fax: 360-412-6189 **Website:** www.stmartin.edu **ACT Code:** 4474

This private school, affiliated with the Roman Catholic Church, was founded in 1895. It has a 300 acre campus.

RATINGS

Admissions Selectivity Rating: 75   Fire Safety Rating: 60*   Green Rating: 60*

STUDENTS AND FACULTY

Enrollment: 1,307. **Student Body:** 54% female, 46% male, 27% out-of-state, 4% international (8 countries represented). Asian 9%, African American 6%, Caucasian 46%, Hispanic 15%, Native American 1%, Pacific Islander 5%, Two or more races 10%, Race unknown 9%.
Retention and Graduation: 77% freshmen return for sophomore year. 58% freshmen graduate within 4 years. 67% freshmen graduate within 6 years.
Faculty: Student/faculty ratio 12:1. 84 full-time faculty, 90% hold PhDs, 18% are members of minority groups, 43% are women. 0% of classes are taught by teaching assistants.

ACADEMICS

Degrees: Bachelor's; Certificate; Master's; Post-bachelor's certificate; Post-master's certificate. **Classes:** Most classes have fewer than 10 students. Most lab/discussion sessions have 20–29 students. **Most popular majors:** Mechanical Engineering; Biology/Biological Sciences, General; Business Administration and Management, General. **Special Study Options:** Distance learning; Double major; English as a Second Language (ESL); Exchange student program (domestic); Independent study; Internships; Study abroad; Teacher certification program. **Combined degree programs:** BA/MEng. **Disability Services offered:** Note-taking services; Reader services; Tape recorders; Tutors. **Career**

services: Alumni network; Alumni services; Career assessment; Career/job search classes; Internships; Regional alumni.

FACILITIES

Housing: Apartments for single students; Coed dorms; Special housing for disabled students; 85% of campus accessible to physically disabled. **Campus Network:** 100% of classrooms, 100% of dorms, 100% of student union, 100% of libraries, 100% of dining areas, 50% of common outdoor areas have wireless network access.

CAMPUS LIFE

Environment: Town. **Activities:** Campus Ministries; Choral groups; Concert band; Dance; Drama/theater; International Student Organization; Jazz band; Model UN; Music ensembles; Musical theater; Pep band; Student government; Student newspaper. 41 registered organizations, 3 honor societies, 3 religious organizations on campus. **Athletics (Intercollegiate):** *Men:* baseball, basketball, cross-country, golf, track/field (outdoor), track/field (indoor). *Women:* basketball, cross-country, golf, softball, track/field (outdoor), track/field (indoor), volleyball. **On-Campus Highlights:** O'Grady Library.

ADMISSIONS

Freshman Academic Profile: Average high school GPA 3.4. 27% in top 10% of high school class, 57% in top 25% of high school class, 88% in top 50% of high school class. 50% from public high schools. **Test Scores:** SAT Math middle 50% range 490–580. SAT EBRW middle 50% range 480–590. ACT middle 50% range 17–24. **Basis for Candidate Selection:** *Very important factors include:* rigor of secondary school record, academic GPA. *Important factors include:* application essay, standardized test scores, recommendation(s), extracurricular activities, character/personal qualities, volunteer work. *Other factors include:* class rank, talent/ability, alumni/ae relation, work experience. **Freshman Admission Requirements:** High school diploma is required and GED is accepted. *Academic units recommended:* 4 English, 3 math, 3 science, 1 science lab, 2 foreign language, 2 social studies, 3 academic electives. **Freshman Admission Statistics:** 1,614 applied, 96% admitted, 22% enrolled. **Transfer Admission Requirements:** College transcript(s), essay or personal statement. Minimum college GPA of 2.25 required. Lowest grade transferable C-. **General Admission Information:** Priority deadline 11/1. Regular application deadline 7/31. Non-fall registration accepted. Admission may be deferred for a maximum of one year.

COSTS AND FINANCIAL AID

Annual tuition $39,500. Room and board $12,410. Required fees $440. Average book and supplies expense $1,000. **Required Forms and Deadlines:** FAFSA. **Notification of Awards:** Applicants will be notified of awards on a rolling basis beginning 11/21. **Types of Aid:** *Need-based scholarships/grants:* College/university scholarship or grant aid from institutional funds; Federal Pell; Private scholarships; SEOG; State scholarships/grants. *Loans:* Direct PLUS loans; Direct Subsidized Stafford Loans; Direct Unsubsidized Stafford Loans. **Student Employment:** Federal Work-Study Program available. Institutional employment available. **Financial Aid Statistics:** 100% needy freshmen, 99% needy undergrads receive need-based scholarship or grant aid. 16% freshmen, 18% undergrads receive non-need-based scholarship or grant aid. 68% freshmen, 70% undergrads receive need-based self-help aid. 6% freshmen, 7% undergrads receive athletic scholarships. 66% undergrads borrow to pay for school. Average cumulative indebtedness $30,672. **Criteria awarding aid:** *Need-based:* Academics, Alumni affiliation, Art, Leadership, Minority status, Music/drama, Religious affiliation. *Non-need-based:* Academics, Alumni affiliation, Art, Athletics, Leadership, Minority status, Music/drama, Religious affiliation, State/district residency.

SAINT MARY-OF-THE-WOODS COLLEGE

Office of Admission, Saint Mary-of-the-Woods, IN 47876-0068
Phone: 812-535-5106 **Financial Aid Phone:** 812-535-5100
E-mail: smwcadms@smwc.edu **CEEB Code:** 1704
Fax: 812-535-5010 **Website:** www.smwc.edu **ACT Code:** 1242

This private school, affiliated with the Roman Catholic Church, was founded in 1840. It has a 67 acre campus.

RATINGS

Admissions Selectivity Rating: 80 **Fire Safety Rating:** 99 **Green Rating:** 60*

STUDENTS AND FACULTY

Enrollment: 1,176. **Student Body:** 97% female, 3% male, 30% out-of-state, 5 countries represented.

Retention and Graduation: 77% freshmen return for sophomore year. 18% grads go on to further study within 1 year. 15% grads pursue arts and sciences degrees. 1% grads pursue law degrees. 1% grads pursue business degrees. 1% grads pursue medical degrees. **Faculty:** Student/faculty ratio 8:1. 67 full-time faculty, 54% hold PhDs, 6% are members of minority groups, 66% are women. 0% of classes are taught by teaching assistants.

ACADEMICS

Degrees: Associate; Bachelor's; Certificate; Master's; Post-bachelor's certificate; Post-master's certificate; Transfer Associate. **Classes:** Most classes have 10–19 students. **Most popular majors:** Biology/Biological Sciences, General; Elementary Education and Teaching; Equestrian/Equine Studies. **Special Study Options:** Accelerated program; Cross-registration; Distance learning; Double major; External degree program; Honors program; Independent study; Internships; Student-designed major; Study abroad; Teacher certification program. **Disability Services offered:** Tutors. **Career services:** Alumni network; Alumni services; Career assessment; Career/job search classes; Internships; Regional alumni.

FACILITIES

Housing: Special housing for disabled students; Women's dorms; 100% of campus accessible to physically disabled. **Special Academic Facilities/Equipment:** Cecilian Auditorium and Conservatory of Music; SMWC Art Gallery.

CAMPUS LIFE

Environment: Town. **Activities:** Campus Ministries; Choral groups; Concert band; Dance; Drama/theater; International Student Organization; Jazz band; Literary magazine; Music ensembles; Musical theater; Student government; Student newspaper; Yearbook. 30 registered organizations, 6 honor societies, 1 religious organization on campus. **Athletics (Intercollegiate):** *Women:* basketball, equestrian sports, golf, soccer, softball, track/field (outdoor). **On-Campus Highlights:** Le Fer Hall (residence hall). **Environmental Initiatives:** Recycling.

ADMISSIONS

Freshman Academic Profile: Average high school GPA 3.3. 85% from public high schools. **Test Scores:** SAT Math middle 50% range 410–520. SAT EBRW middle 50% range 430–540. ACT middle 50% range 18–25. **Basis for Candidate Selection:** *Important factors include:* rigor of secondary school record, class rank, academic GPA, application essay, standardized test scores, recommendation(s). *Other factors include:* interview, talent/ability, character/personal qualities, level of applicant's interest. **Freshman Admission Requirements:** High school diploma is required and GED is accepted. *Academic units required:* 8 English, 6 math, 6 science, 2 science labs, 4 foreign language, 4 social studies, 2 history, 10 academic electives. *Academic units recommended:* 8 English, 8 math, 8 science, 4 science labs, 6 foreign language, 6 social studies, 4 history, 7 academic electives. **Freshman Admission Statistics:** 268 applied, 78% admitted, 62% enrolled. **Transfer Admission Requirements:** College transcript(s), essay or personal statement. Minimum college GPA of 2.0 required. Lowest grade transferable C. **General Admission Information:** Application fee $30. Regular application deadline 8/8. Non-fall registration accepted. Admission may be deferred for a maximum of 1 year.

COSTS AND FINANCIAL AID

Annual tuition $20,900. Room and board $7,890. Required fees $650. Average book and supplies expense $900. **Required Forms and Deadlines:** FAFSA. **Notification of Awards:** Applicants will be notified of awards on a rolling basis beginning 12/1. **Types of Aid:** *Need-based scholarships/grants:* College/university scholarship or grant aid from institutional funds; Federal Pell; Private scholarships; SEOG; State scholarships/grants. **Student Employment:** Federal Work-Study Program available. Institutional employment available. **Financial Aid Statistics:** 77% needy freshmen, 92% needy undergrads receive need-based scholarship or grant aid. 76% freshmen, 12% undergrads receive non-need-based scholarship or grant aid. 49% freshmen, 82% undergrads receive need-based self-help aid. 10% freshmen, 4% undergrads receive athletic scholarships. 98% freshmen, 96% undergrads receive any aid. **Criteria awarding aid:** *Need-based:* Academics, Alumni affiliation, Art, Athletics, Leadership, Music/drama. *Non-need-based:* Academics, Alumni affiliation, Art, Athletics, Leadership, Music/drama.

SAINT MARY'S COLLEGE (IN)

Admission office, Notre Dame, IN 46556
Phone: 574-284-4587 **Financial Aid Phone:** 574-284-4557
E-mail: admission@saintmarys.edu **CEEB Code:** 1702
Fax: 574-284-4841 **Website:** www.saintmarys.edu **ACT Code:** 1244

This private school, affiliated with the Roman Catholic Church, was founded in 1844. It has a 100 acre campus.

RATINGS

Admissions Selectivity Rating: 80   Fire Safety Rating: 90   Green Rating: 77

STUDENTS AND FACULTY

Enrollment: 1,489. **Student Body:** 100% female, 0% male, 70% out-of-state, 1% international (10 countries represented). Asian 2%, African American 2%, Caucasian 78%, Hispanic 11%, Native American <1%, Pacific Islander <1%, Two or more races 3%, Race unknown 2%.
Retention and Graduation: 84% freshmen return for sophomore year. 73% freshmen graduate within 4 years. 80% freshmen graduate within 6 years. 33% grads go on to further study within 1 year. 9% grads pursue arts and sciences degrees. 1% grads pursue law degrees. 2% grads pursue business degrees. 1% grads pursue medical degrees. **Faculty:** Student/faculty ratio 9:1. 144 full-time faculty, 92% hold PhDs, 15% are members of minority groups, 72% are women. 0% of classes are taught by teaching assistants.

ACADEMICS

Degrees: Bachelor's; Doctoral degree—professional practice; Master's. **Classes:** Most classes have 20–29 students. Most lab/discussion sessions have 10–19 students. **Most popular majors:** Registered Nursing/Registered Nurse; Biology/Biological Sciences, General; Business Administration and Management, General. **Special Study Options:** Cross-registration; Distance learning; Double major; Exchange student program (domestic); Independent study; Internships; Liberal arts/career combination; Student-designed major; Study abroad; Teacher certification program. **Disability Services offered:** Note-taking services; Reader services; Tape recorders; Tutors. **Career services:** Alumni network; Alumni services; Career assessment; Career/job search classes; Internships; Regional alumni.

FACILITIES

Housing: Apartments for single students; Special housing for disabled students; Women's dorms; 100% of campus accessible to physically disabled. **Special Academic Facilities/Equipment:** Greenhouse; animal facility; chemical instrumentation lab; incubators; cold room; assorted biological research equipment.

CAMPUS LIFE

Environment: City. **Activities:** Campus Ministries; Choral groups; Concert band; Dance; Drama/theater; International Student Organization; Literary magazine; Marching band; Music ensembles; Musical theater; Opera; Pep band; Radio station; Student government; Student newspaper; Television station; Yearbook. 75 registered organizations, 14 honor societies, 8 religious organizations on campus. **Athletics (Intercollegiate):** *Women:* basketball, cross-country, diving, golf, soccer, softball, swimming, tennis, volleyball. **On-Campus Highlights:** Student Center/Noble Family Dining hall. **Environmental Initiatives:** Campus Recycling Program.

ADMISSIONS

Freshman Academic Profile: Average high school GPA 3.8. 28% in top 10% of high school class, 64% in top 25% of high school class, 93% in top 50% of high school class. 55% from public high schools. **Test Scores:** SAT Math middle 50% range 500–620. SAT EBRW middle 50% range 530–630. ACT middle 50% range 23–29. **Basis for Candidate Selection:** *Important factors include:* rigor of secondary school record, academic GPA, standardized test scores. *Other factors include:* class rank, application essay, recommendation(s), interview, extracurricular activities, talent/ability, character/personal qualities, first generation, alumni/ae relation, geographical residence, state residency, racial/ethnic status, volunteer work, work experience, level of applicant's interest. **Freshman Admission Requirements:** High school diploma is required and GED is accepted. *Academic units required:* 4 English, 3 math, 2 science, 2 science labs, 2 foreign language, 3 history. *Academic units recommended:* 4 English, 4 math, 4 science, 2 science labs, 4 foreign language, 2 social studies. **Freshman Admission Statistics:** 1,830 applied, 78% admitted, 25% enrolled. **Transfer Admission Requirements:** High school transcript, college transcript(s), essay or personal statement, standardized test scores, statement of good standing from prior institution(s). Minimum college GPA of 3.0 required. Lowest grade transferable C. **General Admission Information:** Priority deadline 2/15. Non-fall registration accepted.

COSTS AND FINANCIAL AID

Annual tuition $41,380. Room and board $12,580. Required fees $840. Average book and supplies expense $1,100. **Required Forms and Deadlines:** FAFSA. **Types of Aid:** *Need-based scholarships/grants:* College/university scholarship or grant aid from institutional funds; Federal Pell; Private scholarships; SEOG; State scholarships/grants. *Loans:* Direct PLUS loans; Direct Subsidized Stafford Loans; Direct Unsubsidized Stafford Loans. **Student Employment:** Federal Work-Study Program available. Institutional employment available. **Financial Aid Statistics:** 99% needy freshmen, 97% needy undergrads receive need-based scholarship or grant aid. 26% freshmen, 37% undergrads receive non-need-based scholarship or grant aid. 85% freshmen, 86% undergrads receive need-based self-help aid. 0% freshmen, 0% undergrads receive athletic scholarships. 100% freshmen, 99% undergrads receive any aid. 71% undergrads borrow to pay for school. Average cumulative indebtedness $33,698. **Criteria awarding aid:** *Need-based:* Academics. *Non-need-based:* Academics, Art, Music/drama.

SAINT MARY'S COLLEGE OF CALIFORNIA

1928 St. Mary's Rd, PMB 4800, Moraga, CA 94575-4800
Phone: 925-631-4224 **Financial Aid Phone:** 925-631-4370
E-mail: smcadmit@stmarys-ca.edu **CEEB Code:** 4675
Fax: 925-376-7193 **Website:** www.stmarys-ca.edu **ACT Code:** 386

This private school, affiliated with the Roman Catholic Church, was founded in 1863. It has a 420 acre campus.

RATINGS

Admissions Selectivity Rating: 76   Fire Safety Rating: 95   Green Rating: 93

STUDENTS AND FACULTY

Enrollment: 2,632. **Student Body:** 57% female, 43% male, 13% out-of-state, 3% international (20 countries represented). Asian 12%, African American 4%, Caucasian 42%, Hispanic 28%, Native American <1%, Pacific Islander 2%, Two or more races 8%, Race unknown 2%.
Retention and Graduation: 83% freshmen return for sophomore year. 69% freshmen graduate within 4 years. 76% freshmen graduate within 6 years. 30% grads go on to further study within 1 year. 4% grads pursue arts and sciences degrees. 2% grads pursue law degrees. 3% grads pursue business degrees. 2% grads pursue medical degrees. **Faculty:** Student/faculty ratio 10:1. 193 full-time faculty, 99% hold PhDs, 31% are members of minority groups, 56% are women. 0% of classes are taught by teaching assistants.

ACADEMICS

Degrees: Bachelor's; Certificate; Doctoral degree—other; Master's. **Classes:** Most classes have 10–19 students. Most lab/discussion sessions have 10–19 students. **Most popular majors:** Communication and Media Studies, Other; Business Administration, Management and Operations, Other; Liberal Arts and Sciences, General Studies and Humanities. **Special Study Options:** Accelerated program; Cross-registration; Double major; Dual enrollment; Exchange student program (domestic); Honors program; Independent study; Internships; Liberal arts/career combination; Student-designed major; Study abroad; Teacher certification program. **Honors programs:** Honor Program. **Combined degree programs:** BA/MA. **Disability Services offered:** Note-taking services; Reader services; Tape recorders; Tutors. **Career services:** Alumni network; Alumni services; Career assessment; Career/job search classes; Internships.

FACILITIES

Housing: Apartments for single students; Coed dorms; Cooperative housing; Men's dorms; Special housing for disabled students; Special housing for international students; Theme housing; Women's dorms; 80% of campus accessible to physically disabled. **Special Academic Facilities/Equipment:** Saint Mary's Museum Brousseau Hall, Science Building Geissberger Observatory.

CAMPUS LIFE

Environment: Village. **Activities:** Campus Ministries; Choral groups; Concert band; Dance; Drama/theater; International Student Organization; Jazz band; Literary magazine; Music ensembles; Musical theater; Pep band; Radio station; Student government; Student newspaper. 50 registered organizations, 1 honor society, 3 religious organizations on campus. **Athletics (Intercollegiate):** *Men:* baseball, basketball, cheerleading, cross-country, golf, soccer, tennis. *Women:* basketball, cheerleading, crew/rowing, cross-country, lacrosse, soccer, softball, tennis, volleyball. **On-Campus Highlights:** The 1928 Pub. **Environmental Initiatives:** Members of the Sustainability Committee, particularly the Policy and Operations Subcommittees, are volunteering their time to develop a Climate Action Plan for the College. The Plan addresses the unique challenges and opportunities Saint Mary's faces in trying to reduce greenhouse gas emissions.

ADMISSIONS

Freshman Academic Profile: Average high school GPA 3.5. 52% from public high schools. **Test Scores:** SAT Math middle 50% range 520–620. SAT EBRW middle 50% range 540–630. ACT middle 50% range 22–28. **Basis for Candidate Selection:** *Very important factors include:* rigor of secondary school record, academic GPA. *Important factors include:* standardized test scores, first generation. *Other factors include:* class rank, application essay, recommendation(s), interview, extracurricular activities, talent/ability, character/personal qualities, alumni/ae relation, geographical residence, volunteer work, work experience, level of applicant's interest. **Freshman Admission Requirements:** High school diploma is required and GED is accepted. *Academic units required:* 4 English, 3 math, 3 science, 1 science lab, 2 foreign language, 2 social studies, 1 history. *Academic units recommended:* 4 English, 4 math, 4 science, 1 science lab, 3 foreign language, 2 social studies, 1 history. **Freshman Admission Statistics:** 6,069 applied, 81% admitted, 10% enrolled. **Transfer Admission Requirements:** High school transcript, college transcript(s), essay or personal statement. Minimum college GPA of 2.3 required. Lowest grade transferable C-. **General Admission Information:** Application fee $60. Priority deadline 11/15. Regular application deadline 1/15. Non-fall registration accepted. Admission may be deferred for a maximum of 12 months.

COSTS AND FINANCIAL AID

Annual tuition $50,460. Room and board $15,706. Required fees $200. Average book and supplies expense $1,080. **Required Forms and Deadlines:** FAFSA. **Notification of Awards:** Applicants will be notified of awards on a rolling basis beginning 12/16. **Types of Aid:** *Need-based scholarships/grants:* College/university scholarship or grant aid from institutional funds; Federal Pell; Private scholarships; SEOG; State scholarships/grants. *Loans:* Direct PLUS loans; Direct Subsidized Stafford Loans; Direct Unsubsidized Stafford Loans. **Student Employment:** Federal Work-Study Program available. Institutional employment available. **Financial Aid Statistics:** 61% needy freshmen, 70% needy undergrads receive need-based scholarship or grant aid. 100% freshmen, 86% undergrads receive non-need-based scholarship or grant aid. 70% freshmen, 78% undergrads receive need-based self-help aid. 8% freshmen, 7% undergrads receive athletic scholarships. 99% freshmen, 92% undergrads receive any aid. 85% undergrads borrow to pay for school. Average cumulative indebtedness $30,693. **Criteria awarding aid:** *Need-based:* Alumni affiliation, Minority status. *Non-need-based:* Academics, Athletics, Leadership, Music/drama, Religious affiliation.

ST. MARY'S COLLEGE OF MARYLAND

Best Colleges

47645 College Drive, St. Mary's City, MD 20686-3001
Phone: 240-895-5000 **Financial Aid Phone:** 240-895-3000
E-mail: admissions@smcm.edu **CEEB Code:** 5601
Fax: 240-895-5001 **Website:** www.smcm.edu **ACT Code:** 1736

This public school was founded in 1840. It has a 361 acre campus.

RATINGS

| Admissions Selectivity Rating: 77 | Fire Safety Rating: 88 | Green Rating: 99 |

STUDENTS AND FACULTY

Enrollment: 1,466. **Student Body:** 59% female, 41% male, 5% out-of-state, <1% international (4 countries represented). Asian 4%, African American 10%,

Caucasian 71%, Hispanic 7%, Native American <1%, Pacific Islander <1%, Two or more races 6%, Race unknown 2%.
Retention and Graduation: 85% freshmen return for sophomore year. 68% freshmen graduate within 4 years. 77% freshmen graduate within 6 years. 31% grads go on to further study within 1 year. 10% grads pursue arts and sciences degrees. 1% grads pursue law degrees. <1% grads pursue business degrees. <1% grads pursue medical degrees. **Faculty:** Student/faculty ratio 9:1. 131 full-time faculty, 98% hold PhDs, 14% are members of minority groups, 50% are women. 0% of classes are taught by teaching assistants.

ACADEMICS

Degrees: Bachelor's; Master's. **Classes:** Most classes have 10–19 students. Most lab/discussion sessions have 10–19 students. **Most popular majors:** English Language and Literature, General; Biology/Biological Sciences, General; Psychology, General. **Special Study Options:** Cross-registration; Double major; Dual enrollment; Exchange student program (domestic); Independent study; Internships; Student-designed major; Study abroad. **Disability Services offered:** Note-taking services; Reader services; Tape recorders; Tutors. **Career services:** Alumni network; Alumni services; Career assessment; Career/job search classes; Internships; Regional alumni.

FACILITIES

Housing: Apartments for single students; Coed dorms; Men's dorms; Special housing for disabled students; Special housing for international students; Theme housing; Wellness housing; Women's dorms; 95% of campus accessible to physically disabled. **Special Academic Facilities/Equipment:** Archaeological site of Historic St. Mary's City, electron microscope, marine research vessel, fresh and salt water research facilities, comprehensive neuroscience laboratory facilities. **Campus Network:** 100% of classrooms, 100% of libraries have wireless network access.

CAMPUS LIFE

Environment: Rural. **Activities:** Campus Ministries; Choral groups; Dance; Drama/theater; Jazz band; Literary magazine; Music ensembles; Radio station; Student government; Student newspaper; Symphony orchestra. 99 registered organizations, 12 honor societies, 4 religious organizations on campus. **Athletics (Intercollegiate):** *Men:* baseball, basketball, cross-country, lacrosse, sailing, soccer, swimming, tennis. *Women:* basketball, cross-country, field hockey, lacrosse, sailing, soccer, swimming, tennis, volleyball. **On-Campus Highlights:** Campus Center **Environmental Initiatives:** Purchasing approximately 80% of the school's total energy use in RECs to offset our carbon output.

ADMISSIONS

Freshman Academic Profile: Average high school GPA 3.4. 26% in top 10% of high school class, 55% in top 25% of high school class, 83% in top 50% of high school class. 81% from public high schools. **Test Scores:** SAT Math middle 50% range 520–640. SAT EBRW middle 50% range 540–650. ACT middle 50% range 21–29. **Basis for Candidate Selection:** *Very important factors include:* rigor of secondary school record, academic GPA, application essay, standardized test scores, recommendation(s). *Important factors include:* class rank, extracurricular activities, talent/ability, character/personal qualities. *Other factors include:* interview, first generation, alumni/ae relation, geographical residence, state residency, racial/ethnic status, work experience, level of applicant's interest. **Freshman Admission Requirements:** High school diploma is required and GED is accepted. *Academic units required:* 4 English, 3 math, 3 science, 2 science labs, 2 social studies, 1 history. *Academic units recommended:* 4 math, 4 foreign language, 3 social studies. **Freshman Admission Statistics:** 1,621 applied, 84% admitted, 23% enrolled. **Transfer Admission Requirements:** College transcript(s), essay or personal statement. Minimum college GPA of 3.0 required. Lowest grade transferable C-. **General Admission Information:** Application fee $50. Priority deadline 11/1. Regular application deadline 1/5. Non-fall registration accepted. Admission may be deferred for a maximum of 1 year.

COSTS AND FINANCIAL AID

Annual in-state tuition $12,116. Annual out-of-state tuition $28,192. Room and board $13,595. Required fees $3,008. Average book and supplies expense $800. **Required Forms and Deadlines:** FAFSA. **Notification of Awards:** Applicants will be notified of awards on a rolling basis beginning 12/15. **Types of Aid:** *Need-based scholarships/grants:* College/university scholarship or grant aid from institutional funds; Federal Pell; Private scholarships; SEOG; State scholarships/grants. *Loans:* Direct PLUS loans; Direct Subsidized Stafford Loans; Direct Unsubsidized Stafford Loans. **Student Employment:** Federal Work-Study Program available. Institutional employment available. **Financial Aid Statistics:** 87% needy freshmen, 86% needy undergrads receive need-based scholarship or grant aid. 78% freshmen, 65% undergrads receive non-need-based scholarship or grant aid. 60% freshmen, 70% undergrads receive need-based self-help aid. 0% freshmen, 0% undergrads receive athletic scholarships. 92% freshmen, 83% undergrads receive any aid. 52% undergrads borrow to pay for school. Average cumulative indebtedness $25,579. **Criteria awarding aid:** *Non-need-based:* Academics, Leadership.

ST. MARY'S UNIVERSITY

One Camino Santa Maria, San Antonio, TX 78228-8503
Phone: 210.436.3126 **Financial Aid Phone:** 210-436-3141
E-mail: uadm@stmarytx.edu **CEEB Code:** 6637
Fax: 210.431.6742 **Website:** http://www.stmarytx.edu/ **ACT Code:** 4158

This private school, affiliated with the Roman Catholic Church, was founded in 1852. It has a 135 acre campus.

RATINGS
Admissions Selectivity Rating: 80 **Fire Safety Rating:** 87 **Green Rating:** 68

STUDENTS AND FACULTY
Enrollment: 2,367. **Student Body:** 55% female, 45% male, 8% out-of-state, 8% international (34 countries represented). Asian 2%, African American 3%, Caucasian 15%, Hispanic 67%, Native American <1%, Pacific Islander <1%, Two or more races 1%, Race unknown 3%.
Retention and Graduation: 75% freshmen return for sophomore year. 44% freshmen graduate within 4 years. % freshmen graduate within 6 years. **Faculty:** Student/faculty ratio 11:1. 220 full-time faculty, 95% hold PhDs, 30% are members of minority groups, 39% are women. 0% of classes are taught by teaching assistants.

ACADEMICS
Degrees: Bachelor's; Doctoral degree research/scholarship; Master's; Post-bachelor's certificate; Post-master's certificate. **Classes:** Most classes have 10–19 students. Most lab/discussion sessions have 10–19 students. **Most popular majors:** Biology/Biological Sciences, General; Exercise Science and Kinesiology; Psychology, General. **Special Study Options:** Accelerated program; Cross-registration; Distance learning; Double major; Dual enrollment; English as a Second Language (ESL); Exchange student program (domestic); Honors program; Independent study; Internships; Study abroad; Teacher certification program. **Honors programs:** The Honors Program offers an academically challenging and personally enriching course of study designed to cultivate critical analysis, clear oral and written expression, aesthetic awareness and ethical judgment. In and out of the classroom we seek to prepare our future graduates for lives of leadership and service to their communities. **Combined degree programs:** BA/JD; BA/MA. **Disability Services offered:** Note-taking services; Reader services; Tape recorders; Tutors. **Career services:** Alumni network; Alumni services; Career assessment; Career/job search classes; Internships; Regional alumni.

FACILITIES
Housing: Coed dorms; Theme housing; 80% of campus accessible to physically disabled. **Special Academic Facilities/Equipment:** St. Mary's has many unique facilities available to our undergraduate students. Our Charles Cotrell Learning Commons includes extensive access to technology and on-site technological assistance, extended library hours and a Starbucks coffee shop. The space is popular with students who use the area for group and individual studying, socializing, and breaks between classes. Students interested in fitness and recreation can visit our full-size gym, indoor track, rock-climbing wall, indoor swimming pool, racquetball courts, fitness studio, and multiple fields and basketball courts. Our science department houses Earth Science museum on the second floor which houses over 1,300 samples of minerals, rocks, fossils, maps, and scientific instruments used for research purposes of undergraduates enrolled in the program. For our students interested in the arts, we offer art displays, a music and drama theatre, and an amphitheater. And in our Greehey School of Business, St. Mary's has a trading room that features a Trans-Lux LED jet ticker, a Trans-Lux data board, and a 57-inch LCD television for up-to-date financial information.

CAMPUS LIFE
Environment: Metropolis. **Activities:** Campus Ministries; Choral groups; Concert band; Dance; Drama/theater; International Student Organization; Jazz band; Literary magazine; Model UN; Music ensembles; Musical theater; Opera; Student government; Student newspaper. 74 registered organizations, 10 honor societies, 8 fraternities, 5 sororities on campus. **Athletics (Intercollegiate):**

Men: baseball, basketball, cheerleading, golf, soccer, tennis. *Women:* basketball, cheerleading, cross-country, golf, soccer, softball, tennis, volleyball. **On-Campus Highlights:** Alumni Athletics and Convocation Center. **Environmental Initiatives:** Energy efficiency electric motors, chillers, lighting, Demand Energy Limiting.

ADMISSIONS
Freshman Academic Profile: Average high school GPA 3.6. 34% in top 10% of high school class, 58% in top 25% of high school class, 83% in top 50% of high school class. 75% from public high schools. **Test Scores:** SAT Math middle 50% range 520–620. SAT EBRW middle 50% range 530–630. ACT middle 50% range 21–27. **Basis for Candidate Selection:** *Very important factors include:* rigor of secondary school record, academic GPA. *Important factors include:* standardized test scores. *Other factors include:* application essay, recommendation(s), interview, extracurricular activities, talent/ability, character/personal qualities, volunteer work, work experience, level of applicant's interest. **Freshman Admission Requirements:** High school diploma is required and GED is accepted. *Academic units required:* 4 English, 3 math, 3 science, 2 foreign language, 3 social studies, 1 academic elective. *Academic units recommended:* 4 English, 4 math, 4 science, 3 foreign language, 4 social studies. **Freshman Admission Statistics:** 5,350 applied, 75% admitted, 16% enrolled. **Transfer Admission Requirements:** College transcript(s). Minimum college GPA of 2.5 required. Lowest grade transferable C-. **General Admission Information:** Priority deadline 1/15. Regular application deadline 8/31. Non-fall registration accepted. Admission may be deferred for a maximum of 1 year.

COSTS AND FINANCIAL AID
Required Forms and Deadlines: FAFSA. **Notification of Awards:** Applicants will be notified of awards on a rolling basis beginning 12/1. **Types of Aid:** *Need-based scholarships/grants:* College/university scholarship or grant aid from institutional funds; Federal Pell; Private scholarships; SEOG; State scholarships/grants. *Loans:* Direct PLUS loans; Direct Subsidized Stafford Loans; Direct Unsubsidized Stafford Loans. **Student Employment:** Federal Work-Study Program available. Institutional employment available. **Financial Aid Statistics:** 99% needy freshmen, 98% needy undergrads receive need-based scholarship or grant aid. 8% freshmen, 7% undergrads receive non-need-based scholarship or grant aid. 82% freshmen, 83% undergrads receive need-based self-help aid. 4% freshmen, 6% undergrads receive athletic scholarships. 98.9% freshmen, 94% undergrads receive any aid. 77% undergrads borrow to pay for school. Average cumulative indebtedness $37,866. **Criteria awarding aid:** *Need-based:* Academics. *Non-need-based:* Academics, Alumni affiliation, Athletics, Music/drama, Religious affiliation, State/district residency.

SAINT MARY'S UNIVERSITY OF MINNESOTA

700 Terrace Heights #2, Winona, MN 55987-1399
Phone: 507-457-1700 **Financial Aid Phone:** (612) 238-4552
E-mail: admission@smumn.edu **CEEB Code:** 6632
Fax: 507-457-1722 **Website:** www.smumn.edu **ACT Code:** 2148

This private school, affiliated with the Roman Catholic Church, was founded in 1912. It has a 350 acre campus.

RATINGS
Admissions Selectivity Rating: 75 **Fire Safety Rating:** 94 **Green Rating:** 60*

STUDENTS AND FACULTY
Enrollment: 1,409. **Student Body:** 57% female, 43% male, 46% out-of-state, 3% international. Asian 3%, African American 9%, Caucasian 68%, Hispanic 8%, Native American <1%, Pacific Islander <1%, Two or more races <1%, Race unknown 8%.
Retention and Graduation: 82% freshmen return for sophomore year. 54% freshmen graduate within 4 years. 58% freshmen graduate within 6 years. 11% grads go on to further study within 1 year. **Faculty:** Student/faculty ratio 18:1. 100 full-time faculty, 89% hold PhDs, 6% are members of minority groups, 38% are women. 0% of classes are taught by teaching assistants.

ACADEMICS
Degrees: Bachelor's; Certificate; Diploma; Doctoral degree—professional practice; Doctoral degree research/scholarship; Master's; Post-bachelor's certificate; Post-master's certificate. **Classes:** Most classes have 10–19 students. Most lab/discussion sessions have 10–19 students. **Most popular majors:** Elementary Education and Teaching; Biology/Biological Sciences, General; Marketing/Marketing Management, General. **Special Study Options:**

Cooperative education program; Cross-registration; Distance learning; Double major; Dual enrollment; English as a Second Language (ESL); Honors program; Independent study; Internships; Student-designed major; Study abroad; Teacher certification program. **Honors programs:** The Lasallian Honors Program is the general education core program for honors students. It is designed to provide an intellectually stimulating experience for bright and motivated students who wish to engage in "shared inquiry" in small, interdisciplinary classes. The hallmarks of the Honors Program are in-depth discussions of the Great Books and other notable texts of the Western and Eastern cultural traditions; service learning with organizations in the community; experiential learning in the fine arts; and participation in a community of learners who desire to grow intellectually, spiritually, and creatively. The program is grounded in the university mission and the Lasallian dispositions of faith, zeal, service, and community. The ultimate goal of the Lasallian Honors Program is to awaken and nurture the intellectual, spiritual, and personal development of learners in preparation for lives of servant leadership and appreciation of the world's intellectual and cultural heritages. **Disability Services offered:** Note-taking services; Reader services; Tape recorders; Tutors. **Career services:** Alumni network; Alumni services; Career assessment; Career/job search classes; Internships.

FACILITIES

Housing: Apartments for married students; Apartments for single students; Coed dorms; Men's dorms; Special housing for disabled students; Women's dorms; 93% of campus accessible to physically disabled. **Special Academic Facilities/Equipment:** Art gallery, performance center, laboratories, observatory.

CAMPUS LIFE

Environment: Town. **Activities:** Campus Ministries; Choral groups; Concert band; Dance; Drama/theater; International Student Organization; Jazz band; Literary magazine; Music ensembles; Musical theater; Radio station; Student government; Student newspaper; Student-run film society; Symphony orchestra; Yearbook. 80 registered organizations, 13 honor societies, 6 religious organizations on campus. **Athletics (Intercollegiate):** *Men:* baseball, basketball, cross-country, diving, golf, ice hockey, skiing (Nordic/cross-country), soccer, swimming, tennis, track/field (outdoor), track/field (indoor). *Women:* basketball, cross-country, diving, golf, ice hockey, skiing (Nordic/cross-country), soccer, softball, swimming, tennis, track/field (outdoor), track/field (indoor), volleyball. **On-Campus Highlights:** Brother Leopold Hall. **Environmental Initiatives:** ISO 14001 Certified Environmental Management System (EMS).

ADMISSIONS

Freshman Academic Profile: 65% from public high schools. **Test Scores:** SAT Math middle 50% range 510–620. SAT EBRW middle 50% range 520–620. ACT middle 50% range 20–26. **Basis for Candidate Selection:** *Very important factors include:* rigor of secondary school record, academic GPA. *Important factors include:* standardized test scores, talent/ability, character/personal qualities. *Other factors include:* class rank, application essay, recommendation(s), interview, extracurricular activities, alumni/ae relation, volunteer work, level of applicant's interest. **Freshman Admission Requirements:** High school diploma is required and GED is accepted. *Academic units required:* 4 English, 3 math, 3 science, 2 science labs, 2 social studies, 6 academic electives. *Academic units recommended:* 2 foreign language. **Freshman Admission Statistics:** 1,641 applied, 92% admitted, 20% enrolled. **Transfer Admission Requirements:** High school transcript, college transcript(s), statement of good standing from prior institution(s). Minimum college GPA of 2.0 required. Lowest grade transferable C. **General Admission Information:** Application fee $25. Priority deadline 4/1. Regular application deadline 5/1. Non-fall registration accepted. Admission may be deferred for a maximum of 1 year.

COSTS AND FINANCIAL AID

Required Forms and Deadlines: FAFSA. **Notification of Awards:** Applicants will be notified of awards on a rolling basis beginning 1/1. **Types of Aid:** *Need-based scholarships/grants:* College/university scholarship or grant aid from institutional funds; Federal Pell; Private scholarships; SEOG; State scholarships/grants. *Loans:* Direct PLUS loans; Direct Subsidized Stafford Loans; Direct Unsubsidized Stafford Loans. **Student Employment:** Federal Work-Study Program available. Institutional employment available. **Financial Aid Statistics:** 100% needy freshmen, 95% needy undergrads receive need-based scholarship or grant aid. 0% freshmen, 0% undergrads receive non-need-based scholarship or grant aid. 99% freshmen, 93% undergrads receive need-based self-help aid. 0% freshmen, 0% undergrads receive athletic scholarships. 99% freshmen, 96% undergrads receive any aid. 78% undergrads borrow to pay for school. Average cumulative indebtedness $34,917. **Criteria awarding aid:** *Need-based:* Academics. *Non-need-based:* Academics, Alumni affiliation, Art, Leadership, Music/drama.

SAINT MICHAEL'S COLLEGE

One Winooski Park, Box 7, Colchester, VT 05439
Phone: 802-654-3000 **Financial Aid Phone:** 802-654-3243
E-mail: admission@smcvt.edu **CEEB Code:** 3757
Fax: 802-654-2906 **Website:** www.smcvt.edu **ACT Code:** 4312

This private school, affiliated with the Roman Catholic Church, was founded in 1904. It has a 440 acre campus.

RATINGS

Admissions Selectivity Rating: 77   **Fire Safety Rating:** 89   **Green Rating:** 82

STUDENTS AND FACULTY

Enrollment: 1,551. **Student Body:** 54% female, 46% male, 85% out-of-state, 4% international (34 countries represented). Asian 1%, African American 2%, Caucasian 82%, Hispanic 6%, Native American <1%, Pacific Islander <1%, Two or more races 2%, Race unknown 3%.
Retention and Graduation: 83% freshmen return for sophomore year. 77% freshmen graduate within 4 years. 83% freshmen graduate within 6 years. 12% grads go on to further study within 1 year. 3% grads pursue arts and sciences degrees. 1% grads pursue law degrees. 2% grads pursue business degrees. 4% grads pursue medical degrees. **Faculty:** Student/faculty ratio 13:1. 117 full-time faculty, 87% hold PhDs, 5% are members of minority groups, 44% are women. 0% of classes are taught by teaching assistants.

ACADEMICS

Degrees: Bachelor's; Master's; Post-bachelor's certificate; Post-master's certificate. **Classes:** Most classes have 10–19 students. Most lab/discussion sessions have 10–19 students. **Most popular majors:** Biology/Biological Sciences, General; Psychology, General; Business/Commerce, General. **Special Study Options:** Accelerated program; Cross-registration; Distance learning; Double major; Dual enrollment; English as a Second Language (ESL); Exchange student program (domestic); Honors program; Independent study; Internships; Liberal arts/career combination; Student-designed major; Study abroad; Teacher certification program. **Honors programs:** The Honors Program at Saint Michael's provides additional challenges and opportunities to outstanding students through small group discussion, research and extra-curricular activities. Saint Michael's also has chapters of several national honors societies on campus including Phi Beta Kappa, and Delta Epsilon Sigma. **Combined degree programs:** BA/JD; BA/MA. **Disability Services offered:** Note-taking services; Reader services; Tape recorders; Tutors. **Career services:** Alumni network; Alumni services; Career assessment; Career/job search classes; Internships; Regional alumni.

FACILITIES

Housing: Apartments for single students; Coed dorms; Men's dorms; Special housing for disabled students; Special housing for international students; Theme housing; Wellness housing; Women's dorms; 75% of campus accessible to physically disabled. **Special Academic Facilities/Equipment:** Holcomb Observatory, McCarthy Arts Center Gallery, Maker Space.

CAMPUS LIFE

Environment: City. **Activities:** Campus Ministries; Choral groups; Concert band; Dance; Drama/theater; International Student Organization; Jazz band; Literary magazine; Music ensembles; Musical theater; Radio station; Student government; Student newspaper; Yearbook. 40 registered organizations, 11 honor societies, 1 religious organization on campus. **Athletics (Intercollegiate):** *Men:* baseball, basketball, cross-country, diving, golf, ice hockey, lacrosse, skiing (downhill/Alpine), skiing (Nordic/cross-country), soccer, swimming, tennis. *Women:* basketball, cross-country, diving, field hockey, ice hockey, lacrosse, skiing (downhill/Alpine), skiing (Nordic/cross-country), soccer, softball, swimming, tennis, volleyball. **On-Campus Highlights:** Dion Family Student Center. **Environmental Initiatives:** Energy Efficiency Programs: "Three Degree Challenge" to further reduce campus wide building temperatures by turning down thermostats to reduce energy consumption (in addition to reducing energy consumption, all new major appliances must be energy star certified); new building aims for LEED certification; all campus buildings on an Energy Management System to ensure efficient use of energy.

ADMISSIONS

Freshman Academic Profile: Average high school GPA 3.3. 21% in top 10% of high school class, 49% in top 25% of high school class, 79% in top 50% of high school class. 73% from public high schools. **Test Scores:** SAT Math middle 50% range 570–650. SAT EBRW middle 50% range 585–660. ACT middle 50% range 25–29. **Basis for Candidate Selection:** *Very important factors include:* rigor of secondary school record, class rank, academic GPA. *Important factors include:* application essay, standardized test scores, recommendation(s), talent/ability, character/personal qualities. *Other factors include:* interview, extracurricular activities, first generation, alumni/ae relation, geographical residence, state residency, racial/ethnic status, volunteer work, work experience, level of applicant's interest. **Freshman Admission Requirements:** High school diploma is required and GED is accepted. *Academic units required:* 4 English, 4 math, 3 science, 2 science labs, 2 foreign language, 3 social studies, 3 history. *Academic units recommended:* 4 English, 4 math, 4 science, 3 science labs, 4 foreign language, 4 social studies, 4 history. **Freshman Admission Statistics:** 3,967 applied, 83% admitted, 12% enrolled. **Transfer Admission Requirements:** High school transcript, college transcript(s), essay or personal statement, standardized test scores. Minimum college GPA of 2.8 required. Lowest grade transferable C-. **General Admission Information:** Application fee $50. Priority deadline 11/1. Regular application deadline 2/1. Non-fall registration accepted.

COSTS AND FINANCIAL AID

Annual tuition $46,175. Room and board $13,600. Required fees $2,000. Average book and supplies expense $1,250. **Required Forms and Deadlines:** FAFSA. **Notification of Awards:** Applicants will be notified of awards on a rolling basis beginning 2/1. **Types of Aid:** *Need-based scholarships/grants:* Federal Pell; Private scholarships; SEOG; State scholarships/grants. *Loans:* Direct PLUS loans; Direct Subsidized Stafford Loans; Direct Unsubsidized Stafford Loans. **Student Employment:** Federal Work-Study Program available. Institutional employment available. **Financial Aid Statistics:** 99% needy freshmen, 99% needy undergrads receive need-based scholarship or grant aid. 19% freshmen, 17% undergrads receive non-need-based scholarship or grant aid. 80% freshmen, 81% undergrads receive need-based self-help aid. 2% freshmen, 2% undergrads receive athletic scholarships. 100% freshmen, 98% undergrads receive any aid. 72% undergrads borrow to pay for school. Average cumulative indebtedness $38,040. **Criteria awarding aid:** *Non-need-based:* Academics, Art, Athletics, Music/drama.

ST. NORBERT COLLEGE

100 Grant Street, De Pere, WI 54115-2099
Phone: 920-403-3005 **Financial Aid Phone:** 920-403-3071
E-mail: admit@snc.edu **CEEB Code:** 1706
Fax: 920-403-4072 **Website:** www.snc.edu **ACT Code:** 4644

This private school, affiliated with the Roman Catholic Church, was founded in 1898. It has a 113 acre campus.

RATINGS

Admissions Selectivity Rating: 76   **Fire Safety Rating:** 79   **Green Rating:** 69

STUDENTS AND FACULTY

Enrollment: 1,974. **Student Body:** 58% female, 42% male, 22% out-of-state, 1% international (14 countries represented). Asian 1%, African American 2%, Caucasian 87%, Hispanic 5%, Native American 1%, Pacific Islander <1%, Two or more races 1%, Race unknown 1%.
Retention and Graduation: 82% freshmen return for sophomore year. 70% freshmen graduate within 4 years. 74% freshmen graduate within 6 years. 26% grads go on to further study within 1 year. **Faculty:** Student/faculty ratio 13:1. 138 full-time faculty, 91% hold PhDs, 12% are members of minority groups, 46% are women. 0% of classes are taught by teaching assistants.

ACADEMICS

Degrees: Bachelor's; Master's. **Classes:** Most classes have 20–29 students. Most lab/discussion sessions have 20–29 students. **Most popular majors:** Elementary Education and Teaching; Business/Commerce, General; Biology/Biological Sciences, General. **Special Study Options:** Distance learning; Double major; English as a Second Language (ESL); Honors program; Independent study; Internships; Student-designed major; Study abroad; Teacher certification program. **Honors programs:** The Honors Program at St. Norbert College offers a sophisticated and demanding program of studies and readings to provide the

most academically talented students with an enriched academic curriculum that is stimulating and challenging. **Disability Services offered:** Note-taking services; Reader services; Tape recorders; Tutors. **Career services:** Alumni network; Alumni services; Career assessment; Internships; Regional alumni.

FACILITIES

Housing: Apartments for single students; Coed dorms; Special housing for disabled students; Wellness housing; Women's dorms; 82% of campus accessible to physically disabled. **Special Academic Facilities/Equipment:** Innovation studio; center for women's and gender studies; center for peace, justice, and public understanding; marina; on-campus hotel and conference center; fine and performing arts centers; center for international education; center for leadership and service; children's center; Strategic Research Institute; center for Norbertine studies.

CAMPUS LIFE

Environment: Town. **Activities:** Campus Ministries; Choral groups; Concert band; Dance; Drama/theater; International Student Organization; Jazz band; Literary magazine; Music ensembles; Musical theater; Opera; Pep band; Radio station; Student government; Student newspaper; Student-run film society; Television station; Yearbook. 105 registered organizations, 11 honor societies, 5 religious organizations, 3 fraternities, 4 sororities on campus. **Athletics (Intercollegiate):** *Men:* baseball, basketball, cross-country, football, golf, ice hockey, soccer, tennis, track/field (outdoor), track/field (indoor). *Women:* basketball, cross-country, golf, ice hockey, soccer, softball, tennis, track/field (outdoor), track/field (indoor), volleyball. **On-Campus Highlights:** The Ray Van Den Heuvel Campus Center. **Environmental Initiatives:** Designed new Mulva Library with solar water heating system.

ADMISSIONS

Freshman Academic Profile: Average high school GPA 3.6. 26% in top 10% of high school class, 57% in top 25% of high school class, 85% in top 50% of high school class. 72% from public high schools. **Test Scores:** ACT middle 50% range 21–27. **Basis for Candidate Selection:** *Very important factors include:* academic GPA. *Important factors include:* rigor of secondary school record, application essay, standardized test scores, recommendation(s), extracurricular activities, talent/ability, character/personal qualities, volunteer work. *Other factors include:* class rank, interview, alumni/ae relation. **Freshman Admission Requirements:** High school diploma is required and GED is accepted. *Academic units required:* 4 English, 2 math, 3 science, 3 science labs, 1 social studies, 2 history, 4 academic electives. *Academic units recommended:* 4 English, 3 math, 3 science, 3 science labs, 2 foreign language, 2 social studies, 2 history, 4 academic electives, 1 computer science, 1 visual/performing arts. **Freshman Admission Statistics:** 3,355 applied, 80% admitted, 20% enrolled. **Transfer Admission Requirements:** High school transcript, college transcript(s), essay or personal statement, standardized test scores. Minimum college GPA of 2.5 required. Lowest grade transferable C. **General Admission Information:** Priority deadline 4/1. Non-fall registration accepted. Admission may be deferred for a maximum of 1 year.

COSTS AND FINANCIAL AID

Annual tuition $40,070. Room and board $10,885. Required fees $815. Average book and supplies expense $950. **Required Forms and Deadlines:** FAFSA. **Notification of Awards:** Applicants will be notified of awards on a rolling basis beginning 1/1. **Types of Aid:** *Need-based scholarships/grants:* College/university scholarship or grant aid from institutional funds; Federal Pell; Private scholarships; SEOG; State scholarships/grants. *Loans:* Direct PLUS loans; Direct Subsidized Stafford Loans; Direct Unsubsidized Stafford Loans. **Student Employment:** Federal Work-Study Program available. Institutional employment available. **Financial Aid Statistics:** 97% needy freshmen, 97% needy undergrads receive need-based scholarship or grant aid. 3% freshmen, 3% undergrads receive non-need-based scholarship or grant aid. 79% freshmen, 79% undergrads receive need-based self-help aid. 0% freshmen, 0% undergrads receive athletic scholarships. 100% freshmen, 96% undergrads receive any aid. 77% undergrads borrow to pay for school. Average cumulative indebtedness $40,265. **Criteria awarding aid:** *Need-based:* Academics, Art, Leadership, Minority status, Music/drama. *Non-need-based:* Academics, Art, Leadership, Minority status, Music/drama, State/district residency.

ST. OLAF COLLEGE

1520 St. Olaf Avenue, Northfield, MN 55057
Phone: 507-786-3025 **Financial Aid Phone:** 507-786-3019
E-mail: admissions@stolaf.edu **CEEB Code:** 6638
Fax: 507-786-3832 **Website:** http://wp.stolaf.edu **ACT Code:** 2150

This private school, affiliated with the Lutheran Church, was founded in 1874. It has a 300 acre campus.

RATINGS

Admissions Selectivity Rating: 89   Fire Safety Rating: 82   Green Rating: 60*

STUDENTS AND FACULTY

Enrollment: 3,031. **Student Body:** 57% female, 43% male, 53% out-of-state, 10% international (80 countries represented). Asian 7%, African American 3%, Caucasian 70%, Hispanic 7%, Native American <1%, Pacific Islander <1%, Two or more races 3%, Race unknown 1%.
Retention and Graduation: 91% freshmen return for sophomore year. 85% freshmen graduate within 4 years. 88% freshmen graduate within 6 years. 23% grads go on to further study within 1 year. 17% grads pursue arts and sciences degrees. 3% grads pursue medical degrees. **Faculty:** Student/faculty ratio 12:1. 209 full-time faculty, 97% hold PhDs, 16% are members of minority groups, 48% are women. 0% of classes are taught by teaching assistants.

ACADEMICS

Degrees: Bachelor's. **Classes:** Most classes have 10–19 students. **Most popular majors:** Biology/Biological Sciences, General; Mathematics, General; Economics, General. **Special Study Options:** Cross-registration; Double major; Dual enrollment; Independent study; Internships; Student-designed major; Study abroad; Teacher certification program. **Disability Services offered:** Note-taking services; Reader services; Tape recorders; Tutors. **Career services:** Alumni network; Alumni services; Career assessment; Career/job search classes; Internships; Regional alumni.

FACILITIES

Housing: Coed dorms; Special housing for disabled students; Theme housing; 80% of campus accessible to physically disabled. **Special Academic Facilities/Equipment:** Kierkegaard Library, Flaten Art Museum, Norwegian American Historical Association archives. **Campus Network:** 100% of classrooms, 100% of dorms, 100% of student union, 100% of libraries, 100% of dining areas, 98% of common outdoor areas have wireless network access.

CAMPUS LIFE

Environment: Village. **Activities:** Campus Ministries; Choral groups; Concert band; Dance; Drama/theater; International Student Organization; Jazz band; Literary magazine; Model UN; Music ensembles; Musical theater; Opera; Pep band; Radio station; Student government; Student newspaper; Student-run film society; Symphony orchestra. 221 registered organizations, 20 honor societies, 15 religious organizations on campus. **Athletics (Intercollegiate):** *Men:* baseball, basketball, cross-country, diving, football, golf, ice hockey, skiing (downhill/Alpine), skiing (Nordic/cross-country), soccer, swimming, tennis, track/field (outdoor), track/field (indoor), wrestling. *Women:* basketball, cross-country, diving, golf, ice hockey, skiing (downhill/Alpine), skiing (Nordic/cross-country), soccer, softball, swimming, tennis, track/field (outdoor), track/field (indoor), volleyball. **On-Campus Highlights:** Fireside Lounge, Buntrock Commons.

ADMISSIONS

Freshman Academic Profile: Average high school GPA 3.7. 41% in top 10% of high school class, 72% in top 25% of high school class, 96% in top 50% of high school class. 70% from public high schools. **Test Scores:** SAT Math middle 50% range 590–710. SAT EBRW middle 50% range 600–700. ACT middle 50% range 25–32. **Basis for Candidate Selection:** *Very important factors include:* rigor of secondary school record, academic GPA, application essay. *Important factors include:* class rank, standardized test scores, recommendation(s), interview, extracurricular activities, talent/ability, character/personal qualities. *Other factors include:* first generation, alumni/ae relation, geographical residence, state residency, religious affiliation/commitment, racial/ethnic status, volunteer work, work experience, level of applicant's interest. **Freshman Admission Requirements:** High school diploma is required and GED is accepted. *Academic units recommended:* 4 English, 4 math, 4 science, 2 science labs, 4 foreign language, 4 social studies. **Freshman Admission Statistics:** 5,496 applied, 50% admitted, 29% enrolled. **Transfer Admission Requirements:** High school transcript, college transcript(s), essay or personal statement, standardized test scores, statement of good standing from prior institution(s). Minimum college GPA of 2.50 required. Lowest grade transferable C. **General Admission Information:** Regular application deadline 1/15. Admission may be deferred for a maximum of 1 year.

COSTS AND FINANCIAL AID

Annual tuition $49,710. Room and board $11,270. Average book and supplies expense $1,000. **Required Forms and Deadlines:** CSS/Financial Aid PROFILE; FAFSA; Noncustodial PROFILE. **Notification of Awards:** Applicants will be notified of awards on or about 4/1. **Types of Aid:** *Need-based scholarships/grants:* College/university scholarship or grant aid from institutional funds; Federal Pell; Private scholarships; SEOG; State scholarships/grants. *Loans:* Direct Subsidized Stafford Loans; Direct Unsubsidized Stafford Loans. **Student Employment:** Federal Work-Study Program available. Institutional employment available. **Financial Aid Statistics:** 100% needy freshmen, 100% needy undergrads receive need-based scholarship or grant aid. 35% freshmen, 26% undergrads receive non-need-based scholarship or grant aid. 90% freshmen, 96% undergrads receive need-based self-help aid. 0% freshmen, 0% undergrads receive athletic scholarships. 97% freshmen, 97% undergrads receive any aid. 64% undergrads borrow to pay for school. Average cumulative indebtedness $29,907. **Criteria awarding aid:** *Non-need-based:* Academics, Art, Leadership, Music/drama.

SAINT PETER'S UNIVERSITY

2641 Kennedy Boulevard, Office of Admiss, Jersey City, NJ 07306
Phone: 201-761-7100 **Financial Aid Phone:** 201-761-6071
E-mail: admissions@saintpeters.edu **CEEB Code:** 2806
Website: www.saintpeters.edu **ACT Code:** 2604

This private school, affiliated with the Roman Catholic-Jesuit Church, was founded in 1872. It has a 10 acre campus.

RATINGS

Admissions Selectivity Rating: 77   Fire Safety Rating: 60*   Green Rating: 64

STUDENTS AND FACULTY

Enrollment: 2,512. **Student Body:** 64% female, 36% male, 9% out-of-state, 3% international (56 countries represented). Asian 8%, African American 21%, Caucasian 14%, Hispanic 46%, Native American <1%, Pacific Islander <1%, Two or more races 2%, Race unknown 6%.
Retention and Graduation: 82% freshmen return for sophomore year. 38% freshmen graduate within 4 years. 54% freshmen graduate within 6 years. 27% grads go on to further study within 1 year. 9% grads pursue arts and sciences degrees. 5% grads pursue law degrees. 6% grads pursue business degrees. 7% grads pursue medical degrees. **Faculty:** Student/faculty ratio 13:1. 119 full-time faculty, 85% hold PhDs, 18% are members of minority groups, 47% are women. 0% of classes are taught by teaching assistants.

ACADEMICS

Degrees: Associate; Bachelor's; Certificate; Doctoral degree—professional practice; Master's; Post-bachelor's certificate; Post-master's certificate. **Classes:** Most classes have 10–19 students. Most lab/discussion sessions have fewer than 10 students. **Most popular majors:** Registered Nursing/Registered Nurse; Biology/Biological Sciences, General; Business Administration and Management, General. **Special Study Options:** Accelerated program; Cooperative education program; Cross-registration; Distance learning; Double major; Dual enrollment; English as a Second Language (ESL); Exchange student program (domestic); Honors program; Independent study; Internships; Student-designed major; Study abroad; Teacher certification program; Weekend college. **Honors programs:** While Honors provides academic enrichment for highly motivated students, it is not a formal major or minor. Students enrolled in the program must complete a minimum of 30 credits designated as Honors courses, which include Honors core course seminars, Honors advanced electives, and 6 credits of Honors Thesis: research and independent study. Independent study projects must be approved by the Honors Program and the respective chairs of the student's major department. Independent study projects may carry departmental as well as Honors credit. **Combined degree programs:** BA/JD; BA/MD. **Disability Services offered:** Note-taking services; Reader services; Tape recorders; Tutors. **Career services:** Career/job search classes; Internships.

FACILITIES

Housing: Coed dorms; Special housing for disabled students; Wellness housing. **Special Academic Facilities/Equipment:** TV production facilities, center for government affairs, radio station.

CAMPUS LIFE

Environment: City. **Activities:** Campus Ministries; Choral groups; Dance; Drama/theater; International Student Organization; Literary magazine; Model UN; Musical theater; Radio station; Student government; Student newspaper; Yearbook. 50 registered organizations, 17 honor societies on campus. **Athletics (Intercollegiate):** *Men:* baseball, basketball, cheerleading, cross-country, diving, football, golf, soccer, swimming, tennis, track/field (outdoor). *Women:* basketball, bowling, cheerleading, cross-country, diving, soccer, softball, swimming, tennis, track/field (outdoor), volleyball. **On-Campus Highlights:** MacMahon Student Center. **Environmental Initiatives:** Use of solar and wind energy.

ADMISSIONS

Freshman Academic Profile: Average high school GPA 3.3. 14% in top 10% of high school class, 42% in top 25% of high school class, 73% in top 50% of high school class. **Test Scores:** SAT Math middle 50% range 470–560. SAT EBRW middle 50% range 470–560. ACT middle 50% range 17–22. **Basis for Candidate Selection:** *Very important factors include:* rigor of secondary school record, academic GPA. *Important factors include:* application essay, recommendation(s). *Other factors include:* class rank, standardized test scores, interview, extracurricular activities, character/personal qualities, first generation, alumni/ae relation, geographical residence, state residency, volunteer work, work experience, level of applicant's interest. **Freshman Admission Requirements:** High school diploma is required and GED is accepted. *Academic units required:* 4 English, 3 math, 2 science, 1 science lab, 2 foreign language, 2 history. **Freshman Admission Statistics:** 4,040 applied, 74% admitted, 19% enrolled. **Transfer Admission Requirements:** College transcript(s), essay or personal statement. Minimum college GPA of 2.0 required. Lowest grade transferable C. **General Admission Information:** Priority deadline 12/15. Non-fall registration accepted. Admission may be deferred for a maximum of 1 year.

COSTS AND FINANCIAL AID

Required Forms and Deadlines: FAFSA; State aid form. **Notification of Awards:** Applicants will be notified of awards on a rolling basis beginning 1/1. **Types of Aid:** *Need-based scholarships/grants:* College/university scholarship or grant aid from institutional funds; Federal Pell; Private scholarships; SEOG; State scholarships/grants. *Loans:* Direct PLUS loans; Direct Subsidized Stafford Loans; Direct Unsubsidized Stafford Loans. **Student Employment:** Federal Work-Study Program available. Institutional employment available. **Financial Aid Statistics:** 99% needy freshmen, 99% needy undergrads receive need-based scholarship or grant aid. 7% freshmen, 7% undergrads receive non-need-based scholarship or grant aid. 54% freshmen, 62% undergrads receive need-based self-help aid. 3% freshmen, 2% undergrads receive athletic scholarships. 98% freshmen, 90% undergrads receive any aid. 73% undergrads borrow to pay for school. Average cumulative indebtedness $22,317. **Criteria awarding aid:** *Need-based:* Academics, Athletics *Non-need-based:* Academics, Athletics.

ST. THOMAS AQUINAS COLLEGE

125 Route 340, Sparkill, NY 10976
Phone: 845-398-4100 **Financial Aid Phone:** 845-398-4106
E-mail: admissions@stac.edu **CEEB Code:** 2807
Fax: 845-398-4372 **Website:** www.stac.edu **ACT Code:** 2897

This private school was founded in 1952. It has a 47 acre campus.

RATINGS

Admissions Selectivity Rating: 76   **Fire Safety Rating:** 97   **Green Rating:** 70

STUDENTS AND FACULTY

Enrollment: 1,180. **Student Body:** 48% female, 52% male, 18% out-of-state, 5% international (18 countries represented). Asian 3%, African American 11%, Caucasian 50%, Hispanic 24%, Native American <1%, Pacific Islander 0%, Two or more races 1%, Race unknown 7%.
Retention and Graduation: 81% freshmen return for sophomore year. 41% freshmen graduate within 4 years. **Faculty:** Student/faculty ratio 14:1. 50 full-time faculty, 86% hold PhDs, 6% are members of minority groups, 56% are women. 0% of classes are taught by teaching assistants.

ACADEMICS

Degrees: Associate; Bachelor's; Master's; Post-bachelor's certificate; Post-master's certificate. **Classes:** Most classes have 20–29 students. Most lab/discussion sessions have fewer than 10 students. **Most popular majors:** Education, General; Special Education and Teaching, General; Psychology, General. **Special Study Options:** Accelerated program; Cooperative education program; Cross-registration; Double major; Dual enrollment; English as a Second Language (ESL); Exchange student program (domestic); Honors program; Independent study; Internships; Liberal arts/career combination; Study abroad; Teacher certification program. **Honors programs:** Highly selective honors program with maximum 20 student each class. Honor students receive full scholarship. **Combined degree programs:** BA/MA. **Disability Services offered:** Note-taking services; Tape recorders; Tutors. **Career services:** Alumni network; Alumni services; Career assessment; Career/job search classes; Internships; Regional alumni.

FACILITIES

Housing: Apartments for single students; Men's dorms; Women's dorms; 80% of campus accessible to physically disabled. **Special Academic Facilities/Equipment:** Azarian-McCullough Art Gallery, Sullivan Theatre, Spellman Technology Corridor, Costello Hall Science and Technology Center.

CAMPUS LIFE

Environment: Village. **Activities:** Campus Ministries; Choral groups; Concert band; Dance; Drama/theater; Literary magazine; Music ensembles; Musical theater; Radio station; Student government; Student newspaper; Yearbook. 35 registered organizations, 8 honor societies on campus. **Athletics (Intercollegiate):** *Men:* baseball, basketball, cross-country, golf, soccer, tennis, track/field (outdoor), track/field (indoor). *Women:* basketball, cross-country, lacrosse, soccer, softball, tennis, track/field (outdoor). **On-Campus Highlights:** The College Commons.

ADMISSIONS

Freshman Academic Profile: Average high school GPA 3.0. 10% in top 10% of high school class, 23% in top 25% of high school class, 53% in top 50% of high school class. **Test Scores:** SAT Math middle 50% range 450–560. SAT EBRW middle 50% range 460–560. ACT middle 50% range 18–25. **Basis for Candidate Selection:** *Very important factors include:* rigor of secondary school record. *Important factors include:* recommendation(s), interview, extracurricular activities, talent/ability. *Other factors include:* academic GPA, application essay, standardized test scores, alumni/ae relation, volunteer work, work experience, level of applicant's interest. **Freshman Admission Requirements:** High school diploma is required and GED is accepted. *Academic units required:* 4 English, 3 math, 3 science, 2 science labs, 3 foreign language, 4 social studies, 2 history, 1 academic elective. *Academic units recommended:* 4 English, 3 math, 3 science, 2 science labs, 3 foreign language, 4 social studies, 2 history, 1 academic elective. **Freshman Admission Statistics:** 1,758 applied, 76% admitted, 20% enrolled. **Transfer Admission Requirements:** College transcript(s), statement of good standing from prior institution(s). Minimum college GPA of 2.0 required. Lowest grade transferable C. **General Admission Information:** Application fee $30. Non-fall registration accepted. Admission may be deferred for a maximum of one year.

COSTS AND FINANCIAL AID

Annual tuition $31,150. Room and board $13,250. Required fees $800. Average book and supplies expense $1,250. **Required Forms and Deadlines:** FAFSA; State aid form. **Notification of Awards:** Applicants will be notified of awards on a rolling basis beginning 11/1. **Types of Aid:** *Need-based scholarships/grants:* College/university scholarship or grant aid from institutional funds; Federal Pell; Private scholarships; SEOG; State scholarships/grants. *Loans:* Direct PLUS loans; Direct Subsidized Stafford Loans; Direct Unsubsidized Stafford Loans. **Student Employment:** Federal Work-Study Program available. Institutional employment available. **Financial Aid Statistics:** 100% needy freshmen, 99% needy undergrads receive need-based scholarship or grant aid. 64% freshmen, 74% undergrads receive non-need-based scholarship or grant aid. 74% freshmen, 95% undergrads receive need-based self-help aid. 7% freshmen, 7% undergrads receive athletic scholarships. 80% freshmen, 75% undergrads receive any aid. 70% undergrads borrow to pay for school. Average cumulative indebtedness $31,000. **Criteria awarding aid:** *Need-based:* Academics, Athletics, Job skills, Minority status. *Non-need-based:* Academics, Alumni affiliation, Art, Athletics, Leadership, Minority status, Music/drama, Religious affiliation.

ST. THOMAS UNIVERSITY (FL)

16401 Northwest 37th Avenue, Miami Gardens, FL 33054
Phone: 305-628-6546 **Financial Aid Phone:** 305-628-6547
E-mail: signup@stu.edu **CEEB Code:** 5076
Fax: 305-628-6591 **Website:** www.stu.edu **ACT Code:** 719

This private school, affiliated with the Roman Catholic Church, was founded in 1961. It has a 140 acre campus.

RATINGS

Admissions Selectivity Rating: 89   **Fire Safety Rating:** 81   **Green Rating:** 60*

STUDENTS AND FACULTY

Enrollment: 1,111. **Student Body:** 55% female, 45% male, 92% out-of-state, 15% international (57 countries represented). Asian 1%, African American 23%, Caucasian 12%, Hispanic 40%, Native American <1%, Pacific Islander 0%, Two or more races 1%, Race unknown 8%.
Retention and Graduation: 70% freshmen return for sophomore year.
Faculty: Student/faculty ratio 14:1. 105 full-time faculty, 89% hold PhDs, 30% are members of minority groups, 47% are women. 0% of classes are taught by teaching assistants.

ACADEMICS

Degrees: Bachelor's; Certificate; Doctoral degree—professional practice; Doctoral degree research/scholarship; Master's; Post-bachelor's certificate; Post-master's certificate. **Classes:** Most classes have 10–19 students. Most lab/discussion sessions have 10–19 students. **Most popular majors:** Organizational Behavior Studies; Business Administration and Management, General; Psychology, General. **Special Study Options:** Distance learning; Double major; Dual enrollment; English as a Second Language (ESL); Honors program; Independent study; Internships; Liberal arts/career combination; Teacher certification program. **Honors programs:** The St. Thomas University Honors Program is designed to provide an intensive and stimulating alternative for students who wish to enhance their college academic experience. Qualified students are offered the opportunity to take Honors courses in the subjects of their choice, and, if they desire, to work for an Honors degree. **Combined degree programs:** BA/JD. **Disability Services offered:** Note-taking services; Reader services; Tape recorders; Tutors. **Career services:** Career assessment; Career/job search classes; Internships.

FACILITIES

Housing: Men's dorms; Women's dorms; 80% of campus accessible to physically disabled. **Special Academic Facilities/Equipment:** Multimedia computer equipment, TV studio, Art Atrium Gallery. **Campus Network:** 100% of classrooms, 100% of dorms, 100% of student union, 100% of libraries, 100% of dining areas, 100% of common outdoor areas have wireless network access.

CAMPUS LIFE

Environment: Metropolis. **Activities:** Campus Ministries; Choral groups; International Student Organization; Literary magazine; Radio station; Student government; Television station; Yearbook. 26 registered organizations, 4 honor societies, 2 religious organizations on campus. **Athletics (Intercollegiate):** *Men:* baseball, basketball, cross-country, golf, soccer, tennis. *Women:* basketball, cross-country, soccer, softball, tennis, volleyball. **On-Campus Highlights:** Campus Chapel.

ADMISSIONS

Freshman Academic Profile: Average high school GPA 3.0. 6% in top 10% of high school class, 17% in top 25% of high school class, 53% in top 50% of high school class. **Test Scores:** SAT Math middle 50% range 408–500. SAT EBRW middle 50% range 410–510. ACT middle 50% range 16–21. **Basis for Candidate Selection:** *Very important factors include:* class rank, academic GPA, standardized test scores. *Important factors include:* rigor of secondary school record, application essay, recommendation(s), alumni/ae relation. *Other factors include:* extracurricular activities, talent/ability, character/personal qualities, volunteer work, work experience. **Freshman Admission Requirements:** High school diploma is required and GED is accepted. *Academic units required:* 4 English, 3 math, 2 science, 3 social studies, 6 academic electives. **Freshman Admission Statistics:** 727 applied, 46% admitted, 63% enrolled. **Transfer Admission Requirements:** College transcript(s), essay or personal statement, statement of good standing from prior institution(s). Minimum college GPA of 2.0 required. Lowest grade transferable C-. **General Admission Information:** Application fee $40. Non-fall registration accepted. Admission may be deferred for a maximum of one year.

COSTS AND FINANCIAL AID

Required Forms and Deadlines: FAFSA. **Notification of Awards:** Applicants will be notified of awards on a rolling basis beginning 3/1. **Types of Aid:** *Need-based scholarships/grants:* College/university scholarship or grant aid from institutional funds; Federal Pell; Private scholarships; SEOG; State scholarships/grants. *Loans:* Direct PLUS loans; Direct Subsidized Stafford Loans; Direct Unsubsidized Stafford Loans. **Student Employment:** Federal Work-Study Program available. Institutional employment available. **Financial Aid Statistics:** 77% needy freshmen, 76% needy undergrads receive need-based scholarship or grant aid. 0% freshmen, 0% undergrads receive non-need-based scholarship or grant aid. 72% freshmen, 71% undergrads receive need-based self-help aid. 12% freshmen, 15% undergrads receive athletic scholarships. **Criteria awarding aid:** *Need-based:* Academics. *Non-need-based:* Academics, Athletics, Leadership.

ST. THOMAS UNIVERSITY (NB)

Admissions Office, St. Thomas University, Fredericton, NB E3B 5G3
Phone: 506-452-0532
E-mail: admissions@stu.ca
Fax: 506-452-0617 **Website:** http://www.stu.ca

This private school, affiliated with the Roman Catholic Church, was founded in 1910. It has a 21 acre campus.

RATINGS

Admissions Selectivity Rating: 68   **Fire Safety Rating:** 95   **Green Rating:** 60*

STUDENTS AND FACULTY

Enrollment: 2,475. **Student Body:** 66% female, 34% male, 27% out-of-state, 5% international (42 countries represented). Asian 0%, African American 0%, Caucasian 0%, Hispanic 0%, Native American 0%, Race unknown 95%.
Retention and Graduation: 69% freshmen return for sophomore year.
Faculty: Student/faculty ratio 19:1. 109 full-time faculty, 95% hold PhDs, 0% are members of minority groups, 39% are women. 0% of classes are taught by teaching assistants.

ACADEMICS

Degrees: Bachelor's; Certificate; Post-bachelor's certificate. **Classes:** Most classes have 10–19 students. **Most popular majors:** English Language and Literature, General; Criminology; Psychology, General. **Special Study Options:** Accelerated program; Cross-registration; Double major; English as a Second Language (ESL); Exchange student program (domestic); Honors program; Independent study; Student-designed major; Study abroad; Teacher certification program. **Disability Services offered:** Note-taking services; Reader services; Tape recorders; Tutors. **Career services:** Career assessment; Career/job search classes; Internships.

FACILITIES

Housing: Coed dorms; Women's dorms; 80% of campus accessible to physically disabled.

CAMPUS LIFE

Environment: Town. **Activities:** Campus Ministries; Choral groups; Drama/theater; International Student Organization; Jazz band; Model UN; Music ensembles; Musical theater; Radio station; Student government; Student newspaper; Student-run film society; Yearbook. 5 religious organizations on campus. **Athletics (Intercollegiate):** *Men:* basketball, cross-country, golf, ice hockey, rugby, soccer, volleyball. *Women:* basketball, cross-country, golf, ice hockey, rugby, soccer, volleyball. **On-Campus Highlights:** Margaret Norrie McCain Hall. **Environmental Initiatives:** Recycle bins in all areas.

ADMISSIONS

Freshman Academic Profile: Average high school GPA 3.3. **Basis for Candidate Selection:** *Very important factors include:* academic GPA. *Other factors include:* application essay, standardized test scores, recommendation(s). **Freshman Admission Requirements:** High school diploma is required and GED is not accepted. **Freshman Admission Statistics:** 1,345 applied, 81% admitted, 58% enrolled. **Transfer Admission Requirements:** College transcript(s), statement of good standing from prior institution(s). Lowest grade transferable D. **General Admission Information:** Application fee $35. Regular application deadline 8/31. Non-fall registration accepted. Admission may be deferred for a maximum of 1 year.

COSTS AND FINANCIAL AID

Average book and supplies expense $1,000.

SAINT VINCENT COLLEGE

Office of Admission and Financial Aid, Latrobe, PA 15650-2690
Phone: 724-805-2500 **Financial Aid Phone:** 800-782-5549
E-mail: admission@stvincent.edu **CEEB Code:** 2808
Fax: 724-532-5069 **Website:** www.stvincent.edu **ACT Code:** 3686

This private school, affiliated with the Roman Catholic Church, was founded in 1846. It has a 200 acre campus.

RATINGS
Admissions Selectivity Rating: 84   **Fire Safety Rating:** 69   **Green Rating:** 60*

STUDENTS AND FACULTY
Enrollment: 1,506. **Student Body:** 46% female, 54% male, 22% out-of-state, 1% international (15 countries represented). Asian 1%, African American 6%, Caucasian 83%, Hispanic 4%, Native American <1%, Pacific Islander <1%, Two or more races 2%, Race unknown 3%.
Retention and Graduation: 81% freshmen return for sophomore year. 66% freshmen graduate within 4 years. 69% freshmen graduate within 6 years. 30% grads go on to further study within 1 year. **Faculty:** Student/faculty ratio 11:1. 104 full-time faculty, 94% hold PhDs, 5% are members of minority groups, 34% are women. 0% of classes are taught by teaching assistants.

ACADEMICS
Degrees: Bachelor's; Certificate; Doctoral degree—professional practice; Master's; Post-bachelor's certificate. **Classes:** Most classes have 20–29 students. Most lab/discussion sessions have fewer than 10 students. **Most popular majors:** History, General; Biology/Biological Sciences, General; Psychology, General. **Special Study Options:** Accelerated program; Cooperative education program; Cross-registration; Distance learning; Double major; Dual enrollment; English as a Second Language (ESL); External degree program; Honors program; Independent study; Internships; Liberal arts/career combination; Study abroad; Teacher certification program. **Honors programs:** Professors design Honors classes to challenge and reward students who seek substantial intellectual development in college. The quality, not the quantity of work, distinguishes Honors classes from other courses. As part of their coursework in Honors classes, all students are required to submit a short reflective essay and sample of their work at the end of each Honors class. Dinner and evening discussions based on a reading, or attendance of a play, a film, an art exhibit, etc., on campus provide a special, congenial setting for intellectual exchange as part of a course or an extracurricular event. All Honors students and faculty are regularly invited to attend a play, film, art exhibit, etc. Extended trips within the U.S. or abroad may be planned during breaks or the summer. Senior Capstone Projects Honors students in majors with a senior research or capstone project will be strongly encouraged to present their work in a special colloquium at Saint Vincent and at professional meetings in their research areas. **Combined degree programs:** BA/JD; BA/MEng. **Disability Services offered:** Note-taking services; Tutors. **Career services:** Alumni network; Alumni services; Career assessment; Internships; Regional alumni.

FACILITIES
Housing: Apartments for single students; Coed dorms; 95% of campus accessible to physically disabled. **Special Academic Facilities/Equipment:** Art gallery, life sciences research center, spectrophotometer, spectrometer, physiograph work stations, data acquisition work station, planetarium, observatory, radio telescope, instructional technology resource center.

CAMPUS LIFE
Environment: Village. **Activities:** Campus Ministries; Choral groups; Dance; Drama/theater; International Student Organization; Literary magazine; Marching band; Music ensembles; Musical theater; Pep band; Radio station; Student government; Student newspaper; Television station; Yearbook. 43 registered organizations, 12 honor societies, 2 religious organizations on campus. **Athletics (Intercollegiate): Men:** baseball, basketball, cross-country, football, golf, lacrosse, soccer, swimming, tennis, track/field (outdoor). *Women:* basketball, cross-country, field hockey, golf, lacrosse, soccer, softball, swimming, tennis, volleyball. **On-Campus Highlights:** Library. **Environmental Initiatives:** New construction on campus, including a current building project, will be green.

ADMISSIONS
Freshman Academic Profile: Average high school GPA 3.6. 20% in top 10% of high school class, 46% in top 25% of high school class, 74% in top 50% of high school class. 67% from public high schools. **Test Scores:** SAT Math middle 50% range 510–620. SAT EBRW middle 50% range 520–620. ACT middle 50% range 20–27. **Basis for Candidate Selection:** *Very important factors include:* rigor of secondary school record, academic GPA. *Important factors include:* application essay, standardized test scores, character/personal qualities. *Other factors include:* class rank, recommendation(s), interview, extracurricular activities, talent/ability, first generation. **Freshman Admission Requirements:** High school diploma is required and GED is accepted. *Academic units required:* 4 English, 3 math, 1 science, 1 science lab, 3 social studies, 5 academic electives. *Academic units recommended:* 4 English, 3 math, 3 science, 1 science lab, 2 foreign language, 3 social studies, 5 academic electives. **Freshman Admission Statistics:** 2,025 applied, 68% admitted, 26% enrolled. **Transfer Admission Requirements:** High school transcript, college transcript(s), essay or personal statement, statement of good standing from prior institution(s). Minimum college GPA of 2.5 required. Lowest grade transferable C-. **General Admission Information:** Application fee $25. Priority deadline 2/1. Regular application deadline 5/1. Non-fall registration accepted. Admission may be deferred for a maximum of 1 year.

COSTS AND FINANCIAL AID
Annual tuition $35,520. Room and board $7,542. Average book and supplies expense $1,350. **Required Forms and Deadlines:** FAFSA. **Notification of Awards:** Applicants will be notified of awards on a rolling basis beginning 3/1. **Types of Aid:** *Need-based scholarships/grants:* College/university scholarship or grant aid from institutional funds; Federal Pell; Private scholarships; SEOG; State scholarships/grants; United Negro College Fund. *Loans:* Direct PLUS loans; Direct Subsidized Stafford Loans; Direct Unsubsidized Stafford Loans. **Student Employment:** Federal Work-Study Program available. Institutional employment available. **Financial Aid Statistics:** 67% needy freshmen, 70% needy undergrads receive need-based scholarship or grant aid. 100% freshmen, 96% undergrads receive non-need-based scholarship or grant aid. 74% freshmen, 80% undergrads receive need-based self-help aid. 0% freshmen, 0% undergrads receive athletic scholarships. 99% freshmen, 96% undergrads receive any aid. 80% undergrads borrow to pay for school. Average cumulative indebtedness $36,745. **Criteria awarding aid:** *Need-based:* Alumni affiliation. *Non-need-based:* Academics, Alumni affiliation, Leadership, Minority status, Music/drama.

SAINT XAVIER UNIVERSITY

3700 West 103rd Street., Chicago, IL 60655
Phone: 773-298-3050
E-mail: admissions@sxu.edu **CEEB Code:** 1708
Fax: 773-298-3076 **Website:** www.sxu.edu **ACT Code:** 1134

This private school, affiliated with the Roman Catholic Church, was founded in 1847. It has a 70 acre campus.

RATINGS
Admissions Selectivity Rating: 75   **Fire Safety Rating:** 60*   **Green Rating:** 60*

STUDENTS AND FACULTY
Enrollment: 2,897. **Student Body:** 67% female, 33% male, 5% out-of-state, <1% international. Asian 3%, African American 16%, Caucasian 50%, Hispanic 23%, Native American <1%, Pacific Islander 0%, Two or more races 2%, Race unknown 5%.
Retention and Graduation: 75% freshmen return for sophomore year. 10% grads go on to further study within 1 year. **Faculty:** Student/faculty ratio 13:1. 168 full-time faculty, 86% hold PhDs, 13% are members of minority groups, 57% are women. 0% of classes are taught by teaching assistants.

ACADEMICS
Degrees: Bachelor's; Certificate; Master's; Post-bachelor's certificate; Post-master's certificate. **Classes:** Most classes have 20–29 students. Most lab/discussion sessions have 20–29 students. **Most popular majors:** Business/Commerce, General; Elementary Education and Teaching; Nursing/Registered Nurse (Rn, Asn, Bsn, Msn). **Special Study Options:** Accelerated program; Cooperative education program; Distance learning; Double major; Dual enrollment; English as a Second Language (ESL); External degree program; Honors program; Independent study; Internships; Liberal arts/career combination; Student-designed major; Study abroad; Teacher certification program; Weekend college. **Disability Services offered:** Note-taking services; Reader services; Tape recorders; Tutors. **Career services:** Alumni services; Career assessment; Career/job search classes; Internships.

FACILITIES

Housing: Apartments for single students; Coed dorms; Special housing for disabled students; 98% of campus accessible to physically disabled. **Campus Network:** 85% of classrooms, 65% of dorms, 85% of student union, 100% of libraries, 85% of dining areas, 50% of common outdoor areas have wireless network access.

CAMPUS LIFE

Environment: Metropolis. **Activities:** Campus Ministries; Choral groups; Concert band; Dance; Drama/theater; International Student Organization; Jazz band; Literary magazine; Marching band; Music ensembles; Pep band; Radio station; Student government; Student newspaper; Student-run film society; Symphony orchestra; Yearbook. 41 registered organizations, 2 honor societies, 2 religious organizations on campus. **Athletics (Intercollegiate):** *Men:* baseball, basketball, football, soccer. *Women:* basketball, cross-country, soccer, softball, volleyball. **On-Campus Highlights:** Convocation and Athletic Center.

ADMISSIONS

Freshman Academic Profile: 25% in top 10% of high school class, 54% in top 25% of high school class, 84% in top 50% of high school class. 55% from public high schools. **Test Scores:** SAT Math middle 50% range 440–545. SAT EBRW middle 50% range 455–570. ACT middle 50% range 19–24. **Basis for Candidate Selection:** *Very important factors include:* academic GPA, application essay, standardized test scores. *Important factors include:* rigor of secondary school record. *Other factors include:* recommendation(s), interview, extracurricular activities, talent/ability, character/personal qualities, volunteer work, work experience, level of applicant's interest. **Freshman Admission Requirements:** High school diploma is required and GED is accepted. *Academic units recommended:* 4 English, 3 math, 2 foreign language, 3 academic electives. **Freshman Admission Statistics:** 6,693 applied, 79% admitted, 11% enrolled. **Transfer Admission Requirements:** College transcript(s). Minimum college GPA of 2.5 required. Lowest grade transferable C. **General Admission Information:** Application fee $25. Non-fall registration accepted.

COSTS AND FINANCIAL AID

Annual tuition $29,990. Room and board $10,320. Average book and supplies expense $1,200. **Required Forms and Deadlines:** FAFSA. **Notification of Awards:** Applicants will be notified of awards on a rolling basis beginning 2/15. **Types of Aid:** *Need-based scholarships/grants:* College/university scholarship or grant aid from institutional funds; Federal Pell; Private scholarships; SEOG; State scholarships/grants. **Student Employment:** Federal Work-Study Program available. Institutional employment available. **Financial Aid Statistics:** 100% needy freshmen, 99% needy undergrads receive need-based scholarship or grant aid. 98% freshmen, 92% undergrads receive non-need-based scholarship or grant aid. 84% freshmen, 87% undergrads receive need-based self-help aid. 12% freshmen, 9% undergrads receive athletic scholarships. **Criteria awarding aid:** *Non-need-based:* Academics, Athletics, Music/drama.

SALEM COLLEGE

PO Box 10548, Winston-Salem, NC 27108
Phone: 336-721-2621 **Financial Aid Phone:** 336-721-2808
E-mail: admissions@salem.edu **CEEB Code:** 5607
Fax: 336-917-5572 **Website:** www.salem.edu **ACT Code:** 3156

This private school, affiliated with the Moravian Church, was founded in 1772. It has a 57 acre campus.

RATINGS

Admissions Selectivity Rating: 85 **Fire Safety Rating:** 86 **Green Rating:** 60*

STUDENTS AND FACULTY

Enrollment: 741. **Student Body:** 98% female, 2% male, 23% out-of-state, 13% international (22 countries represented). Asian 1%, African American 19%, Caucasian 60%, Hispanic 4%, Native American <1%, Race unknown 4%. **Retention and Graduation:** 78% freshmen return for sophomore year. 30% grads go on to further study within 1 year. 25% grads pursue arts and sciences degrees. 3% grads pursue law degrees. 5% grads pursue business degrees. **Faculty:** Student/faculty ratio 12:1. 57 full-time faculty, 86% hold PhDs, 9% are members of minority groups, 61% are women. 0% of classes are taught by teaching assistants.

ACADEMICS

Degrees: Bachelor's; Master's. **Classes:** Most classes have 10–19 students. Most lab/discussion sessions have 10–19 students. **Most popular majors:** Business/

Commerce, General; Sociology, General. **Special Study Options:** Cross-registration; Double major; Dual enrollment; Honors program; Independent study; Internships; Liberal arts/career combination; Student-designed major; Study abroad; Teacher certification program. **Career services:** Alumni network; Internships.

FACILITIES

Housing: Apartments for single students; Women's dorms; 75% of campus accessible to physically disabled. **Special Academic Facilities/Equipment:** Art gallery, fine arts center, Center for Women Writers, videoconferencing center. **Campus Network:** 100% of classrooms, 100% of dorms, 100% of student union, 100% of libraries, 100% of dining areas, 100% of common outdoor areas have wireless network access.

CAMPUS LIFE

Environment: City. **Activities:** Choral groups; Dance; Drama/theater; Literary magazine; Marching band; Music ensembles; Musical theater; Student government; Student newspaper; Yearbook. 26 registered organizations, 14 honor societies, 7 religious organizations on campus. **Athletics (Intercollegiate):** *Women:* basketball, cross-country, field hockey, swimming, tennis, volleyball. **On-Campus Highlights:** Back porch of Main Hall. **Environmental Initiatives:** Recycle commitment—all residence halls and academic buildings have paper, plastic, and aluminum containers.

ADMISSIONS

Freshman Academic Profile: Average high school GPA 3.7. 39% in top 10% of high school class, 67% in top 25% of high school class, 94% in top 50% of high school class. **Test Scores:** SAT Math middle 50% range 480–630. SAT EBRW middle 50% range 490–650. ACT middle 50% range 20–25. **Basis for Candidate Selection:** *Very important factors include:* rigor of secondary school record, academic GPA. *Important factors include:* class rank, application essay, standardized test scores, recommendation(s), extracurricular activities, talent/ability, character/personal qualities. *Other factors include:* interview, first generation, alumni/ae relation, volunteer work, level of applicant's interest. **Freshman Admission Requirements:** High school diploma is required and GED is accepted. *Academic units required:* 4 English, 3 math, 3 science, 2 foreign language, 2 history. **Freshman Admission Statistics:** 435 applied, 69% admitted, 40% enrolled. **Transfer Admission Requirements:** High school transcript, college transcript(s), essay or personal statement, statement of good standing from prior institution(s). Minimum college GPA of 2.0 required. Lowest grade transferable C-. **General Admission Information:** Application fee $30. Priority deadline 3/1. Non-fall registration accepted. Admission may be deferred for a maximum of 1 year.

COSTS AND FINANCIAL AID

Annual tuition $18,850. Room and board $10,050. Required fees $340. Average book and supplies expense $900. **Required Forms and Deadlines:** FAFSA. **Notification of Awards:** Applicants will be notified of awards on a rolling basis beginning 3/1. **Types of Aid:** *Need-based scholarships/grants:* College/university scholarship or grant aid from institutional funds; Federal Pell; Private scholarships; SEOG; State scholarships/grants. **Financial Aid Statistics:** 80% needy freshmen, 71% needy undergrads receive need-based scholarship or grant aid. 96% freshmen, 95% undergrads receive non-need-based scholarship or grant aid. 88% freshmen, 83% undergrads receive need-based self-help aid. 0% freshmen, 0% undergrads receive athletic scholarships. **Criteria awarding aid:** *Non-need-based:* Academics, Alumni affiliation, Leadership, Minority status, Music/drama, State/district residency.

SALEM STATE UNIVERSITY

352 Lafayette Street, Salem, MA 01970
Phone: 978-542-6210 **Financial Aid Phone:** 978-542-6112
E-mail: admissions@salemstate.edu **CEEB Code:** 3522
Fax: 978-542-6893 **Website:** www.salemstate.edu

This public school was founded in 1854. It has a 108 acre campus.

RATINGS

Admissions Selectivity Rating: 84 **Fire Safety Rating:** 78 **Green Rating:** 60*

STUDENTS AND FACULTY

Enrollment: 7,296. **Student Body:** 61% female, 39% male, 3% out-of-state, 3% international. Asian 3%, African American 9%, Caucasian 76%, Hispanic 7%, Native American <1%, Pacific Islander 0%, Two or more races 0%, Race unknown 2%.

Faculty: Student/faculty ratio 14:1. 333 full-time faculty, 0% hold PhDs, 10% are members of minority groups, 54% are women. 0% of classes are taught by teaching assistants.

ACADEMICS

Degrees: Bachelor's; Certificate; Master's; Post-bachelor's certificate; Post-master's certificate. **Classes:** Most classes have 10–19 students. Most lab/discussion sessions have 10–19 students. **Most popular majors:** Education, General; Business/Commerce, General; Criminal Justice/Law Enforcement Administration. **Special Study Options:** Accelerated program; Cross-registration; Distance learning; Double major; Dual enrollment; English as a Second Language (ESL); Honors program; Independent study; Internships; Student-designed major; Study abroad; Teacher certification program. **Disability Services offered:** Reader services; Tape recorders.

FACILITIES

Housing: Coed dorms; 100% of campus accessible to physically disabled. **Special Academic Facilities/Equipment:** Aquaculture center, On-campus elementary school, color TV studio, instructional media center.

CAMPUS LIFE

Environment: Village. **Activities:** Choral groups; Concert band; Dance; Drama/theater; Jazz band; Literary magazine; Music ensembles; Musical theater; Radio station; Student government; Student newspaper. 149 registered organizations, 13 honor societies, 3 religious organizations on campus. **Athletics (Intercollegiate):** *Men:* baseball, basketball, cross-country, diving, golf, ice hockey, lacrosse, soccer, swimming, tennis, track/field (outdoor). *Women:* basketball, cross-country, diving, field hockey, lacrosse, soccer, softball, swimming, tennis, track/field (outdoor), volleyball.

ADMISSIONS

Test Scores: SAT Math middle 50% range 450–540. SAT EBRW middle 50% range 440–550. **Basis for Candidate Selection:** *Very important factors include:* rigor of secondary school record, academic GPA, standardized test scores. *Other factors include:* recommendation(s), interview, extracurricular activities, talent/ability, character/personal qualities, volunteer work, work experience, level of applicant's interest. **Freshman Admission Requirements:** High school diploma is required and GED is accepted. *Academic units required:* 4 English, 3 math, 3 science, 2 science labs, 2 foreign language, 2 social studies, 1 history, 2 academic electives, 1 computer science, 1 visual/performing arts. *Academic units recommended:* 4 English, 3 math, 3 science, 2 science labs, 2 foreign language, 2 social studies, 3 history, 2 academic electives, 1 computer science, 1 visual/performing arts. **Freshman Admission Statistics:** 5,697 applied, 57% admitted, 31% enrolled. **Transfer Admission Requirements:** College transcript(s). Minimum college GPA of 2.0 required. Lowest grade transferable C-. **General Admission Information:** Application fee $75. Priority deadline 3/1. Regular application deadline 4/15. Non-fall registration accepted. Admission may be deferred for a maximum of 1 semester.

COSTS AND FINANCIAL AID

Required Forms and Deadlines: FAFSA. **Notification of Awards:** Applicants will be notified of awards on a rolling basis beginning 6/1. **Financial Aid Statistics:** 73% freshmen, 75% undergrads receive any aid.

SALISBURY UNIVERSITY

1101 Camden Avenue, Salisbury, MD 21801
Phone: 410-543-6161 **Financial Aid Phone:** 410-543-6165
E-mail: https://www.salisbury.edu/admissions/ **CEEB Code:** 2091
Fax: 410-546-6016 **Website:** https://www.salisbury.edu/ **ACT Code:** 1716

This public school was founded in 1925. It has a 184.8 acre campus.

RATINGS

Admissions Selectivity Rating: 82   **Fire Safety Rating:** 96   **Green Rating:** 98

STUDENTS AND FACULTY

Enrollment: 7,426. **Student Body:** 56% female, 44% male, 13% out-of-state, 1% international (30 countries represented). Asian 4%, African American 14%, Caucasian 70%, Hispanic 5%, Native American 1%, Pacific Islander <1%, Two or more races 2%, Race unknown 3%.

Retention and Graduation: 81% freshmen return for sophomore year. 52% freshmen graduate within 4 years. 70% freshmen graduate within 6 years. **Faculty:** Student/faculty ratio 15:1. 446 full-time faculty, 83% hold PhDs, 17% are members of minority groups, 52% are women. 2% of classes are taught by teaching assistants.

ACADEMICS

Degrees: Bachelor's; Certificate; Doctoral degree—professional practice; Doctoral degree research/scholarship; Master's; Post-bachelor's certificate; Post-master's certificate. **Classes:** Most classes have 20–29 students. Most lab/discussion sessions have 20–29 students. **Most popular majors:** Speech Communication and Rhetoric; Exercise Science and Kinesiology; Registered Nursing/Registered Nurse. **Special Study Options:** Accelerated program; Cooperative education program; Cross-registration; Distance learning; Double major; Dual enrollment; English as a Second Language (ESL); Exchange student program (domestic); Honors program; Independent study; Internships; Student-designed major; Study abroad; Teacher certification program. **Honors programs:** Honors College (https://www.salisbury.edu/academic-offices/honors/index.aspx). **Disability Services offered:** Note-taking services; Reader services; Tape recorders; Tutors. **Career services:** Alumni network; Alumni services; Career assessment; Career/job search classes; Internships; Regional alumni.

FACILITIES

Housing: Apartments for single students; Coed dorms; Special housing for disabled students; Special housing for international students; Theme housing; Wellness housing; 95% of campus accessible to physically disabled. **Special Academic Facilities/Equipment:** Arboretum, Atrium Gallery, University Galleries, Delmarva History and Culture Research Center, Small Business Development Center, Ward Museum of Wildfowl Art, Blackbox Theatre, Perdue Museum of Business & Entrepreneurship, Guerrieri Academic Commons, Guerrieri University Center. **Campus Network:** 90% of classrooms, 100% of dorms, 100% of student union, 100% of libraries, 100% of dining areas, 40% of common outdoor areas have wireless network access.

CAMPUS LIFE

Environment: Town. **Activities:** Campus Ministries; Choral groups; Concert band; Dance; Drama/theater; International Student Organization; Jazz band; Literary magazine; Model UN; Music ensembles; Musical theater; Opera; Pep band; Radio station; Student government; Student newspaper; Student-run film society; Symphony orchestra; Television station. 121 registered organizations, 30 honor societies, 9 religious organizations, 11 fraternities, 7 sororities on campus. **Athletics (Intercollegiate):** *Men:* baseball, basketball, cross-country, football, lacrosse, soccer, swimming, tennis, track/field (outdoor). *Women:* basketball, cross-country, field hockey, lacrosse, soccer, softball, swimming, tennis, track/field (outdoor), volleyball. **On-Campus Highlights:** Guerrieri Academic Commons. **Environmental Initiatives:** Construction of solar parking canopy that produces 765,000 Kwh annually.

ADMISSIONS

Freshman Academic Profile: Average high school GPA 3.7. 15% in top 10% of high school class, 45% in top 25% of high school class, 81% in top 50% of high school class. 85% from public high schools. **Test Scores:** SAT Math middle 50% range 550–640. SAT EBRW middle 50% range 570–640. ACT middle 50% range 19–23. **Basis for Candidate Selection:** *Very important factors include:* rigor of secondary school record, academic GPA. *Important factors include:* class rank, standardized test scores. *Other factors include:* application essay, recommendation(s), extracurricular activities, talent/ability, character/personal qualities, first generation, alumni/ae relation, geographical residence, state residency, racial/ethnic status, volunteer work, work experience, level of applicant's interest. **Freshman Admission Requirements:** High school diploma is required and GED is accepted. *Academic units required:* 4 English, 4 math, 3 science, 2 science labs, 2 foreign language, 3 social studies. *Academic units recommended:* 4 English, 4 math, 4 science, 3 science labs, 3 foreign language, 3 social studies, 3 academic electives. **Freshman Admission Statistics:** 8,421 applied, 74% admitted, 24% enrolled. **Transfer Admission Requirements:** College transcript(s). Minimum college GPA of 2.0 required. Lowest grade transferable C. **General Admission Information:** Application fee $50. Regular application deadline 1/15. Non-fall registration accepted. Admission may be deferred for a maximum of 1 year.

COSTS AND FINANCIAL AID

Annual in-state tuition $7,264. Annual out-of-state tuition $17,330. Room and board $12,360. Required fees $2,780. Average book and supplies expense $1,300. **Required Forms and Deadlines:** FAFSA. **Notification of Awards:** Applicants will be notified of awards on or about 3/15. **Types of Aid:** *Need-based scholarships/grants:* College/university scholarship or grant aid from institutional funds; Federal Pell; Private scholarships; SEOG; State scholarships/grants. *Loans:* Direct PLUS loans; Direct Subsidized Stafford Loans; Direct

Unsubsidized Stafford Loans. **Student Employment:** Federal Work-Study Program available. Institutional employment available. **Financial Aid Statistics:** 90% needy freshmen, 80% needy undergrads receive need-based scholarship or grant aid. 45% freshmen, 36% undergrads receive non-need-based scholarship or grant aid. 63% freshmen, 74% undergrads receive need-based self-help aid. 0% freshmen, 0% undergrads receive athletic scholarships. 87% freshmen, 78% undergrads receive any aid. 57% undergrads borrow to pay for school. Average cumulative indebtedness $26,521. **Criteria awarding aid:** *Need-based:* Academics, Job skills. *Non-need-based:* Academics, Alumni affiliation, Art, Leadership, Music/drama, State/district residency.

SALVE REGINA UNIVERSITY

100 Ochre Point Avenue, Newport, RI 02840-4192
Phone: 401-341-2908 **Financial Aid Phone:** 401-341-2140
E-mail: admissions@salve.edu **CEEB Code:** 3759
Fax: 401-848-2823 **Website:** www.salve.edu **ACT Code:** 3816

This private school, affiliated with the Roman Catholic Church, was founded in 1947. It has a 80 acre campus.

RATINGS
Admissions Selectivity Rating: 80   Fire Safety Rating: 94   Green Rating: 64

STUDENTS AND FACULTY
Enrollment: 2,140. **Student Body:** 65% female, 35% male, 84% out-of-state, 2% international (16 countries represented). Asian 1%, African American 2%, Caucasian 82%, Hispanic 7%, Native American <1%, Pacific Islander <1%, Two or more races 3%, Race unknown 3%.
Retention and Graduation: 85% freshmen return for sophomore year. 73% freshmen graduate within 4 years. 78% freshmen graduate within 6 years. 25% grads go on to further study within 1 year. 51% grads pursue arts and sciences degrees. 4% grads pursue law degrees. 41% grads pursue business degrees. 0% grads pursue medical degrees. **Faculty:** Student/faculty ratio 13:1. 128 full-time faculty, 84% hold PhDs, 7% are members of minority groups, 60% are women. 0% of classes are taught by teaching assistants.

ACADEMICS
Degrees: Associate; Bachelor's; Doctoral degree—professional practice; Doctoral degree research/scholarship; Master's; Post-bachelor's certificate; Post-master's certificate. **Classes:** Most classes have 20–29 students. Most lab/discussion sessions have 10–19 students. **Most popular majors:** Elementary Education and Teaching; Criminal Justice/Law Enforcement Administration; Registered Nursing/Registered Nurse. **Special Study Options:** Accelerated program; Distance learning; Double major; English as a Second Language (ESL); Honors program; Independent study; Internships; Liberal arts/career combination; Study abroad; Teacher certification program. **Honors programs:** The Pell Honors Program is open to students from all majors who receive the Trustee's, Presidential, or McAuley Scholarships, or who are nominated by Salve Regina faculty or the Admissions Office staff. The goal of the Pell Honors Program is to create a learning community of students from different disciplines. The honors education is an enhancement of the core curriculum. Students are required to take classes together and participate in either an internship or study abroad experience. **Combined degree programs:** BA/MA. **Disability Services offered:** Note-taking services; Reader services; Tape recorders; Tutors. **Career services:** Alumni network; Alumni services; Career assessment; Career/job search classes; Internships; Regional alumni.

FACILITIES
Housing: Apartments for single students; Coed dorms; Men's dorms; Special housing for disabled students; Special housing for international students; Theme housing; Women's dorms; 85% of campus accessible to physically disabled. **Special Academic Facilities/Equipment:** Hamilton Gallery, The Casino Theatre, Munroe Technology Center, Pell Center for International Relations and Public Policy, McKillop Library, Antone Academic Center, O'Hare Academic Center, Mercy Chapel & Spiritual Life Center.

CAMPUS LIFE
Environment: Town. **Activities:** Campus Ministries; Choral groups; Concert band; Dance; Drama/theater; International Student Organization; Jazz band; Literary magazine; Model UN; Music ensembles; Pep band; Radio station; Student government; Student newspaper; Student-run film society; Yearbook. 63 registered organizations, 19 honor societies, 3 religious organizations on campus. **Athletics (Intercollegiate):** *Men:* baseball, basketball, cross-country,

football, ice hockey, lacrosse, soccer, tennis. *Women:* basketball, field hockey, ice hockey, lacrosse, soccer, softball, tennis, track/field (outdoor), volleyball. **On-Campus Highlights:** Miley Hall Starbucks. **Environmental Initiatives:** Recycling.

ADMISSIONS
Freshman Academic Profile: Average high school GPA 3.5. 18% in top 10% of high school class, 43% in top 25% of high school class, 81% in top 50% of high school class. 69% from public high schools. **Test Scores:** SAT Math middle 50% range 540–620. SAT EBRW middle 50% range 560–640. ACT middle 50% range 24–28. **Basis for Candidate Selection:** *Very important factors include:* rigor of secondary school record, class rank, academic GPA. *Important factors include:* application essay, standardized test scores, recommendation(s). *Other factors include:* extracurricular activities, talent/ability, character/personal qualities, alumni/ae relation, racial/ethnic status, volunteer work, work experience, level of applicant's interest. **Freshman Admission Requirements:** High school diploma is required and GED is accepted. *Academic units required:* 4 English, 3 math, 2 science, 2 science labs, 2 foreign language, 1 social studies, 4 academic electives. **Freshman Admission Statistics:** 4,888 applied, 74% admitted, 18% enrolled. **Transfer Admission Requirements:** High school transcript, college transcript(s), essay or personal statement, statement of good standing from prior institution(s). Minimum college GPA of 2.7 required. Lowest grade transferable C. **General Admission Information:** Application fee $50. Priority deadline 2/1. Non-fall registration accepted. Admission may be deferred for a maximum of 12 months.

COSTS AND FINANCIAL AID
Annual tuition $40,750. Room and board $14,960. Required fees $700. Average book and supplies expense $1,450. **Required Forms and Deadlines:** FAFSA. **Notification of Awards:** Applicants will be notified of awards on a rolling basis beginning 1/3. **Types of Aid:** *Need-based scholarships/grants:* College/university scholarship or grant aid from institutional funds; Federal Pell; Private scholarships; SEOG; State scholarships/grants. *Loans:* Direct PLUS loans; Direct Subsidized Stafford Loans; Direct Unsubsidized Stafford Loans. **Student Employment:** Federal Work-Study Program available. Institutional employment available. **Financial Aid Statistics:** 100% needy freshmen, 100% needy undergrads receive need-based scholarship or grant aid. 18% freshmen, 11% undergrads receive non-need-based scholarship or grant aid. 80% freshmen, 86% undergrads receive need-based self-help aid. 0% freshmen, 0% undergrads receive athletic scholarships. 99% freshmen, 99% undergrads receive any aid. **Criteria awarding aid:** *Non-need-based:* Academics, Alumni affiliation, Art.

SAMFORD UNIVERSITY

800 Lakeshore Drive, Birmingham, AL 35229
Phone: 205-726-3673 **Financial Aid Phone:** (205)726-2905
E-mail: admissions@samford.edu **CEEB Code:** 1302
Website: www.samford.edu **ACT Code:** 0016

This private school, affiliated with the Baptist Church, was founded in 1841. It has a 247.31 acre campus.

RATINGS
Admissions Selectivity Rating: 80   Fire Safety Rating: 95   Green Rating: 72

STUDENTS AND FACULTY
Enrollment: 3,585. **Student Body:** 67% female, 33% male, 68% out-of-state, 1% international (24 countries represented). Asian 1%, African American 7%, Caucasian 85%, Hispanic 3%, Native American <1%, Pacific Islander <1%, Two or more races 2%, Race unknown <1%.
Retention and Graduation: 89% freshmen return for sophomore year. 65% freshmen graduate within 4 years. 76% freshmen graduate within 6 years. **Faculty:** Student/faculty ratio 13:1. 368 full-time faculty, 86% hold PhDs, 12% are members of minority groups, 51% are women. 0% of classes are taught by teaching assistants.

ACADEMICS
Degrees: Bachelor's; Certificate; Doctoral degree—professional practice; Doctoral degree research/scholarship; Master's; Post-bachelor's certificate; Post-master's certificate. **Classes:** Most classes have 10–19 students. Most lab/discussion sessions have 10–19 students. **Most popular majors:** Journalism; Registered Nursing/Registered Nurse; Health Professions And Related

Programs. **Special Study Options:** Accelerated program; Distance learning; Double major; Dual enrollment; Exchange student program (domestic); Honors program; Independent study; Internships; Study abroad; Teacher certification program. **Honors programs:** University Fellows is Samford's university-wide honors program. The program offers an interdisciplinary Great Books core curriculum, international study in Italy, funding for academic enrichment and a four-year University Fellows scholarship. Admission to the program is highly competitive. Applicants should be intellectually curious, ambitious students who want to make connections across disciplines. The program is open to students from all Samford undergraduate majors, but students must be admitted as high school seniors. Micah Fellows is a four-year service-oriented, honors program grounded in the wisdom of Micah 6:8: "And what does the Lord require of you? To act justly, and to love mercy, and to walk humbly with your God." As part of an inspired community called to serve others, Micah Fellows devote their minds and talents to making Birmingham, and the world beyond, a better place. Through innovative course work, high-impact community engagement and service learning abroad, the Micah Fellows program will provide an intentional university experience connected to the world around you. **Disability Services offered:** Note-taking services; Reader services; Tape recorders. **Career services:** Alumni network; Alumni services; Career assessment; Career/job search classes; Internships; Regional alumni.

FACILITIES

Housing: Fraternity/sorority housing; Men's dorms; Women's dorms; 100% of campus accessible to physically disabled. **Special Academic Facilities/Equipment:** Divinity school Global Center, Samford University Global Drug Information Center, Nursing school state-of-the-art human sumulation center, Medicinal Plant Conservatory, Business School Investment Trading Room, Sciencenter. **Campus Network:** 100% of classrooms, 100% of dorms, 100% of student union, 100% of libraries, 100% of dining areas, 50% of common outdoor areas have wireless network access.

CAMPUS LIFE

Environment: Town. **Activities:** Campus Ministries; Choral groups; Dance; International Student Organization; Model UN; Musical theater; Student government; Student newspaper; Student-run film society; Yearbook. 109 registered organizations, 17 honor societies, 8 religious organizations, 6 fraternities, 9 sororities on campus. **Athletics (Intercollegiate):** *Men:* baseball, basketball, cross-country, football, golf, tennis, track/field (outdoor). *Women:* basketball, cross-country, golf, soccer, softball, tennis, track/field (outdoor), volleyball. **On-Campus Highlights:** University Center. **Environmental Initiatives:** Along with Johnson Controls, invested $31 million in energy upgrades.

ADMISSIONS

Freshman Academic Profile: Average high school GPA 3.8. 33% in top 10% of high school class, 61% in top 25% of high school class, 87% in top 50% of high school class. 49% from public high schools. **Test Scores:** SAT Math middle 50% range 520–610. SAT EBRW middle 50% range 550–640. ACT middle 50% range 23–29. **Basis for Candidate Selection:** *Important factors include:* rigor of secondary school record, academic GPA, application essay, standardized test scores, recommendation(s). *Other factors include:* character/personal qualities, level of applicant's interest. **Freshman Admission Requirements:** High school diploma is required and GED is accepted. *Academic units required:* 4 English, 3 math, 2 science, 2 science labs, 2 foreign language, 2 history. *Academic units recommended:* 4 English, 4 math, 3 science, 3 science labs, 2 foreign language, 3 history. **Freshman Admission Statistics:** 3,912 applied, 83% admitted, 28% enrolled. **Transfer Admission Requirements:** College transcript(s), essay or personal statement, statement of good standing from prior institution(s). Minimum college GPA of 2.5 required. Lowest grade transferable C-. **General Admission Information:** Application fee $40. Priority deadline 2/15. Admission may be deferred for a maximum of 1 year.

COSTS AND FINANCIAL AID

Annual tuition $32,000. Room and board $10,980. Required fees $850. Average book and supplies expense $1,000. **Required Forms and Deadlines:** FAFSA; Institution's own financial aid form; State aid form. **Notification of Awards:** Applicants will be notified of awards on or about 3/15. **Types of Aid:** *Need-based scholarships/grants:* College/university scholarship or grant aid from institutional funds; Federal Nursing Scholarships; Federal Pell; Private scholarships; SEOG; State scholarships/grants; United Negro College Fund. *Loans:* Direct PLUS loans; Direct Subsidized Stafford Loans; Direct Unsubsidized Stafford Loans. **Student Employment:** Federal Work-Study Program available. Institutional employment available. **Financial Aid Statistics:** 100% needy freshmen, 97% needy undergrads receive need-based scholarship or grant aid. 24% freshmen, 21% undergrads receive non-need-based

scholarship or grant aid. 70% freshmen, 75% undergrads receive need-based self-help aid. 3% freshmen, 5% undergrads receive athletic scholarships. 99% freshmen, 96% undergrads receive any aid. 32% undergrads borrow to pay for school. Average cumulative indebtedness $29,676. **Criteria awarding aid:** *Non-need-based:* Academics, Alumni affiliation, Art, Athletics, Leadership, Minority status, Music/drama, Religious affiliation, State/district residency.

SAM HOUSTON STATE UNIVERSITY

Box 2418, Huntsville, TX 77341-2418
Phone: 936-294-1828 **Financial Aid Phone:** 936-294-1774
E-mail: admissions@shsu.edu **CEEB Code:** 6643
Website: www.shsu.edu **ACT Code:** 4162

This public school was founded in 1879. It has a 272 acre campus.

RATINGS

Admissions Selectivity Rating: 84   **Fire Safety Rating:** 92   **Green Rating:** 60*

STUDENTS AND FACULTY

Enrollment: 15,611. **Student Body:** 58% female, 42% male, 1% out-of-state, 1% international (59 countries represented). Asian 1%, African American 17%, Caucasian 58%, Hispanic 17%, Native American <1%, Pacific Islander <1%, Two or more races 2%, Race unknown 2%.
Faculty: Student/faculty ratio 25:1. 620 full-time faculty, 79% hold PhDs, 16% are members of minority groups, 45% are women. 5% of classes are taught by teaching assistants.

ACADEMICS

Degrees: Bachelor's; Diploma; Doctoral degree—professional practice; Doctoral degree research/scholarship; Master's. **Classes:** Most classes have 20–29 students. Most lab/discussion sessions have 20–29 students. **Most popular majors:** Criminal Justice/Safety Studies; Business/Commerce, General; Multi-/Interdisciplinary Studies, Other. **Special Study Options:** Accelerated program; Distance learning; Double major; Dual enrollment; English as a Second Language (ESL); Honors program; Independent study; Internships; Study abroad; Teacher certification program. **Honors programs:** The Honors student earns Honors credit in a variety of specially designated classes, and works toward the distinction of graduating "With Honors" or "With Highest Honors." To qualify for graduation with honors, a student must have been a participant in the Honors Program and have completed 24 hours of Honors class credit, including participation in two interdisciplinary Honors seminars. To qualify for graduation 'With Highest Honors' a student must, in addition, complete a senior thesis in an approved discipline under the direction of a faculty member of his/her choice. The student will receive 6 credit hours of departmental course credit when completing the senior thesis. **Disability Services offered:** Note-taking services; Reader services; Tape recorders. **Career services:** Alumni network; Alumni services; Career assessment; Career/job search classes; Internships; Regional alumni.

FACILITIES

Housing: Apartments for single students; Coed dorms; Fraternity/sorority housing; Men's dorms; Special housing for disabled students; Theme housing; Women's dorms 85% of campus accessible to physically disabled. **Special Academic Facilities/Equipment:** Sam Houston Memorial Museum, on-campus elementary school, communications center for photography, radio, TV, and film, agricultural complex and university farm.

CAMPUS LIFE

Environment: Town. **Activities:** Campus Ministries; Choral groups; Concert band; Dance; Drama/theater; International Student Organization; Jazz band; Marching band; Music ensembles; Musical theater; Pep band; Radio station; Student government; Student newspaper; Symphony orchestra; Television station. 233 registered organizations, 19 honor societies, 19 religious organizations, 13 fraternities, 11 sororities on campus. **Athletics (Intercollegiate):** *Men:* baseball, basketball, cheerleading, cross-country, equestrian sports, football, golf, rodeo, soccer, softball, tennis, track/field (outdoor), track/field (indoor). *Women:* basketball, cheerleading, cross-country, equestrian sports, golf, rodeo, soccer, softball, tennis, track/field (outdoor), track/field (indoor), volleyball. **On-Campus Highlights:** Lowman Student Center. **Environmental Initiatives:** Hired an Energy Manager.

ADMISSIONS

Freshman Academic Profile: 13% in top 10% of high school class, 42% in top 25% of high school class, 85% in top 50% of high school class. **Test Scores:** SAT Math middle 50% range 470–550. SAT EBRW middle 50% range 450–540. ACT middle 50% range 19–23. **Basis for Candidate Selection:** *Very important factors include:* class rank, standardized test scores. *Important factors include:* academic GPA. *Other factors include:* rigor of secondary school record, recommendation(s), extracurricular activities, talent/ability, character/personal qualities, volunteer work. **Freshman Admission Requirements:** High school diploma is required and GED is accepted. *Academic units required:* 4 English, 4 math, 4 science, 2 science labs, 2 foreign language, 2 social studies, 2 history, 6 academic electives, 1 computer science, 1 visual/performing arts, 2 unit from above areas or other academic areas. *Academic units recommended:* 4 English, 4 math, 4 science, 2 science labs, 2 foreign language, 2 social studies, 2 history, 6 academic electives, 1 computer science, 1 visual/performing arts. **Freshman Admission Statistics:** 9,315 applied, 65% admitted, 40% enrolled. **Transfer Admission Requirements:** College transcript(s), statement of good standing from prior institution(s). Minimum college GPA of 2.0 required. Lowest grade transferable D. **General Admission Information:** Application fee $45. Priority deadline 6/15. Regular application deadline 8/1. Non-fall registration accepted.

COSTS AND FINANCIAL AID

Annual in-state tuition $5,850. Annual out-of-state tuition $16,470. Room and board $8,324. Required fees $2,744. Average book and supplies expense $1,124. **Required Forms and Deadlines:** FAFSA. **Notification of Awards:** Applicants will be notified of awards on a rolling basis beginning 3/15. **Types of Aid:** *Need-based scholarships/grants:* College/university scholarship or grant aid from institutional funds; Federal Pell; SEOG; State scholarships/grants. *Loans:* Direct PLUS loans; Direct Subsidized Stafford Loans; Direct Unsubsidized Stafford Loans. **Student Employment:** Federal Work-Study Program available. Institutional employment available. **Financial Aid Statistics:** 86% needy freshmen, 80% needy undergrads receive need-based scholarship or grant aid. 3% freshmen, 1% undergrads receive non-need-based scholarship or grant aid. 75% freshmen, 81% undergrads receive need-based self-help aid. 2% freshmen, 2% undergrads receive athletic scholarships. 79% freshmen, 71% undergrads receive any aid. **Criteria awarding aid:** *Need-based:* Academics, Art, Music/drama. *Non-need-based:* Academics, Alumni affiliation, Art, Athletics, Job skills, Leadership, Music/drama, Religious affiliation, State/district residency.

SAN DIEGO STATE UNIVERSITY

5500 Campanile Drive, San Diego, CA 92182-7455
Phone: 619-594-6336 **Financial Aid Phone:** 619-594-6323
CEEB Code: 4682
Website: www.sdsu.edu **ACT Code:** 398

This public school was founded in 1897. It has a 288 acre campus.

RATINGS

Admissions Selectivity Rating: 91 **Fire Safety Rating:** 95 **Green Rating:** 89

STUDENTS AND FACULTY

Enrollment: 30,612. **Student Body:** 55% female, 45% male, 11% out-of-state, 7% international (117 countries represented). Asian 13%, African American 4%, Caucasian 34%, Hispanic 32%, Native American <1%, Pacific Islander <1%, Two or more races 6%, Race unknown 4%.
Retention and Graduation: 89% freshmen return for sophomore year. 40% freshmen graduate within 4 years. 74% freshmen graduate within 6 years. 15% grads go on to further study within 1 year. **Faculty:** Student/faculty ratio 25:1. 947 full-time faculty, 88% hold PhDs, 30% are members of minority groups, 46% are women.

ACADEMICS

Degrees: Bachelor's; Doctoral degree—other; Doctoral degree—professional practice; Doctoral degree research/scholarship; Master's; Post-bachelor's certificate. **Classes:** Most classes have 20–29 students. Most lab/discussion sessions have 20–29 students. **Most popular majors:** Psychology, General; Business Administration and Management, General; Sports, Kinesiology, and Physical Education/Fitness, General. **Special Study Options:** Cross-registration; Distance learning; Double major; English as a Second Language (ESL); Exchange student program (domestic); External degree program; Honors program; Independent study; Internships; Liberal arts/career combination; Student-designed major; Study abroad; Teacher certification program. **Honors programs:** The Weber Honors College provides an academic environment in which students experience a dynamic, interactive, and engaged education. The objective of the Weber Honors College is to provide the richest possible intellectual experience by helping students become conversant in multiple disciplines, think flexibly, solve problems and pursue the creative expression of ideas. The Weber Honors College features a unique interdisciplinary curriculum made up of small, discussion-based seminars and innovative teaching techniques that promote active engagement in the subject area and prepare students for high-impact educational experiences beyond the classroom, including study abroad, research, leadership, service, and creative activity; and for future graduate work and successful careers regardless of their chosen field of study. **Combined degree programs:** BA/MA; BA/MEng. **Disability Services offered:** Note-taking services; Reader services; Tape recorders; Tutors. **Career services:** Alumni network; Alumni services; Career assessment; Career/job search classes; Internships; Regional alumni.

FACILITIES

Housing: Apartments for single students; Coed dorms; Fraternity/sorority housing; Special housing for disabled students; Special housing for international students; Theme housing; Wellness housing; 99% of campus accessible to physically disabled. **Special Academic Facilities/Equipment:** Observatory, electron microscope facility, open-air theater, aquatic center, International Student Center, American language institute, recital hall, field studies stations (off-campus), multimedia interactive fine arts lab, MRI machine, engineering and interdisciplinary sciences complex, art gallery, Black Resource Center, Women's Resource Center, Children's Center, Student Ability Success Center, Undocumented Resource Center, Pride Center, Veterans Center.

CAMPUS LIFE

Environment: Metropolis. **Activities:** Campus Ministries; Choral groups; Concert band; Dance; Drama/theater; International Student Organization; Jazz band; Literary magazine; Marching band; Music ensembles; Musical theater; Opera; Pep band; Radio station; Student government; Student newspaper; Student-run film society; Symphony orchestra; Television station. 385 registered organizations, 27 honor societies, 17 religious organizations, 22 fraternities, 22 sororities on campus. **Athletics (Intercollegiate):** *Men:* baseball, basketball, football, golf, soccer, tennis. *Women:* basketball, crew/rowing, cross-country, diving, golf, soccer, softball, swimming, tennis, track/field (outdoor), track/field (indoor), volleyball, water polo. **On-Campus Highlights:** Aztec Student Union.

ADMISSIONS

Freshman Academic Profile: Average high school GPA 3.8. 33% in top 10% of high school class, 70% in top 25% of high school class, 94% in top 50% of high school class. 92% from public high schools. **Test Scores:** SAT Math middle 50% range 550–670. SAT EBRW middle 50% range 560–650. ACT middle 50% range 22–29. **Basis for Candidate Selection:** *Very important factors include:* rigor of secondary school record, academic GPA, standardized test scores. *Important factors include:* geographical residence, state residency. **Freshman Admission Requirements:** High school diploma is required and GED is accepted. *Academic units required:* 4 English, 3 math, 2 science, 2 science labs, 2 foreign language, 1 social studies, 1 history, 1 academic elective, 1 visual/performing arts. *Academic units recommended:* 4 math. **Freshman Admission Statistics:** 69,842 applied, 34% admitted, 22% enrolled. **Transfer Admission Requirements:** College transcript(s). Lowest grade transferable D-. **General Admission Information:** Application fee $70. Regular application deadline 11/30.

COSTS AND FINANCIAL AID

Annual in-state tuition $5,742. Annual out-of-state tuition $17,622. Room and board $17,752. Required fees $1,768. Average book and supplies expense $1,969. **Required Forms and Deadlines:** FAFSA; State aid form. **Notification of Awards:** Applicants will be notified of awards on a rolling basis beginning 3/15. **Types of Aid:** *Need-based scholarships/grants:* College/university scholarship or grant aid from institutional funds; Federal Pell; Private scholarships; SEOG; State scholarships/grants. *Loans:* Direct PLUS loans; Direct Subsidized Stafford Loans; Direct Unsubsidized Stafford Loans. **Student Employment:** Federal Work-Study Program available. Institutional employment available. **Financial Aid Statistics:** 63% needy freshmen, 71% needy undergrads receive need-based scholarship or grant aid. 48% freshmen, 41% undergrads receive non-need-based scholarship or grant aid. 100% freshmen, 94% undergrads receive need-based self-help aid. 2% freshmen, 1% undergrads receive athletic scholarships. 57% freshmen, 59% undergrads receive any aid. 44% undergrads borrow to pay for school. Average cumulative indebtedness $21,172. **Criteria awarding aid:** *Need-based:* Academics, Alumni affiliation, Art, Leadership, Music/drama. *Non-need-based:* Academics, Alumni affiliation, Art, Athletics, Leadership, Music/drama, State/district residency.

SAN FRANCISCO STATE UNIVERSITY

1600 Holloway Avenue, San Francisco, CA 93132
Phone: 415-338-6486 **Financial Aid Phone:** (415) 338-7000
E-mail: ugadmit@sfsu.edu **CEEB Code:** 4684
Fax: 415-338-3880 **Website:** www.sfsu.edu

This public school was founded in 1899. It has a 142 acre campus.

RATINGS

Admissions Selectivity Rating: 77   **Fire Safety Rating:** 88   **Green Rating:** 95

STUDENTS AND FACULTY

Enrollment: 25,903. **Student Body:** 56% female, 44% male, 1% out-of-state, 6% international (75 countries represented). Asian 26%, African American 5%, Caucasian 18%, Hispanic 33%, Native American <1%, Pacific Islander <1%, Two or more races 6%, Race unknown 4%.
Retention and Graduation: 79% freshmen return for sophomore year.
Faculty: Student/faculty ratio 23:1. 1,054 full-time faculty, 63% hold PhDs, 38% are members of minority groups, 56% are women.

ACADEMICS

Degrees: Bachelor's; Certificate; Doctoral degree—other; Doctoral degree—professional practice; Doctoral degree research/scholarship; Master's; Post-bachelor's certificate; Post-master's certificate. **Classes:** Most classes have 20–29 students. Most lab/discussion sessions have 20–29 students. **Most popular majors:** Marketing/Marketing Management, General; Communication and Media Studies; Communication and Media Studies. **Special Study Options:** Accelerated program; Cooperative education program; Cross-registration; Distance learning; Double major; Dual enrollment; English as a Second Language (ESL); Exchange student program (domestic); Honors program; Independent study; Internships; Liberal arts/career combination; Student-designed major; Study abroad; Teacher certification program. **Disability Services offered:** Note-taking services; Reader services; Tape recorders; Tutors. **Career services:** Alumni services; Career assessment; Career/job search classes; Internships.

FACILITIES

Housing: Apartments for married students; Apartments for single students; Coed dorms; Special housing for disabled students; Special housing for international students; Theme housing; Wellness housing; Women's dorms. **Special Academic Facilities/Equipment:** Treganza Anthropology Museum, Moss Landing Marine Laboratories, Romberg Tiburon Center for Environmental Studies, Sierra Nevada Field Campus, Sutro Egyptian Collection.

CAMPUS LIFE

Environment: Metropolis. **Activities:** Choral groups; Concert band; Dance; Drama/theater; International Student Organization; Jazz band; Literary magazine; Marching band; Music ensembles; Musical theater; Opera; Radio station; Student government; Student newspaper; Student-run film society; Symphony orchestra; Television station. 127 registered organizations, 8 honor societies, 14 religious organizations, 12 fraternities, 18 sororities on campus. **Athletics (Intercollegiate):** *Men:* baseball, basketball, cross-country, soccer, wrestling. *Women:* basketball, cross-country, soccer, softball, track/field (outdoor), track/field (indoor), volleyball. **On-Campus Highlights:** J. Paul Leonard Library. **Environmental Initiatives:** SF State is dedicated to reducing the campus' use of resources and its impact on climate change. Some of the projects that demonstrate that are: the Buy Recycled Campaign, purchasing 20% renewable energy, implementing a green cleaning program, hiring a Sustainability Programs Manager and a Sustainability Coordinator, offering alternative transportation incentives, pursuing LEED Gold for its new Rec and Wellness Center and diverting over 75% of the waste from the landfill.

ADMISSIONS

Freshman Academic Profile: Average high school GPA 3.2. 88% from public high schools. **Test Scores:** SAT Math middle 50% range 430–550. SAT EBRW middle 50% range 430–540. ACT middle 50% range 18–24. **Basis for Candidate Selection:** *Very important factors include:* rigor of secondary school record, academic GPA, standardized test scores. *Important factors include:* state residency. *Other factors include:* geographical residence. **Freshman Admission Requirements:** High school diploma is required and GED is accepted. *Academic units required:* 4 English, 3 math, 2 science, 2 science labs, 2 foreign language, 1 social studies, 1 history, 1 academic elective, 1 visual/performing arts. *Academic units recommended:* 4 English, 4 math, 2 science, 2 science labs, 2 foreign language, 1 social studies, 1 history, 1 academic elective, 1 visual/performing arts. **Freshman Admission Statistics:** 34,524 applied, 70% admitted, 18% enrolled. **Transfer Admission Requirements:** College transcript(s), statement of good standing from prior institution(s). Minimum college GPA of 2.0 required. Lowest grade transferable D. **General Admission Information:** Application fee $55. Priority deadline 10/1. Regular application deadline 11/30. Non-fall registration accepted.

COSTS AND FINANCIAL AID

Annual in-state tuition $5,472. Annual out-of-state tuition $16,632. Room and board $12,698. Required fees $1,012. Average book and supplies expense $1,900. **Required Forms and Deadlines:** FAFSA. **Notification of Awards:** Applicants will be notified of awards on a rolling basis beginning 4/15. **Types of Aid:** *Need-based scholarships/grants:* College/university scholarship or grant aid from institutional funds; Federal Pell; Private scholarships; SEOG; State scholarships/grants. *Loans:* Direct PLUS loans; Direct Subsidized Stafford Loans; Direct Unsubsidized Stafford Loans. **Student Employment:** Federal Work-Study Program available. Institutional employment available. **Financial Aid Statistics:** 93% needy freshmen, 91% needy undergrads receive need-based scholarship or grant aid. 26% freshmen, 14% undergrads receive non-need-based scholarship or grant aid. 75% freshmen, 67% undergrads receive need-based self-help aid. 1% freshmen, 1% undergrads receive athletic scholarships. 45% undergrads borrow to pay for school. Average cumulative indebtedness $19,347. **Criteria awarding aid:** *Need-based:* Academics, Athletics. *Non-need-based:* Academics, Athletics.

SAN JOSE STATE UNIVERSITY

One Washington Square, San Jose, CA 95192-0016
Phone: 408-283-7500 **Financial Aid Phone:** 408-283-7500
E-mail: admissions@sjsu.edu **CEEB Code:** 4687
Fax: 408-924-2050 **Website:** www.sjsu.edu

This public school was founded in 1857. It has a 154 acre campus.

RATINGS

Admissions Selectivity Rating: 87   **Fire Safety Rating:** 60*   **Green Rating:** 97

STUDENTS AND FACULTY

Enrollment: 27,327. **Student Body:** 49% female, 51% male, 1% out-of-state, 8% international (93 countries represented). Asian 36%, African American 3%, Caucasian 15%, Hispanic 28%, Native American <1%, Pacific Islander <1%, Two or more races 5%, Race unknown 4%.
Retention and Graduation: 83% freshmen return for sophomore year. 14% freshmen graduate within 4 years. 65% freshmen graduate within 6 years.
Faculty: Student/faculty ratio 26:1. 720 full-time faculty, 0% hold PhDs, 11% are members of minority groups, 50% are women. 1% of classes are taught by teaching assistants.

ACADEMICS

Degrees: Bachelor's; Certificate; Doctoral degree—professional practice; Master's; Post-bachelor's certificate. **Classes:** Most classes have 20–29 students. Most lab/discussion sessions have 20–29 students. **Special Study Options:** Cooperative education program; Cross-registration; Distance learning; Double major; Dual enrollment; Honors program; Independent study; Internships; Liberal arts/career combination; Student-designed major; Study abroad; Teacher certification program; Weekend college. **Disability Services offered:** Note-taking services; Reader services; Tutors. **Career services:** Alumni network; Alumni services; Career assessment; Career/job search classes; Internships; Regional alumni.

FACILITIES

Housing: Apartments for single students; Coed dorms; Fraternity/sorority housing; Men's dorms; Special housing for international students; Women's dorms; 100% of campus accessible to physically disabled. **Special Academic Facilities/Equipment:** Martin Luther King, Jr. Library (Joint with City); Child development lab; Chicano resource center; Beethoven studies center; John Steinbeck research center; art metal foundry; natural history living museum (science education); science resource center; deep-sea research ship; electro-acoustical/recording studios; nuclear science and engineering labs.

CAMPUS LIFE

Environment: Metropolis. **Activities:** Campus Ministries; Choral groups; Concert band; Dance; Drama/theater; International Student Organization; Jazz band; Literary magazine; Marching band; Model UN; Music ensembles; Opera; Pep band; Radio station; Student government; Student newspaper; Student-run film society; Symphony orchestra. 450 registered organizations, 13 honor societies, 20 religious organizations, 26 fraternities, 19 sororities on campus. **Athletics (Intercollegiate):** *Men:* baseball, basketball, cheerleading, cross-country, diving, football, golf, soccer, softball, swimming, volleyball, water polo. *Women:* basketball, cheerleading, cross-country, diving, golf, gymnastics, soccer, softball, swimming, tennis, volleyball, water polo. **On-Campus Highlights:** Martin Luther King, Jr. Library.

ADMISSIONS

Freshman Academic Profile: Average high school GPA 3.5. 89% from public high schools. **Test Scores:** SAT Math middle 50% range 520–640. SAT EBRW middle 50% range 520–620. ACT middle 50% range 19–26. **Basis for Candidate Selection:** *Very important factors include:* rigor of secondary school record, academic GPA, standardized test scores. *Important factors include:* geographical residence, state residency. **Freshman Admission Requirements:** High school diploma is required and GED is accepted. *Academic units required:* 4 English, 3 math, 2 science, 2 science labs, 2 foreign language, 1 social studies, 1 history, 1 academic elective, 1 visual/performing arts. *Academic units recommended:* 4 math, 3 science, 3 science labs. **Freshman Admission Statistics:** 36,243 applied, 55% admitted, 19% enrolled. **Transfer Admission Requirements:** College transcript(s), statement of good standing from prior institution(s). Minimum college GPA of 2.0 required. Lowest grade transferable 2. **General Admission Information:** Application fee $55. Regular application deadline 12/15.

COSTS AND FINANCIAL AID

Annual in-state tuition $5,742. Annual out-of-state tuition $17,622. Room and board $14,535. Required fees $2,054. Average book and supplies expense $2,002. **Required Forms and Deadlines:** FAFSA; State aid form. **Notification of Awards:** Applicants will be notified of awards on a rolling basis beginning 3/1. **Types of Aid:** *Need-based scholarships/grants:* College/university scholarship or grant aid from institutional funds; Federal Pell; Private scholarships; SEOG; State scholarships/grants. *Loans:* Direct PLUS loans; Direct Subsidized Stafford Loans; Direct Unsubsidized Stafford Loans. **Student Employment:** Federal Work-Study Program available. Institutional employment available. **Financial Aid Statistics:** 92% needy freshmen, 76% needy undergrads receive need-based scholarship or grant aid. 8% freshmen, 4% undergrads receive non-need-based scholarship or grant aid. 88% freshmen, 73% undergrads receive need-based self-help aid. 2% freshmen, 1% undergrads receive athletic scholarships. 66.34% freshmen, 64.09% undergrads receive any aid. 44% undergrads borrow to pay for school. Average cumulative indebtedness $18,925. **Criteria awarding aid:** *Need-based:* Academics, Art, Athletics, Job skills, Leadership, Music/drama. *Non-need-based:* Academics, Art, Athletics, Job skills, Leadership, Music/drama, State/district residency.

SANTA CLARA UNIVERSITY

500 El Camino Real, Santa Clara, CA 95053
Phone: 408-554-4700 **Financial Aid Phone:** (408) 551-1000
E-mail: Admission@scu.edu **CEEB Code:** 4851
Fax: 408-554-5255 **Website:** www.scu.edu

This private school, affiliated with the Roman Catholic Church, was founded in 1851. It has a 106 acre campus.

RATINGS

Admissions Selectivity Rating: 91   **Fire Safety Rating:** 96   **Green Rating:** 96

STUDENTS AND FACULTY

Enrollment: 5,676. **Student Body:** 50% female, 50% male, 42% out-of-state, 4% international (40 countries represented). Asian 18%, African American 3%, Caucasian 47%, Hispanic 18%, Native American <1%, Pacific Islander <1%, Two or more races 8%, Race unknown 2%.

Retention and Graduation: 94% freshmen return for sophomore year. 87% freshmen graduate within 4 years. 19% grads go on to further study within 1 year. 14% grads pursue arts and sciences degrees. 2% grads pursue law degrees. <1% grads pursue business degrees. 2% grads pursue medical degrees. **Faculty:** Student/faculty ratio 10:1. 571 full-time faculty, 94% hold PhDs, 28% are members of minority groups, 46% are women. 0% of classes are taught by teaching assistants.

ACADEMICS

Degrees: Bachelor's; Doctoral degree—professional practice; Doctoral degree research/scholarship; Master's; Post-bachelor's certificate; Post-master's certificate. **Classes:** Most classes have 10–19 students. Most lab/discussion sessions have 10–19 students. **Most popular majors:** Economics, General; Finance, General; Speech Communication and Rhetoric. **Special Study Options:** Cooperative education program; Distance learning; Double major; Exchange student program (domestic); Honors program; Independent study; Internships; Student-designed major; Study abroad. **Honors programs:** The University Honors Program provides small, seminar-style classes that emphasize critical thinking, analytical rigor, effective expression, and interaction among professors and students. Honors classes inspire and enable intellectual risk-taking and lifelong learning and develop globally aware and engaged student leaders for the university community and beyond. The Honors educational experience culminates in a focused, meaningful, and collaborative thesis in senior year. Honors classes are designed to fit within the curricula of the humanities, natural and social sciences, business, and engineering. Honors students can major in any undergraduate field offered at Santa Clara University. The University Honors Program welcomes students from diverse geographic, ethnic, and religious backgrounds. **Combined degree programs:** BA/MEng. **Disability Services offered:** Note-taking services; Reader services; Tape recorders; Tutors. **Career services:** Alumni network; Alumni services; Career assessment; Career/job search classes; Internships; Regional alumni.

FACILITIES

Housing: Apartments for single students; Coed dorms; Theme housing; 95% of campus accessible to physically disabled. **Special Academic Facilities/Equipment:** Dowd Art and Art History, museum (de Saisset), Mission Church, Mayer Theatre, Harrington Learning Commons, Sobrato Technology Center and Orradre Library, engineering labs, Markkula Center for Applied Ethics, Miller Center for Social Entrepreneurship, Ignatian Center for Jesuit Education.

CAMPUS LIFE

Environment: City. **Activities:** Campus Ministries; Choral groups; Concert band; Dance; Drama/theater; International Student Organization; Jazz band; Literary magazine; Model UN; Music ensembles; Musical theater; Opera; Pep band; Radio station; Student government; Student newspaper; Student-run film society; Symphony orchestra; Yearbook. 160 registered organizations, 28 honor societies, 11 religious organizations on campus. **Athletics (Intercollegiate):** *Men:* baseball, basketball, crew/rowing, cross-country, golf, soccer, tennis, track/field (outdoor), water polo. *Women:* basketball, crew/rowing, cross-country, golf, soccer, softball, tennis, track/field (outdoor), volleyball, water polo. **On-Campus Highlights:** Historic Mission Church; Mission Gardens.

ADMISSIONS

Freshman Academic Profile: Average high school GPA 3.7. 52% in top 10% of high school class, 88% in top 25% of high school class, 99% in top 50% of high school class. 50% from public high schools. **Test Scores:** SAT Math middle 50% range 650–740. SAT EBRW middle 50% range 630–700. ACT middle 50% range 28–32. **Basis for Candidate Selection:** *Very important factors include:* rigor of secondary school record, academic GPA, application essay. *Important factors include:* class rank, standardized test scores, recommendation(s), extracurricular activities, talent/ability, character/personal qualities, first generation, alumni/ae relation. *Other factors include:* geographical residence, state residency, religious affiliation/commitment, work experience, level of applicant's interest. **Freshman Admission Requirements:** High school diploma is required and GED is accepted. *Academic units required:* 4 English, 3 math, 2 science, 2 foreign language, 3 social studies. *Academic units recommended:* 4 English, 4 math, 3 science, 3 foreign language, 3 social studies, 1 visual/performing arts. **Freshman Admission Statistics:** 16,300 applied, 49% admitted, 17% enrolled. **Transfer Admission Requirements:** College transcript(s), essay or personal statement. Lowest grade transferable C. **General Admission Information:** Application fee $60. Regular application deadline 1/7. Admission may be deferred for a maximum of One year, unless serving required military service or mission work.

COSTS AND FINANCIAL AID

Required Forms and Deadlines: CSS/Financial Aid PROFILE; FAFSA. **Notification of Awards:** Applicants will be notified of awards on or about 4/1.

Types of Aid: *Need-based scholarships/grants:* College/university scholarship or grant aid from institutional funds; Federal Pell; Private scholarships; SEOG; State scholarships/grants. *Loans:* Direct PLUS loans; Direct Subsidized Stafford Loans; Direct Unsubsidized Stafford Loans. **Student Employment:** Federal Work-Study Program available. Institutional employment available. **Financial Aid Statistics:** 83% needy freshmen, 71% needy undergrads receive need-based scholarship or grant aid. 41% freshmen, 34% undergrads receive non-need-based scholarship or grant aid. 47% freshmen, 40% undergrads receive need-based self-help aid. 3% freshmen, 4% undergrads receive athletic scholarships. 70% freshmen, 72% undergrads receive any aid. 35% undergrads borrow to pay for school. Average cumulative indebtedness $26,603. **Criteria awarding aid:** *Need-based:* Academics, Alumni affiliation. *Non-need-based:* Academics, Athletics, Music/drama.

SANTA FE UNIVERSITY OF ART AND DESIGN

1600 St. Michaels Drive, Santa Fe, NM 87505-7634
Phone: 505-473-6937 **Financial Aid Phone:** 505-473-6318
E-mail: admissions@santafeuniversity.edu
Fax: 505-473-6127 **Website:** www.santafeuniversity.edu

This proprietary school was founded in 1874. It has a 65 acre campus.

RATINGS

Admissions Selectivity Rating: 64   **Fire Safety Rating:** 98   **Green Rating:** 65

STUDENTS AND FACULTY

Enrollment: 839. **Student Body:** 52% female, 48% male, 78% out-of-state, 5% international (21 countries represented). Asian 2%, African American 7%, Caucasian 45%, Hispanic 28%, Native American 3%, Pacific Islander 2%, Two or more races 8%, Race unknown 1%.
Retention and Graduation: 64% freshmen return for sophomore year.
Faculty: Student/faculty ratio 15:1.

ACADEMICS

Degrees: Bachelor's; Certificate; Master's. **Classes:** Most classes have 10–19 students. Most lab/discussion sessions have fewer than 10 students. **Most popular majors:** Graphic Design; Drama and Dramatics/Theatre Arts, General; Film/Cinema/Media Studies. **Special Study Options:** Distance learning; Double major; Dual enrollment; Exchange student program (domestic); Honors program; Independent study; Internships; Student-designed major; Study abroad. **Disability Services offered:** Note-taking services; Reader services; Tape recorders; Tutors. **Career services:** Alumni services; Career assessment; Internships.

FACILITIES

Housing: Apartments for single students; Coed dorms; Men's dorms; Special housing for disabled students; Women's dorms. **Special Academic Facilities/Equipment:** Thaw Art History Library, Marion Center Photographic Library, Garson Studios, Visual Art Center, Greer Garson Theatre Centre.

CAMPUS LIFE

Environment: Town. **Activities:** Campus Ministries; Choral groups; Dance; Drama/theater; Jazz band; Literary magazine; Music ensembles; Musical theater; Student government; Student newspaper; Student-run film society. 10 registered organizations, 1 honor society on campus. **Athletics (Intercollegiate):** *Men:* tennis. *Women:* tennis. **On-Campus Highlights:** Visual Arts Center.

ADMISSIONS

Basis for Candidate Selection: *Very important factors include:* academic GPA, talent/ability. *Other factors include:* application essay, recommendation(s). **Freshman Admission Requirements:** High school diploma is required and GED is accepted. *Academic units required:* 4 English, 2 math, 2 science, 2 science labs, 2 social studies. *Academic units recommended:* 4 English, 2 math, 2 science, 2 science labs, 2 foreign language, 2 social studies, 4 academic electives. **Freshman Admission Statistics:** 608 applied, 100% admitted, 41% enrolled. **Transfer Admission Requirements:** High school transcript, college transcript(s), essay or personal statement. Lowest grade transferable C-. **General Admission Information:** Application fee $50. Non-fall registration accepted. Admission may be deferred for a maximum of 1 year.

COSTS AND FINANCIAL AID

Annual tuition $28,836. Room and board $8,984. Required fees $1,300. Average book and supplies expense $1,400. **Required Forms and Deadlines:** FAFSA. **Notification of Awards:** Applicants will be notified of awards on

a rolling basis beginning 3/1. **Types of Aid:** *Need-based scholarships/grants:* College/university scholarship or grant aid from institutional funds; Federal Pell; Private scholarships; SEOG. *Loans:* Direct PLUS loans; Direct Subsidized Stafford Loans; Direct Unsubsidized Stafford Loans. **Student Employment:** Federal Work-Study Program available. **Financial Aid Statistics:** 100% needy freshmen, 100% needy undergrads receive need-based scholarship or grant aid. 4% freshmen, 4% undergrads receive non-need-based scholarship or grant aid. 94% freshmen, 91% undergrads receive need-based self-help aid. 0% freshmen, 0% undergrads receive athletic scholarships. 99% freshmen receive any aid. **Criteria awarding aid:** *Non-need-based:* Academics, Art, Music/drama.

SARAH LAWRENCE COLLEGE

1 Mead Way, Bronxville, NY 10708-5999
Phone: 914-395-2510 **Financial Aid Phone:** (914) 395 2570
E-mail: slcadmit@sarahlawrence.edu **CEEB Code:** 2810
Fax: 914-395-2515 **Website:** www.sarahlawrence.edu **ACT Code:** 2904

This private school was founded in 1926. It has a 44 acre campus.

RATINGS

Admissions Selectivity Rating: 89   **Fire Safety Rating:** 96   **Green Rating:** 63

STUDENTS AND FACULTY

Enrollment: 1,364. **Student Body:** 75% female, 25% male, 78% out-of-state, 11% international (38 countries represented). Asian 5%, African American 4%, Caucasian 61%, Hispanic 9%, Native American <1%, Pacific Islander 0%, Two or more races 5%, Race unknown 5%.
Retention and Graduation: 83% freshmen return for sophomore year. 68% freshmen graduate within 4 years. 78% freshmen graduate within 6 years. 21% grads go on to further study within 1 year. **Faculty:** Student/faculty ratio 9:1. 111 full-time faculty, 88% hold PhDs, 19% are members of minority groups, 49% are women. 0% of classes are taught by teaching assistants.

ACADEMICS

Degrees: Bachelor's; Master's. **Classes:** Most classes have 10–19 students. **Most popular majors:** Liberal Arts and Sciences/Liberal Studies. **Special Study Options:** Double major; Exchange student program (domestic); Independent study; Internships; Student-designed major; Study abroad; Teacher certification program. **Combined degree programs:** BA/MA. **Disability Services offered:** Note-taking services; Reader services; Tape recorders; Tutors. **Career services:** Alumni network; Alumni services; Career assessment; Career/job search classes; Internships.

FACILITIES

Housing: Coed dorms; Men's dorms; Special housing for disabled students; Theme housing; Wellness housing; Women's dorms; 60% of campus accessible to physically disabled. **Special Academic Facilities/Equipment:** Performing arts center including a concert hall, dance studios, and theatres; visual arts center including studios, gallery, film theatre, sound stage, visual resources library; music building including music library; science center, early childhood center, open-air Greek amphitheater. The Barbara Walters Campus Center. Center for the Urban River at Beczak.

CAMPUS LIFE

Environment: Metropolis. **Activities:** Campus Ministries; Choral groups; Dance; Drama/theater; International Student Organization; Jazz band; Literary magazine; Model UN; Music ensembles; Musical theater; Radio station; Student government; Student newspaper; Student-run film society; Symphony orchestra; Yearbook. 123 registered organizations, 6 religious organizations on campus. **Athletics (Intercollegiate):** *Men:* basketball, crew/rowing, cross-country, equestrian sports, soccer, tennis. *Women:* crew/rowing, cross-country, equestrian sports, softball, swimming, tennis, volleyball. **On-Campus Highlights:** Barbara Walters Campus Center. **Environmental Initiatives:** A sustainable living residence and a green roof on another dorm.

ADMISSIONS

Freshman Academic Profile: Average high school GPA 3.7. 36% in top 10% of high school class, 67% in top 25% of high school class, 93% in top 50% of high school class. 50% from public high schools. **Test Scores:** SAT Math middle 50% range 600–702. SAT EBRW middle 50% range 640–720. ACT middle 50% range 28–31. **Basis for Candidate Selection:** *Very important factors include:* rigor of secondary school record, application essay, recommendation(s). *Important factors include:* academic GPA, extracurricular activities, talent/ability, character/personal qualities. *Other factors include:* class rank, standardized test scores, interview, first generation, alumni/ae relation, geographical residence, racial/ethnic status, volunteer work, work experience, level of applicant's interest. **Freshman Admission Requirements:** High school diploma is required and GED is accepted. *Academic units required:* 4 English, 2 math, 2 science, 2 foreign language, 2 history. *Academic units recommended:* 4 math, 4 science, 4 foreign language, 4 social studies, 4 history. **Freshman Admission Statistics:** 4,053 applied, 53% admitted, 18% enrolled. **Transfer Admission Requirements:** High school transcript, college transcript(s), essay or personal statement, statement of good standing from prior institution(s). Lowest grade transferable C. **General Admission Information:** Application fee $60. Regular application deadline 1/15. Admission may be deferred for a maximum of 2 years.

COSTS AND FINANCIAL AID

Annual tuition $56,020. Room and board $15,820. Required fees $1,500. Average book and supplies expense $600. **Required Forms and Deadlines:** FAFSA; State aid form. **Notification of Awards:** Applicants will be notified of awards on or about 4/1. *Types of Aid: Need-based scholarships/grants:* College/university scholarship or grant aid from institutional funds; Federal Pell; Private scholarships; SEOG; State scholarships/grants. *Loans:* Direct PLUS loans; Direct Subsidized Stafford Loans; Direct Unsubsidized Stafford Loans. **Student Employment:** Federal Work-Study Program available. Institutional employment available. **Financial Aid Statistics:** 90% needy freshmen, 97% needy undergrads receive need-based scholarship or grant aid. 15% freshmen, 13% undergrads receive non-need-based scholarship or grant aid. 74% freshmen, 81% undergrads receive need-based self-help aid. 0% freshmen, 0% undergrads receive athletic scholarships. 83% freshmen, 78% undergrads receive any aid. 55% undergrads borrow to pay for school. Average cumulative indebtedness $26,808. **Criteria awarding aid:** *Need-based:* Academics, Leadership. *Non-need-based:* Academics, Leadership.

SAVANNAH COLLEGE OF ART AND DESIGN

PO Box 3146, Savannah, GA 31402-3146
Phone: 912-525-5100 **Financial Aid Phone:** 800-869-7223
E-mail: admission@scad.edu **CEEB Code:** 5631
Fax: 912-525-5986 **Website:** www.scad.edu **ACT Code:** 0855

This private school was founded in 1978.

RATINGS

Admissions Selectivity Rating: 80   **Fire Safety Rating:** 85   **Green Rating:** 60*

STUDENTS AND FACULTY

Enrollment: 10,483. **Student Body:** 67% female, 33% male, 79% out-of-state, 21% international (115 countries represented). Asian 5%, African American 10%, Caucasian 52%, Hispanic 8%, Native American 1%, Pacific Islander <1%, Two or more races <1%, Race unknown 3%.
Retention and Graduation: 85% freshmen return for sophomore year.
Faculty: Student/faculty ratio 19:1. 532 full-time faculty, 80% hold PhDs, 18% are members of minority groups, 40% are women. 0% of classes are taught by teaching assistants.

ACADEMICS

Degrees: Bachelor's; Certificate; Master's; Post-master's certificate. **Classes:** Most classes have 10–19 students. **Most popular majors:** Animation, Interactive Technology, Video Graphics and Special Effects; Fashion/Apparel Design; Graphic Design. **Special Study Options:** Accelerated program; Cooperative education program; Cross-registration; Distance learning; Double major; Dual enrollment; English as a Second Language (ESL); Independent study; Internships; Study abroad. **Disability Services offered:** Note-taking services; Tape recorders; Tutors. **Career services:** Alumni network; Alumni services; Career assessment; Career/job search classes; Internships; Regional alumni.

FACILITIES

Housing: Coed dorms; Special housing for disabled students; Women's dorms; 82% of campus accessible to physically disabled. **Special Academic Facilities/Equipment:** Art galleries; computer, video, photography, and design labs; SCAD Museum of Art. **Campus Network:** 100% of classrooms, 0% of dorms, 100% of student union, 100% of libraries, 100% of dining areas, 100% of common outdoor areas have wireless network access.

CAMPUS LIFE

Environment: City. **Activities:** Campus Ministries; Choral groups; Dance; Drama/theater; International Student Organization; Literary magazine; Music ensembles; Musical theater; Radio station; Student newspaper; Television station. 105 registered organizations, 2 honor societies, 5 religious organizations on campus. **Athletics (Intercollegiate):** *Men:* baseball, basketball, cross-country, equestrian sports, golf, lacrosse, soccer, swimming, tennis. *Women:* basketball, cross-country, equestrian sports, golf, lacrosse, soccer, softball, swimming, tennis, volleyball. **On-Campus Highlights:** SCAD Museum of Art.

ADMISSIONS

Freshman Academic Profile: Average high school GPA 3.5. **Test Scores:** SAT Math middle 50% range 460–580. SAT EBRW middle 50% range 490–610. ACT middle 50% range 21–27. **Basis for Candidate Selection:** *Very important factors include:* academic GPA. *Important factors include:* rigor of secondary school record, standardized test scores, level of applicant's interest. *Other factors include:* class rank, application essay, recommendation(s), interview, extracurricular activities, talent/ability, character/personal qualities. **Freshman Admission Requirements:** High school diploma is required and GED is accepted. **Freshman Admission Statistics:** 11,723 applied, 71% admitted, 28% enrolled. **Transfer Admission Requirements:** College transcript(s). Minimum college GPA of 2.0 required. Lowest grade transferable C. **General Admission Information:** Application fee $40. Non-fall registration accepted. Admission may be deferred for a maximum of 2 quarters.

COSTS AND FINANCIAL AID

Annual tuition $35,190. Room and board $13,905. Required fees $500. Average book and supplies expense $2,025. **Required Forms and Deadlines:** FAFSA; State aid form. **Notification of Awards:** Applicants will be notified of awards on a rolling basis beginning 3/1. *Types of Aid: Need-based scholarships/grants:* College/university scholarship or grant aid from institutional funds; Federal Pell; Private scholarships; SEOG; State scholarships/grants; United Negro College Fund. *Loans:* Direct PLUS loans; Direct Subsidized Stafford Loans; Direct Unsubsidized Stafford Loans. **Student Employment:** Federal Work-Study Program available. Institutional employment available. **Financial Aid Statistics:** 61% needy freshmen, 63% needy undergrads receive need-based scholarship or grant aid. 98% freshmen, 91% undergrads receive non-need-based scholarship or grant aid. 88% freshmen, 92% undergrads receive need-based self-help aid. 1% freshmen, 1% undergrads receive athletic scholarships. 58% undergrads borrow to pay for school. Average cumulative indebtedness $40,718. **Criteria awarding aid:** *Need-based:* Academics, Art, Music/drama. *Non-need-based:* Academics, Alumni affiliation, Art, Athletics, Job skills, Leadership, Minority status, Music/drama.

SCHOOL OF THE ART INSTITUTE OF CHICAGO

36 South Wabash Avenue, Chicago, IL 60603
Phone: 312-629-6100 **Financial Aid Phone:** 312-629-6600
E-mail: admiss@saic.edu **CEEB Code:** 1713
Fax: 312-629-6101 **Website:** www.saic.edu **ACT Code:** 1136

This private school was founded in 1866.

RATINGS

Admissions Selectivity Rating: 87   **Fire Safety Rating:** 83   **Green Rating:** 60*

STUDENTS AND FACULTY

Enrollment: 2,893. **Student Body:** 75% female, 25% male, 70% out-of-state, 33% international (68 countries represented). Asian 10%, African American 4%, Caucasian 34%, Hispanic 11%, Native American <1%, Pacific Islander <1%, Two or more races 3%, Race unknown 5%.
Retention and Graduation: 81% freshmen return for sophomore year.
Faculty: Student/faculty ratio 11:1. 172 full-time faculty, 63% hold PhDs, 22% are members of minority groups, 46% are women.

ACADEMICS

Degrees: Bachelor's; Master's; Post-bachelor's certificate. **Special Study Options:** Cooperative education program; Cross-registration; Double major; English as a Second Language (ESL); Exchange student program (domestic); Independent study; Internships; Student-designed major; Study abroad; Teacher certification program. **Disability Services offered:** Note-taking services; Reader services; Tape recorders; Tutors. **Career services:** Alumni network; Alumni services; Career assessment; Career/job search classes; Internships.

FACILITIES

Housing: Coed dorms; Special housing for disabled students; 99% of campus accessible to physically disabled. **Special Academic Facilities/Equipment:** SAIC is directly affiliated with the Art Institute of Chicago. Other resources include: The Gene Siskel Film Center; Fashion Resource Center, John M. Flaxman Library and Screening Room Galleries (Betty Rymer, Sullivan Galleries, Student Union Galleries, project space and Gallery X), Joan Flasch Artists' Book Collection, Poetry Center, Roger Brown Resources, Video Data Bank, The Poetry Center, Visiting Artists' Program, Media Center. **Campus Network:** 100% of classrooms, 100% of dorms, 100% of student union, 100% of libraries, 100% of dining areas, 100% of common outdoor areas have wireless network access.

CAMPUS LIFE

Environment: Metropolis. **Activities:** Campus Ministries; Dance; Drama/theater; International Student Organization; Literary magazine; Radio station; Student government; Student newspaper; Student-run film society; Television station. 49 registered organizations, 4 religious organizations on campus. **On-Campus Highlights:** Leroy Neiman Student Center. **Environmental Initiatives:** Incandescent light bulbs in dorm rooms have been replaced with CFLs and new low-flow restrictions have been installed in all dorm room showers and sinks. Expected results are 206 metric tons of CO_2 not being release into the atmosphere and 1.7 million gallons of water saved annually.

ADMISSIONS

Freshman Academic Profile: Average high school GPA 3.5. **Test Scores:** SAT Math middle 50% range 540–680. SAT EBRW middle 50% range 580–660. ACT middle 50% range 22–28. **Basis for Candidate Selection:** *Very important factors include:* rigor of secondary school record, application essay, standardized test scores, recommendation(s), talent/ability, character/personal qualities, level of applicant's interest. *Important factors include:* class rank, academic GPA, extracurricular activities, first generation. *Other factors include:* interview, alumni/ae relation, geographical residence, state residency, work experience. **Freshman Admission Requirements:** High school diploma is required and GED is accepted. **Freshman Admission Statistics:** 5,993 applied, 59% admitted, 18% enrolled. **Transfer Admission Requirements:** High school transcript, college transcript(s), essay or personal statement. Lowest grade transferable C. **General Admission Information:** Application fee $65. Priority deadline 11/15. Regular application deadline 4/15. Non-fall registration accepted. Admission may be deferred for a maximum of 1 year.

COSTS AND FINANCIAL AID

Annual tuition $48,390. Room and board $15,890. Required fees $880. Average book and supplies expense $1,770. **Required Forms and Deadlines:** FAFSA. **Notification of Awards:** Applicants will be notified of awards on a rolling basis beginning 3/1. **Types of Aid:** *Need-based scholarships/grants:* College/university scholarship or grant aid from institutional funds; Federal Pell; Private scholarships; SEOG; State scholarships/grants. **Student Employment:** Federal Work-Study Program available. Institutional employment available. **Financial Aid Statistics:** 98% freshmen, 99% undergrads receive any aid. **Criteria awarding aid:** *Need-based:* Academics, Art. *Non-need-based:* Academics, Art.

SCHOOL OF THE MUSEUM OF FINE ARTS

230 The Fenway, Boston, MA 02115
Phone: 617-369-3626 **Financial Aid Phone:** 617-369-3684
E-mail: admissions@smfa.edu **CEEB Code:** 3794
Fax: 617-369-4264 **ACT Code:** 1895

This private school was founded in 1876. It has a 14 acre campus.

RATINGS
Admissions Selectivity Rating: 65   **Fire Safety Rating:** 90   **Green Rating:** 61

STUDENTS AND FACULTY
Enrollment: 278. **Student Body:** 73% female, 27% male, 53% out-of-state, 12% international (19 countries represented). Asian 3%, African American 2%, Caucasian 48%, Hispanic 12%, Native American 0%, Pacific Islander 0%, Two or more races 4%, Race unknown 18%.
Retention and Graduation: 78% freshmen return for sophomore year.
Faculty: Student/faculty ratio 8:1. 40 full-time faculty, 85% hold PhDs, 13% are members of minority groups, 68% are women. 5% of classes are taught by teaching assistants.

ACADEMICS

Degrees: Bachelor's; Certificate; Diploma; Master's; Post-bachelor's certificate. **Classes:** Most classes have 10–19 students. Most lab/discussion sessions have 10–19 students. **Most popular majors:** Fine/Studio Arts, General; Fine Arts and Art Studies, Other. **Special Study Options:** Cross-registration; Double major; Dual enrollment; Exchange student program (domestic); Independent study; Internships; Liberal arts/career combination; Student-designed major; Study abroad; Teacher certification program. **Honors programs:** We have some additional awards for first year students based on the strength of their application. http://www.smfa.edu/awards-grants-fellowships. **Career services:** Alumni network; Alumni services; Career/job search classes; Internships.

FACILITIES

Housing: Coed dorms; 100% of campus accessible to physically disabled. **Special Academic Facilities/Equipment:** Museum of Fine Arts, Boston; Art galleries; welding equipment; darkrooms; digital equipment; kilns; and more.

CAMPUS LIFE

Environment: Metropolis. **Activities:** International Student Organization; Student government; Student-run film society. 12 registered organizations on campus. **On-Campus Highlights:** Classrooms and Studios. **Environmental Initiatives:** Installed a new state of the art HVAC ventilation system, which includes interior vents and hoods customized for specific art making practices.

ADMISSIONS

Freshman Academic Profile: Average high school GPA 3.5. **Basis for Candidate Selection:** *Important factors include:* academic GPA, application essay, talent/ability, level of applicant's interest. *Other factors include:* rigor of secondary school record, class rank, recommendation(s), interview, extracurricular activities, character/personal qualities, volunteer work, work experience. **Freshman Admission Requirements:** High school diploma is required and GED is accepted. *Academic units recommended:* 4 English, 3 math, 3 science, 2 science labs, 2 foreign language, 2 social studies, 2 history, 2 academic electives, 1 computer science, 2 visual/performing arts. **Freshman Admission Statistics:** 371 applied, 83% admitted, 12% enrolled. **Transfer Admission Requirements:** College transcript(s), essay or personal statement. Minimum college GPA of 1.75 required. Lowest grade transferable C-. **General Admission Information:** Application fee $65. Priority deadline 2/17. Non-fall registration accepted. Admission may be deferred for a maximum of 1 year.

COSTS AND FINANCIAL AID

Annual tuition $39,928. Room and board $14,850. Required fees $1,425. Average book and supplies expense $1,600. **Required Forms and Deadlines:** FAFSA. **Notification of Awards:** Applicants will be notified of awards on a rolling basis beginning 4/1. **Types of Aid:** *Need-based scholarships/grants:* College/university scholarship or grant aid from institutional funds; Federal Pell; Private scholarships; SEOG; State scholarships/grants. *Loans:* Direct PLUS loans; Direct Subsidized Stafford Loans; Direct Unsubsidized Stafford Loans. **Student Employment:** Federal Work-Study Program available. Institutional employment available. **Financial Aid Statistics:** 95% needy freshmen, 94% needy undergrads receive need-based scholarship or grant aid. 100% freshmen, 99% undergrads receive non-need-based scholarship or grant aid. 95% freshmen, 89% undergrads receive need-based self-help aid. 0% freshmen, 0% undergrads receive athletic scholarships. 99% freshmen, 99% undergrads receive any aid. 69% undergrads borrow to pay for school. Average cumulative indebtedness $33,176. **Criteria awarding aid:** *Non-need-based:* Art.

SCHOOL OF VISUAL ARTS

209 East 23rd Street, New York, NY 10010
Phone: 212-592-2100 **Financial Aid Phone:** 212-592-2030
E-mail: admissions@sva.edu **CEEB Code:** 2835
Fax: 212-592-2116 **Website:** www.sva.edu **ACT Code:** 2895

This proprietary school was founded in 1947.

RATINGS
Admissions Selectivity Rating: 82   **Fire Safety Rating:** 99   **Green Rating:** 60*

STUDENTS AND FACULTY
Enrollment: 3,332. **Student Body:** 55% female, 45% male, 57% out-of-state, 15% international (55 countries represented). Asian 13%, African American 3%, Caucasian 49%, Hispanic 10%, Native American 1%, Race unknown 9%.

Retention and Graduation: 86% freshmen return for sophomore year. **Faculty:** Student/faculty ratio 9:1. 163 full-time faculty, 24% hold PhDs, 4% are members of minority groups, 31% are women.

ACADEMICS

Degrees: Bachelor's; Master's. **Classes:** Most classes have 10–19 students. **Most popular majors:** Photography; Film/Video and Photographic Arts, Other; Graphic Design. **Special Study Options:** English as a Second Language (ESL); Exchange student program (domestic); Honors program; Internships; Liberal arts/career combination; Study abroad; Teacher certification program. **Honors programs:** SVA offers an honors program for incoming freshmen; program involves a two year commitment, with an optional third year. **Disability Services offered:** Note-taking services; Reader services; Tape recorders; Tutors. **Career services:** Alumni network; Alumni services; Internships.

FACILITIES

Housing: Coed dorms; Women's dorms; 100% of campus accessible to physically disabled. **Special Academic Facilities/Equipment:** Visual Art Museum, Milton Glaser Design Study Center and Archives, 8 student galleries.

CAMPUS LIFE

Environment: Metropolis. **Activities:** Literary magazine; Radio station; Student government; Student-run film society; Yearbook. 23 registered organizations, 3 religious organizations on campus. **On-Campus Highlights:** Visual Arts Gallery. **Environmental Initiatives:** We recycle our trash off site. Due to space limitations we don't have an area to collect and sort out recyclables from our trash, nor do we have the space to store the recyclables prior to shipment to an appropriate recycler. To accomplish this we rely on an outside contractor to collect our trash and sort it at their facilities. They ensure that anything that can be recycled from our trash finds its way to the recyclers.

ADMISSIONS

Freshman Academic Profile: Average high school GPA 3.1. 60% from public high schools. **Test Scores:** SAT Math middle 50% range 460–590. SAT EBRW middle 50% range 450–580. ACT middle 50% range 20–25. **Basis for Candidate Selection:** *Very important factors include:* rigor of secondary school record, academic GPA, application essay, interview, talent/ability, level of applicant's interest. *Other factors include:* standardized test scores, recommendation(s), extracurricular activities, alumni/ae relation, volunteer work, work experience. **Freshman Admission Requirements:** High school diploma is required and GED is accepted. *Academic units recommended:* 4 English, 4 social studies, 4 history, 2 visual/performing arts. **Freshman Admission Statistics:** 2,530 applied, 69% admitted, 38% enrolled. **Transfer Admission Requirements:** College transcript(s), essay or personal statement, statement of good standing from prior institution(s). Minimum college GPA of 2.0 required. Lowest grade transferable C. **General Admission Information:** Application fee $50. Priority deadline 2/1. Admission may be deferred for a maximum of 1 year.

COSTS AND FINANCIAL AID

Annual tuition $26,800. Room and board $12,700. Average book and supplies expense $3,150. **Required Forms and Deadlines:** FAFSA; State aid form. **Notification of Awards:** Applicants will be notified of awards on a rolling basis beginning 2/15. **Types of Aid:** *Need-based scholarships/grants:* College/university scholarship or grant aid from institutional funds; Federal Pell; Private scholarships; SEOG; State scholarships/grants. **Student Employment:** Federal Work-Study Program available. **Financial Aid Statistics:** 68% needy freshmen, 68% needy undergrads receive need-based scholarship or grant aid. 19% freshmen, 19% undergrads receive non-need-based scholarship or grant aid. 95% freshmen, 95% undergrads receive need-based self-help aid. 0% freshmen, 0% undergrads receive athletic scholarships. 60% freshmen, 55% undergrads receive any aid. **Criteria awarding aid:** *Non-need-based:* Art.

SCHREINER UNIVERSITY

2100 Memorial Boulevard, Kerrville, TX 78028-5697
Phone: 830-792-7217 **Financial Aid Phone:** 830-792-7217
E-mail: admissions@schreiner.edu **CEEB Code:** 6647
Fax: (830) 792-7226 **Website:** www.schreiner.edu **ACT Code:** 4168

This private school, affiliated with the Presbyterian Church, was founded in 1923. It has a 205 acre campus.

RATINGS

Admissions Selectivity Rating: 75 **Fire Safety Rating:** 62 **Green Rating:** 60*

STUDENTS AND FACULTY

Enrollment: 1,207. **Student Body:** 57% female, 43% male, 2% out-of-state, 1% international. Asian 1%, African American 5%, Caucasian 49%, Hispanic 42%, Native American <1%, Pacific Islander <1%, Two or more races 2%, Race unknown 0%.

Retention and Graduation: 61% freshmen return for sophomore year. 41% freshmen graduate within 4 years. 48% freshmen graduate within 6 years. 21% grads go on to further study within 1 year. **Faculty:** Student/faculty ratio 13:1. 73 full-time faculty, 62% hold PhDs, 18% are members of minority groups, 51% are women. 0% of classes are taught by teaching assistants.

ACADEMICS

Degrees: Associate; Bachelor's; Certificate; Master's. **Classes:** Most classes have 10–19 students. Most lab/discussion sessions have 10–19 students. **Most popular majors:** Registered Nursing/Registered Nurse; Exercise Science and Kinesiology; Psychology, General. **Special Study Options:** Accelerated program; Cooperative education program; Distance learning; Double major; Dual enrollment; Exchange student program (domestic); Honors program; Independent study; Internships; Liberal arts/career combination; Student-designed major; Study abroad; Teacher certification program. **Disability Services offered:** Note-taking services; Reader services; Tape recorders; Tutors. **Career services:** Alumni network; Alumni services; Career assessment; Career/job search classes; Internships; Regional alumni.

FACILITIES

Housing: Apartments for married students; Apartments for single students; Coed dorms; Special housing for disabled students; Theme housing; Wellness housing; 97% of campus accessible to physically disabled. **Campus Network:** 100% of classrooms, 100% of dorms, 100% of student union, 100% of libraries, 100% of dining areas, 90% of common outdoor areas have wireless network access.

CAMPUS LIFE

Environment: Town. **Activities:** Campus Ministries; Choral groups; Dance; Drama/theater; Literary magazine; Music ensembles; Musical theater; Pep band; Student government; Student newspaper; Symphony orchestra. 38 registered organizations, 3 honor societies, 7 religious organizations, 2 fraternities, 2 sororities on campus. **Athletics (Intercollegiate):** *Men:* baseball, basketball, golf, soccer, tennis. *Women:* basketball, cheerleading, golf, soccer, softball, tennis, volleyball. **On-Campus Highlights:** Caillioux Campus Activity Center.

ADMISSIONS

Freshman Academic Profile: Average high school GPA 3.5. 12% in top 10% of high school class, 33% in top 25% of high school class, 67% in top 50% of high school class. 98% from public high schools. **Test Scores:** SAT Math middle 50% range 480–560. SAT EBRW middle 50% range 480–570. ACT middle 50% range 18–23. **Basis for Candidate Selection:** *Very important factors include:* class rank, academic GPA, standardized test scores. *Important factors include:* rigor of secondary school record, application essay, character/personal qualities, volunteer work, work experience, level of applicant's interest. *Other factors include:* recommendation(s), interview, extracurricular activities, talent/ability. **Freshman Admission Requirements:** High school diploma is required and GED is accepted. *Academic units recommended:* 4 English, 3 math, 3 science, 2 science labs, 2 foreign language, 2 social studies, 2 history, 3.5 academic electives, 1 computer science, 1 visual/performing arts. **Freshman Admission Statistics:** 1,184 applied, 91% admitted, 33% enrolled. **Transfer Admission Requirements:** College transcript(s). Minimum college GPA of 2.0 required. Lowest grade transferable D. **General Admission Information:** Application fee $25. Priority deadline 5/1. Regular application deadline 8/1. Non-fall registration accepted. Admission may be deferred for a maximum of 1 semester.

COSTS AND FINANCIAL AID

Annual tuition $29,500. Room and board $10,442. Required fees $970. Average book and supplies expense $100. **Required Forms and Deadlines:** FAFSA. **Notification of Awards:** Applicants will be notified of awards on a rolling basis beginning 2/15. **Types of Aid:** *Need-based scholarships/grants:* College/university scholarship or grant aid from institutional funds; Federal Pell; Private scholarships; SEOG; State scholarships/grants. *Loans:* Direct PLUS loans; Direct Subsidized Stafford Loans; Direct Unsubsidized Stafford Loans. **Student Employment:** Federal Work-Study Program available. Institutional employment available. **Financial Aid Statistics:** 80% needy freshmen, 81% needy undergrads receive need-based scholarship or grant aid. 91% freshmen, 96% undergrads receive non-need-based scholarship or grant aid. 74% freshmen, 73% undergrads receive need-based self-help aid. 0% freshmen, 0% undergrads receive athletic scholarships. 99% freshmen, 97% undergrads receive any aid. 74% undergrads borrow to pay for school. Average cumulative indebtedness $37,071. **Criteria awarding aid:** *Non-need-based:* Academics, Art, Leadership, Music/drama, Religious affiliation.

SCRIPPS COLLEGE

1030 Columbia Avenue, Claremont, CA 91711
Phone: 909-621-8149 **Financial Aid Phone:** 909-621-8275
E-mail: admission@scrippscollege.edu **CEEB Code:** 4693
Website: www.scrippscollege.edu **ACT Code:** 426

This private school was founded in 1926. It has a 37 acre campus.

RATINGS

Admissions Selectivity Rating: 97   **Fire Safety Rating:** 79   **Green Rating:** 72

STUDENTS AND FACULTY

Enrollment: 1,083. **Student Body:** 100% female, 0% male, 56% out-of-state, 5% international (24 countries represented). Asian 16%, African American 4%, Caucasian 53%, Hispanic 14%, Native American 0%, Pacific Islander <1%, Two or more races 7%, Race unknown 2%.
Retention and Graduation: 93% freshmen return for sophomore year. 86% freshmen graduate within 4 years. 90% freshmen graduate within 6 years.
Faculty: Student/faculty ratio 10:1. 102 full-time faculty, 98% hold PhDs, 34% are members of minority groups, 57% are women. 0% of classes are taught by teaching assistants.

ACADEMICS

Degrees: Bachelor's; Post-bachelor's certificate. **Classes:** Most classes have 10–19 students. **Most popular majors:** Biology/Biological Sciences, General; Psychology, General. **Special Study Options:** Accelerated program; Cross-registration; Double major; Independent study; Internships; Student-designed major; Study abroad. **Combined degree programs:** BA/MA. **Disability Services offered:** Note-taking services; Reader services; Tape recorders; Tutors. **Career services:** Alumni network; Alumni services; Career assessment; Career/job search classes; Internships; Regional alumni.

FACILITIES

Housing: Apartments for single students; Special housing for disabled students; Women's dorms. **Special Academic Facilities/Equipment:** Art center, music complex, dance studio, humanities museum and institute, science center, biological field station, and Tiernan Field House. The Tiernan Field House is a state-of-the art 24,000-square foot facility with an aerobics studio, cardio machine room, weight room, and other spaces for fitness and health education.

CAMPUS LIFE

Environment: Town. **Activities:** Campus Ministries; Choral groups; Dance; Drama/theater; International Student Organization; Literary magazine; Model UN; Music ensembles; Radio station; Student government; Student newspaper; Symphony orchestra; Yearbook. 7 honor societies, 12 religious organizations on campus. **Athletics (Intercollegiate):** *Women:* basketball, cross-country, diving, golf, lacrosse, soccer, softball, swimming, tennis, track/field (outdoor), volleyball, water polo. **On-Campus Highlights:** Ruth Chandler Williamson Gallery. **Environmental Initiatives:** Establishment of a sustainability committee to serve as an advisory counsel to president regarding campus

operations. Provided guidance and roadmap to signing the Second Nature Carbon Commitment.

ADMISSIONS

Freshman Academic Profile: Average high school GPA 4.2. 78% in top 10% of high school class, 98% in top 25% of high school class, 100% in top 50% of high school class. **Test Scores:** SAT Math middle 50% range 660–750. SAT EBRW middle 50% range 673–740. ACT middle 50% range 30–33. **Basis for Candidate Selection:** *Very important factors include:* rigor of secondary school record, class rank, academic GPA, application essay, standardized test scores, recommendation(s), extracurricular activities, talent/ability, character/personal qualities. *Other factors include:* interview, first generation, alumni/ae relation, geographical residence, racial/ethnic status, volunteer work, work experience. **Freshman Admission Requirements:** High school diploma is required and GED is accepted. *Academic units required:* 4 English, 3 math, 3 science, 3 foreign language, 3 social studies. **Freshman Admission Statistics:** 3,022 applied, 32% admitted, 29% enrolled. **Transfer Admission Requirements:** High school transcript, college transcript(s), essay or personal statement, standardized test scores, statement of good standing from prior institution(s). Minimum college GPA of 3.0 required. Lowest grade transferable C. **General Admission Information:** Application fee $60. Regular application deadline 1/3. Admission may be deferred for a maximum of 1 year.

COSTS AND FINANCIAL AID

Annual tuition $56,970. Room and board $17,600. Required fees $218. Average book and supplies expense $800. **Required Forms and Deadlines:** Business/Farm Supplement; CSS/Financial Aid PROFILE; FAFSA; Noncustodial PROFILE; State aid form. **Notification of Awards:** Applicants will be notified of awards on or about 5/1. **Types of Aid:** *Need-based scholarships/grants:* College/university scholarship or grant aid from institutional funds; Federal Pell; Private scholarships; SEOG; State scholarships/grants. *Loans:* Direct PLUS loans; Direct Subsidized Stafford Loans; Direct Unsubsidized Stafford Loans. **Student Employment:** Federal Work-Study Program available. Institutional employment available. **Financial Aid Statistics:** 98% needy freshmen, 99% needy undergrads receive need-based scholarship or grant aid. 0% freshmen, 0% undergrads receive non-need-based scholarship or grant aid. 69% freshmen, 80% undergrads receive need-based self-help aid. 0% freshmen, 0% undergrads receive athletic scholarships. 32% undergrads borrow to pay for school. Average cumulative indebtedness $30,150. **Criteria awarding aid:** *Non-need-based:* Academics, Leadership.

SEATTLE PACIFIC UNIVERSITY

3307 3rd Avenue West, Seattle, WA 98119-1997
Phone: 206-281-2021 **Financial Aid Phone:** 206-281-2061
E-mail: admissions@spu.edu **CEEB Code:** 4694
Fax: 206-281-2669 **Website:** www.spu.edu **ACT Code:** 4476

This private school, affiliated with the Free Methodist Church, was founded in 1891. It has a 40.77 acre campus.

RATINGS

Admissions Selectivity Rating: 74   **Fire Safety Rating:** 60*   **Green Rating:** 60*

STUDENTS AND FACULTY

Enrollment: 2,709. **Student Body:** 66% female, 34% male, 40% out-of-state, 6% international. Asian 13%, African American 5%, Caucasian 48%, Hispanic 14%, Native American <1%, Pacific Islander 1%, Two or more races 9%, Race unknown 3%.
Retention and Graduation: 80% freshmen return for sophomore year. 53% freshmen graduate within 4 years. 68% freshmen graduate within 6 years.
Faculty: Student/faculty ratio 13:1. 199 full-time faculty, 82% hold PhDs, 21% are members of minority groups, 49% are women. 0% of classes are taught by teaching assistants.

ACADEMICS

Degrees: Bachelor's; Master's; Post-master's certificate. **Classes:** Most classes have 10–19 students. Most lab/discussion sessions have 10–19 students. **Most popular majors:** Registered Nursing/Registered Nurse; Business/Commerce, General; Psychology, General. **Special Study Options:** Distance learning; Double major; Exchange student program (domestic); Honors program; Independent study; Internships; Liberal arts/career combination; Student-designed major; Study abroad; Teacher certification program. **Honors programs:** University Scholars. **Disability Services offered:** Note-taking services; Reader services; Tape recorders. **Career services:** Alumni network; Alumni services; Career assessment; Career/job search classes; Internships.

FACILITIES
Housing: Apartments for married students; Apartments for single students; Coed dorms; Special housing for disabled students. **Special Academic Facilities/Equipment:** Art gallery, theatre facilities. **Campus Network:** 100% of classrooms, 100% of dorms, 100% of student union, 100% of libraries, 100% of dining areas, 30% of common outdoor areas have wireless network access.

CAMPUS LIFE
Environment: Metropolis. **Activities:** Campus Ministries; Choral groups; Concert band; Dance; Drama/theater; International Student Organization; Jazz band; Literary magazine; Music ensembles; Musical theater; Radio station; Student government; Student newspaper; Student-run film society; Symphony orchestra; Yearbook. **Athletics (Intercollegiate):** *Men:* badminton, basketball, bowling, crew/rowing, cross-country, football, soccer, softball, table tennis, tennis, track/field (outdoor), track/field (indoor), volleyball, weight lifting. *Women:* badminton, basketball, bowling, crew/rowing, cross-country, football, gymnastics, soccer, softball, table tennis, tennis, track/field (outdoor), track/field (indoor), volleyball, weight lifting. **On-Campus Highlights:** Common Grounds. **Environmental Initiatives:** June 2010 completion of a solar photovoltaic installation atop our physics and engineering building. The installation was conceived as part of a senior honors project and returns to the grid the approximate amount of electricity consumed by our electric maintenance vehicles. A visible production meter in the second floor hallway allows students in the recently created Appropriate and Sustainable Engineering major to monitor its production.

ADMISSIONS
Freshman Academic Profile: Average high school GPA 3.5. **Test Scores:** SAT Math middle 50% range 510–620. SAT EBRW middle 50% range 510–630. ACT middle 50% range 19–26. **Basis for Candidate Selection:** *Very important factors include:* rigor of secondary school record, academic GPA, application essay, standardized test scores, recommendation(s). *Important factors include:* interview, extracurricular activities, talent/ability, character/ personal qualities, first generation, state residency. *Other factors include:* class rank, alumni/ae relation, geographical residence, level of applicant's interest. **Freshman Admission Requirements:** High school diploma is required and GED is accepted. *Academic units recommended:* 4 English, 3 math, 3 science, 3 foreign language, 2 history. **Freshman Admission Statistics:** 4,387 applied, 91% admitted, 16% enrolled. **Transfer Admission Requirements:** College transcript(s), essay or personal statement. Minimum college GPA of 2.5 required. Lowest grade transferable C. **General Admission Information:** Application fee $50. Regular application deadline 2/1. Non-fall registration accepted.

COSTS AND FINANCIAL AID
Annual tuition $44,604. Room and board $12,285. Required fees $474. Average book and supplies expense $900. **Required Forms and Deadlines:** FAFSA. **Notification of Awards:** Applicants will be notified of awards on a rolling basis beginning 3/15. **Types of Aid:** *Need-based scholarships/grants:* College/university scholarship or grant aid from institutional funds; Federal Pell; Private scholarships; SEOG; State scholarships/grants. *Loans:* Direct PLUS loans; Direct Subsidized Stafford Loans; Direct Unsubsidized Stafford Loans. **Student Employment:** Federal Work-Study Program available. Institutional employment available. **Financial Aid Statistics:** 100% needy freshmen, 99% needy undergrads receive need-based scholarship or grant aid. 0% freshmen, 0% undergrads receive non-need-based scholarship or grant aid. 92% freshmen, 92% undergrads receive need-based self-help aid. 1% freshmen, 2% undergrads receive athletic scholarships. 65% undergrads borrow to pay for school. Average cumulative indebtedness $29,782. **Criteria awarding aid:** *Non-need-based:* Academics, Alumni affiliation, Art, Athletics, Leadership, Minority status, Music/drama, Religious affiliation.

SEATTLE UNIVERSITY

Admissions Office, Seattle, WA 98122-1090
Phone: 206-296-2000 **Financial Aid Phone:** 206-296-8020
E-mail: admissions@seattleu.edu **CEEB Code:** 4695
Fax: 206-296-5656 **Website:** www.seattleu.edu **ACT Code:** 4478

This private school, affiliated with the Roman Catholic-Jesuit Church, was founded in 1891. It has a 50 acre campus.

RATINGS
Admissions Selectivity Rating: 82   **Fire Safety Rating:** 97   **Green Rating:** 99

STUDENTS AND FACULTY
Enrollment: 4,751. **Student Body:** 61% female, 39% male, 59% out-of-state, 11% international (80 countries represented). Asian 16%, African American 3%, Caucasian 42%, Hispanic 12%, Native American <1%, Pacific Islander 1%, Two or more races 8%, Race unknown 6%.
Retention and Graduation: 85% freshmen return for sophomore year. 61% freshmen graduate within 4 years. 73% freshmen graduate within 6 years. 14% grads go on to further study within 1 year. **Faculty:** Student/faculty ratio 11:1. 510 full-time faculty, 88% hold PhDs, 23% are members of minority groups, 52% are women. 0% of classes are taught by teaching assistants.

ACADEMICS
Degrees: Bachelor's; Doctoral degree—professional practice; Master's; Post-bachelor's certificate; Post-master's certificate. **Classes:** Most classes have 10–19 students. Most lab/discussion sessions have 10–19 students. **Most popular majors:** Liberal Arts and Sciences, General Studies and Humanities, Other; Business/Commerce, General; Registered Nursing/Registered Nurse. **Special Study Options:** Cross-registration; Distance learning; Double major; Honors program; Independent study; Internships; Liberal arts/career combination; Student-designed major; Study abroad; Teacher certification program. **Honors programs:** The university Honors program provides students of high ability and motivation the opportunity to join a small, select, two-year-long learning community. The program is taken in the freshman and sophomore years and fulfills most of the university's Core curriculum requirements. Students admitted to the program also receive a four-year Honors scholarship. Honors programs are also offered within majors such as History and English. The History Department offers a year-long, cohort model Honors program for qualified majors. It has the following distinctive features: • Highly selective • Students and faculty work together for full year • Thematic focus based on faculty expertise that changes annually • Students expected to present work at National History Honor Society's regional conference • Students required to present work to university community • At least three faculty review and approve final theses • Students in the History Honors track complete an original research project that often, according to faculty reviews at the regional conference, "represents master's level work." • Students' theses have won regional and national undergraduate History awards and several students have gone on to graduate work at well-known research institutions. The English Department's Honors program is a two-quarter opportunity for top seniors in literary studies and creative writing. As they pursue their original research and advanced creative work, qualified students receive one-on-one attention from faculty mentors who guide projects through all stages of development, including their presentation at Seattle University's Undergraduate Research Conference and other regional and national conferences. The curriculum of this program aims to deepen students' understanding of a topic of their choice, either for its own sake or in preparation for graduate school, to help them learn advanced research and composition methods. **Disability Services offered:** Note-taking services; Reader services; Tape recorders; Tutors. **Career services:** Alumni network; Alumni services; Career assessment; Career/job search classes; Internships; Regional alumni.

FACILITIES
Housing: Apartments for single students; Coed dorms; Special housing for disabled students; Theme housing; Wellness housing; 95% of campus accessible to physically disabled. **Special Academic Facilities/Equipment:** Laser spectroscopy user facility in chemistry and mechanical engineering; Award-winning Chapel of St. Ignatius, designed by architect Steven Holl—the spiritual center of campus;

SU is a pesticide-free campus, officially a Backyard Wildlife Sanctuary and features a Healing Garden, where plants have current or historical medicinal value, in front of the College of Nursing.

CAMPUS LIFE

Environment: Metropolis. **Activities:** Campus Ministries; Choral groups; Dance; Drama/theater; International Student Organization; Jazz band; Literary magazine; Model UN; Music ensembles; Pep band; Radio station; Student government; Student newspaper. 119 registered organizations, 10 honor societies, 1 religious organization on campus. **Athletics (Intercollegiate):** *Men:* baseball, basketball, cross-country, golf, soccer, swimming, tennis, track/field (outdoor), track/field (indoor). *Women:* basketball, cross-country, golf, soccer, softball, swimming, tennis, track/field (outdoor), track/field (indoor), volleyball. **On-Campus Highlights:** William F. Eisiminger Fitness Center, a modern fitness/wellness facility. **Environmental Initiatives:** Plastic bottled water is not sold anywhere on campus including: the bookstore, vending machines, athletics concession stands, restaurants, and catered events. Free, filtered water and bottle fillers are available at over 30 water fountains throughout campus. The Bookstore is selling a 27 ounce, steel water bottle at a discounted price to make owning a bottle affordable.

ADMISSIONS

Freshman Academic Profile: Average high school GPA 3.6. 27% in top 10% of high school class, 64% in top 25% of high school class, 94% in top 50% of high school class. 62% from public high schools. **Test Scores:** SAT Math middle 50% range 560–660. SAT EBRW middle 50% range 570–660. ACT middle 50% range 24–30. **Basis for Candidate Selection:** *Very important factors include:* rigor of secondary school record, academic GPA, standardized test scores, character/personal qualities. *Important factors include:* application essay, recommendation(s), extracurricular activities. *Other factors include:* class rank, interview, talent/ability, first generation, alumni/ae relation, geographical residence, state residency, religious affiliation/commitment, racial/ethnic status, volunteer work, work experience. **Freshman Admission Requirements:** High school diploma is required and GED is accepted. *Academic units required:* 4 English, 3 math, 2 science, 2 science labs, 2 foreign language, 3 social studies, 1 history, 2 academic electives. *Academic units recommended:* 4 English, 3 math, 2 science, 2 science labs, 2 foreign language, 3 social studies, 1 history, 2 academic electives. **Freshman Admission Statistics:** 8,640 applied, 76% admitted, 17% enrolled. **Transfer Admission Requirements:** College transcript(s), essay or personal statement, statement of good standing from prior institution(s). Minimum college GPA of 2.25 required. Lowest grade transferable C-. **General Admission Information:** Application fee $55. Priority deadline 1/15. Non-fall registration accepted. Admission may be deferred for a maximum of 1 year.

COSTS AND FINANCIAL AID

Annual tuition $45,765. Room and board $12,531. Required fees $825. Average book and supplies expense $1,200. **Required Forms and Deadlines:** FAFSA. **Notification of Awards:** Applicants will be notified of awards on a rolling basis beginning 3/1. **Types of Aid:** *Need-based scholarships/grants:* College/university scholarship or grant aid from institutional funds; Federal Nursing Scholarships; Federal Pell; Private scholarships; SEOG; State scholarships/grants. *Loans:* Direct PLUS loans; Direct Subsidized Stafford Loans; Direct Unsubsidized Stafford Loans. **Student Employment:** Federal Work-Study Program available. Institutional employment available. **Financial Aid Statistics:** 81% needy freshmen, 89% needy undergrads receive need-based scholarship or grant aid. 82% freshmen, 61% undergrads receive non-need-based scholarship or grant aid. 69% freshmen, 72% undergrads receive need-based self-help aid. 7% freshmen, 5% undergrads receive athletic scholarships. 98% freshmen, 86% undergrads receive any aid. 66% undergrads borrow to pay for school. Average cumulative indebtedness $36,140. **Criteria awarding aid:** *Need-based:* Academics, Athletics, Leadership, Minority status, Music/drama. *Non-need-based:* Academics, Alumni affiliation, Athletics, Leadership, Minority status, Music/drama, State/district residency.

SETON HALL UNIVERSITY

Office of Admission, Seton Hall, South Orange, NJ 07079
Phone: (800) THE HALL **Financial Aid Phone:** 973-761-9332
E-mail: thehall@shu.edu **CEEB Code:** 2811
Fax: 973-275-2339 **Website:** http://admissions.shu.edu/ **ACT Code:** 2606

This private school, affiliated with the Roman Catholic Church, was founded in 1856. It has a 58 acre campus.

RATINGS

Admissions Selectivity Rating: 77 **Fire Safety Rating:** 92 **Green Rating:** 60*

STUDENTS AND FACULTY

Enrollment: 5,295. **Student Body:** 59% female, 41% male, 22% out-of-state, 2% international (71 countries represented). Asian 8%, African American 13%, Caucasian 51%, Hispanic 16%, Native American <1%, Pacific Islander <1%, Two or more races 2%, Race unknown 7%.
Retention and Graduation: 85% freshmen return for sophomore year. 30% grads go on to further study within 1 year. 9% grads pursue arts and sciences degrees. 7% grads pursue law degrees. 5% grads pursue business degrees. 9% grads pursue medical degrees. **Faculty:** 4% of classes are taught by teaching assistants.

ACADEMICS

Degrees: Bachelor's; Doctoral degree—professional practice; Doctoral degree research/scholarship; Master's; Post-master's certificate. **Most popular majors:** Criminal Justice/Safety Studies; Communication, Journalism, and Related Programs, Other; Speech Communication and Rhetoric. **Special Study Options:** Accelerated program; Cross-registration; Distance learning; Double major; Dual enrollment; English as a Second Language (ESL); Honors program; Independent study; Internships; Liberal arts/career combination; Study abroad; Teacher certification program. **Honors programs:** University Honors Program fosters intellectual development through academic challenge. A structured sequence of colloquia and seminars helps to develop critical thinking abilities. Students study the great texts of the past and also have the opportunity to attend operas, theater, museums, concerts, and other cultural events. **Combined degree programs:** BA/MA; BA/MEng. **Disability Services offered:** Note-taking services; Reader services; Tape recorders; Tutors. **Career services:** Alumni network; Alumni services; Career assessment; Career/job search classes; Internships; Regional alumni.

FACILITIES

94% of campus accessible to physically disabled. **Special Academic Facilities/ Equipment:** Art studios, theatre-in-the-round, TV studio, radio station, Market Research Center, Trading Room, Sport Polling Center, Science and Technology Center, Nursing SIM laboratories (mock ER), art gallery, language labs, Academic Resource Center (tutoring center), Writing Center, Green House, organic garden, and observatory.

CAMPUS LIFE

Environment: Village. 100 registered organizations, 13 honor societies, 3 religious organizations, 11 fraternities, 11 sororities on campus. **Athletics (Intercollegiate):** *Men:* baseball, basketball, cross-country, diving, golf, soccer, swimming, track/field (outdoor). *Women:* basketball, cross-country, diving, soccer, softball, swimming, tennis, track/field (outdoor). **On-Campus Highlights:** University Center.

ADMISSIONS

Freshman Academic Profile: Average high school GPA 3.5. 37% in top 10% of high school class, 61% in top 25% of high school class, 86% in top 50% of high school class. 70% from public high schools. **Test Scores:** SAT Math middle 50% range 510–610. SAT EBRW middle 50% range 490–590. ACT middle 50% range 22–27. **Basis for Candidate Selection: Freshman Admission Requirements:** High school diploma is required and GED is accepted. *Academic units required:* 4 English, 3 math, 1 science, 1 science lab, 2 foreign language, 2 social studies, 4 academic electives. **Freshman Admission Statistics:** 10,180 applied, 84% admitted, 17% enrolled. **General Admission Information:** Application fee $55. Priority deadline 3/1. Non-fall registration accepted. Admission may be deferred for a maximum of 1 year.

COSTS AND FINANCIAL AID

Annual tuition $35,940. Room and board $11,522. Required fees $1,782. **Required Forms and Deadlines:** FAFSA. **Student Employment:** Federal Work-Study Program available. Institutional employment available. **Financial Aid Statistics:** 97% freshmen, 97% undergrads receive any aid. **Criteria awarding aid:** *Non-need-based:* Academics, Alumni affiliation, Athletics, Leadership, Music/drama.

SETON HILL UNIVERSITY

1 Seton Hill Drive, Greensburg, PA 15601
Phone: 724-838-4255 **Financial Aid Phone:** 724-838-4293
E-mail: admit@setonhill.edu **CEEB Code:** 2812
Fax: 724-830-1294 **Website:** www.setonhill.edu **ACT Code:** 3688

This private school, affiliated with the Roman Catholic Church, was founded in 1883. It has a 200 acre campus.

RATINGS

Admissions Selectivity Rating: 79   **Fire Safety Rating:** 88   **Green Rating:** 60*

STUDENTS AND FACULTY

Enrollment: 1,660. **Student Body:** 64% female, 36% male, 23% out-of-state, 2% international (17 countries represented). Asian 1%, African American 9%, Caucasian 79%, Hispanic 4%, Native American <1%, Pacific Islander <1%, Two or more races 3%, Race unknown <1%.
Retention and Graduation: 82% freshmen return for sophomore year. 47% freshmen graduate within 4 years. 57% freshmen graduate within 6 years. 30% grads go on to further study within 1 year. 20% grads pursue arts and sciences degrees. 1% grads pursue law degrees. 3% grads pursue business degrees. 1% grads pursue medical degrees. **Faculty:** Student/faculty ratio 14:1. 100 full-time faculty, 82% hold PhDs, 4% are members of minority groups, 55% are women. 0% of classes are taught by teaching assistants.

ACADEMICS

Degrees: Bachelor's; Certificate; Master's; Post-bachelor's certificate; Post-master's certificate. **Classes:** Most classes have 10–19 students. **Most popular majors:** Business/Commerce, General; Fine/Studio Arts, General; Psychology, General. **Special Study Options:** Accelerated program; Cross-registration; Distance learning; Double major; Dual enrollment; English as a Second Language (ESL); Honors program; Independent study; Internships; Liberal arts/career combination; Student-designed major; Study abroad; Teacher certification program; Weekend college. **Honors programs:** Honors Program has designated curriculum components. **Combined degree programs:** BA/JD. **Disability Services offered:** Note-taking services; Reader services; Tape recorders; Tutors. **Career services:** Alumni network; Alumni services; Career assessment; Internships; Regional alumni.

FACILITIES

Housing: Coed dorms; 95% of campus accessible to physically disabled. **Special Academic Facilities/Equipment:** Art gallery, concert hall, theatre, Child Development Center, Performing Arts Center, Visual Arts Center, smart classrooms, Game System Center/MediaSphere, Recording Rooms.

CAMPUS LIFE

Environment: Town. **Activities:** Campus Ministries; Choral groups; Concert band; Dance; Drama/theater; International Student Organization; Jazz band; Literary magazine; Marching band; Model UN; Music ensembles; Musical theater; Pep band; Student government; Student newspaper; Symphony orchestra. 40 registered organizations, 4 honor societies, 6 religious organizations on campus. **Athletics (Intercollegiate):** *Men:* baseball, basketball, cross-country, football, lacrosse, soccer, track/field (outdoor), track/field (indoor), wrestling. *Women:* basketball, cross-country, equestrian sports, field hockey, golf, lacrosse, soccer, softball, tennis, track/field (outdoor), track/field (indoor), volleyball. **On-Campus Highlights:** Griffin's Cove. **Environmental Initiatives:** Association of Independent Colleges and Universities of Pennsylvania self/peer assessment program.

ADMISSIONS

Freshman Academic Profile: Average high school GPA 3.7. 19% in top 10% of high school class, 45% in top 25% of high school class, 77% in top 50% of high school class. **Test Scores:** SAT Math middle 50% range 510–610. SAT EBRW middle 50% range 510–630. ACT middle 50% range 21–27. **Basis for Candidate Selection:** *Very important factors include:* rigor of secondary school

record, academic GPA. *Important factors include:* class rank, standardized test scores, extracurricular activities, talent/ability, character/personal qualities. *Other factors include:* application essay, recommendation(s), interview, volunteer work, work experience. **Freshman Admission Requirements:** High school diploma is required and GED is accepted. *Academic units required:* 4 English, 2 math, 1 science, 1 science lab, 3 social studies, 4 academic electives. *Academic units recommended:* 2 foreign language. **Freshman Admission Statistics:** 2,471 applied, 75% admitted, 21% enrolled. **Transfer Admission Requirements:** High school transcript, college transcript(s), statement of good standing from prior institution(s). Minimum college GPA of 2.0 required. Lowest grade transferable C-. **General Admission Information:** Priority deadline 5/1. Regular application deadline 8/15. Non-fall registration accepted. Admission may be deferred for a maximum of 12 months.

COSTS AND FINANCIAL AID

Annual tuition $36,306. Room and board $12,212. Required fees $550. Average book and supplies expense $1,200. **Required Forms and Deadlines:** FAFSA; Institution's own financial aid form; State aid form. **Notification of Awards:** Applicants will be notified of awards on a rolling basis beginning 10/30. **Types of Aid:** *Need-based scholarships/grants:* College/university scholarship or grant aid from institutional funds; Federal Pell; Private scholarships; SEOG; State scholarships/grants. *Loans:* Direct PLUS loans; Direct Subsidized Stafford Loans; Direct Unsubsidized Stafford Loans. **Student Employment:** Federal Work-Study Program available. Institutional employment available. **Financial Aid Statistics:** 99% needy freshmen, 97% needy undergrads receive need-based scholarship or grant aid. 20% freshmen, 15% undergrads receive non-need-based scholarship or grant aid. 75% freshmen, 80% undergrads receive need-based self-help aid. 13% freshmen, 11% undergrads receive athletic scholarships. 100% freshmen, 82% undergrads receive any aid. 85% undergrads borrow to pay for school. Average cumulative indebtedness $39,892. **Criteria awarding aid:** *Need-based:* Job skills, Leadership, Minority status, Religious affiliation. *Non-need-based:* Academics, Alumni affiliation, Art, Athletics, Music/drama.

SHAWNEE STATE UNIVERSITY

940 Second Street, Portsmouth, OH 45662
Phone: 740-351-4778 **Financial Aid Phone:** 740-351-4357
E-mail: to_ssu@shawnee.edu **CEEB Code:** 1790
Fax: 740-351-3111 **Website:** www.shawnee.edu **ACT Code:** 3336

This public school was founded in 1986. It has a 50 acre campus.

RATINGS

Admissions Selectivity Rating: 79   **Fire Safety Rating:** 95   **Green Rating:** 63

STUDENTS AND FACULTY

Enrollment: 3,756. **Student Body:** 56% female, 44% male, 11% out-of-state, 1% international (20 countries represented). Asian <1%, African American 6%, Caucasian 87%, Hispanic 1%, Native American 1%, Pacific Islander <1%, Two or more races 2%, Race unknown 3%.
Retention and Graduation: 57% freshmen return for sophomore year.
Faculty: Student/faculty ratio 18:1. 145 full-time faculty, 59% hold PhDs, 10% are members of minority groups, 41% are women. 0% of classes are taught by teaching assistants.

ACADEMICS

Degrees: Associate; Bachelor's; Certificate; Master's. **Classes:** Most classes have 10–19 students. Most lab/discussion sessions have 20–29 students. **Most popular majors:** Biological and Biomedical Sciences, Other; Business Administration and Management, General; Psychology, General. **Special Study Options:** Accelerated program; Distance learning; Double major; Dual enrollment; English as a Second Language (ESL); Honors program; Independent study; Internships; Student-designed major; Study abroad; Teacher certification program. **Disability Services offered:** Note-taking services; Reader services; Tape recorders; Tutors. **Career services:** Alumni services; Career assessment; Career/job search classes; Internships.

FACILITIES

Housing: Coed dorms; Theme housing; 100% of campus accessible to physically disabled. **Special Academic Facilities/Equipment:** Vern Riffe Center for the Arts; Clark Planetarium. **Campus Network:** 100% of classrooms, 100% of dorms, 100% of student union, 100% of libraries, 100% of dining areas, 50% of common outdoor areas have wireless network access.

CAMPUS LIFE

Environment: Town. **Activities:** Campus Ministries; Choral groups; Drama/theater; International Student Organization; Literary magazine; Music ensembles; Musical theater; Student government; Student newspaper. 31 registered organizations, 2 honor societies, 3 religious organizations, 1 fraternity, 1 sorority on campus. **Athletics (Intercollegiate):** *Men:* baseball, basketball, cross-country, golf, soccer. *Women:* basketball, cross-country, soccer, softball, tennis, volleyball. **On-Campus Highlights:** Vern Riffe Center for the Arts. **Environmental Initiatives:** Geo-thermal chiller plant for new building.

ADMISSIONS

Freshman Academic Profile: 12% in top 10% of high school class, 33% in top 25% of high school class, 63% in top 50% of high school class. **Test Scores:** SAT Math middle 50% range 433–628. SAT EBRW middle 50% range 440–588. ACT middle 50% range 18–24. **Freshman Admission Requirements:** High school diploma is required and GED is accepted. *Academic units recommended:* 4 English, 3 math, 3 science, 2 foreign language, 3 social studies, 1 visual/performing arts. **Freshman Admission Statistics:** 3,686 applied, 74% admitted, 35% enrolled. **Transfer Admission Requirements:** High school transcript, college transcript(s). Minimum college GPA of 1.0 required. Lowest grade transferable D. **General Admission Information:** Non-fall registration accepted.

COSTS AND FINANCIAL AID

Annual in-state tuition $6,251. Annual out-of-state tuition $11,504. Room and board $9,552. Required fees $1,113. Average book and supplies expense $1,440. **Required Forms and Deadlines:** FAFSA. **Notification of Awards:** Applicants will be notified of awards on a rolling basis beginning 3/15. **Types of Aid:** *Need-based scholarships/grants:* College/university scholarship or grant aid from institutional funds; Federal Pell; Private scholarships; SEOG; State scholarships/grants. *Loans:* Direct PLUS loans; Direct Subsidized Stafford Loans; Direct Unsubsidized Stafford Loans. **Student Employment:** Federal Work-Study Program available. Institutional employment available.

SHAW UNIVERSITY

118 East South Street, Raleigh, NC 27601
Phone: 919-546-8275 **Financial Aid Phone:** 919-546-8565
E-mail: admissions@shawu.edu **CEEB Code:** 5612
Fax: 919-546-8271 **Website:** www.shawu.edu **ACT Code:** 3158

This private school, affiliated with the Baptist Church, was founded in 1865. It has a 30 acre campus.

RATINGS

Admissions Selectivity Rating: 78   **Fire Safety Rating:** 60*   **Green Rating:** 60*

STUDENTS AND FACULTY

Enrollment: 1,302. **Student Body:** 58% female, 42% male, 42% out-of-state, 5% international (16 countries represented). Asian 6%, African American 65%, Caucasian 1%, Hispanic 3%, Native American <1%, Pacific Islander 1%, Two or more races 9%, Race unknown 10%.
Retention and Graduation: 47% freshmen return for sophomore year.
Faculty: Student/faculty ratio 17:1. 73 full-time faculty, 0% hold PhDs, 71% are members of minority groups, 42% are women. 0% of classes are taught by teaching assistants.

ACADEMICS

Degrees: Bachelor's; Certificate; Master's. **Classes:** Most classes have 20–29 students. Most lab/discussion sessions have fewer than 10 students. **Most popular majors:** Social Work; Sociology, General; Business Administration and Management, General. **Special Study Options:** Accelerated program; Cross-registration; Distance learning; Double major; Dual enrollment; Honors program; Independent study; Internships; Liberal arts/career combination; Student-designed major; Study abroad; Teacher certification program; Weekend college. **Honors programs:** The Honors College of Shaw University nurtures excellence in select students who are highly motivated, talented and gifted, and who demonstrate a commitment to the learning process in reaching their potential to become scholars, leaders and role models. It is an innovative, multifaceted program designed to enhance the success of student scholars at Shaw University. Its initiative and activities concentrate on the growth and development of students' intellectual, ethical, and leadership skills. **Disability Services offered:** Note-taking services; Reader services; Tape recorders; Tutors. **Career services:** Career assessment; Career/job search classes; Internships.

FACILITIES

Housing: Men's dorms; Women's dorms. **Special Academic Facilities/Equipment:** TV and film production facilities. Curriculum and Materials Center. **Campus Network:** 100% of classrooms, 10% of dorms, 100% of student union, 100% of libraries, 100% of dining areas, 50% of common outdoor areas have wireless network access.

CAMPUS LIFE

Environment: City. **Activities:** Campus Ministries; Choral groups; Concert band; Dance; Drama/theater; Jazz band; Marching band; Music ensembles; Musical theater; Pep band; Radio station; Student government; Student newspaper; Yearbook. 4 honor societies, 4 fraternities, 4 sororities on campus. **Athletics (Intercollegiate):** *Men:* baseball, basketball, cross-country, football, golf, tennis, track/field (outdoor), track/field (indoor). *Women:* basketball, bowling, cross-country, softball, tennis, track/field (outdoor), track/field (indoor), volleyball.

ADMISSIONS

Freshman Academic Profile: Average high school GPA 2.6. 1% in top 10% of high school class, 6% in top 25% of high school class, 26% in top 50% of high school class. 90% from public high schools. **Test Scores:** SAT Math middle 50% range 380–450. SAT EBRW middle 50% range 400–460. ACT middle 50% range 13–16. **Basis for Candidate Selection:** *Very important factors include:* rigor of secondary school record, academic GPA, recommendation(s), level of applicant's interest. *Important factors include:* class rank, application essay, standardized test scores, extracurricular activities, talent/ability, character/personal qualities, alumni/ae relation. *Other factors include:* geographical residence, state residency, volunteer work, work experience. **Freshman Admission Requirements:** High school diploma is required and GED is accepted. *Academic units required:* 3 English, 2 math, 2 science, 2 social studies, 9 academic electives. **Freshman Admission Statistics:** 12,157 applied, 52% admitted, 6% enrolled. **Transfer Admission Requirements:** College transcript(s). Lowest grade transferable C. **General Admission Information:** Application fee $25. Priority deadline 7/3. Regular application deadline 7/30. Non-fall registration accepted. Admission may be deferred for a maximum of indefinite.

COSTS AND FINANCIAL AID

Annual tuition $11,808. Room and board $8,514. Required fees $4,672. Average book and supplies expense $1,300. **Required Forms and Deadlines:** FAFSA; Institution's own financial aid form; State aid form. **Notification of Awards:** Applicants will be notified of awards on a rolling basis beginning 2/1. **Types of Aid:** *Need-based scholarships/grants:* College/university scholarship or grant aid from institutional funds; Federal Pell; Private scholarships; SEOG; State scholarships/grants; United Negro College Fund. *Loans:* Direct PLUS loans; Direct Subsidized Stafford Loans; Direct Unsubsidized Stafford Loans. **Student Employment:** Federal Work-Study Program available. Institutional employment available. **Financial Aid Statistics:** 97% freshmen, 96% undergrads receive any aid. **Criteria awarding aid:** *Need-based:* Alumni affiliation, Religious affiliation. *Non-need-based:* Academics, Alumni affiliation, Art, Athletics, Music/drama, Religious affiliation.

SHENANDOAH UNIVERSITY

1460 University Drive, Winchester, VA 22601-5195
Phone: 540.665.4581 **Financial Aid Phone:** 540.665.4621
E-mail: admit@su.edu **CEEB Code:** 5613
Fax: 540.665.4627 **Website:** www.su.edu **ACT Code:** 4396

This private school, affiliated with the Methodist Church, was founded in 1875. It has a 359 acre campus.

RATINGS

Admissions Selectivity Rating: 82   **Fire Safety Rating:** 98   **Green Rating:** 86

STUDENTS AND FACULTY

Enrollment: 2,022. **Student Body:** 60% female, 40% male, 40% out-of-state, 2% international (28 countries represented). Asian 3%, African American 10%, Caucasian 59%, Hispanic 6%, Native American 1%, Pacific Islander <1%, Two or more races 1%, Race unknown 16%.
Retention and Graduation: 83% freshmen return for sophomore year. 53% freshmen graduate within 4 years. 63% freshmen graduate within 6 years. 17% grads go on to further study within 1 year. **Faculty:** Student/faculty ratio 10:1.

270 full-time faculty, 77% hold PhDs, 12% are members of minority groups, 60% are women. 0% of classes are taught by teaching assistants.

ACADEMICS

Degrees: Bachelor's; Certificate; Doctoral degree—professional practice; Doctoral degree research/scholarship; Master's; Post-bachelor's certificate; Post-master's certificate. **Classes:** Most classes have 10–19 students. Most lab/discussion sessions have fewer than 10 students. **Most popular majors:** Registered Nursing/Registered Nurse; Business Administration and Management, General. **Special Study Options:** Accelerated program; Distance learning; Double major; Dual enrollment; English as a Second Language (ESL); Independent study; Internships; Study abroad; Teacher certification program; Weekend college. **Honors programs:** The College of Arts and Sciences has a multidisciplinary Honors Program that encourages students to use creativity to solve problems. The program requires students to complete 12 credits of Honors courses and 3 credits of Honors seminars that include multi-disciplinary instruction and practice developing advanced communication skills. Both the non-academic and academic components of the Honors Program help students develop leadership and critical thinking skills through problem solving and program event planning. **Disability Services offered:** Note-taking services; Reader services; Tape recorders; Tutors. **Career services:** Alumni network; Alumni services; Career assessment; Career/job search classes; Internships.

FACILITIES

Housing: Apartments for married students; Apartments for single students; Coed dorms; Special housing for disabled students; 91% of campus accessible to physically disabled. **Special Academic Facilities/Equipment:** Pharmacy Apothecary Museum; Environmental Studies green rooftop garden; cadaver lab and nursing simulation suite in the Health & Life Sciences Building; Claude Moore Center for Literacy in the School of Education & Human Development (SEHD); a model computer classroom in SEHD, as well as the Academic Enrichment Center; Children's Literature Center and Media Center in the Alson H. Smith, Jr. Library. The campus employs a WEPA (wireless everywhere, print anywhere) printing system. The Shenandoah River Campus at Cool Spring Battlefield is 195 acres of land along the Shenandoah River which serves as a field site where students learn by exploring history, environmental studies, and other disciplines in ways that supplement and reinforce classroom and laboratory learning. Shenandoah Conservatory has three academic observation rooms: a recording studio, a music therapy clinic, and the Collins Music Learning Suite, an innovative learning space for undergraduate and graduate music education students. The conservatory also provides a designated Mac Lab, which is a specialized music technology classroom; two classrooms designated for class piano; specialized rooms for film and acting; and specialized equipment for voice and a voice science lab.

CAMPUS LIFE

Environment: Town. **Activities:** Campus Ministries; Choral groups; Concert band; Dance; Drama/theater; International Student Organization; Jazz band; Literary magazine; Music ensembles; Musical theater; Pep band; Radio station; Student government; Student newspaper; Symphony orchestra. 105 registered organizations, 7 honor societies, 7 religious organizations on campus. **Athletics (Intercollegiate):** *Men:* baseball, basketball, cross-country, football, golf, lacrosse, soccer, tennis. *Women:* basketball, cross-country, field hockey, lacrosse, soccer, softball, tennis, volleyball. **On-Campus Highlights:** Brandt Student Center. **Environmental Initiatives:** Continued refitting of lights, from incandescent to CF or LED.

ADMISSIONS

Freshman Academic Profile: Average high school GPA 3.5. 25% in top 10% of high school class, 52% in top 25% of high school class, 80% in top 50% of high school class. 100% from public high schools. **Test Scores:** SAT Math middle 50% range 480–590. SAT EBRW middle 50% range 500–600. ACT middle 50% range 21–26. **Basis for Candidate Selection:** *Very important factors include:* academic GPA. *Important factors include:* rigor of secondary school record, standardized test scores, extracurricular activities, talent/ability. *Other factors include:* application essay, recommendation(s), interview, character/personal qualities, first generation, volunteer work, work experience, level of applicant's interest. **Freshman Admission Requirements:** High school diploma is required and GED is accepted. *Academic units required:* 4 English, 3 math, 2 science, 1 science lab. *Academic units recommended:* 2 foreign language. **Freshman Admission Statistics:** 2,225 applied, 70% admitted, 28% enrolled. **Transfer Admission Requirements:** College transcript(s), statement of good standing from prior institution(s). Minimum college GPA of 2.0 required. Lowest grade transferable C. **General Admission Information:** Application fee $30. Priority deadline 2/4. Non-fall registration accepted. Admission may be deferred for a maximum of 12 months.

COSTS AND FINANCIAL AID

Annual tuition $31,890. Room and board $10,570. Required fees $1,280. Average book and supplies expense $1,500. **Required Forms and Deadlines:** FAFSA; State aid form. **Notification of Awards:** Applicants will be notified of awards on a rolling basis beginning 1/1. **Types of Aid:** *Need-based scholarships/grants:* College/university scholarship or grant aid from institutional funds; Federal Pell; Private scholarships; SEOG; State scholarships/grants. *Loans:* Direct PLUS loans; Direct Subsidized Stafford Loans; Direct Unsubsidized Stafford Loans. **Student Employment:** Federal Work-Study Program available. Institutional employment available. **Financial Aid Statistics:** 73% needy freshmen, 87% needy undergrads receive need-based scholarship or grant aid. 100% freshmen, 98% undergrads receive non-need-based scholarship or grant aid. 81% freshmen, 82% undergrads receive need-based self-help aid. 0% freshmen, 0% undergrads receive athletic scholarships. 100% freshmen, 100% undergrads receive any aid. 71% undergrads borrow to pay for school. Average cumulative indebtedness $41,587. **Criteria awarding aid:** *Non-need-based:* Academics, Music/drama, Religious affiliation.

SHEPHERD UNIVERSITY

Office of Admissions, Shepherdstown, WV 25443-5000
Phone: 304-876-5212 **Financial Aid Phone:** 304-876-5470
E-mail: admission@shepherd.edu **CEEB Code:** 5615
Fax: 304-876-5165 **Website:** www.shepherd.edu **ACT Code:** 4532

This public school was founded in 1871. It has a 323 acre campus.

RATINGS

Admissions Selectivity Rating: 74   **Fire Safety Rating:** 87   **Green Rating:** 66

STUDENTS AND FACULTY

Enrollment: 2,631. **Student Body:** 59% female, 41% male, 32% out-of-state, 1% international (16 countries represented). Asian 1%, African American 8%, Caucasian 75%, Hispanic 7%, Native American <1%, Pacific Islander <1%, Two or more races 4%, Race unknown 2%.
Retention and Graduation: 71% freshmen return for sophomore year. 31% freshmen graduate within 4 years. 49% freshmen graduate within 6 years.
Faculty: Student/faculty ratio 14:1. 140 full-time faculty, 86% hold PhDs, 11% are members of minority groups, 48% are women. 0% of classes are taught by teaching assistants.

ACADEMICS

Degrees: Bachelor's; Doctoral degree—professional practice; Master's. **Classes:** Most classes have 10–19 students. Most lab/discussion sessions have 10–19 students. **Most popular majors:** Secondary Education and Teaching; Registered Nursing/Registered Nurse; Business Administration and Management, General. **Special Study Options:** Cooperative education program; Double major; Dual enrollment; English as a Second Language (ESL); Honors program; Independent study; Internships; Study abroad; Teacher certification program. **Honors programs:** See Honors Program at www.shepherd.edu/honors. **Disability Services offered:** Reader services; Tape recorders; Tutors. **Career services:** Alumni network; Alumni services; Career assessment; Career/job search classes; Internships.

FACILITIES

Housing: Apartments for single students; Coed dorms; Special housing for disabled students; Special housing for international students; Theme housing; 90% of campus accessible to physically disabled. **Special Academic Facilities/Equipment:** Nursery school, elementary education lab, art gallery, theaters, Steinway Concert Grand Piano, George Tyler Moore Center for the Study of the Civil War, Robert C. Byrd Center for Congressional History and Education, Stubblefield Institute for Civil Political Communications, campus radio station, television production studio, veterans center, wellness center, business innovation lab.

CAMPUS LIFE

Environment: Village. **Activities:** Campus Ministries; Choral groups; Concert band; Dance; Drama/theater; International Student Organization; Jazz band; Literary magazine; Marching band; Model UN; Music ensembles; Musical theater; Radio station; Student government; Student newspaper; Symphony orchestra. 88 registered organizations, 14 honor societies, 8 religious organizations, 5 fraternities, 3 sororities on campus. **Athletics (Intercollegiate):** *Men:* baseball, basketball, football, golf, soccer, tennis. *Women:* basketball, lacrosse, soccer, softball, tennis, volleyball. **On-Campus Highlights:** Potomac Place. **Environmental Initiatives:** Recycling.

ADMISSIONS

Freshman Academic Profile: Average high school GPA 3.5. 90% from public high schools. **Test Scores:** SAT Math middle 50% range 480–570. SAT EBRW middle 50% range 490–600. ACT middle 50% range 19–26. **Basis for Candidate Selection:** *Very important factors include:* rigor of secondary school record, academic GPA, standardized test scores. *Important factors include:* talent/ability. *Other factors include:* class rank, application essay, recommendation(s), interview, extracurricular activities, character/personal qualities, alumni/ae relation, level of applicant's interest. **Freshman Admission Requirements:** High school diploma is required and GED is accepted. *Academic units required:* 4 English, 4 math, 3 science, 3 science labs, 2 foreign language, 2 social studies, 1 history, 1 visual/performing arts. **Freshman Admission Statistics:** 1,370 applied, 96% admitted, 37% enrolled. **Transfer Admission Requirements:** College transcript(s). Minimum college GPA of 2.0 required. Lowest grade transferable D. **General Admission Information:** Application fee $45. Priority deadline 2/1. Regular application deadline 8/19. Non-fall registration accepted. Admission may be deferred for a maximum of 12 months.

COSTS AND FINANCIAL AID

Annual in-state tuition $7,784. Annual out-of-state tuition $18,224. Room and board $10,776. Average book and supplies expense $1,000. **Required Forms and Deadlines:** FAFSA; Institution's own financial aid form; State aid form. **Notification of Awards:** Applicants will be notified of awards on a rolling basis beginning 12/15. **Types of Aid:** *Need-based scholarships/grants:* College/university scholarship or grant aid from institutional funds; Federal Pell; Private scholarships; SEOG; State scholarships/grants. *Loans:* Direct PLUS loans; Direct Subsidized Stafford Loans; Direct Unsubsidized Stafford Loans. **Student Employment:** Federal Work-Study Program available. Institutional employment available. **Financial Aid Statistics:** 66% needy freshmen, 71% needy undergrads receive need-based scholarship or grant aid. 57% freshmen, 44% undergrads receive non-need-based scholarship or grant aid. 57% freshmen, 63% undergrads receive need-based self-help aid. 13% freshmen, 9% undergrads receive athletic scholarships. 64.5% freshmen, 62% undergrads receive any aid. 67% undergrads borrow to pay for school. Average cumulative indebtedness $28,371. **Criteria awarding aid:** *Need-based:* Academics. *Non-need-based:* Academics, Art, Athletics, Job skills, Leadership, Minority status, Music/drama, State/district residency.

SHIPPENSBURG UNIVERSITY OF PENNSYLVANIA

Old Main 105, Shippensburg, PA 17257-2299
Phone: 717-477-1231 **Financial Aid Phone:** 717-477-1131
E-mail: admiss@ship.edu **CEEB Code:** 2657
Fax: 717-477-4016 **Website:** www.ship.edu **ACT Code:** 3714

This public school was founded in 1871. It has a 200 acre campus.

RATINGS

Admissions Selectivity Rating: 74   Fire Safety Rating: 98   Green Rating: 73

STUDENTS AND FACULTY

Enrollment: 5,120. **Student Body:** 52% female, 48% male, 7% out-of-state, 1% international (15 countries represented). Asian 1%, African American 13%, Caucasian 74%, Hispanic 6%, Native American <1%, Pacific Islander 0%, Two or more races 5%, Race unknown 1%.
Retention and Graduation: 75% freshmen return for sophomore year. 40% freshmen graduate within 4 years. 58% freshmen graduate within 6 years.

ACADEMICS

Degrees: Bachelor's; Certificate; Doctoral degree—professional practice; Master's; Post-bachelor's certificate; Post-master's certificate. **Classes:** Most classes have 10–19 students. Most lab/discussion sessions have 10–19 students. **Most popular majors:** Biology/Biological Sciences, General; Psychology, General; Criminal Justice/Safety Studies. **Special Study Options:** Accelerated program; Cooperative education program; Distance learning; Double major; Dual enrollment; Honors program; Independent study; Internships; Study abroad; Teacher certification program. **Honors programs:** The Wood Honors College at Shippensburg University offers academically talented and motivated students an enriched undergraduate experience that is tailored to their

academic, personal, and professional goals. Honor College students enroll in unique Honors seminars and have access to specialized Honors leadership, research, study abroad, and service-learning opportunities. Shippensburg Honors students come from a variety of backgrounds, and they have diverse academic interests. What they share is their desire to make a difference on campus, in our local and national communities, and on a global scale. **Disability Services offered:** Note-taking services; Reader services; Tutors. **Career services:** Alumni network; Alumni services; Career assessment; Career/job search classes; Internships; Regional alumni.

FACILITIES

Housing: Apartments for single students; Coed dorms; Theme housing; Wellness housing; 92% of campus accessible to physically disabled. **Special Academic Facilities/Equipment:** Art gallery, vertebrate museum, on-campus elementary school, planetarium, electron microscope, NMR spectrometer, greenhouse, herbarium, Fashion Archives, Women's Center, Closed Circuit TV.

CAMPUS LIFE

Environment: Village. **Activities:** Campus Ministries; Choral groups; Concert band; Dance; Drama/theater; International Student Organization; Jazz band; Literary magazine; Marching band; Music ensembles; Musical theater; Pep band; Radio station; Student government; Student newspaper; Television station; Yearbook. 133 registered organizations, 20 honor societies, 4 religious organizations, 12 fraternities, 8 sororities on campus. **Athletics (Intercollegiate): Men:** baseball, basketball, cross-country, football, soccer, swimming, track/field (outdoor), track/field (indoor), wrestling. *Women:* basketball, cross-country, field hockey, lacrosse, soccer, softball, swimming, tennis, track/field (outdoor), track/field (indoor), volleyball. **On-Campus Highlights:** Ceddia Union Building.

ADMISSIONS

Freshman Academic Profile: Average high school GPA 3.2. 10% in top 10% of high school class, 26% in top 25% of high school class, 59% in top 50% of high school class. 88% from public high schools. **Test Scores:** SAT Math middle 50% range 460–570. SAT EBRW middle 50% range 470–580. ACT middle 50% range 16–23. **Basis for Candidate Selection:** *Very important factors include:* rigor of secondary school record, class rank, academic GPA, standardized test scores. *Other factors include:* application essay, recommendation(s), interview, extracurricular activities, talent/ability, character/personal qualities, volunteer work, work experience, level of applicant's interest. **Freshman Admission Requirements:** High school diploma is required and GED is accepted. *Academic units recommended:* 4 English, 3 math, 3 science, 3 science labs, 3 foreign language. **Freshman Admission Statistics:** 5,927 applied, 91% admitted, 22% enrolled. **Transfer Admission Requirements:** College transcript(s), statement of good standing from prior institution(s). Minimum college GPA of 2.2 required. Lowest grade transferable C. **General Admission Information:** Application fee $45. Non-fall registration accepted. Admission may be deferred for a maximum of 1 year.

COSTS AND FINANCIAL AID

Annual in-state tuition $9,570. Annual out-of-state tuition $17,362. Room and board $12,114. Required fees $3,174. Average book and supplies expense $1,200. **Required Forms and Deadlines:** FAFSA. **Types of Aid:** *Need-based scholarships/grants:* College/university scholarship or grant aid from institutional funds; Federal Pell; Private scholarships; SEOG; State scholarships/grants. *Loans:* Direct PLUS loans; Direct Subsidized Stafford Loans; Direct Unsubsidized Stafford Loans. **Student Employment:** Federal Work-Study Program available. Institutional employment available. **Financial Aid Statistics:** 86% needy freshmen, 79% needy undergrads receive need-based scholarship or grant aid. 6% freshmen, 5% undergrads receive non-need-based scholarship or grant aid. 91% freshmen, 91% undergrads receive need-based self-help aid. 6% freshmen, 6% undergrads receive athletic scholarships. 97% freshmen, 91% undergrads receive any aid. 80% undergrads borrow to pay for school. Average cumulative indebtedness $37,130. **Criteria awarding aid:** *Need-based:* Academics. *Non-need-based:* Academics, Athletics.

SHORTER UNIVERSITY

315 Shorter Avenue, Rome, GA 30165
Phone: 706-233-7319 **Financial Aid Phone:** 706-233-7227
E-mail: admissions@shorter.edu **CEEB Code:** 5616
Fax: 706-233-7224 **Website:** www.shorter.edu **ACT Code:** 860

This private school, affiliated with the Southern Baptist Church, was founded in 1873. It has a 150 acre campus.

RATINGS
Admissions Selectivity Rating: 81   **Fire Safety Rating:** 86   **Green Rating:** 60*

STUDENTS AND FACULTY
Enrollment: 1,581. **Student Body:** 55% female, 45% male, 12% out-of-state, 3% international (22 countries represented). Asian 1%, African American 17%, Caucasian 69%, Hispanic 4%, Native American <1%, Pacific Islander <1%, Two or more races 1%, Race unknown 4%.
Retention and Graduation: 68% freshmen return for sophomore year. 30% grads go on to further study within 1 year. **Faculty:** Student/faculty ratio 13:1. 92 full-time faculty, 70% hold PhDs, 9% are members of minority groups, 50% are women. 0% of classes are taught by teaching assistants.

ACADEMICS
Degrees: Associate; Bachelor's. **Classes:** Most classes have 20–29 students. Most lab/discussion sessions have 20–29 students. **Most popular majors:** Education, General; Visual and Performing Arts, General; Business Administration and Management, General. **Special Study Options:** Cross-registration; Double major; Dual enrollment; Honors program; Independent study; Internships; Student-designed major; Study abroad; Teacher certification program; Weekend college. **Honors programs:** Academy of Aristaeus: a four-year honors program featuring seminar discussions and a research project. **Disability Services offered:** Note-taking services; Reader services; Tape recorders; Tutors. **Career services:** Career assessment; Career/job search classes; Internships.

FACILITIES
Housing: Apartments for single students; Men's dorms; Women's dorms; 70% of campus accessible to physically disabled. **Special Academic Facilities/Equipment:** Shorter History Museum. **Campus Network:** 100% of classrooms, 100% of dorms, 100% of student union, 100% of libraries, 100% of dining areas, 100% of common outdoor areas have wireless network access.

CAMPUS LIFE
Environment: Town. **Activities:** Campus Ministries; Choral groups; Concert band; Dance; Drama/theater; International Student Organization; Literary magazine; Marching band; Model UN; Music ensembles; Musical theater; Opera; Pep band; Radio station; Student government; Student newspaper; Student-run film society; Yearbook. 29 registered organizations, 10 honor societies, 3 religious organizations, 3 fraternities, 3 sororities on campus.
Athletics (Intercollegiate): *Men:* baseball, basketball, cheerleading, cross-country, football, golf, soccer, tennis, track/field (outdoor). *Women:* basketball, cheerleading, cross-country, golf, lacrosse, soccer, softball, tennis, track/field (outdoor), volleyball. **On-Campus Highlights:** Fitton Student Union.

ADMISSIONS
Freshman Academic Profile: Average high school GPA 3.3. 21% in top 10% of high school class, 47% in top 25% of high school class, 77% in top 50% of high school class. 95% from public high schools. **Test Scores:** SAT Math middle 50% range 430–550. SAT EBRW middle 50% range 420–550. ACT middle 50% range 18–24. **Basis for Candidate Selection:** *Very important factors include:* academic GPA, standardized test scores. *Important factors include:* rigor of secondary school record, class rank, application essay, talent/ability. *Other factors include:* recommendation(s), interview, extracurricular activities, character/personal qualities, first generation, alumni/ae relation, volunteer work, work experience, level of applicant's interest. **Freshman Admission Requirements:** High school diploma is required and GED is accepted. *Academic units required:* 4 English, 4 math, 3 science, 2 foreign language, 3 history. **Freshman Admission Statistics:** 1,944 applied, 65% admitted, 32% enrolled. **Transfer Admission Requirements:** College transcript(s), statement of good standing from prior institution(s). Minimum college GPA of 2.0 required. Lowest grade transferable C. **General Admission Information:** Application fee $25. Non-fall registration accepted. Admission may be deferred for a maximum of 2 years.

COSTS AND FINANCIAL AID
Annual tuition $17,500. Room and board $8,600. Required fees $370. Average book and supplies expense $1,200. **Required Forms and Deadlines:** FAFSA; Institution's own financial aid form; State aid form. **Notification of Awards:** Applicants will be notified of awards on a rolling basis beginning 4/1. **Types of Aid:** *Need-based scholarships/grants:* College/university scholarship or grant aid from institutional funds; Federal Pell; Private scholarships; SEOG; State scholarships/grants. **Student Employment:** Federal Work-Study Program available. Institutional employment available. **Financial Aid Statistics:** 99% needy freshmen, 99% needy undergrads receive need-based scholarship or grant aid. 16% freshmen, 15% undergrads receive non-need-based scholarship or grant aid. 79% freshmen, 75% undergrads receive need-based self-help aid. 15% freshmen, 11% undergrads receive athletic scholarships. 99% freshmen, 99% undergrads receive any aid. **Criteria awarding aid:** *Need-based:* Academics, Art, Athletics, Music/drama, Religious affiliation. *Non-need-based:* Academics, Art, Athletics, Music/drama, Religious affiliation.

SIENA COLLEGE

Siena College Admissions Office, Loudonville, NY 12211-1462
Phone: 518-783-2423 **Financial Aid Phone:** 518-783-2427
E-mail: admissions@siena.edu **CEEB Code:** 2814
Fax: 518-783-2436 **Website:** https://www.siena.edu **ACT Code:** 2878

This private school, affiliated with the Roman Catholic Church, was founded in 1937. It has a 175.3 acre campus.

RATINGS
Admissions Selectivity Rating: 76   **Fire Safety Rating:** 91   **Green Rating:** 67

STUDENTS AND FACULTY
Enrollment: 3,146. **Student Body:** 57% female, 43% male, 18% out-of-state, 3% international (45 countries represented). Asian 5%, African American 3%, Caucasian 77%, Hispanic 8%, Native American <1%, Pacific Islander <1%, Two or more races 3%, Race unknown 1%.
Retention and Graduation: 86% freshmen return for sophomore year. 75% freshmen graduate within 4 years. 80% freshmen graduate within 6 years. 30% grads go on to further study within 1 year. 15% grads pursue arts and sciences degrees. 4% grads pursue law degrees. 5% grads pursue business degrees. 4% grads pursue medical degrees. **Faculty:** Student/faculty ratio 12:1. 214 full-time faculty, 93% hold PhDs, 10% are members of minority groups, 47% are women. 0% of classes are taught by teaching assistants.

ACADEMICS
Degrees: Bachelor's; Certificate; Master's; Post-bachelor's certificate. **Classes:** Most classes have 20–29 students. Most lab/discussion sessions have 10–19 students. **Most popular majors:** Biology, General; Psychology, General; Accounting. **Special Study Options:** Cross-registration; Double major; Dual enrollment; English as a Second Language (ESL); Honors program; Independent study; Internships; Student-designed major; Study abroad; Teacher certification program. **Honors programs:** College-wide Honors program. **Combined degree programs:** BA/DDS; BA/JD; BA/MA; BA/MD; BA/MEng. **Disability Services offered:** Note-taking services; Reader services; Tape recorders; Tutors. **Career services:** Alumni network; Alumni services; Career assessment; Career/job search classes; Internships; Regional alumni.

FACILITIES
Housing: Apartments for single students; Coed dorms; Special housing for disabled students; 90% of campus accessible to physically disabled. **Special Academic Facilities/Equipment:** Center for Academic Community Engagement, Center for Undergraduate Research and Creative Activity, Stack Center for Innovation and Entrepreneurship, Stewart's Advanced Instrumentation and Technology Center, Breyo Observatory.

CAMPUS LIFE
Environment: City. **Activities:** Campus Ministries; Choral groups; Dance; Drama/theater; International Student Organization; Literary magazine; Model UN; Music ensembles; Musical theater; Opera; Pep band; Radio station; Student government; Student newspaper; Student-run film society; Symphony orchestra; Television station; Yearbook. 86 registered organizations, 21 honor

societies, 2 religious organizations on campus. **Athletics (Intercollegiate):** *Men:* baseball, basketball, cross-country, golf, lacrosse, soccer, tennis. *Women:* basketball, cross-country, field hockey, golf, lacrosse, soccer, softball, swimming, tennis, volleyball, water polo. **On-Campus Highlights:** Sarazen Student Union.

ADMISSIONS

Freshman Academic Profile: Average high school GPA 3.5. 19% in top 10% of high school class, 51% in top 25% of high school class, 88% in top 50% of high school class. 77% from public high schools. **Test Scores:** SAT Math middle 50% range 540–650. SAT EBRW middle 50% range 530–630. ACT middle 50% range 22–28. **Basis for Candidate Selection:** *Very important factors include:* rigor of secondary school record, academic GPA. *Important factors include:* recommendation(s), interview. *Other factors include:* class rank, application essay, standardized test scores, extracurricular activities, talent/ability, character/personal qualities, first generation, alumni/ae relation, geographical residence, racial/ethnic status, volunteer work, work experience, level of applicant's interest. **Freshman Admission Requirements:** High school diploma is required and GED is accepted. *Academic units required:* 4 English, 3 math, 3 science, 3 science labs, 2 foreign language, 2 social studies, 2 history. *Academic units recommended:* 4 English, 4 math, 4 science, 4 science labs, 3 foreign language, 2 social studies, 2 history. **Freshman Admission Statistics:** 7,728 applied, 81% admitted, 13% enrolled. **Transfer Admission Requirements:** College transcript(s), statement of good standing from prior institution(s). Minimum college GPA of 2.5 required. Lowest grade transferable C+. **General Admission Information:** Application fee $50. Regular application deadline 3/1. Non-fall registration accepted. Admission may be deferred for a maximum of 1 academic year.

COSTS AND FINANCIAL AID

Annual tuition $39,200. Room and board $15,915. Required fees $975. Average book and supplies expense $1,293. **Required Forms and Deadlines:** FAFSA; State aid form. **Notification of Awards:** Applicants will be notified of awards on or about 12/15. **Types of Aid:** *Need-based scholarships/grants:* College/university scholarship or grant aid from institutional funds; Federal Pell; Private scholarships; SEOG; State scholarships/grants. *Loans:* Direct Subsidized Stafford Loans; Direct Unsubsidized Stafford Loans. **Student Employment:** Federal Work-Study Program available. Institutional employment available. **Financial Aid Statistics:** 100% needy freshmen, 100% needy undergrads receive need-based scholarship or grant aid. 97% freshmen, 96% undergrads receive non-need-based scholarship or grant aid. 73% freshmen, 77% undergrads receive need-based self-help aid. 8% freshmen, 8% undergrads receive athletic scholarships. 98% freshmen, 93% undergrads receive any aid. **Criteria awarding aid:** *Need-based:* Academics, Alumni affiliation, Art, Athletics, Job skills, Leadership, Minority status, Music/drama. *Non-need-based:* Academics, Athletics, Leadership, Minority status, State/district residency.

SIENA HEIGHTS UNIVERSITY

1247 E. Siena Heights Drive, Adrian, MI 49221
Phone: 517-264-7180 **Financial Aid Phone:** 517-264-7110
E-mail: admissions@sienaheights.edu **CEEB Code:** 2316
Fax: 517-264-7744 **Website:** www.sienaheights.edu **ACT Code:** 2052

This private school, affiliated with the Roman Catholic Church, was founded in 1919. It has a 55 acre campus.

RATINGS

Admissions Selectivity Rating: 78   **Fire Safety Rating:** 67   **Green Rating:** 75

STUDENTS AND FACULTY

Enrollment: 2,307. **Student Body:** 57% female, 43% male, 12% out-of-state, <1% international (6 countries represented). Asian 1%, African American 13%, Caucasian 76%, Hispanic 5%, Native American 1%, Pacific Islander <1%, Two or more races 2%, Race unknown 2%.
Retention and Graduation: 59% freshmen return for sophomore year.
Faculty: 0% of classes are taught by teaching assistants.

ACADEMICS

Degrees: Associate; Bachelor's; Certificate; Master's; Post-master's certificate.
Classes: Most classes have 10–19 students. Most lab/discussion sessions have 10–19 students. **Most popular majors:** Medical Radiologic Technology/Science—Radiation Therapist; Biology/Biological Sciences, General; Business Administration and Management, General. **Special Study Options:** Cooperative education program; Distance learning; Double major; Dual

enrollment; English as a Second Language (ESL); Independent study; Internships; Student-designed major; Study abroad; Teacher certification program. **Disability Services offered:** Note-taking services; Reader services; Tape recorders; Tutors. **Career services:** Alumni network; Alumni services; Career assessment; Career/job search classes; Internships; Regional alumni.

FACILITIES

Housing: Apartments for married students; Coed dorms; Special housing for international students; 90% of campus accessible to physically disabled. **Special Academic Facilities/Equipment:** Klemm Gallery, Francoeur Theater, Stubnitz Lab Theater. **Campus Network:** 100% of classrooms, 100% of dorms, 100% of student union, 100% of libraries, 100% of dining areas, 15% of common outdoor areas have wireless network access.

CAMPUS LIFE

Environment: Village. **Activities:** Campus Ministries; Choral groups; Concert band; Dance; Drama/theater; International Student Organization; Literary magazine; Marching band; Music ensembles; Musical theater; Pep band; Student government; Symphony orchestra. **On-Campus Highlights:** McLaughlin University Center.

ADMISSIONS

Freshman Academic Profile: Average high school GPA 3.2. 8% in top 10% of high school class, 22% in top 25% of high school class, 68% in top 50% of high school class. **Test Scores:** ACT middle 50% range 19–23. **Basis for Candidate Selection:** *Very important factors include:* rigor of secondary school record, academic GPA, standardized test scores. *Important factors include:* class rank, application essay. **Freshman Admission Requirements:** High school diploma is required and GED is accepted. **Freshman Admission Statistics:** 1,422 applied, 68% admitted, 31% enrolled. **General Admission Information:** Application fee $25. Non-fall registration accepted.

COSTS AND FINANCIAL AID

Annual tuition $21,250. Room and board $8,710. Required fees $640. **Types of Aid:** *Need-based scholarships/grants:* College/university scholarship or grant aid from institutional funds; Federal Pell; Private scholarships; SEOG; State scholarships/grants. *Loans:* Direct PLUS loans; Direct Subsidized Stafford Loans; Direct Unsubsidized Stafford Loans. **Student Employment:** Federal Work-Study Program available. **Financial Aid Statistics:** 99% freshmen receive any aid.

SIERRA NEVADA COLLEGE

999 Tahoe Blvd., Incline Village, NV 89451
Phone: 775-831-1314 **Financial Aid Phone:** 775 8311314 x 7404
E-mail: admissions@sierraneveda.edu **CEEB Code:** 9192
Fax: 775-831-6223 **Website:** www.sierraneveda.edu **ACT Code:** 2497

This private school was founded in 1969. It has a 25 acre campus.

RATINGS

Admissions Selectivity Rating: 73   **Fire Safety Rating:** 96   **Green Rating:** 75

STUDENTS AND FACULTY

Enrollment: 516. **Student Body:** 41% female, 59% male, 84% out-of-state, 7% international (14 countries represented). Asian 1%, African American 1%, Caucasian 72%, Hispanic 1%, Native American 3%, Pacific Islander 1%, Two or more races 0%, Race unknown 15%.
Retention and Graduation: 71% freshmen return for sophomore year.
Faculty: Student/faculty ratio 11:1. 36 full-time faculty, 61% hold PhDs, 14% are members of minority groups, 58% are women. 0% of classes are taught by teaching assistants.

ACADEMICS

Degrees: Bachelor's; Certificate; Diploma; Master's. **Classes:** Most classes have 10–19 students. **Most popular majors:** Multi/Interdisciplinary Studies, Other; Business, Management, Marketing, and Related Support Services, Other. **Special Study Options:** Accelerated program; Distance learning; Double major; English as a Second Language (ESL); Honors program; Independent study; Internships; Student-designed major; Study abroad. **Honors programs:** The Honors Program is designed to challenge and engage high-achieving students in study and co-curricular activities that foster their scholarship, initiative, and leadership. **Combined degree programs:** BA/MA. **Disability Services offered:** Note-taking services; Tutors. **Career services:** Career assessment; Career/job search classes; Internships.

FACILITIES

Housing: Coed dorms; 99% of campus accessible to physically disabled. **Special Academic Facilities/Equipment:** McLean Observatory.

CAMPUS LIFE

Environment: Village. **Activities:** Choral groups; International Student Organization; Literary magazine; Student government; Student newspaper. 10 registered organizations, 1 honor society, 2 religious organizations on campus. **Athletics (Intercollegiate):** *Men:* equestrian sports, skiing (downhill/Alpine). *Women:* equestrian sports, skiing (downhill/Alpine). **On-Campus Highlights:** Tahoe Center for Environmental Sciences. **Environmental Initiatives:** Sierra Nevada College's four Core Themes are Sustainability, Professional Preparedness, Entrepreneurship, and Liberal Arts.

ADMISSIONS

Freshman Academic Profile: Average high school GPA 3.0. 0% in top 10% of high school class, 20% in top 25% of high school class, 50% in top 50% of high school class. 80% from public high schools. **Test Scores:** SAT Math middle 50% range 430–530. SAT EBRW middle 50% range 440–540. ACT middle 50% range 17–25. **Basis for Candidate Selection:** *Important factors include:* academic GPA, application essay, recommendation(s). *Other factors include:* rigor of secondary school record, class rank, standardized test scores, interview, extracurricular activities, talent/ability, character/personal qualities, first generation, alumni/ae relation, geographical residence, state residency, religious affiliation/commitment, racial/ethnic status, volunteer work, work experience, level of applicant's interest. **Freshman Admission Requirements:** High school diploma is required and GED is accepted. *Academic units recommended:* 4 English, 3 math, 2 science, 2 science labs, 2 social studies. **Freshman Admission Statistics:** 604 applied, 87% admitted, 17% enrolled. **Transfer Admission Requirements:** College transcript(s), essay or personal statement. Lowest grade transferable C. **General Admission Information:** Priority deadline 2/15. Regular application deadline 8/28. Non-fall registration accepted. Admission may be deferred for a maximum of 1 year.

COSTS AND FINANCIAL AID

Annual tuition $28,170. Room and board $12,066. Required fees $979. Average book and supplies expense $1,600. **Required Forms and Deadlines:** FAFSA. **Types of Aid:** *Need-based scholarships/grants:* College/university scholarship or grant aid from institutional funds; Federal Pell; Private scholarships; SEOG; State scholarships/grants. *Loans:* Direct PLUS loans; Direct Subsidized Stafford Loans; Direct Unsubsidized Stafford Loans. **Student Employment:** Federal Work-Study Program available. Institutional employment available. **Financial Aid Statistics:** 100% needy freshmen, 100% needy undergrads receive need-based scholarship or grant aid. 100% freshmen, 100% undergrads receive non-need-based scholarship or grant aid. 100% freshmen, 100% undergrads receive need-based self-help aid. 0% freshmen, 1% undergrads receive athletic scholarships. 62% freshmen, 65% undergrads receive any aid. **Criteria awarding aid:** *Non-need-based:* Academics, Alumni affiliation, Athletics, State/district residency.

SIMMONS UNIVERSITY

300 The Fenway, Boston, MA 02115
Phone: 617-521-2051 **Financial Aid Phone:** 617-521-2037
E-mail: ugadm@simmons.edu **CEEB Code:** 3761
Fax: 617-521-3190 **Website:** www.simmons.edu **ACT Code:** 1892

This private school was founded in 1899. It has a 12 acre campus.

RATINGS

Admissions Selectivity Rating: 82   **Fire Safety Rating:** 85   **Green Rating:** 67

STUDENTS AND FACULTY

Enrollment: 1,751. **Student Body:** 100% female, 0% male, 38% out-of-state, 5% international (11 countries represented). Asian 11%, African American 7%, Caucasian 62%, Hispanic 8%, Native American 0%, Pacific Islander 0%, Two or more races 5%, Race unknown 3%.
Retention and Graduation: 83% freshmen return for sophomore year. 72% freshmen graduate within 4 years. 81% freshmen graduate within 6 years. 23% grads go on to further study within 1 year. **Faculty:** Student/faculty ratio 8:1.

231 full-time faculty, 60% hold PhDs, 20% are members of minority groups, 72% are women. 0% of classes are taught by teaching assistants.

ACADEMICS

Degrees: Bachelor's; Doctoral degree—professional practice; Doctoral degree research/scholarship; Master's; Post-master's certificate. **Classes:** Most classes have 10–19 students. Most lab/discussion sessions have fewer than 10 students. **Most popular majors:** Nursing Practice. **Special Study Options:** Accelerated program; Cross-registration; Distance learning; Double major; Exchange student program (domestic); Honors program; Independent study; Internships; Liberal arts/career combination; Student-designed major; Study abroad; Teacher certification program. **Honors programs:** The Simmons Honors Program is an interdisciplinary program that develops thought leaders for the 21st century through rigorous curricular and experiential programming. The Honors Program engages motivated students, enhancing the undergraduate experience of students in all majors by guiding them through complex intellectual tasks and problems. All Honors students are advised to seek depth in their major discipline and to enhance this knowledge through exploration of other departments and programs. Students in the Honors Program are part of a "community of scholars" and offered an enriched curriculum that is presented in small seminars and team-taught courses. This community includes professors who are teacher/scholars, bringing their own research and community engagement into the classroom and creating intellectual settings that challenge Honors students to push themselves beyond what they thought possible. Outside of the classroom, the Honors Program gives opportunities for students to expand their knowledge through study abroad opportunities, access to undergraduate research programs, connections to Honors alumnae/i, and engagement with the city of Boston. **Combined degree programs:** BA/MA. **Disability Services offered:** Note-taking services; Reader services; Tape recorders; Tutors. **Career services:** Alumni network; Alumni services; Career assessment; Career/job search classes; Internships; Regional alumni.

FACILITIES

Housing: Special housing for disabled students; Theme housing; Wellness housing; Women's dorms; 90% of campus accessible to physically disabled. **Special Academic Facilities/Equipment:** Trustman Art Gallery, Nursing Simulation Lab, Rowing practice tanks in Sports Center, Comm Lab, Computer Labs.

CAMPUS LIFE

Environment: Metropolis. **Activities:** Campus Ministries; Choral groups; Concert band; Dance; Drama/theater; International Student Organization; Jazz band; Literary magazine; Model UN; Music ensembles; Musical theater; Radio station; Student government; Student newspaper; Symphony orchestra; Yearbook. 78 registered organizations, 4 religious organizations on campus. **Athletics (Intercollegiate):** *Women:* basketball, crew/rowing, diving, field hockey, lacrosse, soccer, softball, swimming, tennis, volleyball. **On-Campus Highlights:** Sports Center. **Environmental Initiatives:** We are committed to maximizing recycling and composting opportunities to minimize landfill waste.

ADMISSIONS

Freshman Academic Profile: Average high school GPA 3.9. 28% in top 10% of high school class, 69% in top 25% of high school class, 72% in top 50% of high school class. 84% from public high schools. **Test Scores:** SAT Math middle 50% range 540–630. SAT EBRW middle 50% range 570–660. ACT middle 50% range 23–29. **Basis for Candidate Selection:** *Very important factors include:* rigor of secondary school record, class rank, academic GPA, application essay, standardized test scores, recommendation(s). *Important factors include:* extracurricular activities. *Other factors include:* interview, volunteer work, work experience. **Freshman Admission Requirements:** High school diploma is required and GED is accepted. *Academic units required:* 4 English, 4 math, 3 science, 3 foreign language, 3 social studies, 3 history. **Freshman Admission Statistics:** 2,933 applied, 73% admitted, 20% enrolled. **Transfer Admission Requirements:** High school transcript, college transcript(s), essay or personal statement, statement of good standing from prior institution(s). Minimum college GPA of 2.8 required. Lowest grade transferable C+. **General Admission Information:** Application fee $55. Priority deadline 11/1. Regular application deadline 2/1. Non-fall registration accepted. Admission may be deferred for a maximum of 1 year.

COSTS AND FINANCIAL AID

Annual tuition $42,080. Room and board $15,660. Required fees $1,250. Average book and supplies expense $1,280. **Required Forms and Deadlines:** FAFSA. **Notification of Awards:** Applicants will be notified of awards on a rolling basis beginning 12/19. **Types of Aid:** *Need-based scholarships/grants:* College/university scholarship or grant aid from institutional funds; Federal Pell; Private scholarships; SEOG; State scholarships/grants. *Loans:* Direct PLUS loans; Direct Subsidized Stafford Loans; Direct Unsubsidized Stafford Loans. **Student Employment:** Federal Work-Study Program available. **Financial Aid Statistics:** 99% needy freshmen, 100% needy undergrads receive need-based scholarship or grant aid. 29% freshmen, 15% undergrads receive non-need-based scholarship or grant aid. 68% freshmen, 81% undergrads receive need-based self-help aid. 0% freshmen, 0% undergrads receive athletic scholarships. 82% freshmen, 75% undergrads receive any aid. 77% undergrads borrow to pay for school. Average cumulative indebtedness $37,935. **Criteria awarding aid:** *Non-need-based:* Academics, Alumni affiliation.

SKIDMORE COLLEGE

815 North Broadway, Saratoga Springs, NY 12866-1632
Phone: 518-580-5570 **Financial Aid Phone:** 518-580-5750
E-mail: admissions@skidmore.edu **CEEB Code:** 2815
Fax: 518-580-5584 **Website:** www.skidmore.edu **ACT Code:** 2906

This private school was founded in 1903. It has a 890 acre campus.

RATINGS
Admissions Selectivity Rating: 94   **Fire Safety Rating:** 98   **Green Rating:** 94

STUDENTS AND FACULTY
Enrollment: 2,649. **Student Body:** 60% female, 40% male, 66% out-of-state, 11% international (65 countries represented). Asian 6%, African American 5%, Caucasian 62%, Hispanic 9%, Native American 0%, Pacific Islander 0%, Two or more races 5%, Race unknown 2%.
Retention and Graduation: 91% freshmen return for sophomore year. 85% freshmen graduate within 4 years. 89% freshmen graduate within 6 years. 14% grads go on to further study within 1 year. 73% grads pursue arts and sciences degrees. 10% grads pursue law degrees. 6% grads pursue business degrees. 4% grads pursue medical degrees. **Faculty:** Student/faculty ratio 8:1. 286 full-time faculty, 87% hold PhDs, 20% are members of minority groups, 54% are women. 0% of classes are taught by teaching assistants.

ACADEMICS
Degrees: Bachelor's. **Classes:** Most classes have 10–19 students. Most lab/discussion sessions have 10–19 students. **Most popular majors:** English Language and Literature, General; Psychology, General; Business/Commerce, General. **Special Study Options:** Accelerated program; Cross-registration; Distance learning; Double major; Dual enrollment; Exchange student program (domestic); Honors program; Independent study; Internships; Liberal arts/career combination; Student-designed major; Study abroad; Teacher certification program. **Honors programs:** Honors Forum. **Disability Services offered:** Note-taking services; Reader services; Tape recorders; Tutors. **Career services:** Alumni network; Alumni services; Career assessment; Career/job search classes; Internships; Regional alumni.

FACILITIES
Housing: Apartments for single students; Coed dorms; Special housing for disabled students; Theme housing; Wellness housing; 75% of campus accessible to physically disabled. **Special Academic Facilities/Equipment:** Arthur Zankel Music Center; Electronic Music Lab; Frances Young Tang Museum and Art Gallery; DocLab (audiovisual media and documentary storytelling tools); GIS Center for Interdisciplinary Research Lab; Skidmore Community Garden; Human-Performance Lab; First Responder Health and Safety Lab; Gene Expression Lab; Microscopy Imaging Center; Early Childhood Center (lab school affiliated with Education Department); Van Lennep Riding Center; Math-Computer Science Lab (MCS); Community Ecology Lab (includes adjacent North Woods); Skidmore Analytical Interdisciplinary Lab (SAIL).

CAMPUS LIFE
Environment: Town. **Activities:** Campus Ministries; Choral groups; Concert band; Dance; Drama/theater; International Student Organization; Jazz band; Literary magazine; Model UN; Music ensembles; Musical theater; Opera; Radio station; Student government; Student newspaper; Student-run film society; Symphony orchestra; Television station. 128 registered organizations, 16 honor societies, 4 religious organizations on campus. **Athletics (Intercollegiate):** *Men:* baseball, basketball, crew/rowing, diving, golf, ice hockey, lacrosse, soccer, swimming, tennis. *Women:* basketball, crew/rowing, diving, equestrian

sports, field hockey, lacrosse, soccer, softball, swimming, tennis, volleyball. **On-Campus Highlights:** Case Student Center. **Environmental Initiatives:** Skidmore is a leader in geothermal heating and cooling energy among higher education institutions. Currently, 40% of campus is heated and cooled using geothermal energy.

ADMISSIONS
Freshman Academic Profile: 32% in top 10% of high school class, 62% in top 25% of high school class, 90% in top 50% of high school class. 58% from public high schools. **Test Scores:** SAT Math middle 50% range 610–700. SAT EBRW middle 50% range 610–700. ACT middle 50% range 28–32. **Basis for Candidate Selection:** *Very important factors include:* rigor of secondary school record. *Important factors include:* class rank, academic GPA, application essay, recommendation(s), extracurricular activities, talent/ability, character/personal qualities, volunteer work. *Other factors include:* standardized test scores, interview, first generation, alumni/ae relation, geographical residence, racial/ethnic status. **Freshman Admission Requirements:** High school diploma is required and GED is accepted. *Academic units recommended:* 4 English, 4 math, 4 science, 3 science labs, 4 foreign language, 4 social studies. **Freshman Admission Statistics:** 11,102 applied, 30% admitted, 22% enrolled. **Transfer Admission Requirements:** High school transcript, college transcript(s), essay or personal statement, standardized test scores, statement of good standing from prior institution(s). Minimum college GPA of 2.7 required. Lowest grade transferable C. **General Admission Information:** Application fee $65. Regular application deadline 1/15. Admission may be deferred for a maximum of 2 years.

COSTS AND FINANCIAL AID
Annual tuition $55,136. Room and board $15,000. Required fees $1,186. Average book and supplies expense $1,300. **Required Forms and Deadlines:** CSS/Financial Aid PROFILE; Noncustodial PROFILE. **Notification of Awards:** Applicants will be notified of awards on or about 4/1. **Types of Aid:** *Need-based scholarships/grants:* College/university scholarship or grant aid from institutional funds; Federal Pell; Private scholarships; SEOG; State scholarships/grants. *Loans:* Direct PLUS loans; Direct Subsidized Stafford Loans; Direct Unsubsidized Stafford Loans. **Student Employment:** Federal Work-Study Program available. Institutional employment available. **Financial Aid Statistics:** 100% needy freshmen, 100% needy undergrads receive need-based scholarship or grant aid. 4% freshmen, 4% undergrads receive non-need-based scholarship or grant aid. 94% freshmen, 92% undergrads receive need-based self-help aid. 0% freshmen, 0% undergrads receive athletic scholarships. 63% freshmen, 53% undergrads receive any aid. 34% undergrads borrow to pay for school. Average cumulative indebtedness $31,381. **Criteria awarding aid:** *Need-based:* Academics, Leadership. *Non-need-based:* Music/drama.

SLIPPERY ROCK UNIVERSITY OF PENNSYLVANIA

146 North Hall Welcome Center, Slippery Rock, PA 16057
Phone: 724-738-2015 **Financial Aid Phone:** 724-738-2220
E-mail: asktherock@sru.edu **CEEB Code:** 2658
Fax: 724-738-2913 **Website:** http://www.sru.edu **ACT Code:** 3716

This public school was founded in 1889. It has a 660 acre campus.

RATINGS
Admissions Selectivity Rating: 84   **Fire Safety Rating:** 98   **Green Rating:** 87

STUDENTS AND FACULTY
Enrollment: 7,395. **Student Body:** 56% female, 44% male, 8% out-of-state, 1% international (32 countries represented). Asian 1%, African American 5%, Caucasian 86%, Hispanic 3%, Native American <1%, Pacific Islander <1%, Two or more races 4%, Race unknown 1%.
Retention and Graduation: 83% freshmen return for sophomore year. 54% freshmen graduate within 4 years. 68% freshmen graduate within 6 years. **Faculty:** Student/faculty ratio 19:1. 381 full-time faculty, 88% hold PhDs, 18% are members of minority groups, 50% are women. 0% of classes are taught by teaching assistants.

ACADEMICS
Degrees: Bachelor's; Certificate; Doctoral degree—other; Doctoral degree—professional practice; Master's; Post-bachelor's certificate. **Classes:** Most classes have 20–29 students. Most lab/discussion sessions have 20–29 students. **Most popular majors:** Special Education and Teaching, General; Occupational Safety and Health Technology/Technician; Health and Wellness, General. **Special**

Study Options: Distance learning; Double major; Dual enrollment; English as a Second Language (ESL); Exchange student program (domestic); Honors program; Independent study; Internships; Liberal arts/career combination; Student-designed major; Study abroad; Teacher certification program. **Honors programs:** Undergraduate Honors Program. **Combined degree programs:** BA/MA. **Disability Services offered:** Note-taking services; Reader services; Tape recorders; Tutors. **Career services:** Alumni services; Career assessment; Internships; Regional alumni.

FACILITIES

Housing: Apartments for single students; Coed dorms; Special housing for disabled students; 90% of campus accessible to physically disabled. **Special Academic Facilities/Equipment:** Environmental education centers, planetarium, herbarium, artificial intelligence & robotics lab, 3-D printer, math emporium, SCALE-UP collaborative classroom, psychophysiology teaching system, sustainable enterprise accelerator, equestrian center, crime scene investigation room, counselor training & observation equipment, historic inn and museum of rural life, one-room schoolhouse museum. Residence halls offer Living Learning Communities (LLCs) with access to special facilities and equipment, formal and informal interaction with professors, opportunities for professional networking, and social & cultural activities.

CAMPUS LIFE

Environment: Rural. **Activities:** Campus Ministries; Choral groups; Concert band; Dance; Drama/theater; International Student Organization; Jazz band; Literary magazine; Marching band; Model UN; Music ensembles; Musical theater; Radio station; Student government; Student newspaper; Student-run film society; Symphony orchestra; Television station. 160 registered organizations, 10 honor societies, 6 religious organizations, 11 fraternities, 8 sororities on campus. **Athletics (Intercollegiate):** *Men:* baseball, basketball, cheerleading, cross-country, football, soccer, track/field (outdoor), track/field (indoor). *Women:* basketball, cheerleading, cross-country, field hockey, lacrosse, soccer, softball, tennis, track/field (outdoor), track/field (indoor), volleyball. **On-Campus Highlights:** Aebersold Recreation Center.

ADMISSIONS

Freshman Academic Profile: Average high school GPA 3.4. 11% in top 10% of high school class, 35% in top 25% of high school class, 71% in top 50% of high school class. 93% from public high schools. **Test Scores:** SAT Math middle 50% range 500–580. SAT EBRW middle 50% range 500–590. ACT middle 50% range 19–24. **Basis for Candidate Selection:** *Important factors include:* rigor of secondary school record, class rank, academic GPA, standardized test scores. *Other factors include:* application essay, recommendation(s), talent/ability. **Freshman Admission Requirements:** High school diploma is required and GED is accepted. *Academic units recommended:* 4 English, 3 math, 3 science, 1 science lab, 2 foreign language, 3 social studies, 3 history. **Freshman Admission Statistics:** 5,807 applied, 70% admitted, 39% enrolled. **Transfer Admission Requirements:** College transcript(s). Minimum college GPA of 2.0 required. Lowest grade transferable C. **General Admission Information:** Application fee $30. Non-fall registration accepted. Admission may be deferred for a maximum of 1 year.

COSTS AND FINANCIAL AID

Annual in-state tuition $7,716. Annual out-of-state tuition $15,432. Room and board $10,446. Required fees $2,791. Average book and supplies expense $1,590. **Required Forms and Deadlines:** FAFSA. **Notification of Awards:** Applicants will be notified of awards on a rolling basis beginning 12/12. **Types of Aid:** *Need-based scholarships/grants:* College/university scholarship or grant aid from institutional funds; Federal Pell; Private scholarships; SEOG; State scholarships/grants. *Loans:* Direct PLUS loans; Direct Subsidized Stafford Loans; Direct Unsubsidized Stafford Loans. **Student Employment:** Federal Work-Study Program available. Institutional employment available. **Financial Aid Statistics:** 70% needy freshmen, 69% needy undergrads receive need-based scholarship or grant aid. 50% freshmen, 34% undergrads receive non-need-based scholarship or grant aid. 90% freshmen, 87% undergrads receive need-based self-help aid. 4% freshmen, 4% undergrads receive athletic scholarships. 91% freshmen, 93% undergrads receive any aid. 82% undergrads borrow to pay for school. Average cumulative indebtedness $37,450. **Criteria awarding aid:** *Need-based:* Academics, Minority status. *Non-need-based:* Academics, Alumni affiliation, Art, Athletics, Job skills, Leadership, Minority status, Music/drama, State/district residency.

SMITH COLLEGE

Best Colleges

7 College Lane, Northampton, MA 01063
Phone: 413-585-2500 **Financial Aid Phone:** 413-585-2530
E-mail: admission@smith.edu **CEEB Code:** 3762
Fax: 413-585-2527 **Website:** www.smith.edu **ACT Code:** 1894

This private school was founded in 1871. It has a 147 acre campus.

RATINGS
Admissions Selectivity Rating: 96   **Fire Safety Rating:** 84   **Green Rating:** 91

STUDENTS AND FACULTY
Enrollment: 2,484. **Student Body:** 100% female, 0% male, 81% out-of-state, 14% international (59 countries represented). Asian 9%, African American 7%, Caucasian 48%, Hispanic 12%, Native American <1%, Pacific Islander <1%, Two or more races 5%, Race unknown 6%.
Retention and Graduation: 93% freshmen return for sophomore year. 82% freshmen graduate within 4 years. 88% freshmen graduate within 6 years. **Faculty:** Student/faculty ratio 8:1. 290 full-time faculty, 98% hold PhDs, 21% are members of minority groups, 57% are women. 0% of classes are taught by teaching assistants.

ACADEMICS
Degrees: Bachelor's; Doctoral degree research/scholarship; Master's; Post-bachelor's certificate; Post-master's certificate. **Classes:** Most classes have 10–19 students. **Most popular majors:** Economics, General; Political Science and Government, General; Psychology, General. **Special Study Options:** Accelerated program; Cross-registration; Double major; Exchange student program (domestic); Honors program; Independent study; Internships; Student-designed major; Study abroad; Teacher certification program. **Disability Services offered:** Note-taking services; Reader services; Tape recorders; Tutors. **Career services:** Alumni network; Alumni services; Career assessment; Career/job search classes; Internships; Regional alumni.

FACILITIES
Housing: Cooperative housing; Wellness housing; Women's dorms; 85% of campus accessible to physically disabled. **Special Academic Facilities/Equipment:** Art museum, printing, darkroom, and sculpture facilities, dance, electronic music, television, and theatre studios, recital hall, rehearsal rooms, multimedia language lab, early childhood/elementary education campus school, two electronic classrooms, physiology and horticultural labs, animal care facilities, two electron microscopes, greenhouses, observatories.

CAMPUS LIFE
Environment: Town. **Activities:** Campus Ministries; Choral groups; Concert band; Dance; Drama/theater; International Student Organization; Jazz band; Literary magazine; Model UN; Music ensembles; Musical theater; Radio station; Student government; Student newspaper; Symphony orchestra; Television station; Yearbook. 100 registered organizations, 3 honor societies, 9 religious organizations on campus. **Athletics (Intercollegiate):** *Women:* basketball, crew/rowing, cross-country, diving, equestrian sports, field hockey, lacrosse, skiing (downhill/Alpine), soccer, softball, squash, swimming, tennis, track/field (outdoor), track/field (indoor), volleyball. **On-Campus Highlights:** Smith Art Museum. **Environmental Initiatives:** A natural gas fired cogeneration facility went online in October 2008, which generates most campus electric use and achieves 80% efficiency with new absorption chillers.

ADMISSIONS
Freshman Academic Profile: Average high school GPA 4.0. 72% in top 10% of high school class, 96% in top 25% of high school class, 100% in top 50% of high school class. 62% from public high schools. **Test Scores:** SAT Math middle 50% range 670–770. SAT EBRW middle 50% range 670–750. ACT middle 50% range 31–34. **Basis for Candidate Selection:** *Very important factors include:* rigor of secondary school record, academic GPA, application essay, recommendation(s), character/personal qualities. *Important factors include:* class rank, interview, extracurricular activities, talent/ability. *Other factors include:* standardized test scores, first generation, alumni/ae relation, racial/ethnic status, volunteer work, work experience. **Freshman Admission Requirements:** High school diploma or equivalent is not required *Academic units recommended:* 4 English, 3 math, 3 science, 3 science labs, 3 foreign language, 2 history,

1 academic elective. **Freshman Admission Statistics:** 5,780 applied, 31% admitted, 36% enrolled. **Transfer Admission Requirements:** High school transcript, college transcript(s), essay or personal statement, statement of good standing from prior institution(s). Lowest grade transferable C. **General Admission Information:** Regular application deadline 1/15. Admission may be deferred for a maximum of 1 year.

COSTS AND FINANCIAL AID
Annual tuition $53,940. Room and board $18,130. Required fees $284. Average book and supplies expense $800. **Required Forms and Deadlines:** CSS/Financial Aid PROFILE; FAFSA; Institution's own financial aid form; Noncustodial PROFILE;. **Notification of Awards:** Applicants will be notified of awards on or about 4/1. **Types of Aid:** *Need-based scholarships/grants:* College/university scholarship or grant aid from institutional funds; Federal Pell; Private scholarships; SEOG; State scholarships/grants. *Loans:* Direct PLUS loans; Direct Subsidized Stafford Loans; Direct Unsubsidized Stafford Loans. **Student Employment:** Federal Work-Study Program available. Institutional employment available. **Financial Aid Statistics:** 96% needy freshmen, 97% needy undergrads receive need-based scholarship or grant aid. 3% freshmen, 2% undergrads receive non-need-based scholarship or grant aid. 90% freshmen, 93% undergrads receive need-based self-help aid. 0% freshmen, 0% undergrads receive athletic scholarships. 70.4% freshmen, 71.2% undergrads receive any aid. 58% undergrads borrow to pay for school. Average cumulative indebtedness $22,083. **Criteria awarding aid:** *Non-need-based:* Academics, State/district residency.

SOKA UNIVERSITY OF AMERICA

1 University Drive, Aliso Viejo, CA 92656-8081
Phone: (949) 480-4150 **Financial Aid Phone:** 949-480-4112
E-mail: admission@soka.edu **CEEB Code:** 4066
Fax: (949) 480-4151 **Website:** www.soka.edu **ACT Code:** 467

This private school was founded in 1987. It has a 103 acre campus.

RATINGS
Admissions Selectivity Rating: 94   **Fire Safety Rating:** 96   **Green Rating:** 73

STUDENTS AND FACULTY
Enrollment: 405. **Student Body:** 65% female, 35% male, 55% out-of-state, 45% international (36 countries represented). Asian 14%, African American 3%, Caucasian 18%, Hispanic 11%, Native American 0%, Pacific Islander 1%, Two or more races 5%, Race unknown 3%.
Retention and Graduation: 94% freshmen return for sophomore year. 88% freshmen graduate within 4 years. 89% freshmen graduate within 6 years. 21% grads go on to further study within 1 year. 67% grads pursue arts and sciences degrees. 10% grads pursue law degrees. 0% grads pursue business degrees. 2% grads pursue medical degrees. **Faculty:** Student/faculty ratio 7:1. 51 full-time faculty, 98% hold PhDs, 33% are members of minority groups, 45% are women. 0% of classes are taught by teaching assistants.

ACADEMICS
Degrees: Bachelor's; Master's. **Classes:** Most classes have 10–19 students. Most lab/discussion sessions have 40–49 students. **Most popular majors:** Liberal Arts and Sciences/Liberal Studies. **Special Study Options:** Independent study; Internships; Study abroad. **Disability Services offered:** Note-taking services; Reader services; Tape recorders; Tutors. **Career services:** Alumni network; Alumni services; Career assessment; Career/job search classes; Internships.

FACILITIES
Housing: Coed dorms; Special housing for disabled students; Theme housing; Wellness housing; 100% of campus accessible to physically disabled. **Special Academic Facilities/Equipment:** Performing Arts Center, Black Box Theater, Art Gallery, Conference Center, Library, Information Technology Center, Science Hall.

CAMPUS LIFE
Environment: Town. **Activities:** Choral groups; Concert band; Dance; Drama/theater; International Student Organization; Jazz band; Literary magazine; Model UN; Music ensembles; Musical theater; Student government; Student newspaper; Symphony orchestra. 39 registered organizations on campus.
Athletics (Intercollegiate): *Men:* cross-country, diving, soccer, swimming, track/field (outdoor). *Women:* cross-country, diving, soccer, swimming, track/field (outdoor). **On-Campus Highlights:** Residence Halls.

ADMISSIONS
Freshman Academic Profile: Average high school GPA 3.7. 62% in top 10% of high school class, 38% in top 25% of high school class, 100% in top 50% of high school class. 97% from public high schools. **Test Scores:** SAT Math middle 50% range 650–750. SAT EBRW middle 50% range 590–680. ACT middle 50% range 26–32. **Basis for Candidate Selection:** *Very important factors include:* rigor of secondary school record, academic GPA, application essay, standardized test scores, recommendation(s), extracurricular activities, character/personal qualities. *Important factors include:* talent/ability. *Other factors include:* class rank, interview, first generation, geographical residence, state residency, racial/ethnic status, work experience. **Freshman Admission Requirements:** High school diploma is required and GED is accepted. *Academic units recommended:* 4 English, 3 math, 2 science, 2 science labs, 2 foreign language, 1 social studies, 2 history. **Freshman Admission Statistics:** 504 applied, 40% admitted, 53% enrolled. **General Admission Information:** Application fee $45. Priority deadline 11/1. Regular application deadline 1/15. Admission may be deferred for a maximum of 1 year.

COSTS AND FINANCIAL AID
Annual tuition $33,320. Room and board $13,422. Required fees $1,912. Average book and supplies expense $1,080. **Required Forms and Deadlines:** FAFSA; Institution's own financial aid form; State aid form. **Notification of Awards:** Applicants will be notified of awards on or about 3/15. **Types of Aid:** *Need-based scholarships/grants:* College/university scholarship or grant aid from institutional funds; Federal Pell; Private scholarships; SEOG; State scholarships/grants. *Loans:* Direct PLUS loans; Direct Subsidized Stafford Loans; Direct Unsubsidized Stafford Loans. **Student Employment:** Federal Work-Study Program available. Institutional employment available. **Financial Aid Statistics:** 100% needy freshmen, 100% needy undergrads receive need-based scholarship or grant aid. 100% freshmen, 100% undergrads receive non-need-based scholarship or grant aid. 71% freshmen, 80% undergrads receive need-based self-help aid. 4% freshmen, 3% undergrads receive athletic scholarships. 100% freshmen, 100% undergrads receive any aid. 52% undergrads borrow to pay for school. Average cumulative indebtedness $18,098. **Criteria awarding aid:** *Need-based:* Academics. *Non-need-based:* Academics, Athletics, Leadership, Minority status.

SONOMA STATE UNIVERSITY

1801 East Cotati Avenue, Rohnert Park, CA 94928
Phone: 707-664-2778 **Financial Aid Phone:** (707)664-2389
E-mail: student.outreach@sonoma.edu **CEEB Code:** 4723
Fax: 707-664-2060 **Website:** www.sonoma.edu **ACT Code:** 431

This public school was founded in 1960. It has a 269 acre campus.

RATINGS
Admissions Selectivity Rating: 74   **Fire Safety Rating:** 92   **Green Rating:** 70

STUDENTS AND FACULTY
Enrollment: 8,532. **Student Body:** 61% female, 39% male, 3% international. Asian 5%, African American 2%, Caucasian 43%, Hispanic 33%, Native American <1%, Pacific Islander <1%, Two or more races 6%, Race unknown 6%.
Retention and Graduation: 80% freshmen return for sophomore year. 29% freshmen graduate within 4 years. 58% freshmen graduate within 6 years. **Faculty:** Student/faculty ratio 23:1. 251 full-time faculty, 98% hold PhDs, 22% are members of minority groups, 49% are women. 1% of classes are taught by teaching assistants.

ACADEMICS
Degrees: Bachelor's; Master's. **Classes:** Most classes have 20–29 students. Most lab/discussion sessions have 20–29 students. **Most popular majors:** Liberal Arts and Sciences, General Studies and Humanities, Other; Business/Commerce, General. **Special Study Options:** Accelerated program; Cross-registration; Distance learning; Double major; Dual enrollment; English as a Second Language (ESL); Exchange student program (domestic); External degree program; Honors program; Independent study; Internships; Liberal arts/career combination; Student-designed major; Study abroad; Teacher certification

program. **Combined degree programs:** BA/MA. **Disability Services offered:** Note-taking services; Reader services; Tape recorders; Tutors. **Career services:** Career/job search classes; Internships.

FACILITIES

Housing: Apartments for single students; Coed dorms; 99% of campus accessible to physically disabled. **Special Academic Facilities/Equipment:** Performing arts center, observatory, electron microscope, seismograph, information technology center, environmental technology center, high technology high school, nature preserve.

CAMPUS LIFE

Environment: Town. **Activities:** Choral groups; Dance; Drama/theater; Jazz band; Literary magazine; Music ensembles; Musical theater; Opera; Pep band; Radio station; Student government; Student newspaper; Symphony orchestra. 109 registered organizations, 2 honor societies, 4 religious organizations, 8 fraternities, 10 sororities on campus. **Athletics (Intercollegiate):** *Men:* baseball, basketball, soccer, tennis. *Women:* basketball, cross-country, soccer, softball, tennis, track/field (outdoor), volleyball. **On-Campus Highlights:** Schultz Information Center. **Environmental Initiatives:** Energy efficiency.

ADMISSIONS

Freshman Academic Profile: Average high school GPA 3.2. **Test Scores:** SAT Math middle 50% range 490–580. SAT EBRW middle 50% range 490–590. ACT middle 50% range 18–23. **Basis for Candidate Selection:** *Very important factors include:* academic GPA, standardized test scores. *Other factors include:* geographical residence. **Freshman Admission Requirements:** High school diploma is required and GED is accepted. *Academic units required:* 4 English, 3 math, 2 science, 1 science lab, 2 foreign language, 2 history, 1 academic elective, 1 visual/performing arts, 1 unit from above areas or other academic areas. **Freshman Admission Statistics:** 14,129 applied, 92% admitted, 14% enrolled. **Transfer Admission Requirements:** College transcript(s). Minimum college GPA of 2.0 required. Lowest grade transferable D. **General Admission Information:** Application fee $55. Priority deadline 3/1. Regular application deadline 11/30. Non-fall registration accepted.

COSTS AND FINANCIAL AID

Annual in-state tuition $5,742. Annual out-of-state tuition $17,622. Room and board $13,960. Required fees $2,056. Average book and supplies expense $1,916. **Required Forms and Deadlines:** FAFSA. **Notification of Awards:** Applicants will be notified of awards on a rolling basis beginning 3/25. **Types of Aid:** *Need-based scholarships/grants:* College/university scholarship or grant aid from institutional funds; Federal Pell; Private scholarships; SEOG; State scholarships/grants; United Negro College Fund. *Loans:* Direct PLUS loans; Direct Subsidized Stafford Loans; Direct Unsubsidized Stafford Loans. **Student Employment:** Federal Work-Study Program available. Institutional employment available. **Financial Aid Statistics:** 71% needy freshmen, 73% needy undergrads receive need-based scholarship or grant aid. 36% freshmen, 36% undergrads receive non-need-based scholarship or grant aid. 54% freshmen, 55% undergrads receive need-based self-help aid. 0% freshmen, 0% undergrads receive athletic scholarships. 59% freshmen, 51% undergrads receive any aid. **Criteria awarding aid:** *Need-based:* Academics, Minority status. *Non-need-based:* Academics, Alumni affiliation, Art, Athletics, Leadership, Minority status, Music/drama.

SOUTH DAKOTA SCHOOL OF MINES AND TECHNOLOGY

501 East St. Joseph Street, Rapid City, SD 57701-3995
Phone: 605-394-2414 **Financial Aid Phone:** 605-394-2274
E-mail: admissions@sdsmt.edu **CEEB Code:** 3470
Fax: 605-394-1979 **Website:** www.sdsmt.edu **ACT Code:** 3922

This public school was founded in 1885. It has a 120 acre campus.

RATINGS

Admissions Selectivity Rating: 80   **Fire Safety Rating:** 95   **Green Rating:** 74

STUDENTS AND FACULTY

Enrollment: 2,353. **Student Body:** 20% female, 80% male, 53% out-of-state, 3% international (25 countries represented). Asian 1%, African American 2%, Caucasian 84%, Hispanic 5%, Native American 2%, Pacific Islander <1%, Two or more races 3%, Race unknown 1%.
Retention and Graduation: 78% freshmen return for sophomore year. 21% grads go on to further study within 1 year. 3% grads pursue arts and sciences

degrees. 1% grads pursue law degrees. 1% grads pursue business degrees. 2% grads pursue medical degrees. **Faculty:** Student/faculty ratio 15:1. 151 full-time faculty, 85% hold PhDs, 15% are members of minority groups, 26% are women.

ACADEMICS

Degrees: Associate; Bachelor's; Certificate; Doctoral degree research/scholarship; Master's; Post-bachelor's certificate. **Classes:** Most classes have 20–29 students. **Most popular majors:** Civil Engineering, General; Chemical Engineering; Mechanical Engineering. **Special Study Options:** Cooperative education program; Cross-registration; Distance learning; Double major; Dual enrollment; English as a Second Language (ESL); Independent study; Internships; Study abroad. **Disability Services offered:** Note-taking services; Reader services; Tape recorders; Tutors. **Career services:** Alumni network; Alumni services; Career assessment; Career/job search classes; Internships; Regional alumni.

FACILITIES

Housing: Apartments for married students; Apartments for single students; Coed dorms; Fraternity/sorority housing; Special housing for disabled students; Wellness housing; 81% of campus accessible to physically disabled. **Special Academic Facilities/Equipment:** Museum of geology and paleontology, electron microscope, engineering/mining experiment station, supersonic wind tunnel, 3-D visualization lab, polymer processing lab, friction stir welding lab, high-frequency microwave lab, tech development lab, fluid computational dynamics lab, robotics lab, clean manufacturing lab, institute atmospheric science, paleontology research center and other research institutes. **Campus Network:** 100% of classrooms, 100% of dorms, 100% of dining areas, 100% of common outdoor areas have wireless network access.

CAMPUS LIFE

Environment: Town. **Activities:** Campus Ministries; Choral groups; Concert band; Dance; Drama/theater; International Student Organization; Jazz band; Music ensembles; Pep band; Radio station; Student government; Student newspaper. 82 registered organizations, 5 honor societies, 7 religious organizations, 1 fraternity, 1 sorority on campus. **Athletics (Intercollegiate):** *Men:* basketball, cross-country, football, golf, track/field (outdoor), track/field (indoor). *Women:* basketball, cross-country, golf, track/field (outdoor), track/field (indoor), volleyball. **On-Campus Highlights:** Surbeck Student Center. **Environmental Initiatives:** A minimun of LEED Silver is required on all new construction or renovation.

ADMISSIONS

Freshman Academic Profile: Average high school GPA 3.6. 24% in top 10% of high school class, 56% in top 25% of high school class, 86% in top 50% of high school class. **Test Scores:** SAT Math middle 50% range 550–660. SAT EBRW middle 50% range 490–630. ACT middle 50% range 24–29. **Basis for Candidate Selection:** *Very important factors include:* rigor of secondary school record, class rank, academic GPA, standardized test scores. *Other factors include:* extracurricular activities, talent/ability, character/personal qualities, volunteer work, work experience. **Freshman Admission Requirements:** High school diploma is required and GED is accepted. *Academic units required:* 4 English, 4 math, 4 science, 3 science labs, 2 foreign language, 3 social studies, 0.5 computer science, 1 visual/performing arts. *Academic units recommended:* 4 English, 4 math, 4 science, 3 science labs, 2 foreign language, 3 social studies, 0.5 computer science, 1 visual/performing arts. **Freshman Admission Statistics:** 1,368 applied, 85% admitted, 43% enrolled. **Transfer Admission Requirements:** College transcript(s), statement of good standing from prior institution(s). Minimum college GPA of 2.0 required. Lowest grade transferable D. **General Admission Information:** Application fee $20. Non-fall registration accepted. Admission may be deferred for a maximum of 1 semester.

COSTS AND FINANCIAL AID

Annual in-state tuition $7,340. Annual out-of-state tuition $11,500. Room and board $7,720. Required fees $3,820. Average book and supplies expense $2,000. **Required Forms and Deadlines:** FAFSA. **Notification of Awards:** Applicants will be notified of awards on a rolling basis beginning 4/15. **Types of Aid:** *Need-based scholarships/grants:* College/university scholarship or grant aid from institutional funds; Federal Pell; Private scholarships; SEOG; State scholarships/grants. *Loans:* Direct PLUS loans; Direct Subsidized Stafford Loans; Direct Unsubsidized Stafford Loans. **Student Employment:** Federal Work-Study Program available. Institutional employment available. **Financial Aid Statistics:** 77% needy freshmen, 65% needy undergrads receive need-based scholarship or grant aid. 60% freshmen, 38% undergrads receive non-need-based scholarship or grant aid. 79% freshmen, 84% undergrads receive need-based self-help aid. 4% freshmen, 4% undergrads receive athletic scholarships. 90% freshmen, 79% undergrads receive any aid. **Criteria awarding aid:** *Non-need-based:* Academics, Athletics, Leadership, Minority status.

SOUTH DAKOTA STATE UNIVERSITY

Enrollment Services Center, Brookings, SD 57007
Phone: 605-688-4121 **Financial Aid Phone:** 605-688-4695
E-mail: sdsu.admissions@sdstate.edu **CEEB Code:** 6653
Fax: 605-688-6891 **Website:** www.sdstate.edu **ACT Code:** 3924

This public school was founded in 1881. It has a 363 acre campus.

RATINGS
Admissions Selectivity Rating: 73   **Fire Safety Rating:** 91   **Green Rating:** 84

STUDENTS AND FACULTY
Enrollment: 9,317. **Student Body:** 52% female, 48% male, 46% out-of-state, 4% international. Asian 1%, African American 2%, Caucasian 87%, Hispanic 3%, Native American 1%, Pacific Islander <1%, Two or more races 2%, Race unknown <1%.
Retention and Graduation: 76% freshmen return for sophomore year. 36% freshmen graduate within 4 years. **Faculty:** Student/faculty ratio 17:1. 541 full-time faculty, 73% hold PhDs, 15% are members of minority groups, 48% are women.

ACADEMICS
Degrees: Associate; Bachelor's; Certificate; Doctoral degree—professional practice; Doctoral degree research/scholarship; Master's; Post-bachelor's certificate; Post-master's certificate. **Classes:** Most classes have 20–29 students. Most lab/discussion sessions have 10–19 students. **Special Study Options:** Accelerated program; Cross-registration; Distance learning; Double major; Dual enrollment; English as a Second Language (ESL); Exchange student program (domestic); Honors program; Independent study; Internships; Study abroad; Teacher certification program. **Honors programs:** Van D. and Barbara B. Fishback Honors College: http://www.sdstate.edu/Honors/index.cfm. **Disability Services offered:** Note-taking services; Reader services; Tape recorders; Tutors. **Career services:** Career assessment; Career/job search classes; Internships.

FACILITIES
Housing: Apartments for married students; Apartments for single students; Coed dorms; Fraternity/sorority housing; Special housing for disabled students; Wellness housing; 99% of campus accessible to physically disabled. **Special Academic Facilities/Equipment:** South Dakota Art Museum, South Dakota Agricultural Heritage Museum, Northern Plains Bio-stress Laboratory, Animal Disease Research and Diagnostic Lab, McCrory Gardens Education and Visitor Center.

CAMPUS LIFE
Environment: Village. **Activities:** Campus Ministries; Choral groups; Concert band; Dance; Drama/theater; International Student Organization; Jazz band; Literary magazine; Marching band; Model UN; Music ensembles; Musical theater; Pep band; Radio station; Student government; Student newspaper; Symphony orchestra. 200 registered organizations, 8 fraternities, 5 sororities on campus. **Athletics (Intercollegiate):** *Men:* baseball, basketball, cross-country, diving, football, golf, swimming, tennis, track/field (outdoor), track/field (indoor), wrestling. *Women:* basketball, cross-country, diving, equestrian sports, golf, soccer, softball, swimming, tennis, track/field (outdoor), track/field (indoor), volleyball. **On-Campus Highlights:** Performing Arts Center. **Environmental Initiatives:** Establishment of environmental stewardship and sustainability shared governance committee.

ADMISSIONS
Test Scores: SAT Math middle 50% range 520–640. SAT EBRW middle 50% range 490–620. ACT middle 50% range 20–26. **Basis for Candidate Selection:** *Very important factors include:* rigor of secondary school record, class rank, academic GPA, standardized test scores. *Other factors include:* application essay, recommendation(s). **Freshman Admission Requirements:** High school diploma is required and GED is accepted. *Academic units required:* 4 English, 3 math, 3 science, 3 science labs, 3 social studies, 1 visual/performing arts. **Freshman Admission Statistics:** 5,390 applied, 92% admitted, enrolled. **Transfer Admission Requirements:** High school transcript, college transcript(s), statement of good standing from prior institution(s). Minimum college GPA of 2.0 required. Lowest grade transferable D. **General Admission Information:** Application fee $20. Non-fall registration accepted.

COSTS AND FINANCIAL AID
Annual in-state tuition $7,451. Annual out-of-state tuition $10,815. Room and board $7,896. Average book and supplies expense $1,500. **Required Forms and**

Deadlines: FAFSA. **Notification of Awards:** Applicants will be notified of awards on a rolling basis beginning 4/1. **Types of Aid:** *Need-based scholarships/grants:* College/university scholarship or grant aid from institutional funds; Federal Pell; Private scholarships; SEOG; State scholarships/grants. *Loans:* Direct PLUS loans; Direct Subsidized Stafford Loans; Direct Unsubsidized Stafford Loans. **Student Employment:** Federal Work-Study Program available. Institutional employment available. **Financial Aid Statistics:** 37% needy undergrads receive need-based scholarship or grant aid. 43% undergrads receive non-need-based scholarship or grant aid. 5% undergrads receive need-based self-help aid. 0% undergrads receive athletic scholarships. Average cumulative indebtedness $35,201. **Criteria awarding aid:** *Non-need-based:* Academics, Alumni affiliation, Art, Athletics, Leadership, Minority status, Music/drama, State/district residency.

SOUTHEASTERN BIBLE COLLEGE

2545 Valleydale Road, Birmingham, AL 35244
Phone: (205) 970-9211
E-mail: info@sebc.edu
Fax: (205) 970-9207 **Website:** www.sebc.edu

This private school was founded in 1935.

RATINGS
Admissions Selectivity Rating: 75   **Fire Safety Rating:** 60*   **Green Rating:** 60*

STUDENTS AND FACULTY
Enrollment: 143. **Student Body:** 28% female, 72% male, 12% out-of-state. **Retention and Graduation:** 67% freshmen return for sophomore year. **Faculty:** Student/faculty ratio 8:1. 8 full-time faculty, 75% hold PhDs, 0% are members of minority groups, 25% are women. 0% of classes are taught by teaching assistants.

ACADEMICS
Degrees: Associate; Bachelor's; Diploma. **Classes:** Most classes have fewer than 10 students. Most lab/discussion sessions have fewer than 10 students. **Most popular majors:** Bible/Biblical Studies. **Special Study Options:** Double major; Dual enrollment; Internships; Study abroad. **Disability Services offered:** Note-taking services; Tape recorders.

FACILITIES
Housing: Men's dorms; Special housing for disabled students; Women's dorms; 100% of campus accessible to physically disabled. **Campus Network:** 100% of classrooms, 100% of student union, 100% of libraries, 100% of dining areas have wireless network access.

CAMPUS LIFE
Environment: Metropolis. **Activities:** Campus Ministries; Music ensembles; Student government.

ADMISSIONS
Test Scores: ACT middle 50% range 18–23. **Basis for Candidate Selection:** *Very important factors include:* application essay, recommendation(s), interview, religious affiliation/commitment. *Important factors include:* character/personal qualities. *Other factors include:* academic GPA, standardized test scores. **Freshman Admission Requirements:** High school diploma is required and GED is accepted. *Academic units recommended:* 4 English, 4 math, 4 science, 4 social studies, 8 academic electives. **Freshman Admission Statistics:** 18 applied, 100% admitted, 83% enrolled. **Transfer Admission Requirements:** High school transcript, college transcript(s), essay or personal statement. Minimum college GPA of 2.0 required. Lowest grade transferable C. **General Admission Information:** Application fee $30. Priority deadline 8/1. Non-fall registration accepted. Admission may be deferred for a maximum of 1 year.

COSTS AND FINANCIAL AID
Required Forms and Deadlines: FAFSA; Institution's own financial aid form. **Types of Aid:** *Need-based scholarships/grants:* College/university scholarship or grant aid from institutional funds; Federal Pell; SEOG. *Loans:* Direct PLUS loans; Direct Subsidized Stafford Loans; Direct Unsubsidized Stafford Loans. **Student Employment:** Federal Work-Study Program available. **Criteria awarding aid:** *Need-based:* Academics, Leadership. *Non-need-based:* Academics, Leadership.

SOUTHEASTERN LOUISIANA UNIVERSITY

SLU 10752, Hammond, LA 70402
Phone: 985-549-2066 **Financial Aid Phone:** 985-549-2030
E-mail: admissions@southeastern.edu **CEEB Code:** 6656
Fax: 985-549-5632 **Website:** www.southeastern.edu **ACT Code:** 1608

This public school was founded in 1925. It has a 365 acre campus.

RATINGS

Admissions Selectivity Rating: 77   **Fire Safety Rating:** 95   **Green Rating:** 73

STUDENTS AND FACULTY

Enrollment: 10,993. **Student Body:** 63% female, 37% male, 4% out-of-state, 1% international (55 countries represented). Asian 1%, African American 22%, Caucasian 63%, Hispanic 7%, Native American <1%, Pacific Islander <1%, Two or more races 5%, Race unknown 1%.
Retention and Graduation: 67% freshmen return for sophomore year. 41% freshmen graduate within 6 years. **Faculty:** Student/faculty ratio 19:1. 501 full-time faculty, 64% hold PhDs, 13% are members of minority groups, 57% are women. 0% of classes are taught by teaching assistants.

ACADEMICS

Degrees: Associate; Bachelor's; Doctoral degree—professional practice; Doctoral degree research/scholarship; Master's; Post-bachelor's certificate; Post-master's certificate. **Classes:** Most classes have 20–29 students. **Most popular majors:** Registered Nursing/Registered Nurse; Biology/Biological Sciences, General; Business Administration and Management, General. **Special Study Options:** Accelerated program; Cross-registration; Distance learning; Double major; Dual enrollment; English as a Second Language (ESL); Honors program; Independent study; Internships; Study abroad; Teacher certification program. **Honors programs:** Reduced classe size, scholarships, honors residence hall, achievement awards, and honor academic credit shown on the transcript. **Disability Services offered:** Note-taking services; Reader services; Tutors. **Career services:** Alumni network; Alumni services; Career assessment; Internships.

FACILITIES

Housing: Apartments for single students; Coed dorms; Fraternity/sorority housing; Women's dorms; 95% of campus accessible to physically disabled. **Special Academic Facilities/Equipment:** Contemporary Art Gallery; Radio Station; Television Station; Columbia Theatre; Maritime Museum. **Campus Network:** 100% of dorms, 100% of student union, 100% of libraries have wireless network access.

CAMPUS LIFE

Environment: Village. **Activities:** Choral groups; Concert band; Dance; Drama/theater; International Student Organization; Jazz band; Literary magazine; Marching band; Music ensembles; Musical theater; Opera; Pep band; Radio station; Student government; Student newspaper; Symphony orchestra; Television station; Yearbook. 105 registered organizations, 16 honor societies, 12 religious organizations, 11 fraternities, 9 sororities on campus. **Athletics (Intercollegiate):** *Men:* baseball, basketball, cross-country, football, golf, track/field (outdoor), track/field (indoor). *Women:* basketball, cross-country, soccer, softball, tennis, track/field (outdoor), track/field (indoor), volleyball. **On-Campus Highlights:** Student Union. **Environmental Initiatives:** Renewable Energy—investment in solar power, on site waste oil biodiesel fuel production, proactive energy usage reduction management. The university has focused on these areas to reduce both waste and the need for grid power.

ADMISSIONS

Freshman Academic Profile: Average high school GPA 3.3. 12% in top 10% of high school class, 34% in top 25% of high school class, 68% in top 50% of high school class. **Test Scores:** ACT middle 50% range 20–25. **Basis for Candidate Selection:** *Very important factors include:* rigor of secondary school record, academic GPA, standardized test scores. **Freshman Admission Requirements:** High school diploma is required and GED is accepted. *Academic units required:* 4 English, 4 math, 4 science, 2 foreign language, 4 social studies, 1 visual/performing arts. **Freshman Admission Statistics:** 4,248 applied, 90% admitted, 70% enrolled. **Transfer Admission Requirements:** College transcript(s), statement of good standing from prior institution(s). Minimum college GPA of 2.0 required. Lowest grade transferable D. **General Admission Information:** Application fee $20. Priority deadline 7/15. Regular application deadline 8/1. Non-fall registration accepted. Admission may be deferred for a maximum of 1 year.

COSTS AND FINANCIAL AID

Annual in-state tuition $5,777. Annual out-of-state tuition $18,255. Room and board $8,420. Required fees $2,388. Average book and supplies expense $1,300. **Required Forms and Deadlines:** FAFSA. **Notification of Awards:** Applicants will be notified of awards on a rolling basis beginning 4/1. **Types of Aid:** *Need-based scholarships/grants:* College/university scholarship or grant aid from institutional funds; Federal Pell; Private scholarships; SEOG; State scholarships/grants. *Loans:* Direct PLUS loans; Direct Subsidized Stafford Loans; Direct Unsubsidized Stafford Loans. **Student Employment:** Federal Work-Study Program available. Institutional employment available. **Financial Aid Statistics:** 65% needy freshmen, 69% needy undergrads receive need-based scholarship or grant aid. 74% freshmen, 54% undergrads receive non-need-based scholarship or grant aid. 54% freshmen, 65% undergrads receive need-based self-help aid. 1% freshmen, 0% undergrads receive athletic scholarships. 95% freshmen, 76% undergrads receive any aid. 59% undergrads borrow to pay for school. Average cumulative indebtedness $19,736. **Criteria awarding aid:** *Need-based:* Academics, Job skills, Leadership. *Non-need-based:* Academics, Athletics, Job skills, Leadership, Music/drama, State/district residency.

SOUTHEASTERN OKLAHOMA STATE UNIVERSITY

1405 North 4th Avenue, Durant, OK 74701-0609
Phone: 580-745-2060 **Financial Aid Phone:** 580-745-2186
E-mail: admissions@se.edu **CEEB Code:** 6657
Fax: 580-745-4502 **ACT Code:** 3438

This public school was founded in 1909. It has a 268 acre campus.

RATINGS

Admissions Selectivity Rating: 76   **Fire Safety Rating:** 88   **Green Rating:** 60*

STUDENTS AND FACULTY

Enrollment: 3,465. **Student Body:** 55% female, 45% male, 22% out-of-state, 1% international (28 countries represented). Asian 1%, African American 5%, Caucasian 59%, Hispanic 3%, Native American 31%, Race unknown 0%.
Retention and Graduation: 58% freshmen return for sophomore year.
Faculty: Student/faculty ratio 18:1. 143 full-time faculty, 74% hold PhDs, 17% are members of minority groups, 41% are women. 0% of classes are taught by teaching assistants.

ACADEMICS

Degrees: Bachelor's; Master's; Post-master's certificate. **Classes:** Most classes have 20–29 students. Most lab/discussion sessions have 20–29 students. **Most popular majors:** Occupational Safety and Health Technology/Technician; Elementary Education and Teaching; Psychology, General. **Special Study Options:** Distance learning; Double major; Honors program; Independent study; Internships; Teacher certification program. **Honors programs:** Our Honors program offers six different scholarships ranging in value from $6,400 to $26,400 over four years. **Disability Services offered:** Note-taking services; Reader services; Tape recorders; Tutors. **Career services:** Alumni network; Career assessment; Career/job search classes; Internships.

FACILITIES

Housing: Apartments for single students; Coed dorms; 100% of campus accessible to physically disabled. **Special Academic Facilities/Equipment:** Visual and Performing Arts Gallery.

CAMPUS LIFE

Environment: Village. **Activities:** Campus Ministries; Choral groups; Concert band; Dance; Drama/theater; International Student Organization; Jazz band; Literary magazine; Marching band; Music ensembles; Musical theater; Opera; Pep band; Radio station; Student government; Student newspaper; Yearbook. 70 registered organizations, 12 honor societies, 8 religious organizations, 2 fraternities, 2 sororities on campus. **Athletics (Intercollegiate):** *Men:* baseball, basketball, football, golf, tennis. *Women:* basketball, cross-country, softball, tennis, volleyball. **On-Campus Highlights:** Shearer Hall and Suites (New Apartments).

ADMISSIONS

Freshman Academic Profile: Average high school GPA 3.3. 16% in top 10% of high school class, 40% in top 25% of high school class, 77% in top 50% of high school class. 99% from public high schools. **Test Scores:** ACT middle 50% range 18–23. **Basis for Candidate Selection:** *Very important factors include:* class rank, academic GPA, standardized test scores. *Other factors* *include:* rigor of secondary school record, recommendation(s), interview, talent/ability, character/personal qualities, state residency, level of applicant's interest. **Freshman Admission Requirements:** High school diploma is required and GED is accepted. *Academic units required:* 4 English, 3 math, 2 science, 2 science labs, 3 history, 2 academic electives. *Academic units recommended:* 1 foreign language, 1 social studies, 1 computer science. **Freshman Admission Statistics:** 922 applied, 88% admitted, 75% enrolled. **Transfer Admission Requirements:** College transcript(s). Minimum college GPA of 2.0 required. Lowest grade transferable D. **General Admission Information:** Application fee $20. Non-fall registration accepted.

COSTS AND FINANCIAL AID

Annual in-state tuition $3,639. Annual out-of-state tuition $10,010. Room and board $2,005. Average book and supplies expense $800. **Required Forms and Deadlines:** FAFSA; Institution's own financial aid form. **Notification of Awards:** Applicants will be notified of awards on a rolling basis beginning 4/15. **Types of Aid:** *Need-based scholarships/grants:* College/university scholarship or grant aid from institutional funds; Federal Pell; Private scholarships; SEOG; State scholarships/grants. **Student Employment:** Federal Work-Study Program available. Institutional employment available. **Financial Aid Statistics:** 71% needy freshmen, 81% needy undergrads receive need-based scholarship or grant aid. 44% freshmen, 32% undergrads receive non-need-based scholarship or grant aid. 36% freshmen, 58% undergrads receive need-based self-help aid. 10% freshmen, 7% undergrads receive athletic scholarships. 66% freshmen, 65% undergrads receive any aid. **Criteria awarding aid:** *Non-need-based:* Academics, Alumni affiliation, Art, Athletics, Leadership, Minority status, Music/drama, State/district residency.

SOUTHEASTERN UNIVERSITY

1000 Longfellow Blvd., Lakeland, FL 33801
Phone: 863-667-5018 **Financial Aid Phone:** 800-500-8760
E-mail: admission@seu.edu
Fax: 863-667-5200 **Website:** http://www.seu.edu/

This private school, affiliated with the Assemblies of God Church, was founded in 1935. It has a 87 acre campus.

RATINGS

Admissions Selectivity Rating: 89   **Fire Safety Rating:** 99   **Green Rating:** 60*

STUDENTS AND FACULTY

Enrollment: 2,946. **Student Body:** 55% female, 45% male, 32% out-of-state, 2% international. Asian 1%, African American 15%, Caucasian 61%, Hispanic 17%, Native American <1%, Pacific Islander <1%, Two or more races 1%, Race unknown 4%.
Retention and Graduation: 66% freshmen return for sophomore year.
Faculty: Student/faculty ratio 19:1. 118 full-time faculty, 72% hold PhDs, 16% are members of minority groups, 37% are women.

ACADEMICS

Degrees: Associate; Bachelor's; Certificate; Master's; Post-bachelor's certificate. **Classes:** Most classes have 10–19 students. **Most popular majors:** Theology and Religious Vocations, Other; Elementary Education and Teaching; Psychology, General. **Special Study Options:** Distance learning; Double major; Dual enrollment; Honors program; Independent study; Internships; Study abroad; Teacher certification program. **Honors programs:** Honors Program. **Disability Services offered:** Tutors. **Career services:** Career assessment; Internships.

FACILITIES

Housing: Men's dorms; Women's dorms; 100% of campus accessible to physically disabled. **Campus Network:** 100% of classrooms, 100% of dorms, 100% of student union, 100% of libraries, 100% of dining areas, 100% of common outdoor areas have wireless network access.

CAMPUS LIFE

Environment: City. **Activities:** Campus Ministries; Choral groups; Concert band; Dance; Drama/theater; International Student Organization; Jazz band; Music ensembles; Musical theater; Opera; Radio station; Student government; Student newspaper; Television station; Yearbook. **On-Campus Highlights:** Portico Coffeehouse.

ADMISSIONS

Freshman Academic Profile: 77% from public high schools. **Test Scores:** SAT Math middle 50% range 410–520. SAT EBRW middle 50% range 430–560. ACT middle 50% range 18–23. **Basis for Candidate Selection:** *Very important factors include:* character/personal qualities, religious affiliation/commitment. *Important factors include:* academic GPA, application essay, standardized test scores, recommendation(s). *Other factors include:* rigor of secondary school record, class rank, interview, extracurricular activities, talent/ability, first generation, alumni/ae relation, volunteer work, work experience. **Freshman Admission Requirements:** High school diploma is required and GED is accepted. *Academic units recommended:* 4 English, 4 math, 4 science, 1 science lab, 2 foreign language, 4 social studies. **Freshman Admission Statistics:** 3,402 applied, 44% admitted, 61% enrolled. **General Admission Information:** Application fee $40. Regular application deadline 5/1. Non-fall registration accepted.

COSTS AND FINANCIAL AID

Required Forms and Deadlines: FAFSA; Institution's own financial aid form; State aid form. **Notification of Awards:** Applicants will be notified of awards on a rolling basis beginning 1/1. **Types of Aid:** *Need-based scholarships/grants:* College/university scholarship or grant aid from institutional funds; Federal Pell; Private scholarships; SEOG; State scholarships/grants. **Student Employment:** Federal Work-Study Program available. Institutional employment available. **Financial Aid Statistics:** 95% needy freshmen, 96% needy undergrads receive need-based scholarship or grant aid. 10% freshmen, 9% undergrads receive non-need-based scholarship or grant aid. 85% freshmen, 86% undergrads receive need-based self-help aid. 4% freshmen, 3% undergrads receive athletic scholarships. 90% freshmen, 94% undergrads receive any aid. **Criteria awarding aid:** *Non-need-based:* Academics, Athletics, Leadership, Music/drama, State/district residency.

SOUTHEAST MISSOURI STATE UNIVERSITY

One University Plaza, Cape Girardeau, MO 63701
Phone: 573-651-2590 **Financial Aid Phone:** (573) 651-2253
E-mail: admissions@semo.edu **CEEB Code:** 6655
Fax: 573-651-5936 **Website:** www.semo.edu **ACT Code:** 2366

This public school was founded in 1873. It has a 400 acre campus.

RATINGS

Admissions Selectivity Rating: 76   **Fire Safety Rating:** 93   **Green Rating:** 60*

STUDENTS AND FACULTY

Enrollment: 8,000. **Student Body:** 59% female, 41% male, 21% out-of-state, 4% international (41 countries represented). Asian 1%, African American 9%, Caucasian 80%, Hispanic 2%, Native American <1%, Pacific Islander <1%, Two or more races 2%, Race unknown 1%.
Retention and Graduation: 75% freshmen return for sophomore year. 30% freshmen graduate within 4 years. 50% freshmen graduate within 6 years.
Faculty: Student/faculty ratio 19:1. 392 full-time faculty, 75% hold PhDs, 18% are members of minority groups, 53% are women. 12% of classes are taught by teaching assistants.

ACADEMICS

Degrees: Associate; Bachelor's; Certificate; Master's; Post-bachelor's certificate; Post-master's certificate. **Classes:** Most classes have 10–19 students. **Most popular majors:** General Studies; Registered Nursing/Registered Nurse; Business Administration and Management, General. **Special Study Options:** Accelerated program; Distance learning; Double major; Dual enrollment; English as a Second Language (ESL); Honors program; Independent study; Internships; Liberal arts/career combination; Student-designed major; Study abroad; Teacher certification program. **Honors programs:** The Jane Stephens Honors Program encourages intellectual perspective, addresses needs of outstanding students and contributes to the general advancement of learning. Honors students may choose from a variety of honors classes each semester and have the opportunity to work with an Honors Faculty mentor on a capstone, senior project. Honors students receive early registration in the Sophomore and Junior years. The Honors House on campus offers a computer lab, conference room, classroom, lounge, full kitchen and study areas for the use of honors students. Leadership opportunities in the program are available on the Student Honors Council, and our Honors Floor offers honors students suite-style housing in one of our newest residence halls. **Disability Services offered:**

Note-taking services; Reader services; Tape recorders; Tutors. **Career services:** Alumni network; Alumni services; Career assessment; Career/job search classes; Internships; Regional alumni.

FACILITIES

Housing: Coed dorms; Fraternity/sorority housing; Special housing for disabled students; Theme housing; 100% of campus accessible to physically disabled. **Special Academic Facilities/Equipment:** River Campus at Southeast; Crisp Museum; Bedell Performance Hall; Center for Faulkner Studies; Center for Scholarship in Teaching and Learning; Missouri Statewide Early Literacy Intervention Program (MSELIP); Writing Center; University Demonstration Farm; 4 corporate video studios, 2 radio stations; Southeast Explorer; SHOW (Southeast Health on Wheels); Linda Godwin Center for Science and Math Education.

CAMPUS LIFE

Environment: Town. **Activities:** Campus Ministries; Choral groups; Concert band; Dance; Drama/theater; International Student Organization; Jazz band; Literary magazine; Marching band; Music ensembles; Musical theater; Opera; Pep band; Radio station; Student government; Student newspaper; Symphony orchestra. 258 registered organizations, 11 honor societies, 10 religious organizations, 16 fraternities, 13 sororities on campus. **Athletics (Intercollegiate):** *Men:* baseball, basketball, cheerleading, cross-country, football, track/field (outdoor), track/field (indoor). *Women:* basketball, cheerleading, cross-country, gymnastics, soccer, softball, tennis, track/field (outdoor), track/field (indoor), volleyball. **On-Campus Highlights:** River Campus (Visual/Performing Arts).

ADMISSIONS

Freshman Academic Profile: Average high school GPA 3.5. 15% in top 10% of high school class, 42% in top 25% of high school class, 78% in top 50% of high school class. **Test Scores:** SAT Math middle 50% range 500–590. SAT EBRW middle 50% range 500–600. ACT middle 50% range 19–25. **Basis for Candidate Selection:** *Very important factors include:* rigor of secondary school record, academic GPA. *Important factors include:* standardized test scores. *Other factors include:* class rank. **Freshman Admission Requirements:** High school diploma is required and GED is accepted. *Academic units required:* 4 English, 3 math, 3 science, 1 science lab, 2 social studies, 1 history, 3 academic electives, 1 visual/performing arts. **Freshman Admission Statistics:** 4,785 applied, 86% admitted, 37% enrolled. **Transfer Admission Requirements:** College transcript(s). Minimum college GPA of 2.0 required. Lowest grade transferable D. **General Admission Information:** Application fee $30. Priority deadline 12/1. Regular application deadline 7/1. Non-fall registration accepted.

COSTS AND FINANCIAL AID

Annual in-state tuition $6,254. Annual out-of-state tuition $11,991. Room and board $8,935. Required fees $1,164. Average book and supplies expense $520. **Required Forms and Deadlines:** FAFSA. **Notification of Awards:** Applicants will be notified of awards on a rolling basis beginning 2/1. **Types of Aid:** *Need-based scholarships/grants:* College/university scholarship or grant aid from institutional funds; Federal Pell; Private scholarships; SEOG; State scholarships/grants. *Loans:* Direct PLUS loans; Direct Subsidized Stafford Loans; Direct Unsubsidized Stafford Loans. **Student Employment:** Federal Work-Study Program available. Institutional employment available. **Financial Aid Statistics:** 95% needy freshmen, 88% needy undergrads receive need-based scholarship or grant aid. 12% freshmen, 8% undergrads receive non-need-based scholarship or grant aid. 65% freshmen, 69% undergrads receive need-based self-help aid. 2% freshmen, 2% undergrads receive athletic scholarships. 89% freshmen, 83% undergrads receive any aid. 62% undergrads borrow to pay for school. Average cumulative indebtedness $25,380. **Criteria awarding aid:** *Need-based:* Academics, Minority status. *Non-need-based:* Academics, Alumni affiliation, Art, Athletics, Job skills, Leadership, Minority status, Music/drama, State/district residency.

SOUTHERN ADVENTIST UNIVERSITY

P.O. Box 370, Collegedale, TN 37315
Phone: 423-236-2835 **Financial Aid Phone:** 423-236-2894
E-mail: admissions@southern.edu **CEEB Code:** 3518
Fax: 423-236-1835 **ACT Code:** 4006

This private school, affiliated with the Seventh Day Adventist Church, was founded in 1892. It has a 1000 acre campus.

RATINGS

Admissions Selectivity Rating: 80   **Fire Safety Rating:** 94   **Green Rating:** 60*

STUDENTS AND FACULTY

Enrollment: 2,584. **Student Body:** 55% female, 45% male, 69% out-of-state, 5% international. Asian 6%, African American 12%, Caucasian 58%, Hispanic 19%, Native American <1%, Pacific Islander 1%, Two or more races <1%, Race unknown 0%.
Retention and Graduation: 72% freshmen return for sophomore year. 15% grads go on to further study within 1 year. 10% grads pursue arts and sciences degrees. 0% grads pursue law degrees. 1% grads pursue business degrees. 3% grads pursue medical degrees. **Faculty:** Student/faculty ratio 15:1. 146 full-time faculty, 64% hold PhDs, 12% are members of minority groups, 42% are women. 0% of classes are taught by teaching assistants.

ACADEMICS

Degrees: Associate; Bachelor's; Certificate; Master's; Post-master's certificate. **Most popular majors:** Business/Commerce, General; Biology/Biological Sciences, General. **Special Study Options:** Double major; Dual enrollment; English as a Second Language (ESL); Honors program; Independent study; Internships; Study abroad; Teacher certification program. **Honors programs:** Southern Scholars program includes special projects, inter-disciplinary studies, and designated honors courses to provide a challenging and intellectually stimulating educational experience. **Combined degree programs:** BA/MA. **Disability Services offered:** Note-taking services; Reader services; Tape recorders; Tutors.

FACILITIES

Housing: Apartments for married students; Apartments for single students; Men's dorms; Women's dorms; 70% of campus accessible to physically disabled. **Special Academic Facilities/Equipment:** Near-Eastern archaeology teaching collection **Campus Network:** 100% of classrooms, 100% of dorms, 100% of student union, 100% of libraries, 100% of dining areas have wireless network access.

CAMPUS LIFE

Environment: Rural. **Activities:** Campus Ministries; Choral groups; Concert band; Drama/theater; International Student Organization; Jazz band; Music ensembles; Radio station; Student government; Student newspaper; Student-run film society; Symphony orchestra; Television station; Yearbook. 30 registered organizations, 8 honor societies, 3 religious organizations on campus. **On-Campus Highlights:** Student Center. **Environmental Initiatives:** Establishing environmental sustainability committee.

ADMISSIONS

Freshman Academic Profile: Average high school GPA 3.4. 18% from public high schools. **Test Scores:** SAT Math middle 50% range 430–560. SAT EBRW middle 50% range 460–580. ACT middle 50% range 19–25. **Basis for Candidate Selection:** *Very important factors include:* rigor of secondary school record, academic GPA, standardized test scores. **Freshman Admission Requirements:** High school diploma is required and GED is accepted. *Academic units required:* 3 English, 2 math, 2 science, 1 social studies, 1 history, 9 academic electives. *Academic units recommended:* 4 English, 3 math, 3 science, 2 foreign language, 1 social studies, 2 history, 9 academic electives, 1 unit from above areas or other academic areas. **Freshman Admission Statistics:** 1,452 applied, 80% admitted, 54% enrolled. **Transfer Admission Requirements:** College transcript(s). Minimum college GPA of 2 required. Lowest grade transferable D. **General Admission Information:** Application fee $40. Regular application deadline 9/8. Non-fall registration accepted. Admission may be deferred for a maximum of 1 year.

COSTS AND FINANCIAL AID

Annual tuition $17,534. Room and board $5,786. Required fees $790. Average book and supplies expense $1,100. **Required Forms and Deadlines:** FAFSA. **Notification of Awards:** Applicants will be notified of awards on a rolling basis beginning 2/15. **Types of Aid:** *Need-based scholarships/grants:* College/

university scholarship or grant aid from institutional funds; Federal Pell; Private scholarships; SEOG; State scholarships/grants. **Student Employment:** Federal Work-Study Program available. Institutional employment available. **Financial Aid Statistics:** 99% needy freshmen, 98% needy undergrads receive need-based scholarship or grant aid. 82% freshmen, 55% undergrads receive non-need-based scholarship or grant aid. 82% freshmen, 85% undergrads receive need-based self-help aid. 0% freshmen, 0% undergrads receive athletic scholarships. 95% undergrads receive any aid. **Criteria awarding aid:** *Need-based:* Academics, Art. *Non-need-based:* Academics, Alumni affiliation, Art, Leadership, Music/drama.

SOUTHERN CALIFORNIA INSTITUTE OF ARCHITECTURE

SCI-Arc Office of Admissions, Los Angeles, CA 90013-1822
Phone: 213.356.5320 **Financial Aid Phone:** 213-356-5346
E-mail: admissions@sciarc.edu
Fax: 213-613-2260 **Website:** www.sciarc.edu

This private school was founded in 1972.

RATINGS
Admissions Selectivity Rating: 70   **Fire Safety Rating:** 60*   **Green Rating:** 60*

STUDENTS AND FACULTY
Enrollment: 245. **Student Body:** 40% female, 60% male, 40% out-of-state, 20% international (45 countries represented). Asian 24%, African American 1%, Caucasian 30%, Hispanic 18%, Native American 0%, Race unknown 7%. **Retention and Graduation:** 93% freshmen return for sophomore year. **Faculty:** Student/faculty ratio 11:1. 33 full-time faculty,

ACADEMICS
Degrees: Bachelor's; Master's; Post-master's certificate. **Special Study Options:** Internships; Study abroad. **Career services:** Alumni network; Internships.

FACILITIES
Special Academic Facilities/Equipment: SCI-Arc gallery, Wood/Metal Shop, Digital Fabrication shop.

CAMPUS LIFE
Environment: Metropolis. **Activities:** Student government. **On-Campus Highlights:** SCI-Arc Gallery.

ADMISSIONS
Basis for Candidate Selection: *Very important factors include:* academic GPA, character/personal qualities, level of applicant's interest. *Important factors include:* rigor of secondary school record, application essay, standardized test scores. *Other factors include:* recommendation(s), extracurricular activities, talent/ability, volunteer work, work experience. **Freshman Admission Requirements:** High school diploma is required and GED is accepted. **Freshman Admission Statistics:** 276 applied, 55% admitted, 21% enrolled. **Transfer Admission Requirements:** College transcript(s), essay or personal statement. Lowest grade transferable C. **General Admission Information:** Application fee $85. Priority deadline 1/15. Regular application deadline 7/1.

COSTS AND FINANCIAL AID
Annual tuition $27,500. **Required Forms and Deadlines:** FAFSA; Institution's own financial aid form. **Types of Aid:** *Need-based scholarships/grants:* College/university scholarship or grant aid from institutional funds; Federal Pell; SEOG; State scholarships/grants. **Student Employment:** Federal Work-Study Program available. **Criteria awarding aid:** *Need-based:* Academics. *Non-need-based:* Academics, State/district residency.

SOUTHERN CONNECTICUT STATE UNIVERSITY

SCSU-Admissions House, New Haven, CT 06515-1202
Phone: 203-392-5644 **CEEB Code:** 3662
Fax: 203-392-5727 **Website:** www.southernct.edu

This public school was founded in 1893. It has a 168 acre campus.

RATINGS
Admissions Selectivity Rating: 77   **Fire Safety Rating:** 60*   **Green Rating:** 60*

STUDENTS AND FACULTY
Enrollment: 8,525. **Student Body:** 60% female, 40% male, 4% out-of-state, <1% international (39 countries represented). Asian 3%, African American 16%, Caucasian 62%, Hispanic 10%, Native American <1%, Pacific Islander 0%, Two or more races 2%, Race unknown 6%. **Retention and Graduation:** 27% grads go on to further study within 1 year. **Faculty:** Student/faculty ratio 17:1. 403 full-time faculty, 90% hold PhDs, 14% are members of minority groups, 45% are women.

ACADEMICS
Degrees: Bachelor's; Doctoral degree—other; Master's; Post-master's certificate. **Classes:** Most classes have 20–29 students. Most lab/discussion sessions have 10–19 students. **Special Study Options:** Accelerated program; Cooperative education program; Cross-registration; Distance learning; Double major; Dual enrollment; Exchange student program (domestic); External degree program; Honors program; Independent study; Internships; Liberal arts/career combination; Student-designed major; Study abroad; Teacher certification program. **Disability Services offered:** Note-taking services; Reader services; Tape recorders; Tutors. **Career services:** Career/job search classes; Internships.

FACILITIES
Housing: Apartments for single students; Coed dorms; Special housing for disabled students; Theme housing; 95% of campus accessible to physically disabled. **Special Academic Facilities/Equipment:** Art gallery, language lab, child development center, communication disorders center, planetarium and observatory, closed-circuit TV center.

CAMPUS LIFE
Environment: Village. **Activities:** Campus Ministries; Choral groups; Dance; Drama/theater; International Student Organization; Literary magazine; Music ensembles; Musical theater; Pep band; Radio station; Student government; Student newspaper; Television station; Yearbook. 63 registered organizations, 12 honor societies, 4 religious organizations, 5 fraternities, 6 sororities on campus. **Athletics (Intercollegiate):** *Men:* baseball, basketball, cross-country, football, golf, gymnastics, ice hockey, rugby, soccer, softball, swimming, track/field (outdoor), track/field (indoor), volleyball, wrestling. *Women:* basketball, cheerleading, cross-country, field hockey, golf, gymnastics, rugby, soccer, softball, swimming, track/field (outdoor), track/field (indoor), volleyball.

ADMISSIONS
Freshman Academic Profile: 5% in top 10% of high school class, 21% in top 25% of high school class, 60% in top 50% of high school class. 88% from public high schools. **Test Scores:** SAT Math middle 50% range 410–530. SAT EBRW middle 50% range 420–520. ACT middle 50% range 17–22. **Basis for Candidate Selection:** *Very important factors include:* rigor of secondary school record, academic GPA. *Important factors include:* class rank, application essay, standardized test scores, recommendation(s). *Other factors include:* extracurricular activities, talent/ability, character/personal qualities, first generation, volunteer work, work experience. **Freshman Admission Requirements:** High school diploma is required and GED is accepted. *Academic units required:* 4 English, 3 math, 2 science, 1 science lab, 2 foreign language, 2 social studies, 2 history. *Academic units recommended:* 4 English, 4 math, 3 science, 4 foreign language, 3 social studies, 3 history. **Freshman Admission Statistics:** 4,978 applied, 75% admitted, 37% enrolled. **Transfer Admission Requirements:** College transcript(s), essay or personal statement, statement of good standing from prior institution(s). Minimum college GPA of 2.0 required. Lowest grade transferable C-. **General Admission Information:** Application fee $50. Regular application deadline 4/1. Non-fall registration accepted. Admission may be deferred for a maximum of 2 years.

COSTS AND FINANCIAL AID
Annual in-state tuition $4,285. Annual out-of-state tuition $15,137. Room and board $10,687. Required fees $4,256. Average book and supplies expense $1,400. **Required Forms and Deadlines:** FAFSA. **Types of Aid:** *Need-based scholarships/grants:* College/university scholarship or grant aid from institutional

funds; Federal Pell; SEOG; State scholarships/grants. **Student Employment:** Federal Work-Study Program available. Institutional employment available. **Financial Aid Statistics:** 75% needy freshmen, 76% needy undergrads receive need-based scholarship or grant aid. 24% freshmen, 14% undergrads receive non-need-based scholarship or grant aid. 75% freshmen, 83% undergrads receive need-based self-help aid. 1% freshmen, 2% undergrads receive athletic scholarships. **Criteria awarding aid:** *Non-need-based:* Academics, Alumni affiliation, Athletics.

SOUTHERN ILLINOIS UNIVERSITY—CARBONDALE

Undergraduate Admissions, Mailcode 4710, Carbondale, IL 62901
Phone: 618-536-4405 **Financial Aid Phone:** 618-453-4334
E-mail: admissions@siu.edu **CEEB Code:** 1726
Fax: 618-453-4609 **Website:** www.siu.edu **ACT Code:** 1144

This public school was founded in 1869. It has a 1136 acre campus.

RATINGS
Admissions Selectivity Rating: 77   **Fire Safety Rating:** 95   **Green Rating:** 75

STUDENTS AND FACULTY
Enrollment: 8,311. **Student Body:** 47% female, 53% male, 18% out-of-state, 3% international (47 countries represented). Asian 2%, African American 14%, Caucasian 68%, Hispanic 10%, Native American <1%, Pacific Islander <1%, Two or more races 3%, Race unknown <1%.
Retention and Graduation: 75% freshmen return for sophomore year. 32% freshmen graduate within 4 years. 48 graduate within 6 years. **Faculty:** Student/faculty ratio 12:1. 765 full-time faculty, 70% hold PhDs, 21% are members of minority groups, 43% are women. 10% of classes are taught by teaching assistants.

ACADEMICS
Degrees: Associate; Bachelor's; Certificate; Doctoral degree—professional practice; Doctoral degree research/scholarship; Master's; Post-bachelor's certificate. **Classes:** Most classes have 10–19 students. Most lab/discussion sessions have 10–19 students. **Most popular majors:** Psychology, General; Industrial Technology/Technician; Automotive Engineering Technology/Technician. **Special Study Options:** Distance learning; Double major; English as a Second Language (ESL); Honors program; Internships; Student-designed major; Study abroad; Teacher certification program. **Honors programs:** University Honors Program—to reward its best undergraduates for their high academic achievement, the Honors Program offers the experience of a small liberal arts college within a large research public university. Students are mentored individually to tailor curricular and co-curricular activities that are uniquely suited to their goals. Classes are small, specially designed for University Honors by outstanding SIUC faculty. **Disability Services offered:** Note-taking services; Reader services; Tape recorders; Tutors. **Career services:** Alumni network; Alumni services; Career assessment; Career/job search classes; Internships; Regional alumni.

FACILITIES
Housing: Apartments for married students; Apartments for single students; Coed dorms; Men's dorms; Special housing for disabled students; Theme housing; Women's dorms; 98% of campus accessible to physically disabled. **Special Academic Facilities/Equipment:** University press, coal research center, university museum, materials technology center, outdoor education laboratory, university farms, center for study of crime, electron microscopy center, cooperative wildlife research laboratory, cooperative fisheries research laboratory, vivarium, airport training facility, laboratory theater, center for archaeological investigations, small business incubator, public policy institute, dental and medical clinics, environmental center, media center. **Campus Network:** 100% of classrooms, 100% of dorms, 100% of student union, 100% of libraries, 100% of dining areas, 90% of common outdoor areas have wireless network access.

CAMPUS LIFE
Environment: Town. **Activities:** Campus Ministries; Choral groups; Concert band; Dance; Drama/theater; International Student Organization; Jazz band; Literary magazine; Marching band; Model UN; Music ensembles; Musical theater; Opera; Pep band; Radio station; Student government; Student newspaper; Student-run film society; Symphony orchestra; Television station. 299 registered organizations, 22 honor societies, 10 religious organizations, 20 fraternities, 10 sororities on campus. **Athletics (Intercollegiate):** *Men:* baseball,

basketball, cheerleading, cross-country, diving, football, golf, swimming, tennis, track/field (outdoor), track/field (indoor). *Women:* basketball, cheerleading, cross-country, diving, golf, softball, swimming, tennis, track/field (outdoor), track/field (indoor), volleyball. **On-Campus Highlights:** Morris Library. **Environmental Initiatives:** $4.0M campus-wide energy efficiency and conservation project to reduce purchased utilities.

ADMISSIONS
Freshman Academic Profile: Average high school GPA 3.3. 20% in top 10% of high school class, 47% in top 25% of high school class, 79% in top 50% of high school class. **Test Scores:** SAT Math middle 50% range 530–710. SAT EBRW middle 50% range 540–710. ACT middle 50% range 21–28. **Basis for Candidate Selection:** *Very important factors include:* academic GPA, standardized test scores. *Important factors include:* rigor of secondary school record. *Other factors include:* class rank, application essay, recommendation(s), extracurricular activities, talent/ability, character/personal qualities, volunteer work. **Freshman Admission Requirements:** High school diploma is required and GED is accepted. *Academic units required:* 4 English, 3 math, 3 science, 3 science labs, 3 social studies, 2 academic electives. *Academic units recommended:* 4 English, 4 math, 3 science, 3 science labs, 3 social studies, 2 academic electives. **Freshman Admission Statistics:** 5,377 applied, 66% admitted, 29% enrolled. **Transfer Admission Requirements:** College transcript(s), statement of good standing from prior institution(s). Minimum college GPA of 2.0 required. Lowest grade transferable D. **General Admission Information:** Application fee $40. Priority deadline 12/1. Non-fall registration accepted.

COSTS AND FINANCIAL AID
Required Forms and Deadlines: FAFSA. **Notification of Awards:** Applicants will be notified of awards on a rolling basis beginning 2/1. **Types of Aid:** *Need-based scholarships/grants:* College/university scholarship or grant aid from institutional funds; Federal Pell; Private scholarships; SEOG; State scholarships/grants. *Loans:* Direct PLUS loans; Direct Subsidized Stafford Loans; Direct Unsubsidized Stafford Loans. **Student Employment:** Federal Work-Study Program available. Institutional employment available. **Financial Aid Statistics:** 60% needy freshmen, 65% needy undergrads receive need-based scholarship or grant aid. 53% freshmen, 40% undergrads receive non-need-based scholarship or grant aid. 73% freshmen, 78% undergrads receive need-based self-help aid. 7% freshmen, 4% undergrads receive athletic scholarships. 84% freshmen, 80% undergrads receive any aid. 67% undergrads borrow to pay for school. Average cumulative indebtedness $30,292. **Criteria awarding aid:** *Need-based:* Academics. *Non-need-based:* Academics, Alumni affiliation, Art, Athletics, Leadership, Minority status, Music/drama, State/district residency.

SOUTHERN ILLINOIS UNIVERSITY—EDWARDSVILLE

SIUE Office of Admissions, Edwardsville, IL 62026-1047
Phone: 618-650-3705 **Financial Aid Phone:** 618-650-3880
E-mail: admissions@siue.edu **CEEB Code:** 1759
Fax: 618-650-5013 **Website:** www.siue.edu **ACT Code:** 1147

This public school was founded in 1957. It has a 2660 acre campus.

RATINGS
Admissions Selectivity Rating: 75   **Fire Safety Rating:** 93   **Green Rating:** 62

STUDENTS AND FACULTY
Enrollment: 11,339. **Student Body:** 53% female, 47% male, 12% out-of-state, 1% international (39 countries represented). Asian 2%, African American 14%, Caucasian 74%, Hispanic 5%, Native American <1%, Pacific Islander <1%, Two or more races 3%, Race unknown 1%.
Retention and Graduation: 73% freshmen return for sophomore year. 27% freshmen graduate within 4 years. % freshmen graduate within 6 years. 31% grads go on to further study within 1 year. **Faculty:** Student/faculty ratio 20:1. 595 full-time faculty, 80% hold PhDs, 21% are members of minority groups, 48% are women. 4% of classes are taught by teaching assistants.

ACADEMICS
Degrees: Bachelor's; Doctoral degree—other; Doctoral degree—professional practice; Doctoral degree research/scholarship; Master's; Post-bachelor's certificate; Post-master's certificate. **Classes:** Most classes have 10–19 students. Most lab/discussion sessions have 20–29 students. **Most popular majors:** Registered Nursing/Registered Nurse; Business Administration and Management, General; Psychology, General. **Special Study Options:** Accelerated program; Cooperative education program; Distance learning;

Double major; English as a Second Language (ESL); Honors program; Independent study; Internships; Student-designed major; Study abroad; Teacher certification program. **Honors programs:** URCA, Honors Program. **Disability Services offered:** Note-taking services; Reader services; Tape recorders. **Career services:** Alumni network; Alumni services; Career assessment; Career/job search classes; Internships; Regional alumni.

FACILITIES

Housing: Apartments for married students; Apartments for single students; Coed dorms; Special housing for disabled students; Wellness housing; 100% of campus accessible to physically disabled. **Special Academic Facilities/ Equipment:** Art gallery, anthropology museum, language lab, center for advanced manufacturing and production, technology commercialization center, electron microscope, psychomotorskills lab, new engineering building and lab, observatory. **Campus Network:** 80% of classrooms, 100% of dorms, 100% of student union, 100% of libraries, 100% of dining areas, 25% of common outdoor areas have wireless network access.

CAMPUS LIFE

Environment: Town. **Activities:** Campus Ministries; Choral groups; Concert band; Dance; Drama/theater; International Student Organization; Jazz band; Literary magazine; Music ensembles; Musical theater; Opera; Pep band; Radio station; Student government; Student newspaper; Symphony orchestra. 302 registered organizations, 18 honor societies, 10 religious organizations, 13 fraternities, 9 sororities on campus. **Athletics (Intercollegiate):** *Men:* baseball, basketball, cross-country, golf, soccer, tennis, track/field (outdoor), track/field (indoor), wrestling. *Women:* basketball, cross-country, golf, soccer, softball, tennis, track/field (outdoor), track/field (indoor), volleyball. **On-Campus Highlights:** Morris University Center.

ADMISSIONS

Freshman Academic Profile: Average high school GPA 3.4. 17% in top 10% of high school class, 43% in top 25% of high school class, 76% in top 50% of high school class. **Test Scores:** SAT Math middle 50% range 495–600. SAT EBRW middle 50% range 485–625. ACT middle 50% range 20–26. **Basis for Candidate Selection:** *Very important factors include:* academic GPA, standardized test scores. *Important factors include:* rigor of secondary school record, class rank. **Freshman Admission Requirements:** High school diploma is required and GED is accepted. *Academic units required:* 4 English, 3 math, 3 science, 3 science labs, 3 social studies, 2 academic electives. *Academic units recommended:* 2 foreign language. **Freshman Admission Statistics:** 6,273 applied, 90% admitted, 32% enrolled. **Transfer Admission Requirements:** College transcript(s). Minimum college GPA of 2 required. Lowest grade transferable D. **General Admission Information:** Application fee $40. Priority deadline 12/1. Regular application deadline 7/19. Non-fall registration accepted.

COSTS AND FINANCIAL AID

Annual in-state tuition $8,770. Annual out-of-state tuition $21,930. Room and board $9,481. Required fees $2,721. Average book and supplies expense $853. **Required Forms and Deadlines:** FAFSA. **Notification of Awards:** Applicants will be notified of awards on a rolling basis beginning 12/15. **Types of Aid:** *Need-based scholarships/grants:* College/university scholarship or grant aid from institutional funds; Federal Nursing Scholarships; Federal Pell; Private scholarships; SEOG; State scholarships/grants. *Loans:* Direct PLUS loans; Direct Subsidized Stafford Loans; Direct Unsubsidized Stafford Loans. **Student Employment:** Federal Work-Study Program available. Institutional employment available. **Financial Aid Statistics:** 89% needy freshmen, 75% needy undergrads receive need-based scholarship or grant aid. 70% freshmen, 34% undergrads receive non-need-based scholarship or grant aid. 77% freshmen, 81% undergrads receive need-based self-help aid. 1% freshmen, 1% undergrads receive athletic scholarships. 75% freshmen, 67% undergrads receive any aid. **Criteria awarding aid:** *Non-need-based:* Academics, Art, Athletics, Leadership, Minority status, Music/drama.

SOUTHERN MAINE COMMUNITY COLLEGE

2 Fort Road, South Portland, ME 04106
Phone: (207) 741-5800
E-mail: admissions@smccme.edu
Fax: 207-741-5760 **Website:** http://www.smccme.edu

This public school was founded in 1946. It has a 80 acre campus.

RATINGS

Admissions Selectivity Rating: 60*   **Fire Safety Rating:** 60*   **Green Rating:** 60*

STUDENTS AND FACULTY

Enrollment: 4,962. **Student Body:** 54% female, 46% male, 1% international. Asian 2%, African American 8%, Caucasian 80%, Hispanic 3%, Native American 1%, Pacific Islander <1%, Two or more races 3%, Race unknown 3%.
Faculty: Student/faculty ratio 18:1. 0% of classes are taught by teaching assistants.

ACADEMICS

Degrees: Associate; Certificate; Terminal Associate; Transfer Associate. **Special Study Options:** Cross-registration; Distance learning; Double major; Dual enrollment; English as a Second Language (ESL); Honors program; Independent study; Internships; Liberal arts/career combination; Study abroad. **Disability Services offered:** Note-taking services.

FACILITIES

Housing: Coed dorms; Men's dorms.

CAMPUS LIFE

Environment: Town. **Activities:** Choral groups; Drama/theater; Literary magazine; Student government; Student newspaper. 1 honor society on campus. **On-Campus Highlights:** Campus Center (offices, coffee shop, library, tutoring center).

ADMISSIONS

Basis for Candidate Selection: *Other factors include:* state residency. **Freshman Admission Requirements:** High school diploma is required and GED is accepted. **General Admission Information:** Application fee $20. Non-fall registration accepted.

COSTS AND FINANCIAL AID

Required Forms and Deadlines: FAFSA. **Types of Aid:** *Need-based scholarships/grants:* College/university scholarship or grant aid from institutional funds; Federal Pell; Private scholarships; State scholarships/grants. *Loans:* Direct PLUS loans; Direct Subsidized Stafford Loans; Direct Unsubsidized Stafford Loans.

SOUTHERN METHODIST UNIVERSITY

PO Box 750181, Dallas, TX 75275-0181
Phone: 214-768-2058 **Financial Aid Phone:** 214-768-3417
E-mail: ugadmission@smu.edu **CEEB Code:** 6660
Fax: 214-768-0103 **Website:** www.smu.edu **ACT Code:** 4171

This private school, affiliated with the Methodist Church, was founded in 1911. It has a 234 acre campus.

RATINGS

Admissions Selectivity Rating: 91   **Fire Safety Rating:** 97   **Green Rating:** 60*

STUDENTS AND FACULTY

Enrollment: 6,679. **Student Body:** 49% female, 51% male, 55% out-of-state, 7% international (60 countries represented). Asian 7%, African American 4%, Caucasian 64%, Hispanic 12%, Native American <1%, Pacific Islander <1%, Two or more races 4%, Race unknown <1%.
Retention and Graduation: 91% freshmen return for sophomore year. 72% freshmen graduate within 4 years. 81% freshmen graduate within 6 years.
Faculty: Student/faculty ratio 11:1. 754 full-time faculty, 85% hold PhDs, 19% are members of minority groups, 40% are women.

ACADEMICS

Degrees: Bachelor's; Doctoral degree—professional practice; Doctoral degree research/scholarship; Master's; Post-bachelor's certificate; Post-master's certificate. **Classes:** Most classes have 10–19 students. Most lab/discussion sessions have 30–39 students. **Most popular majors:** Economics, General; Accounting; Finance, General. **Special Study Options:** Accelerated program; Cooperative education program; Distance learning; Double major; Dual enrollment; English as a Second Language (ESL); Exchange student program (domestic); Honors program; Independent study; Internships; Liberal arts/career combination; Student-designed major; Study abroad; Teacher certification program; Weekend college. **Honors programs:** The University Honors Program is designed to prepare Honors students for a new millennium to ensure that they can cope with the challenges of rapid change while taking advantage of the possibilities such a volatile and versatile world presents. The BBA Honors Program, which is separate from the University Honors Program, is composed of special sections of courses in accounting, finance, statistics, operations management, marketing, and management. Advertising Honors Program: A student may apply for the Temerlin Advertising Institute Honors program after completion of his or her first semester as a declared Advertising major. **Combined degree programs:** BA/MEng. **Disability Services offered:** Note-taking services; Reader services; Tape recorders; Tutors. **Career services:** Alumni network; Alumni services; Career assessment; Career/job search classes; Internships; Regional alumni.

FACILITIES

Housing: Apartments for married students; Apartments for single students; Coed dorms; Cooperative housing; Fraternity/sorority housing; Theme housing; 95% of campus accessible to physically disabled. **Special Academic Facilities/Equipment:** Art, natural history, and paleontology museums, southwest film/video archives, sculpture garden, performing arts theatres, pollen analysis and geothermal labs, electron microbe lab, microscopy lab, seismological observatory, institute of technology services, TV studio. **Campus Network:** 100% of classrooms, 100% of dorms, 100% of student union, 100% of libraries, 100% of dining areas, 25% of common outdoor areas have wireless network access.

CAMPUS LIFE

Environment: Metropolis. **Activities:** Campus Ministries; Choral groups; Concert band; Dance; Drama/theater; International Student Organization; Jazz band; Literary magazine; Marching band; Model UN; Music ensembles; Musical theater; Opera; Pep band; Radio station; Student government; Student newspaper; Student-run film society; Symphony orchestra; Television station; Yearbook. 180 registered organizations, 16 honor societies, 27 religious organizations, 15 fraternities, 13 sororities on campus. **Athletics (Intercollegiate): Men:** basketball, diving, football, golf, soccer, swimming, tennis, volleyball, water polo. **Women:** basketball, crew/rowing, cross-country, diving, equestrian sports, golf, soccer, swimming, tennis, track/field (outdoor), volleyball, water polo. **On-Campus Highlights:** Dallas Hall. **Environmental Initiatives:** Broad academic commitment: research from Geothermal Energy Lab has revealed widespread availability of green energy source. Geothermal Lab's partnership with Google.org has resulted in sophisticated mapping of geothermal resources across North America. Lab hosts annual geothermal conference attended by the international community. Undergraduate and Graduate environmental degrees available through three portals: the Environmental Studies and Environmental Science programs in Dedman College of Science and Humanities, and the Environmental and Civil Engineering Department of the Lyle School of Engineering.

ADMISSIONS

Freshman Academic Profile: Average high school GPA 3.6. 49% in top 10% of high school class, 79% in top 25% of high school class, 97% in top 50% of high school class. 42% from public high schools. **Test Scores:** SAT Math middle 50% range 660–760. SAT EBRW middle 50% range 640–720. ACT middle 50% range 29–33. **Basis for Candidate Selection:** *Very important factors include:* rigor of secondary school record, academic GPA, application essay, standardized test scores, recommendation(s). *Important factors include:* class rank, extracurricular activities, talent/ability, character/personal qualities. *Other factors include:* first generation, alumni/ae relation, racial/ethnic status, volunteer work, work experience, level of applicant's interest. **Freshman Admission Requirements:** High school diploma is required and GED is not accepted. *Academic units required:* 4 English, 3 math, 3 science, 2 science labs, 2 foreign language, 3 social studies. *Academic units recommended:* 4 English, 4 math, 3 science, 2 science labs, 3 foreign language, 3 history, 3 academic electives. **Freshman Admission Statistics:** 13,959 applied, 47% admitted, 23% enrolled. **Transfer Admission Requirements:** College transcript(s), essay or personal statement. Minimum college GPA of 2.7 required. Lowest grade transferable C-. **General Admission Information:** Application fee $60. Priority deadline 1/15. Regular application deadline 7/31. Non-fall registration accepted. Admission may be deferred for a maximum of 1 year.

COSTS AND FINANCIAL AID

Annual tuition $51,958. Room and board $17,110. Average book and supplies expense $800. **Required Forms and Deadlines:** CSS/Financial Aid PROFILE; FAFSA; Noncustodial PROFILE. **Notification of Awards:** Applicants will be notified of awards on or about 1/20. **Types of Aid:** *Need-based scholarships/grants:* College/university scholarship or grant aid from institutional funds; Federal Pell; Private scholarships; SEOG; State scholarships/grants. *Loans:* Direct PLUS loans; Direct Subsidized Stafford Loans; Direct Unsubsidized Stafford Loans. **Student Employment:** Federal Work-Study Program available. Institutional employment available. **Financial Aid Statistics:** 63% needy freshmen, 71% needy undergrads receive need-based scholarship or grant aid. 77% freshmen, 69% undergrads receive non-need-based scholarship or grant aid. 71% freshmen, 76% undergrads receive need-based self-help aid. 4% freshmen, 5% undergrads receive athletic scholarships. 77.7% freshmen, 73.7% undergrads receive any aid. 28% undergrads borrow to pay for school. Average cumulative indebtedness $30,697. **Criteria awarding aid:** *Need-based:* Religious affiliation. *Non-need-based:* Academics, Alumni affiliation, Art, Athletics, Leadership, Music/drama.

SOUTHERN NEW HAMPSHIRE UNIVERSITY

2500 North River Road, Manchester, NH 03106-1045
Phone: 603-645-9611 **Financial Aid Phone:** 603-645-9645
E-mail: admission@snhu.edu **CEEB Code:** 3649
Fax: 603-645-9693 **Website:** www.snhu.edu **ACT Code:** 2514

This private school was founded in 1932. It has a 300 acre campus.

RATINGS

Admissions Selectivity Rating: 74 **Fire Safety Rating:** 97 **Green Rating:** 60*

STUDENTS AND FACULTY

Enrollment: 1,929. **Student Body:** 52% female, 48% male, 55% out-of-state, 5% international (79 countries represented). Asian 1%, African American 1%, Caucasian 75%, Hispanic 2%, Native American <1%, Race unknown 15%. **Retention and Graduation:** 68% freshmen return for sophomore year. 12% grads go on to further study within 1 year. **Faculty:** Student/faculty ratio 16:1. 120 full-time faculty, 76% hold PhDs, 12% are members of minority groups, 38% are women. 0% of classes are taught by teaching assistants.

ACADEMICS

Degrees: Associate; Bachelor's; Certificate; Master's; Post-bachelor's certificate; Post-master's certificate. **Classes:** Most classes have 10–19 students. **Most popular majors:** Culinary Arts/Chef Training; Business Administration and Management, General; Psychology, General. **Special Study Options:** Accelerated program; Cooperative education program; Distance learning; Double major; Dual enrollment; English as a Second Language (ESL); Honors program; Independent study; Internships; Student-designed major; Study abroad; Teacher certification program; Weekend college. **Honors programs:** Three-Year Honors Program (B.S. in Business Administration) and our traditional four-year honors program (available in conjunction with most majors). **Disability Services offered:** Note-taking services; Reader services; Tape recorders; Tutors. **Career services:** Alumni network; Alumni services; Career assessment; Career/job search classes; Internships.

FACILITIES

Housing: Apartments for single students; Coed dorms; Special housing for disabled students; Theme housing; Wellness housing; 85% of campus accessible to physically disabled. **Special Academic Facilities/Equipment:** Art Gallery. **Campus Network:** 100% of classrooms, 100% of dorms, 100% of student union, 100% of libraries, 100% of dining areas, 100% of common outdoor areas have wireless network access.

CAMPUS LIFE

Environment: City. **Activities:** Campus Ministries; Choral groups; Concert band; Dance; Drama/theater; International Student Organization; Jazz band; Literary magazine; Model UN; Musical theater; Radio station; Student government; Student newspaper; Television station; Yearbook. 58 registered organizations, 7 honor societies, 1 religious organization, 3 fraternities, 3 sororities on campus. **Athletics (Intercollegiate): Men:** baseball, basketball, cheerleading, cross-country, golf, ice hockey, lacrosse, soccer, tennis. *Women:* basketball, cheerleading, cross-country, lacrosse, soccer, softball, tennis, volleyball. **On-Campus Highlights:** Center for Financial Studies. **Environmental Initiatives:** Renewable Energy Hedge from 2007–2022 based on 17,500 megawatt hours of wind power output with PPM Energy Inc. By a financial swap, the hedge will flatline SNHU energy budget, and 100% offset energy green house gas use in the voluntary market with RECs, and provide the wind developer a consistent stream of income to facilitate more wind construction. This represents a new sustainable model of utility cost control based on long-term agreements between energy users and renewable developers.

ADMISSIONS

Freshman Academic Profile: Average high school GPA 3.0. 88% from public high schools. **Test Scores:** SAT Math middle 50% range 440–540. SAT EBRW middle 50% range 440–520. ACT middle 50% range 18–24. **Basis for Candidate Selection:** *Very important factors include:* rigor of secondary school record, academic GPA. *Important factors include:* application essay, recommendation(s), extracurricular activities, character/personal qualities, first generation. *Other factors include:* class rank, standardized test scores, interview, talent/ability, alumni/ae relation, volunteer work, work experience. **Freshman Admission Requirements:** High school diploma is required and GED is accepted. *Academic units required:* 4 English, 3 math, 3 science, 2 science labs, 2 foreign language, 2 social studies, 2 history. **Freshman Admission Statistics:** 3,124 applied, 84% admitted, 18% enrolled. **Transfer Admission Requirements:** High school transcript, college transcript(s), essay or personal statement. Minimum college GPA of 2.50 required. Lowest grade transferable C-. **General Admission Information:** Application fee $40. Priority deadline 3/15. Non-fall registration accepted. Admission may be deferred for a maximum of 1 year.

COSTS AND FINANCIAL AID

Required Forms and Deadlines: FAFSA. **Notification of Awards:** Applicants will be notified of awards on a rolling basis beginning 3/1. **Types of Aid:** *Need-based scholarships/grants:* College/university scholarship or grant aid from institutional funds; Federal Pell; Private scholarships; SEOG; State scholarships/grants. *Loans:* Direct PLUS loans; Direct Subsidized Stafford Loans; Direct Unsubsidized Stafford Loans. **Student Employment:** Federal Work-Study Program available. Institutional employment available. **Financial Aid Statistics:** 94% freshmen, 93% undergrads receive any aid. **Criteria awarding aid:** *Need-based:* Academics. *Non-need-based:* Academics, Alumni affiliation, Athletics, Leadership, State/district residency.

SOUTHERN OREGON UNIVERSITY

Office of Admissions, Ashland, OR 97520-5032
Phone: 541-552-6411 **Financial Aid Phone:** (541)552-6600
E-mail: admissions@sou.edu **CEEB Code:** 4702
Fax: 541-552-8403 **Website:** www.sou.edu **ACT Code:** 3496

This public school was founded in 1926. It has a 175 acre campus.

RATINGS

Admissions Selectivity Rating: 76   Fire Safety Rating: 88   Green Rating: 92

STUDENTS AND FACULTY

Enrollment: 4,064. **Student Body:** 59% female, 41% male, 40% out-of-state, 3% international (12 countries represented). Asian 2%, African American 2%, Caucasian 59%, Hispanic 12%, Native American 1%, Pacific Islander 1%, Two or more races 10%, Race unknown 10%.
Retention and Graduation: 68% freshmen return for sophomore year.
Faculty: Student/faculty ratio 21:1. 167 full-time faculty, 67% hold PhDs, 17% are members of minority groups, 44% are women. 0% of classes are taught by teaching assistants.

ACADEMICS

Degrees: Bachelor's; Certificate; Master's; Post-bachelor's certificate. **Classes:** Most classes have 10–19 students. Most lab/discussion sessions have 10–19 students. **Most popular majors:** Visual and Performing Arts, General; Business Administration and Management, General; Psychology, General. **Special Study Options:** Accelerated program; Cross-registration; Distance learning; Double major; Dual enrollment; English as a Second Language (ESL); Exchange student program (domestic); Honors program; Independent study; Internships; Student-designed major; Study abroad; Teacher certification program. **Honors programs:** SOU established an Honors College in Fall 2013 with a mission &

vision of combing real world projects with intellectual rigor, aiming to provide a challenging learning environment. Our creative curricula will take advantage of the university's unique location by drawing on the rich natural, cultural, and artistic resources that are Southern Oregon. Southern Oregon University seeks to create a community of learners prepared for a lifetime of intellectual curiosity, inquiry, scholarship, and service. The Honors College accepts students from every major and allows for a truly customizable academic plan. You are unique, so why stick with a generic course of study? If you think one major just isn't enough for you, you can work with professors and advisors to create your own interdisciplinary major. Every Honors student will work with a community mentor: a local professional working in a field of your interest. With your mentor's guidance, you will conduct an applied research or a creative project and present it to a group composed of all those who helped you along the way. You can do corporate internships, write a groundbreaking sonnet cycle or one-act play, help a local business get on its feet, seek to disprove a popular theorem, and more. This is more than just networking; it's an exploration of the uncharted world some call "life after college." You will graduate with the necessary skills and experience to feel at home in your professional environment of choice. **Disability Services offered:** Note-taking services; Reader services; Tape recorders; Tutors. **Career services:** Alumni network; Alumni services; Career assessment; Career/job search classes; Internships; Regional alumni.

FACILITIES

Housing: Apartments for married students; Apartments for single students; Coed dorms; Special housing for disabled students; Special housing for international students; Theme housing; Wellness housing; 80% of campus accessible to physically disabled. **Special Academic Facilities/Equipment:** Art and history museums, art galleries, on-campus preschool and kindergarten, National Guard armory, United States Wildlife Forensics Lab.

CAMPUS LIFE

Environment: Town. **Activities:** Campus Ministries; Choral groups; Concert band; Dance; Drama/theater; International Student Organization; Jazz band; Literary magazine; Music ensembles; Musical theater; Pep band; Radio station; Student government; Student newspaper; Student-run film society; Symphony orchestra; Television station. 64 registered organizations, 13 honor societies, 5 religious organizations on campus. **Athletics (Intercollegiate):** *Men:* basketball, cross-country, football, track/field (outdoor), wrestling. *Women:* basketball, cross-country, soccer, softball, tennis, track/field (outdoor), volleyball. **On-Campus Highlights:** Hannon Library. **Environmental Initiatives:** Through the student-initiated Green Energy Fee, SOU purchases Renewable Energy Certificates (RECs) to offset 100% of its electricity consumption and carbon offsets to offset 100% of its natural gas consumption. Among the 54 colleges and universities that are U.S. EPA Green Power Partners, SOU ranked #12 on the EPA's April 6, 2010 Top 20 College & University list.

ADMISSIONS

Freshman Academic Profile: Average high school GPA 3.3. 90% from public high schools. **Test Scores:** SAT Math middle 50% range 440–550. SAT EBRW middle 50% range 460–580. ACT middle 50% range 19–25. **Basis for Candidate Selection:** *Very important factors include:* academic GPA, standardized test scores. *Other factors include:* rigor of secondary school record, application essay, recommendation(s), interview, extracurricular activities, geographical residence, state residency, volunteer work. **Freshman Admission Requirements:** High school diploma is required and GED is accepted. *Academic units required:* 4 English, 3 math, 2 science, 1 science lab, 2 foreign language, 3 social studies. **Freshman Admission Statistics:** 2,766 applied, 78% admitted, 31% enrolled. **Transfer Admission Requirements:** College transcript(s). Minimum college GPA of 2.2 required. Lowest grade transferable D-. **General Admission Information:** Application fee $60. Priority deadline 2/15. Non-fall registration accepted. Admission may be deferred for a maximum of 1 year.

COSTS AND FINANCIAL AID

Annual in-state tuition $6,813. Annual out-of-state tuition $21,460. Room and board $11,610. Required fees $1,710. Average book and supplies expense $999. **Required Forms and Deadlines:** FAFSA. **Notification of Awards:** Applicants will be notified of awards on a rolling basis beginning 3/2. **Types of Aid:** *Need-based scholarships/grants:* College/university scholarship or grant aid from institutional funds; Federal Pell; Private scholarships; SEOG; State scholarships/grants. *Loans:* Direct PLUS loans; Direct Subsidized Stafford Loans; Direct Unsubsidized Stafford Loans. **Student Employment:** Federal Work-Study Program available. Institutional employment available. **Financial Aid Statistics:** 77% needy freshmen, 43% needy undergrads receive need-based scholarship or grant aid. 57% freshmen, 43% undergrads receive non-need-based scholarship or grant aid. 71% freshmen, 40% undergrads receive need-based self-help aid. 7% freshmen, 5% undergrads receive athletic scholarships. 70% freshmen,

81% undergrads receive any aid. 89% undergrads borrow to pay for school. Average cumulative indebtedness $24,179. **Criteria awarding aid:** *Need-based:* Academics. *Non-need-based:* Academics, Athletics, State/district residency.

SOUTHERN UNIVERSITY AND A&M COLLEGE

P.O. Box 9901, Baton Rouge, LA 70813
Phone: 225-771-2430 **Financial Aid Phone:** 225-771-2790
E-mail: admit@subr.edu **CEEB Code:** 6663
Fax: 225-771-2500 **Website:** subr.edu **ACT Code:** 1610

This public school was founded in 1880. It has a 884 acre campus.

RATINGS

Admissions Selectivity Rating: 83   Fire Safety Rating: 82   Green Rating: 60*

STUDENTS AND FACULTY

Enrollment: 6,830. **Student Body:** 61% female, 39% male, 19% out-of-state, 2% international (48 countries represented). Asian <1%, African American 95%, Caucasian 3%, Hispanic <1%, Native American <1%, Race unknown 0%.
Retention and Graduation: 65% freshmen return for sophomore year. 16% grads go on to further study within 1 year. 15% grads pursue arts and sciences degrees. 1% grads pursue law degrees. 0% grads pursue business degrees. 0% grads pursue medical degrees. **Faculty:** Student/faculty ratio 16:1. 405 full-time faculty, 66% hold PhDs, 85% are members of minority groups, 47% are women. 0% of classes are taught by teaching assistants.

ACADEMICS

Degrees: Associate; Bachelor's; Master's; Post-master's certificate. **Classes:** Most classes have 20–29 students. Most lab/discussion sessions have 10–19 students. **Most popular majors:** Biology/Biological Sciences, General; Business Administration and Management, General; Nursing/Registered Nurse (Rn, Asn, Bsn, Msn). **Special Study Options:** Cooperative education program; Cross-registration; Distance learning; Double major; Dual enrollment; Exchange student program (domestic); Honors program; Independent study; Internships; Study abroad; Teacher certification program; Weekend college. **Honors programs:** The Honors College provides an enhanced educational experience for students who have a history of strong academic achievement and who have demonstrated exceptional creativity or talent. The College also provides cultural and intellectual opportunities that are designed to motivae students to perform at the highest level of excellence that they are capable of and through which they may become knowledgeable and effective leaders. **Disability Services offered:** Note-taking services; Tape recorders; Tutors. **Career services:** Career/job search classes; Internships.

FACILITIES

Housing: Men's dorms; Special housing for disabled students; Women's dorms; 100% of campus accessible to physically disabled. **Special Academic Facilities/Equipment:** Jazz institute Southern Museum of Art.

CAMPUS LIFE

Environment: Metropolis. **Activities:** Choral groups; Concert band; Dance; Drama/theater; Jazz band; Literary magazine; Marching band; Music ensembles; Musical theater; Pep band; Student government; Student newspaper; Yearbook. 88 registered organizations, 11 honor societies, 6 religious organizations, 4 fraternities, 4 sororities on campus. **Athletics (Intercollegiate):** *Men:* baseball, basketball, cross-country, football, golf, tennis, track/field (outdoor). *Women:* basketball, cross-country, golf, softball, tennis, track/field (outdoor), volleyball. **On-Campus Highlights:** SUBR Museum of Art. **Environmental Initiatives:** MS4-Stormwater Permit with the Parish of East Baton Rouge.

ADMISSIONS

Freshman Academic Profile: Average high school GPA 2.8. 3% in top 10% of high school class, 13% in top 25% of high school class, 40% in top 50% of high school class. **Test Scores:** SAT Math middle 50% range 380–460. ACT middle 50% range 15–18. **Basis for Candidate Selection:** *Very important factors include:* rigor of secondary school record, class rank, academic GPA, standardized test scores. *Other factors include:* talent/ability. **Freshman Admission Requirements:** High school diploma is required and GED is accepted. *Academic units required:* 4 English, 3 math, 3 science, 2 foreign language, 2 social studies, 1 history, 1 unit from above areas or other academic areas. **Freshman Admission Statistics:** 4,703 applied, 53% admitted, 45% enrolled. **Transfer Admission Requirements:** High school transcript, college

transcript(s), standardized test scores, statement of good standing from prior institution(s). Minimum college GPA of 2.0 required. Lowest grade transferable C. **General Admission Information:** Application fee $20. Regular application deadline 7/1. Non-fall registration accepted. Admission may be deferred for a maximum of 2 semesters.

COSTS AND FINANCIAL AID

Annual in-state tuition $3,666. Annual out-of-state tuition $9,458. Room and board $5,784. Average book and supplies expense $1,200. **Required Forms and Deadlines:** FAFSA; Institution's own financial aid form. **Notification of Awards:** Applicants will be notified of awards on a rolling basis beginning 6/30. **Types of Aid:** *Need-based scholarships/grants:* College/university scholarship or grant aid from institutional funds; Federal Pell; Private scholarships; SEOG; State scholarships/grants. *Loans:* Direct PLUS loans; Direct Subsidized Stafford Loans; Direct Unsubsidized Stafford Loans. **Student Employment:** Federal Work-Study Program available. Institutional employment available. **Financial Aid Statistics:** 80% needy freshmen, 77% needy undergrads receive need-based scholarship or grant aid. 21% freshmen, 18% undergrads receive non-need-based scholarship or grant aid. 79% freshmen, 87% undergrads receive need-based self-help aid. 5% freshmen, 3% undergrads receive athletic scholarships. 89% freshmen, 85% undergrads receive any aid. **Criteria awarding aid:** *Need-based:* Academics, Alumni affiliation, Athletics, Music/drama. *Non-need-based:* Academics, Athletics.

SOUTHERN UTAH UNIVERSITY

351 W University Blvd, Cedar City, UT 84720
Phone: 435-586-7740 **Financial Aid Phone:** 435-586-7735
E-mail: adminfo@suu.edu **CEEB Code:** 4092
Fax: 435-865-8223 **Website:** www.suu.edu **ACT Code:** 4271

This public school was founded in 1897. It has a 113 acre campus.

RATINGS

Admissions Selectivity Rating: 77   Fire Safety Rating: 60*   Green Rating: 60*

STUDENTS AND FACULTY

Enrollment: 7,293. **Student Body:** 55% female, 45% male, 18% out-of-state, 6% international (51 countries represented). Asian 1%, African American 3%, Caucasian 74%, Hispanic 7%, Native American 1%, Pacific Islander 1%, Two or more races <1%, Race unknown 6%.
Retention and Graduation: 73% freshmen return for sophomore year. 19% freshmen graduate within 4 years. 37% freshmen graduate within 6 years. **Faculty:** Student/faculty ratio 19:1. 340 full-time faculty, 55% hold PhDs, 9% are members of minority groups, 32% are women. 0% of classes are taught by teaching assistants.

ACADEMICS

Degrees: Associate; Bachelor's; Certificate; Diploma; Master's; Terminal Associate; Transfer Associate. **Classes:** Most classes have 20–29 students. Most lab/discussion sessions have 20–29 students. **Most popular majors:** General Studies; Biology/Biological Sciences, General; Psychology, General. **Special Study Options:** Cooperative education program; Distance learning; Double major; Dual enrollment; English as a Second Language (ESL); Exchange student program (domestic); Honors program; Independent study; Internships; Liberal arts/career combination; Student-designed major; Study abroad; Teacher certification program. **Disability Services offered:** Note-taking services; Reader services; Tape recorders; Tutors. **Career services:** Alumni services; Career assessment; Career/job search classes; Internships.

FACILITIES

Housing: Apartments for single students; Coed dorms; Special housing for disabled students; Special housing for international students; Theme housing. **Special Academic Facilities/Equipment:** SUMA, Art gallery, natural history museum, farm and ranch, TV studio. **Campus Network:** 100% of classrooms, 100% of dorms, 100% of student union, 100% of libraries, 100% of dining areas, 100% of common outdoor areas have wireless network access.

CAMPUS LIFE

Environment: Village. **Activities:** Campus Ministries; Choral groups; Concert band; Dance; Drama/theater; International Student Organization; Jazz band; Literary magazine; Marching band; Music ensembles; Musical theater; Opera; Pep band; Radio station; Student government; Student newspaper; Student-run film society; Symphony orchestra; Television station. **Athletics**

For more free content, visit PrincetonReview.com

(Intercollegiate): *Men:* baseball, basketball, cross-country, football, golf, track/field (outdoor). *Women:* basketball, cross-country, gymnastics, softball, tennis, track/field (outdoor). **On-Campus Highlights:** SUMA.

ADMISSIONS

Freshman Academic Profile: Average high school GPA 3.6. 19% in top 10% of high school class, 47% in top 25% of high school class, 79% in top 50% of high school class. **Test Scores:** SAT Math middle 50% range 500–610. SAT EBRW middle 50% range 510–640. ACT middle 50% range 21–27. **Basis for Candidate Selection:** *Very important factors include:* academic GPA, standardized test scores. *Important factors include:* level of applicant's interest. **Freshman Admission Requirements:** High school diploma is required and GED is accepted. *Academic units recommended:* 4 English, 3 math, 3 science, 1 science lab, 2 foreign language, 3 social studies. **Freshman Admission Statistics:** 12,435 applied, 79% admitted, 21% enrolled. **Transfer Admission Requirements:** College transcript(s). Minimum college GPA of 2.25 required. Lowest grade transferable D. **General Admission Information:** Application fee $50. Priority deadline 12/1. Regular application deadline 5/1. Non-fall registration accepted. Admission may be deferred for a maximum of 5 semesters.

COSTS AND FINANCIAL AID

Annual in-state tuition $6,006. Annual out-of-state tuition $19,822. Room and board $7,349. Required fees $764. Average book and supplies expense $1,600. **Required Forms and Deadlines:** FAFSA; Institution's own financial aid form. **Notification of Awards:** Applicants will be notified of awards on a rolling basis beginning 3/14. **Types of Aid:** *Need-based scholarships/grants:* College/university scholarship or grant aid from institutional funds; Federal Pell; Private scholarships; SEOG; State scholarships/grants. *Loans:* Direct PLUS loans; Direct Subsidized Stafford Loans; Direct Unsubsidized Stafford Loans. **Student Employment:** Federal Work-Study Program available. Institutional employment available. **Financial Aid Statistics:** 51% needy freshmen, 68% needy undergrads receive need-based scholarship or grant aid. 50% freshmen, 39% undergrads receive non-need-based scholarship or grant aid. 84% freshmen, 85% undergrads receive need-based self-help aid. 5% freshmen, 6% undergrads receive athletic scholarships. 44% undergrads borrow to pay for school. Average cumulative indebtedness $18,185. **Criteria awarding aid:** *Non-need-based:* Academics, Alumni affiliation, Art, Athletics, Job skills, Leadership, Minority status, Music/drama, State/district residency.

SOUTHERN WESLEYAN UNIVERSITY

Wesleyan Drive, Central, SC 29630-1020
Phone: 864-644-5550 **Financial Aid Phone:** 864-644-5500
E-mail: admissions@swu.edu **CEEB Code:** 5896
Fax: 864-644-5972 **Website:** www.swu.edu **ACT Code:** 3837

This private school, affiliated with the Wesleyan Church, was founded in 1906. It has a 330 acre campus.

RATINGS

Admissions Selectivity Rating: 73   Fire Safety Rating: 77   Green Rating: 60*

STUDENTS AND FACULTY

Enrollment: 1,444. **Student Body:** 60% female, 40% male, 28% out-of-state, 1% international (9 countries represented). Asian <1%, African American 27%, Caucasian 61%, Hispanic 2%, Native American 1%, Pacific Islander 0%, Two or more races 0%, Race unknown 8%. **Retention and Graduation:** 70% freshmen return for sophomore year. **Faculty:** Student/faculty ratio 18:1. 58 full-time faculty, 72% hold PhDs, 12% are members of minority groups, 31% are women. 0% of classes are taught by teaching assistants.

ACADEMICS

Degrees: Associate; Bachelor's; Master's. **Classes:** Most classes have 10–19 students. Most lab/discussion sessions have 10–19 students. **Most popular majors:** Business/Commerce, General; Religion/Religious Studies; Elementary Education and Teaching. **Special Study Options:** Cross-registration; Distance learning; Double major; Dual enrollment; English as a Second Language (ESL); Honors program; Independent study; Internships; Student-designed major; Study abroad; Teacher certification program. **Honors programs:** The honors program consists of specialized coursework, non-credit academic experiences, and service opportunities. Honors students must complete a research-based Honors Major Project in their Junior or Senior years. **Disability Services**

offered: Note-taking services; Reader services; Tape recorders; Tutors. **Career services:** Career assessment; Career/job search classes; Internships.

FACILITIES

Housing: Apartments for single students; Coed dorms; Special housing for disabled students; Women's dorms; 90% of campus accessible to physically disabled. **Special Academic Facilities/Equipment:** Freedom's Hill Historic Site, a restored abolitionist church founded in 1848 in Alamance County, NC: The church has many artifacts from its time as a site along the Underground Railroad including bullet holes in the door, evidence of the many attempts to frighten the congregation and impede their abolitionist activities. The Eleanor Gardner Collection: a collection of brass rubbings from medieval burial coverings, the earliest dating from the 12th century. The Faith Clayton Collection: extensive genealogical records from South Carolina and the southeast region of the U.S. The Wesleyana Collection: a compilation of classic theological works from the Wesleyan and Holiness denominational traditions. The Evatt Heritage Center, the university's historical museum and archive. **Campus Network:** 100% of classrooms, 100% of dorms, 100% of student union, 100% of libraries, 100% of dining areas, 50% of common outdoor areas have wireless network access.

CAMPUS LIFE

Environment: Town. **Activities:** Campus Ministries; Choral groups; Concert band; Drama/theater; Jazz band; Literary magazine; Music ensembles; Musical theater; Student government; Yearbook. 12 registered organizations, 2 honor societies, 3 religious organizations on campus. **Athletics (Intercollegiate):** *Men:* baseball, basketball, cross-country, golf, soccer. *Women:* basketball, cross-country, soccer, softball, volleyball. **On-Campus Highlights:** Jennings Campus Center. **Environmental Initiatives:** Voluntary recycling of paper and plastic in residence halls and academic buildings. Materials are collected by the city.

ADMISSIONS

Freshman Academic Profile: Average high school GPA 3.5. 13% in top 10% of high school class, 34% in top 25% of high school class, 75% in top 50% of high school class. **Test Scores:** SAT Math middle 50% range 445–550. SAT EBRW middle 50% range 430–540. ACT middle 50% range 18–22. **Basis for Candidate Selection:** *Very important factors include:* academic GPA, standardized test scores. *Important factors include:* rigor of secondary school record, class rank, talent/ability, character/personal qualities. *Other factors include:* recommendation(s). **Freshman Admission Requirements:** High school diploma is required and GED is accepted. *Academic units recommended:* 4 English, 2 math, 2 science, 2 social studies. **Freshman Admission Statistics:** 575 applied, 94% admitted, 31% enrolled. **Transfer Admission Requirements:** College transcript(s). Minimum college GPA of 2.0 required. Lowest grade transferable C. **General Admission Information:** Application fee $25. Regular application deadline 8/1. Non-fall registration accepted. Admission may be deferred for a maximum of 1 semester.

COSTS AND FINANCIAL AID

Annual tuition $19,950. Room and board $8,410. Required fees $600. Average book and supplies expense $1,020. **Required Forms and Deadlines:** FAFSA; Institution's own financial aid form. **Notification of Awards:** Applicants will be notified of awards on a rolling basis beginning 2/1. **Types of Aid:** *Need-based scholarships/grants:* College/university scholarship or grant aid from institutional funds; Federal Pell; Private scholarships; SEOG; State scholarships/grants. *Loans:* Direct PLUS loans; Direct Subsidized Stafford Loans; Direct Unsubsidized Stafford Loans. **Student Employment:** Federal Work-Study Program available. Institutional employment available. **Financial Aid Statistics:** 100% needy freshmen, 91% needy undergrads receive need-based scholarship or grant aid. 16% freshmen, 8% undergrads receive non-need-based scholarship or grant aid. 73% freshmen, 80% undergrads receive need-based self-help aid. 5% freshmen, 2% undergrads receive athletic scholarships. 100% freshmen, 99% undergrads receive any aid. **Criteria awarding aid:** *Non-need-based:* Academics, Athletics, Music/drama, Religious affiliation.

SOUTHWEST BAPTIST UNIVERSITY

1600 University Avenue, Bolivar, MO 65613-2597
Phone: 417-328-1810 **Financial Aid Phone:** 417-328-1823
E-mail: admitme@sbuniv.edu **CEEB Code:** 6664
Fax: 417-328-1808 **ACT Code:** 2368

This private school, affiliated with the Southern Baptist Church, was founded in 1878. It has a 180 acre campus.

RATINGS
Admissions Selectivity Rating: 74 **Fire Safety Rating:** 77 **Green Rating:** 60*

STUDENTS AND FACULTY
Enrollment: 2,646. **Student Body:** 66% female, 34% male, 29% out-of-state, 1% international (16 countries represented). Asian 1%, African American 4%, Caucasian 86%, Hispanic 1%, Native American 1%, Race unknown 6%. **Retention and Graduation:** 70% freshmen return for sophomore year. **Faculty:** Student/faculty ratio 13:1. 116 full-time faculty, 59% hold PhDs, 2% are members of minority groups, 41% are women. 0% of classes are taught by teaching assistants.

ACADEMICS
Degrees: Associate; Bachelor's; Certificate; Doctoral degree—professional practice; Master's; Post-master's certificate. **Classes:** Most classes have fewer than 10 students. Most lab/discussion sessions have 10–19 students. **Most popular majors:** Business Administration and Management, General; Elementary Education and Teaching; Psychology, General. **Special Study Options:** Cooperative education program; Distance learning; Double major; Dual enrollment; Exchange student program (domestic); Honors program; Independent study; Internships; Student-designed major; Study abroad; Teacher certification program. **Honors programs:** Our academic honors program consists of the following components: academics, servant leadership, intercultural experiences, spiritual growth, and enrichment opportunities. **Disability Services offered:** Note-taking services; Reader services; Tutors. **Career services:** Career assessment; Career/job search classes.

FACILITIES
Housing: Apartments for single students; Men's dorms; Special housing for disabled students; Women's dorms; 95% of campus accessible to physically disabled. **Special Academic Facilities/Equipment:** The Driskell Art Gallery; Jester Learning and Performance Center; Meyer Wellness and Sports Center. **Campus Network:** 100% of classrooms, 100% of dorms, 100% of student union, 100% of libraries, 100% of dining areas, 60% of common outdoor areas have wireless network access.

CAMPUS LIFE
Environment: Village. **Activities:** Campus Ministries; Choral groups; Concert band; Drama/theater; Jazz band; Music ensembles; Musical theater; Opera; Pep band; Student government; Student newspaper; Symphony orchestra; Yearbook. 34 registered organizations, 8 honor societies, 10 religious organizations on campus. **Athletics (Intercollegiate): Men:** baseball, basketball, cheerleading, cross-country, football, golf, tennis, track/field (outdoor), track/field (indoor). *Women:* basketball, cheerleading, cross-country, soccer, softball, tennis, track/field (outdoor), track/field (indoor), volleyball. **On-Campus Highlights:** Meyer Wellness and Sports Center.

ADMISSIONS
Freshman Academic Profile: Average high school GPA 3.5. 22% in top 10% of high school class, 41% in top 25% of high school class, 67% in top 50% of high school class. **Test Scores:** SAT Math middle 50% range 450–600. SAT EBRW middle 50% range 410–560. ACT middle 50% range 20–26. **Basis for Candidate Selection:** *Very important factors include:* class rank, academic GPA, standardized test scores. *Important factors include:* rigor of secondary school record, application essay, recommendation(s). *Other factors include:* interview, talent/ability, character/personal qualities. **Freshman Admission Requirements:** High school diploma is required and GED is accepted. *Academic units recommended:* 4 English, 3 math, 2 science, 2 social studies, 2 unit from above areas or other academic areas. **Freshman Admission Statistics:** 1,617 applied, 92% admitted, 31% enrolled. **Transfer Admission Requirements:** High school transcript, college transcript(s), standardized test scores. Minimum college GPA of 2.0 required. Lowest grade transferable D. **General Admission Information:** Application fee $30. Non-fall registration accepted. Admission may be deferred for a maximum of 1 year.

COSTS AND FINANCIAL AID
Annual tuition $16,500. Room and board $5,720. Required fees $780. Average book and supplies expense $1,000. **Required Forms and Deadlines:** FAFSA; Institution's own financial aid form. **Notification of Awards:** Applicants will be notified of awards on a rolling basis beginning 3/1. **Types of Aid:** *Need-based scholarships/grants:* College/university scholarship or grant aid from institutional funds; Federal Pell; Private scholarships; SEOG; State scholarships/grants. **Student Employment:** Federal Work-Study Program available. Institutional employment available. **Financial Aid Statistics:** 66% needy freshmen, 68% needy undergrads receive need-based scholarship or grant aid. 93% freshmen, 80% undergrads receive non-need-based scholarship or grant aid. 80% freshmen, 84% undergrads receive need-based self-help aid. 16% freshmen, 12% undergrads receive athletic scholarships. 88% freshmen, 71% undergrads receive any aid. **Criteria awarding aid:** *Non-need-based:* Academics, Alumni affiliation, Art, Athletics, Job skills, Leadership, Minority status, Music/drama, Religious affiliation, State/district residency.

SOUTHWESTERN COLLEGE (KS)

100 College Street, Winfield, KS 67156
Phone: 620-229-6236 **Financial Aid Phone:** (620)229-6215
E-mail: scadmit@sckans.edu **CEEB Code:** 6670
Fax: 620-229-6344 **Website:** www.sckans.edu **ACT Code:** 1464

This private school, affiliated with the Methodist Church, was founded in 1885. It has a 85 acre campus.

RATINGS
Admissions Selectivity Rating: 75 **Fire Safety Rating:** 85 **Green Rating:** 60*

STUDENTS AND FACULTY
Enrollment: 1,471. **Student Body:** 48% female, 52% male, 34% out-of-state, 1% international (12 countries represented). Asian 2%, African American 8%, Caucasian 63%, Hispanic 6%, Native American 2%, Race unknown 18%. **Retention and Graduation:** 70% freshmen return for sophomore year. **Faculty:** Student/faculty ratio 12:1. 47 full-time faculty, 60% hold PhDs, 6% are members of minority groups, 38% are women. 0% of classes are taught by teaching assistants.

ACADEMICS
Degrees: Bachelor's; Master's; Post-bachelor's certificate; Post-master's certificate. **Classes:** Most classes have 10–19 students. Most lab/discussion sessions have fewer than 10 students. **Most popular majors:** Business Administration and Management, General; Elementary Education and Teaching; Nursing/Registered Nurse (Rn, Asn, Bsn, Msn). **Special Study Options:** Accelerated program; Distance learning; Double major; Honors program; Independent study; Internships; Student-designed major; Teacher certification program. **Disability Services offered:** Reader services; Tape recorders; Tutors.

FACILITIES
Housing: Apartments for married students; Apartments for single students; Coed dorms; Men's dorms; Women's dorms; 90% of campus accessible to physically disabled. **Special Academic Facilities/Equipment:** Ruth Warren Abbott Horticulture Lab; Floyd and Ethel Moore Biological Field Station; Norman E. Hege Education Center. **Campus Network:** 100% of classrooms, 100% of dorms, 100% of student union, 100% of libraries, 100% of dining areas, 10% of common outdoor areas have wireless network access.

CAMPUS LIFE
Environment: Village. **Activities:** Campus Ministries; Choral groups; Concert band; Dance; Drama/theater; International Student Organization; Jazz band; Music ensembles; Musical theater; Pep band; Radio station; Student government; Student newspaper; Symphony orchestra; Television station; Yearbook. 25 registered organizations, 2 honor societies, 7 religious organizations, 2 fraternities on campus. **Athletics (Intercollegiate): Men:** basketball, cheerleading, cross-country, football, golf, soccer, tennis, track/field (outdoor), track/field (indoor). *Women:* basketball, cheerleading, cross-country, golf, soccer, softball, tennis, track/field (outdoor), track/field (indoor), volleyball. **On-Campus Highlights:** Brand new Women's residence hall. **Environmental Initiatives:** Kansas Envirothon.

ADMISSIONS

Freshman Academic Profile: Average high school GPA 3.3. 16% in top 10% of high school class, 44% in top 25% of high school class, 73% in top 50% of high school class. 95% from public high schools. **Test Scores:** SAT Math middle 50% range 430–550. SAT EBRW middle 50% range 380–540. ACT middle 50% range 19–24. **Basis for Candidate Selection:** *Very important factors include:* rigor of secondary school record, academic GPA, standardized test scores. *Important factors include:* application essay, *Other factors include:* class rank, recommendation(s), interview, extracurricular activities, talent/ ability, character/personal qualities, alumni/ae relation. **Freshman Admission Requirements:** High school diploma is required and GED is accepted. *Academic units required:* 4 English, 3 math, 2 science, 1 science lab, 2.5 social studies, 1 history. **Freshman Admission Statistics:** 293 applied, 90% admitted, 45% enrolled. **Transfer Admission Requirements:** College transcript(s), essay or personal statement. Minimum college GPA of 2.25 required. Lowest grade transferable C. **General Admission Information:** Application fee $25. Regular application deadline 8/25. Non-fall registration accepted.

COSTS AND FINANCIAL AID

Annual tuition $19,530. Room and board $5,750. Required fees $150. Average book and supplies expense $600. **Required Forms and Deadlines:** FAFSA. **Types of Aid:** *Need-based scholarships/grants:* College/university scholarship or grant aid from institutional funds; Federal Pell; SEOG; State scholarships/ grants. *Loans:* Direct PLUS loans; Direct Subsidized Stafford Loans; Direct Unsubsidized Stafford Loans. **Student Employment:** Federal Work-Study Program available. Institutional employment available. **Financial Aid Statistics:** 100% needy freshmen, 98% needy undergrads receive need-based scholarship or grant aid. 9% freshmen, 7% undergrads receive non-need-based scholarship or grant aid. 82% freshmen, 85% undergrads receive need-based self-help aid. 25% freshmen, 25% undergrads receive athletic scholarships. 100% freshmen, 99% undergrads receive any aid. **Criteria awarding aid:** *Non-need-based:* Academics, Athletics, Leadership, Minority status, Music/drama.

SOUTHWESTERN UNIVERSITY

Admission Office, Georgetown, TX 78627-0770
Phone: 512-863-1200 **Financial Aid Phone:** (512) 863 - 1259
E-mail: admission@southwestern.edu **CEEB Code:** 6674
Fax: 512-863-9601 **Website:** www.southwestern.edu **ACT Code:** 4186

This private school, affiliated with the Methodist Church, was founded in 1840. It has a 703 acre campus.

RATINGS

Admissions Selectivity Rating: 89   **Fire Safety Rating:** 96   **Green Rating:** 89

STUDENTS AND FACULTY

Enrollment: 1,428. **Student Body:** 55% female, 45% male, 9% out-of-state, 1% international (12 countries represented). Asian 3%, African American 5%, Caucasian 61%, Hispanic 24%, Native American <1%, Pacific Islander 0%, Two or more races 4%, Race unknown 1%. **Retention and Graduation:** 81% freshmen return for sophomore year. 67% freshmen graduate within 4 years. 74% freshmen graduate within 6 years. 25% grads go on to further study within 1 year. 15% grads pursue arts and sciences degrees. 3% grads pursue law degrees. 1% grads pursue business degrees. 5% grads pursue medical degrees. **Faculty:** Student/faculty ratio 12:1. 110 full-time faculty, 98% hold PhDs, 21% are members of minority groups, 54% are women. 0% of classes are taught by teaching assistants.

ACADEMICS

Degrees: Bachelor's. **Classes:** Most classes have 10–19 students. Most lab/ discussion sessions have 10–19 students. **Most popular majors:** Psychology, General; Business/Commerce, General; Exercise Science and Kinesiology. **Special Study Options:** Double major; Honors program; Independent study; Internships; Liberal arts/career combination; Student-designed major; Study abroad; Teacher certification program. **Honors programs:** Departmental honors, which are reflected on the diploma and transcript, are awarded after successful completion of a two semester honors course. **Disability Services offered:** Note-taking services; Reader services; Tape recorders; Tutors. **Career**

services: Alumni network; Alumni services; Career assessment; Internships; Regional alumni.

FACILITIES

Housing: Apartments for single students; Coed dorms; Fraternity/sorority housing; Men's dorms; Special housing for disabled students; Women's dorms; 90% of campus accessible to physically disabled. **Special Academic Facilities/ Equipment:** Alma Thomas Fine Arts Center; Red and Charline McCombs Campus Center; Corbin J. Robertson Center for Fitness and Wellness; Fountainwood Astronomical Observatory.

CAMPUS LIFE

Environment: Town. **Activities:** Campus Ministries; Choral groups; Concert band; Dance; Drama/theater; Jazz band; Model UN; Music ensembles; Musical theater; Opera; Radio station; Student government; Student newspaper; Symphony orchestra. 94 registered organizations, 17 honor societies, 10 religious organizations, 4 fraternities, 4 sororities on campus. **Athletics (Intercollegiate):** *Men:* baseball, basketball, cross-country, diving, golf, lacrosse, soccer, swimming, tennis, track/field (outdoor). *Women:* basketball, cross-country, diving, golf, soccer, softball, swimming, tennis, track/field (outdoor), volleyball. **On-Campus Highlights:** Robertson Center-indoor olympic size pool. **Environmental Initiatives:** 100% wind power. Formation of the Green Fund, specifically used to fund environmental and sustainable projects/ initiatives on campus. Signing of the Talloires Declaration.

ADMISSIONS

Freshman Academic Profile: 34% in top 10% of high school class, 70% in top 25% of high school class, 94% in top 50% of high school class. 74% from public high schools. **Test Scores:** SAT Math middle 50% range 550–650. SAT EBRW middle 50% range 580–680. ACT middle 50% range 23–29. **Basis for Candidate Selection:** *Very important factors include:* rigor of secondary school record, class rank, academic GPA, application essay, standardized test scores, recommendation(s). *Important factors include:* interview, extracurricular activities, talent/ability, character/personal qualities, first generation, alumni/ae relation, geographical residence, state residency, racial/ethnic status, volunteer work. *Other factors include:* religious affiliation/commitment, work experience, level of applicant's interest. **Freshman Admission Requirements:** High school diploma is required and GED is accepted. *Academic units required:* 4 English, 4 math, 3 science, 2 science labs, 2 foreign language, 2 social studies, 1 history, 1 academic elective. *Academic units recommended:* 4 English, 4 math, 4 science, 3 science labs, 3 foreign language, 3 social studies, 1 history, 1 academic elective. **Freshman Admission Statistics:** 4,551 applied, 45% admitted, 22% enrolled. **Transfer Admission Requirements:** High school transcript, college transcript(s), essay or personal statement, statement of good standing from prior institution(s). Minimum college GPA of 3.0 required. Lowest grade transferable C. **General Admission Information:** Priority deadline 2/1. Regular application deadline 2/1. Admission may be deferred for a maximum of 1 year.

COSTS AND FINANCIAL AID

Annual tuition $43,560. Room and board $12,320. Average book and supplies expense $1,300. **Required Forms and Deadlines:** FAFSA. **Notification of Awards:** Applicants will be notified of awards on a rolling basis beginning 11/15. **Types of Aid:** *Need-based scholarships/grants:* College/ university scholarship or grant aid from institutional funds; Federal Pell; Private scholarships; SEOG; State scholarships/grants. *Loans:* Direct PLUS loans; Direct Subsidized Stafford Loans; Direct Unsubsidized Stafford Loans. **Student Employment:** Federal Work-Study Program available. Institutional employment available. **Financial Aid Statistics:** 100% needy freshmen, 99% needy undergrads receive need-based scholarship or grant aid. 100% freshmen, 98% undergrads receive non-need-based scholarship or grant aid. 79% freshmen, 83% undergrads receive need-based self-help aid. 0% freshmen, 0% undergrads receive athletic scholarships. 100% freshmen, 98% undergrads receive any aid. 61% undergrads borrow to pay for school. Average cumulative indebtedness $34,133. **Criteria awarding aid:** *Need-based:* Academics. *Non-need-based:* Academics, Alumni affiliation, Art, Leadership, Minority status, Music/drama, Religious affiliation.

SPELMAN COLLEGE

Best Colleges

350 Spelman Lane, Atlanta, GA 30314-4399
Phone: 404-270-5193 **Financial Aid Phone:** 404-270-5212
E-mail: admiss@spelman.edu **CEEB Code:** 5628
Fax: 404-270-5201 **Website:** www.spelman.edu **ACT Code:** 0794

This private school was founded in 1881. It has a 39.1 acre campus.

RATINGS
Admissions Selectivity Rating: 89   **Fire Safety Rating:** 87   **Green Rating:** 60*

STUDENTS AND FACULTY
Enrollment: 2,166. **Student Body:** 100% female, 0% male, 74% out-of-state, 1% international (7 countries represented). Asian <1%, African American 97%, Caucasian <1%, Hispanic <1%, Native American 2%, Pacific Islander 0%, Two or more races <1%, Race unknown 0%.
Retention and Graduation: 91% freshmen return for sophomore year. 69% freshmen graduate within 4 years. 75% freshmen graduate within 6 years. 15% grads go on to further study within 1 year. 69% grads pursue arts and sciences degrees. 16% grads pursue law degrees. 5% grads pursue medical degrees. **Faculty:** Student/faculty ratio 11:1. 177 full-time faculty, 90% hold PhDs, 87% are members of minority groups, 74% are women. 0% of classes are taught by teaching assistants.

ACADEMICS
Degrees: Bachelor's. **Classes:** Most classes have 10–19 students. Most lab/discussion sessions have 10–19 students. **Most popular majors:** Psychology, General; Political Science and Government, General. **Special Study Options:** Cooperative education program; Cross-registration; Double major; Dual enrollment; Exchange student program (domestic); Honors program; Independent study; Internships; Student-designed major; Study abroad; Teacher certification program. **Honors programs:** Founded in 1980, the Spelman College Honors Program, named for scholar-teacher Ethel Waddell Githii, is interdisciplinary in design and recognizes the diversity of our faculty expertise and student creative scholarship. The Githii Honors Program creates original programming and targeted support for our member students, and collaborates with academic departments and programs to provide a rich array of scholarly and creative venues. These include our annual reading and lecture series, special programs and workshops for the broader campus and the Atlanta community, and cultural engagements on and beyond the campus. The Program spotlights intellectual leadership as a habit of mind and a quality of the ethical citizen. **Disability Services offered:** Note-taking services; Reader services; Tape recorders; Tutors. **Career services:** Career assessment; Career/job search classes; Internships.

FACILITIES
Housing: Theme housing; Women's dorms; 95% of campus accessible to physically disabled. **Special Academic Facilities/Equipment:** Spelman College Museum of Fine Art, language lab, electron microscope. **Campus Network:** 100% of classrooms, 100% of student union, 100% of libraries, 100% of dining areas, 100% of common outdoor areas have wireless network access.

CAMPUS LIFE
Environment: Metropolis. **Activities:** Campus Ministries; Choral groups; Dance; Drama/theater; International Student Organization; Student government; Student newspaper; Yearbook. 80 registered organizations, 2 religious organizations, 4 sororities on campus. **Athletics (Intercollegiate):** *Women:* basketball, cross-country, golf, soccer, softball, tennis, volleyball. **On-Campus Highlights:** Sister's Chapel.

ADMISSIONS
Freshman Academic Profile: Average high school GPA 3.7. 10% in top 10% of high school class, 25% in top 25% of high school class, 50% in top 50% of high school class. **Test Scores:** SAT Math middle 50% range 520–590. SAT EBRW middle 50% range 560–630. ACT middle 50% range 22–26. **Basis for Candidate Selection:** *Very important factors include:* rigor of secondary school record, academic GPA, application essay, standardized test scores, recommendation(s), character/personal qualities. *Important factors include:* class rank, extracurricular activities, volunteer work. *Other factors include:* talent/ability, alumni/ae relation, geographical residence, work experience, level of

applicant's interest. **Freshman Admission Requirements:** High school diploma is required and GED is accepted. *Academic units required:* 4 English, 2 math, 2 science, 1 science lab, 2 foreign language, 2 social studies, 2 history, 1 academic elective. *Academic units recommended:* 4 English, 4 math, 4 science, 2 science labs, 2 foreign language, 3 social studies. **Freshman Admission Statistics:** 9,451 applied, 39% admitted, 15% enrolled. **Transfer Admission Requirements:** High school transcript, college transcript(s). Minimum college GPA of 2.0 required. Lowest grade transferable C. **General Admission Information:** Application fee $40. Regular application deadline 2/1. Non-fall registration accepted. Admission may be deferred for a maximum of one year.

COSTS AND FINANCIAL AID
Annual tuition $25,942. Room and board $14,338. Required fees $4,280. Average book and supplies expense $3,000. **Required Forms and Deadlines:** FAFSA. **Notification of Awards:** Applicants will be notified of awards on a rolling basis beginning 12/15. **Types of Aid:** *Need-based scholarships/grants:* College/university scholarship or grant aid from institutional funds; Federal Pell; Private scholarships; SEOG; State scholarships/grants; United Negro College Fund. *Loans:* Direct PLUS loans; Direct Subsidized Stafford Loans; Direct Unsubsidized Stafford Loans. **Student Employment:** Federal Work-Study Program available. Institutional employment available. **Financial Aid Statistics:** 99% needy freshmen, 89% needy undergrads receive need-based scholarship or grant aid. 10% freshmen, 13% undergrads receive non-need-based scholarship or grant aid. 85% freshmen, 85% undergrads receive need-based self-help aid. 0% freshmen, 0% undergrads receive athletic scholarships. 26% freshmen, 90% undergrads receive any aid. 82% undergrads borrow to pay for school. Average cumulative indebtedness $35,582. **Criteria awarding aid:** *Need-based:* Academics, Alumni affiliation, Leadership, Music/drama, Religious affiliation. *Non-need-based:* Academics, Alumni affiliation, Music/drama, State/district residency.

SPRING ARBOR UNIVERSITY

106 East Main Street, Spring Arbor, MI 49283-9799
Phone: 517-750-6458 **Financial Aid Phone:** 800-968-0011
E-mail: admissions@admin.arbor.edu **CEEB Code:** 1732
Fax: 517-750-6620 **Website:** www.arbor.edu **ACT Code:** 2056

This private school, affiliated with the Free Methodist Church, was founded in 1873. It has a 100 acre campus.

RATINGS
Admissions Selectivity Rating: 82   **Fire Safety Rating:** 86   **Green Rating:** 60*

STUDENTS AND FACULTY
Enrollment: 2,603. **Student Body:** 69% female, 31% male, 12% out-of-state, 10 countries represented.
Retention and Graduation: 78% freshmen return for sophomore year. 22% grads go on to further study within 1 year. 8% grads pursue arts and sciences degrees. 0% grads pursue law degrees. 3% grads pursue business degrees. 8% grads pursue medical degrees. **Faculty:** Student/faculty ratio 15:1. 81 full-time faculty, 72% hold PhDs, 11% are members of minority groups, 32% are women. 0% of classes are taught by teaching assistants.

ACADEMICS
Degrees: Associate; Bachelor's; Master's; Post-bachelor's certificate. **Classes:** Most classes have 10–19 students. Most lab/discussion sessions have 10–19 students. **Most popular majors:** Elementary Education and Teaching; Secondary Education and Teaching; Psychology, General. **Special Study Options:** Accelerated program; Cross-registration; Distance learning; Double major; Dual enrollment; English as a Second Language (ESL); Honors program; Independent study; Internships; Student-designed major; Study abroad; Teacher certification program; Weekend college. **Combined degree programs:** BA/MEng. **Disability Services offered:** Note-taking services; Reader services; Tape recorders; Tutors. **Career services:** Alumni network; Alumni services; Career assessment; Career/job search classes; Internships; Regional alumni.

FACILITIES
Housing: Apartments for married students; Apartments for single students; Men's dorms; Special housing for disabled students; Special housing for international students; Women's dorms; 80% of campus accessible to physically disabled. **Special Academic Facilities/Equipment:** State-of-the-art academic building (Poling Center); the Poling Center features the CP Federal Credit Union Trading Center and is equipped with some of the same technology that

is used daily on Wall Street including: An electronic wrap-around ticker, large light emitting diode (LED) financial data board, Bloomberg terminal, and continuous financial news feeds. Radio and TV studios, commercial writing/computer graphics lab, science center, art gallery.

CAMPUS LIFE

Environment: Rural. **Activities:** Campus Ministries; Choral groups; Concert band; Drama/theater; International Student Organization; Jazz band; Literary magazine; Model UN; Music ensembles; Musical theater; Opera; Pep band; Radio station; Student government; Student newspaper; Student-run film society; Symphony orchestra; Television station; Yearbook. **Athletics (Intercollegiate):** *Men:* baseball, basketball, cross-country, golf, soccer, tennis, track/field (outdoor), track/field (indoor). *Women:* basketball, cross-country, soccer, softball, tennis, track/field (outdoor), track/field (indoor), volleyball. **On-Campus Highlights:** Sacred Grounds (Starbucks).

ADMISSIONS

Freshman Academic Profile: Average high school GPA 3.4. 22% in top 10% of high school class, 48% in top 25% of high school class, 77% in top 50% of high school class. 80% from public high schools. **Test Scores:** SAT Math middle 50% range 460–580. SAT EBRW middle 50% range 480–585. ACT middle 50% range 20–26. **Basis for Candidate Selection:** *Very important factors include:* rigor of secondary school record, standardized test scores, character/personal qualities. *Important factors include:* academic GPA. *Other factors include:* class rank, application essay, recommendation(s), interview, extracurricular activities, talent/ability, religious affiliation/commitment. **Freshman Admission Requirements:** High school diploma is required and GED is accepted. *Academic units required:* 4 English, 3 math, 3 science, 3 science labs, 3 history, 1 unit from above areas or other academic areas. *Academic units recommended:* 2 foreign language, 1 computer science. **Freshman Admission Statistics:** 2,698 applied, 65% admitted, 21% enrolled. **Transfer Admission Requirements:** High school transcript, college transcript(s), essay or personal statement. Minimum college GPA of 2.0 required. Lowest grade transferable C. **General Admission Information:** Application fee $30. Priority deadline 2/15. Regular application deadline 8/1. Non-fall registration accepted. Admission may be deferred indefinitely.

COSTS AND FINANCIAL AID

Annual tuition $21,998. Room and board $7,900. Required fees $540. Average book and supplies expense $800. **Required Forms and Deadlines:** FAFSA. **Notification of Awards:** Applicants will be notified of awards on a rolling basis beginning 3/1. **Types of Aid:** *Need-based scholarships/grants:* College/university scholarship or grant aid from institutional funds; Federal Pell; Private scholarships; SEOG. *Loans:* Direct PLUS loans; Direct Subsidized Stafford Loans; Direct Unsubsidized Stafford Loans. **Student Employment:** Federal Work-Study Program available. Institutional employment available. **Financial Aid Statistics:** 100% needy freshmen, 99% needy undergrads receive need-based scholarship or grant aid. 10% freshmen, 10% undergrads receive non-need-based scholarship or grant aid. 83% freshmen, 84% undergrads receive need-based self-help aid. 22% freshmen, 19% undergrads receive athletic scholarships. 97% freshmen, 93% undergrads receive any aid. **Criteria awarding aid:** *Non-need-based:* Academics, Art, Athletics, Minority status, Religious affiliation.

SPRING HILL COLLEGE

4000 Dauphin Street, Mobile, AL 36608
Phone: 251-380-3030 **Financial Aid Phone:** (251) 380-2253
E-mail: admit@shc.edu **CEEB Code:** 1733
Fax: 251-460-2186 **Website:** www.shc.edu **ACT Code:** 42

This private school, affiliated with the Roman Catholic-Jesuit Church, was founded in 1830. It has a 381 acre campus.

RATINGS

Admissions Selectivity Rating: 78   **Fire Safety Rating:** 84   **Green Rating:** 60*

STUDENTS AND FACULTY

Enrollment: 1,252. **Student Body:** 61% female, 39% male, 58% out-of-state, 5% international (26 countries represented). Asian 1%, African American 16%, Caucasian 66%, Hispanic 3%, Native American 1%, Pacific Islander <1%, Two or more races 4%, Race unknown 4%.
Retention and Graduation: 72% freshmen return for sophomore year. 44% freshmen graduate within 4 years. 53% freshmen graduate within 6 years.

Faculty: Student/faculty ratio 13:1. 88 full-time faculty, 93% hold PhDs, 7% are members of minority groups, 48% are women. 0% of classes are taught by teaching assistants.

ACADEMICS

Degrees: Bachelor's; Certificate; Master's; Post-bachelor's certificate; Post-master's certificate. **Classes:** Most classes have 10–19 students. Most lab/discussion sessions have 10–19 students. **Most popular majors:** Biology/Biological Sciences, General; Psychology, General; Business Administration, Management and Operations, Other. **Special Study Options:** Accelerated program; Distance learning; Double major; Dual enrollment; Honors program; Independent study; Internships; Student-designed major; Study abroad; Teacher certification program. **Honors programs:** SHC's 4-year Honors Program offers a challenging and rewarding course of study to academically gifted and motivated students. It is comprised of academic courses; seminar experiences; and additional opportunities for service, leadership, cultural exploration, and social interaction both on and off campus. Honors courses cover material in greater depth, use primary materials when possible, stress student participation and responsibility, and encourage high individual achievement. **Disability Services offered:** Tutors. **Career services:** Alumni network; Alumni services; Career assessment; Career/job search classes; Internships; Regional alumni.

FACILITIES

Housing: Apartments for single students; Coed dorms; Theme housing; 90% of campus accessible to physically disabled. **Special Academic Facilities/Equipment:** Theater. **Campus Network:** 100% of classrooms, 100% of dorms, 100% of student union, 100% of libraries, 100% of dining areas, 25% of common outdoor areas have wireless network access.

CAMPUS LIFE

Environment: Metropolis. **Activities:** Campus Ministries; Choral groups; Dance; Drama/theater; Jazz band; Literary magazine; Student government; Student newspaper; Yearbook. 54 registered organizations, 17 honor societies, 5 religious organizations, 4 fraternities, 7 sororities on campus. **Athletics (Intercollegiate):** *Men:* baseball, basketball, cross-country, golf, soccer, tennis. *Women:* basketball, cross-country, golf, soccer, softball, tennis, volleyball. **On-Campus Highlights:** Student Center.

ADMISSIONS

Freshman Academic Profile: Average high school GPA 3.6. 19% in top 10% of high school class, 51% in top 25% of high school class, 81% in top 50% of high school class. **Test Scores:** SAT Math middle 50% range 510–590. SAT EBRW middle 50% range 505–595. ACT middle 50% range 20–25. **Basis for Candidate Selection:** *Very important factors include:* rigor of secondary school record, academic GPA, standardized test scores. *Important factors include:* class rank, recommendation(s), interview. *Other factors include:* application essay, extracurricular activities, talent/ability, character/personal qualities, alumni/ae relation, volunteer work. **Freshman Admission Requirements:** High school diploma is required and GED is accepted. *Academic units recommended:* 4 English, 3 math, 3 science, 1 science lab, 2 foreign language, 2 social studies, 1 history, 1 academic elective. **Freshman Admission Statistics:** 8,587 applied, 66% admitted, 5% enrolled. **Transfer Admission Requirements:** College transcript(s), statement of good standing from prior institution(s). Minimum college GPA of 2.5 required. Lowest grade transferable C-. **General Admission Information:** Application fee $25. Priority deadline 1/15. Regular application deadline 7/15. Non-fall registration accepted. Admission may be deferred for a maximum of 1 year.

COSTS AND FINANCIAL AID

Required Forms and Deadlines: FAFSA; State aid form. **Notification of Awards:** Applicants will be notified of awards on a rolling basis beginning 2/15. **Types of Aid:** *Need-based scholarships/grants:* College/university scholarship or grant aid from institutional funds; Federal Pell; Private scholarships; SEOG; State scholarships/grants. *Loans:* Direct PLUS loans; Direct Subsidized Stafford Loans; Direct Unsubsidized Stafford Loans. **Student Employment:** Federal Work-Study Program available. Institutional employment available. **Criteria awarding aid:** *Need-based:* Academics, Alumni affiliation, Athletics, Job skills, Leadership, Minority status. *Non-need-based:* Academics, Alumni affiliation, Art, Athletics, Job skills, Leadership, Minority status, State/district residency.

STANFORD UNIVERSITY

Undergraduate Admission, Stanford, CA 94305-6106
Phone: 650-723-2091 **Financial Aid Phone:** 650-723-3058
E-mail: admission@stanford.edu **CEEB Code:** 4704
Fax: 650-723-6050 **Website:** www.stanford.edu **ACT Code:** 434

This private school was founded in 1885. It has a 8180 acre campus.

RATINGS
Admissions Selectivity Rating: 99 **Fire Safety Rating:** 89 **Green Rating:** 99

STUDENTS AND FACULTY
Enrollment: 6,994. **Student Body:** 50% female, 50% male, 61% out-of-state, 11% international (90 countries represented). Asian 23%, African American 7%, Caucasian 32%, Hispanic 17%, Native American 1%, Pacific Islander <1%, Two or more races 9%, Race unknown <1%.
Retention and Graduation: 99% freshmen return for sophomore year. 73% freshmen graduate within 4 years. 94% freshmen graduate within 6 years. 25% grads go on to further study within 1 year. **Faculty:** Student/faculty ratio 5:1. 1,679 full-time faculty, 78% hold PhDs, 23% are members of minority groups, 35% are women. 6% of classes are taught by teaching assistants.

ACADEMICS
Degrees: Bachelor's; Doctoral degree—professional practice; Doctoral degree research/scholarship; Master's; Post-bachelor's certificate. **Classes:** Most classes have 10–19 students. Most lab/discussion sessions have fewer than 10 students. **Most popular majors:** Engineering, General; Human Biology; Computer Science. **Special Study Options:** Distance learning; Double major; Exchange student program (domestic); Honors program; Independent study; Internships; Student-designed major; Study abroad; Teacher certification program. **Honors programs:** About 100 students annually participate in Bing Honors College. About 25 percent of each graduating class earn departmental honors. **Combined degree programs:** BA/MA. **Disability Services offered:** Note-taking services; Reader services; Tape recorders; Tutors. **Career services:** Alumni network; Alumni services; Career assessment; Career/job search classes; Internships; Regional alumni.

FACILITIES
Housing: Apartments for married students; Apartments for single students; Coed dorms; Cooperative housing; Fraternity/sorority housing; Special housing for disabled students; Theme housing; Women's dorms; 98% of campus accessible to physically disabled. **Special Academic Facilities/Equipment:** Three art museums, marine station, two observatories, biological preserve, linear accelerator, concert hall.

CAMPUS LIFE
Environment: City. **Activities:** Campus Ministries; Choral groups; Concert band; Dance; Drama/theater; International Student Organization; Jazz band; Literary magazine; Marching band; Model UN; Music ensembles; Musical theater; Opera; Pep band; Radio station; Student government; Student newspaper; Student-run film society; Symphony orchestra; Television station; Yearbook. 600 registered organizations, 35 religious organizations, 16 fraternities, 14 sororities on campus. **Athletics (Intercollegiate):** *Men:* baseball, basketball, crew/rowing, cross-country, diving, fencing, football, golf, gymnastics, sailing, soccer, swimming, tennis, track/field (outdoor), volleyball, water polo, wrestling. *Women:* basketball, crew/rowing, cross-country, diving, fencing, field hockey, golf, gymnastics, lacrosse, sailing, soccer, softball, squash, swimming, synchronized swimming, tennis, track/field (outdoor), volleyball, water polo. **On-Campus Highlights:** Cantor Center for the Visual Arts.
Environmental Initiatives: Stanford Energy System Innovations—(SESI) Between 1987 and 2015, Stanford relied on a natural gas-fired combined heat and power (CHP) plant for virtually all its energy demand. Although efficient, its fossil-fuel based source caused the CHP to produce 90% of Stanford's GHG emissions and consume 25% of the campus' potable water supply. As a result, Stanford's GHG reduction strategy focused primarily on transforming the university's energy supply through a new Central Energy Facility (CEF). The new CEF, which came online in April 2015, includes three large water tanks for thermal energy storage and a high voltage substation that receives electricity from the grid. A key feature of the CEF is an innovative heat recovery system that takes advantage of Stanford's overlap in heating and cooling needs. In

addition to the CEF, the SESI project converted the heat supply of all buildings from steam to hot water. This new system is 70% more efficient than the CHP plant. The efficiencies gained from the new CEF and hot water conversion, along with the introduction of a 67 MW off-site solar plant and 4.5 MW of on-site solar, have reduced the university's overall GHG emissions by approximately 68% between 2011 and 2017.

ADMISSIONS
Freshman Academic Profile: Average high school GPA 4.0. 98% in top 10% of high school class, 100% in top 25% of high school class, 100% in top 50% of high school class. 61% from public high schools. **Test Scores:** SAT Math middle 50% range 740–800. SAT EBRW middle 50% range 700–770. ACT middle 50% range 32–35. **Basis for Candidate Selection:** *Very important factors include:* rigor of secondary school record, class rank, academic GPA, application essay, standardized test scores, recommendation(s), extracurricular activities, talent/ability, character/personal qualities. *Other factors include:* interview, first generation, alumni/ae relation, geographical residence, racial/ethnic status, volunteer work, work experience. **Freshman Admission Requirements:** High school diploma is required and GED is accepted. *Academic units recommended:* 4 English, 4 math, 3 science, 3 science labs, 3 foreign language, 3 social studies. **Freshman Admission Statistics:** 47,498 applied, 4% admitted, 82% enrolled. **Transfer Admission Requirements:** High school transcript, college transcript(s), essay or personal statement, standardized test scores, statement of good standing from prior institution(s). Lowest grade transferable C-. **General Admission Information:** Application fee $90. Regular application deadline 1/2. Admission may be deferred for a maximum of 2 years.

COSTS AND FINANCIAL AID
Annual tuition $55,473. Room and board $17,255. Required fees $696. Average book and supplies expense $1,290. **Required Forms and Deadlines:** CSS/Financial Aid PROFILE; FAFSA; Noncustodial PROFILE. **Notification of Awards:** Applicants will be notified of awards on a rolling basis beginning 4/1. **Types of Aid:** *Need-based scholarships/grants:* College/university scholarship or grant aid from institutional funds; Federal Pell; Private scholarships; SEOG; State scholarships/grants. *Loans:* Direct PLUS loans; Direct Subsidized Stafford Loans; Direct Unsubsidized Stafford Loans. **Student Employment:** Federal Work-Study Program available. Institutional employment available. **Financial Aid Statistics:** 98% needy freshmen, 98% needy undergrads receive need-based scholarship or grant aid. 3% freshmen, 4% undergrads receive non-need-based scholarship or grant aid. 67% freshmen, 74% undergrads receive need-based self-help aid. 6% freshmen, 7% undergrads receive athletic scholarships. 86% freshmen, 85% undergrads receive any aid. 17% undergrads borrow to pay for school. Average cumulative indebtedness $22,897. **Criteria awarding aid:** *Non-need-based:* Athletics.

STATE UNIVERSITY OF NEW YORK—ALFRED STATE COLLEGE

Huntington Administration Bldg., Alfred, NY 14802
Phone: 607-587-4215 **Financial Aid Phone:** 607-587-3979
E-mail: admissions@alfredstate.edu **CEEB Code:** 2522
Fax: 607-587-4299 **Website:** www.alfredstate.edu **ACT Code:** 2910

This public school was founded in 1908. It has a 840 acre campus.

RATINGS
Admissions Selectivity Rating: 81 **Fire Safety Rating:** 92 **Green Rating:** 60*

STUDENTS AND FACULTY
Enrollment: 3,760. **Student Body:** 37% female, 63% male, 4% out-of-state, <1% international (7 countries represented). Asian 1%, African American 13%, Caucasian 72%, Hispanic 9%, Native American <1%, Pacific Islander <1%, Two or more races 3%, Race unknown 2%.
Retention and Graduation: 78% freshmen return for sophomore year. 53% freshmen graduate within 4 years. 68% freshmen graduate within 6 years. 33% grads go on to further study within 1 year. **Faculty:** Student/faculty ratio 18:1. 167 full-time faculty, 38% hold PhDs, 6% are members of minority groups, 30% are women. 0% of classes are taught by teaching assistants.

ACADEMICS
Degrees: Associate; Bachelor's; Certificate; Terminal Associate; Transfer Associate. **Classes:** Most classes have 10–19 students. Most lab/discussion sessions have 10–19 students. **Most popular majors:** Mechanical/Mechanical Engineering Technology/Technician; Business, Management, Marketing, and Related Support Services, Other; Registered Nursing/Registered Nurse. **Special**

Study Options: Accelerated program; Cooperative education program; Cross-registration; Distance learning; Double major; English as a Second Language (ESL); Honors program; Independent study; Internships; Liberal arts/career combination; Student-designed major; Study abroad. **Honors programs:** Participants complete a series of seminars, as well as a substantial honors project and 10 hours of volunteer community service. **Disability Services offered:** Note-taking services; Reader services; Tape recorders; Tutors. **Career services:** Alumni network; Career assessment; Career/job search classes.

FACILITIES
Housing: Apartments for single students; Coed dorms; Cooperative housing; Fraternity/sorority housing; Special housing for disabled students; Special housing for international students; Theme housing; Wellness housing; 100% of campus accessible to physically disabled.

CAMPUS LIFE
Environment: Rural. **Activities:** Campus Ministries; Choral groups; Concert band; Dance; Drama/theater; International Student Organization; Jazz band; Literary magazine; Music ensembles; Musical theater; Pep band; Radio station; Student government; Student newspaper; Symphony orchestra; Yearbook. 125 registered organizations, 5 honor societies, 4 religious organizations, 6 fraternities, 6 sororities on campus. **Athletics (Intercollegiate):** *Men:* baseball, basketball, cheerleading, cross-country, football, lacrosse, soccer, swimming, track/field (outdoor), wrestling. *Women:* basketball, cheerleading, cross-country, soccer, softball, swimming, track/field (outdoor), volleyball. **On-Campus Highlights:** Student Leadership Center. **Environmental Initiatives:** Energy conservation, greenhouse gas inventory, and shrinking our carbon footprint through renewable energy.

ADMISSIONS
Test Scores: SAT Math middle 50% range 470–590. SAT EBRW middle 50% range 470–580. ACT middle 50% range 18–25. **Basis for Candidate Selection:** *Very important factors include:* rigor of secondary school record, academic GPA, standardized test scores. *Other factors include:* application essay, recommendation(s), interview, extracurricular activities, talent/ability, character/personal qualities, volunteer work, work experience, level of applicant's interest. **Freshman Admission Requirements:** High school diploma is required and GED is accepted. **Freshman Admission Statistics:** 6,683 applied, 67% admitted, 26% enrolled. **Transfer Admission Requirements:** High school transcript, college transcript(s), statement of good standing from prior institution(s). Minimum college GPA of 2.4 required. Lowest grade transferable C. **General Admission Information:** Application fee $50. Non-fall registration accepted. Admission may be deferred for a maximum of 1 year.

COSTS AND FINANCIAL AID
Annual in-state tuition $7,070. Annual out-of-state tuition $11,040. Room and board $13,060. Required fees $1,782. Average book and supplies expense $1,200. **Required Forms and Deadlines:** FAFSA; State aid form. **Notification of Awards:** Applicants will be notified of awards on a rolling basis beginning 11/1. **Types of Aid:** *Need-based scholarships/grants:* College/university scholarship or grant aid from institutional funds; Federal Pell; Private scholarships; SEOG; State scholarships/grants. *Loans:* Direct PLUS loans; Direct Subsidized Stafford Loans; Direct Unsubsidized Stafford Loans. **Student Employment:** Federal Work-Study Program available. Institutional employment available. **Financial Aid Statistics:** 84% needy freshmen, 83% needy undergrads receive need-based scholarship or grant aid. 45% freshmen, 36% undergrads receive non-need-based scholarship or grant aid. 81% freshmen, 82% undergrads receive need-based self-help aid. 0% freshmen, 0% undergrads receive athletic scholarships. 93.26% freshmen, 90.07% undergrads receive any aid. 100% undergrads borrow to pay for school. Average cumulative indebtedness $34,177. **Criteria awarding aid:** *Non-need-based:* Academics, Alumni affiliation, Job skills, Music/drama, State/district residency.

STATE UNIVERSITY OF NEW YORK— BINGHAMTON UNIVERSITY

PO Box 6001, Binghamton, NY 13902-6001
Phone: 607-777-2171 **Financial Aid Phone:** 607-777-2428
E-mail: admit@binghamton.edu **CEEB Code:** 2535
Fax: 607-777-4445 **Website:** www.binghamton.edu **ACT Code:** 2956

This public school was founded in 1946. It has a 930 acre campus.

RATINGS
Admissions Selectivity Rating: 92 **Fire Safety Rating:** 95 **Green Rating:** 95

STUDENTS AND FACULTY
Enrollment: 13,693. **Student Body:** 49% female, 51% male, 7% out-of-state, 8% international (97 countries represented). Asian 14%, African American 5%, Caucasian 57%, Hispanic 11%, Native American <1%, Pacific Islander <1%, Two or more races 2%, Race unknown 2%.
Retention and Graduation: 91% freshmen return for sophomore year. 71% freshmen graduate within 4 years. 83% freshmen graduate within 6 years. 57% grads go on to further study within 1 year. 2% grads pursue law degrees. 9% grads pursue business degrees. 6% grads pursue medical degrees. **Faculty:** Student/faculty ratio 19:1. 754 full-time faculty, 92% hold PhDs, 30% are members of minority groups, 44% are women. 7% of classes are taught by teaching assistants.

ACADEMICS
Degrees: Bachelor's; Doctoral degree—professional practice; Doctoral degree research/scholarship; Master's; Post-master's certificate. **Classes:** Most classes have 10–19 students. Most lab/discussion sessions have 20–29 students. **Most popular majors:** Engineering, General; Business Administration and Management, General; Psychology, General. **Special Study Options:** Accelerated program; Cross-registration; Distance learning; Double major; Dual enrollment; English as a Second Language (ESL); Exchange student program (domestic); Honors program; Independent study; Internships; Liberal arts/career combination; Student-designed major; Study abroad; Teacher certification program. **Honors programs:** Binghamton University Scholars Program—See http://scholars.binghamton.edu. Each academic department offers an honors program. Binghamton also has a PricewaterhouseCoopers Scholars program for students in the School of Management. **Combined degree programs:** BA/MA. **Disability Services offered:** Note-taking services; Reader services; Tape recorders. **Career services:** Alumni network; Alumni services; Career assessment; Career/job search classes; Internships; Regional alumni.

FACILITIES
Housing: Apartments for single students; Coed dorms; Special housing for disabled students; Theme housing; Wellness housing 95% of campus accessible to physically disabled. **Special Academic Facilities/Equipment:** Art museum & gallery, 10,000+ square foot fitness facility, performing arts center, indoor/outdoor theater, multi-climate and teaching greenhouse, sculpture foundry, 8,000-seat Events Center, Analytical and Diagnostics Laboratory, Electron Microscopy Facility, modular labs in Innovative Technologies Complex buildings, Public Archaeology Facility, 187-acre Nature Preserve, NYS Center of Excellence in Small Scale Systems Integration and Packaging.

CAMPUS LIFE
Environment: City. **Activities:** Campus Ministries; Choral groups; Concert band; Dance; Drama/theater; International Student Organization; Jazz band; Literary magazine; Model UN; Music ensembles; Musical theater; Opera; Radio station; Student government; Student newspaper; Student-run film society; Symphony orchestra; Television station; Yearbook. 373 registered organizations, 28 honor societies, 14 religious organizations, 36 fraternities, 17 sororities on campus. **Athletics (Intercollegiate):** *Men:* baseball, basketball, cross-country, diving, golf, lacrosse, soccer, swimming, tennis, track/field (outdoor), track/field (indoor), wrestling. *Women:* basketball, cross-country, diving, lacrosse, soccer, softball, swimming, tennis, track/field (outdoor), track/field (indoor), volleyball. **On-Campus Highlights:** Union (The MarketPlace, Late Nite Binghamton, bookstore) **Environmental Initiatives:** Binghamton University designs, constructs, operates and maintains all new buildings following guidelines

set forth by the U.S. Green Building Council's LEED rating system. Since 2004, Binghamton has obtained multiple LEED certifications under the New Construction program including 2 LEED, 3 LEED Silver, 7 LEED Gold, and 1 LEED Platinum for a total of 1,690,183 square feet of building space. This represents 27% of total building space owned by Binghamton University.

ADMISSIONS

Freshman Academic Profile: Average high school GPA 3.7. 90% from public high schools. **Test Scores:** SAT Math middle 50% range 650–720. SAT EBRW middle 50% range 640–711. ACT middle 50% range 28–31. **Basis for Candidate Selection:** *Very important factors include:* rigor of secondary school record, academic GPA, standardized test scores. *Important factors include:* class rank, application essay, recommendation(s), extracurricular activities. *Other factors include:* talent/ability, character/personal qualities, first generation, alumni/ae relation, geographical residence, state residency, racial/ethnic status, volunteer work, work experience, level of applicant's interest. **Freshman Admission Requirements:** High school diploma is required and GED is accepted. *Academic units required:* 4 English, 3 math, 2 science, 3 foreign language, 2 social studies. *Academic units recommended:* 4 math, 4 science, 4 social studies, 4 history. **Freshman Admission Statistics:** 33,467 applied, 40% admitted, 20% enrolled. **Transfer Admission Requirements:** College transcript(s). Lowest grade transferable C-. **General Admission Information:** Application fee $50. Priority deadline 1/15. Non-fall registration accepted. Admission may be deferred for a maximum of varies, 1yr.

COSTS AND FINANCIAL AID

Annual in-state tuition $6,870. Annual out-of-state tuition $23,710. Room and board $15,058. Required fees $2,934. Average book and supplies expense $1,000. **Required Forms and Deadlines:** FAFSA; State aid form. **Notification of Awards:** Applicants will be notified of awards on a rolling basis beginning 1/31. **Types of Aid:** *Need-based scholarships/grants:* College/university scholarship or grant aid from institutional funds; Federal Pell; Private scholarships; SEOG; State scholarships/grants. *Loans:* Direct PLUS loans; Direct Subsidized Stafford Loans; Direct Unsubsidized Stafford Loans. **Student Employment:** Federal Work-Study Program available. Institutional employment available. **Financial Aid Statistics:** 83% needy freshmen, 83% needy undergrads receive need-based scholarship or grant aid. 14% freshmen, 8% undergrads receive non-need-based scholarship or grant aid. 98% freshmen, 98% undergrads receive need-based self-help aid. 2% freshmen, 2% undergrads receive athletic scholarships. 87% freshmen, 73% undergrads receive any aid. 50% undergrads borrow to pay for school. Average cumulative indebtedness $27,470. **Criteria awarding aid:** *Need-based:* Academics, Art, Athletics, Leadership, Minority status, Music/drama. *Non-need-based:* Academics, Art, Athletics, Leadership, Minority status, Music/drama, State/district residency.

STATE UNIVERSITY OF NEW YORK— BUFFALO STATE COLLEGE

1300 Elmwood Avenue, Buffalo, NY 14222
Phone: 716-878-4017 **Financial Aid Phone:** 716-878-4902
E-mail: admissions@buffalostate.edu **CEEB Code:** 2533
Fax: 716-878-6100 **ACT Code:** 2930

This public school was founded in 1871. It has a 115 acre campus.

RATINGS

Admissions Selectivity Rating: 71 **Fire Safety Rating:** 81 **Green Rating:** 61

STUDENTS AND FACULTY

Enrollment: 7,962. **Student Body:** 57% female, 43% male, 6% out-of-state, 1% international (44 countries represented). Asian 4%, African American 34%, Caucasian 44%, Hispanic 13%, Native American <1%, Pacific Islander <1%, Two or more races 4%, Race unknown <1%.
Retention and Graduation: 61% freshmen return for sophomore year. 27% freshmen graduate within 4 years. 47% freshmen graduate within 6 years. 25% grads go on to further study within 1 year. 24% grads pursue arts and sciences degrees. 1% grads pursue law degrees. 3% grads pursue business degrees. 0% grads pursue medical degrees. **Faculty:** Student/faculty ratio 15:1. 363 full-time faculty, 85% hold PhDs, 23% are members of minority groups, 49% are women. 0% of classes are taught by teaching assistants.

ACADEMICS

Degrees: Bachelor's; Master's; Post-master's certificate. **Classes:** Most classes have 20–29 students. Most lab/discussion sessions have fewer than 10 students. **Most popular majors:** Business/Commerce, General; Communication, Journalism, and Related Programs, Other; Criminal Justice/Law Enforcement Administration. **Special Study Options:** Cooperative education program; Cross-registration; Distance learning; Double major; Dual enrollment; English as a Second Language (ESL); Exchange student program (domestic); Honors program; Independent study; Internships; Liberal arts/career combination; Study abroad; Teacher certification program. **Disability Services offered:** Note-taking services; Reader services; Tape recorders; Tutors. **Career services:** Alumni network; Alumni services; Career assessment; Career/job search classes; Internships.

FACILITIES

Housing: Coed dorms; Special housing for international students; 100% of campus accessible to physically disabled. **Special Academic Facilities/Equipment:** Burchfield Penney Art center, anthropology museum, concert hall with pipe organ, nature preserve.

CAMPUS LIFE

Environment: City. **Activities:** Choral groups; Concert band; Dance; Drama/theater; International Student Organization; Jazz band; Literary magazine; Music ensembles; Radio station; Student government; Student newspaper; Student-run film society; Television station; Yearbook. 120 registered organizations, 1 honor society, 5 religious organizations, 12 fraternities, 12 sororities on campus. **Athletics (Intercollegiate):** *Men:* basketball, cross-country, diving, football, ice hockey, soccer, swimming, track/field (outdoor), track/field (indoor). *Women:* basketball, cheerleading, cross-country, diving, ice hockey, lacrosse, soccer, softball, swimming, tennis, track/field (outdoor), track/field (indoor), volleyball. **On-Campus Highlights:** Burchfield Penny Art Center. **Environmental Initiatives:** 1) Creation of a campuswide recycling program for plastic, glass, metal, paper, cardboard, light bulbs, electronics, electronic media, batteries, shrink wrap, bubble wrap, and many other miscellaneous items. This was applied to every building on campus including the residential halls.

ADMISSIONS

Freshman Academic Profile: Average high school GPA 3.1. **Test Scores:** SAT Math middle 50% range 420–560. SAT EBRW middle 50% range 440–570. **Basis for Candidate Selection:** *Very important factors include:* rigor of secondary school record, academic GPA, standardized test scores. *Important factors include:* class rank. *Other factors include:* application essay, recommendation(s), interview, extracurricular activities, talent/ability, character/personal qualities, first generation, volunteer work, work experience. **Freshman Admission Requirements:** High school diploma is required and GED is accepted. *Academic units required:* 2 math, 2 science. *Academic units recommended:* 4 English, 3 math, 3 science, 3 foreign language, 4 history. **Transfer Admission Requirements:** College transcript(s), statement of good standing from prior institution(s). Minimum college GPA of 2.0 required. Lowest grade transferable C. **General Admission Information:** Application fee $50. Non-fall registration accepted. Admission may be deferred for a maximum of 1 year.

COSTS AND FINANCIAL AID

Annual in-state tuition $6,870. Annual out-of-state tuition $16,650. Room and board $13,890. Required fees $1,340. Average book and supplies expense $1,038. **Required Forms and Deadlines:** FAFSA. **Notification of Awards:** Applicants will be notified of awards on a rolling basis beginning 5/1. **Types of Aid:** *Need-based scholarships/grants:* Federal Pell; SEOG; State scholarships/grants. **Student Employment:** Federal Work-Study Program available. **Financial Aid Statistics:** 88% needy freshmen, 88% needy undergrads receive need-based scholarship or grant aid. 17% freshmen, 14% undergrads receive non-need-based scholarship or grant aid. 67% freshmen, 67% undergrads receive need-based self-help aid. 0% freshmen, 0% undergrads receive athletic scholarships. 79% undergrads receive any aid. 79% undergrads borrow to pay for school. Average cumulative indebtedness $26,495. **Criteria awarding aid:** *Non-need-based:* Academics, Minority status.

STATE UNIVERSITY OF NEW YORK—COBLESKILL

Knapp Hall, Cobleskill, NY 12043
Phone: 518-255-5525 **Financial Aid Phone:** 518-255-5623
E-mail: admissions@cobleskill.edu **CEEB Code:** 2524
Fax: 518-255-6769 **Website:** www.cobleskill.edu **ACT Code:** 2914

This public school was founded in 1916. It has a 750 acre campus.

RATINGS

Admissions Selectivity Rating: 76 **Fire Safety Rating:** 87 **Green Rating:** 70

STUDENTS AND FACULTY

Enrollment: 2,421. **Student Body:** 52% female, 48% male, 10% out-of-state, 1% international (11 countries represented). Asian 1%, African American 12%, Caucasian 74%, Hispanic 7%, Native American <1%, Pacific Islander 0%, Two or more races 0%, Race unknown 5%.
Retention and Graduation: 74% freshmen return for sophomore year. 63% grads go on to further study within 1 year. **Faculty:** Student/faculty ratio 18:1. 100 full-time faculty, 46% hold PhDs, 7% are members of minority groups, 33% are women. 0% of classes are taught by teaching assistants.

ACADEMICS

Degrees: Associate; Bachelor's; Certificate; Terminal Associate; Transfer Associate. **Classes:** Most classes have 20–29 students. Most lab/discussion sessions have 10–19 students. **Most popular majors:** Business Administration and Management, General; Wildlife, Fish and Wildlands Science and Management; Animal Sciences, General. **Special Study Options:** Accelerated program; Distance learning; English as a Second Language (ESL); Honors program; Independent study; Internships; Study abroad; Weekend college. **Disability Services offered:** Note-taking services; Reader services; Tape recorders; Tutors. **Career services:** Alumni services; Career assessment; Career/job search classes; Internships.

FACILITIES

Housing: Coed dorms; Special housing for disabled students; Special housing for international students. **Special Academic Facilities/Equipment:** Art museum, 650-acre agricultural campus, distance learning classrooms, ski area, adult study center. **Campus Network:** 100% of dorms, 100% of libraries have wireless network access.

CAMPUS LIFE

Environment: Village. **Activities:** Campus Ministries; Choral groups; Drama/theater; International Student Organization; Jazz band; Student government. 40 registered organizations, 1 honor society, 1 religious organization on campus. **Athletics (Intercollegiate):** *Men:* baseball, basketball, cross-country, diving, equestrian sports, golf, lacrosse, soccer, swimming, tennis, track/field (outdoor), volleyball. *Women:* basketball, cross-country, diving, equestrian sports, golf, soccer, softball, swimming, tennis, track/field (outdoor), volleyball. **On-Campus Highlights:** Bouck Hall/Student Union. **Environmental Initiatives:** Recycling.

ADMISSIONS

Freshman Academic Profile: 6% in top 10% of high school class, 22% in top 25% of high school class, 56% in top 50% of high school class. 98% from public high schools. **Test Scores:** SAT Math middle 50% range 380–500. SAT EBRW middle 50% range 380–500. ACT middle 50% range 17–22. **Basis for Candidate Selection:** *Very important factors include:* rigor of secondary school record, academic GPA, standardized test scores, level of applicant's interest. *Other factors include:* class rank, application essay, recommendation(s), interview, extracurricular activities, talent/ability, character/personal qualities, first generation, alumni/ae relation, geographical residence, state residency, volunteer work, work experience. **Freshman Admission Requirements:** High school diploma is required and GED is accepted. *Academic units recommended:* 3 English, 3 math, 3 science, 3 science labs, 1 foreign language, 3 social studies, 3 history, 3 academic electives. **Freshman Admission Statistics:** 2,765 applied, 73% admitted, 39% enrolled. **Transfer Admission Requirements:** College transcript(s). Minimum college GPA of 2.25 required. Lowest grade transferable D. **General Admission Information:** Application fee $50. Non-fall registration accepted. Admission may be deferred for a maximum of 1 year.

COSTS AND FINANCIAL AID

Annual in-state tuition $5,870. Annual out-of-state tuition $15,320. Room and board $11,720. Required fees $1,279. Average book and supplies expense $1,200. **Required Forms and Deadlines:** FAFSA; State aid form. **Notification of Awards:** Applicants will be notified of awards on a rolling basis beginning 3/15. **Types of Aid:** *Need-based scholarships/grants:* College/university scholarship or grant aid from institutional funds; Federal Pell; Private scholarships; SEOG; State scholarships/grants. *Loans:* Direct PLUS loans; Direct Subsidized Stafford Loans; Direct Unsubsidized Stafford Loans. **Student Employment:** Federal Work-Study Program available. Institutional employment available. **Financial Aid Statistics:** 100% needy freshmen, 99% needy undergrads receive need-based scholarship or grant aid. 33% freshmen, 22% undergrads receive non-need-based scholarship or grant aid. 84% freshmen, 80% undergrads receive need-based self-help aid. 0% freshmen, 0% undergrads receive athletic scholarships. 81% freshmen, 75% undergrads receive any aid. **Criteria awarding aid:** *Non-need-based:* Academics, Alumni affiliation, Leadership, State/district residency.

STATE UNIVERSITY OF NEW YORK— THE COLLEGE AT BROCKPORT

Office of Undergraduate Admissions, Brockport, NY 14420
Phone: 585-395-2751 **Financial Aid Phone:** 585-395-2501
E-mail: admit@brockport.edu **CEEB Code:** 2537
Fax: 585-395-5452 **Website:** https://www.brockport.edu/ **ACT Code:** 2928

This public school was founded in 1835. It has a 464 acre campus.

RATINGS

Admissions Selectivity Rating: 86 **Fire Safety Rating:** 85 **Green Rating:** 87

STUDENTS AND FACULTY

Enrollment: 6,623. **Student Body:** 57% female, 43% male, 1% out-of-state, 1% international (21 countries represented). Asian 2%, African American 12%, Caucasian 70%, Hispanic 8%, Native American <1%, Pacific Islander <1%, Two or more races 3%, Race unknown 5%.
Retention and Graduation: 74% freshmen return for sophomore year. 47% freshmen graduate within 4 years. 64% freshmen graduate within 6 years. **Faculty:** Student/faculty ratio 17:1. 327 full-time faculty, 86% hold PhDs, 18% are members of minority groups, 52% are women.

ACADEMICS

Degrees: Bachelor's; Certificate; Master's; Post-bachelor's certificate; Post-master's certificate. **Classes:** Most classes have 20–29 students. Most lab/discussion sessions have fewer than 10 students. **Most popular majors:** Registered Nursing/Registered Nurse; Business Administration and Management, General; Psychology, General. **Special Study Options:** Accelerated program; Cross-registration; Distance learning; Double major; Dual enrollment; English as a Second Language (ESL); Exchange student program (domestic); External degree program; Honors program; Independent study; Internships; Liberal arts/career combination; Student-designed major; Study abroad; Teacher certification program. **Honors programs:** 1. Honors College: In addition to providing an enriched learning environment for completing the General Education Program, the Honors College enables each student to reach his or her full academic potential within their chosen major. Honors students may pursue any academic major of their choice. Experiential learning opportunities such as internships, study abroad programs, and community service projects are also offered to students. During the final year of undergraduate study, the Honors Senior Thesis provides exceptional preparation for pursuing graduate study or launching a career. Honors courses are integrated into each student's program of study, including those who wish to graduate in three years. Honors first-year and sophomore students fulfill their lower-division General Education requirements by enrolling in special Honors courses. Transfer students and others who join the program in their junior year may complete upper-division Honors requirements within two years. 2. Delta College is a unique program that can be found exclusively at The College at Brockport. Delta College takes its name from the ancient Greek symbol for change. Delta College provides an unconventional education that equips students with the knowledge and skills to be the agents of change in an ever-changing world. Delta College functions as a "college within the College," where the cutting edge ideas of higher education are applied. Delta classes consist of 25 students or fewer because we believe students succeed in an intimate learning environment where they feel known and supported. Our curriculum also satisfies the College's General Education requirements. Courses are taught by dedicated and involved faculty. Instead of taking courses in a large lecture hall, our students walk into a community. **Combined degree programs:** BA/MA. **Disability Services offered:** Note-taking services; Reader services;

Tape recorders; Tutors. **Career services:** Alumni network; Alumni services; Career assessment; Career/job search classes; Internships; Regional alumni.

FACILITIES

Housing: Apartments for single students; Coed dorms; Special housing for disabled students; Theme housing. **Special Academic Facilities/Equipment:** Indoor track and event space, theater and black box performance space, modern dance facilities, art studios, greenhouse, planetarium, electron microscope, nuclear magnetic resonance spectrometer, Faraday cage, geographic information systems lab with Doppler radar station, aquaculture ponds, environmental science deciduous woodlot, computer labs, smart classrooms, student learning center, weather information system, resolution germanium detector, research vessel on Lake Ontario, vacuum deposition lab, physics lab, supercomputer.

CAMPUS LIFE

Environment: Village. **Activities:** Campus Ministries; Concert band; Dance; Drama/theater; International Student Organization; Jazz band; Literary magazine; Model UN; Music ensembles; Musical theater; Pep band; Radio station; Student government; Student newspaper; Symphony orchestra; Television station. 132 registered organizations, 10 honor societies, 7 religious organizations, 3 fraternities, 4 sororities on campus. **Athletics (Intercollegiate):** *Men:* baseball, basketball, cross-country, diving, football, ice hockey, lacrosse, soccer, swimming, track/field (outdoor), track/field (indoor), wrestling. *Women:* basketball, cross-country, diving, field hockey, gymnastics, lacrosse, soccer, softball, swimming, tennis, track/field (outdoor), track/field (indoor), volleyball. **On-Campus Highlights:** Seymour College Union. **Environmental Initiatives:** We received the 2010 Pollution Prevention Award from the Rochester Business Journal for our comprehensive programs and continuing efforts to improve our sustainability performance.

ADMISSIONS

Freshman Academic Profile: Average high school GPA 3.0. 11% in top 10% of high school class, 32% in top 25% of high school class, 74% in top 50% of high school class. **Test Scores:** SAT Math middle 50% range 510–600. SAT EBRW middle 50% range 500–590. ACT middle 50% range 19–24. **Basis for Candidate Selection:** *Very important factors include:* rigor of secondary school record. *Important factors include:* academic GPA, standardized test scores, extracurricular activities, character/personal qualities, volunteer work, work experience. *Other factors include:* application essay, recommendation(s), talent/ability, level of applicant's interest. **Freshman Admission Requirements:** High school diploma is required and GED is accepted. *Academic units required:* 4 English, 3 math, 3 science, 1 science lab, 1 foreign language, 3 social studies, 1 history, 3.5 academic electives, 1 visual/performing arts, 2.5 unit from above areas or other academic areas. *Academic units recommended:* 4 English, 4 math, 3 science, 1 science lab, 2 foreign language, 3 social studies, 1 history, 3.5 academic electives, 1 visual/performing arts. **Freshman Admission Statistics:** 9,672 applied, 55% admitted, 20% enrolled. **Transfer Admission Requirements:** College transcript(s). Minimum college GPA of 2.5 required. Lowest grade transferable D-. **General Admission Information:** Application fee $50. Regular application deadline 8/1. Non-fall registration accepted. Admission may be deferred for a maximum of 1 year.

COSTS AND FINANCIAL AID

Annual in-state tuition $7,270. Annual out-of-state tuition $17,180. Room and board $14,160. Required fees $1,656. Average book and supplies expense $800. **Required Forms and Deadlines:** FAFSA; State aid form. **Notification of Awards:** Applicants will be notified of awards on a rolling basis beginning 1/1. **Types of Aid:** *Need-based scholarships/grants:* College/university scholarship or grant aid from institutional funds; Federal Pell; Private scholarships; SEOG; State scholarships/grants. *Loans:* Direct PLUS loans; Direct Subsidized Stafford Loans; Direct Unsubsidized Stafford Loans. **Student Employment:** Federal Work-Study Program available. Institutional employment available. **Financial Aid Statistics:** 83% needy freshmen, 80% needy undergrads receive need-based scholarship or grant aid. 50% freshmen, 32% undergrads receive non-need-based scholarship or grant aid. 78% freshmen, 78% undergrads receive need-based self-help aid. 0% freshmen, 0% undergrads receive athletic scholarships. 90.9% freshmen, 83.2% undergrads receive any aid. 81% undergrads borrow to pay for school. Average cumulative indebtedness $31,695. **Criteria awarding aid:** *Non-need-based:* Academics, Alumni affiliation, Art, Leadership, Minority status, Music/drama.

STATE UNIVERSITY OF NEW YORK— THE COLLEGE AT OLD WESTBURY

PO Box 307, Old Westbury, NY 11568-0307
Phone: 516-876-3073 **Financial Aid Phone:** 516-876-3247
E-mail: enroll@oldwestbury.edu **CEEB Code:** 2866
Fax: 516-876-3307 **Website:** www.oldwestbury.edu **ACT Code:** 2939

This public school was founded in 1968. It has a 605 acre campus.

RATINGS

Admissions Selectivity Rating: 76   **Fire Safety Rating:** 88   **Green Rating:** 60*

STUDENTS AND FACULTY

Enrollment: 5,109. **Student Body:** 61% female, 39% male, 1% out-of-state, 3% international (58 countries represented). Asian 30%, African American 82%, Caucasian 79%, Hispanic 76%, Native American 1%, Pacific Islander 1%, Two or more races 7%, Race unknown 4%.
Retention and Graduation: 81% freshmen return for sophomore year. 20% freshmen graduate within 4 years. 43% freshmen graduate within 6 years. **Faculty:** Student/faculty ratio 19:1. 164 full-time faculty, 91% hold PhDs, 38% are members of minority groups, 57% are women. 0% of classes are taught by teaching assistants.

ACADEMICS

Degrees: Bachelor's; Certificate; Master's; Post-master's certificate. **Classes:** Most classes have 20–29 students. Most lab/discussion sessions have 20–29 students. **Most popular majors:** Accounting; Biology/Biological Sciences, General; Psychology, General. **Special Study Options:** Cross-registration; Distance learning; Double major; English as a Second Language (ESL); Exchange student program (domestic); Honors program; Independent study; Internships; Liberal arts/career combination; Study abroad; Teacher certification program. **Honors programs:** The Honors College teaches students to integrate learning methods by using in-depth primary source material and complex and intellectually challenging secondary sources. The program emphasizes critical thinking and experiential learning. **Disability Services offered:** Note-taking services; Reader services; Tape recorders; Tutors. **Career services:** Alumni network; Alumni services; Career assessment; Career/job search classes; Internships; Regional alumni.

FACILITIES

Housing: Coed dorms; 90% of campus accessible to physically disabled.

CAMPUS LIFE

Environment: Village. **Activities:** Campus Ministries; Choral groups; Dance; Drama/theater; International Student Organization; Music ensembles; Radio station; Student government; Student newspaper; Student-run film society; Yearbook. **Athletics (Intercollegiate):** *Men:* baseball, basketball, cross-country, golf, soccer, swimming, ultimate frisbee, volleyball. *Women:* basketball, cross-country, soccer, softball, swimming, ultimate frisbee, volleyball. **On-Campus Highlights:** Student Union.

ADMISSIONS

Freshman Academic Profile: Average high school GPA 3.1. 85% from public high schools. **Test Scores:** SAT Math middle 50% range 470–560. SAT EBRW middle 50% range 490–560. ACT middle 50% range 19–21. **Basis for Candidate Selection:** *Very important factors include:* academic GPA, application essay, standardized test scores, recommendation(s). *Other factors include:* interview, character/personal qualities, alumni/ae relation. **Freshman Admission Requirements:** High school diploma is required and GED is accepted. *Academic units required:* 4 English, 3 math, 3 science, 2 science labs, 1 foreign language, 3 social studies, 3.5 academic electives, 1 visual/performing arts, 2.5 unit from above areas or other academic areas. *Academic units recommended:* 4 English, 3 math, 3 science, 3 science labs, 3 foreign language, 4 social studies, 3 academic electives, 1 computer science. **Freshman Admission Statistics:** 4,756 applied, 78% admitted, 19% enrolled. **Transfer Admission Requirements:** College transcript(s), essay or personal statement. Minimum college GPA of 2.0 required. Lowest grade transferable C. **General Admission Information:** Application fee $50. Priority deadline 12/1. Non-fall registration accepted. Admission may be deferred for a maximum of one year.

COSTS AND FINANCIAL AID

Annual in-state tuition $6,870. Annual out-of-state tuition $16,650. Room and board $11,530. Required fees $2,546. Average book and supplies expense $2,500. **Required Forms and Deadlines:** FAFSA; Institution's own financial aid form; State aid form. **Notification of Awards:** Applicants will be notified of awards on or about 4/15. **Types of Aid:** *Need-based scholarships/grants:* College/university scholarship or grant aid from institutional funds; Federal Pell; Private scholarships; SEOG; State scholarships/grants. *Loans:* Direct PLUS loans; Direct Subsidized Stafford Loans; Direct Unsubsidized Stafford Loans. **Student Employment:** Federal Work-Study Program available. Institutional employment available. **Financial Aid Statistics:** 91% needy freshmen, 89% needy undergrads receive need-based scholarship or grant aid. 50% freshmen, 5% undergrads receive non-need-based scholarship or grant aid. 50% freshmen, 51% undergrads receive need-based self-help aid. 0% freshmen, 0% undergrads receive athletic scholarships. 72% freshmen, 67% undergrads receive any aid. 57% undergrads borrow to pay for school. Average cumulative indebtedness $18,307. **Criteria awarding aid:** *Need-based:* Academics. *Non-need-based:* Academics, State/district residency.

STATE UNIVERSITY OF NEW YORK—COLLEGE OF ENVIRONMENTAL SCIENCE AND FORESTRY

Office of Undergraduate Admissions, Syracuse, NY 13210
Phone: 315-470-6600 **Financial Aid Phone:** 315-470-6706
E-mail: esfinfo@esf.edu **CEEB Code:** 2530
Fax: 315-470-6933 **Website:** www.esf.edu **ACT Code:** 2948

This public school was founded in 1911. It has a 25000 acre campus.

RATINGS
Admissions Selectivity Rating: 87   **Fire Safety Rating:** 98   **Green Rating:** 98

STUDENTS AND FACULTY
Enrollment: 1,854. **Student Body:** 47% female, 53% male, 19% out-of-state, 3% international (7 countries represented). Asian 4%, African American 1%, Caucasian 78%, Hispanic 6%, Native American <1%, Pacific Islander 0%, Two or more races 3%, Race unknown 4%.
Retention and Graduation: 83% freshmen return for sophomore year. 74% freshmen graduate within 6 years. **Faculty:** Student/faculty ratio 15:1. 128 full-time faculty, 92% hold PhDs, 16% are members of minority groups, 36% are women. 0% of classes are taught by teaching assistants.

ACADEMICS
Degrees: Associate; Bachelor's; Doctoral degree research/scholarship; Master's; Post-bachelor's certificate. **Classes:** Most classes have 10–19 students. Most lab/discussion sessions have 20–29 students. **Most popular majors:** Environmental Biology; Landscape Architecture; Environmental Science. **Special Study Options:** Cooperative education program; Cross-registration; Distance learning; Double major; Dual enrollment; Honors program; Independent study; Internships; Study abroad. **Honors programs:** Lower Division Honors Program: Freshmen & sophomores, all academic programs, highly selective, associated scholarship, mentoring, honors seminar, honors writing course. Upper Division Thesis Honors Program: Juniors and seniors, 16 of 20 academic programs eligible, intensive research or creative projects guided by faculty mentors, thesis exploration seminar, related coursework, Honors Thesis/Project course. Undergraduate research grants available. **Disability Services offered:** Note-taking services; Reader services; Tape recorders; Tutors. **Career services:** Alumni network; Alumni services; Career assessment; Career/job search classes; Internships; Regional alumni.

FACILITIES
Housing: Apartments for single students; Coed dorms; Fraternity/sorority housing; Special housing for disabled students; Wellness housing; 95% of campus accessible to physically disabled. **Special Academic Facilities/ Equipment:** Plant and animal growth and environmental simulation chambers, wildlife collection, electron microscope, paper making facility, photogrammetric and geodetic facilities, hydrology flumes, weather measurement, biotechnology and bio-process engineering labs, landscape architecture computing lab and design studios, extensive green house facilities.

CAMPUS LIFE
Environment: City. **Activities:** Campus Ministries; Choral groups; Concert band; Dance; Drama/theater; International Student Organization; Jazz band;

Literary magazine; Marching band; Model UN; Music ensembles; Musical theater; Pep band; Radio station; Student government; Student newspaper; Student-run film society; Symphony orchestra; Television station; Yearbook. 300 registered organizations, 1 honor society, 13 religious organizations, 26 fraternities, 21 sororities on campus. **Athletics (Intercollegiate):** *Men:* cross-country, golf, soccer. *Women:* cross-country, golf, soccer. **On-Campus Highlights:** Centennial Residence Hall **Environmental Initiatives:** (1) Biomass fueled power plant in Student Center provides up to 65% of campus heating and 20% of electricity; (2) Photovoltaic arrays/green roof; (3) College owns and manages 25,000 acres of forest (providing carbon offsets).

ADMISSIONS
Freshman Academic Profile: Average high school GPA 3.7. 25% in top 10% of high school class, 63% in top 25% of high school class, 95% in top 50% of high school class. 90% from public high schools. **Test Scores:** SAT Math middle 50% range 560–650. SAT EBRW middle 50% range 560–660. ACT middle 50% range 23–29. **Basis for Candidate Selection:** *Very important factors include:* rigor of secondary school record, academic GPA, application essay, standardized test scores, level of applicant's interest. *Important factors include:* class rank, recommendation(s), extracurricular activities, talent/ability. *Other factors include:* interview, character/personal qualities, first generation, alumni/ae relation, geographical residence, state residency, racial/ethnic status, volunteer work, work experience. **Freshman Admission Requirements:** High school diploma is required and GED is accepted. *Academic units required:* 4 English, 3 math, 3 science, 3 social studies, 1 history. *Academic units recommended:* 4 math, 4 science, 3 science labs, 3 foreign language. **Freshman Admission Statistics:** 2,018 applied, 61% admitted, 31% enrolled. **Transfer Admission Requirements:** High school transcript, college transcript(s). Minimum college GPA of 2.25 required. Lowest grade transferable C. **General Admission Information:** Application fee $50. Priority deadline 2/1. Non-fall registration accepted. Admission may be deferred for a maximum of 2 semesters.

COSTS AND FINANCIAL AID
Annual in-state tuition $7,070. Annual out-of-state tuition $16,980. Room and board $16,270. Required fees $2,045. Average book and supplies expense $1,200. **Required Forms and Deadlines:** FAFSA; State aid form. **Notification of Awards:** Applicants will be notified of awards on a rolling basis beginning 2/1. **Types of Aid:** *Need-based scholarships/grants:* College/university scholarship or grant aid from institutional funds; Federal Pell; Private scholarships; SEOG; State scholarships/grants. *Loans:* Direct PLUS loans; Direct Subsidized Stafford Loans; Direct Unsubsidized Stafford Loans. **Student Employment:** Federal Work-Study Program available. Institutional employment available. **Financial Aid Statistics:** 98% needy freshmen, 92% needy undergrads receive need-based scholarship or grant aid. 72% freshmen, 65% undergrads receive non-need-based scholarship or grant aid. 69% freshmen, 66% undergrads receive need-based self-help aid. 0% freshmen, 0% undergrads receive athletic scholarships. 91% freshmen, 93% undergrads receive any aid. 68% undergrads borrow to pay for school. Average cumulative indebtedness $26,679. **Criteria awarding aid:** *Need-based:* Academics, Alumni affiliation, Leadership, Minority status. *Non-need-based:* Academics, Alumni affiliation, Leadership, Minority status, State/district residency.

STATE UNIVERSITY OF NEW YORK—CORTLAND

PO Box 2000, Cortland, NY 13045-0900
Phone: 607-753-4711 **Financial Aid Phone:** 607-753-4717
E-mail: admissions@cortland.edu **CEEB Code:** 2538
Fax: 607-753-5998 **Website:** http://www2.cortland.edu/home/ **ACT Code:** 2932

This public school was founded in 1868. It has a 191 acre campus.

RATINGS
Admissions Selectivity Rating: 88   **Fire Safety Rating:** 65   **Green Rating:** 96

STUDENTS AND FACULTY
Enrollment: 6,333. **Student Body:** 56% female, 44% male, 4% out-of-state, 1% international (14 countries represented). Asian 1%, African American 6%, Caucasian 73%, Hispanic 13%, Native American <1%, Pacific Islander <1%, Two or more races 2%, Race unknown 4%.
Retention and Graduation: 80% freshmen return for sophomore year. 56% freshmen graduate within 4 years. 75% freshmen graduate within 6 years. **Faculty:** Student/faculty ratio 16:1. 309 full-time faculty, 76% hold PhDs, 12% are members of minority groups, 54% are women. 0% of classes are taught by teaching assistants.

ACADEMICS

Degrees: Bachelor's; Master's; Post-bachelor's certificate; Post-master's certificate. **Classes:** Most classes have 20–29 students. Most lab/discussion sessions have 20–29 students. **Special Study Options:** Cooperative education program; Cross-registration; Distance learning; Double major; Dual enrollment; Exchange student program (domestic); Honors program; Independent study; Internships; Liberal arts/career combination; Student-designed major; Study abroad; Teacher certification program. **Disability Services offered:** Note-taking services; Reader services; Tape recorders; Tutors.

FACILITIES

Housing: Apartments for single students; Coed dorms; Cooperative housing; Special housing for disabled students; Special housing for international students; Wellness housing; 75% of campus accessible to physically disabled. **Special Academic Facilities/Equipment:** Natural science museum, greenhouse, center for speech and hearing disorders, classrooms with integrated technologies, specialized labs to support various program offerings.

CAMPUS LIFE

Environment: Village. **Activities:** Campus Ministries; Choral groups; Dance; Drama/theater; International Student Organization; Literary magazine; Model UN; Music ensembles; Musical theater; Radio station; Student government; Student newspaper; Symphony orchestra; Television station. 100 registered organizations, 16 honor societies, 3 religious organizations, 2 fraternities, 5 sororities on campus. **Athletics (Intercollegiate):** *Men:* baseball, basketball, cheerleading, cross-country, diving, football, gymnastics, ice hockey, lacrosse, soccer, swimming, track/field (outdoor), track/field (indoor), wrestling. *Women:* basketball, cheerleading, cross-country, diving, field hockey, golf, gymnastics, ice hockey, lacrosse, soccer, softball, swimming, tennis, track/field (outdoor), track/field (indoor), volleyball. **On-Campus Highlights:** Corey Union.

ADMISSIONS

Freshman Academic Profile: Average high school GPA 3.4. 11% in top 10% of high school class, 42% in top 25% of high school class, 89% in top 50% of high school class. 91% from public high schools. **Test Scores:** SAT Math middle 50% range 530–600. SAT EBRW middle 50% range 520–600. ACT middle 50% range 22–25. **Basis for Candidate Selection:** *Very important factors include:* rigor of secondary school record, academic GPA, standardized test scores. *Important factors include:* application essay, recommendation(s), extracurricular activities, talent/ability. *Other factors include:* class rank, interview, alumni/ae relation, geographical residence, state residency, racial/ethnic status, volunteer work, work experience, level of applicant's interest. **Freshman Admission Requirements:** High school diploma is required and GED is accepted. *Academic units required:* 4 English, 3 math, 3 science, 3 science labs, 3 foreign language, 4 social studies. *Academic units recommended:* 4 English, 4 math, 4 science, 4 science labs, 4 foreign language, 4 social studies. **Freshman Admission Statistics:** 12,909 applied, 44% admitted, 23% enrolled. **Transfer Admission Requirements:** High school transcript, college transcript(s). Minimum college GPA of 2.5 required. Lowest grade transferable C-. **General Admission Information:** Application fee $50. Priority deadline 12/1. Non-fall registration accepted. Admission may be deferred for a maximum of 1 year.

COSTS AND FINANCIAL AID

Annual in-state tuition $7,070. Annual out-of-state tuition $16,980. Room and board $12,700. Required fees $1,736. Average book and supplies expense $1,000. **Required Forms and Deadlines:** FAFSA; State aid form. **Notification of Awards:** Applicants will be notified of awards on a rolling basis beginning 3/15. **Types of Aid:** *Need-based scholarships/grants:* College/university scholarship or grant aid from institutional funds; Federal Pell; Private scholarships; SEOG; State scholarships/grants. *Loans:* Direct PLUS loans; Direct Subsidized Stafford Loans; Direct Unsubsidized Stafford Loans. **Financial Aid Statistics:** 73% needy freshmen, 74% needy undergrads receive need-based scholarship or grant aid. 33% freshmen, 24% undergrads receive non-need-based scholarship or grant aid. 81% freshmen, 81% undergrads receive need-based self-help aid. 0% freshmen, 0% undergrads receive athletic scholarships. 75% undergrads borrow to pay for school. Average cumulative indebtedness $29,906. **Criteria awarding aid:** *Need-based:* Academics, Art, Leadership, Music/drama. *Non-need-based:* Academics, Art, Leadership, Minority status, Music/drama, State/district residency.

STATE UNIVERSITY OF NEW YORK—EMPIRE STATE COLLEGE

Two Union Avenue, Saratoga, NY 12866
Phone: 518-587-2100 **Financial Aid Phone:** 518-587-2100
E-mail: admissions@esc.edu **CEEB Code:** 2214
Fax: 518-587-9759 **Website:** esc.edu **ACT Code:** 2737

This public school was founded in 1971.

RATINGS

Admissions Selectivity Rating: 68   **Fire Safety Rating:** 60*   **Green Rating:** 60*

STUDENTS AND FACULTY

Enrollment: 10,128. **Student Body:** 62% female, 38% male, 8% out-of-state, 0% international. Asian 2%, African American 18%, Caucasian 66%, Hispanic 5%, Native American 1%, Pacific Islander 0%, Two or more races 1%, Race unknown 7%.
Faculty: Student/faculty ratio 9:1. 202 full-time faculty, 96% hold PhDs, 19% are members of minority groups, 64% are women. 0% of classes are taught by teaching assistants.

ACADEMICS

Degrees: Associate; Bachelor's; Certificate; Master's; Post-bachelor's certificate. **Most popular majors:** Business/Commerce, General; Physical Sciences, Other; Community Organization and Advocacy. **Special Study Options:** Cross-registration; Distance learning; Double major; Dual enrollment; External degree program; Independent study; Internships; Student-designed major. **Combined degree programs:** BA/MA.

FACILITIES

Campus Network: 100% of classrooms, 100% of dorms, 100% of student union, 100% of libraries, 100% of dining areas, 100% of common outdoor areas have wireless network access.

CAMPUS LIFE

Environment: Village. **Activities:** Literary magazine.

ADMISSIONS

Basis for Candidate Selection: *Very important factors include:* application essay, character/personal qualities. *Other factors include:* rigor of secondary school record, recommendation(s), talent/ability. **Freshman Admission Requirements:** High school diploma is required and GED is accepted. **Freshman Admission Statistics:** 1,536 applied, 79% admitted, 72% enrolled. **Transfer Admission Requirements:** High school transcript, essay or personal statement. Lowest grade transferable C. **General Admission Information:** Priority deadline 6/1. Non-fall registration accepted. Admission may be deferred for a maximum of 3 years.

COSTS AND FINANCIAL AID

Annual in-state tuition $5,570. Annual out-of-state tuition $14,820. Required fees $395. **Required Forms and Deadlines:** FAFSA; State aid form. **Types of Aid:** *Need-based scholarships/grants:* College/university scholarship or grant aid from institutional funds; Federal Pell; Private scholarships; SEOG; State scholarships/grants. *Loans:* Direct PLUS loans; Direct Subsidized Stafford Loans; Direct Unsubsidized Stafford Loans. **Student Employment:** Federal Work-Study Program available. **Financial Aid Statistics:** 62.9% undergrads receive any aid. **Criteria awarding aid:** *Need-based:* Academics, Minority status.

STATE UNIVERSITY OF NEW YORK— FARMINGDALE STATE COLLEGE

Admissions Office, Farmingdale, NY 11735
Phone: 631-420-2200 **Financial Aid Phone:** 631-420-2578
E-mail: admissions@farmingdale.edu **CEEB Code:** 2526
Fax: 631-420-2633 **Website:** www.farmingdale.edu **ACT Code:** 2918

This public school was founded in 1912. It has a 380 acre campus.

RATINGS
Admissions Selectivity Rating: 88   **Fire Safety Rating:** 98   **Green Rating:** 78

STUDENTS AND FACULTY
Enrollment: 9,394. **Student Body:** 43% female, 57% male, 2% international (77 countries represented). Asian 9%, African American 9%, Caucasian 55%, Hispanic 22%, Native American <1%, Pacific Islander <1%, Two or more races 3%, Race unknown <1%.
Retention and Graduation: 84% freshmen return for sophomore year. 29% freshmen graduate within 4 years. 53% freshmen graduate within 6 years. **Faculty:** Student/faculty ratio 20:1. 250 full-time faculty, 77% hold PhDs, 0% are members of minority groups, 48% are women. 0% of classes are taught by teaching assistants.

ACADEMICS
Degrees: Associate; Bachelor's; Certificate; Master's. **Classes:** Most classes have 20–29 students. Most lab/discussion sessions have 20–29 students. **Most popular majors:** Registered Nursing/Registered Nurse; Business Administration and Management, General; Computer Programming/Programmer, General. **Special Study Options:** Cross-registration; Distance learning; Double major; Dual enrollment; Independent study; Internships; Study abroad. **Disability Services offered:** Reader services; Tutors. **Career services:** Alumni services; Career assessment; Career/job search classes; Internships.

FACILITIES
Housing: Coed dorms; 90% of campus accessible to physically disabled. **Special Academic Facilities/Equipment:** Memorial Gallery; Aviation Center; Teaching Gardens; Smart Energy House.

CAMPUS LIFE
Environment: Town. **Activities:** Dance; Drama/theater; International Student Organization; Model UN; Musical theater; Radio station; Student government; Student newspaper; Yearbook. 66 registered organizations, 12 honor societies, 2 religious organizations, 4 fraternities, 3 sororities on campus. **Athletics (Intercollegiate): Men:** baseball, basketball, cross-country, golf, lacrosse, soccer, track/field (outdoor), track/field (indoor). **Women:** basketball, cross-country, soccer, softball, track/field (outdoor), track/field (indoor), volleyball. **On-Campus Highlights:** Campus Center. **Environmental Initiatives:** A 80-KW solar car port and the 7.2 KW wind farm.

ADMISSIONS
Freshman Academic Profile: Average high school GPA 3.2. 9% in top 10% of high school class, 31% in top 25% of high school class, 71% in top 50% of high school class. 93% from public high schools. **Test Scores:** SAT Math middle 50% range 510–580. SAT EBRW middle 50% range 500–580. ACT middle 50% range 20–24. **Basis for Candidate Selection:** *Very important factors include:* academic GPA. *Important factors include:* rigor of secondary school record, application essay, standardized test scores, recommendation(s). *Other factors include:* interview, extracurricular activities, talent/ability, character/personal qualities, first generation, alumni/ae relation, volunteer work, work experience, level of applicant's interest. **Freshman Admission Requirements:** High school diploma is required and GED is accepted. *Academic units required:* 4 English, 3 math, 3 science, 4 social studies. *Academic units recommended:* 1 foreign language. **Freshman Admission Statistics:** 7,500 applied, 46% admitted, 39% enrolled. **Transfer Admission Requirements:** High school transcript, college transcript(s), statement of good standing from prior institution(s). Minimum college GPA of 2.0 required. Lowest grade transferable C. **General Admission Information:** Application fee $50. Priority deadline 1/1. Regular application deadline 5/1. Non-fall registration accepted. Admission may be deferred for a maximum of 1 year.

COSTS AND FINANCIAL AID
Annual in-state tuition $6,870. Annual out-of-state tuition $16,650. Room and board $13,238. Required fees $1,436. Average book and supplies expense $1,200. **Required Forms and Deadlines:** FAFSA. **Notification of Awards:**

Applicants will be notified of awards on a rolling basis beginning 3/1. **Types of Aid:** *Need-based scholarships/grants:* College/university scholarship or grant aid from institutional funds; Federal Pell; Private scholarships; SEOG; State scholarships/grants. *Loans:* Direct PLUS loans; Direct Subsidized Stafford Loans; Direct Unsubsidized Stafford Loans. **Student Employment:** Federal Work-Study Program available. Institutional employment available. **Financial Aid Statistics:** 85% needy freshmen, 81% needy undergrads receive need-based scholarship or grant aid. 1% freshmen, 1% undergrads receive non-need-based scholarship or grant aid. 34% freshmen, 47% undergrads receive need-based self-help aid. 0% freshmen, 0% undergrads receive athletic scholarships. 49% undergrads borrow to pay for school. Average cumulative indebtedness $22,047.

STATE UNIVERSITY OF NEW YORK—FREDONIA

280 Central Avenue, Fredonia, NY 14063
Phone: 716-673-3251 **Financial Aid Phone:** 716-673-3253
E-mail: admissions@fredonia.edu **CEEB Code:** 2539
Fax: 716-673-3249 **Website:** www.fredonia.edu **ACT Code:** 2934

This public school was founded in 1826. It has a 249 acre campus.

RATINGS
Admissions Selectivity Rating: 82   **Fire Safety Rating:** 83   **Green Rating:** 89

STUDENTS AND FACULTY
Enrollment: 4,204. **Student Body:** 57% female, 43% male, 3% out-of-state, 2% international (17 countries represented). Asian 2%, African American 9%, Caucasian 71%, Hispanic 10%, Native American 1%, Pacific Islander <1%, Two or more races 3%, Race unknown 1%.
Retention and Graduation: 70% freshmen return for sophomore year. 49% freshmen graduate within 4 years. 64% freshmen graduate within 6 years. 45% grads go on to further study within 1 year. **Faculty:** Student/faculty ratio 14:1. 246 full-time faculty, 87% hold PhDs, 11% are members of minority groups, 42% are women. 0% of classes are taught by teaching assistants.

ACADEMICS
Degrees: Bachelor's; Master's; Post-master's certificate. **Classes:** Most classes have 10–19 students. Most lab/discussion sessions have 10–19 students. **Most popular majors:** Elementary Education and Teaching; Music, Other; Business/Commerce, General. **Special Study Options:** Accelerated program; Cooperative education program; Cross-registration; Distance learning; Double major; Dual enrollment; English as a Second Language (ESL); Exchange student program (domestic); Honors program; Independent study; Internships; Student-designed major; Study abroad; Teacher certification program. **Honors programs:** The honors program challenges and supports student learning through a series of specially designed seminars. Each seminar offers a unique educational experience, enabling students to work with some of the finest faculty members on campus in a small class setting. Honors students take four seminars, ideally within their freshman and sophomore years, which fulfill part of the university's general education requirements. We offer courses in the Arts, Humanities, Social Sciences, and Natural Sciences. Students are also encouraged to participate in the honors colloquium and to take part in the many organized learning experiences outside of the classroom. **Combined degree programs:** BA/DDS; BA/MD. **Disability Services offered:** Note-taking services; Reader services; Tape recorders; Tutors. **Career services:** Alumni network; Alumni services; Career assessment; Career/job search classes; Internships; Regional alumni.

FACILITIES
Housing: Apartments for single students; Coed dorms; Men's dorms; Special housing for international students; Theme housing; Wellness housing; Women's dorms; 85% of campus accessible to physically disabled. **Special Academic Facilities/Equipment:** Art center, education and local history museums, teacher education research center, developmental reading center, Sheldon Communications Lab, SMART classrooms, greenhouse.

CAMPUS LIFE
Environment: Village. **Activities:** Campus Ministries; Choral groups; Concert band; Dance; Drama/theater; International Student Organization; Jazz band; Literary magazine; Model UN; Music ensembles; Musical theater; Opera; Pep band; Radio station; Student government; Student newspaper; Student-run film society; Symphony orchestra; Television station. 180 registered organizations, 22 honor societies, 5 religious organizations, 3 fraternities, 3 sororities on campus. **Athletics (Intercollegiate): Men:** baseball, basketball, cross-country,

diving, ice hockey, soccer, swimming, track/field (outdoor), track/field (indoor). *Women:* basketball, cheerleading, cross-country, diving, lacrosse, soccer, softball, swimming, tennis, track/field (outdoor), track/field (indoor), volleyball. **On-Campus Highlights:** University Commons. **Environmental Initiatives:** Campus owned gas well.

ADMISSIONS

Freshman Academic Profile: Average high school GPA 3.2. 15% in top 10% of high school class, 41% in top 25% of high school class, 70% in top 50% of high school class. 95% from public high schools. **Test Scores:** SAT Math middle 50% range 490–590. SAT EBRW middle 50% range 500–610. ACT middle 50% range 19–25. **Basis for Candidate Selection:** *Very important factors include:* rigor of secondary school record, academic GPA. *Important factors include:* class rank, application essay, standardized test scores, recommendation(s). *Other factors include:* extracurricular activities, talent/ability, character/personal qualities, alumni/ae relation, volunteer work, work experience. **Freshman Admission Requirements:** High school diploma is required and GED is accepted. *Academic units required:* 4 English, 3 math, 3 science, 3 science labs, 3 foreign language, 4 social studies. *Academic units recommended:* 4 English, 4 math, 4 science, 4 science labs, 3 foreign language, 4 social studies, 1 academic elective. **Freshman Admission Statistics:** 6,277 applied, 66% admitted, 24% enrolled. **Transfer Admission Requirements:** College transcript(s). Minimum college GPA of 2.0 required. Lowest grade transferable D. **General Admission Information:** Application fee $50. Non-fall registration accepted. Admission may be deferred for a maximum of 1 year.

COSTS AND FINANCIAL AID

Annual in-state tuition $7,070. Annual out-of-state tuition $16,980. Room and board $12,830. Required fees $1,647. Average book and supplies expense $1,000. **Required Forms and Deadlines:** FAFSA; State aid form. **Notification of Awards:** Applicants will be notified of awards on a rolling basis beginning 12/1. **Types of Aid:** *Need-based scholarships/grants:* College/university scholarship or grant aid from institutional funds; Federal Pell; Private scholarships; SEOG; State scholarships/grants. *Loans:* Direct PLUS loans; Direct Subsidized Stafford Loans; Direct Unsubsidized Stafford Loans. **Student Employment:** Federal Work-Study Program available. Institutional employment available. **Financial Aid Statistics:** 87% needy freshmen, 82% needy undergrads receive need-based scholarship or grant aid. 60% freshmen, 39% undergrads receive non-need-based scholarship or grant aid. 80% freshmen, 78% undergrads receive need-based self-help aid. 0% freshmen, 0% undergrads receive athletic scholarships. 96% freshmen, 90% undergrads receive any aid. 91% undergrads borrow to pay for school. Average cumulative indebtedness $26,722. **Criteria awarding aid:** *Non-need-based:* Academics, Alumni affiliation, Art, Leadership, Minority status, Music/drama, State/district residency.

STATE UNIVERSITY OF NEW YORK—GENESEO

1 College Circle, Geneseo, NY 14454
Phone: 585-245-5571 **Financial Aid Phone:** 585-245-5731
E-mail: admissions@geneseo.edu **CEEB Code:** 2540
Fax: 585-245-5550 **Website:** www.geneseo.edu **ACT Code:** 2936

This public school was founded in 1871. It has a 220 acre campus.

RATINGS

Admissions Selectivity Rating: 85   **Fire Safety Rating:** 98   **Green Rating:** 77

STUDENTS AND FACULTY

Enrollment: 5,425. **Student Body:** 61% female, 39% male, 2% out-of-state, 1% international (26 countries represented). Asian 6%, African American 3%, Caucasian 76%, Hispanic 9%, Native American <1%, Pacific Islander <1%, Two or more races 3%, Race unknown 3%. **Retention and Graduation:** 85% freshmen return for sophomore year. 68% freshmen graduate within 4 years. 77% freshmen graduate within 6 years. 23% grads go on to further study within 1 year. 4% grads pursue arts and sciences degrees. 2% grads pursue law degrees. 2% grads pursue business degrees. 3% grads pursue medical degrees. **Faculty:** Student/faculty ratio 18:1. 256 full-time faculty, 88% hold PhDs, 17% are members of minority groups, 45% are women. 0% of classes are taught by teaching assistants.

ACADEMICS

Degrees: Bachelor's; Master's. **Classes:** Most classes have 20–29 students. Most lab/discussion sessions have 10–19 students. **Most popular majors:** Biology, General; Psychology, General; Business Administration and Management, General. **Special Study Options:** Cross-registration; Distance learning; Double major; English as a Second Language (ESL); Honors program; Independent study; Internships; Study abroad; Teacher certification program. **Honors programs:** The Edgar Fellows Program is designed to enhance the academic experience of a small number of especially dedicated and accomplished students through specially designed seminar courses, research opportunities, close work with program advisors, and co-curricular activities. It is dedicated to its founder and longtime director, William J. Edgar. In the spirit of its founder, the Program values and fosters critical inquiry and the lively interchange of ideas between and among students and faculty. **Combined degree programs:** BA/DDS; BA/MA; BA/MEng. **Disability Services offered:** Note-taking services; Reader services. **Career services:** Alumni network; Alumni services; Career assessment; Career/job search classes; Internships.

FACILITIES

Housing: Coed dorms; Special housing for disabled students; Special housing for international students; Theme housing; 95% of campus accessible to physically disabled. **Special Academic Facilities/Equipment:** Four theatres, electron microscopes, Integrated Science Center, Wave tank, planetarium, particle accelerator, 3D printers, Trading Room, eGarden.

CAMPUS LIFE

Environment: Village. **Activities:** Campus Ministries; Choral groups; Dance; Drama/theater; International Student Organization; Jazz band; Literary magazine; Model UN; Music ensembles; Musical theater; Pep band; Radio station; Student government; Student newspaper; Symphony orchestra. 190 registered organizations, 7 honor societies, 6 religious organizations, 13 fraternities, 13 sororities on campus. **Athletics (Intercollegiate):** *Men:* basketball, cross-country, diving, ice hockey, lacrosse, soccer, swimming, track/field (outdoor), track/field (indoor). *Women:* basketball, cross-country, diving, equestrian sports, field hockey, lacrosse, soccer, softball, swimming, tennis, track/field (outdoor), track/field (indoor), volleyball. **On-Campus Highlights:** MacVittie College Union. **Environmental Initiatives:** Signing of the Presidents Climate Commitment.

ADMISSIONS

Freshman Academic Profile: Average high school GPA 3.6. 26% in top 10% of high school class, 60% in top 25% of high school class, 93% in top 50% of high school class. **Test Scores:** SAT Math middle 50% range 560–650. SAT EBRW middle 50% range 560–650. ACT middle 50% range 24–28. **Basis for Candidate Selection:** *Very important factors include:* rigor of secondary school record, standardized test scores. *Important factors include:* class rank, academic GPA, application essay, recommendation(s), extracurricular activities, talent/ability. *Other factors include:* character/personal qualities, first generation, alumni/ae relation, state residency, volunteer work, work experience, level of applicant's interest. **Freshman Admission Requirements:** High school diploma is required and GED is accepted. *Academic units recommended:* 4 English, 4 math, 4 science, 4 foreign language, 4 social studies. **Freshman Admission Statistics:** 10,048 applied, 68% admitted, 20% enrolled. **Transfer Admission Requirements:** High school transcript, college transcript(s). Minimum college GPA of 3.0 required. Lowest grade transferable D. **General Admission Information:** Application fee $50. Regular application deadline 1/1. Non-fall registration accepted. Admission may be deferred for a maximum of 1 year.

COSTS AND FINANCIAL AID

Annual in-state tuition $6,670. Annual out-of-state tuition $16,320. Room and board $13,214. Required fees $1,738. Average book and supplies expense $1,000. **Required Forms and Deadlines:** FAFSA; State aid form. **Notification of Awards:** Applicants will be notified of awards on a rolling basis beginning 3/15. **Types of Aid:** *Need-based scholarships/grants:* Federal Pell; SEOG; State scholarships/grants. *Loans:* Direct PLUS loans; Direct Subsidized Stafford Loans; Direct Unsubsidized Stafford Loans. **Student Employment:** Federal Work-Study Program available. Institutional employment available. **Financial Aid Statistics:** 80% needy freshmen, 78% needy undergrads receive need-based scholarship or grant aid. 23% freshmen, 22% undergrads receive non-need-based scholarship or grant aid. 80% freshmen, 74% undergrads receive need-based self-help aid. 0% freshmen, 0% undergrads receive athletic scholarships. 82% freshmen, 74% undergrads receive any aid. 59% undergrads borrow to pay for school. Average cumulative indebtedness $22,854. **Criteria awarding aid:** *Need-based:* Academics. *Non-need-based:* Academics, Art, Leadership, Minority status, Music/drama, Religious affiliation, State/district residency.

STATE UNIVERSITY OF NEW YORK—MARITIME COLLEGE

6 Pennyfield Ave, Throggs Neck, NY 10465
Phone: 718-409-7200 **Financial Aid Phone:** 718-409-7227
E-mail: admissions@sunymaritime.edu
Fax: (718) 409-7465 **Website:** www.sunymaritime.edu **ACT Code:** 2954

This public school was founded in 1874. It has a 56 acre campus.

RATINGS
Admissions Selectivity Rating: 83   **Fire Safety Rating:** 89   **Green Rating:** 65

STUDENTS AND FACULTY
Enrollment: 1,510. **Student Body:** 14% female, 86% male, 23% out-of-state, 1% international (33 countries represented). Asian 4%, African American 5%, Caucasian 67%, Hispanic 17%, Native American <1%, Pacific Islander 0%, Two or more races 2%, Race unknown 3%.
Retention and Graduation: 78% freshmen return for sophomore year. 76% freshmen graduate within 6 years. 5% grads go on to further study within 1 year. **Faculty:** Student/faculty ratio 15:1. 92 full-time faculty, 50% hold PhDs, 12% are members of minority groups, 22% are women. 0% of classes are taught by teaching assistants.

ACADEMICS
Degrees: Associate; Bachelor's; Certificate; Master's; Post-bachelor's certificate. **Classes:** Most classes have 20–29 students. Most lab/discussion sessions have 10–19 students. **Most popular majors:** Business, Management, Marketing, and Related Support Services, Other; Mechanical Engineering; Marine Science/Merchant Marine Officer. **Special Study Options:** Distance learning; Double major; Exchange student program (domestic); Independent study; Internships; Study abroad. **Disability Services offered:** Note-taking services; Reader services; Tape recorders; Tutors. **Career services:** Alumni network; Alumni services; Career assessment; Career/job search classes; Internships; Regional alumni.

FACILITIES
Housing: Coed dorms; 81% of campus accessible to physically disabled. **Special Academic Facilities/Equipment:** Maritime Industry Museum, Fort Schuyler (National Historic Landmark), Bridge Simulator, Liquid Cargo Simulator, 565-ft. Training Ship (Empire State VI), Diesel Simulator, 2 Research Ships, State-of-the-Art Electrical Engineering Lab, NY State Strategic Center for Port and Maritime Security (224-ft USS Stalwart), Computerized Weather Station, Maritime College Waterfront Sailboat Fleet: 20 Vanguard 420's, 6 Vanguard FJ's, 1 Laser, J-105, J-35, J-24, Colgate 26.

CAMPUS LIFE
Environment: Metropolis. **Activities:** Campus Ministries; Choral groups; International Student Organization; Marching band; Music ensembles; Pep band; Student government; Yearbook. 63 registered organizations, 1 honor society, 3 religious organizations on campus. **Athletics (Intercollegiate):** *Men:* baseball, basketball, cross-country, football, ice hockey, lacrosse, riflery, soccer, swimming. *Women:* basketball, crew/rowing, cross-country, lacrosse, riflery, soccer, softball, swimming, volleyball. **On-Campus Highlights:** Fort Schuyler. **Environmental Initiatives:** Energy Reduction Programs with NYPA.

ADMISSIONS
Freshman Academic Profile: Average high school GPA 3.3. 0% in top 10% of high school class, 33% in top 25% of high school class, 100% in top 50% of high school class. **Test Scores:** SAT Math middle 50% range 550–640. SAT EBRW middle 50% range 540–620. ACT middle 50% range 22–28. **Basis for Candidate Selection:** *Very important factors include:* rigor of secondary school record, academic GPA. *Important factors include:* standardized test scores, recommendation(s). *Other factors include:* class rank, application essay, interview, extracurricular activities, talent/ability, character/personal qualities, first generation, alumni/ae relation, geographical residence, state residency, racial/ethnic status, volunteer work, work experience, level of applicant's interest. **Freshman Admission Requirements:** High school diploma is required and GED is accepted. *Academic units required:* 3 English, 3 math, 3 science, 1 science lab, 1 foreign language, 3 social studies, 3 history. *Academic units recommended:* 4 English, 3 math, 4 science, 1 foreign language, 4 social studies. **Freshman Admission Statistics:** 1,323 applied, 74% admitted, 35% enrolled. **Transfer Admission Requirements:** High school transcript, college transcript(s). Minimum college GPA of 2.5 required. Lowest grade transferable 2. **General Admission Information:** Application fee $50. Regular application deadline 1/31. Non-fall registration accepted.

COSTS AND FINANCIAL AID
Annual in-state tuition $7,070. Annual out-of-state tuition $16,980. Room and board $13,256. Required fees $1,438. Average book and supplies expense $1,500. **Required Forms and Deadlines:** FAFSA. **Notification of Awards:** Applicants will be notified of awards on a rolling basis beginning 3/15. **Types of Aid:** *Need-based scholarships/grants:* College/university scholarship or grant aid from institutional funds; Federal Pell; Private scholarships; SEOG; State scholarships/grants. *Loans:* Direct PLUS loans; Direct Subsidized Stafford Loans; Direct Unsubsidized Stafford Loans. **Student Employment:** Federal Work-Study Program available. Institutional employment available. **Financial Aid Statistics:** 85% needy freshmen, 82% needy undergrads receive need-based scholarship or grant aid. 0% freshmen, 0% undergrads receive non-need-based scholarship or grant aid. 94% freshmen, 91% undergrads receive need-based self-help aid. 0% freshmen, 0% undergrads receive athletic scholarships. 60% freshmen, 52% undergrads receive any aid. 67% undergrads borrow to pay for school. Average cumulative indebtedness $34,716. **Criteria awarding aid:** *Need-based:* Academics, Leadership. *Non-need-based:* Academics, Leadership, Minority status, State/district residency.

STATE UNIVERSITY OF NEW YORK—NEW PALTZ

100 Hawk Drive, New Paltz, NY 12561
Phone: 845-257-3200 **Financial Aid Phone:** (845) 257-3250
E-mail: admissions@newpaltz.edu **CEEB Code:** 2541
Fax: 845-257-3209 **Website:** www.newpaltz.edu **ACT Code:** 2938

This public school was founded in 1828. It has a 216 acre campus.

RATINGS
Admissions Selectivity Rating: 88   **Fire Safety Rating:** 94   **Green Rating:** 83

STUDENTS AND FACULTY
Enrollment: 6,672. **Student Body:** 63% female, 37% male, 2% out-of-state, 2% international (37 countries represented). Asian 5%, African American 6%, Caucasian 59%, Hispanic 21%, Native American <1%, Pacific Islander <1%, Two or more races 3%, Race unknown 3%.
Retention and Graduation: 85% freshmen return for sophomore year. 62% freshmen graduate within 4 years. 76% freshmen graduate within 6 years. 20% grads go on to further study within 1 year. **Faculty:** Student/faculty ratio 15:1. 344 full-time faculty, 85% hold PhDs, 18% are members of minority groups, 53% are women. 3% of classes are taught by teaching assistants.

ACADEMICS
Degrees: Bachelor's; Master's; Post-bachelor's certificate; Post-master's certificate. **Classes:** Most classes have 20–29 students. Most lab/discussion sessions have 10–19 students. **Most popular majors:** Elementary Education and Teaching; Psychology, General; Sociology, General. **Special Study Options:** Accelerated program; Cross-registration; Distance learning; Double major; Dual enrollment; English as a Second Language (ESL); Honors program; Independent study; Internships; Student-designed major; Study abroad; Teacher certification program. **Honors programs:** The mission of the SUNY New Paltz Honors Program is to provide an enhanced intellectual experience in a climate conducive to interaction among highly motivated students and faculty. This experience will seek to develop and intensify skills from a conceptual point of view in a diverse multidisciplinary analytical environment that nurtures independent thinking, creativity, respect and social responsibility. **Disability Services offered:** Note-taking services; Reader services; Tape recorders; Tutors. **Career services:** Alumni services; Career assessment; Career/job search classes; Internships.

FACILITIES
Housing: Coed dorms; Special housing for disabled students; Special housing for international students; Theme housing; Wellness housing; 90% of campus accessible to physically disabled. **Special Academic Facilities/Equipment:** Hudson Valley Advanced Manufacturing Center for 3D Printing, Samuel Dorsky Museum of Art, John Kirk Planetarium, Smolen Observatory, Resnick Engineering Hall, Coykendall Media Center, Communication Disorders Training Center and Clinic; Music Therapy Training Center and Clinic; Shepherd Recital Hall, Honors Center; Martin Luther King, Jr. Study Center.

CAMPUS LIFE
Environment: Village. **Activities:** Campus Ministries; Choral groups; Concert band; Dance; Drama/theater; International Student Organization; Jazz band;

Literary magazine; Model UN; Music ensembles; Musical theater; Opera; Radio station; Student government; Student newspaper; Symphony orchestra; Television station. 200 registered organizations, 10 religious organizations, 9 fraternities, 15 sororities on campus. **Athletics (Intercollegiate):** *Men:* baseball, basketball, cross-country, diving, soccer, swimming, tennis, volleyball. *Women:* basketball, cross-country, diving, field hockey, lacrosse, soccer, softball, swimming, tennis, volleyball. **On-Campus Highlights:** Samuel Dorsky Museum of Art. **Environmental Initiatives:** Investing $2 million in a campus-wide submetering system for electricity, natural gas, high temp hot water, and domestic water.

ADMISSIONS

Freshman Academic Profile: Average high school GPA 3.6. 18% in top 10% of high school class, 58% in top 25% of high school class, 88% in top 50% of high school class. 92% from public high schools. **Test Scores:** SAT Math middle 50% range 540–640. SAT EBRW middle 50% range 550–640. ACT middle 50% range 23–28. **Basis for Candidate Selection:** *Very important factors include:* rigor of secondary school record, academic GPA, standardized test scores. *Important factors include:* application essay, recommendation(s). *Other factors include:* extracurricular activities, talent/ability, volunteer work, work experience, level of applicant's interest. **Freshman Admission Requirements:** High school diploma is required and GED is accepted. *Academic units required:* 4 English, 3 math, 3 science, 2 science labs, 2 foreign language, 4 social studies, 1 history. *Academic units recommended:* 4 English, 4 math, 4 science, 4 science labs, 4 foreign language, 4 social studies, 1 history. **Freshman Admission Statistics:** 14,425 applied, 45% admitted, 17% enrolled. **Transfer Admission Requirements:** College transcript(s), statement of good standing from prior institution(s). Minimum college GPA of 2.75 required. Lowest grade transferable C-. **General Admission Information:** Application fee $50. Regular application deadline 4/1.

COSTS AND FINANCIAL AID

Annual in-state tuition $7,070. Annual out-of-state tuition $16,980. Room and board $13,928. Required fees $1,432. Average book and supplies expense $1,500. **Required Forms and Deadlines:** FAFSA; State aid form. **Notification of Awards:** Applicants will be notified of awards on a rolling basis beginning 4/1. **Types of Aid:** *Need-based scholarships/grants:* College/university scholarship or grant aid from institutional funds; Federal Pell; Private scholarships; SEOG; State scholarships/grants. *Loans:* Direct PLUS loans; Direct Subsidized Stafford Loans; Direct Unsubsidized Stafford Loans. **Student Employment:** Federal Work-Study Program available. Institutional employment available. **Financial Aid Statistics:** 55% needy freshmen, 78% needy undergrads receive need-based scholarship or grant aid. 35% freshmen, 26% undergrads receive non-need-based scholarship or grant aid. 80% freshmen, 82% undergrads receive need-based self-help aid. 0% freshmen, 0% undergrads receive athletic scholarships. 58% freshmen, 58% undergrads receive any aid. 62% undergrads borrow to pay for school. Average cumulative indebtedness $26,771. **Criteria awarding aid:** *Need-based:* Academics, Alumni affiliation, Art. *Non-need-based:* Academics, Alumni affiliation, Art, Music/drama.

STATE UNIVERSITY OF NEW YORK—ONEONTA

116 Alumni Hall, Oneonta, NY 13820
Phone: 607-436-2524 **Financial Aid Phone:** 607-436-2532
E-mail: admissions@oneonta.edu **CEEB Code:** 2542
Fax: 607-436-3074 **Website:** www.oneonta.edu **ACT Code:** 2940

This public school was founded in 1889. It has a 250 acre campus.

RATINGS

Admissions Selectivity Rating: 88   **Fire Safety Rating:** 91   **Green Rating:** 87

STUDENTS AND FACULTY

Enrollment: 5,804. **Student Body:** 60% female, 40% male, 1% out-of-state, 2% international (18 countries represented). Asian 1%, African American 3%, Caucasian 81%, Hispanic 4%, Native American <1%, Pacific Islander 0%, Two or more races 7%, Race unknown 2%.
Retention and Graduation: 84% freshmen return for sophomore year.
Faculty: Student/faculty ratio 18:1. 259 full-time faculty, 86% hold PhDs, 17% are members of minority groups, 43% are women. 0% of classes are taught by teaching assistants.

ACADEMICS

Degrees: Bachelor's; Master's; Post-bachelor's certificate; Post-master's certificate. **Classes:** Most classes have 20–29 students. **Most popular majors:** Elementary Education and Teaching; Secondary Education and Teaching; Family and Consumer Sciences/Home Economics Teacher Education. **Special Study Options:** Cross-registration; Distance learning; Double major; English as a Second Language (ESL); Independent study; Internships; Liberal arts/career combination; Study abroad; Teacher certification program. **Combined degree programs:** BA/MA; BA/MEng. **Disability Services offered:** Note-taking services; Reader services; Tape recorders; Tutors. **Career services:** Alumni network; Alumni services; Career assessment; Career/job search classes; Internships; Regional alumni.

FACILITIES

Housing: Coed dorms; Special housing for international students; Wellness housing.

CAMPUS LIFE

Environment: Village. **Activities:** Campus Ministries; Choral groups; Concert band; Dance; Drama/theater; International Student Organization; Jazz band; Literary magazine; Model UN; Music ensembles; Musical theater; Opera; Pep band; Radio station; Student government; Student newspaper; Student-run film society; Symphony orchestra; Television station; Yearbook. **Athletics (Intercollegiate):** *Men:* baseball, basketball, cross-country, diving, lacrosse, soccer, swimming, tennis, track/field (outdoor), track/field (indoor), wrestling. *Women:* basketball, cross-country, diving, field hockey, lacrosse, soccer, softball, swimming, tennis, track/field (outdoor), track/field (indoor), volleyball. **On-Campus Highlights:** Alumni Field House.

ADMISSIONS

Test Scores: SAT Math middle 50% range 520–600. SAT EBRW middle 50% range 500–580. ACT middle 50% range 22–26. **Basis for Candidate Selection:** *Very important factors include:* rigor of secondary school record, academic GPA, standardized test scores. *Important factors include:* application essay, recommendation(s), talent/ability, character/personal qualities, volunteer work, work experience. *Other factors include:* class rank, interview, extracurricular activities, first generation, racial/ethnic status, level of applicant's interest. **Freshman Admission Requirements:** High school diploma is required and GED is accepted. *Academic units required:* 4 English, 4 math, 4 science, 3 foreign language, 4 social studies. *Academic units recommended:* 4 foreign language. **Freshman Admission Statistics:** 12,031 applied, 43% admitted, 22% enrolled. **Transfer Admission Requirements:** College transcript(s). Minimum college GPA of 2.5 required. Lowest grade transferable C-. **General Admission Information:** Application fee $50. Non-fall registration accepted. Admission may be deferred for a maximum of 12 months.

COSTS AND FINANCIAL AID

Required Forms and Deadlines: FAFSA; Noncustodial PROFILE. **Notification of Awards:** Applicants will be notified of awards on a rolling basis beginning 3/1. **Types of Aid:** *Need-based scholarships/grants:* College/university scholarship or grant aid from institutional funds; Federal Pell; Private scholarships; SEOG; State scholarships/grants. *Loans:* Direct PLUS loans; Direct Subsidized Stafford Loans; Direct Unsubsidized Stafford Loans. **Student Employment:** Federal Work-Study Program available. Institutional employment available. **Financial Aid Statistics:** 73% needy freshmen, 95% needy undergrads receive need-based scholarship or grant aid. 26% freshmen, 0% undergrads receive non-need-based scholarship or grant aid. 84% freshmen, 81% undergrads receive need-based self-help aid. 0% freshmen, 0% undergrads receive athletic scholarships. 83% freshmen, 66% undergrads receive any aid. **Criteria awarding aid:** *Need-based:* Academics, Leadership, Minority status, Music/drama. *Non-need-based:* Academics, Leadership, Minority status, Music/drama, State/district residency.

STATE UNIVERSITY OF NEW YORK—OSWEGO

229 Sheldon Hall, Oswego, NY 13126-3599
Phone: 315-312-2250 **Financial Aid Phone:** 315-312-2248
E-mail: admiss@oswego.edu **CEEB Code:** 2543
Fax: 315-312-3260 **Website:** www.oswego.edu **ACT Code:** 2942

This public school was founded in 1861. It has a 696 acre campus.

RATINGS
Admissions Selectivity Rating: 87   **Fire Safety Rating:** 86   **Green Rating:** 89

STUDENTS AND FACULTY
Enrollment: 6,881. **Student Body:** 51% female, 49% male, 3% out-of-state, 3% international (39 countries represented). Asian 2%, African American 10%, Caucasian 68%, Hispanic 13%, Native American <1%, Pacific Islander <1%, Two or more races 3%, Race unknown <1%.
Retention and Graduation: 77% freshmen return for sophomore year. 64% freshmen graduate within 6 years. 29% grads go on to further study within 1 year. 22% grads pursue arts and sciences degrees. 4% grads pursue law degrees. 6% grads pursue business degrees. 5% grads pursue medical degrees. **Faculty:** 363 full-time faculty, 88% hold PhDs, 18% are members of minority groups, 47% are women. 0% of classes are taught by teaching assistants.

ACADEMICS
Degrees: Bachelor's; Master's; Post-bachelor's certificate; Post-master's certificate. **Classes:** Most classes have 10–19 students. Most lab/discussion sessions have 10–19 students. **Most popular majors:** Accounting; Business Administration and Management, General; Mass Communication/Media Studies. **Special Study Options:** Accelerated program; Cooperative education program; Cross-registration; Distance learning; Double major; Dual enrollment; English as a Second Language (ESL); Exchange student program (domestic); External degree program; Honors program; Independent study; Internships; Liberal arts/career combination; Study abroad; Teacher certification program. **Honors programs:** Over 250 students participate in our campus wide Honors Program. Students will take smaller courses based on the program's core multidisciplinary courses in the social sciences, the natural sciences, the humanities, and philosophy, as well as several other courses in math, English, and a foreign language. The courses emphasize the interrelatedness of the disciplines, their historical and intellectual origins, their roles in modern society, and their impact on life in the future. **Combined degree programs:** BA/MA. **Disability Services offered:** Note-taking services; Reader services; Tape recorders; Tutors. **Career services:** Alumni network; Alumni services; Career assessment; Career/job search classes; Internships; Regional alumni.

FACILITIES
Housing: Coed dorms; Theme housing; Wellness housing; 95% of campus accessible to physically disabled. **Special Academic Facilities/Equipment:** Tyler Hall Art Galleries, Rice Creek Biological Field Station, curriculum materials center, electron microscopy lab, planetarium.

CAMPUS LIFE
Environment: Village. **Activities:** Choral groups; Concert band; Dance; Drama/theater; International Student Organization; Jazz band; Literary magazine; Music ensembles; Musical theater; Opera; Radio station; Student government; Student newspaper; Student-run film society; Symphony orchestra; Television station; Yearbook. 179 registered organizations, 14 honor societies, 6 religious organizations, 11 fraternity, 9 sororities on campus. **Athletics (Intercollegiate):** *Men:* baseball, basketball, cross-country, diving, golf, ice hockey, lacrosse, soccer, swimming, tennis, track/field (outdoor), track/field (indoor), wrestling. *Women:* basketball, cross-country, diving, field hockey, ice hockey, lacrosse, soccer, softball, swimming, tennis, track/field (outdoor), track/field (indoor), volleyball. **On-Campus Highlights:** Marano Campus Center. **Environmental Initiatives:** All major renovation and new construction to be LEED Gold certified.

ADMISSIONS
Freshman Academic Profile: Average high school GPA 3.5. 11% in top 10% of high school class, 50% in top 25% of high school class, 84% in top 50% of high school class. **Test Scores:** SAT Math middle 50% range 530–620. SAT EBRW middle 50% range 540–620. ACT middle 50% range 21–26. **Basis for Candidate Selection:** *Very important factors include:* rigor of secondary school record, academic GPA. *Important factors include:* standardized test scores. *Other factors include:* class rank, application essay, recommendation(s), interview, extracurricular activities, talent/ability, character/personal qualities,

first generation, alumni/ae relation, geographical residence, racial/ethnic status, volunteer work, work experience, level of applicant's interest. **Freshman Admission Requirements:** High school diploma is required and GED is accepted. *Academic units required:* 4 English, 3 math, 3 science, 2 science labs, 2 foreign language, 4 social studies. *Academic units recommended:* 4 English, 4 math, 4 science, 3 science labs, 4 foreign language, 4 social studies. **Freshman Admission Statistics:** 12,669 applied, 54% admitted, 21% enrolled. **Transfer Admission Requirements:** college transcript(s). Minimum college GPA of 2.5 required. Lowest grade transferable D. **General Admission Information:** Application fee $50. Priority deadline 1/15. Non-fall registration accepted. Admission may be deferred for a maximum of 12 months.

COSTS AND FINANCIAL AID
Annual in-state tuition $7,070. Annual out-of-state tuition $16,980. Room and board $14,290. Required fees $1,647. Average book and supplies expense $1,000. **Required Forms and Deadlines:** FAFSA; State aid form. **Notification of Awards:** Applicants will be notified of awards on a rolling basis beginning 1/15. **Types of Aid:** *Need-based scholarships/grants:* College/university scholarship or grant aid from institutional funds; Federal Pell; Private scholarships; SEOG; State scholarships/grants. *Loans:* Direct PLUS loans; Direct Subsidized Stafford Loans; Direct Unsubsidized Stafford Loans. **Student Employment:** Federal Work-Study Program available. Institutional employment available. **Financial Aid Statistics:** 82% needy freshmen, 83% needy undergrads receive need-based scholarship or grant aid. 2% freshmen, 2% undergrads receive non-need-based scholarship or grant aid. 75% freshmen, 74% undergrads receive need-based self-help aid. 0% freshmen, 0% undergrads receive athletic scholarships. 78% freshmen, 72% undergrads receive any aid. **Criteria awarding aid:** *Need-based:* Academics. *Non-need-based:* Academics, State/district residency.

STATE UNIVERSITY OF NEW YORK— POLYTECHNIC INSTITUTE

PO Box 3050, Utica, NY 13504
Phone: 315-792-7500 **Financial Aid Phone:** 315-792-7210
E-mail: admissions@sunyit.edu **CEEB Code:** 2896
Fax: 315-792-7837 **Website:** www.sunyit.edu **ACT Code:** 2953

This public school was founded in 1966. It has a 850 acre campus.

RATINGS
Admissions Selectivity Rating: 86   **Fire Safety Rating:** 60*   **Green Rating:** 69

STUDENTS AND FACULTY
Enrollment: 1,893. **Student Body:** 38% female, 62% male, 1% out-of-state, 1% international (13 countries represented). Asian 3%, African American 8%, Caucasian 79%, Hispanic 7%, Native American <1%, Pacific Islander <1%, Two or more races 2%, Race unknown <1%.
Retention and Graduation: 84% freshmen return for sophomore year. **Faculty:** Student/faculty ratio 18:1. 131 full-time faculty, 87% hold PhDs, 22% are members of minority groups, 32% are women.

ACADEMICS
Degrees: Bachelor's; Master's; Post-bachelor's certificate; Post-master's certificate. **Classes:** Most classes have 10–19 students. **Most popular majors:** Computer and Information Sciences, General; Mechanical/Mechanical Engineering Technology/Technician; Business Administration and Management, General. **Special Study Options:** Accelerated program; Cross-registration; Distance learning; Double major; Independent study; Internships; Study abroad. **Disability Services offered:** Note-taking services; Reader services; Tape recorders; Tutors. **Career services:** Alumni network; Alumni services; Career assessment; Career/job search classes; Internships; Regional alumni.

FACILITIES
Housing: Coed dorms; Special housing for disabled students; Special housing for international students; 98% of campus accessible to physically disabled. **Special Academic Facilities/Equipment:** Gannett Gallery.

CAMPUS LIFE
Environment: Village. **Activities:** Campus Ministries; Dance; Drama/theater; International Student Organization; Literary magazine; Radio station; Student government; Student newspaper; Television station; Yearbook. 38 registered organizations, 2 honor societies, 1 religious organization on campus.

Athletics (Intercollegiate): *Men:* baseball, basketball, golf, lacrosse, soccer. *Women:* basketball, cross-country, golf, soccer, softball, volleyball. **On-Campus Highlights:** Student Center.

ADMISSIONS

Freshman Academic Profile: 17% in top 10% of high school class, 43% in top 25% of high school class, 83% in top 50% of high school class. 98% from public high schools. **Test Scores:** SAT Math middle 50% range 460–650. SAT EBRW middle 50% range 460–610. ACT middle 50% range 22–28. **Basis for Candidate Selection:** *Very important factors include:* rigor of secondary school record, academic GPA, standardized test scores, recommendation(s). *Important factors include:* class rank, application essay, interview, extracurricular activities. *Other factors include:* talent/ability, character/personal qualities, first generation, volunteer work, work experience. **Freshman Admission Requirements:** High school diploma is required and GED is accepted. *Academic units required:* 4 English, 3 math, 3 science, 3 science labs, 2 social studies, 2 history. *Academic units recommended:* 4 math, 4 science, 4 science labs, 3 foreign language, 2 academic electives. **Freshman Admission Statistics:** 2,233 applied, 57% admitted, 27% enrolled. **Transfer Admission Requirements:** College transcript(s), statement of good standing from prior institution(s). Minimum college GPA of 2.5 required. Lowest grade transferable D. **General Admission Information:** Application fee $50. Priority deadline 3/1. Regular application deadline 7/15. Non-fall registration accepted. Admission may be deferred for a maximum of 1 year.

COSTS AND FINANCIAL AID

Annual in-state tuition $6,170. Annual out-of-state tuition $15,820. Room and board $12,250. Required fees $1,270. Average book and supplies expense $1,500. **Required Forms and Deadlines:** FAFSA; State aid form. **Notification of Awards:** Applicants will be notified of awards on a rolling basis beginning 3/15. **Types of Aid:** *Need-based scholarships/grants:* College/university scholarship or grant aid from institutional funds; Federal Pell; Private scholarships; SEOG; State scholarships/grants. *Loans:* Direct PLUS loans; Direct Subsidized Stafford Loans; Direct Unsubsidized Stafford Loans. **Student Employment:** Federal Work-Study Program available. Institutional employment available. **Financial Aid Statistics:** 90% needy freshmen, 87% needy undergrads receive need-based scholarship or grant aid. 63% freshmen, 30% undergrads receive non-need-based scholarship or grant aid. 98% freshmen, 99% undergrads receive need-based self-help aid. 0% freshmen, 0% undergrads receive athletic scholarships. **Criteria awarding aid:** *Non-need-based:* Academics.

STATE UNIVERSITY OF NEW YORK—POTSDAM

44 Pierrepont Avenue, Potsdam, NY 13676
Phone: 315-267-2180 **Financial Aid Phone:** 315-267-2162
E-mail: admissions@potsdam.edu **CEEB Code:** 2545
Fax: 315-267-2163 **Website:** www.potsdam.edu **ACT Code:** 2946

This public school was founded in 1816. It has a 240 acre campus.

RATINGS

Admissions Selectivity Rating: 83   **Fire Safety Rating:** 89   **Green Rating:** 80

STUDENTS AND FACULTY

Enrollment: 3,055. **Student Body:** 62% female, 38% male, 4% out-of-state, <1% international (6 countries represented). Asian 2%, African American 12%, Caucasian 64%, Hispanic 14%, Native American 1%, Pacific Islander <1%, Two or more races 3%, Race unknown 3%.
Retention and Graduation: 73% freshmen return for sophomore year. 45% freshmen graduate within 4 years. 61% freshmen graduate within 6 years. 41% grads go on to further study within 1 year. 32% grads pursue arts and sciences degrees. 0% grads pursue law degrees. 0% grads pursue business degrees. 1% grads pursue medical degrees. **Faculty:** Student/faculty ratio 11:1. 252 full-time faculty, 87% hold PhDs, 17% are members of minority groups, 50% are women.

ACADEMICS

Degrees: Bachelor's; Master's; Post-master's certificate. **Classes:** Most classes have 10–19 students. Most lab/discussion sessions have 10–19 students. **Most popular majors:** Psychology, General; Business Administration and Management, General; Music Teacher Education. **Special Study Options:** Cross-registration; Distance learning; Double major; Dual enrollment; Exchange student program (domestic); Honors program; Independent study; Internships; Liberal arts/career combination; Student-designed major; Study abroad; Teacher certification program. **Honors programs:** The Honors Program offers special curricular, co-curricular, and extracurricular opportunities for our college's most academically talented students. Benefits include priority registration, honors courses, field trips, undergraduate research, housing, and select study abroad options. **Combined degree programs:** BA/MA. **Disability Services offered:** Note-taking services; Reader services; Tape recorders; Tutors. **Career services:** Alumni network; Alumni services; Career assessment; Career/job search classes; Internships.

FACILITIES

Housing: Apartments for single students; Coed dorms; Special housing for disabled students; Theme housing; Wellness housing; 95% of campus accessible to physically disabled. **Special Academic Facilities/Equipment:** Art gallery, anthropology museum, ecology museum, three performance halls, theatre, synthesizer music studios, planetarium, electron microscope, nuclear magnetic resonator, seismograph.

CAMPUS LIFE

Environment: Village. **Activities:** Campus Ministries; Choral groups; Concert band; Dance; Drama/theater; International Student Organization; Jazz band; Literary magazine; Music ensembles; Musical theater; Opera; Pep band; Radio station; Student government; Student newspaper; Symphony orchestra. 90 registered organizations, 21 honor societies, 6 religious organizations, 2 fraternities, 7 sororities on campus. **Athletics (Intercollegiate):** *Men:* basketball, cross-country, diving, equestrian sports, golf, ice hockey, lacrosse, soccer, swimming. *Women:* basketball, cross-country, diving, equestrian sports, ice hockey, lacrosse, soccer, softball, swimming, tennis, volleyball. **On-Campus Highlights:** Performing Arts Center. **Environmental Initiatives:** Promote sustainability education through eco rep program.

ADMISSIONS

Freshman Academic Profile: 10% in top 10% of high school class, 30% in top 25% of high school class, 70% in top 50% of high school class. 94% from public high schools. **Test Scores:** SAT Math middle 50% range 510–620. SAT EBRW middle 50% range 520–625. ACT middle 50% range 20–27. **Basis for Candidate Selection:** *Important factors include:* rigor of secondary school record, academic GPA, application essay, recommendation(s). *Other factors include:* standardized test scores, interview, extracurricular activities, talent/ability, character/personal qualities, volunteer work, work experience, level of applicant's interest. **Freshman Admission Requirements:** High school diploma is required and GED is accepted. *Academic units recommended:* 4 English, 3 math, 3 science, 3 foreign language, 4 social studies, 1 visual/performing arts. **Freshman Admission Statistics:** 5,079 applied, 68% admitted, 18% enrolled. **Transfer Admission Requirements:** College transcript(s). Minimum college GPA of 2.0 required. Lowest grade transferable D. **General Admission Information:** Application fee $50. Non-fall registration accepted. Admission may be deferred for a maximum of 1 year.

COSTS AND FINANCIAL AID

. Average book and supplies expense $900. **Required Forms and Deadlines:** FAFSA; State aid form. **Notification of Awards:** Applicants will be notified of awards on a rolling basis beginning 12/15. **Types of Aid:** *Need-based scholarships/grants:* College/university scholarship or grant aid from institutional funds; Federal Pell; Private scholarships; SEOG; State scholarships/grants. *Loans:* Direct PLUS loans; Direct Subsidized Stafford Loans; Direct Unsubsidized Stafford Loans. **Student Employment:** Federal Work-Study Program available. Institutional employment available. **Financial Aid Statistics:** 79% needy freshmen, 82% needy undergrads receive need-based scholarship or grant aid. 66% freshmen, 52% undergrads receive non-need-based scholarship or grant aid. 79% freshmen, 79% undergrads receive need-based self-help aid. 0% freshmen, 0% undergrads receive athletic scholarships. 98% freshmen, 85% undergrads receive any aid. 84% undergrads borrow to pay for school. Average cumulative indebtedness $30,057. **Criteria awarding aid:** *Non-need-based:* Academics, Art, Leadership, Music/drama.

STATE UNIVERSITY OF NEW YORK—PURCHASE COLLEGE

735 Anderson Hill Rd., Purchase, NY
Phone: 914-251-6300
E-mail: admissions@purchase.edu **CEEB Code:** 2878
Fax: 914-251-6314 **Website:** www.purchase.edu **ACT Code:** 2931

This public school was founded in 1967. It has a 550 acre campus.

RATINGS
Admissions Selectivity Rating: 87   **Fire Safety Rating:** 60*   **Green Rating:** 92

STUDENTS AND FACULTY
Enrollment: 3,978. **Student Body:** 58% female, 42% male, 13% out-of-state, 2% international (39 countries represented). Asian 4%, African American 12%, Caucasian 51%, Hispanic 25%, Native American <1%, Pacific Islander <1%, Two or more races 5%, Race unknown 1%.
Retention and Graduation: 81% freshmen return for sophomore year. 53% freshmen graduate within 4 years. 61% freshmen graduate within 6 years. **Faculty:** Student/faculty ratio 14:1. 189 full-time faculty, 23% are members of minority groups, 53% are women. 1% of classes are taught by teaching assistants.

ACADEMICS
Degrees: Bachelor's; Certificate; Master's; Post-bachelor's certificate; Post-master's certificate. **Classes:** Most classes have 10–19 students. Most lab/discussion sessions have 10–19 students. **Most popular majors:** Arts, Entertainment,and Media Management; Liberal Arts and Sciences/Liberal Studies; Psychology. **Special Study Options:** Cross-registration; Distance learning; Double major; English as a Second Language (ESL); Independent study; Internships; Liberal arts/career combination; Student-designed major; Study abroad. **Disability Services offered:** Note-taking services; Reader services; Tape recorders; Tutors. **Career services:** Alumni services; Career assessment; Career/job search classes; Internships.

FACILITIES
Housing: Apartments for single students; Coed dorms; Special housing for disabled students; Special housing for international students; Theme housing; Wellness housing; 100% of campus accessible to physically disabled. **Special Academic Facilities/Equipment:** Museum, four-theatre performing arts center, visual arts facility, children's center, recording studio, electron microscopes.

CAMPUS LIFE
Environment: Town. **Activities:** Choral groups; Dance; Drama/theater; International Student Organization; Jazz band; Literary magazine; Music ensembles; Musical theater; Radio station; Student government; Student newspaper; Student-run film society; Television station. 30 registered organizations on campus. **Athletics (Intercollegiate):** *Men:* baseball, basketball, cross-country, golf, soccer, tennis, volleyball. *Women:* basketball, cross-country, soccer, softball, tennis, volleyball. **On-Campus Highlights:** The Performing Arts Center. **Environmental Initiatives:** Committed to reduce GHG emissions by 80% by 2050 (Presidents Climate Commitment).

ADMISSIONS
Freshman Academic Profile: Average high school GPA 3.3. **Test Scores:** SAT Math middle 50% range 520–620. SAT EBRW middle 50% range 540–640. ACT middle 50% range 23–30. **Basis for Candidate Selection:** *Very important factors include:* academic GPA, application essay, talent/ability. *Important factors include:* rigor of secondary school record. *Other factors include:* class rank, standardized test scores, recommendation(s), interview, extracurricular activities, character/personal qualities. **Freshman Admission Requirements:** High school diploma is required and GED is accepted. *Academic units recommended:* 4 English, 4 math, 3 science, 3 foreign language, 4 social studies, 2 academic electives. **Freshman Admission Statistics:** 6,486 applied, 52% admitted, 24% enrolled. **Transfer Admission Requirements:** College transcript(s). Minimum college GPA of 3.0 required. Lowest grade transferable D. **General Admission Information:** Application fee $50. Regular application deadline 7/1. Non-fall registration accepted. Admission may be deferred for a maximum of 1 year.

COSTS AND FINANCIAL AID
Annual in-state tuition $7,070. Annual out-of-state tuition $16,980. Room and board $14,548. Required fees $2,093. Average book and supplies expense

$1,240. **Required Forms and Deadlines:** FAFSA; State aid form. **Notification of Awards:** Applicants will be notified of awards on a rolling basis beginning 3/1. **Types of Aid:** *Need-based scholarships/grants:* College/university scholarship or grant aid from institutional funds; Federal Pell; Private scholarships; SEOG; State scholarships/grants. *Loans:* Direct PLUS loans; Direct Subsidized Stafford Loans; Direct Unsubsidized Stafford Loans. **Student Employment:** Federal Work-Study Program available. Institutional employment available. **Financial Aid Statistics:** 95% needy freshmen, 98% needy undergrads receive need-based scholarship or grant aid. 14% freshmen, 18% undergrads receive non-need-based scholarship or grant aid. 82% freshmen, 88% undergrads receive need-based self-help aid. 0% freshmen, 0% undergrads receive athletic scholarships. 68% undergrads borrow to pay for school. Average cumulative indebtedness $23,987. **Criteria awarding aid:** *Need-based:* Academics, Art, Minority status, Music/drama. *Non-need-based:* Academics, Art, Minority status, Music/drama.

STATE UNIVERSITY OF NEW YORK—STONY BROOK UNIVERSITY

Office of Undergraduate Admissions, Stony Brook, NY 11794-1901
Phone: 631-632-6868 **Financial Aid Phone:** 631-632-6840
E-mail: enroll@stonybrook.edu **CEEB Code:** 2548
Fax: 631-632-9898 **Website:** www.stonybrook.edu/ **ACT Code:** 2952

This public school was founded in 1957. It has a 1450 acre campus.

RATINGS
Admissions Selectivity Rating: 91   **Fire Safety Rating:** 90   **Green Rating:** 97

STUDENTS AND FACULTY
Enrollment: 17,767. **Student Body:** 49% female, 51% male, 6% out-of-state, 14% international (120 countries represented). Asian 27%, African American 7%, Caucasian 30%, Hispanic 13%, Native American <1%, Pacific Islander <1%, Two or more races 3%, Race unknown 6%.
Retention and Graduation: 89% freshmen return for sophomore year. 59% freshmen graduate within 4 years. 76% freshmen graduate within 6 years. 29% grads go on to further study within 1 year. **Faculty:** Student/faculty ratio 19:1. 1,066 full-time faculty, 91% hold PhDs, 22% are members of minority groups, 38% are women.

ACADEMICS
Degrees: Bachelor's; Doctoral degree—professional practice; Doctoral degree research/scholarship; Master's; Post-bachelor's certificate; Post-master's certificate. **Classes:** Most classes have 10–19 students. Most lab/discussion sessions have 20–29 students. **Most popular majors:** Biology/Biological Sciences, General; Health Professions And Related Programs; Business Administration and Management, General. **Special Study Options:** Cooperative education program; Cross-registration; Distance learning; Double major; Dual enrollment; English as a Second Language (ESL); Exchange student program (domestic); Honors program; Independent study; Internships; Liberal arts/career combination; Student-designed major; Study abroad; Teacher certification program; Weekend college. **Honors programs:** BA/MD. **Combined degree programs:** BA/MA. **Disability Services offered:** Note-taking services; Reader services; Tape recorders; Tutors. **Career services:** Alumni network; Alumni services; Career assessment; Career/job search classes; Internships; Regional alumni.

FACILITIES
Housing: Apartments for married students; Apartments for single students; Coed dorms; Wellness housing; 75% of campus accessible to physically disabled. **Special Academic Facilities/Equipment:** SAC Gallery, Staller Gallery, Wang Center, Tabler Center for the Arts.

CAMPUS LIFE
Environment: Town. **Activities:** Campus Ministries; Choral groups; Concert band; Dance; Drama/theater; International Student Organization; Jazz band; Literary magazine; Marching band; Model UN; Music ensembles; Musical theater; Opera; Pep band; Radio station; Student government; Student newspaper; Student-run film society; Symphony orchestra; Television station. 351 registered organizations, 8 honor societies, 19 religious organizations, 15

fraternities, 13 sororities on campus. **Athletics (Intercollegiate):** *Men:* baseball, basketball, cross-country, diving, football, lacrosse, soccer, swimming, tennis, track/field (outdoor), track/field (indoor). *Women:* basketball, cross-country, diving, lacrosse, soccer, softball, swimming, tennis, track/field (outdoor), track/field (indoor), volleyball. **On-Campus Highlights:** Staller Center for the Arts **Environmental Initiatives:** Commitment to obtain carbon neutrality by 2050.

ADMISSIONS
Freshman Academic Profile: Average high school GPA 3.8. 51% in top 10% of high school class, 80% in top 25% of high school class, 96% in top 50% of high school class. 90% from public high schools. **Test Scores:** SAT Math middle 50% range 640–750. SAT EBRW middle 50% range 590–690. ACT middle 50% range 26–32. **Basis for Candidate Selection:** *Very important factors include:* rigor of secondary school record, academic GPA, standardized test scores. *Important factors include:* application essay, recommendation(s). *Other factors include:* class rank, interview, extracurricular activities, talent/ability, character/personal qualities, first generation, alumni/ae relation, geographical residence, state residency, volunteer work, work experience, level of applicant's interest. **Freshman Admission Requirements:** High school diploma is required and GED is accepted. *Academic units required:* 4 English, 4 math, 4 science, 4 social studies. *Academic units recommended:* 4 English, 4 math, 4 science, 3 foreign language, 4 social studies. **Freshman Admission Statistics:** 37,079 applied, 44% admitted, 21% enrolled. **Transfer Admission Requirements:** College transcript(s). Minimum college GPA of 3.0 required. Lowest grade transferable C. **General Admission Information:** Application fee $50. Priority deadline 1/15. Regular application deadline 1/15. Non-fall registration accepted. Admission may be deferred for a maximum of 2 semesters.

COSTS AND FINANCIAL AID
Annual in-state tuition $7,070. Annual out-of-state tuition $24,740. Room and board $14,278. Required fees $3,105. Average book and supplies expense $900. **Required Forms and Deadlines:** FAFSA; State aid form. **Notification of Awards:** Applicants will be notified of awards on a rolling basis beginning 4/1. **Types of Aid:** *Need-based scholarships/grants:* College/university scholarship or grant aid from institutional funds; Federal Pell; Private scholarships; SEOG; State scholarships/grants. *Loans:* Direct PLUS loans; Direct Subsidized Stafford Loans; Direct Unsubsidized Stafford Loans. **Student Employment:** Federal Work-Study Program available. Institutional employment available. **Financial Aid Statistics:** 91% needy freshmen, 87% needy undergrads receive need-based scholarship or grant aid. 10% freshmen, 7% undergrads receive non-need-based scholarship or grant aid. 89% freshmen, 88% undergrads receive need-based self-help aid. 2% freshmen, 1% undergrads receive athletic scholarships. 79% freshmen, 70% undergrads receive any aid. 49% undergrads borrow to pay for school. Average cumulative indebtedness $25,678. **Criteria awarding aid:** *Need-based:* Academics, Leadership, Minority status *Non-need-based:* Academics, Alumni affiliation, Art, Athletics, Job skills, Leadership, Music/drama.

STATE UNIVERSITY OF NEW YORK— UNIVERSITY AT ALBANY

Office of Undergraduate Admissions, Albany, NY 12222
Phone: 518-442-5435 **Financial Aid Phone:** (518) 442-8037
E-mail: ugadmissions@albany.edu **CEEB Code:** 2532
Fax: 518-442-5383 **Website:** www.albany.edu **ACT Code:** 2926

This public school was founded in 1844. It has a 795 acre campus.

RATINGS
Admissions Selectivity Rating: 86   Fire Safety Rating: 79   Green Rating: 95

STUDENTS AND FACULTY
Enrollment: 13,153. **Student Body:** 52% female, 48% male, 4% out-of-state, 5% international (84 countries represented). Asian 9%, African American 19%, Caucasian 44%, Hispanic 18%, Native American <1%, Pacific Islander <1%, Two or more races 4%, Race unknown 2%.
Retention and Graduation: 82% freshmen return for sophomore year. 56% freshmen graduate within 4 years. 63% freshmen graduate within 6 years.
Faculty: Student/faculty ratio 18:1. 685 full-time faculty, 95% hold PhDs, 30% are members of minority groups, 40% are women. 10% of classes are taught by teaching assistants.

ACADEMICS
Degrees: Bachelor's; Doctoral degree research/scholarship; Master's; Post-bachelor's certificate; Post-master's certificate. **Classes:** Most classes have 10–19

students. Most lab/discussion sessions have 10–19 students. **Most popular majors:** English Language and Literature, General; Business Administration and Management, General; Psychology, General. **Special Study Options:** Accelerated program; Cross-registration; Distance learning; Double major; Dual enrollment; English as a Second Language (ESL); Honors program; Independent study; Internships; Liberal arts/career combination; Student-designed major; Study abroad. **Honors programs:** Our Presidential Scholars program combines merit scholarships, honors courses, priority registration, special housing, and faculty mentor opportunities. **Combined degree programs:** BA/JD; BA/MA; BA/MEng. **Disability Services offered:** Tutors. **Career services:** Alumni network; Alumni services; Career assessment; Career/job search classes; Internships; Regional alumni.

FACILITIES
Housing: Coed dorms; Special housing for international students; Theme housing; Wellness housing; 99% of campus accessible to physically disabled. **Special Academic Facilities/Equipment:** Performing Arts Center, Art Museum, art and dance studios, sculpture foundry, nuclear accelerator and advanced materials facilities, a peptide synthesis facility, recombinatnt DNA sequencing laboratories, Drone Lab, Cybersecurity Lab, and atmospheric science's Whiteface Mountain observational facility.

CAMPUS LIFE
Environment: City. **Activities:** Campus Ministries; Choral groups; Concert band; Dance; Drama/theater; International Student Organization; Jazz band; Literary magazine; Marching band; Model UN; Music ensembles; Musical theater; Pep band; Radio station; Student government; Student newspaper; Student-run film society; Symphony orchestra; Television station; Yearbook. 210 registered organizations, 22 honor societies, 15 religious organizations, 17 fraternities, 17 sororities on campus. **Athletics (Intercollegiate):** *Men:* baseball, basketball, cross-country, football, lacrosse, soccer, track/field (outdoor), track/field (indoor). *Women:* basketball, cross-country, field hockey, golf, lacrosse, soccer, softball, tennis, track/field (outdoor), track/field (indoor), volleyball. **On-Campus Highlights:** Campus Center with bookstore, cafés, and lounges. **Environmental Initiatives:** Energy conservation.

ADMISSIONS
Freshman Academic Profile: Average high school GPA 3.3. 18% in top 10% of high school class, 46% in top 25% of high school class, 82% in top 50% of high school class. **Test Scores:** SAT Math middle 50% range 540–630. SAT EBRW middle 50% range 550–620. ACT middle 50% range 22–28. **Basis for Candidate Selection:** *Very important factors include:* rigor of secondary school record, class rank, academic GPA, standardized test scores, recommendation(s), character/personal qualities. *Important factors include:* application essay, *Other factors include:* extracurricular activities, talent/ability, first generation, alumni/ae relation, geographical residence, volunteer work, work experience, level of applicant's interest. **Freshman Admission Requirements:** High school diploma is required and GED is accepted. *Academic units required:* 4 English, 2 math, 2 science, 2 science labs, 1 foreign language, 3 social studies, 2 history, 4 academic electives. *Academic units recommended:* 4 math, 3 science, 3 science labs, 3 foreign language. **Freshman Admission Statistics:** 27,529 applied, 54% admitted, 18% enrolled. **Transfer Admission Requirements:** College transcript(s), essay or personal statement, statement of good standing from prior institution(s). Minimum college GPA of 2.5 required. Lowest grade transferable C. **General Admission Information:** Application fee $50. Priority deadline 3/1. Regular application deadline 3/1. Non-fall registration accepted. Admission may be deferred for a maximum of 1 year.

COSTS AND FINANCIAL AID
Annual in-state tuition $7,070. Annual out-of-state tuition $24,660. Room and board $14,640. Required fees $2,956. Average book and supplies expense $1,000. **Required Forms and Deadlines:** FAFSA;. **Notification of Awards:** Applicants will be notified of awards on a rolling basis beginning 3/2. **Types of Aid:** *Need-based scholarships/grants:* College/university scholarship or grant aid from institutional funds; Federal Pell; Private scholarships; SEOG; State scholarships/grants. *Loans:* Direct PLUS loans; Direct Subsidized Stafford Loans; Direct Unsubsidized Stafford Loans. **Student Employment:** Federal Work-Study Program available. Institutional employment available. **Financial Aid Statistics:** 87% needy freshmen, 86% needy undergrads receive need-based scholarship or grant aid. 4% freshmen, 3% undergrads receive non-need-based scholarship or grant aid. 70% freshmen, 73% undergrads receive need-based self-help aid. 1% freshmen, 1% undergrads receive athletic scholarships. 69% freshmen, 66% undergrads receive any aid. 64% undergrads borrow to pay for school. Average cumulative indebtedness $27,555. **Criteria awarding aid:** *Non-need-based:* Academics, Athletics, State/district residency.

STATE UNIVERSITY OF NEW YORK—
UNIVERSITY AT BUFFALO

12 Capen Hall, Buffalo, NY 14260-1660
Phone: 716-645-6900 **Financial Aid Phone:** 716-645-2450
E-mail: ub-admissions@buffalo.edu **CEEB Code:** 2925
Fax: 716-645-6411 **Website:** www.buffalo.edu **ACT Code:** 2978

This public school was founded in 1846. It has a 1346 acre campus.

RATINGS

Admissions Selectivity Rating: 86   **Fire Safety Rating:** 62   **Green Rating:** 98

STUDENTS AND FACULTY

Enrollment: 21,760. **Student Body:** 44% female, 56% male, 2% out-of-state, 14% international (87 countries represented). Asian 15%, African American 8%, Caucasian 47%, Hispanic 7%, Native American <1%, Pacific Islander <1%, Two or more races 2%, Race unknown 5%.
Retention and Graduation: 86% freshmen return for sophomore year. 60% freshmen graduate within 4 years. 76% freshmen graduate within 6 years.
Faculty: Student/faculty ratio 15:1. 1,314 full-time faculty, 97% hold PhDs, 28% are members of minority groups, 40% are women.

ACADEMICS

Degrees: Bachelor's; Certificate; Doctoral degree—professional practice; Doctoral degree research/scholarship; Master's; Post-master's certificate.
Most popular majors: Engineering, General; Business Administration and Management, General; Social Sciences, General. **Special Study Options:** Accelerated program; Cooperative education program; Cross-registration; Distance learning; Double major; Dual enrollment; English as a Second Language (ESL); Exchange student program (domestic); External degree program; Honors program; Independent study; Internships; Liberal arts/career combination; Student-designed major; Study abroad; Teacher certification program. **Honors programs:** There is a University Honors College as well as honors programs within the majors. Undergraduate research is an option in a variety of disciplines and often affords the student an opportunity to participate in cutting-edge research activities. See Website: http://honors.buffalo.edu.
Combined degree programs: BA/MA. **Disability Services offered:** Note-taking services; Reader services; Tape recorders; Tutors. **Career services:** Alumni network; Alumni services; Career/job search classes; Internships.

FACILITIES

Housing: Apartments for married students; Apartments for single students; Coed dorms; Special housing for disabled students; Theme housing; 90% of campus accessible to physically disabled. **Special Academic Facilities/Equipment:** UB Art Gallery at the Center for the Arts, Slee Concert Hall, Marian E. White Anthropology Research Museum, The School of Pharmacy and Pharmaceutical Sciences Apothecary and Historical Exhibits, The Museum of Radiology and Medical Physics, The Museum of Neuroanatomy, Anderson Gallery, New York State Center of Excellence in Bioinformatics & Life Sciences (CBLS), Center for Computational Research (CCR), Center of Excellence for Document Analysis and Recognition (CEDAR), Center of Excellence in Materials Informatics, Buffalo Clinical and Translational Research Center (CTRC), New York State Center for Engineering Design and Industrial Innovation (NYSCEDII), Electronic Poetry Center, The Archaeological Survey, and numerous research centers.

CAMPUS LIFE

Environment: City. **Activities:** Campus Ministries; Choral groups; Concert band; Dance; Drama/theater; International Student Organization; Jazz band; Literary magazine; Marching band; Model UN; Music ensembles; Musical theater; Opera; Pep band; Radio station; Student government; Student newspaper; Student-run film society; Symphony orchestra; Television station. 651 registered organizations, 33 honor societies, 35 religious organizations, 19 fraternities, 13 sororities on campus. **Athletics (Intercollegiate):** *Men:* baseball, basketball, cross-country, football, soccer, swimming, tennis, track/field (outdoor), wrestling. *Women:* basketball, crew/rowing, cross-country, soccer, softball, swimming, tennis, track/field (outdoor), volleyball. **On-Campus Highlights:** Center for the Arts.

ADMISSIONS

Freshman Academic Profile: 30% in top 10% of high school class, 65% in top 25% of high school class, 94% in top 50% of high school class.
Test Scores: SAT Math middle 50% range 590–690. SAT EBRW middle 50% range 570–650. ACT middle 50% range 24–29. **Basis for Candidate Selection:** *Very important factors include:* rigor of secondary school record, academic GPA, standardized test scores. *Important factors include:* class rank, recommendation(s), interview. *Other factors include:* application essay, extracurricular activities, talent/ability, character/personal qualities, first generation, geographical residence, racial/ethnic status, volunteer work, work experience. **Freshman Admission Requirements:** High school diploma is required and GED is accepted. *Academic units recommended:* 4 English, 3 math, 3 science, 3 foreign language, 4 social studies. **Freshman Admission Statistics:** 29,900 applied, 61% admitted, 23% enrolled. **Transfer Admission Requirements:** High school transcript, college transcript(s), essay or personal statement. Minimum college GPA of 2.5 required. Lowest grade transferable D. **General Admission Information:** Application fee $50. Priority deadline 11/15. Non-fall registration accepted.

COSTS AND FINANCIAL AID

Annual in-state tuition $7,070. Annual out-of-state tuition $24,740. Room and board $14,631. Required fees $3,454. Average book and supplies expense $1,203. **Required Forms and Deadlines:** FAFSA. **Notification of Awards:** Applicants will be notified of awards on a rolling basis beginning 2/1. **Types of Aid:** *Need-based scholarships/grants:* College/university scholarship or grant aid from institutional funds; Federal Nursing Scholarships; Federal Pell; Private scholarships; SEOG; State scholarships/grants. *Loans:* Direct PLUS loans; Direct Subsidized Stafford Loans; Direct Unsubsidized Stafford Loans. **Student Employment:** Federal Work-Study Program available. Institutional employment available. **Financial Aid Statistics:** 77% needy freshmen, 78% needy undergrads receive need-based scholarship or grant aid. 37% freshmen, 26% undergrads receive non-need-based scholarship or grant aid. 85% freshmen, 88% undergrads receive need-based self-help aid. 0% freshmen, 0% undergrads receive athletic scholarships. 57% undergrads borrow to pay for school. Average cumulative indebtedness $25,157. **Criteria awarding aid:** *Need-based:* Academics, Minority status, Music/drama. *Non-need-based:* Academics, Art, Athletics, Minority status, Music/drama, State/district residency.

STATE UNIVERSITY OF NEW YORK—
UPSTATE MEDICAL UNIVERSITY

766 Irving Avenue, Syracuse, NY 13210
Phone: 315-464-4570 **Financial Aid Phone:** 315-464-4329
E-mail: admiss@upstate.edu **CEEB Code:** 2547
Fax: 315-464-8867 **ACT Code:** 2981

This public school was founded in 1850. It has a 25 acre campus.

RATINGS

Admissions Selectivity Rating: 60*   **Fire Safety Rating:** 85   **Green Rating:** 60*

STUDENTS AND FACULTY

Enrollment: 328. **Student Body:** 75% female, 25% male, 9% out-of-state.
Faculty: 43 full-time faculty, 60% hold PhDs, 2% are members of minority groups, 70% are women. 0% of classes are taught by teaching assistants.

ACADEMICS

Degrees: Bachelor's; Doctoral degree—other; Doctoral degree—professional practice; Doctoral degree research/scholarship; Master's; Post-master's certificate.
Classes: Most classes have 10–19 students. **Special Study Options:** Accelerated program; Distance learning; Independent study; Internships. **Disability Services offered:** Note-taking services; Reader services; Tape recorders; Tutors.
Career services: Alumni network; Regional alumni.

FACILITIES

Housing: Apartments for married students; Apartments for single students; Coed dorms; 100% of campus accessible to physically disabled. **Special Academic Facilities/Equipment:** 350 bed Tertiary Care Hospital.

CAMPUS LIFE

Environment: City. **Activities:** Dance; International Student Organization; Student government. 59 registered organizations, 3 religious organizations on campus. **On-Campus Highlights:** Weiskotten Hall.

ADMISSIONS

Freshman Admission Requirements: High school diploma is required and GED is accepted. **Transfer Admission Requirements:** High school transcript, college transcript(s), essay or personal statement, interview. Minimum college GPA of 2.0 required. Lowest grade transferable C-. **General Admission Information:** Application fee $50. Admission may be deferred for a maximum of 1 year.

COSTS AND FINANCIAL AID
Annual in-state tuition $4,970. Annual out-of-state tuition $13,380. Room and board $10,422. Required fees $575. Average book and supplies expense $1,070. **Required Forms and Deadlines:** FAFSA. **Types of Aid:** *Need-based scholarships/grants:* College/university scholarship or grant aid from institutional funds; Federal Pell; Private scholarships; SEOG; State scholarships/grants. *Loans:* Direct PLUS loans; Direct Subsidized Stafford Loans; Direct Unsubsidized Stafford Loans. **Student Employment:** Federal Work-Study Program available. Institutional employment available. **Financial Aid Statistics:** 18% needy undergrads receive need-based scholarship or grant aid. 27% undergrads receive non-need-based scholarship or grant aid. 13% undergrads receive need-based self-help aid. undergrads receive athletic scholarships. 78% freshmen receive any aid. **Criteria awarding aid:** *Need-based:* Academics.

STEPHENS COLLEGE

1200 East Broadway, Columbia, MO 65215
Phone: 573-876-7207 **Financial Aid Phone:** 573-876-7106
E-mail: apply@stephens.edu **CEEB Code:** 6683
Fax: 573-876-7237 **Website:** http://www.stephens.edu/ **ACT Code:** 2374

This private school was founded in 1833. It has a 47 acre campus.

RATINGS
Admissions Selectivity Rating: 83   Fire Safety Rating: 84   Green Rating: 66

STUDENTS AND FACULTY
Enrollment: 724. **Student Body:** 99% female, 1% male, 37% out-of-state, <1% international (1 countries represented). Asian 2%, African American 13%, Caucasian 69%, Hispanic 4%, Native American 1%, Pacific Islander <1%, Two or more races 6%, Race unknown 4%.
Retention and Graduation: 69% freshmen return for sophomore year.
Faculty: Student/faculty ratio 9:1. 54 full-time faculty, 57% hold PhDs, 9% are members of minority groups, 74% are women. 0% of classes are taught by teaching assistants.

ACADEMICS
Degrees: Associate; Bachelor's; Master's; Post-bachelor's certificate; Post-master's certificate. **Classes:** Most classes have fewer than 10 students. **Most popular majors:** Biology/Biological Sciences, General; Fashion/Apparel Design; Health Professions And Related Programs. **Special Study Options:** Accelerated program; Cross-registration; Distance learning; Double major; Dual enrollment; External degree program; Honors program; Independent study; Internships; Liberal arts/career combination; Student-designed major; Study abroad; Teacher certification program. **Combined degree programs:** BA/JD; BA/MA. **Disability Services offered:** Note-taking services; Tutors. **Career services:** Alumni network; Alumni services; Career assessment; Career/job search classes; Internships; Regional alumni.

FACILITIES
Housing: Apartments for single students; Fraternity/sorority housing; Special housing for disabled students; Theme housing; Women's dorms; 80% of campus accessible to physically disabled. **Special Academic Facilities/Equipment:** Art gallery and historical costume collections, on-campus preschool, kindergarten, and elementary school, language lab.

CAMPUS LIFE
Environment: City. **Activities:** Campus Ministries; Choral groups; Dance; Drama/theater; Literary magazine; Music ensembles; Musical theater; Radio station; Student government; Student newspaper; Student-run film society; Television station; Yearbook. 30 registered organizations, 4 honor societies, 1 religious organization, 2 sororities on campus. **Athletics (Intercollegiate):** *Women:* basketball, cross-country, softball, swimming, tennis, volleyball.
On-Campus Highlights: Kaldi's @ Stars Café. **Environmental Initiatives:** Recycling.

ADMISSIONS
Freshman Academic Profile: Average high school GPA 3.3. 14% in top 10% of high school class, 44% in top 25% of high school class, 79% in top 50% of high school class. 80% from public high schools. **Test Scores:** SAT Math middle 50% range 440–570. SAT EBRW middle 50% range 450–620. ACT middle 50% range 20–25. **Basis for Candidate Selection:** *Very important factors include:* rigor of secondary school record, academic GPA, standardized test scores. *Important factors include:* recommendation(s), extracurricular activities, talent/ability, character/personal qualities. *Other factors include:* class rank, application essay, interview, volunteer work, work experience, level of applicant's interest. **Freshman Admission Requirements:** High school diploma is required and GED is accepted. *Academic units recommended:* 4 English, 3 math, 2 science, 2 foreign language, 1 social studies. **Freshman Admission Statistics:** 1,168 applied, 61% admitted, 22% enrolled. **Transfer Admission Requirements:** High school transcript, college transcript(s), essay or personal statement. Minimum college GPA of 2.0 required. Lowest grade transferable C-. **General Admission Information:** Application fee $50. Priority deadline 1/18. Non-fall registration accepted. Admission may be deferred for a maximum of 1 year.

COSTS AND FINANCIAL AID
Annual tuition $30,144. Room and board $10,424. Average book and supplies expense $1,000. **Required Forms and Deadlines:** FAFSA. **Notification of Awards:** Applicants will be notified of awards on a rolling basis beginning 10/1. **Types of Aid:** *Need-based scholarships/grants:* College/university scholarship or grant aid from institutional funds; Federal Pell; Private scholarships; SEOG; State scholarships/grants. *Loans:* Direct PLUS loans; Direct Subsidized Stafford Loans; Direct Unsubsidized Stafford Loans. **Student Employment:** Federal Work-Study Program available. Institutional employment available. **Financial Aid Statistics:** 100% needy freshmen, 100% needy undergrads receive need-based scholarship or grant aid. 84% freshmen, 93% undergrads receive non-need-based scholarship or grant aid. 100% freshmen, 100% undergrads receive need-based self-help aid. 1% freshmen, 2% undergrads receive athletic scholarships. 100% freshmen, 98% undergrads receive any aid. 93% undergrads borrow to pay for school. Average cumulative indebtedness $9,238. **Criteria awarding aid:** *Non-need-based:* Academics, Alumni affiliation, Athletics, Leadership, Music/drama, State/district residency.

STERLING COLLEGE (KS)

125 W. Cooper, Sterling, KS 67579
Phone: 620-278-4275 **Financial Aid Phone:** 620-278-4207
E-mail: admissions@sterling.edu **CEEB Code:** 6684
Fax: 620-869-9021 **Website:** www.sterling.edu **ACT Code:** 1466

This private school, affiliated with the Presbyterian Church, was founded in 1887. It has a 42 acre campus.

RATINGS
Admissions Selectivity Rating: 87   Fire Safety Rating: 71   Green Rating: 60*

STUDENTS AND FACULTY
Enrollment: 657. **Student Body:** 47% female, 53% male, 63% out-of-state, 0% international (6 countries represented). Asian 2%, African American 12%, Caucasian 66%, Hispanic 15%, Native American 3%, Pacific Islander 0%, Two or more races 0%, Race unknown 3%.
Retention and Graduation: 62% freshmen return for sophomore year.
Faculty: Student/faculty ratio 12:1. 40 full-time faculty, 45% hold PhDs, 15% are members of minority groups, 35% are women. 0% of classes are taught by teaching assistants.

ACADEMICS
Degrees: Bachelor's. **Classes:** Most classes have 10–19 students. **Most popular majors:** Business/Commerce, General; Elementary Education and Teaching; Sports, Kinesiology, and Physical Education/Fitness, General. **Special Study Options:** Distance learning; Double major; Dual enrollment; Honors program; Independent study; Internships; Student-designed major; Study abroad; Teacher certification program. **Honors programs:** Honors level general education classes are offered in interdisciplinary history, literature, religious. **Disability Services offered:** Tutors. **Career services:** Alumni network; Alumni services; Career assessment; Internships.

FACILITIES

Housing: Men's dorms; Women's dorms; 80% of campus accessible to physically disabled. **Special Academic Facilities/Equipment:** History/cultural museum within Mabee Library.

CAMPUS LIFE

Environment: Rural. **Activities:** Campus Ministries; Choral groups; Concert band; Drama/theater; Jazz band; Literary magazine; Music ensembles; Musical theater; Radio station; Student government; Student newspaper; Television station; Yearbook. 16 registered organizations, 4 honor societies, 2 religious organizations on campus. **Athletics (Intercollegiate):** *Men:* baseball, basketball, cross-country, football, golf, soccer, track/field (outdoor). *Women:* basketball, cheerleading, cross-country, golf, soccer, softball, track/field (outdoor), volleyball. **On-Campus Highlights:** Gleason Phy. Educ. Center.

ADMISSIONS

Freshman Academic Profile: Average high school GPA 3.3. 8% in top 10% of high school class, 17% in top 25% of high school class, 45% in top 50% of high school class. 80% from public high schools. **Test Scores:** SAT Math middle 50% range 420–510. SAT EBRW middle 50% range 400–520. ACT middle 50% range 19–24. **Basis for Candidate Selection:** *Very important factors include:* rigor of secondary school record, standardized test scores, character/personal qualities. *Important factors include:* academic GPA, application essay, recommendation(s), interview, extracurricular activities, religious affiliation/commitment, volunteer work. *Other factors include:* class rank, talent/ability, first generation, alumni/ae relation, work experience. **Freshman Admission Requirements:** High school diploma is required and GED is accepted. *Academic units recommended:* 4 English, 3 math, 3 science, 2 science labs, 2 foreign language, 1 social studies, 2 history, 1 academic elective, 1 computer science. **Freshman Admission Statistics:** 1,118 applied, 41% admitted, 30% enrolled. **Transfer Admission Requirements:** College transcript(s), essay or personal statement. Minimum college GPA of 2.2 required. Lowest grade transferable C-. **General Admission Information:** Application fee $25. Priority deadline 3/1. Non-fall registration accepted. Admission may be deferred for a maximum of 1 semester.

COSTS AND FINANCIAL AID

Annual tuition $23,400. Room and board $8,580. Required fees $100. Average book and supplies expense $700. **Required Forms and Deadlines:** FAFSA. **Notification of Awards:** Applicants will be notified of awards on a rolling basis beginning 1/1. **Types of Aid:** *Need-based scholarships/grants:* College/university scholarship or grant aid from institutional funds; Federal Pell; Private scholarships; SEOG; State scholarships/grants. **Student Employment:** Federal Work-Study Program available. Institutional employment available. **Financial Aid Statistics:** 0% freshmen, 0% undergrads receive athletic scholarships. 100% freshmen, 96% undergrads receive any aid. **Criteria awarding aid:** *Non-need-based:* Academics, Art, Athletics, Leadership, Music/drama.

STERLING COLLEGE (VT)

PO Box 72, Craftsbury Common, VT 05827
Phone: 802-586-7711 **Financial Aid Phone:** 802-586-7711 x 103
E-mail: admission@sterlingcollege.edu **CEEB Code:** 3752
Fax: 802-586-2596 **Website:** www.sterlingcollege.edu **ACT Code:** 6946

This private school was founded in 1958. It has a 430 acre campus.

RATINGS

Admissions Selectivity Rating: 73   **Fire Safety Rating:** 94   **Green Rating:** 60*

STUDENTS AND FACULTY

Enrollment: 121. **Student Body:** 49% female, 51% male, 80% out-of-state, 3% international (4 countries represented). Asian 1%, African American 4%, Caucasian 83%, Hispanic 2%, Native American 0%, Pacific Islander 0%, Two or more races 2%, Race unknown 6%.
Retention and Graduation: 52% freshmen return for sophomore year. 3% grads go on to further study within 1 year. **Faculty:** Student/faculty ratio 6:1. 18 full-time faculty, 22% hold PhDs, 0% are members of minority groups, 50% are women. 0% of classes are taught by teaching assistants.

ACADEMICS

Degrees: Bachelor's. **Classes:** Most classes have fewer than 10 students. Most lab/discussion sessions have fewer than 10 students. **Most popular majors:** Agroecology and Sustainable Agriculture. **Special Study Options:** Double major; Dual enrollment; Exchange student program (domestic); Independent study; Internships; Student-designed major; Study abroad. **Disability Services offered:** Tutors. **Career services:** Alumni network; Alumni services; Career assessment; Career/job search classes; Internships; Regional alumni.

FACILITIES

Housing: Apartments for married students; Coed dorms; Cooperative housing; Theme housing; Wellness housing. **Special Academic Facilities/Equipment:** Library serves as art gallery. There is a 6–8 week rotation of Vermont artist displays. Campus also includes wind and solar-powered barns that serve as instructional facilities and labs, a greenhouse provides a working lab for plant and soil studies. Other facilities include: a woodshop, logging shop, sugarhouse, root cellar, darkroom, certified organic gardens, and a 32' tall climbing wall provides students with the ability to develop leadership and technical rock-climbing skills. **Campus network:** 50% of classrooms, 20% of dorms, 100% of student union, 100% of libraries, 100% of dining areas, 50% of common outdoor areas have wireless network access.

CAMPUS LIFE

Environment: Rural. **Activities:** Choral groups; Dance; Drama/theater; Literary magazine; Music ensembles; Student government; Student-run film society. 35 registered organizations on campus. **On-Campus Highlights:** Houston House Gardens. **Environmental Initiatives:** Curriculum is completely devoted to environmental stewardship.

ADMISSIONS

Freshman Academic Profile: Average high school GPA 3.2. 20% in top 10% of high school class, 33% in top 25% of high school class, 74% in top 50% of high school class. 64% from public high schools. **Basis for Candidate Selection:** *Very important factors include:* rigor of secondary school record, academic GPA, application essay, recommendation(s), interview, level of applicant's interest. *Important factors include:* class rank, extracurricular activities, talent/ability, character/personal qualities, volunteer work. *Other factors include:* alumni/ae relation, geographical residence, work experience. **Freshman Admission Requirements:** High school diploma is required and GED is accepted. *Academic units required:* 4 English, 3 math, 2 science, 2 science labs, 2 social studies, 2 history. *Academic units recommended:* 4 English, 4 math, 3 science, 3 science labs, 2 foreign language, 2 social studies, 2 history. **Freshman Admission Statistics:** 101 applied, 72% admitted, 55% enrolled. **Transfer Admission Requirements:** High school transcript, college transcript(s), essay or personal statement. Minimum college GPA of 2.0 required. Lowest grade transferable C. **General Admission Information:** Application fee $35. Regular application deadline 4/1. Non-fall registration accepted. Admission may be deferred for a maximum of one year.

COSTS AND FINANCIAL AID

Annual tuition $32,592. Room and board $8,796. Required fees $3,700. Average book and supplies expense $900. **Required Forms and Deadlines:** FAFSA; Institution's own financial aid form; State aid form. **Notification of Awards:** Applicants will be notified of awards on a rolling basis beginning 2/1. **Types of Aid:** *Need-based scholarships/grants:* College/university scholarship or grant aid from institutional funds; Federal Pell; Private scholarships; SEOG; State scholarships/grants. *Loans:* Direct PLUS loans; Direct Subsidized Stafford Loans; Direct Unsubsidized Stafford Loans. **Student Employment:** Federal Work-Study Program available. Institutional employment available. **Financial Aid Statistics:** 100% needy freshmen, 100% needy undergrads receive need-based scholarship or grant aid. 0% freshmen, 22% undergrads receive non-need-based scholarship or grant aid. 100% freshmen, 100% undergrads receive need-based self-help aid. 0% freshmen, 0% undergrads receive athletic scholarships. 100% freshmen, 100% undergrads receive any aid. **Criteria awarding aid:** *Need-based:* Academics, Leadership. *Non-need-based:* Academics, Leadership, State/district residency.

STETSON UNIVERSITY

421 N. Woodland Blvd, DeLand, FL 32723
Phone: 386-822-7100 **Financial Aid Phone:** 800-688-7120
E-mail: admissions@stetson.edu **CEEB Code:** 5630
Fax: 386-822-7112 **Website:** stetson.edu **ACT Code:** 756

This private school was founded in 1883. It has a 159 acre campus.

RATINGS

Admissions Selectivity Rating: 80   **Fire Safety Rating:** 81   **Green Rating:** 76

STUDENTS AND FACULTY

Enrollment: 3,135. **Student Body:** 57% female, 43% male, 25% out-of-state, 6% international (58 countries represented). Asian 2%, African American 8%, Caucasian 58%, Hispanic 18%, Native American <1%, Pacific Islander <1%, Two or more races 5%, Race unknown 1%.
Retention and Graduation: 77% freshmen return for sophomore year. 60% freshmen graduate within 4 years. 65% freshmen graduate within 6 years. 19% grads go on to further study within 1 year. 10% grads pursue arts and sciences degrees. 2% grads pursue law degrees. 6% grads pursue business degrees. 1% grads pursue medical degrees. **Faculty:** Student/faculty ratio 13:1. 269 full-time faculty, 94% hold PhDs, 16% are members of minority groups, 49% are women. 0% of classes are taught by teaching assistants.

ACADEMICS

Degrees: Bachelor's; Doctoral degree—professional practice; Master's; Post-master's certificate. **Classes:** Most classes have 10–19 students. Most lab/discussion sessions have 10–19 students. **Most popular majors:** Psychology, General; Health Professions And Related Programs; Business Administration and Management, General. **Special Study Options:** Accelerated program; Distance learning; Double major; Honors program; Independent study; Internships; Liberal arts/career combination; Student-designed major; Study abroad; Teacher certification program. **Honors programs:** Stetson University Honors Program. **Combined degree programs:** BA/JD. **Disability Services offered:** Note-taking services; Reader services; Tape recorders; Tutors. **Career services:** Alumni network; Alumni services; Career assessment; Career/job search classes; Internships; Regional alumni.

FACILITIES

Housing: Apartments for married students; Apartments for single students; Coed dorms; Fraternity/sorority housing; Men's dorms; Theme housing; Wellness housing; Women's dorms; 80% of campus accessible to physically disabled. **Special Academic Facilities/Equipment:** Language lab, art gallery, greenhouse with growth chambers, mineral museum, electron microscopes.

CAMPUS LIFE

Environment: Town. **Activities:** Campus Ministries; Choral groups; Concert band; Dance; Drama/theater; International Student Organization; Jazz band; Literary magazine; Marching band; Music ensembles; Musical theater; Opera; Pep band; Radio station; Student government; Student newspaper; Student-run film society; Symphony orchestra. 114 registered organizations, 17 honor societies, 11 religious organization, 9 fraternities, 6 sororities on campus. **Athletics (Intercollegiate):** *Men:* baseball, basketball, crew/rowing, cross-country, golf, soccer, tennis. *Women:* basketball, crew/rowing, cross-country, golf, soccer, softball, tennis, volleyball. **On-Campus Highlights:** Palm Court and John B Stetson statue. **Environmental Initiatives:** The Stetson College of Law is home to the Institute for Biodiversity Law and Policy. The Institute serves as an interdisciplinary focal point for education, research and service activities related to biodiversity issues, and is committed to environmental education and service from the local to the global scale. Each semester, the Institute sponsors several biodiversity lectures.

ADMISSIONS

Freshman Academic Profile: Average high school GPA 3.9. 23% in top 10% of high school class, 56% in top 25% of high school class, 87% in top 50% of high school class. 75% from public high schools. **Test Scores:** SAT Math middle 50% range 540–640. SAT EBRW middle 50% range 570–660. ACT middle 50% range 22–29. **Basis for Candidate Selection:** *Very important factors include:* rigor of secondary school record, academic GPA. *Important factors include:* class rank, application essay, standardized test scores,

recommendation(s), interview, extracurricular activities, talent/ability, character/personal qualities. *Other factors include:* alumni/ae relation, geographical residence, state residency, racial/ethnic status. **Freshman Admission Requirements:** High school diploma is required and GED is accepted. *Academic units required:* 4 English, 3 math, 3 science, 2 foreign language, 2 social studies. **Freshman Admission Statistics:** 13,005 applied, 72% admitted, 10% enrolled. **Transfer Admission Requirements:** High school transcript, college transcript(s), essay or personal statement, standardized test scores, statement of good standing from prior institution(s). Minimum college GPA of 2.0 required. Lowest grade transferable C. **General Admission Information:** Application fee $50. Priority deadline 11/1. Non-fall registration accepted.

COSTS AND FINANCIAL AID

Annual tuition $49,140. Room and board $14,540. Required fees $360. Average book and supplies expense $1,200. **Required Forms and Deadlines:** FAFSA. **Notification of Awards:** Applicants will be notified of awards on a rolling basis beginning 12/1. **Types of Aid:** *Need-based scholarships/grants:* College/university scholarship or grant aid from institutional funds; Federal Pell; Private scholarships; SEOG; State scholarships/grants. *Loans:* Direct PLUS loans; Direct Subsidized Stafford Loans; Direct Unsubsidized Stafford Loans. **Student Employment:** Federal Work-Study Program available. Institutional employment available. **Financial Aid Statistics:** 100% needy freshmen, 99% needy undergrads receive need-based scholarship or grant aid. 25% freshmen, 20% undergrads receive non-need-based scholarship or grant aid. 75% freshmen, 75% undergrads receive need-based self-help aid. 4% freshmen, 5% undergrads receive athletic scholarships. 100% freshmen, 98% undergrads receive any aid. 65% undergrads borrow to pay for school. Average cumulative indebtedness $32,601. **Criteria awarding aid:** *Need-based:* Academics, Alumni affiliation, Art, Athletics, Leadership, Minority status, Music/drama, Religious affiliation. *Non-need-based:* Academics, Alumni affiliation, Art, Athletics, Leadership, Minority status, Music/drama, Religious affiliation, State/district residency.

STEVENS INSTITUTE OF TECHNOLOGY

One Castle Point Terrace, Hoboken, NJ 07030
Phone: 201-216-5194 **Financial Aid Phone:** 201-216-8142
E-mail: admissions@stevens.edu **CEEB Code:** 2819
Fax: 201-216-8348 **Website:** http://www.stevens.edu/princetonreview **ACT Code:** 2610

This private school was founded in 1870. It has a 55 acre campus.

RATINGS

Admissions Selectivity Rating: 94   **Fire Safety Rating:** 99   **Green Rating:** 95

STUDENTS AND FACULTY

Enrollment: 3,420. **Student Body:** 29% female, 71% male, 38% out-of-state, 4% international (24 countries represented). Asian 15%, African American 2%, Caucasian 64%, Hispanic 11%, Native American <1%, Pacific Islander 0%, Two or more races 0%, Race unknown 4%.
Retention and Graduation: 95% freshmen return for sophomore year. 42% freshmen graduate within 4 years. 83% freshmen graduate within 6 years. **Faculty:** Student/faculty ratio 10:1. 264 full-time faculty, 95% hold PhDs, 21% are members of minority groups, 26% are women. 0% of classes are taught by teaching assistants.

ACADEMICS

Degrees: Bachelor's; Master's; Post-bachelor's certificate. **Classes:** Most classes have 20–29 students. Most lab/discussion sessions have 20–29 students. **Most popular majors:** Computer Science; Computer Engineering, General; Mechanical Engineering. **Special Study Options:** Accelerated program; Cooperative education program; Cross-registration; Distance learning; Double major; Dual enrollment; Honors program; Independent study; Study abroad. **Honors programs:** The Scholars Program allows high-achieving students to participate in research over the summer or take up to four tuition-free courses each summer. Scholars students may also complete their Bachelor's in three years or a combined Bachelor's and Master's in four years at no extra cost. **Combined degree programs:** BA/DDS; BA/JD; BA/MD. **Disability Services offered:** Note-taking services; Reader services; Tape recorders; Tutors. **Career**

services: Alumni network; Alumni services; Career assessment; Career/job search classes; Internships; Regional alumni.

FACILITIES

Housing: Apartments for single students; Coed dorms; Fraternity/sorority housing; Theme housing; Women's dorms; 100% of campus accessible to physically disabled. **Special Academic Facilities/Equipment:** Art museum, electron microscope, ocean engineering lab, HDTV research facility, advanced telecommunications institute, environmental lab, design/manufacturing institute, wind tunnel, robotics lab, product management center, polymer processing institute. DeBaun Theater, a multi-media facility, wireless campus network.

CAMPUS LIFE

Environment: Town. **Activities:** Campus Ministries; Choral groups; Concert band; Dance; Drama/theater; International Student Organization; Jazz band; Music ensembles; Musical theater; Radio station; Student government; Student newspaper; Symphony orchestra; Television station; Yearbook. 125 registered organizations, 11 honor societies, 4 religious organizations, 13 fraternities, 7 sororities on campus. **Athletics (Intercollegiate):** *Men:* baseball, basketball, cross-country, fencing, lacrosse, soccer, swimming, tennis, track/field (outdoor), track/field (indoor), volleyball, wrestling. *Women:* basketball, cross-country, equestrian sports, fencing, field hockey, lacrosse, soccer, swimming, tennis, track/field (outdoor), track/field (indoor), volleyball. **On-Campus Highlights:** Schaefer Athletic Center. **Environmental Initiatives:** Green minor.

ADMISSIONS

Freshman Academic Profile: Average high school GPA 3.9. 72% in top 10% of high school class, 96% in top 25% of high school class, 100% in top 50% of high school class. **Test Scores:** SAT Math middle 50% range 690–770. SAT EBRW middle 50% range 640–710. ACT middle 50% range 30–33. **Basis for Candidate Selection:** *Very important factors include:* rigor of secondary school record, academic GPA, standardized test scores. *Important factors include:* talent/ability, character/personal qualities. *Other factors include:* class rank, application essay, recommendation(s), interview, extracurricular activities, first generation, alumni/ae relation, geographical residence, state residency, racial/ethnic status, volunteer work, work experience, level of applicant's interest. **Freshman Admission Requirements:** High school diploma is required and GED is accepted. *Academic units required:* 4 English, 4 math, 3 science, 3 science labs. *Academic units recommended:* 4 science, 4 science labs, 2 foreign language, 2 social studies, 2 history, 4 academic electives. **Freshman Admission Statistics:** 9,265 applied, 41% admitted, 26% enrolled. **Transfer Admission Requirements:** High school transcript, college transcript(s), essay or personal statement, interview. Minimum college GPA of 3.0 required. Lowest grade transferable C. **General Admission Information:** Application fee $70. Regular application deadline 1/15. Admission may be deferred for a maximum of 1 year.

COSTS AND FINANCIAL AID

Annual tuition $52,134. Room and board $15,770. Required fees $1,880. Average book and supplies expense $1,200. **Required Forms and Deadlines:** CSS/Financial Aid PROFILE; FAFSA. **Types of Aid:** *Need-based scholarships/grants:* College/university scholarship or grant aid from institutional funds; Federal Pell; Private scholarships; SEOG; State scholarships/grants; United Negro College Fund. *Loans:* Direct PLUS loans; Direct Subsidized Stafford Loans; Direct Unsubsidized Stafford Loans. **Student Employment:** Federal Work-Study Program available. Institutional employment available. **Financial Aid Statistics:** 71% needy freshmen, 65% needy undergrads receive need-based scholarship or grant aid. 99% freshmen, 96% undergrads receive non-need-based scholarship or grant aid. 78% freshmen, 78% undergrads receive need-based self-help aid. 0% freshmen, 0% undergrads receive athletic scholarships. 99% freshmen, 94% undergrads receive any aid. 64% undergrads borrow to pay for school. Average cumulative indebtedness $40,588. **Criteria awarding aid:** *Non-need-based:* Academics, Leadership, Minority status, Music/drama.

STEVENSON UNIVERSITY

1525 Greenspring Valley Road, Stevenson, MD 21153-0641
Phone: 410-486-7001 **Financial Aid Phone:** 443-352-4369
E-mail: admissions@stevenson.edu **CEEB Code:** 2107
Fax: 443-352-4440 **Website:** http://www.stevenson.edu **ACT Code:** 1753

This private school was founded in 1947. It has a 168 acre campus.

RATINGS

Admissions Selectivity Rating: 83   **Fire Safety Rating:** 79   **Green Rating:** 60*

STUDENTS AND FACULTY

Enrollment: 3,826. **Student Body:** 65% female, 35% male, 21% out-of-state, 0% international (7 countries represented). Asian 3%, African American 29%, Caucasian 57%, Hispanic 4%, Native American <1%, Pacific Islander <1%, Two or more races 2%, Race unknown 4%.
Retention and Graduation: 75% freshmen return for sophomore year. 17% grads go on to further study within 1 year. **Faculty:** Student/faculty ratio 15:1. 130 full-time faculty, 74% hold PhDs, 15% are members of minority groups, 54% are women. 0% of classes are taught by teaching assistants.

ACADEMICS

Degrees: Bachelor's; Master's. **Classes:** Most classes have 10–19 students. **Most popular majors:** Registered Nursing/Registered Nurse; Business Administration and Management, General; Legal Assistant/Paralegal. **Special Study Options:** Accelerated program; Cooperative education program; Cross-registration; Distance learning; Double major; Dual enrollment; Honors program; Independent study; Internships; Liberal arts/career combination; Student-designed major; Study abroad; Teacher certification program. **Honors programs:** Consistent with its mission, the Stevenson University Honors Program seeks to admit academically outstanding students who are interested in challenging themselves through a unique and stimulating curriculum that extends beyond traditional academic boundaries. **Disability Services offered:** Note-taking services; Reader services; Tape recorders; Tutors. **Career services:** Alumni network; Alumni services; Career assessment; Internships; Regional alumni.

FACILITIES

Housing: Apartments for single students; Theme housing; Wellness housing; 100% of campus accessible to physically disabled. **Special Academic Facilities/Equipment:** Art gallery and theatre. **Campus network:** 100% of classrooms, 100% of dorms, 100% of student union, 100% of libraries, 100% of dining areas, 100% of common outdoor areas have wireless network access.

CAMPUS LIFE

Environment: Village. **Activities:** Campus Ministries; Choral groups; Dance; Drama/theater; International Student Organization; Jazz band; Literary magazine; Marching band; Music ensembles; Pep band; Radio station; Student government; Student newspaper; Symphony orchestra. 48 registered organizations, 10 honor societies, 2 religious organizations, 2 sororities on campus. **Athletics (Intercollegiate):** *Men:* baseball, basketball, cheerleading, cross-country, golf, lacrosse, soccer, tennis, track/field (indoor), volleyball. *Women:* basketball, cheerleading, cross-country, field hockey, lacrosse, soccer, softball, tennis, track/field (indoor), volleyball. **On-Campus Highlights:** Rockland Center (Dining Hall/Student Center).

ADMISSIONS

Freshman Academic Profile: Average high school GPA 3.2. 11% in top 10% of high school class, 31% in top 25% of high school class, 58% in top 50% of high school class. 70% from public high schools. **Test Scores:** SAT Math middle 50% range 450–560. SAT EBRW middle 50% range 440–540. ACT middle 50% range 18–23. **Basis for Candidate Selection:** *Very important factors include:* rigor of secondary school record, academic GPA. *Important factors include:* application essay, standardized test scores, recommendation(s), extracurricular activities, talent/ability, character/personal qualities. *Other factors include:* class rank, interview, first generation, alumni/ae relation, geographical residence, volunteer work, work experience, level of applicant's interest. **Freshman Admission Requirements:** High school diploma is required and GED is accepted. *Academic units required:* 4 English, 3 math, 3 science, 2 science labs, 2 social studies, 1 history, 4 academic electives. *Academic units recommended:* 4 English, 3 math, 3 science, 2 science labs, 2 foreign language, 2 social studies, 1 history, 4 academic electives. **Freshman Admission Statistics:** 5,318 applied, 60% admitted, 24% enrolled. **Transfer Admission Requirements:** College transcript(s), statement of good standing from prior institution(s). Minimum college GPA of 2.5 required. Lowest grade transferable C. **General Admission Information:** Application fee $40. Priority deadline 3/1. Non-fall registration accepted.

COSTS AND FINANCIAL AID
Annual tuition $25,210. Room and board $12,290. Required fees $1,872. Average book and supplies expense $1,250. **Required Forms and Deadlines:** FAFSA. **Notification of Awards:** Applicants will be notified of awards on a rolling basis beginning 3/15. **Types of Aid:** *Need-based scholarships/grants:* College/university scholarship or grant aid from institutional funds; Federal Pell; Private scholarships; SEOG; State scholarships/grants. *Loans:* Direct PLUS loans; Direct Subsidized Stafford Loans; Direct Unsubsidized Stafford Loans. **Student Employment:** Federal Work-Study Program available. Institutional employment available. **Financial Aid Statistics:** 99% needy freshmen, 96% needy undergrads receive need-based scholarship or grant aid. 9% freshmen, 8% undergrads receive non-need-based scholarship or grant aid. 78% freshmen, 78% undergrads receive need-based self-help aid. 0% freshmen, 0% undergrads receive athletic scholarships. **Criteria awarding aid:** *Need-based:* Leadership, Minority status. *Non-need-based:* Academics, Art, Leadership, Music/drama.

STOCKTON UNIVERSITY

101 Vera King Farris Drive, Galloway, NJ 08205
Phone: 609-652-4261 **Financial Aid Phone:** 609-652-4203
E-mail: admissions@stockton.edu **CEEB Code:** 2889
Fax: 609-748-5541 **Website:** www.stockton.edu

This public school was founded in 1969. It has a 2000 acre campus.

RATINGS
Admissions Selectivity Rating: 80   Fire Safety Rating: 97   Green Rating: 87

STUDENTS AND FACULTY
Enrollment: 8,873. **Student Body:** 59% female, 41% male, 3% out-of-state, 1% international (6 countries represented). Asian 7%, African American 9%, Caucasian 65%, Hispanic 15%, Native American <1%, Pacific Islander <1%, Two or more races 3%, Race unknown 1%. **Retention and Graduation:** 83% freshmen return for sophomore year. 61% freshmen graduate within 4 years. 77% freshmen graduate within 6 years. 33% grads go on to further study within 1 year. 71% grads pursue arts and sciences degrees. 5% grads pursue law degrees. 6% grads pursue business degrees. 4% grads pursue medical degrees. **Faculty:** Student/faculty ratio 17:1. 353 full-time faculty, 91% hold PhDs, 25% are members of minority groups, 56% are women. 0% of classes are taught by teaching assistants.

ACADEMICS
Degrees: Bachelor's; Doctoral degree—professional practice; Doctoral degree research/scholarship; Master's; Post-bachelor's certificate; Post-master's certificate. **Classes:** Most classes have 20–29 students. Most lab/discussion sessions have 10–19 students. **Most popular majors:** Criminology; Health Professions And Related Programs; Business Administration and Management, General. **Special Study Options:** Accelerated program; Cross-registration; Distance learning; Double major; Dual enrollment; English as a Second Language (ESL); Honors program; Independent study; Internships; Liberal arts/career combination; Student-designed major; Study abroad; Teacher certification program. **Honors programs:** Stockton Honors Program. **Combined degree programs:** BA/MA. **Disability Services offered:** Note-taking services; Reader services; Tape recorders; Tutors. **Career services:** Alumni network; Alumni services; Career assessment; Career/job search classes; Internships; Regional alumni.

FACILITIES
Housing: Apartments for single students; Coed dorms; Special housing for disabled students; Theme housing; Wellness housing 100% of campus accessible to physically disabled. **Special Academic Facilities/Equipment:** Observatory, Nacote Creek field station, Holocaust Resource Center, Seaview Resort, The Sam Azeez Museum of Woodbine Heritage.

CAMPUS LIFE
Environment: Town. **Activities:** Campus Ministries; Choral groups; Concert band; Dance; Drama/theater; International Student Organization; Jazz band; Literary magazine; Model UN; Music ensembles; Musical theater; Pep band; Radio station; Student government; Student newspaper; Television station; Yearbook. 111 registered organizations, 22 honor societies, 10

religious organizations, 13 fraternities, 13 sororities on campus. **Athletics (Intercollegiate):** *Men:* baseball, basketball, cheerleading, cross-country, lacrosse, soccer, track/field (outdoor), track/field (indoor). *Women:* basketball, cheerleading, crew/rowing, cross-country, field hockey, soccer, softball, tennis, track/field (outdoor), track/field (indoor), volleyball. **On-Campus Highlights:** Campus Center. **Environmental Initiatives:** 1200 KW capacity arrays operating on campus. This includes rooftop installations and shade canopies over parking lots. Additionally, the GEOTHERMAL PROJECT provides up to 1650 tons of cooling capacity and allows portions of the building to be heated and cooled using the same equipment. Solar hot water heating has been installed on the roof of the newest residential facility, which accommodates 390 students.

ADMISSIONS
Freshman Academic Profile: 20% in top 10% of high school class, 47% in top 25% of high school class, 82% in top 50% of high school class. 88% from public high schools. **Test Scores:** SAT Math middle 50% range 510–600. SAT EBRW middle 50% range 510–610. ACT middle 50% range 20–26. **Basis for Candidate Selection:** *Very important factors include:* rigor of secondary school record, academic GPA. *Other factors include:* class rank, application essay, standardized test scores, recommendation(s), extracurricular activities, talent/ability, character/personal qualities, first generation, alumni/ae relation, volunteer work, work experience, level of applicant's interest. **Freshman Admission Requirements:** High school diploma is required and GED is accepted. *Academic units required:* 4 English, 3 math, 2 science, 2 science labs, 2 social studies, 5 academic electives. *Academic units recommended:* 2 foreign language. **Freshman Admission Statistics:** 6,914 applied, 76% admitted, 29% enrolled. **Transfer Admission Requirements:** Minimum college GPA of 2.5 required. Lowest grade transferable C. **General Admission Information:** Application fee $50. Priority deadline 5/1. Regular application deadline 8/15. Non-fall registration accepted. Admission may be deferred for a maximum of 1 year.

COSTS AND FINANCIAL AID
Annual in-state tuition $12,005. Annual out-of-state tuition $19,293. Room and board $12,496. Required fees $2,043. Average book and supplies expense $1,600. **Required Forms and Deadlines:** FAFSA. **Notification of Awards:** Applicants will be notified of awards on a rolling basis beginning 4/1. **Types of Aid:** *Need-based scholarships/grants:* College/university scholarship or grant aid from institutional funds; Federal Pell; Private scholarships; SEOG; State scholarships/grants. *Loans:* Direct PLUS loans; Direct Subsidized Stafford Loans; Direct Unsubsidized Stafford Loans. **Student Employment:** Federal Work-Study Program available. Institutional employment available. **Financial Aid Statistics:** 89% needy freshmen, 69% needy undergrads receive need-based scholarship or grant aid. 26% freshmen, 28% undergrads receive non-need-based scholarship or grant aid. 76% freshmen, 75% undergrads receive need-based self-help aid. 0% freshmen, 0% undergrads receive athletic scholarships. 86% freshmen, 84% undergrads receive any aid. 76% undergrads borrow to pay for school. Average cumulative indebtedness $31,470. **Criteria awarding aid:** *Non-need-based:* Academics, Art, Leadership, Minority status, Music/drama, State/district residency.

STONEHILL COLLEGE

320 Washington Street, Easton, MA 02357-5610
Phone: (508) 565-1373 **Financial Aid Phone:** 508-565-1088
E-mail: admission@stonehill.edu **CEEB Code:** 3770
Fax: (508) 565-1545 **Website:** www.stonehill.edu **ACT Code:** 1918

This private school, affiliated with the Roman Catholic Church, was founded in 1948. It has a 384 acre campus.

RATINGS
Admissions Selectivity Rating: 84   Fire Safety Rating: 98   Green Rating: 84

STUDENTS AND FACULTY
Enrollment: 2,486. **Student Body:** 59% female, 41% male, 35% out-of-state, 1% international (15 countries represented). Asian 2%, African American 4%,

Caucasian 83%, Hispanic 5%, Native American <1%, Pacific Islander 0%, Two or more races 2%, Race unknown 3%.
Retention and Graduation: 83% freshmen return for sophomore year. 77% freshmen graduate within 4 years. 82% freshmen graduate within 6 years. 14% grads go on to further study within 1 year. 10% grads pursue arts and sciences degrees. 1% grads pursue law degrees. 2% grads pursue business degrees. 1% grads pursue medical degrees. **Faculty:** Student/faculty ratio 12:1. 170 full-time faculty, 92% hold PhDs, 15% are members of minority groups, 46% are women. 0% of classes are taught by teaching assistants.

ACADEMICS
Degrees: Bachelor's; Master's. **Classes:** Most classes have 20–29 students. Most lab/discussion sessions have 10–19 students. **Most popular majors:** Psychology, General; Finance, General; Criminology. **Special Study Options:** Cross-registration; Double major; Dual enrollment; Exchange student program (domestic); Honors program; Independent study; Internships; Liberal arts/career combination; Student-designed major; Study abroad; Teacher certification program. **Honors programs:** Students are accepted into the program as first-year students. The Moreau Honors Program requires 5 honors courses over their 4-year matriculation at the college as well as an introductory 1-credit course (Honors 100) in their first year, and a "capstone" 1-credit Honors 400 Senior seminar in their final year. **Disability Services offered:** Note-taking services; Reader services; Tape recorders; Tutors. **Career services:** Alumni network; Alumni services; Career assessment; Career/job search classes; Internships.

FACILITIES
Housing: Coed dorms; Men's dorms; Special housing for disabled students; Theme housing; Wellness housing; Women's dorms; 95% of campus accessible to physically disabled. **Special Academic Facilities/Equipment:** Joseph W. Martin, Jr. Institute for Law and Society; Thomas and Mary Shields Science Center; Stonehill Industrial History Collection (aka, shovel museum); Cushing-Martin Hall (art gallery and industrial history gallery); Center for Nonprofit Management; Hemingway Theatre; MacPhaidin Library; Sally Ames Blair Sports Complex; Thomas and Donna May Pavilion Ice Rink (seasonal); and observatory.

CAMPUS LIFE
Environment: Village. **Activities:** Campus Ministries; Choral groups; Concert band; Dance; Drama/theater; International Student Organization; Literary magazine; Model UN; Music ensembles; Musical theater; Radio station; Student government; Student newspaper; Student-run film society; Yearbook. 65 registered organizations, 24 honor societies, 3 religious organizations on campus. **Athletics (Intercollegiate):** *Men:* baseball, basketball, cross-country, football, ice hockey, soccer, tennis, track/field (outdoor), track/field (indoor). *Women:* basketball, cross-country, equestrian sports, field hockey, lacrosse, soccer, softball, tennis, track/field (outdoor), track/field (indoor), volleyball. **On-Campus Highlights:** Leo J. Meehan School of Business. **Environmental Initiatives:** Stonehill College enrolls second-Year students in a Learning Community (LC) of their choice. Every year, Stonehill offers LCs that focus on the environment and food politics. These LCs explore the social, economic, and environmental dimensions of these topics. Stonehill's LCs exemplify our commitment to creating a flexible student-centered climate that promotes academic challenge, cooperative learning and authentic community. Our LCs feature linked or collaboratively taught classes from different disciplines or perspectives that are designed to foster students' ability to integrate learning across courses, over time and between campus and community life. Students in LCs address real-world problems that are unscripted and broad, requiring multiple modes of inquiry and perspective. An example of an LC that provides a sustainability-focused immersive experience is The Story of Stonehill's Water. This LC examines Stonehill College uses over 27 million gallons of water per year. This learning community will explore where that water comes from and where it goes after being "used" by the college. More broadly, this course will examine the health of the Taunton River watershed. At the completion of this class, students will be prepared to make recommendations about how to reduce Stonehill's water usage.

ADMISSIONS
Freshman Academic Profile: Average high school GPA 3.3. 19% in top 10% of high school class, 51% in top 25% of high school class, 88% in top 50% of high school class. 67% from public high schools. **Test Scores:** SAT Math middle 50% range 550–640. SAT EBRW middle 50% range 570–650. ACT middle 50% range 24–29. **Basis for Candidate Selection:** *Very important factors include:* rigor of secondary school record, class rank, academic GPA, talent/ability. *Important factors include:* application essay, recommendation(s), extracurricular activities. *Other factors include:* standardized test scores, interview, character/personal qualities, first generation, alumni/ae relation,

geographical residence, religious affiliation/commitment, racial/ethnic status, volunteer work, work experience, level of applicant's interest. **Freshman Admission Requirements:** High school diploma is required and GED is accepted. *Academic units required:* 4 English, 3 math, 3 science, 3 science labs, 3 foreign language, 3 history. *Academic units recommended:* 4 English, 4 math, 4 science, 3 science labs, 4 foreign language, 4 history. **Freshman Admission Statistics:** 6,961 applied, 66% admitted, 14% enrolled. **Transfer Admission Requirements:** High school transcript, college transcript(s), essay or personal statement, statement of good standing from prior institution(s). Minimum college GPA of 2.0 required. Lowest grade transferable C. **General Admission Information:** Application fee $60. Regular application deadline 1/15. Non-fall registration accepted. Admission may be deferred for a maximum of 1 year.

COSTS AND FINANCIAL AID
Annual tuition $44,420. Room and board $16,620. Average book and supplies expense $893. **Required Forms and Deadlines:** CSS/Financial Aid PROFILE; FAFSA; Noncustodial PROFILE. **Notification of Awards:** Applicants will be notified of awards on or about 4/1. **Types of Aid:** *Need-based scholarships/grants:* College/university scholarship or grant aid from institutional funds; Federal Pell; Private scholarships; SEOG; State scholarships/grants. *Loans:* Direct PLUS loans; Direct Subsidized Stafford Loans; Direct Unsubsidized Stafford Loans. **Student Employment:** Federal Work-Study Program available. Institutional employment available. **Financial Aid Statistics:** 99% needy freshmen, 99% needy undergrads receive need-based scholarship or grant aid. 33% freshmen, 35% undergrads receive non-need-based scholarship or grant aid. 64% freshmen, 64% undergrads receive need-based self-help aid. 4% freshmen, 4% undergrads receive athletic scholarships. 100% freshmen, 98% undergrads receive any aid. 71% undergrads borrow to pay for school. Average cumulative indebtedness $38,359. **Criteria awarding aid:** *Need-based:* Academics, Leadership. *Non-need-based:* Academics, Athletics, Leadership.

SUFFOLK UNIVERSITY

8 Ashburton Place, Boston, MA 02108
Phone: (617) 573 8460 **Financial Aid Phone:** 617-573-8470
E-mail: admission@suffolk.edu **CEEB Code:** 3771
Fax: (617) 557 1574 **Website:** www.suffolk.edu **ACT Code:** 1920

This private school was founded in 1906.

RATINGS
Admissions Selectivity Rating: 76   **Fire Safety Rating:** 99   **Green Rating:** 64

STUDENTS AND FACULTY
Enrollment: 4,923. **Student Body:** 56% female, 44% male, 32% out-of-state, 20% international (98 countries represented). Asian 7%, African American 5%, Caucasian 48%, Hispanic 13%, Native American <1%, Pacific Islander <1%, Two or more races 3%, Race unknown 4%.
Retention and Graduation: 77% freshmen return for sophomore year. 42% freshmen graduate within 4 years. 58% freshmen graduate within 6 years. 12% grads go on to further study within 1 year. 2% grads pursue arts and sciences degrees. <1% grads pursue law degrees. 4% grads pursue business degrees. 0% grads pursue medical degrees. **Faculty:** Student/faculty ratio 15:1. 382 full-time faculty, 74% hold PhDs, 19% are members of minority groups, 49% are women.

ACADEMICS
Degrees: Associate; Bachelor's; Certificate; Diploma; Doctoral degree—professional practice; Doctoral degree research/scholarship; Master's; Post-bachelor's certificate; Post-master's certificate. **Classes:** Most classes have 20–29 students. Most lab/discussion sessions have 10–19 students. **Most popular majors:** Finance, General; Business Administration and Management, General; Marketing/Marketing Management, General. **Special Study Options:** Accelerated program; Cooperative education program; Cross-registration; Distance learning; Double major; Dual enrollment; English as a Second Language (ESL); Exchange student program (domestic); Honors program; Independent study; Internships; Liberal arts/career combination; Student-designed major; Study abroad. **Honors programs:** Suffolk University honors students work in collaboration with their school's program director and

advisory committee to plan events that bring the honors community together on a regular basis outside of the classroom. Lectures by Suffolk University scholars or by noted intellectuals outside of the University, a variety of social events, visits to cultural and historical sites, and public service projects offer intellectual challenge, promote leadership, and offer opportunities to develop networking skills with faculty, alumni, community, business, and government leaders. The program provides honors scholars with a broader context for their academic pursuits, while strengthening their sense of community. Honors scholars are eligible for a full tuition scholarship. In addition, honors scholars enjoy guaranteed housing in University residence halls through the sophomore year; priority course registration; special honors program advisors; application assistance, when applicable, for Fulbright, Marshall, Rhodes, and other post-graduate academic and scholarship programs; Honors Program designation on official academic transcript; special listing in commencement program; and other benefits. Read more: https://www.suffolk.edu/undergraduate-admission/information-for/freshman/honors-program. **Combined degree programs:** BA/JD; BA/MA. **Disability Services offered:** Note-taking services; Reader services; Tape recorders; Tutors. **Career services:** Alumni services; Career assessment; Career/job search classes; Internships.

FACILITIES
Housing: Apartments for single students; Coed dorms; Special housing for disabled students. **Special Academic Facilities/Equipment:** Marine biology field station in Maine, NESAD art gallery, Adams art gallery, and the Modern Theatre.

CAMPUS LIFE
Environment: Metropolis. **Activities:** Campus Ministries; Choral groups; Dance; Drama/theater; International Student Organization; Jazz band; Literary magazine; Model UN; Music ensembles; Musical theater; Radio station; Student government; Student newspaper; Television station; Yearbook. 106 registered organizations, 18 honor societies, 3 religious organizations, 1 fraternity, 2 sororities on campus. **Athletics (Intercollegiate):** *Men:* baseball, basketball, cross-country, golf, ice hockey, soccer, tennis. *Women:* basketball, cross-country, softball, tennis, volleyball. **On-Campus Highlights:** Sawyer Library (Stahl Building).

ADMISSIONS
Freshman Academic Profile: Average high school GPA 3.3. 15% in top 10% of high school class, 43% in top 25% of high school class, 81% in top 50% of high school class. 64% from public high schools. **Test Scores:** SAT Math middle 50% range 510–600. SAT EBRW middle 50% range 510–610. ACT middle 50% range 21–26. **Basis for Candidate Selection:** *Very important factors include:* rigor of secondary school record, academic GPA. *Important factors include:* application essay, recommendation(s), character/personal qualities. *Other factors include:* class rank, standardized test scores, interview, extracurricular activities, talent/ability, first generation, alumni/ae relation, volunteer work, work experience, level of applicant's interest. **Freshman Admission Requirements:** High school diploma is required and GED is accepted. *Academic units required:* 4 English, 3 math, 2 science, 1 science labs, 2 foreign language, 1 social studies, 1 history, 4 academic electives. *Academic units recommended:* 4 English, 4 math, 4 science, 3 science labs, 4 foreign language, 2 social studies, 3 history, 4 academic electives. **Freshman Admission Statistics:** 8,362 applied, 84% admitted, 16% enrolled. **Transfer Admission Requirements:** High school transcript, college transcript(s), essay or personal statement. Minimum college GPA of 2.5 required. Lowest grade transferable C. **General Admission Information:** Application fee $50. Priority deadline 2/15. Non-fall registration accepted. Admission may be deferred for a maximum of 1 year.

COSTS AND FINANCIAL AID
Annual tuition $41,242. Room and board $18,134. Required fees $666. Average book and supplies expense $1,200. **Required Forms and Deadlines:** FAFSA. **Notification of Awards:** Applicants will be notified of awards on a rolling basis beginning 2/1. **Types of Aid:** *Need-based scholarships/grants:* College/university scholarship or grant aid from institutional funds; Federal Pell; Private scholarships; SEOG; State scholarships/grants. *Loans:* Direct PLUS loans; Direct Subsidized Stafford Loans; Direct Unsubsidized Stafford Loans. **Student Employment:** Federal Work-Study Program available. Institutional employment available. **Financial Aid Statistics:** 91% needy freshmen, 88% needy undergrads receive need-based scholarship or grant aid. 93% freshmen, 93% undergrads receive non-need-based scholarship or grant aid. 87% freshmen, 85% undergrads receive need-based self-help aid. 0% freshmen, 0% undergrads receive athletic scholarships. 95% freshmen, 87% undergrads receive any aid. 73% undergrads borrow to pay for school. Average cumulative indebtedness $28,582. **Criteria awarding aid:** *Need-based:* Academics. *Non-need-based:* Academics, Alumni affiliation.

SUSQUEHANNA UNIVERSITY

514 University Avenue, Selinsgrove, PA 17870
Phone: 570-372-4260 **Financial Aid Phone:** 570-372-4450
E-mail: suadmiss@susqu.edu **CEEB Code:** 2820
Fax: 570-372-2722 **Website:** www.susqu.edu **ACT Code:** 3720

This private school, affiliated with the Lutheran Church, was founded in 1858. It has a 325 acre campus.

RATINGS
Admissions Selectivity Rating: 78   **Fire Safety Rating:** 98   **Green Rating:** 81

STUDENTS AND FACULTY
Enrollment: 2,198. **Student Body:** 56% female, 44% male, 35% out-of-state, 2% international (21 countries represented). Asian 2%, African American 6%, Caucasian 79%, Hispanic 7%, Native American <1%, Pacific Islander <1%, Two or more races 3%, Race unknown 1%.
Retention and Graduation: 87% freshmen return for sophomore year. 69% freshmen graduate within 4 years. 72% freshmen graduate within 6 years. 14% grads go on to further study within 1 year. <1% grads pursue law degrees. 4% grads pursue medical degrees. **Faculty:** Student/faculty ratio 13:1. 138 full-time faculty, 25% are members of minority groups, 49% are women. 0% of classes are taught by teaching assistants.

ACADEMICS
Degrees: Bachelor's; Master's. **Classes:** Most classes have 10–19 students. Most lab/discussion sessions have 10–19 students. **Most popular majors:** Communication and Media Studies; Business/Commerce, General; Creative Writing. **Special Study Options:** Accelerated program; Cross-registration; Distance learning; Double major; Dual enrollment; English as a Second Language (ESL); Honors program; Independent study; Internships; Student-designed major; Study abroad; Teacher certification program. **Honors programs:** The Honors Program at Susquehanna offers a challenging curriculum to students interested in a more self-directed and interdisciplinary approach at the undergraduate level. The program is well suited to the intensely curious, active learner who values breadth of study and multiple perspectives. Discussion groups, lectures, off-campus visits, and residential programs complement Honors Program courses. **Combined degree programs:** BA/DDS. **Disability Services offered:** Note-taking services; Reader services; Tape recorders; Tutors. **Career services:** Alumni network; Alumni services; Career assessment; Career/job search classes; Internships; Regional alumni.

FACILITIES
Housing: Apartments for single students; Coed dorms; Cooperative housing; Fraternity/sorority housing; Special housing for disabled students; Special housing for international students; Theme housing; 90% of campus accessible to physically disabled. **Special Academic Facilities/Equipment:** Lore Degenstein Art Gallery; Blough-Weis Library, including rare books room; Natural Sciences Center; Stretansky Music Hall; electronic music studio; studio art building; child development center; foreign language broadcast system; teaching theatre; greenhouse; campus garden; ecological field station; electron microscope; reflecting telescope; fluorescent microscopes; video conference center; student investment center including Bloomberg Terminals; graphic design studio; freshwater research institute; multimedia production lab; editing and publishing suite; language classroom equipped for class exchanges with students in other countries.

CAMPUS LIFE
Environment: Town. **Activities:** Campus Ministries; Choral groups; Concert band; Dance; Drama/theater; International Student Organization; Jazz band; Literary magazine; Model UN; Music ensembles; Musical theater; Opera; Pep band; Radio station; Student government; Student newspaper; Symphony orchestra; Yearbook. 156 registered organizations, 25 honor societies, 10 religious organizations, 6 fraternities, 5 sororities on campus. **Athletics (Intercollegiate):** *Men:* baseball, basketball, crew/rowing, cross-country, football, golf, lacrosse, soccer, swimming, tennis, track/field (outdoor), track/field (indoor). *Women:* basketball, crew/rowing, cross-country, field hockey, golf, lacrosse, soccer, softball, swimming, tennis, track/field (outdoor), track/field (indoor), volleyball. **On-Campus Highlights:** Sports and Fitness Complex. **Environmental Initiatives:** New science facility and new student housing are

LEED certified. This housing and two units built in 2010 utilize geo-thermal energy for heating and cooling.

ADMISSIONS

Freshman Academic Profile: Average high school GPA 3.7. 25% in top 10% of high school class, 63% in top 25% of high school class, 88% in top 50% of high school class. 85% from public high schools. **Test Scores:** SAT Math middle 50% range 540–640. SAT EBRW middle 50% range 560–650. ACT middle 50% range 22–28. **Basis for Candidate Selection:** *Very important factors include:* rigor of secondary school record, academic GPA. *Important factors include:* class rank, application essay, standardized test scores, recommendation(s), interview, extracurricular activities, talent/ability, character/personal qualities, alumni/ae relation. *Other factors include:* first generation, geographical residence, state residency. **Freshman Admission Requirements:** High school diploma is required and GED is accepted. *Academic units required:* 4 English, 3 math, 2 science, 2 science labs, 2 foreign language, 2 social studies, 2 history, 2 academic electives. *Academic units recommended:* 4 English, 4 math, 3 science, 3 science labs, 4 foreign language, 4 social studies, 2 history, 3 academic electives. **Freshman Admission Statistics:** 4,863 applied, 85% admitted, 15% enrolled. **Transfer Admission Requirements:** High school transcript, college transcript(s), essay or personal statement, statement of good standing from prior institution(s). Minimum college GPA of 2.0 required. Lowest grade transferable C-. **General Admission Information:** Non-fall registration accepted. Admission may be deferred for a maximum of one year.

COSTS AND FINANCIAL AID

. **Required Forms and Deadlines:** FAFSA; State aid form. **Notification of Awards:** Applicants will be notified of awards on a rolling basis beginning 11/15. **Types of Aid:** *Need-based scholarships/grants:* College/university scholarship or grant aid from institutional funds; Federal Pell; Private scholarships; SEOG; State scholarships/grants. *Loans:* Direct PLUS loans; Direct Subsidized Stafford Loans; Direct Unsubsidized Stafford Loans. **Student Employment:** Federal Work-Study Program available. Institutional employment available. **Financial Aid Statistics:** 100% needy freshmen, 100% needy undergrads receive need-based scholarship or grant aid. 23% freshmen, 18% undergrads receive non-need-based scholarship or grant aid. 74% freshmen, 80% undergrads receive need-based self-help aid. 0% freshmen, 0% undergrads receive athletic scholarships. 98.5% freshmen, 100% undergrads receive any aid. 84% undergrads borrow to pay for school. Average cumulative indebtedness $40,455. **Criteria awarding aid:** *Non-need-based:* Academics, Alumni affiliation, Leadership, Minority status, Music/drama.

SWARTHMORE COLLEGE

500 College Avenue, Swarthmore, PA 19081
Phone: 610-328-8300 **Financial Aid Phone:** 610-328-8358
E-mail: admissions@swarthmore.edu **CEEB Code:** 2821
Fax: 610-328-8580 **Website:** www.swarthmore.edu **ACT Code:** 3722

This private school was founded in 1864. It has a 425 acre campus.

RATINGS

Admissions Selectivity Rating: 98 **Fire Safety Rating:** 92 **Green Rating:** 94

STUDENTS AND FACULTY

Enrollment: 1,657. **Student Body:** 51% female, 49% male, 88% out-of-state, 14% international (70 countries represented). Asian 16%, African American 8%, Caucasian 38%, Hispanic 13%, Native American <1%, Pacific Islander <1%, Two or more races 8%, Race unknown 4%.
Retention and Graduation: 98% freshmen return for sophomore year. 86% freshmen graduate within 4 years. 94% freshmen graduate within 6 years. 26% grads go on to further study within 1 year. 10% grads pursue arts and sciences degrees. 2% grads pursue law degrees. 1% grads pursue business degrees. 2% grads pursue medical degrees. **Faculty:** Student/faculty ratio 8:1. 197 full-time faculty, 100% hold PhDs, 24% are members of minority groups, 49% are women. 0% of classes are taught by teaching assistants.

ACADEMICS

Degrees: Bachelor's. **Classes:** Most classes have 10–19 students. Most lab/discussion sessions have 10–19 students. **Most popular majors:** Economics, General; Biology/Biological Sciences, General; Political Science and Government, General. **Special Study Options:** Accelerated program; Cross-registration; Double major; Exchange student program (domestic); Honors program; Independent study; Internships; Student-designed major; Study abroad; Teacher certification program. **Honors programs:** Modeled after the tutorial system at Oxford, the Swarthmore Honors Program brims with intellectual exploration. This engaging and dynamic program features small-group interaction with peers and faculty, a free and spirited exchange of ideas, independent research, and special projects. Students delve deeply into major and minor areas of study while being challenged to learn and lead discussions across disciplines. The program extolls independent evaluation, bringing more than 100 outside scholars to campus each year to assess students. This rare opportunity to go one-on-one with esteemed scholars, artists, and thinkers is a fitting capstone to the only undergraduate honors program of its kind in the United States. **Disability Services offered:** Note-taking services; Reader services; Tape recorders; Tutors. **Career services:** Alumni network; Alumni services; Career assessment; Career/job search classes; Internships.

FACILITIES

Housing: Apartments for single students; Coed dorms; Men's dorms; Special housing for disabled students; Theme housing; Women's dorms; 90% of campus accessible to physically disabled. **Special Academic Facilities/Equipment:** When you step onto the Swarthmore campus, you engage the world. A world of intellect and action, collaboration and connection. One where idyllic lawns and hills mark your journey to a class on robotics or international cinema. One with a dynamic array of arts spaces to enjoy—or stage—a performance. A place that crackles with diversity of culture and thought, whether it's chatting with a classmate from another continent in one of the campus coffee bars or listening to a Rhodes Scholar in the LEED-certified Science Center. A place replete with avenues of exploration, where you can immerse yourself in the Language Resource Center's many offerings, in the stars when at the College's observatory, or with any number of cultural experiences in center city Philadelphia, just a short train ride away. Whatever you make of your time at Swarthmore, you'll become equipped to excel in our rapidly changing world, attaining fulfillment as a person and citizen. Opportunity abounds.

CAMPUS LIFE

Environment: Village. **Activities:** Campus Ministries; Choral groups; Dance; Drama/theater; International Student Organization; Jazz band; Literary magazine; Music ensembles; Musical theater; Radio station; Student government; Student newspaper; Student-run film society; Symphony orchestra; Yearbook. 150 registered organizations, 3 honor societies, 14 religious organizations, 2 fraternities, 1 sorority on campus. **Athletics (Intercollegiate):** *Men:* baseball, basketball, cross-country, golf, lacrosse, soccer, swimming, tennis, track/field (outdoor), track/field (indoor). *Women:* badminton, basketball, cross-country, field hockey, lacrosse, soccer, softball, swimming, tennis, track/field (outdoor), track/field (indoor), volleyball. **On-Campus Highlights:** Kohlberg & Eldridge Commons Coffee Bars. **Environmental Initiatives:** 100% of the College's electrical demands are met by renewable energy credits and the College has made the decision to burn natural gas as it's primary fuel and convert the heat plant from #6 fuel oil to #2 fuel oil as it's back-up reserve.

ADMISSIONS

Freshman Academic Profile: 87% in top 10% of high school class, 100% in top 25% of high school class, 100% in top 50% of high school class. 59% from public high schools. **Test Scores:** SAT Math middle 50% range 700–790. SAT EBRW middle 50% range 680–750. ACT middle 50% range 31–35. **Basis for Candidate Selection:** *Very important factors include:* rigor of secondary school record, class rank, academic GPA, application essay, recommendation(s), character/personal qualities. *Important factors include:* standardized test scores, extracurricular activities. *Other factors include:* interview, talent/ability, first generation, alumni/ae relation, geographical residence, state residency, religious affiliation/commitment, racial/ethnic status, volunteer work, work experience, level of applicant's interest. **Freshman Admission Requirements:** High school diploma or equivalent is not required. *Academic units recommended:* 4 English, 3 math, 3 science, 3 foreign language, 3 social studies, 3 history. **Freshman Admission Statistics:** 11,442 applied, 9% admitted, 41% enrolled. **Transfer Admission Requirements:** High school transcript, college transcript(s), essay or personal statement, standardized test scores, statement of good standing from prior institution(s). Lowest grade transferable C. **General Admission Information:** Application fee $60. Regular application deadline 1/1. Admission may be deferred for a maximum of 1 year.

COSTS AND FINANCIAL AID

Annual tuition $54,256. Room and board $16,088. Required fees $400. Average book and supplies expense $1,400. **Required Forms and Deadlines:** CSS/Financial Aid PROFILE; FAFSA; Noncustodial PROFILE; State aid form.

Notification of Awards: Applicants will be notified of awards on or about 4/1. **Types of Aid:** *Need-based scholarships/grants:* College/university scholarship or grant aid from institutional funds; Federal Pell; Private scholarships; SEOG; State scholarships/grants. *Loans:* Direct PLUS loans; Direct Subsidized Stafford Loans; Direct Unsubsidized Stafford Loans. **Student Employment:** Federal Work-Study Program available. Institutional employment available. **Financial Aid Statistics:** 99% needy freshmen, 100% needy undergrads receive need-based scholarship or grant aid. 0% freshmen, 0% undergrads receive non-need-based scholarship or grant aid. 97% freshmen, 97% undergrads receive need-based self-help aid. 0% freshmen, 0% undergrads receive athletic scholarships. 58% freshmen, 52% undergrads receive any aid. 26% undergrads borrow to pay for school. Average cumulative indebtedness $24,099. **Criteria awarding aid:** *Non-need-based:* Academics, Leadership, State/district residency.

SWEET BRIAR COLLEGE

P. O. Box 1052, Sweet Briar, VA 24595
Phone: 434-381-6142
E-mail: admissions@sbc.edu **CEEB Code:** 5634
Fax: 434-381-6152 **Website:** www.sbc.edu **ACT Code:** 4406

This private school was founded in 1901. It has a 3250 acre campus.

RATINGS
Admissions Selectivity Rating: 74   **Fire Safety Rating:** 91   **Green Rating:** 60*

STUDENTS AND FACULTY
Enrollment: 281. **Student Body:** 100% female, 0% male, 47% out-of-state, <1% international (1 countries represented). Asian 2%, African American 9%, Caucasian 73%, Hispanic 10%, Native American 0%, Pacific Islander <1%, Two or more races 4%, Race unknown 1%.
Retention and Graduation: 72% freshmen return for sophomore year. 55% freshmen graduate within 4 years. 61% freshmen graduate within 6 years.
Faculty: Student/faculty ratio 5:1. 59 full-time faculty, 93% hold PhDs, 8% are members of minority groups, 51% are women. 0% of classes are taught by teaching assistants.

ACADEMICS
Degrees: Bachelor's; Master's. **Classes:** Most classes have fewer than 10 students. **Most popular majors:** Business/Commerce, General; Biology/Biological Sciences, General; Psychology, General. **Special Study Options:** Accelerated program; Cross-registration; Double major; Dual enrollment; Exchange student program (domestic); Honors program; Independent study; Internships; Liberal arts/career combination; Student-designed major; Study abroad; Teacher certification program. **Honors programs:** The Honors Program at Sweet Briar is dedicated to enriching the intellectual life of the entire College community. The program is designed to engage all programs and academic disciplines and to provide opportunities for motivated students that emphasize both breadth and depth of study. The program offers recognition to those students who perform academically at an honors level, but also encourages the participation of all interested students in honors courses and co-curricular activities. **Career services:** Alumni network; Alumni services; Career assessment; Career/job search classes; Internships; Regional alumni.

FACILITIES
Housing: Apartments for single students; Special housing for disabled students; Special housing for international students; Theme housing; Women's dorms.
Special Academic Facilities/Equipment: Art museum and galleries, college and local history museums, environmental education/nature center, equestrian center and trails, butterfly garden, community garden, 18 miles of hiking and biking trails, two lakes and a boathouse.

CAMPUS LIFE
Environment: Rural. **Activities:** Campus Ministries; Choral groups; Dance; Drama/theater; International Student Organization; Jazz band; Literary magazine; Music ensembles; Musical theater; Radio station; Student government; Student newspaper. 35 registered organizations, 11 honor societies on campus. **Athletics (Intercollegiate):** *Women:* field hockey, horseback riding, lacrosse, soccer, softball, swimming, tennis, volleyball. **Environmental Initiatives:** Collegiate Clean Energy coalition: http://sbc.edu/news/uncategorized/virginia-private-colleges-announce-sustainability-initiative/.

ADMISSIONS
Freshman Academic Profile: Average high school GPA 3.3. 17% in top 10% of high school class, 32% in top 25% of high school class, 68% in top 50% of high school class. **Test Scores:** SAT Math middle 50% range 463–550. SAT EBRW middle 50% range 530–630. ACT middle 50% range 20–28. **Basis for Candidate Selection:** *Very important factors include:* rigor of secondary school record, academic GPA. *Important factors include:* application essay, standardized test scores, recommendation(s). *Other factors include:* class rank, interview, extracurricular activities, talent/ability, character/personal qualities, first generation, alumni/ae relation, volunteer work, work experience. **Freshman Admission Requirements:** High school diploma is required and GED is accepted. *Academic units required:* 4 English, 3 math, 3 science, 2 science labs, 2 foreign language, 3 social studies. *Academic units recommended:* 4 English, 4 math, 4 science, 3 science labs, 4 foreign language, 4 social studies. **Freshman Admission Statistics:** 361 applied, 93% admitted, 24% enrolled. **Transfer Admission Requirements:** High school transcript, college transcript(s), essay or personal statement, standardized test scores, statement of good standing from prior institution(s). Minimum college GPA of 2.5 required. Lowest grade transferable C-. **General Admission Information:** Non-fall registration accepted. Admission may be deferred for a maximum of 1 year.

COSTS AND FINANCIAL AID
Annual tuition $21,000. Room and board $13,000. Average book and supplies expense $1,250. **Required Forms and Deadlines:** FAFSA. **Types of Aid:** *Need-based scholarships/grants:* College/university scholarship or grant aid from institutional funds; Federal Pell; Private scholarships; SEOG; State scholarships/grants; United Negro College Fund. *Loans:* Direct PLUS loans; Direct Subsidized Stafford Loans; Direct Unsubsidized Stafford Loans. **Student Employment:** Federal Work-Study Program available. Institutional employment available. **Financial Aid Statistics:** 100% needy freshmen, 99% needy undergrads receive need-based scholarship or grant aid. 32% freshmen, 26% undergrads receive non-need-based scholarship or grant aid. 77% freshmen, 75% undergrads receive need-based self-help aid. 0% freshmen, 0% undergrads receive athletic scholarships. 80% undergrads borrow to pay for school. Average cumulative indebtedness $31,269. **Criteria awarding aid:** *Need-based:* Alumni affiliation. *Non-need-based:* Academics, Art, Leadership, Music/drama, State/district residency.

SYRACUSE UNIVERSITY

100 Crouse-Hinds Hall, Syracuse, NY 13244-2130
Phone: 315-443-3611 **Financial Aid Phone:** 315-443-1513
E-mail: orange@syr.edu **CEEB Code:** 2823
Fax: 315-443-4226 **Website:** https://www.syracuse.edu **ACT Code:** 2968

This private school was founded in 1870. It has a 721 acre campus.

RATINGS
Admissions Selectivity Rating: 90   **Fire Safety Rating:** 96   **Green Rating:** 97

STUDENTS AND FACULTY
Enrollment: 14,854. **Student Body:** 53% female, 47% male, 63% out-of-state, 15% international (98 countries represented). Asian 6%, African American 7%, Caucasian 56%, Hispanic 10%, Native American 1%, Pacific Islander <1%, Two or more races 3%, Race unknown 3%.
Retention and Graduation: 92% freshmen return for sophomore year. 72% freshmen graduate within 4 years. 83% freshmen graduate within 6 years.
Faculty: Student/faculty ratio 15:1. 1,138 full-time faculty, 92% hold PhDs, 22% are members of minority groups, 43% are women.

ACADEMICS
Degrees: Associate; Bachelor's; Certificate; Doctoral degree—professional practice; Doctoral degree research/scholarship; Master's; Post-bachelor's certificate; Post-master's certificate. **Classes:** Most classes have 10–19 students. Most lab/discussion sessions have 20–29 students. **Most popular majors:** Speech Communication and Rhetoric; Information Science/Studies; Architectural and Building Sciences/Technology. **Special Study Options:** Accelerated program; Cooperative education program; Cross-registration; Distance learning; Double major; Dual enrollment; English as a Second Language (ESL); Honors program; Independent study; Internships; Liberal arts/career combination; Student-designed major; Study abroad; Teacher certification program. **Honors programs:** The Renee Crown University Honors

Program provides a compelling educational experience for accomplished students. Individuals who seek academic challenge and are prepared to invest the extra effort required to meet that challenge will flourish in this demanding and rewarding program. Syracuse University has had an Honors program since 1963. Our current program reflects the University's emphasis on enriched intellectual breadth and depth, command of language, collaborative capacity, global awareness, and civic engagement. While students pursue their chosen academic course of study in their individual departments, schools, and colleges, they immerse themselves in curricular enrichment and innovative scholarship offered by the program's seminars, cultural events, and close contact with faculty and other Honors students. The program is open to qualified students in all of the University's undergraduate schools and colleges. **Combined degree programs:** BA/JD. **Disability Services offered:** Note-taking services; Reader services; Tape recorders; Tutors. **Career services:** Alumni network; Alumni services; Career assessment; Career/job search classes; Internships; Regional alumni.

FACILITIES

Housing: Apartments for single students; Coed dorms; Fraternity/sorority housing; Special housing for disabled students; Theme housing; Wellness housing; 95% of campus accessible to physically disabled. **Special Academic Facilities/Equipment:** SUArt Galleries; The Warehouse Gallery; digital media convergence center; Syracuse Center of Excellence in Environmental and Energy Systems; Fidelity MOTUS 622i flight simulator for aerospace engineering; Ballentine Investment Institute; Community Darkrooms; Syracuse Stage professional equity theater; Bernice M. Wright Child Development Laboratory School; Belfer Audio Laboratory and Archive; Gebbie Speech, Language, and Hearing Clinic; SU Library Special Collections Research Center; UPSTATE: A Center for Design, Research and Real Estate at the SU School of Architecture; Center on Human Policy; Center for Emerging Network Technologies and many other research centers; in addition, the Daniel and Gayle D'Aniello Building, home to the National Veterans Resource Center.

CAMPUS LIFE

Environment: City. **Activities:** Campus Ministries; Choral groups; Concert band; Dance; Drama/theater; International Student Organization; Jazz band; Literary magazine; Marching band; Model UN; Music ensembles; Musical theater; Opera; Pep band; Radio station; Student government; Student newspaper; Student-run film society; Symphony orchestra; Television station; Yearbook. 311 registered organizations, 34 honor societies, 28 religious organizations, 26 fraternities, 22 sororities on campus. **Athletics (Intercollegiate):** *Men:* basketball, cheerleading, crew/rowing, cross-country, diving, football, lacrosse, soccer, swimming, track/field (outdoor). *Women:* basketball, cheerleading, crew/rowing, cross-country, diving, field hockey, ice hockey, lacrosse, soccer, softball, swimming, tennis, track/field (outdoor), volleyball. **On-Campus Highlights:** Barnes Center at the Arch.

ADMISSIONS

Freshman Academic Profile: Average high school GPA 3.6. 33% in top 10% of high school class, 66% in top 25% of high school class, 91% in top 50% of high school class. 61% from public high schools. **Test Scores:** SAT Math middle 50% range 600–710. SAT EBRW middle 50% range 580–670. ACT middle 50% range 26–30. **Basis for Candidate Selection:** *Very important factors include:* rigor of secondary school record, class rank, academic GPA, application essay, standardized test scores, recommendation(s), interview, extracurricular activities, talent/ability, character/personal qualities, volunteer work, level of applicant's interest. *Other factors include:* first generation, alumni/ae relation, geographical residence, state residency, racial/ethnic status, work experience. **Freshman Admission Requirements:** High school diploma is required and GED is accepted. *Academic units recommended:* 4 English, 4 math, 4 science, 4 science labs, 3 foreign language, 4 social studies, 4 history. **Freshman Admission Statistics:** 35,299 applied, 44% admitted, 23% enrolled. **Transfer Admission Requirements:** College transcript(s), essay or personal statement, statement of good standing from prior institution(s). Lowest grade transferable C. **General Admission Information:** Application fee $85. Priority deadline 11/15. Regular application deadline 1/1. Non-fall registration accepted. Admission may be deferred for a maximum of 1 year.

COSTS AND FINANCIAL AID

Required Forms and Deadlines: CSS/Financial Aid PROFILE; FAFSA; Noncustodial PROFILE. **Notification of Awards:** Applicants will be notified of awards on or about 3/15. *Types of Aid:* *Need-based scholarships/grants:* College/university scholarship or grant aid from institutional funds; Federal Pell; Private scholarships; SEOG; State scholarships/grants. *Loans:* Direct PLUS loans; Direct Subsidized Stafford Loans; Direct Unsubsidized Stafford Loans. **Student Employment:** Federal Work-Study Program available. Institutional employment available. **Financial Aid Statistics:** 97% needy freshmen, 97% needy undergrads receive need-based scholarship or grant aid. 18% freshmen, 12% undergrads receive non-need-based scholarship or grant aid. 87% freshmen, 91% undergrads receive need-based self-help aid. 2% freshmen, 2% undergrads receive athletic scholarships. 87% freshmen, 80% undergrads receive any aid. 54% undergrads borrow to pay for school. Average cumulative indebtedness $37,563. **Criteria awarding aid:** *Need-based:* Academics, Athletics. *Non-need-based:* Academics, Art, Athletics, Music/drama.

TALLADEGA COLLEGE

627 West Battle Street, Talladega, AL 35160
Phone: 205-761-6235 **Financial Aid Phone:** 256-761-6341
E-mail: admissions@talladega.edu **CEEB Code:** 001046
Fax: 205-362-0274 **Website:** www.talladega.edu **ACT Code:** 0026

This private school, affiliated with the United Church of Christ, was founded in 1867. It has a 50 acre campus.

RATINGS

Admissions Selectivity Rating: 86   **Fire Safety Rating:** 91   **Green Rating:** 60*

STUDENTS AND FACULTY

Enrollment: 601. **Student Body:** 58% female, 42% male, 48% out-of-state, 0% international. Asian 0%, African American 95%, Caucasian <1%, Hispanic 4%, Native American 0%, Race unknown 0%.
Retention and Graduation: 43% freshmen return for sophomore year. 25% grads go on to further study within 1 year. 25% grads pursue arts and sciences degrees. 25% grads pursue law degrees. 25% grads pursue business degrees. 25% grads pursue medical degrees. **Faculty:** Student/faculty ratio 16:1. 29 full-time faculty, 62% hold PhDs, 66% are members of minority groups, 45% are women. 0% of classes are taught by teaching assistants.

ACADEMICS

Degrees: Bachelor's. **Classes:** Most classes have fewer than 10 students. Most lab/discussion sessions have fewer than 10 students. **Most popular majors:** Business/Commerce, General; Biology/Biological Sciences, General; Psychology, General. **Special Study Options:** Double major; Dual enrollment; Independent study; Internships; Teacher certification program. **Disability Services offered:** Note-taking services; Tape recorders; Tutors. **Career services:** Alumni network; Alumni services; Career assessment; Internships.

FACILITIES

Housing: Men's dorms; Women's dorms; 100% of campus accessible to physically disabled. **Special Academic Facilities/Equipment:** Savery Library, Home of the famous Amistad Murals; historic Swayne Hall, which is listed on the National Register; DeForest Chapel, which has the stained glass windows by famous artist David Driskell; Goodnow Art Building. **Campus network:** 100% of classrooms, 100% of dorms, 100% of libraries, 100% of dining areas, 100% of common outdoor areas have wireless network access.

CAMPUS LIFE

Environment: Rural. **Activities:** Choral groups; Concert band; Dance; Drama/theater; Jazz band; Student government; Student newspaper; Yearbook. 40 registered organizations, 8 honor societies, 1 religious organization, 4 fraternities, 4 sororities on campus. **Athletics (Intercollegiate):** *Men:* baseball, basketball, golf. *Women:* basketball, cheerleading, volleyball. **On-Campus Highlights:** Savery Library.

ADMISSIONS

Freshman Academic Profile: Average high school GPA 2.7. 90% from public high schools. **Test Scores:** SAT Math middle 50% range 340–410. SAT EBRW middle 50% range 320–460. ACT middle 50% range 16–19. **Basis for Candidate Selection:** *Very important factors include:* rigor of secondary school record, application essay, standardized test scores, recommendation(s), extracurricular activities, talent/ability, character/personal qualities, volunteer work, work experience. *Important factors include:* class rank. *Other factors include:* interview. **Freshman Admission Requirements:** High school diploma is required and GED is accepted. *Academic units required:* 4 English, 2 math, 2 science, 3 social studies, 2 unit from above areas or other academic areas. **Freshman Admission Statistics:** 1,960 applied, 38% admitted, 40% enrolled. **Transfer Admission Requirements:** High school transcript, college transcript(s), essay or personal statement, standardized test scores, statement of good standing from prior institution(s). Minimum college GPA of 2.0 required.

Lowest grade transferable C. **General Admission Information:** Application fee $25. Non-fall registration accepted. Admission may be deferred for a maximum of 2 years.

COSTS AND FINANCIAL AID
Annual tuition $12,130. Room and board $8,684. Required fees $1,441. Average book and supplies expense $1,000. **Required Forms and Deadlines:** CSS/Financial Aid PROFILE; FAFSA; Institution's own financial aid form; State aid form. **Notification of Awards:** Applicants will be notified of awards on or about 4/1. **Types of Aid:** *Need-based scholarships/grants:* College/university scholarship or grant aid from institutional funds; Federal Pell; Private scholarships; SEOG; State scholarships/grants; United Negro College Fund. **Financial Aid Statistics:** 100% needy freshmen, 100% needy undergrads receive need-based scholarship or grant aid. 100% freshmen, 79% undergrads receive non-need-based scholarship or grant aid. 55% freshmen, 21% undergrads receive need-based self-help aid. 0% freshmen, 0% undergrads receive athletic scholarships. 90% freshmen, 90% undergrads receive any aid. 100% undergrads borrow to pay for school. Average cumulative indebtedness $7,460. **Criteria awarding aid:** *Need-based:* Leadership, Minority status, Religious affiliation. *Non-need-based:* Academics, Alumni affiliation, Art, Athletics, Music/drama.

TARLETON STATE UNIVERSITY

PO Box T-0030, Stephenville, TX 76402
Phone: 254-968-9125 **Financial Aid Phone:** 254-968-9070
E-mail: uadm@tarleton.edu **CEEB Code:** 6817
Fax: 254-968-9951 **ACT Code:** 4204

This public school was founded in 1899. It has a 125 acre campus.

RATINGS
Admissions Selectivity Rating: 78   **Fire Safety Rating:** 60*   **Green Rating:** 60*

STUDENTS AND FACULTY
Enrollment: 11,283. **Student Body:** 61% female, 39% male, 2% out-of-state, <1% international (33 countries represented). Asian 1%, African American 8%, Caucasian 66%, Hispanic 20%, Native American 1%, Pacific Islander <1%, Two or more races 3%, Race unknown 1%.
Retention and Graduation: 67% freshmen return for sophomore year. 24% freshmen graduate within 4 years. 43% freshmen graduate within 6 years. **Faculty:** Student/faculty ratio 17:1. 393 full-time faculty, 0% hold PhDs, 19% are members of minority groups, 52% are women. 2% of classes are taught by teaching assistants.

ACADEMICS
Degrees: Associate; Bachelor's; Master's. **Classes:** Most classes have 20–29 students. Most lab/discussion sessions have 10–19 students. **Most popular majors:** Multi-/Interdisciplinary Studies, Other; Exercise Science and Kinesiology; Psychology, General. **Special Study Options:** Accelerated program; Distance learning; Double major; Dual enrollment; Honors program; Internships; Study abroad; Teacher certification program. **Honors programs:** Honors classes are offered in core curriculum subjects, including English, history, political science, chemistry, biology, geology, and speech. These courses offer intellectually challenging material, innovative approaches to the subject, increased opportunities for honing critical thinking and writing skills, and the opportunity to interact closely with similarly motivated students and with outstanding faculty. **Disability Services offered:** Note-taking services; Reader services; Tape recorders; Tutors. **Career services:** Alumni services; Career assessment; Career/job search classes; Internships.

FACILITIES
Housing: Apartments for married students; Apartments for single students; Coed dorms; Men's dorms; Special housing for disabled students; Women's dorms; 100% of campus accessible to physically disabled. **Special Academic Facilities/Equipment:** Planetarium in Science Bldg.; W.K. Gordon Center for Industrial History of Texas. **Campus network:** 100% of classrooms, 100% of dorms, 100% of student union, 100% of libraries, 100% of dining areas, 100% of common outdoor areas have wireless network access.

CAMPUS LIFE
Environment: Village. **Activities:** Campus Ministries; Choral groups; Concert band; Dance; Drama/theater; International Student Organization; Jazz band; Literary magazine; Marching band; Music ensembles; Musical theater; Pep band; Radio station; Student government; Student newspaper; Symphony orchestra; Yearbook. 120 registered organizations, 13 honor societies, 12 religious organizations, 9 fraternities, 9 sororities on campus. **Athletics (Intercollegiate):** *Men:* baseball, basketball, cheerleading, cross-country, football, rodeo, track/field (outdoor). *Women:* basketball, cheerleading, cross-country, golf, rodeo, softball, tennis, track/field (outdoor), volleyball. **On-Campus Highlights:** Barry B. Thompson Student Center. **Environmental Initiatives:** 15% Electricity from wind.

ADMISSIONS
Freshman Academic Profile: 10% in top 10% of high school class, 29% in top 25% of high school class, 88% in top 50% of high school class. 97% from public high schools. **Test Scores:** SAT Math middle 50% range 480–560. SAT EBRW middle 50% range 480–570. ACT middle 50% range 18–23. **Basis for Candidate Selection:** *Very important factors include:* rigor of secondary school record, academic GPA, standardized test scores. *Important factors include:* class rank. **Freshman Admission Requirements:** High school diploma is required and GED is accepted. *Academic units required:* 4 English, 3 math, 2 science, 2 social studies, 1 history, 2 academic electives. *Academic units recommended:* 3 science, 2 foreign language, 4 academic electives. **Freshman Admission Statistics:** 7,158 applied, 74% admitted, 33% enrolled. **Transfer Admission Requirements:** College transcript(s). Minimum college GPA of 2.0 required. Lowest grade transferable D. **General Admission Information:** Application fee $45. Priority deadline 12/1. Regular application deadline 6/1. Non-fall registration accepted.

COSTS AND FINANCIAL AID
Annual in-state tuition $4,876. Annual out-of-state tuition $17,200. Room and board $8,880. Required fees $6,435. **Required Forms and Deadlines:** FAFSA. **Notification of Awards:** Applicants will be notified of awards on a rolling basis beginning 5/1. **Types of Aid:** *Need-based scholarships/grants:* College/university scholarship or grant aid from institutional funds; Federal Pell; SEOG; State scholarships/grants. *Loans:* Direct PLUS loans; Direct Subsidized Stafford Loans; Direct Unsubsidized Stafford Loans. **Student Employment:** Federal Work-Study Program available. Institutional employment available. **Financial Aid Statistics:** 91% needy freshmen, 88% needy undergrads receive need-based scholarship or grant aid. 0% freshmen, 1% undergrads receive non-need-based scholarship or grant aid. 73% freshmen, 78% undergrads receive need-based self-help aid. 0% freshmen, 0% undergrads receive athletic scholarships. 68% freshmen, 63% undergrads receive any aid. 72% undergrads borrow to pay for school. Average cumulative indebtedness $25,725. **Criteria awarding aid:** *Non-need-based:* Academics, Alumni affiliation, Athletics, Leadership, Music/drama.

TAYLOR UNIVERSITY

236 West Reade Avenue, Upland, IN 46989-1001
Phone: 765-998-5134 **Financial Aid Phone:** 765-998-5358
E-mail: admissions@tayloru.edu **CEEB Code:** 1802
Fax: 765-998-4925 **Website:** www.taylor.edu **ACT Code:** 1248

This private school, affiliated with the Evangelical Christian Interdenominational Church, was founded in 1846. It has a 952 acre campus.

RATINGS
Admissions Selectivity Rating: 85   **Fire Safety Rating:** 95   **Green Rating:** 64

STUDENTS AND FACULTY
Enrollment: 1,835. **Student Body:** 54% female, 46% male, 45% out-of-state, 5% international (31 countries represented). Asian 3%, African American 3%, Caucasian 83%, Hispanic 4%, Native American <1%, Pacific Islander <1%, Two or more races 1%, Race unknown 0%.
Retention and Graduation: 85% freshmen return for sophomore year. 69% freshmen graduate within 4 years. 77% freshmen graduate within 6 years. 14% grads go on to further study within 1 year. 3% grads pursue arts and sciences degrees. 1% grads pursue law degrees. 1% grads pursue business degrees. 4% grads pursue medical degrees. **Faculty:** Student/faculty ratio 13:1. 134 full-time faculty, 87% hold PhDs, 9% are members of minority groups, 34% are women. 0% of classes are taught by teaching assistants.

ACADEMICS
Degrees: Associate; Bachelor's; Diploma; Master's. **Classes:** Most classes have 10–19 students. Most lab/discussion sessions have 10–19 students. **Most popular majors:** Elementary Education and Teaching; Biology/Biological Sciences, General; Cinematography and Film/Video Production. **Special**

Study Options: Cooperative education program; Distance learning; Double major; Dual enrollment; English as a Second Language (ESL); Exchange student program (domestic); Honors program; Independent study; Internships; Student-designed major; Study abroad; Teacher certification program. **Honors programs:** Honors Program emphasizes to a greater extent than the general curriculum, integration of faith and learning, ideas and values in content and discussion, and student initiative in format. We also offer a Freshmen Irish Studies Program in Ireland. **Disability Services offered:** Note-taking services; Reader services; Tape recorders; Tutors. **Career services:** Alumni network; Alumni services; Career assessment; Internships; Regional alumni.

FACILITIES

Housing: Apartments for married students; Apartments for single students; Men's dorms; Wellness housing; Women's dorms; 95% of campus accessible to physically disabled. **Special Academic Facilities/Equipment:** Compton Art Gallery; Edwin W. Brown Collection/CS Lewis and Friends; Euler Science Complex provides 10kW Photo-Voltaic Solar Array. **Campus network:** 100% of classrooms, 100% of dorms, 100% of student union, 100% of libraries, 100% of dining areas, 50% of common outdoor areas have wireless network access.

CAMPUS LIFE

Environment: Rural. **Activities:** Campus Ministries; Choral groups; Concert band; Dance; Drama/theater; International Student Organization; Jazz band; Literary magazine; Music ensembles; Musical theater; Opera; Pep band; Radio station; Student government; Student newspaper; Student-run film society; Symphony orchestra; Television station; Yearbook. 50 registered organizations, 7 honor societies, 23 religious organizations on campus. **Athletics (Intercollegiate):** *Men:* baseball, basketball, cross-country, football, golf, soccer, tennis, track/field (outdoor), track/field (indoor). *Women:* basketball, cross-country, soccer, softball, tennis, track/field (outdoor), track/field (indoor), volleyball. **On-Campus Highlights:** LaRita R. Boren Campus Center. **Environmental Initiatives:** The 127,000-sq. ft. Euler Science Complex, was completed in the summer of 2012, and subsequently obtained LEED status. This facility includes innovative sustainability features including a 10kW photovoltaic system.

ADMISSIONS

Freshman Academic Profile: Average high school GPA 3.8. 35% in top 10% of high school class, 63% in top 25% of high school class, 88% in top 50% of high school class. 80% from public high schools. **Test Scores:** SAT Math middle 50% range 540–660. SAT EBRW middle 50% range 540–650. ACT middle 50% range 22–28. **Basis for Candidate Selection:** *Very important factors include:* rigor of secondary school record, academic GPA, application essay, standardized test scores, recommendation(s), character/personal qualities, religious affiliation/commitment. *Important factors include:* class rank, interview, extracurricular activities. *Other factors include:* talent/ability, first generation, alumni/ae relation, geographical residence, state residency, racial/ethnic status, work experience. **Freshman Admission Requirements:** High school diploma is required and GED is accepted. *Academic units required:* 4 English, 3 math, 3 science, 3 science labs, 2 social studies, 3 academic electives. *Academic units recommended:* 4 math, 4 science, 4 science labs, 2 foreign language, 3 social studies, 1 computer science, 1 visual/performing arts. **Freshman Admission Statistics:** 2,341 applied, 68% admitted, 31% enrolled. **Transfer Admission Requirements:** High school transcript, college transcript(s), essay or personal statement, standardized test scores, statement of good standing from prior institution(s). Minimum college GPA of 2.5 required. Lowest grade transferable C+. **General Admission Information:** Application fee $15. Priority deadline 2/1. Regular application deadline 8/1. Non-fall registration accepted. Admission may be deferred for a maximum of 2 years.

COSTS AND FINANCIAL AID

Annual tuition $35,050. Room and board $9,950. Required fees $255. Average book and supplies expense $1,600. **Required Forms and Deadlines:** FAFSA. **Notification of Awards:** Applicants will be notified of awards on a rolling basis beginning 11/1. **Types of Aid:** *Need-based scholarships/grants:* College/university scholarship or grant aid from institutional funds; Federal Pell; Private scholarships; SEOG; State scholarships/grants. *Loans:* Direct PLUS loans; Direct Subsidized Stafford Loans; Direct Unsubsidized Stafford Loans. **Student Employment:** Federal Work-Study Program available. Institutional employment available. **Financial Aid Statistics:** 100% needy freshmen, 100% needy undergrads receive need-based scholarship or grant aid. 25% freshmen, 21% undergrads receive non-need-based scholarship or grant aid. 75% freshmen, 79% undergrads receive need-based self-help aid. 4% freshmen, 6% undergrads receive athletic scholarships. 99% freshmen, 96% undergrads receive any aid. 58% undergrads borrow to pay for school. Average cumulative indebtedness $26,009. **Criteria awarding aid:** *Need-based:* Art, Athletics,

Leadership, Minority status, Music/drama, Religious affiliation *Non-need-based:* Academics, Alumni affiliation, Art, Athletics, Leadership, Minority status, Music/drama, Religious affiliation, State/district residency.

TECNOLÓGICO DE MONTERREY

Av. Eugenio Garza Sada 2501 Sur, Monterrey, Mexico
Phone: +52 (81) 8158-2269
E-mail: admisiones.mty@itesm.mx
Website: www.itesm.mx

This is a private school.

RATINGS

Admissions Selectivity Rating: 68   **Fire Safety Rating:** 60*   **Green Rating:** 60*

STUDENTS AND FACULTY

Enrollment: 55,015. **Student Body:** 43% female, 57% male, 22% out-of-state. **Retention and Graduation:** 90% freshmen return for sophomore year. **Faculty:** Student/faculty ratio 15:1. 1,609 full-time faculty, 57% hold PhDs, 0% are members of minority groups, 38% are women.

ACADEMICS

Degrees: Bachelor's; Doctoral degree research/scholarship; Master's. **Classes:** Most classes have 20–29 students.

ADMISSIONS

Freshman Admission Statistics: 15,717 applied, 86% admitted, 74% enrolled.

TEMPLE UNIVERSITY

1801 North Broad Street (041-09), Philadelphia, PA 19122
Phone: 215-204-7200 **Financial Aid Phone:** (215) 204-2244
E-mail: askanowl@temple.edu **CEEB Code:** 2906
Fax: 215-204-5694 **Website:** www.temple.edu **ACT Code:** 3724

This public school was founded in 1888. It has a 384 acre campus.

RATINGS

Admissions Selectivity Rating: 87   **Fire Safety Rating:** 98   **Green Rating:** 91

STUDENTS AND FACULTY

Enrollment: 28,272. **Student Body:** 54% female, 46% male, 21% out-of-state, 5% international (109 countries represented). Asian 12%, African American 13%, Caucasian 55%, Hispanic 8%, Native American <1%, Pacific Islander <1%, Two or more races 4%, Race unknown 2%. **Retention and Graduation:** 89% freshmen return for sophomore year. 52% freshmen graduate within 4 years. 74% freshmen graduate within 6 years. **Faculty:** Student/faculty ratio 13:1. 1,582 full-time faculty, 91% hold PhDs, 21% are members of minority groups, 43% are women.

ACADEMICS

Degrees: Associate; Bachelor's; Certificate; Diploma; Doctoral degree—professional practice; Doctoral degree research/scholarship; Master's; Post-bachelor's certificate; Post-master's certificate. **Classes:** Most classes have 10–19 students. Most lab/discussion sessions have 20–29 students. **Most popular majors:** Liberal Arts and Sciences/Liberal Studies; Biology/Biological Sciences, General; Psychology, General. **Special Study Options:** Accelerated program; Cooperative education program; Distance learning; Double major; Dual enrollment; English as a Second Language (ESL); Honors program; Independent study; Internships; Study abroad; Teacher certification program. **Honors programs:** The honors program at Temple University promotes intellectual curiosity and social courage, valuing academic excellence and integrity in leadership. It is a community and network of scholars comprised of high-achieving undergraduate students, nationally recognized advisors and staff, faculty celebrated both for teaching and research, and impressive alumni at the top of their fields. Honors provides its students with enriching academic opportunities, guides then through co-curricular experiences, cultivates a dynamic and inclusive community, and offers strong encouragement and support. **Combined degree programs:** BA/MA; BA/MD. **Disability Services offered:** Note-taking services; Reader services; Tape recorders; Tutors. **Career services:** Alumni services; Career assessment; Career/job search classes; Internships.

FACILITIES

Housing: Apartments for single students; Coed dorms; Special housing for disabled students; Special housing for international students; Theme housing; 99% of campus accessible to physically disabled. **Special Academic Facilities/Equipment:** Charles L. Blockson Afro-American Collection, Urban Archives, Technology Center, Temple Gallery at Tyler School of Art, Charles Library.

CAMPUS LIFE

Environment: Metropolis. **Activities:** Campus Ministries; Choral groups; Concert band; Dance; Drama/theater; International Student Organization; Jazz band; Literary magazine; Marching band; Model UN; Music ensembles; Musical theater; Opera; Pep band; Radio station; Student government; Student newspaper; Student-run film society; Symphony orchestra; Television station; Yearbook. 361 registered organizations, 19 honor societies, 34 religious organizations, 16 fraternities, 15 sororities on campus. **Athletics (Intercollegiate):** *Men:* baseball, basketball, cheerleading, crew/rowing, cross-country, football, golf, gymnastics, soccer, table tennis, tennis, track/field (outdoor), track/field (indoor). *Women:* basketball, cheerleading, crew/rowing, cross-country, fencing, field hockey, gymnastics, lacrosse, soccer, softball, table tennis, tennis, track/field (outdoor), track/field (indoor), volleyball. **On-Campus Highlights:** The TECH Center.

ADMISSIONS

Freshman Academic Profile: Average high school GPA 3.5. 36% in top 10% of high school class, 76% in top 25% of high school class, 92% in top 50% of high school class. **Test Scores:** SAT Math middle 50% range 550–660. SAT EBRW middle 50% range 570–660. ACT middle 50% range 24–30. **Basis for Candidate Selection:** *Very important factors include:* rigor of secondary school record, academic GPA. *Other factors include:* class rank, application essay, standardized test scores, recommendation(s), extracurricular activities, talent/ability, character/personal qualities, first generation, alumni/ae relation, geographical residence, state residency, volunteer work, work experience. **Freshman Admission Requirements:** High school diploma is required and GED is accepted. *Academic units required:* 4 English, 3 math, 2 science, 1 science labs, 2 foreign language, 2 social studies, 1 history, 1 academic elective, 1 visual/performing arts. *Academic units recommended:* 4 English, 4 math, 3 science, 2 science labs, 2 foreign language, 2 social studies, 1 history, 3 academic electives, 1 visual/performing arts. **Freshman Admission Statistics:** 35,599 applied, 60% admitted, 23% enrolled. **Transfer Admission Requirements:** High school transcript, college transcript(s), essay or personal statement. Minimum college GPA of 2.50 required. Lowest grade transferable C. **General Admission Information:** Application fee $55. Priority deadline 11/1. Regular application deadline 2/1. Non-fall registration accepted. Admission may be deferred for a maximum of one year.

COSTS AND FINANCIAL AID

Required Forms and Deadlines: FAFSA; State aid form. **Notification of Awards:** Applicants will be notified of awards on a rolling basis beginning 2/14. **Types of Aid:** *Need-based scholarships/grants:* College/university scholarship or grant aid from institutional funds; Federal Nursing Scholarships; Federal Pell; Private scholarships; SEOG; State scholarships/grants; United Negro College Fund. *Loans:* Direct PLUS loans; Direct Subsidized Stafford Loans; Direct Unsubsidized Stafford Loans. **Student Employment:** Federal Work-Study Program available. Institutional employment available. **Financial Aid Statistics:** 96% needy freshmen, 91% needy undergrads receive need-based scholarship or grant aid. 65% freshmen, 52% undergrads receive non-need-based scholarship or grant aid. 80% freshmen, 83% undergrads receive need-based self-help aid. 2% freshmen, 2% undergrads receive athletic scholarships. 89.7% freshmen, 81.6% undergrads receive any aid. 71% undergrads borrow to pay for school. Average cumulative indebtedness $38,634. **Criteria awarding aid:** *Non-need-based:* Academics, Art, Athletics, Music/drama.

TENNESSEE STATE UNIVERSITY

3500 John Merritt Boulevard, Nashville, TN 37209-1561
Phone: 615-963-3101
E-mail: jcade@tnstate.edu
Fax: 615-963-5108 **Website:** www.tnstate.edu

This is a public school.

RATINGS

Admissions Selectivity Rating: 91   **Fire Safety Rating:** 60*   **Green Rating:** 60*

STUDENTS AND FACULTY

Enrollment: 7,000. **Student Body:** 63% female, 37% male, 49% out-of-state, 1% international. Asian 1%, African American 83%, Caucasian 15%, Hispanic 1%, Native American 0%, Race unknown 0%.
Retention and Graduation: 77% freshmen return for sophomore year.
Faculty: Student/faculty ratio 22:1. 383 full-time faculty, 74% hold PhDs, 37% are members of minority groups, 42% are women.

ACADEMICS

Degrees: Associate; Bachelor's; Master's. **Classes:** Most classes have fewer than 10 students. Most lab/discussion sessions have 10–19 students. **Special Study Options:** Cooperative education program; Cross-registration; Double major; Exchange student program (domestic); Honors program; Independent study; Internships; Liberal arts/career combination; Teacher certification program.

FACILITIES

Housing: Apartments for single students; Coed dorms; Men's dorms; Women's dorms. **Campus network:** 100% of classrooms, 100% of dorms, 100% of student union, 100% of libraries, 100% of dining areas have wireless network access.

CAMPUS LIFE

Activities: Choral groups; Drama/theater; Jazz band; Marching band; Music ensembles; Radio station; Student government; Student newspaper; Yearbook.

ADMISSIONS

Freshman Academic Profile: Average high school GPA 3.0. 90% from public high schools. **Test Scores:** SAT Math middle 50% range 430–510. SAT EBRW middle 50% range 430–510. ACT middle 50% range 18–21. **Basis for Candidate Selection:** *Very important factors include:* standardized test scores, state residency. *Important factors include:* rigor of secondary school record, class rank, recommendation(s), geographical residence. *Other factors include:* extracurricular activities, talent/ability, character/personal qualities, alumni/ae relation. **Freshman Admission Requirements:** High school diploma is required and GED is accepted. *Academic units required:* 4 English, 3 math, 2 science, 1 science labs, 2 foreign language, 1 social studies, 1 history, 1 academic elective. **Freshman Admission Statistics:** 6,344 applied, 35% admitted, 59% enrolled. **Transfer Admission Requirements:** college transcript(s). Minimum college GPA of 2.9 required. Lowest grade transferable C. **General Admission Information:** Application fee $15. Regular application deadline 8/1.

COSTS AND FINANCIAL AID

Annual in-state tuition $3,272. Annual out-of-state tuition $10,230. Room and board $3,060. Required fees $150. Average book and supplies expense $850. **Required Forms and Deadlines:** CSS/Financial Aid PROFILE; FAFSA; Noncustodial PROFILE. **Types of Aid:** *Need-based scholarships/grants:* Federal Pell; SEOG. *Loans:* Direct PLUS loans; Direct Subsidized Stafford Loans; Direct Unsubsidized Stafford Loans. **Financial Aid Statistics:** 66% needy freshmen, 64% needy undergrads receive need-based scholarship or grant aid. 24% freshmen, 23% undergrads receive non-need-based scholarship or grant aid. 75% freshmen, 75% undergrads receive need-based self-help aid. 1% freshmen receive athletic scholarships. **Criteria awarding aid:** *Need-based:* Academics, Athletics.

TENNESSEE TECHNOLOGICAL UNIVERSITY

PO Box 5006, Cookeville, TN 38505
Phone: (931) 372-3888 **Financial Aid Phone:** 931-372-3073
E-mail: admissions@tntech.edu **CEEB Code:** 1804
Fax: (931) 372-6250 **Website:** www.tntech.edu **ACT Code:** 4012

This public school was founded in 1915. It has a 235 acre campus.

RATINGS

Admissions Selectivity Rating: 75   **Fire Safety Rating:** 80   **Green Rating:** 85

STUDENTS AND FACULTY

Enrollment: 9,647. **Student Body:** 45% female, 55% male, 3% out-of-state, 6% international. Asian 1%, African American 4%, Caucasian 84%, Hispanic 2%, Native American <1%, Pacific Islander <1%, Two or more races 2%, Race unknown <1%.
Retention and Graduation: 70% freshmen return for sophomore year.
Faculty: Student/faculty ratio 21:1. 389 full-time faculty, 72% hold PhDs, 13% are members of minority groups, 40% are women. 1% of classes are taught by teaching assistants.

ACADEMICS

Degrees: Bachelor's; Master's; Post-master's certificate. **Classes:** Most classes have 20–29 students. Most lab/discussion sessions have 20–29 students. **Most popular majors:** Business/Commerce, General; Elementary Education and Teaching; Mechanical Engineering. **Special Study Options:** Cooperative education program; Distance learning; Double major; Dual enrollment; English as a Second Language (ESL); Honors program; Internships; Study abroad; Teacher certification program. **Disability Services offered:** Note-taking services; Reader services; Tape recorders; Tutors. **Career services:** Alumni network; Alumni services; Career/job search classes; Internships; Regional alumni.

FACILITIES

Housing: Apartments for married students; Apartments for single students; Coed dorms; Men's dorms; Special housing for disabled students; Special housing for international students; Theme housing; Women's dorms; 99% of campus accessible to physically disabled. **Special Academic Facilities/Equipment:** 300-acre farm lab, electric power center, water resources center, manufacturing center. **Campus network:** 100% of classrooms, 100% of dorms, 100% of student union, 100% of libraries, 100% of dining areas, 100% of common outdoor areas have wireless network access.

CAMPUS LIFE

Environment: Rural. **Activities:** Campus Ministries; Choral groups; Concert band; Dance; Drama/theater; Jazz band; Literary magazine; Marching band; Music ensembles; Musical theater; Opera; Pep band; Radio station; Student government; Student newspaper; Symphony orchestra; Television station; Yearbook. 182 registered organizations, 26 honor societies, 16 religious organizations, 12 fraternities, 8 sororities on campus. **Athletics (Intercollegiate):** *Men:* baseball, basketball, cheerleading, cross-country, football, golf, riflery, tennis. *Women:* basketball, cheerleading, cross-country, golf, riflery, soccer, softball, tennis, track/field (outdoor), track/field (indoor), volleyball. **On-Campus Highlights:** Recreation/ Fitness Center.

ADMISSIONS

Freshman Academic Profile: Average high school GPA 3.4. 24% in top 10% of high school class, 50% in top 25% of high school class, 82% in top 50% of high school class. 80% from public high schools. **Test Scores:** SAT Math middle 50% range 490–640. SAT EBRW middle 50% range 480–600. ACT middle 50% range 20–26. **Basis for Candidate Selection:** *Very important factors include:* rigor of secondary school record, academic GPA, standardized test scores. *Other factors include:* application essay, recommendation(s), interview, extracurricular activities, character/personal qualities, alumni/ae relation. **Freshman Admission Requirements:** High school diploma is required and GED is accepted. *Academic units required:* 4 English, 3 math, 2 science, 1 science labs, 2 foreign language, 1 social studies, 1 history, 1 unit from above areas or other academic areas. **Freshman Admission Statistics:** 4,553 applied, 94% admitted, 45% enrolled. **Transfer Admission Requirements:** College transcript(s). Minimum college GPA of 2.0 required. Lowest grade transferable D. **General Admission Information:** Application fee $25. Priority deadline 12/15. Regular application deadline 8/1. Non-fall registration accepted. Admission may be deferred for a maximum of 1 semester.

COSTS AND FINANCIAL AID

Annual in-state tuition $5,004. Annual out-of-state tuition $18,000. Room and board $7,382. Required fees $1,034. Average book and supplies expense $1,500. **Required Forms and Deadlines:** FAFSA. **Notification of Awards:** Applicants will be notified of awards on a rolling basis beginning 3/15. **Types of Aid:** *Need-based scholarships/grants:* College/university scholarship or grant aid from institutional funds; Federal Pell; Private scholarships; SEOG; State scholarships/grants; United Negro College Fund. *Loans:* Direct PLUS loans; Direct Subsidized Stafford Loans; Direct Unsubsidized Stafford Loans. **Financial Aid Statistics:** 61% needy freshmen, 63% needy undergrads receive need-based scholarship or grant aid. 91% freshmen, 67% undergrads receive non-need-based scholarship or grant aid. 49% freshmen, 57% undergrads receive need-based self-help aid. 2% freshmen, 2% undergrads receive athletic scholarships. 91% freshmen, 89% undergrads receive any aid. **Criteria awarding aid:** *Need-based:* Academics, Athletics. *Non-need-based:* Academics, Alumni affiliation, Art, Athletics, Leadership, Minority status, Music/drama.

TEXAS A&M UNIVERSITY—COLLEGE STATION

Best Colleges

P.O. Box 30014, College Station, TX 77843-3014
Phone: (979) 845-1060 **Financial Aid Phone:** 979-845-3236
E-mail: admissions@tamu.edu **CEEB Code:** 6003
Fax: (979) 458-1808 **Website:** www.tamu.edu **ACT Code:** 4198

This public school was founded in 1876. It has a 5200 acre campus.

RATINGS

Admissions Selectivity Rating: 90   **Fire Safety Rating:** 95   **Green Rating:** 91

STUDENTS AND FACULTY

Enrollment: 53,123. **Student Body:** 47% female, 53% male, 4% out-of-state, 1% international (77 countries represented). Asian 9%, African American 3%, Caucasian 59%, Hispanic 25%, Native American <1%, Pacific Islander <1%, Two or more races 3%, Race unknown <1%.
Retention and Graduation: 93% freshmen return for sophomore year. 55% freshmen graduate within 4 years. 82% freshmen graduate within 6 years.
Faculty: Student/faculty ratio 19:1. 3,159 full-time faculty, 79% hold PhDs, 21% are members of minority groups, 38% are women. 10% of classes are taught by teaching assistants.

ACADEMICS

Degrees: Bachelor's; Doctoral degree—professional practice; Doctoral degree research/scholarship; Master's; Post-bachelor's certificate; Post-master's certificate. **Classes:** Most classes have 20–29 students. Most lab/discussion sessions have 10–19 students. **Most popular majors:** Engineering, General; Biomedical Sciences, General; Business Administration and Management, General. **Special Study Options:** Accelerated program; Cooperative education program; Cross-registration; Distance learning; Double major; Dual enrollment; English as a Second Language (ESL); Honors program; Independent study; Internships; Liberal arts/career combination; Study abroad; Teacher certification program. **Disability Services offered:** Note-taking services; Reader services; Tape recorders; Tutors. **Career services:** Alumni network; Alumni services; Career assessment; Career/job search classes; Internships; Regional alumni.

FACILITIES

Housing: Apartments for married students; Apartments for single students; Coed dorms; Cooperative housing; Fraternity/sorority housing; Men's dorms; Special housing for international students; Theme housing; Women's dorms; 85% of campus accessible to physically disabled. **Special Academic Facilities/Equipment:** Bush Library/Museum; Jordan International Collection; Corps of Cadets Center/Museum; Forsyth Center Gallary; MSC Visual Arts Gallary; J. Wayne Stark University Center; Gallaries Oran W. Nicks Low Speed Wind Tunnel; Astronomical Observatory; Ocean Drilling Program Building.

CAMPUS LIFE

Environment: City. **Activities:** Campus Ministries; Choral groups; Concert band; Dance; Drama/theater; International Student Organization; Jazz band; Literary magazine; Marching band; Music ensembles; Musical theater; Radio station; Student government; Student newspaper; Student-run film society; Symphony orchestra; Television station; Yearbook. 1111 registered organizations, 33 honor societies, 86 religious organizations, 30 fraternities, 28 sororities on campus. **Athletics (Intercollegiate):** *Men:* baseball, basketball, cross-country, diving, football, golf, riflery, swimming, tennis, track/field (outdoor), track/field (indoor). *Women:* basketball, cross-country, diving, equestrian sports, golf, riflery, soccer, softball, swimming, tennis, track/field (outdoor), track/field (indoor), volleyball. **On-Campus Highlights:** Student Recreation Center. **Environmental Initiatives:** Energy Stewardship Program.

ADMISSIONS

Freshman Academic Profile: 70% in top 10% of high school class, 93% in top 25% of high school class, 99% in top 50% of high school class. **Test Scores:** SAT Math middle 50% range 580–710. SAT EBRW middle 50% range 580–680. ACT middle 50% range 26–31. **Basis for Candidate Selection:** *Very important factors include:* rigor of secondary school record, class rank, academic GPA, standardized test scores, extracurricular activities, talent/ability. *Important factors include:* application essay, first generation, geographical residence, state residency, volunteer work. *Other factors include:* recommendation(s), character/personal qualities, level of applicant's interest. **Freshman Admission Requirements:** High school diploma is required and GED is accepted. *Academic units required:* 4 English, 3 math, 3 science, 1 science labs, 2 foreign language, 3 social studies, 5 academic electives, 1 visual/performing arts, 1 unit from above areas or other academic areas. *Academic units recommended:* 4 English, 4 math, 4 science, 2 science labs, 2 foreign language, 4 social studies, 7 academic electives, 1 visual/performing arts. **Freshman Admission Statistics:** 42,899 applied, 58% admitted, 43% enrolled. **Transfer Admission Requirements:** High school transcript, college transcript(s). Minimum college GPA of 2.5 required. Lowest grade transferable D. **General Admission Information:** Application fee $75. Regular application deadline 12/1. Non-fall registration accepted.

COSTS AND FINANCIAL AID

Annual in-state tuition $7,579. Annual out-of-state tuition $34,073. Room and board $10,400. Required fees $3,652. Average book and supplies expense $1,222. **Required Forms and Deadlines:** FAFSA. **Notification of Awards:** Applicants will be notified of awards on a rolling basis beginning 2/25. **Types of Aid:** *Need-based scholarships/grants:* College/university scholarship or grant aid from institutional funds; Federal Pell; Private scholarships; SEOG; State scholarships/grants. *Loans:* Direct PLUS loans; Direct Subsidized Stafford Loans; Direct Unsubsidized Stafford Loans. **Student Employment:** Federal Work-Study Program available. Institutional employment available. **Financial Aid Statistics:** 90% needy freshmen, 86% needy undergrads receive need-based scholarship or grant aid. 10% freshmen, 7% undergrads receive non-need-based scholarship or grant aid. 46% freshmen, 56% undergrads receive need-based self-help aid. 0% freshmen, 0% undergrads receive athletic scholarships. 76% freshmen, 70% undergrads receive any aid. 43% undergrads borrow to pay for school. Average cumulative indebtedness $24,590. **Criteria awarding aid:** *Need-based:* Academics. *Non-need-based:* Academics, Alumni affiliation, Art, Athletics, Job skills, Leadership, Music/drama, Religious affiliation, State/district residency.

TEXAS A&M UNIVERSITY—GALVESTON

Admissions Office, Galveston, TX 77553
Phone: 409-740-4414 **Financial Aid Phone:** 409-740-4418
E-mail: seaaggie@tamug.edu **CEEB Code:** 6835
Fax: 409-740-4731 **Website:** www.tamug.edu **ACT Code:** 6592

This public school was founded in 1963. It has a 150 acre campus.

RATINGS

Admissions Selectivity Rating: 88   **Fire Safety Rating:** 92   **Green Rating:** 69

STUDENTS AND FACULTY

Enrollment: 50,392. **Student Body:** 49% female, 51% male, 13% out-of-state, 1% international (19 countries represented). Asian 6%, African American 3%, Caucasian 63%, Hispanic 23%, Native American <1%, Pacific Islander <1%, Two or more races 3%, Race unknown <1%.
Retention and Graduation: 91% freshmen return for sophomore year.
Faculty: Student/faculty ratio 15:1. 105 full-time faculty, 61% hold PhDs, 21% are members of minority groups, 33% are women. 3% of classes are taught by teaching assistants.

ACADEMICS

Degrees: Bachelor's; Master's. **Classes:** Most classes have 10–19 students. **Most popular majors:** Naval Architecture and Marine Engineering; Marine Biology and Biological Oceanography. **Special Study Options:** Accelerated program; Cooperative education program; Double major; Dual enrollment; Independent study; Internships; Study abroad. **Disability Services offered:** Note-taking services; Reader services; Tutors. **Career services:** Alumni network; Career assessment; Internships; Regional alumni.

FACILITIES

Housing: Coed dorms; Special housing for disabled students; 90% of campus accessible to physically disabled. **Special Academic Facilities/Equipment:** USTS Texas Clipper II, Radar School/Ship Bridge Simulator, Engineering Laboratory Building, Sea Camp, Center for Bioacoustics, Center for Marine Training and Safety/TEEX, Laboratory for Oceanographic and Environmental Research, Galveston Bay Information Center, Center for Ports and Waterways, Coastal Zone Laboratory, GulfCet, Marine Mammal Research Program, Naval Science, Texas State Maritime Academy, Texas Institute of Oceanography, Texas Marine Mammal Stranding Network, Sea Turtle/Fisheries Ecology Lab.

CAMPUS LIFE

Environment: Town. **Activities:** Choral groups; Dance; Drama/theater; Literary magazine; Student government; Student newspaper; Yearbook. 35 registered organizations, 2 honor societies, 3 religious organizations on campus. **Athletics (Intercollegiate):** *Men:* crew/rowing, sailing. *Women:* crew/rowing, sailing. **On-Campus Highlights:** Mary Moody Northen Student Center.

ADMISSIONS

Freshman Academic Profile: 66% in top 10% of high school class, 90% in top 25% of high school class, 99% in top 50% of high school class. 81% from public high schools. **Test Scores:** SAT Math middle 50% range 550–670. SAT EBRW middle 50% range 520–640. ACT middle 50% range 24–30. **Basis for Candidate Selection:** *Very important factors include:* rigor of secondary school record, class rank, academic GPA, standardized test scores, extracurricular activities, talent/ability. *Important factors include:* application essay, first generation, geographical residence, state residency, volunteer work. *Other factors include:* recommendation(s), character/personal qualities, level of applicant's interest. **Freshman Admission Requirements:** High school diploma is required and GED is accepted. *Academic units required:* 4 English, 3 math, 3 science, 1 science labs, 2 foreign language, 3 social studies, 5 academic electives, 1 visual/performing arts, 1 unit from above areas or other academic areas. *Academic units recommended:* 4 English, 4 math, 4 science, 2 science labs, 2 foreign language, 4 social studies, 7 academic electives, 1 visual/performing arts. **Freshman Admission Statistics:** 34,780 applied, 67% admitted, 43% enrolled. **Transfer Admission Requirements:** High school transcript, college transcript(s), essay or personal statement. Minimum college GPA of 2.5 required. Lowest grade transferable C. **General Admission Information:** Application fee $75. Priority deadline 12/1. Non-fall registration accepted.

COSTS AND FINANCIAL AID

Average book and supplies expense $1,246. **Required Forms and Deadlines:** FAFSA. **Notification of Awards:** Applicants will be notified of awards on or about 3/15. **Types of Aid:** *Need-based scholarships/grants:* College/university scholarship or grant aid from institutional funds; Federal Pell; Private scholarships; SEOG; State scholarships/grants. *Loans:* Direct PLUS loans; Direct Subsidized Stafford Loans; Direct Unsubsidized Stafford Loans. **Student Employment:** Federal Work-Study Program available. Institutional employment available. **Financial Aid Statistics:** 75% needy freshmen, 74% needy undergrads receive need-based scholarship or grant aid. 35% freshmen, 28% undergrads receive non-need-based scholarship or grant aid. 72% freshmen, 76% undergrads receive need-based self-help aid. 0% freshmen, 0% undergrads receive athletic scholarships. 45% freshmen, 56% undergrads receive any aid. **Criteria awarding aid:** *Need-based:* Academics, Leadership. *Non-need-based:* Academics, Leadership, State/district residency.

TEXAS A&M UNIVERSITY—KINGSVILLE

MSC 105, Kingsville, TX 78363
Phone: 361-593-2315
E-mail: ksossrx@tamuk.edu **CEEB Code:** 003639
Fax: 361-593-2195 **Website:** www.tamuk.edu **ACT Code:** 4212

This is a public school.

RATINGS
Admissions Selectivity Rating: 63   **Fire Safety Rating:** 60*   **Green Rating:** 60*

STUDENTS AND FACULTY
Enrollment: 5,087. **Student Body:** 47% female, 53% male, 2% out-of-state, 1% international. Asian 1%, African American 5%, Caucasian 27%, Hispanic 66%, Native American <1%, Race unknown <1%.
Retention and Graduation: 59% freshmen return for sophomore year.
Faculty: Student/faculty ratio 15:1. 276 full-time faculty, 70% hold PhDs, 24% are members of minority groups, 35% are women.

ACADEMICS
Degrees: Bachelor's; Master's; Post-bachelor's certificate; Post-master's certificate. **Classes:** Most classes have 10–19 students. Most lab/discussion sessions have 10–19 students. **Special Study Options:** Accelerated program; Cooperative education program; Distance learning; Double major; English as a Second Language (ESL); Honors program; Internships; Study abroad; Teacher certification program.

FACILITIES
Housing: Apartments for married students; Coed dorms; Men's dorms; Women's dorms.

CAMPUS LIFE
Activities: Choral groups; Concert band; Dance; Drama/theater; Jazz band; Marching band; Music ensembles; Musical theater; Pep band; Radio station; Student government; Student newspaper; Television station.

ADMISSIONS
Basis for Candidate Selection: *Important factors include:* rigor of secondary school record, class rank, standardized test scores. **Freshman Admission Requirements:** *Academic units recommended:* 4 English, 3 math, 3 science, 3 foreign language, 4 social studies, 3 history, 3 academic electives. **Freshman Admission Statistics:** 2,105 applied, 99% admitted, 43% enrolled. **Transfer Admission Requirements:** Minimum college GPA of 2.0 required. **General Admission Information:** Application fee $15. Admission may be deferred for a maximum of varies.

COSTS AND FINANCIAL AID
Annual in-state tuition $1,380. Annual out-of-state tuition $7,590. Room and board $3,966. Required fees $1,602. Average book and supplies expense $614. **Required Forms and Deadlines:** FAFSA. **Financial Aid Statistics:** 92% needy freshmen, 100% needy undergrads receive need-based scholarship or grant aid. 31% freshmen, 71% undergrads receive non-need-based scholarship or grant aid. 87% freshmen, 82% undergrads receive need-based self-help aid. 0% freshmen, 0% undergrads receive athletic scholarships.

TEXAS A&M UNIVERSITY—SAN ANTONIO

One University Way, San Antonio, Texas 78224
Phone: (210) 784-1300
E-mail: admissions.office@tamusa.edu or graduateadmissions@tamusa.edu
CEEB Code: 5996
Fax: (210) 784-1492 **Website:** www.tamusa.edu **ACT Code:** 5350

This is a public school.

RATINGS
Admissions Selectivity Rating: 88   **Fire Safety Rating:** 60*   **Green Rating:** 60*

STUDENTS AND FACULTY
Enrollment: 5,455. **Student Body:** 60% female, 40% male, 1% out-of-state, 1% international. Asian 1%, African American 6%, Caucasian 18%, Hispanic 71%, Native American <1%, Pacific Islander <1%, Two or more races 2%, Race unknown <1%.

Retention and Graduation: 59% freshmen return for sophomore year.
Faculty: 163 full-time faculty, 33% are members of minority groups, 50% are women.

ACADEMICS
Degrees: Bachelor's; Master's. **Classes:** Most classes have 20–29 students. Most lab/discussion sessions have 20–29 students. **Special Study Options:** Distance learning; Double major; Independent study; Internships; Teacher certification program; Weekend college.

FACILITIES
Housing: Coed dorms.

CAMPUS LIFE
Activities: Choral groups; Student government; Student newspaper.

ADMISSIONS
Freshman Academic Profile: Average high school GPA 3.3. 6% in top 10% of high school class, 21% in top 25% of high school class, 55% in top 50% of high school class. **Test Scores:** SAT Math middle 50% range 450–530. SAT EBRW middle 50% range 460–530. ACT middle 50% range 17–20. **Basis for Candidate Selection:** *Very important factors include:* class rank, academic GPA, standardized test scores. *Other factors include:* rigor of secondary school record, application essay, recommendation(s), extracurricular activities, talent/ability, character/personal qualities, volunteer work, work experience. **Freshman Admission Requirements:** High school diploma is required and GED is accepted. *Academic units required:* 4 English, 4 math, 4 science, 2 foreign language, 4 social studies. **Freshman Admission Statistics:** 6,912 applied, 35% admitted, 23% enrolled. **General Admission Information:** Application fee $15. Priority deadline 1/15. Regular application deadline 6/30. Non-fall registration accepted.

COSTS AND FINANCIAL AID
Annual in-state tuition $4,292. Annual out-of-state tuition $16,742. Room and board $10,326. Required fees $3,924. Average book and supplies expense $1,342. **Required Forms and Deadlines:** FAFSA; State aid form. **Types of Aid:** *Need-based scholarships/grants:* College/university scholarship or grant aid from institutional funds; Federal Pell; Private scholarships; SEOG; State scholarships/grants. *Loans:* Direct PLUS loans; Direct Subsidized Stafford Loans; Direct Unsubsidized Stafford Loans.

TEXAS A&M UNIVERSITY—TEXARKANA

P.O. Box 5518, Texarkana, TX 75505
Phone: (903) 223-3069
E-mail: admissions@tamut.edu
Fax: (903) 223-3140

This public school was founded in 1971. It has a 1 acre campus.

RATINGS
Admissions Selectivity Rating: 60*   **Fire Safety Rating:** 60*   **Green Rating:** 60*

STUDENTS AND FACULTY
Enrollment: 1,030. **Student Body:** 71% female, 29% male, <1% international. Asian 1%, African American 15%, Caucasian 76%, Hispanic 6%, Native American 1%, Race unknown <1%.
Faculty: Student/faculty ratio 13:1. 59 full-time faculty, 0% hold PhDs, 15% are members of minority groups, 41% are women.

ACADEMICS
Degrees: Bachelor's; Master's. **Most popular majors:** Accounting; Multi-/Interdisciplinary Studies, Other; General Studies. **Special Study Options:** Cross-registration; Distance learning; Independent study; Internships; Liberal arts/career combination; Study abroad; Teacher certification program. **Disability Services offered:** Note-taking services; Tape recorders. **Career services:** Career/job search classes.

FACILITIES
100% of campus accessible to physically disabled.

CAMPUS LIFE
Environment: Village. **Activities:** Student government; Student newspaper. 20 registered organizations, 5 honor societies, 1 religious organization on campus.

ADMISSIONS

Transfer Admission Requirements: College transcript(s). Minimum college GPA of 2.0 required. Lowest grade transferable D.

COSTS AND FINANCIAL AID

Required Forms and Deadlines: FAFSA; Institution's own financial aid form. **Notification of Awards:** Applicants will be notified of awards on or about 6/1. **Types of Aid:** *Need-based scholarships/grants:* College/university scholarship or grant aid from institutional funds; Federal Pell; Private scholarships; SEOG; State scholarships/grants. **Student Employment:** Federal Work-Study Program available. **Financial Aid Statistics:** 0% undergrads receive athletic scholarships. **Criteria awarding aid:** *Need-based:* Academics. *Non-need-based:* Academics, Alumni affiliation, Leadership, State/district residency.

TEXAS CHRISTIAN UNIVERSITY

TCU, Fort Worth, TX 76129
Phone: 817-257-7490 **Financial Aid Phone:** 817-257-7858
E-mail: frogmail@tcu.edu **CEEB Code:** 6820
Fax: 817-257-7268 **Website:** www.tcu.edu **ACT Code:** 4206

This private school, affiliated with the Disciples of Christ Church, was founded in 1873. It has a 289.42 acre campus.

RATINGS

Admissions Selectivity Rating: 89   **Fire Safety Rating:** 98   **Green Rating:** 75

STUDENTS AND FACULTY

Enrollment: 9,442. **Student Body:** 58% female, 42% male, 46% out-of-state, 5% international (70 countries represented). Asian 3%, African American 5%, Caucasian 68%, Hispanic 15%, Native American 1%, Pacific Islander <1%, Two or more races 2%, Race unknown 1%.
Retention and Graduation: 91% freshmen return for sophomore year. 71% freshmen graduate within 4 years. 82% freshmen graduate within 6 years. 26% grads go on to further study within 1 year. 29% grads pursue arts and sciences degrees. 13% grads pursue law degrees. 18% grads pursue business degrees. 4% grads pursue medical degrees. **Faculty:** Student/faculty ratio 13:1. 715 full-time faculty, 87% hold PhDs, 19% are members of minority groups, 49% are women. 1% of classes are taught by teaching assistants.

ACADEMICS

Degrees: Bachelor's; Certificate; Diploma; Doctoral degree—professional practice; Doctoral degree research/scholarship; Master's; Post-bachelor's certificate; Post-master's certificate. **Most popular majors:** Registered Nursing/Registered Nurse; Finance, General; Public Relations, Advertising, and Applied Communication. **Special Study Options:** Accelerated program; Distance learning; Double major; English as a Second Language (ESL); Honors program; Independent study; Internships; Liberal arts/career combination; Student-designed major; Study abroad; Teacher certification program. **Honors programs:** The John V. Roach Honors College offers academic programs for students of all majors. Students who complete requirements for both lower-division and upper-division Honors graduate as John V. Roach Honors College Laureates and are recognized at an academic hooding ceremony prior to university commencement. Students may also choose to complete only lower-division Honors (15 credit hours of specialized Honors courses linked to the core curriculum) or only upper-division Honors (either Departmental Honors earned through a research/creative project or University Honors achieved through successful work in three interdisciplinary colloquium courses). **Disability Services offered:** Note-taking services. **Career services:** Alumni network; Alumni services; Career assessment; Career/job search classes; Internships; Regional alumni.

FACILITIES

Housing: Apartments for single students; Coed dorms; Fraternity/sorority housing; Special housing for disabled students; Theme housing; Women's dorms; 100% of campus accessible to physically disabled. **Special Academic Facilities/Equipment:** Geological center for remote sensing, nuclear magnetic resonance facility, observatory, film library, performance complex, behavioral research institute, meteorite collection, speech and hearing clinic, transmission electron microscope, Beowulf computing cluster, optical spectroscopy and microscopy laboratory, health professions learning center, new media writing center,

multimedia editing suites, high-end computing lab, 3-D printing lab, radio station, cable TV studio, institute providing instruction for care and treatment of vulnerable children, Art exhibition hall, special collections, alumni and visitors center, Heritage Center, and a variety of athletic facilities.

CAMPUS LIFE

Environment: Metropolis. **Activities:** Campus Ministries; Choral groups; Concert band; Dance; Drama/theater; International Student Organization; Jazz band; Literary magazine; Marching band; Model UN; Music ensembles; Musical theater; Opera; Pep band; Radio station; Student government; Student newspaper; Symphony orchestra; Yearbook. 274 registered organizations, 48 honor societies, 17 religious organizations, 21 fraternity, 21 sorority on campus. **Athletics (Intercollegiate):** *Men:* baseball, basketball, cross-country, diving, football, golf, swimming, tennis, track/field (outdoor), track/field (indoor). *Women:* basketball, cross-country, diving, equestrian sports, golf, riflery, soccer, swimming, tennis, track/field (outdoor), track/field (indoor), volleyball. **On-Campus Highlights:** Campus Commons & Frog Fountain.

ADMISSIONS

Freshman Academic Profile: 47% in top 10% of high school class, 75% in top 25% of high school class, 95% in top 50% of high school class. 57% from public high schools. **Test Scores:** SAT Math middle 50% range 570–680. SAT EBRW middle 50% range 580–670. ACT middle 50% range 25–31. **Basis for Candidate Selection:** *Very important factors include:* rigor of secondary school record, academic GPA. *Important factors include:* application essay, standardized test scores, recommendation(s), extracurricular activities, character/personal qualities, first generation, alumni/ae relation. *Other factors include:* class rank, interview, talent/ability, geographical residence, state residency, religious affiliation/commitment, level of applicant's interest. **Freshman Admission Requirements:** High school diploma is required and GED is not accepted. *Academic units required:* 4 English, 3 math, 3 science, 1 science labs, 2 foreign language, 3 social studies, 2 academic electives. *Academic units recommended:* 4 English, 4 math, 4 science, 1 science labs, 4 foreign language, 4 social studies. **Freshman Admission Statistics:** 19,028 applied, 47% admitted, 24% enrolled. **Transfer Admission Requirements:** College transcript(s), essay or personal statement. Minimum college GPA of 2.0 required. Lowest grade transferable C. **General Admission Information:** Application fee $50. Regular application deadline 2/1. Non-fall registration accepted. Admission may be deferred for a maximum of 1 year (with exceptions).

COSTS AND FINANCIAL AID

Annual tuition $49,160. Room and board $13,200. Required fees $90. Average book and supplies expense $900. **Required Forms and Deadlines:** CSS/Financial Aid PROFILE; FAFSA; Noncustodial PROFILE. **Notification of Awards:** Applicants will be notified of awards on a rolling basis beginning 12/15. **Types of Aid:** *Need-based scholarships/grants:* College/university scholarship or grant aid from institutional funds; Federal Pell; Private scholarships; SEOG; State scholarships/grants. *Loans:* Direct PLUS loans; Direct Subsidized Stafford Loans; Direct Unsubsidized Stafford Loans. **Student Employment:** Federal Work-Study Program available. Institutional employment available. **Financial Aid Statistics:** 94% needy freshmen, 94% needy undergrads receive need-based scholarship or grant aid. 74% freshmen, 68% undergrads receive non-need-based scholarship or grant aid. 72% freshmen, 73% undergrads receive need-based self-help aid. 82% freshmen, 78% undergrads receive any aid. 34% undergrads borrow to pay for school. Average cumulative indebtedness $47,931. **Criteria awarding aid:** *Non-need-based:* Academics, Alumni affiliation, Art, Minority status, Music/drama, Religious affiliation, State/district residency.

TEXAS LUTHERAN UNIVERSITY

1000 West Court Street, Seguin, TX 78155
Phone: 830-372-8050 **Financial Aid Phone:** 830-372-8078
E-mail: admissions@tlu.edu **CEEB Code:** 6823
Fax: 830-372-8096 **Website:** www.tlu.edu **ACT Code:** 4214

This private school, affiliated with the Lutheran Church, was founded in 1891. It has a 184 acre campus.

RATINGS

Admissions Selectivity Rating: 86   **Fire Safety Rating:** 87   **Green Rating:** 60*

STUDENTS AND FACULTY

Enrollment: 1,407. **Student Body:** 51% female, 49% male, 2% out-of-state, 1% international (12 countries represented). Asian 1%, African American 9%,

Caucasian 46%, Hispanic 40%, Native American <1%, Pacific Islander <1%, Two or more races 2%, Race unknown 1%.

Retention and Graduation: 73% freshmen return for sophomore year. 38% freshmen graduate within 4 years. 56% freshmen graduate within 6 years. **Faculty:** Student/faculty ratio 14:1. 85 full-time faculty, 84% hold PhDs, 14% are members of minority groups, 55% are women. 0% of classes are taught by teaching assistants.

ACADEMICS

Degrees: Bachelor's; Master's. **Classes:** Most classes have 20–29 students. **Most popular majors:** Education, General; Business/Commerce, General; Exercise Science and Kinesiology. **Special Study Options:** Double major; Dual enrollment; Exchange student program (domestic); Honors program; Independent study; Internships; Study abroad; Teacher certification program. **Disability Services offered:** Note-taking services; Reader services; Tutors. **Career services:** Alumni network; Alumni services; Career/job search classes; Internships.

FACILITIES

Housing: Apartments for married students; Apartments for single students; Coed dorms; Special housing for disabled students 95% of campus accessible to physically disabled. **Special Academic Facilities/Equipment:** Mexican-American studies center, geological museum, Women's Studies Center.

CAMPUS LIFE

Environment: Town. **Activities:** Campus Ministries; Choral groups; Concert band; Drama/theater; International Student Organization; Jazz band; Literary magazine; Marching band; Music ensembles; Musical theater; Pep band; Student government; Student newspaper; Symphony orchestra. 47 registered organizations, 6 honor societies, 5 religious organizations, 3 fraternities, 5 sororities on campus. **Athletics (Intercollegiate):** *Men:* baseball, basketball, football, golf, soccer, tennis. *Women:* basketball, cross-country, golf, soccer, softball, tennis, track/field (outdoor), track/field (indoor), volleyball. **On-Campus Highlights:** Tschoepe Hall. **Environmental Initiatives:** Installation of more efficient HVAC system campus wide.

ADMISSIONS

Freshman Academic Profile: Average high school GPA 3.6. 11% in top 10% of high school class, 42% in top 25% of high school class, 78% in top 50% of high school class. **Test Scores:** SAT Math middle 50% range 490–580. SAT EBRW middle 50% range 500–580. ACT middle 50% range 20–24. **Basis for Candidate Selection:** *Very important factors include:* rigor of secondary school record, class rank, academic GPA, application essay, standardized test scores. *Important factors include:* recommendation(s), interview, talent/ability, character/personal qualities, alumni/ae relation, volunteer work. *Other factors include:* extracurricular activities, work experience, level of applicant's interest. **Freshman Admission Requirements:** High school diploma is required and GED is accepted. *Academic units required:* 4 English, 3 math, 3 science, 2 science labs, 2 foreign language, 3 social studies, 1 academic elective. *Academic units recommended:* 4 English, 4 math, 4 science, 2 science labs, 3 foreign language, 4 social studies, 1 computer science. **Freshman Admission Statistics:** 3,000 applied, 56% admitted, 25% enrolled. **Transfer Admission Requirements:** High school transcript, college transcript(s), essay or personal statement, statement of good standing from prior institution(s). Minimum college GPA of 2.25 required. Lowest grade transferable C. **General Admission Information:** Regular application deadline 2/1. Non-fall registration accepted. Admission may be deferred for a maximum of 1 year.

COSTS AND FINANCIAL AID

Annual tuition $30,550. Room and board $10,440. Required fees $310. Average book and supplies expense $1,000. **Required Forms and Deadlines:** FAFSA. **Notification of Awards:** Applicants will be notified of awards on a rolling basis beginning 3/1. **Types of Aid:** *Need-based scholarships/grants:* College/university scholarship or grant aid from institutional funds; Federal Pell; Private scholarships; SEOG; State scholarships/grants. *Loans:* Direct PLUS loans; Direct Subsidized Stafford Loans; Direct Unsubsidized Stafford Loans. **Student Employment:** Federal Work-Study Program available. Institutional employment available. **Financial Aid Statistics:** 100% needy freshmen, 100% needy undergrads receive need-based scholarship or grant aid. 15% freshmen, 16% undergrads receive non-need-based scholarship or grant aid. 79% freshmen, 74% undergrads receive need-based self-help aid. 0% freshmen, 0% undergrads receive athletic scholarships. 100% freshmen, 95% undergrads receive any aid. 76% undergrads borrow to pay for school. Average cumulative indebtedness $29,735. **Criteria awarding aid:** *Non-need-based:* Academics, Alumni affiliation, Art, Leadership, Minority status, Music/drama, Religious affiliation.

TEXAS STATE UNIVERSITY

429 North Guadalupe St., San Marcos, TX 78666
Phone: 512-245-2364 **Financial Aid Phone:** (512) 245 2315
E-mail: admissions@txstate.edu **CEEB Code:** 6667
Fax: 512-245-8044 **Website:** www.txstate.edu **ACT Code:** 4178

This public school was founded in 1899. It has a 491 acre campus.

RATINGS

Admissions Selectivity Rating: 82   **Fire Safety Rating:** 95   **Green Rating:** 79

STUDENTS AND FACULTY

Enrollment: 33,917. **Student Body:** 58% female, 42% male, 2% out-of-state, <1% international (50 countries represented). Asian 3%, African American 9%, Caucasian 43%, Hispanic 40%, Native American <1%, Pacific Islander <1%, Two or more races 4%, Race unknown <1%.

Retention and Graduation: 76% freshmen return for sophomore year. 29% freshmen graduate within 4 years. 54% freshmen graduate within 6 years. 10% grads go on to further study within 1 year. 9% grads pursue arts and sciences degrees. 2% grads pursue law degrees. 12% grads pursue business degrees. 1% grads pursue medical degrees. **Faculty:** Student/faculty ratio 20:1. 1,399 full-time faculty, 75% hold PhDs, 26% are members of minority groups, 50% are women. 4% of classes are taught by teaching assistants.

ACADEMICS

Degrees: Bachelor's; Doctoral degree—professional practice; Doctoral degree research/scholarship; Master's; Post-bachelor's certificate. **Classes:** Most classes have 20–29 students. Most lab/discussion sessions have 10–19 students. **Most popular majors:** Multi-/Interdisciplinary Studies, Other; Exercise Science and Kinesiology; Psychology, General. **Special Study Options:** Accelerated program; Cooperative education program; Distance learning; Double major; Dual enrollment; English as a Second Language (ESL); Exchange student program (domestic); Honors program; Independent study; Internships; Study abroad; Teacher certification program; Weekend college. **Honors programs:** To graduate in the University Honors Program, a student must complete at least five Honors Classes (including the Honors Thesis course) and maintain a minimum GPA of 3.25. Honors courses substitute for certain general education core curriculum and individual departmental requirements and thus become integral parts of the degree program. **Combined degree programs:** BA/DDS. **Disability Services offered:** Note-taking services; Reader services; Tape recorders; Tutors. **Career services:** Alumni network; Alumni services; Career assessment; Career/job search classes; Internships.

FACILITIES

Housing: Apartments for single students; Coed dorms; Fraternity/sorority housing; Men's dorms; Theme housing; Women's dorms; 90% of campus accessible to physically disabled. **Special Academic Facilities/Equipment:** Child development center, aquifer research center, two demonstration farms, physical anthropology and archaeology laboratories. Southwestern Writer's Collection. Observatory with a 17-inch telescope. Anthropology forensics body farm. Clean room for microchip processing and development.

CAMPUS LIFE

Environment: Town. **Activities:** Campus Ministries; Choral groups; Concert band; Dance; Drama/theater; International Student Organization; Jazz band; Literary magazine; Marching band; Model UN; Music ensembles; Musical theater; Opera; Pep band; Radio station; Student government; Student newspaper; Student-run film society; Symphony orchestra; Yearbook. 455 registered organizations, 22 honor societies, 42 religious organizations, 19 fraternities, 13 sororities on campus. **Athletics (Intercollegiate):** *Men:* baseball, basketball, cheerleading, cross-country, football, golf, track/field (outdoor). *Women:* basketball, cheerleading, cross-country, golf, soccer, softball, tennis, track/field (outdoor), volleyball. **On-Campus Highlights:** LBJ Student Center. **Environmental Initiatives:** Our programs and projects demonstrate our deep commitment to the careful stewardship of the world's freshwater resources. Through collaborative research, public advocacy, and education on river systems, the Institute affirms the unique role of water in our lives. As one of the earth's most remarkable resources, we are dedicated to preserving and protecting this irreplaceable gift—water.

ADMISSIONS

Freshman Academic Profile: 12% in top 10% of high school class, 46% in top 25% of high school class, 90% in top 50% of high school class. 98% from public high schools. **Test Scores:** SAT Math middle 50% range 500–580. SAT EBRW middle 50% range 510–600. ACT middle 50% range 19–25. **Basis for Candidate Selection:** *Very important factors include:* class rank, standardized test scores. *Other factors include:* rigor of secondary school record, application essay, extracurricular activities, talent/ability, first generation. **Freshman Admission Requirements:** High school diploma is required and GED is accepted. *Academic units required:* 4 English, 4 math, 4 science, 2 science labs, 2 foreign language, 2 social studies, 2 history, 6 academic electives, 1 visual/ performing arts, 1 unit from above areas or other academic areas. *Academic units recommended:* 4 English, 4 math, 4 science, 2 science labs, 2 foreign language, 2 social studies, 2 history, 6 academic electives, 1 visual/performing arts. **Freshman Admission Statistics:** 23,583 applied, 81% admitted, 33% enrolled. **Transfer Admission Requirements:** College transcript(s), statement of good standing from prior institution(s). Minimum college GPA of 2.2 required. Lowest grade transferable D. **General Admission Information:** Application fee $75. Priority deadline 3/1. Regular application deadline 5/1. Non-fall registration accepted. Admission may be deferred indefinitely, fee required.

COSTS AND FINANCIAL AID

Annual in-state tuition $8,627. Annual out-of-state tuition $21,287. Room and board $11,102. Required fees $2,630. Average book and supplies expense $800. **Required Forms and Deadlines:** FAFSA. **Notification of Awards:** Applicants will be notified of awards on a rolling basis beginning 5/1. **Types of Aid:** *Need-based scholarships/grants:* College/university scholarship or grant aid from institutional funds; Federal Pell; Private scholarships; SEOG; State scholarships/ grants. *Loans:* Direct PLUS loans; Direct Subsidized Stafford Loans; Direct Unsubsidized Stafford Loans. **Student Employment:** Federal Work-Study Program available. Institutional employment available. **Financial Aid Statistics:** 82% needy freshmen, 80% needy undergrads receive need-based scholarship or grant aid. 18% freshmen, 9% undergrads receive non-need-based scholarship or grant aid. 76% freshmen, 77% undergrads receive need-based self-help aid. 1% freshmen, 1% undergrads receive athletic scholarships. 77% freshmen, 70% undergrads receive any aid. 65% undergrads borrow to pay for school. Average cumulative indebtedness $24,950. **Criteria awarding aid:** *Need-based:* Academics, Art, Leadership, Minority status, Music/drama. *Non-need-based:* Academics, Art, Athletics, Leadership, Minority status, Music/drama, State/ district residency.

TEXAS TECH UNIVERSITY

Box 45005, Lubbock, TX 79409-5005
Phone: 806-742-1480 **Financial Aid Phone:** 806-742-3681
E-mail: admissions@ttu.edu **CEEB Code:** 6827
Fax: 806-742-0062 **Website:** www.ttu.edu **ACT Code:** 4220

This public school was founded in 1923. It has a 1839 acre campus.

RATINGS

Admissions Selectivity Rating: 85	Fire Safety Rating: 97	Green Rating: 82

STUDENTS AND FACULTY

Enrollment: 31,172. **Student Body:** 48% female, 52% male, 6% out-of-state, 3% international (103 countries represented). Asian 3%, African American 6%, Caucasian 55%, Hispanic 29%, Native American <1%, Pacific Islander <1%, Two or more races 3%, Race unknown 1%.
Retention and Graduation: 87% freshmen return for sophomore year. 34% freshmen graduate within 4 years. % freshmen graduate within 6 years. **Faculty:** 13% of classes are taught by teaching assistants.

ACADEMICS

Degrees: Bachelor's; Doctoral degree—professional practice; Doctoral degree research/scholarship; Master's; Post-bachelor's certificate. **Classes:** Most classes have 20–29 students. Most lab/discussion sessions have 20–29 students. **Most popular majors:** Mechanical Engineering; Multi-/Interdisciplinary Studies, Other; Exercise Science and Kinesiology. **Special Study Options:** Accelerated program; Cooperative education program; Cross-registration; Distance learning; Double major; Dual enrollment; English as a Second Language (ESL); Exchange student program (domestic); External degree program; Honors program; Independent study; Internships; Student-designed major; Study abroad; Teacher certification program; Weekend college. **Honors**

programs: Honors Studies is a special program under our Honors College for highly motivated and academically talented students who want to maximize their college education. **Combined degree programs:** BA/MA. **Disability Services offered:** Note-taking services; Tape recorders; Tutors. **Career services:** Alumni network; Alumni services; Career assessment; Career/job search classes; Internships; Regional alumni.

FACILITIES

Housing: Apartments for single students; Coed dorms; Men's dorms; Special housing for disabled students; Women's dorms; 100% of campus accessible to physically disabled. **Special Academic Facilities/Equipment:** Burkhart Center for Autism Education & Research, Center for the Integration of STEM Education & Research, Child Development Research Center, Fiber and Biopolymer Research Institute, Innovation Hub, Institute of Environmental & Human Health, International Center for Arid and Semi-Arid Land Studies, Lubbock Lake Landmark archaeological dig/state park, Moody Planetarium, Museum of Texas Tech, Nano Tech Center, National Ranching Heritage Center, National Wind Institute, Natural Science Research Laboratory, Preston Gott Observatory, Southwest Collection/Special Collections Library, Vietnam Center and Archive.

CAMPUS LIFE

Environment: Metropolis. **Activities:** Campus Ministries; Choral groups; Concert band; Dance; Drama/theater; International Student Organization; Jazz band; Literary magazine; Marching band; Model UN; Music ensembles; Musical theater; Opera; Pep band; Radio station; Student government; Student newspaper; Student-run film society; Symphony orchestra; Television station; Yearbook. 576 registered organizations, 33 honor societies, 47 religious organizations, 34 fraternities, 23 sororities on campus. **Athletics (Intercollegiate):** *Men:* baseball, basketball, cross-country, football, golf, tennis, track/field (outdoor), track/field (indoor). *Women:* basketball, cross-country, golf, soccer, softball, tennis, track/field (outdoor), track/field (indoor), volleyball. **On-Campus Highlights:** Student Union Building.

ADMISSIONS

Freshman Academic Profile: Average high school GPA 3.6. 19% in top 10% of high school class, 53% in top 25% of high school class, 88% in top 50% of high school class. 88% from public high schools. **Test Scores:** SAT Math middle 50% range 530–630. SAT EBRW middle 50% range 540–630. ACT middle 50% range 22–27. **Basis for Candidate Selection:** *Very important factors include:* rigor of secondary school record, class rank, academic GPA, standardized test scores. *Important factors include:* application essay, recommendation(s), extracurricular activities, talent/ability, character/personal qualities, volunteer work. *Other factors include:* first generation, geographical residence, level of applicant's interest. **Freshman Admission Requirements:** High school diploma is required and GED is accepted. *Academic units required:* 4 English, 3 math, 3 science, 3 science labs, 2 foreign language, 5 academic electives, 1 visual/performing arts, 4 unit from above areas or other academic areas. *Academic units recommended:* 4 English, 4 math, 4 science, 4 science labs, 2 foreign language, 6 academic electives, 1 visual/performing arts. **Freshman Admission Statistics:** 25,384 applied, 69% admitted, 35% enrolled. **Transfer Admission Requirements:** College transcript(s), statement of good standing from prior institution(s). Minimum college GPA of 2.25 required. Lowest grade transferable D-. **General Admission Information:** Application fee $75. Priority deadline 2/1. Regular application deadline 8/1. Non-fall registration accepted.

COSTS AND FINANCIAL AID

Annual in-state tuition $8,430. Annual out-of-state tuition $20,880. Room and board $9,772. Required fees $2,890. Average book and supplies expense $1,200. **Required Forms and Deadlines:** FAFSA. **Notification of Awards:** Applicants will be notified of awards on a rolling basis beginning 12/1. **Types of Aid:** *Need-based scholarships/grants:* College/university scholarship or grant aid from institutional funds; Federal Pell; Private scholarships; SEOG; State scholarships/grants; United Negro College Fund. *Loans:* Direct PLUS loans; Direct Subsidized Stafford Loans; Direct Unsubsidized Stafford Loans. **Student Employment:** Federal Work-Study Program available. Institutional employment available. **Criteria awarding aid:** *Need-based:* Academics, Leadership, Music/drama. *Non-need-based:* Academics, Art, Athletics, Job skills, Leadership, Music/drama.

TEXAS WOMAN'S UNIVERSITY

P.O. Box 425589, Denton, TX 76204-5589
Phone: 940-898-3188 Financial Aid Phone: (940) 898-3050
E-mail: admissions@twu.edu CEEB Code: 6826
Fax: 940-898-3081 Website: www.twu.edu ACT Code: 4224

This public school was founded in 1901. It has a 270 acre campus.

RATINGS
Admissions Selectivity Rating: 74   Fire Safety Rating: 99   Green Rating: 60*

STUDENTS AND FACULTY
Enrollment: 8,668. **Student Body:** 90% female, 10% male, <1% out-of-state, 1% international (62 countries represented). Asian 8%, African American 21%, Caucasian 40%, Hispanic 25%, Native American <1%, Pacific Islander <1%, Two or more races 4%, Race unknown 1%.
Retention and Graduation: 73% freshmen return for sophomore year. 4% grads go on to further study within 1 year. **Faculty:** Student/faculty ratio 14:1. 413 full-time faculty, 0% hold PhDs, 17% are members of minority groups, 76% are women.

ACADEMICS
Degrees: Bachelor's; Doctoral degree—professional practice; Doctoral degree research/scholarship; Master's; Post-bachelor's certificate; Post-master's certificate. **Classes:** Most classes have 10–19 students. Most lab/discussion sessions have 10–19 students. **Special Study Options:** Accelerated program; Cooperative education program; Cross-registration; Distance learning; Double major; Dual enrollment; External degree program; Honors program; Independent study; Internships; Study abroad; Teacher certification program; Weekend college. **Honors programs:** Honors Scholars Program www.twu.edu/honors/index.html. **Combined degree programs:** BA/MEng. **Disability Services offered:** Note-taking services; Reader services; Tape recorders; Tutors. **Career services:** Internships.

FACILITIES
Housing: Apartments for married students; Apartments for single students; Coed dorms; Fraternity/sorority housing; Special housing for disabled students; Theme housing; Women's dorms; 100% of campus accessible to physically disabled. **Special Academic Facilities/Equipment:** Museum, radiation lab, language lab, Texas First Ladies Gown Collection; Texas Women's Hall of Fame. **Campus network:** 100% of classrooms, 100% of dorms, 100% of student union, 100% of libraries, 100% of dining areas, 75% of common outdoor areas have wireless network access.

CAMPUS LIFE
Environment: City. **Activities:** Campus Ministries; Choral groups; Dance; Drama/theater; International Student Organization; Jazz band; Music ensembles; Opera; Pep band; Student government; Student newspaper. 94 registered organizations, 16 honor societies, 10 religious organizations, 9 sororities on campus. **Athletics (Intercollegiate):** *Women:* basketball, gymnastics, soccer, softball, volleyball. **On-Campus Highlights:** Student Union.

ADMISSIONS
Freshman Academic Profile: Average high school GPA 3.1. 14% in top 10% of high school class, 29% in top 25% of high school class, 79% in top 50% of high school class. 93% from public high schools. **Test Scores:** SAT Math middle 50% range 430–530. SAT EBRW middle 50% range 410–530. ACT middle 50% range 17–17. **Basis for Candidate Selection:** *Very important factors include:* rigor of secondary school record, class rank, academic GPA. *Important factors include:* standardized test scores. *Other factors include:* recommendation(s), first generation. **Freshman Admission Requirements:** High school diploma is required and GED is accepted. *Academic units required:* 4 English, 3 math, 3 science, 3 social studies, 1 academic elective. *Academic units recommended:* 4 English, 4 math, 4 science, 2 foreign language, 3.5 social studies, 5.5 academic electives, 1 computer science, 1 visual/performing arts. **Freshman Admission Statistics:** 4,582 applied, 85% admitted, 29% enrolled. **Transfer Admission Requirements:** College transcript(s). Minimum college GPA of 2.0 required. Lowest grade transferable D. **General Admission Information:** Application fee $50. Priority deadline 3/1. Regular application deadline 7/15. Non-fall registration accepted. Admission may be deferred for a maximum of two years.

COSTS AND FINANCIAL AID
Annual in-state tuition $5,650. Annual out-of-state tuition $16,510. Room and board $6,780. Required fees $2,345. Average book and supplies expense $1,050. **Required Forms and Deadlines:** FAFSA; Institution's own financial aid form. **Notification of Awards:** Applicants will be notified of awards on a rolling basis beginning 3/1. **Types of Aid:** *Need-based scholarships/grants:* College/university scholarship or grant aid from institutional funds; Federal Nursing Scholarships; Federal Pell; Private scholarships; SEOG; State scholarships/grants; United Negro College Fund. **Financial Aid Statistics:** 94% needy freshmen, 91% needy undergrads receive need-based scholarship or grant aid. 30% freshmen, 24% undergrads receive non-need-based scholarship or grant aid. 69% freshmen, 82% undergrads receive need-based self-help aid. 0% freshmen, 0% undergrads receive athletic scholarships. 77% freshmen, 85% undergrads receive any aid. **Criteria awarding aid:** *Need-based:* Academics, Art, Athletics, Music/drama.

THIEL COLLEGE

75 College Avenue, Greenville, PA 16125
Phone: 724-589-2345 Financial Aid Phone: 724-589-2178
E-mail: admissions@thiel.edu CEEB Code: 2910
Fax: 724-589-2013 Website: www.thiel.edu ACT Code: 3730

This private school, affiliated with the Lutheran Church, was founded in 1866. It has a 135 acre campus.

RATINGS
Admissions Selectivity Rating: 77   Fire Safety Rating: 88   Green Rating: 78

STUDENTS AND FACULTY
Enrollment: 1,019. **Student Body:** 43% female, 57% male, 37% out-of-state, 3% international (14 countries represented). Asian <1%, African American 6%, Caucasian 69%, Hispanic 2%, Native American <1%, Pacific Islander 0%, Two or more races 1%, Race unknown 18%.
Retention and Graduation: 67% freshmen return for sophomore year. 13% grads go on to further study within 1 year. 86% grads pursue arts and sciences degrees. 1% grads pursue law degrees. 12% grads pursue business degrees. 1% grads pursue medical degrees. **Faculty:** Student/faculty ratio 13:1. 64 full-time faculty, 73% hold PhDs, 8% are members of minority groups, 41% are women. 0% of classes are taught by teaching assistants.

ACADEMICS
Degrees: Associate; Bachelor's. **Classes:** Most classes have 10–19 students. Most lab/discussion sessions have 10–19 students. **Most popular majors:** Business/Commerce, General; Biology/Biological Sciences, General; Elementary Education and Teaching. **Special Study Options:** Cooperative education program; Distance learning; Double major; Dual enrollment; English as a Second Language (ESL); Honors program; Independent study; Internships; Liberal arts/career combination; Study abroad; Teacher certification program. **Honors programs:** Four year Honors Program with special courses for honors students. **Disability Services offered:** Note-taking services; Reader services; Tape recorders; Tutors. **Career services:** Alumni network; Career assessment; Career/job search classes; Internships.

FACILITIES
Housing: Apartments for single students; Coed dorms; Fraternity/sorority housing; Theme housing; 90% of campus accessible to physically disabled. **Special Academic Facilities/Equipment:** Art Gallery, Blackbox Theater, Star Bucks Bistro.

CAMPUS LIFE
Environment: Rural. **Activities:** Campus Ministries; Choral groups; Concert band; Dance; Drama/theater; International Student Organization; Jazz band; Literary magazine; Marching band; Music ensembles; Musical theater; Pep band; Radio station; Student government; Student newspaper; Symphony orchestra; Television station; Yearbook. 40 registered organizations, 8 honor societies, 4 religious organizations, 3 fraternities, 4 sororities on campus. **Athletics (Intercollegiate):** *Men:* baseball, basketball, cheerleading, cross-country, football, golf, soccer, track/field (outdoor), track/field (indoor), wrestling. *Women:* basketball, cheerleading, cross-country, soccer, softball, track/field (outdoor), track/field (indoor), volleyball. **On-Campus Highlights:** Howard Miller Student Center.

ADMISSIONS

Freshman Academic Profile: Average high school GPA 3.0. 12% in top 10% of high school class, 25% in top 25% of high school class, 46% in top 50% of high school class. 88% from public high schools. **Test Scores:** SAT Math middle 50% range 420–520. SAT EBRW middle 50% range 410–510. ACT middle 50% range 18–23. **Basis for Candidate Selection:** *Very important factors include:* rigor of secondary school record, academic GPA, application essay, standardized test scores, recommendation(s), level of applicant's interest. *Important factors include:* class rank, character/personal qualities. *Other factors include:* interview, extracurricular activities, talent/ability, volunteer work, work experience. **Freshman Admission Requirements:** High school diploma is required and GED is accepted. *Academic units recommended:* 4 English, 2 math, 2 science, 2 science labs, 2 foreign language, 3 social studies, 1 academic elective. **Freshman Admission Statistics:** 1,856 applied, 68% admitted, 28% enrolled. **Transfer Admission Requirements:** High school transcript, college transcript(s), essay or personal statement, interview, standardized test scores, statement of good standing from prior institution(s). Minimum college GPA of 2.0 required. Lowest grade transferable C. **General Admission Information:** Application fee $35. Priority deadline 4/1. Regular application deadline 7/1. Non-fall registration accepted. Admission may be deferred for a maximum of 1 year.

COSTS AND FINANCIAL AID

Required Forms and Deadlines: FAFSA; State aid form. **Notification of Awards:** Applicants will be notified of awards on a rolling basis beginning 2/15. **Types of Aid:** *Need-based scholarships/grants:* College/university scholarship or grant aid from institutional funds; Federal Pell; Private scholarships; SEOG; State scholarships/grants. *Loans:* Direct PLUS loans; Direct Subsidized Stafford Loans; Direct Unsubsidized Stafford Loans. **Student Employment:** Federal Work-Study Program available. Institutional employment available. **Financial Aid Statistics:** 100% needy undergrads receive need-based scholarship or grant aid. 100% undergrads receive need-based self-help aid. 0% freshmen, 0% undergrads receive athletic scholarships. **Criteria awarding aid:** *Need-based:* Academics, Alumni affiliation, Leadership, Religious affiliation. *Non-need-based:* Academics, Alumni affiliation, Leadership, Religious affiliation, State/district residency.

THOMAS AQUINAS COLLEGE

10000 Ojai Road, Santa Paula, CA 93060
Phone: 805-525-4417 **Financial Aid Phone:** 800-634-9797
E-mail: admissions@thomasaquinas.edu **CEEB Code:** 4828
Fax: 805-421-5905 **Website:** www.thomasaquinas.edu **ACT Code:** 0425

This private school, affiliated with the Roman Catholic Church, was founded in 1971. It has a 131 acre campus.

RATINGS

Admissions Selectivity Rating: 88   **Fire Safety Rating:** 94   **Green Rating:** 60*

STUDENTS AND FACULTY

Enrollment: 381. **Student Body:** 53% female, 47% male, 60% out-of-state, 1% international (6 countries represented). Asian 3%, African American <1%, Caucasian 75%, Hispanic 15%, Native American 1%, Pacific Islander <1%, Two or more races 4%, Race unknown 1%.
Retention and Graduation: 94% freshmen return for sophomore year. 6% freshmen graduate within 4 years. 84% freshmen graduate within 6 years. **Faculty:** Student/faculty ratio 11:1. 30 full-time faculty, 83% hold PhDs, 0% are members of minority groups, 10% are women. 0% of classes are taught by teaching assistants.

ACADEMICS

Degrees: Bachelor's. **Classes:** Most classes have 10–19 students. **Most popular majors:** Liberal Arts and Sciences/Liberal Studies. **Career services:** Alumni network; Alumni services; Career assessment; Career/job search classes; Internships; Regional alumni.

FACILITIES

Housing: Men's dorms; Women's dorms; 100% of campus accessible to physically disabled. **Special Academic Facilities/Equipment:** St. Bernardine of Siena Library; Albertus Magnus Science Hall, St. Cecilia Performing Arts Hall.

CAMPUS LIFE

Environment: Rural. **Activities:** Campus Ministries; Choral groups; Dance; Drama/theater; Literary magazine; Music ensembles; Musical theater. 3 religious organizations on campus. **On-Campus Highlights:** St. Joseph Commons.

ADMISSIONS

Freshman Academic Profile: Average high school GPA 3.8. 25% in top 10% of high school class, 67% in top 25% of high school class, 83% in top 50% of high school class. 10% from public high schools. **Test Scores:** SAT Math middle 50% range 570–680. SAT EBRW middle 50% range 590–710. ACT middle 50% range 27–31. **Basis for Candidate Selection:** *Very important factors include:* rigor of secondary school record, application essay, standardized test scores, recommendation(s), character/personal qualities, level of applicant's interest. *Important factors include:* academic GPA. *Other factors include:* class rank, interview, extracurricular activities, talent/ability, religious affiliation/commitment, volunteer work, work experience. **Freshman Admission Requirements:** High school diploma is required and GED is accepted. *Academic units required:* 4 English, 3 math, 2 science, 2 foreign language, 2 history. *Academic units recommended:* 4 English, 4 math, 3 science, 2 science labs, 2 history, 3 academic electives. **Freshman Admission Statistics:** 170 applied, 76% admitted, 73% enrolled. **General Admission Information:** Admission may be deferred for a maximum of 1 year.

COSTS AND FINANCIAL AID

Annual tuition $26,000. Room and board $9,400. **Required Forms and Deadlines:** CSS/Financial Aid PROFILE; FAFSA; Noncustodial PROFILE; State aid form. **Notification of Awards:** Applicants will be notified of awards on a rolling basis beginning 2/1. **Types of Aid:** *Need-based scholarships/grants:* College/university scholarship or grant aid from institutional funds; Federal Pell; Private scholarships; State scholarships/grants. *Loans:* Direct PLUS loans; Direct Subsidized Stafford Loans; Direct Unsubsidized Stafford Loans. **Student Employment:** Institutional employment available. **Financial Aid Statistics:** 91% needy freshmen, 83% needy undergrads receive need-based scholarship or grant aid. 0% freshmen, 0% undergrads receive non-need-based scholarship or grant aid. 97% freshmen, 99% undergrads receive need-based self-help aid. 0% freshmen, 0% undergrads receive athletic scholarships. 79% freshmen, 77% undergrads receive any aid. 82% undergrads borrow to pay for school. Average cumulative indebtedness $18,967.

THOMAS COLLEGE

180 West River Road, Waterville, ME 04901
Phone: 207-859-1101 **Financial Aid Phone:** (207) 859-1105
E-mail: admiss@thomas.edu **CEEB Code:** 2052
Fax: 207-859-1114 **Website:** www.thomas.edu **ACT Code:** 1663

This private school was founded in 1894. It has a 120 acre campus.

RATINGS

Admissions Selectivity Rating: 77   **Fire Safety Rating:** 96   **Green Rating:** 60*

STUDENTS AND FACULTY

Enrollment: 739. **Student Body:** 49% female, 51% male, 20% out-of-state, <1% international. Asian 1%, African American 2%, Caucasian 88%, Hispanic 1%, Native American <1%, Race unknown 9%.
Retention and Graduation: 63% freshmen return for sophomore year. 7% grads go on to further study within 1 year. 7% grads pursue business degrees. **Faculty:** Student/faculty ratio 18:1. 21 full-time faculty, 48% hold PhDs, 0% are members of minority groups, 38% are women. 0% of classes are taught by teaching assistants.

ACADEMICS

Degrees: Associate; Bachelor's; Master's; Terminal Associate; Transfer Associate. **Classes:** Most classes have 10–19 students. **Most popular majors:** Accounting; Sport and Fitness Administration/Management; Accounting and Business/Management. **Special Study Options:** Cross-registration; Distance learning; Double major; Internships; Study abroad; Teacher certification program. **Career services:** Career assessment; Internships.

648

FACILITIES

Housing: Coed dorms; 71% of campus accessible to physically disabled.

CAMPUS LIFE

Environment: Rural. **Activities:** Choral groups; Dance; Drama/theater; Student government; Student newspaper; Yearbook. 26 registered organizations, 3 honor societies, 1 fraternity, 1 sorority on campus. **Athletics (Intercollegiate):** *Men:* baseball, basketball, golf, lacrosse, soccer, tennis. *Women:* basketball, field hockey, lacrosse, soccer, softball, volleyball.

ADMISSIONS

Freshman Academic Profile: Average high school GPA 2.7. 7% in top 10% of high school class, 19% in top 25% of high school class, 54% in top 50% of high school class. **Test Scores:** SAT Math middle 50% range 390–510. SAT EBRW middle 50% range 400–500. ACT middle 50% range 13–22. **Basis for Candidate Selection:** *Very important factors include:* rigor of secondary school record, class rank, academic GPA, application essay, standardized test scores, recommendation(s). *Important factors include:* interview, extracurricular activities, character/personal qualities. *Other factors include:* talent/ability, first generation, alumni/ae relation, volunteer work, work experience, level of applicant's interest. **Freshman Admission Requirements:** High school diploma is required and GED is accepted. *Academic units recommended:* 4 English, 3 math, 3 science, 2 foreign language, 2 social studies, 2 history. **Freshman Admission Statistics:** 483 applied, 83% admitted, 62% enrolled. **Transfer Admission Requirements:** High school transcript, college transcript(s), essay or personal statement. Minimum college GPA of 2.0 required. Lowest grade transferable C. **General Admission Information:** Application fee $50. Non-fall registration accepted. Admission may be deferred for a maximum of 2 years.

COSTS AND FINANCIAL AID

Annual tuition $17,280. Room and board $7,430. Required fees $450. Average book and supplies expense $800. **Required Forms and Deadlines:** FAFSA. **Notification of Awards:** Applicants will be notified of awards on a rolling basis beginning 3/15. **Types of Aid:** *Need-based scholarships/grants:* College/university scholarship or grant aid from institutional funds; Federal Pell; Private scholarships; SEOG; State scholarships/grants. *Loans:* Direct PLUS loans; Direct Subsidized Stafford Loans; Direct Unsubsidized Stafford Loans. **Student Employment:** Federal Work-Study Program available. Institutional employment available. **Financial Aid Statistics:** 100% needy freshmen, 98% needy undergrads receive need-based scholarship or grant aid. 31% freshmen, 19% undergrads receive non-need-based scholarship or grant aid. 90% freshmen, 89% undergrads receive need-based self-help aid. 0% freshmen, 0% undergrads receive athletic scholarships. 95% freshmen, 90% undergrads receive any aid. **Criteria awarding aid:** *Need-based:* Academics. *Non-need-based:* Academics.

THOMAS EDISON STATE UNIVERSITY

111 West State Street, Trenton, NJ 08608-1176
Phone: 888-442-8372 **Financial Aid Phone:** 609-633-9658
E-mail: admissions@tesu.edu **CEEB Code:** 2612
Fax: 609-984-8447 **Website:** www.tesu.edu **ACT Code:** 274872

This public school was founded in 1972. It has a 2 acre campus.

RATINGS

Admissions Selectivity Rating: 60* **Fire Safety Rating:** 60* **Green Rating:** 60*

STUDENTS AND FACULTY

Enrollment: 16,506. **Student Body:** 44% female, 56% male, 1% international (63 countries represented). Asian 4%, African American 15%, Caucasian 51%, Hispanic 9%, Native American 1%, Pacific Islander 1%, Two or more races 2%, Race unknown 16%.

ACADEMICS

Degrees: Associate; Bachelor's; Certificate; Master's; Post-bachelor's certificate. **Special Study Options:** Accelerated program; Distance learning; Dual enrollment; External degree program; Independent study; Student-designed major. **Career services:** Alumni network.

CAMPUS LIFE

Environment: City. **Activities:** Student newspaper.

ADMISSIONS

Basis for Candidate Selection: *Other factors include:* state residency. **Freshman Admission Requirements:** High school diploma is required and GED is accepted. **Transfer Admission Requirements:** College transcript(s). Lowest grade transferable D. **General Admission Information:** Application fee $75. Admission may be deferred for a maximum of 6 months.

COSTS AND FINANCIAL AID

Annual in-state tuition $6,350. Annual out-of-state tuition $9,352. **Required Forms and Deadlines:** FAFSA; Institution's own financial aid form. **Notification of Awards:** Applicants will be notified of awards on a rolling basis beginning 3/1. **Types of Aid:** *Need-based scholarships/grants:* Federal Pell; Private scholarships; State scholarships/grants.

THOMAS JEFFERSON UNIVERSITY

130 South 9th Street, Philadelphia, PA 19107
Phone: 215-503-8890 **Financial Aid Phone:** 215 9552867
E-mail: jchp@jefferson.edu **CEEB Code:** 2903
Fax: 215-503-7241 **Website:** www.jefferson.edu/jchp **ACT Code:** 3668

This private school was founded in 1967.

RATINGS

Admissions Selectivity Rating: 60* **Fire Safety Rating:** 79 **Green Rating:** 60*

STUDENTS AND FACULTY

Enrollment: 827. **Student Body:** 83% female, 17% male, 27% out-of-state, 1% international. Asian 8%, African American 9%, Caucasian 71%, Hispanic 3%, Native American <1%, Race unknown 7%.
Faculty: Student/faculty ratio 14:1. 82 full-time faculty, 43% hold PhDs, 12% are members of minority groups, 85% are women.

ACADEMICS

Degrees: Associate; Bachelor's; Master's; Post-bachelor's certificate; Post-master's certificate; Transfer Associate. **Most popular majors:** Clinical Laboratory Science/Medical Technology/Technologist; Health Professions And Related Programs; Health Professions And Related Programs. **Special Study Options:** Accelerated program; Distance learning; Double major; Independent study; Internships; Study abroad. **Disability Services offered:** Note-taking services; Reader services; Tutors. **Career services:** Alumni network; Alumni services; Career assessment; Career/job search classes; Regional alumni.

FACILITIES

Housing: Apartments for married students; Apartments for single students; Coed dorms; Special housing for disabled students; 80% of campus accessible to physically disabled. **Special Academic Facilities/Equipment:** Copy of the famous Gross Clinic, New building with simulation labs. Located in the heart of Center City close to all historical sights as well as cultural events and museums.

CAMPUS LIFE

Environment: Metropolis. **Activities:** Choral groups; International Student Organization; Student government; Yearbook. **On-Campus Highlights:** New Education and Research Building.

ADMISSIONS

Freshman Admission Requirements: High school diploma is required and GED is accepted. **Transfer Admission Requirements:** College transcript(s), essay or personal statement, statement of good standing from prior institution(s). Minimum college GPA of 2.5 required. Lowest grade transferable C. **General Admission Information:** Application fee $50. Priority deadline 3/1. Non-fall registration accepted.

COSTS AND FINANCIAL AID

Annual tuition $23,685. Room and board $8,280. Required fees $400. Average book and supplies expense $1,495. **Required Forms and Deadlines:** FAFSA; Institution's own financial aid form. **Types of Aid:** *Need-based scholarships/grants:* College/university scholarship or grant aid from institutional funds; Federal Nursing Scholarships; Federal Pell; Private scholarships; SEOG; State scholarships/grants. *Loans:* Direct Subsidized Stafford Loans; Direct Unsubsidized Stafford Loans. **Student Employment:** Federal Work-Study Program available. Institutional employment available. **Criteria awarding aid:** *Need-based:* Academics. *Non-need-based:* Academics, Leadership, State/district residency.

THOMAS MORE COLLEGE

333 Thomas More Pkwy., Crestview Hills, KY 41017-3495
Phone: 859-344-3332 **Financial Aid Phone:** 859-344-3319
E-mail: admissions@thomasmore.edu **CEEB Code:** 3892
Fax: 859-344-3444 **Website:** www.thomasmore.edu **ACT Code:** 1560

This private school, affiliated with the Roman Catholic Church, was founded in 1921. It has a 100 acre campus.

RATINGS
Admissions Selectivity Rating: 72   **Fire Safety Rating:** 62   **Green Rating:** 60*

STUDENTS AND FACULTY
Enrollment: 1,399. **Student Body:** 49% female, 51% male, 47% out-of-state, 1% international. Asian 1%, African American 8%, Caucasian 76%, Hispanic 2%, Native American <1%, Pacific Islander <1%, Two or more races 5%, Race unknown 7%.
Retention and Graduation: 67% freshmen return for sophomore year. 17% grads go on to further study within 1 year. **Faculty:** Student/faculty ratio 16:1. 83 full-time faculty, 73% hold PhDs, 6% are members of minority groups, 49% are women. 0% of classes are taught by teaching assistants.

ACADEMICS
Degrees: Associate; Bachelor's; Certificate; Master's. **Classes:** Most classes have 10–19 students. Most lab/discussion sessions have 10–19 students. **Most popular majors:** Business Administration and Management, General; Registered Nursing/Registered Nurse; Psychology, General. **Special Study Options:** Accelerated program; Cooperative education program; Cross-registration; Distance learning; Double major; Dual enrollment; Honors program; Independent study; Internships; Liberal arts/career combination; Student-designed major; Study abroad; Teacher certification program. **Honors programs:** Thomas More Honors Program. **Disability Services offered:** Note-taking services; Reader services; Tape recorders; Tutors. **Career services:** Alumni services; Career assessment; Career/job search classes; Internships; Regional alumni.

FACILITIES
Housing: Men's dorms; Women's dorms; 99% of campus accessible to physically disabled. **Special Academic Facilities/Equipment:** Observatory; Biology Field Station. **Campus network:** 100% of classrooms, 100% of dorms, 100% of student union, 100% of libraries, 100% of dining areas, 15% of common outdoor areas have wireless network access.

CAMPUS LIFE
Environment: Village. **Activities:** Campus Ministries; Choral groups; Dance; Drama/theater; International Student Organization; Literary magazine; Marching band; Music ensembles; Student government. 40 registered organizations, 10 honor societies, 1 religious organization, 1 fraternity on campus.

ADMISSIONS
Test Scores: ACT middle 50% range 19–24. **Basis for Candidate Selection:** *Very important factors include:* academic GPA, standardized test scores. *Important factors include:* rigor of secondary school record. *Other factors include:* class rank, application essay, recommendation(s), interview, extracurricular activities, talent/ability, character/personal qualities, volunteer work. **Freshman Admission Requirements:** High school diploma is required and GED is accepted. *Academic units required:* 4 English, 3 math, 3 science, 1 science labs, 2 foreign language, 3 social studies. *Academic units recommended:* 2 visual/performing arts. **Freshman Admission Statistics:** 2,416 applied, 91% admitted, 16% enrolled. **General Admission Information:** Priority deadline 3/15. Non-fall registration accepted.

COSTS AND FINANCIAL AID
Annual tuition $28,850. Room and board $7,592. **Required Forms and Deadlines:** FAFSA; Institution's own financial aid form. **Notification of Awards:** Applicants will be notified of awards on a rolling basis beginning 3/1. **Types of Aid:** *Need-based scholarships/grants:* College/university scholarship or grant aid from institutional funds; Federal Pell; Private scholarships; SEOG; United Negro College Fund. **Financial Aid Statistics:** 96% needy freshmen, 90% needy undergrads receive need-based scholarship or grant aid. 0% freshmen, 0% undergrads receive non-need-based scholarship or grant aid. 66% freshmen, 61% undergrads receive need-based self-help aid. 0% freshmen, 0% undergrads receive athletic scholarships. 90% freshmen, 74% undergrads receive any aid.

THOMAS MORE COLLEGE OF LIBERAL ARTS

6 Manchester Street, Merrimack, NH 03054-4818
Phone: 603-880-8308
E-mail: admissions@thomasmorecollege.edu **CEEB Code:** 002001
Fax: 603-880-9280 **Website:** www.thomasmorecollege.edu **ACT Code:** 3892

This private school, affiliated with the Roman Catholic Church, was founded in 1978. It has a 13 acre campus.

RATINGS
Admissions Selectivity Rating: 74   **Fire Safety Rating:** 60*   **Green Rating:** 60*

STUDENTS AND FACULTY
Enrollment: 92. **Student Body:** 48% female, 52% male, 84% out-of-state, 6% international. Asian 0%, African American 0%, Caucasian 72%, Hispanic 1%, Native American 0%, Pacific Islander 0%, Two or more races 0%, Race unknown 21%.
Retention and Graduation: 60% freshmen return for sophomore year. 52% grads go on to further study within 1 year. 48% grads pursue arts and sciences degrees. 8% grads pursue law degrees. 2% grads pursue business degrees. 2% grads pursue medical degrees. **Faculty:** Student/faculty ratio 12:1. 5 full-time faculty, 100% hold PhDs, 0% are members of minority groups, 20% are women. 0% of classes are taught by teaching assistants.

ACADEMICS
Degrees: Bachelor's. **Classes:** Most classes have 10–19 students. **Most popular majors:** Business/Commerce, General; Computer and Information Sciences, General. **Special Study Options:** Internships; Study abroad.

FACILITIES
Housing: Men's dorms; Women's dorms; 70% of campus accessible to physically disabled. **Campus network:** 90% of classrooms, 100% of dorms, 100% of student union, 100% of libraries, 100% of dining areas, 25% of common outdoor areas have wireless network access.

CAMPUS LIFE
Environment: Village. **Activities:** Choral groups; Drama/theater.

ADMISSIONS
Freshman Academic Profile: 12% from public high schools. **Basis for Candidate Selection:** *Very important factors include:* application essay, recommendation(s), interview, character/personal qualities. *Important factors include:* talent/ability. *Other factors include:* rigor of secondary school record, class rank, academic GPA, standardized test scores, extracurricular activities, religious affiliation/commitment, level of applicant's interest. **Freshman Admission Requirements:** High school diploma is required and GED is accepted. *Academic units required:* 4 English, 3 math, 2 science, 2 science labs, 2 foreign language, 2 social studies, 2 history. *Academic units recommended:* 2 unit from above areas or other academic areas. **Freshman Admission Statistics:** 75 applied, 55% admitted, 63% enrolled. **Transfer Admission Requirements:** College transcript(s), essay or personal statement. Lowest grade transferable C. **General Admission Information:** Non-fall registration accepted.

COSTS AND FINANCIAL AID
Annual tuition $11,100. Room and board $8,000. Average book and supplies expense $525. **Required Forms and Deadlines:** FAFSA. **Notification of Awards:** Applicants will be notified of awards on a rolling basis beginning 3/15. **Types of Aid:** *Need-based scholarships/grants:* College/university scholarship or grant aid from institutional funds; Federal Pell; Private scholarships; SEOG; State scholarships/grants. **Financial Aid Statistics:** 100% needy freshmen, 100% needy undergrads receive need-based scholarship or grant aid. 0% freshmen, 0% undergrads receive non-need-based scholarship or grant aid. 70% freshmen, 62% undergrads receive need-based self-help aid. 0% freshmen, 0% undergrads receive athletic scholarships. **Criteria awarding aid:** *Non-need-based:* Academics.

TIFFIN UNIVERSITY

155 Miami Street, Tiffin, OH 44883
Phone: 419-448-3423 **Financial Aid Phone:** 419-448-3415
E-mail: admiss@tiffin.edu **CEEB Code:** 1817
Fax: 419-443-5006 **Website:** www.tiffin.edu/ **ACT Code:** 3334

This private school was founded in 1888. It has a 110 acre campus.

RATINGS
Admissions Selectivity Rating: 77   **Fire Safety Rating:** 87   **Green Rating:** 60*

STUDENTS AND FACULTY
Enrollment: 2,001. **Student Body:** 48% female, 52% male, 22% out-of-state, 11% international (34 countries represented). Asian <1%, African American 9%, Caucasian 34%, Hispanic 3%, Native American <1%, Pacific Islander <1%, Two or more races 2%, Race unknown 41%.
Retention and Graduation: 67% freshmen return for sophomore year. 35% freshmen graduate within 4 years. 45% freshmen graduate within 6 years. 25% grads go on to further study within 1 year. **Faculty:** Student/faculty ratio 15:1. 77 full-time faculty, 70% hold PhDs, 16% are members of minority groups, 43% are women. 0% of classes are taught by teaching assistants.

ACADEMICS
Degrees: Associate; Bachelor's; Certificate; Doctoral degree—professional practice; Master's; Post-bachelor's certificate; Post-master's certificate. **Classes:** Most classes have 20–29 students. Most lab/discussion sessions have 10–19 students. **Most popular majors:** Marketing/Marketing Management, General; Business Administration and Management, General. **Special Study Options:** Accelerated program; Cross-registration; Distance learning; Double major; Dual enrollment; English as a Second Language (ESL); Honors program; Independent study; Internships; Liberal arts/career combination; Student-designed major; Study abroad. **Honors programs:** We offer a Freshman Honors Program. **Disability Services offered:** Reader services; Tape recorders; Tutors. **Career services:** Alumni network; Alumni services; Career assessment; Career/job search classes; Internships; Regional alumni.

FACILITIES
Housing: Apartments for single students; Coed dorms; Fraternity/sorority housing; Men's dorms; Women's dorms; 85% of campus accessible to physically disabled. **Special Academic Facilities/Equipment:** University Art Gallery; Multi-Media Lab. **Campus network:** 100% of classrooms, 100% of dorms, 100% of student union, 100% of libraries, 100% of dining areas, 100% of common outdoor areas have wireless network access.

CAMPUS LIFE
Environment: Village. **Activities:** Campus Ministries; Choral groups; Concert band; Dance; Drama/theater; International Student Organization; Jazz band; Literary magazine; Marching band; Model UN; Music ensembles; Musical theater; Pep band; Student government; Student newspaper; Symphony orchestra. 40 registered organizations, 1 honor societies, 2 religious organizations, 3 fraternities, 4 sororities on campus. **Athletics (Intercollegiate):** *Men:* baseball, basketball, cheerleading, cross-country, equestrian sports, football, golf, soccer, tennis, track/field (outdoor), track/field (indoor). *Women:* basketball, cheerleading, cross-country, equestrian sports, golf, lacrosse, soccer, softball, tennis, track/field (outdoor), track/field (indoor), volleyball. **On-Campus Highlights:** Gillmor Student Center. **Environmental Initiatives:** Establishment of a Green Committee and formation of a Green Technologies Minor and Concentration.

ADMISSIONS
Freshman Academic Profile: Average high school GPA 3.0. 75% from public high schools. **Test Scores:** SAT Math middle 50% range 450–550. SAT EBRW middle 50% range 450–550. ACT middle 50% range 17–22. **Basis for Candidate Selection:** *Very important factors include:* rigor of secondary school record, academic GPA, standardized test scores. *Important factors include:* class rank, application essay, recommendation(s), extracurricular activities, geographical residence, state residency. *Other factors include:* interview, talent/ability, character/personal qualities, first generation, alumni/ae relation, work experience, level of applicant's interest. **Freshman Admission Requirements:** High school diploma is required and GED is accepted. *Academic units required:* 4 English, 4 math, 3 science, 1 science labs, 3 social studies, 0.5 history, 5 academic electives, 1 visual/performing arts. **Freshman Admission Statistics:** 3,977 applied, 69% admitted, 18% enrolled. **Transfer Admission Requirements:** High school transcript, college transcript(s). Minimum

college GPA of 2.0 required. Lowest grade transferable C. **General Admission Information:** Non-fall registration accepted. Admission may be deferred for a maximum of 1 year.

COSTS AND FINANCIAL AID
Annual tuition $25,710. Room and board $11,540. Required fees $400. Average book and supplies expense $3,000. **Required Forms and Deadlines:** FAFSA. **Notification of Awards:** Applicants will be notified of awards on a rolling basis beginning 11/15. **Types of Aid:** *Need-based scholarships/grants:* College/university scholarship or grant aid from institutional funds; Federal Pell; Private scholarships; SEOG; State scholarships/grants. *Loans:* Direct PLUS loans; Direct Subsidized Stafford Loans; Direct Unsubsidized Stafford Loans. **Student Employment:** Federal Work-Study Program available. Institutional employment available. **Financial Aid Statistics:** 100% needy freshmen, 96% needy undergrads receive need-based scholarship or grant aid. 11% freshmen, 9% undergrads receive non-need-based scholarship or grant aid. 88% freshmen, 89% undergrads receive need-based self-help aid. 10% freshmen, 10% undergrads receive athletic scholarships. 95% freshmen, 95% undergrads receive any aid. 76% undergrads borrow to pay for school. Average cumulative indebtedness $38,036. **Criteria awarding aid:** *Non-need-based:* Academics, Art, Athletics, Leadership, Music/drama, State/district residency.

TOCCOA FALLS COLLEGE

107 Kincaid Drive, Toccoa Falls, GA 30598
Phone: 888-785-5624 **Financial Aid Phone:** 706-886-6831
E-mail: admissions@tfc.edu **CEEB Code:** 5799
Fax: (706) 282-6012 **Website:** www.tfc.edu **ACT Code:** 0868

This private school, affiliated with the Christian & Missionary Alliance Church, was founded in 1907. It has a 1100 acre campus.

RATINGS
Admissions Selectivity Rating: 86   **Fire Safety Rating:** 70   **Green Rating:** 60*

STUDENTS AND FACULTY
Enrollment: 796. **Student Body:** 53% female, 47% male, 23% out-of-state, 1% international. Asian 8%, African American 7%, Caucasian 72%, Hispanic 4%, Native American <1%, Pacific Islander <1%, Two or more races 2%, Race unknown 6%.
Retention and Graduation: 72% freshmen return for sophomore year. **Faculty:** Student/faculty ratio 14:1. 42 full-time faculty, 60% hold PhDs, 12% are members of minority groups, 31% are women. 0% of classes are taught by teaching assistants.

ACADEMICS
Degrees: Associate; Bachelor's; Certificate. **Classes:** Most classes have fewer than 10 students. **Most popular majors:** Missions/Missionary Studies; Counseling Psychology; Elementary Education and Teaching. **Special Study Options:** Distance learning; Double major; Dual enrollment; Independent study; Internships; Study abroad; Teacher certification program. **Disability Services offered:** Note-taking services; Reader services; Tutors. **Career services:** Career assessment.

FACILITIES
Housing: Apartments for married students; Men's dorms; Special housing for international students; Wellness housing; Women's dorms; 70% of campus accessible to physically disabled. **Campus network:** 100% of classrooms, 100% of dorms, 100% of student union, 100% of libraries, 100% of dining areas, 75% of common outdoor areas have wireless network access.

CAMPUS LIFE
Environment: Village. **Activities:** Campus Ministries; Choral groups; Concert band; Drama/theater; International Student Organization; Jazz band; Music ensembles; Radio station; Student government; Student newspaper; Yearbook. **Athletics (Intercollegiate):** *Men:* baseball, basketball, cross-country, golf, soccer, tennis. *Women:* basketball, cheerleading, cross-country, golf, soccer, tennis, volleyball. **On-Campus Highlights:** The Waterfall.

ADMISSIONS
Freshman Academic Profile: Average high school GPA 3.4. 10% in top 10% of high school class, 28% in top 25% of high school class, 63% in top 50% of high school class. 60% from public high schools. **Test Scores:** SAT Math middle 50% range 410–550. SAT EBRW middle 50% range 410–560. ACT middle 50% range 17–24. **Basis for Candidate Selection:**

Very important factors include: rigor of secondary school record, academic GPA, application essay, standardized test scores, character/personal qualities, religious affiliation/commitment. *Other factors include:* recommendation(s), interview, extracurricular activities, talent/ability, volunteer work, work experience, level of applicant's interest. **Freshman Admission Requirements:** High school diploma is required and GED is accepted. *Academic units recommended:* 4 English, 3 math, 3 science, 2 science labs, 3 social studies, 6 academic electives. **Freshman Admission Statistics:** 879 applied, 54% admitted, 42% enrolled. **Transfer Admission Requirements:** College transcript(s), essay or personal statement. Minimum college GPA of 2.0 required. Lowest grade transferable C-. **General Admission Information:** Application fee $25. Regular application deadline 8/1. Non-fall registration accepted. Admission may be deferred for a maximum of 2 years.

COSTS AND FINANCIAL AID

Annual tuition $22,669. Room and board $7,934. Required fees $770. Average book and supplies expense $1,000. **Required Forms and Deadlines:** FAFSA; Institution's own financial aid form; State aid form. **Notification of Awards:** Applicants will be notified of awards on a rolling basis beginning 11/1. **Types of Aid:** *Need-based scholarships/grants:* College/university scholarship or grant aid from institutional funds; Federal Pell; Private scholarships; SEOG; State scholarships/grants. *Loans:* Direct PLUS loans; Direct Subsidized Stafford Loans; Direct Unsubsidized Stafford Loans. **Financial Aid Statistics:** 100% needy freshmen, 100% needy undergrads receive need-based scholarship or grant aid. 9% freshmen, 8% undergrads receive non-need-based scholarship or grant aid. 83% freshmen, 82% undergrads receive need-based self-help aid. 0% freshmen, 0% undergrads receive athletic scholarships. 100% freshmen, 98% undergrads receive any aid. 78% undergrads borrow to pay for school. Average cumulative indebtedness $29,977. **Criteria awarding aid:** *Need-based:* Academics, Leadership. *Non-need-based:* Academics, Alumni affiliation, Leadership, Music/drama, Religious affiliation, State/district residency.

TOWSON UNIVERSITY

8000 York Road, Towson, MD 21252-0001
Phone: 410-704-2113 **Financial Aid Phone:** 410-704-4236
E-mail: admissions@towson.edu **CEEB Code:** 5404
Fax: 410-704-3030 **Website:** www.towson.edu **ACT Code:** 1718

This public school was founded in 1866. It has a 329 acre campus.

RATINGS

Admissions Selectivity Rating: 80   **Fire Safety Rating:** 92   **Green Rating:** 96

STUDENTS AND FACULTY

Enrollment: 19,458. **Student Body:** 59% female, 41% male, 11% out-of-state, 2% international (75 countries represented). Asian 7%, African American 24%, Caucasian 52%, Hispanic 9%, Native American <1%, Pacific Islander <1%, Two or more races 5%, Race unknown 1%.
Retention and Graduation: 86% freshmen return for sophomore year. 48% freshmen graduate within 4 years. 71% freshmen graduate within 6 years. 17% grads go on to further study within 1 year. **Faculty:** Student/faculty ratio 16:1. 920 full-time faculty, 78% hold PhDs, 25% are members of minority groups, 58% are women. 0% of classes are taught by teaching assistants.

ACADEMICS

Degrees: Bachelor's; Doctoral degree—professional practice; Doctoral degree research/scholarship; Master's; Post-bachelor's certificate; Post-master's certificate. **Classes:** Most classes have 20–29 students. Most lab/discussion sessions have 20–29 students. **Most popular majors:** Biology/Biological Sciences, General; Psychology, General; Business Administration and Management, General. **Special Study Options:** Accelerated program; Cross-registration; Distance learning; Double major; Dual enrollment; English as a Second Language (ESL); Exchange student program (domestic); Honors program; Independent study; Internships; Liberal arts/career combination; Student-designed major; Study abroad; Teacher certification program. **Honors programs:** Honors College. **Disability Services offered:** Note-taking services; Reader services; Tape recorders. **Career services:** Alumni network; Alumni services; Career assessment; Career/job search classes; Internships; Regional alumni.

FACILITIES

Housing: Apartments for single students; Coed dorms; Special housing for disabled students; Special housing for international students; 80% of campus accessible to physically disabled. **Special Academic Facilities/Equipment:** Asian Arts & Culture Center; Burdick Hall (recreation/fitness facility); Center for the Arts; Gallery Media Center; Stephens Hall Theatre; Watson-King Planetarium; Nursing Simulation Center; Towson University Biodiversity Center (TUBC); [TU Herbarium (BALT) & Entomological Collection]; T.Rowe Price Finance Lab; Behavioral Lab (Tobii Eye Tracking Technology); Urban Environmental Biogeochemistry Laboratory (Research Facility); Microscope Lab; Laser ablation system; Discrete Analyzer; Ion Chromatograph X-ray spectrometer; Microwave digestion system; Electron microscope; Stream table. **Campus network:** 75% of classrooms, 100% of dorms, 100% of student union, 100% of libraries, 100% of dining areas, 100% of common outdoor areas have wireless network access.

CAMPUS LIFE

Environment: Metropolis. **Activities:** Campus Ministries; Choral groups; Concert band; Dance; Drama/theater; International Student Organization; Jazz band; Literary magazine; Marching band; Model UN; Music ensembles; Musical theater; Opera; Pep band; Radio station; Student government; Student newspaper; Student-run film society; Symphony orchestra; Television station. 323 registered organizations, 22 honor societies, 27 religious organizations, 25 fraternities, 17 sororities on campus. **Athletics (Intercollegiate):** *Men:* baseball, basketball, cheerleading, cross-country, diving, football, golf, lacrosse, soccer, swimming, tennis. *Women:* basketball, cheerleading, cross-country, diving, field hockey, gymnastics, lacrosse, soccer, softball, swimming, tennis, track/field (outdoor), volleyball. **On-Campus Highlights:** Johnny Unitas Stadium/SECU Arena. **Environmental Initiatives:** Towson University is committed to creating changes, not just on campus, but in the larger Baltimore Metropolitan region. The Baltimore + Towson University (BTU) Partnership allows Towson University to work with over 300 organizations in Greater Baltimore and throughout Maryland to create positive impacts. BTU is about elevating the work that TU is already doing to better address the needs of the regions in areas such as high-quality and equitable education, lifelong health and well being, strong neighborhoods and sustainable communities, a thriving and competitive economy, and vibrant arts and cultural community.

ADMISSIONS

Freshman Academic Profile: Average high school GPA 3.7. 15% in top 10% of high school class, 42% in top 25% of high school class, 79% in top 50% of high school class. 85% from public high schools. **Test Scores:** SAT Math middle 50% range 520–600. SAT EBRW middle 50% range 540–620. ACT middle 50% range 20–25. **Basis for Candidate Selection:** *Very important factors include:* academic GPA, standardized test scores. *Important factors include:* rigor of secondary school record. *Other factors include:* class rank, application essay, recommendation(s), talent/ability, first generation. **Freshman Admission Requirements:** High school diploma is required and GED is accepted. *Academic units required:* 4 English, 4 math, 3 science, 2 science labs, 2 foreign language, 3 social studies, 6 academic electives. **Freshman Admission Statistics:** 12,678 applied, 76% admitted, 29% enrolled. **Transfer Admission Requirements:** College transcript(s). Minimum college GPA of 2.0 required. Lowest grade transferable D. **General Admission Information:** Application fee $45. Priority deadline 12/1. Regular application deadline 1/15. Non-fall registration accepted. Admission may be deferred for a maximum of 1 year.

COSTS AND FINANCIAL AID

Annual in-state tuition $6,962. Annual out-of-state tuition $21,098. Room and board $13,446. Required fees $3,236. Average book and supplies expense $1,080. **Required Forms and Deadlines:** FAFSA; State aid form. **Notification of Awards:** Applicants will be notified of awards on a rolling basis beginning 3/15. **Types of Aid:** *Need-based scholarships/grants:* College/university scholarship or grant aid from institutional funds; Federal Pell; Private scholarships; SEOG; State scholarships/grants. *Loans:* Direct PLUS loans; Direct Subsidized Stafford Loans; Direct Unsubsidized Stafford Loans. **Student Employment:** Federal Work-Study Program available. Institutional employment available. **Financial Aid Statistics:** 57% needy freshmen, 63% needy undergrads receive need-based scholarship or grant aid. 39% freshmen, 25% undergrads receive non-need-based scholarship or grant aid. 68% freshmen, 69% undergrads receive need-based self-help aid. 3% freshmen, 2% undergrads receive athletic scholarships. 81% freshmen, 75% undergrads receive any aid. 60% undergrads borrow to pay for school. Average cumulative indebtedness $27,610. **Criteria awarding aid:** *Non-need-based:* Academics, Alumni affiliation, Art, Athletics, Leadership, Music/drama, State/district residency.

TRANSYLVANIA UNIVERSITY

300 North Broadway, Lexington, KY 40508-1797
Phone: 859-233-8242 **Financial Aid Phone:** 859-233-8239
E-mail: admissions@transy.edu **CEEB Code:** 1808
Fax: 859-281-3649 **Website:** www.transy.edu **ACT Code:** 1550

This private school, affiliated with the Disciples of Christ Church, was founded in 1780. It has a 36 acre campus.

RATINGS
Admissions Selectivity Rating: 77   **Fire Safety Rating:** 90   **Green Rating:** 60*

STUDENTS AND FACULTY
Enrollment: 989. **Student Body:** 60% female, 40% male, 21% out-of-state, 0% international (8 countries represented). Asian 2%, African American 5%, Caucasian 80%, Hispanic 4%, Native American <1%, Pacific Islander 0%, Two or more races 5%, Race unknown 5%.
Retention and Graduation: 82% freshmen return for sophomore year. 69% freshmen graduate within 4 years. 75% freshmen graduate within 6 years. 41% grads go on to further study within 1 year. 55% grads pursue arts and sciences degrees. 23% grads pursue law degrees. 0% grads pursue business degrees. 7% grads pursue medical degrees. **Faculty:** Student/faculty ratio 11:1. 83 full-time faculty, 96% hold PhDs, 6% are members of minority groups, 48% are women. 0% of classes are taught by teaching assistants.

ACADEMICS
Degrees: Bachelor's. **Classes:** Most classes have 10–19 students. Most lab/discussion sessions have 10–19 students. **Most popular majors:** Business/Commerce, General; Accounting; Psychology, General. **Special Study Options:** Double major; Independent study; Internships; Liberal arts/career combination; Student-designed major; Study abroad; Teacher certification program. **Disability Services offered:** Note-taking services; Reader services; Tape recorders; Tutors. **Career services:** Alumni network; Alumni services; Career assessment; Career/job search classes; Internships; Regional alumni.

FACILITIES
Housing: Apartments for single students; Coed dorms; Men's dorms; Women's dorms; 90% of campus accessible to physically disabled. **Special Academic Facilities/Equipment:** Art gallery, museum of early scientific apparatus, medical museum, language lab, transmission electron microscope.

CAMPUS LIFE
Environment: Metropolis. **Activities:** Campus Ministries; Choral groups; Concert band; Dance; Drama/theater; Jazz band; Literary magazine; Music ensembles; Musical theater; Opera; Radio station; Student government; Student newspaper. 55 registered organizations, 10 honor societies, 3 religious organizations, 4 fraternities, 4 sororities on campus. **Athletics (Intercollegiate):** *Men:* baseball, basketball, cheerleading, cross-country, diving, golf, soccer, swimming, tennis, track/field (outdoor). *Women:* basketball, cheerleading, cross-country, diving, field hockey, golf, soccer, softball, swimming, tennis, track/field (outdoor), volleyball. **On-Campus Highlights:** Cowgill Center. **Environmental Initiatives:** Developing a comprehensive sustainability master plan.

ADMISSIONS
Freshman Academic Profile: Average high school GPA 3.7. 30% in top 10% of high school class, 67% in top 25% of high school class, 90% in top 50% of high school class. 78% from public high schools. **Test Scores:** SAT Math middle 50% range 540–670. SAT EBRW middle 50% range 560–640. ACT middle 50% range 24–30. **Basis for Candidate Selection:** *Very important factors include:* rigor of secondary school record, academic GPA, application essay, standardized test scores. *Important factors include:* recommendation(s), extracurricular activities, talent/ability, character/personal qualities. *Other factors include:* class rank, interview, first generation, alumni/ae relation, geographical residence, racial/ethnic status, volunteer work, work experience. **Freshman Admission Requirements:** High school diploma is required and GED is accepted. *Academic units required:* 4 English, 3 math, 3 science, 2 science labs, 2 foreign language, 2 social studies, 2 academic electives. *Academic units recommended:* 4 English, 4 math, 4 science, 3 science labs, 2 foreign language, 2 social studies, 1 history, 2 academic electives. **Freshman Admission**

Statistics: 1,662 applied, 89% admitted, 20% enrolled. **Transfer Admission Requirements:** High school transcript, college transcript(s), essay or personal statement. Minimum college GPA of 2.75 required. Lowest grade transferable C-. **General Admission Information:** Priority deadline 11/1. Non-fall registration accepted. Admission may be deferred for a maximum of 12 months.

COSTS AND FINANCIAL AID
Annual tuition $38,570. Room and board $10,770. Required fees $1,640. Average book and supplies expense $1,000. **Required Forms and Deadlines:** FAFSA. **Notification of Awards:** Applicants will be notified of awards on or about 12/1. **Types of Aid:** *Need-based scholarships/grants:* College/university scholarship or grant aid from institutional funds; Federal Pell; Private scholarships; SEOG; State scholarships/grants. *Loans:* Direct PLUS loans; Direct Subsidized Stafford Loans; Direct Unsubsidized Stafford Loans. **Student Employment:** Federal Work-Study Program available. Institutional employment available. **Financial Aid Statistics:** 100% needy freshmen, 100% needy undergrads receive need-based scholarship or grant aid. 17% freshmen, 16% undergrads receive non-need-based scholarship or grant aid. 76% freshmen, 76% undergrads receive need-based self-help aid. 0% freshmen, 0% undergrads receive athletic scholarships. 99% freshmen, 98% undergrads receive any aid. 55% undergrads borrow to pay for school. Average cumulative indebtedness $33,037. **Criteria awarding aid:** *Need-based:* Academics, Minority status, Religious affiliation. *Non-need-based:* Academics, Art, Minority status, Music/drama, Religious affiliation, State/district residency.

TREVECCA NAZARENE UNIVERSITY

333 Murfreesboro Road, Nashville, TN 37210
Phone: 615-248-1320 **Financial Aid Phone:** 615-248-1242
E-mail: admissions_und@trevecca.edu **CEEB Code:** 003526
Fax: 615-248-7406 **Website:** www.trevecca.edu **ACT Code:** 4016

This private school, affiliated with the Nazarene Church, was founded in 1901. It has a 80 acre campus.

RATINGS
Admissions Selectivity Rating: 86   **Fire Safety Rating:** 60*   **Green Rating:** 60*

STUDENTS AND FACULTY
Enrollment: 2,263. **Student Body:** 61% female, 39% male, 40% out-of-state, 10% international (23 countries represented). Asian 1%, African American 13%, Caucasian 60%, Hispanic 10%, Native American <1%, Pacific Islander <1%, Two or more races 3%, Race unknown 3%.
Retention and Graduation: 76% freshmen return for sophomore year. 49% freshmen graduate within 4 years. 54% freshmen graduate within 6 years. **Faculty:** Student/faculty ratio 24:1. 108 full-time faculty, 88% hold PhDs, 9% are members of minority groups, 44% are women.

ACADEMICS
Degrees: Associate; Bachelor's; Certificate; Doctoral degree research/scholarship; Master's; Post-master's certificate. **Classes:** Most classes have 10–19 students. **Most popular majors:** Psychology, General; Registered Nursing/Registered Nurse; Theology and Religious Vocations, Other. **Special Study Options:** Distance learning; Double major; Dual enrollment; Internships; Study abroad; Teacher certification program. **Disability Services offered:** Note-taking services; Reader services; Tutors. **Career services:** Alumni services; Internships.

FACILITIES
Housing: Men's dorms; Women's dorms.

CAMPUS LIFE
Environment: Metropolis. **Activities:** Campus Ministries; Choral groups; Concert band; Drama/theater; International Student Organization; Jazz band; Literary magazine; Marching band; Music ensembles; Musical theater; Pep band; Student government; Student newspaper; Symphony orchestra; Yearbook. **Athletics (Intercollegiate):** *Men:* baseball, basketball, golf, soccer. *Women:* basketball, golf, soccer, softball, volleyball. **On-Campus Highlights:** Library.

ADMISSIONS
Freshman Academic Profile: Average high school GPA 3.5. **Test Scores:** SAT Math middle 50% range 490–590. SAT EBRW middle 50% range 510–620. ACT middle 50% range 19–26. **Basis for Candidate Selection:** *Very important factors include:* academic GPA, standardized test scores, character/personal qualities. *Important factors include:* level of applicant's interest. *Other factors include:* rigor of secondary school record, class rank, application

---

essay, recommendation(s), extracurricular activities, talent/ability. **Freshman Admission Requirements:** High school diploma is required and GED is accepted. *Academic units recommended:* 4 English, 2 math, 1 science, 2 foreign language, 1 social studies, 1 history, 4 academic electives. **Freshman Admission Statistics:** 1,662 applied, 62% admitted, 38% enrolled. **Transfer Admission Requirements:** College transcript(s). Lowest grade transferable D. **General Admission Information:** Application fee $25. Priority deadline 4/1. Regular application deadline 8/1. Non-fall registration accepted. Admission may be deferred for a maximum of 1 year.

COSTS AND FINANCIAL AID
Annual tuition $25,998. Room and board $9,100. Required fees $900. **Notification of Awards:** Applicants will be notified of awards on a rolling basis beginning 12/1. **Types of Aid:** *Need-based scholarships/grants:* College/university scholarship or grant aid from institutional funds; Federal Pell; Private scholarships; SEOG; State scholarships/grants. *Loans:* Direct PLUS loans; Direct Subsidized Stafford Loans; Direct Unsubsidized Stafford Loans. **Student Employment:** Federal Work-Study Program available. Institutional employment available. **Financial Aid Statistics:** 98% undergrads receive any aid. 56% undergrads borrow to pay for school. Average cumulative indebtedness $24,895. **Criteria awarding aid:** *Non-need-based:* Academics, Alumni affiliation, Athletics, Leadership, Minority status, Music/drama, Religious affiliation.

TRINE UNIVERSITY

1 University Avenue, Angola, IN 46703
Phone: 260-665-4100 **Financial Aid Phone:** 260-664-4158
E-mail: admit@trine.edu **CEEB Code:** 1811
Fax: 260-665-4578 **Website:** www.trine.edu **ACT Code:** 1250

This private school was founded in 1884. It has a 400 acre campus.

RATINGS
Admissions Selectivity Rating: 79   **Fire Safety Rating:** 87   **Green Rating:** 60*

STUDENTS AND FACULTY
Enrollment: 2,059. **Student Body:** 31% female, 69% male, 21% out-of-state, 4% international (24 countries represented). Asian 1%, African American 4%, Caucasian 80%, Hispanic 5%, Native American <1%, Pacific Islander <1%, Two or more races 3%, Race unknown 2%.
Retention and Graduation: 79% freshmen return for sophomore year. 43% freshmen graduate within 4 years. 54% freshmen graduate within 6 years.
Faculty: Student/faculty ratio 15:1. 122 full-time faculty, 63% hold PhDs, 35% are women. 0% of classes are taught by teaching assistants.

ACADEMICS
Degrees: Associate; Bachelor's; Doctoral degree—professional practice; Master's. **Classes:** Most classes have 20–29 students. Most lab/discussion sessions have 20–29 students. **Most popular majors:** Civil Engineering, General. **Special Study Options:** Accelerated program; Cooperative education program; Distance learning; Double major; Dual enrollment; Honors program; Independent study; Internships; Liberal arts/career combination; Student-designed major; Study abroad; Teacher certification program. **Honors programs:** Honors program began with Fall 2006 entering class of freshmen. **Combined degree programs:** BA/MA; BA/MEng. **Disability Services offered:** Reader services; Tape recorders; Tutors. **Career services:** Alumni network; Alumni services; Career assessment; Internships; Regional alumni.

FACILITIES
Housing: Coed dorms; Fraternity/sorority housing; Men's dorms; Special housing for disabled students; Theme housing; Women's dorms; 95% of campus accessible to physically disabled. **Special Academic Facilities/Equipment:** Lewis Hershey Museum; Wells Gallery of Engravings; Zollner Golf Course.

CAMPUS LIFE
Environment: Village. **Activities:** Campus Ministries; Choral groups; Concert band; Dance; Drama/theater; International Student Organization; Jazz band; Literary magazine; Marching band; Music ensembles; Pep band; Radio station; Student government; Yearbook. 51 registered organizations, 9 honor societies, 2 religious organizations, 8 fraternities, 5 sororities on campus. **Athletics (Intercollegiate):** *Men:* baseball, basketball, cross-country, football, golf, lacrosse, soccer, tennis, track/field (outdoor), track/field (indoor), wrestling. *Women:* basketball, cross-country, golf, lacrosse, soccer, softball, tennis, track/

field (outdoor), track/field (indoor), volleyball. **On-Campus Highlights:** University Center.

ADMISSIONS
Freshman Academic Profile: Average high school GPA 3.5. 18% in top 10% of high school class, 46% in top 25% of high school class, 79% in top 50% of high school class. **Test Scores:** SAT Math middle 50% range 510–620. SAT EBRW middle 50% range 500–610. ACT middle 50% range 21–27. **Basis for Candidate Selection:** *Very important factors include:* rigor of secondary school record, class rank, academic GPA, standardized test scores. *Important factors include:* recommendation(s), extracurricular activities. *Other factors include:* talent/ability, character/personal qualities, volunteer work, work experience. **Freshman Admission Requirements:** High school diploma is required and GED is accepted. *Academic units recommended:* 4 English, 3 math, 3 science, 3 social studies. **Freshman Admission Statistics:** 3,993 applied, 73% admitted, 21% enrolled. **Transfer Admission Requirements:** High school transcript, college transcript(s), statement of good standing from prior institution(s). Minimum college GPA of 2.0 required. Lowest grade transferable C. **General Admission Information:** Priority deadline 6/1. Regular application deadline 8/1. Non-fall registration accepted. Admission may be deferred for a maximum of 12 months.

COSTS AND FINANCIAL AID
Annual tuition $31,700. Room and board $10,810. Required fees $476. Average book and supplies expense $1,200. **Required Forms and Deadlines:** FAFSA. **Notification of Awards:** Applicants will be notified of awards on a rolling basis beginning 1/15. **Types of Aid:** *Need-based scholarships/grants:* College/university scholarship or grant aid from institutional funds; Federal Pell; Private scholarships; SEOG; State scholarships/grants. *Loans:* Direct PLUS loans; Direct Subsidized Stafford Loans; Direct Unsubsidized Stafford Loans. **Student Employment:** Federal Work-Study Program available. Institutional employment available. **Financial Aid Statistics:** 100% needy freshmen, 98% needy undergrads receive need-based scholarship or grant aid. 12% freshmen, 22% undergrads receive non-need-based scholarship or grant aid. 88% freshmen, 86% undergrads receive need-based self-help aid. 0% freshmen, 0% undergrads receive athletic scholarships. 77% undergrads borrow to pay for school. Average cumulative indebtedness $36,421. **Criteria awarding aid:** *Non-need-based:* Academics, Alumni affiliation, Minority status, Music/drama.

TRINITY CHRISTIAN COLLEGE

6601 West College Drive, Palos Heights, IL 60463
Phone: (708) 239-4708 **Financial Aid Phone:** (708) 239-4872
E-mail: admissions@trnty.edu **CEEB Code:** 1820
Fax: (708) 239-4826 **Website:** www.trnty.edu **ACT Code:** 1165

This private school was founded in 1959. It has a 60 acre campus.

RATINGS
Admissions Selectivity Rating: 76   **Fire Safety Rating:** 88   **Green Rating:** 60*

STUDENTS AND FACULTY
Enrollment: 789. **Student Body:** 69% female, 31% male, 31% out-of-state, 13% international (12 countries represented). Asian 1%, African American 9%, Caucasian 60%, Hispanic 12%, Native American <1%, Pacific Islander <1%, Two or more races 1%, Race unknown 4%.
Retention and Graduation: 86% freshmen return for sophomore year. 60% freshmen graduate within 4 years. 68% freshmen graduate within 6 years. 12% grads go on to further study within 1 year. 4% grads pursue arts and sciences degrees. 1% grads pursue law degrees. 1% grads pursue business degrees. 2% grads pursue medical degrees. **Faculty:** Student/faculty ratio 10:1. 70 full-time faculty, 66% hold PhDs, 9% are members of minority groups, 60% are women. 0% of classes are taught by teaching assistants.

ACADEMICS
Degrees: Bachelor's; Master's; Post-master's certificate. **Classes:** Most classes have 10–19 students. Most lab/discussion sessions have 10–19 students. **Most popular majors:** Business/Commerce, General; Registered Nursing/Registered Nurse; Elementary Education and Teaching. **Special Study Options:** Accelerated program; Distance learning; Double major; Dual enrollment; English as a Second Language (ESL); Honors program; Independent study; Internships; Liberal arts/career combination; Study abroad; Teacher certification program. **Honors programs:** The Trinity Honors Program challenges and academically supports gifted students through seminars, unique opportunities

within the major program, and participation in co-curricular activities. **Disability Services offered:** Reader services; Tape recorders; Tutors. **Career services:** Alumni network; Alumni services; Career assessment; Internships; Regional alumni.

FACILITIES

Housing: Coed dorms; 98% of campus accessible to physically disabled. **Special Academic Facilities/Equipment:** Dutch Heritage Center. **Campus network:** 100% of classrooms, 100% of dorms, 100% of student union, 100% of libraries, 100% of dining areas have wireless network access.

CAMPUS LIFE

Environment: Metropolis. **Activities:** Campus Ministries; Choral groups; Drama/theater; Jazz band; Literary magazine; Music ensembles; Musical theater; Student government; Student newspaper; Yearbook. 15 registered organizations, 2 honor societies, 1 religious organization on campus. **Athletics (Intercollegiate):** *Men:* baseball, basketball, cross-country, soccer, track/field (outdoor), track/field (indoor). *Women:* basketball, cross-country, soccer, softball, track/field (outdoor), track/field (indoor), volleyball. **On-Campus Highlights:** Bootsma Bookstore/Café. **Environmental Initiatives:** Recycling of paper, aluminum, and glass.

ADMISSIONS

Freshman Academic Profile: Average high school GPA 3.4. 11% in top 10% of high school class, 24% in top 25% of high school class, 66% in top 50% of high school class. 54% from public high schools. **Test Scores:** SAT Math middle 50% range 510–600. SAT EBRW middle 50% range 545–595. ACT middle 50% range 19–26. **Basis for Candidate Selection:** *Very important factors include:* rigor of secondary school record, academic GPA, standardized test scores. *Important factors include:* application essay, recommendation(s), interview, extracurricular activities, talent/ability, character/personal qualities, religious affiliation/commitment. *Other factors include:* class rank, first generation, alumni/ae relation, geographical residence, volunteer work, work experience, level of applicant's interest. **Freshman Admission Requirements:** High school diploma is required and GED is accepted. *Academic units required:* 6 English, 3 math, 2 science, 2 social studies. *Academic units recommended:* 4 English, 4 math, 3 science, 2 foreign language, 3 social studies, 2 history. **Freshman Admission Statistics:** 889 applied, 83% admitted, 26% enrolled. **Transfer Admission Requirements:** College transcript(s), essay or personal statement, interview, statement of good standing from prior institution(s). Minimum college GPA of 2.0 required. Lowest grade transferable C. **General Admission Information:** Application fee $30. Priority deadline 1/15. Non-fall registration accepted. Admission may be deferred for a maximum of 1 semester.

COSTS AND FINANCIAL AID

Annual tuition $29,700. Room and board $9,790. Required fees $475. Average book and supplies expense $1,100. **Required Forms and Deadlines:** FAFSA. **Notification of Awards:** Applicants will be notified of awards on a rolling basis beginning 12/15. **Types of Aid:** *Need-based scholarships/grants:* College/university scholarship or grant aid from institutional funds; Federal Nursing Scholarships; Federal Pell; Private scholarships; SEOG; State scholarships/grants. *Loans:* Direct PLUS loans; Direct Subsidized Stafford Loans; Direct Unsubsidized Stafford Loans. **Student Employment:** Federal Work-Study Program available. Institutional employment available. **Financial Aid Statistics:** 100% needy freshmen, 99% needy undergrads receive need-based scholarship or grant aid. 13% freshmen, 11% undergrads receive non-need-based scholarship or grant aid. 75% freshmen, 80% undergrads receive need-based self-help aid. 9% freshmen, 6% undergrads receive athletic scholarships. 100% freshmen, 98% undergrads receive any aid. 78% undergrads borrow to pay for school. **Criteria awarding aid:** *Need-based:* Leadership. *Non-need-based:* Academics, Alumni affiliation, Art, Athletics, Leadership, Minority status, Music/drama, Religious affiliation.

TRINITY COLLEGE (CT)

300 Summit Street, Hartford, CT 06016
Phone: 860-297-2180 **Financial Aid Phone:** 860-297-2047
E-mail: admissions.office@trincoll.edu **CEEB Code:** 3899
Fax: 860-297-2287 **Website:** www.trincoll.edu **ACT Code:** 598

This private school was founded in 1823. It has a 100 acre campus.

RATINGS

Admissions Selectivity Rating: 92   **Fire Safety Rating:** 95   **Green Rating:** 76

STUDENTS AND FACULTY

Enrollment: 2,225. **Student Body:** 48% female, 52% male, 80% out-of-state, 10% international (62 countries represented). Asian 4%, African American 6%, Caucasian 65%, Hispanic 7%, Native American <1%, Pacific Islander 0%, Two or more races 3%, Race unknown 5%.
Retention and Graduation: 90% freshmen return for sophomore year. 19% grads go on to further study within 1 year. 10% grads pursue arts and sciences degrees. 4% grads pursue law degrees. 1% grads pursue business degrees. 1% grads pursue medical degrees. **Faculty:** Student/faculty ratio 9:1. 207 full-time faculty, 92% hold PhDs, 18% are members of minority groups, 46% are women. 0% of classes are taught by teaching assistants.

ACADEMICS

Degrees: Bachelor's; Master's. **Classes:** Most classes have 10–19 students. Most lab/discussion sessions have 10–19 students. **Most popular majors:** English Language and Literature, General; Economics, General; Political Science and Government, General. **Special Study Options:** Accelerated program; Cross-registration; Double major; Exchange student program (domestic); Honors program; Independent study; Internships; Student-designed major; Study abroad; Teacher certification program. **Combined degree programs:** BA/MEng. **Disability Services offered:** Note-taking services; Reader services; Tape recorders; Tutors. **Career services:** Alumni network; Alumni services; Career assessment; Career/job search classes; Internships; Regional alumni.

FACILITIES

Housing: Coed dorms; Fraternity/sorority housing; Special housing for disabled students; Theme housing; Wellness housing 60% of campus accessible to physically disabled. **Special Academic Facilities/Equipment:** Watkinson Library; Austin Arts Center.

CAMPUS LIFE

Environment: Metropolis. **Activities:** Campus Ministries; Choral groups; Dance; Drama/theater; International Student Organization; Jazz band; Literary magazine; Model UN; Music ensembles; Musical theater; Radio station; Student government; Student newspaper; Student-run film society; Yearbook. 105 registered organizations, 5 honor societies, 6 religious organizations, 7 fraternities, 3 sororities on campus. **Athletics (Intercollegiate):** *Men:* baseball, basketball, crew/rowing, cross-country, diving, football, golf, ice hockey, lacrosse, soccer, squash, swimming, tennis, track/field (outdoor), track/field (indoor), wrestling. *Women:* basketball, crew/rowing, cross-country, diving, field hockey, ice hockey, lacrosse, soccer, softball, squash, swimming, tennis, track/field (outdoor), track/field (indoor), volleyball. **On-Campus Highlights:** The Learning Corridor. **Environmental Initiatives:** Reduced energy consumption in the dining halls through automated lighting and low-draw fume hoods as well as a new Building Automation System to increase control of temperatures on campus.

ADMISSIONS

Freshman Academic Profile: 50% in top 10% of high school class, 78% in top 25% of high school class, 96% in top 50% of high school class. 42% from public high schools. **Test Scores:** SAT Math middle 50% range 610–690. SAT EBRW middle 50% range 600–680. ACT middle 50% range 28–32. **Basis for Candidate Selection:** *Very important factors include:* rigor of secondary school record, character/personal qualities. *Important factors include:* academic GPA, application essay, recommendation(s), extracurricular activities, talent/ability. *Other factors include:* class rank, standardized test scores, interview, first generation, alumni/ae relation, racial/ethnic status, volunteer work, work experience. **Freshman Admission Requirements:** High school diploma is required and GED is accepted. *Academic units required:* 4 English, 3 math, 2 science, 2 science labs, 3 foreign language, 2 history. **Freshman Admission Statistics:** 6,073 applied, 34% admitted, 28% enrolled. **Transfer Admission Requirements:** High school transcript, college transcript(s), essay or personal statement, standardized test scores, statement of good standing from prior institution(s). Minimum college GPA of 3.0 required. Lowest grade transferable C-. **General Admission Information:** Application fee $65. Regular application deadline 1/1. Non-fall registration accepted. Admission may be deferred for a maximum of 1 year.

COSTS AND FINANCIAL AID

Annual tuition $52,280. Room and board $14,200. Required fees $2,490. Average book and supplies expense $1,000. **Required Forms and Deadlines:** CSS/Financial Aid PROFILE; FAFSA; Noncustodial PROFILE. **Notification of Awards:** Applicants will be notified of awards on or about 4/1. **Types of Aid:** *Need-based scholarships/grants:* College/university scholarship or grant aid from institutional funds; Federal Pell; Private scholarships; SEOG; State scholarships/grants. *Loans:* Direct PLUS loans; Direct Subsidized Stafford Loans; Direct Unsubsidized Stafford Loans. **Student Employment:** Federal Work-Study Program available. Institutional employment available. **Financial Aid Statistics:** 97% needy freshmen, 97% needy undergrads receive need-based scholarship or grant aid. 4% freshmen, 6% undergrads receive non-need-based scholarship or grant aid. 59% freshmen, 68% undergrads receive need-based self-help aid. 0% freshmen, 0% undergrads receive athletic scholarships. 49% freshmen, 45% undergrads receive any aid. 43% undergrads borrow to pay for school. Average cumulative indebtedness $29,506. **Criteria awarding aid:** *Non-need-based:* Academics, Leadership.

TRINITY COLLEGE DUBLIN

Academic Registry, Watts Building, Dublin, IR
Phone: 35318964500
E-mail: academic.registry@tcd.ie
Website: www.tcd.ie

This public school was founded in 1592. It has a 47 acre campus.

RATINGS

Admissions Selectivity Rating: 87   **Fire Safety Rating:** 90   **Green Rating:** 64

STUDENTS AND FACULTY

Enrollment: 11,839. **Student Body:** 60% female, 40% male, 15% out-of-state,(122 countries represented).
Retention and Graduation: 91% freshmen return for sophomore year.
Faculty: Student/faculty ratio 17:1. 864 full-time faculty, 8% hold PhDs, 0% are members of minority groups, 0% are women. 10% of classes are taught by teaching assistants.

ACADEMICS

Degrees: Bachelor's; Doctoral degree—professional practice; Doctoral degree research/scholarship; Master's; Post-master's certificate. **Special Study Options:** Cross-registration; Double major; English as a Second Language (ESL); Exchange student program (domestic); Honors program; Internships; Liberal arts/career combination; Study abroad; Teacher certification program. **Honors programs:** All degrees conferred by the University of Dublin are Honors Degrees. There are over 400 four-year full-time degree programs on offer at the University for undergraduate students. **Disability Services offered:** Note-taking services; Reader services; Tape recorders; Tutors. **Career services:** Alumni network; Alumni services; Career assessment; Career/job search classes; Internships; Regional alumni.

FACILITIES

Housing: Apartments for married students; Apartments for single students; Coed dorms; Special housing for disabled students; Special housing for international students. **Special Academic Facilities/Equipment:** Science Gallery (www.sciencegallery.com). Zoology Museum (http://www.tcd.ie/Zoology/museum/). Geology Museum(http://www.tcd.ie/Geology/museum/). Douglas Hyde Art Gallery (www.douglashydegallery.com). Book of Kells Exhibition (http://www.tcd.ie/Library/bookofkells/).

CAMPUS LIFE

Environment: Metropolis. **Activities:** Campus Ministries; Choral groups; Concert band; Dance; Drama/theater; International Student Organization; Jazz band; Literary magazine; Music ensembles; Musical theater; Radio station; Student government; Student newspaper; Student-run film society; Symphony

orchestra; Television station. 160 registered organizations on campus. **On-Campus Highlights:** Science Gallery

ADMISSIONS

Basis for Candidate Selection: *Very important factors include:* rigor of secondary school record, academic GPA, standardized test scores. *Important factors include:* application essay, recommendation(s). *Other factors include:* extracurricular activities, character/personal qualities, volunteer work, work experience, level of applicant's interest. **Freshman Admission Requirements:** High school diploma is required and GED is not accepted. **Freshman Admission Statistics:** 18,995 applied, 16% admitted, 93% enrolled. **General Admission Information:** Application fee $35. Priority deadline 2/1. Regular application deadline 6/1. Admission may be deferred for a maximum of 1 year.

COSTS AND FINANCIAL AID

Annual in-state tuition $19,000. Room and board $9,300. **Required Forms and Deadlines:** FAFSA. **Types of Aid:** *Need-based scholarships/grants:* Private scholarships; State scholarships/grants. *Loans:* Direct PLUS loans; Direct Subsidized Stafford Loans; Direct Unsubsidized Stafford Loans. **Criteria awarding aid:** *Non-need-based:* Academics, Leadership.

TRINITY COLLEGE OF FLORIDA

2430 Welbilt Boulevard, Trinity, FL 34655
Phone: 727-569-1411 **Financial Aid Phone:** 727-569-1413
E-mail: admissions@trinitycollege.edu **CEEB Code:** 030282
Fax: 727-569-1410 **Website:** www.trinitycollege.edu **ACT Code:** 4876

This private school, affiliated with the Interdenominational, was founded in 1932. It has a 40 acre campus.

RATINGS

Admissions Selectivity Rating: 76   **Fire Safety Rating:** 86   **Green Rating:** 60*

STUDENTS AND FACULTY

Enrollment: 210. **Student Body:** 39% female, 61% male, 28% out-of-state, 1% international (2 countries represented). Asian <1%, African American 18%, Caucasian 64%, Hispanic 16%, Native American <1%, Race unknown 0%.
Retention and Graduation: 67% freshmen return for sophomore year. 14% grads go on to further study within 1 year. **Faculty:** Student/faculty ratio 14:1. 6 full-time faculty, 83% hold PhDs, 0% are members of minority groups, 17% are women. 0% of classes are taught by teaching assistants.

ACADEMICS

Degrees: Associate; Bachelor's; Certificate; Terminal Associate. **Classes:** Most classes have fewer than 10 students. **Most popular majors:** Pastoral Studies/Counseling; Youth Ministry; Pre-Theology/Pre-Ministerial Studies. **Special Study Options:** Accelerated program; Double major; Dual enrollment; Honors program; Independent study; Internships; Weekend college. **Honors programs:** Our honors program consists of 4 Great Books Seminars. **Disability Services offered:** Tutors. **Career services:** Career assessment; Internships.

FACILITIES

Housing: Men's dorms; Special housing for disabled students; Women's dorms; 100% of campus accessible to physically disabled.

CAMPUS LIFE

Environment: City. **Activities:** Campus Ministries; Choral groups; Drama/theater; Student government; Yearbook. 4 religious organizations on campus. **Athletics (Intercollegiate):** *Men:* basketball. *Women:* volleyball. **On-Campus Highlights:** Epiphanies Coffee Shop.

ADMISSIONS

Freshman Academic Profile: Average high school GPA 2.8. **Test Scores:** SAT Math middle 50% range 370–480. SAT EBRW middle 50% range 460–550. ACT middle 50% range 19–23. **Basis for Candidate Selection:** *Very important factors include:* academic GPA, application essay, standardized test scores, recommendation(s), religious affiliation/commitment. *Important factors include:* character/personal qualities. *Other factors include:* extracurricular activities. **Freshman Admission Requirements:** High school diploma is required and GED is accepted. *Academic units required:* 4 English, 4 math, 4 science, 2 foreign language, 2 social studies, 2 history. **Freshman Admission Statistics:** 79 applied, 85% admitted, 49% enrolled. **Transfer Admission Requirements:** High school transcript, college transcript(s), essay or personal statement. Minimum college GPA of 2.0 required. Lowest grade transferable C. **General**

Admission Information: Application fee $25. Regular application deadline 8/2. Non-fall registration accepted. Admission may be deferred for a maximum of 1 year.

COSTS AND FINANCIAL AID
Annual tuition $11,024. Room and board $6,656. Required fees $800. Average book and supplies expense $1,185. **Required Forms and Deadlines:** FAFSA; Institution's own financial aid form. **Types of Aid:** *Need-based scholarships/grants:* College/university scholarship or grant aid from institutional funds; Federal Pell; Private scholarships; SEOG; State scholarships/grants. **Student Employment:** Federal Work-Study Program available. Institutional employment available. **Financial Aid Statistics:** 100% needy freshmen, 86% needy undergrads receive need-based scholarship or grant aid. 100% freshmen, 74% undergrads receive non-need-based scholarship or grant aid. 75% freshmen, 79% undergrads receive need-based self-help aid. 0% freshmen, 0% undergrads receive athletic scholarships. 99% freshmen, 99% undergrads receive any aid. **Criteria awarding aid:** *Need-based:* Academics. *Non-need-based:* Academics, Music/drama.

TRINITY INTERNATIONAL UNIVERSITY

2065 Half Day Road, Deerfield, IL 60015
Phone: 847-317-7000 **Financial Aid Phone:** 847-317-7033
E-mail: tcadmissions@tiu.edu **CEEB Code:** 1810
Fax: 847-317-8097 **Website:** www.tiu.edu **ACT Code:** 1150

This private school was founded in 1897. It has a 111 acre campus.

RATINGS
Admissions Selectivity Rating: 76   **Fire Safety Rating:** 82   **Green Rating:** 60*

STUDENTS AND FACULTY
Enrollment: 950. **Student Body:** 57% female, 43% male, 41% out-of-state, 1% international (38 countries represented). Asian 5%, African American 17%, Caucasian 63%, Hispanic 4%, Native American <1%, Pacific Islander, Two or more races, Race unknown 10%.
Retention and Graduation: 66% freshmen return for sophomore year. 32% grads go on to further study within 1 year. **Faculty:** Student/faculty ratio 12:1. 43 full-time faculty, 84% hold PhDs, 14% are members of minority groups, 42% are women. 0% of classes are taught by teaching assistants.

ACADEMICS
Degrees: Bachelor's; Certificate; Master's; Post-bachelor's certificate. **Classes:** Most classes have 10–19 students. Most lab/discussion sessions have 10–19 students. **Most popular majors:** Business/Commerce, General; Theology and Religious Vocations, Other; Elementary Education and Teaching. **Special Study Options:** Cross-registration; Double major; Dual enrollment; Honors program; Independent study; Internships; Study abroad; Teacher certification program. **Honors programs:** Trinity has adopted a model for an Honors Program that is intended to enhance the breadth and depth of your liberal-arts learning, but without the burden of many additional requirements. Hence, you will do honors work in the areas of your disciplinary major, general education, and special interdisciplinary classes, but virtually all of your honors work will also fulfill regular Trinity requirements. **Combined degree programs:** BA/MA. **Disability Services offered:** Note-taking services; Reader services; Tape recorders; Tutors. **Career services:** Alumni services; Career assessment; Career/job search classes; Internships.

FACILITIES
Housing: Apartments for married students; Apartments for single students; Men's dorms; Special housing for disabled students; Women's dorms; 75% of campus accessible to physically disabled.

CAMPUS LIFE
Environment: Village. **Activities:** Campus Ministries; Choral groups; Concert band; Drama/theater; Jazz band; Music ensembles; Musical theater; Pep band; Student government; Student newspaper; Symphony orchestra; Yearbook. 33 registered organizations, 2 honor societies on campus. **Athletics (Intercollegiate):** *Men:* baseball, basketball, football, soccer. *Women:* basketball, soccer, softball, volleyball. **On-Campus Highlights:** Lew Student Center.

ADMISSIONS
Freshman Academic Profile: Average high school GPA 3.3. 37% in top 10% of high school class, 43% in top 25% of high school class, 68% in top 50% of high school class. 69% from public high schools. **Test Scores:** SAT Math

middle 50% range 440–600. SAT EBRW middle 50% range 445–610. ACT middle 50% range 19–26. **Basis for Candidate Selection:** *Very important factors include:* class rank, academic GPA, application essay, standardized test scores, recommendation(s), character/personal qualities, religious affiliation/commitment. *Other factors include:* rigor of secondary school record, extracurricular activities, talent/ability, first generation. **Freshman Admission Requirements:** High school diploma is required and GED is accepted. *Academic units required:* 4 English, 2 math, 2 science, 1 science labs, 2 foreign language, 2 social studies, 2 history, 2 visual/performing arts. **Freshman Admission Statistics:** 466 applied, 80% admitted, 36% enrolled. **Transfer Admission Requirements:** High school transcript, college transcript(s), essay or personal statement, statement of good standing from prior institution(s). Minimum college GPA of 2.0 required. Lowest grade transferable C-. **General Admission Information:** Application fee $25. Non-fall registration accepted. Admission may be deferred for a maximum of 12 months.

COSTS AND FINANCIAL AID
Annual tuition $21,980. Room and board $7,430. Required fees $390. **Required Forms and Deadlines:** FAFSA. **Notification of Awards:** Applicants will be notified of awards on a rolling basis beginning 2/15. **Types of Aid:** *Need-based scholarships/grants:* College/university scholarship or grant aid from institutional funds; Federal Pell; Private scholarships; SEOG; State scholarships/grants. **Student Employment:** Federal Work-Study Program available. Institutional employment available. **Financial Aid Statistics:** 95% needy freshmen, 95% needy undergrads receive need-based scholarship or grant aid. 95% freshmen, 95% undergrads receive non-need-based scholarship or grant aid. 82% freshmen, 78% undergrads receive need-based self-help aid. 0% freshmen, 0% undergrads receive athletic scholarships. 90% freshmen, 86% undergrads receive any aid. **Criteria awarding aid:** *Non-need-based:* Academics, Alumni affiliation, Athletics, Minority status, Music/drama, Religious affiliation.

TRINITY UNIVERSITY

Northrup Hall Room 140, San Antonio, TX 78212-7200
Phone: 210-999-7207 **Financial Aid Phone:** (210) 999-8898
E-mail: admissions@trinity.edu **CEEB Code:** 6831
Fax: 210-999-8164 **Website:** www.trinity.edu **ACT Code:** 4226

This private school, affiliated with the Presbyterian Church, was founded in 1869. It has a 117 acre campus.

RATINGS
Admissions Selectivity Rating: 93   **Fire Safety Rating:** 94   **Green Rating:** 72

STUDENTS AND FACULTY
Enrollment: 2,465. **Student Body:** 53% female, 47% male, 24% out-of-state, 5% international (61 countries represented). Asian 7%, African American 4%, Caucasian 57%, Hispanic 21%, Native American 1%, Pacific Islander <1%, Two or more races 4%, Race unknown 2%.
Retention and Graduation: 91% freshmen return for sophomore year. 72% freshmen graduate within 4 years. 80% freshmen graduate within 6 years. 27% grads go on to further study within 1 year. 1% grads pursue law degrees. 2% grads pursue medical degrees. **Faculty:** Student/faculty ratio 9:1. 253 full-time faculty, 95% hold PhDs, 22% are members of minority groups, 43% are women. 0% of classes are taught by teaching assistants.

ACADEMICS
Degrees: Bachelor's; Master's. **Classes:** Most classes have 10–19 students. Most lab/discussion sessions have 10–19 students. **Most popular majors:** Business Administration and Management, General; Finance, General; Mass Communication/Media Studies. **Special Study Options:** Accelerated program; Double major; Honors program; Independent study; Internships; Liberal arts/career combination; Student-designed major; Study abroad; Teacher certification program. **Honors programs:** Honors Program. **Combined degree programs:** BA/MA. **Disability Services offered:** Note-taking services; Reader services; Tape recorders; Tutors. **Career services:** Alumni network; Alumni services; Career assessment; Career/job search classes; Internships; Regional alumni.

FACILITIES

Housing: Coed dorms; Fraternity/sorority housing; Special housing for disabled students; Theme housing; Wellness housing; 99% of campus accessible to physically disabled. **Special Academic Facilities/Equipment:** Center for the Sciences & Innovation, Steiren Theatre, Richardson Communication Center, KRTU Radio Station, TigerTV Television Station, Ruth Taylor Arts Complex including art gallery, Laurie Auditorium.

CAMPUS LIFE

Environment: Metropolis. **Activities:** Campus Ministries; Choral groups; Concert band; Dance; Drama/theater; International Student Organization; Jazz band; Literary magazine; Model UN; Music ensembles; Musical theater; Opera; Pep band; Radio station; Student government; Student newspaper; Student-run film society; Symphony orchestra; Television station; Yearbook. 92 registered organizations, 7 honor societies, 10 religious organizations, 7 fraternities, 7 sororities on campus. **Athletics (Intercollegiate):** *Men:* baseball, basketball, cross-country, diving, football, golf, soccer, swimming, tennis, track/field (outdoor). *Women:* basketball, cross-country, diving, golf, soccer, softball, swimming, tennis, track/field (outdoor), volleyball. **On-Campus Highlights:** Center for the Sciences and Innovation.

ADMISSIONS

Freshman Academic Profile: Average high school GPA 3.6. 42% in top 10% of high school class, 76% in top 25% of high school class, 96% in top 50% of high school class. 68% from public high schools. **Test Scores:** SAT Math middle 50% range 630–720. SAT EBRW middle 50% range 630–710. ACT middle 50% range 28–32. **Basis for Candidate Selection:** *Very important factors include:* rigor of secondary school record, class rank, academic GPA, standardized test scores. *Important factors include:* application essay, recommendation(s), interview, extracurricular activities, talent/ability, character/personal qualities. *Other factors include:* first generation, alumni/ae relation, geographical residence, volunteer work, work experience, level of applicant's interest. **Freshman Admission Requirements:** High school diploma is required and GED is accepted. *Academic units required:* 4 English, 3 math, 3 science, 2 science labs, 2 foreign language, 3 social studies. *Academic units recommended:* 4 English, 3 math, 3 science, 2 science labs, 2 foreign language, 3 social studies. **Freshman Admission Statistics:** 8,654 applied, 34% admitted, 23% enrolled. **Transfer Admission Requirements:** High school transcript, college transcript(s), essay or personal statement, statement of good standing from prior institution(s). Minimum college GPA of 3.0 required. Lowest grade transferable C-. **General Admission Information:** Regular application deadline 2/1. Non-fall registration accepted.

COSTS AND FINANCIAL AID

Annual tuition $42,360. Room and board $13,464. Required fees $616. Average book and supplies expense $1,000. **Required Forms and Deadlines:** CSS/Financial Aid PROFILE; FAFSA. **Notification of Awards:** Applicants will be notified of awards on or about 3/15. **Types of Aid:** *Need-based scholarships/grants:* College/university scholarship or grant aid from institutional funds; Federal Pell; Private scholarships; SEOG; State scholarships/grants. *Loans:* Direct PLUS loans; Direct Subsidized Stafford Loans; Direct Unsubsidized Stafford Loans. **Student Employment:** Federal Work-Study Program available. Institutional employment available. **Financial Aid Statistics:** 100% needy freshmen, 99% needy undergrads receive need-based scholarship or grant aid. 31% freshmen, 19% undergrads receive non-need-based scholarship or grant aid. 55% freshmen, 62% undergrads receive need-based self-help aid. 0% freshmen, 0% undergrads receive athletic scholarships. 99% freshmen, 97% undergrads receive any aid. 44% undergrads borrow to pay for school. Average cumulative indebtedness $42,036. **Criteria awarding aid:** *Need-based:* Academics. *Non-need-based:* Academics, Art, Leadership, Music/drama.

TROY UNIVERSITY

111 Adams Administration, Troy, AL 36082
Phone: 334-670-3179 **Financial Aid Phone:** 334-670-3186
E-mail: admit@troy.edu **CEEB Code:** 1738
Fax: 334-670-3733 **Website:** www.troy.edu **ACT Code:** 48

This public school was founded in 1887. It has a 906 acre campus.

RATINGS

Admissions Selectivity Rating: 74   **Fire Safety Rating:** 94   **Green Rating:** 60*

STUDENTS AND FACULTY

Enrollment: 13,147. **Student Body:** 62% female, 38% male, 29% out-of-state, 5% international. Asian 1%, African American 31%, Caucasian 52%, Hispanic 4%, Native American 1%, Pacific Islander <1%, Two or more races 3%, Race unknown 4%.
Retention and Graduation: 73% freshmen return for sophomore year. 18% freshmen graduate within 4 years. 39% freshmen graduate within 6 years.
Faculty: Student/faculty ratio 17:1. 534 full-time faculty, 76% hold PhDs, 10% are members of minority groups, 51% are women. 1% of classes are taught by teaching assistants.

ACADEMICS

Degrees: Associate; Bachelor's; Certificate; Doctoral degree—professional practice; Master's; Post-bachelor's certificate; Post-master's certificate. **Classes:** Most classes have fewer than 10 students. Most lab/discussion sessions have 20–29 students. **Most popular majors:** Psychology, General; Business Administration and Management, General; Accounting. **Special Study Options:** Accelerated program; Cross-registration; Distance learning; Double major; Dual enrollment; English as a Second Language (ESL); External degree program; Honors program; Independent study; Internships; Study abroad; Teacher certification program; Weekend college. **Honors programs:** The University Honors Program, open to students in all undergraduate divisions of the university, is administered by the Honors Council and the director of university honors. The purpose of the University Honors Program is to offer the academically superior student a specially designed program, within a supportive community, that fosters critical thinking, intellectual development and social responsibility. This enhanced program is designed to provide a balance of common experience and flexibility addressed to individual achievement as well as a comprehensive framework on which to build disciplinary studies. The Honors Program also has an honors house on campus which houses both male and female students. Students should consult with the director of the University Honors Program and the director of University Housing for availabilities and stipulations. The house serves as a residence and a focal point for meetings and activities with the Honors Alliance, faculty and staff in the Honors Program. The official student voice within the program is the University Honors Alliance. Membership to the University Honors Alliance is offered to any student with a 3.3 grade point average or higher. There is an annual membership fee of $5. **Disability Services offered:** Note-taking services; Reader services; Tape recorders; Tutors. **Career services:** Alumni network; Alumni services; Career assessment; Career/job search classes.

FACILITIES

Housing: Apartments for married students; Apartments for single students; Coed dorms; Fraternity/sorority housing; Men's dorms; Special housing for international students; Women's dorms; 95% of campus accessible to physically disabled. **Special Academic Facilities/Equipment:** Art museum, recording studio. **Campus network:** 100% of classrooms, 100% of dorms, 100% of student union, 100% of libraries, 100% of dining areas, 100% of common outdoor areas have wireless network access.

CAMPUS LIFE

Environment: Town. **Activities:** Campus Ministries; Choral groups; Concert band; Dance; Drama/theater; International Student Organization; Jazz band; Literary magazine; Marching band; Music ensembles; Musical theater; Pep band; Radio station; Student government; Student newspaper; Student-run film society; Symphony orchestra; Television station; Yearbook. 125 registered organizations, 27 honor societies, 11 religious organization, 13 fraternities, 9 sororities on campus. **Athletics (Intercollegiate):** *Men:* baseball, basketball, cheerleading, cross-country, football, golf, rodeo, tennis, track/field (outdoor). *Women:* basketball, cheerleading, cross-country, golf, rodeo, soccer, softball, tennis, track/field (outdoor), volleyball. **On-Campus Highlights:** Veterans Memorial Stadium. **Environmental Initiatives:** Recycling.

ADMISSIONS

Freshman Academic Profile: Average high school GPA 3.4. **Test Scores:** SAT Math middle 50% range 470–565. ACT middle 50% range 18–24. **Basis for Candidate Selection:** *Very important factors include:* rigor of secondary school record, academic GPA, standardized test scores. **Freshman Admission Requirements:** High school diploma is required and GED is accepted. *Academic units required:* 3 English. **Freshman Admission Statistics:** 7,332 applied, 88% admitted, 30% enrolled. **Transfer Admission Requirements:** College transcript(s). Minimum college GPA of 2.0 required. Lowest grade transferable D. **General Admission Information:** Application fee $30. Non-fall registration accepted. Admission may be deferred for a maximum of 1 year.

COSTS AND FINANCIAL AID

Annual in-state tuition $10,415. Annual out-of-state tuition $20,830. Room and board $8,185. Required fees $2,045. Average book and supplies expense $1,138. **Required Forms and Deadlines:** FAFSA; Institution's own financial aid form. **Notification of Awards:** Applicants will be notified of awards on a rolling basis beginning 5/1. **Types of Aid:** *Need-based scholarships/grants:* College/university scholarship or grant aid from institutional funds; Federal Pell; Private scholarships; SEOG; State scholarships/grants. **Student Employment:** Federal Work-Study Program available. **Financial Aid Statistics:** 56% needy freshmen, 62% needy undergrads receive need-based scholarship or grant aid. 63% freshmen, 51% undergrads receive non-need-based scholarship or grant aid. 99% freshmen, 99% undergrads receive need-based self-help aid. 2% freshmen, 2% undergrads receive athletic scholarships. 96% freshmen, 90% undergrads receive any aid. 50% undergrads borrow to pay for school. Average cumulative indebtedness $3,048. **Criteria awarding aid:** *Need-based:* Academics. *Non-need-based:* Academics, Athletics, Leadership, Music/drama.

TRUMAN STATE UNIVERSITY

100 E. Normal Ave., Kirksville, MO 63501
Phone: 660-785-4114 **Financial Aid Phone:** 660-785-4130
E-mail: admissions@truman.edu **CEEB Code:** 6483
Fax: 660-785-7456 **Website:** http://www.truman.edu **ACT Code:** 2336

This public school was founded in 1867. It has a 140 acre campus.

RATINGS

Admissions Selectivity Rating: 89   **Fire Safety Rating:** 98   **Green Rating:** 60*

STUDENTS AND FACULTY

Enrollment: 4,384. **Student Body:** 60% female, 40% male, 15% out-of-state, 8% international (48 countries represented). Asian 3%, African American 4%, Caucasian 77%, Hispanic 3%, Native American <1%, Pacific Islander <1%, Two or more races 4%, Race unknown 1%.
Retention and Graduation: 84% freshmen return for sophomore year. 60% freshmen graduate within 4 years. 75% freshmen graduate within 6 years. 31% grads go on to further study within 1 year. **Faculty:** Student/faculty ratio 15:1. 295 full-time faculty, 86% hold PhDs, 14% are members of minority groups, 43% are women. 1% of classes are taught by teaching assistants.

ACADEMICS

Degrees: Bachelor's; Master's; Post-bachelor's certificate. **Classes:** Most classes have 20–29 students. Most lab/discussion sessions have 10–19 students. **Most popular majors:** Biology/Biological Sciences, General; Business Administration and Management, General; Exercise Science and Kinesiology. **Special Study Options:** Double major; Dual enrollment; English as a Second Language (ESL); Honors program; Independent study; Internships; Student-designed major; Study abroad; Teacher certification program. **Honors programs:** Honors Scholar Program: Students must complete five upper-level courses in math, social science, science, and humanities with a 3.5 GPA in these 5 courses. Departmental honors are also available in some disciplines. **Disability Services offered:** Note-taking services; Reader services; Tape recorders; Tutors. **Career services:** Alumni network; Alumni services; Career assessment; Career/job search classes; Internships; Regional alumni.

FACILITIES

Housing: Apartments for married students; Apartments for single students; Coed dorms; Fraternity/sorority housing; Theme housing; 99% of campus accessible to physically disabled. **Special Academic Facilities/Equipment:** Planetarium, art gallery, local history and artifacts museum, human performance lab, greenhouse, observatory, and convergent media center (TV studio, newspaper, and radio station). **Campus network:** 100% of classrooms, 100% of dorms, 100% of student union, 100% of libraries, 100% of dining areas, 60% of common outdoor areas have wireless network access.

CAMPUS LIFE

Environment: Village. **Activities:** Campus Ministries; Choral groups; Concert band; Dance; Drama/theater; International Student Organization; Jazz band; Literary magazine; Marching band; Model UN; Music ensembles; Musical theater; Opera; Pep band; Radio station; Student government; Student newspaper; Student-run film society; Symphony orchestra; Television station. 247 registered organizations, 18 honor societies, 17 religious organizations, 12 fraternities, 6 sororities on campus. **Athletics (Intercollegiate):** *Men:* baseball, basketball, cross-country, football, golf, soccer, swimming, tennis, track/field (outdoor), track/field (indoor), wrestling. *Women:* basketball, cross-country, golf, soccer, softball, swimming, tennis, track/field (outdoor), track/field (indoor), volleyball. **On-Campus Highlights:** Student Recreation Center.

ADMISSIONS

Freshman Academic Profile: Average high school GPA 3.8. 57% in top 10% of high school class, 82% in top 25% of high school class, 97% in top 50% of high school class. 86% from public high schools. **Test Scores:** SAT Math middle 50% range 570–670. SAT EBRW middle 50% range 580–680. ACT middle 50% range 24–31. **Basis for Candidate Selection:** *Very important factors include:* rigor of secondary school record, class rank, academic GPA, standardized test scores. *Important factors include:* application essay, *Other factors include:* recommendation(s), extracurricular activities, talent/ability, character/personal qualities, first generation, alumni/ae relation, geographical residence, state residency, racial/ethnic status, volunteer work, work experience, level of applicant's interest. **Freshman Admission Requirements:** High school diploma is required and GED is accepted. *Academic units required:* 4 English, 3 math, 3 science, 2 science labs, 2 foreign language, 2 social studies, 1 history, 5 academic electives, 1 visual/performing arts, 3 unit from above areas or other academic areas. *Academic units recommended:* 4 English, 4 math, 3 science, 2 science labs, 2 foreign language, 2 social studies, 1 history, 5 academic electives, 1 visual/performing arts, 3 unit from above areas or other academic areas. **Freshman Admission Statistics:** 4,595 applied, 63% admitted, 31% enrolled. **Transfer Admission Requirements:** College transcript(s), essay or personal statement. **General Admission Information:** Priority deadline 12/1. Non-fall registration accepted.

COSTS AND FINANCIAL AID

Annual in-state tuition $7,796. Annual out-of-state tuition $14,990. Room and board $9,012. Required fees $674. Average book and supplies expense $1,000. **Required Forms and Deadlines:** FAFSA. **Notification of Awards:** Applicants will be notified of awards on a rolling basis beginning 1/1. **Types of Aid:** *Need-based scholarships/grants:* College/university scholarship or grant aid from institutional funds; Federal Pell; Private scholarships; SEOG; State scholarships/grants. *Loans:* Direct PLUS loans; Direct Subsidized Stafford Loans; Direct Unsubsidized Stafford Loans. **Student Employment:** Federal Work-Study Program available. Institutional employment available. **Financial Aid Statistics:** 99% needy freshmen, 95% needy undergrads receive need-based scholarship or grant aid. 98% freshmen, 82% undergrads receive non-need-based scholarship or grant aid. 67% freshmen, 76% undergrads receive need-based self-help aid. 7% freshmen, 6% undergrads receive athletic scholarships. 99.36% freshmen, 84.71% undergrads receive any aid. 52% undergrads borrow to pay for school. Average cumulative indebtedness $25,660. **Criteria awarding aid:** *Need-based:* Academics. *Non-need-based:* Academics, Alumni affiliation, Art, Athletics, Leadership, Minority status, Music/drama, State/district residency.

TUFTS UNIVERSITY

Bendetson Hall, Medford, MA 02155
Phone: 617-627-3170 **Financial Aid Phone:** 617-627-2000
E-mail: undergraduate.admissions@tufts.edu **CEEB Code:** 3901
Fax: 617-627-3860 **Website:** www.tufts.edu **ACT Code:** 1922

This private school was founded in 1852. It has a 150 acre campus.

RATINGS

Admissions Selectivity Rating: 98   **Fire Safety Rating:** 99   **Green Rating:** 88

STUDENTS AND FACULTY

Enrollment: 5,828. **Student Body:** 53% female, 47% male, 75% out-of-state, 11% international (74 countries represented). Asian 14%, African American 4%, Caucasian 53%, Hispanic 7%, Native American <1%, Pacific Islander <1%, Two or more races 5%, Race unknown 4%.
Retention and Graduation: 96% freshmen return for sophomore year. 88% freshmen graduate within 4 years. 94% freshmen graduate within 6 years. 14% grads go on to further study within 1 year. **Faculty:** Student/faculty ratio 9:1. 653 full-time faculty, 93% hold PhDs, 21% are members of minority groups, 47% are women. 1% of classes are taught by teaching assistants.

ACADEMICS

Degrees: Bachelor's; Certificate; Doctoral degree—professional practice; Doctoral degree research/scholarship; Master's; Post-bachelor's certificate; Post-master's certificate. **Classes:** Most classes have 10–19 students. Most lab/discussion sessions have 10–19 students. **Most popular majors:** International Relations and Affairs; Economics; Computer Science. **Special Study Options:** Cooperative education program; Cross-registration; Double major; Dual enrollment; Exchange student program (domestic); Independent study; Internships; Liberal arts/career combination; Student-designed major; Study abroad; Teacher certification program. **Combined degree programs:** BA/DDS; BA/MA; BA/MD; BA/MEng. **Disability Services offered:** Note-taking services; Reader services; Tape recorders; Tutors. **Career services:** Alumni network; Alumni services; Career assessment; Career/job search classes; Internships; Regional alumni.

FACILITIES

Housing: Apartments for single students; Coed dorms; Cooperative housing; Fraternity/sorority housing; Special housing for disabled students; Special housing for international students; Theme housing; Wellness housing; Women's dorms **Special Academic Facilities/Equipment:** Language lab, nutrition institute, research lab for physical electronics, bioelectrical and biochemical labs, computer-aided design (CAD) facility, electro-optics technology and environmental management centers.

CAMPUS LIFE

Environment: Metropolis. **Activities:** Campus Ministries; Choral groups; Concert band; Dance; Drama/theater; International Student Organization; Jazz band; Literary magazine; Model UN; Music ensembles; Musical theater; Opera; Pep band; Radio station; Student government; Student newspaper; Student-run film society; Symphony orchestra; Television station; Yearbook. 325 registered organizations, 5 honor societies, 20 religious organizations, 7 fraternities, 3 sororities on campus. **Athletics (Intercollegiate):** *Men:* baseball, basketball, crew/rowing, cross-country, diving, football, golf, ice hockey, lacrosse, sailing, soccer, squash, swimming, tennis, track/field (outdoor), track/field (indoor). *Women:* basketball, cheerleading, crew/rowing, cross-country, diving, fencing, field hockey, golf, lacrosse, sailing, soccer, softball, squash, swimming, tennis, track/field (outdoor), track/field (indoor), volleyball. **On-Campus Highlights:** The Aidekman Arts Center. **Environmental Initiatives:** Reduced green house gas emissions to below 1998 levels, working to further that with the creation of a new power plant that will decrease energy usage.

ADMISSIONS

Freshman Academic Profile: 80% in top 10% of high school class, 95% in top 25% of high school class, 99% in top 50% of high school class. 55% from public high schools. **Test Scores:** SAT Math middle 50% range 710–790. SAT EBRW middle 50% range 680–750. ACT middle 50% range 32–34. **Basis for Candidate Selection:** *Very important factors include:* rigor of secondary school record, class rank, academic GPA, application essay, standardized test scores, recommendation(s), character/personal qualities. *Important factors include:*

extracurricular activities, talent/ability. *Other factors include:* interview, first generation, alumni/ae relation, geographical residence, racial/ethnic status, volunteer work, work experience, level of applicant's interest. **Freshman Admission Requirements:** High school diploma is required and GED is accepted. *Academic units required:* 4 English, 4 math, 4 science, 3 foreign language, 4 social studies. *Academic units recommended:* 4 foreign language. **Freshman Admission Statistics:** 22,766 applied, 15% admitted, 47% enrolled. **Transfer Admission Requirements:** High school transcript, college transcript(s), essay or personal statement, standardized test scores, statement of good standing from prior institution(s). Lowest grade transferable C. **General Admission Information:** Application fee $75. Regular application deadline 1/1. Admission may be deferred for a maximum of 1 year.

COSTS AND FINANCIAL AID

Annual tuition $57,324. Room and board $15,086. Required fees $1,254. Average book and supplies expense $1,000. **Required Forms and Deadlines:** CSS/Financial Aid PROFILE; FAFSA; Noncustodial PROFILE. **Notification of Awards:** Applicants will be notified of awards on or about 4/1. **Types of Aid:** *Need-based scholarships/grants:* College/university scholarship or grant aid from institutional funds; Federal Pell; Private scholarships; SEOG; State scholarships/grants. *Loans:* Direct PLUS loans; Direct Subsidized Stafford Loans; Direct Unsubsidized Stafford Loans. **Student Employment:** Federal Work-Study Program available. Institutional employment available. **Financial Aid Statistics:** 92% needy freshmen, 92% needy undergrads receive need-based scholarship or grant aid. 3% freshmen, 4% undergrads receive non-need-based scholarship or grant aid. 84% freshmen, 88% undergrads receive need-based self-help aid. 0% freshmen, 0% undergrads receive athletic scholarships. 38% freshmen, 36% undergrads receive any aid. 33% undergrads borrow to pay for school. Average cumulative indebtedness $28,014. **Criteria awarding aid:** *Non-need-based:* Academics.

TULANE UNIVERSITY

6823 St. Charles Avenue, New Orleans, LA 70118
Phone: 504-865-5731 **Financial Aid Phone:** 504-865-5723
E-mail: https://admission.tulane.edu/ **CEEB Code:** 6832
Fax: 504-862-8715 **Website:** www.tulane.edu **ACT Code:** 1614

This private school was founded in 1834. It has a 110 acre campus.

RATINGS

Admissions Selectivity Rating: 97   **Fire Safety Rating:** 96   **Green Rating:** 70

STUDENTS AND FACULTY

Enrollment: 6,968. **Student Body:** 59% female, 41% male, 80% out-of-state, 5% international (62 countries represented). Asian 6%, African American 5%, Caucasian 71%, Hispanic 7%, Native American <1%, Pacific Islander <1%, Two or more races 4%, Race unknown 1%.
Retention and Graduation: 93% freshmen return for sophomore year. 77% freshmen graduate within 4 years. 86% freshmen graduate within 6 years. **Faculty:** Student/faculty ratio 8:1. 804 full-time faculty, 95% hold PhDs, 21% are members of minority groups, 44% are women.

ACADEMICS

Degrees: Bachelor's; Certificate; Doctoral degree—professional practice; Doctoral degree research/scholarship; Master's; Post-bachelor's certificate. **Special Study Options:** Accelerated program; Cross-registration; Distance learning; Double major; English as a Second Language (ESL); Exchange student program (domestic); Honors program; Independent study; Internships; Liberal arts/career combination; Student-designed major; Study abroad; Teacher certification program. **Honors programs:** Tulane Honors Program. **Combined degree programs:** BA/JD; BA/MA; BA/MD. **Disability Services offered:** Note-taking services; Reader services; Tape recorders; Tutors. **Career services:** Alumni network; Alumni services; Career assessment; Career/job search classes; Internships; Regional alumni.

FACILITIES

Housing: Apartments for married students; Apartments for single students; Coed dorms; Fraternity/sorority housing; Special housing for disabled students; Theme housing; Wellness housing; Women's dorms 60% of campus accessible to physically disabled. **Special Academic Facilities/Equipment:**

Newcomb Art Gallery, Amistad Research Center, Latin American Library, Maxwell Music Library, Hogan Jazz Archives, Louisiana Special Collection, Manuscripts Department, Koch Herbarium, Tulane Museum of Natural History, Government Documents, ByWater Institute. **Campus network:** 100% of classrooms, 100% of dorms, 100% of libraries, 100% of dining areas, 100% of common outdoor areas have wireless network access.

CAMPUS LIFE

Environment: Metropolis. **Activities:** Campus Ministries; Choral groups; Concert band; Dance; Drama/theater; International Student Organization; Jazz band; Literary magazine; Marching band; Model UN; Music ensembles; Musical theater; Pep band; Radio station; Student government; Student newspaper; Student-run film society; Symphony orchestra; Television station; Yearbook. 250 registered organizations, 43 honor societies, 11 religious organization, 12 fraternities, 12 sororities on campus. **Athletics (Intercollegiate):** *Men:* baseball, basketball, cross-country, football, tennis, track/field (outdoor). *Women:* basketball, cross-country, diving, golf, swimming, tennis, track/field (outdoor), track/field (indoor), volleyball. **On-Campus Highlights:** Amistad Research Center.

ADMISSIONS

Freshman Academic Profile: Average high school GPA 3.6. 64% in top 10% of high school class, 88% in top 25% of high school class, 97% in top 50% of high school class. 64% from public high schools. **Test Scores:** SAT Math middle 50% range 700–770. SAT EBRW middle 50% range 660–750. ACT middle 50% range 31–33. **Basis for Candidate Selection:** *Very important factors include:* rigor of secondary school record, class rank, academic GPA, standardized test scores. *Important factors include:* application essay, recommendation(s), character/personal qualities. *Other factors include:* interview, extracurricular activities, talent/ability, first generation, alumni/ae relation, volunteer work, work experience, level of applicant's interest. **Freshman Admission Requirements:** High school diploma is required and GED is accepted. *Academic units recommended:* 4 English, 3 math, 3 science, 3 science labs, 3 foreign language, 3 social studies. **Freshman Admission Statistics:** 42,185 applied, 13% admitted, 34% enrolled. **Transfer Admission Requirements:** High school transcript, college transcript(s), essay or personal statement. Minimum college GPA of 2.5 required. Lowest grade transferable C. **General Admission Information:** Priority deadline 11/1. Regular application deadline 11/15. Non-fall registration accepted. Admission may be deferred for a maximum of 1 year.

COSTS AND FINANCIAL AID

Annual tuition $52,760. Room and board $16,464. Required fees $4,040. Average book and supplies expense $1,200. **Required Forms and Deadlines:** Business/Farm Supplement; CSS/Financial Aid PROFILE; FAFSA; Noncustodial PROFILE. **Notification of Awards:** Applicants will be notified of awards on a rolling basis beginning 12/15. **Types of Aid:** *Need-based scholarships/grants:* College/university scholarship or grant aid from institutional funds; Federal Pell; Private scholarships; SEOG; State scholarships/grants. *Loans:* Direct PLUS loans; Direct Subsidized Stafford Loans; Direct Unsubsidized Stafford Loans. **Student Employment:** Federal Work-Study Program available. Institutional employment available. **Financial Aid Statistics:** 98% needy freshmen, 97% needy undergrads receive need-based scholarship or grant aid. 32% freshmen, 26% undergrads receive non-need-based scholarship or grant aid. 71% freshmen, 72% undergrads receive need-based self-help aid. 2% freshmen, 2% undergrads receive athletic scholarships. 94% freshmen, 93% undergrads receive any aid. 34% undergrads borrow to pay for school. Average cumulative indebtedness $31,306. **Criteria awarding aid:** *Non-need-based:* Academics, Athletics, Leadership, Music/drama, State/district residency.

TUSCULUM COLLEGE

PO Box 5051, Greeneville, TN 37743
Phone: 423-636-7300
E-mail: admissions@tusculum.edu **CEEB Code:** 1812
Fax: 423-638-7166 **Website: ACT Code:** 4018

This private school, affiliated with the Presbyterian Church, was founded in 1794. It has a 142 acre campus.

RATINGS

Admissions Selectivity Rating: 73   **Fire Safety Rating:** 60*   **Green Rating:** 60*

STUDENTS AND FACULTY

Enrollment: 1,484. **Student Body:** 51% female, 49% male, 30% out-of-state, 5% international (8 countries represented). Asian <1%, African American 17%, Caucasian 70%, Hispanic 4%, Native American <1%, Pacific Islander <1%, Two or more races 2%, Race unknown 2%.
Retention and Graduation: 65% freshmen return for sophomore year. **Faculty:** Student/faculty ratio 17:1. 72 full-time faculty, 61% hold PhDs, 10% are members of minority groups, 49% are women.

ACADEMICS

Degrees: Associate; Bachelor's; Master's. **Classes:** Most classes have fewer than 10 students. **Most popular majors:** Education, General; Business Administration and Management, General; Family Practice Nurse/Nursing. **Special Study Options:** Cross-registration; Distance learning; Double major; Dual enrollment; Honors program; Independent study; Internships; Student-designed major; Study abroad; Teacher certification program.

FACILITIES

Housing: Coed dorms; Men's dorms; Special housing for disabled students; Theme housing; Women's dorms. **Campus network:** 100% of classrooms, 100% of dorms, 100% of student union, 100% of libraries, 100% of dining areas, 50% of common outdoor areas have wireless network access.

CAMPUS LIFE

Environment: Village. **Activities:** Campus Ministries; Choral groups; Concert band; Dance; Drama/theater; Jazz band; Literary magazine; Marching band; Music ensembles; Musical theater; Pep band; Radio station; Student government; Student newspaper; Yearbook.

ADMISSIONS

Test Scores: SAT Math middle 50% range 440–540. SAT EBRW middle 50% range 440–540. ACT middle 50% range 17–24. **Basis for Candidate Selection:** *Very important factors include:* rigor of secondary school record, application essay, standardized test scores. *Important factors include:* academic GPA, recommendation(s), character/personal qualities. *Other factors include:* class rank, interview, extracurricular activities, talent/ability, first generation, alumni/ae relation, geographical residence, state residency, religious affiliation/commitment, racial/ethnic status, work experience. **Freshman Admission Requirements:** High school diploma is required and GED is accepted. *Academic units recommended:* 4 English, 3 math, 2 science, 2 social studies, 2 history. **Freshman Admission Statistics:** 2,139 applied, 89% admitted, 17% enrolled. **General Admission Information:** Application fee $20. Non-fall registration accepted.

TUSKEGEE UNIVERSITY

Margaret Murray Washington Hall, Tuskegee, AL 36088
Phone: 334-727-8500 **Financial Aid Phone:** 334-727-8088
E-mail: admissions@mytu.tuskegee.edu **CEEB Code:** 1813
Fax: 334-727-5750 **Website:** www.tuskegee.edu **ACT Code:** 50

This private school was founded in 1881. It has a 5200 acre campus.

RATINGS
Admissions Selectivity Rating: 84   **Fire Safety Rating:** 97   **Green Rating:** 60*

STUDENTS AND FACULTY
Enrollment: 2,480. **Student Body:** 61% female, 39% male, 70% out-of-state, <1% international (19 countries represented). Asian <1%, African American 78%, Caucasian <1%, Hispanic <1%, Native American <1%, Pacific Islander 0%, Two or more races 0%, Race unknown 21%.
Retention and Graduation: 73% freshmen return for sophomore year. 23% grads go on to further study within 1 year. 11% grads pursue arts and sciences degrees. 2% grads pursue law degrees. 4% grads pursue business degrees. 3% grads pursue medical degrees. **Faculty:** Student/faculty ratio 14:1. 194 full-time faculty, 87% hold PhDs, 84% are members of minority groups, 32% are women. 0% of classes are taught by teaching assistants.

ACADEMICS
Degrees: Bachelor's; Doctoral degree—professional practice; Doctoral degree research/scholarship; Master's. **Classes:** Most classes have 10–19 students. **Most popular majors:** Electrical and Electronics Engineering. **Special Study Options:** Cooperative education program; Distance learning; Double major; Dual enrollment; Honors program; Independent study; Internships; Study abroad; Teacher certification program. **Honors programs:** Co-Curricular Honors Program. **Disability Services offered:** Note-taking services; Reader services; Tape recorders; Tutors. **Career services:** Alumni network; Career assessment; Career/job search classes; Internships; Regional alumni.

FACILITIES
Housing: Apartments for married students; Apartments for single students; Coed dorms; Men's dorms; Women's dorms; 33% of campus accessible to physically disabled. **Special Academic Facilities/Equipment:** Agricultural and natural history museum, electron microscopes, two nursery schools.

CAMPUS LIFE
Environment: Rural. **Activities:** Campus Ministries; Choral groups; Concert band; Dance; Drama/theater; International Student Organization; Jazz band; Marching band; Pep band; Student government; Student newspaper; Symphony orchestra; Yearbook. 36 registered organizations, 22 honor societies, 6 religious organizations, 5 fraternities, 6 sororities on campus. **Athletics (Intercollegiate):** *Men:* baseball, basketball, cheerleading, cross-country, diving, fencing, football, golf, gymnastics, riflery, soccer, swimming, tennis, track/field (outdoor), track/field (indoor), volleyball. *Women:* basketball, cheerleading, cross-country, diving, fencing, golf, gymnastics, riflery, soccer, swimming, tennis, track/field (outdoor), track/field (indoor), volleyball. **On-Campus Highlights:** George Washington Carver Museum.

ADMISSIONS
Freshman Academic Profile: Average high school GPA 3.2. 20% in top 10% of high school class, 60% in top 25% of high school class, 100% in top 50% of high school class. 88% from public high schools. **Test Scores:** SAT Math middle 50% range 420–520. SAT EBRW middle 50% range 440–510. ACT middle 50% range 18–23. **Basis for Candidate Selection:** *Very important factors include:* rigor of secondary school record, class rank, academic GPA, standardized test scores, recommendation(s), talent/ability. *Important factors include:* character/personal qualities, alumni/ae relation. *Other factors include:* application essay, interview, extracurricular activities, first generation, geographical residence, state residency, volunteer work, work experience. **Freshman Admission Requirements:** High school diploma is required and GED is accepted. *Academic units required:* 4 English, 3 math, 2 science, 3 social studies, 4 academic electives. **Freshman Admission Statistics:** 9,582 applied, 36% admitted, 17% enrolled. **Transfer Admission Requirements:** College transcript(s). Minimum college GPA of 2.0 required. Lowest grade transferable C. **General Admission Information:** Application fee $25. Priority deadline 3/31. Regular application deadline 7/15. Non-fall registration accepted. Admission may be deferred for a maximum of 12 months.

COSTS AND FINANCIAL AID
Annual tuition $18,100. Room and board $8,510. Required fees $3,525. Average book and supplies expense $1,282. **Required Forms and Deadlines:** CSS/Financial Aid PROFILE; FAFSA; Institution's own financial aid form. **Types of Aid:** *Need-based scholarships/grants:* College/university scholarship or grant aid from institutional funds; Federal Nursing Scholarships; Federal Pell; Private scholarships; SEOG; State scholarships/grants; United Negro College Fund. *Loans:* Direct PLUS loans; Direct Subsidized Stafford Loans; Direct Unsubsidized Stafford Loans. **Student Employment:** Federal Work-Study Program available. Institutional employment available. **Financial Aid Statistics:** 100% needy freshmen, 100% needy undergrads receive need-based scholarship or grant aid. 17% freshmen, 22% undergrads receive non-need-based scholarship or grant aid. 100% freshmen, 68% undergrads receive need-based self-help aid. 7% freshmen, 9% undergrads receive athletic scholarships. 90% freshmen, 92% undergrads receive any aid. 49% undergrads borrow to pay for school. Average cumulative indebtedness $18,100. **Criteria awarding aid:** *Need-based:* Academics, Athletics. *Non-need-based:* Academics, Athletics, State/district residency.

UNION COLLEGE (KY)

310 College Street, Barbourville, KY 40906
Phone: 606-546-1229 **Financial Aid Phone:** 606-546-1224
E-mail: enrollme@unionky.edu **CEEB Code:** 001825
Fax: 606-546-1667 **Website:** www.unionky.edu **ACT Code:** 015520

This private school, affiliated with the Methodist Church, was founded in 1879. It has a 100 acre campus.

RATINGS
Admissions Selectivity Rating: 77   **Fire Safety Rating:** 65   **Green Rating:** 60*

STUDENTS AND FACULTY
Enrollment: 794. **Student Body:** 47% female, 53% male, 26% out-of-state, 8% international (19 countries represented). Asian 1%, African American 12%, Caucasian 72%, Hispanic 2%, Native American <1%, Pacific Islander <1%, Two or more races 5%, Race unknown 1%.
Retention and Graduation: 56% freshmen return for sophomore year. **Faculty:** Student/faculty ratio 12:1. 56 full-time faculty, 45% hold PhDs, 11% are members of minority groups, 45% are women. 0% of classes are taught by teaching assistants.

ACADEMICS
Degrees: Bachelor's; Master's; Post-bachelor's certificate. **Classes:** Most classes have fewer than 10 students. **Most popular majors:** Special Education and Teaching, General; Business Administration and Management, General; Psychology, General. **Special Study Options:** Distance learning; Double major; Honors program; Independent study; Internships; Liberal arts/career combination; Student-designed major; Study abroad; Teacher certification program. **Combined degree programs:** BA/MA. **Disability Services offered:** Reader services; Tape recorders; Tutors. **Career services:** Alumni network; Career assessment; Career/job search classes; Internships; Regional alumni.

FACILITIES
Housing: Apartments for married students; Apartments for single students; Men's dorms; Women's dorms; 50% of campus accessible to physically disabled.

CAMPUS LIFE
Environment: Rural. **Activities:** Choral groups; Drama/theater; Literary magazine; Pep band; Student government; Television station; Yearbook. 23 registered organizations, 2 honor societies, 2 religious organizations on campus. **Athletics (Intercollegiate):** *Men:* baseball, basketball, bowling, cheerleading, cross-country, cycling, football, golf, soccer, swimming, tennis, track/field (outdoor). *Women:* basketball, bowling, cheerleading, cross-country, cycling, golf, soccer, softball, swimming, tennis, track/field (outdoor), volleyball. **On-Campus Highlights:** Student Center.

ADMISSIONS
Test Scores: SAT Math middle 50% range 453–553. SAT EBRW middle 50% range 433–508. ACT middle 50% range 18–23. **Basis for Candidate Selection:** *Important factors include:* rigor of secondary school record, class rank, academic GPA, standardized test scores. *Other factors include:*

recommendation(s), extracurricular activities, talent/ability, character/personal qualities, first generation, alumni/ae relation, geographical residence, volunteer work. **Freshman Admission Requirements:** High school diploma is required and GED is accepted. *Academic units recommended:* 4 English, 3 math, 2 science, 2 science labs, 1 foreign language, 2 social studies. **Freshman Admission Statistics:** 1,332 applied, 69% admitted, 23% enrolled. **Transfer Admission Requirements:** College transcript(s). Minimum college GPA of 2.0 required. Lowest grade transferable 2. **General Admission Information:** Application fee $10. Non-fall registration accepted.

COSTS AND FINANCIAL AID
Annual tuition $22,720. Room and board $7,000. Required fees $640. **Required Forms and Deadlines:** FAFSA. **Notification of Awards:** Applicants will be notified of awards on a rolling basis beginning 3/1. **Types of Aid:** *Need-based scholarships/grants:* College/university scholarship or grant aid from institutional funds; Federal Pell; Private scholarships; SEOG; State scholarships/grants. *Loans:* Direct PLUS loans; Direct Subsidized Stafford Loans; Direct Unsubsidized Stafford Loans. **Student Employment:** Federal Work-Study Program available. Institutional employment available. **Financial Aid Statistics:** 98% needy freshmen, 95% needy undergrads receive need-based scholarship or grant aid. 7% freshmen, 11% undergrads receive non-need-based scholarship or grant aid. 87% freshmen, 78% undergrads receive need-based self-help aid. 0% freshmen, 0% undergrads receive athletic scholarships. 100% freshmen, 100% undergrads receive any aid. **Criteria awarding aid:** *Need-based:* Academics, Alumni affiliation, Athletics, Job skills. *Non-need-based:* Academics, Athletics, Job skills, Religious affiliation, State/district residency.

UNION COLLEGE (NY)

Grant Hall, Schenectady, NY 12308
Phone: 518-388-6112 **Financial Aid Phone:** 518-388-6123
E-mail: admissions@union.edu **CEEB Code:** 2920
Fax: 518-388-6986 **Website:** www.union.edu **ACT Code:** 2970

This private school was founded in 1795. It has a 100 acre campus.

RATINGS
Admissions Selectivity Rating: 93   **Fire Safety Rating:** 98   **Green Rating:** 94

STUDENTS AND FACULTY
Enrollment: 2,161. **Student Body:** 46% female, 54% male, 66% out-of-state, 10% international (37 countries represented). Asian 6%, African American 4%, Caucasian 68%, Hispanic 9%, Native American <1%, Pacific Islander 0%, Two or more races 3%, Race unknown <1%.
Retention and Graduation: 93% freshmen return for sophomore year. 78% freshmen graduate within 4 years. 82% freshmen graduate within 6 years. 24% grads go on to further study within 1 year. **Faculty:** Student/faculty ratio 10:1. 209 full-time faculty, 96% hold PhDs, 16% are members of minority groups, 43% are women. 0% of classes are taught by teaching assistants.

ACADEMICS
Degrees: Bachelor's. **Classes:** Most classes have 10–19 students. Most lab/discussion sessions have 10–19 students. **Most popular majors:** Mechanical Engineering; Psychology, General; Biology/Biological Sciences, General. **Special Study Options:** Accelerated program; Cross-registration; Double major; Dual enrollment; Honors program; Independent study; Internships; Liberal arts/career combination; Student-designed major; Study abroad; Teacher certification program. **Honors programs:** The Union Scholars program offers selected students the opportunity to take full advantage of the diverse intellectual experiences at Union. Specific features of the program are an enriched two-term version of First-Year Preceptorial; a sophomore independent study project with a professor of the student's choosing; the option to participate as a junior in a program in which students take a leadership role in the College's intellectual and social life; and a Scholars Colloquium run by students for presenting faculty and student research, in the senior year. Union Scholars use their extra courses to create an enriched program that meets their specific needs and interests. **Combined degree programs:** BA/JD. **Disability Services offered:** Note-taking services; Reader services; Tape recorders. **Career**

services: Alumni network; Alumni services; Career assessment; Career/job search classes; Internships; Regional alumni.

FACILITIES
Housing: Apartments for single students; Coed dorms; Fraternity/sorority housing; Theme housing; 80% of campus accessible to physically disabled. **Special Academic Facilities/Equipment:** The Nott Memorial and its Mandeville Gallery; Yulman Theater; Burns Arts Atrium; Taylor Music Center and its Emerson Auditorium; Special Collections at Schaffer Library; Memorial Chapel; Jackson's Garden, an eight-acre formal garden and woodland. Academic facilities include the F.W. Olin Center, with high technology classrooms and laboratories, a multi-media auditorium, collaborative computer classrooms, and a 20-inch remote-controlled telescope. Science and engineering facilities include superconducting nuclear magnetic resonance spectrometer, two electron microscopes, tandem pelletron positive ion accelerator, a fully accessible machine lab, and Aerogel fabrication and analysis lab.

CAMPUS LIFE
Environment: Town. **Activities:** Campus Ministries; Choral groups; Concert band; Dance; Drama/theater; International Student Organization; Jazz band; Literary magazine; Model UN; Music ensembles; Pep band; Radio station; Student government; Student newspaper; Student-run film society; Symphony orchestra; Television station; Yearbook. 101 registered organizations, 14 honor societies, 11 religious organization, 11 fraternity, 7 sororities on campus. **Athletics (Intercollegiate):** *Men:* baseball, basketball, crew/rowing, cross-country, diving, football, ice hockey, lacrosse, soccer, swimming, tennis, track/field (outdoor), track/field (indoor). *Women:* basketball, crew/rowing, cross-country, diving, field hockey, ice hockey, lacrosse, soccer, softball, swimming, tennis, track/field (outdoor), track/field (indoor), volleyball. **On-Campus Highlights:** The Nott Memorial. **Environmental Initiatives:** Incorporation of Sustainability into Union College's Mission, Presidential Priority & Strategic Plan.

ADMISSIONS
Freshman Academic Profile: Average high school GPA 3.5. 63% in top 10% of high school class, 86% in top 25% of high school class, 98% in top 50% of high school class. **Test Scores:** SAT Math middle 50% range 620–740. SAT EBRW middle 50% range 600–680. ACT middle 50% range 27–32. **Basis for Candidate Selection:** *Very important factors include:* rigor of secondary school record, class rank, academic GPA. *Important factors include:* application essay, standardized test scores, recommendation(s), extracurricular activities, talent/ability, character/personal qualities. *Other factors include:* interview, first generation, alumni/ae relation, geographical residence, state residency, racial/ethnic status, level of applicant's interest. **Freshman Admission Requirements:** High school diploma is required and GED is not accepted. *Academic units required:* 4 English, 3 math, 2 science, 2 science labs, 2 foreign language, 1 social studies, 1 history. *Academic units recommended:* 4 English, 4 math, 4 science, 4 science labs, 4 foreign language, 2 social studies, 2 history. **Freshman Admission Statistics:** 6,086 applied, 43% admitted, 21% enrolled. **Transfer Admission Requirements:** High school transcript, college transcript(s), essay or personal statement, statement of good standing from prior institution(s). Minimum college GPA of 3.0 required. Lowest grade transferable C. **General Admission Information:** Regular application deadline 1/15. Non-fall registration accepted. Admission may be deferred for a maximum of 2 years.

COSTS AND FINANCIAL AID
Required Forms and Deadlines: CSS/Financial Aid PROFILE; FAFSA; Noncustodial PROFILE; State aid form. **Notification of Awards:** Applicants will be notified of awards on or about 3/25. **Types of Aid:** *Need-based scholarships/grants:* College/university scholarship or grant aid from institutional funds; Federal Pell; Private scholarships; SEOG; State scholarships/grants. *Loans:* Direct PLUS loans; Direct Subsidized Stafford Loans; Direct Unsubsidized Stafford Loans. **Student Employment:** Federal Work-Study Program available. Institutional employment available. **Financial Aid Statistics:** 100% needy freshmen, 100% needy undergrads receive need-based scholarship or grant aid. 4% freshmen, 6% undergrads receive non-need-based scholarship or grant aid. 97% freshmen, 97% undergrads receive need-based self-help aid. 0% freshmen, 0% undergrads receive athletic scholarships. 82% freshmen, 80% undergrads receive any aid. 53% undergrads borrow to pay for school. Average cumulative indebtedness $36,921. **Criteria awarding aid:** *Need-based:* Academics. *Non-need-based:* Academics.

UNION INSTITUTE & UNIVERSITY

440 East McMillan Street, Cincinnati, OH 45206
Phone: 513-861-6400 **Financial Aid Phone:** 800-486-3116
E-mail: admissions@myunion.edu **CEEB Code:** 010923
Fax: 513-861-3238 **Website:** www.myunion.edu

This private school was founded in 1964.

RATINGS
Admissions Selectivity Rating: 60*   **Fire Safety Rating:** 60*   **Green Rating:** 60*

STUDENTS AND FACULTY
Enrollment: 1,101. **Student Body:** 53% female, 47% male, 16% out-of-state, 0% international (24 countries represented). Asian 1%, African American 26%, Caucasian 33%, Hispanic 13%, Native American 1%, Pacific Islander <1%, Two or more races 2%, Race unknown 24%.
Retention and Graduation: 90% freshmen return for sophomore year.
Faculty: Student/faculty ratio 9:1. 31 full-time faculty, 84% hold PhDs, 19% are members of minority groups, 52% are women. 0% of classes are taught by teaching assistants.

ACADEMICS
Degrees: Bachelor's; Doctoral degree research/scholarship; Master's. **Classes:** Most classes have fewer than 10 students. **Most popular majors:** Liberal Arts and Sciences, General Studies and Humanities, Other; Criminal Justice/Law Enforcement Administration; Child Development. **Special Study Options:** Cross-registration; Distance learning; Independent study; Internships; Teacher certification program. **Career services:** Alumni services; Career assessment.

FACILITIES
100% of campus accessible to physically disabled. **Campus network:** 100% of classrooms, 100% of dorms, 100% of student union, 100% of libraries, 100% of dining areas, 75% of common outdoor areas have wireless network access.

CAMPUS LIFE
Environment: Metropolis.

ADMISSIONS
Basis for Candidate Selection: *Important factors include:* application essay, recommendation(s), interview, level of applicant's interest. *Other factors include:* extracurricular activities, talent/ability, character/personal qualities, volunteer work, work experience. **Freshman Admission Requirements:** High school diploma is required and GED is accepted. **Transfer Admission Requirements:** College transcript(s), essay or personal statement, interview. Lowest grade transferable D. **General Admission Information:** Non-fall registration accepted. Admission may be deferred for a maximum of 12 months.

COSTS AND FINANCIAL AID
Required Forms and Deadlines: FAFSA; Institution's own financial aid form. **Notification of Awards:** Applicants will be notified of awards on a rolling basis beginning 5/1. **Types of Aid:** *Need-based scholarships/grants:* College/university scholarship or grant aid from institutional funds; Federal Pell; Private scholarships; SEOG; State scholarships/grants. **Student Employment:** Federal Work-Study Program available. **Criteria awarding aid:** *Need-based:* Academics. *Non-need-based:* Academics, State/district residency.

UNION UNIVERSITY

1050 Union University Drive, Jackson, TN 38305-3697
Phone: 731-661-5000
E-mail: rgraves@uu.edu **CEEB Code:** 1826
Fax: 731-661-5017 **ACT Code:** 4020

This private school, affiliated with the Southern Baptist Church, was founded in 1823. It has a 360 acre campus.

RATINGS
Admissions Selectivity Rating: 60*   **Fire Safety Rating:** 86   **Green Rating:** 64

STUDENTS AND FACULTY
Enrollment: 3,377.
Faculty: Student/faculty ratio 10:1. 0% of classes are taught by teaching assistants.

ACADEMICS
Degrees: Associate; Bachelor's; Certificate; Diploma; Doctoral degree—other; Doctoral degree—professional practice; Doctoral degree research/scholarship; Master's; Post-master's certificate; Transfer Associate. **Most popular majors:** Elementary Education and Teaching; Christian Studies; Nursing/Registered Nurse (Rn, Asn, Bsn, Msn). **Special Study Options:** Accelerated program; Cooperative education program; Cross-registration; Distance learning; Double major; Dual enrollment; English as a Second Language (ESL); Exchange student program (domestic); Honors program; Independent study; Internships; Study abroad; Teacher certification program. **Honors programs:** General Honors plus discipline-specific honors in Art, Biology, Business, Chemistry, Education, English, History, Math, Political Science, and Theology. **Disability Services offered:** Note-taking services; Reader services; Tape recorders; Tutors. **Career services:** Alumni network; Alumni services; Career assessment; Career/job search classes; Internships; Regional alumni.

FACILITIES
Housing: Apartments for married students; Men's dorms; Special housing for disabled students; Women's dorms; 98% of campus accessible to physically disabled. **Special Academic Facilities/Equipment:** Elementary education lab, 21st-century classroom, TV communications truck, nursing/health assessment labs, health and wellness center, art gallery. **Campus network:** 60% of classrooms, 100% of dorms, 100% of student union, 95% of libraries, 70% of dining areas, 10% of common outdoor areas have wireless network access.

CAMPUS LIFE
Environment: City. **Activities:** Campus Ministries; Choral groups; Concert band; Drama/theater; International Student Organization; Jazz band; Literary magazine; Music ensembles; Musical theater; Pep band; Radio station; Student government; Student newspaper; Student-run film society; Symphony orchestra; Television station; Yearbook. 90 registered organizations on campus. **Athletics (Intercollegiate):** *Men:* baseball, basketball, cheerleading, cross-country, golf, soccer. *Women:* basketball, cheerleading, cross-country, soccer, softball, volleyball. **On-Campus Highlights:** Bowld Commons. **Environmental Initiatives:** Campus-wide recycling campaign for aluminum, plastics and paper. This includes pick up from all student residential areas as well as all buildings/offices.

ADMISSIONS
Freshman Academic Profile: Average high school GPA 3.8. 57% from public high schools. **Basis for Candidate Selection:** *Very important factors include:* rigor of secondary school record, academic GPA, character/personal qualities, level of applicant's interest. *Important factors include:* class rank, standardized test scores, interview, extracurricular activities, talent/ability, religious affiliation/commitment. *Other factors include:* application essay, recommendation(s), first generation, alumni/ae relation, volunteer work, work experience. **Freshman Admission Requirements:** High school diploma is required and GED is accepted. *Academic units required:* 4 English, 3 math, 3 science, 2 science labs, 1 foreign language, 2 social studies, 1 history, 1 academic elective. *Academic units recommended:* 4 English, 4 math, 4 science, 2 science labs, 2 foreign language, 2 social studies, 2 history, 4 academic electives, 1 computer science, 1 visual/performing arts. **Freshman Admission Statistics:** 2,184 applied, admitted, enrolled. **Transfer Admission Requirements:** College transcript(s), statement of good standing from prior institution(s). Minimum college GPA of 2.3 required. Lowest grade transferable C. **General Admission Information:** Application fee $35. Priority deadline 12/1. Regular application deadline 8/1. Non-fall registration accepted. Admission may be deferred for a maximum of 1 year.

COSTS AND FINANCIAL AID
Annual tuition $32,650. Required fees $1,100. **Required Forms and Deadlines:** FAFSA; Institution's own financial aid form. **Notification of Awards:** Applicants will be notified of awards on a rolling basis beginning 12/1. **Types of Aid:** *Need-based scholarships/grants:* College/university scholarship or grant aid from institutional funds; Federal Nursing Scholarships; Federal Pell; Private scholarships; SEOG; State scholarships/grants. *Loans:* Direct PLUS loans; Direct Subsidized Stafford Loans; Direct Unsubsidized Stafford Loans. **Student Employment:** Federal Work-Study Program available. Institutional employment available. **Financial Aid Statistics:** 99% freshmen, 99% undergrads receive any aid. **Criteria awarding aid:** *Need-based:* Job skills, Minority status. *Non-need-based:* Academics, Alumni affiliation, Art, Athletics, Job skills, Leadership, Minority status, Music/drama, Religious affiliation.

UNITED STATES AIR FORCE ACADEMY

HQ USAFA/ RRS, USAF Academy, CO 80840-5025
Phone: 719-333-2520
E-mail: rr_admissions@usafa.edu **CEEB Code:** 4830
Fax: 719-333-3012 **Website:** www.academyadmissions.com/about-the-academy
ACT Code: 0530

This public school was founded in 1954. It has a 18000 acre campus.

RATINGS
Admissions Selectivity Rating: 99   **Fire Safety Rating:** 99   **Green Rating:** 83

STUDENTS AND FACULTY
Enrollment: 4,336. **Student Body:** 27% female, 73% male, 93% out-of-state, 1% international (27 countries represented). Asian 6%, African American 6%, Caucasian 63%, Hispanic 11%, Native American <1%, Pacific Islander 1%, Two or more races 8%, Race unknown 4%.
Retention and Graduation: 96% freshmen return for sophomore year. 77% freshmen graduate within 4 years. 78% freshmen graduate within 6 years. 11% grads go on to further study within 1 year. 11% grads pursue arts and sciences degrees. <1% grads pursue law degrees. <1% grads pursue business degrees. <1% grads pursue medical degrees. **Faculty:** Student/faculty ratio 7:1. 537 full-time faculty, 57% hold PhDs, 10% are members of minority groups, 24% are women. 0% of classes are taught by teaching assistants.

ACADEMICS
Degrees: Bachelor's. **Classes:** Most classes have 10–19 students. Most lab/discussion sessions have 20–29 students. **Most popular majors:** Aerospace, Aeronautical, and Astronautical/Space Engineering, General; Systems Engineering; Business Administration and Management, General. **Special Study Options:** Double major; English as a Second Language (ESL); Exchange student program (domestic); Honors program; Independent study; Internships; Liberal arts/career combination; Study abroad. **Honors programs:** The Academy Scholars Program offers participating cadets a four-year experience featuring core substitute and upper-division courses. In addition to course offerings, the Academy Scholars Program also provides many opportunities beyond the curriculum, including participation in the National Collegiate Honors Council and the Aspen Institute. **Career services:** Alumni network; Alumni services; Career assessment; Internships; Regional alumni.

FACILITIES
Housing: Coed dorms. **Special Academic Facilities/Equipment:** Planetarium; Polaris Hall; Aircraft Simulators; Center for Character and Leadership Development; CyberWorx Innovation Center, teaching creative problem solving techniques to improve leadership and innovation; Consolidated Education and Training Facility (CETF) Building; Human Performance Lab; Cadet Gym; Language learning center; laser and optics research center; Dept. of Engineering Mechanics Lab; US Air Force Academy visitor's center; consolidated educational training facility; Air Force Academy cadet chapel; American Legion Memorial Tower; Clune area athletic and speaking events (seats 6,000); Air Garden; Falcon Stadium; Holaday Athletic Center Aeronautics Lab; Meteorology Lab; Arnold Hall Broadway Theater ballroom, conference rooms and historical displays; Visitors Center; Cadet Demographic Map as well as cadet life film.

CAMPUS LIFE
Environment: Metropolis. **Activities:** Campus Ministries; Choral groups; Concert band; Dance; Drama/theater; International Student Organization; Marching band; Music ensembles; Musical theater; Pep band; Radio station; Student government; Symphony orchestra; Yearbook. 93 registered organizations, 4 honor societies, 17 religious organizations on campus. **Athletics (Intercollegiate):** *Men:* baseball, basketball, boxing, cheerleading, cross-country, diving, fencing, football, golf, gymnastics, ice hockey, lacrosse, riflery, soccer, swimming, tennis, track/field (outdoor), track/field (indoor), water polo, wrestling. *Women:* basketball, cheerleading, cross-country, diving, fencing, gymnastics, riflery, soccer, swimming, tennis, track/field (outdoor), track/field (indoor), volleyball. **On-Campus Highlights:** USAF Academy Visitor Center and Planetarium. **Environmental Initiatives:** Solar.

ADMISSIONS
Freshman Academic Profile: Average high school GPA 3.8. 53% in top 10% of high school class, 82% in top 25% of high school class, 98% in top 50%

of high school class. 76% from public high schools. **Test Scores:** SAT Math middle 50% range 620–720. SAT EBRW middle 50% range 610–690. ACT middle 50% range 28–33. **Basis for Candidate Selection:** *Very important factors include:* rigor of secondary school record, class rank, academic GPA, application essay, standardized test scores, recommendation(s), interview, extracurricular activities, character/personal qualities, level of applicant's interest. *Important factors include:* talent/ability, geographical residence, volunteer work. *Other factors include:* first generation, alumni/ae relation, racial/ethnic status. **Freshman Admission Requirements:** High school diploma is required and GED is accepted. *Academic units required:* 4 English, 4 math, 4 science, 3 social studies, 1 history. *Academic units recommended:* 4 English, 4 math, 4 science, 2 science labs, 2 foreign language, 4 social studies, 3 history, 1 computer science. **Freshman Admission Statistics:** 10,726 applied, 11% admitted, 98% enrolled. **Transfer Admission Requirements:** High school transcript, college transcript(s), essay or personal statement, interview, standardized test scores. Minimum college GPA of 2.0 required. **General Admission Information:** Regular application deadline 12/31.

UNITED STATES COAST GUARD ACADEMY

31 Mohegan Avenue, New London, CT 06320-8103
Phone: 860-444-8500
E-mail: USCGA.Admissions@uscga.edu **CEEB Code:** 5807
Fax: 860-701-6700 **Website:** www.uscga.edu **ACT Code:** 0600

This public school was founded in 1876. It has a 103 acre campus.

RATINGS
Admissions Selectivity Rating: 97   **Fire Safety Rating:** 91   **Green Rating:** 61

STUDENTS AND FACULTY
Enrollment: 898. **Student Body:** 35% female, 65% male, 95% out-of-state, 2% international (12 countries represented). Asian 7%, African American 4%, Caucasian 67%, Hispanic 10%, Native American <1%, Pacific Islander <1%, Two or more races 8%, Race unknown 2%.
Retention and Graduation: 90% freshmen return for sophomore year. **Faculty:** Student/faculty ratio 8:1. 115 full-time faculty, 56% hold PhDs, 12% are members of minority groups, 28% are women. 0% of classes are taught by teaching assistants.

ACADEMICS
Degrees: Bachelor's. **Classes:** Most classes have 10–19 students. Most lab/discussion sessions have 10–19 students. **Most popular majors:** Business Administration and Management, General; Oceanography, Chemical and Physical; Political Science and Government, General. **Special Study Options:** Cross-registration; Double major; English as a Second Language (ESL); Exchange student program (domestic); Honors program; Independent study; Internships. **Career services:** Alumni network; Career assessment; Regional alumni.

FACILITIES
Housing: Coed dorms; Wellness housing; 95% of campus accessible to physically disabled. **Special Academic Facilities/Equipment:** CG Museum; Library; Visitors Center; Alumni Center.

CAMPUS LIFE
Environment: City. **Activities:** Campus Ministries; Choral groups; Concert band; Dance; Drama/theater; International Student Organization; Jazz band; Marching band; Model UN; Music ensembles; Musical theater; Pep band; Student government; Yearbook. 65 registered organizations, 3 honor societies, 7 religious organizations on campus. **Athletics (Intercollegiate):** *Men:* baseball, basketball, crew/rowing, cross-country, diving, football, pistol, riflery, sailing, soccer, swimming, tennis, track/field (outdoor), track/field (indoor), wrestling. *Women:* basketball, cheerleading, crew/rowing, cross-country, diving, pistol, riflery, sailing, soccer, softball, swimming, track/field (outdoor), track/field (indoor), volleyball. **On-Campus Highlights:** Coast Guard Barque EAGLE. **Environmental Initiatives:** Federal Electronic Recycling Challenge Participant and winner 2008 and 2009.

ADMISSIONS

Freshman Academic Profile: Average high school GPA 3.8. 45% in top 10% of high school class, 79% in top 25% of high school class, 96% in top 50% of high school class. 76% from public high schools. **Test Scores:** SAT Math middle 50% range 610–690. SAT EBRW middle 50% range 570–660. ACT middle 50% range 26–31. **Basis for Candidate Selection:** *Very important factors include:* rigor of secondary school record, class rank, academic GPA, standardized test scores, extracurricular activities, character/personal qualities. *Important factors include:* application essay, recommendation(s), talent/ability. *Other factors include:* interview, first generation, alumni/ae relation, geographical residence, state residency, religious affiliation/commitment, racial/ethnic status, volunteer work, work experience, level of applicant's interest. **Freshman Admission Requirements:** High school diploma is required and GED is accepted. *Academic units required:* 4 English, 4 math, 3 science, 3 science labs. *Academic units recommended:* 4 English, 4 math, 4 science, 3 science labs. **Freshman Admission Statistics:** 2,214 applied, 18% admitted, 75% enrolled. **Transfer Admission Requirements:** High school transcript, essay or personal statement, standardized test scores, statement of good standing from prior institution(s). **General Admission Information:** Priority deadline 11/15. Regular application deadline 2/1. Admission may be deferred for a maximum of 1 year.

COSTS AND FINANCIAL AID

Required fees $978. Average book and supplies expense $2,199.

UNITED STATES MERCHANT MARINE ACADEMY

Office of Admissions, Kings Point, NY 11024-1699
Phone: 516-726-5643 **Financial Aid Phone:** 516-773-5295
E-mail: admissions@usmma.edu **CEEB Code:** 2923
Fax: 516-773-5390 **Website:** www.usmma.edu **ACT Code:** 2974

This public school was founded in 1943. It has a 82 acre campus.

RATINGS

Admissions Selectivity Rating: 96   **Fire Safety Rating:** 98   **Green Rating:** 63

STUDENTS AND FACULTY

Enrollment: 952. **Student Body:** 17% female, 83% male, 87% out-of-state, 1% international (4 countries represented). Asian 8%, African American 3%, Caucasian 75%, Hispanic 10%, Native American 1%, Pacific Islander <1%, Two or more races 0%, Race unknown 3%.
Retention and Graduation: 89% freshmen return for sophomore year. 81% freshmen graduate within 4 years. % freshmen graduate within 6 years. **Faculty:** Student/faculty ratio 8:1. 113 full-time faculty, 9% are members of minority groups, 15% are women.

ACADEMICS

Degrees: Bachelor's; Master's. **Classes:** Most classes have 20–29 students. **Most popular majors:** Naval Architecture and Marine Engineering; Engineering, General; Transportation and Materials Moving, Other. **Special Study Options:** Honors program; Independent study; Internships; Study abroad. **Career services:** Alumni network; Alumni services; Career assessment; Career/job search classes; Internships.

FACILITIES

Housing: Coed dorms **Special Academic Facilities/Equipment:** American Merchant Marine Museum.

CAMPUS LIFE

Environment: Town. **Activities:** Campus Ministries; Choral groups; Concert band; Marching band; Pep band; Student government; Student newspaper; Yearbook. 38 registered organizations, 2 honor societies, 2 religious organizations on campus. **Athletics (Intercollegiate):** *Men:* baseball, basketball, crew/rowing, cross-country, diving, football, golf, lacrosse, riflery, sailing, soccer, swimming, tennis, track/field (outdoor), volleyball, water polo, wrestling. *Women:* basketball, crew/rowing, cross-country, diving, golf, riflery, sailing, softball, swimming, tennis, track/field (outdoor), volleyball. **On-Campus Highlights:** American Merchant Marine Museum.

ADMISSIONS

Freshman Academic Profile: 22% in top 10% of high school class, 64% in top 25% of high school class, 96% in top 50% of high school class. 75% from public high schools. **Test Scores:** SAT Math middle 50% range 630–660. SAT EBRW middle 50% range 570–660. **Basis for Candidate Selection:** *Very important factors include:* rigor of secondary school record, class rank, standardized test scores, extracurricular activities, character/personal qualities. *Important factors include:* academic GPA, application essay, recommendation(s), talent/ability. *Other factors include:* interview, first generation, geographical residence, state residency, racial/ethnic status, volunteer work, work experience. **Freshman Admission Requirements:** High school diploma is required and GED is accepted. *Academic units required:* 3 English, 3 math, 1 science, 1 science labs, 8 academic electives. *Academic units recommended:* 4 English, 4 math, 3 science, 2 science labs, 2 foreign language. **Freshman Admission Statistics:** 1,855 applied, 22% admitted, 68% enrolled. **Transfer Admission Requirements:** High school transcript, college transcript(s), essay or personal statement, standardized test scores, statement of good standing from prior institution(s). Minimum college GPA of 2.5 required. **General Admission Information:** Regular application deadline 3/1.

COSTS AND FINANCIAL AID

Required fees $1,050. Average book and supplies expense $2,880. **Required Forms and Deadlines:** FAFSA. **Notification of Awards:** Applicants will be notified of awards on a rolling basis beginning 5/1. **Types of Aid:** *Need-based scholarships/grants:* Federal Pell; Private scholarships; State scholarships/grants. *Loans:* Direct PLUS loans; Direct Subsidized Stafford Loans; Direct Unsubsidized Stafford Loans. **Financial Aid Statistics:** 33% freshmen, 30% undergrads receive any aid.

UNITED STATES MILITARY ACADEMY

646 Swift Road, West Point, NY 10996-1905
Phone: 845-938-4041
E-mail: admissions@usma.edu **CEEB Code:** 2924
Fax: 845-938-3021 **Website:** www.westpoint.edu **ACT Code:** 2976

This public school was founded in 1802. It has a 16080 acre campus.

RATINGS

Admissions Selectivity Rating: 99   **Fire Safety Rating:** 91   **Green Rating:** 60*

STUDENTS AND FACULTY

Enrollment: 4,491. **Student Body:** 22% female, 78% male, 94% out-of-state, 1% international (29 countries represented). Asian 8%, African American 12%, Caucasian 62%, Hispanic 10%, Native American 1%, Pacific Islander <1%, Two or more races 3%, Race unknown 1%.
Retention and Graduation: 98% freshmen return for sophomore year. 83% freshmen graduate within 4 years. 85% freshmen graduate within 6 years. 38% grads go on to further study within 1 year. 1% grads pursue arts and sciences degrees. 2% grads pursue medical degrees. **Faculty:** Student/faculty ratio 7:1. 611 full-time faculty, 52% hold PhDs, 10% are members of minority groups, 20% are women. 0% of classes are taught by teaching assistants.

ACADEMICS

Degrees: Bachelor's. **Classes:** Most classes have 10–19 students. Most lab/discussion sessions have 10–19 students. **Most popular majors:** Engineering/Industrial Management; Economics, General; Business Administration and Management, General. **Special Study Options:** Double major; Exchange student program (domestic); Honors program; Independent study; Internships; Study abroad. **Honors programs:** Thayer Honors Program, offers a broad umbrella to provide comprehensive academic development for cadets with outstanding potential. The program offers systematic and sustained intellectual challenge, while affording and encouraging opportunities outside West Point's curricular path. The Thayer Honors Program is a powerful instrument to attract, retain, and develop young leaders of the highest caliber. Cadets in the program likewise serve as ambassadors for the military to their civilian counterparts, whether at academic conferences presenting their research, interning during summers, or for those who receive nationally-competitive scholarships, in graduate school following commissioning.

FACILITIES

Housing: Coed dorms. **Special Academic Facilities/Equipment:** West Point Museum, American Revolutionary-era Fort Putnam, 4,500-seat Eisenhower Hall, 18-hole Golf Course, Victor Constant Ski Slope, Arvin Cadet Physical Development Center, Michie Stadium, Christi Arena, Gillis Field House, and Jefferson Hall Library.

CAMPUS LIFE

Environment: Village. **Activities:** Campus Ministries; Choral groups; Drama/theater; International Student Organization; Literary magazine; Model UN; Music ensembles; Pep band; Radio station; Student government; Student-run film society; Television station; Yearbook. 86 registered organizations, 15 honor societies, 12 religious organizations on campus. **Athletics (Intercollegiate):** *Men:* baseball, basketball, cross-country, football, golf, gymnastics, ice hockey, lacrosse, riflery, soccer, swimming, tennis, track/field (outdoor), track/field (indoor), wrestling. *Women:* basketball, cross-country, riflery, soccer, softball, swimming, tennis, track/field (outdoor), track/field (indoor), volleyball. **On-Campus Highlights:** Cadet Chapel.

ADMISSIONS

Freshman Academic Profile: 46% in top 10% of high school class, 74% in top 25% of high school class, 94% in top 50% of high school class. 80% from public high schools. **Test Scores:** SAT Math middle 50% range 600–710. SAT EBRW middle 50% range 585–690. ACT middle 50% range 23–28. **Basis for Candidate Selection:** *Very important factors include:* rigor of secondary school record, class rank, academic GPA, standardized test scores, extracurricular activities, character/personal qualities. *Important factors include:* application essay, recommendation(s), talent/ability, level of applicant's interest. *Other factors include:* interview, first generation, racial/ethnic status, volunteer work, work experience. **Freshman Admission Requirements:** High school diploma is required and GED is accepted. *Academic units recommended:* 4 English, 4 math, 4 science, 2 science labs, 2 foreign language, 3 social studies, 1 history, 3 academic electives. **Freshman Admission Statistics:** 12,973 applied, 10% admitted, 98% enrolled. **General Admission Information:** Regular application deadline 2/28.

UNITED STATES NAVAL ACADEMY

52 King George Street, Annapolis, MD 21402
Phone: 410-293-1858
E-mail: inquire@usna.edu **CEEB Code:** 5809
Fax: 410-293-4348 **Website:** www.usna.edu **ACT Code:** 1742

This public school was founded in 1845. It has a 338 acre campus.

RATINGS

Admissions Selectivity Rating: 98   **Fire Safety Rating:** 77   **Green Rating:** 60*

STUDENTS AND FACULTY

Enrollment: 4,512. **Student Body:** 28% female, 72% male, 94% out-of-state, 1% international (29 countries represented). Asian 7%, African American 7%, Caucasian 63%, Hispanic 12%, Native American <1%, Pacific Islander 1%, Two or more races 9%, Race unknown 1%.
Retention and Graduation: 97% freshmen return for sophomore year. 90% freshmen graduate within 4 years. 91% freshmen graduate within 6 years. 10% grads go on to further study within 1 year. 9% grads pursue arts and sciences degrees. 0% grads pursue law degrees. 0% grads pursue business degrees. 1% grads pursue medical degrees. **Faculty:** Student/faculty ratio 8:1. 542 full-time faculty, 66% hold PhDs, 13% are members of minority groups, 32% are women. 0% of classes are taught by teaching assistants.

ACADEMICS

Degrees: Bachelor's; Diploma. **Classes:** Most classes have 10–19 students. **Most popular majors:** Econometrics and Quantitative Economics; Political Science and Government, General; Mechatronics, Robotics, and Automation Engineering. **Special Study Options:** Double major; Exchange student program (domestic); Honors program; Independent study; Study abroad. **Career services:** Alumni network; Alumni services.

FACILITIES

Housing: Coed dorms. **Special Academic Facilities/Equipment:** 34,000-seat stadium, 5,700-seat basketball arena, Olympic pool with a diving well for 10-meter diving boards, wrestling arena, hydraulically banked 200-meter indoor track, 400-meter outdoor track, indoor ice rink, 6 nautilus and weight rooms, facilities for gymnastics, boxing, volleyball, swimming, water polo, racquetball, basketball and personal conditioning, squash courts, climbing wall, baseball stadium, crew house, 18-hole golf course, soccer facility, a sailing center, indoor and outdoor tennis courts, and 2 athletic field houses. **Campus network:** 100% of classrooms, 100% of dorms, 100% of student union, 100% of libraries, 100% of dining areas, 90% of common outdoor areas have wireless network access.

CAMPUS LIFE

Environment: Town. **Activities:** Campus Ministries; Choral groups; Concert band; Dance; Drama/theater; International Student Organization; Jazz band; Literary magazine; Marching band; Model UN; Music ensembles; Musical theater; Pep band; Radio station; Student government; Student-run film society; Symphony orchestra; Yearbook. 100 registered organizations, 8 honor societies, 8 religious organizations on campus. **Athletics (Intercollegiate):** *Men:* baseball, basketball, crew/rowing, cross-country, diving, football, golf, gymnastics, lacrosse, light weight football, riflery, sailing, soccer, squash, swimming, tennis, track/field (outdoor), track/field (indoor), water polo, wrestling. *Women:* basketball, crew/rowing, cross-country, diving, lacrosse, riflery, sailing, soccer, swimming, tennis, track/field (outdoor), track/field (indoor), volleyball. **On-Campus Highlights:** Bancroft Hall.

ADMISSIONS

Freshman Academic Profile: Average high school GPA 4.1. 57% in top 10% of high school class, 81% in top 25% of high school class, 96% in top 50% of high school class. 60% from public high schools. **Test Scores:** SAT Math middle 50% range 590–690. SAT EBRW middle 50% range 560–680. ACT middle 50% range 26–32. **Basis for Candidate Selection:** *Very important factors include:* rigor of secondary school record, class rank, academic GPA, application essay, recommendation(s), interview, extracurricular activities, character/personal qualities, level of applicant's interest. *Important factors include:* standardized test scores, talent/ability. *Other factors include:* first generation, alumni/ae relation, geographical residence, state residency, racial/ethnic status, volunteer work, work experience. **Freshman Admission Requirements:** High school diploma or equivalent is not required. *Academic units recommended:* 4 English, 4 math, 2 science, 1 science labs, 2 foreign language, 2 history, 1 unit from above areas or other academic areas. **Freshman Admission Statistics:** 16,086 applied, 9% admitted, 87% enrolled. **General Admission Information:** Regular application deadline 1/31.

UNITY COLLEGE

PO Box 532, Unity, ME 04988
Phone: 800.624.1024 **Financial Aid Phone:** 207-948-3131 ext 235
E-mail: admissions@unity.edu **CEEB Code:** 3925
Fax: 207.948.9776 **Website:** www.unity.edu **ACT Code:** 3925

This private school was founded in 1965. It has a 225 acre campus.

RATINGS

Admissions Selectivity Rating: 85   **Fire Safety Rating:** 94   **Green Rating:** 95

STUDENTS AND FACULTY

Enrollment: 574. **Student Body:** 55% female, 45% male, 75% out-of-state, 0% international. Asian 1%, African American 1%, Caucasian 93%, Hispanic 2%, Native American 2%, Pacific Islander 0%, Two or more races 1%, Race unknown 0%.
Retention and Graduation: 83% freshmen return for sophomore year. 24% grads go on to further study within 1 year. 22% grads pursue arts and sciences degrees. 1% grads pursue law degrees. **Faculty:** Student/faculty ratio 12:1. 37 full-time faculty, 89% hold PhDs, 0% are members of minority groups, 54% are women. 0% of classes are taught by teaching assistants.

ACADEMICS

Degrees: Associate; Bachelor's. **Classes:** Most classes have 10–19 students. Most lab/discussion sessions have 10–19 students. **Most popular majors:** Environmental/Natural Resources Law Enforcement and Protective Services; Wildlife Biology; Wildlife, Fish and Wildlands Science and Management. **Special Study Options:** Accelerated program; Double major; Independent study; Internships; Study abroad; Teacher certification program. **Honors**

programs: Juniors and Seniors with a cumulative grade point average of 3.75 or higher may take one additional credit for no tuition charge. **Disability Services offered:** Note-taking services; Reader services; Tape recorders; Tutors. **Career services:** Alumni network; Alumni services; Career assessment; Internships.

FACILITIES
Housing: Coed dorms; Cooperative housing; Men's dorms; Special housing for disabled students; Theme housing; Women's dorms.

CAMPUS LIFE
Environment: Rural. **Activities:** Drama/theater; Literary magazine; Student government. 20 registered organizations on campus. **On-Campus Highlights:** Terra Haus. **Environmental Initiatives:** We only offer environmental degree programs and every student studies sustainability through our Environmental Stewardship Core curriculum. Campus sustainability efforts are an outgrowth of our academic focus.

ADMISSIONS
Freshman Academic Profile: Average high school GPA 3.3. 14% in top 10% of high school class, 33% in top 25% of high school class, 55% in top 50% of high school class. 97% from public high schools. **Test Scores:** SAT Math middle 50% range 490–560. SAT EBRW middle 50% range 480–560. ACT middle 50% range 22–25. **Basis for Candidate Selection:** *Very important factors include:* rigor of secondary school record, academic GPA, application essay, level of applicant's interest. *Important factors include:* recommendation(s), extracurricular activities, talent/ability, character/personal qualities. *Other factors include:* class rank, standardized test scores, interview. **Freshman Admission Requirements:** High school diploma is required and GED is accepted. *Academic units required:* 4 English, 3 math, 2 science, 2 science labs, 3 social studies, 3 history. *Academic units recommended:* 4 math, 3 science, 3 science labs, 2 foreign language. **Freshman Admission Statistics:** 737 applied, 61% admitted, 38% enrolled. **General Admission Information:** Application fee $25. Priority deadline 12/15. Regular application deadline 2/15. Non-fall registration accepted. Admission may be deferred for a maximum of 3 years.

COSTS AND FINANCIAL AID
Annual tuition $22,440. Room and board $8,380. Required fees $800. Average book and supplies expense $500. **Required Forms and Deadlines:** FAFSA. **Types of Aid:** *Need-based scholarships/grants:* College/university scholarship or grant aid from institutional funds; Federal Pell; Private scholarships; SEOG; State scholarships/grants. *Loans:* Direct PLUS loans; Direct Subsidized Stafford Loans; Direct Unsubsidized Stafford Loans. **Student Employment:** Federal Work-Study Program available. Institutional employment available. **Financial Aid Statistics:** 100% needy freshmen, 100% needy undergrads receive need-based scholarship or grant aid. 8% freshmen, 3% undergrads receive non-need-based scholarship or grant aid. 91% freshmen, 95% undergrads receive need-based self-help aid. 0% freshmen, 0% undergrads receive athletic scholarships. 98% freshmen, 98% undergrads receive any aid. **Criteria awarding aid:** *Non-need-based:* Academics, Leadership, Minority status.

UNIVERSITY OF ADVANCING TECHNOLOGY (UAT)

2625 W. Baseline Rd., Tempe, AZ 85283-1056
Phone: 602-383-8228 **Financial Aid Phone:** 602-383-8228
E-mail: admissions@uat.edu
Fax: 602-383-8222 **Website:** www.uat.edu

This proprietary school was founded in 1983.

RATINGS
Admissions Selectivity Rating: 60*   **Fire Safety Rating:** 60*   **Green Rating:** 60*

STUDENTS AND FACULTY
Enrollment: 1,090. **Student Body:** 10% female, 90% male, 6% out-of-state, <1% international. Asian 4%, African American 7%, Caucasian 61%, Hispanic 6%, Native American 1%, Pacific Islander 0%, Two or more races 0%, Race unknown 21%.
Faculty: Student/faculty ratio 12:1. 31 full-time faculty, 16% hold PhDs, 0% are members of minority groups, 35% are women. 0% of classes are taught by teaching assistants.

ACADEMICS
Degrees: Associate; Bachelor's; Master's. **Special Study Options:** Accelerated program; Cooperative education program; Distance learning; Double major;

Independent study; Internships; Student-designed major. **Career services:** Alumni network; Alumni services; Career assessment; Career/job search classes; Internships; Regional alumni.

FACILITIES
100% of campus accessible to physically disabled. **Campus network:** 90% of classrooms, 100% of dorms, 100% of student union, 100% of libraries, 20% of dining areas, 40% of common outdoor areas have wireless network access.

CAMPUS LIFE
Environment: Metropolis. **Activities:** Student government. 1 religious organization on campus. **On-Campus Highlights:** The Café.

ADMISSIONS
Basis for Candidate Selection: *Very important factors include:* interview, talent/ability, character/personal qualities, level of applicant's interest. *Important factors include:* rigor of secondary school record. *Other factors include:* academic GPA, standardized test scores, volunteer work. **Freshman Admission Requirements:** High school diploma is required and GED is accepted. **Transfer Admission Requirements:** High school transcript, college transcript(s). Minimum college GPA of 2.0 required. Lowest grade transferable C. **General Admission Information:** Non-fall registration accepted. Admission may be deferred for a maximum of 1 year.

COSTS AND FINANCIAL AID
Annual tuition $19,400. Average book and supplies expense $1,000. **Required Forms and Deadlines:** FAFSA. **Types of Aid:** *Need-based scholarships/grants:* College/university scholarship or grant aid from institutional funds; Federal Pell; Private scholarships; SEOG. **Student Employment:** Federal Work-Study Program available.

THE UNIVERSITY OF AKRON

The University of Akron, Akron, OH 44325-2001
Phone: 330-972-7100 **Financial Aid Phone:** 800-621-3847
E-mail: admissions@uakron.edu **CEEB Code:** 1829
Fax: 330-972-7022 **Website:** www.uakron.edu **ACT Code:** 3338

This public school was founded in 1870. It has a 223 acre campus.

RATINGS
Admissions Selectivity Rating: 75   **Fire Safety Rating:** 92   **Green Rating:** 60*

STUDENTS AND FACULTY
Enrollment: 18,137. **Student Body:** 47% female, 53% male, 4% out-of-state, 2% international (61 countries represented). Asian 2%, African American 13%, Caucasian 74%, Hispanic 2%, Native American <1%, Pacific Islander <1%, Two or more races 3%, Race unknown 3%.
Retention and Graduation: 74% freshmen return for sophomore year. **Faculty:** Student/faculty ratio 19:1. 792 full-time faculty, 79% hold PhDs, 21% are members of minority groups, 42% are women. 4% of classes are taught by teaching assistants.

ACADEMICS
Degrees: Associate; Bachelor's; Certificate; Doctoral degree—professional practice; Doctoral degree research/scholarship; Master's; Post-bachelor's certificate; Post-master's certificate. **Classes:** Most classes have 10–19 students. Most lab/discussion sessions have 20–29 students. **Most popular majors:** Marketing/Marketing Management, General; Biology/Biological Sciences, General; Mechanical Engineering. **Special Study Options:** Accelerated program; Cooperative education program; Distance learning; Double major; English as a Second Language (ESL); External degree program; Honors program; Independent study; Internships; Student-designed major; Study abroad; Teacher certification program; Weekend college. **Honors programs:** Honors Delegates, Engineering Program, Emerging Leaders Program. **Combined degree programs:** BA/MD. **Disability Services offered:** Note-taking services; Reader services; Tape recorders; Tutors. **Career services:** Alumni services; Career assessment; Career/job search classes; Internships.

FACILITIES
Housing: Coed dorms; Fraternity/sorority housing; Men's dorms; Special housing for disabled students; Special housing for international students; Women's dorms; 90% of campus accessible to physically disabled. **Special Academic Facilities/Equipment:** Performing arts hall, nursery center, language lab, speech and hearing center, nursing learning resource labs, institute of

polymer science and engineering, chemical lab, institute for health and social policy, Bliss Institute of Applied Politics. **Campus network:** 100% of classrooms, 100% of dorms, 100% of student union, 100% of libraries, 100% of dining areas, 85% of common outdoor areas have wireless network access.

CAMPUS LIFE

Environment: City. **Activities:** Campus Ministries; Choral groups; Concert band; Dance; Drama/theater; International Student Organization; Jazz band; Marching band; Music ensembles; Musical theater; Pep band; Radio station; Student government; Student newspaper; Symphony orchestra; Television station; Yearbook. 254 registered organizations, 34 honor societies, 13 religious organizations, 16 fraternities, 14 sororities on campus. **Athletics (Intercollegiate):** *Men:* baseball, basketball, cheerleading, cross-country, football, golf, riflery, soccer, track/field (outdoor), track/field (indoor). *Women:* basketball, cheerleading, cross-country, diving, riflery, soccer, softball, swimming, tennis, track/field (outdoor), track/field (indoor), volleyball. **On-Campus Highlights:** Recreation Center.

ADMISSIONS

Freshman Academic Profile: Average high school GPA 3.2. 13% in top 10% of high school class, 38% in top 25% of high school class, 66% in top 50% of high school class. **Test Scores:** SAT Math middle 50% range 450–620. SAT EBRW middle 50% range 450–580. ACT middle 50% range 19–26. **Basis for Candidate Selection:** *Very important factors include:* rigor of secondary school record, class rank, academic GPA, standardized test scores. *Other factors include:* application essay, recommendation(s), extracurricular activities, talent/ability, volunteer work, level of applicant's interest. **Freshman Admission Requirements:** High school diploma is required and GED is accepted. *Academic units recommended:* 4 English, 3 math, 3 science, 2 foreign language, 3 social studies. **Freshman Admission Statistics:** 13,109 applied, 87% admitted, 32% enrolled. **Transfer Admission Requirements:** College transcript(s), statement of good standing from prior institution(s). Lowest grade transferable D-. **General Admission Information:** Application fee $45. Regular application deadline 7/1. Non-fall registration accepted. Admission may be deferred for a maximum of 2 semesters.

COSTS AND FINANCIAL AID

Annual in-state tuition $8,618. Annual out-of-state tuition $17,149. Room and board $11,322. Required fees $1,891. Average book and supplies expense $1,000. **Required Forms and Deadlines:** FAFSA; Institution's own financial aid form. **Notification of Awards:** Applicants will be notified of awards on a rolling basis beginning 4/1. **Types of Aid:** *Need-based scholarships/grants:* Federal Pell; SEOG. *Loans:* Direct PLUS loans; Direct Subsidized Stafford Loans; Direct Unsubsidized Stafford Loans. **Student Employment:** Federal Work-Study Program available. Institutional employment available. **Financial Aid Statistics:** 55% needy freshmen, 53% needy undergrads receive need-based scholarship or grant aid. 62% freshmen, 52% undergrads receive non-need-based scholarship or grant aid. 74% freshmen, 72% undergrads receive need-based self-help aid. 0% freshmen, 0% undergrads receive athletic scholarships. 78% freshmen, 81% undergrads receive any aid. **Criteria awarding aid:** *Non-need-based:* Academics, Art, Athletics, Leadership, Music/drama, State/district residency.

THE UNIVERSITY OF ALABAMA—BIRMINGHAM

Office of Undergraduate Admissions, Birmingham, AL 35294-4412
Phone: 205-934-8221 **Financial Aid Phone:** 205-934-8223
E-mail: chooseuab@uab.edu **CEEB Code:** 1856
Fax: 205-975-7114 **Website:** www.uab.edu **ACT Code:** 56

This public school was founded in 1969. It has a 275 acre campus.

RATINGS

Admissions Selectivity Rating: 78   **Fire Safety Rating:** 95   **Green Rating:** 84

STUDENTS AND FACULTY

Enrollment: 13,328. **Student Body:** 61% female, 39% male, 13% out-of-state, 2% international (53 countries represented). Asian 7%, African American 24%, Caucasian 56%, Hispanic 6%, Native American <1%, Pacific Islander <1%, Two or more races 4%, Race unknown 1%.

Retention and Graduation: 83% freshmen return for sophomore year. 40% freshmen graduate within 4 years. 63% freshmen graduate within 6 years. **Faculty:** Student/faculty ratio 19:1. 902 full-time faculty, 87% hold PhDs, 23% are members of minority groups, 51% are women. 4% of classes are taught by teaching assistants.

ACADEMICS

Degrees: Bachelor's; Certificate; Doctoral degree—other; Doctoral degree—professional practice; Doctoral degree research/scholarship; Master's; Post-bachelor's certificate; Post-master's certificate. **Classes:** Most classes have 10–19 students. Most lab/discussion sessions have 20–29 students. **Most popular majors:** Biology/Biological Sciences, General; Psychology, General; Accounting. **Special Study Options:** Accelerated program; Cooperative education program; Cross-registration; Distance learning; Double major; Dual enrollment; English as a Second Language (ESL); Exchange student program (domestic); Honors program; Independent study; Internships; Student-designed major; Study abroad; Teacher certification program. **Honors programs:** The University Honors Program is designed for students who want to satisfy their intellectual curiosity both inside and outside the classroom. The program is limited in size to 200 students who represent a wide variety of disciplines, backgrounds and interests. Without delaying progress toward a degree, the Honors College provides students an opportunity to participate in a community of committed scholars, to form close relationships with faculty, to explore new ideas, and to share their ideas, interests, and lives on a daily basis in the Honors House. Students have opportunities to work on independent projects, to travel, and to participate in special extracurricular activities. Those who complete the program are recognized with the designation "With University Honors" on their transcripts and in the graduation program. Please visit our Univeristy Honors Program website for more information: http://main.uab.edu/Sites/undergraduate-programs/honors_college/. **Combined degree programs:** BA/MA; BA/MD. **Disability Services offered:** Note-taking services; Reader services; Tape recorders. **Career services:** Alumni network; Alumni services; Career assessment; Career/job search classes; Internships; Regional alumni.

FACILITIES

Housing: Apartments for married students; Apartments for single students; Coed dorms; Special housing for disabled students; Special housing for international students; Theme housing; 100% of campus accessible to physically disabled. **Special Academic Facilities/Equipment:** Museum of health sciences, Alys Stephens Center for the performing arts, Samuel Ullman Museum, Abroms-Engel Institute for the Visual Arts. **Campus network:** 100% of classrooms, 100% of dorms, 100% of student union have wireless network access.

CAMPUS LIFE

Environment: Metropolis. **Activities:** Campus Ministries; Choral groups; Concert band; Dance; Drama/theater; International Student Organization; Jazz band; Literary magazine; Marching band; Model UN; Music ensembles; Musical theater; Opera; Pep band; Radio station; Student government; Student newspaper; Student-run film society; Television station. 250 registered organizations, 17 honor societies, 13 fraternities, 13 sororities on campus. **Athletics (Intercollegiate):** *Men:* baseball, basketball, football, golf, soccer, tennis. *Women:* basketball, cross-country, golf, riflery, soccer, softball, synchronized swimming, tennis, track/field (outdoor), track/field (indoor), volleyball. **On-Campus Highlights:** Student Recreation Center. **Environmental Initiatives:** Recycling.

ADMISSIONS

Freshman Academic Profile: Average high school GPA 3.8. 29% in top 10% of high school class, 57% in top 25% of high school class, 87% in top 50% of high school class. **Test Scores:** SAT Math middle 50% range 530–685. SAT EBRW middle 50% range 560–680. ACT middle 50% range 22–29. **Basis for Candidate Selection:** *Very important factors include:* rigor of secondary school record, academic GPA, standardized test scores. **Freshman Admission Requirements:** High school diploma is required and GED is accepted. *Academic units required:* 4 English, 3 math, 3 science, 2 science labs, 1 foreign language, 3 social studies, 3 academic electives. **Freshman Admission Statistics:** 8,298 applied, 74% admitted, 38% enrolled. **Transfer Admission Requirements:** College transcript(s). Minimum college GPA of 2.0 required. **General Admission Information:** Application fee $30. Priority deadline 6/1. Non-fall registration accepted. Admission may be deferred for a maximum of 1 year.

COSTS AND FINANCIAL AID

Annual in-state tuition $10,710. Annual out-of-state tuition $25,500. Room and board $10,910. Average book and supplies expense $1,200. **Required Forms and Deadlines:** FAFSA. **Notification of Awards:** Applicants will be notified of awards on a rolling basis beginning 3/15. **Types of Aid:** *Need-based scholarships/grants:* College/university scholarship or grant aid from institutional funds; Federal Pell; Private scholarships; SEOG; State scholarships/grants; United Negro College Fund. *Loans:* Direct PLUS loans; Direct Subsidized Stafford Loans; Direct Unsubsidized Stafford Loans. **Student Employment:** Federal Work-Study Program available. Institutional employment available. **Financial Aid Statistics:** 56% needy freshmen, 63% needy undergrads receive need-based scholarship or grant aid. 78% freshmen, 50% undergrads receive non-need-based scholarship or grant aid. 24% freshmen, 14% undergrads receive need-based self-help aid. 3% freshmen, 3% undergrads receive athletic scholarships. 60% undergrads borrow to pay for school. Average cumulative indebtedness $29,914. **Criteria awarding aid:** *Need-based:* Academics, Alumni affiliation, Minority status. *Non-need-based:* Academics, Alumni affiliation, Art, Athletics, Leadership, Minority status, Music/drama.

THE UNIVERSITY OF ALABAMA—HUNTSVILLE

UAH Office of Admissions, Huntsville, AL 35899
Phone: 256-824-2773 **Financial Aid Phone:** 256-824-2761
E-mail: uahadmissions@uah.edu **CEEB Code:** 1854
Fax: 256-824-4539 **Website:** www.uah.edu **ACT Code:** 53

This public school was founded in 1950. It has a 400 acre campus.

RATINGS

Admissions Selectivity Rating: 83   Fire Safety Rating: 96   Green Rating: 71

STUDENTS AND FACULTY
Enrollment: 6,338. **Student Body:** 42% female, 58% male, 16% out-of-state, 3% international (75 countries represented). Asian 4%, African American 11%, Caucasian 72%, Hispanic 4%, Native American 1%, Pacific Islander 0%, Two or more races 2%, Race unknown 3%.
Retention and Graduation: 83% freshmen return for sophomore year.
Faculty: Student/faculty ratio 17:1. 326 full-time faculty, 79% hold PhDs, 25% are members of minority groups, 43% are women. 3% of classes are taught by teaching assistants.

ACADEMICS
Degrees: Bachelor's; Certificate; Doctoral degree—professional practice; Doctoral degree research/scholarship; Master's; Post-bachelor's certificate; Post-master's certificate. **Classes:** Most classes have 20–29 students. Most lab/discussion sessions have fewer than 10 students. **Most popular majors:** Registered Nursing/Registered Nurse; Biology/Biological Sciences, General; Mechanical Engineering. **Special Study Options:** Cooperative education program; Cross-registration; Distance learning; Double major; Dual enrollment; English as a Second Language (ESL); Honors program; Independent study; Internships; Student-designed major; Study abroad; Teacher certification program. **Honors programs:** The Honors College at UAH provides academically talented undergraduate students with opportunities to develop their special talents and skills within an expanded and enriched version of the curriculum leading to an Honors Diploma. Honors coursework parallels regular offerings in all majors and programs. The courses include special interdisciplinary seminars, and opportunities for independent study and research/creative work, including the opportunity to work closely with faculty on special student projects. Students may participate in an Honors internship that offers active involvement in a business enterprise, professional organization, or government agency that has particular interest and relevance to the student's course of study. Participating students also benefit from the interaction the Honors College affords with other talented and highly motivated students. See http://honors.uah.edu for more information. **Combined degree programs:** BA/MA; BA/MEng. **Disability Services offered:** Note-taking services; Reader services; Tutors. **Career services:** Alumni services; Career assessment; Career/job search classes; Internships.

FACILITIES
Housing: Apartments for married students; Apartments for single students; Coed dorms; Cooperative housing; Fraternity/sorority housing; Special housing for disabled students; Theme housing; 98% of campus accessible to physically disabled. **Special Academic Facilities/Equipment:** UAH has an art museum and galleries, an optical observatory, a radio telescope, and a rooftop greenhouse used for research and lab experiences. The National Space and Technology Center located on our campus is shared between UAH, NASA, and the National Weather Service. **Campus network:** 100% of classrooms, 100% of

dorms, 100% of student union, 100% of libraries, 100% of dining areas, 100% of common outdoor areas have wireless network access.

CAMPUS LIFE
Environment: City. **Activities:** Campus Ministries; Choral groups; Concert band; Dance; Drama/theater; International Student Organization; Jazz band; Model UN; Music ensembles; Musical theater; Opera; Pep band; Student government; Student newspaper. 125 registered organizations, 15 honor societies, 9 religious organizations, 6 fraternities, 6 sororities on campus. **Athletics (Intercollegiate):** *Men:* baseball, basketball, cheerleading, cross-country, ice hockey, soccer, tennis, track/field (outdoor), track/field (indoor). *Women:* basketball, cheerleading, cross-country, soccer, softball, tennis, track/field (outdoor), track/field (indoor), volleyball. **On-Campus Highlights:** Charger Union **Environmental Initiatives:** A hazard chemical waste and waste minimization program has been in effect for over 15 years. Improved environmental awareness communications and training/learning opportunities will soon be available on the OEHS web site.

ADMISSIONS
Freshman Academic Profile: Average high school GPA 3.8. 29% in top 10% of high school class, 56% in top 25% of high school class, 85% in top 50% of high school class. 90% from public high schools. **Test Scores:** SAT Math middle 50% range 540–680. SAT EBRW middle 50% range 520–650. ACT middle 50% range 25–31. **Basis for Candidate Selection:** *Very important factors include:* academic GPA, standardized test scores. *Other factors include:* level of applicant's interest. **Freshman Admission Requirements:** High school diploma is required and GED is accepted. *Academic units required:* 4 English, 3 math, 3 science, 4 social studies, 6 academic electives. *Academic units recommended:* 4 English, 4 math, 4 science, 2 science labs, 2 foreign language, 4 social studies, 6 academic electives. **Freshman Admission Statistics:** 4,545 applied, 76% admitted, 35% enrolled. **Transfer Admission Requirements:** College transcript(s), statement of good standing from prior institution(s). Minimum college GPA of 2.0 required. Lowest grade transferable D. **General Admission Information:** Application fee $30. Regular application deadline 8/20. Non-fall registration accepted. Admission may be deferred for a maximum of 1 year.

COSTS AND FINANCIAL AID
Annual in-state tuition $8,996. Annual out-of-state tuition $19,766. Room and board $9,603. Required fees $846. Average book and supplies expense $1,688. **Required Forms and Deadlines:** FAFSA. **Notification of Awards:** Applicants will be notified of awards on a rolling basis beginning 4/1. **Types of Aid:** *Need-based scholarships/grants:* College/university scholarship or grant aid from institutional funds; Federal Nursing Scholarships; Federal Pell; Private scholarships; SEOG; State scholarships/grants. *Loans:* Direct PLUS loans; Direct Subsidized Stafford Loans; Direct Unsubsidized Stafford Loans. **Student Employment:** Federal Work-Study Program available. Institutional employment available. **Financial Aid Statistics:** 91% needy freshmen, 84% needy undergrads receive need-based scholarship or grant aid. 26% freshmen, 10% undergrads receive non-need-based scholarship or grant aid. 66% freshmen, 79% undergrads receive need-based self-help aid. 6% freshmen, 4% undergrads receive athletic scholarships. 88% freshmen, 78% undergrads receive any aid. 54% undergrads borrow to pay for school. Average cumulative indebtedness $35,009. **Criteria awarding aid:** *Non-need-based:* Academics, Art, Athletics, Leadership, Minority status, Music/drama.

THE UNIVERSITY OF ALABAMA—TUSCALOOSA

Box 870132, Tuscaloosa, AL 35487-0132
Phone: 205-348-5666 **Financial Aid Phone:** 205-348-7949
E-mail: admissions@ua.edu **CEEB Code:** 1830
Fax: 205-348-9046 **Website:** www.ua.edu **ACT Code:** 52

This public school was founded in 1831. It has a 1026 acre campus.

RATINGS
Admissions Selectivity Rating: 84   Fire Safety Rating: 83   Green Rating: 60*

STUDENTS AND FACULTY
Enrollment: 31,900. **Student Body:** 55% female, 45% male, 61% out-of-state, 2% international (57 countries represented). Asian 1%, African American 10%,

Caucasian 77%, Hispanic 5%, Native American <1%, Pacific Islander <1%, Two or more races 4%, Race unknown <1%. **Retention and Graduation:** 87% freshmen return for sophomore year. 50% freshmen graduate within 4 years. 71% freshmen graduate within 6 years. 25% grads go on to further study within 1 year. 5% grads pursue arts and sciences degrees. 3% grads pursue law degrees. 7% grads pursue business degrees. 2% grads pursue medical degrees. **Faculty:** 1,466 full-time faculty, 86% hold PhDs, 19% are members of minority groups, 45% are women. 10% of classes are taught by teaching assistants.

ACADEMICS
Degrees: Bachelor's; Doctoral degree—professional practice; Doctoral degree research/scholarship; Master's; Post-master's certificate. **Classes:** Most classes have 20–29 students. Most lab/discussion sessions have 20–29 students. **Most popular majors:** Business Administration and Management, General; Marketing/Marketing Management, General; Finance, General. **Special Study Options:** Accelerated program; Cooperative education program; Cross-registration; Distance learning; Double major; Dual enrollment; English as a Second Language (ESL); Exchange student program (domestic); External degree program; Honors program; Independent study; Internships; Liberal arts/career combination; Student-designed major; Study abroad; Teacher certification program; Weekend college. **Honors programs:** The Honors College serves its students through the core Honors experience and other specialized programs, including the Randall Research Scholars Program and the University Fellows Experience. The Honors College also collaborates with other Colleges to create departmental honors programs and unique program offerings throughout the University, which allows Honors students to major in any discipline and add to the diversity of their Honors experience. Selected students concentrating their studies in either a STEM discipline or in a traditionally creative discipline have the opportunity to complete coursework to earn an MBA from the Manderson Graduate School of Business in one additional year beyond the completion of an undergraduate degree. The STEM Path to the MBA and CREATE Path to the MBA programs are centered around innovative solutions to real-world problems and run in parallel to one another. The Accelerated Masters Program (AMP) allows Honors students to earn up to 15 dual-credit hours towards a bachelors and masters degrees. **Combined degree programs:** BA/MA; BA/MEng. **Disability Services offered:** Note-taking services; Reader services; Tape recorders; Tutors. **Career services:** Alumni network; Alumni services; Career assessment; Career/job search classes; Internships; Regional alumni.

FACILITIES
Housing: Apartments for single students; Coed dorms; Fraternity/sorority housing; Men's dorms; Special housing for disabled students; Special housing for international students; Theme housing; Women's dorms; 99% of campus accessible to physically disabled. **Special Academic Facilities/Equipment:** Art gallery, natural history museum, concert hall, archaeologic site and museum, arboretum, observatory, simulated coal mine, robotics lab, wind tunnel, artificial intelligence lab, jet propulsion engine mini-lab, special collections building. **Campus network:** 100% of classrooms, 50% of dorms, 100% of student union, 100% of libraries, 100% of dining areas, 50% of common outdoor areas have wireless network access.

CAMPUS LIFE
Environment: City. **Activities:** Campus Ministries; Choral groups; Concert band; Dance; Drama/theater; International Student Organization; Jazz band; Literary magazine; Marching band; Model UN; Music ensembles; Musical theater; Opera; Pep band; Radio station; Student government; Student newspaper; Student-run film society; Symphony orchestra; Television station. 583 registered organizations, 44 honor societies, 73 religious organizations, 43 fraternities, 24 sororities on campus. **Athletics (Intercollegiate):** *Men:* baseball, basketball, cross-country, diving, football, golf, swimming, tennis, track/field (outdoor), track/field (indoor). *Women:* basketball, crew/rowing, cross-country, diving, golf, gymnastics, soccer, softball, swimming, tennis, track/field (outdoor), track/field (indoor), volleyball. **On-Campus Highlights:** Ferguson Center Student Union **Environmental Initiatives:** Recycling has increased by 181% over fiscal year 2008. Currently we are recycling over 1,300 tons of recyclable material.

ADMISSIONS
Freshman Academic Profile: Average high school GPA 3.8. 40% in top 10% of high school class, 61% in top 25% of high school class, 84% in top 50% of high school class. **Test Scores:** SAT Math middle 50% range 530–680. SAT EBRW middle 50% range 550–660. ACT middle 50% range 23–31. **Basis for Candidate Selection:** *Very important factors include:* rigor of secondary school record, academic GPA, standardized test scores. *Important factors include:* class rank. *Other factors include:* application essay, recommendation(s), interview, extracurricular activities, talent/ability, character/personal qualities, first

generation, alumni/ae relation, volunteer work, work experience. **Freshman Admission Requirements:** High school diploma is required and GED is accepted. *Academic units required:* 4 English, 3 math, 3 science, 2 science labs, 1 foreign language, 4 social studies, 5 academic electives. *Academic units recommended:* 4 English, 3 math, 3 science, 2 science labs, 2 foreign language, 4 social studies, 5 academic electives. **Freshman Admission Statistics:** 38,505 applied, 83% admitted, 21% enrolled. **Transfer Admission Requirements:** College transcript(s). Minimum college GPA of 2.0 required. Lowest grade transferable D. **General Admission Information:** Application fee $40. Priority deadline 2/1. Non-fall registration accepted. Admission may be deferred for a maximum of one year.

COSTS AND FINANCIAL AID
Annual in-state tuition $10,780. Annual out-of-state tuition $30,250. Room and board $10,836. Average book and supplies expense $1,000. **Required Forms and Deadlines:** FAFSA. **Notification of Awards:** Applicants will be notified of awards on a rolling basis beginning 4/1. **Types of Aid:** *Need-based scholarships/grants:* College/university scholarship or grant aid from institutional funds; Federal Nursing Scholarships; Federal Pell; Private scholarships; SEOG; State scholarships/grants. *Loans:* Direct PLUS loans; Direct Subsidized Stafford Loans; Direct Unsubsidized Stafford Loans. **Student Employment:** Institutional employment available. **Financial Aid Statistics:** 77% needy freshmen, 75% needy undergrads receive need-based scholarship or grant aid. 63% freshmen, 54% undergrads receive non-need-based scholarship or grant aid. 63% freshmen, 73% undergrads receive need-based self-help aid. 1% freshmen, 2% undergrads receive athletic scholarships. 81.3% freshmen, 73.7% undergrads receive any aid. 47% undergrads borrow to pay for school. Average cumulative indebtedness $34,975. **Criteria awarding aid:** *Need-based:* Academics. *Non-need-based:* Academics, Alumni affiliation, Art, Athletics, Leadership, Minority status, Music/drama, State/district residency.

UNIVERSITY OF ALASKA ANCHORAGE

3211 Providence Drive, Anchorage, AK 99508-8046
Phone: 907-786-1480
E-mail: enroll@uaa.alaska.edu **CEEB Code:** 4896
Fax: 907-786-4888 **Website:** www.uaa.alaska.edu/ **ACT Code:** 137

This public school was founded in 1954. It has a 384 acre campus.

RATINGS
Admissions Selectivity Rating: 73   **Fire Safety Rating:** 75   **Green Rating:** 60*

STUDENTS AND FACULTY
Enrollment: 13,390. **Student Body:** 58% female, 42% male, 10% out-of-state, <1% international (35 countries represented). Asian 7%, African American 4%, Caucasian 58%, Hispanic 7%, Native American 12%, Pacific Islander 1%, Two or more races 3%, Race unknown 6%.
Retention and Graduation: 73% freshmen return for sophomore year.
Faculty: Student/faculty ratio 12:1. 680 full-time faculty, 53% hold PhDs, 12% are members of minority groups, 52% are women. 0% of classes are taught by teaching assistants.

ACADEMICS
Degrees: Associate; Bachelor's; Certificate; Master's; Post-bachelor's certificate; Post-master's certificate. **Classes:** Most classes have 10–19 students. Most lab/discussion sessions have 10–19 students. **Special Study Options:** Accelerated program; Cooperative education program; Cross-registration; Distance learning; Double major; Dual enrollment; English as a Second Language (ESL); Exchange student program (domestic); Honors program; Independent study; Internships; Liberal arts/career combination; Student-designed major; Study abroad; Teacher certification program. **Honors programs:** University Honors Program. **Disability Services offered:** Note-taking services; Reader services; Tape recorders. **Career services:** Alumni services; Career assessment; Career/job search classes; Internships.

FACILITIES
Housing: Apartments for single students; Coed dorms; Special housing for disabled students; Special housing for international students; Wellness housing; 95% of campus accessible to physically disabled. **Special Academic Facilities/Equipment:** Kimura and student Center Galleries.

CAMPUS LIFE

Environment: City. **Activities:** Campus Ministries; Choral groups; Dance; Drama/theater; International Student Organization; Jazz band; Literary magazine; Model UN; Music ensembles; Musical theater; Opera; Radio station; Student government; Student newspaper; Student-run film society. 70 registered organizations, 5 honor societies, 5 religious organizations, 1 fraternity, 2 sororities on campus. **Athletics (Intercollegiate):** *Men:* basketball, cross-country, ice hockey, skiing (downhill/Alpine), skiing (Nordic/cross-country). *Women:* basketball, cross-country, gymnastics, skiing (downhill/Alpine), skiing (Nordic/cross-country), volleyball. **On-Campus Highlights:** Campus Center.

ADMISSIONS

Freshman Academic Profile: 13% in top 10% of high school class, 32% in top 25% of high school class, 62% in top 50% of high school class. 95% from public high schools. **Test Scores:** SAT Math middle 50% range 440–570. SAT EBRW middle 50% range 430–580. **Basis for Candidate Selection:** *Very important factors include:* rigor of secondary school record. *Other factors include:* class rank, standardized test scores, talent/ability. **Freshman Admission Requirements:** High school diploma is required and GED is accepted. **Freshman Admission Statistics:** 2,976 applied, 100% admitted, 43% enrolled. **Transfer Admission Requirements:** College transcript(s), statement of good standing from prior institution(s). Minimum college GPA of 2.0 required. Lowest grade transferable C. **General Admission Information:** Application fee $50. Regular application deadline 7/1. Non-fall registration accepted. Admission may be deferred for a maximum of 1 years.

COSTS AND FINANCIAL AID

Annual in-state tuition $4,950. Annual out-of-state tuition $17,400. Room and board $9,827. Average book and supplies expense $1,575. **Required Forms and Deadlines:** FAFSA; Institution's own financial aid form. **Notification of Awards:** Applicants will be notified of awards on a rolling basis beginning 3/15. **Types of Aid:** *Need-based scholarships/grants:* College/university scholarship or grant aid from institutional funds; Federal Pell; Private scholarships; SEOG; State scholarships/grants. **Student Employment:** Federal Work-Study Program available. Institutional employment available. **Financial Aid Statistics:** 84% needy freshmen, 74% needy undergrads receive need-based scholarship or grant aid. 10% freshmen, 3% undergrads receive non-need-based scholarship or grant aid. 63% freshmen, 71% undergrads receive need-based self-help aid. 2% freshmen, 1% undergrads receive athletic scholarships. **Criteria awarding aid:** *Need-based:* Academics, Leadership, Minority status. *Non-need-based:* Academics, Athletics.

UNIVERSITY OF ALASKA FAIRBANKS

PO Box 757480, Fairbanks, AK 99775-7480
Phone: 907-474-7500 **Financial Aid Phone:** 888-474-7256
E-mail: admissions@uaf.edu **CEEB Code:** 4866
Fax: 907-474-5379 **Website:** www.uaf.edu **ACT Code:** 64

This public school was founded in 1917. It has a 2250 acre campus.

RATINGS

Admissions Selectivity Rating: 86   **Fire Safety Rating:** 93   **Green Rating:** 60*

STUDENTS AND FACULTY

Enrollment: 5,445. **Student Body:** 55% female, 45% male, 14% out-of-state, 1% international (29 countries represented). Asian 1%, African American 2%, Caucasian 42%, Hispanic 6%, Native American 14%, Pacific Islander <1%, Two or more races 4%, Race unknown 29%.
Retention and Graduation: 75% freshmen return for sophomore year.
Faculty: Student/faculty ratio 11:1. 357 full-time faculty, 76% hold PhDs, 20% are members of minority groups, 43% are women.

ACADEMICS

Degrees: Associate; Bachelor's; Certificate; Doctoral degree research/scholarship; Master's; Post-bachelor's certificate; Terminal Associate; Transfer Associate. **Classes:** Most classes have 10–19 students. Most lab/discussion sessions have 10–19 students. **Most popular majors:** Biology/Biological Sciences, General; Business Administration and Management, General; Mechanical Engineering. **Special Study Options:** Accelerated program; Cooperative education program; Distance learning; Double major; Dual enrollment; English as a Second Language (ESL); Exchange student program (domestic); External degree program; Honors program; Independent study; Internships; Student-designed major; Study abroad; Teacher certification program. **Honors programs:** The

Honors Program at UAF provides superior undergraduate students with intellectual opportunities greater than those generally found in university lecture halls. Honors students experience small classes, direct contact with top faculty members, a flexible curriculum and great encouragement to pursue their own intellectual interests. **Disability Services offered:** Note-taking services; Reader services; Tape recorders; Tutors. **Career services:** Alumni network; Alumni services; Career assessment; Career/job search classes; Internships.

FACILITIES

Housing: Apartments for married students; Apartments for single students; Coed dorms; Special housing for disabled students; Wellness housing; 90% of campus accessible to physically disabled. **Special Academic Facilities/ Equipment:** Museum of natural/cultural history of Alaska and the North, Super Computer, extensive telecommunication network, Geophysical Institute, NASA earth station, Poker Flat Research Range, electron microscope, microprobe, International Arctic Research Center, Institute of Arctic Biology, Institute of Northern Engineering, Arctic Region Supercomputing Center, Institute of Marine Biology, Agriculture and Forestry Experiment Station, Office of Electronic Miniaturization, Alaska Native Language Center, Georgeson Botanical Gardens, Cold Climate Housing Research Center, Large Animal Research Station.

CAMPUS LIFE

Environment: City. **Activities:** Campus Ministries; Choral groups; Dance; Drama/theater; International Student Organization; Jazz band; Literary magazine; Model UN; Music ensembles; Radio station; Student government; Student newspaper; Symphony orchestra. 134 registered organizations, 7 honor societies, 7 religious organizations, 1 fraternity, 1 sorority on campus. **Athletics (Intercollegiate):** *Men:* basketball, cross-country, ice hockey, riflery, skiing (Nordic/cross-country). *Women:* basketball, cross-country, riflery, skiing (Nordic/cross-country), volleyball. **On-Campus Highlights:** Wood Center (includes food court).

ADMISSIONS

Freshman Academic Profile: Average high school GPA 3.3. 18% in top 10% of high school class, 38% in top 25% of high school class, 69% in top 50% of high school class. **Test Scores:** SAT Math middle 50% range 480–610. SAT EBRW middle 50% range 480–610. ACT middle 50% range 18–26. **Basis for Candidate Selection:** *Very important factors include:* academic GPA, standardized test scores. **Freshman Admission Requirements:** High school diploma is required and GED is not accepted. *Academic units required:* 4 English, 3 math, 3 science, 1 science labs, 3 social studies. *Academic units recommended:* 2 foreign language. **Freshman Admission Statistics:** 1,554 applied, 73% admitted, 70% enrolled. **Transfer Admission Requirements:** College transcript(s). Minimum college GPA of 2.0 required. Lowest grade transferable C. **General Admission Information:** Application fee $50. Priority deadline 2/15. Regular application deadline 6/15. Non-fall registration accepted. Admission may be deferred for a maximum of 1 year.

COSTS AND FINANCIAL AID

Annual in-state tuition $6,360. Annual out-of-state tuition $21,030. Room and board $8,380. Required fees $1,424. Average book and supplies expense $1,400. **Required Forms and Deadlines:** FAFSA; Institution's own financial aid form. **Notification of Awards:** Applicants will be notified of awards on a rolling basis beginning 3/1. **Types of Aid:** *Need-based scholarships/grants:* College/university scholarship or grant aid from institutional funds; Federal Pell; Private scholarships; SEOG; State scholarships/grants. *Loans:* Direct PLUS loans; Direct Subsidized Stafford Loans; Direct Unsubsidized Stafford Loans. **Student Employment:** Federal Work-Study Program available. Institutional employment available. **Financial Aid Statistics:** 89% needy freshmen, 87% needy undergrads receive need-based scholarship or grant aid. 14% freshmen, 9% undergrads receive non-need-based scholarship or grant aid. 43% freshmen, 58% undergrads receive need-based self-help aid. 2% freshmen, 3% undergrads receive athletic scholarships. 79% freshmen, 68% undergrads receive any aid. 48% undergrads borrow to pay for school. Average cumulative indebtedness $27,805. **Criteria awarding aid:** *Need-based:* Academics. *Non-need-based:* Academics, Art, Athletics, Music/drama, State/district residency.

UNIVERSITY OF ARIZONA

PO Box 210073, Tucson, AZ 85721-0073
Phone: 520-621-3237 **Financial Aid Phone:** 520-621-1858
E-mail: admissions@arizona.edu **CEEB Code:** 4832
Fax: 520-621-9799 **Website:** http://www.arizona.edu **ACT Code:** 96

This public school was founded in 1885. It has a 392 acre campus.

RATINGS
Admissions Selectivity Rating: 82   **Fire Safety Rating:** 91   **Green Rating:** 95

STUDENTS AND FACULTY
Enrollment: 34,591. **Student Body:** 54% female, 46% male, 39% out-of-state, 6% international (120 countries represented). Asian 5%, African American 4%, Caucasian 49%, Hispanic 27%, Native American 1%, Pacific Islander <1%, Two or more races 5%, Race unknown 2%.
Retention and Graduation: 83% freshmen return for sophomore year. 47% freshmen graduate within 4 years. 65% freshmen graduate within 6 years. 21% grads go on to further study within 1 year. 3% grads pursue arts and sciences degrees. 1% grads pursue law degrees. 2% grads pursue business degrees. 4% grads pursue medical degrees. **Faculty:** Student/faculty ratio 15:1. 2,118 full-time faculty, 94% hold PhDs, 25% are members of minority groups, 41% are women. 17% of classes are taught by teaching assistants.

ACADEMICS
Degrees: Bachelor's; Certificate; Doctoral degree—professional practice; Doctoral degree research/scholarship; Master's; Post-bachelor's certificate; Post-master's certificate. **Classes:** Most classes have 10–19 students. Most lab/discussion sessions have 20–29 students. **Most popular majors:** Psychology, General; Public Health, General; Registered Nursing/Registered Nurse. **Special Study Options:** Accelerated program; Cooperative education program; Cross-registration; Distance learning; Double enrollment; Dual enrollment; English as a Second Language (ESL); Exchange student program (domestic); Honors program; Independent study; Internships; Liberal arts/career combination; Study abroad; Teacher certification program. **Honors programs:** For information on our Honors College, visit: https://honors.arizona.edu/. **Combined degree programs:** BA/JD; BA/MA. **Disability Services offered:** Note-taking services; Reader services; Tape recorders; Tutors. **Career services:** Alumni network; Alumni services; Career assessment; Career/job search classes; Internships; Regional alumni.

FACILITIES
Housing: Apartments for married students; Apartments for single students; Coed dorms; Fraternity/sorority housing; Special housing for disabled students; Special housing for international students; Theme housing; Wellness housing; Women's dorms; 100% of campus accessible to physically disabled. **Special Academic Facilities/Equipment:** Art, photography, and natural history museums, tree-ring lab, planetarium, optical sciences center, nuclear reactor.

CAMPUS LIFE
Environment: Metropolis. **Activities:** Campus Ministries; Choral groups; Concert band; Dance; Drama/theater; International Student Organization; Jazz band; Literary magazine; Marching band; Model UN; Music ensembles; Musical theater; Opera; Pep band; Radio station; Student government; Student newspaper; Symphony orchestra; Television station; Yearbook. 920 registered organizations, 49 honor societies, 69 religious organizations, 25 fraternities, 24 sororities on campus. **Athletics (Intercollegiate):** *Men:* baseball, basketball, cross-country, diving, football, golf, swimming, tennis, track/field (outdoor). *Women:* basketball, cross-country, diving, golf, gymnastics, soccer, softball, swimming, tennis, track/field (outdoor), track/field (indoor), volleyball. **On-Campus Highlights:** Flandrau Science Center. **Environmental Initiatives:** The University of Arizona's top environmental commitments are conducting comprehensive research on environmental issues ranging from biodiversity, management, and global change.

ADMISSIONS
Freshman Academic Profile: Average high school GPA 3.4. 36% in top 10% of high school class, 65% in top 25% of high school class, 88% in top 50% of high school class. 99% from public high schools. **Test Scores:** SAT Math middle 50% range 550–690. SAT EBRW middle 50% range 560–670. ACT middle 50% range 21–29. **Basis for Candidate Selection:** *Very important factors include:* rigor of secondary school record, academic GPA. *Important factors include:* standardized test scores, extracurricular activities, talent/ability, character/personal qualities, level of applicant's interest. *Other factors include:* class rank, application essay, recommendation(s), volunteer work, work experience. **Freshman Admission Requirements:** High school diploma is required and GED is accepted. *Academic units required:* 4 English, 4 math, 3 science, 3 science labs, 2 foreign language, 2 social studies, 1 visual/performing arts. *Academic units recommended:* 4 English, 4 math, 3 science, 3 science labs, 2 foreign language, 2 social studies, 1 visual/performing arts. **Freshman Admission Statistics:** 40,854 applied, 85% admitted, 22% enrolled. **Transfer Admission Requirements:** College transcript(s). Lowest grade transferable C. **General Admission Information:** Application fee $50. Priority deadline 5/1. Regular application deadline 5/1. Non-fall registration accepted.

COSTS AND FINANCIAL AID
Annual in-state tuition $11,299. Annual out-of-state tuition $35,326. Room and board $13,050. Required fees $1,412. Average book and supplies expense $800. **Required Forms and Deadlines:** FAFSA; Institution's own financial aid form. **Notification of Awards:** Applicants will be notified of awards on a rolling basis beginning 2/1. **Types of Aid:** *Need-based scholarships/grants:* College/university scholarship or grant aid from institutional funds; Federal Pell; Private scholarships; SEOG; State scholarships/grants. *Loans:* Direct PLUS loans; Direct Subsidized Stafford Loans; Direct Unsubsidized Stafford Loans. **Student Employment:** Federal Work-Study Program available. Institutional employment available. **Financial Aid Statistics:** 96% needy freshmen, 91% needy undergrads receive need-based scholarship or grant aid. 17% freshmen, 11% undergrads receive non-need-based scholarship or grant aid. 46% freshmen, 58% undergrads receive need-based self-help aid. 1% freshmen, 1% undergrads receive athletic scholarships. 92% freshmen, 80% undergrads receive any aid. 45% undergrads borrow to pay for school. Average cumulative indebtedness $26,414. **Criteria awarding aid:** *Need-based:* Academics. *Non-need-based:* Academics, Art, Athletics, Music/drama.

UNIVERSITY OF ARKANSAS AT PINE BLUFF

1200 N. University Drive, Pine Bluff, AR 71601
Phone: (870) 575-8492 **Financial Aid Phone:** (870) 575-8302
E-mail: fultone@uapb.edu **CEEB Code:** 6004
Fax: (870) 575-4608 **Website:** http://www.uapb.edu **ACT Code:** 0108

This is a public school.

RATINGS
Admissions Selectivity Rating: 81   **Fire Safety Rating:** 60*   **Green Rating:** 60*

STUDENTS AND FACULTY
Enrollment: 3,048. **Student Body:** 58% female, 42% male, 33% out-of-state, <1% international. Asian <1%, African American 96%, Caucasian 3%, Hispanic <1%, Native American 0%, Race unknown <1%.
Retention and Graduation: 57% freshmen return for sophomore year.
Faculty: Student/faculty ratio 18:1. 164 full-time faculty, 0% hold PhDs, 46% are members of minority groups, 54% are women.

ACADEMICS
Degrees: Associate; Bachelor's; Certificate; Master's. **Classes:** Most classes have 20–29 students. **Special Study Options:** Cooperative education program; Distance learning; Double major; Dual enrollment; Honors program; Internships; Study abroad; Teacher certification program.

FACILITIES
Housing: Men's dorms; Women's dorms.

CAMPUS LIFE
Activities: Choral groups; Concert band; Drama/theater; Jazz band; Marching band; Radio station; Student government; Student newspaper; Television station; Yearbook.

ADMISSIONS
Freshman Academic Profile: 93% from public high schools. **Test Scores:** SAT Math middle 50% range 350–450. SAT EBRW middle 50% range 350–440. ACT middle 50% range 14–18. **Basis for Candidate Selection:** *Very important factors include:* rigor of secondary school record, standardized test scores. *Important factors include:* academic GPA. **Freshman Admission Requirements:** High school diploma is required and GED is accepted. *Academic units required:*

4 English, 3 math, 3 science, 2 science labs, 2 foreign language, 1 social studies, 2 history, 4 academic electives. **Freshman Admission Statistics:** 2,169 applied, 64% admitted, 59% enrolled. **Transfer Admission Requirements:** High school transcript, college transcript(s). **General Admission Information:** Priority deadline 8/1. Non-fall registration accepted.

COSTS AND FINANCIAL AID
Annual in-state tuition $3,300. Annual out-of-state tuition $7,710. Room and board $6,070. Required fees $1,199. Average book and supplies expense $1,000. **Required Forms and Deadlines:** FAFSA. **Types of Aid:** *Need-based scholarships/grants:* College/university scholarship or grant aid from institutional funds; Federal Pell; Private scholarships; SEOG; State scholarships/grants.

UNIVERSITY OF ARKANSAS—FAYETTEVILLE

232 Silas H. Hunt Hall, Fayetteville, AR 72701
Phone: 479-575-5346 **Financial Aid Phone:** (479) 575-3806
E-mail: uofa@uark.edu **CEEB Code:** 6866
Fax: 479-575-7515 **Website:** http://www.uark.edu **ACT Code:** 144

This public school was founded in 1871. It has a 718 acre campus.

RATINGS
Admissions Selectivity Rating: 83   **Fire Safety Rating:** 94   **Green Rating:** 91

STUDENTS AND FACULTY
Enrollment: 22,757. **Student Body:** 54% female, 46% male, 46% out-of-state, 3% international (77 countries represented). Asian 3%, African American 4%, Caucasian 76%, Hispanic 9%, Native American 1%, Pacific Islander <1%, Two or more races 4%, Race unknown 1%.
Retention and Graduation: 84% freshmen return for sophomore year. 49% freshmen graduate within 4 years. 66% freshmen graduate within 6 years. 20% grads go on to further study within 1 year. 5% grads pursue arts and sciences degrees. 2% grads pursue law degrees. 1% grads pursue business degrees. 2% grads pursue medical degrees. **Faculty:** Student/faculty ratio 18:1. 1,206 full-time faculty, 83% hold PhDs, 22% are members of minority groups, 41% are women. 15% of classes are taught by teaching assistants.

ACADEMICS
Degrees: Bachelor's; Certificate; Doctoral degree—professional practice; Doctoral degree research/scholarship; Master's; Post-bachelor's certificate; Post-master's certificate. **Classes:** Most classes have 10–19 students. Most lab/discussion sessions have 20–29 students. **Most popular majors:** Registered Nursing/Registered Nurse; Finance, General; Marketing/Marketing Management, General. **Special Study Options:** Accelerated program; Cooperative education program; Cross-registration; Distance learning; Double major; Dual enrollment; English as a Second Language (ESL); Honors program; Independent study; Internships; Liberal arts/career combination; Student-designed major; Study abroad; Teacher certification program. **Honors programs:** The Honors College admitted 1,139 freshman in Fall 2019. Each year the Honors College awards up to 90 freshman fellowships that provide $72,000 over four years, and more than $1 million in study abroad and undergraduate research grants. The Honors College is nationally recognized for the high caliber of students it admits and graduates. Honors students enjoy small, in-depth seminars on cutting-edge topics, taught by top professors and leaders on campus and in the community. Honors programs are offered in all disciplines, tailored to students' academic interests, with interdisciplinary collaborations encouraged. One hundred percent of Honors College graduates have engaged in mentored research. **Combined degree programs:** BA/DDS; BA/JD; BA/MD. **Disability Services offered:** Note-taking services; Reader services; Tape recorders; Tutors. **Career services:** Alumni network; Alumni services; Career assessment; Career/job search classes; Internships.

FACILITIES
Housing: Apartments for single students; Coed dorms; Fraternity/sorority housing; Special housing for disabled students; Special housing for international students; Theme housing; Women's dorms; 100% of campus accessible to physically disabled. **Special Academic Facilities/Equipment:** High

performance computing, nanoscale science & engineering building, center for space and planetary sciences, chamber for planetary & asteroid simulation, national center for reliable electric power, high density electronics research center, poultry research center, art galleries, Brewer Family Entrepreneurship Hub, McMillon Family Retail & Innovation Lab, Business Behavioral Research Lab, Faulkner Performing Arts Center, Honors College networking area, equine pavilion, animal science center, optical network.

CAMPUS LIFE
Environment: City. **Activities:** Campus Ministries; Choral groups; Concert band; Dance; Drama/theater; International Student Organization; Jazz band; Marching band; Model UN; Music ensembles; Musical theater; Opera; Pep band; Radio station; Student government; Student newspaper; Symphony orchestra; Television station; Yearbook. 443 registered organizations, 47 honor societies, 19 fraternities, 15 sororities on campus. **Athletics (Intercollegiate):** *Men:* baseball, basketball, cross-country, football, golf, tennis, track/field (outdoor), track/field (indoor). *Women:* basketball, cross-country, diving, golf, gymnastics, soccer, softball, swimming, tennis, track/field (outdoor), track/field (indoor), volleyball. **On-Campus Highlights:** Old Main: Iconic Image of Higher Education in the State of Arkansas. **Environmental Initiatives:** ACUPCC Signatory, GHG inventory, climate action plan.

ADMISSIONS
Freshman Academic Profile: Average high school GPA 3.7. 25% in top 10% of high school class, 52% in top 25% of high school class, 83% in top 50% of high school class. 82% from public high schools. **Test Scores:** SAT Math middle 50% range 550–650. SAT EBRW middle 50% range 570–650. ACT middle 50% range 23–30. **Basis for Candidate Selection:** *Very important factors include:* academic GPA, standardized test scores. *Other factors include:* rigor of secondary school record, class rank, application essay, recommendation(s), extracurricular activities, talent/ability, character/personal qualities, first generation, alumni/ae relation, geographical residence, state residency, volunteer work, work experience. **Freshman Admission Requirements:** High school diploma is required and GED is accepted. *Academic units required:* 4 English, 4 math, 3 science, 1 science labs, 1 social studies, 2 history, 2 academic electives. *Academic units recommended:* 4 English, 4 math, 3 science, 1 science labs, 2 foreign language, 1 social studies, 2 history, 2 academic electives. **Freshman Admission Statistics:** 17,913 applied, 77% admitted, 33% enrolled. **Transfer Admission Requirements:** College transcript(s). Minimum college GPA of 2.0 required. Lowest grade transferable C-. **General Admission Information:** Application fee $40. Priority deadline 11/1. Regular application deadline 8/1. Non-fall registration accepted.

COSTS AND FINANCIAL AID
Annual in-state tuition $7,384. Annual out-of-state tuition $23,422. Room and board $11,020. Required fees $1,746. Average book and supplies expense $1,046. **Required Forms and Deadlines:** FAFSA. **Notification of Awards:** Applicants will be notified of awards on or about 4/1. **Types of Aid:** *Need-based scholarships/grants:* College/university scholarship or grant aid from institutional funds; Federal Pell; Private scholarships; SEOG; State scholarships/grants. *Loans:* Direct PLUS loans; Direct Subsidized Stafford Loans; Direct Unsubsidized Stafford Loans. **Student Employment:** Federal Work-Study Program available. Institutional employment available. **Financial Aid Statistics:** 78% needy freshmen, 75% needy undergrads receive need-based scholarship or grant aid. 10% freshmen, 8% undergrads receive non-need-based scholarship or grant aid. 65% freshmen, 68% undergrads receive need-based self-help aid. 2% freshmen, 2% undergrads receive athletic scholarships. 77% freshmen, 70% undergrads receive any aid. 47% undergrads borrow to pay for school. Average cumulative indebtedness $26,242. **Criteria awarding aid:** *Need-based:* Academics, Alumni affiliation, Leadership, Minority status. *Non-need-based:* Academics, Alumni affiliation, Art, Athletics, Leadership, Minority status, Music/drama, State/district residency.

UNIVERSITY OF BALTIMORE

1420 North Charles Street, Baltimore, MD 21201
Phone: 410-837-4777 **Financial Aid Phone:** (410)837-4763
E-mail: admissions@ubmall.ubalt.edu **CEEB Code:** 5810
Fax: 410-837-4793 **Website:** http://www.ubalt.edu/admission/ **ACT Code:** 1744

This public school was founded in 1925. It has a 11.3 acre campus.

RATINGS
Admissions Selectivity Rating: 84   Fire Safety Rating: 60*   Green Rating: 60*

STUDENTS AND FACULTY
Enrollment: 3,526. **Student Body:** 57% female, 43% male, 4% out-of-state, 3% international. Asian 4%, African American 38%, Caucasian 42%, Hispanic 4%, Native American <1%, Pacific Islander <1%, Two or more races 3%, Race unknown 5%.
Retention and Graduation: 18% grads go on to further study within 1 year. 10% grads pursue arts and sciences degrees. 2% grads pursue law degrees. 9% grads pursue business degrees. **Faculty:** Student/faculty ratio 16:1. 182 full-time faculty, 85% hold PhDs, 23% are members of minority groups, 45% are women. 0% of classes are taught by teaching assistants.

ACADEMICS
Degrees: Bachelor's; Certificate; Master's; Post-bachelor's certificate; Post-master's certificate. **Classes:** Most classes have 20–29 students. **Most popular majors:** Digital Communication and Media/Multimedia; Criminal Justice/Law Enforcement Administration; Business Administration and Management, General. **Special Study Options:** Accelerated program; Cooperative education program; Distance learning; Honors program; Independent study; Internships; Student-designed major; Study abroad. **Combined degree programs:** BA/JD; BA/MA. **Disability Services offered:** Note-taking services; Reader services; Tape recorders; Tutors. **Career services:** Alumni network; Alumni services; Career assessment; Career/job search classes; Internships; Regional alumni.

FACILITIES
Housing: 100% of campus accessible to physically disabled. **Campus network:** 100% of classrooms, 100% of dorms, 95% of student union, 95% of libraries, 95% of dining areas, 25% of common outdoor areas have wireless network access.

CAMPUS LIFE
Environment: Metropolis. **Activities:** Drama/theater; International Student Organization; Literary magazine; Student government; Student newspaper. 60 registered organizations, 11 honor societies, 2 religious organizations on campus. **On-Campus Highlights:** Student Union. **Environmental Initiatives:** 30% energy reduction contract with Energy Systems Group.

ADMISSIONS
Freshman Academic Profile: Average high school GPA 3.0. **Test Scores:** SAT Math middle 50% range 410–540. SAT EBRW middle 50% range 420–560. ACT middle 50% range 17–21. **Basis for Candidate Selection:** *Important factors include:* rigor of secondary school record, class rank, academic GPA, standardized test scores. *Other factors include:* application essay, recommendation(s), extracurricular activities, talent/ability, character/personal qualities, first generation, alumni/ae relation, volunteer work, work experience. **Freshman Admission Requirements:** High school diploma is required and GED is accepted. *Academic units required:* 4 English, 3 math, 3 science, 2 science labs, 3 social studies, 6 academic electives. **Freshman Admission Statistics:** 730 applied, 64% admitted, 51% enrolled. **Transfer Admission Requirements:** College transcript(s). Minimum college GPA of 2.0 required. Lowest grade transferable D. **General Admission Information:** Application fee $30. Priority deadline 2/15. Non-fall registration accepted. Admission may be deferred for a maximum of 1 year.

COSTS AND FINANCIAL AID
Annual in-state tuition $5,992. Annual out-of-state tuition $16,550. Required fees $1,846. **Required Forms and Deadlines:** FAFSA. **Types of Aid:** *Need-based scholarships/grants:* College/university scholarship or grant aid from institutional funds; Federal Pell; Private scholarships; SEOG; State scholarships/grants. *Loans:* Direct PLUS loans; Direct Subsidized Stafford Loans; Direct Unsubsidized Stafford Loans. **Student Employment:** Federal Work-Study Program available. Institutional employment available. **Financial Aid Statistics:** 90% needy freshmen, 91% needy undergrads receive need-based scholarship or grant aid. 0% freshmen, 0% undergrads receive non-need-based scholarship

---

or grant aid. 65% freshmen, 72% undergrads receive need-based self-help aid. 0% freshmen, 0% undergrads receive athletic scholarships. 97% freshmen, 86% undergrads receive any aid. **Criteria awarding aid:** *Need-based:* Academics. *Non-need-based:* Academics, State/district residency.

UNIVERSITY OF BRIDGEPORT

126 Park Avenue, Bridgeport, CT 06604
Phone: 203-576-4552 **Financial Aid Phone:** 203-576-4568
E-mail: admit@.bridgeport.edu **CEEB Code:** 3914
Fax: 203-576-4941 **ACT Code:** 602

This private school was founded in 1927. It has a 86 acre campus.

RATINGS
Admissions Selectivity Rating: 77 · Fire Safety Rating: 91   Green Rating: 60*

STUDENTS AND FACULTY
Enrollment: 2,688. **Student Body:** 68% female, 32% male, 38% out-of-state, 11% international (74 countries represented). Asian 3%, African American 37%, Caucasian 27%, Hispanic 18%, Native American 1%, Pacific Islander <1%, Two or more races 3%, Race unknown 0%.
Retention and Graduation: 62% freshmen return for sophomore year. 15% grads go on to further study within 1 year. 5% grads pursue arts and sciences degrees. 10% grads pursue law degrees. 10% grads pursue business degrees. 5% grads pursue medical degrees. **Faculty:** Student/faculty ratio 17:1. 121 full-time faculty, 79% hold PhDs, 19% are members of minority groups, 38% are women. 0% of classes are taught by teaching assistants.

ACADEMICS
Degrees: Associate; Bachelor's; Certificate; Doctoral degree—professional practice; Doctoral degree research/scholarship; Master's; Post-bachelor's certificate; Post-master's certificate. **Classes:** Most classes have 10–19 students. **Most popular majors:** Business/Commerce, General; Dental Hygiene/Hygienist; Psychology, General. **Special Study Options:** Accelerated program; Cooperative education program; Cross-registration; Distance learning; Double major; English as a Second Language (ESL); Honors program; Independent study; Internships; Liberal arts/career combination; Student-designed major; Study abroad; Teacher certification program; Weekend college. **Disability Services offered:** Note-taking services; Reader services; Tape recorders; Tutors. **Career services:** Alumni network; Alumni services; Career assessment; Career/job search classes; Internships; Regional alumni.

FACILITIES
Housing: Coed dorms; 80% of campus accessible to physically disabled.

CAMPUS LIFE
Environment: City. **Activities:** Campus Ministries; Choral groups; Dance; International Student Organization; Literary magazine; Model UN; Music ensembles; Student government; Student newspaper; Yearbook. 48 registered organizations, 15 honor societies, 4 religious organizations, 2 fraternities, 3 sororities on campus. **Athletics (Intercollegiate):** *Men:* baseball, basketball, cross-country, soccer, swimming. *Women:* basketball, cross-country, gymnastics, lacrosse, soccer, softball, swimming, volleyball. **On-Campus Highlights:** Arnold Bernhard Center.

ADMISSIONS
Freshman Academic Profile: Average high school GPA 3.0. 1% in top 10% of high school class, 32% in top 25% of high school class, 69% in top 50% of high school class. 90% from public high schools. **Test Scores:** SAT Math middle 50% range 410–500. SAT EBRW middle 50% range 410–490. ACT middle 50% range 18–21. **Basis for Candidate Selection:** *Very important factors include:* rigor of secondary school record, academic GPA, standardized test scores. *Important factors include:* class rank, application essay, recommendation(s), talent/ability, character/personal qualities, level of applicant's interest. *Other factors include:* interview, extracurricular activities, volunteer work, work experience. **Freshman Admission Requirements:** High school diploma is required and GED is accepted. *Academic units required:* 4 English, 3 math, 2 science, 2 science labs, 2 social studies, 5 academic electives. *Academic units recommended:* 4 English, 3 math, 2 science, 2 science labs, 2 social studies, 5 academic electives. **Freshman Admission Statistics:** 5,736 applied, 63% admitted, 16% enrolled. **Transfer Admission Requirements:** College transcript(s), essay or personal statement. Minimum college GPA of

2.0 required. Lowest grade transferable C-. **General Admission Information:** Application fee $25. Priority deadline 4/1. Non-fall registration accepted. Admission may be deferred for a maximum of 1 year.

COSTS AND FINANCIAL AID

Annual tuition $25,950. Room and board $12,050. Required fees $2,190. Average book and supplies expense $1,500. **Required Forms and Deadlines:** FAFSA. **Notification of Awards:** Applicants will be notified of awards on a rolling basis beginning 3/1. **Types of Aid:** *Need-based scholarships/grants:* College/university scholarship or grant aid from institutional funds; Federal Pell; Private scholarships; SEOG; State scholarships/grants. *Loans:* Direct PLUS loans; Direct Subsidized Stafford Loans; Direct Unsubsidized Stafford Loans. **Student Employment:** Federal Work-Study Program available. Institutional employment available. **Financial Aid Statistics:** 85% needy freshmen, 87% needy undergrads receive need-based scholarship or grant aid. 95% freshmen, 88% undergrads receive non-need-based scholarship or grant aid. 85% freshmen, 87% undergrads receive need-based self-help aid. 3% freshmen, 8% undergrads receive athletic scholarships. 98% freshmen, 98% undergrads receive any aid. **Criteria awarding aid:** *Non-need-based:* Academics, Art, Athletics, Leadership, Music/drama, State/district residency.

THE UNIVERSITY OF BRITISH COLUMBIA

Room 2016, Vancouver, BC V6T 1Z1
Phone: 1-604-822-3014 **Financial Aid Phone:** 604-822-5111
E-mail: askme@interchange.ubc.ca **CEEB Code:** 0965
Fax: 604-822-3599 **Website:** www.ubc.ca **ACT Code:** 5259

This public school was founded in 1908. It has a 1000 acre campus.

RATINGS

Admissions Selectivity Rating: 72   **Fire Safety Rating:** 79   **Green Rating:** 60*

STUDENTS AND FACULTY

Enrollment: 29,717. **Student Body:** 54% female, 46% male.
Retention and Graduation: 91% freshmen return for sophomore year. 50% grads go on to further study within 1 year. **Faculty:** Student/faculty ratio 15:1.

ACADEMICS

Degrees: Bachelor's; Certificate; Diploma; Doctoral degree—professional practice; Master's. **Classes:** Most classes have 50–99 students. Most lab/discussion sessions have 20–29 students. **Most popular majors:** Computer and Information Sciences, General; Biological and Physical Sciences; Psychology, General. **Special Study Options:** Cooperative education program; Distance learning; Double major; Dual enrollment; English as a Second Language (ESL); Exchange student program (domestic); Honors program; Internships; Liberal arts/career combination; Student-designed major; Study abroad; Teacher certification program. **Honors programs:** UBC offers many honors programs for academically strong undergraduates. **Disability Services offered:** Note-taking services; Reader services; Tape recorders; Tutors. **Career services:** Alumni network; Alumni services; Career assessment; Career/job search classes; Internships; Regional alumni.

FACILITIES

Housing: Apartments for married students; Apartments for single students; Coed dorms; Fraternity/sorority housing; Men's dorms; Special housing for disabled students; Special housing for international students; Theme housing; Women's dorms; 90% of campus accessible to physically disabled. **Special Academic Facilities/Equipment:** Museum of Anthropology; Barber Learning Centre; Beaty Biodiversity Museum; Geological Museum; TRIUMF, sub-atomic particle research; Botanical Gardens; Nitobe Garden; Old Auditorium Opera Theatre; Belkin Art Gallery; Chan Centre for Performing Arts; Frederick Wood Theatre; Irving K Barber Centre of Learning; Liu International Studies Centre; Green College (Graduate College); St. John's College (Graduate College); Centre for Intergrated Systems Research; Wall Centre for Interdisciplinary Studies; Model Crop Farm. **Campus network:** 100% of classrooms, 100% of dorms, 100% of student union, 100% of libraries, 100% of dining areas, 65% of common outdoor areas have wireless network access.

CAMPUS LIFE

Environment: Metropolis. **Activities:** Campus Ministries; Choral groups; Concert band; Dance; Drama/theater; International Student Organization; Literary magazine; Model UN; Music ensembles; Musical theater; Opera; Radio station; Student government; Student newspaper; Student-run film society;

Symphony orchestra. 250 registered organizations, 1 honor society, 7 religious organizations, 9 fraternities, 8 sororities on campus. **Athletics (Intercollegiate):** *Men:* baseball, basketball, crew/rowing, cross-country, field hockey, football, golf, ice hockey, rugby, soccer, swimming, track/field (outdoor), volleyball. *Women:* basketball, crew/rowing, cross-country, field hockey, golf, ice hockey, rugby, soccer, swimming, track/field (outdoor), volleyball. **On-Campus Highlights:** Koerner Library. **Environmental Initiatives:** UBC is a signatory to the Talloires Declaration. It has integrated sustainability into its vision statement and strategic plan and formed a President's Advisory Council on Sustainability. The UBC Sustainability Office opened in 1998—the first of its kind in a Canadian university. UBC has created an advisory committee of faculty, staff, students, and alumni on socially responsible investing. The committee advises the Board of Governors on issues of transparency, proxy votes, and socially responsible investment practices.

ADMISSIONS

Basis for Candidate Selection: *Very important factors include:* rigor of secondary school record, academic GPA. *Important factors include:* application essay. *Other factors include:* standardized test scores, recommendation(s), extracurricular activities, talent/ability, character/personal qualities, volunteer work, work experience, level of applicant's interest. **Freshman Admission Requirements:** High school diploma is required and GED is not accepted. *Academic units required:* 4 English, 3 math, 2 academic electives. **Freshman Admission Statistics:** 27,134 applied, 49% admitted, 48% enrolled. **Transfer Admission Requirements:** College transcript(s), statement of good standing from prior institution(s). **General Admission Information:** Application fee $102. Priority deadline 1/31. Regular application deadline 1/31. Non-fall registration accepted. Admission may be deferred for a maximum of up to one year.

COSTS AND FINANCIAL AID

Required Forms and Deadlines: Institution's own financial aid form. *Loans:* Direct PLUS loans; Direct Subsidized Stafford Loans; Direct Unsubsidized Stafford Loans. **Student Employment:** Institutional employment available. **Criteria awarding aid:** *Need-based:* Academics, Athletics, Leadership. *Non-need-based:* Academics, Athletics, Leadership.

UNIVERSITY OF CALIFORNIA—BERKELEY

110 Sproul Hall, Berkeley, CA 94720-5800
Phone: 510-642-6000
CEEB Code: 4833
Website: www.berkeley.edu **ACT Code:** 444

This public school was founded in 1868. It has a 1232 acre campus.

RATINGS

Admissions Selectivity Rating: 97   **Fire Safety Rating:** 96   **Green Rating:** 99

STUDENTS AND FACULTY

Enrollment: 30,602. **Student Body:** 53% female, 47% male, 16% out-of-state, 13% international. Asian 35%, African American 2%, Caucasian 25%, Hispanic 15%, Native American <1%, Pacific Islander <1%, Two or more races 6%, Race unknown 4%.
Retention and Graduation: 97% freshmen return for sophomore year. 75% freshmen graduate within 4 years. **Faculty:** Student/faculty ratio 20:1. 1,621 full-time faculty, 99% hold PhDs, 22% are members of minority groups, 36% are women. 0% of classes are taught by teaching assistants.

ACADEMICS

Degrees: Bachelor's; Doctoral degree—professional practice; Doctoral degree research/scholarship; Master's; Post-bachelor's certificate. **Classes:** Most classes have 10–19 students. Most lab/discussion sessions have 20–29 students. **Most popular majors:** English Language and Literature, General; Computer Engineering, General; Political Science and Government, General. **Special Study Options:** Accelerated program; Cross-registration; Double major; Dual enrollment; English as a Second Language (ESL); Exchange student program (domestic); Honors program; Independent study; Internships; Student-designed major; Study abroad. **Disability Services offered:** Note-taking services; Reader services; Tape recorders; Tutors. **Career services:** Alumni services; Career assessment; Career/job search classes; Internships.

FACILITIES

Housing: Apartments for married students; Apartments for single students; Coed dorms; Cooperative housing; Fraternity/sorority housing; Men's dorms; Special housing for disabled students; Special housing for international students; Theme housing; Women's dorms; 95% of campus accessible to physically disabled. **Special Academic Facilities/Equipment:** Lawrence Berkeley National Lab, Pacific Film Archive, Earthquake Data Center, Museums of art, anthropology, natural history, paleontology, Botanical Garden.

CAMPUS LIFE

Environment: City. **Activities:** Campus Ministries; Choral groups; Concert band; Dance; Drama/theater; International Student Organization; Jazz band; Literary magazine; Marching band; Model UN; Music ensembles; Musical theater; Pep band; Radio station; Student government; Student newspaper; Student-run film society; Symphony orchestra; Television station; Yearbook. 300 registered organizations, 6 honor societies, 28 religious organizations, 38 fraternities, 19 sororities on campus. **Athletics (Intercollegiate):** *Men:* baseball, basketball, crew/rowing, cross-country, diving, football, golf, gymnastics, rugby, sailing, soccer, swimming, tennis, track/field (outdoor), water polo. *Women:* basketball, crew/rowing, cross-country, diving, field hockey, golf, gymnastics, lacrosse, sailing, soccer, softball, swimming, tennis, track/field (outdoor), volleyball, water polo. **On-Campus Highlights:** Botanical Gardens. **Environmental Initiatives:** The popular Cool Campus Challenge returned to UC in April 2019, and UC Berkeley took the overall honor as the Coolest UC, achieving the most carbon-saving points of any UC campus or medical center. Engaging more than 4,200 participants, or 7.5 percent of the campus, UC Berkeley is saving tons of carbon dioxide from participants' actions, equivalent to taking 500 cars off the road for an entire year. Also in support of carbon reduction action, UC Berkeley's chancellor, in coordination with students, signed a memorandum of understanding committing the Berkeley campus to 100 percent clean, renewable energy by 2050.

ADMISSIONS

Freshman Academic Profile: Average high school GPA 3.9. 98% in top 10% of high school class, 100% in top 25% of high school class, 100% in top 50% of high school class. **Test Scores:** SAT Math middle 50% range 660–790. SAT EBRW middle 50% range 640–740. ACT middle 50% range 28–34. **Basis for Candidate Selection:** *Very important factors include:* rigor of secondary school record, academic GPA, application essay, standardized test scores. *Important factors include:* extracurricular activities, character/personal qualities. *Other factors include:* recommendation(s), first generation, state residency. **Freshman Admission Requirements:** High school diploma is required and GED is accepted. *Academic units required:* 4 English, 3 math, 2 science, 2 science labs, 2 foreign language, 2 history, 1 academic elective, 1 visual/performing arts. *Academic units recommended:* 4 English, 4 math, 3 science, 3 science labs, 3 foreign language, 2 history, 1 academic elective, 1 visual/performing arts. **Freshman Admission Statistics:** 86,779 applied, 15% admitted, 47% enrolled. **Transfer Admission Requirements:** Essay or personal statement. Minimum college GPA of 2.4 required. Lowest grade transferable D. **General Admission Information:** Application fee $70. Regular application deadline 11/30. Non-fall registration accepted.

COSTS AND FINANCIAL AID

Annual in-state tuition $11,442. Annual out-of-state tuition $41,196. Room and board $17,220. Required fees $3,009. Average book and supplies expense $870. **Required Forms and Deadlines:** FAFSA; State aid form. **Notification of Awards:** Applicants will be notified of awards on or about 3/31. **Types of Aid:** *Need-based scholarships/grants:* College/university scholarship or grant aid from institutional funds; Federal Pell; Private scholarships; SEOG; State scholarships/grants. *Loans:* Direct PLUS loans; Direct Subsidized Stafford Loans; Direct Unsubsidized Stafford Loans. **Student Employment:** Federal Work-Study Program available. Institutional employment available. **Financial Aid Statistics:** 92% needy freshmen, 94% needy undergrads receive need-based scholarship or grant aid. 3% freshmen, 2% undergrads receive non-need-based scholarship or grant aid. 67% freshmen, 69% undergrads receive need-based self-help aid. 1% freshmen, 1% undergrads receive athletic scholarships. 34% undergrads borrow to pay for school. Average cumulative indebtedness $18,225. **Criteria awarding aid:** *Need-based:* Academics. *Non-need-based:* Academics, Athletics, Leadership.

UNIVERSITY OF CALIFORNIA—DAVIS

178 Mrak Hall, One Shields Ave, Davis, CA 95616
Phone: 530-752-2971 **Financial Aid Phone:** 530-752-2396
E-mail: undergraduateadmissions@ucdavis.edu **CEEB Code:** 4834
Fax: 530-752-1280 **Website:** www.ucdavis.edu **ACT Code:** 454

This public school was founded in 1908. It has a 5200 acre campus.

RATINGS

Admissions Selectivity Rating: 90   **Fire Safety Rating:** 97   **Green Rating:** 95

STUDENTS AND FACULTY

Enrollment: 30,636. **Student Body:** 60% female, 40% male, 5% out-of-state, 17% international (121 countries represented). Asian 27%, African American 2%, Caucasian 24%, Hispanic 22%, Native American <1%, Pacific Islander <1%, Two or more races 5%, Race unknown 2%.
Retention and Graduation: 92% freshmen return for sophomore year. 58% freshmen graduate within 4 years. 85% freshmen graduate within 6 years. 40% grads go on to further study within 1 year. 23% grads pursue arts and sciences degrees. 4% grads pursue law degrees. 1% grads pursue business degrees. 12% grads pursue medical degrees. **Faculty:** Student/faculty ratio 19:1. 1,702 full-time faculty, 98% hold PhDs, 25% are members of minority groups, 39% are women.

ACADEMICS

Degrees: Bachelor's; Doctoral degree—professional practice; Doctoral degree research/scholarship; Master's; Post-bachelor's certificate; Post-master's certificate. **Classes:** Most classes have 20–29 students. Most lab/discussion sessions have 20–29 students. **Most popular majors:** Economics, General; Biology/Biological Sciences, General; Psychology, General. **Special Study Options:** Accelerated program; Cross-registration; Double major; Dual enrollment; English as a Second Language (ESL); Honors program; Independent study; Internships; Student-designed major; Study abroad; Teacher certification program. **Honors programs:** The Davis Honors Challenge (DHC) is an innovative, open-application, campuswide honors program for highly motivated students. In addition to a mentor program and a residential living-learning option for first-year students, DHC offers students the opportunity to participate in an honors program for four years. Integrated Studies Honors Program (ISHP), the oldest continuous residential learning community in the UC system, is an invitational, residential honors program for first-year students. ISHP provides an academic residential community similar to those of the best small colleges and helps students integrate knowledge from the arts and humanities, natural sciences and engineering, and social sciences. **Disability Services offered:** Note-taking services; Reader services; Tape recorders; Tutors.

FACILITIES

Housing: Apartments for married students; Apartments for single students; Coed dorms; Cooperative housing; Special housing for disabled students; Theme housing; Wellness housing; Women's dorms. **Special Academic Facilities/Equipment:** Art galleries, 150-acre university arboretum, equestrian center, craft center, student experimental farm, nuclear lab, human performance lab, natural reserves, early childhood lab, raptor center, primate research center.

CAMPUS LIFE

Environment: Town. **Activities:** Campus Ministries; Choral groups; Concert band; Dance; Drama/theater; International Student Organization; Jazz band; Literary magazine; Marching band; Model UN; Music ensembles; Musical theater; Pep band; Radio station; Student government; Student newspaper; Student-run film society; Symphony orchestra; Television station; Yearbook. 364 registered organizations, 1 honor society, 50 religious organizations, 28 fraternities, 21 sorority on campus. **Athletics (Intercollegiate):** *Men:* baseball, basketball, cross-country, diving, football, golf, soccer, swimming, tennis, track/field (outdoor), track/field (indoor), water polo, wrestling. *Women:* basketball, crew/rowing, cross-country, diving, field hockey, golf, gymnastics, lacrosse, soccer, softball, swimming, tennis, track/field (outdoor), track/field (indoor), volleyball, water polo. **On-Campus Highlights:** Mondavi Center for the Performing Arts. **Environmental Initiatives:** UC Davis is taking action to reduce greenhouse gas emissions and energy use on campus through programs like the Strategic Energy Partnership Program, which is improving energy conservation and energy efficiency on campus and has identified retrofit and recommissioning projects that will save more than 28 million kilowatt-hours and 2 million therms. The campus installed a 756kW solar photovoltaic system, which generates over 1 million kilowatt-hours a year. UC Davis has also embarked on an ambitious initiative to reduce lighting energy use by 60% in five years, which will reduce energy use and greenhouse gas emissions (www.sustainability.ucdavis.edu/news/2010/november/smart_lighting.html) and is pursuing a project to build an on-campus anaerobic biodigester that will generate about 2 million kilowatt-hours a year of clean, renewable electricity from campus organic wastes (news.ucdavis.edu/search/news_detail.lasso?id=10202). Work on climate issues at UC Davis includes everything from studying pollution in the Arctic atmosphere and building global climate models to the campus Climate Action Plan (CAP) and energy use reduction. UC Davis faculty and student research on climate change spans a wide range of investigation from basic inquiry to solution-based engineering work (climatechange.ucdavis.edu/). The CAP analyzes campus issues around greenhouse gas emissions reductions, energy use and energy sourcing (www.sustainability.ucdavis.edu/progress/climate/index.html).

ADMISSIONS

Freshman Academic Profile: Average high school GPA 4.0. 84% from public high schools. **Test Scores:** SAT Math middle 50% range 580–740. SAT EBRW middle 50% range 570–670. ACT middle 50% range 25–31. **Basis for Candidate Selection:** *Very important factors include:* rigor of secondary school record, academic GPA, application essay, standardized test scores. *Important factors include:* extracurricular activities, talent/ability, character/personal qualities. *Other factors include:* first generation, state residency, work experience. **Freshman Admission Requirements:** High school diploma is required and GED is accepted. *Academic units required:* 4 English, 3 math, 2 science, 2 science labs, 2 foreign language, 2 history, 1 academic elective, 1 visual/performing arts. *Academic units recommended:* 4 English, 4 math, 3 science, 3 science labs, 3 foreign language, 2 history, 1 academic elective, 1 visual/performing arts. **Freshman Admission Statistics:** 76,647 applied, 41% admitted, 20% enrolled. **Transfer Admission Requirements:** High school transcript, college transcript(s), essay or personal statement, statement of good standing from prior institution(s). Lowest grade transferable D-. **General Admission Information:** Application fee $70. Regular application deadline 11/30. Admission may be deferred for a maximum of up to 1 year/3 qtrs.

COSTS AND FINANCIAL AID

Annual in-state tuition $11,442. Annual out-of-state tuition $40,434. Room and board $15,863. Required fees $3,050. Average book and supplies expense $1,159. **Required Forms and Deadlines:** FAFSA; State aid form. **Notification of Awards:** Applicants will be notified of awards on a rolling basis beginning 3/10. **Types of Aid:** *Need-based scholarships/grants:* College/university scholarship or grant aid from institutional funds; Federal Pell; Private scholarships; SEOG; State scholarships/grants. *Loans:* Direct PLUS loans; Direct Subsidized Stafford Loans; Direct Unsubsidized Stafford Loans. **Student Employment:** Federal Work-Study Program available. Institutional employment available. **Financial Aid Statistics:** 96% needy freshmen, 97% needy undergrads receive need-based scholarship or grant aid. 2% freshmen, 2% undergrads receive non-need-based scholarship or grant aid. 53% freshmen, 51% undergrads receive need-based self-help aid. 1% freshmen, 1% undergrads receive athletic scholarships. 67% freshmen, 71% undergrads receive any aid. 48% undergrads borrow to pay for school. Average cumulative indebtedness $18,575. **Criteria awarding aid:** *Need-based:* Academics, Athletics. *Non-need-based:* Academics, Athletics.

UNIVERSITY OF CALIFORNIA—IRVINE

Office of Admissions and Relations with Schools, Irvine, CA 92697-1075
Phone: 949-824-6703 **Financial Aid Phone:** 949-824-5337
E-mail: admissions@uci.edu **CEEB Code:** 4859
Fax: 949-824-2951 **Website:** www.uci.edu **ACT Code:** 0446

This public school was founded in 1965. It has a 1500 acre campus.

RATINGS

Admissions Selectivity Rating: 95   **Fire Safety Rating:** 88   **Green Rating:** 99

STUDENTS AND FACULTY

Enrollment: 30,382. **Student Body:** 52% female, 48% male, 2% out-of-state, 17% international (80 countries represented). Asian 36%, African American 2%, Caucasian 13%, Hispanic 26%, Native American <1%, Pacific Islander <1%, Two or more races 4%, Race unknown 1%.

Retention and Graduation: 94% freshmen return for sophomore year. 69% freshmen graduate within 4 years. 84% freshmen graduate within 6 years. **Faculty:** 1,413 full-time faculty, 98% hold PhDs, 31% are members of minority groups, 39% are women.

ACADEMICS

Degrees: Bachelor's; Doctoral degree—professional practice; Doctoral degree research/scholarship; Master's; Post-bachelor's certificate. **Classes:** Most classes have 10–19 students. Most lab/discussion sessions have 20–29 students. **Most popular majors:** Computer Science; Biology/Biological Sciences, General; Business/Managerial Economics. **Special Study Options:** Accelerated program; Cross-registration; Distance learning; Double major; Dual enrollment; English as a Second Language (ESL); Honors program; Independent study; Internships; Study abroad; Teacher certification program. **Honors programs:** Campuswide Honors Program (CHP). **Disability Services offered:** Note-taking services; Reader services; Tape recorders; Tutors. **Career services:** Alumni network; Alumni services; Career assessment; Career/job search classes; Internships.

FACILITIES

Housing: Apartments for married students; Apartments for single students; Coed dorms; Fraternity/sorority housing; Men's dorms; Special housing for disabled students; Special housing for international students; Theme housing; Women's dorms; 95% of campus accessible to physically disabled. **Special Academic Facilities/Equipment:** Museum of systemic biology, freshwater marsh reserve, electron microscope, nuclear reactor, laser institute, research facilities.

CAMPUS LIFE

Environment: City. **Activities:** Campus Ministries; Choral groups; Concert band; Dance; Drama/theater; International Student Organization; Jazz band; Literary magazine; Marching band; Model UN; Music ensembles; Musical theater; Opera; Pep band; Radio station; Student government; Student newspaper; Student-run film society; Symphony orchestra; Yearbook. 654 registered organizations, 15 honor societies, 59 religious organizations, 24 fraternities, 24 sororities on campus. **Athletics (Intercollegiate):** *Men:* baseball, basketball, cross-country, golf, sailing, soccer, tennis, track/field (outdoor), volleyball, water polo. *Women:* basketball, cross-country, golf, sailing, soccer, tennis, track/field (outdoor), volleyball, water polo. **On-Campus Highlights:** Anteater Recreation Center. **Environmental Initiatives:** The University of California is a leader in water conservation and water efficiency. Every UC campus, including UCI, has committed to reducing per capita potable water consumption 20 percent by 2020 and 36 percent by 2025. The UCI Water Resources Working Group (WRWG) assembled the campus's first Water Action Plan in 2013, identifying strategies to achieve this goal. Since 2013 significant progress has been made in potable water reduction with more than 78 million gallons saved annually, largely due to plumbing fixture upgrades, landscape irrigation reduction, and replacement of once-through cooling equipment in labs. UCI is currently exceeding the 36 percent use reduction goal, achieving a current use reduction of 40 percent. In 2017, UCI set a stretch goal of reducing per capita water usage by 50 percent by 2025, with the 2017 Water Action Plan Update identifying strategies to reach this goal. A key strategy is a collaborative project with the Irvine Ranch Water District to replace potable water use in the central plant's cooling towers with recycled water. The project has conserved approximately 80 million gallons of potable water annually and increase per capita water savings to a remarkable 54 percent. UCI's strong performance in water-wise operations is more than matched by the campus's academic expertise on this front. In addition to individual faculty research, a number of research centers are focused on water issues and/or host water-focused seminars throughout the year.

ADMISSIONS

Freshman Academic Profile: 98% in top 10% of high school class, 100% in top 25% of high school class, 100% in top 50% of high school class. 75% from public high schools. **Test Scores:** SAT Math middle 50% range 590–750. SAT EBRW middle 50% range 570–690. **Basis for Candidate Selection:** *Very important factors include:* rigor of secondary school record, academic GPA, application essay, standardized test scores, extracurricular activities, talent/ability, volunteer work, work experience. *Important factors include:* character/personal qualities. *Other factors include:* first generation, geographical residence, state residency. **Freshman Admission Requirements:** High school diploma is required and GED is accepted. *Academic units required:* 4 English, 3 math, 2 science, 2 science labs, 2 foreign language, 2 history, 1 academic elective, 1 visual/performing arts. *Academic units recommended:* 4 English, 4 math, 3 science, 3 science labs, 3 foreign language, 2 history, 1 academic elective, 1 visual/performing arts. **Freshman Admission Statistics:** 95,568 applied, 27% admitted, 24% enrolled. **Transfer Admission Requirements:** High school transcript, college transcript(s), essay or personal statement. Minimum college GPA of

2.0 required. Lowest grade transferable C. **General Admission Information:** Application fee $70. Regular application deadline 11/30.

COSTS AND FINANCIAL AID
Annual in-state tuition $11,442. Annual out-of-state tuition $41,196. Room and board $16,135. Required fees $2,285. Average book and supplies expense $1,390. **Required Forms and Deadlines:** FAFSA; State aid form. **Types of Aid:** *Need-based scholarships/grants:* College/university scholarship or grant aid from institutional funds; Federal Pell; Private scholarships; SEOG; State scholarships/grants. *Loans:* Direct PLUS loans; Direct Subsidized Stafford Loans; Direct Unsubsidized Stafford Loans. **Student Employment:** Federal Work-Study Program available. Institutional employment available. **Financial Aid Statistics:** 94% needy freshmen, 95% needy undergrads receive need-based scholarship or grant aid. 3% freshmen, 2% undergrads receive non-need-based scholarship or grant aid. 64% freshmen, 58% undergrads receive need-based self-help aid. 1% freshmen, 0% undergrads receive athletic scholarships. 53% undergrads borrow to pay for school. Average cumulative indebtedness $19,039.

UNIVERSITY OF CALIFORNIA—LOS ANGELES

1147 Murphy Hall, Los Angeles, CA 90095-1436
Phone: 310-825-3101 **Financial Aid Phone:** 310-206-0400
CEEB Code: 4837
Fax: 310-206-1206 **Website:** www.ucla.edu **ACT Code:** 448

This public school was founded in 1919. It has a 419 acre campus.

RATINGS
Admissions Selectivity Rating: 98   **Fire Safety Rating:** 92   **Green Rating:** 93

STUDENTS AND FACULTY
Enrollment: 31,441. **Student Body:** 58% female, 42% male, 13% out-of-state, 11% international (116 countries represented). Asian 28%, African American 3%, Caucasian 26%, Hispanic 22%, Native American <1%, Pacific Islander <1%, Two or more races 6%, Race unknown 3%.
Retention and Graduation: 96% freshmen return for sophomore year. 79% freshmen graduate within 4 years. 91% freshmen graduate within 6 years. **Faculty:** Student/faculty ratio 18:1. 3,102 full-time faculty, 98% hold PhDs, 30% are members of minority groups, 39% are women. 0% of classes are taught by teaching assistants.

ACADEMICS
Degrees: Bachelor's; Doctoral degree—professional practice; Doctoral degree research/scholarship; Master's. **Classes:** Most classes have 10–19 students. Most lab/discussion sessions have 20–29 students. **Most popular majors:** Biology/Biological Sciences, General; Psychology, General; Business/Managerial Economics. **Special Study Options:** Accelerated program; Double major; Honors program; Independent study; Internships; Student-designed major; Study abroad. **Honors programs:** The College Honors Program. **Disability Services offered:** Note-taking services; Reader services; Tape recorders; Tutors. **Career services:** Alumni network; Alumni services; Career assessment; Career/job search classes; Internships; Regional alumni.

FACILITIES
Housing: Apartments for married students; Apartments for single students; Coed dorms; Cooperative housing; Fraternity/sorority housing; Special housing for disabled students; Theme housing; Wellness housing; 100% of campus accessible to physically disabled. **Special Academic Facilities/Equipment:** Fowler Museum, Costen Institute of Archeology facility, Hammer Museum, Film and Television Archive, Embedded and Reconfigurable Systems Lab, Graphics & Vision Lab, Animation Lab, Ethnomusicology Archive, Jonsson Comprehensive Cancer Center labs, Basic Plasma Science facility, Planeterrella Aurora Simulator, Neuropsychiatric Institute labs, Brain Research Institute for Neuroscience and Genetics Research Labs, California NanoSystems Institute (CNSI) Labs, Broad Stem Cell Center Labs, Institute for Cell Mimetic Space Exploration facility, Particle Beam Physics lab, Southern California Particle Center, Simulation Center at the David Geffen School of Medicine, Ronald

Regan Medical Center, Mattel Children's Hospital, Center for Population Research facility, California Census Research Data Center, LaKretz Center for California Conservation Science, Institute of Environmental and Sustainability facility, Stunt Ranch Reserve and Education Center, Luskin Conference Center, Lake Arrowhead Conference Center, Mildred E. Mathias Botanical Garden, Division of Laboratory Animal Medicine, Biological Collections, Grunwald Center for Graphic Arts, Franklin D. Murphy Sculpture Garden, Meteorite Collection and Gallery. **Campus network:** 100% of classrooms, 100% of dorms, 100% of student union, 100% of libraries, 100% of dining areas have wireless network access.

CAMPUS LIFE
Environment: Metropolis. **Activities:** Campus Ministries; Choral groups; Concert band; Dance; Drama/theater; International Student Organization; Jazz band; Literary magazine; Marching band; Model UN; Music ensembles; Musical theater; Opera; Pep band; Radio station; Student government; Student newspaper; Student-run film society; Symphony orchestra; Television station; Yearbook. 850 registered organizations, 21 honor societies, 35 fraternities, 35 sororities on campus. **Athletics (Intercollegiate):** *Men:* baseball, basketball, cross-country, football, golf, soccer, tennis, track/field (outdoor), track/field (indoor), volleyball, water polo. *Women:* basketball, crew/rowing, cross-country, diving, golf, gymnastics, soccer, softball, swimming, tennis, track/field (outdoor), track/field (indoor), volleyball, water polo. **On-Campus Highlights:** UCLA Library. **Environmental Initiatives:** Through a combination of energy efficiency, renewable energy, sustainable transportation programs and offsets, UCLA reduced greenhouse gas emissions to below 1990 levels in 2014, achieving the 2020 goal six years ahead of schedule.

ADMISSIONS
Freshman Academic Profile: Average high school GPA 3.9. 97% in top 10% of high school class, 100% in top 25% of high school class, 100% in top 50% of high school class. 74% from public high schools. **Test Scores:** SAT Math middle 50% range 640–790. SAT EBRW middle 50% range 640–740. ACT middle 50% range 27–34. **Basis for Candidate Selection:** *Very important factors include:* rigor of secondary school record, academic GPA, application essay, standardized test scores. *Important factors include:* extracurricular activities, talent/ability, character/personal qualities. *Other factors include:* first generation, geographical residence, state residency. **Freshman Admission Requirements:** High school diploma is required and GED is accepted. *Academic units required:* 4 English, 3 math, 2 science, 2 science labs, 2 foreign language, 2 history, 1 academic elective, 1 visual/performing arts. *Academic units recommended:* 4 English, 4 math, 3 science, 3 science labs, 3 foreign language, 2 history, 1 academic elective, 1 visual/performing arts. **Freshman Admission Statistics:** 111,322 applied, 12% admitted, 43% enrolled. **Transfer Admission Requirements:** College transcript(s), essay or personal statement, statement of good standing from prior institution(s). Minimum college GPA of 2.4 required. Lowest grade transferable D. **General Admission Information:** Application fee $70. Regular application deadline 11/30.

COSTS AND FINANCIAL AID
Annual in-state tuition $11,442. Annual out-of-state tuition $40,434. Room and board $15,902. Required fees $1,784. Average book and supplies expense $1,464. **Required Forms and Deadlines:** FAFSA. **Notification of Awards:** Applicants will be notified of awards on a rolling basis beginning 3/15. **Types of Aid:** *Need-based scholarships/grants:* College/university scholarship or grant aid from institutional funds; Federal Pell; Private scholarships; SEOG; State scholarships/grants. *Loans:* Direct PLUS loans; Direct Subsidized Stafford Loans; Direct Unsubsidized Stafford Loans. **Student Employment:** Federal Work-Study Program available. Institutional employment available. **Financial Aid Statistics:** 96% needy freshmen, 96% needy undergrads receive need-based scholarship or grant aid. 4% freshmen, 2% undergrads receive non-need-based scholarship or grant aid. 54% freshmen, 55% undergrads receive need-based self-help aid. 1% freshmen, 1% undergrads receive athletic scholarships. 53% freshmen, 54% undergrads receive any aid. 42% undergrads borrow to pay for school. Average cumulative indebtedness $22,390. **Criteria awarding aid:** *Non-need-based:* Academics, Art, Job skills.

UNIVERSITY OF CALIFORNIA—MERCED

5200 Lake Rd., Merced, CA 95343, CA
Phone: 209-228-7178 **Financial Aid Phone:** 209 228-7178
E-mail: admissions@ucmerced.edu **CEEB Code:** 041271
Fax: 209-228-4244 **Website:** http://www.ucmerced.edu **ACT Code:** 0450

This public school was founded in 2005. It has a 815 acre campus.

RATINGS
Admissions Selectivity Rating: 77   **Fire Safety Rating:** 97   **Green Rating:** 99

STUDENTS AND FACULTY
Enrollment: 8,088. **Student Body:** 52% female, 48% male, 1% out-of-state, 8% international (7 countries represented). Asian 19%, African American 4%, Caucasian 9%, Hispanic 56%, Native American <1%, Pacific Islander 1%, Two or more races 3%, Race unknown 1%.
Retention and Graduation: 85% freshmen return for sophomore year. 45% freshmen graduate within 4 years. 69% freshmen graduate within 6 years. 17% grads go on to further study within 1 year. 43% grads pursue arts and sciences degrees. 3% grads pursue law degrees. 7% grads pursue business degrees. 1% grads pursue medical degrees. **Faculty:** Student/faculty ratio 19:1. 389 full-time faculty, 83% hold PhDs, 26% are members of minority groups, 45% are women.

ACADEMICS
Degrees: Bachelor's; Doctoral degree research/scholarship; Master's. **Classes:** Most classes have 20–29 students. Most lab/discussion sessions have 20–29 students. **Most popular majors:** Psychology, General; Biology/Biological Sciences, General; Computer Engineering, General. **Special Study Options:** Accelerated program; Double major; Independent study; Internships; Study abroad. **Disability Services offered:** Note-taking services; Reader services; Tape recorders. **Career services:** Alumni network; Alumni services; Career assessment; Internships; Regional alumni.

FACILITIES
Housing: Apartments for married students; Apartments for single students; Coed dorms; Special housing for disabled students; Theme housing.

CAMPUS LIFE
Environment: City. **Activities:** Campus Ministries; Choral groups; Dance; Pep band; Radio station; Student government; Student newspaper; Student-run film society; Yearbook. 200 registered organizations, 2 honor societies, 11 religious organization, 6 fraternities, 7 sororities on campus.

ADMISSIONS
Freshman Academic Profile: Average high school GPA 3.6. **Test Scores:** SAT Math middle 50% range 490–590. SAT EBRW middle 50% range 490–590. ACT middle 50% range 17–22. **Basis for Candidate Selection:** *Very important factors include:* rigor of secondary school record, academic GPA, application essay, standardized test scores. *Important factors include:* extracurricular activities, talent/ability. *Other factors include:* recommendation(s), character/personal qualities, first generation, geographical residence, state residency, volunteer work, work experience. **Freshman Admission Requirements:** High school diploma is required and GED is accepted. *Academic units required:* 4 English, 3 math, 2 science, 2 science labs, 2 foreign language, 2 history, 1 academic elective, 1 visual/performing arts. *Academic units recommended:* 4 math, 3 science, 3 science labs, 3 foreign language. **Freshman Admission Statistics:** 25,368 applied, 72% admitted, 12% enrolled. **General Admission Information:** Application fee $70. Regular application deadline 11/30. Non-fall registration accepted. Admission may be deferred for a maximum of 1 year.

COSTS AND FINANCIAL AID
Annual in-state tuition $11,502. Annual out-of-state tuition $39,516. Room and board $16,454. Required fees $2,125. Average book and supplies expense $1,106. **Student Employment:** Federal Work-Study Program available. Institutional employment available. **Financial Aid Statistics:** 99% needy freshmen, 98% needy undergrads receive need-based scholarship or grant aid. 1% freshmen, 1% undergrads receive non-need-based scholarship or grant aid. 69% freshmen, 62% undergrads receive need-based self-help aid. 0% freshmen, 0% undergrads receive athletic scholarships. 94% freshmen, 90% undergrads receive any aid. 71% undergrads borrow to pay for school. Average cumulative indebtedness $18,187.

UNIVERSITY OF CALIFORNIA—RIVERSIDE

3106 Student Services Building, Riverside, CA 92521
Phone: 951-827-3411 **Financial Aid Phone:** (951) 827-3878
E-mail: admissions@ucr.edu **CEEB Code:** 4839
Fax: 951-827-6344 **Website:** www.ucr.edu **ACT Code:** 0456

This public school was founded in 1954. It has a 1200 acre campus.

RATINGS
Admissions Selectivity Rating: 92   **Fire Safety Rating:** 94   **Green Rating:** 97

STUDENTS AND FACULTY
Enrollment: 22,020. **Student Body:** 54% female, 46% male, 0% out-of-state, 4% international (90 countries represented). Asian 34%, African American 3%, Caucasian 11%, Hispanic 42%, Native American <1%, Pacific Islander <1%, Two or more races 6%, Race unknown 1%.
Retention and Graduation: 90% freshmen return for sophomore year. 56% freshmen graduate within 4 years. 76% freshmen graduate within 6 years. **Faculty:** Student/faculty ratio 22:1. 1,000 full-time faculty, 98% hold PhDs, 46% are members of minority groups, 37% are women. 0% of classes are taught by teaching assistants.

ACADEMICS
Degrees: Bachelor's; Doctoral degree—professional practice; Doctoral degree research/scholarship; Master's. **Classes:** Most classes have 20–29 students. Most lab/discussion sessions have 20–29 students. **Most popular majors:** Psychology, General; Business Administration and Management, General; Biology/Biological Sciences, General. **Special Study Options:** Accelerated program; Cross-registration; Distance learning; Double major; English as a Second Language (ESL); Exchange student program (domestic); Honors program; Independent study; Internships; Study abroad; Teacher certification program. **Honors programs:** University Honors is designed for students who have shown through their own high achievement that they value intellectual challenges and want to be a part of an innovative, diverse, and demanding learning community. Students benefit from close interaction with Honors Faculty in small class settings, and with Professional Staff who provide developmental advising to help them optimize their educational experience at UCR. High impact, experiential learning opportunities available to Honors students include; undergraduate research, scholarly and creative work, internships, service learning, and faculty-led co-curricular activities. In addition Honors students are supported by a strong peer leader support system, faculty mentorship, Honors scholarship opportunities, and preparation for prestigious scholarships and awards. These experiences are designed to prepare students for participation in a senior thesis project that advances knowledge in their discipline, culminating in an Honors Thesis. **Combined degree programs:** BA/MA. **Disability Services offered:** Note-taking services; Reader services; Tape recorders; Tutors. **Career services:** Alumni services; Career assessment; Career/job search classes; Internships.

FACILITIES
Housing: Apartments for married students; Apartments for single students; Coed dorms; Special housing for disabled students; Special housing for international students; Theme housing. **Special Academic Facilities/Equipment:** Art gallery, photography museum, botanical gardens, audio-visual resource center/studios, media resource center, statistical consulting center, citrus research center and agricultural experiment station, air pollution research center, center for environmental research and technology, water resources center, geophysics and planetary physics institute, center for bibliographical studies, center for family studies, center for crime and justice studies, natural reserve system, water resources center, salinity lab.

CAMPUS LIFE
Environment: City. **Activities:** Campus Ministries; Choral groups; Concert band; Dance; Drama/theater; International Student Organization; Jazz band; Literary magazine; Model UN; Music ensembles; Musical theater; Pep band; Radio station; Student government; Student newspaper; Student-run film society; Symphony orchestra. 512 registered organizations, 11 honor societies, 28 religious organizations, 16 fraternities, 16 sororities on campus. **Athletics (Intercollegiate):** *Men:* baseball, basketball, cross-country, golf, soccer, tennis, track/field (outdoor), track/field (indoor). *Women:* basketball, cross-country, golf, soccer, softball, tennis, track/field (outdoor), track/field

(indoor), volleyball. **On-Campus Highlights:** The Highlander Union Building (HUB). **Environmental Initiatives:** UCR has a funded non-restrictive Office of Sustainability charged with coordinating sustainability initiatives throughout the campus supported by the Chancellor's Committee on Sustainability with the Chancellor serving as chair.

ADMISSIONS
Freshman Academic Profile: Average high school GPA 3.8. 94% in top 10% of high school class, 100% in top 25% of high school class, 100% in top 50% of high school class. 90% from public high schools. **Test Scores:** SAT Math middle 50% range 550–690. SAT EBRW middle 50% range 560–650. ACT middle 50% range 24–30. **Basis for Candidate Selection:** *Very important factors include:* academic GPA, application essay, standardized test scores. *Important factors include:* rigor of secondary school record. *Other factors include:* first generation, state residency. **Freshman Admission Requirements:** High school diploma is required and GED is accepted. *Academic units required:* 4 English, 3 math, 2 science, 2 science labs, 2 foreign language, 2 history, 1 academic elective, 1 visual/performing arts. *Academic units recommended:* 4 English, 4 math, 3 science, 3 science labs, 3 foreign language, 2 history, 1 academic elective, 1 visual/performing arts. **Freshman Admission Statistics:** 49,518 applied, 57% admitted, 17% enrolled. **Transfer Admission Requirements:** College transcript(s), essay or personal statement, statement of good standing from prior institution(s). Minimum college GPA of 2.4 required. Lowest grade transferable D-. **General Admission Information:** Application fee $70. Regular application deadline 11/30.

COSTS AND FINANCIAL AID
Required Forms and Deadlines: FAFSA; State aid form. **Notification of Awards:** Applicants will be notified of awards on a rolling basis beginning 3/1. **Types of Aid:** *Need-based scholarships/grants:* College/university scholarship or grant aid from institutional funds; Federal Pell; Private scholarships; SEOG; State scholarships/grants. *Loans:* Direct PLUS loans; Direct Subsidized Stafford Loans; Direct Unsubsidized Stafford Loans. **Student Employment:** Federal Work-Study Program available. Institutional employment available. **Financial Aid Statistics:** 96% needy freshmen, 96% needy undergrads receive need-based scholarship or grant aid. 2% freshmen, 2% undergrads receive non-need-based scholarship or grant aid. 81% freshmen, 68% undergrads receive need-based self-help aid. 0% freshmen, 0% undergrads receive athletic scholarships. 89% freshmen, 87% undergrads receive any aid. 62% undergrads borrow to pay for school. Average cumulative indebtedness $20,779. **Criteria awarding aid:** *Need-based:* Academics. *Non-need-based:* Academics, Alumni affiliation, Art, Athletics, Leadership.

UNIVERSITY OF CALIFORNIA—SAN DIEGO

9500 Gilman Drive, La Jolla, CA 92093-0021
Phone: 858-534-4831 **Financial Aid Phone:** (858) 534-4480
E-mail: admissionsinfo@ucsd.edu **CEEB Code:** 4836
Fax: 858-534-5723 **Website:** www.ucsd.edu **ACT Code:** 0459

This public school was founded in 1960. It has a 1976 acre campus.

RATINGS
Admissions Selectivity Rating: 97   **Fire Safety Rating:** 85   **Green Rating:** 97

STUDENTS AND FACULTY
Enrollment: 30,645. **Student Body:** 50% female, 50% male, 7% out-of-state, 18% international (120 countries represented). Asian 36%, African American 3%, Caucasian 19%, Hispanic 21%, Native American <1%, Pacific Islander <1%, Two or more races 0%, Race unknown 2%.
Retention and Graduation: 93% freshmen return for sophomore year. 55% freshmen graduate within 4 years. 85% freshmen graduate within 6 years. 42% grads go on to further study within 1 year. 36% grads pursue arts and sciences degrees. 17% grads pursue law degrees. 9% grads pursue business degrees. 17% grads pursue medical degrees. **Faculty:** Student/faculty ratio 19:1. 1,230 full-time faculty, 90% hold PhDs, 30% are members of minority groups, 33% are women. 0% of classes are taught by teaching assistants.

ACADEMICS
Degrees: Bachelor's; Doctoral degree—professional practice; Doctoral degree research/scholarship; Master's. **Classes:** Most classes have 10–19 students. Most lab/discussion sessions have 10–19 students. **Special Study Options:** Accelerated program; Cooperative education program; Cross-registration; Double major; English as a Second Language (ESL); Exchange student program (domestic); Honors program; Independent study; Internships; Liberal arts/career combination; Student-designed major; Study abroad; Teacher certification program. **Honors programs:** Each of UCSDs six colleges offers an honors program. Honors programs differ from college to college and year to year. Honors programs at John Muir College have been established to provide outstanding students with enhanced educational experiences through close interaction with faculty and other honors students. The Muir 90 Honors Seminar is by invitation and focuses primarily on entering freshmen. **Combined degree programs:** BA/MA; BA/MD; BA/MEng. **Disability Services offered:** Note-taking services; Reader services; Tape recorders; Tutors. **Career services:** Alumni network; Alumni services; Career assessment; Career/job search classes; Internships; Regional alumni.

FACILITIES
Housing: Apartments for married students; Apartments for single students; Coed dorms; Special housing for disabled students; Special housing for international students; Theme housing; Wellness housing. **Special Academic Facilities/Equipment:** Art galleries, center for U.S.-Mexican studies, music recording studio, audiovisual center, center for music experimentation, aquarium, structural lab, San Diego supercomputer center,electron microscopes lab, the UC San Diego Medical Center, Scripps Institution of Oceanography, California Institute for Telecommunications and Information Technology (Calit2), Institute for Global Conflict and Cooperation; Institute of the Americas. **Campus network:** 100% of classrooms, 100% of dorms, 100% of student union, 100% of libraries, 100% of dining areas, 100% of common outdoor areas have wireless network access.

CAMPUS LIFE
Environment: Metropolis. **Activities:** Campus Ministries; Choral groups; Concert band; Dance; Drama/theater; International Student Organization; Jazz band; Literary magazine; Marching band; Model UN; Music ensembles; Musical theater; Opera; Pep band; Radio station; Student government; Student newspaper; Student-run film society; Symphony orchestra; Television station; Yearbook. 531 registered organizations, 4 honor societies, 36 religious organizations, 16 fraternities, 12 sororities on campus. **Athletics (Intercollegiate):** *Men:* baseball, basketball, crew/rowing, cross-country, diving, fencing, golf, soccer, swimming, tennis, track/field (outdoor), volleyball, water polo. *Women:* basketball, crew/rowing, cross-country, diving, fencing, soccer, softball, swimming, tennis, track/field (outdoor), volleyball, water polo. **On-Campus Highlights:** Geisel Library. **Environmental Initiatives:** The LEED Gold Certified Sustainability Resource Center (SRC), completed November 20, 2009, was constructed to provide a centralized, collaborative space in which to realize the common goals of maximizing campus environmental, social, and economic stewardship and sustainability; reducing the campus impact on the environment; maximizing campus and local outreach and participation; and, establishing a model for contributing to local, national, and global sustainability. The SRC houses the Sustainability Program Office, Student Sustainability Collective and provides workspace for a variety of student, faculty, and staff sustainability-related work groups such as AQUAholics Anonymous, Green Campus, CalPIRG, Net Impact, Sustainable Food Project, Student Sustainability Collective, Association of Environmental Professionals, San Diego Alliance for Campus Sustainability, University Extension, UCSD Composting, and many more.

ADMISSIONS
Freshman Academic Profile: Average high school GPA 4.1. 100% in top 10% of high school class, 100% in top 25% of high school class, 100% in top 50% of high school class. **Test Scores:** SAT Math middle 50% range 620–780. SAT EBRW middle 50% range 610–710. ACT middle 50% range 24–33. **Basis for Candidate Selection:** *Very important factors include:* rigor of secondary school record, academic GPA, application essay, standardized test scores. *Important factors include:* extracurricular activities, talent/ability, character/personal qualities, state residency, volunteer work. *Other factors include:* first generation, geographical residence, work experience. **Freshman Admission Requirements:** High school diploma is required and GED is accepted. *Academic units required:* 4 English, 3 math, 2 science, 2 science labs, 2 foreign language, 2 history, 1 academic elective, 1 visual/performing arts. *Academic units recommended:* 4 English, 4 math, 3 science, 3 science labs, 3 foreign language, 2 history, 1 academic elective, 1 visual/performing arts. **Freshman Admission Statistics:** 99,133 applied, 32% admitted, 19% enrolled. **Transfer Admission**

Requirements: College transcript(s), essay or personal statement, statement of good standing from prior institution(s). Minimum college GPA of 2.4 required. Lowest grade transferable D. **General Admission Information:** Application fee $125. Regular application deadline 11/30.

COSTS AND FINANCIAL AID
Annual in-state tuition $12,570. Annual out-of-state tuition $42,324. Room and board $14,295. Required fees $2,046. Average book and supplies expense $1,128. **Required Forms and Deadlines:** FAFSA; State aid form. **Notification of Awards:** Applicants will be notified of awards on a rolling basis beginning 3/15. **Types of Aid:** *Need-based scholarships/grants:* College/university scholarship or grant aid from institutional funds; Federal Pell; Private scholarships; SEOG; State scholarships/grants. *Loans:* Direct PLUS loans; Direct Subsidized Stafford Loans; Direct Unsubsidized Stafford Loans. **Student Employment:** Federal Work-Study Program available. Institutional employment available. **Financial Aid Statistics:** 94% needy freshmen, 95% needy undergrads receive need-based scholarship or grant aid. 3% freshmen, 2% undergrads receive non-need-based scholarship or grant aid. 69% freshmen, 70% undergrads receive need-based self-help aid. 0% freshmen, 0% undergrads receive athletic scholarships. 77% freshmen, 63% undergrads receive any aid. 45% undergrads borrow to pay for school. Average cumulative indebtedness $21,061. **Criteria awarding aid:** *Need-based:* Academics, Art, Leadership, Minority status, Music/drama. *Non-need-based:* Academics, Art, Athletics, Leadership, Minority status, Music/drama.

UNIVERSITY OF CALIFORNIA—SANTA BARBARA

Office of Admissions, Santa Barbara, CA 93106-2014
Phone: 805-893-2881 **Financial Aid Phone:** (805) 893-2432
E-mail: admissions@sa.ucsb.edu **CEEB Code:** 4835
Fax: 805-893-2676 **Website:** www.ucsb.edu **ACT Code:** 004835

This public school was founded in 1909. It has a 989 acre campus.

RATINGS
Admissions Selectivity Rating: 95   Fire Safety Rating: 95   Green Rating: 98

STUDENTS AND FACULTY
Enrollment: 22,186. **Student Body:** 54% female, 46% male, 4% out-of-state, 8% international (82 countries represented). Asian 21%, African American 2%, Caucasian 34%, Hispanic 26%, Native American <1%, Pacific Islander <1%, Two or more races 6%, Race unknown 1%.
Retention and Graduation: 92% freshmen return for sophomore year. 72% freshmen graduate within 4 years. 88% freshmen graduate within 6 years.
Faculty: Student/faculty ratio 17:1. 922 full-time faculty, 100% hold PhDs, 20% are members of minority groups, 38% are women.

ACADEMICS
Degrees: Bachelor's; Doctoral degree research/scholarship; Master's; Post-bachelor's certificate; Post-master's certificate. **Classes:** Most classes have 20–29 students. Most lab/discussion sessions have 20–29 students. **Most popular majors:** Economics, General; Biology/Biological Sciences, General; Psychology, General. **Special Study Options:** Accelerated program; Cross-registration; Double major; Dual enrollment; English as a Second Language (ESL); Exchange student program (domestic); Honors program; Independent study; Internships; Student-designed major; Study abroad; Teacher certification program. **Honors programs:** The Letters & Science Honors Program is designed to give students in the College of Letters and Science the opportunity to pursue their interests as part of a small community of scholars. The program connects such students to the resources of a large university, while providing an intimate collegiate atmosphere where students work closely with peers and professors in small classes, research laboratories, and special program and activities. **Combined degree programs:** BA/MA. **Disability Services offered:** Note-taking services; Reader services; Tape recorders; Tutors. **Career services:** Career assessment; Career/job search classes; Internships.

FACILITIES
Housing: Apartments for married students; Apartments for single students; Coed dorms; Cooperative housing; Fraternity/sorority housing; Special housing for international students; Theme housing; Wellness housing; 100% of campus

accessible to physically disabled. **Special Academic Facilities/Equipment:** Art museum; centers for black studies, Chicano studies, and study of developing nations; institutes for applied behavioral sciences, community/organizational research, marine science, and theoretical physics; Channel Islands field station.

CAMPUS LIFE
Environment: City. **Activities:** Campus Ministries; Choral groups; Concert band; Dance; Drama/theater; International Student Organization; Jazz band; Literary magazine; Model UN; Music ensembles; Musical theater; Opera; Pep band; Radio station; Student government; Student newspaper; Student-run film society; Symphony orchestra; Television station; Yearbook. 404 registered organizations, 13 honor societies, 16 religious organizations, 12 fraternities, 20 sororities on campus. **Athletics (Intercollegiate):** *Men:* baseball, basketball, cross-country, diving, golf, gymnastics, soccer, swimming, tennis, track/field (outdoor), volleyball, water polo. *Women:* basketball, cross-country, diving, gymnastics, soccer, softball, swimming, tennis, track/field (outdoor), volleyball, water polo. **On-Campus Highlights:** Storke Tower Plaza/University Center. **Environmental Initiatives:** 1) Green buildings: minimum silver and strive for gold LEED certification. Six buildings are currently certified, including San Clemente Villages Graduate Housing, one of the largest Gold certified housing projects in the US, and Bren Hall, the first building in the US to receive two Platinum ratings for new construction and existing buildings. Plus, 24 additional existing buildings scheduled to be certified in the next couple years through the USGBC Portfolio Program. UCSB has the most LEED EB buildings in the UC System. We created Low Environmental Impact Cleaning Policy for the campus custodial services. All cleaning products and soaps used by the custodial staff are Green Seal certified. Plus toilet tissue, seat covers, and brown paper towels have 100% recycled content. Housing & Residential Services, supports solar water heating providing hot water for dorms, recycling used cooking oil from dining commons for biofuel, extensive recycling program including composting of food waste, purchasing local and/or organic foods for dining commons, using Green Seal cleaning products for custodial duties.

ADMISSIONS
Freshman Academic Profile: Average high school GPA 4.1. 100% in top 10% of high school class, 100% in top 25% of high school class, 100% in top 50% of high school class. 80% from public high schools. **Test Scores:** SAT Math middle 50% range 620–760. SAT EBRW middle 50% range 620–710. ACT middle 50% range 26–32. **Basis for Candidate Selection:** *Very important factors include:* academic GPA, application essay, standardized test scores. *Important factors include:* rigor of secondary school record. *Other factors include:* extracurricular activities, talent/ability, character/personal qualities, first generation, geographical residence, state residency, volunteer work, work experience. **Freshman Admission Requirements:** High school diploma is required and GED is accepted. *Academic units required:* 4 English, 3 math, 2 science, 2 science labs, 2 foreign language, 2 history, 1 academic elective, 1 visual/performing arts. *Academic units recommended:* 4 English, 4 math, 3 science, 3 science labs, 3 foreign language, 2 history, 1 academic elective, 1 visual/performing arts. **Freshman Admission Statistics:** 80,319 applied, 33% admitted, 17% enrolled. **Transfer Admission Requirements:** High school transcript, college transcript(s), essay or personal statement. Minimum college GPA of 2.4 required. Lowest grade transferable D. **General Admission Information:** Application fee $70. Regular application deadline 11/30.

COSTS AND FINANCIAL AID
Annual in-state tuition $12,570. Annual out-of-state tuition $42,324. Room and board $15,111. Required fees $1,875. Average book and supplies expense $1,143. **Required Forms and Deadlines:** FAFSA. **Types of Aid:** *Need-based scholarships/grants:* College/university scholarship or grant aid from institutional funds; Federal Pell; SEOG; State scholarships/grants. *Loans:* Direct PLUS loans; Direct Subsidized Stafford Loans; Direct Unsubsidized Stafford Loans. **Student Employment:** Federal Work-Study Program available. Institutional employment available. **Financial Aid Statistics:** 94% needy freshmen, 95% needy undergrads receive need-based scholarship or grant aid. 1% freshmen, 1% undergrads receive athletic scholarships. 61% freshmen, 59% undergrads receive any aid. 50% undergrads borrow to pay for school. Average cumulative indebtedness $20,004. **Criteria awarding aid:** *Need-based:* Academics, Alumni affiliation, Art, Athletics, Music/drama. *Non-need-based:* Academics, Alumni affiliation, Athletics.

UNIVERSITY OF CALIFORNIA—SANTA CRUZ

Office of Admissions, Cook House, Santa Cruz, CA 95064
Phone: 831-459-4008 **Financial Aid Phone:** 831-459-2963
E-mail: admissions@ucsc.edu **CEEB Code:** 4860
Fax: 831-459-4452 **Website:** www.ucsc.edu **ACT Code:** 0460

This public school was founded in 1965. It has a 2000 acre campus.

RATINGS
Admissions Selectivity Rating: 94   **Fire Safety Rating:** 80   **Green Rating:** 97

STUDENTS AND FACULTY
Enrollment: 17,517. **Student Body:** 48% female, 52% male, 4% out-of-state, 9% international (55 countries represented). Asian 22%, African American 2%, Caucasian 31%, Hispanic 26%, Native American <1%, Pacific Islander <1%, Two or more races 8%, Race unknown 2%.
Retention and Graduation: 52% freshmen graduate within 4 years. 75% freshmen graduate within 6 years. **Faculty:** 0% of classes are taught by teaching assistants.

ACADEMICS
Degrees: Bachelor's; Doctoral degree research/scholarship; Master's. **Most popular majors:** Computer Science; Psychology, General; Business/Managerial Economics. **Special Study Options:** Cooperative education program; Distance learning; Double major; Exchange student program (domestic); Honors program; Independent study; Internships; Student-designed major; Study abroad; Teacher certification program. **Honors programs:** UCSC provides a variety of honors programs which are described on the following website: http://honors.ucsc.edu/honors-programs/index.html. **Combined degree programs:** BA/MA. **Disability Services offered:** Note-taking services; Reader services; Tape recorders; Tutors. **Career services:** Alumni network; Alumni services; Career assessment; Career/job search classes; Internships.

FACILITIES
Housing: Apartments for married students; Apartments for single students; Coed dorms; Men's dorms; Special housing for international students; Theme housing; Wellness housing; Women's dorms; 100% of campus accessible to physically disabled. **Special Academic Facilities/Equipment:** Eloise Pickard Smith Gallery; Mary Porter Sesnon Gallery; Center for Agroecology; Wellness Center; Long Marine Laboratory; Arboretum.

CAMPUS LIFE
Environment: City. **Activities:** Campus Ministries; Choral groups; Dance; Drama/theater; International Student Organization; Jazz band; Literary magazine; Model UN; Music ensembles; Musical theater; Opera; Radio station; Student government; Student newspaper; Student-run film society; Symphony orchestra; Television station. 176 registered organizations, 4 honor societies, 6 religious organizations, 7 fraternities, 13 sororities on campus. **Athletics (Intercollegiate):** *Men:* basketball, diving, soccer, swimming, tennis, volleyball. *Women:* basketball, cross-country, diving, golf, soccer, swimming, tennis, volleyball. **On-Campus Highlights:** Arboretum.

ADMISSIONS
Freshman Academic Profile: Average high school GPA 3.6. 96% in top 10% of high school class, 100% in top 25% of high school class, 100% in top 50% of high school class. 81% from public high schools. **Test Scores:** SAT Math middle 50% range 600–710. SAT EBRW middle 50% range 590–680. ACT middle 50% range 24–30. **Basis for Candidate Selection:** *Very important factors include:* rigor of secondary school record, academic GPA, application essay, standardized test scores, state residency. *Important factors include:* extracurricular activities, talent/ability, character/personal qualities, first generation, geographical residence. *Other factors include:* volunteer work, work experience. **Freshman Admission Requirements:** High school diploma is required and GED is accepted. *Academic units required:* 4 English, 3 math, 2 science, 2 science labs, 2 foreign language, 1 social studies, 1 history, 1 academic elective, 1 visual/performing arts. *Academic units recommended:* 4 English, 4 math, 3 science, 3 science labs, 3 foreign language, 1 social studies, 1 history, 1 academic elective, 1 visual/performing arts. **Freshman Admission Statistics:** 55,866 applied, 52% admitted, 13% enrolled. **Transfer Admission Requirements:** College transcript(s), essay or personal statement, statement of good standing from prior institution(s). Minimum college GPA of 2.4 required.

Lowest grade transferable D. **General Admission Information:** Application fee $70. Regular application deadline 11/30.

COSTS AND FINANCIAL AID
Annual in-state tuition $11,442. Annual out-of-state tuition $40,434. Room and board $16,916. Required fees $2,612. Average book and supplies expense $1,085. **Required Forms and Deadlines:** FAFSA; State aid form. **Notification of Awards:** Applicants will be notified of awards on a rolling basis beginning 4/1. **Types of Aid:** *Need-based scholarships/grants:* College/university scholarship or grant aid from institutional funds; Federal Pell; Private scholarships; SEOG; State scholarships/grants. *Loans:* Direct PLUS loans; Direct Subsidized Stafford Loans; Direct Unsubsidized Stafford Loans. **Student Employment:** Federal Work-Study Program available. Institutional employment available. **Financial Aid Statistics:** 92% needy freshmen, 93% needy undergrads receive need-based scholarship or grant aid. 2% freshmen, 1% undergrads receive non-need-based scholarship or grant aid. 73% freshmen, 71% undergrads receive need-based self-help aid. 0% freshmen, 0% undergrads receive athletic scholarships. 51% freshmen, 57% undergrads receive any aid. 58% undergrads borrow to pay for school. Average cumulative indebtedness $22,092. **Criteria awarding aid:** *Need-based:* Academics, Alumni affiliation, Art, Leadership, Music/drama. *Non-need-based:* Academics, Alumni affiliation, Art, Leadership, Music/drama.

UNIVERSITY OF CENTRAL ARKANSAS

201 Donaghey Avenue, Conway, AR 72035
Phone: 501-450-3128 **Financial Aid Phone:** 501-450-3140
E-mail: admissions@uca.edu **CEEB Code:** 6012
Fax: 501-450-5228 **Website:** www.uca.edu/ **ACT Code:** 118

This public school was founded in 1907. It has a 350 acre campus.

RATINGS
Admissions Selectivity Rating: 75   **Fire Safety Rating:** 62   **Green Rating:** 61

STUDENTS AND FACULTY
Enrollment: 7,626. **Student Body:** 54% female, 46% male, 10% out-of-state, 4% international (73 countries represented). Asian 5%, African American 16%, Caucasian 64%, Hispanic 5%, Native American <1%, Pacific Islander <1%, Two or more races 4%, Race unknown <1%.
Retention and Graduation: 74% freshmen return for sophomore year. 41% freshmen graduate within 6 years. **Faculty:** 558 full-time faculty, 72% hold PhDs, 16% are members of minority groups, 52% are women. 0% of classes are taught by teaching assistants.

ACADEMICS
Degrees: Associate; Bachelor's; Certificate; Doctoral degree—professional practice; Doctoral degree research/scholarship; Master's; Post-bachelor's certificate; Post-master's certificate. **Classes:** Most classes have 20–29 students. **Special Study Options:** Accelerated program; Cooperative education program; Distance learning; Double major; Dual enrollment; English as a Second Language (ESL); Honors program; Independent study; Internships; Liberal arts/career combination; Study abroad; Teacher certification program. **Disability Services offered:** Note-taking services; Reader services; Tape recorders. **Career services:** Alumni network; Career/job search classes; Internships; Regional alumni.

FACILITIES
Housing: Apartments for single students; Coed dorms; Fraternity/sorority housing; Special housing for disabled students; Special housing for international students; Women's dorms. **Special Academic Facilities/Equipment:** Greenhouse, Baum Gellery, HPER Center, Planetarium, Technology Plaza, Smartboards, H.L. Minton Center for Geospatial Analysis and Research. **Campus network:** 100% of classrooms, 100% of dorms, 100% of student union, 100% of libraries, 100% of dining areas, 65% of common outdoor areas have wireless network access.

CAMPUS LIFE
Environment: Town. **Activities:** Campus Ministries; Choral groups; Concert band; Dance; Drama/theater; International Student Organization; Jazz band; Marching band; Model UN; Music ensembles; Musical theater; Pep band; Radio station; Student government; Student newspaper; Symphony orchestra; Television station; Yearbook. 231 registered organizations, 20 honor societies, 18 religious organizations, 13 fraternities, 9 sororities on campus. **Athletics (Intercollegiate):** *Men:* baseball, basketball, cheerleading, cross-country,

football, golf, soccer, tennis, track/field (outdoor), track/field (indoor). *Women:* basketball, cheerleading, cross-country, golf, soccer, softball, tennis, track/field (outdoor), track/field (indoor), volleyball. **On-Campus Highlights:** Student Center.

ADMISSIONS
Freshman Academic Profile: Average high school GPA 3.5. 21% in top 10% of high school class, 49% in top 25% of high school class, 81% in top 50% of high school class. **Test Scores:** SAT Math middle 50% range 490–590. SAT EBRW middle 50% range 480–580. ACT middle 50% range 21–27. **Basis for Candidate Selection:** *Very important factors include:* academic GPA, standardized test scores. **Freshman Admission Requirements:** High school diploma is required and GED is accepted. *Academic units recommended:* 4 English, 4 math, 3 science, 3 social studies, 6 academic electives, 1 unit from above areas or other academic areas. **Freshman Admission Statistics:** 5,541 applied, 91% admitted, 40% enrolled. **Transfer Admission Requirements:** College transcript(s), statement of good standing from prior institution(s). Minimum college GPA of 2.0 required. Lowest grade transferable C. **General Admission Information:** Application fee $25. Non-fall registration accepted.

COSTS AND FINANCIAL AID
Student Employment: Federal Work-Study Program available. Institutional employment available.

UNIVERSITY OF CENTRAL FLORIDA

Best Colleges

P.O. Box 160111, Orlando, FL 32816-0111
Phone: 407-823-3000 **Financial Aid Phone:** 407-823-2827
E-mail: admission@ucf.edu **CEEB Code:** 5233
Fax: 407-823-5625 **Website:** www.ucf.edu **ACT Code:** 735

This public school was founded in 1963. It has a 1415 acre campus.

RATINGS
Admissions Selectivity Rating: 91   **Fire Safety Rating:** 94   **Green Rating:** 90

STUDENTS AND FACULTY
Enrollment: 58,998. **Student Body:** 55% female, 45% male, 7% out-of-state, 3% international (140 countries represented). Asian 6%, African American 11%, Caucasian 47%, Hispanic 28%, Native American <1%, Pacific Islander <1%, Two or more races 4%, Race unknown 1%.
Retention and Graduation: 92% freshmen return for sophomore year. 44% freshmen graduate within 4 years. 72% freshmen graduate within 6 years. **Faculty:** Student/faculty ratio 30:1. 1,660 full-time faculty, 85% hold PhDs, 29% are members of minority groups, 44% are women. 5% of classes are taught by teaching assistants.

ACADEMICS
Degrees: Associate; Bachelor's; Certificate; Doctoral degree—professional practice; Doctoral degree research/scholarship; Master's; Post-bachelor's certificate; Post-master's certificate. **Classes:** Most classes have 20–29 students. Most lab/discussion sessions have 30–39 students. **Most popular majors:** Psychology, General; Health Professions And Related Programs; Business Administration and Management, General. **Special Study Options:** Accelerated program; Cooperative education program; Distance learning; Double major; Dual enrollment; English as a Second Language (ESL); Honors program; Independent study; Internships; Study abroad; Teacher certification program.
Honors programs: The Burnett Honors College (BHC) fosters an environment of academic excellence and intellectual inquiry that gives students the best of both worlds — an intimate, welcoming place to study and make new friends as well as access to the resources of one of the nation's largest and most innovative metropolitan research universities. BHC focuses on developing highly skilled graduates distinctively prepared for tomorrow's complex challenges, while being mindful of today's changing demographics and the importance of access to opportunity. The college creates a diverse learning community that cultivates talent and inspires excellence. The Burnett Honors College offers two main program tracks, University Honors and Honors Undergraduate Thesis. University Honors provides a special course of study geared toward incoming freshmen or students transferring from one of the five partner community colleges with an Honors A.A. degree. Students of all majors participate in the

University Honors program, which is based on nearly 240 distinctive, small honors classes generally capped at about 20 students. The honors curriculum, which consists of honors courses, interdisciplinary seminars and the honors symposium, takes place over the student's undergraduate career. Though a thesis is not required, the program provides breadth, depth, and engagement with the learning process. All honors courses meet UCF General Education and major-specific requirements. Honors interdisciplinary seminars allow students to explore topics outside the confines of their discipline. As students participate in the University Honors program, they are encouraged to not only pursue rigorous coursework inside and outside the major but also to engage in research, internships, and study abroad programs. Honors Undergraduate Thesis is a two-semester program that allows motivated and talented juniors and seniors to serve as principal investigators and independent scholars while carrying out an original research project or creative activity. Students who successfully complete an honors thesis in their academic major earn the Honors in the Major distinction. Students may also choose to write an honors thesis in another discipline, earning Honors in Research or Honors in Creative Inquiry. Students work under the supervision of a faculty committee, and their published thesis is available to scholars worldwide through the UCF Library. **Combined degree programs:** BA/JD; BA/MA. **Disability Services offered:** Note-taking services; Reader services; Tape recorders; Tutors. **Career services:** Career assessment; Career/job search classes; Internships.

FACILITIES
Housing: Apartments for married students; Apartments for single students; Coed dorms; Fraternity/sorority housing; Theme housing; Wellness housing; 97% of campus accessible to physically disabled. **Campus network:** 100% of classrooms, 100% of dorms, 100% of student union, 100% of libraries, 100% of dining areas, 100% of common outdoor areas have wireless network access.

CAMPUS LIFE
Environment: City. **Activities:** Campus Ministries; Choral groups; Concert band; Dance; Drama/theater; International Student Organization; Jazz band; Literary magazine; Marching band; Model UN; Music ensembles; Musical theater; Pep band; Radio station; Student government; Student-run film society; Symphony orchestra; Television station. 612 registered organizations, 34 honor societies, 45 religious organizations, 21 fraternity, 20 sororities on campus. **Athletics (Intercollegiate):** *Men:* baseball, basketball, cheerleading, cross-country, football, golf, soccer, tennis. *Women:* basketball, cheerleading, crew/rowing, cross-country, golf, soccer, softball, tennis, track/field (outdoor), track/field (indoor), volleyball. **On-Campus Highlights:** Student Union.

ADMISSIONS
Freshman Academic Profile: Average high school GPA 4.1. 36% in top 10% of high school class, 74% in top 25% of high school class, 97% in top 50% of high school class. **Test Scores:** SAT Math middle 50% range 580–670. SAT EBRW middle 50% range 590–670. ACT middle 50% range 25–30. **Basis for Candidate Selection:** *Very important factors include:* rigor of secondary school record, academic GPA, standardized test scores. *Important factors include:* application essay, *Other factors include:* class rank, extracurricular activities, talent/ability, character/personal qualities, first generation, alumni/ae relation, geographical residence, state residency, volunteer work, work experience, level of applicant's interest. **Freshman Admission Requirements:** High school diploma is required and GED is accepted. *Academic units required:* 4 English, 4 math, 3 science, 2 science labs, 2 foreign language, 3 social studies, 2 academic electives. **Freshman Admission Statistics:** 45,118 applied, 44% admitted, 37% enrolled. **Transfer Admission Requirements:** College transcript(s). Minimum college GPA of 2.0 required. Lowest grade transferable D. **General Admission Information:** Application fee $30. Priority deadline 1/1. Regular application deadline 5/1. Non-fall registration accepted.

COSTS AND FINANCIAL AID
Annual in-state tuition $6,368. Annual out-of-state tuition $22,467. Room and board $9,850. Average book and supplies expense $1,200. **Required Forms and Deadlines:** FAFSA. **Notification of Awards:** Applicants will be notified of awards on a rolling basis beginning 3/15. **Types of Aid:** *Need-based scholarships/grants:* College/university scholarship or grant aid from institutional funds; Federal Pell; Private scholarships; SEOG; State scholarships/grants. *Loans:* Direct PLUS loans; Direct Subsidized Stafford Loans; Direct Unsubsidized Stafford Loans. **Student Employment:** Federal Work-Study Program available. Institutional employment available. **Financial Aid Statistics:** 68% needy freshmen, 74% needy undergrads receive need-based scholarship or grant aid. 80% freshmen, 41% undergrads receive non-need-based scholarship or grant aid. 36% freshmen, 49% undergrads receive need-based self-help aid. 1% freshmen, 1% undergrads receive athletic scholarships. 85.4% freshmen, 74.29% undergrads receive any aid. 49% undergrads borrow to pay for school. Average cumulative indebtedness $22,561. **Criteria awarding aid:** *Need-based:*

Academics, Athletics, Leadership, Minority status, Music/drama. *Non-need-based:* Academics, Alumni affiliation, Athletics, Leadership, State/district residency.

UNIVERSITY OF CENTRAL MISSOURI

Office of Admissions, Warrensburg, MO 64093
Phone: 660-543-4290 **Financial Aid Phone:** 660-543-8266
E-mail: admit@ucmo.edu **CEEB Code:** 6090
Fax: 660-543-8517 **Website:** www.ucmo.edu **ACT Code:** 2272

This public school was founded in 1871. It has a 1561 acre campus.

RATINGS
Admissions Selectivity Rating: 74   **Fire Safety Rating:** 62   **Green Rating:** 60*

STUDENTS AND FACULTY
Enrollment: 8,099. **Student Body:** 55% female, 45% male, 12% out-of-state, 2% international (60 countries represented). Asian 1%, African American 10%, Caucasian 76%, Hispanic 5%, Native American <1%, Pacific Islander <1%, Two or more races 4%, Race unknown 1%.
Retention and Graduation: 69% freshmen return for sophomore year. 29% freshmen graduate within 4 years. 49% freshmen graduate within 6 years.
Faculty: Student/faculty ratio 16:1. 463 full-time faculty, 72% hold PhDs, 13% are members of minority groups, 47% are women.

ACADEMICS
Degrees: Bachelor's; Certificate; Master's; Post-bachelor's certificate; Post-master's certificate. **Classes:** Most classes have 10–19 students. Most lab/discussion sessions have 10–19 students. **Most popular majors:** Education, General; Marketing/Marketing Management, General; Criminal Justice/Law Enforcement Administration. **Special Study Options:** Accelerated program; Cooperative education program; Cross-registration; Distance learning; Double major; Dual enrollment; English as a Second Language (ESL); Exchange student program (domestic); Honors program; Independent study; Internships; Liberal arts/career combination; Study abroad; Teacher certification program; Weekend college. **Disability Services offered:** Note-taking services; Reader services; Tape recorders; Tutors.

FACILITIES
Housing: Apartments for married students; Apartments for single students; Coed dorms; Fraternity/sorority housing; Men's dorms; Special housing for disabled students; Women's dorms; 95% of campus accessible to physically disabled. **Special Academic Facilities/Equipment:** Art gallery, Nance Museum and Library of Antiquities, natural history museum, English language center, child development lab, speech and hearing lab, 260-acre farm, Missouri Safety center, National Police Institute, driving/safety range, center for technology and business research, airport for aviation program. Extended campus, Lee's Summit, MO.KCMW-FM, KMOS-TV, Public Broadcasting Stations. **Campus network:** 100% of classrooms, 100% of dorms, 100% of libraries have wireless network access.

CAMPUS LIFE
Environment: Village. **Activities:** Campus Ministries; Choral groups; Concert band; Dance; Drama/theater; International Student Organization; Jazz band; Literary magazine; Marching band; Model UN; Music ensembles; Musical theater; Opera; Pep band; Radio station; Student government; Student newspaper; Student-run film society; Symphony orchestra; Television station. 150 registered organizations, 24 honor societies, 14 religious organizations, 9 fraternities, 10 sororities on campus. **Athletics (Intercollegiate):** *Men:* baseball, basketball, bowling, cross-country, football, golf, soccer, track/field (outdoor), wrestling. *Women:* basketball, bowling, cross-country, soccer, softball, track/field (outdoor), volleyball. **On-Campus Highlights:** Union Commons.

ADMISSIONS
Freshman Academic Profile: Average high school GPA 3.4. 12% in top 10% of high school class, 36% in top 25% of high school class, 70% in top 50% of high school class. 90% from public high schools. **Test Scores:** ACT middle 50% range 19–24. **Basis for Candidate Selection:** *Very important factors include:* class rank, academic GPA, standardized test scores. *Other factors include:* rigor of secondary school record, application essay. **Freshman Admission Requirements:** High school diploma is required and GED is accepted. *Academic units required:* 4 English, 3 math, 2 science, 1 science labs, 3 social studies, 3 academic electives, 1 visual/performing arts. **Freshman Admission**

Statistics: 4,867 applied, 86% admitted, 36% enrolled. **Transfer Admission Requirements:** College transcript(s). Minimum college GPA of 2.0 required. Lowest grade transferable C. **General Admission Information:** Application fee $30. Non-fall registration accepted. Admission may be deferred for a maximum of 3 semesters.

COSTS AND FINANCIAL AID
Annual in-state tuition $7,128. Annual out-of-state tuition $14,256. Room and board $8,962. Required fees $915. Average book and supplies expense $1,000. **Required Forms and Deadlines:** FAFSA; Institution's own financial aid form. **Notification of Awards:** Applicants will be notified of awards on or about 3/1. **Types of Aid:** *Need-based scholarships/grants:* College/university scholarship or grant aid from institutional funds; Federal Pell; Private scholarships; SEOG; State scholarships/grants. *Loans:* Direct PLUS loans; Direct Subsidized Stafford Loans; Direct Unsubsidized Stafford Loans. **Student Employment:** Federal Work-Study Program available. Institutional employment available. **Financial Aid Statistics:** 62% needy freshmen, 62% needy undergrads receive need-based scholarship or grant aid. 98% freshmen, 95% undergrads receive non-need-based scholarship or grant aid. 75% freshmen, 75% undergrads receive need-based self-help aid. 6% freshmen, 5% undergrads receive athletic scholarships. 70% undergrads borrow to pay for school. Average cumulative indebtedness $28,543. **Criteria awarding aid:** *Non-need-based:* Academics, Alumni affiliation, Art, Athletics, Leadership, Minority status, Music/drama, Religious affiliation, State/district residency.

UNIVERSITY OF CENTRAL OKLAHOMA

100 North University Drive, Edmond, OK 73034
Phone: 405-974-2727 **Financial Aid Phone:** 405-974-2727
E-mail: onestop@uco.edu **CEEB Code:** 6091
Fax: 405-974-3841 **Website:** http://www.uco.edu **ACT Code:** 3390

This public school was founded in 1890. It has a 200 acre campus.

RATINGS
Admissions Selectivity Rating: 84   **Fire Safety Rating:** 84   **Green Rating:** 60*

STUDENTS AND FACULTY
Enrollment: 14,788. **Student Body:** 58% female, 42% male, 3% out-of-state, 7% international (67 countries represented). Asian 3%, African American 9%, Caucasian 58%, Hispanic 9%, Native American 4%, Pacific Islander <1%, Two or more races 9%, Race unknown 1%.
Retention and Graduation: 62% freshmen return for sophomore year.
Faculty: Student/faculty ratio 19:1. 513 full-time faculty, 78% hold PhDs, 13% are members of minority groups, 50% are women. 1% of classes are taught by teaching assistants.

ACADEMICS
Degrees: Associate; Bachelor's; Certificate; Master's. **Classes:** Most classes have 20–29 students. Most lab/discussion sessions have 10–19 students. **Most popular majors:** Psychology, General. **Special Study Options:** Accelerated program; Distance learning; Double major; Dual enrollment; English as a Second Language (ESL); Honors program; Independent study; Internships; Study abroad; Teacher certification program; Weekend college. **Disability Services offered:** Note-taking services; Reader services; Tape recorders; Tutors. **Career services:** Alumni services; Career assessment; Career/job search classes; Internships.

FACILITIES
Housing: Apartments for married students; Apartments for single students; Coed dorms; Fraternity/sorority housing; Men's dorms; Women's dorms; 95% of campus accessible to physically disabled. **Special Academic Facilities/Equipment:** Melton Gallery, Donna Nigh Gallery, Design Gallery, Evan Hall Interior Design Gallery, African Art Collection, Archives Photography Collection, Bob Burke Collection, Thatcher Hall Gallery, Will Rogers Room Collection, Library Archives, Forensic Science Institute, Center for Transformative Learning, UCO Boathouse.

CAMPUS LIFE
Environment: Metropolis. **Activities:** Campus Ministries; Choral groups; Concert band; Dance; Drama/theater; International Student Organization; Jazz band; Marching band; Model UN; Music ensembles; Musical theater; Pep band; Radio station; Student government; Student newspaper; Symphony orchestra; Television station; Yearbook. 250 registered organizations, 27 honor societies,

16 religious organizations, 10 fraternities, 11 sorority on campus. **Athletics (Intercollegiate):** *Men:* baseball, basketball, football, golf, wrestling. *Women:* basketball, cross-country, golf, soccer, softball, tennis, volleyball. **On-Campus Highlights:** Starbucks. **Environmental Initiatives:** Use 100% wind power.

ADMISSIONS

Freshman Academic Profile: Average high school GPA 3.3. 11% in top 10% of high school class, 35% in top 25% of high school class, 68% in top 50% of high school class. 91% from public high schools. **Test Scores:** ACT middle 50% range 19–24. **Basis for Candidate Selection:** *Very important factors include:* rigor of secondary school record, class rank, academic GPA, standardized test scores. *Other factors include:* extracurricular activities, talent/ability. **Freshman Admission Requirements:** High school diploma is required and GED is accepted. *Academic units required:* 4 English, 3 math, 3 science, 3 science labs, 1 social studies, 2 history. *Academic units recommended:* 4 English, 4 math, 3 science, 3 science labs, 2 foreign language, 1 social studies, 3 history, 1 computer science. **Freshman Admission Statistics:** 5,122 applied, 70% admitted, 69% enrolled. **Transfer Admission Requirements:** College transcript(s), statement of good standing from prior institution(s). Minimum college GPA of 2.0 required. Lowest grade transferable D. **General Admission Information:** Application fee $90. Non-fall registration accepted. Admission may be deferred for a maximum of 1 semester.

COSTS AND FINANCIAL AID

Annual in-state tuition $5,157. Annual out-of-state tuition $14,033. Room and board $7,130. Required fees $939. Average book and supplies expense $1,200. **Required Forms and Deadlines:** FAFSA; Institution's own financial aid form. **Notification of Awards:** Applicants will be notified of awards on a rolling basis beginning 5/1. **Types of Aid:** *Need-based scholarships/grants:* College/university scholarship or grant aid from institutional funds; Federal Pell; Private scholarships; SEOG; State scholarships/grants. **Student Employment:** Federal Work-Study Program available. Institutional employment available. **Financial Aid Statistics:** 66% freshmen, 75% undergrads receive any aid. **Criteria awarding aid:** *Need-based:* Academics, Alumni affiliation, Art, Athletics, Leadership, Minority status, Music/drama. *Non-need-based:* Academics, Alumni affiliation, Art, Athletics, Leadership, Minority status, Music/drama, State/district residency.

UNIVERSITY OF CHARLESTON

2300 MacCorkle Ave SE, Charleston, WV 25304
Phone: 304-357-4750 **Financial Aid Phone:** 304-357-4950
E-mail: admissions@ucwv.edu **CEEB Code:** 5419
Fax: 304-357-4781 **Website:** http://www.ucwv.edu/ **ACT Code:** 4528

This private school was founded in 1888. It has a 24 acre campus.

RATINGS

Admissions Selectivity Rating: 77   Fire Safety Rating: 98   Green Rating: 61

STUDENTS AND FACULTY

Enrollment: 1,810. **Student Body:** 45% female, 55% male, 48% out-of-state, 7% international (40 countries represented). Asian 1%, African American 9%, Caucasian 48%, Hispanic 2%, Native American 1%, Pacific Islander <1%, Two or more races 0%, Race unknown 31%.
Retention and Graduation: 58% freshmen return for sophomore year.
Faculty: Student/faculty ratio 15:1. 116 full-time faculty, 0% hold PhDs, 9% are members of minority groups, 67% are women.

ACADEMICS

Degrees: Associate; Bachelor's; Doctoral degree—professional practice; Master's. **Classes:** Most classes have 10–19 students. Most lab/discussion sessions have fewer than 10 students. **Most popular majors:** Registered Nursing/Registered Nurse; Biology/Biological Sciences, General; Business Administration and Management, General. **Special Study Options:** Accelerated program; Distance learning; Double major; Dual enrollment; English as a Second Language (ESL); Independent study; Internships; Liberal arts/career combination; Student-designed major; Study abroad; Teacher certification program. **Disability Services offered:** Note-taking services; Reader services; Tape recorders; Tutors. **Career services:** Alumni network; Alumni services; Career assessment; Internships; Regional alumni.

FACILITIES

Housing: Apartments for married students; Apartments for single students; Coed dorms; Special housing for disabled students; Theme housing. **Special**

Academic Facilities/Equipment: Erma Byrd Art Gallery. **Campus network:** 100% of classrooms, 100% of dorms, 100% of student union, 100% of libraries, 100% of dining areas, 100% of common outdoor areas have wireless network access.

CAMPUS LIFE

Environment: City. **Activities:** Campus Ministries; Choral groups; International Student Organization; Pep band; Student government; Student newspaper. 39 registered organizations, 8 honor societies, 3 religious organizations, 2 sororities on campus. **Athletics (Intercollegiate):** *Men:* baseball, basketball, football, golf, soccer, tennis. *Women:* basketball, crew/rowing, cross-country, golf, soccer, softball, tennis, track/field (outdoor), volleyball. **On-Campus Highlights:** Fitness Center. **Environmental Initiatives:** Recycling on campus.

ADMISSIONS

Freshman Academic Profile: Average high school GPA 3.3. **Test Scores:** SAT Math middle 50% range 420–510. SAT EBRW middle 50% range 440–520. ACT middle 50% range 18–22. **Basis for Candidate Selection:** *Very important factors include:* academic GPA. *Important factors include:* rigor of secondary school record. *Other factors include:* class rank, standardized test scores, recommendation(s), alumni/ae relation. **Freshman Admission Requirements:** High school diploma is required and GED is accepted. *Academic units required:* 4 English, 4 math, 2 science, 2 science labs, 1 social studies, 1 history, 1 computer science. *Academic units recommended:* 1 foreign language, 1 visual/performing arts. **Freshman Admission Statistics:** 2,740 applied, 65% admitted, 19% enrolled. **Transfer Admission Requirements:** College transcript(s). Minimum college GPA of 2.25 required. Lowest grade transferable C. **General Admission Information:** Application fee $25. Priority deadline 5/1. Non-fall registration accepted.

COSTS AND FINANCIAL AID

Annual tuition $29,900. Room and board $9,180. Required fees $1,000. Average book and supplies expense $1,800. **Required Forms and Deadlines:** FAFSA; Institution's own financial aid form; State aid form. **Notification of Awards:** Applicants will be notified of awards on a rolling basis beginning 3/1. **Types of Aid:** *Need-based scholarships/grants:* College/university scholarship or grant aid from institutional funds; Federal Pell; Private scholarships; SEOG; State scholarships/grants. *Loans:* Direct Subsidized Stafford Loans; Direct Unsubsidized Stafford Loans. **Student Employment:** Federal Work-Study Program available. Institutional employment available. **Financial Aid Statistics:** 100% needy freshmen, 81% needy undergrads receive need-based scholarship or grant aid. 100% freshmen, 100% undergrads receive non-need-based scholarship or grant aid. 100% freshmen, 81% undergrads receive need-based self-help aid. 49% freshmen, 34% undergrads receive athletic scholarships. 100% freshmen receive any aid. **Criteria awarding aid:** *Need-based:* Minority status. *Non-need-based:* Academics, Alumni affiliation, Art, Athletics, Leadership, Music/drama.

THE UNIVERSITY OF CHICAGO

1101 E 58th Street, Chicago, IL 60637
Phone: 773-702-8650 **Financial Aid Phone:** 773-702-8666
E-mail: collegeadmissions@uchicago.edu **CEEB Code:** 1832
Fax: 773-702-4199 **Website:** uchicago.edu **ACT Code:** 1152

This private school was founded in 1890. It has a 217 acre campus.

RATINGS

Admissions Selectivity Rating: 99   Fire Safety Rating: 97   Green Rating: 87

STUDENTS AND FACULTY

Enrollment: 6,734. **Student Body:** 49% female, 51% male, 82% out-of-state, 15% international (125 countries represented). Asian 19%, African American 6%, Caucasian 37%, Hispanic 14%, Native American <1%, Pacific Islander <1%, Two or more races 7%, Race unknown 2%.
Retention and Graduation: 99% freshmen return for sophomore year. 90% freshmen graduate within 4 years. 95% freshmen graduate within 6 years.
Faculty: Student/faculty ratio 5:1. 1,508 full-time faculty, 100% hold PhDs, 23% are members of minority groups, 35% are women.

ACADEMICS

Degrees: Bachelor's; Doctoral degree—professional practice; Doctoral degree research/scholarship; Master's; Post-bachelor's certificate. **Classes:** Most classes have fewer than 10 students. Most lab/discussion sessions have 10–19 students. **Most popular majors:** Biology/Biological Sciences, General; Mathematics, General; Econometrics and Quantitative Economics. **Special Study Options:** Cross-registration; Double major; Dual enrollment; English as a Second Language (ESL); Exchange student program (domestic); Honors program; Independent study; Internships; Liberal arts/career combination; Study abroad; Teacher certification program. **Combined degree programs:** BA/MA; BA/MD. **Disability Services offered:** Note-taking services; Reader services; Tape recorders. **Career services:** Alumni network; Alumni services; Career assessment; Career/job search classes; Internships; Regional alumni.

FACILITIES

Housing: Coed dorms; Special housing for disabled students. **Special Academic Facilities/Equipment:** Joe and Rika Mansueto Library, Arts Incubator, Logan Center, Smart Museum of Art, Renaissance Society, Oriental Institute Museum, D'Angelo Law Library, John Crerar Library, Joseph Regenstein Library, Social Services Administration Library, Laboratory Schools (PreK-12), Court Theater, Neubauer Collegium for Culture and Society, Robie House, The Renaissance Society.

CAMPUS LIFE

Environment: Metropolis. **Activities:** Campus Ministries; Choral groups; Concert band; Dance; Drama/theater; International Student Organization; Jazz band; Literary magazine; Model UN; Music ensembles; Musical theater; Pep band; Radio station; Student government; Student newspaper; Student-run film society; Symphony orchestra; Television station. 392 registered organizations, 2 honor societies, 20 religious organizations on campus. **Athletics (Intercollegiate):** *Men:* baseball, basketball, cross-country, diving, football, soccer, swimming, tennis, track/field (outdoor), track/field (indoor), volleyball, wrestling. *Women:* basketball, cross-country, diving, soccer, softball, swimming, tennis, track/field (outdoor), track/field (indoor), volleyball. **On-Campus Highlights:** Logan Arts Center.

ADMISSIONS

Freshman Academic Profile: Average high school GPA 4.2. 99% in top 10% of high school class, 100% in top 25% of high school class, 100% in top 50% of high school class. **Test Scores:** SAT Math middle 50% range 770–800. SAT EBRW middle 50% range 730–770. ACT middle 50% range 33–35. **Basis for Candidate Selection:** *Very important factors include:* rigor of secondary school record, application essay, recommendation(s), extracurricular activities, talent/ability, character/personal qualities. *Other factors include:* class rank, academic GPA, standardized test scores, first generation, alumni/ae relation, geographical residence, state residency, religious affiliation/commitment, racial/ethnic status, volunteer work, work experience, level of applicant's interest. **Freshman Admission Requirements:** High school diploma is required and GED is accepted. *Academic units recommended:* 4 English, 4 math, 4 science, 3 foreign language, 2 social studies, 2 history. **Freshman Admission Statistics:** 34,641 applied, 6% admitted, 81% enrolled. **Transfer Admission Requirements:** High school transcript, college transcript(s), essay or personal statement, standardized test scores, statement of good standing from prior institution(s). Minimum college GPA of 3.0 required. Lowest grade transferable 2. **General Admission Information:** Application fee $75. Regular application deadline 1/4. Admission may be deferred for a maximum of 2 years.

COSTS AND FINANCIAL AID

Annual tuition $55,425. Room and board $16,350. Required fees $2,805. Average book and supplies expense $1,800. **Required Forms and Deadlines:** CSS/Financial Aid PROFILE; FAFSA; Institution's own financial aid form. **Notification of Awards:** Applicants will be notified of awards on or about 3/15. **Types of Aid:** *Need-based scholarships/grants:* College/university scholarship or grant aid from institutional funds; Federal Pell; Private scholarships; SEOG; State scholarships/grants. *Loans:* Direct PLUS loans; Direct Subsidized Stafford Loans; Direct Unsubsidized Stafford Loans. **Student Employment:** Federal Work-Study Program available. Institutional employment available. **Financial Aid Statistics:** 99% needy freshmen, 99% needy undergrads receive need-based scholarship or grant aid. 22% freshmen, 16% undergrads receive non-need-based scholarship or grant aid. 72% freshmen, 74% undergrads receive need-based self-help aid. 0% freshmen, 0% undergrads receive athletic scholarships. 56% freshmen, 57% undergrads receive any aid. 17% undergrads borrow to pay for school. Average cumulative indebtedness $26,619. **Criteria awarding aid:** *Non-need-based:* Academics, Leadership.

UNIVERSITY OF CINCINNATI

P.O. Box 210091, Cincinnati, OH 45221-0091
Phone: 513-556-1100 **Financial Aid Phone:** 513-556-1000
E-mail: admissions@uc.edu **CEEB Code:** 1833
Fax: 513-556-1105 **Website:** www.uc.edu **ACT Code:** 3340

This public school was founded in 1819. It has a 473 acre campus.

RATINGS

Admissions Selectivity Rating: 83   **Fire Safety Rating:** 96   **Green Rating:** 93

STUDENTS AND FACULTY

Enrollment: 26,731. **Student Body:** 50% female, 50% male, 17% out-of-state, 4% international (7 countries represented). Asian 4%, African American 7%, Caucasian 75%, Hispanic 3%, Native American <1%, Pacific Islander <1%, Two or more races 4%, Race unknown 2%. **Retention and Graduation:** 86% freshmen return for sophomore year. 35% freshmen graduate within 4 years. 23% grads go on to further study within 1 year. 0% grads pursue arts and sciences degrees. 27% grads pursue law degrees. 2% grads pursue business degrees. 33% grads pursue medical degrees. **Faculty:** 2,201 full-time faculty, 84% hold PhDs, 22% are members of minority groups, 44% are women. 2% of classes are taught by teaching assistants.

ACADEMICS

Degrees: Associate; Bachelor's; Certificate; Doctoral degree—professional practice; Doctoral degree research/scholarship; Master's; Post-bachelor's certificate; Post-master's certificate; Terminal Associate; Transfer Associate. **Classes:** Most classes have 20–29 students. Most lab/discussion sessions have 20–29 students. **Most popular majors:** Communication and Media Studies; Nursing/Registered Nurse (Rn, Asn, Bsn, Msn). **Special Study Options:** Accelerated program; Cooperative education program; Cross-registration; Distance learning; Double major; Dual enrollment; English as a Second Language (ESL); Honors program; Independent study; Internships; Liberal arts/career combination; Student-designed major; Study abroad; Teacher certification program. **Honors programs:** The University Honors Program's (UHP) vision is to develop students into global citizen scholars who lead innovative efforts toward solving the world's complex problems. The UHP is built around an innovative pedagogical approach to honors education. It is focused on experiential, reflective and integrative learning as well as the following thematic areas: community engagement, creativity, global studies, leadership and research. The UHP is comprised of students in the top 5% of UC's undergraduate baccalaureate seeking population. The University Honors Program is committed to offering students an individualized, student-centered approach to a meaningful undergraduate experience. To that end, we are dedicated to: • Promoting activities that lead students to discover their passions and enhance their gifts and talents. • Coaching students to purposefully engage in experiential learning opportunities and reflection to maximize and integrate their learning. • Fostering a community that prioritizes transformational personal development, civic participation, and global responsibility. The college experience of these academically talented and motivated students is enriched through their honors experiences–honors seminars and honors experiential learning projects–and the compilation of a learning portfolio throughout their time in the UHP. http://www.uc.edu/honors honors@uc.edu 513-556-6254. **Combined degree programs:** BA/MA. **Disability Services offered:** Note-taking services; Reader services; Tape recorders; Tutors. **Career services:** Alumni network; Alumni services; Career assessment; Career/job search classes; Internships; Regional alumni.

FACILITIES

Housing: Apartments for married students; Apartments for single students; Coed dorms; Fraternity/sorority housing; Special housing for international students; Theme housing; 100% of campus accessible to physically disabled. **Special Academic Facilities/Equipment:** Art museum, language lab, observatory. **Campus network:** 100% of classrooms, 100% of dorms, 100% of student union, 100% of libraries, 100% of dining areas, 60% of common outdoor areas have wireless network access.

CAMPUS LIFE

Environment: Metropolis. **Activities:** Campus Ministries; Choral groups; Concert band; Dance; Drama/theater; International Student Organization;

Jazz band; Marching band; Model UN; Music ensembles; Musical theater; Opera; Pep band; Radio station; Student government; Student newspaper; Student-run film society; Symphony orchestra. 981 registered organizations, 25 honor societies, 13 religious organizations, 28 fraternities, 17 sororities on campus. **Athletics (Intercollegiate):** *Men:* baseball, basketball, cheerleading, cross-country, diving, football, golf, soccer, swimming, track/field (outdoor). *Women:* basketball, cheerleading, cross-country, diving, golf, lacrosse, soccer, swimming, tennis, track/field (outdoor), track/field (indoor), volleyball. **On-Campus Highlights:** Tangeman University Center (TUC). **Environmental Initiatives:** UC has commited to a policy that all new construction and major renovations on campus will be built to LEED standards, striving for at least Silver certification levels.

ADMISSIONS

Freshman Academic Profile: Average high school GPA 3.7. 24% in top 10% of high school class, 51% in top 25% of high school class, 83% in top 50% of high school class. **Test Scores:** SAT Math middle 50% range 560–690. SAT EBRW middle 50% range 560–660. ACT middle 50% range 23–29. **Basis for Candidate Selection:** *Very important factors include:* rigor of secondary school record, academic GPA, standardized test scores. *Important factors include:* application essay, recommendation(s), talent/ability. *Other factors include:* class rank, extracurricular activities, character/personal qualities, first generation, geographical residence, state residency, racial/ethnic status, volunteer work, work experience. **Freshman Admission Requirements:** High school diploma is required and GED is not accepted. *Academic units required:* 4 English, 4 math, 3 science, 3 social studies, 5 unit from above areas or other academic areas. *Academic units recommended:* 2 foreign language. **Freshman Admission Statistics:** 23,609 applied, 77% admitted, 30% enrolled. **General Admission Information:** Application fee $50. Priority deadline 12/1. Regular application deadline 3/1. Non-fall registration accepted. Admission may be deferred for a maximum of 1 year.

COSTS AND FINANCIAL AID

Annual in-state tuition $9,982. Annual out-of-state tuition $25,316. Room and board $11,530. Required fees $1,678. Average book and supplies expense $1,200. **Required Forms and Deadlines:** FAFSA. **Notification of Awards:** Applicants will be notified of awards on a rolling basis beginning 3/1. **Types of Aid:** *Need-based scholarships/grants:* College/university scholarship or grant aid from institutional funds; Federal Pell; Private scholarships; SEOG; State scholarships/grants; United Negro College Fund. *Loans:* Direct PLUS loans; Direct Subsidized Stafford Loans; Direct Unsubsidized Stafford Loans. **Student Employment:** Federal Work-Study Program available. Institutional employment available. **Criteria awarding aid:** *Non-need-based:* Academics, Alumni affiliation, Art, Athletics, Leadership, Minority status, Music/drama, State/district residency.

UNIVERSITY OF COLORADO—BOULDER

552 UCB, Boulder, CO 80309-0552
Phone: 303-492-6301 **Financial Aid Phone:** 303-492-5091
CEEB Code: 4841
Fax: 303-735-2501 **Website:** www.colorado.edu/ **ACT Code:** 532

This public school was founded in 1876. It has a 600 acre campus.

RATINGS

Admissions Selectivity Rating: 81   **Fire Safety Rating:** 95   **Green Rating:** 88

STUDENTS AND FACULTY

Enrollment: 30,673. **Student Body:** 45% female, 55% male, 42% out-of-state, 6% international (76 countries represented). Asian 6%, African American 2%, Caucasian 67%, Hispanic 13%, Native American <1%, Pacific Islander <1%, Two or more races 6%, Race unknown 1%.
Retention and Graduation: 87% freshmen return for sophomore year. 46% freshmen graduate within 4 years. 69% freshmen graduate within 6 years. 14% grads go on to further study within 1 year. **Faculty:** Student/faculty ratio 18:1. 1,667 full-time faculty, 87% hold PhDs, 18% are members of minority groups, 40% are women. 12% of classes are taught by teaching assistants.

ACADEMICS

Degrees: Bachelor's; Doctoral degree—professional practice; Doctoral degree research/scholarship; Master's; Post-master's certificate. **Classes:** Most classes have 10–19 students. Most lab/discussion sessions have 20–29 students. **Most popular majors:** Psychology, General; Finance, General; Public Relations, Advertising, and Applied Communication. **Special Study Options:** Accelerated program; Cooperative education program; Cross-registration; Distance learning; Double major; Dual enrollment; English as a Second Language (ESL); Exchange student program (domestic); Honors program; Independent study; Internships; Liberal arts/career combination; Student-designed major; Study abroad; Teacher certification program. **Honors programs:** The CU Honors Program offers a wide-ranging curriculum supported by thoughtful advising and close contact with faculty. The program aspires to provide the best education possible for the leaders of the future. The Honors Residential Academic Program (HRAP) is a co-educational living-learning community open to Honors-qualified freshmen and returning students in all majors in the College of Arts & Sciences. The Engineering Honors Residential Academic Program is open to qualified students in the college of Engineering and Applied Science. In these living and learning environments, students experience all of the advantages of a small college environment while also enjoying the diverse resources of a major university. The Norlin Scholars Program is a community of students with a broad, synthetic view of education that embraces active learning, creativity, and interdisciplinary scholarship. Norlin Scholars participate in small, specialized courses and other small-group experiences emphasizing critical thinking, collaboration, and written and oral communications skills. They also engage in research or creative work with faculty mentors. The Presidents Leadership Class (PLC) offers a unique opportunity to those students who want to make a difference for themselves and their community. The core of PLC is an academic program focusing on leadership development, personal development, and community service initiatives. PLC scholars receive a four-year scholarship. **Combined degree programs:** BA/MA. **Disability Services offered:** Note-taking services; Reader services; Tape recorders; Tutors. **Career services:** Alumni network; Alumni services; Career assessment; Career/job search classes; Internships; Regional alumni.

FACILITIES

Housing: Apartments for married students; Apartments for single students; Coed dorms; Fraternity/sorority housing; Special housing for disabled students; Theme housing; 87.5% of campus accessible to physically disabled. **Special Academic Facilities/Equipment:** Art museum and galleries, natural history museum, heritage center, observatory, planetarium and science center, electron microscopes, outdoor theater, video interactive foreign language laboratory, mountain research station, centrifuge laboratory, hands-on teaching and learning laboratory for engineering, production and performance studios with advanced technologies, multipurpose cultural/athletics/educational events and conference center, a premier concert hall and an innovative multi-disciplinary Information Technology center.

CAMPUS LIFE

Environment: City. **Activities:** Campus Ministries; Choral groups; Concert band; Dance; Drama/theater; International Student Organization; Jazz band; Literary magazine; Marching band; Model UN; Music ensembles; Musical theater; Opera; Pep band; Radio station; Student government; Student newspaper; Student-run film society; Symphony orchestra. 576 registered organizations, 32 honor societies, 30 religious organizations, 31 fraternity, 18 sororities on campus. **Athletics (Intercollegiate):** *Men:* basketball, cross-country, football, golf, skiing (downhill/Alpine), skiing (Nordic/cross-country), track/field (outdoor), track/field (indoor). *Women:* basketball, cross-country, golf, skiing (downhill/Alpine), skiing (Nordic/cross-country), soccer, tennis, track/field (outdoor), track/field (indoor), volleyball. **On-Campus Highlights:** Center for Community. **Environmental Initiatives:** Education and Research: Campus commitment to environmental education and research has helped CU Boulder become one of the nation's top environmental research universities. CU Boulder's reputation and performance as a national leader in environmental issues and sustainability helps recruit and retain faculty with the recognized expertise to win leading-edge research awards, to contribute to the global sustainability knowledge base, and to enhance an already respected environmental studies department—one with integrated environmental content across the campus. Environmental Studies is an interdisciplinary program that draws from curricula in the earth and natural sciences as well as the social sciences. Undergraduate students have the opportunity to participate in three residential academic programs (RAPs) that emphasize environmental studies and sustainability. All offer smaller courses in the residences halls. The Baker RAP consists of a cohort of students with interest in the environment and in future careers in working on environmental problems, such as sustainable use of our resources. The Sustainable by Design RAP includes students with an interest in resource-efficient design, renewable energy, and environmental and social impacts of community development. The Sustainability and Social Innovation RAP guides students in developing innovative, self-sustaining solutions for addressing critical social and environmental issues around the globe.

ADMISSIONS

Freshman Academic Profile: Average high school GPA 3.7. 26% in top 10% of high school class, 56% in top 25% of high school class, 86% in top 50% of high school class. 86% from public high schools. **Test Scores:** SAT Math middle 50% range 560–690. SAT EBRW middle 50% range 580–670. ACT middle 50% range 25–31. **Basis for Candidate Selection:** *Very important factors include:* rigor of secondary school record, academic GPA, standardized test scores. *Important factors include:* application essay, recommendation(s), extracurricular activities, talent/ability, character/personal qualities, first generation. *Other factors include:* class rank, alumni/ae relation, geographical residence, state residency, racial/ethnic status, volunteer work, work experience. **Freshman Admission Requirements:** High school diploma is required and GED is accepted. *Academic units required:* 4 English, 4 math, 3 science, 2 science labs, 3 foreign language, 3 social studies, 1 history, 1 unit from above areas or other academic areas. **Freshman Admission Statistics:** 40,740 applied, 79% admitted, 22% enrolled. **Transfer Admission Requirements:** High school transcript, college transcript(s), essay or personal statement. Lowest grade transferable C-. **General Admission Information:** Application fee $50. Priority deadline 11/15. Regular application deadline 1/15. Non-fall registration accepted. Admission may be deferred for a maximum of 12 months.

COSTS AND FINANCIAL AID

Annual in-state tuition $10,728. Annual out-of-state tuition $36,546. Room and board $14,778. Required fees $1,772. Average book and supplies expense $1,200. **Required Forms and Deadlines:** FAFSA. **Notification of Awards:** Applicants will be notified of awards on a rolling basis beginning 3/15. **Types of Aid:** *Need-based scholarships/grants:* College/university scholarship or grant aid from institutional funds; Federal Pell; Private scholarships; SEOG; State scholarships/grants. *Loans:* Direct PLUS loans; Direct Subsidized Stafford Loans; Direct Unsubsidized Stafford Loans. **Student Employment:** Federal Work-Study Program available. Institutional employment available. **Financial Aid Statistics:** 77% needy freshmen, 74% needy undergrads receive need-based scholarship or grant aid. 6% freshmen, 4% undergrads receive non-need-based scholarship or grant aid. 84% freshmen, 83% undergrads receive need-based self-help aid. 1% freshmen, 1% undergrads receive athletic scholarships. 77% freshmen, 60% undergrads receive any aid. 40% undergrads borrow to pay for school. Average cumulative indebtedness $27,568. **Criteria awarding aid:** *Need-based:* Academics, Alumni affiliation, Art, Athletics, Leadership, Music/drama. *Non-need-based:* Academics, Alumni affiliation, Art, Athletics, Leadership, Music/drama, State/district residency.

UNIVERSITY OF COLORADO—COLORADO SPRINGS

1420 Austin Bluffs Parkway, Colorado Springs, CO 80918
Phone: 719-255-3084 **Financial Aid Phone:** 719-262-3460
E-mail: go@uccs.edu **CEEB Code:** 4874
Website: www.uccs.edu **ACT Code:** 535

This public school was founded in 1965. It has a 550 acre campus.

RATINGS

Admissions Selectivity Rating: 74   **Fire Safety Rating:** 60*   **Green Rating:** 99

STUDENTS AND FACULTY

Enrollment: 8,868. **Student Body:** 53% female, 47% male, 11% out-of-state, 1% international (35 countries represented). Asian 3%, African American 4%, Caucasian 69%, Hispanic 14%, Native American 1%, Pacific Islander <1%, Two or more races 6%, Race unknown 3%.
Retention and Graduation: 71% freshmen return for sophomore year.
Faculty: Student/faculty ratio 17:1. 371 full-time faculty. 73% hold PhDs, 14% are members of minority groups, 51% are women.

ACADEMICS

Degrees: Bachelor's; Doctoral degree—professional practice; Doctoral degree research/scholarship; Master's. **Classes:** Most classes have 10–19 students. Most lab/discussion sessions have fewer than 10 students. **Special Study Options:** Cross-registration; Distance learning; Double major; Dual enrollment; English as a Second Language (ESL); Exchange student program (domestic); Honors program; Independent study; Internships; Study abroad; Teacher certification

program; Weekend college. **Honors programs:** The University of Colorado-Colorado Springs (UCCS) Honors Program serves rigorously trained students who share a desire to become intentional learners. Honors at UCCS offers students a choice of two levels of participation: University Honors or Mountain Lion Honors. Read more at http://www.uccs.edu/~honors/. **Combined degree programs:** BA/MA. **Disability Services offered:** Note-taking services; Reader services; Tape recorders; Tutors. **Career services:** Alumni network; Alumni services; Career assessment; Career/job search classes.

FACILITIES

Housing: Apartments for single students; Coed dorms; Men's dorms; Special housing for disabled students; Theme housing; Women's dorms. **Special Academic Facilities/Equipment:** Gallery of contemporary art.

CAMPUS LIFE

Environment: Metropolis. **Activities:** Choral groups; Dance; Drama/theater; International Student Organization; Literary magazine; Pep band; Radio station; Student government; Student newspaper; Television station. 55 registered organizations, 4 honor societies, 7 religious organizations, 1 sorority on campus. **Athletics (Intercollegiate):** *Men:* basketball, cross-country, golf, soccer, tennis, track/field (outdoor). *Women:* basketball, cross-country, softball, tennis, track/field (outdoor), volleyball. **On-Campus Highlights:** Kraemer Family Library.

ADMISSIONS

Freshman Academic Profile: Average high school GPA 3.3. 13% in top 10% of high school class, 36% in top 25% of high school class, 70% in top 50% of high school class. **Test Scores:** SAT Math middle 50% range 472–600. SAT EBRW middle 50% range 470–590. ACT middle 50% range 21–25. **Basis for Candidate Selection:** *Very important factors include:* rigor of secondary school record, class rank, academic GPA, standardized test scores. *Other factors include:* application essay, recommendation(s). **Freshman Admission Requirements:** High school diploma is required and GED is accepted. *Academic units required:* 4 English, 4 math, 3 science, 2 science labs, 1 foreign language, 3 social studies, 1 history, 2 academic electives. *Academic units recommended:* 4 English, 4 math, 3 science, 2 science labs, 1 foreign language, 3 social studies, 1 history, 2 academic electives. **Freshman Admission Statistics:** 7,352 applied, 89% admitted, 25% enrolled. **Transfer Admission Requirements:** High school transcript, college transcript(s). Minimum college GPA of 2.0 required. Lowest grade transferable C. **General Admission Information:** Application fee $50. Non-fall registration accepted. Admission may be deferred for a maximum of 3 terms.

COSTS AND FINANCIAL AID

Average book and supplies expense $1,800. **Required Forms and Deadlines:** FAFSA. **Notification of Awards:** Applicants will be notified of awards on a rolling basis beginning 4/15. **Types of Aid:** *Need-based scholarships/grants:* College/university scholarship or grant aid from institutional funds; Federal Pell; Private scholarships; SEOG; State scholarships/grants. *Loans:* Direct PLUS loans; Direct Subsidized Stafford Loans; Direct Unsubsidized Stafford Loans. **Financial Aid Statistics:** 58% needy freshmen, 65% needy undergrads receive need-based scholarship or grant aid. 35% freshmen, 23% undergrads receive non-need-based scholarship or grant aid. 70% freshmen, 78% undergrads receive need-based self-help aid. 2% freshmen, 2% undergrads receive athletic scholarships. **Criteria awarding aid:** *Need-based:* Academics, Alumni affiliation, Athletics. *Non-need-based:* Academics, Alumni affiliation, Athletics, Leadership, State/district residency.

UNIVERSITY OF COLORADO—DENVER

P.O. Box 173364, Denver, CO 80217
Phone: 303-556-2704 **Financial Aid Phone:** 303-556-2886
E-mail: admissions@cudenver.edu **CEEB Code:** 4875
Fax: 303-556-4838 **Website:** www.cudenver.edu **ACT Code:** 533

This public school was founded in 1912. It has a 127 acre campus.

RATINGS

Admissions Selectivity Rating: 85   **Fire Safety Rating:** 60*   **Green Rating:** 60*

STUDENTS AND FACULTY

Enrollment: 8,327. **Student Body:** 55% female, 45% male, 4% out-of-state, 1% international (57 countries represented). Asian 10%, African American 5%, Caucasian 64%, Hispanic 12%, Native American 1%, Pacific Islander 0%, Two or more races 0%, Race unknown 8%.

Retention and Graduation: 71% freshmen return for sophomore year. 7% grads go on to further study within 1 year. 19% grads pursue arts and sciences degrees. 8% grads pursue business degrees. **Faculty:** Student/faculty ratio 15:1. 2,186 full-time faculty, 81% hold PhDs, 11% are members of minority groups, 47% are women.

ACADEMICS

Degrees: Bachelor's; Master's; Post-master's certificate. **Classes:** Most classes have 20–29 students. Most lab/discussion sessions have 20–29 students. **Most popular majors:** Business/Commerce, General; Biology/Biological Sciences, General; Psychology, General. **Special Study Options:** Accelerated program; Cooperative education program; Cross-registration; Distance learning; Double major; English as a Second Language (ESL); Honors program; Independent study; Internships; Student-designed major; Study abroad; Teacher certification program; Weekend college. **Disability Services offered:** Note-taking services; Reader services; Tape recorders; Tutors. **Career services:** Alumni services; Career assessment; Internships.

FACILITIES

Housing: Coed dorms; 100% of campus accessible to physically disabled. **Special Academic Facilities/Equipment:** Emmanual Gallery. **Campus network:** 100% of classrooms, 100% of dorms, 100% of student union, 100% of libraries, 100% of dining areas, 10% of common outdoor areas have wireless network access.

CAMPUS LIFE

Environment: Metropolis. **Activities:** Choral groups; Dance; Drama/theater; Jazz band; Music ensembles; Musical theater; Student government; Student newspaper. 77 registered organizations, 5 honor societies, 4 religious organizations on campus. **On-Campus Highlights:** PE/Events Center and Emmanuel Gallery.

ADMISSIONS

Freshman Academic Profile: Average high school GPA 3.3. 17% in top 10% of high school class, 43% in top 25% of high school class, 78% in top 50% of high school class. **Test Scores:** SAT Math middle 50% range 490–590. SAT EBRW middle 50% range 490–600. ACT middle 50% range 19–25. **Basis for Candidate Selection:** *Very important factors include:* rigor of secondary school record, class rank, academic GPA, standardized test scores. *Important factors include:* application essay, recommendation(s), level of applicant's interest. *Other factors include:* extracurricular activities, talent/ability, character/personal qualities. **Freshman Admission Requirements:** High school diploma is required and GED is accepted. *Academic units required:* 4 English, 3 math, 3 science, 2 foreign language, 2 social studies, 1 academic elective. *Academic units recommended:* 4 English, 3 math, 3 science, 2 science labs, 2 foreign language, 2 social studies, 1 history, 1 academic elective. **Freshman Admission Statistics:** 2,968 applied, 69% admitted, 52% enrolled. **Transfer Admission Requirements:** College transcript(s), statement of good standing from prior institution(s). Minimum college GPA of 2.4 required. Lowest grade transferable C-. **General Admission Information:** Application fee $50. Priority deadline 7/22. Non-fall registration accepted. Admission may be deferred for a maximum of 12 months.

COSTS AND FINANCIAL AID

Annual in-state tuition $5,054. Annual out-of-state tuition $17,010. Room and board $9,990. Required fees $878. Average book and supplies expense $1,700. **Required Forms and Deadlines:** FAFSA; Institution's own financial aid form. **Notification of Awards:** Applicants will be notified of awards on a rolling basis beginning 5/1. **Types of Aid:** *Need-based scholarships/grants:* College/university scholarship or grant aid from institutional funds; Federal Nursing Scholarships; Federal Pell; Private scholarships; SEOG; State scholarships/grants. *Loans:* Direct PLUS loans; Direct Subsidized Stafford Loans; Direct Unsubsidized Stafford Loans. **Student Employment:** Federal Work-Study Program available. **Financial Aid Statistics:** 97% needy freshmen, 86% needy undergrads receive need-based scholarship or grant aid. 12% freshmen, 5% undergrads receive non-need-based scholarship or grant aid. 72% freshmen, 85% undergrads receive need-based self-help aid. 0% freshmen, 0% undergrads receive athletic scholarships. **Criteria awarding aid:** *Need-based:* Academics, Minority status. *Non-need-based:* Academics, Art, Leadership, Music/drama.

UNIVERSITY OF CONNECTICUT

2131 Hillside Road, Storrs, CT 06268-3088
Phone: 860-486-3137 **Financial Aid Phone:** 860-486-2819
E-mail: beahusky@uconn.edu **CEEB Code:** 3915
Fax: 860-486-1476 **Website:** www.uconn.edu **ACT Code:** 0604

This public school was founded in 1881. It has a 4109 acre campus.

RATINGS
Admissions Selectivity Rating: 89   **Fire Safety Rating:** 96   **Green Rating:** 99

STUDENTS AND FACULTY
Enrollment: 19,030. **Student Body:** 50% female, 50% male, 22% out-of-state, 6% international (71 countries represented). Asian 11%, African American 6%, Caucasian 60%, Hispanic 10%, Native American <1%, Pacific Islander <1%, Two or more races 3%, Race unknown 5%.
Retention and Graduation: 92% freshmen return for sophomore year. 70% freshmen graduate within 4 years. 82 28% grads go on to further study within 1 year. 13% grads pursue arts and sciences degrees. 1% grads pursue law degrees. 2% grads pursue business degrees. 5% grads pursue medical degrees. **Faculty:** Student/faculty ratio 16:1. 1,262 full-time faculty, 93% hold PhDs, 24% are members of minority groups, 40% are women. 19% of classes are taught by teaching assistants.

ACADEMICS
Degrees: Associate; Bachelor's; Diploma; Doctoral degree—professional practice; Doctoral degree research/scholarship; Master's; Post-bachelor's certificate; Post-master's certificate; Terminal Associate; Transfer Associate. **Classes:** Most classes have 10–19 students. Most lab/discussion sessions have 10–19 students. **Most popular majors:** Economics, General; Communication and Media Studies; Psychology, General. **Special Study Options:** Accelerated program; Cooperative education program; Cross-registration; Distance learning; Double major; Dual enrollment; English as a Second Language (ESL); Exchange student program (domestic); External degree program; Honors program; Independent study; Internships; Liberal arts/career combination; Student-designed major; Study abroad; Teacher certification program. **Honors programs:** Honors Scholar Program for all Undergraduates. **Combined degree programs:** BA/DDS; BA/JD; BA/MA; BA/MD. **Disability Services offered:** Note-taking services; Tape recorders; Tutors. **Career services:** Alumni services; Career assessment; Internships.

FACILITIES
Housing: Apartments for married students; Apartments for single students; Coed dorms; Fraternity/sorority housing; Men's dorms; Special housing for disabled students; Special housing for international students; Theme housing; Wellness housing; Women's dorms; 90% of campus accessible to physically disabled. **Special Academic Facilities/Equipment:** Art and natural history museums, child development labs, national undersea research center, arboretum, institute for social inquiry, institute of materials science, electron microscope labs.

CAMPUS LIFE
Environment: Town. **Activities:** Campus Ministries; Choral groups; Concert band; Dance; Drama/theater; International Student Organization; Jazz band; Literary magazine; Marching band; Model UN; Music ensembles; Musical theater; Opera; Pep band; Radio station; Student government; Student newspaper; Student-run film society; Symphony orchestra; Television station; Yearbook. 765 registered organizations, 23 honor societies, 30 religious organizations, 23 fraternities, 13 sororities on campus. **Athletics (Intercollegiate):** *Men:* baseball, basketball, cross-country, diving, football, golf, ice hockey, soccer, swimming, tennis, track/field (outdoor), track/field (indoor). *Women:* basketball, crew/rowing, cross-country, diving, field hockey, ice hockey, lacrosse, soccer, softball, swimming, tennis, track/field (outdoor), track/field (indoor), volleyball. **On-Campus Highlights:** William Benton Museum of Art. **Environmental Initiatives:** 1. In January 2017, President Susan Herbst endorsed UConn's 2020 Vision Plan for Campus Sustainability and Climate Leadership, which outlines a number of specific environmental goals and strategies, including: • Increase the percentage of purchased power system-wide that consists of renewable energy from 40% to 100% • Increase the university's waste diversion rate from 47% to 60% • Increase the percentage

of locally-grown food or community-based food from 35% to 40% • Reduce average daily potable water use by 30% Shortly after endorsing the 2020 Vision, President Herbst also joined more than 2,300 top executives and officials in the Grand Coalition's We Are Still In pledge, promising to continue pursuing ambitious climate action goals.

ADMISSIONS

Freshman Academic Profile: 51% in top 10% of high school class, 84% in top 25% of high school class, 98% in top 50% of high school class. 88% from public high schools. **Test Scores:** SAT Math middle 50% range 610–710. SAT EBRW middle 50% range 600–680. ACT middle 50% range 26–31. **Basis for Candidate Selection:** *Very important factors include:* rigor of secondary school record, class rank, academic GPA, standardized test scores. *Important factors include:* application essay, recommendation(s), extracurricular activities, talent/ability, character/personal qualities, first generation. *Other factors include:* alumni/ae relation, geographical residence, state residency, racial/ethnic status, work experience, level of applicant's interest. **Freshman Admission Requirements:** High school diploma is required and GED is accepted. *Academic units required:* 4 English, 3 math, 2 science, 2 science labs, 2 foreign language, 2 social studies, 3 academic electives. *Academic units recommended:* 3 foreign language. **Freshman Admission Statistics:** 35,980 applied, 49% admitted, 22% enrolled. **Transfer Admission Requirements:** High school transcript, college transcript(s), essay or personal statement. Minimum college GPA of 2.7 required. Lowest grade transferable C. **General Admission Information:** Application fee $80. Regular application deadline 1/15. Non-fall registration accepted. Admission may be deferred for a maximum of 1 semester.

COSTS AND FINANCIAL AID

Annual in-state tuition $13,798. Annual out-of-state tuition $36,466. Room and board $13,258. Required fees $3,428. Average book and supplies expense $950. **Required Forms and Deadlines:** FAFSA. **Notification of Awards:** Applicants will be notified of awards on a rolling basis beginning 3/1. **Types of Aid:** *Need-based scholarships/grants:* College/university scholarship or grant aid from institutional funds; Federal Pell; Private scholarships; SEOG; State scholarships/grants. *Loans:* Direct PLUS loans; Direct Subsidized Stafford Loans; Direct Unsubsidized Stafford Loans. **Student Employment:** Federal Work-Study Program available. Institutional employment available. **Financial Aid Statistics:** 67% needy freshmen, 71% needy undergrads receive need-based scholarship or grant aid. 40% freshmen, 33% undergrads receive non-need-based scholarship or grant aid. 62% freshmen, 72% undergrads receive need-based self-help aid. 3% freshmen, 2% undergrads receive athletic scholarships. 49% freshmen, 48% undergrads receive any aid. 59% undergrads borrow to pay for school. Average cumulative indebtedness $28,028. **Criteria awarding aid:** *Non-need-based:* Academics, Art, Athletics, Leadership, Minority status, Music/drama.

UNIVERSITY OF DALLAS

1845 East Northgate Drive, Irving, TX 75062
Phone: 972-721-5266 **Financial Aid Phone:** 972-721-5266
CEEB Code: 6868
Website: www.udallas.edu **ACT Code:** 4234

This private school, affiliated with the Roman Catholic Church, was founded in 1956. It has a 450 acre campus.

RATINGS

Admissions Selectivity Rating: 89   **Fire Safety Rating:** 95   **Green Rating:** 60*

STUDENTS AND FACULTY

Enrollment: 1,469. **Student Body:** 53% female, 47% male, 48% out-of-state, 3% international (41 countries represented). Asian 7%, African American 2%, Caucasian 59%, Hispanic 25%, Native American <1%, Pacific Islander <1%, Two or more races 3%, Race unknown 1%.
Retention and Graduation: 85% freshmen return for sophomore year. 68% freshmen graduate within 4 years. 71% freshmen graduate within 6 years. 28% grads go on to further study within 1 year. 34% grads pursue arts and sciences degrees. 5% grads pursue law degrees. 15% grads pursue business degrees. 8% grads pursue medical degrees. **Faculty:** Student/faculty ratio 11:1. 150 full-time faculty, 90% hold PhDs, 13% are members of minority groups, 39% are women. 0% of classes are taught by teaching assistants.

ACADEMICS

Degrees: Bachelor's; Certificate; Doctoral degree research/scholarship; Master's; Post-bachelor's certificate. **Classes:** Most classes have 10–19 students. Most lab/discussion sessions have 10–19 students. **Most popular majors:** English Language and Literature, General; Biology/Biological Sciences, General. **Special Study Options:** Double major; Dual enrollment; Independent study; Internships; Liberal arts/career combination; Student-designed major; Study abroad; Teacher certification program. **Honors programs:** At UD, the academic rigor of our Core Curriculum is analogous to an Honors program so we do not have a separate program or focus for that purpose. **Combined degree programs:** BA/MA. **Disability Services offered:** Note-taking services; Reader services; Tape recorders; Tutors. **Career services:** Alumni network; Alumni services; Career assessment; Career/job search classes; Internships.

FACILITIES

Housing: Apartments for single students; Coed dorms; Men's dorms; Women's dorms. **Special Academic Facilities/Equipment:** Art gallery, theater, language science and computer labs, observatory. **Campus network:** 100% of classrooms, 100% of dorms, 100% of student union, 100% of libraries, 100% of dining areas, 0% of common outdoor areas have wireless network access.

CAMPUS LIFE

Environment: City. **Activities:** Campus Ministries; Choral groups; Dance; Drama/theater; International Student Organization; Literary magazine; Music ensembles; Musical theater; Student government; Student newspaper; Student-run film society; Yearbook. 54 registered organizations, 4 honor societies, 6 religious organizations on campus. **Athletics (Intercollegiate):** *Men:* baseball, basketball, cross-country, golf, lacrosse, soccer, track/field (outdoor). *Women:* basketball, cross-country, lacrosse, soccer, softball, track/field (outdoor), volleyball. **On-Campus Highlights:** Church of the Incarnation. **Environmental Initiatives:** Student Government recycling committee and Environmental Alliance Club. SG provides recycling receptacles for cans and papers.

ADMISSIONS

Freshman Academic Profile: Average high school GPA 3.8. 32% in top 10% of high school class, 66% in top 25% of high school class, 91% in top 50% of high school class. 45% from public high schools. **Test Scores:** SAT Math middle 50% range 540–660. SAT EBRW middle 50% range 590–700. ACT middle 50% range 24–30. **Basis for Candidate Selection:** *Very important factors include:* rigor of secondary school record, academic GPA, application essay, standardized test scores, recommendation(s), character/personal qualities. *Important factors include:* class rank, talent/ability. *Other factors include:* interview, extracurricular activities, first generation, alumni/ae relation, volunteer work, work experience, level of applicant's interest. **Freshman Admission Requirements:** High school diploma is required and GED is accepted. *Academic units required:* 4 English, 3 math, 3 science, 2 foreign language, 3 social studies, 3 history, 3 academic electives, 1 visual/performing arts. *Academic units recommended:* 4 English, 4 math, 4 science, 3 science labs, 3 foreign language, 4 social studies, 4 history, 4 academic electives, 2 visual/performing arts. **Freshman Admission Statistics:** 4,676 applied, 45% admitted, 18% enrolled. **Transfer Admission Requirements:** College transcript(s), essay or personal statement, statement of good standing from prior institution(s). Minimum college GPA of 2.5 required. Lowest grade transferable C-. **General Admission Information:** Application fee $50. Priority deadline 12/1. Regular application deadline 8/1. Non-fall registration accepted. Admission may be deferred for a maximum of 2 years.

COSTS AND FINANCIAL AID

Annual tuition $41,660. Room and board $13,080. Required fees $3,150. Average book and supplies expense $1,040. **Required Forms and Deadlines:** FAFSA. **Notification of Awards:** Applicants will be notified of awards on a rolling basis beginning 12/1. **Types of Aid:** *Need-based scholarships/grants:* College/university scholarship or grant aid from institutional funds; Federal Pell; Private scholarships; SEOG; State scholarships/grants. *Loans:* Direct PLUS loans; Direct Subsidized Stafford Loans; Direct Unsubsidized Stafford Loans. **Student Employment:** Federal Work-Study Program available. Institutional employment available. **Financial Aid Statistics:** 97% needy freshmen, 99% needy undergrads receive need-based scholarship or grant aid. 17% freshmen, 15% undergrads receive non-need-based scholarship or grant aid. 63% freshmen, 68% undergrads receive need-based self-help aid. 0% freshmen, 0% undergrads receive athletic scholarships. 99% freshmen, 98% undergrads receive any aid. 60% undergrads borrow to pay for school. Average cumulative indebtedness $34,205. **Criteria awarding aid:** *Non-need-based:* Academics, Alumni affiliation, Art, Leadership, Minority status, Music/drama, Religious affiliation, State/district residency.

UNIVERSITY OF DAYTON

300 College Park, Dayton, OH 45469-1669
Phone: 937-229-4411 **Financial Aid Phone:** 800-427-5029
E-mail: admission@udayton.edu **CEEB Code:** 1834
Fax: 937-229-4729 **Website:** www.udayton.edu **ACT Code:** 3342

This private school, affiliated with the Roman Catholic Church, was founded in 1850. It has a 388 acre campus.

RATINGS

Admissions Selectivity Rating: 81   **Fire Safety Rating:** 81   **Green Rating:** 91

STUDENTS AND FACULTY

Enrollment: 8,508. **Student Body:** 48% female, 52% male, 51% out-of-state, 5% international (36 countries represented). Asian 1%, African American 3%, Caucasian 79%, Hispanic 6%, Native American <1%, Pacific Islander <1%, Two or more races 5%, Race unknown 1%.
Retention and Graduation: 91% freshmen return for sophomore year. 21% grads go on to further study within 1 year. 37% grads pursue arts and sciences degrees. 6% grads pursue law degrees. 20% grads pursue business degrees. 7% grads pursue medical degrees. **Faculty:** Student/faculty ratio 14:1. 609 full-time faculty, 88% hold PhDs, 20% are members of minority groups, 44% are women. 4% of classes are taught by teaching assistants.

ACADEMICS

Degrees: Bachelor's; Doctoral degree—professional practice; Doctoral degree research/scholarship; Master's; Post-bachelor's certificate. **Classes:** Most classes have 20–29 students. Most lab/discussion sessions have 10–19 students. **Most popular majors:** Mechanical Engineering; Liberal Arts and Sciences, General Studies and Humanities, Other; Marketing/Marketing Management, General. **Special Study Options:** Accelerated program; Cooperative education program; Cross-registration; Distance learning; Double major; Dual enrollment; English as a Second Language (ESL); Exchange student program (domestic); Honors program; Independent study; Internships; Liberal arts/career combination; Student-designed major; Study abroad; Teacher certification program; Weekend college. **Honors programs:** The University Honors Program offers courses, programming, fellowship advising, funding, guidance, and benefits to undergraduates who have superior academic records, culminating in an Honors-designated diploma. Through the Honors Program, students can develop their academic talents, explore the world, undertake extensive, self-directed research, and apply their knowledge for the benefit of others. **Combined degree programs:** BA/MA. **Disability Services offered:** Note-taking services; Reader services; Tutors. **Career services:** Alumni network; Alumni services; Career assessment; Career/job search classes; Internships; Regional alumni.

FACILITIES

Housing: Apartments for single students; Coed dorms; Cooperative housing; Fraternity/sorority housing; Special housing for disabled students; Special housing for international students; Theme housing; Wellness housing; 90% of campus accessible to physically disabled. **Special Academic Facilities/Equipment:** UD Research Institute, Bombeck Family Learning Center, Learning Teaching Center, Davis Center for Portfolio Management, Marian Library, ArtStreet living-learning complex, RecPlex.

CAMPUS LIFE

Environment: City. **Activities:** Campus Ministries; Choral groups; Concert band; Dance; Drama/theater; International Student Organization; Jazz band; Literary magazine; Marching band; Model UN; Music ensembles; Musical theater; Opera; Pep band; Radio station; Student government; Student newspaper; Symphony orchestra; Television station; Yearbook. 267 registered organizations, 16 honor societies, 11 religious organization, 10 fraternities, 11 sorority on campus. **Athletics (Intercollegiate):** *Men:* baseball, basketball, cheerleading, cross-country, football, golf, soccer, tennis. *Women:* basketball, cheerleading, crew/rowing, cross-country, golf, soccer, softball, tennis, track/field (outdoor), track/field (indoor), volleyball. **On-Campus Highlights:** John F. Kennedy Memorial Union. **Environmental Initiatives:** Composting program that has eliminated ~90% of waste from all campus dining halls complete with a total conversion to compostable disposable products for takeout and washable service ware for dine-in customers.

ADMISSIONS

Freshman Academic Profile: Average high school GPA 3.8. 26% in top 10% of high school class, 58% in top 25% of high school class, 85% in top 50% of high school class. 43% from public high schools. **Test Scores:** SAT Math middle 50% range 560–610. SAT EBRW middle 50% range 570–610. ACT middle 50% range 24–27. **Basis for Candidate Selection:** *Very important factors include:* rigor of secondary school record, class rank, academic GPA, application essay, standardized test scores. *Important factors include:* recommendation(s), extracurricular activities, character/personal qualities, alumni/ae relation. *Other factors include:* talent/ability, first generation, racial/ethnic status, volunteer work, work experience. **Freshman Admission Requirements:** High school diploma is required and GED is accepted. *Academic units recommended:* 4 English, 4 math, 4 science, 1 science labs, 2 foreign language, 4 social studies, 4 history, 4 computer science, 4 visual/performing arts. **Freshman Admission Statistics:** 16,693 applied, 72% admitted, 18% enrolled. **Transfer Admission Requirements:** High school transcript, college transcript(s), essay or personal statement. Minimum college GPA of 2.0 required. Lowest grade transferable C-. **General Admission Information:** Priority deadline 11/1. Regular application deadline 3/1. Non-fall registration accepted.

COSTS AND FINANCIAL AID

Annual tuition $44,100. Room and board $14,050. Average book and supplies expense $1,000. **Required Forms and Deadlines:** FAFSA. **Types of Aid:** *Need-based scholarships/grants:* College/university scholarship or grant aid from institutional funds; Federal Pell; Private scholarships; SEOG; State scholarships/grants. **Student Employment:** Federal Work-Study Program available. Institutional employment available. **Financial Aid Statistics:** 99% needy freshmen, 97% needy undergrads receive need-based scholarship or grant aid. 8% freshmen, 8% undergrads receive non-need-based scholarship or grant aid. 73% freshmen, 79% undergrads receive need-based self-help aid. 1% freshmen, 1% undergrads receive athletic scholarships. 99% freshmen, 98% undergrads receive any aid. 57% undergrads borrow to pay for school. Average cumulative indebtedness $37,533. **Criteria awarding aid:** *Need-based:* Academics, Alumni affiliation, Art, Athletics, Leadership, Minority status, Music/drama, Religious affiliation. *Non-need-based:* Academics, Alumni affiliation, Art, Athletics, Leadership, Minority status, Music/drama, Religious affiliation, State/district residency.

UNIVERSITY OF DELAWARE

210 South College Ave., Newark, DE 19716
Phone: 302-831-8123 **Financial Aid Phone:** 302-831-0520
E-mail: admissions@udel.edu **CEEB Code:** 5811
Fax: 302-831-6905 **Website:** http://www.udel.edu **ACT Code:** 634

This public school was founded in 1743. It has a 1000 acre campus.

RATINGS

Admissions Selectivity Rating: 87   **Fire Safety Rating:** 98   **Green Rating:** 86

STUDENTS AND FACULTY

Enrollment: 18,144. **Student Body:** 58% female, 42% male, 62% out-of-state, 5% international (81 countries represented). Asian 5%, African American 5%, Caucasian 72%, Hispanic 8%, Native American <1%, Pacific Islander <1%, Two or more races 3%, Race unknown 1%.
Retention and Graduation: 91% freshmen return for sophomore year. 71% freshmen graduate within 4 years. 83% freshmen graduate within 6 years. 28% grads go on to further study within 1 year. 23% grads pursue arts and sciences degrees. 6% grads pursue law degrees. 9% grads pursue business degrees. 15% grads pursue medical degrees. **Faculty:** Student/faculty ratio 13:1. 1,247 full-time faculty, 90% hold PhDs, 22% are members of minority groups, 44% are women. 5% of classes are taught by teaching assistants.

ACADEMICS

Degrees: Associate; Bachelor's; Doctoral degree—professional practice; Doctoral degree research/scholarship; Master's. **Classes:** Most classes have 20–29 students. Most lab/discussion sessions have 20–29 students. **Most popular majors:** Registered Nursing/Registered Nurse; Biology/Biological Sciences, General; Finance, General. **Special Study Options:** Accelerated program; Cooperative education program; Distance learning; Double major;

Dual enrollment; English as a Second Language (ESL); Honors program; Independent study; Internships; Liberal arts/career combination; Student-designed major; Study abroad; Teacher certification program. **Honors programs:** University Honors Program, http://honors.udel.edu/. **Disability Services offered:** Note-taking services; Reader services; Tape recorders; Tutors. **Career services:** Alumni network; Alumni services; Career assessment; Career/job search classes; Internships; Regional alumni.

FACILITIES

Housing: Apartments for married students; Apartments for single students; Coed dorms; Fraternity/sorority housing; Special housing for disabled students; Theme housing; Women's dorms; 95% of campus accessible to physically disabled. **Special Academic Facilities/Equipment:** University Museums, including the Old College Gallery, Mechanical Hall Gallery, and Mineralogical Museum; the Historic Costume and Textile Collection; a variety of state-of-the-art research facilities serving several disciplines, including the Center for Composite Materials, Delaware Biotechnology Institute, Allen Biotechnology Laboratory, a coastal research vessel—the Hugh R. Sharp, art conservation laboratories at Winterthur Museum and Gardens, and more than 40 research centers and institutes; a 350-acre Agricultural Teaching and Research Complex, including botanical gardens, livestock arena, working farm, botanical gardens, and a 35-acre woodlot harboring numerous wild species of animals and birds; the University of Delaware Library, 6-acre research library containing over 2.8 million books and over 300 networked databases; 28 micro-computing sites; two student centers; athletic facilities, including the 23,000-seat Delaware Football Stadium, two ice arenas, the 5,000-seat Bob Carpenter Sports/Convocation Center, indoor and outdoor swimming pools, Fred Rullo Stadium and a variety of playing fields and training and recreational spaces; and a student-run restaurant, Vita Nova, and campus hotel that serves as a training site for students in the hotel, restaurant and institutional management department. **Campus network:** 95% of classrooms, 100% of dorms, 98% of student union, 95% of libraries, 100% of dining areas, 5% of common outdoor areas have wireless network access.

CAMPUS LIFE

Environment: Town. **Activities:** Campus Ministries; Choral groups; Concert band; Dance; Drama/theater; International Student Organization; Jazz band; Literary magazine; Marching band; Model UN; Music ensembles; Musical theater; Opera; Pep band; Radio station; Student government; Student newspaper; Student-run film society; Symphony orchestra; Television station. 350 registered organizations, 16 honor societies, 20 religious organizations, 24 fraternities, 19 sororities on campus. **Athletics (Intercollegiate):** *Men:* baseball, basketball, cross-country, diving, football, golf, lacrosse, soccer, swimming, tennis, track/field (outdoor). *Women:* basketball, crew/rowing, cross-country, diving, field hockey, lacrosse, soccer, softball, swimming, tennis, track/field (outdoor), track/field (indoor), volleyball. **On-Campus Highlights:** Interdisciplinary Science Engineering Lab. **Environmental Initiatives:** The University of Delaware is launching a revolving energy loan fund dedicated to increasing energy efficiency of campus buildings.

ADMISSIONS

Freshman Academic Profile: Average high school GPA 3.7. 32% in top 10% of high school class, 66% in top 25% of high school class, 93% in top 50% of high school class. 80% from public high schools. **Test Scores:** SAT Math middle 50% range 570–670. SAT EBRW middle 50% range 580–660. ACT middle 50% range 25–29. **Basis for Candidate Selection:** *Very important factors include:* rigor of secondary school record, academic GPA, state residency. *Important factors include:* application essay, standardized test scores, recommendation(s), extracurricular activities, talent/ability, character/personal qualities, volunteer work, work experience. *Other factors include:* class rank, interview, first generation, alumni/ae relation, geographical residence, racial/ethnic status, level of applicant's interest. **Freshman Admission Requirements:** High school diploma is required and GED is accepted. *Academic units required:* 4 English, 3 math, 3 science, 2 science labs, 2 foreign language, 2 social studies, 2 history, 2 academic electives. *Academic units recommended:* 4 English, 4 math, 4 science, 3 science labs, 4 foreign language, 2 social studies, 2 history, 2 academic electives. **Freshman Admission Statistics:** 27,803 applied, 60% admitted, 26% enrolled. **Transfer Admission Requirements:** High school transcript, college transcript(s), essay or personal statement, statement of good standing from prior institution(s). Minimum college GPA of 2.5 required. Lowest grade transferable C. **General Admission Information:** Application fee $75. Regular application deadline 1/15. Non-fall registration accepted. Admission may be deferred for a maximum of 1 year.

COSTS AND FINANCIAL AID

Annual in-state tuition $12,730. Annual out-of-state tuition $34,160. Room and board $13,208. Required fees $1,550. Average book and supplies expense $1,000. **Required Forms and Deadlines:** FAFSA. **Notification of Awards:** Applicants will be notified of awards on a rolling basis beginning 2/1. **Types of Aid:** *Need-based scholarships/grants:* College/university scholarship or grant aid from institutional funds; Federal Pell; Private scholarships; SEOG; State scholarships/grants. *Loans:* Direct PLUS loans; Direct Subsidized Stafford Loans; Direct Unsubsidized Stafford Loans. **Student Employment:** Federal Work-Study Program available. Institutional employment available. **Financial Aid Statistics:** 92% needy freshmen, 83% needy undergrads receive need-based scholarship or grant aid. 8% freshmen, 6% undergrads receive non-need-based scholarship or grant aid. 75% freshmen, 81% undergrads receive need-based self-help aid. 2% freshmen, 2% undergrads receive athletic scholarships. 83% freshmen, 76% undergrads receive any aid. 62% undergrads borrow to pay for school. Average cumulative indebtedness $34,144. **Criteria awarding aid:** *Need-based:* Academics, Art. *Non-need-based:* Academics, Alumni affiliation, Art, Athletics, Leadership, Minority status, Music/drama, State/district residency.

UNIVERSITY OF DENVER

Office of Admission, Denver, CO 80208
Phone: (303) 871-2036 **Financial Aid Phone:** 303-871-4020
E-mail: admission@du.edu **CEEB Code:** 4842
Fax: 303-871-3301 **Website:** http://www.du.edu **ACT Code:** 0534

This private school was founded in 1864. It has a 125 acre campus.

RATINGS

Admissions Selectivity Rating: 82   **Fire Safety Rating:** 82   **Green Rating:** 60*

STUDENTS AND FACULTY

Enrollment: 5,755. **Student Body:** 54% female, 46% male, 63% out-of-state, 6% international (52 countries represented). Asian 4%, African American 2%, Caucasian 68%, Hispanic 12%, Native American <1%, Pacific Islander <1%, Two or more races 5%, Race unknown 2%.
Retention and Graduation: 86% freshmen return for sophomore year. 67% freshmen graduate within 4 years. 77% freshmen graduate within 6 years.
Faculty: Student/faculty ratio 12:1. 733 full-time faculty, 90% hold PhDs, 20% are members of minority groups, 48% are women. 3% of classes are taught by teaching assistants.

ACADEMICS

Degrees: Bachelor's; Certificate; Doctoral degree—professional practice; Doctoral degree research/scholarship; Master's; Post-bachelor's certificate; Post-master's certificate. **Classes:** Most classes have 10–19 students. Most lab/discussion sessions have 10–19 students. **Most popular majors:** Speech Communication and Rhetoric, Psychology, General. **Special Study Options:** Accelerated program; Cooperative education program; Distance learning; Double major; Dual enrollment; English as a Second Language (ESL); Honors program; Independent study; Internships; Student-designed major; Study abroad; Teacher certification program; Weekend college. **Honors programs:** The University of Denver offers a challenging Honors Program for talented students who seek an advanced liberal education, lively dialogue with their peers and faculty on important issues, study abroad in first-rate universities, and inspiring in-depth work in their majors. The aim of the program is to challenge students to cultivate strong habits of critical thinking, creativity, and scholarship and to offer close support for advanced work. Students in the Honors Program have the best of both worlds: the small classes and close community of a liberal arts college and the opportunities and resources of a research university. **Combined degree programs:** BA/JD; BA/MA. **Disability Services offered:** Note-taking services; Reader services; Tape recorders; Tutors. **Career services:** Alumni network; Alumni services; Career assessment; Career/job search classes; Internships; Regional alumni.

FACILITIES

Housing: Apartments for married students; Apartments for single students; Coed dorms; Fraternity/sorority housing; Theme housing; Wellness housing; 85% of campus accessible to physically disabled.

CAMPUS LIFE

Environment: Metropolis. **Activities:** Campus Ministries; Choral groups; Concert band; Dance; Drama/theater; International Student Organization;

Jazz band; Literary magazine; Marching band; Model UN; Music ensembles; Musical theater; Opera; Pep band; Radio station; Student government; Student newspaper; Student-run film society; Symphony orchestra. **Athletics (Intercollegiate):** *Men:* basketball, diving, golf, ice hockey, lacrosse, skiing (downhill/Alpine), skiing (Nordic/cross-country), soccer, swimming, tennis. *Women:* basketball, diving, golf, gymnastics, lacrosse, skiing (downhill/Alpine), skiing (Nordic/cross-country), soccer, swimming, tennis, volleyball. **On-Campus Highlights:** Campus Green (Driscoll Lawn).

ADMISSIONS

Basis for Candidate Selection: *Very important factors include:* rigor of secondary school record, academic GPA, standardized test scores. *Important factors include:* application essay, recommendation(s), extracurricular activities, talent/ability, character/personal qualities. *Other factors include:* first generation, alumni/ae relation, geographical residence, racial/ethnic status, volunteer work, work experience, level of applicant's interest. **Freshman Admission Requirements:** High school diploma is required and GED is accepted. *Academic units recommended:* 4 English, 4 math, 4 science, 2 science labs, 4 foreign language, 4 social studies. **Freshman Admission Statistics:** 21,028 applied, 59% admitted, 11% enrolled. **Transfer Admission Requirements:** College transcript(s), essay or personal statement, statement of good standing from prior institution(s). Lowest grade transferable C. **General Admission Information:** Application fee $65. Regular application deadline 1/15. Non-fall registration accepted. Admission may be deferred for a maximum of 12 months.

COSTS AND FINANCIAL AID

Annual tuition $52,596. Room and board $14,178. Average book and supplies expense $1,000. **Required Forms and Deadlines:** CSS/Financial Aid PROFILE; FAFSA; Noncustodial PROFILE. **Notification of Awards:** Applicants will be notified of awards on or about 3/1. **Types of Aid:** *Need-based scholarships/grants:* College/university scholarship or grant aid from institutional funds; Federal Pell; Private scholarships; SEOG; State scholarships/grants. *Loans:* Direct PLUS loans; Direct Subsidized Stafford Loans; Direct Unsubsidized Stafford Loans. **Student Employment:** Federal Work-Study Program available. Institutional employment available. **Financial Aid Statistics:** 99% needy freshmen, 99% needy undergrads receive need-based scholarship or grant aid. 25% freshmen, 23% undergrads receive non-need-based scholarship or grant aid. 68% freshmen, 68% undergrads receive need-based self-help aid. 3% freshmen, 4% undergrads receive athletic scholarships. 85% freshmen, 85% undergrads receive any aid. 44% undergrads borrow to pay for school. Average cumulative indebtedness $27,938. **Criteria awarding aid:** *Need-based:* Academics, Art, Athletics, Leadership, Music/drama. *Non-need-based:* Academics, Art, Athletics, Leadership, Music/drama.

UNIVERSITY OF DETROIT MERCY

4001 W McNichols Rd, Detroit, MI 48221-3038
Phone: 313-993-1245 **Financial Aid Phone:** 313-993-3350
E-mail: admissions@udmercy.edu **CEEB Code:** 1835
Fax: 313-993-3326 **Website:** www.udmercy.edu **ACT Code:** 2060

RATINGS

Admissions Selectivity Rating: 76   **Fire Safety Rating:** 60*   **Green Rating:** 60*

STUDENTS AND FACULTY

Enrollment: 2,754. **Student Body:** 63% female, 37% male, 6% out-of-state, 8% international. Asian 6%, African American 13%, Caucasian 60%, Hispanic 6%, Native American <1%, Pacific Islander <1%, Two or more races 2%, Race unknown 4%.
Retention and Graduation: 83% freshmen return for sophomore year. 46% freshmen graduate within 4 years. 62% freshmen graduate within 6 years. 20% grads go on to further study within 1 year. 5% grads pursue arts and sciences degrees. 4% grads pursue law degrees. 8% grads pursue business degrees. 3% grads pursue medical degrees. **Faculty:** Student/faculty ratio 10:1. 330 full-time faculty, 92% hold PhDs, 15% are members of minority groups, 52% are women. 0% of classes are taught by teaching assistants.

ACADEMICS

Degrees: Bachelor's; Certificate; Doctoral degree—professional practice; Doctoral degree research/scholarship; Master's; Post-bachelor's certificate; Post-master's certificate. **Classes:** Most classes have 10–19 students. Most lab/discussion sessions have 10–19 students. **Most popular majors:** Registered Nursing/Registered Nurse; Biology/Biological Sciences, General; Business

Administration and Management, General. **Special Study Options:** Accelerated program; Cooperative education program; Cross-registration; Distance learning; Double major; Dual enrollment; English as a Second Language (ESL); Honors program; Independent study; Internships; Study abroad; Teacher certification program. **Honors programs:** Please see the honors website for information. http://www.udmercy.edu/academics/special/honors/. **Combined degree programs:** BA/DDS; BA/MA; BA/MEng. **Disability Services offered:** Note-taking services; Reader services; Tutors. **Career services:** Alumni services; Career assessment; Career/job search classes; Internships.

FACILITIES

Housing: Coed dorms; 5% of campus accessible to physically disabled. **Campus network:** 100% of classrooms, 100% of dorms, 100% of student union, 100% of libraries, 100% of dining areas, 100% of common outdoor areas have wireless network access.

CAMPUS LIFE

Environment: Metropolis. **Activities:** Campus Ministries; Choral groups; Dance; Drama/theater; International Student Organization; Literary magazine; Musical theater; Pep band; Radio station; Student government; Student newspaper; Student-run film society. 90 registered organizations, 23 honor societies, 4 religious organizations, 12 fraternities, 6 sororities on campus.

ADMISSIONS

Freshman Academic Profile: Average high school GPA 3.6. 19% in top 10% of high school class, 47% in top 25% of high school class, 81% in top 50% of high school class. **Test Scores:** SAT Math middle 50% range 520–630. SAT EBRW middle 50% range 530–620. ACT middle 50% range 21–27. **Basis for Candidate Selection:** *Very important factors include:* rigor of secondary school record, academic GPA, standardized test scores. *Important factors include:* class rank, application essay, recommendation(s), interview, extracurricular activities, character/personal qualities, volunteer work. *Other factors include:* talent/ability, first generation, alumni/ae relation, work experience, level of applicant's interest. **Freshman Admission Requirements:** High school diploma is required and GED is accepted. **Freshman Admission Statistics:** 3,760 applied, 83% admitted, 19% enrolled. **General Admission Information:** Priority deadline 12/1. Regular application deadline 3/1. Non-fall registration accepted. Admission may be deferred for a maximum of 1 year.

COSTS AND FINANCIAL AID

Annual tuition $28,000. Room and board $9,736. Average book and supplies expense $1,230. **Required Forms and Deadlines:** FAFSA. **Types of Aid:** *Need-based scholarships/grants:* College/university scholarship or grant aid from institutional funds; Federal Nursing Scholarships; Federal Pell; Private scholarships; SEOG; State scholarships/grants. *Loans:* Direct PLUS loans; Direct Subsidized Stafford Loans; Direct Unsubsidized Stafford Loans. **Student Employment:** Federal Work-Study Program available. Institutional employment available. **Financial Aid Statistics:** 100% needy freshmen, 100% needy undergrads receive need-based scholarship or grant aid. 4% freshmen, 3% undergrads receive non-need-based scholarship or grant aid. 71% freshmen, 75% undergrads receive need-based self-help aid. 11% freshmen, 11% undergrads receive athletic scholarships. 97% freshmen, 92% undergrads receive any aid. 70% undergrads borrow to pay for school. Average cumulative indebtedness $44,180.

UNIVERSITY OF DUBUQUE

2000 University Avenue, Dubuque, IA 52001-5050
Phone: 319-589-3200 **Financial Aid Phone:** 563-589-3396
E-mail: admssns@dbq.edu **CEEB Code:** 6869
Fax: 319-589-3690 **Website:** www.dbq.edu **ACT Code:** 1358

This private school, affiliated with the Presbyterian Church, was founded in 1852. It has a 77 acre campus.

RATINGS

Admissions Selectivity Rating: 77   **Fire Safety Rating:** 96   **Green Rating:** 60*

STUDENTS AND FACULTY

Enrollment: 1,542. **Student Body:** 44% female, 56% male, 53% out-of-state, 1% international. Asian 2%, African American 12%, Caucasian 73%, Hispanic 3%, Native American 1%, Pacific Islander <1%, Two or more races 0%, Race unknown 8%.

Retention and Graduation: 68% freshmen return for sophomore year. 20% grads go on to further study within 1 year. 10% grads pursue arts and sciences degrees. 2% grads pursue law degrees. 3% grads pursue business degrees. 2% grads pursue medical degrees. **Faculty:** Student/faculty ratio 14:1. 87 full-time faculty, 56% hold PhDs, 6% are members of minority groups, 39% are women. 0% of classes are taught by teaching assistants.

ACADEMICS

Degrees: Bachelor's; Doctoral degree—professional practice; Master's. **Classes:** Most classes have 10–19 students. Most lab/discussion sessions have fewer than 10 students. **Most popular majors:** Business/Commerce, General; Animation, Interactive Technology, Video Graphics and Special Effects; Airline/Commercial/Professional Pilot and Flight Crew. **Special Study Options:** Accelerated program; Cooperative education program; Cross-registration; Distance learning; Double major; Dual enrollment; Honors program; Independent study; Internships; Liberal arts/career combination; Student-designed major; Study abroad; Teacher certification program. **Combined degree programs:** BA/MA. **Disability Services offered:** Note-taking services; Reader services; Tape recorders; Tutors. **Career services:** Alumni network; Alumni services; Career assessment; Career/job search classes; Internships; Regional alumni.

FACILITIES

Housing: Apartments for married students; Apartments for single students; Coed dorms; Special housing for disabled students; 50% of campus accessible to physically disabled. **Special Academic Facilities/Equipment:** Art gallery, language labs, electron microscope, gas chromatograph/mass spectrometer, floating science lab on the Mississippi River, computer graphics/interactive media studios, multimedia project production studio in the new Charles C. Myers Library. **Campus network:** 100% of classrooms, 100% of libraries, 100% of dining areas, 100% of common outdoor areas have wireless network access.

CAMPUS LIFE

Environment: Town. **Activities:** Campus Ministries; Choral groups; Dance; Drama/theater; International Student Organization; Jazz band; Literary magazine; Music ensembles; Musical theater; Pep band; Student government; Student newspaper; Student-run film society; Yearbook. 50 registered organizations, 4 honor societies, 2 religious organizations, 6 fraternities, 4 sororities on campus. **Athletics (Intercollegiate):** *Men:* baseball, basketball, cross-country, football, golf, soccer, tennis, track/field (outdoor), track/field (indoor), wrestling. *Women:* basketball, cross-country, golf, soccer, softball, tennis, track/field (outdoor), track/field (indoor), volleyball. **On-Campus Highlights:** Coffee Shop. **Environmental Initiatives:** Campus-wide recycling.

ADMISSIONS

Freshman Academic Profile: Average high school GPA 3.0. 7% in top 10% of high school class, 24% in top 25% of high school class, 54% in top 50% of high school class. 85% from public high schools. **Test Scores:** SAT Math middle 50% range 420–550. SAT EBRW middle 50% range 440–550. ACT middle 50% range 18–23. **Basis for Candidate Selection:** *Very important factors include:* rigor of secondary school record, class rank, application essay, standardized test scores, recommendation(s), character/personal qualities. *Other factors include:* interview, extracurricular activities, talent/ability, alumni/ae relation, volunteer work, work experience. **Freshman Admission Requirements:** High school diploma is required and GED is accepted. *Academic units required:* 4 English, 3 math, 3 science, 3 social studies, 3 academic electives. *Academic units recommended:* 4 English, 3 math, 3 science, 3 social studies, 3 academic electives. **Freshman Admission Statistics:** 1,288 applied, 76% admitted, 42% enrolled. **Transfer Admission Requirements:** College transcript(s). Minimum college GPA of 2.0 required. Lowest grade transferable C. **General Admission Information:** Application fee $25. Non-fall registration accepted. Admission may be deferred for a maximum of 1 year.

COSTS AND FINANCIAL AID

Annual tuition $21,000. Room and board $7,370. Required fees $590. Average book and supplies expense $950. **Required Forms and Deadlines:** FAFSA. **Notification of Awards:** Applicants will be notified of awards on a rolling basis beginning 3/1. **Types of Aid:** *Need-based scholarships/grants:* College/university scholarship or grant aid from institutional funds; Federal Pell; Private scholarships; SEOG; State scholarships/grants. *Loans:* Direct PLUS loans; Direct Subsidized Stafford Loans; Direct Unsubsidized Stafford Loans. **Student Employment:** Federal Work-Study Program available. Institutional employment available. **Financial Aid Statistics:** 99% needy freshmen, 98% needy undergrads receive need-based scholarship or grant aid. 16% freshmen, 12% undergrads receive non-need-based scholarship or grant aid. 80% freshmen, 83% undergrads receive need-based self-help aid. 0% freshmen, 0%

undergrads receive athletic scholarships. 85% freshmen, 85% undergrads receive any aid. **Criteria awarding aid:** *Need-based:* Academics, Alumni affiliation, Minority status, Music/drama, Religious affiliation. *Non-need-based:* Academics, Alumni affiliation, Leadership, Music/drama, State/district residency.

UNIVERSITY OF EVANSVILLE

1800 Lincoln Avenue, Evansville, IN 47722
Phone: 812-488-2468 **Financial Aid Phone:** 812-488-2364
E-mail: admission@evansville.edu **CEEB Code:** 1208
Fax: 812-488-4076 **Website:** www.evansville.edu **ACT Code:** 1188

This private school, affiliated with the Methodist Church, was founded in 1854. It has a 75 acre campus.

RATINGS

Admissions Selectivity Rating: 82   Fire Safety Rating: 64   Green Rating: 60*

STUDENTS AND FACULTY

Enrollment: 2,164. **Student Body:** 54% female, 46% male, 39% out-of-state, 15% international (55 countries represented). Asian 2%, African American 3%, Caucasian 71%, Hispanic 4%, Native American <1%, Pacific Islander 0%, Two or more races 2%, Race unknown 3%.
Retention and Graduation: 89% freshmen return for sophomore year. 18% grads go on to further study within 1 year. **Faculty:** Student/faculty ratio 12:1. 169 full-time faculty, 86% hold PhDs, 12% are members of minority groups, 41% are women. 0% of classes are taught by teaching assistants.

ACADEMICS

Degrees: Associate; Bachelor's; Doctoral degree—professional practice; Master's. **Classes:** Most classes have 10–19 students. **Most popular majors:** Registered Nursing/Registered Nurse; Drama and Dramatics/Theatre Arts, General; Exercise Science and Kinesiology. **Special Study Options:** Cooperative education program; Double major; Dual enrollment; English as a Second Language (ESL); Honors program; Independent study; Internships; Study abroad; Teacher certification program. **Honors programs:** The Honors Program is designed to enhance one's academic and social experience at the University. Special honors courses are offered each semester, as is the opportunity to create an honors experience from virtually any non-honors course. An honors project serves as the program capstone and is expressed through research, publication, or performance. Special honors events include guest lectures, book and movie discussions, an annual philanthropic event, and off-campus trips. Honors students enjoy many benefits, such as priority class registration, honors campus housing, opportunity to apply for undergraduate research funds, and access to a 24-hour honors lounge equipped with computers and printers. The Honors Program is structured to allow students in each of the University's colleges and schools to participate. **Disability Services offered:** Note-taking services; Tutors. **Career services:** Alumni network; Alumni services; Career assessment; Career/job search classes; Internships; Regional alumni.

FACILITIES

Housing: Apartments for single students; Coed dorms; Fraternity/sorority housing; Men's dorms; Theme housing; Women's dorms; 87% of campus accessible to physically disabled.

CAMPUS LIFE

Environment: City. **Activities:** Campus Ministries; Choral groups; Concert band; Dance; Drama/theater; International Student Organization; Jazz band; Literary magazine; Model UN; Music ensembles; Musical theater; Opera; Pep band; Radio station; Student government; Student newspaper; Student-run film society; Symphony orchestra; Yearbook. 144 registered organizations, 17 honor societies, 9 religious organizations, 6 fraternities, 5 sororities on campus. **Athletics (Intercollegiate):** *Men:* baseball, basketball, cross-country, diving, golf, soccer, swimming. *Women:* basketball, cross-country, diving, golf, soccer, softball, swimming, tennis, volleyball. **On-Campus Highlights:** Koch Center.

ADMISSIONS

Freshman Academic Profile: Average high school GPA 3.7. 34% in top 10% of high school class, 68% in top 25% of high school class, 90% in top 50% of high school class. **Test Scores:** SAT Math middle 50% range 500–620. SAT EBRW middle 50% range 490–600. ACT middle 50% range 23–29. **Basis for Candidate Selection:** *Very important factors include:* academic GPA, standardized test scores, talent/ability. *Important factors include:* rigor of secondary school record, alumni/ae relation. *Other factors include:* class rank, application essay, recommendation(s), interview, extracurricular activities, character/personal qualities, first generation, geographical residence, state residency, religious affiliation/commitment, racial/ethnic status, volunteer work, work experience. **Freshman Admission Requirements:** High school diploma is required and GED is accepted. *Academic units required:* 4 English, 3 math, 3 science, 2 social studies, 1 history. *Academic units recommended:* 4 math, 3 science labs, 2 foreign language. **Freshman Admission Statistics:** 4,033 applied, 71% admitted, 19% enrolled. **Transfer Admission Requirements:** High school transcript, college transcript(s), statement of good standing from prior institution(s). Minimum college GPA of 2.0 required. Lowest grade transferable C. **General Admission Information:** Non-fall registration accepted. Admission may be deferred for a maximum of 1 year.

COSTS AND FINANCIAL AID
Annual tuition $34,300. Room and board $12,160. Required fees $1,096. Average book and supplies expense $1,200. **Required Forms and Deadlines:** FAFSA. **Notification of Awards:** Applicants will be notified of awards on a rolling basis beginning 12/15. **Types of Aid:** *Need-based scholarships/grants:* College/university scholarship or grant aid from institutional funds; Federal Pell; Private scholarships; SEOG; State scholarships/grants. *Loans:* Direct PLUS loans; Direct Subsidized Stafford Loans; Direct Unsubsidized Stafford Loans. **Student Employment:** Federal Work-Study Program available. Institutional employment available. **Financial Aid Statistics:** 99% needy freshmen, 96% needy undergrads receive need-based scholarship or grant aid. 24% freshmen, 21% undergrads receive non-need-based scholarship or grant aid. 66% freshmen, 67% undergrads receive need-based self-help aid. 5% freshmen, 6% undergrads receive athletic scholarships. 98.3% freshmen, 93.7% undergrads receive any aid. 65% undergrads borrow to pay for school. Average cumulative indebtedness $35,346. **Criteria awarding aid:** *Need-based:* Job skills. *Non-need-based:* Academics, Alumni affiliation, Art, Athletics, Job skills, Music/drama, Religious affiliation.

THE UNIVERSITY OF FINDLAY

1000 North Main Street, Findlay, OH 45840
Phone: 419-434-4732 **Financial Aid Phone:** 419-434-4791
E-mail: admissions@findlay.edu **CEEB Code:** 1223
Fax: 419-434-4898 **Website:** www.findlay.edu **ACT Code:** 3272

This private school was founded in 1882. It has a 175 acre campus.

RATINGS
Admissions Selectivity Rating: 78 **Fire Safety Rating:** 88 **Green Rating:** 60*

STUDENTS AND FACULTY
Enrollment: 2,277. **Student Body:** 67% female, 33% male, 6% international (42 countries represented). Asian 1%, African American 4%, Caucasian 78%, Hispanic 3%, Native American <1%, Pacific Islander <1%, Two or more races 2%, Race unknown 5%.
Retention and Graduation: 76% freshmen return for sophomore year. 53% freshmen graduate within 4 years. 65% graduate within 6 years. 35% grads go on to further study within 1 year. 55% grads pursue arts and sciences degrees. 1% grads pursue law degrees. 4% grads pursue business degrees. 0% grads pursue medical degrees. **Faculty:** Student/faculty ratio 16:1. 231 full-time faculty, 66% hold PhDs, 9% are members of minority groups, 52% are women. 10% of classes are taught by teaching assistants.

ACADEMICS
Degrees: Associate; Bachelor's; Certificate; Doctoral degree—professional practice; Master's; Terminal Associate. **Classes:** Most classes have 10–19 students. Most lab/discussion sessions have 10–19 students. **Most popular majors:** Equestrian/Equine Studies; Business Administration and Management, General. **Special Study Options:** Accelerated program; Distance learning; Double major; Dual enrollment; English as a Second Language (ESL); Honors program; Independent study; Internships; Liberal arts/career combination; Student-designed major; Study abroad; Teacher certification program; Weekend college. **Disability Services offered:** Note-taking services; Reader services; Tape recorders; Tutors. **Career services:** Alumni services; Career/job search classes; Internships.

FACILITIES
Housing: Apartments for single students; Coed dorms; Fraternity/sorority housing; Theme housing; Women's dorms; 85% of campus accessible to physically disabled. **Special Academic Facilities/Equipment:** The Mazza

Museum International Art from Picture Books is the world's first and largest teaching museum devoted to literacy and the art of children's picture books. Founded in 1982, the Mazza Museum now contains more than 3,000 original artworks. The Havens Resource Center contains more than 5,000 volumes. **Campus network:** 95% of classrooms, 100% of dorms, 100% of student union, 100% of libraries, 100% of dining areas, 75% of common outdoor areas have wireless network access.

CAMPUS LIFE
Environment: Town. **Activities:** Campus Ministries; Choral groups; Concert band; Drama/theater; Jazz band; Literary magazine; Marching band; Music ensembles; Pep band; Radio station; Student government; Student newspaper; Symphony orchestra; Television station. 90 registered organizations, 28 honor societies, 3 religious organizations, 1 fraternity, 2 sororities on campus. **On-Campus Highlights:** Center for Student Life and College of Business.

ADMISSIONS
Freshman Academic Profile: Average high school GPA 3.6. 22% in top 10% of high school class, 54% in top 25% of high school class, 84% in top 50% of high school class. 89% from public high schools. **Test Scores:** SAT Math middle 50% range 520–620. SAT EBRW middle 50% range 520–643. ACT middle 50% range 21–26. **Basis for Candidate Selection:** *Very important factors include:* rigor of secondary school record, academic GPA, standardized test scores. *Important factors include:* character/personal qualities. *Other factors include:* class rank, application essay, recommendation(s), interview, extracurricular activities, talent/ability, first generation, volunteer work, work experience. **Freshman Admission Requirements:** High school diploma is required and GED is accepted. *Academic units required:* 4 English, 4 math, 3 science, 3 social studies, 5 academic electives, 1 unit from above areas or other academic areas. *Academic units recommended:* 4 English, 4 math, 4 science, 2 foreign language, 4 social studies, 2 history, 5 academic electives, 2 computer science, 2 visual/performing arts, 1 unit from above areas or other academic areas. **Freshman Admission Statistics:** 3,376 applied, 77% admitted, 20% enrolled. **General Admission Information:** Non-fall registration accepted. Admission may be deferred for a maximum of 1 year.

COSTS AND FINANCIAL AID
Annual tuition $34,200. Room and board $10,200. Required fees $1,210. Average book and supplies expense $1,375. **Required Forms and Deadlines:** FAFSA. **Notification of Awards:** Applicants will be notified of awards on a rolling basis beginning 3/1. **Types of Aid:** *Need-based scholarships/grants:* College/university scholarship or grant aid from institutional funds; Federal Pell; Private scholarships; SEOG; State scholarships/grants. *Loans:* Direct PLUS loans; Direct Subsidized Stafford Loans; Direct Unsubsidized Stafford Loans. **Student Employment:** Federal Work-Study Program available. Institutional employment available. **Financial Aid Statistics:** 100% needy freshmen, 100% needy undergrads receive need-based scholarship or grant aid. 100% freshmen, 100% undergrads receive non-need-based scholarship or grant aid. 100% freshmen, 100% undergrads receive need-based self-help aid. 13% freshmen, 10% undergrads receive athletic scholarships. 99% undergrads receive any aid.

UNIVERSITY OF FLORIDA

201 Criser Hall, Gainesville, FL 32611-4000
Phone: 352-392-1365 **Financial Aid Phone:** (352) 294-3226
E-mail: https://admissions.ufl.edu/staff **CEEB Code:** 5812
Fax: 352-392-2115 **Website:** www.ufl.edu

This public school was founded in 1853. It has a 2000 acre campus.

RATINGS
Admissions Selectivity Rating: 96 **Fire Safety Rating:** 88 **Green Rating:** 93

STUDENTS AND FACULTY
Enrollment: 34,523. **Student Body:** 56% female, 44% male, 8% out-of-state, 2% international (114 countries represented). Asian 9%, African American 6%, Caucasian 52%, Hispanic 23%, Native American <1%, Pacific Islander <1%, Two or more races 4%, Race unknown 3%.
Faculty: 22% of classes are taught by teaching assistants.

ACADEMICS

Degrees: Associate; Bachelor's; Certificate; Doctoral degree—other; Doctoral degree—professional practice; Doctoral degree research/scholarship; Master's; Post-bachelor's certificate; Post-master's certificate. **Most popular majors:** Biology/Biological Sciences, General; Psychology, General; Finance, General. **Special Study Options:** Accelerated program; Cooperative education program; Cross-registration; Distance learning; Double major; Dual enrollment; English as a Second Language (ESL); Exchange student program (domestic); Honors program; Independent study; Internships; Liberal arts/career combination; Student-designed major; Study abroad; Teacher certification program. **Honors programs:** The University of Florida Honors Program blends the vast resources of a research university with the individualized attention often available only at small liberal arts colleges. With small classes taught by the top faculty at the university, the program offers students the opportunity to make the most of their educational experience. Close interaction with faculty often leads to undergraduate research projects, and students are encouraged to pursue such activities. Students in the Honors Program have the opportunity to live in the Honors Residential College at Hume Hall where they will be surrounded by like-minded individuals and engage in a unique living-learning community. **Disability Services offered:** Note-taking services; Reader services; Tape recorders. **Career services:** Alumni services; Career assessment; Career/job search classes; Internships; Regional alumni.

FACILITIES

Housing: Apartments for married students; Apartments for single students; Coed dorms; Fraternity/sorority housing; Special housing for disabled students; Special housing for international students; Theme housing; 90% of campus accessible to physically disabled. **Special Academic Facilities/Equipment:** Natural history museum, art museum, art gallery, center for the performing arts, Aeolian Skinner organ, cast-bell carillon, citrus research center, coastal engineering wave tank, 100-kilowatt training and research reactor, academic computing center, microkelvin lab, self-contained intensive care hyperbaric chamber, Butterfly Rainforest.

CAMPUS LIFE

Environment: City. **Activities:** Campus Ministries; Choral groups; Concert band; Dance; Drama/theater; International Student Organization; Jazz band; Literary magazine; Marching band; Model UN; Music ensembles; Musical theater; Opera; Pep band; Radio station; Student government; Student newspaper; Student-run film society; Symphony orchestra; Television station; Yearbook. 925 registered organizations, 25 honor societies, 46 religious organizations, 36 fraternities, 28 sororities on campus. **Athletics (Intercollegiate):** *Men:* baseball, basketball, cross-country, diving, football, golf, swimming, tennis, track/field (outdoor), track/field (indoor). *Women:* basketball, cross-country, diving, golf, gymnastics, lacrosse, soccer, softball, swimming, tennis, track/field (outdoor), track/field (indoor), volleyball. **On-Campus Highlights:** Southwest Recreation Center. **Environmental Initiatives:** As a result of Dr. Machen's goal for Zero Waste by 2015, UF now recycles over 6,500 tons of material annually, approximately 43% of the waste stream. Additionally, UF strives to recycle at least 75% of its deconstruction debris and has instituted an Electronics Reuse/Recycling Policy and accompanying step-by-step guide for disposal and recycling. Indoor collection of paper, cans & bottles is institution-wide. UF initiated a Tail-gator recycling program for home game days in 2006 and the program has diverted more than 350,000 pounds of recyclables from the landfill since then. This program continues to grow through self-service stations and other outreach on campus and within the stadium. In 2013, UF began composting efforts on campus by taking the stadium "zero waste" through the football season, diverting an additional 50,000 pounds of organic waste from the landfill. UF researchers recycle Helium on campus and the Veterinary Medical Center repurposes animal waste through a composting partnership with the Forestry Service.

ADMISSIONS

Freshman Academic Profile: Average high school GPA 4.5. 81% in top 10% of high school class, 98% in top 25% of high school class, 100% in top 50% of high school class. 84% from public high schools. **Test Scores:** SAT Math middle 50% range 660–750. SAT EBRW middle 50% range 650–720. ACT middle 50% range 28–33. **Basis for Candidate Selection:** *Very important factors include:* rigor of secondary school record, academic GPA, application essay, extracurricular activities, talent/ability, character/personal qualities, volunteer work. *Important factors include:* standardized test scores, first generation. *Other factors include:* class rank, geographical residence, state residency, level of applicant's interest. **Freshman Admission Requirements:** High school diploma is required and GED is accepted. *Academic units required:* 4 English, 4 math, 3 science, 2 science labs, 2 foreign language, 3 social studies. **Freshman Admission Statistics:** 38,069 applied, 37% admitted, 47% enrolled. **Transfer Admission Requirements:** High school transcript, college

transcript(s), standardized test scores. Minimum college GPA of 2.0 required. **General Admission Information:** Application fee $30. Priority deadline 11/1. Regular application deadline 3/1.

COSTS AND FINANCIAL AID

Annual in-state tuition $6,381. Annual out-of-state tuition $28,658. Room and board $10,220. Average book and supplies expense $850. **Required Forms and Deadlines:** FAFSA. **Notification of Awards:** Applicants will be notified of awards on a rolling basis beginning 2/22. **Types of Aid:** *Need-based scholarships/grants:* College/university scholarship or grant aid from institutional funds; Federal Pell; Private scholarships; SEOG; State scholarships/grants; United Negro College Fund. *Loans:* Direct PLUS loans; Direct Subsidized Stafford Loans; Direct Unsubsidized Stafford Loans. **Student Employment:** Federal Work-Study Program available. Institutional employment available. **Financial Aid Statistics:** 53% needy freshmen, 62% needy undergrads receive need-based scholarship or grant aid. 88% freshmen, 68% undergrads receive non-need-based scholarship or grant aid. 28% freshmen, 41% undergrads receive need-based self-help aid. 2% freshmen, 2% undergrads receive athletic scholarships. 90% freshmen, 85% undergrads receive any aid. 38% undergrads borrow to pay for school. Average cumulative indebtedness $21,800. **Criteria awarding aid:** *Need-based:* Academics. *Non-need-based:* Academics, Alumni affiliation, Art, Athletics, Leadership, Minority status, Music/drama, State/district residency.

UNIVERSITY OF GEORGIA

Terrell Hall, 210 South Jackson Street, Athens, GA 30602-1633
Phone: 706-542-8776 **Financial Aid Phone:** (706)542-6147
E-mail: adm-info@uga.edu **CEEB Code:** 5813
Website: www.uga.edu **ACT Code:** 872

This public school was founded in 1785. It has a 767 acre campus.

RATINGS

Admissions Selectivity Rating: 90 **Fire Safety Rating:** 88 **Green Rating:** 95

STUDENTS AND FACULTY

Enrollment: 22,919. **Student Body:** 56% female, 44% male, 11% out-of-state, 2% international (90 countries represented). Asian 10%, African American 8%, Caucasian 69%, Hispanic 6%, Native American <1%, Pacific Islander <1%, Two or more races 4%, Race unknown 1%.
Retention and Graduation: 96% freshmen return for sophomore year. 63% freshmen graduate within 4 years. % freshmen graduate within 6 years. **Faculty:** Student/faculty ratio 17:1. 2,028 full-time faculty, 94% hold PhDs, 19% are members of minority groups, 39% are women. 15% of classes are taught by teaching assistants.

ACADEMICS

Degrees: Bachelor's; Certificate; Doctoral degree—professional practice; Doctoral degree research/scholarship; Master's; Post-bachelor's certificate; Post-master's certificate. **Classes:** Most classes have 10–19 students. **Most popular majors:** Biology/Biological Sciences, General; Finance, General; Psychology, General. **Special Study Options:** Accelerated program; Cooperative education program; Cross-registration; Distance learning; Double major; Dual enrollment; Exchange student program (domestic); Honors program; Independent study; Internships; Liberal arts/career combination; Student-designed major; Study abroad; Teacher certification program. **Honors programs:** General Honors Program (university-wide), Foundation Fellows, Center for Undergraduate Research Summer Research Fellows, CURO Apprentice Program. **Disability Services offered:** Note-taking services; Reader services; Tape recorders; Tutors. **Career services:** Alumni network; Alumni services; Career assessment; Career/job search classes; Internships; Regional alumni.

FACILITIES

Housing: Apartments for married students; Apartments for single students; Coed dorms; Fraternity/sorority housing; Special housing for disabled students; Special housing for international students; Theme housing; Women's dorms; 90% of campus accessible to physically disabled. **Special Academic Facilities/Equipment:** Miller Learning Center, Georgia Museum of Art, Georgia Museum of Natural History, Ramsey Student Center for Physical Activities,

Performing Arts Center, Tate Student Center, Richard B. Russell Building for Special Collections Libraries, Science Learning Center.

CAMPUS LIFE

Environment: City. **Activities:** Campus Ministries; Choral groups; Concert band; Dance; Drama/theater; International Student Organization; Jazz band; Literary magazine; Marching band; Model UN; Music ensembles; Musical theater; Opera; Pep band; Radio station; Student government; Student newspaper; Student-run film society; Symphony orchestra; Yearbook. 746 registered organizations, 28 honor societies, 64 religious organizations, 37 fraternities, 29 sororities on campus. **Athletics (Intercollegiate):** *Men:* baseball, basketball, cross-country, diving, football, golf, swimming, tennis, track/field (outdoor), track/field (indoor). *Women:* basketball, cross-country, diving, equestrian sports, golf, gymnastics, soccer, softball, swimming, tennis, track/field (outdoor), track/field (indoor), volleyball. **On-Campus Highlights:** Zell B. Miller Learning Center.

ADMISSIONS

Freshman Academic Profile: Average high school GPA 4.0. 54% in top 10% of high school class, 90% in top 25% of high school class, 99% in top 50% of high school class. 65% from public high schools. **Test Scores:** SAT Math middle 50% range 590–680. SAT EBRW middle 50% range 610–690. ACT middle 50% range 26–31. **Basis for Candidate Selection:** *Very important factors include:* rigor of secondary school record, academic GPA. *Important factors include:* standardized test scores. *Other factors include:* application essay, recommendation(s), extracurricular activities, talent/ability, character/personal qualities, first generation, volunteer work, work experience. **Freshman Admission Requirements:** High school diploma is required and GED is accepted. *Academic units required:* 4 English, 4 math, 4 science, 2 science labs, 2 foreign language, 3 social studies. *Academic units recommended:* 4 English, 4 math, 4 science, 2 science labs, 3 foreign language, 3 social studies, 1 academic elective. **Freshman Admission Statistics:** 24,165 applied, 54% admitted, 45% enrolled. **Transfer Admission Requirements:** College transcript(s). Lowest grade transferable D. **General Admission Information:** Application fee $60. Priority deadline 10/15. Regular application deadline 1/1. Non-fall registration accepted. Admission may be deferred for a maximum of one academic year.

COSTS AND FINANCIAL AID

Annual in-state tuition $12,080. Annual out-of-state tuition $31,120. Room and board $10,314. Average book and supplies expense $986. **Required Forms and Deadlines:** FAFSA. **Notification of Awards:** Applicants will be notified of awards on a rolling basis beginning 5/1. **Types of Aid:** *Need-based scholarships/grants:* College/university scholarship or grant aid from institutional funds; Federal Pell; Private scholarships; SEOG; State scholarships/grants. *Loans:* Direct PLUS loans; Direct Subsidized Stafford Loans; Direct Unsubsidized Stafford Loans. **Student Employment:** Federal Work-Study Program available. Institutional employment available. **Financial Aid Statistics:** 97% needy freshmen, 92% needy undergrads receive need-based scholarship or grant aid. 25% freshmen, 18% undergrads receive non-need-based scholarship or grant aid. 43% freshmen, 50% undergrads receive need-based self-help aid. 2% freshmen, 2% undergrads receive athletic scholarships. 45.6% freshmen, 44.9% undergrads receive any aid. 43% undergrads borrow to pay for school. Average cumulative indebtedness $22,872. **Criteria awarding aid:** *Non-need-based:* Academics, Athletics, State/district residency.

UNIVERSITY OF GREAT FALLS

1301 20th Street South, Great Falls, MT 59405
Phone: 406-791-5200 **Financial Aid Phone:** 406-791-5235
E-mail: enroll@ugf.edu **CEEB Code:** 4058
Fax: 406-791-5209 **Website:** www.ugf.edu **ACT Code:** 2410

This private school, affiliated with the Roman Catholic Church, was founded in 1932. It has a 44 acre campus.

RATINGS

Admissions Selectivity Rating: 83   **Fire Safety Rating:** 60*   **Green Rating:** 60*

STUDENTS AND FACULTY

Enrollment: 612. **Student Body:** 63% female, 37% male, 20% out-of-state. **Retention and Graduation:** 59% freshmen return for sophomore year. 20% grads pursue arts and sciences degrees. 100% grads pursue medical degrees. **Faculty:** Student/faculty ratio 12:1. 33 full-time faculty, 61% hold PhDs, 6% are members of minority groups, 33% are women. 0% of classes are taught by teaching assistants.

ACADEMICS

Degrees: Associate; Bachelor's; Master's; Terminal Associate; Transfer Associate. **Classes:** Most classes have 10–19 students. **Most popular majors:** Criminal Justice/Safety Studies; Elementary Education and Teaching; Psychology, General. **Special Study Options:** Cooperative education program; Distance learning; Double major; Independent study; Internships; Liberal arts/career combination; Teacher certification program. **Disability Services offered:** Note-taking services; Reader services; Tape recorders; Tutors. **Career services:** Alumni network; Alumni services; Career/job search classes; Internships.

FACILITIES

Housing: Apartments for married students; Apartments for single students; Coed dorms; 85% of campus accessible to physically disabled. **Special Academic Facilities/Equipment:** Art museum; Dr. Hong Herbarium.

CAMPUS LIFE

Environment: Town. **Activities:** Campus Ministries; Choral groups; Concert band; Dance; Drama/theater; Jazz band; Music ensembles; Musical theater; Pep band; Radio station; Student government; Student newspaper; Symphony orchestra. 10 registered organizations, 2 honor societies, 1 religious organization on campus. **Athletics (Intercollegiate):** *Men:* basketball, cheerleading, cross-country, golf, track/field (outdoor), wrestling. *Women:* basketball, cheerleading, cross-country, golf, soccer, softball, track/field (outdoor), volleyball. **On-Campus Highlights:** Student Center.

ADMISSIONS

Freshman Academic Profile: Average high school GPA 3.4. 87% from public high schools. **Test Scores:** SAT Math middle 50% range 360–490. SAT EBRW middle 50% range 330–430. ACT middle 50% range 18–24. **Basis for Candidate Selection:** *Important factors include:* rigor of secondary school record, academic GPA, application essay, standardized test scores, interview, character/personal qualities, religious affiliation/commitment, level of applicant's interest. *Other factors include:* class rank, recommendation(s), extracurricular activities, talent/ability, first generation, racial/ethnic status, volunteer work, work experience. **Freshman Admission Requirements:** High school diploma is required and GED is accepted. *Academic units required:* 4 English, 3 math, 3 science, 1 science labs, 1 social studies, 3 history, 5 academic electives. *Academic units recommended:* 4 English, 3 math, 3 science, 1 science labs, 2 foreign language, 2 social studies, 3 history, 3 academic electives. **Freshman Admission Statistics:** 278 applied, 73% admitted, 73% enrolled. **Transfer Admission Requirements:** College transcript(s), essay or personal statement. Minimum college GPA of 2.0 required. Lowest grade transferable C. **General Admission Information:** Application fee $35. Priority deadline 6/1. Regular application deadline 8/30. Non-fall registration accepted. Admission may be deferred for a maximum of 2 semesters.

COSTS AND FINANCIAL AID

Annual tuition $15,500. Room and board $6,490. Required fees $900. Average book and supplies expense $500. **Required Forms and Deadlines:** FAFSA. **Notification of Awards:** Applicants will be notified of awards on a rolling basis beginning 3/1. **Types of Aid:** *Need-based scholarships/grants:* College/university scholarship or grant aid from institutional funds; Federal Pell; Private scholarships; SEOG; State scholarships/grants. **Student Employment:** Federal Work-Study Program available. Institutional employment available. **Financial Aid Statistics:** 69% needy freshmen, 73% needy undergrads receive need-based scholarship or grant aid. 92% freshmen, 92% undergrads receive non-need-based scholarship or grant aid. 90% freshmen, 93% undergrads receive need-based self-help aid. 47% freshmen, 38% undergrads receive athletic scholarships. 46% freshmen, 50% undergrads receive any aid. **Criteria awarding aid:** *Need-based:* Job skills, Minority status, Religious affiliation. *Non-need-based:* Academics, Alumni affiliation, Art, Athletics, Job skills, Leadership, Minority status, Music/drama, Religious affiliation, State/district residency.

For more free content, visit PrincetonReview.com

UNIVERSITY OF HARTFORD

200 Bloomfield Avenue, West Hartford, CT 06117
Phone: 860-768-4296 **Financial Aid Phone:** 800-947-4303
E-mail: admissions@mail.hartford.edu **CEEB Code:** 3436
Fax: 860-768-4961 **Website:** www.hartford.edu **ACT Code:** 606

This private school was founded in 1877. It has a 320 acre campus.

RATINGS
Admissions Selectivity Rating: 77 **Fire Safety Rating:** 78 **Green Rating:** 60*

STUDENTS AND FACULTY
Enrollment: 4,924. **Student Body:** 51% female, 49% male, 51% out-of-state, 6% international (50 countries represented). Asian 3%, African American 16%, Caucasian 56%, Hispanic 12%, Native American <1%, Pacific Islander <1%, Two or more races 3%, Race unknown 4%.
Retention and Graduation: 75% freshmen return for sophomore year. 22% grads go on to further study within 1 year. 39% grads pursue arts and sciences degrees. 2% grads pursue law degrees. 14% grads pursue business degrees. 2% grads pursue medical degrees. **Faculty:** Student/faculty ratio 9:1. 366 full-time faculty, 71% hold PhDs, 14% are members of minority groups, 42% are women. 0% of classes are taught by teaching assistants.

ACADEMICS
Degrees: Associate; Bachelor's; Certificate; Diploma; Doctoral degree—professional practice; Doctoral degree research/scholarship; Master's; Post-bachelor's certificate; Post-master's certificate. **Classes:** Most classes have 10–19 students. Most lab/discussion sessions have 10–19 students. **Most popular majors:** Architectural Engineering Technologies/Technicians; Psychology, General. **Special Study Options:** Accelerated program; Cross-registration; Distance learning; Double major; Dual enrollment; English as a Second Language (ESL); Exchange student program (domestic); Honors program; Independent study; Internships; Liberal arts/career combination; Student-designed major; Study abroad; Teacher certification program; Weekend college. **Disability Services offered:** Note-taking services; Reader services; Tutors.

FACILITIES
Housing: Apartments for single students; Coed dorms; Special housing for disabled students; Theme housing; Wellness housing; Women's dorms. **Special Academic Facilities/Equipment:** Museum of presidential memorabilia, Art Gallery, off-campus child care center for student teaching, learning skills and language lab, audio-visual aids center, 8,000-acre environmental center. **Campus network:** 100% of classrooms, 100% of dorms, 100% of student union, 100% of libraries, 100% of dining areas, 60% of common outdoor areas have wireless network access.

CAMPUS LIFE
Environment: Metropolis. **Activities:** Campus Ministries; Choral groups; Concert band; Dance; Drama/theater; International Student Organization; Jazz band; Literary magazine; Music ensembles; Musical theater; Opera; Pep band; Radio station; Student government; Student newspaper; Student-run film society; Symphony orchestra; Television station; Yearbook. 93 registered organizations, 22 honor societies, 7 religious organizations, 16 fraternities, 14 sororities on campus. **Athletics (Intercollegiate):** *Men:* baseball, basketball, cross-country, golf, lacrosse, soccer, tennis, track/field (outdoor), track/field (indoor). *Women:* basketball, cross-country, golf, soccer, softball, tennis, track/field (outdoor), track/field (indoor), volleyball. **On-Campus Highlights:** Museum of American Political Life.

ADMISSIONS
Test Scores: SAT Math middle 50% range 460–580. SAT EBRW middle 50% range 460–580. ACT middle 50% range 20–26. **Basis for Candidate Selection:** *Very important factors include:* rigor of secondary school record. *Important factors include:* class rank, academic GPA, standardized test scores. *Other factors include:* application essay, recommendation(s), interview, extracurricular activities, talent/ability, character/personal qualities. **Freshman Admission Requirements:** High school diploma is required and GED is accepted. *Academic units required:* 4 English, 2 math, 2 science, 2 social studies, 2 history, 4 academic electives. *Academic units recommended:* 3 math, 3 science, 2 foreign language. **Freshman Admission Statistics:** 15,526 applied, 72% admitted, 12% enrolled. **Transfer Admission Requirements:** College transcript(s). Minimum college GPA of 2.2 required. Lowest grade transferable C-. **General Admission Information:** Application fee $35. Non-fall registration accepted. Admission may be deferred for a maximum of 1 year.

COSTS AND FINANCIAL AID
Annual tuition $36,088. Room and board $12,346. Required fees $2,822. Average book and supplies expense $1,020. **Required Forms and Deadlines:** FAFSA. **Notification of Awards:** Applicants will be notified of awards on a rolling basis beginning 3/1. **Types of Aid:** *Need-based scholarships/grants:* College/university scholarship or grant aid from institutional funds; Federal Pell; Private scholarships; SEOG; State scholarships/grants. *Loans:* Direct PLUS loans; Direct Subsidized Stafford Loans; Direct Unsubsidized Stafford Loans. **Financial Aid Statistics:** 97% freshmen, 95% undergrads receive any aid. **Criteria awarding aid:** *Non-need-based:* Academics, Art, Athletics, Music/drama, State/district residency.

UNIVERSITY OF HAWAII—HILO

200 West Kawili Street, Hilo, HI 96720-4091
Phone: 808-974-7414 **Financial Aid Phone:** 808-974-7323
E-mail: uhhadm@hawaii.edu **CEEB Code:** 001611
Fax: 808-933-0861 **ACT Code:** 904

This public school was founded in 1970. It has a 225 acre campus.

RATINGS
Admissions Selectivity Rating: 81 **Fire Safety Rating:** 60* **Green Rating:** 60*

STUDENTS AND FACULTY
Enrollment: 3,385. **Student Body:** 59% female, 41% male, 35% out-of-state, 5% international. Asian 19%, African American 1%, Caucasian 24%, Hispanic 10%, Native American 1%, Pacific Islander 12%, Two or more races 27%, Race unknown <1%.
Retention and Graduation: 69% freshmen return for sophomore year. **Faculty:** Student/faculty ratio 14:1. 227 full-time faculty, 0% hold PhDs, 0% are members of minority groups, 44% are women. 0% of classes are taught by teaching assistants.

ACADEMICS
Degrees: Bachelor's; Certificate; Master's; Post-bachelor's certificate. **Classes:** Most classes have 10–19 students. **Most popular majors:** Business, Management, Marketing, and Related Support Services, Other; Psychology, General. **Special Study Options:** Cross-registration; Distance learning; Double major; Dual enrollment; English as a Second Language (ESL); Exchange student program (domestic); Honors program; Independent study; Internships; Student-designed major; Study abroad; Teacher certification program. **Disability Services offered:** Note-taking services; Reader services; Tape recorders; Tutors. **Career services:** Alumni network; Alumni services; Career assessment; Internships.

FACILITIES
Housing: Apartments for married students; Apartments for single students; Coed dorms; Special housing for disabled students; 90% of campus accessible to physically disabled. **Campus network:** 100% of classrooms, 100% of dorms, 100% of student union, 100% of libraries, 100% of dining areas, 100% of common outdoor areas have wireless network access.

CAMPUS LIFE
Environment: Town. **Activities:** Choral groups; Dance; Drama/theater; Jazz band; Literary magazine; Music ensembles; Radio station; Student government; Student newspaper. 43 registered organizations, 4 religious organizations on campus. **Athletics (Intercollegiate):** *Men:* baseball, basketball, cross-country, golf, tennis. *Women:* cross-country, softball, tennis, volleyball. **On-Campus Highlights:** University Classroom Building.

ADMISSIONS
Freshman Academic Profile: Average high school GPA 3.3. 17% in top 10% of high school class, 47% in top 25% of high school class, 82% in top 50% of high school class. **Test Scores:** SAT Math middle 50% range 440–600. SAT EBRW middle 50% range 440–560. ACT middle 50% range 17–24. **Basis for Candidate Selection:** *Very important factors include:* rigor of secondary school record. *Important factors include:* class rank, academic GPA, standardized test scores. *Other factors include:* application essay, recommendation(s), extracurricular activities, talent/ability. **Freshman Admission Requirements:** High school diploma is required and GED is accepted. *Academic units required:* 4 English, 3 math, 3 science, 3 science labs, 7 academic electives. *Academic units recommended:* 4 English, 4 math, 4 science, 3 science labs, 2 foreign language, 2 social studies, 2 history. **Freshman Admission Statistics:** 1,500 applied, 72% admitted, 44% enrolled. **Transfer Admission Requirements:** College

transcript(s). Minimum college GPA of 2.0 required. Lowest grade transferable C. **General Admission Information:** Application fee $50. Priority deadline 3/1. Regular application deadline 7/1. Non-fall registration accepted. Admission may be deferred for a maximum of 1 semester.

COSTS AND FINANCIAL AID

Annual in-state tuition $5,640. Annual out-of-state tuition $17,112. Room and board $7,134. Average book and supplies expense $1,017. **Required Forms and Deadlines:** FAFSA. **Notification of Awards:** Applicants will be notified of awards on a rolling basis beginning 4/12. **Types of Aid:** *Need-based scholarships/grants:* College/university scholarship or grant aid from institutional funds; Federal Pell; Private scholarships; SEOG; State scholarships/grants. **Student Employment:** Federal Work-Study Program available. Institutional employment available. **Financial Aid Statistics:** 78% needy freshmen, 79% needy undergrads receive need-based scholarship or grant aid. 15% freshmen, 17% undergrads receive non-need-based scholarship or grant aid. 56% freshmen, 65% undergrads receive need-based self-help aid. 3% freshmen, 3% undergrads receive athletic scholarships. **Criteria awarding aid:** *Need-based:* Academics. *Non-need-based:* Academics, Art, Athletics, Leadership, Minority status, Music/drama.

UNIVERSITY OF HAWAII—MANOA

2600 Campus Road, Honolulu, HI 96822
Phone: 808-956-8975 **Financial Aid Phone:** 808-956-7251
E-mail: manoa.admissions@hawaii.edu **CEEB Code:** 4867
Fax: 808-956-4148 **Website:** http://manoa.hawaii.edu **ACT Code:** 902

This public school was founded in 1907. It has a 320 acre campus.

RATINGS

Admissions Selectivity Rating: 77   **Fire Safety Rating:** 89   **Green Rating:** 60*

STUDENTS AND FACULTY

Enrollment: 12,609. **Student Body:** 57% female, 43% male, 28% out-of-state, 3% international (67 countries represented). Asian 40%, African American 2%, Caucasian 20%, Hispanic 2%, Native American <1%, Pacific Islander 17%, Two or more races 16%, Race unknown <1%.
Retention and Graduation: 79% freshmen return for sophomore year. 32% freshmen graduate within 4 years. **Faculty:** Student/faculty ratio 10:1. 1,149 full-time faculty, 88% hold PhDs, 46% are members of minority groups, 46% are women.

ACADEMICS

Degrees: Bachelor's; Doctoral degree—professional practice; Doctoral degree research/scholarship; Master's; Post-bachelor's certificate. **Classes:** Most classes have 10–19 students. Most lab/discussion sessions have 10–19 students. **Most popular majors:** Registered Nursing/Registered Nurse; Biology/Biological Sciences, General; Psychology, General. **Special Study Options:** Cooperative education program; Distance learning; Double major; English as a Second Language (ESL); Exchange student program (domestic); Honors program; Independent study; Internships; Student-designed major; Study abroad; Teacher certification program. **Honors programs:** Selected Studies Program. **Disability Services offered:** Note-taking services; Reader services; Tape recorders. **Career services:** Alumni services; Career assessment; Career/job search classes; Internships.

FACILITIES

Housing: Apartments for married students; Apartments for single students; Coed dorms; Special housing for disabled students; Theme housing; 40% of campus accessible to physically disabled. **Special Academic Facilities/Equipment:** UH Art and Commons Galleries, John Young Museum, John F. Kennedy Theatre, Lyon Arboretum, Waikiki Aquarium, Sunset (travel industry) Library, Chuck Gee Technology Learning Center, Advanced Computing Research Laboratory, Environmental Engineering Lab, Hawaii Center for Advanced Communications, Coral Reef Science Laboratory, traditionally designed Korean Studies Building, Coconut Island marine biology labs, Wong Audio-Visual Center, language lab, speech and hearing and dental hygiene clinics, law library, Hawaiian lo'i(garden), electron microscope and laser laboratories, ship and submersible research fleet, and Maui Super Computer,

Jakuan Tea House. **Campus network:** 100% of classrooms, 100% of student union, 100% of libraries, 100% of dining areas have wireless network access.

CAMPUS LIFE

Environment: Metropolis. **Activities:** Campus Ministries; Choral groups; Concert band; Dance; Drama/theater; International Student Organization; Jazz band; Literary magazine; Marching band; Music ensembles; Musical theater; Pep band; Radio station; Student government; Student newspaper; Student-run film society; Symphony orchestra. 270 registered organizations, 5 honor societies, 28 religious organizations, 2 fraternities, 3 sororities on campus. **Athletics (Intercollegiate):** *Men:* baseball, basketball, cheerleading, diving, football, golf, sailing, swimming, tennis, volleyball. *Women:* basketball, cheerleading, cross-country, diving, golf, sailing, soccer, softball, swimming, tennis, track/field (outdoor), track/field (indoor), volleyball, water polo. **On-Campus Highlights:** Campus Center. **Environmental Initiatives:** Creation & convening of Manoa Sustainability Corps.

ADMISSIONS

Freshman Academic Profile: Average high school GPA 3.6. 25% in top 10% of high school class, 54% in top 25% of high school class, 86% in top 50% of high school class. **Test Scores:** SAT Math middle 50% range 525–620. SAT EBRW middle 50% range 530–620. ACT middle 50% range 20–25. **Basis for Candidate Selection:** *Very important factors include:* rigor of secondary school record, academic GPA, standardized test scores. *Important factors include:* class rank, state residency. *Other factors include:* application essay, recommendation(s), interview, extracurricular activities, talent/ability, geographical residence. **Freshman Admission Requirements:** High school diploma is required and GED is accepted. *Academic units required:* 4 English, 3 math, 3 science, 3 social studies, 5 academic electives. **Freshman Admission Statistics:** 9,350 applied, 83% admitted, 28% enrolled. **Transfer Admission Requirements:** College transcript(s). Minimum college GPA of 2.5 required. Lowest grade transferable D. **General Admission Information:** Application fee $70. Priority deadline 1/5. Regular application deadline 3/1. Non-fall registration accepted.

COSTS AND FINANCIAL AID

Annual in-state tuition $11,088. Annual out-of-state tuition $33,120. Room and board $12,686. Required fees $882. Average book and supplies expense $1,040. **Required Forms and Deadlines:** FAFSA. **Notification of Awards:** Applicants will be notified of awards on a rolling basis beginning 4/1. **Types of Aid:** *Need-based scholarships/grants:* College/university scholarship or grant aid from institutional funds; Federal Pell; Private scholarships; SEOG; State scholarships/grants. *Loans:* Direct PLUS loans; Direct Subsidized Stafford Loans; Direct Unsubsidized Stafford Loans. **Student Employment:** Federal Work-Study Program available. Institutional employment available. **Financial Aid Statistics:** 99% needy freshmen, 95% needy undergrads receive need-based scholarship or grant aid. 27% freshmen, 22% undergrads receive non-need-based scholarship or grant aid. 52% freshmen, 57% undergrads receive need-based self-help aid. 3% freshmen, 2% undergrads receive athletic scholarships. 56% freshmen, 59% undergrads receive any aid. 45% undergrads borrow to pay for school. Average cumulative indebtedness $24,233. **Criteria awarding aid:** *Need-based:* Academics. *Non-need-based:* Academics, Alumni affiliation, Art, Athletics, Leadership, Music/drama, State/district residency.

UNIVERSITY OF HAWAII—WEST OAHU

91-1001 Farrington Hwy, Kapolei, HI 96707
Phone: 808-689-2900 **Financial Aid Phone:** 808-454-4700
E-mail: uhwo.admissions@hawaii.edu **CEEB Code:** 1042
Fax: 808-689-2901 **Website:** www.uhwo.hawaii.edu **ACT Code:** 6465

This public school was founded in 1976.

RATINGS

Admissions Selectivity Rating: 73   **Fire Safety Rating:** 60*   **Green Rating:** 60*

STUDENTS AND FACULTY

Enrollment: 1,950. **Student Body:** 67% female, 33% male, 2% out-of-state, <1% international (16 countries represented). Asian 41%, African American 1%, Caucasian 14%, Hispanic 1%, Native American <1%, Pacific Islander 27%, Two or more races 14%, Race unknown <1%.
Retention and Graduation: 67% freshmen return for sophomore year. **Faculty:** Student/faculty ratio 18:1. 51 full-time faculty, 92% hold PhDs, 51%

are members of minority groups, 41% are women. 0% of classes are taught by teaching assistants.

ACADEMICS

Degrees: Bachelor's; Certificate. **Classes:** Most classes have 20–29 students. Most lab/discussion sessions have fewer than 10 students. **Most popular majors:** Business/Commerce, General; Elementary Education and Teaching; Psychology, General. **Special Study Options:** Distance learning; Double major; Teacher certification program. **Disability Services offered:** Note-taking services; Reader services; Tape recorders.

FACILITIES

100% of campus accessible to physically disabled.

CAMPUS LIFE

Environment: Town. **Activities:** Student government. 14 registered organizations, 1 honor societies on campus. **Environmental Initiatives:** All buildings being constructed at new campus are LEED Silver Certified or above.

ADMISSIONS

Freshman Academic Profile: 74% from public high schools. **Basis for Candidate Selection:** *Very important factors include:* academic GPA. *Important factors include:* rigor of secondary school record. *Other factors include:* application essay, standardized test scores, recommendation(s), interview, extracurricular activities, first generation, geographical residence, state residency. **Freshman Admission Requirements:** High school diploma is required and GED is accepted. *Academic units required:* 4 English, 3 math, 3 science, 3 social studies, 5 academic electives, 4 unit from above areas or other academic areas. **Freshman Admission Statistics:** 908 applied, 51% admitted, 64% enrolled. Minimum college GPA of 2.0 required. Lowest grade transferable D. **General Admission Information:** Application fee $50. Priority deadline 3/1. Regular application deadline 8/1. Non-fall registration accepted. Admission may be deferred for a maximum of 1 semester.

COSTS AND FINANCIAL AID

Annual in-state tuition $5,592. Annual out-of-state tuition $16,656. **Required Forms and Deadlines:** FAFSA. **Notification of Awards:** Applicants will be notified of awards on a rolling basis beginning 4/15. **Types of Aid:** *Need-based scholarships/grants:* Federal Pell; Private scholarships; SEOG; State scholarships/grants. *Loans:* Direct PLUS loans; Direct Subsidized Stafford Loans; Direct Unsubsidized Stafford Loans. **Student Employment:** Federal Work-Study Program available. Institutional employment available. **Financial Aid Statistics:** 40% needy freshmen, 69% needy undergrads receive need-based scholarship or grant aid. 70% freshmen, 10% undergrads receive non-need-based scholarship or grant aid. 20% freshmen, 62% undergrads receive need-based self-help aid. 0% freshmen, 0% undergrads receive athletic scholarships. **Criteria awarding aid:** *Need-based:* Academics. *Non-need-based:* Academics.

UNIVERSITY OF HOUSTON

Office of Admissions, Houston, TX 77204-2023
Phone: 713-743-1010 **Financial Aid Phone:** 713-743-1010
E-mail: admissions@uh.edu **CEEB Code:** 6870
Fax: 713-743-7542 **Website:** www.uh.edu **ACT Code:** 4236

This public school was founded in 1927. It has a 594 acre campus.

RATINGS

Admissions Selectivity Rating: 86 **Fire Safety Rating:** 96 **Green Rating:** 88

STUDENTS AND FACULTY

Enrollment: 37,689. **Student Body:** 50% female, 50% male, 2% out-of-state, 4% international (106 countries represented). Asian 23%, African American 10%, Caucasian 22%, Hispanic 36%, Native American <1%, Pacific Islander <1%, Two or more races 3%, Race unknown 2%. **Retention and Graduation:** 85% freshmen return for sophomore year. 32% freshmen graduate within 4 years. 61% freshmen graduate within 6 years. **Faculty:** Student/faculty ratio 23:1. 1,533 full-time faculty, 88% hold PhDs, 33% are members of minority groups, 42% are women. 1% of classes are taught by teaching assistants.

ACADEMICS

Degrees: Bachelor's; Doctoral degree—professional practice; Doctoral degree research/scholarship; Master's. **Classes:** Most classes have 20–29 students. Most lab/discussion sessions have 20–29 students. **Most popular majors:** Biology/Biological Sciences, General; Psychology, General; Business Administration and Management, General. **Special Study Options:** Accelerated program; Cooperative education program; Cross-registration; Distance learning; Double major; Dual enrollment; English as a Second Language (ESL); Exchange student program (domestic); Honors program; Independent study; Internships; Student-designed major; Study abroad; Teacher certification program; Weekend college. **Honors programs:** The Honors College at the University of Houston is a nationally recognized, intellectually stimulating learning community. As a vibrant, leading presence within the University, the Honors College attracts highly talented and motivated students and educators to a collegial environment where tradition is honored and possibilities are both created and realized. **Disability Services offered:** Note-taking services; Reader services; Tape recorders. **Career services:** Alumni network; Alumni services; Career assessment; Career/job search classes; Internships.

FACILITIES

Housing: Apartments for single students; Coed dorms; Fraternity/sorority housing; Special housing for disabled students; Theme housing; Wellness housing; 98% of campus accessible to physically disabled. **Special Academic Facilities/Equipment:** Blaffer Art gallery; University Hilton (the coffee shop and cafe staffed by students in College of Hotel and Restaurant Management); Moores School of Music Opera House; Alley Theatre.

CAMPUS LIFE

Environment: Metropolis. **Activities:** Campus Ministries; Choral groups; Concert band; Dance; Drama/theater; International Student Organization; Jazz band; Literary magazine; Marching band; Music ensembles; Musical theater; Opera; Pep band; Radio station; Student government; Student newspaper; Student-run film society; Symphony orchestra; Television station; Yearbook. 491 registered organizations, 28 honor societies, 57 religious organizations, 22 fraternities, 18 sororities on campus. **Athletics (Intercollegiate):** *Men:* baseball, basketball, cross-country, football, golf, track/field (outdoor), track/field (indoor). *Women:* basketball, cross-country, diving, soccer, softball, swimming, tennis, track/field (outdoor), track/field (indoor), volleyball. **On-Campus Highlights:** Student Center. **Environmental Initiatives:** Education of the campus community through communications, events, and campus as a living laboratory: One of the main goals of our sustainability program is to create a culture of sustainability on campus. The Office of Sustainability hosts numerous events throughout the year to show members of the campus community what resources and behaviors they can utilize to become more sustainable in their everyday lives. These include theme speakers, documentary screenings, workshops, competitions and Sustainability Fest, our largest annual event that features over 30 sustainability-themed community and campus organizations and departments. The festival attracts hundreds of attendees, who get to explore all the resources and opportunities offered by a wide range of exhibitors. Additionally, the Office of Sustainability works with the Auxiliary Services marketing team to publish university press releases and share various articles and events via social media, as well as through a monthly newsletter that is sent to over 2,000 subscribers. Lastly, several parts of the campus serve as a living laboratory for students and researchers. Our pocket prairie, known as Shasta's Prairie, was established in May 2016. It serves as a habitat for pollinators and native grass species, as well as a study site for students in the biology and ecology programs at The University.

ADMISSIONS

Freshman Academic Profile: Average high school GPA 3.7. 32% in top 10% of high school class, 64% in top 25% of high school class, 88% in top 50% of high school class. 94% from public high schools. **Test Scores:** SAT Math middle 50% range 570–660. SAT EBRW middle 50% range 570–650. ACT middle 50% range 22–27. **Basis for Candidate Selection:** *Very important factors include:* rigor of secondary school record, class rank, academic GPA, standardized test scores. *Other factors include:* application essay, recommendation(s), extracurricular activities, talent/ability, first generation, volunteer work, work experience. **Freshman Admission Requirements:** High school diploma is required and GED is accepted. *Academic units required:* 4 English, 3 math, 3 science, 2 science labs, 3 social studies. *Academic units recommended:* 4 math, 4 science, 2 foreign language, 1 history, 1 visual/performing arts. **Freshman Admission Statistics:** 25,393 applied, 65% admitted, 34% enrolled. **Transfer Admission Requirements:** College transcript(s). Minimum college GPA of 2.0 required. Lowest grade transferable C-. **General Admission Information:** Application fee $75. Priority deadline 11/15. Regular application deadline 6/1. Non-fall registration accepted.

COSTS AND FINANCIAL AID

Annual in-state tuition $10,274. Annual out-of-state tuition $25,934. Room and board $9,368. Required fees $1,002. Average book and supplies expense $1,338. **Required Forms and Deadlines:** FAFSA. **Notification of Awards:** Applicants will be notified of awards on a rolling basis beginning 2/1. **Types of Aid:** *Need-based scholarships/grants:* College/university scholarship or grant aid from institutional funds; Federal Pell; Private scholarships; SEOG; State scholarships/grants. *Loans:* Direct PLUS loans; Direct Subsidized Stafford Loans; Direct Unsubsidized Stafford Loans. **Student Employment:** Federal Work-Study Program available. Institutional employment available. **Financial Aid Statistics:** 88% needy freshmen, 84% needy undergrads receive need-based scholarship or grant aid. 4% freshmen, 3% undergrads receive non-need-based scholarship or grant aid. 49% freshmen, 53% undergrads receive need-based self-help aid. 0% freshmen, 0% undergrads receive athletic scholarships. 83% freshmen, 77% undergrads receive any aid. 44% undergrads borrow to pay for school. Average cumulative indebtedness $22,858. **Criteria awarding aid:** *Need-based:* Academics, Leadership. *Non-need-based:* Academics, Alumni affiliation, Art, Athletics, Job skills, Leadership, Music/drama, State/district residency.

UNIVERSITY OF HOUSTON—CLEAR LAKE

2700 Bay Area Boulevard, Houston, TX 77058-1098
Phone: 281-283-2500 **Financial Aid Phone:** 281-283-2480
E-mail: admissions@uhcl.edu **CEEB Code:** 6916
Fax: 281-283-2522 **Website:** https://www.uhcl.edu **ACT Code:** 4171

This public school was founded in 1974. It has a 524 acre campus.

RATINGS

Admissions Selectivity Rating: 60* **Fire Safety Rating:** 60* **Green Rating:** 60*

STUDENTS AND FACULTY

Enrollment: 4,689. **Student Body:** 68% female, 32% male, 0% out-of-state, 2% international (45 countries represented). Asian 6%, African American 9%, Caucasian 49%, Hispanic 32%, Native American <1%, Pacific Islander <1%, Two or more races <1%, Race unknown 1%.
Faculty: Student/faculty ratio 17:1. 247 full-time faculty, 86% hold PhDs, 27% are members of minority groups, 46% are women.

ACADEMICS

Degrees: Bachelor's; Certificate; Master's; Post-bachelor's certificate; Post-master's certificate. **Most popular majors:** Accounting; Multi-/Interdisciplinary Studies, Other; Psychology, General. **Special Study Options:** Cooperative education program; Distance learning; Double major; Dual enrollment; English as a Second Language (ESL); Independent study; Internships; Study abroad; Teacher certification program; Weekend college. **Disability Services offered:** Note-taking services; Reader services; Tape recorders; Tutors. **Career services:** Alumni network; Alumni services; Career assessment; Career/job search classes; Internships.

FACILITIES

Housing: 100% of campus accessible to physically disabled. **Special Academic Facilities/Equipment:** Student Art Gallery; Fitness Center/Fitness Zone.

CAMPUS LIFE

Environment: Metropolis. **Activities:** International Student Organization; Literary magazine; Student government; Student newspaper; Student-run film society. 73 registered organizations, 8 honor societies, 5 religious organizations on campus. **On-Campus Highlights:** Student Serivce Building.

ADMISSIONS

Freshman Admission Requirements: High school diploma is required and GED is accepted. **Transfer Admission Requirements:** College transcript(s), standardized test scores, statement of good standing from prior institution(s). Minimum college GPA of 2.0 required. Lowest grade transferable D-. **General Admission Information:** Application fee $45. Regular application deadline 6/1. Non-fall registration accepted. Admission may be deferred for a maximum of 1 year.

COSTS AND FINANCIAL AID

Annual in-state tuition $5,142. Annual out-of-state tuition $16,992. **Types of Aid:** *Need-based scholarships/grants:* College/university scholarship or grant aid from institutional funds; Federal Pell; SEOG; State scholarships/grants. *Loans:*

Direct PLUS loans; Direct Subsidized Stafford Loans; Direct Unsubsidized Stafford Loans. **Student Employment:** Federal Work-Study Program available. Institutional employment available. **Financial Aid Statistics:** 41% undergrads receive any aid. **Criteria awarding aid:** *Need-based:* Academics, Art, Leadership, Minority status.

UNIVERSITY OF HOUSTON—DOWNTOWN

One Main Street, Office of Admissions, Houston, TX 77002-1001
Phone: 713-221-8522 **Financial Aid Phone:** 713-221-8041
E-mail: uhdadmit@uhd.edu **CEEB Code:** 3612
Fax: 713-221-8522 **Website:** www.uhd.edu **ACT Code:** 4170

This public school was founded in 1974. It has a 24 acre campus.

RATINGS

Admissions Selectivity Rating: 75 **Fire Safety Rating:** 60* **Green Rating:** 60*

STUDENTS AND FACULTY

Enrollment: 12,313. **Student Body:** 61% female, 39% male, 1% out-of-state, 5% international (65 countries represented). Asian 9%, African American 20%, Caucasian 16%, Hispanic 48%, Native American <1%, Pacific Islander <1%, Two or more races 1%, Race unknown 1%.
Retention and Graduation: 72% freshmen return for sophomore year. 3% freshmen graduate within 4 years. **Faculty:** Student/faculty ratio 19:1. 376 full-time faculty, 84% hold PhDs, 39% are members of minority groups, 47% are women. 0% of classes are taught by teaching assistants.

ACADEMICS

Degrees: Bachelor's; Master's; Post-bachelor's certificate. **Classes:** Most classes have 20–29 students. Most lab/discussion sessions have 10–19 students. **Most popular majors:** Accounting; Multi-/Interdisciplinary Studies, Other; Psychology, General. **Special Study Options:** Distance learning; Double major; Dual enrollment; English as a Second Language (ESL); Honors program; Independent study; Internships; Study abroad; Teacher certification program; Weekend college. **Honors programs:** The UHD Scholars Academy promotes scholarship and student success for students in the Science, Technology, Engineering and Mathematics (STEM) fields. The Academy supports 160 students annually through scholarships, mentoring, and broadening experiences student success components. The program addresses UHD's commitment to increase the number of underrepresented graduating with STEM degrees and increasing advancement qualifications and preparation into graduate/professional degrees and the STEM workforce. About 39% of the 500+ alumni from the Academy have pursued advanced degrees. 91% remain in STEM after graduation in roles involving graduate/professional schools/programs or in the workforce. **Disability Services offered:** Note-taking services; Tape recorders; Tutors. **Career services:** Alumni services; Career assessment; Career/job search classes; Internships.

FACILITIES

95% of campus accessible to physically disabled. **Special Academic Facilities/Equipment:** O'Kane Gallery.

CAMPUS LIFE

Environment: Metropolis. **Activities:** Campus Ministries; Drama/theater; International Student Organization; Jazz band; Literary magazine; Model UN; Student government; Student newspaper. 63 registered organizations, 12 honor societies, 3 religious organizations, 4 fraternities, 6 sororities on campus. **Athletics (Intercollegiate):** *Men:* badminton, basketball, bowling, football, soccer, softball, tennis, volleyball, weight lifting. *Women:* badminton, basketball, bowling, soccer, softball, tennis, volleyball, weight lifting. **On-Campus Highlights:** 40,000 Windows Café.

ADMISSIONS

Freshman Academic Profile: 6% in top 10% of high school class, 32% in top 25% of high school class, 76% in top 50% of high school class. 86% from public high schools. **Test Scores:** SAT Math middle 50% range 460–540. SAT EBRW middle 50% range 460–538. ACT middle 50% range 17–21. **Basis for Candidate Selection:** *Very important factors include:* class rank, academic GPA, standardized test scores. *Important factors include:* rigor of secondary school record. **Freshman Admission Requirements:** High school diploma is required and GED is accepted. *Academic units required:* 4 English, 4 math, 4 science, 2 foreign language, 2 social studies, 2 history, 5.5 academic electives, 1 visual/performing arts, 1.5 unit from above areas or other academic areas. **Freshman**

Admission Statistics: 3,931 applied, 84% admitted, 29% enrolled. **Transfer Admission Requirements:** College transcript(s). Lowest grade transferable C. **General Admission Information:** Application fee $50. Regular application deadline 7/1. Non-fall registration accepted.

COSTS AND FINANCIAL AID
Annual in-state tuition $18,315. Annual out-of-state tuition $18,315. Required fees $1,166. **Required Forms and Deadlines:** FAFSA. **Types of Aid:** *Need-based scholarships/grants:* College/university scholarship or grant aid from institutional funds; Federal Pell; Private scholarships; SEOG; State scholarships/grants. *Loans:* Direct PLUS loans; Direct Subsidized Stafford Loans; Direct Unsubsidized Stafford Loans. **Student Employment:** Federal Work-Study Program available. Institutional employment available. **Financial Aid Statistics:** 81% needy freshmen, 75% needy undergrads receive need-based scholarship or grant aid. 0% freshmen, 0% undergrads receive non-need-based scholarship or grant aid. 26% freshmen, 53% undergrads receive need-based self-help aid. 0% freshmen, 0% undergrads receive athletic scholarships. 81% freshmen, 78% undergrads receive any aid. 53% undergrads borrow to pay for school. Average cumulative indebtedness $25,747. **Criteria awarding aid:** *Need-based:* Academics, Leadership. *Non-need-based:* Leadership.

UNIVERSITY OF HOUSTON—VICTORIA

Admissions and Records, Victoria, TX 77901-4450
Phone: 361-570-4110 **Financial Aid Phone:** 316-570-4131
E-mail: admissions@uhv.edu
Fax: 361-580-5500 **Website:** www.uhv.edu **ACT Code:** 4255

This public school was founded in 1973.

RATINGS
Admissions Selectivity Rating: 80   **Fire Safety Rating:** 60*   **Green Rating:** 60*

STUDENTS AND FACULTY
Enrollment: 2,991. **Student Body:** 66% female, 34% male, 2% international (39 countries represented). Asian 8%, African American 16%, Caucasian 37%, Hispanic 34%, Native American <1%, Pacific Islander <1%, Two or more races 2%, Race unknown 1%.
Retention and Graduation: 55% freshmen return for sophomore year.
Faculty: Student/faculty ratio 18:1. 136 full-time faculty, 87% hold PhDs, 32% are members of minority groups, 49% are women. 0% of classes are taught by teaching assistants.

ACADEMICS
Degrees: Bachelor's; Master's; Post-bachelor's certificate; Post-master's certificate. **Classes:** Most classes have 20–29 students. **Most popular majors:** Education, General; Business/Commerce, General; Multi-/Interdisciplinary Studies, Other. **Special Study Options:** Accelerated program; Distance learning; Double major; Dual enrollment; Independent study; Internships; Study abroad; Teacher certification program. **Disability Services offered:** Note-taking services; Tutors. **Career services:** Alumni services; Career assessment; Career/job search classes; Internships.

FACILITIES
Housing: Coed dorms; 100% of campus accessible to physically disabled. **Campus network:** 100% of classrooms, 100% of dorms, 100% of student union, 100% of libraries, 100% of dining areas, 75% of common outdoor areas have wireless network access.

CAMPUS LIFE
Environment: City. **Activities:** International Student Organization; Literary magazine; Student government. 24 registered organizations on campus. **Athletics (Intercollegiate):** *Men:* baseball. *Women:* softball. **On-Campus Highlights:** Jaguar Village.

ADMISSIONS
Test Scores: SAT Math middle 50% range 390–480. SAT EBRW middle 50% range 380–460. ACT middle 50% range 15–19. **Basis for Candidate Selection:** *Very important factors include:* rigor of secondary school record. *Important factors include:* class rank, academic GPA, standardized test scores. *Other factors include:* application essay, recommendation(s), interview, extracurricular activities, talent/ability, character/personal qualities, first generation, alumni/ae relation, geographical residence, state residency, level of applicant's interest. **Freshman Admission Requirements:** High school diploma is required and GED is accepted. **Freshman Admission Statistics:** 3,950

applied, 56% admitted, 16% enrolled. **Transfer Admission Requirements:** College transcript(s), standardized test scores. Minimum college GPA of 2.0 required. Lowest grade transferable C. **General Admission Information:** Non-fall registration accepted.

COSTS AND FINANCIAL AID
Annual in-state tuition $9,632. Annual out-of-state tuition $19,264. Room and board $7,853. Required fees $1,567. Average book and supplies expense $1,129. **Required Forms and Deadlines:** FAFSA; Institution's own financial aid form. **Notification of Awards:** Applicants will be notified of awards on a rolling basis beginning 3/30. **Types of Aid:** *Need-based scholarships/grants:* College/university scholarship or grant aid from institutional funds; Federal Pell; Private scholarships; SEOG; State scholarships/grants. *Loans:* Direct PLUS loans; Direct Subsidized Stafford Loans; Direct Unsubsidized Stafford Loans. **Student Employment:** Federal Work-Study Program available. Institutional employment available. **Financial Aid Statistics:** 73% undergrads receive any aid. **Criteria awarding aid:** *Need-based:* Academics. *Non-need-based:* Academics, Athletics, Leadership, State/district residency.

UNIVERSITY OF IDAHO

UI Admissions Office, Moscow, ID 83844-4264
Phone: (208) 885-6326 **Financial Aid Phone:** 208-885-6312
E-mail: admappl@uidaho.edu **CEEB Code:** 4843
Fax: (208) 885-9119 **Website:** http://www.uidaho.edu/ **ACT Code:** 928

This public school was founded in 1889. It has a 810 acre campus.

RATINGS
Admissions Selectivity Rating: 78   **Fire Safety Rating:** 89   **Green Rating:** 97

STUDENTS AND FACULTY
Enrollment: 7,227. **Student Body:** 49% female, 51% male, 23% out-of-state, 4% international (45 countries represented). Asian 2%, African American 1%, Caucasian 75%, Hispanic 11%, Native American 1%, Pacific Islander <1%, Two or more races 4%, Race unknown 2%.
Retention and Graduation: 77% freshmen return for sophomore year. 35% freshmen graduate within 4 years. 56 11% grads go on to further study within 1 year. **Faculty:** Student/faculty ratio 16:1. 587 full-time faculty, 88% hold PhDs, 15% are members of minority groups, 36% are women. 8% of classes are taught by teaching assistants.

ACADEMICS
Degrees: Bachelor's; Certificate; Doctoral degree—professional practice; Doctoral degree research/scholarship; Master's; Post-bachelor's certificate; Post-master's certificate. **Classes:** Most classes have 10–19 students. Most lab/discussion sessions have 10–19 students. **Most popular majors:** Mechanical Engineering; Psychology, General; Marketing/Marketing Management, General. **Special Study Options:** Accelerated program; Cooperative education program; Cross-registration; Distance learning; Double major; Dual enrollment; English as a Second Language (ESL); Exchange student program (domestic); Honors program; Independent study; Internships; Study abroad; Teacher certification program. **Honors programs:** Established in 1983, the University Honors Program offers a stimulating course of study and the advantages of an enriched learning community for over 500 students from all colleges and majors. The UHP's diverse curriculum, including special topic courses and innovative seminars, serves a variety of needs and interests. Beyond the classroom, the program's extracurricular opportunities include concerts, plays, films, lectures, and other off-campus excursions that foster cultural enrichment, friendship, and learning. Honors classes offer opportunities to explore subjects and methods in significant depth—students find that their education and their academic performance are enhanced by strong mentoring relationships with faculty devoted to enabling each student to fulfill his or her potential, and by the lively, participation-based modes of learning in small classes. Lower-division honors core courses enable students to learn with their peers in small classes taught by honors faculty. Moreover, each year the program offers innovative upper-division seminars, with each class limited to fifteen students. Honors students are frequently interested in and encouraged to apply for exchanges to other American universities or to universities abroad. As part of a dynamic,

broad-based education, members are also encouraged to participate in domestic or international exchange programs, and to take advantage of opportunities to engage in laboratory or field-based research programs as well as internships and other forms of cooperative education. **Combined degree programs:** BA/MA. **Disability Services offered:** Note-taking services; Reader services; Tape recorders; Tutors. **Career services:** Alumni network; Alumni services; Career assessment; Career/job search classes; Internships; Regional alumni.

FACILITIES

Housing: Apartments for married students; Apartments for single students; Coed dorms; Cooperative housing; Fraternity/sorority housing; Men's dorms; Special housing for disabled students; Special housing for international students; Theme housing; Women's dorms; 87% of campus accessible to physically disabled. **Special Academic Facilities/Equipment:** Arboretum & Botanical Garden, Integrated Research and Innovation Center (IRIC), Lionel Hampton International Jazz Collection, experimental forest, Optical Imaging Center, electron microscope, 3D Modeling (CAVE) Technology, Anechoic chamber, on-campus preschool.

CAMPUS LIFE

Environment: Town. **Activities:** Campus Ministries; Choral groups; Concert band; Dance; Drama/theater; International Student Organization; Jazz band; Literary magazine; Marching band; Model UN; Music ensembles; Musical theater; Opera; Pep band; Radio station; Student government; Student newspaper; Student-run film society; Symphony orchestra; Television station. 200 registered organizations, 10 honor societies, 9 religious organizations, 18 fraternities, 10 sororities on campus. **Athletics (Intercollegiate):** *Men:* basketball, cross-country, football, golf, track/field (outdoor), track/field (indoor). *Women:* basketball, cross-country, golf, soccer, swimming, track/field (outdoor), track/field (indoor), volleyball. **On-Campus Highlights:** Idaho Commons -common areas, food and meeting rooms.

ADMISSIONS

Freshman Academic Profile: Average high school GPA 3.5. 18% in top 10% of high school class, 44% in top 25% of high school class, 75% in top 50% of high school class. **Test Scores:** SAT Math middle 50% range 500–610. SAT EBRW middle 50% range 510–630. ACT middle 50% range 20–27. **Basis for Candidate Selection:** *Very important factors include:* academic GPA, standardized test scores. **Freshman Admission Requirements:** High school diploma is required and GED is accepted. *Academic units required:* 4 English, 3 math, 3 science, 1 science labs, 2.5 social studies, 1.5 academic electives, 1 unit from above areas or other academic areas. **Freshman Admission Statistics:** 8,071 applied, 78% admitted, 24% enrolled. **Transfer Admission Requirements:** College transcript(s). Minimum college GPA of 2.0 required. Lowest grade transferable D. **General Admission Information:** Application fee $60. Priority deadline 2/15. Regular application deadline 8/1. Non-fall registration accepted. Admission may be deferred for a maximum of 4 years.

COSTS AND FINANCIAL AID

Annual in-state tuition $6,182. Annual out-of-state tuition $25,418. Room and board $9,080. Required fees $2,122. Average book and supplies expense $1,130. **Required Forms and Deadlines:** FAFSA. **Notification of Awards:** Applicants will be notified of awards on a rolling basis beginning 12/20. **Types of Aid:** *Need-based scholarships/grants:* College/university scholarship or grant aid from institutional funds; Federal Pell; Private scholarships; SEOG; State scholarships/grants. *Loans:* Direct PLUS loans; Direct Subsidized Stafford Loans; Direct Unsubsidized Stafford Loans. **Student Employment:** Federal Work-Study Program available. Institutional employment available. **Financial Aid Statistics:** 57% needy freshmen, 65% needy undergrads receive need-based scholarship or grant aid. 81% freshmen, 67% undergrads receive non-need-based scholarship or grant aid. 68% freshmen, 70% undergrads receive need-based self-help aid. 4% freshmen, 4% undergrads receive athletic scholarships. 93% freshmen, 81% undergrads receive any aid. 61% undergrads borrow to pay for school. Average cumulative indebtedness $23,105. **Criteria awarding aid:** *Need-based:* Academics. *Non-need-based:* Academics, Alumni affiliation, Art, Athletics, Leadership, Minority status, Music/drama, State/district residency.

UNIVERSITY OF ILLINOIS—CHICAGO

Suite 100, SSB, 1200 W. Harrison St., Chicago, IL 60607-7161
Phone: 312-996-4350 **Financial Aid Phone:** 312-996-5563
E-mail: uicadmit@uic.edu **CEEB Code:** 1851
Fax: 312-413-7628 **Website:** http://www.uic.edu **ACT Code:** 1155

This public school was founded in 1982. It has a 240 acre campus.

RATINGS

Admissions Selectivity Rating: 81   **Fire Safety Rating:** 98   **Green Rating:** 91

STUDENTS AND FACULTY

Enrollment: 19,204. **Student Body:** 51% female, 49% male, 3% out-of-state, 4% international (65 countries represented). Asian 24%, African American 0%, Caucasian 33%, Hispanic 36%, Native American <1%, Pacific Islander <1%, Two or more races 3%, Race unknown 1%.
Retention and Graduation: 80% freshmen return for sophomore year. 30% freshmen graduate within 4 years. 57% freshmen graduate within 6 years. **Faculty:** Student/faculty ratio 17:1. 1,200 full-time faculty, 88% hold PhDs, 25% are members of minority groups, 48% are women.

ACADEMICS

Degrees: Bachelor's; Doctoral degree—professional practice; Doctoral degree research/scholarship; Master's; Post-bachelor's certificate; Post-master's certificate. **Classes:** Most classes have 20–29 students. Most lab/discussion sessions have 20–29 students. **Special Study Options:** Accelerated program; Cooperative education program; Cross-registration; Distance learning; Double major; Dual enrollment; Honors program; Independent study; Internships; Student-designed major; Study abroad; Teacher certification program. **Honors programs:** Guaranteed Preferred Program Admission Honors College. President Award Program "PAP" and President Award Program Honors. **Combined degree programs:** BA/DDS; BA/MD. **Disability Services offered:** Note-taking services; Tutors. **Career services:** Alumni network; Alumni services; Career assessment; Career/job search classes; Internships; Regional alumni.

FACILITIES

Housing: Apartments for married students; Apartments for single students; Coed dorms; Special housing for disabled students; Special housing for international students; Theme housing; 80% of campus accessible to physically disabled. **Special Academic Facilities/Equipment:** Jane Addams Hull House Museum; Richard J. Daley Library.

CAMPUS LIFE

Environment: Metropolis. **Activities:** Campus Ministries; Choral groups; Concert band; Dance; Drama/theater; International Student Organization; Jazz band; Literary magazine; Music ensembles; Musical theater; Pep band; Radio station; Student government; Student newspaper. 287 registered organizations, 23 honor societies, 19 religious organizations, 16 fraternities, 15 sororities on campus. **Athletics (Intercollegiate):** *Men:* baseball, basketball, cross-country, diving, gymnastics, soccer, swimming, tennis, track/field (outdoor). *Women:* basketball, cross-country, diving, gymnastics, softball, swimming, tennis, track/field (outdoor), volleyball. **On-Campus Highlights:** Student Center East. **Environmental Initiatives:** Establishment of Office of Sustainability.

ADMISSIONS

Freshman Academic Profile: Average high school GPA 3.3. 25% in top 10% of high school class, 58% in top 25% of high school class, 89% in top 50% of high school class. 76% from public high schools. **Test Scores:** SAT Math middle 50% range 550–680. SAT EBRW middle 50% range 530–650. ACT middle 50% range 20–26. **Basis for Candidate Selection:** *Very important factors include:* rigor of secondary school record, class rank, academic GPA, standardized test scores. *Important factors include:* application essay, *Other factors include:* recommendation(s), extracurricular activities, level of applicant's interest. **Freshman Admission Requirements:** High school diploma is required and GED is accepted. *Academic units required:* 4 English, 3 math, 3 science, 2 foreign language, 3 social studies. *Academic units recommended:* 4 math. **Freshman Admission Statistics:** 18,768 applied, 77% admitted, 28% enrolled. **Transfer Admission Requirements:** College transcript(s). Minimum college GPA of 2.5 required. **General Admission Information:** Application fee $50. Regular application deadline 1/15.

COSTS AND FINANCIAL AID

Annual in-state tuition $10,584. Annual out-of-state tuition $23,440. Room and board $10,960. Required fees $3,120. Average book and supplies expense $1,400. **Required Forms and Deadlines:** FAFSA. **Notification of Awards:**

Applicants will be notified of awards on a rolling basis beginning 3/15. **Types of Aid:** *Need-based scholarships/grants:* College/university scholarship or grant aid from institutional funds; Federal Pell; Private scholarships; SEOG; State scholarships/grants. *Loans:* Direct PLUS loans; Direct Subsidized Stafford Loans; Direct Unsubsidized Stafford Loans. **Student Employment:** Federal Work-Study Program available. Institutional employment available. **Financial Aid Statistics:** 83% needy freshmen, 82% needy undergrads receive need-based scholarship or grant aid. 3% freshmen, 2% undergrads receive non-need-based scholarship or grant aid. 71% freshmen, 79% undergrads receive need-based self-help aid. 0% freshmen, 1% undergrads receive athletic scholarships. 61% freshmen, 61% undergrads receive any aid. 63% undergrads borrow to pay for school. Average cumulative indebtedness $23,076. **Criteria awarding aid:** *Need-based:* Music/drama. *Non-need-based:* Academics, Art, Athletics.

UNIVERSITY OF ILLINOIS—SPRINGFIELD

One University Plaza, Springfield, IL 62703-5407
Phone: 217-206-4847 **Financial Aid Phone:** 217-206-6724
E-mail: admissions@uis.edu **CEEB Code:** 834
Fax: 217-206-6620 **Website:** www.uis.edu **ACT Code:** 1137

This public school was founded in 1969. It has a 746 acre campus.

RATINGS
Admissions Selectivity Rating: 88   **Fire Safety Rating:** 90   **Green Rating:** 96

STUDENTS AND FACULTY
Enrollment: 2,613. **Student Body:** 51% female, 49% male, 12% out-of-state, 3% international (25 countries represented). Asian 4%, African American 15%, Caucasian 63%, Hispanic 11%, Native American <1%, Pacific Islander <1%, Two or more races 4%, Race unknown 1%.
Retention and Graduation: 79% freshmen return for sophomore year. 42% freshmen graduate within 4 years. % freshmen graduate within 6 years. **Faculty:** Student/faculty ratio 13:1. 206 full-time faculty, 84% hold PhDs, 9% are members of minority groups, 45% are women.

ACADEMICS
Degrees: Bachelor's; Doctoral degree research/scholarship; Master's; Post-bachelor's certificate; Post-master's certificate. **Classes:** Most classes have 10–19 students. Most lab/discussion sessions have 10–19 students. **Most popular majors:** Computer Science; Business Administration and Management, General; Psychology, General. **Special Study Options:** Distance learning; English as a Second Language (ESL); Honors program; Independent study; Internships; Study abroad; Teacher certification program. **Honors programs:** Interdisciplinary four-year baccalaureate experience for highly qualified freshman. **Disability Services offered:** Note-taking services; Reader services; Tape recorders. **Career services:** Alumni network; Alumni services; Career assessment; Career/job search classes; Internships; Regional alumni.

FACILITIES
Housing: Apartments for married students; Apartments for single students; Coed dorms; Special housing for disabled students; Special housing for international students; Theme housing; Wellness housing; 99% of campus accessible to physically disabled. **Special Academic Facilities/Equipment:** Norris L. Brookens Library, Sangamon Auditorium, Observatory. **Campus network:** 100% of classrooms have wireless network access.

CAMPUS LIFE
Environment: City. **Activities:** Campus Ministries; Choral groups; Concert band; Dance; Drama/theater; International Student Organization; Jazz band; Model UN; Music ensembles; Pep band; Radio station; Student government; Student newspaper; Student-run film society. 85 registered organizations, 8 honor societies, 8 religious organizations, 6 fraternities, 5 sororities on campus. **Athletics (Intercollegiate):** *Men:* basketball, golf, soccer, tennis. *Women:* basketball, cheerleading, golf, soccer, softball, tennis, volleyball. **On-Campus Highlights:** Student Union. **Environmental Initiatives:** New student union is being designed to LEED Gold standards.

ADMISSIONS
Freshman Academic Profile: Average high school GPA 3.7. 21% in top 10% of high school class, 45% in top 25% of high school class, 82% in top 50% of high school class. 88% from public high schools. **Test Scores:** SAT Math middle 50% range 495–610. SAT EBRW middle 50% range 500–610. ACT middle 50% range 19–26. **Basis for Candidate Selection:** *Very important*

factors include: rigor of secondary school record, academic GPA, standardized test scores. *Important factors include:* class rank. *Other factors include:* application essay, recommendation(s), extracurricular activities, character/personal qualities, volunteer work, work experience, level of applicant's interest. **Freshman Admission Requirements:** High school diploma is required and GED is accepted. *Academic units required:* 4 English, 3 math, 3 science, 1 science labs, 2 foreign language, 3 social studies. *Academic units recommended:* 4 English, 4 math, 3 science, 1 science labs, 2 foreign language, 3 social studies, 3 history. **Freshman Admission Statistics:** 4,165 applied, 39% admitted, 23% enrolled. **Transfer Admission Requirements:** College transcript(s). Minimum college GPA of 2.0 required. Lowest grade transferable D. **General Admission Information:** Application fee $50. Priority deadline 5/1. Non-fall registration accepted. Admission may be deferred for a maximum of 1 year.

COSTS AND FINANCIAL AID
Annual in-state tuition $9,405. Annual out-of-state tuition $18,930. Room and board $11,660. Required fees $2,408. Average book and supplies expense $1,200. **Required Forms and Deadlines:** FAFSA. **Notification of Awards:** Applicants will be notified of awards on a rolling basis beginning 1/1. **Types of Aid:** *Need-based scholarships/grants:* College/university scholarship or grant aid from institutional funds; Federal Pell; Private scholarships; SEOG; State scholarships/grants. *Loans:* Direct PLUS loans; Direct Subsidized Stafford Loans; Direct Unsubsidized Stafford Loans. **Student Employment:** Federal Work-Study Program available. Institutional employment available. **Financial Aid Statistics:** 94% needy freshmen, 87% needy undergrads receive need-based scholarship or grant aid. 23% freshmen, 15% undergrads receive non-need-based scholarship or grant aid. 73% freshmen, 77% undergrads receive need-based self-help aid. 9% freshmen, 6% undergrads receive athletic scholarships. 81% freshmen, 71% undergrads receive any aid. 66% undergrads borrow to pay for school. Average cumulative indebtedness $22,248. **Criteria awarding aid:** *Need-based:* Academics, Alumni affiliation, Art, Athletics, Job skills, Leadership, Minority status, Music/drama. *Non-need-based:* Academics, Alumni affiliation, Art, Athletics, Job skills, Leadership, Minority status, Music/drama, State/district residency.

UNIVERSITY OF ILLINOIS—URBANA-CHAMPAIGN

901 West Illinois Street, Champaign, IL 61801-3028
Phone: 217-333-0302 **Financial Aid Phone:** 217-333-0100
E-mail: http://admissions.illinois.edu/contact_u **CEEB Code:** 4607
Fax: 217-244-4614 **Website:** illinois.edu **ACT Code:** 1154

This public school was founded in 1867. It has a 1783 acre campus.

RATINGS
Admissions Selectivity Rating: 89   **Fire Safety Rating:** 60*   **Green Rating:** 98

STUDENTS AND FACULTY
Enrollment: 32,884. **Student Body:** 46% female, 54% male, 14% out-of-state, 16% international (90 countries represented). Asian 18%, African American 6%, Caucasian 45%, Hispanic 11%, Native American <1%, Pacific Islander <1%, Two or more races 3%, Race unknown <1%.
Retention and Graduation: 92% freshmen return for sophomore year. 70% freshmen graduate within 4 years. 85% freshmen graduate within 6 years. **Faculty:** 1,930 full-time faculty, 93% hold PhDs, 27% are members of minority groups, 35% are women.

ACADEMICS
Degrees: Bachelor's; Certificate; Doctoral degree—professional practice; Doctoral degree research/scholarship; Master's; Post-bachelor's certificate; Post-master's certificate. **Classes:** Most classes have 10–19 students. Most lab/discussion sessions have 20–29 students. **Special Study Options:** Cooperative education program; Cross-registration; Distance learning; Double major; English as a Second Language (ESL); Honors program; Independent study; Internships; Student-designed major; Study abroad; Teacher certification program. **Honors programs:** http://admissions.illinois.edu/Discover/Academics/honors. **Disability Services offered:** Note-taking services; Reader services; Tape recorders; Tutors. **Career services:** Alumni network; Alumni services; Career assessment; Career/job search classes; Internships; Regional alumni.

FACILITIES

Housing: Apartments for married students; Coed dorms; Cooperative housing; Fraternity/sorority housing; Special housing for disabled students; Theme housing; Women's dorms; 100% of campus accessible to physically disabled. **Special Academic Facilities/Equipment:** Art, cultural and natural history museums, performing arts center, National Center for Supercomputing Applications, Beckman Institute, Siebel Computer Science Center, University Library (37 separate libraries and centers on campus), Japan House and Gardens, State Farm Center for large concerts, Allerton Park and Conference Center, Arboretum, and the Illini Student Union.

CAMPUS LIFE

Environment: City. **Activities:** Choral groups; Concert band; Dance; Drama/theater; International Student Organization; Jazz band; Literary magazine; Marching band; Music ensembles; Musical theater; Opera; Pep band; Radio station; Student government; Student newspaper; Student-run film society; Symphony orchestra; Television station; Yearbook. 1400 registered organizations on campus. **Athletics (Intercollegiate):** *Men:* baseball, basketball, cheerleading, cross-country, football, golf, gymnastics, tennis, track/field (outdoor), wrestling. *Women:* basketball, cheerleading, cross-country, diving, golf, gymnastics, soccer, softball, swimming, tennis, track/field (outdoor), volleyball. **Environmental Initiatives:** The state-of-the-art Business Instructional Facility at the University of Illinois has earned the world's highest honor for sustainable, environmentally friendly construction and design. The building is the first business facility at a public university anywhere in the world to earn platinum certification.

ADMISSIONS

Freshman Academic Profile: 49% in top 10% of high school class, 82% in top 25% of high school class, 99% in top 50% of high school class. **Test Scores:** SAT Math middle 50% range 700–790. SAT EBRW middle 50% range 580–690. ACT middle 50% range 26–32. **Basis for Candidate Selection:** *Very important factors include:* rigor of secondary school record, academic GPA. *Important factors include:* application essay, standardized test scores, extracurricular activities, talent/ability. *Other factors include:* class rank, character/personal qualities, first generation, geographical residence, state residency, racial/ethnic status, volunteer work, work experience. **Freshman Admission Requirements:** High school diploma is required and GED is accepted. *Academic units required:* 4 English, 3 math, 2 science, 2 science labs, 2 foreign language, 2 social studies, 2 academic electives. *Academic units recommended:* 4 English, 4 math, 4 science, 4 science labs, 4 foreign language, 4 social studies, 4 academic electives. **Freshman Admission Statistics:** 38,093 applied, 60% admitted, 33% enrolled. **Transfer Admission Requirements:** College transcript(s), essay or personal statement. Lowest grade transferable D. **General Admission Information:** Application fee $50. Priority deadline 11/1. Regular application deadline 12/1. Admission may be deferred for a maximum of 1 year.

COSTS AND FINANCIAL AID

Annual in-state tuition $12,036. Annual out-of-state tuition $28,156. Room and board $11,308. Required fees $3,832. Average book and supplies expense $1,200. **Required Forms and Deadlines:** FAFSA. **Notification of Awards:** Applicants will be notified of awards on a rolling basis beginning 3/10. **Types of Aid:** *Need-based scholarships/grants:* College/university scholarship or grant aid from institutional funds; Federal Pell; Private scholarships; SEOG; State scholarships/grants; United Negro College Fund. *Loans:* Direct PLUS loans; Direct Subsidized Stafford Loans; Direct Unsubsidized Stafford Loans. **Student Employment:** Federal Work-Study Program available. Institutional employment available. **Financial Aid Statistics:** 81% needy freshmen, 64% needy undergrads receive need-based scholarship or grant aid. 17% freshmen, 8% undergrads receive non-need-based scholarship or grant aid. 74% freshmen, 60% undergrads receive need-based self-help aid. 0% freshmen, 1% undergrads receive athletic scholarships. 47% undergrads borrow to pay for school. Average cumulative indebtedness $25,222. **Criteria awarding aid:** *Need-based:* Academics, Art, Athletics, Leadership, Minority status, Music/drama *Non-need-based:* Academics, Alumni affiliation, Art, Athletics, Leadership, Minority status, Music/drama, State/district residency.

1400 East Hanna Avenue, Indianapolis, IN 46227-3697
Phone: 317-788-3216 **Financial Aid Phone:** 317-788-3217
E-mail: admissions@uindy.edu **CEEB Code:** 1321
Fax: 317-788-3300 **Website:** www.uindy.edu **ACT Code:** 1204

This private school, affiliated with the Methodist Church, was founded in 1902. It has a 65 acre campus.

RATINGS

Admissions Selectivity Rating: 75   **Fire Safety Rating:** 72   **Green Rating:** 60*

STUDENTS AND FACULTY

Enrollment: 4,138. **Student Body:** 68% female, 32% male, 9% out-of-state, 5% international (47 countries represented). Asian 1%, African American 13%, Caucasian 73%, Hispanic 2%, Native American <1%, Pacific Islander <1%, Two or more races 2%, Race unknown 4%. **Retention and Graduation:** 74% freshmen return for sophomore year. **Faculty:** Student/faculty ratio 15:1. 218 full-time faculty, 76% hold PhDs, 6% are members of minority groups, 57% are women. 0% of classes are taught by teaching assistants.

ACADEMICS

Degrees: Associate; Bachelor's; Doctoral degree—professional practice; Doctoral degree research/scholarship; Master's. **Classes:** Most classes have 10–19 students. Most lab/discussion sessions have 20–29 students. **Most popular majors:** Business/Commerce, General; Registered Nursing/Registered Nurse; Psychology, General. **Special Study Options:** Accelerated program; Cross-registration; Distance learning; Double major; Dual enrollment; English as a Second Language (ESL); Honors program; Independent study; Internships; Liberal arts/career combination; Student-designed major; Study abroad; Teacher certification program. **Disability Services offered:** Note-taking services; Reader services; Tape recorders; Tutors. **Career services:** Internships; Regional alumni.

FACILITIES

Housing: Apartments for married students; Apartments for single students; Coed dorms; Women's dorms 90% of campus accessible to physically disabled. **Special Academic Facilities/Equipment:** Developmental preschool, art gallery, observatory.

CAMPUS LIFE

Environment: Metropolis. **Activities:** Campus Ministries; Choral groups; Concert band; Dance; Drama/theater; International Student Organization; Jazz band; Literary magazine; Music ensembles; Musical theater; Opera; Pep band; Radio station; Student government; Student newspaper; Television station; Yearbook. 53 registered organizations, 14 honor societies, 4 religious organizations on campus. **Athletics (Intercollegiate):** *Men:* baseball, basketball, cross-country, diving, football, golf, soccer, swimming, tennis, track/field (outdoor), wrestling. *Women:* basketball, cross-country, diving, golf, soccer, softball, swimming, tennis, track/field (outdoor), volleyball. **On-Campus Highlights:** Ruth Lilly Fitness Center.

ADMISSIONS

Freshman Academic Profile: Average high school GPA 3.4. 27% in top 10% of high school class, 56% in top 25% of high school class, 88% in top 50% of high school class. **Test Scores:** SAT Math middle 50% range 460–570. SAT EBRW middle 50% range 450–560. ACT middle 50% range 19–25. **Basis for Candidate Selection:** *Very important factors include:* rigor of secondary school record, academic GPA. *Important factors include:* standardized test scores. *Other factors include:* class rank, recommendation(s), interview, talent/ability. **Freshman Admission Requirements:** High school diploma is required and GED is accepted. *Academic units required:* 4 English, 3 math, 2 science, 1 science labs, 2 foreign language, 2 social studies, 1 history, 3 academic electives, 1 computer science, 2 visual/performing arts. *Academic units recommended:* 4 English, 3 math, 3 science, 2 science labs, 3 foreign language, 2 social studies, 1 history, 3 academic electives, 1 computer science, 2 visual/performing arts. **Freshman Admission Statistics:** 5,396 applied, 79% admitted, 19% enrolled. **Transfer Admission Requirements:** High school transcript, college transcript(s), standardized test scores, statement of good standing from prior institution(s). Minimum college GPA of 2.0 required. Lowest grade transferable C-. **General Admission Information:** Application fee $25. Regular application deadline 8/20. Non-fall registration accepted.

COSTS AND FINANCIAL AID

Annual tuition $23,590. Room and board $9,090. Required fees $240. Average book and supplies expense $1,076. **Required Forms and Deadlines:** FAFSA; Institution's own financial aid form. **Notification of Awards:** Applicants will be notified of awards on a rolling basis beginning 3/1. **Types of Aid:** *Need-based scholarships/grants:* College/university scholarship or grant aid from institutional funds; Federal Pell; Private scholarships; SEOG; State scholarships/grants. *Loans:* Direct PLUS loans; Direct Subsidized Stafford Loans; Direct Unsubsidized Stafford Loans. **Student Employment:** Federal Work-Study Program available. Institutional employment available. **Financial Aid Statistics:** 57% needy freshmen, 68% needy undergrads receive need-based scholarship or grant aid. 99% freshmen, 69% undergrads receive non-need-based scholarship or grant aid. 78% freshmen, 78% undergrads receive need-based self-help aid. 8% freshmen, 8% undergrads receive athletic scholarships. 99% freshmen, 98% undergrads receive any aid. **Criteria awarding aid:** *Non-need-based:* Academics, Alumni affiliation, Art, Athletics, Job skills, Music/drama, Religious affiliation, State/district residency.

UNIVERSITY OF IOWA

107 Calvin Hall, Iowa City, IA 52242
Phone: 319-335-3847 **Financial Aid Phone:** 319-335-1450
E-mail: admissions@uiowa.edu **CEEB Code:** 6681
Fax: 319-333-1535 **Website:** www.uiowa.edu **ACT Code:** 1356

This public school was founded in 1847. It has a 1700 acre campus.

RATINGS

Admissions Selectivity Rating: 82   **Fire Safety Rating:** 92   **Green Rating:** 91

STUDENTS AND FACULTY

Enrollment: 22,920. **Student Body:** 54% female, 46% male, 32% out-of-state, 5% international (59 countries represented). Asian 4%, African American 3%, Caucasian 74%, Hispanic 8%, Native American <1%, Pacific Islander <1%, Two or more races 3%, Race unknown 2%.
Retention and Graduation: 86% freshmen return for sophomore year. 54% freshmen graduate within 4 years. 72% freshmen graduate within 6 years.
Faculty: Student/faculty ratio 15:1. 1,454 full-time faculty, 89% hold PhDs, 19% are members of minority groups, 44% are women. 10% of classes are taught by teaching assistants.

ACADEMICS

Degrees: Bachelor's; Doctoral degree—professional practice; Doctoral degree research/scholarship; Master's; Post-bachelor's certificate; Post-master's certificate. **Classes:** Most classes have 10–19 students. Most lab/discussion sessions have 20–29 students. **Most popular majors:** Pre-Medicine/Pre-Medical Studies; Business/Commerce, General; Engineering, General. **Special Study Options:** Accelerated program; Cooperative education program; Distance learning; Double major; Dual enrollment; English as a Second Language (ESL); Exchange student program (domestic); External degree program; Honors program; Independent study; Internships; Liberal arts/career combination; Student-designed major; Study abroad; Teacher certification program. **Honors programs:** Honors Students enjoy ample opportunities for original research, cultural exploration, artistic invention, political action, community service, and more. Students can design their own programs of study, choose from a rich array of Iowa innovations, or learn almost any discipline in the world. To feed sparks from its students, Honors adds superb advisers, events, facilities, grants, and projects. **Combined degree programs:** BA/DDS; BA/MA; BA/MEng. **Disability Services offered:** Note-taking services; Reader services; Tape recorders; Tutors. **Career services:** Alumni services; Career assessment; Career/job search classes; Internships; Regional alumni.

FACILITIES

Housing: Apartments for married students; Apartments for single students; Coed dorms; Fraternity/sorority housing; Theme housing; Wellness housing; 99% of campus accessible to physically disabled. **Special Academic Facilities/Equipment:** National Advanced Driving Simulator, electron microscope, laser facility, Oakdale Research park, UI Hygienic Lab, UI Center for Biocatalysis & Bioprocessing, UI Research Foundation, survey research facilities, natural

history museum, Medical Museum, Old Capitol Museum, Main Library and 7 departmental libraries, information arcade, newspaper production lab, TV lab, UI Technology Innovation Center, Project Art, Fraternal Order of Eagles Diabetes Research Center, and Center for the Book. **Campus network:** 100% of classrooms, 100% of dorms, 100% of student union, 100% of libraries, 100% of dining areas, 100% of common outdoor areas have wireless network access.

CAMPUS LIFE

Environment: City. **Activities:** Campus Ministries; Choral groups; Concert band; Dance; Drama/theater; International Student Organization; Jazz band; Literary magazine; Marching band; Model UN; Music ensembles; Musical theater; Opera; Pep band; Radio station; Student government; Student newspaper; Student-run film society; Symphony orchestra; Television station. 500 registered organizations, 18 honor societies, 21 religious organization, 27 fraternities, 23 sororities on campus. **Athletics (Intercollegiate):** *Men:* baseball, basketball, cheerleading, cross-country, diving, football, golf, gymnastics, swimming, tennis, track/field (outdoor), track/field (indoor), wrestling. *Women:* basketball, cheerleading, crew/rowing, cross-country, diving, field hockey, golf, gymnastics, soccer, softball, swimming, tennis, track/field (outdoor), track/field (indoor), volleyball. **On-Campus Highlights:** Kinnick Stadium/Carver Hawkeye Arena. **Environmental Initiatives:** The University of Iowa has established seven 2020 Sustainability Targets that include goals for energy conservation, renewable energy, waste diversion, reduced carbon impact of transportation, increasing student opportunities to learn and practice sustainability principles, support sustainability research and develop partnerships to advance collaborative initiatives. The UI was the first certified Tree Campus in Iowa. The number of LEED-Accredited Professionals on staff in Facilities Management tripled to total 17.

ADMISSIONS

Freshman Academic Profile: Average high school GPA 3.8. 32% in top 10% of high school class, 63% in top 25% of high school class, 93% in top 50% of high school class. 90% from public high schools. **Test Scores:** SAT Math middle 50% range 570–680. SAT EBRW middle 50% range 560–660. ACT middle 50% range 22–29. **Basis for Candidate Selection:** *Very important factors include:* rigor of secondary school record, class rank, academic GPA, standardized test scores. *Other factors include:* recommendation(s), talent/ability, character/personal qualities, state residency. **Freshman Admission Requirements:** High school diploma is required and GED is accepted. *Academic units required:* 4 English, 3 math, 3 science, 2 foreign language, 3 social studies. *Academic units recommended:* 4 math. **Freshman Admission Statistics:** 25,928 applied, 83% admitted, 23% enrolled. **Transfer Admission Requirements:** High school transcript, college transcript(s). Minimum college GPA of 2.5 required. Lowest grade transferable D. **General Admission Information:** Application fee $40. Regular application deadline 5/1. Non-fall registration accepted. Admission may be deferred for a maximum of 1 year.

COSTS AND FINANCIAL AID

Annual in-state tuition $8,073. Annual out-of-state tuition $30,036. Room and board $11,400. Required fees $1,533. Average book and supplies expense $950. **Required Forms and Deadlines:** FAFSA. **Notification of Awards:** Applicants will be notified of awards on a rolling basis beginning 11/15. **Types of Aid:** *Need-based scholarships/grants:* College/university scholarship or grant aid from institutional funds; Federal Pell; Private scholarships; SEOG; State scholarships/grants. *Loans:* Direct PLUS loans; Direct Subsidized Stafford Loans; Direct Unsubsidized Stafford Loans. **Student Employment:** Federal Work-Study Program available. Institutional employment available. **Financial Aid Statistics:** 83% needy freshmen, 82% needy undergrads receive need-based scholarship or grant aid. 47% freshmen, 10% undergrads receive non-need-based scholarship or grant aid. 78% freshmen, 78% undergrads receive need-based self-help aid. 2% freshmen, 2% undergrads receive athletic scholarships. 91% freshmen, 78% undergrads receive any aid. 48% undergrads borrow to pay for school. Average cumulative indebtedness $28,328. **Criteria awarding aid:** *Need-based:* Academics. *Non-need-based:* Academics, Alumni affiliation, Art, Athletics, Leadership, Music/drama, State/district residency.

UNIVERSITY OF JAMESTOWN

6081 College Lane, Jamestown, ND 58405-0001
Phone: 701-252-3467 **Financial Aid Phone:** 701-252-3467
E-mail: admissions@uj.edu
Fax: 701-253-4318 **Website:** www.uj.edu **ACT Code:** 3200

This private school, affiliated with the Presbyterian Church, was founded in 1883. It has a 110 acre campus.

RATINGS
Admissions Selectivity Rating: 82   **Fire Safety Rating:** 89   **Green Rating:** 60*

STUDENTS AND FACULTY
Enrollment: 905. **Student Body:** 45% female, 55% male, 60% out-of-state, 9% international (20 countries represented). Asian 1%, African American 6%, Caucasian 72%, Hispanic 10%, Native American <1%, Pacific Islander 1%, Two or more races 3%, Race unknown 0%.
Retention and Graduation: 70% freshmen return for sophomore year. 30% freshmen graduate within 4 years. 45% freshmen graduate within 6 years. 19% grads go on to further study within 1 year. 5% grads pursue arts and sciences degrees. 1% grads pursue law degrees. 1% grads pursue business degrees. 8% grads pursue medical degrees. **Faculty:** Student/faculty ratio 10:1. 76 full-time faculty, 62% hold PhDs, 11% are members of minority groups, 53% are women. 0% of classes are taught by teaching assistants.

ACADEMICS
Degrees: Bachelor's; Doctoral degree—professional practice; Master's.
Classes: Most classes have 10–19 students. Most lab/discussion sessions have 10–19 students. **Most popular majors:** Elementary Education and Teaching; Registered Nursing/Registered Nurse; Business/Commerce, General. **Special Study Options:** Cooperative education program; Distance learning; Double major; Dual enrollment; Honors program; Independent study; Internships; Liberal arts/career combination; Student-designed major; Study abroad; Teacher certification program. **Honors programs:** Character and Leadership Program. The heart of the Character in Leadership program is its academic core. Each student who participates will receive a minor in leadership. University of Jamestown values its reputation for quality education and therefore is committed through its Character in Leadership Program to providing a broad and sound intellectual foundation that will enable its students to provide ethical leadership in an ever-changing world. **Disability Services offered:** Note-taking services; Reader services; Tape recorders; Tutors. **Career services:** Alumni network; Alumni services; Career assessment; Career/job search classes; Internships.

FACILITIES
Housing: Apartments for married students; Apartments for single students; Coed dorms; Special housing for disabled students; Wellness housing; 80% of campus accessible to physically disabled.

CAMPUS LIFE
Environment: Village. **Activities:** Campus Ministries; Choral groups; Concert band; Drama/theater; International Student Organization; Jazz band; Literary magazine; Music ensembles; Musical theater; Pep band; Student government; Student newspaper. 26 registered organizations, 5 honor societies, 2 religious organizations on campus. **Athletics (Intercollegiate):** *Men:* baseball, basketball, cross-country, football, golf, track/field (outdoor), track/field (indoor), wrestling. *Women:* basketball, cross-country, golf, soccer, softball, track/field (outdoor), track/field (indoor), volleyball, wrestling. **On-Campus Highlights:** Nafus Student Center—Java Hut.

ADMISSIONS
Freshman Academic Profile: Average high school GPA 3.4. 15% in top 10% of high school class, 35% in top 25% of high school class, 73% in top 50% of high school class. **Test Scores:** SAT Math middle 50% range 470–560. SAT EBRW middle 50% range 480–560. ACT middle 50% range 19–25.
Basis for Candidate Selection: *Very important factors include:* academic GPA, standardized test scores. *Important factors include:* rigor of secondary school record. *Other factors include:* class rank, application essay, recommendation(s), alumni/ae relation, level of applicant's interest. **Freshman Admission Requirements:** High school diploma is required and GED is accepted. *Academic units recommended:* 4 English, 3 math, 4 science, 2 foreign language, 3 social studies. **Freshman Admission Statistics:** 1,106 applied, 69% admitted, 34% enrolled. **Transfer Admission Requirements:** High school transcript, college transcript(s), statement of good standing from prior institution(s).

Minimum college GPA of 2.5 required. Lowest grade transferable C. **General Admission Information:** Priority deadline 5/1. Non-fall registration accepted.

COSTS AND FINANCIAL AID
Annual tuition $22,718. Room and board $8,316. Required fees $780. Average book and supplies expense $1,300. **Required Forms and Deadlines:** FAFSA. **Notification of Awards:** Applicants will be notified of awards on a rolling basis beginning 2/1. **Types of Aid:** *Need-based scholarships/grants:* Federal Pell; Private scholarships; SEOG; State scholarships/grants. *Loans:* Direct PLUS loans; Direct Subsidized Stafford Loans; Direct Unsubsidized Stafford Loans. **Student Employment:** Federal Work-Study Program available. Institutional employment available. **Financial Aid Statistics:** 100% needy freshmen, 100% needy undergrads receive need-based scholarship or grant aid. 27% freshmen, 22% undergrads receive non-need-based scholarship or grant aid. 71% freshmen, 76% undergrads receive need-based self-help aid. 33% freshmen, 30% undergrads receive athletic scholarships. 100% freshmen, 99% undergrads receive any aid. 62% undergrads borrow to pay for school. Average cumulative indebtedness $28,889. **Criteria awarding aid:** *Non-need-based:* Academics, Alumni affiliation, Art, Athletics, Job skills, Leadership, Music/drama, Religious affiliation.

UNIVERSITY OF KANSAS

Office of Admissions, Lawrence, KS 66045-7576
Phone: 785-864-3911 **Financial Aid Phone:** 785-864-4700
E-mail: adm@ku.edu **CEEB Code:** 6871
Fax: 785-864-5017 **Website:** https://www.ku.edu/ **ACT Code:** 1470

This public school was founded in 1865. It has a 1000 acre campus.

RATINGS
Admissions Selectivity Rating: 76   **Fire Safety Rating:** 97   **Green Rating:** 79

STUDENTS AND FACULTY
Enrollment: 19,003. **Student Body:** 52% female, 48% male, 29% out-of-state, 5% international (109 countries represented). Asian 5%, African American 4%, Caucasian 71%, Hispanic 9%, Native American <1%, Pacific Islander <1%, Two or more races 5%, Race unknown <1%.
Retention and Graduation: 86% freshmen return for sophomore year. 48% freshmen graduate within 4 years. 66% freshmen graduate within 6 years. 31% grads go on to further study within 1 year. **Faculty:** Student/faculty ratio 17:1. 1,438 full-time faculty, 92% hold PhDs, 21% are members of minority groups, 42% are women. 16% of classes are taught by teaching assistants.

ACADEMICS
Degrees: Bachelor's; Certificate; Doctoral degree—professional practice; Doctoral degree research/scholarship; Master's; Post-bachelor's certificate; Post-master's certificate. **Classes:** Most classes have 10–19 students. Most lab/discussion sessions have 10–19 students. **Most popular majors:** Biology/Biological Sciences, General; Business/Commerce, General; Engineering, General. **Special Study Options:** Accelerated program; Cooperative education program; Distance learning; Double major; Dual enrollment; English as a Second Language (ESL); Honors program; Independent study; Internships; Liberal arts/career combination; Study abroad; Teacher certification program. **Honors programs:** The University Honors Program is one of the oldest and best Honors programs in the country. It provides enriched educational opportunities to academically talented, promising, and motivated undergraduate students. These opportunities include priority enrollment, small honors courses with top faculty, specialized advising, experiential learning (research, internships, study abroad, cultural and social activities and community service) and special programs. Web site at http://honors.ku.edu/. **Combined degree programs:** BA/JD. **Disability Services offered:** Note-taking services; Reader services; Tape recorders; Tutors. **Career services:** Alumni network; Alumni services; Career assessment; Career/job search classes; Internships; Regional alumni.

FACILITIES
Housing: Apartments for single students; Coed dorms; Cooperative housing; Fraternity/sorority housing; Theme housing; Women's dorms; 95% of campus accessible to physically disabled. **Special Academic Facilities/Equipment:** 12

libraries (including art and architecture, engineering, law, medical, music and dance, rare research materials, special collections, and science), performing arts center, organ recital hall, museums (art, anthropology, classical, entomology, invertebrate paleontology, and natural history), film studio, student operated radio and television stations, public radio station, herbarium, space technology center, observatory, Robert J. Dole Institute for Politics, Hall Center for the Humanities, Center for International Business Education and Research, ecological reserves, Biological Survey, Geological Survey, Information and Telecommunication Technology Center, energy research center, flight research lab, Transportation Research Center, 400+ bed hospital for clinical learning, Hoglund Brain Imaging Center, Center on Aging.

CAMPUS LIFE

Environment: City. **Activities:** Choral groups; Concert band; Dance; Drama/theater; International Student Organization; Jazz band; Literary magazine; Marching band; Model UN; Music ensembles; Musical theater; Opera; Pep band; Radio station; Student government; Student newspaper; Symphony orchestra; Television station. 582 registered organizations, 28 honor societies, 39 religious organizations, 26 fraternities, 17 sororities on campus. **Athletics (Intercollegiate):** *Men:* baseball, basketball, cross-country, football, golf, track/field (outdoor), track/field (indoor). *Women:* basketball, crew/rowing, cross-country, diving, golf, soccer, softball, swimming, tennis, track/field (outdoor), track/field (indoor), volleyball. **On-Campus Highlights:** Spencer Museum of Art.

ADMISSIONS

Freshman Academic Profile: Average high school GPA 3.6. 29% in top 10% of high school class, 55% in top 25% of high school class, 83% in top 50% of high school class. **Test Scores:** ACT middle 50% range 22–29. **Basis for Candidate Selection:** *Very important factors include:* academic GPA, standardized test scores. *Other factors include:* rigor of secondary school record, class rank, application essay, extracurricular activities, talent/ability, character/personal qualities, first generation, alumni/ae relation, geographical residence, state residency, racial/ethnic status, volunteer work, work experience, level of applicant's interest. **Freshman Admission Requirements:** High school diploma is required and GED is accepted. *Academic units required:* 4 English, 3 math, 3 science, 1 science labs, 3 social studies, 3 academic electives. *Academic units recommended:* 4 English, 4 math, 3 science, 3 social studies, 3 academic electives. **Freshman Admission Statistics:** 15,093 applied, 93% admitted, 29% enrolled. **Transfer Admission Requirements:** College transcript(s). Minimum college GPA of 2.5 required. Lowest grade transferable C. **General Admission Information:** Application fee $40. Priority deadline 2/1. Regular application deadline 8/19. Non-fall registration accepted. Admission may be deferred for a maximum of 1 year.

COSTS AND FINANCIAL AID

Annual in-state tuition $10,092. Annual out-of-state tuition $26,960. Room and board $10,350. Required fees $1,074. Average book and supplies expense $1,212. **Required Forms and Deadlines:** FAFSA. **Types of Aid:** *Need-based scholarships/grants:* College/university scholarship or grant aid from institutional funds; Federal Pell; Private scholarships; SEOG; State scholarships/grants. *Loans:* Direct PLUS loans; Direct Subsidized Stafford Loans; Direct Unsubsidized Stafford Loans. **Student Employment:** Federal Work-Study Program available. Institutional employment available. **Financial Aid Statistics:** 90% needy freshmen, 80% needy undergrads receive need-based scholarship or grant aid. 15% freshmen, 9% undergrads receive non-need-based scholarship or grant aid. 65% freshmen, 70% undergrads receive need-based self-help aid. 2% freshmen, 2% undergrads receive athletic scholarships. 80% freshmen, 67% undergrads receive any aid. 53% undergrads borrow to pay for school. Average cumulative indebtedness $28,176. **Criteria awarding aid:** *Need-based:* Academics, Alumni affiliation, Art, Job skills, Leadership, Minority status, Music/drama. *Non-need-based:* Academics, Alumni affiliation, Art, Athletics, Leadership, Minority status, Music/drama, State/district residency.

UNIVERSITY OF KENTUCKY

100 W.D. Funkhouser Building, Lexington, KY 40506
Phone: 859-257-2000 **Financial Aid Phone:** (859) 257-3172
E-mail: admissions@uky.edu **CEEB Code:** 1837
Fax: (859) 257-3823 **Website:** www.uky.edu **ACT Code:** 1554

This public school was founded in 1865. It has a 687 acre campus.

RATINGS

Admissions Selectivity Rating: 76   **Fire Safety Rating:** 91   **Green Rating:** 93

STUDENTS AND FACULTY

Enrollment: 22,078. **Student Body:** 55% female, 45% male, 31% out-of-state, 2% international (117 countries represented). Asian 3%, African American 8%, Caucasian 76%, Hispanic 5%, Native American <1%, Pacific Islander <1%, Two or more races 4%, Race unknown 3%.
Retention and Graduation: 83% freshmen return for sophomore year. 38% freshmen graduate within 4 years. 64% freshmen graduate within 6 years.
Faculty: Student/faculty ratio 17:1. 1,392 full-time faculty, 93% hold PhDs, 18% are members of minority groups, 41% are women. 20% of classes are taught by teaching assistants.

ACADEMICS

Degrees: Bachelor's; Certificate; Doctoral degree—professional practice; Doctoral degree research/scholarship; Master's; Post-bachelor's certificate; Post-master's certificate. **Classes:** Most classes have 20–29 students. **Special Study Options:** Accelerated program; Cooperative education program; Distance learning; Double major; Dual enrollment; English as a Second Language (ESL); Exchange student program (domestic); Honors program; Independent study; Internships; Student-designed major; Study abroad; Teacher certification program; Weekend college. **Combined degree programs:** BA/MA. **Disability Services offered:** Note-taking services; Reader services.

FACILITIES

Housing: Apartments for single students; Coed dorms; Fraternity/sorority housing; Men's dorms 95% of campus accessible to physically disabled. **Special Academic Facilities/Equipment:** Anthropology and art museums, center for the humanities, centers for equine research, cancer research, and robotics, pharmacy manufacturing lab. **Campus network:** 100% of classrooms, 100% of dorms, 80% of student union, 90% of libraries, 100% of dining areas, 50% of common outdoor areas have wireless network access.

CAMPUS LIFE

Environment: City. **Activities:** Campus Ministries; Choral groups; Concert band; Dance; Drama/theater; International Student Organization; Jazz band; Literary magazine; Marching band; Model UN; Music ensembles; Musical theater; Opera; Pep band; Radio station; Student government; Student newspaper; Symphony orchestra; Television station; Yearbook. 348 registered organizations, 28 honor societies, 20 religious organizations, 19 fraternities, 16 sororities on campus. **Athletics (Intercollegiate):** *Men:* baseball, basketball, cheerleading, cross-country, diving, football, golf, riflery, soccer, swimming, tennis, track/field (outdoor), track/field (indoor). *Women:* basketball, cheerleading, cross-country, diving, golf, gymnastics, riflery, soccer, softball, swimming, tennis, track/field (outdoor), track/field (indoor), volleyball. **On-Campus Highlights:** W.T. Young Library.

ADMISSIONS

Freshman Academic Profile: Average high school GPA 3.7. 29% in top 10% of high school class, 58% in top 25% of high school class, 86% in top 50% of high school class. **Test Scores:** SAT Math middle 50% range 530–660. SAT EBRW middle 50% range 550–660. ACT middle 50% range 22–28. **Basis for Candidate Selection:** *Very important factors include:* rigor of secondary school record, academic GPA, standardized test scores. *Important factors include:* application essay, recommendation(s). *Other factors include:* class rank, interview, extracurricular activities, talent/ability, character/personal qualities, alumni/ae relation, geographical residence, state residency, volunteer work. **Freshman Admission Requirements:** High school diploma is required and GED is accepted. *Academic units required:* 4 English, 3 math, 3 science, 1 science labs, 3 foreign language, 3 social studies, 7 academic electives, 1 visual/performing arts, 1 unit from above areas or other academic areas. **Freshman Admission Statistics:** 18,925 applied, 96% admitted, 27% enrolled. **Transfer**

Admission Requirements: College transcript(s). Minimum college GPA of 2.0 required. Lowest grade transferable D. **General Admission Information:** Application fee $50. Priority deadline 2/15. Regular application deadline 2/15. Non-fall registration accepted. Admission may be deferred for a maximum of 1 year.

COSTS AND FINANCIAL AID

Annual in-state tuition $10,896. Annual out-of-state tuition $27,750. Room and board $12,982. Required fees $1,349. Average book and supplies expense $1,000. **Required Forms and Deadlines:** FAFSA. **Notification of Awards:** Applicants will be notified of awards on a rolling basis beginning 3/15. **Types of Aid:** *Need-based scholarships/grants:* College/university scholarship or grant aid from institutional funds; Federal Pell; Private scholarships; SEOG; State scholarships/grants. *Loans:* Direct PLUS loans; Direct Subsidized Stafford Loans; Direct Unsubsidized Stafford Loans. **Student Employment:** Federal Work-Study Program available. **Financial Aid Statistics:** 42% needy freshmen, 47% needy undergrads receive need-based scholarship or grant aid. 62% freshmen, 76% undergrads receive non-need-based scholarship or grant aid. 58% freshmen, 53% undergrads receive need-based self-help aid. 11% freshmen, 3% undergrads receive athletic scholarships. 40% freshmen, 38% undergrads receive any aid. 54% undergrads borrow to pay for school. Average cumulative indebtedness $42,090. **Criteria awarding aid:** *Need-based:* Academics, Alumni affiliation, Minority status. *Non-need-based:* Academics, Alumni affiliation, Art, Athletics, Job skills, Leadership, Minority status, Music/drama, State/district residency.

UNIVERSITY OF KING'S COLLEGE

Registrars Office, Halifax, NS B3H 2A1
Phone: 902-422-1271
E-mail: admissions@ukings.ns.ca
Fax: 902-423-3357 Website: www.ukings.ca

This public school was founded in 1789. It has a 3 acre campus.

RATINGS

Admissions Selectivity Rating: 76   Fire Safety Rating: 60*   Green Rating: 60*

STUDENTS AND FACULTY

Enrollment: 1,137. **Student Body:** 57% female, 43% male, 53% out-of-state, (6 countries represented).
Faculty: Student/faculty ratio 25:1. 51 full-time faculty, 71% hold PhDs, 0% are members of minority groups, 31% are women. 0% of classes are taught by teaching assistants.

ACADEMICS

Degrees: Bachelor's. **Most popular majors:** English Language and Literature, General; Psychology, General; Sociology, General. **Special Study Options:** Cooperative education program; Double major; Honors program; Internships; Study abroad. **Career services:** Career assessment; Career/job search classes.

FACILITIES

Housing: Coed dorms; Men's dorms; Women's dorms.

CAMPUS LIFE

Environment: Metropolis. **Activities:** Choral groups; Dance; Drama/theater; Literary magazine; Radio station; Student government; Student newspaper; Student-run film society; Yearbook. **Athletics (Intercollegiate):** *Men:* badminton, basketball, soccer, volleyball. *Women:* badminton, basketball, soccer, volleyball. **On-Campus Highlights:** The Pit.

ADMISSIONS

Basis for Candidate Selection: *Very important factors include:* rigor of secondary school record, standardized test scores. **Freshman Admission Requirements:** High school diploma is required and GED is not accepted. **Freshman Admission Statistics:** 904 applied, 47% admitted, 83% enrolled. **Transfer Admission Requirements:** College transcript(s). Lowest grade transferable C. **General Admission Information:** Application fee $45. Priority deadline 3/1. Regular application deadline 6/1. Admission may be deferred for a maximum of one year.

COSTS AND FINANCIAL AID

Average book and supplies expense $1,000.

UNIVERSITY OF LA VERNE

1950 Third Street, La Verne, CA 91750
Phone: (800) 876-4858 Financial Aid Phone: 1-800-649-0160
E-mail: admission@laverne.edu CEEB Code: 4381
Fax: (909) 392-2714 Website: www.laverne.edu ACT Code: 295

This private school was founded in 1891. It has a 66 acre campus.

RATINGS

Admissions Selectivity Rating: 87   Fire Safety Rating: 93   Green Rating: 98

STUDENTS AND FACULTY

Enrollment: 2,859. **Student Body:** 59% female, 41% male, 4% out-of-state, 5% international (24 countries represented). Asian 6%, African American 5%, Caucasian 25%, Hispanic 51%, Native American <1%, Pacific Islander 1%, Two or more races 5%, Race unknown 2%.
Retention and Graduation: 85% freshmen return for sophomore year.
Faculty: Student/faculty ratio 13:1. 233 full-time faculty, 0% hold PhDs, 0% are members of minority groups, 0% are women. 0% of classes are taught by teaching assistants.

ACADEMICS

Degrees: Bachelor's; Certificate; Doctoral degree—professional practice; Doctoral degree research/scholarship; Master's; Post-bachelor's certificate.
Classes: Most classes have 10–19 students. Most lab/discussion sessions have fewer than 10 students. **Most popular majors:** Biology/Biological Sciences, General; Business Administration and Management, General; Psychology, General. **Special Study Options:** Distance learning; Double major; English as a Second Language (ESL); Exchange student program (domestic); Honors program; Independent study; Internships; Liberal arts/career combination; Student-designed major; Study abroad; Teacher certification program; Weekend college. **Honors programs:** The La Verne Honors Program offers a challenging intellectual experience that complements any major at the university. Open to students with proven academic success in high school, the rigorous curriculum is taught by passionate and knowledgeable professors, and allows students an opportunity to complete most general education requirements in accelerated fashion. **Disability Services offered:** Note-taking services; Reader services; Tape recorders; Tutors. **Career services:** Alumni services; Career assessment; Career/job search classes; Internships; Regional alumni.

FACILITIES

Housing: Coed dorms; Men's dorms; Special housing for disabled students; Special housing for international students; Women's dorms. **Special Academic Facilities/Equipment:** Greenhouse and Animal Care Facility; Montana Field Station—Magpie Ranch; Photography and Art galleries; The Microscopy and Imaging Center; Jeagar science specimen Museum.

CAMPUS LIFE

Environment: Town. **Activities:** Campus Ministries; Choral groups; Dance; Drama/theater; International Student Organization; Literary magazine; Model UN; Music ensembles; Musical theater; Radio station; Student government; Student newspaper; Student-run film society; Television station. 66 registered organizations, 4 honor societies, 5 religious organizations, 2 fraternities, 4 sororities on campus. **Athletics (Intercollegiate):** *Men:* baseball, basketball, cross-country, diving, football, golf, soccer, swimming, tennis, track/field (outdoor), water polo. *Women:* basketball, cross-country, diving, soccer, softball, swimming, tennis, track/field (outdoor), volleyball, water polo. **On-Campus Highlights:** Campus Center. **Environmental Initiatives:** Total Recycling Program.

ADMISSIONS

Freshman Academic Profile: Average high school GPA 3.5. 18% in top 10% of high school class, 54% in top 25% of high school class, 86% in top 50% of high school class. **Test Scores:** SAT Math middle 50% range 470–570. SAT EBRW middle 50% range 470–560. ACT middle 50% range 20–24. **Basis for Candidate Selection:** *Very important factors include:* rigor of secondary school record, academic GPA, application essay, standardized test scores, recommendation(s), extracurricular activities, character/personal qualities. *Important factors include:* class rank. *Other factors include:* interview, talent/ability, first generation, alumni/ae relation, geographical residence, volunteer work, work experience, level of applicant's interest. **Freshman Admission Requirements:** High school diploma is required and GED is accepted. *Academic units required:* 4 English, 3 math, 2 science, 1 science labs, 2 social studies, 3 history. *Academic units recommended:* 4 English, 4 math, 2 science, 2 science labs, 2 foreign language, 2 social studies, 3 history, 2 academic electives. **Freshman Admission Statistics:** 8,179 applied, 47% admitted, 19% enrolled. **Transfer Admission Requirements:** College transcript(s), essay or personal statement. Minimum college GPA of 2.7 required. Lowest grade transferable C-. **General Admission Information:** Application fee $50. Priority deadline 2/1. Non-fall registration accepted. Admission may be deferred for a maximum of 1 year.

COSTS AND FINANCIAL AID
Annual tuition $37,100. Room and board $12,510. Required fees $1,460. Average book and supplies expense $1,746. **Required Forms and Deadlines:** FAFSA; State aid form. **Types of Aid:** *Need-based scholarships/grants:* College/university scholarship or grant aid from institutional funds; Federal Pell; Private scholarships; SEOG; State scholarships/grants. *Loans:* Direct PLUS loans; Direct Subsidized Stafford Loans; Direct Unsubsidized Stafford Loans. **Student Employment:** Federal Work-Study Program available. Institutional employment available. **Financial Aid Statistics:** 70% needy freshmen, 67% needy undergrads receive need-based scholarship or grant aid. 99% freshmen, 99% undergrads receive non-need-based scholarship or grant aid. 93% freshmen, 93% undergrads receive need-based self-help aid. 0% freshmen, 0% undergrads receive athletic scholarships. 87% freshmen, 83% undergrads receive any aid. 82% undergrads borrow to pay for school. Average cumulative indebtedness $30,844. **Criteria awarding aid:** *Need-based:* Academics. *Non-need-based:* Academics, Alumni affiliation, Art, Leadership, Minority status, Music/drama, Religious affiliation.

THE UNIVERSITY OF LETHBRIDGE

4401 University Drive, Lethbridge, AB T1K 3M4
Phone: 403-382-7134 **Financial Aid Phone:** 403-329-2585
E-mail: admissions@uleth.ca
Fax: 403-329-5159 **Website:** www.uleth.ca **ACT Code:** 5202

This public school was founded in 1967. It has a 576 acre campus.

RATINGS
Admissions Selectivity Rating: 66   **Fire Safety Rating:** 60*   **Green Rating:** 60*

STUDENTS AND FACULTY
Enrollment: 7,737.
Retention and Graduation: 81% freshmen return for sophomore year.

ACADEMICS
Degrees: Bachelor's; Certificate; Diploma; Master's; Post-bachelor's certificate; Post-master's certificate. **Most popular majors:** Accounting; Registered Nursing/Registered Nurse; Business Administration and Management, General. **Special Study Options:** Accelerated program; Cooperative education program; Double major; Dual enrollment; English as a Second Language (ESL); Exchange student program (domestic); Independent study; Internships; Student-designed major; Study abroad; Teacher certification program. **Disability Services offered:** Note-taking services; Reader services; Tape recorders; Tutors. **Career services:** Alumni services; Career assessment; Career/job search classes; Internships.

FACILITIES
Housing: Apartments for married students; Apartments for single students; Coed dorms; Special housing for disabled students; 100% of campus accessible to physically disabled. **Special Academic Facilities/Equipment:** Art Gallery, Theatres.

CAMPUS LIFE
Environment: City. **Activities:** Choral groups; Concert band; Dance; Drama/theater; International Student Organization; Jazz band; Literary magazine; Music ensembles; Musical theater; Opera; Radio station; Student government; Student newspaper; Student-run film society; Symphony orchestra. 2 fraternities, 1 sorority on campus. **Athletics (Intercollegiate):** *Men:* basketball, ice hockey, soccer, swimming, track/field (outdoor). *Women:* basketball, ice hockey, rugby, soccer, swimming, track/field (outdoor).

ADMISSIONS
Basis for Candidate Selection: *Very important factors include:* rigor of secondary school record. *Other factors include:* class rank, standardized test scores. **Freshman Admission Requirements:** High school diploma is required and GED is not accepted. **Freshman Admission Statistics:** 2,997 applied,

84% admitted, 49% enrolled. **Transfer Admission Requirements:** College transcript(s). **General Admission Information:** Application fee $100. Priority deadline 3/1. Regular application deadline 6/30. Non-fall registration accepted. Admission may be deferred for a maximum of 1 semester.

COSTS AND FINANCIAL AID
Annual in-state tuition $4,974. Annual out-of-state tuition $4,974. Room and board $6,268. **Required Forms and Deadlines:** Institution's own financial aid form. **Student Employment:** Institutional employment available. **Criteria awarding aid:** *Non-need-based:* Academics, Athletics, Leadership.

UNIVERSITY OF LOUISIANA AT LAFAYETTE

P.O. Drawer 41210, Lafayette, LA 70504
Phone: 337-482-6553 **Financial Aid Phone:** 337-482-6506
E-mail: enroll@louisiana.edu **CEEB Code:** 6672
Fax: 337-482-1112 **Website:** www.louisiana.edu **ACT Code:** 1612

This public school was founded in 1898. It has a 1375 acre campus.

RATINGS
Admissions Selectivity Rating: 85   **Fire Safety Rating:** 94   **Green Rating:** 60*

STUDENTS AND FACULTY
Enrollment: 13,639. **Student Body:** 57% female, 43% male, 6% out-of-state, 1% international (101 countries represented). Asian 3%, African American 21%, Caucasian 64%, Hispanic 6%, Native American <1%, Pacific Islander <1%, Two or more races 3%, Race unknown 3%.
Retention and Graduation: 76% freshmen return for sophomore year. 23% freshmen graduate within 4 years. 51% freshmen graduate within 6 years.
Faculty: Student/faculty ratio 20:1. 664 full-time faculty, 70% hold PhDs, 19% are members of minority groups, 45% are women.

ACADEMICS
Degrees: Bachelor's; Doctoral degree—professional practice; Master's; Post-bachelor's certificate; Post-master's certificate. **Classes:** Most classes have 20–29 students. **Most popular majors:** Biology/Biological Sciences, General; Business Administration and Management, General; Nursing/Registered Nurse (Rn, Asn, Bsn, Msn). **Special Study Options:** Accelerated program; Cooperative education program; Cross-registration; Distance learning; Double major; Dual enrollment; Exchange student program (domestic); Honors program; Independent study; Internships; Student-designed major; Study abroad; Teacher certification program. **Honors programs:** Honors Baccalaureate degree is available. **Disability Services offered:** Note-taking services; Reader services; Tape recorders; Tutors. **Career services:** Career assessment; Career/job search classes.

FACILITIES
Housing: Apartments for married students; Apartments for single students; Fraternity/sorority housing; Men's dorms; Women's dorms; 85% of campus accessible to physically disabled. **Special Academic Facilities/Equipment:** Art museum, experimental farm, primate center, CAD/CAM laboratory, marine research facility on campus restaurant and hotel with instructional facilities, 2 nuclear accelerators, 2 electron microscopes, radio station and television production studio, nursery school laboratory, Louisiana Emersive Technologies Enterprise.

CAMPUS LIFE
Environment: City. **Activities:** Campus Ministries; Choral groups; Concert band; Dance; Drama/theater; International Student Organization; Jazz band; Literary magazine; Marching band; Music ensembles; Musical theater; Opera; Radio station; Student government; Student newspaper; Symphony orchestra; Yearbook. 155 registered organizations, 14 honor societies, 8 religious organizations, 11 fraternity, 9 sororities on campus. **Athletics (Intercollegiate):** *Men:* baseball, basketball, cheerleading, cross-country, football, golf, tennis, track/field (outdoor), track/field (indoor). *Women:* basketball, cheerleading, cross-country, soccer, softball, tennis, track/field (outdoor), track/field (indoor), volleyball. **On-Campus Highlights:** University Museum.

ADMISSIONS

Freshman Academic Profile: Average high school GPA 3.4. 17% in top 10% of high school class, 38% in top 25% of high school class, 65% in top 50% of high school class. **Test Scores:** SAT Math middle 50% range 510–650. SAT EBRW middle 50% range 510–618. ACT middle 50% range 21–26. **Basis for Candidate Selection:** *Very important factors include:* rigor of secondary school record, class rank, academic GPA, standardized test scores. *Other factors include:* state residency. **Freshman Admission Requirements:** High school diploma is required and GED is accepted. *Academic units required:* 4 English, 4 math, 3 science, 2 foreign language, 1 social studies, 2 history, 1 visual/performing arts, 1 unit from above areas or other academic areas. **Freshman Admission Statistics:** 9,138 applied, 68% admitted, 41% enrolled. **Transfer Admission Requirements:** College transcript(s). Lowest grade transferable D. **General Admission Information:** Application fee $25. Priority deadline 7/2. Non-fall registration accepted. Admission may be deferred for a maximum of 1 semester.

COSTS AND FINANCIAL AID

Annual in-state tuition $5,407. Annual out-of-state tuition $19,135. Room and board $10,708. Required fees $4,975. Average book and supplies expense $1,220. **Required Forms and Deadlines:** FAFSA. **Notification of Awards:** Applicants will be notified of awards on a rolling basis beginning 4/1. **Types of Aid:** *Need-based scholarships/grants:* College/university scholarship or grant aid from institutional funds; Federal Nursing Scholarships; Federal Pell; Private scholarships; SEOG; State scholarships/grants. **Student Employment:** Federal Work-Study Program available. Institutional employment available. **Financial Aid Statistics:** 96% needy freshmen, 88% needy undergrads receive need-based scholarship or grant aid. 15% freshmen, 9% undergrads receive non-need-based scholarship or grant aid. 48% freshmen, 59% undergrads receive need-based self-help aid. 2% freshmen, 3% undergrads receive athletic scholarships. 87% freshmen, 72% undergrads receive any aid. **Criteria awarding aid:** *Need-based:* Job skills.

UNIVERSITY OF LOUISVILLE

Admissions Office, Louisville, KY 40292
Phone: 502-852-6531 **Financial Aid Phone:** (502) 852-5511
E-mail: admitme@louisville.edu **CEEB Code:** 1838
Fax: 502-852-4776 **Website:** www.louisville.edu **ACT Code:** 1556

This public school was founded in 1798. It has a 640.12 acre campus.

RATINGS

Admissions Selectivity Rating: 83   **Fire Safety Rating:** 98   **Green Rating:** 97

STUDENTS AND FACULTY

Enrollment: 14,303. **Student Body:** 53% female, 47% male, 18% out-of-state, 1% international (60 countries represented). Asian 4%, African American 12%, Caucasian 70%, Hispanic 6%, Native American <1%, Pacific Islander <1%, Two or more races 6%, Race unknown <1%. **Retention and Graduation:** 80% freshmen return for sophomore year. 37% freshmen graduate within 4 years. 59% freshmen graduate within 6 years. 25% grads go on to further study within 1 year. 41% grads pursue arts and sciences degrees. 7% grads pursue law degrees. 14% grads pursue business degrees. 20% grads pursue medical degrees. **Faculty:** Student/faculty ratio 14:1. 896 full-time faculty, 87% hold PhDs, 23% are members of minority groups, 43% are women. 3% of classes are taught by teaching assistants.

ACADEMICS

Degrees: Associate; Bachelor's; Certificate; Doctoral degree—professional practice; Doctoral degree research/scholarship; Master's; Post-bachelor's certificate; Post-master's certificate. **Classes:** Most classes have 20–29 students. **Most popular majors:** Biology/Biological Sciences, General; Registered Nursing/Registered Nurse; Psychology, General. **Special Study Options:** Accelerated program; Cooperative education program; Cross-registration; Distance learning; Double major; English as a Second Language (ESL); Exchange student program (domestic); Honors program; Independent study; Internships; Study abroad; Teacher certification program. **Combined degree programs:** BA/MA. **Disability Services offered:** Note-taking services; Reader

services; Tape recorders; Tutors. **Career services:** Alumni services; Career assessment; Career/job search classes; Internships.

FACILITIES

Housing: Apartments for married students; Apartments for single students; Coed dorms; Fraternity/sorority housing; Men's dorms; Special housing for disabled students; Theme housing; 95% of campus accessible to physically disabled. **Special Academic Facilities/Equipment:** Planetarium, computer-aided engineering building with robotics laboratory, rapid prototype facility with Sinterstation 2000 system, photographic archives, Speed Art Museum.

CAMPUS LIFE

Environment: Metropolis. **Activities:** Campus Ministries; Choral groups; Concert band; Drama/theater; International Student Organization; Jazz band; Literary magazine; Marching band; Music ensembles; Musical theater; Opera; Pep band; Student government; Student newspaper; Symphony orchestra. 450 registered organizations, 16 honor societies, 51 religious organization, 20 fraternities, 13 sororities on campus. **Athletics (Intercollegiate):** *Men:* baseball, basketball, cheerleading, cross-country, diving, football, golf, soccer, swimming, tennis, track/field (outdoor). *Women:* basketball, cheerleading, crew/rowing, cross-country, diving, field hockey, golf, lacrosse, soccer, softball, swimming, tennis, track/field (outdoor), volleyball. **On-Campus Highlights:** Floyd Theatre.

ADMISSIONS

Freshman Academic Profile: Average high school GPA 3.6. 88% from public high schools. **Test Scores:** ACT middle 50% range 22–29. **Basis for Candidate Selection:** *Very important factors include:* rigor of secondary school record, academic GPA, standardized test scores. *Other factors include:* class rank, recommendation(s), extracurricular activities, talent/ability, state residency, racial/ethnic status, volunteer work, work experience. **Freshman Admission Requirements:** High school diploma is required and GED is accepted. *Academic units required:* 4 English, 3 math, 3 science, 1 science labs, 2 foreign language, 3 social studies, 5 academic electives, 1 visual/performing arts, 5 unit from above areas or other academic areas. *Academic units recommended:* 4 math, 4 science, 3 foreign language. **Freshman Admission Statistics:** 14,447 applied, 70% admitted, 28% enrolled. **Transfer Admission Requirements:** College transcript(s). Minimum college GPA of 2.0 required. Lowest grade transferable D. **General Admission Information:** Application fee $25. Priority deadline 2/15. Regular application deadline 8/1. Non-fall registration accepted.

COSTS AND FINANCIAL AID

Annual in-state tuition $11,732. Annual out-of-state tuition $27,758. Room and board $9,452. Required fees $196. Average book and supplies expense $1,200. **Required Forms and Deadlines:** FAFSA. **Types of Aid:** *Need-based scholarships/grants:* College/university scholarship or grant aid from institutional funds; Federal Nursing Scholarships; Federal Pell; Private scholarships; SEOG; State scholarships/grants. *Loans:* Direct PLUS loans; Direct Subsidized Stafford Loans; Direct Unsubsidized Stafford Loans. **Student Employment:** Federal Work-Study Program available. Institutional employment available. **Financial Aid Statistics:** 98% needy freshmen, 92% needy undergrads receive need-based scholarship or grant aid. 16% freshmen, 11% undergrads receive non-need-based scholarship or grant aid. 55% freshmen, 60% undergrads receive need-based self-help aid. 4% freshmen, 4% undergrads receive athletic scholarships. 67% freshmen, 61% undergrads receive any aid. 51% undergrads borrow to pay for school. Average cumulative indebtedness $24,840. **Criteria awarding aid:** *Non-need-based:* Academics, Art, Athletics, Leadership, Minority status, Music/drama, State/district residency.

For more free content, visit <u>PrincetonReview.com</u>

UNIVERSITY OF LYNCHBURG

1501 Lakeside Drive, Lynchburg, VA 24501
Phone: 434-544-8300 **Financial Aid Phone:** (434) 544-8230
E-mail: admissions@lynchburg.edu **CEEB Code:** 5372
Fax: 434-544-8653 **Website:** www.lynchburg.edu **ACT Code:** 4368

This private school, affiliated with the Disciples of Christ Church, was founded in 1903. It has a 264 acre campus.

RATINGS
Admissions Selectivity Rating: 73   **Fire Safety Rating:** 80   **Green Rating:** 60*

STUDENTS AND FACULTY
Enrollment: 1,985. **Student Body:** 60% female, 40% male, 29% out-of-state, 1% international (15 countries represented). Asian 2%, African American 11%, Caucasian 76%, Hispanic 5%, Native American 1%, Pacific Islander <1%, Two or more races 3%, Race unknown 2%.
Retention and Graduation: 79% freshmen return for sophomore year. 51% freshmen graduate within 4 years. 59% freshmen graduate within 6 years. 18% grads go on to further study within 1 year. 21% grads pursue arts and sciences degrees. 12% grads pursue business degrees. **Faculty:** Student/faculty ratio 11:1. 187 full-time faculty, 88% hold PhDs, 5% are members of minority groups, 51% are women. 0% of classes are taught by teaching assistants.

ACADEMICS
Degrees: Bachelor's; Doctoral degree—other; Doctoral degree—professional practice; Doctoral degree research/scholarship; Master's; Post-bachelor's certificate; Post-master's certificate. **Classes:** Most classes have 10–19 students. Most lab/discussion sessions have 10–19 students. **Most popular majors:** Registered Nursing, Nursing Administration, Nursing Research and Clinical Nursing; Teacher Education and Professional Development, Specific Levels and Methods, Other; Speech Communication and Rhetoric. **Special Study Options:** Cross-registration; Distance learning; Double major; English as a Second Language (ESL); Honors program; Independent study; Internships; Study abroad; Teacher certification program. **Honors programs:** Westover Honors Program. **Disability Services offered:** Note-taking services; Reader services; Tape recorders; Tutors. **Career services:** Alumni network; Alumni services; Career assessment; Career/job search classes; Internships; Regional alumni.

FACILITIES
Housing: Apartments for single students; Coed dorms; Fraternity/sorority housing; Men's dorms; Special housing for disabled students; Special housing for international students; Theme housing; Wellness housing; Women's dorms; 90% of campus accessible to physically disabled. **Special Academic Facilities/Equipment:** Daura Art Gallery, Claytor Nature Study Center, Ramsey-Freer Herbarium, cadaver lab; Schewel Hall audio-visual and television studios, Dillard Fine Arts Center, Belk Observatory. **Campus network:** 95% of classrooms, 95% of dorms, 100% of student union, 100% of libraries, 100% of dining areas, 95% of common outdoor areas have wireless network access.

CAMPUS LIFE
Environment: City. **Activities:** Campus Ministries; Choral groups; Concert band; Dance; Drama/theater; International Student Organization; Jazz band; Literary magazine; Model UN; Music ensembles; Musical theater; Pep band; Student government; Student newspaper; Symphony orchestra. 80 registered organizations, 14 honor societies, 10 religious organizations, 5 fraternities, 6 sororities on campus. **Athletics (Intercollegiate):** *Men:* baseball, basketball, cheerleading, cross-country, golf, lacrosse, soccer, tennis, track/field (outdoor), track/field (indoor). *Women:* basketball, cheerleading, cross-country, equestrian sports, field hockey, lacrosse, soccer, softball, tennis, track/field (outdoor), track/field (indoor), volleyball. **On-Campus Highlights:** Shellenberger Field. **Environmental Initiatives:** Recovery of College Lake. Working with the Army Corp of Engineers, and the state of Virginia, Lynchburg College is attempting to restore College Lake.

ADMISSIONS
Freshman Academic Profile: Average high school GPA 3.4. 13% in top 10% of high school class, 22% in top 25% of high school class, 69% in top 50% of high school class. 80% from public high schools. **Test Scores:** SAT Math middle 50% range 580–480. SAT EBRW middle 50% range 500–605. ACT middle 50% range 19–26. **Basis for Candidate Selection:** *Very important factors include:* rigor of secondary school record, academic GPA, standardized test scores. *Important factors include:* interview. *Other factors include:* application essay, recommendation(s), extracurricular activities, talent/ability, character/personal qualities, volunteer work, work experience, level of applicant's interest. **Freshman Admission Requirements:** High school diploma is required and GED is accepted. *Academic units required:* 4 English, 3 math, 3 science, 2 science labs, 2 foreign language, 2 social studies, 2 history. *Academic units recommended:* 4 English, 4 math, 4 science, 2 science labs, 3 foreign language, 2 social studies, 2 history, 1 academic elective. **Freshman Admission Statistics:** 3,937 applied, 97% admitted, 14% enrolled. **Transfer Admission Requirements:** College transcript(s). Minimum college GPA of 2.0 required. Lowest grade transferable C. **General Admission Information:** Application fee $30. Non-fall registration accepted.

COSTS AND FINANCIAL AID
Annual tuition $38,560. Room and board $10,800. Required fees $970. Average book and supplies expense $1,200. **Required Forms and Deadlines:** FAFSA; State aid form. **Notification of Awards:** Applicants will be notified of awards on a rolling basis beginning 12/1. **Types of Aid:** *Need-based scholarships/grants:* College/university scholarship or grant aid from institutional funds; Federal Pell; SEOG. *Loans:* Direct PLUS loans; Direct Subsidized-Stafford Loans; Direct Unsubsidized Stafford Loans. **Student Employment:** Federal Work-Study Program available. Institutional employment available. **Financial Aid Statistics:** 100% needy freshmen, 100% needy undergrads receive need-based scholarship or grant aid. 18% freshmen, 16% undergrads receive non-need-based scholarship or grant aid. 82% freshmen, 81% undergrads receive need-based self-help aid. 0% freshmen, 0% undergrads receive athletic scholarships. 80% freshmen, 76% undergrads receive any aid. 80% undergrads borrow to pay for school. Average cumulative indebtedness $36,076. **Criteria awarding aid:** *Need-based:* Minority status, Religious affiliation. *Non-need-based:* Academics, Art, Leadership, Music/drama, Religious affiliation, State/district residency.

UNIVERSITY OF MAINE

5713 Chadbourne Hall, Orono, ME 04469-5713
Phone: 207-581-1561 **Financial Aid Phone:** 207-581-1324
E-mail: umaineadmissions@maine.edu **CEEB Code:** 3916
Fax: 207-581-1213 **Website:** www.umaine.edu **ACT Code:** 1664

This public school was founded in 1865. It has a 660 acre campus.

RATINGS
Admissions Selectivity Rating: 75   **Fire Safety Rating:** 99   **Green Rating:** 91

STUDENTS AND FACULTY
Enrollment: 8,832. **Student Body:** 46% female, 54% male, 33% out-of-state, 2% international (51 countries represented). Asian 2%, African American 2%, Caucasian 84%, Hispanic 4%, Native American 1%, Pacific Islander <1%, Two or more races 4%, Race unknown 2%.
Retention and Graduation: 74% freshmen return for sophomore year. 38% freshmen graduate within 4 years. 57% freshmen graduate within 6 years. **Faculty:** Student/faculty ratio 15:1. 535 full-time faculty, 87% hold PhDs, 11% are members of minority groups, 41% are women. 7% of classes are taught by teaching assistants.

ACADEMICS
Degrees: Bachelor's; Doctoral degree research/scholarship; Master's; Post-bachelor's certificate; Post-master's certificate. **Classes:** Most classes have 10–19 students. Most lab/discussion sessions have 10–19 students. **Most popular majors:** Psychology, General; Registered Nursing/Registered Nurse; Business Administration and Management, General. **Special Study Options:** Accelerated program; Cooperative education program; Distance learning; Double major; Dual enrollment; English as a Second Language (ESL); Exchange student program (domestic); Honors program; Independent study; Internships; Liberal arts/career combination; Study abroad; Teacher certification program. **Honors programs:** UMaine's Honors College is a dynamic program offering students from Maine and beyond the advantages of both a great research university

and a rigorous liberal arts education within a tight-knit community. Named a UMaine Signature Program "for strengths in research and education," the Honors College provides exemplary student-centered and community-engaged learning experiences for undergraduates as it prepares them for the 21st century workplace and society. One of the oldest and most respected Honors programs in the country, the tradition of personalized teaching of legendary Maine professors like Vincent Hartgen and Robert Thomson has been adapted to meet the needs of a growing number of in-state and out-of-state students. The intellectual breadth and scholarly depth of the highly interdisciplinary faculty provide unique opportunities for our students. Small classes combined with the living-learning communities of Colvin and Balentine Halls provide Honors students with opportunities for engaged, interdisciplinary learning. The College continues to innovate, build capacity, create partnerships and enhance the lives of future leaders in business, science, education, and the arts. **Combined degree programs:** BA/MA; BA/MEng. **Disability Services offered:** Note-taking services; Reader services; Tape recorders; Tutors. **Career services:** Alumni network; Alumni services; Career assessment; Career/job search classes; Internships; Regional alumni.

FACILITIES

Housing: Apartments for married students; Apartments for single students; Coed dorms; Fraternity/sorority housing; Special housing for disabled students; Special housing for international students; Theme housing; Wellness housing; 90% of campus accessible to physically disabled. **Special Academic Facilities/Equipment:** Emera Astronomy Center; Hudson Museum; Lord Hall Gallery; Innovative Media, Research and Commercialization Center; Wyeth Family Studio Art Center; Collins Center for the Arts; Minsky Recital Hall; Cyrus Pavilion; Fay Hyland Arboretum; Lyle E. Littlefield Ornamentals Trial Garden; Page Farm and Home Museum; Demeritt Forest; Alfond Arena and Stadium; New Balance Recreation Center; Advanced Manufacturing Center; Foster Center for Student Innovation; Virtual Environment and Multimodal Interaction Laboratory; and the Advanced Structures and Composites Center.

CAMPUS LIFE

Environment: Village. **Activities:** Campus Ministries; Choral groups; Concert band; Dance; Drama/theater; International Student Organization; Jazz band; Literary magazine; Marching band; Model UN; Music ensembles; Musical theater; Opera; Pep band; Radio station; Student government; Student newspaper; Student-run film society; Symphony orchestra. 168 registered organizations, 11 honor societies, 8 religious organizations, 17 fraternities, 9 sororities on campus. **Athletics (Intercollegiate):** *Men:* baseball, basketball, cross-country, diving, football, ice hockey, soccer, swimming, track/field (outdoor), track/field (indoor). *Women:* basketball, cross-country, diving, field hockey, ice hockey, soccer, softball, swimming, track/field (outdoor), track/field (indoor), volleyball. **On-Campus Highlights:** New Balance Student Recreation Center. **Environmental Initiatives:** UMaine has developed a master plan centered on sustainability, restoring habitat, avoiding sprawl, maximizing solar orientation, and reducing carbon emissions.

ADMISSIONS

Freshman Academic Profile: Average high school GPA 3.3. 20% in top 10% of high school class, 46% in top 25% of high school class, 79% in top 50% of high school class. **Test Scores:** SAT Math middle 50% range 520–620. SAT EBRW middle 50% range 530–630. ACT middle 50% range 21–27. **Basis for Candidate Selection:** *Very important factors include:* rigor of secondary school record, class rank, academic GPA, standardized test scores. *Important factors include:* application essay, recommendation(s). *Other factors include:* interview, extracurricular activities, talent/ability, character/personal qualities, volunteer work, work experience. **Freshman Admission Requirements:** High school diploma is required and GED is accepted. *Academic units required:* 4 English, 3 math, 2 science, 2 science labs, 2 social studies, 4 academic electives. *Academic units recommended:* 4 English, 4 math, 4 science, 3 science labs, 2 foreign language, 2 social studies, 1 history, 4 academic electives. **Freshman Admission Statistics:** 13,118 applied, 90% admitted, 18% enrolled. **Transfer Admission Requirements:** High school transcript, college transcript(s), essay or personal statement. Minimum college GPA of 2.0 required. Lowest grade transferable C-. **General Admission Information:** Priority deadline 2/1. Regular application deadline 2/1. Non-fall registration accepted. Admission may be deferred for a maximum of 2 semesters.

COSTS AND FINANCIAL AID

Annual in-state tuition $9,000. Annual out-of-state tuition $29,310. Room and board $10,966. Required fees $2,438. Average book and supplies expense $1,000. **Required Forms and Deadlines:** FAFSA. **Notification of Awards:** Applicants will be notified of awards on a rolling basis beginning 1/1. **Types of Aid:** *Need-based scholarships/grants:* College/university scholarship or grant aid from institutional funds; Federal Pell; Private scholarships; SEOG; State

scholarships/grants. *Loans:* Direct PLUS loans; Direct Subsidized Stafford Loans; Direct Unsubsidized Stafford Loans. **Student Employment:** Federal Work-Study Program available. Institutional employment available. **Financial Aid Statistics:** 99% needy freshmen, 94% needy undergrads receive need-based scholarship or grant aid. 14% freshmen, 10% undergrads receive non-need-based scholarship or grant aid. 76% freshmen, 79% undergrads receive need-based self-help aid. 2% freshmen, 2% undergrads receive athletic scholarships. 99% freshmen, 93% undergrads receive any aid. 75% undergrads borrow to pay for school. Average cumulative indebtedness $34,703. **Criteria awarding aid:** *Need-based:* Academics, Alumni affiliation, Art, Athletics, Job skills, Leadership, Minority status, Music/drama, Religious affiliation. *Non-need-based:* Academics, Alumni affiliation, Art, Athletics, Job skills, Leadership, Minority status, Music/drama, Religious affiliation, State/district residency.

UNIVERSITY OF MAINE—AUGUSTA

46 University Drive, Augusta, ME 04330
Phone: 207-621-3465 **Financial Aid Phone:** 207-621-3455
E-mail: umaadm@maine.edu **CEEB Code:** 3929
Fax: 207-621-3333 **Website:** www.uma.edu **ACT Code:** 1641

This public school was founded in 1965. It has a 159 acre campus.

RATINGS

Admissions Selectivity Rating: 65   **Fire Safety Rating:** 60*   **Green Rating:** 60*

STUDENTS AND FACULTY

Enrollment: 4,523. **Student Body:** 73% female, 27% male, 3% out-of-state, <1% international (5 countries represented). Asian 1%, African American 1%, Caucasian 85%, Hispanic 1%, Native American 2%, Pacific Islander <1%, Two or more races 2%, Race unknown 8%.
Retention and Graduation: 53% freshmen return for sophomore year. 40% grads go on to further study within 1 year. **Faculty:** Student/faculty ratio 18:1. 103 full-time faculty, 56% hold PhDs, 0% are members of minority groups, 58% are women. 0% of classes are taught by teaching assistants.

ACADEMICS

Degrees: Associate; Bachelor's; Certificate; Terminal Associate; Transfer Associate. **Classes:** Most classes have 10–19 students. Most lab/discussion sessions have 10–19 students. **Most popular majors:** Business/Commerce, General; Social Sciences, General; Health Professions And Related Programs. **Special Study Options:** Cross-registration; Distance learning; Double major; Dual enrollment; Honors program; Independent study; Internships; Liberal arts/career combination; Student-designed major; Study abroad; Teacher certification program. **Honors programs:** UMA Honors Program—augments a student's academic and co-curricular experience. **Disability Services offered:** Note-taking services. **Career services:** Career assessment; Career/job search classes.

FACILITIES

99% of campus accessible to physically disabled. **Special Academic Facilities/Equipment:** Jewett Gallery, Katz Library, Student Center **Campus network:** 100% of classrooms, 100% of dorms, 100% of student union, 100% of libraries, 100% of dining areas, 10% of common outdoor areas have wireless network access.

CAMPUS LIFE

Environment: Village. **Activities:** Drama/theater; International Student Organization; Jazz band; Literary magazine; Music ensembles; Pep band; Student government; Student newspaper. 23 registered organizations, 1 honor society, 1 religious organization on campus. **Athletics (Intercollegiate):** *Men:* basketball, golf. *Women:* basketball, golf, soccer. **On-Campus Highlights:** Katz Library. **Environmental Initiatives:** Reduce - Reuse - Recycle program in place since 1990.

ADMISSIONS

Freshman Academic Profile: 95% from public high schools. **Basis for Candidate Selection:** *Important factors include:* rigor of secondary school record, academic GPA. *Other factors include:* class rank, application essay, standardized test scores, recommendation(s), interview, extracurricular activities, talent/ability, character/personal qualities, first generation. **Freshman Admission Requirements:** High school diploma is required and GED is accepted. *Academic units required:* 4 English, 2 math, 2 science, 2 science labs, 2 social studies, 2 history. *Academic units recommended:* 3 math, 3 science.

Freshman Admission Statistics: 875 applied, 93% admitted, 63% enrolled. **Transfer Admission Requirements:** College transcript(s). Minimum college GPA of 2.0 required. Lowest grade transferable C. **General Admission Information:** Application fee $40. Priority deadline 6/15. Regular application deadline 8/15. Non-fall registration accepted. Admission may be deferred for a maximum of 12 months.

COSTS AND FINANCIAL AID

Annual in-state tuition $6,510. Annual out-of-state tuition $15,750. Required fees $938. **Required Forms and Deadlines:** FAFSA. **Notification of Awards:** Applicants will be notified of awards on a rolling basis beginning 3/15. **Types of Aid:** *Need-based scholarships/grants:* College/university scholarship or grant aid from institutional funds; Federal Pell; Private scholarships; SEOG; State scholarships/grants. *Loans:* Direct PLUS loans; Direct Subsidized Stafford Loans; Direct Unsubsidized Stafford Loans. **Student Employment:** Federal Work-Study Program available. Institutional employment available. **Financial Aid Statistics:** 87% needy freshmen, 86% needy undergrads receive need-based scholarship or grant aid. 0% freshmen, 1% undergrads receive non-need-based scholarship or grant aid. 79% freshmen, 89% undergrads receive need-based self-help aid. 0% freshmen, 0% undergrads receive athletic scholarships. 64% freshmen, 72% undergrads receive any aid. **Criteria awarding aid:** *Non-need-based:* Academics, Athletics, Leadership, Music/drama, State/district residency.

UNIVERSITY OF MAINE—FARMINGTON

246 Main Street, Farmington, ME 04938
Phone: 207-778-7050 **Financial Aid Phone:** 207-778-7100
E-mail: umfadmit@maine.edu **CEEB Code:** 3506
Fax: 207-778-8182 **Website:** www.umf.maine.edu **ACT Code:** 1640

This public school was founded in 1863. It has a 55 acre campus.

RATINGS

Admissions Selectivity Rating: 74   **Fire Safety Rating:** 91   **Green Rating:** 66

STUDENTS AND FACULTY

Enrollment: 1,567. **Student Body:** 67% female, 33% male, 17% out-of-state, <1% international (9 countries represented). Asian 1%, African American 3%, Caucasian 88%, Hispanic 3%, Native American 1%, Pacific Islander <1%, Two or more races 3%, Race unknown 2%.
Retention and Graduation: 73% freshmen return for sophomore year. 46% freshmen graduate within 4 years. 58% freshmen graduate within 6 years. **Faculty:** Student/faculty ratio 11:1. 117 full-time faculty, 90% hold PhDs, 4% are members of minority groups, 62% are women. 0% of classes are taught by teaching assistants.

ACADEMICS

Degrees: Bachelor's; Certificate; Master's; Post-bachelor's certificate. **Classes:** Most classes have 10–19 students. Most lab/discussion sessions have fewer than 10 students. **Most popular majors:** Elementary Education and Teaching; Secondary Education and Teaching; Psychology, General. **Special Study Options:** Accelerated program; Cross-registration; Distance learning; Double major; Dual enrollment; Exchange student program (domestic); Honors program; Independent study; Internships; Liberal arts/career combination; Student-designed major; Study abroad; Teacher certification program. **Honors programs:** UMF Honors Program. **Disability Services offered:** Note-taking services; Reader services; Tape recorders; Tutors. **Career services:** Alumni network; Alumni services; Career assessment; Career/job search classes; Internships; Regional alumni.

FACILITIES

Housing: Coed dorms; Cooperative housing; Special housing for disabled students; Theme housing; Wellness housing; Women's dorms; 95% of campus accessible to physically disabled. **Special Academic Facilities/Equipment:** Astronomy Observatory, Alice James Books poetry journal, assistive learning center, and on-site nursery school and day care as a teaching environment.

CAMPUS LIFE

Environment: Village. **Activities:** Campus Ministries; Choral groups; Dance; Drama/theater; International Student Organization; Literary magazine; Music ensembles; Musical theater; Radio station; Student government; Student newspaper; Symphony orchestra; Television station; Yearbook. 60 registered organizations, 14 honor societies, 2 religious organizations on campus. **Athletics (Intercollegiate):** *Men:* baseball, basketball, cross-country, golf, soccer.

Women: basketball, cross-country, field hockey, soccer, softball, volleyball. **On-Campus Highlights:** Recreation and Fitness Center **Environmental Initiatives:** Completion of two LEED-certified buildings and a third building which meets most qualifications for LEED standard.

ADMISSIONS

Freshman Academic Profile: Average high school GPA 3.1. 15% in top 10% of high school class, 37% in top 25% of high school class, 72% in top 50% of high school class. **Test Scores:** SAT Math middle 50% range 460–560. SAT EBRW middle 50% range 480–600. ACT middle 50% range 20–26. **Basis for Candidate Selection:** *Very important factors include:* rigor of secondary school record, academic GPA. *Important factors include:* class rank, application essay, recommendation(s), talent/ability, character/personal qualities. *Other factors include:* standardized test scores, interview, extracurricular activities, first generation, alumni/ae relation, geographical residence, state residency, volunteer work, work experience, level of applicant's interest. **Freshman Admission Requirements:** High school diploma is required and GED is accepted. *Academic units required:* 4 English, 3 math, 3 science, 2 science labs, 3 social studies. *Academic units recommended:* 2 foreign language. **Freshman Admission Statistics:** 1,744 applied, 91% admitted, 24% enrolled. **Transfer Admission Requirements:** High school transcript, college transcript(s), essay or personal statement. Minimum college GPA of 2.5 required. Lowest grade transferable C. **General Admission Information:** Non-fall registration accepted. Admission may be deferred for a maximum of one academic year.

COSTS AND FINANCIAL AID

Annual in-state tuition $8,220. Annual out-of-state tuition $17,700. Room and board $9,626. Required fees $898. Average book and supplies expense $900. **Required Forms and Deadlines:** FAFSA. **Notification of Awards:** Applicants will be notified of awards on a rolling basis beginning 2/1. **Types of Aid:** *Need-based scholarships/grants:* College/university scholarship or grant aid from institutional funds; Federal Pell; Private scholarships; SEOG; State scholarships/grants. *Loans:* Direct PLUS loans; Direct Subsidized Stafford Loans; Direct Unsubsidized Stafford Loans. **Student Employment:** Federal Work-Study Program available. Institutional employment available. **Financial Aid Statistics:** 99% needy freshmen, 96% needy undergrads receive need-based scholarship or grant aid. 8% freshmen, 5% undergrads receive non-need-based scholarship or grant aid. 86% freshmen, 87% undergrads receive need-based self-help aid. 0% freshmen, 0% undergrads receive athletic scholarships. 85% undergrads borrow to pay for school. Average cumulative indebtedness $30,315. **Criteria awarding aid:** *Non-need-based:* Academics, Leadership, Minority status, Music/drama, State/district residency.

UNIVERSITY OF MAINE—FORT KENT

23 University Drive, Fort Kent, ME 04743
Phone: 888-879-8635 **Financial Aid Phone:** 207-834-7607
E-mail: umfkadm@maine.maine.edu **CEEB Code:** 3393
Fax: 207-834-7609 **Website:** www.umfk.maine.edu **ACT Code:** 1642

This public school was founded in 1878. It has a 52 acre campus.

RATINGS

Admissions Selectivity Rating: 72   **Fire Safety Rating:** 99   **Green Rating:** 63

STUDENTS AND FACULTY

Enrollment: 1,036. **Student Body:** 73% female, 27% male, 14% out-of-state, 7% international. Asian 1%, African American 3%, Caucasian 79%, Hispanic 3%, Native American 1%, Pacific Islander <1%, Two or more races 3%, Race unknown 3%.
Retention and Graduation: 61% freshmen return for sophomore year. 21% freshmen graduate within 4 years. 33% freshmen graduate within 6 years. 5% grads go on to further study within 1 year. 3% grads pursue arts and sciences degrees. **Faculty:** Student/faculty ratio 14:1. 34 full-time faculty, 44% hold PhDs, 3% are members of minority groups, 41% are women. 0% of classes are taught by teaching assistants.

ACADEMICS

Degrees: Associate; Bachelor's; Certificate. **Classes:** Most classes have 10–19 students. Most lab/discussion sessions have fewer than 10 students. **Most popular majors:** Behavioral Sciences; Business/Commerce, General; Registered Nursing, Nursing Administration, Nursing Research and Clinical Nursing. **Special Study Options:** Cross-registration; Distance learning; Double major; Independent study; Internships; Student-designed major; Study abroad; Teacher certification program. **Disability Services offered:** Note-taking services; Reader services; Tape recorders; Tutors. **Career services:** Alumni services; Career assessment; Career/job search classes; Internships.

FACILITIES
Housing: Coed dorms; 90% of campus accessible to physically disabled.

CAMPUS LIFE
Environment: Rural. **Activities:** Campus Ministries; Drama/theater; Student government. 25 registered organizations, 1 fraternity, 1 sorority on campus. **Athletics (Intercollegiate):** *Men:* basketball, cross-country, golf, skiing (downhill/Alpine), skiing (Nordic/cross-country), soccer. *Women:* basketball, cross-country, golf, skiing (downhill/Alpine), skiing (Nordic/cross-country), soccer, volleyball. **On-Campus Highlights:** Bengal's Lair.

ADMISSIONS
Freshman Academic Profile: Average high school GPA 3.0. 9% in top 10% of high school class, 24% in top 25% of high school class, 68% in top 50% of high school class. 96% from public high schools. **Test Scores:** SAT Math middle 50% range 410–560. SAT EBRW middle 50% range 450–550. ACT middle 50% range 17–22. **Basis for Candidate Selection:** *Very important factors include:* level of applicant's interest. *Important factors include:* rigor of secondary school record, class rank, academic GPA, application essay, recommendation(s), talent/ability, character/personal qualities, first generation, geographical residence, state residency, volunteer work. *Other factors include:* standardized test scores, interview, extracurricular activities, alumni/ae relation, work experience. **Freshman Admission Requirements:** High school diploma is required and GED is accepted. *Academic units required:* 4 English, 2 math, 2 science, 2 science labs. *Academic units recommended:* 2 foreign language. **Freshman Admission Statistics:** 572 applied, 97% admitted, 24% enrolled. **Transfer Admission Requirements:** High school transcript, college transcript(s), essay or personal statement. Lowest grade transferable C-. **General Admission Information:** Application fee $40. Regular application deadline 8/15. Non-fall registration accepted.

COSTS AND FINANCIAL AID
Annual in-state tuition $6,990. Annual out-of-state tuition $11,190. Room and board $7,910. Required fees $1,125. Average book and supplies expense $500. **Required Forms and Deadlines:** CSS/Financial Aid PROFILE; FAFSA; Institution's own financial aid form; State aid form. **Notification of Awards:** Applicants will be notified of awards on a rolling basis beginning 3/15. **Types of Aid:** *Need-based scholarships/grants:* College/university scholarship or grant aid from institutional funds; Federal Nursing Scholarships; Federal Pell; Private scholarships; SEOG; State scholarships/grants. *Loans:* Direct PLUS loans; Direct Subsidized Stafford Loans; Direct Unsubsidized Stafford Loans. **Student Employment:** Federal Work-Study Program available. Institutional employment available. **Financial Aid Statistics:** 94% needy freshmen, 86% needy undergrads receive need-based scholarship or grant aid. 2% freshmen, 2% undergrads receive non-need-based scholarship or grant aid. 70% freshmen, 81% undergrads receive need-based self-help aid. 0% freshmen, 0% undergrads receive athletic scholarships. 78% freshmen receive any aid. 76% undergrads borrow to pay for school. Average cumulative indebtedness $24,096. **Criteria awarding aid:** *Need-based:* Academics, Leadership. *Non-need-based:* Academics, Alumni affiliation, Job skills, Leadership, State/district residency.

UNIVERSITY OF MAINE—MACHIAS

Office of Admissions, Machias, ME 04654
Phone: 207-255-1318 **Financial Aid Phone:** 207-255-1203
E-mail: ummadmissions@maine.edu **CEEB Code:** 3956
Fax: 207-255-1363 **Website:** www.umm.maine.edu **ACT Code:** 1666

This public school was founded in 1909. It has a 42 acre campus.

RATINGS
Admissions Selectivity Rating: 73 **Fire Safety Rating:** 76 **Green Rating:** 60*

STUDENTS AND FACULTY
Enrollment: 554. **Student Body:** 65% female, 35% male, 24% out-of-state, 4% international (18 countries represented). Asian 1%, African American 1%, Caucasian 88%, Hispanic 2%, Native American 4%, Race unknown 0%. **Retention and Graduation:** 73% freshmen return for sophomore year. **Faculty:** Student/faculty ratio 15:1. 30 full-time faculty, 73% hold PhDs, 3% are members of minority groups, 33% are women. 0% of classes are taught by teaching assistants.

ACADEMICS
Degrees: Bachelor's. **Classes:** Most classes have 10–19 students. Most lab/discussion sessions have 10–19 students. **Most popular majors:** Elementary Education and Teaching; Marine Biology and Biological Oceanography; Parks, Recreation and Leisure Facilities Management, General. **Special Study Options:** Cooperative education program; Distance learning; Double major; Dual enrollment; Honors program; Independent study; Internships; Student-designed major; Study abroad; Teacher certification program. **Disability Services offered:** Reader services; Tape recorders; Tutors. **Career services:** Career assessment; Internships.

FACILITIES
Housing: Coed dorms; 85% of campus accessible to physically disabled. **Special Academic Facilities/Equipment:** Art Gallery; Book Arts Print Shop; Geographic Information Systems Laboratory and Service Center.

CAMPUS LIFE
Environment: Rural. **Activities:** Campus Ministries; Choral groups; Dance; Drama/theater; Literary magazine; Music ensembles; Musical theater; Pep band; Radio station; Student government. 38 registered organizations, 2 religious organizations, 5 fraternities, 4 sororities on campus. **Athletics (Intercollegiate):** *Men:* basketball, soccer. *Women:* basketball, soccer, volleyball. **On-Campus Highlights:** Aquatics/Fitness Center/Gymnasium. **Environmental Initiatives:** Green Council.

ADMISSIONS
Freshman Academic Profile: 13% in top 10% of high school class, 24% in top 25% of high school class, 63% in top 50% of high school class. **Test Scores:** SAT Math middle 50% range 400–530. SAT EBRW middle 50% range 440–530. ACT middle 50% range 15–25. **Basis for Candidate Selection:** *Very important factors include:* rigor of secondary school record, application essay, recommendation(s), interview. *Important factors include:* class rank, standardized test scores, extracurricular activities. *Other factors include:* talent/ability, character/personal qualities, volunteer work, work experience. **Freshman Admission Requirements:** High school diploma is required and GED is accepted. *Academic units required:* 4 English, 3 math, 2 science, 2 science labs, 2 social studies. *Academic units recommended:* 2 foreign language, 3 academic electives. **Freshman Admission Statistics:** 381 applied, 92% admitted, 32% enrolled. **Transfer Admission Requirements:** High school transcript, college transcript(s), statement of good standing from prior institution(s). Minimum college GPA of 2.0 required. Lowest grade transferable C-. **General Admission Information:** Application fee $40. Regular application deadline 8/15. Non-fall registration accepted. Admission may be deferred for a maximum of 1 year.

COSTS AND FINANCIAL AID
Annual in-state tuition $6,410. Annual out-of-state tuition $16,550. Room and board $6,574. Average book and supplies expense $650. **Required Forms and Deadlines:** FAFSA. **Notification of Awards:** Applicants will be notified of awards on a rolling basis beginning 3/1. **Types of Aid:** *Need-based scholarships/grants:* College/university scholarship or grant aid from institutional funds; Federal Pell; Private scholarships; SEOG; State scholarships/grants. **Student Employment:** Federal Work-Study Program available. Institutional employment available. **Financial Aid Statistics:** 97% needy freshmen, 87% needy undergrads receive need-based scholarship or grant aid. 9% freshmen, 5% undergrads receive non-need-based scholarship or grant aid. 81% freshmen, 79% undergrads receive need-based self-help aid. 0% freshmen, 0% undergrads receive athletic scholarships. 82% freshmen, 74% undergrads receive any aid. **Criteria awarding aid:** *Need-based:* Academics, Art, Leadership. *Non-need-based:* Academics, Alumni affiliation, Art, Leadership, Minority status, Music/drama, State/district residency.

UNIVERSITY OF MAINE—PRESQUE ISLE

Office of Admissions, Presque Isle, ME 04769
Phone: 207-768-9532 **Financial Aid Phone:** 207-768-9510
E-mail: admissions@umpi.edu **CEEB Code:** 3008
Fax: 207-768-9777 **Website:** www.umpi.edu **ACT Code:** 1630

This public school was founded in 1903. It has a 150 acre campus.

RATINGS
Admissions Selectivity Rating: 75 **Fire Safety Rating:** 84 **Green Rating:** 63

STUDENTS AND FACULTY
Enrollment: 833. **Student Body:** 62% female, 38% male, 4% out-of-state, 8% international (3 countries represented). Asian <1%, African American 3%,

Caucasian 79%, Hispanic 2%, Native American 3%, Pacific Islander 0%, Two or more races 3%, Race unknown 4%.
Retention and Graduation: 65% freshmen return for sophomore year. **Faculty:** Student/faculty ratio 15:1. 42 full-time faculty, 64% hold PhDs, 5% are members of minority groups, 48% are women. 0% of classes are taught by teaching assistants.

ACADEMICS

Degrees: Associate; Bachelor's; Certificate. **Classes:** Most classes have 10–19 students. Most lab/discussion sessions have 10–19 students. **Most popular majors:** Business/Commerce, General; Liberal Arts and Sciences/Liberal Studies; Elementary Education and Teaching. **Special Study Options:** Accelerated program; Distance learning; Double major; Dual enrollment; Exchange student program (domestic); Honors program; Independent study; Internships; Study abroad; Teacher certification program. **Disability Services offered:** Note-taking services; Reader services; Tape recorders; Tutors. **Career services:** Alumni services; Career assessment; Career/job search classes; Internships.

FACILITIES

Housing: Apartments for married students; Coed dorms; Special housing for disabled students; 100% of campus accessible to physically disabled. **Special Academic Facilities/Equipment:** Art Gallery and Gentile Hall.

CAMPUS LIFE

Environment: Village. **Activities:** Campus Ministries; Dance; International Student Organization; Radio station; Student government; Student newspaper. 30 registered organizations, 1 honor society, 1 religious organization, 1 fraternity, 1 sorority on campus. **Athletics (Intercollegiate):** *Men:* baseball, basketball, cross-country, golf, skiing (Nordic/cross-country), soccer. *Women:* basketball, cross-country, skiing (Nordic/cross-country), soccer, softball, volleyball. **On-Campus Highlights:** Caroline D. Gentile Hall.

ADMISSIONS

Freshman Academic Profile: Average high school GPA 3.0. 3% in top 10% of high school class, 15% in top 25% of high school class, 45% in top 50% of high school class. **Test Scores:** SAT Math middle 50% range 397–532. SAT EBRW middle 50% range 394–528. ACT middle 50% range 18–23. **Basis for Candidate Selection:** *Very important factors include:* rigor of secondary school record. *Important factors include:* academic GPA, application essay, recommendation(s). *Other factors include:* class rank, standardized test scores, interview, extracurricular activities, talent/ability, character/personal qualities, first generation, alumni/ae relation, volunteer work, work experience, level of applicant's interest. **Freshman Admission Requirements:** High school diploma is required and GED is accepted. *Academic units recommended:* 4 English, 3 math, 2 science, 2 science labs, 2 foreign language, 3 social studies, 2 academic electives. **Freshman Admission Statistics:** 1,442 applied, 77% admitted, 18% enrolled. **Transfer Admission Requirements:** High school transcript, college transcript(s), essay or personal statement, statement of good standing from prior institution(s). Minimum college GPA of 2.0 required. Lowest grade transferable C-. **General Admission Information:** Application fee $40. Non-fall registration accepted.

COSTS AND FINANCIAL AID

Annual in-state tuition $6,600. Annual out-of-state tuition $9,900. Room and board $8,044. Required fees $700. Average book and supplies expense $900. **Required Forms and Deadlines:** FAFSA. **Notification of Awards:** Applicants will be notified of awards on a rolling basis beginning 3/1. **Types of Aid:** *Need-based scholarships/grants:* College/university scholarship or grant aid from institutional funds; Federal Pell; Private scholarships; SEOG; State scholarships/grants. *Loans:* Direct PLUS loans; Direct Subsidized Stafford Loans; Direct Unsubsidized Stafford Loans. **Student Employment:** Federal Work-Study Program available. Institutional employment available. **Financial Aid Statistics:** 99% needy freshmen, 98% needy undergrads receive need-based scholarship or grant aid. 7% freshmen, 5% undergrads receive non-need-based scholarship or grant aid. 74% freshmen, 77% undergrads receive need-based self-help aid. 0% freshmen, 0% undergrads receive athletic scholarships. 83% freshmen, 76% undergrads receive any aid. 84% undergrads borrow to pay for school. Average cumulative indebtedness $25,713. **Criteria awarding aid:** *Non-need-based:* Academics.

UNIVERSITY OF MARY HARDIN-BAYLOR

UMHB Box 8004, Belton, TX 76513
Phone: 254-295-4520 **Financial Aid Phone:** 254-295-4517
E-mail: admissions@umhb.edu **CEEB Code:** 3588
Fax: 254-295-5049 **Website:** www.umhb.edu **ACT Code:** 4128

This private school, affiliated with the Baptist Church, was founded in 1845. It has a 125 acre campus.

RATINGS

Admissions Selectivity Rating: 75   **Fire Safety Rating:** 79   **Green Rating:** 60*

STUDENTS AND FACULTY

Enrollment: 3,173. **Student Body:** 63% female, 37% male, 2% out-of-state, 2% international (12 countries represented). Asian 2%, African American 15%, Caucasian 57%, Hispanic 20%, Native American 1%, Pacific Islander <1%, Two or more races 3%, Race unknown 1%.
Retention and Graduation: 69% freshmen return for sophomore year. **Faculty:** Student/faculty ratio 19:1. 167 full-time faculty, 74% hold PhDs, 14% are members of minority groups, 55% are women. 0% of classes are taught by teaching assistants.

ACADEMICS

Degrees: Bachelor's; Doctoral degree—professional practice; Doctoral degree research/scholarship; Master's; Post-master's certificate. **Classes:** Most classes have 10–19 students. Most lab/discussion sessions have 20–29 students. **Most popular majors:** Registered Nursing/Registered Nurse; Elementary Education and Teaching. **Special Study Options:** Distance learning; Double major; Dual enrollment; English as a Second Language (ESL); Honors program; Independent study; Internships; Study abroad; Teacher certification program. **Honors programs:** Lower Level Honors Program—approximately the top 10% of UMHB's entering freshman class. Freshman year offerings include English and religion, and sophomore year offerings are interdisciplinary courses in the humanities and social sciences. Upper Level Honors Program—Minimum requirements for completion of this program include the completion of three upper level courses designated as honors level and the completion of HNRS 3110 "Great Books and Ideas" and HNRS 3120 "Living Issues." Successful completion of these requirements will allow the student to graduate with the cum laude designation. To receive the higher designations of magna cum laude or summa cum laude, the student must also successfully complete an Honors Research Project. This project must include original research and both written and oral presentations of that research to the Honors Committee. **Disability Services offered:** Note-taking services; Reader services; Tape recorders; Tutors. **Career services:** Alumni network; Alumni services; Career assessment; Career/job search classes; Internships; Regional alumni.

FACILITIES

Housing: Apartments for single students; Men's dorms; Special housing for disabled students; Women's dorms; 85% of campus accessible to physically disabled. **Special Academic Facilities/Equipment:** Language lab.

CAMPUS LIFE

Environment: Town. **Activities:** Campus Ministries; Choral groups; Concert band; Drama/theater; International Student Organization; Jazz band; Literary magazine; Model UN; Music ensembles; Musical theater; Opera; Pep band; Student government; Student newspaper; Student-run film society; Yearbook. 51 registered organizations, 5 honor societies, 7 religious organizations on campus. **Athletics (Intercollegiate):** *Men:* baseball, basketball, football, golf, soccer, tennis. *Women:* basketball, golf, soccer, softball, tennis, volleyball. **On-Campus Highlights:** Isabelle Rutherford Meyer Nursing Education Center.

ADMISSIONS

Freshman Academic Profile: Average high school GPA 3.6. 20% in top 10% of high school class, 50% in top 25% of high school class, 84% in top 50% of high school class. **Test Scores:** SAT Math middle 50% range 470–570. SAT EBRW middle 50% range 460–560. ACT middle 50% range 20–26. **Basis for Candidate Selection:** *Very important factors include:* class rank, standardized test scores. *Important factors include:* academic GPA. *Other factors include:* rigor of secondary school record, application essay, recommendation(s), interview, extracurricular activities, talent/ability, character/personal qualities, first generation, alumni/ae relation, geographical residence, state residency, religious affiliation/commitment, racial/ethnic status, volunteer work, work experience, level of applicant's interest. **Freshman Admission Requirements:** High school diploma is required and GED is accepted. *Academic units required:* 4 English,

3 math, 3 science, 2 foreign language, 3.5 social studies. **Freshman Admission Statistics:** 7,504 applied, 80% admitted, 12% enrolled. **Transfer Admission Requirements:** College transcript(s). Minimum college GPA of 2.0 required. Lowest grade transferable C. **General Admission Information:** Application fee $35. Non-fall registration accepted. Admission may be deferred for a maximum of 1 semester.

COSTS AND FINANCIAL AID

Required Forms and Deadlines: FAFSA. **Notification of Awards:** Applicants will be notified of awards on a rolling basis beginning 2/15. **Types of Aid:** *Need-based scholarships/grants:* College/university scholarship or grant aid from institutional funds; Federal Nursing Scholarships; Federal Pell; Private scholarships; SEOG; State scholarships/grants. *Loans:* Direct PLUS loans; Direct Subsidized Stafford Loans; Direct Unsubsidized Stafford Loans. **Student Employment:** Federal Work-Study Program available. Institutional employment available. **Financial Aid Statistics:** 100% needy freshmen, 99% needy undergrads receive need-based scholarship or grant aid. 7% freshmen, 5% undergrads receive non-need-based scholarship or grant aid. 83% freshmen, 84% undergrads receive need-based self-help aid. 0% freshmen, 0% undergrads receive athletic scholarships. 84% freshmen, 87% undergrads receive any aid. 78% undergrads borrow to pay for school. Average cumulative indebtedness $35,011. **Criteria awarding aid:** *Need-based:* Academics, Alumni affiliation, Art, Job skills, Leadership, Music/drama, Religious affiliation.

UNIVERSITY OF MARYLAND, BALTIMORE COUNTY

1000 Hilltop Circle, Baltimore, MD 21250
Phone: 410-455-2292 **Financial Aid Phone:** 410-455-2387
E-mail: admissions@umbc.edu **CEEB Code:** 5835
Fax: 410-455-1094 **Website:** www.umbc.edu **ACT Code:** 1751

This public school was founded in 1966. It has a 530 acre campus.

RATINGS

Admissions Selectivity Rating: 87 Fire Safety Rating: 65 Green Rating: 92

STUDENTS AND FACULTY

Enrollment: 10,955. **Student Body:** 45% female, 55% male, 5% out-of-state, 4% international (82 countries represented). Asian 22%, African American 19%, Caucasian 39%, Hispanic 8%, Native American <1%, Pacific Islander <1%, Two or more races 5%, Race unknown 2%.
Retention and Graduation: 87% freshmen return for sophomore year. 42% freshmen graduate within 4 years. 71% freshmen graduate within 6 years. 41% grads go on to further study within 1 year. 35% grads pursue arts and sciences degrees. 1% grads pursue law degrees. 1% grads pursue business degrees. 1% grads pursue medical degrees. **Faculty:** Student/faculty ratio 17:1. 555 full-time faculty, 85% hold PhDs, 28% are members of minority groups, 48% are women. 2% of classes are taught by teaching assistants.

ACADEMICS

Degrees: Bachelor's; Certificate; Doctoral degree research/scholarship; Master's; Post-bachelor's certificate; Post-master's certificate. **Classes:** Most classes have 10–19 students. Most lab/discussion sessions have 20–29 students.
Most popular majors: Biology/Biological Sciences, General; Management Information Systems and Services; Psychology. **Special Study Options:** Accelerated program; Cooperative education program; Cross-registration; Double major; Dual enrollment; English as a Second Language (ESL); Honors program; Independent study; Internships; Liberal arts/career combination; Student-designed major; Study abroad; Teacher certification program.
Honors programs: UMBC Honors College, Meyerhoff (Science, Technology, Engineering, and Mathematics), Scholars Program, Sherman Teacher Education Scholars Program, Sondheim Scholars Programs, Center for Women and Information Technology (CWIT) Scholars Program, Humanities Scholars Program, Linehan Scholars Program, Cyber Scholars Program. **Combined degree programs:** BA/MA. **Disability Services offered:** Note-taking services; Reader services; Tape recorders; Tutors. **Career services:** Alumni network; Alumni services; Career assessment; Career/job search classes; Internships; Regional alumni.

FACILITIES

Housing: Apartments for single students; Coed dorms; Special housing for disabled students; Special housing for international students; Theme housing; 95% of campus accessible to physically disabled. **Special Academic Facilities/Equipment:** Albin O. Kuhn Library and Gallery, Center for Art and Visual Culture, Women's Center, Center for Environmental Science, Center for Photonics Technology, Center for Women and Information Technology, Center on Research and Teaching in Social Work, Howard Hughes Medical Institute at UMBC, Imaging Research Center, Institute for Global Electronic Commerce, Joint Center for Earth Systems Technology, Laboratory for Healthcare Informatics, Maryland Center for Telecommunications Research, Maryland Institute for Policy Analysis and Research, bwtech@umbc Research and Technology Park and Incubator and Accelerator, Shriver Center, UMBC Technology Center, Goddard Earth Science and Technology Center.

CAMPUS LIFE

Environment: Metropolis. **Activities:** Campus Ministries; Choral groups; Concert band; Dance; Drama/theater; International Student Organization; Jazz band; Literary magazine; Marching band; Model UN; Music ensembles; Musical theater; Opera; Pep band; Radio station; Student government; Student newspaper; Symphony orchestra; Television station. 255 registered organizations, 7 honor societies, 16 religious organizations, 11 fraternity, 6 sororities on campus. **Athletics (Intercollegiate):** *Men:* baseball, basketball, cheerleading, cross-country, diving, lacrosse, soccer, swimming, tennis, track/field (outdoor), track/field (indoor). *Women:* basketball, cheerleading, cross-country, diving, lacrosse, soccer, softball, swimming, tennis, track/field (outdoor), track/field (indoor), volleyball. **On-Campus Highlights:** Albin O. Kuhn Library and Gallery. **Environmental Initiatives:** Climate Commitment Task Force (students, faculty, staff) will commence implementation of its Climate Action Plan and reduce our carbon footprint.

ADMISSIONS

Freshman Academic Profile: Average high school GPA 3.9. 21% in top 10% of high school class, 51% in top 25% of high school class, 83% in top 50% of high school class. 91% from public high schools. **Test Scores:** SAT Math middle 50% range 590–690. SAT EBRW middle 50% range 590–670. ACT middle 50% range 24–29. **Basis for Candidate Selection:** *Very important factors include:* rigor of secondary school record, academic GPA, application essay, standardized test scores, recommendation(s). *Important factors include:* class rank, talent/ability. *Other factors include:* extracurricular activities, character/personal qualities, first generation, volunteer work, work experience. **Freshman Admission Requirements:** High school diploma is required and GED is accepted. *Academic units required:* 4 English, 4 math, 3 science, 2 foreign language, 3 social studies, 3 history, 3 unit from above areas or other academic areas. *Academic units recommended:* 4 English, 4 math, 3 science, 2 foreign language. **Freshman Admission Statistics:** 11,842 applied, 61% admitted, 24% enrolled. **Transfer Admission Requirements:** College transcript(s), statement of good standing from prior institution(s). Minimum college GPA of 2.5 required. Lowest grade transferable D. **General Admission Information:** Application fee $75. Priority deadline 11/1. Regular application deadline 2/1. Non-fall registration accepted. Admission may be deferred for a maximum of 1 year.

COSTS AND FINANCIAL AID

Annual in-state tuition $8,704. Annual out-of-state tuition $24,338. Room and board $12,000. Required fees $3,324. Average book and supplies expense $1,200. **Required Forms and Deadlines:** FAFSA. **Notification of Awards:** Applicants will be notified of awards on a rolling basis beginning 3/25. **Types of Aid:** *Need-based scholarships/grants:* College/university scholarship or grant aid from institutional funds; Federal Pell; Private scholarships; SEOG; State scholarships/grants; United Negro College Fund. *Loans:* Direct PLUS loans; Direct Subsidized Stafford Loans; Direct Unsubsidized Stafford Loans. **Student Employment:** Federal Work-Study Program available. Institutional employment available. **Financial Aid Statistics:** 88% needy freshmen, 78% needy undergrads receive need-based scholarship or grant aid. 35% freshmen, 13% undergrads receive non-need-based scholarship or grant aid. 42% freshmen, 56% undergrads receive need-based self-help aid. 2% freshmen, 1% undergrads receive athletic scholarships. 89% freshmen, 62% undergrads receive any aid. 49% undergrads borrow to pay for school. Average cumulative indebtedness $26,315. **Criteria awarding aid:** *Non-need-based:* Academics, Alumni affiliation, Art, Athletics, Music/drama.

UNIVERSITY OF MARYLAND, COLLEGE PARK

Mitchell Building, College Park, MD 20742-5235
Phone: 301-314-8385 **Financial Aid Phone:** 301-314-9000
E-mail: ApplyMaryland@umd.edu **CEEB Code:** 5814
Fax: 301-314-9693 **Website:** http://www.umd.edu **ACT Code:** 1746

This public school was founded in 1856. It has a 1335 acre campus.

RATINGS
Admissions Selectivity Rating: 94   **Fire Safety Rating:** 90   **Green Rating:** 98

STUDENTS AND FACULTY
Enrollment: 29,905. **Student Body:** 48% female, 52% male, 23% out-of-state, 4% international (66 countries represented). Asian 18%, African American 11%, Caucasian 49%, Hispanic 9%, Native American <1%, Pacific Islander <1%, Two or more races 5%, Race unknown 3%.
Retention and Graduation: 95% freshmen return for sophomore year. 69% freshmen graduate within 4 years. 87% freshmen graduate within 6 years. **Faculty:** Student/faculty ratio 18:1. 1,867 full-time faculty, 92% hold PhDs, 26% are members of minority groups, 40% are women. 12% of classes are taught by teaching assistants.

ACADEMICS
Degrees: Bachelor's; Certificate; Doctoral degree—professional practice; Doctoral degree research/scholarship; Master's; Post-bachelor's certificate; Post-master's certificate. **Classes:** Most classes have 10–19 students. Most lab/discussion sessions have 20–29 students. **Most popular majors:** Computer Science; Biology/Biological Sciences, General. **Special Study Options:** Accelerated program; Cooperative education program; Cross-registration; Distance learning; Double major; Dual enrollment; English as a Second Language (ESL); Exchange student program (domestic); External degree program; Honors program; Independent study; Internships; Liberal arts/career combination; Student-designed major; Study abroad; Teacher certification program. **Honors programs:** Gemstone, Honors, Honors Humanities. **Combined degree programs:** BA/JD; BA/MA; BA/MEng. **Disability Services offered:** Note-taking services; Reader services; Tape recorders; Tutors. **Career services:** Alumni network; Alumni services; Career assessment; Career/job search classes; Internships; Regional alumni.

FACILITIES
Housing: Apartments for married students; Apartments for single students; Coed dorms; Cooperative housing; Fraternity/sorority housing; Special housing for disabled students; Special housing for international students; Theme housing; Wellness housing; Women's dorms. **Special Academic Facilities/Equipment:** Aerospace buoyancy lab, art gallery, international piano archives, center for architectural design and research, model nuclear reactor, wind tunnel. **Campus network:** 100% of classrooms, 100% of dorms, 100% of student union, 100% of libraries, 100% of dining areas, 95% of common outdoor areas have wireless network access.

CAMPUS LIFE
Environment: Metropolis. **Activities:** Campus Ministries; Choral groups; Concert band; Dance; Drama/theater; International Student Organization; Jazz band; Literary magazine; Marching band; Model UN; Music ensembles; Musical theater; Opera; Pep band; Radio station; Student government; Student newspaper; Student-run film society; Symphony orchestra; Television station; Yearbook. 724 registered organizations, 49 honor societies, 52 religious organizations, 32 fraternities, 24 sororities on campus. **Athletics (Intercollegiate):** *Men:* baseball, basketball, cross-country, football, golf, lacrosse, soccer, swimming, tennis, track/field (outdoor), track/field (indoor), wrestling. *Women:* basketball, cheerleading, cross-country, field hockey, golf, gymnastics, lacrosse, soccer, softball, swimming, tennis, track/field (outdoor), track/field (indoor), volleyball, water polo. **On-Campus Highlights:** Clarice Smith Performing Arts Center. **Environmental Initiatives:** The Green Office Program engages staff, faculty and students in a voluntary, self-guided initiative that promotes best environmental practices at the University of Maryland. The program supports and promotes offices that are taking steps toward reducing their environmental footprint. Learn more at http://www.sustainability.umd.edu/content/culture/green_offices.php.

ADMISSIONS
Freshman Academic Profile: Average high school GPA 4.3. 69% in top 10% of high school class, 89% in top 25% of high school class, 99% in top 50% of high school class. **Test Scores:** SAT Math middle 50% range 650–760. SAT EBRW middle 50% range 630–720. ACT middle 50% range 29–33. **Basis for Candidate Selection:** *Very important factors include:* rigor of secondary school record, academic GPA, standardized test scores. *Important factors include:* class rank, application essay, recommendation(s), talent/ability, first generation, state residency. *Other factors include:* extracurricular activities, character/personal qualities, alumni/ae relation, geographical residence, racial/ethnic status, volunteer work, work experience. **Freshman Admission Requirements:** High school diploma is required and GED is accepted. *Academic units required:* 4 English, 4 math, 3 science, 2 science labs, 2 foreign language, 3 social studies. *Academic units recommended:* 4 English, 4 math, 3 science, 2 science labs, 2 foreign language, 3 social studies. **Freshman Admission Statistics:** 32,987 applied, 44% admitted, 29% enrolled. **Transfer Admission Requirements:** College transcript(s), essay or personal statement, statement of good standing from prior institution(s). Lowest grade transferable C. **General Admission Information:** Application fee $75. Priority deadline 11/1. Regular application deadline 1/20. Non-fall registration accepted. Admission may be deferred for a maximum of 1 year.

COSTS AND FINANCIAL AID
Annual in-state tuition $8,824. Annual out-of-state tuition $34,936. Room and board $12,935. Required fees $1,955. Average book and supplies expense $1,250. **Required Forms and Deadlines:** FAFSA. **Notification of Awards:** Applicants will be notified of awards on a rolling basis beginning 4/1. **Types of Aid:** *Need-based scholarships/grants:* College/university scholarship or grant aid from institutional funds; Federal Pell; Private scholarships; SEOG; State scholarships/grants. *Loans:* Direct PLUS loans; Direct Subsidized Stafford Loans; Direct Unsubsidized Stafford Loans. **Student Employment:** Federal Work-Study Program available. Institutional employment available. **Financial Aid Statistics:** 78% needy freshmen, 75% needy undergrads receive need-based scholarship or grant aid. 10% freshmen, 5% undergrads receive non-need-based scholarship or grant aid. 84% freshmen, 91% undergrads receive need-based self-help aid. 2% freshmen, 2% undergrads receive athletic scholarships. 86.4% freshmen, 71.7% undergrads receive any aid. 39% undergrads borrow to pay for school. Average cumulative indebtedness $29,133. **Criteria awarding aid:** *Need-based:* Academics. *Non-need-based:* Academics, Art, Athletics, Leadership, Music/drama, State/district residency.

UNIVERSITY OF MARY WASHINGTON

1301 College Avenue, Fredericksburg, VA 22401
Phone: 540-654-2000 **Financial Aid Phone:** 540-654-1682
E-mail: admit@umw.edu **CEEB Code:** 5398
Fax: 540-654-1857 **Website:** www.umw.edu **ACT Code:** 4414

This public school was founded in 1908. It has a 234 acre campus.

RATINGS
Admissions Selectivity Rating: 82   **Fire Safety Rating:** 93   **Green Rating:** 91

STUDENTS AND FACULTY
Enrollment: 4,371. **Student Body:** 64% female, 36% male, 9% out-of-state, 1% international (50 countries represented). Asian 4%, African American 8%, Caucasian 68%, Hispanic 10%, Native American <1%, Pacific Islander <1%, Two or more races 6%, Race unknown 3%.
Retention and Graduation: 82% freshmen return for sophomore year. 60% freshmen graduate within 4 years. 71% freshmen graduate within 6 years. 15% grads go on to further study within 1 year. 10% grads pursue arts and sciences degrees. 1% grads pursue law degrees. 1% grads pursue business degrees. 1% grads pursue medical degrees. **Faculty:** Student/faculty ratio 14:1. 254 full-time faculty, 91% hold PhDs, 20% are members of minority groups, 48% are women. 0% of classes are taught by teaching assistants.

ACADEMICS
Degrees: Bachelor's; Certificate; Master's; Post-bachelor's certificate. **Classes:** Most classes have 20–29 students. Most lab/discussion sessions have 20–29

students. **Most popular majors:** Biology/Biological Sciences, General; Business Administration and Management, General; Psychology, General. **Special Study Options:** Accelerated program; Distance learning; Double major; Honors program; Independent study; Internships; Student-designed major; Study abroad; Teacher certification program. **Honors programs:** UMW's honors program offers highly motivated and advanced undergraduates the opportunity to enhance their intellectual growth through rigorous honors-designated coursework, interdisciplinary seminars, strong internship experiences, extended research and creative projects, and intriguing community service endeavors. **Career services:** Alumni network; Alumni services; Career assessment; Career/job search classes; Internships; Regional alumni.

FACILITIES

Housing: Apartments for single students; Coed dorms; Men's dorms; Special housing for disabled students; Special housing for international students; Theme housing; Wellness housing; Women's dorms; 75% of campus accessible to physically disabled. **Special Academic Facilities/Equipment:** Two art galleries, Center for Historic Preservation, language labs, Leidecker Center for Asian Studies, cartography lab, greenhouse.

CAMPUS LIFE

Environment: City. **Activities:** Campus Ministries; Choral groups; Concert band; Dance; Drama/theater; International Student Organization; Jazz band; Literary magazine; Model UN; Music ensembles; Musical theater; Radio station; Student government; Student newspaper; Student-run film society; Symphony orchestra; Yearbook. 161 registered organizations, 22 honor societies, 12 religious organizations on campus. **Athletics (Intercollegiate):** *Men:* baseball, basketball, crew/rowing, cross-country, equestrian sports, lacrosse, soccer, swimming, tennis, track/field (outdoor), track/field (indoor). *Women:* basketball, crew/rowing, cross-country, equestrian sports, field hockey, lacrosse, soccer, softball, swimming, tennis, track/field (outdoor), track/field (indoor), volleyball. **On-Campus Highlights:** Ball Circle. **Environmental Initiatives:** In July 2010, UMW adopted sustainability policies and practices committing to reducing solid waste, conserving energy and water, encouraging the purchasing of products to promote sustainability and promote alternative methods of transportation.

ADMISSIONS

Freshman Academic Profile: Average high school GPA 3.6. 16% in top 10% of high school class, 46% in top 25% of high school class, 81% in top 50% of high school class. 79% from public high schools. **Test Scores:** SAT Math middle 50% range 510–620. SAT EBRW middle 50% range 540–649. ACT middle 50% range 22–29. **Basis for Candidate Selection:** *Very important factors include:* rigor of secondary school record, academic GPA, standardized test scores. *Important factors include:* class rank, application essay, recommendation(s). *Other factors include:* interview, extracurricular activities, talent/ability, character/personal qualities, first generation, alumni/ae relation, geographical residence, state residency, racial/ethnic status, volunteer work, work experience, level of applicant's interest. **Freshman Admission Requirements:** High school diploma is required and GED is accepted. *Academic units required:* 4 English, 3 math, 3 science, 3 science labs, 3 foreign language, 3 social studies. *Academic units recommended:* 4 English, 4 math, 4 science, 4 science labs, 4 foreign language, 2 social studies, 2 history. **Freshman Admission Statistics:** 5,909 applied, 72% admitted, 22% enrolled. **Transfer Admission Requirements:** High school transcript, college transcript(s), essay or personal statement, statement of good standing from prior institution(s). Minimum college GPA of 2.0 required. Lowest grade transferable C. **General Admission Information:** Application fee $50. Priority deadline 2/1. Regular application deadline 2/1. Non-fall registration accepted. Admission may be deferred for a maximum of one year.

COSTS AND FINANCIAL AID

Annual in-state tuition $6,522. Annual out-of-state tuition $23,014. Room and board $11,612. Required fees $6,576. Average book and supplies expense $1,200. **Required Forms and Deadlines:** FAFSA. **Notification of Awards:** Applicants will be notified of awards on a rolling basis beginning 12/1. **Types of Aid:** *Need-based scholarships/grants:* College/university scholarship or grant aid from institutional funds; Federal Pell; Private scholarships; SEOG; State scholarships/grants. *Loans:* Direct PLUS loans; Direct Subsidized Stafford Loans; Direct Unsubsidized Stafford Loans. **Student Employment:** Federal Work-Study Program available. Institutional employment available. **Financial Aid Statistics:** 68% needy freshmen, 67% needy undergrads receive need-based scholarship or grant aid. 82% freshmen, 57% undergrads receive non-need-based scholarship or grant aid. 69% freshmen, 75% undergrads receive need-based self-help aid. 0% freshmen, 0% undergrads receive athletic scholarships. 93% freshmen, 81% undergrads receive any aid. 56% undergrads borrow to pay for school. Average cumulative indebtedness $32,820. **Criteria awarding aid:**

Need-based: Academics, Art, Music/drama. *Non-need-based:* Academics, Alumni affiliation, Art, Leadership, Music/drama, State/district residency.

UNIVERSITY OF MASSACHUSETTS—AMHERST

University Admissions Center, Amherst, MA 01003
Phone: 413-545-0222 **Financial Aid Phone:** 413-545-0801
E-mail: mail@admissions.umass.edu **CEEB Code:** 3917
Fax: 413-545-4312 **Website:** www.umass.edu **ACT Code:** 1924

This public school was founded in 1863. It has a 1463 acre campus.

RATINGS

Admissions Selectivity Rating: 86   **Fire Safety Rating:** 93   **Green Rating:** 96

STUDENTS AND FACULTY

Enrollment: 23,907. **Student Body:** 50% female, 50% male, 17% out-of-state, 7% international (86 countries represented). Asian 11%, African American 5%, Caucasian 61%, Hispanic 8%, Native American <1%, Pacific Islander <1%, Two or more races 3%, Race unknown 5%.
Retention and Graduation: 91% freshmen return for sophomore year. 74% freshmen graduate within 4 years. 82% freshmen graduate within 6 years. 21% grads go on to further study within 1 year. 1% grads pursue law degrees. <1% grads pursue business degrees. 2% grads pursue medical degrees. **Faculty:** Student/faculty ratio 17:1. 1,461 full-time faculty, 93% hold PhDs, 22% are members of minority groups, 45% are women.

ACADEMICS

Degrees: Associate; Bachelor's; Certificate; Doctoral degree—professional practice; Doctoral degree research/scholarship; Master's; Post-bachelor's certificate. **Classes:** Most classes have 10–19 students. Most lab/discussion sessions have 20–29 students. **Most popular majors:** Biology/Biological Sciences, General; Psychology, General; Public Health, General. **Special Study Options:** Accelerated program; Cooperative education program; Cross-registration; Distance learning; Double major; Dual enrollment; English as a Second Language (ESL); Exchange student program (domestic); Honors program; Independent study; Internships; Liberal arts/career combination; Student-designed major; Study abroad; Teacher certification program. **Honors programs:** Commonwealth Honors College provides a diverse community of academically talented students at the University of Massachusetts Amherst with extensive opportunities for analysis, research, professional development, and international experience. Small Honors classes foster intellectual exchange and close interaction with faculty, offering the advantages of a small scholarly community alongside all the resources of a nationally recognized research university. The Honors Curriculum promotes education that is both broad and deep. Through Honors General Education courses, Honors College students reach beyond the boundaries of their academic majors, while advanced scholarship tracks provide students opportunities to delve deeply into topics of interest and contribute new and original knowledge to their fields of study. The Honors Thesis is the culminating experience of the Commonwealth Honors College academic journey. The Honors Thesis centers around an original investigation of a topic of the student's choice and is traditionally completed over two semesters in the senior year. In addition, Commonwealth Honors College offers an array of professional development opportunities, community-engaged research, special lectures, and international programs—all designed to foster global perspectives, encourage diverse viewpoints, and promote dialogue on social justice. **Combined degree programs:** BA/MA. **Disability Services offered:** Note-taking services; Reader services; Tape recorders. **Career services:** Alumni network; Alumni services; Career assessment; Career/job search classes; Internships.

FACILITIES

Housing: Apartments for married students; Apartments for single students; Coed dorms; Fraternity/sorority housing; Special housing for disabled students; Special housing for international students; Theme housing; Wellness housing. **Special Academic Facilities/Equipment:** Computer Science Complex, Polymer Research Institute, Herter (Art) Gallery, University Museum of Contemporary Art, Natural History Museum, Fine Arts Center, Mullins Center (sports and entertainment arena), Integrative Learning Center, Integrated Sciences Building,

Isenberg Business Hub, John W. Olver Design Building, Learning Commons, Botanical Gardens, Astronomical Observatory, Historic Old Chapel.

CAMPUS LIFE

Environment: Town. **Activities:** Campus Ministries; Choral groups; Concert band; Dance; Drama/theater; International Student Organization; Jazz band; Literary magazine; Marching band; Model UN; Music ensembles; Musical theater; Opera; Pep band; Radio station; Student government; Student newspaper; Student-run film society; Symphony orchestra; Television station. 500 registered organizations, 38 honor societies, 22 religious organizations, 22 fraternities, 14 sororities on campus. **Athletics (Intercollegiate):** *Men:* baseball, basketball, cross-country, diving, football, ice hockey, lacrosse, soccer, swimming, track/field (outdoor), track/field (indoor). *Women:* basketball, crew/rowing, cross-country, diving, field hockey, lacrosse, soccer, softball, swimming, tennis, track/field (outdoor), track/field (indoor). **On-Campus Highlights:** The Campus Center & Student Union. **Environmental Initiatives:** The UMass Amherst School of Earth & Sustainability (SES) is a cross-disciplinary partnership between the Departments of Environmental Conservation, Geosciences, Landscape Architecture & Regional Planning and Stockbridge School of Agriculture as well as the Environmental Microbiology group from the Department of Microbiology. SES joins diverse academic programs, research, and outreach that share a common focus on earth, sustainability, and environmental sciences. Together, our community includes over 100 world-class faculty, 1,300 undergraduate students, 320 graduate students as well as many research scientists, technicians and support staff. The SES provides UMass with a learning community dedicated to training the next generation of scholars and environmental leaders who will increase our understanding of how the planet works and solve the global challenges of sustainability. www.umass.edu/ses.

ADMISSIONS

Freshman Academic Profile: Average high school GPA 3.9. 31% in top 10% of high school class, 70% in top 25% of high school class, 96% in top 50% of high school class. **Test Scores:** SAT Math middle 50% range 600–710. SAT EBRW middle 50% range 590–680. ACT middle 50% range 26–32. **Basis for Candidate Selection:** *Very important factors include:* rigor of secondary school record, academic GPA, standardized test scores. *Important factors include:* class rank, application essay, recommendation(s), extracurricular activities, talent/ability, character/personal qualities, first generation. *Other factors include:* alumni/ae relation, geographical residence, state residency, racial/ethnic status, volunteer work. **Freshman Admission Requirements:** High school diploma is required and GED is accepted. *Academic units required:* 4 English, 4 math, 3 science, 2 science labs, 2 foreign language, 2 social studies, 2 academic electives. **Freshman Admission Statistics:** 42,157 applied, 64% admitted, 21% enrolled. **Transfer Admission Requirements:** College transcript(s), essay or personal statement. Minimum college GPA of 2.5 required. Lowest grade transferable C-. **General Admission Information:** Application fee $80. Regular application deadline 1/15. Non-fall registration accepted. Admission may be deferred for a maximum of 1 year.

COSTS AND FINANCIAL AID

Required Forms and Deadlines: FAFSA. **Notification of Awards:** Applicants will be notified of awards on a rolling basis beginning 12/15. **Types of Aid:** *Need-based scholarships/grants:* College/university scholarship or grant aid from institutional funds; Federal Pell; Private scholarships; SEOG; State scholarships/grants. *Loans:* Direct PLUS loans; Direct Subsidized Stafford Loans; Direct Unsubsidized Stafford Loans. **Student Employment:** Federal Work-Study Program available. Institutional employment available. **Financial Aid Statistics:** 92% needy freshmen, 90% needy undergrads receive need-based scholarship or grant aid. 8% freshmen, 6% undergrads receive non-need-based scholarship or grant aid. 86% freshmen, 90% undergrads receive need-based self-help aid. 1% freshmen, 1% undergrads receive athletic scholarships. 90.4% freshmen, 90.8% undergrads receive any aid. 62% undergrads borrow to pay for school. Average cumulative indebtedness $31,755. **Criteria awarding aid:** *Non-need-based:* Academics, Art, Athletics, Music/drama, State/district residency.

UNIVERSITY OF MASSACHUSETTS—BOSTON

UMass Boston Undergraduate Processing Center PO Box, Boston, MA 02358
Phone: 617-287-6100 **Financial Aid Phone:** 617-287-6300
E-mail: undergrad.admissions@umb.edu **CEEB Code:** 3924
Fax: 617-287-5999 **Website:** www.umb.edu

This public school was founded in 1964. It has a 120 acre campus.

RATINGS
Admissions Selectivity Rating: 77   **Fire Safety Rating:** 60*   **Green Rating:** 96

STUDENTS AND FACULTY
Enrollment: 12,192. **Student Body:** 55% female, 45% male, 5% out-of-state, 10% international (150 countries represented). Asian 14%, African American 17%, Caucasian 34%, Hispanic 17%, Native American <1%, Pacific Islander <1%, Two or more races 3%, Race unknown 5%.
Retention and Graduation: 75% freshmen return for sophomore year. 24% freshmen graduate within 4 years. 49% freshmen graduate within 6 years. **Faculty:** Student/faculty ratio 16:1. 689 full-time faculty, 87% hold PhDs, 28% are members of minority groups, 50% are women. 0% of classes are taught by teaching assistants.

ACADEMICS
Degrees: Bachelor's; Certificate; Doctoral degree—professional practice; Doctoral degree research/scholarship; Master's; Post-bachelor's certificate; Post-master's certificate. **Classes:** Most classes have 20–29 students. Most lab/discussion sessions have fewer than 10 students. **Most popular majors:** Management Science. **Special Study Options:** Cooperative education program; Cross-registration; Distance learning; Double major; Dual enrollment; English as a Second Language (ESL); Exchange student program (domestic); Honors program; Independent study; Internships; Liberal arts/career combination; Student-designed major; Study abroad; Teacher certification program. **Honors programs:** The University Honors Program seeks to meet the needs of students who thrive on intellectual challenge by offering special interdisciplinary academic opportunities outside the major. **Combined degree programs:** BA/MA. **Disability Services offered:** Note-taking services; Reader services; Tape recorders; Tutors. **Career services:** Alumni network; Alumni services; Career assessment; Career/job search classes; Internships; Regional alumni.

FACILITIES
Housing: Coed dorms; 100% of campus accessible to physically disabled. **Special Academic Facilities/Equipment:** In 2019, UMass Boston inaugurated its first ever LEED Gold Residence Halls—the 1,077-bed, $120 million, 260,000-square-foot complex was built through a public-private partnership, the first of its kind for the UMass system. A variety of green construction and operations features include a 500-seat Dining Commons featuring zero-waste dining with non-disposable dinnerware and numerous sustainable dining, single stream recycling and composting along with outdoors access for walkability, outdoors recycling, bike racks, access to the harbor and marine recreational and learning facilities. Other cutting edge new construction and amenities include the Campus' 1st LEED Gold Academic Bldg (ISC, 2015), Campus' Second LEED Gold bldg. (Univ Hall, 2016), UMass Harbor Walk, Harbor Art gallery, Art installation and sculpture inside buildings and outdoors, Greenhouse, Solar photo-voltaic installation on top of Wheatley Hall, adaptive computer lab, Healey library gallery space and special collections displays, Nantucket Field Station for immersive environmental studies, Marine sailing vessels at UMB Fox Point Pavilion for faculty,student and community marine education opportunities. Life on campus offers many opportunities as listed here: https://www.umb.edu/life_on_campus.

CAMPUS LIFE
Environment: Metropolis. **Activities:** Campus Ministries; Choral groups; Concert band; Dance; Drama/theater; International Student Organization; Jazz band; Literary magazine; Model UN; Music ensembles; Musical theater; Radio station; Student government; Student newspaper; Student-run film society; Symphony orchestra. 152 registered organizations, 4 honor societies, 4 religious organizations, 2 fraternities, 1 sorority on campus. **Athletics (Intercollegiate):** *Men:* baseball, basketball, cross-country, ice hockey, lacrosse, soccer, tennis, track/field (outdoor), track/field (indoor). *Women:* basketball, cross-country, ice hockey, soccer, softball, tennis, track/field (outdoor), track/field (indoor), volleyball. **On-Campus Highlights:** New Campus Center. **Environmental Initiatives:** Green Building Design and Strategic Sustainability Planning: UMass Boston's was awarded three consecutive LEED GOLD certifications for its first ever Dorms (Residence Halls, 2019) as well as for University Hall, 2016, and

the Integrated Sciences Complex, 2015, representing 18% of the campus as certified green building space. The harbor campus is an award-winning campus for green transportation options and walkability. In 2019, UMass Boston neared completion on one of the largest campus transformational projects, the UCRR project which included a new utility corridor to support future buildings and provide reliable and efficient utility services to the campus as well as a new two-way roadway network to provide various amenities including 3 miles of bike lanes, tree lawns of about 600 trees, and 6 miles of walkways sidewalks throughout the campus.

ADMISSIONS

Freshman Academic Profile: Average high school GPA 3.1. 15% in top 10% of high school class, 41% in top 25% of high school class, 76% in top 50% of high school class. **Test Scores:** SAT Math middle 50% range 510–610. SAT EBRW middle 50% range 500–610. ACT middle 50% range 20–27. **Basis for Candidate Selection:** *Very important factors include:* rigor of secondary school record, academic GPA. *Important factors include:* application essay, recommendation(s), character/personal qualities. *Other factors include:* standardized test scores, extracurricular activities, talent/ability, first generation, volunteer work, work experience. **Freshman Admission Requirements:** High school diploma is required and GED is accepted. *Academic units required:* 4 English, 4 math, 3 science, 3 science labs, 2 foreign language, 1 social studies, 1 history, 2 academic electives. **Freshman Admission Statistics:** 13,649 applied, 76% admitted, 20% enrolled. **Transfer Admission Requirements:** College transcript(s), essay or personal statement, statement of good standing from prior institution(s). Minimum college GPA of 2.5 required. Lowest grade transferable C-. **General Admission Information:** Application fee $60. Priority deadline 11/1. Regular application deadline 3/1. Non-fall registration accepted. Admission may be deferred for a maximum of 1 year.

COSTS AND FINANCIAL AID

Annual in-state tuition $14,187. Annual out-of-state tuition $34,649. Room and board $16,902. Required fees $426. Average book and supplies expense $800. **Required Forms and Deadlines:** FAFSA. **Notification of Awards:** Applicants will be notified of awards on a rolling basis beginning 12/15. **Types of Aid:** *Need-based scholarships/grants:* College/university scholarship or grant aid from institutional funds; Federal Pell; Private scholarships; SEOG; State scholarships/grants; United Negro College Fund. *Loans:* Direct PLUS loans; Direct Subsidized Stafford Loans; Direct Unsubsidized Stafford Loans. **Financial Aid Statistics:** 91% needy freshmen, 90% needy undergrads receive need-based scholarship or grant aid. 7% freshmen, 3% undergrads receive non-need-based scholarship or grant aid. 86% freshmen, 91% undergrads receive need-based self-help aid. 0% freshmen, 0% undergrads receive athletic scholarships. 59% undergrads borrow to pay for school. Average cumulative indebtedness $27,109. **Criteria awarding aid:** *Need-based:* Academics. *Non-need-based:* Academics, Leadership, State/district residency.

UNIVERSITY OF MASSACHUSETTS—DARTMOUTH

285 Old Westport Road, North Dartmouth, MA 02747-2300
Phone: (508) 999-8605 **Financial Aid Phone:** 508-999-8643
E-mail: admissions@umassd.edu **CEEB Code:** 3786
Fax: (508) 999-8755 **Website:** http://www.umassd.edu/ **ACT Code:** 001906

This public school was founded in 1895. It has a 710 acre campus.

RATINGS

Admissions Selectivity Rating: 77   **Fire Safety Rating:** 92   **Green Rating:** 91

STUDENTS AND FACULTY

Enrollment: 6,649. **Student Body:** 49% female, 51% male, 9% out-of-state, 2% international (36 countries represented). Asian 4%, African American 16%, Caucasian 59%, Hispanic 10%, Native American <1%, Pacific Islander <1%, Two or more races 4%, Race unknown 4%.
Retention and Graduation: 71% freshmen return for sophomore year. 30% freshmen graduate within 4 years. 49% freshmen graduate within 6 years. 19% grads go on to further study within 1 year. 33% grads pursue arts and sciences degrees. 4% grads pursue law degrees. 16% grads pursue business degrees. 11% grads pursue medical degrees. **Faculty:** Student/faculty ratio 16:1. 402 full-time faculty, 22% are members of minority groups, 48% are women. 3% of classes are taught by teaching assistants.

ACADEMICS

Degrees: Bachelor's; Certificate; Doctoral degree—professional practice; Doctoral degree research/scholarship; Master's; Post-bachelor's certificate; Post-master's certificate. **Classes:** Most classes have 10–19 students. Most lab/discussion sessions have 10–19 students. **Most popular majors:** Registered Nursing, Nursing Administration, Nursing Research and Clinical Nursing, Other; Psychology, General; Liberal Arts and Sciences, General Studies and Humanities, Other. **Special Study Options:** Accelerated program; Cooperative education program; Cross-registration; Distance learning; Double major; Dual enrollment; English as a Second Language (ESL); Exchange student program (domestic); Honors program; Independent study; Internships; Student-designed major; Study abroad; Teacher certification program. **Honors programs:** Honors Program. **Combined degree programs:** BA/MA. **Disability Services offered:** Note-taking services; Reader services; Tape recorders; Tutors. **Career services:** Alumni network; Career/job search classes; Internships.

FACILITIES

Housing: Apartments for single students; Coed dorms; Special housing for disabled students; Theme housing; Wellness housing; 97% of campus accessible to physically disabled. **Special Academic Facilities/Equipment:** Art gallery, language center, center for Jewish culture, Robert F. Kennedy assassination archives, electron microscope, observatory, marine research vessels, Business Innovation Research Center, School of Marine Science and Technology, Portuguese archives.

CAMPUS LIFE

Environment: Town. **Activities:** Campus Ministries; Choral groups; Concert band; Dance; Drama/theater; International Student Organization; Jazz band; Literary magazine; Model UN; Music ensembles; Radio station; Student government; Student newspaper; Symphony orchestra; Yearbook. 165 registered organizations, 4 honor societies, 3 religious organizations, 7 fraternities, 6 sororities on campus. **Athletics (Intercollegiate):** *Men:* baseball, basketball, cross-country, diving, football, golf, ice hockey, lacrosse, soccer, swimming, tennis, track/field (outdoor), track/field (indoor). *Women:* basketball, cheerleading, cross-country, diving, equestrian sports, field hockey, golf, lacrosse, soccer, softball, swimming, tennis, track/field (outdoor), track/field (indoor), volleyball. **On-Campus Highlights:** Tripp Athletic Center. **Environmental Initiatives:** Large scale energy performance.

ADMISSIONS

Freshman Academic Profile: Average high school GPA 3.3. 14% in top 10% of high school class, 34% in top 25% of high school class, 68% in top 50% of high school class. 88% from public high schools. **Test Scores:** SAT Math middle 50% range 500–590. SAT EBRW middle 50% range 490–600. ACT middle 50% range 19–26. **Basis for Candidate Selection:** *Very important factors include:* rigor of secondary school record, academic GPA, standardized test scores. *Other factors include:* application essay, recommendation(s), extracurricular activities, talent/ability, character/personal qualities, first generation, alumni/ae relation, volunteer work, work experience. **Freshman Admission Requirements:** High school diploma is required and GED is accepted. *Academic units required:* 4 English, 4 math, 3 science, 3 science labs, 2 foreign language, 1 social studies, 1 history, 2 academic electives. **Freshman Admission Statistics:** 8,697 applied, 78% admitted, 21% enrolled. **Transfer Admission Requirements:** College transcript(s), essay or personal statement. Minimum college GPA of 2.5 required. Lowest grade transferable C-. **General Admission Information:** Application fee $60. Priority deadline 3/1. Non-fall registration accepted. Admission may be deferred for a maximum of 2 semesters.

COSTS AND FINANCIAL AID

Required Forms and Deadlines: FAFSA. **Notification of Awards:** Applicants will be notified of awards on a rolling basis beginning 12/27. **Types of Aid:** *Need-based scholarships/grants:* College/university scholarship or grant aid from institutional funds; Federal Pell; Private scholarships; SEOG; State scholarships/grants. *Loans:* Direct PLUS loans; Direct Subsidized Stafford Loans; Direct Unsubsidized Stafford Loans. **Student Employment:** Federal Work-Study Program available. Institutional employment available. **Financial Aid Statistics:** 92% needy freshmen, 88% needy undergrads receive need-based scholarship or grant aid. 5% freshmen, 3% undergrads receive non-need-based scholarship or grant aid. 84% freshmen, 87% undergrads receive need-based self-help aid. 0% freshmen, 0% undergrads receive athletic scholarships. 92% freshmen, 87% undergrads receive any aid. 95% undergrads borrow to pay for school. Average cumulative indebtedness $29,000. **Criteria awarding aid:** *Non-need-based:* Academics, Minority status, State/district residency.

UNIVERSITY OF MASSACHUSETTS—LOWELL

University Crossing Suite 420, Lowell, MA 01854-2874
Phone: 978-934-3931 **Financial Aid Phone:** 978-934-4220
E-mail: admissions@uml.edu **CEEB Code:** 3911
Fax: 978-934-3086 **Website:** www.uml.edu **ACT Code:** 1854

This public school was founded in 1894. It has a 150 acre campus.

RATINGS

Admissions Selectivity Rating: 84   **Fire Safety Rating:** 97   **Green Rating:** 95

STUDENTS AND FACULTY

Enrollment: 13,386. **Student Body:** 39% female, 61% male, 8% out-of-state, 4% international (66 countries represented). Asian 11%, African American 6%, Caucasian 60%, Hispanic 12%, Native American <1%, Pacific Islander <1%, Two or more races 3%, Race unknown 4%.
Retention and Graduation: 85% freshmen return for sophomore year. 38% freshmen graduate within 4 years. 63% freshmen graduate within 6 years. **Faculty:** Student/faculty ratio 17:1. 637 full-time faculty, 90% hold PhDs, 26% are members of minority groups, 45% are women. 2% of classes are taught by teaching assistants.

ACADEMICS

Degrees: Associate; Bachelor's; Certificate; Doctoral degree—professional practice; Doctoral degree research/scholarship; Master's; Post-bachelor's certificate; Post-master's certificate; Terminal Associate; Transfer Associate. **Classes:** Most classes have 10–19 students. Most lab/discussion sessions have greater than 100 students. **Most popular majors:** Information Science/Studies; Criminal Justice/Law Enforcement Administration; Business Administration and Management, General. **Special Study Options:** Accelerated program; Cooperative education program; Cross-registration; Distance learning; Double major; Dual enrollment; Honors program; Independent study; Internships; Study abroad; Teacher certification program. **Honors programs:** The Honors College at UMass Lowell offers high-achieving students individualized instruction in small groups, often in seminar format; opportunities for undergraduate research; special "Commonwealth Honors Program Scholar" designation on transcripts and diplomas, upon completion of program requirements; opportunity to live on one of the Honors floors in the residence halls; and Honors Program social events. **Combined degree programs:** BA/MA; BA/MEng. **Disability Services offered:** Note-taking services; Reader services; Tape recorders; Tutors. **Career services:** Alumni network; Alumni services; Career assessment; Career/job search classes; Internships; Regional alumni.

FACILITIES

Housing: Apartments for single students; Coed dorms; Theme housing; Wellness housing; 90% of campus accessible to physically disabled. **Special Academic Facilities/Equipment:** Language lab, media center, audio-visual department, Centers for Learning, Center for field studies, Center for Performing and Visual Arts, Center for Health Promotion, Research Nuclear Reactor. New $19.5 million recreation center which includes multi court gymnasium, 1/8 mile indoor elevated track, aerobics room, game rooms, locker rooms, and a sauna. Also included are meeting rooms and an indoor/outdoor food court.

CAMPUS LIFE

Environment: City. **Activities:** Campus Ministries; Choral groups; Concert band; Dance; Drama/theater; International Student Organization; Jazz band; Literary magazine; Marching band; Model UN; Music ensembles; Pep band; Radio station; Student government; Student newspaper; Student-run film society; Symphony orchestra; Yearbook. 250 registered organizations, 5 honor societies, 8 religious organizations, 4 fraternities, 4 sororities on campus. **Athletics (Intercollegiate):** *Men:* baseball, basketball, crew/rowing, cross-country, golf, ice hockey, soccer, track/field (outdoor), track/field (indoor). *Women:* basketball, crew/rowing, cross-country, field hockey, soccer, softball, track/field (outdoor), track/field (indoor), volleyball. **On-Campus Highlights:** University Crossing.

ADMISSIONS

Freshman Academic Profile: Average high school GPA 3.6. 25% in top 10% of high school class, 56% in top 25% of high school class, 88% in top 50% of high school class. 88% from public high schools. **Test Scores:** SAT Math middle 50% range 580–670. SAT EBRW middle 50% range 570–650. ACT middle 50% range 24–29. **Basis for Candidate Selection:** *Very important*

factors include: rigor of secondary school record, academic GPA. *Important factors include:* application essay, standardized test scores, recommendation(s), character/personal qualities. *Other factors include:* class rank, extracurricular activities, talent/ability, first generation, alumni/ae relation, geographical residence, state residency, racial/ethnic status, volunteer work, work experience, level of applicant's interest. **Freshman Admission Requirements:** High school diploma is required and GED is accepted. *Academic units required:* 4 English, 4 math, 3 science, 3 science labs, 2 foreign language, 1 social studies, 1 history, 2 academic electives. *Academic units recommended:* 4 English, 4 math, 4 science, 3 science labs, 2 foreign language, 1 social studies, 1 history, 2 academic electives. **Freshman Admission Statistics:** 12,117 applied, 72% admitted, 24% enrolled. **Transfer Admission Requirements:** College transcript(s). Minimum college GPA of 2.0 required. Lowest grade transferable C-. **General Admission Information:** Application fee $60. Priority deadline 11/1. Regular application deadline 2/1. Non-fall registration accepted. Admission may be deferred for a maximum of 12 months.

COSTS AND FINANCIAL AID

Required Forms and Deadlines: FAFSA. **Notification of Awards:** Applicants will be notified of awards on a rolling basis beginning 1/1. **Types of Aid:** *Need-based scholarships/grants:* College/university scholarship or grant aid from institutional funds; Federal Pell; Private scholarships; SEOG; State scholarships/grants. *Loans:* Direct PLUS loans; Direct Subsidized Stafford Loans; Direct Unsubsidized Stafford Loans. **Financial Aid Statistics:** 91% needy freshmen, 85% needy undergrads receive need-based scholarship or grant aid. 5% freshmen, 4% undergrads receive non-need-based scholarship or grant aid. 91% freshmen, 92% undergrads receive need-based self-help aid. 2% freshmen, 1% undergrads receive athletic scholarships. 77% undergrads borrow to pay for school. Average cumulative indebtedness $32,178. **Criteria awarding aid:** *Need-based:* Academics. *Non-need-based:* Academics, Alumni affiliation, Art, Athletics, Leadership, Minority status, Music/drama, State/district residency.

THE UNIVERSITY OF MEMPHIS

101 Wilder Tower, Memphis, TN 38152
Phone: 901-678-2111 **Financial Aid Phone:** 901-678-4825
E-mail: recruitment@memphis.edu **CEEB Code:** 1459
Fax: 901-678-3053 **Website:** www.memphis.edu **ACT Code:** 3992

This public school was founded in 1912. It has a 1160 acre campus.

RATINGS

Admissions Selectivity Rating: 86   **Fire Safety Rating:** 92   **Green Rating:** 60*

STUDENTS AND FACULTY

Enrollment: 16,741. **Student Body:** 61% female, 39% male, 10% out-of-state, 1% international (53 countries represented). Asian 3%, African American 40%, Caucasian 49%, Hispanic 3%, Native American <1%, Pacific Islander <1%, Two or more races 3%, Race unknown 1%.
Retention and Graduation: 76% freshmen return for sophomore year. **Faculty:** Student/faculty ratio 14:1. 136 full-time faculty, 59% hold PhDs, 14% are members of minority groups, 57% are women.

ACADEMICS

Degrees: Bachelor's; Doctoral degree—professional practice; Doctoral degree research/scholarship; Master's; Post-bachelor's certificate; Post-master's certificate. **Classes:** Most classes have 20–29 students. Most lab/discussion sessions have 10–19 students. **Most popular majors:** Biology/Biological Sciences, General; General Studies; Psychology, General. **Special Study Options:** Accelerated program; Cooperative education program; Cross-registration; Distance learning; Double major; Dual enrollment; English as a Second Language (ESL); Exchange student program (domestic); External degree program; Honors program; Independent study; Internships; Liberal arts/career combination; Student-designed major; Study abroad; Teacher certification program. **Honors programs:** The Honors Program offers students the opportunity to take small classes and interdisciplinary seminars with the University's most outstanding faculty. The program also includes many wonderful opportunities beyond the classroom such as study abroad, independent research, and co-curricular activities. Honors students also have the chance to participate in nationally recognized undergraduate research conferences and extend their learning through internships and public service. **Disability Services offered:** Note-taking services; Reader services;

Tape recorders. **Career services:** Alumni network; Alumni services; Career assessment; Career/job search classes; Internships; Regional alumni.

FACILITIES

Housing: Apartments for married students; Apartments for single students; Coed dorms; Cooperative housing; Fraternity/sorority housing; Men's dorms; Special housing for disabled students; Women's dorms; 95% of campus accessible to physically disabled. **Special Academic Facilities/Equipment:** Center for Earthquake Research & Information; Institute of Egyptian Art & Archaeology; Bureau of Business and Economic Research. **Campus network:** 100% of classrooms have wireless network access.

CAMPUS LIFE

Environment: Metropolis. **Activities:** Campus Ministries; Choral groups; Concert band; Dance; Drama/theater; International Student Organization; Jazz band; Literary magazine; Marching band; Music ensembles; Musical theater; Opera; Pep band; Radio station; Student government; Student newspaper; Symphony orchestra. 186 registered organizations, 20 honor societies, 15 religious organizations, 15 fraternities, 10 sororities on campus. **Athletics (Intercollegiate): Men:** baseball, basketball, cross-country, football, golf, riflery, soccer, tennis, track/field (outdoor). **Women:** basketball, cross-country, golf, riflery, soccer, softball, tennis, track/field (outdoor), volleyball. **On-Campus Highlights:** Rose Theater Lecture Hall. **Environmental Initiatives:** Energy Conservation.

ADMISSIONS

Freshman Academic Profile: Average high school GPA 3.3. 1% in top 10% of high school class, 42% in top 25% of high school class, 79% in top 50% of high school class. **Test Scores:** SAT Math middle 50% range 440–590. SAT EBRW middle 50% range 440–570. ACT middle 50% range 20–25. **Basis for Candidate Selection:** *Very important factors include:* rigor of secondary school record, academic GPA, standardized test scores. *Other factors include:* application essay, recommendation(s), talent/ability, character/personal qualities, first generation, work experience. **Freshman Admission Requirements:** High school diploma is required and GED is accepted. *Academic units required:* 4 English, 3 math, 2 science, 1 science labs, 2 foreign language, 1 social studies, 1 history, 1 visual/performing arts. **Freshman Admission Statistics:** 6,798 applied, 62% admitted, 53% enrolled. **Transfer Admission Requirements:** College transcript(s), standardized test scores. Lowest grade transferable C. **General Admission Information:** Application fee $25. Regular application deadline 7/1. Non-fall registration accepted.

COSTS AND FINANCIAL AID

Required Forms and Deadlines: FAFSA. **Notification of Awards:** Applicants will be notified of awards on a rolling basis beginning 3/15. **Types of Aid:** *Need-based scholarships/grants:* College/university scholarship or grant aid from institutional funds; Federal Pell; Private scholarships; SEOG; State scholarships/grants. *Loans:* Direct PLUS loans; Direct Subsidized Stafford Loans; Direct Unsubsidized Stafford Loans. **Student Employment:** Federal Work-Study Program available. Institutional employment available. **Financial Aid Statistics:** 67% needy freshmen, 71% needy undergrads receive need-based scholarship or grant aid. 46% freshmen, 54% undergrads receive non-need-based scholarship or grant aid. 56% freshmen, 72% undergrads receive need-based self-help aid. 3% freshmen, 2% undergrads receive athletic scholarships. 95% freshmen, 91% undergrads receive any aid. **Criteria awarding aid:** *Need-based:* Academics, Leadership, Minority status. *Non-need-based:* Academics, Alumni affiliation, Art, Athletics, Leadership, Music/drama, State/district residency.

UNIVERSITY OF MIAMI

P.O. Box 248025, Coral Gables, FL 33124-4616
Phone: 305-284-4323 **Financial Aid Phone:** 305-284-2270
E-mail: admission@miami.edu **CEEB Code:** 5815
Fax: 305-284-2507 **Website:** www.miami.edu **ACT Code:** 0760

This private school was founded in 1925. It has a 239 acre campus.

RATINGS

Admissions Selectivity Rating: 93   **Fire Safety Rating:** 91   **Green Rating:** 93

STUDENTS AND FACULTY

Enrollment: 10,868. **Student Body:** 52% female, 48% male, 60% out-of-state, 15% international (107 countries represented). Asian 5%, African American 8%, Caucasian 42%, Hispanic 22%, Native American <1%, Pacific Islander <1%, Two or more races 3%, Race unknown 4%.
Retention and Graduation: 92% freshmen return for sophomore year. 72% freshmen graduate within 4 years. 84% freshmen graduate within 6 years. 34% grads go on to further study within 1 year. 9% grads pursue arts and sciences degrees. 5% grads pursue law degrees. 1% grads pursue business degrees. 7% grads pursue medical degrees. **Faculty:** Student/faculty ratio 12:1. 1,125 full-time faculty, 86% hold PhDs, 36% are members of minority groups, 41% are women. 7% of classes are taught by teaching assistants.

ACADEMICS

Degrees: Bachelor's; Certificate; Doctoral degree—professional practice; Doctoral degree research/scholarship; Master's; Post-bachelor's certificate; Post-master's certificate. **Classes:** Most classes have 10–19 students. Most lab/discussion sessions have fewer than 10 students. **Most popular majors:** Biology/Biological Sciences, General; Psychology, General; Finance, General. **Special Study Options:** Accelerated program; Cooperative education program; Distance learning; Double major; Dual enrollment; English as a Second Language (ESL); Honors program; Independent study; Internships; Liberal arts/career combination; Student-designed major; Study abroad; Teacher certification program; Weekend college. **Honors programs:** The Foote Fellows Honors Program allows students to pursue their interests and explore the topics they are most passionate about by exempting them from general education requirements. Invitation to the program is offered only to the highest achieving admitted students in each school and college. There are also Dual-Degree Programs in Medicine, Law, Latin American Studies, Marine Geology, Biology, Biochemistry & Molecular Biology, Exercise Physiology and Computer Science. **Combined degree programs:** BA/JD; BA/MA; BA/MD; BA/MEng. **Disability Services offered:** Note-taking services; Reader services; Tape recorders; Tutors. **Career services:** Alumni services; Career assessment; Career/job search classes; Internships.

FACILITIES

Housing: Apartments for single students; Coed dorms; Fraternity/sorority housing; Special housing for disabled students; Theme housing. **Special Academic Facilities/Equipment:** Lowe Art Museum, Gusman Concert Hall, Clarke Recital Hall, Jerry Herman Ring Theatre, Bill Cosford Cinema, Sheldon and Myrna Palley Pavillion for Contemporary Glass and Studio Arts, BankUnited Center, Martha and Austin Weeks Music Library and Technology Center, Wellness Center, state-of-the-art computer labs, digital television studios, film sound stage, a radio station, a new Student Activities Center, a new seawater research facility, and new North and South studio wings at our Frost School of Music. **Campus network:** 100% of classrooms, 100% of dorms, 100% of student union, 100% of libraries, 100% of dining areas, 100% of common outdoor areas have wireless network access.

CAMPUS LIFE

Environment: Town. **Activities:** Campus Ministries; Choral groups; Concert band; Dance; Drama/theater; International Student Organization; Jazz band; Literary magazine; Marching band; Model UN; Music ensembles; Musical theater; Opera; Pep band; Radio station; Student government; Student newspaper; Student-run film society; Symphony orchestra; Television station; Yearbook. 290 registered organizations, 33 honor societies, 25 religious organizations, 18 fraternities, 12 sororities on campus. **Athletics (Intercollegiate): Men:** baseball, basketball, cheerleading, cross-country, football, tennis, track/field (outdoor), track/field (indoor). **Women:** basketball, cheerleading, crew/rowing, cross-country, diving, golf, soccer, swimming, tennis, track/field (outdoor), track/field (indoor), volleyball. **On-Campus Highlights:** Student Center Complex (student union). **Environmental Initiatives:** The President signed the ACUPCC. The University also hired a sustainability coordinator.

ADMISSIONS

Freshman Academic Profile: Average high school GPA 3.6. 55% in top 10% of high school class, 83% in top 25% of high school class, 95% in top 50% of high school class. 62% from public high schools. **Test Scores:** SAT Math middle 50% range 630–740. SAT EBRW middle 50% range 620–690. ACT middle 50% range 29–32. **Basis for Candidate Selection:** *Very important factors include:* rigor of secondary school record, class rank, academic GPA, application essay, standardized test scores, recommendation(s), extracurricular activities, character/personal qualities. *Important factors include:* talent/ ability. *Other factors include:* first generation, alumni/ae relation, geographical residence, state residency, racial/ethnic status, level of applicant's interest. **Freshman Admission Requirements:** High school diploma is required and GED is accepted. *Academic units recommended:* 4 English, 4 math, 3 science, 2 science labs, 2 foreign language, 2 social studies. **Freshman Admission Statistics:** 34,279 applied, 32% admitted, 21% enrolled. **Transfer Admission Requirements:** College transcript(s), statement of good standing from prior institution(s). Lowest grade transferable C. **General Admission Information:** Application fee $70. Regular application deadline 1/1. Non-fall registration accepted. Admission may be deferred for a maximum of 1 year.

COSTS AND FINANCIAL AID

Annual tuition $48,720. Room and board $14,108. Required fees $1,506. Average book and supplies expense $1,000. **Required Forms and Deadlines:** Business/Farm Supplement; CSS/Financial Aid PROFILE; FAFSA; Noncustodial PROFILE. **Notification of Awards:** Applicants will be notified of awards on a rolling basis beginning 1/20. **Types of Aid:** *Need-based scholarships/ grants:* College/university scholarship or grant aid from institutional funds; Federal Pell; Private scholarships; SEOG; State scholarships/grants. *Loans:* Direct PLUS loans; Direct Subsidized Stafford Loans; Direct Unsubsidized Stafford Loans. **Student Employment:** Federal Work-Study Program available. Institutional employment available. **Financial Aid Statistics:** 76% needy freshmen, 75% needy undergrads receive need-based scholarship or grant aid. 48% freshmen, 40% undergrads receive non-need-based scholarship or grant aid. 57% freshmen, 61% undergrads receive need-based self-help aid. 2% freshmen, 2% undergrads receive athletic scholarships. 70% freshmen, 72% undergrads receive any aid. 36% undergrads borrow to pay for school. Average cumulative indebtedness $22,000. **Criteria awarding aid:** *Need-based:* Alumni affiliation, Art, Job skills, Leadership, Minority status. *Non-need-based:* Academics, Athletics, Music/drama, State/district residency.

UNIVERSITY OF MICHIGAN—ANN ARBOR

515 E. Jefferson St, Ann Arbor, MI 48109-1316
Phone: 734-764-7433 **Financial Aid Phone:** 734-763-6600
CEEB Code: 1839
Fax: 734-936-0740 **Website:** umich.edu **ACT Code:** 2062

This public school was founded in 1817. It has a 3207 acre campus.

RATINGS

Admissions Selectivity Rating: 97   **Fire Safety Rating:** 88   **Green Rating:** 91

STUDENTS AND FACULTY

Enrollment: 31,046. **Student Body:** 50% female, 50% male, 41% out-of-state, 7% international (100 countries represented). Asian 16%, African American 4%, Caucasian 57%, Hispanic 7%, Native American <1%, Pacific Islander <1%, Two or more races 5%, Race unknown 3%.
Retention and Graduation: 97% freshmen return for sophomore year. 80% freshmen graduate within 4 years. 93% freshmen graduate within 6 years. **Faculty:** Student/faculty ratio 15:1. 2,925 full-time faculty, 92% hold PhDs, 24% are members of minority groups, 43% are women. 36% of classes are taught by teaching assistants.

ACADEMICS

Degrees: Bachelor's; Doctoral degree—professional practice; Doctoral degree research/scholarship; Master's; Post-bachelor's certificate; Post-master's certificate. **Classes:** Most classes have 10–19 students. Most lab/discussion sessions have 20–29 students. **Most popular majors:** Computer and Information Sciences, General; Economics, General; Business Administration and Management, General. **Special Study Options:** Accelerated program; Cooperative education program; Cross-registration; Distance learning; Double major; Dual enrollment; English as a Second Language (ESL); Exchange student program (domestic); External degree program; Honors program; Independent study; Internships; Liberal arts/career combination; Student-designed major; Study abroad; Teacher certification program; Weekend college. **Honors programs:** Honors Programs offered by several schools and departments. **Combined degree programs:** BA/MA; BA/MEng. **Disability Services offered:** Note-taking services; Reader services; Tape recorders; Tutors. **Career services:** Alumni network; Alumni services; Career assessment; Career/ job search classes; Internships.

FACILITIES

Housing: Apartments for married students; Apartments for single students; Coed dorms; Cooperative housing; Fraternity/sorority housing; Special housing for disabled students; Theme housing; Wellness housing; Women's dorms; 95% of campus accessible to physically disabled. **Special Academic Facilities/ Equipment:** Anthropology, archaeology, art, dentistry, natural science, musical instruments, paleontology, and zoology museums; planetarium; electron microscope; athletic campus; medical center; nuclear lab; botanical garden; herbarium; arboretum. **Campus network:** 40% of classrooms, 100% of dorms, 100% of student union, 100% of libraries, 100% of dining areas have wireless network access.

CAMPUS LIFE

Environment: City. **Activities:** Campus Ministries; Choral groups; Concert band; Dance; Drama/theater; International Student Organization; Jazz band; Literary magazine; Marching band; Model UN; Music ensembles; Musical theater; Opera; Pep band; Radio station; Student government; Student newspaper; Student-run film society; Symphony orchestra; Television station; Yearbook. 1500 registered organizations, 38 honor societies, 89 religious organizations, 29 fraternities, 28 sororities on campus. **Athletics (Intercollegiate):** *Men:* baseball, basketball, cheerleading, cross-country, diving, football, golf, gymnastics, ice hockey, swimming, tennis, track/field (outdoor), track/field (indoor), wrestling. *Women:* basketball, cheerleading, crew/rowing, cross-country, diving, field hockey, golf, gymnastics, soccer, softball, swimming, tennis, track/field (outdoor), track/field (indoor), volleyball, water polo. **On-Campus Highlights:** Michigan Stadium. **Environmental Initiatives:** Establishment and tracking of Campus Sustainability goals. http://sustainability. umich.edu/ocs/goals.

ADMISSIONS

Freshman Academic Profile: Average high school GPA 3.9. **Test Scores:** SAT Math middle 50% range 680–790. SAT EBRW middle 50% range 660–740. ACT middle 50% range 31–34. **Basis for Candidate Selection:** *Very important factors include:* rigor of secondary school record, academic GPA. *Important factors include:* application essay, standardized test scores, recommendation(s), character/personal qualities, first generation. *Other factors include:* extracurricular activities, talent/ability, alumni/ae relation, geographical residence, state residency, volunteer work, work experience, level of applicant's interest. **Freshman Admission Requirements:** High school diploma is required and GED is accepted. *Academic units required:* 4 English, 3 math, 3 science, 1 science labs, 2 foreign language, 1 social studies, 3 history. *Academic units recommended:* 4 English, 4 math, 4 science, 1 science labs, 4 foreign language, 1 social studies, 3 history, 1 computer science, 2 visual/performing arts. **Freshman Admission Statistics:** 64,917 applied, 23% admitted, 46% enrolled. **Transfer Admission Requirements:** High school transcript, college transcript(s), essay or personal statement, statement of good standing from prior institution(s). Minimum college GPA of 3.0 required. Lowest grade transferable C. **General Admission Information:** Application fee $75. Priority deadline 11/1. Regular application deadline 2/1. Non-fall registration accepted. Admission may be deferred for a maximum of 1 year.

COSTS AND FINANCIAL AID

Annual in-state tuition $16,212. Annual out-of-state tuition $52,669. Room and board $11,996. Required fees $328. Average book and supplies expense $1,048. **Required Forms and Deadlines:** CSS/Financial Aid PROFILE; FAFSA. **Notification of Awards:** Applicants will be notified of awards on a rolling basis beginning 3/15. **Types of Aid:** *Need-based scholarships/grants:* College/university scholarship or grant aid from institutional funds; Federal Pell; Private scholarships; SEOG; State scholarships/grants. *Loans:* Direct PLUS loans; Direct Subsidized Stafford Loans; Direct Unsubsidized Stafford Loans. **Student Employment:** Federal Work-Study Program available. Institutional employment available. **Financial Aid Statistics:** 76% needy freshmen, 81% needy undergrads receive need-based scholarship or grant aid. 70% freshmen, 66% undergrads receive non-need-based scholarship or grant aid. 68% freshmen, 73% undergrads receive need-based self-help aid. 2% freshmen, 3% undergrads receive athletic scholarships. 70% freshmen, 59% undergrads receive any aid. 38% undergrads borrow to pay for school. Average cumulative indebtedness $25,777. **Criteria awarding aid:** *Need-based:* Academics. *Non-need-based:* Academics, Alumni affiliation, Art, Athletics, Leadership, Music/drama, Religious affiliation, State/district residency.

UNIVERSITY OF MICHIGAN—DEARBORN

4901 Evergreen Road, Dearborn, MI 48128-1491
Phone: 313-593-5100 **Financial Aid Phone:** 734-763-6600
E-mail: admissions@umd.umich.edu **CEEB Code:** 1861
Fax: 313-436-9167 **Website:** umdearborn.edu **ACT Code:** 2074

This public school was founded in 1959. It has a 230 acre campus.

RATINGS
Admissions Selectivity Rating: 84 **Fire Safety Rating:** 60* **Green Rating:** 60*

STUDENTS AND FACULTY
Enrollment: 6,843. **Student Body:** 48% female, 52% male, 4% out-of-state, 2% international (27 countries represented). Asian 7%, African American 10%, Caucasian 69%, Hispanic 6%, Native American <1%, Pacific Islander <1%, Two or more races 3%, Race unknown 3%.
Retention and Graduation: 81% freshmen return for sophomore year. 27% grads go on to further study within 1 year. 10% grads pursue arts and sciences degrees. 3% grads pursue law degrees. 4% grads pursue business degrees. 1% grads pursue medical degrees. **Faculty:** Student/faculty ratio 15:1. 322 full-time faculty, 87% hold PhDs, 34% are members of minority groups, 41% are women. 0% of classes are taught by teaching assistants.

ACADEMICS
Degrees: Bachelor's; Doctoral degree—professional practice; Master's; Post-bachelor's certificate. **Classes:** Most classes have 20–29 students. Most lab/discussion sessions have 20–29 students. **Most popular majors:** Biology/Biological Sciences, General; Mechanical Engineering; Psychology, General. **Special Study Options:** Cooperative education program; Cross-registration; Distance learning; Double major; Dual enrollment; Honors program; Independent study; Internships; Liberal arts/career combination; Student-designed major; Study abroad; Teacher certification program. **Honors programs:** Honors Transfers Innovators. **Disability Services offered:** Note-taking services; Reader services; Tutors.

FACILITIES
100% of campus accessible to physically disabled.

CAMPUS LIFE
Environment: City. **Activities:** Campus Ministries; Choral groups; International Student Organization; Literary magazine; Radio station; Student government; Student newspaper. 130 registered organizations, 10 honor societies, 7 religious organizations, 6 fraternities, 5 sororities on campus. **On-Campus Highlights:** McKinley Cafe/University Center.

ADMISSIONS
Freshman Academic Profile: Average high school GPA 4.0. 28% in top 10% of high school class, 59% in top 25% of high school class, 90% in top 50% of high school class. **Test Scores:** ACT middle 50% range 21–27. **Basis for Candidate Selection:** *Very important factors include:* academic GPA, standardized test scores. *Other factors include:* application essay, interview, alumni/ae relation. **Freshman Admission Requirements:** High school diploma is required and GED is accepted. *Academic units recommended:* 4 English, 4 math, 2 science, 1 science labs, 2 foreign language, 4 social studies, 4 history. **Freshman Admission Statistics:** 5,312 applied, 62% admitted, 29% enrolled. **Transfer Admission Requirements:** High school transcript, college transcript(s). Lowest grade transferable C. **General Admission Information:** Application fee $30. Regular application deadline 5/1. Non-fall registration accepted. Admission may be deferred for a maximum of 1 year.

COSTS AND FINANCIAL AID
Annual in-state tuition $14,982. Annual out-of-state tuition $46,676. Room and board $10,872. Required fees $328. Average book and supplies expense

$1,048. **Required Forms and Deadlines:** FAFSA. **Notification of Awards:** Applicants will be notified of awards on a rolling basis beginning 3/15. **Types of Aid:** *Need-based scholarships/grants:* College/university scholarship or grant aid from institutional funds; Federal Pell; Private scholarships; SEOG; State scholarships/grants. *Loans:* Direct PLUS loans; Direct Subsidized Stafford Loans; Direct Unsubsidized Stafford Loans. **Student Employment:** Federal Work-Study Program available. Institutional employment available. **Financial Aid Statistics:** 90% needy freshmen, 84% needy undergrads receive need-based scholarship or grant aid. 50% freshmen, 34% undergrads receive non-need-based scholarship or grant aid. 86% freshmen, 91% undergrads receive need-based self-help aid. 2% freshmen, 2% undergrads receive athletic scholarships. 67% freshmen, 60% undergrads receive any aid. 65% undergrads borrow to pay for school. Average cumulative indebtedness $27,346. **Criteria awarding aid:** *Need-based:* Leadership. *Non-need-based:* Academics, Alumni affiliation, Art, Athletics, Job skills, Leadership, Minority status, Music/drama, State/district residency.

UNIVERSITY OF MICHIGAN—FLINT

303 E. Kearsley St., Flint, MI 48502
Phone: 810-762-3300 **Financial Aid Phone:** 810-762-3444
E-mail: admissions@umflint.edu **CEEB Code:** 1853
Fax: 810-762-3272 **Website:** www.umflint.edu **ACT Code:** 2063

This public school was founded in 1956. It has a 76 acre campus.

RATINGS
Admissions Selectivity Rating: 82 **Fire Safety Rating:** 96 **Green Rating:** 70

STUDENTS AND FACULTY
Enrollment: 5,499. **Student Body:** 65% female, 35% male, 2% out-of-state, 3% international (26 countries represented). Asian 2%, African American 13%, Caucasian 70%, Hispanic 6%, Native American 1%, Pacific Islander <1%, Two or more races 4%, Race unknown 4%.
Retention and Graduation: 74% freshmen return for sophomore year. 16% freshmen graduate within 4 years. 40% freshmen graduate within 6 years. **Faculty:** Student/faculty ratio 14:1. 302 full-time faculty, 78% hold PhDs, 21% are members of minority groups, 53% are women. 0% of classes are taught by teaching assistants.

ACADEMICS
Degrees: Bachelor's; Doctoral degree—professional practice; Doctoral degree research/scholarship; Master's; Post-bachelor's certificate; Post-master's certificate. **Classes:** Most classes have 10–19 students. Most lab/discussion sessions have 10–19 students. **Most popular majors:** Health Professions And Related Programs; Mechanical Engineering; Psychology, General. **Special Study Options:** Accelerated program; Cooperative education program; Distance learning; Double major; Dual enrollment; English as a Second Language (ESL); Honors program; Independent study; Internships; Student-designed major; Study abroad; Teacher certification program. **Honors programs:** 4-yr University Honors Scholar Program; 2-yr Phase I Freshman/Sophmore Honors Scholar Program; 2-yr Phase II Junior/Senior Honors Scholar Program. **Disability Services offered:** Note-taking services; Reader services; Tape recorders; Tutors. **Career services:** Alumni services; Career assessment; Career/job search classes; Internships.

FACILITIES
Housing: Coed dorms; 97% of campus accessible to physically disabled. **Special Academic Facilities/Equipment:** Frances Wilson Thompson Library.

CAMPUS LIFE
Environment: City. **Activities:** Choral groups; Concert band; Dance; Drama/theater; International Student Organization; Jazz band; Literary magazine; Music ensembles; Musical theater; Student government; Student newspaper. 112 registered organizations, 5 honor societies, 4 religious organizations, 6 fraternities, 6 sororities on campus. **On-Campus Highlights:** Recreation Center. **Environmental Initiatives:** Recycling and Waste Minimization.

ADMISSIONS
Freshman Academic Profile: Average high school GPA 3.5. 19% in top 10% of high school class, 41% in top 25% of high school class, 77% in top 50% of high school class. 91% from public high schools. **Test Scores:** SAT Math middle 50% range 470–600. SAT EBRW middle 50% range 500–620. ACT middle 50% range 20–26. **Basis for Candidate Selection:** *Very important*

factors include: academic GPA, standardized test scores. *Important factors include:* extracurricular activities. *Other factors include:* class rank, application essay, recommendation(s), interview, talent/ability, first generation. **Freshman Admission Requirements:** High school diploma is required and GED is accepted. *Academic units recommended:* 4 English, 4 math, 3 science, 3 foreign language, 3 history. **Freshman Admission Statistics:** 4,254 applied, 66% admitted, 22% enrolled. **Transfer Admission Requirements:** High school transcript, college transcript(s). Minimum college GPA of 2.0 required. Lowest grade transferable 2. **General Admission Information:** Application fee $55. Priority deadline 5/1. Regular application deadline 8/22. Non-fall registration accepted. Admission may be deferred for a maximum of 1 year.

COSTS AND FINANCIAL AID
Annual in-state tuition $11,952. Annual out-of-state tuition $23,238. Room and board $9,092. Required fees $454. Average book and supplies expense $1,000. **Required Forms and Deadlines:** FAFSA. **Notification of Awards:** Applicants will be notified of awards on a rolling basis beginning 12/1. **Types of Aid:** *Need-based scholarships/grants:* College/university scholarship or grant aid from institutional funds; Federal Pell; Private scholarships; SEOG; State scholarships/grants. *Loans:* Direct PLUS loans; Direct Subsidized Stafford Loans; Direct Unsubsidized Stafford Loans. **Student Employment:** Federal Work-Study Program available. Institutional employment available. **Financial Aid Statistics:** 73% needy freshmen, 74% needy undergrads receive need-based scholarship or grant aid. 69% freshmen, 39% undergrads receive non-need-based scholarship or grant aid. 62% freshmen, 73% undergrads receive need-based self-help aid. 0% freshmen, 0% undergrads receive athletic scholarships. 92% freshmen, 69% undergrads receive any aid. 66% undergrads borrow to pay for school. Average cumulative indebtedness $29,645. **Criteria awarding aid:** *Need-based:* Academics, Art. *Non-need-based:* Academics, Art, Leadership, Music/drama.

UNIVERSITY OF MINNESOTA—CROOKSTON

University of Minnesota, Crookston, Crookston, MN 56716-5001
Phone: 218-281-8569 **Financial Aid Phone:** 218-281-8563
E-mail: UMCinfo@umn.edu **CEEB Code:** 6893
Fax: 218-281-8575 **Website:** http://www1.crk.umn.edu/ **ACT Code:** 2129

This public school was founded in 1966. It has a 37 acre campus.

RATINGS
Admissions Selectivity Rating: 77   **Fire Safety Rating:** 99   **Green Rating:** 73

STUDENTS AND FACULTY
Enrollment: 1,876. **Student Body:** 50% female, 50% male, 28% out-of-state, 4% international (35 countries represented). Asian 2%, African American 7%, Caucasian 80%, Hispanic 3%, Native American <1%, Pacific Islander <1%, Two or more races 1%, Race unknown 2%.
Retention and Graduation: 66% freshmen return for sophomore year. 12% grads go on to further study within 1 year. **Faculty:** Student/faculty ratio 20:1. 66 full-time faculty, 53% hold PhDs, 6% are members of minority groups, 41% are women. 0% of classes are taught by teaching assistants.

ACADEMICS
Degrees: Bachelor's; Certificate. **Classes:** Most classes have 10–19 students. Most lab/discussion sessions have 10–19 students. **Most popular majors:** Natural Resources/Conservation, General; Business Administration and Management, General; Animal Sciences, General. **Special Study Options:** Cooperative education program; Cross-registration; Distance learning; Double major; Dual enrollment; English as a Second Language (ESL); Honors program; Independent study; Internships; Student-designed major; Study abroad; Teacher certification program. **Honors programs:** The UMC Honors Program was developed to inspire and transform students' writing, discussion, and critical thinking skills in such a way that reflects high expectations for academically successful students. The program nurtures and challenges students to explore ideas, assess values, and develop leadership skills. Honors coursework addresses the diverse and global atmosphere in which we live. In addition, students in the Honors Program will have the opportunity for various social outings outside of the normal campus experience. Key features of the program consist of a required course that introduces the student to the rigors of the Honors Program; final requirements which include an honors proposal course that culminates in an honors essay; and a research or creative project that requires a public defense. The Honors Program includes the following components: 1. Honors courses

(courses developed or to be developed include leadership, orientation courses, global perspective courses, composition courses) 2. Honors options (faculty-mentored, student-organized discussion groups) 3. Honors contracts (honors activities incorporated into "regular" courses) 4. Honors colloquia, leadership development, and cultural enrichment 5. Honors national or international experience 6. Honors essay, research or creative project (capstone experience). **Disability Services offered:** Note-taking services; Reader services; Tape recorders; Tutors. **Career services:** Alumni services; Career assessment; Career/job search classes; Internships.

FACILITIES
Housing: Apartments for single students; Coed dorms; Special housing for disabled students; 90% of campus accessible to physically disabled. **Special Academic Facilities/Equipment:** The new Immersive Visualization and Informatics Lab, one of only two in the Upper Midwest, allows faculty members and software engineering students to develop 3-D computer models and simulations; the Equine Arena and Stables feature a 90 x 120 ft. heated indoor riding arena, 45-stall horse stables, training pen, round pen, breeding phantom and stocks, and tack room; the Alseth NWSA Business Board Room is a classroom featuring state-of-the-art technology for business and marketing students; the Early Childhood Development Center provides students the opportunity to observe and participate in a teacher-training laboratory at a fully operational child care facility; the Production Horticulture Building and Greenhouse Complex is a production horticulture lab where horticulture students gain direct experience with the culture, care, and growth of commercial horticulture crops; the Bergland Laboratory is center for teaching, applied student lab experiences, and research in the agronomic, botanical, and horticultural sciences; located adjacent to campus, the 85-acre Red River Valley Natural History Area contains prairie, marshland, and forest ecosystems and is used extensively for practice in conservation techniques and nature observation.

CAMPUS LIFE
Environment: Village. **Activities:** Campus Ministries; Choral groups; Drama/theater; International Student Organization; Jazz band; Musical theater; Pep band; Student government. 38 registered organizations, 1 honor society, 2 religious organizations, 1 fraternity, 1 sorority on campus. **Athletics (Intercollegiate):** *Men:* baseball, basketball, football, golf, ice hockey. *Women:* basketball, equestrian sports, golf, soccer, softball, tennis, volleyball. **On-Campus Highlights:** Sargeant Student Center. **Environmental Initiatives:** Evaluate the reduction of coal as a primary feedstock for the campus energy and supplement with renewable fuels.

ADMISSIONS
Freshman Academic Profile: Average high school GPA 3.2. 12% in top 10% of high school class, 31% in top 25% of high school class, 65% in top 50% of high school class. **Test Scores:** SAT Math middle 50% range 470–510. SAT EBRW middle 50% range 430–480. ACT middle 50% range 19–24. **Basis for Candidate Selection:** *Very important factors include:* rigor of secondary school record, class rank, academic GPA, standardized test scores. *Other factors include:* application essay, recommendation(s). **Freshman Admission Requirements:** High school diploma is required and GED is accepted. *Academic units required:* 4 English, 3 math, 3 science, 2 science labs, 3 social studies. *Academic units recommended:* 2 foreign language. **Freshman Admission Statistics:** 927 applied, 71% admitted, 41% enrolled. **Transfer Admission Requirements:** College transcript(s). Minimum college GPA of 2.0 required. Lowest grade transferable D. **General Admission Information:** Application fee $30. Non-fall registration accepted. Admission may be deferred for a maximum of 1 semester.

COSTS AND FINANCIAL AID
Annual in-state tuition $10,180. Annual out-of-state tuition $10,180. Room and board $8,418. Required fees $1,520. Average book and supplies expense $1,200. **Required Forms and Deadlines:** FAFSA. **Notification of Awards:** Applicants will be notified of awards on a rolling basis beginning 3/1. **Types of Aid:** *Need-based scholarships/grants:* College/university scholarship or grant aid from institutional funds; Federal Pell; Private scholarships; SEOG; State scholarships/grants. *Loans:* Direct PLUS loans; Direct Subsidized Stafford Loans; Direct Unsubsidized Stafford Loans. **Student Employment:** Federal Work-Study Program available. Institutional employment available. **Financial Aid Statistics:** 95% needy freshmen, 90% needy undergrads receive need-based scholarship or grant aid. 11% freshmen, 8% undergrads receive non-need-based scholarship or grant aid. 74% freshmen, 76% undergrads receive need-based self-help aid. 9% freshmen, 4% undergrads receive athletic scholarships. 88% freshmen, 48% undergrads receive any aid. 80% undergrads borrow to pay for school. Average cumulative indebtedness $28,309. **Criteria awarding aid:** *Non-need-based:* Academics, Alumni affiliation, Athletics, Leadership, Minority status, Music/drama, State/district residency.

UNIVERSITY OF MINNESOTA—DULUTH

25 Solon Campus Center, Duluth, MN 55812-3000
Phone: 218-726-7171 **Financial Aid Phone:** (218) 726-8000
E-mail: umdadmis@d.umn.edu **CEEB Code:** 6873
Fax: 218-726-7040 **Website:** www.d.umn.edu **ACT Code:** 2157

This public school was founded in 1947. It has a 247 acre campus.

RATINGS

Admissions Selectivity Rating: 79   **Fire Safety Rating:** 93   **Green Rating:** 97

STUDENTS AND FACULTY

Enrollment: 9,051. **Student Body:** 45% female, 55% male, 12% out-of-state, 2% international (42 countries represented). Asian 3%, African American 2%, Caucasian 85%, Hispanic 3%, Native American 1%, Pacific Islander <1%, Two or more races 3%, Race unknown 1%.
Retention and Graduation: 78% freshmen return for sophomore year. 16% grads go on to further study within 1 year. **Faculty:** Student/faculty ratio 18:1. 508 full-time faculty, 74% hold PhDs, 18% are members of minority groups, 45% are women.

ACADEMICS

Degrees: Bachelor's; Certificate; Doctoral degree—professional practice; Master's; Post-bachelor's certificate. **Classes:** Most classes have 20–29 students. Most lab/discussion sessions have 10–19 students. **Most popular majors:** Biology/Biological Sciences, General; Business Administration and Management, General; Elementary Education and Teaching. **Special Study Options:** Accelerated program; Cooperative education program; Cross-registration; Distance learning; Double major; Dual enrollment; English as a Second Language (ESL); Exchange student program (domestic); Honors program; Independent study; Internships; Liberal arts/career combination; Student-designed major; Study abroad; Teacher certification program; Weekend college. **Honors programs:** The Honors Program offers motivated students who are serious about their intellectual and personal growth a variety of special classes enhanced by cultural events and activities, as well as leadership and research opportunities. **Disability Services offered:** Note-taking services; Reader services; Tape recorders; Tutors. **Career services:** Alumni services; Career assessment; Career/job search classes; Internships.

FACILITIES

Housing: Apartments for single students; Coed dorms; Men's dorms; Special housing for disabled students; Theme housing; Women's dorms; 100% of campus accessible to physically disabled. **Special Academic Facilities/Equipment:** Art museum, planetarium, music performance hall, theatre.

CAMPUS LIFE

Environment: Village. **Activities:** Campus Ministries; Choral groups; Concert band; Dance; Drama/theater; International Student Organization; Jazz band; Marching band; Music ensembles; Musical theater; Opera; Pep band; Radio station; Student government; Student newspaper; Student-run film society; Symphony orchestra. 150 registered organizations, 10 honor societies, 7 religious organizations, 2 fraternities, 2 sororities on campus. **Athletics (Intercollegiate):** *Men:* baseball, basketball, cross-country, football, ice hockey, track/field (outdoor), track/field (indoor). *Women:* basketball, cross-country, ice hockey, soccer, softball, tennis, track/field (outdoor), track/field (indoor), volleyball. **On-Campus Highlights:** Solon Campus Center. **Environmental Initiatives:** LEED.

ADMISSIONS

Freshman Academic Profile: Average high school GPA 3.5. 17% in top 10% of high school class, 42% in top 25% of high school class, 85% in top 50% of high school class. 94% from public high schools. **Test Scores:** SAT Math middle 50% range 500–610. SAT EBRW middle 50% range 450–590. ACT middle 50% range 22–26. **Basis for Candidate Selection:** *Very important factors include:* academic GPA, standardized test scores. *Important factors include:* rigor of secondary school record. *Other factors include:* class rank, application essay, recommendation(s), extracurricular activities, talent/ability, character/personal qualities, first generation, alumni/ae relation, geographical residence, state residency, racial/ethnic status, volunteer work, work experience. **Freshman Admission Requirements:** High school diploma is required and GED is accepted. *Academic units required:* 4 English, 4 math, 3 science, 2 foreign language, 3 social studies, 1 visual/performing arts. **Freshman Admission Statistics:** 7,973 applied, 77% admitted, 35% enrolled. **Transfer Admission Requirements:** High school transcript, college transcript(s). Minimum college

GPA of 2.0 required. Lowest grade transferable D. **General Admission Information:** Application fee $40. Priority deadline 12/1. Regular application deadline 6/15. Non-fall registration accepted.

COSTS AND FINANCIAL AID

Required Forms and Deadlines: FAFSA. **Notification of Awards:** Applicants will be notified of awards on a rolling basis beginning 2/1. **Types of Aid:** *Need-based scholarships/grants:* College/university scholarship or grant aid from institutional funds; Federal Pell; Private scholarships; SEOG; State scholarships/grants. *Loans:* Direct PLUS loans; Direct Subsidized Stafford Loans; Direct Unsubsidized Stafford Loans. **Student Employment:** Federal Work-Study Program available. Institutional employment available. **Financial Aid Statistics:** 87% needy freshmen, 85% needy undergrads receive need-based scholarship or grant aid. 16% freshmen, 15% undergrads receive non-need-based scholarship or grant aid. 82% freshmen, 84% undergrads receive need-based self-help aid. 2% freshmen, 2% undergrads receive athletic scholarships. 85% freshmen, 81% undergrads receive any aid. 73% undergrads borrow to pay for school. Average cumulative indebtedness $30,579. **Criteria awarding aid:** *Need-based:* Alumni affiliation, Athletics, Minority status. *Non-need-based:* Academics, Alumni affiliation, Art, Athletics, Leadership, Minority status, Music/drama, State/district residency.

UNIVERSITY OF MINNESOTA—MORRIS

600 E 4th St, Morris, MN 56267
Phone: 320-589-6035 **Financial Aid Phone:** 800-992-8863 / 320-589-6046
E-mail: http://admissions.morris.umn.edu/contact **CEEB Code:** 6890
Fax: 320-589-6051 **Website:** www.morris.umn.edu **ACT Code:** 2155

This public school was founded in 1959. It has a 130 acre campus.

RATINGS

Admissions Selectivity Rating: 86   **Fire Safety Rating:** 98   **Green Rating:** 98

STUDENTS AND FACULTY

Enrollment: 1,552. **Student Body:** 56% female, 44% male, 17% out-of-state, 11% international (21 countries represented). Asian 3%, African American 2%, Caucasian 58%, Hispanic 5%, Native American 8%, Pacific Islander 0%, Two or more races 13%, Race unknown <1%.
Retention and Graduation: 80% freshmen return for sophomore year. 50% freshmen graduate within 4 years. 64% freshmen graduate within 6 years. 20% grads go on to further study within 1 year. 81% grads pursue arts and sciences degrees. 0% grads pursue law degrees. 2% grads pursue business degrees. 5% grads pursue medical degrees. **Faculty:** Student/faculty ratio 11:1. 125 full-time faculty, 93% hold PhDs, 12% are members of minority groups, 44% are women. 0% of classes are taught by teaching assistants.

ACADEMICS

Degrees: Bachelor's. **Classes:** Most classes have 10–19 students. Most lab/discussion sessions have 10–19 students. **Most popular majors:** Biology/Biological Sciences, General; Psychology, General. **Special Study Options:** Cross-registration; Distance learning; Double major; Dual enrollment; English as a Second Language (ESL); Exchange student program (domestic); Honors program; Independent study; Internships; Student-designed major; Study abroad; Teacher certification program. **Honors programs:** The University of Minnesota, Morris Honors Program provides motivated, high-achieving students a distinctive, academically challenging intellectual experience amplifying and complementing the Morris liberal arts education. Successful completion of the Honors Program, an interdisciplinary curriculum team-taught by faculty from across the campus, provides the student a Morris degree "with Honors" in recognition of their achievement. **Disability Services offered:** Note-taking services; Reader services; Tape recorders; Tutors. **Career services:** Alumni network; Alumni services; Career assessment; Career/job search classes; Internships.

FACILITIES

Housing: Apartments for single students; Coed dorms; Special housing for disabled students; Theme housing; 70% of campus accessible to physically disabled. **Special Academic Facilities/Equipment:** Morrison Art Gallery, conservatory, observatory.

CAMPUS LIFE

Environment: Rural. **Activities:** Campus Ministries; Choral groups; Concert band; Dance; Drama/theater; International Student Organization; Jazz band; Literary magazine; Music ensembles; Musical theater; Radio station;

Student government; Student newspaper; Symphony orchestra. 100 registered organizations, 5 honor societies, 12 religious organizations on campus. **Athletics (Intercollegiate):** *Men:* baseball, basketball, football, golf, tennis, track/field (outdoor), track/field (indoor). *Women:* basketball, cross-country, diving, golf, soccer, softball, swimming, tennis, track/field (outdoor), track/field (indoor), volleyball. **On-Campus Highlights:** Student Center — KUMM, Turtle Mountain café. **Environmental Initiatives:** Morris is actively working to become a sustainable and low-carbon community, and renewable energy research and demonstration is a big part of that effort. Morris receives power from two 1.65 MW University of Minnesota wind turbines. We receive 60% of our annual electricity from wind. We have an on-campus biomass gasification research and demonstration platform. We have solar thermal and solar PV projects on campus. And we have completed a multi-million dollar energy service contract to retrofit the campus for conservation.

ADMISSIONS

Freshman Academic Profile: Average high school GPA 3.6. 24% in top 10% of high school class, 49% in top 25% of high school class, 84% in top 50% of high school class. 95% from public high schools. **Test Scores:** SAT Math middle 50% range 590–710. SAT EBRW middle 50% range 560–680. ACT middle 50% range 22–28. **Basis for Candidate Selection:** *Very important factors include:* rigor of secondary school record, class rank, academic GPA, standardized test scores. *Important factors include:* extracurricular activities, talent/ability, character/personal qualities, volunteer work, work experience. *Other factors include:* application essay, recommendation(s), interview, first generation. **Freshman Admission Requirements:** High school diploma is required and GED is accepted. *Academic units required:* 4 English, 4 math, 3 science, 2 foreign language, 3 social studies. **Freshman Admission Statistics:** 3,211 applied, 64% admitted, 17% enrolled. **Transfer Admission Requirements:** College transcript(s), essay or personal statement, statement of good standing from prior institution(s). Minimum college GPA of 2.5 required. Lowest grade transferable D. **General Admission Information:** Application fee $35. Priority deadline 12/15. Regular application deadline 3/15. Non-fall registration accepted. Admission may be deferred for a maximum of 1 year.

COSTS AND FINANCIAL AID

Required Forms and Deadlines: FAFSA. **Notification of Awards:** Applicants will be notified of awards on a rolling basis beginning 4/1. **Types of Aid:** *Need-based scholarships/grants:* College/university scholarship or grant aid from institutional funds; Federal Pell; Private scholarships; SEOG; State scholarships/grants. *Loans:* Direct PLUS loans; Direct Subsidized Stafford Loans; Direct Unsubsidized Stafford Loans. **Student Employment:** Federal Work-Study Program available. Institutional employment available. **Financial Aid Statistics:** 97% needy freshmen, 96% needy undergrads receive need-based scholarship or grant aid. 6% freshmen, 9% undergrads receive non-need-based scholarship or grant aid. 56% freshmen, 59% undergrads receive need-based self-help aid. 0% freshmen, 0% undergrads receive athletic scholarships. 98% freshmen, 96% undergrads receive any aid. 72% undergrads borrow to pay for school. Average cumulative indebtedness $24,189. **Criteria awarding aid:** *Non-need-based:* Academics.

UNIVERSITY OF MINNESOTA—TWIN CITIES

240 Williamson Hall, Minneapolis, MN 55455-0213
Phone: 612-625-2008 **Financial Aid Phone:** 612-624-1111 or 1-800-400-8636
CEEB Code: 6874
Fax: 612-626-1693 **Website:** https://twin-cities.umn.edu/ **ACT Code:** 2156

This public school was founded in 1851. It has a 2000 acre campus.

RATINGS

Admissions Selectivity Rating: 89   **Fire Safety Rating:** 88   **Green Rating:** 96

STUDENTS AND FACULTY

Enrollment: 31,367. **Student Body:** 53% female, 47% male, 27% out-of-state, 8% international (147 countries represented). Asian 10%, African American 5%, Caucasian 65%, Hispanic 5%, Native American <1%, Pacific Islander <1%, Two or more races 4%, Race unknown 2%.

Retention and Graduation: 93% freshmen return for sophomore year. 69% freshmen graduate within 4 years. 83% freshmen graduate within 6 years. **Faculty:** Student/faculty ratio 17:1. 2,673 full-time faculty, 78% hold PhDs, 18% are members of minority groups, 45% are women.

ACADEMICS

Degrees: Bachelor's; Certificate; Diploma; Doctoral degree—professional practice; Doctoral degree research/scholarship; Master's; Post-bachelor's certificate; Post-master's certificate. **Classes:** Most classes have 20–29 students. Most lab/discussion sessions have 10–19 students. **Most popular majors:** Journalism; Psychology, General; Computer Science. **Special Study Options:** Accelerated program; Cooperative education program; Cross-registration; Distance learning; Double major; Dual enrollment; English as a Second Language (ESL); Exchange student program (domestic); External degree program; Honors program; Independent study; Internships; Liberal arts/career combination; Student-designed major; Study abroad; Teacher certification program. **Honors programs:** Honors, Undergraduate Research Opportunities Program. **Combined degree programs:** BA/MA; BA/MD. **Disability Services offered:** Note-taking services; Reader services; Tape recorders; Tutors. **Career services:** Alumni network; Alumni services; Career assessment; Career/job search classes; Internships; Regional alumni.

FACILITIES

Housing: Apartments for married students; Apartments for single students; Coed dorms; Cooperative housing; Fraternity/sorority housing; Special housing for disabled students; Special housing for international students; Theme housing; Wellness housing. **Special Academic Facilities/Equipment:** Frederick R. Weisman Art Museum, Bell Museum of Natural History, Ted Mann Concert Hall, Recreational Sports Center, Civil Engineering Building, Basic Sciences/Biomedical Engineering Building, Coffman Memorial Union, West Bank Arts Quarter, Goldstein Gallery, Arboretum.

CAMPUS LIFE

Environment: Metropolis. **Activities:** Choral groups; Concert band; Dance; Drama/theater; International Student Organization; Jazz band; Literary magazine; Marching band; Model UN; Music ensembles; Musical theater; Opera; Pep band; Radio station; Student government; Student newspaper; Student-run film society; Symphony orchestra; Television station. 800 registered organizations, 14 religious organizations, 31 fraternity, 12 sororities on campus. **Athletics (Intercollegiate):** *Men:* baseball, basketball, cross-country, diving, football, golf, gymnastics, ice hockey, swimming, tennis, track/field (outdoor), track/field (indoor), wrestling. *Women:* basketball, cheerleading, cross-country, diving, golf, gymnastics, ice hockey, soccer, softball, swimming, tennis, track/field (outdoor), track/field (indoor), volleyball. **On-Campus Highlights:** Weisman Art Museum. **Environmental Initiatives:** In 2013, a new gaming feature was piloted in order to make sustainability fun and effortless. A list of green acts was promoted among students, showing how they could help create a more sustainable campus, community and world. The pilot resulted in over 7,000 acts of green, saving 125 tons of carbon, over 97,000 gallons of water and 252,000kWh electricity. The University Services Sustainability Office collaborates with faculty to raise awareness of the campus CAP. For example, the Sustainability Director presented on the CAP, which was featured in Architecture 5750—Planning and Design of the University, a course offered through College of Design. The Sustainability Office participated on the steering committee and work teams to update the City of Minneapolis Climate Action Plan, which provides a roadmap to guide Minneapolis towards greenhouse gas emissions reduction targets. The Twin Cities and Morris campuses, Twin Cities Sustainability Education program and Institute on the Environmental provided space and some support for the Next Generation Congress—a group of students who developed long term environmental policy recommendations and delivered them to the Governor's Environmental Congress. The recommendations included addressing climate impacts by supporting renewable energy and sustainable energy and building practices. Some of these students connected through programs and education the University offered to raised awareness about energy and climate, such as It All Adds Up and the Sustainability Minor. The student leaders who helped organize the efforts received the Assn. for the Advancement of Sustainability in Higher Education (AASHE) Student Leadership Award. Links: http://italladdsup.umn.edu/news/platinum.award_03132013.php http://ow.ly/tDUAt http://ow.ly/tDUWF.

ADMISSIONS

Freshman Academic Profile: 50% in top 10% of high school class, 83% in top 25% of high school class, 98% in top 50% of high school class. **Test Scores:** SAT Math middle 50% range 660–770. SAT EBRW middle 50% range 600–710. ACT middle 50% range 26–31. **Basis for Candidate Selection:** *Very important factors include:* rigor of secondary school record, class rank, academic GPA, standardized test scores. *Other factors include:* extracurricular activities, talent/ability, character/personal qualities, first generation, alumni/ae relation, geographical residence, racial/ethnic status, volunteer work, work experience. **Freshman Admission Requirements:** High school diploma is required and GED is accepted. *Academic units required:* 4 English, 4 math, 3 science, 1 science labs, 2 foreign language, 3 social studies, 1 visual/performing arts. *Academic units recommended:* 4 English, 4 math, 4 science, 1 science labs, 2 foreign language, 3 social studies, 1 visual/performing arts. **Freshman Admission Statistics:** 40,673 applied, 57% admitted, 27% enrolled. **Transfer Admission Requirements:** College transcript(s). Minimum college GPA of 2.0 required. Lowest grade transferable D. **General Admission Information:** Application fee $55. Non-fall registration accepted.

COSTS AND FINANCIAL AID

Annual in-state tuition $13,318. Annual out-of-state tuition $31,616. Room and board $10,768. Required fees $1,709. Average book and supplies expense $1,000. **Required Forms and Deadlines:** FAFSA; Institution's own financial aid form. **Notification of Awards:** Applicants will be notified of awards on a rolling basis beginning 2/15. **Types of Aid:** *Need-based scholarships/grants:* College/university scholarship or grant aid from institutional funds; Federal Nursing Scholarships; Federal Pell; Private scholarships; SEOG; State scholarships/grants. *Loans:* Direct PLUS loans; Direct Subsidized Stafford Loans; Direct Unsubsidized Stafford Loans. **Student Employment:** Federal Work-Study Program available. Institutional employment available. **Financial Aid Statistics:** 88% needy freshmen, 86% needy undergrads receive need-based scholarship or grant aid. 10% freshmen, 7% undergrads receive non-need-based scholarship or grant aid. 78% freshmen, 80% undergrads receive need-based self-help aid. 0% freshmen, 0% undergrads receive athletic scholarships. 55% undergrads borrow to pay for school. Average cumulative indebtedness $27,077. **Criteria awarding aid:** *Non-need-based:* Academics, Art, Athletics, Job skills, Leadership, Minority status, Music/drama, State/district residency.

UNIVERSITY OF MISSISSIPPI

145 Martindale, University, MS 38677
Phone: 662-915-7226 **Financial Aid Phone:** 800-891-4596
E-mail: admissions@olemiss.edu **CEEB Code:** 1840
Fax: 662-915-5869 **Website:** www.olemiss.edu **ACT Code:** 2250

This public school was founded in 1844. It has a 3391 acre campus.

RATINGS

Admissions Selectivity Rating: 76 **Fire Safety Rating:** 90 **Green Rating:** 69

STUDENTS AND FACULTY

Enrollment: 16,932. **Student Body:** 57% female, 43% male, 44% out-of-state, 1% international. Asian 2%, African American 12%, Caucasian 78%, Hispanic 4%, Native American <1%, Pacific Islander <1%, Two or more races 2%, Race unknown <1%.
Retention and Graduation: 85% freshmen return for sophomore year. 37% freshmen graduate within 4 years. 60% freshmen graduate within 6 years.
Faculty: Student/faculty ratio 18:1. 1,075 full-time faculty, 86% hold PhDs, 17% are members of minority groups, 49% are women.

ACADEMICS

Degrees: Bachelor's; Doctoral degree—professional practice; Doctoral degree research/scholarship; Master's; Post-bachelor's certificate; Post-master's certificate. **Classes:** Most classes have 10–19 students. Most lab/discussion sessions have 20–29 students. **Most popular majors:** Accounting; Marketing/Marketing Management, General. **Special Study Options:** Accelerated program; Cooperative education program; Distance learning; Double major; Dual enrollment; English as a Second Language (ESL); Exchange student program (domestic); Honors program; Independent study; Internships; Study abroad; Teacher certification program. **Honors programs:** Sally McDonnell-Barksdale Honors College. **Disability Services offered:** Note-taking services; Reader services; Tape recorders. **Career services:** Alumni services; Career assessment; Career/job search classes; Internships.

FACILITIES

Housing: Apartments for married students; Apartments for single students; Fraternity/sorority housing; Men's dorms; Special housing for international students; Theme housing; Wellness housing; Women's dorms. **Special Academic Facilities/Equipment:** Sally McDonnell-Barksdale Honors College, Croft Institute for International Studies, National Food Service Management Institute, Mississippi Center for Supercomputing Research, Art and archaeology museums, Sarah Isom Center for Women & Gender Studies, Center for Study of Southern Culture, William Faulkner home, Marine Minerals Research Institute, National Center for Physical Acoustics, National Center for Natural Products Research, Biological Field Station, Barksdale Reading Institute, Ford Center for the Performing Arts, William Winter Institutue for Racial Reconciliation, Paris-Yates Chapel, Trent Lott Leadership Institute, Living Blues Archive, Student Media Center, Center for Inclusion and Cross-Cultural Engagement, Mary Buie Museum, Luckyday Residential College. **Campus network:** 90% of classrooms, 95% of dorms, 90% of student union, 95% of libraries, 90% of dining areas, 90% of common outdoor areas have wireless network access.

CAMPUS LIFE

Environment: Village. **Activities:** Campus Ministries; Choral groups; Concert band; Dance; Drama/theater; International Student Organization; Jazz band; Marching band; Music ensembles; Musical theater; Opera; Pep band; Radio station; Student government; Student newspaper; Symphony orchestra; Television station; Yearbook. 312 registered organizations, 23 honor societies, 24 religious organizations, 20 fraternities, 15 sororities on campus. **Athletics (Intercollegiate):** *Men:* baseball, basketball, cheerleading, cross-country, football, golf, tennis, track/field (outdoor), track/field (indoor). *Women:* basketball, cheerleading, cross-country, golf, riflery, soccer, softball, tennis, track/field (outdoor), track/field (indoor), volleyball. **On-Campus Highlights:** The Grove. **Environmental Initiatives:** UM is installing SmartMeters on the majority of campus buildings.

ADMISSIONS

Freshman Academic Profile: Average high school GPA 3.6. 25% in top 10% of high school class, 49% in top 25% of high school class, 76% in top 50% of high school class. **Test Scores:** SAT Math middle 50% range 500–620. SAT EBRW middle 50% range 520–630. ACT middle 50% range 21–29. **Basis for Candidate Selection:** *Important factors include:* academic GPA, standardized test scores. *Other factors include:* rigor of secondary school record, class rank. **Freshman Admission Requirements:** High school diploma is required and GED is accepted. *Academic units required:* 4 English, 3 math, 3 science, 2 science labs, 2 foreign language, 3 social studies, 0.5 computer science, 1 visual/performing arts. *Academic units recommended:* 4 English, 4 math, 4 science, 2 science labs, 2 foreign language, 4 social studies, 0.5 computer science, 1 visual/performing arts, 2 unit from above areas or other academic areas. **Freshman Admission Statistics:** 16,253 applied, 88% admitted, 23% enrolled. **Transfer Admission Requirements:** College transcript(s). Minimum college GPA of 2.0 required. Lowest grade transferable D. **General Admission Information:** Application fee $40. Priority deadline 4/1. Non-fall registration accepted. Admission may be deferred for a maximum of two years.

COSTS AND FINANCIAL AID

Annual in-state tuition $8,550. Annual out-of-state tuition $24,504. Room and board $10,696. Required fees $100. Average book and supplies expense $1,200. **Required Forms and Deadlines:** FAFSA. **Notification of Awards:** Applicants will be notified of awards on a rolling basis beginning 4/1. **Types of Aid:** *Need-based scholarships/grants:* College/university scholarship or grant aid from institutional funds; Federal Pell; Private scholarships; SEOG; State scholarships/grants. *Loans:* Direct PLUS loans; Direct Subsidized Stafford Loans; Direct Unsubsidized Stafford Loans. **Student Employment:** Federal Work-Study Program available. Institutional employment available. **Financial Aid Statistics:** 91% needy freshmen, 85% needy undergrads receive need-based scholarship or grant aid. 15% freshmen, 10% undergrads receive non-need-based scholarship or grant aid. 63% freshmen, 71% undergrads receive need-based self-help aid. 2% freshmen, 1% undergrads receive athletic scholarships. 86% freshmen, 80% undergrads receive any aid. 50% undergrads borrow to pay for school. Average cumulative indebtedness $30,731. **Criteria awarding aid:** *Need-based:* Academics, Leadership. *Non-need-based:* Academics, Alumni affiliation, Art, Athletics, Leadership, Music/drama, State/district residency.

UNIVERSITY OF MISSOURI

230 Jesse Hall, Columbia, MO 65211
Phone: 573-882-7786 **Financial Aid Phone:** 573-882-7506
E-mail: MU4U@missouri.edu **CEEB Code:** 260735
Fax: 573-882-7887 **Website:** www.missouri.edu **ACT Code:** 2382

This public school was founded in 1839. It has a 1262 acre campus.

RATINGS
Admissions Selectivity Rating: 82   **Fire Safety Rating:** 81   **Green Rating:** 94

STUDENTS AND FACULTY
Enrollment: 21,933. **Student Body:** 53% female, 47% male, 20% out-of-state, 2% international (38 countries represented). Asian 3%, African American 7%, Caucasian 78%, Hispanic 5%, Native American <1%, Pacific Islander <1%, Two or more races 4%, Race unknown 1%.
Retention and Graduation: 88% freshmen return for sophomore year. 48% freshmen graduate within 4 years. 71% freshmen graduate within 6 years.
Faculty: Student/faculty ratio 17:1. 1,191 full-time faculty, 90% hold PhDs, 26% are members of minority groups, 42% are women.

ACADEMICS
Degrees: Bachelor's; Certificate; Doctoral degree—professional practice; Doctoral degree research/scholarship; Master's; Post-bachelor's certificate. **Classes:** Most classes have 20–29 students. Most lab/discussion sessions have 20–29 students. **Most popular majors:** Journalism; Health Professions And Related Programs; Business/Commerce, General. **Special Study Options:** Accelerated program; Cooperative education program; Cross-registration; Distance learning; Double major; English as a Second Language (ESL); Exchange student program (domestic); External degree program; Honors program; Independent study; Internships; Liberal arts/career combination; Student-designed major; Study abroad; Teacher certification program. **Honors programs:** The Honors College has its own highly-developed curriculum and works closely with departments and colleges on campus to provide a wide range of exciting, engaging, and challenging honors courses, academic programs, and extra-curricular events and activities. We call this exciting and varied set of offerings, the "Honors Experience." **Combined degree programs:** BA/MA. **Disability Services offered:** Note-taking services; Reader services; Tape recorders; Tutors. **Career services:** Alumni network; Alumni services; Career assessment; Career/job search classes; Internships; Regional alumni.

FACILITIES
Housing: Apartments for married students; Apartments for single students; Coed dorms; Fraternity/sorority housing; Men's dorms; Theme housing; Women's dorms; 100% of campus accessible to physically disabled. **Special Academic Facilities/Equipment:** Life Sciences Center for Research Tiger Place, a licensed care facility; Department of Nursing; James B Nutter Family Information; Ellis Library; Museum of Anthropology; Museum of Art and Archeology; World's most powerful university research reactor for Nuclear Medicine; one of 15 European Union Centers on college campuses; MU Botanic Garden. **Campus network:** 20% of classrooms, 0% of dorms, 100% of student union, 100% of libraries, 0% of dining areas, 0% of common outdoor areas have wireless network access.

CAMPUS LIFE
Environment: City. **Activities:** Campus Ministries; Choral groups; Concert band; Dance; Drama/theater; International Student Organization; Jazz band; Literary magazine; Marching band; Model UN; Music ensembles; Musical theater; Opera; Pep band; Radio station; Student government; Student newspaper; Student-run film society; Symphony orchestra; Television station; Yearbook. 600 registered organizations, 31 honor societies, 40 religious organizations, 31 fraternity, 23 sororities on campus. **Athletics (Intercollegiate):** *Men:* baseball, basketball, cross-country, diving, football, golf, swimming, track/field (outdoor), track/field (indoor), wrestling. *Women:* basketball, cheerleading, cross-country, diving, golf, gymnastics, soccer, softball, swimming, tennis, track/field (outdoor), track/field (indoor), volleyball. **On-Campus Highlights:** MU Student Center.

ADMISSIONS
Freshman Academic Profile: 33% in top 10% of high school class, 63% in top 25% of high school class, 91% in top 50% of high school class. **Test**

Scores: SAT Math middle 50% range 560–680. SAT EBRW middle 50% range 560–660. ACT middle 50% range 23–29. **Basis for Candidate Selection:** *Very important factors include:* class rank, academic GPA, standardized test scores. *Other factors include:* rigor of secondary school record, application essay, recommendation(s), talent/ability. **Freshman Admission Requirements:** High school diploma is required and GED is accepted. *Academic units required:* 4 English, 4 math, 3 science, 1 science labs, 2 foreign language, 3 social studies, 1 unit from above areas or other academic areas. **Freshman Admission Statistics:** 20,015 applied, 81% admitted, 34% enrolled. **Transfer Admission Requirements:** College transcript(s). Minimum college GPA of 2.5 required. **General Admission Information:** Application fee $55. Non-fall registration accepted.

COSTS AND FINANCIAL AID
Annual in-state tuition $9,120. Annual out-of-state tuition $26,991. Room and board $11,618. Required fees $1,357. Average book and supplies expense $1,232. **Required Forms and Deadlines:** FAFSA. **Notification of Awards:** Applicants will be notified of awards on a rolling basis beginning 12/15. **Types of Aid:** *Need-based scholarships/grants:* College/university scholarship or grant aid from institutional funds; Federal Nursing Scholarships; Federal Pell; Private scholarships; SEOG; State scholarships/grants. *Loans:* Direct PLUS loans; Direct Subsidized Stafford Loans; Direct Unsubsidized Stafford Loans. **Student Employment:** Federal Work-Study Program available. Institutional employment available. **Financial Aid Statistics:** 85% freshmen, 77% undergrads receive any aid. **Criteria awarding aid:** *Need-based:* Academics, Alumni affiliation, Art, Athletics, Leadership, Minority status, Music/drama. *Non-need-based:* Academics, Alumni affiliation, Art, Athletics, Leadership, Minority status, Music/drama, State/district residency.

UNIVERSITY OF MISSOURI—KANSAS CITY

5100 Rockhill Road, Kansas City, MO 64114
Phone: 816-235-1111 **Financial Aid Phone:** 816-235-1154
E-mail: admissions@umkc.edu **CEEB Code:** 6872
Fax: 816-235-5544 **Website:** www.umkc.edu **ACT Code:** 2380

This public school was founded in 1929. It has a 191 acre campus.

RATINGS
Admissions Selectivity Rating: 60*   **Fire Safety Rating:** 98   **Green Rating:** 60*

STUDENTS AND FACULTY
Enrollment: 7,426. **Student Body:** 57% female, 43% male, 21% out-of-state, 5% international (55 countries represented). Asian 9%, African American 12%, Caucasian 56%, Hispanic 10%, Native American <1%, Pacific Islander <1%, Two or more races 5%, Race unknown 3%.
Retention and Graduation: 76% freshmen return for sophomore year. 23% freshmen graduate within 4 years. 47% freshmen graduate within 6 years. 24% grads go on to further study within 1 year.

ACADEMICS
Degrees: Bachelor's; Certificate; Doctoral degree—professional practice; Doctoral degree research/scholarship; Master's; Post-bachelor's certificate; Post-master's certificate. **Most popular majors:** Business/Commerce, General; Liberal Arts and Sciences/Liberal Studies; Health Professions And Related Programs. **Special Study Options:** Accelerated program; Distance learning; Double major; Dual enrollment; English as a Second Language (ESL); Honors program; Independent study; Internships; Liberal arts/career combination; Student-designed major; Study abroad; Teacher certification program; Weekend college. **Honors programs:** UMKC Honors College. **Combined degree programs:** BA/JD; BA/MD. **Disability Services offered:** Note-taking services; Reader services; Tape recorders; Tutors. **Career services:** Alumni network; Alumni services; Career assessment; Career/job search classes; Internships; Regional alumni.

FACILITIES
Housing: Apartments for married students; Apartments for single students; Coed dorms; Fraternity/sorority housing; Special housing for disabled students; 100% of campus accessible to physically disabled. **Special Academic Facilities/Equipment:** Unique facilities at UMKC include an observatory, national museum of toys and miniatures, geosciences museum, art gallery, and repertory theatre.

CAMPUS LIFE

Environment: Metropolis. **Activities:** Campus Ministries; Choral groups; Concert band; Dance; Drama/theater; International Student Organization; Jazz band; Literary magazine; Model UN; Music ensembles; Musical theater; Opera; Pep band; Radio station; Student government; Student newspaper; Student-run film society; Symphony orchestra. 338 registered organizations, 32 honor societies, 13 religious organizations, 5 fraternities, 7 sororities on campus. **Athletics (Intercollegiate):** *Men:* basketball, cheerleading, cross-country, golf, riflery, soccer, tennis, track/field (outdoor). *Women:* basketball, cheerleading, cross-country, golf, riflery, softball, tennis, track/field (outdoor), volleyball. **On-Campus Highlights:** UMKC Student Union. **Environmental Initiatives:** Recycling.

ADMISSIONS

Basis for Candidate Selection: *Very important factors include:* rigor of secondary school record, class rank, academic GPA. *Other factors include:* application essay, standardized test scores, recommendation(s), interview, extracurricular activities, talent/ability, character/personal qualities, first generation, volunteer work, work experience. **Freshman Admission Requirements:** High school diploma is required and GED is accepted. *Academic units required:* 4 English, 4 math, 3 science, 1 science labs, 2 foreign language, 3 social studies, 1 visual/performing arts. **Transfer Admission Requirements:** College transcript(s). Minimum college GPA of 2.0 required. Lowest grade transferable D. **General Admission Information:** Application fee $45. Priority deadline 4/1. Regular application deadline 6/1. Non-fall registration accepted. Admission may be deferred for a maximum of 2 semesters.

COSTS AND FINANCIAL AID

Annual in-state tuition $8,844. Room and board $10,864. Average book and supplies expense $770. **Required Forms and Deadlines:** FAFSA. **Notification of Awards:** Applicants will be notified of awards on a rolling basis beginning 4/15. **Types of Aid:** *Need-based scholarships/grants:* College/university scholarship or grant aid from institutional funds; Federal Nursing Scholarships; Federal Pell; Private scholarships; SEOG; State scholarships/grants; United Negro College Fund. *Loans:* Direct PLUS loans; Direct Subsidized Stafford Loans; Direct Unsubsidized Stafford Loans. **Student Employment:** Federal Work-Study Program available. Institutional employment available. **Financial Aid Statistics:** 92% freshmen receive any aid. **Criteria awarding aid:** *Need-based:* Academics, Alumni affiliation, Art, Athletics, Leadership, Minority status, Music/drama. *Non-need-based:* Academics, Alumni affiliation, Art, Athletics, Leadership, Minority status, Music/drama, State/district residency.

UNIVERSITY OF MISSOURI—SAINT LOUIS

351 Millenium Student Center, St. Louis, MO 63121-4400
Phone: 314-516-5451 **Financial Aid Phone:** 314-516-5526
E-mail: admissions@umsl.edu **CEEB Code:** 6889
Fax: 314-516-5310 **Website:** www.umsl.edu **ACT Code:** 2383

This public school was founded in 1963. It has a 350 acre campus.

RATINGS

Admissions Selectivity Rating: 80 **Fire Safety Rating:** 85 **Green Rating:** 60*

STUDENTS AND FACULTY

Enrollment: 6,703. **Student Body:** 55% female, 45% male, 11% out-of-state, 3% international (44 countries represented). Asian 5%, African American 15%, Caucasian 61%, Hispanic 3%, Native American <1%, Pacific Islander <1%, Two or more races 4%, Race unknown 9%.
Retention and Graduation: 77% freshmen return for sophomore year. 39% freshmen graduate within 4 years. 13% grads go on to further study within 1 year. 35% grads pursue arts and sciences degrees. 3% grads pursue law degrees. 30% grads pursue business degrees. 1% grads pursue medical degrees. **Faculty:** Student/faculty ratio 19:1. 389 full-time faculty, 76% hold PhDs, 23% are members of minority groups, 56% are women. 22% of classes are taught by teaching assistants.

ACADEMICS

Degrees: Bachelor's; Certificate; Doctoral degree—professional practice; Doctoral degree research/scholarship; Master's; Post-bachelor's certificate; Post-master's certificate. **Classes:** Most classes have 10–19 students. Most lab/discussion sessions have fewer than 10 students. **Most popular majors:** Psychology, General; Registered Nursing/Registered Nurse; Business/

Commerce, General. **Special Study Options:** Accelerated program; Cooperative education program; Cross-registration; Distance learning; Double major; Dual enrollment; English as a Second Language (ESL); Exchange student program (domestic); External degree program; Honors program; Independent study; Internships; Student-designed major; Study abroad; Teacher certification program. **Honors programs:** Pierre Laclede Honors College offers a four-year and a two-year honors program through which students can meet their General Education and other graduation requirements (e.g., advanced composition, global awareness, cultural diversity). Instruction is in small seminars (average enrollment is 15). There is a six-hour independent study requirement which includes internship and study abroad options and a writing program which engages all students and includes a capstone which aids students in job and graduate school applications. Students in the four year program take a first-year Cultural Traditions seminar, and all students have the option of living in an honors living-learning community. **Combined degree programs:** BA/MA. **Disability Services offered:** Note-taking services; Reader services; Tape recorders. **Career services:** Alumni services; Career assessment; Internships.

FACILITIES

Housing: Apartments for married students; Apartments for single students; Coed dorms; Fraternity/sorority housing; Special housing for disabled students; Theme housing; Wellness housing; 100% of campus accessible to physically disabled. **Special Academic Facilities/Equipment:** Art galleries, language, writing labs, math labs Mercantile Library, and observatory, radio station. **Campus network:** 100% of classrooms, 100% of student union, 100% of libraries, 100% of common outdoor areas have wireless network access.

CAMPUS LIFE

Environment: Metropolis. **Activities:** Campus Ministries; Choral groups; Concert band; Dance; Drama/theater; International Student Organization; Jazz band; Literary magazine; Model UN; Music ensembles; Musical theater; Opera; Pep band; Radio station; Student government; Student newspaper; Student-run film society. 100 registered organizations, 25 honor societies, 8 religious organizations, 3 fraternities, 4 sororities on campus. **Athletics (Intercollegiate):** *Men:* baseball, basketball, golf, soccer, tennis. *Women:* basketball, golf, soccer, softball, tennis, volleyball. **On-Campus Highlights:** Millennium Student Center. **Environmental Initiatives:** Energy Conservation.

ADMISSIONS

Freshman Academic Profile: Average high school GPA 3.5. 32% in top 10% of high school class, 64% in top 25% of high school class, 91% in top 50% of high school class. 84% from public high schools. **Test Scores:** SAT Math middle 50% range 520–520. SAT EBRW middle 50% range 510–610. ACT middle 50% range 21–27. **Basis for Candidate Selection:** *Very important factors include:* rigor of secondary school record, class rank, academic GPA, standardized test scores. *Other factors include:* application essay, recommendation(s). **Freshman Admission Requirements:** High school diploma is required and GED is accepted. *Academic units required:* 4 English, 4 math, 3 science, 1 science labs, 2 foreign language, 3 social studies, 1 unit from above areas or other academic areas. **Freshman Admission Statistics:** 2,452 applied, 73% admitted, 25% enrolled. **Transfer Admission Requirements:** College transcript(s). Minimum college GPA of 2.0 required. Lowest grade transferable D. **General Admission Information:** Application fee $35. Regular application deadline 8/21. Non-fall registration accepted. Admission may be deferred for a maximum of 3 semesters.

COSTS AND FINANCIAL AID

Annual in-state tuition $11,079. Annual out-of-state tuition $29,295. Room and board $9,550. Average book and supplies expense $1,000. **Required Forms and Deadlines:** FAFSA. **Notification of Awards:** Applicants will be notified of awards on a rolling basis beginning 12/1. **Types of Aid:** *Need-based scholarships/grants:* College/university scholarship or grant aid from institutional funds; Federal Nursing Scholarships; Federal Pell; Private scholarships; SEOG; State scholarships/grants; United Negro College Fund. *Loans:* Direct PLUS loans; Direct Subsidized Stafford Loans; Direct Unsubsidized Stafford Loans. **Student Employment:** Federal Work-Study Program available. Institutional employment available. **Financial Aid Statistics:** 97% needy freshmen, 87% needy undergrads receive need-based scholarship or grant aid. 13% freshmen, 6% undergrads receive non-need-based scholarship or grant aid. 64% freshmen, 80% undergrads receive need-based self-help aid. 1% freshmen, 0% undergrads receive athletic scholarships. 93.33% freshmen, 79.61% undergrads receive any aid. 58% undergrads borrow to pay for school. Average cumulative indebtedness $25,110. **Criteria awarding aid:** *Need-based:* Academics, Alumni affiliation, Art, Leadership, Minority status, Music/drama. *Non-need-based:* Academics, Alumni affiliation, Art, Athletics, Music/drama, State/district residency.

UNIVERSITY OF MOBILE

5735 College Parkway, Mobile, AL 36613-2842
Phone: 251-442-2222 **Financial Aid Phone:** 251-442-2222
E-mail: enrollmentservices@umobile.edu **CEEB Code:** 1515
Website: www.umobile.edu **ACT Code:** 29

This private school, affiliated with the Southern Baptist Church, was founded in 1961. It has a 880 acre campus.

RATINGS

Admissions Selectivity Rating: 87   **Fire Safety Rating:** 90   **Green Rating:** 60*

STUDENTS AND FACULTY

Enrollment: 1,276. **Student Body:** 63% female, 37% male, 23% out-of-state, 3% international (28 countries represented). Asian 1%, African American 19%, Caucasian 57%, Hispanic 2%, Native American 1%, Pacific Islander <1%, Two or more races 3%, Race unknown 13%.
Retention and Graduation: 69% freshmen return for sophomore year. 25% freshmen graduate within 4 years. 17% grads go on to further study within 1 year. 5% grads pursue arts and sciences degrees. 2% grads pursue law degrees. 5% grads pursue business degrees. 1% grads pursue medical degrees. **Faculty:** Student/faculty ratio 14:1. 73 full-time faculty, 59% hold PhDs, 7% are members of minority groups, 58% are women. 0% of classes are taught by teaching assistants.

ACADEMICS

Degrees: Associate; Bachelor's; Master's. **Classes:** Most classes have 10–19 students. Most lab/discussion sessions have fewer than 10 students. **Most popular majors:** Registered Nursing/Registered Nurse; Business Administration and Management, General; Elementary Education and Teaching. **Special Study Options:** Accelerated program; Distance learning; Double major; Dual enrollment; Honors program; Independent study; Internships; Study abroad; Teacher certification program. **Honors programs:** Exploring the great books and the enduring questions; join a community of enthusiastic students like yourself; take courses designed not to make you do more work, but do the kind of work that will help you become a thinking leader; earn the "Honors Scholar" designation and seal on your diploma and transcript; participate in special events, such as an annual honor dinner hosted by President Foley; have frequent access to honors faculty; benefit from honors roundtable designed to help students prepare for and apply to graduate school, seek grants and scholarships, and pursue post-graduate career opportunities. **Combined degree programs:** BA/MA. **Disability Services offered:** Tutors. **Career services:** Alumni services; Career assessment; Career/job search classes; Internships.

FACILITIES

Housing: Apartments for single students; Men's dorms; Women's dorms; 100% of campus accessible to physically disabled. **Special Academic Facilities/Equipment:** Donald Art Gallery and Recording Studio.

CAMPUS LIFE

Environment: City. **Activities:** Campus Ministries; Choral groups; Concert band; Drama/theater; International Student Organization; Jazz band; Music ensembles; Musical theater; Opera; Pep band; Student government; Symphony orchestra. 25 registered organizations, 10 honor societies, 3 religious organizations on campus. **Athletics (Intercollegiate):** *Men:* baseball, basketball, cross-country, golf, soccer, tennis. *Women:* basketball, cheerleading, cross-country, golf, soccer, softball, tennis, volleyball. **On-Campus Highlights:** Newly renovated School of Nursing & science labs. **Environmental Initiatives:** Recycling.

ADMISSIONS

Freshman Academic Profile: Average high school GPA 3.5. 23% in top 10% of high school class, 53% in top 25% of high school class, 80% in top 50% of high school class. **Test Scores:** SAT Math middle 50% range 450–540. SAT EBRW middle 50% range 460–560. ACT middle 50% range 20–25. **Basis for Candidate Selection:** *Very important factors include:* academic GPA, standardized test scores. **Freshman Admission Requirements:** High school diploma is required and GED is accepted. *Academic units recommended:* 4 English, 3 math, 3 science, 2 foreign language, 3 social studies, 3 history. **Freshman Admission Statistics:** 1,493 applied, 47% admitted, 32% enrolled. **Transfer Admission Requirements:** college transcript(s). Minimum college GPA of 2.75 required. Lowest grade transferable C. **General Admission Information:** Application fee $25. Non-fall registration accepted. Admission may be deferred for a maximum of 1 year.

COSTS AND FINANCIAL AID

Required Forms and Deadlines: FAFSA; Institution's own financial aid form; State aid form. **Notification of Awards:** Applicants will be notified of awards on a rolling basis beginning 12/1. **Types of Aid:** *Need-based scholarships/grants:* College/university scholarship or grant aid from institutional funds; Federal Nursing Scholarships; Federal Pell; Private scholarships; SEOG; State scholarships/grants. *Loans:* Direct PLUS loans; Direct Subsidized Stafford Loans; Direct Unsubsidized Stafford Loans. **Student Employment:** Federal Work-Study Program available. Institutional employment available. **Financial Aid Statistics:** 67% needy freshmen, 66% needy undergrads receive need-based scholarship or grant aid. 99% freshmen, 89% undergrads receive non-need-based scholarship or grant aid. 45% freshmen, 6% undergrads receive need-based self-help aid. 1% freshmen, 4% undergrads receive athletic scholarships. 98% freshmen, 99% undergrads receive any aid. 68% undergrads borrow to pay for school. Average cumulative indebtedness $28,574. **Criteria awarding aid:** *Non-need-based:* Academics, Alumni affiliation, Athletics, Music/drama, Religious affiliation.

THE UNIVERSITY OF MONTANA—MISSOULA

Best Colleges

Lommasson Center 101, Missoula, MT 59812
Phone: 406-243-6266 **Financial Aid Phone:** 406-243-5373
E-mail: admiss@umontana.edu **CEEB Code:** 4489
Fax: 406-243-5711 **Website:** www.umt.edu **ACT Code:** 2422

This public school was founded in 1893. It has a 220 acre campus.

RATINGS

Admissions Selectivity Rating: 75   **Fire Safety Rating:** 90   **Green Rating:** 82

STUDENTS AND FACULTY

Enrollment: 7,515. **Student Body:** 56% female, 44% male, 30% out-of-state, 1% international (43 countries represented). Asian 1%, African American 1%, Caucasian 78%, Hispanic 5%, Native American 3%, Pacific Islander <1%, Two or more races 5%, Race unknown 5%.
Retention and Graduation: 71% freshmen return for sophomore year. 30% freshmen graduate within 4 years. 49% freshmen graduate within 6 years. **Faculty:** Student/faculty ratio 16:1. 465 full-time faculty, 79% hold PhDs, 8% are members of minority groups, 40% are women. 5% of classes are taught by teaching assistants.

ACADEMICS

Degrees: Associate; Bachelor's; Certificate; Doctoral degree—professional practice; Doctoral degree research/scholarship; Master's; Post-bachelor's certificate; Post-master's certificate; Terminal Associate; Transfer Associate. **Classes:** Most classes have 10–19 students. Most lab/discussion sessions have 10–19 students. **Most popular majors:** Business Administration and Management, General; Forest Management/Forest Resources Management; Psychology, General. **Special Study Options:** Cooperative education program; Cross-registration; Distance learning; Double major; Dual enrollment; English as a Second Language (ESL); Exchange student program (domestic); External degree program; Honors program; Independent study; Internships; Study abroad; Teacher certification program. **Honors programs:** The Davidson Honors College offers talented and motivated students an academic and social community as an important part of their undergraduate experience at the University of Montana, regardless of their major disciplines. Honors courses are taught by many of the best scholars on campus and are generally limited to 20 students. The Honors College encourages its students to participate in community service activities, international educational experiences and undergraduate research. **Combined degree programs:** BA/JD. **Disability Services offered:** Note-taking services; Reader services; Tape recorders; Tutors. **Career services:** Alumni network; Alumni services; Career assessment; Career/job search classes; Internships; Regional alumni.

FACILITIES

Housing: Apartments for married students; Apartments for single students; Coed dorms; Fraternity/sorority housing; Men's dorms; Special housing for disabled students; Special housing for international students; Theme housing; Women's dorms 87% of campus accessible to physically disabled. **Special Academic Facilities/Equipment:** On main campus: clinical psychology center;

environmental studies lab; geology field camp; several biological, biomedical, kinesiology, physiology, forestry-related, and other research labs or centers; art galleries; broadcast media center (public radio and television) and performing arts-radio-television building; practical ethics center; extensive presentation technology equipment and services, and others. Other locations: biological station, experimental forest, two-year college of technology (two locations), Fort Missoula field research center, and others.

CAMPUS LIFE

Environment: City. **Activities:** Campus Ministries; Choral groups; Concert band; Dance; Drama/theater; International Student Organization; Jazz band; Literary magazine; Marching band; Model UN; Music ensembles; Musical theater; Opera; Pep band; Radio station; Student government; Student newspaper; Symphony orchestra; Television station. 150 registered organizations, 6 fraternities, 4 sororities on campus. **Athletics (Intercollegiate):** *Men:* basketball, cheerleading, cross-country, football, tennis, track/field (outdoor), track/field (indoor). *Women:* basketball, cheerleading, cross-country, golf, soccer, tennis, track/field (outdoor), track/field (indoor), volleyball. **On-Campus Highlights:** Adams Center (sports, entertainment, etc.). **Environmental Initiatives:** Climate Action Plan to reach carbon neutrality by 2020 and biannual Greenhouse Gas Inventories are completed by a full-time Sustainability Coordinator and the Sustainable Campus Committee.

ADMISSIONS

Freshman Academic Profile: Average high school GPA 3.4. 16% in top 10% of high school class, 40% in top 25% of high school class, 73% in top 50% of high school class. **Test Scores:** SAT Math middle 50% range 520–610. SAT EBRW middle 50% range 535–635. ACT middle 50% range 20–26. **Basis for Candidate Selection:** *Very important factors include:* rigor of secondary school record, class rank, academic GPA, standardized test scores. *Important factors include:* extracurricular activities, talent/ability. **Freshman Admission Requirements:** High school diploma is required and GED is accepted. *Academic units required:* 4 English, 3 math, 2 science, 2 science labs, 3 social studies, 2 history. *Academic units recommended:* 2 foreign language, 2 computer science, 2 visual/performing arts. **Freshman Admission Statistics:** 4,910 applied, 94% admitted, 32% enrolled. **Transfer Admission Requirements:** College transcript(s). Minimum college GPA of 2.0 required. Lowest grade transferable D. **General Admission Information:** Application fee $30. Priority deadline 3/1. Non-fall registration accepted. Admission may be deferred for a maximum of 1 year.

COSTS AND FINANCIAL AID

Annual in-state tuition $5,352. Annual out-of-state tuition $24,144. Room and board $9,966. Required fees $2,002. Average book and supplies expense $1,100. **Required Forms and Deadlines:** FAFSA. **Notification of Awards:** Applicants will be notified of awards on a rolling basis beginning 3/16. **Types of Aid:** *Need-based scholarships/grants:* College/university scholarship or grant aid from institutional funds; Federal Pell; Private scholarships; SEOG; State scholarships/grants. *Loans:* Direct PLUS loans; Direct Subsidized Stafford Loans; Direct Unsubsidized Stafford Loans. **Student Employment:** Federal Work-Study Program available. Institutional employment available. **Financial Aid Statistics:** 56% needy freshmen, 61% needy undergrads receive need-based scholarship or grant aid. 80% freshmen, 52% undergrads receive non-need-based scholarship or grant aid. 95% freshmen, 91% undergrads receive need-based self-help aid. 3% freshmen, 3% undergrads receive athletic scholarships. 74% freshmen, 63% undergrads receive any aid. 58% undergrads borrow to pay for school. Average cumulative indebtedness $27,132. **Criteria awarding aid:** *Need-based:* Academics, Minority status. *Non-need-based:* Academics, Athletics, Leadership, Music/drama, State/district residency.

THE UNIVERSITY OF MONTANA—WESTERN

710 South Atlantic, Dillon, MT 59725
Phone: 406-683-7331
E-mail: admissions@umwestern.edu **CEEB Code:** 4945
Fax: 406-683-7493 **Website:** https://w.umwestern.edu/ **ACT Code:** 2428

This public school was founded in 1893. It has a 34 acre campus.

RATINGS

Admissions Selectivity Rating: 85   **Fire Safety Rating:** 60*   **Green Rating:** 60*

STUDENTS AND FACULTY

Enrollment: 1,467. **Student Body:** 61% female, 39% male, 24% out-of-state, 0% international (1 countries represented). Asian 1%, African American 1%,

Caucasian 86%, Hispanic 4%, Native American 3%, Pacific Islander <1%, Two or more races 2%, Race unknown 3%.
Retention and Graduation: 68% freshmen return for sophomore year. 50% grads go on to further study within 1 year. **Faculty:** Student/faculty ratio 19:1. 62 full-time faculty, 87% hold PhDs, 0% are members of minority groups, 48% are women. 0% of classes are taught by teaching assistants.

ACADEMICS

Degrees: Associate; Bachelor's; Certificate. **Classes:** Most classes have 10–19 students. **Most popular majors:** Business/Commerce, General; Elementary Education and Teaching. **Special Study Options:** Cooperative education program; Distance learning; Double major; Dual enrollment; Honors program; Independent study; Internships; Study abroad; Teacher certification program. **Disability Services offered:** Note-taking services; Reader services; Tape recorders; Tutors. **Career services:** Alumni services; Career assessment; Career/job search classes; Internships.

FACILITIES

Housing: Apartments for married students; Apartments for single students; Coed dorms; Men's dorms; Special housing for disabled students; Special housing for international students; Women's dorms; 90% of campus accessible to physically disabled. **Special Academic Facilities/Equipment:** Art gallery, outdoor education center, learning center.

CAMPUS LIFE

Environment: Rural. **Activities:** Campus Ministries; Choral groups; Drama/theater; Music ensembles; Musical theater; Radio station; Student government. 25 registered organizations, 2 honor societies, 2 religious organizations on campus. **Athletics (Intercollegiate):** *Men:* basketball, cheerleading, football, golf, rodeo. *Women:* basketball, cheerleading, golf, rodeo, volleyball. **On-Campus Highlights:** SUB (Sudent Union Building).

ADMISSIONS

Freshman Academic Profile: Average high school GPA 3.1. 7% in top 10% of high school class, 23% in top 25% of high school class, 51% in top 50% of high school class. 96% from public high schools. **Test Scores:** SAT Math middle 50% range 420–530. SAT EBRW middle 50% range 430–540. ACT middle 50% range 17–22. **Basis for Candidate Selection:** *Very important factors include:* rigor of secondary school record, class rank, academic GPA, standardized test scores. **Freshman Admission Requirements:** High school diploma is required and GED is accepted. *Academic units required:* 4 English, 3 math, 2 science, 2 science labs, 2 social studies, 1 history, 2 academic electives. *Academic units recommended:* 4 English, 4 math, 3 science, 2 science labs, 2 social studies, 1 history, 3 academic electives. **Freshman Admission Statistics:** 785 applied, 68% admitted, 63% enrolled. **Transfer Admission Requirements:** College transcript(s). Minimum college GPA of 2.0 required. Lowest grade transferable C. **General Admission Information:** Application fee $30. Priority deadline 7/1. Non-fall registration accepted. Admission may be deferred for a maximum of 1 year.

COSTS AND FINANCIAL AID

Required Forms and Deadlines: FAFSA. **Notification of Awards:** Applicants will be notified of awards on a rolling basis beginning 3/1. **Types of Aid:** *Need-based scholarships/grants:* College/university scholarship or grant aid from institutional funds; Federal Pell; Private scholarships; SEOG; State scholarships/grants. *Loans:* Direct PLUS loans; Direct Subsidized Stafford Loans; Direct Unsubsidized Stafford Loans. **Student Employment:** Federal Work-Study Program available. Institutional employment available. **Financial Aid Statistics:** 70% needy freshmen, 66% needy undergrads receive need-based scholarship or grant aid. 33% freshmen, 29% undergrads receive non-need-based scholarship or grant aid. 70% freshmen, 66% undergrads receive need-based self-help aid. 8% freshmen, 3% undergrads receive athletic scholarships. 77% undergrads borrow to pay for school. Average cumulative indebtedness $29,779. **Criteria awarding aid:** *Need-based:* Academics, Alumni affiliation, Art, Leadership, Minority status. *Non-need-based:* Academics, Alumni affiliation, Art, Athletics, Leadership, State/district residency.

UNIVERSITY OF MONTEVALLO

Station 6030, Montevallo, AL 35115
Phone: 205-665-6030 **Financial Aid Phone:** 205-665-6050
E-mail: admissions@montevallo.edu **CEEB Code:** 1004
Fax: 205-665-6032 **Website:** http://www.montevallo.edu/ **ACT Code:** 4

This public school was founded in 1896. It has a 160 acre campus.

RATINGS
Admissions Selectivity Rating: 86   **Fire Safety Rating:** 82   **Green Rating:** 76

STUDENTS AND FACULTY
Enrollment: 2,201. **Student Body:** 65% female, 35% male, 3% international (23 countries represented). Asian 1%, African American 16%, Caucasian 68%, Hispanic 5%, Native American <1%, Pacific Islander <1%, Two or more races 4%, Race unknown 2%.
Retention and Graduation: 74% freshmen return for sophomore year. 33% freshmen graduate within 4 years. 55% freshmen graduate within 6 years.
Faculty: Student/faculty ratio 13:1. 159 full-time faculty, 94% hold PhDs, 13% are members of minority groups, 50% are women. 0% of classes are taught by teaching assistants.

ACADEMICS
Degrees: Bachelor's; Master's; Post-master's certificate. **Classes:** Most classes have 10–19 students. Most lab/discussion sessions have 20–29 students.
Most popular majors: Business Administration and Management, General; Elementary Education and Teaching; Sports, Kinesiology, and Physical Education/Fitness, General. **Special Study Options:** Accelerated program; Cross-registration; Distance learning; Double major; Dual enrollment; Honors program; Independent study; Internships; Study abroad; Teacher certification program. **Honors programs:** The Mission of the University of Montevallo's Honors Program is to provide intellectually talented students with specially designed academic offerings, co-curricular activities, and recognition. The Honors Program provides students with three special features in their college experience: (1) classes with limited enrollment, specially designed and taught by demanding and supportive faculty to elicit the students' powers, (2) time spent in one another's company, and (3) encouragement, public and private, to persevere. The Honors Program provides these features through a spectrum of academic offerings, opportunities for recognition, and extracurricular activities. The Honors Program is designed to enhance a students' University experience. Students pursue a major and minor in their area of interest, while taking honors courses at specific times during their academic career. **Disability Services offered:** Note-taking services; Reader services; Tape recorders; Tutors. **Career services:** Alumni services; Career assessment.

FACILITIES
Housing: Apartments for married students; Coed dorms; Fraternity/sorority housing; Men's dorms; Special housing for disabled students; Women's dorms. **Special Academic Facilities/Equipment:** Art gallery, child development, speech and hearing, traffic safety, and undergraduate liberal studies centers, mass communications center with cable TV broadcasting capabilities. **Campus network:** 100% of classrooms, 100% of dorms, 100% of student union, 100% of libraries, 100% of dining areas, 100% of common outdoor areas have wireless network access.

CAMPUS LIFE
Environment: Rural. **Activities:** Campus Ministries; Choral groups; Concert band; Dance; Drama/theater; International Student Organization; Jazz band; Model UN; Music ensembles; Musical theater; Student government; Student newspaper; Television station; Yearbook. 75 registered organizations, 26 honor societies, 8 religious organizations, 6 fraternities, 8 sororities on campus. **Athletics (Intercollegiate):** *Men:* baseball, basketball, golf, soccer. *Women:* basketball, cross-country, golf, soccer, tennis, volleyball. **On-Campus Highlights:** Cafeteria. **Environmental Initiatives:** Campus lighting retrofit to energy saving bulbs.

ADMISSIONS
Freshman Academic Profile: Average high school GPA 3.6. 90% from public high schools. **Test Scores:** SAT Math middle 50% range 510–620. SAT EBRW middle 50% range 520–620. ACT middle 50% range 20–25. **Basis for Candidate Selection:** *Very important factors include:* rigor of secondary school record. *Other factors include:* class rank, academic GPA, interview, extracurricular activities, talent/ability. **Freshman Admission Requirements:** High school diploma is required and GED is accepted. *Academic units required:*

4 English, 2 math, 2 science, 4 social studies, 4 academic electives. **Freshman Admission Statistics:** 5,553 applied, 53% admitted, 17% enrolled. **Transfer Admission Requirements:** College transcript(s). Minimum college GPA of 2.0 required. Lowest grade transferable D. **General Admission Information:** Application fee $30. Regular application deadline 8/1. Non-fall registration accepted.

COSTS AND FINANCIAL AID
Annual in-state tuition $9,990. Annual out-of-state tuition $20,550. Room and board $6,400. Required fees $670. Average book and supplies expense $2,050. **Required Forms and Deadlines:** FAFSA. **Notification of Awards:** Applicants will be notified of awards on a rolling basis beginning 3/25. **Types of Aid:** *Need-based scholarships/grants:* College/university scholarship or grant aid from institutional funds; Federal Pell; Private scholarships; SEOG; State scholarships/grants. *Loans:* Direct PLUS loans; Direct Subsidized Stafford Loans; Direct Unsubsidized Stafford Loans. **Student Employment:** Federal Work-Study Program available. Institutional employment available. **Financial Aid Statistics:** 85% needy freshmen, 84% needy undergrads receive need-based scholarship or grant aid. 18% freshmen, 10% undergrads receive non-need-based scholarship or grant aid. 77% freshmen, 84% undergrads receive need-based self-help aid. 4% freshmen, 4% undergrads receive athletic scholarships. 87% freshmen, 77% undergrads receive any aid. **Criteria awarding aid:** *Need-based:* Academics. *Non-need-based:* Academics, Alumni affiliation, Art, Athletics, Leadership, Minority status, Music/drama.

UNIVERSITY OF MOUNT UNION

1972 Clark Avenue, Alliance, OH 44601-3993
Phone: 330-823-2590 **Financial Aid Phone:** 877-543-9185
E-mail: admission@mountunion.edu **CEEB Code:** 1492
Fax: 330-823-5097 **Website:** www.mountunion.edu **ACT Code:** 3298

This private school, affiliated with the Methodist Church, was founded in 1846. It has a 123 acre campus.

RATINGS
Admissions Selectivity Rating: 77   **Fire Safety Rating:** 90   **Green Rating:** 87

STUDENTS AND FACULTY
Enrollment: 1,987. **Student Body:** 48% female, 52% male, 19% out-of-state, 2% international (12 countries represented). Asian 1%, African American 7%, Caucasian 80%, Hispanic 4%, Native American <1%, Pacific Islander <1%, Two or more races 4%, Race unknown 2%.
Retention and Graduation: 72% freshmen return for sophomore year. 66% freshmen graduate within 6 years. 15% grads go on to further study within 1 year. 10% grads pursue arts and sciences degrees. 1% grads pursue law degrees. 1% grads pursue business degrees. **Faculty:** Student/faculty ratio 12:1. 0% of classes are taught by teaching assistants.

ACADEMICS
Degrees: Bachelor's; Doctoral degree—other; Master's. **Classes:** Most classes have 10–19 students. Most lab/discussion sessions have 10–19 students. **Most popular majors:** Early Childhood Education and Teaching; Sport and Fitness Administration/Management; Business Administration and Management, General. **Special Study Options:** Accelerated program; Cooperative education program; Double major; Dual enrollment; English as a Second Language (ESL); Honors program; Independent study; Internships; Liberal arts/career combination; Student-designed major; Study abroad; Teacher certification program. **Honors programs:** The Honors Program at the University of Mount Union offers integrated learning opportunities and challenges for motivated students with exceptional academic potential. The program is designed to foster intellectual curiosity, leadership, initiative, creativity, civic-mindedness and a high standard of performance. Two honors tracks are available: University Honors and Honors in the Major. A qualified student may participate in either or both tracks. The first, University Honors, fulfills a student's Integrative Core requirements and includes a First Year Seminar, three Honors Foundations courses plus an elective in the fourth Foundations area, an Honors Theme, which comprises one Honors theme course plus a Theme project to be completed in conjunction with an upper-level course of the student's choosing, and an Honors Capstone. The Honors in the Major Program offers the opportunity for intensive, individual study in a major. Honors in the Major is earned by completing honors projects in regular courses. Although the nature of honors work will vary, it should involve intellectual creativity and may take

such forms as research, investigation, or artistic effort. The student initiates and plans the honors project and works closely with one or more faculty members in carrying it out. The University of Mount Union Honors Program offers eligible students an exceptional educational opportunity and a supportive community of students focused on academic achievement and social responsibility. **Disability Services offered:** Note-taking services; Reader services; Tutors. **Career services:** Alumni network; Alumni services; Career assessment; Career/job search classes; Internships; Regional alumni.

FACILITIES

Housing: Apartments for single students; Coed dorms; Fraternity/sorority housing; Men's dorms; Special housing for disabled students; Special housing for international students; Theme housing; Women's dorms; 95% of campus accessible to physically disabled. **Special Academic Facilities/Equipment:** Art gallery, ecological center, observatory, educational media center.

CAMPUS LIFE

Environment: Town. **Activities:** Campus Ministries; Choral groups; Concert band; Dance; Drama/theater; International Student Organization; Jazz band; Literary magazine; Marching band; Model UN; Music ensembles; Musical theater; Pep band; Radio station; Student government; Student newspaper; Symphony orchestra; Television station. 80 registered organizations, 16 honor societies, 10 religious organizations, 4 fraternities, 4 sororities on campus. **Athletics (Intercollegiate):** *Men:* baseball, basketball, cross-country, diving, football, golf, soccer, swimming, tennis, track/field (outdoor), track/field (indoor), wrestling. *Women:* basketball, cheerleading, cross-country, diving, golf, soccer, softball, swimming, tennis, track/field (outdoor), track/field (indoor), volleyball. **On-Campus Highlights:** Hoover Price Campus Center. **Environmental Initiatives:** Sustainability (Climate Action) Plan.

ADMISSIONS

Freshman Academic Profile: 88% from public high schools. **Test Scores:** SAT Math middle 50% range 498–590. SAT EBRW middle 50% range 490–603. ACT middle 50% range 20–25. **Basis for Candidate Selection:** *Very important factors include:* academic GPA, standardized test scores. *Other factors include:* rigor of secondary school record, class rank, application essay, recommendation(s), extracurricular activities. **Freshman Admission Requirements:** High school diploma is required and GED is accepted. *Academic units recommended:* 4 English, 3 math, 3 science, 2 science labs, 2 foreign language, 3 social studies. **Freshman Admission Statistics:** 3,007 applied, 78% admitted, 23% enrolled. **Transfer Admission Requirements:** High school transcript, college transcript(s), essay or personal statement, statement of good standing from prior institution(s). Minimum college GPA of 2.0 required. Lowest grade transferable C. **General Admission Information:** Priority deadline 3/1. Non-fall registration accepted. Admission may be deferred for a maximum of one semester.

COSTS AND FINANCIAL AID

Annual tuition $32,200. Room and board $10,700. Required fees $400. Average book and supplies expense $1,100. **Required Forms and Deadlines:** FAFSA. **Notification of Awards:** Applicants will be notified of awards on a rolling basis beginning 12/1. **Types of Aid:** *Need-based scholarships/grants:* College/university scholarship or grant aid from institutional funds; Federal Pell; Private scholarships; SEOG; State scholarships/grants. *Loans:* Direct PLUS loans; Direct Subsidized Stafford Loans; Direct Unsubsidized Stafford Loans. **Student Employment:** Federal Work-Study Program available. Institutional employment available. **Financial Aid Statistics:** 88% freshmen, 90% undergrads receive any aid. **Criteria awarding aid:** *Need-based:* Religious affiliation. *Non-need-based:* Academics, Alumni affiliation, Art, Job skills, Leadership, Minority status, Music/drama, Religious affiliation, State/district residency.

UNIVERSITY OF NEBRASKA—OMAHA

Office of Admissions, Omaha, NE 68182
Phone: 402-554-2393 **Financial Aid Phone:** 402-554-2327
E-mail: unoadmissions@unomaha.edu **CEEB Code:** 6420
Fax: 402-554-3472 **Website:** www.unomaha.edu **ACT Code:** 2464

This public school was founded in 1908. It has a 577 acre campus.

RATINGS

Admissions Selectivity Rating: 83   **Fire Safety Rating:** 97   **Green Rating:** 90

STUDENTS AND FACULTY

Enrollment: 12,153. **Student Body:** 52% female, 48% male, 7% out-of-state, 3% international (62 countries represented). Asian 3%, African American 7%, Caucasian 72%, Hispanic 9%, Native American <1%, Pacific Islander <1%, Two or more races 3%, Race unknown 3%.
Retention and Graduation: 75% freshmen return for sophomore year. 21% grads go on to further study within 1 year. **Faculty:** Student/faculty ratio 17:1. 520 full-time faculty, 83% hold PhDs, 18% are members of minority groups, 44% are women. 4% of classes are taught by teaching assistants.

ACADEMICS

Degrees: Bachelor's; Doctoral degree—other; Master's; Post-bachelor's certificate; Post-master's certificate. **Classes:** Most classes have 20–29 students. Most lab/discussion sessions have 20–29 students. **Most popular majors:** Criminal Justice/Safety Studies; Business Administration and Management, General. **Special Study Options:** Cooperative education program; Cross-registration; Distance learning; Double major; Dual enrollment; English as a Second Language (ESL); Exchange student program (domestic); Honors program; Independent study; Internships; Student-designed major; Study abroad; Teacher certification program. **Honors programs:** UNO Honors Program includes many opportunities such as Early Registration, Honors-only courses, Honors-priority Housing, Honors domestic and international semesters, Honors internships, and a Washington Center affiliation. **Disability Services offered:** Note-taking services; Reader services; Tape recorders; Tutors. **Career services:** Career assessment; Career/job search classes; Internships.

FACILITIES

Housing: Coed dorms; 99% of campus accessible to physically disabled. **Special Academic Facilities/Equipment:** Center for Afghanistan studies, physical education facility, Strauss Performing Arts Center, Speech Center, Writing Center, Math/Science Center, Peter Kiewit Information Technology Building, and Career Center.

CAMPUS LIFE

Environment: Metropolis. **Activities:** Campus Ministries; Choral groups; Concert band; Dance; Drama/theater; International Student Organization; Jazz band; Literary magazine; Marching band; Model UN; Music ensembles; Musical theater; Opera; Pep band; Radio station; Student government; Student newspaper; Student-run film society; Symphony orchestra; Television station. 153 registered organizations, 23 honor societies, 14 religious organizations, 6 fraternities, 8 sororities on campus. **Athletics (Intercollegiate):** *Men:* baseball, basketball, football, ice hockey, wrestling. *Women:* basketball, cross-country, diving, golf, soccer, softball, swimming, tennis, track/field (outdoor), track/field (indoor), volleyball. **On-Campus Highlights:** University Library. **Environmental Initiatives:** To identify sustainability opportunities and to develop a recommended action plan for each.

ADMISSIONS

Freshman Academic Profile: Average high school GPA 3.4. 15% in top 10% of high school class, 40% in top 25% of high school class, 75% in top 50% of high school class. 90% from public high schools. **Test Scores:** ACT middle 50% range 20–26. **Basis for Candidate Selection:** *Very important factors include:* rigor of secondary school record, class rank, standardized test scores. *Other factors include:* character/personal qualities. **Freshman Admission Requirements:** High school diploma is required and GED is accepted. *Academic units required:* 4 English, 3 math, 3 science, 1 science labs, 2 foreign language, 1 social studies, 2 history, 1 academic elective. **Freshman Admission Statistics:** 4,955 applied, 71% admitted, 54% enrolled. **Transfer Admission Requirements:** College transcript(s), statement of good standing from prior institution(s). Minimum college GPA of 2.0 required. Lowest grade transferable C-. **General Admission Information:** Application fee $45. Regular application deadline 8/1. Non-fall registration accepted.

COSTS AND FINANCIAL AID

Annual in-state tuition $5,180. Annual out-of-state tuition $15,520. Room and board $8,090. Required fees $1,370. Average book and supplies expense $1,000. **Required Forms and Deadlines:** FAFSA. **Notification of Awards:** Applicants will be notified of awards on a rolling basis beginning 4/15. **Types of Aid:** *Need-based scholarships/grants:* College/university scholarship or grant aid from institutional funds; Federal Pell; Private scholarships; SEOG; State scholarships/grants. *Loans:* Direct PLUS loans; Direct Subsidized Stafford Loans; Direct Unsubsidized Stafford Loans. **Student Employment:** Federal Work-Study Program available. Institutional employment available. **Financial Aid Statistics:** 60% needy freshmen, 64% needy undergrads receive need-based scholarship or grant aid. 12% freshmen, 13% undergrads receive non-need-based scholarship or grant aid. 52% freshmen, 65% undergrads receive need-based self-help aid. 3% freshmen, 2% undergrads receive athletic scholarships. 80% freshmen, 81% undergrads receive any aid. **Criteria awarding aid:** *Need-based:* Academics, Leadership. *Non-need-based:* Academics, Alumni affiliation, Art, Athletics, Leadership, Music/drama, State/district residency.

UNIVERSITY OF NEBRASKA—LINCOLN

1410 Q Street, Lincoln, NE 68588-0417
Phone: 402-472-2023 **Financial Aid Phone:** 402-472-2030
E-mail: admissions@unl.edu **CEEB Code:** 6877
Fax: 402-472-0670 **Website:** http://www.unl.edu **ACT Code:** 2482

This public school was founded in 1869. It has a 623 acre campus.

RATINGS

Admissions Selectivity Rating: 83   **Fire Safety Rating:** 86   **Green Rating:** 81

STUDENTS AND FACULTY

Enrollment: 20,253. **Student Body:** 48% female, 52% male, 25% out-of-state, 8% international (100 countries represented). Asian 3%, African American 3%, Caucasian 75%, Hispanic 7%, Native American <1%, Pacific Islander <1%, Two or more races 3%, Race unknown 1%.
Retention and Graduation: 81% freshmen return for sophomore year. 40% freshmen graduate within 4 years. 63% freshmen graduate within 6 years. 25% grads go on to further study within 1 year. **Faculty:** Student/faculty ratio 17:1. 1,333 full-time faculty, 77% hold PhDs, 20% are members of minority groups, 37% are women.

ACADEMICS

Degrees: Bachelor's; Doctoral degree—professional practice; Doctoral degree research/scholarship; Master's; Post-bachelor's certificate; Post-master's certificate. **Classes:** Most classes have 20–29 students. Most lab/discussion sessions have 20–29 students. **Most popular majors:** Public Relations, Advertising, and Applied Communication; Psychology, General; Business Administration and Management, General. **Special Study Options:** Accelerated program; Cooperative education program; Cross-registration; Distance learning; Double major; Dual enrollment; English as a Second Language (ESL); Exchange student program (domestic); Honors program; Independent study; Internships; Liberal arts/career combination; Student-designed major; Study abroad; Teacher certification program. **Honors programs:** The University Honors Program (UHP) equips high-ability students from all UNL undergraduate colleges with the skills and mindsets to be ready for an uncertain, globalized world and a competitive, evolving workforce. Honors develops students to be globally aware and engaged citizens by providing a continuum of experiences and academic opportunities, including: • Small, interactive and discussion-based interdisciplinary seminars • Short, pop-up courses that allow students to explore new disciplines and gain exposure to new skills and experiences in a low-stakes setting • Experientially-infused and tailored tracks for students in years 3 and 4 to provide students with a shared experience and a professional network • Honors Dialogues, which facilitate global experiences through an emphasis on dialogue and problem solving • Honors afterschool clubs that allow students to create and teach their passions to low-income Nebraska youth • The Honors Cooperative, which connects students to work-based experiences through partnerships on campus, in Lincoln, and in communities across Nebraska • Leadership development and experiences through three active student organizations • Engagement in research/creative activity via completion of a senior project or thesis. In 2019, the university Honors program moved to the Knoll Residence Hall, one of the newest residence halls with three newly renovated classrooms designed to support interactive and global engagement. The Jeffrey S. Raikes School of Computer Science & Management is a highly selective academic and scholarship program that educates tomorrow's business and technology leaders through a focused curriculum of computer science, business and real-world projects. Design Studio teams are mentored by industry professionals from the community, helping teams more effectively communicate, overcome technical challenges, and drive innovation for their partners. Students in the Raikes School may receive partial scholarships for room and board in the Kauffman Residential Center, networking opportunities with current business leaders, and top internship placement at companies such as Google, Microsoft, Amazon, Hudl, Ameritrade, Gallup, and Kiewit. Sixty percent of Raikes school graduates have internships for two summers, half of which are through Design Studio sponsors, and 95% of graduates have jobs within three months of graduation. The College of Business Administration Honors Academy is a unique, four-year cohort-based learning environment for high-ability students with demonstrated leadership potential. CBA Honors students solve real-world business problems in a small-class team environment led by top faculty, develop network and mentor relationships with business leaders, and compete in regional and national business competitions. In the class of 2019, 100% of CBA honors students attained internships and averaged a 3.8 grade point average. A $2,500 study abroad scholarship is available to CBA Honors students. **Combined degree programs:** BA/DDS; BA/JD; BA/MD; BA/MEng. **Disability Services offered:** Note-taking services; Reader services; Tape recorders; Tutors. **Career services:** Alumni network; Alumni services; Career assessment; Career/job search classes; Internships.

FACILITIES

Housing: Apartments for married students; Apartments for single students; Coed dorms; Cooperative housing; Fraternity/sorority housing; Special housing for disabled students; Special housing for international students; Theme housing; Women's dorms; 95% of campus accessible to physically disabled. **Special Academic Facilities/Equipment:** Art museum; state natural history museum; planetarium; observatory; center for performing arts; arboretum; Center for Great Plains Studies; center for biomaterials and genetic research; international quilt study center and museum; diocles laser/extreme light lab; midwest roadside safety facility; food industries complex; center for mass spectrometry; animal science complex; veterinary animal research/diagnosis center; center for brain, biology and behavior; Nebraska Innovation Campus; Adele Coryell Hall Learning Commons. **Campus network:** 50% of classrooms, 100% of dorms, 100% of student union, 100% of libraries, 75% of dining areas, 25% of common outdoor areas have wireless network access.

CAMPUS LIFE

Environment: City. **Activities:** Campus Ministries; Choral groups; Concert band; Dance; Drama/theater; International Student Organization; Jazz band; Literary magazine; Marching band; Model UN; Music ensembles; Musical theater; Opera; Pep band; Radio station; Student government; Student newspaper; Student-run film society; Symphony orchestra; Television station. 535 registered organizations, 29 honor societies, 31 religious organization, 33 fraternities, 23 sororities on campus. **Athletics (Intercollegiate):** *Men:* baseball, basketball, cross-country, football, golf, gymnastics, rodeo, tennis, track/field (outdoor), track/field (indoor), wrestling. *Women:* basketball, bowling, cross-country, diving, golf, gymnastics, riflery, rodeo, soccer, softball, swimming, tennis, track/field (outdoor), track/field (indoor), volleyball. **On-Campus Highlights:** Student Union. **Environmental Initiatives:** Centralized Renewable Energy System (CRES)—The University of Nebraska-Lincoln's Innovation Campus sustainably warms and cools buildings by exchanging thermal energy from treated wastewater through City of Lincoln's waste water treatment plant.

ADMISSIONS

Freshman Academic Profile: Average high school GPA 3.6. 28% in top 10% of high school class, 56% in top 25% of high school class, 87% in top 50% of high school class. **Test Scores:** SAT Math middle 50% range 560–690. SAT EBRW middle 50% range 560–670. ACT middle 50% range 22–28. **Basis for Candidate Selection:** *Very important factors include:* class rank, academic GPA, standardized test scores. *Important factors include:* rigor of secondary school record. **Freshman Admission Requirements:** High school diploma is required and GED is accepted. *Academic units required:* 4 English, 4 math, 3 science, 1 science labs, 2 foreign language, 1 social studies, 2 history. **Freshman Admission Statistics:** 16,829 applied, 78% admitted, 36% enrolled. **Transfer Admission Requirements:** High school transcript, college transcript(s). Minimum college GPA of 2.0 required. Lowest grade transferable D. **General Admission Information:** Application fee $45. Priority deadline 3/1. Regular application deadline 5/1. Non-fall registration accepted.

COSTS AND FINANCIAL AID

Annual in-state tuition $7,560. Annual out-of-state tuition $24,000. Room and board $11,330. Required fees $1,806. Average book and supplies expense $1,044. **Required Forms and Deadlines:** FAFSA. **Notification of Awards:** Applicants will be notified of awards on a rolling basis beginning 12/15. **Types of Aid:** *Need-based scholarships/grants:* College/university scholarship or grant aid from institutional funds; Federal Pell; Private scholarships; SEOG; State scholarships/grants. *Loans:* Direct PLUS loans; Direct Subsidized Stafford Loans; Direct Unsubsidized Stafford Loans. **Student Employment:** Federal Work-Study Program available. Institutional employment available. **Financial Aid Statistics:** 91% needy freshmen, 85% needy undergrads receive need-based scholarship or grant aid. 12% freshmen, 8% undergrads receive non-need-based scholarship or grant aid. 64% freshmen, 64% undergrads receive need-based self-help aid. 3% freshmen, 3% undergrads receive athletic scholarships. 93% freshmen, 77% undergrads receive any aid. 55% undergrads borrow to pay for school. Average cumulative indebtedness $22,290. **Criteria awarding aid:** *Need-based:* Music/drama. *Non-need-based:* Academics, Alumni affiliation, Art, Athletics, Leadership, Music/drama, State/district residency.

UNIVERSITY OF NEBRASKA MEDICAL CENTER

984230 Nebr Med Ctr, Omaha, NE 68198-4230
Phone: 402-559-6864 **Financial Aid Phone:** 402-559-4109
E-mail: ttonjes@unmc.edu
Fax: 402-559-6796 **Website:** http://www.unmc.edu/

This public school was founded in 1902.

RATINGS

Admissions Selectivity Rating: 60*   **Fire Safety Rating:** 60*   **Green Rating:** 60*

STUDENTS AND FACULTY

Enrollment: 812. **Student Body:** 88% female, 12% male, 12% out-of-state, 1% international. Asian 1%, African American 1%, Caucasian 93%, Hispanic 3%, Native American 1%, Race unknown 0%.
Faculty: 768 full-time faculty, 90% hold PhDs, 14% are members of minority groups, 39% are women.

ACADEMICS

Degrees: Bachelor's; Master's; Post-bachelor's certificate; Post-master's certificate. **Most popular majors:** Pharmacy; Medicine; Nursing/Registered Nurse (Rn, Asn, Bsn, Msn). **Special Study Options:** Accelerated program; Distance learning; Honors program; Independent study. **Disability Services offered:** Note-taking services; Tutors.

FACILITIES

Campus network: 95% of classrooms, 100% of dorms, 100% of student union, 100% of libraries, 100% of dining areas, 100% of common outdoor areas have wireless network access.

CAMPUS LIFE

Environment: Metropolis. **Activities:** Student government; Student newspaper.

ADMISSIONS

Transfer Admission Requirements: College transcript(s). Lowest grade transferable C.

COSTS AND FINANCIAL AID

Annual in-state tuition $6,450. Annual out-of-state tuition $18,900. Average book and supplies expense $950. **Required Forms and Deadlines:** FAFSA; Institution's own financial aid form. **Notification of Awards:** Applicants will be notified of awards on or about 4/1. **Types of Aid:** *Need-based scholarships/grants:* College/university scholarship or grant aid from institutional funds; Federal Pell; Private scholarships; SEOG; State scholarships/grants. **Student Employment:** Federal Work-Study Program available. Institutional employment available. **Financial Aid Statistics:** 79% needy undergrads receive need-based scholarship or grant aid. 4% undergrads receive non-need-based scholarship or grant aid. 88% undergrads receive need-based self-help aid. 0% undergrads receive athletic scholarships. **Criteria awarding aid:** *Non-need-based:* Academics, Leadership, Minority status.

UNIVERSITY OF NEVADA, LAS VEGAS

4505 Maryland Parkway, Las Vegas, NV 89154-1021
Phone: 702-774-8658
E-mail: admissions@unlv.edu **CEEB Code:** 4861
Fax: 702-774-8008 **Website:** www.unlv.edu **ACT Code:** 2496

This public school was founded in 1957. It has a 337 acre campus.

RATINGS

Admissions Selectivity Rating: 76   **Fire Safety Rating:** 60*   **Green Rating:** 60*

STUDENTS AND FACULTY

Enrollment: 23,329. **Student Body:** 56% female, 44% male, 11% out-of-state, 4% international (84 countries represented). Asian 15%, African American 8%, Caucasian 35%, Hispanic 26%, Native American <1%, Pacific Islander 1%, Two or more races 9%, Race unknown 1%.
Retention and Graduation: 74% freshmen return for sophomore year.
Faculty: Student/faculty ratio 20:1. 776 full-time faculty, 90% hold PhDs, 18% are members of minority groups, 33% are women. 11% of classes are taught by teaching assistants.

ACADEMICS

Degrees: Bachelor's; Certificate; Doctoral degree—professional practice; Doctoral degree research/scholarship; Master's; Post-bachelor's certificate; Post-master's certificate. **Classes:** Most classes have 20–29 students. Most lab/discussion sessions have 20–29 students. **Most popular majors:** Hospitality Administration/Management, General; Elementary Education and Teaching; Psychology, General. **Special Study Options:** Accelerated program; Cooperative education program; Double major; Dual enrollment; English as a Second Language (ESL); Exchange student program (domestic); Honors program; Independent study; Internships; Student-designed major; Study abroad; Teacher certification program. **Disability Services offered:** Note-taking services; Reader services; Tape recorders; Tutors. **Career services:** Alumni network; Alumni services; Career assessment; Career/job search classes; Internships; Regional alumni.

FACILITIES

Housing: Coed dorms; Special housing for disabled students; Special housing for international students. **Special Academic Facilities/Equipment:** Art galleries, national supercomputing center for energy and environment, natural history museum, arboretum, 3 theaters, concert hall, law school, dental school, international gaming institute, professional practice school for teachers.

CAMPUS LIFE

Environment: Metropolis. **Activities:** Campus Ministries; Choral groups; Concert band; Dance; Drama/theater; International Student Organization; Jazz band; Literary magazine; Marching band; Model UN; Music ensembles; Musical theater; Opera; Pep band; Radio station; Student government; Student newspaper; Student-run film society; Symphony orchestra; Television station; Yearbook. 24 honor societies, 14 religious organizations, 8 fraternities, 6 sororities on campus. **Athletics (Intercollegiate):** *Men:* baseball, basketball, football, golf, soccer, swimming, tennis. *Women:* basketball, cross-country, equestrian sports, golf, soccer, softball, swimming, tennis, track/field (outdoor), volleyball. **On-Campus Highlights:** Lied Library.

ADMISSIONS

Freshman Academic Profile: Average high school GPA 3.3. 23% in top 10% of high school class, 52% in top 25% of high school class, 82% in top 50% of high school class. **Test Scores:** SAT Math middle 50% range 450–560. SAT EBRW middle 50% range 440–560. ACT middle 50% range 18–25. **Basis for Candidate Selection:** *Very important factors include:* rigor of secondary school record, academic GPA. *Important factors include:* standardized test scores. **Freshman Admission Requirements:** High school diploma is required and GED is not accepted. *Academic units required:* 4 English, 3 math, 3 science, 2 science labs, 3 social studies. **Freshman Admission Statistics:** 7,666 applied, 88% admitted, 56% enrolled. **Transfer Admission Requirements:** College transcript(s). Minimum college GPA of 2.0 required. Lowest grade transferable D-. **General Admission Information:** Application fee $60. Priority deadline 2/1. Regular application deadline 7/1. Non-fall registration accepted. Admission may be deferred for a maximum of 1 year.

COSTS AND FINANCIAL AID

Average book and supplies expense $1,224. **Required Forms and Deadlines:** FAFSA. **Types of Aid:** *Need-based scholarships/grants:* College/university scholarship or grant aid from institutional funds; Federal Pell; Private scholarships; SEOG; State scholarships/grants. *Loans:* Direct PLUS loans; Direct Subsidized Stafford Loans; Direct Unsubsidized Stafford Loans. **Student Employment:** Federal Work-Study Program available. Institutional employment available. **Financial Aid Statistics:** 64% needy freshmen, 67% needy undergrads receive need-based scholarship or grant aid. 73% freshmen, 46% undergrads receive non-need-based scholarship or grant aid. 80% freshmen, 88% undergrads receive need-based self-help aid. 2% freshmen, 2% undergrads receive athletic scholarships. 41% undergrads borrow to pay for school. Average cumulative indebtedness $24,891. **Criteria awarding aid:** *Need-based:* Academics, Alumni affiliation. *Non-need-based:* Academics, Alumni affiliation, Athletics, Music/drama.

UNIVERSITY OF NEW ENGLAND

11 Hills Beach Road, Biddeford, ME 04005-9599
Phone: 207-602-2847 **Financial Aid Phone:** 207-602-2342
E-mail: admissions@une.edu **CEEB Code:** 3751
Fax: 207-602-5900 **Website:** www.une.edu **ACT Code:** 3751

This private school was founded in 1831. It has a 550 acre campus.

RATINGS

Admissions Selectivity Rating: 76   **Fire Safety Rating:** 99   **Green Rating:** 93

STUDENTS AND FACULTY

Enrollment: 2,449. **Student Body:** 69% female, 31% male, 73% out-of-state, 7 countries represented.
Retention and Graduation: 82% freshmen return for sophomore year. 59% freshmen graduate within 4 years. 68% freshmen graduate within 6 years. 31% grads go on to further study within 1 year. **Faculty:** Student/faculty ratio 13:1. 299 full-time faculty, 9% are members of minority groups, 58% are women. 0% of classes are taught by teaching assistants.

ACADEMICS

Degrees: Bachelor's; Doctoral degree—professional practice; Doctoral degree research/scholarship; Master's; Post-bachelor's certificate; Post-master's certificate. **Classes:** Most classes have 10–19 students. Most lab/discussion sessions have 10–19 students. **Most popular majors:** Biomedical Sciences, General; Exercise Science and Kinesiology; Registered Nursing/Registered Nurse. **Special Study Options:** Accelerated program; Cooperative education program; Cross-registration; Double major; Dual enrollment; Honors program; Independent study; Internships; Liberal arts/career combination; Study abroad; Teacher certification program. **Honors programs:** The College of Arts and Sciences offers an honors program to qualified applicants. **Disability Services offered:** Note-taking services; Tape recorders. **Career services:** Alumni services; Career assessment; Career/job search classes.

FACILITIES

Housing: Coed dorms; Special housing for disabled students; Theme housing; Wellness housing; Women's dorms. **Special Academic Facilities/Equipment:** Payson Art Gallery; Maine Women Writers Collection; Marine Science Center; Performance Enhancement and Evaluation Center for health sciences (PEEC); Center for Health Ethics, Law and Policy; Center for Transcultural Health; and New England Institute of Cognitive Science and Evolutionary Psychology.

CAMPUS LIFE

Environment: Town. **Activities:** Campus Ministries; Dance; Drama/theater; International Student Organization; Jazz band; Literary magazine; Music ensembles; Musical theater; Pep band; Student government; Student newspaper; Yearbook. 70 registered organizations, 3 honor societies, 6 religious organizations on campus. **Athletics (Intercollegiate):** *Men:* basketball, cross-country, golf, lacrosse, soccer. *Women:* basketball, cross-country, field hockey, golf, lacrosse, soccer, softball, swimming, volleyball. **On-Campus Highlights:** Marine Science Center. **Environmental Initiatives:** UNE joined as an institutional member of the Planetary Health Alliance in April 2017. Interested faculty and staff from UNE have formed a University Planetary Health Steering Committee to explore how UNE can contribute to the field of Planetary Health and how Planetary Health concepts can be more fully integrated into our curriculum and student learning experience. In 2019 the Planetary Health Council was formalized through the Office of Academic Affairs. UNE is

uniquely positioned to contribute to the field of planetary health due to the wide breadth of expertise in the College of Arts and Sciences and the more human-health focused colleges of Pharmacy, Osteopathic Medicine, and the Westbrook College of Health Professions. The Planetary Health Alliance was founded on the premise that we are entrenched in a new era, the Anthropocene, where our industrial society has firmly implanted itself into the deep ranks of time. In this era, problems occurring in our environment are problems impacting human health—and they must be looked at as a singular issue with a unified solution.

ADMISSIONS

Freshman Academic Profile: Average high school GPA 3.4. **Test Scores:** SAT Math middle 50% range 520–610. SAT EBRW middle 50% range 520–620. ACT middle 50% range 21–27. **Basis for Candidate Selection:** *Very important factors include:* rigor of secondary school record, academic GPA. *Important factors include:* class rank. *Other factors include:* application essay, standardized test scores, recommendation(s), extracurricular activities, talent/ability, character/personal qualities, alumni/ae relation, geographical residence, volunteer work, work experience. **Freshman Admission Requirements:** High school diploma is required and GED is accepted. *Academic units required:* 4 English, 3 math, 3 science, 2 science labs, 2 social studies, 2 history. *Academic units recommended:* 4 math, 4 science, 3 science labs, 2 foreign language, 4 social studies, 4 history, 4 academic electives. **Freshman Admission Statistics:** 5,175 applied, 84% admitted, 16% enrolled. **Transfer Admission Requirements:** College transcript(s). Minimum college GPA of 2.0 required. Lowest grade transferable C-. **General Admission Information:** Application fee $40. Priority deadline 12/1. Regular application deadline 2/15. Non-fall registration accepted. Admission may be deferred for a maximum of 12 months.

COSTS AND FINANCIAL AID

Average book and supplies expense $1,400. **Required Forms and Deadlines:** FAFSA. **Notification of Awards:** Applicants will be notified of awards on a rolling basis beginning 12/1. **Types of Aid:** *Need-based scholarships/grants:* College/university scholarship or grant aid from institutional funds; Federal Pell; Private scholarships; SEOG; State scholarships/grants. *Loans:* Direct PLUS loans; Direct Subsidized Stafford Loans; Direct Unsubsidized Stafford Loans. **Student Employment:** Federal Work-Study Program available. Institutional employment available. **Financial Aid Statistics:** 78% needy freshmen, 72% needy undergrads receive need-based scholarship or grant aid. 100% freshmen, 100% undergrads receive non-need-based scholarship or grant aid. 93% freshmen, 91% undergrads receive need-based self-help aid. freshmen, undergrads receive athletic scholarships. 98% undergrads receive any aid. 94% undergrads borrow to pay for school. Average cumulative indebtedness $40,683.

UNIVERSITY OF NEW HAMPSHIRE

UNH Office of Admissions, Durham, NH 03824
Phone: 603-862-1360 **Financial Aid Phone:** 603-862-3600
E-mail: admissions@unh.edu **CEEB Code:** 3918
Fax: 603-862-0077 **Website:** www.unh.edu **ACT Code:** 2524

This public school was founded in 1866. It has a 2600 acre campus.

RATINGS

Admissions Selectivity Rating: 76   **Fire Safety Rating:** 90   **Green Rating:** 99

STUDENTS AND FACULTY

Enrollment: 12,103. **Student Body:** 56% female, 44% male, 52% out-of-state, 3% international (37 countries represented). Asian 3%, African American 1%, Caucasian 83%, Hispanic 4%, Native American <1%, Pacific Islander <1%, Two or more races 2%, Race unknown 4%.
Retention and Graduation: 86% freshmen return for sophomore year. 68% freshmen graduate within 4 years. 77% freshmen graduate within 6 years. 21% grads go on to further study within 1 year. 5% grads pursue arts and sciences degrees. <1% grads pursue law degrees. 2% grads pursue business degrees. <1% grads pursue medical degrees. **Faculty:** Student/faculty ratio 17:1. 746 full-time faculty, 81% hold PhDs, 14% are members of minority groups, 51% are women. 3% of classes are taught by teaching assistants.

ACADEMICS

Degrees: Associate; Bachelor's; Doctoral degree—professional practice; Doctoral degree research/scholarship; Master's; Post-bachelor's certificate. **Classes:** Most classes have 20–29 students. Most lab/discussion sessions have 10–19 students. **Most popular majors:** Biomedical Sciences, General; Psychology, General; Business Administration and Management, General. **Special Study Options:** Accelerated program; Cross-registration; Distance learning; Double major; Dual enrollment; English as a Second Language (ESL); Exchange student program (domestic); Honors program; Independent study; Internships; Student-designed major; Study abroad; Teacher certification program. **Honors programs:** The UNH honors program serves students looking for an especially challenging academic curriculum. The program focuses on small, discussion-based courses, interdisciplinary approaches, and individualized advising. It also provides opportunities for research, supports students who seek to study overseas or elsewhere in the U.S., and offers a close and supportive community. **Combined degree programs:** BA/MA; BA/MEng. **Disability Services offered:** Note-taking services; Reader services; Tape recorders; Tutors. **Career services:** Alumni network; Alumni services; Career assessment; Career/job search classes; Internships; Regional alumni.

FACILITIES

Housing: Apartments for married students; Apartments for single students; Coed dorms; Fraternity/sorority housing; Special housing for disabled students; Special housing for international students; Theme housing; 88% of campus accessible to physically disabled. **Special Academic Facilities/Equipment:** Art gallery, radio station, optical observatory, marine research labs (coastal, estuarine, island), interoperability lab, experiential learning center with challenge course, electron microscope, child development center, journalism lab, writing center, experimental wind tunnel, agricultural and equine facilities including an organic research dairy farm and sustainable agriculture facilities, advanced manufacturing center, nursing simulation lab, instructional climbing wall, exercise physiology lab, sawmill, language labs, performing arts center, survey center, nature preserve and university museum. **Campus network:** 100% of classrooms, 100% of dorms, 100% of student union, 100% of libraries, 100% of dining areas, 50% of common outdoor areas have wireless network access.

CAMPUS LIFE

Environment: Village. **Activities:** Campus Ministries; Choral groups; Concert band; Dance; Drama/theater; International Student Organization; Jazz band; Literary magazine; Marching band; Model UN; Music ensembles; Musical theater; Opera; Pep band; Radio station; Student government; Student newspaper; Student-run film society; Symphony orchestra; Yearbook. 271 registered organizations, 25 honor societies, 9 religious organizations, 12 fraternities, 8 sororities on campus. **Athletics (Intercollegiate):** *Men:* basketball, cross-country, football, ice hockey, skiing (downhill/Alpine), skiing (Nordic/cross-country), soccer, track/field (outdoor), track/field (indoor). *Women:* basketball, cross-country, diving, field hockey, gymnastics, ice hockey, lacrosse, skiing (downhill/Alpine), skiing (Nordic/cross-country), soccer, swimming, track/field (outdoor), track/field (indoor), volleyball. **On-Campus Highlights:** Dimond Library **Environmental Initiatives:** UNH's greenhouse gas footprint is down 51% from our 2001 baseline. This is thanks in part to our CoGen plant being fueled by local landfill gas, which prevents thousands of tons of harmful methane emissions annually. We've invested heavily in renewables, including 100% renewable electricity. Our partnership with three New Hampshire micro-hydroelectric plants supports renewable energy generation. We have also invested more than $500,000 through a revolving energy efficiency fund each year.

ADMISSIONS

Freshman Academic Profile: Average high school GPA 3.5. 22% in top 10% of high school class, 49% in top 25% of high school class, 85% in top 50% of high school class. **Test Scores:** SAT Math middle 50% range 530–630. SAT EBRW middle 50% range 540–640. ACT middle 50% range 22–28. **Basis for Candidate Selection:** *Very important factors include:* rigor of secondary school record, academic GPA. *Important factors include:* recommendation(s). *Other factors include:* class rank, application essay, standardized test scores, extracurricular activities, talent/ability, character/personal qualities, first generation, alumni/ae relation, geographical residence, state residency, racial/ethnic status, volunteer work, work experience. **Freshman Admission Requirements:** High school diploma is required and GED is accepted. *Academic units required:* 4 English, 3 math, 3 science, 2 science labs, 2 foreign language, 3 social studies. *Academic units recommended:* 4 English, 4 math, 4 science, 3 science labs, 3 foreign language, 3 social studies, 1 visual/performing arts. **Freshman Admission Statistics:** 18,040 applied, 84% admitted, 18% enrolled. **Transfer Admission Requirements:** High school transcript, college

transcript(s), essay or personal statement, interview, standardized test scores. Minimum college GPA of 2.8 required. Lowest grade transferable C. **General Admission Information:** Application fee $50. Regular application deadline 2/1. Non-fall registration accepted. Admission may be deferred for a maximum of 1 year.

COSTS AND FINANCIAL AID

Annual in-state tuition $15,520. Annual out-of-state tuition $32,050. Room and board $11,942. Required fees $3,359. Average book and supplies expense $1,000. **Required Forms and Deadlines:** FAFSA. **Notification of Awards:** Applicants will be notified of awards on a rolling basis beginning 12/1. **Types of Aid:** *Need-based scholarships/grants:* College/university scholarship or grant aid from institutional funds; Federal Pell; Private scholarships; SEOG; State scholarships/grants. *Loans:* Direct PLUS loans; Direct Subsidized Stafford Loans; Direct Unsubsidized Stafford Loans. **Student Employment:** Federal Work-Study Program available. Institutional employment available. **Financial Aid Statistics:** 9% needy freshmen, 82% needy undergrads receive need-based scholarship or grant aid. 12% freshmen, 8% undergrads receive non-need-based scholarship or grant aid. 93% freshmen, 94% undergrads receive need-based self-help aid. 2% freshmen, 2% undergrads receive athletic scholarships. 91% freshmen, 81% undergrads receive any aid. 80% undergrads borrow to pay for school. Average cumulative indebtedness $42,246. **Criteria awarding aid:** *Need-based:* Academics, Alumni affiliation, Art, Athletics, Minority status. *Non-need-based:* Academics, Art, Athletics, Leadership, Music/drama.

UNIVERSITY OF NEW HAVEN

300 Boston Post Road, West Haven, CT 06516
Financial Aid Phone: 203-479-4520
E-mail: admissions@newhaven.edu **CEEB Code:** 3663
Fax: 203-931-6093 **Website:** www.newhaven.edu **ACT Code:** 0576

This private school was founded in 1920. It has a 82 acre campus.

RATINGS

Admissions Selectivity Rating: 76 **Fire Safety Rating:** 60* **Green Rating:** 75

STUDENTS AND FACULTY

Enrollment: 4,863. **Student Body:** 56% female, 44% male, 57% out-of-state, 3% international (31 countries represented). Asian 4%, African American 12%, Caucasian 64%, Hispanic 13%, Native American <1%, Pacific Islander <1%, Two or more races 1%, Race unknown 3%.
Retention and Graduation: 77% freshmen return for sophomore year. 51% freshmen graduate within 4 years. 61% freshmen graduate within 6 years.
Faculty: Student/faculty ratio 16:1. 265 full-time faculty, 87% hold PhDs, 26% are members of minority groups, 37% are women.

ACADEMICS

Degrees: Associate; Bachelor's; Certificate; Doctoral degree research/scholarship; Master's; Post-master's certificate. **Classes:** Most classes have 10–19 students. Most lab/discussion sessions have 10–19 students. **Most popular majors:** Criminal Justice/Law Enforcement Administration; Psychology, General. **Special Study Options:** Accelerated program; Cooperative education program; Cross-registration; Distance learning; Double major; Dual enrollment; English as a Second Language (ESL); Exchange student program (domestic); Honors program; Independent study; Internships; Study abroad. **Disability Services offered:** Note-taking services; Reader services; Tape recorders; Tutors. **Career services:** Alumni network; Alumni services; Career assessment; Career/job search classes; Internships.

FACILITIES

Housing: Apartments for single students; Coed dorms; Special housing for disabled students; Theme housing; Wellness housing. **Special Academic Facilities/Equipment:** Henry C. Lee Institute; Fire Science Laboratories; Dental Hygiene Center; Bergami Learning Center for Finance & Technology.

CAMPUS LIFE

Environment: Town. **Activities:** Campus Ministries; Dance; Drama/theater; International Student Organization; Marching band; Model UN; Music ensembles; Pep band; Radio station; Student government; Student newspaper;

Television station; Yearbook. 165 registered organizations on campus. **Athletics (Intercollegiate):** *Men:* baseball, basketball, cross-country, golf, lacrosse, soccer, track/field (outdoor), track/field (indoor), volleyball. *Women:* basketball, cheerleading, cross-country, lacrosse, soccer, softball, tennis, volleyball.

ADMISSIONS

Freshman Academic Profile: Average high school GPA 3.5. 17% in top 10% of high school class, 42% in top 25% of high school class, 75% in top 50% of high school class. **Test Scores:** SAT Math middle 50% range 510–600. SAT EBRW middle 50% range 520–620. ACT middle 50% range 21–27. **Basis for Candidate Selection:** *Very important factors include:* academic GPA. *Important factors include:* application essay, recommendation(s). *Other factors include:* rigor of secondary school record, standardized test scores, interview, extracurricular activities, character/personal qualities, volunteer work, work experience, level of applicant's interest. **Freshman Admission Requirements:** High school diploma is required and GED is accepted. *Academic units recommended:* 4 English, 3 math, 3 science, 2 science labs, 2 foreign language, 3 social studies. **Freshman Admission Statistics:** 10,997 applied, 83% admitted, 14% enrolled. **Transfer Admission Requirements:** High school transcript, college transcript(s). Minimum college GPA of 2.5 required. Lowest grade transferable C. **General Admission Information:** Application fee $50. Priority deadline 3/1. Non-fall registration accepted.

COSTS AND FINANCIAL AID

Required Forms and Deadlines: FAFSA. **Notification of Awards:** Applicants will be notified of awards on a rolling basis beginning 1/15. **Types of Aid:** *Need-based scholarships/grants:* College/university scholarship or grant aid from institutional funds; Federal Pell; Private scholarships; SEOG; State scholarships/grants. *Loans:* Direct PLUS loans; Direct Subsidized Stafford Loans; Direct Unsubsidized Stafford Loans. **Student Employment:** Federal Work-Study Program available. Institutional employment available. **Financial Aid Statistics:** 100% needy freshmen, 99% needy undergrads receive need-based scholarship or grant aid. 12% freshmen, 12% undergrads receive non-need-based scholarship or grant aid. 80% freshmen, 81% undergrads receive need-based self-help aid. 1% freshmen, 0% undergrads receive athletic scholarships. 78% undergrads borrow to pay for school. Average cumulative indebtedness $47,457. **Criteria awarding aid:** *Non-need-based:* Academics, Art, Athletics.

UNIVERSITY OF NEW MEXICO

Office of Admissions, Albuquerque, NM 86131
Phone: 505-277-2446 **Financial Aid Phone:** 505-277-8900
E-mail: apply@unm.edu **CEEB Code:** 4845
Fax: 505-277-6686 **Website:** www.unm.edu **ACT Code:** 2650

This public school was founded in 1889. It has a 769 acre campus.

RATINGS

Admissions Selectivity Rating: 89   **Fire Safety Rating:** 80   **Green Rating:** 60*

STUDENTS AND FACULTY

Enrollment: 18,913. **Student Body:** 56% female, 44% male, 13% out-of-state, 2% international (92 countries represented). Asian 4%, African American 2%, Caucasian 32%, Hispanic 49%, Native American 6%, Pacific Islander <1%, Two or more races 4%, Race unknown 1%.
Retention and Graduation: 16% freshmen graduate within 4 years. 44% freshmen graduate within 6 years. **Faculty:** Student/faculty ratio 16:1. 1,103 full-time faculty, 78% hold PhDs, 23% are members of minority groups, 49% are women.

ACADEMICS

Degrees: Associate; Bachelor's; Certificate; Doctoral degree—professional practice; Doctoral degree research/scholarship; Master's; Post-bachelor's certificate; Post-master's certificate. **Classes:** Most classes have 10–19 students. Most lab/discussion sessions have 20–29 students. **Most popular majors:** Biology/Biological Sciences, General; Business Administration and Management, General; Psychology, General. **Special Study Options:** Accelerated program; Cooperative education program; Distance learning; Double major; Dual enrollment; English as a Second Language (ESL); Exchange student program (domestic); Honors program; Independent study;

Internships; Student-designed major; Study abroad; Teacher certification program; Weekend college. **Honors programs:** The University Honors Program offers the chance to explore major contemporary ideas and values in small interdisciplinary seminars with the additional benefits of personal interaction with outstanding UNM faculty, opportunities for upper-division independent research, social and cultural events, lecture series, and opportunities to participate in regional and national honors conferences. UHP students do not major in University Honors. They graduate with a degree from one of UNM's degree-granting colleges or schools. **Combined degree programs:** BA/MD; BA/MEng. **Disability Services offered:** Note-taking services; Reader services; Tape recorders; Tutors. **Career services:** Alumni network; Alumni services; Career assessment; Career/job search classes; Internships; Regional alumni.

FACILITIES

Housing: Apartments for married students; Apartments for single students; Coed dorms; Fraternity/sorority housing; Special housing for disabled students; Special housing for international students; Theme housing; 100% of campus accessible to physically disabled. **Special Academic Facilities/Equipment:** Museums of art, anthropology, geology, and Southwestern biology; lithography institute; meteoritics institute; electron and electron scanning microscopes; nuclear reactor; robotics lab; observatory; planetarium; Science and Technology Park. **Campus network:** 100% of classrooms have wireless network access.

CAMPUS LIFE

Environment: Metropolis. **Activities:** Campus Ministries; Choral groups; Concert band; Dance; Drama/theater; International Student Organization; Jazz band; Literary magazine; Marching band; Model UN; Music ensembles; Musical theater; Opera; Pep band; Radio station; Student government; Student newspaper; Student-run film society; Symphony orchestra; Television station. 400 registered organizations, 17 honor societies, 30 religious organizations, 10 fraternities, 10 sororities on campus. **Athletics (Intercollegiate):** *Men:* baseball, basketball, cross-country, football, golf, skiing (downhill/Alpine), skiing (Nordic/cross-country), soccer, tennis, track/field (outdoor), track/field (indoor). *Women:* basketball, cross-country, diving, golf, skiing (downhill/Alpine), skiing (Nordic/cross-country), soccer, softball, swimming, tennis, track/field (outdoor), track/field (indoor), volleyball. **On-Campus Highlights:** SUB (Student Union Building). **Environmental Initiatives:** In November 2009, UNM submitted its first Climate Action Plan to the American College and University Presidents Climate Commitment website and set a climate neutrality target date of year 2050. UNM will use a multi-tiered approach to reducing our greenhouse gas emissions. The tiers are behavior-based energy conservation, technological improvements in utilities production and consumption, renewable energy, and alternative transportation.

ADMISSIONS

Freshman Academic Profile: Average high school GPA 3.4. **Test Scores:** SAT Math middle 50% range 470–580. SAT EBRW middle 50% range 460–590. ACT middle 50% range 19–25. **Basis for Candidate Selection:** *Very important factors include:* rigor of secondary school record, academic GPA. *Important factors include:* standardized test scores. *Other factors include:* application essay, interview, extracurricular activities, talent/ability, volunteer work, work experience. **Freshman Admission Requirements:** High school diploma is required and GED is accepted. *Academic units required:* 4 English, 4 math, 3 science, 2 science labs, 2 foreign language, 2 social studies, 1 history. **Freshman Admission Statistics:** 11,347 applied, 49% admitted, 57% enrolled. **Transfer Admission Requirements:** College transcript(s). Minimum college GPA of 2.0 required. Lowest grade transferable C. **General Admission Information:** Application fee $25. Priority deadline 5/1. Non-fall registration accepted.

COSTS AND FINANCIAL AID

Room and board $8,690. **Required Forms and Deadlines:** FAFSA. **Notification of Awards:** Applicants will be notified of awards on a rolling basis beginning 4/15. **Types of Aid:** *Need-based scholarships/grants:* College/university scholarship or grant aid from institutional funds; Federal Nursing Scholarships; Federal Pell; Private scholarships; SEOG; State scholarships/grants; United Negro College Fund. *Loans:* Direct PLUS loans; Direct Subsidized Stafford Loans; Direct Unsubsidized Stafford Loans. **Student Employment:** Federal Work-Study Program available. **Criteria awarding aid:** *Need-based:* Minority status. *Non-need-based:* Academics, Alumni affiliation, Art, Athletics, Job skills, Leadership, Minority status, Music/drama, Religious affiliation, State/district residency.

UNIVERSITY OF NEW ORLEANS

University of New Orleans Privateer Enrollment Center, New Orleans, LA 70148
Phone: 504-280-6595 **Financial Aid Phone:** 504-280-6603
E-mail: admissions@uno.edu **CEEB Code:** 6379
Fax: 504-280-3973 **Website:** www.uno.edu **ACT Code:** 1591

This public school was founded in 1958. It has a 195 acre campus.

RATINGS
Admissions Selectivity Rating: 87   **Fire Safety Rating:** 89   **Green Rating:** 60*

STUDENTS AND FACULTY
Enrollment: 5,917. **Student Body:** 49% female, 51% male, 4% international (62 countries represented). Asian 9%, African American 15%, Caucasian 52%, Hispanic 13%, Native American <1%, Pacific Islander <1%, Two or more races 4%, Race unknown 3%.
Retention and Graduation: 62% freshmen return for sophomore year. 15% freshmen graduate within 4 years. 36% freshmen graduate within 6 years. **Faculty:** Student/faculty ratio 22:1. 262 full-time faculty, 84% hold PhDs, 19% are members of minority groups, 34% are women.

ACADEMICS
Degrees: Bachelor's; Doctoral degree research/scholarship; Master's; Post-bachelor's certificate. **Classes:** Most classes have 10–19 students. Most lab/discussion sessions have 20–29 students. **Most popular majors:** Biology/Biological Sciences, General; Multi-/Interdisciplinary Studies, Other; Business Administration and Management, General. **Special Study Options:** Accelerated program; Cooperative education program; Cross-registration; Distance learning; Double major; Dual enrollment; English as a Second Language (ESL); Exchange student program (domestic); Honors program; Independent study; Internships; Study abroad; Teacher certification program. **Disability Services offered:** Note-taking services; Reader services; Tape recorders; Tutors. **Career services:** Alumni network; Alumni services; Career assessment; Career/job search classes; Internships; Regional alumni.

FACILITIES
Housing: Apartments for married students; Coed dorms; Theme housing; 100% of campus accessible to physically disabled. **Special Academic Facilities/Equipment:** Performing Arts Center, Nims Center Studios (motion picture and television production facility), Eisenhower leadership studies center, Louisiana and Special Collections, The Cove (a student dining and entertainment center that is home to Jazz at the Sandbar, a unique performance series in which students are paired with professional jazz musicians). **Campus network:** 100% of classrooms, 100% of dorms, 100% of student union, 100% of libraries, 100% of dining areas, 0% of common outdoor areas have wireless network access.

CAMPUS LIFE
Environment: Metropolis. **Activities:** Campus Ministries; Choral groups; Concert band; Dance; Drama/theater; International Student Organization; Jazz band; Literary magazine; Model UN; Music ensembles; Musical theater; Pep band; Radio station; Student government; Student newspaper; Student-run film society. 101 registered organizations, 9 honor societies, 5 religious organizations, 8 fraternities, 7 sororities on campus. **Athletics (Intercollegiate):** *Men:* baseball, basketball, diving, golf, swimming, tennis. *Women:* basketball, diving, swimming, tennis, volleyball. **On-Campus Highlights:** Recreation and Fitness Center.

ADMISSIONS
Freshman Academic Profile: Average high school GPA 3.2. 15% in top 10% of high school class, 34% in top 25% of high school class, 64% in top 50% of high school class. **Test Scores:** SAT Math middle 50% range 510–610. SAT EBRW middle 50% range 520–640. ACT middle 50% range 20–25. **Basis for Candidate Selection:** *Very important factors include:* academic GPA, standardized test scores. **Freshman Admission Requirements:** High school diploma is required and GED is accepted. *Academic units required:* 4 English, 4 math, 4 science, 2 foreign language, 4 social studies, 1 visual/performing arts. **Freshman Admission Statistics:** 3,736 applied, 57% admitted, 45% enrolled. **Transfer Admission Requirements:** college transcript(s). Minimum college GPA of 2.25 required. Lowest grade transferable D. **General Admission**

Information: Application fee $25. Priority deadline 12/15. Regular application deadline 7/15. Non-fall registration accepted.

COSTS AND FINANCIAL AID
Annual in-state tuition $6,090. Annual out-of-state tuition $10,926. Room and board $10,575. Required fees $2,394. Average book and supplies expense $1,300. **Required Forms and Deadlines:** FAFSA; Institution's own financial aid form. **Notification of Awards:** Applicants will be notified of awards on or about 1/15. **Types of Aid:** *Need-based scholarships/grants:* College/university scholarship or grant aid from institutional funds; Federal Pell; Private scholarships; SEOG; State scholarships/grants; United Negro College Fund. *Loans:* Direct PLUS loans; Direct Subsidized Stafford Loans; Direct Unsubsidized Stafford Loans. **Student Employment:** Federal Work-Study Program available. Institutional employment available. **Financial Aid Statistics:** 80% needy freshmen, 78% needy undergrads receive need-based scholarship or grant aid. 65% freshmen, 51% undergrads receive non-need-based scholarship or grant aid. 55% freshmen, 56% undergrads receive need-based self-help aid. 4% freshmen, 3% undergrads receive athletic scholarships. 48% undergrads borrow to pay for school. Average cumulative indebtedness $20,723. **Criteria awarding aid:** *Need-based:* Academics, Alumni affiliation, Art, Athletics, Job skills, Leadership, Minority status, Music/drama. *Non-need-based:* Academics, Athletics, Music/drama.

THE UNIVERSITY OF NORTH CAROLINA—ASHEVILLE

One University Heights, Asheville, NC 28804-8502
Phone: 828-251-6481 **Financial Aid Phone:** 828-251-6535
E-mail: admissions@unca.edu **CEEB Code:** 5013
Fax: 828-251-6482 **Website:** www.unca.edu **ACT Code:** 3064

This public school was founded in 1927. It has a 365 acre campus.

RATINGS
Admissions Selectivity Rating: 76   **Fire Safety Rating:** 97   **Green Rating:** 91

STUDENTS AND FACULTY
Enrollment: 3,286. **Student Body:** 57% female, 43% male, 11% out-of-state, 1% international (15 countries represented). Asian 2%, African American 5%, Caucasian 74%, Hispanic 9%, Native American <1%, Pacific Islander <1%, Two or more races 4%, Race unknown 4%.
Retention and Graduation: 73% freshmen return for sophomore year. 39% freshmen graduate within 4 years. 59% freshmen graduate within 6 years. 12% grads go on to further study within 1 year. 84% grads pursue arts and sciences degrees. 2% grads pursue law degrees. 6% grads pursue business degrees. 6% grads pursue medical degrees. **Faculty:** Student/faculty ratio 13:1. 220 full-time faculty, 88% hold PhDs, 17% are members of minority groups, 46% are women. 0% of classes are taught by teaching assistants.

ACADEMICS
Degrees: Bachelor's; Master's; Post-bachelor's certificate. **Classes:** Most classes have 10–19 students. Most lab/discussion sessions have 10–19 students. **Most popular majors:** Environmental Studies; Psychology, General; Business Administration and Management, General. **Special Study Options:** Cooperative education program; Cross-registration; Distance learning; Double major; Dual enrollment; Honors program; Independent study; Internships; Student-designed major; Study abroad; Teacher certification program.
Honors programs: Designed for talented and motivated students, the Honors curriculum complements the core general education curriculum and major curricula. Successful completion of the Honors Program enables the student to graduate with Distinction as a University Scholar. (See http://honors.unca.edu for further information.) The Undergraduate Research Program at UNCA seeks to encourage the establishment of faculty/student research pairs who work together on a project of mutual interest. Research may be performed in any discipline on campus. Students who have made oral presentations at symposia and have had their work reviewed and published can receive recognition as University Research Scholars. (See http://www.unca.edu/urp/ for more information.) **Disability Services offered:** Note-taking services; Reader services; Tape recorders; Tutors. **Career services:** Alumni network; Alumni services; Career assessment; Career/job search classes; Internships; Regional alumni.

FACILITIES

Housing: Apartments for single students; Coed dorms; Special housing for disabled students; Special housing for international students; Theme housing; Wellness housing; 95% of campus accessible to physically disabled. **Special Academic Facilities/Equipment:** STEAM Studio for science, technology, engineering, art and math; Bob Moog Electric Music Studio (Dr. Moog, inventor of the Moog Synthesizer, was Research Professor of Music at UNC Asheville); N.C. Center for Health & Wellness, including BodPod, Balance Lab, Biofeedback Lab, Meditation Space; Lookout Observatory and optical telescope for astronomical research; Botanical Gardens. **Campus network:** 10% of classrooms, 100% of dorms, 50% of student union, 100% of libraries, 10% of dining areas, 10% of common outdoor areas have wireless network access.

CAMPUS LIFE

Environment: Town. **Activities:** Campus Ministries; Choral groups; Concert band; Dance; Drama/theater; International Student Organization; Jazz band; Literary magazine; Model UN; Music ensembles; Musical theater; Pep band; Radio station; Student government; Student newspaper; Student-run film society. 79 registered organizations, 2 honor societies, 9 religious organizations, 2 fraternities, 2 sororities on campus. **Athletics (Intercollegiate):** *Men:* baseball, basketball, cheerleading, cross-country, soccer, tennis, track/field (outdoor). *Women:* basketball, cheerleading, cross-country, soccer, tennis, track/field (outdoor), volleyball. **On-Campus Highlights:** Sherrill Center for Health and Wellness. **Environmental Initiatives:** Sustainability has been enshrined in our current strategic plan as one of the 3 core values of the institution: "We must continue our commitment to sustainability and support of the natural environment, human communities, and the financial health of the institution. Our commitment to sustainability includes building and strengthening alliances on campus and beyond by encouraging active participation with community organizations and partners, promoting enduring alumni engagement, and facilitating inclusive discussions about a sustainable future. We must sustain affordable higher education and continue to identify new sources of support while also operating effectively and efficiently. We educate students about all dimensions of sustainability by integrating environmental literacy throughout the curriculum and by modeling sustainable campus practices. We will continue to build our students' capacities to strengthen the health and resilience of our community and environment, at the local and global levels, by providing high quality instructional expertise and by supporting sustainability-related learning opportunities."

ADMISSIONS

Freshman Academic Profile: Average high school GPA 3.4. 14% in top 10% of high school class, 39% in top 25% of high school class, 78% in top 50% of high school class. 87% from public high schools. **Test Scores:** SAT Math middle 50% range 530–620. SAT EBRW middle 50% range 560–650. ACT middle 50% range 22–27. **Basis for Candidate Selection:** *Very important factors include:* rigor of secondary school record, class rank, academic GPA, application essay, standardized test scores, recommendation(s). *Important factors include:* extracurricular activities, talent/ability, character/personal qualities. *Other factors include:* first generation, alumni/ae relation, geographical residence, state residency, racial/ethnic status, volunteer work, work experience, level of applicant's interest. **Freshman Admission Requirements:** High school diploma is required and GED is not accepted. *Academic units required:* 4 English, 4 math, 3 science, 1 science labs, 2 foreign language, 2 social studies. **Freshman Admission Statistics:** 3,750 applied, 84% admitted, 21% enrolled. **Transfer Admission Requirements:** College transcript(s). Minimum college GPA of 2.50 required. Lowest grade transferable C. **General Admission Information:** Application fee $75. Regular application deadline 8/1. Non-fall registration accepted. Admission may be deferred for a maximum of one year.

COSTS AND FINANCIAL AID

Annual in-state tuition $4,246. Annual out-of-state tuition $21,594. Room and board $9,950. Average book and supplies expense $1,200. **Required Forms and Deadlines:** FAFSA. **Notification of Awards:** Applicants will be notified of awards on a rolling basis beginning 2/15. **Types of Aid:** *Need-based scholarships/grants:* College/university scholarship or grant aid from institutional funds; Federal Pell; Private scholarships; SEOG; State scholarships/grants. *Loans:* Direct PLUS loans; Direct Subsidized Stafford Loans; Direct Unsubsidized Stafford Loans. **Student Employment:** Federal Work-Study Program available. Institutional employment available. **Financial Aid Statistics:** 95% needy freshmen, 88% needy undergrads receive need-based scholarship or grant aid. 41% freshmen, 23% undergrads receive non-need-based scholarship or grant aid. 68% freshmen, 69% undergrads receive need-based self-help aid. 3% freshmen, 3% undergrads receive athletic scholarships. 83% freshmen, 73% undergrads receive any aid. 59% undergrads borrow to pay for school. Average cumulative indebtedness $24,476. **Criteria awarding aid:**

Need-based: Academics, Job skills, Leadership, Music/drama. *Non-need-based:* Academics, Alumni affiliation, Art, Athletics, Job skills, Leadership, Music/drama, State/district residency.

UNIVERSITY OF NORTH CAROLINA—CHAPEL HILL

Jackson Hall, Chapel Hill, NC 27599-2200
Phone: 919-962-2211 **Financial Aid Phone:** 919-962-8396
E-mail: unchelp@admissions.unc.edu **CEEB Code:** 5816
Fax: 919-962-3045 **Website:** www.unc.edu **ACT Code:** 3162

This public school was founded in 1789. It has a 729 acre campus.

RATINGS

Admissions Selectivity Rating: 97   **Fire Safety Rating:** 97   **Green Rating:** 96

STUDENTS AND FACULTY

Enrollment: 19,034. **Student Body:** 60% female, 40% male, 14% out-of-state, 4% international (103 countries represented). Asian 11%, African American 8%, Caucasian 59%, Hispanic 9%, Native American <1%, Pacific Islander <1%, Two or more races 5%, Race unknown 4%.
Retention and Graduation: 96% freshmen return for sophomore year. 84% freshmen graduate within 4 years. 91% freshmen graduate within 6 years. 32% grads go on to further study within 1 year. **Faculty:** Student/faculty ratio 13:1. 1,643 full-time faculty, 84% hold PhDs, 22% are members of minority groups, 46% are women. 23% of classes are taught by teaching assistants.

ACADEMICS

Degrees: Bachelor's; Certificate; Doctoral degree—professional practice; Doctoral degree research/scholarship; Master's; Post-bachelor's certificate; Post-master's certificate. **Classes:** Most classes have 10–19 students. Most lab/discussion sessions have 10–19 students. **Most popular majors:** Biology/Biological Sciences, General; Psychology, General; Business Administration and Management, General. **Special Study Options:** Cross-registration; Distance learning; Double major; Dual enrollment; Honors program; Independent study; Internships; Student-designed major; Study abroad; Teacher certification program. **Honors programs:** See http://www.honors.unc.edu/. **Combined degree programs:** BA/MA. **Disability Services offered:** Note-taking services; Reader services; Tape recorders; Tutors. **Career services:** Alumni services; Career assessment; Career/job search classes; Internships.

FACILITIES

Housing: Apartments for married students; Apartments for single students; Coed dorms; Fraternity/sorority housing; Men's dorms; Special housing for disabled students; Special housing for international students; Theme housing; Wellness housing; Women's dorms; 97% of campus accessible to physically disabled. **Special Academic Facilities/Equipment:** Ackland Art Museum, Be A Maker Space (BeAM), Kenan-Flagler Business Capital Markets Lab, Carolina Basketball Museum, Institute of Latin American Studies, Ida B. Wells Society for Investigative Reporting, Institute of Marine Sciences, Center for the Study of the American South, Morehead Planetarium, Historic Playmakers Theater, 1789 Venture Lab for Entrepreneurship, Joint Applied Mathematics and Marine Sciences Fluids Lab, Sonja Haynes Stone Center for Black Culture and History, Matthew Gfeller Sport-Related Traumatic Brain Injury Research Center.

CAMPUS LIFE

Environment: Town. **Activities:** Campus Ministries; Choral groups; Concert band; Dance; Drama/theater; International Student Organization; Jazz band; Literary magazine; Marching band; Model UN; Music ensembles; Musical theater; Opera; Pep band; Radio station; Student government; Student newspaper; Student-run film society; Symphony orchestra; Television station; Yearbook. 836 registered organizations, 30 honor societies, 47 religious organizations, 30 fraternities, 24 sororities on campus. **Athletics (Intercollegiate):** *Men:* baseball, basketball, cross-country, diving, fencing, football, golf, lacrosse, soccer, swimming, tennis, track/field (outdoor), track/field (indoor), wrestling. *Women:* basketball, crew/rowing, cross-country, diving, fencing, field hockey, golf, gymnastics, lacrosse, soccer, softball, swimming, tennis, track/field (outdoor), track/field (indoor), volleyball. **On-Campus Highlights:** The Old Well. **Environmental Initiatives:** Partnered with Orange (County) Water and Sewer Authority (OWASA) to install a water reclamation and reuse system that replaced 218 million gallons of potable water in FY 2016. Started in summer 2009, the system provides makeup water at campus cooling towers, irrigates athletic fields and grounds, and flushes toilets in new buildings adjacent to the distribution network.

ADMISSIONS

Freshman Academic Profile: Average high school GPA 4.4. 78% in top 10% of high school class, 95% in top 25% of high school class, 99% in top 50% of high school class. 82% from public high schools. **Test Scores:** SAT Math middle 50% range 650–760. SAT EBRW middle 50% range 650–730. ACT middle 50% range 27–33. **Basis for Candidate Selection:** *Very important factors include:* rigor of secondary school record, application essay, standardized test scores, recommendation(s), extracurricular activities, talent/ability, character/personal qualities, state residency. *Important factors include:* class rank, academic GPA, volunteer work, work experience. *Other factors include:* first generation, alumni/ae relation, racial/ethnic status. **Freshman Admission Requirements:** High school diploma is required and GED is not accepted. *Academic units required:* 4 English, 4 math, 3 science, 1 science labs, 2 foreign language, 1 social studies, 1 history, 1 academic elective. **Freshman Admission Statistics:** 42,466 applied, 23% admitted, 44% enrolled. **Transfer Admission Requirements:** High school transcript, college transcript(s), essay or personal statement, statement of good standing from prior institution(s). Minimum college GPA of 2.0 required. Lowest grade transferable C. **General Admission Information:** Application fee $85. Priority deadline 10/15. Regular application deadline 1/15. Admission may be deferred for a maximum of 1 year.

COSTS AND FINANCIAL AID

Annual in-state tuition $7,019. Annual out-of-state tuition $34,198. Room and board $11,526. Required fees $2,027. Average book and supplies expense $972. **Required Forms and Deadlines:** CSS/Financial Aid PROFILE; FAFSA. **Notification of Awards:** Applicants will be notified of awards on a rolling basis beginning 3/15. **Types of Aid:** *Need-based scholarships/grants:* College/university scholarship or grant aid from institutional funds; Federal Pell; Private scholarships; SEOG; State scholarships/grants. *Loans:* Direct PLUS loans; Direct Subsidized Stafford Loans; Direct Unsubsidized Stafford Loans. **Student Employment:** Federal Work-Study Program available. Institutional employment available. **Financial Aid Statistics:** 93% needy freshmen, 91% needy undergrads receive need-based scholarship or grant aid. 7% freshmen, 4% undergrads receive non-need-based scholarship or grant aid. 59% freshmen, 65% undergrads receive need-based self-help aid. 2% freshmen, 2% undergrads receive athletic scholarships. 64.5% freshmen, 62.8% undergrads receive any aid. 40% undergrads borrow to pay for school. Average cumulative indebtedness $22,466. **Criteria awarding aid:** *Need-based:* Academics, Leadership. *Non-need-based:* Academics, Alumni affiliation, Art, Athletics, Leadership, Music/drama, Religious affiliation, State/district residency.

UNIVERSITY OF NORTH CAROLINA—CHARLOTTE

9201 University City Boulevard, Charlotte, NC 28223-0001
Phone: 704-687-5507 **Financial Aid Phone:** 704-687-5504
E-mail: admissions@uncc.edu **CEEB Code:** 5105
Fax: 704-687-6483 **Website:** www.uncc.edu **ACT Code:** 3163

This public school was founded in 1946. It has a 1000 acre campus.

RATINGS

Admissions Selectivity Rating: 86   **Fire Safety Rating:** 97   **Green Rating:** 85

STUDENTS AND FACULTY

Enrollment: 23,939. **Student Body:** 47% female, 53% male, 5% out-of-state, 2% international (92 countries represented). Asian 7%, African American 16%, Caucasian 57%, Hispanic 10%, Native American <1%, Pacific Islander <1%, Two or more races 5%, Race unknown 2%.
Retention and Graduation: 82% freshmen return for sophomore year. 29% freshmen graduate within 4 years. 54% freshmen graduate within 6 years.
Faculty: Student/faculty ratio 19:1. 1,169 full-time faculty, 84% hold PhDs, 23% are members of minority groups, 48% are women. 5% of classes are taught by teaching assistants.

ACADEMICS

Degrees: Bachelor's; Doctoral degree—professional practice; Doctoral degree research/scholarship; Master's; Post-bachelor's certificate; Post-master's certificate.
Classes: Most classes have 20–29 students. Most lab/discussion sessions have 20–29 students. **Most popular majors:** Computer Science; Business Administration

and Management, General; Psychology, General. **Special Study Options:** Accelerated program; Cooperative education program; Cross-registration; Distance learning; Double major; Dual enrollment; English as a Second Language (ESL); Exchange student program (domestic); External degree program; Honors program; Independent study; Internships; Study abroad; Teacher certification program. **Honors programs:** A variety of honors programs are available in the College of Arts and Architecture, Belk College of Business, College of Computing and Informatics, College of Education, and the College of Engineering. Honors programs are also available in the following departments: Anthropology, Art History, Biological Sciences, Chemistry, Communication Studies, Criminal Justice, English, Geography & Earth Science, History, Kinesiology, Languages & Culture Studies, Latin American Studies, Mathematics, Philosophy, Physics & Optical Science, Political Science, Psychology, Religious Studies, and Sociology. There is also a University Honors Program in the Honors College. The University Honors Program is a four year program that welcomes students from any major. **Disability Services offered:** Note-taking services; Reader services; Tape recorders; Tutors. **Career services:** Alumni network; Alumni services; Career assessment; Career/job search classes; Internships; Regional alumni.

FACILITIES

Housing: Apartments for single students; Coed dorms; Fraternity/sorority housing; Special housing for disabled students; Special housing for international students; Theme housing; Wellness housing; 90% of campus accessible to physically disabled. **Special Academic Facilities/Equipment:** Largest research library in the Southern Piedmont region with more than three million volumes; NC's Urban Research University; Energy Production and Infrastructure Center; renovated fitness gymnasium; two botanical gardens that span 10 acres; McMillan greenhouse with a tropical conservatory; PORTAL which stands for Partnership, Outreach and Research to Accelerate Learning, is a business incubator and corporate innovation center that offers a unique and flexible environment for emerging enterprises, Center City building, Engineering Early College High School, Charlotte Research Institute.

CAMPUS LIFE

Environment: Metropolis. **Activities:** Campus Ministries; Choral groups; Concert band; Dance; Drama/theater; International Student Organization; Jazz band; Literary magazine; Marching band; Model UN; Music ensembles; Musical theater; Opera; Pep band; Radio station; Student government; Student newspaper; Student-run film society; Symphony orchestra; Television station. 363 registered organizations, 14 honor societies, 47 religious organizations, 22 fraternities, 16 sororities on campus. **Athletics (Intercollegiate):** *Men:* baseball, basketball, cross-country, golf, soccer, tennis, track/field (outdoor). *Women:* basketball, cross-country, soccer, softball, tennis, track/field (outdoor), volleyball. **On-Campus Highlights:** Popp Martin Student Union. **Environmental Initiatives:** Energy and Water Conservation initiatives led by a full-time Energy Manager.

ADMISSIONS

Freshman Academic Profile: Average high school GPA 4.1. 17% in top 10% of high school class, 47% in top 25% of high school class, 86% in top 50% of high school class. 86% from public high schools. **Test Scores:** SAT Math middle 50% range 560–640. SAT EBRW middle 50% range 560–630. ACT middle 50% range 21–26. **Basis for Candidate Selection:** *Very important factors include:* rigor of secondary school record, academic GPA, standardized test scores. *Other factors include:* extracurricular activities, talent/ability, character/personal qualities, geographical residence, state residency, work experience, level of applicant's interest. **Freshman Admission Requirements:** High school diploma is required and GED is accepted. *Academic units required:* 4 English, 4 math, 3 science, 1 science labs, 2 foreign language, 1 social studies, 1 history. *Academic units recommended:* 3 foreign language. **Freshman Admission Statistics:** 17,119 applied, 67% admitted, 32% enrolled. **Transfer Admission Requirements:** High school transcript, college transcript(s), statement of good standing from prior institution(s). Minimum college GPA of 2.0 required. Lowest grade transferable C. **General Admission Information:** Application fee $60. Regular application deadline 6/1. Non-fall registration accepted.

COSTS AND FINANCIAL AID

Annual in-state tuition $3,812. Annual out-of-state tuition $17,246. Room and board $11,100. Required fees $3,232. Average book and supplies expense $1,250. **Required Forms and Deadlines:** FAFSA. **Notification of Awards:** Applicants will be notified of awards on or about 3/1. **Types of Aid:** *Need-based scholarships/grants:* College/university scholarship or grant aid from institutional funds; Federal Pell; Private scholarships; SEOG; State scholarships/grants; United Negro College Fund. *Loans:* Direct PLUS loans; Direct Subsidized Stafford Loans; Direct Unsubsidized Stafford Loans. **Student Employment:** Federal Work-Study Program available. Institutional employment available. **Financial Aid Statistics:** 75% needy freshmen, 77% needy undergrads receive need-based scholarship or grant aid. 8% freshmen, 6% undergrads receive non-need-based scholarship or grant aid. 97% freshmen, 95% undergrads receive need-based self-help aid. 2% freshmen, 2% undergrads receive athletic scholarships. 82.32% freshmen, 71.83% undergrads receive any aid. 64% undergrads borrow to pay for school. Average cumulative indebtedness $28,080. **Criteria awarding aid:** *Non-need-based:* Academics, Alumni affiliation, Art, Athletics, Job skills, Leadership, Minority status, Music/drama, Religious affiliation, State/district residency.

UNIVERSITY OF NORTH CAROLINA—GREENSBORO

P O Box 26170, Greensboro, NC 27402-6170
Phone: 336-334-5243 **Financial Aid Phone:** 336-334-5702
E-mail: admissions@uncg.edu **CEEB Code:** 5913
Fax: 336-334-4180 **Website:** www.uncg.edu **ACT Code:** 3166

This public school was founded in 1891. It has a 357 acre campus.

RATINGS

Admissions Selectivity Rating: 77   Fire Safety Rating: 99   Green Rating: 93

STUDENTS AND FACULTY

Enrollment: 16,106. **Student Body:** 67% female, 33% male, 3% out-of-state, 1% international (70 countries represented). Asian 5%, African American 30%, Caucasian 46%, Hispanic 12%, Native American <1%, Pacific Islander <1%, Two or more races 5%, Race unknown 1%.
Retention and Graduation: 75% freshmen return for sophomore year. 46% freshmen graduate within 4 years. 59% freshmen graduate within 6 years.
Faculty: Student/faculty ratio 16:1. 863 full-time faculty, 73% hold PhDs, 28% are members of minority groups, 55% are women. 8% of classes are taught by teaching assistants.

ACADEMICS

Degrees: Bachelor's; Doctoral degree—professional practice; Doctoral degree research/scholarship; Master's; Post-bachelor's certificate; Post-master's certificate. **Classes:** Most classes have 20–29 students. Most lab/discussion sessions have 20–29 students. **Most popular majors:** Biology/Biological Sciences, General; Psychology, General; Business Administration and Management, General. **Special Study Options:** Accelerated program; Cross-registration; Distance learning; Double major; Dual enrollment; English as a Second Language (ESL); Honors program; Independent study; Internships; Liberal arts/career combination; Student-designed major; Study abroad; Teacher certification program. **Honors programs:** The International Honors Program is geared towards motivated, high-achieving incoming first-year students and current UNCG students who have completed fewer than 30 hours, pursuing all majors. New first-year students take a 1-credit Honors Colloquium, which introduces them to the Honors experience and to UNCG, and a 3-credit 100-level Honors First-Year Seminar. (Current students substitute a 200-level seminar for the 100-level seminar.) In order to complete the requirements of the program, by graduation, students need to complete three additional 200-level International Honors seminars, achieve proficiency (the 204 level) of a second language, and study abroad, typically for a semester at one of UNCG's 100+ exchange partner institutions. Honors students in good standing receive a travel scholarship, currently $1,300, which helps offset the cost of plane fare. The International Honors Program is very flexible, and teaches students to think and read critically, to craft clear arguments, and to find their place in an increasingly interdependent world. Once you begin taking courses in your major field, you can enroll in the Disciplinary Honors Program. Program requirements vary by academic department, but in general, you complete special coursework in your major field of study and have the option of studying overseas. You also undertake a Senior Honors Project–typically a major research paper, project, or performance. To be eligible to enroll in this program you must have a UNCG GPA of at least 3.30. Students who successfully complete the requirements of both the International Honors Program and Disciplinary Honors Programs are awarded Full University Honors upon graduation. This award constitutes the University's highest academic honor. **Combined degree programs:** BA/MA. **Disability Services offered:** Note-taking services; Reader services; Tape recorders; Tutors. **Career services:** Alumni network; Alumni services; Career assessment; Career/job search classes; Internships.

FACILITIES

Housing: Apartments for single students; Coed dorms; Fraternity/sorority housing; Special housing for disabled students; Special housing for international students; Theme housing; Women's dorms; 95% of campus accessible to physically disabled. **Special Academic Facilities/Equipment:** Weatherspoon Art Gallery, 45,000-sq.ft. Student Center, Music Building, Sullivan Building, 216,000-sq.ft. recreation facility, recreation field, outdoor courts, track, tennis courts, golf greens, Piney Lake park, Gatewood Gallery, UNCG Auditorium, Taylor Theater.

CAMPUS LIFE

Environment: City. **Activities:** Campus Ministries; Choral groups; Concert band; Dance; Drama/theater; International Student Organization; Jazz band; Literary magazine; Music ensembles; Musical theater; Opera; Pep band; Radio station; Student government; Student newspaper; Student-run film society; Symphony orchestra. 195 registered organizations, 39 honor societies, 36 religious organizations, 39 fraternities, 36 sororities on campus. **Athletics (Intercollegiate):** *Men:* baseball, basketball, cross-country, golf, soccer, tennis, wrestling. *Women:* basketball, cross-country, golf, soccer, softball, tennis, volleyball. **On-Campus Highlights:** Kaplan Center for Wellness. **Environmental Initiatives:** Commitment to become carbon neutral by 2050.

ADMISSIONS

Freshman Academic Profile: Average high school GPA 3.7. 13% in top 10% of high school class, 39% in top 25% of high school class, 77% in top 50% of high school class. 94% from public high schools. **Test Scores:** SAT Math middle 50% range 500–570. SAT EBRW middle 50% range 500–590. ACT middle 50% range 19–24. **Basis for Candidate Selection:** *Very important factors include:* rigor of secondary school record, academic GPA. *Important factors include:* standardized test scores. *Other factors include:* class rank, application essay, recommendation(s), extracurricular activities, volunteer work. **Freshman Admission Requirements:** High school diploma is required and GED is accepted. *Academic units required:* 4 English, 4 math, 3 science, 1 science labs, 2 foreign language, 2 social studies. **Freshman Admission Statistics:** 9,972 applied, 82% admitted, 33% enrolled. **Transfer Admission Requirements:** High school transcript, college transcript(s), standardized test scores, statement of good standing from prior institution(s). Minimum college GPA of 2.0 required. Lowest grade transferable 2. **General Admission Information:** Application fee $65. Priority deadline 12/1. Regular application deadline 3/1. Non-fall registration accepted.

COSTS AND FINANCIAL AID

Room and board $9,264. **Required Forms and Deadlines:** FAFSA. **Notification of Awards:** Applicants will be notified of awards on a rolling basis beginning 3/15. **Types of Aid:** *Need-based scholarships/grants:* College/university scholarship or grant aid from institutional funds; Federal Pell; Private scholarships; SEOG; State scholarships/grants. *Loans:* Direct PLUS loans; Direct Subsidized Stafford Loans; Direct Unsubsidized Stafford Loans. **Student Employment:** Federal Work-Study Program available. Institutional employment available. **Financial Aid Statistics:** 85% needy freshmen, 80% needy undergrads receive need-based scholarship or grant aid. 13% freshmen, 16% undergrads receive non-need-based scholarship or grant aid. 74% freshmen, 76% undergrads receive need-based self-help aid. 2% freshmen, 1% undergrads receive athletic scholarships. 74% freshmen, 68% undergrads receive any aid. 71% undergrads borrow to pay for school. Average cumulative indebtedness $23,317. **Criteria awarding aid:** *Need-based:* Academics. *Non-need-based:* Academics, Athletics, Music/drama, Religious affiliation, State/district residency.

THE UNIVERSITY OF NORTH CAROLINA—PEMBROKE

One University Drive, Pembroke, NC 28372
Phone: 910-521-6262 **Financial Aid Phone:** 910-521-6255
E-mail: admissions@uncp.edu **CEEB Code:** 5534
Fax: 910-521-6497 **Website:** www.uncp.edu **ACT Code:** 3138

This public school was founded in 1887. It has a 264 acre campus.

RATINGS

Admissions Selectivity Rating: 74   Fire Safety Rating: 97   Green Rating: 60*

STUDENTS AND FACULTY

Enrollment: 5,508. **Student Body:** 60% female, 40% male, 2% out-of-state, 1% international (20 countries represented). Asian 2%, African American 36%,

Caucasian 37%, Hispanic 6%, Native American 15%, Pacific Islander <1%, Two or more races 2%, Race unknown 2%.

Retention and Graduation: 67% freshmen return for sophomore year. **Faculty:** Student/faculty ratio 16:1. 295 full-time faculty, 79% hold PhDs, 25% are members of minority groups, 51% are women. 0% of classes are taught by teaching assistants.

ACADEMICS

Degrees: Bachelor's; Master's. **Classes:** Most classes have 20–29 students. Most lab/discussion sessions have 10–19 students. **Most popular majors:** Criminal Justice/Safety Studies; Business Administration and Management, General; Sociology, General. **Special Study Options:** Accelerated program; Cross-registration; Distance learning; Double major; Dual enrollment; English as a Second Language (ESL); Exchange student program (domestic); Honors program; Independent study; Internships; Study abroad; Teacher certification program. **Honors programs:** The Esther G. Maynor Honors College began in 2001 to attract top scholars to UNCP and provide an environment that stimulates academic and personal growth. **Combined degree programs:** BA/MA. **Disability Services offered:** Note-taking services; Reader services; Tape recorders; Tutors. **Career services:** Alumni network; Alumni services; Career assessment; Career/job search classes; Internships.

FACILITIES

Housing: Apartments for single students; Coed dorms; Men's dorms; Women's dorms; 99% of campus accessible to physically disabled. **Special Academic Facilities/Equipment:** Native American Resources Center and Museum; Nursing's Clinical Learning Center. **Campus network:** 100% of classrooms, 100% of dorms, 100% of student union, 100% of libraries, 100% of dining areas, 10% of common outdoor areas have wireless network access.

CAMPUS LIFE

Environment: Rural. **Activities:** Campus Ministries; Choral groups; Concert band; Dance; Drama/theater; International Student Organization; Jazz band; Marching band; Music ensembles; Musical theater; Radio station; Student government; Student newspaper; Television station; Yearbook. 90 registered organizations, 8 honor societies, 7 religious organizations, 8 fraternities, 8 sororities on campus. **Athletics (Intercollegiate):** *Men:* baseball, basketball, cheerleading, cross-country, football, golf, soccer, track/field (outdoor), wrestling. *Women:* basketball, cheerleading, cross-country, golf, soccer, softball, tennis, track/field (outdoor), volleyball. **On-Campus Highlights:** English E. Jones Health and Physical Education Center. **Environmental Initiatives:** Planning & Construction Dept. mandates all new facilities to be LEED certified.

ADMISSIONS

Freshman Academic Profile: Average high school GPA 3.4. 11% in top 10% of high school class, 34% in top 25% of high school class, 73% in top 50% of high school class. 95% from public high schools. **Test Scores:** SAT Math middle 50% range 420–500. SAT EBRW middle 50% range 410–490. ACT middle 50% range 18–22. **Basis for Candidate Selection:** *Very important factors include:* rigor of secondary school record, academic GPA, standardized test scores. *Other factors include:* class rank, geographical residence, state residency. **Freshman Admission Requirements:** High school diploma is required and GED is accepted. *Academic units required:* 4 English, 4 math, 3 science, 1 science labs, 2 foreign language, 1 social studies, 1 history. **Freshman Admission Statistics:** 4,596 applied, 74% admitted, enrolled. **Transfer Admission Requirements:** High school transcript, college transcript(s), statement of good standing from prior institution(s). Minimum college GPA of 2.0 required. Lowest grade transferable C. **General Admission Information:** Application fee $45. Priority deadline 7/15. Regular application deadline 7/31. Non-fall registration accepted. Admission may be deferred for a maximum of 1 year.

COSTS AND FINANCIAL AID

Annual in-state tuition $3,531. Annual out-of-state tuition $14,475. Room and board $8,790. Required fees $2,285. Average book and supplies expense $1,505. **Required Forms and Deadlines:** FAFSA. **Notification of Awards:** Applicants will be notified of awards on a rolling basis beginning 4/15. **Types of Aid:** *Need-based scholarships/grants:* College/university scholarship or grant aid from institutional funds; Federal Pell; SEOG; State scholarships/grants. *Loans:* Direct PLUS loans; Direct Subsidized Stafford Loans; Direct Unsubsidized Stafford Loans. **Student Employment:** Federal Work-Study Program available. **Financial Aid Statistics:** 86% needy freshmen, 84% needy undergrads receive need-based scholarship or grant aid. 14% freshmen, 12% undergrads receive non-need-based scholarship or grant aid. 85% freshmen, 84% undergrads receive need-based self-help aid. 1% freshmen, 1% undergrads receive athletic scholarships. 79.23% freshmen, 74.56% undergrads receive any aid. 82% undergrads borrow to pay for school. Average cumulative indebtedness

$24,169. **Criteria awarding aid:** *Need-based:* Academics, Alumni affiliation, Art, Athletics, Music/drama. *Non-need-based:* Academics, Alumni affiliation, Art, Athletics, Minority status, Music/drama.

UNIVERSITY OF NORTH CAROLINA—WILMINGTON

601 South College Rd, Wilmington, NC 28403-5904
Phone: 910-962-3243 **Financial Aid Phone:** 910-962-3177
E-mail: admissions@uncw.edu **CEEB Code:** 5907
Fax: 910-962-3038 **Website:** www.uncw.edu **ACT Code:** 3174

This public school was founded in 1947. It has a 661 acre campus.

RATINGS

Admissions Selectivity Rating: 87 **Fire Safety Rating:** 97 **Green Rating:** 68

STUDENTS AND FACULTY

Enrollment: 14,076. **Student Body:** 62% female, 38% male, 11% out-of-state, 1% international (53 countries represented). Asian 2%, African American 4%, Caucasian 78%, Hispanic 7%, Native American <1%, Pacific Islander <1%, Two or more races 4%, Race unknown 3%.

Retention and Graduation: 83% freshmen return for sophomore year. 54% freshmen graduate within 4 years. 72% freshmen graduate within 6 years. 24% grads go on to further study within 1 year. **Faculty:** Student/faculty ratio 17:1. 688 full-time faculty, 83% hold PhDs, 15% are members of minority groups, 52% are women. 1% of classes are taught by teaching assistants.

ACADEMICS

Degrees: Bachelor's; Doctoral degree—professional practice; Doctoral degree research/scholarship; Master's; Post-bachelor's certificate; Post-master's certificate. **Classes:** Most classes have 20–29 students. Most lab/discussion sessions have 10–19 students. **Most popular majors:** Psychology, General; Registered Nursing/Registered Nurse; Business Administration and Management, General. **Special Study Options:** Accelerated program; Distance learning; Double major; Dual enrollment; English as a Second Language (ESL); Honors program; Independent study; Internships; Study abroad; Teacher certification program. **Honors programs:** The Honors Scholars College at UNCW offers an immediate community for motivated and creative students to discover and pursue their academic passions. The curriculum is built to develop students into well-rounded, interdisciplinary thinkers—citizen-scholars—who can examine topics from multiple perspectives and take ownership of their own questions and how to answer them. Honors Scholars cultivate a larger context around their academic major, allowing them to draw important links to other disciplines and to reach audiences beyond their academic major(s). Honors College classes are small—usually fewer than 20 students—providing personal attention with the opportunity to engage with faculty on a level similar to that enjoyed by graduate students at other universities. In their freshman and sophomore years, students take special interdisciplinary honors seminars and honors sections of general education courses. In any given semester, an honors scholar will enroll in both honors and other university classes, enhancing his or her experiences in many academic areas with a wide variety of students. Honors classes emphasize applied learning, including travel opportunities. In their junior and senior years, honors students propose and carry out an honors "capstone experience"—a scholarly project related to the student's major. This involves independent work and close interaction with a faculty sponsor. Many of these have led to publication and presentations at professional conferences. Overall, the program encourages curiosity, critical thinking, and independent work skills by offering exciting academic and cultural activities as well as the opportunity for close working and social relationships with the faculty. **Combined degree programs:** BA/MA. **Disability Services offered:** Note-taking services; Tape recorders. **Career services:** Alumni network; Alumni services; Career assessment; Internships; Regional alumni.

FACILITIES

Housing: Coed dorms; Fraternity/sorority housing; Special housing for disabled students; Theme housing; 96% of campus accessible to physically disabled. **Special Academic Facilities/Equipment:** Upperman African American Cultural Arts Center, N.C. Teachers Legacy Hall, Ev-Henwood Nature Preserve, Center for Marine Science at Myrtle Grove, Almkuist-Nixon Sports Medicine Building, Museum of World Cultures, Claude Howell Gallery, UNCW Library Archives and Special Collections.

CAMPUS LIFE

Environment: City. **Activities:** Campus Ministries; Choral groups; Concert band; Dance; Drama/theater; International Student Organization; Literary magazine; Model UN; Music ensembles; Pep band; Radio station; Student government; Student newspaper; Student-run film society; Television station. 272 registered organizations, 15 honor societies, 19 religious organizations, 15 fraternities, 14 sororities on campus. **Athletics (Intercollegiate):** *Men:* baseball, basketball, cheerleading, cross-country, diving, golf, soccer, swimming, tennis, track/field (outdoor). *Women:* basketball, cheerleading, cross-country, diving, golf, soccer, softball, swimming, tennis, track/field (outdoor), volleyball. **On-Campus Highlights:** Fisher Student Center. **Environmental Initiatives:** UNCW Campus Dining's Dub's Café is named Wilmington's first Certified Green Restaurant®.

ADMISSIONS

Freshman Academic Profile: Average high school GPA 4.2. 24% in top 10% of high school class, 60% in top 25% of high school class, 92% in top 50% of high school class. **Test Scores:** SAT Math middle 50% range 600–660. SAT EBRW middle 50% range 590–660. ACT middle 50% range 23–27. **Basis for Candidate Selection:** *Very important factors include:* rigor of secondary school record, academic GPA, application essay, standardized test scores, recommendation(s). *Important factors include:* class rank. *Other factors include:* extracurricular activities, talent/ability, character/personal qualities, first generation, alumni/ae relation, geographical residence, state residency, racial/ethnic status, volunteer work, work experience, level of applicant's interest. **Freshman Admission Requirements:** High school diploma is required and GED is accepted. *Academic units required:* 4 English, 4 math, 3 science, 1 science labs, 2 foreign language, 1 social studies, 1 history. **Freshman Admission Statistics:** 13,117 applied, 61% admitted, 27% enrolled. **Transfer Admission Requirements:** High school transcript, college transcript(s), essay or personal statement. Minimum college GPA of 2.5 required. Lowest grade transferable C. **General Admission Information:** Application fee $80. Priority deadline 11/1. Regular application deadline 2/1. Non-fall registration accepted. Admission may be deferred for a maximum of 1 year.

COSTS AND FINANCIAL AID

Annual in-state tuition $4,443. Annual out-of-state tuition $18,508. Room and board $10,686. Required fees $2,648. Average book and supplies expense $1,126. **Required Forms and Deadlines:** FAFSA; Institution's own financial aid form. **Notification of Awards:** Applicants will be notified of awards on or about 3/29. **Types of Aid:** *Need-based scholarships/grants:* College/university scholarship or grant aid from institutional funds; Federal Nursing Scholarships; Federal Pell; Private scholarships; SEOG; State scholarships/grants; United Negro College Fund. *Loans:* Direct PLUS loans; Direct Subsidized Stafford Loans; Direct Unsubsidized Stafford Loans. **Student Employment:** Federal Work-Study Program available. Institutional employment available. **Financial Aid Statistics:** 89% needy freshmen, 81% needy undergrads receive need-based scholarship or grant aid. 33% freshmen, 19% undergrads receive non-need-based scholarship or grant aid. 69% freshmen, 73% undergrads receive need-based self-help aid. 3% freshmen, 2% undergrads receive athletic scholarships. 76% freshmen, 65% undergrads receive any aid. 58% undergrads borrow to pay for school. Average cumulative indebtedness $26,315. **Criteria awarding aid:** *Need-based:* Academics, Alumni affiliation, Art, Athletics, Minority status, Music/drama. *Non-need-based:* Academics, Alumni affiliation, Art, Athletics, Leadership, Minority status, Music/drama.

UNIVERSITY OF NORTH DAKOTA

3501 University Avenue Stop 8357, Grand Forks, ND 58202
Phone: 701-777-3000 **Financial Aid Phone:** 701-777-3121
E-mail: admissions@UND.edu **CEEB Code:** 6878
Fax: 701-777-2721 **Website:** http://und.edu **ACT Code:** 3218

This public school was founded in 1883. It has a 521 acre campus.

RATINGS

Admissions Selectivity Rating: 77   **Fire Safety Rating:** 87   **Green Rating:** 83

STUDENTS AND FACULTY

Enrollment: 9,519. **Student Body:** 44% female, 56% male, 62% out-of-state, 5% international (78 countries represented). Asian 2%, African American 2%, Caucasian 80%, Hispanic 4%, Native American 1%, Pacific Islander <1%, Two or more races 5%, Race unknown 1%.

Retention and Graduation: 78% freshmen return for sophomore year. 32% freshmen graduate within 4 years. 1% freshmen graduate within 6 years. 17% grads go on to further study within 1 year. 8% grads pursue arts and sciences degrees. 1% grads pursue law degrees. 1% grads pursue business degrees. 5% grads pursue medical degrees. **Faculty:** Student/faculty ratio 21:1. 677 full-time faculty, 73% hold PhDs, 10% are members of minority groups, 44% are women.

ACADEMICS

Degrees: Bachelor's; Certificate; Doctoral degree—professional practice; Doctoral degree research/scholarship; Master's; Post-bachelor's certificate; Post-master's certificate. **Classes:** Most classes have 20–29 students. Most lab/discussion sessions have 10–19 students. **Most popular majors:** Business, Management, Marketing, And Related Support Services; Engineering; Health Professions And Related Programs. **Special Study Options:** Accelerated program; Cooperative education program; Cross-registration; Distance learning; Double major; Dual enrollment; English as a Second Language (ESL); Exchange student program (domestic); External degree program; Honors program; Independent study; Internships; Liberal arts/career combination; Student-designed major; Study abroad; Teacher certification program; Weekend college. **Honors programs:** Students may participate in the Honors Program throughout their undergraduate career. Students in any college of the University may enroll in the Honors Program. Most students graduate from the Program as "Scholars in the Honors Program" while also fulfilling a major in the Colleges, but the Honors Program also offers the option of creating an individually designed program of study through Honors. This option may result in either a B.A. or a B.S. degree earned through the College of Arts and Sciences. **Disability Services offered:** Note-taking services; Reader services; Tape recorders. **Career services:** Alumni network; Alumni services; Career assessment; Career/job search classes; Internships; Regional alumni.

FACILITIES

Housing: Apartments for married students; Apartments for single students; Coed dorms; Fraternity/sorority housing; Men's dorms; Special housing for disabled students; Theme housing; Wellness housing; Women's dorms; 99% of campus accessible to physically disabled. **Special Academic Facilities/Equipment:** Hughes Fine Arts Center, Burtness Theatre, North Dakota Museum of Art, Chester Fritz Auditorium, mining/mineral resources research institute/energy and environmental research center, remote sensing institute, aviation facilities, meteorology data center, Ralph Engelstad Arena, Center for Innovation, Research Institute for Autonomous Systems (RIAS) Human Nutrition Research Center, Biology Field Prairie & Wetland Stations, Computational Research Center.

CAMPUS LIFE

Environment: Town. **Activities:** Campus Ministries; Choral groups; Concert band; Dance; Drama/theater; International Student Organization; Jazz band; Marching band; Music ensembles; Musical theater; Pep band; Student government; Student newspaper; Symphony orchestra. 248 registered organizations, 20 honor societies, 3 religious organizations, 13 fraternities, 7 sororities on campus. **Athletics (Intercollegiate):** *Men:* baseball, basketball, cross-country, diving, football, golf, ice hockey, swimming, track/field (outdoor), track/field (indoor). *Women:* basketball, cross-country, diving, golf, ice hockey, soccer, softball, swimming, tennis, track/field (outdoor), track/field (indoor), volleyball. **On-Campus Highlights:** Ralph Engelstad Arena. **Environmental Initiatives:** Recycling.

ADMISSIONS

Freshman Academic Profile: Average high school GPA 3.5. 18% in top 10% of high school class, 43% in top 25% of high school class, 74% in top 50% of high school class. 92% from public high schools. **Test Scores:** SAT Math middle 50% range 500–630. SAT EBRW middle 50% range 480–600. ACT middle 50% range 21–27. **Basis for Candidate Selection:** *Very important factors include:* academic GPA, standardized test scores. *Important factors include:* rigor of secondary school record. *Other factors include:* recommendation(s). **Freshman Admission Requirements:** High school diploma is required and GED is accepted. *Academic units required:* 4 English, 3 math, 3 science, 2 science labs, 3 social studies. **Freshman Admission Statistics:** 4,964 applied, 81% admitted, 42% enrolled. **Transfer Admission Requirements:** College transcript(s). Minimum college GPA of 2.0 required. **General Admission Information:** Application fee $35. Priority deadline 5/1. Non-fall registration accepted. Admission may be deferred for a maximum of 1 term.

COSTS AND FINANCIAL AID

Annual in-state tuition $8,212. Annual out-of-state tuition $12,318. Room and board $9,544. Required fees $1,524. Average book and supplies expense $1,000. **Required Forms and Deadlines:** FAFSA. **Notification of Awards:**

Applicants will be notified of awards on a rolling basis beginning 2/1. **Types of Aid:** *Need-based scholarships/grants:* College/university scholarship or grant aid from institutional funds; Federal Pell; Private scholarships; SEOG; State scholarships/grants. *Loans:* Direct PLUS loans; Direct Subsidized Stafford Loans; Direct Unsubsidized Stafford Loans. **Student Employment:** Federal Work-Study Program available. Institutional employment available. **Financial Aid Statistics:** 87% needy freshmen, 76% needy undergrads receive need-based scholarship or grant aid. 10% freshmen, 6% undergrads receive non-need-based scholarship or grant aid. 79% freshmen, 80% undergrads receive need-based self-help aid. 1% freshmen, 0% undergrads receive athletic scholarships. 92% freshmen, 77% undergrads receive any aid. 69% undergrads borrow to pay for school. Average cumulative indebtedness $35,320.

UNIVERSITY OF NORTHERN COLORADO

UNC Admissions, Greeley, CO 80639
Phone: 970-351-2881 **Financial Aid Phone:** 970-351-2502
E-mail: admissions@unco.edu **CEEB Code:** 4074
Fax: 970-351-2984 **Website:** www.unco.edu **ACT Code:** 0502

This public school was founded in 1890. It has a 243 acre campus.

RATINGS

Admissions Selectivity Rating: 74 **Fire Safety Rating:** 96 **Green Rating:** 63

STUDENTS AND FACULTY

Enrollment: 8,446. **Student Body:** 67% female, 33% male, 14% out-of-state, 1% international (41 countries represented). Asian 2%, African American 4%, Caucasian 63%, Hispanic 24%, Native American <1%, Pacific Islander <1%, Two or more races 5%, Race unknown 1%.
Retention and Graduation: 72% freshmen return for sophomore year. 31% freshmen graduate within 4 years. 52% freshmen graduate within 6 years. 23% grads go on to further study within 1 year. 11% grads pursue arts and sciences degrees. 1% grads pursue law degrees. 2% grads pursue business degrees. 3% grads pursue medical degrees. **Faculty:** Student/faculty ratio 17:1. 482 full-time faculty, 85% hold PhDs, 13% are members of minority groups, 52% are women. 10% of classes are taught by teaching assistants.

ACADEMICS

Degrees: Bachelor's; Doctoral degree—professional practice; Doctoral degree research/scholarship; Master's. **Classes:** Most classes have 20–29 students. Most lab/discussion sessions have 20–29 students. **Most popular majors:** Registered Nursing/Registered Nurse; Business Administration and Management, General; Elementary Education and Teaching. **Special Study Options:** Cooperative education program; Cross-registration; Distance learning; Double major; Dual enrollment; English as a Second Language (ESL); Exchange student program (domestic); External degree program; Honors program; Independent study; Internships; Student-designed major; Study abroad; Teacher certification program. **Honors programs:** The University Honors Program, Life of the Mind, McNair Scholars Program, President's Leadership Program, Reisher Family Scholarship Program and Stryker Institute for Leadership Development each has its own eligibility requirements and distinctive program characteristics. The Schulze Endowment fosters a university-wide interest in interdisciplinary studies with various activities. Collectively, the seven programs provide a broad spectrum of academic enrichment opportunities for students on the university campus. **Combined degree programs:** BA/MA. **Disability Services offered:** Note-taking services; Reader services; Tape recorders. **Career services:** Alumni network; Alumni services; Career assessment; Internships; Regional alumni.

FACILITIES

Housing: Apartments for married students; Apartments for single students; Coed dorms; Fraternity/sorority housing; Special housing for disabled students; Special housing for international students; Theme housing; Women's dorms; 100% of campus accessible to physically disabled. **Special Academic Facilities/Equipment:** Art Galleries, UNC Cancer Rehabilitation Institute, Social Research Laboratory, Speech Language, Pathology Audiology Clinic, FETCH Lab for animal hearing, Music Library, Michener Collection. **Campus network:** 50% of classrooms, 100% of dorms, 100% of student union, 100% of libraries, 50% of dining areas, 75% of common outdoor areas have wireless network access.

CAMPUS LIFE

Environment: City. **Activities:** Campus Ministries; Choral groups; Concert band; Dance; Drama/theater; International Student Organization; Jazz band; Literary magazine; Marching band; Music ensembles; Musical theater; Opera; Student government; Student newspaper; Student-run film society; Symphony orchestra; Television station. 154 registered organizations, 34 honor societies, 14 religious organizations, 10 fraternities, 13 sororities on campus. **Athletics (Intercollegiate):** *Men:* baseball, basketball, football, golf, tennis, track/field (outdoor), wrestling. *Women:* basketball, cross-country, diving, golf, soccer, softball, swimming, tennis, track/field (outdoor), volleyball. **On-Campus Highlights:** Campus Commons and Pie Café.

ADMISSIONS

Freshman Academic Profile: Average high school GPA 3.4. 13% in top 10% of high school class, 37% in top 25% of high school class, 73% in top 50% of high school class. **Test Scores:** SAT Math middle 50% range 480–590. SAT EBRW middle 50% range 490–610. ACT middle 50% range 19–26. **Basis for Candidate Selection:** *Very important factors include:* class rank, academic GPA, standardized test scores. *Other factors include:* rigor of secondary school record, interview, extracurricular activities, talent/ability, character/personal qualities, first generation, alumni/ae relation, geographical residence, state residency, volunteer work, work experience, level of applicant's interest. **Freshman Admission Requirements:** High school diploma is required and GED is accepted. *Academic units recommended:* 4 English, 4 math, 3 science, 2 science labs, 1 foreign language, 2 social studies, 1 history, 2 academic electives. **Freshman Admission Statistics:** 9,275 applied, 91% admitted, 22% enrolled. **Transfer Admission Requirements:** College transcript(s), statement of good standing from prior institution(s). Minimum college GPA of 2.4 required. Lowest grade transferable C. **General Admission Information:** Application fee $50. Priority deadline 3/1. Regular application deadline 8/1. Non-fall registration accepted. Admission may be deferred for a maximum of 1 year.

COSTS AND FINANCIAL AID

Annual in-state tuition $7,830. Annual out-of-state tuition $19,902. Room and board $11,204. Required fees $2,358. Average book and supplies expense $1,200. **Required Forms and Deadlines:** FAFSA. **Notification of Awards:** Applicants will be notified of awards on a rolling basis beginning 1/1. **Types of Aid:** *Need-based scholarships/grants:* College/university scholarship or grant aid from institutional funds; Federal Pell; Private scholarships; SEOG; State scholarships/grants. *Loans:* Direct PLUS loans; Direct Subsidized Stafford Loans; Direct Unsubsidized Stafford Loans. **Student Employment:** Federal Work-Study Program available. Institutional employment available. **Financial Aid Statistics:** 88% needy freshmen, 79% needy undergrads receive need-based scholarship or grant aid. 91% freshmen, 74% undergrads receive non-need-based scholarship or grant aid. 93% freshmen, 93% undergrads receive need-based self-help aid. 4% freshmen, 4% undergrads receive athletic scholarships. 94% freshmen, 90% undergrads receive any aid. 62% undergrads borrow to pay for school. Average cumulative indebtedness $23,967. **Criteria awarding aid:** *Need-based:* Academics. *Non-need-based:* Academics, Athletics, Music/drama.

UNIVERSITY OF NORTHERN IOWA

1227 West 27th Street, Cedar Falls, IA 50614-0018
Phone: 319-273-2281 **Financial Aid Phone:** 319-273-2722
E-mail: admissions@uni.edu **CEEB Code:** 6307
Fax: 319-273-2885 **Website:** www.uni.edu **ACT Code:** 1322

This public school was founded in 1876. It has a 910 acre campus.

RATINGS

Admissions Selectivity Rating: 76 **Fire Safety Rating:** 89 **Green Rating:** 97

STUDENTS AND FACULTY

Enrollment: 8,796. **Student Body:** 59% female, 41% male, 6% out-of-state, 2% international (47 countries represented). Asian 1%, African American 2%, Caucasian 83%, Hispanic 4%, Native American <1%, Pacific Islander <1%, Two or more races 3%, Race unknown 4%.
Retention and Graduation: 83% freshmen return for sophomore year. 43% freshmen graduate within 4 years. 67% freshmen graduate within 6 years. 13% grads go on to further study within 1 year. 7% grads pursue arts and sciences degrees. 5% grads pursue law degrees. 1% grads pursue business degrees. 4% grads pursue medical degrees. **Faculty:** Student/faculty ratio 17:1. 515 full-time faculty, 80% hold PhDs, 18% are members of minority groups, 50% are women. 1% of classes are taught by teaching assistants.

ACADEMICS

Degrees: Bachelor's; Certificate; Doctoral degree—other; Master's; Post-master's certificate. **Classes:** Most classes have 20–29 students. Most lab/discussion sessions have 20–29 students. **Most popular majors:** Elementary Education and Teaching; Accounting; Business Administration and Management, General. **Special Study Options:** Accelerated program; Cooperative education program; Distance learning; Double major; Dual enrollment; English as a Second Language (ESL); Exchange student program (domestic); External degree program; Honors program; Independent study; Internships; Liberal arts/career combination; Student-designed major; Study abroad; Teacher certification program; Weekend college. **Honors programs:** University Honors Program—includes all 4 colleges and is open to all majors. www.uni.edu/honors. **Disability Services offered:** Note-taking services; Reader services; Tape recorders; Tutors. **Career services:** Alumni network; Alumni services; Career assessment; Career/job search classes; Internships; Regional alumni.

FACILITIES

Housing: Apartments for married students; Apartments for single students; Coed dorms; Cooperative housing; Fraternity/sorority housing; Men's dorms; Theme housing; Wellness housing; Women's dorms; 95% of campus accessible to physically disabled. **Special Academic Facilities/Equipment:** Natural history museum, art gallery, greenhouse and biological preserves, Lakeside biology lab and field lab for conservation problems, Tallgrass Prairie Center, Arctic Social and Environmental Systems (ARCSES) Research Lab, speech and hearing clinic, Small Business Development Center, Iowa Waste Reduction Center, Center for Applied Research in Metal Casting, Performing Arts Center, Center for Energy and Environmental Education, Center for Social and Behavioral Research. **Campus network:** 100% of classrooms, 100% of dorms, 100% of student union, 100% of libraries, 100% of dining areas, 30% of common outdoor areas have wireless network access.

CAMPUS LIFE

Environment: Town. **Activities:** Campus Ministries; Choral groups; Concert band; Dance; Drama/theater; International Student Organization; Jazz band; Literary magazine; Marching band; Model UN; Music ensembles; Musical theater; Opera; Pep band; Radio station; Student government; Student newspaper; Symphony orchestra; Yearbook. 260 registered organizations, 17 honor societies, 17 religious organizations, 4 fraternities, 5 sororities on campus. **Athletics (Intercollegiate):** *Men:* basketball, cross-country, football, golf, track/field (outdoor), track/field (indoor), wrestling. *Women:* basketball, cross-country, diving, golf, soccer, softball, swimming, tennis, track/field (outdoor), track/field (indoor), volleyball. **On-Campus Highlights:** Wellness Recreation Center. **Environmental Initiatives:** The University of Northern Iowa (UNI) has a long history of incorporating sustainability-related topics across the academy. In the past, this has occurred through a combination of individual and group efforts. The most recent step undertaken to strategically advance and elevate these efforts was the creation of the inaugural Provost's Fellow for Sustainability, designed to help shepherd these faculty initiatives. This past academic year, UNI named Dr. Michael Childers as the first Fellow to serve in this role. The Fellow was a vital investment by the university into the faculty's ownership of UNI Strategic Plan's call to create a vibrant and sustainable campus community. An assistant professor in the history department, Dr. Childers spent the year facilitating campus-wide sustainability initiatives within the academy and providing leadership in furthering sustainability-related curriculum. Childers began the fellowship by holding a series of one-on-one conversations with facility and staff to gather their visions of what direction UNI should take on issues of sustainability. He quickly discovered that while sustainability enjoys broad support from across campus, there was a lack of awareness and cohesion which hindered efforts in sustainability education and other initiatives. Building upon his conversations, Childers implemented a plan to bridge those communication gaps and build greater faculty leadership. After reaching out to other universities which had addressed similar issues, he worked with individuals throughout campus to establish a faculty sustainability board. Comprised of eleven faculty from nine different departments, the new board will work to expand UNI's Sustainability Certificate and provide leadership in the university's implementing a fundamental awareness of need for environmental, economic, and cultural sustainability for all UNI graduates. Childers is looking forward to his second year as sustainability fellow in working with the advisory board to further sustainability education across UNI's curriculum.

ADMISSIONS

Freshman Academic Profile: Average high school GPA 3.6. 20% in top 10% of high school class, 45% in top 25% of high school class, 84% in top 50% of high school class. 94% from public high schools. **Test Scores:** ACT middle 50% range 20–25. **Basis for Candidate Selection:** *Very important factors include:* rigor of secondary school record, class rank, academic GPA, standardized test scores. *Other factors include:* application essay, recommendation(s), interview, talent/ability, first generation. **Freshman Admission Requirements:** High school diploma is required and GED is accepted. *Academic units required:* 4 English, 3 math, 3 science, 3 social studies, 2 academic electives. *Academic units recommended:* 1 science labs, 2 foreign language. **Freshman Admission Statistics:** 4,701 applied, 79% admitted, 39% enrolled. **Transfer Admission Requirements:** College transcript(s), Lowest grade transferable D. **General Admission Information:** Application fee $40. Non-fall registration accepted. Admission may be deferred indefinitely.

COSTS AND FINANCIAL AID

Annual in-state tuition $7,666. Annual out-of-state tuition $18,207. Room and board $9,160. Required fees $1,273. Average book and supplies expense $900. **Required Forms and Deadlines:** FAFSA. **Notification of Awards:** Applicants will be notified of awards on a rolling basis beginning 1/31. **Types of Aid:** *Need-based scholarships/grants:* College/university scholarship or grant aid from institutional funds; Federal Pell; Private scholarships; SEOG; State scholarships/grants. *Loans:* Direct PLUS loans; Direct Subsidized Stafford Loans; Direct Unsubsidized Stafford Loans. **Student Employment:** Federal Work-Study Program available. Institutional employment available. **Financial Aid Statistics:** 57% needy freshmen, 58% needy undergrads receive need-based scholarship or grant aid. 71% freshmen, 53% undergrads receive non-need-based scholarship or grant aid. 65% freshmen, 66% undergrads receive need-based self-help aid. 2% freshmen, 2% undergrads receive athletic scholarships. 93% freshmen, 93% undergrads receive any aid. 68% undergrads borrow to pay for school. Average cumulative indebtedness $23,671. **Criteria awarding aid:** *Need-based:* Academics, Minority status. *Non-need-based:* Academics, Alumni affiliation, Art, Athletics, Leadership, Minority status, Music/drama, State/district residency.

UNIVERSITY OF NORTH FLORIDA

1 UNF Drive, Jacksonville, FL 32224-7699
Phone: 904-620-5555 **Financial Aid Phone:** 904-620-2698
E-mail: admissions@unf.edu **CEEB Code:** 9841
Fax: 904-620-2414 **Website:** www.unf.edu **ACT Code:** 5490

This public school was founded in 1965. It has a 1300 acre campus.

RATINGS

Admissions Selectivity Rating: 82   **Fire Safety Rating:** 80   **Green Rating:** 60*

STUDENTS AND FACULTY

Enrollment: 14,405. **Student Body:** 57% female, 43% male, 4% out-of-state, 2% international (112 countries represented). Asian 5%, African American 9%, Caucasian 64%, Hispanic 14%, Native American <1%, Pacific Islander <1%, Two or more races 5%, Race unknown <1%.
Retention and Graduation: 83% freshmen return for sophomore year. 33% freshmen graduate within 4 years. **Faculty:** Student/faculty ratio 19:1. 554 full-time faculty, 79% hold PhDs, 19% are members of minority groups, 48% are women. 0% of classes are taught by teaching assistants.

ACADEMICS

Degrees: Associate; Bachelor's; Doctoral degree—professional practice; Doctoral degree research/scholarship; Master's; Post-bachelor's certificate; Post-master's certificate. **Classes:** Most classes have 20–29 students. Most lab/discussion sessions have 20–29 students. **Most popular majors:** Registered Nursing/Registered Nurse; Psychology, General; Mass Communication/Media Studies. **Special Study Options:** Accelerated program; Cooperative education program; Distance learning; Double major; Dual enrollment; English as a Second Language (ESL); Exchange student program (domestic); Honors program; Independent study; Internships; Study abroad; Teacher certification program; Weekend college. **Honors programs:** The Honors Program at the University of North Florida offers talented students a unique approach to higher education. Averaging only 20 students, Honors seminars apply active learning in interdisciplinary settings. The goal is to build a community of learners who have the power to take their learning outside the classroom, enabling them to take what they read in their text and apply it to the outside world. In addition, Honors students are offered special funding opportunities to enable them to learn through travel, internships, and research. The Honors Program provides students with a personalized education that is usually only available at small liberal arts colleges but at the price of a state university tuition. **Disability Services offered:** Note-taking services; Reader services; Tape recorders. **Career services:** Alumni network; Alumni services; Career assessment; Career/job search classes; Internships.

FACILITIES

Housing: Apartments for single students; Coed dorms; Special housing for disabled students. **Special Academic Facilities/Equipment:** Art gallery, bird sanctuary, Fine Arts Center.

CAMPUS LIFE

Environment: Metropolis. **Activities:** Campus Ministries; Choral groups; Concert band; Drama/theater; International Student Organization; Jazz band; Literary magazine; Music ensembles; Radio station; Student government; Student newspaper; Television station. 254 registered organizations, 2 honor societies, 26 religious organizations, 14 fraternities, 12 sororities on campus. **Athletics (Intercollegiate):** *Men:* baseball, basketball, cheerleading, cross-country, golf, soccer, tennis, track/field (outdoor), track/field (indoor). *Women:* basketball, cheerleading, cross-country, diving, soccer, softball, swimming, tennis, track/field (outdoor), track/field (indoor), volleyball. **On-Campus Highlights:** Student Union. **Environmental Initiatives:** Requiring LEED Silver or comparable compliance.

ADMISSIONS

Freshman Academic Profile: Average high school GPA 3.9. 15% in top 10% of high school class, 40% in top 25% of high school class, 77% in top 50% of high school class. 83% from public high schools. **Test Scores:** SAT Math middle 50% range 530–620. SAT EBRW middle 50% range 560–640. ACT middle 50% range 20–25. **Basis for Candidate Selection:** *Very important factors include:* rigor of secondary school record, academic GPA, standardized test scores. *Other factors include:* class rank, application essay, recommendation(s), extracurricular activities, talent/ability, volunteer work, work experience, level of applicant's interest. **Freshman Admission Requirements:** High school diploma is required and GED is accepted. *Academic units required:* 4 English, 4 math, 3 science, 1 science labs, 2 foreign language, 3 social studies, 2 academic electives. **Freshman Admission Statistics:** 16,305 applied, 72% admitted, 22% enrolled. **Transfer Admission Requirements:** College transcript(s). Minimum college GPA of 2.0 required. Lowest grade transferable D. **General Admission Information:** Application fee $30. Priority deadline 11/16. Non-fall registration accepted. Admission may be deferred for a maximum of 2 semesters.

COSTS AND FINANCIAL AID

Annual in-state tuition $4,281. Annual out-of-state tuition $17,999. Room and board $9,720. Required fees $2,108. Average book and supplies expense $1,200. **Required Forms and Deadlines:** FAFSA. **Notification of Awards:** Applicants will be notified of awards on a rolling basis beginning 3/15. **Types of Aid:** *Need-based scholarships/grants:* College/university scholarship or grant aid from institutional funds; Federal Pell; Private scholarships; SEOG; State scholarships/grants. *Loans:* Direct PLUS loans; Direct Subsidized Stafford Loans; Direct Unsubsidized Stafford Loans. **Student Employment:** Federal Work-Study Program available. Institutional employment available. **Financial Aid Statistics:** 67% needy freshmen, 67% needy undergrads receive need-based scholarship or grant aid. 54% freshmen, 41% undergrads receive non-need-based scholarship or grant aid. 38% freshmen, 45% undergrads receive need-based self-help aid. 1% freshmen, 2% undergrads receive athletic scholarships. 81% freshmen, 68% undergrads receive any aid. 47% undergrads borrow to pay for school. Average cumulative indebtedness $19,388. **Criteria awarding aid:** *Need-based:* Academics. *Non-need-based:* Academics, Athletics, Leadership, Minority status, Music/drama, State/district residency.

UNIVERSITY OF NORTH GEORGIA

Office of Undergraduate Admissions, Dahlonega, GA 30503
Phone: 706-864-1800 **Financial Aid Phone:** 706-864-1412
E-mail: admissions@ung.edu **CEEB Code:** 5497
Fax: 706-864-1478 **Website:** www.ung.edu **ACT Code:** 848

This public school was founded in 1873. It has a 781 acre campus.

RATINGS

Admissions Selectivity Rating: 84   **Fire Safety Rating:** 95   **Green Rating:** 60*

STUDENTS AND FACULTY

Enrollment: 17,490. **Student Body:** 56% female, 44% male, 4% out-of-state, 1% international (94 countries represented). Asian 3%, African American 4%, Caucasian 73%, Hispanic 14%, Native American <1%, Pacific Islander <1%, Two or more races 3%, Race unknown 1%.

Retention and Graduation: 79% freshmen return for sophomore year. 29% freshmen graduate within 4 years. 55% freshmen graduate within 6 years. **Faculty:** Student/faculty ratio 20:1. 714 full-time faculty, 73% hold PhDs, 25% are members of minority groups, 51% are women. 0% of classes are taught by teaching assistants.

ACADEMICS

Degrees: Associate; Bachelor's; Certificate; Doctoral degree—professional practice; Doctoral degree research/scholarship; Master's; Post-bachelor's certificate; Post-master's certificate. **Classes:** Most classes have 20–29 students. Most lab/discussion sessions have 20–29 students. **Most popular majors:** Biology/Biological Sciences, General; Research and Experimental Psychology, Other; Business Administration, Management and Operations, Other. **Special Study Options:** Accelerated program; Cooperative education program; Distance learning; Double major; Dual enrollment; English as a Second Language (ESL); Honors program; Internships; Liberal arts/career combination; Study abroad; Teacher certification program. **Honors programs:** UNG's Honors Program provides selected students the opportunity to obtain an education designed to foster maximum intellectual growth while, at the same time, encouraging the development of the whole person. Honors Program students take courses designed to expand such capabilities as writing, speaking, quantitative reasoning, ethical reasoning, critical and creative thinking, and the ability to engage technology. The program emphasizes independent learning, teamwork, initiative, responsibility, and respect for all persons. **Disability Services offered:** Note-taking services; Reader services; Tape recorders; Tutors. **Career services:** Alumni services; Career assessment; Career/job search classes; Internships.

FACILITIES

Housing: Apartments for single students; Men's dorms; Theme housing; Women's dorms. **Special Academic Facilities/Equipment:** Planetarium; 2 Art galleries; Hall of fame; North Georgia museum.

CAMPUS LIFE

Environment: Village. **Activities:** Campus Ministries; Choral groups; Concert band; Dance; Drama/theater; International Student Organization; Jazz band; Literary magazine; Marching band; Model UN; Music ensembles; Musical theater; Radio station; Student government; Student newspaper; Student-run film society; Symphony orchestra. 278 registered organizations, 25 honor societies, 29 religious organizations, 7 fraternities, 6 sororities on campus. **Athletics (Intercollegiate):** *Men:* baseball, basketball, cross-country, football, golf, riflery, soccer, table tennis, tennis, track/field (outdoor), volleyball, water polo. *Women:* basketball, cheerleading, cross-country, golf, riflery, soccer, softball, table tennis, tennis, track/field (outdoor), volleyball, water polo. **On-Campus Highlights:** Library Technology Center.

ADMISSIONS

Freshman Academic Profile: Average high school GPA 3.6. 17% in top 10% of high school class, 48% in top 25% of high school class, 85% in top 50% of high school class. **Test Scores:** SAT Math middle 50% range 520–600. SAT EBRW middle 50% range 578–661. ACT middle 50% range 23–27. **Basis for Candidate Selection:** *Very important factors include:* rigor of secondary school record, academic GPA, standardized test scores. **Freshman Admission Requirements:** High school diploma is required and GED is accepted. *Academic units required:* 4 English, 4 math, 4 science, 2 science labs, 2 foreign language, 3 social studies. *Academic units recommended:* 4 English, 4 math, 4 science, 2 science labs, 2 foreign language, 3 social studies. **Freshman Admission Statistics:** 6,498 applied, 74% admitted, 40% enrolled. **Transfer Admission Requirements:** college transcript(s), statement of good standing from prior institution(s). Minimum college GPA of 2.0 required. Lowest grade transferable C. **General Admission Information:** Application fee $30. Regular application deadline 2/15. Non-fall registration accepted.

COSTS AND FINANCIAL AID

Annual in-state tuition $5,700. Annual out-of-state tuition $20,150. Room and board $11,510. Average book and supplies expense $1,420. **Required Forms and Deadlines:** FAFSA. **Notification of Awards:** Applicants will be notified of awards on a rolling basis beginning 4/1. **Types of Aid:** *Need-based scholarships/grants:* College/university scholarship or grant aid from institutional funds; Federal Pell; Private scholarships; SEOG; State scholarships/grants. *Loans:* Direct PLUS loans; Direct Subsidized Stafford Loans; Direct Unsubsidized Stafford Loans. **Student Employment:** Federal Work-Study Program available. Institutional employment available. **Financial Aid Statistics:** 57% needy freshmen, 57% needy undergrads receive need-based scholarship or grant aid. 57% freshmen, 64% undergrads receive non-need-based scholarship or grant aid. 81% freshmen, 82% undergrads receive need-based self-help aid. 1% freshmen, 1% undergrads receive athletic scholarships. 89% freshmen,

84% undergrads receive any aid. 50% undergrads borrow to pay for school. Average cumulative indebtedness $15,011. **Criteria awarding aid:** *Need-based:* Academics, Leadership, Religious affiliation. *Non-need-based:* Academics, Alumni affiliation, Art, Athletics, Leadership, Music/drama, State/district residency.

UNIVERSITY OF NORTH TEXAS

1155 Union Circle #311277, Denton, TX 76203-5017
Phone: 940-565-2681 **Financial Aid Phone:** 940-565-3901
E-mail: undergrad@unt.edu **CEEB Code:** 6481
Fax: 940-565-2408 **Website:** www.unt.edu **ACT Code:** 4136

This public school was founded in 1890. It has a 875 acre campus.

RATINGS
Admissions Selectivity Rating: 86   Fire Safety Rating: 93   Green Rating: 95

STUDENTS AND FACULTY
Enrollment: 29,481. **Student Body:** 52% female, 48% male, 4% out-of-state, 3% international (164 countries represented). Asian 6%, African American 13%, Caucasian 53%, Hispanic 20%, Native American 1%, Pacific Islander <1%, Two or more races 3%, Race unknown 1%.
Retention and Graduation: 76% freshmen return for sophomore year.
Faculty: Student/faculty ratio 23:1. 963 full-time faculty, 81% hold PhDs, 30% are members of minority groups, 40% are women. 11% of classes are taught by teaching assistants.

ACADEMICS
Degrees: Bachelor's; Doctoral degree—professional practice; Doctoral degree research/scholarship; Master's; Post-bachelor's certificate. **Classes:** Most classes have 20–29 students. Most lab/discussion sessions have 20–29 students. **Most popular majors:** Business/Commerce, General; Multi-/Interdisciplinary Studies, Other; Biology/Biological Sciences, General. **Special Study Options:** Distance learning; Double major; Dual enrollment; English as a Second Language (ESL); Exchange student program (domestic); Honors program; Independent study; Internships; Student-designed major; Study abroad; Teacher certification program. **Honors programs:** University of North Texas Honors College. **Combined degree programs:** BA/MA. **Disability Services offered:** Note-taking services; Reader services; Tape recorders; Tutors. **Career services:** Alumni network; Alumni services; Career assessment; Career/job search classes; Internships; Regional alumni.

FACILITIES
Housing: Apartments for single students; Coed dorms; Fraternity/sorority housing; Men's dorms; Special housing for disabled students; Special housing for international students; Theme housing; Wellness housing; Women's dorms; 90% of campus accessible to physically disabled. **Special Academic Facilities/ Equipment:** Laser, observatory, accelerators, recreational facility, music facilities, environmental sciences building, planetarium, art galleries.

CAMPUS LIFE
Environment: City. **Activities:** Campus Ministries; Choral groups; Concert band; Dance; Drama/theater; International Student Organization; Jazz band; Literary magazine; Marching band; Model UN; Music ensembles; Musical theater; Opera; Pep band; Radio station; Student government; Student newspaper; Student-run film society; Symphony orchestra; Television station. 340 registered organizations, 25 honor societies, 26 religious organizations, 24 fraternities, 18 sororities on campus. **Athletics (Intercollegiate):** *Men:* basketball, cross-country, football, golf, softball, track/field (indoor). *Women:* basketball, cross-country, diving, golf, soccer, softball, swimming, tennis, track/field (indoor), volleyball. **On-Campus Highlights:** UNT Housing. **Environmental Initiatives:** In 2011 UNT completed construction on three community sized wind turbine's located at the university's Eagle Point. The project was funded through a 2.2 million dollar grant awarded by the State Energy Conservation Office. Since their completion, the wind turbines have generated 284,182 kWh of energy.

ADMISSIONS
Freshman Academic Profile: 20% in top 10% of high school class, 52% in top 25% of high school class, 90% in top 50% of high school class. 95% from public high schools. **Test Scores:** SAT Math middle 50% range 510–610. SAT

EBRW middle 50% range 490–600. ACT middle 50% range 20–26. **Basis for Candidate Selection:** *Very important factors include:* rigor of secondary school record, class rank, academic GPA, standardized test scores. *Important factors include:* application essay, recommendation(s). *Other factors include:* extracurricular activities, talent/ability, character/personal qualities, first generation, geographical residence, volunteer work, work experience, level of applicant's interest. **Freshman Admission Requirements:** High school diploma is required and GED is accepted. *Academic units required:* 4 English, 4 math, 4 science, 4 science labs, 2 foreign language, 2 social studies, 2 history, 3.5 academic electives, 1 computer science, 1 visual/performing arts. **Freshman Admission Statistics:** 16,326 applied, 61% admitted, 44% enrolled. **Transfer Admission Requirements:** College transcript(s), statement of good standing from prior institution(s). Minimum college GPA of 2.5 required. Lowest grade transferable D. **General Admission Information:** Application fee $60. Priority deadline 3/1. Regular application deadline 8/1. Non-fall registration accepted.

COSTS AND FINANCIAL AID
Annual in-state tuition $6,834. Annual out-of-state tuition $17,364. Room and board $7,356. Required fees $2,590. Average book and supplies expense $1,000. **Required Forms and Deadlines:** FAFSA. **Notification of Awards:** Applicants will be notified of awards on a rolling basis beginning 4/1. **Types of Aid:** *Need-based scholarships/grants:* College/university scholarship or grant aid from institutional funds; Federal Pell; Private scholarships; SEOG; State scholarships/grants. *Loans:* Direct PLUS loans; Direct Subsidized Stafford Loans; Direct Unsubsidized Stafford Loans. **Student Employment:** Federal Work-Study Program available. Institutional employment available. **Financial Aid Statistics:** 82% needy freshmen, 74% needy undergrads receive need-based scholarship or grant aid. 49% freshmen, 26% undergrads receive non-need-based scholarship or grant aid. 78% freshmen, 81% undergrads receive need-based self-help aid. 0% freshmen, 1% undergrads receive athletic scholarships. 88% freshmen, 71% undergrads receive any aid.

UNIVERSITY OF NOTRE DAME

220 Main Building, Notre Dame, IN 46556
Phone: 574-631-7505 **Financial Aid Phone:** 574-631-6436
E-mail: admissions@nd.edu **CEEB Code:** 1841
Fax: 574-631-8865 **Website:** www.nd.edu **ACT Code:** 1252

This private school, affiliated with the Roman Catholic Church, was founded in 1842. It has a 1250 acre campus.

RATINGS
Admissions Selectivity Rating: 98   Fire Safety Rating: 98   Green Rating: 92

STUDENTS AND FACULTY
Enrollment: 8,568. **Student Body:** 48% female, 52% male, 92% out-of-state, 6% international (68 countries represented). Asian 5%, African American 4%, Caucasian 68%, Hispanic 11%, Native American <1%, Pacific Islander <1%, Two or more races 5%, Race unknown 1%.
Retention and Graduation: 98% freshmen return for sophomore year. 92% freshmen graduate within 4 years. 95% freshmen graduate within 6 years. 22% grads go on to further study within 1 year. **Faculty:** Student/faculty ratio 10:1. 1,216 full-time faculty, 91% hold PhDs, 20% are members of minority groups, 32% are women. 9% of classes are taught by teaching assistants.

ACADEMICS
Degrees: Bachelor's; Doctoral degree—professional practice; Doctoral degree research/scholarship; Master's. **Classes:** Most classes have 10–19 students. **Most popular majors:** Psychology, General; Political Science and Government, General; Finance, General. **Special Study Options:** Cross-registration; Double major; Exchange student program (domestic); Honors program; Independent study; Internships; Liberal arts/career combination; Student-designed major; Study abroad. **Disability Services offered:** Note-taking services; Reader services; Tape recorders; Tutors. **Career services:** Alumni network; Alumni services; Career assessment; Career/job search classes; Internships.

FACILITIES
Housing: Apartments for married students; Men's dorms; Women's dorms; 95% of campus accessible to physically disabled. **Special Academic Facilities/**

Equipment: Snite Museum of Art; DeBartolo Performing Arts Center; Stinson-Remick engineering clean room; LOBUND Laboratory for germ-free research; Radiation Laboratory. **Campus network:** 100% of classrooms, 50% of dorms, 100% of student union, 100% of libraries, 100% of dining areas, 100% of common outdoor areas have wireless network access.

CAMPUS LIFE

Environment: City. **Activities:** Campus Ministries; Choral groups; Concert band; Dance; Drama/theater; International Student Organization; Jazz band; Literary magazine; Marching band; Model UN; Music ensembles; Musical theater; Opera; Pep band; Radio station; Student government; Student newspaper; Student-run film society; Symphony orchestra; Television station; Yearbook. 440 registered organizations, 10 honor societies, 9 religious organizations on campus. **Athletics (Intercollegiate):** *Men:* baseball, basketball, cross-country, diving, fencing, football, golf, ice hockey, lacrosse, soccer, swimming, tennis, track/field (outdoor). *Women:* basketball, crew/rowing, cross-country, diving, fencing, golf, lacrosse, soccer, softball, swimming, tennis, track/field (outdoor), volleyball. **On-Campus Highlights:** Grotto. **Environmental Initiatives:** Expansion of Office of Sustainability to include 3 full time staff and 7 interns; development of metrics and quantitative goals in 7 key sustainability areas.

ADMISSIONS

Freshman Academic Profile: 89% in top 10% of high school class, 98% in top 25% of high school class, 100% in top 50% of high school class. 42% from public high schools. **Test Scores:** SAT Math middle 50% range 710–790. SAT EBRW middle 50% range 690–760. ACT middle 50% range 33–35. **Basis for Candidate Selection:** *Very important factors include:* rigor of secondary school record. *Important factors include:* class rank, academic GPA, application essay, standardized test scores, recommendation(s), extracurricular activities, talent/ability, character/personal qualities, alumni/ae relation, volunteer work. *Other factors include:* first generation, religious affiliation/commitment, racial/ethnic status, work experience, level of applicant's interest. **Freshman Admission Requirements:** High school diploma is required and GED is accepted. *Academic units required:* 4 English, 3 math, 2 science, 2 science labs, 2 foreign language, 2 history, 3 academic electives. *Academic units recommended:* 4 English, 4 math, 4 science, 2 science labs, 4 foreign language, 4 history. **Freshman Admission Statistics:** 20,371 applied, 18% admitted, 57% enrolled. **Transfer Admission Requirements:** High school transcript, college transcript(s), essay or personal statement, standardized test scores, statement of good standing from prior institution(s). Minimum college GPA of 3.0 required. Lowest grade transferable C. **General Admission Information:** Application fee $75. Regular application deadline 1/1. Non-fall registration accepted. Admission may be deferred for a maximum of 12 months.

COSTS AND FINANCIAL AID

Annual tuition $55,046. Room and board $15,640. Required fees $507. Average book and supplies expense $1,050. **Required Forms and Deadlines:** CSS/Financial Aid PROFILE; FAFSA; Noncustodial PROFILE. **Notification of Awards:** Applicants will be notified of awards on a rolling basis beginning 2/15. **Types of Aid:** *Need-based scholarships/grants:* College/university scholarship or grant aid from institutional funds; Federal Pell; Private scholarships; SEOG; State scholarships/grants. *Loans:* Direct PLUS loans; Direct Subsidized Stafford Loans; Direct Unsubsidized Stafford Loans. **Student Employment:** Federal Work-Study Program available. Institutional employment available. **Financial Aid Statistics:** 96% needy freshmen, 97% needy undergrads receive need-based scholarship or grant aid. 30% freshmen, 28% undergrads receive non-need-based scholarship or grant aid. 86% freshmen, 87% undergrads receive need-based self-help aid. 5% freshmen, 5% undergrads receive athletic scholarships. 63% freshmen, 75% undergrads receive any aid. 42% undergrads borrow to pay for school. Average cumulative indebtedness $27,686. **Criteria awarding aid:** *Need-based:* Academics. *Non-need-based:* Academics, Athletics.

UNIVERSITY OF OKLAHOMA

1000 Asp Aveune, Norman, OK 73019
Phone: 405-325-2251 **Financial Aid Phone:** (405) 325-5505
E-mail: admissions@ou.edu **CEEB Code:** 6879
Fax: 405-325-7124 **Website:** www.ou.edu **ACT Code:** 3442

This public school was founded in 1890. It has a 4138.39 acre campus.

RATINGS

Admissions Selectivity Rating: 81   **Fire Safety Rating:** 97   **Green Rating:** 93

STUDENTS AND FACULTY

Enrollment: 22,143. **Student Body:** 52% female, 48% male, 34% out-of-state, 3% international (119 countries represented). Asian 7%, African American 4%, Caucasian 61%, Hispanic 11%, Native American 4%, Pacific Islander <1%, Two or more races 9%, Race unknown 2%.
Retention and Graduation: 88% freshmen return for sophomore year. 44% freshmen graduate within 4 years. 70% freshmen graduate within 6 years. **Faculty:** Student/faculty ratio 17:1. 1,537 full-time faculty, 83% hold PhDs, 23% are members of minority groups, 44% are women. 12% of classes are taught by teaching assistants.

ACADEMICS

Degrees: Bachelor's; Doctoral degree—professional practice; Doctoral degree research/scholarship; Master's; Post-bachelor's certificate; Post-master's certificate. **Classes:** Most classes have 10–19 students. Most lab/discussion sessions have 20–29 students. **Most popular majors:** Zoology/Animal Biology; Registered Nursing/Registered Nurse; Psychology, General. **Special Study Options:** Accelerated program; Cooperative education program; Distance learning; Double major; Dual enrollment; English as a Second Language (ESL); External degree program; Honors program; Independent study; Internships; Liberal arts/career combination; Student-designed major; Study abroad; Teacher certification program; Weekend college. **Honors programs:** Honors at Oxford: This summer program enables students to study at Oxford (while living at Brasenose College). While there, students work in private tutorials with distinguished Oxford dons. Students can earn up to 6 hours of honors credit in one of our four classes that are offered. Honors in Germany: Honors student travel to Leipzig, Germany in June, live at the University of Leipzig, study German, and take a course on German-American literary relations. Students also focus on experiencing and exploring major sites for the history and memory of WWII in Germany by taking day trips from Leipzig to major WWII-related sites and Germany. Students earn up to six hours of Honors credit. Honors Undergraduate Research Assistant Program: Honors Undergraduate Research Assistant Program provides undergraduates the opportunity to work with professors as research assistants on specific projects. Student assistants are expected to work 10 hours a week for 10 weeks for $6 an hour. Honors College students with at least 15 hours of college credit and a 3.4+ GPA are eligible to apply. Medical Humanities Scholars Program: The Honors College and the University of Oklahoma College of Medicine have created a special pathway (through a bachelor of arts degree leading to a medical doctorate) for up to five high school students each year who wish to study the humanistic aspects of medicine as undergraduates. Through a special admissions process, the Medical Humanities Scholars are accepted at the medical school as part of their application to OU's undergraduate honors program. The Honors College has also created a Medical Humanities Minor open to all honors students wishing to study medicine from the perspectives of history, sociology, anthropology, bioethics, literature, and economics. **Combined degree programs:** BA/MA; BA/MEng. **Disability Services offered:** Note-taking services; Reader services; Tutors. **Career services:** Alumni services; Career assessment; Career/job search classes; Internships; Regional alumni.

FACILITIES

Housing: Apartments for married students; Apartments for single students; Coed dorms; Fraternity/sorority housing; Men's dorms; Special housing for disabled students; Special housing for international students; Women's dorms; 95% of campus accessible to physically disabled. **Special Academic Facilities/Equipment:** Norman Campus National Weather Center Radar Innovations Laboratory; Lin Hall (home of the Center for Quantum Research and Technology); Gallogly Hall (home of Stephenson School of Biomedical Engineering); Sarkeys Energy Center (home of the Mewbourne College of

Earth and Energy); Stephenson Life Sciences Center; Stephenson Research and Technology Center; Gould Hall (home of the Christopher C. Gibbs College of Architecture and The American School); Fred Jones Jr. Museum of Art; Sam Noble Museum of Natural History; Donald W. Reynolds Performing Arts Center; Bizzell Memorial Library; Gaylord Family—Oklahoma Memorial Stadium; Tulsa OU Physicians Schusterman Center; Clinic Founders Student Center; Tandy Education Center (Simulation Center); Schusterman Center Library (digital information gallery); Telecommunications Interoperability Lab; Stanton L. Young Walk (although not a building it is nice place of interest); University Health Club (basketball, weight lifting, swimming, racquetball, etc.); Health Sciences Center; Stephenson Cancer Center; Harold Hamm Diabetes Center; Robert M. Bird Health Sciences Library; Stanton L. Young Biomedical Research Center; Dean A. McGee Eyes Institute; OU Medical Center; OU Children's Hospital; Andrews Academic Tower (administrative home of the departments of medicine, surgery, obstetrics and gynecology, orthopedic surgery and rehabilitation, and otolaryngology-head and neck surgery); The Clinical Skills Education and Testing Center; Biomedical Sciences Education Building; OU Medical Center; Adult Patient Tower, Norman campus.

CAMPUS LIFE

Environment: City. **Activities:** Campus Ministries; Choral groups; Concert band; Dance; Drama/theater; International Student Organization; Literary magazine; Marching band; Model UN; Music ensembles; Musical theater; Opera; Pep band; Radio station; Student government; Student newspaper; Student-run film society; Symphony orchestra; Television station; Yearbook. 437 registered organizations, 9 honor societies, 36 religious organizations, 29 fraternities, 26 sororities on campus. **Athletics (Intercollegiate):** Men: baseball, basketball, cross-country, football, golf, gymnastics, tennis, track/field (outdoor), track/field (indoor), wrestling. Women: basketball, crew/rowing, cross-country, golf, gymnastics, soccer, softball, tennis, track/field (outdoor), track/field (indoor), volleyball. **On-Campus Highlights:** Fred Jones Jr. Museum of Art. **Environmental Initiatives:** 1. Wind Power Commitment—On September 10, 2008, the University signed an agreement with Oklahoma Gas & Electric Company (OG&E) to acquire 100% of our purchased electricity from renewable energy sources by 2013. This project was instrumental in enabling OG&E to build the OU Spirit Wind Farm—along with the required transmission lines to the grid—in northwestern Oklahoma. The 101 megawatt "OU Spirit" wind farm features 44 2.3 MW turbines. Since entering our power purchase program with OG&E, the University has purchased over one billion kwh of renewable energy. Compared to regular electric service, choosing to purchase 100% renewable energy has the greenhouse gas benefit equivalent of more than 700,000 metric tons.

ADMISSIONS

Freshman Academic Profile: Average high school GPA 3.6. 33% in top 10% of high school class, 61% in top 25% of high school class, 89% in top 50% of high school class. **Test Scores:** SAT Math middle 50% range 550–660. SAT EBRW middle 50% range 560–650. ACT middle 50% range 23–29. **Basis for Candidate Selection:** Very important factors include: rigor of secondary school record, class rank, academic GPA, standardized test scores. Important factors include: application essay, recommendation(s). Other factors include: interview, extracurricular activities, talent/ability, character/personal qualities, alumni/ ae relation, volunteer work, work experience, level of applicant's interest. **Freshman Admission Requirements:** High school diploma is required and GED is accepted. Academic units required: 4 English, 3 math, 3 science, 3 science labs, 1 social studies, 2 history, 2 academic electives. Academic units recommended: 4 math, 4 science, 2 foreign language, 1 computer science. **Freshman Admission Statistics:** 15,673 applied, 80% admitted, 36% enrolled. **Transfer Admission Requirements:** College transcript(s). Lowest grade transferable D. **General Admission Information:** Application fee $40. Priority deadline 12/15. Regular application deadline 2/1. Non-fall registration accepted. Admission may be deferred for a maximum of one academic year, must make a formal request of update prior to the new term's deadline.

COSTS AND FINANCIAL AID

Annual in-state tuition $4,788. Annual out-of-state tuition $20,169. Room and board $10,994. Required fees $6,975. Average book and supplies expense $667. **Required Forms and Deadlines:** FAFSA. **Notification of Awards:** Applicants will be notified of awards on a rolling basis beginning 3/15. **Types of Aid:** Need-based scholarships/grants: College/university scholarship or grant aid from institutional funds; Federal Pell; Private scholarships; SEOG; State scholarships/grants; United Negro College Fund. Loans: Direct PLUS loans; Direct Subsidized Stafford Loans; Direct Unsubsidized Stafford Loans. **Student Employment:** Federal Work-Study Program available. Institutional employment available. **Financial Aid Statistics:** 50% needy freshmen, 57% needy undergrads receive need-based scholarship or grant aid. 58% freshmen,

51% undergrads receive non-need-based scholarship or grant aid. 64% freshmen, 67% undergrads receive need-based self-help aid. 1% freshmen, 1% undergrads receive athletic scholarships. 88% freshmen, 81% undergrads receive any aid. 43% undergrads borrow to pay for school. Average cumulative indebtedness $30,258. **Criteria awarding aid:** Need-based: Academics. Non-need-based: Academics, Alumni affiliation, Art, Athletics, Leadership, Music/drama, Religious affiliation.

UNIVERSITY OF OREGON

1217 University of Oregon, Eugene, OR 97403-1217
Phone: 541-346-3201 **Financial Aid Phone:** 541-346-3221
E-mail: uoadmit@uoregon.edu **CEEB Code:** 4846
Fax: 541-346-5815 **Website:** www.uoregon.edu **ACT Code:** 3498

This public school was founded in 1876. It has a 295 acre campus.

RATINGS
Admissions Selectivity Rating: 80 **Fire Safety Rating:** 93 **Green Rating:** 96

STUDENTS AND FACULTY
Enrollment: 18,743. **Student Body:** 54% female, 46% male, 43% out-of-state, 7% international (74 countries represented). Asian 6%, African American 2%, Caucasian 59%, Hispanic 14%, Native American 1%, Pacific Islander <1%, Two or more races 8%, Race unknown 2%.
Retention and Graduation: 86% freshmen return for sophomore year. 56% freshmen graduate within 4 years. 74% freshmen graduate within 6 years.
Faculty: Student/faculty ratio 16:1. 1,215 full-time faculty, 95% hold PhDs, 16% are members of minority groups, 46% are women. 14% of classes are taught by teaching assistants.

ACADEMICS
Degrees: Bachelor's; Doctoral degree—professional practice; Doctoral degree research/scholarship; Master's; Post-bachelor's certificate; Post-master's certificate. **Classes:** Most classes have 10–19 students. Most lab/discussion sessions have 20–29 students. **Most popular majors:** Business/Commerce, General; Social Sciences, General; Economics, General. **Special Study Options:** Distance learning; Double major; Dual enrollment; English as a Second Language (ESL); Exchange student program (domestic); Honors program; Independent study; Internships; Liberal arts/career combination; Student-designed major; Study abroad; Teacher certification program. **Honors programs:** Robert D. Clark Honors College, Professional Distinctions program, Dean's List, Junior Scholars, and 21 honor societies based on scholarship, leadership, and service. **Disability Services offered:** Note-taking services; Reader services; Tape recorders; Tutors. **Career services:** Alumni network; Alumni services; Career assessment; Career/job search classes; Internships; Regional alumni.

FACILITIES
Housing: Apartments for married students; Apartments for single students; Coed dorms; Cooperative housing; Fraternity/sorority housing; Theme housing; Wellness housing; 98% of campus accessible to physically disabled. **Special Academic Facilities/Equipment:** Jordan Schnitzer Museum of Art; Museum of Natural and Cultural History; James Warsaw Sports Marketing Center; Lundquist Center for Entrepreneurship; University of Oregon Many Nations Longhouse; Green Chemistry Laboratory and Alice C. Tyler Instrumentation Center; Future Music Oregon, a computer music center in the School of Music; Pine Mountain Observatory (Bend, Oregon); Oregon Institute of Marine Biology (Oregon Coast); Central Oregon programs affiliated with the Oregon University System Cascades Campus (Bend, Oregon); Urban Architecture program and BetterBricks Daylighting Laboratory at the University of Oregon Portland Center (Portland, Oregon).

CAMPUS LIFE
Environment: City. **Activities:** Campus Ministries; Choral groups; Concert band; Dance; Drama/theater; International Student Organization; Jazz band; Literary magazine; Marching band; Music ensembles; Musical theater; Opera; Pep band; Radio station; Student government; Student newspaper; Student-run film society; Symphony orchestra; Television station. 250 registered organizations, 21 honor societies, 19 fraternities, 18 sororities on campus.

Athletics (Intercollegiate): *Men:* baseball, basketball, cross-country, football, golf, tennis, track/field (outdoor). *Women:* basketball, cross-country, golf, gymnastics, lacrosse, soccer, softball, tennis, track/field (outdoor), volleyball. **On-Campus Highlights:** University of Oregon Duck Store. **Environmental Initiatives:** Created the Oregon Model for Sustainable Development which puts a cap on building energy consumption.

ADMISSIONS

Freshman Academic Profile: Average high school GPA 3.7. 26% in top 10% of high school class, 57% in top 25% of high school class, 86% in top 50% of high school class. **Test Scores:** SAT Math middle 50% range 540–650. SAT EBRW middle 50% range 560–660. ACT middle 50% range 22–28. **Basis for Candidate Selection:** *Very important factors include:* rigor of secondary school record, academic GPA. *Important factors include:* application essay, standardized test scores. *Other factors include:* class rank, recommendation(s), extracurricular activities, talent/ability, character/personal qualities, first generation, geographical residence, state residency, racial/ethnic status, volunteer work, work experience. **Freshman Admission Requirements:** High school diploma is required and GED is accepted. *Academic units required:* 4 English, 3 math, 3 science, 2 foreign language, 3 social studies. *Academic units recommended:* 1 science labs, 1 visual/performing arts. **Freshman Admission Statistics:** 27,358 applied, 82% admitted, 20% enrolled. **Transfer Admission Requirements:** College transcript(s). Minimum college GPA of 2.25 required. Lowest grade transferable D-. **General Admission Information:** Application fee $65. Regular application deadline 1/15. Non-fall registration accepted. Admission may be deferred for a maximum of 1 year.

COSTS AND FINANCIAL AID

Annual in-state tuition $10,440. Annual out-of-state tuition $34,335. Room and board $13,482. Required fees $2,280. Average book and supplies expense $1,178. **Required Forms and Deadlines:** FAFSA. **Notification of Awards:** Applicants will be notified of awards on a rolling basis beginning 4/15. **Types of Aid:** *Need-based scholarships/grants:* College/university scholarship or grant aid from institutional funds; Federal Pell; Private scholarships; SEOG; State scholarships/grants. *Loans:* Direct PLUS loans; Direct Subsidized Stafford Loans; Direct Unsubsidized Stafford Loans. **Student Employment:** Federal Work-Study Program available. Institutional employment available. **Financial Aid Statistics:** 75% needy freshmen, 72% needy undergrads receive need-based scholarship or grant aid. 4% freshmen, 4% undergrads receive non-need-based scholarship or grant aid. 62% freshmen, 66% undergrads receive need-based self-help aid. 2% freshmen, 2% undergrads receive athletic scholarships. 69% freshmen, 65% undergrads receive any aid. 44% undergrads borrow to pay for school. Average cumulative indebtedness $26,548. **Criteria awarding aid:** *Need-based:* Academics, Athletics, Leadership, Minority status, Music/drama. *Non-need-based:* Academics, Athletics, Leadership, Minority status, Music/drama, State/district residency.

UNIVERSITY OF PENNSYLVANIA

1 College Hall, Philadelphia, PA 19104
Phone: 215-898-7507 **Financial Aid Phone:** 215-898-1988
E-mail: info@admissions.upenn.edu **CEEB Code:** 2926
Fax: 215-898-7507 **Website:** www.upenn.edu **ACT Code:** 3732

This private school was founded in 1740. It has a 279 acre campus.

RATINGS

Admissions Selectivity Rating: 99   Fire Safety Rating: 84   Green Rating: 94

STUDENTS AND FACULTY

Enrollment: 10,019. **Student Body:** 52% female, 48% male, 81% out-of-state, 13% international (126 countries represented). Asian 22%, African American 8%, Caucasian 39%, Hispanic 10%, Native American <1%, Pacific Islander <1%, Two or more races 5%, Race unknown 2%.
Retention and Graduation: 98% freshmen return for sophomore year. 86% freshmen graduate within 4 years. 96% freshmen graduate within 6 years. 20% grads go on to further study within 1 year. 5% grads pursue arts and sciences degrees. 4% grads pursue law degrees. 1% grads pursue business degrees. 5% grads pursue medical degrees. **Faculty:** Student/faculty ratio 6:1. 1,570 full-time faculty, 100% hold PhDs, 22% are members of minority groups, 41% are women. 5% of classes are taught by teaching assistants.

ACADEMICS

Degrees: Associate; Bachelor's; Certificate; Doctoral degree—other; Doctoral degree—professional practice; Doctoral degree research/scholarship; Master's; Post-bachelor's certificate; Post-master's certificate; Terminal Associate. **Classes:** Most classes have 10–19 students. **Most popular majors:** Economics, General; Registered Nursing/Registered Nurse; Finance, General. **Special Study Options:** Accelerated program; Cross-registration; Distance learning; Double major; Dual enrollment; English as a Second Language (ESL); Exchange student program (domestic); Honors program; Independent study; Internships; Liberal arts/career combination; Student-designed major; Study abroad; Teacher certification program. **Honors programs:** Penn's general honors program is called the Benjamin Franklin Scholars program, although the honors program for students in business is called Joseph Wharton Scholars. There are specialized honors programs including Fisher Program in Management and Technology, the Huntsman Program in International Studies and Business, the Vagelos Scholars Program in Molecular Life Sciences, and the Civic Scholars Program which offers opportunities to integrate community service and academics. The University Scholars Program is open to already matriculated students who are interested in engaging in high-level research. **Combined degree programs:** BA/DDS; BA/JD; BA/MA; BA/MEng. **Disability Services offered:** Note-taking services; Reader services; Tape recorders; Tutors. **Career services:** Alumni network; Alumni services; Career assessment; Internships; Regional alumni.

FACILITIES

Housing: Apartments for married students; Apartments for single students; Coed dorms; Fraternity/sorority housing; Special housing for disabled students; Theme housing; Wellness housing; 92% of campus accessible to physically disabled. **Special Academic Facilities/Equipment:** Art gallery, anthropology museum, institute for contemporary art, language lab, large animal research center, primate research center, arboretum, observatory, wind tunnel, electron microscope.

CAMPUS LIFE

Environment: Metropolis. **Activities:** Campus Ministries; Choral groups; Concert band; Dance; Drama/theater; International Student Organization; Jazz band; Literary magazine; Marching band; Model UN; Music ensembles; Musical theater; Opera; Pep band; Radio station; Student government; Student newspaper; Student-run film society; Symphony orchestra; Television station; Yearbook. 350 registered organizations, 9 honor societies, 18 religious organizations, 36 fraternities, 13 sororities on campus. **Athletics (Intercollegiate):** *Men:* baseball, basketball, crew/rowing, cross-country, diving, fencing, football, golf, lacrosse, light weight football, soccer, squash, swimming, tennis, track/field (outdoor), track/field (indoor), wrestling. *Women:* basketball, crew/rowing, cross-country, diving, fencing, field hockey, golf, gymnastics, lacrosse, soccer, softball, squash, swimming, tennis, track/field (outdoor), track/field (indoor), volleyball. **On-Campus Highlights:** University of Pennsylvania Museum. **Environmental Initiatives:** Building optimization implementation, a program to optimize building systems in high-energy-use buildings to reduce their utility use and carbon footprint. This effort is enhanced by Penn's comprehensive building metering program.

ADMISSIONS

Freshman Academic Profile: Average high school GPA 3.9. 96% in top 10% of high school class, 98% in top 25% of high school class, 100% in top 50% of high school class. 60% from public high schools. **Test Scores:** SAT Math middle 50% range 750–800. SAT EBRW middle 50% range 700–760. ACT middle 50% range 33–35. **Basis for Candidate Selection:** *Very important factors include:* rigor of secondary school record, academic GPA, application essay, standardized test scores, recommendation(s), character/personal qualities. *Important factors include:* class rank, interview, extracurricular activities, talent/ability. *Other factors include:* first generation, alumni/ae relation, geographical residence, state residency, racial/ethnic status, volunteer work, work experience, level of applicant's interest. **Freshman Admission Requirements:** High school diploma or equivalent is not required. *Academic units recommended:* 4 English, 4 math, 3 science, 3 science labs, 4 foreign language, 2 social studies, 3 history. **Freshman Admission Statistics:** 44,961 applied, 8% admitted, 70% enrolled. **Transfer Admission Requirements:** High school transcript, college transcript(s), essay or personal statement, standardized test scores, statement of good standing from prior institution(s). Lowest grade transferable C. **General Admission Information:** Application fee $75. Regular application deadline 1/5. Admission may be deferred for a maximum of 1 year.

COSTS AND FINANCIAL AID
Annual tuition $51,156. Room and board $16,190. Required fees $6,614. Average book and supplies expense $1,358. **Required Forms and Deadlines:** Business/Farm Supplement; CSS/Financial Aid PROFILE; FAFSA; Institution's own financial aid form; Noncustodial PROFILE. **Notification of Awards:** Applicants will be notified of awards on or about 4/1. **Types of Aid:** *Need-based scholarships/grants:* College/university scholarship or grant aid from institutional funds; Federal Pell; Private scholarships; SEOG; State scholarships/grants. *Loans:* Direct PLUS loans; Direct Subsidized Stafford Loans; Direct Unsubsidized Stafford Loans. **Student Employment:** Federal Work-Study Program available. Institutional employment available. **Financial Aid Statistics:** 99% needy freshmen, 99% needy undergrads receive need-based scholarship or grant aid. 100% freshmen, 100% undergrads receive non-need-based scholarship or grant aid. 100% freshmen, 100% undergrads receive need-based self-help aid. 0% freshmen, 0% undergrads receive athletic scholarships. 47% freshmen, 45% undergrads receive any aid. 22% undergrads borrow to pay for school. Average cumulative indebtedness $23,009.

UNIVERSITY OF PHOENIX

4035 S. Riverpoint Parkway, Phoenix, AZ 85040
Phone: 480-446-4600 **Financial Aid Phone:** 1-800-921-1904
Website: www.phoenix.edu

This proprietary school was founded in 1976.

RATINGS
Admissions Selectivity Rating: 60*   **Fire Safety Rating:** 60*   **Green Rating:** 60*

STUDENTS AND FACULTY
Enrollment: 332,377. **Student Body:** 69% female, 31% male, 3% international. Asian 2%, African American 18%, Caucasian 39%, Hispanic 9%, Native American 1%, Pacific Islander 0%, Two or more races 0%, Race unknown 28%.
Retention and Graduation: 39% freshmen return for sophomore year. **Faculty:** Student/faculty ratio 43:1. 1,410 full-time faculty, 23% hold PhDs, 19% are members of minority groups, 46% are women. 0% of classes are taught by teaching assistants.

ACADEMICS
Degrees: Associate; Bachelor's; Certificate; Master's; Post-bachelor's certificate; Post-master's certificate; Transfer Associate. **Most popular majors:** Accounting; Business Administration and Management, General; Health/Health Care Administration/Management. **Special Study Options:** Accelerated program; Distance learning; Independent study. **Disability Services offered:** Tape recorders. **Career services:** Alumni network.

FACILITIES
100% of campus accessible to physically disabled.

CAMPUS LIFE
Environment: Metropolis. 2 honor societies on campus.

ADMISSIONS
Basis for Candidate Selection: *Very important factors include:* work experience. *Other factors include:* recommendation(s). **Freshman Admission Requirements:** High school diploma is required and GED is accepted. **Transfer Admission Requirements:** College transcript(s). **General Admission Information:** Non-fall registration accepted.

UNIVERSITY OF PIKEVILLE

Admissions Office, Pikeville, KY 41501
Phone: 606-218-5251 **Financial Aid Phone:** 606-218-5247
E-mail: wewantyou@upike.edu **CEEB Code:** 1980
Fax: 606-218-5255 **Website:** http://www.upike.edu/ **ACT Code:** 1540

This private school, affiliated with the Presbyterian Church, was founded in 1889. It has a 25 acre campus.

RATINGS
Admissions Selectivity Rating: 70   **Fire Safety Rating:** 87   **Green Rating:** 60*

STUDENTS AND FACULTY
Enrollment: 1,244. **Student Body:** 51% female, 49% male, 20% out-of-state, 4% international (22 countries represented). Asian 1%, African American 12%, Caucasian 81%, Hispanic 2%, Native American <1%, Pacific Islander <1%, Two or more races 0%, Race unknown 0%.
Retention and Graduation: 58% freshmen return for sophomore year. 32% grads go on to further study within 1 year. 0% grads pursue arts and sciences degrees. 0% grads pursue law degrees. 75% grads pursue business degrees. 0% grads pursue medical degrees. **Faculty:** Student/faculty ratio 15:1. 69 full-time faculty, 59% hold PhDs, 4% are members of minority groups, 57% are women. 0% of classes are taught by teaching assistants.

ACADEMICS
Degrees: Associate; Bachelor's; Doctoral degree—professional practice; Master's; Terminal Associate. **Classes:** Most classes have 10–19 students. **Most popular majors:** Criminal Justice/Safety Studies; Business/Commerce, General; Biology, General. **Special Study Options:** Double major; Dual enrollment; English as a Second Language (ESL); Internships; Liberal arts/career combination; Student-designed major; Study abroad; Teacher certification program. **Disability Services offered:** Reader services; Tape recorders; Tutors. **Career services:** Career/job search classes.

FACILITIES
Housing: Coed dorms; Men's dorms; Theme housing; Women's dorms 97% of campus accessible to physically disabled. **Campus network:** 100% of classrooms, 100% of dorms, 100% of student union, 100% of libraries, 100% of dining areas, 100% of common outdoor areas have wireless network access.

CAMPUS LIFE
Environment: Village. **Activities:** Campus Ministries; Choral groups; Dance; Pep band; Student government; Student newspaper; Television station. 30 registered organizations, 6 honor societies, 3 religious organizations on campus. **Athletics (Intercollegiate):** *Men:* baseball, basketball, bowling, cheerleading, cross-country, football, golf, soccer, tennis. *Women:* basketball, bowling, cheerleading, cross-country, golf, soccer, softball, tennis, volleyball. **On-Campus Highlights:** Coal Building.

ADMISSIONS
Freshman Academic Profile: Average high school GPA 3.1. 14% in top 10% of high school class, 27% in top 25% of high school class, 61% in top 50% of high school class. 99% from public high schools. **Test Scores:** SAT Math middle 50% range 400–470. SAT EBRW middle 50% range 410–460. ACT middle 50% range 18–23. **Basis for Candidate Selection: Freshman Admission Requirements:** High school diploma is required and GED is accepted. *Academic units recommended:* 4 English, 3 math, 3 science, 2 social studies, 1 history. **Freshman Admission Statistics:** 2,408 applied, 100% admitted, 13% enrolled. **Transfer Admission Requirements:** High school transcript, college transcript(s), standardized test scores, statement of good standing from prior institution(s). Lowest grade transferable C. **General Admission Information:** Regular application deadline 8/15. Non-fall registration accepted.

COSTS AND FINANCIAL AID
Annual tuition $19,600. Room and board $8,376. Average book and supplies expense $2,500. **Required Forms and Deadlines:** FAFSA. **Notification of Awards:** Applicants will be notified of awards on a rolling basis beginning 2/1. **Types of Aid:** *Need-based scholarships/grants:* College/university scholarship or grant aid from institutional funds; Federal Pell; Private scholarships; SEOG; State scholarships/grants. *Loans:* Direct PLUS loans; Direct Subsidized Stafford Loans; Direct Unsubsidized Stafford Loans. **Student Employment:** Federal Work-Study Program available. **Financial Aid Statistics:** 100% needy freshmen, 100% needy undergrads receive need-based scholarship or grant aid. 58% freshmen, 48% undergrads receive non-need-based scholarship or

grant aid. 86% freshmen, 84% undergrads receive need-based self-help aid. 0% freshmen, 0% undergrads receive athletic scholarships. 100% freshmen, 97% undergrads receive any aid. 76% undergrads borrow to pay for school. Average cumulative indebtedness $27,645. **Criteria awarding aid:** *Need-based:* Academics, Alumni affiliation, Athletics, Music/drama.

UNIVERSITY OF PITTSBURGH—BRADFORD

Office of Admissions - Hanley Library, Bradford, PA 16701
Phone: 814-362-7555 **Financial Aid Phone:** 814-362-7550
E-mail: Admissions@upb.pitt.edu **CEEB Code:** 2935
Fax: 814-362-5150 **Website:** www.upb.pitt.edu **ACT Code:** 3731

This public school was founded in 1963. It has a 317 acre campus.

RATINGS

Admissions Selectivity Rating: 86 **Fire Safety Rating:** 94 **Green Rating:** 76

STUDENTS AND FACULTY

Enrollment: 1,260. **Student Body:** 56% female, 44% male, 26% out-of-state, 2% international (13 countries represented). Asian 3%, African American 13%, Caucasian 67%, Hispanic 6%, Native American 1%, Pacific Islander <1%, Two or more races 4%, Race unknown 4%.
Retention and Graduation: 69% freshmen return for sophomore year. 33% freshmen graduate within 4 years. 43% freshmen graduate within 6 years. 33% grads go on to further study within 1 year. 7% grads pursue arts and sciences degrees. 4% grads pursue law degrees. 2% grads pursue business degrees. 2% grads pursue medical degrees. **Faculty:** Student/faculty ratio 16:1. 75 full-time faculty, 68% hold PhDs, 19% are members of minority groups, 39% are women. 0% of classes are taught by teaching assistants.

ACADEMICS

Degrees: Associate; Bachelor's; Terminal Associate; Transfer Associate. **Classes:** Most classes have 10–19 students. Most lab/discussion sessions have 10–19 students. **Most popular majors:** Biology/Biological Sciences, General; Information Technology; Business/Commerce, General. **Special Study Options:** Cross-registration; Distance learning; Double major; Dual enrollment; Exchange student program (domestic); Independent study; Internships; Student-designed major; Study abroad; Teacher certification program. **Honors programs:** The University of Pittsburgh at Bradford offers the Scholars Program which is designed to create a learning community for outstanding students at Pitt-Bradford. **Disability Services offered:** Note-taking services; Reader services; Tape recorders; Tutors. **Career services:** Alumni network; Alumni services; Career assessment; Internships; Regional alumni.

FACILITIES

Housing: Apartments for single students; Coed dorms; Special housing for disabled students; 99% of campus accessible to physically disabled. **Special Academic Facilities/Equipment:** Ceramics Studio, Biodiesal Lab, Television and Radio Broadcast Labs, Marilyn Horne Museum.

CAMPUS LIFE

Environment: Village. **Activities:** Campus Ministries; Choral groups; Dance; Drama/theater; International Student Organization; Literary magazine; Music ensembles; Pep band; Radio station; Student government; Student newspaper. 60 registered organizations, 7 honor societies, 1 religious organization, 4 fraternities, 2 sororities on campus. **Athletics (Intercollegiate):** *Men:* baseball, basketball, cross-country, golf, soccer, swimming, tennis. *Women:* basketball, cross-country, golf, soccer, softball, swimming, tennis, volleyball. **On-Campus Highlights:** Sport and Fitness Center. **Environmental Initiatives:** Installation of a 2.6 kW solar array to power a sustainability information center in the student commons which connects to energy monitors that were installed on every building on campus.

ADMISSIONS

Freshman Academic Profile: Average high school GPA 3.3. 10% in top 10% of high school class, 33% in top 25% of high school class, 70% in top 50% of high school class. 88% from public high schools. **Test Scores:** SAT Math middle 50% range 490–580. SAT EBRW middle 50% range 490–580. ACT middle 50% range 18–24. **Basis for Candidate Selection:** *Very important factors include:* level of applicant's interest. *Important factors include:* rigor of secondary school record, academic GPA, standardized test scores, interview. *Other factors include:* class rank, application essay, recommendation(s), extracurricular activities, talent/ability, character/personal qualities, volunteer

work, work experience. **Freshman Admission Requirements:** High school diploma is required and GED is accepted. *Academic units required:* 4 English, 2 math, 1 science, 1 science labs, 2 foreign language, 1 history, 5 academic electives. *Academic units recommended:* 4 English, 2.5 math, 2 science, 2 science labs, 2 foreign language, 1 history, 5 academic electives. **Freshman Admission Statistics:** 3,135 applied, 51% admitted, 22% enrolled. **Transfer Admission Requirements:** College transcript(s), statement of good standing from prior institution(s). Minimum college GPA of 2.0 required. Lowest grade transferable C-. **General Admission Information:** Priority deadline 5/1. Non-fall registration accepted. Admission may be deferred for a maximum of 1 year.

COSTS AND FINANCIAL AID

Annual in-state tuition $12,940. Annual out-of-state tuition $24,184. Room and board $10,222. Required fees $960. Average book and supplies expense $785. **Required Forms and Deadlines:** FAFSA. **Notification of Awards:** Applicants will be notified of awards on a rolling basis beginning 4/1. **Types of Aid:** *Need-based scholarships/grants:* College/university scholarship or grant aid from institutional funds; Federal Pell; Private scholarships; SEOG; State scholarships/grants. *Loans:* Direct PLUS loans; Direct Subsidized Stafford Loans; Direct Unsubsidized Stafford Loans. **Student Employment:** Federal Work-Study Program available. Institutional employment available. **Financial Aid Statistics:** 97% needy freshmen, 95% needy undergrads receive need-based scholarship or grant aid. 7% freshmen, 6% undergrads receive non-need-based scholarship or grant aid. 85% freshmen, 87% undergrads receive need-based self-help aid. 0% freshmen, 0% undergrads receive athletic scholarships. 93.6% freshmen, 89.1% undergrads receive any aid. 90% undergrads borrow to pay for school. Average cumulative indebtedness $37,735. **Criteria awarding aid:** *Need-based:* Minority status. *Non-need-based:* Academics, Alumni affiliation, State/district residency.

UNIVERSITY OF PITTSBURGH—GREENSBURG

150 Finoli Drive, Greensburg, PA 15601
Phone: 724-836-9880 **Financial Aid Phone:** 724-836-9881
E-mail: upgadmit@pitt.edu **CEEB Code:** 2936
Fax: 724-836-7471 **Website:** www.greensburg.pitt.edu **ACT Code:** 3733

This public school was founded in 1963. It has a 217 acre campus.

RATINGS

Admissions Selectivity Rating: 76 **Fire Safety Rating:** 60* **Green Rating:** 60*

STUDENTS AND FACULTY

Enrollment: 1,578. **Student Body:** 52% female, 48% male, 2% out-of-state, 1% international. Asian 4%, African American 6%, Caucasian 79%, Hispanic 4%, Native American <1%, Pacific Islander <1%, Two or more races 3%, Race unknown 3%.
Retention and Graduation: 76% freshmen return for sophomore year. 26% grads go on to further study within 1 year. 11% grads pursue arts and sciences degrees. 1% grads pursue law degrees. 2% grads pursue business degrees. 1% grads pursue medical degrees. **Faculty:** Student/faculty ratio 20:1. 76 full-time faculty, 83% hold PhDs, 13% are members of minority groups, 57% are women. 0% of classes are taught by teaching assistants.

ACADEMICS

Degrees: Bachelor's; Certificate. **Classes:** Most classes have 20–29 students. Most lab/discussion sessions have 20–29 students. **Most popular majors:** Biology/Biological Sciences, General; Management Information Systems, General; Psychology, General. **Special Study Options:** Cross-registration; Double major; Dual enrollment; Exchange student program (domestic); Independent study; Internships; Liberal arts/career combination; Student-designed major; Study abroad; Teacher certification program. **Disability Services offered:** Note-taking services; Reader services; Tape recorders; Tutors. **Career services:** Alumni network; Alumni services; Career assessment; Career/job search classes; Internships; Regional alumni.

FACILITIES

Housing: Coed dorms; Theme housing; 95% of campus accessible to physically disabled. **Campus network:** 100% of classrooms, 100% of dorms, 85% of student union, 100% of libraries, 75% of dining areas, 10% of common outdoor areas have wireless network access.

CAMPUS LIFE

Environment: Village. **Activities:** Campus Ministries; Choral groups; Dance; Drama/theater; International Student Organization; Literary magazine; Musical theater; Student government; Student newspaper. 25 registered organizations, 11 honor societies, 3 religious organizations on campus. **Athletics (Intercollegiate):** *Men:* baseball, basketball, cross-country, golf, soccer, tennis. *Women:* basketball, cross-country, golf, soccer, softball, volleyball. **On-Campus Highlights:** Academic Village.

ADMISSIONS

Freshman Academic Profile: Average high school GPA 3.5. 15% in top 10% of high school class, 47% in top 25% of high school class, 84% in top 50% of high school class. 95% from public high schools. **Test Scores:** SAT Math middle 50% range 460–560. SAT EBRW middle 50% range 460–550. ACT middle 50% range 18–24. **Basis for Candidate Selection:** *Very important factors include:* rigor of secondary school record, class rank, academic GPA, standardized test scores. *Other factors include:* application essay, recommendation(s), interview, extracurricular activities, talent/ability, character/ personal qualities, volunteer work, level of applicant's interest. **Freshman Admission Requirements:** High school diploma is required and GED is accepted. *Academic units required:* 4 English, 2 math, 1 science, 1 science labs, 4 foreign language, 2 social studies, 2 history, 1 academic elective. *Academic units recommended:* 4 English, 4 math, 2 science, 4 foreign language, 2 social studies, 2 history, 3 academic electives, 1 computer science. **Freshman Admission Statistics:** 1,538 applied, 81% admitted, 35% enrolled. **Transfer Admission Requirements:** High school transcript, college transcript(s), statement of good standing from prior institution(s). Minimum college GPA of 2.0 required. Lowest grade transferable C. **General Admission Information:** Application fee $45. Non-fall registration accepted. Admission may be deferred for a maximum of 12 months.

COSTS AND FINANCIAL AID

Annual in-state tuition $12,452. Annual out-of-state tuition $23,268. Room and board $9,490. Required fees $920. **Required Forms and Deadlines:** FAFSA; State aid form. **Notification of Awards:** Applicants will be notified of awards on a rolling basis beginning 3/15. **Types of Aid:** *Need-based scholarships/ grants:* College/university scholarship or grant aid from institutional funds; Federal Pell; Private scholarships; SEOG; State scholarships/grants; United Negro College Fund. *Loans:* Direct PLUS loans; Direct Subsidized Stafford Loans; Direct Unsubsidized Stafford Loans. **Student Employment:** Federal Work-Study Program available. Institutional employment available. **Financial Aid Statistics:** 83% needy freshmen, 79% needy undergrads receive need-based scholarship or grant aid. 8% freshmen, 4% undergrads receive non-need-based scholarship or grant aid. 81% freshmen, 85% undergrads receive need-based self-help aid. 0% freshmen, 0% undergrads receive athletic scholarships. **Criteria awarding aid:** *Non-need-based:* Academics, Leadership, Minority status.

UNIVERSITY OF PITTSBURGH—JOHNSTOWN

157 Blackington Hall, Johnstown, PA 15904
Phone: 814-269-7050 **Financial Aid Phone:** 814-269-7045
E-mail: upjadmit@pitt.edu **CEEB Code:** 2934
Fax: 814-269-7044 **Website:** www.upj.pitt.edu **ACT Code:** 3735

This public school was founded in 1927. It has a 655 acre campus.

RATINGS

Admissions Selectivity Rating: 75   **Fire Safety Rating:** 88   **Green Rating:** 60*

STUDENTS AND FACULTY

Enrollment: 2,814. **Student Body:** 45% female, 55% male, 2% out-of-state, 2% international (20 countries represented). Asian 1%, African American 3%, Caucasian 87%, Hispanic 1%, Native American <1%, Pacific Islander <1%, Two or more races 2%, Race unknown 3%.
Retention and Graduation: 82% freshmen return for sophomore year. 8% grads pursue arts and sciences degrees. 1% grads pursue law degrees. 1% grads pursue business degrees. 2% grads pursue medical degrees. **Faculty:** 0% of classes are taught by teaching assistants.

ACADEMICS

Degrees: Associate; Bachelor's; Certificate. **Classes:** Most classes have 10–19 students. Most lab/discussion sessions have 10–19 students. **Most popular majors:** Electrical, Electronic, and Communications Engineering Technology/ Technician; Business/Commerce, General; Mechanical/Mechanical Engineering Technology/Technician. **Special Study Options:** Accelerated program; Cross-registration; Double major; Dual enrollment; Independent study; Internships; Liberal arts/career combination; Student-designed major; Study abroad; Teacher certification program. **Disability Services offered:** Note-taking services; Reader services; Tutors. **Career services:** Alumni network; Alumni services; Career/job search classes; Internships; Regional alumni.

FACILITIES

Housing: Coed dorms; Fraternity/sorority housing; Special housing for disabled students; Theme housing; 100% of campus accessible to physically disabled. **Special Academic Facilities/Equipment:** Art museum, performing arts center, language lab, Idea Lab, Mountain Cat Mission Control—The Region's First Social Media Training Center.

CAMPUS LIFE

Environment: City. **Activities:** Campus Ministries; Choral groups; Concert band; Dance; Drama/theater; Literary magazine; Model UN; Music ensembles; Musical theater; Radio station; Student government; Student newspaper; Television station. 110 registered organizations, 13 honor societies, 3 religious organizations, 5 fraternities, 4 sororities on campus. **Athletics (Intercollegiate):** *Men:* baseball, basketball, golf, soccer, wrestling. *Women:* basketball, cheerleading, cross-country, golf, soccer, track/field (outdoor), volleyball. **On-Campus Highlights:** Student Union Building.

ADMISSIONS

Freshman Academic Profile: Average high school GPA 3.5. 14% in top 10% of high school class, 40% in top 25% of high school class, 72% in top 50% of high school class. **Test Scores:** SAT Math middle 50% range 460–570. SAT EBRW middle 50% range 450–550. ACT middle 50% range 20–25. **Basis for Candidate Selection:** *Very important factors include:* rigor of secondary school record, class rank, academic GPA. *Important factors include:* standardized test scores, interview, extracurricular activities, talent/ability, volunteer work, level of applicant's interest. *Other factors include:* application essay, recommendation(s), character/personal qualities, racial/ethnic status, work experience. **Freshman Admission Requirements:** High school diploma is required and GED is accepted. *Academic units required:* 4 English, 2 math, 2 science, 1 science labs, 2 foreign language, 4 social studies. **Freshman Admission Statistics:** 3,456 applied, 81% admitted, 26% enrolled. **Transfer Admission Requirements:** High school transcript, college transcript(s). Minimum college GPA of 2.0 required. Lowest grade transferable C. **General Admission Information:** Regular application deadline 5/1. Non-fall registration accepted. Admission may be deferred for a maximum of 12 months.

COSTS AND FINANCIAL AID

Required Forms and Deadlines: FAFSA. **Notification of Awards:** Applicants will be notified of awards on a rolling basis beginning 3/1. **Types of Aid:** *Need-based scholarships/grants:* College/university scholarship or grant aid from institutional funds; Federal Pell; Private scholarships; SEOG; State scholarships/ grants. *Loans:* Direct PLUS loans; Direct Subsidized Stafford Loans; Direct Unsubsidized Stafford Loans. **Student Employment:** Federal Work-Study Program available. Institutional employment available. **Financial Aid Statistics:** 85% needy freshmen, 77% needy undergrads receive need-based scholarship or grant aid. 6% freshmen, 4% undergrads receive non-need-based scholarship or grant aid. 83% freshmen, 85% undergrads receive need-based self-help aid. 3% freshmen, 2% undergrads receive athletic scholarships. 80% freshmen, 80% undergrads receive any aid. 85% undergrads borrow to pay for school. Average cumulative indebtedness $34,127. **Criteria awarding aid:** *Need-based:* Academics, Athletics, Minority status, Music/drama. *Non-need-based:* Academics, Alumni affiliation, Athletics, Leadership, State/district residency.

UNIVERSITY OF PITTSBURGH—PITTSBURGH CAMPUS

4227 Fifth Avenue, Pittsburgh, PA 15260
Phone: 412-624-7488 **Financial Aid Phone:** 412-624-7488
E-mail: oafa@pitt.edu **CEEB Code:** 2927
Fax: 412-648-8815 **Website:** www.pitt.edu **ACT Code:** 3734

This public school was founded in 1787. It has a 145 acre campus.

RATINGS
Admissions Selectivity Rating: 89   **Fire Safety Rating:** 91   **Green Rating:** 93

STUDENTS AND FACULTY
Enrollment: 19,017. **Student Body:** 53% female, 47% male, 31% out-of-state, 5% international (58 countries represented). Asian 11%, African American 5%, Caucasian 68%, Hispanic 5%, Native American <1%, Pacific Islander <1%, Two or more races 4%, Race unknown 1%.
Retention and Graduation: 93% freshmen return for sophomore year. 65% freshmen graduate within 4 years. 83% freshmen graduate within 6 years. 31% grads go on to further study within 1 year. 37% grads pursue arts and sciences degrees. 8% grads pursue law degrees. 3% grads pursue business degrees. 10% grads pursue medical degrees. **Faculty:** Student/faculty ratio 15:1. 1,791 full-time faculty, 94% hold PhDs, 21% are members of minority groups, 45% are women.

ACADEMICS
Degrees: Associate; Bachelor's; Certificate; Doctoral degree—professional practice; Doctoral degree research/scholarship; Master's; Post-bachelor's certificate; Post-master's certificate. **Classes:** Most classes have 10–19 students. Most lab/discussion sessions have 20–29 students. **Most popular majors:** Biology/Biological Sciences, General; Psychology, General; Registered Nursing/Registered Nurse. **Special Study Options:** Accelerated program; Cooperative education program; Cross-registration; Distance learning; Double major; Dual enrollment; English as a Second Language (ESL); Exchange student program (domestic); External degree program; Honors program; Independent study; Internships; Liberal arts/career combination; Student-designed major; Study abroad; Teacher certification program; Weekend college. **Honors programs:** University Honors College - see http://www.honorscollege.pitt.edu/. **Combined degree programs:** BA/DDS; BA/JD; BA/MD. **Disability Services offered:** Note-taking services. **Career services:** Alumni network; Alumni services; Career assessment; Career/job search classes; Internships; Regional alumni.

FACILITIES
Housing: Apartments for single students; Coed dorms; Cooperative housing; Fraternity/sorority housing; Special housing for disabled students; Theme housing; Wellness housing; 90% of campus accessible to physically disabled. **Special Academic Facilities/Equipment:** Stephen Foster Memorial, Allegheny Observatory, Jazz Hall of Fame.

CAMPUS LIFE
Environment: City. **Activities:** Campus Ministries; Choral groups; Concert band; Dance; Drama/theater; International Student Organization; Jazz band; Literary magazine; Marching band; Model UN; Music ensembles; Musical theater; Opera; Pep band; Radio station; Student government; Student newspaper; Student-run film society; Symphony orchestra; Television station. 649 registered organizations, 30 honor societies, 24 fraternities, 12 sororities on campus. **Athletics (Intercollegiate):** *Men:* baseball, basketball, cross-country, diving, football, soccer, swimming, track/field (outdoor), wrestling. *Women:* basketball, cross-country, diving, gymnastics, soccer, softball, swimming, tennis, track/field (outdoor), volleyball. **On-Campus Highlights:** Cathedral of Learning. **Environmental Initiatives:** Energy Center: The Facilities Management Division recently consolidated all energy-related operations to a single location. The newly constructed Energy Center space is designed to increase collaboration among energy managers, engineers, utility analysts, and energy management system personnel. These personnel will use new and existing controls and diagnostic tools to place an even greater focus on ensuring optimal building operations and incorporating new technologies into building system designs to further energy conservation on campus. A new command center provides technicians and managers with consolidated access to the building automation system and other diagnostic tools.

ADMISSIONS
Freshman Academic Profile: Average high school GPA 4.1. 53% in top 10% of high school class, 86% in top 25% of high school class, 98% in top 50% of high school class. **Test Scores:** SAT Math middle 50% range 630–740. SAT EBRW middle 50% range 630–700. ACT middle 50% range 28–33. **Basis for Candidate Selection:** *Very important factors include:* rigor of secondary school record, academic GPA, standardized test scores. *Important factors include:* application essay. *Other factors include:* class rank, recommendation(s), interview, extracurricular activities, talent/ability, character/personal qualities, first generation, alumni/ae relation, geographical residence, state residency, racial/ethnic status, volunteer work, work experience, level of applicant's interest. **Freshman Admission Requirements:** High school diploma is required and GED is not accepted. *Academic units required:* 4 English, 3 math, 3 science, 3 science labs, 2 foreign language, 2 social studies, 3 academic electives. *Academic units recommended:* 4 English, 4 math, 4 science, 4 science labs, 3 foreign language, 3 social studies, 5 academic electives. **Freshman Admission Statistics:** 32,091 applied, 57% admitted, 22% enrolled. **Transfer Admission Requirements:** High school transcript, college transcript(s), essay or personal statement. Lowest grade transferable C. **General Admission Information:** Application fee $55. Non-fall registration accepted. Admission may be deferred for a maximum of 1 year.

COSTS AND FINANCIAL AID
Annual in-state tuition $18,628. Annual out-of-state tuition $32,656. Room and board $11,050. Required fees $1,090. Average book and supplies expense $755. **Required Forms and Deadlines:** FAFSA; State aid form. **Notification of Awards:** Applicants will be notified of awards on a rolling basis beginning 2/1. **Types of Aid:** *Need-based scholarships/grants:* College/university scholarship or grant aid from institutional funds; Federal Nursing Scholarships; Federal Pell; Private scholarships; SEOG; State scholarships/grants. *Loans:* Direct PLUS loans; Direct Subsidized Stafford Loans; Direct Unsubsidized Stafford Loans. **Student Employment:** Federal Work-Study Program available. Institutional employment available. **Financial Aid Statistics:** 79% needy freshmen, 73% needy undergrads receive need-based scholarship or grant aid. 11% freshmen, 8% undergrads receive non-need-based scholarship or grant aid. 72% freshmen, 78% undergrads receive need-based self-help aid. 1% freshmen, 0% undergrads receive athletic scholarships. 61.6% freshmen, 54.2% undergrads receive any aid. 61% undergrads borrow to pay for school. Average cumulative indebtedness $39,417. **Criteria awarding aid:** *Non-need-based:* Academics, Athletics, Minority status.

UNIVERSITY OF PORTLAND

5000 N. Willamette Blvd., Portland, OR 97203-5798
Phone: 503-943-7147 **Financial Aid Phone:** 503-943-7311
E-mail: admissions@up.edu **CEEB Code:** 4847
Fax: 503-943-7315 **Website:** www.up.edu **ACT Code:** 3500

This private school, affiliated with the Roman Catholic Church, was founded in 1901. It has a 130 acre campus.

RATINGS
Admissions Selectivity Rating: 81   **Fire Safety Rating:** 65   **Green Rating:** 60*

STUDENTS AND FACULTY
Enrollment: 3,758. **Student Body:** 60% female, 40% male, 73% out-of-state, 3% international (38 countries represented). Asian 14%, African American 1%, Caucasian 57%, Hispanic 13%, Native American <1%, Pacific Islander 2%, Two or more races 8%, Race unknown 2%.
Retention and Graduation: 90% freshmen return for sophomore year. 74% freshmen graduate within 4 years. 82% freshmen graduate within 6 years. 15% grads go on to further study within 1 year. **Faculty:** Student/faculty ratio 12:1. 244 full-time faculty, 84% hold PhDs, 10% are members of minority groups, 54% are women. 0% of classes are taught by teaching assistants.

ACADEMICS
Degrees: Bachelor's; Doctoral degree—professional practice; Master's; Post-master's certificate. **Classes:** Most classes have 20–29 students. Most lab/discussion sessions have 10–19 students. **Most popular majors:** Biology/Biological Sciences, General; Registered Nursing, Nursing Administration, Nursing Research and Clinical Nursing; Mechanical Engineering. **Special Study Options:** Cross-registration; Distance learning; Double major; Honors program; Independent study; Internships; Liberal arts/career combination;

Study abroad; Teacher certification program. **Honors programs:** The honors program provides an exciting intellectual challenge for highly motivated students with above average high school records. The program is designed to facilitate learning through special small classes which permit a high level of student-faculty interaction. Honors students may be enrolled in any major. **Disability Services offered:** Note-taking services; Reader services; Tutors. **Career services:** Alumni network; Alumni services; Career assessment; Career/job search classes; Internships; Regional alumni.

FACILITIES

Housing: Coed dorms; Men's dorms; Theme housing; Women's dorms; 80% of campus accessible to physically disabled. **Special Academic Facilities/Equipment:** Art gallery, observatory.

CAMPUS LIFE

Environment: Metropolis. **Activities:** Campus Ministries; Choral groups; Concert band; Dance; Drama/theater; International Student Organization; Jazz band; Literary magazine; Model UN; Music ensembles; Musical theater; Pep band; Radio station; Student government; Student newspaper; Student-run film society; Symphony orchestra; Yearbook. 64 registered organizations, 16 honor societies, 9 religious organizations on campus. **Athletics (Intercollegiate):** *Men:* baseball, basketball, cross-country, golf, soccer, tennis, track/field (outdoor). *Women:* basketball, cross-country, golf, soccer, tennis, track/field (outdoor), volleyball. **On-Campus Highlights:** The Commons. **Environmental Initiatives:** Food for Thought (with Michael Pollan), April 2011; Confluences, Water and Justice (with Maude Barlow), May 2010; Portland host and active participant of Focus the Nation, January 30, 2008.

ADMISSIONS

Freshman Academic Profile: Average high school GPA 3.7. 60% from public high schools. **Test Scores:** SAT Math middle 50% range 560–660. SAT EBRW middle 50% range 580–660. ACT middle 50% range 23–28. **Basis for Candidate Selection:** *Very important factors include:* rigor of secondary school record, academic GPA. *Important factors include:* class rank, application essay, standardized test scores, recommendation(s), extracurricular activities, talent/ability. *Other factors include:* interview, character/personal qualities, first generation, alumni/ae relation, geographical residence, religious affiliation/commitment, racial/ethnic status, level of applicant's interest. **Freshman Admission Requirements:** High school diploma is required and GED is accepted. *Academic units required:* 4 English, 3 math, 3 science, 2 foreign language, 3 social studies, 2 history, 7 academic electives. *Academic units recommended:* 4 English, 4 math, 4 science, 3 foreign language, 4 social studies, 4 history, 7 academic electives. **Freshman Admission Statistics:** 10,666 applied, 75% admitted, 12% enrolled. **Transfer Admission Requirements:** College transcript(s), essay or personal statement. Minimum college GPA of 2.5 required. Lowest grade transferable C. **General Admission Information:** Application fee $50. Priority deadline 11/15. Regular application deadline 1/15. Non-fall registration accepted. Admission may be deferred for a maximum of 1 year.

COSTS AND FINANCIAL AID

Annual tuition $47,478. Room and board $13,968. Required fees $340. Average book and supplies expense $75. **Required Forms and Deadlines:** FAFSA. **Notification of Awards:** Applicants will be notified of awards on a rolling basis beginning 3/1. **Types of Aid:** *Need-based scholarships/grants:* College/university scholarship or grant aid from institutional funds; Federal Nursing Scholarships; Federal Pell; Private scholarships; SEOG; State scholarships/grants. *Loans:* Direct PLUS loans; Direct Subsidized Stafford Loans; Direct Unsubsidized Stafford Loans. **Student Employment:** Federal Work-Study Program available. **Financial Aid Statistics:** 80% needy freshmen, 79% needy undergrads receive need-based scholarship or grant aid. 96% freshmen, 93% undergrads receive non-need-based scholarship or grant aid. 68% freshmen, 70% undergrads receive need-based self-help aid. 2% freshmen, 3% undergrads receive athletic scholarships. 98% freshmen, 95% undergrads receive any aid. 57% undergrads borrow to pay for school. Average cumulative indebtedness $29,186. **Criteria awarding aid:** *Need-based:* Academics, Minority status. *Non-need-based:* Academics, Athletics, Leadership, Minority status, Music/drama.

UNIVERSITY OF PUGET SOUND

1500 North Warner Street CMB 1062, Tacoma, WA 98416-1062
Phone: 253-879-3211 **Financial Aid Phone:** 253-879-3214
E-mail: admission@pugetsound.edu **CEEB Code:** 4067
Fax: 253-879-3993 **Website:** www.pugetsound.edu **ACT Code:** 4450

This private school was founded in 1888. It has a 97 acre campus.

RATINGS

Admissions Selectivity Rating: 83   **Fire Safety Rating:** 91   **Green Rating:** 78

STUDENTS AND FACULTY

Enrollment: 2,298. **Student Body:** 59% female, 41% male, 75% out-of-state, <1% international (9 countries represented). Asian 7%, African American 2%, Caucasian 67%, Hispanic 10%, Native American <1%, Pacific Islander <1%, Two or more races 10%, Race unknown 3%.
Retention and Graduation: 81% freshmen return for sophomore year. 65% freshmen graduate within 4 years. 76% freshmen graduate within 6 years.
Faculty: Student/faculty ratio 11:1. 229 full-time faculty, 90% hold PhDs, 15% are members of minority groups, 50% are women. 0% of classes are taught by teaching assistants.

ACADEMICS

Degrees: Bachelor's; Doctoral degree—professional practice; Master's. **Classes:** Most classes have 10–19 students. Most lab/discussion sessions have 10–19 students. **Most popular majors:** Biology/Biological Sciences, General; Psychology, General; Business Administration and Management, General. **Special Study Options:** Cooperative education program; Double major; Honors program; Independent study; Internships; Liberal arts/career combination; Student-designed major; Study abroad; Teacher certification program. **Honors programs:** Business Leadership Program; Honors Program. **Disability Services offered:** Note-taking services; Reader services; Tape recorders; Tutors. **Career services:** Alumni network; Alumni services; Career assessment; Career/job search classes; Internships; Regional alumni.

FACILITIES

Housing: Apartments for single students; Coed dorms; Fraternity/sorority housing; Special housing for disabled students; Theme housing; Wellness housing. **Special Academic Facilities/Equipment:** Art gallery, natural history museum, concert hall, transmission and scanning electron microscopes, spectrometers, exercise science lab, observatory, paleomagnetic and X-ray lab, physiology labs, and DNA Sequencer.

CAMPUS LIFE

Environment: City. **Activities:** Campus Ministries; Choral groups; Concert band; Dance; Drama/theater; International Student Organization; Jazz band; Literary magazine; Model UN; Music ensembles; Musical theater; Opera; Pep band; Radio station; Student government; Student newspaper; Student-run film society; Symphony orchestra; Yearbook. 105 registered organizations, 14 honor societies, 17 religious organizations, 4 fraternities, 5 sororities on campus. **Athletics (Intercollegiate):** *Men:* baseball, basketball, crew/rowing, cross-country, football, golf, soccer, swimming, tennis, track/field (outdoor), track/field (indoor). *Women:* basketball, crew/rowing, cross-country, golf, lacrosse, soccer, softball, swimming, tennis, track/field (outdoor), track/field (indoor), volleyball. **On-Campus Highlights:** Diversions Café. **Environmental Initiatives:** In 2005, President Thomas established the Sustainability Advisory Committee (SAC), which reports to the president through the Vice President of Student Affairs and the Vice President for Finance and Administration. The president empowered the committee to advise on and implement sustainability policies and programs on campus and collaboratively with our regional community. The committee addresses sustainability across the institution and in partnership with external organizations. It also uniquely engages students, faculty, and staff in comprehensive, collaborative, and strategic sustainability endeavors.

ADMISSIONS

Freshman Academic Profile: Average high school GPA 3.6. 30% in top 10% of high school class, 64% in top 25% of high school class, 91% in top 50% of high school class. 72% from public high schools. **Test Scores:** SAT Math middle 50% range 560–680. SAT EBRW middle 50% range 590–690. ACT middle 50% range 25–30. **Basis for Candidate Selection:** *Very important*

factors include: rigor of secondary school record, academic GPA, application essay, character/personal qualities. *Important factors include:* recommendation(s), extracurricular activities, talent/ability. *Other factors include:* class rank, standardized test scores, interview, first generation, alumni/ae relation, racial/ethnic status, volunteer work, work experience, level of applicant's interest. **Freshman Admission Requirements:** High school diploma is required and GED is accepted. *Academic units recommended:* 4 English, 4 math, 4 science, 4 science labs, 3 foreign language, 3 social studies, 3 history, 1 visual/performing arts. **Freshman Admission Statistics:** 5,181 applied, 84% admitted, 14% enrolled. **Transfer Admission Requirements:** College transcript(s), essay or personal statement, statement of good standing from prior institution(s). Minimum college GPA of 2.0 required. Lowest grade transferable D. **General Admission Information:** Application fee $60. Priority deadline 1/15. Regular application deadline 1/15. Non-fall registration accepted. Admission may be deferred for a maximum of 1 year.

COSTS AND FINANCIAL AID

Annual tuition $53,520. Room and board $13,480. Required fees $280. Average book and supplies expense $1,000. **Required Forms and Deadlines:** FAFSA. **Notification of Awards:** Applicants will be notified of awards on or about 3/15. **Types of Aid:** *Need-based scholarships/grants:* College/university scholarship or grant aid from institutional funds; Federal Pell; Private scholarships; SEOG; State scholarships/grants. *Loans:* Direct PLUS loans; Direct Subsidized Stafford Loans; Direct Unsubsidized Stafford Loans. **Student Employment:** Federal Work-Study Program available. Institutional employment available. **Financial Aid Statistics:** 99% needy freshmen, 99% needy undergrads receive need-based scholarship or grant aid. 16% freshmen, 12% undergrads receive non-need-based scholarship or grant aid. 78% freshmen, 78% undergrads receive need-based self-help aid. 0% freshmen, 0% undergrads receive athletic scholarships. 100% freshmen, 99% undergrads receive any aid. 48% undergrads borrow to pay for school. Average cumulative indebtedness $36,290. **Criteria awarding aid:** *Need-based:* Academics, Minority status, Religious affiliation. *Non-need-based:* Academics, Alumni affiliation, Art, Leadership, Music/drama, Religious affiliation.

UNIVERSITY OF REDLANDS

1200 E. Colton Avenue, Redlands, CA 92373
Phone: 909-748-8074 **Financial Aid Phone:** 909-748-8047
E-mail: admissions@redlands.edu **CEEB Code:** 4848
Fax: 909-335-4089 **Website:** www.redlands.edu **ACT Code:** 464

This private school was founded in 1907. It has a 160 acre campus.

RATINGS

Admissions Selectivity Rating: 77   **Fire Safety Rating:** 86   **Green Rating:** 60*

STUDENTS AND FACULTY

Enrollment: 2,402. **Student Body:** 58% female, 42% male, 30% out-of-state, 2% international (45 countries represented). Asian 6%, African American 3%, Caucasian 52%, Hispanic 25%, Native American 1%, Pacific Islander 1%, Two or more races 6%, Race unknown 4%.
Retention and Graduation: 87% freshmen return for sophomore year. 19% grads go on to further study within 1 year. 5% grads pursue law degrees. 20% grads pursue business degrees. 2% grads pursue medical degrees. **Faculty:** Student/faculty ratio 12:1. 169 full-time faculty, 0% hold PhDs, 0% are members of minority groups, 0% are women. 0% of classes are taught by teaching assistants.

ACADEMICS

Degrees: Bachelor's; Certificate; Diploma; Doctoral degree research/scholarship; Master's; Post-bachelor's certificate; Post-master's certificate. **Classes:** Most classes have 10–19 students. Most lab/discussion sessions have fewer than 10 students. **Most popular majors:** Business/Commerce, General; Liberal Arts and Sciences/Liberal Studies; Psychology, General. **Special Study Options:** Accelerated program; Cross-registration; Distance learning; Double major; Exchange student program (domestic); Honors program; Independent study; Internships; Liberal arts/career combination; Student-designed major; Study abroad; Teacher certification program. **Honors programs:** The Johnston

Center for Integrative Studies allows students to design their own majors in consultation with faculty advisors. Students write contracts for their courses and receive narrative evaluations in lieu of traditional grades. The center has received national acclaim for its innovative approaches to education. **Disability Services offered:** Note-taking services; Reader services; Tutors. **Career services:** Alumni services; Career/job search classes; Regional alumni.

FACILITIES

Housing: Apartments for married students; Apartments for single students; Coed dorms; Fraternity/sorority housing; Special housing for disabled students; Special housing for international students; Theme housing; Women's dorms; 75% of campus accessible to physically disabled. **Special Academic Facilities/Equipment:** Art gallery, Far East art collection, Southwest collection, center for communicative disorders, language lab, Helen and Vernon Farquar Anthropology Lab, Physics Laser Photonics Lab, Irvine Map Library, Geographic Information System lab.

CAMPUS LIFE

Environment: Town. **Activities:** Campus Ministries; Choral groups; Concert band; Dance; Drama/theater; International Student Organization; Jazz band; Literary magazine; Music ensembles; Musical theater; Opera; Radio station; Student government; Student newspaper; Symphony orchestra; Yearbook. 105 registered organizations, 8 honor societies, 8 religious organizations, 5 fraternities, 5 sororities on campus. **Athletics (Intercollegiate):** *Men:* baseball, basketball, cross-country, diving, football, golf, soccer, swimming, tennis, track/field (outdoor), water polo. *Women:* basketball, cross-country, diving, golf, lacrosse, soccer, softball, swimming, tennis, track/field (outdoor), volleyball, water polo. **On-Campus Highlights:** Armacost Library. **Environmental Initiatives:** Co-Generation facility to provide power to much of the campus.

ADMISSIONS

Freshman Academic Profile: Average high school GPA 3.5. 22% in top 10% of high school class, 55% in top 25% of high school class, 88% in top 50% of high school class. **Test Scores:** SAT Math middle 50% range 490–600. SAT EBRW middle 50% range 490–590. ACT middle 50% range 22–27. **Basis for Candidate Selection:** *Very important factors include:* academic GPA. *Important factors include:* rigor of secondary school record, application essay, standardized test scores, recommendation(s). *Other factors include:* class rank, interview, extracurricular activities, talent/ability, character/personal qualities, first generation, alumni/ae relation, geographical residence, racial/ethnic status, volunteer work, work experience. **Freshman Admission Requirements:** High school diploma is required and GED is accepted. *Academic units required:* 4 English, 3 math, 2 science, 2 science labs, 2 foreign language, 2 social studies. *Academic units recommended:* 3 science, 3 foreign language, 3 social studies. **Freshman Admission Statistics:** 4,562 applied, 75% admitted, 17% enrolled. **Transfer Admission Requirements:** High school transcript, college transcript(s), essay or personal statement. Minimum college GPA of 2.5 required. Lowest grade transferable C. **General Admission Information:** Application fee $30. Priority deadline 11/15. Regular application deadline 1/15. Non-fall registration accepted. Admission may be deferred for a maximum of 2 semesters.

COSTS AND FINANCIAL AID

Annual tuition $47,722. Room and board $13,862. Required fees $350. Average book and supplies expense $1,850. **Required Forms and Deadlines:** FAFSA. **Notification of Awards:** Applicants will be notified of awards on a rolling basis beginning 2/17. **Types of Aid:** *Need-based scholarships/grants:* College/university scholarship or grant aid from institutional funds; Federal Pell; Private scholarships; SEOG; State scholarships/grants. *Loans:* Direct PLUS loans; Direct Subsidized Stafford Loans; Direct Unsubsidized Stafford Loans. **Student Employment:** Federal Work-Study Program available. **Financial Aid Statistics:** 100% needy freshmen, 99% needy undergrads receive need-based scholarship or grant aid. 23% freshmen, 21% undergrads receive non-need-based scholarship or grant aid. 81% freshmen, 82% undergrads receive need-based self-help aid. 0% freshmen, 0% undergrads receive athletic scholarships. 94% freshmen, 94% undergrads receive any aid. 68% undergrads borrow to pay for school. Average cumulative indebtedness $32,662. **Criteria awarding aid:** *Non-need-based:* Academics, Art, Music/drama.

UNIVERSITY OF RHODE ISLAND

Newman Hall, Kingston, RI 02881
Phone: 401-874-7100 **Financial Aid Phone:** 401-874-7530
E-mail: admission@uri.edu **CEEB Code:** 3919
Fax: 401-874-5523 **Website:** www.uri.edu **ACT Code:** 3818

This public school was founded in 1892. It has a 1300 acre campus.

RATINGS
Admissions Selectivity Rating: 82   **Fire Safety Rating:** 89   **Green Rating:** 67

STUDENTS AND FACULTY
Enrollment: 13,671. **Student Body:** 56% female, 44% male, 49% out-of-state, 1% international (41 countries represented). Asian 3%, African American 5%, Caucasian 73%, Hispanic 11%, Native American <1%, Pacific Islander <1%, Two or more races 3%, Race unknown 3%.
Retention and Graduation: 86% freshmen return for sophomore year. 52% freshmen graduate within 4 years. 69% freshmen graduate within 6 years.
Faculty: Student/faculty ratio 16:1. 766 full-time faculty, 85% hold PhDs, 22% are members of minority groups, 51% are women.

ACADEMICS
Degrees: Bachelor's; Certificate; Doctoral degree—other; Doctoral degree—professional practice; Doctoral degree research/scholarship; Master's; Post-bachelor's certificate. **Classes:** Most classes have 10–19 students. Most lab/discussion sessions have 10–19 students. **Most popular majors:** Psychology, General; Registered Nursing/Registered Nurse. **Special Study Options:** Accelerated program; Cooperative education program; Distance learning; Double major; Dual enrollment; Exchange student program (domestic); Honors program; Independent study; Internships; Student-designed major; Study abroad; Teacher certification program. **Honors programs:** The Honors Program at URI features small classes, a nationally renowned Honors Colloquium, National Scholarships and Fellowships for upper class students, advising, including pre-health professions advising, and honors housing for upper class students. **Combined degree programs:** BA/MA; BA/MEng. **Disability Services offered:** Note-taking services; Reader services; Tape recorders; Tutors. **Career services:** Alumni network; Alumni services; Career assessment; Career/job search classes; Internships.

FACILITIES
Housing: Apartments for married students; Apartments for single students; Coed dorms; Fraternity/sorority housing; Special housing for disabled students; Special housing for international students; Theme housing; Wellness housing 90% of campus accessible to physically disabled. **Special Academic Facilities/Equipment:** Center for robotic research, animal science farm, planetarium, Watson House Museum, Narragansett Bay Campus for Marine Sciences, American historic textiles museum, aquaculture center, fisheries and marine technology laboratory, center for biotechnology and life sciences, human performance laboratory.

CAMPUS LIFE
Environment: Village. **Activities:** Campus Ministries; Choral groups; Concert band; Dance; Drama/theater; International Student Organization; Jazz band; Literary magazine; Marching band; Model UN; Music ensembles; Musical theater; Opera; Pep band; Radio station; Student government; Student newspaper; Student-run film society; Symphony orchestra; Television station; Yearbook. 100 registered organizations, 40 honor societies, 12 religious organizations, 15 fraternities, 10 sororities on campus. **Athletics (Intercollegiate):** *Men:* baseball, basketball, cheerleading, cross-country, football, golf, soccer, track/field (outdoor), track/field (indoor). *Women:* basketball, cheerleading, crew/rowing, cross-country, diving, soccer, softball, swimming, tennis, track/field (outdoor), track/field (indoor), volleyball. **On-Campus Highlights:** Ryan Center and Boss Ice Arena. **Environmental Initiatives:** Development of a sustainability component to the general education requirements for all undergraduate students.

ADMISSIONS
Freshman Academic Profile: Average high school GPA 3.5. 18% in top 10% of high school class, 49% in top 25% of high school class, 85% in top 50% of high school class. **Test Scores:** SAT Math middle 50% range 501–677. SAT

EBRW middle 50% range 511–668. ACT middle 50% range 20–29. **Basis for Candidate Selection:** *Very important factors include:* rigor of secondary school record, academic GPA. *Important factors include:* standardized test scores. *Other factors include:* class rank, application essay, recommendation(s), extracurricular activities, talent/ability, character/personal qualities, first generation, alumni/ae relation, geographical residence, state residency, racial/ethnic status, volunteer work, work experience, level of applicant's interest. **Freshman Admission Requirements:** High school diploma is required and GED is accepted. *Academic units required:* 4 English, 3 math, 2 science, 1 science labs, 2 foreign language, 2 social studies, 5 academic electives. **Freshman Admission Statistics:** 21,259 applied, 72% admitted, 21% enrolled. **Transfer Admission Requirements:** College transcript(s), essay or personal statement, statement of good standing from prior institution(s). Minimum college GPA of 2.5 required. Lowest grade transferable C. **General Admission Information:** Application fee $65. Regular application deadline 2/1. Non-fall registration accepted. Admission may be deferred for a maximum of 1 year.

COSTS AND FINANCIAL AID
Annual in-state tuition $12,590. Annual out-of-state tuition $29,710. Room and board $12,510. Required fees $1,976. Average book and supplies expense $1,250. **Required Forms and Deadlines:** FAFSA. **Notification of Awards:** Applicants will be notified of awards on a rolling basis beginning 3/15. **Types of Aid:** *Need-based scholarships/grants:* College/university scholarship or grant aid from institutional funds; Federal Pell; Private scholarships; SEOG; State scholarships/grants; United Negro College Fund. *Loans:* Direct PLUS loans; Direct Subsidized Stafford Loans; Direct Unsubsidized Stafford Loans. **Student Employment:** Federal Work-Study Program available. Institutional employment available. **Financial Aid Statistics:** 94% needy freshmen, 87% needy undergrads receive need-based scholarship or grant aid. 21% freshmen, 12% undergrads receive non-need-based scholarship or grant aid. 82% freshmen, 69% undergrads receive need-based self-help aid. 1% freshmen, 0% undergrads receive athletic scholarships. 91% freshmen, 90% undergrads receive any aid. 63% undergrads borrow to pay for school. Average cumulative indebtedness $35,883. **Criteria awarding aid:** *Need-based:* Alumni affiliation, Art, Minority status, Music/drama. *Non-need-based:* Academics, Alumni affiliation, Art, Athletics, Music/drama.

UNIVERSITY OF RICHMOND

Queally Center: 142 UR Drive, University of Richmond, VA 23173
Phone: 804-289-8640 **Financial Aid Phone:** 804-289-8438
E-mail: admission@richmond.edu **CEEB Code:** 5569
Fax: 804-287-6003 **Website:** www.richmond.edu **ACT Code:** 4410

This private school was founded in 1830. It has a 350 acre campus.

RATINGS
Admissions Selectivity Rating: 95   **Fire Safety Rating:** 94   **Green Rating:** 95

STUDENTS AND FACULTY
Enrollment: 3,069. **Student Body:** 52% female, 48% male, 76% out-of-state, 9% international (63 countries represented). Asian 7%, African American 7%, Caucasian 58%, Hispanic 9%, Native American <1%, Pacific Islander <1%, Two or more races 5%, Race unknown 4%.
Retention and Graduation: 94% freshmen return for sophomore year. 84% freshmen graduate within 4 years. 89% freshmen graduate within 6 years. 24% grads go on to further study within 1 year. 9% grads pursue arts and sciences degrees. 2% grads pursue law degrees. 2% grads pursue business degrees. 4% grads pursue medical degrees. **Faculty:** Student/faculty ratio 8:1. 406 full-time faculty, 93% hold PhDs, 16% are members of minority groups, 45% are women. 0% of classes are taught by teaching assistants.

ACADEMICS
Degrees: Bachelor's; Certificate; Doctoral degree—professional practice; Master's; Post-bachelor's certificate; Post-master's certificate. **Classes:** Most classes have 10–19 students. Most lab/discussion sessions have 10–19 students. **Most popular majors:** Biology/Biological Sciences, General; Business Administration and Management, General; Organizational Behavior Studies. **Special Study Options:** Cross-registration; Double major; English as a Second

Language (ESL); Exchange student program (domestic); Honors program; Independent study; Internships; Student-designed major; Study abroad; Teacher certification program. **Disability Services offered:** Note-taking services; Reader services; Tape recorders; Tutors. **Career services:** Alumni network; Alumni services; Career assessment; Career/job search classes; Internships; Regional alumni.

FACILITIES

Housing: Apartments for single students; Coed dorms; Men's dorms; Special housing for disabled students; Theme housing; Women's dorms; 93% of campus accessible to physically disabled. **Special Academic Facilities/Equipment:** Museum of art and print study center, greenhouse, electron microscope, radionuclide complex, neuroscience research lab, music technology lab, art technology lab, spatial analysis lab, herbarium, high field nuclear magnetic resonance spectrometer, gallery of design from nature, ancient world gallery, real-time stock trading floor, digital scholarship lab, center for pro bono law clinic, Virginia Baptist Historical Society museum, Speech Center, Jepson School of Leadership, Center for Civic Engagement. **Campus network:** 100% of classrooms, 100% of dorms, 100% of student union, 100% of libraries, 100% of dining areas, 70% of common outdoor areas have wireless network access.

CAMPUS LIFE

Environment: City. **Activities:** Campus Ministries; Choral groups; Concert band; Dance; Drama/theater; International Student Organization; Jazz band; Literary magazine; Model UN; Music ensembles; Musical theater; Pep band; Radio station; Student government; Student newspaper; Student-run film society; Symphony orchestra. 163 registered organizations, 7 honor societies, 14 religious organizations, 8 fraternities, 8 sororities on campus. **Athletics (Intercollegiate):** *Men:* baseball, basketball, cross-country, football, golf, soccer, tennis, track/field (outdoor), track/field (indoor). *Women:* basketball, cross-country, diving, field hockey, golf, lacrosse, soccer, swimming, tennis, track/field (outdoor), track/field (indoor). **On-Campus Highlights:** Boatwright Memorial Library and 8:15 Coffee Shop. **Environmental Initiatives:** The University of Richmond is committed to being carbon neutral by 2050 with interim goals of 30% below 2008 levels by 2020 and 65% below 2008 levels by 2035. As of our last GHG accounting in 2017, we have reduced our greenhouse gas emissions 24% below 2008 levels. We accomplished this by installing a 205 kW rooftop solar array, transitioning from coal to natural gas for heating, completing dozens of energy efficiency upgrades, and setting a LEED Silver minimum requirement on all new construction.

ADMISSIONS

Freshman Academic Profile: 59% in top 10% of high school class, 86% in top 25% of high school class, 96% in top 50% of high school class. 59% from public high schools. **Test Scores:** SAT Math middle 50% range 650–750. SAT EBRW middle 50% range 640–710. ACT middle 50% range 30–33. **Basis for Candidate Selection:** *Very important factors include:* rigor of secondary school record, academic GPA. *Important factors include:* class rank, application essay, standardized test scores, recommendation(s), extracurricular activities, talent/ability, character/personal qualities. *Other factors include:* first generation, alumni/ae relation, geographical residence, state residency, racial/ethnic status, volunteer work, work experience, level of applicant's interest. **Freshman Admission Requirements:** High school diploma is required and GED is accepted. *Academic units required:* 4 English, 3 math, 2 science, 2 science labs, 2 foreign language, 2 history. *Academic units recommended:* 4 English, 4 math, 4 science, 4 science labs, 4 foreign language, 4 history. **Freshman Admission Statistics:** 12,356 applied, 28% admitted, 23% enrolled. **Transfer Admission Requirements:** High school transcript, college transcript(s), essay or personal statement, statement of good standing from prior institution(s). Minimum college GPA of 2.0 required. Lowest grade transferable C. **General Admission Information:** Application fee $50. Regular application deadline 1/15. Admission may be deferred for a maximum of 1 year.

COSTS AND FINANCIAL AID

Annual tuition $56,860. Room and board $13,430. Average book and supplies expense $1,100. **Required Forms and Deadlines:** CSS/Financial Aid PROFILE; FAFSA; Noncustodial PROFILE. **Notification of Awards:** Applicants will be notified of awards on or about 4/1. **Types of Aid:** *Need-based scholarships/grants:* College/university scholarship or grant aid from institutional funds; Federal Pell; Private scholarships; SEOG; State scholarships/grants. *Loans:* Direct PLUS loans; Direct Subsidized Stafford Loans; Direct Unsubsidized Stafford Loans. **Student Employment:** Federal Work-Study Program available. Institutional employment available. **Financial Aid Statistics:** 99% needy freshmen, 98% needy undergrads receive need-based scholarship or

grant aid. 24% freshmen, 19% undergrads receive non-need-based scholarship or grant aid. 72% freshmen, 78% undergrads receive need-based self-help aid. 8% freshmen, 8% undergrads receive athletic scholarships. 61% freshmen, 68% undergrads receive any aid. 41% undergrads borrow to pay for school. Average cumulative indebtedness $28,341. **Criteria awarding aid:** *Non-need-based:* Academics, Art, Athletics, Leadership, Music/drama.

UNIVERSITY OF RIO GRANDE

218 North College Avenue, Rio Grande, OH 45774
Phone: 740-245-7206 **Financial Aid Phone:** 740-245-7219
E-mail: admissions@rio.edu **CEEB Code:** 1663
Fax: 740-245-7260 **Website:** rio.edu **ACT Code:** 3324

This private school was founded in 1876. It has a 190 acre campus.

RATINGS

Admissions Selectivity Rating: 76   **Fire Safety Rating:** 87   **Green Rating:** 60*

STUDENTS AND FACULTY

Enrollment: 1,165. **Student Body:** 65% female, 35% male, 4% out-of-state, 2% international. Asian <1%, African American 5%, Caucasian 81%, Hispanic 1%, Native American <1%, Pacific Islander <1%, Two or more races <1%, Race unknown 10%.
Retention and Graduation: 50% freshmen return for sophomore year. 0% grads go on to further study within 1 year. **Faculty:** Student/faculty ratio 20:1. 77 full-time faculty, 45% hold PhDs, 4% are members of minority groups, 44% are women. 0% of classes are taught by teaching assistants.

ACADEMICS

Degrees: Associate; Bachelor's; Certificate; Master's. **Classes:** Most classes have fewer than 10 students. Most lab/discussion sessions have 10–19 students. **Most popular majors:** Business/Office Automation/Technology/Data Entry; Elementary Education and Teaching. **Special Study Options:** Accelerated program; Cooperative education program; Distance learning; Double major; Dual enrollment; English as a Second Language (ESL); Honors program; Independent study; Internships; Liberal arts/career combination; Student-designed major; Study abroad; Teacher certification program. **Disability Services offered:** Note-taking services; Reader services; Tape recorders; Tutors. **Career services:** Alumni services; Career assessment; Internships.

FACILITIES

Housing: Coed dorms; Men's dorms; Special housing for disabled students; Wellness housing; Women's dorms 75% of campus accessible to physically disabled. **Special Academic Facilities/Equipment:** Archives of local and college history, art museum, fine woodworking, theater, art annex, Greer Museum for history and art. **Campus network:** 100% of classrooms, 100% of dorms, 100% of student union, 100% of libraries, 100% of dining areas, 100% of common outdoor areas have wireless network access.

CAMPUS LIFE

Environment: Rural. **Activities:** Campus Ministries; Choral groups; Concert band; Dance; Drama/theater; Jazz band; Literary magazine; Music ensembles; Musical theater; Pep band; Radio station; Student government; Student newspaper; Television station. 36 registered organizations, 4 honor societies, 3 religious organizations, 4 fraternities, 5 sororities on campus. **Athletics (Intercollegiate):** *Men:* baseball, basketball, cross-country, soccer, track/field (outdoor), track/field (indoor). *Women:* basketball, cheerleading, cross-country, soccer, softball, track/field (outdoor), track/field (indoor), volleyball. **On-Campus Highlights:** Food Court. **Environmental Initiatives:** Recycling program, some solar powered equipment, energy usage reduction program, trayless Tuesdays in the cafeteria.

ADMISSIONS

Freshman Academic Profile: Average high school GPA 2.9. 5% in top 10% of high school class, 20% in top 25% of high school class, 49% in top 50% of high school class. 95% from public high schools. **Test Scores:** ACT middle 50% range 17–22. **Basis for Candidate Selection:** *Other factors include:* class rank, academic GPA, standardized test scores. **Freshman Admission Requirements:** High school diploma is required and GED is accepted. *Academic units required:* 4 English, 3 math, 3 science, 1 science labs, 3 social studies, 7 academic electives. *Academic units recommended:* 2 science labs, 2 foreign language, 2 history, 9 academic electives. **Freshman Admission Statistics:** 1,909 applied, 69% admitted, 35% enrolled. **Transfer Admission**

Requirements: High school transcript, college transcript(s), statement of good standing from prior institution(s). Lowest grade transferable D. **General Admission Information:** Application fee $25. Non-fall registration accepted.

COSTS AND FINANCIAL AID
Annual tuition $23,260. Room and board $9,920. Required fees $600. Average book and supplies expense $1,200. **Required Forms and Deadlines:** FAFSA; Institution's own financial aid form. **Notification of Awards:** Applicants will be notified of awards on a rolling basis beginning 1/15. **Types of Aid:** *Need-based scholarships/grants:* College/university scholarship or grant aid from institutional funds; Federal Pell; Private scholarships; SEOG; State scholarships/grants. *Loans:* Direct PLUS loans; Direct Subsidized Stafford Loans; Direct Unsubsidized Stafford Loans. **Student Employment:** Federal Work-Study Program available. Institutional employment available. **Financial Aid Statistics:** 69% needy freshmen, 68% needy undergrads receive need-based scholarship or grant aid. 68% freshmen, 69% undergrads receive non-need-based scholarship or grant aid. 56% freshmen, 59% undergrads receive need-based self-help aid. 79% freshmen, 28% undergrads receive athletic scholarships. 78% freshmen, 77% undergrads receive any aid. 74% undergrads borrow to pay for school. Average cumulative indebtedness $32,722. **Criteria awarding aid:** *Need-based:* Academics. *Non-need-based:* Academics, Alumni affiliation, Athletics, Leadership, Music/drama, State/district residency.

UNIVERSITY OF ROCHESTER

300 Wilson Blvd, Rochester, NY 14627
Phone: 585-275-3221 **Financial Aid Phone:** 585-275-3226
E-mail: admit@admissions.rochester.edu **CEEB Code:** 2928
Fax: 585-461-4595 **Website:** www.rochester.edu **ACT Code:** 2980

This private school was founded in 1850. It has a 655 acre campus.

RATINGS
Admissions Selectivity Rating: 94   Fire Safety Rating: 95   Green Rating: 86

STUDENTS AND FACULTY
Enrollment: 6,348. **Student Body:** 49% female, 51% male, 59% out-of-state, 27% international (114 countries represented). Asian 11%, African American 5%, Caucasian 42%, Hispanic 7%, Native American <1%, Pacific Islander <1%, Two or more races 3%, Race unknown 5%.
Retention and Graduation: 95% freshmen return for sophomore year. 34% grads go on to further study within 1 year. **Faculty:** Student/faculty ratio 10:1. 368 full-time faculty, 0% hold PhDs, 0% are members of minority groups, 0% are women.

ACADEMICS
Degrees: Bachelor's; Doctoral degree—professional practice; Doctoral degree research/scholarship; Master's; Post-bachelor's certificate; Post-master's certificate. **Most popular majors:** Economics, General; Biology/Biological Sciences, General; Psychology, General. **Special Study Options:** Accelerated program; Cooperative education program; Cross-registration; Double major; Dual enrollment; English as a Second Language (ESL); Honors program; Independent study; Internships; Liberal arts/career combination; Student-designed major; Study abroad; Teacher certification program. **Honors programs:** Exceptional undergraduates interested in studying medicine, engineering, or education may pursue one of the following Combined-Admission Programs (CAP), which guarantee admission to professional or graduate school upon successful completion of undergraduate studies: • Rochester Early Medical Scholars (REMS), an eight-year BA/BS–MD program. Admitted students enter the University with a guarantee of admission to the School of Medicine and Dentistry. • Graduate Engineering at Rochester (GEAR), a five-year BS-MS program. Admitted students enter the University with assurance of admission into one of seven engineering master's programs at the Hajim School of Engineering. • Guaranteed Rochester Accelerated Degree in Education (GRADE), a five-year BA/BS–MS program. Admitted students enter the University with a guarantee of admission to the Margaret Warner Graduate School of Education. **Combined degree programs:** BA/MA; BA/MD. **Disability Services offered:** Note-taking services; Reader services; Tape recorders; Tutors. **Career services:** Alumni network; Alumni services; Career assessment; Internships.

FACILITIES
Housing: Apartments for married students; Apartments for single students; Coed dorms; Fraternity/sorority housing; Men's dorms; Special housing for disabled students; Special housing for international students; Theme housing; Wellness housing; Women's dorms; 90% of campus accessible to physically disabled. **Special Academic Facilities/Equipment:** Anthony Center for Women's Leadership, Arthur Kornberg Medical Research Building, C.E.K. Mees Observatory, Center for Biomedical Ultrasound, Center for Electronic Imaging Systems, Center for Future Health, Center for Visual Science, Clinical and Translational Sciences Building, Eastman Theatre, Frederick Douglas Institute for African and African-American, Institute for Popular Music, Institute of Optics, Laboratory for Laser Energetics, Medical Center, Memorial Art Gallery, Omega Laser Facility, Sign Language Research Center, Skalny Center for Polish and Central European Studies, W. Allen Wallis Institute of Political Economy.

CAMPUS LIFE
Environment: City. **Activities:** Campus Ministries; Choral groups; Concert band; Dance; Drama/theater; International Student Organization; Jazz band; Literary magazine; Marching band; Model UN; Music ensembles; Musical theater; Opera; Pep band; Radio station; Student government; Student newspaper; Student-run film society; Symphony orchestra; Television station; Yearbook. 260 registered organizations, 6 honor societies, 13 religious organizations, 18 fraternities, 15 sororities on campus. **Athletics (Intercollegiate):** *Men:* baseball, basketball, cross-country, diving, football, golf, soccer, squash, swimming, tennis, track/field (outdoor), track/field (indoor). *Women:* basketball, crew/rowing, cross-country, diving, field hockey, golf, lacrosse, soccer, softball, swimming, tennis, track/field (outdoor), track/field (indoor), volleyball. **On-Campus Highlights:** Eastman Theater. **Environmental Initiatives:** For the fourth year in a row, the University of Rochester has been recognized as a Tree Campus USA by the Arbor Day Foundation. The program recognizes college campuses that have made a commitment to effective urban forest management by planting, preserving, and protecting tree resources and that engage staff, students, and the community in conservation goals. To become a Tree Campus, the University must maintain five standards—have a campus tree advisory committee, a campus tree care plan, dedicated annual expenditures, Arbor Day observance, and a service learning project. This past year, Dan Schied, manager of Horticulture and Grounds, gave several "tree tours" around campus, as well as lead two new tree planting ceremonies with students on campus in celebration of Earth Day and Arbor Day.

ADMISSIONS
Freshman Academic Profile: Average high school GPA 3.8. 74% from public high schools. **Test Scores:** SAT Math middle 50% range 710–790. SAT EBRW middle 50% range 630–710. ACT middle 50% range 29–34. **Basis for Candidate Selection:** *Very important factors include:* rigor of secondary school record, recommendation(s), character/personal qualities. *Important factors include:* academic GPA, application essay, standardized test scores, interview, extracurricular activities, talent/ability. *Other factors include:* class rank, first generation, alumni/ae relation, geographical residence, racial/ethnic status, volunteer work, work experience, level of applicant's interest. **Freshman Admission Requirements:** High school diploma is required and GED is accepted. **Freshman Admission Statistics:** 18,915 applied, 31% admitted, 23% enrolled. **Transfer Admission Requirements:** College transcript(s), essay or personal statement. Lowest grade transferable C. **General Admission Information:** Application fee $50. Regular application deadline 1/5. Non-fall registration accepted.

COSTS AND FINANCIAL AID
Annual tuition $55,040. Room and board $15,938. Required fees $990. Average book and supplies expense $1,310. **Required Forms and Deadlines:** CSS/Financial Aid PROFILE; FAFSA; Noncustodial PROFILE; State aid form. **Notification of Awards:** Applicants will be notified of awards on or about 4/1. **Types of Aid:** *Need-based scholarships/grants:* College/university scholarship or grant aid from institutional funds; Federal Pell; Private scholarships; SEOG; State scholarships/grants. *Loans:* Direct PLUS loans; Direct Subsidized Stafford Loans; Direct Unsubsidized Stafford Loans. **Student Employment:** Federal Work-Study Program available. Institutional employment available. **Financial Aid Statistics:** 99% needy freshmen, 100% needy undergrads receive need-based scholarship or grant aid. 12% freshmen, 12% undergrads receive non-need-based scholarship or grant aid. 82% freshmen, 83% undergrads receive need-based self-help aid. 0% freshmen, 0% undergrads receive athletic scholarships. 85% freshmen receive any aid. 51% undergrads borrow to pay for school. Average cumulative indebtedness $29,553. **Criteria awarding aid:** *Need-based:* Academics, Music/drama. *Non-need-based:* Academics, Alumni affiliation, Art, Leadership, Music/drama.

UNIVERSITY OF ST. FRANCIS (IL)

500 Wilcox Street, Joliet, IL 60435
Phone: 815-740-5037 **Financial Aid Phone:** 866-890-8331
E-mail: admissions@stfrancis.edu **CEEB Code:** 1130
Fax: 815-740-5078 **Website:** www.stfrancis.edu **ACT Code:** 1000

This private school, affiliated with the Roman Catholic Church, was founded in 1920. It has a 18 acre campus.

RATINGS
Admissions Selectivity Rating: 88   **Fire Safety Rating:** 99   **Green Rating:** 86

STUDENTS AND FACULTY
Enrollment: 1,648. **Student Body:** 66% female, 34% male, 9% out-of-state, 3% international (14 countries represented). Asian 3%, African American 9%, Caucasian 58%, Hispanic 22%, Native American <1%, Pacific Islander <1%, Two or more races 3%, Race unknown 1%.
Retention and Graduation: 81% freshmen return for sophomore year. 42% freshmen graduate within 4 years. 62% freshmen graduate within 6 years. 21% grads go on to further study within 1 year. **Faculty:** Student/faculty ratio 13:1. 99 full-time faculty, 74% hold PhDs, 15% are members of minority groups, 63% are women. 0% of classes are taught by teaching assistants.

ACADEMICS
Degrees: Bachelor's; Certificate; Doctoral degree—other; Doctoral degree research/scholarship; Master's; Post-bachelor's certificate; Post-master's certificate. **Classes:** Most classes have 10–19 students. Most lab/discussion sessions have 10–19 students. **Most popular majors:** Registered Nursing/Registered Nurse; Business/Commerce, General. **Special Study Options:** Distance learning; Double major; Dual enrollment; English as a Second Language (ESL); Honors program; Independent study; Internships; Student-designed major; Study abroad; Teacher certification program. **Honors programs:** Duns Scotus Fellow/Scholars Program is designed to create a learning community of motivated students who are challenged to excel academically. **Disability Services offered:** Note-taking services; Reader services; Tape recorders. **Career services:** Alumni network; Alumni services; Career assessment; Career/job search classes; Internships; Regional alumni.

FACILITIES
Housing: Apartments for single students; Coed dorms; Men's dorms; Special housing for disabled students; Theme housing; Wellness housing; Women's dorms; 100% of campus accessible to physically disabled. **Special Academic Facilities/Equipment:** Wireless and multimedia classrooms, numerous science laboratories, testing centers, private music practice and instruction rooms, digital audio and recording arts studio, 2D/3D design labs and equipment, medical and skills simulation labs, a cadaver lab, a mock trial courtroom, a business incubator, an art & design complex with studio spaces for senior students, an international student center, golf studio, a greenhouse, numerous multi-purpose spaces, on-campus beehives, butterfly garden, two greenhouses, and an outdoor challenge course.

CAMPUS LIFE
Environment: City. **Activities:** Campus Ministries; Choral groups; Dance; Drama/theater; International Student Organization; Music ensembles; Musical theater; Opera; Radio station; Student government; Student newspaper; Symphony orchestra; Television station. 65 registered organizations, 19 honor societies, 2 religious organizations, 1 fraternity, 1 sorority on campus. **Athletics (Intercollegiate):** *Men:* baseball, basketball, cross-country, football, golf, soccer, tennis, track/field (outdoor), track/field (indoor). *Women:* basketball, cheerleading, cross-country, golf, soccer, softball, tennis, track/field (outdoor), track/field (indoor), volleyball. **On-Campus Highlights:** Bistro. **Environmental Initiatives:** 1. Campus wide recycling; 2. Two large on-campus bee and butterfly garden: monarch way station and bee and butterfly pollinator certified; 3. Two beehives on campus, university community garden.

ADMISSIONS
Freshman Academic Profile: Average high school GPA 3.6. 83% from public high schools. **Test Scores:** SAT Math middle 50% range 510–620. SAT EBRW middle 50% range 520–600. ACT middle 50% range 20–27. **Basis for Candidate Selection:** *Very important factors include:* rigor of secondary school record, academic GPA, standardized test scores. *Other factors include:* class rank, application essay, recommendation(s), interview. **Freshman Admission Requirements:** High school diploma is required and GED is accepted. *Academic units required:* 4 English, 3 math, 2 science, 1 science labs, 2 social

studies, 3 academic electives, 3 unit from above areas or other academic areas. **Freshman Admission Statistics:** 2,273 applied, 46% admitted, 23% enrolled. **Transfer Admission Requirements:** College transcript(s), statement of good standing from prior institution(s). Minimum college GPA of 2.5 required. **General Admission Information:** Regular application deadline 8/1. Admission may be deferred for a maximum of 1 year.

COSTS AND FINANCIAL AID
Annual tuition $35,000. Room and board $10,210. Average book and supplies expense $800. **Required Forms and Deadlines:** FAFSA; Institution's own financial aid form. **Notification of Awards:** Applicants will be notified of awards on a rolling basis beginning 10/15. **Types of Aid:** *Need-based scholarships/grants:* College/university scholarship or grant aid from institutional funds; Federal Pell; Private scholarships; SEOG; State scholarships/grants; United Negro College Fund. *Loans:* Direct PLUS loans; Direct Subsidized Stafford Loans; Direct Unsubsidized Stafford Loans. **Student Employment:** Federal Work-Study Program available. Institutional employment available. **Financial Aid Statistics:** 100% needy freshmen, 99% needy undergrads receive need-based scholarship or grant aid. 28% freshmen, 15% undergrads receive non-need-based scholarship or grant aid. 60% freshmen, 93% undergrads receive need-based self-help aid. 8% freshmen, 7% undergrads receive athletic scholarships. 99% freshmen, 89% undergrads receive any aid. 75% undergrads borrow to pay for school. Average cumulative indebtedness $30,274. **Criteria awarding aid:** *Need-based:* Academics, Art, Athletics, Leadership, Minority status, Music/drama, Religious affiliation. *Non-need-based:* Academics, Alumni affiliation, Art, Athletics, Leadership, Minority status, Music/drama, Religious affiliation, State/district residency.

UNIVERSITY OF SAINT FRANCIS (IN)

2701 Spring Street, Fort Wayne, IN 46808
Phone: 260-399-8000 **Financial Aid Phone:** 260-399-8003
E-mail: admis@sf.edu **CEEB Code:** 1693
Website: www.sf.edu **ACT Code:** 1238

This private school, affiliated with the Roman Catholic Church, was founded in 1890. It has a 100 acre campus.

RATINGS
Admissions Selectivity Rating: 73   **Fire Safety Rating:** 97   **Green Rating:** 60*

STUDENTS AND FACULTY
Enrollment: 1,741. **Student Body:** 70% female, 30% male, 11% out-of-state, 1% international (8 countries represented). Asian 2%, African American 9%, Caucasian 74%, Hispanic 10%, Native American <1%, Pacific Islander 0%, Two or more races 3%, Race unknown 1%.
Retention and Graduation: 69% freshmen return for sophomore year. 44% freshmen graduate within 4 years. 53% freshmen graduate within 6 years. 18% grads go on to further study within 1 year. 2% grads pursue arts and sciences degrees. 0% grads pursue law degrees. 2% grads pursue business degrees. 1% grads pursue medical degrees. **Faculty:** Student/faculty ratio 11:1. 128 full-time faculty, 51% hold PhDs, 8% are members of minority groups, 60% are women. 0% of classes are taught by teaching assistants.

ACADEMICS
Degrees: Associate; Bachelor's; Certificate; Doctoral degree—professional practice; Master's; Post-master's certificate. **Classes:** Most classes have 10–19 students. Most lab/discussion sessions have fewer than 10 students. **Most popular majors:** Biology/Biological Sciences, General; Health and Wellness, General; Registered Nursing/Registered Nurse. **Special Study Options:** Cooperative education program; Cross-registration; Distance learning; Double major; Honors program; Independent study; Internships; Student-designed major; Teacher certification program. **Honors programs:** John Duns Scotus Honors Program. **Disability Services offered:** Note-taking services; Reader services; Tape recorders; Tutors. **Career services:** Alumni network; Alumni services; Career assessment; Internships.

FACILITIES
Housing: Apartments for single students; Coed dorms; Men's dorms; Special housing for disabled students; Women's dorms. **Special Academic Facilities/Equipment:** Five art galleries (John P. Weatherhead Gallery, The Goldfish Gallery, The Artist Spotlight Gallery, Lupke Gallery, Rolland Gallery); Robert Goldstine Performing Arts Center; Health Sciences Simulation Lab; North Campus Auditorium; music technology digital recording studio; School

of Creative Arts specialized facilities and studios; nature preserve. **Campus network:** 100% of classrooms, 100% of dorms, 100% of student union, 100% of libraries, 100% of dining areas, 100% of common outdoor areas have wireless network access.

CAMPUS LIFE

Environment: City. **Activities:** Campus Ministries; Choral groups; Concert band; Dance; Drama/theater; Jazz band; Literary magazine; Marching band; Music ensembles; Musical theater; Pep band; Student government; Student-run film society. 36 registered organizations, 6 honor societies, 1 religious organization on campus. **On-Campus Highlights:** Pope John Paul II Center.

ADMISSIONS

Freshman Academic Profile: Average high school GPA 3.4. 17% in top 10% of high school class, 46% in top 25% of high school class, 75% in top 50% of high school class. 84% from public high schools. **Test Scores:** SAT Math middle 50% range 470–580. SAT EBRW middle 50% range 478–590. ACT middle 50% range 18–25. **Basis for Candidate Selection:** *Very important factors include:* rigor of secondary school record, academic GPA, standardized test scores. *Important factors include:* class rank. *Other factors include:* application essay, recommendation(s), interview, extracurricular activities, volunteer work, work experience, level of applicant's interest. **Freshman Admission Requirements:** High school diploma is required and GED is accepted. *Academic units required:* 4 English, 3 math, 2 science, 2 social studies, 1 history, 1 academic elective. *Academic units recommended:* 4 English, 4 math, 3 science, 3 social studies, 1 history, 4 academic electives. **Freshman Admission Statistics:** 1,587 applied, 96% admitted, 26% enrolled. **General Admission Information:** Non-fall registration accepted. Admission may be deferred for a maximum of one semester.

COSTS AND FINANCIAL AID

Annual tuition $31,290. Room and board $10,490. Required fees $1,130. Average book and supplies expense $1,200. **Required Forms and Deadlines:** FAFSA. **Notification of Awards:** Applicants will be notified of awards on a rolling basis beginning 12/1. **Types of Aid:** *Need-based scholarships/grants:* College/university scholarship or grant aid from institutional funds; Federal Pell; Private scholarships; SEOG; State scholarships/grants. *Loans:* Direct PLUS loans; Direct Subsidized Stafford Loans; Direct Unsubsidized Stafford Loans. **Student Employment:** Federal Work-Study Program available. Institutional employment available. **Financial Aid Statistics:** 100% needy freshmen, 99% needy undergrads receive need-based scholarship or grant aid. 17% freshmen, 14% undergrads receive non-need-based scholarship or grant aid. 81% freshmen, 81% undergrads receive need-based self-help aid. 11% freshmen, 11% undergrads receive athletic scholarships. 99% freshmen, 94% undergrads receive any aid. 83% undergrads borrow to pay for school. Average cumulative indebtedness $42,336. **Criteria awarding aid:** *Need-based:* Academics, Art, Athletics, Music/drama. *Non-need-based:* Academics, Art, Athletics, Music/drama, State/district residency.

UNIVERSITY OF SAINT JOSEPH

1678 Asylum Avenue, West Hartford, CT 06117
Phone: 860-231-5216 **Financial Aid Phone:** 860-231-5223
E-mail: admissions@usj.edu **CEEB Code:** 3754
Fax: 860-231-5744 **Website:** www.usj.edu

This private school, affiliated with the Roman Catholic Church, was founded in 1932. It has a 90 acre campus.

RATINGS

Admissions Selectivity Rating: 82   **Fire Safety Rating:** 99   **Green Rating:** 60*

STUDENTS AND FACULTY

Enrollment: 871. **Student Body:** 80% female, 20% male, 95% out-of-state, 1% international. Asian 6%, African American 14%, Caucasian 57%, Hispanic 15%, Native American <1%, Pacific Islander <1%, Two or more races 3%, Race unknown 3%.
Retention and Graduation: 79% freshmen return for sophomore year. 57% freshmen graduate within 4 years. 63% freshmen graduate within 6 years.
Faculty: Student/faculty ratio 10:1. 134 full-time faculty, 94% hold PhDs, 22% are members of minority groups, 72% are women. 0% of classes are taught by teaching assistants.

ACADEMICS

Degrees: Bachelor's; Certificate; Doctoral degree—professional practice; Master's; Post-bachelor's certificate; Post-master's certificate. **Classes:** Most classes have 10–19 students. Most lab/discussion sessions have 10–19 students. **Most popular majors:** Social Work; Registered Nursing/Registered Nurse; Psychology, General. **Special Study Options:** Accelerated program; Distance learning; Double major; Honors program; Independent study; Internships; Liberal arts/career combination; Student-designed major; Study abroad; Teacher certification program; Weekend college. **Combined degree programs:** BA/MA. **Career services:** Alumni services; Career assessment; Career/job search classes; Internships; Regional alumni.

FACILITIES

Housing: Apartments for single students; Coed dorms; Special housing for disabled students; Theme housing; Women's dorms. **Special Academic Facilities/Equipment:** Art Museum' 2 Lab Schools.

CAMPUS LIFE

Environment: Town. **Activities:** Campus Ministries; Choral groups; Dance; Drama/theater; International Student Organization; Literary magazine; Student government. 17 registered organizations, 4 religious organizations on campus. **Athletics (Intercollegiate):** . *Women:* basketball, cross-country, diving, lacrosse, soccer, softball, swimming, tennis, volleyball. **On-Campus Highlights:** Hoffman Auditorium.

ADMISSIONS

Freshman Academic Profile: Average high school GPA 3.3. 31% in top 10% of high school class, 54% in top 25% of high school class, 84% in top 50% of high school class. **Test Scores:** SAT Math middle 50% range 510–590. SAT EBRW middle 50% range 520–620. ACT middle 50% range 20–25. **Basis for Candidate Selection:** *Very important factors include:* rigor of secondary school record, academic GPA. *Important factors include:* class rank, application essay, standardized test scores, recommendation(s), volunteer work. *Other factors include:* extracurricular activities, talent/ability, character/personal qualities, alumni/ae relation. **Freshman Admission Requirements:** High school diploma is required and GED is accepted. **Freshman Admission Statistics:** 1,646 applied, 77% admitted, 16% enrolled. **Transfer Admission Requirements:** High school transcript, college transcript(s). Lowest grade transferable C. **General Admission Information:** Non-fall registration accepted. Admission may be deferred for a maximum of 2 semesters.

COSTS AND FINANCIAL AID

Annual tuition $38,482. Room and board $11,771. Required fees $1,804. Average book and supplies expense $1,000. **Required Forms and Deadlines:** FAFSA. **Notification of Awards:** Applicants will be notified of awards on a rolling basis beginning 11/15. **Types of Aid:** *Need-based scholarships/grants:* College/university scholarship or grant aid from institutional funds; Federal Nursing Scholarships; Federal Pell; Private scholarships; SEOG; State scholarships/grants. *Loans:* Direct PLUS loans; Direct Subsidized Stafford Loans; Direct Unsubsidized Stafford Loans. **Student Employment:** Federal Work-Study Program available. Institutional employment available. **Financial Aid Statistics:** 33% needy freshmen, 97% needy undergrads receive need-based scholarship or grant aid. 2% freshmen, 3% undergrads receive non-need-based scholarship or grant aid. 85% freshmen, 87% undergrads receive need-based self-help aid. 0% freshmen, 0% undergrads receive athletic scholarships. 100% freshmen, 93% undergrads receive any aid. 86% undergrads borrow to pay for school. Average cumulative indebtedness $36,700. **Criteria awarding aid:** *Non-need-based:* Academics, Leadership, Minority status.

UNIVERSITY OF SAINT MARY (KS)

4100 South Fourth Street, Leavenworth, KS 66048
Phone: 913-682-5151 **Financial Aid Phone:** 913-758-4303
E-mail: admiss@stmary.edu **CEEB Code:** 6630
Fax: 913-758-6140 **Website:** www.stmary.edu **ACT Code:** 1458

This private school, affiliated with the Roman Catholic Church, was founded in 1923. It has a 240 acre campus.

RATINGS

Admissions Selectivity Rating: 84   **Fire Safety Rating:** 60*   **Green Rating:** 60*

STUDENTS AND FACULTY

Enrollment: 732. **Student Body:** 48% female, 52% male, 49% out-of-state, 1% international (5 countries represented). Asian 1%, African American 12%,

Caucasian 50%, Hispanic 11%, Native American 1%, Pacific Islander 1%, Two or more races 1%, Race unknown 23%.
Retention and Graduation: 62% freshmen return for sophomore year. 33% freshmen graduate within 4 years. 44% freshmen graduate within 6 years.
Faculty: Student/faculty ratio 11:1. 67 full-time faculty, 79% hold PhDs, 18% are members of minority groups, 61% are women. 0% of classes are taught by teaching assistants.

ACADEMICS

Degrees: Associate; Bachelor's; Doctoral degree—professional practice; Master's. **Classes:** Most classes have 10–19 students. **Most popular majors:** Biology/ Biological Sciences, General; Sport and Fitness Administration/Management; Registered Nursing/Registered Nurse. **Special Study Options:** Accelerated program; Distance learning; Double major; Honors program; Independent study; Internships; Study abroad; Teacher certification program. **Honors programs:** USM Honors Program. **Disability Services offered:** Note-taking services; Tutors.

FACILITIES

Housing: Coed dorms. **Special Academic Facilities/Equipment:** Lincoln Library Collection, Art Gallery, Craig Scripture Collection, Civil War Collection.

CAMPUS LIFE

Environment: Town. **Activities:** Campus Ministries; Choral groups; Concert band; Dance; Drama/theater; Student government. 16 registered organizations, 3 religious organizations on campus. **Athletics (Intercollegiate):** *Men:* baseball, basketball, football, soccer. *Women:* basketball, soccer, softball, volleyball. **On-Campus Highlights:** De Paul Library and the Active Learning Center.

ADMISSIONS

Freshman Academic Profile: Average high school GPA 3.3. 9% in top 10% of high school class, 30% in top 25% of high school class, 63% in top 50% of high school class. 80% from public high schools. **Test Scores:** SAT Math middle 50% range 490–575. SAT EBRW middle 50% range 485–595. ACT middle 50% range 19–23. **Basis for Candidate Selection:** *Very important factors include:* academic GPA, standardized test scores. *Other factors include:* rigor of secondary school record, class rank, recommendation(s). **Freshman Admission Requirements:** High school diploma is required and GED is accepted. *Academic units required:* 4 English, 2 math, 2 science, 2 academic electives. *Academic units recommended:* 4 English, 4 math, 4 science, 2 science labs, 2 foreign language, 2 social studies, 2 history, 4 academic electives. **Freshman Admission Statistics:** 996 applied, 61% admitted, 22% enrolled. **Transfer Admission Requirements:** College transcript(s). Minimum college GPA of 2.0 required. Lowest grade transferable C. **General Admission Information:** Application fee $25. Non-fall registration accepted.

COSTS AND FINANCIAL AID

Annual tuition $27,880. Room and board $8,140. Required fees $810. Average book and supplies expense $2,550. **Required Forms and Deadlines:** FAFSA; State aid form. **Notification of Awards:** Applicants will be notified of awards on a rolling basis beginning 2/15. **Types of Aid:** *Need-based scholarships/grants:* College/university scholarship or grant aid from institutional funds; Federal Pell; Private scholarships; SEOG; State scholarships/grants. *Loans:* Direct PLUS loans; Direct Subsidized Stafford Loans; Direct Unsubsidized Stafford Loans. **Student Employment:** Federal Work-Study Program available. **Financial Aid Statistics:** 78% needy freshmen, 75% needy undergrads receive need-based scholarship or grant aid. 95% freshmen, 88% undergrads receive non-need-based scholarship or grant aid. 69% freshmen, 77% undergrads receive need-based self-help aid. 74% freshmen, 59% undergrads receive athletic scholarships. 100% undergrads borrow to pay for school. Average cumulative indebtedness $27,141. **Criteria awarding aid:** *Non-need-based:* Academics, Alumni affiliation, Art, Athletics, Leadership, Music/drama, Religious affiliation.

UNIVERSITY OF SAINT THOMAS (MN)

2115 Summit Avenue, St. Paul, MN 55105
Phone: (651) 962-6150 **Financial Aid Phone:** 651-962-6550
E-mail: admissions@stthomas.edu **CEEB Code:** 6110
Fax: (651) 962-6160 **Website:** www.stthomas.edu **ACT Code:** 2102

This private school, affiliated with the Roman Catholic Church, was founded in 1885. It has a 78 acre campus.

RATINGS

Admissions Selectivity Rating: 78   **Fire Safety Rating:** 60*   **Green Rating:** 89

STUDENTS AND FACULTY

Enrollment: 6,299. **Student Body:** 47% female, 53% male, 20% out-of-state, 3% international (71 countries represented). Asian 5%, African American 4%, Caucasian 76%, Hispanic 6%, Native American <1%, Pacific Islander <1%, Two or more races 3%, Race unknown 3%.
Retention and Graduation: 87% freshmen return for sophomore year.
Faculty: Student/faculty ratio 14:1. 440 full-time faculty, 91% hold PhDs, 18% are members of minority groups, 41% are women. 0% of classes are taught by teaching assistants.

ACADEMICS

Degrees: Associate; Bachelor's; Certificate; Doctoral degree—other; Doctoral degree—professional practice; Doctoral degree research/scholarship; Master's; Post-bachelor's certificate; Post-master's certificate. **Classes:** Most classes have 20–29 students. Most lab/discussion sessions have 10–19 students. **Special Study Options:** Cross-registration; Distance learning; Double major; English as a Second Language (ESL); Honors program; Independent study; Internships; Student-designed major; Study abroad; Teacher certification program. **Honors programs:** The Aquinas Scholars Program is the undergraduate honors program. Its purpose is to provide opportunities for motivated and curious students to deepen and enrich their undergraduate education. **Combined degree programs:** BA/MEng. **Disability Services offered:** Note-taking services; Reader services; Tape recorders; Tutors. **Career services:** Alumni network; Alumni services; Career assessment; Career/job search classes; Internships; Regional alumni.

FACILITIES

Housing: Apartments for single students; Coed dorms; Men's dorms; Special housing for disabled students; Special housing for international students; Theme housing; Wellness housing; Women's dorms; 5% of campus accessible to physically disabled.

CAMPUS LIFE

Environment: Metropolis. **Activities:** Campus Ministries; Choral groups; Concert band; Dance; Drama/theater; International Student Organization; Jazz band; Literary magazine; Music ensembles; Musical theater; Pep band; Radio station; Student government; Student newspaper; Student-run film society; Television station. 140 registered organizations, 2 honor societies, 12 religious organizations, 1 fraternity on campus. **Athletics (Intercollegiate):** *Men:* baseball, basketball, cross-country, diving, football, golf, ice hockey, soccer, swimming, tennis, track/field (outdoor), track/field (indoor). *Women:* basketball, cross-country, diving, golf, ice hockey, soccer, softball, swimming, tennis, track/field (outdoor), track/field (indoor), volleyball. **On-Campus Highlights:** Anderson Student Center. **Environmental Initiatives:** The University of St. Thomas recently received a three-year foundation grant of $575,000 to support an integrated university-wide system and culture of sustainability. The grant enabled the university to hire a full time staff member to coordinate campus sustainability initiatives.

ADMISSIONS

Freshman Academic Profile: Average high school GPA 3.6. 21% in top 10% of high school class, 49% in top 25% of high school class, 84% in top 50% of high school class. 73% from public high schools. **Test Scores:** SAT Math middle 50% range 590–690. SAT EBRW middle 50% range 570–660. ACT middle 50% range 24–29. **Basis for Candidate Selection:** *Very important factors include:* rigor of secondary school record, academic GPA, application essay, standardized test scores. *Important factors include:* class rank, recommendation(s). *Other factors include:* extracurricular activities, talent/ability, character/personal qualities, alumni/ae relation, geographical residence, racial/ethnic status, volunteer work, work experience, level of applicant's interest. **Freshman Admission Requirements:** High school diploma is required and GED is accepted. *Academic units required:* 3 math. *Academic units recommended:* 4 English, 4 math, 2 science, 4 foreign language. **Freshman**

Admission Statistics: 6,718 applied, 83% admitted, 25% enrolled. Transfer Admission Requirements: High school transcript, college transcript(s), essay or personal statement, statement of good standing from prior institution(s). Minimum college GPA of 2.3 required. Lowest grade transferable C-. General Admission Information: Non-fall registration accepted. Admission may be deferred for a maximum of Fall to Spring.

COSTS AND FINANCIAL AID
Student Employment: Federal Work-Study Program available. Institutional employment available. Financial Aid Statistics: 94% undergrads receive any aid. Criteria awarding aid: Non-need-based: Academics, Music/drama.

UNIVERSITY OF ST. THOMAS (TX)

3800 Montrose Boulevard, Houston, TX 77006-4696
Phone: 713-525-3500 Financial Aid Phone: 713-525-2151
E-mail: admissions@stthom.edu CEEB Code: 6880
Fax: 713-525-3558 Website: www.stthom.edu ACT Code: 4238

This private school, affiliated with the Roman Catholic Church, was founded in 1947. It has a 23 acre campus.

RATINGS
Admissions Selectivity Rating: 79   Fire Safety Rating: 95   Green Rating: 60*

STUDENTS AND FACULTY
Enrollment: 1,942. Student Body: 63% female, 37% male, 2% out-of-state, 8% international (38 countries represented). Asian 12%, African American 7%, Caucasian 21%, Hispanic 47%, Native American <1%, Pacific Islander <1%, Two or more races 2%, Race unknown 2%.
Retention and Graduation: 82% freshmen return for sophomore year. 33% freshmen graduate within 4 years. 63% freshmen graduate within 6 years. Faculty: Student/faculty ratio 11:1. 154 full-time faculty, 90% hold PhDs, 19% are members of minority groups, 46% are women. 0% of classes are taught by teaching assistants.

ACADEMICS
Degrees: Diploma; Doctoral degree—professional practice; Doctoral degree research/scholarship; Master's; Post-bachelor's certificate; Post-master's certificate. Classes: Most classes have 20–29 students. Most lab/discussion sessions have 10–19 students. Most popular majors: Registered Nursing/Registered Nurse; Biology/Biological Sciences, General; Psychology, General. Special Study Options: Accelerated program; Distance learning; Double major; Dual enrollment; Honors program; Independent study; Internships; Liberal arts/career combination; Student-designed major; Study abroad; Teacher certification program; Weekend college. Honors programs: The Honors Program at the University of St. Thomas is a four-year interdisciplinary program for students of exceptional intellectual ability, motivation, and curiosity. It is designed not simply to provoke students to master specific disciplines such as philosophy, history, mathematics, and natural science but to offer an experience which integrates, on the deepest and most profound level, the intellectual, cultural, and spiritual foundations of a liberal arts education. Combined degree programs: BA/MA. Disability Services offered: Note-taking services; Reader services; Tape recorders; Tutors. Career services: Alumni network; Alumni services; Career assessment; Internships.

FACILITIES
Housing: Apartments for married students; Apartments for single students; Coed dorms; Men's dorms; Women's dorms; 90% of campus accessible to physically disabled. Special Academic Facilities/Equipment: Tutorial Services Center, Chapel of St. Basil, Doherty Library, Link-Lee Mansion, Little Art Gallery.

CAMPUS LIFE
Environment: Metropolis. Activities: Campus Ministries; Choral groups; Drama/theater; International Student Organization; Jazz band; Literary magazine; Music ensembles; Musical theater; Opera; Student government; Student newspaper. 80 registered organizations, 21 honor societies, 13 religious organizations on campus. Athletics (Intercollegiate): Men: basketball, soccer. Women: volleyball. On-Campus Highlights: Jerabeck Activity and Athletic Center Environmental Initiatives: Campus Recycling of glass, aluminum, plastic & paper.

ADMISSIONS
Freshman Academic Profile: Average high school GPA 3.6. 23% in top 10% of high school class, 52% in top 25% of high school class, 81% in top 50% of high school class. 70% from public high schools. Test Scores: SAT Math middle 50% range 530–620. SAT EBRW middle 50% range 540–630. ACT middle 50% range 22–25. Basis for Candidate Selection: *Very important factors include:* academic GPA, standardized test scores. *Important factors include:* rigor of secondary school record, application essay, *Other factors include:* recommendation(s), interview, extracurricular activities, talent/ability, character/personal qualities, first generation, alumni/ae relation, volunteer work, work experience, level of applicant's interest. Freshman Admission Requirements: High school diploma is required and GED is accepted. *Academic units required:* 4 English, 3 math, 3 science, 2 science labs, 2 foreign language, 2 social studies, 1 history, 3 unit from above areas or other academic areas. *Academic units recommended:* 4 English, 3 math, 3 science, 2 science labs, 2 foreign language, 2 social studies, 1 history. Freshman Admission Statistics: 1,216 applied, 82% admitted, 36% enrolled. Transfer Admission Requirements: College transcript(s). Minimum college GPA of 2.50 required. Lowest grade transferable C. General Admission Information: Non-fall registration accepted. Admission may be deferred for a maximum of 1 year.

COSTS AND FINANCIAL AID
Annual tuition $30,800. Room and board $9,300. Required fees $660. Average book and supplies expense $1,094. Required Forms and Deadlines: FAFSA. Notification of Awards: Applicants will be notified of awards on a rolling basis beginning 2/15. Types of Aid: *Need-based scholarships/grants:* College/university scholarship or grant aid from institutional funds; Federal Pell; Private scholarships; SEOG; State scholarships/grants. *Loans:* Direct PLUS loans; Direct Subsidized Stafford Loans; Direct Unsubsidized Stafford Loans. Student Employment: Federal Work-Study Program available. Institutional employment available. Financial Aid Statistics: 99% needy freshmen, 98% needy undergrads receive need-based scholarship or grant aid. 7% freshmen, 5% undergrads receive non-need-based scholarship or grant aid. 34% freshmen, 47% undergrads receive need-based self-help aid. 4% freshmen, 3% undergrads receive athletic scholarships. 95% freshmen, 88% undergrads receive any aid. 55% undergrads borrow to pay for school. Average cumulative indebtedness $29,896. Criteria awarding aid: *Non-need-based:* Academics, Athletics, Music/drama, Religious affiliation.

UNIVERSITY OF SAN DIEGO

5998 Alcala Park, San Diego, CA 92110-2492
Phone: 619-260-4506 Financial Aid Phone: 619-260-4514
E-mail: admissions@sandiego.edu CEEB Code: 4849
Fax: 619-260-6836 Website: www.sandiego.edu ACT Code: 394

This private school, affiliated with the Roman Catholic Church, was founded in 1949. It has a 180 acre campus.

RATINGS
Admissions Selectivity Rating: 88   Fire Safety Rating: 93   Green Rating: 99

STUDENTS AND FACULTY
Enrollment: 5,820. Student Body: 55% female, 45% male, 39% out-of-state, 9% international (57 countries represented). Asian 7%, African American 3%, Caucasian 50%, Hispanic 21%, Native American <1%, Pacific Islander <1%, Two or more races 7%, Race unknown 3%.
Retention and Graduation: 92% freshmen return for sophomore year. 66% freshmen graduate within 4 years. 81% freshmen graduate within 6 years. 16% grads go on to further study within 1 year. 35% grads pursue arts and sciences degrees. 11% grads pursue law degrees. 22% grads pursue business degrees. 16% grads pursue medical degrees. Faculty: Student/faculty ratio 13:1. 484 full-time faculty, 94% hold PhDs, 26% are members of minority groups, 48% are women. 0% of classes are taught by teaching assistants.

ACADEMICS
Degrees: Bachelor's; Doctoral degree—other; Doctoral degree—professional practice; Doctoral degree research/scholarship; Master's; Post-bachelor's certificate. Classes: Most classes have 20–29 students. Most lab/discussion

sessions have 10–19 students. **Most popular majors:** Finance, General; Marketing/Marketing Management, General; Business Administration and Management, General. **Special Study Options:** Double major; English as a Second Language (ESL); Honors program; Independent study; Internships; Liberal arts/career combination; Study abroad; Teacher certification program. **Honors programs:** Phi Beta Kappa, Honors Program. **Disability Services offered:** Note-taking services; Reader services; Tape recorders. **Career services:** Alumni network; Alumni services; Career assessment; Career/job search classes; Internships; Regional alumni.

FACILITIES

Housing: Apartments for single students; Coed dorms; Men's dorms; Special housing for disabled students; Theme housing; Women's dorms; 85% of campus accessible to physically disabled. **Special Academic Facilities/Equipment:** Art gallery, peace and justice institute, child development center, language labs.

CAMPUS LIFE

Environment: Metropolis. **Activities:** Campus Ministries; Choral groups; Concert band; Dance; Drama/theater; International Student Organization; Jazz band; Marching band; Model UN; Music ensembles; Musical theater; Pep band; Radio station; Student government; Student newspaper; Student-run film society; Television station. 170 registered organizations, 22 honor societies, 3 religious organizations, 8 fraternities, 9 sororities on campus. **Athletics (Intercollegiate):** *Men:* baseball, basketball, crew/rowing, cross-country, football, golf, soccer, tennis. *Women:* basketball, cheerleading, crew/rowing, cross-country, diving, soccer, softball, swimming, tennis, track/field (outdoor), volleyball. **On-Campus Highlights:** Aromas Coffee House. **Environmental Initiatives:** The University of San Diego's E-waste center helps reduce the greenhouse gases, and landfill waste generated by the community as well as recycling E-waste produced by students, staff and the institution. The E-waste Center collects unwanted electronics from the community and recycles them. The usable components in these electronics are separated and sold, and the rest is processed and sent for recycling. This reduces landfill waste, hazardous waste, and greenhouse gas emissions of the community. As the ownership of these material is transferred to the E-waste center, the emissions reductions once they are recycled safely is 'owned' by USD. The E-waste center is managed as a non-profit and employs students, who can use the opportunity to earn and income while learning about recycling electronic waste.

ADMISSIONS

Freshman Academic Profile: Average high school GPA 3.9. 33% in top 10% of high school class, 74% in top 25% of high school class, 97% in top 50% of high school class. 52% from public high schools. **Test Scores:** SAT Math middle 50% range 590–690. SAT EBRW middle 50% range 600–680. ACT middle 50% range 26–31. **Basis for Candidate Selection:** *Very important factors include:* rigor of secondary school record, academic GPA, standardized test scores. *Important factors include:* class rank, application essay, recommendation(s), extracurricular activities, talent/ability, character/personal qualities, alumni/ae relation, religious affiliation/commitment, volunteer work. *Other factors include:* interview, first generation, geographical residence, racial/ethnic status, work experience, level of applicant's interest. **Freshman Admission Requirements:** High school diploma is required and GED is accepted. *Academic units required:* 4 English, 3 math, 3 science, 2 science labs, 3 foreign language, 2 social studies. *Academic units recommended:* 4 English, 4 math, 4 science, 3 science labs, 4 foreign language, 3 social studies. **Freshman Admission Statistics:** 13,287 applied, 53% admitted, 16% enrolled. **Transfer Admission Requirements:** High school transcript, college transcript(s), essay or personal statement. Minimum college GPA of 3.0 required. Lowest grade transferable C. **General Admission Information:** Application fee $55. Regular application deadline 12/15. Non-fall registration accepted. Admission may be deferred for a maximum of one year.

COSTS AND FINANCIAL AID

Annual tuition $50,450. Room and board $14,126. Required fees $736. Average book and supplies expense $1,970. **Required Forms and Deadlines:** FAFSA. **Notification of Awards:** Applicants will be notified of awards on a rolling basis beginning 3/1. **Types of Aid:** *Need-based scholarships/grants:* College/university scholarship or grant aid from institutional funds; Federal Nursing Scholarships; Federal Pell; Private scholarships; SEOG; State scholarships/grants. *Loans:* Direct PLUS loans; Direct Subsidized Stafford Loans; Direct Unsubsidized Stafford Loans. **Student Employment:** Federal Work-Study Program available. Institutional employment available. **Financial Aid Statistics:** 98% needy freshmen, 97% needy undergrads receive need-based scholarship or grant aid. 54% freshmen, 51% undergrads receive non-need-based scholarship or grant aid. 70% freshmen, 74% undergrads receive need-

based self-help aid. 2% freshmen, 2% undergrads receive athletic scholarships. 82% freshmen, 76% undergrads receive any aid. 45% undergrads borrow to pay for school. Average cumulative indebtedness $30,497. **Criteria awarding aid:** *Need-based:* Academics, Leadership, Religious affiliation. *Non-need-based:* Academics, Athletics, Leadership, Music/drama, Religious affiliation.

UNIVERSITY OF SAN FRANCISCO

2130 Fulton Street, San Francisco, CA 94117
Phone: 415-422-6563 **Financial Aid Phone:** (415) 422-3387
E-mail: admission@usfca.edu **CEEB Code:** 1325
Fax: 415-422-2217 **Website:** www.usfca.edu **ACT Code:** 0466

This private school, affiliated with the Roman Catholic Church, was founded in 1855. It has a 55 acre campus.

RATINGS

Admissions Selectivity Rating: 85   **Fire Safety Rating:** 90   **Green Rating:** 73

STUDENTS AND FACULTY

Enrollment: 6,510. **Student Body:** 62% female, 38% male, 33% out-of-state, 13% international (75 countries represented). Asian 24%, African American 5%, Caucasian 25%, Hispanic 22%, Native American <1%, Pacific Islander 1%, Two or more races 9%, Race unknown 2%.
Retention and Graduation: 85% freshmen return for sophomore year. 66% freshmen graduate within 4 years. 75% freshmen graduate within 6 years.
Faculty: Student/faculty ratio 13:1. 471 full-time faculty, 96% hold PhDs, 30% are members of minority groups, 54% are women. 0% of classes are taught by teaching assistants.

ACADEMICS

Degrees: Bachelor's; Doctoral degree—professional practice; Doctoral degree research/scholarship; Master's; Post-bachelor's certificate; Post-master's certificate. **Classes:** Most classes have 10–19 students. Most lab/discussion sessions have 10–19 students. **Most popular majors:** Biology/Biological Sciences, General; Psychology, General; Registered Nursing/Registered Nurse. **Special Study Options:** Cooperative education program; Cross-registration; Distance learning; Double major; English as a Second Language (ESL); Exchange student program (domestic); External degree program; Honors program; Independent study; Internships; Liberal arts/career combination; Study abroad; Teacher certification program. **Honors programs:** The Honors College offers high-achieving students in all majors a rigorous core curriculum that connects them with world-renowned scholars, writers, artists, and scientists through small seminars, special events, and workshops. Honors students can also apply for scholarships to attend conferences and immersion trips, or to study abroad. **Combined degree programs:** BA/JD; BA/MA; BA/MEng. **Disability Services offered:** Note-taking services; Reader services; Tape recorders; Tutors. **Career services:** Alumni network; Alumni services; Career assessment; Career/job search classes; Internships; Regional alumni.

FACILITIES

Housing: Apartments for single students; Coed dorms; Special housing for disabled students; Special housing for international students; Theme housing; Women's dorms; 100% of campus accessible to physically disabled. **Special Academic Facilities/Equipment:** Rare Book Room, Ricci Institute for Chinese-Western Cultural History. **Campus network:** 100% of classrooms, 100% of dorms, 100% of student union, 100% of libraries, 100% of dining areas, 75% of common outdoor areas have wireless network access.

CAMPUS LIFE

Environment: Metropolis. **Activities:** Campus Ministries; Choral groups; Dance; Drama/theater; International Student Organization; Jazz band; Literary magazine; Marching band; Music ensembles; Musical theater; Pep band; Radio station; Student government; Student newspaper; Television station; Yearbook. 149 registered organizations, 7 honor societies, 3 religious organizations, 4 fraternities, 6 sororities on campus. **Athletics (Intercollegiate):** *Men:* baseball, basketball, cross-country, golf, riflery, soccer, tennis, track/field (outdoor). *Women:* basketball, cross-country, golf, riflery, soccer, tennis, track/field (outdoor), volleyball. **On-Campus Highlights:** Koret Health and Recreation Center. **Environmental Initiatives:** Sustainability. Placed 5th in National competition in Recyclemania. Currently, USF's co-generation plant produces about half of lower campus' peak energy needs. Located in the basement of Gleeson Library, the plant converts natural gas into electricity. Although the conversion of natural gas to energy does produce some emissions, natural gas is considered the cleanest of the fossil fuels. The plant gets its co-generation designation because it also captures heat lost during the conversion process and uses that to provide some of the heat lower campus uses. The plant provides about 38 percent of lower campus' heating needs. Additionally, the university uses thermal panels on top of Phelan, Gillson, and Hayes-Healy halls. The panels differ from solar panels in that they heat water directly rather than producing electricity, providing some of the hot water needed in those halls.

ADMISSIONS

Freshman Academic Profile: Average high school GPA 3.5. 32% in top 10% of high school class, 66% in top 25% of high school class, 95% in top 50% of high school class. 59% from public high schools. **Test Scores:** SAT Math middle 50% range 560–670. SAT EBRW middle 50% range 570–660. ACT middle 50% range 23–29. **Basis for Candidate Selection:** *Very important factors include:* rigor of secondary school record, academic GPA. *Important factors include:* application essay, character/personal qualities, volunteer work. *Other factors include:* class rank, standardized test scores, recommendation(s), interview, extracurricular activities, talent/ability, first generation, alumni/ae relation, racial/ethnic status, work experience, level of applicant's interest. **Freshman Admission Requirements:** High school diploma is required and GED is accepted. *Academic units required:* 4 English, 3 math, 2 science, 2 science labs, 2 foreign language, 3 social studies, 6 academic electives. **Freshman Admission Statistics:** 21,867 applied, 64% admitted, 9% enrolled. **Transfer Admission Requirements:** college transcript(s), essay or personal statement. Minimum college GPA of 2.5 required. Lowest grade transferable C. **General Admission Information:** Application fee $70. Priority deadline 1/15. Regular application deadline 1/15. Non-fall registration accepted. Admission may be deferred for a maximum of 2 semesters.

COSTS AND FINANCIAL AID

Annual tuition $51,930. Room and board $15,990. Required fees $552. Average book and supplies expense $1,600. **Required Forms and Deadlines:** FAFSA; State aid form. **Notification of Awards:** Applicants will be notified of awards on or about 4/1. **Types of Aid:** *Need-based scholarships/grants:* College/university scholarship or grant aid from institutional funds; Federal Pell; Private scholarships; SEOG; State scholarships/grants. *Loans:* Direct PLUS loans; Direct Subsidized Stafford Loans; Direct Unsubsidized Stafford Loans. **Student Employment:** Federal Work-Study Program available. Institutional employment available. **Financial Aid Statistics:** 99% needy freshmen, 98% needy undergrads receive need-based scholarship or grant aid. 8% freshmen, 6% undergrads receive non-need-based scholarship or grant aid. 76% freshmen, 75% undergrads receive need-based self-help aid. 2% freshmen, 2% undergrads receive athletic scholarships. 87% freshmen, 81% undergrads receive any aid. 49% undergrads borrow to pay for school. Average cumulative indebtedness $33,752. **Criteria awarding aid:** *Need-based:* Academics, Alumni affiliation, Athletics, Minority status. *Non-need-based:* Academics, Athletics, Minority status.

UNIVERSITY OF SCIENCE & ARTS OF OKLAHOMA

1727 West Alabama, Chickasha, OK 73018
Phone: 405-574-1357 **Financial Aid Phone:** 405-574-1240
E-mail: usao-admissions@usao.edu **CEEB Code:** 6544
Fax: 405-574-1220 **Website:** www.usao.edu **ACT Code:** 3418

This public school was founded in 1908. It has a 75 acre campus.

RATINGS

Admissions Selectivity Rating: 82   **Fire Safety Rating:** 96   **Green Rating:** 60*

STUDENTS AND FACULTY

Enrollment: 847. **Student Body:** 66% female, 34% male, 14% out-of-state, 8% international (22 countries represented). Asian 1%, African American 5%, Caucasian 63%, Hispanic 7%, Native American 14%, Pacific Islander 0%, Two or more races 0%, Race unknown 2%.
Retention and Graduation: 78% freshmen return for sophomore year.
Faculty: Student/faculty ratio 12:1. 54 full-time faculty, 87% hold PhDs, 11% are members of minority groups, 52% are women. 0% of classes are taught by teaching assistants.

ACADEMICS

Degrees: Bachelor's. **Classes:** Most classes have 10–19 students. Most lab/discussion sessions have 10–19 students. **Most popular majors:** Business Administration and Management, General; Elementary Education and Teaching; Psychology, General. **Special Study Options:** Accelerated program; Double major; Independent study; Internships; Liberal arts/career combination; Student-designed major; Study abroad; Teacher certification program. **Disability Services offered:** Note-taking services; Tutors. **Career services:** Career assessment; Career/job search classes; Internships.

FACILITIES

Housing: Apartments for single students; Coed dorms; Special housing for disabled students 100% of campus accessible to physically disabled. **Special Academic Facilities/Equipment:** Language labs, speech and hearing clinic, multiple computer labs, herbarium.

CAMPUS LIFE

Environment: Village. **Activities:** Campus Ministries; Choral groups; Concert band; Dance; Drama/theater; International Student Organization; Jazz band; Literary magazine; Music ensembles; Musical theater; Pep band; Student government; Student newspaper. 24 registered organizations, 7 honor societies, 4 religious organizations, 1 fraternity, 1 sorority on campus. **Athletics (Intercollegiate):** *Men:* baseball, basketball, cheerleading, soccer. *Women:* basketball, cheerleading, soccer, softball. **On-Campus Highlights:** Lawson Court.

ADMISSIONS

Freshman Academic Profile: Average high school GPA 3.4. 25% in top 10% of high school class, 47% in top 25% of high school class, 78% in top 50% of high school class. 90% from public high schools. **Test Scores:** SAT Math middle 50% range 410–510. SAT EBRW middle 50% range 390–490. ACT middle 50% range 19–24. **Basis for Candidate Selection:** *Very important factors include:* class rank, academic GPA, standardized test scores. *Other factors include:* recommendation(s), talent/ability. **Freshman Admission Requirements:** High school diploma is required and GED is accepted. *Academic units required:* 4 English, 3 math, 3 science, 3 science labs, 2 social studies, 1 history, 2 academic electives. *Academic units recommended:* 4 English, 4 math, 4 science, 4 science labs, 2 foreign language, 2 social studies, 1 history, 2 academic electives, 1 computer science, 2 visual/performing arts. **Freshman Admission Statistics:** 706 applied, 66% admitted, 48% enrolled. **Transfer Admission Requirements:** College transcript(s). Minimum college GPA of 2.0 required. Lowest grade transferable D. **General Admission Information:** Application fee $40. Regular application deadline 9/2. Non-fall registration accepted. Admission may be deferred for a maximum of 1 year.

COSTS AND FINANCIAL AID

Required Forms and Deadlines: FAFSA. **Notification of Awards:** Applicants will be notified of awards on a rolling basis beginning 3/1. **Types of Aid:** *Need-based scholarships/grants:* College/university scholarship or grant aid from institutional funds; Federal Pell; Private scholarships; SEOG; State scholarships/grants. *Loans:* Direct PLUS loans; Direct Subsidized Stafford Loans; Direct Unsubsidized Stafford Loans. **Student Employment:** Federal Work-Study Program available. Institutional employment available. **Financial Aid Statistics:** 93% needy freshmen, 92% needy undergrads receive need-based scholarship or grant aid. 13% freshmen, 11% undergrads receive non-need-based scholarship or grant aid. 62% freshmen, 67% undergrads receive need-based self-help aid. 12% freshmen, 11% undergrads receive athletic scholarships. 93% freshmen, 89% undergrads receive any aid. 52% undergrads borrow to pay for school. Average cumulative indebtedness $24,460. **Criteria awarding aid:** *Need-based:* Academics, Art, Athletics, Leadership, Music/drama. *Non-need-based:* Academics, Art, Athletics, Leadership, Music/drama, State/district residency.

THE UNIVERSITY OF SCRANTON

800 Linden Street, Scranton, PA 18510
Phone: 570-941-7540 **Financial Aid Phone:** 570-941-7701
E-mail: admissions@scranton.edu **CEEB Code:** 2929
Fax: 570-941-5928 **Website:** www.scranton.edu **ACT Code:** 3736

This private school, affiliated with the Roman Catholic-Jesuit Church, was founded in 1888. It has a 58 acre campus.

RATINGS

Admissions Selectivity Rating: 83   **Fire Safety Rating:** 96   **Green Rating:** 77

STUDENTS AND FACULTY

Enrollment: 3,675. **Student Body:** 57% female, 43% male, 58% out-of-state, 1% international (15 countries represented). Asian 3%, African American 2%, Caucasian 78%, Hispanic 10%, Native American <1%, Pacific Islander <1%, Two or more races 2%, Race unknown 3%.
Retention and Graduation: 88% freshmen return for sophomore year. 79% freshmen graduate within 4 years. 83% freshmen graduate within 6 years. 39% grads go on to further study within 1 year. 74% grads pursue arts and sciences degrees. 3% grads pursue law degrees. 8% grads pursue business degrees. 10% grads pursue medical degrees. **Faculty:** Student/faculty ratio 13:1. 280 full-time faculty, 87% hold PhDs, 11% are members of minority groups, 42% are women. 2% of classes are taught by teaching assistants.

ACADEMICS

Degrees: Associate; Bachelor's; Certificate; Doctoral degree—professional practice; Doctoral degree research/scholarship; Master's; Post-bachelor's certificate; Post-master's certificate. **Classes:** Most classes have 10–19 students. Most lab/discussion sessions have 10–19 students. **Most popular majors:** Biology/Biological Sciences, General; Exercise Science and Kinesiology; Registered Nursing/Registered Nurse. **Special Study Options:** Accelerated program; Cross-registration; Distance learning; Double major; Dual enrollment; Exchange student program (domestic); Honors program; Independent study; Internships; Student-designed major; Study abroad; Teacher certification program. **Honors programs:** The Special Jesuit Liberal Arts Honors Program (SJLA) provides an alternative approach to satisfying general education requirements by pairing selected students with designated faculty in a curriculum that is deeply rooted in philosophy and dedicated to serving the common good. The Honors Program students take seminars together and work one-on-one with professors in tutorials. The program culminates with a senior creative or research project. The Business Leadership Honors Program is a highly selective program in which students explore concepts of leadership through special seminars and courses in management, ethics, strategy and analysis. The Business Honors Program offers four years of honors-level academic curriculum and a series of service and career building activities to develop skills needed for success in business. The Magis Honors Program in STEM provides undergraduate students with a more intense, interdisciplinary experience of research in STEM fields. Participants are enrolled in a special first-year seminar and a series of 1.5-credit seminar courses culminating in a senior thesis project. **Combined degree programs:** BA/MA. **Disability Services offered:** Note-taking services; Reader services; Tape recorders; Tutors. **Career services:** Alumni network; Alumni services; Career assessment; Career/job search classes; Internships; Regional alumni.

FACILITIES

Housing: Apartments for single students; Coed dorms; Men's dorms; Special housing for disabled students; Theme housing; Women's dorms; 100% of campus accessible to physically disabled. **Special Academic Facilities/Equipment:** Hope Horn Gallery in Hyland Hall; Scranton Heritage Room, Weinberg Memorial Library; The Estate; Houlihan-McLean Center.

CAMPUS LIFE

Environment: City. **Activities:** Campus Ministries; Choral groups; Concert band; Dance; Drama/theater; International Student Organization; Jazz band; Literary magazine; Music ensembles; Musical theater; Radio station; Student government; Student newspaper; Symphony orchestra; Television station; Yearbook. 78 registered organizations, 35 honor societies, 9 religious organizations on campus. **Athletics (Intercollegiate):** *Men:* baseball, basketball, cross-country, golf, ice hockey, lacrosse, soccer, swimming, tennis, wrestling. *Women:* basketball, cross-country, field hockey, lacrosse, soccer, softball, swimming, tennis, volleyball.

On-Campus Highlights: Loyola Science Center, state-of-the-art facility for the natural sciences. **Environmental Initiatives:** We have incorporated energy efficient technology in our new construction and renovations over the past 20 years. We had one LEED Silver building, one LEED Gold building, and then recently opened 117,421 GSF Leahy Hall which is LEED silver. All of our campus is using green cleaning supplies and practices.

ADMISSIONS

Freshman Academic Profile: Average high school GPA 3.6. 34% in top 10% of high school class, 68% in top 25% of high school class, 92% in top 50% of high school class. **Test Scores:** SAT Math middle 50% range 550–660. SAT EBRW middle 50% range 570–650. ACT middle 50% range 24–29. **Basis for Candidate Selection:** *Very important factors include:* rigor of secondary school record, class rank, academic GPA, standardized test scores. *Important factors include:* extracurricular activities. *Other factors include:* application essay, recommendation(s), interview, talent/ability, character/personal qualities, alumni/ae relation, volunteer work, work experience, level of applicant's interest. **Freshman Admission Requirements:** High school diploma is required and GED is accepted. *Academic units required:* 4 English, 3 math, 1 science, 2 foreign language, 2 history, 4 unit from above areas or other academic areas. *Academic units recommended:* 4 English, 4 math, 2 science, 2 foreign language, 3 history. **Freshman Admission Statistics:** 9,545 applied, 76% admitted, 14% enrolled. **Transfer Admission Requirements:** High school transcript, college transcript(s). Minimum college GPA of 2.75 required. Lowest grade transferable C. **General Admission Information:** Priority deadline 11/15. Regular application deadline 3/1. Non-fall registration accepted. Admission may be deferred for a maximum of 1 year.

COSTS AND FINANCIAL AID

Annual tuition $44,132. Room and board $15,182. Required fees $400. Average book and supplies expense $1,300. **Required Forms and Deadlines:** FAFSA; State aid form. **Notification of Awards:** Applicants will be notified of awards on a rolling basis beginning 1/15. **Types of Aid:** *Need-based scholarships/grants:* College/university scholarship or grant aid from institutional funds; Federal Pell; Private scholarships; SEOG; State scholarships/grants. *Loans:* Direct PLUS loans; Direct Subsidized Stafford Loans; Direct Unsubsidized Stafford Loans. **Student Employment:** Federal Work-Study Program available. Institutional employment available. **Financial Aid Statistics:** 81% needy freshmen, 82% needy undergrads receive need-based scholarship or grant aid. 83% freshmen, 74% undergrads receive non-need-based scholarship or grant aid. 75% freshmen, 78% undergrads receive need-based self-help aid. 0% freshmen, 0% undergrads receive athletic scholarships. 99% freshmen, 94% undergrads receive any aid. 75% undergrads borrow to pay for school. Average cumulative indebtedness $41,570. **Criteria awarding aid:** *Need-based:* Minority status. *Non-need-based:* Academics, Minority status.

THE UNIVERSITY OF THE SOUTH

735 University Avenue, Sewanee, TN 37383-1000
Phone: 931-598-1238 **Financial Aid Phone:** 931-598-1312
E-mail: admiss@sewanee.edu **CEEB Code:** 1842
Fax: 931-538-3248 **Website:** www.sewanee.edu **ACT Code:** 4024

This private school, affiliated with the Episcopal Church, was founded in 1857. It has a 13000 acre campus.

RATINGS

Admissions Selectivity Rating: 85   **Fire Safety Rating:** 98   **Green Rating:** 80

STUDENTS AND FACULTY

Enrollment: 1,669. **Student Body:** 51% female, 49% male, 79% out-of-state, 4% international (21 countries represented). Asian 1%, African American 4%, Caucasian 82%, Hispanic 5%, Native American <1%, Pacific Islander 0%, Two or more races 3%, Race unknown 0%.
Retention and Graduation: 88% freshmen return for sophomore year. 72% freshmen graduate within 4 years. 79% freshmen graduate within 6 years. 19% grads go on to further study within 1 year. 8% grads pursue arts and sciences degrees. 4% grads pursue law degrees. 1% grads pursue business degrees. <1% grads pursue medical degrees. **Faculty:** Student/faculty ratio 10:1. 173 full-time faculty, 93% hold PhDs, 16% are members of minority groups, 45% are women. 0% of classes are taught by teaching assistants.

ACADEMICS

Degrees: Bachelor's; Doctoral degree—professional practice; Master's; Post-bachelor's certificate; Post-master's certificate. **Classes:** Most classes have 10–19 students. Most lab/discussion sessions have 10–19 students. **Most popular majors:** English Language and Literature, General; Psychology, General; Economics, General. **Special Study Options:** Double major; Independent study; Internships; Student-designed major; Study abroad. **Combined degree programs:** BA/MEng. **Disability Services offered:** Note-taking services; Tape recorders; Tutors. **Career services:** Alumni network; Alumni services; Career assessment; Career/job search classes; Internships; Regional alumni.

FACILITIES

Housing: Apartments for married students; Coed dorms; Fraternity/sorority housing; Men's dorms; Theme housing; Wellness housing; Women's dorms; 90% of campus accessible to physically disabled. **Special Academic Facilities/Equipment:** Art gallery, observatory, keyboard collection, materials analysis lab with electron microscope, Landscape Analysis Lab, Ralston Music Listening Library. **Campus Network:** 100% of classrooms, 100% of dorms, 100% of student union, 100% of libraries, 100% of dining areas, 4% of common outdoor areas have wireless network access.

CAMPUS LIFE

Environment: Village. **Activities:** Campus Ministries; Choral groups; Dance; Drama/theater; International Student Organization; Jazz band; Literary magazine; Model UN; Music ensembles; Musical theater; Pep band; Radio station; Student government; Student newspaper; Student-run film society; Symphony orchestra; Yearbook. 107 registered organizations, 10 honor societies, 10 religious organizations, 12 fraternities, 10 sororities on campus. **Athletics (Intercollegiate):** *Men:* baseball, basketball, cross-country, diving, equestrian sports, football, golf, lacrosse, soccer, swimming, tennis, track/field (outdoor), track/field (indoor). *Women:* basketball, cheerleading, cross-country, diving, equestrian sports, field hockey, golf, lacrosse, soccer, softball, swimming, tennis, track/field (outdoor), track/field (indoor), volleyball. **On-Campus Highlights:** Outdoor recreation on Sewanee's 13,000 acre campus. **Environmental Initiatives:** In pursuit of a goal from our 2008 Strategic Planning Addendum, Sewanee's Sustainability Steering Committee developed a Sustainability Master Plan that has been formerly adopted. The plan, the first of its kind at Sewanee, is a blueprint for the institution's commitment to sustainability as we move forward, empowering Sewanee to teach and lead by example.

ADMISSIONS

Freshman Academic Profile: 32% in top 10% of high school class, 60% in top 25% of high school class, 86% in top 50% of high school class. 46% from public high schools. **Test Scores:** SAT Math middle 50% range 570–660. SAT EBRW middle 50% range 580–680. ACT middle 50% range 25–30. **Basis for Candidate Selection:** *Very important factors include:* rigor of secondary school record, academic GPA, recommendation(s). *Important factors include:* application essay, extracurricular activities, character/personal qualities, volunteer work. *Other factors include:* class rank, standardized test scores, interview, talent/ability, first generation, alumni/ae relation, geographical residence, level of applicant's interest. **Freshman Admission Requirements:** High school diploma is required and GED is not accepted *Academic units required:* 4 English, 3 math, 2 science, 2 science labs, 2 foreign language, 1 social studies, 1 history. *Academic units recommended:* 4 English, 4 math, 4 science, 3 science labs, 4 foreign language, 2 social studies, 2 history. **Freshman Admission Statistics:** 3,545 applied, 67% admitted, 19% enrolled. **Transfer Admission Requirements:** High school transcript, college transcript(s), essay or personal statement, standardized test scores, statement of good standing from prior institution(s). Minimum college GPA of 3.00 required. Lowest grade transferable C. **General Admission Information:** Regular application deadline 2/1. Non-fall registration accepted. Admission may be deferred for a maximum of one year.

COSTS AND FINANCIAL AID

Annual tuition $47,708. Room and board $13,700. Required fees $272. Average book and supplies expense $1,200. **Required Forms and Deadlines:** CSS/Financial Aid PROFILE; FAFSA. **Notification of Awards:** Applicants will be notified of awards on a rolling basis beginning 2/1. **Types of Aid:** *Need-based scholarships/grants:* College/university scholarship or grant aid from institutional funds; Federal Pell; Private scholarships; SEOG; State scholarships/grants. *Loans:* Direct PLUS loans; Direct Subsidized Stafford Loans; Direct Unsubsidized Stafford Loans. **Student Employment:** Federal Work-Study Program available. Institutional employment available. **Financial Aid Statistics:** 98% needy freshmen, 98% needy undergrads receive need-based scholarship or grant aid. 22% freshmen, 20% undergrads receive non-need-based scholarship or grant aid. 76% freshmen, 72% undergrads receive need-based self-help aid.

0% freshmen, 0% undergrads receive athletic scholarships. 95.9% freshmen, 93.4% undergrads receive any aid. 44% undergrads borrow to pay for school. Average cumulative indebtedness $31,737. **Criteria awarding aid:** *Need-based:* Academics, Religious affiliation. *Non-need-based:* Academics, Art, Religious affiliation, State/district residency.

UNIVERSITY OF SOUTH ALABAMA

University of South Alabama Meisler Hall, Mobile, AL 36688-0002
Phone: 251-460-6141 **Financial Aid Phone:** (251) 460-6231
E-mail: recruitment@southalabama.edu **CEEB Code:** 1880
Fax: 251-460-7876 **Website:** www.southalabama.edu **ACT Code:** 0059

This public school was founded in 1963. It has a 1225 acre campus.

RATINGS
Admissions Selectivity Rating: 80   **Fire Safety Rating:** 65   **Green Rating:** 65

STUDENTS AND FACULTY

Enrollment: 10,035. **Student Body:** 59% female, 41% male, 18% out-of-state, 3% international (67 countries represented). Asian 3%, African American 23%, Caucasian 61%, Hispanic 4%, Native American 1%, Pacific Islander <1%, Two or more races 4%, Race unknown 2%.
Retention and Graduation: 74% freshmen return for sophomore year. 22% freshmen graduate within 4 years. 43% freshmen graduate within 6 years. **Faculty:** Student/faculty ratio 18:1. 590 full-time faculty, 78% hold PhDs, 17% are members of minority groups, 52% are women.

ACADEMICS

Degrees: Bachelor's; Certificate; Doctoral degree—professional practice; Doctoral degree research/scholarship; Master's; Post-bachelor's certificate; Post-master's certificate. **Classes:** Most classes have 10–19 students. Most lab/discussion sessions have 30–39 students. **Most popular majors:** Elementary Education and Teaching; Health/Medical Preparatory Programs, Other; Registered Nursing/Registered Nurse. **Special Study Options:** Accelerated program; Cooperative education program; Cross-registration; Distance learning; Double major; Dual enrollment; English as a Second Language (ESL); Exchange student program (domestic); Honors program; Independent study; Internships; Student-designed major; Study abroad; Teacher certification program. **Honors programs:** Honors College. **Disability Services offered:** Note-taking services; Reader services; Tape recorders. **Career services:** Alumni services; Career assessment; Career/job search classes; Internships.

FACILITIES

Housing: Apartments for single students; Coed dorms; Fraternity/sorority housing; Special housing for disabled students; Theme housing; Wellness housing. **Special Academic Facilities/Equipment:** Museum/gallery complex, three hospitals, center for clinical education in health programs, engineering labs. **Campus Network:** 100% of classrooms, 100% of dorms, 100% of student union, 100% of libraries, 100% of dining areas, 0% of common outdoor areas have wireless network access.

CAMPUS LIFE

Environment: City. **Activities:** Campus Ministries; Choral groups; Concert band; Dance; Drama/theater; International Student Organization; Jazz band; Literary magazine; Marching band; Music ensembles; Musical theater; Opera; Pep band; Radio station; Student government; Student newspaper; Student-run film society; Symphony orchestra; Television station. 207 registered organizations, 17 honor societies, 14 religious organizations, 12 fraternities, 9 sororities on campus. **Athletics (Intercollegiate):** *Men:* baseball, basketball, cross-country, football, golf, tennis, track/field (outdoor). *Women:* basketball, cross-country, golf, soccer, softball, tennis, track/field (outdoor), volleyball. **On-Campus Highlights:** Mitchell Center (arena).

ADMISSIONS

Freshman Academic Profile: Average high school GPA 3.6. 85% from public high schools. **Test Scores:** SAT Math middle 50% range 510–610. SAT EBRW middle 50% range 530–630. ACT middle 50% range 21–27. **Basis for Candidate Selection:** *Very important factors include:* academic GPA, standardized test scores. **Freshman Admission Requirements:** High school diploma is required and GED is accepted. *Academic units required:* 4 English, 3 math, 3 science, 2 science labs, 3 social studies, 3 academic electives. **Freshman Admission Statistics:** 6,688 applied, 79% admitted, 36% enrolled. **Transfer Admission Requirements:** College transcript(s). Minimum college GPA of

2.0 required. Lowest grade transferable D. **General Admission Information:** Application fee $45. Regular application deadline 7/15. Non-fall registration accepted. Admission may be deferred for a maximum of 2 years.

COSTS AND FINANCIAL AID

Annual in-state tuition $9,870. Annual out-of-state tuition $19,740. Room and board $7,620. Average book and supplies expense $1,300. **Required Forms and Deadlines:** FAFSA. **Notification of Awards:** Applicants will be notified of awards on or about 2/15. **Types of Aid:** *Need-based scholarships/grants:* College/university scholarship or grant aid from institutional funds; Federal Pell; Private scholarships; SEOG; State scholarships/grants. *Loans:* Direct PLUS loans; Direct Subsidized Stafford Loans; Direct Unsubsidized Stafford Loans. **Student Employment:** Federal Work-Study Program available. Institutional employment available. **Financial Aid Statistics:** 91% needy freshmen, 83% needy undergrads receive need-based scholarship or grant aid. 91% freshmen, 83% undergrads receive non-need-based scholarship or grant aid. 90% freshmen, 95% undergrads receive need-based self-help aid. 4% freshmen, 4% undergrads receive athletic scholarships. 80% freshmen, 60% undergrads receive any aid. **Criteria awarding aid:** *Non-need-based:* Academics, Alumni affiliation, Art, Athletics, Job skills, Leadership, Minority status, Music/drama, State/district residency.

UNIVERSITY OF SOUTH CAROLINA—AIKEN

471 University Parkway, Aiken, SC 29801
Phone: 803-641-3366 **Financial Aid Phone:** 803-641-3476
E-mail: admit@usca.edu **CEEB Code:** 5840
Fax: 803-641-3727 **Website:** www.usca.edu **ACT Code:** 3879

This public school was founded in 1961. It has a 453 acre campus.

RATINGS

Admissions Selectivity Rating: 85   Fire Safety Rating: 95   Green Rating: 84

STUDENTS AND FACULTY

Enrollment: 3,131. **Student Body:** 64% female, 36% male, 11% out-of-state, 4% international (30 countries represented). Asian 1%, African American 27%, Caucasian 58%, Hispanic 4%, Native American 1%, Pacific Islander <1%, Two or more races 4%, Race unknown 1%.
Retention and Graduation: 72% freshmen return for sophomore year.
Faculty: Student/faculty ratio 15:1. 152 full-time faculty, 79% hold PhDs, 16% are members of minority groups, 48% are women. 0% of classes are taught by teaching assistants.

ACADEMICS

Degrees: Bachelor's; Master's. **Classes:** Most classes have 20–29 students. Most lab/discussion sessions have 20–29 students. **Most popular majors:** Registered Nursing/Registered Nurse; Business Administration and Management, General; Exercise Science and Kinesiology. **Special Study Options:** Cooperative education program; Distance learning; Double major; Dual enrollment; English as a Second Language (ESL); Honors program; Independent study; Internships; Student-designed major; Study abroad; Teacher certification program. **Honors programs:** The USCA Honors Program is designed to increase the educational opportunities for the academically well qualified and highly motivated student. Designed in accordance with the principles of the National Collegiate Honors Council, the USC Aiken Honors Program provides an enriched academic experience, both in and out of the classroom, for outstanding students committed to reaching their highest potential as scholars and creative thinkers. For details on our Honors Program or the other high quality academic opportunities awaiting you at USC Aiken, please call on our Office of Admissions toll free at 888.WOW.USCA or locally at 803.641.3366. The Honors Director may be reached at 803.641.3291. **Disability Services offered:** Note-taking services; Reader services; Tape recorders. **Career services:** Alumni network; Alumni services; Career assessment; Career/job search classes; Internships; Regional alumni.

FACILITIES

Housing: Apartments for single students; Coed dorms; Special housing for disabled students; Theme housing; 100% of campus accessible to physically disabled. **Special Academic Facilities/Equipment:** Ruth Patrick Science Education Center Etherredge Center (Fine Arts Center) Wellness Center Planetarium Natatorium. **Campus Network:** 100% of classrooms, 100% of dorms, 100% of libraries, 100% of dining areas have wireless network access.

CAMPUS LIFE

Environment: Town. **Activities:** Campus Ministries; Choral groups; Concert band; Dance; Drama/theater; International Student Organization; Jazz band; Literary magazine; Music ensembles; Musical theater; Pep band; Student government; Student newspaper; Yearbook. 90 registered organizations, 15 honor societies, 6 religious organizations, 7 fraternities, 7 sororities on campus. **Athletics (Intercollegiate):** *Men:* baseball, basketball, cheerleading, golf, soccer, tennis. *Women:* basketball, cheerleading, cross-country, soccer, softball, tennis, volleyball. **On-Campus Highlights:** DuPont Planetarium in the Ruth Patrick Science Education Center. **Environmental Initiatives:** Obtain State Energy Department stimulus funding approval to 'jump start' significant energy conservation actions. The energy conservation projects will reduce each building's energy use (kWh) by 18%—reducing the carbon footprint from purchased electricity by at least 20%.

ADMISSIONS

Freshman Academic Profile: Average high school GPA 3.8. 15% in top 10% of high school class, 40% in top 25% of high school class, 80% in top 50% of high school class. 92% from public high schools. **Test Scores:** SAT Math middle 50% range 420–530. SAT EBRW middle 50% range 430–530. ACT middle 50% range 18–23. **Basis for Candidate Selection:** *Very important factors include:* rigor of secondary school record, class rank, academic GPA, standardized test scores. **Freshman Admission Requirements:** High school diploma is required and GED is accepted. *Academic units required:* 4 English, 4 math, 3 science, 3 science labs, 2 foreign language, 2 social studies, 1 history, 4 academic electives. *Academic units recommended:* 1 computer science, 1 visual/performing arts. **Freshman Admission Statistics:** 2,177 applied, 61% admitted, 47% enrolled. **Transfer Admission Requirements:** College transcript(s), statement of good standing from prior institution(s). Minimum college GPA of 2.0 required. Lowest grade transferable C. **General Admission Information:** Application fee $45. Priority deadline 6/1. Regular application deadline 8/1. Non-fall registration accepted. Admission may be deferred for a maximum of 1 year.

COSTS AND FINANCIAL AID

Annual in-state tuition $9,882. Annual out-of-state tuition $19,788. Room and board $7,466. Required fees $314. Average book and supplies expense $1,656. **Required Forms and Deadlines:** FAFSA. **Notification of Awards:** Applicants will be notified of awards on a rolling basis beginning 4/20. **Types of Aid:** *Need-based scholarships/grants:* College/university scholarship or grant aid from institutional funds; Federal Pell; Private scholarships; SEOG; State scholarships/grants. *Loans:* Direct PLUS loans; Direct Subsidized Stafford Loans; Direct Unsubsidized Stafford Loans. **Student Employment:** Federal Work-Study Program available. Institutional employment available. **Financial Aid Statistics:** 94% needy freshmen, 83% needy undergrads receive need-based scholarship or grant aid. 10% freshmen, 8% undergrads receive non-need-based scholarship or grant aid. 70% freshmen, 77% undergrads receive need-based self-help aid. 4% freshmen, 4% undergrads receive athletic scholarships. 72% freshmen, 70% undergrads receive any aid. 75% undergrads borrow to pay for school. Average cumulative indebtedness $31,289. **Criteria awarding aid:** *Need-based:* Leadership. *Non-need-based:* Academics, Alumni affiliation, Art, Athletics, Leadership, Minority status, Music/drama, State/district residency.

UNIVERSITY OF SOUTH CAROLINA—BEAUFORT

1 University Boulevard, Bluffton, SC 29909
Phone: 843-208-8000 **Financial Aid Phone:** 843-521-3104
E-mail: admissions@uscb.edu **CEEB Code:** 5845
Fax: 843-208-8290 **Website:** www.uscb.edu **ACT Code:** 3835

This public school was founded in 1959. It has a 213 acre campus.

RATINGS

Admissions Selectivity Rating: 67   Fire Safety Rating: 60*   Green Rating: 60*

STUDENTS AND FACULTY

Enrollment: 1,773. **Student Body:** 63% female, 37% male, 22% out-of-state, international (14 countries represented).
Retention and Graduation: 54% freshmen return for sophomore year.
Faculty: Student/faculty ratio 18:1. 59 full-time faculty, 76% hold PhDs, 15% are members of minority groups, 47% are women.

ACADEMICS

Degrees: Associate; Bachelor's. **Classes:** Most classes have 10–19 students. **Most popular majors:** Registered Nursing, Nursing Administration, Nursing Research and Clinical Nursing; Business Administration and Management, General; Hospitality Administration/Management, General. **Special Study Options:** Cooperative education program; Cross-registration; Distance learning; Dual enrollment; Independent study; Internships; Study abroad; Teacher certification program; Weekend college. **Disability Services offered:** Note-taking services; Reader services; Tape recorders; Tutors. **Career services:** Career/job search classes; Internships.

FACILITIES

Housing: Apartments for single students; Coed dorms; Special housing for disabled students. **Special Academic Facilities/Equipment:** Science and Technology building; Center for the Arts.

CAMPUS LIFE

Environment: Village. **Activities:** Choral groups; Drama/theater; Literary magazine; Music ensembles; Musical theater; Student government; Student newspaper. 11 registered organizations on campus. **Athletics (Intercollegiate):** *Men:* baseball, cross-country, golf, track/field (outdoor). **On-Campus Highlights:** Sandbar Café.

ADMISSIONS

Basis for Candidate Selection: *Very important factors include:* rigor of secondary school record, academic GPA, standardized test scores. *Important factors include:* class rank. **Freshman Admission Requirements:** High school diploma is required and GED is accepted. *Academic units required:* 4 English, 4 math, 3 science, 3 science labs, 2 foreign language, 2 social studies, 1 history, 1 academic electives, 1 visual/performing arts, 1 unit from above areas or other academic areas. *Academic units recommended:* 1 computer science. **Freshman Admission Statistics:** 1,434 applied, 75% admitted, 38% enrolled. **Transfer Admission Requirements:** College transcript(s). Minimum college GPA of 2.0 required. Lowest grade transferable C-. **General Admission Information:** Application fee $40. Non-fall registration accepted.

COSTS AND FINANCIAL AID

Required Forms and Deadlines: FAFSA. **Notification of Awards:** Applicants will be notified of awards on a rolling basis beginning 5/31. **Types of Aid:** *Need-based scholarships/grants:* College/university scholarship or grant aid from institutional funds; Federal Pell; Private scholarships; SEOG; State scholarships/grants. **Student Employment:** Federal Work-Study Program available. **Financial Aid Statistics:** 35% freshmen, 65% undergrads receive any aid. **Criteria awarding aid:** *Need-based:* Academics. *Non-need-based:* Academics, State/district residency.

UNIVERSITY OF SOUTH CAROLINA—COLUMBIA

Office of Undergraduate Admissions, Columbia, SC 29208
Phone: 803-777-7700 **Financial Aid Phone:** (803) 777-8134
E-mail: admissions-ugrad@sc.edu **CEEB Code:** 5818
Fax: 803-777-0101 **Website:** www.sc.edu **ACT Code:** 3880

This public school was founded in 1801. It has a 444 acre campus.

RATINGS

Admissions Selectivity Rating: 86 **Fire Safety Rating:** 96 **Green Rating:** 60*

STUDENTS AND FACULTY

Enrollment: 27,066. **Student Body:** 54% female, 46% male, 39% out-of-state, 3% international (115 countries represented). Asian 3%, African American 8%, Caucasian 76%, Hispanic 5%, Native American <1%, Pacific Islander <1%, Two or more races 4%, Race unknown 1%. **Retention and Graduation:** 89% freshmen return for sophomore year. 64% freshmen graduate within 4 years. 77% freshmen graduate within 6 years. **Faculty:** Student/faculty ratio 17:1. 1,555 full-time faculty, 90% hold PhDs, 21% are members of minority groups, 45% are women.

ACADEMICS

Degrees: Associate; Bachelor's; Certificate; Doctoral degree—professional practice; Doctoral degree research/scholarship; Master's; Post-bachelor's

certificate; Post-master's certificate. **Classes:** Most classes have 10–19 students. Most lab/discussion sessions have 20–29 students. **Most popular majors:** Criminal Justice/Law Enforcement Administration; Experimental Psychology; Registered Nursing, Nursing Administration, Nursing Research and Clinical Nursing. **Special Study Options:** Accelerated program; Cooperative education program; Cross-registration; Distance learning; Double major; Dual enrollment; English as a Second Language (ESL); Exchange student program (domestic); External degree program; Honors program; Independent study; Internships; Student-designed major; Study abroad; Teacher certification program; Weekend college. **Honors programs:** The Honors College is a small college of about 1,000 students, all of whom excel in academics. What makes the Honors College different is its ability to weave engaging, exciting course offerings into any undergraduate major. You choose your major and set up your course schedule just like any other student at the University. But your choices include classes especially for Honors College students over 100 courses each semester. **Disability Services offered:** Note-taking services; Reader services; Tape recorders. **Career services:** Alumni services; Career assessment; Career/job search classes; Internships.

FACILITIES

Housing: Apartments for single students; Coed dorms; Fraternity/sorority housing; Men's dorms; Special housing for disabled students; Special housing for international students; Wellness housing; Women's dorms; 85% of campus accessible to physically disabled. **Special Academic Facilities/Equipment:** Art gallery, movie theater, McKissick Museum, South Caroliniana Library, Melton Observatory, Gibbes Planetarium, Melton Observatory, Filtration Research Engineering Demonstration Unit, Belser Arboretum, A.C. Moore Gardens. **Campus Network:** 50% of classrooms, 100% of dorms, 100% of student union, 75% of libraries, 100% of dining areas, 25% of common outdoor areas have wireless network access.

CAMPUS LIFE

Environment: City. **Activities:** Campus Ministries; Choral groups; Concert band; Dance; Drama/theater; International Student Organization; Jazz band; Literary magazine; Marching band; Music ensembles; Musical theater; Opera; Pep band; Radio station; Student government; Student newspaper; Student-run film society; Symphony orchestra; Television station. 387 registered organizations, 28 honor societies, 31 religious organizations, 22 fraternities, 16 sororities on campus. **Athletics (Intercollegiate):** *Men:* baseball, basketball, diving, football, golf, racquetball, soccer, softball, swimming, tennis, track/field (outdoor). *Women:* basketball, cross-country, diving, equestrian sports, golf, racquetball, soccer, softball, swimming, tennis, track/field (outdoor), volleyball. **On-Campus Highlights:** Strom Thurmond Wellness & Fitness Center. **Environmental Initiatives:** Sustainable Carolina represents all the sustainability efforts on campus and utilizes over 40 student interns to implement the campus sustainability plan. The program is based on leadership development and allows students to apply sustainability practices on campus. Last year students put in nearly 20,000 hours working, learning and training on sustainability issues.

ADMISSIONS

Freshman Academic Profile: Average high school GPA 4.0. 28% in top 10% of high school class, 59% in top 25% of high school class, 90% in top 50% of high school class. **Test Scores:** SAT Math middle 50% range 580–690. SAT EBRW middle 50% range 600–680. ACT middle 50% range 25–31. **Basis for Candidate Selection:** *Very important factors include:* rigor of secondary school record, academic GPA, standardized test scores. *Other factors include:* class rank, application essay, recommendation(s), extracurricular activities, talent/ability, character/personal qualities, first generation, state residency, racial/ethnic status, volunteer work, work experience. **Freshman Admission Requirements:** High school diploma is required and GED is accepted. *Academic units required:* 4 English, 4 math, 3 science, 3 science labs, 2 foreign language, 2 social studies, 1 history, 2 academic electives, 1 visual/performing arts, 1 unit from above areas or other academic areas. **Freshman Admission Statistics:** 31,268 applied, 69% admitted, 29% enrolled. **Transfer Admission Requirements:** College transcript(s). Minimum college GPA of 2.25 required. Lowest grade transferable C-. **General Admission Information:** Application fee $65. Priority deadline 12/1. Regular application deadline 12/1. Non-fall registration accepted. Admission may be deferred for a maximum of 1 year.

COSTS AND FINANCIAL AID

Required Forms and Deadlines: FAFSA. **Notification of Awards:** Applicants will be notified of awards on a rolling basis beginning 4/1. **Types of Aid:** *Need-based scholarships/grants:* College/university scholarship or grant aid from institutional funds; Federal Nursing Scholarships; Federal Pell; Private scholarships; SEOG; State scholarships/grants; United Negro College Fund. *Loans:* Direct PLUS loans; Direct Subsidized Stafford Loans; Direct Unsubsidized Stafford Loans. **Student Employment:** Federal Work-Study

Program available. Institutional employment available. **Financial Aid Statistics:** 35% needy freshmen, 43% needy undergrads receive need-based scholarship or grant aid. 93% freshmen, 70% undergrads receive non-need-based scholarship or grant aid. 72% freshmen, 78% undergrads receive need-based self-help aid. 2% freshmen, 2% undergrads receive athletic scholarships. 96% freshmen, 87% undergrads receive any aid. 52% undergrads borrow to pay for school. Average cumulative indebtedness $30,449. **Criteria awarding aid:** *Non-need-based:* Academics, Alumni affiliation, Art, Athletics, Job skills, Leadership, Minority status, Music/drama, Religious affiliation, State/district residency.

THE UNIVERSITY OF SOUTH DAKOTA

414 East Clark, Vermillion, SD 57069
Phone: 605-677-5434 **Financial Aid Phone:** 605-677-5446
E-mail: admissions@usd.edu **CEEB Code:** 6881
Fax: 605-677-6323 **Website:** www.usd.edu **ACT Code:** 3928

This public school was founded in 1862. It has a 273 acre campus.

RATINGS

Admissions Selectivity Rating: 77   **Fire Safety Rating:** 98   **Green Rating:** 64

STUDENTS AND FACULTY

Enrollment: 6,228. **Student Body:** 63% female, 37% male, 35% out-of-state, 2% international (46 countries represented). Asian 1%, African American 3%, Caucasian 83%, Hispanic 4%, Native American 2%, Pacific Islander <1%, Two or more races 4%, Race unknown <1%.
Retention and Graduation: 77% freshmen return for sophomore year. 39% freshmen graduate within 4 years. 57% freshmen graduate within 6 years. 48% grads go on to further study within 1 year. 26% grads pursue arts and sciences degrees. 9% grads pursue law degrees. 9% grads pursue business degrees. 9% grads pursue medical degrees. **Faculty:** Student/faculty ratio 16:1. 386 full-time faculty, 66% hold PhDs, 16% are members of minority groups, 51% are women. 8% of classes are taught by teaching assistants.

ACADEMICS

Degrees: Associate; Bachelor's; Certificate; Doctoral degree—professional practice; Doctoral degree research/scholarship; Master's; Post-bachelor's certificate. **Classes:** Most classes have 10–19 students. Most lab/discussion sessions have 10–19 students. **Most popular majors:** Education, General; Business/Commerce, General; Psychology, General. **Special Study Options:** Accelerated program; Cross-registration; Distance learning; Double major; Dual enrollment; English as a Second Language (ESL); Exchange student program (domestic); External degree program; Honors program; Independent study; Internships; Liberal arts/career combination; Student-designed major; Study abroad; Teacher certification program. **Honors programs:** University Honors Program. The program has its own core curriculum that replaces the University's general education requirements. Thesis Scholars Program, Alumni Student Scholars Program, Law Honors Scholars Program. **Combined degree programs:** BA/MA. **Disability Services offered:** Note-taking services; Reader services; Tape recorders; Tutors. **Career services:** Alumni network; Alumni services; Career assessment; Career/job search classes; Internships.

FACILITIES

Housing: Apartments for single students; Coed dorms; Fraternity/sorority housing; Special housing for disabled students; Theme housing; 96% of campus accessible to physically disabled. **Special Academic Facilities/Equipment:** W.H. Over Museum, The National Music Museum, Oscar Howe Art Gallery, Center for Instructional Design and Delivery, Institute of American Indian Studies, Native American Cultural Center, Disaster Mental Health Institute, Neuharth Center for Excellence in Journalism, Missouri River Institute.
Campus Network: 100% of classrooms, 100% of dorms, 100% of student union, 100% of libraries, 100% of dining areas, 50% of common outdoor areas have wireless network access.

CAMPUS LIFE

Environment: Village. **Activities:** Campus Ministries; Choral groups; Concert band; Dance; Drama/theater; International Student Organization; Jazz band; Literary magazine; Marching band; Music ensembles; Musical theater; Opera; Pep band; Radio station; Student government; Student newspaper; Student-

run film society; Symphony orchestra; Television station. 144 registered organizations, 6 honor societies, 6 religious organizations, 7 fraternities, 3 sororities on campus. **Athletics (Intercollegiate):** *Men:* basketball, cross-country, diving, football, golf, swimming, track/field (outdoor), track/field (indoor). *Women:* basketball, cross-country, diving, golf, soccer, softball, swimming, tennis, track/field (outdoor), track/field (indoor), volleyball. **On-Campus Highlights:** Al Neuharth Media Center. **Environmental Initiatives:** Creation of the Sustainability Task Force for evaluation, monitoring and policy creation.

ADMISSIONS

Freshman Academic Profile: Average high school GPA 3.4. 13% in top 10% of high school class, 37% in top 25% of high school class, 68% in top 50% of high school class. 75% from public high schools. **Test Scores:** SAT Math middle 50% range 510–640. SAT EBRW middle 50% range 520–620. ACT middle 50% range 20–25. **Basis for Candidate Selection:** *Very important factors include:* rigor of secondary school record, class rank, academic GPA, standardized test scores. *Other factors include:* application essay, recommendation(s). **Freshman Admission Requirements:** High school diploma is required and GED is accepted. *Academic units required:* 4 English, 3 math, 3 science labs, 3 social studies. *Academic units recommended:* 4 math, 4 science, 2 foreign language. **Freshman Admission Statistics:** 4,119 applied, 86% admitted, 41% enrolled. **Transfer Admission Requirements:** High school transcript, college transcript(s). Minimum college GPA of 2.0 required. Lowest grade transferable D. **General Admission Information:** Application fee $20. Non-fall registration accepted.

COSTS AND FINANCIAL AID

Annual in-state tuition $7,697. Annual out-of-state tuition $11,172. Room and board $8,409. Required fees $1,635. Average book and supplies expense $1,200. **Required Forms and Deadlines:** FAFSA. **Types of Aid:** *Need-based scholarships/grants:* College/university scholarship or grant aid from institutional funds; Federal Pell; Private scholarships; SEOG; State scholarships/grants; United Negro College Fund. *Loans:* Direct PLUS loans; Direct Subsidized Stafford Loans; Direct Unsubsidized Stafford Loans. **Student Employment:** Federal Work-Study Program available. Institutional employment available. **Financial Aid Statistics:** 45% needy freshmen, 46% needy undergrads receive need-based scholarship or grant aid. 73% freshmen, 57% undergrads receive non-need-based scholarship or grant aid. 80% freshmen, 84% undergrads receive need-based self-help aid. 7% freshmen, 6% undergrads receive athletic scholarships. 94% freshmen, 81% undergrads receive any aid. 73% undergrads borrow to pay for school. Average cumulative indebtedness $29,548. **Criteria awarding aid:** *Non-need-based:* Academics, Art, Athletics, Leadership, Minority status, Music/drama.

UNIVERSITY OF SOUTHERN CALIFORNIA

Office of Admission (University Park Campus), Los Angeles, CA 90089-0911
Phone: 213-740-1111 **Financial Aid Phone:** 213-740-4444
E-mail: admitusc@usc.edu **CEEB Code:** 4852
Fax: 213-821-0200 **Website:** www.usc.edu **ACT Code:** 470

This private school was founded in 1880. It has a 229 acre campus.

RATINGS

Admissions Selectivity Rating: 98   **Fire Safety Rating:** 97   **Green Rating:** 86

STUDENTS AND FACULTY

Enrollment: 19,908. **Student Body:** 52% female, 48% male, 35% out-of-state, 13% international (114 countries represented). Asian 21%, African American 5%, Caucasian 37%, Hispanic 16%, Native American <1%, Pacific Islander <1%, Two or more races 6%, Race unknown 2%.
Retention and Graduation: 96% freshmen return for sophomore year. 77% freshmen graduate within 4 years. 92% freshmen graduate within 6 years. **Faculty:** Student/faculty ratio 8:1. 2,133 full-time faculty, 91% hold PhDs, 30% are members of minority groups, 40% are women.

ACADEMICS

Degrees: Bachelor's; Doctoral degree—other; Doctoral degree—professional practice; Doctoral degree research/scholarship; Master's; Post-bachelor's certificate; Post-master's certificate. **Classes:** Most classes have 10–19 students. Most lab/discussion sessions have 20–29 students. **Most popular majors:** Visual and Performing Arts, General; Business Administration and Management, General; Social Sciences, General. **Special Study Options:** Cooperative education program; Distance learning; Double major; English as a Second Language (ESL); Exchange student program (domestic); Honors program; Independent study; Internships; Liberal arts/career combination; Student-designed major; Study abroad. **Honors programs:** Thematic Option Program Multimedia Scholarship. **Combined degree programs:** BA/MA; BA/MEng. **Disability Services offered:** Note-taking services; Reader services; Tape recorders; Tutors. **Career services:** Alumni network; Alumni services; Career assessment; Internships; Regional alumni.

FACILITIES

Housing: Apartments for married students; Apartments for single students; Coed dorms; Cooperative housing; Fraternity/sorority housing; Special housing for disabled students; Special housing for international students; Theme housing; Wellness housing; 97% of campus accessible to physically disabled. **Special Academic Facilities/Equipment:** USC Fisher Museum of Art; Hancock Memorial Museum; specialized architecture and fine arts galleries, studios, and labs; media labs; cinema scoring sound stage; recording studios; theatres and recital halls; exercise physiology lab; specialized engineering laboratories; biomedical imaging labs; Center for Electron Microscopy and Microanalysis; genomic research facilities; GIS research lab; USC Shoah Foundation Institute visual history archive; Archival Research Center; High-Performance Computing Center; public computing centers and labs; extensive wireless access to the USC network; classrooms outfitted with multiple webcams and microphones. **Campus Network:** 100% of classrooms, 100% of dorms, 100% of student union, 100% of libraries, 100% of dining areas, 50% of common outdoor areas have wireless network access.

CAMPUS LIFE

Environment: Metropolis. **Activities:** Campus Ministries; Choral groups; Concert band; Dance; Drama/theater; International Student Organization; Jazz band; Literary magazine; Marching band; Model UN; Music ensembles; Musical theater; Opera; Pep band; Radio station; Student government; Student newspaper; Student-run film society; Symphony orchestra; Television station; Yearbook. 850 registered organizations, 46 honor societies, 87 religious organizations, 32 fraternities, 26 sororities on campus. **Athletics (Intercollegiate):** *Men:* baseball, basketball, diving, football, golf, swimming, tennis, track/field (outdoor), volleyball, water polo. *Women:* basketball, crew/rowing, cross-country, diving, golf, soccer, swimming, tennis, track/field (outdoor), volleyball, water polo. **On-Campus Highlights:** Tutor Campus Center. **Environmental Initiatives:** Energy Efficiency & Innovation: USC employs a full time Director of Energy Services to manage energy programs including lighting retrofits, equipment upgrades, and a recent retrofit of chillers, cooling towers, and pumps throughout the University, including a three million gallon centralized thermal energy storage tank installed belowground. The 3 million-gallon thermal energy water storage (TES) system was built 40 feet below ground. It is estimated that the new system conserves about 4,500 megawatt-hours of electricity a year by circulating chilled water to air conditioning systems throughout the University Park Campus, significantly expanding the capacity of the campus' existing chilled-water system while reducing utility use. The warmer water coming back through pipes has a chance to chill overnight before it is recirculated which allows USC to shift much of the kilowatt-hour usage to off-peak hours when electricity is more available. The entire system was conceived in 2001 and completed in 2005.

ADMISSIONS

Freshman Academic Profile: Average high school GPA 3.8. 54% from public high schools. **Test Scores:** SAT Math middle 50% range 690–790. SAT EBRW middle 50% range 670–740. ACT middle 50% range 31–34. **Basis for Candidate Selection:** *Very important factors include:* rigor of secondary school record, academic GPA, application essay, standardized test scores, recommendation(s). *Important factors include:* extracurricular activities, talent/ability, character/personal qualities. *Other factors include:* first generation, alumni/ae relation, racial/ethnic status, volunteer work, work experience. **Freshman Admission Requirements:** High school diploma is required and GED is not accepted. *Academic units required:* 4 English, 3 math, 2 science, 2 science labs, 2 foreign language, 2 social studies, 3 academic electives. *Academic units recommended:* 4 English, 4 math, 3 science, 3 science labs, 3 foreign language, 3 social studies, 3 academic electives. **Freshman Admission Statistics:** 66,198 applied, 11% admitted, 42% enrolled. **Transfer Admission Requirements:** High school transcript, college transcript(s), essay or personal statement. Lowest grade transferable C-. **General Admission Information:** Application fee $85. Priority deadline 12/1. Regular application deadline 1/15.

Non-fall registration accepted. Admission may be deferred for a maximum of one year.

COSTS AND FINANCIAL AID

Annual tuition $58,133. Room and board $15,916. Required fees $1,389. Average book and supplies expense $1,200. **Required Forms and Deadlines:** Business/Farm Supplement; CSS/Financial Aid PROFILE; FAFSA; Noncustodial PROFILE. **Notification of Awards:** Applicants will be notified of awards on or about 4/1. **Types of Aid:** *Need-based scholarships/grants:* College/university scholarship or grant aid from institutional funds; Federal Pell; Private scholarships; SEOG; State scholarships/grants. *Loans:* Direct PLUS loans; Direct Subsidized Stafford Loans; Direct Unsubsidized Stafford Loans. **Student Employment:** Federal Work-Study Program available. Institutional employment available. **Financial Aid Statistics:** 85% needy freshmen, 89% needy undergrads receive need-based scholarship or grant aid. 74% freshmen, 55% undergrads receive non-need-based scholarship or grant aid. 89% freshmen, 93% undergrads receive need-based self-help aid. 3% freshmen, 2% undergrads receive athletic scholarships. 68% freshmen, 65% undergrads receive any aid. 35% undergrads borrow to pay for school. Average cumulative indebtedness $28,228. **Criteria awarding aid:** *Non-need-based:* Academics, Alumni affiliation, Art, Athletics, Leadership, Music/drama.

UNIVERSITY OF SOUTHERN INDIANA

8600 University Boulevard, Evansville, IN 47712
Phone: 812-464-1765 **Financial Aid Phone:** 812-464-1767
E-mail: enroll@usi.edu **CEEB Code:** 1335
Fax: 812-465-7154 **Website:** www.usi.edu **ACT Code:** 1207

This public school was founded in 1965. It has a 1400 acre campus.

RATINGS
Admissions Selectivity Rating: 75   **Fire Safety Rating:** 80   **Green Rating:** 75

STUDENTS AND FACULTY
Enrollment: 7,476. **Student Body:** 62% female, 38% male, 15% out-of-state, 2% international (60 countries represented). Asian 1%, African American 4%, Caucasian 86%, Hispanic 4%, Native American <1%, Pacific Islander <1%, Two or more races 2%, Race unknown <1%.
Retention and Graduation: 72% freshmen return for sophomore year. 21% freshmen graduate within 4 years. 40% freshmen graduate within 6 years. 25% grads go on to further study within 1 year. **Faculty:** Student/faculty ratio 16:1. 362 full-time faculty, 72% hold PhDs, 10% are members of minority groups, 54% are women. 0% of classes are taught by teaching assistants.

ACADEMICS
Degrees: Associate; Bachelor's; Certificate; Doctoral degree—professional practice; Doctoral degree research/scholarship; Master's; Post-bachelor's certificate; Post-master's certificate; Transfer Associate. **Classes:** Most classes have 20–29 students. Most lab/discussion sessions have 20–29 students.
Most popular majors: Registered Nursing/Registered Nurse; Business Administration and Management, General; Psychology, General. **Special Study Options:** Accelerated program; Cooperative education program; Distance learning; Double major; Dual enrollment; English as a Second Language (ESL); Honors program; Independent study; Internships; Study abroad; Teacher certification program. **Honors programs:** The Honors Program at the University of Southern Indiana offers a selective, demanding, and rewarding program for students who are searching for an intellectual challenge and are prepared to invest extra effort to meet that challenge. Honors students benefit from smaller classes, close contact with faculty, grants to study abroad, research opportunities, exciting extracurricular activities, and the Honors living learning community. The Honors Program provides students with a supportive community of fellow Honors students who are academically motivated and talented. The USI Honors Program offers a broad range of opportunities for personal and academic growth. The most outstanding feature of the program is the students themselves. Their motivation and creativity stimulate the entire University campus. **Disability Services offered:** Note-taking services; Reader services; Tape recorders; Tutors. **Career services:** Alumni network; Alumni services; Career assessment; Career/job search classes; Internships.

FACILITIES
Housing: Apartments for single students; Coed dorms; Fraternity/sorority housing; Special housing for disabled students; Special housing for international students; Theme housing; 95% of campus accessible to physically disabled.

Special Academic Facilities/Equipment: The McCutchan Art Center, Pace Galleries, Griffin Center, Bent Twig Outdoor Education Center. **Campus Network:** 100% of classrooms, 100% of dorms, 100% of student union, 100% of libraries, 100% of dining areas, 10% of common outdoor areas have wireless network access.

CAMPUS LIFE

Environment: City. **Activities:** Campus Ministries; Choral groups; Dance; Drama/theater; International Student Organization; Jazz band; Literary magazine; Pep band; Radio station; Student government; Student newspaper; Television station. 151 registered organizations, 9 honor societies, 11 religious organizations, 6 fraternities, 7 sororities on campus. **Athletics (Intercollegiate):** *Men:* baseball, basketball, cross-country, golf, soccer, tennis, track/field (outdoor), track/field (indoor). *Women:* basketball, cross-country, golf, soccer, softball, tennis, track/field (outdoor), track/field (indoor), volleyball. **On-Campus Highlights:** University Center. **Environmental Initiatives:** Established environmental stewardship committee.

ADMISSIONS

Freshman Academic Profile: Average high school GPA 3.4. 14% in top 10% of high school class, 34% in top 25% of high school class, 69% in top 50% of high school class. 86% from public high schools. **Test Scores:** SAT Math middle 50% range 490–590. SAT EBRW middle 50% range 490–590. ACT middle 50% range 19–25. **Basis for Candidate Selection:** *Very important factors include:* academic GPA, standardized test scores. *Important factors include:* class rank. *Other factors include:* rigor of secondary school record, application essay, recommendation(s), interview, extracurricular activities, talent/ability, character/personal qualities, volunteer work. **Freshman Admission Requirements:** High school diploma is required and GED is accepted *Academic units recommended:* 4 English, 4 math, 2 science, 2 foreign language, 2 social studies, 2 history, 2 academic electives. **Freshman Admission Statistics:** 4,461 applied, 95% admitted, 39% enrolled. **Transfer Admission Requirements:** High school transcript, college transcript(s). Minimum college GPA of 2.0 required. Lowest grade transferable C-. **General Admission Information:** Application fee $40. Regular application deadline 8/15. Non-fall registration accepted. Admission may be deferred for a maximum of 1 semester term.

COSTS AND FINANCIAL AID

Annual in-state tuition $8,349. Annual out-of-state tuition $19,437. Room and board $9,102. Required fees $520. Average book and supplies expense $1,140. **Required Forms and Deadlines:** FAFSA. **Notification of Awards:** Applicants will be notified of awards on a rolling basis beginning 4/1. **Types of Aid:** *Need-based scholarships/grants:* College/university scholarship or grant aid from institutional funds; Federal Nursing Scholarships; Federal Pell; Private scholarships; SEOG; State scholarships/grants; United Negro College Fund. *Loans:* Direct PLUS loans; Direct Subsidized Stafford Loans; Direct Unsubsidized Stafford Loans. **Student Employment:** Federal Work-Study Program available. Institutional employment available. **Financial Aid Statistics:** 88% needy freshmen, 90% needy undergrads receive need-based scholarship or grant aid. 98% freshmen, 96% undergrads receive non-need-based scholarship or grant aid. 79% freshmen, 82% undergrads receive need-based self-help aid. 2% freshmen, 2% undergrads receive athletic scholarships. 84% freshmen, 75% undergrads receive any aid. 65% undergrads borrow to pay for school. Average cumulative indebtedness $24,074. **Criteria awarding aid:** *Need-based:* Academics. *Non-need-based:* Academics, Art, Athletics, Leadership, Music/drama, State/district residency.

UNIVERSITY OF SOUTHERN MAINE

PO Box 9300, Portland, ME 04104
Phone: 207-780-5670 **Financial Aid Phone:** 207-780-5250
E-mail: usmadm@usm.maine.edu **CEEB Code:** 9762
Fax: 207-780-5640 **Website:** www.usm.maine.edu **ACT Code:** 1644

This public school was founded in 1878. It has a 144 acre campus.

RATINGS

Admissions Selectivity Rating: 74   **Fire Safety Rating:** 85   **Green Rating:** 60*

STUDENTS AND FACULTY

Enrollment: 5,359. **Student Body:** 57% female, 43% male, 11% out-of-state, 1% international (19 countries represented). Asian 2%, African American 4%, Caucasian 82%, Hispanic 2%, Native American 1%, Pacific Islander <1%, Two or more races 3%, Race unknown 5%.

Retention and Graduation: 63% freshmen return for sophomore year. **Faculty:** Student/faculty ratio 16:1. 248 full-time faculty, 84% hold PhDs, 7% are members of minority groups, 48% are women. 0% of classes are taught by teaching assistants.

ACADEMICS

Degrees: Bachelor's; Certificate; Doctoral degree—professional practice; Doctoral degree research/scholarship; Master's; Post-bachelor's certificate; Post-master's certificate. **Classes:** Most classes have 10–19 students. Most lab/discussion sessions have 10–19 students. **Most popular majors:** Registered Nursing/Registered Nurse; Biology/Biological Sciences, General; Business Administration and Management, General. **Special Study Options:** Cooperative education program; Cross-registration; Distance learning; Double major; Dual enrollment; English as a Second Language (ESL); Exchange student program (domestic); Honors program; Independent study; Internships; Liberal arts/career combination; Student-designed major; Study abroad; Teacher certification program; Weekend college. **Honors programs:** Russell Scholars—living/learning community, USM honors program, Pioneers program. **Disability Services offered:** Note-taking services; Reader services; Tape recorders; Tutors. **Career services:** Alumni network; Alumni services; Career/job search classes; Internships.

FACILITIES

Housing: Apartments for married students; Apartments for single students; Coed dorms; Fraternity/sorority housing; Special housing for disabled students; Special housing for international students; Theme housing; Wellness housing; 90% of campus accessible to physically disabled. **Special Academic Facilities/Equipment:** Southworth Planetarium, Osher Map Collection and Smith Center for Cartographic Education, WMPG (radio station), Free Press (campus newspaper), various art galleries on all three campuses.

CAMPUS LIFE

Environment: City. **Activities:** Campus Ministries; Choral groups; Concert band; Dance; Drama/theater; International Student Organization; Jazz band; Literary magazine; Model UN; Music ensembles; Musical theater; Opera; Radio station; Student government; Student newspaper; Symphony orchestra. 100 registered organizations, 8 honor societies, 7 religious organizations, 4 fraternities, 3 sororities on campus. **Athletics (Intercollegiate):** *Men:* baseball, basketball, cheerleading, cross-country, golf, ice hockey, lacrosse, soccer, tennis, track/field (outdoor), track/field (indoor), wrestling. *Women:* basketball, cheerleading, cross-country, field hockey, golf, ice hockey, lacrosse, soccer, softball, tennis, track/field (outdoor), track/field (indoor), volleyball. **On-Campus Highlights:** Art Gallery.

ADMISSIONS

Freshman Academic Profile: Average high school GPA 3.0. 5% in top 10% of high school class, 26% in top 25% of high school class, 61% in top 50% of high school class. **Test Scores:** SAT Math middle 50% range 440–550. SAT EBRW middle 50% range 420–550. ACT middle 50% range 19–25. **Basis for Candidate Selection:** *Very important factors include:* rigor of secondary school record, class rank, academic GPA. *Important factors include:* application essay, standardized test scores. *Other factors include:* recommendation(s), interview, extracurricular activities, talent/ability, character/personal qualities, first generation, alumni/ae relation, geographical residence, state residency, racial/ethnic status, volunteer work, work experience, level of applicant's interest. **Freshman Admission Requirements:** High school diploma is required and GED is accepted. *Academic units required:* 4 English, 3 math, 2 science, 2 science labs, 2 social studies, 1 history. *Academic units recommended:* 3 science, 3 science labs, 3 social studies, 1 history. **Freshman Admission Statistics:** 3,402 applied, 88% admitted, 24% enrolled. **Transfer Admission Requirements:** High school transcript, college transcript(s), essay or personal statement. Minimum college GPA of 2.0 required. Lowest grade transferable C-. **General Admission Information:** Application fee $40. Non-fall registration accepted.

COSTS AND FINANCIAL AID

Annual in-state tuition $7,590. Annual out-of-state tuition $19,950. Room and board $9,400. Required fees $1,330. Average book and supplies expense $1,220. **Required Forms and Deadlines:** FAFSA. **Notification of Awards:** Applicants will be notified of awards on a rolling basis beginning 3/15. **Types of Aid:** *Need-based scholarships/grants:* College/university scholarship or grant aid from institutional funds; Federal Pell; Private scholarships; SEOG; State scholarships/grants. *Loans:* Direct PLUS loans; Direct Subsidized Stafford Loans; Direct Unsubsidized Stafford Loans. **Student Employment:** Federal Work-Study Program available. Institutional employment available. **Financial Aid Statistics:** 94% needy freshmen, 84% needy undergrads receive need-based scholarship or grant aid. 5% freshmen, 3% undergrads receive non-need-based scholarship or grant aid. 79% freshmen, 87% undergrads receive need-based self-help aid. 0% freshmen, 0% undergrads receive athletic scholarships. **Criteria awarding aid:** *Need-based:* Academics, Music/drama *Non-need-based:* Academics, Music/drama, State/district residency.

UNIVERSITY OF SOUTHERN MISSISSIPPI

118 College Drive #5166, Hattiesburg, MS 39406
Phone: 601-266-5000 **Financial Aid Phone:** (601) 266-4774
E-mail: admissions@usm.edu **CEEB Code:** 1479
Fax: 601-266-5148 **Website:** www.usm.edu **ACT Code:** 2218

This public school was founded in 1910. It has a 1090 acre campus.

RATINGS

Admissions Selectivity Rating: 89   Fire Safety Rating: 90   Green Rating: 60*

STUDENTS AND FACULTY

Enrollment: 11,689. **Student Body:** 63% female, 37% male, 16% out-of-state, 2% international. Asian 1%, African American 29%, Caucasian 61%, Hispanic 3%, Native American <1%, Pacific Islander <1%, Two or more races 2%, Race unknown 1%.
Retention and Graduation: 74% freshmen return for sophomore year.
Faculty: Student/faculty ratio 17:1. 687 full-time faculty, 79% hold PhDs, 16% are members of minority groups, 48% are women.

ACADEMICS

Degrees: Bachelor's; Certificate; Master's; Post-bachelor's certificate; Post-master's certificate. **Classes:** Most classes have 10–19 students. Most lab/discussion sessions have 10–19 students. **Most popular majors:** Elementary Education and Teaching; Psychology, General; Nursing/Registered Nurse (Rn, Asn, Bsn, Msn). **Special Study Options:** Distance learning; Double major; Dual enrollment; English as a Second Language (ESL); Exchange student program (domestic); Honors program; Internships; Study abroad; Teacher certification program. **Disability Services offered:** Note-taking services; Reader services; Tape recorders; Tutors. **Career services:** Alumni services; Career assessment; Career/job search classes; Internships.

FACILITIES

Housing: Fraternity/sorority housing; Men's dorms; Special housing for disabled students; Theme housing; Women's dorms. **Special Academic Facilities/Equipment:** Museum of Art. **Campus Network:** 100% of classrooms, 100% of dorms, 100% of student union, 100% of libraries, 100% of dining areas, 30% of common outdoor areas have wireless network access.

CAMPUS LIFE

Environment: City. **Activities:** Campus Ministries; Choral groups; Concert band; Dance; Drama/theater; International Student Organization; Jazz band; Literary magazine; Marching band; Music ensembles; Musical theater; Opera; Pep band; Radio station; Student government; Student newspaper; Student-run film society; Symphony orchestra; Yearbook. 8 honor societies, 20 religious organizations, 15 fraternities, 11 sororities, on campus. **Athletics (Intercollegiate):** *Men:* baseball, basketball, football, golf, tennis, track/field (outdoor), track/field (indoor). *Women:* basketball, cross-country, golf, soccer, softball, tennis, track/field (outdoor), track/field (indoor); volleyball. **On-Campus Highlights:** Starbucks. **Environmental Initiatives:** Recycling (12+ years).

ADMISSIONS

Freshman Academic Profile: Average high school GPA 3.3. 88% from public high schools. **Test Scores:** SAT Math middle 50% range 510–650. SAT EBRW middle 50% range 430–540. ACT middle 50% range 20–26. **Basis for Candidate Selection:** *Very important factors include:* academic GPA, standardized test scores. *Important factors include:* class rank. **Freshman Admission Requirements:** High school diploma is required and GED is accepted. *Academic units required:* 4 English, 3 math, 3 science, 3 science labs, 1 foreign language, 3 social studies, 2 academic electives, 0.5 computer science. *Academic units recommended:* 4 English, 4 math, 4 science, 3 science labs, 1 foreign language, 4 social studies, 2 academic electives, 0.5 computer science, 1 visual/performing arts. **Freshman Admission Statistics:** 6,607 applied, 46% admitted, 52% enrolled. **Transfer Admission Requirements:** College transcript(s), statement of good standing from prior institution(s). Minimum college GPA of 2.0 required. Lowest grade transferable D. **General Admission Information:** Application fee $40. Non-fall registration accepted.

COSTS AND FINANCIAL AID

Annual in-state tuition $7,854. Annual out-of-state tuition $9,854. Room and board $9,012. Average book and supplies expense $1,200. **Required Forms and Deadlines:** FAFSA. **Notification of Awards:** Applicants will be notified of awards on a rolling basis beginning 12/15. **Types of Aid:** *Need-based scholarships/grants:* College/university scholarship or grant aid from institutional funds; Federal Pell; Private scholarships; SEOG; State scholarships/grants. *Loans:* Direct PLUS loans; Direct Subsidized Stafford Loans; Direct Unsubsidized Stafford Loans. **Student Employment:** Federal Work-Study Program available. Institutional employment available. **Financial Aid Statistics:** 70% needy freshmen, 68% needy undergrads receive need-based scholarship or grant aid. 69% freshmen, 55% undergrads receive non-need-based scholarship or grant aid. 68% freshmen, 74% undergrads receive need-based self-help aid. 6% freshmen, 4% undergrads receive athletic scholarships. 62% freshmen, 63% undergrads receive any aid. 68% undergrads borrow to pay for school. Average cumulative indebtedness $28,700. **Criteria awarding aid:** *Need-based:* Academics. *Non-need-based:* Academics, Alumni affiliation, Art, Athletics, Leadership, Music/drama, State/district residency.

UNIVERSITY OF SOUTH FLORIDA

4202 East Fowler Avenue, Tampa, FL 33620-9951
Phone: 813-974-3350 **Financial Aid Phone:** 813-974-3039
E-mail: admissions@usf.edu **CEEB Code:** 5828
Fax: 813-974-9689 **Website:** www.usf.edu **ACT Code:** 761

This public school was founded in 1956. It has a 1562 acre campus.

RATINGS

Admissions Selectivity Rating: 89   Fire Safety Rating: 98   Green Rating: 92

STUDENTS AND FACULTY

Enrollment: 31,766. **Student Body:** 55% female, 45% male, 6% out-of-state, 7% international (141 countries represented). Asian 7%, African American 10%, Caucasian 46%, Hispanic 22%, Native American <1%, Pacific Islander <1%, Two or more races 4%, Race unknown 4%.
Faculty: Student/faculty ratio 23:1. 1,308 full-time faculty, 82% hold PhDs, 32% are members of minority groups, 45% are women. 15% of classes are taught by teaching assistants.

ACADEMICS

Degrees: Associate; Bachelor's; Doctoral degree—professional practice; Doctoral degree research/scholarship; Master's. **Classes:** Most classes have 10–19 students. Most lab/discussion sessions have 20–29 students. **Most popular majors:** Biomedical Sciences, General; Health Professions And Related Programs; Psychology, General. **Special Study Options:** Accelerated program; Cooperative education program; Distance learning; Double major; Dual enrollment; English as a Second Language (ESL); Exchange student program (domestic); Honors program; Independent study; Internships; Study abroad; Teacher certification program. **Honors programs:** Honors College: http://honors.usf.edu/. **Combined degree programs:** BA/MA; BA/MD; BA/MEng. **Disability Services offered:** Note-taking services; Reader services; Tape recorders. **Career services:** Alumni services; Career assessment; Career/job search classes; Internships.

FACILITIES

Housing: Apartments for married students; Apartments for single students; Coed dorms; Fraternity/sorority housing; Men's dorms; Special housing for disabled students; Theme housing; Wellness housing; Women's dorms; 100% of campus accessible to physically disabled. **Special Academic Facilities/Equipment:** Art museum and galleries, contemporary art museum, graphic studio, anthropology museum, fitness center, par course. **Campus Network:** 100% of classrooms, 100% of dorms, 100% of student union, 100% of libraries, 100% of dining areas, 100% of common outdoor areas have wireless network access.

CAMPUS LIFE

Environment: Metropolis. **Activities:** Campus Ministries; Choral groups; Concert band; Dance; Drama/theater; International Student Organization; Jazz band; Literary magazine; Marching band; Model UN; Music ensembles;

Musical theater; Opera; Pep band; Radio station; Student government; Student newspaper; Student-run film society; Symphony orchestra; Television station; Yearbook. 600 registered organizations, 3 honor societies, 14 religious organizations, 34 fraternities, 29 sororities on campus. **Athletics (Intercollegiate): Men:** baseball, basketball, cheerleading, cross-country, football, golf, sailing, soccer, tennis, track/field (outdoor), track/field (indoor). *Women:* basketball, cheerleading, cross-country, golf, sailing, soccer, softball, tennis, track/field (outdoor), track/field (indoor), volleyball. **On-Campus Highlights:** Marshall Center. **Environmental Initiatives:** USF's 2008 Going Green Tampa Bay sustainability EXPO which drew over 3,000 visitors.

ADMISSIONS

Freshman Academic Profile: Average high school GPA 4.0. 34% in top 10% of high school class, 68% in top 25% of high school class, 92% in top 50% of high school class. **Test Scores:** SAT Math middle 50% range 580–670. SAT EBRW middle 50% range 590–660. ACT middle 50% range 25–29. **Basis for Candidate Selection:** *Very important factors include:* academic GPA, standardized test scores. *Important factors include:* rigor of secondary school record. *Other factors include:* class rank, talent/ability, first generation, geographical residence. **Freshman Admission Requirements:** High school diploma is required and GED is accepted. *Academic units required:* 4 English, 4 math, 3 science, 2 science labs, 2 foreign language, 3 social studies, 2 academic electives. **Freshman Admission Statistics:** 36,986 applied, 48% admitted, 29% enrolled. **Transfer Admission Requirements:** College transcript(s), statement of good standing from prior institution(s). Minimum college GPA of 2.3 required. Lowest grade transferable D. **General Admission Information:** Application fee $30. Priority deadline 12/1. Regular application deadline 4/1. Non-fall registration accepted. Admission may be deferred for a maximum of 3 academic terms.

COSTS AND FINANCIAL AID

Annual in-state tuition $4,559. Annual out-of-state tuition $15,473. Room and board $11,836. Average book and supplies expense $1,100. **Required Forms and Deadlines:** FAFSA. **Notification of Awards:** Applicants will be notified of awards on a rolling basis beginning 3/1. **Types of Aid:** *Need-based scholarships/grants:* College/university scholarship or grant aid from institutional funds; Federal Pell; Private scholarships; SEOG; State scholarships/grants. *Loans:* Direct PLUS loans; Direct Subsidized Stafford Loans; Direct Unsubsidized Stafford Loans. **Student Employment:** Federal Work-Study Program available. Institutional employment available. **Financial Aid Statistics:** 93% needy freshmen, 84% needy undergrads receive need-based scholarship or grant aid. 14% freshmen, 6% undergrads receive non-need-based scholarship or grant aid. 40% freshmen, 53% undergrads receive need-based self-help aid. 2% freshmen, 1% undergrads receive athletic scholarships. 80% freshmen, 66% undergrads receive any aid. 50% undergrads borrow to pay for school. Average cumulative indebtedness $21,463. **Criteria awarding aid:** *Need-based:* Academics *Non-need-based:* Academics, Art, Athletics, Leadership, Music/drama, State/district residency.

UNIVERSITY OF SOUTH FLORIDA—ST. PETERSBURG

140 Seventh Avenue South, St. Petersburg, FL 33701-5016
Phone: 727-873-4142 **Financial Aid Phone:** (727) 873-4128
E-mail: admissions@usfsp.edu
Fax: 813-873-4525 **Website:** http://www.usfsp.edu **ACT Code:** 0761

This public school was founded in 1965. It has a 48 acre campus.

RATINGS

Admissions Selectivity Rating: 93   **Fire Safety Rating:** 99   **Green Rating:** 60*

STUDENTS AND FACULTY

Enrollment: 3,810. **Student Body:** 64% female, 36% male, 4% out-of-state, 1% international (58 countries represented). Asian 4%, African American 7%, Caucasian 63%, Hispanic 18%, Native American <1%, Pacific Islander <1%, Two or more races 4%, Race unknown 3%.
Retention and Graduation: 74% freshmen return for sophomore year. 21% freshmen graduate within 4 years. 36% freshmen graduate within 6 years.
Faculty: Student/faculty ratio 18:1. 142 full-time faculty, 85% hold PhDs, 27% are members of minority groups, 49% are women. 0% of classes are taught by teaching assistants.

ACADEMICS

Degrees: Associate; Bachelor's; Master's; Post-master's certificate. **Classes:** Most classes have 20–29 students. Most lab/discussion sessions have 10–19 students.

Most popular majors: Biology/Biological Sciences, General; Psychology, General; Accounting. **Special Study Options:** Distance learning; Double major; Dual enrollment; Honors program; Independent study; Internships; Study abroad; Teacher certification program. **Disability Services offered:** Note-taking services; Reader services; Tape recorders; Tutors. **Career services:** Alumni services; Career assessment; Career/job search classes; Internships.

FACILITIES

Housing: Coed dorms; Special housing for disabled students; Theme housing.

CAMPUS LIFE

Environment: City. **Activities:** Campus Ministries; Choral groups; Dance; Radio station; Student government; Student newspaper. 100 registered organizations, 6 honor societies, on campus. **On-Campus Highlights:** Waterfront.

ADMISSIONS

Freshman Academic Profile: Average high school GPA 3.9. 22% in top 10% of high school class, 61% in top 25% of high school class, 90% in top 50% of high school class. 85% from public high schools. **Test Scores:** SAT Math middle 50% range 550–625. SAT EBRW middle 50% range 590–650. ACT middle 50% range 24–29. **Basis for Candidate Selection:** *Other factors include:* rigor of secondary school record, academic GPA, standardized test scores, volunteer work. **Freshman Admission Requirements:** High school diploma is required and GED is accepted. *Academic units required:* 4 English, 4 math, 3 science, 2 science labs, 2 foreign language, 3 social studies, 2 academic electives. **Freshman Admission Statistics:** 3,396 applied, 27% admitted, 34% enrolled. **General Admission Information:** Application fee $30. Priority deadline 1/15. Regular application deadline 5/1. Non-fall registration accepted.

COSTS AND FINANCIAL AID

Annual in-state tuition $4,206. Annual out-of-state tuition $15,473. Room and board $11,836. Required fees $1,615. Average book and supplies expense $1,100. **Required Forms and Deadlines:** FAFSA. **Notification of Awards:** Applicants will be notified of awards on a rolling basis beginning 3/1. **Types of Aid:** *Need-based scholarships/grants:* College/university scholarship or grant aid from institutional funds; Federal Pell; Private scholarships; SEOG; State scholarships/grants. *Loans:* Direct PLUS loans; Direct Subsidized Stafford Loans; Direct Unsubsidized Stafford Loans. **Student Employment:** Federal Work-Study Program available. Institutional employment available. **Financial Aid Statistics:** 86% needy freshmen, 82% needy undergrads receive need-based scholarship or grant aid. 6% freshmen, 3% undergrads receive non-need-based scholarship or grant aid. 44% freshmen, 52% undergrads receive need-based self-help aid. freshmen, undergrads receive athletic scholarships. 72% freshmen, 57% undergrads receive any aid. 50% undergrads borrow to pay for school. Average cumulative indebtedness $19,853.

UNIVERSITY OF TAMPA

401 West Kennedy Boulevard, Tampa, FL 33606-1490
Phone: 813-253-6211 **Financial Aid Phone:** (813) 253-6219
E-mail: admissions@ut.edu **CEEB Code:** 5819
Fax: 813-258-7398 **Website:** www.ut.edu **ACT Code:** 762

This private school was founded in 1931. It has a 110 acre campus.

RATINGS

Admissions Selectivity Rating: 88   **Fire Safety Rating:** 98   **Green Rating:** 62

STUDENTS AND FACULTY

Enrollment: 8,685. **Student Body:** 58% female, 42% male, 69% out-of-state, 8% international (132 countries represented). Asian 2%, African American 4%, Caucasian 61%, Hispanic 12%, Native American <1%, Pacific Islander <1%, Two or more races 3%, Race unknown 9%.
Retention and Graduation: 78% freshmen return for sophomore year. 49% freshmen graduate within 4 years. 58% freshmen graduate within 6 years. 14% grads go on to further study within 1 year. 4% grads pursue arts and sciences degrees. 1% grads pursue law degrees. 4% grads pursue business degrees. 3% grads pursue medical degrees. **Faculty:** Student/faculty ratio 17:1. 394 full-time faculty, 90% hold PhDs, 16% are members of minority groups, 47% are women. 0% of classes are taught by teaching assistants.

ACADEMICS

Degrees: Bachelor's; Doctoral degree—professional practice; Master's; Post-master's certificate. **Classes:** Most classes have 20–29 students. Most lab/discussion sessions have 10–19 students. **Most popular majors:** Marketing/Marketing Management, General; Criminology; Finance, General. **Special Study Options:** Double major; Honors program; Independent study; Internships; Study abroad; Teacher certification program. **Honors programs:** UT's Honors Program offers special classes that are developed to enhance creative thinking processes while meeting general distribution requirements. **Disability Services offered:** Note-taking services; Reader services; Tutors. **Career services:** Alumni network; Alumni services; Career assessment; Career/job search classes; Internships.

FACILITIES

Housing: Apartments for single students; Coed dorms; Special housing for disabled students; Theme housing; Wellness housing; 100% of campus accessible to physically disabled. **Special Academic Facilities/Equipment:** Victorian art and furniture museum, theatres, studios, music center, language lab, H.B.Plant Museum, marine science research center on Tampa Bay, an entrepreneurship center, a fully equipped research vessel for marine science studies, a music facility, writing and language labs, an academic center for excellence, a graphic design studio, a marine science lab, and art studios.

CAMPUS LIFE

Environment: Metropolis. **Activities:** Campus Ministries; Choral groups; Concert band; Dance; Drama/theater; International Student Organization; Jazz band; Literary magazine; Model UN; Music ensembles; Musical theater; Pep band; Radio station; Student government; Student newspaper; Student-run film society; Symphony orchestra; Television station; Yearbook. 267 registered organizations, 15 honor societies, 7 religious organizations, 15 fraternities, 12 sororities on campus. **Athletics (Intercollegiate):** *Men:* baseball, basketball, cross-country, golf, soccer, swimming. *Women:* basketball, crew/rowing, cross-country, soccer, softball, swimming, tennis, volleyball. **On-Campus Highlights:** Vaughn Student Center.

ADMISSIONS

Freshman Academic Profile: Average high school GPA 3.4. 19% in top 10% of high school class, 47% in top 25% of high school class, 81% in top 50% of high school class. 75% from public high schools. **Test Scores:** SAT Math middle 50% range 550–620. SAT EBRW middle 50% range 550–630. ACT middle 50% range 23–28. **Basis for Candidate Selection:** *Very important factors include:* rigor of secondary school record, academic GPA, standardized test scores. *Important factors include:* application essay, recommendation(s), talent/ability. *Other factors include:* class rank, interview, extracurricular activities, character/personal qualities, first generation, alumni/ae relation, volunteer work, work experience, level of applicant's interest. **Freshman Admission Requirements:** High school diploma is required and GED is accepted. *Academic units required:* 4 English, 3 math, 3 science, 2 science labs, 2 foreign language, 3 social studies, 3 academic electives. **Freshman Admission Statistics:** 23,341 applied, 44% admitted, 20% enrolled. **Transfer Admission Requirements:** College transcript(s). Minimum college GPA of 2.2 required. Lowest grade transferable C. **General Admission Information:** Application fee $40. Priority deadline 11/15. Non-fall registration accepted. Admission may be deferred for a maximum of 1 term.

COSTS AND FINANCIAL AID

Annual tuition $28,802. Room and board $11,526. Required fees $2,082. **Required Forms and Deadlines:** FAFSA. **Notification of Awards:** Applicants will be notified of awards on a rolling basis beginning 3/1. **Types of Aid:** *Need-based scholarships/grants:* College/university scholarship or grant aid from institutional funds; Federal Nursing Scholarships; Federal Pell; Private scholarships; SEOG; State scholarships/grants. *Loans:* Direct PLUS loans; Direct Subsidized Stafford Loans; Direct Unsubsidized Stafford Loans. **Student Employment:** Federal Work-Study Program available. Institutional employment available. **Financial Aid Statistics:** 98% needy freshmen, 97% needy undergrads receive need-based scholarship or grant aid. 96% freshmen, 95% undergrads receive non-need-based scholarship or grant aid. 82% freshmen, 84% undergrads receive need-based self-help aid. 3% freshmen, 3% undergrads receive athletic scholarships. 96% freshmen, 93% undergrads receive any aid. 58% undergrads borrow to pay for school. Average cumulative indebtedness $35,046. **Criteria awarding aid:** *Non-need-based:* Academics, Art, Athletics, Leadership, Music/drama.

UNIVERSITY OF TENNESSEE—CHATTANOOGA

615 McCallie Avenue, Chattanooga, TN 37403
Phone: 423-425-4662 **Financial Aid Phone:** 423-425-4677
E-mail: utcmocs@utc.edu **CEEB Code:** 1831
Fax: 423-425-4157 **Website:** www.utc.edu **ACT Code:** 4022

This public school was founded in 1886. It has a 134 acre campus.

RATINGS

Admissions Selectivity Rating: 77   **Fire Safety Rating:** 96   **Green Rating:** 76

STUDENTS AND FACULTY

Enrollment: 10,097. **Student Body:** 56% female, 44% male, 6% out-of-state, 1% international (26 countries represented). Asian 2%, African American 10%, Caucasian 76%, Hispanic 4%, Native American <1%, Pacific Islander <1%, Two or more races 4%, Race unknown 2%.
Retention and Graduation: 73% freshmen return for sophomore year. 21% freshmen graduate within 4 years. 44% freshmen graduate within 6 years.
Faculty: Student/faculty ratio 14:1. 469 full-time faculty, 81% hold PhDs, 17% are members of minority groups, 49% are women.

ACADEMICS

Degrees: Bachelor's; Doctoral degree—professional practice; Doctoral degree research/scholarship; Master's; Post-bachelor's certificate; Post-master's certificate. **Classes:** Most classes have 10–19 students. Most lab/discussion sessions have 20–29 students. **Most popular majors:** Biology/Biological Sciences, General; Exercise Science and Kinesiology; Business Administration and Management, General. **Special Study Options:** Accelerated program; Cooperative education program; Cross-registration; Distance learning; Double major; Dual enrollment; English as a Second Language (ESL); Exchange student program (domestic); Honors program; Independent study; Internships; Liberal arts/career combination; Student-designed major; Study abroad; Teacher certification program. **Honors programs:** The University Honors College offers two honors programs. The first is the Brock Scholars Program, a four-year program that delivers a classical liberal arts education with a curriculum based on fulfilling most general education categories with honors seminars. The second is the Departmental Honors Program, a program in which eligible students from any UTC department can complete an honors thesis project in their major area of study. http://www.utc.edu/Academic/UniversityHonors/. **Disability Services offered:** Note-taking services; Reader services; Tape recorders; Tutors. **Career services:** Alumni services; Career/job search classes; Internships.

FACILITIES

Housing: Apartments for single students; Coed dorms; Special housing for disabled students; Special housing for international students; Theme housing; 95% of campus accessible to physically disabled. **Special Academic Facilities/Equipment:** Walker Teaching Resource Center; Jones Observatory; Institute of Archaeology; Odor Research Center; SIM Center; Challenger Center; Center for Applied Social Research; The Ochs Center for Metropolitan Studies.

CAMPUS LIFE

Environment: City. **Activities:** Campus Ministries; Choral groups; Concert band; Dance; Drama/theater; International Student Organization; Jazz band; Literary magazine; Marching band; Model UN; Music ensembles; Musical theater; Opera; Pep band; Radio station; Student government; Student newspaper; Student-run film society; Symphony orchestra; Television station. 125 registered organizations, 34 honor societies, 8 religious organizations, 14 fraternities, 11 sororities on campus. **Athletics (Intercollegiate):** *Men:* basketball, cross-country, football, golf, tennis, track/field (outdoor), wrestling. *Women:* basketball, cross-country, golf, soccer, softball, tennis, track/field (outdoor), volleyball. **On-Campus Highlights:** Aquatic and Recreation Center. **Environmental Initiatives:** Central Plan Improvements.

ADMISSIONS

Freshman Academic Profile: Average high school GPA 3.5. 75% from public high schools. **Test Scores:** SAT Math middle 50% range 510–610. SAT EBRW middle 50% range 530–630. ACT middle 50% range 21–26. **Basis for Candidate Selection:** *Very important factors include:* rigor of secondary school record, academic GPA, standardized test scores. *Important factors include:* character/personal qualities. *Other factors include:* application essay, recommendation(s), extracurricular activities, talent/ability, volunteer work, work experience. **Freshman Admission Requirements:** High school diploma is required and GED is accepted. *Academic units required:* 4 English, 4 math,

3 science, 3 science labs, 2 foreign language, 2 history, 1 visual/performing arts. **Freshman Admission Statistics:** 7,235 applied, 83% admitted, 36% enrolled. **Transfer Admission Requirements:** College transcript(s). Minimum college GPA of 2.0 required. Lowest grade transferable D. **General Admission Information:** Application fee $30. Regular application deadline 5/1. Non-fall registration accepted. Admission may be deferred for a maximum of 1 semester.

COSTS AND FINANCIAL AID
Annual in-state tuition $6,888. Annual out-of-state tuition $23,006. Room and board $8,786. Average book and supplies expense $1,400. **Required Forms and Deadlines:** FAFSA. **Notification of Awards:** Applicants will be notified of awards on a rolling basis beginning 1/20. **Types of Aid:** *Need-based scholarships/grants:* College/university scholarship or grant aid from institutional funds; Federal Pell; Private scholarships; SEOG; State scholarships/grants. *Loans:* Direct PLUS loans; Direct Subsidized Stafford Loans; Direct Unsubsidized Stafford Loans. **Student Employment:** Federal Work-Study Program available. Institutional employment available. **Financial Aid Statistics:** 96% needy freshmen, 87% needy undergrads receive need-based scholarship or grant aid. 1% freshmen, 3% undergrads receive non-need-based scholarship or grant aid. 73% freshmen, 75% undergrads receive need-based self-help aid. 2% freshmen, 1% undergrads receive athletic scholarships. 64% freshmen, 61% undergrads receive any aid. 56% undergrads borrow to pay for school. Average cumulative indebtedness $22,293. **Criteria awarding aid:** *Need-based:* Academics *Non-need-based:* Academics, Alumni affiliation, Art, Athletics, Leadership, Music/drama, State/district residency.

UNIVERSITY OF TENNESSEE—KNOXVILLE

320 Student Service Building, Knoxville, TN 37996-0230
Phone: 865-974-1111 **Financial Aid Phone:** (865) 974-1111
E-mail: admissions@utk.edu **CEEB Code:** 1843
Website: http://www.utk.edu **ACT Code:** 4026

This public school was founded in 1794. It has a 600 acre campus.

RATINGS
Admissions Selectivity Rating: 84   **Fire Safety Rating:** 96   **Green Rating:** 90

STUDENTS AND FACULTY
Enrollment: 23,152. **Student Body:** 51% female, 49% male, 18% out-of-state, 1% international (55 countries represented). Asian 4%, African American 6%, Caucasian 78%, Hispanic 5%, Native American <1%, Pacific Islander 0%, Two or more races 4%, Race unknown 2%.
Retention and Graduation: 87% freshmen return for sophomore year. 52% freshmen graduate within 4 years. 72% freshmen graduate within 6 years.
Faculty: Student/faculty ratio 17:1. 1,625 full-time faculty, 86% hold PhDs, 20% are members of minority groups, 45% are women.

ACADEMICS
Degrees: Bachelor's; Doctoral degree—professional practice; Doctoral degree research/scholarship; Master's; Post-bachelor's certificate. **Classes:** Most classes have 20–29 students. **Most popular majors:** Biology/Biological Sciences, General; Psychology, General; Logistics, Materials, and Supply Chain Management. **Special Study Options:** Accelerated program; Cooperative education program; Distance learning; Double major; Dual enrollment; English as a Second Language (ESL); Exchange student program (domestic); External degree program; Honors program; Independent study; Internships; Liberal arts/career combination; Student-designed major; Study abroad; Teacher certification program. **Honors programs:** Chancellor's Honors Program; Haslam Scholars Program; Honors Leadership Program; 1794 Scholars Program; College Scholars Program; Global Leadership Scholars Program; Tickle College of Engineering Honors Program; Cook Grand Challenge Honors Program; Herbert College of Agriculture Honors Program; College of Social Work Honors Program; Howard H. Baker Jr. Center for Public Policy's Baker Scholars Program; The Math Honors Program; Additional departmental honors programs. **Combined degree programs:** BA/DDS; BA/JD; BA/MA. **Disability Services offered:** Note-taking services; Reader services; Tape recorders; Tutors. **Career services:** Alumni network; Alumni services; Career assessment; Career/job search classes; Internships; Regional alumni.

FACILITIES
Housing: Apartments for single students; Coed dorms; Fraternity/sorority housing; Men's dorms; Special housing for disabled students; Theme housing; Women's dorms; 95% of campus accessible to physically disabled. **Special Academic Facilities/Equipment:** McClung Museum of Natural History and Culture has collections in anthropology, archaeology, decorative arts, local history, and natural history. Exhibits showcase the geologic, historical, and artistic past of Tennessee as well as cultures from around the globe. The campus is adjacent to a thriving historic downtown. The UT Downtown Gallery and the Ewing Gallery of Art on campus exhibit a wide range of art, media, graphic design, architectural drawings, and photographs. The UT Gardens is a living outdoor laboratory featuring trees, shrubs, annual and perennial flowers, and ornamental grasses, and links to Knoxville's more than 112 miles of trails and greenways. The Natalie L. Haslam Music Center and the Cox Auditorium in the Alumni Memorial Building host hundreds of shows every year ranging from UT Opera and choral groups to string, wind, and jazz ensembles and a wide variety of bands. With a dual mission to train the next generation of theatre artists and to provide top quality professional theatre, the Clarence Brown Theatre is one of only 12 academic LORT (League of Resident Theatre) institutions in the nation. The CBT season runs from August through May and features eight productions ranging from musicals to drama. The International House is a multicultural gathering and programming facility where individuals from all over the globe come together to share experiences. The Howard H. Baker Jr. Center for Public Policy is a nonpartisan institute devoted to education, scholarship, and civic engagement. Through classes, public lectures, research, and outreach programs, the center provides policy makers, citizens, scholars, and students with the information and skills needed to work effectively within our political system. **Campus Network:** 100% of classrooms, 100% of dorms, 100% of student union, 100% of libraries, 100% of dining areas, 70% of common outdoor areas have wireless network access.

CAMPUS LIFE
Environment: City. **Activities:** Campus Ministries; Choral groups; Concert band; Dance; Drama/theater; International Student Organization; Jazz band; Literary magazine; Marching band; Model UN; Music ensembles; Musical theater; Opera; Pep band; Radio station; Student government; Student newspaper; Student-run film society; Symphony orchestra; Television station; Yearbook. 481 registered organizations, 14 honor societies, 42 religious organizations, 25 fraternities, 20 sororities on campus. **Athletics (Intercollegiate):** *Men:* baseball, basketball, cheerleading, cross-country, diving, football, golf, swimming, tennis, track/field (outdoor), track/field (indoor). *Women:* basketball, cheerleading, crew/rowing, cross-country, diving, golf, soccer, softball, swimming, tennis, track/field (outdoor), track/field (indoor), volleyball. **On-Campus Highlights:** Neyland Stadium. **Environmental Initiatives:** Climate Action Plan.

ADMISSIONS
Freshman Academic Profile: Average high school GPA 4.0. 35% in top 10% of high school class, 63% in top 25% of high school class, 88% in top 50% of high school class. **Test Scores:** SAT Math middle 50% range 570–670. SAT EBRW middle 50% range 580–660. ACT middle 50% range 24–30. **Basis for Candidate Selection:** *Very important factors include:* academic GPA, standardized test scores. *Important factors include:* rigor of secondary school record, application essay, *Other factors include:* class rank, recommendation(s), extracurricular activities, talent/ability, character/personal qualities, first generation, alumni/ae relation, geographical residence, state residency, racial/ethnic status, volunteer work, work experience, level of applicant's interest. **Freshman Admission Requirements:** High school diploma is required and GED is accepted *Academic units recommended:* 4 English, 4 math, 3 science, 3 science labs, 2 foreign language, 1 social studies, 1 history, 1 visual/performing arts. **Freshman Admission Statistics:** 21,764 applied, 79% admitted, 31% enrolled. **Transfer Admission Requirements:** High school transcript, college transcript(s), statement of good standing from prior institution(s). Minimum college GPA of 2.0 required. Lowest grade transferable C. **General Admission Information:** Application fee $50. Regular application deadline 8/20. Non-fall registration accepted. Admission may be deferred for a maximum of 1 year.

COSTS AND FINANCIAL AID
Annual in-state tuition $11,332. Annual out-of-state tuition $29,522. Room and board $11,482. Required fees $1,932. Average book and supplies expense $1,598. **Required Forms and Deadlines:** FAFSA. **Notification of Awards:** Applicants will be notified of awards on a rolling basis beginning 2/15. **Types of Aid:** *Need-based scholarships/grants:* College/university scholarship or grant aid from institutional funds; Federal Pell; Private scholarships; SEOG; State scholarships/grants. *Loans:* Direct PLUS loans; Direct Subsidized Stafford Loans; Direct Unsubsidized Stafford Loans. **Student Employment:** Federal

Work-Study Program available. **Financial Aid Statistics:** 92% needy freshmen, 87% needy undergrads receive need-based scholarship or grant aid. 0% freshmen, 0% undergrads receive non-need-based scholarship or grant aid. 99% freshmen, 98% undergrads receive need-based self-help aid. 2% freshmen, 2% undergrads receive athletic scholarships. 93.43% freshmen, 87.63% undergrads receive any aid. 50% undergrads borrow to pay for school. Average cumulative indebtedness $27,060. **Criteria awarding aid:** *Need-based:* Academics, Minority status *Non-need-based:* Academics, Art, Athletics, Leadership, Minority status, Music/drama, State/district residency.

UNIVERSITY OF TENNESSEE—MARTIN

201 Hall-Moody, Martin, TN 38238
Phone: 731-881-7020 **Financial Aid Phone:** 731-881-7031
E-mail: admitme@utm.edu
Fax: 731-881-7029 **Website:** www.utm.edu **ACT Code:** 4032

This public school was founded in 1900. It has a 930 acre campus.

RATINGS
Admissions Selectivity Rating: 80   Fire Safety Rating: 85   Green Rating: 72

STUDENTS AND FACULTY
Enrollment: 5,228. **Student Body:** 60% female, 40% male, 9% out-of-state, 1% international (21 countries represented). Asian 1%, African American 13%, Caucasian 79%, Hispanic 3%, Native American <1%, Pacific Islander 0%, Two or more races 3%, Race unknown 0%.
Retention and Graduation: 74% freshmen return for sophomore year. 26% freshmen graduate within 4 years. 47 21% grads go on to further study within 1 year. **Faculty:** Student/faculty ratio 15:1. 285 full-time faculty, 71% hold PhDs, 11% are members of minority groups, 45% are women. 0% of classes are taught by teaching assistants.

ACADEMICS
Degrees: Bachelor's; Master's. **Classes:** Most classes have 10–19 students. Most lab/discussion sessions have 10–19 students. **Most popular majors:** Agricultural/Animal/Plant/Veterinary Science and Related Fields; Sports, Kinesiology, and Physical Education/Fitness, General; Registered Nursing/Registered Nurse. **Special Study Options:** Accelerated program; Cooperative education program; Cross-registration; Distance learning; Double major; Dual enrollment; English as a Second Language (ESL); Honors program; Independent study; Internships; Student-designed major; Study abroad; Teacher certification program. **Honors programs:** University Scholars Honors Seminar. **Disability Services offered:** Note-taking services; Reader services; Tape recorders; Tutors. **Career services:** Alumni network; Alumni services; Career assessment; Career/job search classes; Internships; Regional alumni.

FACILITIES
Housing: Apartments for married students; Apartments for single students; Coed dorms; Men's dorms; Special housing for disabled students; Women's dorms; 100% of campus accessible to physically disabled. **Special Academic Facilities/Equipment:** Paul Meek Library contains Houston Gordon University Museum. **Campus Network:** 100% of classrooms, 100% of dorms, 100% of student union, 100% of libraries, 100% of dining areas, 100% of common outdoor areas have wireless network access.

CAMPUS LIFE
Environment: Village. **Activities:** Campus Ministries; Choral groups; Concert band; Dance; Drama/theater; International Student Organization; Jazz band; Literary magazine; Marching band; Model UN; Music ensembles; Musical theater; Pep band; Radio station; Student government; Student newspaper; Student-run film society; Television station; Yearbook. 170 registered organizations, 18 honor societies, 12 religious organizations, 11 fraternities, 9 sororities on campus. **Athletics (Intercollegiate):** *Men:* baseball, basketball, cross-country, football, golf, riflery, rodeo. *Women:* basketball, cheerleading, cross-country, equestrian sports, riflery, rodeo, soccer, softball, tennis, volleyball. **On-Campus Highlights:** Boling University Center. **Environmental Initiatives:** UTM Center for Sustainability and Recycling Center.

ADMISSIONS
Freshman Academic Profile: Average high school GPA 3.6. 15% in top 10% of high school class, 43% in top 25% of high school class, 80% in top 50% of high school class. 94% from public high schools. **Test Scores:** ACT middle 50% range 21–26. **Basis for Candidate Selection:** *Very important factors*

include: rigor of secondary school record, academic GPA, standardized test scores. **Freshman Admission Requirements:** High school diploma is required and GED is accepted *Academic units required:* 4 English, 4 math, 3 science, 1 science labs, 2 foreign language, 1 social studies, 1 history, 1 visual/performing arts. **Freshman Admission Statistics:** 9,158 applied, 64% admitted, 20% enrolled. **Transfer Admission Requirements:** High school transcript, college transcript(s). Minimum college GPA of 2.0 required. Lowest grade transferable D. **General Admission Information:** Application fee $30. Priority deadline 8/1. Non-fall registration accepted. Admission may be deferred for a maximum of year.

COSTS AND FINANCIAL AID
Annual in-state tuition $8,214. Annual out-of-state tuition $14,254. Room and board $6,396. Required fees $1,534. Average book and supplies expense $1,400. **Required Forms and Deadlines:** FAFSA. **Notification of Awards:** Applicants will be notified of awards on a rolling basis beginning 3/15. **Types of Aid:** *Need-based scholarships/grants:* College/university scholarship or grant aid from institutional funds; Federal Pell; Private scholarships; SEOG; State scholarships/grants. *Loans:* Direct PLUS loans; Direct Subsidized Stafford Loans; Direct Unsubsidized Stafford Loans. **Student Employment:** Federal Work-Study Program available. Institutional employment available. **Financial Aid Statistics:** 70% needy freshmen, 68% needy undergrads receive need-based scholarship or grant aid. 91% freshmen, 68% undergrads receive non-need-based scholarship or grant aid. 55% freshmen, 58% undergrads receive need-based self-help aid. 4% freshmen, 3% undergrads receive athletic scholarships. 98.1% freshmen, 85.9% undergrads receive any aid. 62% undergrads borrow to pay for school. Average cumulative indebtedness $24,096. **Criteria awarding aid:** *Need-based:* Academics. *Non-need-based:* Academics, Alumni affiliation, Art, Athletics, Leadership, Minority status, Music/drama, State/district residency.

THE UNIVERSITY OF TEXAS AT ARLINGTON

Office of Admissions, Arlington, TX 76019-0111
Phone: 817-272-6287 **Financial Aid Phone:** 817-272-3561
E-mail: admissions@uta.edu **CEEB Code:** 6013
Fax: 817-272-3435 **Website:** www.uta.edu **ACT Code:** 4200

This public school was founded in 1895. It has a 420 acre campus.

RATINGS
Admissions Selectivity Rating: 86   Fire Safety Rating: 96   Green Rating: 60*

STUDENTS AND FACULTY
Enrollment: 25,414. **Student Body:** 56% female, 44% male, 3% out-of-state, 4% international (123 countries represented). Asian 12%, African American 15%, Caucasian 40%, Hispanic 26%, Native American <1%, Pacific Islander <1%, Two or more races 3%, Race unknown 1%.
Retention and Graduation: 74% freshmen return for sophomore year. **Faculty:** Student/faculty ratio 22:1. 941 full-time faculty, 0% hold PhDs, 28% are members of minority groups, 42% are women. 16% of classes are taught by teaching assistants.

ACADEMICS
Degrees: Bachelor's; Doctoral degree—professional practice; Doctoral degree research/scholarship; Master's; Post-bachelor's certificate; Post-master's certificate. **Classes:** Most classes have 20–29 students. **Most popular majors:** Registered Nursing/Registered Nurse; Business Administration and Management, General. **Special Study Options:** Cross-registration; Distance learning; Double major; Dual enrollment; English as a Second Language (ESL); Honors program; Independent study; Internships; Student-designed major; Study abroad; Teacher certification program. **Honors programs:** We have the only Honors College in N. Texas. Freshmen interest groups, honors study abroad. **Combined degree programs:** BA/MD. **Disability Services offered:** Note-taking services; Reader services; Tape recorders; Tutors. **Career services:** Alumni services; Career assessment; Career/job search classes; Internships.

FACILITIES
Housing: Apartments for married students; Apartments for single students; Coed dorms; Fraternity/sorority housing; Men's dorms; Women's dorms 95% of campus accessible to physically disabled. **Special Academic Facilities/Equipment:** Cartographic history library with maps collection, minority cultures collection, library of Texana and Mexican war; Continuing Education

Work Force Development Center; Planetarium, Automation and Robotics Research institute; Wave Scattering Research Center.

CAMPUS LIFE

Environment: Metropolis. **Activities:** Campus Ministries; Choral groups; Concert band; Dance; Drama/theater; International Student Organization; Jazz band; Literary magazine; Marching band; Music ensembles; Opera; Radio station; Student government; Student newspaper; Student-run film society; Symphony orchestra. 256 registered organizations, 28 honor societies, 24 religious organizations, 20 fraternities, 11 sororities on campus. **Athletics (Intercollegiate):** *Men:* baseball, basketball, cross-country, golf, tennis, track/field (outdoor). *Women:* basketball, cross-country, softball, tennis, track/field (outdoor), volleyball. **On-Campus Highlights:** Click Cafe in Library. **Environmental Initiatives:** Transportation programs like car sharing, ride share, bike program.

ADMISSIONS

Freshman Academic Profile: 28% in top 10% of high school class, 75% in top 25% of high school class, 98% in top 50% of high school class. **Test Scores:** SAT Math middle 50% range 500–620. SAT EBRW middle 50% range 460–580. ACT middle 50% range 20–26. **Basis for Candidate Selection:** *Very important factors include:* class rank, academic GPA, standardized test scores. *Important factors include:* rigor of secondary school record. *Other factors include:* application essay, recommendation(s), extracurricular activities, talent/ability, character/personal qualities, first generation, volunteer work, work experience, level of applicant's interest. **Freshman Admission Requirements:** High school diploma is required and GED is not accepted. *Academic units required:* 4 English, 3 math, 3 science, 2 foreign language, 3 social studies, 5 academic electives, 5 unit from above areas or other academic areas. *Academic units recommended:* 4 English, 4 math, 3 science, 3 foreign language, 4 social studies, 5 academic electives. **Freshman Admission Statistics:** 10,679 applied, 60% admitted, 42% enrolled. **Transfer Admission Requirements:** High school transcript, college transcript(s). Minimum college GPA of 2.25 required. Lowest grade transferable C. **General Admission Information:** Application fee $50. Priority deadline 6/1. Non-fall registration accepted. Admission may be deferred for a maximum of 1 year.

COSTS AND FINANCIAL AID

Annual in-state tuition $8,878. Annual out-of-state tuition $19,497. Room and board $7,864. Average book and supplies expense $1,160. **Required Forms and Deadlines:** FAFSA. **Notification of Awards:** Applicants will be notified of awards on a rolling basis beginning 4/1. **Types of Aid:** *Need-based scholarships/grants:* College/university scholarship or grant aid from institutional funds; Federal Pell; Private scholarships; SEOG; State scholarships/grants; United Negro College Fund. *Loans:* Direct PLUS loans; Direct Subsidized Stafford Loans; Direct Unsubsidized Stafford Loans. **Student Employment:** Federal Work-Study Program available. Institutional employment available. **Financial Aid Statistics:** 74% needy freshmen, 80% needy undergrads receive need-based scholarship or grant aid. 50% freshmen, 31% undergrads receive non-need-based scholarship or grant aid. 94% freshmen, 95% undergrads receive need-based self-help aid. 0% freshmen, 0% undergrads receive athletic scholarships. 65.28% freshmen, 68.34% undergrads receive any aid. **Criteria awarding aid:** *Need-based:* Academics, Athletics *Non-need-based:* Academics, Art, Athletics, Leadership, Music/drama.

THE UNIVERSITY OF TEXAS AT AUSTIN

P.O. Box 8058, Austin, TX 78713-8058
Phone: 512-475-7399 **Financial Aid Phone:** (512) 475-6282
E-mail: admissions@austin.utexas.edu **CEEB Code:** 6882
Fax: 512-475-7478 **Website:** http://www.utexas.edu **ACT Code:** 4240

This public school was founded in 1883. It has a 436 acre campus.

RATINGS

Admissions Selectivity Rating: 95   **Fire Safety Rating:** 84   **Green Rating:** 83

STUDENTS AND FACULTY

Enrollment: 39,783. **Student Body:** 55% female, 45% male, 5% out-of-state, 5% international (103 countries represented). Asian 23%, African American 4%, Caucasian 39%, Hispanic 24%, Native American <1%, Pacific Islander <1%, Two or more races 4%, Race unknown 1%.
Retention and Graduation: 96% freshmen return for sophomore year. 66% freshmen graduate within 4 years. 86% freshmen graduate within 6 years.
Faculty: Student/faculty ratio 18:1. 2,534 full-time faculty, 90% hold PhDs, 26% are members of minority groups, 41% are women.

ACADEMICS

Degrees: Bachelor's; Certificate; Doctoral degree—professional practice; Doctoral degree research/scholarship; Master's; Post-bachelor's certificate. **Classes:** Most classes have 10–19 students. Most lab/discussion sessions have 10–19 students. **Most popular majors:** Biology/Biological Sciences, General; Economics, General; Psychology, General. **Special Study Options:** Accelerated program; Cooperative education program; Cross-registration; Distance learning; Double major; Dual enrollment; English as a Second Language (ESL); Exchange student program (domestic); Honors program; Independent study; Internships; Liberal arts/career combination; Student-designed major; Study abroad; Teacher certification program. **Honors programs:** Canfield Business Honors Program, Engineering Honors Program, Liberal Arts Honors Program, Moody College Honors Program, Plan II Honors Program, Texas Honors Computer Science and Business, Natural Sciences Honors Programs: Dean's Scholars, Health Science Scholars, Polymathic Scholars, Turing Scholars Program in Computer Science, and Human Ecology Honors. **Disability Services offered:** Note-taking services; Reader services; Tape recorders; Tutors. **Career services:** Alumni network; Alumni services; Career assessment; Internships; Regional alumni.

FACILITIES

Housing: Apartments for married students; Apartments for single students; Coed dorms; Men's dorms; Special housing for disabled students; Special housing for international students; Theme housing; Wellness housing; Women's dorms. **Special Academic Facilities/Equipment:** Blanton Museum of Art, Lyndon Baines Johnson Presidential Library/Museum, Performing Arts Center, Texas Memorial Museum, Harry Ransom Humanities Research Center.

CAMPUS LIFE

Environment: Metropolis. **Activities:** Campus Ministries; Choral groups; Concert band; Dance; Drama/theater; International Student Organization; Jazz band; Literary magazine; Marching band; Model UN; Music ensembles; Musical theater; Opera; Pep band; Radio station; Student government; Student newspaper; Student-run film society; Symphony orchestra; Television station; Yearbook. 1055 registered organizations, 5 honor societies, 96 religious organizations on campus. **Athletics (Intercollegiate):** *Men:* baseball, basketball, cross-country, diving, football, golf, swimming, tennis, track/field (outdoor). *Women:* basketball, crew/rowing, cross-country, diving, golf, soccer, softball, swimming, tennis, track/field (outdoor), volleyball. **On-Campus Highlights:** The Tower. **Environmental Initiatives:** Incorporation of sustainability principles throughout the institution's approved Campus Master Plan (May 2013).

ADMISSIONS

Freshman Academic Profile: 87% in top 10% of high school class, 96% in top 25% of high school class, 99% in top 50% of high school class. **Test Scores:** SAT Math middle 50% range 610–760. SAT EBRW middle 50% range 620–720. ACT middle 50% range 27–33. **Basis for Candidate Selection:** *Very important factors include:* rigor of secondary school record, class rank, academic GPA, application essay, standardized test scores, recommendation(s), extracurricular activities, talent/ability, character/personal qualities, first generation, geographical residence, state residency, religious affiliation/commitment, racial/ethnic status, volunteer work, work experience. **Freshman Admission Requirements:** High school diploma is required and GED is accepted *Academic units required:* 4 English, 4 math, 4 science, 2 foreign language, 4 social studies, 6 academic electives. **Freshman Admission Statistics:** 53,525 applied, 32% admitted, 48% enrolled. **Transfer Admission Requirements:** College transcript(s), essay or personal statement. Minimum college GPA of 3.0 required. Lowest grade transferable C. **General Admission Information:** Application fee $75. Priority deadline 11/1. Regular application deadline 12/1. Non-fall registration accepted.

COSTS AND FINANCIAL AID

Annual in-state tuition $10,824. Annual out-of-state tuition $38,326. Room and board $11,812. Average book and supplies expense $700. **Required Forms and Deadlines:** FAFSA; Institution's own financial aid form. **Notification of Awards:** Applicants will be notified of awards on a rolling basis beginning 1/15. **Types of Aid:** *Need-based scholarships/grants:* College/university scholarship or grant aid from institutional funds; Federal Pell; Private scholarships; SEOG;

State scholarships/grants. *Loans:* Direct PLUS loans; Direct Subsidized Stafford Loans; Direct Unsubsidized Stafford Loans. **Student Employment:** Federal Work-Study Program available. Institutional employment available. **Financial Aid Statistics:** 72% needy freshmen, 77% needy undergrads receive need-based scholarship or grant aid. 53% freshmen, 27% undergrads receive non-need-based scholarship or grant aid. 61% freshmen, 65% undergrads receive need-based self-help aid. 11% freshmen, 7% undergrads receive athletic scholarships. 40% undergrads borrow to pay for school. Average cumulative indebtedness $24,244. **Criteria awarding aid:** *Need-based:* Academics, Art, Leadership, Music/drama *Non-need-based:* Academics, Art, Athletics, Leadership, Music/drama, State/district residency.

THE UNIVERSITY OF TEXAS AT BROWNSVILLE

80 Fort Brown, Brownsville, TX 78520
Phone: 956-882-8295 **Financial Aid Phone:** 956-882-8814
E-mail: admissions@utb.edu **CEEB Code:** 6825
Fax: 956-882-7810 **Website:** www.utb.edu

This public school was founded in 1926.

RATINGS
Admissions Selectivity Rating: 65   **Fire Safety Rating:** 60*   **Green Rating:** 60*

STUDENTS AND FACULTY
Enrollment: 10,145. **Student Body:** 60% female, 40% male, 4% out-of-state, 4% international (21 countries represented). Asian <1%, African American <1%, Caucasian 5%, Hispanic 90%, Native American <1%, Race unknown 1%.
Faculty: 366 full-time faculty, 59% hold PhDs, 46% are members of minority groups, 43% are women. 0% of classes are taught by teaching assistants.

ACADEMICS
Degrees: Associate; Bachelor's; Certificate; Master's; Terminal Associate; Transfer Associate. **Most popular majors:** Business/Commerce, General; Multi-/Interdisciplinary Studies, Other; Psychology, General. **Special Study Options:** Cooperative education program; Distance learning; Double major; Dual enrollment; English as a Second Language (ESL); Independent study; Internships; Teacher certification program. **Disability Services offered:** Note-taking services; Reader services; Tape recorders; Tutors.

FACILITIES
Housing: Apartments for single students; Coed dorms; Men's dorms; Special housing for disabled students; Women's dorms. **Campus Network:** 100% of classrooms, 70% of dorms, 100% of student union, 100% of libraries, 100% of dining areas, 80% of common outdoor areas, have wireless network access.

CAMPUS LIFE
Environment: City. **Activities:** Choral groups; Concert band; Dance; Drama/theater; Jazz band; Music ensembles; Opera; Radio station; Student government; Student newspaper. 56 registered organizations, 6 honor societies, on campus. **Athletics (Intercollegiate):** *Men:* baseball, golf. *Women:* golf, volleyball.

ADMISSIONS
Freshman Academic Profile: Average high school GPA 2.6. 10% in top 10% of high school class, 27% in top 25% of high school class, 57% in top 50% of high school class. 95% from public high schools. **Basis for Candidate Selection: Freshman Admission Requirements:** High school diploma or equivalent is not required. *Academic units required:* 4 English, 2 math, 2 science, 2 science labs, 2 foreign language, 4 social studies, 2 history, 1 academic electives, 3 unit from above areas or other academic areas. *Academic units recommended:* 4 English, 4 math, 3 science, 3 science labs, 3 foreign language, 4 social studies, 2 history, 4 academic electives, 3 unit from above areas or other academic areas. **Freshman Admission Statistics:** 3,594 applied, 100% admitted, 50% enrolled. **Transfer Admission Requirements:** High school transcript, college transcript(s). Minimum college GPA of 2.0 required. Lowest grade transferable C. **General Admission Information:** Priority deadline 4/1. Regular application deadline 7/1. Non-fall registration accepted. Admission may be deferred for a maximum of 1 year.

COSTS AND FINANCIAL AID
Average book and supplies expense $615. **Required Forms and Deadlines:** FAFSA. **Notification of Awards:** Applicants will be notified of awards on or about 5/1. **Types of Aid:** *Need-based scholarships/grants:* College/university

scholarship or grant aid from institutional funds; Federal Pell; Private scholarships; SEOG; State scholarships/grants. **Criteria awarding aid:** *Need-based:* Academics. *Non-need-based:* Academics, Art, Athletics, Leadership, Music/drama.

THE UNIVERSITY OF TEXAS AT DALLAS

Admission & Enrollment, Richardson, TX 75080-3021
Phone: 972-883-2270 **Financial Aid Phone:** 972-883-2941
E-mail: admission@utdallas.edu **CEEB Code:** 6897
Fax: 972-883-2599 **Website:** www.utdallas.edu **ACT Code:** 4243

This public school was founded in 1969. It has a 500 acre campus.

RATINGS
Admissions Selectivity Rating: 86   **Fire Safety Rating:** 95   **Green Rating:** 94

STUDENTS AND FACULTY
Enrollment: 20,771. **Student Body:** 43% female, 57% male, 5% out-of-state, 5% international (68 countries represented). Asian 33%, African American 6%, Caucasian 31%, Hispanic 19%, Native American <1%, Pacific Islander <1%, Two or more races 4%, Race unknown 2%.
Retention and Graduation: 88% freshmen return for sophomore year. 53% freshmen graduate within 4 years. 71% freshmen graduate within 6 years.
Faculty: Student/faculty ratio 24:1. 932 full-time faculty, 87% hold PhDs, 28% are members of minority groups, 33% are women. 2% of classes are taught by teaching assistants.

ACADEMICS
Degrees: Bachelor's; Doctoral degree—professional practice; Doctoral degree research/scholarship; Master's; Post-bachelor's certificate. **Classes:** Most classes have 40–49 students. Most lab/discussion sessions have 20–29 students. **Most popular majors:** Computer and Information Sciences, General; Mechanical Engineering; Biology/Biological Sciences, General.
Special Study Options: Accelerated program; Cooperative education program; Cross-registration; Distance learning; Double major; Dual enrollment; Exchange student program (domestic); Honors program; Independent study; Internships; Liberal arts/career combination; Student-designed major; Study abroad; Teacher certification program. **Honors programs:** UTD's Honors College offers small classes, innovative instruction, world class faculty, bright and inquisitive colleagues, and an array of extracurricular events to provide special opportunities for professional and personal growth. **Combined degree programs:** BA/MA. **Disability Services offered:** Note-taking services; Reader services; Tape recorders; Tutors. **Career services:** Alumni network; Alumni services; Career assessment; Career/job search classes; Internships.

FACILITIES
Housing: Apartments for married students; Apartments for single students; Coed dorms; 100% of campus accessible to physically disabled. **Special Academic Facilities/Equipment:** McDermott Library Special Collections, History of Aviation Collection, Wineburgh Philatelic Research Library, Louise B. Belsterling Botanical Library, SP/N Art Gallery, Nebula Art Gallery, O'Donnell Theater. **Campus Network:** 100% of classrooms, 100% of dorms, 100% of student union, 100% of libraries, 100% of dining areas, 1% of common outdoor areas have wireless network access.

CAMPUS LIFE
Environment: Metropolis. **Activities:** Choral groups; Concert band; Dance; Drama/theater; International Student Organization; Jazz band; Literary magazine; Model UN; Music ensembles; Musical theater; Pep band; Radio station; Student government; Student newspaper; Student-run film society; Symphony orchestra; Television station. 461 registered organizations, 12 honor societies, 45 religious organizations, 12 fraternities, 11 sororities on campus. **Athletics (Intercollegiate):** *Men:* baseball, basketball, cross-country, golf, soccer, tennis. *Women:* basketball, cross-country, golf, soccer, softball, tennis, volleyball. **On-Campus Highlights:** The Pub (coffeehouse). **Environmental Initiatives:** Campus recycling program.

ADMISSIONS

Freshman Academic Profile: 39% in top 10% of high school class, 71% in top 25% of high school class, 95% in top 50% of high school class. 95% from public high schools. **Test Scores:** SAT Math middle 50% range 630–750. SAT EBRW middle 50% range 610–710. ACT middle 50% range 26–33. **Basis for Candidate Selection:** *Very important factors include:* rigor of secondary school record, class rank, academic GPA, standardized test scores. *Important factors include:* application essay, *Other factors include:* recommendation(s), extracurricular activities, talent/ability, character/personal qualities, geographical residence, state residency, volunteer work, work experience, level of applicant's interest. **Freshman Admission Requirements:** High school diploma is required and GED is accepted *Academic units required:* 4 English, 4 math, 3 science, 3 science labs, 2 foreign language, 3 social studies, 1.5 academic electives, 0.5 visual/performing arts. *Academic units recommended:* 4 English, 4 math, 3 science, 3 science labs, 3 foreign language, 4 social studies, 2.5 academic electives, 1 computer science, 1 visual/performing arts. **Freshman Admission Statistics:** 14,327 applied, 79% admitted, 36% enrolled. **Transfer Admission Requirements:** College transcript(s). Minimum college GPA of 2.5 required. Lowest grade transferable C. **General Admission Information:** Application fee $50. Priority deadline 12/1. Regular application deadline 5/1. Non-fall registration accepted. Admission may be deferred for a maximum of one year.

COSTS AND FINANCIAL AID

Annual in-state tuition $13,442. Annual out-of-state tuition $38,168. Room and board $12,076. Average book and supplies expense $1,200. **Required Forms and Deadlines:** FAFSA. **Notification of Awards:** Applicants will be notified of awards on a rolling basis beginning 3/1. **Types of Aid:** *Need-based scholarships/grants:* College/university scholarship or grant aid from institutional funds; Federal Pell; Private scholarships; SEOG; State scholarships/grants. *Loans:* Direct PLUS loans; Direct Subsidized Stafford Loans; Direct Unsubsidized Stafford Loans. **Student Employment:** Federal Work-Study Program available. Institutional employment available. **Financial Aid Statistics:** 87% needy freshmen, 88% needy undergrads receive need-based scholarship or grant aid. 13% freshmen, 6% undergrads receive non-need-based scholarship or grant aid. 82% freshmen, 88% undergrads receive need-based self-help aid. 0% freshmen, 0% undergrads receive athletic scholarships. 72% freshmen, 65% undergrads receive any aid. 32% undergrads borrow to pay for school. Average cumulative indebtedness $23,176. **Criteria awarding aid:** *Need-based:* Academics. *Non-need-based:* Academics.

THE UNIVERSITY OF TEXAS AT EL PASO

Mike Loya Academic Services Bldg., #102, El Paso, TX 79968-0510
Phone: 915-747-5890
E-mail: CEEB Code: 6829
Fax: 915-747-8893 **Website:** http://www.utep.edu/ **ACT Code:** 4223

This public school was founded in 1913. It has a 330 acre campus.

RATINGS

Admissions Selectivity Rating: 75   **Fire Safety Rating:** 75   **Green Rating:** 60*

STUDENTS AND FACULTY

Enrollment: 19,078. **Student Body:** 54% female, 46% male, 3% out-of-state, 5% international (65 countries represented). Asian 1%, African American 3%, Caucasian 8%, Hispanic 81%, Native American <1%, Pacific Islander <1%, Two or more races <1%, Race unknown 2%.
Retention and Graduation: 72% freshmen return for sophomore year.
Faculty: Student/faculty ratio 21:1. 2% of classes are taught by teaching assistants.

ACADEMICS

Degrees: Bachelor's; Doctoral degree—professional practice; Doctoral degree research/scholarship; Master's; Post-bachelor's certificate; Post-master's certificate. **Classes:** Most classes have 20–29 students. Most lab/discussion sessions have 10–19 students. **Most popular majors:** Criminal Justice/Safety Studies; Multi-/Interdisciplinary Studies, Other; Psychology, General. **Special Study Options:** Accelerated program; Cooperative education program; Distance learning; Double major; English as a Second Language (ESL); Exchange student program (domestic); Honors program; Independent study; Internships; Student-designed major; Study abroad; Teacher certification program. **Combined degree programs:** BA/MA. **Disability Services offered:**

Note-taking services; Reader services; Tape recorders. **Career services:** Alumni services; Career assessment; Internships.

FACILITIES

90% of campus accessible to physically disabled. **Special Academic Facilities/Equipment:** Cross-cultural ethnic study center, natural history and cultural museum, solar pond and solar house, electron microscope, atmospheric and acoustic research lab, seismic observatory.

CAMPUS LIFE

Environment: Metropolis. **Activities:** Choral groups; Concert band; Dance; Drama/theater; International Student Organization; Jazz band; Marching band; Music ensembles; Musical theater; Radio station; Student government; Student newspaper. 1 honor societies, 1 religious organizations, 6 fraternities, 4 sororities, on campus. **Athletics (Intercollegiate):** *Men:* basketball, cross-country, football, golf, track/field (outdoor), track/field (indoor). *Women:* basketball, cross-country, golf, riflery, soccer, softball, tennis, track/field (outdoor), track/field (indoor), volleyball.

ADMISSIONS

Freshman Academic Profile: Average high school GPA 3.2. 17% in top 10% of high school class, 40% in top 25% of high school class, 69% in top 50% of high school class. 94% from public high schools. **Test Scores:** SAT Math middle 50% range 420–530. SAT EBRW middle 50% range 390–500. ACT middle 50% range 17–22. **Basis for Candidate Selection:** *Important factors include:* rigor of secondary school record, class rank, academic GPA, standardized test scores. **Freshman Admission Requirements:** High school diploma is required and GED is accepted. *Academic units required:* 4 English, 4 math, 4 science, 4 science labs, 2 social studies, 4 history, 6 computer science, 1 visual/performing arts, 1.5 unit from above areas or other academic areas. **Freshman Admission Statistics:** 6,240 applied, 100% admitted, 70% enrolled. **Transfer Admission Requirements:** College transcript(s). Minimum college GPA of 2.0 required. Lowest grade transferable D. **General Admission Information:** Non-fall registration accepted. Admission may be deferred for a maximum of 1 semester.

COSTS AND FINANCIAL AID

Annual in-state tuition $5,565. Annual out-of-state tuition $16,095. Room and board $8,924. Required fees $1,649. Average book and supplies expense $1,160. **Student Employment:** Federal Work-Study Program available. Institutional employment available. **Financial Aid Statistics:** 88% needy freshmen, 88% needy undergrads receive need-based scholarship or grant aid. 25% freshmen, 14% undergrads receive non-need-based scholarship or grant aid. 81% freshmen, 85% undergrads receive need-based self-help aid. 1% freshmen, 1% undergrads receive athletic scholarships. 77% freshmen, 65% undergrads receive any aid.

THE UNIVERSITY OF TEXAS MEDICAL BRANCH AT GALVESTON

301 University Boulevard, Galveston, TX 77555-1305
Phone: 409-772-1215 **Financial Aid Phone:** 409-772-1215
E-mail: enrollment.services@utmb.edu **CEEB Code:** 6887
Fax: 409-772-4466 **Website:** www.utmb.edu

This public school was founded in 1891. It has a 85 acre campus.

RATINGS

Admissions Selectivity Rating: 60*   **Fire Safety Rating:** 60*   **Green Rating:** 60*

STUDENTS AND FACULTY

Enrollment: 492. **Student Body:** 80% female, 20% male, 1% out-of-state, 2% international (34 countries represented). Asian 18%, African American 18%, Caucasian 42%, Hispanic 14%, Native American 1%, Race unknown 5%.

ACADEMICS

Degrees: Bachelor's; Doctoral degree—professional practice; Doctoral degree research/scholarship; Master's; Post-master's certificate. **Most popular majors:** Respiratory Care Therapy/Therapist; Clinical Laboratory Science/Medical Technology/Technologist; Nursing/Registered Nurse (Rn, Asn, Bsn, Msn). **Special Study Options:** Distance learning; Independent study; Internships. **Disability Services offered:** Note-taking services; Reader services; Tape recorders; Tutors. **Career services:** Alumni network; Alumni services; Internships.

FACILITIES

Housing: Apartments for married students; Apartments for single students; Coed dorms; Fraternity/sorority housing 100% of campus accessible to physically disabled. **Special Academic Facilities/Equipment:** Moody Medical Library. **Campus Network:** 90% of classrooms, 100% of libraries, have wireless network access.

CAMPUS LIFE

Environment: Town. **Activities:** Student government; Student newspaper; Yearbook. 94 registered organizations, 4 honor societies, 7 religious organizations, 5 fraternities on campus. **On-Campus Highlights:** Joe Jamail Student Center.

ADMISSIONS

Transfer Admission Requirements: College transcript(s). Minimum college GPA of 2.0 required. Lowest grade transferable C.

COSTS AND FINANCIAL AID

Required Forms and Deadlines: FAFSA. **Types of Aid:** *Need-based scholarships/grants:* College/university scholarship or grant aid from institutional funds; Federal Pell; Private scholarships; SEOG; State scholarships/grants. *Loans:* Direct PLUS loans; Direct Subsidized Stafford Loans; Direct Unsubsidized Stafford Loans. **Student Employment:** Federal Work-Study Program available. Institutional employment available. **Criteria awarding aid:** *Need-based:* Academics, Minority status. *Non-need-based:* Academics, Minority status, State/district residency.

THE UNIVERSITY OF TEXAS AT RIO GRANDE VALLEY

1201 West University Drive, Edinburg, TX 78539-2999
Phone: (956) 665-2999 **Financial Aid Phone:** 956-665-2501
E-mail: admissions@utrgv.edu **CEEB Code:** 6570
Fax: (956) 665-2687 **Website:** www.utrgv.edu **ACT Code:** 4142

This public school was founded in 1927. It has a 331 acre campus.

RATINGS

Admissions Selectivity Rating: 79   **Fire Safety Rating:** 79   **Green Rating:** 86

STUDENTS AND FACULTY

Enrollment: 24,596. **Student Body:** 57% female, 43% male, 1% out-of-state, 2% international (25 countries represented). Asian 1%, African American <1%, Caucasian 2%, Hispanic 91%, Native American <1%, Pacific Islander <1%, Two or more races <1%, Race unknown 3%.
Retention and Graduation: 71% freshmen return for sophomore year.

ACADEMICS

Degrees: Bachelor's; Doctoral degree research/scholarship; Master's; Post-bachelor's certificate. **Classes:** Most classes have 20–29 students. Most lab/discussion sessions have 20–29 students. **Most popular majors:** Multi-/Interdisciplinary Studies, Other; Biology/Biological Sciences, General; Business Administration and Management, General. **Special Study Options:** Accelerated program; Distance learning; Double major; Dual enrollment; English as a Second Language (ESL); Exchange student program (domestic); Honors program; Independent study; Internships; Study abroad; Teacher certification program. **Honors programs:** Pre-Medical Honors College with Baylor College of Medicine. **Combined degree programs:** BA/MA. **Disability Services offered:** Note-taking services; Reader services; Tape recorders; Tutors. **Career services:** Alumni services; Career assessment; Internships.

FACILITIES

Housing: Apartments for married students; Apartments for single students; Men's dorms; Special housing for disabled students; Women's dorms; 95% of campus accessible to physically disabled.

CAMPUS LIFE

Environment: Town. **Activities:** Campus Ministries; Choral groups; Concert band; Dance; Drama/theater; International Student Organization; Jazz band; Literary magazine; Music ensembles; Musical theater; Opera; Pep band; Radio station; Student government; Student newspaper; Student-run film society; Symphony orchestra; Television station; Yearbook. 218 registered organizations, 9 honor societies, 7 religious organizations, 9 fraternities, 6 sororities on campus. **Athletics (Intercollegiate):** *Men:* baseball, basketball, cross-country, golf, tennis, track/field (outdoor). *Women:* basketball, cross-

country, golf, tennis, track/field (outdoor), volleyball. **On-Campus Highlights:** Visitors Center. **Environmental Initiatives:** The direction of disposal of hazardous waste streams toward recycling or reuse.

ADMISSIONS

Freshman Academic Profile: 22% in top 10% of high school class, 51% in top 25% of high school class, 80% in top 50% of high school class. 99% from public high schools. **Test Scores:** SAT Math middle 50% range 470–550. SAT EBRW middle 50% range 480–570. ACT middle 50% range 17–22. **Basis for Candidate Selection:** *Very important factors include:* class rank, academic GPA, standardized test scores. *Important factors include:* rigor of secondary school record, application essay, level of applicant's interest. *Other factors include:* recommendation(s), extracurricular activities, talent/ability, character/personal qualities, volunteer work, work experience. **Freshman Admission Requirements:** High school diploma is required and GED is accepted *Academic units required:* 4 English, 3 math, 2 science, 3 social studies, 7.5 academic electives, 1 visual/performing arts, 1.5 unit from above areas or other academic areas. *Academic units recommended:* 4 English, 4 math, 4 science, 2 foreign language, 4 social studies, 5.5 academic electives, 1 visual/performing arts. **Freshman Admission Statistics:** 10,710 applied, 81% admitted, 53% enrolled. **Transfer Admission Requirements:** College transcript(s). Minimum college GPA of 2.0 required. Lowest grade transferable D. **General Admission Information:** Priority deadline 2/1. Regular application deadline 7/1. Non-fall registration accepted.

COSTS AND FINANCIAL AID

Annual in-state tuition $6,345. Annual out-of-state tuition $18,795. Room and board $8,124. Required fees $1,468. Average book and supplies expense $1,218. **Required Forms and Deadlines:** FAFSA. **Types of Aid:** *Need-based scholarships/grants:* College/university scholarship or grant aid from institutional funds; Federal Pell; Private scholarships; SEOG; State scholarships/grants. *Loans:* Direct PLUS loans; Direct Subsidized Stafford Loans; Direct Unsubsidized Stafford Loans. **Student Employment:** Federal Work-Study Program available. Institutional employment available. **Financial Aid Statistics:** 98% needy freshmen, 96% needy undergrads receive need-based scholarship or grant aid. 1% freshmen, 1% undergrads receive non-need-based scholarship or grant aid. 25% freshmen, 44% undergrads receive need-based self-help aid. 0% freshmen, 0% undergrads receive athletic scholarships. 58% undergrads borrow to pay for school. Average cumulative indebtedness $16,067. **Criteria awarding aid:** *Need-based:* Academics, Athletics *Non-need-based:* Academics, Alumni affiliation, Art, Athletics.

THE UNIVERSITY OF TEXAS AT SAN ANTONIO

One UTSA Circle, San Antonio, TX 78249-0617
Phone: (210) 458-8000 **Financial Aid Phone:** 210-458-8000
E-mail: prospects@utsa.edu **CEEB Code:** 6919
Fax: 210-458-7857 **Website:** http://www.utsa.edu/ **ACT Code:** 4239

This public school was founded in 1969. It has a 725 acre campus.

RATINGS

Admissions Selectivity Rating: 80   **Fire Safety Rating:** 84   **Green Rating:** 60*

STUDENTS AND FACULTY

Enrollment: 25,709. **Student Body:** 50% female, 50% male, 2% out-of-state, 2% international (74 countries represented). Asian 6%, African American 9%, Caucasian 23%, Hispanic 55%, Native American <1%, Pacific Islander <1%, Two or more races 3%, Race unknown 1%.
Retention and Graduation: 74% freshmen return for sophomore year. 13% freshmen graduate within 4 years. 35% freshmen graduate within 6 years.
Faculty: Student/faculty ratio 25:1. 885 full-time faculty, 86% hold PhDs, 35% are members of minority groups, 38% are women.

ACADEMICS

Degrees: Bachelor's; Certificate; Doctoral degree research/scholarship; Master's; Post-bachelor's certificate. **Classes:** Most classes have 20–29 students. Most lab/discussion sessions have 10–19 students. **Most popular majors:** Biology/Biological Sciences, General; Exercise Science and Kinesiology; Psychology, General. **Special Study Options:** Distance learning; Double major; Dual enrollment; English as a Second Language (ESL); Honors program; Independent study; Internships; Student-designed major; Study abroad; Teacher certification program. **Honors programs:** http://utsa.edu/honors/programs/index.html. **Disability Services offered:** Note-taking services; Reader services; Tape recorders; Tutors. **Career services:** Alumni network; Alumni services; Career assessment; Career/job search classes; Internships; Regional alumni.

FACILITIES
Housing: Apartments for single students; Coed dorms; Theme housing; 85% of campus accessible to physically disabled. **Special Academic Facilities/ Equipment:** The Institute of Texan Cultures.

CAMPUS LIFE
Environment: Metropolis. **Activities:** Campus Ministries; Choral groups; Concert band; Dance; International Student Organization; Jazz band; Literary magazine; Marching band; Model UN; Music ensembles; Musical theater; Opera; Pep band; Student government; Student newspaper; Television station. 364 registered organizations, 44 honor societies, 38 religious organizations on campus. **Athletics (Intercollegiate):** *Men:* baseball, basketball, cross-country, golf, tennis, track/field (outdoor), track/field (indoor). *Women:* basketball, cross-country, soccer, softball, tennis, track/field (outdoor), track/field (indoor), volleyball. **On-Campus Highlights:** Sombrilla.

ADMISSIONS
Freshman Academic Profile: 17% in top 10% of high school class, 58% in top 25% of high school class, 90% in top 50% of high school class. **Test Scores:** SAT Math middle 50% range 510–600. SAT EBRW middle 50% range 520–610. ACT middle 50% range 20–25. **Basis for Candidate Selection:** *Very important factors include:* rigor of secondary school record, class rank, academic GPA, standardized test scores. *Important factors include:* application essay, recommendation(s), extracurricular activities, talent/ability. *Other factors include:* first generation, volunteer work, work experience. **Freshman Admission Requirements:** High school diploma is required and GED is accepted. *Academic units required:* 4 English, 3 math, 3 science, 2 foreign language, 3 social studies, 3 history, 2 computer science, 1 visual/performing arts, 1 unit from above areas or other academic areas. **Freshman Admission Statistics:** 15,973 applied, 79% admitted, 40% enrolled. **Transfer Admission Requirements:** College transcript(s). Minimum college GPA of 2.0 required. Lowest grade transferable D. **General Admission Information:** Application fee $60. Priority deadline 3/1. Regular application deadline 6/1. Non-fall registration accepted.

COSTS AND FINANCIAL AID
Annual in-state tuition $6,635. Annual out-of-state tuition $20,634. Room and board $7,190. Required fees $2,745. Average book and supplies expense $1,500. **Required Forms and Deadlines:** FAFSA. **Notification of Awards:** Applicants will be notified of awards on a rolling basis beginning 3/1. **Types of Aid:** *Need-based scholarships/grants:* College/university scholarship or grant aid from institutional funds; Federal Pell; Private scholarships; SEOG; State scholarships/grants. *Loans:* Direct PLUS loans; Direct Subsidized Stafford Loans; Direct Unsubsidized Stafford Loans. **Student Employment:** Federal Work-Study Program available. Institutional employment available. **Financial Aid Statistics:** 77% needy freshmen, 82% needy undergrads receive need-based scholarship or grant aid. 1% freshmen, 1% undergrads receive non-need-based scholarship or grant aid. 64% freshmen, 69% undergrads receive need-based self-help aid. 1% freshmen, 1% undergrads receive athletic scholarships. 67% freshmen, 67% undergrads receive any aid. 63% undergrads borrow to pay for school. Average cumulative indebtedness $26,089. **Criteria awarding aid:** *Non-need-based:* Academics, Alumni affiliation; Art, Athletics, Job skills, Leadership, Music/drama, State/district residency.

THE UNIVERSITY OF TEXAS AT TYLER

3900 University Blvd., Tyler, TX 75799
Phone: 903-566-7203 **Financial Aid Phone:** 903-566-7180
E-mail: admrequest@uttyler.edu
Fax: 903-566-7068 **Website:** www.uttyler.edu

This public school was founded in 1971. It has a 204 acre campus.

RATINGS
Admissions Selectivity Rating: 86   **Fire Safety Rating:** 93   **Green Rating:** 60*

STUDENTS AND FACULTY
Enrollment: 6,059. **Student Body:** 57% female, 43% male, 1% out-of-state, 2% international (45 countries represented). Asian 3%, African American 9%,

Caucasian 58%, Hispanic 16%, Native American <1%, Pacific Islander <1%, Two or more races 8%, Race unknown 3%.
Retention and Graduation: 62% freshmen return for sophomore year. 14% grads go on to further study within 1 year.

ACADEMICS
Degrees: Bachelor's; Doctoral degree—professional practice; Doctoral degree research/scholarship; Master's; Post-master's certificate. **Classes:** Most classes have 20–29 students. **Most popular majors:** Multi-/Interdisciplinary Studies, Other; Business/Managerial Economics; Nursing/Registered Nurse (Rn, Asn, Bsn, Msn). **Special Study Options:** Cooperative education program; Distance learning; Double major; Dual enrollment; Honors program; Independent study; Internships; Student-designed major; Study abroad; Teacher certification program. **Disability Services offered:** Note-taking services; Reader services. **Career services:** Career assessment; Career/job search classes.

FACILITIES
Housing: Coed dorms.

CAMPUS LIFE
Environment: City. **Activities:** Choral groups; International Student Organization; Jazz band; Model UN; Music ensembles; Pep band; Student government; Student newspaper. 73 registered organizations, 6 honor societies, 4 fraternities, 4 sororities, on campus. **Athletics (Intercollegiate):** *Men:* baseball, basketball, cheerleading, cross-country, golf, soccer, tennis. *Women:* basketball, cheerleading, cross-country, golf, soccer, tennis, volleyball. **On-Campus Highlights:** Herrington Patriot Center.

ADMISSIONS
Freshman Academic Profile: Average high school GPA 3.4. 10% in top 10% of high school class, 35% in top 25% of high school class, 64% in top 50% of high school class. **Test Scores:** SAT Math middle 50% range 490–590. SAT EBRW middle 50% range 480–570. ACT middle 50% range 20–25. **Basis for Candidate Selection:** *Very important factors include:* rigor of secondary school record, class rank, academic GPA, standardized test scores, level of applicant's interest. *Important factors include:* extracurricular activities, talent/ ability, character/personal qualities, first generation, volunteer work. *Other factors include:* work experience. **Freshman Admission Requirements:** High school diploma is required and GED is accepted *Academic units required:* 4 English, 3 math, 3 science, 2 foreign language, 3 social studies. *Academic units recommended:* 4 math, 4 science, 3 science labs, 4 social studies, 4 history. **Freshman Admission Statistics:** 2,468 applied, 64% admitted, 49% enrolled. **Transfer Admission Requirements:** College transcript(s). Minimum college GPA of 2.0 required. Lowest grade transferable C. **General Admission Information:** Regular application deadline 8/24. Non-fall registration accepted. Admission may be deferred for a maximum of 1 year.

COSTS AND FINANCIAL AID
Required Forms and Deadlines: FAFSA; Institution's own financial aid form. **Types of Aid:** *Need-based scholarships/grants:* College/university scholarship or grant aid from institutional funds; Federal Pell; Private scholarships; SEOG; State scholarships/grants. **Criteria awarding aid:** *Non-need-based:* Academics, Art, Music/drama.

UNIVERSITY OF THE ARTS

320 South Broad Street, Philadelphia, PA 19102
Phone: 215-717-6049 **Financial Aid Phone:** 215-717-6170
E-mail: admissions@uarts.edu **CEEB Code:** 2664
Fax: 215-717-6045 **Website:** www.uarts.edu **ACT Code:** 3664

This private school was founded in 1876. It has a 18 acre campus.

RATINGS
Admissions Selectivity Rating: 79   **Fire Safety Rating:** 60*   **Green Rating:** 60*

STUDENTS AND FACULTY
Enrollment: 1,865. **Student Body:** 58% female, 42% male, 62% out-of-state, 5% international (19 countries represented). Asian 3%, African American 13%, Caucasian 62%, Hispanic 9%, Native American <1%, Pacific Islander 1%, Two or more races 4%, Race unknown 4%.
Retention and Graduation: 82% freshmen return for sophomore year.
Faculty: Student/faculty ratio 8:1. 113 full-time faculty, 0% hold PhDs, 0% are members of minority groups, 0% are women. 0% of classes are taught by teaching assistants.

ACADEMICS

Degrees: Bachelor's; Diploma; Master's; Post-bachelor's certificate. **Classes:** Most classes have 10–19 students. **Most popular majors:** Illustration; Graphic Design; Dance, General. **Special Study Options:** Cross-registration; Double major; Dual enrollment; English as a Second Language (ESL); Exchange student program (domestic); Honors program; Independent study; Internships; Liberal arts/career combination; Study abroad; Teacher certification program. **Honors programs:** The University Honors Program at the University of the Arts is an integrative model that asks scholars to seek out and understand the connections between all of their coursework, connecting what they discover in their studio, labor, rehearsal room with cultural and historical underpinnings they investigate in their liberal arts courses. **Disability Services offered:** Note-taking services; Reader services; Tape recorders; Tutors. **Career services:** Alumni network; Alumni services; Career assessment; Career/job search classes; Internships.

FACILITIES

Housing: Apartments for single students; Coed dorms; 85% of campus accessible to physically disabled. **Special Academic Facilities/Equipment:** Rosenwald-Wolf Gallery, Merriam Theater, Arts Bank, Borowsky Center for Publication arts, Gershman Y.

CAMPUS LIFE

Environment: Metropolis. **Activities:** Choral groups; Dance; Drama/theater; International Student Organization; Jazz band; Literary magazine; Music ensembles; Musical theater; Student government; Student-run film society. 19 registered organizations, 1 religious organization on campus. **On-Campus Highlights:** Merriam Theater.

ADMISSIONS

Test Scores: SAT Math middle 50% range 440–550. SAT EBRW middle 50% range 450–580. ACT middle 50% range 18–25. **Basis for Candidate Selection:** *Very important factors include:* rigor of secondary school record, interview, talent/ability. *Important factors include:* class rank, academic GPA, application essay, standardized test scores, extracurricular activities. *Other factors include:* recommendation(s), alumni/ae relation, racial/ethnic status, volunteer work, work experience. **Freshman Admission Requirements:** High school diploma is required and GED is accepted *Academic units required:* 4 English. *Academic units recommended:* 3 math, 2 science, 2 foreign language, 2 social studies, 2 history. **Freshman Admission Statistics:** 1,479 applied, 75% admitted, 41% enrolled. **Transfer Admission Requirements:** High school transcript, college transcript(s), essay or personal statement, standardized test scores. Minimum college GPA of 2.0 required. Lowest grade transferable C. **General Admission Information:** Application fee $60. Priority deadline 3/15. Non-fall registration accepted. Admission may be deferred for a maximum of 12 months.

COSTS AND FINANCIAL AID

Annual tuition $39,908. Room and board $14,552. **Required Forms and Deadlines:** FAFSA. **Notification of Awards:** Applicants will be notified of awards on a rolling basis beginning 3/15. **Types of Aid:** *Need-based scholarships/grants:* College/university scholarship or grant aid from institutional funds; Federal Pell; Private scholarships; SEOG; State scholarships/grants. *Loans:* Direct PLUS loans; Direct Subsidized Stafford Loans; Direct Unsubsidized Stafford Loans. **Student Employment:** Federal Work-Study Program available. Institutional employment available. **Financial Aid Statistics:** 95% needy freshmen, 94% needy undergrads receive need-based scholarship or grant aid. 10% freshmen, 5% undergrads receive non-need-based scholarship or grant aid. 99% freshmen, 98% undergrads receive need-based self-help aid. 0% freshmen, 0% undergrads receive athletic scholarships. % freshmen, 80% undergrads receive any aid. **Criteria awarding aid:** *Non-need-based:* Academics, Art, Music/drama.

UNIVERSITY OF THE INCARNATE WORD

4301 Broadway, San Antonio, TX 78209-6397
Phone: 210-829-6005 **Financial Aid Phone:** 210-829-6008
E-mail: admis@uiwtx.edu **CEEB Code:** 6303
Fax: 210-829-3921 **Website:** www.uiw.edu **ACT Code:** 4106

This private school, affiliated with the Roman Catholic Church, was founded in 1881. It has a 154 acre campus.

RATINGS

Admissions Selectivity Rating: 73   **Fire Safety Rating:** 93   **Green Rating:** 64

STUDENTS AND FACULTY

Enrollment: 5,055. **Student Body:** 61% female, 39% male, 5% out-of-state, 4% international (34 countries represented). Asian 2%, African American 7%, Caucasian 18%, Hispanic 59%, Native American <1%, Pacific Islander <1%, Two or more races 2%, Race unknown 6%.
Retention and Graduation: 73% freshmen return for sophomore year. 32% freshmen graduate within 4 years. 52% freshmen graduate within 6 years. **Faculty:** Student/faculty ratio 14:1. 340 full-time faculty, 37% are members of minority groups, 55% are women.

ACADEMICS

Degrees: Associate; Bachelor's; Certificate; Doctoral degree—professional practice; Doctoral degree research/scholarship; Master's. **Classes:** Most classes have 10–19 students. Most lab/discussion sessions have 10–19 students. **Most popular majors:** Business Administration and Management, General; Health Professions And Related Programs; Psychology, General. **Special Study Options:** Accelerated program; Cross-registration; Distance learning; Double major; English as a Second Language (ESL); Exchange student program (domestic); Honors program; Independent study; Internships; Study abroad; Teacher certification program. **Honors programs:** The UIW Honors Program. Participation in the unique opportunities of the Honors Program exposes the student to new ideas and academic challenges, develops your critical thinking, and enhances their professional development. **Combined degree programs:** BA/MA. **Disability Services offered:** Note-taking services; Reader services; Tape recorders; Tutors. **Career services:** Alumni services; Career assessment; Career/job search classes; Internships.

FACILITIES

Housing: Coed dorms; Men's dorms; Special housing for disabled students; Special housing for international students; Women's dorms.

CAMPUS LIFE

Environment: Metropolis. **Activities:** Campus Ministries; Choral groups; Concert band; Dance; Drama/theater; International Student Organization; Jazz band; Literary magazine; Marching band; Music ensembles; Pep band; Radio station; Student government; Student newspaper; Symphony orchestra; Television station. 104 registered organizations, 7 honor societies, 2 religious organizations, 4 fraternities, 3 sororities on campus. **Athletics (Intercollegiate):** *Men:* baseball, basketball, cross-country, football, golf, soccer, swimming, tennis, track/field (outdoor). *Women:* basketball, cross-country, golf, soccer, softball, swimming, synchronized swimming, tennis, track/field (outdoor), volleyball. **On-Campus Highlights:** Student Engagement Center.

ADMISSIONS

Freshman Academic Profile: Average high school GPA 3.6. 18% in top 10% of high school class, 27% in top 25% of high school class, 29% in top 50% of high school class. **Test Scores:** SAT Math middle 50% range 470–570. SAT EBRW middle 50% range 480–590. ACT middle 50% range 18–23. **Basis for Candidate Selection:** *Very important factors include:* rigor of secondary school record, academic GPA, standardized test scores. *Important factors include:* class rank. *Other factors include:* application essay, recommendation(s), interview, extracurricular activities, talent/ability, character/personal qualities, first generation, alumni/ae relation, volunteer work, work experience, level of applicant's interest. **Freshman Admission Requirements:** High school diploma is required and GED is accepted. *Academic units required:* 4 English, 3 math, 3 science, 2 foreign language, 3 social studies, 1 visual/performing arts. *Academic units recommended:* 4 English, 4 math, 3 science, 2 foreign language, 4 social studies, 1 visual/performing arts. **Freshman Admission Statistics:** 6,291 applied, 94% admitted, 17% enrolled. **Transfer Admission Requirements:** College transcript(s). Minimum college GPA of 2.50 required. Lowest grade transferable C. **General Admission Information:** Application fee $20. Priority deadline 2/1. Non-fall registration accepted. Admission may be deferred for a maximum of 1 term.

COSTS AND FINANCIAL AID

Annual tuition $29,900. Room and board $12,824. Required fees $2,676. Average book and supplies expense $1,400. **Required Forms and Deadlines:** FAFSA. **Notification of Awards:** Applicants will be notified of awards on a rolling basis beginning 2/15. **Types of Aid:** *Need-based scholarships/ grants:* College/university scholarship or grant aid from institutional funds; Federal Nursing Scholarships; Federal Pell; Private scholarships; SEOG; State scholarships/grants. *Loans:* Direct PLUS loans; Direct Subsidized Stafford Loans; Direct Unsubsidized Stafford Loans. **Student Employment:** Federal Work-Study Program available. Institutional employment available. **Financial Aid Statistics:** 99% needy freshmen, 96% needy undergrads receive need-based scholarship or grant aid. 7% freshmen, 5% undergrads receive non-need-based scholarship or grant aid. 72% freshmen, 74% undergrads receive need-based self-help aid. 4% freshmen, 4% undergrads receive athletic scholarships. 99% freshmen receive any aid. 70% undergrads borrow to pay for school. Average cumulative indebtedness $36,147. **Criteria awarding aid:** *Non-need-based:* Academics, Alumni affiliation, Art, Athletics, Leadership, Music/drama, Religious affiliation, State/district residency.

UNIVERSITY OF THE OZARKS

415 N College Avenue, Clarksville, AR 72830
Phone: 479-979-1227 **Financial Aid Phone:** 479-979-1221
E-mail: admiss@ozarks.edu **CEEB Code:** 6111
Fax: 479-979-1417 **Website:** www.ozarks.edu **ACT Code:** 120

This private school, affiliated with the Presbyterian Church, was founded in 1834. It has a 50 acre campus.

RATINGS

Admissions Selectivity Rating: 83   **Fire Safety Rating:** 93   **Green Rating:** 60*

STUDENTS AND FACULTY

Enrollment: 615. **Student Body:** 55% female, 45% male, 29% out-of-state, 14% international (13 countries represented). Asian 1%, African American 4%, Caucasian 71%, Hispanic 6%, Native American 2%, Pacific Islander 0%, Two or more races 1%, Race unknown 1%.
Retention and Graduation: 64% freshmen return for sophomore year.
Faculty: Student/faculty ratio 11:1. 49 full-time faculty, 69% hold PhDs, 8% are members of minority groups, 37% are women. 0% of classes are taught by teaching assistants.

ACADEMICS

Degrees: Bachelor's. **Most popular majors:** Physical Education Teaching and Coaching; Biology/Biological Sciences, General; Business Administration and Management, General. **Special Study Options:** Cooperative education program; Double major; Dual enrollment; Independent study; Internships; Liberal arts/career combination; Study abroad; Teacher certification program. **Disability Services offered:** Note-taking services; Reader services; Tape recorders; Tutors. **Career services:** Alumni network; Alumni services; Career assessment; Career/job search classes; Internships; Regional alumni.

FACILITIES

Housing: Apartments for married students; Apartments for single students; Coed dorms; Men's dorms; Women's dorms 100% of campus accessible to physically disabled. **Special Academic Facilities/Equipment:** Walton Fine Arts Center; Stephens Gallery; Smith-Broyles Science Center; Walker Hall Teacher Education and Communications Center; Rogers Conference Center. **Campus Network:** 100% of classrooms, 80% of dorms, 90% of student union, 100% of libraries, 100% of dining areas, 60% of common outdoor areas have wireless network access.

CAMPUS LIFE

Environment: Village. **Activities:** Campus Ministries; Choral groups; Drama/ theater; International Student Organization; Literary magazine; Music ensembles; Radio station; Student government; Student-run film society; Television station; Yearbook. 40 registered organizations, 6 honor societies, 7 religious organizations on campus. **Athletics (Intercollegiate):** *Men:* baseball, basketball, cheerleading, cross-country, soccer, tennis. *Women:* basketball, cheerleading, cross-country, soccer, softball, tennis. **On-Campus Highlights:** Seay Student Center.

ADMISSIONS

Freshman Academic Profile: Average high school GPA 3.3. 18% in top 10% of high school class, 44% in top 25% of high school class, 76% in top 50% of high school class. 92% from public high schools. **Test Scores:** SAT Math middle 50% range 443–560. SAT EBRW middle 50% range 450–570. ACT middle 50% range 19–25. **Basis for Candidate Selection:** *Important factors include:* standardized test scores. *Other factors include:* rigor of secondary school record, academic GPA, application essay, recommendation(s), interview, extracurricular activities, talent/ability, character/personal qualities, alumni/ ae relation, volunteer work, work experience, level of applicant's interest.
Freshman Admission Requirements: High school diploma is required and GED is accepted *Academic units recommended:* 4 English, 4 math, 3 science, 2 science labs, 2 foreign language, 1 social studies, 2 history. **Freshman Admission Statistics:** 1,372 applied, 59% admitted, 25% enrolled. **Transfer Admission Requirements:** College transcript(s). Minimum college GPA of 2.0 required. Lowest grade transferable C. **General Admission Information:** Application fee $30. Priority deadline 4/1. Non-fall registration accepted.

COSTS AND FINANCIAL AID

Annual tuition $21,450. Room and board $6,500. Required fees $600. Average book and supplies expense $800. **Required Forms and Deadlines:** FAFSA. **Notification of Awards:** Applicants will be notified of awards on a rolling basis beginning 3/1. **Types of Aid:** *Need-based scholarships/grants:* College/university scholarship or grant aid from institutional funds; Federal Nursing Scholarships; Federal Pell; Private scholarships; SEOG; State scholarships/grants; United Negro College Fund. **Student Employment:** Federal Work-Study Program available. Institutional employment available. **Financial Aid Statistics:** 97% needy freshmen, 97% needy undergrads receive need-based scholarship or grant aid. 0% freshmen, 0% undergrads receive non-need-based scholarship or grant aid. 82% freshmen, 85% undergrads receive need-based self-help aid. 0% freshmen, 0% undergrads receive athletic scholarships. 100% freshmen, 98% undergrads receive any aid. **Criteria awarding aid:** *Need-based:* Academics, Alumni affiliation, Art, Leadership, Minority status, Music/drama, Religious affiliation. *Non-need-based:* Academics, Alumni affiliation, Art, Leadership, Minority status, Music/drama, Religious affiliation, State/district residency.

UNIVERSITY OF THE PACIFIC

3601 Pacific Avenue, Stockton, CA 95211
Phone: 209-946-2211 **Financial Aid Phone:** 209-946-2421
E-mail: admissions@pacific.edu **CEEB Code:** 4065
Fax: 209-946-4213 **Website:** www.pacific.edu **ACT Code:** 240

This private school was founded in 1851. It has a 175 acre campus.

RATINGS

Admissions Selectivity Rating: 82   **Fire Safety Rating:** 93   **Green Rating:** 60*

STUDENTS AND FACULTY

Enrollment: 3,474. **Student Body:** 53% female, 47% male, 7% out-of-state, 6% international (66 countries represented). Asian 37%, African American 3%, Caucasian 25%, Hispanic 19%, Native American <1%, Pacific Islander <1%, Two or more races 5%, Race unknown 4%.
Retention and Graduation: 82% freshmen return for sophomore year.
Faculty: Student/faculty ratio 12:1. 443 full-time faculty, 91% hold PhDs, 22% are members of minority groups, 43% are women.

ACADEMICS

Degrees: Bachelor's; Doctoral degree—professional practice; Doctoral degree research/scholarship; Master's. **Classes:** Most classes have 10–19 students. Most lab/discussion sessions have 10–19 students. **Most popular majors:** Business/Commerce, General; Engineering, General; Biology/Biological Sciences, General. **Special Study Options:** Accelerated program; Cooperative education program; Distance learning; Double major; Dual enrollment; English as a Second Language (ESL); Exchange student program (domestic); Honors program; Independent study; Internships; Liberal arts/career combination; Student-designed major; Study abroad; Teacher certification program. **Honors programs:** Freshman Honors Program, Powell Scholars, Pacific Legal Scholars, Humanities Scholars. **Combined degree programs:** BA/DDS. **Disability Services offered:** Note-taking services; Reader services; Tape recorders; Tutors.

FACILITIES

Housing: Apartments for married students; Apartments for single students; Coed dorms; Cooperative housing; Fraternity/sorority housing; Special housing for international students; Theme housing; 90% of campus accessible to physically disabled. **Special Academic Facilities/Equipment:** John Muir Collection, Dave and Iola Brubeck Collection, Brubeck Institute for Jazz Studies, Reynolds Art Gallery

CAMPUS LIFE

Environment: City. **Activities:** Campus Ministries; Choral groups; Concert band; Dance; Drama/theater; International Student Organization; Jazz band; Literary magazine; Model UN; Music ensembles; Musical theater; Opera; Pep band; Radio station; Student government; Student newspaper; Student-run film society; Yearbook. 100 registered organizations, 14 honor societies, 10 religious organizations, 8 fraternities, 7 sororities on campus. **Athletics (Intercollegiate):** *Men:* baseball, basketball, golf, swimming, tennis, volleyball, water polo. *Women:* basketball, cross-country, field hockey, soccer, softball, swimming, tennis, volleyball, water polo. **On-Campus Highlights:** Brubeck Istitute for Jazz Studies. **Environmental Initiatives:** Natural Resource Institute.

ADMISSIONS

Freshman Academic Profile: Average high school GPA 3.5. 37% in top 10% of high school class, 40% in top 25% of high school class, 92% in top 50% of high school class. 82% from public high schools. **Test Scores:** SAT Math middle 50% range 530–670. SAT EBRW middle 50% range 500–630. ACT middle 50% range 23–30. **Basis for Candidate Selection:** *Very important factors include:* rigor of secondary school record. *Important factors include:* academic GPA, standardized test scores, extracurricular activities, first generation. *Other factors include:* class rank, application essay, recommendation(s), talent/ability, character/personal qualities, alumni/ae relation, geographical residence, racial/ethnic status, volunteer work, work experience. **Freshman Admission Requirements:** High school diploma is required and GED is accepted. *Academic units recommended:* 4 English, 4 math, 3 science labs, 2 foreign language, 2 social studies, 1 history, 1 academic electives, 1 visual/performing arts. **Freshman Admission Statistics:** 8,870 applied, 66% admitted, 12% enrolled. **Transfer Admission Requirements:** College transcript(s), statement of good standing from prior institution(s). Minimum college GPA of 3.0 required. Lowest grade transferable C. **General Admission Information:** Application fee $35. Priority deadline 11/15. Regular application deadline 8/15. Non-fall registration accepted. Admission may be deferred for a maximum of 1 year.

COSTS AND FINANCIAL AID

Annual tuition $47,480. Room and board $13,650. Required fees $560. Average book and supplies expense $1,917. **Required Forms and Deadlines:** FAFSA. **Notification of Awards:** Applicants will be notified of awards on a rolling basis beginning 3/1. **Types of Aid:** *Need-based scholarships/grants:* College/university scholarship or grant aid from institutional funds; Federal Pell; Private scholarships; SEOG; State scholarships/grants. *Loans:* Direct PLUS loans; Direct Subsidized Stafford Loans; Direct Unsubsidized Stafford Loans. **Financial Aid Statistics:** 99% needy freshmen, 97% needy undergrads receive need-based scholarship or grant aid. 0% freshmen, 0% undergrads receive non-need-based scholarship or grant aid. 91% freshmen, 94% undergrads receive need-based self-help aid. 3% freshmen, 4% undergrads receive athletic scholarships. 91% freshmen, 83% undergrads receive any aid. 67% undergrads borrow to pay for school. Average cumulative indebtedness $28,759. **Criteria awarding aid:** *Need-based:* Academics. *Non-need-based:* Academics, Athletics, Leadership, Music/drama, Religious affiliation.

UNIVERSITY OF THE SCIENCES IN PHILADELPHIA

600 South 43rd Street, Philadelphia, PA 19104-4495
Phone: 215-596-8810 **Financial Aid Phone:** (215)596-8894
E-mail: admit@usciences.edu **CEEB Code:** 2663
Fax: 215-596-8821 **Website: ACT Code:** 3671

This private school was founded in 1821. It has a 35 acre campus.

RATINGS

Admissions Selectivity Rating: 87 **Fire Safety Rating:** 80 **Green Rating:** 60*

STUDENTS AND FACULTY

Enrollment: 2,427. **Student Body:** 61% female, 39% male, 59% out-of-state, 2% international. Asian 36%, African American 5%, Caucasian 46%, Hispanic 2%, Native American <1%, Pacific Islander <1%, Two or more races 2%, Race unknown 7%.

Retention and Graduation: 88% freshmen return for sophomore year. **Faculty:** Student/faculty ratio 10:1. 191 full-time faculty, 82% hold PhDs, 20% are members of minority groups, 52% are women.

ACADEMICS

Degrees: Bachelor's; Certificate; Doctoral degree—professional practice; Doctoral degree research/scholarship; Master's. **Classes:** Most classes have 20–29 students. Most lab/discussion sessions have 10–19 students. **Most popular majors:** Pharmacy; Physical Therapy/Therapist; Biology/Biological Sciences, General. **Special Study Options:** Cross-registration; Double major; Honors program; Independent study; Internships; Study abroad. **Honors programs:** The Honors Program at University of the Sciences offers exceptional students the opportunity for specialized, intensive learning experiences both inside and outside the classroom. As an honors student, you will take part in special honors classes and recitations. The workload for these classes is not harder than others at University of the Sciences, but different. For example you may do smaller, more advanced experiments in a lab course. You may tour historic sites for a history class, or meet with a visiting author in your writing class. You will work in smaller classes and have more independent and group projects. **Disability Services offered:** Note-taking services; Reader services; Tape recorders; Tutors. **Career services:** Alumni services; Career assessment; Career/job search classes; Internships.

FACILITIES

Housing: Apartments for single students; Coed dorms; Fraternity/sorority housing; Wellness housing. **Special Academic Facilities/Equipment:** The USciences campus is the perfect setting for the University's close-knit community of scholars of all ages. Nestled in the heart of University City, just west of Center City Philadelphia, the campus is bordered by the neighborhood's stately, tree-lined streets and sits adjacent to sprawling, picturesque Clark Park. The University's 23 buildings, sitting on 36 acres, are comprised of both historic structures and modern facilities, including more than 100 laboratories open to students, the leading-edge McNeil Science and Technology Center, three residence halls, and the Athletic/Recreation Center. The campus is also home to the Integrated Professional Education Complex (IPEX), a 57,000-square-foot building that provides an interprofessional education model for students from several disciplines, including pharmacy, physical therapy, occupational therapy, exercise science, psychology, and healthcare business and policy, to obtain traditional and hands-on experience. To better meet the needs of its students, the University has constructed a new, mixed-use residence hall at 46th Street and Woodland Avenue. The 426-bed Living & Learning Commons is a live-learn community that incorporates numerous sustainable features to achieve Green Globe certification.

CAMPUS LIFE

Environment: Metropolis. **Activities:** Choral groups; Concert band; Dance; Drama/theater; Literary magazine; Musical theater; Student government; Student newspaper; Yearbook. 75 registered organizations, 7 honor societies, 5 religious organizations, 7 fraternities, 5 sororities on campus. **Athletics (Intercollegiate):** *Men:* baseball, basketball, cross-country, golf, riflery, tennis. *Women:* basketball, cross-country, golf, riflery, softball, tennis, volleyball. **On-Campus Highlights:** McNeil Science and Technology Center. **Environmental Initiatives:** All "On the Go" containers are fully recyclable.

ADMISSIONS

Freshman Academic Profile: Average high school GPA 3.6. 45% in top 10% of high school class, 80% in top 25% of high school class, 98% in top 50% of high school class. **Test Scores:** SAT Math middle 50% range 550–650. SAT EBRW middle 50% range 520–590. ACT middle 50% range 22–27. **Basis for Candidate Selection:** *Very important factors include:* rigor of secondary school record, class rank, academic GPA, standardized test scores. *Other factors include:* application essay, recommendation(s), interview, extracurricular activities, character/personal qualities, alumni/ae relation, volunteer work, work experience, level of applicant's interest. **Freshman Admission Requirements:** High school diploma is required and GED is accepted *Academic units required:* 4 English, 3 math, 3 science, 2 science labs, 1 social studies, 1 history, 4 academic electives. *Academic units recommended:* 4 English, 4 math, 3 science, 3 science labs, 1 social studies, 1 history, 4 academic electives. **Freshman Admission Statistics:** 4,099 applied, 61% admitted, 18% enrolled. **Transfer Admission Requirements:** College transcript(s), standardized test scores. Minimum college GPA of 3.0 required. Lowest grade transferable C. **General Admission Information:** Application fee $45. Admission may be deferred for a maximum of 12 months.

COSTS AND FINANCIAL AID

Annual tuition $34,336. Room and board $14,108. Required fees $1,760. Average book and supplies expense $1,050. **Required Forms and Deadlines:**

FAFSA. **Notification of Awards:** Applicants will be notified of awards on a rolling basis beginning 2/15. **Types of Aid:** *Need-based scholarships/grants:* College/university scholarship or grant aid from institutional funds; Federal Pell; Private scholarships; SEOG; State scholarships/grants. *Loans:* Direct PLUS loans; Direct Subsidized Stafford Loans; Direct Unsubsidized Stafford Loans. **Student Employment:** Federal Work-Study Program available. Institutional employment available. **Financial Aid Statistics:** 81% needy freshmen, 82% needy undergrads receive need-based scholarship or grant aid. 97% freshmen, 89% undergrads receive non-need-based scholarship or grant aid. 77% freshmen, 84% undergrads receive need-based self-help aid. 1% freshmen, 7% undergrads receive athletic scholarships. **Criteria awarding aid:** *Need-based:* Academics, Athletics *Non-need-based:* Academics, Athletics.

UNIVERSITY OF TORONTO

172 St. George Street, Toronto, ON M5R 0A3
Phone: 416-978-2190
E-mail: admissions.help@utoronto.ca **CEEB Code:** 982
Fax: 416-978-7022 **Website:** www.utoronto.ca

This public school was founded in 1827. It has a 1767 acre campus.

RATINGS

Admissions Selectivity Rating: 60*   **Fire Safety Rating:** 79   **Green Rating:** 60*

STUDENTS AND FACULTY

Enrollment: 65,151. **Student Body:** 56% female, 44% male, 22% out-of-state, international (166 countries represented).
Retention and Graduation: 91% freshmen return for sophomore year.
Faculty: Student/faculty ratio 6:1. 14,332 full-time faculty.

ACADEMICS

Degrees: Bachelor's; Certificate; Diploma; Doctoral degree—other; Doctoral degree—professional practice; Doctoral degree research/scholarship; Master's; Post-bachelor's certificate; Post-master's certificate. **Special Study Options:** Cooperative education program; Double major; English as a Second Language (ESL); Exchange student program (domestic); Honors program; Independent study; Internships; Study abroad; Teacher certification program. **Disability Services offered:** Note-taking services; Reader services; Tape recorders. **Career services:** Alumni services; Career assessment; Career/job search classes; Internships.

FACILITIES

Housing: Apartments for married students; Coed dorms; Cooperative housing; Women's dorms.

CAMPUS LIFE

Environment: Metropolis. **Activities:** Choral groups; Concert band; Dance; Drama/theater; International Student Organization; Jazz band; Literary magazine; Model UN; Music ensembles; Opera; Radio station; Student government; Student newspaper; Student-run film society; Symphony orchestra. 1000 registered organizations, 50 religious organizations, on campus. **Athletics (Intercollegiate):** *Men:* badminton, baseball, basketball, crew/rowing, cross-country, curling, fencing, football, golf, ice hockey, lacrosse, mountain biking, rugby, skiing (Nordic/cross-country), soccer, squash, swimming, tennis, track/field (outdoor), track/field (indoor), volleyball, water polo, wrestling. *Women:* badminton, basketball, crew/rowing, cross-country, curling, fencing, field hockey, ice hockey, lacrosse, mountain biking, rugby, skiing (Nordic/cross-country), soccer, squash, swimming, tennis, track/field (outdoor), track/field (indoor), volleyball, water polo, wrestling. **On-Campus Highlights:** Hart House.

ADMISSIONS

Basis for Candidate Selection: *Very important factors include:* academic GPA, standardized test scores. *Other factors include:* rigor of secondary school record. **Freshman Admission Requirements:** High school diploma is required and GED is accepted. **Freshman Admission Statistics:** 80,262 applied, admitted, enrolled. **Transfer Admission Requirements:** High school transcript, college transcript(s), standardized test scores. **General Admission Information:** Application fee $225. Priority deadline 11/1. Regular application deadline 1/16. Admission may be deferred for a maximum of 12 months.

COSTS AND FINANCIAL AID

Annual in-state tuition $6,900. Annual out-of-state tuition $6,900. Room and board $13,000. Average book and supplies expense $1,000.

THE UNIVERSITY OF TULSA

Best Colleges

800 South Tucker Drive, Tulsa, OK 74104
Phone: 918-631-2307 **Financial Aid Phone:** 918-631-2526
E-mail: admission@utulsa.edu **CEEB Code:** 6883
Fax: 918-631-5003 **Website:** utulsa.edu **ACT Code:** 3444

This private school, affiliated with the Presbyterian Church, was founded in 1894. It has a 209 acre campus.

RATINGS

Admissions Selectivity Rating: 93   **Fire Safety Rating:** 97   **Green Rating:** 83

STUDENTS AND FACULTY

Enrollment: 3,316. **Student Body:** 44% female, 56% male, 41% out-of-state, 19% international (53 countries represented). Asian 5%, African American 5%, Caucasian 57%, Hispanic 6%, Native American 3%, Pacific Islander <1%, Two or more races 3%, Race unknown 2%.
Retention and Graduation: 88% freshmen return for sophomore year. 58% freshmen graduate within 4 years. 73% freshmen graduate within 6 years. 34% grads go on to further study within 1 year. 15% grads pursue arts and sciences degrees. 2% grads pursue law degrees. 9% grads pursue business degrees. 5% grads pursue medical degrees. **Faculty:** Student/faculty ratio 11:1. 350 full-time faculty, 95% hold PhDs, 18% are members of minority groups, 34% are women. 4% of classes are taught by teaching assistants.

ACADEMICS

Degrees: Bachelor's; Doctoral degree—professional practice; Doctoral degree research/scholarship; Master's; Post-bachelor's certificate. **Classes:** Most classes have 10–19 students. Most lab/discussion sessions have 10–19 students. **Most popular majors:** Computer Science; Psychology, General; Business Statistics. **Special Study Options:** Accelerated program; Distance learning; Double major; English as a Second Language (ESL); Honors program; Independent study; Internships; Liberal arts/career combination; Student-designed major; Study abroad; Teacher certification program. **Honors programs:** The Honors Program is a four-year course of study consisting of 18 hours of academic credit. In small classes and individual tutorials, students pursue a critical examination of the moral and political commitments, scientific achievments, and artistic sensibilities that have shaped the modern world. The program culminates in the senior year with students designing and executing individual research projects. The Tulsa Undergraduate Research Challenge (TURC) is an innovative program that enables undergraduates to take challenging courses and conduct advanced research with the guidance of top professors. Its aim is to create leaders in scholarship, research, and public life. The centerpiece of the program is research; the goal of such research may be to deliver papers at academic conferences, to produce publishable articles, or to initiate meaningful community projects. **Combined degree programs:** BA/JD; BA/MA; BA/MEng. **Disability Services offered:** Note-taking services; Reader services; Tape recorders; Tutors. **Career services:** Alumni network; Alumni services; Career assessment; Career/job search classes; Internships; Regional alumni.

FACILITIES

Housing: Apartments for married students; Apartments for single students; Coed dorms; Fraternity/sorority housing; Men's dorms; Special housing for disabled students; Theme housing; Women's dorms; 97% of campus accessible to physically disabled. **Special Academic Facilities/Equipment:** Alexandre Hogue Art Gallery; Biotechnology Institute; Center for Communicative Disorders; Gilcrease Art Museum; Charge-Coupled Camera Microscope; Donald W. Reynolds Center (site of a state-of-the-art athletic training program); Education Technology Lab; Electron Microscopes; Kendall Theatre; McFarlin Library Special Collections (focus on American, British, and Irish Literature of the late 19th and early 20th centuries, and on Native American History and Law); Multimedia "board-room" style classrooms (3); ONEOK Multimedia Auditorium; Sadie Adwan Communication Lab; Sidney Born Technical Library (contains an outstanding collection concerning energy, most notably petroleum); Sun Computer Work Stations; World's largest research flow-loop in Petroleum Engr. North Campus Research Lab (dedicated to petroleum engineering research with specialized areas for undergraduate and graduate research studies); Boulder Building for Oxley College of Health Sciences (newly funded area for research in the area of health and behavioral sciences located in the downtown Tulsa OK area around other businesses, the labs in this building are fully fitted with state of the art lab and medical testing equipment).

CAMPUS LIFE

Environment: Metropolis. **Activities:** Campus Ministries; Choral groups; Concert band; Dance; Drama/theater; International Student Organization; Jazz band; Literary magazine; Marching band; Music ensembles; Musical theater; Opera; Pep band; Radio station; Student government; Student newspaper; Student-run film society; Symphony orchestra; Television station. 200 registered organizations, 35 honor societies, 19 religious organizations, 7 fraternities, 8 sororities on campus. **Athletics (Intercollegiate):** *Men:* basketball, cheerleading, cross-country, football, golf, soccer, tennis, track/field (outdoor), track/field (indoor). *Women:* basketball, cheerleading, crew/rowing, cross-country, golf, soccer, softball, tennis, track/field (outdoor), track/field (indoor), volleyball. **On-Campus Highlights:** Collins Fitness Center. **Environmental Initiatives:** The School of Engineering and Natural Sciences partnered with the local utility company to develop and install a 300kW Solar Panel array on top of our Tennis facility. The project was completed in September of 2016. It produces enough energy to cover the usage of the tennis sporting complex. Overall, students were able to analyze real world data and work with the installing contractor. This project was our first step in establishing a greener footprint. Over the past 5 years we have decreased energy consumption by more than 10% while adding more than 450,000 new square feet of academic and living areas. We continue to invest and install new green technologies. In Aug 2016, we installed our first dual-port hybrid vehicle charging station on campus and made it free for the community to use.

ADMISSIONS

Freshman Academic Profile: Average high school GPA 3.9. 70% in top 10% of high school class, 85% in top 25% of high school class, 97% in top 50% of high school class. 72% from public high schools. **Test Scores:** SAT Math middle 50% range 560–720. SAT EBRW middle 50% range 590–720. ACT middle 50% range 25–32. **Basis for Candidate Selection:** *Very important factors include:* rigor of secondary school record, academic GPA, standardized test scores. *Important factors include:* class rank, application essay, recommendation(s), interview. *Other factors include:* extracurricular activities, talent/ability, character/personal qualities, first generation, alumni/ae relation, racial/ethnic status, volunteer work, work experience. **Freshman Admission Requirements:** High school diploma is required and GED is accepted *Academic units recommended:* 4 English, 4 math, 3 science, 3 science labs, 2 foreign language, 3 social studies, 1 computer science, 1 visual/performing arts. **Freshman Admission Statistics:** 7,869 applied, 39% admitted, 24% enrolled. **Transfer Admission Requirements:** College transcript(s), essay or personal statement, statement of good standing from prior institution(s). Minimum college GPA of 2.5 required. Lowest grade transferable C. **General Admission Information:** Application fee $50. Priority deadline 1/15. Non-fall registration accepted. Admission may be deferred for a maximum of 1 year.

COSTS AND FINANCIAL AID

Annual tuition $40,484. Room and board $11,116. Required fees $1,025. Average book and supplies expense $1,200. **Required Forms and Deadlines:** FAFSA. **Notification of Awards:** Applicants will be notified of awards on a rolling basis beginning 2/1. **Types of Aid:** *Need-based scholarships/grants:* College/university scholarship or grant aid from institutional funds; Federal Pell; Private scholarships; SEOG; State scholarships/grants. *Loans:* Direct PLUS loans; Direct Subsidized Stafford Loans; Direct Unsubsidized Stafford Loans. **Student Employment:** Federal Work-Study Program available. Institutional employment available. **Financial Aid Statistics:** 92% needy freshmen, 89% needy undergrads receive need-based scholarship or grant aid. 99% freshmen, 94% undergrads receive non-need-based scholarship or grant aid. 58% freshmen, 62% undergrads receive need-based self-help aid. 11% freshmen, 10% undergrads receive athletic scholarships. 96% freshmen, 88% undergrads receive any aid. 50% undergrads borrow to pay for school. Average cumulative indebtedness $34,869. **Criteria awarding aid:** *Need-based:* Minority status. *Non-need-based:* Academics, Alumni affiliation, Art, Athletics, Leadership, Minority status, Music/drama, Religious affiliation.

UNIVERSITY OF UTAH

201 South 1460 East, Salt Lake City, UT 84112
Phone: 801-581-8761 **Financial Aid Phone:** 801-581-6211
E-mail: admissions@utah.edu **CEEB Code:** 4853
Fax: 801-585-7864 **Website:** www.utah.edu **ACT Code:** 4274

This public school was founded in 1850. It has a 1535 acre campus.

RATINGS

Admissions Selectivity Rating: 87   **Fire Safety Rating:** 96   **Green Rating:** 94

STUDENTS AND FACULTY

Enrollment: 23,432. **Student Body:** 47% female, 53% male, 22% out-of-state, 5% international (97 countries represented). Asian 6%, African American 1%, Caucasian 67%, Hispanic 13%, Native American <1%, Pacific Islander <1%, Two or more races 6%, Race unknown 1%.
Retention and Graduation: 89% freshmen return for sophomore year. 33% freshmen graduate within 4 years. 70% freshmen graduate within 6 years. 17% grads go on to further study within 1 year. 4% grads pursue arts and sciences degrees. 1% grads pursue law degrees. 1% grads pursue business degrees. 1% grads pursue medical degrees. **Faculty:** Student/faculty ratio 17:1. 1,439 full-time faculty, 87% hold PhDs, 16% are members of minority groups, 38% are women. 11% of classes are taught by teaching assistants.

ACADEMICS

Degrees: Bachelor's; Doctoral degree—professional practice; Doctoral degree research/scholarship; Master's; Post-bachelor's certificate; Post-master's certificate. **Classes:** Most classes have 20–29 students. Most lab/discussion sessions have 20–29 students. **Most popular majors:** Communication and Media Studies; Psychology, General; Economics, General. **Special Study Options:** Accelerated program; Cross-registration; Distance learning; Double major; Dual enrollment; English as a Second Language (ESL); Exchange student program (domestic); Honors program; Independent study; Internships; Student-designed major; Study abroad; Teacher certification program. **Honors programs:** For more than fifty years, the University of Utah has offered Honors programs. The Honors College Curriculum and Community give students unique opportunities to learn to think critically and to develop excellent communication skills and problem solving skills applicable to any and all fields of study and careers. Special Honors-only opportunities include year-long theory into practice (Praxis) Labs, close work with faculty, and thesis projects grounded in a student's major. Only students in the Honors College have the opportunity to earn an Honors Bachelor degree from the U of U, the highest degree conferred on an undergraduate. **Combined degree programs:** BA/MEng. **Disability Services offered:** Note-taking services; Reader services; Tape recorders; Tutors. **Career services:** Alumni network; Alumni services; Career assessment; Career/job search classes; Internships.

FACILITIES

Housing: Apartments for married students; Apartments for single students; Coed dorms; Fraternity/sorority housing; Men's dorms; Special housing for disabled students; Theme housing; Women's dorms; 97% of campus accessible to physically disabled. **Special Academic Facilities/Equipment:** Utah Museum of Fine Arts, Natural History Museum of Utah, Red Butte Garden & Arboretum, Art & Art History Galleries.

CAMPUS LIFE

Environment: Metropolis. **Activities:** Campus Ministries; Choral groups; Concert band; Dance; Drama/theater; International Student Organization; Jazz band; Literary magazine; Marching band; Model UN; Music ensembles; Musical theater; Opera; Pep band; Radio station; Student government; Student newspaper; Student-run film society; Symphony orchestra; Television station. 513 registered organizations, 27 honor societies, 14 religious organizations, 11 fraternities, 7 sororities on campus. **Athletics (Intercollegiate):** *Men:* baseball, basketball, cheerleading, diving, football, golf, skiing (downhill/Alpine), skiing (Nordic/cross-country), swimming, tennis. *Women:* basketball, cheerleading, cross-country, diving, gymnastics, skiing (downhill/Alpine), skiing (Nordic/cross-country), soccer, softball, swimming, tennis, track/field (outdoor), track/field (indoor), volleyball. **On-Campus Highlights:** Rice Eccles Stadium. **Environmental Initiatives:** Transportation: Free public transportation

(Ed-Pass) for all students, staff and faculty; gas-electric hybrid, biodiesel, and natural gas-powered campus vehicles.

ADMISSIONS

Freshman Academic Profile: Average high school GPA 3.7. 91% from public high schools. **Test Scores:** SAT Math middle 50% range 570–700. SAT EBRW middle 50% range 573–680. ACT middle 50% range 22–29. **Basis for Candidate Selection:** *Very important factors include:* rigor of secondary school record, academic GPA. *Important factors include:* standardized test scores. *Other factors include:* class rank, interview, extracurricular activities, talent/ability, character/personal qualities, first generation, alumni/ae relation, geographical residence, state residency, racial/ethnic status, volunteer work, work experience. **Freshman Admission Requirements:** High school diploma is required and GED is accepted. *Academic units required:* 4 English, 2 math, 3 science, 1 science labs, 2 foreign language, 1 history, 4 academic electives. **Freshman Admission Statistics:** 24,404 applied, 62% admitted, 28% enrolled. **Transfer Admission Requirements:** College transcript(s), statement of good standing from prior institution(s). Minimum college GPA of 2.6 required. Lowest grade transferable D-. **General Admission Information:** Application fee $55. Priority deadline 11/1. Regular application deadline 4/1. Non-fall registration accepted. Admission may be deferred for a maximum of 7 consecutive semesters.

COSTS AND FINANCIAL AID

Required Forms and Deadlines: FAFSA. **Notification of Awards:** Applicants will be notified of awards on a rolling basis beginning 3/1. **Types of Aid:** *Need-based scholarships/grants:* College/university scholarship or grant aid from institutional funds; Federal Nursing Scholarships; Federal Pell; Private scholarships; SEOG; State scholarships/grants. *Loans:* Direct PLUS loans; Direct Subsidized Stafford Loans; Direct Unsubsidized Stafford Loans. **Student Employment:** Federal Work-Study Program available. Institutional employment available. **Financial Aid Statistics:** 91% needy freshmen, 85% needy undergrads receive need-based scholarship or grant aid. 20% freshmen, 10% undergrads receive non-need-based scholarship or grant aid. 75% freshmen, 84% undergrads receive need-based self-help aid. 2% freshmen, 2% undergrads receive athletic scholarships. 46% freshmen, 44% undergrads receive any aid. 46% undergrads borrow to pay for school. Average cumulative indebtedness $19,656. **Criteria awarding aid:** *Non-need-based:* Academics, Alumni affiliation, Art, Athletics, Leadership, Minority status, Music/drama, State/district residency.

UNIVERSITY OF VERMONT

University of Vermont Admissions, Burlington, VT 05401-3596
Phone: 802-656-3370 **Financial Aid Phone:** (802) 656-5700
E-mail: admissions@uvm.edu **CEEB Code:** 3920
Website: www.uvm.edu **ACT Code:** 4322

This public school was founded in 1791. It has a 460 acre campus.

RATINGS

Admissions Selectivity Rating: 87 **Fire Safety Rating:** 98 **Green Rating:** 95

STUDENTS AND FACULTY

Enrollment: 10,700. **Student Body:** 59% female, 41% male, 72% out-of-state, 4% international (43 countries represented). Asian 3%, African American 1%, Caucasian 82%, Hispanic 4%, Native American <1%, Pacific Islander 0%, Two or more races 3%, Race unknown 3%. **Retention and Graduation:** 87% freshmen return for sophomore year. 65% freshmen graduate within 4 years. 76% freshmen graduate within 6 years. 20% grads go on to further study within 1 year. 13% grads pursue arts and sciences degrees. <1% grads pursue law degrees. 1% grads pursue business degrees. <1% grads pursue medical degrees. **Faculty:** Student/faculty ratio 18:1. 622 full-time faculty, 84% hold PhDs, 14% are members of minority groups, 49% are women. 3% of classes are taught by teaching assistants.

ACADEMICS

Degrees: Bachelor's; Doctoral degree—professional practice; Doctoral degree research/scholarship; Master's; Post-bachelor's certificate; Post-master's certificate. **Classes:** Most classes have 10–19 students. Most lab/discussion sessions have 10–19 students. **Most popular majors:** Psychology, General;

Business Administration and Management, General; Environmental Science. **Special Study Options:** Cooperative education program; Cross-registration; Distance learning; Double major; Dual enrollment; English as a Second Language (ESL); Exchange student program (domestic); Honors program; Independent study; Internships; Liberal arts/career combination; Student-designed major; Study abroad; Teacher certification program. **Honors programs:** The Honors College is a residential learning community where students live together and take classes in one of UVM's newest residence halls. Honors College students are simultaneously enrolled in one of seven other UVM undergraduate colleges or schools. Honors College courses comprise approximately 20% of a students overall coursework and include a year-long common first year seminar, a choice of a variety of sophomore seminars, a junior year thesis prep course, and a senior year thesis, creative project or practicum. Upon graduation, program completers are designated as Honors College Scholars. **Combined degree programs:** BA/JD. **Disability Services offered:** Note-taking services; Reader services; Tape recorders; Tutors. **Career services:** Alumni network; Alumni services; Career assessment; Career/job search classes; Internships.

FACILITIES

Housing: Apartments for married students; Apartments for single students; Coed dorms; Fraternity/sorority housing; Theme housing; Wellness housing 90% of campus accessible to physically disabled. **Special Academic Facilities/Equipment:** Art/ethnography museum, chemistry/physics library, medical library, on-campus preschool, government research and world affairs centers, agricultural experiment station, horse farm, multinuclear magnetic resonance spectrometers, mass spectrometer.

CAMPUS LIFE

Environment: Town. **Activities:** Campus Ministries; Choral groups; Concert band; Dance; Drama/theater; International Student Organization; Jazz band; Literary magazine; Music ensembles; Musical theater; Pep band; Radio station; Student government; Student newspaper; Student-run film society; Symphony orchestra; Television station. 214 registered organizations, 29 honor societies, 7 religious organizations, 8 fraternities, 6 sororities, on campus. **Athletics (Intercollegiate):** *Men:* basketball, cross-country, ice hockey, lacrosse, skiing (downhill/Alpine), skiing (Nordic/cross-country), soccer, track/field (outdoor), track/field (indoor). *Women:* basketball, cross-country, diving, field hockey, ice hockey, lacrosse, skiing (downhill/Alpine), skiing (Nordic/cross-country), soccer, swimming, track/field (outdoor), track/field (indoor). **On-Campus Highlights:** Dudley H. Davis Student Center. **Environmental Initiatives:** Reporting jointly to the Associate Vice Provost for Teaching & Learning and the VP for Finance, the Office of Sustainability supports the infusion of sustainability into operations, student life, curriculum, and communications, managing University commitments for energy, food, and sustainability education.

ADMISSIONS

Freshman Academic Profile: Average high school GPA 3.7. 34% in top 10% of high school class, 75% in top 25% of high school class, 98% in top 50% of high school class. 74% from public high schools. **Test Scores:** SAT Math middle 50% range 580–680. SAT EBRW middle 50% range 600–680. ACT middle 50% range 26–31. **Basis for Candidate Selection:** *Very important factors include:* rigor of secondary school record. *Important factors include:* class rank, academic GPA, application essay, standardized test scores, character/personal qualities, state residency. *Other factors include:* recommendation(s), extracurricular activities, talent/ability, first generation, alumni/ae relation, geographical residence, racial/ethnic status, volunteer work, work experience, level of applicant's interest. **Freshman Admission Requirements:** High school diploma is required and GED is accepted *Academic units required:* 4 English, 3 math, 2 science, 1 science labs, 2 foreign language, 3 social studies. **Freshman Admission Statistics:** 19,233 applied, 67% admitted, 20% enrolled. **Transfer Admission Requirements:** High school transcript, college transcript(s), essay or personal statement. Minimum college GPA of 2.5 required. Lowest grade transferable C. **General Admission Information:** Regular application deadline 1/15. Non-fall registration accepted.

COSTS AND FINANCIAL AID

Annual in-state tuition $16,392. Annual out-of-state tuition $41,280. Room and board $12,916. Required fees $2,410. Average book and supplies expense $1,200. **Required Forms and Deadlines:** FAFSA. **Notification of Awards:** Applicants will be notified of awards on a rolling basis beginning 3/15. **Types of Aid:** *Need-based scholarships/grants:* College/university scholarship or grant aid from institutional funds; Federal Pell; Private scholarships; SEOG; State scholarships/grants. *Loans:* Direct PLUS loans; Direct Subsidized Stafford Loans; Direct Unsubsidized Stafford Loans. **Student Employment:** Federal

Work-Study Program available. Institutional employment available. **Financial Aid Statistics:** 98% needy freshmen, 96% needy undergrads receive need-based scholarship or grant aid. 13% freshmen, 11% undergrads receive non-need-based scholarship or grant aid. 64% freshmen, 68% undergrads receive need-based self-help aid. 2% freshmen, 2% undergrads receive athletic scholarships. 96% freshmen, 87% undergrads receive any aid. 57% undergrads borrow to pay for school. Average cumulative indebtedness $31,684. **Criteria awarding aid:** *Need-based:* Academics, Athletics, Leadership, Minority status, Music/drama *Non-need-based:* Academics, Alumni affiliation, Athletics, Leadership, Minority status, Music/drama, State/district residency.

UNIVERSITY OF VIRGINIA

Best Colleges

Office of Admission, Charlottesville, VA 22903
Phone: 434-982-3200 **Financial Aid Phone:** 434-982-4757
E-mail: undergradadmission@virginia.edu **CEEB Code:** 5820
Fax: 434-924-3587 **Website:** www.virginia.edu **ACT Code:** 4412

This public school was founded in 1819. It has a 1167 acre campus.

RATINGS

Admissions Selectivity Rating: 98   Fire Safety Rating: 92   Green Rating: 96

STUDENTS AND FACULTY

Enrollment: 16,593. **Student Body:** 55% female, 45% male, 28% out-of-state, 4% international (122 countries represented). Asian 15%, African American 7%, Caucasian 56%, Hispanic 7%, Native American <1%, Pacific Islander <1%, Two or more races 5%, Race unknown 5%.
Retention and Graduation: 97% freshmen return for sophomore year. 89% freshmen graduate within 4 years. 95% freshmen graduate within 6 years. **Faculty:** Student/faculty ratio 14:1. 1,523 full-time faculty, 94% hold PhDs, 17% are members of minority groups, 40% are women. 7% of classes are taught by teaching assistants.

ACADEMICS

Degrees: Bachelor's; Certificate; Doctoral degree—professional practice; Doctoral degree research/scholarship; Master's; Post-bachelor's certificate; Post-master's certificate. **Classes:** Most classes have 10–19 students. Most lab/discussion sessions have 20–29 students. **Most popular majors:** Business/Commerce, General; Economics, General; Biology/Biological Sciences, General. **Special Study Options:** Accelerated program; Cooperative education program; Distance learning; Double major; English as a Second Language (ESL); Exchange student program (domestic); Honors program; Independent study; Internships; Liberal arts/career combination; Student-designed major; Study abroad; Teacher certification program. **Honors programs:** Jefferson Scholars: Full scholarship given to approximately 30 students per year. Special lectures and discussions with distinguished University faculty; all first year Jefferson Scholars take part in an outdoor leadership experience; all rising-second year Jefferson Scholars, prior to the beginning of school, participate in a two-week Institute for Leadership and Citizenship designed to foster a deeper understanding of the art of leadership and the importance of citizenship. Additionally, all Jefferson Scholars are granted an opportunity to travel and study abroad between their second and third year. Scholars may elect to spend three weeks of study at either Regent's College in England or the Erasmus Institute in Tuscany, Italy. Following the structured tutorial, each Scholar designs and completes two weeks of travel and independent inquiry. Echols Scholars-School of Arts and Sciences. Separate dormitory, with Rodman Scholars, for first-year students. Flexible degree requirements; exemption from some requirements; preference for courses. Rodman Scholars-School of Engineering and Applied Sciences. Separate dormitory, with Echols Scholars, for first-year students. Special courses designed only for Rodman Scholars in first two years. **Disability Services offered:** Note-taking services; Reader services; Tape recorders; Tutors. **Career services:** Alumni network; Alumni services; Career assessment; Career/job search classes; Internships; Regional alumni.

FACILITIES

Housing: Apartments for married students; Apartments for single students; Coed dorms; Fraternity/sorority housing; Special housing for international students; 100% of campus accessible to physically disabled. **Special Academic Facilities/Equipment:** 15 libraries, art museum, experimental farm, biological station, observatory/planetarium, nuclear information center, media center (multimedia editing).

CAMPUS LIFE

Environment: City. **Activities:** Choral groups; Concert band; Dance; Drama/theater; International Student Organization; Jazz band; Literary magazine; Marching band; Model UN; Music ensembles; Musical theater; Opera; Pep band; Radio station; Student government; Student newspaper; Student-run film society; Symphony orchestra; Television station; Yearbook. 7 honor societies, 31 fraternities, 16 sororities, on campus. **Athletics (Intercollegiate):** *Men:* baseball, basketball, cross-country, diving, football, golf, lacrosse, soccer, swimming, tennis, track/field (outdoor), track/field (indoor), wrestling. *Women:* basketball, crew/rowing, cross-country, diving, field hockey, golf, lacrosse, soccer, softball, swimming, tennis, track/field (outdoor), track/field (indoor), volleyball. **On-Campus Highlights:** Rotunda/Academical Village (orig campus). **Environmental Initiatives:** Academics: The University of Virginia offers 70+ courses in 8 different schools with significant focus on sustainability, including a global sustainability course, a new course model cross listed and taught jointly by faculty from Engineering, Architecture, and Commerce. In Spring 2011, the University created the interdisciplinary Global Sustainability minor.

ADMISSIONS

Freshman Academic Profile: Average high school GPA 4.3. 90% in top 10% of high school class, 98% in top 25% of high school class, 99% in top 50% of high school class. 73% from public high schools. **Test Scores:** SAT Math middle 50% range 670–780. SAT EBRW middle 50% range 670–740. ACT middle 50% range 30–34. **Basis for Candidate Selection:** *Very important factors include:* rigor of secondary school record, class rank, academic GPA, recommendation(s), character/personal qualities, state residency. *Important factors include:* application essay, standardized test scores, extracurricular activities, talent/ability. *Other factors include:* first generation, alumni/ae relation, geographical residence, racial/ethnic status, volunteer work, work experience. **Freshman Admission Requirements:** High school diploma is required and GED is accepted *Academic units required:* 4 English, 4 math, 2 science, 2 foreign language, 1 social studies. *Academic units recommended:* 5 math, 5 science, 5 foreign language, 5 social studies. **Freshman Admission Statistics:** 40,839 applied, 24% admitted, 40% enrolled. **Transfer Admission Requirements:** High school transcript, college transcript(s), essay or personal statement, standardized test scores, statement of good standing from prior institution(s). Minimum college GPA of 2.0 required. Lowest grade transferable C. **General Admission Information:** Application fee $70. Regular application deadline 1/1. Admission may be deferred for a maximum of 1 year.

COSTS AND FINANCIAL AID

Annual in-state tuition $15,848. Annual out-of-state tuition $50,516. Room and board $12,350. Required fees $3,120. Average book and supplies expense $1,356. **Required Forms and Deadlines:** CSS/Financial Aid PROFILE; FAFSA. **Notification of Awards:** Applicants will be notified of awards on or about 4/5. **Types of Aid:** *Need-based scholarships/grants:* College/university scholarship or grant aid from institutional funds; Federal Nursing Scholarships; Federal Pell; Private scholarships; SEOG; State scholarships/grants. *Loans:* Direct PLUS loans; Direct Subsidized Stafford Loans; Direct Unsubsidized Stafford Loans. **Student Employment:** Federal Work-Study Program available. Institutional employment available. **Financial Aid Statistics:** 88% needy freshmen, 87% needy undergrads receive need-based scholarship or grant aid. 9% freshmen, 7% undergrads receive non-need-based scholarship or grant aid. 57% freshmen, 61% undergrads receive need-based self-help aid. 3% freshmen, 3% undergrads receive athletic scholarships. 57.6% freshmen, 52.2% undergrads receive any aid. 33% undergrads borrow to pay for school. Average cumulative indebtedness $26,023. **Criteria awarding aid:** *Need-based:* Academics, Leadership, Minority status. *Non-need-based:* Academics, Athletics, Leadership, Minority status, Music/drama, State/district residency.

UNIVERSITY OF VIRGINIA'S COLLEGE AT WISE

1 College Avenue, Wise, VA 24293
Phone: 276-328-0102 **Financial Aid Phone:**
E-mail: admissions@uvawise.edu **CEEB Code:** 5124
Fax: 276-328-0251 **Website:** www.uvawise.edu **ACT Code:** 4343

This public school was founded in 1954. It has a 367 acre campus.

RATINGS
Admissions Selectivity Rating: 79   **Fire Safety Rating:** 60*   **Green Rating:** 60*

STUDENTS AND FACULTY
Enrollment: 1,629. **Student Body:** 52% female, 48% male, 5% out-of-state, <1% international. Asian 1%, African American 7%, Caucasian 90%, Hispanic 2%, Native American <1%, Race unknown 0%.
Retention and Graduation: 73% freshmen return for sophomore year. 14% grads go on to further study within 1 year. 7% grads pursue arts and sciences degrees. 6% grads pursue law degrees. 4% grads pursue business degrees. 1% grads pursue medical degrees. **Faculty:** Student/faculty ratio 16:1. 91 full-time faculty, 29% hold PhDs, 13% are members of minority groups, 41% are women. 0% of classes are taught by teaching assistants.

ACADEMICS
Degrees: Bachelor's. **Classes:** Most classes have 10–19 students. Most lab/discussion sessions have 10–19 students. **Special Study Options:** Accelerated program; Cooperative education program; Distance learning; Double major; Dual enrollment; Honors program; Independent study; Internships; Student-designed major; Study abroad; Teacher certification program. **Disability Services offered:** Note-taking services; Reader services; Tape recorders; Tutors. **Career services:** Alumni services; Career assessment; Career/job search classes; Internships.

FACILITIES
Housing: Apartments for single students; Coed dorms; Men's dorms; Special housing for disabled students; Women's dorms; 95% of campus accessible to physically disabled. **Campus Network:** 100% of classrooms, 100% of dorms, 100% of student union, 100% of libraries, 100% of dining areas, 100% of common outdoor areas have wireless network access.

CAMPUS LIFE
Environment: Rural. **Activities:** Choral groups; Concert band; Dance; Drama/theater; Literary magazine; Music ensembles; Musical theater; Pep band; Radio station; Student government; Student newspaper; Television station; Yearbook. 40 registered organizations, 3 honor societies, 3 religious organizations, 3 fraternities, 2 sororities on campus. **Athletics (Intercollegiate):** *Men:* baseball, basketball, cross-country, football, golf, tennis, track/field (outdoor). *Women:* basketball, cross-country, softball, tennis, track/field (outdoor), volleyball.

ADMISSIONS
Freshman Academic Profile: Average high school GPA 3.3. 18% in top 10% of high school class, 40% in top 25% of high school class, 78% in top 50% of high school class. 99% from public high schools. **Test Scores:** SAT Math middle 50% range 430–530. SAT EBRW middle 50% range 420–530, ACT middle 50% range 16–21. **Basis for Candidate Selection:** *Very important factors include:* rigor of secondary school record, class rank. *Important factors include:* standardized test scores, talent/ability. *Other factors include:* application essay, recommendation(s), interview, extracurricular activities, character/personal qualities, racial/ethnic status, volunteer work, work experience. **Freshman Admission Requirements:** High school diploma is required and GED is accepted *Academic units required:* 4 English, 3 math, 2 science, 2 science labs, 2 foreign language, 1 social studies, 1 history, 5 academic electives. **Freshman Admission Statistics:** 987 applied, 78% admitted, 52% enrolled. **Transfer Admission Requirements:** College transcript(s). Minimum college GPA of 2.3 required. Lowest grade transferable C-. **General Admission Information:** Application fee $25. Priority deadline 4/1. Regular application deadline 8/1. Non-fall registration accepted. Admission may be deferred for a maximum of 1 year.

COSTS AND FINANCIAL AID
Required Forms and Deadlines: FAFSA. **Notification of Awards:** Applicants will be notified of awards on a rolling basis beginning 4/1. **Types of Aid:** *Need-based scholarships/grants:* College/university scholarship or grant aid from institutional funds; Federal Pell; Private scholarships; SEOG; State scholarships/grants. **Student Employment:** Federal Work-Study Program available. Institutional employment available. **Criteria awarding aid:** *Need-based:*

Academics, Alumni affiliation, Athletics, Leadership, Minority status *Non-need-based:* Academics, Alumni affiliation, Art, Athletics, Job skills, Leadership, Music/drama, State/district residency.

UNIVERSITY OF WASHINGTON

1410 NE Campus Parkway, Seattle, WA 98195-5852
Phone: 206-543-9686 **Financial Aid Phone:** 206-543-6101
CEEB Code: 4854
Fax: 206-685-3655 **Website:** www.washington.edu **ACT Code:** 4484

This public school was founded in 1861. It has a 634 acre campus.

RATINGS
Admissions Selectivity Rating: 89   **Fire Safety Rating:** 95   **Green Rating:** 98

STUDENTS AND FACULTY
Enrollment: 31,042. **Student Body:** 54% female, 46% male, 19% out-of-state, 16% international (76 countries represented). Asian 26%, African American 3%, Caucasian 37%, Hispanic 9%, Native American <1%, Pacific Islander <1%, Two or more races 8%, Race unknown 1%.
Retention and Graduation: 95% freshmen return for sophomore year. 66% freshmen graduate within 4 years. 84% freshmen graduate within 6 years. **Faculty:** Student/faculty ratio 21:1. 1,842 full-time faculty, 82% hold PhDs, 18% are members of minority groups, 45% are women.

ACADEMICS
Degrees: Bachelor's; Doctoral degree—professional practice; Doctoral degree research/scholarship; Master's; Post-master's certificate. **Classes:** Most classes have 20–29 students. Most lab/discussion sessions have 20–29 students. **Most popular majors:** Engineering, General; Business Administration and Management, General; Computer Science. **Special Study Options:** Cooperative education program; Cross-registration; Distance learning; Double major; Dual enrollment; English as a Second Language (ESL); Exchange student program (domestic); Honors program; Independent study; Internships; Student-designed major; Study abroad; Teacher certification program. **Honors programs:** We have a University Honors Program, as well as departmental honors options. **Disability Services offered:** Note-taking services; Reader services; Tape recorders; Tutors. **Career services:** Alumni network; Alumni services; Career assessment; Career/job search classes; Internships; Regional alumni.

FACILITIES
Housing: Apartments for married students; Apartments for single students; Coed dorms; Fraternity/sorority housing; Special housing for disabled students; Theme housing 100% of campus accessible to physically disabled. **Special Academic Facilities/Equipment:** Multiple art galleries, an anthropology and natural history museum, arboretum, closed-circuit TV studio.

CAMPUS LIFE
Environment: Metropolis. **Activities:** Campus Ministries; Choral groups; Concert band; Dance; Drama/theater; International Student Organization; Jazz band; Literary magazine; Marching band; Model UN; Music ensembles; Musical theater; Opera; Pep band; Radio station; Student government; Student newspaper; Student-run film society; Symphony orchestra; Television station. 800 registered organizations, 13 honor societies, 54 religious organizations, 32 fraternities, 16 sororities, on campus. **Athletics (Intercollegiate):** *Men:* baseball, basketball, crew/rowing, cross-country, football, golf, soccer, tennis, track/field (outdoor). *Women:* basketball, crew/rowing, cross-country, golf, gymnastics, soccer, softball, tennis, track/field (outdoor), volleyball. **On-Campus Highlights:** Henry Art Gallery. **Environmental Initiatives:** College of the Environment http://coenv.washington.edu/.

ADMISSIONS
Freshman Academic Profile: Average high school GPA 3.8. **Test Scores:** SAT Math middle 50% range 620–770. SAT EBRW middle 50% range 600–700. ACT middle 50% range 27–33. **Basis for Candidate Selection:** *Very important factors include:* rigor of secondary school record, academic GPA, application essay. *Important factors include:* standardized test scores, extracurricular activities, talent/ability, first generation. *Other factors include:* character/personal qualities, state residency. **Freshman Admission Requirements:**

High school diploma or equivalent is not required *Academic units required:* 4 English, 3 math, 2 science, 2 science labs, 2 foreign language, 3 social studies, 0.5 academic electives, 1 visual/performing arts. *Academic units recommended:* 4 English, 4 math, 4 science, 3 science labs, 3 foreign language, 4 social studies, 1 history, 1 computer science, 1 visual/performing arts. **Freshman Admission Statistics:** 45,579 applied, 52% admitted, 30% enrolled. **Transfer Admission Requirements:** High school transcript, college transcript(s), essay or personal statement. Minimum college GPA of 2.5 required. Lowest grade transferable .7. **General Admission Information:** Application fee $80. Regular application deadline 11/15.

COSTS AND FINANCIAL AID
Annual in-state tuition $10,370. Annual out-of-state tuition $37,071. Room and board $13,296. Required fees $1,095. Average book and supplies expense $900. **Required Forms and Deadlines:** FAFSA. **Notification of Awards:** Applicants will be notified of awards on or about 4/1. **Types of Aid:** *Need-based scholarships/grants:* College/university scholarship or grant aid from institutional funds; Federal Pell; Private scholarships; SEOG; State scholarships/grants. *Loans:* Direct PLUS loans; Direct Subsidized Stafford Loans; Direct Unsubsidized Stafford Loans. **Student Employment:** Federal Work-Study Program available. Institutional employment available. **Financial Aid Statistics:** 85% needy freshmen, 87% needy undergrads receive need-based scholarship or grant aid. 4% freshmen, 3% undergrads receive non-need-based scholarship or grant aid. 40% freshmen, 47% undergrads receive need-based self-help aid. 1% freshmen, 1% undergrads receive athletic scholarships. 38% freshmen, 39% undergrads receive any aid. 33% undergrads borrow to pay for school. Average cumulative indebtedness $19,198. **Criteria awarding aid:** *Need-based:* Academics, Art, Leadership, Music/drama *Non-need-based:* Academics, Alumni affiliation, Art, Athletics, Leadership, Music/drama, State/district residency.

UNIVERSITY OF WASHINGTON—BOTHELL

Office of Admissions, Bothell, WA 98011
Phone: 425-352-5000 **Financial Aid Phone:** 425-352-5240
E-mail: uwbinfo@uw.edu **CEEB Code:** 4467
Fax: 425-352-5455 **Website:** www.uwb.edu **ACT Code:** 4497

This public school was founded in 1990. It has a 128 acre campus.

RATINGS
Admissions Selectivity Rating: 80 **Fire Safety Rating:** 78 **Green Rating:** 60*

STUDENTS AND FACULTY
Enrollment: 5,332. **Student Body:** 48% female, 52% male, 2% out-of-state, 8% international (24 countries represented). Asian 31%, African American 7%, Caucasian 35%, Hispanic 10%, Native American <1%, Pacific Islander <1%, Two or more races 6%, Race unknown 1%.
Retention and Graduation: 83% freshmen return for sophomore year. 45% freshmen graduate within 4 years. 69% freshmen graduate within 6 years.
Faculty: Student/faculty ratio 20:1. 194 full-time faculty, 82% hold PhDs, 24% are members of minority groups, 50% are women.

ACADEMICS
Degrees: Bachelor's; Master's; Post-bachelor's certificate. **Classes:** Most classes have 20–29 students. Most lab/discussion sessions have 20–29 students. **Most popular majors:** Health Professions And Related Programs; Business/Commerce, General; Computer and Information Sciences, General. **Special Study Options:** Cross-registration; Double major; English as a Second Language (ESL); Independent study; Internships; Student-designed major; Study abroad; Teacher certification program. **Honors programs:** We have a University Honors Program, as well as departmental honors options. **Disability Services offered:** Note-taking services; Reader services; Tape recorders; Tutors. **Career services:** Alumni network; Alumni services; Career assessment; Career/job search classes; Internships; Regional alumni.

FACILITIES
Housing: Coed dorms; Special housing for disabled students; Theme housing; 100% of campus accessible to physically disabled. **Special Academic Facilities/Equipment:** The Sarah Simonds Green Conservatory was completed in the summer of 2013. This 2,800 square foot complex on the western edge of the wetlands houses a 1,600 square foot greenhouse, classroom, and support space for education, research, and public outreach.

CAMPUS LIFE
Environment: City. **Activities:** Campus Ministries; Dance; International Student Organization; Literary magazine; Radio station; Student government; Student newspaper; Student-run film society. 32 registered organizations on campus. **On-Campus Highlights:** STEM buildings.

ADMISSIONS
Freshman Academic Profile: Average high school GPA 3.4. **Test Scores:** SAT Math middle 50% range 520–633. SAT EBRW middle 50% range 500–620. ACT middle 50% range 19–28. **Basis for Candidate Selection:** *Very important factors include:* rigor of secondary school record, academic GPA, application essay, standardized test scores, extracurricular activities, character/personal qualities. *Important factors include:* level of applicant's interest. *Other factors include:* talent/ability, volunteer work, work experience. **Freshman Admission Requirements:** High school diploma is required and GED is accepted *Academic units required:* 4 English, 3 math, 2 science, 2 science labs, 2 foreign language, 3 social studies, 0.5 academic electives, 0.5 visual/performing arts. *Academic units recommended:* 4 English, 4 math, 4 science, 3 science labs, 2 foreign language, 4 social studies, 1 visual/performing arts. **Freshman Admission Statistics:** 4,242 applied, 74% admitted, 26% enrolled. **General Admission Information:** Application fee $60. Priority deadline 1/15. Admission may be deferred by petition.

COSTS AND FINANCIAL AID
Annual in-state tuition $10,370. Annual out-of-state tuition $37,071. Room and board $12,636. Required fees $1,020. Average book and supplies expense $900. **Required Forms and Deadlines:** FAFSA. **Notification of Awards:** Applicants will be notified of awards on or about 4/1. **Types of Aid:** *Need-based scholarships/grants:* College/university scholarship or grant aid from institutional funds; Federal Pell; Private scholarships; SEOG; State scholarships/grants. *Loans:* Direct PLUS loans; Direct Subsidized Stafford Loans; Direct Unsubsidized Stafford Loans. **Student Employment:** Federal Work-Study Program available. Institutional employment available. **Financial Aid Statistics:** 83% needy freshmen, 86% needy undergrads receive need-based scholarship or grant aid. 2% freshmen, 1% undergrads receive non-need-based scholarship or grant aid. 43% freshmen, 45% undergrads receive need-based self-help aid. 0% freshmen, 0% undergrads receive athletic scholarships. 54% freshmen, 53% undergrads receive any aid. 39% undergrads borrow to pay for school. Average cumulative indebtedness $18,449. **Criteria awarding aid:** *Need-based:* Academics, Art, Leadership, Music/drama *Non-need-based:* Academics, Alumni affiliation, Art, Athletics, Leadership, Music/drama, State/district residency.

UNIVERSITY OF WASHINGTON—TACOMA

1900 Commerce Campus, Tacoma, WA 98402-3100
Phone: 253.692.4742 **Financial Aid Phone:** 253-692-4374
E-mail: uwtinfo@uw.edu **CEEB Code:** 4445
Fax: 253.692.4414 **Website:** http://www.tacoma.uw.edu/ **ACT Code:** 4493

This is a public school.

RATINGS
Admissions Selectivity Rating: 76 **Fire Safety Rating:** 60* **Green Rating:** 60*

STUDENTS AND FACULTY
Enrollment: 4,565. **Student Body:** 52% female, 48% male, 2% out-of-state, 3% international (17 countries represented). Asian 21%, African American 9%, Caucasian 39%, Hispanic 15%, Native American 1%, Pacific Islander 1%, Two or more races 8%, Race unknown 2%.
Retention and Graduation: 80% freshmen return for sophomore year. 41% freshmen graduate within 4 years. 56% freshmen graduate within 6 years.
Faculty: Student/faculty ratio 15:1. 251 full-time faculty, 73% hold PhDs, 20% are members of minority groups, 54% are women.

ACADEMICS
Degrees: Bachelor's; Doctoral degree research/scholarship; Master's; Post-bachelor's certificate. **Classes:** Most classes have 20–29 students. Most lab/discussion sessions have 20–29 students. **Most popular majors:** Computer And Information Sciences And Support Services; Psychology; Business, Management, Marketing, And Related Support Services. **Special Study Options:** Cross-registration; Distance learning; Double major; Dual enrollment; Honors program; Independent study; Internships; Student-designed major; Study abroad; Teacher certification program. **Honors programs:** We have a University Honors Program, as well as departmental honors options. **Disability Services offered:** Note-taking services; Reader

services; Tape recorders; Tutors. **Career services:** Alumni network; Alumni services; Career assessment; Career/job search classes; Internships; Regional alumni.

FACILITIES

Housing: Apartments for single students; 100% of campus accessible to physically disabled.

CAMPUS LIFE

Environment: City. **Activities:** Campus Ministries; Drama/theater; International Student Organization; Literary magazine; Student government; Student newspaper. 60 registered organizations, 8 honor societies, on campus. **On-Campus Highlights:** Mattress Factory.

ADMISSIONS

Freshman Academic Profile: Average high school GPA 3.4. **Test Scores:** SAT Math middle 50% range 490–590. SAT EBRW middle 50% range 490–600. ACT middle 50% range 16–24. **Basis for Candidate Selection:** *Very important factors include:* rigor of secondary school record, academic GPA. *Important factors include:* application essay, standardized test scores. *Other factors include:* extracurricular activities, talent/ability, character/personal qualities, first generation, volunteer work, work experience, level of applicant's interest. **Freshman Admission Requirements:** High school diploma or equivalent is not required *Academic units required:* 4 English, 3 math, 2 science, 2 science labs, 2 foreign language, 3 social studies, 0.5 academic electives, 0.5 visual/performing arts, 1 unit from above areas or other academic areas. **Freshman Admission Statistics:** 2,026 applied, 87% admitted, 37% enrolled. **General Admission Information:** Application fee $60. Priority deadline 1/15. Regular application deadline 6/30. Non-fall registration accepted. Admission may be deferred for a maximum of 4 quarters.

COSTS AND FINANCIAL AID

Annual in-state tuition $10,370. Annual out-of-state tuition $37,071. Room and board $11,748. Required fees $1,269. Average book and supplies expense $900. **Required Forms and Deadlines:** FAFSA;. **Notification of Awards:** Applicants will be notified of awards on or about 4/1. **Types of Aid:** *Need-based scholarships/grants:* College/university scholarship or grant aid from institutional funds; Federal Pell; Private scholarships; SEOG; State scholarships/grants. *Loans:* Direct PLUS loans; Direct Subsidized Stafford Loans; Direct Unsubsidized Stafford Loans. **Student Employment:** Federal Work-Study Program available. Institutional employment available. **Financial Aid Statistics:** 92% needy freshmen, 89% needy undergrads receive need-based scholarship or grant aid. 5% freshmen, 2% undergrads receive non-need-based scholarship or grant aid. 31% freshmen, 47% undergrads receive need-based self-help aid. 0% freshmen, 0% undergrads receive athletic scholarships. 71% freshmen, 69% undergrads receive any aid. 45% undergrads borrow to pay for school. Average cumulative indebtedness $16,716. **Criteria awarding aid:** *Need-based:* Academics, Art, Leadership, Music/drama *Non-need-based:* Academics, Alumni affiliation, Art, Athletics, Leadership, Music/drama, State/district residency.

UNIVERSITY OF WEST ALABAMA

Station 4, Livingston, AL 35470
Phone: 205-652-3578 **Financial Aid Phone:** 205-652-3576
E-mail: admissions@uwa.edu
Fax: 205-652-3522 **Website:** http://www.uwa.edu/ **ACT Code:** 0024

This public school was founded in 1835. It has a 514 acre campus.

RATINGS

Admissions Selectivity Rating: 85   **Fire Safety Rating:** 87   **Green Rating:** 66

STUDENTS AND FACULTY

Enrollment: 2,157. **Student Body:** 58% female, 42% male, 19% out-of-state, 5% international (24 countries represented). Asian <1%, African American 43%, Caucasian 43%, Hispanic 2%, Native American <1%, Pacific Islander <1%, Two or more races 3%, Race unknown 3%.
Retention and Graduation: 62% freshmen return for sophomore year. 13% freshmen graduate within 4 years. 32% freshmen graduate within 6 years.
Faculty: Student/faculty ratio 14:1. 118 full-time faculty, 66% hold PhDs, 20% are members of minority groups, 58% are women. 0% of classes are taught by teaching assistants.

ACADEMICS

Degrees: Associate; Bachelor's; Certificate; Doctoral degree—professional practice; Master's; Post-master's certificate. **Classes:** Most classes have fewer

than 10 students. Most lab/discussion sessions have 10–19 students. **Most popular majors:** Teacher Education, Multiple Levels; Multi/Interdisciplinary Studies; Business Administration and Management, General. **Special Study Options:** Accelerated program; Cooperative education program; Distance learning; Double major; Dual enrollment; English as a Second Language (ESL); Honors program; Independent study; Internships; Student-designed major; Study abroad; Teacher certification program. **Combined degree programs:** BA/MEng. **Disability Services offered:** Tutors. **Career services:** Alumni services; Career assessment; Internships.

FACILITIES

Housing: Apartments for single students; Coed dorms; Theme housing; Wellness housing; 90% of campus accessible to physically disabled. **Campus Network:** 100% of classrooms, 100% of dorms, 100% of student union, 100% of libraries, 100% of dining areas, 100% of common outdoor areas have wireless network access.

CAMPUS LIFE

Environment: Rural. **Activities:** Campus Ministries; Choral groups; Concert band; Dance; Drama/theater; International Student Organization; Jazz band; Marching band; Music ensembles; Pep band; Student government; Student newspaper; Television station; Yearbook. 64 registered organizations, 9 honor societies, 2 religious organizations, 6 fraternities, 6 sororities on campus. **Athletics (Intercollegiate):** *Men:* baseball, basketball, cheerleading, cross-country, football, rodeo. *Women:* basketball, cheerleading, cross-country, rodeo, softball, volleyball. **On-Campus Highlights:** Student Union Building (SUB).

ADMISSIONS

Basis for Candidate Selection: *Very important factors include:* rigor of secondary school record, academic GPA, standardized test scores. **Freshman Admission Requirements:** High school diploma is required and GED is accepted *Academic units required:* 3 English, 3 math, 3 science, 3 social studies, 3 academic electives. **Freshman Admission Statistics:** 8,870 applied, 40% admitted, 12% enrolled. **Transfer Admission Requirements:** College transcript(s), statement of good standing from prior institution(s). Minimum college GPA of 2.0 required. Lowest grade transferable C. **General Admission Information:** Application fee $40. Non-fall registration accepted. Admission may be deferred for a maximum of 1 year.

COSTS AND FINANCIAL AID

Annual in-state tuition $8,450. Annual out-of-state tuition $16,900. Room and board $8,116. Required fees $1,590. Average book and supplies expense $1,216. **Required Forms and Deadlines:** FAFSA. **Notification of Awards:** Applicants will be notified of awards on a rolling basis beginning 4/15. **Types of Aid:** *Need-based scholarships/grants:* College/university scholarship or grant aid from institutional funds; Federal Pell; Private scholarships; SEOG; State scholarships/grants; United Negro College Fund. *Loans:* Direct PLUS loans; Direct Subsidized Stafford Loans; Direct Unsubsidized Stafford Loans. **Student Employment:** Federal Work-Study Program available. Institutional employment available. **Financial Aid Statistics:** 73% needy freshmen, 73% needy undergrads receive need-based scholarship or grant aid. 68% freshmen, 44% undergrads receive non-need-based scholarship or grant aid. 3% freshmen, 5% undergrads receive need-based self-help aid. 10% freshmen, 13% undergrads receive athletic scholarships. 95% freshmen, 95% undergrads receive any aid. 73% undergrads borrow to pay for school. Average cumulative indebtedness $21,562. **Criteria awarding aid:** *Non-need-based:* Academics, Alumni affiliation, Art, Athletics, Leadership, Music/drama, State/district residency.

UNIVERSITY OF WEST FLORIDA

11000 University Parkway, Pensacola, FL 32514-5750
Phone: 850-474-2230 **Financial Aid Phone:** 850-474-2400
E-mail: admissions@uwf.edu **CEEB Code:** 5833
Fax: 850-474-3360 **Website:** http://uwf.edu **ACT Code:** 771

This public school was founded in 1963. It has a 1600 acre campus.

RATINGS

Admissions Selectivity Rating: 89   **Fire Safety Rating:** 89   **Green Rating:** 60*

STUDENTS AND FACULTY

Enrollment: 9,786. **Student Body:** 57% female, 43% male, 9% out-of-state, 2% international (71 countries represented). Asian 3%, African American 13%,

Caucasian 65%, Hispanic 9%, Native American <1%, Pacific Islander <1%, Two or more races 5%, Race unknown 2%.
Retention and Graduation: 72% freshmen return for sophomore year.
Faculty: Student/faculty ratio 22:1. 338 full-time faculty, 0% hold PhDs, 17% are members of minority groups, 44% are women.

ACADEMICS

Degrees: Associate; Bachelor's; Certificate; Master's; Post-master's certificate. **Classes:** Most classes have 20–29 students. Most lab/discussion sessions have 20–29 students. **Most popular majors:** Accounting; Biology/Biological Sciences, General; Psychology, General. **Special Study Options:** Cooperative education program; Distance learning; Dual enrollment; English as a Second Language (ESL); Exchange student program (domestic); Honors program; Independent study; Internships; Study abroad; Teacher certification program. **Disability Services offered:** Note-taking services; Reader services; Tape recorders; Tutors. **Career services:** Alumni services; Career assessment; Career/job search classes; Internships.

FACILITIES

Housing: Apartments for married students; Apartments for single students; Coed dorms; Fraternity/sorority housing; Special housing for disabled students; 80% of campus accessible to physically disabled. **Special Academic Facilities/Equipment:** Archeology museum; instructional media center; biology, chemistry, physics, and psychology labs; property on the Gulf of Mexico for marine and ecology research. **Campus Network:** 100% of classrooms, 100% of dorms, 100% of student union, 100% of libraries, 100% of dining areas, 100% of common outdoor areas have wireless network access.

CAMPUS LIFE

Environment: City. **Activities:** Campus Ministries; Choral groups; Concert band; Dance; Drama/theater; International Student Organization; Jazz band; Music ensembles; Musical theater; Pep band; Radio station; Student government; Student newspaper; Symphony orchestra; Television station. 154 registered organizations, 7 honor societies, 10 religious organizations, 9 fraternities, 7 sororities on campus. **Athletics (Intercollegiate):** *Men:* baseball, basketball, cross-country, golf, soccer, tennis. *Women:* basketball, cross-country, golf, soccer, softball, tennis, volleyball. **On-Campus Highlights:** The Commons (has cafeteria and bookstore). **Environmental Initiatives:** All new buildings must be at least L.E.E.D Silver Certified.

ADMISSIONS

Freshman Academic Profile: Average high school GPA 3.6. 14% in top 10% of high school class, 38% in top 25% of high school class, 74% in top 50% of high school class. **Test Scores:** SAT Math middle 50% range 460–550. SAT EBRW middle 50% range 470–570. ACT middle 50% range 20–26. **Basis for Candidate Selection:** *Very important factors include:* rigor of secondary school record, academic GPA, standardized test scores. *Other factors include:* application essay, recommendation(s), extracurricular activities, talent/ability, character/personal qualities, first generation, alumni/ae relation, geographical residence, state residency, volunteer work, work experience. **Freshman Admission Requirements:** High school diploma is required and GED is accepted *Academic units required:* 4 English, 3 math, 3 science, 2 science labs, 2 foreign language, 3 social studies, 4 academic electives. **Freshman Admission Statistics:** 7,104 applied, 42% admitted, 44% enrolled. **Transfer Admission Requirements:** College transcript(s). Minimum college GPA of 2.0 required. Lowest grade transferable D. **General Admission Information:** Application fee $30. Regular application deadline 6/30. Non-fall registration accepted. Admission may be deferred for a maximum of one year.

COSTS AND FINANCIAL AID

Annual in-state tuition $6,360. Annual out-of-state tuition $19,241. Room and board $9,912. Average book and supplies expense $1,200. **Required Forms and Deadlines:** FAFSA. **Notification of Awards:** Applicants will be notified of awards on a rolling basis beginning 3/1. **Types of Aid:** *Need-based scholarships/grants:* College/university scholarship or grant aid from institutional funds; Federal Pell; Private scholarships; SEOG; State scholarships/grants. *Loans:* Direct PLUS loans; Direct Subsidized Stafford Loans; Direct Unsubsidized Stafford Loans. **Student Employment:** Federal Work-Study Program available. Institutional employment available. **Financial Aid Statistics:** 92% needy freshmen, 85% needy undergrads receive need-based scholarship or grant aid. 3% freshmen, 2% undergrads receive non-need-based scholarship or grant aid. 61% freshmen, 65% undergrads receive need-based self-help aid. 2% freshmen, 2% undergrads receive athletic scholarships. **Criteria awarding aid:** *Need-based:* Academics, Leadership *Non-need-based:* Academics, Alumni affiliation, Art, Athletics, Leadership, Minority status, Music/drama.

UNIVERSITY OF WEST GEORGIA

1601 Maple Street, Carrollton, GA 30118
Phone: 678-839-5600 **Financial Aid Phone:** 678-839-6421
E-mail: admiss@westga.edu **CEEB Code:** 5900
Fax: 678-839-4747 **Website:** www.westga.edu **ACT Code:** 878

This public school was founded in 1906. It has a 645 acre campus.

RATINGS
Admissions Selectivity Rating: 82   **Fire Safety Rating:** 79   **Green Rating:** 78

STUDENTS AND FACULTY

Enrollment: 10,411. **Student Body:** 64% female, 36% male, 5% out-of-state, 1% international (40 countries represented). Asian 1%, African American 37%, Caucasian 47%, Hispanic 8%, Native American <1%, Pacific Islander <1%, Two or more races 4%, Race unknown 1%.
Retention and Graduation: 69% freshmen return for sophomore year. 19% freshmen graduate within 4 years. **Faculty:** Student/faculty ratio 18:1. 460 full-time faculty, 75% hold PhDs, 22% are members of minority groups, 58% are women. 0% of classes are taught by teaching assistants.

ACADEMICS

Degrees: Bachelor's; Doctoral degree research/scholarship; Master's; Post-bachelor's certificate; Post-master's certificate. **Classes:** Most classes have 10–19 students. Most lab/discussion sessions have 20–29 students. **Special Study Options:** Accelerated program; Cooperative education program; Cross-registration; Distance learning; Double major; Dual enrollment; External degree program; Honors program; Independent study; Internships; Study abroad; Teacher certification program. **Honors programs:** http://www.westga.edu/~honors/. The Donald R. Wagner Honors College welcomes applications from all interested students, including high school seniors and undergraduates already enrolled at the University of West Georgia. The students come from a wide variety of backgrounds and have diverse academic and social interests. Honors students' majors include all academic undergraduate degree programs offered by the University. **Disability Services offered:** Note-taking services; Reader services; Tape recorders; Tutors. **Career services:** Alumni services; Career assessment; Internships.

FACILITIES

Housing: Apartments for married students; Apartments for single students; Coed dorms; Fraternity/sorority housing; Special housing for disabled students; Special housing for international students; Theme housing; Wellness housing 80% of campus accessible to physically disabled. **Special Academic Facilities/Equipment:** Archaeology Lab, West Georgia Observatory, Bruce Bobick Art Gallery, Townsend Center for the Performing Arts, Richard Dangle Theatre, Kathy Cashen Recital Hall, TV studio. **Campus Network:** 100% of classrooms, 100% of dorms, 100% of student union, 100% of libraries, 100% of dining areas, 33% of common outdoor areas, have wireless network access.

CAMPUS LIFE

Environment: City. **Activities:** Campus Ministries; Choral groups; Concert band; Dance; Drama/theater; International Student Organization; Jazz band; Literary magazine; Marching band; Music ensembles; Musical theater; Pep band; Radio station; Student government; Student newspaper; Television station. 160 registered organizations, 6 honor societies, 15 religious organizations, 14 fraternities, 12 sororities, on campus. **Athletics (Intercollegiate):** *Men:* baseball, basketball, cheerleading, cross-country, football, golf. *Women:* basketball, cheerleading, cross-country, golf, soccer, softball, volleyball. **On-Campus Highlights:** Technology Enhanced Learning Center (TLC).

ADMISSIONS

Freshman Academic Profile: Average high school GPA 3.2. 95% from public high schools. **Test Scores:** SAT Math middle 50% range 430–510. ACT middle 50% range 18–22. **Basis for Candidate Selection:** *Very important factors include:* academic GPA, standardized test scores. **Freshman Admission Requirements:** High school diploma is required and GED is accepted *Academic units required:* 4 English, 4 math, 4 science, 2 science labs, 2 foreign language, 1 social studies, 2 history. **Freshman Admission Statistics:** 7,272 applied, 59% admitted, 43% enrolled. **Transfer Admission Requirements:** College transcript(s). Minimum college GPA of 2.0 required. Lowest grade transferable D. **General Admission Information:** Application fee $40. Priority deadline 2/1. Regular application deadline 6/1. Non-fall registration accepted. Admission may be deferred for a maximum of 1 year.

COSTS AND FINANCIAL AID

Annual in-state tuition $5,464. Annual out-of-state tuition $19,282. Room and board $10,340. Required fees $2,024. Average book and supplies expense $1,500. **Required Forms and Deadlines:** FAFSA. **Notification of Awards:** Applicants will be notified of awards on a rolling basis beginning 5/1. **Types of Aid:** *Need-based scholarships/grants:* College/university scholarship or grant aid from institutional funds; Federal Nursing Scholarships; Federal Pell; Private scholarships; SEOG; State scholarships/grants; United Negro College Fund. *Loans:* Direct PLUS loans; Direct Subsidized Stafford Loans; Direct Unsubsidized Stafford Loans. **Student Employment:** Federal Work-Study Program available. Institutional employment available. **Financial Aid Statistics:** 68% needy freshmen, 70% needy undergrads receive need-based scholarship or grant aid. 22% freshmen, 18% undergrads receive non-need-based scholarship or grant aid. 87% freshmen, 88% undergrads receive need-based self-help aid. 4% freshmen, 3% undergrads receive athletic scholarships. 78% undergrads borrow to pay for school. Average cumulative indebtedness $26,376. **Criteria awarding aid:** *Need-based:* Academics, Alumni affiliation, Art, Job skills, Leadership, Minority status, Music/drama, Religious affiliation. *Non-need-based:* Academics, Alumni affiliation, Art, Athletics, Job skills, Leadership, Minority status, Music/drama, Religious affiliation.

UNIVERSITY OF WINDSOR

Office of the Registrar, Windsor, ON N9B3P4
Phone: 519-253-3000 **Financial Aid Phone:** 519-253-3000
E-mail: registrar@uwindsor.ca
Fax: 519-971-3653 **Website:** www.uwindsor.ca

This public school was founded in 1857. It has a 125 acre campus.

RATINGS

Admissions Selectivity Rating: 66   **Fire Safety Rating:** 88   **Green Rating:** 84

STUDENTS AND FACULTY

Enrollment: 12,180. **Student Body:** 52% female, 48% male, international (83 countries represented). Asian, African American, Caucasian, Hispanic, Native American, Pacific Islander, Two or more races, Race unknown.
Faculty: Student/faculty ratio 23:1. 573 full-time faculty, 84% hold PhDs, 0% are members of minority groups, 39% are women.

ACADEMICS

Degrees: Bachelor's; Certificate; Master's. **Most popular majors:** Social Sciences, Other; Engineering, General; Registered Nursing, Nursing Administration, Nursing Research and Clinical Nursing, Other. **Special Study Options:** Cooperative education program; Distance learning; Double major; English as a Second Language (ESL); Exchange student program (domestic); Honors program; Independent study; Internships; Study abroad; Teacher certification program. **Honors programs:** As a comprehensive university we have distinguished ourselves at many levels, with program offerings across a broad array of academic and professional programs. Our Outstanding Scholars Program, entrance and in-course awards, Deans' Honour Rolls, and President's Medal are among the many opportunities that exist to motivate you to fulfill your academic potential. **Disability Services offered:** Note-taking services; Reader services; Tape recorders; Tutors. **Career services:** Alumni network; Alumni services; Career assessment; Career/job search classes; Internships.

FACILITIES

Housing: Apartments for married students; Apartments for single students; Coed dorms; Cooperative housing; Fraternity/sorority housing; Special housing for disabled students; Special housing for international students; 85% of campus accessible to physically disabled. **Special Academic Facilities/Equipment:** Ed Lumley Centre for Engineering Innovation(CEI); C.A.R.E. (Centre for Automotive Research and Education); GLIER (Great Lakes Institute for Environemntal Research); Jackman Dramatic Art Centre (Theatrical space); Bio-Learning Centre (BLC); Biotechnology Laboratory; Odette School of Business; Financial Markets lab; and Entrepreneurship Practice & Innovation Centre (EPICentre). **Campus Network:** 100% of classrooms, 25% of dorms, 100% of student union, 100% of libraries, 100% of dining areas, 100% of common outdoor areas, have wireless network access.

CAMPUS LIFE

Environment: City. **Activities:** Campus Ministries; Choral groups; Dance; Drama/theater; International Student Organization; Jazz band; Literary magazine; Model UN; Music ensembles; Musical theater; Radio station; Student government; Student newspaper; Student-run film society;

Television station. 160 registered organizations, 4 honor societies, 14 religious organizations on campus. **Athletics (Intercollegiate):** *Men:* basketball, cross-country, football, ice hockey, soccer, track/field (outdoor), track/field (indoor), volleyball. *Women:* basketball, cross-country, ice hockey, soccer, track/field (outdoor), track/field (indoor), volleyball. **On-Campus Highlights:** CAW Student Centre. **Environmental Initiatives:** In January 2013, the Environmental Advocate was appointed, the University of Windsor Joined AASHE, and the sustainability website was created. The Environmental Advocate is also a member of the Ontario College and University Sustainability Professionals.

ADMISSIONS

Basis for Candidate Selection: *Very important factors include:* rigor of secondary school record, academic GPA. *Other factors include:* standardized test scores, recommendation(s), interview, extracurricular activities, geographical residence. **Freshman Admission Requirements:** High school diploma is required and GED is not accepted **Freshman Admission Statistics:** 9,470 applied, 74% admitted, 33% enrolled. **Transfer Admission Requirements:** College transcript(s). **General Admission Information:** Application fee $120. Non-fall registration accepted.

COSTS AND FINANCIAL AID

Annual in-state tuition $7,197. Room and board $10,604. **Required Forms and Deadlines:** FAFSA; Institution's own financial aid form. **Notification of Awards:** Applicants will be notified of awards on a rolling basis beginning 8/1. **Types of Aid:** *Loans:* Direct PLUS loans; Direct Subsidized Stafford Loans; Direct Unsubsidized Stafford Loans. **Criteria awarding aid:** *Need-based:* Academics, Athletics, Leadership *Non-need-based:* Academics, Athletics, Leadership.

UNIVERSITY OF WISCONSIN—EAU CLAIRE

105 Garfield Avenue, Eau Claire, WI 54701
Phone: 715-836-5415 **Financial Aid Phone:** 715-836-5606
E-mail: admissions@uwec.edu **CEEB Code:** 1913
Fax: 715-831-4799 **Website:** www.uwec.edu **ACT Code:** 4670

This public school was founded in 1916. It has a 337 acre campus.

RATINGS

Admissions Selectivity Rating: 77   **Fire Safety Rating:** 91   **Green Rating:** 82

STUDENTS AND FACULTY

Enrollment: 9,993. **Student Body:** 62% female, 38% male, 31% out-of-state, 2% international (26 countries represented). Asian 3%, African American 1%, Caucasian 86%, Hispanic 4%, Native American <1%, Pacific Islander <1%, Two or more races 3%, Race unknown <1%.
Retention and Graduation: 82% freshmen return for sophomore year. 40% freshmen graduate within 4 years. 67% freshmen graduate within 6 years. 14% grads go on to further study within 1 year. 19% grads pursue arts and sciences degrees. 6% grads pursue law degrees. 1% grads pursue business degrees. 2% grads pursue medical degrees. **Faculty:** Student/faculty ratio 22:1. 407 full-time faculty, 84% hold PhDs, 21% are members of minority groups, 51% are women. 0% of classes are taught by teaching assistants.

ACADEMICS

Degrees: Associate; Bachelor's; Certificate; Doctoral degree—professional practice; Master's; Post-bachelor's certificate; Post-master's certificate; Transfer Associate. **Classes:** Most classes have 20–29 students. Most lab/discussion sessions have 20–29 students. **Most popular majors:** Registered Nursing/Registered Nurse; Management Information Systems, General; Marketing/Marketing Management, General. **Special Study Options:** Accelerated program; Distance learning; Double major; Dual enrollment; English as a Second Language (ESL); Exchange student program (domestic); External degree program; Honors program; Independent study; Internships; Student-designed major; Study abroad; Teacher certification program. **Honors programs:** University Honors provides an array of high-impact, leadership, and innovative exploration options for students to engage in as they build a program to meet their personal, professional, and academic goals. These personalized pathways include taking innovative Honors colloquia and elective courses, developing independent inquiry/research projects, leadership opportunities, departmental honors programs, Honors experience related to study abroad or NSE, and Senior Honors thesis option. **Combined degree programs:** BA/MA. **Disability Services offered:** Note-taking services; Reader services; Tape recorders; Tutors.

Career services: Alumni network; Alumni services; Career assessment; Career/job search classes; Internships; Regional alumni.

FACILITIES
Housing: Apartments for single students; Coed dorms; Theme housing; Wellness housing; 90% of campus accessible to physically disabled. **Special Academic Facilities/Equipment:** Art Gallery, Greenhouses, Bird Museum, Communication and Journalism Center, Human Development Center, Materials Science Center (wide array of instrumentation for materials imaging, elemental/chemical analysis, physical/mechanical properties analysis, and sample preparation), Natural Preserve, Nursing Clinical Simulation/Skills Lab, Planetarium, Ropes Course, Special Collections (including John L. Buchholz Jazz Library and the Frederick G. and Joan Christopherson Schmidt Robert Frost Collection). **Campus Network:** 100% of classrooms, 100% of dorms, 100% of student union, 100% of libraries, 100% of dining areas, 100% of common outdoor areas have wireless network access.

CAMPUS LIFE
Environment: City. **Activities:** Campus Ministries; Choral groups; Concert band; Dance; Drama/theater; International Student Organization; Jazz band; Literary magazine; Marching band; Model UN; Music ensembles; Musical theater; Opera; Pep band; Radio station; Student government; Student newspaper; Student-run film society; Symphony orchestra; Television station. 230 registered organizations, 17 honor societies, 10 religious organizations, 3 fraternities, 3 sororities on campus. **Athletics (Intercollegiate):** *Men:* basketball, cross-country, diving, football, golf, ice hockey, swimming, tennis, track/field (outdoor), track/field (indoor), wrestling. *Women:* basketball, cross-country, diving, golf, gymnastics, ice hockey, soccer, softball, swimming, tennis, track/field (outdoor), track/field (indoor), volleyball. **On-Campus Highlights:** Chippewa River Footbridge/Garfield Ave. **Environmental Initiatives:** Creation of an energy performance contract to provide $3.4 million in energy conservation measures across campus, including heating and ventilation, lighting, water conservation, etc.

ADMISSIONS
Freshman Academic Profile: Average high school GPA 3.4. 17% in top 10% of high school class, 48% in top 25% of high school class, 88% in top 50% of high school class. **Test Scores:** SAT Math middle 50% range 540–660. SAT EBRW middle 50% range 510–650. ACT middle 50% range 21–26. **Basis for Candidate Selection:** *Very important factors include:* rigor of secondary school record, class rank, academic GPA, standardized test scores. *Important factors include:* application essay, *Other factors include:* recommendation(s), interview, extracurricular activities, talent/ability, character/personal qualities, first generation, geographical residence, state residency, racial/ethnic status, volunteer work, work experience, level of applicant's interest. **Freshman Admission Requirements:** High school diploma is required and GED is accepted. *Academic units required:* 4 English, 3 math, 3 science, 3 social studies, 4 academic electives. *Academic units recommended:* 4 English, 4 math, 4 science, 4 social studies. **Freshman Admission Statistics:** 5,568 applied, 89% admitted, 47% enrolled. **Transfer Admission Requirements:** High school transcript, college transcript(s), statement of good standing from prior institution(s). Minimum college GPA of 2.0 required. Lowest grade transferable D-. **General Admission Information:** Application fee $50. Priority deadline 12/1. Regular application deadline 8/20. Non-fall registration accepted.

COSTS AND FINANCIAL AID
Annual in-state tuition $7,361. Annual out-of-state tuition $15,637. Room and board $8,216. Required fees $1,479. Average book and supplies expense $400. **Required Forms and Deadlines:** FAFSA. **Notification of Awards:** Applicants will be notified of awards on a rolling basis beginning 4/15. **Types of Aid:** *Need-based scholarships/grants:* College/university scholarship or grant aid from institutional funds; Federal Pell; Private scholarships; SEOG; State scholarships/grants. *Loans:* Direct PLUS loans; Direct Subsidized Stafford Loans; Direct Unsubsidized Stafford Loans. **Student Employment:** Federal Work-Study Program available. Institutional employment available. **Financial Aid Statistics:** 83% needy freshmen, 78% needy undergrads receive need-based scholarship or grant aid. 5% freshmen, 3% undergrads receive non-need-based scholarship or grant aid. 90% freshmen, 92% undergrads receive need-based self-help aid. 0% freshmen, 0% undergrads receive athletic scholarships. 82.3% freshmen, 82.9% undergrads receive any aid. 68% undergrads borrow to pay for school. Average cumulative indebtedness $27,129. **Criteria awarding aid:** *Need-based:* Academics, Minority status. *Non-need-based:* Academics, Art, Leadership, Minority status, Music/drama, State/district residency.

UNIVERSITY OF WISCONSIN—GREEN BAY

2420 Nicolet Drive, Green Bay, WI 53411-7001
Phone: 920-465-2111 **Financial Aid Phone:** (920)465-2075
E-mail: admissions@uwgb.edu **CEEB Code:** 1859
Fax: 920-465-5754 **Website:** http://www.uwgb.edu/ **ACT Code:** 4688

This public school was founded in 1965. It has a 700 acre campus.

RATINGS
Admissions Selectivity Rating: 75   **Fire Safety Rating:** 88   **Green Rating:** 74

STUDENTS AND FACULTY
Enrollment: 5,492. **Student Body:** 66% female, 34% male, 9% out-of-state, 1% international (27 countries represented). Asian 3%, African American 2%, Caucasian 84%, Hispanic 5%, Native American 1%, Pacific Islander <1%, Two or more races 3%, Race unknown <1%.
Retention and Graduation: 73% freshmen return for sophomore year. 24% freshmen graduate within 4 years. 49% freshmen graduate within 6 years. 15% grads go on to further study within 1 year. 7% grads pursue arts and sciences degrees. 1% grads pursue law degrees. 3% grads pursue business degrees. 1% grads pursue medical degrees. **Faculty:** Student/faculty ratio 23:1. 182 full-time faculty, 87% hold PhDs, 22% are members of minority groups, 49% are women. 0% of classes are taught by teaching assistants.

ACADEMICS
Degrees: Associate; Bachelor's; Doctoral degree—professional practice; Master's. **Classes:** Most classes have 20–29 students. Most lab/discussion sessions have 20–29 students. **Most popular majors:** Multi-/Interdisciplinary Studies, Other; Accounting and Related Services; Business Administration and Management, General. **Special Study Options:** Cross-registration; Distance learning; Double major; Exchange student program (domestic); External degree program; Independent study; Internships; Liberal arts/career combination; Student-designed major; Study abroad; Teacher certification program. **Disability Services offered:** Note-taking services; Reader services; Tape recorders. **Career services:** Alumni network; Alumni services; Career/job search classes; Internships.

FACILITIES
Housing: Apartments for single students; Coed dorms; 99% of campus accessible to physically disabled. **Special Academic Facilities/Equipment:** 290-acre arboretum, Herbarium, regional Performing Arts Center.

CAMPUS LIFE
Environment: City. **Activities:** Campus Ministries; Choral groups; Concert band; Dance; Drama/theater; International Student Organization; Jazz band; Literary magazine; Music ensembles; Musical theater; Pep band; Radio station; Student government; Student newspaper; Student-run film society; Television station. 106 registered organizations, 7 honor societies, 5 religious organizations, 2 fraternities, 2 sororities on campus. **Athletics (Intercollegiate):** *Men:* basketball, cheerleading, cross-country, diving, golf, skiing (Nordic/cross-country), soccer, swimming, tennis. *Women:* basketball, cheerleading, cross-country, diving, golf, skiing (Nordic/cross-country), soccer, softball, swimming, tennis, volleyball. **On-Campus Highlights:** Weidner Center for Performing Arts. **Environmental Initiatives:** Building integrated photovoltaics in Mary Ann Cofrin Hall (http://www.buildingsolar.com/index.html).

ADMISSIONS
Freshman Academic Profile: Average high school GPA 3.3. 95% from public high schools. **Test Scores:** SAT Math middle 50% range 465–555. SAT EBRW middle 50% range 450–595. ACT middle 50% range 20–25. **Basis for Candidate Selection:** *Very important factors include:* rigor of secondary school record, academic GPA, level of applicant's interest. *Important factors include:* application essay, standardized test scores, extracurricular activities. *Other factors include:* recommendation(s), interview, talent/ability, character/personal qualities, geographical residence, state residency, racial/ethnic status. **Freshman Admission Requirements:** High school diploma is required and GED is accepted *Academic units required:* 4 English, 3 math, 3 science, 1 science labs, 3 social studies, 4 academic electives. *Academic units recommended:* 4 English, 3 math, 3 science, 1 science labs, 2 foreign language, 3 social studies, 4 academic electives. **Freshman Admission Statistics:** 2,151 applied, 95% admitted, 48% enrolled. **Transfer Admission Requirements:** College transcript(s). Minimum college GPA of 2.0 required. Lowest grade transferable D. **General Admission Information:** Application fee $50. Priority deadline 4/15. Non-fall registration accepted. Admission may be deferred for a maximum of 1 year.

COSTS AND FINANCIAL AID

Annual in-state tuition $6,298. Annual out-of-state tuition $14,148. Room and board $7,306. Required fees $1,792. Average book and supplies expense $800. **Required Forms and Deadlines:** FAFSA. **Notification of Awards:** Applicants will be notified of awards on a rolling basis beginning 1/1. **Types of Aid:** *Need-based scholarships/grants:* College/university scholarship or grant aid from institutional funds; Federal Pell; Private scholarships; SEOG; State scholarships/grants. *Loans:* Direct PLUS loans; Direct Subsidized Stafford Loans; Direct Unsubsidized Stafford Loans. **Student Employment:** Federal Work-Study Program available. Institutional employment available. **Financial Aid Statistics:** 80% needy freshmen, 78% needy undergrads receive need-based scholarship or grant aid. 3% freshmen, 5% undergrads receive non-need-based scholarship or grant aid. 76% freshmen, 72% undergrads receive need-based self-help aid. 3% freshmen, 2% undergrads receive athletic scholarships. 88% freshmen, 76% undergrads receive any aid. 72% undergrads borrow to pay for school. Average cumulative indebtedness $22,664. **Criteria awarding aid:** *Non-need-based:* Academics, Art, Athletics, Leadership, Minority status, Music/drama.

UNIVERSITY OF WISCONSIN—LA CROSSE

1725 State Street, La Crosse, WI 54601-3742
Phone: 608-785-8939 **Financial Aid Phone:** 608-785-8604
E-mail: admissions@uwlax.edu **CEEB Code:** 1914
Fax: 608-785-8940 **Website:** www.uwlax.edu **ACT Code:** 4672

This public school was founded in 1909. It has a 120 acre campus.

RATINGS

Admissions Selectivity Rating: 84   Fire Safety Rating: 62   Green Rating: 60*

STUDENTS AND FACULTY

Enrollment: 9,416. **Student Body:** 56% female, 44% male, 18% out-of-state, <1% international (23 countries represented). Asian 2%, African American 1%, Caucasian 89%, Hispanic 4%, Native American <1%, Pacific Islander <1%, Two or more races 3%, Race unknown <1%.
Retention and Graduation: 84% freshmen return for sophomore year. 40% freshmen graduate within 4 years. 69% freshmen graduate within 6 years.
Faculty: Student/faculty ratio 19:1. 468 full-time faculty, 81% hold PhDs, 18% are members of minority groups, 47% are women. 0% of classes are taught by teaching assistants.

ACADEMICS

Degrees: Associate; Bachelor's; Doctoral degree—professional practice; Doctoral degree research/scholarship; Master's; Post-bachelor's certificate; Post-master's certificate. **Classes:** Most classes have 20–29 students. Most lab/discussion sessions have 20–29 students. **Most popular majors:** Biology/Biological Sciences, General; Exercise Science and Kinesiology; Psychology, General. **Special Study Options:** Cross-registration; Distance learning; Double major; Dual enrollment; Exchange student program (domestic); Independent study; Internships; Study abroad; Teacher certification program. **Honors programs:** We do not offer a university honors program. There are honors programs within some majors; individual majors have information about participation in these programs. **Disability Services offered:** Note-taking services; Reader services; Tape recorders. **Career services:** Alumni services; Career assessment; Career/job search classes; Internships.

FACILITIES

Housing: Apartments for single students; Coed dorms; Special housing for disabled students; Special housing for international students; Theme housing; 98% of campus accessible to physically disabled. **Special Academic Facilities/Equipment:** Planetarium, Health Science Center, Mississippi Valley Archaeology Center, River Studies Center, Small Business Development Center. **Campus Network:** 100% of classrooms, 100% of dorms, 100% of libraries, 100% of dining areas have wireless network access.

CAMPUS LIFE

Environment: City. **Activities:** Campus Ministries; Choral groups; Concert band; Dance; Drama/theater; International Student Organization; Jazz band; Literary magazine; Marching band; Model UN; Music ensembles; Musical theater; Radio station; Student government; Student newspaper; Symphony orchestra; Television station. 222 registered organizations, 15 honor societies, 7 religious organizations, 5 fraternities, 3 sororities on campus. **Athletics (Intercollegiate):** *Men:* baseball, basketball, cross-country, diving, football, swimming, tennis, track/field (outdoor), track/field (indoor), wrestling. *Women:*

basketball, cross-country, diving, gymnastics, soccer, softball, swimming, tennis, track/field (outdoor), track/field (indoor), volleyball. **On-Campus Highlights:** The Student Union.

ADMISSIONS

Freshman Academic Profile: 22% in top 10% of high school class, 57% in top 25% of high school class, 96% in top 50% of high school class. **Test Scores:** SAT Math middle 50% range 560–660. SAT EBRW middle 50% range 560–645. ACT middle 50% range 23–27. **Basis for Candidate Selection:** *Very important factors include:* rigor of secondary school record, class rank, academic GPA, standardized test scores. *Important factors include:* application essay, extracurricular activities. *Other factors include:* recommendation(s), interview, talent/ability, character/personal qualities, first generation, alumni/ae relation, geographical residence, state residency, racial/ethnic status, work experience. **Freshman Admission Requirements:** High school diploma is required and GED is accepted *Academic units required:* 4 English, 3 math, 3 science, 2 science labs, 3 social studies, 4 academic electives. *Academic units recommended:* 4 English, 4 math, 4 science, 3 science labs, 3 foreign language, 4 social studies. **Freshman Admission Statistics:** 5,843 applied, 80% admitted, 47% enrolled. **Transfer Admission Requirements:** College transcript(s), statement of good standing from prior institution(s). Minimum college GPA of 3.0 required. Lowest grade transferable D-. **General Admission Information:** Application fee $50. Priority deadline 2/1. Non-fall registration accepted.

COSTS AND FINANCIAL AID

Required Forms and Deadlines: FAFSA. **Types of Aid:** *Need-based scholarships/grants:* College/university scholarship or grant aid from institutional funds; Federal Pell; Private scholarships; SEOG; State scholarships/grants. *Loans:* Direct PLUS loans; Direct Subsidized Stafford Loans; Direct Unsubsidized Stafford Loans. **Student Employment:** Federal Work-Study Program available. Institutional employment available. **Financial Aid Statistics:** 64% needy freshmen, 62% needy undergrads receive need-based scholarship or grant aid. 17% freshmen, 12% undergrads receive non-need-based scholarship or grant aid. 75% freshmen, 78% undergrads receive need-based self-help aid. 0% freshmen, 0% undergrads receive athletic scholarships. 66% undergrads borrow to pay for school. Average cumulative indebtedness $25,926. **Criteria awarding aid:** *Non-need-based:* Academics, Alumni affiliation, Art, Leadership, Minority status, Music/drama.

UNIVERSITY OF WISCONSIN—MADISON

702 West Johnson Street, Suite 101, Madison, WI 53715Å–1007
Phone: 608-262-3961 **Financial Aid Phone:** 608-262-3060
E-mail: onwisconsin@admissions.wisc.edu **CEEB Code:** 1846
Fax: 608-262-7706 **Website:** www.wisc.edu **ACT Code:** 4656

This public school was founded in 1848. It has a 936 acre campus.

RATINGS

Admissions Selectivity Rating: 93   Fire Safety Rating: 83   Green Rating: 86

STUDENTS AND FACULTY

Enrollment: 31,185. **Student Body:** 52% female, 48% male, 38% out-of-state, 10% international (81 countries represented). Asian 7%, African American 2%, Caucasian 69%, Hispanic 5%, Native American <1%, Pacific Islander <1%, Two or more races 4%, Race unknown 2%.
Retention and Graduation: 95% freshmen return for sophomore year. 63% freshmen graduate within 4 years. 88% freshmen graduate within 6 years.
Faculty: Student/faculty ratio 17:1. 2,514 full-time faculty, 91% hold PhDs, 22% are members of minority groups, 42% are women.

ACADEMICS

Degrees: Bachelor's; Doctoral degree—professional practice; Doctoral degree research/scholarship; Master's; Post-bachelor's certificate. **Classes:** Most classes have 10–19 students. Most lab/discussion sessions have 20–29 students. **Most popular majors:** Computer and Information Sciences, General; Biology/Biological Sciences, General; Economics, General. **Special Study Options:** Accelerated program; Cooperative education program; Distance learning; Double major; Dual enrollment; English as a Second Language (ESL);

Exchange student program (domestic); Honors program; Independent study; Internships; Liberal arts/career combination; Student-designed major; Study abroad; Teacher certification program. **Disability Services offered:** Note-taking services; Reader services; Tape recorders; Tutors. **Career services:** Alumni network; Alumni services; Career assessment; Career/job search classes; Internships.

FACILITIES

Housing: Coed dorms; Cooperative housing; Fraternity/sorority housing; Men's dorms; Theme housing; Wellness housing; Women's dorms 90% of campus accessible to physically disabled. **Special Academic Facilities/ Equipment:** Art, physics, and geology museums; nuclear reactor; arboretum; botanical gardens; observatory; campus dairy store (campus-made ice cream and cheese); american indian burial mounds. **Campus Network:** 100% of classrooms, 100% of dorms, 100% of student union, 100% of libraries, 100% of dining areas, 100% of common outdoor areas, have wireless network access.

CAMPUS LIFE

Environment: City. **Activities:** Choral groups; Concert band; Dance; Drama/ theater; International Student Organization; Jazz band; Literary magazine; Marching band; Music ensembles; Musical theater; Opera; Pep band; Radio station; Student government; Student newspaper; Student-run film society; Symphony orchestra; Television station; Yearbook. 986 registered organizations, 27 honor societies, 26 fraternities, 11 sororities on campus. **Athletics (Intercollegiate):** *Men:* basketball, cheerleading, crew/rowing, cross-country, football, golf, ice hockey, soccer, swimming, tennis, track/ field (outdoor), wrestling. *Women:* basketball, cheerleading, crew/rowing, cross-country, golf, ice hockey, soccer, softball, swimming, tennis, track/field (outdoor), volleyball. **On-Campus Highlights:** Allen Centennial Gardens. **Environmental Initiatives:** Our conservation efforts in the last four years have reduced campus energy consumption by over 1 trillion BTUs and water consumption by 178,000,000 gallons annually.

ADMISSIONS

Freshman Academic Profile: Average high school GPA 3.9. 57% in top 10% of high school class, 90% in top 25% of high school class, 100% in top 50% of high school class. **Test Scores:** SAT Math middle 50% range 680–780. SAT EBRW middle 50% range 630–710. ACT middle 50% range 27–32. **Basis for Candidate Selection:** *Very important factors include:* rigor of secondary school record, application essay. *Important factors include:* academic GPA, standardized test scores, state residency. *Other factors include:* class rank, recommendation(s), extracurricular activities, talent/ability, character/personal qualities, first generation, racial/ethnic status, volunteer work, work experience, level of applicant's interest. **Freshman Admission Requirements:** High school diploma is required and GED is accepted *Academic units required:* 4 English, 4 math, 3 science, 3 foreign language, 3 social studies, 2 unit from above areas or other academic areas. *Academic units recommended:* 4 English, 4 math, 4 science, 2 science labs, 4 foreign language, 4 social studies, 2 unit from above areas or other academic areas. **Freshman Admission Statistics:** 43,921 applied, 53% admitted, 32% enrolled. **Transfer Admission Requirements:** High school transcript, college transcript(s), essay or personal statement. Lowest grade transferable D. **General Admission Information:** Application fee $60. Regular application deadline 2/1. Non-fall registration accepted. Admission may be deferred for a maximum of 1 year.

COSTS AND FINANCIAL AID

Annual in-state tuition $9,273. Annual out-of-state tuition $36,333. Room and board $11,114. Average book and supplies expense $1,200. **Required Forms and Deadlines:** FAFSA. **Notification of Awards:** Applicants will be notified of awards on a rolling basis beginning 3/1. **Types of Aid:** *Need-based scholarships/ grants:* College/university scholarship or grant aid from institutional funds; Federal Pell; Private scholarships; SEOG; State scholarships/grants. *Loans:* Direct PLUS loans; Direct Subsidized Stafford Loans; Direct Unsubsidized Stafford Loans. **Student Employment:** Federal Work-Study Program available. Institutional employment available. **Financial Aid Statistics:** 75% needy freshmen, 76% needy undergrads receive need-based scholarship or grant aid. 10% freshmen, 9% undergrads receive non-need-based scholarship or grant aid. 71% freshmen, 72% undergrads receive need-based self-help aid. 1% freshmen, 1% undergrads receive athletic scholarships. Average cumulative indebtedness $27,973. **Criteria awarding aid:** *Need-based:* Academics, Alumni affiliation, Minority status. *Non-need-based:* Academics, Alumni affiliation, Art, Athletics, Leadership, Minority status, Music/drama, State/district residency.

UNIVERSITY OF WISCONSIN—MILWAUKEE

Department of Admissions and Recruitment, Milwaukee, WI 53211
Phone: 414-229-2222 **Financial Aid Phone:** 414-229-4541
E-mail: uwmlook@uwm.edu **CEEB Code:** 1473
Fax: 414-229-6940 **Website:** www4.uwm.edu **ACT Code:** 4658

This public school was founded in 1956. It has a 93 acre campus.

RATINGS
Admissions Selectivity Rating: 70   **Fire Safety Rating:** 97   **Green Rating:** 93

STUDENTS AND FACULTY
Enrollment: 20,000. **Student Body:** 51% female, 49% male, 11% out-of-state, 4% international (88 countries represented). Asian 7%, African American 8%, Caucasian 67%, Hispanic 10%, Native American <1%, Pacific Islander <1%, Two or more races 4%, Race unknown <1%.
Retention and Graduation: 72% freshmen return for sophomore year.
Faculty: Student/faculty ratio 19:1. 1,010 full-time faculty, 73% hold PhDs, 22% are members of minority groups, 46% are women.

ACADEMICS
Degrees: Bachelor's; Certificate; Doctoral degree—professional practice; Doctoral degree research/scholarship; Master's; Post-bachelor's certificate; Post-master's certificate. **Classes:** Most classes have 20–29 students. Most lab/ discussion sessions have 10–19 students. **Most popular majors:** Education, General; Marketing/Marketing Management, General; Psychology, General. **Special Study Options:** Accelerated program; Cooperative education program; Cross-registration; Distance learning; Double major; Dual enrollment; English as a Second Language (ESL); External degree program; Honors program; Independent study; Internships; Liberal arts/career combination; Student-designed major; Study abroad; Teacher certification program; Weekend college. **Honors programs:** UWM Honors College. **Combined degree programs:** BA/MA; BA/MEng. **Disability Services offered:** Note-taking services; Reader services; Tape recorders; Tutors. **Career services:** Alumni network; Alumni services; Career assessment; Career/job search classes; Internships.

FACILITIES
Housing: Apartments for single students; Coed dorms; Special housing for disabled students. **Special Academic Facilities/Equipment:** Art and geology museums, childhood education center, foreign language resource center, Great Lakes research facility and environmental studies field station, planetarium. **Campus Network:** 100% of classrooms, 100% of dorms, 100% of student union, 100% of libraries, 100% of dining areas have wireless network access.

CAMPUS LIFE
Environment: Metropolis. **Activities:** Campus Ministries; Choral groups; Concert band; Dance; Drama/theater; International Student Organization; Jazz band; Literary magazine; Model UN; Music ensembles; Musical theater; Opera; Pep band; Radio station; Student government; Student newspaper; Student-run film society; Symphony orchestra. 296 registered organizations, 4 honor societies, 18 religious organizations, 10 fraternities, 7 sororities on campus. **Athletics (Intercollegiate):** *Men:* baseball, basketball, cross-country, diving, soccer, swimming, track/field (outdoor). *Women:* basketball, cross-country, soccer, swimming, tennis, track/field (outdoor), volleyball. **On-Campus Highlights:** The Grind Coffee Shop.

ADMISSIONS
Freshman Academic Profile: Average high school GPA 3.1. 9% in top 10% of high school class, 19% in top 25% of high school class, 67% in top 50% of high school class. **Basis for Candidate Selection:** *Very important factors include:* rigor of secondary school record, academic GPA, standardized test scores. *Important factors include:* application essay, *Other factors include:* class rank, recommendation(s), interview, extracurricular activities, talent/ability, character/personal qualities, first generation, racial/ethnic status, volunteer work, work experience. **Freshman Admission Requirements:** High school diploma is required and GED is accepted. *Academic units required:* 4 English, 3 math, 3 science, 1 science labs, 3 social studies, 4 academic electives. *Academic units recommended:* 4 English, 4 math, 4 science, 1 science labs, 2 foreign language, 4 social studies, 4 academic electives. **Freshman Admission Statistics:** 9,834 applied, 72% admitted, 44% enrolled. **Transfer Admission Requirements:** High school transcript, college transcript(s). Minimum college GPA of 2.0 required. Lowest grade transferable D-. **General Admission Information:** Application fee $50. Priority deadline 3/1. Regular application deadline 8/11. Non-fall registration accepted. Admission may be deferred for a maximum of 1 year.

COSTS AND FINANCIAL AID
Annual in-state tuition $8,090. Annual out-of-state tuition $9,685. Room and board $10,560. Required fees $1,444. Average book and supplies expense $800. **Required Forms and Deadlines:** FAFSA. **Notification of Awards:** Applicants will be notified of awards on a rolling basis beginning 3/15. **Types of Aid:** *Need-based scholarships/grants:* College/university scholarship or grant aid from institutional funds; Federal Pell; Private scholarships; SEOG; State scholarships/grants. *Loans:* Direct PLUS loans; Direct Subsidized Stafford Loans; Direct Unsubsidized Stafford Loans. **Student Employment:** Federal Work-Study Program available. Institutional employment available. **Financial Aid Statistics:** 58% needy freshmen, 57% needy undergrads receive need-based scholarship or grant aid. 28% freshmen, 17% undergrads receive non-need-based scholarship or grant aid. 76% freshmen, 65% undergrads receive need-based self-help aid. 1% freshmen, 4% undergrads receive athletic scholarships. 90% freshmen, 92% undergrads receive any aid. 76% undergrads borrow to pay for school. Average cumulative indebtedness $36,945. **Criteria awarding aid:** *Need-based:* Academics, Music/drama *Non-need-based:* Academics, Art, Athletics, Leadership.

UNIVERSITY OF WISCONSIN—OSHKOSH

Dempsey Hall 135, Oshkosh, WI 54901
Phone: 920-424-0202 **Financial Aid Phone:** 920-424-4025
E-mail: oshadmuw@uwosh.edu **CEEB Code:** 1916
Fax: 920-424-1098 **Website:** http://www.uwosh.edu/home **ACT Code:** 4674

This public school was founded in 1871. It has a 192 acre campus.

RATINGS
Admissions Selectivity Rating: 81   **Fire Safety Rating:** 60*   **Green Rating:** 98

STUDENTS AND FACULTY
Enrollment: 10,771. **Student Body:** 57% female, 43% male, 3% out-of-state, 1% international (32 countries represented). Asian 4%, African American 2%, Caucasian 88%, Hispanic 3%, Native American 1%, Pacific Islander <1%, Two or more races 1%, Race unknown <1%.
Retention and Graduation: 75% freshmen return for sophomore year.
Faculty: Student/faculty ratio 22:1. 416 full-time faculty, 84% hold PhDs, 12% are members of minority groups, 47% are women. 0% of classes are taught by teaching assistants.

ACADEMICS
Degrees: Associate; Bachelor's; Certificate; Master's. **Classes:** Most classes have 20–29 students. Most lab/discussion sessions have 20–29 students. **Most popular majors:** Business/Commerce, General; Elementary Education and Teaching; Registered Nursing, Nursing Administration, Nursing Research and Clinical Nursing, Other. **Special Study Options:** Accelerated program; Cooperative education program; Distance learning; Double major; Dual enrollment; English as a Second Language (ESL); Exchange student program (domestic); Honors program; Independent study; Internships; Liberal arts/career combination; Student-designed major; Study abroad; Teacher certification program; Weekend college. **Disability Services offered:** Note-taking services; Reader services; Tape recorders; Tutors. **Career services:** Alumni network; Career assessment; Career/job search classes; Internships.

FACILITIES
Housing: Coed dorms; Fraternity/sorority housing; Men's dorms; Special housing for disabled students; Theme housing; Women's dorms. **Special Academic Facilities/Equipment:** Art gallery, ceramics lab, aquatic research laboratory, electron microscope.

CAMPUS LIFE
Environment: City. **Activities:** Campus Ministries; Choral groups; Concert band; Dance; Drama/theater; International Student Organization; Jazz band; Literary magazine; Model UN; Music ensembles; Musical theater; Pep band; Radio station; Student government; Student newspaper; Student-run film society; Television station. 175 registered organizations, 15 honor societies, 6 religious organizations, 8 fraternities, 5 sororities on campus. **Athletics (Intercollegiate):** *Men:* baseball, basketball, cross-country, diving, football, soccer, swimming, tennis, track/field (outdoor), track/field (indoor), wrestling. *Women:* basketball, cross-country, diving, golf, gymnastics, soccer, softball, swimming, tennis, track/field (outdoor), track/field (indoor), volleyball. **On-Campus Highlights:** Sage Hall—LEEDS certification. **Environmental Initiatives:** Leadership in adopting renewable energy, from 2003 as the largest purchaser of renewable electricity in

the State of Wisconsin to the recent construction of the first commercial-scale dry anerobic biodigester in the Western Hemisphere.

ADMISSIONS
Freshman Academic Profile: Average high school GPA 3.3. 10% in top 10% of high school class, 37% in top 25% of high school class, 84% in top 50% of high school class. 90% from public high schools. **Basis for Candidate Selection:** *Very important factors include:* rigor of secondary school record, class rank, academic GPA, standardized test scores. *Important factors include:* application essay, recommendation(s), first generation. *Other factors include:* interview, extracurricular activities, talent/ability, character/personal qualities, alumni/ae relation, volunteer work, work experience. **Freshman Admission Requirements:** High school diploma is required and GED is accepted. *Academic units required:* 4 English, 3 math, 3 science, 3 science labs, 3 social studies, 2 history, 4 academic electives. *Academic units recommended:* 4 math, 4 science, 4 science labs, 2 foreign language, 4 social studies, 1 history, 1 visual/performing arts. **Freshman Admission Statistics:** 6,052 applied, 68% admitted, 44% enrolled. **Transfer Admission Requirements:** College transcript(s). Minimum college GPA of 2.50 required. Lowest grade transferable D. **General Admission Information:** Application fee $44. Non-fall registration accepted.

COSTS AND FINANCIAL AID
Annual in-state tuition $7,360. Annual out-of-state tuition $14,934. Room and board $6,926. Average book and supplies expense $1,000. **Required Forms and Deadlines:** FAFSA. **Notification of Awards:** Applicants will be notified of awards on or about 4/15. **Types of Aid:** *Need-based scholarships/grants:* College/university scholarship or grant aid from institutional funds; Federal Nursing Scholarships; Federal Pell; Private scholarships; SEOG; State scholarships/grants; United Negro College Fund. *Loans:* Direct PLUS loans; Direct Subsidized Stafford Loans; Direct Unsubsidized Stafford Loans. **Student Employment:** Federal Work-Study Program available. Institutional employment available. **Financial Aid Statistics:** 53% needy freshmen, 55% needy undergrads receive need-based scholarship or grant aid. 34% freshmen, 20% undergrads receive non-need-based scholarship or grant aid. 28% freshmen, 20% undergrads receive need-based self-help aid. 0% freshmen, 0% undergrads receive athletic scholarships. **Criteria awarding aid:** *Need-based:* Academics, Art, Job skills, Leadership, Minority status, Music/drama *Non-need-based:* Academics, Art, Job skills, Leadership, Minority status, Music/drama, State/district residency.

UNIVERSITY OF WISCONSIN—PLATTEVILLE

1 University Plaza, Platteville, WI 53818
Phone: (608)342-1125 **Financial Aid Phone:** 608-342-6188
E-mail: admit@uwplatt.edu **CEEB Code:** 1917
Fax: (608)342-1122 **Website:** www.uwplatt.edu **ACT Code:** 4676

This public school was founded in 1866. It has a 820 acre campus.

RATINGS
Admissions Selectivity Rating: 85   **Fire Safety Rating:** 78   **Green Rating:** 89

STUDENTS AND FACULTY
Enrollment: 7,427. **Student Body:** 33% female, 67% male, 24% out-of-state, 1% international (10 countries represented). Asian 1%, African American 1%, Caucasian 89%, Hispanic 3%, Native American <1%, Pacific Islander <1%, Two or more races 3%, Race unknown 1%.
Retention and Graduation: 79% freshmen return for sophomore year. 19% freshmen graduate within 4 years. 53% freshmen graduate within 6 years.
Faculty: Student/faculty ratio 21:1. 316 full-time faculty, 75% hold PhDs, 22% are members of minority groups, 37% are women. 0% of classes are taught by teaching assistants.

ACADEMICS
Degrees: Associate; Bachelor's; Certificate; Master's; Post-bachelor's certificate. **Classes:** Most classes have 20–29 students. Most lab/discussion sessions have 20–29 students. **Most popular majors:** Mechanical Engineering; Criminal Justice/Safety Studies; Business Administration and Management, General. **Special Study Options:** Cooperative education program; Distance learning; Double major; Dual enrollment; Exchange student program (domestic); External degree program; Honors program; Independent study; Internships; Study abroad; Teacher certification program. **Honors programs:** N/A. **Disability Services offered:** Note-taking services; Reader services; Tape recorders; Tutors. **Career services:** Alumni services.

FACILITIES

Housing: Apartments for single students; Coed dorms; Men's dorms; Special housing for disabled students; Wellness housing; Women's dorms; 95% of campus accessible to physically disabled. **Special Academic Facilities/ Equipment:** Electron microscope; Nohr Art Gallery; Southwest Wisconsin Room/Archives; North American Manx Museum; Forensic Investigation Crime Scene House; Pioneer Farm. **Campus Network:** 100% of classrooms, 100% of dorms, 100% of student union, 100% of libraries, 100% of dining areas, 100% of common outdoor areas have wireless network access.

CAMPUS LIFE

Environment: Village. **Activities:** Campus Ministries; Choral groups; Concert band; Dance; Drama/theater; International Student Organization; Jazz band; Literary magazine; Marching band; Music ensembles; Musical theater; Pep band; Radio station; Student government; Student newspaper; Symphony orchestra; Television station. 270 registered organizations, 12 honor societies, 7 religious organizations, 9 fraternities, 6 sororities on campus. **On-Campus Highlights:** Markee Pioneer Student Center.

ADMISSIONS

Freshman Academic Profile: 13% in top 10% of high school class, 37% in top 25% of high school class, 76% in top 50% of high school class. 94% from public high schools. **Test Scores:** SAT Math middle 50% range 605–655. SAT EBRW middle 50% range 542–688. ACT middle 50% range 20–25. **Basis for Candidate Selection:** *Very important factors include:* rigor of secondary school record, class rank, academic GPA, application essay, standardized test scores, talent/ability, character/personal qualities, level of applicant's interest. *Important factors include:* extracurricular activities, first generation, alumni/ae relation, volunteer work. *Other factors include:* recommendation(s), geographical residence, racial/ethnic status. **Freshman Admission Requirements:** High school diploma is required and GED is accepted *Academic units required:* 4 English, 3 math, 3 science, 2 science labs, 3 social studies, 4 academic electives. **Freshman Admission Statistics:** 3,711 applied, 79% admitted, 48% enrolled. **General Admission Information:** Application fee $50. Non-fall registration accepted.

COSTS AND FINANCIAL AID

Annual in-state tuition $6,298. Annual out-of-state tuition $14,148. Room and board $7,160. Required fees $1,245. Average book and supplies expense $550. **Required Forms and Deadlines:** FAFSA. **Types of Aid:** *Need-based scholarships/grants:* State scholarships/grants.

UNIVERSITY OF WISCONSIN—RIVER FALLS

410 S. Third Street, River Falls, WI 54022
Phone: 715-425-3500 **Financial Aid Phone:** 715-425-3141
E-mail: admissions@uwrf.edu **CEEB Code:** 1918
Website: www.uwrf.edu **ACT Code:** 4678

This public school was founded in 1874. It has a 226 acre campus.

RATINGS

Admissions Selectivity Rating: 83   **Fire Safety Rating:** 77   **Green Rating:** 97

STUDENTS AND FACULTY

Enrollment: 5,399. **Student Body:** 64% female, 36% male, 50% out-of-state, 1% international (15 countries represented). Asian 3%, African American 1%, Caucasian 88%, Hispanic 4%, Native American <1%, Pacific Islander <1%, Two or more races 3%, Race unknown <1%.
Retention and Graduation: 74% freshmen return for sophomore year. 37% freshmen graduate within 4 years. 58% freshmen graduate within 6 years. 8% grads go on to further study within 1 year. 3% grads pursue arts and sciences degrees. 0% grads pursue law degrees. <1% grads pursue business degrees. 3% grads pursue medical degrees. **Faculty:** Student/faculty ratio 21:1. 221 full-time faculty, 86% hold PhDs, 15% are members of minority groups, 43% are women. 0% of classes are taught by teaching assistants.

ACADEMICS

Degrees: Associate; Bachelor's; Certificate; Master's; Post-bachelor's certificate; Post-master's certificate. **Classes:** Most classes have 20–29 students. Most lab/discussion sessions have 10–19 students. **Most popular majors:** Animal Sciences, General; Elementary Education and Teaching; Business Administration and Management, General. **Special Study Options:** Accelerated program; Cooperative education program; Cross-registration;

Distance learning; Double major; Dual enrollment; English as a Second Language (ESL); External degree program; Honors program; Independent study; Internships; Study abroad; Teacher certification program. **Honors programs:** The Honors Program at UWRF provides an academic and social community for students who have outstanding records of academic achievement and who seize opportunities to pursue knowledge in a variety of subjects, interact socially with like-minded students, engage with their communities, and develop leadership skills and leadership potential. **Disability Services offered:** Note-taking services; Reader services; Tape recorders; Tutors. **Career services:** Alumni network; Alumni services; Career assessment; Career/ job search classes; Internships; Regional alumni.

FACILITIES

Housing: Coed dorms; Special housing for disabled students; Theme housing; Women's dorms; 100% of campus accessible to physically disabled. **Special Academic Facilities/Equipment:** Art Gallery, Campus Farm, Campus Greenhouse, C.H.I.L.D. Child Care Center, Digital Dome Planetarium, Falcon Center, GIS Lab, Tissue and Cellular Innovation Center, University Archives and Area Research Center, University Preschool, University Theatre, UWRF Observatory, William Abbott Concert Hall, WRFW-FM radio station, Writing Center. **Campus Network:** 100% of classrooms, 100% of dorms, 100% of student union, 100% of libraries, 100% of dining areas, 100% of common outdoor areas have wireless network access.

CAMPUS LIFE

Environment: Village. **Activities:** Campus Ministries; Choral groups; Concert band; Dance; Drama/theater; International Student Organization; Jazz band; Literary magazine; Model UN; Music ensembles; Musical theater; Pep band; Radio station; Student government; Student newspaper; Symphony orchestra; Television station. 144 registered organizations, 4 honor societies, 8 religious organizations, 3 fraternities, 5 sororities on campus. **Athletics (Intercollegiate):** *Men:* basketball, cross-country, football, ice hockey, swimming, track/field (outdoor), track/field (indoor). *Women:* basketball, cross-country, golf, ice hockey, soccer, softball, swimming, tennis, track/field (outdoor), track/field (indoor), volleyball. **On-Campus Highlights:** University Center student center.

ADMISSIONS

Freshman Academic Profile: Average high school GPA 3.4. 9% in top 10% of high school class, 31% in top 25% of high school class, 73% in top 50% of high school class. 85% from public high schools. **Test Scores:** SAT Math middle 50% range 500–620. SAT EBRW middle 50% range 520–620. ACT middle 50% range 20–25. **Basis for Candidate Selection:** *Very important factors include:* rigor of secondary school record, class rank, standardized test scores. *Important factors include:* academic GPA, application essay, *Other factors include:* recommendation(s), extracurricular activities, talent/ability, character/ personal qualities, first generation, racial/ethnic status, volunteer work, work experience. **Freshman Admission Requirements:** High school diploma is required and GED is accepted. *Academic units required:* 4 English, 3 math, 3 science, 3 social studies, 4 academic electives. *Academic units recommended:* 4 English, 4 math, 4 science, 1 science labs, 2 foreign language, 4 social studies, 4 academic electives. **Freshman Admission Statistics:** 2,969 applied, 79% admitted, 51% enrolled. **Transfer Admission Requirements:** College transcript(s), statement of good standing from prior institution(s). Minimum college GPA of 2.6 required. Lowest grade transferable D. **General Admission Information:** Application fee $50. Non-fall registration accepted. Admission may be deferred for a maximum of 1 year.

COSTS AND FINANCIAL AID

Annual in-state tuition $6,428. Annual out-of-state tuition $14,001. Room and board $6,600. Required fees $1,609. Average book and supplies expense $400. **Required Forms and Deadlines:** FAFSA. **Notification of Awards:** Applicants will be notified of awards on a rolling basis beginning 2/2. **Types of Aid:** *Need-based scholarships/grants:* College/university scholarship or grant aid from institutional funds; Federal Pell; Private scholarships; SEOG; State scholarships/ grants. *Loans:* Direct PLUS loans; Direct Subsidized Stafford Loans; Direct Unsubsidized Stafford Loans. **Student Employment:** Federal Work-Study Program available. Institutional employment available. **Financial Aid Statistics:** 56% needy freshmen, 58% needy undergrads receive need-based scholarship or grant aid. 39% freshmen, 28% undergrads receive non-need-based scholarship or grant aid. 69% freshmen, 74% undergrads receive need-based self-help aid. 0% freshmen, 0% undergrads receive athletic scholarships. 85% freshmen, 79% undergrads receive any aid. 65% undergrads borrow to pay for school. Average cumulative indebtedness $26,814. **Criteria awarding aid:** *Need-based:* Academics, Art, Leadership, Minority status, Music/drama *Non-need-based:* Academics, Art, Leadership, Minority status, Music/drama, State/district residency.

UNIVERSITY OF WISCONSIN—STEVENS POINT

1108 Fremont St., Stevens Point, WI 54481
Phone: 715-346-2441 **Financial Aid Phone:** 715-346-4771
E-mail: admiss@uwsp.edu **CEEB Code:** 1919
Fax: 715-346-3296 **Website:** www.uwsp.edu **ACT Code:** 4680

This public school was founded in 1894. It has a 335 acre campus.

RATINGS
Admissions Selectivity Rating: 70   **Fire Safety Rating:** 79   **Green Rating:** 97

STUDENTS AND FACULTY
Enrollment: 7,310. **Student Body:** 53% female, 47% male, 13% out-of-state, 1% international (37 countries represented). Asian 3%, African American 2%, Caucasian 87%, Hispanic 4%, Native American <1%, Pacific Islander <1%, Two or more races 2%, Race unknown 1%.
Retention and Graduation: 72% freshmen return for sophomore year. 33% freshmen graduate within 4 years. 65% freshmen graduate within 6 years. 14% grads go on to further study within 1 year. 20% grads pursue arts and sciences degrees. <1% grads pursue law degrees. 1% grads pursue business degrees. <1% grads pursue medical degrees. **Faculty:** Student/faculty ratio 18:1. 391 full-time faculty, 73% hold PhDs, 13% are members of minority groups, 47% are women. 0% of classes are taught by teaching assistants.

ACADEMICS
Degrees: Associate; Bachelor's; Doctoral degree—professional practice; Master's. **Classes:** Most classes have 20–29 students. Most lab/discussion sessions have 20–29 students. **Most popular majors:** Natural Resources/Conservation, General; Biological and Physical Sciences; Business/Commerce, General. **Special Study Options:** Accelerated program; Distance learning; Double major; Dual enrollment; English as a Second Language (ESL); Honors program; Independent study; Internships; Student-designed major; Study abroad; Teacher certification program. **Disability Services offered:** Note-taking services; Reader services; Tape recorders; Tutors. **Career services:** Alumni network; Alumni services; Career assessment; Career/job search classes; Internships; Regional alumni.

FACILITIES
Housing: Coed dorms; Men's dorms; Special housing for international students; Theme housing; Wellness housing; Women's dorms; 100% of campus accessible to physically disabled. **Special Academic Facilities/Equipment:** Art galleries, costume and goblet collections, museum of natural history, early childhood study institute, communicative disorders center, map center, observatory, planetarium, Foucault pendulum, nature preserve, environmental station, groundwater center, herbarium, aviary, wellness institute.

CAMPUS LIFE
Environment: Town. **Activities:** Campus Ministries; Choral groups; Dance; Drama/theater; International Student Organization; Jazz band; Model UN; Music ensembles; Musical theater; Opera; Pep band; Radio station; Student government; Student newspaper; Student-run film society; Symphony orchestra; Television station. 185 registered organizations, 11 honor societies, 10 religious organizations, 5 fraternities, 3 sororities on campus. **Athletics (Intercollegiate): Men:** baseball, basketball, cross-country, diving, football, ice hockey, swimming, track/field (outdoor), wrestling. **Women:** basketball, cross-country, diving, golf, ice hockey, soccer, softball, swimming, tennis, track/field (outdoor), volleyball. **On-Campus Highlights:** University Center/Brewhouse. **Environmental Initiatives:** In December 2012, UWSP hired an energy service company (ESCO) through the WI Performance Contracting Program. Work was completed in 2016 so we are currently evaluating results. In 2012, we received LEED-NC Gold for a residence hall. We are in the final construction stages of a science building that was built to LEED-Gold equivalency.

ADMISSIONS
Freshman Academic Profile: Average high school GPA 3.4. 10% in top 10% of high school class, 24% in top 25% of high school class, 74% in top 50% of high school class. **Test Scores:** ACT middle 50% range 20–25. **Basis for Candidate Selection:** *Very important factors include:* rigor of secondary school record, class rank, academic GPA, standardized test scores. *Important factors include:* application essay, recommendation(s), talent/ability, first generation. *Other factors include:* interview, extracurricular activities, character/personal qualities, alumni/ae relation, geographical residence, state residency, racial/ethnic status, volunteer work, work experience. **Freshman Admission Requirements:** High school diploma is required and GED is accepted.

Academic units required: 4 English, 3 math, 3 science, 3 social studies, 4 academic electives. *Academic units recommended:* 4 English, 4 math, 4 science, 4 social studies, 4 academic electives. **Transfer Admission Requirements:** High school transcript, college transcript(s), statement of good standing from prior institution(s). Minimum college GPA of 2.25 required. Lowest grade transferable D. **General Admission Information:** Application fee $50. Non-fall registration accepted.

COSTS AND FINANCIAL AID
Annual in-state tuition $8,239. Annual out-of-state tuition $16,506. Room and board $5,519. Required fees $1,541. Average book and supplies expense $500. **Required Forms and Deadlines:** FAFSA. **Notification of Awards:** Applicants will be notified of awards on a rolling basis beginning 3/1. **Types of Aid:** *Need-based scholarships/grants:* College/university scholarship or grant aid from institutional funds; Federal Pell; Private scholarships; SEOG; State scholarships/grants. *Loans:* Direct PLUS loans; Direct Subsidized Stafford Loans; Direct Unsubsidized Stafford Loans. **Student Employment:** Federal Work-Study Program available. Institutional employment available. **Financial Aid Statistics:** 71% needy freshmen, 71% needy undergrads receive need-based scholarship or grant aid. 61% freshmen, 62% undergrads receive non-need-based scholarship or grant aid. 90% freshmen, 90% undergrads receive need-based self-help aid. 0% freshmen, 0% undergrads receive athletic scholarships. 65.09% freshmen, 67.96% undergrads receive any aid. 78% undergrads borrow to pay for school. Average cumulative indebtedness $25,030. **Criteria awarding aid:** *Non-need-based:* Academics, Alumni affiliation, Art, Music/drama.

UNIVERSITY OF WISCONSIN—STOUT

Admissions UW-Stout, Menomonie, WI 54751
Phone: 715-232-1232 **Financial Aid Phone:** 715-232-1363
E-mail: admissions@uwstout.edu **CEEB Code:** 1740
Fax: 715-232-1667 **Website:** www.uwstout.edu **ACT Code:** 4652

This public school was founded in 1891. It has a 110 acre campus.

RATINGS
Admissions Selectivity Rating: 76   **Fire Safety Rating:** 62   **Green Rating:** 60*

STUDENTS AND FACULTY
Enrollment: 7,935. **Student Body:** 43% female, 57% male, 33% out-of-state, 2% international (28 countries represented). Asian 3%, African American 2%, Caucasian 87%, Hispanic 1%, Native American <1%, Pacific Islander <1%, Two or more races 4%, Race unknown <1%.
Retention and Graduation: 69% freshmen return for sophomore year. 21% freshmen graduate within 4 years. 54% freshmen graduate within 6 years. 9% grads go on to further study within 1 year. **Faculty:** Student/faculty ratio 20:1. 391 full-time faculty, 76% hold PhDs, 13% are members of minority groups, 45% are women. 0% of classes are taught by teaching assistants.

ACADEMICS
Degrees: Bachelor's; Certificate; Doctoral degree—professional practice; Master's; Post-bachelor's certificate; Post-master's certificate. **Classes:** Most classes have 20–29 students. Most lab/discussion sessions have 20–29 students. **Most popular majors:** Business/Commerce, General; Design and Applied Arts, Other; Hospitality Administration/Management, General. **Special Study Options:** Accelerated program; Cooperative education program; Cross-registration; Distance learning; Double major; Dual enrollment; English as a Second Language (ESL); Exchange student program (domestic); External degree program; Honors program; Independent study; Internships; Study abroad; Teacher certification program. **Honors programs:** The University Honors Program (UHP) is designed to enhance the education of students, challenging them to think in more depth and detail and to provide the opportunity to meet other students while doing so. **Disability Services offered:** Note-taking services; Reader services; Tutors. **Career services:** Alumni services; Career/job search classes; Internships.

FACILITIES
Housing: Apartments for single students; Coed dorms; Special housing for disabled students; Wellness housing 100% of campus accessible to physically disabled. **Special Academic Facilities/Equipment:** Specialized labs support degree programs throughout the campus. Furlong Art Gallery in Micheal's Hall.

CAMPUS LIFE

Environment: Village. **Activities:** Campus Ministries; Choral groups; Concert band; Dance; Drama/theater; International Student Organization; Jazz band; Literary magazine; Marching band; Model UN; Music ensembles; Musical theater; Pep band; Radio station; Student government; Student newspaper; Student-run film society. 120 registered organizations, 1 honor societies, 12 religious organizations, 5 fraternities, 3 sororities on campus. **Athletics (Intercollegiate):** *Men:* baseball, basketball, cross-country, football, ice hockey, track/field (outdoor). *Women:* basketball, cross-country, gymnastics, soccer, softball, tennis, track/field (outdoor), volleyball. **On-Campus Highlights:** Millenium Hall.

ADMISSIONS

Freshman Academic Profile: Average high school GPA 3.2. 9% in top 10% of high school class, 31% in top 25% of high school class, 64% in top 50% of high school class. **Test Scores:** ACT middle 50% range 19–25. **Basis for Candidate Selection:** *Very important factors include:* class rank, academic GPA, standardized test scores. *Important factors include:* rigor of secondary school record, application essay. *Other factors include:* recommendation(s), interview, extracurricular activities, talent/ability, character/personal qualities, first generation, alumni/ae relation, racial/ethnic status, volunteer work, work experience, level of applicant's interest. **Freshman Admission Requirements:** *Academic units required:* 4 English, 3 math, 3 science, 3 social studies, 4 academic electives. *Academic units recommended:* 4 math. **Freshman Admission Statistics:** 3,267 applied, 86% admitted, 54% enrolled. **Transfer Admission Requirements:** College transcript(s), statement of good standing from prior institution(s). Minimum college GPA of 2.5 required. Lowest grade transferable D-. **General Admission Information:** Application fee $50. Priority deadline 1/1.

COSTS AND FINANCIAL AID

Annual in-state tuition $7,014. Annual out-of-state tuition $14,981. Room and board $6,744. Required fees $2,442. Average book and supplies expense $408. **Notification of Awards:** Applicants will be notified of awards on a rolling basis beginning 1/27. **Types of Aid:** *Loans:* Direct Subsidized Stafford Loans. **Student Employment:** Federal Work-Study Program available. Institutional employment available. **Financial Aid Statistics:** 52% needy freshmen, 55% needy undergrads receive need-based scholarship or grant aid. 40% freshmen, 27% undergrads receive non-need-based scholarship or grant aid. 89% freshmen, 91% undergrads receive need-based self-help aid. 0% freshmen, 0% undergrads receive athletic scholarships. 71% freshmen, 74% undergrads receive any aid. 73% undergrads borrow to pay for school. Average cumulative indebtedness $30,409. **Criteria awarding aid:** *Non-need-based:* Academics.

UNIVERSITY OF WISCONSIN—SUPERIOR

Belknap and Catlin, P.O. Box 2000, Superior, WI 54880-4500
Phone: 715-394-8230 **Financial Aid Phone:** 715-394-8200
E-mail: admissions@uwsuper.edu **CEEB Code:** 1920
Fax: 715-394-8454 **Website:** www.uwsuper.edu **ACT Code:** 4682

This public school was founded in 1893. It has a 230 acre campus.

RATINGS

Admissions Selectivity Rating: 83   **Fire Safety Rating:** 84   **Green Rating:** 60*

STUDENTS AND FACULTY

Enrollment: 2,140. **Student Body:** 63% female, 37% male, 46% out-of-state, 9% international (42 countries represented). Asian 1%, African American 2%, Caucasian 80%, Hispanic 3%, Native American 2%, Pacific Islander 0%, Two or more races 4%, Race unknown <1%.
Retention and Graduation: 64% freshmen return for sophomore year. 27% freshmen graduate within 4 years. 48% freshmen graduate within 6 years.
Faculty: Student/faculty ratio 14:1. 118 full-time faculty, 71% hold PhDs, 11% are members of minority groups, 48% are women. 0% of classes are taught by teaching assistants.

ACADEMICS

Degrees: Associate; Bachelor's; Certificate; Master's; Post-bachelor's certificate; Post-master's certificate. **Classes:** Most classes have 10–19 students. Most lab/discussion sessions have 10–19 students. **Most popular majors:** Elementary Education and Teaching; Physical Education Teaching and Coaching; Business Administration and Management, General. **Special Study Options:** Accelerated program; Cooperative education program; Cross-registration;

Distance learning; Double major; Dual enrollment; English as a Second Language (ESL); Exchange student program (domestic); External degree program; Independent study; Internships; Liberal arts/career combination; Student-designed major; Study abroad; Teacher certification program. **Disability Services offered:** Note-taking services; Reader services; Tape recorders; Tutors. **Career services:** Alumni network; Alumni services; Career assessment; Career/job search classes; Internships; Regional alumni.

FACILITIES

Housing: Apartments for married students; Coed dorms; Special housing for disabled students; Special housing for international students; 95% of campus accessible to physically disabled. **Special Academic Facilities/Equipment:** Observatory, Oexemann Greenhouse, Art Galleries (2), Thorpe Langley Auditorium, Webb Recital Hall, rehearsal hall, Manion Theatre, Developmental Theatre, KUWS, recording studio, Lake Superior National Estuarine Research Reserve, Lake Superior Research Institute, Montreal Pier Testing Facility, Transportation and Logistics Research Center, Great Lakes Maritime Research Institute, Pruitt Center for Mindfulness and Well-Being, Climbing Wall, Ropes Course.

CAMPUS LIFE

Environment: City. **Activities:** Campus Ministries; Choral groups; Concert band; Dance; Drama/theater; International Student Organization; Jazz band; Literary magazine; Music ensembles; Musical theater; Opera; Pep band; Radio station; Student government; Student newspaper; Symphony orchestra. 52 registered organizations, 3 honor societies, 5 religious organizations on campus. **Athletics (Intercollegiate):** *Men:* baseball, basketball, cross-country, ice hockey, soccer, track/field (outdoor), track/field (indoor). *Women:* basketball, cross-country, golf, ice hockey, soccer, softball, track/field (outdoor), track/field (indoor), volleyball. **On-Campus Highlights:** Health and Wellness Center. **Environmental Initiatives:** LEED certification for new buildings.

ADMISSIONS

Freshman Academic Profile: Average high school GPA 3.2. 8% in top 10% of high school class, 24% in top 25% of high school class, 55% in top 50% of high school class. **Test Scores:** SAT Math middle 50% range 520–670. SAT EBRW middle 50% range 510–590. ACT middle 50% range 18–23. **Basis for Candidate Selection:** *Very important factors include:* rigor of secondary school record. *Important factors include:* class rank, academic GPA, standardized test scores. *Other factors include:* application essay, recommendation(s), interview, extracurricular activities, talent/ability, character/personal qualities, first generation, racial/ethnic status, volunteer work, work experience. **Freshman Admission Requirements:** High school diploma is required and GED is accepted *Academic units required:* 4 English, 3 math, 3 science, 3 social studies, 4 academic electives. *Academic units recommended:* 4 math, 4 science, 2 foreign language, 4 social studies. **Freshman Admission Statistics:** 897 applied, 78% admitted, 47% enrolled. **Transfer Admission Requirements:** College transcript(s). Minimum college GPA of 2.0 required. Lowest grade transferable D. **General Admission Information:** Application fee $44. Priority deadline 4/1. Regular application deadline 8/1. Non-fall registration accepted.

COSTS AND FINANCIAL AID

Annual in-state tuition $6,535. Annual out-of-state tuition $14,108. Room and board $6,730. Required fees $1,575. Average book and supplies expense $1,000. **Required Forms and Deadlines:** FAFSA. **Notification of Awards:** Applicants will be notified of awards on a rolling basis beginning 2/2. **Types of Aid:** *Need-based scholarships/grants:* College/university scholarship or grant aid from institutional funds; Federal Pell; Private scholarships; SEOG; State scholarships/grants. *Loans:* Direct PLUS loans; Direct Subsidized Stafford Loans; Direct Unsubsidized Stafford Loans. **Student Employment:** Federal Work-Study Program available. Institutional employment available. **Financial Aid Statistics:** 68% needy freshmen, 69% needy undergrads receive need-based scholarship or grant aid. 53% freshmen, 29% undergrads receive non-need-based scholarship or grant aid. 80% freshmen, 85% undergrads receive need-based self-help aid. 0% freshmen, 0% undergrads receive athletic scholarships. 58% freshmen, 59% undergrads receive any aid. 63% undergrads borrow to pay for school. Average cumulative indebtedness $31,490. **Criteria awarding aid:** *Need-based:* Academics, Art, Minority status, Music/drama *Non-need-based:* Academics, Alumni affiliation, Art, Leadership, Minority status, Music/drama, State/district residency.

UNIVERSITY OF WISCONSIN—WHITEWATER

800 West Main Street, Whitewater, WI 53190-1791
Phone: 262-472-1440 **Financial Aid Phone:** 262-472-1130
E-mail: uwwadmit@uww.edu **CEEB Code:** 1921
Fax: 262-472-1515 **Website:** http://www.uww.edu/ **ACT Code:** 4684

This public school was founded in 1868. It has a 385 acre campus.

RATINGS
Admissions Selectivity Rating: 77 **Fire Safety Rating:** 84 **Green Rating:** 88

STUDENTS AND FACULTY
Enrollment: 8,999. **Student Body:** 50% female, 50% male, 4% out-of-state, <1% international (69 countries represented). Asian 2%, African American 4%, Caucasian 90%, Hispanic 2%, Native American <1%, Race unknown <1%. **Retention and Graduation:** 74% freshmen return for sophomore year. **Faculty:** Student/faculty ratio 22:1. 392 full-time faculty, 85% hold PhDs, 18% are members of minority groups, 44% are women. 0% of classes are taught by teaching assistants.

ACADEMICS
Degrees: Associate; Bachelor's; Master's. **Classes:** Most classes have 30–39 students. **Most popular majors:** Physical Education Teaching and Coaching; Elementary Education and Teaching. **Special Study Options:** Accelerated program; Cooperative education program; Cross-registration; Distance learning; Double major; Dual enrollment; English as a Second Language (ESL); Exchange student program (domestic); External degree program; Honors program; Independent study; Internships; Liberal arts/career combination; Student-designed major; Study abroad; Teacher certification program; Weekend college. **Honors programs:** General academic honors program. **Disability Services offered:** Note-taking services; Reader services; Tape recorders; Tutors. **Career services:** Career assessment; Career/job search classes; Internships.

FACILITIES
Housing: Coed dorms; Special housing for disabled students; Special housing for international students; Women's dorms 100% of campus accessible to physically disabled. **Special Academic Facilities/Equipment:** Two electron microscopes, State of the Art Theater/Auditorium.

CAMPUS LIFE
Environment: Village. **Activities:** Choral groups; Concert band; Dance; Drama/theater; Jazz band; Literary magazine; Marching band; Music ensembles; Musical theater; Opera; Radio station; Student government; Student newspaper; Symphony orchestra; Television station. 130 registered organizations, 4 honor societies, 8 religious organizations, 9 fraternities, 8 sororities on campus. **Athletics (Intercollegiate):** *Men:* baseball, basketball, cross-country, diving, football, soccer, swimming, tennis, track/field (outdoor), track/field (indoor), wrestling. *Women:* basketball, bowling, cross-country, diving, golf, gymnastics, soccer, softball, swimming, tennis, track/field (outdoor), track/field (indoor), volleyball. **On-Campus Highlights:** New Kachel Field House.

ADMISSIONS
Freshman Academic Profile: 9% in top 10% of high school class, 32% in top 25% of high school class, 77% in top 50% of high school class. 90% from public high schools. **Test Scores:** SAT Math middle 50% range 480–600. ACT middle 50% range 20–24. **Basis for Candidate Selection:** *Very important factors include:* rigor of secondary school record, class rank, standardized test scores. *Other factors include:* academic GPA, application essay, recommendation(s), interview, extracurricular activities, talent/ability, character/personal qualities, first generation, geographical residence, state residency, racial/ethnic status, volunteer work, work experience, level of applicant's interest. **Freshman Admission Requirements:** High school diploma is required and GED is accepted *Academic units required:* 4 English, 3 math, 3 science, 1 science labs, 3 social studies, 4 academic electives. *Academic units recommended:* 4 math, 4 science, 2 foreign language, 4 social studies. **Freshman Admission Statistics:** 5,570 applied, 76% admitted, 43% enrolled. **Transfer Admission Requirements:** High school transcript, college transcript(s). Minimum college GPA of 2.0 required. Lowest grade transferable D-. **General Admission Information:** Application fee $35. Priority deadline 1/1. Non-fall registration accepted. Admission may be deferred for a maximum of 3 terms.

COSTS AND FINANCIAL AID
Annual in-state tuition $5,568. Annual out-of-state tuition $13,042. Room and board $4,322. Required fees $710. Average book and supplies expense $170. **Required Forms and Deadlines:** FAFSA. **Notification of Awards:** Applicants will be notified of awards on a rolling basis beginning 4/1. **Types of Aid:** *Need-based scholarships/grants:* College/university scholarship or grant aid from institutional funds; Federal Pell; Private scholarships; SEOG; State scholarships/grants. *Loans:* Direct PLUS loans; Direct Subsidized Stafford Loans; Direct Unsubsidized Stafford Loans. **Financial Aid Statistics:** 38% needy freshmen, 44% needy undergrads receive need-based scholarship or grant aid. 27% freshmen, 13% undergrads receive non-need-based scholarship or grant aid. 85% freshmen, 84% undergrads receive need-based self-help aid. 0% freshmen, 0% undergrads receive athletic scholarships. 52% freshmen, 42% undergrads receive any aid. **Criteria awarding aid:** *Need-based:* Academics, Leadership, Minority status. *Non-need-based:* Academics, Alumni affiliation, Art, Leadership, Minority status, Music/drama, State/district residency.

UNIVERSITY OF WYOMING

Dept 3435, Laramie, WY 82071
Phone: 307-766-5160 **Financial Aid Phone:** 307-766-2116
E-mail: admissions@uwyo.edu **CEEB Code:** 4855
Fax: 307-766-4042 **Website:** www.uwyo.edu **ACT Code:** 5006

This public school was founded in 1886. It has a 785 acre campus.

RATINGS
Admissions Selectivity Rating: 75 **Fire Safety Rating:** 91 **Green Rating:** 74

STUDENTS AND FACULTY
Enrollment: 9,854. **Student Body:** 51% female, 49% male, 34% out-of-state, 4% international (64 countries represented). Asian 1%, African American 1%, Caucasian 72%, Hispanic 7%, Native American 1%, Pacific Islander <1%, Two or more races 4%, Race unknown 11%. **Retention and Graduation:** 78% freshmen return for sophomore year. 26% freshmen graduate within 4 years. 58% freshmen graduate within 6 years. 24% grads go on to further study within 1 year. 3% grads pursue arts and sciences degrees. 1% grads pursue law degrees. 1% grads pursue business degrees. 0% grads pursue medical degrees. **Faculty:** Student/faculty ratio 15:1. 730 full-time faculty, 79% hold PhDs, 9% are members of minority groups, 42% are women. 10% of classes are taught by teaching assistants.

ACADEMICS
Degrees: Bachelor's; Certificate; Doctoral degree—professional practice; Doctoral degree research/scholarship; Master's; Post-bachelor's certificate. **Classes:** Most classes have 20–29 students. Most lab/discussion sessions have 20–29 students. **Most popular majors:** Mechanical Engineering; Psychology, General; Elementary Education and Teaching. **Special Study Options:** Accelerated program; Distance learning; Double major; English as a Second Language (ESL); Exchange student program (domestic); External degree program; Honors program; Independent study; Internships; Study abroad. **Honors programs:** The University Honors Program provides highly motivated students a series of curricular and extracurricular opportunities. Most students are selected for the program prior to their freshman year, although the program welcomes UW and transfer students up to the beginning of the junior year. Each year the Honors Program awards scholarships to qualifying students who are beginning their undergraduate education or who are entering the University as transfer students. The honors students organize extracurricular activities, have a student lounge and computers for their use, and have the option of living on one of the honors floors in the residence halls or in the Honors House. Courses offered in the honors program are restricted to honors program students; exceptions must be approved by the Honors program office. **Combined degree programs:** BA/MEng. **Disability Services offered:** Note-taking services; Reader services; Tape recorders; Tutors. **Career services:** Alumni network; Alumni services; Career assessment; Career/job search classes; Internships; Regional alumni.

FACILITIES

Housing: Apartments for married students; Apartments for single students; Coed dorms; Fraternity/sorority housing; Men's dorms; Special housing for disabled students; Theme housing; Women's dorms; 95% of campus accessible to physically disabled. **Special Academic Facilities/Equipment:** Art gallery, Geology museum, American Heritage Center, Rocky Mountain Herbarium, Solheim Mycology Herbarium, art museum, planetarium, environmental biology lab, anthropology museum, on-site elementary school, state veterinary lab, infrared telescope observatory, lysimeter lab, insect museum and gallery room, Wyoming Geographic Information Science Center, Writing Center, Wyoming Cooperative Fishery and Wildlife Research Unit.

CAMPUS LIFE

Environment: Town. **Activities:** Campus Ministries; Choral groups; Concert band; Dance; Drama/theater; International Student Organization; Jazz band; Literary magazine; Marching band; Model UN; Music ensembles; Musical theater; Opera; Pep band; Radio station; Student government; Student newspaper; Student-run film society; Symphony orchestra; Television station. 195 registered organizations, 41 honor societies, 11 religious organizations, 9 fraternities, 5 sororities, on campus. **Athletics (Intercollegiate):** *Men:* basketball, cheerleading, cross-country, diving, football, golf, swimming, track/field (outdoor), track/field (indoor), wrestling. *Women:* basketball, cheerleading, cross-country, diving, golf, soccer, swimming, tennis, track/field (outdoor), track/field (indoor), volleyball. **On-Campus Highlights:** Wyoming Student Union **Environmental Initiatives:** Campus Sustainability Committee.

ADMISSIONS

Freshman Academic Profile: Average high school GPA 3.5. 21% in top 10% of high school class, 48% in top 25% of high school class, 80% in top 50% of high school class. **Test Scores:** SAT Math middle 50% range 520–640. SAT EBRW middle 50% range 530–640. ACT middle 50% range 22–28. **Basis for Candidate Selection:** *Very important factors include:* rigor of secondary school record, academic GPA, standardized test scores. *Other factors include:* application essay. **Freshman Admission Requirements:** High school diploma is required and GED is accepted *Academic units required:* 4 English, 4 math, 4 science, 3 science labs, 2 foreign language, 3 social studies, 2 academic electives, 2 unit from above areas or other academic areas. *Academic units recommended:* 4 English, 4 math, 4 science, 3 science labs, 2 foreign language, 3 social studies, 2 academic electives. **Freshman Admission Statistics:** 5,293 applied, 96% admitted, 37% enrolled. **Transfer Admission Requirements:** College transcript(s). Minimum college GPA of 2.0 required. Lowest grade transferable D. **General Admission Information:** Application fee $40. Regular application deadline 8/10. Non-fall registration accepted. Admission may be deferred for a maximum of 1 year.

COSTS AND FINANCIAL AID

Annual in-state tuition $4,020. Annual out-of-state tuition $16,110. Room and board $10,320. Required fees $1,380. Average book and supplies expense $1,200. **Required Forms and Deadlines:** FAFSA. **Notification of Awards:** Applicants will be notified of awards on a rolling basis beginning 12/20. **Types of Aid:** *Need-based scholarships/grants:* College/university scholarship or grant aid from institutional funds; Federal Pell; Private scholarships; SEOG; State scholarships/grants. *Loans:* Direct PLUS loans; Direct Subsidized Stafford Loans; Direct Unsubsidized Stafford Loans. **Student Employment:** Federal Work-Study Program available. Institutional employment available. **Financial Aid Statistics:** 64% needy freshmen, 67% needy undergrads receive need-based scholarship or grant aid. 88% freshmen, 70% undergrads receive non-need-based scholarship or grant aid. 50% freshmen, 57% undergrads receive need-based self-help aid. 4% freshmen, 4% undergrads receive athletic scholarships. 44.7% freshmen, 84% undergrads receive any aid. 46% undergrads borrow to pay for school. Average cumulative indebtedness $24,474. **Criteria awarding aid:** *Need-based:* Academics, Athletics, Job skills, Minority status. *Non-need-based:* Academics, Alumni affiliation, Art, Athletics, Leadership, Minority status, Music/drama, State/district residency.

UPPER IOWA UNIVERSITY

Parker Fox Hall Box 1859, Fayette, IA 52142-1859
Phone: 800-553-4150 **Financial Aid Phone:** 800-553-4150
E-mail: admission@uiu.edu
Fax: 563-425-5277 **ACT Code:** 1360

This private school was founded in 1857. It has a 80 acre campus.

RATINGS

Admissions Selectivity Rating: 72   **Fire Safety Rating:** 84   **Green Rating:** 66

STUDENTS AND FACULTY

Enrollment: 3,859. **Student Body:** 62% female, 38% male, 55% out-of-state, 2% international (30 countries represented). Asian 1%, African American 20%, Caucasian 66%, Hispanic 6%, Native American <1%, Pacific Islander <1%, Two or more races 2%, Race unknown 3%.
Retention and Graduation: 63% freshmen return for sophomore year. 25% grads go on to further study within 1 year. 29% grads pursue arts and sciences degrees. 1% grads pursue law degrees. 17% grads pursue business degrees. 5% grads pursue medical degrees. **Faculty:** Student/faculty ratio 17:1. 78 full-time faculty, 59% hold PhDs, 3% are members of minority groups, 55% are women. 0% of classes are taught by teaching assistants.

ACADEMICS

Degrees: Associate; Bachelor's; Certificate; Master's; Terminal Associate; Transfer Associate. **Classes:** Most classes have fewer than 10 students. Most lab/discussion sessions have fewer than 10 students. **Most popular majors:** Public Administration And Social Service Professions; Human Resources Management/Personnel Administration, General; Public Administration And Social Service Professions. **Special Study Options:** Accelerated program; Distance learning; Double major; Dual enrollment; English as a Second Language (ESL); External degree program; Honors program; Independent study; Internships; Liberal arts/career combination; Student-designed major; Study abroad; Teacher certification program. **Disability Services offered:** Note-taking services; Reader services; Tape recorders; Tutors. **Career services:** Alumni services; Career assessment; Career/job search classes; Internships; Regional alumni.

FACILITIES

Housing: Coed dorms; Men's dorms; Special housing for disabled students; Women's dorms; 70% of campus accessible to physically disabled. **Special Academic Facilities/Equipment:** Bing Art Gallery, Library archives. **Campus Network:** 100% of classrooms, 100% of dorms, 100% of student union, 100% of libraries, 100% of dining areas, 90% of common outdoor areas have wireless network access.

CAMPUS LIFE

Environment: Rural. **Activities:** Campus Ministries; Choral groups; Dance; Drama/theater; International Student Organization; Literary magazine; Radio station; Student government; Student newspaper; Yearbook. 29 registered organizations, 1 honor societies, 2 religious organizations, 3 fraternities, 8 sororities on campus. **Athletics (Intercollegiate):** *Men:* baseball, basketball, cross-country, football, golf, soccer, wrestling. *Women:* basketball, cross-country, golf, soccer, softball, tennis, volleyball. **On-Campus Highlights:** Student Center. **Environmental Initiatives:** Geothermal Heating/Cooling.

ADMISSIONS

Freshman Academic Profile: Average high school GPA 3.1. 22% in top 10% of high school class, 27% in top 25% of high school class, 57% in top 50% of high school class. **Test Scores:** ACT middle 50% range 17–24. **Basis for Candidate Selection:** *Very important factors include:* academic GPA, standardized test scores. *Other factors include:* rigor of secondary school record, class rank, recommendation(s). **Freshman Admission Requirements:** High school diploma is required and GED is accepted **Freshman Admission Statistics:** 1,121 applied, 94% admitted, 20% enrolled. **Transfer Admission Requirements:** High school transcript, college transcript(s). Lowest grade transferable D-. **General Admission Information:** Non-fall registration accepted. Admission may be deferred for a maximum of two years.

COSTS AND FINANCIAL AID

Annual tuition $28,850. Room and board $8,370. Required fees $750. Average book and supplies expense $1,500. **Required Forms and Deadlines:** FAFSA. **Notification of Awards:** Applicants will be notified of awards on a rolling basis beginning 3/1. **Types of Aid:** *Need-based scholarships/grants:* College/university scholarship or grant aid from institutional funds; Federal Pell; Private scholarships; SEOG; State scholarships/grants. *Loans:* Direct PLUS loans; Direct Subsidized Stafford Loans; Direct Unsubsidized Stafford Loans. **Student Employment:** Federal Work-Study Program available. **Financial Aid Statistics:** 95% needy freshmen, 85% needy undergrads receive need-based scholarship or grant aid. 3% freshmen, 7% undergrads receive non-need-based scholarship or grant aid. 96% freshmen, 94% undergrads receive need-based self-help aid. 0% freshmen, 0% undergrads receive athletic scholarships. 100% freshmen, 90% undergrads receive any aid. 96% undergrads borrow to pay for school. Average cumulative indebtedness $18,863. **Criteria awarding aid:** *Need-based:* Academics, Alumni affiliation. *Non-need-based:* Academics, Alumni affiliation, Athletics.

URSINUS COLLEGE

Best Colleges

601 E. Main Street, Collegeville, PA 19426
Phone: 610-409-3200 **Financial Aid Phone:** 610-409-3600
E-mail: admission@ursinus.edu **CEEB Code:** 2931
Fax: 610-409-3197 **Website:** www.ursinus.edu **ACT Code:** 3738

This private school was founded in 1869. It has a 170 acre campus.

RATINGS
Admissions Selectivity Rating: 80   Fire Safety Rating: 97   Green Rating: 86

STUDENTS AND FACULTY
Enrollment: 1,458. **Student Body:** 50% female, 50% male, 38% out-of-state, 1% international (8 countries represented). Asian 4%, African American 8%, Caucasian 73%, Hispanic 8%, Native American <1%, Pacific Islander <1%, Two or more races 3%, Race unknown 3%.
Retention and Graduation: 87% freshmen return for sophomore year. 77% freshmen graduate within 4 years. 81% freshmen graduate within 6 years. 23% grads go on to further study within 1 year. 14% grads pursue arts and sciences degrees. 1% grads pursue law degrees. 1% grads pursue business degrees. 5% grads pursue medical degrees. **Faculty:** Student/faculty ratio 10:1. 123 full-time faculty, 91% hold PhDs, 15% are members of minority groups, 59% are women. 0% of classes are taught by teaching assistants.

ACADEMICS
Degrees: Bachelor's. **Classes:** Most classes have 10–19 students. Most lab/discussion sessions have 10–19 students. **Most popular majors:** Biology/Biological Sciences, General; Psychology, General. **Special Study Options:** Double major; Dual enrollment; Exchange student program (domestic); Honors program; Independent study; Internships; Student-designed major; Study abroad; Teacher certification program. **Honors programs:** Students can participate in Summer Fellows, a unique program where students from any subject get paid to do independent work on a subject they come up with. That work often leads to an Honors Project: a year-long, in-depth project that is the ultimate conclusion to a student's career at Ursinus. **Disability Services offered:** Note-taking services; Reader services; Tape recorders; Tutors. **Career services:** Alumni network; Alumni services; Career assessment; Career/job search classes; Internships; Regional alumni.

FACILITIES
Housing: Coed dorms; Men's dorms; Special housing for disabled students; Special housing for international students; Theme housing; Women's dorms; 95% of campus accessible to physically disabled. **Special Academic Facilities/Equipment:** The Philip and Muriel Berman Museum of Art; The Kaleidoscope Performing Arts Center; F.W. Olin Hall for Humanities; Bomberger Hall; Innovation and Discovery Center; Thomas Hall; Floy Lewis Bakes Field House; Mossbauer Spectrometer.

CAMPUS LIFE
Environment: Town. **Activities:** Campus Ministries; Choral groups; Concert band; Dance; Drama/theater; International Student Organization; Jazz band; Literary magazine; Model UN; Music ensembles; Musical theater; Pep band; Radio station; Student government; Student newspaper; Student-run film society; Television station; Yearbook. 100 registered organizations, 17 honor societies, 5 religious organizations, 7 fraternities, 5 sororities on campus.
Athletics (Intercollegiate): *Men:* baseball, basketball, cross-country, football, golf, lacrosse, soccer, swimming, tennis, track/field (outdoor), track/field (indoor), wrestling. *Women:* basketball, cross-country, field hockey, golf, gymnastics, lacrosse, soccer, softball, swimming, tennis, track/field (outdoor), track/field (indoor), volleyball. **On-Campus Highlights:** The Kaleidoscope Performing Arts Center. **Environmental Initiatives:** Environmental education, both academic and co-curricular, through our ENV department and our Office of Sustainability.

ADMISSIONS
Freshman Academic Profile: Average high school GPA 3.4. 21% in top 10% of high school class, 50% in top 25% of high school class, 83% in top 50% of high school class. 74% from public high schools. **Test Scores:** SAT Math middle 50% range 570–680. SAT EBRW middle 50% range 580–670. ACT middle 50% range 24–30. **Basis for Candidate Selection:** *Very important factors include:* rigor of secondary school record, academic GPA, character/personal qualities. *Important factors include:* class rank, application essay, recommendation(s), interview, extracurricular activities, talent/ability. *Other factors include:* standardized test scores, first generation, alumni/ae relation, geographical residence, state residency, racial/ethnic status, volunteer work, work experience, level of applicant's interest. **Freshman Admission Requirements:** High school diploma is required and GED is accepted. *Academic units required:* 4 English, 3 math, 1 science, 1 science labs, 2 foreign language, 1 social studies, 5 academic electives. *Academic units recommended:* 4 English, 4 math, 4 science, 3 science labs, 3 foreign language, 4 social studies. **Freshman Admission Statistics:** 3,530 applied, 79% admitted, 15% enrolled. **Transfer Admission Requirements:** High school transcript, college transcript(s), essay or personal statement, standardized test scores. Minimum college GPA of 3.0 required. Lowest grade transferable C. **General Admission Information:** Regular application deadline 2/1. Non-fall registration accepted. Admission may be deferred for a maximum of 1 year.

COSTS AND FINANCIAL AID
Annual tuition $55,210. Room and board $13,530. Average book and supplies expense $1,000. **Required Forms and Deadlines:** FAFSA; State aid form. **Notification of Awards:** Applicants will be notified of awards on or about 3/15. **Types of Aid:** *Need-based scholarships/grants:* College/university scholarship or grant aid from institutional funds; Federal Pell; Private scholarships; SEOG; State scholarships/grants. *Loans:* Direct PLUS loans; Direct Subsidized Stafford Loans; Direct Unsubsidized Stafford Loans. **Student Employment:** Federal Work-Study Program available. Institutional employment available. **Financial Aid Statistics:** 98% needy freshmen, 99% needy undergrads receive need-based scholarship or grant aid. 21% freshmen, 17% undergrads receive non-need-based scholarship or grant aid. 75% freshmen, 77% undergrads receive need-based self-help aid. 0% freshmen, 0% undergrads receive athletic scholarships. 99% freshmen, 99% undergrads receive any aid. 70% undergrads borrow to pay for school. Average cumulative indebtedness $41,654. **Criteria awarding aid:** *Need-based:* Academics. *Non-need-based:* Academics, Alumni affiliation, Leadership, Minority status, Music/drama, State/district residency.

URSULINE COLLEGE

2550 Lander Road, Pepper Pike, OH 44124-4398
Phone: 440-449-4203 **Financial Aid Phone:** 440-646-8309
E-mail: admission@ursuline.edu **CEEB Code:** 1848
Fax: 440-684-6138 **Website:** www.ursuline.edu

This private school, affiliated with the Roman Catholic Church, was founded in 1871. It has a 110 acre campus.

RATINGS
Admissions Selectivity Rating: 74   Fire Safety Rating: 88   Green Rating: 60*

STUDENTS AND FACULTY
Enrollment: 641. **Student Body:** 93% female, 7% male, 8% out-of-state, 2% international (6 countries represented). Asian 1%, African American 26%, Caucasian 62%, Hispanic 3%, Native American 0%, Pacific Islander 0%, Two or more races 3%, Race unknown 4%.
Retention and Graduation: 59% freshmen return for sophomore year. 5% grads go on to further study within 1 year. **Faculty:** Student/faculty ratio 7:1. 66 full-time faculty, 68% hold PhDs, 9% are members of minority groups, 85% are women. 0% of classes are taught by teaching assistants.

ACADEMICS
Degrees: Bachelor's; Certificate; Doctoral degree—professional practice; Master's; Post-bachelor's certificate; Post-master's certificate. **Classes:** Most

classes have 10–19 students. Most lab/discussion sessions have 10–19 students. **Most popular majors:** Business Administration, Management and Operations, Other; Psychology, General; Health Professions And Related Programs. **Special Study Options:** Accelerated program; Cross-registration; Double major; Dual enrollment; Independent study; Internships; Teacher certification program. **Disability Services offered:** Note-taking services; Reader services; Tape recorders; Tutors. **Career services:** Career assessment; Internships.

FACILITIES

Housing: Coed dorms; Theme housing; Women's dorms 98% of campus accessible to physically disabled. **Special Academic Facilities/Equipment:** Fritsche Gallery (Art); New Athletic Center. **Campus Network:** 100% of classrooms, 100% of dorms, 100% of student union, 100% of libraries, 100% of dining areas, 100% of common outdoor areas, have wireless network access.

CAMPUS LIFE

Environment: City. **Activities:** Campus Ministries; Drama/theater; Literary magazine; Student government. 23 registered organizations, 4 honor societies, on campus. **Athletics (Intercollegiate):** *Women:* basketball, bowling, cross-country, golf, soccer, softball, swimming, tennis, track/field (outdoor), volleyball. **On-Campus Highlights:** Bishop Anthony M. Pilla Student Learning Center. **Environmental Initiatives:** Increased Recycling; Energy Conservation; Renewable Energy.

ADMISSIONS

Freshman Academic Profile: Average high school GPA 3.3. 16% in top 10% of high school class, 45% in top 25% of high school class, 74% in top 50% of high school class. 94% from public high schools. **Test Scores:** SAT Math middle 50% range 440–535. SAT EBRW middle 50% range 425–590. ACT middle 50% range 19–24. **Basis for Candidate Selection:** *Very important factors include:* academic GPA, standardized test scores. *Other factors include:* rigor of secondary school record, class rank, application essay, recommendation(s), interview, alumni/ae relation. **Freshman Admission Requirements:** High school diploma is required and GED is accepted *Academic units recommended:* 4 English, 3 math, 3 science, 2 science labs, 2 foreign language, 3 social studies, 1 visual/performing arts. **Freshman Admission Statistics:** 723 applied, 88% admitted, 18% enrolled. **Transfer Admission Requirements:** College transcript(s), essay or personal statement. Minimum college GPA of 2.5 required. Lowest grade transferable C. **General Admission Information:** Regular application deadline 2/1. Non-fall registration accepted. Admission may be deferred for a maximum of 1 year.

COSTS AND FINANCIAL AID

Required Forms and Deadlines: FAFSA. **Notification of Awards:** Applicants will be notified of awards on a rolling basis beginning 2/15. **Types of Aid:** *Need-based scholarships/grants:* College/university scholarship or grant aid from institutional funds; Federal Nursing Scholarships; Federal Pell; Private scholarships; SEOG; State scholarships/grants. *Loans:* Direct PLUS loans; Direct Subsidized Stafford Loans; Direct Unsubsidized Stafford Loans. **Student Employment:** Federal Work-Study Program available. **Financial Aid Statistics:** 100% needy freshmen, 96% needy undergrads receive need-based scholarship or grant aid. 20% freshmen, 13% undergrads receive non-need-based scholarship or grant aid. 84% freshmen, 88% undergrads receive need-based self-help aid. 17% freshmen, 12% undergrads receive athletic scholarships. 100% freshmen, 80% undergrads receive any aid. 98% undergrads borrow to pay for school. Average cumulative indebtedness $37,900. **Criteria awarding aid:** *Need-based:* Athletics, Minority status. *Non-need-based:* Academics, Alumni affiliation, Art, Athletics, Job skills, Minority status.

UTAH STATE UNIVERSITY

0160 Old Main Hill, Logan, UT 84322-0160
Phone: 435-797-1079 **Financial Aid Phone:** 435-797-0173
E-mail: admit@usu.edu
Fax: 435-797-3708 **Website:** www.usu.edu **ACT Code:** 4276

This public school was founded in 1888. It has a 400 acre campus.

RATINGS

Admissions Selectivity Rating: 76   **Fire Safety Rating:** 82   **Green Rating:** 89

STUDENTS AND FACULTY

Enrollment: 20,913. **Student Body:** 54% female, 46% male, 27% out-of-state, 1% international (59 countries represented). Asian 1%, African American 1%, Caucasian 83%, Hispanic 6%, Native American 2%, Pacific Islander <1%, Two or more races 2%, Race unknown 4%.
Retention and Graduation: 74% freshmen return for sophomore year. 28% freshmen graduate within 4 years. 54% freshmen graduate within 6 years. **Faculty:** Student/faculty ratio 20:1. 1,010 full-time faculty, 79% hold PhDs, 11% are members of minority groups, 39% are women. 4% of classes are taught by teaching assistants.

ACADEMICS

Degrees: Associate; Bachelor's; Certificate; Doctoral degree—professional practice; Doctoral degree research/scholarship; Master's; Post-bachelor's certificate; Terminal Associate; Transfer Associate. **Classes:** Most classes have 20–29 students. Most lab/discussion sessions have 10–19 students. **Most popular majors:** Communication Sciences and Disorders, General; Economics, General; Business Administration and Management, General. **Special Study Options:** Accelerated program; Cooperative education program; Cross-registration; Distance learning; Double major; Dual enrollment; English as a Second Language (ESL); Exchange student program (domestic); Honors program; Independent study; Internships; Liberal arts/career combination; Student-designed major; Study abroad; Teacher certification program; Weekend college. **Honors programs:** The Honors Program is a community of scholars whose curiosity, creativity, and enthusiasm for learning foster educational achievement and personal growth. Our students are going places—graduate school, professional school, terrific jobs. Honors offers undergraduate students intensive seminars, experimental and interdisciplinary courses, writing projects, leadership opportunities, artistic and social activities. Our classes are smaller, allowing students to get to know professors and encouraging classroom interaction and discussion. We allow students to define their own interests and pursue them through "contracts" with professors, fostering close contact with professors. Other advantages include priority registration, an Honors-only computer lab, the Honors lounge and study areas. **Disability Services offered:** Note-taking services; Reader services; Tape recorders. **Career services:** Alumni network; Alumni services; Career assessment; Career/job search classes; Internships; Regional alumni.

FACILITIES

Housing: Apartments for married students; Apartments for single students; Coed dorms; Fraternity/sorority housing; Men's dorms; Special housing for disabled students; Special housing for international students; Theme housing; Women's dorms; 97% of campus accessible to physically disabled. **Special Academic Facilities/Equipment:** Art gallery, agricultural and engineering experiment station, water research lab, wildlife and fishery research unit, on-campus school, intermountain herbarium, electron microscope, space dynamics lab.

CAMPUS LIFE

Environment: Town. **Activities:** Campus Ministries; Choral groups; Concert band; Dance; Drama/theater; International Student Organization; Jazz band; Marching band; Music ensembles; Musical theater; Opera; Pep band; Radio station; Student government; Student newspaper; Student-run film society; Symphony orchestra; Television station. 32 honor societies, 8 religious organizations, 5 fraternities, 3 sororities on campus. **Athletics (Intercollegiate):** *Men:* basketball, cross-country, football, golf, tennis, track/field (outdoor), track/field (indoor). *Women:* basketball, cross-country, gymnastics, soccer, softball, tennis, track/field (outdoor), track/field (indoor), volleyball. **On-Campus Highlights:** Aggie Recreation Center. **Environmental Initiatives:** Increased efficiency — All new buildings on campus are LEED Silver or higher, and projects must achieve EA Credit 3, enhanced commissioning. According to LEED, this can result in 5%–10% improvements in energy efficiency, ensure personnel know how to operate key building systems, and catch mistakes like incorrectly installed equipment. Many buildings have been retro-commisioned to ensure existing buildings are operating efficiently. Non-potable water is used for irrigation. Irrigation systems use central computer controls to maximize efficiency, and water lines are regularly inspected for leaks. Campus housing has installed 6500 LEDs and water efficient shower heads.

ADMISSIONS

Freshman Academic Profile: Average high school GPA 3.6. 23% in top 10% of high school class, 49% in top 25% of high school class, 79% in top 50% of high school class. **Test Scores:** SAT Math middle 50% range 520–650. SAT EBRW middle 50% range 530–660. ACT middle 50% range 21–28. **Basis for Candidate Selection:** *Very important factors include:* academic GPA, standardized test scores. *Other factors include:* rigor of secondary school record, class rank, recommendation(s). **Freshman Admission Requirements:** High school diploma is required and GED is accepted *Academic units recommended:* 4 English, 4 math, 3 science, 3 science labs, 2 foreign language, 3.5 social studies. **Freshman Admission Statistics:** 15,276 applied, 91% admitted, 32%

enrolled. **Transfer Admission Requirements:** College transcript(s). Minimum college GPA of 2.2 required. Lowest grade transferable D. **General Admission Information:** Application fee $50. Non-fall registration accepted. Admission may be deferred for a maximum of 2 years+ one semester.

COSTS AND FINANCIAL AID
Annual in-state tuition $6,549. Annual out-of-state tuition $21,087. Room and board $5,770. Required fees $1,110. Average book and supplies expense $868. **Required Forms and Deadlines:** FAFSA. **Notification of Awards:** Applicants will be notified of awards on a rolling basis beginning 4/1. **Types of Aid:** *Need-based scholarships/grants:* College/university scholarship or grant aid from institutional funds; Federal Pell; Private scholarships; SEOG; State scholarships/grants. *Loans:* Direct PLUS loans; Direct Subsidized Stafford Loans; Direct Unsubsidized Stafford Loans. **Student Employment:** Federal Work-Study Program available. Institutional employment available. **Financial Aid Statistics:** 62% needy freshmen, 72% needy undergrads receive need-based scholarship or grant aid. 77% freshmen, 48% undergrads receive non-need-based scholarship or grant aid. 85% freshmen, 93% undergrads receive need-based self-help aid. 3% freshmen, 2% undergrads receive athletic scholarships. 75% freshmen, 72% undergrads receive any aid. 45% undergrads borrow to pay for school. Average cumulative indebtedness $21,080. **Criteria awarding aid:** *Non-need-based:* Academics, Alumni affiliation, Art, Athletics, Leadership, Minority status, Music/drama, Religious affiliation, State/district residency.

UTICA COLLEGE

1600 Burrstone Road, Utica, NY 13502-4892
Phone: 315-792-3006 **Financial Aid Phone:** 315-792-3179
E-mail: admiss@utica.edu **CEEB Code:** 2932
Fax: 315-792-3003 **Website:** www.utica.edu **ACT Code:** 2932

This private school was founded in 1946. It has a 128 acre campus.

RATINGS
Admissions Selectivity Rating: 76   **Fire Safety Rating:** 88   **Green Rating:** 69

STUDENTS AND FACULTY
Enrollment: 3,602. **Student Body:** 59% female, 41% male, 12% out-of-state, 1% international (40 countries represented). Asian 4%, African American 10%, Caucasian 69%, Hispanic 9%, Native American <1%, Pacific Islander <1%, Two or more races 2%, Race unknown 5%.
Retention and Graduation: 70% freshmen return for sophomore year. 35% freshmen graduate within 4 years. 49% freshmen graduate within 6 years. 46% grads go on to further study within 1 year. 1% grads pursue medical degrees.
Faculty: Student/faculty ratio 13:1. 149 full-time faculty, 87% hold PhDs, 11% are members of minority groups, 46% are women. 0% of classes are taught by teaching assistants.

ACADEMICS
Degrees: Bachelor's; Certificate; Doctoral degree—professional practice; Master's; Post-bachelor's certificate. **Classes:** Most classes have 10–19 students. Most lab/discussion sessions have 10–19 students. **Most popular majors:** Business/Commerce, General; Corrections and Criminal Justice, Other; Health Professions And Related Programs. **Special Study Options:** Accelerated program; Distance learning; Double major; English as a Second Language (ESL); Honors program; Independent study; Internships; Study abroad; Teacher certification program; Weekend college. **Honors programs:** http://www.utica.edu/academic/opportunities/honors.cfm. **Disability Services offered:** Note-taking services; Reader services; Tape recorders; Tutors. **Career services:** Alumni network; Alumni services; Career assessment; Career/job search classes; Internships.

FACILITIES
Housing: Apartments for single students; Coed dorms; Special housing for disabled students; Special housing for international students; Theme housing; 85% of campus accessible to physically disabled. **Special Academic Facilities/Equipment:** Edith Langley Barrett Art Gallery.

CAMPUS LIFE
Environment: City. **Activities:** Campus Ministries; Choral groups; Concert band; Dance; Drama/theater; International Student Organization; Jazz band; Literary magazine; Music ensembles; Radio station; Student government; Student newspaper; Television station; Yearbook. 80 registered organizations, 8

honor societies, 3 religious organizations, 3 fraternities, 4 sororities on campus. **Athletics (Intercollegiate):** *Men:* baseball, basketball, cross-country, diving, football, golf, ice hockey, lacrosse, soccer, swimming, tennis, track/field (outdoor). *Women:* basketball, cross-country, diving, field hockey, ice hockey, lacrosse, soccer, softball, swimming, tennis, track/field (outdoor), volleyball, water polo. **On-Campus Highlights:** Strebel Student Center and Lounge **Environmental Initiatives:** Committee on sustainability formed in 2007.

ADMISSIONS
Freshman Academic Profile: Average high school GPA 3.2. 13% in top 10% of high school class, 35% in top 25% of high school class, 66% in top 50% of high school class. **Test Scores:** SAT Math middle 50% range 520–620. SAT EBRW middle 50% range 510–600. ACT middle 50% range 20–26. **Basis for Candidate Selection:** *Very important factors include:* rigor of secondary school record, academic GPA. *Important factors include:* application essay, standardized test scores. *Other factors include:* class rank, recommendation(s), interview, extracurricular activities, talent/ability, character/personal qualities, first generation, alumni/ae relation, volunteer work, work experience. **Freshman Admission Requirements:** High school diploma is required and GED is accepted *Academic units required:* 4 English, 3 math, 3 science, 1 foreign language, 4 social studies, 3.5 academic electives, 1 visual/performing arts, 2.5 unit from above areas or other academic areas. **Freshman Admission Statistics:** 4,224 applied, 84% admitted, 16% enrolled. **Transfer Admission Requirements:** College transcript(s), essay or personal statement. Minimum college GPA of 2.50 required. Lowest grade transferable C. **General Admission Information:** Application fee $40. Priority deadline 3/1. Non-fall registration accepted. Admission may be deferred for a maximum of one year.

COSTS AND FINANCIAL AID
Annual tuition $20,127. Room and board $10,828. Required fees $550. Average book and supplies expense $1,400. **Required Forms and Deadlines:** FAFSA; State aid form. **Notification of Awards:** Applicants will be notified of awards on a rolling basis beginning 2/1. **Types of Aid:** *Need-based scholarships/grants:* College/university scholarship or grant aid from institutional funds; Federal Pell; Private scholarships; SEOG; State scholarships/grants. *Loans:* Direct PLUS loans; Direct Subsidized Stafford Loans; Direct Unsubsidized Stafford Loans. **Student Employment:** Federal Work-Study Program available. Institutional employment available. **Financial Aid Statistics:** 98% needy freshmen, 86% needy undergrads receive need-based scholarship or grant aid. 13% freshmen, 8% undergrads receive non-need-based scholarship or grant aid. 97% freshmen, 95% undergrads receive need-based self-help aid. 0% freshmen, 0% undergrads receive athletic scholarships. 96% freshmen, 95% undergrads receive any aid. 85% undergrads borrow to pay for school. Average cumulative indebtedness $29,054. **Criteria awarding aid:** *Non-need-based:* Academics, Alumni affiliation, Minority status.

VALDOSTA STATE UNIVERSITY

1500 North Patterson Street, Valdosta, GA 31698
Phone: 229-333-5791 **Financial Aid Phone:** 229-333-5935
E-mail: admissions@valdosta.edu **CEEB Code:** 5855
Fax: 229-333-5482 **Website:** http://www.valdosta.edu/ **ACT Code:** 874

This public school was founded in 1906. It has a 180 acre campus.

RATINGS
Admissions Selectivity Rating: 86   **Fire Safety Rating:** 63   **Green Rating:** 60*

STUDENTS AND FACULTY
Enrollment: 10,638. **Student Body:** 60% female, 40% male, 4% out-of-state, 1% international (73 countries represented). Asian 1%, African American 34%, Caucasian 54%, Hispanic 4%, Native American <1%, Pacific Islander <1%, Two or more races 3%, Race unknown 2%.
Retention and Graduation: 67% freshmen return for sophomore year.
Faculty: Student/faculty ratio 23:1. 489 full-time faculty, 77% hold PhDs, 15% are members of minority groups, 48% are women. 2% of classes are taught by teaching assistants.

ACADEMICS
Degrees: Associate; Bachelor's; Master's; Post-master's certificate. **Classes:** Most classes have 20–29 students. Most lab/discussion sessions have 20–29 students. **Most popular majors:** Registered Nursing/Registered Nurse; Biology/

Biological Sciences, General; Psychology, General. **Special Study Options:** Accelerated program; Cooperative education program; Distance learning; Double major; Dual enrollment; English as a Second Language (ESL); External degree program; Honors program; Independent study; Internships; Study abroad; Teacher certification program; Weekend college. **Honors programs:** Valdosta State University Honors College. **Disability Services offered:** Note-taking services; Reader services; Tape recorders; Tutors. **Career services:** Alumni services; Career assessment; Career/job search classes; Internships.

FACILITIES
Housing: Apartments for single students; Coed dorms; Special housing for disabled students; Special housing for international students; Theme housing; 100% of campus accessible to physically disabled. **Special Academic Facilities/ Equipment:** Planetarium; Herbarium; Art Gallery; VSU Archives. **Campus Network:** 100% of classrooms, 100% of dorms, 100% of student union, 100% of libraries, 100% of dining areas, 10% of common outdoor areas have wireless network access.

CAMPUS LIFE
Environment: City. **Activities:** Campus Ministries; Choral groups; Concert band; Dance; Drama/theater; International Student Organization; Jazz band; Literary magazine; Marching band; Model UN; Music ensembles; Opera; Pep band; Radio station; Student government; Student newspaper; Symphony orchestra; Television station; Yearbook. 183 registered organizations, 18 honor societies, 19 religious organizations, 14 fraternities, 10 sororities on campus. **Athletics (Intercollegiate):** *Men:* baseball, basketball, cross-country, football, golf, tennis. *Women:* basketball, cheerleading, cross-country, softball, tennis, volleyball. **On-Campus Highlights:** Student Recreation Center. **Environmental Initiatives:** Recycling.

ADMISSIONS
Freshman Academic Profile: Average high school GPA 3.1. **Test Scores:** SAT Math middle 50% range 460–540. SAT EBRW middle 50% range 470–540. ACT middle 50% range 20–23. **Basis for Candidate Selection:** *Very important factors include:* academic GPA, standardized test scores. *Important factors include:* rigor of secondary school record, class rank, extracurricular activities, talent/ability, character/personal qualities. **Freshman Admission Requirements:** High school diploma is required and GED is not accepted *Academic units required:* 4 English, 4 math, 3 science, 2 science labs, 2 foreign language, 3 social studies. **Freshman Admission Statistics:** 7,950 applied, 58% admitted, 48% enrolled. **Transfer Admission Requirements:** College transcript(s). Minimum college GPA of 2.0 required. Lowest grade transferable D. **General Admission Information:** Application fee $40. Regular application deadline 6/1. Non-fall registration accepted. Admission may be deferred for a maximum of 1 year.

COSTS AND FINANCIAL AID
Annual in-state tuition $3,787. Annual out-of-state tuition $13,368. Room and board $6,850. Required fees $1,910. Average book and supplies expense $1,200. **Required Forms and Deadlines:** FAFSA. **Notification of Awards:** Applicants will be notified of awards on a rolling basis beginning 4/15. **Types of Aid:** *Need-based scholarships/grants:* College/university scholarship or grant aid from institutional funds; Federal Nursing Scholarships; Federal Pell; Private scholarships; SEOG; State scholarships/grants. *Loans:* Direct PLUS loans; Direct Subsidized Stafford Loans; Direct Unsubsidized Stafford Loans. **Student Employment:** Federal Work-Study Program available. Institutional employment available. **Financial Aid Statistics:** 89% needy freshmen, 82% needy undergrads receive need-based scholarship or grant aid. 6% freshmen, 5% undergrads receive non-need-based scholarship or grant aid. 87% freshmen, 76% undergrads receive need-based self-help aid. 1% freshmen, 0% undergrads receive athletic scholarships. 76% freshmen, 70% undergrads receive any aid. **Criteria awarding aid:** *Need-based:* Art, Athletics, Minority status, Music/ drama. *Non-need-based:* Academics, Art, Athletics, Minority status, Music/ drama, State/district residency.

VALPARAISO UNIVERSITY

Duesenberg Welcome Center, Valparaiso, IN 46383
Phone: 219-464-5011 **Financial Aid Phone:** 219-464-5015
E-mail: undergrad.admission@valpo.edu **CEEB Code:** 1874
Fax: 219-464-6898 **Website:** https://www.valpo.edu **ACT Code:** 1256

This private school, affiliated with the Lutheran Church, was founded in 1859. It has a 350 acre campus.

RATINGS
Admissions Selectivity Rating: 81   **Fire Safety Rating:** 84   **Green Rating:** 80

STUDENTS AND FACULTY
Enrollment: 2,982. **Student Body:** 56% female, 44% male, 54% out-of-state, 3% international (38 countries represented). Asian 2%, African American 5%, Caucasian 72%, Hispanic 11%, Native American <1%, Pacific Islander <1%, Two or more races 3%, Race unknown 3%.
Retention and Graduation: 84% freshmen return for sophomore year. 62% freshmen graduate within 4 years. 71% freshmen graduate within 6 years. 17% grads go on to further study within 1 year. 10% grads pursue arts and sciences degrees. 10% grads pursue law degrees. 1% grads pursue business degrees. <1% grads pursue medical degrees. **Faculty:** Student/faculty ratio 10:1. 290 full-time faculty, 90% hold PhDs, 9% are members of minority groups, 45% are women. 0% of classes are taught by teaching assistants.

ACADEMICS
Degrees: Associate; Bachelor's; Certificate; Doctoral degree—professional practice; Master's; Post-bachelor's certificate; Post-master's certificate; Terminal Associate. **Classes:** Most classes have 10–19 students. Most lab/discussion sessions have 10–19 students. **Most popular majors:** Mechanical Engineering; Biology/Biological Sciences, General; Registered Nursing/Registered Nurse. **Special Study Options:** Accelerated program; Cooperative education program; Cross-registration; Distance learning; Double major; Dual enrollment; Exchange student program (domestic); Honors program; Independent study; Internships; Liberal arts/career combination; Student-designed major; Study abroad; Teacher certification program. **Honors programs:** Christ College, VU's honors college, provides an honors-level liberal arts curriculum dedicated to the study and practice of the basic arts of inquiry and committed to educational processes that enable students to achieve a measure of intellectual independence. **Combined degree programs:** BA/MA. **Disability Services offered:** Note-taking services; Reader services; Tape recorders; Tutors. **Career services:** Alumni network; Alumni services; Career assessment; Career/job search classes; Internships; Regional alumni.

FACILITIES
Housing: Apartments for single students; Coed dorms; Fraternity/sorority housing; Special housing for disabled students; Theme housing; Women's dorms; 60% of campus accessible to physically disabled. **Special Academic Facilities/Equipment:** Art Museum, Galleries, Language Lab, Planetarium, Electron Microscope, Observatory, TV Studio, Weather Station, Virtual Nursing Learning Center, VisBox, Non-linear Video Editing, Christopher Center for Learning and Information Resources, Doppler Radar Facility, Solar Energy Center, Writing Center, Center for the Sciences, Fites Engineering.

CAMPUS LIFE
Environment: Town. **Activities:** Campus Ministries; Choral groups; Concert band; Dance; Drama/theater; International Student Organization; Jazz band; Literary magazine; Music ensembles; Musical theater; Pep band; Radio station; Student government; Student newspaper; Symphony orchestra; Television station; Yearbook. 100 registered organizations, 35 honor societies, 8 religious organizations, 10 fraternities, 7 sororities on campus. **Athletics (Intercollegiate):** *Men:* baseball, basketball, cross-country, diving, football, golf, soccer, swimming, tennis, track/field (outdoor), track/field (indoor). *Women:* basketball, bowling, cross-country, diving, golf, soccer, softball, swimming, tennis, track/field (outdoor), track/field (indoor), volleyball. **On-Campus Highlights:** Harre Union.

ADMISSIONS
Freshman Academic Profile: Average high school GPA 3.8. 36% in top 10% of high school class, 65% in top 25% of high school class, 93% in top 50% of high school class. **Test Scores:** SAT Math middle 50% range 530–650. SAT EBRW middle 50% range 540–640. ACT middle 50% range 22–29. **Basis for Candidate Selection:** *Very important factors include:* rigor of secondary school record, academic GPA, standardized test scores. *Important factors include:*

class rank, extracurricular activities, talent/ability, character/personal qualities, alumni/ae relation. *Other factors include:* application essay, recommendation(s), interview, first generation, religious affiliation/commitment, racial/ethnic status, volunteer work, level of applicant's interest. **Freshman Admission Requirements:** High school diploma is required and GED is accepted *Academic units required:* 4 English, 3 math, 2 science, 2 science labs, 2 foreign language, 2 history, 3 academic electives. *Academic units recommended:* 4 English, 4 math, 3 science, 3 science labs, 2 foreign language, 1 social studies, 2 history, 3 academic electives. **Freshman Admission Statistics:** 5,491 applied, 86% admitted, 14% enrolled. **Transfer Admission Requirements:** College transcript(s), essay or personal statement, statement of good standing from prior institution(s). Minimum college GPA of 2.0 required. Lowest grade transferable C-. **General Admission Information:** Priority deadline 12/1. Non-fall registration accepted. Admission may be deferred for a maximum of 1 year.

COSTS AND FINANCIAL AID

Annual tuition $41,940. Room and board $12,620. Required fees $1,346. Average book and supplies expense $1,200. **Required Forms and Deadlines:** FAFSA. **Notification of Awards:** Applicants will be notified of awards on a rolling basis beginning 12/15. **Types of Aid:** *Need-based scholarships/grants:* College/university scholarship or grant aid from institutional funds; Federal Pell; Private scholarships; SEOG; State scholarships/grants. *Loans:* Direct PLUS loans; Direct Subsidized Stafford Loans; Direct Unsubsidized Stafford Loans. **Student Employment:** Federal Work-Study Program available. Institutional employment available. **Financial Aid Statistics:** 100% needy freshmen, 100% needy undergrads receive need-based scholarship or grant aid. 25% freshmen, 19% undergrads receive non-need-based scholarship or grant aid. 42% freshmen, 63% undergrads receive need-based self-help aid. 2% freshmen, 3% undergrads receive athletic scholarships. 99% freshmen, 97% undergrads receive any aid. 72% undergrads borrow to pay for school. Average cumulative indebtedness $35,968. **Criteria awarding aid:** *Need-based:* Religious affiliation. *Non-need-based:* Academics, Alumni affiliation, Art, Athletics, Leadership, Music/drama, Religious affiliation, State/district residency.

VANDERBILT UNIVERSITY

2305 West End Ave., Nashville, TN 37203
Phone: 615-322-2561 **Financial Aid Phone:** 800-288-0204
E-mail: admissions@vanderbilt.edu **CEEB Code:** 1871
Fax: 615-343-7765 **Website:** www.vanderbilt.edu **ACT Code:** 4036

This private school was founded in 1873. It has a 323 acre campus.

RATINGS

Admissions Selectivity Rating: 99   Fire Safety Rating: 91   Green Rating: 99

STUDENTS AND FACULTY

Enrollment: 6,871. **Student Body:** 52% female, 48% male, 89% out-of-state, 10% international (51 countries represented). Asian 14%, African American 11%, Caucasian 44%, Hispanic 10%, Native American <1%, Pacific Islander <1%, Two or more races 6%, Race unknown 5%.
Retention and Graduation: 97% freshmen return for sophomore year. 90% freshmen graduate within 4 years. 93% freshmen graduate within 6 years. 32% grads go on to further study within 1 year. 11% grads pursue arts and sciences degrees. 9% grads pursue law degrees. 25% grads pursue business degrees. 9% grads pursue medical degrees. **Faculty:** Student/faculty ratio 7:1. 974 full-time faculty, 96% hold PhDs, 17% are members of minority groups, 41% are women.

ACADEMICS

Degrees: Bachelor's; Doctoral degree—professional practice; Doctoral degree research/scholarship; Master's; Post-master's certificate. **Classes:** Most classes have 10–19 students. Most lab/discussion sessions have 10–19 students. **Most popular majors:** Engineering Science; Multi-/Interdisciplinary Studies, Other; Social Sciences, General. **Special Study Options:** Accelerated program; Double major; Dual enrollment; English as a Second Language (ESL); Honors program; Independent study; Internships; Liberal arts/career combination; Student-designed major; Study abroad; Teacher certification program. **Honors programs:** Alpha Lambda Delta, Phi Eta Sigma, Lotus Eaters Sophomore

Honor Society, Athenian Honorary, Omicron Delta Kappa, Mortar Board. **Combined degree programs:** BA/MA. **Disability Services offered:** Note-taking services; Reader services; Tape recorders; Tutors. **Career services:** Alumni network; Career assessment; Career/job search classes; Internships.

FACILITIES

Housing: Apartments for single students; Coed dorms; Fraternity/sorority housing; Men's dorms; Special housing for disabled students; Theme housing; Women's dorms; 95% of campus accessible to physically disabled. **Special Academic Facilities/Equipment:** Freedom Forum First Amendment Center, Biological Sciences/Medical Research Building III, Dyer Observatory, Kennedy Center, Martha Rivers Ingram Center for the Performing Arts, E. Bronson Ingram Studio Arts Center, Student Life Center. **Campus Network:** 100% of classrooms, 40% of dorms, 100% of student union, 100% of libraries, 100% of dining areas, 0% of common outdoor areas have wireless network access.

CAMPUS LIFE

Environment: Metropolis. **Activities:** Campus Ministries; Choral groups; Concert band; Dance; Drama/theater; International Student Organization; Jazz band; Literary magazine; Marching band; Model UN; Music ensembles; Musical theater; Opera; Pep band; Radio station; Student government; Student newspaper; Student-run film society; Symphony orchestra; Television station; Yearbook. 467 registered organizations, 16 honor societies, 14 religious organizations, 17 fraternities, 15 sororities on campus. **Athletics (Intercollegiate):** *Men:* baseball, basketball, cross-country, football, golf, tennis. *Women:* basketball, cross-country, golf, lacrosse, soccer, tennis, track/field (outdoor). **On-Campus Highlights:** The Commons. **Environmental Initiatives:** 1. Greenhouse gas emissions reduction—Overall greenhouse gas emissions from Vanderbilt's campus and medical center decreased by 12% from an all-time high reached in 2008—and by 7% from 2005 to 2011—even though Vanderbilt has seen significant growth in square footage, staff, students, and research dollars over the last four years. GHG emissions per square foot have gone down 21% over the past seven years, which reflects a lot of hard work to improve the energy efficiency of existing buildings, some that are very old, as well as new construction and renovation projects that have incorporated excellent energy efficiency. GHG emissions per person, per student, per research dollar, per inpatient day and per ambulatory visit also have trended significantly in a positive direction since 2005. Most university greenhouse gas inventory reports do not include research and/or patient care activity, making Vanderbilt's report more comprehensive than most and also more comprehensive than what is now required by the Environmental Protection Agency.

ADMISSIONS

Freshman Academic Profile: Average high school GPA 3.8. 90% in top 10% of high school class, 7% in top 25% of high school class, 2% in top 50% of high school class. 64% from public high schools. **Test Scores:** SAT Math middle 50% range 750–800. SAT EBRW middle 50% range 710–760. ACT middle 50% range 33–35. **Basis for Candidate Selection:** *Very important factors include:* rigor of secondary school record, class rank, academic GPA, application essay, standardized test scores, extracurricular activities, character/personal qualities. *Important factors include:* recommendation(s), talent/ability. *Other factors include:* interview, first generation, alumni/ae relation, geographical residence, state residency, racial/ethnic status, volunteer work, work experience. **Freshman Admission Requirements:** *Academic units required:* 4 English, 3 math, 3 science, 2 science labs, 2 foreign language, 2 social studies, 1 history, 3 academic electives. *Academic units recommended:* 4 English, 4 math, 4 science, 3 science labs, 2 foreign language, 3 social studies, 1 history, 3 academic electives. **Freshman Admission Statistics:** 37,310 applied, 9% admitted, 47% enrolled. **Transfer Admission Requirements:** College transcript(s), essay or personal statement, statement of good standing from prior institution(s). Lowest grade transferable C. **General Admission Information:** Application fee $50. Priority deadline 1/1. Regular application deadline 1/1. Admission may be deferred for a maximum of 2 years.

COSTS AND FINANCIAL AID

Annual tuition $50,800. Room and board $16,910. Required fees $2,106. Average book and supplies expense $1,294. **Required Forms and Deadlines:** CSS/Financial Aid PROFILE; FAFSA. **Notification of Awards:** Applicants will be notified of awards on or about 4/1. **Types of Aid:** *Need-based scholarships/grants:* College/university scholarship or grant aid from institutional funds; Federal Pell; Private scholarships; SEOG; State scholarships/grants; United Negro College Fund. *Loans:* Direct PLUS loans; Direct Subsidized Stafford Loans; Direct Unsubsidized Stafford Loans. **Student Employment:** Federal Work-Study Program available. Institutional employment available. **Financial Aid Statistics:** 98% needy freshmen, 99% needy undergrads receive need-based scholarship or grant aid. 10% freshmen, 5% undergrads receive non-need-based scholarship or grant aid. 49% freshmen, 54% undergrads receive need-based self-help aid. 4% freshmen, 4% undergrads receive athletic scholarships. 54% freshmen receive any aid. 22% undergrads borrow to pay for school. Average cumulative indebtedness $22,727. **Criteria awarding aid:** *Need-based:* Academics, Leadership, Music/drama *Non-need-based:* Academics, Athletics, Leadership, Music/drama, State/district residency.

VANDERCOOK COLLEGE OF MUSIC

3140 South Federal Street, Chicago, IL 60616-3731
Phone: 312-788-1120 **Financial Aid Phone:** 312-788-1146
E-mail: admissions@vandercook.edu **CEEB Code:** 1872
Fax: 312-225-5211 **Website:** www.vandercook.edu **ACT Code:** 1156

This private school was founded in 1909. It has a 1 acre campus.

RATINGS

Admissions Selectivity Rating: 74   Fire Safety Rating: 62   Green Rating: 60*

STUDENTS AND FACULTY

Enrollment: 90. **Student Body:** 47% female, 53% male, 23% out-of-state, 2% international (2 countries represented). African American 3%, Caucasian 59%, Hispanic 24%, Native American 0%, Pacific Islander 1%, Two or more races 3%, Race unknown 7%.
Retention and Graduation: 73% freshmen return for sophomore year. 41% freshmen graduate within 4 years. 59% freshmen graduate within 6 years. **Faculty:** Student/faculty ratio 3:1. 13 full-time faculty, 54% hold PhDs, 23% are members of minority groups, 62% are women. 0% of classes are taught by teaching assistants.

ACADEMICS

Degrees: Bachelor's; Master's. **Classes:** Most classes have fewer than 10 students. **Most popular majors:** Teacher certification program. **Career services:** Alumni services; Career/job search classes.

FACILITIES

Housing: Apartments for married students; Apartments for single students; Coed dorms; Fraternity/sorority housing. **Campus Network:** 95% of classrooms, 5% of dorms, 100% of student union, 100% of libraries, 100% of dining areas have wireless network access.

CAMPUS LIFE

Environment: Metropolis. **Activities:** Choral groups; Concert band; Jazz band; Music ensembles; Musical theater; Radio station; Symphony orchestra. 5 registered organizations, 1 fraternities, 1 sororities, on campus.

ADMISSIONS

Freshman Academic Profile: Average high school GPA 3.0. 100% in top 50% of high school class. 80% from public high schools. **Test Scores:** SAT Math middle 50% range 450–540. SAT EBRW middle 50% range 430–530. ACT middle 50% range 21–29. **Basis for Candidate Selection:** *Very important factors include:* academic GPA, application essay, standardized test scores, recommendation(s), interview, talent/ability, character/personal qualities. *Important factors include:* extracurricular activities, alumni/ae relation. *Other factors include:* rigor of secondary school record, class rank, first generation. **Freshman Admission Requirements:** High school diploma is required and GED is accepted. *Academic units recommended:* 3 English, 2 math, 2 science, 2 foreign language, 3 social studies, 3 unit from above areas or other academic areas. **Freshman Admission Statistics:** 38 applied, 100% admitted, 39% enrolled. **Transfer Admission Requirements:** High school transcript, college transcript(s), essay or personal statement, interview, standardized test scores. Minimum college GPA of 2.5 required. Lowest grade transferable C. **General Admission Information:** Application fee $35. Priority deadline 4/1. Non-fall registration accepted. Admission may be deferred for a maximum of 1 year.

COSTS AND FINANCIAL AID

Annual tuition $26,458. Room and board $12,074. Required fees $1,886. Average book and supplies expense $1,900. **Required Forms and Deadlines:** FAFSA. **Notification of Awards:** Applicants will be notified of awards on a rolling basis beginning 3/1. **Types of Aid:** *Need-based scholarships/grants:* College/university scholarship or grant aid from institutional funds; Federal Pell; Private scholarships; SEOG; State scholarships/grants; United Negro College Fund. *Loans:* Direct PLUS loans; Direct Subsidized Stafford Loans; Direct Unsubsidized Stafford Loans. **Student Employment:** Federal Work-Study Program available. Institutional employment available. **Financial Aid Statistics:** 78% needy freshmen, 61% needy undergrads receive need-based

scholarship or grant aid. 100% freshmen, 100% undergrads receive non-need-based scholarship or grant aid. 89% freshmen, 96% undergrads receive need-based self-help aid. 0% freshmen, 0% undergrads receive athletic scholarships. 100% freshmen, 97% undergrads receive any aid. 78% undergrads borrow to pay for school. Average cumulative indebtedness $42,886. **Criteria awarding aid:** *Non-need-based:* Academics, Alumni affiliation, Music/drama.

VASSAR COLLEGE

Box 10, 124 Raymond Avenue, Poughkeepsie, NY 12604
Phone: 845-437-7300 **Financial Aid Phone:** 845-437-5320
E-mail: admissions@vassar.edu **CEEB Code:** 2956
Website: www.vassar.edu **ACT Code:** 2982

This private school was founded in 1861. It has a 1000 acre campus.

RATINGS

Admissions Selectivity Rating: 96   Fire Safety Rating: 89   Green Rating: 89

STUDENTS AND FACULTY

Enrollment: 2,436. **Student Body:** 59% female, 41% male, 72% out-of-state, 9% international (54 countries represented). Asian 12%, African American 4%, Caucasian 56%, Hispanic 11%, Native American <1%, Pacific Islander 0%, Two or more races 8%, Race unknown <1%.
Retention and Graduation: 95% freshmen return for sophomore year. 85% freshmen graduate within 4 years. 90% freshmen graduate within 6 years. 20% grads go on to further study within 1 year. 8% grads pursue arts and sciences degrees. 2% grads pursue law degrees. 1% grads pursue business degrees. 1% grads pursue medical degrees. **Faculty:** Student/faculty ratio 8:1. 283 full-time faculty, 91% hold PhDs, 26% are members of minority groups, 47% are women. 0% of classes are taught by teaching assistants.

ACADEMICS

Degrees: Bachelor's; Master's. **Classes:** Most classes have 10–19 students. Most lab/discussion sessions have 10–19 students. **Most popular majors:** Economics, General; Political Science and Government, General; Research and Experimental Psychology, Other. **Special Study Options:** Cooperative education program; Cross-registration; Double major; Exchange student program (domestic); Independent study; Internships; Liberal arts/career combination; Student-designed major; Study abroad; Teacher certification program. **Combined degree programs:** BA/MA. **Disability Services offered:** Note-taking services; Reader services; Tape recorders. **Career services:** Alumni network; Alumni services; Career assessment; Career/job search classes; Internships; Regional alumni.

FACILITIES

Housing: Apartments for single students; Coed dorms; Cooperative housing; Special housing for disabled students; Special housing for international students; Wellness housing; Women's dorms 75% of campus accessible to physically disabled. **Special Academic Facilities/Equipment:** Art center, theatres, nursery school, environmental field station, geology museum, electron microscope, observatory, Skinner Music Hall, Fitness Center.

CAMPUS LIFE

Environment: Town. **Activities:** Campus Ministries; Choral groups; Concert band; Dance; Drama/theater; International Student Organization; Jazz band; Literary magazine; Model UN; Music ensembles; Musical theater; Opera; Radio station; Student government; Student newspaper; Student-run film society; Symphony orchestra; Yearbook. 145 registered organizations, 5 honor societies, 12 religious organizations, on campus. **Athletics (Intercollegiate):** *Men:* baseball, basketball, crew/rowing, cross-country, diving, fencing, lacrosse, soccer, squash, swimming, tennis, track/field (outdoor), volleyball. *Women:* basketball, crew/rowing, cross-country, diving, fencing, field hockey, golf, lacrosse, soccer, squash, swimming, tennis, track/field (outdoor), volleyball. **On-Campus Highlights:** Library.

ADMISSIONS

Freshman Academic Profile: 61% in top 10% of high school class, 91% in top 25% of high school class, 98% in top 50% of high school class. 64% from public high schools. **Test Scores:** SAT Math middle 50% range 690–770. SAT

EBRW middle 50% range 680–740. ACT middle 50% range 31–33. **Basis for Candidate Selection:** *Very important factors include:* rigor of secondary school record, academic GPA. *Important factors include:* class rank, application essay, standardized test scores, recommendation(s), extracurricular activities, talent/ability, character/personal qualities. *Other factors include:* interview, first generation, alumni/ae relation, geographical residence, racial/ethnic status, volunteer work, work experience. **Freshman Admission Requirements:** High school diploma is required and GED is accepted. *Academic units recommended:* 4 English, 4 math, 4 science, 3 science labs, 4 foreign language, 2 social studies, 2 history. **Freshman Admission Statistics:** 8,312 applied, 25% admitted, 34% enrolled. **Transfer Admission Requirements:** High school transcript, college transcript(s), essay or personal statement, standardized test scores, statement of good standing from prior institution(s). Minimum college GPA of 3.0 required. Lowest grade transferable C. **General Admission Information:** Application fee $65. Regular application deadline 1/1. Admission may be deferred for a maximum of 1 year.

COSTS AND FINANCIAL AID
Annual tuition $54,410. Room and board $12,900. Required fees $800. Average book and supplies expense $900. **Required Forms and Deadlines:** CSS/Financial Aid PROFILE; FAFSA; Noncustodial PROFILE. **Types of Aid:** *Need-based scholarships/grants:* College/university scholarship or grant aid from institutional funds; Federal Pell; Private scholarships; SEOG; State scholarships/grants. *Loans:* Direct PLUS loans; Direct Subsidized Stafford Loans; Direct Unsubsidized Stafford Loans. **Student Employment:** Federal Work-Study Program available. Institutional employment available. **Financial Aid Statistics:** 99% needy freshmen, 99% needy undergrads receive need-based scholarship or grant aid. 0% freshmen, 0% undergrads receive non-need-based scholarship or grant aid. 95% freshmen, 97% undergrads receive need-based self-help aid. 0% freshmen, 0% undergrads receive athletic scholarships. 64% freshmen, 66% undergrads receive any aid. 49% undergrads borrow to pay for school. Average cumulative indebtedness $21,473.

VAUGHN COLLEGE OF AERONAUTICS AND TECHNOLOGY

86-01 23rd Avenue, Flushing, NY 11369
Phone: 718-429-6600 **Financial Aid Phone:** 718-429-6600
E-mail: admitme@vaughn.edu **CEEB Code:** 2001
Fax: 718-779-2231 **Website:** www.vaughn.edu

This private school was founded in 1932. It has a 6 acre campus.

RATINGS
Admissions Selectivity Rating: 81   **Fire Safety Rating:** 96   **Green Rating:** 60*

STUDENTS AND FACULTY
Enrollment: 1,605. **Student Body:** 13% female, 87% male, 11% out-of-state, 2% international. Asian 12%, African American 22%, Caucasian 13%, Hispanic 38%, Native American <1%, Pacific Islander 3%, Two or more races 5%, Race unknown 5%.
Retention and Graduation: 66% freshmen return for sophomore year. 0% grads pursue business degrees. **Faculty:** Student/faculty ratio 15:1. 41 full-time faculty, 49% hold PhDs, 37% are members of minority groups, 20% are women. 0% of classes are taught by teaching assistants.

ACADEMICS
Degrees: Associate; Bachelor's; Certificate; Master's. **Classes:** Most classes have fewer than 10 students. Most lab/discussion sessions have 20–29 students. **Most popular majors:** Airframe Mechanics and Aircraft Maintenance Technology/Technician; Airline/Commercial/Professional Pilot and Flight Crew; Aeronautics/Aviation/Aerospace Science and Technology, General. **Special Study Options:** Accelerated program; Distance learning; Independent study; Internships; Liberal arts/career combination. **Disability Services offered:** Tutors. **Career services:** Alumni network; Alumni services; Career assessment; Career/job search classes; Internships.

FACILITIES
Housing: Coed dorms; Special housing for disabled students; Theme housing; Wellness housing; 100% of campus accessible to physically disabled. **Campus Network:** 100% of classrooms, 100% of dorms, 100% of student union, 100% of libraries, 100% of dining areas, 90% of common outdoor areas have wireless network access.

CAMPUS LIFE
Environment: Metropolis. **Activities:** Dance; International Student Organization; Student government. 11 registered organizations, 1 honor society on campus. **Athletics (Intercollegiate):** *Men:* basketball, soccer. *Women:* tennis. **On-Campus Highlights:** Flight Simulator Complex.

ADMISSIONS
Test Scores: SAT Math middle 50% range 459–560. SAT EBRW middle 50% range 432–533. ACT middle 50% range 19–24. **Basis for Candidate Selection:** *Very important factors include:* rigor of secondary school record, academic GPA. *Important factors include:* standardized test scores, extracurricular activities, volunteer work, level of applicant's interest. *Other factors include:* application essay, recommendation(s), interview, talent/ability, character/personal qualities, work experience. **Freshman Admission Requirements:** High school diploma is required and GED is accepted. *Academic units required:* 4 English, 3 math, 2 science, 2 science labs, 1 social studies. *Academic units recommended:* 4 English, 4 math, 3 science, 3 science labs, 4 social studies. **Freshman Admission Statistics:** 813 applied, 75% admitted, 51% enrolled. **Transfer Admission Requirements:** College transcript(s). Minimum college GPA of 2.0 required. Lowest grade transferable C. **General Admission Information:** Application fee $40. Priority deadline 3/1. Non-fall registration accepted. Admission may be deferred for a maximum of 1 year.

COSTS AND FINANCIAL AID
Annual tuition $20,840. Room and board $13,265. Required fees $960. Average book and supplies expense $2,160. **Required Forms and Deadlines:** FAFSA; State aid form. **Notification of Awards:** Applicants will be notified of awards on a rolling basis beginning 4/15. **Types of Aid:** *Need-based scholarships/grants:* College/university scholarship or grant aid from institutional funds; Federal Pell; Private scholarships; SEOG; State scholarships/grants. *Loans:* Direct PLUS loans; Direct Subsidized Stafford Loans; Direct Unsubsidized Stafford Loans. **Student Employment:** Federal Work-Study Program available. Institutional employment available. **Financial Aid Statistics:** 99% needy freshmen, 91% needy undergrads receive need-based scholarship or grant aid. 29% freshmen, 23% undergrads receive non-need-based scholarship or grant aid. 96% freshmen, 76% undergrads receive need-based self-help aid. 0% freshmen, 0% undergrads receive athletic scholarships. 94% freshmen, 95% undergrads receive any aid. **Criteria awarding aid:** *Need-based:* Academics, Leadership. *Non-need-based:* Academics, Alumni affiliation, Leadership.

VERMONT TECHNICAL COLLEGE

PO Box 500, Randolph Ctr, VT 05061
Phone: 802-728-1444 **Financial Aid Phone:** 800-965-8790
E-mail: admissions@vtc.edu **CEEB Code:** 3941
Fax: 8027281321 **Website:** http://www.vtc.edu/ **ACT Code:** 4323

This is a public school.

RATINGS
Admissions Selectivity Rating: 86   **Fire Safety Rating:** 60*   **Green Rating:** 64

STUDENTS AND FACULTY
Enrollment: 1,434. **Student Body:** 48% female, 52% male, 19% out-of-state, 1% international (25 countries represented). Asian 1%, African American 1%, Caucasian 63%, Hispanic 2%, Native American <1%, Pacific Islander 0%, Two or more races 30%, Race unknown 1%.
Retention and Graduation: 71% freshmen return for sophomore year. 33% freshmen graduate within 4 years. 46% freshmen graduate within 6 years. **Faculty:** Student/faculty ratio 8:1. 82 full-time faculty, 33% hold PhDs, 4% are members of minority groups, 52% are women. 0% of classes are taught by teaching assistants.

ACADEMICS
Degrees: Associate; Bachelor's; Certificate; Diploma; Master's. **Classes:** Most classes have 10–19 students. Most lab/discussion sessions have fewer than 10 students. **Most popular majors:** Licensed Practical/Vocational Nurse Training (Lpn, Lvn, Cert, Dipl, Aas); Nursing/Registered Nurse (Rn, Asn, Bsn, Msn); Air Transportation. **Special Study Options:** Cooperative education program; Cross-registration; Distance learning; Double major; Dual enrollment; Independent study; Internships. **Disability Services offered:** Note-taking services; Reader services; Tape recorders; Tutors. **Career services:** Alumni network; Alumni services; Career assessment; Internships.

FACILITIES

Housing: Coed dorms; Men's dorms; Special housing for disabled students; Women's dorms.

CAMPUS LIFE

Environment: Rural. **Activities:** Campus Ministries; International Student Organization; Model UN; Radio station; Student government; Student-run film society. **On-Campus Highlights:** SHAPE (athletic facility).

ADMISSIONS

Freshman Academic Profile: Average high school GPA 3.1. **Test Scores:** SAT Math middle 50% range 500–580. SAT EBRW middle 50% range 480–590. ACT middle 50% range 17–23. **Basis for Candidate Selection:** *Very important factors include:* rigor of secondary school record. *Important factors include:* academic GPA, standardized test scores. *Other factors include:* class rank, application essay, recommendation(s). **Freshman Admission Requirements:** High school diploma is required and GED is accepted *Academic units required:* 4 English, 3 math, 2 science, 1 science labs, 2 social studies. *Academic units recommended:* 4 math, 4 science, 1 history. **Freshman Admission Statistics:** 1,087 applied, 68% admitted, 39% enrolled. **General Admission Information:** Application fee $47. Non-fall registration accepted.

COSTS AND FINANCIAL AID

Annual in-state tuition $14,304. Annual out-of-state tuition $27,336. Room and board $11,020. Required fees $1,667. Average book and supplies expense $800. **Required Forms and Deadlines:** FAFSA; State aid form. **Types of Aid:** *Need-based scholarships/grants:* College/university scholarship or grant aid from institutional funds; Federal Nursing Scholarships; Federal Pell; Private scholarships; SEOG; State scholarships/grants. *Loans:* Direct PLUS loans; Direct Subsidized Stafford Loans; Direct Unsubsidized Stafford Loans. **Student Employment:** Federal Work-Study Program available. Institutional employment available. **Financial Aid Statistics:** 73% needy freshmen, 76% needy undergrads receive need-based scholarship or grant aid. 40% freshmen, 26% undergrads receive non-need-based scholarship or grant aid. 77% freshmen, 75% undergrads receive need-based self-help aid. 0% freshmen, 0% undergrads receive athletic scholarships. 80% freshmen, 80% undergrads receive any aid. 84% undergrads borrow to pay for school. Average cumulative indebtedness $24,410.

VILLA MARIA COLLEGE OF BUFFALO

240 Pine Ridge Road, Buffalo, NY 14225
Phone: 716-961-1805 **Financial Aid Phone:** 716-961-1850
E-mail: admissions@villa.edu
Fax: 716-896-0705 **ACT Code:** 2983

This private school, affiliated with the Roman Catholic Church, was founded in 1960. It has a 9 acre campus.

RATINGS

Admissions Selectivity Rating: 68   **Fire Safety Rating:** 60*   **Green Rating:** 60*

STUDENTS AND FACULTY

Enrollment: 469. **Student Body:** 68% female, 32% male, 3% out-of-state, 0% international (0 countries represented). Asian 1%, African American 26%, Caucasian 61%, Hispanic 6%, Native American <1%, Pacific Islander <1%, Two or more races 5%, Race unknown <1%.
Retention and Graduation: 59% freshmen return for sophomore year. **Faculty:** Student/faculty ratio 8:1. 29 full-time faculty, 52% hold PhDs, 0% are members of minority groups, 59% are women. 0% of classes are taught by teaching assistants.

ACADEMICS

Degrees: Associate; Bachelor's; Certificate. **Classes:** Most classes have 10–19 students. Most lab/discussion sessions have fewer than 10 students. **Most popular majors:** Visual and Performing Arts, General; Physical Therapy Assistant. **Special Study Options:** Cross-registration; Double major; Dual enrollment; Internships; Liberal arts/career combination. **Disability Services offered:** Tutors. **Career services:** Alumni services; Career assessment; Career/job search classes; Internships.

FACILITIES

Housing: 80% of campus accessible to physically disabled. **Special Academic Facilities/Equipment:** Art Gallery, Music Building, Recording Studio, Student Center, Athletic Center, Art Shop.

CAMPUS LIFE

Environment: City. **Activities:** Campus Ministries; Choral groups; Jazz band; Literary magazine; Music ensembles; Student government. 1 honor society on campus. **On-Campus Highlights:** Athletic/Student Center.

ADMISSIONS

Freshman Academic Profile: Average high school GPA 3.0. 28% in top 25% of high school class, 52% in top 50% of high school class. 93% from public high schools. **Basis for Candidate Selection:** *Very important factors include:* academic GPA, application essay, interview, talent/ability. *Important factors include:* level of applicant's interest. *Other factors include:* rigor of secondary school record, standardized test scores, recommendation(s), volunteer work, work experience. **Freshman Admission Requirements:** High school diploma is required and GED is accepted. *Academic units recommended:* 4 English, 3 math, 3 science, 4 social studies, 4 history. **Freshman Admission Statistics:** 248 applied, 80% admitted, 55% enrolled. **Transfer Admission Requirements:** College transcript(s), interview. Lowest grade transferable C. **General Admission Information:** Non-fall registration accepted. Admission may be deferred for a maximum of 2 semesters.

COSTS AND FINANCIAL AID

Annual tuition $18,520. **Required Forms and Deadlines:** FAFSA. **Notification of Awards:** Applicants will be notified of awards on a rolling basis beginning 2/15. **Types of Aid:** *Need-based scholarships/grants:* College/university scholarship or grant aid from institutional funds; Federal Pell; Private scholarships; SEOG; State scholarships/grants. **Student Employment:** Federal Work-Study Program available. **Financial Aid Statistics:** 98% needy freshmen, 99% needy undergrads receive need-based scholarship or grant aid. 49% freshmen, 78% undergrads receive non-need-based scholarship or grant aid. 19% freshmen, 15% undergrads receive need-based self-help aid. 0% freshmen, 0% undergrads receive athletic scholarships. 99% freshmen, 92% undergrads receive any aid. **Criteria awarding aid:** *Need-based:* Academics, Alumni affiliation, Art, Leadership. *Non-need-based:* Academics, Alumni affiliation, Art, Leadership.

VILLANOVA UNIVERSITY

Best Colleges

Austin Hall, 800 Lancaster Avenue, Villanova, PA 19085
Phone: 610-519-4000 **Financial Aid Phone:** 610-519-4010
E-mail: gotovu@villanova.edu **CEEB Code:** 2959
Fax: 610-519-6450 **Website:** www.villanova.edu **ACT Code:** 3744

This private school, affiliated with the Roman Catholic Church, was founded in 1842. It has a 254 acre campus.

RATINGS

Admissions Selectivity Rating: 95   **Fire Safety Rating:** 97   **Green Rating:** 93

STUDENTS AND FACULTY

Enrollment: 6,857. **Student Body:** 53% female, 47% male, 79% out-of-state, 2% international (49 countries represented). Asian 6%, African American 5%, Caucasian 74%, Hispanic 8%, Native American <1%, Pacific Islander 0%, Two or more races 3%, Race unknown 2%.
Retention and Graduation: 95% freshmen return for sophomore year. 87% freshmen graduate within 4 years. 90% freshmen graduate within 6 years. 23% grads go on to further study within 1 year. 7% grads pursue arts and sciences degrees. 5% grads pursue law degrees. 1% grads pursue business degrees. 2% grads pursue medical degrees. **Faculty:** Student/faculty ratio 12:1. 618 full-time faculty, 16% are members of minority groups, 40% are women. 1% of classes are taught by teaching assistants.

ACADEMICS

Degrees: Associate; Bachelor's; Doctoral degree—professional practice; Doctoral degree research/scholarship; Master's; Post-bachelor's certificate; Post-master's certificate. **Most popular majors:** Registered Nursing/Registered Nurse; Finance, General; Mass Communication/Media Studies. **Special Study Options:** Accelerated program; Cooperative education program; Cross-registration; Distance learning; Double major; Dual enrollment; English as a Second Language (ESL); External degree program; Honors program; Independent study; Internships; Liberal arts/career combination; Student-designed major; Study abroad; Teacher certification program. **Honors programs:** The Honors Program at Villanova stands at the forefront of Villanova's long commitment to excellence. Our outstanding faculty educate our gifted students to be the transformative leaders the world needs. We prepare our students for distinguished careers in law, politics, education, business, medicine, and many other fields. We encourage our Honors students to actively engage in the creation of culture, at Villanova and beyond. We inspire them to connect their rich talents with a strong sense of their responsibility to lives of service. We are a community of learners who delight in the life of the mind and in each other. Honors students across all colleges at Villanova are challenged by a rigorous four-year comprehensive program of studies. They attend small, discussion-based seminars, undertake original research projects, and are mentored by nationally-renowned scholars. Our community values diverse backgrounds and perspectives, as well as international study. In short, Villanova is one of the nation's premier Catholic universities, and Honors students enjoy the best Villanova has to offer. The Honors Program seeks leaders who display sharp, critical intelligence; a passion for service; and a broad range of intellectual interests. Visit www.honorsprogram.villanova.edu to learn more about the opportunities an Honors education at Villanova affords. **Combined degree programs:** BA/MA. **Disability Services offered:** Note-taking services; Reader services; Tape recorders; Tutors. **Career services:** Alumni network; Alumni services; Career assessment; Career/job search classes; Internships; Regional alumni.

FACILITIES

Housing: Apartments for single students; Coed dorms; Special housing for disabled students; 95% of campus accessible to physically disabled. **Special Academic Facilities/Equipment:** Driscoll Hall, home of the Villanova College of Nursing; the Villanova School of Business Applied Finance Lab; the Structural Engineering Teaching and Research Laboratory; the Augustinian Historical Museum, and the Villanova Observatory.

CAMPUS LIFE

Environment: Village. **Activities:** Campus Ministries; Choral groups; Concert band; Dance; Drama/theater; International Student Organization; Jazz band; Literary magazine; Marching band; Model UN; Music ensembles; Musical theater; Pep band; Radio station; Student government; Student newspaper; Student-run film society; Symphony orchestra; Television station; Yearbook. 250 registered organizations, 36 honor societies, 15 religious organizations, 14 fraternities, 14 sororities on campus. **Athletics (Intercollegiate):** *Men:* baseball, basketball, cheerleading, cross-country, diving, football, golf, lacrosse, soccer, swimming, tennis, track/field (outdoor), track/field (indoor). *Women:* basketball, cheerleading, crew/rowing, cross-country, diving, field hockey, lacrosse, soccer, softball, swimming, tennis, track/field (outdoor), track/field (indoor), volleyball, water polo. **On-Campus Highlights:** St. Thomas of Villanova Church. **Environmental Initiatives:** Academic programs: The master's degree in sustainable engineering; the first-year environmental leadership learning community; bachelor's degrees in environmental science and environmental studies; an undergraduate minor in sustainability; a biology master's degree, graduate certificate, and advanced graduate certificate with a concentration in ecology, evolution, and organismal biology; a master's degree in water resources and environmental engineering, and a graduate certificate in urban water resources design.

ADMISSIONS

Freshman Academic Profile: Average high school GPA 4.1. 65% in top 10% of high school class, 95% in top 25% of high school class, 98% in top 50% of high school class. 53% from public high schools. **Test Scores:** SAT Math middle 50% range 630–730. SAT EBRW middle 50% range 620–710. ACT middle 50% range 30–33. **Basis for Candidate Selection:** *Very important factors include:* rigor of secondary school record, class rank, academic GPA, standardized test scores. *Important factors include:* application essay, recommendation(s), extracurricular activities, talent/ability, character/personal qualities. *Other factors include:* first generation, alumni/ae relation, geographical residence, state residency, racial/ethnic status, level of applicant's interest. **Freshman Admission Requirements:** High school diploma is required and GED is accepted. *Academic units required:* 4 English, 4 math, 4 science, 2 science labs, 2 foreign language, 2 academic electives, 4 unit from above areas or other academic areas. *Academic units recommended:* 4 English, 4 math, 4 science, 3 science labs, 4 foreign language, 2 academic electives. **Freshman Admission Statistics:** 21,112 applied, 36% admitted, 23% enrolled. **Transfer Admission Requirements:** High school transcript, college transcript(s), essay or personal statement, standardized test scores, statement of good standing from prior institution(s). Lowest grade transferable C. **General Admission Information:** Application fee $80. Priority deadline 12/15. Regular application deadline 1/15. Admission may be deferred for a maximum of 1 year.

COSTS AND FINANCIAL AID

Annual tuition $52,578. Room and board $14,020. Required fees $820. Average book and supplies expense $1,100. **Required Forms and Deadlines:** CSS/Financial Aid PROFILE; FAFSA; Noncustodial PROFILE. **Notification of Awards:** Applicants will be notified of awards on or about 4/1. **Types of Aid:** *Need-based scholarships/grants:* College/university scholarship or grant aid from institutional funds; Federal Pell; Private scholarships; SEOG; State scholarships/grants. *Loans:* Direct PLUS loans; Direct Subsidized Stafford Loans; Direct Unsubsidized Stafford Loans. **Student Employment:** Federal Work-Study Program available. Institutional employment available. **Financial Aid Statistics:** 92% needy freshmen, 90% needy undergrads receive need-based scholarship or grant aid. 7% freshmen, 4% undergrads receive non-need-based scholarship or grant aid. 92% freshmen, 92% undergrads receive need-based self-help aid. 3% freshmen, 3% undergrads receive athletic scholarships. 65% freshmen, 68% undergrads receive any aid. 53% undergrads borrow to pay for school. Average cumulative indebtedness $35,552. **Criteria awarding aid:** *Need-based:* Religious affiliation. *Non-need-based:* Academics, Alumni affiliation, Athletics, Leadership, Minority status, Religious affiliation.

VIRGINIA COMMONWEALTH UNIVERSITY

821 West Franklin Street, Richmond, VA 23284
Phone: 804-828-1222 **Financial Aid Phone:** 804-828-6669
E-mail: upgrad@vcu.edu **CEEB Code:** 5570
Fax: 804-828-1899 **Website:** www.vcu.edu

This public school was founded in 1838. It has a 150.2 acre campus.

RATINGS

Admissions Selectivity Rating: 80   Fire Safety Rating: 95   Green Rating: 97

STUDENTS AND FACULTY

Enrollment: 22,268. **Student Body:** 61% female, 39% male, 7% out-of-state, 2% international (81 countries represented). Asian 14%, African American 19%, Caucasian 43%, Hispanic 11%, Native American <1%, Pacific Islander <1%, Two or more races 7%, Race unknown 3%.
Retention and Graduation: 83% freshmen return for sophomore year. 45% freshmen graduate within 4 years. 67% freshmen graduate within 6 years.
Faculty: Student/faculty ratio 17:1. 1,276 full-time faculty, 72% hold PhDs, 22% are members of minority groups, 49% are women.

ACADEMICS

Degrees: Bachelor's; Certificate; Doctoral degree—professional practice; Doctoral degree research/scholarship; Master's; Post-bachelor's certificate; Post-master's certificate. **Classes:** Most classes have 10–19 students. Most lab/discussion sessions have 20–29 students. **Most popular majors:** Biology/Biological Sciences, General; Sports, Kinesiology, and Physical Education/Fitness, General; Psychology, General. **Special Study Options:** Accelerated program; Cooperative education program; Distance learning; Double major; Dual enrollment; English as a Second Language (ESL); Honors program; Independent study; Internships; Student-designed major; Study abroad; Teacher certification program. **Honors programs:** VCU Honors College—students gain a small, liberal arts college experience while being fully engaged in a large, urban university. The students will be part of a diverse and supportive community of students, faculty, and staff who will ease your transition from high school to college. Take small, discussion-based classes in place of larger, more lecture-oriented classes, giving you the opportunity to engage more closely with your classmates and more meaningfully with our outstanding faculty. Engage in local community service and have unique study-abroad options. Have an Honors advisor in addition to the advisor in your major. Gain access to special housing and scholarships. Students receive early registration privileges and enjoy unique professional development opportunities. Students come from all majors and participate in a wide variety of activities and organizations on and off campus, typically in leadership positions. **Disability Services offered:** Note-taking services; Reader services; Tape recorders; Tutors. **Career services:** Alumni network; Alumni services; Career assessment; Career/job search classes; Internships; Regional alumni.

FACILITIES

Housing: Apartments for single students; Coed dorms; Special housing for disabled students; Special housing for international students; Theme housing; Wellness housing; 90% of campus accessible to physically disabled. **Special Academic Facilities/Equipment:** Anderson Gallery, Student Art Gallery,

Larrick Student Center, Shafer Ct. Dining Facilities, Student Commons, Siegel Center, Cabell Library, Biotech Research Bldgs., Tompkins McCaw Library, VCU Bookstores and the Rice Center. **Campus Network:** 100% of classrooms, 100% of dorms, 100% of student union, 100% of libraries, 100% of dining areas, 75% of common outdoor areas have wireless network access.

CAMPUS LIFE

Environment: Metropolis. **Activities:** Campus Ministries; Choral groups; Concert band; Dance; Drama/theater; International Student Organization; Jazz band; Literary magazine; Model UN; Music ensembles; Musical theater; Opera; Pep band; Radio station; Student government; Student newspaper; Student-run film society; Symphony orchestra. 432 registered organizations, 16 honor societies, 32 religious organizations, 22 fraternities, 23 sororities on campus. **Athletics (Intercollegiate):** *Men:* baseball, basketball, cross-country, golf, soccer, tennis, track/field (outdoor). *Women:* basketball, cross-country, field hockey, soccer, tennis, track/field (outdoor), volleyball. **On-Campus Highlights:** Student Commons.

ADMISSIONS

Freshman Academic Profile: Average high school GPA 3.7. 18% in top 10% of high school class, 45% in top 25% of high school class, 79% in top 50% of high school class. **Test Scores:** SAT Math middle 50% range 520–620. SAT EBRW middle 50% range 550–640. ACT middle 50% range 21–28. **Basis for Candidate Selection:** *Very important factors include:* rigor of secondary school record, academic GPA. *Important factors include:* application essay, *Other factors include:* class rank, standardized test scores, recommendation(s), extracurricular activities, talent/ability, character/personal qualities, first generation, geographical residence, state residency, volunteer work. **Freshman Admission Requirements:** High school diploma is required and GED is accepted. *Academic units required:* 4 English, 3 math, 3 science, 1 science labs, 2 foreign language, 1 social studies, 2 history. *Academic units recommended:* 4 English, 4 math, 4 science, 1 science labs, 3 foreign language, 1 social studies, 3 history, 1 visual/performing arts. **Freshman Admission Statistics:** 19,199 applied, 78% admitted, 30% enrolled. **Transfer Admission Requirements:** College transcript(s). Minimum college GPA of 2.25 required. Lowest grade transferable C. **General Admission Information:** Application fee $70. Priority deadline 1/15. Non-fall registration accepted.

COSTS AND FINANCIAL AID

Required Forms and Deadlines: FAFSA; State aid form. **Notification of Awards:** Applicants will be notified of awards on a rolling basis beginning 4/1. **Types of Aid:** *Need-based scholarships/grants:* College/university scholarship or grant aid from institutional funds; Federal Nursing Scholarships; Federal Pell; Private scholarships; SEOG; State scholarships/grants; United Negro College Fund. *Loans:* Direct PLUS loans; Direct Subsidized Stafford Loans; Direct Unsubsidized Stafford Loans. **Student Employment:** Federal Work-Study Program available. Institutional employment available. **Financial Aid Statistics:** 87% needy freshmen, 78% needy undergrads receive need-based scholarship or grant aid. 4% freshmen, 3% undergrads receive non-need-based scholarship or grant aid. 73% freshmen, 78% undergrads receive need-based self-help aid. 1% freshmen, 1% undergrads receive athletic scholarships. 81.54% freshmen, 73.72% undergrads receive any aid. 64% undergrads borrow to pay for school. Average cumulative indebtedness $32,163. **Criteria awarding aid:** *Need-based:* Academics. *Non-need-based:* Academics, Alumni affiliation, Art, Athletics, Leadership, Music/drama.

VIRGINIA MILITARY INSTITUTE

VMI Office of Admissions, Lexington, VA 24450-0304
Phone: 540-464-7211 **Financial Aid Phone:** 540-464-7208
E-mail: admissions@vmi.edu **CEEB Code:** 5858
Fax: 540-464-7746 **Website:** www.vmi.edu **ACT Code:** 4418

This public school was founded in 1839. It has a 140 acre campus.

RATINGS

Admissions Selectivity Rating: 90 **Fire Safety Rating:** 79 **Green Rating:** 60*

STUDENTS AND FACULTY

Enrollment: 1,722. **Student Body:** 12% female, 88% male, 36% out-of-state, 2% international (9 countries represented). Asian 4%, African American 6%, Caucasian 79%, Hispanic 7%, Native American 1%, Pacific Islander <1%, Two or more races 1%, Race unknown <1%.

Retention and Graduation: 87% freshmen return for sophomore year. 64% freshmen graduate within 4 years. 78% freshmen graduate within 6 years. 8% grads go on to further study within 1 year. 3% grads pursue arts and sciences degrees. 2% grads pursue law degrees. 1% grads pursue business degrees. 1% grads pursue medical degrees. **Faculty:** Student/faculty ratio 11:1. 136 full-time faculty, 97% hold PhDs, 14% are members of minority groups, 35% are women. 0% of classes are taught by teaching assistants.

ACADEMICS

Degrees: Bachelor's. **Classes:** Most classes have 10–19 students. **Most popular majors:** History, General; Business/Managerial Economics; Mechanical Engineering. **Special Study Options:** Cross-registration; Double major; Honors program; Independent study; Internships; Study abroad. **Honors programs:** Institute Honors Program, departmental honors programs. **Career services:** Alumni network; Career assessment; Career/job search classes; Internships.

FACILITIES

Housing: 50% of campus accessible to physically disabled. **Special Academic Facilities/Equipment:** VMI Museum; George C. Marshall Museum. **Campus Network:** 100% of classrooms, 100% of dorms, 100% of student union, 100% of libraries, 100% of dining areas, 80% of common outdoor areas, have wireless network access.

CAMPUS LIFE

Environment: Village. **Activities:** Campus Ministries; Choral groups; Concert band; Dance; Drama/theater; International Student Organization; Jazz band; Literary magazine; Marching band; Music ensembles; Musical theater; Pep band; Student government; Student newspaper; Yearbook. 50 registered organizations, 11 honor societies, 3 religious organizations, on campus. **Athletics (Intercollegiate):** *Men:* baseball, basketball, cross-country, football, golf, lacrosse, riflery, soccer, swimming, track/field (outdoor), track/field (indoor), wrestling. *Women:* cross-country, riflery, soccer, swimming, track/field (outdoor), track/field (indoor). **On-Campus Highlights:** VMI Museum.

ADMISSIONS

Freshman Academic Profile: Average high school GPA 3.7. 15% in top 10% of high school class, 45% in top 25% of high school class, 81% in top 50% of high school class. 84% from public high schools. **Test Scores:** SAT Math middle 50% range 540–640. SAT EBRW middle 50% range 560–640. ACT middle 50% range 23–28. **Basis for Candidate Selection:** *Very important factors include:* rigor of secondary school record, class rank, standardized test scores, character/personal qualities. *Important factors include:* interview, extracurricular activities, state residency. *Other factors include:* application essay, recommendation(s), talent/ability, alumni/ae relation, geographical residence, work experience, level of applicant's interest. **Freshman Admission Requirements:** High school diploma is required and GED is not accepted. *Academic units required:* 4 English, 3 math, 3 science, 3 science labs, 3 foreign language, 2 social studies, 1 history. *Academic units recommended:* 4 English, 4 math, 4 science, 4 science labs, 4 foreign language, 2 social studies, 1 history. **Freshman Admission Statistics:** 1,718 applied, 53% admitted, 49% enrolled. **Transfer Admission Requirements:** High school transcript, college transcript(s), standardized test scores. Minimum college GPA of 2.0 required. Lowest grade transferable C. **General Admission Information:** Application fee $40. Regular application deadline 2/1.

COSTS AND FINANCIAL AID

Average book and supplies expense $1,000. **Required Forms and Deadlines:** FAFSA; Institution's own financial aid form. **Notification of Awards:** Applicants will be notified of awards on or about 3/15. **Types of Aid:** *Need-based scholarships/grants:* College/university scholarship or grant aid from institutional funds; Federal Pell; Private scholarships; SEOG; State scholarships/grants. *Loans:* Direct PLUS loans; Direct Subsidized Stafford Loans; Direct Unsubsidized Stafford Loans. **Financial Aid Statistics:** 88% needy freshmen, 76% needy undergrads receive need-based scholarship or grant aid. 41% freshmen, 52% undergrads receive non-need-based scholarship or grant aid. 83% freshmen, 84% undergrads receive need-based self-help aid. 15% freshmen, 15% undergrads receive athletic scholarships. 85% freshmen, 82% undergrads receive any aid. 66% undergrads borrow to pay for school. Average cumulative indebtedness $30,367. **Criteria awarding aid:** *Need-based:* Academics. *Non-need-based:* Academics, Alumni affiliation, Athletics, Leadership, Music/drama.

VIRGINIA STATE UNIVERSITY

One Hayden Drive, Petersburg, VA 23806
Phone: 804-524-5902 **Financial Aid Phone:** (804) 524-5990
E-mail: admiss@vsu.edu **CEEB Code:** 5860
Fax: 804-524-5055 **Website:** www.vsu.edu **ACT Code:** 4424

This public school was founded in 1882. It has a 246 acre campus.

RATINGS
Admissions Selectivity Rating: 74   **Fire Safety Rating:** 60*   **Green Rating:** 60*

STUDENTS AND FACULTY
Enrollment: 4,481. **Student Body:** 60% female, 40% male, 32% out-of-state, <1% international (29 countries represented). Asian <1%, African American 85%, Caucasian 3%, Hispanic 2%, Native American <1%, Pacific Islander 0%, Two or more races 0%, Race unknown 9%.
Retention and Graduation: 61% freshmen return for sophomore year.
Faculty: Student/faculty ratio 13:1. 296 full-time faculty, 0% hold PhDs, 0% are members of minority groups, 42% are women. 0% of classes are taught by teaching assistants.

ACADEMICS
Degrees: Associate; Bachelor's; Doctoral degree research/scholarship; Master's; Post-bachelor's certificate. **Most popular majors:** Physical Education Teaching and Coaching; Liberal Arts and Sciences/Liberal Studies; Sociology, General.
Special Study Options: Cooperative education program; Double major; Dual enrollment; Honors program; Independent study; Internships; Study abroad; Teacher certification program. **Disability Services offered:** Note-taking services; Reader services; Tutors. **Career services:** Alumni network; Internships.

FACILITIES
Housing: Apartments for single students; Coed dorms; Men's dorms; Women's dorms; 90% of campus accessible to physically disabled. **Campus Network:** 100% of classrooms, 100% of dorms, 100% of student union, 100% of libraries, 100% of dining areas, 1% of common outdoor areas, have wireless network access.

CAMPUS LIFE
Environment: Town. **Activities:** Campus Ministries; Choral groups; Concert band; Dance; Drama/theater; Jazz band; Literary magazine; Marching band; Music ensembles; Pep band; Radio station; Student government; Student newspaper; Television station; Yearbook. 70 registered organizations, 6 honor societies, 4 religious organizations, 5 fraternities, 4 sororities, on campus.
Athletics (Intercollegiate): *Men:* baseball, basketball, cheerleading, cross-country, football, golf, tennis, track/field (outdoor), track/field (indoor). *Women:* basketball, bowling, cheerleading, cross-country, golf, softball, tennis, track/field (outdoor), track/field (indoor), volleyball.

ADMISSIONS
Freshman Academic Profile: Average high school GPA 2.9. 3% in top 10% of high school class, 17% in top 25% of high school class, 53% in top 50% of high school class. **Test Scores:** SAT Math middle 50% range 380–460. SAT EBRW middle 50% range 380–460. ACT middle 50% range 15–19. **Basis for Candidate Selection:** *Very important factors include:* rigor of secondary school record, academic GPA, standardized test scores. *Important factors include:* application essay, recommendation(s). *Other factors include:* extracurricular activities, talent/ability, character/personal qualities, first generation, alumni/ae relation, geographical residence, state residency, volunteer work, work experience. **Freshman Admission Requirements:** High school diploma is required and GED is accepted. *Academic units required:* 4 English, 3 math, 2 science, 1 science labs, 2 history. *Academic units recommended:* 2 foreign language, 2 social studies. **Freshman Admission Statistics:** 5,923 applied, 80% admitted, 19% enrolled. **Transfer Admission Requirements:** College transcript(s), essay or personal statement, statement of good standing from prior institution(s). Minimum college GPA of 2.0 required. Lowest grade transferable C. **General Admission Information:** Application fee $25. Priority deadline 3/31. Regular application deadline 5/1. Non-fall registration accepted.

COSTS AND FINANCIAL AID
Annual in-state tuition $4,876. Annual out-of-state tuition $14,132. Room and board $10,128. Average book and supplies expense $1,300. **Required Forms and Deadlines:** FAFSA; Institution's own financial aid form. **Notification of Awards:** Applicants will be notified of awards on a rolling basis beginning 3/1. **Types of Aid:** *Need-based scholarships/grants:* College/university scholarship or grant aid from institutional funds; Federal Pell; Private scholarships; SEOG;

State scholarships/grants. *Loans:* Direct PLUS loans; Direct Subsidized Stafford Loans; Direct Unsubsidized Stafford Loans. **Student Employment:** Federal Work-Study Program available. Institutional employment available.
Financial Aid Statistics: 80% needy freshmen, 80% needy undergrads receive need-based scholarship or grant aid. 22% freshmen, 22% undergrads receive non-need-based scholarship or grant aid. 72% freshmen, 72% undergrads receive need-based self-help aid. 3% freshmen, 3% undergrads receive athletic scholarships. **Criteria awarding aid:** *Need-based:* Academics, Alumni affiliation, Art, Athletics, Leadership, Minority status. *Non-need-based:* Academics, Alumni affiliation, Art, Athletics, Job skills, Leadership, Minority status, Music/drama, Religious affiliation.

VIRGINIA TECH

925 Prices Fork Road, Blacksburg, VA 24061
Phone: 540-231-6267 **Financial Aid Phone:** 540-231-5179
E-mail: admissions@vt.edu **CEEB Code:** 5859
Fax: 540-231-3242 **Website:** www.vt.edu **ACT Code:** 4420

This public school was founded in 1872. It has a 2600 acre campus.

RATINGS
Admissions Selectivity Rating: 87   **Fire Safety Rating:** 94   **Green Rating:** 97

STUDENTS AND FACULTY
Enrollment: 27,730. **Student Body:** 43% female, 57% male, 24% out-of-state, 7% international (116 countries represented). Asian 10%, African American 4%, Caucasian 65%, Hispanic 6%, Native American <1%, Pacific Islander <1%, Two or more races 5%, Race unknown 3%.
Retention and Graduation: 63% freshmen graduate within 4 years. 84% freshmen graduate within 6 years. 31% grads go on to further study within 1 year. **Faculty:** Student/faculty ratio 14:1. 1,841 full-time faculty, 90% hold PhDs, 20% are members of minority groups, 34% are women.

ACADEMICS
Degrees: Associate; Bachelor's; Doctoral degree—professional practice; Doctoral degree research/scholarship; Master's; Post-bachelor's certificate; Post-master's certificate. **Classes:** Most classes have 20–29 students. Most lab/discussion sessions have 20–29 students. **Most popular majors:** Mechanical Engineering; Biology/Biological Sciences, General; Management Science.
Special Study Options: Accelerated program; Cooperative education program; Distance learning; Double major; English as a Second Language (ESL); Honors program; Independent study; Internships; Liberal arts/career combination; Study abroad; Teacher certification program. **Combined degree programs:** BA/MA. **Disability Services offered:** Note-taking services; Reader services; Tape recorders; Tutors. **Career services:** Career assessment; Career/job search classes; Internships.

FACILITIES
Housing: Coed dorms; Fraternity/sorority housing; Men's dorms; Special housing for disabled students; Theme housing; Wellness housing; Women's dorms; 60% of campus accessible to physically disabled. **Special Academic Facilities/Equipment:** Art gallery, digital music facilities, multimedia labs, Black Cultural Center, television studio, anaerobic lab, CAD-CAM labs, observatory, wind tunnel, farms, Math Emporium, the CAVE (virtual reality learning facility), Moss Arts Center.

CAMPUS LIFE
Environment: Town. **Activities:** Campus Ministries; Choral groups; Concert band; Dance; Drama/theater; International Student Organization; Jazz band; Literary magazine; Marching band; Model UN; Music ensembles; Musical theater; Opera; Pep band; Radio station; Student government; Student newspaper; Student-run film society; Television station; Yearbook. 849 registered organizations, 13 honor societies, 90 religious organizations, 30 fraternities, 21 sororities on campus. **Athletics (Intercollegiate):** *Men:* baseball, basketball, cheerleading, cross-country, diving, football, golf, soccer, swimming, tennis, track/field (outdoor), track/field (indoor), ultimate frisbee, water polo. *Women:* basketball, cheerleading, cross-country, diving, lacrosse, soccer, softball, swimming, tennis, track/field (outdoor), track/field (indoor), ultimate frisbee, volleyball, water polo. **On-Campus Highlights:** The Pylons. **Environmental**

Initiatives: Virginia Tech is committed to being a Leader in Campus Sustainability. In April 2008 former Virginia Tech President Charles W. Steger charged the Energy and Sustainability Committee to develop a climate commitment and accompanying sustainability plan that was unique to our university. The "Virginia Tech Climate Action Commitment & Sustainability Plan (VTCAC&SP)" was developed as a comprehensive working document that addressed specific actions to be implemented in six broad sustainability categories to include: administrative structure and governance, facilities infrastructure, facilities operations, transportation, behavior and campus life, and academic programs. On June 1, 2009 the Virginia Tech Board of Visitors unanimously approved "The Virginia Tech Climate Action Commitment" and it became university policy (Presidential Policy Memorandum No. 262). The VTCAC contained 14 specific points and included the establishment of greenhouse gas emission reduction targets, the pursuit of USGBC LEED Silver ratings or higher for all future new construction and major renovations projects, and the creation of a sustainability office to oversee the implementation of our sustainability plan and to coordinate programs for campus sustainability and outreach. The Office of Energy and Sustainability established and maintained a comprehensive system to track our sustainability progress in over 100 specific areas of interest. During academic year 2012–13 the Energy and Sustainability Committee revised the VTCAC to take advantage of the many successes achieved and lessons learned in the initial three years of implementation. On May 6, 2013 University Council approved the "Update to the Virginia Tech Climate Action Commitment" (Presidential Policy Memorandum No. 262, Rev 1). See: http://www.it.vpas.vt.edu/docs/sust/op18/PPM262rev1.pdf Virginia Tech is a charter member of the AASHE's "Sustainability, Tracking, Assessment, and Rating System (STARS)." STARS is nationally recognized in higher education as the best management and reporting tool available to evaluate the effectiveness of your sustainability program. During academic year 2014–15, the Energy and Sustainability Committee reviewed and updated the VTCAC&SP. In the "2014 Update and Supplement to the 2009 VTCAC&SP" the university has decided to have the AASHE STARS Program serve as our primary "Sustainability Plan" with additions based on initiatives that are unique to Virginia Tech. See: http://www.it.vpas.vt.edu/docs/sust/PA2/2014_SP_SupplementWithAppendices.pdf On October 15, 2014 Virginia Tech received a STARS "Gold Rating" (version 1.2). Our overall score of 71.02 points placed the university in the top 10% of the nearly 300 colleges and universities having received a STARS rating as of that point in time. See: https://stars.aashe.org/institutions/virginia-tech-va/report/2014-10-15/ In addition to receiving recognition at the national level, Virginia Tech is the recipient of six Governor's Environment Excellence Awards during the period 2008 through 2015 (two Gold and four Bronze), and this represents the most of any college or university in the Commonwealth of Virginia.

ADMISSIONS

Freshman Academic Profile: Average high school GPA 4.0. 38% in top 10% of high school class, 77% in top 25% of high school class, 97% in top 50% of high school class. **Test Scores:** SAT Math middle 50% range 590–710. SAT EBRW middle 50% range 590–680. ACT middle 50% range 25–31. **Basis for Candidate Selection:** *Very important factors include:* rigor of secondary school record, academic GPA, application essay, standardized test scores. *Other factors include:* extracurricular activities, talent/ability, character/personal qualities, first generation, alumni/ae relation, geographical residence, state residency, racial/ethnic status, volunteer work, work experience, level of applicant's interest. **Freshman Admission Requirements:** High school diploma is required and GED is accepted. *Academic units required:* 4 English, 3 math, 2 science, 2 science labs, 1 social studies, 1 history, 4 academic electives. *Academic units recommended:* 4 math, 3 science, 3 foreign language. **Freshman Admission Statistics:** 31,936 applied, 65% admitted, 30% enrolled. **Transfer Admission Requirements:** High school transcript, college transcript(s). Minimum college GPA of 3.0 required. Lowest grade transferable C. **General Admission Information:** Application fee $60. Regular application deadline 1/15. Non-fall registration accepted. Admission may be deferred for a maximum of 1 year.

COSTS AND FINANCIAL AID

Annual in-state tuition $11,420. Annual out-of-state tuition $29,960. Room and board $9,342. Required fees $2,271. Average book and supplies expense $1,100. **Required Forms and Deadlines:** FAFSA. **Notification of Awards:** Applicants will be notified of awards on or about 4/1. **Types of Aid:** *Need-based scholarships/grants:* College/university scholarship or grant aid from institutional funds; Federal Pell; Private scholarships; SEOG; State scholarships/grants; United Negro College Fund. *Loans:* Direct PLUS loans; Direct Subsidized Stafford Loans; Direct Unsubsidized Stafford Loans. **Student Employment:** Federal Work-Study Program available. Institutional employment available. **Financial Aid Statistics:** 60% needy freshmen, 69% needy undergrads receive need-based scholarship or grant aid. 49% freshmen, 34% undergrads receive

non-need-based scholarship or grant aid. 68% freshmen, 71% undergrads receive need-based self-help aid. 1% freshmen, 2% undergrads receive athletic scholarships. 65% freshmen, 75% undergrads receive any aid. 48% undergrads borrow to pay for school. Average cumulative indebtedness $31,494. **Criteria awarding aid:** *Need-based:* Academics, Art, Leadership, Minority status, Music/drama *Non-need-based:* Academics, Art, Athletics, Leadership, Minority status, Music/drama, State/district residency.

VIRGINIA WESLEYAN UNIVERSITY

5817 Wesleyan Drive, Virginia Beach, VA 23455
Phone: 757-455-3208 **Financial Aid Phone:** 757-455-3345
E-mail: admissions@vwu.edu **CEEB Code:** 5867
Fax: 757-461-5238 **Website:** www.vwu.edu **ACT Code:** 4429

This private school, affiliated with the Methodist Church, was founded in 1961. It has a 300 acre campus.

RATINGS
Admissions Selectivity Rating: 79 **Fire Safety Rating:** 79 **Green Rating:** 87

STUDENTS AND FACULTY
Enrollment: 1,369. **Student Body:** 60% female, 40% male, 26% out-of-state, 1% international (9 countries represented). Asian 1%, African American 27%, Caucasian 49%, Hispanic 9%, Native American 1%, Pacific Islander <1%, Two or more races 7%, Race unknown 5%.
Retention and Graduation: 63% freshmen return for sophomore year. 37% freshmen graduate within 4 years. 44% freshmen graduate within 6 years. 32% grads go on to further study within 1 year. 1% grads pursue law degrees. 1% grads pursue business degrees. **Faculty:** Student/faculty ratio 12:1. 91 full-time faculty, 92% hold PhDs, 11% are members of minority groups, 46% are women. 0% of classes are taught by teaching assistants.

ACADEMICS
Degrees: Bachelor's; Certificate; Master's. **Classes:** Most classes have 10–19 students. **Most popular majors:** Criminal Justice/Safety Studies; Business Administration and Management, General; Social Sciences, General. **Special Study Options:** Cross-registration; Double major; Honors program; Independent study; Internships; Liberal arts/career combination; Student-designed major; Study abroad; Teacher certification program. **Honors programs:** Wesleyan Scholars is an honors program which is designed for applicants with superior high school achievement records. The Honors and Scholars program, including Wesleyan Scholars, offers academically challenging honors courses and stimulating co-curricular experiences. Program enhancement is also offered through PORTfolio, a selective program designed to integrate the liberal arts with experiential learning opportunities available in Hampton Roads. **Disability Services offered:** Note-taking services; Reader services; Tape recorders; Tutors. **Career services:** Alumni network; Career/job search classes; Internships; Regional alumni.

FACILITIES
Housing: Apartments for single students; Coed dorms; Fraternity/sorority housing; Special housing for disabled students; Theme housing; Wellness housing; Women's dorms; 90% of campus accessible to physically disabled. **Special Academic Facilities/Equipment:** Greer Environmental Science Center, language lab, teleconferencing facility, social science teach and learn lab, radio station, TV studio, Barclay Sheaks Art Gallery, computerized classrooms, Internet access in all classrooms, 24-hr. computer lab, Lambuth M. Clarke Hall with state-of-the-art teaching technologies, three academic villages combining residences and campus offices and services. **Campus Network:** 100% of classrooms, 100% of dorms, 100% of student union, 100% of libraries, 100% of dining areas, 100% of common outdoor areas have wireless network access.

CAMPUS LIFE
Environment: Metropolis. **Activities:** Campus Ministries; Choral groups; Dance; Drama/theater; International Student Organization; Literary magazine; Marching band; Model UN; Music ensembles; Musical theater; Radio station; Student government; Student newspaper; Yearbook. 60 registered organizations, 19 honor societies, 4 religious organizations, 4 fraternities, 4 sororities on campus. **Athletics (Intercollegiate):** *Men:* baseball, basketball,

cross-country, golf, lacrosse, soccer, tennis, track/field (outdoor), track/field (indoor). *Women:* basketball, cheerleading, cross-country, field hockey, lacrosse, soccer, softball, tennis, track/field (outdoor), track/field (indoor), volleyball. **On-Campus Highlights:** Jane P. Batten Student Center. **Environmental Initiatives:** Green Roof.

ADMISSIONS
Freshman Academic Profile: Average high school GPA 3.2. 15% in top 10% of high school class, 33% in top 25% of high school class, 63% in top 50% of high school class. 86% from public high schools. **Test Scores:** SAT Math middle 50% range 463–570. SAT EBRW middle 50% range 490–590. ACT middle 50% range 19–25. **Basis for Candidate Selection:** *Very important factors include:* rigor of secondary school record, academic GPA, standardized test scores, level of applicant's interest. *Important factors include:* extracurricular activities. *Other factors include:* recommendation(s), interview, talent/ability, character/personal qualities, first generation, alumni/ae relation, volunteer work, work experience. **Freshman Admission Requirements:** High school diploma is required and GED is accepted. *Academic units required:* 4 English, 3 math, 2 science, 2 science labs, 2 foreign language, 1 history, 1 computer science. *Academic units recommended:* 4 English, 3 math, 2 science, 2 science labs, 2 foreign language, 1 history, 4 academic electives, 1 computer science. **Freshman Admission Statistics:** 2,200 applied, 71% admitted, 27% enrolled. **Transfer Admission Requirements:** High school transcript, college transcript(s), essay or personal statement, statement of good standing from prior institution(s). Minimum college GPA of 2.5 required. Lowest grade transferable C. **General Admission Information:** Priority deadline 3/1. Non-fall registration accepted. Admission may be deferred for a maximum of 1 term.

COSTS AND FINANCIAL AID
Annual tuition $36,010. Room and board $9,988. Required fees $850. Average book and supplies expense $1,500. **Required Forms and Deadlines:** FAFSA; State aid form. **Notification of Awards:** Applicants will be notified of awards on a rolling basis beginning 10/15. **Types of Aid:** *Need-based scholarships/ grants:* College/university scholarship or grant aid from institutional funds; Federal Pell; Private scholarships; SEOG; State scholarships/grants. *Loans:* Direct PLUS loans; Direct Subsidized Stafford Loans; Direct Unsubsidized Stafford Loans. **Student Employment:** Federal Work-Study Program available. Institutional employment available. **Financial Aid Statistics:** 100% needy freshmen, 99% needy undergrads receive need-based scholarship or grant aid. 14% freshmen, 17% undergrads receive non-need-based scholarship or grant aid. 79% freshmen, 77% undergrads receive need-based self-help aid. 0% freshmen, 0% undergrads receive athletic scholarships. 99.3% freshmen, 97.6% undergrads receive any aid. 86% undergrads borrow to pay for school. Average cumulative indebtedness $32,404. **Criteria awarding aid:** *Need-based:* Art, Job skills, Music/drama *Non-need-based:* Academics, Alumni affiliation, Leadership, Religious affiliation, State/district residency.

VITERBO UNIVERSITY

900 Viterbo Drive, La Crosse, WI 54601
Phone: 608-796-3010 **Financial Aid Phone:** 608-496-3900
E-mail: admission@viterbo.edu **CEEB Code:** 1878
Fax: 608-796-3020 **ACT Code:** 4662

This private school, affiliated with the Roman Catholic Church, was founded in 1890. It has a 25 acre campus.

RATINGS
Admissions Selectivity Rating: 74   **Fire Safety Rating:** 73   **Green Rating:** 60*

STUDENTS AND FACULTY
Enrollment: 1,922. **Student Body:** 71% female, 29% male, 19% out-of-state, 1% international (15 countries represented). Asian 1%, African American 1%, Caucasian 93%, Hispanic 1%, Native American 1%, Race unknown 2%.
Retention and Graduation: 74% freshmen return for sophomore year. 7% grads go on to further study within 1 year. 4% grads pursue arts and sciences degrees. 1% grads pursue law degrees. 0% grads pursue business degrees. 2% grads pursue medical degrees. **Faculty:** Student/faculty ratio 13:1. 110 full-time faculty, 56% hold PhDs, 4% are members of minority groups, 56% are women. 0% of classes are taught by teaching assistants.

ACADEMICS
Degrees: Associate; Bachelor's; Master's; Post-bachelor's certificate; Terminal Associate; Transfer Associate. **Classes:** Most classes have 10–19 students. Most lab/discussion sessions have 10–19 students. **Most popular majors:**

Business Administration and Management, General; Elementary Education and Teaching; Nursing/Registered Nurse (Rn, Asn, Bsn, Msn). **Special Study Options:** Accelerated program; Cross-registration; Distance learning; Double major; Dual enrollment; Honors program; Independent study; Internships; Liberal arts/career combination; Student-designed major; Study abroad; Teacher certification program; Weekend college. **Honors programs:** The mission of the Viterbo University Honors Program is to provide a supportive, enriched learning environment responsive to the educational needs of highly able and exceptionally motivated undergraduate students who are committed to achieving academic excellence. The program provides honors sections of regular, general education courses, honors credit within regular sections, interdisciplinary Honors Capstone courses, oversight of senior honors projects, and increased opportunity for undergraduate research and creative activity. The program complements and enhances the Liberal Arts mission of the university. Together, honors students and faculty constitute a community of scholars. **Disability Services offered:** Note-taking services; Reader services; Tape recorders; Tutors. **Career services:** Alumni network; Alumni services; Career assessment; Career/job search classes; Internships; Regional alumni.

FACILITIES
Housing: Apartments for single students; Coed dorms; 90% of campus accessible to physically disabled. **Special Academic Facilities/Equipment:** Fine Arts Center; Center for Ethics, Science, and Technology with distance education labs and video conferencing; Nursing center with labs and simulated equipment; new recreation and education center co-sponsored by Viterbo University and the Boys and Girls Club. **Campus Network:** 100% of classrooms, 100% of dorms, 100% of student union, 100% of libraries, 100% of dining areas, 50% of common outdoor areas have wireless network access.

CAMPUS LIFE
Environment: Town. **Activities:** Choral groups; Dance; Drama/theater; Literary magazine; Music ensembles; Musical theater; Opera; Pep band; Student government; Student newspaper. 22 registered organizations, 2 honor societies, 2 religious organizations on campus. **Athletics (Intercollegiate):** *Men:* baseball, basketball, golf, soccer. *Women:* basketball, golf, soccer, softball, volleyball. **On-Campus Highlights:** Reinhart Center for Ethics, Science and Technology.

ADMISSIONS
Freshman Academic Profile: Average high school GPA 3.3. 13% in top 10% of high school class, 39% in top 25% of high school class, 73% in top 50% of high school class. 97% from public high schools. **Test Scores:** ACT middle 50% range 20–24. **Basis for Candidate Selection:** *Very important factors include:* rigor of secondary school record, academic GPA, standardized test scores, character/personal qualities, level of applicant's interest. *Important factors include:* class rank, interview, talent/ability. *Other factors include:* application essay, recommendation(s), extracurricular activities, first generation, alumni/ ae relation, volunteer work. **Freshman Admission Requirements:** High school diploma is required and GED is accepted *Academic units required:* 3 English, 2 math, 2 science, 2 social studies, 5 academic electives. *Academic units recommended:* 4 English, 2 math, 2 science, 2 science labs, 2 foreign language, 2 social studies, 5 academic electives. **Freshman Admission Statistics:** 1,107 applied, 89% admitted, 37% enrolled. **Transfer Admission Requirements:** High school transcript, college transcript(s), statement of good standing from prior institution(s). Minimum college GPA of 2.0 required. Lowest grade transferable C-. **General Admission Information:** Application fee $25. Priority deadline 8/1. Non-fall registration accepted. Admission may be deferred for a maximum of Two years.

COSTS AND FINANCIAL AID
Annual tuition $18,170. Room and board $6,140. Required fees $420. Average book and supplies expense $800. **Required Forms and Deadlines:** FAFSA; Institution's own financial aid form. **Notification of Awards:** Applicants will be notified of awards on a rolling basis beginning 4/1. **Types of Aid:** *Need-based scholarships/grants:* College/university scholarship or grant aid from institutional funds; Federal Pell; Private scholarships; SEOG; State scholarships/grants. **Student Employment:** Federal Work-Study Program available. Institutional employment available. **Financial Aid Statistics:** 98% needy freshmen, 97% needy undergrads receive need-based scholarship or grant aid. 6% freshmen, 6% undergrads receive non-need-based scholarship or grant aid. 94% freshmen, 93% undergrads receive need-based self-help aid. 0% freshmen, 1% undergrads receive athletic scholarships. 98% freshmen, 89% undergrads receive any aid. **Criteria awarding aid:** *Need-based:* Academics, Alumni affiliation *Non-need-based:* Academics, Alumni affiliation, Art, Athletics, Leadership, Minority status, Music/drama.

WABASH COLLEGE

P.O. Box 352, Crawfordsville, IN 47933
Phone: 765-361-6225 **Financial Aid Phone:** 765-361-6375
E-mail: admissions@wabash.edu **CEEB Code:** 1895
Fax: 765-361-6437 **Website:** www.wabash.edu **ACT Code:** 1260

This private school was founded in 1832. It has a 60 acre campus.

RATINGS
Admissions Selectivity Rating: 86 **Fire Safety Rating:** 89 **Green Rating:** 71

STUDENTS AND FACULTY
Enrollment: 866. **Student Body:** 0% female, 100% male, 20% out-of-state, 5% international (20 countries represented). Asian 1%, African American 5%, Caucasian 76%, Hispanic 9%, Native American 0%, Pacific Islander 0%, Two or more races 3%, Race unknown 2%.
Retention and Graduation: 91% freshmen return for sophomore year. 71% freshmen graduate within 4 years. 74% freshmen graduate within 6 years. 32% grads go on to further study within 1 year. 41% grads pursue arts and sciences degrees. 26% grads pursue law degrees. 8% grads pursue business degrees. 21% grads pursue medical degrees. **Faculty:** Student/faculty ratio 10:1. 82 full-time faculty, 100% hold PhDs, 13% are members of minority groups, 39% are women. 0% of classes are taught by teaching assistants.

ACADEMICS
Degrees: Bachelor's. **Classes:** Most classes have fewer than 10 students. Most lab/discussion sessions have fewer than 10 students. **Most popular majors:** Rhetoric and Composition; Economics, General; History, General. **Special Study Options:** Double major; Independent study; Internships; Student-designed major; Study abroad. **Combined degree programs:** BA/MEng. **Disability Services offered:** Note-taking services; Reader services; Tape recorders; Tutors. **Career services:** Alumni network; Alumni services; Career assessment; Career/job search classes; Internships; Regional alumni.

FACILITIES
Housing: Apartments for single students; Fraternity/sorority housing; Men's dorms; 70% of campus accessible to physically disabled. **Special Academic Facilities/Equipment:** Malcolm X Institute of Black Studies; two art galleries; language lab; electron microscope; atomic absorption, nuclear, and infrared spectrometers; Beowulf Supercomputer; Center of Inquiry in the Liberal Arts; Wabash Center for Teaching and Learning in Theology and Religion; Ramsey Archival Center. **Campus Network:** 100% of classrooms, 100% of dorms, 100% of student union, 100% of libraries, 100% of dining areas, 70% of common outdoor areas have wireless network access.

CAMPUS LIFE
Environment: Village. **Activities:** Campus Ministries; Choral groups; Dance; Drama/theater; International Student Organization; Jazz band; Literary magazine; Music ensembles; Pep band; Radio station; Student government; Student newspaper; Student-run film society; Yearbook. 66 registered organizations, 9 honor societies, 3 religious organizations, 10 fraternities on campus. **Athletics (Intercollegiate):** *Men:* baseball, basketball, cross-country, diving, football, golf, soccer, swimming, tennis, track/field (outdoor), track/field (indoor), wrestling. **On-Campus Highlights:** Allen Athletics and Recreation Center. **Environmental Initiatives:** Printing Quota that saved 240,000 sheets of paper in the first semester (among 900 students).

ADMISSIONS
Freshman Academic Profile: Average high school GPA 3.8. 25% in top 10% of high school class, 60% in top 25% of high school class, 92% in top 50% of high school class. 73% from public high schools. **Test Scores:** SAT Math middle 50% range 560–670. SAT EBRW middle 50% range 560–650. ACT middle 50% range 23–29. **Basis for Candidate Selection:** *Very important factors include:* rigor of secondary school record, class rank, academic GPA, level of applicant's interest. *Important factors include:* standardized test scores, interview, extracurricular activities, talent/ability. *Other factors include:* application essay, recommendation(s), character/personal qualities, first generation, alumni/ae relation, geographical residence, racial/ethnic status, volunteer work, work experience. **Freshman Admission Requirements:** High school diploma is required and GED is accepted. *Academic units recommended:*

4 English, 4 math, 2 science, 2 science labs, 2 foreign language, 2 social studies, 2 history, 2 academic electives. **Freshman Admission Statistics:** 1,307 applied, 64% admitted, 27% enrolled. **Transfer Admission Requirements:** High school transcript, college transcript(s), essay or personal statement, standardized test scores, statement of good standing from prior institution(s). Lowest grade transferable C. **General Admission Information:** Application fee $50. Priority deadline 12/1. Regular application deadline 7/1. Non-fall registration accepted.

COSTS AND FINANCIAL AID
Annual tuition $45,000. Room and board $10,900. Required fees $850. Average book and supplies expense $950. **Required Forms and Deadlines:** FAFSA. **Notification of Awards:** Applicants will be notified of awards on a rolling basis beginning 12/15. **Types of Aid:** *Need-based scholarships/grants:* College/university scholarship or grant aid from institutional funds; Federal Pell; Private scholarships; SEOG; State scholarships/grants; United Negro College Fund. *Loans:* Direct PLUS loans; Direct Subsidized Stafford Loans; Direct Unsubsidized Stafford Loans. **Student Employment:** Federal Work-Study Program available. Institutional employment available. **Financial Aid Statistics:** 99% needy freshmen, 99% needy undergrads receive need-based scholarship or grant aid. 25% freshmen, 16% undergrads receive non-need-based scholarship or grant aid. 75% freshmen, 82% undergrads receive need-based self-help aid. 0% freshmen, 0% undergrads receive athletic scholarships. 100% freshmen, 99.9% undergrads receive any aid. 72% undergrads borrow to pay for school. Average cumulative indebtedness $35,273. **Criteria awarding aid:** *Need-based:* Academics. *Non-need-based:* Academics, Art, Leadership, Music/drama.

WAGNER COLLEGE

One Campus Road, Staten Island, NY 10301
Phone: 718-390-3411 **Financial Aid Phone:** 718-390-3183
E-mail: adm@wagner.edu **CEEB Code:** 2966
Fax: 718-390-3105 **Website:** www.wagner.edu **ACT Code:** 2984

This private school was founded in 1883. It has a 110 acre campus.

RATINGS
Admissions Selectivity Rating: 83 **Fire Safety Rating:** 98 **Green Rating:** 60*

STUDENTS AND FACULTY
Enrollment: 1,752. **Student Body:** 65% female, 35% male, 46% out-of-state, 4% international. Asian 5%, African American 8%, Caucasian 62%, Hispanic 13%, Native American <1%, Pacific Islander <1%, Two or more races 3%, Race unknown 5%.
Retention and Graduation: 81% freshmen return for sophomore year. 63% freshmen graduate within 4 years. 70% freshmen graduate within 6 years. 42% grads go on to further study within 1 year. 23% grads pursue arts and sciences degrees. 4% grads pursue law degrees. 26% grads pursue business degrees. 6% grads pursue medical degrees. **Faculty:** Student/faculty ratio 13:1. 110 full-time faculty, 87% hold PhDs, 10% are members of minority groups, 50% are women. 0% of classes are taught by teaching assistants.

ACADEMICS
Degrees: Bachelor's; Doctoral degree—professional practice; Master's; Post-master's certificate. **Classes:** Most classes have 10–19 students. Most lab/discussion sessions have 10–19 students. **Most popular majors:** Visual and Performing Arts, General; Business/Commerce, General; Nursing Science. **Special Study Options:** Accelerated program; Double major; Exchange student program (domestic); Honors program; Independent study; Internships; Liberal arts/career combination; Student-designed major; Study abroad; Teacher certification program; Weekend college. **Disability Services offered:** Note-taking services; Reader services; Tape recorders; Tutors. **Career services:** Alumni network; Alumni services; Internships.

FACILITIES
Housing: Coed dorms; Fraternity/sorority housing; Special housing for disabled students; Theme housing; Wellness housing; 50% of campus accessible to physically disabled. **Special Academic Facilities/Equipment:** Art gallery, early childhood center, nursing resource center, planetarium, two electron microscopes, solar energy project, theater, blackbox theatre.

CAMPUS LIFE

Environment: Metropolis. **Activities:** Campus Ministries; Choral groups; Concert band; Dance; Drama/theater; International Student Organization; Jazz band; Marching band; Model UN; Music ensembles; Musical theater; Radio station; Student government; Student newspaper; Yearbook. 66 registered organizations, 10 honor societies, 4 religious organizations, 5 fraternities, 4 sororities, on campus. **Athletics (Intercollegiate):** *Men:* baseball, basketball, cross-country, football, golf, lacrosse, tennis, track/field (outdoor), track/field (indoor). *Women:* basketball, cross-country, golf, lacrosse, soccer, softball, swimming, tennis, track/field (outdoor), track/field (indoor), water polo. **On-Campus Highlights:** Wagner Student Union.

ADMISSIONS

Freshman Academic Profile: Average high school GPA 3.5. 20% in top 10% of high school class, 49% in top 25% of high school class, 80% in top 50% of high school class. 67% from public high schools. **Test Scores:** SAT Math middle 50% range 530–630. SAT EBRW middle 50% range 540–640. ACT middle 50% range 22–28. **Basis for Candidate Selection:** *Very important factors include:* rigor of secondary school record, class rank, academic GPA. *Important factors include:* application essay, recommendation(s), interview, extracurricular activities, talent/ability, character/personal qualities. *Other factors include:* standardized test scores, volunteer work, work experience, level of applicant's interest. **Freshman Admission Requirements:** High school diploma is required and GED is accepted. *Academic units required:* 4 English, 3 math, 2 science, 1 science labs, 2 foreign language, 3 history, 7 academic electives. **Freshman Admission Statistics:** 2,898 applied, 70% admitted, 21% enrolled. **Transfer Admission Requirements:** College transcript(s), essay or personal statement, statement of good standing from prior institution(s). Minimum college GPA of 3.0 required. Lowest grade transferable C. **General Admission Information:** Application fee $60. Priority deadline 12/1. Regular application deadline 2/15. Non-fall registration accepted. Admission may be deferred for a maximum of 1 year.

COSTS AND FINANCIAL AID

Annual tuition $47,300. Room and board $14,575. Required fees $950. Average book and supplies expense $850. **Required Forms and Deadlines:** FAFSA; State aid form. **Notification of Awards:** Applicants will be notified of awards on a rolling basis beginning 1/31. **Types of Aid:** *Need-based scholarships/grants:* College/university scholarship or grant aid from institutional funds; Federal Pell; Private scholarships; SEOG; State scholarships/grants. *Loans:* Direct PLUS loans; Direct Subsidized Stafford Loans; Direct Unsubsidized Stafford Loans. **Student Employment:** Federal Work-Study Program available. Institutional employment available. **Financial Aid Statistics:** 100% needy freshmen, 100% needy undergrads receive need-based scholarship or grant aid. 0% freshmen, 0% undergrads receive non-need-based scholarship or grant aid. 67% freshmen, 78% undergrads receive need-based self-help aid. 6% freshmen, 8% undergrads receive athletic scholarships. 99% freshmen, 93% undergrads receive any aid. **Criteria awarding aid:** *Non-need-based:* Academics, Athletics, Leadership, Music/drama.

WAKE FOREST UNIVERSITY

P.O. Box 7305 Reynolda Station, Winston Salem, NC 27109
Phone: 336-758-5201 **Financial Aid Phone:** (336)758-5154
E-mail: admissions@wfu.edu **CEEB Code:** 5885
Fax: 336-758-4324 **Website:** www.wfu.edu **ACT Code:** 3168

This private school was founded in 1834. It has a 340 acre campus.

RATINGS

Admissions Selectivity Rating: 96   **Fire Safety Rating:** 96   **Green Rating:** 94

STUDENTS AND FACULTY

Enrollment: 5,101. **Student Body:** 54% female, 46% male, 78% out-of-state, 10% international (27 countries represented). Asian 4%, African American 7%, Caucasian 70%, Hispanic 7%, Native American <1%, Pacific Islander <1%, Two or more races 3%, Race unknown <1%.
Retention and Graduation: 94% freshmen return for sophomore year. 84% freshmen graduate within 4 years. 88% freshmen graduate within 6 years. 32% grads go on to further study within 1 year. 28% grads pursue arts and sciences

degrees. 16% grads pursue law degrees. 36% grads pursue business degrees. 17% grads pursue medical degrees. **Faculty:** Student/faculty ratio 11:1. 579 full-time faculty, 93% hold PhDs, 17% are members of minority groups, 43% are women. 0% of classes are taught by teaching assistants.

ACADEMICS

Degrees: Bachelor's; Doctoral degree—professional practice; Doctoral degree research/scholarship; Master's; Post-bachelor's certificate. **Classes:** Most classes have 10–19 students. Most lab/discussion sessions have 10–19 students. **Most popular majors:** Business/Commerce, General; Political Science and Government, General; Psychology, General. **Special Study Options:** Cross-registration; Distance learning; Double major; Dual enrollment; Honors program; Independent study; Internships; Study abroad; Teacher certification program. **Honors programs:** For highly qualified students, a series of interdisciplinary honors courses are offered. Additionally, for students especially talented in individual areas of study, most departments in the College offer special studies leading to graduation with honors in a particular discipline. **Disability Services offered:** Note-taking services; Reader services; Tape recorders; Tutors. **Career services:** Alumni network; Alumni services; Career assessment; Career/job search classes; Internships; Regional alumni.

FACILITIES

Housing: Apartments for single students; Coed dorms; Fraternity/sorority housing; Theme housing; Wellness housing. **Special Academic Facilities/Equipment:** Museum of Anthropology; Charlotte and Philip Hanes Art Gallery; Scales Fine Arts Center; Reynolda House, Museum of American Art; Laser and Electron Microscope Labs. **Campus Network:** 100% of classrooms, 100% of dorms, 100% of student union, 100% of libraries, 100% of dining areas, 100% of common outdoor areas have wireless network access.

CAMPUS LIFE

Environment: City. **Activities:** Campus Ministries; Choral groups; Concert band; Dance; Drama/theater; International Student Organization; Jazz band; Literary magazine; Marching band; Model UN; Music ensembles; Musical theater; Pep band; Radio station; Student government; Student newspaper; Student-run film society; Symphony orchestra; Television station; Yearbook. 168 registered organizations, 16 honor societies, 16 religious organizations, 14 fraternities, 9 sororities, on campus. **Athletics (Intercollegiate):** *Men:* baseball, basketball, cheerleading, cross-country, football, golf, soccer, tennis, track/field (outdoor), track/field (indoor). *Women:* basketball, cheerleading, cross-country, field hockey, golf, soccer, tennis, track/field (outdoor), track/field (indoor), volleyball. **On-Campus Highlights:** Charlotte and Philip Hanes Art Gallery. **Environmental Initiatives:** Campus Master Plan: Wake Forest has completed a new campus master plan that will guide development over the next 50 years. Heavily integrated into that plan are tenents for sustainable design (e.g., LEED) as well as stormwater management and biohabitat protection. This new master plan will guide the campus in integrating sustainability within the built and natural environments for the years ahead.

ADMISSIONS

Freshman Academic Profile: 77% in top 10% of high school class, 93% in top 25% of high school class, 98% in top 50% of high school class. 65% from public high schools. **Test Scores:** SAT Math middle 50% range 630–730. SAT EBRW middle 50% range 630–710. ACT middle 50% range 28–32. **Basis for Candidate Selection:** *Very important factors include:* rigor of secondary school record, class rank, academic GPA, application essay, character/personal qualities. *Important factors include:* recommendation(s), interview, extracurricular activities, talent/ability. *Other factors include:* standardized test scores, first generation, alumni/ae relation, geographical residence, state residency, religious affiliation/commitment, racial/ethnic status, volunteer work, level of applicant's interest. **Freshman Admission Requirements:** High school diploma is required and GED is accepted. *Academic units required:* 4 English, 3 math, 1 science, 2 foreign language, 2 social studies. *Academic units recommended:* 4 English, 4 math, 4 science, 4 foreign language, 4 social studies. **Freshman Admission Statistics:** 13,071 applied, 28% admitted, 37% enrolled. **Transfer Admission Requirements:** High school transcript, college transcript(s), essay or personal statement, statement of good standing from prior institution(s). Minimum college GPA of 2.0 required. Lowest grade transferable C. **General Admission Information:** Application fee $65. Regular application deadline 1/1.

COSTS AND FINANCIAL AID

Annual tuition $54,430. Room and board $16,740. Required fees $1,010. Average book and supplies expense $1,500. **Required Forms and Deadlines:** CSS/Financial Aid PROFILE; FAFSA; Noncustodial PROFILE; State aid form. **Notification of Awards:** Applicants will be notified of awards on a rolling basis beginning 4/1. **Types of Aid:** *Need-based scholarships/grants:* College/university scholarship or grant aid from institutional funds; Federal Pell;

For more free content, visit PrincetonReview.com

Private scholarships; SEOG; State scholarships/grants; United Negro College Fund. *Loans:* Direct PLUS loans; Direct Subsidized Stafford Loans; Direct Unsubsidized Stafford Loans. **Student Employment:** Federal Work-Study Program available. Institutional employment available. **Financial Aid Statistics:** 94% needy freshmen, 96% needy undergrads receive need-based scholarship or grant aid. 82% freshmen, 59% undergrads receive non-need-based scholarship or grant aid. 91% freshmen, 94% undergrads receive need-based self-help aid. 3% freshmen, 4% undergrads receive athletic scholarships. 39% freshmen, 34% undergrads receive any aid. 30% undergrads borrow to pay for school. Average cumulative indebtedness $36,863. **Criteria awarding aid:** *Non-need-based:* Academics, Alumni affiliation, Art, Athletics, Leadership, Music/drama, Religious affiliation, State/district residency.

WALLA WALLA UNIVERSITY

Office of Admissions, College Place, WA 99324-1198
Phone: (509) 527-2615 **Financial Aid Phone:** (509) 527-2815
E-mail: info@wallawalla.edu **CEEB Code:** 4940
Fax: (509) 527-2253 **Website:** www.wallawalla.edu **ACT Code:** 4486

This private school, affiliated with the Seventh Day Adventist Church, was founded in 1892. It has a 77 acre campus.

RATINGS
Admissions Selectivity Rating: 67   **Fire Safety Rating:** 62   **Green Rating:** 60*

STUDENTS AND FACULTY
Enrollment: 1,549. **Student Body:** 50% female, 50% male, 59% out-of-state, 3% international (30 countries represented). Asian 0%, African American 3%, Caucasian 74%, Hispanic 10%, Native American 1%, Pacific Islander 7%, Two or more races 0%, Race unknown 1%.
Retention and Graduation: 78% freshmen return for sophomore year.
Faculty: 112 full-time faculty, 69% hold PhDs, 6% are members of minority groups, 39% are women. 0% of classes are taught by teaching assistants.

ACADEMICS
Degrees: Associate; Bachelor's; Diploma; Master's. **Classes:** Most classes have 10–19 students. Most lab/discussion sessions have 10–19 students. **Most popular majors:** Social Work; Business/Commerce, General; Engineering, General. **Special Study Options:** Cooperative education program; Distance learning; Double major; Honors program; Independent study; Internships; Liberal arts/career combination; Study abroad; Teacher certification program. **Disability Services offered:** Note-taking services; Reader services; Tape recorders; Tutors. **Career services:** Alumni network; Career assessment; Career/job search classes; Internships.

FACILITIES
Housing: Apartments for married students; Apartments for single students; Men's dorms; Special housing for international students; Wellness housing; Women's dorms; 75% of campus accessible to physically disabled. **Special Academic Facilities/Equipment:** Marine station on the Rosario Strait of the Puget Sound in Washington state.

CAMPUS LIFE
Environment: Town. **Activities:** Campus Ministries; Choral groups; Concert band; Drama/theater; International Student Organization; Jazz band; Literary magazine; Music ensembles; Radio station; Student government; Student newspaper; Symphony orchestra; Television station; Yearbook. 33 registered organizations, 7 honor societies, 6 religious organizations, on campus. **Athletics (Intercollegiate):** *Men:* basketball, golf, soccer, volleyball. *Women:* basketball, softball, volleyball. **On-Campus Highlights:** The Dairy Express.

ADMISSIONS
Freshman Academic Profile: 9% from public high schools. **Basis for Candidate Selection:** *Very important factors include:* rigor of secondary school record, academic GPA, recommendation(s). *Important factors include:* character/personal qualities, level of applicant's interest. *Other factors include:* class rank, standardized test scores, extracurricular activities, talent/ability. **Freshman Admission Requirements:** High school diploma is required and GED is accepted. *Academic units required:* 4 English, 3 math, 2 science, 2 science labs, 2 history. *Academic units recommended:* 4 English, 4 math, 3 science, 2 science labs, 2 foreign language, 1 social studies, 2 history. **Freshman Admission Statistics:** 626 applied, 89% admitted, 54% enrolled. **Transfer Admission Requirements:** College transcript(s). Minimum college GPA of 2.0 required.

Lowest grade transferable D-. **General Admission Information:** Application fee $40. Non-fall registration accepted.

COSTS AND FINANCIAL AID
Annual tuition $23,670. Room and board $5,655. Required fees $528. Average book and supplies expense $1,068. **Required Forms and Deadlines:** FAFSA; Institution's own financial aid form. **Notification of Awards:** Applicants will be notified of awards on a rolling basis beginning 3/1. **Types of Aid:** *Need-based scholarships/grants:* College/university scholarship or grant aid from institutional funds; Federal Nursing Scholarships; Federal Pell; Private scholarships; SEOG; State scholarships/grants. *Loans:* Direct PLUS loans; Direct Subsidized Stafford Loans; Direct Unsubsidized Stafford Loans. **Student Employment:** Federal Work-Study Program available. Institutional employment available. **Financial Aid Statistics:** 79% needy freshmen, 79% needy undergrads receive need-based scholarship or grant aid. 99% freshmen, 80% undergrads receive non-need-based scholarship or grant aid. 89% freshmen, 93% undergrads receive need-based self-help aid. 0% freshmen, 0% undergrads receive athletic scholarships. 84% freshmen, 83% undergrads receive any aid. **Criteria awarding aid:** *Need-based:* Academics, Alumni affiliation. *Non-need-based:* Academics, Leadership, Music/drama.

WALSH COLLEGE

3838 Livernois Road, Troy, MI 48007-7006
Phone: 248-823-1610 **Financial Aid Phone:** 248-823-1285
E-mail: admissions@walshcollege.edu
Fax: 248-823-1611 **Website:** www.walshcollege.edu

This private school was founded in 1922. It has a 20 acre campus.

RATINGS
Admissions Selectivity Rating: 60*   **Fire Safety Rating:** 60*   **Green Rating:** 60*

STUDENTS AND FACULTY
Enrollment: 929. **Student Body:** 47% female, 53% male, <1% out-of-state, 2% international (46 countries represented). Asian 4%, African American 6%, Caucasian 84%, Hispanic 2%, Native American <1%, Pacific Islander <1%, Two or more races 1%, Race unknown 1%.
Faculty: Student/faculty ratio 13:1. 23 full-time faculty, 78% hold PhDs, 4% are members of minority groups, 52% are women. 0% of classes are taught by teaching assistants.

ACADEMICS
Degrees: Bachelor's; Master's; Post-bachelor's certificate; Post-master's certificate. **Classes:** Most classes have 20–29 students. **Most popular majors:** Pharmacy; Biology/Biological Sciences, General. **Special Study Options:** Distance learning; Double major; Independent study; Internships. **Disability Services offered:** Note-taking services; Reader services; Tape recorders; Tutors. **Career services:** Alumni network; Alumni services; Career assessment; Career/job search classes; Internships.

FACILITIES
100% of campus accessible to physically disabled. **Campus Network:** 90% of libraries, 90% of dining areas have wireless network access.

CAMPUS LIFE
Environment: City. **Activities:** International Student Organization. 6 registered organizations, 1 honor society on campus. **On-Campus Highlights:** Barry Center.

ADMISSIONS
Transfer Admission Requirements: College transcript(s). Minimum college GPA of 2.0 required. Lowest grade transferable C. **General Admission Information:** Application fee $25.

COSTS AND FINANCIAL AID
Annual tuition $9,850. **Required Forms and Deadlines:** FAFSA. **Types of Aid:** *Need-based scholarships/grants:* College/university scholarship or grant aid from institutional funds; Federal Pell; SEOG; State scholarships/grants. **Student Employment:** Federal Work-Study Program available. **Financial Aid Statistics:** 64% needy undergrads receive need-based scholarship or grant aid. 18% undergrads receive non-need-based scholarship or grant aid. 100% undergrads receive need-based self-help aid. 0% undergrads receive athletic scholarships. **Criteria awarding aid:** *Need-based:* Academics, Minority status. *Non-need-based:* Academics.

WALSH UNIVERSITY

2020 East Maple St, North Canton, OH 44720-3396
Phone: 330-490-7172 **Financial Aid Phone:** 330-490-7367
E-mail: admissions@walsh.edu **CEEB Code:** 1926
Fax: 330-490-7165 **Website:** www.walsh.edu **ACT Code:** 3349

This private school, affiliated with the Roman Catholic Church, was founded in 1958. It has a 140 acre campus.

RATINGS
Admissions Selectivity Rating: 77   **Fire Safety Rating:** 92   **Green Rating:** 60*

STUDENTS AND FACULTY
Enrollment: 2,157. **Student Body:** 61% female, 39% male, 7% out-of-state, 4% international (30 countries represented). Asian 1%, African American 6%, Caucasian 75%, Hispanic 3%, Native American <1%, Pacific Islander <1%, Two or more races 2%, Race unknown 9%.
Retention and Graduation: 80% freshmen return for sophomore year. 16% grads go on to further study within 1 year. 9% grads pursue arts and sciences degrees. 1% grads pursue law degrees. 3% grads pursue business degrees. 2% grads pursue medical degrees. **Faculty:** Student/faculty ratio 13:1. 132 full-time faculty, 67% hold PhDs, 7% are members of minority groups, 55% are women. 0% of classes are taught by teaching assistants.

ACADEMICS
Degrees: Associate; Bachelor's; Certificate; Doctoral degree—professional practice; Master's. **Classes:** Most classes have 10–19 students. Most lab/discussion sessions have fewer than 10 students. **Most popular majors:** Registered Nursing/Registered Nurse; Biology/Biological Sciences, General; Business Administration and Management, General. **Special Study Options:** Accelerated program; Distance learning; Double major; Dual enrollment; English as a Second Language (ESL); Exchange student program (domestic); External degree program; Honors program; Independent study; Internships; Liberal arts/career combination; Study abroad; Teacher certification program. **Honors programs:** Honors Program students may pursue any major and have opportunity annually to attend the national honors conference, where Walsh students frequently present their research. The Blouin Scholars Program in Global Studies at Walsh University provides students with a unique opportunity to become part of a community of students and faculty dedicated to using scholarship and service to address major global issues. As a Blouin Scholar, you will live and take classes with a cohort of students who are similarly dedicated to become leaders in service to the global community. All classes are built into the Walsh University core curriculum—you still choose your own majors and minors—and center on a common global theme. You will be supported with opportunities such as global learning in Africa and Europe, special lectures and co-curricular activities, and priority registration and advising procedures. **Combined degree programs:** BA/MA. **Disability Services offered:** Reader services; Tape recorders; Tutors. **Career services:** Alumni network; Alumni services; Career assessment; Internships; Regional alumni.

FACILITIES
Housing: Apartments for single students; Coed dorms; Special housing for disabled students; Special housing for international students; Wellness housing; 100% of campus accessible to physically disabled. **Special Academic Facilities/Equipment:** Bioinformatics lab, Hoover Historical Center (corporate and local history), human cadaver lab (prosection for undergrad), Gathering Garden for Education activities with schoolchildren, Religious Education Center, two Anatomage virtual dissection tables that display 3D images of human anatomy with stunning detail in a multitude of layers, views and perspectives. **Campus Network:** 100% of classrooms, 100% of dorms, 100% of student union, 100% of libraries, 100% of dining areas, 100% of common outdoor areas have wireless network access.

CAMPUS LIFE
Environment: City. **Activities:** Campus Ministries; Choral groups; Dance; Drama/theater; International Student Organization; Literary magazine; Marching band; Music ensembles; Pep band; Radio station; Student government; Student newspaper; Yearbook. 38 registered organizations, 14 honor societies, 13 religious organizations on campus. **Athletics (Intercollegiate):** *Men:* baseball, basketball, cheerleading, cross-country, football, golf, soccer, tennis, track/field (outdoor), track/field (indoor). *Women:* basketball, cheerleading, cross-country, golf, soccer, softball, tennis, track/field (outdoor), track/field (indoor), volleyball. **On-Campus Highlights:** David

Campus Center. **Environmental Initiatives:** HVAC & electrical managament system.

ADMISSIONS
Freshman Academic Profile: Average high school GPA 3.4. 17% in top 10% of high school class, 43% in top 25% of high school class, 76% in top 50% of high school class. 71% from public high schools. **Test Scores:** SAT Math middle 50% range 430–620. SAT EBRW middle 50% range 450–630. ACT middle 50% range 18–27. **Basis for Candidate Selection:** *Very important factors include:* rigor of secondary school record, academic GPA. *Important factors include:* recommendation(s). *Other factors include:* class rank, application essay, standardized test scores, interview, extracurricular activities, character/personal qualities, volunteer work, work experience. **Freshman Admission Requirements:** High school diploma is required and GED is accepted. *Academic units recommended:* 4 English, 3 math, 3 science, 2 foreign language, 3 social studies, 1 academic electives. **Freshman Admission Statistics:** 1,480 applied, 81% admitted, 37% enrolled. **Transfer Admission Requirements:** High school transcript, college transcript(s). Minimum college GPA of 2.0 required. Lowest grade transferable C. **General Admission Information:** Application fee $25. Regular application deadline 8/15. Non-fall registration accepted. Admission may be deferred for a maximum of 1 year.

COSTS AND FINANCIAL AID
Annual tuition $26,300. Room and board $9,920. Required fees $1,410. Average book and supplies expense $1,104. **Required Forms and Deadlines:** FAFSA. **Notification of Awards:** Applicants will be notified of awards on a rolling basis beginning 2/15. **Types of Aid:** *Need-based scholarships/grants:* College/university scholarship or grant aid from institutional funds; Federal Pell; Private scholarships; SEOG; State scholarships/grants. *Loans:* Direct PLUS loans; Direct Subsidized Stafford Loans; Direct Unsubsidized Stafford Loans. **Student Employment:** Federal Work-Study Program available. Institutional employment available. **Financial Aid Statistics:** 80% needy freshmen, 79% needy undergrads receive need-based scholarship or grant aid. 100% freshmen, 87% undergrads receive non-need-based scholarship or grant aid. 81% freshmen, 78% undergrads receive need-based self-help aid. 18% freshmen, 19% undergrads receive athletic scholarships. 99% freshmen, 93% undergrads receive any aid. 85% undergrads borrow to pay for school. Average cumulative indebtedness $29,702. **Criteria awarding aid:** *Non-need-based:* Academics, Alumni affiliation, Athletics, Music/drama, Religious affiliation, State/district residency.

WARNER PACIFIC COLLEGE

Office of Admissions, Portland, OR 97215
Phone: 503-517-1020 **Financial Aid Phone:** 503-517-1091
E-mail: admissions@warnerpacific.edu **CEEB Code:** 4595
Fax: 503-517-1540 **Website:** http://www.warnerpacific.edu/

This private school, affiliated with the Church of God, was founded in 1937. It has a 15 acre campus.

RATINGS
Admissions Selectivity Rating: 84   **Fire Safety Rating:** 73   **Green Rating:** 60*

STUDENTS AND FACULTY
Enrollment: 501. **Student Body:** 56% female, 44% male, 35% out-of-state, 0% international (12 countries represented). Asian 4%, African American 7%, Caucasian 66%, Hispanic 9%, Native American <1%, Pacific Islander 2%, Two or more races 6%, Race unknown 5%.
Retention and Graduation: 32% freshmen return for sophomore year. 7% grads go on to further study within 1 year. 2% grads pursue arts and sciences degrees. 2% grads pursue business degrees. 1% grads pursue medical degrees. **Faculty:** Student/faculty ratio 11:1. 31 full-time faculty, 68% hold PhDs, 10% are members of minority groups, 35% are women. 0% of classes are taught by teaching assistants.

ACADEMICS
Degrees: Associate; Bachelor's; Certificate; Master's. **Classes:** Most classes have 10–19 students. Most lab/discussion sessions have fewer than 10 students. **Most popular majors:** Business Administration, Management and Operations, Other; Human Development and Family Studies, General; Biology/Biological Sciences, General. **Special Study Options:** Double major; Exchange student program (domestic); Independent study; Internships; Liberal arts/career combination; Student-designed major; Study abroad; Teacher certification

program. **Disability Services offered:** Note-taking services; Reader services; Tape recorders; Tutors. **Career services:** Alumni network; Alumni services; Career assessment; Internships.

FACILITIES

Housing: Apartments for married students; Apartments for single students; Men's dorms; Special housing for disabled students; Women's dorms; 50% of campus accessible to physically disabled. **Special Academic Facilities/Equipment:** Early learning center. **Campus Network:** 100% of classrooms, 100% of dorms, 100% of student union, 100% of libraries, 100% of dining areas, 100% of common outdoor areas have wireless network access.

CAMPUS LIFE

Environment: Metropolis. **Activities:** Campus Ministries; Choral groups; Concert band; Drama/theater; International Student Organization; Jazz band; Literary magazine; Music ensembles; Student government; Student newspaper; Yearbook. 20 registered organizations, 2 religious organizations on campus. **Athletics (Intercollegiate):** *Men:* basketball, cross-country, golf, soccer, track/field (outdoor), track/field (indoor). *Women:* basketball, cross-country, golf, soccer, track/field (outdoor), track/field (indoor), volleyball. **On-Campus Highlights:** Tabor Grind Coffee Shop.

ADMISSIONS

Freshman Academic Profile: Average high school GPA 3.2. 8% in top 10% of high school class, 25% in top 25% of high school class, 77% in top 50% of high school class. **Test Scores:** SAT Math middle 50% range 410–550. SAT EBRW middle 50% range 420–550. ACT middle 50% range 16–22. **Basis for Candidate Selection:** *Very important factors include:* academic GPA, standardized test scores. *Other factors include:* application essay, recommendation(s), religious affiliation/commitment. **Freshman Admission Requirements:** High school diploma is required and GED is accepted. *Academic units recommended:* 4 English, 2 math, 2 science, 2 science labs, 3 social studies. **Freshman Admission Statistics:** 948 applied, 53% admitted, 15% enrolled. **Transfer Admission Requirements:** College transcript(s), essay or personal statement. Minimum college GPA of 2.5 required. Lowest grade transferable D. **General Admission Information:** Non-fall registration accepted. Admission may be deferred for a maximum of 3 years.

COSTS AND FINANCIAL AID

Annual tuition $18,370. Room and board $7,690. Required fees $660. Average book and supplies expense $1,300. **Required Forms and Deadlines:** FAFSA. **Notification of Awards:** Applicants will be notified of awards on a rolling basis beginning 3/1. **Types of Aid:** *Need-based scholarships/grants:* College/university scholarship or grant aid from institutional funds; Federal Pell; Private scholarships; SEOG; State scholarships/grants. *Loans:* Direct PLUS loans; Direct Subsidized Stafford Loans; Direct Unsubsidized Stafford Loans. **Student Employment:** Federal Work-Study Program available. Institutional employment available. **Financial Aid Statistics:** 97% needy freshmen, 93% needy undergrads receive need-based scholarship or grant aid. 95% freshmen, 89% undergrads receive non-need-based scholarship or grant aid. 94% freshmen, 91% undergrads receive need-based self-help aid. 9% freshmen, 5% undergrads receive athletic scholarships. 99% freshmen, 99% undergrads receive any aid. **Criteria awarding aid:** *Non-need-based:* Academics, Alumni affiliation, Athletics, Leadership, Music/drama, Religious affiliation, State/district residency.

WARREN WILSON COLLEGE

PO Box 9000, Asheville, NC 28815-9000
Phone: 828-771-2073 **Financial Aid Phone:** 828-771-2082
E-mail: admit@warren-wilson.edu **CEEB Code:** 5886
Fax: 828-298-1440 **Website:** www.warren-wilson.edu **ACT Code:** 3170

This private school was founded in 1894. It has a 1100 acre campus.

RATINGS

Admissions Selectivity Rating: 75   **Fire Safety Rating:** 69   **Green Rating:** 76

STUDENTS AND FACULTY

Enrollment: 635. **Student Body:** 64% female, 36% male, 66% out-of-state, 2% international (14 countries represented). Asian 1%, African American 7%, Caucasian 76%, Hispanic 7%, Native American 1%, Pacific Islander 0%, Two or more races 4%, Race unknown 2%.
Retention and Graduation: 65% freshmen return for sophomore year. 49% freshmen graduate within 4 years. 53% freshmen graduate within 6 years.
Faculty: Student/faculty ratio 10:1. 53 full-time faculty, 96% hold PhDs, 11% are members of minority groups, 53% are women. 0% of classes are taught by teaching assistants.

ACADEMICS

Degrees: Bachelor's; Master's. **Classes:** Most classes have 10–19 students. **Most popular majors:** Environmental Studies; Biology/Biological Sciences, General; Psychology, General. **Special Study Options:** Cross-registration; Double major; English as a Second Language (ESL); Exchange student program (domestic); Honors program; Independent study; Internships; Liberal arts/career combination; Student-designed major; Study abroad. **Honors programs:** Natural Sciences Honors Program; English Honors Program. **Disability Services offered:** Tutors. **Career services:** Alumni network; Alumni services; Career assessment; Career/job search classes; Internships; Regional alumni.

FACILITIES

Housing: Coed dorms; Cooperative housing; Men's dorms; Special housing for disabled students; Theme housing; Wellness housing; Women's dorms 90% of campus accessible to physically disabled. **Special Academic Facilities/Equipment:** Bannerman Technology Center, WWC Tech Lab, Geographic Information Systems Lab, Warren Wilson Archaeological Site, Environmental Leadership Center, Holden Visual Arts Center & Gallery, Kittredge Theatre and Community Arts Center, Amphitheatre, Gossman/Cannon Climbing Tower, Blacksmithing Shop, Fine Woodworking Shop, Fiber Arts Studio, 3D Studio (ceramics, sculpture, kiln and foundry), and the Lucy Fletcher Studios (painting, drawing, senior studio spaces, photography darkrooms).

CAMPUS LIFE

Environment: City. **Activities:** Campus Ministries; Choral groups; Dance; Drama/theater; International Student Organization; Jazz band; Literary magazine; Music ensembles; Musical theater; Student government; Student newspaper. 35 registered organizations, 3 honor societies, 6 religious organizations on campus. **Athletics (Intercollegiate):** *Men:* basketball, cross-country, diving, kayaking, mountain biking, soccer, swimming, ultimate frisbee. *Women:* basketball, cross-country, diving, kayaking, mountain biking, soccer, swimming, ultimate frisbee. **On-Campus Highlights:** Sage café. **Environmental Initiatives:** Warren Wilson College made significant progress in 2019 preparing future leaders and serving as an educational hub for sustainable land management practices in the region. To accomplish these goals, the College continued to strengthen and align its institutional framework. The College's new 2022 Strategic Plan directs us to "prepare graduates to engage in groundbreaking scholarship, pursue meaningful careers with professionalism, and lead purposeful lives dedicated to fostering a just, equitable, and sustainable world." Its strategic imperatives represent the broad range of sustainability concerns with such goals as diversity, equity, inclusion, land and environmental sustainability, "with a focus on the well-being of individuals in our community."

ADMISSIONS

Freshman Academic Profile: 80% from public high schools. **Test Scores:** ACT middle 50% range 21–28. **Basis for Candidate Selection:** *Very important factors include:* rigor of secondary school record, recommendation(s). *Important factors include:* academic GPA, application essay, interview, volunteer work, work experience. *Other factors include:* class rank, standardized test scores, extracurricular activities, talent/ability, character/personal qualities, first generation. **Freshman Admission Requirements:** High school diploma is required and GED is accepted. *Academic units recommended:* 4 English, 3 math, 2 science, 2 science labs, 2 foreign language, 3 social studies. **Freshman Admission Statistics:** 1,013 applied, 86% admitted, 29% enrolled. **Transfer Admission Requirements:** High school transcript, college transcript(s), standardized test scores. Minimum college GPA of 3.0 required. Lowest grade transferable C. **General Admission Information:** Priority deadline 2/1. Non-fall registration accepted. Admission may be deferred for a maximum of 1 year/2 sem.

COSTS AND FINANCIAL AID

Annual tuition $36,600. Room and board $11,300. Required fees $764. Average book and supplies expense $850. **Required Forms and Deadlines:** FAFSA; State aid form. **Notification of Awards:** Applicants will be notified of awards on a rolling basis beginning 3/1. **Types of Aid:** *Need-based scholarships/grants:* College/university scholarship or grant aid from institutional funds; Federal Pell; Private scholarships; SEOG; State scholarships/grants. *Loans:* Direct PLUS loans; Direct Subsidized Stafford Loans; Direct Unsubsidized Stafford Loans. **Student Employment:** Federal Work-Study Program available. Institutional employment available. **Financial Aid Statistics:** 100% freshmen, 95% undergrads receive any aid. **Criteria awarding aid:** *Need-based:* Academics. *Non-need-based:* Academics, Art, Leadership.

WARTBURG COLLEGE

100 Wartburg Blvd., Waverly, IA 50677-0903
Phone: 319-352-8264 **Financial Aid Phone:** 319-352-8262
E-mail: admissions@wartburg.edu **CEEB Code:** 6926
Fax: 319-352-8579 **Website:** www.wartburg.edu **ACT Code:** 1364

This private school, affiliated with the Lutheran Church, was founded in 1852. It has a 118 acre campus.

RATINGS
Admissions Selectivity Rating: 77   **Fire Safety Rating:** 86   **Green Rating:** 60*

STUDENTS AND FACULTY
Enrollment: 1,478. **Student Body:** 55% female, 45% male, 31% out-of-state, 8% international (62 countries represented). Asian 1%, African American 4%, Caucasian 78%, Hispanic 5%, Native American <1%, Pacific Islander <1%, Two or more races 3%, Race unknown 1%.
Retention and Graduation: 78% freshmen return for sophomore year. 58% freshmen graduate within 4 years. 62% freshmen graduate within 6 years. 18% grads go on to further study within 1 year. 62% grads pursue arts and sciences degrees. 4% grads pursue law degrees. 9% grads pursue business degrees. 23% grads pursue medical degrees. **Faculty:** Student/faculty ratio 11:1. 92 full-time faculty, 89% hold PhDs, 12% are members of minority groups, 48% are women. 0% of classes are taught by teaching assistants.

ACADEMICS
Degrees: Bachelor's; Master's; Post-bachelor's certificate. **Classes:** Most classes have 20–29 students. Most lab/discussion sessions have 10–19 students. **Most popular majors:** Biology/Biological Sciences, General; Business, Management, Marketing, and Related Support Services, Other; Elementary Education and Teaching. **Special Study Options:** Accelerated program; Distance learning; Double major; Dual enrollment; Honors program; Independent study; Internships; Student-designed major; Study abroad; Teacher certification program. **Honors programs:** Scholars Program—features small seminar classes, distinguished speaker series, sophomore-year program of lectures, concerts, and performances, student involvement in designing courses and activities, variety of social and travel opportunities, student-designed senior project. **Combined degree programs:** BA/JD; BA/MA; BA/MEng. **Disability Services offered:** Note-taking services; Reader services; Tape recorders; Tutors. **Career services:** Alumni network; Alumni services; Career assessment; Career/job search classes; Internships; Regional alumni.

FACILITIES
Housing: Apartments for single students; Coed dorms; Men's dorms; Special housing for disabled students; Theme housing; Women's dorms 85% of campus accessible to physically disabled. **Special Academic Facilities/Equipment:** Waldemar A. Schmidt Art Gallery, Bachman Fine Arts Center, Institute for Leadership Education, Platte Observatory, prairie preserve learning space, state-of-the-art library study spaces, Center for Community Engagement, Wartburg-Waverly Sports & Wellness Center. **Campus Network:** 100% of classrooms, 100% of dorms, 100% of student union, 100% of libraries, 100% of dining areas, 100% of common outdoor areas have wireless network access.

CAMPUS LIFE
Environment: Village. **Activities:** Campus Ministries; Choral groups; Concert band; Dance; Drama/theater; International Student Organization; Jazz band; Literary magazine; Model UN; Music ensembles; Musical theater; Opera; Pep band; Radio station; Student government; Student newspaper; Student-run film society; Symphony orchestra; Television station; Yearbook. 87 registered organizations, 17 honor societies, 7 religious organizations on campus.
Athletics (Intercollegiate): *Men:* baseball, basketball, cross-country, football, golf, soccer, tennis, track/field (outdoor), track/field (indoor), wrestling. *Women:* basketball, cross-country, golf, soccer, softball, tennis, track/field (outdoor), track/field (indoor), volleyball. **On-Campus Highlights:** Konditorei Coffee Shop/Vogel Library.

ADMISSIONS
Freshman Academic Profile: Average high school GPA 3.6. 21% in top 10% of high school class, 56% in top 25% of high school class, 80% in top 50% of

high school class. **Test Scores:** SAT Math middle 50% range 520–600. SAT EBRW middle 50% range 520–620. ACT middle 50% range 21–26. **Basis for Candidate Selection:** *Very important factors include:* rigor of secondary school record, class rank, academic GPA, standardized test scores, recommendation(s). *Important factors include:* interview, character/personal qualities. *Other factors include:* extracurricular activities, talent/ability, volunteer work, work experience, level of applicant's interest. **Freshman Admission Requirements:** High school diploma is required and GED is accepted *Academic units required:* 4 English, 3 math, 3 science, 2 foreign language, 2 social studies. *Academic units recommended:* 1 computer science. **Freshman Admission Statistics:** 4,018 applied, 75% admitted, 13% enrolled. **Transfer Admission Requirements:** High school transcript, college transcript(s), standardized test scores, statement of good standing from prior institution(s). Minimum college GPA of 2.0 required. Lowest grade transferable C-. **General Admission Information:** Priority deadline 12/1. Non-fall registration accepted.

COSTS AND FINANCIAL AID
Annual tuition $43,500. Room and board $9,592. Required fees $2,180. Average book and supplies expense $1,100. **Required Forms and Deadlines:** FAFSA. **Notification of Awards:** Applicants will be notified of awards on a rolling basis beginning 1/15. **Types of Aid:** *Need-based scholarships/grants:* College/university scholarship or grant aid from institutional funds; Federal Pell; Private scholarships; SEOG; State scholarships/grants. *Loans:* Direct PLUS loans; Direct Subsidized Stafford Loans; Direct Unsubsidized Stafford Loans. **Student Employment:** Federal Work-Study Program available. Institutional employment available. **Financial Aid Statistics:** 100% needy freshmen, 100% needy undergrads receive need-based scholarship or grant aid. 24% freshmen, 21% undergrads receive non-need-based scholarship or grant aid. 72% freshmen, 76% undergrads receive need-based self-help aid. 0% freshmen, 0% undergrads receive athletic scholarships. 99.6% freshmen, 97.6% undergrads receive any aid. 75% undergrads borrow to pay for school. Average cumulative indebtedness $39,849. **Criteria awarding aid:** *Need-based:* Minority status. *Non-need-based:* Academics, Alumni affiliation, Leadership, Music/drama, Religious affiliation.

WASHBURN UNIVERSITY

1700 SW College Ave, Topeka, KS 66621
Phone: 785-670-1030
E-mail: admissions@washburn.edu **CEEB Code:** 001949
Fax: 785-670-1113 **Website:** www.washburn.edu **ACT Code:** 1474

This is a public school.

RATINGS
Admissions Selectivity Rating: 74   **Fire Safety Rating:** 60*   **Green Rating:** 60*

STUDENTS AND FACULTY
Enrollment: 4,900. **Student Body:** 59% female, 41% male, 7% out-of-state.
Retention and Graduation: 68% freshmen return for sophomore year.
Faculty: Student/faculty ratio 13:1. 286 full-time faculty, 84% hold PhDs, 14% are members of minority groups, 55% are women.

ACADEMICS
Degrees: Associate; Bachelor's; Certificate; Doctoral degree—professional practice; Master's; Post-bachelor's certificate; Post-master's certificate. **Classes:** Most classes have 10–19 students. Most lab/discussion sessions have 20–29 students. **Special Study Options:** Cooperative education program; Cross-registration; Distance learning; Double major; Dual enrollment; English as a Second Language (ESL); Honors program; Independent study; Internships; Liberal arts/career combination; Student-designed major; Study abroad; Teacher certification program.

FACILITIES
Housing: Apartments for single students; Coed dorms; Fraternity/sorority housing; Wellness housing.

CAMPUS LIFE
Activities: Campus Ministries; Choral groups; Concert band; Dance; Drama/theater; International Student Organization; Jazz band; Literary magazine; Marching band; Model UN; Music ensembles; Musical theater; Pep band; Student government; Student newspaper; Student-run film society; Symphony orchestra; Television station; Yearbook.

ADMISSIONS

Freshman Academic Profile: Average high school GPA 3.4. 13% in top 10% of high school class, 34% in top 25% of high school class, 67% in top 50% of high school class. 96% from public high schools. **Test Scores:** ACT middle 50% range 19–25. **Basis for Candidate Selection:** *Very important factors include:* rigor of secondary school record, academic GPA, standardized test scores. **Freshman Admission Requirements:** High school diploma is required and GED is accepted. *Academic units recommended:* 4 English, 3 math, 3 science, 2 foreign language, 3 social studies, 1 history, 1 computer science. **Freshman Admission Statistics:** 1,458 applied, 99% admitted, 56% enrolled. **Transfer Admission Requirements:** College transcript(s), statement of good standing from prior institution(s). Minimum college GPA of 2.0 required. Lowest grade transferable 1. **General Admission Information:** Application fee $20. Regular application deadline 8/1. Non-fall registration accepted.

COSTS AND FINANCIAL AID

Annual in-state tuition $7,800. Annual out-of-state tuition $17,640. Room and board $6,830. Required fees $110. Average book and supplies expense $1,000. **Required Forms and Deadlines:** FAFSA. **Notification of Awards:** Applicants will be notified of awards on a rolling basis beginning 4/1. **Types of Aid:** *Need-based scholarships/grants:* College/university scholarship or grant aid from institutional funds; Federal Pell; Private scholarships; SEOG; State scholarships/grants. *Loans:* Direct PLUS loans; Direct Subsidized Stafford Loans; Direct Unsubsidized Stafford Loans. **Financial Aid Statistics:** 60% needy freshmen, 63% needy undergrads receive need-based scholarship or grant aid. 68% freshmen, 50% undergrads receive non-need-based scholarship or grant aid. 70% freshmen, 73% undergrads receive need-based self-help aid. 5% freshmen, 4% undergrads receive athletic scholarships. 68% undergrads borrow to pay for school. Average cumulative indebtedness $24,665. **Criteria awarding aid:** *Non-need-based:* Academics, Alumni affiliation, Art, Athletics, Job skills, Leadership, Minority status, Music/drama, Religious affiliation, State/district residency.

WASHINGTON ADVENTIST UNIVERSITY

7600 Flower Avenue, Takoma Park, MD 20912
Phone: 301-891-4080 **Financial Aid Phone:** 301-891-4005
E-mail: enroll@wau.edu **CEEB Code:** 5890
Fax: 301-891-4230 **ACT Code:** 1687

This private school, affiliated with the Seventh Day Adventist Church, was founded in 1904. It has a 19 acre campus.

RATINGS

Admissions Selectivity Rating: 74   **Fire Safety Rating:** 60*   **Green Rating:** 60*

STUDENTS AND FACULTY

Enrollment: 986. **Student Body:** 65% female, 35% male, 57% out-of-state, 0% international (47 countries represented). Asian 6%, African American 52%, Caucasian 11%, Hispanic 11%, Native American <1%, Pacific Islander, Two or more races, Race unknown 20%.
Retention and Graduation: 61% freshmen return for sophomore year.
Faculty: Student/faculty ratio 14:1. 41 full-time faculty, 51% hold PhDs, 44% are members of minority groups, 51% are women. 0% of classes are taught by teaching assistants.

ACADEMICS

Degrees: Associate; Bachelor's; Certificate; Master's. **Classes:** Most classes have fewer than 10 students. Most lab/discussion sessions have 30–39 students.
Most popular majors: Business/Commerce, General; Nursing/Registered Nurse (Rn, Asn, Bsn, Msn). **Special Study Options:** Accelerated program; Cooperative education program; Cross-registration; Distance learning; Double major; Dual enrollment; English as a Second Language (ESL); External degree program; Honors program; Independent study; Internships; Liberal arts/career combination; Student-designed major; Study abroad; Teacher certification program. **Honors programs:** The Honors Program at CUC strives to provide academically talented students the opportunity to engage and explore subject material in greater depth. This does not mean more work, it means a different kind of work, with more individual attention. The honors classes are different in design as each class explores the topic from an interdisciplinary perspective, where areas of study are combined into one course. **Disability Services offered:** Reader services; Tutors. **Career services:** Career assessment; Internships.

FACILITIES

Housing: Apartments for married students; Apartments for single students; Men's dorms; Women's dorms; 30% of campus accessible to physically disabled. **Special Academic Facilities/Equipment:** Hospital adjacent to campus for students in health fields, performing arts at adjacent large church auditorium, learning center, radio station, playing fields and gymnasium. **Campus Network:** 100% of classrooms, 100% of dorms, 100% of student union, 100% of libraries, 100% of dining areas, 100% of common outdoor areas have wireless network access.

CAMPUS LIFE

Environment: Metropolis. **Activities:** Campus Ministries; Choral groups; Concert band; International Student Organization; Jazz band; Literary magazine; Music ensembles; Musical theater; Pep band; Radio station; Student government; Student newspaper; Symphony orchestra; Yearbook. 6 honor societies on campus. **Athletics (Intercollegiate):** *Men:* baseball, basketball, cross-country, soccer, track/field (outdoor). *Women:* basketball, cross-country, soccer, softball, track/field (outdoor).

ADMISSIONS

Freshman Academic Profile: 53% from public high schools. **Basis for Candidate Selection:** *Very important factors include:* academic GPA, standardized test scores. *Important factors include:* recommendation(s), character/personal qualities. *Other factors include:* rigor of secondary school record, application essay, talent/ability, religious affiliation/commitment. **Freshman Admission Requirements:** High school diploma is required and GED is accepted. *Academic units required:* 4 English, 2 math, 2 science, 2 science labs, 4 history, 4 academic electives. *Academic units recommended:* 4 English, 4 math, 4 science, 4 science labs, 2 foreign language, 2 social studies, 4 history, 4 academic electives, 1 computer science. **Freshman Admission Statistics:** 1,293 applied, 41% admitted, 27% enrolled. **Transfer Admission Requirements:** College transcript(s). Minimum college GPA of 2.0 required. Lowest grade transferable C. **General Admission Information:** Application fee $25. Priority deadline 7/1. Regular application deadline 8/1. Non-fall registration accepted. Admission may be deferred for a maximum of 1 year.

COSTS AND FINANCIAL AID

Annual tuition $18,200. Room and board $7,530. Average book and supplies expense $1,200. **Required Forms and Deadlines:** FAFSA; State aid form. **Notification of Awards:** Applicants will be notified of awards on a rolling basis beginning 5/1. **Types of Aid:** *Need-based scholarships/grants:* Federal Pell; Private scholarships; SEOG; State scholarships/grants. *Loans:* Direct PLUS loans; Direct Subsidized Stafford Loans; Direct Unsubsidized Stafford Loans. **Student Employment:** Federal Work-Study Program available. Institutional employment available. **Criteria awarding aid:** *Non-need-based:* Academics, Athletics, Music/drama.

WASHINGTON & JEFFERSON COLLEGE

60 South Lincoln Street, Washington, PA 15301
Phone: 724-223-6025 **Financial Aid Phone:** 724-223-6019
E-mail: admission@washjeff.edu **CEEB Code:** 2967
Fax: 724-223-6534 **Website:** www.washjeff.edu **ACT Code:** 3746

This private school was founded in 1781. It has a 60 acre campus.

RATINGS

Admissions Selectivity Rating: 76   **Fire Safety Rating:** 95   **Green Rating:** 78

STUDENTS AND FACULTY

Enrollment: 1,246. **Student Body:** 52% female, 48% male, 23% out-of-state, 3% international (29 countries represented). Asian 2%, African American 7%, Caucasian 74%, Hispanic 6%, Native American 0%, Pacific Islander 0%, Two or more races 3%, Race unknown 6%.
Retention and Graduation: 83% freshmen return for sophomore year. 69% freshmen graduate within 4 years. 75% freshmen graduate within 6 years. 33% grads go on to further study within 1 year. 51% grads pursue arts and sciences degrees. 23% grads pursue law degrees. 6% grads pursue business degrees. 17% grads pursue medical degrees. **Faculty:** Student/faculty ratio 10:1. 113 full-

time faculty, 93% hold PhDs, 16% are members of minority groups, 52% are women. 0% of classes are taught by teaching assistants.

ACADEMICS
Degrees: Bachelor's; Master's; Post-bachelor's certificate. **Classes:** Most classes have 10–19 students. Most lab/discussion sessions have 10–19 students. **Most popular majors:** Business/Commerce, General; Accounting; Psychology, General. **Special Study Options:** Accelerated program; Double major; Dual enrollment; English as a Second Language (ESL); Honors program; Independent study; Internships; Liberal arts/career combination; Student-designed major; Study abroad; Teacher certification program. **Honors programs:** The Magellan program allows outstanding students to pursue independent research during the summer that is funded by the College. **Combined degree programs:** BA/JD; BA/MD; BA/MEng. **Disability Services offered:** Note-taking services; Reader services; Tape recorders; Tutors. **Career services:** Alumni network; Alumni services; Career assessment; Career/job search classes; Internships; Regional alumni.

FACILITIES
Housing: Apartments for single students; Coed dorms; Fraternity/sorority housing; Men's dorms; Special housing for disabled students; Special housing for international students; Theme housing; Wellness housing; Women's dorms; 90% of campus accessible to physically disabled. **Special Academic Facilities/Equipment:** Abernathy Field Station, Olin Fine Arts Center, laser scanning confocal microscope facility, atomic force microscope, 3-D printers, mass spectrometer/gas chromatograph, microplate reader, cell culture labs, isolator lab, X-ray diffraction unit, neuropsychology lab, atomic absorption unit, nuclear magnetic resonance (NMR) lab, refrigerated centrifuge, global learning unit, language lab, spectrometers.

CAMPUS LIFE
Environment: Village. **Activities:** Campus Ministries; Choral groups; Concert band; Dance; Drama/theater; International Student Organization; Jazz band; Literary magazine; Model UN; Music ensembles; Musical theater; Pep band; Radio station; Student government; Student newspaper; Student-run film society; Yearbook. 93 registered organizations, 22 honor societies, 4 religious organizations, 5 fraternities, 4 sororities on campus. **Athletics (Intercollegiate):** *Men:* baseball, basketball, cheerleading, cross-country, diving, football, golf, lacrosse, soccer, swimming, tennis, track/field (outdoor), track/field (indoor), water polo, wrestling. *Women:* basketball, cheerleading, cross-country, diving, field hockey, golf, lacrosse, soccer, softball, swimming, tennis, track/field (outdoor), track/field (indoor), volleyball, water polo. **On-Campus Highlights:** The Hub (Student Center). **Environmental Initiatives:** Signed the ACUPCC, created the Sustainability Committee and a Climate Action Plan, which outlines many past accomplishments and current initiatives.

ADMISSIONS
Freshman Academic Profile: Average high school GPA 3.7. 24% in top 10% of high school class, 48% in top 25% of high school class, 85% in top 50% of high school class. 81% from public high schools. **Test Scores:** SAT Math middle 50% range 540–640. SAT EBRW middle 50% range 550–640. ACT middle 50% range 22–28. **Basis for Candidate Selection:** *Very important factors include:* rigor of secondary school record, class rank, academic GPA, application essay, recommendation(s), interview, character/personal qualities. *Important factors include:* extracurricular activities. *Other factors include:* standardized test scores, talent/ability, alumni/ae relation, geographical residence, state residency, racial/ethnic status, volunteer work, work experience, level of applicant's interest. **Freshman Admission Requirements:** High school diploma is required and GED is accepted. *Academic units required:* 3 English, 3 math, 1 science, 1 science labs, 2 foreign language, 6 academic electives. *Academic units recommended:* 4 English, 4 math, 2 science, 2 science labs, 3 foreign language, 6 academic electives. **Freshman Admission Statistics:** 2,722 applied, 85% admitted, 13% enrolled. **Transfer Admission Requirements:** High school transcript, college transcript(s), essay or personal statement, standardized test scores, statement of good standing from prior institution(s). Minimum college GPA of 2.50 required. Lowest grade transferable C. **General Admission Information:** Priority deadline 1/15. Regular application deadline 3/1. Non-fall registration accepted. Admission may be deferred for a maximum of 1 year.

COSTS AND FINANCIAL AID
Annual tuition $48,758. Room and board $13,044. Required fees $550. Average book and supplies expense $1,000. **Required Forms and Deadlines:** FAFSA. **Notification of Awards:** Applicants will be notified of awards on a rolling basis beginning 12/15. **Types of Aid:** *Need-based scholarships/grants:* College/university scholarship or grant aid from institutional funds; Federal Pell; Private scholarships; SEOG; State scholarships/grants; United Negro College Fund. *Loans:* Direct PLUS loans; Direct Subsidized Stafford Loans; Direct Unsubsidized Stafford Loans. **Student Employment:** Federal Work-Study Program available. Institutional employment available. **Financial Aid Statistics:** 100% needy freshmen, 97% needy undergrads receive need-based scholarship or grant aid. 10% freshmen, 38% undergrads receive non-need-based scholarship or grant aid. 80% freshmen, 80% undergrads receive need-based self-help aid. 0% freshmen, 0% undergrads receive athletic scholarships. 100% freshmen, 100% undergrads receive any aid. 83% undergrads borrow to pay for school. Average cumulative indebtedness $48,582. **Criteria awarding aid:** *Need-based:* Academics. *Non-need-based:* Academics, Alumni affiliation, Leadership.

WASHINGTON AND LEE UNIVERSITY

204 W. Washington Street, Lexington, VA 24450-0303
Phone: 540-458-8710. **Financial Aid Phone:** 540-458-8720
E-mail: admissions@wlu.edu **CEEB Code:** 5887
Fax: 540-458-8062 **Website:** www.wlu.edu **ACT Code:** 4430

This private school was founded in 1749. It has a 430 acre campus.

RATINGS
Admissions Selectivity Rating: 97   **Fire Safety Rating:** 60*   **Green Rating:** 88

STUDENTS AND FACULTY
Enrollment: 1,822. **Student Body:** 50% female, 50% male, 84% out-of-state, 4% international (30 countries represented). Asian 4%, African American 3%, Caucasian 81%, Hispanic 5%, Native American 0%, Pacific Islander 0%, Two or more races 4%, Race unknown 1%.
Retention and Graduation: 96% freshmen return for sophomore year. 89% freshmen graduate within 4 years. 92% freshmen graduate within 6 years. 20% grads go on to further study within 1 year. 5% grads pursue law degrees. 3% grads pursue business degrees. 3% grads pursue medical degrees. **Faculty:** Student/faculty ratio 8:1. 242 full-time faculty, 95% hold PhDs, 13% are members of minority groups, 39% are women. 0% of classes are taught by teaching assistants.

ACADEMICS
Degrees: Bachelor's; Doctoral degree—professional practice. **Classes:** Most classes have 10–19 students. Most lab/discussion sessions have 20–29 students. **Most popular majors:** Economics, General; Accounting and Business/Management; Political Science and Government, General. **Special Study Options:** Double major; Exchange student program (domestic); Honors program; Independent study; Internships; Liberal arts/career combination; Student-designed major; Study abroad; Teacher certification program. **Honors programs:** University Scholars, Bonner Scholars, Johnson Scholars. **Disability Services offered:** Note-taking services; Reader services; Tape recorders; Tutors. **Career services:** Alumni network; Career assessment; Career/job search classes; Internships; Regional alumni.

FACILITIES
Housing: Apartments for single students; Coed dorms; Fraternity/sorority housing; Special housing for disabled students; Special housing for international students; Theme housing; 80% of campus accessible to physically disabled. **Special Academic Facilities/Equipment:** Center for International Education IQ Center; Collaborative Teaching and Learning Space; History and porcelain museums; Lenfest Performing Arts Center; Communications labs; Nuclear science lab; Scanning electron microscope. **Campus Network:** 100% of classrooms, 100% of dorms, 100% of student union, 100% of libraries, 100% of dining areas, 100% of common outdoor areas have wireless network access.

CAMPUS LIFE
Environment: Village. **Activities:** Campus Ministries; Choral groups; Concert band; Dance; Drama/theater; International Student Organization; Jazz band; Literary magazine; Model UN; Music ensembles; Musical theater; Pep band; Radio station; Student government; Student newspaper; Student-run film society; Symphony orchestra; Television station; Yearbook. 168 registered organizations, 17 honor societies, 10 religious organizations, 11 fraternities, 6 sororities on campus. **Athletics (Intercollegiate):** *Men:* baseball, basketball, cross-country, equestrian sports, football, golf, lacrosse, soccer, swimming, tennis, track/field (outdoor), track/field (indoor), wrestling. *Women:* basketball, cheerleading, cross-country, equestrian sports, field hockey, lacrosse, soccer, swimming, tennis, track/field (outdoor), track/field (indoor), volleyball. **On-Campus Highlights:** The Village.

ADMISSIONS

Freshman Academic Profile: 83% in top 10% of high school class, 97% in top 25% of high school class, 100% in top 50% of high school class. 52% from public high schools. **Test Scores:** SAT Math middle 50% range 678–760. SAT EBRW middle 50% range 670–730. ACT middle 50% range 31–34. **Basis for Candidate Selection:** *Very important factors include:* rigor of secondary school record, class rank, extracurricular activities, character/personal qualities. *Important factors include:* academic GPA, application essay, standardized test scores, recommendation(s). *Other factors include:* interview, talent/ability, first generation, alumni/ae relation, geographical residence, state residency, racial/ethnic status, volunteer work, work experience, level of applicant's interest. **Freshman Admission Requirements:** High school diploma is required and GED is accepted. *Academic units required:* 4 English, 3 math, 1 science, 1 science labs, 3 foreign language, 1 social studies, 1 history, 4 academic electives. *Academic units recommended:* 4 English, 4 math, 4 science, 4 foreign language, 2 social studies, 2 history, 4 academic electives. **Freshman Admission Statistics:** 5,855 applied, 21% admitted, 38% enrolled. **Transfer Admission Requirements:** High school transcript, college transcript(s), essay or personal statement, standardized test scores, statement of good standing from prior institution(s). Minimum college GPA of 2.0 required. Lowest grade transferable C. **General Admission Information:** Application fee $60. Regular application deadline 1/1. Admission may be deferred for a maximum of 1 year.

COSTS AND FINANCIAL AID

Annual tuition $51,420. Room and board $13,925. Required fees $1,035. Average book and supplies expense $1,950. **Required Forms and Deadlines:** CSS/Financial Aid PROFILE; FAFSA; Noncustodial PROFILE;. **Notification of Awards:** Applicants will be notified of awards on or about 4/1. **Types of Aid:** *Need-based scholarships/grants:* College/university scholarship or grant aid from institutional funds; Federal Pell; Private scholarships; SEOG; State scholarships/grants. *Loans:* Direct PLUS loans; Direct Subsidized Stafford Loans; Direct Unsubsidized Stafford Loans. **Student Employment:** Federal Work-Study Program available. Institutional employment available. **Financial Aid Statistics:** 100% needy freshmen, 100% needy undergrads receive need-based scholarship or grant aid. 34% freshmen, 28% undergrads receive non-need-based scholarship or grant aid. 64% freshmen, 66% undergrads receive need-based self-help aid. 0% freshmen, 0% undergrads receive athletic scholarships. 49% freshmen, 43% undergrads receive any aid. 31% undergrads borrow to pay for school. Average cumulative indebtedness $21,758. **Criteria awarding aid:** *Need-based:* Academics. *Non-need-based:* Academics.

WASHINGTON COLLEGE

300 Washington Avenue, Chestertown, MD 21620
Phone: 410-778-7700 **Financial Aid Phone:** 410-778-7214
E-mail: wc_admissions@washcoll.edu **CEEB Code:** 5888
Fax: 410-778-7287 **Website:** www.washcoll.edu **ACT Code:** 1754

This private school was founded in 1782. It has a 144 acre campus.

RATINGS

Admissions Selectivity Rating: 81   **Fire Safety Rating:** 94   **Green Rating:** 63

STUDENTS AND FACULTY

Enrollment: 1,266. **Student Body:** 60% female, 40% male, 58% out-of-state, 5% international (22 countries represented). Asian 3%, African American 11%, Caucasian 69%, Hispanic 6%, Native American <1%, Pacific Islander <1%, Two or more races <1%, Race unknown 5%.
Retention and Graduation: 81% freshmen return for sophomore year. 69% freshmen graduate within 4 years. 73% freshmen graduate within 6 years. 50% grads go on to further study within 1 year. 12% grads pursue arts and sciences degrees. 4% grads pursue law degrees. 8% grads pursue business degrees. 3% grads pursue medical degrees. **Faculty:** Student/faculty ratio 10:1. 105 full-time faculty, 96% hold PhDs, 18% are members of minority groups, 55% are women. 0% of classes are taught by teaching assistants.

ACADEMICS

Degrees: Bachelor's. **Classes:** Most classes have 10–19 students. Most lab/discussion sessions have 10–19 students. **Most popular majors:** Biology/

Biological Sciences, General; Business Administration and Management, General; Psychology, General. **Special Study Options:** Cross-registration; Double major; Dual enrollment; Exchange student program (domestic); Honors program; Independent study; Internships; Liberal arts/career combination; Student-designed major; Study abroad; Teacher certification program. **Honors programs:** The Douglass Cater Society of Junior Fellows is the College's flagship academic enrichment program—one that rewards creativity, initiative, and intellectual curiosity with competitive grants to support self-directed undergraduate research and scholarship anywhere in the world. The intent is to bring together the best and brightest in what founder Douglass Cater called "a companionship of learning." **Career services:** Alumni network; Alumni services; Career assessment; Career/job search classes; Internships; Regional alumni.

FACILITIES

Housing: Apartments for single students; Coed dorms; Fraternity/sorority housing; Men's dorms; Theme housing; Wellness housing; Women's dorms; 90% of campus accessible to physically disabled. **Special Academic Facilities/Equipment:** Language lab, computer classroom, C.V. Starr Center for the Study of the American Experience, The Center for the Environment and Society, O'Neill Literary House, Eastern Shore Food Lab **Campus Network:** 100% of classrooms, 100% of dorms, 100% of student union, 100% of libraries, 100% of dining areas, 100% of common outdoor areas have wireless network access.

CAMPUS LIFE

Environment: Rural. **Activities:** Campus Ministries; Choral groups; Concert band; Dance; Drama/theater; International Student Organization; Jazz band; Literary magazine; Model UN; Music ensembles; Musical theater; Student government; Student newspaper; Yearbook. 50 registered organizations, 13 honor societies, 4 religious organizations, 4 fraternities, 3 sororities on campus. **Athletics (Intercollegiate):** *Men:* baseball, basketball, crew/rowing, lacrosse, sailing, soccer, swimming, tennis. *Women:* basketball, crew/rowing, field hockey, lacrosse, sailing, soccer, softball, swimming, tennis, volleyball. **On-Campus Highlights:** Miller Library. **Environmental Initiatives:** George Goes Green (G3) is Washington College's initiative for stewardship and sustainability. Situated on Maryland's Eastern Shore, the College is surrounded by the coastal and inland waters of the Chesapeake Bay, which informs our sense of history, our sense of self, and our sense of place. Our benefactor George Washington promoted sustainable economic cycles by advocating compost as a method to amend damaged soils. Today, Washington College is nationally renowned for promoting sustainability. Green at a Glance: Chesapeake Semester composting recycling environmentally-friendly products local foods native plant landscaping green facilities.

ADMISSIONS

Freshman Academic Profile: Average high school GPA 3.4. 28% in top 10% of high school class, 53% in top 25% of high school class, 83% in top 50% of high school class. **Test Scores:** SAT Math middle 50% range 530–640. SAT EBRW middle 50% range 560–660. ACT middle 50% range 20–29. **Basis for Candidate Selection:** *Very important factors include:* rigor of secondary school record, academic GPA, interview, level of applicant's interest. *Important factors include:* class rank, application essay, standardized test scores. *Other factors include:* recommendation(s), extracurricular activities, talent/ability, character/personal qualities, first generation, alumni/ae relation, geographical residence, state residency, racial/ethnic status, volunteer work, work experience. **Freshman Admission Requirements:** High school diploma is required and GED is accepted. *Academic units required:* 4 English, 3 math, 3 science, 2 science labs, 2 foreign language, 2 social studies, 2 history. *Academic units recommended:* 4 English, 4 math, 4 science, 3 science labs, 4 foreign language, 2 social studies, 2 history. **Freshman Admission Statistics:** 2,224 applied, 92% admitted, 16% enrolled. **Transfer Admission Requirements:** High school transcript, college transcript(s), essay or personal statement, statement of good standing from prior institution(s). **General Admission Information:** Regular application deadline 2/15. Non-fall registration accepted.

COSTS AND FINANCIAL AID

Annual tuition $48,678. Room and board $13,038. Average book and supplies expense $1,400. **Required Forms and Deadlines:** FAFSA. **Notification of Awards:** Applicants will be notified of awards on a rolling basis beginning 2/1. **Types of Aid:** *Need-based scholarships/grants:* College/university scholarship or grant aid from institutional funds; Federal Pell; Private scholarships; SEOG; State scholarships/grants. *Loans:* Direct PLUS loans; Direct Subsidized Stafford Loans; Direct Unsubsidized Stafford Loans. **Student Employment:** Federal Work-Study Program available. Institutional employment available. **Financial Aid Statistics:** 99% needy freshmen, 100% needy undergrads receive need-based scholarship or grant aid. 18% freshmen, 15% undergrads receive non-need-based scholarship or grant aid. 71% freshmen, 72% undergrads receive need-based self-help aid. 0% freshmen, 0% undergrads receive athletic scholarships. 99.1% freshmen, 96.4% undergrads receive any aid. 65% undergrads borrow to pay for school. Average cumulative indebtedness $34,903. **Criteria awarding aid:** *Non-need-based:* Academics, Art, Music/drama.

WASHINGTON STATE UNIVERSITY

PO Box 641067, Pullman, WA 99164-1067
Phone: 509-335-5586 **Financial Aid Phone:** 509-335-9711
E-mail: admissions@wsu.edu **CEEB Code:** 3800
Fax: 509-335-4902 **Website:** www.wsu.edu **ACT Code:** 4482

This public school was founded in 1890. It has a 1745 acre campus.

RATINGS
Admissions Selectivity Rating: 80   Fire Safety Rating: 92   Green Rating: 97

STUDENTS AND FACULTY
Enrollment: 25,562. **Student Body:** 53% female, 47% male, 15% out-of-state, 4% international (85 countries represented). Asian 6%, African American 3%, Caucasian 61%, Hispanic 16%, Native American 1%, Pacific Islander <1%, Two or more races 7%, Race unknown 2%.
Retention and Graduation: 79% freshmen return for sophomore year. 37% freshmen graduate within 4 years. 60% freshmen graduate within 6 years. **Faculty:** Student/faculty ratio 16:1. 1,311 full-time faculty, 87% hold PhDs, 15% are members of minority groups, 44% are women. 9% of classes are taught by teaching assistants.

ACADEMICS
Degrees: Bachelor's; Certificate; Doctoral degree—professional practice; Doctoral degree research/scholarship; Master's; Post-bachelor's certificate; Post-master's certificate. **Classes:** Most classes have 20–29 students. **Special Study Options:** Accelerated program; Cooperative education program; Cross-registration; Distance learning; Double major; Dual enrollment; English as a Second Language (ESL); Exchange student program (domestic); External degree program; Honors program; Independent study; Internships; Liberal arts/career combination; Student-designed major; Study abroad; Teacher certification program. **Honors programs:** The Washington State University Honors College is one of the oldest and most highly regarded public university honors colleges in the country. It attracts top students in all majors from throughout the United States and around the world. The Honors College curriculum emphasizes global awareness and international impact. It immerses students in the study of international issues, builds their proficiency in a second language, and encourages them to study abroad. Instead of lecturing, professors teach courses interactively, inspiring discussions among students. Honors students conduct research as undergraduates, exploring an academic question of importance to them, documenting their analysis and conclusions, and orally presenting their work to faculty. The Honors College deepens students' intellectual curiosity and builds a lifelong love of learning, as well as skills in critical thinking, writing, public presentation, and information literacy. Graduates emerge with the tools required to become leaders in their fields. **Disability Services offered:** Note-taking services; Reader services; Tape recorders; Tutors. **Career services:** Alumni network; Alumni services; Career assessment; Career/job search classes; Internships.

FACILITIES
Housing: Apartments for married students; Apartments for single students; Coed dorms; Cooperative housing; Fraternity/sorority housing; Men's dorms; Special housing for disabled students; Special housing for international students; Theme housing; Wellness housing; Women's dorms; 95% of campus accessible to physically disabled. **Special Academic Facilities/Equipment:** Museums, displays, and collections, including a natural history museum, museum of art, museum of anthropology, an entomological collection, a veterinary anatomy teaching museum, and geology museums. Livestock centers, labs, and barns, including beef and dairy centers, a cattle feeding lab, a meats lab, and feed plant. Radio and TV stations. Digital recording studio. Music listening library. Fine arts studio facilities with specialized equipment. International center for exchanging cultural knowledge. Child development lab. Financial markets lab (trading room). Food sensory evaluation lab. Culinary lab and teaching kitchen. social and economic sciences research center. Planetarium and astronomical observatory. Specialized teaching and research labs for science and engineering, including a bio-molecular X-ray crystallography center, a genomics and gene sequencing lab, a virtual reality computer-integrated manufacturing lab, a hydraulics lab, laboratory for atmospheric research, and more. Wildlife center. Ecological reserves. Greenhouses, vivaria, and herbaria. Agronomic research farms, a horticultural orchard, and an organic teaching farm. On-campus market for locally grown, alumni-grown, and organic produce. Veterinary teaching hospital. Human anatomy lab. Water research center. Nuclear radiation center.

CAMPUS LIFE
Environment: Town. **Activities:** Campus Ministries; Choral groups; Concert band; Dance; Drama/theater; International Student Organization; Jazz band; Literary magazine; Marching band; Model UN; Music ensembles; Musical theater; Opera; Pep band; Radio station; Student government; Student newspaper; Student-run film society; Symphony orchestra; Television station; Yearbook. 456 registered organizations, 10 honor societies, 23 religious organizations, 27 fraternities, 14 sororities, on campus. **Athletics (Intercollegiate):** *Men:* baseball, basketball, cross-country, football, golf, track/field (outdoor). *Women:* basketball, crew/rowing, cross-country, golf, soccer, swimming, tennis, track/field (outdoor), volleyball. **On-Campus Highlights:** Compton Union Building (CUB). **Environmental Initiatives:** The Sustainability & Environment Committee, established by the President of WSU, meets monthly and has campus-wide representation.

ADMISSIONS
Freshman Academic Profile: Average high school GPA 3.5. % in top 10% of high school class, % in top 25% of high school class, % in top 50% of high school class. **Test Scores:** SAT Math middle 50% range 510–610. SAT EBRW middle 50% range 510–620. ACT middle 50% range 20–26. **Basis for Candidate Selection:** *Very important factors include:* academic GPA, standardized test scores. *Important factors include:* rigor of secondary school record, class rank. *Other factors include:* application essay, recommendation(s), extracurricular activities, talent/ability, character/personal qualities, volunteer work, work experience. **Freshman Admission Requirements:** High school diploma is required and GED is accepted *Academic units required:* 4 English, 3 math, 2 science, 2 foreign language, 3 social studies, 1 visual/performing arts, 1 unit from above areas or other academic areas. *Academic units recommended:* 4 English, 4 math, 2 science, 2 foreign language, 3 social studies, 1 visual/performing arts. **Freshman Admission Statistics:** 21,434 applied, 76% admitted, 30% enrolled. **Transfer Admission Requirements:** College transcript(s). Minimum college GPA of 2.5 required. Lowest grade transferable D. **General Admission Information:** Application fee $50. Priority deadline 1/31. Non-fall registration accepted.

COSTS AND FINANCIAL AID
Annual in-state tuition $9,953. Annual out-of-state tuition $24,531. Room and board $11,648. Required fees $1,888. Average book and supplies expense $960. **Required Forms and Deadlines:** FAFSA; State aid form. **Notification of Awards:** Applicants will be notified of awards on a rolling basis beginning 4/15. **Types of Aid:** *Need-based scholarships/grants:* College/university scholarship or grant aid from institutional funds; Federal Nursing Scholarships; Federal Pell; Private scholarships; SEOG; State scholarships/grants. *Loans:* Direct PLUS loans; Direct Subsidized Stafford Loans; Direct Unsubsidized Stafford Loans. **Student Employment:** Federal Work-Study Program available. Institutional employment available. **Financial Aid Statistics:** 92% needy freshmen, 87% needy undergrads receive need-based scholarship or grant aid. 75% freshmen, 50% undergrads receive non-need-based scholarship or grant aid. 62% freshmen, 65% undergrads receive need-based self-help aid. 2% freshmen, 1% undergrads receive athletic scholarships. 86% freshmen, 76% undergrads receive any aid. 57% undergrads borrow to pay for school. Average cumulative indebtedness $25,899. **Criteria awarding aid:** *Need-based:* Academics *Non-need-based:* Academics, Alumni affiliation, Art, Athletics, Job skills, Leadership, Minority status, Music/drama, Religious affiliation, State/district residency.

WASHINGTON UNIVERSITY IN ST. LOUIS

Best Colleges

Campus Box 1089, St. Louis, MO 63130-4899
Phone: 314-935-6000 **Financial Aid Phone:** 888-547-6670
E-mail: admissions@wustl.edu **CEEB Code:** 6929
Fax: 314-935-4290 **Website:** wustl.edu **ACT Code:** 2386

This private school was founded in 1853. It has a 169 acre campus.

RATINGS
Admissions Selectivity Rating: 99   **Fire Safety Rating:** 97   **Green Rating:** 96

STUDENTS AND FACULTY
Enrollment: 7,404. **Student Body:** 53% female, 47% male, 89% out-of-state, 8% international (47 countries represented). Asian 16%, African American 9%, Caucasian 49%, Hispanic 10%, Native American <1%, Pacific Islander <1%, Two or more races 5%, Race unknown 2%.
Retention and Graduation: 97% freshmen return for sophomore year. 89% freshmen graduate within 4 years. 95% freshmen graduate within 6 years. 21% grads go on to further study within 1 year. 5% grads pursue arts and sciences degrees. 2% grads pursue law degrees. 1% grads pursue business degrees. 6% grads pursue medical degrees. **Faculty:** Student/faculty ratio 7:1. 1,012 full-time faculty, 93% hold PhDs, 26% are members of minority groups, 39% are women.

ACADEMICS
Degrees: Associate; Bachelor's; Certificate; Doctoral degree—professional practice; Doctoral degree research/scholarship; Master's; Post-bachelor's certificate; Post-master's certificate. **Classes:** Most classes have 10–19 students. Most lab/discussion sessions have 10–19 students. **Most popular majors:** Engineering, General; Business Administration and Management, General; Social Sciences, General. **Special Study Options:** Accelerated program; Cooperative education program; Cross-registration; Double major; Dual enrollment; English as a Second Language (ESL); Independent study; Internships; Liberal arts/career combination; Student-designed major; Study abroad; Teacher certification program. **Combined degree programs:** BA/MA; BA/MEng. **Disability Services offered:** Note-taking services; Reader services; Tape recorders; Tutors. **Career services:** Alumni network; Alumni services; Career assessment; Career/job search classes; Internships; Regional alumni.

FACILITIES
Housing: Apartments for married students; Apartments for single students; Coed dorms; Cooperative housing; Fraternity/sorority housing; Special housing for disabled students; Special housing for international students; Theme housing; 95% of campus accessible to physically disabled. **Special Academic Facilities/Equipment:** 12 university-wide and 56 school-based research centers and institutes, 59-acre medical campus, observatory, plant growth facility, international writer's center, laboratory science building, theater, art museum, maker space, state-of-the-art recreation facility, center for entrepreneurship and innovation, career centers, and state-of-the-art architecture and art studios.

CAMPUS LIFE
Environment: City. **Activities:** Campus Ministries; Choral groups; Concert band; Dance; Drama/theater; International Student Organization; Jazz band; Literary magazine; Model UN; Music ensembles; Musical theater; Opera; Pep band; Radio station; Student government; Student newspaper; Student-run film society; Symphony orchestra; Television station. 380 registered organizations, 22 honor societies, 20 religious organizations, 15 fraternities, 10 sororities, on campus. **Athletics (Intercollegiate):** *Men:* baseball, basketball, cross-country, diving, football, soccer, swimming, tennis, track/field (outdoor), track/field (indoor). *Women:* basketball, cross-country, diving, golf, soccer, softball, swimming, tennis, track/field (outdoor), track/field (indoor), volleyball. **On-Campus Highlights:** Kemper Art Museum.

ADMISSIONS
Freshman Academic Profile: Average high school GPA 4.2. 84% in top 10% of high school class, 96% in top 25% of high school class, 100% in top 50% of high school class. 58% from public high schools. **Test Scores:** SAT Math middle 50% range 760–800. SAT EBRW middle 50% range 720–760. ACT middle 50% range 33–35. **Basis for Candidate Selection:** *Very important factors include:* rigor of secondary school record, class rank, academic GPA,

application essay, standardized test scores, recommendation(s), extracurricular activities, talent/ability, character/personal qualities, volunteer work, work experience, level of applicant's interest. *Important factors include:* first generation. *Other factors include:* interview, alumni/ae relation, geographical residence, state residency, racial/ethnic status. **Freshman Admission Requirements:** High school diploma is required and GED is accepted *Academic units required:* 4 English, 3 math, 3 science, 2 science labs, 2 foreign language, 2 social studies, 2 history. *Academic units recommended:* 4 English, 4 math, 4 science, 4 science labs, 4 foreign language, 4 social studies, 4 history. **Freshman Admission Statistics:** 25,426 applied, 14% admitted, 49% enrolled. **Transfer Admission Requirements:** College transcript(s), essay or personal statement, statement of good standing from prior institution(s). Lowest grade transferable C. **General Admission Information:** Application fee $75. Regular application deadline 1/2. Admission may be deferred for a maximum of 2 years.

COSTS AND FINANCIAL AID
Annual tuition $56,300. Room and board $17,402. Required fees $1,086. Average book and supplies expense $1,144. **Required Forms and Deadlines:** CSS/Financial Aid PROFILE; FAFSA; Noncustodial PROFILE;. **Notification of Awards:** Applicants will be notified of awards on or about 4/1. **Types of Aid:** *Need-based scholarships/grants:* College/university scholarship or grant aid from institutional funds; Federal Pell; Private scholarships; SEOG; State scholarships/grants; United Negro College Fund. *Loans:* Direct PLUS loans; Direct Subsidized Stafford Loans; Direct Unsubsidized Stafford Loans. **Student Employment:** Federal Work-Study Program available. Institutional employment available. **Financial Aid Statistics:** 97% needy freshmen, 98% needy undergrads receive need-based scholarship or grant aid. 9% freshmen, 5% undergrads receive non-need-based scholarship or grant aid. 74% freshmen, 67% undergrads receive need-based self-help aid. 0% freshmen, 0% undergrads receive athletic scholarships. 52% freshmen, 50% undergrads receive any aid. 28% undergrads borrow to pay for school. Average cumulative indebtedness $24,247. **Criteria awarding aid:** *Need-based:* Academics. *Non-need-based:* Academics, Art, Leadership.

WATKINS COLLEGE OF ART, DESIGN & FILM

2298 Rosa L Parks Blvd, Nashville, TN 37228
Phone: 615-277-7418 **Financial Aid Phone:** 615-277-7421
E-mail: admissions@watkins.edu
Fax: 615-383-4849 **Website:** www.watkins.edu **ACT Code:** 4027

This private school was founded in 1895. It has a 13 acre campus.

RATINGS
Admissions Selectivity Rating: 77   **Fire Safety Rating:** 96   **Green Rating:** 60*

STUDENTS AND FACULTY
Enrollment: 396. **Student Body:** 52% female, 48% male, 30% out-of-state, 1% international (4 countries represented). Asian 2%, African American 9%, Caucasian 78%, Hispanic 2%, Native American <1%, Pacific Islander <1%, Two or more races 3%, Race unknown 5%.
Retention and Graduation: 53% freshmen return for sophomore year. 10% grads go on to further study within 1 year. 10% grads pursue arts and sciences degrees. **Faculty:** Student/faculty ratio 7:1. 20 full-time faculty, 60% hold PhDs, 0% are members of minority groups, 50% are women. 0% of classes are taught by teaching assistants.

ACADEMICS
Degrees: Bachelor's; Post-bachelor's certificate. **Classes:** Most classes have 10–19 students. Most lab/discussion sessions have 10–19 students. **Most popular majors:** Graphic Design; Fine/Studio Arts, General; Film/Cinema/Media Studies. **Special Study Options:** Cooperative education program; Dual enrollment; Independent study; Internships; Study abroad. **Disability Services offered:** Note-taking services; Reader services; Tape recorders; Tutors. **Career services:** Alumni network; Alumni services; Career assessment; Career/job search classes; Internships.

FACILITIES
Housing: Apartments for single students; Coed dorms; Special housing for disabled students; Women's dorms; 100% of campus accessible to physically disabled. **Special Academic Facilities/Equipment:** Brownlee O. Currey Gallery.

CAMPUS LIFE

Environment: Metropolis. **Activities:** Student-run film society. **Environmental Initiatives:** Recycling Program.

ADMISSIONS

Freshman Academic Profile: 60% from public high schools. **Test Scores:** ACT middle 50% range 20–25. **Basis for Candidate Selection:** *Very important factors include:* application essay, talent/ability, level of applicant's interest. *Important factors include:* academic GPA, standardized test scores, recommendation(s), character/personal qualities. *Other factors include:* rigor of secondary school record, class rank, interview, extracurricular activities, volunteer work. **Freshman Admission Requirements:** High school diploma is required and GED is accepted. *Academic units recommended:* 3 English, 2 math, 2 science, 1 foreign language, 3 social studies, 3 history, 3 computer science, 4 visual/performing arts. **Freshman Admission Statistics:** 113 applied, 83% admitted, 61% enrolled. **Transfer Admission Requirements:** College transcript(s), essay or personal statement. Minimum college GPA of 3.0 required. Lowest grade transferable C. **General Admission Information:** Application fee $50. Priority deadline 5/1. Regular application deadline 7/15. Non-fall registration accepted. Admission may be deferred for a maximum of 1 semester.

COSTS AND FINANCIAL AID

Annual tuition $18,900. Room and board $6,200. Average book and supplies expense $1,500. **Required Forms and Deadlines:** FAFSA; Institution's own financial aid form. **Notification of Awards:** Applicants will be notified of awards on a rolling basis beginning 5/1. **Types of Aid:** *Need-based scholarships/grants:* College/university scholarship or grant aid from institutional funds; Federal Pell; Private scholarships; SEOG; State scholarships/grants. **Student Employment:** Federal Work-Study Program available. Institutional employment available. **Financial Aid Statistics:** 68% needy freshmen, 83% needy undergrads receive need-based scholarship or grant aid. 37% freshmen, 10% undergrads receive non-need-based scholarship or grant aid. 100% freshmen, 83% undergrads receive need-based self-help aid. 0% freshmen, 0% undergrads receive athletic scholarships. 50% freshmen, 40% undergrads receive any aid. **Criteria awarding aid:** *Non-need-based:* Academics, Art.

WAYLAND BAPTIST UNIVERSITY

1900 West 7th Street, Plainview, TX 79072
Phone: 806-291-3500 **Financial Aid Phone:** 806-291-3520
E-mail: admityou@wbu.edu
Fax: 806-291-1963 **ACT Code:** 4246

This private school, affiliated with the Southern Baptist Church, was founded in 1908. It has a 80 acre campus.

RATINGS

Admissions Selectivity Rating: 74   **Fire Safety Rating:** 88   **Green Rating:** 60*

STUDENTS AND FACULTY

Enrollment: 3,715. **Student Body:** 48% female, 52% male, 31% out-of-state, 1% international (20 countries represented). Asian 2%, African American 16%, Caucasian 43%, Hispanic 28%, Native American 1%, Pacific Islander 1%, Two or more races 4%, Race unknown 4%.
Retention and Graduation: 45% freshmen return for sophomore year.
Faculty: Student/faculty ratio 8:1. 174 full-time faculty, 78% hold PhDs, 14% are members of minority groups, 34% are women. 0% of classes are taught by teaching assistants.

ACADEMICS

Degrees: Associate; Bachelor's; Certificate; Doctoral degree research/scholarship; Master's; Transfer Associate. **Classes:** Most classes have 10–19 students. **Most popular majors:** Liberal Arts and Sciences, General Studies and Humanities, Other; Criminal Justice/Law Enforcement Administration; Business Administration and Management, General. **Special Study Options:** Accelerated program; Distance learning; Double major; External degree program; Honors program; Internships; Study abroad; Teacher certification program. **Honors programs:** The Honors Program offered by Wayland is designed to challenge the academically superior student to develop initiative and abilities beyond what is expected in a normal course of study. Electing an Honors program offers breadth and depth of content through independent study and research, aiding the student in preparation for entering a career upon graduation or attending graduate school in a field of choice. Honors

work represents the highest level of academic work available at Wayland on the undergraduate level. **Disability Services offered:** Note-taking services; Reader services; Tutors. **Career services:** Career assessment.

FACILITIES

Housing: Apartments for married students; Apartments for single students; Men's dorms; Women's dorms; 100% of campus accessible to physically disabled. **Special Academic Facilities/Equipment:** Llano Estacado Museum.

CAMPUS LIFE

Environment: Town. **Activities:** Campus Ministries; Choral groups; Concert band; Dance; Drama/theater; International Student Organization; Marching band; Music ensembles; Musical theater; Pep band; Radio station; Student government; Student newspaper; Television station; Yearbook. 34 registered organizations, 7 honor societies, 7 religious organizations, 1 fraternity, 1 sorority on campus. **Athletics (Intercollegiate):** *Men:* baseball, basketball, cheerleading, cross-country, golf, soccer, track/field (outdoor), track/field (indoor). *Women:* basketball, cheerleading, cross-country, golf, soccer, track/field (outdoor), track/field (indoor), volleyball. **On-Campus Highlights:** McClung University Center. **Environmental Initiatives:** Installed energy efficient lighting campuswide.

ADMISSIONS

Freshman Academic Profile: Average high school GPA 3.3. 9% in top 10% of high school class, 29% in top 25% of high school class, 60% in top 50% of high school class. 86% from public high schools. **Test Scores:** SAT Math middle 50% range 420–530. SAT EBRW middle 50% range 390–520. ACT middle 50% range 18–23. **Basis for Candidate Selection:** *Very important factors include:* class rank, standardized test scores. *Important factors include:* rigor of secondary school record. **Freshman Admission Requirements:** High school diploma is required and GED is accepted *Academic units required:* 3 English, 2 math, 2 science, 2 history. *Academic units recommended:* 3 math, 3 science. **Freshman Admission Statistics:** 548 applied, 97% admitted, 59% enrolled. **Transfer Admission Requirements:** College transcript(s), statement of good standing from prior institution(s). Minimum college GPA of 2.0 required. Lowest grade transferable D. **General Admission Information:** Application fee $35. Priority deadline 8/1. Non-fall registration accepted.

COSTS AND FINANCIAL AID

Annual tuition $14,850. Room and board $6,072. Required fees $1,080. Average book and supplies expense $1,650. **Required Forms and Deadlines:** FAFSA; Institution's own financial aid form; State aid form. **Notification of Awards:** Applicants will be notified of awards on a rolling basis beginning 2/1. **Types of Aid:** *Need-based scholarships/grants:* College/university scholarship or grant aid from institutional funds; Federal Pell; Private scholarships; SEOG; State scholarships/grants. *Loans:* Direct PLUS loans; Direct Subsidized Stafford Loans; Direct Unsubsidized Stafford Loans. **Student Employment:** Federal Work-Study Program available. Institutional employment available. **Financial Aid Statistics:** 99% needy freshmen, 97% needy undergrads receive need-based scholarship or grant aid. 11% freshmen, 9% undergrads receive non-need-based scholarship or grant aid. 68% freshmen, 77% undergrads receive need-based self-help aid. 13% freshmen, 8% undergrads receive athletic scholarships. 66.48% freshmen, 64.78% undergrads receive any aid. **Criteria awarding aid:** *Need-based:* Academics. *Non-need-based:* Academics, Alumni affiliation, Art, Athletics, Leadership, Music/drama, Religious affiliation.

WAYNESBURG UNIVERSITY

51 West College Street, Waynesburg, PA 15370
Phone: 724-852-3248 **Financial Aid Phone:** 724-852-3208
E-mail: admissions@waynesburg.edu **CEEB Code:** 2969
Fax: 724-627-8124 **Website:** www.waynesburg.edu **ACT Code:** 3748

This private school, affiliated with the Presbyterian Church, was founded in 1849. It has a 30 acre campus.

RATINGS

Admissions Selectivity Rating: 74   **Fire Safety Rating:** 96   **Green Rating:** 60*

STUDENTS AND FACULTY

Enrollment: 1,322. **Student Body:** 57% female, 43% male, 22% out-of-state, <1% international (4 countries represented). Asian 1%, African American 4%, Caucasian 87%, Hispanic 2%, Native American <1%, Pacific Islander <1%, Two or more races 3%, Race unknown 3%.

Retention and Graduation: 78% freshmen return for sophomore year. 60% freshmen graduate within 4 years. % freshmen graduate within 6 years. 95% grads go on to further study within 1 year. **Faculty:** Student/faculty ratio 13:1. 79 full-time faculty, 68% hold PhDs, 0% are members of minority groups, 52% are women. 0% of classes are taught by teaching assistants.

ACADEMICS

Degrees: Bachelor's; Doctoral degree—professional practice; Doctoral degree research/scholarship; Master's. **Classes:** Most classes have 10–19 students. Most lab/discussion sessions have 10–19 students. **Most popular majors:** Criminal Justice/Law Enforcement Administration; Registered Nursing/Registered Nurse; Business Administration and Management, General. **Special Study Options:** Accelerated program; Distance learning; Double major; Dual enrollment; Honors program; Independent study; Internships; Student-designed major; Study abroad; Teacher certification program. **Honors programs:** The Waynesburg University Honors Program exists to foster the further development of students who have demonstrated a commitment to academic excellence. Through enhanced learning opportunities both in and out of the classroom, the Honors Program seeks to develop the intellect of such students by emphasizing the pursuit of intellectual curiosity, reflective and meditative engagement with significant texts, and critical thinking across the disciplines. The goal of the program is the intellectual development of engaged and thoughtful Christian leaders through the pursuit of a challenging liberal arts experience. Through a course of study emphasizing rigorous academic and experiential inquiry, Honors Students may complete the program through a combination of traditional coursework and opportunities outside the classroom. These include interdisciplinary projects, Honors Colloquia, campus leadership, and independent research, among many others. These opportunities are designed to foster the curiosity and critical thinking skills of Honors Students, and to build a community of scholars. The Honors Program at Waynesburg University serves as a model of and laboratory for excellence in interdisciplinary learning, service to the community, intercultural awareness, and leadership development. **Combined degree programs:** BA/MA. **Disability Services offered:** Note-taking services; Reader services; Tape recorders; Tutors. **Career services:** Alumni network; Alumni services; Career assessment; Career/job search classes; Internships; Regional alumni.

FACILITIES

Housing: Men's dorms; Special housing for disabled students; Women's dorms; 98% of campus accessible to physically disabled. **Special Academic Facilities/Equipment:** Geology, biology, archaeology, and ceramics museum; arboretum; 174-acre farm; Center for Research and Economic Development.

CAMPUS LIFE

Environment: Village. **Activities:** Campus Ministries; Choral groups; Concert band; Drama/theater; Jazz band; Literary magazine; Music ensembles; Musical theater; Pep band; Radio station; Student government; Student newspaper; Television station; Yearbook. 51 registered organizations, 17 honor societies on campus. **Athletics (Intercollegiate):** *Men:* baseball, basketball, cross-country, football, golf, soccer, tennis, track/field (outdoor), wrestling. *Women:* basketball, cross-country, golf, lacrosse, soccer, softball, tennis, track/field (outdoor), volleyball. **On-Campus Highlights:** Roberts Chapel.

ADMISSIONS

Freshman Academic Profile: Average high school GPA 3.6. 11% in top 10% of high school class, 37% in top 25% of high school class, 72% in top 50% of high school class. 85% from public high schools. **Test Scores:** SAT Math middle 50% range 480–570. SAT EBRW middle 50% range 500–580. ACT middle 50% range 19–25. **Basis for Candidate Selection:** *Very important factors include:* rigor of secondary school record, class rank, academic GPA, standardized test scores, interview. *Important factors include:* extracurricular activities. *Other factors include:* application essay, recommendation(s), character/personal qualities, alumni/ae relation, volunteer work, work experience, level of applicant's interest. **Freshman Admission Requirements:** High school diploma is required and GED is accepted *Academic units required:* 4 English, 3 math, 2 science, 2 science labs, 2 social studies, 5 academic electives. *Academic units recommended:* 3 science, 2 foreign language. **Freshman Admission Statistics:** 1,590 applied, 91% admitted, 22% enrolled. **Transfer Admission Requirements:** High school transcript, college transcript(s), statement of good standing from prior institution(s). Minimum college GPA of 2.5 required. Lowest grade transferable C. **General Admission Information:** Application fee $20. Non-fall registration accepted.

COSTS AND FINANCIAL AID

Annual tuition $23,970. Room and board $10,160. Required fees $850. Average book and supplies expense $1,400. **Required Forms and Deadlines:** FAFSA. **Notification of Awards:** Applicants will be notified of awards on

a rolling basis beginning 2/15. **Types of Aid:** *Need-based scholarships/grants:* College/university scholarship or grant aid from institutional funds; Federal Pell; Private scholarships; SEOG; State scholarships/grants. *Loans:* Direct PLUS loans; Direct Subsidized Stafford Loans; Direct Unsubsidized Stafford Loans. **Student Employment:** Federal Work-Study Program available. Institutional employment available. **Financial Aid Statistics:** 100% needy freshmen, 98% needy undergrads receive need-based scholarship or grant aid. 10% freshmen, 11% undergrads receive non-need-based scholarship or grant aid. 83% freshmen, 84% undergrads receive need-based self-help aid. 0% freshmen, 0% undergrads receive athletic scholarships. 100% freshmen, 96% undergrads receive any aid. 45% undergrads borrow to pay for school. Average cumulative indebtedness $22,088. **Criteria awarding aid:** *Need-based:* Academics, Job skills, Leadership, Religious affiliation. *Non-need-based:* Academics, Alumni affiliation, Job skills, Leadership, Religious affiliation, State/district residency.

WAYNE STATE COLLEGE

1111 Main Street, Wayne, NE 68787
Phone: 402-375-7234 **Financial Aid Phone:** 402-375-7230
E-mail: admit1@wsc.edu **CEEB Code:** 6469
Fax: 402-375-7204 **Website:** www.wsc.edu **ACT Code:** 2472

This public school was founded in 1909. It has a 128 acre campus.

RATINGS

Admissions Selectivity Rating: 72   **Fire Safety Rating:** 60*   **Green Rating:** 60*

STUDENTS AND FACULTY

Enrollment: 2,829. **Student Body:** 58% female, 42% male, 16% out-of-state, 3% international (36 countries represented). Asian 1%, African American 3%, Caucasian 78%, Hispanic 10%, Native American 1%, Pacific Islander 0%, Two or more races 3%, Race unknown 1%.
Retention and Graduation: 69% freshmen return for sophomore year. 34% freshmen graduate within 4 years. 51% freshmen graduate within 6 years. **Faculty:** Student/faculty ratio 21:1. 121 full-time faculty, 88% hold PhDs, 7% are members of minority groups, 47% are women.

ACADEMICS

Degrees: Bachelor's; Master's; Post-master's certificate. **Classes:** Most classes have 20–29 students. Most lab/discussion sessions have 10–19 students. **Special Study Options:** Cooperative education program; Distance learning; Double major; Dual enrollment; English as a Second Language (ESL); Honors program; Independent study; Internships; Study abroad; Teacher certification program. **Disability Services offered:** Note-taking services; Reader services; Tape recorders; Tutors. **Career services:** Alumni network; Alumni services; Career assessment; Career/job search classes; Internships.

FACILITIES

Housing: Coed dorms. **Special Academic Facilities/Equipment:** Art gallery, fine arts center, planetarium, recreation center, telecommunications network. **Campus Network:** 100% of classrooms, 100% of dorms, 100% of student union, 100% of libraries, 100% of dining areas, 100% of common outdoor areas have wireless network access.

CAMPUS LIFE

Environment: Rural. **Activities:** Campus Ministries; Choral groups; Concert band; Dance; Drama/theater; International Student Organization; Jazz band; Literary magazine; Marching band; Music ensembles; Musical theater; Pep band; Radio station; Student government; Student newspaper; Television station. 100 registered organizations, on campus. **Athletics (Intercollegiate):** *Men:* baseball, basketball, cross-country, football, golf, track/field (outdoor), track/field (indoor). *Women:* basketball, cross-country, golf, soccer, softball, track/field (outdoor), track/field (indoor), volleyball.

ADMISSIONS

Freshman Academic Profile: Average high school GPA 3.3. 12% in top 10% of high school class, 32% in top 25% of high school class, 62% in top 50% of high school class. **Test Scores:** ACT middle 50% range 18–25. **Freshman Admission Requirements:** High school diploma is required and GED is accepted. *Academic units recommended:* 4 English, 3 math, 2 science, 2 foreign language, 3 social studies, 2 computer science, 2 visual/performing arts. **Freshman Admission Statistics:** 2,060 applied, 100% admitted, 35% enrolled. **Transfer Admission Requirements:** College transcript(s). Minimum college GPA of 2.0 required. Lowest grade transferable C-. **General Admission**

Information: Priority deadline 12/1. Regular application deadline 8/24. Non-fall registration accepted.

COSTS AND FINANCIAL AID

Required Forms and Deadlines: FAFSA. **Notification of Awards:** Applicants will be notified of awards on a rolling basis beginning 2/1. **Types of Aid:** *Need-based scholarships/grants:* College/university scholarship or grant aid from institutional funds; Federal Pell; Private scholarships; SEOG; State scholarships/grants. *Loans:* Direct PLUS loans; Direct Subsidized Stafford Loans; Direct Unsubsidized Stafford Loans. **Student Employment:** Federal Work-Study Program available. Institutional employment available. **Financial Aid Statistics:** 71% needy freshmen, 69% needy undergrads receive need-based scholarship or grant aid. 80% freshmen, 57% undergrads receive non-need-based scholarship or grant aid. 77% freshmen, 74% undergrads receive need-based self-help aid. 7% freshmen, 7% undergrads receive athletic scholarships. **Criteria awarding aid:** *Non-need-based:* Academics, Art, Athletics, Leadership, Minority status, Music/drama, Religious affiliation, State/district residency.

WAYNE STATE UNIVERSITY

42 West Warren, Detroit, MI 48202
Phone: 313-577-2100 **Financial Aid Phone:** 313-577-2100
E-mail: studentservice@wayne.edu **CEEB Code:** 1898
Website: www.wayne.edu **ACT Code:** 2064

This public school was founded in 1868. It has a 200 acre campus.

RATINGS

Admissions Selectivity Rating: 81 **Fire Safety Rating:** 84 **Green Rating:** 63

STUDENTS AND FACULTY

Enrollment: 17,114. **Student Body:** 57% female, 43% male, 2% out-of-state, 2% international (40 countries represented). Asian 10%, African American 16%, Caucasian 59%, Hispanic 5%, Native American <1%, Pacific Islander <1%, Two or more races 4%, Race unknown 3%.
Retention and Graduation: 79% freshmen return for sophomore year. 19% freshmen graduate within 4 years. 47% freshmen graduate within 6 years.
Faculty: Student/faculty ratio 16:1. 1,028 full-time faculty, 0% hold PhDs, 27% are members of minority groups, 46% are women.

ACADEMICS

Degrees: Bachelor's; Certificate; Doctoral degree—professional practice; Doctoral degree research/scholarship; Master's; Post-bachelor's certificate; Post-master's certificate. **Classes:** Most classes have 10–19 students. Most lab/discussion sessions have 20–29 students. **Most popular majors:** Biology/Biological Sciences, General; Psychology, General; Health Professions and Related Clinical Sciences, Other. **Special Study Options:** Accelerated program; Cooperative education program; Distance learning; Double major; Dual enrollment; English as a Second Language (ESL); Honors program; Independent study; Internships; Study abroad; Teacher certification program. **Honors programs:** The Irvin D. Reid Honors College is city-based and service-oriented; we promote excellence and challenge our students to engage the world around them as problem-solvers and leaders. Our curriculum requires that students inform themselves about what it means to be citizens, of this city, this country, and the world; we give our students tools, tools to be catalysts for innovation and improvement, and the skills necessary to create powerful solutions. Honors also offers a number of pre-professional programs such as MedStart, HealthPro Start and BStart, designed to prepare and transition students into graduate and professional programs in medicine, health sciences, and business. **Combined degree programs:** BA/MA; BA/MD; BA/MEng. **Disability Services offered:** Note-taking services; Reader services; Tape recorders; Tutors. **Career services:** Career assessment; Career/job search classes; Internships.

FACILITIES

Housing: Apartments for married students; Apartments for single students; Coed dorms; Special housing for disabled students; Theme housing; 100% of campus accessible to physically disabled. **Special Academic Facilities/Equipment:** Detroit Institute of Arts; Detroit Historical Museum; Michigan Science Center; Charles H Wright Museum of African American History; Planetarium. **Campus Network:** 100% of classrooms, 50% of dorms, 100% of libraries, 100% of dining areas, 75% of common outdoor areas have wireless network access.

CAMPUS LIFE

Environment: Metropolis. **Activities:** Campus Ministries; Choral groups; Concert band; Dance; Drama/theater; International Student Organization; Jazz band; Marching band; Model UN; Music ensembles; Musical theater; Pep band; Radio station; Student government; Student newspaper; Student-run film society; Symphony orchestra. 543 registered organizations, 5 honor societies, 35 religious organizations, 15 fraternities, 15 sororities on campus. **Athletics (Intercollegiate):** *Men:* baseball, basketball, cross-country, diving, fencing, football, golf, ice hockey, swimming, tennis. *Women:* basketball, cross-country, diving, fencing, ice hockey, softball, swimming, tennis, volleyball. **On-Campus Highlights:** Recreation and Fitness Center. **Environmental Initiatives:** Past and ongoing LEED certified buildings being constructed.

ADMISSIONS

Freshman Academic Profile: Average high school GPA 3.4. 18% in top 10% of high school class, 45% in top 25% of high school class, 78% in top 50% of high school class. **Test Scores:** SAT Math middle 50% range 500–600. SAT EBRW middle 50% range 510–610. ACT middle 50% range 21–27. **Basis for Candidate Selection:** *Very important factors include:* academic GPA, standardized test scores. *Other factors include:* rigor of secondary school record, application essay, recommendation(s). **Freshman Admission Requirements:** High school diploma is required and GED is accepted *Academic units recommended:* 4 English, 4 math, 3 science, 2 foreign language, 3 social studies, 2 visual/performing arts. **Freshman Admission Statistics:** 16,210 applied, 71% admitted, 26% enrolled. **Transfer Admission Requirements:** College transcript(s). Minimum college GPA of 2.0 required. Lowest grade transferable C. **General Admission Information:** Application fee $25. Regular application deadline 8/1. Non-fall registration accepted. Admission may be deferred for a maximum of 1 year.

COSTS AND FINANCIAL AID

Annual in-state tuition $12,620. Annual out-of-state tuition $28,967. Room and board $10,502. Required fees $1,805. Average book and supplies expense $1,212. **Required Forms and Deadlines:** FAFSA. **Notification of Awards:** Applicants will be notified of awards on a rolling basis beginning 3/31. **Types of Aid:** *Need-based scholarships/grants:* College/university scholarship or grant aid from institutional funds; Federal Pell; Private scholarships; SEOG; State scholarships/grants; United Negro College Fund. *Loans:* Direct PLUS loans; Direct Subsidized Stafford Loans; Direct Unsubsidized Stafford Loans. **Student Employment:** Federal Work-Study Program available. Institutional employment available. **Financial Aid Statistics:** 75% needy freshmen, 72% needy undergrads receive need-based scholarship or grant aid. 65% freshmen, 65% undergrads receive non-need-based scholarship or grant aid. 56% freshmen, 65% undergrads receive need-based self-help aid. 1% freshmen, 1% undergrads receive athletic scholarships. 93% freshmen, 86% undergrads receive any aid. 88% undergrads borrow to pay for school. Average cumulative indebtedness $25,433. **Criteria awarding aid:** *Need-based:* Academics, Art, Leadership *Non-need-based:* Academics, Art, Athletics, Leadership, Music/drama.

WEBBER INTERNATIONAL UNIVERSITY

PO Box 96, Babson Park, FL 33827
Phone: 863-628-2910 **Financial Aid Phone:** 863-638-2930
E-mail: admissions@webber.edu **CEEB Code:** 5893
Fax: 863-638-1591 **Website:** www.webber.edu **ACT Code:** 773

This private school was founded in 1927. It has a 110 acre campus.

RATINGS

Admissions Selectivity Rating: 89 **Fire Safety Rating:** 91 **Green Rating:** 60*

STUDENTS AND FACULTY

Enrollment: 681. **Student Body:** 31% female, 69% male, 13% out-of-state, 24% international (45 countries represented). Asian 1%, African American 22%, Caucasian 39%, Hispanic 11%, Native American <1%, Pacific Islander 0%, Two or more races 2%, Race unknown 1%.
Retention and Graduation: 7% grads go on to further study within 1 year. 0% grads pursue arts and sciences degrees. 2% grads pursue law degrees. 5% grads pursue business degrees. 0% grads pursue medical degrees. **Faculty:** Student/faculty ratio 23:1. 21 full-time faculty, 71% hold PhDs, 10% are members of minority groups, 33% are women. 0% of classes are taught by teaching assistants.

ACADEMICS

Degrees: Associate; Bachelor's; Master's. **Classes:** Most classes have 20–29 students. **Most popular majors:** Business/Commerce, General; Business Administration and Management, General; Parks, Recreation and Leisure Facilities Management, General. **Special Study Options:** Cooperative education program; Cross-registration; Distance learning; Double major; Dual enrollment; English as a Second Language (ESL); Exchange student program (domestic); External degree program; Independent study; Internships; Weekend college. **Disability Services offered:** Tutors. **Career services:** Career assessment; Career/job search classes; Internships.

FACILITIES

Housing: Men's dorms; Women's dorms; 90% of campus accessible to physically disabled. **Campus Network:** 100% of classrooms, 100% of dorms, 100% of student union, 100% of libraries, 100% of dining areas, 25% of common outdoor areas have wireless network access.

CAMPUS LIFE

Environment: Rural. **Activities:** International Student Organization; Marching band; Student government; Student newspaper. 11 registered organizations, 1 religious organizations, on campus. **Athletics (Intercollegiate):** *Men:* baseball, basketball, bowling, cheerleading, cross-country, football, golf, soccer, tennis, track/field (outdoor). *Women:* basketball, bowling, cheerleading, cross-country, golf, soccer, softball, tennis, track/field (outdoor), volleyball. **On-Campus Highlights:** Student Union.

ADMISSIONS

Freshman Academic Profile: Average high school GPA 3.1. 72% in top 10% of high school class, 100% in top 25% of high school class, 0% in top 50% of high school class. 75% from public high schools. **Test Scores:** SAT Math middle 50% range 430–530. SAT EBRW middle 50% range 430–510. ACT middle 50% range 17–23. **Basis for Candidate Selection:** *Very important factors include:* academic GPA, standardized test scores. *Important factors include:* rigor of secondary school record. *Other factors include:* class rank, application essay, recommendation(s), interview, character/personal qualities, alumni/ae relation. **Freshman Admission Requirements:** High school diploma is required and GED is accepted *Academic units required:* 4 English, 2 math, 1 science, 2 social studies, 2 unit from above areas or other academic areas. *Academic units recommended:* 3 math, 3 science, 1 foreign language, 2 history, 4 academic electives. **Freshman Admission Statistics:** 710 applied, 51% admitted, 42% enrolled. **Transfer Admission Requirements:** College transcript(s), statement of good standing from prior institution(s). Minimum college GPA of 2.0 required. Lowest grade transferable C. **General Admission Information:** Application fee $35.

COSTS AND FINANCIAL AID

Annual tuition $21,686. Room and board $8,462. Average book and supplies expense $1,148. **Required Forms and Deadlines:** FAFSA; Institution's own financial aid form. **Types of Aid:** *Need-based scholarships/grants:* College/university scholarship or grant aid from institutional funds; Federal Pell; Private scholarships; SEOG; State scholarships/grants. *Loans:* Direct PLUS loans; Direct Subsidized Stafford Loans; Direct Unsubsidized Stafford Loans. **Student Employment:** Federal Work-Study Program available. Institutional employment available. **Financial Aid Statistics:** 98% needy freshmen, 97% needy undergrads receive need-based scholarship or grant aid. 5% freshmen, 6% undergrads receive non-need-based scholarship or grant aid. 82% freshmen, 80% undergrads receive need-based self-help aid. 10% freshmen, 16% undergrads receive athletic scholarships. 97% freshmen, 96% undergrads receive any aid. **Criteria awarding aid:** *Need-based:* Academics, Athletics, Leadership. *Non-need-based:* Academics, Athletics, Leadership.

WEBB INSTITUTE

298 Crescent Beach Road, Glen Cove, NY 11542
Phone: 516-671-8355 **Financial Aid Phone:** 516-403-5928
E-mail: admissions@webb.edu **CEEB Code:** 2970
Fax: 516-674-9838 **Website:** www.webb.edu **ACT Code:** 2987

This private school was founded in 1889. It has a 26 acre campus.

RATINGS

Admissions Selectivity Rating: 97   **Fire Safety Rating:** 87   **Green Rating:** 60*

STUDENTS AND FACULTY

Enrollment: 104. **Student Body:** 24% female, 76% male, 72% out-of-state, 0% international (1 countries represented). Asian 11%, African American 0%, Caucasian 81%, Hispanic 2%, Native American 0%, Pacific Islander 0%, Two or more races 6%, Race unknown 1%.
Retention and Graduation: 100% freshmen return for sophomore year. 73% freshmen graduate within 4 years. % freshmen graduate within 6 years. 10% grads go on to further study within 1 year. **Faculty:** Student/faculty ratio 9:1. 10 full-time faculty, 50% hold PhDs, 0% are members of minority groups, 10% are women. 0% of classes are taught by teaching assistants.

ACADEMICS

Degrees: Bachelor's. **Classes:** Most classes have 20–29 students. Most lab/discussion sessions have 20–29 students. **Special Study Options:** Double major; Independent study; Internships; Study abroad. **Career services:** Alumni network; Alumni services; Career/job search classes; Internships; Regional alumni.

FACILITIES

Housing: Coed dorms; Men's dorms; Women's dorms 70% of campus accessible to physically disabled. **Special Academic Facilities/Equipment:** Towing tank for model testing, marine engineering lab, other state-of-the-art laboratories.

CAMPUS LIFE

Environment: Village. **Activities:** Choral groups; Jazz band; Music ensembles; Student government; Yearbook. 4 registered organizations, on campus. **Athletics (Intercollegiate):** *Men:* basketball, cross-country, sailing, soccer, tennis, volleyball. *Women:* basketball, cross-country, sailing, soccer, tennis, volleyball. **On-Campus Highlights:** Stevenson Taylor Hall.

ADMISSIONS

Freshman Academic Profile: Average high school GPA 4.0. 78% in top 10% of high school class, 100% in top 25% of high school class, 0% in top 50% of high school class. 72% from public high schools. **Test Scores:** SAT Math middle 50% range 720–790. SAT EBRW middle 50% range 680–760. ACT middle 50% range 32–34. **Basis for Candidate Selection:** *Very important factors include:* rigor of secondary school record, class rank, academic GPA, application essay, standardized test scores, recommendation(s), interview, character/personal qualities, level of applicant's interest. *Important factors include:* extracurricular activities, talent/ability. *Other factors include:* volunteer work, work experience. **Freshman Admission Requirements:** High school diploma is required and GED is not accepted *Academic units required:* 4 English, 4 math, 2 science, 2 science labs, 2 social studies, 4 academic electives. **Freshman Admission Statistics:** 99 applied, 33% admitted, 76% enrolled. **Transfer Admission Requirements:** High school transcript, college transcript(s), interview, standardized test scores. Minimum college GPA of 3.5 required. **General Admission Information:** Application fee $60. Priority deadline 10/15. Regular application deadline 2/1. Admission may be deferred for a maximum of 1 year.

COSTS AND FINANCIAL AID

Annual tuition $51,240. Room and board $15,400. Required fees $450. Average book and supplies expense $700. **Required Forms and Deadlines:** Business/Farm Supplement; FAFSA; Institution's own financial aid form. **Notification of Awards:** Applicants will be notified of awards on or about 6/1. **Types of Aid:** *Need-based scholarships/grants:* College/university scholarship or grant aid from institutional funds; Federal Pell; Private scholarships; State scholarships/grants. *Loans:* Direct PLUS loans; Direct Subsidized Stafford Loans; Direct Unsubsidized Stafford Loans. **Financial Aid Statistics:** 100%

needy freshmen, 100% needy undergrads receive need-based scholarship or grant aid. 100% freshmen, 97% undergrads receive non-need-based scholarship or grant aid. 100% freshmen, 100% undergrads receive need-based self-help aid. 0% freshmen, 0% undergrads receive athletic scholarships. 27% freshmen, 31% undergrads receive any aid. 41% undergrads borrow to pay for school. Average cumulative indebtedness $22,700. **Criteria awarding aid:** *Non-need-based:* Academics.

WEBER STATE UNIVERSITY

1137 University Circle, Ogden, UT 84408-1137
Phone: 801-626-6743 **Financial Aid Phone:** 801-626-7569
E-mail: admissions@weber.edu **CEEB Code:** 4941
Fax: 801-626-6747 **Website:** weber.edu/ **ACT Code:** 4282

This public school was founded in 1889. It has a 508.9 acre campus.

RATINGS
Admissions Selectivity Rating: 73   **Fire Safety Rating:** 98   **Green Rating:** 92

STUDENTS AND FACULTY
Enrollment: 17,728. **Student Body:** 57% female, 43% male, 10% out-of-state, 1% international (61 countries represented). Asian 2%, African American 2%, Caucasian 74%, Hispanic 12%, Native American 1%, Pacific Islander 1%, Two or more races 4%, Race unknown 3%.
Retention and Graduation: 65% freshmen return for sophomore year. 12% freshmen graduate within 4 years. 34% freshmen graduate within 6 years. 18% grads go on to further study within 1 year. **Faculty:** Student/faculty ratio 21:1. 531 full-time faculty, 58% hold PhDs, 11% are members of minority groups, 46% are women. 0% of classes are taught by teaching assistants.

ACADEMICS
Degrees: Associate; Bachelor's; Certificate; Doctoral degree—other; Master's; Post-bachelor's certificate; Post-master's certificate; Terminal Associate; Transfer Associate. **Classes:** Most classes have 20–29 students. Most lab/discussion sessions have fewer than 10 students. **Most popular majors:** Computer Science; Registered Nursing/Registered Nurse; Business Administration and Management, General. **Special Study Options:** Accelerated program; Cooperative education program; Distance learning; Double major; Dual enrollment; English as a Second Language (ESL); Exchange student program (domestic); External degree program; Honors program; Independent study; Internships; Student-designed major; Study abroad; Teacher certification program. **Honors programs:** Weber State University's Honors Program offers you small, challenging, and creative courses, as well as opportunities for leadership and social interaction. An "Honors" designation on your transcript and diploma makes you more attractive to employers, graduate schools, and professional programs. **Combined degree programs:** BA/MA. **Disability Services offered:** Note-taking services; Reader services; Tape recorders; Tutors. **Career services:** Alumni network; Alumni services; Career assessment; Career/job search classes; Internships; Regional alumni.

FACILITIES
Housing: Apartments for single students; Coed dorms; Men's dorms; Special housing for disabled students; Wellness housing; Women's dorms; 99% of campus accessible to physically disabled. **Special Academic Facilities/Equipment:** Art gallery, language lab, TV studio, communication arts/technologies facilities, natural science museum, herbarium, planetarium, aerospace technology equipment for developing satellite projects, dental hygiene clinic.

CAMPUS LIFE
Environment: City. **Activities:** Campus Ministries; Choral groups; Concert band; Dance; Drama/theater; International Student Organization; Jazz band; Literary magazine; Marching band; Model UN; Music ensembles; Musical theater; Opera; Pep band; Radio station; Student government; Student newspaper; Student-run film society; Symphony orchestra; Television station. 218 registered organizations, 9 honor societies, 6 religious organizations, 3 fraternities, 4 sororities on campus. **Athletics (Intercollegiate):** *Men:* basketball, cheerleading, cross-country, football, golf, tennis, track/field (outdoor), track/field (indoor). *Women:* basketball, cheerleading, cross-country, golf, soccer, tennis, track/field (outdoor), track/field (indoor), volleyball. **On-Campus Highlights:** Health and Physical Education Center. **Environmental Initiatives:** Weber State University is in the process of upgrading all interior and exterior campus lighting to high-efficiency flourescents, CLFs and LEDs in some applications. This project began last year and will continue for another 3 years.

ADMISSIONS
Freshman Academic Profile: Average high school GPA 3.4. 99% from public high schools. **Test Scores:** ACT middle 50% range 18–24. **Basis for Candidate Selection:** *Other factors include:* standardized test scores. **Freshman Admission Requirements:** High school diploma is required and GED is accepted. *Academic units recommended:* 4 English, 2 math, 2 science, 2 foreign language, 1 history, 4 academic electives. **Freshman Admission Statistics:** 6,853 applied, 100% admitted, 46% enrolled. **Transfer Admission Requirements:** College transcript(s). Minimum college GPA of 2.0 required. Lowest grade transferable C. **General Admission Information:** Application fee $30. Priority deadline 3/15. Regular application deadline 8/31. Non-fall registration accepted. Admission may be deferred for a maximum of 1 year.

COSTS AND FINANCIAL AID
Annual in-state tuition $5,986. Annual out-of-state tuition $15,968. Room and board $9,900. Required fees $996. Average book and supplies expense $1,400. **Required Forms and Deadlines:** FAFSA; Institution's own financial aid form. **Notification of Awards:** Applicants will be notified of awards on a rolling basis beginning 3/15. **Types of Aid:** *Need-based scholarships/grants:* College/university scholarship or grant aid from institutional funds; Federal Pell; Private scholarships; SEOG; State scholarships/grants. *Loans:* Direct PLUS loans; Direct Subsidized Stafford Loans; Direct Unsubsidized Stafford Loans. **Student Employment:** Federal Work-Study Program available. Institutional employment available. **Financial Aid Statistics:** 63% needy freshmen, 72% needy undergrads receive need-based scholarship or grant aid. 20% freshmen, 31% undergrads receive non-need-based scholarship or grant aid. 43% freshmen, 45% undergrads receive need-based self-help aid. 3% freshmen, 3% undergrads receive athletic scholarships. 47% freshmen, 47% undergrads receive any aid. 40% undergrads borrow to pay for school. Average cumulative indebtedness $21,690. **Criteria awarding aid:** *Need-based:* Academics, Alumni affiliation, Art, Job skills, Minority status, Music/drama *Non-need-based:* Academics, Alumni affiliation, Art, Athletics, Job skills, Leadership, Minority status, Music/drama, State/district residency.

WEBSTER UNIVERSITY

470 East Lockwood Avenue, Saint Louis, MO 63119-3194
Phone: 314-246-7800 **Financial Aid Phone:** 314-968-6992
E-mail: admit@webster.edu **CEEB Code:** 6933
Fax: 314-246-7116 **Website:** www.webster.edu **ACT Code:** 2388

This private school was founded in 1915. It has a 47 acre campus.

RATINGS
Admissions Selectivity Rating: 86   **Fire Safety Rating:** 89   **Green Rating:** 60*

STUDENTS AND FACULTY
Enrollment: 2,721. **Student Body:** 55% female, 45% male, 27% out-of-state, 5% international (56 countries represented). Asian 2%, African American 13%, Caucasian 64%, Hispanic 5%, Native American <1%, Pacific Islander <1%, Two or more races 3%, Race unknown 8%.
Retention and Graduation: 78% freshmen return for sophomore year. 14% grads go on to further study within 1 year. **Faculty:** Student/faculty ratio 9:1. 200 full-time faculty, 85% hold PhDs, 16% are members of minority groups, 48% are women. 0% of classes are taught by teaching assistants.

ACADEMICS
Degrees: Bachelor's; Certificate; Doctoral degree—other; Doctoral degree research/scholarship; Master's; Post-bachelor's certificate; Post-master's certificate. **Classes:** Most classes have 10–19 students. **Most popular majors:** Registered Nursing/Registered Nurse; Business Administration and Management, General; Psychology, General. **Special Study Options:** Cooperative education program; Cross-registration; Distance learning; Double major; English as a Second Language (ESL); Independent study; Internships; Liberal arts/career combination; Student-designed major; Study abroad; Teacher certification program. **Combined degree programs:** BA/MA. **Disability Services offered:** Note-taking services; Reader services; Tape recorders; Tutors. **Career services:** Alumni network; Alumni services; Career assessment; Internships.

FACILITIES
Housing: Apartments for single students; Coed dorms; Special housing for disabled students; Special housing for international students; 85% of campus accessible to physically disabled. **Campus Network:** 100% of classrooms, 100%

of dorms, 100% of student union, 100% of libraries, 100% of dining areas, 70% of common outdoor areas have wireless network access.

CAMPUS LIFE

Environment: Metropolis. **Activities:** Campus Ministries; Choral groups; Dance; Drama/theater; International Student Organization; Jazz band; Literary magazine; Music ensembles; Musical theater; Opera; Radio station; Student government; Student newspaper; Student-run film society; Symphony orchestra; Television station. 82 registered organizations, 1 sorority on campus. **Athletics (Intercollegiate):** *Men:* baseball, basketball, cross-country, golf, soccer, tennis, track/field (outdoor). *Women:* basketball, cross-country, soccer, softball, tennis, track/field (outdoor), volleyball.

ADMISSIONS

Freshman Academic Profile: Average high school GPA 3.5. 20% in top 10% of high school class, 47% in top 25% of high school class, 76% in top 50% of high school class. **Test Scores:** ACT middle 50% range 21–27. **Basis for Candidate Selection:** *Very important factors include:* academic GPA, standardized test scores. *Important factors include:* rigor of secondary school record, class rank, talent/ability. *Other factors include:* application essay, recommendation(s), interview, extracurricular activities, character/personal qualities, first generation, alumni/ae relation, geographical residence, volunteer work, work experience, level of applicant's interest. **Freshman Admission Requirements:** High school diploma is required and GED is accepted. *Academic units recommended:* 4 English, 3 math, 3 science, 2 science labs, 2 foreign language, 3 social studies, 3 academic electives, 1 visual/performing arts. **Freshman Admission Statistics:** 1,994 applied, 56% admitted, 37% enrolled. **Transfer Admission Requirements:** College transcript(s), essay or personal statement. Minimum college GPA of 2.5 required. Lowest grade transferable C. **General Admission Information:** Application fee $35. Priority deadline 3/1. Regular application deadline 8/1. Non-fall registration accepted. Admission may be deferred for a maximum of 12 months.

COSTS AND FINANCIAL AID

Annual tuition $25,300. Room and board $10,860. Required fees $325. Average book and supplies expense $1,000. **Required Forms and Deadlines:** FAFSA; Institution's own financial aid form. **Notification of Awards:** Applicants will be notified of awards on a rolling basis beginning 2/1. **Types of Aid:** *Need-based scholarships/grants:* College/university scholarship or grant aid from institutional funds; Federal Pell; Private scholarships; SEOG; State scholarships/grants. *Loans:* Direct PLUS loans; Direct Subsidized Stafford Loans; Direct Unsubsidized Stafford Loans. **Student Employment:** Federal Work-Study Program available. Institutional employment available. **Financial Aid Statistics:** 98% needy freshmen, 90% needy undergrads receive need-based scholarship or grant aid. 94% freshmen, 87% undergrads receive non-need-based scholarship or grant aid. 96% freshmen, 90% undergrads receive need-based self-help aid. 0% freshmen, 0% undergrads receive athletic scholarships. 78% undergrads borrow to pay for school. Average cumulative indebtedness $31,548. **Criteria awarding aid:** *Need-based:* Minority status. *Non-need-based:* Academics, Art, Leadership, Music/drama.

WELLESLEY COLLEGE

Admission Office, Wellesley, MA 02481-8203
Phone: 781-283-2270 **Financial Aid Phone:** 781-283-2360
E-mail: admission@wellesley.edu **CEEB Code:** 3957
Fax: 781-283-3678 **Website:** www.wellesley.edu **ACT Code:** 1926

This private school was founded in 1870. It has a 500 acre campus.

RATINGS

Admissions Selectivity Rating: 97   **Fire Safety Rating:** 98   **Green Rating:** 92

STUDENTS AND FACULTY

Enrollment: 2,392. **Student Body:** 100% female, 0% male, 86% out-of-state, 14% international (88 countries represented). Asian 22%, African American 7%, Caucasian 38%, Hispanic 13%, Native American <1%, Pacific Islander, Two or more races 6%, Race unknown <1%.
Retention and Graduation: 96% freshmen return for sophomore year. 78% freshmen graduate within 4 years. 90% freshmen graduate within 6 years. 18% grads go on to further study within 1 year. 24% grads pursue arts and sciences

degrees. 13% grads pursue law degrees. 3% grads pursue business degrees. 10% grads pursue medical degrees. **Faculty:** Student/faculty ratio 8:1. 300 full-time faculty, 93% hold PhDs, 24% are members of minority groups, 62% are women. 0% of classes are taught by teaching assistants.

ACADEMICS

Degrees: Bachelor's. **Classes:** Most classes have 10–19 students. Most lab/discussion sessions have 10–19 students. **Most popular majors:** Economics, General; Psychology, General; Computer Science. **Special Study Options:** Cooperative education program; Cross-registration; Distance learning; Double major; Exchange student program (domestic); Honors program; Independent study; Internships; Student-designed major; Study abroad; Teacher certification program. **Combined degree programs:** BA/MA. **Disability Services offered:** Note-taking services; Reader services; Tape recorders; Tutors. **Career services:** Alumni network; Alumni services; Career assessment; Career/job search classes; Internships; Regional alumni.

FACILITIES

Housing: Apartments for single students; Cooperative housing; Theme housing; Women's dorms; 85% of campus accessible to physically disabled. **Special Academic Facilities/Equipment:** Clapp Library; Davis Museum and Cultural Center; Harambee House; Houghton Memorial Chapel; Hunnewell Arboretum, Alexandra Botanic Gardens, and Ferguson Greenhouses; Jewett Art Museum; Keohane Sports Center; Knapp Media and Technology Center; Knapp Social Science Center; Lake Waban Pforzheimer Learning and Teaching Center; Ruth Nagel Jones Theatre; Science Center; Slater International Center; Wang Campus Center; Wellesley Centers for Women; Whitin Observatory, including 3 telescopes.

CAMPUS LIFE

Environment: Town. **Activities:** Campus Ministries; Choral groups; Concert band; Dance; Drama/theater; International Student Organization; Jazz band; Literary magazine; Model UN; Music ensembles; Radio station; Student government; Student newspaper; Student-run film society; Symphony orchestra; Television station; Yearbook. 160 registered organizations, 7 honor societies, 30 religious organizations, on campus. **Athletics (Intercollegiate):** *Women:* basketball, crew/rowing, cross-country, diving, fencing, field hockey, golf, lacrosse, soccer, softball, squash, swimming, tennis, track/field (outdoor), track/field (indoor), volleyball. **On-Campus Highlights:** Wang Campus Center.

ADMISSIONS

Freshman Academic Profile: 83% in top 10% of high school class, 96% in top 25% of high school class, 99% in top 50% of high school class. 62% from public high schools. **Test Scores:** SAT Math middle 50% range 660–780. SAT EBRW middle 50% range 670–740. ACT middle 50% range 30–34. **Basis for Candidate Selection:** *Very important factors include:* rigor of secondary school record, academic GPA, recommendation(s), character/personal qualities. *Important factors include:* class rank, application essay, standardized test scores, extracurricular activities, talent/ability. *Other factors include:* interview, first generation, alumni/ae relation, geographical residence, state residency, racial/ethnic status, volunteer work, work experience, level of applicant's interest. **Freshman Admission Requirements:** High school diploma or equivalent is not required. *Academic units recommended:* 4 English, 4 math, 3 science, 2 science labs, 4 foreign language, 4 social studies, 4 history. **Freshman Admission Statistics:** 6,631 applied, 20% admitted, 47% enrolled. **Transfer Admission Requirements:** High school transcript, college transcript(s), essay or personal statement, interview, standardized test scores, statement of good standing from prior institution(s). Lowest grade transferable C. **General Admission Information:** Application fee $50. Regular application deadline 1/15. Admission may be deferred for a maximum of 1 year.

COSTS AND FINANCIAL AID

Annual tuition $53,408. Room and board $16,468. Required fees $324. Average book and supplies expense $800. **Required Forms and Deadlines:** CSS/Financial Aid PROFILE; FAFSA; Noncustodial PROFILE. **Notification of Awards:** Applicants will be notified of awards on or about 4/1. **Types of Aid:** *Need-based scholarships/grants:* College/university scholarship or grant aid from institutional funds; Federal Pell; Private scholarships; SEOG; State scholarships/grants; United Negro College Fund. *Loans:* Direct PLUS loans; Direct Subsidized Stafford Loans; Direct Unsubsidized Stafford Loans. **Student Employment:** Federal Work-Study Program available. Institutional employment available. **Financial Aid Statistics:** 97% needy freshmen, 95% needy undergrads receive need-based scholarship or grant aid. 8% freshmen, 7% undergrads receive non-need-based scholarship or grant aid. 93% freshmen, 94% undergrads receive need-based self-help aid. 0% freshmen, 0% undergrads receive athletic scholarships. 60% freshmen, 63% undergrads receive any aid. 52% undergrads borrow to pay for school. Average cumulative indebtedness $16,122.

WELLS COLLEGE

170 Main Street, Aurora, NY 13026
Phone: 315-364-3264 **Financial Aid Phone:** 315-364-3289
E-mail: admissions@wells.edu **CEEB Code:** 2971
Fax: 315-364-3227 **Website:** www.wells.edu **ACT Code:** 2971

This private school was founded in 1868. It has a 365 acre campus.

RATINGS
Admissions Selectivity Rating: 75   **Fire Safety Rating:** 90   **Green Rating:** 93

STUDENTS AND FACULTY
Enrollment: 413. **Student Body:** 65% female, 35% male, 29% out-of-state, 2% international (6 countries represented). Asian 2%, African American 13%, Caucasian 61%, Hispanic 16%, Native American 1%, Pacific Islander 0%, Two or more races 3%, Race unknown 2%.
Retention and Graduation: 71% freshmen return for sophomore year. 54% freshmen graduate within 4 years. 55% freshmen graduate within 6 years. 28% grads go on to further study within 1 year. 5% grads pursue law degrees. 4% grads pursue medical degrees. **Faculty:** Student/faculty ratio 10:1. 37 full-time faculty, 95% hold PhDs, 16% are members of minority groups, 54% are women. 0% of classes are taught by teaching assistants.

ACADEMICS
Degrees: Bachelor's. **Classes:** Most classes have 10–19 students. Most lab/discussion sessions have fewer than 10 students. **Most popular majors:** Psychology, General; Biology, General; Business Administration and Management, General. **Special Study Options:** Accelerated program; Cross-registration; Double major; Independent study; Internships; Liberal arts/career combination; Student-designed major; Study abroad; Teacher certification program. **Disability Services offered:** Note-taking services; Reader services; Tape recorders; Tutors. **Career services:** Alumni network; Alumni services; Career assessment; Internships; Regional alumni.

FACILITIES
Housing: Apartments for single students; Coed dorms; Wellness housing; Women's dorms; 65% of campus accessible to physically disabled. **Special Academic Facilities/Equipment:** Two greenhouses, environmentally regulated animal room, the college theatre (Phillips Auditorium), recital hall, electronic music studio, 15 pianos, a Dowd harpsichord, an early instrument collection, a sculpture and ceramics studio, dark rooms, painting and drawing studio, a Book Arts Center, lithography presses, an extensive art library, art gallery, general and specialized clusters for the social sciences, foreign languages, and natural and mathematical sciences.

CAMPUS LIFE
Environment: Rural. **Activities:** Choral groups; Concert band; Dance; Drama/theater; International Student Organization; Jazz band; Literary magazine; Model UN; Music ensembles; Musical theater; Student government; Student-run film society; Symphony orchestra; Yearbook. 35 registered organizations, 2 honor societies, 2 religious organizations on campus. **Athletics (Intercollegiate):** *Men:* basketball, cross-country, golf, lacrosse, soccer, swimming. *Women:* basketball, cross-country, field hockey, golf, lacrosse, soccer, softball, swimming, tennis. **On-Campus Highlights:** Sommer Center.

ADMISSIONS
Freshman Academic Profile: Average high school GPA 3.4. 19% in top 10% of high school class, 37% in top 25% of high school class, 66% in top 50% of high school class. **Test Scores:** SAT Math middle 50% range 470–610. SAT EBRW middle 50% range 480–630. ACT middle 50% range 18–22. **Basis for Candidate Selection:** *Very important factors include:* rigor of secondary school record, academic GPA. *Important factors include:* application essay, recommendation(s). *Other factors include:* class rank, standardized test scores, interview, extracurricular activities, talent/ability, character/personal qualities, first generation, alumni/ae relation, volunteer work, work experience, level of applicant's interest. **Freshman Admission Requirements:** High school diploma is required and GED is accepted. *Academic units required:* 4 English, 3 math, 2 science, 2 science labs, 1 foreign language, 1 social studies, 3 history. *Academic units recommended:* 4 English, 4 math, 4 science, 2 science labs, 2 foreign language, 3 social studies, 3 history, 2 visual/performing arts. **Freshman Admission Statistics:** 1,848 applied, 83% admitted, 9% enrolled. **Transfer Admission Requirements:** High school transcript, college transcript(s), essay or personal statement, standardized test scores, statement of good standing

from prior institution(s). Minimum college GPA of 2.0 required. Lowest grade transferable C-. **General Admission Information:** Priority deadline 12/15. Regular application deadline 3/1. Non-fall registration accepted. Admission may be deferred for a maximum of 12 months.

COSTS AND FINANCIAL AID
Annual tuition $30,300. Room and board $14,500. Required fees $1,500. Average book and supplies expense $1,050. **Required Forms and Deadlines:** FAFSA; State aid form. **Notification of Awards:** Applicants will be notified of awards on a rolling basis beginning 12/15. **Types of Aid:** *Need-based scholarships/grants:* College/university scholarship or grant aid from institutional funds; Federal Pell; Private scholarships; SEOG; State scholarships/grants. *Loans:* Direct PLUS loans; Direct Subsidized Stafford Loans; Direct Unsubsidized Stafford Loans. **Student Employment:** Federal Work-Study Program available. Institutional employment available. **Financial Aid Statistics:** 100% needy freshmen, 100% needy undergrads receive need-based scholarship or grant aid. 100% freshmen, 100% undergrads receive non-need-based scholarship or grant aid. 94% freshmen, 96% undergrads receive need-based self-help aid. 0% freshmen, 0% undergrads receive athletic scholarships. 96% freshmen, 95% undergrads receive any aid. 92% undergrads borrow to pay for school. Average cumulative indebtedness $39,010. **Criteria awarding aid:** *Non-need-based:* Academics, Alumni affiliation, Leadership.

WENTWORTH INSTITUTE OF TECHNOLOGY

550 Huntington Avenue, Boston, MA 02115-5998
Phone: 617-989-4000 **Financial Aid Phone:** 617-989-4174
E-mail: admissions@wit.edu **CEEB Code:** 3958
Fax: 617-989-4010 **Website:** www.wit.edu

This private school was founded in 1904. It has a 31 acre campus.

RATINGS
Admissions Selectivity Rating: 77   **Fire Safety Rating:** 97   **Green Rating:** 89

STUDENTS AND FACULTY
Enrollment: 4,254. **Student Body:** 21% female, 79% male, 33% out-of-state, 7% international (53 countries represented). Asian 8%, African American 6%, Caucasian 63%, Hispanic 7%, Native American <1%, Pacific Islander <1%, Two or more races 4%, Race unknown 6%.
Retention and Graduation: 83% freshmen return for sophomore year. 52% freshmen graduate within 4 years. 67% freshmen graduate within 6 years. 17% grads go on to further study within 1 year. 11% grads pursue arts and sciences degrees. 2% grads pursue business degrees. **Faculty:** Student/faculty ratio 18:1. 160 full-time faculty, 0% hold PhDs, 23% are members of minority groups, 29% are women. 0% of classes are taught by teaching assistants.

ACADEMICS
Degrees: Associate; Bachelor's; Certificate; Master's. **Classes:** Most classes have 20–29 students. Most lab/discussion sessions have 10–19 students. **Most popular majors:** Architecture; Construction Management, General; Mechanical Engineering. **Special Study Options:** Accelerated program; Cooperative education program; Distance learning; Double major; Dual enrollment; English as a Second Language (ESL); Independent study; Study abroad; Weekend college. **Disability Services offered:** Note-taking services; Reader services; Tape recorders; Tutors. **Career services:** Alumni network; Alumni services; Career assessment; Career/job search classes; Internships.

FACILITIES
Housing: Apartments for single students; Coed dorms; Special housing for disabled students; Special housing for international students; 75% of campus accessible to physically disabled.

CAMPUS LIFE
Environment: Metropolis. **Activities:** Campus Ministries; Choral groups; Concert band; Dance; Drama/theater; International Student Organization; Jazz band; Marching band; Model UN; Music ensembles; Musical theater; Radio station; Student government; Symphony orchestra. 40 registered organizations, 4 honor societies, 2 religious organizations on campus. **Athletics (Intercollegiate):** *Men:* baseball, basketball, golf, ice hockey, lacrosse, riflery, soccer, tennis, volleyball. *Women:* basketball, golf, riflery, soccer, softball, tennis, volleyball. **On-Campus Highlights:** 525 Huntington Avenue (newest residence hall).

ADMISSIONS

Freshman Academic Profile: Average high school GPA 3.1. 16% in top 10% of high school class, 40% in top 25% of high school class, 73% in top 50% of high school class. **Test Scores:** SAT Math middle 50% range 550–650. SAT EBRW middle 50% range 530–620. ACT middle 50% range 22–27. **Basis for Candidate Selection:** *Important factors include:* rigor of secondary school record, academic GPA, application essay, standardized test scores, recommendation(s). *Other factors include:* extracurricular activities, talent/ability, character/personal qualities, first generation, alumni/ae relation, geographical residence, racial/ethnic status, volunteer work, work experience, level of applicant's interest. **Freshman Admission Requirements:** High school diploma is required and GED is accepted. *Academic units required:* 4 English, 3 math, 2 science, 1 science labs. *Academic units recommended:* 4 English, 4 math, 2 science, 1 science labs. **Freshman Admission Statistics:** 7,109 applied, 78% admitted, 19% enrolled. **Transfer Admission Requirements:** High school transcript, college transcript(s), essay or personal statement, Lowest grade transferable C. **General Admission Information:** Application fee $50. Priority deadline 2/15. Non-fall registration accepted. Admission may be deferred for a maximum of 1 academic year.

COSTS AND FINANCIAL AID

Annual tuition $33,950. Room and board $14,190. Average book and supplies expense $1,500. **Required Forms and Deadlines:** FAFSA. **Notification of Awards:** Applicants will be notified of awards on a rolling basis beginning 5/1. **Types of Aid:** *Need-based scholarships/grants:* College/university scholarship or grant aid from institutional funds; Federal Pell; Private scholarships; SEOG; State scholarships/grants; United Negro College Fund. *Loans:* Direct PLUS loans; Direct Subsidized Stafford Loans; Direct Unsubsidized Stafford Loans. **Student Employment:** Federal Work-Study Program available. Institutional employment available. **Financial Aid Statistics:** 82% needy freshmen, 88% needy undergrads receive need-based scholarship or grant aid. 36% freshmen, 29% undergrads receive non-need-based scholarship or grant aid. 85% freshmen, 84% undergrads receive need-based self-help aid. 0% freshmen, 0% undergrads receive athletic scholarships. 99% freshmen, 90% undergrads receive any aid. 78% undergrads borrow to pay for school. Average cumulative indebtedness $41,429. **Criteria awarding aid:** *Non-need-based:* Academics, Leadership, State/district residency.

WESLEYAN COLLEGE

4760 Forsyth Road, Macon, GA 31210-4462
Phone: 478-757-5206 **Financial Aid Phone:** 478-757-5167
E-mail: admissions@wesleyancollege.edu **CEEB Code:** 5895
Fax: 478-757-4030 **Website:** https://www.wesleyancollege.edu/ **ACT Code:** 876

This private school, affiliated with the Methodist Church, was founded in 1836. It has a 200 acre campus.

RATINGS

Admissions Selectivity Rating: 89   **Fire Safety Rating:** 96   **Green Rating:** 91

STUDENTS AND FACULTY

Enrollment: 584. **Student Body:** 100% female, 0% male, 7% out-of-state, 7% international (20 countries represented). Asian 1%, African American 37%, Caucasian 45%, Hispanic 5%, Native American <1%, Pacific Islander 0%, Two or more races 4%, Race unknown 2%. **Retention and Graduation:** 68% freshmen return for sophomore year. 42% freshmen graduate within 4 years. 50% freshmen graduate within 6 years. 30% grads go on to further study within 1 year. 10% grads pursue arts and sciences degrees. 1% grads pursue law degrees. 15% grads pursue business degrees. 4% grads pursue medical degrees. **Faculty:** Student/faculty ratio 8:1. 53 full-time faculty, 77% hold PhDs, 6% are members of minority groups, 68% are women. 0% of classes are taught by teaching assistants.

ACADEMICS

Degrees: Bachelor's; Master's. **Classes:** Most classes have 10–19 students. Most lab/discussion sessions have fewer than 10 students. **Most popular majors:** Business Administration, Management and Operations, Other; Accounting; Registered Nursing/Registered Nurse. **Special Study Options:** Accelerated program; Cross-registration; Distance learning; Double major;

Dual enrollment; Honors program; Independent study; Internships; Student-designed major; Study abroad; Teacher certification program. **Honors programs:** Honors Thesis. **Disability Services offered:** Note-taking services; Reader services; Tape recorders; Tutors. **Career services:** Alumni network; Career assessment; Career/job search classes; Internships; Regional alumni.

FACILITIES

Housing: Apartments for single students; Special housing for disabled students; Women's dorms; 89% of campus accessible to physically disabled. **Special Academic Facilities/Equipment:** Art and history museums, special collection of Georgiana and Americana, Confucius Institute, equestrian center. **Campus Network:** 100% of classrooms, 100% of dorms, 100% of student union, 100% of libraries, 100% of dining areas have wireless network access.

CAMPUS LIFE

Environment: City. **Activities:** Campus Ministries; Choral groups; Dance; Drama/theater; International Student Organization; Literary magazine; Model UN; Music ensembles; Musical theater; Student government. 26 registered organizations, 12 honor societies, 4 religious organizations on campus. **Athletics (Intercollegiate):** *Women:* basketball, cross-country, equestrian sports, soccer, softball, tennis, volleyball. **On-Campus Highlights:** Library with 24 hour access. **Environmental Initiatives:** Plastic Bottle Policy.

ADMISSIONS

Freshman Academic Profile: Average high school GPA 3.4. 80% from public high schools. **Test Scores:** SAT Math middle 50% range 470–540. SAT EBRW middle 50% range 470–580. ACT middle 50% range 17–22. **Basis for Candidate Selection:** *Very important factors include:* academic GPA. *Important factors include:* rigor of secondary school record, class rank, standardized test scores. *Other factors include:* recommendation(s), interview, extracurricular activities, talent/ability, character/personal qualities, alumni/ae relation, volunteer work, work experience. **Freshman Admission Requirements:** High school diploma is required and GED is accepted. *Academic units recommended:* 4 English, 3 math, 3 science, 3 science labs, 2 foreign language, 4 social studies, 4 academic electives, 2 visual/performing arts. **Freshman Admission Statistics:** 737 applied, 44% admitted, 42% enrolled. **Transfer Admission Requirements:** College transcript(s), essay or personal statement, statement of good standing from prior institution(s). Minimum college GPA of 2.5 required. Lowest grade transferable C. **General Admission Information:** Non-fall registration accepted. Admission may be deferred for a maximum of 1 year.

COSTS AND FINANCIAL AID

Annual tuition $23,990. Room and board $10,365. Required fees $1,200. **Required Forms and Deadlines:** FAFSA. **Notification of Awards:** Applicants will be notified of awards on a rolling basis beginning 10/1. **Types of Aid:** *Need-based scholarships/grants:* College/university scholarship or grant aid from institutional funds; Federal Pell; Private scholarships; SEOG; State scholarships/grants. *Loans:* Direct PLUS loans; Direct Subsidized Stafford Loans; Direct Unsubsidized Stafford Loans. **Student Employment:** Federal Work-Study Program available. Institutional employment available. **Financial Aid Statistics:** 99% needy freshmen, 100% needy undergrads receive need-based scholarship or grant aid. 12% freshmen, 16% undergrads receive non-need-based scholarship or grant aid. 68% freshmen, 72% undergrads receive need-based self-help aid. 0% freshmen, 0% undergrads receive athletic scholarships. 96% freshmen, 88% undergrads receive any aid. 74% undergrads borrow to pay for school. Average cumulative indebtedness $28,882. **Criteria awarding aid:** *Need-based:* Academics, Alumni affiliation, Job skills, Religious affiliation *Non-need-based:* Academics, Alumni affiliation, Art, Job skills, Leadership, Music/drama, Religious affiliation, State/district residency.

WESLEYAN UNIVERSITY

70 Wyllys Avenue, Middletown, CT 06459
Phone: 860-685-3000 **Financial Aid Phone:** 860-685-2800
E-mail: admission@wesleyan.edu **CEEB Code:** 3959
Fax: 860-685-3001 **Website:** www.wesleyan.edu **ACT Code:** 0614

This private school was founded in 1831. It has a 316 acre campus.

RATINGS

Admissions Selectivity Rating: 97 **Fire Safety Rating:** 93 **Green Rating:** 94

STUDENTS AND FACULTY

Enrollment: 2,933. **Student Body:** 55% female, 45% male, 92% out-of-state, 14% international (56 countries represented). Asian 7%, African American 5%, Caucasian 54%, Hispanic 11%, Native American <1%, Pacific Islander <1%, Two or more races 6%, Race unknown 2%.
Retention and Graduation: 97% freshmen return for sophomore year. 88% freshmen graduate within 4 years. 92% freshmen graduate within 6 years. 11% grads go on to further study within 1 year. 6% grads pursue arts and sciences degrees. 2% grads pursue law degrees. 0% grads pursue business degrees. 1% grads pursue medical degrees. **Faculty:** Student/faculty ratio 8:1. 372 full-time faculty, 92% hold PhDs, 22% are members of minority groups, 46% are women. 0% of classes are taught by teaching assistants.

ACADEMICS

Degrees: Bachelor's; Doctoral degree research/scholarship; Master's; Post-master's certificate. **Classes:** Most classes have 10–19 students. Most lab/discussion sessions have 10–19 students. **Most popular majors:** Psychology, General; Econometrics and Quantitative Economics; Political Science and Government, General. **Special Study Options:** Accelerated program; Cross-registration; Double major; Dual enrollment; Exchange student program (domestic); Honors program; Independent study; Internships; Student-designed major; Study abroad. **Combined degree programs:** BA/MA. **Disability Services offered:** Note-taking services; Reader services; Tape recorders; Tutors. **Career services:** Alumni network; Alumni services; Career assessment; Career/job search classes; Internships; Regional alumni.

FACILITIES

Housing: Apartments for single students; Coed dorms; Fraternity/sorority housing; Men's dorms; Special housing for disabled students; Theme housing; Wellness housing; Women's dorms; 56% of campus accessible to physically disabled. **Special Academic Facilities/Equipment:** Art center, art galleries, Center for Afro-American studies, East Asian Studies Center, Cinema Archives, concert hall, public affairs center, language lab, electron microscope, observatory, nuclear magnetic resonance spectrometers.

CAMPUS LIFE

Environment: Town. **Activities:** Campus Ministries; Choral groups; Concert band; Dance; Drama/theater; International Student Organization; Jazz band; Literary magazine; Model UN; Music ensembles; Musical theater; Pep band; Radio station; Student government; Student newspaper; Student-run film society; Symphony orchestra; Yearbook. 234 registered organizations, 2 honor societies, 10 religious organizations, 4 fraternities, 1 sorority on campus. **Athletics (Intercollegiate):** *Men:* baseball, basketball, crew/rowing, cross-country, diving, football, golf, ice hockey, lacrosse, soccer, squash, swimming, tennis, track/field (outdoor), track/field (indoor), wrestling. *Women:* basketball, crew/rowing, cross-country, diving, field hockey, ice hockey, lacrosse, soccer, softball, squash, swimming, tennis, track/field (outdoor), track/field (indoor), volleyball. **On-Campus Highlights:** Center for the Arts. **Environmental Initiatives:** Energy conservation activities resulting in a 28% reduction of energy consumption campus wide and the construction of 3 PV solar system with a combined output of 215 kW.

ADMISSIONS

Freshman Academic Profile: 67% in top 10% of high school class, 94% in top 50% of high school class. 52% from public high schools. **Test Scores:** SAT Math middle 50% range 670–770. SAT EBRW middle 50% range 650–740. ACT middle 50% range 31–34. **Basis for Candidate Selection:** *Very important factors include:* rigor of secondary school record. *Important factors include:* class rank, academic GPA, application essay, recommendation(s), talent/ability,

character/personal qualities, first generation, racial/ethnic status. *Other factors include:* standardized test scores, interview, extracurricular activities, alumni/ae relation, geographical residence, volunteer work, work experience. **Freshman Admission Requirements:** High school diploma is required and GED is accepted. *Academic units recommended:* 4 English, 4 math, 4 science, 3 science labs, 4 foreign language, 4 social studies, 4 history. **Freshman Admission Statistics:** 13,264 applied, 16% admitted, 35% enrolled. **Transfer Admission Requirements:** High school transcript, college transcript(s), essay or personal statement, standardized test scores, statement of good standing from prior institution(s). Lowest grade transferable C-. **General Admission Information:** Application fee $55. Regular application deadline 1/1.

COSTS AND FINANCIAL AID

Annual tuition $56,704. Room and board $15,724. Required fees $300. Average book and supplies expense $1,200. **Required Forms and Deadlines:** CSS/Financial Aid PROFILE; FAFSA; Noncustodial PROFILE;. **Notification of Awards:** Applicants will be notified of awards on or about 4/1. **Types of Aid:** *Need-based scholarships/grants:* College/university scholarship or grant aid from institutional funds; Federal Pell; Private scholarships; SEOG; State scholarships/grants. *Loans:* Direct PLUS loans; Direct Subsidized Stafford Loans; Direct Unsubsidized Stafford Loans. **Student Employment:** Federal Work-Study Program available. Institutional employment available. **Financial Aid Statistics:** 100% needy freshmen, 99% needy undergrads receive need-based scholarship or grant aid. 4% freshmen, 3% undergrads receive non-need-based scholarship or grant aid. 98% freshmen, 99% undergrads receive need-based self-help aid. 0% freshmen, 0% undergrads receive athletic scholarships. 48% freshmen, 47% undergrads receive any aid. 36% undergrads borrow to pay for school. Average cumulative indebtedness $26,016.

WEST CHESTER UNIVERSITY OF PENNSYLVANIA

Messikomer Hall, West Chester, PA 19383
Phone: 610-436-3411 **Financial Aid Phone:** 610-436-2627
CEEB Code: 3328
Fax: 610-436-2907 **Website:** www.wcupa.edu **ACT Code:** 3750

This public school was founded in 1871. It has a 409.05 acre campus.

RATINGS

Admissions Selectivity Rating: 80 **Fire Safety Rating:** 98 **Green Rating:** 91

STUDENTS AND FACULTY

Enrollment: 14,328. **Student Body:** 59% female, 41% male, 10% out-of-state, <1% international (83 countries represented). Asian 2%, African American 11%, Caucasian 74%, Hispanic 6%, Native American <1%, Pacific Islander <1%, Two or more races 4%, Race unknown 2%.
Retention and Graduation: 86% freshmen return for sophomore year. 54% freshmen graduate within 4 years. 77% freshmen graduate within 6 years. **Faculty:** 0% of classes are taught by teaching assistants.

ACADEMICS

Degrees: Bachelor's; Doctoral degree—professional practice; Doctoral degree research/scholarship; Master's; Post-bachelor's certificate; Post-master's certificate. **Classes:** Most classes have 20–29 students. Most lab/discussion sessions have 20–29 students. **Most popular majors: Special Study Options:** Accelerated program; Cross-registration; Distance learning; Double major; Dual enrollment; English as a Second Language (ESL); Exchange student program (domestic); Honors program; Independent study; Internships; Liberal arts/career combination; Student-designed major; Study abroad; Teacher certification program. **Honors programs:** The Honors College has two distinct academic programs. The Honors Core Program for incoming First Year Students with a maximum of 80 seats offered each fall and the Honors Seminar Program geared toward transfer students and WCU students with a minimum of 30 earned credits. The Honors College also offers a Minor in Civic and Professional Leadership. **Disability Services offered:** Note-taking services; Reader services; Tape recorders; Tutors. **Career services:** Alumni network; Alumni services; Career assessment; Internships; Regional alumni.

FACILITIES

Housing: Apartments for single students; Coed dorms; Special housing for disabled students; Special housing for international students; Theme housing; 95% of campus accessible to physically disabled. **Special Academic Facilities/Equipment:** HEAT (Heat Illness Evaluation Avoidance and Treatment) Institute, Geology Museum, Planetarium, Observatory, Darlington Herbarium,

Robert B. Gordon Natural Area for Environmental Studies, Emilie K. Asplundh Concert Hall, The John Baker Gallery at The E.O. Bull Center for the Arts, E. O. Bull Main Stage Theatre, J. Peter Adler Studio Theatre, Madeleine Wing Adler Theatre, Knauer Gallery, Gates Family Recital Hall, Outdoor Classroom & Native Plant & Ornithology Lab, Presser Music Library, Harvey Green Library, Speech and Hearing Clinic, Sturzebecker Health Science Center, Swope Music Building and the Performing Arts Center, The Poetry Center, Southeastern Pennsylvania Autism Resource Center and D-CAP (DubC Autism Program).

CAMPUS LIFE

Environment: Town. **Activities:** Campus Ministries; Choral groups; Concert band; Dance; Drama/theater; International Student Organization; Jazz band; Literary magazine; Marching band; Model UN; Music ensembles; Musical theater; Opera; Pep band; Radio station; Student government; Student newspaper; Student-run film society; Symphony orchestra; Television station; Yearbook. 294 registered organizations, 41 honor societies, 13 religious organizations, 17 fraternities, 16 sororities on campus. **Athletics (Intercollegiate):** *Men:* baseball, basketball, cross-country, diving, football, golf, soccer, swimming, tennis, track/field (outdoor). *Women:* basketball, cheerleading, cross-country, diving, field hockey, golf, gymnastics, lacrosse, rugby, soccer, softball, swimming, tennis, track/field (outdoor), volleyball. **On-Campus Highlights:** Student Recreation Center. **Environmental Initiatives:** West Chester University has invested in one of the largest geo-exchange heating and cooling systems at any North American institution of higher education. Those systems keep almost half of campus building space (over 1.5 million square feet) comfortable year-round, they allowed WCU to decommission its coal-fired boiler plant in 2014, and they reduce our annual carbon emissions by thousands of metric tons of carbon dioxide.

ADMISSIONS

Freshman Academic Profile: Average high school GPA 3.4. 10% in top 10% of high school class, 34% in top 25% of high school class, 69% in top 50% of high school class. 85% from public high schools. **Test Scores:** SAT Math middle 50% range 520–600. SAT EBRW middle 50% range 520–610. ACT middle 50% range 20–26. **Basis for Candidate Selection:** *Very important factors include:* rigor of secondary school record, academic GPA. *Important factors include:* class rank, standardized test scores. *Other factors include:* application essay, recommendation(s), talent/ability, character/personal qualities, state residency, racial/ethnic status. **Freshman Admission Requirements:** High school diploma is required and GED is accepted *Academic units required:* 4 English, 3 math, 3 science, 2 science labs, 2 social studies, 2 history, 2 academic electives. *Academic units recommended:* 4 English, 4 math, 3 science, 2 foreign language, 2 social studies, 2 history, 2 academic electives, 1 visual/performing arts. **Freshman Admission Statistics:** 15,085 applied, 75% admitted, 25% enrolled. **Transfer Admission Requirements:** College transcript(s), essay or personal statement. Minimum college GPA of 2.0 required. Lowest grade transferable C. **General Admission Information:** Application fee $45. Priority deadline 2/1. Non-fall registration accepted.

COSTS AND FINANCIAL AID

Annual in-state tuition $7,716. Annual out-of-state tuition $19,290. Room and board $9,326. Required fees $2,705. Average book and supplies expense $1,200. **Required Forms and Deadlines:** FAFSA. **Notification of Awards:** Applicants will be notified of awards on a rolling basis beginning 3/1. **Types of Aid:** *Need-based scholarships/grants:* College/university scholarship or grant aid from institutional funds; Federal Pell; Private scholarships; SEOG; State scholarships/grants. *Loans:* Direct PLUS loans; Direct Subsidized Stafford Loans; Direct Unsubsidized Stafford Loans. **Student Employment:** Federal Work-Study Program available. Institutional employment available. **Financial Aid Statistics:** 71% needy freshmen, 63% needy undergrads receive need-based scholarship or grant aid. 32% freshmen, 20% undergrads receive non-need-based scholarship or grant aid. 82% freshmen, 83% undergrads receive need-based self-help aid. 1% freshmen, 1% undergrads receive athletic scholarships. 84% freshmen, 75% undergrads receive any aid. 77% undergrads borrow to pay for school. Average cumulative indebtedness $36,469. **Criteria awarding aid:** *Need-based:* Academics, Minority status. *Non-need-based:* Academics, Art, Athletics, Leadership, Music/drama.

WESTERN CAROLINA UNIVERSITY

102 Camp Building, Cullowhee, NC 28723
Phone: 828-227-7317 **Financial Aid Phone:** 828-227-7290
E-mail: admiss@email.wcu.edu **CEEB Code:** 5897
Fax: 828-227-7319 **Website:** www.wcu.edu **ACT Code:** 3172

This public school was founded in 1889. It has a 682 acre campus.

RATINGS
Admissions Selectivity Rating: 89   **Fire Safety Rating:** 87   **Green Rating:** 82

STUDENTS AND FACULTY
Enrollment: 9,835. **Student Body:** 54% female, 46% male, 9% out-of-state, 1% international. Asian 1%, African American 5%, Caucasian 79%, Hispanic 7%, Native American 1%, Pacific Islander <1%, Two or more races 4%, Race unknown 1%.
Retention and Graduation: 80% freshmen return for sophomore year. 40% freshmen graduate within 4 years. 59% freshmen graduate within 6 years.
Faculty: Student/faculty ratio 17:1. 513 full-time faculty, 81% hold PhDs, 10% are members of minority groups, 50% are women.

ACADEMICS
Degrees: Bachelor's; Doctoral degree—professional practice; Doctoral degree research/scholarship; Master's; Post-bachelor's certificate; Post-master's certificate. **Classes:** Most classes have 20–29 students. Most lab/discussion sessions have 10–19 students. **Most popular majors:** Criminal Justice/Safety Studies; Registered Nursing/Registered Nurse; Junior High/Intermediate/Middle School Education and Teaching. **Special Study Options:** Cooperative education program; Distance learning; Double major; Dual enrollment; English as a Second Language (ESL); Exchange student program (domestic); Honors program; Independent study; Internships; Student-designed major; Study abroad; Teacher certification program. **Honors programs:** Western has a residential Honors College designed to enhance the academic and social university experience for high-achieving students. The college consists of honors courses throughout liberal studies with an emphasis on special projects and undergraduate research in the major. Also, special housing, academic, leadership, and social programs are available for honors students. **Disability Services offered:** Note-taking services; Reader services; Tape recorders; Tutors. **Career services:** Alumni network; Alumni services; Career assessment; Internships.

FACILITIES
Housing: Apartments for married students; Coed dorms; Fraternity/sorority housing; Men's dorms; Special housing for disabled students; Theme housing; Wellness housing; Women's dorms; 91% of campus accessible to physically disabled. **Special Academic Facilities/Equipment:** Fine Arts Gallery, Mountain Heritage Center, Reading Center, North Carolina Center for the Advancement of Teaching, Speech/Hearing Center, Center for Applied Technology, CATA Lab (high technology computer lab), Fine and Performing Arts Center, Institute for the Economy and the Future, Public Policy Institute.

CAMPUS LIFE
Environment: Rural. **Activities:** Campus Ministries; Choral groups; Concert band; Dance; Drama/theater; International Student Organization; Jazz band; Literary magazine; Marching band; Model UN; Music ensembles; Musical theater; Pep band; Radio station; Student government; Student newspaper; Student-run film society; Television station. 150 registered organizations, 7 honor societies, 17 religious organizations, 13 fraternities, 9 sororities on campus. **Athletics (Intercollegiate):** *Men:* baseball, basketball, cheerleading, cross-country, football, golf, track/field (outdoor), track/field (indoor). *Women:* basketball, cheerleading, cross-country, golf, soccer, softball, tennis, track/field (outdoor), track/field (indoor), volleyball. **On-Campus Highlights:** University Center.

ADMISSIONS
Freshman Academic Profile: Average high school GPA 3.9. 14% in top 10% of high school class, 41% in top 25% of high school class, 77% in top 50% of high school class. **Test Scores:** SAT Math middle 50% range 510–600. SAT EBRW middle 50% range 520–620. ACT middle 50% range 20–25. **Basis for Candidate Selection:** *Very important factors include:* rigor of secondary school record, class rank, academic GPA, standardized test scores, level of applicant's interest. *Important factors include:* application essay, recommendation(s), extracurricular activities, talent/ability, character/personal qualities. *Other factors include:* interview, first generation, geographical residence, state residency. **Freshman Admission Requirements:** High school diploma is required and

GED is accepted *Academic units required:* 4 English, 4 math, 3 science, 3 science labs, 2 foreign language, 2 social studies, 1 history, 4 academic electives. *Academic units recommended:* 4 English, 4 math, 3 science, 3 science labs, 2 foreign language, 2 social studies, 1 history, 8 academic electives. **Freshman Admission Statistics:** 19,341 applied, 40% admitted, 29% enrolled. **Transfer Admission Requirements:** College transcript(s), statement of good standing from prior institution(s). Minimum college GPA of 2.0 required. Lowest grade transferable C. **General Admission Information:** Application fee $65. Priority deadline 11/15. Regular application deadline 3/1. Non-fall registration accepted.

COSTS AND FINANCIAL AID

Annual in-state tuition $1,000. Annual out-of-state tuition $5,000. Room and board $9,682. Required fees $3,220. Average book and supplies expense $805. **Required Forms and Deadlines:** FAFSA; Institution's own financial aid form. **Notification of Awards:** Applicants will be notified of awards on a rolling basis beginning 4/1. **Types of Aid:** *Need-based scholarships/grants:* College/university scholarship or grant aid from institutional funds; Federal Pell; Private scholarships; SEOG; State scholarships/grants. *Loans:* Direct PLUS loans; Direct Subsidized Stafford Loans; Direct Unsubsidized Stafford Loans. **Student Employment:** Federal Work-Study Program available. Institutional employment available. **Financial Aid Statistics:** 94% needy freshmen, 91% needy undergrads receive need-based scholarship or grant aid. 3% freshmen, 2% undergrads receive non-need-based scholarship or grant aid. 77% freshmen, 79% undergrads receive need-based self-help aid. 1% freshmen, 1% undergrads receive athletic scholarships. 63% undergrads borrow to pay for school. Average cumulative indebtedness $10,038. **Criteria awarding aid:** *Need-based:* Academics, Minority status. *Non-need-based:* Academics, Art, Athletics, Leadership, Music/drama, State/district residency.

WESTERN COLORADO UNIVERSITY

600 N. Adams, Gunnison, CO 81231
Financial Aid Phone: (970) 943-3085
E-mail: discover@western.edu **CEEB Code:** 4946
Fax: (970) 943-2363 **Website:** www.western.edu **ACT Code:** 536

This public school was founded in 1911. It has a 228 acre campus.

RATINGS

Admissions Selectivity Rating: 75   **Fire Safety Rating:** 96   **Green Rating:** 93

STUDENTS AND FACULTY

Enrollment: 1,899. **Student Body:** 41% female, 59% male, 70% out-of-state, <1% international (7 countries represented). Asian 1%, African American 3%, Caucasian 71%, Hispanic 11%, Native American 1%, Pacific Islander <1%, Two or more races 5%, Race unknown 8%.
Retention and Graduation: 64% freshmen return for sophomore year. 21% freshmen graduate within 4 years. % freshmen graduate within 6 years. 15% grads go on to further study within 1 year. **Faculty:** Student/faculty ratio 18:1. 122 full-time faculty, 84% hold PhDs, 4% are members of minority groups, 43% are women. 0% of classes are taught by teaching assistants.

ACADEMICS

Degrees: Bachelor's; Master's; Post-bachelor's certificate. **Classes:** Most classes have 10–19 students. **Most popular majors:** Biology/Biological Sciences, General; Parks, Recreation and Leisure Studies; Business Administration and Management, General. **Special Study Options:** Accelerated program; Distance learning; Double major; Dual enrollment; Exchange student program (domestic); Honors program; Independent study; Internships; Liberal arts/career combination; Study abroad; Teacher certification program. **Honors programs:** Honors Program--based on the National Collegiate Honors Council-modeled City of Text explores urban environments, while the Partners in the Parks: Black Canyon of the Gunnison course immerses students in the ecosystems of one of America's most amazing national parks. **Disability Services offered:** Note-taking services; Reader services; Tape recorders; Tutors. **Career services:** Alumni network; Alumni services; Career assessment; Career/job search classes; Internships; Regional alumni.

FACILITIES

Housing: Apartments for married students; Apartments for single students; Coed dorms; Special housing for disabled students; Theme housing; 80% of campus accessible to physically disabled.

CAMPUS LIFE

Environment: Rural. **Activities:** Campus Ministries; Choral groups; Concert band; Dance; Drama/theater; International Student Organization; Jazz band; Literary magazine; Music ensembles; Pep band; Radio station; Student government; Student newspaper; Symphony orchestra; Television station. 60 registered organizations, 8 honor societies, 5 religious organizations, on campus. **Athletics (Intercollegiate):** *Men:* basketball, cross-country, football, track/field (outdoor), track/field (indoor), wrestling. *Women:* basketball, cross-country, track/field (outdoor), track/field (indoor), volleyball. **On-Campus Highlights:** Unviersity Center—new student center. **Environmental Initiatives:** President's Climate Committment—which is a significant challenge for one of the coldest locations in the nation and the isolated nature of Gunnison.

ADMISSIONS

Freshman Academic Profile: Average high school GPA 3.1. 8% in top 10% of high school class, 25% in top 25% of high school class, 49% in top 50% of high school class. **Test Scores:** SAT Math middle 50% range 500–590. SAT EBRW middle 50% range 500–590. ACT middle 50% range 20–25. **Basis for Candidate Selection:** *Very important factors include:* rigor of secondary school record, class rank, academic GPA, standardized test scores. *Important factors include:* application essay, recommendation(s). *Other factors include:* interview, extracurricular activities, talent/ability, character/personal qualities, first generation, alumni/ae relation, volunteer work, work experience. **Freshman Admission Requirements:** High school diploma is required and GED is accepted. **Freshman Admission Statistics:** 1,955 applied, 86% admitted, 27% enrolled. **Transfer Admission Requirements:** College transcript(s). Minimum college GPA of 2.0 required. Lowest grade transferable C. **General Admission Information:** Application fee $30. Priority deadline 6/1. Non-fall registration accepted.

COSTS AND FINANCIAL AID

Required Forms and Deadlines: FAFSA. **Notification of Awards:** Applicants will be notified of awards on a rolling basis beginning 3/15. **Types of Aid:** *Need-based scholarships/grants:* College/university scholarship or grant aid from institutional funds; Federal Pell; Private scholarships; SEOG; State scholarships/grants. *Loans:* Direct PLUS loans; Direct Subsidized Stafford Loans; Direct Unsubsidized Stafford Loans. **Student Employment:** Federal Work-Study Program available. Institutional employment available. **Financial Aid Statistics:** 93% needy freshmen, 91% needy undergrads receive need-based scholarship or grant aid. 93% freshmen, 46% undergrads receive non-need-based scholarship or grant aid. 69% freshmen, 72% undergrads receive need-based self-help aid. 7% freshmen, 5% undergrads receive athletic scholarships. 85% freshmen, 75% undergrads receive any aid. 60% undergrads borrow to pay for school. Average cumulative indebtedness $24,187. **Criteria awarding aid:** *Non-need-based:* Academics, Art, Athletics, Leadership, Music/drama.

WESTERN CONNECTICUT STATE UNIVERSITY

Undergraduate Admissions Office, Danbury, CT 06810-6855
Phone: 203-837-9000 **Financial Aid Phone:** 203-837-8588
E-mail: admissions@wcsu.edu **CEEB Code:** 3350
Fax: 203-837-8338 **Website:** www.wcsu.edu **ACT Code:** 558

This public school was founded in 1903. It has a 364 acre campus.

RATINGS

Admissions Selectivity Rating: 77   **Fire Safety Rating:** 91   **Green Rating:** 60*

STUDENTS AND FACULTY

Enrollment: 4,872. **Student Body:** 52% female, 48% male, 15% out-of-state, <1% international (10 countries represented). Asian 4%, African American 10%, Caucasian 60%, Hispanic 19%, Native American <1%, Pacific Islander <1%, Two or more races 3%, Race unknown 3%.
Retention and Graduation: 74% freshmen return for sophomore year. 20% freshmen graduate within 4 years. 44% freshmen graduate within 6 years. **Faculty:** Student/faculty ratio 13:1. 223 full-time faculty, 91% hold PhDs, 20% are members of minority groups, 51% are women. 0% of classes are taught by teaching assistants.

ACADEMICS

Degrees: Associate; Bachelor's; Doctoral degree—professional practice; Master's; Post-master's certificate. **Classes:** Most classes have 20–29 students. Most lab/discussion sessions have 10–19 students. **Most popular majors:** Elementary Education and Teaching; Homeland Security, Law Enforcement,

Firefighting And Related Protective Services; Criminal Justice/Police Science. **Special Study Options:** Cooperative education program; Cross-registration; Distance learning; Dual enrollment; Honors program; Independent study; Internships; Student-designed major; Study abroad; Teacher certification program. **Honors programs:** University Scholars Program. **Disability Services offered:** Note-taking services; Reader services; Tape recorders; Tutors. **Career services:** Career assessment; Career/job search classes; Internships.

FACILITIES

Housing: Apartments for single students; Coed dorms; 100% of campus accessible to physically disabled. **Special Academic Facilities/Equipment:** Language lab, observatory, electron microscope, nature preserve, computer-enhanced classrooms, business library, Jane Goodall Institute.

CAMPUS LIFE

Environment: City. **Activities:** Campus Ministries; Choral groups; Concert band; Dance; Drama/theater; International Student Organization; Jazz band; Literary magazine; Music ensembles; Musical theater; Opera; Pep band; Radio station; Student government; Student newspaper; Symphony orchestra. 79 registered organizations, 8 honor societies, 3 religious organizations, 3 fraternities, 4 sororities on campus. **Athletics (Intercollegiate):** *Men:* baseball, basketball, football, lacrosse, soccer, tennis. *Women:* basketball, field hockey, lacrosse, soccer, softball, swimming, tennis, volleyball. **On-Campus Highlights:** Visual and Performing Arts Center. **Environmental Initiatives:** Think Green: Go Blue recycling efforts (with distribution campus wide of an instruction brochure).

ADMISSIONS

Freshman Academic Profile: Average high school GPA 3.1. 7% in top 10% of high school class, 23% in top 25% of high school class, 59% in top 50% of high school class. 90% from public high schools. **Test Scores:** SAT Math middle 50% range 500–600. SAT EBRW middle 50% range 520–620. ACT middle 50% range 20–25. **Basis for Candidate Selection:** *Very important factors include:* rigor of secondary school record, standardized test scores, talent/ability. *Important factors include:* class rank, academic GPA, extracurricular activities. *Other factors include:* application essay, recommendation(s), interview, character/personal qualities, alumni/ae relation, state residency, racial/ethnic status, volunteer work, work experience. **Freshman Admission Requirements:** High school diploma is required and GED is accepted. *Academic units required:* 4 English, 3 math, 2 science, 2 science labs, 2 foreign language, 1 social studies, 1 history. **Freshman Admission Statistics:** 5,375 applied, 79% admitted, 21% enrolled. **Transfer Admission Requirements:** College transcript(s). Minimum college GPA of 2.0 required. Lowest grade transferable C-. **General Admission Information:** Application fee $50. Regular application deadline 4/1. Non-fall registration accepted. Admission may be deferred for a maximum of 1 year.

COSTS AND FINANCIAL AID

Annual in-state tuition $5,642. Annual out-of-state tuition $16,882. Room and board $13,072. Required fees $5,217. Average book and supplies expense $1,300. **Required Forms and Deadlines:** FAFSA; Institution's own financial aid form. **Notification of Awards:** Applicants will be notified of awards on a rolling basis beginning 4/15. **Types of Aid:** *Need-based scholarships/grants:* College/university scholarship or grant aid from institutional funds; Federal Pell; Private scholarships; SEOG; State scholarships/grants. *Loans:* Direct PLUS loans; Direct Subsidized Stafford Loans; Direct Unsubsidized Stafford Loans. **Student Employment:** Federal Work-Study Program available. Institutional employment available. **Financial Aid Statistics:** 90% needy freshmen, 87% needy undergrads receive need-based scholarship or grant aid. 22% freshmen, 17% undergrads receive non-need-based scholarship or grant aid. 74% freshmen, 95% undergrads receive need-based self-help aid. 0% freshmen, 0% undergrads receive athletic scholarships. 62% freshmen, 70% undergrads receive any aid. 74% undergrads borrow to pay for school. Average cumulative indebtedness $35,177. **Criteria awarding aid:** *Need-based:* Academics, Art, Minority status, Music/drama *Non-need-based:* Academics, Art, Minority status, Music/drama.

WESTERN ILLINOIS UNIVERSITY

1 University Circle, Sherman Hall 115, Macomb, IL 61455-1390
Phone: 309-298-3157 **Financial Aid Phone:** 309-298-2446
E-mail: admissions@wiu.edu **CEEB Code:** 1900
Fax: 309-298-3111 **Website:** http://www.wiu.edu **ACT Code:** 1158

This public school was founded in 1899. It has a 1050 acre campus.

RATINGS

Admissions Selectivity Rating: 82   **Fire Safety Rating:** 89   **Green Rating:** 65

STUDENTS AND FACULTY

Enrollment: 6,754. **Student Body:** 52% female, 48% male, 11% out-of-state, 1% international (61 countries represented). Asian 1%, African American 21%, Caucasian 59%, Hispanic 13%, Native American <1%, Pacific Islander <1%, Two or more races 3%, Race unknown 2%.
Retention and Graduation: 65% freshmen return for sophomore year. 30% freshmen graduate within 4 years. 50% freshmen graduate within 6 years.
Faculty: Student/faculty ratio 13:1. 527 full-time faculty, 74% hold PhDs, 13% are members of minority groups, 46% are women. 3% of classes are taught by teaching assistants.

ACADEMICS

Degrees: Bachelor's; Doctoral degree research/scholarship; Master's; Post-bachelor's certificate; Post-master's certificate. **Classes:** Most classes have 10–19 students. Most lab/discussion sessions have 10–19 students. **Most popular majors:** Biology/Biological Sciences, General; Psychology, General; Criminal Justice/Law Enforcement Administration. **Special Study Options:** Distance learning; Double major; Dual enrollment; English as a Second Language (ESL); External degree program; Honors program; Independent study; Internships; Student-designed major; Study abroad; Teacher certification program; Weekend college. **Honors programs:** Illinois Centennial Honors College http://www.wiu.edu/centennial_honors_college/. **Combined degree programs:** BA/MA. **Disability Services offered:** Note-taking services; Reader services; Tape recorders; Tutors. **Career services:** Alumni network; Alumni services; Career assessment; Career/job search classes; Internships.

FACILITIES

Housing: Apartments for married students; Apartments for single students; Coed dorms; Cooperative housing; Fraternity/sorority housing; Special housing for disabled students; Special housing for international students; Theme housing; Wellness housing; 95% of campus accessible to physically disabled. **Special Academic Facilities/Equipment:** Art gallery, Geology museum, electron microscope, multicultural center. **Campus Network:** 100% of classrooms, 100% of dorms, 100% of student union, 100% of libraries, 100% of dining areas, 30% of common outdoor areas have wireless network access.

CAMPUS LIFE

Environment: Village. **Activities:** Campus Ministries; Choral groups; Concert band; Dance; Drama/theater; International Student Organization; Jazz band; Literary magazine; Marching band; Model UN; Music ensembles; Musical theater; Opera; Pep band; Radio station; Student government; Student newspaper; Student-run film society; Symphony orchestra; Television station. 273 registered organizations, 15 honor societies, 11 religious organizations, 16 fraternities, 10 sororities on campus. **Athletics (Intercollegiate):** *Men:* baseball, basketball, cross-country, diving, football, golf, soccer, swimming, tennis, track/field (outdoor), track/field (indoor). *Women:* basketball, cheerleading, cross-country, diving, golf, soccer, softball, swimming, tennis, track/field (outdoor), track/field (indoor), volleyball. **On-Campus Highlights:** University Union. **Environmental Initiatives:** WIU has received numerous energy efficiency grants from the Illinois Department of Commerce and Economic Opportunity, which total over $2,400,000 in the last six years.

ADMISSIONS

Freshman Academic Profile: Average high school GPA 3.3. 11% in top 10% of high school class, 32% in top 25% of high school class, 69% in top 50% of high school class. 91% from public high schools. **Test Scores:** SAT Math middle 50% range 460–550. SAT EBRW middle 50% range 470–560. ACT middle 50% range 18–23. **Basis for Candidate Selection:** *Very important factors include:* academic GPA, standardized test scores. *Other factors include:* rigor of secondary school record. **Freshman Admission Requirements:** High school diploma is required and GED is accepted. *Academic units required:* 4 English, 3 math, 3 science, 3 social studies, 2 academic electives. **Freshman Admission Statistics:** 9,151 applied, 59% admitted, 17% enrolled. **Transfer Admission Requirements:** College transcript(s). Minimum college GPA of

2.0 required. Lowest grade transferable D. **General Admission Information:** Application fee $30. Non-fall registration accepted.

COSTS AND FINANCIAL AID

Annual in-state tuition $8,883. Annual out-of-state tuition $8,883. Room and board $9,630. Required fees $2,783. Average book and supplies expense $1,200. **Required Forms and Deadlines:** FAFSA. **Notification of Awards:** Applicants will be notified of awards on a rolling basis beginning 1/15. **Types of Aid:** *Need-based scholarships/grants:* College/university scholarship or grant aid from institutional funds; Federal Pell; Private scholarships; SEOG; State scholarships/grants. *Loans:* Direct PLUS loans; Direct Subsidized Stafford Loans; Direct Unsubsidized Stafford Loans. **Student Employment:** Federal Work-Study Program available. Institutional employment available. **Financial Aid Statistics:** 80% needy freshmen, 73% needy undergrads receive need-based scholarship or grant aid. 57% freshmen, 51% undergrads receive non-need-based scholarship or grant aid. 87% freshmen, 87% undergrads receive need-based self-help aid. 5% freshmen, 5% undergrads receive athletic scholarships. 90% freshmen, 79% undergrads receive any aid. 86% undergrads borrow to pay for school. Average cumulative indebtedness $31,326. **Criteria awarding aid:** *Non-need-based:* Academics, Alumni affiliation, Art, Athletics, Leadership, Minority status, Music/drama.

WESTERN KENTUCKY UNIVERSITY

Potter Hall 117, Bowling Green, KY 42101-1020
Phone: 270-745-2551 **Financial Aid Phone:** 270-745-2755
E-mail: admission@wku.edu **CEEB Code:** 1901
Fax: 270-745-6133 **Website:** www.wku.edu **ACT Code:** 1562

This public school was founded in 1906. It has a 235 acre campus.

RATINGS

Admissions Selectivity Rating: 74   **Fire Safety Rating:** 98   **Green Rating:** 91

STUDENTS AND FACULTY

Enrollment: 13,139. **Student Body:** 59% female, 41% male, 24% out-of-state, 2% international (50 countries represented). Asian 2%, African American 9%, Caucasian 79%, Hispanic 4%, Native American <1%, Pacific Islander <1%, Two or more races 3%, Race unknown <1%.
Retention and Graduation: 73% freshmen return for sophomore year. 31% freshmen graduate within 4 years. 52% freshmen graduate within 6 years.
Faculty: Student/faculty ratio 18:1. 681 full-time faculty, 79% hold PhDs, 17% are members of minority groups, 51% are women. 1% of classes are taught by teaching assistants.

ACADEMICS

Degrees: Associate; Bachelor's; Certificate; Doctoral degree—other; Doctoral degree—professional practice; Master's; Post-bachelor's certificate; Post-master's certificate. **Classes:** Most classes have 10–19 students. Most lab/discussion sessions have 20–29 students. **Most popular majors:** Registered Nursing/Registered Nurse; Business Administration and Management, General; Biology/Biological Sciences, General. **Special Study Options:** Accelerated program; Cooperative education program; Distance learning; Double major; Dual enrollment; English as a Second Language (ESL); Honors program; Independent study; Internships; Student-designed major; Study abroad; Teacher certification program; Weekend college. **Honors programs:** Mahurin Honors College at WKU and Gatton Academy of Mathematics and Science. **Combined degree programs:** BA/MA. **Disability Services offered:** Note-taking services; Reader services; Tape recorders; Tutors. **Career services:** Alumni network; Alumni services; Career assessment; Career/job search classes; Internships; Regional alumni.

FACILITIES

Housing: Apartments for married students; Apartments for single students; Coed dorms; Fraternity/sorority housing; Men's dorms; Special housing for international students; Theme housing; Wellness housing; Women's dorms. **Special Academic Facilities/Equipment:** Hardin Planetarium, Bell Observatory and Weather Station, Kentucky Museum, Baker Arboretum, Downing Museum, WKU Farm. **Campus Network:** 100% of classrooms, 100% of dorms, 100% of student union, 100% of libraries, 100% of dining areas, 100% of common outdoor areas have wireless network access.

CAMPUS LIFE

Environment: Town. **Activities:** Campus Ministries; Choral groups; Concert band; Dance; Drama/theater; International Student Organization; Jazz band; Literary magazine; Marching band; Model UN; Music ensembles; Musical theater; Opera; Pep band; Radio station; Student government; Student newspaper; Student-run film society; Symphony orchestra; Television station; Yearbook. 366 registered organizations, 25 honor societies, 35 religious organizations, 19 fraternities, 16 sororities on campus. **Athletics (Intercollegiate):** *Men:* baseball, basketball, cross-country, diving, football, golf, riflery, swimming, tennis, track/field (outdoor), track/field (indoor). *Women:* basketball, cross-country, diving, golf, riflery, soccer, swimming, tennis, track/field (outdoor), track/field (indoor), volleyball. **On-Campus Highlights:** Downing Student Union. **Environmental Initiatives:** Sustainability-oriented staff positions and Sustainability Committee, Education for Sustainability resolution adopted 2010, Sustainability in operations, services, and academics included in 2010–2012 University Strategic Plan.

ADMISSIONS

Freshman Academic Profile: Average high school GPA 3.4. 22% in top 10% of high school class, 45% in top 25% of high school class, 74% in top 50% of high school class. **Test Scores:** SAT Math middle 50% range 490–600. SAT EBRW middle 50% range 500–620. ACT middle 50% range 19–27. **Basis for Candidate Selection:** *Very important factors include:* academic GPA, standardized test scores. **Freshman Admission Requirements:** High school diploma is required and GED is accepted. *Academic units required:* 4 English, 3 math, 3 science, 3 social studies, 7 academic electives, 1 visual/performing arts. *Academic units recommended:* 2 foreign language. **Freshman Admission Statistics:** 8,245 applied, 97% admitted, 34% enrolled. **Transfer Admission Requirements:** College transcript(s), statement of good standing from prior institution(s). Minimum college GPA of 2.0 required. Lowest grade transferable D*. **General Admission Information:** Application fee $45. Regular application deadline 8/1. Non-fall registration accepted.

COSTS AND FINANCIAL AID

Annual in-state tuition $10,802. Annual out-of-state tuition $26,496. Room and board $8,432. Average book and supplies expense $1,000. **Required Forms and Deadlines:** FAFSA. **Notification of Awards:** Applicants will be notified of awards on a rolling basis beginning 3/1. **Types of Aid:** *Need-based scholarships/grants:* College/university scholarship or grant aid from institutional funds; Federal Pell; Private scholarships; SEOG; State scholarships/grants; United Negro College Fund. *Loans:* Direct PLUS loans; Direct Subsidized Stafford Loans; Direct Unsubsidized Stafford Loans. **Student Employment:** Federal Work-Study Program available. Institutional employment available. **Financial Aid Statistics:** 59% needy freshmen, 60% needy undergrads receive need-based scholarship or grant aid. 91% freshmen, 79% undergrads receive non-need-based scholarship or grant aid. 58% freshmen, 65% undergrads receive need-based self-help aid. 2% freshmen, 2% undergrads receive athletic scholarships. 97% freshmen, 89% undergrads receive any aid. 57% undergrads borrow to pay for school. Average cumulative indebtedness $26,803. **Criteria awarding aid:** *Non-need-based:* Academics, Alumni affiliation, Art, Athletics, Job skills, Leadership, Minority status, Music/drama, Religious affiliation, State/district residency.

WESTERN MICHIGAN UNIVERSITY

1903 W Michigan Ave, Kalamazoo, MI 49008-5211
Phone: 269-387-2000 **Financial Aid Phone:** 269-387-6000
E-mail: ask-wmu@wmich.edu **CEEB Code:** 1902
Fax: 269-387-2096 **Website:** https://wmich.edu/ **ACT Code:** 2066

This public school was founded in 1903. It has a 1289 acre campus.

RATINGS

Admissions Selectivity Rating: 76   **Fire Safety Rating:** 88   **Green Rating:** 84

STUDENTS AND FACULTY

Enrollment: 16,801. **Student Body:** 49% female, 51% male, 15% out-of-state, 6% international (70 countries represented). Asian 2%, African American 11%, Caucasian 69%, Hispanic 7%, Native American <1%, Pacific Islander <1%, Two or more races 4%, Race unknown 1%.
Retention and Graduation: 78% freshmen return for sophomore year. 27% freshmen graduate within 4 years. 57% freshmen graduate within 6 years.
Faculty: Student/faculty ratio 16:1. 933 full-time faculty, 77% hold PhDs, 21% are members of minority groups, 47% are women. 11% of classes are taught by teaching assistants.

ACADEMICS

Degrees: Bachelor's; Certificate; Doctoral degree—professional practice; Doctoral degree research/scholarship; Master's; Post-bachelor's certificate; Post-master's certificate. **Classes:** Most classes have 20–29 students. Most lab/discussion sessions have 20–29 students. **Most popular majors:** Health and Medical Administrative Services, Other; Registered Nursing/Registered Nurse; Marketing, Other. **Special Study Options:** Accelerated program; Cooperative education program; Cross-registration; Distance learning; Double major; Dual enrollment; English as a Second Language (ESL); Honors program; Independent study; Internships; Student-designed major; Study abroad; Teacher certification program. **Honors programs:** The mission of the Carl and Winifred Lee Honors College is to provide an exceptional undergraduate experience for high achieving students, to inspire in our graduates a thirst for the lifelong pursuit of creative inquiry and discovery, to provide our students with the skill and passion to address critical challenges, and to foster personal responsibility informed by a global perspective. **Combined degree programs:** BA/MA; BA/MEng. **Disability Services offered:** Reader services; Tutors. **Career services:** Alumni network; Career assessment; Career/job search classes; Internships.

FACILITIES

Housing: Apartments for married students; Apartments for single students; Coed dorms; Fraternity/sorority housing; Men's dorms; Special housing for disabled students; Theme housing; Women's dorms; 85% of campus accessible to physically disabled. **Special Academic Facilities/Equipment:** Archives & Regional History Library; Aviation flight simulators; Behavioral research and development center; Business incubator for student entrepreneurs and inventors; Business technology and research park; Center for electron microscopy; Historic farm sustainability living/learning community with permaculture landscape; Nuclear accelerator; Particle accelerator; Pilot plant for manufacturing and printing of paper and fiber recovery; Stock trading room with electronic ticker and terminals. **Campus Network:** 100% of classrooms, 100% of dorms, 100% of student union, 100% of libraries, 100% of dining areas, 10% of common outdoor areas have wireless network access.

CAMPUS LIFE

Environment: City. **Activities:** Campus Ministries; Choral groups; Concert band; Dance; Drama/theater; International Student Organization; Jazz band; Literary magazine; Marching band; Model UN; Music ensembles; Musical theater; Opera; Pep band; Radio station; Student government; Student newspaper; Student-run film society; Symphony orchestra. 418 registered organizations, 17 honor societies, 47 religious organizations, 19 fraternities, 14 sororities on campus. **Athletics (Intercollegiate):** *Men:* baseball, basketball, football, ice hockey, soccer, tennis. *Women:* basketball, cross-country, golf, gymnastics, soccer, softball, tennis, track/field (outdoor), track/field (indoor), volleyball. **On-Campus Highlights:** Bernhard Center. **Environmental Initiatives:** Strategic Planning for Sustainability—Climate Action Plan (2012); University Strategic Plan Implementation utilizing the Sustainability Tracking, Assessment, and Rating System program as an overarching framework for evaluation; Sustainability Across Research & Teaching Survey, Luncheon Series, and Faculty Learning Community; Humanities Center Climate Change Study Group and lecture series; creation of a 7,000 square foot Office for Sustainability building hosting several 2012 events; Office for Sustainability website upgrade: www.wmich.edu/sustainability and http://www.youtube.com/user/WMUSustainability.

ADMISSIONS

Freshman Academic Profile: Average high school GPA 3.5. 13% in top 10% of high school class, 37% in top 25% of high school class, 37% in top 50% of high school class. **Test Scores:** SAT Math middle 50% range 500–600. SAT EBRW middle 50% range 500–610. ACT middle 50% range 19–26. **Basis for Candidate Selection:** *Very important factors include:* academic GPA, standardized test scores. *Important factors include:* rigor of secondary school record. *Other factors include:* application essay, recommendation(s), extracurricular activities. **Freshman Admission Requirements:** High school diploma is required and GED is accepted. *Academic units recommended:* 4 English, 3 math, 3 science, 2 foreign language, 3 social studies. **Freshman Admission Statistics:** 17,689 applied, 80% admitted, 21% enrolled. **Transfer Admission Requirements:** College transcript(s), Minimum college GPA of 2.0 required. Lowest grade transferable C. **General Admission Information:** Application fee $40. Non-fall registration accepted.

COSTS AND FINANCIAL AID

Annual in-state tuition $12,094. Annual out-of-state tuition $15,118. Room and board $10,567. Required fees $923. Average book and supplies expense $987. **Required Forms and Deadlines:** FAFSA. **Notification of Awards:** Applicants will be notified of awards on a rolling basis beginning 12/10. **Types of Aid:** *Need-based scholarships/grants:* College/university scholarship or grant aid from institutional funds; Federal Pell; Private scholarships; SEOG; State scholarships/grants. *Loans:* Direct PLUS loans; Direct Subsidized Stafford Loans; Direct Unsubsidized Stafford Loans. **Student Employment:** Federal Work-Study Program available. Institutional employment available. **Financial Aid Statistics:** 60% needy freshmen, 56% needy undergrads receive need-based scholarship or grant aid. 35% freshmen, 27% undergrads receive non-need-based scholarship or grant aid. 57% freshmen, 55% undergrads receive need-based self-help aid. 2% freshmen, 2% undergrads receive athletic scholarships. 81.5% freshmen, 76.4% undergrads receive any aid. 50% undergrads borrow to pay for school. Average cumulative indebtedness $8,427. **Criteria awarding aid:** *Need-based:* Academics. *Non-need-based:* Academics, Alumni affiliation, Art, Athletics, Music/drama, State/district residency.

WESTERN NEW ENGLAND UNIVERSITY

Admissions Office, Springfield, MA 01119
Phone: 413-782-1321 **Financial Aid Phone:** 413-796-2080
E-mail: learn@wne.edu **CEEB Code:** 3962
Fax: 413-782-1777 **Website:** http://www.wne.edu **ACT Code:** 1930

This private school was founded in 1919. It has a 215 acre campus.

RATINGS

Admissions Selectivity Rating: 76   **Fire Safety Rating:** 71   **Green Rating:** 60*

STUDENTS AND FACULTY

Enrollment: 2,675. **Student Body:** 39% female, 61% male, 48% out-of-state, 3% international (15 countries represented). Asian 3%, African American 4%, Caucasian 75%, Hispanic 9%, Native American <1%, Pacific Islander <1%, Two or more races 3%, Race unknown 3%.
Retention and Graduation: 76% freshmen return for sophomore year. 57% freshmen graduate within 4 years. 65% freshmen graduate within 6 years. 18% grads go on to further study within 1 year. 26% grads pursue arts and sciences degrees. <1% grads pursue law degrees. 14% grads pursue business degrees. <1% grads pursue medical degrees. **Faculty:** Student/faculty ratio 13:1. 225 full-time faculty, 86% hold PhDs, 8% are members of minority groups, 44% are women. 1% of classes are taught by teaching assistants.

ACADEMICS

Degrees: Associate; Bachelor's; Certificate; Doctoral degree—professional practice; Doctoral degree research/scholarship; Master's; Post-bachelor's certificate. **Classes:** Most classes have 10–19 students. Most lab/discussion sessions have 10–19 students. **Most popular majors:** Mechanical Engineering; Psychology, General; Accounting. **Special Study Options:** Accelerated program; Cross-registration; Distance learning; Double major; Dual enrollment; Exchange student program (domestic); Honors program; Independent study; Internships; Liberal arts/career combination; Study abroad; Teacher certification program. **Honors programs:** The Honors Program at Western New England University gives academically qualified and motivated students the opportunity to join a community of like students and participate in challenging courses taught by some of the University's best faculty. Honors students generally take one honors course per semester for their first three years and work on a senior honors project during their final year. **Combined degree programs:** BA/JD; BA/MEng. **Disability Services offered:** Note-taking services; Reader services; Tape recorders. **Career services:** Alumni network; Career assessment; Internships.

FACILITIES

Housing: Apartments for married students; Coed dorms; Special housing for disabled students; Theme housing. **Special Academic Facilities/Equipment:** Art Gallery; Math, Writing and Science Centers.

CAMPUS LIFE

Environment: City. **Activities:** Campus Ministries; Choral groups; Concert band; Dance; Drama/theater; International Student Organization; Jazz band; Literary magazine; Model UN; Music ensembles; Musical theater; Pep band; Radio station; Student government; Student newspaper; Student-run film society; Television station; Yearbook. 70 registered organizations, 14 honor societies, 6 religious organizations on campus. **Athletics (Intercollegiate):** *Men:* baseball, basketball, cross-country, football, golf, ice hockey, lacrosse, soccer, tennis, wrestling. *Women:* basketball, cross-country, field hockey, lacrosse, soccer, softball, swimming, tennis, volleyball. **On-Campus Highlights:** Alumni Healthful Living Center.

ADMISSIONS

Freshman Academic Profile: Average high school GPA 3.6. 22% in top 10% of high school class, 52% in top 25% of high school class, 80% in top 50% of high school class. 91% from public high schools. **Test Scores:** SAT Math middle 50% range 540–622. SAT EBRW middle 50% range 540–620. ACT middle 50% range 23–28. **Basis for Candidate Selection:** *Very important factors include:* academic GPA. *Important factors include:* rigor of secondary school record. *Other factors include:* class rank, application essay, standardized test scores, recommendation(s), interview, extracurricular activities, talent/ability, character/personal qualities, volunteer work, work experience. **Freshman Admission Requirements:** High school diploma is required and GED is accepted. *Academic units required:* 4 English, 2 math, 1 science, 1 science labs, 1 social studies, 1 history. *Academic units recommended:* 4 English, 4 math, 2 science, 2 science labs, 2 foreign language, 2 social studies, 2 history. **Freshman Admission Statistics:** 6,862 applied, 85% admitted, 12% enrolled. **Transfer Admission Requirements:** High school transcript, college transcript(s). Minimum college GPA of 2.3 required. Lowest grade transferable C-. **General Admission Information:** Application fee $40. Non-fall registration accepted. Admission may be deferred for a maximum of 12 months.

COSTS AND FINANCIAL AID

Annual tuition $35,454. Room and board $14,034. Required fees $2,538. Average book and supplies expense $1,305. **Required Forms and Deadlines:** FAFSA. **Notification of Awards:** Applicants will be notified of awards on a rolling basis beginning 12/15. **Types of Aid:** *Need-based scholarships/grants:* College/university scholarship or grant aid from institutional funds; Federal Pell; Private scholarships; SEOG; State scholarships/grants. *Loans:* Direct PLUS loans; Direct Subsidized Stafford Loans; Direct Unsubsidized Stafford Loans. **Student Employment:** Federal Work-Study Program available. Institutional employment available. **Financial Aid Statistics:** 100% needy freshmen, 100% needy undergrads receive need-based scholarship or grant aid. 12% freshmen, 10% undergrads receive non-need-based scholarship or grant aid. 99% freshmen, 95% undergrads receive need-based self-help aid. 0% freshmen, 0% undergrads receive athletic scholarships. 98% freshmen, 97% undergrads receive any aid. 81% undergrads borrow to pay for school. Average cumulative indebtedness $46,591. **Criteria awarding aid:** *Need-based:* Academics, Alumni affiliation, Leadership, Minority status. *Non-need-based:* Academics, Music/drama.

WESTERN OREGON UNIVERSITY

345 N Monmouth Avenue, Monmouth, OR 97361
Phone: 503-838-8211 **Financial Aid Phone:** 877-877-1593
E-mail: wolfgram@wou.edu **CEEB Code:** 4585
Fax: 503-838-8067 **Website:** www.wou.edu **ACT Code:** 3480

This public school was founded in 1856. It has a 157 acre campus.

RATINGS

Admissions Selectivity Rating: 66   **Fire Safety Rating:** 95   **Green Rating:** 60*

STUDENTS AND FACULTY

Enrollment: 4,696. **Student Body:** 62% female, 38% male, 23% out-of-state, 6% international (19 countries represented). Asian 5%, African American 4%, Caucasian 61%, Hispanic 16%, Native American 2%, Pacific Islander 3%, Two or more races <1%, Race unknown 4%.
Retention and Graduation: 72% freshmen return for sophomore year. 22% freshmen graduate within 4 years. 39% freshmen graduate within 6 years. **Faculty:** Student/faculty ratio 15:1. 287 full-time faculty, 71% hold PhDs, 14% are members of minority groups, 54% are women. 0% of classes are taught by teaching assistants.

ACADEMICS

Degrees: Associate; Bachelor's; Certificate; Master's; Post-bachelor's certificate. **Most popular majors:** Business/Commerce, General; Social Sciences, General; Teacher Education, Multiple Levels. **Special Study Options:** Cross-registration; Distance learning; Double major; Dual enrollment; Exchange student program (domestic); Honors program; Independent study; Internships; Student-designed major; Study abroad; Teacher certification program. **Honors programs:** WOU Honors Program. **Disability Services offered:** Note-taking services; Reader services; Tape recorders; Tutors. **Career services:** Career/job search classes; Internships.

FACILITIES

Housing: Apartments for married students; Apartments for single students; Coed dorms; Men's dorms; Special housing for disabled students; Special housing for international students; Theme housing; Wellness housing; Women's dorms; 95% of campus accessible to physically disabled.

CAMPUS LIFE

Environment: Village. **Activities:** Campus Ministries; Choral groups; Concert band; Dance; Drama/theater; International Student Organization; Jazz band; Literary magazine; Marching band; Model UN; Music ensembles; Musical theater; Pep band; Radio station; Student government; Student newspaper. 50 registered organizations, 4 honor societies, 6 religious organizations on campus. **Athletics (Intercollegiate):** *Men:* baseball, basketball, cheerleading, cross-country, football, track/field (outdoor). *Women:* basketball, cheerleading, cross-country, soccer, softball, track/field (outdoor), volleyball. **On-Campus Highlights:** Wayne and Lynn Hamersly Library. **Environmental Initiatives:** Paper recyling.

ADMISSIONS

Freshman Academic Profile: Average high school GPA 3.3. 95% from public high schools. **Basis for Candidate Selection:** *Very important factors include:* rigor of secondary school record, class rank, academic GPA. *Important factors include:* recommendation(s), talent/ability. *Other factors include:* application essay, standardized test scores, character/personal qualities, first generation. **Freshman Admission Requirements:** High school diploma is required and GED is accepted. *Academic units required:* 4 English, 3 math, 2 foreign language, 3 social studies. *Academic units recommended:* 4 English, 3 math, 2 foreign language, 3 social studies. **Freshman Admission Statistics:** 2,942 applied, 81% admitted, 34% enrolled. **Transfer Admission Requirements:** College transcript(s). Minimum college GPA of 2.0 required. Lowest grade transferable D-. **General Admission Information:** Application fee $60. Non-fall registration accepted.

COSTS AND FINANCIAL AID

Annual in-state tuition $7,440. Annual out-of-state tuition $23,895. Room and board $10,203. Required fees $1,758. Average book and supplies expense $1,299. **Required Forms and Deadlines:** FAFSA. **Notification of Awards:** Applicants will be notified of awards on a rolling basis beginning 3/15. **Types of Aid:** *Need-based scholarships/grants:* College/university scholarship or grant aid from institutional funds; Federal Pell; Private scholarships; SEOG; State scholarships/grants; United Negro College Fund. *Loans:* Direct PLUS loans; Direct Subsidized Stafford Loans; Direct Unsubsidized Stafford Loans. **Student Employment:** Federal Work-Study Program available. **Financial Aid Statistics:** 65% freshmen, 58% undergrads receive any aid. **Criteria awarding aid:** *Need-based:* Academics. *Non-need-based:* Academics, Athletics, Leadership, Music/drama.

WESTERN UNIVERSITY

Western Student Services Bldg., RM 1150B, London, ON N6A 3K7
Phone: 519-661-2100 **Financial Aid Phone:** 519-661-2100
E-mail: welcome@uwo.ca
Fax: 519-661-3710 **Website:** www.westernu.ca **ACT Code:** 4837

This public school was founded in 1878. It has a 1200 acre campus.

RATINGS

Admissions Selectivity Rating: 69   **Fire Safety Rating:** 82   **Green Rating:** 66

STUDENTS AND FACULTY

Enrollment: 23,050. **Student Body:** 57% female, 43% male.
Faculty: 1,406 full-time faculty, 0% hold PhDs, 0% are members of minority groups, 36% are women.

ACADEMICS

Degrees: Bachelor's; Certificate; Diploma; Doctoral degree research/scholarship; Master's; Post-bachelor's certificate. **Special Study Options:** Accelerated program; Cooperative education program; Cross-registration; Distance learning; Double major; Dual enrollment; English as a Second Language (ESL); Exchange student program (domestic); Honors program; Independent study; Internships; Liberal arts/career combination; Student-designed major; Study abroad; Teacher certification program. **Honors programs:** Scholar's Electives—http://success.uwo.ca/index.cfm/scholars/scholars-electives/. **Combined degree programs:** BA/JD. **Disability Services**

offered: Note-taking services; Reader services; Tape recorders. **Career services:** Alumni services; Career assessment; Career/job search classes; Internships.

FACILITIES

Housing: Apartments for married students; Apartments for single students; Coed dorms; Men's dorms; Special housing for disabled students; Special housing for international students; Theme housing; Wellness housing; Women's dorms; 93.5% of campus accessible to physically disabled. **Special Academic Facilities/Equipment:** McIntosh Gallery (http://mcintoshgallery. ca/); Hume Cronyn Memorial Observatory (http://cronyn.uwo.ca); Western Student Recreation Centre (http://www.campusrec.uwo.ca); University Hospital—on-campus teaching hospital; The Wind, Engineering and Environment Institute—World's first hexagonal wind tunnel (http://www. eng.uwo.ca/windeee/); Map and Data Centre (https://www.lib.uwo.ca/ madgic); The Sherwood Fox Arboretum (https://www.uwo.ca/biology/research/ biology_facilities/arboretum.html); LEED Gold Certified Claudette Mackay-Lassonde Pavilion (https://www.eng.uwo.ca/departments-units/claudette-mackay-lassonde-pavilion/); Propel—Entrepreneurship centre and student business incubator (http://propel.uwo.ca/); Wellness Education Centre—central hub for students to ask questions and learn about the many health and wellness resources available on and off campus (includes Nutritionist and Sexual Violence Prevention Education)—(https://www.uwo.ca/health/wec/index. html).

CAMPUS LIFE

Environment: Metropolis. **Activities:** Campus Ministries; Choral groups; Concert band; Dance; Drama/theater; International Student Organization; Jazz band; Literary magazine; Marching band; Model UN; Music ensembles; Musical theater; Opera; Radio station; Student government; Student newspaper; Student-run film society; Symphony orchestra; Television station. 221 registered organizations, 11 religious organizations, 8 fraternities, 5 sororities on campus. **Athletics (Intercollegiate):** *Men:* badminton, baseball, basketball, crew/rowing, cross-country, curling, fencing, football, golf, ice hockey, rugby, soccer, squash, swimming, tennis, track/field (outdoor), track/field (indoor), volleyball, water polo, wrestling. *Women:* badminton, basketball, crew/rowing, cross-country, curling, fencing, field hockey, golf, ice hockey, lacrosse, rugby, soccer, squash, swimming, tennis, track/field (outdoor), track/field (indoor), volleyball, wrestling. **On-Campus Highlights:** University Community Centre. **Environmental Initiatives:** Hiring an employee dedicated to sustainability initiatives on campus.

ADMISSIONS

Basis for Candidate Selection: *Very important factors include:* rigor of secondary school record, academic GPA, standardized test scores. *Other factors include:* recommendation(s), extracurricular activities, talent/ability, first generation, volunteer work, work experience. **Freshman Admission Requirements:** High school diploma is required and GED is not accepted. **Freshman Admission Statistics:** 41,053 applied, 56% admitted, 23% enrolled. **Transfer Admission Requirements:** High school transcript, college transcript(s). Lowest grade transferable C. **General Admission Information:** Application fee $156. Priority deadline 3/1. Regular application deadline 6/1. Admission may be deferred for a maximum of 1 year.

COSTS AND FINANCIAL AID

Annual in-state tuition $6,050. Room and board $15,116. Average book and supplies expense $1,500. **Required Forms and Deadlines:** FAFSA; Institution's own financial aid form; State aid form. **Types of Aid:** *Need-based scholarships/grants:* College/university scholarship or grant aid from institutional funds; Private scholarships; State scholarships/grants. **Student Employment:** Institutional employment available. **Criteria awarding aid:** *Need-based:* Academics, Alumni affiliation, Art, Athletics, Leadership, Minority status, Music/drama *Non-need-based:* Academics, Alumni affiliation, Art, Athletics, Leadership, Minority status, Music/drama, State/district residency.

WWU Office of Admissions, Bellingham, WA 98225-9009
Phone: 360-650-3440 **Financial Aid Phone:** 360.650.2422
E-mail: admissions@wwu.edu **CEEB Code:** 4947
Fax: 360-650-7369 **Website:** http://www.wwu.edu/ **ACT Code:** 4490

This public school was founded in 1893. It has a 223 acre campus.

RATINGS

Admissions Selectivity Rating: 76 **Fire Safety Rating:** 86 **Green Rating:** 92

STUDENTS AND FACULTY

Enrollment: 15,098. **Student Body:** 57% female, 43% male, 12% out-of-state, 1% international (42 countries represented). Asian 6%, African American 2%, Caucasian 70%, Hispanic 10%, Native American <1%, Pacific Islander <1%, Two or more races 9%, Race unknown 2%.
Retention and Graduation: 82% freshmen return for sophomore year. 37% freshmen graduate within 4 years. 68% freshmen graduate within 6 years. 21% grads go on to further study within 1 year. 6% grads pursue arts and sciences degrees. 1% grads pursue law degrees. <1% grads pursue business degrees. 1% grads pursue medical degrees. **Faculty:** Student/faculty ratio 19:1. 665 full-time faculty, 88% hold PhDs, 18% are members of minority groups, 47% are women. 1% of classes are taught by teaching assistants.

ACADEMICS

Degrees: Bachelor's; Certificate; Master's; Post-master's certificate. **Classes:** Most classes have 10–19 students. Most lab/discussion sessions have 20–29 students. **Most popular majors:** Computer and Information Sciences, General; Special Education and Teaching, General; Creative Writing. **Special Study Options:** Accelerated program; Cooperative education program; Cross-registration; Distance learning; Double major; English as a Second Language (ESL); Exchange student program (domestic); External degree program; Honors program; Independent study; Internships; Liberal arts/career combination; Student-designed major; Study abroad; Teacher certification program. **Honors programs:** Honors Program features small classes and interaction between students and faculty. It is an exciting opportunity for accomplished students who would like a more intimate college experience within the setting of a larger institution. Honors students are welcome to pursue any academic major, and all students complete a self-designed capstone senior project. **Disability Services offered:** Note-taking services; Reader services; Tape recorders; Tutors. **Career services:** Alumni network; Alumni services; Career assessment; Career/job search classes; Internships; Regional alumni.

FACILITIES

Housing: Apartments for married students; Apartments for single students; Coed dorms; Special housing for disabled students; Special housing for international students; Theme housing; Wellness housing; 100% of campus accessible to physically disabled. **Special Academic Facilities/Equipment:** Outdoor art museum, planetarium, electronic music studio, air pollution lab, motor vehicle research lab, marine lab, wind tunnel, electron microscope, neutron generator lab.

CAMPUS LIFE

Environment: City. **Activities:** Campus Ministries; Choral groups; Concert band; Dance; Drama/theater; International Student Organization; Jazz band; Literary magazine; Model UN; Music ensembles; Musical theater; Opera; Pep band; Radio station; Student government; Student newspaper; Student-run film society; Symphony orchestra. 234 registered organizations, 12 honor societies, 17 religious organizations on campus. **Athletics (Intercollegiate):** *Men:* basketball, cheerleading, crew/rowing, cross-country, golf, soccer, track/field (outdoor), track/field (indoor). *Women:* basketball, cheerleading, crew/rowing, cross-country, golf, soccer, softball, track/field (outdoor), track/field (indoor), volleyball. **On-Campus Highlights:** Viking Union Student Center. **Environmental Initiatives:** WWU Green Energy Fee—The GEF pays for purchase of Renewable Energy Credits to offset 100% of WWU's CO_2 emissions from electrical energy consumption, and pays for approximately $260,000 per year of on-campus sustainability projects. Due to our purchase of Renewable Energy Credits, WWU is ranked 17th by the EPA for largest higher ed. purchase of renewable energy in the U.S. This year's projects include a $167,000 solar array, high-speed hand driers, conversion of parking lot lights to high-efficiency LEDs, a paper towel composting system, and water bottle refilling stations.

ADMISSIONS

Freshman Academic Profile: Average high school GPA 3.4. 21% in top 10% of high school class, 51% in top 25% of high school class, 85% in top 50% of high school class. 91% from public high schools. **Test Scores:** SAT Math middle 50% range 520–630. SAT EBRW middle 50% range 540–650. ACT middle 50% range 22–28. **Basis for Candidate Selection:** *Very important factors include:* rigor of secondary school record, academic GPA, standardized test scores. *Important factors include:* application essay, *Other factors include:* recommendation(s), extracurricular activities, talent/ability, character/personal qualities, first generation, alumni/ae relation, geographical residence, state residency, volunteer work, work experience, level of applicant's interest. **Freshman Admission Requirements:** High school diploma is required and GED is accepted. *Academic units required:* 4 English, 3 math, 2 science, 1 science labs, 2 foreign language, 3 social studies, 0.5 visual/performing arts. **Freshman Admission Statistics:** 10,532 applied, 90% admitted, 33% enrolled. **Transfer Admission Requirements:** College transcript(s), statement of good standing from prior institution(s). Minimum college GPA of 2.0 required. Lowest grade transferable D-. **General Admission Information:** Application fee $60. Regular application deadline 1/31. Non-fall registration accepted. Admission may be deferred for a maximum of 1 year.

COSTS AND FINANCIAL AID

Required Forms and Deadlines: FAFSA. **Notification of Awards:** Applicants will be notified of awards on a rolling basis beginning 3/20. **Types of Aid:** *Need-based scholarships/grants:* College/university scholarship or grant aid from institutional funds; Federal Pell; Private scholarships; SEOG; State scholarships/grants; United Negro College Fund. *Loans:* Direct PLUS loans; Direct Subsidized Stafford Loans; Direct Unsubsidized Stafford Loans. **Student Employment:** Federal Work-Study Program available. Institutional employment available. **Financial Aid Statistics:** 91% needy freshmen, 85% needy undergrads receive need-based scholarship or grant aid. 8% freshmen, 4% undergrads receive non-need-based scholarship or grant aid. 81% freshmen, 85% undergrads receive need-based self-help aid. 1% freshmen, 1% undergrads receive athletic scholarships. 86% freshmen, 66% undergrads receive any aid. 53% undergrads borrow to pay for school. Average cumulative indebtedness $22,466. **Criteria awarding aid:** *Need-based:* Academics, Leadership *Non-need-based:* Academics, Alumni affiliation, Art, Athletics, Job skills, Leadership, Minority status, Music/drama, State/district residency.

WESTFIELD STATE UNIVERSITY

Westfield State University, Westfield, MA 01086-1630
Phone: 413-572-5218 **Financial Aid Phone:** 413-572-8541
E-mail: admissions@westfield.ma.edu **CEEB Code:** 3523
Fax: 413-572-0520 **Website:** www.westfield.ma.edu **ACT Code:** 1912

This public school was founded in 1839. It has a 227 acre campus.

RATINGS

Admissions Selectivity Rating: 75   **Fire Safety Rating:** 87   **Green Rating:** 72

STUDENTS AND FACULTY

Enrollment: 4,779. **Student Body:** 55% female, 45% male, 8% out-of-state, <1% international (12 countries represented). Asian 2%, African American 5%, Caucasian 75%, Hispanic 11%, Native American <1%, Pacific Islander <1%, Two or more races 3%, Race unknown 4%.
Retention and Graduation: 72% freshmen return for sophomore year. 50% freshmen graduate within 4 years. 61% freshmen graduate within 6 years.
Faculty: Student/faculty ratio 17:1. 236 full-time faculty, 92% hold PhDs, 20% are members of minority groups, 51% are women. 0% of classes are taught by teaching assistants.

ACADEMICS

Degrees: Bachelor's; Master's; Post-bachelor's certificate. **Classes:** Most classes have 20–29 students. Most lab/discussion sessions have 10–19 students. **Most popular majors:** Liberal Arts and Sciences/Liberal Studies; Criminal Justice/Safety Studies; Business/Commerce, General. **Special Study Options:** Cross-registration; Distance learning; Double major; Dual enrollment; Exchange student program (domestic); Honors program; Independent study; Internships; Student-designed major; Study abroad; Teacher certification program. **Honors programs:** http://www.westfield.ma.edu/prospective-students/academics/academic-resources/honors-program/. **Combined degree programs:** BA/JD. **Disability Services offered:** Note-taking services; Reader services; Tutors.

Career services: Alumni network; Alumni services; Career assessment; Career/job search classes; Internships.

FACILITIES

Housing: Apartments for single students; Coed dorms; Special housing for disabled students; Special housing for international students; Theme housing; Wellness housing; 75% of campus accessible to physically disabled. **Special Academic Facilities/Equipment:** Art gallery, language lab, electron microscope, television studio, GIS laboratory.

CAMPUS LIFE

Environment: Town. **Activities:** Campus Ministries; Choral groups; Concert band; Dance; Drama/theater; International Student Organization; Jazz band; Literary magazine; Model UN; Music ensembles; Musical theater; Pep band; Radio station; Student government; Student newspaper; Symphony orchestra; Television station; Yearbook. 98 registered organizations, 5 religious organizations on campus. **Athletics (Intercollegiate):** *Men:* baseball, basketball, cross-country, football, golf, soccer, track/field (outdoor). *Women:* basketball, cheerleading, cross-country, field hockey, soccer, softball, swimming, volleyball. **On-Campus Highlights:** Ely Library. **Environmental Initiatives:** RecycleMania: participated in the targeted paper competition in 2015.

ADMISSIONS

Freshman Academic Profile: Average high school GPA 3.2. 8% in top 10% of high school class, 25% in top 25% of high school class, 60% in top 50% of high school class. **Test Scores:** SAT Math middle 50% range 490–570. SAT EBRW middle 50% range 490–580. ACT middle 50% range 18–24. **Basis for Candidate Selection:** *Very important factors include:* rigor of secondary school record, academic GPA, standardized test scores. *Other factors include:* application essay, recommendation(s), extracurricular activities, talent/ability, character/personal qualities, volunteer work, work experience, level of applicant's interest. **Freshman Admission Requirements:** High school diploma is required and GED is accepted. *Academic units required:* 4 English, 4 math, 3 science, 2 science labs, 2 foreign language, 1 social studies, 1 history, 2 academic electives. **Freshman Admission Statistics:** 4,455 applied, 87% admitted, 27% enrolled. **Transfer Admission Requirements:** College transcript(s). Minimum college GPA of 2.0 required. Lowest grade transferable C-. **General Admission Information:** Application fee $50. Regular application deadline 3/1. Non-fall registration accepted. Admission may be deferred for a maximum of 1 semester.

COSTS AND FINANCIAL AID

Annual in-state tuition $970. Annual out-of-state tuition $7,050. Room and board $11,453. Required fees $9,879. Average book and supplies expense $1,142. **Required Forms and Deadlines:** FAFSA. **Notification of Awards:** Applicants will be notified of awards on a rolling basis beginning 2/1. **Types of Aid:** *Need-based scholarships/grants:* College/university scholarship or grant aid from institutional funds; Federal Pell; Private scholarships; SEOG; State scholarships/grants. *Loans:* Direct PLUS loans; Direct Subsidized Stafford Loans; Direct Unsubsidized Stafford Loans. **Student Employment:** Federal Work-Study Program available. Institutional employment available. **Financial Aid Statistics:** 92% needy freshmen, 93% needy undergrads receive need-based scholarship or grant aid. 21% freshmen, 10% undergrads receive non-need-based scholarship or grant aid. 82% freshmen, 86% undergrads receive need-based self-help aid. 0% freshmen, 0% undergrads receive athletic scholarships. 55% freshmen, 58% undergrads receive any aid. 81% undergrads borrow to pay for school. Average cumulative indebtedness $24,121. **Criteria awarding aid:** *Non-need-based:* Academics.

WESTMINSTER COLLEGE (MO)

Champ Auditorium, Westminster College, Fulton, MO 65251
Phone: 573-592-5251 **Financial Aid Phone:** (800) 475-3361
E-mail: admissions@westminster-mo.edu **CEEB Code:** 6937
Fax: 573-592-5255 **Website:** http://www.westminster-mo.edu/ **ACT Code:** 2392

This private school, affiliated with the Presbyterian Church, was founded in 1851. It has a 86 acre campus.

RATINGS

Admissions Selectivity Rating: 75   **Fire Safety Rating:** 87   **Green Rating:** 60*

STUDENTS AND FACULTY

Enrollment: 764. **Student Body:** 44% female, 56% male, 19% out-of-state, 6% international (69 countries represented). Asian 2%, African American 7%,

Caucasian 70%, Hispanic 4%, Native American 2%, Pacific Islander 0%, Two or more races 0%, Race unknown 10%.
Retention and Graduation: 73% freshmen return for sophomore year. 30% grads go on to further study within 1 year. 10% grads pursue arts and sciences degrees. 4% grads pursue law degrees. 6% grads pursue business degrees. 3% grads pursue medical degrees. **Faculty:** Student/faculty ratio 11:1. 46 full-time faculty, 96% hold PhDs, 4% are members of minority groups, 41% are women. 0% of classes are taught by teaching assistants.

ACADEMICS
Degrees: Bachelor's. **Classes:** Most classes have 10–19 students. **Most popular majors:** Business/Commerce, General; Biology/Biological Sciences, General; Political Science and Government, General. **Special Study Options:** Cooperative education program; Cross-registration; Distance learning; Double major; Dual enrollment; English as a Second Language (ESL); Exchange student program (domestic); Honors program; Independent study; Internships; Liberal arts/career combination; Student-designed major; Study abroad; Teacher certification program. **Honors programs:** The new Westminster College Honors Program is exciting for high achieving students, providing high impact, deep learning opportunities. Designed for a limited number of qualified students, the Honors Program includes a highly specialized, dynamic honors curriculum. The program includes an array of experiences that develop academic skills, leadership skills, and global perspectives. **Combined degree programs:** BA/MEng. **Disability Services offered:** Note-taking services; Reader services; Tape recorders; Tutors. **Career services:** Alumni services; Career assessment; Career/job search classes; Internships; Regional alumni.

FACILITIES
Housing: Apartments for single students; Coed dorms; Fraternity/sorority housing; Men's dorms; Special housing for disabled students; Theme housing; Women's dorms 70% of campus accessible to physically disabled. **Special Academic Facilities/Equipment:** Winston Churchill Memorial Museum, Coulter Science Center, language lab, NMR spectrometer, laser equipment. **Campus Network:** 100% of classrooms, 100% of dorms, 100% of libraries, 100% of dining areas, have wireless network access.

CAMPUS LIFE
Environment: Village. **Activities:** Campus Ministries; Choral groups; Dance; Drama/theater; International Student Organization; Jazz band; Literary magazine; Model UN; Music ensembles; Pep band; Student government; Student newspaper. 49 registered organizations, 15 honor societies, 2 religious organizations, 6 fraternities, 3 sororities on campus. **Athletics (Intercollegiate):** *Men:* baseball, basketball, cheerleading, cross-country, football, golf, soccer, tennis, track/field (outdoor). *Women:* basketball, cheerleading, cross-country, golf, soccer, softball, tennis, track/field (outdoor), volleyball. **On-Campus Highlights:** Coulter Science Center.

ADMISSIONS
Freshman Academic Profile: Average high school GPA 3.4. 13% in top 10% of high school class, 26% in top 25% of high school class, 70% in top 50% of high school class. 70% from public high schools. **Test Scores:** SAT Math middle 50% range 515–575. SAT EBRW middle 50% range 500–600. ACT middle 50% range 21–26. **Basis for Candidate Selection:** *Very important factors include:* rigor of secondary school record, standardized test scores, character/personal qualities. *Important factors include:* class rank, academic GPA, recommendation(s), extracurricular activities, volunteer work. *Other factors include:* application essay, interview, talent/ability, alumni/ae relation, work experience. **Freshman Admission Requirements:** High school diploma is required and GED is accepted. *Academic units required:* 4 English, 3 math, 2 science, 2 science labs. *Academic units recommended:* 2 foreign language, 2 social studies, 2 academic electives. **Freshman Admission Statistics:** 1,035 applied, 90% admitted, 19% enrolled. **Transfer Admission Requirements:** College transcript(s). Lowest grade transferable C. **General Admission Information:** Non-fall registration accepted. Admission may be deferred for a maximum of 1 year.

COSTS AND FINANCIAL AID
Annual tuition $25,700. Room and board $10,140. Required fees $1,900. Average book and supplies expense $1,100. **Required Forms and Deadlines:** FAFSA. **Notification of Awards:** Applicants will be notified of awards on a rolling basis beginning 3/15. **Types of Aid:** *Need-based scholarships/grants:* College/university scholarship or grant aid from institutional funds; Federal Pell; Private scholarships; SEOG; State scholarships/grants. *Loans:* Direct PLUS loans; Direct Subsidized Stafford Loans; Direct Unsubsidized Stafford Loans. **Student Employment:** Federal Work-Study Program available. Institutional employment available. **Financial Aid Statistics:** 100% needy freshmen, 100% needy undergrads receive need-based scholarship or grant aid. 0% freshmen,

0% undergrads receive non-need-based scholarship or grant aid. 88% freshmen, 88% undergrads receive need-based self-help aid. 0% freshmen, 0% undergrads receive athletic scholarships. 100% freshmen, 98% undergrads receive any aid. 17% undergrads borrow to pay for school. Average cumulative indebtedness $29,573. **Criteria awarding aid:** *Non-need-based:* Academics, Alumni affiliation, Leadership, Minority status, Music/drama, Religious affiliation.

WESTMINSTER COLLEGE (PA)

319 South Market Street, New Wilmington, PA 16172
Phone: 724-946-7100 **Financial Aid Phone:** (724) 946-6171
E-mail: admis@westminster.edu **CEEB Code:** 2975
Fax: 724-946-7171 **Website:** www.westminster.edu **ACT Code:** 2975

This private school, affiliated with the Presbyterian Church, was founded in 1852. It has a 350 acre campus.

RATINGS
Admissions Selectivity Rating: 71   **Fire Safety Rating:** 97   **Green Rating:** 60*

STUDENTS AND FACULTY
Enrollment: 1,171. **Student Body:** 52% female, 48% male, 28% out-of-state, <1% international (1 countries represented). Asian <1%, African American 5%, Caucasian 70%, Hispanic 2%, Native American 1%, Pacific Islander 0%, Two or more races 1%, Race unknown 21%.
Retention and Graduation: 76% freshmen return for sophomore year. 61% freshmen graduate within 4 years. 69% freshmen graduate within 6 years. 21% grads go on to further study within 1 year. 3% grads pursue law degrees. 2% grads pursue business degrees. 3% grads pursue medical degrees. **Faculty:** Student/faculty ratio 11:1. 90 full-time faculty, 90% hold PhDs, 3% are members of minority groups, 48% are women. 0% of classes are taught by teaching assistants.

ACADEMICS
Degrees: Bachelor's; Master's. **Classes:** Most classes have 10–19 students. Most lab/discussion sessions have 10–19 students. **Most popular majors:** Education, General; Biology/Biological Sciences, General; Business Administration and Management, General. **Special Study Options:** Distance learning; Double major; Dual enrollment; Exchange student program (domestic); Honors program; Independent study; Internships; Liberal arts/career combination; Student-designed major; Study abroad; Teacher certification program. **Honors programs:** The College broadly supports the All-College Honors Program, which is a four-year curriculum. Students enter the program in their first-year, and students from all majors are eligible to participate. **Combined degree programs:** BA/MA. **Disability Services offered:** Note-taking services; Reader services; Tape recorders; Tutors. **Career services:** Alumni network; Alumni services; Career assessment; Career/job search classes; Internships; Regional alumni.

FACILITIES
Housing: Coed dorms; Fraternity/sorority housing; Men's dorms; Special housing for disabled students; Theme housing; Women's dorms; 90% of campus accessible to physically disabled. **Special Academic Facilities/Equipment:** On-campus preschool, Moeller pipe organs, planetarium, observatory, electron microscopes, X-ray diffractor, spectrometer.

CAMPUS LIFE
Environment: Village. **Activities:** Campus Ministries; Choral groups; Concert band; Dance; Drama/theater; Jazz band; Literary magazine; Marching band; Model UN; Music ensembles; Musical theater; Opera; Pep band; Radio station; Student government; Student newspaper; Symphony orchestra; Television station; Yearbook. 81 registered organizations, 16 honor societies, 3 religious organizations, 4 fraternities, 5 sororities on campus. **Athletics (Intercollegiate):** *Men:* baseball, basketball, cheerleading, cross-country, football, golf, soccer, swimming, tennis, track/field (outdoor), track/field (indoor). *Women:* basketball, cheerleading, cross-country, golf, soccer, softball, swimming, tennis, track/field (outdoor), track/field (indoor), volleyball. **On-Campus Highlights:** McKelvey Campus Center.

ADMISSIONS
Freshman Academic Profile: Average high school GPA 3.5. 22% in top 10% of high school class, 42% in top 25% of high school class, 75% in top 50% of high school class. 90% from public high schools. **Basis for Candidate Selection:** *Very important factors include:* rigor of secondary school

record, academic GPA. *Important factors include:* class rank, standardized test scores. *Other factors include:* application essay, recommendation(s), extracurricular activities, talent/ability, character/personal qualities, alumni/ae relation, volunteer work, level of applicant's interest. **Freshman Admission Requirements:** High school diploma is required and GED is accepted. *Academic units required:* 4 English, 3 math, 2 science, 2 science labs, 2 foreign language, 2 social studies, 1 academic electives. **Freshman Admission Statistics:** 3,011 applied, 66% admitted, 17% enrolled. **Transfer Admission Requirements:** High school transcript, college transcript(s), essay or personal statement, interview, standardized test scores. Minimum college GPA of 2.5 required. Lowest grade transferable C. **General Admission Information:** Application fee $35. Regular application deadline 5/1. Non-fall registration accepted. Admission may be deferred for a maximum of 1 year.

COSTS AND FINANCIAL AID

Annual tuition $36,700. Room and board $11,450. Required fees $600. Average book and supplies expense $1,700. **Required Forms and Deadlines:** FAFSA; Institution's own financial aid form. **Notification of Awards:** Applicants will be notified of awards on a rolling basis beginning 12/15. **Types of Aid:** *Need-based scholarships/grants:* College/university scholarship or grant aid from institutional funds; Federal Pell; Private scholarships; SEOG; State scholarships/grants. *Loans:* Direct PLUS loans; Direct Subsidized Stafford Loans; Direct Unsubsidized Stafford Loans. **Student Employment:** Federal Work-Study Program available. **Financial Aid Statistics:** 100% needy freshmen, 99% needy undergrads receive need-based scholarship or grant aid. 98% freshmen, 97% undergrads receive non-need-based scholarship or grant aid. 79% freshmen, 78% undergrads receive need-based self-help aid. 0% freshmen, 0% undergrads receive athletic scholarships. 85% undergrads borrow to pay for school. Average cumulative indebtedness $43,241. **Criteria awarding aid:** *Need-based:* Academics. *Non-need-based:* Academics, Alumni affiliation, Leadership, Minority status, Music/drama, Religious affiliation, State/district residency.

WESTMINSTER COLLEGE (UT)

1840 South 1300 East, Salt Lake City, UT 54105
Phone: 801-832-2200 **Financial Aid Phone:** 801-832-2502
E-mail: admission@westminstercollege.edu **CEEB Code:** 4948
Fax: 801-832-3101 **Website:** www.westminstercollege.edu **ACT Code:** 4284

This private school was founded in 1875. It has a 27 acre campus.

RATINGS

Admissions Selectivity Rating: 75   **Fire Safety Rating:** 95   **Green Rating:** 85

STUDENTS AND FACULTY

Enrollment: 1,946. **Student Body:** 60% female, 40% male, 36% out-of-state, 4% international (43 countries represented). Asian 3%, African American 2%, Caucasian 70%, Hispanic 12%, Native American 1%, Pacific Islander <1%, Two or more races 5%, Race unknown 3%.
Retention and Graduation: 82% freshmen return for sophomore year. 47% freshmen graduate within 4 years. 62% freshmen graduate within 6 years. 6% grads go on to further study within 1 year. 1% grads pursue arts and sciences degrees. <1% grads pursue law degrees. 2% grads pursue business degrees. 2% grads pursue medical degrees. **Faculty:** Student/faculty ratio 8:1. 154 full-time faculty, 91% hold PhDs, 13% are members of minority groups, 51% are women. 0% of classes are taught by teaching assistants.

ACADEMICS

Degrees: Bachelor's; Master's; Post-bachelor's certificate. **Classes:** Most classes have 10–19 students. Most lab/discussion sessions have fewer than 10 students. **Special Study Options:** Accelerated program; Cooperative education program; Cross-registration; Distance learning; Double major; Dual enrollment; English as a Second Language (ESL); Honors program; Independent study; Internships; Liberal arts/career combination; Student-designed major; Study abroad; Teacher certification program; Weekend college. **Honors programs:** https://www.westminstercollege.edu/undergraduate/programs/honors. **Disability Services offered:** Note-taking services; Reader services; Tape recorders; Tutors. **Career services:** Alumni network; Alumni services; Career assessment; Career/job search classes; Internships; Regional alumni.

FACILITIES

Housing: Apartments for single students; Coed dorms; Special housing for disabled students; 98% of campus accessible to physically disabled. **Special Academic Facilities/Equipment:** Emma Eccles Jones Conservatory, Gore School of Business, Giovale Library, Meldrum Science Center, Climbing Wall, Converse Hall, Dolores Dore Eccles Health, Wellness, and Athletic Center. **Campus Network:** 100% of classrooms, 100% of dorms, 100% of student union, 100% of libraries, 100% of dining areas, 100% of common outdoor areas have wireless network access.

CAMPUS LIFE

Environment: Metropolis. **Activities:** Campus Ministries; Concert band; Dance; Drama/theater; International Student Organization; Jazz band; Literary magazine; Music ensembles; Musical theater; Opera; Student government; Student newspaper; Student-run film society; Symphony orchestra. 56 registered organizations, 2 honor societies, 5 religious organizations on campus. **Athletics (Intercollegiate):** *Men:* basketball, cross-country, golf, lacrosse, skiing (downhill/Alpine), snowboarding, soccer, track/field (outdoor), track/field (indoor). *Women:* basketball, cross-country, golf, lacrosse, skiing (downhill/Alpine), snowboarding, soccer, track/field (outdoor), track/field (indoor), volleyball. **On-Campus Highlights:** Shaw Student Center. **Environmental Initiatives:** With guidance from the Environmental Center, students completed the STARS assessment in 2010, achieving a Silver rating. Westminster scored particularly well in co-curricular and curricular sustainability efforts.

ADMISSIONS

Freshman Academic Profile: Average high school GPA 3.6. 21% in top 10% of high school class, 44% in top 25% of high school class, 81% in top 50% of high school class. **Test Scores:** SAT Math middle 50% range 540–620. SAT EBRW middle 50% range 540–640. ACT middle 50% range 21–27. **Basis for Candidate Selection:** *Very important factors include:* rigor of secondary school record, academic GPA, application essay, standardized test scores, recommendation(s). *Important factors include:* class rank, interview, extracurricular activities, talent/ability, character/personal qualities. *Other factors include:* first generation, alumni/ae relation, volunteer work, work experience. **Freshman Admission Requirements:** High school diploma is required and GED is accepted. *Academic units required:* 4 English, 2 math, 3 science, 2 foreign language, 2 social studies, 1 history, 2 academic electives. *Academic units recommended:* 4 English, 3 math, 3 science, 3 foreign language, 2 social studies, 1 history, 3 academic electives. **Freshman Admission Statistics:** 1,864 applied, 93% admitted, 25% enrolled. **Transfer Admission Requirements:** High school transcript, college transcript(s), essay or personal statement. Minimum college GPA of 2.5 required. Lowest grade transferable C-. **General Admission Information:** Non-fall registration accepted. Admission may be deferred for a maximum of 2 years.

COSTS AND FINANCIAL AID

Annual tuition $34,464. Room and board $9,810. Required fees $820. Average book and supplies expense $1,000. **Required Forms and Deadlines:** FAFSA; Institution's own financial aid form. **Notification of Awards:** Applicants will be notified of awards on a rolling basis beginning 1/1. **Types of Aid:** *Need-based scholarships/grants:* College/university scholarship or grant aid from institutional funds; Federal Pell; Private scholarships; SEOG; State scholarships/grants. *Loans:* Direct PLUS loans; Direct Subsidized Stafford Loans; Direct Unsubsidized Stafford Loans. **Student Employment:** Federal Work-Study Program available. Institutional employment available. **Financial Aid Statistics:** 100% needy freshmen, 100% needy undergrads receive need-based scholarship or grant aid. 18% freshmen, 17% undergrads receive non-need-based scholarship or grant aid. 85% freshmen, 86% undergrads receive need-based self-help aid. 3% freshmen, 4% undergrads receive athletic scholarships. 98% freshmen, 97% undergrads receive any aid. 60% undergrads borrow to pay for school. Average cumulative indebtedness $29,713. **Criteria awarding aid:** *Need-based:* Academics, Alumni affiliation, Art, Leadership, Religious affiliation. *Non-need-based:* Academics, Alumni affiliation, Art, Athletics, Leadership, Minority status, Music/drama.

WESTMONT COLLEGE

955 La Paz Road, Santa Barbara, CA 93108
Phone: 805-565-6200 **Financial Aid Phone:** 888-963-4624
E-mail: admissions@westmont.edu **CEEB Code:** 4950
Fax: 805-565-6234 **Website:** www.westmont.edu **ACT Code:** 478

This private school, affiliated with the Christian (Nondenominational) Church, was founded in 1937. It has a 133 acre campus.

RATINGS
Admissions Selectivity Rating: 83 **Fire Safety Rating:** 60* **Green Rating:** 60*

STUDENTS AND FACULTY
Enrollment: 1,289. **Student Body:** 61% female, 39% male, 25% out-of-state, 1% international (8 countries represented). Asian 6%, African American 1%, Caucasian 67%, Hispanic 12%, Native American <1%, Pacific Islander 1%, Two or more races 8%, Race unknown 4%.
Retention and Graduation: 85% freshmen return for sophomore year.
Faculty: Student/faculty ratio 11:1. 96 full-time faculty, 90% hold PhDs, 13% are members of minority groups, 39% are women. 0% of classes are taught by teaching assistants.

ACADEMICS
Degrees: Bachelor's; Post-bachelor's certificate. **Classes:** Most classes have 10–19 students. Most lab/discussion sessions have 10–19 students. **Most popular majors:** English/Language Arts Teacher Education; Cell/Cellular and Molecular Biology. **Special Study Options:** Accelerated program; Cross-registration; Double major; Exchange student program (domestic); Honors program; Independent study; Internships; Liberal arts/career combination; Student-designed major; Study abroad; Teacher certification program. **Honors programs:** Some general education courses are designated as honors courses. **Disability Services offered:** Note-taking services; Reader services; Tape recorders; Tutors. **Career services:** Career assessment; Career/job search classes; Internships.

FACILITIES
Housing: Apartments for single students; Coed dorms 65% of campus accessible to physically disabled. **Special Academic Facilities/Equipment:** Reynolds Art Gallery features the gallery, art studios and classrooms; Carroll Observatory houses a 24-inch reflector telescope; Mericos Whittier Science facility includes state of the art technical equipment such as ultracentrifuge, Fouriertransform NMR spectrometer, etc., as well as the pre-med center; Voskuyl Library holds over 150,000 bound volumes; the physics department is developing advanced experiments for the lab; Ellen Porter Hall of Fine Arts showcases ten to twenty live musical and theatrical performances each year; Physiology Lab and Fitness Center for Kinesiology studies.

CAMPUS LIFE
Environment: City. **Activities:** Campus Ministries; Choral groups; Concert band; Dance; Drama/theater; International Student Organization; Jazz band; Literary magazine; Model UN; Music ensembles; Musical theater; Student government; Student newspaper; Symphony orchestra; Yearbook. 50 registered organizations, 7 honor societies, 40 religious organizations on campus.
Athletics (Intercollegiate): *Men:* baseball, basketball, cross-country, soccer, tennis, track/field (outdoor). *Women:* basketball, cross-country, soccer, tennis, track/field (outdoor), volleyball.

ADMISSIONS
Freshman Academic Profile: Average high school GPA 3.8. 29% in top 10% of high school class, 66% in top 25% of high school class, 94% in top 50% of high school class. 70% from public high schools. **Test Scores:** SAT Math middle 50% range 540–660. SAT EBRW middle 50% range 520–650. ACT middle 50% range 24–29. **Basis for Candidate Selection:** *Very important factors include:* academic GPA, standardized test scores, character/personal qualities. *Important factors include:* rigor of secondary school record, application essay, recommendation(s), interview, extracurricular activities, talent/ability, religious affiliation/commitment. *Other factors include:* class rank, first generation, alumni/ae relation, geographical residence, racial/ethnic status, volunteer work, work experience. **Freshman Admission Requirements:** High school diploma is required and GED is accepted. *Academic units required:* 4 English, 3 math, 3 science, 2 science labs, 2 foreign language, 1 social studies, 1 history, 2 academic electives. *Academic units recommended:* 3 foreign language, 4 academic electives. **Freshman Admission Statistics:** 2,145 applied, 70% admitted, 20% enrolled. **Transfer Admission Requirements:** High school

transcript, college transcript(s), essay or personal statement, statement of good standing from prior institution(s). Lowest grade transferable C-. **General Admission Information:** Application fee $40. Priority deadline 2/15. Regular application deadline 8/15. Non-fall registration accepted.

COSTS AND FINANCIAL AID
Annual tuition $38,960. Room and board $12,580. Required fees $1,030. Average book and supplies expense $1,600. **Required Forms and Deadlines:** FAFSA; Institution's own financial aid form. **Notification of Awards:** Applicants will be notified of awards on a rolling basis beginning 4/1. **Types of Aid:** *Need-based scholarships/grants:* College/university scholarship or grant aid from institutional funds; Federal Pell; Private scholarships; SEOG; State scholarships/grants. *Loans:* Direct PLUS loans; Direct Subsidized Stafford Loans; Direct Unsubsidized Stafford Loans. **Student Employment:** Federal Work-Study Program available. Institutional employment available. **Financial Aid Statistics:** 99% needy freshmen, 99% needy undergrads receive need-based scholarship or grant aid. 11% freshmen, 12% undergrads receive non-need-based scholarship or grant aid. 97% freshmen, 87% undergrads receive need-based self-help aid. freshmen, 6% undergrads receive athletic scholarships. 85% undergrads receive any aid. **Criteria awarding aid:** *Non-need-based:* Academics, Art, Athletics, Music/drama.

WEST SUBURBAN COLLEGE OF NURSING

3 Erie Court, Oak Park, IL 60302
Phone: 708-763-6530 **Financial Aid Phone:** (708) 763-1426
E-mail: admission@wscn.edu
Fax: 708-763-1531 **Website:** www.wscn.edu

This private school, affiliated with the Roman Catholic Church, was founded in 1914.

RATINGS
Admissions Selectivity Rating: 60* **Fire Safety Rating:** 60* **Green Rating:** 60*

STUDENTS AND FACULTY
Enrollment: 236. **Student Body:** 86% female, 14% male, 0% international. Asian 24%, African American 10%, Caucasian 40%, Hispanic 13%, Native American 0%, Race unknown 13%.
Faculty: Student/faculty ratio 10:1. 23 full-time faculty, 17% hold PhDs, 17% are members of minority groups, 100% are women. 0% of classes are taught by teaching assistants.

ACADEMICS
Degrees: Bachelor's; Master's. **Classes:** Most classes have 10–19 students. Most lab/discussion sessions have fewer than 10 students. **Special Study Options:** Accelerated program. **Career services:** Alumni services; Career assessment.

FACILITIES
Campus Network: 100% of classrooms, 100% of dorms, 100% of student union, 100% of libraries, 100% of dining areas, 40% of common outdoor areas have wireless network access.

CAMPUS LIFE
Environment: Metropolis. **Activities:** Student government. 2 registered organizations on campus.

ADMISSIONS
Freshman Admission Requirements: High school diploma is required and GED is accepted. **Transfer Admission Requirements:** College transcript(s), essay or personal statement, standardized test scores. Minimum college GPA of 2.75 required. Lowest grade transferable C. **General Admission Information:** Application fee $30. Regular application deadline 4/1. Admission may be deferred for a maximum of 1 semester.

COSTS AND FINANCIAL AID
Types of Aid: *Need-based scholarships/grants:* College/university scholarship or grant aid from institutional funds; Federal Nursing Scholarships; Federal Pell; Private scholarships; SEOG; State scholarships/grants. **Student Employment:** Federal Work-Study Program available. Institutional employment available. **Financial Aid Statistics:** 100% needy undergrads receive need-based scholarship or grant aid. 18% undergrads receive non-need-based scholarship or grant aid. 79% undergrads receive need-based self-help aid. 0% undergrads receive athletic scholarships. 86% undergrads receive any aid. **Criteria awarding aid:** *Need-based:* Academics. *Non-need-based:* Academics.

WEST TEXAS A&M UNIVERSITY

PO Box 60907, Canyon, TX 79016-0001
Phone: 806-651-2020 **Financial Aid Phone:** 806-651-2055
E-mail: admissions@mail.wtamu.edu **CEEB Code:** 3665
Fax: 806-651-5268 **Website:** www.wtamu.edu **ACT Code:** 4250

This public school was founded in 1910. It has a 135 acre campus.

RATINGS

Admissions Selectivity Rating: 87   **Fire Safety Rating:** 91   **Green Rating:** 66

STUDENTS AND FACULTY

Enrollment: 7,383. **Student Body:** 57% female, 43% male, 14% out-of-state, 2% international (37 countries represented). Asian 2%, African American 5%, Caucasian 58%, Hispanic 28%, Native American <1%, Pacific Islander <1%, Two or more races 3%, Race unknown 2%.
Retention and Graduation: 64% freshmen return for sophomore year. 28% freshmen graduate within 4 years. 44% freshmen graduate within 6 years. 22% grads go on to further study within 1 year. **Faculty:** Student/faculty ratio 20:1. 342 full-time faculty, 63% hold PhDs, 14% are members of minority groups, 46% are women. 4% of classes are taught by teaching assistants.

ACADEMICS

Degrees: Bachelor's; Doctoral degree research/scholarship; Master's. **Classes:** Most classes have 10–19 students. Most lab/discussion sessions have 20–29 students. **Most popular majors:** Business/Commerce, General; Multi-/Interdisciplinary Studies, Other; Registered Nursing/Registered Nurse. **Special Study Options:** Accelerated program; Cooperative education program; Distance learning; Double major; English as a Second Language (ESL); Honors program; Independent study; Internships; Liberal arts/career combination; Study abroad; Teacher certification program. **Honors programs:** The Honors Program at West Texas A&M University is committed to providing exceptional students with challenging academic studies, innovative approaches to instruction; increased opportunities for improving skills in critical thinking, research, developing creative works and writing; expanded cultural knowledge; and the opportunity to interact closely with faculty and similarly motivated students. **Disability Services offered:** Note-taking services; Reader services; Tape recorders; Tutors. **Career services:** Alumni network; Alumni services; Career assessment; Career/job search classes; Internships; Regional alumni.

FACILITIES

Housing: Coed dorms; Fraternity/sorority housing; Men's dorms; Special housing for disabled students; Women's dorms; 100% of campus accessible to physically disabled. **Special Academic Facilities/Equipment:** Regional History Museum, Research Center, Panhandle Plains Historical Museum, Killgore Research Center.

CAMPUS LIFE

Environment: Village. **Activities:** Campus Ministries; Choral groups; Concert band; Dance; Drama/theater; International Student Organization; Jazz band; Literary magazine; Marching band; Music ensembles; Musical theater; Opera; Pep band; Radio station; Student government; Student newspaper; Symphony orchestra; Television station; Yearbook. 145 registered organizations, 13 honor societies, 9 religious organizations, 8 fraternities, 7 sororities on campus. **Athletics (Intercollegiate):** *Men:* baseball, basketball, cross-country, football, golf, soccer. *Women:* basketball, cheerleading, cross-country, equestrian sports, golf, soccer, softball, volleyball. **On-Campus Highlights:** Panhandle-Plains Historical Museum.

ADMISSIONS

Freshman Academic Profile: 15% in top 10% of high school class, 43% in top 25% of high school class, 80% in top 50% of high school class. 97% from public high schools. **Test Scores:** SAT Math middle 50% range 490–580. SAT EBRW middle 50% range 490–590. ACT middle 50% range 19–23. **Basis for Candidate Selection:** *Very important factors include:* class rank, academic GPA, standardized test scores. *Important factors include:* rigor of secondary school record. **Freshman Admission Requirements:** High school diploma is required and GED is accepted. *Academic units required:* 4 English, 4 math, 4 science, 2 foreign language, 3.5 social studies, 6 academic electives, 1 visual/performing arts, 1.5 unit from above areas or other academic areas. **Freshman Admission Statistics:** 6,116 applied, 38% admitted, 53% enrolled. **Transfer Admission Requirements:** College transcript(s). Minimum college GPA of 2.0 required. Lowest grade transferable C. **General Admission Information:** Application fee $40. Priority deadline 8/1. Regular application deadline 8/1. Non-fall registration accepted. Admission may be deferred for a maximum of 1 semester.

COSTS AND FINANCIAL AID

Annual in-state tuition $5,544. Annual out-of-state tuition $6,567. Room and board $7,196. Required fees $2,392. Average book and supplies expense $1,000. **Required Forms and Deadlines:** FAFSA. **Notification of Awards:** Applicants will be notified of awards on a rolling basis beginning 3/1. **Types of Aid:** *Need-based scholarships/grants:* College/university scholarship or grant aid from institutional funds; Federal Pell; Private scholarships; SEOG; State scholarships/grants. *Loans:* Direct PLUS loans; Direct Subsidized Stafford Loans; Direct Unsubsidized Stafford Loans. **Financial Aid Statistics:** 76% needy freshmen, 78% needy undergrads receive need-based scholarship or grant aid. 50% freshmen, 33% undergrads receive non-need-based scholarship or grant aid. 62% freshmen, 68% undergrads receive need-based self-help aid. 3% freshmen, 3% undergrads receive athletic scholarships. 52% freshmen, 53% undergrads receive any aid. 62% undergrads borrow to pay for school. Average cumulative indebtedness $24,525. **Criteria awarding aid:** *Need-based:* Academics. *Non-need-based:* Academics, Art, Athletics, Leadership, Music/drama.

WEST VIRGINIA STATE UNIVERSITY

106 Ferrell Hall, Institute, WV 25112
Phone: 304-766-3033 **Financial Aid Phone:** 304-766-3131
E-mail: admissions@wvstateu.edu **CEEB Code:** 5903
Fax: 304-766-5182 **Website:** www.wvstateu.edu **ACT Code:** 4538

This public school was founded in 1891. It has a 95 acre campus.

RATINGS

Admissions Selectivity Rating: 72   **Fire Safety Rating:** 60*   **Green Rating:** 60*

STUDENTS AND FACULTY

Enrollment: 2,033. **Student Body:** 54% female, 46% male, 8% out-of-state, 1% international (8 countries represented). Asian <1%, African American 14%, Caucasian 65%, Hispanic 1%, Native American <1%, Pacific Islander 0%, Two or more races 10%, Race unknown 9%.
Retention and Graduation: 59% freshmen return for sophomore year. 6% grads go on to further study within 1 year. 3% grads pursue arts and sciences degrees. 1% grads pursue law degrees. 1% grads pursue business degrees. 1% grads pursue medical degrees.

ACADEMICS

Degrees: Bachelor's; Master's. **Most popular majors:** Business Administration and Management, General; Elementary Education and Teaching; General Studies. **Special Study Options:** Cooperative education program; Distance learning; Dual enrollment; English as a Second Language (ESL). **Disability Services offered:** Tutors.

FACILITIES

Housing: Apartments for married students; Coed dorms; Men's dorms; Women's dorms. **Special Academic Facilities/Equipment:** On-campus day-care center, art gallery, ROTC Hall of Fame, Sports Hall of Fame. **Campus Network:** 100% of classrooms, 100% of dorms, 100% of student union, 100% of libraries, 100% of dining areas, 0% of common outdoor areas have wireless network access.

CAMPUS LIFE

Environment: Village. **Activities:** Choral groups; Concert band; Jazz band; Literary magazine; Marching band; Music ensembles; Radio station; Student government; Student newspaper; Television station; Yearbook. 4 honor societies, 2 religious organizations, 6 fraternities, 3 sororities on campus. **Athletics (Intercollegiate):** *Men:* baseball, basketball, cross-country, football, softball, tennis, track/field (outdoor), volleyball. *Women:* basketball, cross-country, softball, tennis, track/field (outdoor), volleyball.

ADMISSIONS

Freshman Academic Profile: 99% from public high schools. **Test Scores:** SAT Math middle 50% range 400–500. SAT EBRW middle 50% range 390–510. ACT middle 50% range 17–22. **Freshman Admission Requirements:** High school diploma is required and GED is accepted; High school diploma is required and GED is not accepted. *Academic units required:* 4 English, 2 math, 2 science, 2 foreign language, 3 social studies, 1 history. **Freshman Admission**

Statistics: 1,439 applied, 94% admitted, 27% enrolled. **Transfer Admission Requirements:** College transcript(s). Minimum college GPA of 2.0 required. Lowest grade transferable D. **General Admission Information:** Application fee $20. Regular application deadline 8/22. Non-fall registration accepted.

COSTS AND FINANCIAL AID
Annual in-state tuition $2,116. Annual out-of-state tuition $5,150. Room and board $4,950. Average book and supplies expense $500. **Required Forms and Deadlines:** FAFSA; Institution's own financial aid form.

WEST VIRGINIA UNIVERSITY

Admissions Office, Morgantown, WV 26506-6009
Phone: 304-293-2121 **Financial Aid Phone:** 304-293-5242
E-mail: go2wvu@mail.wvu.edu **CEEB Code:** 5904
Fax: 304-293-3080 **Website:** www.wvu.edu **ACT Code:** 4540

This public school was founded in 1867. It has a 2800 acre campus.

RATINGS
Admissions Selectivity Rating: 77   **Fire Safety Rating:** 98   **Green Rating:** 80

STUDENTS AND FACULTY
Enrollment: 20,499. **Student Body:** 48% female, 52% male, 48% out-of-state, 6% international (75 countries represented). Asian 2%, African American 4%, Caucasian 80%, Hispanic 4%, Native American <1%, Pacific Islander <1%, Two or more races 4%, Race unknown <1%.
Retention and Graduation: 76% freshmen return for sophomore year. 35% freshmen graduate within 4 years. 58% freshmen graduate within 6 years.
Faculty: Student/faculty ratio 18:1. 1,119 full-time faculty, 76% hold PhDs, 15% are members of minority groups, 44% are women.

ACADEMICS
Degrees: Bachelor's; Doctoral degree—professional practice; Doctoral degree research/scholarship; Master's. **Classes:** Most classes have 20–29 students. Most lab/discussion sessions have 20–29 students. **Most popular majors:** Engineering, General; Business Administration and Management, General; Journalism. **Special Study Options:** Accelerated program; Cooperative education program; Distance learning; Double major; English as a Second Language (ESL); Exchange student program (domestic); External degree program; Honors program; Independent study; Internships; Student-designed major; Study abroad; Teacher certification program. **Honors programs:** Honors Leadership Academy. **Combined degree programs:** BA/MA. **Disability Services offered:** Note-taking services; Reader services; Tape recorders; Tutors. **Career services:** Alumni network; Alumni services; Career assessment; Career/job search classes; Internships.

FACILITIES
Housing: Apartments for married students; Apartments for single students; Coed dorms; Fraternity/sorority housing; Men's dorms; Special housing for disabled students; Special housing for international students; Theme housing; Wellness housing; Women's dorms; 99% of campus accessible to physically disabled. **Special Academic Facilities/Equipment:** Art galleries, creative arts center, arboretum, herbarium, planetarium, concurrent engineering research center, discovery lab (for inventors), Appalachian hardwood center, small business development center, pharmacy museum, coal and energy museum, center for economic research, fluidization center, center for software development. **Campus Network:** 100% of classrooms, 100% of dorms, 100% of student union, 100% of libraries, 100% of dining areas, 65% of common outdoor areas have wireless network access.

CAMPUS LIFE
Environment: Town. **Activities:** Campus Ministries; Choral groups; Concert band; Dance; Drama/theater; International Student Organization; Jazz band; Literary magazine; Marching band; Model UN; Music ensembles; Musical theater; Pep band; Radio station; Student government; Student newspaper; Symphony orchestra. 450 registered organizations, 26 honor societies, 26 religious organizations, 9 fraternities, 8 sororities on campus. **Athletics (Intercollegiate):** *Men:* baseball, basketball, diving, football, riflery, soccer, swimming, wrestling. *Women:* basketball, crew/rowing, cross-country, diving,

gymnastics, riflery, soccer, swimming, tennis, track/field (outdoor), track/field (indoor), volleyball. **On-Campus Highlights:** Student Recreation Center. **Environmental Initiatives:** Energy performance management and emissions reduction through a performance contract (approx. $30 million) between WVU and Siemens Inc. Behavior-based energy management program is currently being implemented to educate and empower faculty, staff, and students to be better stewards of energy resources.

ADMISSIONS
Freshman Academic Profile: Average high school GPA 3.5. 23% in top 10% of high school class, 48% in top 25% of high school class, 78% in top 50% of high school class. **Test Scores:** SAT Math middle 50% range 520–620. SAT EBRW middle 50% range 530–620. ACT middle 50% range 21–27. **Basis for Candidate Selection:** *Very important factors include:* academic GPA, standardized test scores. *Important factors include:* rigor of secondary school record, state residency. *Other factors include:* extracurricular activities, talent/ability. **Freshman Admission Requirements:** High school diploma is required and GED is accepted. *Academic units required:* 4 English, 4 math, 3 science, 3 science labs, 2 foreign language, 3 social studies, 1 visual/performing arts. **Freshman Admission Statistics:** 18,639 applied, 82% admitted, 31% enrolled. **Transfer Admission Requirements:** College transcript(s). Minimum college GPA of 2.0 required. Lowest grade transferable D. **General Admission Information:** Application fee $45. Priority deadline 3/1. Regular application deadline 8/1. Non-fall registration accepted. Admission may be deferred for a maximum of 1 year.

COSTS AND FINANCIAL AID
Annual in-state tuition $8,976. Annual out-of-state tuition $25,320. Room and board $10,918. Average book and supplies expense $950. **Required Forms and Deadlines:** FAFSA. **Notification of Awards:** Applicants will be notified of awards on a rolling basis beginning 12/1. **Types of Aid:** *Need-based scholarships/ grants:* College/university scholarship or grant aid from institutional funds; Federal Nursing Scholarships; Federal Pell; Private scholarships; SEOG. *Loans:* Direct PLUS loans; Direct Subsidized Stafford Loans; Direct Unsubsidized Stafford Loans. **Student Employment:** Federal Work-Study Program available. Institutional employment available. **Financial Aid Statistics:** 81% needy freshmen, 74% needy undergrads receive need-based scholarship or grant aid. 46% freshmen, 39% undergrads receive non-need-based scholarship or grant aid. 69% freshmen, 77% undergrads receive need-based self-help aid. 2% freshmen, 2% undergrads receive athletic scholarships. 72% freshmen, 75% undergrads receive any aid. 61% undergrads borrow to pay for school. Average cumulative indebtedness $32,541. **Criteria awarding aid:** *Need-based:* Academics *Non-need-based:* Academics, Alumni affiliation, Art, Athletics, Job skills, Leadership, Minority status, Music/drama, Religious affiliation, State/district residency.

WEST VIRGINIA UNIVERSITY INSTITUTE OF TECHNOLOGY

Box 10 Old Main, Montgomery, WV 25136
Phone: 304-442-3167
E-mail: admissions@wvutech.edu
Fax: 304-442-3097 **Website:** www.wvutech.edu

This is a public school.

RATINGS
Admissions Selectivity Rating: 77   **Fire Safety Rating:** 60*   **Green Rating:** 60*

STUDENTS AND FACULTY
Enrollment: 2,001. **Student Body:** 39% female, 61% male, 6% out-of-state, 4% international. Asian 1%, African American 8%, Caucasian 87%, Hispanic 1%, Native American <1%, Race unknown 0%.
Retention and Graduation: 62% freshmen return for sophomore year.
Faculty: Student/faculty ratio 16:1. 119 full-time faculty, 47% hold PhDs, 18% are members of minority groups, 28% are women.

ACADEMICS
Degrees: Associate; Bachelor's; Certificate; Master's. **Classes:** Most classes have 10–19 students. Most lab/discussion sessions have 20–29 students. **Special Study Options:** Cooperative education program; Distance learning; Double major; Dual enrollment; Internships; Student-designed major.

FACILITIES
Housing: Coed dorms; Fraternity/sorority housing; Men's dorms; Women's dorms. **Campus Network:** 100% of classrooms, 100% of dorms, 100% of

student union, 100% of libraries, 100% of dining areas, 100% of common outdoor areas have wireless network access.

CAMPUS LIFE

Activities: Choral groups; Concert band; Drama/theater; Jazz band; Marching band; Music ensembles; Pep band; Student government; Student newspaper.

ADMISSIONS

Freshman Academic Profile: Average high school GPA 3.2. 20% in top 10% of high school class, 21% in top 25% of high school class, 43% in top 50% of high school class. 88% from public high schools. **Test Scores:** SAT Math middle 50% range 400–580. SAT EBRW middle 50% range 380–530. ACT middle 50% range 17–23. **Basis for Candidate Selection:** *Very important factors include:* rigor of secondary school record, standardized test scores. *Other factors include:* class rank, recommendation(s), interview, extracurricular activities, talent/ability, character/personal qualities, alumni/ae relation, state residency, volunteer work. **Freshman Admission Requirements:** High school diploma is required and GED is accepted. *Academic units required:* 4 English, 2 math, 2 science, 2 science labs, 3 social studies. *Academic units recommended:* 4 English, 3 math, 2 science, 2 science labs, 2 foreign language, 3 social studies. **Freshman Admission Statistics:** 1,191 applied, 74% admitted, 47% enrolled. **Transfer Admission Requirements:** College transcript(s). Minimum college GPA of 1.7 required. Lowest grade transferable D. **General Admission Information:** Priority deadline 8/3. Non-fall registration accepted. Admission may be deferred for a maximum of 1 semester.

COSTS AND FINANCIAL AID

Annual in-state tuition $3,200. Annual out-of-state tuition $8,400. Room and board $4,896. Average book and supplies expense $800. **Required Forms and Deadlines:** FAFSA; Institution's own financial aid form. **Notification of Awards:** Applicants will be notified of awards on a rolling basis beginning 3/3. **Types of Aid:** *Need-based scholarships/grants:* College/university scholarship or grant aid from institutional funds; Federal Pell; Private scholarships; SEOG; State scholarships/grants. *Loans:* Direct PLUS loans; Direct Subsidized Stafford Loans; Direct Unsubsidized Stafford Loans. **Financial Aid Statistics:** 78% needy freshmen, 78% needy undergrads receive need-based scholarship or grant aid. 70% freshmen, 48% undergrads receive non-need-based scholarship or grant aid. 59% freshmen, 69% undergrads receive need-based self-help aid. 2% freshmen, 6% undergrads receive athletic scholarships. **Criteria awarding aid:** *Need-based:* Academics, Athletics, Music/drama *Non-need-based:* Academics, Alumni affiliation, Art, Athletics, Music/drama.

WEST VIRGINIA WESLEYAN COLLEGE

59 College Avenue, Buckhannon, WV 26201
Phone: 304-473-8510 **Financial Aid Phone:** 304-473-8080
E-mail: admission@wvwc.edu **CEEB Code:** 5905
Fax: 304-473-8108 **Website:** www.wvwc.edu **ACT Code:** 4544

This private school, affiliated with the Methodist Church, was founded in 1890. It has a 180 acre campus.

RATINGS

Admissions Selectivity Rating: 77   **Fire Safety Rating:** 60*   **Green Rating:** 60*

STUDENTS AND FACULTY

Enrollment: 1,304. **Student Body:** 56% female, 44% male, 38% out-of-state, 6% international (22 countries represented). Asian <1%, African American 9%, Caucasian 78%, Hispanic 3%, Native American <1%, Pacific Islander <1%, Two or more races 4%, Race unknown <1%. **Retention and Graduation:** 74% freshmen return for sophomore year. 38% freshmen graduate within 4 years. 50% freshmen graduate within 6 years. 35% grads go on to further study within 1 year. 57% grads pursue arts and sciences degrees. 11% grads pursue law degrees. 16% grads pursue business degrees. 6% grads pursue medical degrees. **Faculty:** Student/faculty ratio 13:1. 83 full-time faculty, 69% hold PhDs, 7% are members of minority groups, 53% are women. 0% of classes are taught by teaching assistants.

ACADEMICS

Degrees: Bachelor's; Master's; Post-bachelor's certificate; Post-master's certificate. **Classes:** Most classes have 10–19 students. Most lab/discussion sessions have fewer than 10 students. **Most popular majors:** Business Administration and Management, General; Elementary Education and Teaching; Exercise Science and Kinesiology. **Special Study Options:** Distance learning; Double major; English as a Second Language (ESL); Exchange

student program (domestic); Honors program; Independent study; Internships; Liberal arts/career combination; Student-designed major; Study abroad; Teacher certification program. **Honors programs:** The Honors Program is offered to recognize and challenge the College's most academically talented students. Participation is voluntary for all qualified students. **Combined degree programs:** BA/MA. **Disability Services offered:** Note-taking services; Reader services; Tape recorders; Tutors. **Career services:** Alumni network; Alumni services; Career/job search classes; Internships.

FACILITIES

Housing: Coed dorms; Fraternity/sorority housing; Men's dorms; Special housing for disabled students; Women's dorms. **Campus Network:** 100% of classrooms, 100% of dorms, 100% of student union, 100% of libraries, 100% of dining areas, 100% of common outdoor areas have wireless network access.

CAMPUS LIFE

Environment: Village. **Activities:** Campus Ministries; Choral groups; Concert band; Dance; Drama/theater; International Student Organization; Jazz band; Literary magazine; Marching band; Music ensembles; Musical theater; Opera; Pep band; Radio station; Student government; Student newspaper; Yearbook. 75 registered organizations, 31 honor societies, 6 religious organizations, 6 fraternities, 5 sororities on campus. **Athletics (Intercollegiate):** *Men:* baseball, basketball, cross-country, football, golf, soccer, softball, swimming, tennis, track/field (outdoor), track/field (indoor). *Women:* basketball, cross-country, golf, lacrosse, soccer, swimming, tennis, track/field (outdoor), track/field (indoor), volleyball. **On-Campus Highlights:** David E. Reemsnyder Research Center.

ADMISSIONS

Freshman Academic Profile: Average high school GPA 3.5. 20% in top 10% of high school class, 49% in top 25% of high school class, 83% in top 50% of high school class. 88% from public high schools. **Test Scores:** SAT Math middle 50% range 485–580. SAT EBRW middle 50% range 470–590. ACT middle 50% range 19–25. **Basis for Candidate Selection:** *Very important factors include:* rigor of secondary school record, academic GPA, talent/ability. *Important factors include:* class rank, standardized test scores, extracurricular activities, character/personal qualities, volunteer work, work experience, level of applicant's interest. *Other factors include:* application essay, recommendation(s), interview. **Freshman Admission Requirements:** High school diploma is required and GED is accepted. *Academic units required:* 4 English, 3 math, 3 science, 1 science labs, 3 social studies. *Academic units recommended:* 2 foreign language. **Freshman Admission Statistics:** 2,272 applied, 71% admitted, 23% enrolled. **Transfer Admission Requirements:** High school transcript, college transcript(s), statement of good standing from prior institution(s). Minimum college GPA of 2.50 required. Lowest grade transferable C-. **General Admission Information:** Application fee $35. Priority deadline 2/1. Regular application deadline 8/15. Non-fall registration accepted. Admission may be deferred for a maximum of 1 year.

COSTS AND FINANCIAL AID

Annual tuition $31,074. Room and board $9,576. Required fees $1,178. Average book and supplies expense $2,500. **Required Forms and Deadlines:** FAFSA. **Notification of Awards:** Applicants will be notified of awards on a rolling basis beginning 3/1. **Types of Aid:** *Need-based scholarships/grants:* College/university scholarship or grant aid from institutional funds; Federal Nursing Scholarships; Federal Pell; Private scholarships; SEOG; State scholarships/grants. *Loans:* Direct PLUS loans; Direct Subsidized Stafford Loans; Direct Unsubsidized Stafford Loans. **Student Employment:** Federal Work-Study Program available. Institutional employment available. **Financial Aid Statistics:** 100% needy freshmen, 100% needy undergrads receive need-based scholarship or grant aid. freshmen, undergrads receive non-need-based scholarship or grant aid. 77% freshmen, 71% undergrads receive need-based self-help aid. 23% freshmen, 23% undergrads receive athletic scholarships. 99% freshmen, 98% undergrads receive any aid. 68% undergrads borrow to pay for school. Average cumulative indebtedness $31,175. **Criteria awarding aid:** *Need-based:* Art, Leadership, Music/drama *Non-need-based:* Academics, Alumni affiliation, Art, Athletics, Leadership, Music/drama, Religious affiliation.

WHEATON COLLEGE (IL)

501 College Avenue, Wheaton, IL 60187
Phone: 630-752-5011 **Financial Aid Phone:** 630-752-5021
E-mail: admissions@wheaton.edu **CEEB Code:** 1905
Fax: 630-752-5285 **Website:** www.wheaton.edu **ACT Code:** 1160

This private school, affiliated with the Christian non-denominational Church, was founded in 1860. It has a 80 acre campus.

RATINGS

Admissions Selectivity Rating: 87   **Fire Safety Rating:** 94   **Green Rating:** 67

STUDENTS AND FACULTY

Enrollment: 2,358. **Student Body:** 54% female, 46% male, 73% out-of-state, 4% international (41 countries represented). Asian 10%, African American 3%, Caucasian 71%, Hispanic 7%, Native American <1%, Pacific Islander <1%, Two or more races 5%, Race unknown <1%.
Retention and Graduation: 93% freshmen return for sophomore year. 82% freshmen graduate within 4 years. 89% freshmen graduate within 6 years. 20% grads go on to further study within 1 year. 12% grads pursue arts and sciences degrees. 1% grads pursue law degrees. <1% grads pursue business degrees. 4% grads pursue medical degrees. **Faculty:** Student/faculty ratio 10:1. 219 full-time faculty, 95% hold PhDs, 19% are members of minority groups, 37% are women. 0% of classes are taught by teaching assistants.

ACADEMICS

Degrees: Bachelor's; Doctoral degree—professional practice; Doctoral degree research/scholarship; Master's; Post-bachelor's certificate. **Classes:** Most classes have 10–19 students. Most lab/discussion sessions have 10–19 students. **Most popular majors:** Speech Communication and Rhetoric; Business/Managerial Economics; Psychology, General. **Special Study Options:** Cross-registration; Double major; Exchange student program (domestic); Independent study; Internships; Liberal arts/career combination; Student-designed major; Study abroad; Teacher certification program. **Honors programs:** Some departments offer qualified students to submit an honors project. **Disability Services offered:** Note-taking services; Reader services; Tape recorders; Tutors. **Career services:** Alumni network; Alumni services; Career assessment; Career/job search classes; Internships; Regional alumni.

FACILITIES

Housing: Apartments for married students; Apartments for single students; Coed dorms; Cooperative housing; Men's dorms; Women's dorms; 97% of campus accessible to physically disabled. **Special Academic Facilities/Equipment:** The Billy Graham Center Museum, The Black Hills Science Station, the Center for Applied Christian Ethics (CACE); HoneyRock is the year-round Northwoods Camp and Campus of Wheaton College. The Wheaton Center for Faith, Politics, and Economics; The Marion E. Wade Center; The Meyer Science Center contains a unique, interactive atrium museum featuring the Perry Mastodon, a geology exhibit, a natural history exhibit, a Foucault pendulum, and additional exhibits.

CAMPUS LIFE

Environment: Town. **Activities:** Campus Ministries; Choral groups; Concert band; Dance; Drama/theater; International Student Organization; Jazz band; Literary magazine; Model UN; Music ensembles; Musical theater; Opera; Pep band; Student government; Student newspaper; Student-run film society; Symphony orchestra. 95 registered organizations, 13 honor societies, 16 religious organizations on campus. **Athletics (Intercollegiate):** *Men:* baseball, basketball, cross-country, football, golf, soccer, swimming, tennis, track/field (outdoor), track/field (indoor), wrestling. *Women:* basketball, cross-country, golf, soccer, softball, swimming, tennis, track/field (outdoor), track/field (indoor), volleyball, water polo. **On-Campus Highlights:** "The Stupe" grill in the Beamer Student Center. **Environmental Initiatives:** Environmental Science Major.

ADMISSIONS

Freshman Academic Profile: Average high school GPA 3.7. 49% in top 10% of high school class, 78% in top 25% of high school class, 92% in top 50% of high school class. 46% from public high schools. **Test Scores:** SAT Math middle 50% range 600–720. SAT EBRW middle 50% range 620–720. ACT middle 50% range 26–32. **Basis for Candidate Selection:** *Very important factors include:* rigor of secondary school record, academic GPA, application essay, standardized test scores, recommendation(s), character/personal qualities, religious affiliation/commitment. *Important factors include:* interview, extracurricular activities, talent/ability. *Other factors include:* class rank, first generation, alumni/ae relation, geographical residence, state residency, racial/ethnic status, work experience, level of applicant's interest. **Freshman Admission Requirements:** High school diploma is required and GED is accepted. *Academic units required:* 4 English, 3 math, 3 science, 2 foreign language, 3 social studies. *Academic units recommended:* 4 English, 4 math, 4 science, 3 foreign language, 4 social studies. **Freshman Admission Statistics:** 1,889 applied, 85% admitted, 38% enrolled. **Transfer Admission Requirements:** High school transcript, college transcript(s), essay or personal statement, Minimum college GPA of 3.0 required. Lowest grade transferable C-. **General Admission Information:** Application fee $50. Regular application deadline 1/10. Non-fall registration accepted. Admission may be deferred for a maximum of 1 year.

COSTS AND FINANCIAL AID

Annual tuition $39,100. Room and board $10,990. Average book and supplies expense $800. **Required Forms and Deadlines:** FAFSA. **Notification of Awards:** Applicants will be notified of awards on a rolling basis beginning 12/31. **Types of Aid:** *Need-based scholarships/grants:* College/university scholarship or grant aid from institutional funds; Federal Pell; Private scholarships; SEOG; State scholarships/grants. *Loans:* Direct PLUS loans; Direct Subsidized Stafford Loans; Direct Unsubsidized Stafford Loans. **Student Employment:** Federal Work-Study Program available. Institutional employment available. **Financial Aid Statistics:** 99% needy freshmen, 97% needy undergrads receive need-based scholarship or grant aid. 10% freshmen, 7% undergrads receive non-need-based scholarship or grant aid. 70% freshmen, 71% undergrads receive need-based self-help aid. 0% freshmen, 0% undergrads receive athletic scholarships. 90% freshmen, 85% undergrads receive any aid. 59% undergrads borrow to pay for school. Average cumulative indebtedness $29,555. **Criteria awarding aid:** *Non-need-based:* Academics, Alumni affiliation, Art, Minority status, Music/drama.

WHEATON COLLEGE (MA)

26 E Main Street, Norton, MA 02766
Phone: 508-286-8251 **Financial Aid Phone:** 508-286-8232
E-mail: admission@wheatoncollege.edu **CEEB Code:** 3963
Fax: 508-286-8271 **Website:** www.wheatoncollege.edu **ACT Code:** 1932

This private school was founded in 1834. It has a 478 acre campus.

RATINGS

Admissions Selectivity Rating: 85   **Fire Safety Rating:** 95   **Green Rating:** 73

STUDENTS AND FACULTY

Enrollment: 1,750. **Student Body:** 61% female, 39% male, 61% out-of-state, 10% international (67 countries represented). Asian 5%, African American 5%, Caucasian 65%, Hispanic 8%, Native American <1%, Pacific Islander 0%, Two or more races 4%, Race unknown 2%.
Retention and Graduation: 87% freshmen return for sophomore year. 72% freshmen graduate within 4 years. 78% freshmen graduate within 6 years. **Faculty:** Student/faculty ratio 11:1. 132 full-time faculty, 92% hold PhDs, 21% are members of minority groups, 55% are women. 0% of classes are taught by teaching assistants.

ACADEMICS

Degrees: Bachelor's. **Classes:** Most classes have 10–19 students. Most lab/discussion sessions have 10–19 students. **Most popular majors:** Psychology, General; Business Administration and Management, General; Film/Cinema/Media Studies. **Special Study Options:** Accelerated program; Cross-registration; Double major; Dual enrollment; Exchange student program (domestic); Honors program; Independent study; Internships; Student-designed major; Study abroad; Teacher certification program. **Combined degree programs:** BA/MA. **Disability Services offered:** Note-taking services; Reader services. **Career services:** Alumni network; Alumni services; Career assessment; Career/job search classes; Internships; Regional alumni.

FACILITIES

Housing: Apartments for single students; Coed dorms; Special housing for disabled students; Special housing for international students; Theme housing; Wellness housing; Women's dorms. **Special Academic Facilities/Equipment:** Art gallery, radio station, planetarium, observatory, language lab, photography darkrooms, dance studio, media center, greenhouse, GIS lab, Imaging Center for Undergraduate Collaboration (ICUC), Graphics Design lab, Wheaton Autonomous Learning Lab (WHALE), on-campus nursery school, early childhood lab.

CAMPUS LIFE

Environment: Village. **Activities:** Campus Ministries; Choral groups; Dance; Drama/theater; International Student Organization; Jazz band; Literary magazine; Model UN; Music ensembles; Musical theater; Radio station; Student government; Student newspaper; Student-run film society; Symphony orchestra; Yearbook. 110 registered organizations, 10 honor societies, 5 religious organizations on campus. **Athletics (Intercollegiate):** *Men:* baseball, basketball, cross-country, diving, lacrosse, soccer, swimming, tennis, track/field (outdoor), track/field (indoor). *Women:* basketball, cross-country, diving, field hockey, lacrosse, soccer, softball, swimming, synchronized swimming, tennis, track/field (outdoor), track/field (indoor), volleyball. **On-Campus Highlights:** Mars Center for Science and Technology. **Environmental Initiatives:** 1.3 MW solar field.

ADMISSIONS

Freshman Academic Profile: Average high school GPA 3.4. 21% in top 10% of high school class, 52% in top 25% of high school class, 84% in top 50% of high school class. 69% from public high schools. **Test Scores:** SAT Math middle 50% range 580–670. SAT EBRW middle 50% range 600–680. ACT middle 50% range 27–31. **Basis for Candidate Selection:** *Very important factors include:* rigor of secondary school record, academic GPA, application essay, recommendation(s), character/personal qualities. *Important factors include:* extracurricular activities, talent/ability, alumni/ae relation. *Other factors include:* class rank, standardized test scores, interview, first generation, geographical residence, state residency, racial/ethnic status, volunteer work, work experience. **Freshman Admission Requirements:** High school diploma is required and GED is accepted. *Academic units required:* 4 English. *Academic units recommended:* 4 math, 4 science, 4 foreign language, 4 social studies, 4 history. **Freshman Admission Statistics:** 3,673 applied, 70% admitted, 19% enrolled. **Transfer Admission Requirements:** High school transcript, college transcript(s), essay or personal statement, statement of good standing from prior institution(s). Minimum college GPA of 3.0 required. Lowest grade transferable C. **General Admission Information:** Application fee $60. Priority deadline 11/1. Regular application deadline 1/1. Non-fall registration accepted. Admission may be deferred for a maximum of 1 year.

COSTS AND FINANCIAL AID

Annual tuition $54,118. Room and board $14,096. Required fees $450. Average book and supplies expense $940. **Required Forms and Deadlines:** Business/Farm Supplement; CSS/Financial Aid PROFILE; FAFSA; Noncustodial PROFILE;. **Notification of Awards:** Applicants will be notified of awards on or about 3/15. **Types of Aid:** *Need-based scholarships/grants:* College/university scholarship or grant aid from institutional funds; Federal Pell; Private scholarships; SEOG; State scholarships/grants. *Loans:* Direct PLUS loans; Direct Subsidized Stafford Loans; Direct Unsubsidized Stafford Loans. **Student Employment:** Federal Work-Study Program available. Institutional employment available. **Financial Aid Statistics:** 100% needy freshmen, 100% needy undergrads receive need-based scholarship or grant aid. 12% freshmen, 8% undergrads receive non-need-based scholarship or grant aid. 76% freshmen, 83% undergrads receive need-based self-help aid. 0% freshmen, 0% undergrads receive athletic scholarships. 99% freshmen, 97% undergrads receive any aid. 69% undergrads borrow to pay for school. Average cumulative indebtedness $34,830. **Criteria awarding aid:** *Need-based:* Academics. *Non-need-based:* Academics.

WHEELING JESUIT UNIVERSITY

316 Washington Avenue, Wheeling, WV 26003
Phone: 304-243-2359 **Financial Aid Phone:** (304) 243-2304
E-mail: admiss@wju.edu **CEEB Code:** 5906
Fax: 304-243-2397 **Website:** www.wju.edu **ACT Code:** 4546

This private school, affiliated with the Roman Catholic-Jesuit Church, was founded in 1954. It has a 65 acre campus.

RATINGS

Admissions Selectivity Rating: 74   **Fire Safety Rating:** 98   **Green Rating:** 69

STUDENTS AND FACULTY

Enrollment: 820. **Student Body:** 45% female, 55% male, 69% out-of-state, 2% international (13 countries represented). Asian <1%, African American 12%, Caucasian 67%, Hispanic 3%, Native American <1%, Pacific Islander 1%, Two or more races 2%, Race unknown 12%.
Retention and Graduation: 68% freshmen return for sophomore year. 58% freshmen graduate within 4 years. 64% freshmen graduate within 6 years. 22% grads go on to further study within 1 year. **Faculty:** Student/faculty ratio 11:1. 53 full-time faculty, 79% hold PhDs, 8% are members of minority groups, 49% are women. 0% of classes are taught by teaching assistants.

ACADEMICS

Degrees: Bachelor's; Doctoral degree—professional practice; Master's; Post-bachelor's certificate; Post-master's certificate. **Classes:** Most classes have 10–19 students. Most lab/discussion sessions have 10–19 students. **Most popular majors:** Psychology, General; Registered Nursing/Registered Nurse; Business Administration and Management, General. **Special Study Options:** Distance learning; Double major; Dual enrollment; Exchange student program (domestic); Honors program; Independent study; Internships; Liberal arts/career combination; Student-designed major; Study abroad; Teacher certification program. **Honors programs:** The Laut Honors program, which is designed to introduce students to aspects of the arts and sciences that are not available in the regular curriculum in order to inspire and awaken curiosity through a variety of enriching experiences offered. **Disability Services offered:** Note-taking services; Reader services; Tutors. **Career services:** Alumni network; Alumni services; Career assessment; Career/job search classes; Internships; Regional alumni.

FACILITIES

Housing: Apartments for single students; Coed dorms; Men's dorms; Special housing for disabled students; Theme housing; Wellness housing; Women's dorms; 85% of campus accessible to physically disabled. **Special Academic Facilities/Equipment:** Mount de Chantal Conservatory of Music, Challenger Learning Center, Lantz Farm.

CAMPUS LIFE

Environment: City. **Activities:** Campus Ministries; Choral groups; Dance; Drama/theater; International Student Organization; Literary magazine; Musical theater; Student government. 29 registered organizations, 10 honor societies, 8 religious organizations on campus. **Athletics (Intercollegiate):** *Men:* baseball, basketball, cross-country, golf, lacrosse, soccer, swimming, track/field (outdoor), track/field (indoor). *Women:* basketball, cross-country, golf, soccer, softball, swimming, track/field (outdoor), track/field (indoor), volleyball. **On-Campus Highlights:** McDonough Center Athletic Complex.

ADMISSIONS

Freshman Academic Profile: Average high school GPA 3.3. 17% in top 10% of high school class, 36% in top 25% of high school class, 69% in top 50% of high school class. 79% from public high schools. **Test Scores:** SAT Math middle 50% range 450–540. SAT EBRW middle 50% range 440–520. ACT middle 50% range 18–23. **Basis for Candidate Selection:** *Very important factors include:* academic GPA, standardized test scores. *Important factors include:* rigor of secondary school record. *Other factors include:* class rank, application essay, recommendation(s), interview, extracurricular activities, talent/ability, character/personal qualities, first generation, alumni/ae relation, volunteer work, work experience, level of applicant's interest. **Freshman Admission Requirements:** High school diploma is required and GED is accepted. *Academic units required:* 4 English, 3 math, 2 science, 2 science labs, 2 social studies, 1 history, 4 academic electives. *Academic units recommended:* 4 English, 3 math, 3 science, 3 science labs, 2 foreign language, 2 social studies, 1 history, 4 academic electives. **Freshman Admission Statistics:** 1,640 applied, 86% admitted, 21% enrolled. **Transfer Admission Requirements:** College transcript(s). Minimum college GPA of 2.3 required. Lowest grade transferable

C. **General Admission Information:** Non-fall registration accepted. Admission may be deferred for a maximum of one semester.

COSTS AND FINANCIAL AID

Annual tuition $29,090. Room and board $9,900. Required fees $200. Average book and supplies expense $1,300. **Required Forms and Deadlines:** FAFSA. **Notification of Awards:** Applicants will be notified of awards on a rolling basis beginning 11/1. **Types of Aid:** *Need-based scholarships/grants:* College/university scholarship or grant aid from institutional funds; Federal Pell; Private scholarships; SEOG; State scholarships/grants. *Loans:* Direct PLUS loans; Direct Subsidized Stafford Loans; Direct Unsubsidized Stafford Loans. **Student Employment:** Federal Work-Study Program available. Institutional employment available. **Financial Aid Statistics:** 67% needy freshmen, 71% needy undergrads receive need-based scholarship or grant aid. 98% freshmen, 93% undergrads receive non-need-based scholarship or grant aid. 76% freshmen, 84% undergrads receive need-based self-help aid. 58% freshmen, 46% undergrads receive athletic scholarships. 91% freshmen, 93% undergrads receive any aid. 74% undergrads borrow to pay for school. Average cumulative indebtedness $34,151. **Criteria awarding aid:** *Non-need-based:* Academics, Alumni affiliation, Athletics, Music/drama, Religious affiliation.

WHITMAN COLLEGE

345 Boyer Ave, Walla Walla, WA 99362
Phone: 509-527-5176 **Financial Aid Phone:** 509-527-5178
E-mail: admission@whitman.edu **CEEB Code:** 4951
Fax: 509-527-4967 **Website:** https://www.whitman.edu **ACT Code:** 4492

This private school was founded in 1883. It has a 117 acre campus.

RATINGS

Admissions Selectivity Rating: 91 **Fire Safety Rating:** 90 **Green Rating:** 98

STUDENTS AND FACULTY

Enrollment: 1,468. **Student Body:** 57% female, 43% male, 66% out-of-state, 7% international (26 countries represented). Asian 5%, African American 2%, Caucasian 69%, Hispanic 7%, Native American 1%, Pacific Islander <1%, Two or more races 7%, Race unknown 2%. **Retention and Graduation:** 94% freshmen return for sophomore year. 83% freshmen graduate within 4 years. 88% freshmen graduate within 6 years. **Faculty:** Student/faculty ratio 9:1. 165 full-time faculty, 93% hold PhDs, 12% are members of minority groups, 50% are women. 0% of classes are taught by teaching assistants.

ACADEMICS

Degrees: Bachelor's. **Classes:** Most classes have 10–19 students. Most lab/discussion sessions have 10–19 students. **Most popular majors:** Biology, General; Biochemistry, Biophysics and Molecular Biology, Other; Psychology, General. **Special Study Options:** Accelerated program; Cooperative education program; Cross-registration; Double major; Dual enrollment; Exchange student program (domestic); Honors program; Independent study; Internships; Liberal arts/career combination; Student-designed major; Study abroad. **Combined degree programs:** BA/JD; BA/MA. **Disability Services offered:** Note-taking services; Reader services; Tape recorders; Tutors. **Career services:** Alumni network; Alumni services; Career assessment; Internships; Regional alumni.

FACILITIES

Housing: Coed dorms; Fraternity/sorority housing; Theme housing; Women's dorms; 96% of campus accessible to physically disabled. **Special Academic Facilities/Equipment:** Art gallery, Asian art collection, anthropology museum, planetarium, outdoor observatory, two electron microscopes, outdoor sculpture walk, technology/video-conferencing center, rock-climbing walls, organic garden.

CAMPUS LIFE

Environment: Town. **Activities:** Campus Ministries; Choral groups; Concert band; Dance; Drama/theater; International Student Organization; Jazz band; Literary magazine; Model UN; Music ensembles; Musical theater; Radio station; Student government; Student newspaper; Student-run film society; Symphony orchestra; Yearbook. 86 registered organizations, 3 honor societies,

4 religious organizations, 4 fraternities, 4 sororities, on campus. **Athletics (Intercollegiate):** *Men:* baseball, basketball, cross-country, golf, soccer, swimming, tennis. *Women:* basketball, cross-country, golf, soccer, swimming, tennis, volleyball. **On-Campus Highlights:** Reid Campus Center.

ADMISSIONS

Freshman Academic Profile: Average high school GPA 3.8. 59% in top 10% of high school class, 88% in top 25% of high school class, 98% in top 50% of high school class. 62% from public high schools. **Test Scores:** SAT Math middle 50% range 510–680. SAT EBRW middle 50% range 510–690. ACT middle 50% range 26–31. **Basis for Candidate Selection:** *Very important factors include:* rigor of secondary school record, academic GPA, application essay. *Important factors include:* recommendation(s), extracurricular activities, talent/ability, character/personal qualities. *Other factors include:* class rank, standardized test scores, interview, first generation, alumni/ae relation, geographical residence, state residency, religious affiliation/commitment, racial/ethnic status, volunteer work, work experience, level of applicant's interest. **Freshman Admission Requirements:** High school diploma is required and GED is accepted. *Academic units recommended:* 4 English, 4 math, 3 science, 3 science labs, 2 foreign language, 2 social studies, 2 history. **Freshman Admission Statistics:** 4,081 applied, 52% admitted, 18% enrolled. **Transfer Admission Requirements:** High school transcript, college transcript(s), essay or personal statement, statement of good standing from prior institution(s). Lowest grade transferable C-. **General Admission Information:** Application fee $50. Priority deadline 11/15. Regular application deadline 1/15. Admission may be deferred for a maximum of 1 year.

COSTS AND FINANCIAL AID

Annual tuition $53,420. Room and board $13,512. Required fees $400. Average book and supplies expense $1,400. **Required Forms and Deadlines:** CSS/Financial Aid PROFILE; FAFSA; Noncustodial PROFILE;. **Notification of Awards:** Applicants will be notified of awards on or about 4/1. **Types of Aid:** *Need-based scholarships/grants:* College/university scholarship or grant aid from institutional funds; Federal Pell; Private scholarships; SEOG; State scholarships/grants. *Loans:* Direct PLUS loans; Direct Subsidized Stafford Loans; Direct Unsubsidized Stafford Loans. **Student Employment:** Federal Work-Study Program available. Institutional employment available. **Financial Aid Statistics:** 100% needy freshmen, 100% needy undergrads receive need-based scholarship or grant aid. 48% freshmen, 33% undergrads receive non-need-based scholarship or grant aid. 79% freshmen, 79% undergrads receive need-based self-help aid. 0% freshmen, 0% undergrads receive athletic scholarships. 83% freshmen, 76% undergrads receive any aid. 46% undergrads borrow to pay for school. Average cumulative indebtedness $23,254. **Criteria awarding aid:** *Need-based:* Academics, Art, Minority status, Music/drama *Non-need-based:* Academics, Art, Minority status, Music/drama.

WHITTIER COLLEGE

13406 E. Philadelphia Street, Whittier, CA 90608
Phone: 562-907-4238 **Financial Aid Phone:** 562-907-4285
E-mail: admissions@whittier.edu **CEEB Code:** 4952
Fax: 562-907-4870 **Website:** www.whittier.edu **ACT Code:** 480

This private school was founded in 1887. It has a 75 acre campus.

RATINGS

Admissions Selectivity Rating: 74 **Fire Safety Rating:** 95 **Green Rating:** 60*

STUDENTS AND FACULTY

Enrollment: 1,664. **Student Body:** 56% female, 44% male, 16% out-of-state, 3% international (24 countries represented). Asian 7%, African American 5%, Caucasian 27%, Hispanic 50%, Native American <1%, Pacific Islander <1%, Two or more races 7%, Race unknown 1%. **Retention and Graduation:** 78% freshmen return for sophomore year. 58% freshmen graduate within 4 years. 63% freshmen graduate within 6 years. 18% grads go on to further study within 1 year. 7% grads pursue arts and sciences degrees. 2% grads pursue law degrees. 3% grads pursue business degrees. 1% grads pursue medical degrees. **Faculty:** Student/faculty ratio 12:1. 119 full-time faculty, 95% hold PhDs, 30% are members of minority groups, 51% are women. 0% of classes are taught by teaching assistants.

ACADEMICS

Degrees: Bachelor's; Doctoral degree—professional practice; Master's. **Classes:** Most classes have 10–19 students. Most lab/discussion sessions have 10–19 students. **Most popular majors:** Business Administration and Management, General; Political Science and Government, General; Psychology, General. **Special Study Options:** Double major; Independent study; Internships; Liberal arts/career combination; Student-designed major; Study abroad; Teacher certification program. **Combined degree programs:** BA/JD. **Disability Services offered:** Note-taking services; Reader services; Tape recorders. **Career services:** Alumni network; Alumni services; Career assessment; Career/job search classes; Internships; Regional alumni.

FACILITIES

Housing: Apartments for single students; Coed dorms; Special housing for disabled students; Theme housing 60% of campus accessible to physically disabled. **Special Academic Facilities/Equipment:** Performing arts center, on-campus pre-school/ elementary school, image processing lab, state-of-the-art nightclub, on-air radio studio and production room, video production room. **Campus Network:** 100% of classrooms, 100% of dorms, 100% of libraries, 100% of dining areas, 50% of common outdoor areas have wireless network access.

CAMPUS LIFE

Environment: City. **Activities:** Campus Ministries; Choral groups; Dance; Drama/theater; International Student Organization; Jazz band; Literary magazine; Model UN; Music ensembles; Radio station; Student government; Student newspaper; Student-run film society; Television station; Yearbook. 60 registered organizations, 17 honor societies, 6 religious organizations, 4 fraternities, 5 sororities on campus. **Athletics (Intercollegiate):** *Men:* baseball, basketball, cross-country, diving, football, golf, lacrosse, soccer, swimming, tennis, track/field (outdoor), water polo. *Women:* basketball, cross-country, diving, lacrosse, soccer, softball, swimming, tennis, track/field (outdoor), volleyball, water polo. **On-Campus Highlights:** The Campus Center. **Environmental Initiatives:** Climate Commitment signatory.

ADMISSIONS

Freshman Academic Profile: Average high school GPA 3.5. 21% in top 10% of high school class, 63% in top 25% of high school class, 92% in top 50% of high school class. **Test Scores:** SAT Math middle 50% range 500–600. SAT EBRW middle 50% range 510–620. ACT middle 50% range 21–27. **Basis for Candidate Selection:** *Very important factors include:* rigor of secondary school record, academic GPA, application essay, recommendation(s), character/personal qualities. *Important factors include:* interview, extracurricular activities, talent/ability. *Other factors include:* class rank, standardized test scores, first generation, alumni/ae relation, geographical residence, state residency, racial/ethnic status, work experience. **Freshman Admission Requirements:** High school diploma is required and GED is accepted. *Academic units required:* 3 English, 2 math, 1 science, 1 science labs, 2 foreign language, 1 social studies. *Academic units recommended:* 4 English, 3 math, 2 science, 3 foreign language, 2 social studies. **Freshman Admission Statistics:** 4,585 applied, 99% admitted, 11% enrolled. **Transfer Admission Requirements:** High school transcript, college transcript(s), essay or personal statement. Lowest grade transferable C-. **General Admission Information:** Application fee $50. Priority deadline 2/1. Non-fall registration accepted. Admission may be deferred for a maximum of 1 year.

COSTS AND FINANCIAL AID

Annual tuition $47,496. Room and board $13,742. Required fees $590. Average book and supplies expense $800. **Required Forms and Deadlines:** FAFSA. **Notification of Awards:** Applicants will be notified of awards on a rolling basis beginning 2/15. **Types of Aid:** *Need-based scholarships/grants:* College/university scholarship or grant aid from institutional funds; Federal Pell; Private scholarships; SEOG; State scholarships/grants. *Loans:* Direct PLUS loans; Direct Subsidized Stafford Loans; Direct Unsubsidized Stafford Loans. **Student Employment:** Federal Work-Study Program available. **Financial Aid Statistics:** 86% needy freshmen, 89% needy undergrads receive need-based scholarship or grant aid. 14% freshmen, 11% undergrads receive non-need-based scholarship or grant aid. 81% freshmen, 82% undergrads receive need-based self-help aid. 0% freshmen, 0% undergrads receive athletic scholarships. 92% freshmen, 89% undergrads receive any aid. 77% undergrads borrow to pay for school. Average cumulative indebtedness $32,167. **Criteria awarding aid:** *Need-based:* Job skills, Leadership, Religious affiliation. *Non-need-based:* Academics, Alumni affiliation, Art, Minority status, Music/drama.

WHITWORTH UNIVERSITY

300 W. Hawthorne Road, Spokane, WA 99251
Phone: 509-777-4786 **Financial Aid Phone:** 509-777-4340
E-mail: admissions@whitworth.edu **CEEB Code:** 4953
Fax: 509-777-3758 **Website:** www.whitworth.edu **ACT Code:** 4494

This private school, affiliated with the Presbyterian Church, was founded in 1890. It has a 200 acre campus.

RATINGS

Admissions Selectivity Rating: 77 **Fire Safety Rating:** 87 **Green Rating:** 60*

STUDENTS AND FACULTY

Enrollment: 2,387. **Student Body:** 58% female, 42% male, 28% out-of-state, 4% international (35 countries represented). Asian 5%, African American 2%, Caucasian 65%, Hispanic 12%, Native American 1%, Pacific Islander 1%, Two or more races 10%, Race unknown 1%. **Retention and Graduation:** 84% freshmen return for sophomore year. 63% freshmen graduate within 4 years. 76% freshmen graduate within 6 years. 18% grads go on to further study within 1 year. **Faculty:** Student/faculty ratio 12:1. 193 full-time faculty, 76% hold PhDs, 30% are members of minority groups, 46% are women. 0% of classes are taught by teaching assistants.

ACADEMICS

Degrees: Bachelor's; Master's; Post-bachelor's certificate; Post-master's certificate. **Classes:** Most classes have 10–19 students. Most lab/discussion sessions have 10–19 students. **Most popular majors:** Education, General; Biology/Biological Sciences, General; Business Administration and Management, General. **Special Study Options:** Accelerated program; Cross-registration; Distance learning; Double major; Dual enrollment; English as a Second Language (ESL); Exchange student program (domestic); Honors program; Independent study; Internships; Liberal arts/career combination; Student-designed major; Study abroad; Teacher certification program. **Honors programs:** Students in the George F. Whitworth Honors Program are challenged to distinguish themselves by developing habits of excellence in learning and life; integrating their studies with a profound sense of purpose; and achieving, as an ultimate goal, a wisdom that integrates mind and heart, faith and reason, and knowledge and service. Opportunities in the program may include honors general education or interdisciplinary courses, honors courses within a major, advanced seminars, honors creative projects, honors research, honors off-campus programs, and honors internships. **Disability Services offered:** Note-taking services; Reader services; Tape recorders. **Career services:** Alumni network; Alumni services; Career assessment; Career/job search classes; Internships; Regional alumni.

FACILITIES

Housing: Coed dorms; Men's dorms; Special housing for disabled students; Theme housing; Women's dorms; 80% of campus accessible to physically disabled.

CAMPUS LIFE

Environment: City. **Activities:** Campus Ministries; Choral groups; Concert band; Dance; Drama/theater; International Student Organization; Jazz band; Literary magazine; Music ensembles; Musical theater; Pep band; Radio station; Student government; Student newspaper; Symphony orchestra; Yearbook. **Athletics (Intercollegiate):** *Men:* baseball, basketball, cheerleading, cross-country, football, golf, soccer, swimming, tennis, track/field (outdoor). *Women:* basketball, cheerleading, cross-country, golf, soccer, softball, swimming, tennis, track/field (outdoor), volleyball. **On-Campus Highlights:** Hixson Student Union Building Mind & Hearth Coffee Shop.

ADMISSIONS

Freshman Academic Profile: Average high school GPA 3.6. 33% in top 10% of high school class, 64% in top 25% of high school class, 92% in top 50% of high school class. 85% from public high schools. **Test Scores:** SAT Math middle 50% range 520–640. SAT EBRW middle 50% range 530–650. ACT middle 50% range 21–29. **Basis for Candidate Selection:** *Very important factors include:* academic GPA, application essay. *Important factors include:* rigor of secondary school record, standardized test scores, interview, extracurricular activities, character/personal qualities. *Other factors include:* recommendation(s), talent/ability, first generation, alumni/ae relation, geographical residence, state residency, racial/ethnic status, volunteer work, work experience, level of applicant's interest. **Freshman Admission Requirements:** High school diploma is required and GED is accepted. *Academic units recommended:* 4 English, 3 math, 3 science, 2 science labs, 2 foreign language, 2 social studies,

2 history. **Freshman Admission Statistics:** 3,817 applied, 91% admitted, 20% enrolled. **Transfer Admission Requirements:** High school transcript, college transcript(s), essay or personal statement, standardized test scores, statement of good standing from prior institution(s). Minimum college GPA of 2.5 required. Lowest grade transferable C-. **General Admission Information:** Priority deadline 3/1. Regular application deadline 8/1. Non-fall registration accepted. Admission may be deferred for a maximum of 1 year.

COSTS AND FINANCIAL AID
Annual tuition $43,800. Room and board $11,800. Required fees $1,140. Average book and supplies expense $912. **Required Forms and Deadlines:** FAFSA. **Notification of Awards:** Applicants will be notified of awards on a rolling basis beginning 1/17. **Types of Aid:** *Need-based scholarships/grants:* College/university scholarship or grant aid from institutional funds; Federal Pell; Private scholarships; SEOG; State scholarships/grants. *Loans:* Direct PLUS loans; Direct Subsidized Stafford Loans; Direct Unsubsidized Stafford Loans. **Student Employment:** Federal Work-Study Program available. Institutional employment available. **Financial Aid Statistics:** 99% needy freshmen, 99% needy undergrads receive need-based scholarship or grant aid. 18% freshmen, 14% undergrads receive non-need-based scholarship or grant aid. 73% freshmen, 75% undergrads receive need-based self-help aid. 0% freshmen, 0% undergrads receive athletic scholarships. 99% freshmen, 99% undergrads receive any aid. 64% undergrads borrow to pay for school. Average cumulative indebtedness $32,607. **Criteria awarding aid:** *Need-based:* Academics, Music/drama *Non-need-based:* Academics, Alumni affiliation, Art, Minority status, Music/drama.

WICHITA STATE UNIVERSITY

1845 Fairmount, Wichita, KS 67260-0124
Phone: 316-978-3085 **Financial Aid Phone:** 1-855-978-1787
E-mail: admissions@wichita.edu **CEEB Code:** 6884
Fax: 316-978-3174 **Website:** www.wichita.edu **ACT Code:** 1472

This public school was founded in 1895. It has a 330 acre campus.

RATINGS
Admissions Selectivity Rating: 86   **Fire Safety Rating:** 84   **Green Rating:** 62

STUDENTS AND FACULTY
Enrollment: 11,204. **Student Body:** 54% female, 46% male, 12% out-of-state, 6% international (81 countries represented). Asian 7%, African American 6%, Caucasian 60%, Hispanic 13%, Native American 1%, Pacific Islander <1%, Two or more races 5%, Race unknown 2%.
Retention and Graduation: 71% freshmen return for sophomore year. 23% freshmen graduate within 4 years. 50% freshmen graduate within 6 years. **Faculty:** Student/faculty ratio 19:1. 551 full-time faculty, 70% hold PhDs, 19% are members of minority groups, 48% are women. 18% of classes are taught by teaching assistants.

ACADEMICS
Degrees: Associate; Bachelor's; Certificate; Doctoral degree—professional practice; Doctoral degree research/scholarship; Master's; Post-bachelor's certificate; Post-master's certificate; Terminal Associate; Transfer Associate. **Classes:** Most classes have 10–19 students. Most lab/discussion sessions have 10–19 students. **Special Study Options:** Accelerated program; Cooperative education program; Cross-registration; Distance learning; Double major; Dual enrollment; English as a Second Language (ESL); Exchange student program (domestic); Honors program; Independent study; Internships; Liberal arts/career combination; Study abroad; Teacher certification program. **Honors programs:** The Dorothy and Bill Cohen Honors College at WSU aims to prepare students for innovative intellectual, creative, and professional work in a complex society. We sit at the heart of an urban university with high research activity and a commitment to benefit the region and beyond. Honors students reflect these characteristics, while seeking to enrich their lives and the lives of others. **Disability Services offered:** Note-taking services; Reader services; Tape recorders; Tutors. **Career services:** Alumni network; Alumni services; Career assessment; Career/job search classes; Internships; Regional alumni.

FACILITIES
Housing: Apartments for married students; Apartments for single students; Coed dorms; Fraternity/sorority housing; 98% of campus accessible to physically disabled. **Special Academic Facilities/Equipment:** Art museum,

performance hall, media resource center, observatory, national institute of aviation research, supersonic wind tunnels, 24-hour study room in library, outdoor sculpture collection. The Innovation Campus has various laboratories, a community maker-space, and a mixed-use area, along with partnerships with companies to give students hands-on experience.

CAMPUS LIFE
Environment: Metropolis. **Activities:** Campus Ministries; Choral groups; Concert band; Dance; Drama/theater; International Student Organization; Jazz band; Literary magazine; Marching band; Model UN; Music ensembles; Musical theater; Opera; Pep band; Radio station; Student government; Student newspaper; Symphony orchestra. 235 registered organizations, 19 honor societies, 16 religious organizations, 11 fraternities, 11 sororities on campus. **Athletics (Intercollegiate):** *Men:* baseball, basketball, bowling, cheerleading, cross-country, golf, rugby, swimming, tennis, track/field (outdoor). *Women:* basketball, bowling, cheerleading, cross-country, golf, softball, swimming, tennis, track/field (outdoor), volleyball. **On-Campus Highlights:** Rhatigan Student Center. **Environmental Initiatives:** Recycle Program.

ADMISSIONS
Freshman Academic Profile: Average high school GPA 3.5. 19% in top 10% of high school class, 47% in top 25% of high school class, 82% in top 50% of high school class. **Test Scores:** SAT Math middle 50% range 530–640. SAT EBRW middle 50% range 510–630. ACT middle 50% range 20–27. **Basis for Candidate Selection:** *Very important factors include:* rigor of secondary school record, academic GPA, standardized test scores. *Important factors include:* class rank. *Other factors include:* extracurricular activities, talent/ability, work experience. **Freshman Admission Requirements:** High school diploma is required and GED is accepted. *Academic units required:* 4 English, 3 math, 3 science, 1 science labs, 3 social studies, 3 history, 3 academic electives. *Academic units recommended:* 4 English, 3 math, 3 science, 1 science labs, 3 foreign language, 3 social studies, 3 history, 3 academic electives, 3 computer science. **Freshman Admission Statistics:** 5,947 applied, 56% admitted, 49% enrolled. **Transfer Admission Requirements:** College transcript(s). Minimum college GPA of 2.0 required. Lowest grade transferable C. **General Admission Information:** Application fee $30. Non-fall registration accepted. Admission may be deferred for a maximum of 2 years.

COSTS AND FINANCIAL AID
Annual in-state tuition $6,708. Annual out-of-state tuition $15,890. Room and board $11,252. Required fees $1,562. Average book and supplies expense $1,250. **Required Forms and Deadlines:** FAFSA; State aid form. **Notification of Awards:** Applicants will be notified of awards on a rolling basis beginning 8/1. **Types of Aid:** *Need-based scholarships/grants:* College/university scholarship or grant aid from institutional funds; Federal Pell; Private scholarships; SEOG; State scholarships/grants; United Negro College Fund. *Loans:* Direct PLUS loans; Direct Subsidized Stafford Loans; Direct Unsubsidized Stafford Loans. **Student Employment:** Federal Work-Study Program available. Institutional employment available. **Financial Aid Statistics:** 66% needy freshmen, 68% needy undergrads receive need-based scholarship or grant aid. 63% freshmen, 46% undergrads receive non-need-based scholarship or grant aid. 64% freshmen, 70% undergrads receive need-based self-help aid. 2% freshmen, 2% undergrads receive athletic scholarships. 87.4% freshmen, 75% undergrads receive any aid. 61% undergrads borrow to pay for school. Average cumulative indebtedness $24,839. **Criteria awarding aid:** *Need-based:* Leadership, Music/drama *Non-need-based:* Academics, Alumni affiliation, Art, Athletics, Job skills.

WIDENER UNIVERSITY

One University Place, Chester, PA 19013
Phone: 610-499-4126 **Financial Aid Phone:** 610-499-4161
E-mail: admissions.office@widener.edu **CEEB Code:** 2642
Fax: 610-499-4676 **Website:** www.widener.edu **ACT Code:** 3652

This private school was founded in 1821. It has a 110 acre campus.

RATINGS
Admissions Selectivity Rating: 80   **Fire Safety Rating:** 60*   **Green Rating:** 60*

STUDENTS AND FACULTY
Enrollment: 3,179. **Student Body:** 57% female, 43% male, 40% out-of-state, 2% international (38 countries represented). Asian 3%, African American 13%, Caucasian 71%, Hispanic 5%, Native American <1%, Pacific Islander 0%, Two or more races 4%, Race unknown 2%.

Retention and Graduation: 78% freshmen return for sophomore year. 44% freshmen graduate within 4 years. 57% freshmen graduate within 6 years. 20% grads go on to further study within 1 year. **Faculty:** Student/faculty ratio 13:1. 271 full-time faculty, 89% hold PhDs, 17% are members of minority groups, 55% are women. 0% of classes are taught by teaching assistants.

ACADEMICS

Degrees: Associate; Bachelor's; Certificate; Doctoral degree—professional practice; Doctoral degree research/scholarship; Master's; Post-bachelor's certificate; Post-master's certificate. **Classes:** Most classes have 10–19 students. Most lab/discussion sessions have 10–19 students. **Most popular majors:** Business/Commerce, General; Registered Nursing/Registered Nurse; Psychology, General. **Special Study Options:** Accelerated program; Cooperative education program; Distance learning; Double major; Dual enrollment; Honors program; Independent study; Internships; Liberal arts/career combination; Student-designed major; Study abroad; Teacher certification program; Weekend college. **Honors programs:** Honors Program in General Education. **Combined degree programs:** BA/MA; BA/MD; BA/MEng. **Disability Services offered:** Note-taking services; Reader services; Tape recorders; Tutors. **Career services:** Alumni network; Alumni services; Career assessment; Career/job search classes; Regional alumni.

FACILITIES

Housing: Coed dorms; Cooperative housing; Fraternity/sorority housing; Men's dorms; Theme housing; Wellness housing; Women's dorms. **Special Academic Facilities/Equipment:** Art gallery, restaurant lab, child development center education lab, recording studio, commercial graphics lab, physical therapy lab, science labs, engineering labs, nursing labs, multimedia classrooms, Media Center.

CAMPUS LIFE

Environment: Town. **Activities:** Campus Ministries; Choral groups; Concert band; Dance; Drama/theater; International Student Organization; Jazz band; Literary magazine; Marching band; Music ensembles; Pep band; Radio station; Student government; Student-run film society; Television station. 80 registered organizations, 29 honor societies, 3 religious organizations, 5 fraternities, 6 sororities on campus. **Athletics (Intercollegiate):** *Men:* baseball, basketball, cross-country, football, golf, lacrosse, soccer, swimming, tennis, track/field (outdoor), track/field (indoor). *Women:* basketball, cheerleading, cross-country, field hockey, lacrosse, soccer, softball, swimming, tennis, track/field (outdoor), track/field (indoor), volleyball. **On-Campus Highlights:** University Center.

ADMISSIONS

Freshman Academic Profile: Average high school GPA 3.5. **Test Scores:** SAT Math middle 50% range 510–600. SAT EBRW middle 50% range 510–600. ACT middle 50% range 20–26. **Basis for Candidate Selection:** *Very important factors include:* rigor of secondary school record, class rank, academic GPA, standardized test scores. *Other factors include:* application essay, recommendation(s), interview, extracurricular activities, talent/ability, character/personal qualities, alumni/ae relation, volunteer work, level of applicant's interest. **Freshman Admission Requirements:** High school diploma is required and GED is accepted. *Academic units required:* 4 English, 3 math, 3 science, 2 foreign language, 3 social studies, 3 academic electives. *Academic units recommended:* 4 English, 4 math, 4 science, 2 science labs, 2 foreign language, 4 social studies, 3 academic electives. **Freshman Admission Statistics:** 6,422 applied, 69% admitted, 17% enrolled. **Transfer Admission Requirements:** College transcript(s). Minimum college GPA of 2.0 required. Lowest grade transferable C. **General Admission Information:** Non-fall registration accepted. Admission may be deferred for a maximum of 1 academic year.

COSTS AND FINANCIAL AID

Annual tuition $45,028. Room and board $14,446. Required fees $920. Average book and supplies expense $1,300. **Required Forms and Deadlines:** FAFSA. **Notification of Awards:** Applicants will be notified of awards on a rolling basis beginning 1/30. **Types of Aid:** *Need-based scholarships/grants:* College/university scholarship or grant aid from institutional funds; Federal Pell; Private scholarships; SEOG; State scholarships/grants. *Loans:* Direct PLUS loans; Direct Subsidized Stafford Loans; Direct Unsubsidized Stafford Loans. **Student Employment:** Federal Work-Study Program available. Institutional employment available. **Financial Aid Statistics:** 98% needy freshmen, 97% needy undergrads receive need-based scholarship or grant aid. 96% freshmen, 93% undergrads receive non-need-based scholarship or grant aid. 93% freshmen, 92% undergrads receive need-based self-help aid. 0% freshmen, 0% undergrads receive athletic scholarships. 99% freshmen, 90% undergrads receive any aid. **Criteria awarding aid:** *Need-based:* Academics. *Non-need-based:* Academics, Leadership, Music/drama.

WILKES UNIVERSITY

84 W South St, Wilkes-Barre, PA 18766
Phone: 570-408-4400 **Financial Aid Phone:** 570-408-2000
E-mail: admissions@wilkes.edu **CEEB Code:** 2977
Fax: 570-408-4904 **Website:** www.wilkes.edu **ACT Code:** 3756

This private school was founded in 1933. It has a 27 acre campus.

RATINGS
Admissions Selectivity Rating: 79   **Fire Safety Rating:** 87   **Green Rating:** 60*

STUDENTS AND FACULTY
Enrollment: 2,358. **Student Body:** 47% female, 53% male, 21% out-of-state, 7% international (13 countries represented). Asian 2%, African American 5%, Caucasian 72%, Hispanic 7%, Native American <1%, Pacific Islander <1%, Two or more races 3%, Race unknown 3%.
Retention and Graduation: 76% freshmen return for sophomore year. 47% freshmen graduate within 4 years. 60% freshmen graduate within 6 years. **Faculty:** Student/faculty ratio 12:1. 193 full-time faculty, 90% hold PhDs, 12% are members of minority groups, 48% are women. 0% of classes are taught by teaching assistants.

ACADEMICS
Degrees: Bachelor's; Doctoral degree—professional practice; Doctoral degree research/scholarship; Master's. **Classes:** Most classes have 10–19 students. Most lab/discussion sessions have 10–19 students. **Most popular majors:** Mechanical Engineering; Biology/Biological Sciences, General; Registered Nursing/Registered Nurse. **Special Study Options:** Accelerated program; Cooperative education program; Cross-registration; Distance learning; Double major; Dual enrollment; English as a Second Language (ESL); External degree program; Honors program; Independent study; Internships; Student-designed major; Study abroad; Teacher certification program; Weekend college. **Disability Services offered:** Note-taking services; Reader services; Tape recorders; Tutors. **Career services:** Alumni network; Alumni services; Career assessment; Career/job search classes; Internships; Regional alumni.

FACILITIES
Housing: Apartments for single students; Coed dorms; Men's dorms; Women's dorms. **Special Academic Facilities/Equipment:** Art gallery, performing arts center, electron microscope, television studio.

CAMPUS LIFE
Environment: City. **Activities:** Campus Ministries; Choral groups; Dance; Drama/theater; International Student Organization; Jazz band; Literary magazine; Marching band; Music ensembles; Musical theater; Pep band; Radio station; Student government; Student newspaper; Television station; Yearbook. 70 registered organizations, 19 honor societies on campus. **Athletics (Intercollegiate):** *Men:* baseball, basketball, cross-country, football, golf, soccer, tennis, wrestling. *Women:* basketball, cross-country, field hockey, lacrosse, soccer, softball, tennis, volleyball.

ADMISSIONS
Freshman Academic Profile: Average high school GPA 3.6. 23% in top 10% of high school class, 51% in top 25% of high school class, 84% in top 50% of high school class. **Test Scores:** SAT Math middle 50% range 520–620. SAT EBRW middle 50% range 530–620. ACT middle 50% range 21–27. **Basis for Candidate Selection:** *Very important factors include:* rigor of secondary school record, class rank. *Important factors include:* academic GPA, standardized test scores, extracurricular activities, character/personal qualities. *Other factors include:* recommendation(s), interview, talent/ability, alumni/ae relation, volunteer work, work experience. **Freshman Admission Requirements:** High school diploma is required and GED is accepted. *Academic units recommended:* 4 English, 3 math, 3 science, 2 science labs, 2 foreign language, 3 social studies, 1 computer science. **Freshman Admission Statistics:** 3,932 applied, 75% admitted, 22% enrolled. **Transfer Admission Requirements:** College transcript(s), statement of good standing from prior institution(s). Minimum college GPA of 2.0 required. Lowest grade transferable C. **General Admission Information:** Application fee $40. Non-fall registration accepted. Admission may be deferred for a maximum of 12 months.

COSTS AND FINANCIAL AID
Annual tuition $35,814. Room and board $14,682. Required fees $1,808. Average book and supplies expense $1,600. **Required Forms and Deadlines:** FAFSA. **Notification of Awards:** Applicants will be notified of awards on a rolling basis beginning 3/1. **Types of Aid:** *Need-based scholarships/grants:*

College/university scholarship or grant aid from institutional funds; Federal Pell; Private scholarships; SEOG; State scholarships/grants. *Loans:* Direct PLUS loans; Direct Subsidized Stafford Loans; Direct Unsubsidized Stafford Loans. **Student Employment:** Federal Work-Study Program available. Institutional employment available. **Financial Aid Statistics:** 100% needy freshmen, 99% needy undergrads receive need-based scholarship or grant aid. 61% freshmen, 75% undergrads receive non-need-based scholarship or grant aid. 88% freshmen, 89% undergrads receive need-based self-help aid. 0% freshmen, 0% undergrads receive athletic scholarships. 99% freshmen, 92% undergrads receive any aid. **Criteria awarding aid:** *Non-need-based:* Academics, Leadership, Minority status, Music/drama.

WILLAMETTE UNIVERSITY

Office of Admission Willamette University, Salem, OR 97301
Phone: 503-370-6303 **Financial Aid Phone:** 503-370-6273
E-mail: bearcat@willamette.edu **CEEB Code:** 4954
Fax: 503-375-5363 **Website:** http://www.willamette.edu **ACT Code:** 3504

This private school, affiliated with the Methodist Church, was founded in 1842. It has a 72 acre campus.

RATINGS
Admissions Selectivity Rating: 89   Fire Safety Rating: 98   Green Rating: 73

STUDENTS AND FACULTY
Enrollment: 1,479. **Student Body:** 59% female, 41% male, 71% out-of-state, 1% international (30 countries represented). Asian 6%, African American 2%, Caucasian 65%, Hispanic 15%, Native American 1%, Pacific Islander <1%, Two or more races 8%, Race unknown 4%.
Retention and Graduation: 84% freshmen return for sophomore year. 62% freshmen graduate within 4 years. 69% freshmen graduate within 6 years. 23% grads go on to further study within 1 year. 18% grads pursue arts and sciences degrees. 1% grads pursue law degrees. 1% grads pursue business degrees. 4% grads pursue medical degrees. **Faculty:** Student/faculty ratio 11:1. 178 full-time faculty, 98% hold PhDs, 24% are members of minority groups, 48% are women. 0% of classes are taught by teaching assistants.

ACADEMICS
Degrees: Bachelor's; Doctoral degree—professional practice; Master's. **Classes:** Most classes have 10–19 students. Most lab/discussion sessions have 10–19 students. **Most popular majors:** Biology/Biological Sciences, General; Psychology, General; Economics, General. **Special Study Options:** Accelerated program; Cross-registration; Double major; Dual enrollment; Exchange student program (domestic); Independent study; Internships; Student-designed major; Study abroad; Teacher certification program. **Honors programs:** Our challenging curriculum includes a variety of opportunities for individualized honors study, for example: Presidential Scholars (senior year), Carson Undergraduate Research Program, Science Collaborative Research Program, various departmental honors programs. **Combined degree programs:** BA/JD. **Disability Services offered:** Note-taking services; Reader services; Tape recorders; Tutors. **Career services:** Alumni network; Career assessment; Career/job search classes; Internships.

FACILITIES
Housing: Apartments for single students; Coed dorms; Fraternity/sorority housing; 95% of campus accessible to physically disabled. **Special Academic Facilities/Equipment:** Student Art purchased annually and displayed in all public access buildings, Hallie Ford Museum of Art, Collections and papers of Congressional leaders from Oregon, Electron Microscope Lab (scanning and transmission), Herbarium, Japanese and Botanical Gardens, Carnegie Library (fully restored).

CAMPUS LIFE
Environment: City. **Activities:** Campus Ministries; Choral groups; Concert band; Dance; Drama/theater; International Student Organization; Jazz band; Literary magazine; Model UN; Music ensembles; Musical theater; Opera; Student government; Student newspaper; Student-run film society; Symphony orchestra; Yearbook. 107 registered organizations, 7 honor societies, 5 religious organizations, 5 fraternities, 4 sororities on campus. **Athletics (Intercollegiate):** *Men:* baseball, basketball, crew/rowing, cross-country, football, golf, soccer, swimming, tennis, track/field (outdoor), track/field (indoor). *Women:* basketball, crew/rowing, cross-country, golf, soccer, softball, swimming, tennis, track/field (outdoor), track/field (indoor), volleyball. **On-Campus Highlights:**

Hallie Ford Museum of Art. **Environmental Initiatives:** Kaneko Commons Residential Hall; Zena Forest—nearby 308-Acre Sustainable forest for research and teaching; New Construction Achieved LEED Gold status in 2007. Photo Voltaic panels, solar hot water heating, rainwater reclamation for flushing toilets, FSC wood products, Indoor Air Quality measures, low/no VOC materials and products, sustainability educational signage, high recycled content materials, energy efficient boilers, lighting control system, Energy Management System controls, 50% reduction in irrigation, low flow plumbing fixtures, use of plate-to-plate heat exchangers, sun shades, 95% recycle of construction waste, reflective roof coatings, use of local materials & labor, FSC cert furnishings, Fat Spaniel PV panel monitoring, electrical use monitoring, FLEX CAR program initiated, purchase of Green Power, energy star appliances, and more.

ADMISSIONS
Freshman Academic Profile: Average high school GPA 3.9. 48% in top 10% of high school class, 78% in top 25% of high school class, 96% in top 50% of high school class. 87% from public high schools. **Test Scores:** SAT Math middle 50% range 560–660. SAT EBRW middle 50% range 580–680. ACT middle 50% range 31–35. **Basis for Candidate Selection:** *Very important factors include:* rigor of secondary school record, class rank, academic GPA, application essay, standardized test scores. *Important factors include:* recommendation(s), interview. *Other factors include:* extracurricular activities, talent/ability, character/personal qualities, first generation, alumni/ae relation, geographical residence, racial/ethnic status. **Freshman Admission Requirements:** High school diploma is required and GED is accepted. *Academic units recommended:* 4 English, 4 math, 4 science, 4 foreign language, 4 social studies, 4 academic electives, 4 visual/performing arts. **Freshman Admission Statistics:** 3,972 applied, 78% admitted, 12% enrolled. **Transfer Admission Requirements:** High school transcript, college transcript(s), essay or personal statement, statement of good standing from prior institution(s). Lowest grade transferable C. **General Admission Information:** Application fee $50. Priority deadline 1/15. Regular application deadline 1/15. Non-fall registration accepted. Admission may be deferred for a maximum of 1 year.

COSTS AND FINANCIAL AID
Annual tuition $53,300. Room and board $13,328. Required fees $324. Average book and supplies expense $1,012. **Required Forms and Deadlines:** FAFSA. **Notification of Awards:** Applicants will be notified of awards on a rolling basis beginning 4/1. **Types of Aid:** *Need-based scholarships/grants:* College/university scholarship or grant aid from institutional funds; Federal Pell; Private scholarships; SEOG; State scholarships/grants. *Loans:* Direct PLUS loans; Direct Subsidized Stafford Loans; Direct Unsubsidized Stafford Loans. **Student Employment:** Federal Work-Study Program available. Institutional employment available. **Financial Aid Statistics:** 99% needy freshmen, 96% needy undergrads receive need-based scholarship or grant aid. 30% freshmen, 18% undergrads receive non-need-based scholarship or grant aid. 84% freshmen, 86% undergrads receive need-based self-help aid. 0% freshmen, 0% undergrads receive athletic scholarships. 100% freshmen, 99% undergrads receive any aid. 61% undergrads borrow to pay for school. Average cumulative indebtedness $26,973. **Criteria awarding aid:** *Need-based:* Academics, Alumni affiliation, Leadership, Minority status, Music/drama, Religious affiliation *Non-need-based:* Academics, Alumni affiliation, Leadership, Minority status, Music/drama, Religious affiliation.

WILLIAM & MARY

Office of Admissions,, Williamsburg, VA 23187-8795
Phone: 757-221-4223 **Financial Aid Phone:** 757-221-2420
E-mail: admission@wm.edu **CEEB Code:** 5115
Fax: 757-221-1242 **Website:** www.wm.edu **ACT Code:** 4344

This public school was founded in 1693. It has a 1200 acre campus.

RATINGS
Admissions Selectivity Rating: 95   Fire Safety Rating: 92   Green Rating: 60*

STUDENTS AND FACULTY
Enrollment: 6,249. **Student Body:** 57% female, 43% male, 31% out-of-state, 6% international (84 countries represented). Asian 8%, African American 7%, Caucasian 59%, Hispanic 9%, Native American <1%, Pacific Islander <1%, Two or more races 5%, Race unknown 6%.
Retention and Graduation: 95% freshmen return for sophomore year. 85% freshmen graduate within 4 years. 92% freshmen graduate within 6 years. 26%

grads go on to further study within 1 year. 48% grads pursue arts and sciences degrees. 6% grads pursue law degrees. 17% grads pursue business degrees. 12% grads pursue medical degrees. **Faculty:** Student/faculty ratio 12:1. 656 full-time faculty, 96% hold PhDs, 13% are members of minority groups, 41% are women. 0% of classes are taught by teaching assistants.

ACADEMICS

Degrees: Bachelor's; Doctoral degree—professional practice; Doctoral degree research/scholarship; Master's; Post-bachelor's certificate; Post-master's certificate. **Classes:** Most classes have 10–19 students. Most lab/discussion sessions have 10–19 students. **Most popular majors:** Political Science and Government, General; Biology/Biological Sciences, General; Psychology, General. **Special Study Options:** Accelerated program; Distance learning; Double major; Dual enrollment; English as a Second Language (ESL); Honors program; Independent study; Internships; Student-designed major; Study abroad; Teacher certification program. **Honors programs:** 1693 Scholars—This is a four-year award for approximately 8 of the College's most academically distinguished entering freshmen each year. 1693 Scholars include both Virginia residents and out-of-state students, and they all receive the full cost of education at the in-state level, including room and board. They enroll for classes early, participate in special seminars and programming, and receive funding and close mentoring for research projects. James Monroe Scholars—About 10% of the most academically distinguished entering freshmen are named Monroe Scholars. First-year Monroe Scholars are given the opportunity to live in Monroe housing and may apply for funding to support a summer research project to be completed the summer after their first year. Every Sophomore/Junior Scholar receives a $3,000 grant to conduct a research project the summer after their sophomore or junior year. All Monroes are invited to participate in the Monroe Enrichment series, which include small group discussions led by faculty members from across campus & various community events for Monroe Scholars. Sharpe Community Scholars—Sharpe is a specialized program for first-year students with the goal of connecting academic work to real-world community action with the intentional partnership of research and community engagement. Students take specially designed seminars that integrate community research projects with the seminars' curricula. The program has a living-learning community that provides a robust academic and co-curricular learning environment that promotes student development. W&M Scholars—The William & Mary Scholars Award is presented each year to a small group of academically distinguished students who have overcome unusual adversity and/or are members of underrepresented groups who would contribute to campus diversity. Many will be the first members of their families to attend college. W&M Scholars participate in workshops and participate in faculty-led research experiences. **Combined degree programs:** BA/MA. **Disability Services offered:** Note-taking services; Reader services; Tape recorders; Tutors. **Career services:** Alumni services; Career assessment; Internships.

FACILITIES

Housing: Apartments for single students; Coed dorms; Fraternity/sorority housing; Special housing for disabled students; Special housing for international students; Theme housing; 95% of campus accessible to physically disabled. **Special Academic Facilities/Equipment:** Observatory, continuous beam accelerator, 3 interdisciplinary centers (humanities, international studies, writing resources), marine science institute, materials processes research center, public policy research center, health policy research center, center for geospatial analysis, center for archeological research, Institute for the Theory and Practice of International Relations, environmental field laboratory, Reves Center for International Studies, Special Collections Research Center, Charles W. Reeder Media Center, Muscarelle Museum of Art, College Woods, Lake Matoaka and Matoaka Trails (10 miles of nature trails surrounding the lake). **Campus Network:** 90% of classrooms, 100% of dorms, 100% of student union, 100% of libraries, 100% of dining areas, 30% of common outdoor areas have wireless network access.

CAMPUS LIFE

Environment: Town. **Activities:** Campus Ministries; Choral groups; Concert band; Dance; Drama/theater; International Student Organization; Jazz band; Literary magazine; Model UN; Music ensembles; Musical theater; Opera; Pep band; Radio station; Student government; Student newspaper; Student-run film society; Symphony orchestra; Television station; Yearbook. 475 registered organizations, 19 honor societies, 30 religious organizations, 19 fraternities, 14 sororities on campus. **Athletics (Intercollegiate):** *Men:* baseball, basketball, cheerleading, cross-country, diving, football, golf, gymnastics, soccer, swimming, tennis, track/field (outdoor), track/field (indoor). *Women:* basketball, cheerleading, cross-country, diving, field hockey, golf, gymnastics, lacrosse, soccer, swimming, tennis, track/field (outdoor), track/field (indoor), volleyball. **On-Campus Highlights:** Wren Building (oldest academic building).

ADMISSIONS

Freshman Academic Profile: Average high school GPA 4.2. 77% in top 10% of high school class, 95% in top 25% of high school class, 99% in top 50% of high school class. 77% from public high schools. **Test Scores:** SAT Math middle 50% range 650–760. SAT EBRW middle 50% range 660–730. ACT middle 50% range 30–33. **Basis for Candidate Selection:** *Very important factors include:* rigor of secondary school record, class rank, academic GPA, application essay, standardized test scores, recommendation(s), extracurricular activities, talent/ability, character/personal qualities, state residency, volunteer work, work experience. *Other factors include:* interview, first generation, alumni/ae relation, geographical residence, racial/ethnic status, level of applicant's interest. **Freshman Admission Requirements:** High school diploma or equivalent is not required. *Academic units recommended:* 4 English, 4 math, 4 science, 3 science labs, 4 foreign language, 4 social studies. **Freshman Admission Statistics:** 14,644 applied, 37% admitted, 29% enrolled. **Transfer Admission Requirements:** High school transcript, college transcript(s), essay or personal statement, statement of good standing from prior institution(s). Minimum college GPA of 3.00 required. Lowest grade transferable C. **General Admission Information:** Application fee $75. Regular application deadline 1/1. Admission may be deferred for a maximum of 1 year.

COSTS AND FINANCIAL AID

Annual in-state tuition $17,434. Annual out-of-state tuition $40,089. Room and board $12,926. Required fees $6,194. Average book and supplies expense $1,000. **Required Forms and Deadlines:** CSS/Financial Aid PROFILE; FAFSA. **Notification of Awards:** Applicants will be notified of awards on or about 3/15. **Types of Aid:** *Need-based scholarships/grants:* College/university scholarship or grant aid from institutional funds; Federal Pell; Private scholarships; SEOG; State scholarships/grants. *Loans:* Direct PLUS loans; Direct Subsidized Stafford Loans; Direct Unsubsidized Stafford Loans. **Student Employment:** Federal Work-Study Program available. Institutional employment available. **Financial Aid Statistics:** 90% needy freshmen, 89% needy undergrads receive need-based scholarship or grant aid. 42% freshmen, 37% undergrads receive non-need-based scholarship or grant aid. 49% freshmen, 58% undergrads receive need-based self-help aid. 5% freshmen, 5% undergrads receive athletic scholarships. 40% freshmen, 36% undergrads receive any aid. 35% undergrads borrow to pay for school. Average cumulative indebtedness $25,409. **Criteria awarding aid:** *Need-based:* Academics, Alumni affiliation, Athletics, Music/drama *Non-need-based:* Academics, Art, Athletics, Music/drama.

WILLIAM JEWELL COLLEGE

500 College Hill, Liberty, MO 64068
Phone: 816-415-7511 **Financial Aid Phone:** 816-415-5973
E-mail: admission@william.jewell.edu **CEEB Code:** 6941
Fax: 816-415-5040 **Website:** www.jewell.edu **ACT Code:** 2394

This private school was founded in 1849. It has a 200 acre campus.

RATINGS

Admissions Selectivity Rating: 89	Fire Safety Rating: 88	Green Rating: 60*

STUDENTS AND FACULTY

Enrollment: 734. **Student Body:** 54% female, 46% male, 37% out-of-state, 2% international (10 countries represented). Asian 1%, African American 5%, Caucasian 78%, Hispanic 7%, Native American <1%, Pacific Islander <1%, Two or more races 4%, Race unknown 2%.
Retention and Graduation: 80% freshmen return for sophomore year. 55% freshmen graduate within 4 years. 63% freshmen graduate within 6 years. 21% grads go on to further study within 1 year. 18% grads pursue arts and sciences degrees. 2% grads pursue law degrees. 1% grads pursue business degrees. 0% grads pursue medical degrees. **Faculty:** Student/faculty ratio 10:1. 69 full-time faculty, 86% hold PhDs, 4% are members of minority groups, 45% are women. 0% of classes are taught by teaching assistants.

ACADEMICS

Degrees: Bachelor's; Master's; Post-bachelor's certificate. **Classes:** Most classes have 10–19 students. Most lab/discussion sessions have fewer than 10 students. **Most popular majors:** Biology/Biological Sciences, General; Registered

Nursing/Registered Nurse; Business Administration and Management, General. **Special Study Options:** Accelerated program; Distance learning; Double major; Honors program; Independent study; Internships; Liberal arts/career combination; Student-designed major; Study abroad; Teacher certification program. **Honors programs:** The Oxbridge Honors Program combines British tutorial methods of instruction with opportunities for a year of study in Oxford, England. For the Honors Institute in Critical Thinking, students must complete Jewell's admission application and check that they are interested in the Honors Institute. The Office of Admission will follow up with details about a video application. Jewell faculty select Fellows from a holistic review rather than identifying candidates solely through standardized test scores and high school achievements. **Disability Services offered:** Note-taking services; Reader services; Tape recorders. **Career services:** Alumni network; Alumni services; Career assessment; Career/job search classes; Internships; Regional alumni.

FACILITIES

Housing: Coed dorms; Fraternity/sorority housing; Men's dorms; Special housing for disabled students; Wellness housing; Women's dorms; 90% of campus accessible to physically disabled. **Special Academic Facilities/Equipment:** Art gallery, observatory, language and computer labs, high-ropes course, greenhouse.

CAMPUS LIFE

Environment: Town. **Activities:** Campus Ministries; Choral groups; Concert band; Dance; Drama/theater; International Student Organization; Jazz band; Literary magazine; Marching band; Music ensembles; Musical theater; Opera; Pep band; Student government; Student newspaper; Symphony orchestra. 50 registered organizations, 14 honor societies, 4 religious organizations, 3 fraternities, 3 sororities on campus. **Athletics (Intercollegiate):** *Men:* baseball, basketball, cheerleading, cross-country, football, golf, soccer, tennis, track/field (outdoor), track/field (indoor). *Women:* basketball, cheerleading, cross-country, golf, soccer, softball, tennis, track/field (outdoor), track/field (indoor), volleyball. **On-Campus Highlights:** Pryor Learning Commons—intellectual and innovative technology center. **Environmental Initiatives:** Campus recycling program.

ADMISSIONS

Freshman Academic Profile: Average high school GPA 3.6. 34% in top 10% of high school class, 61% in top 25% of high school class, 86% in top 50% of high school class. 90% from public high schools. **Test Scores:** SAT Math middle 50% range 540–650. SAT EBRW middle 50% range 540–650. ACT middle 50% range 22–27. **Basis for Candidate Selection:** *Very important factors include:* rigor of secondary school record, academic GPA. *Important factors include:* class rank, standardized test scores, recommendation(s), extracurricular activities, talent/ability, character/personal qualities. *Other factors include:* application essay, interview, first generation, alumni/ae relation, volunteer work, work experience. **Freshman Admission Requirements:** High school diploma is required and GED is accepted. *Academic units required:* 4 English, 3 math, 3 science, 1 science labs, 2 foreign language, 3 social studies. *Academic units recommended:* 4 math, 3 foreign language, 2 academic electives. **Freshman Admission Statistics:** 1,167 applied, 46% admitted, 31% enrolled. **Transfer Admission Requirements:** College transcript(s), statement of good standing from prior institution(s). Minimum college GPA of 2.5 required. Lowest grade transferable C-. **General Admission Information:** Non-fall registration accepted. Admission may be deferred for a maximum of 1 year.

COSTS AND FINANCIAL AID

Annual tuition $33,500. Room and board $10,220. Required fees $950. Average book and supplies expense $800. **Required Forms and Deadlines:** FAFSA. **Notification of Awards:** Applicants will be notified of awards on a rolling basis beginning 11/1. **Types of Aid:** *Need-based scholarships/grants:* College/university scholarship or grant aid from institutional funds; Federal Pell; Private scholarships; SEOG; State scholarships/grants; United Negro College Fund. *Loans:* Direct PLUS loans; Direct Subsidized Stafford Loans; Direct Unsubsidized Stafford Loans. **Student Employment:** Federal Work-Study Program available. Institutional employment available. **Financial Aid Statistics:** 100% needy freshmen, 100% needy undergrads receive need-based scholarship or grant aid. 19% freshmen, 20% undergrads receive non-need-based scholarship or grant aid. 78% freshmen, 76% undergrads receive need-based self-help aid. 15% freshmen, 15% undergrads receive athletic scholarships. 100% freshmen, 99% undergrads receive any aid. 59% undergrads borrow to pay for school. Average cumulative indebtedness $37,322. **Criteria awarding aid:** *Need-based:* Leadership *Non-need-based:* Academics, Alumni affiliation, Athletics, Music/drama.

WILLIAM PATERSON UNIVERSITY

Morrison Hall, Wayne, NJ 07470
Phone: 973-720-2125 **Financial Aid Phone:** 973-720-3945
E-mail: admissions@wpunj.edu **CEEB Code:** 2518
Fax: 973-720-2910 **Website:** www.wpunj.edu **ACT Code:** 2584

This public school was founded in 1855. It has a 370 acre campus.

RATINGS

Admissions Selectivity Rating: 73   **Fire Safety Rating:** 98   **Green Rating:** 85

STUDENTS AND FACULTY

Enrollment: 8,641. **Student Body:** 55% female, 45% male, 2% out-of-state, <1% international (37 countries represented). Asian 7%, African American 19%, Caucasian 37%, Hispanic 32%, Native American <1%, Pacific Islander 0%, Two or more races 3%, Race unknown 1%.
Retention and Graduation: 70% freshmen return for sophomore year. 27% freshmen graduate within 4 years. 55% freshmen graduate within 6 years. 22% grads go on to further study within 1 year. **Faculty:** Student/faculty ratio 14:1. 403 full-time faculty, 92% hold PhDs, 36% are members of minority groups, 50% are women. 0% of classes are taught by teaching assistants.

ACADEMICS

Degrees: Bachelor's; Certificate; Doctoral degree—professional practice; Master's; Post-bachelor's certificate; Post-master's certificate. **Classes:** Most classes have 10–19 students. **Special Study Options:** Accelerated program; Cross-registration; Distance learning; Double major; Dual enrollment; English as a Second Language (ESL); Exchange student program (domestic); Honors program; Independent study; Internships; Liberal arts/career combination; Study abroad; Teacher certification program. **Honors programs:** University Honors College offers honors research tracks as well as honors general education courses. For more information please visit our Honors College http://www.wpunj.edu/honors-program. **Combined degree programs:** BA/MA. **Disability Services offered:** Note-taking services; Reader services; Tape recorders; Tutors. **Career services:** Alumni network; Alumni services; Career assessment; Career/job search classes; Internships.

FACILITIES

Housing: Apartments for single students; Coed dorms; Special housing for disabled students; 88% of campus accessible to physically disabled. **Special Academic Facilities/Equipment:** Art galleries; Collection of NJ State Documents; Collection of William Paterson's private papers; Interactive television classroom; Neurobiology facility; E-Trading Campus Network with ATM technology; Center for Computer Art and Animation; State-of-the-art electron microscopy facility; Teleconference Center with uplink and downlink capabilities; 44,000 square foot, state-of-the-art studio art facility; Center for Electro-Acoustic Music (CEM); E-Trade Financial Learning Center, a real-time simulated trading and financial educational facility; Russ Berrie Institute for Professional Sales including real-time Sales Laboratory.

CAMPUS LIFE

Environment: Town. **Activities:** Campus Ministries; Choral groups; Dance; Drama/theater; Literary magazine; Model UN; Music ensembles; Musical theater; Opera; Pep band; Radio station; Student government; Student newspaper; Student-run film society; Symphony orchestra; Television station; Yearbook. 139 registered organizations, 27 honor societies, 5 religious organizations, 12 fraternities, 11 sororities on campus. **Athletics (Intercollegiate):** *Men:* baseball, basketball, football, soccer, swimming. *Women:* basketball, cheerleading, field hockey, soccer, softball, swimming, volleyball. **On-Campus Highlights:** Student Center: Coffee Cafe (Starbucks). **Environmental Initiatives:** ACUPCC.

ADMISSIONS

Freshman Academic Profile: Average high school GPA 2.9. **Test Scores:** SAT Math middle 50% range 440–540. SAT EBRW middle 50% range 450–550. ACT middle 50% range 16–23. **Basis for Candidate Selection:** *Very important factors include:* rigor of secondary school record, academic GPA. *Other factors include:* application essay, standardized test scores, recommendation(s), interview, extracurricular activities, talent/ability, character/personal qualities, first generation, alumni/ae relation, volunteer work, work experience, level of applicant's interest. **Freshman Admission Requirements:** High school diploma is required and GED is accepted. *Academic units required:* 4 English, 3 math, 2 science, 2 science labs, 2 social studies, 5 academic electives. **Freshman Admission Statistics:** 8,150 applied, 93% admitted, 22% enrolled. **Transfer**

Admission Requirements: College transcript(s). Minimum college GPA of 2.00 required. Lowest grade transferable C. **General Admission Information:** Application fee $50. Priority deadline 12/1. Regular application deadline 6/1. Non-fall registration accepted. Admission may be deferred for a maximum of 1 semester.

COSTS AND FINANCIAL AID

Required Forms and Deadlines: FAFSA. **Notification of Awards:** Applicants will be notified of awards on a rolling basis beginning 2/1. **Types of Aid:** *Need-based scholarships/grants:* College/university scholarship or grant aid from institutional funds; Federal Pell; Private scholarships; SEOG; State scholarships/grants. *Loans:* Direct PLUS loans; Direct Subsidized Stafford Loans; Direct Unsubsidized Stafford Loans. **Student Employment:** Federal Work-Study Program available. Institutional employment available. **Financial Aid Statistics:** 74% needy freshmen, 71% needy undergrads receive need-based scholarship or grant aid. 18% freshmen, 26% undergrads receive non-need-based scholarship or grant aid. 72% freshmen, 72% undergrads receive need-based self-help aid. 0% freshmen, 0% undergrads receive athletic scholarships. 88% freshmen, 77% undergrads receive any aid. 74% undergrads borrow to pay for school. Average cumulative indebtedness $31,105. **Criteria awarding aid:** *Need-based:* Academics. *Non-need-based:* Academics, Art, Music/drama.

WILLIAM PEACE UNIVERSITY

15 East Peace Street, Raleigh, NC 27604
Phone: 919.508.2214 **Financial Aid Phone:** 919.508.2214
E-mail: admissions@peace.edu **CEEB Code:** 002953
Fax: 919.508-2306 **Website:** www.peace.edu **ACT Code:** 3136

This private school, affiliated with the Presbyterian Church, was founded in 1857. It has a 21 acre campus.

RATINGS

Admissions Selectivity Rating: 73 **Fire Safety Rating:** 60* **Green Rating:** 61

STUDENTS AND FACULTY

Enrollment: 1,076. **Student Body:** 72% female, 28% male, 6% out-of-state, <1% international. Asian 2%, African American 34%, Caucasian 43%, Hispanic 4%, Native American 1%, Pacific Islander 0%, Two or more races 5%, Race unknown 11%.
Retention and Graduation: 63% freshmen return for sophomore year.
Faculty: Student/faculty ratio 15:1. 24 full-time faculty, 79% hold PhDs, 4% are members of minority groups, 58% are women. 0% of classes are taught by teaching assistants.

ACADEMICS

Degrees: Bachelor's. **Classes:** Most classes have 10–19 students. Most lab/discussion sessions have 10–19 students. **Special Study Options:** Cross-registration; Distance learning; Double major; Honors program; Independent study; Internships; Liberal arts/career combination; Study abroad; Teacher certification program; Weekend college. **Career services:** Alumni network; Career assessment; Career/job search classes; Internships.

FACILITIES

Housing: Apartments for single students; Coed dorms; Women's dorms. **Campus Network:** 100% of classrooms, 100% of dorms, 100% of student union, 100% of libraries, 100% of dining areas, 0% of common outdoor areas have wireless network access.

CAMPUS LIFE

Environment: Metropolis. **Activities:** Campus Ministries; Choral groups; Dance; Drama/theater; Literary magazine; Music ensembles; Musical theater; Student government; Student newspaper. 30 registered organizations on campus. **On-Campus Highlights:** Hermann Athletic Center.

ADMISSIONS

Freshman Academic Profile: Average high school GPA 3.1. 6% in top 10% of high school class, 26% in top 25% of high school class, 57% in top 50% of high school class. **Test Scores:** SAT Math middle 50% range 400–510. SAT EBRW middle 50% range 410–520. ACT middle 50% range 16–21. **Basis for Candidate Selection:** *Very important factors include:* rigor of secondary school record, academic GPA, standardized test scores. *Important factors include:* application essay, recommendation(s), interview, extracurricular activities, volunteer work. *Other factors include:* class rank, talent/ability, character/

personal qualities, alumni/ae relation, geographical residence, work experience. **Freshman Admission Requirements:** High school diploma is required and GED is accepted. *Academic units required:* 4 English, 3 math, 3 science, 2 science labs, 2 social studies. *Academic units recommended:* 4 math, 2 foreign language. **Freshman Admission Statistics:** 1,083 applied, 91% admitted, 33% enrolled. **General Admission Information:** Application fee $35. Non-fall registration accepted. Admission may be deferred for a maximum of 1 year.

COSTS AND FINANCIAL AID

Annual tuition $24,450. Room and board $9,450. Required fees $400.
Required Forms and Deadlines: FAFSA. **Notification of Awards:** Applicants will be notified of awards on a rolling basis beginning 3/15. **Types of Aid:** *Need-based scholarships/grants:* College/university scholarship or grant aid from institutional funds; Federal Pell; Private scholarships; SEOG; State scholarships/grants. *Loans:* Direct PLUS loans; Direct Subsidized Stafford Loans; Direct Unsubsidized Stafford Loans. **Student Employment:** Federal Work-Study Program available. **Financial Aid Statistics:** 84% needy freshmen, 85% needy undergrads receive need-based scholarship or grant aid. 72% freshmen, 78% undergrads receive non-need-based scholarship or grant aid. 89% freshmen, 89% undergrads receive need-based self-help aid. 0% freshmen, 0% undergrads receive athletic scholarships. 91% freshmen, 91% undergrads receive any aid. **Criteria awarding aid:** *Non-need-based:* Academics, Leadership, Music/drama.

WILLIAM PENN UNIVERSITY

201 Trueblood Avenue, Oskaloosa, IA 52577
Phone: 641-673-1012
E-mail: admissions@wmpenn.edu **CEEB Code:** 6943
Fax: 641-673-2113 **Website:** www.wmpenn.edu **ACT Code:** 1372

This private school, affiliated with the Quaker Church, was founded in 1873. It has a 53 acre campus.

RATINGS

Admissions Selectivity Rating: 73 **Fire Safety Rating:** 60* **Green Rating:** 60*

STUDENTS AND FACULTY

Enrollment: 1,586. **Student Body:** 48% female, 52% male, 28% out-of-state, 2% international. Asian 1%, African American 15%, Caucasian 68%, Hispanic 7%, Native American 1%, Pacific Islander <1%, Two or more races 1%, Race unknown 5%.
Faculty: Student/faculty ratio 14:1. 35 full-time faculty, 49% hold PhDs, 3% are members of minority groups, 29% are women. 0% of classes are taught by teaching assistants.

ACADEMICS

Degrees: Associate; Bachelor's; Master's; Transfer Associate. **Classes:** Most classes have fewer than 10 students. **Most popular majors:** Education, General; Business/Commerce, General; Psychology, General. **Special Study Options:** Cooperative education program; Distance learning; Double major; Independent study; Internships; Study abroad; Teacher certification program. **Disability Services offered:** Tape recorders; Tutors. **Career services:** Alumni services; Career/job search classes; Internships.

FACILITIES

Housing: Apartments for married students; Apartments for single students; Coed dorms; Men's dorms; Special housing for international students; Women's dorms; 75% of campus accessible to physically disabled. **Special Academic Facilities/Equipment:** Foyer Gallery, Mid-East art and artifact collection. **Campus Network:** 100% of classrooms, 100% of dorms, 100% of student union, 100% of libraries, 100% of dining areas, 90% of common outdoor areas have wireless network access.

CAMPUS LIFE

Environment: Village. **Activities:** Campus Ministries; Choral groups; Concert band; Dance; Drama/theater; International Student Organization; Jazz band; Literary magazine; Marching band; Music ensembles; Musical theater; Pep band; Radio station; Student government; Student newspaper; Student-run film society; Yearbook. 34 registered organizations, 3 honor societies, 2 religious organizations, 3 fraternities, 4 sororities on campus. **Athletics (Intercollegiate):** *Men:* baseball, basketball, cheerleading, cross-country, football, golf, soccer, track/field (outdoor), wrestling. *Women:* basketball, cheerleading, cross-country, soccer, softball, track/field (outdoor), volleyball. **On-Campus Highlights:** Penn Activity Center (PAC).

ADMISSIONS

Freshman Academic Profile: 14% in top 25% of high school class, 47% in top 50% of high school class. 97% from public high schools. **Basis for Candidate Selection:** *Very important factors include:* rigor of secondary school record, academic GPA. *Important factors include:* class rank, standardized test scores, character/personal qualities. *Other factors include:* application essay, recommendation(s), interview, extracurricular activities, talent/ability, alumni/ae relation, volunteer work, work experience. **Freshman Admission Requirements:** High school diploma is required and GED is accepted. *Academic units recommended:* 4 English, 3 math, 3 science, 2 foreign language, 2 social studies, 2 history, 2 academic electives. **Freshman Admission Statistics:** 841 applied, 54% admitted, 53% enrolled. **Transfer Admission Requirements:** College transcript(s). Minimum college GPA of 2.0 required. Lowest grade transferable D. **General Admission Information:** Application fee $20. Priority deadline 7/1. Non-fall registration accepted.

COSTS AND FINANCIAL AID

Annual tuition $22,840. Room and board $5,472. Required fees $370. Average book and supplies expense $1,150. **Required Forms and Deadlines:** FAFSA. **Notification of Awards:** Applicants will be notified of awards on a rolling basis beginning 1/1. **Types of Aid:** *Need-based scholarships/grants:* College/university scholarship or grant aid from institutional funds; Federal Pell; Private scholarships; SEOG; State scholarships/grants. **Student Employment:** Federal Work-Study Program available. Institutional employment available. **Criteria awarding aid:** *Need-based:* Academics, Alumni affiliation, Athletics, Leadership, Music/drama, Religious affiliation. *Non-need-based:* Academics, Alumni affiliation, Athletics, Leadership, Music/drama, Religious affiliation.

WILLIAMS COLLEGE

995 Main St., Williamstown, MA 01267
Phone: 413-597-2211 **Financial Aid Phone:** (413) 597-4181
E-mail: admission@williams.edu **CEEB Code:** 3965
Fax: 413-597-4052 **Website:** www.williams.edu **ACT Code:** 1936

This private school was founded in 1793. It has a 450 acre campus.

RATINGS

Admissions Selectivity Rating: 98   **Fire Safety Rating:** 60*   **Green Rating:** 87

STUDENTS AND FACULTY

Enrollment: 2,025. **Student Body:** 50% female, 50% male, 84% out-of-state, 9% international (63 countries represented). Asian 12%, African American 7%, Caucasian 49%, Hispanic 13%, Native American <1%, Pacific Islander <1%, Two or more races 6%, Race unknown 4%.
Retention and Graduation: 97% freshmen return for sophomore year. 88% freshmen graduate within 4 years. 95% freshmen graduate within 6 years.
Faculty: Student/faculty ratio 7:1. 296 full-time faculty, 97% hold PhDs, 26% are members of minority groups, 46% are women. 0% of classes are taught by teaching assistants.

ACADEMICS

Degrees: Bachelor's; Master's. **Classes:** Most classes have 10–19 students. Most lab/discussion sessions have 10–19 students. **Most popular majors:** Econometrics and Quantitative Economics; Mathematics, General; Biology/Biological Sciences, General. **Special Study Options:** Cross-registration; Double major; Independent study; Student-designed major; Study abroad. **Disability Services offered:** Note-taking services; Reader services; Tape recorders; Tutors. **Career services:** Alumni network; Alumni services; Career assessment; Career/job search classes; Internships; Regional alumni.

FACILITIES

Housing: Apartments for married students; Coed dorms; Cooperative housing; Special housing for disabled students **Special Academic Facilities/Equipment:** College art museum, experimental forest, observatory, performing arts center, environmental studies center, rare books library, studio art center, electron scanning microscope, transmission microscopes, nuclear magnetic resonance imager, center for educational technology.

CAMPUS LIFE

Environment: Village. **Activities:** Campus Ministries; Choral groups; Concert band; Dance; Drama/theater; International Student Organization; Jazz band;
Literary magazine; Marching band; Music ensembles; Musical theater; Opera; Pep band; Radio station; Student government; Student newspaper; Student-run film society; Symphony orchestra; Yearbook. 140 registered organizations, 2 honor societies on campus. **Athletics (Intercollegiate):** *Men:* baseball, basketball, crew/rowing, cross-country, diving, football, golf, ice hockey, lacrosse, skiing (downhill/Alpine), skiing (Nordic/cross-country), soccer, squash, swimming, tennis, track/field (outdoor), track/field (indoor), wrestling. *Women:* basketball, crew/rowing, cross-country, diving, field hockey, golf, ice hockey, lacrosse, skiing (downhill/Alpine), skiing (Nordic/cross-country), soccer, softball, squash, swimming, tennis, track/field (outdoor), track/field (indoor), volleyball. **On-Campus Highlights:** Paresky Center. **Environmental Initiatives:** Over the past few years, the Zilkha Center (ZC) has focused on a number of big projects in the built environment, energy, and engagement in particular. The Class of 1966 Environmental Center completed its performance year without fully meeting the requirements of the Living Building Challenge, however the building was Petal Certified and is undergoing further work to become fully certified—the Zilkha Center has overseen this process. The Zilkha Center is coordinating a partnership with four other liberal arts colleges to plan and purchase from a utility scale solar facility that will provide 80–90% of campus purchased electricity. Another main focus has been on reaching more of the community and at a deeper level of engagement. The ZC first year orientation program Root (focusing on sustainability, identity and social justice, started in 2015) has gained traction and enrolls more students each year—it has also aligned itself with further campus engagement opportunities through speakers and events and greater levels of coordination between the Zilkha Center and the Davis Center (the intercultural center, with whom the ZC plans and runs Root). This includes an installation of the Equity Drafting Table in order to get feedback and promote conversation about Equity in the Built Environment. The Zilkha Center is engaging a record number of students through internships on campus—this year we have hired 30 students for either a semester or for the full year, and an additional 8 in the summer. This year marks a new level of cross campus trainings on sustainability—the Zilkha Center staff have instituted trainings with Residential Advisors for first years and upperclassmen, Dining staff, Custodial staff, and new staff through Human Resources. To engage staff and faculty in a deeper and more meaningful way we have launched a Green Offices Program that encourages sustainability habits in the daily operations of staff offices and faculty departments. The Zilkha Center is continually sharing best practices and our work with the broader community through conference presentations, including conferences hosted by NESSBE, NESEA, AASHE, ILFI, NECSC, and more.

ADMISSIONS

Freshman Academic Profile: 85% in top 10% of high school class, 98% in top 25% of high school class, 99% in top 50% of high school class. 52% from public high schools. **Test Scores:** SAT Math middle 50% range 710–790. SAT EBRW middle 50% range 700–760. ACT middle 50% range 32–35. **Basis for Candidate Selection:** *Very important factors include:* rigor of secondary school record, class rank, academic GPA, standardized test scores, recommendation(s), character/personal qualities. *Important factors include:* application essay, extracurricular activities, talent/ability, first generation, alumni/ae relation, racial/ethnic status, volunteer work. *Other factors include:* geographical residence, religious affiliation/commitment. **Freshman Admission Requirements:** High school diploma or equivalent is not required. *Academic units recommended:* 4 English, 4 math, 4 science, 3 science labs, 4 foreign language, 4 social studies. **Freshman Admission Statistics:** 9,715 applied, 13% admitted, 45% enrolled. **Transfer Admission Requirements:** High school transcript, college transcript(s), essay or personal statement, standardized test scores, statement of good standing from prior institution(s). Minimum college GPA of 3.5 required. Lowest grade transferable C-. **General Admission Information:** Application fee $65. Regular application deadline 1/1. Admission may be deferred for a maximum of negotiable.

COSTS AND FINANCIAL AID

Annual tuition $59,350. Room and board $15,000. Average book and supplies expense $800. **Required Forms and Deadlines:** CSS/Financial Aid PROFILE; FAFSA; Noncustodial PROFILE. **Notification of Awards:** Applicants will be notified of awards on or about 4/1. **Types of Aid:** *Need-based scholarships/grants:* College/university scholarship or grant aid from institutional funds; Federal Pell; SEOG; State scholarships/grants. *Loans:* Direct PLUS loans; Direct Subsidized Stafford Loans; Direct Unsubsidized Stafford Loans. **Student Employment:** Federal Work-Study Program available. Institutional employment available. **Financial Aid Statistics:** 100% needy freshmen, 100% needy undergrads receive need-based scholarship or grant aid. 0% freshmen, 0% undergrads receive non-need-based scholarship or grant aid. 87% freshmen, 87% undergrads receive need-based self-help aid. 0% freshmen, 0% undergrads receive athletic scholarships. 52% freshmen, 52% undergrads receive any aid. 33% undergrads borrow to pay for school. Average cumulative indebtedness $15,911.

WILMINGTON COLLEGE (DE)

320 Dupont Highway, New Castle, DE 19720
Phone: 302-328-9401
E-mail: mlee@wilmcoll.edu **CEEB Code:** 5925
Fax: 302-328-5902 **Website:** www.wilmcoll.edu **ACT Code:** 635

This private school was founded in 1967. It has a 15 acre campus.

RATINGS
Admissions Selectivity Rating: 60* **Fire Safety Rating:** 60* **Green Rating:** 60*

STUDENTS AND FACULTY
Enrollment: 4,399. **Student Body:** 53% female, 47% male, 3% out-of-state, 0% international. Asian 1%, African American 14%, Caucasian 64%, Hispanic 2%, Native American <1%, Race unknown 19%.
Retention and Graduation: 87% freshmen return for sophomore year. 50% grads go on to further study within 1 year. 9% grads pursue arts and sciences degrees. 10% grads pursue law degrees. 80% grads pursue business degrees. 1% grads pursue medical degrees. **Faculty:** Student/faculty ratio 18:1. 0% of classes are taught by teaching assistants.

ACADEMICS
Degrees: Associate; Bachelor's; Certificate; Master's; Post-master's certificate. **Most popular majors:** Education, General; Business/Commerce, General. **Special Study Options:** Accelerated program; Cooperative education program; Distance learning; Double major; Independent study; Internships; Teacher certification program; Weekend college. **Disability Services offered:** Tutors. **Career services:** Alumni services; Career assessment; Career/job search classes; Internships.

CAMPUS LIFE
Environment: Village. **Activities:** Student government. 1 honor societies, on campus. **Athletics (Intercollegiate):** *Men:* baseball, basketball, cross-country, soccer. *Women:* basketball, softball.

ADMISSIONS
Basis for Candidate Selection: *Important factors include:* rigor of secondary school record, recommendation(s). **Freshman Admission Requirements:** High school diploma is required and GED is accepted. **Transfer Admission Requirements:** College transcript(s). Minimum college GPA of 2.0 required. Lowest grade transferable C. **General Admission Information:** Application fee $25. Non-fall registration accepted. Admission may be deferred for a maximum of 12 months.

COSTS AND FINANCIAL AID
Annual tuition $6,060. Average book and supplies expense $500. **Required Forms and Deadlines:** FAFSA. **Student Employment:** Federal Work-Study Program available.

WILMINGTON COLLEGE (OH)

1870 Quaker Way #2499, Wilmington, OH
Phone: 937-382-6661
CEEB Code: 1909
Website: www.wilmington.edu **ACT Code:** 3362

This private school, affiliated with the Quaker Church, was founded in 1870. It has a 65 acre campus.

RATINGS
Admissions Selectivity Rating: 80 **Fire Safety Rating:** 60* **Green Rating:** 60*

STUDENTS AND FACULTY
Enrollment: 1,274. **Student Body:** 56% female, 44% male, 6% out-of-state, 1% international. Asian <1%, African American 11%, Caucasian 72%, Hispanic 1%, Native American 1%, Pacific Islander 0%, Two or more races 3%, Race unknown 11%.
Retention and Graduation: 67% freshmen return for sophomore year. **Faculty:** Student/faculty ratio 14:1. 66 full-time faculty, 0% hold PhDs, 0% are members of minority groups, 0% are women. 0% of classes are taught by teaching assistants.

ACADEMICS
Degrees: Bachelor's; Master's. **Classes:** Most classes have 10–19 students. **Most popular majors:** Bible/Biblical Studies; Business Administration and Management, General; Psychology, General. **Special Study Options:** Cross-registration; Double major; Dual enrollment; Honors program; Independent study; Internships; Liberal arts/career combination; Student-designed major; Study abroad; Teacher certification program; Weekend college. **Disability Services offered:** Note-taking services; Reader services; Tape recorders; Tutors. **Career services:** Alumni services; Internships.

FACILITIES
Housing: Apartments for single students; Coed dorms; Fraternity/sorority housing; Men's dorms; Women's dorms; 100% of campus accessible to physically disabled. **Special Academic Facilities/Equipment:** Hiroshima-Nagasaki memorial collection and peace resource center, education lab, language lab, three farms, observatory, electron microscope. **Campus Network:** 100% of classrooms, 100% of dorms, 100% of student union, 100% of libraries, 100% of dining areas, 10% of common outdoor areas have wireless network access.

CAMPUS LIFE
Environment: Rural. **Activities:** Campus Ministries; Choral groups; Drama/theater; Music ensembles; Musical theater; Pep band; Student government; Student newspaper; Yearbook. 48 registered organizations, 3 honor societies, 3 religious organizations, 6 fraternities, 5 sororities on campus. **Athletics (Intercollegiate):** *Men:* baseball, basketball, cheerleading, cross-country, football, golf, soccer, swimming, tennis, track/field (outdoor), wrestling. *Women:* basketball, cheerleading, cross-country, golf, soccer, softball, swimming, tennis, track/field (outdoor), volleyball. **On-Campus Highlights:** Residence Hall room.

ADMISSIONS
Freshman Academic Profile: Average high school GPA 3.2. 11% in top 10% of high school class, 36% in top 25% of high school class, 70% in top 50% of high school class. **Test Scores:** SAT Math middle 50% range 420–550. SAT EBRW middle 50% range 440–560. ACT middle 50% range 18–23. **Basis for Candidate Selection:** *Very important factors include:* academic GPA. *Important factors include:* rigor of secondary school record, class rank, standardized test scores, talent/ability, character/personal qualities, alumni/ae relation. *Other factors include:* recommendation(s), interview, extracurricular activities, volunteer work, level of applicant's interest. **Freshman Admission Requirements:** High school diploma is required and GED is accepted. *Academic units required:* 4 English, 2 math, 2 science, 2 science labs. *Academic units recommended:* 2 foreign language, 2 social studies. **Freshman Admission Statistics:** 1,651 applied, 28% admitted, 45% enrolled. **Transfer Admission Requirements:** College transcript(s), statement of good standing from prior institution(s). Minimum college GPA of 2.0 required. Lowest grade transferable C-. **General Admission Information:** Regular application deadline 8/1. Non-fall registration accepted.

COSTS AND FINANCIAL AID
Annual tuition $25,214. Room and board $8,520. Required fees $500. **Student Employment:** Federal Work-Study Program available. Institutional employment available.

WILSON COLLEGE

1015 Philadelphia Avenue, Chambersburg, PA 17201
Phone: 717-262-2002 **Financial Aid Phone:** 717-262-2016
E-mail: admissions@wilson.edu **CEEB Code:** 2979
Fax: 717-262-2546 **Website:** www.wilson.edu **ACT Code:** 3758

This private school, affiliated with the Presbyterian Church, was founded in 1869. It has a 300 acre campus.

RATINGS
Admissions Selectivity Rating: 74 **Fire Safety Rating:** 87 **Green Rating:** 64

STUDENTS AND FACULTY
Enrollment: 827. **Student Body:** 83% female, 17% male, 28% out-of-state, 3% international (10 countries represented). Asian 1%, African American 7%, Caucasian 74%, Hispanic 6%, Native American <1%, Pacific Islander <1%, Two or more races 2%, Race unknown 6%.
Retention and Graduation: 67% freshmen return for sophomore year. 53% freshmen graduate within 4 years. 64% freshmen graduate within 6 years. 30%

grads go on to further study within 1 year. 6% grads pursue arts and sciences degrees. 9% grads pursue law degrees. 8% grads pursue business degrees. 8% grads pursue medical degrees. **Faculty:** Student/faculty ratio 11:1. 48 full-time faculty, 83% hold PhDs, 4% are members of minority groups, 58% are women. 0% of classes are taught by teaching assistants.

ACADEMICS

Degrees: Associate; Bachelor's; Master's. **Classes:** Most classes have 10–19 students. Most lab/discussion sessions have 10–19 students. **Most popular majors:** Elementary Education and Teaching; Equestrian/Equine Studies. **Special Study Options:** Cross-registration; Distance learning; Double major; Dual enrollment; Honors program; Independent study; Internships; Liberal arts/career combination; Student-designed major; Study abroad; Teacher certification program. **Honors programs:** Wilson Scholars Program. **Disability Services offered:** Note-taking services; Reader services; Tape recorders; Tutors. **Career services:** Alumni network; Alumni services; Career assessment; Career/job search classes; Internships.

FACILITIES

Housing: Coed dorms; Men's dorms; Theme housing; Women's dorms 49% of campus accessible to physically disabled. **Special Academic Facilities/Equipment:** Archives, Bogigian Art gallery, Dance Studio, Helen M. Beach '24 Veterinary Medical Center, Penn Hall Equestrian Center, Natural History Museum, electron microscope, NMR spectrometer.

CAMPUS LIFE

Environment: Village. **Activities:** Campus Ministries; Choral groups; Dance; Drama/theater; International Student Organization; Literary magazine; Pep band; Student government; Student newspaper; Yearbook. 42 registered organizations, 2 honor societies, 3 religious organizations on campus. **Athletics (Intercollegiate):** *Women:* basketball, field hockey, gymnastics, lacrosse, soccer, softball, tennis. **On-Campus Highlights:** Penn Hall Equestrian Center. **Environmental Initiatives:** Organic farm.

ADMISSIONS

Freshman Academic Profile: Average high school GPA 3.5. 10% in top 10% of high school class, 41% in top 25% of high school class, 83% in top 50% of high school class. 84% from public high schools. **Test Scores:** SAT Math middle 50% range 440–580. SAT EBRW middle 50% range 470–610. ACT middle 50% range 19–24. **Basis for Candidate Selection:** *Very important factors include:* rigor of secondary school record, academic GPA, application essay. *Important factors include:* standardized test scores, recommendation(s), character/personal qualities. *Other factors include:* class rank, interview, extracurricular activities, talent/ability, alumni/ae relation, volunteer work, work experience, level of applicant's interest. **Freshman Admission Requirements:** High school diploma is required and GED is accepted. *Academic units recommended:* 4 English, 3 math, 2 science, 2 science labs, 2 foreign language, 4 social studies. **Freshman Admission Statistics:** 806 applied, 93% admitted, 27% enrolled. **Transfer Admission Requirements:** High school transcript, college transcript(s), essay or personal statement. Minimum college GPA of 2.0 required. Lowest grade transferable C. **General Admission Information:** Non-fall registration accepted. Admission may be deferred for a maximum of 1 year.

COSTS AND FINANCIAL AID

Annual tuition $25,200. Room and board $11,716. Required fees $890. Average book and supplies expense $1,100. **Required Forms and Deadlines:** FAFSA. **Notification of Awards:** Applicants will be notified of awards on a rolling basis beginning 11/15. **Types of Aid:** *Need-based scholarships/grants:* College/university scholarship or grant aid from institutional funds; Federal Pell; Private scholarships; SEOG; State scholarships/grants. *Loans:* Direct PLUS loans; Direct Subsidized Stafford Loans; Direct Unsubsidized Stafford Loans. **Student Employment:** Federal Work-Study Program available. Institutional employment available. **Financial Aid Statistics:** 100% needy freshmen, 99% needy undergrads receive need-based scholarship or grant aid. 0% freshmen, 58% undergrads receive non-need-based scholarship or grant aid. 100% freshmen, 89% undergrads receive need-based self-help aid. 0% freshmen, 0% undergrads receive athletic scholarships. 99% freshmen, 97% undergrads receive any aid. 83% undergrads borrow to pay for school. Average cumulative indebtedness $39,090. **Criteria awarding aid:** *Need-based:* Academics, Art, Leadership, Music/drama, Religious affiliation. *Non-need-based:* Academics, Alumni affiliation, Religious affiliation, State/district residency.

WINGATE UNIVERSITY

P.O. Box 159, Wingate, NC 28174
Phone: 704-233-8200 **Financial Aid Phone:** 704-233-8209
E-mail: admit@wingate.edu **CEEB Code:** 5908
Fax: 704-233-8110 **Website:** www.wingate.edu **ACT Code:** 3176

This private school was founded in 1896. It has a 390 acre campus.

RATINGS

Admissions Selectivity Rating: 74   **Fire Safety Rating:** 87   **Green Rating:** 60*

STUDENTS AND FACULTY

Enrollment: 2,721. **Student Body:** 60% female, 40% male, 26% out-of-state, 4% international (21 countries represented). Asian 2%, African American 18%, Caucasian 57%, Hispanic 4%, Native American <1%, Pacific Islander <1%, Two or more races 8%, Race unknown 6%.

Retention and Graduation: 64% freshmen return for sophomore year. 41% freshmen graduate within 4 years. 52% freshmen graduate within 6 years. 20% grads go on to further study within 1 year. 9% grads pursue arts and sciences degrees. 2% grads pursue law degrees. 8% grads pursue business degrees. 1% grads pursue medical degrees. **Faculty:** Student/faculty ratio 16:1. 197 full-time faculty, 86% hold PhDs, 9% are members of minority groups, 58% are women. 0% of classes are taught by teaching assistants.

ACADEMICS

Degrees: Bachelor's; Doctoral degree—professional practice; Doctoral degree research/scholarship; Master's; Post-bachelor's certificate; Post-master's certificate. **Classes:** Most classes have 20–29 students. Most lab/discussion sessions have 20–29 students. **Most popular majors:** Biology/Biological Sciences, General; Psychology, General; Business Administration and Management, General. **Special Study Options:** Cross-registration; Double major; Dual enrollment; Honors program; Independent study; Internships; Study abroad; Teacher certification program. **Honors programs:** Our University Honors program offers students 18 hours of honors courses covering a spectrum of disciplines. Students may travel to New York City as part of the program. **Disability Services offered:** Note-taking services; Tape recorders; Tutors. **Career services:** Alumni network; Career assessment; Career/job search classes; Internships.

FACILITIES

Housing: Apartments for single students; Coed dorms; Fraternity/sorority housing; Men's dorms; Special housing for disabled students; Theme housing; Women's dorms; 95% of campus accessible to physically disabled. **Special Academic Facilities/Equipment:** Batte Fine Arts Center. **Campus Network:** 95% of classrooms, 80% of dorms, 100% of student union, 100% of libraries, 100% of dining areas, 80% of common outdoor areas have wireless network access.

CAMPUS LIFE

Environment: Town. **Activities:** Campus Ministries; Choral groups; Drama/theater; International Student Organization; Literary magazine; Model UN; Music ensembles; Opera; Pep band; Student government; Student newspaper; Yearbook. 45 registered organizations, 10 honor societies, 8 religious organizations, 4 fraternities, 4 sororities on campus. **Athletics (Intercollegiate):** *Men:* baseball, basketball, cheerleading, cross-country, football, golf, lacrosse, soccer, swimming, tennis. *Women:* basketball, cheerleading, cross-country, golf, soccer, softball, swimming, tennis, volleyball. **On-Campus Highlights:** George A. Batte Jr. Fine Arts Center.

ADMISSIONS

Freshman Academic Profile: Average high school GPA 3.3. 15% in top 10% of high school class, 40% in top 25% of high school class, 76% in top 50% of high school class. 85% from public high schools. **Test Scores:** SAT Math middle 50% range 480–580. SAT EBRW middle 50% range 480–590. ACT middle 50% range 19–24. **Basis for Candidate Selection:** *Very important factors include:* academic GPA, standardized test scores. *Important factors include:* rigor of secondary school record, class rank. *Other factors include:* recommendation(s), extracurricular activities, talent/ability, character/personal qualities. **Freshman Admission Requirements:** High school diploma is required and GED is accepted. *Academic units recommended:* 4 English, 3 math, 2 science, 1 science labs, 2 foreign language, 2 social studies. **Freshman Admission Statistics:** 14,784 applied, 85% admitted, 7% enrolled. **Transfer Admission Requirements:** High school transcript, college transcript(s), statement of good standing from prior institution(s). Minimum college GPA of

2.0 required. Lowest grade transferable C. **General Admission Information:** Priority deadline 4/1. Non-fall registration accepted. Admission may be deferred for a maximum of 1 year.

COSTS AND FINANCIAL AID

Annual tuition $35,810. Room and board $10,280. Required fees $100. Average book and supplies expense $2,000. **Required Forms and Deadlines:** FAFSA; State aid form. **Notification of Awards:** Applicants will be notified of awards on a rolling basis beginning 3/1. **Types of Aid:** *Need-based scholarships/ grants:* College/university scholarship or grant aid from institutional funds; Federal Pell; Private scholarships; SEOG; State scholarships/grants. *Loans:* Direct PLUS loans; Direct Subsidized Stafford Loans; Direct Unsubsidized Stafford Loans. **Student Employment:** Federal Work-Study Program available. Institutional employment available. **Financial Aid Statistics:** 89% needy freshmen, 90% needy undergrads receive need-based scholarship or grant aid. 18% freshmen, 17% undergrads receive non-need-based scholarship or grant aid. 73% freshmen, 74% undergrads receive need-based self-help aid. 7% freshmen, 10% undergrads receive athletic scholarships. 97% freshmen, 96% undergrads receive any aid. 59% undergrads borrow to pay for school. Average cumulative indebtedness $28,650. **Criteria awarding aid:** *Need-based:* Athletics *Non-need-based:* Academics, Alumni affiliation, Art, Athletics, Leadership, Music/drama, Religious affiliation.

WINONA STATE UNIVERSITY

175 Mark Street, Winona, MN 55987
Phone: 507-457-5100 **Financial Aid Phone:** 507-457-5090
E-mail: admissions@winona.edu **CEEB Code:** 6680
Fax: 507-457-5620 **Website:** www.winona.edu **ACT Code:** 2162

This public school was founded in 1858. It has a 125 acre campus.

RATINGS

Admissions Selectivity Rating: 83   **Fire Safety Rating:** 93   **Green Rating:** 79

STUDENTS AND FACULTY

Enrollment: 6,789. **Student Body:** 66% female, 34% male, 29% out-of-state, 2% international (44 countries represented). Asian 2%, African American 3%, Caucasian 84%, Hispanic 5%, Native American <1%, Pacific Islander <1%, Two or more races 3%, Race unknown 1%.
Retention and Graduation: 75% freshmen return for sophomore year. 38% freshmen graduate within 4 years. 59% freshmen graduate within 6 years. 11% grads go on to further study within 1 year. **Faculty:** Student/faculty ratio 19:1. 306 full-time faculty, 87% hold PhDs, 14% are members of minority groups, 53% are women. 1% of classes are taught by teaching assistants.

ACADEMICS

Degrees: Associate; Bachelor's; Doctoral degree research/scholarship; Master's; Post-bachelor's certificate; Post-master's certificate. **Classes:** Most classes have 20–29 students. Most lab/discussion sessions have 20–29 students. **Most popular majors:** Elementary Education and Teaching; Biology/Biological Sciences, General; Registered Nursing/Registered Nurse. **Special Study Options:** Distance learning; Double major; Dual enrollment; English as a Second Language (ESL); Independent study; Internships; Student-designed major; Study abroad; Teacher certification program. **Disability Services offered:** Note-taking services; Reader services; Tape recorders. **Career services:** Alumni network; Alumni services; Career assessment; Internships; Regional alumni.

FACILITIES

Housing: Apartments for single students; Coed dorms; Men's dorms; Special housing for disabled students; Theme housing; Women's dorms; 100% of campus accessible to physically disabled. **Special Academic Facilities/ Equipment:** Paul Watkins Art Gallery, KQAL Radio Station, Performing Arts Center. **Campus Network:** 100% of classrooms, 100% of dorms, 100% of student union, 100% of libraries, 100% of dining areas, 100% of common outdoor areas have wireless network access.

CAMPUS LIFE

Environment: Town. **Activities:** Campus Ministries; Choral groups; Concert band; Dance; Drama/theater; International Student Organization; Jazz band; Literary magazine; Model UN; Music ensembles; Musical theater; Pep band; Radio station; Student government; Student newspaper; Student-run film society. 198 registered organizations, 9 honor societies, 8 religious organizations, 7 fraternities, 3 sororities on campus. **Athletics (Intercollegiate):** *Men:* baseball, basketball, cross-country, football, golf. *Women:* basketball, cross-country, golf, gymnastics, soccer, softball, tennis, track/field (outdoor), track/field (indoor), volleyball. **On-Campus Highlights:** The Library. **Environmental Initiatives:** Recycling/Post Consumer Waste Reduction.

ADMISSIONS

Freshman Academic Profile: Average high school GPA 3.4. 9% in top 10% of high school class, 32% in top 25% of high school class, 69% in top 50% of high school class. **Test Scores:** SAT Math middle 50% range 510–630. SAT EBRW middle 50% range 490–580. ACT middle 50% range 19–24. **Basis for Candidate Selection:** *Very important factors include:* rigor of secondary school record, class rank, academic GPA, standardized test scores. **Freshman Admission Requirements:** High school diploma is required and GED is accepted. *Academic units required:* 4 English, 3 math, 3 science, 3 science labs, 2 foreign language, 2 social studies, 1 history, 1 academic electives. **Freshman Admission Statistics:** 7,663 applied, 68% admitted, 30% enrolled. **Transfer Admission Requirements:** College transcript(s). Minimum college GPA of 2.4 required. Lowest grade transferable D. **General Admission Information:** Application fee $20. Regular application deadline 7/1. Non-fall registration accepted. Admission may be deferred for a maximum of 12 months.

COSTS AND FINANCIAL AID

Annual in-state tuition $7,598. Annual out-of-state tuition $13,698. Room and board $9,086. Required fees $2,068. Average book and supplies expense $900. **Required Forms and Deadlines:** FAFSA. **Notification of Awards:** Applicants will be notified of awards on a rolling basis beginning 12/1. **Types of Aid:** *Need-based scholarships/grants:* College/university scholarship or grant aid from institutional funds; Federal Pell; Private scholarships; SEOG; State scholarships/ grants. *Loans:* Direct PLUS loans; Direct Subsidized Stafford Loans; Direct Unsubsidized Stafford Loans. **Student Employment:** Federal Work-Study Program available. Institutional employment available. **Criteria awarding aid:** *Non-need-based:* Academics, Alumni affiliation, Art, Athletics, Minority status, Music/drama.

WINTHROP UNIVERSITY

Admissions, Winthrop University, Rock Hill, SC 29733
Phone: 803-323-2191 **Financial Aid Phone:** 803-323-2189
E-mail: admissions@winthrop.edu **CEEB Code:** 5910
Fax: 803-323-2137 **Website:** www.winthrop.edu **ACT Code:** 3884

This public school was founded in 1886. It has a 445 acre campus.

RATINGS

Admissions Selectivity Rating: 81   **Fire Safety Rating:** 92   **Green Rating:** 79

STUDENTS AND FACULTY

Enrollment: 4,786. **Student Body:** 68% female, 32% male, 8% out-of-state, 2% international (39 countries represented). Asian 1%, African American 30%, Caucasian 58%, Hispanic 4%, Native American <1%, Pacific Islander <1%, Two or more races 4%, Race unknown <1%.
Retention and Graduation: 77% freshmen return for sophomore year. 25% grads go on to further study within 1 year. 6% grads pursue arts and sciences degrees. 0% grads pursue law degrees. 4% grads pursue business degrees. 1% grads pursue medical degrees. **Faculty:** Student/faculty ratio 14:1. 282 full-time faculty, 89% hold PhDs, 14% are members of minority groups, 54% are women. 0% of classes are taught by teaching assistants.

ACADEMICS

Degrees: Bachelor's; Certificate; Master's; Post-bachelor's certificate; Post-master's certificate. **Classes:** Most classes have 10–19 students. Most lab/discussion sessions have 20–29 students. **Most popular majors:** Business/Commerce, General; Biology/Biological Sciences, General; Design and Visual Communications, General. **Special Study Options:** Cooperative education program; Cross-registration; Distance learning; Double major; Dual enrollment; English as a Second Language (ESL); Exchange student program (domestic); Honors program; Independent study; Internships; Liberal arts/career combination; Student-designed major; Study abroad; Teacher certification program. **Honors programs:** The Winthrop University Honors Program is designed to enrich the college experience for highly talented and motivated students. Through interactions with outstanding faculty and peers, a vital community of scholars is created that embraces the pursuit of knowledge for the enhancement of intellectual and personal growth. **Disability Services**

offered: Note-taking services; Reader services; Tape recorders. **Career services:** Alumni network; Alumni services; Career assessment; Career/job search classes; Internships; Regional alumni.

FACILITIES

Housing: Apartments for single students; Coed dorms; Theme housing; Women's dorms; 90% of campus accessible to physically disabled. **Special Academic Facilities/Equipment:** Art gallery, Early Childhood Laboratory School, Music Conservatory, Academic Success Center and Trading Center in the business college. **Campus Network:** 100% of classrooms, 100% of dorms, 100% of student union, 100% of libraries, 100% of dining areas, 100% of common outdoor areas have wireless network access.

CAMPUS LIFE

Environment: Town. **Activities:** Campus Ministries; Choral groups; Concert band; Dance; Drama/theater; International Student Organization; Jazz band; Literary magazine; Marching band; Model UN; Music ensembles; Musical theater; Opera; Pep band; Radio station; Student government; Student newspaper; Television station; Yearbook. 158 registered organizations, 15 honor societies, 19 religious organizations, 7 fraternities, 9 sororities on campus. **Athletics (Intercollegiate):** *Men:* baseball, basketball, cross-country, golf, soccer, tennis, track/field (outdoor). *Women:* basketball, cross-country, golf, soccer, softball, tennis, track/field (outdoor), volleyball. **On-Campus Highlights:** DiGiorgio Campus Center **Environmental Initiatives:** Very strong recycling program.

ADMISSIONS

Freshman Academic Profile: Average high school GPA 3.9. 22% in top 10% of high school class, 51% in top 25% of high school class, 87% in top 50% of high school class. **Test Scores:** SAT Math middle 50% range 450–560. SAT EBRW middle 50% range 460–570. ACT middle 50% range 20–26. **Basis for Candidate Selection:** *Very important factors include:* rigor of secondary school record, academic GPA, standardized test scores. *Other factors include:* application essay, recommendation(s), interview, extracurricular activities, talent/ability, volunteer work. **Freshman Admission Requirements:** High school diploma is required and GED is accepted. *Academic units required:* 4 English, 4 math, 3 science, 3 science labs, 2 foreign language, 2 social studies, 1 history, 1 academic electives, 1 visual/performing arts, 1 unit from above areas or other academic areas. **Freshman Admission Statistics:** 4,876 applied, 67% admitted, 33% enrolled. **Transfer Admission Requirements:** College transcript(s), statement of good standing from prior institution(s). Minimum college GPA of 2.0 required. Lowest grade transferable C. **General Admission Information:** Application fee $40. Regular application deadline 5/1. Non-fall registration accepted.

COSTS AND FINANCIAL AID

Annual in-state tuition $14,510. Annual out-of-state tuition $28,090. Room and board $8,572. Average book and supplies expense $1,000. **Required Forms and Deadlines:** FAFSA. **Notification of Awards:** Applicants will be notified of awards on a rolling basis beginning 3/1. **Types of Aid:** *Need-based scholarships/grants:* College/university scholarship or grant aid from institutional funds; Federal Pell; Private scholarships; SEOG; State scholarships/grants. *Loans:* Direct PLUS loans; Direct Subsidized Stafford Loans; Direct Unsubsidized Stafford Loans. **Student Employment:** Federal Work-Study Program available. Institutional employment available. **Financial Aid Statistics:** 99% needy freshmen, 90% needy undergrads receive need-based scholarship or grant aid. 18% freshmen, 12% undergrads receive non-need-based scholarship or grant aid. 72% freshmen, 80% undergrads receive need-based self-help aid. 2% freshmen, 3% undergrads receive athletic scholarships. 70% freshmen, 83% undergrads receive any aid. **Criteria awarding aid:** *Non-need-based:* Academics, Art, Athletics, Leadership, Music/drama.

WISCONSIN LUTHERAN COLLEGE

8800 West Bluemound Road, Milwaukee, WI 53226
Phone: 414-443-8811 **Financial Aid Phone:** 414-443-8856
E-mail: admissions@wlc.edu **CEEB Code:** 1513
Fax: 414-443-8514 **Website:** www.wlc.edu **ACT Code:** 4699

This private school, affiliated with the Lutheran Church, was founded in 1973. It has a 21 acre campus.

RATINGS
Admissions Selectivity Rating: 77　　**Fire Safety Rating:** 60*　　**Green Rating:** 60*

STUDENTS AND FACULTY

Enrollment: 1,037. **Student Body:** 55% female, 45% male, 27% out-of-state, 1% international (4 countries represented). Asian 2%, African American 6%, Caucasian 81%, Hispanic 7%, Native American <1%, Pacific Islander 0%, Two or more races 3%, Race unknown <1%.
Retention and Graduation: 79% freshmen return for sophomore year. 43% freshmen graduate within 4 years. % freshmen graduate within 6 years. **Faculty:** Student/faculty ratio 11:1. 62 full-time faculty, 65% hold PhDs, 0% are members of minority groups, 39% are women. 0% of classes are taught by teaching assistants.

ACADEMICS

Degrees: Bachelor's; Master's. **Classes:** Most classes have fewer than 10 students. Most lab/discussion sessions have 10–19 students. **Most popular majors:** Business Administration and Management, General; Business Administration, Management and Operations, Other; Registered Nursing/Registered Nurse. **Special Study Options:** Accelerated program; Distance learning; Double major; Dual enrollment; Honors program; Independent study; Internships; Student-designed major; Study abroad; Teacher certification program. **Disability Services offered:** Note-taking services; Reader services; Tape recorders; Tutors. **Career services:** Alumni network; Career assessment; Career/job search classes; Internships.

FACILITIES

Housing: Apartments for single students; Men's dorms; Women's dorms; 90% of campus accessible to physically disabled. **Special Academic Facilities/Equipment:** Center for Arts and Performance, Science Hall. **Campus Network:** 100% of classrooms, 100% of dorms, 100% of student union, 100% of libraries, 100% of dining areas, 100% of common outdoor areas have wireless network access.

CAMPUS LIFE

Environment: Metropolis. **Activities:** Campus Ministries; Choral groups; Concert band; Drama/theater; Jazz band; Music ensembles; Student government; Student newspaper. 40 registered organizations on campus. **Athletics (Intercollegiate):** *Men:* baseball, basketball, cross-country, football, golf, soccer, tennis, track/field (outdoor), track/field (indoor). *Women:* basketball, cross-country, golf, soccer, softball, tennis, track/field (outdoor), track/field (indoor), volleyball.

ADMISSIONS

Freshman Academic Profile: Average high school GPA 3.4. 21% in top 10% of high school class, 47% in top 25% of high school class, 74% in top 50% of high school class. 49% from public high schools. **Test Scores:** SAT Math middle 50% range 513–598. SAT EBRW middle 50% range 503–600. ACT middle 50% range 20–26. **Basis for Candidate Selection:** *Very important factors include:* rigor of secondary school record, academic GPA, standardized test scores. *Other factors include:* application essay, recommendation(s), extracurricular activities, talent/ability, character/personal qualities, alumni/ae relation, religious affiliation/commitment, volunteer work. **Freshman Admission Requirements:** High school diploma is required and GED is accepted *Academic units required:* 4 English, 3 math, 2 science, 1 science labs, 2 foreign language, 2 history, 3 academic electives. *Academic units recommended:* 4 English, 4 math, 3 science, 2 science labs, 4 foreign language, 2 history, 3 academic electives. **Freshman Admission Statistics:** 969 applied, 80% admitted, 37% enrolled. **Transfer Admission Requirements:** College transcript(s), statement of good standing from prior institution(s). Minimum college GPA of 2.5 required. Lowest grade transferable CD. **General Admission Information:** Non-fall registration accepted. Admission may be deferred for a maximum of 1 semester.

COSTS AND FINANCIAL AID

Annual tuition $30,406. Room and board $10,496. Required fees $444. Average book and supplies expense $800. **Required Forms and Deadlines:** FAFSA; Institution's own financial aid form. **Notification of Awards:** Applicants will be notified of awards on a rolling basis beginning 3/15. **Types of Aid:** *Need-based scholarships/grants:* College/university scholarship or grant aid from institutional funds; Federal Pell; Private scholarships; SEOG; State scholarships/grants. *Loans:* Direct PLUS loans; Direct Subsidized Stafford Loans; Direct Unsubsidized Stafford Loans. **Student Employment:** Federal Work-Study Program available. Institutional employment available. **Financial Aid Statistics:** 100% needy freshmen, 99% needy undergrads receive need-based scholarship or grant aid. 18% freshmen, 13% undergrads receive non-need-based scholarship or grant aid. 82% freshmen, 87% undergrads receive need-based self-help aid. 0% freshmen, 0% undergrads receive athletic scholarships. 100% freshmen receive any aid. 85% undergrads borrow to pay for school. Average cumulative indebtedness $31,002. **Criteria awarding aid:** *Need-based:* Academics, Leadership, Minority status. *Non-need-based:* Academics, Art, Leadership, Music/drama.

WITTENBERG UNIVERSITY

PO Box 720, Springfield, OH 45501
Phone: 937-327-6314 **Financial Aid Phone:** 937-327-7321
E-mail: admission@wittenberg.edu **CEEB Code:** 1922
Fax: 937-327-6379 **Website:** www.wittenberg.edu **ACT Code:** 3364

This private school, affiliated with the Lutheran Church, was founded in 1845. It has a 114 acre campus.

RATINGS

Admissions Selectivity Rating: 77   **Fire Safety Rating:** 98   **Green Rating:** 60*

STUDENTS AND FACULTY

Enrollment: 1,701. **Student Body:** 54% female, 46% male, 23% out-of-state, 1% international (12 countries represented). Asian 1%, African American 10%, Caucasian 77%, Hispanic 4%, Native American <1%, Pacific Islander 0%, Two or more races 5%, Race unknown 2%.
Retention and Graduation: 70% freshmen return for sophomore year. 61% freshmen graduate within 4 years. 67% freshmen graduate within 6 years. 28% grads go on to further study within 1 year. 10% grads pursue arts and sciences degrees. 3% grads pursue law degrees. 2% grads pursue business degrees. 2% grads pursue medical degrees. **Faculty:** Student/faculty ratio 12:1. 121 full-time faculty, 91% hold PhDs, 12% are members of minority groups, 45% are women. 0% of classes are taught by teaching assistants.

ACADEMICS

Degrees: Bachelor's; Master's. **Classes:** Most classes have 10–19 students. Most lab/discussion sessions have 10–19 students. **Most popular majors:** Biology/Biological Sciences, General; Business/Commerce, General. **Special Study Options:** Cross-registration; Distance learning; Double major; Dual enrollment; Honors program; Independent study; Internships; Liberal arts/career combination; Student-designed major; Study abroad; Teacher certification program. **Honors programs:** Honors Program, 3–2 Engineering Program, Pre-Health Programs. **Disability Services offered:** Note-taking services; Reader services; Tape recorders; Tutors. **Career services:** Alumni network; Alumni services; Career assessment; Career/job search classes; Internships; Regional alumni.

FACILITIES

Housing: Apartments for married students; Apartments for single students; Coed dorms; Fraternity/sorority housing; Special housing for disabled students; Special housing for international students; Women's dorms; 81% of campus accessible to physically disabled. **Special Academic Facilities/Equipment:** Language lab, electron microscope, observatory.

CAMPUS LIFE

Environment: Town. **Activities:** Campus Ministries; Choral groups; Concert band; Dance; Drama/theater; International Student Organization; Jazz band; Literary magazine; Model UN; Music ensembles; Musical theater; Opera; Pep band; Radio station; Student government; Student newspaper; Student-run

film society; Symphony orchestra; Yearbook. 120 registered organizations, 30 honor societies, 8 religious organizations, 6 fraternities, 5 sororities on campus. **Athletics (Intercollegiate):** *Men:* baseball, basketball, cross-country, diving, football, golf, lacrosse, soccer, swimming, tennis, track/field (outdoor), track/field (indoor). *Women:* basketball, cheerleading, cross-country, diving, field hockey, golf, lacrosse, soccer, softball, swimming, tennis, track/field (outdoor), track/field (indoor), volleyball. **On-Campus Highlights:** HPERC Athletic Center.

ADMISSIONS

Freshman Academic Profile: Average high school GPA 3.5. 16% in top 10% of high school class, 40% in top 25% of high school class, 73% in top 50% of high school class. 85% from public high schools. **Test Scores:** SAT Math middle 50% range 530–620. SAT EBRW middle 50% range 540–650. ACT middle 50% range 22–28. **Basis for Candidate Selection:** *Very important factors include:* rigor of secondary school record, class rank, academic GPA. *Important factors include:* application essay, recommendation(s), extracurricular activities, talent/ability, character/personal qualities, volunteer work. *Other factors include:* standardized test scores, interview, first generation, alumni/ae relation, work experience. **Freshman Admission Requirements:** High school diploma is required and GED is accepted *Academic units required:* 4 English, 3 math, 3 science, 2 science labs, 2 foreign language, 2 history. *Academic units recommended:* 4 English, 4 math, 5 science, 2 science labs, 3 foreign language, 3 history. **Freshman Admission Statistics:** 7,393 applied, 74% admitted, 9% enrolled. **Transfer Admission Requirements:** College transcript(s). Minimum college GPA of 2.0 required. Lowest grade transferable C. **General Admission Information:** Application fee $40. Priority deadline 3/15. Non-fall registration accepted. Admission may be deferred for a maximum of 12 months.

COSTS AND FINANCIAL AID

Annual tuition $39,450. Room and board $10,564. Required fees $890. Average book and supplies expense $1,000. **Required Forms and Deadlines:** FAFSA. **Notification of Awards:** Applicants will be notified of awards on a rolling basis beginning 3/1. **Types of Aid:** *Need-based scholarships/grants:* College/university scholarship or grant aid from institutional funds; Federal Pell; Private scholarships; SEOG; State scholarships/grants; United Negro College Fund. *Loans:* Direct PLUS loans; Direct Subsidized Stafford Loans; Direct Unsubsidized Stafford Loans. **Student Employment:** Federal Work-Study Program available. Institutional employment available. **Financial Aid Statistics:** 100% needy freshmen, 99% needy undergrads receive need-based scholarship or grant aid. 0% freshmen, 0% undergrads receive non-need-based scholarship or grant aid. 99% freshmen, 92% undergrads receive need-based self-help aid. 0% freshmen, 0% undergrads receive athletic scholarships. 99% freshmen, 97% undergrads receive any aid. 73% undergrads borrow to pay for school. Average cumulative indebtedness $37,154. **Criteria awarding aid:** *Need-based:* Academics, Alumni affiliation, Art, Leadership, Minority status, Music/drama, Religious affiliation. *Non-need-based:* Academics, Alumni affiliation, Art, Minority status, Music/drama, Religious affiliation, State/district residency.

WOFFORD COLLEGE

429 North Church Street, Spartanburg, SC 29303-3663
Phone: 864-597-4130 **Financial Aid Phone:** (864) 597-4160
E-mail: admission@wofford.edu **CEEB Code:** 5912
Fax: 864-597-4147 **Website:** www.wofford.edu **ACT Code:** 3886

This private school, affiliated with the Methodist Church, was founded in 1854. It has a 175 acre campus.

RATINGS

Admissions Selectivity Rating: 86   **Fire Safety Rating:** 94   **Green Rating:** 60*

STUDENTS AND FACULTY

Enrollment: 1,582. **Student Body:** 53% female, 47% male, 46% out-of-state, 2% international (24 countries represented). Asian 2%, African American 8%, Caucasian 79%, Hispanic 4%, Native American <1%, Pacific Islander <1%, Two or more races 4%, Race unknown <1%.

Retention and Graduation: 90% freshmen return for sophomore year. 77% freshmen graduate within 4 years. 81% freshmen graduate within 6 years. **Faculty:** Student/faculty ratio 10:1. 146 full-time faculty, 89% hold PhDs, 11% are members of minority groups, 42% are women. 0% of classes are taught by teaching assistants.

ACADEMICS

Degrees: Bachelor's. **Classes:** Most classes have 10–19 students. Most lab/discussion sessions have 10–19 students. **Most popular majors:** Biology/Biological Sciences, General; Business/Managerial Economics; Finance, General. **Special Study Options:** Accelerated program; Cross-registration; Double major; Dual enrollment; Independent study; Internships; Student-designed major; Study abroad; Teacher certification program. **Combined degree programs:** BA/MEng. **Disability Services offered:** Note-taking services; Reader services; Tape recorders; Tutors. **Career services:** Alumni network; Alumni services; Career assessment; Career/job search classes; Internships; Regional alumni.

FACILITIES

Housing: Apartments for single students; Coed dorms; Special housing for disabled students; Wellness housing; 85% of campus accessible to physically disabled. **Special Academic Facilities/Equipment:** In 2017, the Rosalind Sallenger Richardson Center for the Arts opened as the home of academic programs in art history, film and digital media, studio art, and theatre. The building includes several gallery spaces and a 300-seat theatre as well as practice and workshop spaces. Other gallery spaces on campus include the Sandor Teszler Library Gallery and the Martha Cloud Chapman Gallery. The Michael S. Brown Village Center is the home to high-impact programs that blend the curricular with the co-curricular so learning at Wofford happens around the clock and around the globe. The MSBVC includes The Space in the Mungo Center (professional development, internship and entrepreneurship assistance), the Center for Community-Based Learning (a program focused on civic engagement and social impact) and International Programs (the home of Wofford's nationally ranked study abroad program and support for international students and faculty). The college also offers the Goodall Environmental Studies Center located in Glendale Shoals as a laboratory and classroom space where students interact with the local community and environment.

CAMPUS LIFE

Environment: City. **Activities:** Campus Ministries; Choral groups; Concert band; Dance; Drama/theater; International Student Organization; Jazz band; Literary magazine; Music ensembles; Pep band; Radio station; Student government; Student newspaper; Yearbook. 98 registered organizations, 11 honor societies, 10 religious organizations, 6 fraternities, 4 sororities on campus. **Athletics (Intercollegiate):** *Men:* baseball, basketball, cross-country, football, golf, riflery, soccer, tennis, track/field (outdoor), track/field (indoor). *Women:* basketball, cross-country, golf, riflery, soccer, tennis, track/field (outdoor), track/field (indoor), volleyball. **On-Campus Highlights:** The Wofford Village. **Environmental Initiatives:** The Milliken Sustainability Initiative at Wofford College is an innovative program that connects the college with both the Northside and Glendale neighborhoods near Wofford's campus through exploration of community and sustainability. The initiative includes a new energy metering and monitoring system at the college with savings fueling student social entrepreneurs and their sustainable ideas.

ADMISSIONS

Freshman Academic Profile: Average high school GPA 3.7. 43% in top 10% of high school class, 76% in top 25% of high school class, 95% in top 50% of high school class. 63% from public high schools. **Test Scores:** SAT Math middle 50% range 550–650. SAT EBRW middle 50% range 570–660. ACT middle 50% range 24–30. **Basis for Candidate Selection:** *Very important factors include:* rigor of secondary school record, academic GPA. *Important factors include:* class rank, application essay, extracurricular activities, talent/ability, character/personal qualities. *Other factors include:* standardized test scores, recommendation(s), interview, first generation, alumni/ae relation, geographical residence, state residency, religious affiliation/commitment, racial/ethnic status, volunteer work, work experience, level of applicant's interest. **Freshman Admission Requirements:** High school diploma is required and GED is accepted. *Academic units required:* 4 English, 4 math, 3 science, 3 science labs, 3 foreign language, 3 social studies. *Academic units recommended:* 4 English, 4 math, 3 science, 3 science labs, 3 foreign language, 3 social studies, 1 history, 1 academic electives, 1 computer science, 1 visual/performing arts. **Freshman Admission Statistics:** 3,092 applied, 69% admitted, 21% enrolled. **Transfer Admission Requirements:** High school transcript, college transcript(s), essay or personal statement, standardized test scores, statement of good standing from prior institution(s). Minimum college GPA of 2.5 required.

Lowest grade transferable C. **General Admission Information:** Application fee $35. Regular application deadline 1/15. Non-fall registration accepted. Admission may be deferred for a maximum of 1 year.

COSTS AND FINANCIAL AID

Annual tuition $42,335. Room and board $13,045. Required fees $1,510. Average book and supplies expense $1,200. **Required Forms and Deadlines:** FAFSA. **Notification of Awards:** Applicants will be notified of awards on or about 3/15. **Types of Aid:** *Need-based scholarships/grants:* College/university scholarship or grant aid from institutional funds; Federal Pell; Private scholarships; SEOG; State scholarships/grants. *Loans:* Direct PLUS loans; Direct Subsidized Stafford Loans; Direct Unsubsidized Stafford Loans. **Student Employment:** Federal Work-Study Program available. Institutional employment available. **Financial Aid Statistics:** 100% needy freshmen, 100% needy undergrads receive need-based scholarship or grant aid. 40% freshmen, 31% undergrads receive non-need-based scholarship or grant aid. 49% freshmen, 56% undergrads receive need-based self-help aid. 10% freshmen, 11% undergrads receive athletic scholarships. 97.99% freshmen, 94.83% undergrads receive any aid. 50% undergrads borrow to pay for school. Average cumulative indebtedness $32,043. **Criteria awarding aid:** *Need-based:* Job skills *Non-need-based:* Academics, Alumni affiliation, Art, Athletics, Job skills, Leadership, Minority status, Music/drama, Religious affiliation, State/district residency.

WOODBURY UNIVERSITY

7500 N Glenoaks Boulevard, Burbank, CA 91504-1052
Phone: 818-252-5221 **Financial Aid Phone:** 818-252-5273
E-mail: info@woodbury.edu **CEEB Code:** 4955
Website: https://woodbury.edu/ **ACT Code:** 481

This private school was founded in 1884. It has a 22 acre campus.

RATINGS

Admissions Selectivity Rating: 80 **Fire Safety Rating:** 65 **Green Rating:** 60*

STUDENTS AND FACULTY

Enrollment: 1,117. **Student Body:** 52% female, 48% male, 16% out-of-state, 12% international. Asian 10%, African American 3%, Caucasian 34%, Hispanic 37%, Native American <1%, Pacific Islander <1%, Two or more races 3%, Race unknown <1%.
Retention and Graduation: 84% freshmen return for sophomore year. 28% freshmen graduate within 4 years. 54% freshmen graduate within 6 years. **Faculty:** Student/faculty ratio 9:1. 67 full-time faculty, 90% hold PhDs, 21% are members of minority groups, 40% are women. 0% of classes are taught by teaching assistants.

ACADEMICS

Degrees: Bachelor's; Master's. **Classes:** Most classes have 10–19 students. **Special Study Options:** Accelerated program; Double major; Independent study; Internships; Student-designed major; Study abroad. **Disability Services offered:** Note-taking services; Reader services; Tutors. **Career services:** Alumni services; Career assessment; Internships.

FACILITIES

Housing: Coed dorms; 90% of campus accessible to physically disabled. **Special Academic Facilities/Equipment:** Art Gallery; Architecture Gallery. **Campus Network:** 88% of classrooms, 100% of dorms, 100% of student union, 100% of libraries, 100% of dining areas, 75% of common outdoor areas have wireless network access.

CAMPUS LIFE

Environment: City. **Activities:** Literary magazine; Radio station; Student government.

ADMISSIONS

Freshman Academic Profile: Average high school GPA 3.3. **Test Scores:** SAT Math middle 50% range 470–600. SAT EBRW middle 50% range 470–620. ACT middle 50% range 17–27. **Basis for Candidate Selection:** *Very important factors include:* academic GPA. *Important factors include:* rigor of secondary school record. *Other factors include:* application essay, standardized test scores, recommendation(s), volunteer work, work experience, level of applicant's interest. **Freshman Admission Requirements:** High school diploma is required and GED is accepted. *Academic units recommended:* 4 English, 4 math, 4 science, 1 science labs, 2 foreign language, 2 social studies, 2 history, 2 academic electives, 1 computer science, 1 visual/performing arts. **Freshman Admission Statistics:** 1,907 applied, 66% admitted, 16% enrolled. **Transfer Admission Requirements:** College transcript(s). Minimum college GPA of 2.5 required. Lowest grade transferable C. **General Admission Information:** Application fee $85. Priority deadline 3/1. Non-fall registration accepted. Admission may be deferred for a maximum of 1 year.

COSTS AND FINANCIAL AID
Annual tuition $41,102. Room and board $13,331. Required fees $1,726. Average book and supplies expense $1,080. **Required Forms and Deadlines:** FAFSA; Institution's own financial aid form. **Notification of Awards:** Applicants will be notified of awards on a rolling basis beginning 12/1. **Types of Aid:** *Need-based scholarships/grants:* College/university scholarship or grant aid from institutional funds; Federal Pell; Private scholarships; SEOG; State scholarships/grants. *Loans:* Direct PLUS loans; Direct Subsidized Stafford Loans; Direct Unsubsidized Stafford Loans. **Student Employment:** Federal Work-Study Program available. Institutional employment available. **Financial Aid Statistics:** 92% needy freshmen, 96% needy undergrads receive need-based scholarship or grant aid. 7% freshmen, 6% undergrads receive non-need-based scholarship or grant aid. 76% freshmen, 81% undergrads receive need-based self-help aid. 0% freshmen, 0% undergrads receive athletic scholarships. 51% undergrads borrow to pay for school. Average cumulative indebtedness $35,814. **Criteria awarding aid:** *Non-need-based:* Academics.

WORCESTER POLYTECHNIC INSTITUTE

Admissions Office, Bartlett Center, Worcester, MA 01609
Phone: 508-831-5286 **Financial Aid Phone:** 508-831-5469
E-mail: admissions@wpi.edu **CEEB Code:** 3969
Fax: 508-831-5875 **Website:** https://www.wpi.edu/ **ACT Code:** 1942

This private school was founded in 1865. It has a 95 acre campus.

RATINGS
Admissions Selectivity Rating: 94   **Fire Safety Rating:** 77   **Green Rating:** 91

STUDENTS AND FACULTY
Enrollment: 4,655. **Student Body:** 40% female, 60% male, 55% out-of-state, 9% international (62 countries represented). Asian 6%, African American 3%, Caucasian 63%, Hispanic 9%, Native American <1%, Pacific Islander <1%, Two or more races 3%, Race unknown 8%.
Retention and Graduation: 95% freshmen return for sophomore year. 82% freshmen graduate within 4 years. 89% freshmen graduate within 6 years. 23% grads go on to further study within 1 year. 21% grads pursue arts and sciences degrees. <1% grads pursue law degrees. 1% grads pursue business degrees. <1% grads pursue medical degrees. **Faculty:** Student/faculty ratio 14:1. 419 full-time faculty, 90% hold PhDs, 18% are members of minority groups, 30% are women. 0% of classes are taught by teaching assistants.

ACADEMICS
Degrees: Bachelor's; Doctoral degree research/scholarship; Master's; Post-bachelor's certificate. **Classes:** Most classes have 20–29 students. Most lab/discussion sessions have 20–29 students. **Most popular majors:** Computer Science; Mechanical Engineering; Bioengineering and Biomedical Engineering. **Special Study Options:** Accelerated program; Cooperative education program; Cross-registration; Distance learning; Double major; English as a Second Language (ESL); Independent study; Internships; Liberal arts/career combination; Student-designed major; Study abroad; Teacher certification program. **Disability Services offered:** Note-taking services; Reader services; Tape recorders; Tutors. **Career services:** Alumni network; Alumni services; Career assessment; Career/job search classes; Internships; Regional alumni.

FACILITIES
Housing: Apartments for single students; Coed dorms; Fraternity/sorority housing; Special housing for disabled students; 88% of campus accessible to physically disabled. **Special Academic Facilities/Equipment:** State-of-the-art specialized laboratories in all science and engineering research departments, including: two atomic-force microscopes, medical imaging lab, fire science lab, laser holography lab, computer music lab; Life Sciences and Bioengineering Center at Gateway Park.

CAMPUS LIFE
Environment: City. **Activities:** Campus Ministries; Choral groups; Concert band; Dance; Drama/theater; International Student Organization; Jazz band; Literary magazine; Model UN; Music ensembles; Musical theater; Pep band; Radio station; Student government; Student newspaper; Symphony orchestra; Yearbook. 235 registered organizations, 19 honor societies, 10 religious organizations, 13 fraternities, 6 sororities on campus. **Athletics (Intercollegiate):** *Men:* baseball, basketball, crew/rowing, cross-country, diving, football, soccer, swimming, track/field (outdoor), track/field (indoor), wrestling. *Women:* basketball, crew/rowing, cross-country, diving, field hockey, soccer, softball, swimming, track/field (outdoor), track/field (indoor), volleyball. **On-Campus Highlights:** Foisie Innovation Studio.

ADMISSIONS
Freshman Academic Profile: Average high school GPA 3.9. 63% in top 10% of high school class, 96% in top 25% of high school class, 100% in top 50% of high school class. **Test Scores:** SAT Math middle 50% range 680–760. SAT EBRW middle 50% range 630–710. ACT middle 50% range 29–33. **Basis for Candidate Selection:** *Very important factors include:* rigor of secondary school record, academic GPA. *Important factors include:* class rank, standardized test scores, recommendation(s), extracurricular activities, character/personal qualities. *Other factors include:* application essay, interview, talent/ability, first generation, alumni/ae relation, geographical residence, racial/ethnic status, volunteer work, work experience, level of applicant's interest. **Freshman Admission Requirements:** High school diploma is required and GED is accepted. *Academic units required:* 4 English, 4 math, 2 science, 2 science labs. *Academic units recommended:* 4 science, 2 foreign language, 2 social studies, 1 history, 1 computer science. **Freshman Admission Statistics:** 10,645 applied, 49% admitted, 23% enrolled. **Transfer Admission Requirements:** College transcript(s), essay or personal statement, statement of good standing from prior institution(s). Minimum college GPA of 3.0 required. Lowest grade transferable C. **General Admission Information:** Application fee $65. Regular application deadline 1/15. Admission may be deferred for a maximum of 1 year.

COSTS AND FINANCIAL AID
Annual tuition $51,604. Room and board $15,292. Required fees $916. Average book and supplies expense $1,000. **Required Forms and Deadlines:** CSS/Financial Aid PROFILE; FAFSA; Noncustodial PROFILE. **Notification of Awards:** Applicants will be notified of awards on a rolling basis beginning 12/21. **Types of Aid:** *Need-based scholarships/grants:* College/university scholarship or grant aid from institutional funds; Federal Pell; Private scholarships; SEOG; State scholarships/grants. *Loans:* Direct PLUS loans; Direct Subsidized Stafford Loans; Direct Unsubsidized Stafford Loans. **Student Employment:** Federal Work-Study Program available. Institutional employment available. **Financial Aid Statistics:** 100% needy freshmen, 97% needy undergrads receive need-based scholarship or grant aid. 99% freshmen, 47% undergrads receive non-need-based scholarship or grant aid. 44% freshmen, 45% undergrads receive need-based self-help aid. 0% freshmen, 0% undergrads receive athletic scholarships. 98.9% freshmen, 91% undergrads receive any aid. **Criteria awarding aid:** *Need-based:* Academics, Minority status. *Non-need-based:* Academics, Leadership, Minority status.

WORCESTER STATE UNIVERSITY

486 Chandler Street, Worcester, MA 01602-2597
Phone: 508-929-8040 **Financial Aid Phone:** 508-929-8056
E-mail: admissions@worcester.edu **CEEB Code:** 3524
Fax: 508-929-8183 **Website:** www.worcester.edu **ACT Code:** 1914

This public school was founded in 1874. It has a 58 acre campus.

RATINGS
Admissions Selectivity Rating: 81   **Fire Safety Rating:** 91   **Green Rating:** 95

STUDENTS AND FACULTY
Enrollment: 4,996. **Student Body:** 60% female, 40% male, 4% out-of-state, 1% international (19 countries represented). Asian 5%, African American 9%, Caucasian 65%, Hispanic 13%, Native American <1%, Pacific Islander <1%, Two or more races 3%, Race unknown 4%.
Retention and Graduation: 79% freshmen return for sophomore year. 36% freshmen graduate within 4 years. 55% freshmen graduate within 6 years. **Faculty:** Student/faculty ratio 17:1. 208 full-time faculty, 84% hold PhDs, 20% are members of minority groups, 56% are women. 0% of classes are taught by teaching assistants.

ACADEMICS

Degrees: Bachelor's; Master's; Post-bachelor's certificate; Post-master's certificate. **Classes:** Most classes have 10–19 students. Most lab/discussion sessions have 10–19 students. **Most popular majors:** Biology/Biological Sciences, General; Criminal Justice/Safety Studies; Business Administration and Management, General. **Special Study Options:** Accelerated program; Cross-registration; Distance learning; Double major; Dual enrollment; English as a Second Language (ESL); Exchange student program (domestic); Honors program; Independent study; Internships; Liberal arts/career combination; Student-designed major; Study abroad; Teacher certification program. **Honors programs:** The Commonwealth Honors Program at Worcester State University gives high-performing and motivated students opportunities to realize their academic potential and achieve their future goals. We promote scholarly excellence among both students and faculty through our curriculum and events programming. We are a strong community dedicated to sustaining the intellectual and social development of our students and enhancing life at WSU. Our program is part of the Massachusetts Commonwealth Honors Program and a member of the National Collegiate Honors Council. **Combined degree programs:** BA/MA. **Disability Services offered:** Note-taking services; Reader services; Tape recorders; Tutors. **Career services:** Alumni network; Alumni services; Career assessment; Career/job search classes; Internships; Regional alumni.

FACILITIES

Housing: Apartments for single students; Coed dorms; Men's dorms; Special housing for disabled students; Special housing for international students; Theme housing; Women's dorms; 100% of campus accessible to physically disabled. **Special Academic Facilities/Equipment:** Mary Cosgrove Dolphin Gallery (Art Gallery); Worcester Center for Crafts.

CAMPUS LIFE

Environment: City. **Activities:** Campus Ministries; Choral groups; Concert band; Dance; Drama/theater; Jazz band; Literary magazine; Model UN; Music ensembles; Radio station; Student government; Student newspaper; Student-run film society; Television station; Yearbook. 40 registered organizations, 22 honor societies, 1 religious organization on campus. **Athletics (Intercollegiate):** *Men:* baseball, basketball, cheerleading, cross-country, football, golf, ice hockey, soccer, track/field (outdoor), track/field (indoor). *Women:* basketball, cheerleading, cross-country, field hockey, lacrosse, soccer, softball, tennis, track/field (outdoor), track/field (indoor), volleyball. **On-Campus Highlights:** Wellness Center. **Environmental Initiatives:** After years of campaigning, we are finally purchasing 30% recycled content copy paper for all copying (student, faculty, and staff) on campus. While this may seem simple and obvious, due to institutional thinking it was an extremely hard change to make happen.

ADMISSIONS

Freshman Academic Profile: Average high school GPA 3.3. **Test Scores:** SAT Math middle 50% range 510–590. SAT EBRW middle 50% range 500–800. ACT middle 50% range 22–26. **Basis for Candidate Selection:** *Very important factors include:* rigor of secondary school record, academic GPA, standardized test scores. *Important factors include:* class rank, first generation. *Other factors include:* application essay, recommendation(s), extracurricular activities, talent/ability, character/personal qualities, alumni/ae relation, geographical residence, state residency, racial/ethnic status, volunteer work. **Freshman Admission Requirements:** High school diploma is required and GED is accepted. *Academic units required:* 4 English, 4 math, 3 science, 3 science labs, 2 foreign language, 1 social studies, 1 history, 2 academic electives. **Freshman Admission Statistics:** 4,076 applied, 78% admitted, 28% enrolled. **Transfer Admission Requirements:** High school transcript, college transcript(s), statement of good standing from prior institution(s). Minimum college GPA of 2.5 required. Lowest grade transferable C-. **General Admission Information:** Application fee $50. Priority deadline 3/1. Regular application deadline 5/1. Non-fall registration accepted. Admission may be deferred for a maximum of 1 year.

COSTS AND FINANCIAL AID

Annual in-state tuition $970. Annual out-of-state tuition $7,050. Room and board $12,360. Required fees $9,191. Average book and supplies expense $1,368. **Required Forms and Deadlines:** FAFSA. **Notification of Awards:** Applicants will be notified of awards on a rolling basis beginning 12/15. **Types of Aid:** *Need-based scholarships/grants:* College/university scholarship or grant aid from institutional funds; Federal Pell; Private scholarships; SEOG; State scholarships/grants. *Loans:* Direct PLUS loans; Direct Subsidized Stafford Loans; Direct Unsubsidized Stafford Loans. **Student Employment:** Federal Work-Study Program available. Institutional employment available. **Financial Aid Statistics:** 88% needy freshmen, 83% needy undergrads receive need-based scholarship or grant aid. 42% freshmen, 35% undergrads receive non-need-based scholarship or grant aid. 97% freshmen, 93% undergrads receive need-

based self-help aid. 0% freshmen, 0% undergrads receive athletic scholarships. 64.8% freshmen, 59.7% undergrads receive any aid. 79% undergrads borrow to pay for school. Average cumulative indebtedness $28,759. **Criteria awarding aid:** *Non-need-based:* Academics.

WRIGHT STATE UNIVERSITY

3640 Colonel Glenn Highway, Dayton, OH 45435
Phone: 937-775-5700 **Financial Aid Phone:** 937-775-5405
E-mail: admissions@wright.edu **CEEB Code:** 1179
Fax: 937-775-4410 **Website:** www.wright.edu **ACT Code:** 3295

This public school was founded in 1967. It has a 557 acre campus.

RATINGS

Admissions Selectivity Rating: 75   **Fire Safety Rating:** 93   **Green Rating:** 82

STUDENTS AND FACULTY

Enrollment: 11,251. **Student Body:** 52% female, 48% male, 5% out-of-state, 3% international. Asian 3%, African American 11%, Caucasian 75%, Hispanic 4%, Native American <1%, Pacific Islander <1%, Two or more races 4%, Race unknown 1%.
Retention and Graduation: 63% freshmen return for sophomore year. 19% freshmen graduate within 4 years. 35% freshmen graduate within 6 years. **Faculty:** 1% of classes are taught by teaching assistants.

ACADEMICS

Degrees: Bachelor's; Certificate; Doctoral degree—other; Doctoral degree—professional practice; Doctoral degree research/scholarship; Master's; Post-bachelor's certificate; Post-master's certificate. **Most popular majors:** Registered Nursing/Registered Nurse; Biology/Biological Sciences, General; Mechanical Engineering. **Special Study Options:** Cooperative education program; Cross-registration; Distance learning; Double major; Dual enrollment; English as a Second Language (ESL); Honors program; Independent study; Internships; Student-designed major; Study abroad; Teacher certification program; Weekend college. **Honors programs:** The University Honors Program was created in 1972 to meet the needs of the university's brightest, most ambitious students. Approximately 7% of Wright State undergraduates are enrolled in the University Honors Program. It is open to students of all majors and provides a varied, dedicated curriculum, including interdisciplinary courses, service learning, study abroad, and independent research. **Disability Services offered:** Note-taking services; Reader services; Tape recorders; Tutors. **Career services:** Alumni network; Alumni services; Career assessment; Career/job search classes; Internships.

FACILITIES

Housing: Apartments for married students; Apartments for single students; Coed dorms; Special housing for disabled students; Theme housing; 100% of campus accessible to physically disabled. **Special Academic Facilities/Equipment:** Art gallery located in the Creative Arts Center; Tom Hanks Center for Motion Pictures; Student Success Center; Garden of the Senses; Robert and Elaine Stein Galleries; Neuroscience Engineering Collaboration Building. **Campus Network:** 100% of classrooms, 100% of dorms, 100% of student union, 100% of libraries, 100% of dining areas, 100% of common outdoor areas have wireless network access.

CAMPUS LIFE

Environment: City. **Activities:** Campus Ministries; Choral groups; Concert band; Dance; Drama/theater; International Student Organization; Jazz band; Literary magazine; Model UN; Music ensembles; Musical theater; Opera; Pep band; Radio station; Student government; Student newspaper; Symphony orchestra; Television station. 205 registered organizations, 12 honor societies, 18 religious organizations, 9 fraternities, 11 sororities on campus. **Athletics (Intercollegiate):** *Men:* baseball, basketball, cheerleading, cross-country, diving, golf, soccer, swimming, tennis. *Women:* basketball, cheerleading, cross-country, diving, soccer, softball, swimming, tennis, track/field (outdoor), volleyball. **On-Campus Highlights:** Student Union. **Environmental Initiatives:** Matthew O. Diggs III Laboratory for Life Sciences Research achieved LEED Gold status, the first laboratory in Ohio to achieve LEED-NC Gold status.

ADMISSIONS

Freshman Academic Profile: Average high school GPA 3.3. 18% in top 10% of high school class, 40% in top 25% of high school class, 68% in top 50% of high school class. **Test Scores:** SAT Math middle 50% range 490–630. SAT

EBRW middle 50% range 490–640. ACT middle 50% range 19–25. **Basis for Candidate Selection:** *Very important factors include:* rigor of secondary school record, academic GPA, standardized test scores. *Important factors include:* class rank. *Other factors include:* recommendation(s), state residency. **Freshman Admission Requirements:** High school diploma is required and GED is accepted. *Academic units required:* 4 English, 4 math, 3 science, 3 science labs, 3 social studies. *Academic units recommended:* 2 foreign language, 1 visual/performing arts. **Freshman Admission Statistics:** 5,826 applied, 97% admitted, 40% enrolled. **Transfer Admission Requirements:** College transcript(s). Minimum college GPA of 2.0 required. Lowest grade transferable D. **General Admission Information:** Application fee $30. Regular application deadline 8/20. Non-fall registration accepted. Admission may be deferred for a maximum of one year.

COSTS AND FINANCIAL AID

Annual in-state tuition $9,254. Annual out-of-state tuition $18,398. Room and board $11,832. Average book and supplies expense $1,560. **Required Forms and Deadlines:** FAFSA. **Notification of Awards:** Applicants will be notified of awards on or about 2/1. **Types of Aid:** *Need-based scholarships/grants:* College/university scholarship or grant aid from institutional funds; Federal Nursing Scholarships; Federal Pell; Private scholarships; SEOG; State scholarships/grants; United Negro College Fund. *Loans:* Direct PLUS loans; Direct Subsidized Stafford Loans; Direct Unsubsidized Stafford Loans. **Student Employment:** Federal Work-Study Program available. Institutional employment available. **Financial Aid Statistics:** 85% needy freshmen, 84% needy undergrads receive need-based scholarship or grant aid. 12% freshmen, 9% undergrads receive non-need-based scholarship or grant aid. 89% freshmen, 90% undergrads receive need-based self-help aid. 1% freshmen, 2% undergrads receive athletic scholarships. 61% undergrads borrow to pay for school. Average cumulative indebtedness $30,677. **Criteria awarding aid:** *Need-based:* Academics, Art, Minority status, Music/drama. *Non-need-based:* Academics, Alumni affiliation, Art, Athletics, Leadership, Minority status, Music/drama, State/district residency.

XAVIER UNIVERSITY (OH)

3800 Victory Parkway, Cincinnati, OH 45207-5311
Phone: 513-745-3301 **Financial Aid Phone:** 513-745-3142
E-mail: xuadmit@xavier.edu **CEEB Code:** 1965
Fax: 513-745-4319 **Website:** www.xavier.edu **ACT Code:** 3366

This private school, affiliated with the Roman Catholic-Jesuit Church, was founded in 1831. It has a 189 acre campus.

RATINGS

Admissions Selectivity Rating: 78   **Fire Safety Rating:** 87   **Green Rating:** 76

STUDENTS AND FACULTY

Enrollment: 5,010. **Student Body:** 54% female, 46% male, 57% out-of-state, 1% international (45 countries represented). Asian 3%, African American 9%, Caucasian 75%, Hispanic 6%, Native American <1%, Pacific Islander <1%, Two or more races 4%, Race unknown 2%. **Retention and Graduation:** 83% freshmen return for sophomore year. 66% freshmen graduate within 4 years. 73% freshmen graduate within 6 years. 23% grads go on to further study within 1 year. 3% grads pursue arts and sciences degrees. 1% grads pursue law degrees. 1% grads pursue business degrees. 1% grads pursue medical degrees. **Faculty:** Student/faculty ratio 11:1. 385 full-time faculty, 77% hold PhDs, 15% are members of minority groups, 56% are women. 0% of classes are taught by teaching assistants.

ACADEMICS

Degrees: Associate; Bachelor's; Certificate; Doctoral degree—professional practice; Master's; Post-bachelor's certificate; Post-master's certificate; Terminal Associate. **Classes:** Most classes have 20–29 students. Most lab/discussion sessions have 10–19 students. **Special Study Options:** Cooperative education program; Cross-registration; Distance learning; Double major; Dual enrollment; English as a Second Language (ESL); Exchange student program (domestic); Honors program; Independent study; Internships; Study abroad; Teacher certification program; Weekend college. **Honors programs:**

University Scholars Program; Philosophy, Politics and the Public; Honors Bachelors of Arts; Smith Scholars Program. **Disability Services offered:** Note-taking services; Reader services; Tape recorders; Tutors. **Career services:** Alumni network; Alumni services; Career assessment; Career/job search classes; Internships; Regional alumni.

FACILITIES

Housing: Apartments for single students; Coed dorms; Special housing for disabled students; Theme housing; 99% of campus accessible to physically disabled. **Special Academic Facilities/Equipment:** Student-run art gallery, Montessori lab school, The Fifth Third Trading Room, Makerspace, Nursing Simulation labs, and an observatory. **Campus Network:** 100% of classrooms, 100% of dorms, 100% of student union, 100% of libraries, 100% of dining areas, 80% of common outdoor areas have wireless network access.

CAMPUS LIFE

Environment: Metropolis. **Activities:** Campus Ministries; Choral groups; Concert band; Dance; Drama/theater; International Student Organization; Literary magazine; Model UN; Music ensembles; Musical theater; Pep band; Student government; Student newspaper; Television station. 167 registered organizations, 9 honor societies, 4 religious organizations on campus. **Athletics (Intercollegiate):** *Men:* baseball, basketball, cheerleading, cross-country, golf, soccer, swimming, tennis, track/field (outdoor), track/field (indoor). *Women:* basketball, cheerleading, cross-country, golf, soccer, swimming, tennis, track/field (outdoor), track/field (indoor), volleyball. **On-Campus Highlights:** Cintas Center basketball arena. **Environmental Initiatives:** Growth and investment 'All-In': Linking the growth of new undergraduate and Masters programs- with more students, regular field trips, social events, and lecture series—with the leadership team's investment of time and talent participating on and leading local boards: Watershed Council, Economics of Compassion Board, Southwest Ohio sustainable farming board, and Green Business Council.

ADMISSIONS

Freshman Academic Profile: Average high school GPA 3.6. 23% in top 10% of high school class, 52% in top 25% of high school class, 82% in top 50% of high school class. 59% from public high schools. **Test Scores:** SAT Math middle 50% range 530–640. SAT EBRW middle 50% range 540–640. ACT middle 50% range 22–28. **Basis for Candidate Selection:** *Very important factors include:* rigor of secondary school record, academic GPA. *Important factors include:* application essay, standardized test scores, recommendation(s), extracurricular activities, character/personal qualities, volunteer work. *Other factors include:* class rank, talent/ability, first generation, alumni/ae relation, work experience, level of applicant's interest. **Freshman Admission Requirements:** High school diploma is required and GED is accepted. *Academic units recommended:* 4 English, 3 math, 3 science, 2 foreign language, 3 social studies, 5 academic electives, 1 unit from above areas or other academic areas. **Freshman Admission Statistics:** 14,758 applied, 76% admitted, 11% enrolled. **Transfer Admission Requirements:** High school transcript, college transcript(s), statement of good standing from prior institution(s). Minimum college GPA of 2.0 required. Lowest grade transferable C-. **General Admission Information:** Application fee $35. Priority deadline 2/1. Non-fall registration accepted. Admission may be deferred for a maximum of 1 year.

COSTS AND FINANCIAL AID

Annual tuition $42,230. Room and board $13,310. Required fees $230. Average book and supplies expense $1,300. **Required Forms and Deadlines:** FAFSA. **Notification of Awards:** Applicants will be notified of awards on a rolling basis beginning 12/15. **Types of Aid:** *Need-based scholarships/grants:* College/university scholarship or grant aid from institutional funds; Federal Pell; Private scholarships; SEOG; State scholarships/grants; United Negro College Fund. *Loans:* Direct PLUS loans; Direct Subsidized Stafford Loans; Direct Unsubsidized Stafford Loans. **Student Employment:** Federal Work-Study Program available. Institutional employment available. **Financial Aid Statistics:** 60% needy freshmen, 60% needy undergrads receive need-based scholarship or grant aid. 39% freshmen, 31% undergrads receive non-need-based scholarship or grant aid. 55% freshmen, 60% undergrads receive need-based self-help aid. 1% freshmen, 1% undergrads receive athletic scholarships. 99.7% freshmen, 89.3% undergrads receive any aid. 53% undergrads borrow to pay for school. Average cumulative indebtedness $10,348. **Criteria awarding aid:** *Need-based:* Job skills. *Non-need-based:* Academics, Alumni affiliation, Art, Athletics, Leadership, Music/drama, Religious affiliation.

XAVIER UNIVERSITY OF LOUISIANA

1 Drexel Drive, New Orleans, LA 70125
Phone: 504-520-7388 **Financial Aid Phone:** 504-520-7835
E-mail: apply@xula.edu **CEEB Code:** 6975
Fax: 504-520-7941 **Website:** www.xula.edu **ACT Code:** 1618

This private school, affiliated with the Roman Catholic Church, was founded in 1915. It has a 29 acre campus.

RATINGS
Admissions Selectivity Rating: 85   **Fire Safety Rating:** 99   **Green Rating:** 60*

STUDENTS AND FACULTY
Enrollment: 2,515. **Student Body:** 76% female, 24% male, 62% out-of-state, 2% international (13 countries represented). Asian 4%, African American 79%, Caucasian 2%, Hispanic 5%, Native American <1%, Pacific Islander 0%, Two or more races 4%, Race unknown 5%.
Retention and Graduation: 70% freshmen return for sophomore year. 38% freshmen graduate within 4 years. 51% freshmen graduate within 6 years. 31% grads go on to further study within 1 year. **Faculty:** Student/faculty ratio 15:1. 223 full-time faculty, 99% hold PhDs, 63% are members of minority groups, 49% are women. 0% of classes are taught by teaching assistants.

ACADEMICS
Degrees: Bachelor's; Certificate; Doctoral degree—professional practice; Doctoral degree research/scholarship; Master's. **Classes:** Most classes have 20–29 students. Most lab/discussion sessions have 20–29 students. **Most popular majors:** Pre-Medicine/Pre-Medical Studies; Pre-Pharmacy Studies; Psychology, General. **Special Study Options:** Accelerated program; Cooperative education program; Cross-registration; Distance learning; Double major; Dual enrollment; Exchange student program (domestic); Honors program; Independent study; Internships; Study abroad; Teacher certification program. **Combined degree programs:** BA/MEng. **Disability Services offered:** Note-taking services; Reader services; Tape recorders; Tutors. **Career services:** Alumni network; Career assessment; Career/job search classes; Internships.

FACILITIES
Housing: Coed dorms; Men's dorms; Women's dorms; 100% of campus accessible to physically disabled. **Special Academic Facilities/Equipment:** University Library Archives.

CAMPUS LIFE
Environment: Metropolis. **Activities:** Campus Ministries; Choral groups; Concert band; Dance; International Student Organization; Jazz band; Literary magazine; Music ensembles; Opera; Pep band; Radio station; Student government; Student newspaper; Symphony orchestra; Yearbook. 100 registered organizations, 9 honor societies, 1 religious organization, 4 fraternities, 4 sororities on campus. **Athletics (Intercollegiate):** *Men:* basketball, cross-country, tennis, track/field (outdoor), track/field (indoor). *Women:* basketball, cross-country, tennis, track/field (outdoor), track/field (indoor), volleyball. **On-Campus Highlights:** University Center.

ADMISSIONS
Freshman Academic Profile: Average high school GPA 3.7. 30% in top 10% of high school class, 59% in top 25% of high school class, 85% in top 50% of high school class. **Test Scores:** SAT Math middle 50% range 480–580. SAT EBRW middle 50% range 510–580. ACT middle 50% range 20–26. **Basis for Candidate Selection:** *Very important factors include:* rigor of secondary school record, academic GPA, standardized test scores, recommendation(s). *Important factors include:* class rank, application essay, *Other factors include:* interview, extracurricular activities, talent/ability, character/personal qualities, alumni/ae relation, volunteer work, work experience, level of applicant's interest. **Freshman Admission Requirements:** High school diploma is required and GED is accepted. *Academic units required:* 4 English, 2 math, 2 science, 1 social studies, 7 academic electives. *Academic units recommended:* 4 math, 3 science, 1 foreign language, 1 history. **Freshman Admission Statistics:** 9,291 applied, 60% admitted, 15% enrolled. **Transfer Admission Requirements:** College transcript(s). Minimum college GPA of 2.00 required. Lowest grade transferable C. **General Admission Information:** Priority deadline 3/1. Regular application deadline 7/1. Non-fall registration accepted. Admission may be deferred for a maximum of 1 year.

COSTS AND FINANCIAL AID
Annual tuition $22,612. Room and board $9,047. Required fees $2,394. Average book and supplies expense $1,300. **Required Forms and Deadlines:** FAFSA. **Types of Aid:** *Need-based scholarships/grants:* College/university scholarship or grant aid from institutional funds; Federal Pell; SEOG; State scholarships/grants; United Negro College Fund. *Loans:* Direct PLUS loans; Direct Subsidized Stafford Loans; Direct Unsubsidized Stafford Loans. **Student Employment:** Federal Work-Study Program available. Institutional employment available. **Financial Aid Statistics:** 96% needy freshmen, 93% needy undergrads receive need-based scholarship or grant aid. 96% freshmen, 91% undergrads receive need-based self-help aid. 98% freshmen, 94% undergrads receive any aid. **Criteria awarding aid:** *Need-based:* Academics, Art, Athletics, Music/drama.

YALE UNIVERSITY

PO Box 208234, New Haven, CT 06520-8234
Phone: 203-432-9300 **Financial Aid Phone:** 203-432-2700
E-mail: student.questions@yale.edu **CEEB Code:** 3987
Fax: 203-432-9392 **Website:** www.yale.edu **ACT Code:** 618

This private school was founded in 1701. It has a 342 acre campus.

RATINGS
Admissions Selectivity Rating: 99   **Fire Safety Rating:** 62   **Green Rating:** 95

STUDENTS AND FACULTY
Enrollment: 5,963. **Student Body:** 50% female, 50% male, 92% out-of-state, 11% international (118 countries represented). Asian 19%, African American 8%, Caucasian 42%, Hispanic 13%, Native American <1%, Pacific Islander <1%, Two or more races 6%, Race unknown <1%.
Retention and Graduation: 99% freshmen return for sophomore year. 88% freshmen graduate within 4 years. 21% grads go on to further study within 1 year. 7% grads pursue arts and sciences degrees. 4% grads pursue law degrees. 4% grads pursue medical degrees. **Faculty:** Student/faculty ratio 6:1. 1,223 full-time faculty, 93% hold PhDs, 22% are members of minority groups, 39% are women.

ACADEMICS
Degrees: Bachelor's; Certificate; Diploma; Doctoral degree—professional practice; Doctoral degree research/scholarship; Master's; Post-bachelor's certificate; Post-master's certificate. **Classes:** Most classes have 10–19 students. **Most popular majors:** Economics, General; History, General; Political Science and Government, General. **Special Study Options:** Accelerated program; Double major; English as a Second Language (ESL); Honors program; Independent study; Internships; Liberal arts/career combination; Student-designed major; Study abroad. **Combined degree programs:** BA/MA. **Disability Services offered:** Note-taking services; Reader services; Tape recorders; Tutors. **Career services:** Alumni network; Alumni services; Career/job search classes; Internships; Regional alumni.

FACILITIES
Housing: Coed dorms; Special housing for disabled students. **Special Academic Facilities/Equipment:** Yale British Art Museum, Yale Art Gallery, Peabody Museum of Natural History, Jackson Institute for Global Affairs, Center for Engineering Innovation and Design, clean room, wind tunnel, engine testing facility, graphic workstations, robotics labs, nuclear accelerators, nuclear magnetic resonance spectrometers, optical spectroscopy instruments, high-resolution mass spectrometer, X-ray diffraction instruments, scanning electron microscopes, observatories, biospheric studies institute.

CAMPUS LIFE
Environment: City. **Activities:** Choral groups; Concert band; Dance; Drama/theater; Jazz band; Literary magazine; Marching band; Music ensembles; Musical theater; Opera; Pep band; Radio station; Student government; Student newspaper; Student-run film society; Symphony orchestra; Television station; Yearbook. 350 registered organizations on campus. **Athletics (Intercollegiate):** *Men:* baseball, basketball, crew/rowing, cross-country, diving, fencing, football, golf, ice hockey, lacrosse, sailing, soccer, squash, swimming, tennis, track/field (outdoor), track/field (indoor). *Women:* basketball, crew/rowing, cross-country,

diving, fencing, field hockey, golf, gymnastics, ice hockey, lacrosse, sailing, soccer, softball, squash, swimming, tennis, track/field (outdoor), track/field (indoor), volleyball. **On-Campus Highlights:** Old Campus. **Environmental Initiatives:** The university pledged to a greenhouse gas commitment of 43% below 2005 levels by 2020.

ADMISSIONS

Freshman Academic Profile: 95% in top 10% of high school class, 99% in top 25% of high school class, 100% in top 50% of high school class. 57% from public high schools. **Test Scores:** SAT Math middle 50% range 730–790. SAT EBRW middle 50% range 720–770. ACT middle 50% range 33–35. **Basis for Candidate Selection:** *Very important factors include:* rigor of secondary school record, class rank, academic GPA, application essay, standardized test scores, recommendation(s), extracurricular activities, talent/ability, character/personal qualities. *Other factors include:* interview, first generation, alumni/ae relation, geographical residence, state residency, racial/ethnic status, volunteer work, work experience. **Freshman Admission Requirements:** High school diploma is required and GED is accepted. **Freshman Admission Statistics:** 35,307 applied, 6% admitted, 70% enrolled. **Transfer Admission Requirements:** High school transcript, college transcript(s), essay or personal statement, standardized test scores, statement of good standing from prior institution(s). Lowest grade transferable C. **General Admission Information:** Application fee $80. Regular application deadline 1/2. Admission may be deferred for a maximum of one year.

COSTS AND FINANCIAL AID

Annual tuition $55,500. Room and board $16,600. Average book and supplies expense $3,670. **Required Forms and Deadlines:** CSS/Financial Aid PROFILE; FAFSA; Institution's own financial aid form; Noncustodial PROFILE. **Notification of Awards:** Applicants will be notified of awards on or about 4/1. **Types of Aid:** *Need-based scholarships/grants:* College/university scholarship or grant aid from institutional funds; Federal Pell; Private scholarships; SEOG; State scholarships/grants; United Negro College Fund. *Loans:* Direct PLUS loans; Direct Subsidized Stafford Loans; Direct Unsubsidized Stafford Loans. **Student Employment:** Institutional employment available. **Financial Aid Statistics:** 100% needy freshmen, 100% needy undergrads receive need-based scholarship or grant aid. 0% freshmen, 0% undergrads receive non-need-based scholarship or grant aid. 75% freshmen, 85% undergrads receive need-based self-help aid. 0% freshmen, 0% undergrads receive athletic scholarships. 51% freshmen, 52% undergrads receive any aid. 16% undergrads borrow to pay for school. Average cumulative indebtedness $14,575.

YESHIVA UNIVERSITY

500 West 185th Street, New York, NY 10033-3299
Phone: 212-960-5277
E-mail: yuadmit@yu.edu **CEEB Code:** 2990
Fax: 212-960-0086 **Website:** www.yu.edu **ACT Code:** 2992

This private school was founded in 1886. It has a 12 acre campus.

RATINGS

Admissions Selectivity Rating: 89   **Fire Safety Rating:** 60*   **Green Rating:** 60*

STUDENTS AND FACULTY

Enrollment: 2,866. **Student Body:** 46% female, 54% male, 35% out-of-state, 12% international (53 countries represented). Asian <1%, African American <1%, Caucasian 82%, Hispanic 2%, Native American <1%, Race unknown 4%.
Retention and Graduation: 90% freshmen return for sophomore year.
Faculty: Student/faculty ratio 7:1. 0% of classes are taught by teaching assistants.

ACADEMICS

Degrees: Bachelor's; Master's. **Classes:** Most classes have 10–19 students. Most lab/discussion sessions have 10–19 students. **Most popular majors:** Political Science and Government, General; Jewish/Judaic Studies; Psychology, General. **Special Study Options:** Double major; Honors program; Independent study; Internships; Student-designed major; Study abroad; Teacher certification program. **Combined degree programs:** BA/MA. **Career services:** Career assessment; Career/job search classes; Internships.

FACILITIES

Housing: Apartments for married students; Apartments for single students; Men's dorms; Women's dorms. **Special Academic Facilities/Equipment:** Archives and rare book collection, museum of Jewish art, architecture, history, and culture.

CAMPUS LIFE

Activities: Choral groups; Concert band; Drama/theater; Jazz band; Literary magazine; Music ensembles; Musical theater; Radio station; Student government; Student newspaper; Yearbook. **Athletics (Intercollegiate):** *Men:* basketball, tennis, volleyball. *Women:* basketball, tennis.

ADMISSIONS

Freshman Academic Profile: Average high school GPA 3.5. 48% in top 10% of high school class, 77% in top 25% of high school class, 95% in top 50% of high school class. **Test Scores:** SAT Math middle 50% range 550–680. SAT EBRW middle 50% range 550–690. ACT middle 50% range 22–28. **Basis for Candidate Selection:** *Important factors include:* rigor of secondary school record, academic GPA, application essay, standardized test scores, interview, extracurricular activities, talent/ability. *Other factors include:* volunteer work, work experience. **Freshman Admission Requirements:** High school diploma is required and GED is accepted. *Academic units recommended:* 4 English, 2 math, 2 science, 2 foreign language, 2 social studies. **Freshman Admission Statistics:** 2,027 applied, 63% admitted, 65% enrolled. **Transfer Admission Requirements:** High school transcript, college transcript(s), essay or personal statement, interview, standardized test scores. Lowest grade transferable 75. **General Admission Information:** Application fee $40. Regular application deadline 2/15. Non-fall registration accepted.

COSTS AND FINANCIAL AID

Annual tuition $31,594. Room and board $10,380. Average book and supplies expense $1,224. **Required Forms and Deadlines:** Business/Farm Supplement; CSS/Financial Aid PROFILE; FAFSA; Institution's own financial aid form; Noncustodial PROFILE; State aid form. **Types of Aid:** *Need-based scholarships/grants:* College/university scholarship or grant aid from institutional funds; Federal Pell; Private scholarships; SEOG; State scholarships/grants. **Student Employment:** Federal Work-Study Program available. Institutional employment available. **Financial Aid Statistics:** 89% needy freshmen, 85% needy undergrads receive need-based scholarship or grant aid. 13% freshmen, 9% undergrads receive non-need-based scholarship or grant aid. 75% freshmen, 68% undergrads receive need-based self-help aid. 0% freshmen, 0% undergrads receive athletic scholarships. **Criteria awarding aid:** *Non-need-based:* Academics.

YORK COLLEGE

1125 E. 8th Street, York, NE 68467
Phone: 402-363-5627 **Financial Aid Phone:** 402-363-5625
E-mail: enroll@york.edu
Fax: 402-363-5623 **Website:** www.york.edu **ACT Code:** 2484

This private school, affiliated with the Church of Christ, was founded in 1890. It has a 200 acre campus.

RATINGS

Admissions Selectivity Rating: 85   **Fire Safety Rating:** 97   **Green Rating:** 60*

STUDENTS AND FACULTY

Enrollment: 385. **Student Body:** 51% female, 49% male, 69% out-of-state, 1% international (6 countries represented). Asian 2%, African American 5%, Caucasian 73%, Hispanic 4%, Native American 0%, Race unknown 15%.
Retention and Graduation: 55% freshmen return for sophomore year.
Faculty: Student/faculty ratio 7:1. 33 full-time faculty, 36% hold PhDs, 3% are members of minority groups, 27% are women. 0% of classes are taught by teaching assistants.

ACADEMICS

Degrees: Associate; Bachelor's; Transfer Associate. **Classes:** Most classes have fewer than 10 students. **Most popular majors:** Education, General; Business Administration and Management, General; Psychology, General. **Special Study Options:** Double major; Dual enrollment; Internships; Student-designed major; Teacher certification program. **Career services:** Alumni network; Career assessment.

FACILITIES

Housing: Apartments for married students; Men's dorms; Special housing for disabled students; Women's dorms; 60% of campus accessible to physically disabled. **Campus Network:** 100% of classrooms, 100% of dorms, 100% of student union, 100% of libraries, 100% of dining areas, 100% of common outdoor areas have wireless network access.

CAMPUS LIFE

Environment: Village. **Activities:** Campus Ministries; Choral groups; Drama/theater; Literary magazine; Music ensembles; Musical theater; Student government; Student newspaper; Yearbook. 12 registered organizations, 2 honor societies, 1 religious organization, 4 fraternities, 4 sororities on campus. **Athletics (Intercollegiate):** *Men:* baseball, basketball, soccer, wrestling. *Women:* basketball, soccer, softball, volleyball. **On-Campus Highlights:** Mackey Center.

ADMISSIONS

Freshman Academic Profile: Average high school GPA 3.4. 13% in top 10% of high school class, 25% in top 25% of high school class, 60% in top 50% of high school class. **Test Scores:** SAT Math middle 50% range 440–560. SAT EBRW middle 50% range 450–590. ACT middle 50% range 18–26. **Basis for Candidate Selection:** *Very important factors include:* rigor of secondary school record, class rank, academic GPA, standardized test scores. *Other factors include:* application essay, recommendation(s), extracurricular activities, talent/ability, character/personal qualities, first generation, alumni/ae relation, religious affiliation/commitment, volunteer work, level of applicant's interest. **Freshman Admission Requirements:** High school diploma is required and GED is accepted. *Academic units required:* 3 English, 2 math, 2 science, 1 social studies, 1 history. *Academic units recommended:* 4 English, 4 math, 4 science, 3 foreign language, 4 social studies, 4 history. **Freshman Admission Statistics:** 531 applied, 57% admitted, 30% enrolled. **Transfer Admission Requirements:** High school transcript, college transcript(s). Minimum college GPA of 2 required. Lowest grade transferable 1. **General Admission Information:** Application fee $20. Priority deadline 3/31. Regular application deadline 8/31. Non-fall registration accepted.

COSTS AND FINANCIAL AID

Annual tuition $12,500. Room and board $4,500. Required fees $1,500. Average book and supplies expense $1,500. **Required Forms and Deadlines:** FAFSA. **Notification of Awards:** Applicants will be notified of awards on a rolling basis beginning 3/1. **Types of Aid:** *Need-based scholarships/grants:* College/university scholarship or grant aid from institutional funds; Federal Pell; Private scholarships; SEOG; State scholarships/grants. *Loans:* Direct PLUS loans; Direct Subsidized Stafford Loans; Direct Unsubsidized Stafford Loans. **Student Employment:** Federal Work-Study Program available. **Financial Aid Statistics:** 0% freshmen, 0% undergrads receive athletic scholarships. 89% freshmen, 89% undergrads receive any aid. **Criteria awarding aid:** *Non-need-based:* Academics, Athletics, Leadership, Music/drama.

YORK COLLEGE OF PENNSYLVANIA

441 Country Club Road, York, PA 17403-3651
Phone: 717-849-1600 **Financial Aid Phone:** 717-849-1682
E-mail: admissions@ycp.edu **CEEB Code:** 2991
Fax: 717-849-1607 **Website:** www.ycp.edu **ACT Code:** 3762

This private school was founded in 1787. It has a 190 acre campus.

RATINGS

Admissions Selectivity Rating: 76   **Fire Safety Rating:** 97   **Green Rating:** 63

STUDENTS AND FACULTY

Enrollment: 4,847. **Student Body:** 55% female, 45% male, 42% out-of-state, <1% international (32 countries represented). Asian 1%, African American 5%, Caucasian 83%, Hispanic 5%, Native American <1%, Pacific Islander <1%, Two or more races 3%, Race unknown 2%.
Retention and Graduation: 75% freshmen return for sophomore year.
Faculty: Student/faculty ratio 16:1. 189 full-time faculty, 81% hold PhDs, 4% are members of minority groups, 43% are women. 0% of classes are taught by teaching assistants.

ACADEMICS

Degrees: Associate; Bachelor's; Doctoral degree—professional practice; Master's; Post-master's certificate. **Classes:** Most classes have 20–29 students. Most lab/discussion sessions have 10–19 students. **Most popular majors:** Registered Nursing/Registered Nurse; Biology/Biological Sciences, General; Business Administration and Management, General. **Special Study Options:** Cooperative education program; Double major; Dual enrollment; Independent study; Internships; Liberal arts/career combination; Student-designed major; Study abroad; Teacher certification program. **Disability Services offered:** Note-taking services; Reader services; Tutors. **Career services:** Alumni network; Alumni services; Career assessment; Career/job search classes; Internships; Regional alumni.

FACILITIES

Housing: Apartments for single students; Coed dorms; Fraternity/sorority housing; Special housing for disabled students; Theme housing; Wellness housing; 98% of campus accessible to physically disabled. **Special Academic Facilities/Equipment:** Music, arts, and communication center; nursing education center; humanities center.

CAMPUS LIFE

Environment: Town. **Activities:** Campus Ministries; Choral groups; Concert band; Dance; Drama/theater; International Student Organization; Jazz band; Literary magazine; Model UN; Music ensembles; Musical theater; Radio station; Student government; Student newspaper; Symphony orchestra; Television station. 85 registered organizations, 10 honor societies, 4 religious organizations, 8 fraternities, 6 sororities on campus. **Athletics (Intercollegiate):** *Men:* baseball, basketball, cheerleading, cross-country, golf, lacrosse, soccer, swimming, tennis, track/field (outdoor), wrestling. *Women:* basketball, cheerleading, cross-country, field hockey, lacrosse, soccer, softball, swimming, tennis, track/field (outdoor), volleyball. **On-Campus Highlights:** Collegiate Performing Arts Center.

ADMISSIONS

Freshman Academic Profile: Average high school GPA 3.5. 12% in top 10% of high school class, 40% in top 25% of high school class, 77% in top 50% of high school class. **Test Scores:** SAT Math middle 50% range 480–578. SAT EBRW middle 50% range 470–560. ACT middle 50% range 20–25. **Basis for Candidate Selection:** *Very important factors include:* rigor of secondary school record, academic GPA. *Important factors include:* class rank, standardized test scores, character/personal qualities. *Other factors include:* application essay, recommendation(s), interview, extracurricular activities, talent/ability, alumni/ae relation, volunteer work, work experience, level of applicant's interest. **Freshman Admission Requirements:** High school diploma is required and GED is accepted. *Academic units required:* 4 English, 3 math, 3 science, 2 foreign language, 3 social studies. *Academic units recommended:* 4 English, 4 math, 3 science, 2 foreign language, 3 social studies. **Freshman Admission Statistics:** 9,934 applied, 74% admitted, 15% enrolled. **Transfer Admission Requirements:** College transcript(s). Minimum college GPA of 2.0 required. Lowest grade transferable C. **General Admission Information:** Non-fall registration accepted. Admission may be deferred for a maximum of 12 months.

COSTS AND FINANCIAL AID

Annual tuition $15,350. Room and board $9,580. Required fees $1,660. Average book and supplies expense $1,200. **Required Forms and Deadlines:** FAFSA. **Notification of Awards:** Applicants will be notified of awards on a rolling basis beginning 3/1. **Types of Aid:** *Need-based scholarships/grants:* College/university scholarship or grant aid from institutional funds; Federal Pell; Private scholarships; SEOG; State scholarships/grants. *Loans:* Direct PLUS loans; Direct Subsidized Stafford Loans; Direct Unsubsidized Stafford Loans. **Student Employment:** Federal Work-Study Program available. Institutional employment available. **Financial Aid Statistics:** 61% needy freshmen, 67% needy undergrads receive need-based scholarship or grant aid. 99% freshmen, 78% undergrads receive non-need-based scholarship or grant aid. 85% freshmen, 88% undergrads receive need-based self-help aid. 0% freshmen, 0% undergrads receive athletic scholarships. 99% freshmen, 89% undergrads receive any aid. **Criteria awarding aid:** *Need-based:* Minority status. *Non-need-based:* Academics, Alumni affiliation, Minority status, Music/drama.

YORK UNIVERSITY

Bennett Centre for Student Services, Toronto, ON M3J 1P3
Phone: 416-736-5000 **Financial Aid Phone:** 416-872-9675
E-mail: intlenq@yorku.ca **CEEB Code:** 894
Fax: 416-736-5536 **Website:** www.yorku.ca

This public school was founded in 1959. It has a 550 acre campus.

RATINGS
Admissions Selectivity Rating: 60*   **Fire Safety Rating:** 62   **Green Rating:** 60*

STUDENTS AND FACULTY
Enrollment: 48,631. **Student Body:** 59% female, 41% male.
Faculty: Student/faculty ratio 17:1. 1,480 full-time faculty, 0% hold PhDs, 0% are members of minority groups, 46% are women.

ACADEMICS
Degrees: Bachelor's; Certificate; Diploma; Doctoral degree research/scholarship; Master's; Post-bachelor's certificate. **Most popular majors:** Psychology, General. **Special Study Options:** Accelerated program; Distance learning; Double major; English as a Second Language (ESL); Exchange student program (domestic); Honors program; Independent study; Internships; Student-designed major; Study abroad; Teacher certification program. **Disability Services offered:** Note-taking services; Reader services; Tape recorders; Tutors. **Career services:** Career assessment; Career/job search classes; Internships.

FACILITIES
Housing: Apartments for married students; Apartments for single students; Coed dorms; Men's dorms; Special housing for disabled students; Special housing for international students; Theme housing; Women's dorms. **Special Academic Facilities/Equipment:** 5 museums with more than 4.4 million items. Observatory with 2 telescopes. Robotics laboratory. 2 professionally staffed art galleries. 6 student-run art exhibition spaces. 3 theatres. 2 cinemas. 1 screening room. Wide-variety professional standard film and video production facilities.

CAMPUS LIFE
Environment: Metropolis. **Activities:** Choral groups; Concert band; Dance; Drama/theater; International Student Organization; Jazz band; Model UN; Music ensembles; Pep band; Radio station; Student government; Student newspaper; Symphony orchestra; Yearbook. 259 registered organizations, 35 religious organizations on campus. **Athletics (Intercollegiate):** *Men:* badminton, basketball, cross-country, fencing, football, ice hockey, soccer, swimming, tennis, track/field (outdoor), volleyball, water polo. *Women:* badminton, basketball, cross-country, fencing, field hockey, ice hockey, rugby, soccer, swimming, tennis, track/field (outdoor), volleyball, water polo. **On-Campus Highlights:** York Lanes: on-campus mall.

ADMISSIONS
Basis for Candidate Selection: *Very important factors include:* rigor of secondary school record, academic GPA. *Important factors include:* standardized test scores. *Other factors include:* class rank, interview. **Freshman Admission Requirements:** High school diploma is required and GED is not accepted. **Transfer Admission Requirements:** College transcript(s). Minimum college GPA of 2.5 required. Lowest grade transferable C. **General Admission Information:** Application fee $100. Non-fall registration accepted. Admission may be deferred for a maximum of 1 year.

COSTS AND FINANCIAL AID
Annual in-state tuition $6,712. Annual out-of-state tuition $6,712. Room and board $7,702. Average book and supplies expense $1,000. **Required Forms and Deadlines:** FAFSA. **Student Employment:** Institutional employment available. **Criteria awarding aid:** *Need-based:* Leadership. *Non-need-based:* Academics, Art, Music/drama.

YOUNGSTOWN STATE UNIVERSITY

One University Plaza, Youngstown, OH 44555
Phone: 330-941-2000 **Financial Aid Phone:** 330-941-3505
E-mail: enroll@ysu.edu **CEEB Code:** 1975
Fax: 330-941-3674 **Website:** www.ysu.edu **ACT Code:** 3368

This public school was founded in 1908. It has a 160 acre campus.

RATINGS
Admissions Selectivity Rating: 83   **Fire Safety Rating:** 96   **Green Rating:** 60*

STUDENTS AND FACULTY
Enrollment: 9,755. **Student Body:** 53% female, 47% male, 15% out-of-state, 3% international (83 countries represented). Asian 1%, African American 8%, Caucasian 75%, Hispanic 4%, Native American <1%, Pacific Islander <1%, Two or more races 4%, Race unknown 3%.
Retention and Graduation: 74% freshmen return for sophomore year. 19% freshmen graduate within 4 years. 42% freshmen graduate within 6 years.
Faculty: Student/faculty ratio 18:1. 400 full-time faculty, 88% hold PhDs, 17% are members of minority groups, 45% are women.

ACADEMICS
Degrees: Associate; Bachelor's; Certificate; Diploma; Doctoral degree—professional practice; Doctoral degree research/scholarship; Master's; Post-bachelor's certificate; Post-master's certificate; Terminal Associate; Transfer Associate. **Classes:** Most classes have 20–29 students. Most lab/discussion sessions have 10–19 students. **Most popular majors:** Criminal Justice/Safety Studies; Registered Nursing/Registered Nurse; Psychology, General. **Special Study Options:** Accelerated program; Cooperative education program; Cross-registration; Distance learning; Double major; Dual enrollment; English as a Second Language (ESL); Exchange student program (domestic); Honors program; Independent study; Internships; Student-designed major; Study abroad; Teacher certification program. **Honors programs:** The mission of the Youngstown State University Honors College is to provide academically talented students of any discipline with a community of excellence to develop their full intellectual and cultural potential. Through a combination of extraordinary learning experiences in small classes and experiential seminars, living-learning communities, unique and flexible resources for commuter students, leadership and innovative engagement activities, service-learning and traditional volunteer initiatives, interdisciplinary projects, research opportunities, and community, regional, and global perspectives, we fulfill this mission. As a direct outgrowth and articulated in the YSU Mission Statement, the Honors College "places students at our center" of an energized and inclusive community of faculty, staff, and alumni who share in the pursuit of life-long excellence in learning and civic engagement. Eligible students who desire an enriched education may take honors courses and thus participate in the "honors experience" by applying to the Honors College. Students may apply to the Honors College, pursuing excellence in a broad range of subjects. Successful completion of this guided course of study will be acknowledged with a special designation on the commencement program, diploma, and final transcript. Students enjoy the benefits of early registration each semester they are actively participating. Honors students are eligible to live in the Honors College's living and learning center, Cafaro House Residence Hall, or The Courtyards Apartments—Building #2. Course material is covered in much greater depth than in a traditional class. Therefore, Honors students receive a "value-added" education; Members may use the computer facilities in Fok Hall, which includes wireless connectivity, study space, and a student lounge. As reflected by the transcript and diploma, an Honors student has shown the desire and ability to go above and beyond what is traditionally required by the University. This is particularly impressive to graduate and professional schools and potential employers. High-achieving students benefit from the experience of taking classes and learning with some of the most academically talented students in the nation. The program is operated by the Honors Director under the jurisdiction of the Honors Committee of the University Senate. The Honors Director reports to the Special Assistant to the President. **Disability Services offered:** Note-taking services; Reader services; Tape recorders; Tutors. **Career services:** Alumni services; Career assessment; Career/job search classes; Internships; Regional alumni.

FACILITIES

Housing: Apartments for married students; Apartments for single students; Coed dorms; Special housing for disabled students; Women's dorms; 98% of campus accessible to physically disabled. **Special Academic Facilities/ Equipment:** Art museum, human services development center, engineering services center, planetarium, center for urban studies, industrial development center.

CAMPUS LIFE

Environment: City. **Activities:** Campus Ministries; Choral groups; Concert band; Dance; Drama/theater; International Student Organization; Jazz band; Marching band; Model UN; Music ensembles; Musical theater; Opera; Pep band; Radio station; Student government; Student newspaper; Student-run film society; Symphony orchestra; Television station; Yearbook. 212 registered organizations, 30 honor societies, 11 religious organizations, 5 fraternities, 5 sororities on campus. **On-Campus Highlights:** Stambaugh Stadium.

ADMISSIONS

Freshman Academic Profile: Average high school GPA 3.4. 14% in top 10% of high school class, 35% in top 25% of high school class, 68% in top 50% of high school class. **Test Scores:** SAT Math middle 50% range 480–590. SAT EBRW middle 50% range 490–590. ACT middle 50% range 18–25. **Basis for Candidate Selection:** *Very important factors include:* rigor of secondary school record, academic GPA, standardized test scores. *Important factors include:* class rank. **Freshman Admission Requirements:** High school diploma is required and GED is accepted. *Academic units recommended:* 4 English, 4 math, 3 science, 1 science labs, 2 foreign language, 3 social studies, 1 visual/performing arts. **Freshman Admission Statistics:** 9,243 applied, 68% admitted, 32% enrolled. **General Admission Information:** Application fee $45. Regular application deadline 8/1. Non-fall registration accepted. Admission may be deferred for a maximum of 12 months.

COSTS AND FINANCIAL AID

Annual in-state tuition $9,211. Annual out-of-state tuition $15,211. Required fees $68. Average book and supplies expense $1,100. **Required Forms and Deadlines:** FAFSA; Institution's own financial aid form. **Notification of Awards:** Applicants will be notified of awards on a rolling basis beginning 12/15. **Types of Aid:** *Need-based scholarships/grants:* College/university scholarship or grant aid from institutional funds; Federal Pell; Private scholarships; SEOG; State scholarships/grants. *Loans:* Direct PLUS loans; Direct Subsidized Stafford Loans; Direct Unsubsidized Stafford Loans. **Student Employment:** Federal Work-Study Program available. Institutional employment available. **Financial Aid Statistics:** 78% needy freshmen, 76% needy undergrads receive need-based scholarship or grant aid. 65% freshmen, 54% undergrads receive non-need-based scholarship or grant aid. 79% freshmen, 82% undergrads receive need-based self-help aid. 5% freshmen, 5% undergrads receive athletic scholarships. 94% freshmen, 90% undergrads receive any aid. 96% undergrads borrow to pay for school. Average cumulative indebtedness $30,137. **Criteria awarding aid:** *Need-based:* Academics, Art, Athletics, Leadership, Minority status, Music/drama. *Non-need-based:* Academics, Alumni affiliation, Athletics, State/district residency.

SCHOOL SAYS . . .

In this section you'll find hundreds of colleges with extended listings describing admissions, curriculum, internships, and much more. This is your chance to get in-depth information on colleges that interest you. The Princeton Review charges each school a small fee to be listed, and the editorial responsibility is solely that of the college.

ACADEMY OF ART UNIVERSITY

AT A GLANCE

Established in 1929, Academy of Art University is one of the largest private accredited art and design schools in the nation. Located in San Francisco, the epicenter of culture and technology, Academy of Art University offers more than 135 accredited degree programs in the areas of art, design, music, acting, and writing for media and has a diverse population of more than 10,000 students from around the world.

As more and more art and design career opportunities arise, employers are on the hunt for the next generation of talented—and skilled—creative professionals. Academy of Art University classes build all students from the ground up so students with no experience will be able to gain the skills necessary to fill the positions that employers want, helping to bridge the skills gap in a number of exciting fields.

Academy of Art University welcomes:

- Students with All Levels of Experience
- Transfer Students
- International Students
- Continuing Art Education Students
- High School Students for the Pre-college Art Experience Program
- Undergraduate, Graduate, Certificate, and Continuing Education Students (Personal Enrichment)

Requirements:

- AA, BA, BFA, BS, B.Arch and Portfolio Development Programs: High School Diploma or Equivalent. No Portfolio Required.
- MA and MFA Degree Programs: Bachelor's Degree, Submission of Portfolio, and Statement of Intent.

Students who do not speak English as their first language must be tested on their written and spoken proficiency in order to place them in the appropriate ESL courses, if necessary. ESL requirements can be completed concurrently with regular art and design coursework. Each of the foundation classes runs sections specifically for ESL students, led by instructors who are experienced in language assistance.

Applicants may begin classes at the Academy at the start of the spring, fall, or summer sessions. Undergraduate applicants pay a $50 application fee. *Students should be advised that details provided in this profile may change at any time and may be different for international students. In order to receive the most current information, interested students should visit the website (www.academyart.edu) or use the contact information provided below.

Academy of Art University
79 New Montgomery Street
San Francisco, CA 94105
Telephone: 415-274-2222
(Toll Free): 800-544-ARTS (2787)
Fax: 415-618-6287
Website: www.academyart.edu
Email: info@academyart.edu

LOCATION AND ENVIRONMENT

The Academy has over forty-seven facilities that house classrooms, cafes, studios, galleries, and residence halls.

CAMPUS FACILITIES AND EQUIPMENT

Academy of Art University takes its facilities beyond the typical art school. From two green screens for filmmakers and visual effects artists to a bronze-casting foundry for sculptors and jewelry makers to Cintiq labs and the Oculus Rift System, students have the very best at their fingertips to prepare them for dream careers beyond the Academy.

A creative haven Campus housing

Students making their homes in Academy of Art University residence halls live in some of the most unique buildings in San Francisco, but more importantly, they become part of a tightly knit artist community. Making friends with students from other countries and other disciplines is part of becoming a whole artist. Being exposed to different cultures opens students' minds to new perspectives, while working with students in other departments broadens practical skills and knowledge.

ACADEMIC PROGRAMS

Students study in a professional environment from day one at Academy of Art University, with instructors who are working professionals at the top of their industry. The Academy's career services team works tirelessly to assist students in career development. Graduates go on to work at big name companies like Pixar, Disney, Tesla, Adobe, Apple, Blizzard, DreamWorks, Missoni, EA Games, and many more.

Every year, the Academy goes above and beyond to connect students with industry giants in their fields. Industry leaders are flown in to view student work during the school's annual Spring Show. School of Fashion students showcase their collections at New York and San Francisco Fashion Week. Advertising students win record-breaking numbers of awards including the ADDYs, ANDYs, and Clios, catching the attention of top firms.

Flexible online learning

Academy of Art University's accredited online degree programs offer the same high level, hands-on education as the San Francisco campus. The Academy's professional instructors have created flexible, cutting-edge online classes to help students achieve their art and design dreams.

MAJORS AND DEGREES OFFERED

The students, who are admitted through an open-enrollment policy, aspire to earn A.A., B.A., B.S., B.F.A., B.Arch., M.A., M.F.A., or M.Arch. degrees in more than 40 areas of study; as well as continuing art education and certificate programs for those wishing to tailor programs to meet their specific goals; pre-college art experience programs for high school students; and teacher grants.

Classes are available in Acting, Advertising, Studio Production for Advertising & Design, Animation & Visual Effects, Architecture, Art Education, Art History, Art Teaching Credential, Communications & Media Technologies, Fashion Costume Design, Fashion Design, Fashion Journalism, Fashion Marketing, Fashion Marketing & Brand Management, Fashion Merchandising & Management, Fashion Product Development, Fashion Styling, Fashion Visual Merchandising, Footwear & Accessory Design, Knitwear Design, Textile Design, Fine Art, Game Development, Game Programming, Graphic Design, Illustration, Automotive Restoration, Industrial Design, Interior Architecture & Design, Jewelry & Metal Arts, Landscape Architecture, Motion Pictures & Television, Music Production, Music Scoring & Composition, Sound Design, Photography, Visual Development, Web Design & New Media, Writing for Film, Television & Digital Media. Students can study on-site in San Francisco or through the Academy's flexible online programs (in most areas of study).

TUITION, ROOM, BOARD, FEES

Tuition is structured to give students the best value and most flexibility during their academic studies. Tuition is calculated on a per unit basis, and lab fees and course fees are assessed per individual class.

Fall 2020–Summer 2021

- Undergraduate Tuition: $1,011 per unit—3 units per class
- Graduate & Art Teaching Credential: $1,137 per unit—3 units per class

Estimated undergraduate expenses for a full-time student for the academic year (Fall 2020–Spring'2021 undergraduate)

Application Fee = $50
Registration Fee = $50/semester
Enrollment Fee = $95 (first term domestic students only)
Student Activity Fee = $30/semester (onsite only)
Course Fees (average) = $400/semester
Materials/Supplies (average) = $540/semester
Estimated total = $26,399

FINANCIAL AID

Financial aid is available for those students who qualify. The Academy offers a number of scholarships and grants each semester. Interested students learn more by visiting the Academy online here: https://www.academyart.edu/finances/types-of-financial-aid or contact a financial aid representative at financialaid@academyart.edu to learn more. financial aid representatives are committed to helping students achieve their dreams.

Dates
Notification Date
Mar 2

Required Forms
FAFSA
Student Aid Report (SAR)

Financial aid Statistics

Average Freshman Total Need-Based Gift Aid
$11,719

Average Undergraduate Total Need-Based Gift Aid
$11,761

Average Need-Based Loan
$3,921

Undergraduates who have borrowed through any loan program
60%

Average amount of loan debt per graduate
$35,862

Average amount of each freshman scholarship/grant package
$12,892

Financial aid provided to international students
Yes

STUDENT ORGANIZATIONS AND ACTIVITIES

- Total Undergraduate Enrollment: 7,233
- Foreign Countries Represented: 110

Demographics

- 5% Asian
- 6% African-American
- 9% Hispanic
- 15% Caucasian
- 30% Unknown
- 32% International
- 60% female, 40% male
- 53% are out of state
- 57% are full time, 43% are part time

ADMISSIONS PROCESS

Step 1: Contact Academy of Art University

Fill out information form (https://www.academyart.edu/form-request-information/) or call at 1-415-274-2222. Your personal admissions representative will partner with you to answer any questions and set up a guided campus tour.

Step 2: Getting to know you

Your admissions rep will set a time to get a more in-depth view of your interests and career goals. Their objective is to help you discover the degree program that best fits your interests and walk you through the application process.

Step 3: Complete your application

After talking to your personal admissions representatives, you can complete your online application forms. Applying only takes about 15 minutes.

Step 4: Let's talk funding

Once you've applied, your admissions rep will schedule a meeting with one of our financial aid representatives to inform you of financial resources available and your potential options.

Step 5: Register for classes

After speaking with financial aid representatives, you can register for classes and set up your profile on the student portal. Classes fill up fast, so you'll want to register as soon as possible to ensure you get the classes you want.

ARKANSAS STATE UNIVERSITY

AT A GLANCE

Founded in 1909, Arkansas State University is a Carnegie Research 2 institution and the second-largest university in the state. It hosts the first osteopathic medical school in Arkansas, NYIT's College of Osteopathic Medicine, opened the first U.S.-style residential campus in Mexico in fall 2017, and is studying the creation of the first college of veterinary medicine in the state. A-State is the heart of activity for its hometown of Jonesboro, starting with its FBS Division I athletic program, and is the economic and research hub for the region.

Dedicated to teaching, research and service, the university provides students with the broad educational foundations that help them develop critical thinking, decision-making, analytical, and communication skills. With more than 90,000 living alumni, the university is the state's leading provider of nursing graduates, early childhood educators, and agricultural business graduates.

Research opportunities alongside our faculty are not the exception at A-State. Whether it is performing experiments at the Arkansas Biosciences Institute at A-State or assisting with research studies in other laboratory spaces, hands-on work usually associated with graduate school is common for our students. These undergraduate experiences are highlighted by the annual Create@State spring conference. Create@State participants have an advantage in achieving the graduate school of their choice, including continuing to advance degrees at Arkansas State.

LOCATION AND ENVIRONMENT

Located in Jonesboro, Ark., and situated in the northeast corner of Arkansas, A-State is connected by interstate highways 55/555 to Memphis on the east and St. Louis to the north; and is less than two hours by four-lane highway to Little Rock.

Jonesboro is one of the fastest growing cities in Arkansas, and has seen remarkable growth in the medical sector with over $1 billion of new facilities completed or under construction related to health care. The town has one of the lowest unemployment rates in the state. As the commercial hub of the region, Jonesboro's business activity is considered one of the fastest expanding in the state and in the Delta region. The city serves an 18-county retail trade area of a half-million residents.

CAMPUS FACILITIES AND EQUIPMENT

Home to the Arkansas Biosciences Institute, A-State is the location of the first osteopathic medical school in Arkansas with New York Institute of Technology's College of Osteopathic Medicine in historic Wilson Hall. Combined with the College of Nursing and Health Professions, this makes the A-State campus a leader in health professions for the state. One of the largest instructional facilities in higher education in Arkansas opened in 2015 at A-State: the 130,000-square-foot Humanities and Social Sciences Building.

A pedestrian campus, A-State is also the first Bicycle Friendly University in Arkansas. A 2016 national survey ranked Arkansas State as one of the safest residential campuses, and another placed A-State's security in the top 10.

Campus life is currently at an all-time peak with record participation in on-campus activities and groups during the past five years. With residence hall occupancy at historic highs, space for 500 more graduate and undergraduate students was added for fall 2017.

Annual events include the Agribusiness Conference hosted by the College of Agriculture; the Delta Symposium hosted by the College of Liberal Arts and Communication; and the Women's Business Leadership Forum hosted by the Neil Griffin College of Business. Among the major cultural events spanning multiple disciplines are the Delta Symposium and the Johnny Cash Heritage Festival.

OFF-CAMPUS OPPORTUNITIES

Within a one-square mile area of its campus, A-State is the center of cultural, entertainment and tourism for NEA, with the largest concert venue, First National Bank Arena, as well as the largest concert hall and theatre located at Fowler Center. Centennial Bank Stadium is the home of the Red Wolves football program, a FBS Division I athletic program with eight consecutive bowl appearances. Nestled adjacent to all three is the new Red Wolf Convention Center and Embassy Suites Hotel, the first large-scale convention facility in the region. The Bradbury Art Museum is the region's leading visual arts facility, and the Arkansas State University Museum is the only natural science, history and children's museum on a university campus in the state.

ACADEMIC PROGRAMS

As a doctoral granting research university, Arkansas State moved into the national editors of *U.S. News & World Report* magazine in the 2020 edition of "America's Best Colleges." A-State was previously among the top 70 for US News Southern universities. Arkansas State is also ranked in the top Southern universities by Princeton Review. Among our individual academic programs, A-State has notable achievements, including the following:

- Highest ranked national university in Arkansas for undergraduate teaching (76th in country) and social mobility (119th in country) by U.S. News
- One of the nation's top-10 nursing programs according to NurseJournal.org;
- The largest online enrollment in the state of Arkansas with 34 programs delivered 100 percent online;
- Home to an Honors College with an enrollment of almost 1,000 students in the program;
- A veteran-friendly campus, recognized repeatedly by Military Times magazine, sponsors one of America's oldest ROTC units, and home to the Beck Center for Veterans.
- Most A-State faculty members hold the highest possible degrees and are recognized leaders in their fields.

In addition, Arkansas State's First-Year Experience received the Apple Distinguished Program award. Study Abroad is a major component of student experience at A-State. Students outside Arkansas should inquire about Beyond Boundaries scholarship opportunities.

MAJORS AND DEGREES OFFERED

As of fall 2019, Arkansas State had 45 degree programs with 161 major fields of study offered at the doctoral, specialist, master, bachelor, and associate degree levels. Master's degree programs were initiated in 1955, and A-State began offering its first doctoral degree program, educational leadership, in the fall of 1992. Arkansas State has seen continued growth in doctoral programs, adding Environmental Science in 1998, Heritage Studies in 2001, Molecular Biosciences in 2006, Physical Therapy in 2008, Nursing Practice in 2012, and, most recently, Occupational Therapy in 2016.

A-State is a leader in meeting Arkansas's need for educators and health care professionals. The College of Education and Behavioral Science graduates more teachers, counselors, and administrators than any other Arkansas institution, while the College of Nursing and Health Professions is among the state's leaders in graduating nurses with bachelor's degrees. Arkansas State's commitment to excellence in higher education is demonstrated through its accreditation by The Higher Learning Commission of the North Central Association of Colleges and Schools, as well as more than 20 specialized accrediting organizations. A-State also holds membership in national and international organizations that support the highest educational standards.

TUITION, ROOM, BOARD, FEES

One of the best values in the state and region, Arkansas State is sixth out of the 10 in-state four-year universities for undergraduate tuition and fees; one of the lowest cost of attendance among the nation's Research 2 institutions. To provide greater access to students across the country, Arkansas State participates in the Common Application.

FINANCIAL AID

Arkansas State provides in-state tuition to border counties and regions of our state, and alumni families may also apply for in-state tuition waivers. To learn more, go to AState.edu/FinAid

STUDENT ORGANIZATIONS AND ACTIVITIES

With students from almost every state in America and more than 50 countries around the world, Arkansas State has a diverse student body.

More than 200 registered student organizations offer a wide range of events and activities for students at A-State.

ADMISSIONS PROCESS

To achieve admission at Arkansas State, begin by filling out your application at: AState.edu/ApplyNow.

Arkansas State is now a member of the Common Application. Search for Arkansas State in the Common App to add A-State to your universities.

ASSUMPTION COLLEGE

AT A GLANCE

Established in 1904 by the Augustinians of the Assumption, Assumption College is a Catholic coeducational institution known for its classic liberal arts curriculum and strong academic programs.

Assumption College is a place of big ideas and generous hearts, people who inspire you to grow as a student and as a human being. The educational experience is grounded in the rich Catholic intellectual tradition, which cultivates both the intellect and the personal values that students need to meet the demands of a constantly changing world. Undergraduates and graduate students closely interact with faculty members and staff in a thriving community that forms graduates known for critical intelligence, thoughtful citizenship and compassionate service.

At Assumption, 85 percent of our 2,000 undergraduates live on campus and housing is guaranteed for all four years. The campus is lively seven days a week with academic programming, activities sponsored by student clubs and organizations, community service opportunities, campus ministry programs and intercollegiate, intramural and club sports.

LOCATION AND ENVIRONMENT

Assumption College is located on a 185 acre private campus, nestled in a beautiful, residential neighborhood. When you step onto the campus you will feel the immediate sense of community.

The campus is just minutes from downtown Worcester, a bustling metropolitan mecca for the more than 35,000 students attending area colleges and universities. Businesses, government offices and nonprofit organizations provide our students with numerous internships and job opportunities. Assumption students also enjoy access to first-class restaurants and shops, museums, local sports teams and entertainment venues. Students enjoy the best of both worlds—a secure suburban setting with easy access to urban advantages.

Assumption offers a unique study abroad opportunity at its own campus in Rome, Italy. Staffed by full-time Assumption faculty, this semester-long experience lets students explore the country as a "living classroom."

CAMPUS FACILITIES AND EQUIPMENT

Assumption is dedicated to providing enhanced learning and student life facilities.

The new Tsotsis Family Academic Center, a 60,000-square-foot state-of-the-art academic building, contains 13 high-tech, flexible classrooms, seminar rooms, common study spaces, a 400-seat performance hall, a rehearsal room, a multi-purpose space, faculty offices for the Assumption Core Texts and Enduring Questions Program, the Business Studies Department, the Honors Program, the Center for Teaching Excellence, and a new Center for the Study of Ethics.

A new 41,000 square foot Health Sciences building, opening in fall 2020, will feature a nursing floor that includes a nursing skills lab with seven full-sized hospital beds and four simulation labs with hi-fidelity mannequins, and a physician assistant studies floor that includes a practice lab with 11 exam tables, two simulation labs, and four objective structured clinical examination (OSCE) rooms.

More than half a million dollars in renovations were completed in Taylor Dining Hall, the primary dining facility on campus that offers students an array of meal options for breakfast, lunch and dinner.

OFF-CAMPUS OPPORTUNITIES

Assumption encourages students to expand their horizons. In addition to the Rome campus, undergraduates can spend a semester or a year studying abroad—from France and England, to Japan, the Czech Republic and Australia, to name a few locations. Many students also augment their education and hone professional skills through local, regional, national and international internships. Assumption students have worked at diverse organizations around the globe, from the Department of Commerce, Central America Bureau and the Department of State (NAFTA Agreement), to Smith Barney, Fidelity, Morgan Stanley, ABC News, and the Alliance Francaise in Paris.

ACADEMIC PROGRAMS

With majors and minors in business, sciences and professional programs, you are sure to find an academic area of interest to you—whether you enter college knowing what that is, or if you figure it out once you get here. And with a dedicated faculty that will guide you each step of the way, your path to success will be clearly lit.

Assumption offers various areas of study—from diverse major and minor combinations to unique partnership programs, pre-professional to accelerated master's degrees.

Accounting
Accounting—Fraud Examination & Forensic
Actuarial Science
Applied Behavior Analysis
Art History
Biology
Biotechnology & Molecular Biology
Business
Chemistry
Clinical Health Professions
Communications
Communication Sciences and Disorders
Community Service Learning
Computer Science
Creative Writing and Magazine Design
Criminology
Cybersecurity
Data Analytics
Economics
Education (elementary, middle school, secondary)
English
Environmental Science
Finance
French
German Studies
Global Studies
Graphic Design
Health Sciences
History
Human Services and Rehabilitation Studies
Information Technology
International Business
Italian Studies
Latin American and Latino Studies
Law and Economics
Law, Ethics and Constitutional Studies
Management
Marketing
Mathematics
Medieval and Early Modern Studies

Molecular Biology
Music
Neuroscience
Occupational Therapy
Organizational Communication
Philosophy
Physical Therapy
Physics
Political Science
Psychology
Sociology
Spanish
Sport Management
Studio Art
Theology
Women's Studies
Writing

Accelerated Master's Degrees
MBA
Special Education Program M.A.
Rehabilitation Counseling M.A.
Dual Degree Programs
BA / MBA
MA / Physician Assistant M.S.
Special Programs
Common Pursuit of Academic and Social Success (COMPASS)
Honors Program
Pre-professional Programs
    Pre-Law
    Pre-Medical/Pre-Dental/Pre-Vet
Rome, Italy, Campus
SOPHIA (SOPHomore Initiative at Assumption College)
Study Abroad
Articulation Agreements
Optometry
Physical Therapy
Podiatry
Engineering
Environmental Science
Law

MAJORS AND DEGREES OFFERED

Area, Ethnic, Cultural, and Gender Studies
- Italian Studies
- Latin American and Latino Studies
- Women's Studies

Biological and Biomedical Sciences
- Biology/Biological Sciences, General
- Biotechnology
- Molecular Biology

Business, Management, Marketing, and Related Support Services
- Accounting
- Actuarial Science
- Business Administration and Management, General
- Data Analytics
- Finance
- International Business/Trade/Commerce
- Marketing/Management, General

Communication, Journalism, and Related Programs
- Organizational Communication, General

Computer and Information Sciences and Support Services
- Computer Science
- Cybersecurity
- Information Technology

Education
- Teacher Education, Multiple Levels

English Language and Literature/Letters
- English Language and Literature, General

Foreign languages, literatures, and Linguistics
- French Language and Literature
- Linguistic, Comparative, and Related Language Studies and Services
- Spanish Language and Literature

Health Professions and Related Clinical Sciences
- Nursing
- Physician Assistant
- Rehabilitation and Therapeutic Professions

History
- History, General

Mathematics and Statistics
- Mathematics, General

Multi/Interdisciplinary Studies
- International/Global Studies

Natural Resources and Conservation
- Environmental Science

Philosophy and Religious Studies
- Psychology

Physical Sciences
- Chemistry, General

Psychology
- Psychology, General

Social Sciences
- Criminology
- Economics, General
- International Economics
- Political Science and Government, General
- Sociology

Theology and Religious Vocations
- Theology/Theological Studies

Visual and Performing Arts
- Art History, Criticism and Conservation
- Fine/Studio Arts, General
- Graphic Design
- Music, General

TUITION, ROOM, BOARD, FEES

Tuition	$43,178
Room and Board	$13,588
Fees	$1,575

FINANCIAL AID

More than 90 percent of Assumption students receive some form of financial assistance, and we're committed to providing you with a consistent level of institutional grants and scholarships all four years. Assumption College will pair you with a personal financial aid advisor who will work with you and your family throughout your four years to pursue federal, state and private funding. You'll also have access to a variety of payment options, including a 10-month, interest-free payment plan.

The Assumption College Merit Scholarship Program is based on academic and cocurricular merit, not financial need. It reflects the College's commitment to promoting a culture of academic excellence and leadership. All students who are accepted for admission to Assumption College are considered for scholarship awards up to $25,000.

In line with our mission, Assumption's $27,000 Light the Way Scholarship is awarded to up to 50 students who utilize their abilities to Light the Way for others. Whether it's community service to help people in need, innovation to improve society, or volunteering to heal our planet, this scholarship recognizes and supports students who positively impact the world in their own meaningful way.

To apply for financial aid, families must complete the Free Application for Federal Student Aid (FAFSA) by February 15.

STUDENT ORGANIZATIONS AND ACTIVITIES

Our campus buzzes with activity. There is an abundance of events and campus traditions to celebrate as a Greyhound. From attending lectures by renowned speakers, to cheering on the Greyhounds, to grabbing a cup of coffee with friends at the Dunkin' Donuts in Hagan Campus Center, Pup Cup to Spring Concert, Homecoming to Midnight Madness. There's always something happening on the Assumption campus.

Students are encouraged to get involved, you can participate in more than 60 student-run clubs and organizations, whether academic clubs or service groups, theatrical productions or the incredibly popular intramural sports teams.

Accounting Club	Human Services Club
ACTV	Latin Dance
AC Allies	Le Provocateur
ADAPT	Love Your Melon
Advocates for Life	Martial Arts Club
African Dance Club	Medlife
ALANA Network	Men's Club Basketball
Assumption Against Cancer	Men's Club Volleyball
Best Buddies	Moot Court
Campus Activities Board	NSSLHA
Cheerleading	Outdoors Club
Chinese Students and Friends Association	PAWS
Chorale	Phi Sigma Tau
Dance Team	Psychology Club
Equestrian Team	Social Justice Ambassadors
Esports Club	Student Philanthropy
Figure Skating Club	Ultimate Frisbee
Food Recovery Network	Women's Club Basketball
GAME	Women's Club Volleyball
Graphic Design Club	Womens' Studies Club
Greenhounds	Young Conservative's Club
Heights Yearbook	Running Club
Hound Sound	

ADMISSIONS PROCESS

Application Review Process:

The Admissions Committee understands that grading standards vary from school to school, or from one course to another. Class rank provides some context in which to place the grades of students applying from a given school. Some schools also provide grade distribution charts. Finally, the Admissions Committee also considers whether the applicant's grade-point average or rank-in-class is weighted or unweighted.

The number of solid academic courses, including the number of honors or Advanced Placement-level courses, are considered during the application review process. Submission of standardized test scores (SAT-1 or ACT) is optional and applicants who choose not to submit SAT or ACT test scores will not be penalized in the review for admission.

Application Requirements:

- A completed Common Application
- An official high school transcript including senior grades
- A letter of recommendation from a counselor or teacher
- Standardized test scores (optional). Should you want your test scores included in your application review, the school code for the SAT is 3009 and the ACT code is 1782. Test scores must be submitted from the testing center.
- A $50 non-refundable application fee
- ZeeMee video to showcase your personality. Add your ZeeMee link to your Common Application (optional)

Application Deadlines:

Early Decision Deadline is November 1
Early Action Deadline is November 1
Early Action II Deadline is December 15
Regular Decision Deadline is February 15

AUBURN UNIVERSITY

AT A GLANCE

Auburn University is one of the nation's premier public land-grant institutions and in 2019, was ranked in the Top 50 among public universities by *U.S. News and World Report*. Auburn maintains very high levels of research activity as an R1 institution and high standards for teaching excellence, offering bachelor's, master's, and doctor's degrees in the arts and sciences, agriculture, architecture, business, engineering, nursing, pharmacy and veterinary medicine. Organized into 12 academic colleges and schools, we offer more than 150 undergraduate degrees. Our 2019 enrollment of 30,460 students includes 24,594 undergraduates and 5,866 graduate and professional students.

Auburn University has recently been highly ranked by several national publications, including:

- #1 happiest students, *The Princeton Review*, 2019
- Best Value College, *The Princeton Review*, 2020
- #1 university in Alabama, *Forbes*, 2019
- #1 best value in Alabama, *Money*, 2019
- Top 50 Public University in the nation and #1 university in Alabama, *U.S. News and World Report*, 2020
- Top 100 Best Values in Public Colleges and #1 Public in state, *Kiplinger's*
- #1 university in state, Niche.com

The university is nationally recognized for its commitment to academic excellence, its positive work environment, its student engagement and its beautiful campus. As a land-grant institution, Auburn is dedicated to improving the lives of the people of Alabama, the nation and the world through forward-thinking education, life-enhancing research and scholarship and selfless service.

As a Research 1 university, we're among the nation's elite, but we're also known for our "Auburn Family"—the human connection of a quarter of a million alumni around the globe. It's a connected community that also ranks among the 50 most powerful alumni networks in the world. Auburn people will be ready to help you now and throughout your life.

In a survey of recent graduates, 97% feel their Auburn education has enhanced their opportunity for future advancement. Auburn alumni are satisfied with their college choice, with 92% of recent graduates indicating they would choose Auburn again.

LOCATION AND ENVIRONMENT

We have the resources of a large research university set on a collegial, small, friendly, open campus in the rolling hills of east-central Alabama, with a local area population of approximately 65,000. Conveniently located along Interstate 85, Auburn is less than 60 miles northeast of Alabama's capital city of Montgomery and about 30 miles west of Columbus, Georgia. Conveniently located 1.5 hours from the largest airport in the U.S. in Atlanta, Georgia, Auburn is within a reasonable driving distance from many major cities, so students can take easy road trips to Nashville or check-out the beaches in Gulf Shores or the Florida Panhandle.

Southern Living named Auburn one of the South's Best College Towns with its convenient restaurants and shops. Toomer's Corner marks the spot where the university and city intersect, and offers a gathering spot for one of the university's greatest traditions—rolling our famous oak trees after a big win. An easy walk from campus, the city hosts events throughout the year, featuring outdoor concerts, art, food and street parties, especially on home football weekends.

Across from the Jule Collins Smith Museum of Fine Art, the Jay and Susie Gogue Performing Arts Center is a cultural destination offering world-class performances. The Gogue Center and museum create a vibrant arts district for the campus, community and region.

CAMPUS FACILITIES

Auburn is a student-centric campus, so facilities and services are structured to support and encourage students. Our campus growth enhances the academic experience by offering students unparalleled opportunities. A few recent additions include:

- The School of Nursing building is the first facility designed for nursing education and features skills labs and an advanced simulation suite.
- The Delta Air Lines Aviation Education Building houses classrooms, a flight simulator lab and debriefing rooms. Through a partnership with Delta Air Lines, Auburn is helping to solve a nationwide pilot shortage, expand air service for communities and improve how luggage is tracked through RFID technology.
- The Brown-Kopel Engineering Student Achievement Center supports Auburn's vision to provide the nation's best student-centered engineering education experience. It houses classrooms, student study spaces, a wind-tunnel lab, and space for advising, tutoring, studying, professional development and industry relations.
- The new Horton-Hardgrave Hall meets the growing needs of the Harbert College of Business and houses flat-flexible and case study classrooms, a flexible studio lecture hall, an innovation lab, and study pods and team areas.

OFF-CAMPUS OPPORTUNITIES

Just a few miles from campus, students can enjoy several nature getaways, including Chewacla State Park, where hiking to waterfalls, mountain biking and camping are just a few activities to enjoy. From festivals and outdoor concerts to top-ranked golf on the Robert Trent Golf Trail at Grand National, to unique dining experiences, Auburn has much to offer in education, recreation, nature, history, culture and more.

ACADEMIC PROGRAMS

Accelerated Bachelor's/Master's Program

Some schools and colleges offer an accelerated bachelor's/master's program that gives outstanding students the opportunity to earn both the bachelor's and master's degrees in less time and at less cost. Contact the school or college you're interested in to see if it is available for your major.

Faculty Profile Fall 2020

Full-time instruction faculty: 1,426
Faculty with terminal (highest available) degrees: 1,270 (89%)
Minority faculty: 307
Female faculty: 585
Male faculty: 841
Student-to-faculty ratio: 20:1
84% of undergraduate classes have fewer than 50 students

Retention and Graduation Rates

First-year retention rate (2018 cohort): 91.1%
Six-year graduation rate (2013 cohort): 78.8%

These are a few of the top companies and organizations that regularly recruit on campus: Apple, AT&T, BMW, Coca-Cola, CIA, Delta, Exxon Mobil, GE, Honda, Lockheed Martin, NASA, Proctor & Gamble, Ralph Lauren, Target and Wells Fargo.

- Academic Support provides a variety of academic skill development programs that promote self-directed learning strategies and student success. academicsupport.auburn.edu.
- The Miller Writing Center offers free, one-on-one writing consultations. Undergraduate and graduate peer tutors can help with all kinds of writing, whether for class or otherwise, at any stage in the writing process. auburn.edu/writingcenter.
- Academic Coaching allows students to collaborate with a trained coach to progress in areas of academic workload management, time management, testing and more.
- Plainsmen's Prep is a 10-day experience for eligible incoming first-year students. The program provides an opportunity for participants to increase their initial math course placement as dictated by their math ACT/SAT score, bypassing prerequisite courses and supporting timely graduation.
- Study Partners offers peer tutoring by students who have excelled in the course, and encourages students to become independent learners through one-on-one and drop-in tutoring for a number of undergraduate core courses.
- Supplemental Instruction (SI) supports historically difficult classes with weekly active-review sessions facilitated by students who previously excelled in the course.
- First Year Seminar (FYS) courses help new students acclimate to various aspects of university life, learning about academic and personal resources on campus, relevant social issues, opportunities for campus involvement and in the local community, time management, critical thinking skills, study strategies, test preparation, note taking, goal setting, and many other topics and skills vital to college success. auburn.edu/fys
- Learning Community (LC) cohorts are composed of 20 students who share a common interest or major. Students are co-enrolled in a FYS and two to four additional courses (usually core curriculum courses). Students have the benefit of taking the linked courses with the students in their FYS and will be pre-registered for these courses. auburn.edu/lc

MAJORS AND DEGREES OFFERED

From cybersecurity to housing design; from animal-assisted health intervention to graphic design beauty; from new farming methods and additive manufacturing to neuroscience, arctic expeditions and food safety—virtually any area you want to explore, understand and shape, you can take on here. With more than 150 undergraduate majors within 12 colleges and schools, Auburn is at the educational forefront of blending the social sciences, humanities and applied sciences to transform not only the world, but you as a student. There are limitless options to create a unique interdisciplinary studies degree with areas of study in at least two colleges.

According to the National Survey of Student Engagement, Auburn provides a supportive campus environment and our students report higher satisfaction with their overall academic experience than students at peer institutions.

Through active research, internships, service learning, entrepreneurial competitions, co-op programs and hands-on experiences in and out of the classroom, Auburn students gain the work ethic and leadership skills to be successful in the professional world. Recruiters note that our graduates "have an edge with their level of professionalism, communication skills, polish and preparation."

Auburn's Honors College mentors students applying for national prestigious scholarships, such as Rhodes, Goldwater and Fulbright. More than 1,350 students study and intern abroad annually, with programs in 30+ countries ranging from one week to a full semester. Students interested in undergraduate research are able to work on a faculty member's research team and are invited to present their scholarly results and discoveries at the annual Student Research Symposium.

STUDENT ORGANIZATIONS AND ACTIVITIES

Auburn University's 30,460 undergraduate and graduate students hail from all 50 states and 106 countries.

Fall 2019	Count	% of Total Enrollment
Total enrollment	30,460	100.0%
• Undergraduate*	24,594	80.1%
• DVM & PharmD**	1,101	3.6%
• Graduate***	4,765	15.6%
Male students	15,538	51.0%
Female students	14,922	49.0%
Alabama residents	16,574	54.4%
Paying resident tuition	17,341	56.9%
African-American enrollment	1,814	6.0%
Minority enrollment	2,582	8.5%
International enrollment (106 countries)	3,034	10.0%
• Undergraduate (66 countries)	1,757	5.8%
• Graduate (86 countries)	1,277	4.2%
New freshmen****	4,808	

*Undergraduate enrollment includes at least one student from each of the 50 states, as well as from the District of Columbia, the U.S. Virgin Islands, and U.S. citizens living abroad.

** First-professional enrollment includes at least one student from each of 34 states.

***Graduate enrollment includes at least one student from each of the 50 states, as well as from the District of Columbia, Puerto Rico, and U.S. citizens living abroad.

****The fall 2019 new freshman cohort includes at least one student from 48 states (none from Nevada or Wyoming), as well as from the District of Columbia and U.S. citizens living abroad. The cohort also includes 46 international students, representing 14 countries.

If you want heart-thumping school spirit and pride along with the warm welcome of home, you can't beat Auburn. We rank #1 on The Princeton Review's list of "Students Pack the Stadiums." ESPN considered Auburn's eagle flight as the best pregame tradition in the SEC. USA Today's Readers' Choice Travel Award Contest named rolling the Auburn Oaks at Toomer's Corner as the nation's "best sports tradition."

Nearly 20,000 Auburn students are involved in 500+ student organizations on campus. You can find student groups with a huge range of interests such as Advanced Biofuels, the African Students Association, Greek societies, Women in Science and the Auburn Marching Band—organizations focused on athletics, the arts, culture, outdoor adventure, faith, service, professional development, networking and so much more. Through Student Involvement, the university supports students so they can create, organize, lead, finance and advertise the organizations they care about as well as track their own involvement and growth.

Students can participate in more than 40 club and intramural sports, plus enjoy the amenities offered at the Recreation and Wellness Center, named one of the "Coolest College Recreation Centers in America," by Men's Health magazine. The center has two 50-foot climbing towers, a bouldering wall, a 1/3-mile corkscrew track and a leisure pool.

The university offers 32 residence halls in five area, housing 4,800 on-campus residents in suite-style living arrangements or double occupancy rooms. Dining preferences include national restaurants, like Chick-fil-A and Starbucks, as well as convenient food trucks which offer local favorites. Choices range from vegan to meat and potatoes and gluten free, meeting a variety of dietary needs and tastes.

ADMISSIONS PROCESS

Fall 2019 New Freshmen 4,808
% Scoring above 24 on ACT 76%
Average ACT 27.6
Average SAT 1235

BABSON COLLEGE

AT A GLANCE

Babson College shapes the entrepreneurial leaders our world needs most: those with strong functional knowledge and the skills and vision to navigate change, accommodate ambiguity, surmount complexity, and motivate teams in a common purpose to create sustainable economic and social value in organizations of all types and sizes. A global leader in entrepreneurship education, Babson offers undergraduate, graduate, and executive education programs as well as partnership opportunities.

As the No. 1 undergraduate school for entrepreneurship for 23 consecutive years, Babson's Undergraduate School provides a top-ranked education, blending business and liberal arts programs with curricular and cocurricular learning that teaches students to turn ideas into action. Studying business doesn't mean you have to give up on fun. Babson has the classic aspects of a college campus—athletics, Greek life, arts, clubs and organizations. When something doesn't exist, our students take an entrepreneurial approach to create communities, opportunities, and moments that contribute to a vibrant and thriving living and learning environment.

Babson has an undergraduate student population of 2,397 students—including 42% U.S. students of color and 30% international students, underscoring Babson's commitment to diversity.

With a global network of more than 42,000 alumni in 120 countries, Babson graduates prove that you don't need to start a business to be an entrepreneur. Rather, entrepreneurship is a mindset—one that makes students innovative, flexible, creative, and out of the box thinkers. That entrepreneurial mindset can be applied to innovating within a large corporation, solving global social issues, or starting a business in any industry, sectors, or function.

That entrepreneurial mindset gives Babson students an edge in today's evolving global economy. Ninety nine percent of Babson alumni are employed or attending graduate school within six months of graduation, and Payscale has consistently named the College the top business school in the country for salary potential.

LOCATION AND ENVIRONMENT

The Babson campus is located in Wellesley, MA, just 10 miles west of Boston.

CAMPUS FACILITIES AND EQUIPMENT

Babson Recreation and Athletics Complex

From its Olympic lifting platforms to its array of cardio equipment and multipurpose courts, the newly completed Babson Recreation and Athletics Complex (BRAC) is the College's home for community building, serving as a destination for students to pursue health and wellness initiatives, and as a programming space for myriad events. BRAC features three basketball courts, two floors of exercise spaces, and multipurpose recreational rooms, as well as Varsity locker rooms and an enhanced sports medicine area.

The Weissman Foundry

The Weissman Foundry at Babson College is a cutting-edge studio dedicated to fostering creative and collaborative projects led by a community of Babson, Olin, and Wellesley college students. The Foundry's intentional mashup of student disciplines and interests ignites forward-thinking idea exploration, iteration, and design, and facilitates meaningful knowledge transfer between its community members.

Finance Lab at the Stephen D. Cutler Center for Investments and Finance

A new, state of the art finance lab at Babson College sits at the heart of campus and has 42 workstations equipped with Bloomberg terminals, FactSet, and other tools used by industry professionals. The new facility provides students with unique opportunities to learn and lead through signature learning experiences designed to prepare them for successful careers in financial services and a variety of thought leadership events that bring some of the brightest minds in finance to campus.

OFF-CAMPUS OPPORTUNITIES

Access to Boston, MA

Located just 10 miles from downtown Boston, Babson offers a number of opportunities for students to travel to the city for class, or for fun. Boston is rich in history, diversity, food and culture. And with four major sports teams, Boston boasts year-round activities that are sure to keep students busy and entertained outside of class. There is a weekday shuttle between Babson, Olin and Wellesley Colleges; a weekend shuttle to the Woodland MBTA Station and Copley Square in Boston; and a Sunday shuttle to the Woodland MBTA Station.

Students also have the opportunity to take classes in our downtown Boston space.

Venture Beyond Babson

A Babson undergraduate education extends beyond the borders of the Wellesley campus. Students are encouraged to infuse their learning with international experiences, including:

- Spend an academic year, semester, or summer abroad through one of Babson's 100+ approved education abroad programs
- Travel with a Babson faculty member during an academic break on an Elective Abroad
- Hone consulting skills on an international consulting project

Babson partners with top international business schools and organizations to offer academically rigorous and culturally engaging experiences abroad while earning credit toward your degree.

ACADEMIC PROGRAMS

Babson College's academic curriculum blends business fundamentals with liberal arts courses, helping students build critical thinking and communication skills for the modern business world.

Students can customize their degree with optional concentrations. Our 27 concentrations are like majors, but better, requiring fewer courses and allowing students to focus learning on one or more subject areas of interest. They offer a targeted way to customize a Babson degree, connect with specific faculty advisers, and align education with career aspirations.

MAJORS AND DEGREES OFFERED

Babson offers a Bachelor of Science degree to future leaders looking to create social and economic value around the world. The academic experience at Babson is uniquely designed for students who want to study business while developing an entrepreneurial mindset and gaining real-world experience. Our focus on Entrepreneurial Thought and Action® enables you to discover your strengths, pursue your passions, and create your path to success.

At Babson, you learn to:

- Think entrepreneurially, turning ideas into action
- Communicate effectively when writing and speaking
- Understand global and multicultural perspectives
- Lead teams effectively to tackle challenges
- Analyze data to gain insights and develop strategies
- Create socially responsible and ethical business solutions

TUITION, ROOM, BOARD, FEES

2019–2020 total estimated cost: $72,428

Tuition: $52,608
Room: $10,828
Meal Plan: $5,948

FINANCIAL AID

Babson awards $43 million in undergraduate aid; $36 million comes directly from Babson in grants and scholarships. Approximately 50% of Babson's undergraduates receive financial assistance. Babson meets approximately 100% of students' demonstrated need in their first year. Babson commits to each student's level of Babson Grant for four years, provided there are no major changes to the family's financial circumstances or a change in the number of the student's siblings in college.

We require the FAFSA and the CSS Profile in order to be considered for financial aid. In addition to financial aid, we award many scholarships based on merit and other criteria.

STUDENT ORGANIZATIONS AND ACTIVITIES

Babson's co-curricular opportunities reflect a tapestry of emerging student interests and passions that you will have an opportunity to fully immerse in, connect to, and lead. There are more than 100 student clubs and organizations on campus, including the Babson Dance Ensemble, Improv Troupe, Babson Fashion Group, Babson's Community of Developers & Entrepreneurs (CODE), Black Student Union, and Investment Club. Twenty-one percent of the student population participates in Greek Life.

Babson offers 22 NCAA Division III Varsity Athletic Programs—11 for men, 11 for women—club sports, and recreational programming.

ADMISSIONS PROCESS

Babson College bases its acceptance of students on both academic and nonacademic factors. The academic factors include high school record, recommendations, standardized test scores, and essays. The nonacademic factors include extracurricular activities, demonstrated leadership, character/personal qualities, volunteer work, work experience, creativity and enthusiasm, and a willingness to contribute to the Babson community in meaningful ways. Graduation from secondary school is required for admission. The most competitive students have taken approximately 5 solid academic courses per year at the highest available level (Honors, Advanced Placement or International Baccalaureate). The SAT I or ACT is required for admission. The TOEFL or IELTS is required for students who are nonnative English speakers. Babson offers several application programs. Students may apply Early Decision (binding process), Early Action or Regular Decision. The deadline for Early Decision I and Early Action is November 1. The deadline for Early Decision II and Regular Decision is January 2. Transfer students may apply for September entrance by March 15 and for January entrance by October 15.

BARD COLLEGE AT SIMON'S ROCK

AT A GLANCE

Bard College at Simon's Rock is the country's only residential college of the liberal arts and sciences specifically designed to provide highly motivated students with the opportunity to begin college after the 10th or 11th grade. Simon's Rock brings students face-to-face with big ideas, essential texts, deep and high-spirited discussion, advanced research, and the latest scholarship with professors who are tops in their fields. Our students seek opportunities to build on inspiring classroom experiences, develop confidence in who they are as they support those who are different, and most importantly, are committed to creating a better future.

At Simon's Rock, our students work toward a bachelor's degree in a remarkably individualized program. Some choose to transfer after two years with an associate degree that is highly respected by some of the most prestigious colleges and universities. Merit scholarships and need-based aid are available. The average age of entering students is 16.

For fifty years, Simon's Rock has demonstrated that high school-age students are fully capable of college work; that they thrive intellectually and socially in a small-college environment; that serving these students well requires a faculty committed to distinction in teaching and scholarship, as well as active participation in the students' social and personal development; and that a coherent general education in the liberal arts and sciences should be the foundation for early college students. Based on the success of the College and its graduates, Simon's Rock serves as a model for the growing U.S. early college movement.

As a part of the prestigious Bard network, Simon's Rock students also have access to a global consortium of institutions—including numerous civic, scientific, and art organizations. Upperclass students are encouraged to take advantage of the facilities and resources of Bard College's main campus at Annandale-on-Hudson, which offers more than 800 courses each year.

Simon's Rock students build a strong foundation for their future academic pursuits, with most completing a bachelor's degree by age 20, and 80 percent going on to graduate school. A few notable alumni include Ronan Farrow, Pulitzer Prize-winning journalist; Nina Perales, vice president of litigation at Mexican American Legal Defense and Educational Fund, Inc. (MALDEF); and John McWhorter, linguist; author; and political commentator for *The Wall Street Journal*, *The New York Times* and *Los Angeles Times*.

LOCATION AND ENVIRONMENT

Simon's Rock is located in Great Barrington, Massachusetts, named "Best Small Town" in America by Smithsonian magazine, and the perfect home for a dynamic rural college experience.

Built on 275 rolling and wooded acres in the Berkshire Hills of western Massachusetts, the campus is just 2.5 hours from Boston and New York City. The Berkshires' natural beauty and variety of cultural attractions make the area an unusually appealing place in which to live. The terrain is excellent for hiking, bicycling, cross-country and Alpine skiing, canoeing, and climbing. Nationally renowned arts organizations, including the Tanglewood Music Festival, Jacob's Pillow Dance Festival, and Shakespeare and Company are located nearby. Great Barrington is a thriving business community with shops, restaurants, and a variety of schools and service agencies at which Simon's Rock students work and volunteer.

CAMPUS FACILITIES AND EQUIPMENT

Simon's Rock offers an unabashedly intellectual, proudly independent, creative college community, including the facilities that support academic exploration, self-expression, and development of a sense of purpose.

- The Fisher Science and Academic Center houses the College's biology, chemistry, ecology, and physics laboratories; research labs for faculty members and students; classrooms and tutorial rooms; a sixty-seat lecture center; and faculty offices.
- The Daniel Arts Center incorporates a 350-seat theater and concert hall, black box theater, dance studio, and rehearsal facilities; painting, drawing, photography, ceramics, metalworking, printmaking, 3-D, video production, and digital arts studios; exhibition areas; and spaces for large-scale art and set construction.
- A music hall, recording studio, and music practice rooms are also available to students in the arts. The Liebowitz International Center houses faculty and programs focused on global issues, as well as state-of-the-art classrooms.
- The campus library is a unique space, one that combines both academic and social aspects, playing an important role in students' lives. The library provides a comfortable, welcoming place for reading, research, and reflection, as well as room to collaborate and engage with a like-minded community. Simon's Rock students also have access to the Bard College library. An interlibrary loan system provides access to other college and university collections.
- The Kilpatrick Athletic Center includes a basketball court, elevated track, eight-lane swimming pool, sauna, rock-climbing wall, indoor cycling studio, squash courts, and a full-service fitness center.

ACADEMIC PROGRAMS

We take students seriously as scholars and as thinkers. We believe their ideas matter. In small classes with individual attention, students learn through connecting and synthesizing—not memorizing and regurgitating.

The academic program at Simon's Rock combines a core curriculum in the liberal arts and sciences with extensive opportunities for students to pursue their own interests through electives, tutorials, independent studies, internships, and study abroad opportunities.

The core curriculum comprises approximately half of students' total course load during their first two years. Requirements include the Writing and Thinking workshop; first-year, sophomore, and cultural perspectives seminars; and courses in the arts, mathematics, natural sciences, and foreign languages. The College also requires students to participate in the campus Active Community Engagement program, which involves them in athletics, health and wellness education, and community service opportunities on and off campus.

All new students are assigned a faculty adviser, who meets with them weekly during their first semester and regularly throughout the rest of their time at Simon's Rock. Classes are small, faculty members are accessible, and opportunities to pursue individual interests are extensive. After earning the associate degree, many students begin work toward a bachelor's degree in one of dozens of concentrations. Some others transfer to highly competitive colleges and universities in the U.S. and abroad. Through the sophomore planning process, students receive individualized guidance from advisers and faculty as they explore options for their last two years of undergraduate study.

The academic program is supplemented by a number of signature programs. The Simon's Rock/Columbia University Engineering Program offers three years at Simon's Rock and two years at Columbia's School of Engineering and Applied Science, after which students receive both a bachelor of arts from Simon's Rock and a bachelor of science from Columbia University. A similar arrangement exists with the engineering school at Dartmouth University. A partnership with Vermont Law School offers two accelerated degree programs through which students earn a bachelor of arts from Simon's Rock and a master's degree in Environmental Law and Policy, or Energy Regulation and Law, from Vermont Law School, in a total of four years. Additionally, the Simon's Rock/Upstate Medical University program allows students to earn a BA from Simon's Rock—in a pre-med or another concentration—and then matriculate directly into SUNY's Upstate Medical University. The MCAT is waived for students admitted to the BA/MD program.

Through Simon's Rock Scholars at Oxford, a select group of students is admitted each year to spend their junior year at Lincoln College or St Catherine's College of the University of Oxford in England. The College also offers a half-or full-year program in creative writing at the Centre for New Writing at the University of Manchester in the UK and the opportunity to pursue Chinese language immersion study at Qingdao University in China. Students interested in theater can spend a year at London Dramatic Academy; those interested in photography can study at the International Center of Photography in New York City.

MAJORS AND DEGREES OFFERED

At Simon's Rock, we offer associate and bachelor's degrees.

While studying for the associate degree, students take elective courses in areas of special interest while completing courses in a variety of disciplines within the liberal arts. Students may complete the bachelor's degree in a concentration focused on a traditional discipline, or choose one of several interdisciplinary concentrations. Students may also design a second concentration.

TUITION, ROOM, BOARD, FEES

For 2019–20, tuition and fees were $55,292, and room and board were $15,364. Other fees included health services fees of $1409, a student activity fee of $200, and a $650 orientation fee for first-year students.

FINANCIAL AID

Simon's Rock is committed to making an early college education available to a diverse group of highly motivated, academically qualified students. U.S. citizens and permanent residents are eligible for federal and state grant and loan aid, as well as institutional scholarships and grants. International students are eligible to receive Simon's Rock scholarships and grants. Approximately 85 percent of students receive some form of financial aid.

Applications for admission and financial aid are considered on a rolling basis as long as space remains available; early application is encouraged. All applicants will be considered for any non-need-based scholarships for which they are eligible; no additional application is required for non-need-based scholarships.

STUDENT ORGANIZATIONS AND ACTIVITIES

Our students come from all over the world, and they bring a wide range of perspectives and talents. At Simon's Rock, they find a place to belong. One thing students have in common is a love of learning. Not all students are characterized as gifted or advanced, but all are ready and eager to learn among others who are similarly engaged and curious about the world. Some were students who didn't raise their hands during class, who were bored and restless—hiding their curiosity in order to fit in. Others exhausted all the AP classes their high school had to offer and were hungry for more ways to deepen their knowledge and expand their intellect.

On campus, students can choose from a packed schedule of guest speakers and performances; a range of programs designed to explore and promote diversity; a long list of student-run clubs and organizations (like the International Student Association, Pre-Med Society, LGBTQ+ Student Alliance, Black Student Union, Asian Student Association, and Social Justice Committee); a constantly updated schedule of conferences, panels, and visiting artists and scholars; a Community Service Program with extensive ties to local and regional agencies and institutions; and an inventive athletic program—it's all part of our campus-wide commitment to living in smarter, more creative, engaged, and healthier ways.

ADMISSIONS PROCESS

Simon's Rock seeks students who are independent-minded, self-directed, creative, and passionate about learning. The admission staff works closely with prospective students and their parents to ensure that the decision to enter Simon's Rock is the right one. The College understands that students are not defined solely by grades and test scores. For this reason, two essays and a personal interview are required of each applicant. The application also requires an official high school transcript, three letters of recommendation, and a parent statement. Standardized test scores are optional for most applicants; international students for whom English is not a first language must submit TOEFL scores.

Candidates should submit their materials by one of a series of submission dates listed on the Simon's Rock website and will receive a decision by the corresponding notification date, which is typically within six weeks. Applying by one of the earlier dates is strongly encouraged. There is no application fee.

To schedule an interview or request further information, students should contact the Office of Admission at admit@simons-rock.edu or 800-235-7186.

BARNARD COLLEGE

AT A GLANCE

Barnard is the most sought-after liberal arts college for women in the United States. Barnard provides a cosmopolitan setting, dynamic academic programs, access to internships and a unique partnership with Columbia University.

Barnard is a small, highly selective liberal arts college for women located in New York City. The student body of just over 2,650 is part of a diverse and close-knit community and students study with leading scholars who serve as dedicated, accessible mentors and teachers. Founded in 1889, Barnard also engages in a unique partnership with Columbia University, situated directly across the street. Students have access to cross-registration of courses with Columbia, many joint extracurricular activities, participate in NCAA Division I Ivy League athletics and enjoy a fully coed social life. The location in New York City grants students access to thousands of internship opportunities in addition to unparalleled cultural, intellectual and social resources. Barnard's diverse student body includes residents from nearly every state and more than 55 countries worldwide. About 40 percent of the student body identify as students of color, and 11 percent are non-US citizens or permanent residents.

LOCATION AND ENVIRONMENT

Barnard is located north of Central Park on the upper west side of Manhattan, in the student-friendly Morningside Heights neighborhood. The campus occupies 4 acres of urban property along Broadway between 116th and 120th streets, directly across the street from Columbia University and the campus feels like an oasis from the hustle and bustle of New York City. The campus is framed around Futter Field, named after one of the College's former presidents. On warmer days classes are often held there and on any given day you can find outdoor events and students relaxing. The south end of the campus, referred to as the Quad, contains 4 interconnected residence halls surrounding a quaint grassy courtyard; 8 additional residence halls provide apartment-style student housing. Those entering as first-years are guaranteed housing for four years. Housing for transfers is available but not guaranteed.

CAMPUS FACILITIES AND EQUIPMENT

The Quad is located at the south end of campus and includes four residence hall buildings: Brooks, Hewitt, Reid and Sulzberger. The Jan R. and Marley Blue Lewis '05 Parlor is located on the 1st floor of Brooks Hall and is a reading room for quiet study. The Arthur Ross Courtyard is located within the Quad.

The Diana Center, the hub for campus life, is located in the center of campus. Housed within are Liz's Place cafe and the Millicent Carey McIntosh Student Dining Room. The Louise Heublein McCagg in '59 Gallery located on the 4th floor. The gallery hosts student exhibitions coordinated by the Art History and Architecture Departments. The Green Roof, located on the 6th floor of The Diana Center, is used both as a classroom, research area and as an event space. It also has terrific birdseye views of campus and the surrounding neighborhood. There is a black box theatre located on the lower level.

The Milstein Center for Teaching and Learning, which opened in August 2018, serves as the academic hub in the heart of the campus. It includes a library that brings together current technologies and learning spaces in interactive settings, and seven centers offering students the opportunity to explore areas such as media, design, movement, empirical reasoning, computational science and leadership studies. Features include:

- A digital commons with five innovative teaching labs (movement lab, empirical reasoning center, digital humanities lab, creativity lab, and multimedia lab) and a range of flexible learning spaces that utilize new media and digital technologies.
- A computational science center equipped to support students and faculty in pioneering scientific, mathematical, and computational methods research, which physically connects to science classrooms and labs in neighboring Altschul Hall.
- Inviting student spaces that include a variety of active and quiet study areas for individuals and groups.
- Flexible, technologically current classrooms for seminars and large group instruction.
- Conferencing facilities connected to meeting and event spaces in The Diana Center.
- Departmental offices for economics, history, political science and urban studies.
- The Barnard Center for Research on Women
- The Athena Center for Leadership Studies.
- A café, serving coffee and grab-and-go items.
- Accessible outdoor terraces.

INTERNSHIPS AND CAREER DEVELOPMENT

Beyond Barnard provides advising and resources in the areas of career exploration and development, opportunities for experiential education (including internships, externships, post-baccalaureate programs, and civic engagement), preparation for graduate and professional school (including law, medical, and other programs), and support for applications to competitive national and international fellowships. Barnard's location offers its students a variety of work experiences on and off campus. 75% of Barnard students are estimated to complete an internship during their four years at the College. Barnard offered 300 total funded opportunities in Summer 2019.

Top industries for graduating seniors in the Class of 2019 included Journalism, Media & Publishing (11%); Financial Services (11%); Law, Government & Politics (11%); Non-Profit & NGO (10%); and Education (9%)

STUDY ABROAD

Furthermore, Barnard has a rich history and tradition of study abroad dating back to the 1930s. Qualified students are eligible to study in over 100 programs in more than 50 countries worldwide. Students may also participate in a domestic exchange with Spelman College in Atlanta or Howard University in Washington, D.C.

ACADEMIC PROGRAMS

First-Year Experience: The First-Year Experience includes two required seminar courses: First-Year Writing, focusing on reading literary texts critically and writing effectively, and First-Year Seminar, emphasizing disciplinary and interdisciplinary content that challenges students to write and speak persuasively. First-year students are also required to take one course in Physical Education.

FOUNDATIONS

The Distribution Requirements, called Foundations, are designed to expose students to a variety of disciplines, approaches, and skills that, together, form the whole of a liberal arts education. The requirements are designed to be flexible; students choose from a wide spectrum of courses and take two courses each in languages, arts and humanities, social sciences, and sciences (one of which includes a lab). Furthermore, students follow Modes of Thinking that include one course each in the following areas. Courses taken to satisfy the Distribution Requirements can also be used to satisfy the Modes of Thinking requirements:

- *Thinking Locally-New York City*—where students examine the community and environment in which they find themselves as residents of New York City to better understand the significance of local context.
- *Thinking through Global Inquiry*—where students consider communities, places, and experiences beyond their immediate location, expanding their perspectives on the world and their place in it.
- *Thinking about Social Difference*—where students examine how difference is defined, lived, and challenged, and the disparities of power and resources in all their manifestations.
- *Thinking with Historical Perspective*—where students examine the ways in which historical context shapes and conditions the world, challenging them to see the past with fresh eyes.
- *Thinking Quantitatively and Empirically*—where students are exposed to numbers, data, graphs, and mathematical methods, in order to better understand quantitative and empirical approaches to thinking and problem solving.
- *Thinking Technologically and Digitally*—where students discover new ways of learning that open up innovative fields of study, including computational science and coding, digital arts and humanities, geographic information systems, and digital design.

MAJORS AND DEGREES OFFERED

- Africana Studies
- American Studies
- Anthropology
- Architecture
- Art History
- Asian and Middle Eastern Cultures
- Biochemistry
- Biological Sciences
- Chemistry
- Classics and Ancient Studies
- Comparative Literature
- Computer Science
- Dance
- Economic History
- Economics
- Economics and Mathematics
- Education Studies
- English
- Environmental Biology

- Environmental Science
- European Studies
- Film Studies
- French
- German
- History
- Human Rights
- Italian
- Jewish Studies
- Mathematics
- Medieval and Renaissance Studies
- Music
- Neuroscience and Behavior
- Philosophy
- Physics & Astronomy
- Political Science
- Psychology
- Religion
- Russian (Slavic)
- Sociology

- Spanish & Latin American Cultures
- Statistics
- Theatre
- Urban Studies
- Women's, Gender and Sexuality Studies

The College's unique education program leads to teaching certification with a specific urban studies track, and prepares students for programs in health and medicine, law, and business, as well as further study in a variety of graduate programs.

Barnard College also incredible opportunities to apply for double and joint-degree programs in cooperation with other schools within the Columbia community. These include:

- A BA/MS 4+1 pathway in Chemical Engineering, Biomedical Engineering, Mechanical Engineering and Industrial Engineering and Operations Research with the School of Engineering and Applied Science
- A BA/MS 4+1 pathway with Columbia's Mailman School of Public Health
- A BA/MIA or BA/MPA 4+1 pathway in conjunction with the School of International and Public Affairs.
- A BA/MA 4+1 pathway in Quantitative Methods in the social Sciences at Columbia's Graduate School of Arts and Sciences

Through an agreement with List College of the Jewish Theological Seminary, located just north of the campus at 122nd Street, students can apply to simultaneously earn a BA degree from Barnard and a BA at JTS.

Barnard also offers highly-talented music students the opportunity to apply for the Lesson Exchange Program with Juilliard and/or the Cross Registration Program with the Manhattan School of Music. Both programs will require a separate application and audition. The Lesson Exchange at MSM and Juilliard provide private weekly lessons with faculty. It is important to note that the Exchange does not include participation in large ensembles. Students in the Juilliard program can take classes in instrumental or vocal performance (Classical or Jazz) and piano composition. MSM students can take lessons for instrumental or composition only. Barnard does also offer a multitude of music courses, major, private lessons and many performance opportunities through its own music department and at Columbia.

For a select group of scholars who meet specific eligibility requirements, the Arthur O. Eve Higher Education Opportunity Program (HEOP), Barnard Opportunity Program (BOP), and The College Science and Technology Entry program (CSTEP) offer additional pathways for admission to Barnard that include ongoing academic and personal support. A lending library, laptop computers, free tutoring, mentoring, study skills workshops, and graduate school preparation and career guidance are available, in addition to the resources and support they receive as Barnard students. To be considered for HEOP, students must be residents of New York State.

Barnard College's Student Success program, located within the Dean of Studies Office, provides support, training, and programming to the College's highly diverse student body, working with students, faculty, and other campus offices to create a positive experience for underrepresented students, including low income and international students.

TUITION, ROOM, BOARD, FEES

Total Basic Budget 2019–2020
Tuition and Fees: $58,086
Room and Board*: $17,856

Books/Supplies: $1,150
Miscellaneous: $1,370
Total Basic Budget: $78,444

FINANCIAL AID

Barnard College's policies reflect a commitment to making Barnard a realistic financial option for families. Barnard College is 100% need blind in its review of US citizens and permanent residents applying as first-year students. The college is need-aware for transfer students and international citizens. For all admitted students, Barnard will meet 100% of demonstrated need. Note that Barnard does not offer merit or athletic scholarships.

Average Institutional grant: $47,751
% of First year students receiving financial aid: 38%
Pell Grant Recipients (total Population): 18%
Class of 2019 financial aid indebtedness: $16,538
Applications for financial aid follow strict deadlines, listed on the website.

STUDENT ORGANIZATIONS AND ACTIVITIES

Barnard women have access to more than 80 clubs and organizations on the Barnard campus. Add to this list hundreds of additional dually recognized clubs with members from both Barnard and Columbia, provided for through Barnard's partnership with the University. Student groups include performance groups, academic and pre-professional, ethnic and cultural, language, community service, and publications. Social interaction and cooperation between Barnard and Columbia groups is virtually seamless, with Barnard women regularly joining and leading many Columbia organizations.

A sampling of the recognized Barnard Student Organizations and Activities:

PRE-PROFESSIONAL

The Athena Pre-Law Society
Barnard Association of Pre-Dental Students
Barnard Psychology Society
Barnard Chemical Society
Barnard Quantitative Society
CU Pre-Veterinary Society
Network for Pre-Medical Students
Pre-Health Students Organization
Smart Women Lead
Smart Women Securities

CULTURAL

Asian American Alliance
African Students Association
Barnard Organization of Soul Sisters (BOSS)
Caribbean Students Association
Chinese Students Club
Club Bangla
Club Q
Club Zamana
Columbia Japan Society
CU SAFA (South-Asian Feminist Alliance)
Haitian Students' Association
Korean Students Association
Liga Filipina
Mujeres
Organization of Pakistani Students
Sounds of China
Taiwanese American Students Association
Turath, The Arab Students Association

PERFORMANCE

Bacchantae
Bach Society
Barnard Columbia Ancient Drama Group
Barnard Flute Choir

Columbia Musical Theatre Society
CoLab Performing Arts Collective
Columbia Raas
CUPAL
Control Top
CUBE (CU Ballet Ensemble)
CU Dhoom
CU Players
King's Crown Shakespeare Troupe
Latenite Theatre
New Opera Workshop

NOMADS

Orchesis
Philolexian Society
Raw Elementz
Roya Persian Dance Group
Sabor
Taal
Third Wheel Improv
VDay
XMAS!

SPECIAL INTEREST

Barnard Movement Exchange
Barnard Outdoor Adventure Team
Barnard EcoReps
Barnard Writing Collective
Columbia University Sign Language Club
Nightline Peer-Listening Hotline
She's the First
Sprout Up
Take Back the Night
WBAR

PUBLICATIONS

Barnard Bite
Barnard Bulletin
Echoes
Hoot Magazine
HerCampus

ADMISSIONS PROCESS

The Committee on Admissions selects young women of proven academic strength who exhibit the desire to discover their voices, further their intellectual growth and make their mark on the world! Careful consideration is given to candidates' high school records, recommendations, writing skills, standardized test scores, special abilities and interests, all with a consideration for personal and educational context. An interview is optional.

Admission to Barnard is highly selective and candidates for admission to the first-year class are expected to have taken a highly rigorous college-preparatory program. Barnard requires first-year candidates to submit scores from the SAT Reasoning Test or the ACT. Barnard requires students to display English proficiency and may be required to submit scores from the Test of English as a Foreign Language (TOEFL), the International English Language Testing System (IELTS) or the Duolingo English Test. Applicants are eligible to have the English Language Proficiency Requirement waived if they meet certain criteria outlined on the website.

Early decision applications must be submitted by November 1. Regular applications must be received by January 1. There is a non-refundable application fee of $75. Fee waivers are possible. Transfer applications must be submitted by November 1 for consideration for January enrollment and by March 15 for consideration for September enrollment.

Barnard College accepts both the Common Application and the Coalition Application.

BELMONT UNIVERSITY

AT A GLANCE

Belmont University—home of the October 22, 2020 Presidential Debate, the third and final in the election season—sits on 84 historic acres in the heart of Nashville, Tennessee, a thriving metropolis known worldwide as Music City. Belmont University is among the fastest growing Christian universities in the nation with nearly 8,500 students hailing from every state and 36 countries. Belmont University is accredited by the Commission on Colleges of the Southern Association of Colleges and Schools to award baccalaureate, master's, and doctoral degrees. Belmont offers over 95 areas of undergraduate study, more than 25 master's programs and five doctoral degrees through its ten colleges: Jack C. Massey College of Business, Liberal Arts and Social Sciences, Mike Curb College of Entertainment and Music Business, Gordon E. Inman College of Health Sciences and Nursing, Law, Pharmacy, Theology and Christian Ministry, Science and Mathematics, Music and Performing Arts, and O'More College of Architecture, Art and Design.

LOCATION AND ENVIRONMENT

Belmont University occupies an 84-acre campus in Nashville, Tennessee, just two miles from downtown and adjacent to the world-famous Music Row. With more than 1.7 million residents, the metropolitan Nashville area is a cultural, educational, health-care, commercial, and financial center in the mid-South. Practical educational opportunities, offered through diverse curriculums, provide students with the hands-on experience they need in preparation for a meaningful career. The city's location, halfway between the northern and southern boundaries of the United States, with three intersecting interstate highways and an international airport, makes it accessible to students from across the country.

CAMPUS FACILITIES AND EQUIPMENT

Belmont is also consistently growing its number of residential, academic and student spaces on campus, investing more than 650 million dollars on new facilities and building improvements since 2000. The past five years alone have seen the opening of many new and renovated buildings. This includes the expansive Janet Ayers Academic Center—home to three colleges covering a wide span of programs including the Liberal Arts, Social Sciences, Theology, Sciences and Mathematics. The building also houses Belmont's first intentionally-designed chapel and popular dining options.

Other new facilities include the technology-laden R. Milton and Denice Johnson Center—home to the Curb College of Entertainment and Music Business, as well as the vibrant 950-seat Harrington Place Dining Hall. The Massey Business Center—home of the Jack C. Massey College of Business—was renovated to feature state-of-the-art classrooms and learning spaces for Belmont's nationally ranked business programs. Also recently remodeled, the Hitch building, provides new classroom, practice and rehearsal space for the School of Music and also houses the new O'More College of Architecture, Art & Design.

Notably, Belmont's added more than academic spaces. The Gabhart Student Center was revamped to provide expanded student meeting space and centralized student support services. The Gallery of Iconic Guitars, known as the GIG, hails as Music City's premier venue designed to celebrate some of the rarest guitars and stringed instruments in the world. And Tall Hall, Belmont's largest residence hall accommodates more than 600 students, and grows the number of on-campus residence spaces to nearly 3,900. And construction is well underway on Belmont's most ambitious project to date—a new state-of-the-art performing arts center. This 1,700 seat facility, opening in 2021, will serve as a world-class training ground for students both onstage and backstage.

OFF-CAMPUS OPPORTUNITIES

A Christian Community of Learning and Service

Belmont is a student-focused, Christian community of learning and service where students hear from their first visit to campus until the day they graduate that they are created for a purpose in life. The Belmont faculty and staff dedicate themselves to preparing and empowering students to find their passion and use it to change the world. The university seeks to show every student how the love of Christ can compel them to lead lives of disciplined intelligence, compassion, courage and faith.

In fact, Belmont students, faculty and staff are consistently challenged to look at the hardest circumstances and ask, "What can we do?" and are encouraged to engage and transform the world, locally and globally. Students serve locally at various relief and community organizations in Nashville throughout the year, and student-athletes take part annually in sports evangelism mission trips to South Africa, Ukraine and Brazil. Others have taken advantage of what they're learning at Belmont, incorporating their major studies into various service projects around the world, including working with orphans in India and assisting with physical therapy needs in Guatemala.

ACADEMIC PROGRAMS

Intent on being a leader among teaching universities, Belmont brings together the best of liberal arts and professional education in a Christian community of learning and service. Belmont was included on the U.S. News & World Report's 2020 "Most Innovative Schools" list for the twelfth consecutive year, making Belmont the highest ranked university in Tennessee in this category. Both Rolling Stone and Time magazines have hailed Belmont's Mike Curb College of Entertainment & Music Business as one of the best music business programs in the country. The Jack C. Massey Graduate School of Business has been named the best MBA program in the region, while Belmont's business administration and accounting programs have been accredited by AACSB International, the premier accrediting agency in that arena, placing Belmont amongst less than 1% of the world's business schools. Moreover, Belmont University's undergraduate School of Business consistently achieves a Top 100 national ranking in BusinessWeek's annual report on "The Best Undergrad B-Schools" in the U.S. Belmont's Enactus team has won multiple national championships and a World Cup.

Located in the heart of Music City, one of Belmont's consistent success stories is its world-renowned music and music business programs, including songwriting. Several big names in the music industry started their careers at Belmont including, Christian recording artists Ginny Owens and Steven Curtis Chapman, and country stars Trisha Yearwood, Lee Ann Womack, Brad Paisley, Josh Turner and Florida Georgia Line, plus alternative rock band Judah and the Lion. The annual "Christmas at Belmont" concert showcases performing ensembles from many different genres and has been broadcast nationwide on PBS for several years.

Students who have passions outside of the music industry also have a home at Belmont. From international business and accounting to education, theology, nursing, design, journalism and the humanities, Belmont provides avenues of learning for almost any interest. Recent program additions include undergraduate degrees in business systems and analytics, data science, hospitality and tourism management, social media management and architecture, in addition to, a four-year dual PharmD/MBA degree, a Master of Arts in Mental Health Counseling and a Doctor of Nursing Practice program.

Belmont faculty members display a consistent commitment to excellence as well. Multiple professors have been awarded Fulbright awards, including a nursing professor who spent a year in Uganda as a guest lecturer while conducting research on how standards of nursing are adapted to austere conditions. Also, five Belmont professors (Finance, Psychology, Spanish, Philosophy and Mathematics) have been chosen as Tennessee Professor of the Year by CASE/Carnegie Foundation since 2000.

Belmont's boundaries extend beyond the Nashville campus through organized programs such as the Washington Center program and Belmont West in Los Angeles and Belmont East in New York City and Washington D.C. Belmont University ranked no. 17 among U.S. higher education institutions for undergraduate student participation in study abroad, according to the Institute of International Education's (IIE) 2019 Open Doors Report on International Educational Exchange. Belmont's study-abroad programs place students in China, Costa Rica, Great Britain, France, Germany, Italy, Russia, South Africa and Spain, among other foreign nations.

MAJORS AND DEGREES OFFERED

O'More College of Architecture, Art and Design
Architecture*
Art
Art Education
Art History
Design Communications
Experiential Design
Fashion Design
Fashion Merchandising
Interior Design
Studio Art
*Pending SACSCOC approval

Jack C. Massey College of Business
Accounting
Business Systems and Analytics
Economics
Entrepreneurship
Finance
General Business
Hospitality and Tourism Management
International Business
International Economics
Management
Marketing
Social Entrepreneurship

Mike Curb College of Entertainment and Music Business
Audio Engineering Technology
Audio and Video Production
Creative and Entertainment Studies
Journalism
Mass Communication
Motion Pictures
Music Business
Multimedia Production
Publishing
Songwriting
Video Production

Gordon E. Inman College of Health Sciences and Nursing
Exercise Science
Nursing
Public Health
Social Work

College of Liberal Arts and Social Sciences
School of Education
Early Childhood Education
Elementary Education
Secondary Education
School of Humanities
Asian Studies
English
French
German
Philosophy
Spanish
School of Social Sciences
Communication Studies
Corporate Communication
History
International Politics

Political Science
Politics & Public Law
Public Relations
Social Media Management
Sociology
Sport Administration

College of Music and Performing Arts
Department of Theatre and Dance
Theatre Directing
Theatre and Drama
Theatre Education
Theatre Performance
Theatre Production Design

School of Music
Church Music
Commercial Music
Music (Bachelor of Arts)
Music Composition
Music Education
Music Performance
Music Theory
Music Therapy
Music with an Outside Minor
Musical Theatre
Piano Pedagogy

College of Sciences and Mathematics
Applied Mathematics
Biochemistry and Molecular Biology
Biophysics
Biology
Chemistry
Computer Science
Data Science
Engineering Physics
Environmental Science
Mathematics
Neuroscience
Pharmaceutical Studies
Physics
Psychology
Web Programming and Development

College of Theology and Christian Ministry
Biblical Languages
Biblical Studies
Christian Leadership
Church Leadership and Administration
Faith and Social Justice
Philosophy of Religion
Religion and the Arts
Religious Studies
Worship Leadership

Interdisciplinary Programs
Global Leadership Studies
Legal Studies

Pre-Professional Programs Available In:
Pre-Allied Health
Pre-Dental
Pre-Law
Pre-Medical

Pre-Occupational Therapy
Pre-Optometry
Pre-Pharmacy

Pre-Physical Therapy
Pre-Veterinary

TUITION, ROOM, BOARD, FEES

The total cost of attending Belmont is only 80 percent of the national average for a private college. For a full-time undergraduate student living on campus, the total cost for the 2020–2021 academic year is approximately $49,920 which includes tuition, fees, room, and board.

FINANCIAL AID

The financial aid program at Belmont combines merit-based assistance with need-based assistance to make the university education affordable. Institutional merit awards range from highly selective full-tuition Archer Presidential Scholarships to various levels of partial merit awards. Athletic and artistic scholarships are also available. Belmont also administers traditional state and federal financial aid programs. Campus employment is available. A monthly tuition payment plan is available. To apply for need-based financial assistance, the student must complete the Free Application for Federal Student Aid (FAFSA). FAFSA Code: 003479.

STUDENT ORGANIZATIONS AND ACTIVITIES

Belmont's campus life offers 160+ clubs and organizations. The popular intramurals program includes everything from flag football and basketball to wiffleball and dodgeball. With more than half of Belmont's undergrads living on campus there's always something going on from socials, movie nights and concerts to the annual Fall Follies and Curb College Showcase Series.

And in terms of student activities, there's a club or group for nearly every interest. Belmont is home to nationally recognized sororities and fraternities representing NPC, IFC and NPHC. The Bruins are big on giving back, too, logging more than 200,000 hours of community service annually.

ATHLETICS

In addition to celebrating academic excellence and phenomenal growth, Belmont boasts 17 intercollegiate sports teams. The Belmont Bruins men's basketball team won the Ohio Valley Conference regular season championship in 2013, 2014, 2015 and 2019 and made its eighth appearance in the NCAA National Tournament in 2019. The Belmont Bruins women's basketball team has made four consecutive appearances in the NCAA National Tournament during the years 2016–2019. Baseball, both cross country teams, and the volleyball team have earned recent conference titles. Belmont student-athletes excel in the classroom, too, as Belmont has won the conference's All-Academic Trophy multiple times. The award is given annually to the conference school with the greatest percentage of student-athletes who earned a GPA of 3.0 or higher.

ADMISSIONS PROCESS

Belmont's Admissions Committee considers applications based on the total picture that a student's credentials present. High school students will be considered competitive for admission if they present a rigorous course of college-preparatory, academic studies. Students should have an above-average academic and cumulative grade point average and rank in the top half of their graduating class. Any college-level work is also expected to be at the above-average level. A strong correlation between high school grades and entrance examination scores is expected. The essays, list of activities, and recommendations are also strongly considered as indicators of success at Belmont. Additional requirements such as portfolios or auditions are considered in conjunction with the academic credentials for those programs that require them. Each application is considered on an individual basis. No two applicants will present the same credentials or the same "fit" with the university. Our desire is to work with each student to determine the likelihood of that student to enroll in, graduate from, and use the benefits of the Belmont educational experience.

For more information, contact:

Office of Admissions
Belmont University
1900 Belmont Boulevard
Nashville, TN 37212
615-460-6785
800-56ENROLL

Fax: 615-460-5434
admissions@belmont.edu
www.belmont.edu
CEEB Code: 1058
ACT Code: 3946

School Says . . .

BELOIT COLLEGE

AT A GLANCE

Beloit College is a four-year, independent, national college of liberal arts and sciences in southern Wisconsin. Students can expect to receive a premium education from scholars who put teaching first and involve students as much as possible in hands-on research. Small class sizes often result in professors becoming influential mentors, who empower their students to discover what they love to do and put into practice their newfound skills and knowledge to make a remarkable difference in the world. By the time Beloiters graduate, they haven't just accrued a transcript; they've compiled a strong resume that demonstrates an ability to think critically and creatively, communicate clearly, and collaborate effectively with diverse groups of people.

Beloit's 1,275 students come from nearly every state and more than 44 countries. With an incredible breadth of opportunities, a historic campus with modern facilities, a nationally recognized faculty, and creative, motivated students, Beloit is truly a "college that changes lives." Founded in 1846 on the Midwestern frontier, Beloit is Wisconsin's oldest continuously operating.

LOCATION AND ENVIRONMENT

Beloit's 40-acre campus rests just across the Wisconsin-Illinois state line and is conveniently located just a short drive from three major cities: Chicago (90 miles southwest of campus), Madison (50 miles north of campus), and Milwaukee (70 miles northwest of campus). Beloit's academic buildings are clustered around lawns dotted with trees and twenty ancient Native American mounds.

Most students live on campus, as Beloit is a residential college that requires students to live in college-operated residence facilities for at least six semesters of full-time enrollment. Beloiters have a variety of housing options to choose from, including traditional residence halls, fraternities (3) and sororities (3), apartments, and special interest houses. All residences halls are within easy walking distance of classrooms, studio locations, and the college's athletic facilities.

Banks, restaurants, and shops can be found within a short walking distance, in downtown Beloit just two blocks from campus. On Saturdays from May through October, students like to attend the region's most popular farmers' market. For ten days each winter, students, local residents, and visitors flock to the Beloit International Film Festival (BIFF), where more than 100 films are screened in downtown venues. Year-round, active students venture to one of several nearby parks to exercise, or when it's warm, to listen to outdoor concerts.

CAMPUS FACILITIES AND EQUIPMENT

Beloit's academic buildings are both historic and cutting edge and are located toward the southern half of campus. Particularly noteworthy are Beloit's two on-campus teaching museums. The Logan Museum of Anthropology houses approximately 15,000 ethnographic—and over 200,000 archaeological objects— from 129 countries and more than 600 cultural groups. The Wright Museum of Art holds approximately 6,000 works of art in its permanent collection. Significant collections include American Impressionism, Modernist paintings, a collection of 19th century plaster casts, German Expressionism, and Japanese Modern prints. Both museums offer students professional opportunities to conduct real museum work in collaboration with faculty and staff. Beloit's Museum Studies program is renowned.

The Laura Aldrich Neese Performing Arts theatre complex features a large thrust stage theater built to Equity standards, a black box theater with flexible staging, a scenic design studio, costume shop, makeup rooms, dressing rooms, and a greenroom.

The Marjorie and James Sanger Center for the Sciences is a platinum LEED-certified green building that houses the Biology, Chemistry, Geology, Math and Computer Science, Physics, and Psychology departments. Besides its spectacular four-story open foyer roof garden, and rain garden, the Sanger Center features student offices and space for studio format and inquiry-based courses that integrate class, laboratory, and collaborative group work. Special facilities include a visualization lab, a 1,900 square-foot greenhouse with three climate zones, a herbarium, and a rooftop small-telescope astronomy area. Off-campus facilities include Chamberlin Springs, 50 acres of oak and hickory woods and wildlife northwest of the city; the Smith Limnology Lab, a small boat launch and aquatic station on the Rock River; and Newark Road Prairie State Natural Area, a 32.5 acre virgin prairie with more than 300 species of flowering plants.

Several campus buildings are within walking distance downtown: the Hendricks Center for the Arts, a performing arts center; Turtle Creek, the Beloit College bookstore and The Center for Entrepreneurship in Liberal Education (CELEB), a laboratory for entrepreneurship education. Six blocks east of campus, students can head to the Strong Stadium Complex and watch the competition from the 3,000-seat stands; the complex is home to the football, baseball, tennis, softball, track and field, and soccer teams. Back on campus, the entire student body can exercise in the Sports Center, which features two racquetball courts, a weight and training room, three full-sized basketball courts and a six-lane, 25 yard pool.

In February of 2020, Beloit College opened the doors to "the most forward looking concept in the world" and welcomed students for the first time after being converted from a decommissioned powerhouse. The Powerhouse, a facility that provides a spectacular space for the community to come together to work, train, eat and play was once used to provide hydroelectricity to the surrounding area, it will now serve as a hub for student life on campus. The Powerhouse features a plethora of lounging spaces, an auditorium, an indoor running track, multiple fitness classrooms, an eight-lane 25 yard competition pool that features one and three meter diving, a gaming cafe, and alternate dining options. The project is funded entirely by donations and grant money (no student tuition dollars).

OFF-CAMPUS OPPORTUNITIES

Each year, 40% of Beloiters choose to study abroad for one or two semesters and travel to more than 40 countries to do so. Students study worldwide through a combination of college programs, offerings by other institutions and partners, and direct enrollment in universities. Domestic off-campus study programs are also robust. Current North American programs open to Beloit College students are: a semester in environmental science at the Marine Biological Laboratory in Woods Hole, MA; public affairs programs at American University in Washington, D.C.; an arts, entrepreneurship, and urban studies program in Chicago, IL; the Newberry Seminar in Chicago, IL; and the Oak Ridge Science Semester at the Oak Ridge National Laboratory near Knoxville, TN.

The college also offers Cities in Transitions courses, which provide opportunities for students to strengthen their language skills and pursue independent study projects in China, Ecuador, Germany, Japan, Russia, and Senegal. Beloit's Career and Community Engagement Center is a great resource for students, providing them with as much as $400,000 in student project funding annually.

ACADEMIC PROGRAMS

Beloit offers a variety of programs that supplement and complement its curriculum. Channels are Beloit's pioneering approach to connecting college and career. When you dive into a Channel, you sign on to a journey of discovery with dedicated guides. If your answers to the question of what you want to be doing with your life fall somewhere in the range of "curing disease," "seeking justice," "saving the planet," or "bringing new ideas to market," we have a Channel for you. Once you're in a Channel, you'll find yourself with similarly driven students and access to alumni, employers, and other friends of the college who are eager to connect you to new opportunities. As part of a Channel, you receive the most intentional guidance we offer, and you keep the freedom to plot a course all your own.

All Beloiters know that the relationships you build with faculty and staff are key to your success here and beyond. That's why our Advising and Mentoring Program (or AMP) is built around relationships with your academic advisor, your instructors, and all of the many campus members who are here to see you succeed. When you come to Beloit, you are matched with an academic advisor who you can start building a relationship with right away. Advisors help connect new students to resources such as tutoring, health and wellness, library, and more.

In the summer, the Center for Language Studies offers intensive summer language instruction in Chinese, Japanese, and Russian. The anthropology field training program has taken students to excavation sites from Colorado to Chile, and geology field expeditions include trips to Iceland, New Zealand, and Scotland. Each spring, students present their research at a conference-style Student Symposium event, and in the fall, International Symposium Day is a forum set aside for students to present research and projects they have conducted abroad. Beloit students serve on the editorial board of the *Beloit Fiction Journal*. Each year, the college brings as many as six groundbreaking scholars and artists to campus, who join the community for an extended stay as part of a distinguished residency program.

MAJORS AND DEGREES OFFERED

Beloit offers undergraduate degree programs exclusively and confers bachelor of arts and bachelor of science degrees. There are more than 50 fields of study in 31 departments.

Fields of study (possible major and minor concentrations) include: African studies, anthropology, art and art history, biochemistry, biology, chemistry, Chinese language and culture, cognitive science, comparative literature, computer science, critical identity studies, dance, economics, education and youth studies, engineering program, English, environmental studies, European studies, french language and culture, geology, Greek and Latin studies, health and society, history, interdisciplinary studies, international relations, Japanese language and culture, journalism, Latin American and Caribbean studies, law and justice, mathematics, media studies, medieval studies, modern languages and literatures, museum studies, music, philosophy, physics, political science, psychology, religious studies, Russian language and culture, russian studies, sociology, Spanish language and culture, and theatre.

Teacher Certification (BA, BS): Children and schools (middle childhood/early adolescence, grades 1-8); Adolescents and schools (early adolescence/adolescence, grades 6-12); Art education (early childhood-adolescence, ages birth-21).

Pre-professional programs: Engineering programs (3-2 and 4-2); health professions advising; pre-law preparation advising

TUITION, ROOM, BOARD, FEES

$51,050 tuition
$280 Activities fee
$202 Health/Wellness fee
$9,360 for room and board
Total: $60,892

FINANCIAL AID

Overview

Beloit College is committed to making the Beloit experience affordable for all admitted students. During the 2016–2017 academic year, 98% of enrolling first-year students received Beloit gift aid. The average financial aid award (including federal loans and work study) was $36,857.

Bottom line

Full tuition at Beloit costs $51,050 for the academic year. Housing costs an additional $5,332, and a full meal plan runs $4028 (this plan is required for all first year students). In addition, there's also a $280 student activity fee, and a $202 health and wellness charge. Families can expect to pay another $1,690 in estimated health insurance costs. Books and supplies often run around $1,000. Finally, it is recommended that students set aside another $1,352 for personal expenses.

STUDENT ORGANIZATIONS AND ACTIVITIES

Beloit students are remarkably unique, passionate, and involved. They do what needs doing, change what needs changing, and create what needs creating. Students serve on college governance and search committees, establish their own organizations, orchestrate events such as the annual Folk 'n' Blues music festival, and host their own radio and cable TV shows. The college has more than 60 active student clubs ranging in focus from ballroom dance to ultimate frisbee to yoga.

An NCAA Division III school, Beloit competes in the Midwest Conference and has 19 varsity teams. Men's varsity teams include: baseball, basketball, cross country, football, lacrosse, soccer, swimming and diving, and track and field. Women's varsity teams include: basketball, cross country, lacrosse, soccer, softball, swimming and diving, track and field, and volleyball.

ADMISSIONS PROCESS

Beloit adheres to a holistic Admissions Process and aims to get a complete picture of who an applicant is as a person and not just as a prospective student. The committee looks closely at grades and academic history, but also looks for other qualities that indicate students would do well at Beloit, such as strong leadership abilities and unique talents. The college encourages applicants who are interested in getting involved in the campus community and who will leverage their Beloit educations to effect remarkable change in the world.

Review of transfer applications for the fall term begins July 15 and continues through the spring; the deadline for the spring term is December 15. Notification for transfer applications is rolling.

Deadline

Early Decision I	November 1
Early Action I	November 1
Early Action II	December 1
Early Decision II	January 15
Regular Decision	January 15

BENTLEY UNIVERSITY

AT A GLANCE

Bentley is more than just one of the nation's top business schools. We're a transformative living-learning community that prepares ethical students to use their business know-how to make a positive difference in the world. With a blend of business, technology and the arts and sciences, we provide students with critical thinking and practical skills to help them collaborate effectively in different settings and prepare them to lead successful, rewarding careers. If you're interested in changing the world, we'd like to help.

Your education doesn't stop at the classroom door. With a classic New England campus just minutes from Harvard Square and Boston, you'll enjoy a beautiful setting and easy access to Boston's professional networking and cultural opportunities. Seventy-eight percent of our students live on campus, creating a tight-knit bond among neighbors and classmates, and our 11-to-1 student-to-faculty ratio ensures that you'll work directly with professors. You'll be part of a welcoming, inclusive community that embraces diverse perspectives and backgrounds.

Our strong emphasis on engaged, hands-on learning prepares you for today's fast-changing economy. With 25 majors and 34 minors to choose from, you'll be able to follow your curiosity, pursue your specific academic interests and see firsthand why Bentley is consistently recognized among the top business schools in the country.

LOCATION AND ENVIRONMENT

Bentley's location in Waltham, Massachusetts-just minutes west of Boston—puts the city within easy reach. As the country's ultimate university town, Boston's options range from theater to art exhibits, clubs to concerts, and championship sports to world-class shopping. Boston also offers many opportunities for internships and jobs after graduation.

CAMPUS FACILITIES AND EQUIPMENT

The Dana Athletic Center

The Dana Athletic Center has everything you need to play, practice and stay in shape. The facility is equipped for a wide-range of sports and interests, from basketball courts to batting cages, dance studios to saunas, swimming and diving pools-and more.

The Bentley Arena

Build in 2018 and home to Bentley's Division I Hockey team, the Bentley Arena is the first standalone ice arena in the country to receive LEED platinum certification. Students use the facility as a "living lab" for academic projects on everything from data analysis to marketing and sales.

Trading Room (Hughey Center for Financial Services):

State-of-the-art investment research center, featuring 60 workstations, each equipped with real-time data and leading financial technologies, and 24 Bloomberg terminals.

User Experience Center (UXC):

The UXC offers a wide range of user research services aimed at understanding user/customer needs, motivations, and the broader context of use, giving you the data and insights to design a great user experience.

Center for Marketing Technology (CMT):

The CMT is home to high-quality research, collaboration and strategic consulting for corporate clients. Through coursework and corporate immersion projects, you'll get real-life experience supporting some of the world's largest and most influential brands.

Media and Culture Labs and Studio:

A state-of-the-art facility in support of arts and sciences majors and liberal studies concentrations, professionally equipped with media production tools for video, audio, digital photography and design projects.

Computer Information Systems (CIS) Sandbox:

The CIS Sandbox is Bentley University's Technology Social Learning Space that prepares students to succeed in their CIS courses and to thrive in a technology-driven business world. Located in Smith 234, the Sandbox is a campus destination for informal, peer-led technology education.

Center for Languages and International Collaboration (CLIC):

The CLIC is equipped with high-tech conferencing capabilities, multimedia libraries and international satellite broadcasts to give students authentic exposure to other languages, countries and cultures.

Accounting Center for Electronic Learning and Business Measurement (ACELAB):

Home to Bentley's top accounting students, whether they are working on fast-paced tutorials or state-of-the-art software programs, or providing tutoring services to assist their peers.

Eco-Fi-Stat Learning Center:

The Eco-Fi-Stat Learning Center provides a place for students to study and receive help from qualified tutors in economics, finance and statistics. The tutors are able to provide help with 100, 200 and 300-level courses in all three areas.

Mathematics Learning Center:

The Mathematics Learning Center offers drop-in tutoring services to students enrolled in undergraduate mathematics courses and supports all first-year mathematics courses, as well as mathematics electives.

The Writing Center:

The Writing Center is staffed by a writing instructor and peer tutors who offer one-on-one assistance with writing assignments.

English to Speakers of Other Languages (ESOL) Center:

Students whose home language is not English are invited to take advantage of the free tutorial services offered by our ESOL Center. English and Media Studies Department faculty who specialize in teaching English to speakers of other languages (ESOL) provide language support to help students achieve success in their courses across the curriculum.

OFF-CAMPUS OPPORTUNITIES

Hands-on experience is emphasized across the curriculum. Internships, study abroad, service-learning, and other opportunities allow students to apply classroom theory in the community. More than 92% of seniors complete one internship and over 71% complete two or more, building valuable work experience and networking connections. Some of the top internship employers include Fidelity Investments, the TJX Companies, Liberty Mutual, Bain & Company, and all of the Big Four accounting firms.

Bentley students can gain insight into different cultures by studying abroad. Programs take place in more than 25 countries and vary in length from one week to a full academic year. Through Bentley's Service-Learning Center, students build skills in business, communication, and teamwork while assisting nonprofit and community-based organizations both locally and internationally.

ACADEMIC PROGRAMS

At Bentley, we know a modern education has to prepare you for today's complex world. So we've designed the Bentley experience to give you more: Business plus the arts and sciences. Classroom learning plus real-world experience. World-class technology plus a global perspective.

Here, you'll take risks, confront your blind spots, challenge yourself, and discover a better, more complete you. You'll graduate knowing everything you've studied has a place and a purpose, bridging hard and soft skills, right and left brain, your dreams and the reality of today's fast-moving global marketplace. You'll not only be ready to succeed in your adult life but prepared to thrive in everything you do.

Choose from 25 majors in business or the arts and sciences and turn your passion into your future. Majors are easily customized to match your career interests.

If you're earning a Bachelor of Science degree in a business-related field, Bentley has created a one-of-a-kind way for you to develop a more well-rounded education. The Liberal Studies Major (LSM) offers a more thematic approach to your course selection, allowing you to shape your education into something that really reflects you, without giving up the core business knowledge Bentley is famous for.

But the LSM is about more than a new kind of major. It's about a new way of thinking. By creating your own educational path, you'll explore different ways to turn your personal interests and passions into a lifetime of professional success. You'll develop an interdisciplinary approach to problem-solving and communication, learning soft skills that future employers are looking for. And you'll join a community of like-minded faculty members, mentors and fellow students who care about the world like you do.

MAJORS AND DEGREES OFFERED

Bachelor of Science Degree is offered in the following majors:

Accountancy
Actuarial Science
Computer Information Systems
Corporate Finance and Accounting
Creative Industries
Data Analytics
Economics-Finance
Finance
Information Design and Corporate Communication
Information Systems Audit and Control
Management
Managerial Economics
Marketing
Mathematical Sciences
Professional Sales

Bachelor of Arts Degree is offered in the following majors:

English
Health Studies
Hispanic Studies
History
International affairs
Liberal Arts
Media and Culture
Philosophy
Public Policy
Sustainability Science

If you're a Bachelor of Arts student at Bentley, you can also earn a Business Studies Major (or a Business Studies minor). It's a comprehensive program that ensures you graduate with the core knowledge of management, finance, and marketing that only a nationally ranked business university like Bentley can deliver, while giving you the flexibility to customize your degree with electives chosen around a topic of interest or specific discipline.

ACADEMIC PROGRAMS

Business
Liberal Arts

TUITION, ROOM, BOARD, FEES

Your college education is a big investment. That's why we do everything possible to make it as affordable as possible for you and your family, and to provide the kind of return on investment you expect—and deserve.

The value of your education is one of our top priorities. We will work closely with you to identify every appropriate financial aid solution. In most cases, our financial aid program makes the cost of attending Bentley competitive with most private and public institutions—even with the in-state costs. More than 70 percent of Bentley students receive some kind of financial aid. Depending on your circumstances, you might be eligible for grants and scholarships, work opportunities, low-interest student loans or one of several alternative financing programs. Our personalized approach to financial aid has resulted in Bentley graduates defaulting at a rate of less than one percent on their student loans, compared to the national average of 11 percent.

2019–2020 Tuition and Fees for Undergraduate Domestic Students:

$50,060 Tuition
$16,960 Room and Board
$1,300 Books and Supplies
$1,360 Technology Fee
$1,230 Personal Expenditures
$410 Student Activity Fee
$250 New Student Enrollment Fee
$71,570 TOTAL

* A student health insurance fee of $1,919 may also be assessed

FINANCIAL AID

Bentley offers a variety of sources for financial aid, including scholarships, grants, loans, and work opportunities. A financial aid package may include federal and state aid, but approximately 75 percent of financial aid awarded comes from Bentley grant and scholarship resources. Your financial aid package can include many different types of aid.

STUDENT BODY

4,253 Undergraduate Students
3:2 Male-to-female ratio
1,207 Graduate Students
26% Students of color
16% International Students
78% Students living on campus
97% First-year students living on campus
8% Asian
4% African-American
7% Hispanic
58% Caucasian
2% Two or more races

STUDENT ORGANIZATIONS AND ACTIVITIES

Approximately 97 percent of freshmen live on campus. Twenty-three residence halls provide a range of housing options: dorms, suites, and apartments. Housing is provided for all four years; all residence halls are air-conditioned and typically include study lounges, with exercise facilities and game rooms easily accessible on campus.

Students live and learn in a multicultural environment that prepares them to thrive in today's diverse world. International students representing nearly 100 countries make up 16% of the student body and bring valuable perspectives to the Bentley community.

Supporting Bentley's commitment to diversity are offices such as the Multicultural Center, Spiritual Life Center, Center for International Students and Scholars, Equity Center, Center for Women in Business, and the Women's Center.

The newly renovated Student Center is the hub of campus activity and is home to the 921 Dining Room and more than 100 student organizations. These groups represent academics, the arts, media, fraternity and sorority life, and cultural interests.

Athletic programs are a Bentley hallmark and include intramurals, recreational sports, and more than 20 varsity teams in NCAA Divisions I and II. The Dana Athletic Center houses a weight and fitness complex, food court, locker rooms, a gym, a basketball court, volleyball court, and a competition-size pool with a diving tank. Outdoor facilities include soccer and baseball fields, a softball field, and a track. Our brand new arena houses our division 1 hockey team and other campus traditions.

ADMISSIONS PROCESS

At Bentley, we're committed to a caring and holistic review of every application, one that considers everything that makes you the person you are today. The entire application process at Bentley is about you and finding the best fit for your college experience.

Our students come from a variety of experiences, backgrounds, and cultures—aspects that are important to a rich educational experience and your success in college and beyond. Of course, we review the rigor of your curriculum and your achievements in the classroom, but beyond academics, we consider other attributes that define you. We want to know the way you navigated your high school years, your involvement in your community and your commitment to your interests.

Application requirements:

Application form and $75 fee
Official high school transcript or GED score report

Core requirements include 4 years of English, 4 years of Math (including pre-calculus) 3 years of lab science, 3 years of social science and 3 years of foreign language.

College Essay
Senior grades
Two letters of recommendation
Standardized test scores

BOSTON UNIVERSITY

AT A GLANCE

Is Boston University the right place for you? With an average class size of 27 students and a student-to-faculty ratio of 10:1, you'll find yourself in classes taught by Pulitzer Prize winners, Fulbright scholars, or a MacArthur fellow. BU offers more than 300 programs of study to choose from, so you can take classes in subjects as varied as biology, broadcast journalism, business, computer engineering, education, film, international relations, physical therapy, psychology, and theatre, just to name a few. If hands-on research is what interests you, the Undergraduate Research Opportunities Program (UROP) offers hundreds of research opportunities across all areas of study. You'll have the rare opportunity to participate in research across the humanities, arts, and sciences as early as your first year. Add hundreds of extracurricular activities and the exciting city of Boston, and you'll never experience a dull moment as a BU student.

LOCATION AND ENVIRONMENT

Located in the heart of Boston, students experience the city as an extension of the campus. No other city can compete with Boston's remarkable concentration of higher education institutions, world-renowned medical centers, and historic and cultural attractions. The city provides many opportunities for impressive internship and research positions and is home to world-class attractions including the Museum of Fine Arts, Fenway Park, and the Boston Symphony Orchestra. The nation's first transit system runs right down the spine of out 1.3-mile campus, and the Charles River flows by our side. With four years of guaranteed campus housing, and 75 percent of undergraduates living on campus all four years, the campus feels like a true residential community in the heart of Boston.

CAMPUS FACILITIES AND EQUIPMENT

Boston University's academic, research, athletic facilities are some of the best in the country. The Engineering Product Innovation Center (EPIC) is home to a full carpentry and machine shop, 3D printers, a metals foundry, and laboratories. The University's Rajen Kilachand Center for Integrated Life Sciences & Engineering brings together life scientists, engineers, and physicians to speed life-changing developments in the fields of human health, environment, and energy. The BUild Lab: IDG Capital Student Innovation Center fosters innovation and entrepreneurship across the campus. Students can connect with advisers, collaborate with other students, and get help with matters from design and prototyping to legal advice and marketing. The Joan & Edgar Booth Theatre and College of Fine Arts Production Center is home to studio space for visual arts students, practice rooms for music, and a 575-seat music performance center. The Student Village provides first-rate recreation and athletics with the Fitness & Recreation Center and Agganis Arena, as well as high-rise apartments and dining. The University also offers the Yawkey Center for Student Services, which houses the Center for Career Development, Educational Resource Center, Pre-Professional Advising Offices, and two stories of dining in Marciano Commons.

OFF-CAMPUS OPPORTUNITIES

The opportunities to learn outside the classroom are limitless thanks to BU's location in the heart of the city. In fact, 89% of undergraduates participate in at least one internship before graduating. Students can intern with top-tier financial services, biomedical, or engineering companies. The city is also home to world-class museums and art galleries, top-ranked hospitals and health services facilities, numerous advertising and public relations firms, and more. BU's Center for Career Development works to provide students with the resources to secure internships in any number of fields.

Boston University has one of the world's most extensive study abroad programs. Among the University's 100+ programs are language and liberal arts programs; programs that combine studies with internships; fieldwork programs for students wishing to pursue academic or scientific research; and summer programs. Programs are available in Argentina, Australia, Belgium, China, Czech Republic, Denmark, Ecuador, England, France, Germany, Ghana, India, Ireland, Israel, Italy, Japan, Mexico, Morocco, New Zealand, Singapore, South Korea, Spain, Switzerland, Tanzania, and Turkey. There are also programs available in Los Angeles, New York, Silicon Valley, and Washington, D.C.

ACADEMIC PROGRAMS

What does it mean to study at a world-class research university? As a university receiving more than $579 million in research funding in 2019 and a member of the prestigious Association of American Universities (AAU), we expect students to formulate bold questions and seek out the answers. You don't have to be science-minded to thrive in BU's culture of inquiry—research takes place in nearly every academic discipline.

The academic flexibility offered by BU can maximize the value of your degree. Choose from more than 300 programs of study, Dual Degree programs, combined BA/MA programs, and chances to take coursework across schools and colleges. Think psychology and economics, or business and international relations.

Students complete general education requirements through the BU Hub, an innovative general education program that is integrated with majors and minors. Students take courses of interest while exploring areas ranging from global citizenship to scientific and social inquiry to ethical reasoning or digital communication. The Hub is robust in its options for experiential learning and co-curriculars, and its signature feature, the BU Cross-College Challenge, offers an opportunity to work with a team of students from across BU's schools and colleges.

BU's most ambitious and high achieving applicants can apply for admission to the Kilachand Honors College. Kilachand offers a challenging liberal arts education grounded in critical and creative thinking and interdisciplinary problem-solving related to important global, societal, corporate, and geopolitical challenges. The integrated, four-year curriculum is augmented by an extensive series of enrichment experiences, including visits to cultural institutions, arts events, and discussions with leading scientists, artists, and professionals. All Kilachand students complete a substantial work of empirical or scholarly research, creativity, or invention by the close of their senior year and share the outcomes of their work in a celebratory Symposium.

TUITION, ROOM, BOARD, FEES

Tuition for the 2019–20 academic year is $54,720; standard room and board is $16,160. Additional mandatory fees are $1,172. Allowances for the cost of books, supplies, travel, and other incidental expenses brings the total cost of attendance for a student to $75,002.

FINANCIAL AID

Boston University offers expanded financial aid packages that will make up the difference between the cost of attendance and what students can afford. The total cost varies from family to family. BU will calculate your family contribution based on a student's FAFSA and CSS Profile™. This will be subtracted from the full cost of attendance. The difference—your calculated need—will be made up by financial aid. The same amount is guaranteed for each of your undergraduate years through The BU Scholarship Assurance.

STUDENT ORGANIZATIONS AND ACTIVITIES

Boston University is one of the most diverse research universities in the country. Students come from all 50 U.S. states, more than 100 countries, and a myriad of ethnic, cultural, and socioeconomic backgrounds. In fact, BU ranked among the top universities hosting the most international students in the US by Open Doors.

Boston University students are extremely engaged, participating in academic clubs, cultural or religious organizations, and community service groups. There are more than 450 student organizations and more than 40 intramural and club sports that students can participate in. You can get involved with organizations such as Alianza Latina, BU Habitat for Humanity, the Debate Society, or the Alpine Ski Team. A separate student government exists at each school and college to manage student affairs, and the Student Union includes members who represent all schools and colleges within the university.

ADMISSIONS PROCESS

The Board of Admissions evaluates each prospective student holistically. The Board's main focus centers on the rigor of a student's high school record, but required standardized test scores (SAT and ACT)*, personal qualities and integrity, interests, teacher and counselor references, and other relevant attributes are also considered carefully. All candidates must have graduated from high school or earned an equivalency diploma to be considered. For admission to the College of Fine Arts, most students are not required to submit the SAT or ACT but must either audition or submit a portfolio (some programs also require pre-screening). A few select programs require interviews for admission. Boston University accepts either the Common Application or the Coalition Application.

Students should visit www.bu.edu/admissions for additional information. Boston University also considers students with transferable credit from other institutions for admission. Boston University considers transfer applicants for September or January admission, depending on the program of interest.

Boston University offers early decision and early decision 2 (which are binding agreements), and regular decision programs. All applications for early decision must be submitted by November 1. Applications for early decision 2 and regular decision are due in early January. Accelerated Medical Program applications must be submitted by November 15. Applications for admission to qualify for the Presidential or Trustee Scholarships must be submitted by December 1.

Transfer students seeking January admission must submit their application forms by November 1. Those seeking September admission must submit their application forms by March 1.

Transfer students cannot be admitted to the Accelerated Liberal Arts Medical Program; or the nutrition or six-year, combined AT/DPT and DPT programs in the College of Health & Rehabilitation Sciences: Sargent College. Transfer students may not apply for January admission to the School of Theatre in the College of Fine Arts. They also cannot apply as "undeclared" to any school or college.

Boston University accepts qualified applicants regardless of age, color, disability, national origin, race, religion, sexual orientation, or gender to all of its activities and programs.

*Applicants for fall 2021 are not required to submit SAT and ACT scores. For more details, visit go.bu.edu/apply.

BRYANT UNIVERSITY

AT A GLANCE

To make an impact in the real world, you need to go beyond the textbook. You need experience, practice solving real problems, and a set of values you can draw upon to make important, and complicated, decisions.

For more than a century and a half, Bryant University has inspired excellence in an ever-changing world. We empower students to ask Why? What if? and Why not?—to think that anything is possible, that no idea is too big, and that unique paths often lead to the richest rewards.

Bryant offers an innovative model of education that integrates business with the liberal arts and provides you with the world-ready experience and knowhow to stand out after graduation. It's an approach that prepares you for both personal fulfillment and professional success.

Our faculty, whose expertise is sought after around the globe, will engage you in ways that educate the whole person. They'll be your mentors both in the classroom and beyond, and inspire you to reach your fullest potential. Our supportive culture and collegial community will challenge you to achieve more than you ever thought possible.

At Bryant, you'll not only learn how to make your mark, you'll become a change maker and impact thinker.

Competitive Advantage

The nationally recognized programs of Bryant's Amica Center for Career Education will help you develop lifelong career skills and secure the position you want after college. Our 45,000-strong international alumni network will allow you to find a mentor on your path to success.

Ninety-nine percent of Bryant's Class of 2018 was employed—or enrolled in graduate school—within six months of graduation. The median starting salary was $60,000. Most importantly, they were prepared to make a real difference in the world.

LOCATION AND ENVIRONMENT

With 3,259 undergraduate students, Bryant's stunning, secure 435-acre campus in Smithfield, RI, offers a close-knit, friendly community with a warm, small-town atmosphere. More than 80 percent of Bryant's students live on campus, enjoying an exciting and purposeful student life.

Our strategic location, just 15 minutes from downtown Providence, an hour from Boston, and three hours from New York City, provides exciting internship, entertainment, and employment opportunities within driving distance.

CAMPUS FACILITIES AND EQUIPMENT

Bryant is a leader among academic institutions in its use of technology and innovation in support of learning. Bryant has recently invested more than $280 million in facilities built specifically for student success, including our groundbreaking Quinlan/Brown Academic Innovation Center, which fosters creativity in a flexible, interactive environment.

From early access to high-level lab equipment to our state-of-the-industry Bloomberg terminals to our new Data Visualization Lab, we ensure that students have the tools to stay ahead of the field.

OFF-CAMPUS OPPORTUNITIES

Bryant is a community that encourages different perspectives and celebrates racial, cultural, gender-based, and religious diversity. We put an emphasis on global immersion, both on-campus and abroad, so that when you graduate, you will truly be a global citizen—ready to work effectively anywhere in the world.

Bryant's study abroad opportunities range from the traditional semester abroad to our distinctive Sophomore International Experience. Costa Rica, England, Malaysia, Japan, and Singapore are among the more than 270 destinations worldwide where you can study. You can also take advantage of our strategic international partnerships, including Bryant Zhuhai in China—a bridge between nations that inspires mutual understanding.

ACADEMIC PROGRAMS

Bryant's student-centered approach is a hallmark of everything we do. We keep the classes small; there are no large lecture halls, and 100 percent of your classes will be taught by professors—not teaching assistants or graduate students. Our faculty, who are world-class experts and scholars, will be your mentors and coaches, both in class and beyond. An academic advisor will help you plan your future.

Our nationally recognized First-Year Gateway provides the foundation for your success. Through engaging with fundamental questions about the role of the individual in an ever changing world, the interdisciplinary Gateway sets the stage for you to explore the global foundations of character, leadership, culture, and business. Our IDEA (Innovation and Design Thinking Experience for All) program will teach you the proven skills of innovators—creativity, empathy, collaboration, connectivity, and perseverance.

Collaborative and experiential learning are at the heart of a Bryant education. Group projects, practicum experiences, social entrepreneurship, academic competitions, business simulations, and internships are just a few of the ways you'll develop highly marketable skills that will set you apart in the real world.

You'll work with an industry expert in one class and gain valuable experience through a service-learning project in the next, developing a wide range of skills. You'll learn how to innovate—and collaborate—to understand and solve real-world problems.

MAJORS AND DEGREES OFFERED

At Bryant, the possibilities, and roads to success, are endless. You'll graduate with either a major in business and a complementary minor in the liberal arts, or a liberal arts major and a business minor. With more than 195 different major/minor combinations available, ranging from Biology and Marketing to Global Supply Chain Management and Literary and Cultural Studies, you'll be able to create the path that's right for you and prepare for a career you'll love.

Our degrees include:

Undergraduate: Bachelor of Arts, Bachelor of Science, Bachelor of Science in Business Administration, Bachelor of Science in Data Science, and Bachelor of Science in International Business.

Graduate: Master of Business Administration, Professional Master of Business Administration Online, Master of Professional Accountancy, Master of Science in Physician Assistant Studies, and Master of Arts in Communication.

TUITION, ROOM, BOARD, FEES

Tuition 2019–2020: $45,966 (Includes a new laptop)

Room and board: $15,893 (for standard double-occupancy room and standard meal plan of 14 meals per week)

Student fees: $897

FINANCIAL AID

The value of a Bryant education is measured in the academic, professional, cultural, and personal growth opportunities that you students achieve success. Our financial aid counselors know that your education is one of the biggest investments you'll ever make—and that a Bryant education is one of the wisest. They're trained to work with you and your family to create a solution that fits you best.

The University understands that financing a student's education is a vital part of the decision about which college to attend. In the 2018–2019 year, more than 97 percent of Bryant's undergraduate students received institutional aid and the University awarded approximately $62.9 million in grants and scholarships.

STUDENT ORGANIZATIONS AND ACTIVITIES

Bryant University students come from 38 states and territories and from 49 countries. About 62% of the undergraduate student body is male and 38% is female. 8% of our students come from outside the United States.

Bryant is more than an institution, it's a community. Student life here is purposeful, engaging, and inspiring. Our 24/7 learning environment, culture of mentorship, and wide variety of co-curricular experiences will help you to discover your true passion and accelerate your personal and professional growth beyond the classroom.

More than 100 student organizations, including academic clubs, community service groups, club sports teams, and cultural organizations, will help you form lifelong bonds with your classmates and enhance your ability to lead and collaborate. Our 22 Division I varsity sports teams inspire Bulldog pride and bring the community together throughout the school year.

ADMISSIONS PROCESS

We're looking for applicants with strong academic preparation and who are eager to tackle challenges. Students admitted to Bryant also participated in extracurricular activities and submitted strong letters of recommendation.

Students come to us with a diversity of strengths. That's why we offer admission interviews and test-optional alternatives. Show us how you shine and share your big plans. If you'll thrive in a learning environment that places a priority on innovation and collaboration, we can't wait to meet you.

Bryant offers several options to apply for admission. Early applications are accepted under Early Decision 1, Early Action, and Early Decision 2 programs.

To contact the Office of Admission, call 1-800-622-7001 or email admission@bryant.edu

Contact:
Bryant University
(800) 622-7001
admission.bryant.edu

BUCKNELL UNIVERSITY

AT A GLANCE

Bring your natural curiosity to Bucknell University in Pennsylvania, where you'll meet world-class faculty and study in leading-edge lab spaces.

- Bucknell is an innovative University based in the liberal arts. We have three colleges: the College of Arts & Sciences, College of Engineering and the Freeman College of Management
- With more than 60 majors and 70 minors, we help you explore many different interests, meaning you'll graduate with an impressive array of in-demand skills.
- We have a 9-to-1 student-faculty ratio and average class size of 20. Our professors will know you and support you in every aspect of your education.

LOCATION AND ENVIRONMENT

Bucknell's gorgeous campus is located in the heart of central Pennsylvania, a scenic region where you can enjoy the changing beauty of all four seasons in a climate that's neither too hot nor too cold. As college towns go, it's hard to imagine a better one than Lewisburg. Like Bucknell itself, it's the ideal size. So you won't get stuck in traffic, but you won't run out of things to do, either.

CAMPUS FACILITIES AND EQUIPMENT

For many Bucknell students, their most meaningful academic experiences are the research projects they undertake with faculty mentors.

The University provides many opportunities for students to get involved in research, starting the summer before their first semester and continuing through all four years.

Students who take part in research not only learn about their own projects, they build analytical and critical-thinking skills, leaving them better prepared to take on their first job or excel in graduate school.

This happens in state-of-the-art labs and learning spaces that, at other schools, might be off-limits to undergrads or first-year students. At Bucknell, we're all about opening doors and opening minds.

OFF-CAMPUS OPPORTUNITIES

You don't have to travel far to get out and explore nature. There are eight state parks less than an hour from campus—a fact that our adventurous students see as a welcome challenge to hike, swim, climb, fish and paddle. Explore areas rich with geological and paleontological significance. Gaze up at a night sky unsullied by light pollution. Borrow a kayak from Bucknell's rental center and travel down the Susquehanna River.

With so many great options right here in town, you may never want to leave. But if you're craving a weekend getaway, you can get to New York City, Philadelphia, Baltimore, and Washington, D.C., in just three hours.

Plan your visit to campus at bucknell.edu/visit.

ACADEMIC PROGRAMS

At Bucknell, we support our students as they explore their intellectual curiosity, and we empower them to become innovators in whatever field they choose.

It starts in the classroom, where our world-class professors personally guide discovery in small groups. But it doesn't end there.

We are a living-learning community where students explore the ideas and theories they're passionate about. This happens in laboratories, residence hall lounges, the local community and study-abroad programs around the world.

It's why our students graduate ready to make a difference and shape the world they live in.

See more at bucknell.edu/academics.

MAJORS AND DEGREES OFFERED

At Bucknell, you can choose from a much larger selection of majors, minors and courses than other liberal arts colleges and universities.

You can major in English and go to medical school, major in anthropology and become a marketing executive, or major in engineering and become a manager. About 25 percent of our students go one step further and double up on majors. And if you're still deciding, you can apply undeclared—you have until your sophomore year to choose the most appropriate path for you.

That's the beauty of our liberal arts mission and personalized education—you will have the freedom to pursue your interests while staying on target with your future plans.

Discover your path at bucknell.edu/majors.

TUITION, ROOM, BOARD, FEES

For the 2019–20 academic year, tuition and fees are set at:

Tuition: $57,882
Meal plan: $5,530
Room: $8,644
Activity fee: $314
Total comprehensive fee: $72,370

FINANCIAL AID

More than half of our students receive financial assistance. We're here to help you understand all of your options and guide you through the process of applying for grants, loans and work-study opportunities. Our goal is to assist all students and their parents to try and find reasonable ways to pay the costs associated with joining their peers at an exceptional university.

Together we can explore all available aid options at Bucknell and help you on your way to becoming part of the Bucknell family.

- The average total need-based financial aid package for a student in the Class of 2023 is $39,000, including need-based grants and scholarships, loans and work-study.
- About 52 percent of students receive financial aid from Bucknell, and 60 percent receive financial aid of some form.
- The average federal student loan indebtedness upon graduation for those who borrowed was $21,100 (Class of 2019)

Scholarships:

Bucknell University's merit awarding process is comprehensive, holistic and extremely competitive. We're looking for students who have extraordinary academic records and show promise that their talents will enrich our highly personal, transformative learning environment. Explore scholarship opportunities at bucknell.edu/TuitionAndAid

STUDENT ORGANIZATIONS AND ACTIVITIES

Bucknell's undergraduate student body includes 3,600 students from most states and 67 countries. You'll join active students whose voices are valued in the classroom, lab and creative spaces, in student government and throughout the University community.

While here, you can expect something extraordinary from your extracurriculars.

With more than 200 student clubs, you'll find your place. Plunge into your interests with people who share your passion. Explore a new endeavor to reveal a talent you didn't know you had. Or embrace your pioneering spirit and get funding to start your own group.

And it doesn't end there. You'll discover something new on campus every day of the week. Volunteer at the community garden, watch some stand-up comedy, learn yoga. We offer the variety of opportunities found at a larger university but in a personalized setting.

That means that even when you're cheering for one of our 27 Division I sports teams, you're not just a face in the crowd.

See what you can do at bucknell.edu/life-bucknell.

ADMISSIONS PROCESS

An application to Bucknell is an application to a new kind of education—one where learning isn't limited to a classroom and investigation is encouraged. Where your classmates are more than people in a classroom—they are your companions on a quest to discover new truths and invent new possibilities.

At Bucknell University, you can become the most brilliant, most adventurous, most authentic you.

To apply to Bucknell University, choose either the Common Application or the Coalition Application. We encourage each applicant to express their unique personality and diverse array of life experiences through the included essays. We don't require SAT or ACT scores, though you're welcome to submit them if you choose.

Deadlines

- Regular Decision applications should be filed by Jan. 15 for notification by April 1.
- Early Decision candidates may apply for Early Decision I consideration by Nov. 15 or Early Decision II consideration by Jan. 15.
- Transfer student information is available at bucknell.edu/transfer. Applications for transfer students should be submitted by Nov. 1 for spring enrollment and March 15 for fall enrollment.

For detailed information about admissions at Bucknell and to sign up for our mailing list, go to bucknell.edu/admissions.

We also invite you to visit our beautiful campus to learn more about our academic and co-curricular opportunities, meet faculty and students, and see for yourself how you will discover your path to success.

View visit options at bucknell.edu/visit

Take a virtual tour at bucknell.edu/virtualtour

Get in touch with us at admissions@bucknell.edu

CENTRAL CONNECTICUT STATE UNIVERSITY

AT A GLANCE

With the lowest tuition and fees among the comprehensive public universities in the state, Central Connecticut State University is considered the best value.

Dedicated to learning in the liberal arts and sciences, the University comprises five schools: Carol Ammon College of Liberal Arts & Social Sciences; and the schools of Business; Education & Professional Studies; Engineering, Science & Technology; and Graduate Studies. CCSU offers full-and part-time undergraduate programs in more than 100 areas of study.

LOCATION AND ENVIRONMENT

CCSU is located in suburban New Britain, in the center of Connecticut. It's approximately two hours from Boston or New York. The campus has been extensively renovated and continues to expand and upgrade academic and student facilities. The University is surrounded by a pleasant, residential neighborhood, with shopping and dining facilities nearby.

CAMPUS FACILITIES AND EQUIPMENT

With new and renovated buildings CCSU's campus offers the classic collegiate style of architecture. Academic buildings are equipped with "smart classrooms" and seminar rooms. The Student Center provides lounges, dining services, conference and game rooms, information services, and a range of other support services. Three theatres provide space for plays, concerts, and guest lectures. The S.T. Chen Art Gallery hosts shows by students, faculty, and visiting artists. The Student Technology Center features 250 computers plus printers and scanners for student use. Campus-based TV and radio stations provide exciting entertainment as well as opportunities to learn about the professions. The Elihu Burritt Library provides access to over 2 million books through an online catalog, a wide array of electronic databases and online resources, and special collections ranging from the unparalleled collection of Polish American materials to the Equity Archive. The University also offers many athletic facilities, including an Olympic-sized swimming pool, modern exercise equipment, a state-of-the-art fitness center, a weight-training room, and an athletic training center. Approximately 26 percent of the students live on campus in eight residence halls.

OFF-CAMPUS OPPORTUNITIES

The School of Education has many connections to area schools, including several Professional Development Schools, which provide CCSU students opportunities to perfect their teaching skills in a full range of elementary and secondary classrooms.

The School of Engineering, Science & Technology offers a wide array of internship opportunities in area engineering, manufacturing, and technology businesses.

The Center for International Education, nationally recognized for the quality of its Study Abroad programs, offers students a rich variety of study-abroad opportunities at more than 40 locations throughout the world and provides academic and cultural programs that promote a better understanding of peoples and cultures.

The University and the New Britain Museum of American Art (an internationally acclaimed museum) have a partnership allowing students and faculty to visit the museum for free.

ACADEMIC PROGRAMS

CCSU also offers a number of interdisciplinary programs as well as independently designed majors. The Honors Program, a challenging interdisciplinary program of study for academically qualified students, offers half and full-tuition merit scholarships and a variety of other benefits and resources, including a new Honors Lab.

MAJORS AND DEGREES OFFERED

CCSU is accredited by the New England Association of Schools and Colleges (NEASC). The University operates on a two-semester calendar and offers four summer sessions plus one winter session.

Undergraduate programs include: Accounting; Anthropology; Art (Art History); Biochemistry; Biology (Ecology; Biodiversity; Evolutionary; Environmental Science; General); Biomolecular Sciences; Chemistry; Civil Engineering; Civil Engineering Technology; Communication (Media Studies; Strategic Communications); Computer Engineering Technology; Computer Science; Construction Management; Criminology; Dance Education; Design (Graphic/Information); Digital Printing Graphics Technology; Early Childhood Studies & Infant/Toddler Mental Health; Earth Sciences; Economics (General; Operations Research); Education (Elementary; K-12; Secondary; Special Education); Electronics Technology; Engineering & Technology Education; Engineering Technology; English; Entrepreneurship; Exercise Science; Finance; French; Geography (Environmental; General Regional; Planning; Geographic Information Science; Tourism); German; History; Hospitality & Tourism; Industrial Technology (Electro-Mechanical Technology; Environmental & Occupational Safety; Graphics Technology; Manufacturing; Networking Technology; Technology Management); Interdisciplinary Science (Environmental Interpretation; Physical Sciences); International Business; International Studies; Italian; Journalism; Management (Entrepreneurship; Human Resource); Management Information Systems; Manufacturing Engineering Technology; Marketing; Mathematics (Actuarial; Statistics); Mechanical Engineering; Mechanical Engineering Technology; Media Studies; Music; Nursing (BSN & RN to BSN); Philosophy; Physical Education (Exercise Science & Health Promotion); Physics; Political Science (General; Public Administration); Psychology; Robotics & Mechatronics; Social Sciences; Social Work; Sociology; Spanish; Special Studies; Theatre.

Degrees: BA, BFA (Theatre); BS; BSN; BS-RN, Teacher Certification (elementary; secondary; K–12)

TUITION, ROOM, BOARD, FEES

CT Resident

Tuition & fees $11,068
Housing (double occupancy) $7,174
Food (cost varies per meal plan) $5,354
Total $23,596

Out-of-State Resident

Tuition & fees $24,028
Housing (double occupancy) $7,174
Food (cost varies per meal plan) $5,354
Total $36,556

Annual costs for books, travel and personal expenses vary (approx. $2,500).

FINANCIAL AID

Approximately 85% of CCSU's first-time, full-time students receive some form of financial aid. CCSU's office of financial aid works with students to help them meet educational expenses from their first year until graduation. To apply for financial aid students must complete the FAFSA form. For more information, call 860.832.2200, e-mail finaid@ccsu.edu, or visit the website at www.ccsu.edu/finaid.

STUDENT ORGANIZATIONS AND ACTIVITIES

CCSU serves approximately 11,150 students, including 9,050 undergraduate and 2,100 graduate students. Our distinguished alumni include over 70,000 successful men and women, including the first Latina state supreme court justice, CEOs in a wide range of industries and corporations, leading academics at national universities, award-winning educators and educational leaders, trainers and coaches at high schools and colleges as well as top NFL and MLB teams, journalists, novelists, and artists. Each and all demonstrate that success begins with a degree from CCSU.

There are more than 100 student clubs and organizations at CCSU. They cover a broad range of interests including academic—such as the Anthropology or the Investment clubs; athletics—such as the crew or flying clubs; cultural—such as the art club and the jazz band; ethnic—such as the Black Student Union, Latin American Students Organization, and the Muslim Student Association; religious—such as Hillel and the Newman Club; and honors organizations such as Delta Mu Delta, Lambda Delta, and Kappa Delta Pi. On-campus entertainment is also wide and varied, including, most recently, "Devils Den@ 10"—student-run entertainment on Thursday evenings.

ADMISSIONS PROCESS

CCSU is a learning community of students with a broad range of abilities, interests, and backgrounds. We value excellence and achievement in academic scholarship, community involvement, and extracurricular activities. Our Admissions Process evaluates the readiness of applicants to succeed based on past demonstrations of academic and personal successes.

CCSU has a "rolling" admissions policy, not a set admissions deadline, which gives students greater flexibility in applying. The University urges prospective students to apply as early as possible in their senior year. The University begins accepting students for the fall semester in mid-October and will continue to review applications until the class is filled.

First-year applicants are considered on the basis of performance in college preparatory classes, rank in class, SAT or ACT test scores, recommendations, and community and extracurricular involvement and leadership. A personal essay is required. For some applicants an interview with a representative of the Office of Recruitment & Admissions may be necessary. If the applicant ranks in the top 20% of his/her class, is an A-B student, and has SAT scores of 1100 or higher, the student should consider CCSU's Honors Program; call 860-832-2938 for details. CCSU accepts most Advanced Placement (AP) courses for college credit, provided the minimum CCSU required score is achieved. Check with Admissions for the required scores.

Admission criteria include graduation from a regionally accredited secondary school. High school work should include college preparatory courses in: English (four years); Mathematics (covering algebra I, geometry, and algebra II); Science (two years including one-year lab science); Social sciences (two to three years including U.S. history). Coursework in foreign language is recommended (at least three consecutive years of the same foreign language up through the third level will satisfy the foreign language proficiency required of all CCSU-enrolled students). Students whose preparation does not follow this pattern may still qualify for admission if, in the judgment of the Director of Recruitment and Admissions, there is strong evidence that they have the potential to complete a degree program or if they meet other established criteria as authorized by the University President under authority delegated by the Board of Regents of the Connecticut State College & University System. Applicants who are not graduates of a secondary school should submit their secondary school transcript up to the time of withdrawal and a copy of their high school equivalency diploma and scores.

The most important thing for the applicant to remember is to provide as much information as possible achievements, awards, and examples of leadership when applying.

HOW TO APPLY

Students are encouraged to apply online at www.ccsu.edu/apply. For paper applications, please provide the Office of Recruitment & Admissions with 1) completed application for undergraduate admission 2) official high school transcripts, SAT or ACT test scores, recommendations, and essay and 3) a non-refundable application fee of $50. All correspondence should be sent to the Office of Recruitment and Admissions, CCSU, P.O. Box 4010, 1615 Stanley Street, New Britain, CT 06050-4010. Tours and information sessions may be arranged by calling 860.832.2289 or via e-mail at: admissions@ccsu.edu.

CHRISTOPHER NEWPORT UNIVERSITY

AT A GLANCE

At Christopher Newport University we care about minds and hearts. We want our students to choose to lead lives of meaning and consequence and purpose. We call that a life of significance.

At this affordable, public university in Virginia, students study the liberal arts and sciences. Christopher Newport is ranked among the nation's top universities for the value it offers, for its science facilities, for its four-year graduation rate, and for the quality of its business school.

Our classes are small and rigorous, and our professors know their students by name. We offer a nationally respected President's Leadership Program. We celebrate our speaking tradition and honor code. We open doors for each other. Our teams are among the winningest in the nation. Our performing and visual arts facilities are world class. Our campus is stunningly beautiful, close to beaches and big cities and endless opportunities for internships and careers.

Because our students care so much about the world around them, they perform thousands of hours of meaningful community service. Our students lead, serve, engage and get ready to set the world on fire.

LOCATION AND ENVIRONMENT

Located in Southeastern Virginia, Christopher Newport is in the heart of one of the most historic—and beautiful—areas of the United States, convenient to Williamsburg, Busch Gardens, Chesapeake Bay and Virginia Beach. Three airports are close by and so is an Amtrak station. The university is nestled in a suburban area and a short walk to the James River, hiking trails, and history and art museums.

CAMPUS FACILITIES AND EQUIPMENT

Matching Christopher Newport's strong academic reputation is the beauty of campus—a place where students learn in classrooms and labs equipped with the latest technology, and play out their dreams on the stages of the Ferguson Center for the Arts. It was designed by the firm of acclaimed architect I.M. Pei. Since its opening in 2005, more than two million people have attended performances by world-renowned entertainers. An adjoining fine arts center is under construction.

The Paul and Rosemary Trible Library provides an unbeatable atmosphere for research, learning and scholarly interaction. Einstein's Café on the ground floor is a hub of campus activity.

Christopher Newport has nationally acclaimed athletic facilities and recently opened a new lacrosse and field hockey stadium. Nearly 4,000 students live in award-winning residence halls and apartment suites with all the amenities and comforts of home. Every residential room has high-speed internet, satellite cable TV and electronic room access. All rooms are equipped with a microwave and mini-refrigerator or have kitchen access. Residents of on-campus apartments have their own bathroom and an in-unit washer and dryer.

OFF-CAMPUS OPPORTUNITIES

Christopher Newport students participate in internships in Newport News, Norfolk and nearby communities, home to NASA, Langley Air Force Base, Canon, Sentara Health Care and numerous other nonprofit, government and private sector employers. Students also are offered research opportunities at Jefferson Lab, the U.S. Department of Energy Office of Science national laboratory, where scientists utilize the lab's unique particle accelerator to probe the most basic building blocks of matter

ACADEMIC PROGRAMS

Learning Communities

All freshmen are placed into a Learning Community based on their academic interests, which facilitates a successful transition from high school to college. Living together, sharing multiple classes with a small group of students and collaborating with faculty enable learning beyond the classroom while providing extra support.

President's Leadership Program

Make an impact through the President's Leadership Program (PLP). Through challenging courses, public service, foreign study and other targeted opportunities, PLP empowers students to become caring, knowledgeable and effective leaders for America and the world. The President's Leadership Program offers priority registration, annual scholarships and study abroad awards.

Honors Program

This unique program offers students more freedom to customize their academic experience for their personal and professional aspirations. The Honors Program allows more time for interdisciplinary seminar-style courses and challenges students by means of study abroad, independent research, internships, jobs and volunteer experience relevant to their passions. Each student receives an annual residential scholarship (including a study abroad stipend), as well as other exclusive benefits.

Undergraduate Research and Creative Activity

Christopher Newport undergraduates engage in cutting-edge research and creative activities. In all fields of study, students collaborate with faculty mentors on key research, make conference presentations, and publish books and scholarly journal articles with faculty. Each spring the Paideia conference showcases outstanding student research, and the Summer Scholars Program offers paid research assistantships.

Pre-Law Program

Interested in pursuing a career in law? The nation's top law schools seek applicants who have received a well-rounded undergraduate education—one like the liberal arts and sciences curriculum Christopher Newport offers. Many of our pre-law students pursue a philosophy of law minor or an American studies major with a constitutional studies concentration. Regardless of your undergraduate field of study, our Pre-Law Program is designed to help you gain admission to one of the nation's top law schools.

Pre-Med and Pre-Health Program

Medical schools and other graduate programs seek applicants with a well-rounded undergraduate education. The Pre-Med and Pre-Health Program at Christopher Newport assists students pursuing any academic major to prepare for postgraduate study. In addition to the necessary prerequisite coursework, we offer several resources to help you gain admission to your professional school of choice—from academic and career advising to mentoring, clinical internships, workshops and seminars.

Study Abroad

We encourage you to study abroad, either accompanied by Christopher Newport faculty or independently. Learn about different cultures while falling in love with America. You may choose to study for an entire semester, a year or more briefly between academic terms. These rich cultural experiences are as unique as the destinations. With scholarship opportunities available, the world is your classroom! Christopher Newport students have recently spent semesters or full academic years in Australia, Costa Rica, England, France, Germany, Greece, India, Italy, Japan, Mexico, Russia, Scotland, Spain and many other locales.

Bachelor's to Master's Five-Year Programs

Students can obtain a bachelor's and master's degree in the following five-year programs:

- Master of Arts in Teaching
- Master of Science in Applied Physics and Computer Science
- Master of Science in Environmental Science

Center for Academic Success

Throughout the CNU experience, the Center for Academic Success offers tutoring, workshops, seminars and one-on-one assistance to help students improve their academic performance with effective study strategies. Peer writing consultants available in the Writing Center offer specialized help with all stages of the writing process.

Center for Career Planning

The Center for Career Planning directly assists students with academic major exploration, landing a first job or gaining admission to a top graduate school. Workshops, seminars, job fairs, on-campus interviews and career counseling—a full range of services—are available to students and alumni.

Service

Christopher Newport students make a positive difference in the life of our campus, community and world. We offer countless opportunities—from service-learning initiatives and projects like Habitat for Humanity to the philanthropic work of our Greek organizations and student-athletes, among others. Through a partnership with the prestigious Bonner Foundation, Christopher Newport joins a national network of more than 75 colleges and universities who support four-year, service scholarships.

MAJORS AND DEGREES OFFERED

We offer more than 90 areas of study in the liberal arts and sciences, providing a breadth and depth of knowledge that will prepare you to take advantage of any opportunity that presents itself in today's global marketplace. Through Christopher Newport's rigorous curriculum, you will learn to think critically and communicate effectively while developing the tools and skills that will serve you for a lifetime.

Areas of Study

Accounting
African-American Studies
American Studies
- Constitutional Studies
- Humanities
- Social Science

Anthropology
Applied Physics
Asian Studies
Biochemistry
Biology
Biology—Cellular, Molecular and Physiological
Biology—Integrative
Biology—Organismal and Environmental
Chemistry
Childhood Studies
Civic Engagement and Social Justice
Classical Studies
- Classical Languages
- Classical Studies

Communication Studies
Computer Engineering
Computer Science
Cybersecurity
Dance
Digital Humanities
Discrete Mathematics
Economics
- Mathematical Economics

Electrical Engineering
English
- Literature
- Writing

Environmental Studies
Film Studies
Finance
Fine Arts
- Art History
- Studio Art

French
German
Graphic Design
Greek Studies
History
Human Rights and Conflict Resolution
Information Science
Interdisciplinary Studies
International Culture and Business
Judeo-Christian Studies
Latin
Latin American Studies
Leadership Studies

Linguistics
Management
Marketing
Mathematics
Mathematics—Computational and Applied
- Biology and Life Sciences
- Economics
- Physics, Dynamics and Engineering

Medieval and Renaissance Studies
Middle East and North Africa Studies
Military Science (ROTC)
Museum Studies
Music
- Composition
- Creative Studies
- Music Studies

Performance
Pre-Certification Choral
- Pre-Certification Instrumental

Neuroscience
Philosophy
- Pre-Seminary Studies
- Studies in Religion

Philosophy and Religion
Philosophy of Law
Photography and Video Art
Political Science
Psychology
Social Work
Sociology
- Anthropology
- Criminology

Spanish
Theater
- Acting
- Arts Administration
- Design/Technical Theater
- Directing/Dramatic Literature
- Music Theater/Dance
- Theater Studies

U.S. National Security Studies
Women's and Gender Studies
Advising Tracks
Biotechnology and Management
Pre-Health
Pre-Law
Pre-Med

Master's Degrees

Applied Physics and Computer Science
Environmental Science
Financial Analysis
Teaching (MAT)

TUITION, ROOM, BOARD, FEES

Christopher Newport offers exceptional academics, stunning facilities and a vibrant campus life. Yet we recognize paying for college can be a challenge. That's why we distribute nearly $50 million in aid to students each year. Most assistance comes in the form of federal and state grants, scholarships to reward merit and help students with financial need, educational loans, and college work-study programs.

2019–20 Costs per Year

In-State Tuition and Fees: $14,924
In-State Room and Board: $11,760
Total: $26,684

Out-of-State Tuition and Fees: $27,790
Out-of-State Room and Board: $11,760
Total: $39,550

FINANCIAL AID

Important New FAFSA Deadline:

To apply for financial aid or scholarships, submit your FAFSA by the December 15 preferred filing deadline or the March 1 priority filing deadline.

STUDENT ORGANIZATIONS AND ACTIVITIES

Student Clubs

With more than 200 student clubs and organizations, Christopher Newport offers activities in a wide range of interests.

Athletics

One of the nation's most successful NCAA Division III programs

24 Varsity Teams
700+ All-Americans
80 Individual and team championships
Top winning percentage nearly every year among all Virginia schools

ADMISSIONS PROCESS

We encourage students to apply to Christopher Newport as early as possible due to our selective admission standards. We anticipate receiving 8,000 applications for only 1,200 spaces in the fall freshman class. Students applying for Early Decision or Early Action will receive priority consideration for admission as well as academic scholarships.

Early Decision

Deadline to Apply: November 15
Notification Date: December 15

Early Action

Deadline to Apply: December 1
Notification Date: January 15

Regular Decision

Deadline to Apply: February 1
Notification Date: March 15

We accept applications from either The Common Application or Coalition for College. Apply online at freshman.cnu.edu.

Application Review

When reviewing applications we consider each student's academic grades and curriculum, with special attention given to honors, Advanced Placement, International Baccalaureate or dual-enrollment courses. We also look for students who demonstrate leadership ability, a commitment to service and community involvement, exemplary talents, and diverse experiences. As part of the application review, Christopher Newport requires a personal statement or essay of no fewer than 250 words to learn more about you, your goals and ideas.

Admission Interviews

Any high school senior planning to apply is strongly encouraged to interview at Christopher Newport. This personal interaction is an important part of the application process. It is a great way to enhance your admission application and receive a personalized introduction to Christopher Newport. We want to meet you one-on-one to learn about you—your qualities, experiences and goals we can't discern from your test scores or GPA. An interview is required for Honors and PLP applicants.

THE CLEVELAND INSTITUTE OF ART

AT A GLANCE

Cleveland Institute of Art is one of the nation's leading accredited independent colleges of art and design. Offering 15 majors in fine art, craft, design and digital arts, the college has been an educational cornerstone in Ohio since 1882, producing graduates who are leaders in their disciplines as studio artists, designers, photographers, contemporary craftspersons, entrepreneurs, and educators.

LOCATION AND ENVIRONMENT

CIA is located in Cleveland's University Circle, home of the world-renowned Cleveland Museum of Art, Severance Hall, home of the Cleveland Orchestra, as well as spaces for contemporary art, dance, and performance. One of the most culturally dense square miles anywhere in the United States, University Circle was named by *Forbes Magazine* as one of the most beautiful communities in the country. University Circle is also home to Case Western Reserve University and the Cleveland Institute of Music, with a combined enrollment of 11,000 students, offering CIA students the experience of a traditional college campus, and the personal attention of a boutique college.

CAMPUS FACILITIES AND EQUIPMENT

Cleveland Institute of Art's contemporary campus provides students with spaces designed specifically for studying, living, and exhibiting art and design. Its four-story atrium floods the building with natural light, perfect for creating and studying. Our fabrication studios and computer labs have the latest in traditional and new technologies to allow students to execute what they imagine. Students in their majors receive studio spaces that model what life after college will be like, from skylit factory spaces for painters to collaborative design studios.

CIA's campus is home to the Reinberger Gallery, presenting exhibitions of contemporary artists from across the country; the Peter B. Lewis Theater, home of CIA's nationally acclaimed Cinematheque film program; the Jessica R. Gund Memorial Library, which has collections specifically developed for the visual artist and designer; the Stone Flower Cafe; and CIA's Fabrication Studios, offering tools and training in wood, plastic, metal, stone, clay and digital print production.

First and second-year students live on campus in CIA-owned housing. First-year students live in our Uptown Residence Hall, which opened in 2014. Designed in consultation with students, these two-bedroom suites house two students per bedroom, each with their own bath. Bedrooms are connected by a common work area and kitchenette. Second-year students reside in our new upperclass residence hall, featuring four-person suites with individual bedrooms. Both residence halls offer workout spaces, on-site printing, and free laundry.

OFF-CAMPUS OPPORTUNITIES

Cleveland's many diverse neighborhoods are just minutes from our campus via public transportation, where you can sample the city's best restaurants, take in a concert or comedy show, explore its galleries, take art walks, and visit Cleveland's beaches and lush parks. If you're a sports fan, plan on cheering on the Cleveland Indians, Cavaliers, or Browns at their downtown venues.

ACADEMIC PROGRAMS

At CIA, we've made an academic commitment to prepare students for a creative career by engaging them in community-based learning, real-world projects, and social practices. Through a selection of field-based courses, our students graduate with real-world experience working on real-world projects. From our early relationships with the auto industry, to relationships today with NASA, students across all of our disciplines are learning the skills necessary to be successful in the 21st century. Whether you're a performance artist or a product designer, you'll learn to use your creativity to collaborate, communicate your ideas, and solve problems to make work that makes a difference in the world.

MAJORS AND DEGREES OFFERED

Cleveland Institute of Art offers 17 programs in art, design, craft, and digital media. After a foundation year developing strong skills in drawing, design and problem-solving, you'll enter your major spending three intense years building skills and mastering techniques. CIA faculty will encourage you to develop a wider perspective by experimenting with media outside your major through interdisciplinary study.

TUITION, ROOM, BOARD, FEES

Estimated 2019–20 full-time tuition is US$41,490. Estimated fees are $2,895. Estimated housing for incoming first-year students is $8,940 for our apartment-style residence halls, and $2,650 for meal plan.

FINANCIAL AID

Cleveland Institute of Art offers merit and need-based financial aid, as well as federal and state financial aid. 95% of students enrolled in 2019–20 received scholarships. Average financial aid package for 2017–18 was $39,0028

CIA's financial aid officers work with students to craft a personalized financial aid package that combines merit and need-based scholarships, federal loans and grants, scholarships, loans, and work study programs.

STUDENT ORGANIZATIONS AND ACTIVITIES

With approximately 650 students from around the country and the world, CIA offers a personal educational experience with the benefits of a larger institution. Surrounded by creative-minded friends and mentors, CIA students find inspiration inside and outside of the studio. Students also experience a community full of cultural energy, ethnic neighborhoods, and a vibrant downtown, all accessible by public transportation.

When not in the studio, CIA students can enjoy organized activities, annual campus traditions, and various student groups that specialize in topics from academics to religion. Some favorite traditions include late-night breakfasts during finals, the wildly creative Halloween costume party, and the year-end school-wide picnic. Numerous clubs, based on disciplines (printmaking, game design) to interests (LGBTQ, Christian fellowship) offer students opportunities to share experiences, look new skills, and meet leaders in their communities.

ADMISSIONS PROCESS

To be considered for admission, you must follow the application procedures and criteria below.

1. Complete the application online at cia.edu/apply

2. Submit the $40 application fee (fee is waived if you apply online). Make checks payable to the Cleveland Institute of Art.

3. Arrange to have your high school transcripts sent to the Office of Admissions. If you have successfully completed 24 college credits and attended a regionally accredited college or university full time for a year or more, have your college transcripts sent instead.

4. Have one letter of recommendation completed on your behalf. We suggest this be from an art teacher. We also will accept this letter from a counselor or someone who understands your desire to pursue an arts education.

5. Optional: Request SAT or ACT test results be sent to CIA. Our school numbers are: SAT: 1152 and ACT: 3243. International students whose first language is not English must submit the TOEFL with a minimum score of 60 IBT (Internet-based test). We also accept a band score of at least 6.0 on the IELTS or completion of Level 112 of ESL coursework.

6. Submit your portfolio of artwork. All work can be submitted via our online application (go.cia.edu). Your portfolio should consist of no fewer than 12 and no more than 20 pieces of work. Please carefully follow all our portfolio guidelines (https://www.cia.edu/admissions/apply/submitting-your-portfolio).

Application materials should be submitted online. Our mailing address, if paper-based materials need to be forwarded is: Cleveland Institute of Art, Office of Admissions, 11610 Euclid Avenue, Cleveland OH 44106.

Applications can be submitted at any time before the first day of classes and will be considered as long as space is available. However, candidates are encouraged to follow application deadlines to ensure eligibility for merit scholarships and institutional financial aid. Dates and deadlines can be viewed online (https://www.cia.edu/admissions/apply/dates—deadlines).

Applications are welcome from all qualified students. The admissions committee bases its decisions on a careful review of all credentials submitted by the applicant. Acceptance decisions are made without regard to race, color, sex, sexual orientation, gender expression, marital status, age, ethnic or national origin, religion, creed, veteran status, or physical or mental disability in accordance with federal, state, and local laws.

Visit cia.edu/admissions for more info.

COLLEGE OF CHARLESTON

AT A GLANCE

A superior public university with personality to spare.

Located in the heart of historic Charleston, South Carolina, the College of Charleston is a nationally recognized public university. Founded in 1770, the College is among the nation's top universities for quality education, student life and affordability. Its beautiful and historic campus, combined with contemporary facilities, cutting-edge programs and accessible faculty attracts students from across the U.S. and around the world.

Nearly 10,000 undergraduates and approximately 1,000 graduate students at the College enjoy a small-college feel blended with the advantages and diversity of a mid-sized, urban university. Students work with exceptional professors who love to teach, who are focused on student growth and who help them succeed. And the city of Charleston—world-renowned for its history, architecture, culture and coastal environment—serves as a living and learning laboratory for experiences in business, science, technology, teaching, the humanities, languages and the arts.

LOCATION AND ENVIRONMENT

Trying to describe why Charleston's vibe resonates is like trying to explain why your favorite song rocks. It just does. Downtown Charleston is 20 minutes from some of the best beaches in the Southeast and our year-round temperate weather makes the Charleston area ideal for surfing, kayaking, climbing, hiking and camping.

It seems like there's always something going on in Charleston. The annual Spoleto Festival USA is the premier arts festival in the country. The Cooper River Bridge Run has been called the best 10K race in the world. And every March, top chefs and fashion designers flock to the Lowcountry for the Charleston Wine + Food Festival and Charleston Fashion Week.

The College of Charleston campus is smack dab in the middle of one of the most lovingly preserved historic districts in America (look both ways for horse-drawn carriages). It's like going to school in a postcard. The College of Charleston was chosen as America's Most Beautiful College Campus by *Travel + Leisure Magazine*.

The College of Charleston is inseparable from the city of Charleston, and you'll feel like a local no matter where you're from. Charleston is the perfect sized city for the perfect sized college. It's big enough to support a vibrant cultural life—huge concerts and small clubs, dance troupes and opera, historic sites and professional sports—and small enough for students to feel right at home from their very first day

CAMPUS FACILITIES AND EQUIPMENT

The Marlene and Nathan Addlestone Library is the region's top research library. This modern facility has a holding capacity of one million volumes, seats 1,400 people and has 300+ computers.

The library is also the prime study spot on campus. A huge draw is **Rivers Green,** a large, inviting lawn and patio area behind the library that's equipped with tables, chairs and high-speed WiFi. Another "perk" is Starbucks, Addlestone's tasty refueling station for marathon study sessions.

TD Arena, a 5,000-seat, state-of-the-art athletic facility that serves as home to the Cougars men's and women's basketball and women's volleyball teams.

Patriots Point, a 35-acre athletic complex, home to the Cougar soccer, softball and baseball programs.

Avery Research Center for African American History and Culture, Part museum, part research facility, the center plays a central role in Charleston's black community through research opportunities and outreach programs.

The **Center for Entrepreneurship** directs its resources and energies to providing experiential activities that assist students in developing an entrepreneurial mindset. It helps connect students to the wider entrepreneurial ecosystem encapsulating guest speakers, mentors, judges, etc. This focus ties directly into the College's strategic plan to provide enhanced "opportunities for experiential learning" and "contribute to the well-being of the region."

Environmental Campus on the Stono River is a majestic 881-acre property along the Stono River and the Intercoastal Waterway. The myriad ecosystems include pine forests, wetlands, savannahs, tidal marshes, as well as brackish, saltwater and fresh-water ponds. College of Charleston students and faculty of multiple disciplines—from marine biology to forest management and historic preservation—utilize this vibrant living laboratory. This property enables the College of Charleston to educate its students in an unparalleled natural setting; inspire collaboration across campus, industry and governmental agencies; and prepare students and faculty to be leaders in today's environmentally volatile, global society.

Established in 1955, **Grice Marine Laboratory** is a core facility in support of the undergraduate and the graduate degree programs in marine and environmental sciences at the College of Charleston. The lab supports research in marine sciences conducted by faculty members and students.

Part of the School of the Arts at the College of Charleston, the **Halsey Institute of Contemporary Art** is the public face of artistic life at the College. In addition to exhibiting some of the finest contemporary art in the Southeast, HICA sponsors lectures, film series and publications, and serves as an inspiring living laboratory for undergraduate art students.

Harbor Walk, this 45,000-square-foot contemporary complex consists of classrooms, faculty offices and laboratories. Home to the Department of Computer Science and the Computer Science Student Innovation Center, this facility is immediately adjacent to Charleston Harbor.

The Sustainability Literacy Institute (SLI) is the physical, pedagogical, virtual and institutional hub for sustainability literacy efforts at the College. The purpose of SLI is to foster positive social, economic and environmental change by way of a sustainably literate campus community.

OFF-CAMPUS OPPORTUNITIES

Business is booming in Charleston with an explosion of technology startups, a multi-billion-dollar tourism industry and a thriving biomedical community.

The Port of Charleston is a vibrant economic engine, offering a gateway to more than 150 countries and countless internship opportunities.

The city offers endless opportunity for College of Charleston students:

- Hospitality and tourism majors are right in the middle of the number one travel destination in the U.S. (according to Travel + Leisure).
- Marine biology majors study at the Ft. Johnson Marine Science Center, a world-class research facility surrounded by a variety of marine ecosystems on nearby James Island.
- Arts management majors are immersed in a vibrant arts community.
- Computer Science majors work alongside technology business leaders at our Harbor Walk facility

Seventy-four percent of incoming students choose the College of Charleston because of the rich diversity and depth of its study abroad programs. With over 85 **study abroad programs** to choose from, we encourage students to get out and explore the world. We offer programs led by our own faculty to a broad swath of places. You could study global environmental changes in Panama, volcanoes and glaciers in Iceland or culture and art in Costa Rica. Whether for a summer, a semester or a full year, there are so many opportunities to see and explore, and gain a global perspective.

ACADEMIC PROGRAMS

A College of Charleston education is consistently excellent and constantly evolving. We're proud to offer nearly 140 majors and minors, which empower our talented students to explore every inch of the expanding intellectual universe.

The strength of a College of Charleston education is in its deeply rooted liberal arts and sciences tradition. Our goal is to prepare our students to be ethical, open-minded leaders and multidisciplinary problem solvers.

The College of Charleston is a mid-sized university organized around seven schools:

- School of the Arts
- School of Business
- School of Education, Health, and Human Performance
- School of Humanities and Social Sciences
- School of Languages, Cultures, and World Affairs
- School of Professional Studies
- School of Sciences and Mathematics

We also invite you to learn more about our distinctive Honors College, which expands on partnerships between faculty and student by creating a vibrant and diverse living-learning community.

MAJORS AND DEGREES OFFERED

A College of Charleston education is a personalized education. We offer 60+ majors and nearly 80 minors. You'll have the freedom to mix and match your academic interests to create a unique, intellectually stimulating course of study.

We've given you a head start with our 25 interdisciplinary minors such as Environmental and Sustainability Studies and Crime, Law and Society. These programs draw resources from several different schools and departments. We also offer innovative degree programs like data science, the first undergraduate degree program of its kind in the nation.

No matter which major or minor you choose, you'll be taught by exceptional professors whose top priority is your success.

TUITION, ROOM, BOARD, FEES

Undergraduate tuition* is $12,518 (resident) and $32,848 (non-resident). Tuition includes the fall and spring semesters. Average tech and library fees are $425.

Room and board costs include expenses for housing and food. For on-campus and off-campus students the weighted average room and board cost is $11,815, which includes $8,200 for room (housing) and $3,615 for board (food). For students that indicated on the FAFSA living with parents, there is no room allowance, just the surveyed average off-campus board amount of $2,853.

*Tuition includes the fall and spring semesters and are estimated based on the student taking at least 12 hours per semester. All figures are subject to change without notice. Please see the Treasurer's office website for a complete list of charges.

FINANCIAL AID

The College of Charleston recognizes that a college education is a major expense in most family budgets. It is important to know that there are many federal, state, local and institutional sources available to help students meet those expenses. The Office of Financial Assistance and Veterans Affairs administers scholarships, grants, loans, work study and Veterans benefits. Please explore our website for information about those programs.

STUDENT ORGANIZATIONS AND ACTIVITIES

Based upon Fall 2017 enrollment:

- Undergraduate students: 9,895
- Graduate students: 968
- Total: 10,863
- Minority students: 19.8%
- Students living on campus: 31%
- Percentage of in-state students: 69.9%*
- Percentage of out-of-state students: 30.1%*
- U.S. states and territories represented: 51
- Foreign countries represented: 61

*Based on tuition residency

College of Charleston students are film buffs, black belts, environmentalists, deejays and volunteers. We've formed more than 200 student clubs and organizations where you can make new friends, learn from others, serve the community, share your talents, and best of all try something totally new.

Our sport clubs are the perfect place to release your inner athlete or a great excuse to hang out at the beach. Or, you can experience hands-on media training with Cistern Yard Media, an organization that controls our campus television studio, radio station, the newsroom and our award-winning literary magazine, *Miscellany*.

Our students are also dedicated to service. Sign up for Habitat for Humanity, Alternative Spring Break or the always-rockin', never-stoppin' Dance Marathon. Members of the 25 national fraternities and sororities on campus spend serious time volunteering with community groups when they're not planning for Greek Week.

College is a great place to meet people with similar backgrounds or hang out with a whole new crowd. Whatever your preference, we have dozens of religious, international and multicultural organizations to serve our diverse student body.

ADMISSIONS PROCESS

The middle 50 percent of freshmen accepted:

- scored between 1100 and 1250 (in-state), and 1120 and 1280 (out-of-state) on the SAT.
- scored between 21 and 27 (in-state), and 24 and 29 (out-of-state) on the ACT.
- had consistent academic achievement in the A/B range.

You can apply on our website or through the **Common App.**

Know that we'll consider many elements of your application file during our holistic review in addition to GPA and SAT/ACT scores including your:

- overall academic preparedness,
- talents and leadership qualifications, and
- extra-curricular activities and other achievements.

THE COLLEGE OF NEW JERSEY

AT A GLANCE

The College of New Jersey (TCNJ) has created a culture of constant questioning. In small classes, students and faculty members collaborate in a rewarding process. They seek to understand fundamental principles, apply key concepts, reveal new problems and pursue lines of inquiry to gain a fluency of thought in their disciplines. This transformative process is at the core of the educational experience at The College.

In order to enhance student development and empowerment, TCNJ's curriculum is built around five key experiences which permeate every major across seven academic schools. Small classes prioritizing discussion and inquiry create a Personalized, Rigorous, and Collaborative Learning Environment where students and faculty work side by side in developing skills and applying concepts. Undergraduate Research, Mentored Internships, and Field Experiences give TCNJ students opportunities to get out of the classroom, develop their professional skill sets, and discover exciting career paths and academic endeavors. Passion for civic responsibility and a commitment to Community-Engaged Learning ensures that TCNJ graduates enter the professional world as top-notch scholars and citizens. Opportunities for Global Engagement found on campus and facilitated through internationally recognized study-abroad programs allow students to expand their internal scope and frame their academic goals and achievements in a truly global context. Finally, academic and extracurricular programs designed to foster Leadership Development help students build confidence and decision-making skills that they will need to solve the problems of tomorrow and build a brighter future.

TCNJ admits a diverse class each year full of ambitious students, eager to build on their educational foundations and dive into new topics. These students will ultimately find a home away from home on campus, and ninety-five percent of first-year students will return for their second year. The most successful admits are prepared to steer their own academic pursuits toward post-graduation goals of graduate school, professional training, or satisfying careers.

Prestigious graduate schools, including the University of Pennsylvania, Georgetown Law School, Maxwell School at Syracuse University, NYU Law School, and Harvard, Yale, and Northwestern Universities, routinely welcome TCNJ alumni into their ranks. TCNJ graduates boast a 64% acceptance rate into Medical School and an 88% acceptance rate into Law School.

Many top corporations recruit TCNJ graduates, providing avenues into rewarding jobs directly after graduation. Other barometers of student success include the 100 percent pass rate of education majors taking the state teacher preparation test and the 94 percent three-year pass rate for nursing students obtaining their license. The numerous learning opportunities at The College prepare students to prosper in any arena after the completion of their undergraduate career.

LOCATION AND ENVIRONMENT

Neoclassical Georgian Colonial architecture, meticulous landscaping and intentional design merge to meet the evolving needs of the TCNJ community. Students enjoy a campus with 289 acres of trees, lakes, and open spaces within the suburban setting of Ewing Township, New Jersey. Two out of three undergraduate students take part in the on-campus residence hall experience. The residence halls vary in configuration from the first-year towers to suites and townhouse arrangements for upper class students. The College ensures that on-campus housing is available to all students in their first two years, with out-of-state students guaranteed to receive housing for all four years of study.

Nearby cities, such as Princeton, Trenton, Philadelphia, and New York, allow for abundant entertainment, employment, and social options. Many courses incorporate field trips to New York City or Washington DC.

Adding an attractive downtown component to an already appealing campus, Campus Town offers students brand new residential opportunities, a pristine Barnes and Noble bookstore and cafe, and a comprehensive fitness center. Retail and dining establishments such as Panera Bread, Yummy Sushi, and Redberry Yogurt have been incorporated as well.

CAMPUS FACILITIES AND EQUIPMENT

Learning, like everything else, is contextual. The surroundings in which students learn and the tools they use influence their experience. Not surprisingly, the College supports its educational aspirations with careful attention to the quality of its facilities. Since the year 2000, more than $250 million in ongoing and new facilities construction has ensured that TCNJ students continue to thrive in an environment that not only meets their academic, athletic, social and living needs, but extends their reach resulting in higher scholarship, better health and fitness, closer community, and greater comfort.

Recent additions to campus include Campus Town, a newly renovated student center, and a state-of-the-art STEM Complex.

OFF-CAMPUS OPPORTUNITIES

TCNJ fosters global engagement with a robust offering of programs that build students' intercultural competence. For education abroad, TCNJ offers an extensive portfolio of short-term and long-term opportunities through study abroad partnerships, faculty-led programs, global student teaching, and internships. TCNJ welcomes global students and provides support services such as personalized language support and academic advising.

Mentored internships, both on and off campus, expose students to career options as they gain professional skills. With the College's location providing easy access to New York, Philadelphia, and other corporate centers, numerous internships are available either for pay or college credit.

Faculty mentors lend their advice and help students locate and procure appropriate opportunities including fellowships, research positions and internships. Students may also use resources at the Career Center to find positions in New York, Philadelphia, or with one of TCNJ's many corporate, government, or research partners located closer to campus.

ACADEMIC PROGRAMS

A Liberal Learning Curriculum ensures that all students are grounded in the values of civic responsibility, intellectual and scholarly growth, and that they receive a well-rounded education in the liberal arts.

TCNJ's innovative curriculum requires students to complete fewer courses, while adding depth to each course pursued. All courses contain significant out-of-class requirements that provide for student and faculty interaction. Small classes enable dialog between students and TCNJ's accomplished teaching faculty. All courses are led by active faculty; no courses are taught by graduate students or Teacher's Assistants. The College shapes its curricula and educational experiences around the concept of Personalized, Collaborative, and Rigorous Intellectual Development.

The required First-Year Seminar, the cornerstone of The College's Liberal Learning program, introduces students to the habits of mind and the methodologies of research; The seminar format of no more than 15 students reinforces the message that students are not passive recipients of knowledge but rather active contributors in their own learning. Liberal Learning requirements are grouped by diversity and community engagement goals that can be self-designed or designated as interdisciplinary concentrations.

Top students may enroll in TCNJ's Honors Program, designed to provide a core curriculum with additional challenges and opportunities for individualized work. Most honors classes take an interdisciplinary approach and encourage collaboration between faculty and students from multiple academic departments and disciplines. Independent study arrangements fall easily within the parameters of the Honors Program, as well.

In addition to full degree programs, students may also choose to complete a minor in most disciplines offered as majors or in other subject areas, such as Classical Studies, Comparative Literature, Religion, Public Administration, and Communication Disorders.

Specialized Programs

TCNJ offers a number of 5-year combined Master of Arts in Teaching degrees with dual certification in Elementary Education, and either Special Education, Urban Education, or Deaf and Hard-of-Hearing Education. 5-year combined Master's programs are also offered in English and Public Health. Additionally, students may enroll in a 7-year BS/MD degree program with the New Jersey Medical School (Newark) or a 7-year BS/OD degree program with the State University of New York College of Optometry. The College offers a Medical Careers Advisory Committee for premed students and a Pre-Law Advisement Committee for students planning a career in law. 64 percent of TCNJ undergraduates seeking Admission into Medical School and 88 percent of TCNJ undergraduates seeking Admission into Law School are accepted into their top choice programs. Both of these figures significantly exceed national averages.

MAJORS AND DEGREES OFFERED

Accountancy
African-American Studies
Art History
Art Education
Biology
Biomedical Engineering
Business Administration specializations in Finance, Interdisciplinary Business, Management, and Marketing
Chemistry
Civil Engineering
Communication Studies
Computer Engineering
Computer Science
Criminology
Early Childhood Education
Economics
Education of the Deaf and Hard of Hearing
Electrical Engineering
Elementary Education
Engineering Science—specializations in Engineering Management, and Policy & Society
English
Health & Exercise Science

History
Interactive Multimedia
International Studies
Integrative-STEM Education (iSTEM Education)
Journalism and Professional Writing
Mathematics
Mechanical Engineering
Music
Nursing
Philosophy
Physics
Political Science
Psychology
Public Health
Self-Designed Major
Sociology
Spanish
Special Education
Speech Pathology and Audiology
Technology Education / Pre-Engineering
Urban Education
Visual Arts—options available in Fine Arts, Graphic Design, and Lens-Based Art
Women's & Gender Studies

TUITION, ROOM, BOARD, FEES

In-state tuition and fees: $16,942
Out-of-state tuition and fees: $28,921
Room and board (all students): $13,964

FINANCIAL AID

Over 50 percent of full-time undergraduates benefit from financial aid, whether from merit-based scholarships, work-study programs, loans, or government/institutional grants. All students seeking financial aid at the state or federal level must submit the Free Application for Federal Student Aid (FAFSA) form or renewal FAFSA to apply. The Title IV FAFSA Code for The College is 002642.

TCNJ also offers institutional need-based scholarships. Institutional need-based aid considerations are made based on information from the FAFSA.

Students may compete for the College's merit scholarships. These awards are offered to those applicants with top SAT/ACT scores and class rankings. Over the last six years, TCNJ has given scholarships totaling more than $30 million.

STUDENT ORGANIZATIONS AND ACTIVITIES

Classroom learning at TCNJ is complemented by an extensive and acclaimed Leadership Development Program. Life outside the classroom is not something students do on the side. It is an extension of the learning experience. At every turn from the first year on, students blur the boundary between living and learning, closing the gap between "scholar" and "citizen."

More than 250 student organizations flourish at The College. Right off the bat, students are encouraged to discover their passion through the various clubs and activities offered. Anyone can find an intramural sports team, Greek organization, cultural club, or academic group to suit their interests. Many students build friendships as well as personal networks and optimize their leisure time participating in these groups. In addition, the College Union Board-administered by TCNJ students-organizes large-scale events including concerts, performances, and comedy shows.

The College's highly successful Division III athletic programs also provide an opportunity to socialize and cheer on fellow classmates. TCNJ fields ten sports for men and ten for women. With more than 40 national titles, The College holds the record for the highest number of championship and runner-up titles since Division III was implemented in 1979. For those looking for something a little less competitive, intramural and club sports, including flag football, volleyball, softball, floor hockey, and basketball, have thriving coed leagues of their own. Intramural and club teams play in state, regional, and national tournaments.

ADMISSIONS PROCESS

The admissions committee at TCNJ accepts a class of motivated, ambitious, and highly talented students. Most successful applicants have taken 16 college-preparatory units in high school, demonstrating mastery of the core academic areas of Science, Math, Language Arts, Social Sciences, and Foreign Languages. They also show impressive class ranks and SAT/ACT scores. Most students admitted fall within the top 20 percent of their graduating class. The committee also considers extracurricular involvement, individual pursuits, and community participation. Standardized test scores are not required for students applying into the Art or Music disciplines.

The College of New Jersey accepts applications via The Common Application and The Coalition Application. The application deadline for Spring enrollment is November 1. The Regular Decision application deadline for Fall enrollment is February 1. There is a $75 application fee. Candidates who apply only to The College of New Jersey under the Early Decision agreement may apply before November 1 and will be notified on or before December 1. Early Decision applicants unable to complete and submit their application prior to November 1 may also choose to apply before January 1 and receive notification on or before February 1. Students applying to the seven-year Accelerated Medical program must apply by November 1. For Fall enrollment, the College requires incoming students to pay an enrollment deposit of $600 no later than May 1.

For more information, students should contact:

The College of New Jersey
P.O. Box 7718
Ewing, New Jersey 08628-0718
United States
Phone: 609-771-2131
Website: https://tcnj.pages.tcnj.edu

DESALES UNIVERSITY

AT A GLANCE

DeSales University is a medium-sized, Catholic liberal arts university for men and women administered by the Oblates of St. Francis de Sales.

Founded in 1964, DeSales University is a Catholic liberal arts university that offers courses in a wide range of disciplines. DeSales provides personal attention, small class size, and a feeling of community. The University uses a holistic approach to help students develop a "sense of self," enabling all students to reach their personal and academic potential. This student-centered philosophy is conveyed by an enthusiastic, accessible faculty.

LOCATION AND ENVIRONMENT

DeSales University's suburban campus is located 15 minutes south of Bethlehem and Allentown, Pa., and only 1 hour from Philadelphia, 90 minutes from Scranton and Wilkes-Barre, Pa., less than 2 hours from New York City, and 3 hours from Baltimore. The campus is 500 acres with more than 16 major buildings.

CAMPUS FACILITIES AND EQUIPMENT

The Priscilla Payne Hurd Science Center, a 37,500-square-foot facility, is equipped with up-to-date computers, labs, and medical equipment. The Hurd Science Center also features a sterile molecular/cell biology suite, complete with a freezer room, bench room, support room, dark room, and instrument room. An ecology/environmental lab with a growing chamber, an analytical/physical chemistry/inorganic laboratory, and a bioinformatics/physics lab also inhabit the two-story building.

The Labuda Center for the Performing Arts houses the theatre, dance, and TV/Film majors and features a 473-seat main stage theatre, the 187-seat black box theatre, and a TV/film studio with a control room. Dance rehearsal space as well as costume and scene shops are also featured.

The Gambet Center for Business and Health Care Education is a 77,000-square-foot academic building that houses the school's business division and health care majors. It features a simulated trading room for business and finance majors, standardized patient areas, and a gross anatomy lab.

The DeSales University Center features many menu choices—especially for healthy eaters—in a food-court setting. There are three other food venues on campus located in the academic buildings as well as the Dorothy Day Student Union.

Trexler Library has a collection of more than 500,000 items and there are electronic databases of newspapers, journal articles, and the Oxford Dictionary of National Biography. There are computer and multimedia labs and a staff who will help with any research topic. Trexler Library has wireless access both with personal laptops or laptops that can be borrowed to use in the building. The Library's resources can be accessed from anywhere on campus. There is online access to databases and full-text journal articles. Students can also instant message a librarian with a question.

OFF-CAMPUS OPPORTUNITIES

Allentown and Bethlehem are a short 15-minute drive from campus and offer many dining, shopping, and outdoor activities, including the Promenade Shops at Saucon Valley, just minutes from campus. The Lehigh Valley, aka 'College Valley,' boasts beautiful hiking and biking trails, historic sites, museums, cultural festivals, and Dorney Park and Wildwater Kingdom. Skiing at nearby Blue Mountain and other Pocono resorts is just a short drive away. The Poconos also offer white water rafting trips down the Lehigh and Delaware Rivers.

ACADEMIC PROGRAMS

DeSales University defines "global competence" as using an open, inquisitive mind to understand the norms and expectations of other cultures, and using this acquired knowledge to communicate and to work effectively outside of one's usual environment in the promotion of human solidarity. DeSales University presents opportunities for students to enlarge their world view, from activities and concerts to short and long-term study abroad programs.

Study abroad programs through DeSales present the opportunity for our students to live and work in this vibrantly interdependent world, and range from semester-long study to short-stay travel of 10 days. Our students can spend semesters in England, Greece, Italy, Ireland, Switzerland, France, Australia, Tokyo, and Monte Carlo. More importantly, DeSales uses a model of intense hands-on engagement through short-stay co-curricular trips of students, faculty, and staff. Trips to Ireland, Germany, India, Istanbul, South Africa, and Austria for short-stay intensive travel have been combined with academic courses, the activities of student organizations, or out-of-season competition for our athletic teams.

Freshman students are asked to participate in the Character U program, a self-assessment program based on the Golden Counsels of St. Francis de Sales. Each month, University programming addresses one of these Golden Counsels or traits including patience, trust and cooperation, and perseverance. The DeSales Experience offers opportunities to learn and lead outside the classroom. The University's Academic Resource Center can offer assistance in reading comprehension, study skills, time management, and effective writing techniques. Additionally, they can help find a tutor if you need it or provide you with the opportunity to become a peer tutor.

Career Services and Placement

The Career Development Center can help students strategically showcase skills and stand out from a sea of competitors. The Center starts early by helping students define goals and make the right major and career choices. Job shadowing, learning to network, practice for interviews, and preparing resumes are all part of the process.

MAJORS AND DEGREES OFFERED

DeSales University offers more than 35 bachelor's degrees including 8 pre-professional programs, and 8 graduate programs through the divisions of business, liberal arts and social sciences, performing arts, natural sciences, and health care. Our more popular majors include criminal justice, theatre, medical studies, and business administration.

The newest majors are homeland security, neuroscience and special education. New tracks within the business department are financial planning and data analytics AI.

Special Programs

At DeSales, qualified business, nursing, criminal justice, and computer science majors have an option to earn both a bachelor's degree and a master's degree in five years. Qualified health science or medical studies majors are guaranteed an interview into the doctor of physical therapy program or the graduate physician assistant program respectively.

DeSales also has an Exploratory Studies Program, a structured program that helps students determine his or her major. This program includes a 3-credit course called Major Decision Making that will introduce different majors while fulfilling an elective requirement for graduation. Another exploratory course—Career Development and Planning—is available in the spring semester.

TUITION, ROOM, BOARD, FEES

Tuition and Fees (2020–2021): $38,500
Room and Board: $13,300
Student & Technology Fee: $1,500
One-time Orientation Fee: $200
Total: $53,500

FINANCIAL AID

Nine out of 10 DeSales University students receive financial aid in the form of grants, scholarships, work study, and loans. About 85% of the students receive grants directly from DeSales University, and funds are also available from federal and state programs to those who qualify. The amount of aid received and the composition of an aid package will depend on financial need and on academic achievement and potential.

Academic scholarships are also available through DeSales University. All applicants for admission are automatically considered for each of the scholarships offered by the University.

Students can also compete for one of six full-tuition Leadership Scholarships by writing an essay about leadership and service experience and, if selected, participating in an interview.

STUDENT ORGANIZATIONS AND ACTIVITIES

There are more than 1,600 full-time undergraduate students and about 64% live on campus. The male to female ratio is 43% to 57%. More than 11% of our undergraduate students are Hispanic and 8.9% are American minorities. Our students come to DeSales from 25 states and 7 other countries with many coming from Pennsylvania.

DeSales University has more than 30 campus organizations, including the Student Activities crew, which helps plan student events, bus trips, and on-campus performances. The Dorothy Day Student Union includes a student activities lounge open to students for entertainment and socializing and a café that offers another dining option in the form of a Sandella's Cafe. The Dorothy Day Student Union has been renovated to accommodate increased special events such as independent movie nights, comedians, music acts, and expanded space for programs sponsored by various student organizations.

DeSales University has 19 intercollegiate varsity sports teams and all are members of the NCAA Division III, Middle Atlantic States Collegiate Athletic Corporation (MAC) Freedom Conference, and the Eastern College Athletic Conference (ECAC).

The University's men's sports are baseball, basketball, cross-country, golf, lacrosse, soccer, tennis, and indoor and outdoor track and field. Women's sports are basketball, cross-country, field hockey, lacrosse, soccer, softball, indoor and outdoor track and field, tennis, and volleyball. The University also has club sports, including cheerleading, cycling, disc golf, equestrian, ice hockey, and men's volleyball.

There are intramural sports for all seasons, or students can visit the Billera Hall fitness center, which offers aerobic, Nautilus, and free-weight training.

ADMISSIONS PROCESS

To Apply for Admission you need to:

- Complete a DeSales University application and submit it to our Admissions Office.
- Have your high school guidance department send your official high school transcript to our Admissions Office.
- Have your standardized test scores (SAT or ACT) sent to our Admissions Office. Our code number for SAT scores is 2021. Submitting SAT or ACT test scores is strongly encouraged but not required for the following majors: dance, early childhood education, exploratory studies (undeclared), marriage & family studies, philosophy, psychology, Spanish, sport and exercise physiology, sport management, and theology. Students who don't submit test scores will need to have a personal interview with the admissions office.
- Have a guidance counselor and teacher complete the recommendation forms and send to our Admissions Office.

DIGIPEN INSTITUTE OF TECHNOLOGY

AT A GLANCE

DigiPen Institute of Technology is focused on igniting your passion and launching your career in interactive media and video game development. Our strong academic foundation and immersive project-based approach bring together passionate students who collaborate in a rigorous professional studio setting.

As the first school in the world to offer a bachelor's degree in video game programming, DigiPen has advanced the digital entertainment industry by preparing students to become skilled artists, designers, and engineers. Through a combined academic focus on both theory and application, students graduate with a deep foundational knowledge and a portfolio of work that is demonstrative of their practical and creative capabilities. Our bachelor and master's degree graduates thrive in any industry where passion, creativity, and innovation meet.

LOCATION AND ENVIRONMENT

DigiPen's U.S. campus is located in Redmond, Washington, a global hub for game and software development. The region is home to more than 400 interactive media companies, including tech industry giants like Microsoft, Nintendo, Amazon, and several more.

Situated about 10 miles east of Seattle, the Redmond area is home to much more than a wide range of successful economic enterprises. It's a renowned center of artistic excellence, cultural diversity, and beautiful outdoor surroundings.

DigiPen also operates at two international campuses in Singapore and Bilbao, Spain.

CAMPUS FACILITIES AND EQUIPMENT

Students at DigiPen go beyond the textbook—putting knowledge and theory into daily practice through extensive project coursework that brings together multiple areas of study including art, music, design, and computer science. As such, the DigiPen campus features several dedicated lab spaces, including:

- Two large-scale production labs dedicated to game project teams.
- Two music and sound labs, complete with recording studio, instrument practice rooms, and digital audio workstations.
- A Nintendo console development lab with special access to licensed software development kits.
- A computer engineering lab.
- An MFA computer lab.
- Numerous game lab spaces for prototyping and playtesting projects, from board games to video games.

As a testing ground for new ideas, DigiPen students regularly work and experiment with emerging technologies, such as virtual and augmented reality devices. Thanks to industry connections with local technology companies, DigiPen students have been among the first to get their hands on software development kits for products like the HTC Vive, Microsoft HoloLens, and more. Compared to most institutions, DigiPen provides its students with an unparalleled depth of hands-on experience that—combined with their solid knowledge base—gives them a competitive edge when beginning their careers.

In addition to DigiPen's lab and classroom spaces, the DigiPen campus library houses a vast collection of print and digital materials, including books, periodicals, films, and a growing catalogue of over 500 video games and game console equipment—an exceptional resource both for study and amusement.

OFF-CAMPUS OPPORTUNITIES

DigiPen's close proximity to hundreds of game and technology companies doesn't just benefit students after they graduate. It allows them to tap into a deep well of industry experience and begin building their professional network even before they graduate, thanks to a wealth of local off-campus events and internship opportunities.

DigiPen's internship program is a carefully monitored work experience in which students learn about their discipline in a professional development studio under the supervision of an industry veteran. DigiPen interns have earned their names in the credits of published AAA game titles, taken part in Microsoft research projects, and even assisted in the development of the Nintendo Wii controller.

Outside of the classroom, students can take advantage of a mix of fun activities throughout Redmond and the greater Seattle area. At the annual PAX West, a gaming expo that draws tens of thousands of visitors each year, DigiPen students plan, set up, and operate a student game arcade booth where they demo their academic projects to attendees—in the same venue as some of the largest game publishers in the world. The region is also home to other annual events, such as the Emerald City Comicon, Bumbershoot, Geek-GirlCon, and more.

ACADEMIC PROGRAMS

DigiPen's degree programs give students a comprehensive understanding of the academic fundamentals of their field while preparing them with the skills that will allow them to thrive in a professional environment.

While many schools tout their programs as being "interdisciplinary," the concept of an integrated curriculum is more than a buzzword at DigiPen—it's a central component of what students experience every day on campus. Beginning with a strong focus on foundational theory, each program at DigiPen challenges students to apply what they learn in the classroom toward intensive, sometimes year-long projects. Whether working on games, animations, or computer hardware devices, students put their knowledge into practice in a results-driven studio environment where they quickly learn the value of teamwork and communications. By working alongside their peers from other degree programs, students begin to think beyond the boundaries of their individual areas of study and to "speak the language" of the other disciplines. This cooperative method allows them to achieve the kind of standout student work that would be impossible to accomplish alone and prepares them for the challenges and realities of working in the professional industries after they graduate.

By the time they complete their degrees, students are equipped with a portfolio of work that can help them stand out to prospective employers, as well as the industry connections needed to jump-start their job search. More importantly, they leave with a depth of knowledge and experience that allows them to meaningfully contribute to their team from day one on the job.

Faculty Expertise

DigiPen faculty instructors come from a wide range of academic and professional backgrounds. From Ph.D. professors who have worked on Nobel-prize winning physics projects to instructors who cut their teeth on classic video games and blockbuster films, these faculty members bring to the classroom a unique blend of both scholarly and commercial expertise. Instructors at DigiPen are dedicated teachers whose primary motivation is to impart their years of knowledge to a new generation of creators and innovators. And with an impressive student-to-faculty ratio of 10:1, DigiPen students are able to receive individual mentorship and guidance.

MAJORS AND DEGREES OFFERED

DigiPen offers eight bachelor's programs and two master's degree programs in fields relating to computer science and engineering, as well as art, music, and design.

Computer Science

BS in Computer Science in Real-Time Interactive Simulation (an ABET-accredited program)
BS in Computer Science and Game Design
BS in Computer Science and Digital Audio
BS in Computer Science in Machine Learning
BS in Computer Science
MS in Computer Science

Art, Music, and Design

BFA in Digital Art and Animation
BA in Game Design
BA in Music and Sound Design
MFA in Digital Arts

Engineering

BS in Computer Engineering (an ABET-accredited program)

TUITION, ROOM, BOARD, FEES

Tuition and fees for the 2020–21 academic year for undergraduate students is $33,900, which covers the cost of 32–44 course credits per year and access to all of DigiPen's on-campus facilities and support services. There is no additional tuition cost for out-of-state U.S citizens and residents. Housing and meals, for students living in a DigiPen Housing apartment, costs an estimated $10,304.

FINANCIAL AID

There are several types of financial aid available for students who qualify. DigiPen's Office of financial aid is ready to help by connecting students with a range of financial resources, including:

- Scholarships
- Grants
- Loans
- Federal Work Study
- Veterans Benefits

For the 2018–19 academic year, approximately 59% of DigiPen students received financial assistance in the form of scholarships, state grants, and federal grants and loans. The average scholarship awarded that year was $8,209.

DigiPen is committed to helping all students make the most of their financial investment by providing the resources needed to succeed, including one-on-one financial aid counseling to help make the costs of attendance affordable.

ON-CAMPUS EMPLOYMENT

In addition to offering Federal Work Study for students who qualify, DigiPen also provides a number of on-campus employment opportunities. Students can earn income and work experience by applying to student job openings in several academic and administrative departments on campus. Each summer, DigiPen employs hundreds of current students to work as teachers and teaching assistants for DigiPen Academy's summer youth education programs for students in grades 1-12.

STUDENT ORGANIZATIONS AND ACTIVITIES

The student body at DigiPen is a tight-knit community of people who share a passion for games, art, and technology. Students thrive on teamwork, creativity, and a spirit of learning—both in and out of the classroom.

Despite being a small school, DigiPen has attracted an amazing community of students who have come to campus from more than 50 countries. DigiPen is committed to fostering a diverse campus culture that is welcoming and supportive to students of all backgrounds.

A Lasting Network

The shared experience among students doesn't end at graduation. It's not uncommon for DigiPen alumni to be working together as professionals as well, either at major technology companies or at small, entrepreneurial startups. Some DigiPen graduates have also continued to give back to their alma mater by participating in the DigiPen Alumni Mentorship Program, helping current students to effectively prepare for the transition from college to career.

Campus Support Systems

At any time during their education, DigiPen students do not have to look far to receive the support they need. Students have access to a wealth of on-campus services, such as:

- Professional mental health counseling
- Disability support services
- Peer tutors and advisors
- Academic and faculty advisors

While the demands of DigiPen's curriculum can be intense, students also have plenty of ways to relax, unwind, and explore new interests and activities. From organizing clubs and social events to participating in the Student Senate leadership group, students join together to create a vibrant and inclusive campus community.

Speaking of student clubs, there are several to choose from, with brand new groups springing up each year. For those drawn to the friendly competition of Pokemon Club or for anyone looking to become educated on LGBTQ issues through DigiPen's PRISM (People Respecting Individuals and Sexual Minorities) club, these and other campus groups provide a great way to connect with fellow students outside the classroom.

ADMISSIONS PROCESS

Applying to college is an exciting experience, but it can also feel intimidating at first. Our Office of Admissions seeks to make your journey to becoming a DigiPen Dragon as smooth as possible for you and your family. By taking the Admissions Process one step at a time, you could soon be on your way to joining the many ranks of students who make up our unique and exciting community.

DigiPen works on a rolling admissions basis, meaning we accept and evaluate applications as they are submitted to us throughout the year. New students begin in the fall semester each year. Once your application is submitted and you have provided all the required materials, you can typically expect to receive a decision within two-to-four weeks for undergraduate applications or four-to-six weeks for graduate applications. Within our admissions year, we do have several application deadlines, including:

February 1
Priority Application Deadline to submit all application materials by this date for greater access to scholarships and housing.

April 1
General Application Deadline. Submit all application materials by this date to guarantee your placement (upon acceptance) in the Fall 2020 incoming class.

July 1
Final Application Deadline

Apply by this date to be considered for the Fall incoming class.

These deadlines are subject to change. Please check the Admissions section of our website for the most updated information.

Because applicants must select their degree program prior to enrolling, DigiPen encourages all of its prospective students to do as much research as possible before applying. Prospective students can learn more by visiting the website, requesting information, or participating in an on-campus or online informational event.

DigiPen Pre-College Program

DigiPen's Pre-College Program is an intensive college preparatory experience for students who have completed their sophomore, junior, or senior year of high school. Designed for students with strong academic aspirations, this program provides a glimpse into the DigiPen college experience and is an ideal introduction for students who may be interested in attending the Institute. Taught by DigiPen faculty over a four-week period during the summer, the Pre-College Program not only exposes students to DigiPen's academic coursework but also requires students to work together on multidisciplinary project teams.

ELMHURST COLLEGE

AT A GLANCE

A private college in the heart of the Chicago metropolitan area, Elmhurst College is committed to helping students reach their full potential—in college and in the world beyond.

Located in a beautiful suburb just minutes from Chicago, Elmhurst College combines the close-knit learning environment of a small school with the endless opportunities of a world-class city.

Elmhurst ranks in the top 25 regional universities in the Midwest, according to *U.S. News & World Report,* and among the Midwest's Best Values, according to *Forbes.*

Wherever you want to go in life, Elmhurst has an academic program for you. Our 60 + majors and 17 pre-professional programs give you plenty of opportunities to explore your interests and discover your passions. In small classes, your professors will get to know you and help you find your professional path.

Student life at Elmhurst is active and creative, with endless ways to get involved. Our campus is a 48-acre arboretum with nearly 900 trees, but we're also a 30-minute train ride from the bright lights and unlimited opportunities of downtown Chicago.

More than 80 percent of Elmhurst students gain on-the-job experience through internships or service work, and 93 percent of our students find full-time employment or enter graduate school within a year of graduation.

LOCATION AND ENVIRONMENT

The College's gorgeous campus is a green oasis in the heart of a safe, quiet suburb—but it's also just a half-hour train ride from downtown Chicago, giving students unlimited access to world-class cultural and professional opportunities.

A short walk from campus is downtown Elmhurst, where you'll find an eight-screen movie theater, lots of great restaurants and coffee shops, a bowling alley and all the other necessities of college life.

The campus is also a short walk from the Metra commuter train station, where you can catch the train for a 30-minute ride to the Loop. The Chicago region is the Midwest's capital of industry, finance, arts and culture, and scientific discovery. From WGN and Morgan Stanley to the Shedd Aquarium and Lollapalooza, the Chicago area offers plenty of opportunities for internships and fun.

CAMPUS FACILITIES AND EQUIPMENT

The Elmhurst campus combines the high-tech necessities of a modern education with the charm of a classic college campus. The 48-acre grounds are an award-winning arboretum with nearly 900 trees. At the same time, we offer the latest technologies in the sciences and beyond.

The College has a long tradition of responsible stewardship of the environment. From its two active beehives atop the science center to a Gold LEED-certified residence hall, Elmhurst incorporates green principles throughout campus life.

OFF-CAMPUS OPPORTUNITIES

Elmhurst offers international education experiences in 68 countries, including Spain, the Netherlands, Poland, Germany, Bulgaria and England. Students can go abroad for a semester, a year or a month during the College's distinctive January Term.

Other Off-Campus Opportunities include a wealth of internship and job-shadowing experiences at sites ranging from WMAQ-NBC5 to Kraft Foods to WorldChicago to Gray Hunter Stenn LLP. In a typical year, students can choose from more than 2,000 internship options.

ACADEMIC PROGRAMS

Elmhurst offers over 60 majors, ranging from art and music to business, education and nursing. No matter which major you choose, you'll be the faculty's first priority. Our student-to-faculty ratio is only 14:1, and a faculty member—not a teaching assistant—teaches every course. Your professors will get to know you as an individual.

The Honors Program provides additional opportunities for students who are especially motivated and accomplished academically. Students in the Honors Program take part in small, stimulating seminar courses where class discussions are lively and engaging. They also conduct and present professional-level research.

Elmhurst students gain hands-on experience through internships and many other professional opportunities—working with prestigious medical institutions, schools, corporations, not-for-profits and more. The vast majority of Elmhurst undergraduates— more than 80 percent—gain on-the-job experience through internships or service work, with many internships leading to full-time job offers.

TUITION, ROOM, BOARD, FEES

Full-time undergraduate tuition for 2020–2021 is $38,654; basic room and board is $11,452.

FINANCIAL AID

Elmhurst College is committed to making a great education affordable by offering financial aid to nearly all of our full-time students. Financial aid programs include scholarships, grants, loans and federal work-study awards.

SCHOLARSHIPS

Elmhurst offers several merit-based awards to first-year and transfer students. Some awards are based on your academic record, while others are based on your talent (art, music or theater), United Church of Christ membership or other criteria. Scholarship awards range up to $20,000.

Admission decisions at Elmhurst are made independently from any consideration of financial need.

STUDENT ORGANIZATIONS AND ACTIVITIES

Elmhurst attracts students from across the nation and around the world. In small classes, you'll work closely with faculty members who are accomplished scholars and professionals—but above all, they're dedicated teachers.

On campus, students get involved in more than 100 activities, from theater to Greek life to the Mock Trial Team. The student newspaper wins awards; the radio station has been on the air since 1947. The campus regularly hosts performances, concerts, art exhibits and an outstanding array of guest speakers.

Elmhurst's 20 varsity sports teams compete in the CCIW, one of the top conferences in NCAA Division III athletics. Bluejay teams regularly engage in NCAA post-season play, and have won several conference championships in various sports.

ADMISSIONS PROCESS

It's easy to apply to Elmhurst, and there's no application fee. Our non-binding Early Action deadline is November 1. After that, applications are reviewed on a rolling basis.

Learn more at elmhurst.edu/apply.

ELMIRA COLLEGE

AT A GLANCE

Elmira College is a private, coeducational, Phi Beta Kappa college located in Elmira, New York.

Founded in 1855, Elmira was the first college for women with a course of study equal in rigor to the best men's colleges. "Female seminaries" as they were called at the time, were essentially glorified high schools. In contrast, from its very inception, Elmira College offered rigorous academic programs.

Coeducational since 1969, Elmira has an undergraduate enrollment of approximately 800 full-time, mostly residential students today. The College also offers advanced certificates, master degree programs, and non-credit courses for professional development.

LOCATION AND ENVIRONMENT

Elmira, NY, Suburban, 55 Acres, Approximately 800 students.

CAMPUS FACILITIES AND EQUIPMENT

Small college does not mean small on opportunities. At Elmira College, we offer students hands-on, immersive curricular and co-curricular opportunities, and our undergraduates use them day in and day out. From athletics facilities which allow year-round student use, to top of the line research equipment, to a medical school being built on campus, our students have opportunities at every turn.

The Center for Mark Twain Studies at Elmira College is a world class research center. Established in 1983, The Center for Mark Twain Studies awards internationally renowned Twain scholars Quarry Farm fellowships and hosts "The Trouble Begins" lecture series.

Lake Erie College of Osteopathic Medicine (LECOM) will open a new facility on the campus of Elmira College in 2020. Elmira College students already enjoy reserved, early acceptance spots at LECOM sites for EC students who meet the LECOM acceptance requirements. The addition of LECOM at Elmira College will expand the number of reserved medical spots for EC students to 25, the number of reserved pharmacy spots to 20 and the number of reserved dentistry spots to 5, and provide a seamless transition from undergraduate coursework to medical school.

Labs and research:

Facilities at Elmira College for studying biochemistry include laboratories for research, instrumentation, and teaching. Of particular utility to biochemistry students are instruments for amplifying and manipulating DNA, a DNA sequencer, gel electrophoresis apparatuses, a gel imager, and a plate-reader that can analyze various types of information on small samples.

Facilities at Elmira College for studying chemistry include laboratories for research, radioisotope, instrumentation, and teaching. In addition to the standard laboratory equipment, major instruments available to students are: nuclear magnetic resonance, atomic absorption, ultraviolet-visible, infrared, and fluorescent spectrophotometers; gas chromatography; mass spectrometry; ultra-centrifuge; as well as computer and data stations.

Students who study Speech and Language at Elmira College also have access to a brand new Audiometer, courtesy of the students of the Class of 2019 who funded its purchase as their class gift.

The College now offers an environmental science major and students are already involved in a solar and wind feasibility study for the College campus. Thanks to funding received from a private funder, the project features a solar-powered weather station that has the capability to monitor weather quantities crucial for gauging solar and wind power feasibility such as wind speed, wind direction, temperature, humidity, dew point, atmospheric pressure, rainfall, and solar radiation once an hour for approximately a year.

Dunn Field

Dunn Field is now one of the oldest stadiums in college baseball. Formerly home to the Elmira Pioneers, a minor league affiliate of the Boston Red Sox, Dunn Field now hosts the Perfect Game Collegiate League edition of the Elmira Pioneers during the summer months. The 4,020 capacity stadium has been home to several baseball greats including Hall of Famers Earl Weaver and Wade Boggs, legendary manager Lou Piniella, along with Davey Johnson, Don Zimmer, and two-time World Series Champion, Curt Schilling.

MAC

Elmira College also has an off-campus athletic complex, the Murray Athletic Center. Comprised of three geodesic domes, the MAC is the premier location for all other sports EC offers. The Murray Athletic Center has six squash courts, a media room, and a smart classroom used by our athletic teams for film sessions. The world's first geodesic dome athletic complex, the Murray Athletic Center, is nearly unique among athletic facilities in the Northeast. Located fifteen minutes from the main campus, it features a 3,200 seat hockey arena, a 2,000-seat gymnasium, a 38,000 square-foot field house with four indoor tennis courts, six squash courts and two playing fields.

OFF-CAMPUS OPPORTUNITIES

Hiking, Skiing, Boating, Shopping, Theater, Dining

ACADEMIC PROGRAMS

Accounting	Human Services
American Studies	Individualized Studies
Art	International Studies
Biochemistry	Legal Studies
Biology	Mathematics
Business Administration	Music
Chemistry	Nursing
Classical Studies	Philosophy and Religion
Clinical Laboratory Science	Political Science
Communication Sciences and Disorders	Pre-Health
Criminal Justice	Pre-Law
Economics	Psychology
Education	Social Studies
Educational Studies	Sociology and Anthropology
English Literature	Spanish and Hispanic Studies
Environmental Science	Theatre
Finance	Undeclared
History	Women's Studies

TUITION, ROOM, BOARD, FEES

Tuition: $34,578
Comprehensive Fees: $1,650
Standard Room and Board Plan: $13,125

FINANCIAL AID

Elmira College offers merit-based as well as need-based, financial aid. For a full list of grants and scholarships offered by EC please visit https://www.elmira.edu/admissions-aid/Tuition_Aid/Scholarships_and_Aid/index.html

STUDENT ORGANIZATIONS AND ACTIVITIES

More than 800 students, from 23 states and nine foreign countries.

More than 70 student clubs and organizations and 19 NCAA Division III athletic teams.

ADMISSIONS PROCESS

The College offers two admission plans for freshman applicants: Early Action and Regular (Rolling) Admission.

International students may apply only under the Regular Admission program.

Early Action

The Early Action deadline is November 1 and students will receive a decision by November 15.

Regular (Rolling) Admission

Students who self-select or who apply to the College after November 1 will be reviewed on a rolling basis. The College will begin to notify applicants of our decisions in early December. Students typically receive their admission decision within four weeks of the date their application file completes.

How to apply to Elmira College:

- Submit an Application for Admission. We accept the online Common Application or the EC Online Application.
- Submit an official transcript, including senior year courses and grades to date.
- Submit one academic letter of recommendation completed by a teacher or school counselor.
- Send SAT and/or ACT scores to Elmira College (if applicable). As a test-optional institution we do not require the SAT or ACT for admission.

EMERSON COLLEGE

AT A GLANCE

Emerson College in Boston has exceptional programs in comedic arts, communications, communication disorders, visual and media arts, performing arts, journalism, marketing communication, political communication, public relations, sports communication, creative writing and writing, literature and publishing.

Emerson College is the only college in America dedicated exclusively to communication and the arts in a liberal arts context. Established in 1880 as a small regional school of oratory, Emerson has evolved into a diverse, coeducational, and multifaceted institution that educates students to assume positions of leadership in communication and the arts. Emerson is forward thinking, grounded in academic excellence, and committed to advancing the scholarship and creative work that brings innovation, depth, and diversity to those disciplines. Emerson has always been at the forefront of instruction in communications and the arts. Students are taking classes taught by industry professionals while engaging in hands-on projects to put what they learn in the classroom into practice.

LOCATION AND ENVIRONMENT

Emerson's campus is located across from historic Boston Common in the heart of the city's thriving Theatre District, and offers multiple theaters, television and film studios, and cutting-edge technical facilities for students. Emerson's connection with Boston's media, theater, and arts industries, as well as government, hospitals, and businesses, provides many opportunities for student internships and professional growth.

Emerson is home to 14 varsity sport teams, and over 100 student organizations including performance groups, student publications, and honor societies. More than two thirds of the students are housed on-campus, some in learning communities such as the Writers' Block, Film Immersion, and Performing Cultures.

CAMPUS FACILITIES AND EQUIPMENT

Emerson has the highest quality equipment, including sound-treated television studios, digital editing labs, audio post-production suites, industry standard software, a professional marketing research suite, and an integrated digital newsroom for aspiring journalists. Additionally, an 11-story performance and production center houses a theatre design/technology center, makeup lab, and costume shop. The College's Paramount Center opened in 2010 and includes a 560-seat theater, black box, scene shop, film screening room, and sound stage. Emerson is also home to the Robbins Speech, Language and Hearing Center, which provides evaluation and treatment for children and adults with communication challenges and serves as the primary clinical training facility for the Department of Communication Sciences and Disorders.

OFF-CAMPUS OPPORTUNITIES

Internships are popular with Emerson students and hundreds of opportunities exist throughout Boston and in major cities across the country, including exclusive placements in Los Angeles, home to our residential study and internship program.

Emerson's relationship with Los Angeles is long-standing, but Emerson Los Angeles (ELA) is a state-of-the-art facility that houses classrooms, residential space, faculty offices, an auditorium, screening room, event spaces, studios and more. It solidifies Emerson's commitment to their Los Angeles program and to creating opportunities for students and alumni on the west coast. The internship program enrolls approximately 200 students, mostly seniors, during both the fall and spring semesters. Emerson students who participate in the ELA program gain the knowledge, skills, and confidence to pursue their chosen fields before launching their post-graduate lives on the west coast.

In addition to ELA, Emerson owns a restored 14th-century medieval castle, Kasteel Well, which is home to their semester abroad program in The Netherlands. The castle is a national historical monument that provides living accommodations, classrooms, a resource center, and related facilities. Emerson also sponsors a semester in Washington, D.C. and, Beijing (at Communication University of China University), along with our Global Pathways Summer Programs in more than 16 locations including London, Prague, and Greece.

ACADEMIC PROGRAMS

Emerson offers a wide range of undergraduate, graduate, and professional studies programs in communications and the arts. All undergraduate students take part in a robust curriculum including general education and liberal arts courses with advanced, specialized classes that are specific to individual departments and academic programs. Internships for academic credit are available to juniors and seniors, and the College's Institute for Liberal Arts and Interdisciplinary Studies offers first-year seminars, independent study options, and innovative courses that cut across academic disciplines. In addition, students can cross-register for courses with the seven-member ProArts Consortium (Berklee College of Music, Boston Architectural College, Boston Conservatory, Emerson, Massachusetts College of Art, New England Conservatory and the School of the Museum of Fine Arts).

MAJORS AND DEGREES OFFERED

Undergraduate students can earn a Bachelor of Arts, Bachelor of Science, or Bachelor of Fine Arts degree, depending on which major they select. Twenty-five (25) majors are available throughout the departments of Communication Sciences & Disorders, Communication Studies, Journalism, Marketing Communication, Performing Arts, Visual & Media Arts, Writing, Literature & Publishing and Liberal Arts & Interdisciplinary Studies. Students can also minor in several areas, including business, comedy, dance, entrepreneurship, eSports, fiction, hearing and deafness, history, literature, music appreciation, philosophy, photography, poetry, political science, publishing, psychology, radio, sociology, and women's and gender studies.

Emerson is accredited by the New England Association of Schools and Colleges and operates on a two-semester calendar.

TUITION, ROOM, BOARD, FEES

Basic expenses related to attending Emerson for the 2019–2020 academic year are $48,560 (tuition), $18,400 (double room and board), and $872 (Student Services Fee).

FINANCIAL AID

Emerson is committed to offering its students an excellent education at an affordable price. They have consistently set their tuition below their nearest competitors and are seen as a superb value in higher education. Students have all of the benefits of living in a world-class city, working with state-of-the-art equipment and in beautiful facilities, and learning from faculty who are top in their fields. The Office of financial aid will make every effort to help students finance the cost of their education. Emerson offers several types of financial assistance programs: need-based grants, employment, low-interest loans, merit scholarships, and alternative payment plans to help make an Emerson education possible. Each year, approximately two-thirds of the students receive some form of financial assistance. The College makes every effort to help students finance their education and provides need-based support packaged in awards that typically combine grant and scholarship, loan, and college work-study aid.

To apply for financial aid, students must complete the Free Application for Federal Student Assistance (FAFSA) and CSS PROFILE forms. More information can be found online at www2.emerson.edu/financial_aid or by contacting the Office of Student Financial Services at 617-824-8655 or finaid@emerson.edu.

STUDENT ORGANIZATIONS AND ACTIVITIES

In addition to the myriad of activities and events in Boston, student life at Emerson revolves around the more than 80 student-run organizations. These include radio stations, TV networks, publications, performance groups, service clubs, spiritual and cultural organizations, non-residential fraternities and sororities, professional societies, and intercollegiate and recreational athletics. Information about the specific organizations on campus can be found at www2.emerson.edu/student-affairs/campus-life/student-engagement-leadership.

ADMISSIONS PROCESS

Emerson College accepts the Common Application or our Emerson Application and requires an application supplement. Admission is competitive. The college looks for students who present academic promise in their secondary school record, recommendations, and writing competency, as well as personal qualities as seen in extracurricular activities, community involvement, and demonstrated leadership. Emerson is a test optional institution. Applicants may choose not to submit SAT and/or ACT scores unless they feel as though it assists in the review of their application.

Successful candidates typically have four years of English and three years each of mathematics, science, social science, and three years of a single foreign language. The application deadline for September admission is January 15 (Early Action, November 1), and for January admission it is November 1. Transfer applicants should apply by March 15 for September admission, or by November 1 for January admission.

Prospective students are encouraged to visit campus. Tours and information sessions may be scheduled online at www.emerson.edu/ugvisit or by contacting the Admission Office at 617-824-8600 or admission@emerson.edu.

FLORIDA SOUTHERN COLLEGE

AT A GLANCE

Founded in 1883, Florida Southern is the oldest private comprehensive college in the state of Florida. Florida Southern is nationally recognized for excellence in experiential education and guarantees students the opportunity to study abroad, participate in professional internships, and graduate in four years. Offering more than 70 undergraduate and graduate degree programs, the College enrolls 3,000+ students from 50 states and 50 countries.

LOCATION AND ENVIRONMENT

Florida Southern's 113-acre, lakeside campus is ideally located directly between Tampa and Orlando in Lakeland, Florida—named one of the best places to live and fastest growing metropolitan areas. Designated a National Historic Landmark, FSC is also home to the world's largest collection of Frank Lloyd Wright architecture in the world.

CAMPUS FACILITIES AND EQUIPMENT

Consistently named among The Princeton Review's "most beautiful" colleges, our campus facilities provide students with a living and learning experience unlike any other. Experience the Barney Barnett School of Business and Free Enterprise within the walls of the innovative Becker Business Building—a 40,000-square-foot facility with large screens powered by Bloomberg financial software. Biochemistry, microbiology and citrus students work with state-of-the-art equipment inside the Berry Science Building. The three-story Christoverson Humanities building is home to classrooms, computer labs and a theatre. FSC is also home to an esports arena, Barnett Athletic Complex, Wynee Warden Dance Studio, state-of-the-art Nursing facilities, the Sharon and Jim France Admissions Center, and the recently completed Jean and Sal Campisi, Sr. Academic Center for Physical Therapy. In 2020, FSC will open the Carole and Marcus Weinstein Computer Sciences Center for students to experiment with artificial intelligence, autonomous vehicles, and cybersecurity technologies.

OFF-CAMPUS OPPORTUNITIES

Vibrant downtown Lakeland is a short walk from campus and is well-known for its trendy restaurants and unique coffee shops. Community events like First Fridays, the Downtown Farmer's Curb Market, the Lakeland Food Truck Rally, and Pics on the Promenade provide opportunities to gather with friends. Florida Southern is 45-minutes from Walt Disney World and Busch Gardens, putting even more entertainment in easy reach.

ACADEMIC PROGRAMS

Ranked among the nation's top colleges, Florida Southern is nationally recognized for excellence in experiential education and guarantees students the opportunity to participate in professional internships, study abroad, and graduate in four years.

Hands-on learning experiences are built into each degree program and give students a deeper understanding of the curriculum through real-world application of knowledge. Science students conduct research in the field alongside professors and present papers at national conferences; theatre and music students take the stage alongside world-renowned guest performers; political science majors spend a semester interning at a senator's office in Washington, D.C.; and business students analyze problems and present real solutions to executives at major area corporations.

Beyond these opportunities, which are an integral part of the engaged learning experience, each student is guaranteed an internship, a crucial step in gathering resume-building experience prior to graduation.

We also guarantee each student a study-abroad experience. Once a student has completed four full semesters in good standing, they qualify for Junior Journey, often at no additional cost beyond the usual FSC tuition! Junior Journey trips are hosted by faculty members and designed to take education far beyond the classroom: political science and history students travel to Germany to study the history of WWII and the Holocaust; marine biology students head to the Bahamas to study shark conservation and biology; and theatre students travel to New York City for behind-the-scenes tours of Broadway shows. Each semester offers a host of options to suit a multitude of interests and majors, and each trip is a once-in-a-lifetime experience!

To ensure student success in their academic journeys, the Student Solutions Center hosts Academic Fuel, a combination of group peer-tutoring programs including the FSC Writing Center, Scholars Strengthening Scholars, and Peer Assisted Study Sessions (PASS). Academic Fuel is designed to help each student stay on top of their academic progress. The atmosphere is relaxed and friendly; students support each other and professional staff ensure that each student is matched with the best resources for their needs. Students are encouraged to use Academic Fuel programs early and often to stay ahead academically and realize the benefit of connecting with peers.

The Honors Program at Florida Southern offers talented and motivated students the opportunity to work one-on-one with faculty mentors on a senior project of their own design. Honors students also enjoy collaborative, interdisciplinary seminars with exceptional faculty, a series of "supper seminars" that host expert speakers, and specially designated facilities—including classrooms, the Honors Lounge, and special housing—which foster an enriching living-learning environment. All honors students receive priority registration and are able to take course overloads without paying additional fees. For two consecutive years FSC has also been named a Fulbright top producing institution, with students also receiving prestigious academic honors such as the Goldwater Scholarship, which is awarded only to a small group of students across the United States each year.

Florida Southern College courses are taught mostly by full-time faculty members, many of whom hold the highest credentials in their field. Our faculty members have chosen to teach at Florida Southern because they value the opportunity to work one-on-one with students. Here, your professor won't just know your name. They will know you and will take an active interest in helping you achieve your goals.

MAJORS & DEGREES OFFERED

Florida Southern offers more than 70 undergraduate degree programs, including highly successful pre-medical, pre-dental, pre-optometry, pre-physician, pre-veterinary, pre-law, pre-physical therapy, pre-theological, pre-engineering, and pre-pharmacy studies programs.

Bachelor's degree programs are available in accounting, art education, art history, biochemistry and molecular biology, biology, biotechnology, business administration, business and free enterprise, chemistry, citrus/horticulture, communication, computer science, criminology, dance, economics and finance, elementary education, English, environmental studies, exercise science, film, graphic design, history, humanities, marine biology, mathematics, music, music education, music management, music performance, musical theatre, nursing, philosophy, political communication, political economy, political science, psychology, religion, self-designed major, social sciences, Spanish, sport business management, sports communication and marketing, studio art, technical theatre/design, theatre arts, theatre performance, and youth ministry. Many areas are available as concentrations and interdisciplinary minors are available in advertising design, integrated marketing communications, Latin American studies, pre-law, and women and gender studies.

TUITION, ROOM, BOARD, FEES

Full-time (12–18 credits) tuition per semester is $19,490. The standard 20-meal plan, required for all first-year students, is $2,400 per semester. The average cost for housing in a double-occupancy room is $3,603 per semester. Total tuition, fees, and room and board per year for a first-year student averages $50,986.

FINANCIAL AID

Each year, Florida Southern College offers more than $45 million in institutional aid on the basis of academic merit, talent in athletics or fine arts, demonstrated leadership or service, need, and other factors. Combined with federal, state, and other private funding sources, FSC students receive $60 million in overall assistance, and more than 98 percent of FSC students receive some form of aid. It all begins with our net price calculator, available on our website. Answer a few simple questions, and we'll give you an immediate assessment of some of the financial aid options available to you. Additionally, your admissions counselor will work with you to ensure that you are considered for every possible scholarship, grant, and source of aid available.

STUDENT ORGANIZATIONS AND ACTIVITIES

Florida Southern is home to more than 100 student clubs and organizations, 13 Greek Life chapters (six sororities and seven fraternities) and 20 NCAA Division II men's and women's varsity sports teams. The College also hosts four club sports—equestrian, esports, ice hockey, and water skiing.

ADMISSIONS PROCESS

Students may apply for admission as early as May of their junior year in high school. It is free to apply, and students may choose to use FSC's online application or add us to their Common or Coalition Applications. For more application information, please visit flsouthern.edu/applynow.

Application Information

Applying to Florida Southern is the first step in making your college experience one that defines your future success. We strongly encourage you to apply before the priority deadlines to maximize your scholarship and visit opportunities.

Early decision November 1
Regular decision March 1

Students applying via Regular and Early Decision receive decisions approximately two-three weeks from the date their application and all credentials have been received.

Required Application Materials

Application
Essay or Personal Statement
Official High School Transcripts
Official ACT or SAT Scores
Academic Letter of Recommendation
Student Profile

Florida Southern currently has a traditional undergraduate class of about 2,495 students from nearly all states and 36 countries around the world. Incoming freshman average a 3.76 GPA, and the middle 50% range is an 1130–1290 on the SAT and a 23–29 on the ACT. While FSC admits students both above and below our averages, admission is competitive and the College seeks to enroll students who will be involved both inside and outside the classroom. Florida Southern receives more than 7,000 undergraduate applications annually and admits approximately 51% of applicants.

GEORGE MASON UNIVERSITY

AT A GLANCE

George Mason University is Virginia's largest public research university. Located near Washington, D.C., Mason enrolls more than 37,000 students from 130 countries and all 50 states. Mason has grown rapidly over the past half-century and is recognized for its innovation and entrepreneurship, remarkable diversity, and commitment to accessibility. Mason is also one of the best values in higher education, producing graduates who lead all Virginia schools with the highest annual salaries.

LOCATION AND ENVIRONMENT

1. *Location and Environment:* Mason's beautiful 670-acre residential campus in Fairfax, Virginia is just 24 kilometers outside of Washington, D.C. We are one of the most diverse universities in the country. Our diversity has defined and shaped our culture, from how we educate our students, to our sense of responsibility in our communities, and in our world as a whole. Our students represent all races, ethnicities, nationalities, religions, sexual orientations, and gender identities. Hailing from 139 countries and all 50 states, the Mason Nation brings together many different idea and perspectives that contribute to a vibrant and engaging community.

2. *Off-Campus Opportunities:* The universities off-campus team comprised of students and faculty help to provide a centralized resource center and comprehensive offering of academic and social engagement opportunities for students. They work to specifically meet the needs of students living off-campus and those transitioning to off-campus living, contributing to a successful, holistic, and seamless collegiate experience. This includes students who are parenting, student veterans, adult learners over the age of 25, students from the foster care system, fully online learners, and transfer students. Mason has free shuttle bus services that takes students to the mall, various shopping plazas, and more. There are a number of opportunities for students to not only live off campus but to explore various landmarks and destinations in D.C., Maryland, and Virginia.

ACADEMICS

1. *MAJORS AND DEGREES OFFERED:* Mason offers more than 200 degrees and numerous minors and certificate programs to customize your education and meet your career and personal goals.

AGRICULTURE, AGRICULTURE OPERATIONS, AND RELATED SCIENCES.
- Agricultural Business and Management.

AREA, ETHNIC, CULTURAL, GENDER, AND GROUP STUDIES.
- Latin American Studies.
- Russian Studies.

BIOLOGICAL AND BIOMEDICAL SCIENCES.
- Biology/Biological Sciences, General.
- Neuroscience.

BUSINESS, MANAGEMENT, MARKETING, AND RELATED SUPPORT SERVICES.
- Accounting.
- Business Administration and Management, General.
- Finance, General.
- Management Sciences and Quantitative Methods, Other.
- Marketing/Marketing Management, General.
- Tourism and Travel Services Management.

COMMUNICATIONS TECHNOLOGIES/TECHNICIANS AND SUPPORT SERVICES.
- Animation, Interactive Technology, Video Graphics and Special Effects.

COMPUTER AND INFORMATION SCIENCES AND SUPPORT SERVICES.
- Computer and Information Sciences, General.
- Computer Science.
- Information Technology.

EDUCATION.
- Health Teacher Education.
- Physical Education Teaching and Coaching.

ENGINEERING.
- Bioengineering and Biomedical Engineering.
- Civil Engineering, General.
- Computer Engineering, General.
- Electrical and Electronics Engineering
- Mechanical Engineering.
- Systems Engineering.

ENGLISH LANGUAGE AND LITERATURE/LETTERS.
- Creative Writing.
- English Language and Literature, General.
- Rhetoric and Composition.

FAMILY AND CONSUMER SCIENCES/HUMAN SCIENCES.
- Human Development and Family Studies, General.

FOREIGN LANGUAGES, LITERATURES, AND LINGUISTICS.
- Foreign Languages and Literatures, General.

HEALTH PROFESSIONS AND RELATED PROGRAMS.
- Athletic Training/Trainer.
- Clinical Laboratory Science/Medical Technology/Technologist.
- Clinical Nutrition/Nutritionist.
- Community Health and Preventive Medicine.
- Health Professions and Related Clinical Sciences, Other.
- Registered Nursing/Registered Nurse.
- Rehabilitation Science.

HISTORY.
- History, General.

HOMELAND SECURITY, LAW ENFORCEMENT, FIREFIGHTING AND RELATED PROTECTIVE SERVICES.
- Criminal Justice/Police Science.
- Critical Infrastructure Protection.
- Forensic Science and Technology.

LIBERAL ARTS AND SCIENCES, GENERAL STUDIES AND HUMANITIES.
- General Studies.
- Liberal Arts and Sciences, General Studies and Humanities, Other.
- Liberal Arts and Sciences/Liberal Studies.

MATHEMATICS AND STATISTICS.
- Mathematics, General.
- Statistics, General.

MULTI/INTERDISCIPLINARY STUDIES.
- Mathematics and Computer Science.
- Multi-/Interdisciplinary Studies, Other.
- Peace Studies and Conflict Resolution.
- Sustainability Studies.

NATURAL RESOURCES AND CONSERVATION.
- Environmental Science.

PARKS, RECREATION, LEISURE, AND FITNESS STUDIES.
- Kinesiology and Exercise Science.

PHILOSOPHY AND RELIGIOUS STUDIES.
- Philosophy.
- Religion/Religious Studies.

PHYSICAL SCIENCES.
- Astronomy.
- Atmospheric Sciences and Meteorology, General.
- Chemistry, General.
- Geology/Earth Science, General.
- Physics, General.

PSYCHOLOGY.
- Psychology, General.

PUBLIC ADMINISTRATION AND SOCIAL SERVICE PROFESSIONS.
- Public Administration.
- Social Work.

SOCIAL SCIENCES.
- Anthropology.
- Economics, General.
- Geographic Information Science and Cartography.
- Geography.

- International Relations and Affairs.
- Political Science and Government, Other.
- Sociology.

VISUAL AND PERFORMING ARTS.
- Art History, Criticism and Conservation.
- Art/Art Studies, General.
- Cinematography and Film/Video Production.
- Dance, General.
- Drama and Dramatics/Theatre Arts, General.
- Graphic Design.
- Music Performance, General.
- Visual and Performing Arts, General.

Degrees

Bachelor's
Doctoral
Doctoral/Professional
Doctoral/Research
Master's
Post-Bachelor's certificate
Post-Master's certificate

2. *Academic Programs:* Mason's 10 colleges and schools provide the opportunity to craft your own course of study. Whether you're passionate about a certain subject or want to explore your options, we'll provide the advice and guidance to find the best fit.

   1. Arts, Media and Communication
   2. Business, Economics, and Entrepreneurship
   3. Computing
   4. Education and Social Service
   5. Engineering, Technology, and Design
   6. Government, Policy, and International Affairs
   7. Health, Medicine, and Well-Being
   8. People, Culture, and Behavior
   9. Science and Math

Mason's Honors College provides talented students with unique academic and social environments that enhance the college experience. Selected from the most outstanding students invited to the Honors College University Scholars are awarded scholarships covering the full cost of tuition over four years.

ATHLETIC FACILITIES

With three state-of-the-art fitness centers that offer everything from an Olympic- sized pool to group exercise classes, Mason's fitness resources are endless-and free for students.

The **Aquatic and Fitness Center (AFC)** supports a wide range of activities for the University community. Both students and members have access to a variety of fitness and well-being programs and services, including; weight training/strength gallery, cardio gallery, cycle studio, multipurpose room, locker rooms, Olympic size and recreational pool, alongside fitness and aquatic programs.

The 120,000-square foot **Recreation Athletic Complex (RAC)** boasts three gymnasiums, two racquetball courts, two squash courts, and a two-story fitness gallery that spans over 15,000 square feet. The facility is home to the Patriots volleyball and wrestling teams, along with intramural and club sports, ROTC, as well as classroom and offices for the School of Recreation, Health and Tourism.

Skyline Fitness Center which is centrally located on the Fairfax campus features a variety of cardio equipment, weight training/strength equipment, 1 basketball court, basketball checkout, TV lounge, locker rooms, outdoor adventures and outdoor adventure equipment.

LIBRARIES

The five-floor state of the art facility known as **Fenwick Library** is centrally located on the Fairfax Campus. Fenwick is George Mason University's main research library. This facility features the state-of-the-art Special Collections Research Center, learning spaces, digital technology, group study rooms, extended- hours study lounge, Argo tea and then some.

The **Gateway Library** located on the first floor of the Johnson Center, provides dynamic environment for undergraduate learning and research. Through fostering interaction, collaboration and creative work, this library introduces both undergraduates and new students to the University Libraries' resources, services and programs.

STUDENT CENTERS

The **Johnson Center** biggest and busiest Student Centers building cultivates opportunities to engage with members of the Mason Nation. The Johnson Center Atrium food court is the largest on Fairfax campus and brings students together before and after class to share and discover great ideas over great meals. The JC inspires learning and positive change through its library and meeting spaces. Many of the community's events are held in spaces like Dewberry Hall and the Cinema.

STUDENT BODY

1. **Student Body:** Truly embodying an enriched diverse community and culture, Mason continuous rises to the top of the charts as one of the most diverse schools in the nation. The diversity factor continues to play a significant role in the decision-making process for students determining what college or university they will attend. Students here at the university choose and love Mason because of the numerous opportunities it provides to get a taste of the world through interactions with individuals from all across the world.

2. **Student Organizations and Activities:** With over 460 student organizations here at Mason, every student can find a niche, get involved, and meet new friends. There are also opportunities for team activities through Mason's intramural or club teams. Every year, Mason hosts thousands of events on campus, including theater, music, live sports, movies, comedians, and more. There is always something to do.

ADMISSION PROCESSES AND REQUIREMENTS

Freshman General Admission Requirements

The following factors are evaluated in the decision process:

- *Cumulative high school grade point average (GPA)* for work completed in grades 9-12 along with level of difficulty of courses selected, particularly in core academic courses. Request your high school send an official copy of your transcript.
- *SAT or ACT* scores George Mason University uses self-reported SAT and/or ACT test scores throughout the initial Admissions Process to make both admissions and scholarship decisions.
- *Secondary School Report and counselor recommendations.* We suggest sending two letters of recommendation, one from your high school counselor and one from a teacher.
- *An optional, but strongly encouraged Personal Statement of approximately 250 words explaining to the office of Admissions why YOU want to go to college.* Tell us about yourself and your experiences that have led to this decision.
- *Test of English as a Foreign Language (TOEFL) scores* from non-native English-speaking applicants to supplement other standardized test results. If you do not speak English at hoe you are highly encouraged to take the TOEFL.
- *Extracurricular Activities* listed on your online application, common application, or sent within an activity sheet or resume

Important Deadlines

Information about important application deadlines.

Deadline Type	Date	Decisions Mail
Fresh. Non-Binding Early Action Deadline*	November 1	December 15
Fresh. Honors College Consideration*	November 1	December 15
Fresh. University Scholars Consideration*	November 1	Mid-February
Fresh. Merit-Based Scholarship Consideration*	November 1	December 15
Fresh. Regular Decision Deadline*	January 15	Late March
Mason Financial Aid Deadline	January 15	Mid-February
Fresh. Priority Application Deadline (for Spring Semester)	October 1	November 1

*All freshman applicants who apply to Mason by 11:59 pm EST on November 1 will automatically be considered for merit-based scholarships and our non-binding, Early Action decision.

THE GEORGE WASHINGTON UNIVERSITY

AT A GLANCE

The George Washington University, located in downtown Washington, D.C., provides students with invaluable learning experiences on campus, throughout the city and around the world.

Founded in 1821 by an Act of Congress, the George Washington University (GW) offers majors in business, engineering, fine art, the humanities, international affairs, public health, and sciences through seven undergraduate schools.

We go beyond the typical university experience with an education that is deeply connected to our location in the center of Washington, D.C. Our nearly 10,000 undergraduates actively engage the city and the world through hands-on learning experiences, where they study alongside faculty experts, policy leaders and extraordinary individuals in every discipline to shape global progress and define the issues that will shape the present and future.

LOCATION AND ENVIRONMENT

GW maintains two fully integrated campuses in Washington, D.C., with residence halls and classrooms located on both and free shuttle service provided. Through these two different learning environments, students have the ability to create a college experience that is uniquely their own.

Our Foggy Bottom campus is blocks from the major landmarks that make Washington one of the most recognizable cities in the world. Our students can study on the steps of the Lincoln Memorial, jog to the Washington Monument or take a stroll to the White House and Kennedy Center.

Our Mount Vernon campus, just a few miles from the hustle and bustle of downtown, offers a residential liberal arts campus experience while still providing all the opportunities of D.C. Many of GW's living and learning communities and GW Athletic fields are located on this campus.

Explore both campuses in our virtual tour at http://virtualtour.gwu.edu.

CAMPUS FACILITIES AND EQUIPMENT

GW is full of world-class facilities, such as Gelman Library, at the heart of campus, the Smith Center, home of GW Athletics, Lisner Auditorium, which hosts performances and lectures to enrich our community, and the Science and Engineering Hall, full of highly specialized lab facilities. Learn more about our facilities at http://virtualtour.gwu.edu.

OFF-CAMPUS OPPORTUNITIES

What distinguishes a GW education is the way we consistently put knowledge in action through research, internship and service opportunities for students in all academic areas.

Our students have access to innovative facilities and faculty to support their research in all subjects. Students and faculty have worked together on topics including food waste in D.C. public schools, cholesterol transport in HIV and Tangier disease, and how personality affects purchasing.

GW also excels at helping students land internships in the nation's capital and beyond. GW students gain invaluable professional experience and often even security clearance during internships at the White House, U.S. Department of State, Folger Shakespeare Library and NPR, just to name a few.

In addition, we encourage students to give back on the local, national and international levels through university-wide community service, including Welcome Day of Service and Alternative Spring Breaks. That dedication to service continues after graduation, as GW is a top-ranked Peace Corps feeder among medium-sized schools.

Special Interest Programs

Learn more about these programs at https://go.gwu.edu/specialinterest.

Civic House
Mount Vernon Campus Scholars
Politics & Values Program
Seven-Year B.A./M.D. Program
University Honors Program
Women's Leadership Program

MAJORS AND DEGREES OFFERED

With more than 2,000 courses in over 70 majors for undergraduate students, GW offers a wide range of academic opportunities. Our average class size is 29, and 70 percent of classes have fewer than 30 students. Browse all of our majors at http://go.gwu.edu/gwmajors.

Columbian College of Arts & Sciences

Africana Studies
American Studies
Anthropology
Arabic Studies
Archaeology
Astronomy and Astrophysics
Biological Anthropology
Biology
Biophysics
Chemistry
Chinese Language and Literature
Classical Studies
Cognitive Neuroscience
Communication
Criminal Justice
Economics
English
English and Creative Writing
Environmental Studies
French Language and Literature
Geography
Geological Sciences
German Language and Literature
History
Human Services and Social Justice
Japanese Language and Literature
Judaic Studies
Korean Language and Literature
Mathematics
Neuroscience
Organizational Sciences
Peace Studies
Philosophy
Philosophy (Public Affairs)
Physics
Political Science
Political Science (Public Policy)
Psychology
Religion
Russian Language and Literature
Sociology

Spanish and Latin American Languages, Literature and Culture
Speech and Hearing Sciences
Statistics
Women's Studies

Corcoran School of the Arts & Design

Art History
Dance
Fine Art
Graphic Design
Interaction Design
Interior Architecture
Music
Photojournalism
Theatre

Elliott School of International Affairs

Asian Studies
International Affairs
Latin American and Hemispheric Studies
Middle East Studies

School of Media & Public Affairs

Journalism and Mass Communication
Political Communication

Milken Institute School of Public Health

Exercise Science
Nutrition Science
Public Health

School of Business

Accountancy
Business Administration
Finance

School of Engineering & Applied Science

Applied Science and Technology
Biomedical Engineering
Civil Engineering
Computer Engineering
Computer Science
Electrical Engineering
Mechanical Engineering
Systems Engineering

TUITION, ROOM, BOARD, FEES

Earning a GW degree is invaluable, but it takes an investment of time, effort and money. We believe that investment is within reach for every admitted student, and we leverage our resources to make it worthwhile.

Through scholarships and need-based aid, we aim to make a GW education an affordable and realistic option for every admitted student.

GW also invests more than $185 million in financial aid, which is awarded to 70 percent of the incoming first-year class.

We believe that your investment in GW will pay dividends for the rest of your life.

Tuition $56,845
Fees $440
Room and Board $14,360

For up-to-date information on costs, visit https://go.gwu.edu/cost.

FINANCIAL AID

All applicants for admission are automatically considered for scholarships (with the exception of special programs which may require a separate application). Need-based aid is determined by the Office of Student Financial Assistance. For more information, visit http://financialaid.gwu.edu.

STUDENT ORGANIZATIONS AND ACTIVITIES

Our nearly 10,000 undergraduate students come from all across the U.S. and more than 130 countries. While at GW, they participate in more than 450 student organizations and community groups. Students have an open dining plan, which offers options on and off campus, and are required to live on campus for their first 3 years.

450 student clubs and organizations
50 club sports and intramural teams
27 NCAA Division I sports teams
35 Greek life chapters

ADMISSIONS PROCESS

GW strives to recruit a diverse and inclusive class each and every year. We do this through our holistic review process, which takes into account not just overall grades, but also course rigor, essays, recommendation letters and extracurricular activities. This allows us to admit students who have the academic preparation, personal qualities and motivation to thrive in GW's dynamic environment.

GW is test-optional, allowing students to choose whether or not to submit SAT/ACT scores, because we believe that a student's performance throughout high school is the best indication of college readiness.

GETTYSBURG COLLEGE

AT A GLANCE

Gettysburg is a national college of liberal arts and sciences located in the world-famous town of Gettysburg, Pennsylvania. Our 2,600 students are actively involved in an academically rigorous and personally challenging educational experience. With an average class size of 17 and a student-to-faculty ratio of 9:1, everyone plays a role. At Gettysburg College, learning often means doing— doing everything. Students engage in cutting edge research, study across the globe, and serve the community of Gettysburg and beyond. There are no bystanders here.

Gettysburg is a place of variety and diversity, a community where every student has the chance to stand out, take responsibility, and lead. In addition to leading more than 120 student clubs and campus organizations, "Gettysburgians" are mindful of their responsibilities as global citizens. Nearly 60 percent of the student body pursues at least one of the College's extensive study abroad programs, and many become involved with Gettysburg's Center for Public Service.

Gettysburg College inspires students to be great. From the very first semester, when incoming Gettysburg students take an intensive First-Year Seminar, students analyze, discuss, debate, and present. They often collaborate and conduct research with the College's faculty, and they leave Gettysburg prepared to make discoveries, inspire others, and lead lives of impact.

LOCATION AND ENVIRONMENT

Two things make Gettysburg College's location extraordinary—what's here and what happened here. Less than a mile from the sites of the Battle of Gettysburg and the famous Gettysburg Address by Abraham Lincoln, our 200-acre campus connects to a famous and engaging town that offers a variety of options when you decide it's time to head off campus. Downtown you'll find an eclectic array of stores, restaurants, and cultural offerings, including the Majestic Theater, art galleries sponsoring First Friday openings each month, and many other attractions. Outdoor enthusiasts will enjoy the area's kayaking, rock climbing and mountain biking, three nearby ski and snowboard resorts, and outstanding hiking trails, including the Appalachian Trail. And the College offers easy access to three major metropolitan areas: Harrisburg (45 minutes), Baltimore (60 minutes), and Washington, D.C. (80 minutes).

CAMPUS FACILITIES AND EQUIPMENT

The 55,000 square foot John F. Jaeger Center for Athletics, Recreation, and Fitness is a sleek facility with an array of athletic and fitness areas including a fitness center, a bouldering area and rock climbing wall, and a natatorium with eight competition lanes and a four-lane warm-up pool. There are more than 20 fitness classes (some are student-led) each week, from aerobics to spinning to yoga. Nearly all students take advantage of the opportunities for recreation and fitness at Gettysburg.

The Majestic Theater, a renovated and restored 1926 vaudeville theater, seats 830 and features two cinema theatres. The Majestic hosts world-class performances by visiting artists and a stage for College music and theatre performances.

The Science Center, McCreary Hall, and Masters Hall are at the heart of scientific research on campus. The Science Center is a state-of-the-art teaching and research facility and houses two virtual dissection tables, a Multidisciplinary Imaging Suite which includes an atomic force microscope, a greenhouse, a nuclear magnetic resonance spectrometer, and a Geographical Information System lab. McCreary is home to the latest equipment for biology, and there is space for cognitive neuroscience, an infant research lab, and a vivarium. Masters Hall houses the Physics department. Inside are atomic and nuclear physics labs, a planetarium, an accelerator research lab, and a plasma research lab. Across campus in the West Building is the Innovation and Creativity Lab, which houses technology for virtual reality, 3-D printing, and more.

OFF-CAMPUS OPPORTUNITIES

At Gettysburg College, everyone has the option of off-campus study and we encourage every student to consider it. Studying off campus offers many obvious benefits—a more global perspective, fluency in another language, and a deeper firsthand knowledge of critical world issues. There are a rich and diverse range of off-campus study options all over the world: in any given semester, Gettysburg students are on six continents, representing all majors and disciplines. In addition to taking course work toward their major, students abroad may be conducting field research, working as interns, living with local people, and studying languages ranging from Arabic to Zulu. By the time they graduate, nearly 60 percent of Gettysburg students have spent at least a semester abroad. In fact, the Institute of International Education has ranked Gettysburg College 8th in the country and 3rd in Pennsylvania for semester-long study abroad experiences.

ACADEMIC PROGRAMS

Gettysburg's strong academic tradition is rooted in a rigorous liberal arts and science curriculum. The College augments academic excellence with community responsibility and global experiences, provides leadership opportunities and engages with public policy issues. Some of Gettysburg's key distinctive features include:

The Eisenhower Institute—Become a master of global and public policy issues by taking a front row seat to political leaders, the press, and policy experts—both on campus and in Washington, D.C.

Sunderman Conservatory of Music—Undertake a rigorous music curriculum, or get involved in a multitude of performance groups open to everyone, all within the context of a liberal arts and sciences education.

Garthwait Leadership Center—Sharpen your skills through our intellectual and experiential hub for leadership development; take advantage of workshops, retreats, one-on-one mentoring, or even pursue a Leadership Certificate!

Center for Public Service—Engage with community members, faculty and staff to facilitate partnerships, education, critical thinking, and informed action to foster social change in the local and global communities.

Civil War Institute—Immerse yourself in Civil War dialogue through one of the CWI's special programs or fellowships, or pursue the nation's only minor in Civil War Era Studies.

First-Year Seminar Program—Dive into one of over 40 unique seminar courses and share a residential experience with your classmates; topics include everything from "Protest Music & Social Change in the American Experience" to "Food, Water, Shelter, Song: Staying Human on a Planet in Transition."

Center for Global Education—Take advantage of one of Gettysburg's renowned study abroad programs across the globe, ranked 8th in the country by the Institute of International Education. Nearly 60 percent of students study abroad for a semester or more.

Undergraduate Research—Work side-by-side with distinguished professors to investigate cutting-edge developments, and even share your findings in scholarly journals and professional conferences—work often reserved for graduate students.

MAJORS AND DEGREES OFFERED

There are 65 majors and special programs from which to choose a major, a double major, a self-designed major or a major/minor combination. Every student has a senior capstone experience and nearly 60 percent of the students will study abroad before they graduate. There has been an Honor Code in effect since 1957.

More than 95 percent of the faculty has a doctorate or the highest degree in their field. They have earned Fulbright and Luce Fellowships, won NSF grants, and many have gained national and international reputations for their work. However, excellent teaching is central to the College's mission and it is the strong relationship between students and faculty as learners that is the hallmark of a Gettysburg education. At Gettysburg, there is a 9:1 student-faculty ratio and an average class size of 17 students.

TUITION, ROOM, BOARD, FEES

Comprehensive Fee

The cost of attendance at Gettysburg College includes charges for tuition, room and board. Allowances for books and supplies, transportation, and other personal expenses are factored into a student's budget for the purpose of determining aid eligibility. Typical fees are listed below. Various room and board options are available after the first year.

Tuition: $56,390
Room (regular room): $7,220
Meal Plan (unlimited access): $6,240
Total Charges: $69,850

FINANCIAL AID

Gettysburg continues to uphold a long-standing commitment to place the College within reach of each accepted student. Recognized by Kiplinger's Personal Finance as a "Best Value" among private colleges based upon academic quality and affordability, a Gettysburg education is an investment worth making. Need-based financial aid, merit scholarships, and music scholarships are available. Over $72 million in scholarships and grants were awarded from Gettysburg College resources for the 2019–20 academic year. Approximately 65 percent of the student body benefit from these funds.

Merit scholarships range from $15,000 to $40,000 per year. Decisions on merit scholarship recipients are made as part of the Admissions Process for entering first-year students. The four academic merit scholarships (Abraham Lincoln, Presidential, David Wills, and 1832 Founders) are awarded as part of the review process; a separate application is not required; all students including those who apply test optional are considered. The Eisenhower Scholarship, designed to recognize students' commitment to civic engagement, requires a separate application.

Applicants who are applying for financial aid should submit both the Free Application for Federal Student Aid (FAFSA) and the CSS PROFILE by the appropriate deadline dates (November 15 for Early Decision I; January 15 for Early Decision II and Regular Decision). The Gettysburg College Code Number for the PROFILE is 2275 and the Gettysburg College federal school code for the FAFSA is 003268.

STUDENT ORGANIZATIONS AND ACTIVITIES

At Gettysburg, students are "all in;" they engage in a broad range of activities that complement their academics both during the week and on the weekends. With more than 120 student-led clubs and organizations and 24 intercollegiate (NCAA division III) athletic programs, it's not uncommon for students to be involved in as many as three or more organizations. From student government and campus publications, to sports, the fine and performing arts, community service, and outdoor adventure, all clubs and organizations are run by students, creating more than a thousand leadership opportunities on campus. Don't see something you're interested in? Start your own organization!

ADMISSIONS PROCESS

If Gettysburg is your first choice, you are strongly encouraged to apply for Early Decision (ED) admission. Gettysburg offers two Early Decision deadline dates; the ED I application deadline is November 15 and the ED II deadline is January 15. Early Decision admissions decisions are released in student portals and mailed within one month of the deadline date. Regular Decision applications are due by January 15.

The Admissions Process at Gettysburg is highly selective and the admissions staff gives careful consideration to each application. We expect students to make the most of the academic offerings of their high school. Participation in a solid college preparatory program with enriched, accelerated, and advanced placement courses is expected. Grades in academic courses, quality and distribution of subjects, and rank in class (when applicable) are highly significant parts of the applicant's credentials.

The College is also very interested in individuals of character who will make positive contributions to the campus community and beyond. In estimating such qualities, we rely on what students say about themselves through essays, along with the recommendations from secondary school counselors and teachers. In-depth involvement in extracurricular and community service activities both inside and outside of school is favorably considered in the Admissions Process.

An admissions interview is strongly recommended, but not required. Interviews are available from April 1 of the junior year through early February of the senior year. Students applying to the Sunderman Conservatory of Music are required to audition.

Standardized test scores from the SAT or ACT exams are reviewed in the overall context of a student's application and academic record. If a student has taken the SAT or ACT more than once, only their highest section scores across all test dates will be considered as part of the final admissions decision. Gettysburg College accepts self-reported scores on the Common Application. SAT II exams are not required. Strong students who believe that standardized test scores do not accurately reflect the strength of their academic achievements can choose to be considered as test optional in the Admissions Process.

GONZAGA UNIVERSITY

AT A GLANCE

Gonzaga University, founded in 1887, is an independent, comprehensive university with a distinguished background in the Catholic, Jesuit, and humanistic tradition. Gonzaga emphasizes the moral and ethical implications of learning, living, and working in today's global society. Through the University Core Curriculum, each student develops a strong liberal arts foundation, which many alumni cite as a most valuable asset. In addition, students specialize in any of more than 75 academic programs and majors. Gonzaga enrolls approximately 5,300 undergraduates and 2,500 graduate and law students.

Gonzaga's 152-acre campus combines the old and new: College Hall, the original administration building, and DeSmet Residence Hall with the modern architectural structures of the John J. Hemmingson Center, Myrtle Woldson Performing Arts Center, Hughes Life Sciences Building, Jundt Art Center and Museum, and the PACCAR Center for Applied Science. The campus is characterized by sprawling green lawns and majestic evergreen trees. Towering above the campus are the stately spires of St. Aloysius Church, the well-recognized landmark featured in the University logo.

Gonzaga encompasses five undergraduate schools: Arts and Sciences, Business Administration, Education, Engineering and Applied Science, and Nursing and Human Physiology. The University offers the BA, BBA, BEd, BS, BSCE, BSCpE, BSCS, BSEE, BSEM, BSME, and BSN degrees.

Gonzaga offers several unique options for students. The Honors Program provides a rigorous liberal arts curriculum for intellectually curious students who thrive in a competitive academic environment. Business leaders mentor the Hogan Entrepreneurial Leadership Program students, and internships are an integral part of the program. The award-winning Gonzaga Alumni Mentor Program (GAMP) connects current students and recent graduates with alumni in their professional areas of interest. Students in the Comprehensive Leadership Program take a leadership minor curriculum that may be combined with any major, and they participate in valuable, interactive leadership experiences. The Army ROTC unit prepares select women and men as leaders in service of their communities and their country. Gonzaga's nationally ranked debate team includes all skill levels. The Mock Trial Team competes nationally and involves students majoring in many different areas of study. Internships, research with faculty, and community service learning enhance class time while providing students first-hand experience.

LOCATION AND ENVIRONMENT

As the hub of the Inland Northwest, Spokane plays a vital role in shaping the University's character. While offering urban advantages such as museum exhibits, shopping, symphony, Broadway and ballet performances, Spokane still maintains an intimate, friendly, and community atmosphere. Used for running and cycling, part of the 37-mile Centennial Trail, runs through campus and to Coeur d' Alene, Idaho. Within a short distance of campus, students snow and water ski, hike, cycle, rock climb, swim, camp, and golf. With an average rainfall of only 16.7 inches per year, outdoor activities are easily accessible.

The 20 residence halls and apartments on campus, both single-sex and coed, house 40 to 360 students each. First-year and sophomore students are required to live on campus. The Zagweb network provides students round-the-clock electronic access to email, Internet, campus intranet, and library holdings, all directly from residence hall rooms. Additionally, the whole campus is wireless. Resident Directors and Assistants, along with Chaplains and Social Justice Peer Educators, provide a fun, secure, and nurturing environment.

CAMPUS FACILITIES AND EQUIPMENT

The Foley Library contains more than 800,000 volumes and microform titles, with two special collections of material especially rich in the areas of philosophy and classical civilization, as well as the nation's most extensive collection of works concerning the famous Jesuit poet Gerard Manley Hopkins. The historic College Hall houses the Harry & Colleen Magnuson Theatre, a Florentine-style University Chapel, and numerous classrooms and faculty offices including the Office of Admission. Jesuits living and working in the Spokane area reside on campus in the new Della Strada Jesuit Community. Gonzaga is also home to the Bing Crosby House Museum, which houses a large collection of material relating to singer and actor, Bing Crosby, in his original home.

Students are able to produce sophisticated multimedia presentations and research hundreds of libraries across the country from their own residence hall rooms, by accessing campus-wide wireless, or from one of many labs on campus. The Communications Building offers an arts lab for the Bulletin (the weekly student-published newspaper), KAGU, the University's radio station, and GUTV, a state-of-the-art TV production station where students learn all aspects of broadcast studies. The Herak Center for Engineering offers state-of-the-art CAD/CAM, electronic, digital, microwave, and calibration labs, and the PACCAR Center for Applied Science, which received a "Gold" certification rating from the Leadership in Energy and Environmental Design (LEED), adds more classroom space, a robotics lab, a computer science lab with a high-speed cluster computer array, and the rapidly growing Electric Utility Transmission & Distribution program.

The Martin Athletic Centre boasts a 13,000 sq. ft. state-of-the-art fitness center, and next door, the 6000-seat McCarthey Athletic Center houses the men's and women's basketball games as well as concerts and events throughout the year. Washington Trust Field at Patterson Baseball Complex hosts the Gonzaga baseball program. The new Volkar Center for Athletic Achievement is located south of the Martin Centre and is designated to help student-athletes succeed in competition, in the classroom, and in the community.

Gonzaga has committed that any new buildings on campus (including the recent addition of the 167,726 square-foot John J. Hemmingson Center which was certified "Gold") will seek at least "Silver" LEED certification. Additionally, as a signatory of the Presidents' Climate Commitment, Gonzaga has created a Climate Action Plan to reduce its carbon footprint by 20% by 2020 and 50% by 2035 (from 2009 levels).

OFF-CAMPUS OPPORTUNITIES

Recognizing the importance of an international perspective for learning, Gonzaga offers study abroad programs in over 30 countries, including Argentina, Australia, Austria, Belgium, Bhutan, Cambodia, Chile, China, Colombia, Costa Rica, Denmark, Ecuador, England, France, Ghana, India, Ireland, Italy, Japan, Jordan, Kenya, Mexico, New Zealand, Panama, Peru, Scotland, South Africa, Spain, Tanzania, Turkey, Turks and Caicos, and Zambia. Gonzaga's campus in Florence, Italy is the most popular option.

ACADEMIC PROGRAMS

The core curriculum (an intentionally-designed set of courses bookended by the first-year and final year core integration seminars), encourages students to embrace an interdisciplinary mindset. All students take classes in writing, reasoning, scientific inquiry, mathematics, communication & speech, philosophy, religious studies, and English literature, and they further broaden their education with classes in the arts, humanities, social/behavior sciences, social justice, and global studies designated courses. The College of Arts & Sciences adds a requirement in modern or classical language proficiency that complements the core. Often, classes at Gonzaga require oral presentations or use of the written and discussion-based communication skills emphasized in the core curriculum.

MAJORS AND DEGREES OFFERED

Gonzaga offers the following areas of study in the five undergraduate schools. The College of Arts and Sciences offers applied mathematics, art, biochemistry, biology (research), broadcast & electronic media studies, chemistry, classical civilizations, communication studies, computer science and computational thinking, criminology, economics, English (writing concentration), environmental studies, French, history, international studies (including international relations and Asian, European, and Latin American studies), Italian studies, journalism, mathematics, music (including emphases in composition, general studies, performance, and sacred music), music education (choral and instrumental), philosophy (Kossel concentration option), physics, political science, psychology (research), public relations, religious studies (Christian theology and religious pluralism concentrations), sociology, Spanish, and theatre arts (performance and technical concentrations). Additionally, the School offers minors in art history, Asian studies, Catholic studies, critical race & ethnic studies, conducting, dance, German, history of race & ethnic communities, interdisciplinary arts, Italian, jazz performance, Latin American history, leadership studies, Native American studies, solidarity and social justice, visual literacy, women's & gender studies, and writing. Students interested in the following areas take tracks of classes respectively in pre-dentistry, pre-law, pre-health sciences, pre-medicine, pre-physical therapy, and pre-veterinary studies. The School of Business Administration offers majors in accounting or business administration (with concentrations in economics, entrepreneurship and innovation, finance, human resource management, individualized study, international business, law and public policy, management information systems, marketing, and operations and supply chain management). The School of Business also offers the following minors to non-business majors: analytical finance, digital marketing, economics, entrepreneurship & innovation, general business, management information systems, promotion, and sustainable business (available to business majors as well). As well as granting teacher certification on both the elementary and secondary levels, the School of Education offers degrees in community, culture, & language (with an optional teaching certification track), kinesiology and physical education (with a fitness specialist track), special education, and sport management. The School of Engineering and Applied Science offers computer science and civil, computer, electrical, and mechanical engineering degrees, as well as an engineering management degree and a 5-year BSEM/MBA option. Also, The School of Nursing and Human Physiology offers human physiology and nursing degrees at the undergraduate level. Advanced degrees in accounting, business, communication and leadership, education, educational leadership, engineering, law, leadership studies, nursing, organizational leadership, philosophy, teaching English as a second language, and theology and leadership are also offered.

TUITION, ROOM, BOARD, FEES
Tuition for the 2020–2021 academic year is $46,060; room and board is estimated at $12,880. Including tuition, room and board, books, fees, transportation, and living expenses, Gonzaga estimates $64,802 as the total cost of attendance for the 2020–2021 year.

FINANCIAL AID
99% percent of admitted students earn scholarships and/or grants. The average package for 2019–2020 was $33,655 awarded in the form of grants, scholarships, loans, and campus employment. A number of merit-based, merit/need-based, athletic, music, debate, and other program scholarships are awarded to students each year. The Free Application for Federal Student Aid (FAFSA) is available on October 1, and Gonzaga encourages students to apply as close to October 1 as they can and up to December 1 to be eligible for Gonzaga's Priority Awarding Pool. Also, check the website for scholarship information and online applications. Gonzaga is committed to working with students and families to finance their investment in a quality education.

STUDENT ORGANIZATIONS AND ACTIVITIES
GU students enjoy a wide variety of activities on and off campus. The Gonzaga Student Body Association (GSBA) oversees over one hundred academic, social, and cultural clubs and provides the structure of student government. Some of the most popular clubs include the Outdoors Club, THIRST (a non-denominational worship group), the Kennel Club (student cheering section for basketball games), GUTS (an improvisational comedy team), and the Hawaii Pacific Islanders Club. GSBA organizes service and conservation projects, dances, and countless other activities to channel and challenge the talents and passions of motivated men and women who seek to make a difference.

As the leading provider of service hours in the entire city of Spokane, Gonzaga University encourages students to engage with the community at any of the area nonprofit organizations. Mission & Ministry, the Gonzaga Student Body Association, Unity Multicultural Education Center, Lincoln LGBTQ+ Center, and the Center for Community Engagement (CCE) provide organized projects through which students become involved in the greater Spokane community and other cities.

Division I, West Coast Conference sports include baseball (men), basketball, crew, cross-country/track, golf, soccer, tennis, and volleyball (women). Approximately 60% of students participate in intramural and club sports such as ultimate frisbee and rugby. The Harry & Colleen Magnuson Theatre and the Myrtle Woldson Center for Performing Arts host main-stage plays (including musicals), dance recitals, GUTS, sketch comedy, numerous one-acts and student directed scenes as well as professional musical, theatrical, and dance performances and clinics. Gonzaga's musical groups include a nationally recognized University Choir, a Chorale, the GU Symphony, the Jazz Ensemble, the Gonzaga Bulldog Band, The Big Bing Theory-an a cappella group, and numerous other ensembles. GU's students also host programs on Gonzaga's TV and radio stations. Additionally, many students participate in Mission & Ministry events such as retreats, the annual Pilgrimage hike, THIRST, Masses, Christian Life Communities, and interdenominational and/or interfaith services.

ADMISSIONS PROCESS
The University seeks diligent, inquisitive applicants with diverse backgrounds who will benefit from the rigorous Jesuit instruction at Gonzaga as well as enhance the University environment. A Common Application (www.commonapp.org) and the Gonzaga member page, SAT I (Essay Section not required) or ACT scores (Writing Section not required), a transcript, a teacher recommendation, a school report, an activities list or resume, and an essay are required. Transfer students and students with any college credit must submit official transcripts from all colleges. Transfer students must also complete the Gonzaga Application for Transfers (https://apply.gonzaga.edu/apply/), including the Transfer College Report and Academic Evaluation. Transfer application decisions are sent on a rolling basis. International students must also submit official transcripts from all colleges attended. Additionally, international students must submit official results of one of the following: TOEFL, IELTS, SAT, or ACT examination. The Application Deadline for Admission for domestic and international first-year students is December 1, and decisions are sent by the beginning of March. Students can apply up to February 1 for late consideration. After February 1, applications will be accepted only if space is available. Nursing (first-year students only) and Engineering have direct entry admissions, and the limited spaces available make the majors the most competitive.

For more information on Gonzaga, please see: www.gonzaga.edu.

HIGH POINT UNIVERSITY

AT A GLANCE

High Point University is The Premier Life Skills University working to transform the lives of its students.

Innovative educational initiatives like the President's Seminar on Life Skills, a required course for all freshmen, ensures students grow not only in specific academic areas of expertise, but also develop competencies in communication, networking, coachability, fiscal literacy and service. These are among the traits HPU refers to as "life skills," which employers rank as the most critical skills necessary to succeed in the modern workplace.

With 60 majors and 64 minors, HPU offers a broad spectrum of academic coursework, all complemented by experiential learning programs that include internships, undergraduate research, global education and service learning. Their approach to life preparation is perhaps best showcased by their 97% placement rate of graduates employed or enrolled in graduate school within six months of graduating from HPU.

In addition to expert faculty who have been attracted from places like Duke University, Harvard University, Stanford University, Cornell University, Johns Hopkins University and many other impressive institutions, HPU has also attracted global leaders and industry giants to mentor students as part of a unique "In Residence" program designed to foster life skills and leadership development. Examples include:

- Steve Wozniak, Apple Co-founder and HPU's Innovator in Residence
- Marc Randolph, Netflix Co-founder and HPU's Entrepreneur in Residence
- Cynt Marshall, Dallas Mavericks CEO and HPU's Sports Executive in Residence
- Karen Jacobsen, The "GPS Girl," voice of Australian Siri and HPU's Global Artist in Residence
- Joe Michaels, 20-year Veteran Director of NBC's TODAY Show and HPU's Broadcaster in Residence
- Byron Pitts, Journalist and Co-anchor of ABC's "Nightline" and HPU's Journalist in Residence
- Bob Ryan, Famed Sports Columnist for The Boston Globe and HPU's Sports Reporter in Residence

By focusing holistically on the student's transformational education journey, HPU attracts students from all 50 states and nearly 40 countries. Since 2005, HPU has transformed its campus and culture under the leadership of President Nido R. Qubein. HPU has completed a $2 billion investment in academic programs (six new academic schools added), student life facilities (including two student centers), 10 new residential communities, and a $250 million Innovation Corridor. This fall, a 4,500-seat basketball arena and conference center will open.

High Point University is a values-based institution that believes each member of its faculty and staff has the power to enhance the lives of the students entrusted to their care. Their call to action is simple and profound: Choose to be extraordinary! And they live by it every day.

LOCATION AND ENVIRONMENT

With 4,600 undergraduate students, High Point University is a small university with big-school facilities. Its 16 varsity teams play at the NCAA Division I level. Students come to HPU from 50 states and 40 countries, providing the school with great diversity in student history and experience. HPU offers its students a safe community that feels like home, where the average class size is 18, and professors don't just know students' names—they know who they are and who they want to become.

Nestled within the city of High Point, North Carolina, HPU sits in the center of the Piedmont Triad, North Carolina's third largest metropolitan area with more than 1.6 million people. Both Greensboro and Winston-Salem are 20 minutes from campus. East of campus are Raleigh (1.5 hours away) and the Atlantic Ocean (4 hours away); south of campus are Charlotte (1.5 hours away) and Atlanta, Georgia (5 hours away); and west of campus are the Appalachian Mountains (2 hours away).

CAMPUS FACILITIES AND EQUIPMENT

High Point University is committed to providing state-of-the-art facilities across disciplines that meet the needs of extraordinary students. Cottrell Hall, home to the Flanagan Center for Student Success, is a 40,000 square-foot facility that is the central hub of activity for students preparing for job interviews, seeking career development opportunities and looking for ways to diversify their career skills.

The state-of-the-art 220,000 square-foot Congdon Hall features a pharmacology research lab, a gross anatomy lab, a human biomechanics and physiology lab and more than a dozen simulation labs and spaces where real-world scenarios can come to life, including an operating room, an emergency room, a labor and delivery room, eight exam rooms, a pharmacy retail setting and a pharmacy hospital setting.

The Nido R. Qubein School of Communication features a high-definition TV studio, an audio recording studio, a screening theater, editing labs, a student-operated radio station, a nationally-cited survey and research center, a recently updated game design and Esports arena, and various computer labs. The school's Board of Advisors includes leaders in radio, television, newspaper and magazine companies across the nation.

HPU's School of Art and Design emphasizes the importance of hands-on skills combined with technological proficiency in profession-specific software. Students studying in the School of Art and Design have access to cutting-edge equipment including a technology lab and several design-specific computer labs.

The 31,000 square-foot, LEED-Certified Stout School of Education building houses the psychology department and the NCATE-accredited education school. It is equipped with simulated classrooms and clinical labs where psychology majors conduct hands-on testing and experiments.

The Plato S. Wilson School of Commerce houses the Tilley Trading Room, which includes a live stock ticker and allows students to receive real-world, practical learning opportunities. The space also includes teaching and research technology, such as financial databases, investment software, and more.

OFF-CAMPUS OPPORTUNITIES

Together, the cities of High Point, Greensboro and Winston-Salem form the Piedmont Triad, a metropolitan area with a population of more than 1.6 million. High Point University is located within 25 minutes of the Piedmont Triad International Airport.

The Piedmont Triad is a dynamic market that is poised for tremendous growth. Contributing factors are its temperate climate, centralized location affording quick access to major metros, relatively low population density, high quality of life, high education index, diversity and inclusion, and the development of markets to leverage its manufacturing experience.

Downtown High Point revitalization efforts, led by HPU's own President Nido Qubein, are centered on the city's newly finished baseball stadium, BB&T Point, home to the High Point Rockers. The stadium is attracting new energy to downtown High Point, and so are plans for an events center, children's museum and urban park. Already, the city enjoys a vibrant Main Street area with shops, restaurants and gathering places, such as the Downtown Train Depot or The Pit Murals. These features, combined with the twice-yearly bustling furniture market and the new baseball stadium, are attracting new people who want to live in High Point's hub of excitement.

High Point University is fortunate to be located in the furniture capital of the world, the city of High Point. HPU students biannually assist High Point Market exhibitors to prepare for the largest home furnishings industry trade show in the world. With more than 75,000 attendees and 2,000 exhibitors, the biannual event attracts industry leaders from across the globe and provides students with experiential learning opportunities. While supporting an international trade show in the heart of downtown High Point, HPU students gain hands-on experience that helps them hone their professional skills through experiential learning.

Numerous global companies have a large presence here including Ashley Furniture, Bank of America, BB&T, Daimler Buses of North America, DT, Ernst & Young, FedEx, HanesBrands, Honda Aircraft Company, KPMG, Lincoln Financial Group, Old Dominion Freight Lines, Polo Ralph Lauren Corporation, PwC, Qorvo, and Volvo. In addition to internships, the student experience is enhanced through business relationships with activities such as mentoring sessions, speaker events, sales role-plays, experiential learning assignments, business community projects, and a variety of career-related events.

ACADEMIC PROGRAMS

High Point University has 60 majors and 64 undergraduate minors, 12 pre-professional programs and 13 graduate programs to choose from. Students may choose an area of study they've always been passionate about, a subject that they've recently become interested in or a major that they've never considered before. The opportunities are endless at HPU. Some of the most popular undergraduate majors include Business, Exercise Science, Communications, Education, Biology and Interior Design.

STUDENT ORGANIZATIONS AND ACTIVITIES

High Point University's entire campus inspires students to perform at their highest levels academically and socially. There are numerous opportunities for students to be involved, learn, and grow, reinforcing HPU's call to action: Choose to Be Extraordinary! *

HPU's Kester International Promenade is lined with flags representing countries from which students hail. The residential communities are as diverse as the student population and provide opportunities for honors housing, and living and learning communities. All housing is new or recently renovated, with many dorms providing apartment-style living.

The campus is completely wireless, and students are able to check out complimentary iPads or Kindles from the Campus Concierge. Students may also schedule academic tutoring, reserve a bicycle, and receive complimentary tickets to all athletic events, concerts, speakers and films.

HPU is committed to surrounding students with an environment that motivates and inspires learning. The university regularly hosts internationally acclaimed thought leaders who interact with the student body, helping students to discover their own path to personal growth and leadership. These leaders include people like Former U.S. Secretary of State, Condoleezza Rice; Astronaut Buzz Aldrin; Apple Co-founder and HPU's Innovator in Residence, Steve Wozniak; and Former First Lady Laura Bush.

Opportunities for student engagement are abundant at High Point University. With 80% of students coming from out-of-state and 95% living on-campus, the student body has a distinct sense of family. There's no denying the beauty of HPU—most families notice that first. But it isn't about beauty; it's about intentional living. When students have been immersed in professional settings for years, they grow confident and unintimidated. HPU instills in students a growth mindset. They live, learn and grow to understand that intelligence, like a muscle, can be exercised and strengthened. This way of thinking enables students to learn more efficiently and transforms them into lifelong learners—a skill that will stay with them long after they graduate. There are also quotations that provide ideas for reflection. Sculptures of significant historical figures inspire students to pursue their goals. The Mariana H. Qubein Arboretum and Botanical Gardens bring holistic learning to life throughout HPU's 500-acre classroom.

High Point University has nearly 100 clubs and organizations providing students diverse opportunities to get involved on campus! From volunteering in the local community, gaining a leadership position in the Student Government Association, joining a Greek life organization or playing intramural or club sports, every student can find a way to make High Point University their home!

To find a full list of current student clubs and organizations and contact information, visit www.highpoint.edu/studentactivities/.

TUITION, ROOM, BOARD, FEES

Tuition & Fees: $38,080
Room & Dining Plan: $15,438

FINANCIAL AID

The Office of Student Financial Planning works diligently to assist students in their pursuit of postsecondary education at High Point University. Although the financial aid process can be complex, HPU's Financial Planning staff are well trained and highly qualified to make students' experiences positive and rewarding.

Interested students should submit the Free Application for Federal Student Aid (FAFSA) electronically via www.fafsa.ed.gov. The earliest that students may begin filing the FAFSA is October 1 of the senior year prior to entrance to HPU. The HPU school code is 002933.

The results from filing the FAFSA will be electronically transmitted to HPU for review. This form will produce an expected family contribution based on the family's financial data and will determine students' eligibility for HPU's need-based programs.

HPU will not be able to estimate students' eligibility for need-based aid until the FAFSA is filed. While there is not a deadline date for FAFSA, it is important to file as early as possible; HPU releases financial aid package information for students on March 1.

All major High Point University academic scholarships are awarded through the Presidential Scholarship and High Point Scholars programs. Each Early Decision or Early Action undergraduate admissions application also serves as an application for these scholarships.

ADMISSIONS PROCESS

High Point University is an exclusive member of the Common Application, which helps facilitate the application process for you. The Office of Undergraduate Admissions is available to help you throughout the entire application and decision process. If you have any questions about the university or application, we encourage you to reach out.

Complete and submit your application for admission and all required supporting documents online at www.commonapp.org/school/high-point-university.

Ask your guidance or college counselor to send your official high school transcript to the Office of Undergraduate Admissions or upload it to the Common App.

Ask your guidance or college counselor to complete and submit the Common App's School Report Form. Provide one letter of recommendation.

High Point University is test-optional. If you would like to be considered for the Presidential Scholarship Program or Honors Scholar Program, an SAT or ACT score is required. When completing the test, request that the official results of the SAT or ACT be sent to the Office of Undergraduate Admissions. High Point University's SAT code is 5293; the ACT code is 3108.

Application deadlines are as follows:

Early Decision (binding) application deadline: November 1
Admissions notification date: November 23

Early Action (nonbinding) application deadline: November 15
Admissions notification date: December 16

Early Decision II (binding) application deadline: February 1
Admissions notification is within 30 days

Regular Decision Priority: February 1
Admissions notification is within 30 days

Regular Decision application deadline: March 1
Admissions notification is rolling.

Over 85% of enrolled students each year apply using one of the two Early Decision or Early Action November application plans.

HILLSDALE COLLEGE

AT A GLANCE

Hillsdale College offers a traditional, classical, liberal arts education featuring a strong core curriculum and a dedicated faculty.

Hillsdale is a private, independent, nonsectarian Christian institution of higher learning. It was founded in 1844 by men and women who described themselves as "grateful to God for the inestimable blessings" resulting from civil and religious liberty and as "believing that the diffusion of learning is essential to the perpetuity of those blessings." The College has maintained institutional independence since its founding by refusing to accept aid from federal authorities. Private support from a national constituency has enabled Hillsdale to continue its trusteeship of the intellectual and spiritual inheritance tracing to Athens and Jerusalem. The undergraduate enrollment for Fall 2019 was 1,468—52 percent men and 48 percent women—from 49 states and 11 foreign countries. The freshman class entering in Fall 2019 had an average GPA of 3.91, ACT of 31, and SAT of 1381. All Hillsdale students sign an Honor Code encouraging self-government and committing them to honesty, duty, and respect. Students are housed in single-sex dormitories, fraternity and sorority houses, and off-campus houses. Each College-owned residence hall is supervised by a resident director and resident advisers. Special student services provided by the College include career planning and placement counseling, academic advising and tutoring, and a health service staffed by a resident nurse, counselors, and visiting medical professionals.

LOCATION AND ENVIRONMENT

Hillsdale College is located in the south-central Michigan town of Hillsdale (population 8,000) near the Ohio and Indiana borders. Stores, churches, restaurants, and coffee shops are all within walking distance of the campus.

CAMPUS FACILITIES AND EQUIPMENT

The Hillsdale College Mossey Library features a collection of more than 1,500,000 volumes (print and electronic), including rare and special holdings such as the Ludwig von Mises and Russell Kirk collections.

Lane and Kendall Halls contain classroom space and faculty offices for the humanities and social sciences, and Kendall Hall features an experimental psychology laboratory. The Strosacker Science Center and the Herbert Henry Dow Science Building provide classrooms and laboratories for the natural sciences. The Joseph H. Moss Family Laboratory Wing includes a microbiology/cell biology lab, anatomy/physiology lab with human cadaver access, conservation genetics lab, water lab, greenhouse, and organic/general chemistry labs. Slayton Arboretum is a 48-acre garden and bird sanctuary used by students to conduct research.

At the Mary Randall Preschool, nursery school children are taught by students specializing in early childhood education and psychology. Hillsdale Academy, a K–12 private school, provides additional opportunities for classroom observation.

The Roche Sports Complex is available to varsity athletes and the general student body alike. It houses the Dawn Tibbetts Potter Arena, with a student fitness center and basketball/volleyball courts, the John "Jack" McAvoy Natatorium for swimming and diving, an exercise physiology and sports medicine facility, four racquetball courts, extensive locker room space, and a weight/fitness room. Adjacent to the sports complex is the Frank "Muddy" Waters Stadium, which features an artificial surface football field; an all-weather, Olympic-quality eight-lane running track; outdoor tennis courts; and fields for soccer, baseball, and women's softball. The Margot V. Biermann Athletic Center houses four acrylic tennis courts and a six-lane, 200-meter NCAA regulation Mondo surface track. The 113-acre John Anthony Halter Shooting Sports Education Center, located five miles from the main campus, features seven American trap fields, a five-stand sporting clays field, a small arms range, a skeet field for both American and International skeet, an Olympic bunker, an outdoor Olympic archery range, a 20-station sporting clays course, and a lodge and education center.

The Fine Arts Building is home to the departments of art and theatre. It contains studios, classroom space, an exhibition gallery, a prop and scene-construction shop, a sound studio, graphics lab, black box theatre, and Markel Auditorium, a 353-seat performance hall (with orchestra pit). Howard Music Hall houses McNamara Rehearsal Hall, Conrad Recital Hall, studio space for percussion and jazz studies, offices, and student practice rooms.

The Grewcock Student Union houses the cafeteria, bookstore, student mail center, offices for student activities and publications, a lounge with a 100-inch flat screen television, a formal lounge and conference room, AJ's Café, and a game area. Hayden Park sits at the northeastern perimeter of campus and encompasses 190 acres of rolling, partially wooded farmland. In addition to serving as a course for Hillsdale's cross-country teams and offering a driving range for the golf team, it provides a place for mountain biking, cross-country skiing, sand volleyball, and intramural competition, as well as general outdoor recreation. The 27,000-square-foot Christ Chapel opened in 2019 and serves as a performance venue, as a center for campus spiritual life, and as a symbol of Hillsdale's Christian roots and identity.

OFF-CAMPUS OPPORTUNITIES

For more than forty years, the Washington-Hillsdale Internship Program (WHIP) has provided students the opportunity to participate in full-time, academically intensive internships in Washington, D.C. Past interns and fellows have been placed in locations such as the U.S. Senate, the White House, think tanks, news and media outlets, and national security agencies. Students complement their internships with classes at Hillsdale's Allan P. Kirby, Jr. Center for Constitutional Studies and Citizenship. Through the College's affiliations with the Center for Medieval and Renaissance Studies and the Oxford Study Abroad Program, Hillsdale students can study abroad at one of the more than thirty colleges of Oxford University. Hillsdale also offers a summer business program in cooperation with Regent's College in London, England, and the opportunity to study at the University of St. Andrews in St. Andrews, Scotland. Science students benefit from Hillsdale's 685-acre field research laboratory in northern Michigan, as well as from a marine biology program in the Florida Keys and internship opportunities with the Omaha Zoo. Foreign language students frequently study abroad in Argentina, France, Germany, and Spain.

ACADEMIC PROGRAMS

Hillsdale operates on a two-semester schedule. Two 3-week summer sessions are also offered. The College believes that a sound classical liberal arts education includes study in the humanities, natural sciences, and social sciences, and each student is required to complete a structured core of courses in these areas. To graduate, students must complete a minimum 124 hours of coursework and fulfill the requirements of at least one major field. The B.A. program includes a foreign language proficiency requirement. The B.S. program requires additional studies in mathematics and the natural sciences.

The Collegiate Scholars Program enriches the academic experience of high-performing students by providing opportunities to become deeply versed in the contents and methods of inquiry of the liberal arts. A combination of seminars, campus lectures and discussions, retreats, subsidized foreign travel, and the completion of an interdisciplinary senior thesis help to meet this goal.

The Center for Constructive Alternatives conducts four weeklong symposia during the academic year. These programs, with themes ranging from history to politics, business, science, and the arts, bring distinguished scholars and public figures to the campus. All students are required to enroll in at least one seminar for credit during their time at Hillsdale.

MAJORS AND DEGREES OFFERED

Hillsdale awards Bachelor of Arts and Bachelor of Science degrees in accounting, applied mathematics, art, biochemistry, biology, chemistry, classics, economics, English, exercise science, financial management, French, German, Greek, history, Latin, marketing/management, mathematics, music, philosophy, philosophy and religion, physical education, physics, politics, psychology, religion, rhetoric and public address, Spanish, sport management, sport psychology, and theatre. Interdisciplinary majors are also available in American studies, Christian studies, comparative literature, European studies, international studies in business and foreign language, political economy, and sociology and social thought. Pre-professional programs are offered in allied health sciences, chiropractic, dentistry, education, engineering, journalism, law, medicine, ministry, optometry, pharmacy, physical therapy, and veterinary medicine. The Van Andel Graduate School of Statesmanship offers a Doctor of Philosophy in politics and a Master of Arts in politics. In 2019, Hillsdale launched the Steve and Amy Van Andel Graduate School of Government in Washington, D.C., offering an M.A. degree in government.

TUITION, ROOM, BOARD, FEES

Annual tuition for the 2019–20 academic year was $27,090, room was $5,640, board was $5,750, and general fees were $1,278. Books, supplies, and personal expenses (including travel, recreation, and clothing) are estimated at $3,200 per year.

FINANCIAL AID

Academic scholarships are awarded on a competitive basis, regardless of financial need. The priority fall term application deadline for academic scholarship consideration is January 1. The application for admission also serves as the application for merit-based aid. Athletic scholarships are available on a competitive basis in men's baseball, football, and golf; men's and women's basketball, tennis, track, and cross-country; and women's swimming, softball, and volleyball. The departments of art and music also award a select number of scholarships based on strength of portfolio/audition. To apply for aid on the basis of financial need, students are required to file Hillsdale's Confidential Family Financial Statement (CFFS). Because Hillsdale does not accept government funds either directly for its operations or indirectly in the form of student aid, the FAFSA is not applicable; government funds are replaced with private dollars. Grants and loans are available from the College.

STUDENT ORGANIZATIONS AND ACTIVITIES

Four national fraternities, three national sororities, a newspaper and radio station, and more than 100 other social, academic, spiritual, and service organizations provide Hillsdale students with a diverse array of co-curricular opportunities. A resident drama troupe and dance company, a concert choir and chamber chorale, a jazz program with big band and combos, instrumental chamber ensembles from string quartets to percussion ensemble, and a symphony orchestra and band constitute the College's performing arts organizations. Hillsdale's Charger athletes compete in 14 intercollegiate NCAA Division II varsity sports as part of the Great Midwest Athletic Conference (G-MAC). An active intramural program is also available. The Student Activities Board hosts campus-wide social functions throughout the year, including events like Garden Party, Homecoming, President's Ball, and Centralhallapalooza.

ADMISSIONS PROCESS

Important determinants for admission are intellectual curiosity, ambition, leadership, and volunteerism. Accordingly, grade-point average, test scores, strength of curriculum, extracurricular activities, interviews, self-evaluations, writing samples, and recommendations are all reviewed carefully and are important in the evaluation process. An admissions interview is strongly encouraged. A formal application includes a completed application form accompanied by a nonrefundable fee of $35 (free if submitted online) and all required credentials. Transfer students must submit the standard application, including the high school record, SAT, ACT, or CLT scores, transcripts from all colleges previously attended, and a transfer form from the dean of students of the most recent college attended. Applications by transfers are evaluated similarly to non-transfers. Candidates for admission from other countries follow the regular entrance procedures. Students who come from a non-English-speaking country must submit all required documents in English and must complete the SAT, ACT, or CLT to demonstrate proficiency in English as well as academic preparedness. The Test of English as a Foreign Language (TOEFL) or the Michigan Test of English Proficiency are recommended to help further demonstrate English proficiency. Students may apply to Hillsdale College any time after the completion of the junior year of high school. Hillsdale accepts The Common Application.

Students may apply under one of three plans. Early Decision is a binding application deadline, where students are asked to withdraw applications from other institutions should their application be accepted by Hillsdale. The due date for Early Decision candidates is November 1, and notification is early December. The deadline for Regular Decision is April 1, and students are notified of a decision within four weeks of finalizing their application (beginning December 15). Deadline for priority merit scholarship consideration is January 1. Spring Admission candidates should submit application materials by December 15 with priority consideration given to applications completed by November 1, and will receive notification within two weeks of completing their application file (beginning November 15). Hillsdale College has been distinguished since its founding by voluntarily adhering to a nondiscriminatory policy regarding race, religion, sex, and national or ethnic origin.

HOFSTRA UNIVERSITY

AT A GLANCE

Hofstra University is a diverse, dynamic community where you can pursue your passions, with a greater purpose. Our classes are small, and our programs are tailored to empower students to seek, shape, and discover their own educational and career path.

Live, work, and play on a suburban campus with landscaped quads and ivy-covered buildings that's less than an hour by train from New York City, with its countless cultural, recreational, and internship opportunities.

Build leadership skills through varied clubs, organizations, and service projects. Our students log 100,000 volunteer hours every year, and Hofstra has been recognized by the President's Higher Education Community Service Honor Roll for seven consecutive years.

Hofstra University is internationally recognized by *U.S. News & World Report*, The Princeton Review, and PayScale College ROI and Salary Reports. We are the only university to host three consecutive U.S. presidential debates (2008, 2012, and 2016), and one of only three universities in the New York metropolitan area with schools of engineering, medicine, and law.

Our more than 10,000 students come from 51 states and territories and 88 countries, but they share an entrepreneurial spirit, a curiosity about the world, and a desire to make a difference. At Hofstra, you will be challenged, you will be supported, you will discover your best self.

You will be a world changer.

LOCATION AND ENVIRONMENT

Hofstra is a global community just 25 miles east of Manhattan. Our 244-acre campus is a nationally registered arboretum with 75 outdoor sculptures that blooms with thousands of tulips every spring.

Students can choose to live in one of our 35 residence halls, each with a unique flair, community, and life of its own. We also offer 10 living-learning communities, in which students live with classmates in the same programs, or who share the same passion for leadership, health professions, or the arts.

CAMPUS FACILITIES AND EQUIPMENT

Connect with the real world through experiential learning in our cutting-edge facilities, including the Martin B. Greenberg Trading Room; WRHU-88.7 FM, Radio Hofstra University; a big data lab; a robotics and advanced manufacturing lab; a cell and tissue engineering lab; and a Cybersecurity and Innovation Research Center. Hofstra also boasts six theaters, as well as the most historically accurate replica of Shakespeare's original Globe stage in the U.S., which is used for the University's annual Shakespeare Festival.

The David S. Mack Sports and Exhibition Complex is a 5,023-seat arena that is home to the Hofstra Pride men's wrestling team and the men's and women's basketball teams.

Our nationally accredited museum has a permanent collection of more than 5,000 works of art.

OFF-CAMPUS OPPORTUNITIES

Hofstra extends learning beyond the classroom through internship programs, a Co-op program, and study abroad opportunities. Our internship programs capitalize on the University's proximity to New York City, allowing students to gain on-the-job experience in areas such as advertising, business, entertainment, finance, and media. The Co-op program at the Fred DeMatteis School of Engineering and Applied Science offers students paid work experience in a field related to their major.

Study abroad programs are offered in Europe, Asia, South America, and more. Students can explore the world while enhancing their college experience and earning course credits. Learn more at hofstra.edu/studyabroad.

ACADEMIC PROGRAMS

Learn the art of filmmaking from an Emmy Award-winning director. Discuss economic policy with top business leaders and former Cabinet members. Debate political strategy with a former presidential candidate. Participate in faculty research projects sponsored by the National Science Foundation. Our professors are scholars, artists, and scientists who are passionate about their work and dedicated to teaching and training the next generation of leaders.

With an average undergraduate class size of 21 and a student-faculty ratio of 13-to-1, students are encouraged to debate, question, and think critically in an open, collaborative learning environment. Ninety-one percent of our full-time faculty hold the highest degree in their respective fields.

Requirements for graduation vary among schools and majors. A liberal arts core curriculum is integral to all areas of concentration. Hofstra's academic calendar is organized in a traditional fall and spring semester system, and offers an optional January session and three optional summer sessions (between May and August).

Hofstra offers innovative programs to meet the needs of its diverse student body. These include Hofstra University Honors College, Legal Education Accelerated Program (LEAP), Hofstra 4+4 Program (a highly selective BA-BS/MD program), Physician Assistant Studies Program (a highly selective BS/MS program), and First-Year Connections.

Hofstra University Honors College students can study in any of the University's undergraduate programs and are involved in all fields of advanced study.

ILLINOIS INSTITUTE OF TECHNOLOGY

MAJORS AND DEGREES OFFERED

Hofstra holds 29 academic and 33 total accreditations. The University offers six undergraduate degrees—BA, BBA, BE, BFA, BS, and BSEd—and approximately 160 undergraduate program options. Hofstra also offers more than 100 dual-degree programs, which allow students to earn both an undergraduate and graduate degree in less time, and at lower cost, than if each degree was pursued separately.

The University comprises the following schools: Hofstra College of Liberal Arts and Sciences (Peter S. Kalikow School of Government, Public Policy and International Affairs; School of Education; School of Humanities, Fine and Performing Arts; School of Natural Sciences and Mathematics); Hofstra University Honors College; Frank G. Zarb School of Business; The Lawrence Herbert School of Communication; Fred DeMatteis School of Engineering and Applied Science; Academic Health Sciences Center (Donald and Barbara Zucker School of Medicine at Hofstra/Northwell; Hofstra Northwell School of Graduate Nursing and Physician Assistant Studies; School of Health Professions and Human Services); and Maurice A. Deane School of Law.

TUITION, ROOM, BOARD, FEES

The 2019–2020 annual tuition and fees for a full-time undergraduate student were $47,510. The cost of a housing and dining plan was approximately $15,940. Visit hofstra.edu/tuition for the full tuition and fees schedule.

FINANCIAL AID

Hofstra University works hard to make a private college education affordable for students and families, and offers several financial aid options for new undergraduates, including interest-free payment plans and a money-saving four-year locked-in rate for tuition and fees (hofstra.edu/lockedintuitionrate) to help students manage costs from admission through graduation. For details, students should visit hofstra.edu/financialaid.

STUDENT ORGANIZATIONS AND ACTIVITIES

Hofstra is home to 26 local/national fraternities and sororities, and more than 220 academic, media, multicultural, performance, pre-professional, religious, social/political, and sports clubs and organizations. Hofstra also offers 21 intercollegiate athletic programs competing at the NCAA Division I level.

The Student Government Association (SGA) is Hofstra's student-run governing body. Composed of full-time undergraduate students, the SGA is a liaison between students and the University's faculty, administration, and Board of Trustees. The SGA plans and executes multiple programs and initiatives throughout the academic year, and oversees the finances of over 180 clubs and organizations.

ADMISSIONS PROCESS

Hofstra University seeks to enroll students from diverse backgrounds and geographic locations, with varied interests. Applications are accepted for fall and spring admission. The Admission Committee reviews each application individually to assess academic achievement, curricular rigor, leadership potential, depth of extracurricular activities, standardized test scores, and overall interest in attending Hofstra. The application process provides an opportunity for the prospective student to share information that may not be apparent on a transcript or through a test score. Go to hofstra.edu/admission for information about the admission process, or go to hofstra.edu/visit to schedule a campus visit today!

ILLINOIS INSTITUTE OF TECHNOLOGY

AT A GLANCE

Founded in 1890, Illinois Institute of Technology is a private, independent research university that is innovation centered and idea driven. Illinois Tech is Chicago's only tech-focused university and the place where smart students from throughout the world discover, create, and solve.

Ranked as a Best Value School and among the top National Universities by *U.S. News & World Report,* Illinois Tech offers undergraduate and graduate degrees in engineering, science, architecture, business, design, human sciences, applied technology, and law. Our signature hands-on academic programs provide a truly distinctive education.

LOCATION AND ENVIRONMENT

Illinois Tech's location in Chicago provides students the best of both worlds: the excitement of living in an amazing global metropolis, combined with the comfort and small-town feel of attending a private university.

Our Mies Campus is located in the city of Chicago, just 15 minutes from downtown and less a mile away from Lake Michigan. With a total enrollment of 6,840 (2,883 undergraduates), students never feel like just a number.

With endless options come unlimited opportunities to discover: diversity, inspiration, languages, landscapes, viewpoints, technology, history, future, surprises—and most importantly, yourself.

CAMPUS FACILITIES AND EQUIPMENT

Some of the most famous buildings in the world, designed by legendary architects, are located on Illinois Tech's Mies Campus in Chicago. S. R. Crown Hall, an elegant steel-and-glass National Historic Landmark, is a marvel of engineering and simplicity by influential architect and former head of architecture at Illinois Tech, Ludwig Mies van der Rohe. Elevated trains run through the Rem Koolhaas-designed McCormick Tribune Campus Center. And Helmut Jahn's Rowe Village residence hall was named one of the "coolest dorms in the nation" (*U.S. News & World Report*).

Ed Kaplan Family Institute for Innovation and Tech Entrepreneurship is our new home for big ideas. Open in 2018, the Kaplan Institute is the HQ of the IPRO Program, Idea Shop, world-renowned Institute of Design, and work spaces where students' entrepreneurial endeavors can incubate and flourish. Special programming fosters creativity, ideation, and no-holds-barred thinking—and is designed to help students prepare to launch the next great invention.

The Idea Shop has the equipment students need to see their ideas actually take shape, literally and figuratively. The facility is equipped with a state-of-the-art, rapid-prototyping lab featuring 3-D printers and a 3-D scanner, multiple CNC milling machines, a vacuum former, and a laser cutter. Innovations come in all shapes and sizes in this massive innovation hub, but they all have two things in common: they are the byproducts of imagination and the start of something extraordinary.

In the Architecture Design/Build Studio, students experience firsthand the entire life cycle of a small-building project. Students conceptualize, draft, design, and build a structure from the ground up, and they construct their projects around the world. The program has taken students to Indonesia, Ghana, Japan, New Orleans, Chile, Germany, and Puerto Rico, where students built a community building that allows local citizens to cook for themselves and others. The project in Chile earned students a 2018 Small Project Honor Award from the American Institute of Architects Chicago.

The state-of-the-art Illinois Tech Esports and Digital Arts Center opened in August 2018, specially equipping the university's esports community. The lab, featuring 14 Alienware Aurora R7 computer stations with Alienware 25 gaming monitors, is the central hub for competitive teams to practice. The center is open to casual gamers on weekdays, and available for digital arts workshops and special events.

OFF-CAMPUS OPPORTUNITIES

Let Chicago be your playground. Go to a pro game, check out a museum, see your favorite band in concert. You can do it all—and it's just minutes from campus.

Chicago is a great global city (just ask Google, GrubHub, Boeing, Orbitz, or any of the thousands of other companies with headquarters here). What does that mean for Illinois Tech students? Access to jobs in a diverse range of industries including a fast-growing tech sector. Illinois Tech is a pipeline for talent in Chicago, a city where an Illinois Tech degree is recognized and rewarded.

The surrounding Bridgeport and Bronzeville neighborhoods are great for exploring, too. Go to an edgy art gallery, eat at an old-school soul food restaurant or Italian café, or ride your bike along the lakefront (it's less than a mile from campus!). Because of Illinois Tech's proximity to downtown Chicago, you'll find an abundance of convenient transportation on campus. Every Illinois Tech undergraduate receives a Ventra U-Pass, which gives you unlimited access to CTA public transportation citywide.

ACADEMIC PROGRAMS

Undergraduates study in five of Illinois Tech's seven academic divisions. Illinois Tech's signature Interprofessional Projects (IPRO) Program is one of just a few programs like it in the country. IPRO joins students from various majors and backgrounds to work together in teams to solve real-world problems, often on behalf of sponsor companies.

Why stop with one degree? Illinois Tech's accelerated master's program allows students to complete both their bachelor's and master's degrees in as few as five years. You'll keep your undergraduate scholarships in your fifth year and pay the lower undergraduate tuition rate for graduate courses.

It's focused, highly specialized, saves you money—and you can earn your second degree in one of 50 majors.

You can also apply for our combined undergraduate/graduate law program (leading to a B.S./J.D. degree), offered with Illinois Tech's Chicago-Kent College of Law.

If you do not have a planned area of study before entering, you can choose an Undecided path from Armour College of Engineering or the College of Science, or a General Undecided.

Armour College of Engineering

Educating engineers for more than a century, Armour College of Engineering prepares its students to be the innovators and entrepreneurs that will shape the future, educating them to be leaders in the development and use of multidisciplinary approaches and technology to solve complex, socially critical problems. As a twenty-first century engineering student, you'll learn the principles of your profession and work in an interdisciplinary environment that emphasizes hands-on learning, teamwork, and leadership, all through the lens of our four engineering themes—water, health, energy, and security—that highlight issues that are vital today and will be in the future. Research at Armour is aggressively growing, and our focus ensures that students are given the opportunity to explore topics of high priority and relevance to society throughout their academic careers and beyond.

College of Architecture

With more than 800 students from 50 countries and more than 100 faculty members, the College of Architecture represents the global metropolis in miniature. Our faculty are international prize-winning architects, scholars, and engineers. Beyond the college, Chicago provides the inspiration and testing ground for our explorations, as students learn directly from one of the world's greatest cities. The College of Architecture builds on a legacy of disciplined experimentation in materials and technologies to educate and inspire the next generation of architects and landscape architects. From our landmark campus and home at S. R. Crown Hall, the college champions an interdisciplinary approach to education and research that is simultaneously local and global in its impact—and our students are educated to address complex, contemporary challenges of designing and constructing across all scales.

College of Computing

The College of Computing will develop the next generation of talent, tools, and technologies to power the tech community in Chicago and beyond. The college will train its graduates in computing, applied math, and technology and management to have both an immediate impact in their careers and the power to develop into true technology leaders. The college will take on a rare, if not unique, educational mission: to infuse computation and data skills and thinking throughout every major and course on campus. This will equip all students in every discipline to capitalize on computation and data to drive innovation and decision-making while fulfilling Illinois Tech's founding mission to prepare students of all backgrounds for meaningful roles in a changing technological society.

Lewis College of Science and Letters

Technology is playing an increasingly large role in shaping how we look at our world—what we do and how we do it. Within Lewis College of Science and Letters, we explore and explain what is happening as technology reshapes the real and virtual places where we live, work, and play. You are challenged to think critically and will strive to solve complex problems with the aid of sophisticated technology. Lewis College offers challenging and rigorous programs in science and human sciences to ambitious students with a thirst for knowledge and who want to change the world. Rigor and relevance are the two words defining our educational experience. We will give you the tools to solve today's problems and the knowledge to build the new tools to meet tomorrow's challenges.

Stuart School of Business

At Stuart School of Business, we recognize the need to prepare students for a world focused on science, technology, and innovation. We recognize Chicago's leadership in global financial markets, marketing analytics, and sustainable enterprise, and have developed academic programs that prepare our graduates to be outstanding leaders in these industries. Chicago's business community is known for its spirit of entrepreneurship, its leadership in technical innovation, and its concern for the quality of its environment. Stuart's curriculum is designed with these characteristics in mind. You will share the classroom with students from all backgrounds, representing more than 37 different countries. Stuart is committed to creating well-rounded students who are not only armed with expert academic knowledge, but who also possess the interpersonal skills and professional experiences that are critical to academic and career success.

MAJORS AND DEGREES OFFERED

Illinois Tech students describe our programs as challenging, focused, and demanding. What makes our undergraduate education different is a focus on emerging technologies and our hands-on, interdisciplinary, collaborative programs.

Degrees Offered:
Bachelor's
Master's
J.D.
Ph.D./J.S.D.
B.S./D.O./O.D./Pharm.D. Programs

Majors:
Aerospace Engineering
Applied Analytics
Applied Cybersecurity and Information
  Technology
Applied Mathematics
Applied Physics
Architecture
Architectural Engineering
Artificial Intelligence
Astrophysics
Behavioral Health and Wellness
Bioanalytical Chemistry
Biochemistry
Biochemistry and Psychological Science
Bioinformatics
Biology
Biology and Psychological Science
Biomedical Engineering
Business Administration
Chemical Engineering
Chemistry
Civil Engineering
Communication
Computational Chemistry and
  Biochemistry
Computer and Cybersecurity
  Engineering
Computer Engineering
Computer Information Systems
Consumer Research, Analytics, and
  Communication
Computer Science
Digital Humanities
Electrical Engineering

Engineering Management
Environmental Chemistry
Food Science and Nutrition
Forensic Chemistry
Global Studies
Humanities
Industrial Technology and Management
Information Technology and
  Management
Materials Science and Engineering
Mechanical Engineering
Medicinal Chemistry
Molecular Biochemistry and Biophysics
Physics
Psychological Science
Science, Technology, and Society
Social and Economic Development Policy
Statistics
Undecided Computing
Undecided Engineering
Undecided Human Science
Undecided Science

Minors:
Artificial Intelligence
Cybersecurity Foundations
Engineering Graphics and CAS
Entrepreneurship
Environmental Engineering
Game Studies and Design
History
Human Resources
Information Architecture
Internet Application Development
Leadership
Literature
Military/Naval Science
Music
Public Administration
Rehabilitation Services
Urban Studies... and many more!

TUITION, ROOM, BOARD, FEES

2020–21 Academic Year Example Budget—New Undergraduate Student

Tuition
U.S. Citizens/Permanent Residents: $48,670
International Students: $48,670
Fees
U.S. Citizens/Permanent Residents: $1,820
International Students: $1,820
Room and Board
U.S. Citizens/Permanent Residents: $15,328
International Students: $15,328
Health Insurance
U.S. Citizens/Permanent Residents:
International Students: $1,499

Books and Supplies
U.S. Citizens/Permanent Residents: $1,200
International Students: $1,200
Transportation
U.S. Citizens/Permanent Residents: $1,150
International Students: Varies
Personal/Miscellaneous
U.S. Citizens/Permanent Residents: $3,000
International Students: Varies

FINANCIAL AID

Illinois Tech is ranked the #1 Best Value College in Illinois (with aid) by PayScale. At Illinois Tech more than 98 percent of students receive some type of financial aid, whether it be need-based, merit-based, or both. All applicants are considered for merit-based scholarships when they apply before the university's rolling admission deadline, but students are encouraged to apply by the priority scholarship deadline of November 15 for the best chance to receive a scholarship award.

STUDENT ORGANIZATIONS AND ACTIVITIES

Illinois Tech students—composed of more than 6,800 undergraduates and graduate students—are curious, creative, and innovative. All 2,800 of our undergraduates have access to cutting-edge research as early as their freshman year.

Illinois Tech is a global and diverse campus, representing 93 countries, with 19 percent of undergraduate students coming from outside the United States and 26 percent of the undergraduate population composed of African American, Hispanic, American Indian or Alaskan Native, Native Hawaiian, or Pacific Islander students.

Illinois Tech students work hard, but they also find time to take part in a long list of diverse, quirky, and fun student organizations, academic groups, and traditions. Illinois Tech offers more than 150 student groups, from theater to urban farming. Students can help design a quadcoptor in Illinois Tech Robotics, join a fraternity or sorority, or form a team to compete in the university's annual Pumpkin Launch.

Varsity athletics has had a strong and proud legacy at Illinois Tech. The university currently offers 17 NCAA Division III varsity sports, including men's baseball and men's and women's basketball, soccer, lacrosse, track and field, cross country, tennis, volleyball, and swimming and diving.

Illinois Tech also offers club sports including badminton, cricket, cycling, fencing, flag football, lacrosse, martial arts, racquetball, rock climbing, and water polo. Want more? How about a disc golf course and a bowling alley right on campus?

ADMISSIONS PROCESS

Illinois Tech is looking for students of high academic caliber with strong community ties and work ethic. In the application, we evaluate your academic standing and your extracurricular, community-based, and leadership involvement. We also like to hear why you think an education at Illinois Tech would help you pursue your academic and career goals and how you could contribute to the Illinois Tech community. Be specific. We want to hear your story!

Submit your application as early as possible so our admission staff can help you through the process. All applications will be treated and evaluated equally by the Admissions Committee.

STEP 1: APPLICATION FOR ADMISSION
Apply online using the Common Application.

STEP 2: COUNSELOR/TEACHER EVALUATION OR LETTER OF RECOMMENDATION
Select a counselor and/or teacher who knows you well and can write about your strengths as a student. One letter is required but up to three are accepted. This form and letter can be submitted electronically by the teacher through the Common Application.

STEP 3: HIGH SCHOOL/SECONDARY SCHOOL TRANSCRIPTS
Ask your high school counselor to submit your official high school/secondary school transcripts to the Office of Undergraduate Admission.

STEP 4: TEST SCORES
Send official SAT I or ACT scores to the Office of Undergraduate Admissions. Illinois Tech's SAT code is 1318; the ACT code is 1040.

You can email supporting documents to ugaprocessing@iit.edu or mail them to:

Illinois Institute of Technology
Office of Undergraduate Admission
10 West 33rd Street
Perlstein Hall, Room 101
Chicago, IL 60616

High School Requirements
Students engaged in a college preparatory or general education curriculum generally make good candidates for Illinois Tech. Specifically, we recommend the following high school courses be completed:

- 4 years of English
- 4 years of mathematics
- 3 years of science

JOHNS HOPKINS UNIVERSITY

AT A GLANCE

As America's first research institution, Johns Hopkins University has been tackling difficult questions and providing innovative solutions since 1876. Faculty and students work side-by-side in the pursuit of discovery, continuing the university's founding mission to bring knowledge to the world.

From day one, undergraduates are given the freedom to chart their own academic paths and are encouraged to explore their interests both in and outside the classroom. Students across all majors learn how to think critically, analyze problems from different angles, and view the world from a wider lens. This prepares them to innovate in any subject they pursue and make new connections across disciplines. Collaboration—with peers, mentors, and professors—is built into the academic culture at Hopkins and the campus is designed to foster work across academic boundaries. Students get to know their professors and classmates the way they would at a small liberal arts college but have all of the opportunities of a major research institution with a global reach.

Living and learning at Hopkins is multi-dimensional. The Homewood campus brings together scholars with diverse interests and cultivates a dynamic, open-minded environment. Students are engaged beyond academics as leaders, creators, and performers. With over 400 student-run organizations, from fraternities and sororities to performing arts, they find opportunities to get involved on campus and beyond.

The university looks for students who will contribute to the campus community while taking advantage of all Johns Hopkins has to offer.

LOCATION AND ENVIRONMENT

With a traditional campus feel in the heart of big city life, the undergraduate Homewood Campus is an exciting place to live, research, learn, and play. Every week offers lectures, concerts, art and photography exhibitions, theater shows, film screenings, volunteer opportunities, and more. All the while, our students enjoy the bustling, energetic city of Baltimore, Maryland. A short walk or a free shuttle ride leads to museums, concert halls, shops, historic movie-theaters, restaurants, and professional sports stadiums. Hopkins students are involved, engaged, and pursuing the activities that mean the most to them. They create a vibrant community, sharing their interests with one another and participating in about 400 student-run groups on campus that range from dance and performing arts to cultural groups to service-based organizations to club sports and Sorority and Fraternity Life.

CAMPUS FACILITIES AND EQUIPMENT

The Biomedical Engineering Design Studio, Archaeological Museum, Laboratory for Computational Sensing and Robotics, and other state-of-the-art resources on the Homewood campus allow undergraduates to follow their interests beyond papers and projects to make meaningful contributions across disciplines. From labs to libraries to film centers, groundbreaking discoveries happen everywhere at Johns Hopkins.

Collaborative learning is fundamental to the academic environment, and many buildings were designed to foster collaboration across disciplines. The Brody Learning Commons is one of the most popular places for students to gather, study, and work together. Designed with student input, the building contains the latest learning technology to support collaborative work—like interactive projectors that allow students to write on walls and video teleconferencing capabilities. It's also directly connected to the Milton S. Eisenhower Library, part of the university's Sheridan Libraries, which provide one of the most comprehensive learning resources in the world.

The Undergraduate Teaching Labs is a 105,000 square foot facility equipped with the latest lab technology that enables synergistic, cross-disciplinary partnerships and research opportunities. Two on-campus creative centers provide resources for students in the arts. The Mattin Student Arts Center contains theaters, a dance studio, music practice rooms, film and digital labs, darkrooms, and art studios; the Digital Media Center offers digital tools like high-end computers and cameras that enable digital and audio composition and editing, animation, virtual painting, and 3-D modeling workshops for programs like Adobe After Effects. Off campus, just a short shuttle ride away, the Johns Hopkins-MICA Film Centre gives students access to professional-grade production facilities. A collaborative, cross-disciplinary environment open to all Johns Hopkins students, FastForward U is an innovative space that provides training and resources to empower emerging student entrepreneurs to develop ideas and disruptive technologies into successful startups.

The Ralph S. O'Connor Recreation Center houses basketball and volleyball courts, a rock-climbing wall, a weight room, and fitness training and aerobics areas, as well as access to the Athletic Center's swimming facilities. Popular fitness classes include yoga, Pilates, kickboxing, step aerobics, spinning, and sports conditioning.

OFF-CAMPUS OPPORTUNITIES

Baltimore is a vibrant city—an entrepreneurial hub with a rapidly growing technology sector and dynamic arts scene. Students enjoy the fast-paced yet accessible nature of a city like Baltimore, which gives them access to coveted internships and careers. It's the perfect environment for real-world experiences like building professional networks or getting startups off the ground. It's an incubator for scientists, clinicians, artists, legal experts, venture capitalists, philanthropists—and students who want to change the world.

As a part of the Johns Hopkins family, undergraduates have the entirety of an internationally renowned research institution at their fingertips. The medical school and Bloomberg School of Public Health, where many students take classes or have internships, are about 15 minutes away and available by a free shuttle. Peabody, the world-class music conservatory, offers dual degree options as well as classes and private instruction, and is also a free shuttle ride away. There are also other schools and centers throughout Baltimore and in Washington, D.C., including the School of Advanced International Studies and the Applied Physics Lab, which offers a unique internship each year in conjunction with NASA.

ACADEMIC PROGRAMS

See a full list of majors and minors: https://apply.jhu.edu/explore-academics/majors-and-minors/.

MAJORS AND DEGREES OFFERED

Students define their own academic direction within our liberal arts curriculum, often combining multiple majors, minors, and programs. They're active learners who pursue their interests across academic boundaries, discovering new ways to combine their passions as they find their own paths forward. The international studies major is one example of Johns Hopkins' interdisciplinary curriculum that connects diversity of thought in the fields of political science, history, economics, anthropology, sociology, and languages. Students interested in pursuing law or medicine choose any major and minor—from philosophy to physics—but follow a pre-law or pre-med advising track offered through the Office of Pre-Professional Advising. The biomedical engineering (BME) program at Johns Hopkins is widely regarded as one of the best in the world.

TUITION, ROOM, BOARD, FEES

Johns Hopkins University meets 100% of demonstrated financial need for our students for all four years of undergraduate study.

Costs for 2019–2020 are $55,350 for tuition and $16,310 for room and board, plus personal expenses like books and travel. (Expenses such as travel and room and board vary based on choices.)

FINANCIAL AID

The financial aid philosophy at Hopkins is anchored around a simple approach: Enrolling the brightest minds. Hopkins believes students from all backgrounds should have access to the opportunities, resources, and intellectual community where groundbreaking ideas are created. Those opportunities abound on the Homewood campus, and we are proud to support our students—during their time here and after graduation. With the potential to graduate debt-free, equipped with an education that opens doors, students have the freedom to boldly explore ways to apply their knowledge and talents.

The university offers a variety of financial support programs for all types of families as well as personalized guidance through the process of finding the right path for them. Last year, students received over $100 million in Hopkins grant money towards their education, with an average need-based grant for first-year students of $48,000. In the fall of 2018, a landmark gift by Michael R. Bloomberg '64 expanded the university's ability to carry on this mission: Supporting need-blind admissions and meeting 100% of demonstrated need with no-loan financial aid packages.

STUDENT ORGANIZATIONS AND ACTIVITIES

Life at Homewood is much more than a degree; it's about joining a community, meeting people who will change your life, and building a life here. Living and learning at Hopkins is multidimensional, just like the students themselves. As one current Hopkins student put it, students here are "involved in groundbreaking research, contribute to the Baltimore community, start their own clubs and non-profits, wake up at 6am every day for swim practice, and have the desire to learn, discover, meet new people, make a difference, and have fun." It's a collaborative community where you will meet the most curious and driven individuals from all walks of life, who will take your learning and undergraduate experience to the next level.

All Johns Hopkins student groups are governed and managed by students, and there is something for everybody with organizations dedicated to—theater and performing arts, politics, investments, service work, publications, student government, and even fire juggling. Athletics and recreation opportunities fuel school spirit, whether that's on one of our varsity teams at the Division III level and our storied Division I lacrosse teams, or club and intramural sports at our recreation center.

Hopkins students are not just members of our community, but also citizens of Baltimore. Just as they are engaged on our Homewood campus, our students are actively partnering with the rest of the city in important causes. Whether it's through the more than fifty volunteer student groups housed in the Center for Social Concern, each of which focuses on direct service to the city, or independent projects, research, or startups, Hopkins students are excited to contribute to the larger story of the "Charm City." Plus, as an affordable and cosmopolitan East-coast city, Hopkins is a fun and accessible place to live as a college student.

ADMISSIONS PROCESS

Applications are accepted from August through January for the fall semester only; first-year candidates can apply using the Coalition for College application or the Common Application.

Johns Hopkins conducts a context-based review of all pieces of every application, looking at each application individually and evaluating how your current interests and goals will help you thrive in their unique environment. The university seeks students who are eager to contribute to both the academic and campus community at Johns Hopkins. The three main areas considered are academic character, impact and initiative, and overall match. Students who are admitted to Hopkins are strong in all three areas.

- *Academic character:* What's important to you and what your academic passions are help the university get to know what kind of student you might be. Will you see connections between disciplines, enroll in active and dynamic classes, and take advantage of unparalleled access to research, mentorship, internship and study abroad experiences? To get a good idea of where your academic spirit lies, they'll look at your transcripts and testing, but also your teacher and counselor recommendations.

- *Impact and initiative:* Students who thrive at Hopkins are proactive and take ownership in and outside of the classroom—through service, leadership, and innovation. The university wants to see that you're eager to make an impact in a cause or community that is important to you. This includes any jobs, family responsibilities, volunteer work, or other pursuits where you're investing a lot of your time. The admissions committee looks closely at applicants' involvements outside of school, alongside other parts of the application, to envision how you could make an impact on our campus.

- *Making the match:* Hopkins is looking for students who are eager to follow their interests at the college level and are prepared to take advantage of everything the school has to offer—academically, personally, and socially. What personal qualities do you possess that would make you a good fit for our campus? The Johns Hopkins supplemental essay asks about collaboration; when read in the context of all other application components, your response will help the admissions committee get a sense of the kind of classroom and campus community member you would be.

More details about application deadlines and requirements: apply.jhu.edu/application-process/deadlines-and-requirements

KING'S COLLEGE (PA)

AT A GLANCE

King's College is a Catholic, comprehensive college in the liberal arts tradition founded in 1946 by the Congregation of Holy Cross from the University of Notre Dame. King's is located on a small urban campus in Wilkes-Barre, Pennsylvania. King's offers 41 majors in business, the humanities, engineering, social sciences, education, sciences and allied health programs, as well as seven pre-professional programs and 11 special concentrations. With over 50 clubs and activities and 27 NCAA Division III athletic programs for men and women, there is plenty to do outside the classroom.

Small classes and labs allow for meaningful interaction between professors and students. The average class size is 18 students, average lab size is 13 students, and the student/faculty ratio is 12:1. The favorable student-teacher ratio means more opportunities for personal attention, which in turn accounts for King's superior graduation rates.

King's academic programs are accredited by highly respected accrediting agencies, including the following:

- The Association to Advance Collegiate Schools of Business (AACSB) (The William G. McGowan School of Business is one of only 42 undergraduate schools of business nationwide accredited by the AACSB.)
- The Accreditation Review Commission on Education for Physician Assistants
- The Commission on Accreditation of Athletic Training Education
- The American Chemical Society

LOCATION AND ENVIRONMENT

King's College is located in the City of Wilkes-Barre in northeastern Pennsylvania, within driving distance of New York City, Philadelphia, Washington, D.C. and other east coast attractions. The atmosphere is friendly and inviting, with a strong sense of community. The King's campus is easy to navigate and has impressive facilities, equal to those at much larger institutions. Located near the campus are malls, theatres and restaurants. The region hosts a busy schedule of cultural events, ethnic celebrations and festivals.

CAMPUS FACILITIES AND EQUIPMENT

The new Alley Center for Health Sciences, located in the heart of Wilkes-Barre, is home to King's allied health programs. The College features a state-of-the-art sports medicine clinic for its athletic training program. New science labs and equipment enable students to conduct hands-on research. On campus radio and television studios offer audio and video editing equipment for students involved in communications or media. The D. Leonard Corgan Library offers a comprehensive collection of books, periodicals and catalogs, providing students with the informational resources they need to enhance their skills. The College's new food services partner maintains outstanding dining facilities, including a full-service Chick-Fil-A restaurant, located at King's on the Square.

Residence halls offer a variety of living arrangements from single rooms to apartments. Amenities include 24-hour computer labs in several residence halls; each room is equipped with cable TV access. These facilities are all secure, accessible either by student ID card or by the desk attendant on staff 24-hours a day. A state-of-the-art Wi-Fi network is accessible across the entire King's campus.

Athletics Facilities

The 33-acre Robert L. Betzler Fields at McCarthy Stadium is one of the finest facilities in the MAC for football, field hockey, baseball, softball, soccer, lacrosse and track and field. The William S. Scandlon Physical Education Center features the Robert McGrane Basketball Arena. The center also includes a sports medicine clinic, swimming pool, handball and racquetball courts, wrestling room, and new locker rooms. In addition, the recently completed gym expansion project has added a new facility to the Scandlon Center, including three multi-purpose courts as well as new offices, meeting rooms, and additional sports medicine facilities.

OFF-CAMPUS OPPORTUNITIES

It's not all limited to campus, we've got malls, theatres and restaurants minutes away as well as specialty shops, cultural events, ethnic celebrations and festivals. Our bookstore is located in a Barnes & Noble/Starbucks Cafe and is the centerpiece of a bustling downtown.

Core Curriculum

All students at King's College, regardless of their individual majors, participate in the Core Curriculum, a set of courses and experiences designed to help students develop the intellectual maturity and moral strength to lead purposeful, meaningful lives. As the name suggests, the Core is central to a King's liberal arts education in the Catholic tradition.

The Core Curriculum has two basic aims: foundational, in service of students' majors and professional programs; and formative, in service of students' lives more broadly, beyond any one discipline or any one profession. As an integrated curriculum, the Core is an expression of the College's shared mission to be a community of learning, mindful of life's great questions of meaning and purpose.

The Core helps students develop foundational skills and competencies that majors and professional programs build upon, including written and oral communication, quantitative reasoning, critical inquiry and analysis, technological competency, and information literacy. The Core also fosters in our students intellectual virtues such as curiosity, open-mindedness, creativity, perseverance, and independent thinking. Ideally, our graduates consequently demonstrate tolerance for ambiguity and diversity of opinion and thought. They solve problems imaginatively, engage and learn from perspectives and experiences different from their own, and are confident in what they know while recognizing that they always have much to learn.

MAJORS AND DEGREES OFFERED

Athletic Training
Biology
Biochemistry/Molecular Biology
Business
- Accounting
- Finance
- Human Resources Management
- International Business Management
- Marketing

Chemistry
Clinical Laboratory Science/
- Medical Technology

Computers and Information Systems
Computer Science
Criminal Justice
Economics
Education
- Preschool-Grade 4
- Middle Level -Math/Science (Grade 4-8)
- Secondary Level
- Foreign Language (Grades K-12)
- Special Education

Engineering
Civil
MechanicalEngineering (dual degree with University of Notre Dame)
- Chemistry
- Computer Science
- Environmental Science
- Physics

English -Literature
English -Professional Writing
Environmental Science
Environmental Studies
Exercise Science
French
General Science
History

Mass Communications
Mathematics
Neuroscience
Nursing (beginning Fall 2018)
Philosophy
Physician Assistant (five-year master's)
Physics
Political Science
Pre-Health
- Pre-Chiropractic
- Pre-Dental
- Pre-Medical
- Pre-Pharmaceutical
- Pre-Veterinarian

Pre-Law
Pre-Theological
Psychology
Sociology
Spanish
Theatre
Theology

TUITION, ROOM, BOARD, FEES

2019–2020 Costs:

Cost	RESIDENT	COMMUTER
Tuition and Fees (full-time)	$36,774	$36,774
Average Room and Board	$13,464	N/A
Total	$50,238	$36,774

The College encourages every student to apply for financial aid no matter what their family circumstances are. Only after you have applied and been considered for all available assistance will you have a true idea of what your costs will be.

FINANCIAL AID

Over 99% of our first-year students receive financial assistance. We offer numerous scholarship, grant, loan and work-study programs because we believe college is an investment in the future-both yours and ours. In 2018–2019, our average gift aid was $20,117, with average first year financial aid Offer at $28,257.

STUDENT ORGANIZATIONS AND ACTIVITIES

At King's, we're proud of our diverse student body that includes individuals from many ethnic and religious traditions from across the country and around the world. Recognizing that involvement in student clubs and organizations is an important part of the educational experience, King's offers more than 50 student organizations to meet virtually any interest.

More than 82 percent of the King's College faculty has a Ph.D. or equivalent degrees. Faculty members have been entrepreneurs and practitioners, are authors, scientists, and researchers. They engage in scholarly research and ongoing professional development to support and strengthen their primary role of teaching.

The American Association of Colleges and Universities (AACU) Greater Expectations Initiative named King's as one of only 16 Leadership Institutions nationwide as part of an organized effort to influence the future of liberal arts higher education. The Center for Excellence in Learning and Teaching (CELT) gives King's faculty members a wealth of teaching resources. At King's, faculty members take the time to explain the lesson one more time, answer the question you just couldn't bring yourself to ask in class, and listen intently to your theories and opinions. Professors are interested in their students' success as individuals and therefore make themselves available whether it's during scheduled office hours, e-mail or even over coffee.

The Office of Career Planning offers a broad range of services from credit-bearing academic courses, individualized career counseling, and a variety of professional development activities, programs, and events. The Career Resource Center offers up-to date job search information by field and graduate school resources. The Center also sponsors and provides information about recruiting events, including company visits and information about job fairs and professional development seminars.

King's offer a number of special programs to enhance your learning experience. The First-Year Experience helps new students adjust to campus life. Special honors programs give exceptional students additional challenges. King's study abroad programs offer the chance to travel and study different cultures first hand. ROTC programs provide students an opportunity to serve their country. Other programs, such as the McGowan Center for Ethics and Social Responsibility, prepare you intellectually, morally, and spiritually for a satisfying and purposeful life. Guided internships enable you to experience and earn credit while working within your field of study, and the Experiencing the Arts program is designed to help you explore your artistic side.

ADMISSIONS PROCESS

A visit is the best way to get to know our admission and financial aid counselors, our coaches and our faculty members. Let us know you're coming—we'll arrange for you to sit in on a class, spend the night in one of our residence halls and have a meal in our Marketplace café.

You can use this link to schedule a visit (https://www.kings.edu/admissions/admission_events), call 1-888-KINGS-PA, or e-mail admissions@kings.edu.

In the meantime, whether you're applying as a freshman, transfer, international, or graduate student, or as an adult learner or young scholar, please take the time to review our applicant requirements. If you have questions or need further clarification, just call give us a call or send an e-mail.

HIGH SCHOOL STUDENTS must complete the application form in its entirety. You must also complete the top section of the school report form and submit it to your guidance counselor. Be sure to forward your SAT or ACT scores. (We accept either direct reports from the testing services or test scores included on an official high school transcript.) If you are choosing the Test Optional application decision, you must select that option on the application for it to be processed. If applicable, please submit any college/university transcript indicating course work completed.

PARENTS should complete the Free Application for Federal Student Aid (FAFSA) after October 1, 2016. The King's College Federal School Code is 003282 (this code must be entered correctly on the FAFSA in order for King's College to receive access to your federal record). Be sure to accurately report your social security number on the application for admission, financial aid application, and the FAFSA forms. To help, the College has assembled a number of resources to help you navigate the application process, which can be downloaded here: https://www.kings.edu/admissions/application-forms-and-links.

TRANSFER STUDENTS may enroll at King's in the fall or spring semester after completing at least one semester or 12 transferable credits at another school. To apply, submit a completed application and the $30 fee. (Note: The application fee is waived if you apply online at www.kings.edu/admissions/applying_to_kings.) You must also submit official transcript(s) from all post-secondary institutions (including two and four-year colleges), an official transcript from a secondary school or a GED, SAT or ACT scores (if available), and a personal essay.

INTERNATIONAL STUDENTS must complete the International Application for Admission, available here: https://www.kings.edu/non_cms/pdf/international_application.pdf. Be sure to enclose the $50 non-refundable application fee when mailing. Checks should be made payable to King's College. (NOTE: There is no application fee if you apply online at https://www.kings.edu/admissions/applying_to_kings.) You must also submit your official high school transcript. Your official SAT, TOEFL or IELTS scores must also be submitted to the Office of Admission. If you have any questions about the application, please contact the Office of International Student Recruitment at 001-570-208-5834. In special cases we may choose to waive requirements and will process the application with available information.

For all students, we value the opportunity to meet our applicants in person and therefore strongly recommend scheduling a personal interview at your earliest convenience.

For more information, contact the Office of Admission at 1-888-KINGS PA or email admissions@kings.edu.

For all students, we value the opportunity to meet our applicants in person and therefore strongly recommend scheduling a personal interview at your earliest convenience.

For more information, contact the Office of Admission at 1-888-KINGS PA or email admissions@kings.edu.

KNOX COLLEGE

AT A GLANCE

Knox College is an independent-minded, uncannily smart four-year residential college. We're home to transformative teachers, classes, and learning opportunities, plus 1,200 brilliantly original human beings from everywhere on the planet. We believe that every experience is an education, that every new venture, every fantastic idea, every great journey, is human-powered. We also believe you learn the most from the people least like you. Knox is one of the 25 most diverse liberal arts colleges in America, with a campus community of 1,200 students from 45 states and 49 countries, including a wide array of races, ethnicities, ages, cultures, backgrounds, genders and gender identities, and beliefs.

A Knox education is not something you sit and watch—it's something you do. Our students test their knowledge by applying theory to practice both in and out of the classroom. That can take the form of advanced research and creative work, internships, off-campus (sometimes way off-campus) programs, community service, or some combination of your own devising. We help make these experiences possible with a $2,000 Power of Experience Grant available to all incoming students during their junior and senior years.

These experiences, combined with opportunities to live and learn with students from different backgrounds, empower students to find success after Knox. Our students become engaged, innovative, and productive global citizens, ready to lead lives of purpose. They run Fortune 500 companies and grassroots nonprofits, they conduct major research at sites around the world, they found startups and music festivals, they see a human need and they meet it.

Our future is also rooted in our past. The commitment to put learning to use to accomplish both personal and social goals dates back to the founding of the College in 1837. We take particular pride in the College's early commitment to increase access to all qualified students of varied backgrounds, races, and conditions, regardless of financial means.

Today, we continue to expand that historic mission and the tradition of active liberal arts learning. We provide an environment where students and dedicated faculty work closely together and where teaching is characterized by inviting and expecting students to pursue fundamental questions in order to reach their own reflective but independent judgments. Our aim is to foster a lifelong love of learning and a sense of competence, confidence, and proportion that will enable us to live with purpose and to contribute to the well-being of others.

LOCATION AND ENVIRONMENT

Knox is located in Galesburg, Illinois (pop. 33,000), full of enterprising, big-hearted people: Galesburg was founded alongside Knox, surrounded by prairie and farmland. We are at the heart of a national rail network; there's an Amtrak station a few blocks from campus; Chicago (home to many Knox alumni) is three hours away. And two regional airports are less than an hour away.

The Knox campus consists of 90 acres located in the heart of Galesburg. While our campus is home to academic and administrative buildings, both historic and modern, residence halls, and athletic facilities, it also features wide-open spaces that provide beautiful prairie vistas and provides plenty of room for our Ultimate Frisbee team to practice alongside students studying on the lawn. Our own 700-acre Green Oaks Biological Field Station—one of the country's oldest prairie restoration sites—is 20 miles from campus.

And one last slightly esoteric note about this exact place: The land around us is fairly flat. No one lives high on a mountaintop or deep in a valley. There's something deeply democratic about this. We all have power. We all have a voice. We all stand on equal ground.

CAMPUS FACILITIES AND EQUIPMENT

House of Peace and Equity:

The HOPE Center is where faith-based and cultural student organizations meet. Whatever your religion, nationality, race, ethnicity, sexual orientation, or gender identity, you belong there.

Libraries:

Knox College maintains two libraries: Seymour Library and the Science-Mathematics Library, housing more than 350,000 volumes, as well as Special Collections & Archives, which contains primary source materials used by students, faculty, and researchers from around the world.

Arts:

The Ford Center for the Fine Arts houses theatre, dance, and music and features the 600-seat Harbach theatre (with a 360-degree rotating stage), the 325-seat Kresge Recital Hall, the Studio Theatre, as well as dance and music studios. Our new Whitcomb Art Center provides a state-of-the-art facility for students to study, create, and share their art.

Science:

Knox is engaged in multi-year renovation of the Umbeck Science-Mathematics Center, the first phase of which was completed in 2020. The new facilities include technology-enabled teaching spaces and learning commons for interdisciplinary and collaborative study. The centerpiece of the new space is a 55-foot-long fin whale skeleton that was restored, assembled, and mounted for display by Knox faculty and students. Knox continues to expand an equipment roster that includes electron microscopes, NMR, ESR, GC-MS, other spectrometers and chromatographs, X-ray, laser labs, 3D printers, experimental psychology labs, four computer labs, a rooftop observatory, and a greenhouse. Green Oaks Biological Field Station, about 20 miles east of campus, encompasses 700 acres of tallgrass prairie, old-growth oaks, second-growth oak-hickory forest, lakes, and streams.

Athletics:

T. Fleming Fieldhouse provides an indoor six-lane 200-meter track and court space for numerous activities. Andrew Fitness Center offers separate cardio/weight machines and free-weight floors. Knosher Bowl, a true bowl stadium, features artificial turf and one of the best playing surfaces in Division III football. Blodgett Field is a pro-level baseball diamond, with special soil composition. Knox also maintains a main gym and basketball court, a six-lane outdoor track, softball and soccer fields, tennis courts, and natatorium. Golf is played at a nearby private 18-hole course, supplemented with practice in the Schmid Golf Performance Center, a year-round practice facility with a video simulator and high-speed cameras.

OFF-CAMPUS OPPORTUNITIES

A few of the many reasons to like Galesburg:

It knows what it is: It is not Chicago; it is not a tiny farm town. It is a small city (pop. 33,000) that was founded alongside a great liberal arts college, surrounded by prairie and farmland, with 23 city parks, a public beach, and wooded biking/walking trails.

It runs on collective ingenuity: If you have a great idea, it's easy to bring people together to bring it to life. Example: A Knox alumnus wanted to turn Seminary Street into a classic independent shopping district. Now it's home to locally owned cafes, restaurants, a natural foods store, and an antique mall.

People make art here: At the Prairie Players Civic Theatre or in the Knox-Rootabaga Jazz Festival. Plus: The Galesburg Civic Art Center hosts exhibits by local artists. The Knox-Galesburg Symphony Orchestra—featuring many Knox students—performs at the historic Orpheum Theatre.

You can make a difference here: Our students contribute thousands of hours of service in Galesburg every year, through long-standing programs like the Knox Prairie Community Kitchen, our Days of Service, and the groundbreaking KnoxCorps program, which places current students and recent graduates in long-term positions with local organizations.

ACADEMIC PROGRAMS

We believe that every experience is a kind of education. Everything you learn gains value when you apply it. That's why every Knox student will participate in some form of experiential learning before they graduate. All students receive a $2,000 Power of Experience Grant during their junior or senior year to support a qualifying experiential learning opportunity, including research or creative work, an internship, community service, or study abroad.

Our immersion terms allow students to focus on one topic (entrepreneurship, studio art, Japanese language and history, clinical psychology) for an entire term. They all provide hands-on experience—internships, research, travel, creative work. A few examples: In Green Oaks Term, students live at our biological field station, take interdisciplinary coursework in science, anthropology, and the arts, conduct research, and build a community. In Repertory Theatre Term, students research, design, produce, and perform two full-length plays—the most comprehensive undergraduate theatre experience in the country. The newest is StartUp Term, where students develop a business, coming up with a product, developing it, then pitching it to investors.

Knox has a longstanding (and pioneering) commitment to supporting advanced student research—intensive, long-term projects that go beyond coursework. The vast majority of our students (89%) produce research, independent studies, or creative work.

Half of our students study abroad, and our off-campus study programs—more than 80 in total—are designed to work with the Knox experience. You take what you've studied at Knox out into the world; you gather new information, new ideas, new experiences; and you come back with a new way of seeing yourself, your education, and your future.

Our career center helps students find meaningful professional experience by making the most of their education, resources, and connections to secure internships and postgraduate opportunities across the country and around the world.

MAJORS AND DEGREES OFFERED

Knox's program provides a balanced curriculum in the arts, humanities, sciences, and social sciences. Our 3-3 academic calendar—three terms (fall, winter, and spring), three courses per term—allows students to fully explore course subject matter and fulfill research expectations.

With our newest minors—arts management, astronomy, design, health studies, peace and justice studies, and statistics—we offer more than 60 courses of study. Many students double major; you can also design your own major. Choosing a major, and thinking broadly about the work you'll do in college and beyond, is in many ways a collaborative process, involving intensive conversations with peers, professors, counselors, and advisors (who are, in fact, professors).

TUITION, ROOM, BOARD, FEES

Expenses per academic year:

Tuition:	$49,185
Room:	$ 5,040
Board:	$ 5,130
Fees:	$ 789
Total:	$60,144

Average cost for books and supplies: $900

FINANCIAL AID

Knox was founded on the idea that college should be accessible to people regardless of their financial means. We offer more than $40 million in financial aid every year. We're proud to offer a range of scholarships that recognize students' achievements in academics, arts, and leadership.

For more information on scholarships or financial aid, visit knox.edu, or contact us at 800-678-KNOX.

STUDENT ORGANIZATIONS AND ACTIVITIES

Student Organizations: The one quality that binds our 100+ student organizations is that they are all student-driven. Students create and run organizations in response to interests and needs. Some clubs focus on academic disciplines such as chemistry or physics. Others, such as Common Ground, Model United Nations, and Allied Blacks for Liberty and Equality focus on identity, culture, and politics. And, our successful club-level Ultimate Frisbee team and our music, dance, and performance ensembles provide an athletic and creative energy that characterizes Knox.

Intramural Clubs: More than half of our students participate in some kind of organized athletic activity, from club sports (water polo, ultimate frisbee, cricket); to intramurals (basketball, indoor soccer, softball, volleyball); to fitness classes organized and taught by students (a few recent examples: Balinese dancing, yoga).

Student Governance: Our student government actually governs. The Student Senate helps determine how funds from student activity fees are spent, makes student appointments to faculty committees, and serves as a forum for the debate of important issues on campus. Our students shape the future of Knox; their work is a lasting legacy.

Civic Engagement: We pride ourselves on being deeply engaged in the life of a strong, sustainable community—whether that community is local or global. Our students contribute tens of thousands of hours of service every year through established partnerships, special programs, and our KnoxCorps program. Knox was the first college or university in the country to offer an official Peace Corps Preparatory Program; we rank among the top producers of Peace Corps volunteers.

ADMISSIONS PROCESS

Knox seeks students who are active, engaged learners. We value students who demonstrate their appreciation for a variety of educational experiences, both in and out of the classroom. Our admission counselors consider you as an individual when making our admission decisions.

You can apply to Knox online via the Common Application. Deadlines for first-year admission are November 1 for Early Decision and Early Action I, December 1 for Early Action II, and January 15 for Regular Decision. We also accept transfer applications for fall, winter, and spring terms.

For more information, please visit admission online or contact us directly.

Office of Admission
Knox College
2 East South Street
Galesburg, Illinois 61401-4999
United States
Phone: 800-678-KNOX or 309-341-7100

Fax: 309-341-7070
E-mail: admission@knox.edu
Web: knox.edu

LAKE FOREST COLLEGE

AT A GLANCE

Lake Forest offers students a rare combination: an exceptionally beautiful residential campus offering a rigorous curriculum, and the opportunity to tap into the many academic, cultural, and social resources of nearby Chicago.

Founded in 1857, Lake Forest College has a long tradition of academic excellence and is known for its innovative curriculum and focus on career preparation. In addition to majors in the humanities, social sciences, and natural sciences, the College features programs of study in data science, entrepreneurship and innovation, pre-health, pre-law, business, finance, computer science, and still other practical areas. Every first-year student and transfer student is assigned a career advisor, in addition to an academic advisor. Lake Forest prepares students to lead successful lives, and many go on to competitive graduate programs and top jobs. Abundant internships, research opportunities, personal guidance from professors, and connections to nearby Chicago also set Lake Forest apart. Students learn in a rigorous academic environment in small class settings where professors do all the teaching and also serve as advisors and mentors. Professors are accomplished scholars, published authors, and recipients of prestigious grants. Many have come from some of the top PhD programs in the country.

Students represent nearly every state and more than 80 countries around the world. Together they comprise a learning community that prepares them to succeed in a global society. More than eighty student groups provide a host of extracurricular opportunities that develop leadership skills and enhance students' campus experience and post-college prospects. Lake Forest College offers recreational music, art, and theater programs, as well as 23 varsity sports and intramural and club sports. Men's and women's varsity lacrosse will begin in 2021–22. Lake Forest competes in NCAA Division III.

LOCATION AND ENVIRONMENT

Just an hour's train ride to Chicago, the College is located in the town of Lake Forest, Illinois, 30 miles north of the city along the shores of Lake Michigan. The 107-acre residential campus is a safe academic home in a beautiful wooded suburban setting within walking distance to the train to downtown Chicago, historic Lake Forest, and the beaches of Lake Michigan.

The College is only 25 miles from O'Hare International Airport and is also served by Midway Airport and Mitchell International Airport in Milwaukee.

The campus is surrounded by lush wooded neighborhoods, ravines, natural prairies, the beautiful beaches along Lake Michigan, and an extensive network of bike and running trails. Nearby Chicago boasts nearly 70 world-class museums, more than 200 theaters, seven major league sports teams, and one of the nation's top opera companies. Chicago is known for its cleanliness, abundant green space, good transportation system, and friendly people.

CAMPUS FACILITIES AND EQUIPMENT

The new state-of-the-art Lillard Science Center, a $43 million renovation and expansion project, opened in January 2018. The Oppenheimer Center for Entrepreneurship and Innovation, located in the Donnelley and Lee Library, is scheduled to open in fall 2020.

The Sports and Recreation Center is a popular facility on campus and includes multipurpose courts, a suspended running track, aerobic and dance studio, a batting/golf cage, strength, cardio, and fitness spaces, a pool, and an indoor ice rink just next door.

The Mohr Student Center is a student-centered social space that is the hub of social activity on campus. It features pool tables and other games, stage and performance space, large-screen TVs, lounges, deli/snack bar, grocery store, and an outdoor terrace with seating.

Center for Chicago Programs

Chicago provides a hands-on resource for student learning through research, internships, study, and fun. The Center is an on-campus hub for all Chicago-related programming. Students can plan visits to the city and professors can get help incorporating Chicago resources into their classrooms. The Center also brings well-known Chicagoans to the College for lectures and performances.

OFF-CAMPUS OPPORTUNITIES

Lake Forest encourages students to take advantage of study, internship, and research opportunities in Chicago, around the United States, and abroad. Internship opportunities are plentiful in the Chicago area and students have interned at places such as the Art Institute of Chicago, Chicago Blackhawks, Chicago Board of Trade, Chicago Council on Global Affairs, Edelman Public Relations Worldwide, Morgan Stanley, NBC Chicago, Second City, and the John G. Shedd Aquarium, among others. Students can choose to spend a semester living at our modern residential facility in Chicago and interning through the Lake Forest In The Loop program. Our close proximity and relationship with Rosalind Franklin University of Medicine and Science offers many opportunities for students interested in the health professions.

In addition to a well-established internship program, Lake Forest College students gain international experience through access to over 230 study abroad and internship options in more than 70 countries. There are international and/or domestic programs suited for every major, minor, or program, at Lake Forest. Students can choose a program based on major, minor, language ability, and desired semester. Most students' financial aid packages can be applied to the program of choice.

ACADEMIC PROGRAMS

The First-Year Studies Program (FIYS)

First-year studies classes are small in size to encourage interaction and discussion. The FIYS professors also serve as the students' primary academic advisors and help them navigate the College's academic offerings during their first year. With many topics to choose from, first-year studies courses cover a wide range of academic interests from music, art, and politics to neuroscience, terrorism and religion, many with a focus on Chicago or directly utilizing the resources available there. Chicago plays an integral role in the FIYS program. Students travel to the city with their class during orientation week, providing a first-hand introduction to how the educational, cultural, and social resources of Chicago will influence their coursework and experiences during their four years at Lake Forest.

The Richter Scholars Program

This program provides students, early in their academic careers, with the opportunity to conduct independent, individual research with Lake Forest faculty. In the summer after their first year, each student in the Richter Program is employed for a ten-week period and does independent research one-on-one with a faculty member.

Self-Designed Major

This program allows students to develop an academic major of their own, working closely with a faculty advisor, culminating in a thesis or a creative project.

MAJORS AND DEGREES OFFERED

The academic calendar is based on two 15-week semesters, beginning in August and January. Students normally take four four-credit courses per semester (the equivalent of 16 credits).

There are no teaching assistants at the College. Courses are taught in small classroom settings by professors who are experts in their fields and who also serve students as one-on-one advisors. In addition to classroom studies, students are encouraged to complete an internship, conduct original research, and study abroad for a semester.

A Lake Forest graduate will have studied a broad range of ideas; developed real competence in writing, speaking, and quantitative skills; and gained significant experience in humanities, natural sciences and mathematics, and social sciences while completing requirements for a major in an academic department or interdisciplinary program. The College's General Education Curriculum, advising system, and major requirements are designed to support these educational ideals.

Lake Forest awards the bachelor of arts (BA) degree in both traditional academic departments and interdisciplinary programs. Areas of study include: African American studies, American studies, anthropology, area studies, studio art, art history, art education, Asian studies, biology, biochemistry and molecular biology, business (concentrations in accounting and marketing available), chemistry, cinema studies, classical studies, communication, computer science, data science, digital media design, economics, education (elementary and secondary), engineering (dual degree), English (literature and writing), entrepreneurship and innovation, environmental studies, finance, gender, sexuality and women's studies, history, international relations, Islamic world studies, journalism, Latin American studies, legal studies, mathematics, medieval and renaissance studies, modern languages and literatures (Arabic, Chinese, French, German, Italian, Japanese, and Spanish), museum studies, music, music education, neuroscience, philosophy, physics, politics, print and digital publishing, psychology, religion, self-designed major, social justice, sociology, theater, urban studies. Lake Forest also offers pre-professional programs in law, medicine, dentistry, veterinary medicine, nursing, pharmacy, physical therapy.

Accelerated and dual-degree programs are offered. Dual-degree programs are available in law, international studies, pharmacy, and engineering. Lake Forest is affiliated with several competitive law schools that allow students to complete a bachelor's degree and a law degree in a total of six years, rather than the usual seven. Qualified Lake Forest College students may be admitted to the Monterey Institute of International Studies with accelerated status, and can complete their master's degrees with 48 credits as opposed to the 60 normally required. A dual-degree program has been arranged, leading to a bachelor of arts degree in biology from Lake Forest College and a doctor of pharmacy from the Rosalind Franklin University of Medicine and Science. The engineering program is in cooperation with the Sever Institute of Technology at Washington University (St. Louis). Our Health Professions Program, in conjunction with Rosalind Franklin University of Medicine and Science, provides multiple pathways for students to prepare for graduate programs and careers in the field of health care.

TUITION, ROOM, BOARD, FEES

2019–2020 Tuition: $47,680.00
Room: $5,140.00
Board: $5,536.00
Fees: $744.00

FINANCIAL AID

Lake Forest College provides an affordable, high-quality education through maintaining a strong commitment to supporting each student's demonstrated financial need.

The College offers academic scholarships up to $30,000 and talent-based scholarships in music, studio art, and theater.

STUDENT ORGANIZATIONS AND ACTIVITIES

Lake Forest College is a place to study, work, and live. With the diversity of the student body there is an eclectic mix of activities and opportunities outside the classroom.

Student organizations include student government, international interest groups, Greek Life, academic honor societies, community service, publications and media, music and performance, spiritual and religious groups, and many others.

Students have a voice in how the College is run and are actively involved in governance committees such as the College Council and have representation on the Board of Trustees. Student writers and performers can showcase their talents on stage with the Garrick Players, by hosting a show on "WMXM," the College's FM radio station, or through the student newspaper, literary magazines, chorus and instrumental ensembles. Academic honor societies enjoy active student participation as do the community service groups and many special-interest clubs. The College provides and maintains a comprehensive intramural and intercollegiate athletic program. There are four national fraternities and five national sororities, all housed within the residence halls. All students have equal opportunity to take advantage of the richness of the College's programs.

Lake Forest College competes in the NCAA Division III fielding twelve women's and eleven men's intercollegiate varsity teams. Women's teams include basketball, cross-country, golf, handball, ice hockey, soccer, softball, swimming and diving, tennis, volleyball, track (indoor), and track (distance). Men's teams include basketball, cross-country, football, golf, handball, ice hockey, soccer, swimming and diving, tennis, track (indoor), and track (distance). The College also offers an extensive roster of intramural and club sports.

The College's Center for Chicago Programs facilitates engagement with the resources of Chicago which often complements programs for student organizations as well as provides students with information on cultural and social activities happening downtown. The train to Chicago is a short walk from campus and students enjoy traveling to the city for fun and entertainment as well as many class trips with professors. The College shuttle provides service seven days a week to popular shopping areas and destinations around campus.

ADMISSIONS PROCESS

The criteria used for selection include assessment of a student's program of study, academic achievement, aptitude, intellectual curiosity, qualities of character and personality, and activities.

Standardized test scores (ACT/SAT) are optional, except for international or home-schooled candidates, and those applying for some academic scholarships. A personal interview is required for students who do not submit scores.

Request More Information

https://www.lakeforest.edu/admissions/requestinformation.php

Apply Online

https://www.lakeforest.edu/admissions/apply/

Visit Campus

https://www.lakeforest.edu/admissions/visit/

Majors and Minors

https://www.lakeforest.edu/academics/

Scholarships and Financial aid

https://www.lakeforest.edu/admissions/scholarships/

Virtual Tour https://www.lakeforest.edu/about/ourcampus/tour.php

LASALLE COLLEGE VANCOUVER

AT A GLANCE

LaSalle College Vancouver (LCV) is an arts and design school delivering over 30 creative programs with credentials ranging from Bachelor's degrees, Diplomas and Certificates. LCV's objective is to offer high-quality education and to develop your creative potential, while also offering you opportunities to create, experiment, connect, and grow every day. Pursuing your studies at LCV will put you ahead of the game and allow you to discover all the facets of the different career opportunities available in the world of design.

LOCATION AND ENVIRONMENT

Our campus is located in an 80,000-square-foot building in beautiful Vancouver, steps away from the metro. The school prides itself on small class size, a friendly environment, hands-on delivery, and excellent industry-experienced instructors.

At LaSalle College Vancouver, you will find yourself surrounded by people who really get you—from instructors who've made it in their careers outside of the classroom and can inspire you to do the same, to fellow students who share your intensity and push you beyond your expectations.

The professional staff at LaSalle College Vancouver is there to guide you and bring out your full creative potential and give you the broad experience you deserve using state-of-the-art, industry-related technology and equipment. With everything from a surround sound studio, automated music production facility, film soundstage, effects animation labs, games labs, and internet broadcast studio to industrial kitchens, art rooms, and a 40-seat restaurant, you will be provided with the creative environment that enables you to really flex your creative muscles and create your best work.

CAMPUS FACILITIES AND EQUIPMENT

Student Services

The Student Services department at LaSalle College Vancouver is committed to providing comprehensive student services that promotes student engagement, growth, and development for all students. Student Services does this by providing coordinated, intentional services that supports all of our students' individual academic and personal development.

There is a lot to do at LaSalle College Vancouver, such as workshops, guest speakers, career fairs, student socials in addition to the clubs and organizations oriented to students' professional and personal interests. Students can not only enjoy taking part in activities but also gain leadership experience that can contribute to their professional life.

LCV's Student Services department can help students with the following:

- International Student Advising
- Student Clubs, Organizations, and Activities
- Disabilities Support Services
- Mentoring
- Student Engagement Opportunities
- Health & Wellness Counselling
- Student Safety Programs

OFF-CAMPUS OPPORTUNITIES

We're all about helping connect you to a creative career where you do what you love. And a big part of that is connecting you with new people and places and gathering new experiences outside the classroom. We're here to help you explore the campus and the city, and get involved in organizations, clubs and activities, on and off campus. Because all those experiences enrich not only your life, but your creativity.

By being a member of the LCI Education network, students are able to enjoy opportunities to study abroad for one quarter at a selection of the network's campuses, including Montreal, Melbourne, and Barcelona.

MAJORS AND DEGREES OFFERED
PROGRAMS:

Game Design & VFX
- Bachelor of Science in Game Programming
- 3D Modeling for Animation & Games, Diploma
- Animation Art & Design, Diploma
- VFX for Film & Television, Diploma
- Game Art & Design, Diploma
- Visual & Game Programming, Diploma

Graphic Design
- Bachelor of Design in Graphic Design
- Graphic Design, Diploma
- Graphic Design & Foundation for Design, Diploma

Interior Design
- Bachelor of Applied Design in Interior Design
- Interior Design, Diploma

Audio & Film
- Digital Film & Video, Diploma
- Professional Recording Arts, Diploma
- Professional Recording Arts (LIPA), Diploma
- Digital Photography, Diploma

Fashion
- Fashion Design, Diploma
- Fashion Marketing, Diploma
- Jewellery Design, Diploma
- Bachelor of Design in Fashion Design

Culinary
- Culinary Arts, Diploma and Certificate
- Baking & Pastry Arts, Diploma and Certificate
- Entrepreneurship & Restaurant Ownership, Diploma
- Hospitality & Restaurant Business Management, Diploma
- Culinary Arts & Restaurant Ownership, Advanced Diploma

CREDENTIALS:

Bachelors
- Bachelor of Science in Game Programming
- Bachelor of Design in Graphic Design
- Bachelor of Applied Design in Interior Design
- Bachelor of Design in Fashion Design

Diplomas
Certificates
High School Diploma

CAREER SERVICES:

On-campus Career Services available.

Our Career Services team offers a bundle of valuable resources to help you plan and launch your professional future. Some of these resources include job search aid to sharpen your job-search strategy, interview techniques, and resume, as well as the organization of Portfolio Shows designed to put you face-to-face with potential employers from the industry at the end of your studies.

FINANCIAL AID

Need help with budgeting or navigating the world of student financial aid? LaSalle College Vancouver has a dedicated team who assist all students with budgets, student loans, bursary, and scholarship applications.

Scholarships:

LaSalle College Vancouver provides scholarships for Canadian high school students, indigenous students, mature learners, and international students enrolled in our innovative full-time programs. Our scholarships recognize and support students who excel academically, athletically, or creatively by providing up to 50% of their tuition.

ADMISSIONS PROCESS

All LaSalle College Vancouver applicants are evaluated for admission on the basis of their previous education, background, and stated or demonstrated interest in one of our education programs. An applicant must be a high school graduate, possess a recognized high school equivalency, or qualify as a mature student of not less than 19 years of age as of the start date of the program.

LaSalle College Vancouver offers 4 start dates per calendar year. Individuals seeking admission to a full-time program at LaSalle College Vancouver are required to complete and submit the following:

- Proof of Secondary School Graduation
- Admissions Interview (in person or over the phone) with an Admissions Advisor
- English Proficiency: Regardless of country of birth or citizenship, temporary or permanent status, all applicants to LaSalle College Vancouver whose first language is not English must demonstrate competency in the English language.

Each applicant's academic transcript, completed essay, and any other submitted documents will be evaluated by the Admissions Committee. The Committee determines the compatibility of the applicant with the programs at LaSalle College Vancouver and ultimately makes the final decision regarding acceptance to LaSalle College Vancouver.

For a full list of admission requirements please visit LaSalle College Vancouver's website:

https://www.lasallecollegevancouver.com/future-students?utm_source=Princeton_Review&utm_medium=Profile&utm_campaign=Admission_Require

LAWRENCE TECHNOLOGICAL UNIVERSITY

AT A GLANCE

Lawrence Technological University is a private, personally focused university providing students a rigorous, high-quality education–an education that pays off. The Brookings Institution ranks Lawrence Technological University fifth among U.S. colleges and universities for boosting graduates' earning potential. Payscale.com reports that salaries of LTU bachelor's graduates are in the top 11 percent nationally. Some 92 percent of students are employed or registered for graduate school by the date of their graduation, nearly double the national average.

The University, including its graduate programs, is accredited by the Higher Learning Commission and is a member of the North Central Association of Colleges and Schools. In addition to its ranking by the Princeton Review, LTU placed in the top tier of U.S. News and World Report's 2019 America's Best Colleges rankings. Among other distinctions are Best Value Schools, Best Regional University in the Midwest, Best Undergraduate Engineering Programs, Top Schools for Game Design, and the designation as a Military Friendly School by G.I. Jobs.

LTU's student-faculty ratio is 11:1. Most undergraduate classes have 19 or fewer students, and less than 1 percent of the classes enroll more than 50. More than 1000 students live in University Housing. Women make up 26 percent of the student body, and 37 states and 47 nations are represented on campus.

LOCATION AND ENVIRONMENT

The University is situated in Southfield, a dynamic suburb in Oakland County, Michigan. Hundreds of Fortune 500 and international companies are located nearby, and the region has one of the largest concentrations of engineering, architecture, and technology jobs in the world. Southeastern Michigan also offers a rich variety of recreational and cultural activities, with public transportation making most areas accessible to students. Hundreds of major research, manufacturing, scientific, and business enterprises are located nearby, aiding students who work full- or part-time while attending classes, as well as those in co-ops and internships, and participating in professional societies. The campus is close to major freeways and about a 30-minute drive north of downtown Detroit and Detroit Metro Airport.

CAMPUS FACILITIES AND EQUIPMENT

Lawrence Tech's modern 107-acre campus includes a variety of academic, recreational, and housing facilities. Students use advanced, leading-edge facilities, including LTU's acclaimed Center for Innovative Materials Research; an environmental scanning microscope; architectural and design studios; a structural testing lab; a wind tunnel; wood, metal, and model shops; a 4 x 4 chassis dynamometer; labs for alternative energy, robotics, biomedical research, graphics; and the Taubman Engineering, Architecture, and Life Sciences Complex.

High-end personal laptops, customized with all the professional software students need, are provided through the LTuZone. This unique benefit, with an average retail value of $75,000, is the only one of its kind in the nation.

The University's four residence halls feature community living and one and two-bedroom apartment-style suites that accommodate two to four students. All utilities, wifi, basic cable TV, and parking are included.

LTU's library offers a wide selection of print and electronic materials, including numerous online databases, visual resources, digital images, and full-text periodical titles accessible on and off campus. Librarians provide research guidance and instruction. As a key part of the research community in Michigan, LTU's library participates in the reciprocal borrowing and sharing of resources with many other institutions.

The A. Alfred Taubman Student Services Center consolidates all student support services—from admissions through career services—into a convenient one-stop center. This innovative 42,000-square-foot building, which utilizes many energy-efficient and environmentally friendly features and technologies, serves as a "living laboratory" of sustainability, and is part of a regional stormwater management effort.

LTU's Johnson Controls Vehicle Engineering Systems Laboratory provides students opportunities to conduct sponsored research on a unique 4 x 4 vehicle chassis dynamometer.

OFF-CAMPUS OPPORTUNITIES

Students can participate in applied co-ops and internships that offer remarkable hands-on experience. Professional organizations provide additional opportunities to network with industry leaders.

Lawrence Tech's Detroit design programs are housed under one roof at the Detroit Center for Design + Technology, allowing students to explore community-based architectural, urban design, and community development projects. Architecture students regularly build homes for Habitat for Humanity.

LTU's Study-Abroad Program is open to all students. The University has partnerships with universities in China, India, Canada, Brazil, Mexico, Europe, and the Middle East. The Global Engineering Program arranges for engineering students to work and study abroad.

ACADEMIC PROGRAMS

Theory and Practice

LTU provides students the tools they need to compete and succeed within their chosen profession. Whether inside or outside of the classroom, the University's theory and practice approach to learning provides opportunities to combine practical knowledge with real-world applications.

Lawrence Tech is the recipient of numerous grants and awards for the development and implementation of innovative materials and practices that are expected to double the lifespan of concrete bridges and highways, and provide armor protection for soldiers.

Student engineering teams design, build, and race electric, Supermileage, Baja, and Formula-style vehicles. Students also compete in bridge building and assembling and designing zero energy homes, airplanes, robots, and concrete canoes and toboggans.

MAJORS AND DEGREES OFFERED

LTU is a 3,000-student university offering over 100 undergraduate, master's, and doctoral programs in Colleges of Architecture and Design, Arts and Sciences, Business and Information Technology, and Engineering. Most programs are available days or evenings; many are offered on weekends and online. Dual majors and customized degree programs combining either associate and bachelor's programs or bachelor's and master's programs also are available. Pre-professional preparation includes pre-dental, pre-law, and pre-medical programs, as well as a post-baccalaureate certificate in premedical studies.

LTU's College of Architecture and Design offers bachelor's degrees in architecture, architectural studies, game art, graphic design, industrial design, interior architecture, and transportation design. Lawrence Tech remains among the largest colleges of architecture and design in the nation.

LTU's College of Arts and Sciences offers bachelor's degrees in chemical biology, chemistry, computer science (business software development, game software development, scientific software development, and software engineering), English and communication arts, environmental chemistry, mathematical sciences, mathematics and computer science, media communication, molecular and cell biology, nursing, physics, physics and computer science, and psychology (clinical, general and applied, industrial/organizational, and pre-medical/biobehavioral).

Accredited by AACSB International, LTU's College of Business and Information Technology offers undergraduate degrees in business administration (accounting, finance, general business, information technology, and marketing) and information technology.

Bachelor's degrees offered by LTU's College of Engineering are audio engineering technology, biomedical engineering, civil engineering, computer engineering, construction engineering technology and management, electrical engineering (computer engineering, electronics engineering, and power engineering), embedded software engineering, industrial engineering, mechanical and manufacturing engineering technology, mechanical engineering (aeronautical, alternative energy, automotive, manufacturing, nanoscience and nanotechnology, solid mechanics, and thermal fluids), and robotics engineering. A direct-entry master's degree in architectural engineering, combining bachelor's and master's programs, is also offered.

Minors include aeronautical engineering, biology, business, chemistry, computer science, economics, energy engineering, English, general sciences, history, mathematics, media communication, military sciences and leadership (ROTC), nanoscience and nanotechnology, philosophy, physics, psychology, and technical and professional communication.

Associate degrees are offered in general studies, and radio and television broadcasting.

Undergraduate certificates can be earned in building information modeling, computer science, design thinking, electrical power systems, embedded systems, entrepreneurial engineering, entrepreneurial skills, industrial/organizational psychology, technical and professional communication, and television and video production.

TUITION, ROOM, BOARD, FEES

Tuition for all undergrads includes being provided a laptop with all required software. The 2019–20 tuition for students majoring in arts and sciences is $910 per credit hour for basic studies courses. Sophomores, juniors, and seniors in arts and sciences, and business and information technology pay $1160 per credit hour. In architecture and design, tuition for freshmen and sophomores is $1090; for juniors and seniors, it is $1160 per credit hour. Tuition for engineering majors is $1160 per credit hour for all four years.

A normal course load is 12–17 credit hours per semester. The undergraduate registration fee is $200 each semester. International students on temporary visas must have sufficient funds to pay for an entire year of tuition, room and board, and books at the time of first registration. Additional fees for specific labs and studio courses vary.

Room costs vary, but average $7,260 per year. Meal plans are $3,480, per year, with a variety of options.

FINANCIAL AID

Over 74 percent of students receive financial assistance and the University awards more than $42 million in scholarships, grants, loans, and work-study funds each academic year. The average annual, need-based financial aid package is $25,515. Many privately funded scholarships are awarded to qualified students, based on need and/or scholastic performance. Part-time employment is available at the University on a first-come, first-served basis for full-time students. Student loans are also available from a variety of sources—state, federal, and private. Prospective students are urged to contact the Office of financial aid for information on deadlines and requirements for eligibility (www.ltu.edu/financial_aid).

STUDENT ORGANIZATIONS AND ACTIVITIES

More than 60 student clubs and organizations, including fraternities, sororities, honor societies, and student chapters of professional groups are active on campus and sponsor a variety of activities during the year. The Student Government sponsors and supports a variety of campus activities.

LTU features NAIA, ACHA, and USBC varsity and junior varsity athletics in men's and women's sports such as basketball, soccer, lacrosse, ice hockey, and tennis; as well as women's softball, and men's baseball and football. Students can also show their Blue Devil spirit on LTU's marching band and dance team. Intramural leagues and tournaments are active in 30 sports. Club sports include lacrosse, mixed martial arts, and biking. LTU's Don Ridler Field House is open to all students and features a fitness track, gymnasium, racquetball courts, game room, saunas, and weight and conditioning room.

ADMISSIONS PROCESS

Admissions decisions are based on a student's recalculated GPA, ACT/SAT scores, essay, and letters of recommendation. Strong emphasis is placed on grade trends as well as the strength of the curriculum and rigor of a student's senior schedule. A portfolio is required for art and design majors.

Lawrence Tech's ACT code is 2020 and SAT is 1399. Required high school courses vary with the curriculum, and LTU offers a number of basic studies courses designed to augment incoming students' backgrounds if deficiencies exist.

Programs start in August and January, and an optional summer semester begins in May. Entry in the fall semester is advised but not required. Students must submit transcripts from all schools attended, along with a nonrefundable $30 application fee. Students may also fill out a brief survey and apply free at ltu.edu/applyfree. See our campus video at ltu.edu/StudentStories. To learn more, visit ltu.edu or contact:

Lawrence Technological University
Office of Admissions
21000 West Ten Mile Road
Southfield, MI 48075-1058
800.225.5588 or 248.204.3160
admissions@ltu.edu
ltu.edu

LE MOYNE COLLEGE

AT A GLANCE

Le Moyne College is a four-year, coeducational Jesuit college of approximately 2,800 full-time undergraduate students that uniquely balances a comprehensive liberal arts education with preparation for specific career paths or graduate study.

Founded in 1946, Le Moyne is the second youngest of the twenty-eight Jesuit colleges and universities in the United States. Its emphasis is on the education of the whole person and on the search for meaning and value as integral parts of an intellectual life. Learning, leadership and service are the hallmarks of a Le Moyne College education. Those values are evident in the College's undergraduate majors in more than 40 programs of study including pre-professional studies and graduate programs in business administration, arts administration, education, nursing, occupational therapy, information systems and physician assistant studies.

Le Moyne's personal approach to education is reflected in the quality of contact between students and faculty members. With approximately 150 full-time faculty members, Le Moyne has a student-faculty ratio of 13:1 and an average class size of 20.

LOCATION AND ENVIRONMENT

Le Moyne's 160-plus acre, tree-lined campus is located in a residential setting 10 minutes from downtown Syracuse, the heart of New York state, whose metropolitan population is about 700,000. Just a few miles outside the city are the rolling hills, picturesque lakes, and miles of open country for which central New York is renowned.

CAMPUS FACILITIES AND EQUIPMENT

Le Moyne students benefit from an ongoing commitment to technological excellence. The College's 42 buildings are equipped with accounting, biological sciences, chemistry, computer science, physics, psychology, and statistics laboratories.

Le Moyne recently opened a 48,000 square foot addition to its existing science complex, as well as the new Madden School of Business featuring a state-of-the-art live trading floor and analytics lab. The newly refurbished Noreen Reale Falcone Library houses the new Quantitative Reasoning Center, Writing Center and Student Success Center.

The W. Carroll Coyne Center for the Performing Arts houses generous production, performance, and classroom space; the latest light and sound technology; scene and costume shops; an aerobics and dance studio; and rehearsal rooms for instrumental and choral music.

Academic facilities also include an extensively renovated color television studio; a radio/recording studio; a receiver-antenna satellite dish; transmission and scanning electron microscopes; a nuclear magnetic resonance spectrometer; a gas chromatograph/mass spectrophotometer; a 240,000-volume, open-stack library; and extensive on-site computer facilities.

A wireless network allows students easy access to the campus network and Internet. All classrooms are smart classrooms, with multimedia capabilities that expand and enrich the learning process.

Le Moyne students have access to other libraries through the Central New York Library Resources Council, and the campus Academic Support Center is available to students for instructional support.

Athletic facilities include the newly renovated Event Center, new soccer and lacrosse turf field, a new softball field; baseball field, tennis, basketball, and wellness studios; a weight-training and fitness center; practice fields; and two gymnasiums. A recreation center houses an Olympic-size indoor swimming pool, jogging track, indoor tennis and volleyball courts, and additional basketball, racquetball, and fitness areas.

The College also has a plaza, which houses its bookstore, a cafe, and a pizzeria. The Dolphin Den, which features a food court and a convenience store, is a popular space for students to meet, have a bite to eat, or just spend a quiet moment relaxing by the fireplace.

OFF-CAMPUS OPPORTUNITIES

Named "America's Best College Town" in 2014 by Travel + Leisure Magazine, Syracuse is convenient to most major cities throughout the Northeast, New England, and Canada and offers a wide array of shopping centers and restaurants, many near Le Moyne. Syracuse offers year-round entertainment in the form of rock concerts at the Landmark Theatre, professional baseball and hockey, the Bristol Omni-theatre, Syracuse Stage, the Everson Museum of Art, and the Armory Square district downtown, which offers one-of-a-kind eateries, pubs, and coffeehouses in addition to a wide variety of social and cultural events. Central New York is home to an extensive network of state and county parks, recreational areas, and other facilities that offer an abundance of recreational opportunities, including swimming, boating, hiking, downhill and cross-country skiing, snowboarding, and golf.

ACADEMIC PROGRAMS

While each major department has its own sequence requirements for the minimum 120 credit hours needed for the Le Moyne degree, the College is convinced that there is a fundamental intellectual discipline that should characterize the graduate of a superior liberal arts college. Le Moyne's interdisciplinary core curriculum provides the foundation by including studies of English language and literature, mathematics, philosophy, history, theology and religion, natural science, and social science to reflect international trends within a liberal arts education.

For exceptional students, Le Moyne offers an integral honors program that includes an interdisciplinary humanities sequence as well as departmental honors courses. The study-abroad program allows qualified students to spend a semester or year in numerous countries around the world. Thanks in part to a network of Jesuit colleges across the globe, Le Moyne College has virtually unlimited study-abroad programs or affiliations in locations such as Czech Republic, Dominican Republic, England, Germany, Ireland, Scotland, and Spain. Students can also use partner programs to study in locations such as Australia, Costa Rica, Egypt, France, Italy, Japan, and South Africa. Le Moyne is a participant in the sixty-member New York State Visiting Student Program.

As part of the mission of preparing future leaders, Le Moyne College places a strong emphasis on career preparation through internships and other forms of experiential education. Academic departments and the Office of Career Advising and Development both provide programs and services for students interested in interning part time and full time, both locally and in major cities such as New York and Washington, D.C.

The Offices of Service Learning and the Academic Deans are also involved in experiential education to promote learning outside the classroom. In the sciences, students take part in campus research with faculty mentors. Others receive assistance in pursuing outstanding opportunities off campus in leading research laboratories and health-care settings. Through the College's long-standing relationship with The Washington Center for Internships and Academic Seminars, students from all majors complete full-time semester-long internships in Washington, D.C., with government, business, or major nonprofit organizations. Faculty members in the Department of Political Science assist students interested in opportunities in Albany, N.Y., the state's seat of government, with either the State Senate or Assembly. Finally, the education programs at Le Moyne put students into school classrooms starting immediately as freshmen and continuing each year until graduation. Le Moyne students may enroll in Army and Air Force ROTC programs in conjunction with Syracuse University.

MAJORS AND DEGREES OFFERED

Le Moyne College awards the Bachelor of Arts degree in biological sciences, communication and film studies, computer science, criminology, cybersecurity, economics, english (creative writing, literature), French, history, mathematics (actuarial science, applied mathematics, pure mathematics, statistics), peace and global studies, philosophy, physics, political science, psychology, religious studies, sociology (anthropology, criminology, human services, research and theory), software application and system development, Spanish, and theatre arts. The Bachelor of Science degree is awarded in biochemistry, biological sciences, chemistry, economics, environmental science systems, environmental studies, physics, and psychology. The Bachelor of Science in business is awarded in accounting, business analytics, finance, human resource management, information systems, management and leadership, and marketing. A Bachelor of Science in nursing is also offered. Students may minor in advanced writing, arts administration, Catholic studies, classical humanities, film, gender and women's studies, health information systems, Irish literature, Italian, Latin, legal studies, medieval studies, music, or visual arts as well as most of the major fields of study offered. Pre-professional programs are offered in dentistry, law, medicine, optometry, physical therapy, physician assistant studies, podiatry, dental medicine, occupational therapy, and veterinary science. Students may prepare for teaching careers through certification programs in adolescent education, dual adolescent/special education, dual childhood/special education, and TESOL.

Le Moyne College and the L. C. Smith College of Engineering and Computer Science at Syracuse University have a dual-degree program in which students may earn a bachelor's degree from Le Moyne and a master's degree in engineering from Syracuse University in as few as five and a half years. Concentrations include aerospace, bioengineering, chemical, civil/structural, computer, electrical, environmental, geotechnical, and mechanical engineering.

Formal accelerated 3+3 and 3+4 programs are offered in physical therapy, law, optometry, communication, public administration, forensic science, library science, and podiatry in cooperation with the State University of New York at Buffalo School of Dentistry, New York College of Podiatric Medicine, School of Information Studies at Syracuse University, Forensic and National Security Sciences Institute at Syracuse University, S.I. Newhouse School of Public Communication at Syracuse University, Maxwell School of Citizenship and Public Affairs at Syracuse University, and Syracuse University College of Law, among others

TUITION, ROOM, BOARD, FEES

For 2019–20, Le Moyne's tuition is $34,230. Room and board charges are $14,120. Additional fees amount to approximately $1,000.

FINANCIAL AID

Le Moyne has worked tirelessly to contain costs while providing students with an excellent education. The College commits more than $47 million annually to financial aid, which is used to help 95 percent of its students. The average financial aid for a first year student is about $25,000, an amount that includes Le Moyne scholarships, need-based grants from the College, and federal and state grants and loans. The College has earned recognition from the editors at Barron's and U.S. News & World Reports as one of America's "Best Buys in College Education."

There are a number ways in which students can receive help financing their education, including loans, scholarships, grants and work-study opportunities. The College awards numerous merit- and program-based endowed scholarships, as well as athletic scholarships.

A student's eligibility for need-based financial aid is determined from both the Free Application for Federal Student Aid (FAFSA) and the Le Moyne Financial Aid Application Form. It is recommended that these forms be mailed by February 1.

STUDENT ORGANIZATIONS AND ACTIVITIES

A wide range of student-directed activities, athletics, clubs, and service organizations complement the academic experience. Intramural sports are very popular with Le Moyne students; nearly 85 percent of the students participate. Le Moyne also has twenty-one NCAA intercollegiate teams (ten for men and eleven for women). Roughly 85 percent of students live in residence halls, apartments, and town houses on campus. The Residence Hall Councils and the Le Moyne Student Programming Board organize a variety of campus activities, including concerts, dances, a weekly film series, student talent programs, and special lectures as well as off-campus trips and skiing excursions.

The College encourages student leadership in all activities with positions open to students in all class years. Students are represented by a Student Government Association and have formal representation through the senate on most College-wide committees involved in decision making and policy formation.

ADMISSIONS PROCESS

Le Moyne seeks qualified students who are well-prepared for serious academic study. Secondary school preparation must have included at least 17 college-preparatory high school units, 4 of which must be in English, 4 in social studies, 3-4 in mathematics, 3-4 in foreign language, and 3-4 in science. It is also recommended that prospective science and mathematics majors complete 4 units of mathematics and science. Le Moyne is test optional, which means SAT and/or ACT scores are not required for admission. However, test scores must be submitted to be considered for top academic scholarships, for certain programs of study, for students who have been Home Schooled, and for international students for whom English is not a first language. SAT and/or ACT exams should be taken no later than December or January of the senior year in high school for test scores to be submitted as part of the application. Campus visits are strongly recommended, as the admission process is a personal one. As bases for selection, academic achievement and secondary school recommendations are of primary importance. Out-of-state students are encouraged to apply.

Le Moyne offers students the opportunity to apply in two ways: early action or regular admission. The early action program is nonbinding and provides high school students the opportunity to receive an early admission decision. Following early action, regular admission applications are reviewed and admission decisions are made on a rolling basis. The priority deadline for applications is February 1; all students who wish to be considered for academic merit scholarships should have a completed application on file in the Office of Admission before this date. Transfer students are encouraged to apply before August 1 for the fall semester and December 1 for the spring semester. Orientation programs for incoming freshmen take place in June. Transfer student orientation programs are offered throughout the summer.

LEWIS & CLARK COLLEGE

AT A GLANCE

On a stunning campus in one of the most exciting and progressive cities anywhere, the next generation of global thinkers gathers to discard conventional thinking, civic complacency, and outmoded preconceptions. Leaders, visionaries, and problem-solvers, we come together to explore new ways of knowing through classic liberal learning and innovative collaboration.

At Lewis & Clark College in Portland, Oregon, we welcome all who are alive to inquiry, open to diversity, and eager to shape the new global century. Through our undergraduate programs in the arts, humanities, and sciences, and through our graduate and professional studies in education, counseling, and law, we undertake original research, interdisciplinary studies, and community service. We push beyond what is known in order to discover something new every day.

Reflecting the College's national and global reach, approximately 89 percent of Lewis & Clark's 1,901 undergraduate students come from outside Oregon, representing 46 states plus the District of Columbia, Puerto Rico, and the U.S. Virgin Islands, as well as 49 countries.

LOCATION AND ENVIRONMENT

Founded in 1867, Lewis & Clark College moved to its present location in Portland's southwest hills in 1942. The 137-acre campus sits on a wooded hilltop just six miles from Portland's dynamic downtown, offering stunning views of snow-covered Mount Hood.

Portland is a very livable city with an excellent public transportation system that includes buses, light-rail, and the Portland streetcar. In addition, a free Lewis & Clark shuttle runs frequently into the heart of the city and back to campus. The scenic Willamette River bisects metropolitan Portland, which is home to approximately 2.4 million people. There are endless things to do in Portland: 10,477 acres of parks; diverse galleries, museums, music groups, and theater and dance companies; and a nationally recognized food scene. The city also offers professional hockey, soccer, and the NBA's Portland Trail Blazers. Our students take advantage of the many internship and service opportunities available in the Portland metro area.

Just 50 miles east of campus rises Mount Hood with its 10-month-a-year skiing and snow-boarding. The rugged Oregon coastline is just 90 miles to the west. Throughout the state lie innumerable hiking, climbing, and backpacking opportunities.

CAMPUS FACILITIES AND EQUIPMENT

Located on Palatine Hill on a former estate, Lewis & Clark offers students a campus of unmatched physical beauty, along with academic and residential buildings designed to support a rigorous academic environment and strong sense of community.

Academic buildings include the Aubrey R. Watzek library, which is open 24 hours on weekdays during the school year and houses over 800,000 items including books, documents, audiovisual materials, microforms, and periodicals. The library is a member of the Summit consortium, allowing access to approximately 28 million items from the 39 member institutions in the Pacific Northwest. Watzek library also houses the most extensive collection of printed materials known to exist on the Lewis and Clark Expedition. Evans Music Center includes a 410-seat recital hall equipped with an orchestra pit and stage elevator, 22 practice rooms, 43 pianos, 2 harpsichords, a Javanese gamelan, a Baroque organ, and an electronic music studio with digitally-based music production capability. An 85-rank Casavant organ is housed in the college chapel. Fir Acres Theatre houses a

225-seat Main Stage performance/teaching theatre and a black-box experimental theatre (also used as a dance studio) along with a scene shop, costume room, green room and design lab. The Olin Center (physics and chemistry), the Biology-Psychology building, and BoDine (mathematical sciences) all house well-equipped classrooms and extensive laboratory spaces for our natural sciences. Our notable science facilities include a scanning electron microscope, a time-lapse deconvolution microscope, a gas chromatograph/mass spectrometer, a high-pressure liquid chromatograph, a 300 MHz nuclear magnetic resonance spectrometer, an observatory with Newtonian and solar telescopes, an astrophysics lab, an electrical instrumentation lab, a molecular modeling lab, a lab for studying the biomechanics of animal locomotion, and a lab for studying parallel computing. Nearby Tryon Creek State Park and the Columbia River Gorge are frequently used as laboratories for field courses in biology and geology.

Other academic buildings include the Fields Center, which houses studio facilities for drawing, painting, sculpture, ceramics, graphic design, and photography. The Miller Center and Howard Hall are home to the humanities and social sciences and offer state-of-the-art classrooms, small auditoriums, and the Keck Interactive Learning Center, a digital language lab.

Several computer labs are available for student use. These labs house more than 130 computers, along with peripherals such as scanners, laser printers, and digital video editing equipment. Other equipment including digital still and video cameras, digital audio recorders, and more are available for checkout. All residence halls have wireless capability. The institution has a 150 Mbps connection to the internet.

OFF-CAMPUS OPPORTUNITIES

Overseas and off-campus study programs have been a big part of Lewis & Clark for more than 50 years. Each year, about 300 students participate in approximately 30 programs abroad and in selected areas of the United States. During the next few years, programs will be offered in Australia, Chile, China, Cuba, Dominican Republic, East Africa, Ecuador, England, France, Germany, Greece, India, Ireland, Italy, Japan, Mexico, Morocco, New York City, New Zealand, Russia, Senegal, South Korea, Southeast Asia, Spain, Taiwan, and Washington, D.C.

Whether their off-campus study is domestic or abroad, students earn credit (equivalent to a full semester or year) for their academic work. Depending on the specific program content, it is possible to earn General Education and/or major credit during these programs. 60% of students participate in one of these programs prior to graduating from Lewis & Clark. Students can use Lewis & Clark's financial aid and scholarships for assistance in these programs.

ACADEMIC PROGRAMS

A liberal arts education at Lewis & Clark connects classical learning with fresh inquiry and exciting research that pushes the frontiers of knowledge. Lewis & Clark considers the following elements essential to a liberal arts education:

1. Mastery of the fundamental techniques of intellectual inquiry: effective writing and speaking, active reading, and critical and imaginative thinking.

2. Exposure to the major assumptions, knowledge, and approaches in the fine arts, humanities, natural sciences and social sciences.

3. Critical understanding of important contemporary and historical issues.

4. Awareness of international and cross-cultural issues and gender relations.

5. Application of theory and knowledge to the search for informed, thoughtful and responsible solutions to important human problems.

The curriculum combines structure and freedom. Depth and breadth of subject matter are highly valued, but equally important are creativity and critical thinking. There are many opportunities for students to take their learning to a higher level, such as honors projects within academic departments, independent research, and internships. Our fast-growing Bates Center for Entrepreneurship and Leadership offers academic and cocurricular opportunities to translate knowledge and experiences into skills for success beyond college.

Two 15-week semesters make up the academic year, and each semester students normally take four 4-semester-credit courses, and one or more activity courses. The average student course load is 16 credits per semester. The requirement for graduation is 128 semester credits, approximately eight classes each year.

MAJORS AND DEGREES OFFERED

Lewis & Clark offers one degree: the Bachelor of Arts. Students have a wide selection of majors from which to choose: art (studio), art history, Asian studies, biochemistry and molecular biology, biology, chemistry, classics, computer science, computer science and mathematics, economics, English, environmental studies, French, German, Hispanic studies, history, international affairs, mathematics, music, philosophy, physics, political science, psychology, religious studies, rhetoric and media studies, sociology/anthropology, theater, and world languages and literature. Students may also design their own major, pursue a double major, or select from 28 minors. Pre-professional preparation is available in the fields of law, business, education, entrepreneurship, and medicine. Dual degree (3-2 or 4-2) programs in engineering are offered in cooperation with Columbia University, Washington University in St. Louis, and the University of Southern California. A dual degree, BA/MBA program is available in conjunction with the Simon Graduate School of Business at the University of Rochester. A dual degree, 4-1 BA/MAT program is offered through Lewis & Clark's Graduate School of Education and Counseling, and a dual degree, 3-3 BA/JD program is offered through Lewis & Clark's Law School. Outside of the 3-3 BA/JD program, there is a guaranteed admission agreement with the Law School for students meeting certain criteria.

TUITION, ROOM, BOARD, FEES

2020–21 tuition and fees are $55,266, and room and board are $13,324.

FINANCIAL AID

During the 2018–19 academic year, approximately 95 percent of Lewis & Clark students received some form of financial assistance. Institutional, state, and federal resources including grants, loans and work-study may be part of an aid package. Eligibility for need-based funds is based primarily on an analysis of the income and asset information submitted on the Free Application for Federal Student Aid (FAFSA) and the College Board's CSS/Financial aid Profile. To receive priority consideration for all sources of need-based financial aid, students must meet appropriate deadlines for admission and should submit the FAFSA and Profile by the date appropriate for their admissions plan as noted at go.lclark.edu/fao.

STUDENT ORGANIZATIONS AND ACTIVITIES

With over 100 student-run organizations, there's never a lack of things to do at Lewis & Clark. Cultural events include lectures, symposia, art exhibits, plays, musical events, and dance performances. Athletics play an important role on campus, where 19 varsity teams, 6 club teams, and numerous intramural sports keep students physically active. Nature-lovers will enjoy the College Outdoors program, which offers activities such as hiking, backpacking, rafting, skiing, and kayaking in the wilderness of the Pacific Northwest. There are also plenty of opportunities for volunteering in and around the Portland area.

Lewis & Clark is committed to residential education, to creating a community dedicated to the exploration of ideas, values, beliefs and backgrounds, to the discovery of lifelong friendships; and to collaboration, both formal and informal, with peers, faculty, and staff. About 69 percent of undergraduates live on campus in residence halls; most of our residential space is co-ed. Along with personal living space (usually shared by two to four students), the residence halls host several community venues including coffee houses, convenience stores, art centers, outdoor basketball courts, recreation and fitness centers, lounges, and game rooms. Themed communities within the residence halls are also available, including those that focus on visual and performing arts, multicultural engagement, outdoor pursuits, environmental action, holistic wellness, and more. There is no Greek system at Lewis & Clark.

ADMISSIONS PROCESS

Commitment to academic excellence and personal and intellectual growth is imperative for successful Lewis & Clark applicants. Lewis & Clark is very selective, and every part of the application matters: academic records, essays, involvement in activities at school and in the community, leadership, and the strength of recommendations. Students are encouraged to visit our campus. Interviews are available but not required. The best-prepared applicants will have had four years of English, four years of mathematics, three to four years of history or social sciences, three years of laboratory sciences, two to three years of a foreign language, and one year of fine arts. Required credentials include the Common Application with essay and supplemental questions, an official transcript including first term grades from senior year, the school report form, and one academic teacher recommendation. Lewis & Clark requires the SAT or ACT, unless the student is applying via the Test-Optional Portfolio Path (see lclark.edu for details). There is no application fee. Deadlines for first-year applicants are: November 1 for binding Early Decision (notification, December 15), November 1 for non-binding Early Action (notification, January 1), and January 15 for Regular Decision (notification, April 1). Transfer applicants are reviewed on a rolling basis beginning January 1.

LIM COLLEGE

AT A GLANCE

LIM College is exclusively focused on the business side of fashion. We've been a leader and innovator in this space since 1939, and our location in midtown Manhattan is the perfect setting for our immersive "learn by doing" approach. We blend real-life experience with academic study, equipping you with specialized knowledge and skills and giving you countless opportunities to apply them outside the classroom. Through required internships—many paid and with top companies—you'll find out firsthand what it's like to have a career in fashion, applying what you've learned in your courses and making invaluable career connections along the way. This means LIM graduates are prepared for life after college. In fact, 94% of our undergraduate Class of 2019 found employment in fashion and its related fields.

LOCATION AND ENVIRONMENT

At LIM College, New York City is your campus. With three academic buildings within walking distance of each other in midtown Manhattan and a student residence hall on the Upper East Side, you can experience all the opportunities, advantages, and excitement New York City has to offer.

CAMPUS FACILITIES AND EQUIPMENT

Academic facilities include the 5,000-square-foot Adrian G. Marcuse Library, with over 14,700 books, 1,118 librarian-selected e-books, 164 scholarly journals and print magazines, 855 bound volumes of magazine back issues, 1,161 DVDs, an archive of historic materials, and a large collection of fashion, business, and marketing books to assist students in their research. The library also has 42 CAD-enabled computers. The 60 subscription databases located on the library-run web page are available 24/7, on-or off-campus, and can be accessed by computer, tablet, smart phone, or any other Internet-ready device.

Student computer labs (Mac and PC) and lounges are positioned throughout LIM's buildings, and the Fifth Avenue location is equipped with two fashion merchandising studios, two 1,100-square-foot visual merchandising studios, as well as a Color and Materials Lab.

The student residence hall is located in a high-rise building on the Upper East Side of Manhattan and houses approximately 350 LIM students. All rooms have private bathrooms, complimentary wireless Internet access, phone service, and over 100 cable channels. Rooms are also equipped with refrigerators and 25-inch flat-screen televisions. In addition, the residence hall contains a private gym, game room, computer lab, quiet study area, laundry room, and a modern communal kitchen.

OFF-CAMPUS OPPORTUNITIES

At LIM, you'll become part of the fashion business from day one. That's because as you work towards your degree, you gain invaluable hands-on experience and make important professional connections through three required internships, including an intensive full-semester internship in your senior year. Companies LIM students interned for during the 2018-19 academic year include: Chanel, DVF, Kleinfeld Bridal, Marc Jacobs International, Peter Thomas Roth, Sony Music Entertainment, and Tom Ford. LIM College students also volunteer backstage at New York Fashion Week and many other fashion events in New York City throughout the year.

ACADEMIC PROGRAMS

At LIM College, we take an experience-based approach to education. It's the best way to learn how all aspects of the global fashion business work together—while giving you the knowledge and skills you'll need to build a successful career.

No matter your major, you'll learn from faculty with extensive experience in their fields, including many current fashion and business professionals. Core courses will teach you the foundational skills needed in any field, including the ability to think critically, communicate effectively, and analyze data.

You'll also complete required internships, applying and refining your skills while building invaluable professional contacts. Guest speakers, industry competitions and special projects, and visits to fashion companies provide even more opportunities to connect the dots between learning and doing.

Because your time is valuable and flexibility is key, we've structured our programs to ensure you're always making progress toward your degree. Our adaptable curriculum allows you to explore your interests and discover new talents through electives, minors, and study abroad opportunities. Our academic approach also makes changing your major or transferring to LIM, while staying on track for graduation, simple and straightforward. Further, many of our courses—as well as some entire degree programs—are available online.

At LIM College, the true value in your education doesn't lie in a single class, program, or internship. It's the way all these experiences come together to position you for success.

MAJORS AND DEGREES OFFERED

Fashion Merchandising

- Bachelor of Business Administration
- Bachelor of Professional Studies
- Associate in Occupational Studies
- Associate in Applied Science

Fashion Media

- Bachelor of Science

Visual Studies

- Bachelor of Business Administration

International Business

- Bachelor of Science

Management

- Bachelor of Business Administration

Marketing

- Bachelor of Business Administration

The Business of Fashion (*Transfer Students Only*)

- Bachelor of Business Administration

TUITION, ROOM, BOARD, FEES (2020–2021)

Undergraduate:

Tuition: $27,936
Mandatory Fees: $820
Housing: $17,346

FINANCIAL AID

LIM College is committed to helping all students finance their education. 81% of LIM College students receive some type of financial assistance. This may take the form of grants, scholarships, work-study, and/or government or private loans.

STUDENT ORGANIZATIONS AND ACTIVITIES

LIM College's undergraduate students hail from 42 U.S. states and 28 countries. The undergraduate student body is 90% female and the average age is 21. Approximately 350 students live in the College's residence hall on the Upper East Side of Manhattan. Approximately 40% of students transfer in from other colleges and universities. While our study body is geographically and ethnically diverse, LIM students share a love of fashion, an appreciation of life in New York City, and a drive to succeed academically and professionally. Clubs/organizations include:

Blog Club
Book Club
BRAG (diversity in retail)
Corporate Social Responsibility Club
Cosmetics Club
Dance Team
Fashion Show Production Club
Fashion Styling Club
Film & TV Society
Global Students Club
Leadership Initiatives for Males
The Lexington Line (fashion/lifestyle magazine)
LGBTQ+ Alliance
National Retail Federation Student Association
Philanthropy Club
Residence Hall Council
Student Leadership Council
S.L.A.B (Student Life Activities Board)
Sewing Club
Sustainability Club
Vintage Club
Visual Club

ADMISSIONS PROCESS

Admission is done on a rolling basis. All applicants must apply online and submit:

Completed Application
Personal Essay
High School and College (if applicable) Transcripts
Letter of Recommendation
Resume/Activity Sheet
Interview (if applicable)
Application Fee ($40)

LOYOLA UNIVERSITY OF CHICAGO

AT A GLANCE

Annually ranked by *U.S. News & World Report,* Loyola University Chicago will help you prepare for a career with 80+ programs in business, sciences, and other disciplines.

Loyola is the largest Jesuit Catholic university in the United States, enrolling 17,159 students. Incoming freshmen come from 47 states and 48 countries. Loyola offers more than 80 undergraduate majors and more than 140 graduate, professional, and graduate-level certificate programs as well as three professional programs in law, medicine, and nursing.

Loyola helps students prepare for meaningful careers with top academic programs in business, the sciences, and numerous other disciplines, along with opportunities for internships throughout the city of Chicago and beyond. Loyola's well-rounded, transformative education will help students develop as a whole person-intellectually, socially, physically, and spiritually.

LOCATION AND ENVIRONMENT

Loyola gives students the best of campus and city life with diverse living and learning opportunities in the world-class city of Chicago. Located off North Michigan Avenue, Chicago's Magnificent Mile, Loyola's dynamic Water Tower Campus is home to the Quinlan School of Business as well as the Schools of Communication, Continuing and Professional Studies, Education, Law, and Social Work and connects students to myriad internship, job, and service opportunities. Loyola's Lake Shore Campus, home to the College of Arts and Sciences, the Graduate School, and the Marcella Niehoff School of Nursing, is located on the picturesque shore of Lake Michigan and offers students the comforts of a traditional residential campus. The Parkinson School of Health Sciences and Public Health and the Stritch School of Medicine are housed at the Medical Sciences Campus in west suburban Maywood, Illinois.

Exposure to Loyola's three Chicago campuses gives students three diverse experiences: a vibrant urban environment, the comfort of a more traditional collegiate setting, and the bustle of a professional medical environment. At each campus, students have access to computers, study areas, and dining halls, as well as a network of student groups and activities. A free intercampus shuttle is available between the Lake Shore and Water Tower Campuses. Loyola has been offering online learning for 10+ years.

CAMPUS FACILITIES AND EQUIPMENT

The Schreiber Center is home to the Quinlan School of Business. Opened in 2015, the Schreiber Center is a 10-story business learning space designed to foster community, connectivity, and transparency. This sustainable, state-of-the-art building is a landmark on our Water Tower Campus and acts as a networking hub for students, faculty, and alumni.

The 100,000+ sq. ft. Damen Student Center is a LEED Silver certified building. Named after the founder of Loyola University Chicago, the Arnold J. Damen, S.J. Student Center provides students a dedicated space to build community and encourage co-curricular engagement. Damen is the place to relax, study, play pool, watch TV, grab a snack, or hang out with friends.

The Institute of Environmental Sustainability at Loyola is the latest way we are extending our commitment to responsible leadership. The Institute provides practical experiences that will translate to your future workplace, such as working on the student-run farm or in the ecosystem research labs, as well as through degree options in environmental studies and environmental science with concentrations in conservation and restoration, food systems and sustainable agriculture, and public health.

Our student-run biodiesel program is the first and only school operation licensed to sell reclaimed biodiesel fuel In the U.S.

Not only is the recently completed Cuneo Hall a state-of-the-art building with a cutting-edge academic center—but it also uses sustainable technologies to reduce its ecological footprint. Cuneo is LEED Gold certified and will use approximately 60% less energy than comparable academic buildings.

The renovated Mundelein Center offers new options for fine arts programming. For plays and theatre are the Newhart Family Theatre and the Underground Laboratory Theatre. Mundelein Music Hall has been completely renovated as well. These new spaces give students an opportunity to hone their craft in contemporary surroundings.

The School of Communication is in the heart of Chicago's creative and business communities. Located at the Water Tower Campus, the building features generously equipped computer labs, state-of-the-art classrooms and offices, and on-site production facilities, including street-side lab with a TV studio and radio interview sets.

The Information Commons is a four-story lakeside research facility that provides individual and group study space for students, as well as state-of-the-art technology with more than 200 computers, wireless internet connections, and a lakefront café.

Loyola's Michael R. and Marilyn C. Quinlan Life Sciences Education and Research Center provides numerous opportunities for undergraduates to engage in the latest scientific research alongside their professors in modern labs for biology, bioinformatics, chemistry, ecology, and other life sciences.

For information about campus facilities, visit https://www.luc.edu/campus_community.shtml

OFF-CAMPUS OPPORTUNITIES

Students may study abroad at the John Felice Rome Center in Italy, our Vietnam Center in Ho Chi Minh City, or choose from 150 other study abroad programs in 70 countries.

ACADEMIC PROGRAMS

The Core Curriculum is the foundation of Loyola's liberal arts education. Core courses are aimed at increasing students' understanding of themselves and the world while they explore diverse subjects and cultivate new interests. Courses provide a strong base of knowledge, skills, and values that will help students achieve academic, professional, and personal success throughout their lives.

Exceptionally well-qualified students may apply to the Interdisciplinary Honors Program.

Other special academic opportunities include pre-professional programs for law and health professions; 40+ five-year (bachelor's/master's) degree programs; numerous interdisciplinary programs; a six-year, early admission to Loyola's School of Law; and the Loyola/Midwestern University Dual-Acceptance Pharmacy Program.

MAJORS AND DEGREES OFFERED

The College of Arts and Sciences offers undergraduate majors in African Studies and the African Diaspora, anthropology, art history, biochemistry, bioinformatics, biology, biophysics, chemistry, classical civilization, computer science, criminal justice and criminology, cybersecurity, dance, economics, engineering science, English, forensic science, French, global and international studies, Greek (ancient), history, human services, information technology, Italian, Latin, mathematics, mathematics and computer science, mathematics education, music, neuroscience, philosophy, physics, physics and computer science, physics and engineering, political science, psychology, religious studies, sociology, sociology and anthropology, software engineering, Spanish, statistics, studio art, theater, theology, theoretical physics and applied mathematics, visual communication, and women's studies and gender studies.

The Institute of Environmental Sustainability offers majors in Environmental Policy, Environmental Science, and Environmental Studies.

The Quinlan School of Business offers majors in accounting, economics, entrepreneurship, finance, human resource management, information systems, international business, management, marketing, supply chain management, sport management, and a US/Europe Business double degree.

The School of Communication offers majors in advertising creative, advertising and public relations, advocacy and social change, communication studies, film and digital media, and multimedia journalism.

The School of Education offers majors in bilingual/bicultural education, early childhood/special education, elementary education, middle grade education, secondary education, and special education.

The Marcella Niehoff School of Nursing offers the Bachelor of Science in Exercise Science, Bachelor of Science in Nursing, an RN to BSN, and an Accelerated BSN program, which is available to students who have already completed a baccalaureate degree.

The Parkinson School of Health Sciences Offers Bachelor's degrees in Exercise Science, Healthcare Administration, and Public Health.

The School of Social Work offers an undergraduate major in social work and a combined bachelor's and master's degree in social work, which can be completed in five years.

Learn more at LUC.edu/majors.

TUITION, ROOM, BOARD, FEES

Tuition for 2020–2021 entering students (per year): $45,500

Room and board (per year): Room and board cost is dependent on students' selection of residence hall and meal plan (average is $14,820).

Tuition part-time (per credit hour): $840

FINANCIAL AID

At Loyola, we're committed to making a high-quality education affordable. Our financial aid Office works with students and families to address each student's specific situation and needs. Our expert staff evaluates financial aid eligibility for resources such as grants, scholarships, and loans to help make a Loyola education a possibility for students.

Approximately 99% of Loyola freshmen receive some form of financial aid. Students are encouraged to file the Free Application for Federal Student Aid (FAFSA) by February 15 in order to meet Loyola's March 1 priority processing date.

In addition to the many scholarships awarded with admission, students may also explore more than 75 types of additional scholarships. For more information, visit LUC.edu/scholarships.

STUDENT ORGANIZATIONS AND ACTIVITIES

Loyola's total enrollment is 17,159 students, both undergraduate and graduate. The 2019 incoming freshman class consisted of 2,636 students. These students came from 47 states, Puerto Rico, American Samoa, and 48 foreign countries. Of these students, 33% attended private/Catholic high school. Our diverse student population is comprised of 41% African American, Asian American, Latin American, Native American, and Multiracial/Other students. With 45% of our student body identifying as Buddhist, Easter Orthodox, Hindu, Jewish, Muslim, and Protestant, Loyola University Chicago is a home to all faiths.

Loyola offers students the chance to develop leadership and social skills by participating in any of its more than 250+ academic, athletic, cultural, hobby, media, political, social, and spiritual student-run organizations.

ADMISSIONS PROCESS

Students seeking admission to Loyola are evaluated on their overall academic record, including ACT or SAT scores. The freshman class entering in Fall 2019 had middle 50% ACT score ranges between 25 and 30, middle 50% range on the SAT Verbal between 570 and 660, middle 50% range on the SAT Math between 560 and 660, and an average GPA of 3.72. Most Loyola students rank in the upper quarter of their graduating class, but consideration is given to students in the upper half.

Transfer students with 20 credit hours or more are evaluated on the basis of their college work only. The minimum acceptable GPA varies from 2.0 to 2.5, depending upon academic interest. Candidates must also be in good standing at the last college attended.

Loyola notifies applicants on a rolling basis after the application, supporting credentials, and secondary school counselor or teacher recommendation are received. The application is only available online and there is no application fee at LUC.edu/applyluc

Prospective students are encouraged to visit campus by arranging individual appointments and campus tours up to two weeks in advance. Arrange a visit at LUC.edu/visit.

To obtain an application, get more information, or arrange a visit, contact:

Undergraduate Admission Office
Loyola University Chicago
Sullivan Center
6339 N. Sheridan Road
Chicago, IL 60660
Telephone: 773.508.3075 or 800.262.2373 (toll-free)
E-mail: admission@luc.edu
Website: LUC.edu/undergrad

LOYOLA UNIVERSITY OF MARYLAND

AT A GLANCE

Loyola's time-tested, distinctly taught Jesuit approach to education helps you master the tools and develop the traits you'll need to learn, lead, and serve in today's diverse and ever-changing world. Loyola University Maryland is everything Jesuit education should be: rigorous, values oriented, communal, and spiritually uplifting. Your experiences here will be some of the most challenging and transformative of your life—and some of the most rewarding. They will help you become even more than you knew you could be: more knowledgeable, capable, confident, and committed to changing lives—others' and your own.

At Loyola, you will embrace new perspectives and expand your possibilities. Shatter your preconceptions. Find your joy. Divine your truths. So that when you graduate, you'll be ready. Ready to meet the complex demands of today. To anticipate and adapt to the needs of tomorrow. To forge a career that's true to who you are. To build a life you love—and create the world you imagine.

LOCATION AND ENVIRONMENT

Loyola's campus is located in a residential area of north Baltimore, five miles from the city's Inner Harbor area. This location offers students the advantage of quiet residential living with the attractions and amenities of city life. Other colleges and universities in the vicinity help to expand the social calendar and academic life. The fourth-largest metropolitan area in the United States, Baltimore/Washington D.C. has a wide variety of theaters, museums, professional and intercollegiate sports events, and historical points of interest.

The Evergreen campus is, quite simply, what college should be. It is grassy quadrangles filled with Frisbees and picnic lunches, historic academic buildings that inspire you to crack open your books, and comfortable residence halls where you have life-changing conversations, discover new favorite bands, and eat a whole lot of pizza. We invite you to explore our facilities, buildings, and 80 acres of wooded Maryland landscape through our photo gallery. Of course, there's no better way to learn about Loyola than to experience it firsthand—so plan your visit today!

The Loyola campus is like a city within a city. You'll belong to a community that's big enough to challenge and inspire you, yet small enough for you to feel connected, supported, and valued. It's no wonder that 81% of undergraduates choose to live on campus throughout their four years at Loyola.

Unlike many urban campuses, Loyola's campus occupies the best of two worlds: Our beautiful wooded Evergreen campus is distinct from the surrounding city, yet intimately connected to the diverse and quirky metropolis we call home.

You'll draw inspiration and knowledge from Baltimore's unique culture, history, people, neighborhoods, and institutions—and discover ways to make your own mark on a city you'll quickly come to love.

CAMPUS FACILITIES AND EQUIPMENT

Loyola's campus is like a city within a city: theaters, art galleries, and sports arenas. A library, bookstore, student center, and state-of-the-art fitness center. Places of worship. An innovation lab. Great places to eat that offer fresh, made-from-scratch food and multiple student meal plans. A student-run radio station, literary journal, publishing house, and newspaper. Spacious, modern, fully furnished double-room and apartment-style homes—equipped with heating and air conditioning, laundry facilities, vending machines, and recreation areas—provide all the comforts of home...and then some. Loyola's seven residence halls combine the comfort and space of top-notch accommodations with the activity of dorm life.

OFF-CAMPUS OPPORTUNITIES

Anticipation. That's the pulse beating through the heart of Baltimore. Loyola residents and eager newcomers alike are looking toward the future with optimism, excitement, curiosity, and determination.

A burgeoning technology sector. Second to none in biohealth. An expanding culinary and cultural scene. Growing, affordable neighborhoods ideal for young families and professionals. Fertile ground to start a business—at a low relative cost.

Mix in the region's excellent job prospects, and it's easy why college-educated millennials have been streaming into the city at record pace for the past two decades.

The rich soil of Baltimore has been tilled, and it's ready for the innovative ideas and passionate action of Loyola students and graduates.

Loyola University Maryland participates in a cooperative program with Notre Dame of Maryland University, Johns Hopkins University, Goucher College, Morgan State University, Towson University, the Peabody Conservatory of Music, Stevenson University, University of Maryland (Baltimore County), and the Maryland Institute College of Art. Loyola students may cross-register at any of these area colleges and universities.

Students in good academic standing may pursue studies abroad through Loyola's programs in Accra, Ghana; Amsterdam, Netherlands; Athens, Greece; Auckland, New Zealand; Bangkok, Thailand; Beijing, China; Berlin, Germany; Budapest, Hungary; Buenos Aires, Argentina; Cape Town, South Africa; Copenhagen, Denmark; Cork, Ireland; Dubai, United Arab Emirates; Glasgow, Scotland; Leuven, Belgium; Lyon, France; Madrid, Spain; Melbourne, Australia; Montpellier, France; Newcastle, England; Osaka, Japan; Paris, France; Rome, Italy; Santiago, Chile; Seoul, South Korea; Singapore; and Stockholm, Sweden. Loyola also participates in exchange programs with eight other countries, offers summer and winter study tours, and assists students in applying to a variety of non-Loyola affiliated international study programs each year.

ACADEMIC PROGRAMS

There's a simple reason a comprehensive liberal arts experience has been the Jesuit educational standard for nearly 500 years: It works. No other academic program better prepares students to meet the various and complex challenges that await—today, tomorrow, and 20 years from now. No other educational experience better prepares students to lead a life full of intellectual inquiry, creative output, meaning, and professional fulfilment. With a 12:1 student-to-faculty ratio and an average class size of 20, students who experience the Jesuit approach to education Loyola University Maryland graduate with uniquely powerful traits: bright minds, bold hearts, and broad global knowledge. They embrace and thrive—and go on to succeed—in our wondrous, interconnected, and complicated world.

The curriculum at Loyola is divided into three parts: the core, the major, and electives. The core contains courses essential to the liberal arts foundation of a Jesuit education: a classical or foreign language, literature, writing, natural and applied science, social science, fine arts, history, philosophy, ethics, diversity, and theology, and these courses are completed by all students throughout their years. Majors enable students to pursue their specialized area of study in depth. Electives give students the opportunity to broaden their intellectual and cultural background in areas of special interest. To prepare for graduate study, students may enroll in one of three pre-professional programs: pre-health, pre-medical, or pre-law. Through service-learning, research, practicums, field experience, internships, and independent study, students extend classroom learning throughout their coursework and obtain valuable skills and experience.

Messina, Loyola's first-year experience, is designed to help students adjust quickly to college-level work and forge a clear path to success at Loyola and in the life and career that will follow. Messina offers a similarly distinctive and powerful beginning, an opportunity to explore a wide range of academic disciplines, appreciate their interconnectedness, and take to heart the importance of learning in a student's personal and intellectual growth.

MAJORS AND DEGREES OFFERED

Loyola offers more than 30 majors and more than 45 minors. The Bachelor of Arts degree is awarded in art history, classical civilization, classics, communication, comparative cultures and literary studies, computer science, economics, elementary education, English, fine arts, forensic studies, French,, global studies, history, philosophy, political science, psychology, sociology, Spanish, speech-language-hearing sciences, theology, and writing. The Bachelor of Business Administration degree is awarded in accounting, business economics, finance, information systems, international business, management, and marketing. The Bachelor of Science degree is awarded in biology, chemistry, computer science, engineering (with concentrations in mechanical, computer, electrical, and materials), mathematics, statistics, and physics.

TUITION, ROOM, BOARD, FEES

For 2020–2021, tuition for all undergraduate students is $49,700 per year. Housing costs are $10,580 or $11,920, depending upon the specific residence hall in which the student lives. The base meal plan for first-year residential students is $5,240 per year and student fees are estimated at $1,400.

FINANCIAL AID

The University is dedicated to helping students navigate the application process and is committed to making Loyola's Jesuit, private education affordable and accessible for all students. Approximately 92% of undergraduates are receiving some form of aid from federal, state, institutional, and private sources, and the average financial aid package for first time students is $35,650. To apply for need-based financial aid, students must submit the Free Application for Federal Student Aid (FAFSA) and the CSS/Financial Aid Profile through the College Scholarship Service. The financial aid application deadline is January 15.

All students (first-year, transfer, DACA/undocumented, international) are eligible to receive merit-based scholarships, and every student who completes an application for admission is automatically considered for merit scholarship funding. No separate application is required. Students are notified of their merit scholarship at the time of admission.

STUDENT ORGANIZATIONS AND ACTIVITIES

With just over 4,000 undergraduates from 39 states, more than 30 countries, and six continents, Loyola University Maryland is big enough to inspire and challenge students, and small enough for opportunities to be accessible to them. Loyola makes it easy for students to embrace new challenges, feel comfortable taking risks, and connect to the experiences and resources they need to develop as a learner, leader, citizen, and professional. Our students feel called and confident in trying new activities, pursuing their talents, sharing their research, and asking bold questions. Surrounded by people from different backgrounds and with diverse interests, students are members of a student body that is sure to enrich their experience.

At Loyola University Maryland, higher education is as much social, physical, and spiritual as it is intellectual. More than 200 student-led clubs and organizations, collegiate and intramural athletics, service opportunities, lectures, concerts, and on-campus events, Greyhounds have a world of opportunity to get involved, pursue a passion—and even discover a new one. Loyola's offices of student engagement, student activities, and student life offer further opportunities throughout the year for students to get off campus and explore and experience Baltimore and beyond.

As a Jesuit, Catholic university, we foster a community rooted in spirituality that is integrated into daily life through experience, discernment, service, and the promotion of social justice. Loyola students serve on campus, in the local community, and around the globe with myriad programs and partnerships through the Center for Community Service and Justice. Regardless of their religious beliefs, we invite all members of our community to grow in faith through daily Mass and prayer, faith-based student organizations, retreats, reflection, and interfaith dialogue.

ADMISSIONS PROCESS

Loyola's admission process—like our academic philosophy and our graduates—is atypical. Taking a holistic approach, we seek students who are best suited to take advantage of everything Loyola has to offer. Our Jesuit tradition of education is based on the concept of *cura personalis*, or care for the whole person. We consider academic merit as well as all other aspects of your preparation to handle what will be asked of you once you enroll at Loyola University Maryland. That may be extracurricular involvement, athletics, service, leadership, or something totally unique to you. This interest in the whole student is why we've adopted a test-optional admission policy.

First-year students apply online using the Common Application and are required to submit the following materials: official high school transcript(s), high school counselor recommendation letter, high school teacher, recommendation letter, SAT/ACT scores (optional), personal essay, and $60 application fee. Test scores are optional for admission. For detailed information on the first-year admission process, please visit www.loyola.edu/apply-now or contact us at admission@loyola.edu.

Transfer students apply online using the Common Application for transfer students and are required to submit the following material: the college report/Registrar's Report from each institution attended, official high school transcript(s), official college transcript(s) including current semester courses, and $60 application fee. For detailed information on the transfer admission process, please visit www.loyola.edu/transfer or contact us at transferadmission@loyola.edu.

International applicants can apply for first-year or transfer admission and are required to submit additional material with their application. Visit www.loyola.edu/internationaladmission for details.

MACALESTER COLLEGE

AT A GLANCE

Macalester College is one of very few selective liberal arts colleges located in the heart of a major metropolitan area. Macalester's demanding academic program and commitments to internationalism, multiculturalism, and service to society are all amplified by its location in the Twin Cities of Saint Paul and Minneapolis.

Students are curious, highly motivated, serious about their academic pursuits, and supportive of each other. Macalester students are more likely to work together for collective academic success than to compete. Every Macalester student takes a First Year Course (FYC) in their first semester. Seminar-style FYCs are limited to 16 students and the professor is the academic advisor for each student in the class. FYCs set the stage for an academic journey based on small classes, individual attention, and collaboration. Average class size in the fall semester of 2019–2020 was 16.5.

Macalester's location in the heart of a metropolitan area of 3.5 million people augments academic opportunities. Over 60 courses partner with organizations in the Twin Cities of Saint Paul and Minneapolis. Examples classes include

- Legislative Politics, where students intern as legislative aides in the nearby Minnesota State Capitol;
- Cultural Atlas, where students collaborate to create a cultural atlas of Saint Paul (see macalester.edu/curiouscity);
- Community Psychology and Public Health, in which students engage in off-campus shadowing opportunities;
- Drama: Theater and Politics, which incorporates theatrical performances in multiple Twin Cities theaters including the world-class Guthrie Theater.

Students come from more than 90 countries and all 50 states. More than 60% of students study abroad for 15 weeks or more going to over 50 countries, providing time for substantial experience and learning in another culture. The United Nations flag has flown over campus since 1950, a symbol of Macalester's commitment to world peace and understanding.

Campus life is lively, with over one hundred campus organizations providing opportunities for Macalester students to pursue their passions. Activity is focused on campus, especially for students in their first year at Macalester. Theatrical performances, speakers, student media organizations, identity collectives, cultural organizations, concerts, dance, and sporting events flavor campus life.

Opportunities continue off-campus. From internships with Fortune 500 companies and non-profit organizations, to professional sports (Minnesota's new Major League Soccer stadium is less than one mile from campus), to world class theaters and museums, Macalester's best-of-both-worlds location manifests itself in the academic and social lives of students.

LOCATION AND ENVIRONMENT

Macalester's location is one of the most desirable in the Twin Cities. Adjacent to campus, Summit Avenue has the largest concentration of Victorian architecture in the nation. Grand Avenue is home to an abundance of restaurants and shops. Many faculty and staff live on the winding streets adjacent to campus. Minneapolis and St. Paul are known as two of the best biking cities, with numerous scenic bike paths. Within five blocks of Macalester, there are at least twenty restaurants, eight coffee houses, five places of worship, two bookstores, a tea shop, movie theater and stores for art supplies, flowers, bike repairs, pharmacies, and music, as well as Ace Hardware, Breadsmith, Jamba Juice, Patagonia, Whole Foods and more.

CAMPUS FACILITIES AND EQUIPMENT

Macalester offers extraordinary resources for classroom learning, laboratory experience, original research, field work, dining options, athletics, and more. Students work in state-of-the-art labs with impressive equipment. They enjoy a dining hall filled with natural light and healthy food options. They participate in varsity and club sports in an award-winning athletic & wellness complex. And they benefit from a library that has kept pace with the needs of today's students and faculty.

Macalester's facilities and equipment include:

A bronze foundry

Science Center where students conduct cutting-edge research over multiple disciplines with impressive equipment, including these and much more:

- Coherent 899-29 ring laser
- Beckman CEQ Capillary DNA Sequencer
- PANalytical PW2400 X-Ray Fluorescence spectrometer
- Magneto-Optical cryostat
- Fast Protein Liquid Chromatography (FPLC) system
- Beckman Coulter Cytomics FC500 Flow Cytometer
- Leica DMRA2 Fluorescent microscope with advanced image processing
- FEMTOLASERS femtosecond Ti-Sapphire laser

Center for Religious and Spiritual Life

Award-winning library that houses an Idea Lab, film collection, archives, rare books and special collections.

Bikes that can be checked out from the library.

Ordway Field Station, 278 acres to conduct research and advance the protection of natural environments

Observatory with DFM 16″ telescope
Foucault pendulum

Several large dinosaur skeletons

Econometrics lab, Ethnographic lab, and GIS lab

A ballroom for large audiences and student dances

Seven language houses: Arabic, Chinese, French, German, Japanese, Russian, Spanish

Athletic and wellness complex with a fitness center, fieldhouse, performance gym, tennis courts, pole vault, indoor track and natatorium

Campus Center with primary dining hall serving food from around the world, vegetarian meals, stir fry, soups, salad bar, cereals, ice cream and more.

OFF-CAMPUS OPPORTUNITIES

A New York student recently wrote this about Off-Campus Opportunities: "I've been to a Grammy-winning classical performance by the Saint Paul Chamber orchestra and a big pop concert with Pentatonix. I've been to the Super Bowl and seen a show at the Guthrie Theater. I can take a walk by the Mississippi River or Minnehaha Falls, stroll through an art museum like the Walker or the Minneapolis Institute of Art and it's all within a short bus ride or even walking distance from campus. There are so many opportunities within just a few minutes. Our location is also amazing for internships and research."

ACADEMIC PROGRAMS

African Studies
Arabic
Asian Languages and Cultures
Astronomy
Biochemistry
Cognitive Science
Community and Global Health
Creative Writing
Critical Theory
Dance
Data Science
Food, Agriculture and Society
Greek
Hebrew

Human Rights and Humanitarianism
International Development
Latin
Legal Studies
Middle Eastern Studies and Islamic
    Civilization
Performance Design and Technologies
Portuguese
Pre-Engineering
Pre-Law
Pre-Medicine
Statistics
Theater
Urban Studies

MAJORS AND DEGREES OFFERED

Degree offered = Bachelor of Arts

Majors

American Studies
Anthropology
Applied Mathematics and Statistics
Art and Art History
Asian Studies
Biology
Chemistry
Chinese
Classical Mediterranean and Middle East
Computer Science
Economics
Educational Studies
English
Environmental Studies
French
Geography
Geology
German Studies

History
Individually Designed Interdepartmental
International Studies
Japanese
Latin American Studies
Linguistics
Mathematics
Media and Cultural Studies
Music
Neuroscience
Philosophy
Physics
Political Science
Psychology
Religious Studies
Russian Studies
Sociology
Spanish
Theater and Dance
Women's, Gender and Sexuality Studies

TUITION, ROOM, BOARD, FEES

Macalester's 2019–2020 comprehensive fee $68,884 includes tuition & fees of $56,292 and room/dining charges of $12,592.

FINANCIAL AID

Macalester's robust financial aid program supports the enrollment of bright, talented students from around the world, regardless of their family's financial background. Macalester provides a financial aid package equal to 100% of demonstrated financial need for every admitted student.

Two out of three Macalester students receive need-based financial aid. The average total financial aid package for the 2019–2020 school year was $49,047. Financial aid eligibility varies widely with some students receiving much more than the average and some receiving much less.

Students are strongly encouraged to use the financial aid eligibility estimating tools found at macalester.edu/financialaid/estimate for a more specific estimate of financial aid eligibility. Macalester participates in MyinTuition, a quick and easy (6 financial questions, 3 minutes) way to obtain a ballpark estimate of financial aid eligibility.

Macalester also provides a significant merit-based scholarship program. Around half of Macalester students received a merit-based scholarship from Macalester in 2019–2020, averaging $12,625 (most merit scholars also qualified for need-based financial aid). All applicants for admission are considered for Macalester's merit scholarships. No additional application is required.

STUDENT ORGANIZATIONS AND ACTIVITIES

Two current students wrote this about Macalester. "We come from all over the world, every U.S. state, and right down the street. We are from cities and rural towns, upper class communities and first generation families, blue states, swing states, and red states.

Our diversity of backgrounds, identities, and perspectives combine to form a vibrant community united by our dedication to academic excellence, civic engagement, multiculturalism, and internationalism. Every person you meet on campus will, if you let them, talk to you for hours on end about some topic that fascinates and inspires. While we are passionate about many different topics, each of us has at least one subject that drives us forward to discover more, delve deeper, and always ask another question.

We constantly strive to create a better world and find new ways to build bridges across differences. We celebrate time to gather with friends and continue broadening our experiences. We are a community of 2,100 unique students. There is a Macalester identity that seems to transcend difference and unite us under one common, if slightly unconventional roof."

There are over 100 student organizations available. They reflect the diverse interests of our students and range in focus from academic, adventure, art, athletics, chess, comedy, consulting, culture, dance, entrepreneurship, gaming, Habitat for Humanity, investing, Mac radio station, Model United Nations, music, performance, philosophy, politics, Quiz Bowl, recreation, religion, rocketry, scrabble, service, slam poetry, software development, sports, ultimate frisbee, water polo and more.

Macalester has 19 varsity athletic teams as well as club and intramural sports. Most varsity teams compete in the Minnesota Intercollegiate Athletic Conference and football competes in the Midwest Athletic Conference.

ADMISSIONS PROCESS

Seniors and transfer applicants can begin their application and receive a $40 fee waiver by submitting the Macalester Part 1 form by November 15. The form is available at macalester.edu/apply along with detailed instructions for completing the application.

The best preparation for college is a balanced and rigorous high school curriculum. It is important to take classes in all five academic core subjects: English, mathematics, history or social science, laboratory science, and foreign language. Honors, Advanced Placement (AP) or International Baccalaureate (IB) courses should be taken if available.

Macalester evaluates each applicant's record in their high school context, paying particular attention to each applicant's curricular opportunities and performance. There is no minimum GPA because school systems vary a great deal.

Macalester practices holistic admissions review. Factors such as academic performance in high school, teacher recommendations, essays, leadership experience, extracurricular involvement and standardized testing results are thoroughly reviewed by the Admissions Committee.

There is an admissions staff member assigned to every state and region of the world, ready to answer your questions and help you through the application process. Find your counselor at macalester.edu/admissions/connect/.

MAYNOOTH UNIVERSITY

AT A GLANCE

Maynooth University is a modern and dynamic university with a tradition of academic excellence dating back to 1795. Our campus has both historic buildings and state-of-the-art research and teaching facilities. Located in the quaint town of Maynooth with a medieval castle at its gates, students are exposed to two worlds; the charm and tranquility of the student town and the vibrancy of Dublin, located just 15 miles away.

The last two decades have seen Maynooth University grow rapidly in scale, strength and stature. Today, with 13,000 students from more than 90 countries, we are Ireland's fastest growing university. In 2019, Maynooth University placed #50 in the global top 100 universities under 50 years old in the Times Higher Education World University Rankings. Maynooth has a global reputation. Leading international researchers deliver small, friendly classes whilst our curriculum is designed to be flexible and maximize post-graduate success. We have a strong campus community with a student-centered and collegiate ethos. These characteristics together create a student experience that is uniquely Maynooth.

The central elements of our new model of undergraduate education are deep engagement with a student's chosen disciplines; the ability to combine different subjects to create a more tailored educational experience and distinctive degree; time to broaden their perspective through electives, modern languages and multidisciplinary 'Maynooth Modules'; and perhaps most fundamentally, the intellectual skills of analysis, reflection, critical thinking and clear communication that prepare students for today's world of work.

LOCATION AND ENVIRONMENT

Maynooth University has two campuses founded over 200 years apart! Our South Campus includes beautiful historic buildings, green fields, hidden walkways, and even a cemetery! Our North Campus is rapidly expanding and has seen a €250 million investment in recent years. A small road separates them and our modern, airy library marks the midway point. From one end of the South Campus to the other end of the North Campus students can expect to walk a maximum of fifteen minutes.

Maynooth is adjacent to Ireland's 'Silicon Valley'; the university maintains strong links with Intel, HP, Google and over 50 other giants of industry and we have one of the best graduate employment records of any Irish university with a strong track record for commercialisation of research. Bus and train routes make for easy connections into Dublin, the airport and the rest of Ireland!

You will have the opportunity to experience breathtaking land, sky and seascapes as well as an unparalleled cultural and archaeological heritage. All of this is surrounded by 'the world's friendliest people'!

CAMPUS FACILITIES AND EQUIPMENT

Maynooth University provides a wide range of student supports and facilities. These include:

- 7 on-campus eateries
- Free access to our health and counselling service
- Budgeting advice
- A multi-faith worship room and a chaplaincy service
- Academic advisory office
- Maths and writing learning centres
- Learning support services including career development, accessibility supports and an access programme for mature learners
- We boast two libraries-one for rare books and manuscripts and one with over 45,000 items and 16 types of study spaces
- Library information and skills tutorials
- Critical skills classes for first years
- 24-7 campus security
- A fully equipped gym, several bookable sports halls, synthetic pitches, turf pitches and scholarships across six sports
- An on-campus shop, bank and bookstore
- Temporary housing for visiting friends and family

OFF-CAMPUS OPPORTUNITIES

Students can work up to 20 hours a week during term time and up to 40 hours a week during the holidays. More information can be found here: Cost of Living

ACADEMIC PROGRAMS

Maynooth University has an exceptional track record across many disciplines. From Anthropology to Celtic Studies, Robotics to Biomedical Devices, and Design Innovation to Ancient Classics we have a course to suit your interests.

We offer an education that is similar to liberal arts curriculums but a number of our departments focus on more vocational training. These include international development, performance music, digital humanities, equine management, experimental physics and media studies.

Our full range of academic undergraduate courses can be found here: Undergraduate Courses

MAJORS AND DEGREES OFFERED

Maynooth has 34 academic departments across 3 faculties and 8 specialist research institutes. We offer flexible pathways, experiential learning, internships and electives at the undergraduate level and offer a full range of undergraduate and postgraduate programmes.

TUITION, ROOM, BOARD, FEES

€13,500–€15,000 per year. There is more information here: https://www.maynoothuniversity.ie/student-fees-grants/international

Room (including utilities): €4740–€6566 per year

Fees: N/A

FINANCIAL AID

Maynooth University is approved by the US Department of Education to certify loans that fall under the William D. Ford Federal Direct Loan Programme. Veteran Affairs benefits under the G.I Bill and Sallie Mae private loans are also available to US students at Maynooth University. For further details please refer to the US financial aid.

STUDENT ORGANIZATIONS AND ACTIVITIES

Maynooth has a diverse student body, representing many mature, commuter and first-in-the-family students. We cater to the fastest growing student body in Ireland but pride ourselves on our ability to provide a personal and intimate living-learning community. The MSU (Maynooth Students' Union): https://www.msu.ie is a body of over 9,000 students with the numbers rising every year. They answer solely to the student body. Every year the student body elects officers to work on their behalf for the year ahead. MSU has four full time officers and eight part time officers to work on your behalf for the year. They also provide support in regards to education and welfare and organize student-based events during the year to get students involved in the social aspects of college life.

MU has over 100 Clubs and Societies there is bound to be something that interests you. And if not, you can set one up! Further details here: https://www.msu.ie/clubs-socs/list-of-societies.html

ADMISSIONS PROCESS

Applications for undergraduate courses should be submitted online through the Common App or PAC Online Applications. Deadline for applications is July 31st for incoming September cohorts.

Please read the below instructions carefully before completing the online application form.

1. Check the courses available using the Course Finder.

2. For the USA entry requirements are:
   - GPA plus SAT or ACT
   - Minimum High School GPA 3.0/4.0 (3.5/4.0 for certain degrees)
   - Minimum SAT Composite (reading, writing and math): 1000 / 1600 (1200 / 1600 for certain degrees)
   - Minimum ACT Composite: 22 / 36 (26 /36 for certain degrees (writing section not required)
   - Superscoring applies if tests are taken within two years of applying
   - Maynooth University's ACT code is 5483 and our SAT code is 7266.

3. Complete the PAC application, uploading all required documents:
   - All second level (high school) certificates or transcripts
   - Any third level (college) transcript(s)
   - Most recent English language qualifications (where relevant) clearly showing the level achieved (IELTS, TOEFL or PTE)
   - Students wishing to transfer to Maynooth University from another degree programme should provide an official description of the courses they have taken to date as well as up-to-date transcripts, clearly showing all details of your current studies.
   - Any other documentation as specified in the country-specific entry requirements, or as requested by the International Office

MCDANIEL COLLEGE

AT A GLANCE

McDaniel College is a four-year, independent college of the liberal arts and sciences. Founded in 1867 as one of the first coeducational colleges in the nation and the first south of the Mason-Dixon Line, McDaniel is a diverse, student-centered community of 1,600 undergraduates and 1,400 graduate students. Among "Colleges That Change Lives," McDaniel is committed to access and affordability. Students can choose from more than 70 undergraduate programs of study, including pre-professional specializations and student-designed majors, plus over 20 graduate programs. Academics center on the McDaniel Plan, a customized, interdisciplinary curriculum that emphasizes experiential learning and student-faculty collaboration to develop the unique potential in every student. The McDaniel Commitment guarantees every student two experiential learning opportunities, including service learning, study abroad, student-faculty collaborative research, credit-based internship or independent study. Students also enroll in first-year seminars and senior capstone projects. Special opportunities abound through McDaniel's Center for Experience and Opportunity, The Encompass Distinction program in innovation and entrepreneurship, the Honors Program, Military Science (ROTC), and Global Initiatives including the Global Fellows program. Represented by the Green Terror, its 24 athletic teams compete in the NCAA Division III Centennial Conference. Additionally, students are involved in over 100 student organizations, intramural sports, and fraternities and sororities. McDaniel offers access to both Baltimore and Washington, D.C., plus a European campus in Budapest, Hungary.

LOCATION AND ENVIRONMENT

McDaniel's 160-acre suburban campus overlooking downtown Westminster, Md., Carroll County's largest town and county seat, McDaniel offers access to the resources of Baltimore and Washington, D.C.

CAMPUS FACILITIES AND EQUIPMENT

Special collections in Hoover Library include the Nora Roberts American Romance Collection, the Bothe Poetry Lecture Collection, and the Alumni Book Collection; video production laboratory; photography studio; human performance laboratory, neuromuscular performance laboratory, and human anatomy and physiology laboratory; graphics laboratory; observatory; student research science labs; 9-hole golf course and 18-hole FootGolf course.

OFF-CAMPUS OPPORTUNITIES

Study abroad for academic credit at McDaniel's European campus in Budapest, Hungary, or in more than 50 countries, including Belgium, Scotland, and Zimbabwe; The Washington Semester Program administered by American University enables students to study public affairs in the nation's capital; The Gallaudet Visiting Student Program gives students the opportunity to study and/or complete the American Sign Language (ASL) Studies minor by immersion in the language and culture of deaf people; engineering specialization partnership with Washington University in St. Louis.

ACADEMIC PROGRAMS

For the full listing of majors, minors, and specializations, check the college website at www.mcdaniel.edu/academics/programs-degrees.

Majors, Minors, and Specializations include Accounting, Acting, Actuarial Science, Africana Studies, American History, American Politics and Law, American Sign Language (ASL), Applied Mathematics, Arabic and Middle Eastern Studies, Art (Studio Art), Art History, Asian Studies, Athletic Training, Biochemistry, Biology, Biomedical Science, Business Administration, Chemistry, Cinema, Classical Civilizations, Communication, Computer Science, Criminal Justice, Cross-Cultural Studies, Economics, Education (P-12), Elementary Education, Secondary Education, Earth System Science, Engineering, English, Entrepreneurship, Environmental Biology, Environmental Policy and Management, Environmental Studies, European History, European Studies, Financial Economics, Forensic Science, French, Graphic Design, Health Sciences, History, International Studies, Journalism and New Media, Kinesiology, Marketing, Mathematics, Molecular Biology, Performance, Fitness and Conditioning, Philosophy, Physics, Political Science, Popular Literature, Psychology, Religious Studies, Social Work, Sociology, Spanish, Sports Coaching, Sports Management, Student-Designed Major, Theatre Arts, Urban and Community Studies, Women's Studies, Writing and Publishing.

MAJORS AND DEGREES OFFERED

More than 70 undergraduate programs of study, including pre-professional specializations and student-designed majors, plus over 20 graduate programs, as well as five-year BA/MS programs.

TUITION, ROOM, BOARD, FEES

Tuition: $45,876; Room: $5,626; Board: $6,620

FINANCIAL AID

Over 90 percent of students receive some type of financial assistance (need-based and/or academic scholarships). The College invests over $40 million annually in grants and scholarships to ensure that students from all kinds of financial backgrounds are able to experience a McDaniel education. A large percentage of incoming students earn merit scholarships based on scholastic and personal achievement, ranging from $15,000 to $28,000 per year.

STUDENT ORGANIZATIONS AND ACTIVITIES

McDaniel is not just a college or a place, but a 24/7 experience designed to help students develop and realize their unique potentials. With access to a team of mentors, each student can completely tailor and personalize their own path.

Students are involved in more than 100 student organizations and intramural sports, plus fraternities and sororities. More than 20 national and international honor societies, including Phi Beta Kappa, recognize leadership, service, and academic achievement.

ADMISSIONS PROCESS

First time college students have the option to apply using The McDaniel Application for First Year Students or the Common Application and can choose any deadline. In addition to the completed application, first year students are required to submit a personal essay and an official high school transcript. One letter of recommendation and SAT or ACT scores are optional. There is no fee to apply. Because merit scholarship decisions are made along with admission decisions, students should include all honors and activities with the application or attach a resume. Students who file the FAFSA when they submit their application will also receive their need-based financial aid award shortly after they receive their admission and scholarship decisions.

MIDDLE TENNESSEE STATE UNIVERSITY

AT A GLANCE

Middle Tennessee State University is a large public institution established in 1911 as a teacher training college. Over the years MTSU has become a dominant entity in higher education in the Southeast.

With over 130,000 alumni, MTSU is the largest contributor to the workforce in middle Tennessee. Currently, one college degree-holder in five in the greater Nashville area graduated from Middle Tennessee State University.

With a student/faculty ratio of 17:1, students receive a great deal of personal attention from their professors. Students may choose from more than 180 undergraduate programs of study and over 140 graduate programs. Our student body consists of a remarkably diverse population with members from almost every state and 77 foreign countries, where we've established long-term relationships with many other universities. As a state-supported university, our students receive an excellent education for a fraction of the cost when compared to comparable schools across the country.

LOCATION AND ENVIRONMENT

Middle Tennessee State University is on a 515-acre campus located in Murfreesboro, Tennessee, just 35 miles from downtown Nashville, in the heart of one of the fastest-growing and most energetic regions of the country. Our students get the best of both worlds—the resources of a large public university coupled with the personalized student services that you would expect at a small private college. In addition, we also have a 500-acre agricultural lab located just minutes from the primary campus for those studying agriculture and related disciplines. There are numerous opportunities for recreation and entertainment when students want to take a break from their studies. Outdoor activities in this region abound in a beautiful and tranquil setting.

The campus and facilities at MTSU are an undiscovered gem to those who may have never visited here. With over $1 billion dollars invested in new and remodeled infrastructure in the past 10 years, our students benefit from state-of-the-art facilities and resources that are often unavailable at other schools. For example, our 250,000-square-foot Science Building, the centerpiece of the $147 million Science Corridor of Innovation, marked the largest project on a higher education campus approved by the state of Tennessee. We also have built a new College of Education building and a 211,000-square-foot Student Union; have a $39 million College of Behavioral and Health Sciences building opening in Fall 2020 to house our Psychology, Criminal Justice Administration, and Social Work programs and labs; and will start construction soon on a School of Concrete and Construction Management building.

Facilities and Equipment

In 2012, MTSU built the new $65 million, 211,000-square-foot Student Union which houses multiple eateries, the campus bookstore, game rooms, computer labs, a movie theater, conference and seminar rooms, student programming offices, and more. It is the largest of the three student union buildings on campus.

The new Science Building opened in 2014 with more than 250,000 square feet for teaching, faculty and student laboratory research, and collaborative learning. This building is the biggest improvement ever for science education and research at MTSU and for the more than 13,000 students who enroll annually in biology, chemistry, and other science courses. It contains more than 50 separate laboratories for educational use.

MTSU is home to four libraries which provide information, resources, and instructional services to meet the needs of students, faculty, staff, and researchers. They are the James E. Walker Library, Albert Gore Research Center, Center of Popular Music, and Women's Studies Library.

OFF-CAMPUS OPPORTUNITIES

MTSU offers an extensive study abroad program which allows our students to gain new cultural experiences to extend and enhance their on-campus learning. Students often are able to develop customized programs to fit their specific needs and interests.

For six years, our Video and Film Production, Photography, and Audio Production majors have been actively involved in the production of the Bonnaroo Music and Arts Festival which takes place annually on 700 acres in Manchester, Tennessee, about 30 minutes south of our main campus. "Our partnership with Bonnaroo has opened up so many opportunities for our students, and we're now seeing those first students in the program return as professionals," former Media and Entertainment Dean Ken Paulson said. "It's a reminder to all of us that classrooms shouldn't be contained by four walls." This is not a theory class. "MTSU's partnership with Bonnaroo gives our students an amazing hands-on opportunity to engage the world with all of the rich media that we teach," said Media Arts Chair Billy Pittard.

MTSU has been involved with Nashville Fashion Week (NFW) since its inception. As NFW has grown to the third-largest fashion week event in the country, our relationship and the opportunities for our students to gain excellent experience and build professional relationships within the fashion community where many have now found their careers has increased as well.

For the 10th-year anniversary, with the help of the NFW executives, MTSU is expanding its partnerships and will involve a multitude of programs including Fashion Merchandising, Journalism, Interactive Media, Photography, and Tourism and Hospitality Management (which includes an emphasis in event planning).

Many of our other programs provide outstanding opportunities for fieldwork both domestically and internationally.

ACADEMIC PROGRAMS

Middle Tennessee State University is comprised of eight undergraduate colleges as well as a College of Graduate Studies and offers more than 320 undergraduate and graduate degree programs. It boasts a diverse portfolio of programs providing a wide-ranging array of disciplines from which to choose, including some that are not available from other universities.

MTSU is renowned for its Aerospace program, Concrete Industry Management, Recording Industry, and numerous other programs that have gained national and international recognition for excellence. Many of our programs incorporate one or more experiential learning components which allow our students to gain practical real-world experience to build upon the base of superior knowledge and theory earned in the classroom. Our undergraduate students have an opportunity to engage in a strong research program at levels usually reserved for graduate students at most universities. Our faculty of nearly 1,000 professional educators consists of many individuals with business and industry experience directly related to their specialty.

ACADEMIC PROGRAMS

BASIC AND APPLIED SCIENCES PROGRAMS

Actuarial Science
Aerospace
  Aviation Management
  Flight Dispatch
  Maintenance Management
  Professional Pilot
  Technology
  Unmanned Aircraft Systems Operations
Agribusiness*
Animal Science*
  Horse Science
  Pre-Veterinary Medicine
Biochemistry
Biology*
  Genetics and Biotechnology
  Microbiology
  Organismal Biology and Ecology
  Physiology
Chemistry*
  ACS Certified
Computer Science
  Business Applications
  Professional Computer Science
Concrete Industry Management
  Concrete Contracting
  Production, Sales, and Service
Construction Management
  Commercial Construction Mgmt.
  Electrical Construction Mgmt.
  Land Development/Residential
  Building Construction Mgmt.
Engineering Technology
  Computer Engineering Technology
  Electromechanical Engineering Technology
  Mechanical Engineering Technology
  ‡‡ Pre-Engineering
Environmental Science
Fermentation Science
Forensic Science
Geosciences*
  Physical Geography
  Geology
Mathematics

Math Education*
Professional Mathematics
Mechatronics Engineering
Military Science (ROTC) (minor)
Physics
  Applied Physics
  Astronomy
  Physics Teaching*
  Professional Physics
Plant and Soil Science*
Science*
  General Science
  Allied Health Science
    ‡ Pre-Chiropractic
    ‡ Pre-Cytotechnology
    ‡ Pre-Dental
    ‡‡ Pre-Health Information Management
    ‡‡ Pre-Medical
    ‡ Pre-Medical Technology
    ‡‡ Pre-Occupational Therapy
    ‡ Pre-Pharmacy
    ‡‡ Pre-Physical Therapy
  Allied Health Technology
    ‡ Pre-Diagnostic Medical Sonography
    ‡ Pre-Nuclear Medicine Technology
    ‡ Pre-Radiation Therapy Technology
  Medical School Early Acceptance Program with Meharry Medical College
* Tennessee teacher licensure available
‡ 3+1 pre-professional program: Upon acceptance and successful completion of the first year of professional school, the student will have completed requirements for a B.S. degree at MTSU.
‡‡ Suggested coursework that offers preparation

BEHAVIORAL AND HEALTH SCIENCES PROGRAMS

Athletic Training
Community and Public Health*
  Health Education and Lifetime Wellness
  Public Health
Criminal Justice Administration
  Homeland Security
  Law Enforcement
Exercise Science

Family and Consumer Studies*
 Child Development and Family Studies
 Family and Consumer Sciences
  Education
Industrial/Organizational Psychology
Interior Design
Leisure, Sport, and Tourism Studies
Nursing
Nutrition and Food Science
 Dietetics
Physical Education*
 Sport Pedagogy
Psychology
 Pre-Graduate School
Social Work
Speech-Language Pathology and Audiology
Textiles, Merchandising, and Design
 Apparel Design
 Fashion Merchandising
Tourism and Hospitality Management
*Tennessee teacher licensure available

JONES COLLEGE OF BUSINESS PROGRAMS
Accounting
Business Administration
Business Education*
Commerce
Economics
Entrepreneurship
Finance
 Real Estate
Information Systems
Management
 Supply Chain Management
Marketing
 Professional Selling
Risk Management and Insurance
*Tennessee teacher licensure available

COLLEGE OF EDUCATION PROGRAMS
Early Childhood Education*
Elementary Education*
Interdisciplinary Studies*
 Grades 6–8 licensure option
Special Education*
 Comprehensive K–12 licensure option
 Interventionist K–8
 Interventionist 6–12
*Tennessee teacher licensure available

LIBERAL ARTS PROGRAMS
Africana Studies
Anthropology
Art
 Art History
 Graphic Design
 Studio
 Visual Arts
Art Education*
Communication
 Culture and Social Influence

Organizational Communication
Dance
English
 Literary Studies
 Literature and Culture
 Secondary English Teacher Licensure*
 Writing
Foreign Languages*
 French
 German
 Japanese
 Spanish
Global Studies and Human Geography*
 Global Studies
 Human Geography
History*
International Relations
Music
 Instrumental Music Education*
 Instrumental Performance
 Music Industry
 Theory-Composition
 Vocal/General Music Education*
 Voice Performance
Philosophy
Political Science*
 Pre-Law
 Public Policy and Management
Religious Studies
Sociology
 Anthropology
Theatre*
*Tennessee teacher licensure available

MEDIA AND ENTERTAINMENT PROGRAMS
Animation
Audio Production
Interactive Media
Journalism
 Advertising/Public Relations
 Media Studies
 Sports Media
 Visual Communication
Media and Entertainment
 Interdisciplinary Media
 Media Management
 Photography
Recording Industry
 Commercial Songwriting
 Music Business
Video and Film Production

UNIVERSITY COLLEGE PROGRAMS
Integrated Studies
 Applied Leadership
Professional Studies
 Healthcare Administration
 Information Technology
 International Organizational Leadership
 Organizational Leadership

MAJORS AND DEGREES OFFERED
Bachelor of Arts (B.A.)
Bachelor of Business Administration (B.B.A.)
Bachelor of Fine Arts (B.F.A.)
Bachelor of Music (B.M.)
Bachelor of Science (B.S.)
Bachelor of Science in Nursing (B.S.N.)
Bachelor of Social Work (B.S.W.)
Master of Accountancy (M.Acc.)

Master of Arts (M.A.)
Master of Arts in Teaching (M.A.T.)
Master of Business Administration (M.B.A.)
Master of Business Education (M.B.E.)
Master of Criminal Justice (M.C.J.)
Master of Education (M.Ed.)
Master of Fine Arts (M.F.A.)
Master of Library Science (M.L.S)

Master of Music (M.M.)
Master of Professional Studies (M.P.S.)
Master of Public Health (M.P.H.)
Master of Science (M.S.)
Master of Science in Nursing (M.S.N.)

Master of Science in Teaching (M.S.T.)
Master of Social Work (M.S.W.)
Specialist in Education (Ed.S.)
Doctor of Education (Ed.D.)
Doctor of Philosophy (Ph.D.)

TUITION, ROOM, BOARD, FEES
In-state tuition and fees $9,216 (2018–19)
Out-of-state tuition and fees $28,364 (2018–19)
Room and board $9,590 (2018–19)

FINANCIAL AID
At Middle Tennessee State University, 68% of full-time undergraduate students receive some kind of need-based financial aid. New incoming freshmen students meeting certain ACT and GPA minimums are eligible for guaranteed academic scholarships if they complete their applications by Dec. 1 of each year. These scholarships start at a 23 ACT and range from $2,000 per year to $5,000 per year depending upon the score. These scholarships are "stackable" and may be combined with other scholarships.

MTSU also has a Regional Scholars Program which provides students in the surrounding contiguous states the ability to come to MTSU a reduced rate. In addition, our Academic Common Market Program provides in-state for unique programs not available in some states. For more information go to mtsu.edu/regionalscholars or mtsu.edu/acm. To qualify:

- Application for admissions as a new incoming freshman
- Admissions application fee paid
- Qualifying official ACT and/or SAT test score (without the writing subscore)
  - Only ACT/SAT scores on file with MTSU as of the Dec. 1 deadline will be considered. MTSU will not consider writing test subscores or accept test superscores in regard to scholarship consideration.
- Qualifying official sixth-semester high school transcript with cumulative GPA requirement (transcript must reflect GPA through end of junior year)
- Must be U.S. citizen or permanent resident

STUDENT ORGANIZATIONS AND ACTIVITIES
Middle Tennessee State University has a total undergraduate enrollment of 19,523, with a gender distribution of 46% male students and 54% female students. At this school, 17% of the students live in college-owned, -operated or -affiliated housing and 83% of students live off campus.

MTSU currently has more than 300 registered student organizations providing involvement opportunities for diverse interests. Of course, if you don't find what you're looking for you can always create a new organization. Becoming involved in student groups and events will provide you with many opportunities for learning outside of the classroom, meeting people from other cultures, challenging yourself with new programs, and meeting people with similar interests. Being involved can help you meet career goals, develop organizational skills and personal interests, and enrich your sense of self-worth.

ADMISSIONS PROCESS
Apply for admission easily online. mtsu.edu/apply

Guaranteed Admission
First-Time Freshmen
Complete college preparatory courses and have ONE of the following:
- 3.0+ GPA Or
- ACT composite score of 22+ (SAT 1100+) Or
- 2.7+ GPA and ACT score of 19+ (SAT 980+)

Conditional Admission
- If you don't meet guaranteed admission, complete the additional personal statement questions on the application.
- Your academic performance, standardized test scores, special interests and skills, and other nonacademic factors will be considered

To Apply
- Fill out application at mtsu.edu/applynow
- Pay $25 nonrefundable application fee
- Have official high school and/or college, technical school, and GED (if applicable) transcripts sent to:
  MTSU Office of Admissions
  120 Student Services and Admissions Center
  1301 E. Main St.
  Murfreesboro, TN 37132

Submit official ACT or SAT scores if under age 21 (must be on high school transcripts or be sent directly from testing agency)
Questions? Contact the Admissions Office at 615-898-2233 or admissions@mtsu.edu

MOLLOY COLLEGE

AT A GLANCE

Graduate Programs Fuel Careers

Molloy offers a variety of graduate and doctoral programs that provide the opportunity for students to further enhance their career or take a new direction while pursuing a passion. The College's graduate programs include a variety of MBA options, as well as programs in Clinical Mental Health Counseling, Criminal Justice, Music Therapy, Speech-Language Pathology, Education and Nursing.

What's New

Molloy, founded in 1955 by the Sisters of Saint Dominic in Amityville, NY, and home to approximately 4,900 undergraduate and graduate students, recently opened its new facility at 50 Broadway in lower Manhattan. The space serves as the new home of the nationally-ranked Molloy/CAP21 B.F.A. in musical theatre, and also hosts other academic programs and special events. Additionally, Molloy recently opened its newest residence hall, the College's third.

In Fall 2020, Molloy will pilot The Experiential Academy. This two-year program enables students to fulfil their entire general education requirements through hands-on, active, in-the-world learning. A unique opportunity, this program meets only one day a week on campus and uses online modules and assignments to create flexibility in the learning environment. At the end of two years, students will have completed an Associate's degree and have the opportunity to transition into most majors at the College.

The School of Arts and Sciences at Molloy College and the College of Liberal Arts and Sciences at St. John's University have teamed up to provide accelerated pathways for students to achieve their Master's degrees. The alliance permits students across 14 academic disciplines in arts and sciences at Molloy College to earn two degrees in five years, a Bachelor's degree from Molloy College and a Master's degree from St. John's University.

The College continues to expand its flexible learning options for many of its programs, so that students can take evening, weekend, hybrid or online classes. Some of Molloy's newer offerings include an online MBA, as well as a new degree completion program that will enable returning students to easily complete their undergraduate degree.

LOCATION AND ENVIRONMENT

Molloy is located on the South Shore of Long Island in Rockville Centre. Its proximity to New York City, just a short train ride away from the 30-acre campus, enables students to benefit from the cultural and social opportunities that Manhattan has to offer. Molloy's location in the New York metro region provides its students with numerous opportunities for internships and clinical placements, critical for students in landing their first job upon graduation.

Molloy College also offers off campus locations for study at the Suffolk Center in East Farmingdale and at area hospitals and schools, all designed to provide convenience for our graduate and continuing education students. Molloy recently opened a new facility at 50 Broadway in Manhattan's downtown Oculus District. The new building houses the Molloy/CAP21 theatre arts program, in addition to hosting a variety of lectures and other academic programs.

OFF-CAMPUS OPPORTUNITIES

Molloy students are also instilled with the belief that they can make a difference beyond the classroom. As part of Molloy's tradition of service, students become involved in projects that help underserved populations in New York City, New Orleans, Puerto Rico and Haiti, to name but a few locations. Through the College's international education program, students seek enrichment and greater understanding of the world by participating in trips to Europe, Japan, South America and other locales around the globe.

ACADEMIC PROGRAMS

At Molloy, small class size, engaging and experienced faculty and renowned academic programs will help ensure your success, both in the classroom and in your professional life. Our vibrant student life program will help you make a smooth transition to our campus.

We also make it easy for you to take classes when it is convenient for YOU. We offer evening and weekend classes, many in online and hybrid formats, with accelerated schedules designed to accommodate your busy schedule.

A minimum of 128 credit hours is required for a baccalaureate degree; these courses include a strong liberal arts general education curriculum for every major field of study. Students may choose a double major, and many minors are available. Molloy has a 4-1-4 academic calendar.

Students may earn CLEP and CPE credit, and advanced placement credit is granted for a score of 3 or better on the AP Exam. Qualified full-time students may participate in the Army ROTC program at Hofstra University or St. John's University on a cross enrolled basis. Molloy students may also elect Air Force ROTC on a cross enrolled basis with New York Institute of Technology.

The vast majority of students at Molloy enjoy an internship at some point in their academic careers. These real-world experiences are a crucial part of the learning process and ensure that students enter their chosen field ready to make strong contributions. Molloy's location in the New York metro region provides its students with numerous opportunities for all-important internships and clinical placements that can lead to a full-time job upon graduation.

MAJORS AND DEGREES OFFERED

Molloy offers the AA degree in liberal arts; the AAS degree in cardiovascular technology and respiratory care; and the BA or BS degree in accounting, art, biology, business management, communications, computer science, computer information systems, criminal justice, economics, education, English, earth and environmental studies, finance, history, interdisciplinary studies, marketing, mathematics, modern languages, music, music therapy, new media, nuclear medicine technology, nursing, philosophy, political science, psychology, respiratory care, sociology, speech language pathology/audiology, and theology; the BSW degree in Social Work; and the BFA in art, music and theatre arts. Teacher certification programs are available in childhood, adolescence, special education, music education, or visual arts education.

On the graduate level, Molloy offers a Master of Science degree as well as post-master's certification in nursing and education. M.B.A. programs are available in business, accounting, healthcare, marketing and personal financial planning; a master's program in clinical mental health counseling was recently launched as well. A master's in social work is offered through Molloy's partnership with Fordham University. Molloy also offers graduate degrees in criminal justice, music therapy, and speech-language pathology. The College offers three doctoral programs, a Ph.D. in nursing and a Doctor of Nursing Practice (D.N.P.), as well as an Ed.D. in Education.

Students interested in pre-dental, pre-law, pre-medical, or pre-veterinary programs are offered special advisement.

Experienced admissions counselors will evaluate your credits and put you on the path towards completing your degree. Articulation agreements with community colleges and established transfer credit policies ensure ease of transferability.

TUITION, ROOM, BOARD, FEES

For 2019–20, tuition was $31,330 and required fees were $1,270. Students can expect to spend about $1,400 on books.

FINANCIAL AID

Financial aid, which is based on academic achievement and financial need, is awarded to more than 85 percent of the student body. Aid is awarded in the form of scholarships, grants, loans, and Federal Work-Study Program employment. Merit-based scholarships and grants are also available.

Students are required to complete the FAFSA application every year. Full and partial tuition scholarships are available through the following: Molloy Scholars, Presidential Dominican Scholarships, Presidential Business Scholarships, Dean Scholarships, Academic Achievement, Fine Arts Scholarships, Community Service Awards, and other funded scholarships. The Transfer Scholarship Program awards partial tuition scholarships to students transferring into Molloy College with at least a 3.0 cumulative GPA. Nursing transfers are required to have a 3.3 GPA to be eligible for a transfer scholarship. Athletic grants (Division II only) are awarded to full-time students who show superior athletic ability in baseball, basketball, cross-country, equestrian, lacrosse, soccer, softball, tennis, bowling, indoor and outdoor track, field hockey or volleyball.

STUDENT ORGANIZATIONS AND ACTIVITIES

With more than 4,900 undergraduate and graduate students, Molloy has something for everyone. There are more than 50 academic programs, approximately 60 clubs and honor societies, various service opportunities and NCAA Division II athletics, providing abundant opportunities for each student to not only strive for academic excellence, but also explore new interests, pursue athletics and enrich our community.

ADMISSIONS PROCESS

While Molloy is a selective college, admissions counselors respect each individual applicant and consider the whole student-not just test scores-when making admissions decision. Prospective freshmen must submit their high school credentials, SAT or ACT scores, the Molloy application, and a $40 nonrefundable application fee. While not required, a personal interview is strongly suggested. Entrance requirements include graduation from high school or equivalent with 20.5 units, including the following: 4 units of English, 3 units of a foreign language, 3 units of mathematics, 4 units of social studies, and 3 units of science. Those who plan to major in mathematics must have 4 units of high school mathematics and 2 units of science, including either chemistry or physics. Biology majors must have biology, chemistry, physics, and 4 units of mathematics. Nursing majors must have biology and chemistry. Cardio-respiratory science majors must have biology, chemistry, and mathematics. Nuclear medicine majors must have high school algebra and biology. Applicants lacking above requirements are reviewed on an individual basis.

A select group of freshmen are invited to participate in the Molloy College Honors Program. This program offers challenging coursework and encourages reflection and personal growth. Honors students are provided with several special incentives for participating in the program.

The St. Thomas Aquinas program may be an option for students not normally eligible for admission.

Early admission is available. Molloy admits students on a rolling basis and students are advised of the admission decision within a few weeks of completion of the application filing process.

Prospective students should submit the following to the admissions office to be considered for enrollment: a completed application for admission (the Common Application is accepted), a nonrefundable $40 application fee, an official high school transcript or TASC score report, official SAT or ACT score, and official college transcripts (transfer students only).

SAT or ACT score, and official college transcripts (transfer students only).

MONMOUTH UNIVERSITY (NJ)

AT A GLANCE

Monmouth University is a first-tier, private university that empowers students to reach their full potential as leaders who are able to make significant contributions to their community and society.

A comprehensive selection of baccalaureate and graduate degree programs in subject areas that are in demand in the workplace is offered, including a number of unique Bachelor's + Master's programs. Small classes geared toward individual attention, and led by an innovative faculty, provide a transformative learning environment where students are active participants in their education.

Monmouth's academic areas including music industry, communication, homeland security, business, and more can easily be linked with world-class learning experiences in New York City and other nearby major urban areas. Students who are interested in coastal environmental studies can focus on biological, chemical, and physical sciences, together with environmental policy and natural resource conservation and management, by pursuing Monmouth's marine and environmental biology and policy major.

The University is also close to many technology firms, financial institutions, and a business-industrial sector that provides both employment possibilities for graduates and opportunities for undergraduates to gain experience.

Monmouth's location and network provide tremendous academic opportunities to students. For example, students in Monmouth's music industry program interface with industry professionals in and beyond the classroom, managing their own record label, Blue Hawk Records. There is a real spirit of entrepreneurship on campus that comes to life through student activities like the student-managed investment fund Hawk Capital. Marine and environmental biology and policy students benefit from the University's proximity to coastal waterways.

While preparing students for successful careers in leadership roles, Monmouth University believes that a major goal of higher education is to help students develop values. These include senses of citizenship and social responsibility that enable graduates to contribute actively to the societies in which they live. Academic programs and personal development opportunities at Monmouth prepare students to take the lead in an increasingly complex, multicultural world. These opportunities—combined with the myriad of art exhibits, concerts, lectures, and sightseeing trips planned each year—provide students with shared experiences outside the classroom to match the ones they receive inside.

LOCATION AND ENVIRONMENT

Located in the town of West Long Branch, New Jersey, Monmouth is situated on a beautiful, coastal campus that is one mile from the beaches of the Atlantic Ocean and also about one hour from New York City and Philadelphia. The 159-acre campus is home to a diverse student body comprising some 6,400 undergraduate and graduate students. Students come to Monmouth from 34 states and 36 countries to participate in the University's academic programs. A ratio of 12 students to each professor enables a personalized learning environment along with mentoring opportunities.

CAMPUS FACILITIES AND EQUIPMENT

The Monmouth University Library holds approximately 360,000 print and electronic monographs, 74,000 print and electronic periodicals, 180 databases, and 1,200 media assets including CDs and DVDs. All academic programs are amply supported by state-of-the-art computer hardware and software and classroom/laboratory facilities. The major components supporting Monmouth academic programs include Windows, Mac OS, and Unix systems connected via an expansive wired and wireless network, which spans all campus buildings and encompasses more than 2,400 workstations in general and specialty labs and classrooms.

OFF-CAMPUS OPPORTUNITIES

Putting learning into action is what makes education come alive. Experiential education, which includes internships, study abroad, select service learning projects, dedicated experiential coursework, or cooperative learning experiences, is a required part of the undergraduate curriculum. By their senior year, 77 percent of Monmouth undergraduate students have completed a practicum, internship, co-op, or similar real world experience; only forty-nine percent of graduating students at comparable institutions have done this according to the latest National Survey of Student Engagement.

At Monmouth, professional-quality experience comes in many forms, from collaborating on original research with faculty that can be presented at national and international conferences to traveling with the mock trial team and engaging in a wide-variety of academic field experiences. There are service learning and global study opportunities in Australia, England, Italy, Spain, Guatemala, Haiti, and more.

ACADEMIC PROGRAMS

Undergraduate students who are interested in the sciences, if qualified, can be involved in hands-on original research projects with faculty. Monmouth students present award-winning research at regional, national, and international conferences along with earning faculty co-authorship in peer-reviewed publications.

At Monmouth, about 10 percent of first-year students enroll in one of the University's five-year baccalaureate/master's programs. Subject areas for five-year programs are offered in computer science, business, criminal justice, education (select programs), English, history, social work, and software engineering.

Additionally, Graduate Studies at Monmouth University provides high-quality master's degree and certificate programs to students seeking to increase their professional skills and enhance their intellectual development. Monmouth also offers a Doctor of Nursing Practice (DNP) and Doctor of Education in Educational Leadership (EdD). Every program curriculum aims to improve students' leadership qualities and prepare them for career advancement, career changes, or further study.

Graduate students have chances to advance their knowledge and engage in scholarly research with faculty members who are not only impassioned teachers and mentors, but also leaders in their chosen fields. Those enrolled benefit from Monmouth's commitment to personalized attention and a strong bond between students and faculty members.

MAJORS AND DEGREES OFFERED
MAJORS

Anthropology*
Art*: optional concentration in Photography*
Biology*: optional concentration in Molecular Cell Physiology
Business Administration*: concentrations in Accounting*, Economics*, Economics and Finance, Finance*, Finance and Real Estate, International Business, Management and Decision Sciences, Marketing*, Marketing, Management, and Decision Sciences, or Real Estate
Chemistry*: optional concentrations in Advanced Chemistry, Biochemistry, or Chemical Physics
Clinical Laboratory Sciences: concentration in Medical Laboratory Science
Communication*: Communication Studies, Public Relations/Journalism, or Radio/TV
Computer Science*
Criminal Justice*
Education: Early Childhood, Elementary, Middle School, Secondary, English as a Second Language, Teacher of Students with Disabilities
English*: optional concentration in Creative Writing*
Fine Arts: concentrations in Animation or Graphic and Interactive Design
Foreign Language: concentrations in Spanish, Spanish and Communication/Journalism, or Spanish and Communication/Radio and TV
Health and Physical Education (teaching and non-teaching options)
Health Studies*
History*
History and Political Science
Homeland Security*
Marine and Environmental Biology and Policy
Mathematics*: optional concentration in Statistics*
Medical Laboratory Science
Music: optional concentrations in Music Industry and Musical Theater
Nursing (BSN) (direct admit program, freshmen only)
Nursing (RN to BSN) (transfer students with RN license only)
Political Science*: optional concentration in International Relations or Legal Studies*
Psychology*

Social Work
Sociology*
Software Engineering
Spanish and International Business

MINORS

Animation/Motion Design
Archaeology
Art History
Asian Studies
Business of Healthcare
Communication Sciences and Disorders
Forensic Investigation
Gender Studies
General Management
Geographic Information Systems
Geography
Global Sustainability
Graphic and Interactive Design
Information Technology
Interactive Media
Irish Studies
Italian
Journalism
Leadership Communication
Media Production
Musical Theatre
Philosophy
Philosophy and Religious Studies
Physics
Popular Music
Professional Writing
Public Policy
Public Relations
Religious Studies
Screen Studies
Social Justice
Social Services
Spanish
Spanish for Business
Sports Communication
Theatre

FIVE-YEAR BACHELOR'S + MASTER'S PROGRAMS

Business Administration
Computer Science
Criminal Justice
Education (certain programs)
English
History
Social Work
Software Engineering

4+2 BACHELOR'S + MASTER'S PROGRAMS

Health Studies & Communication Sciences and Disorders + Speech-Language Pathology

PRE-PROFESSIONAL ADVISING

Pre-Dentistry
Pre-Law
Pre-Medicine
Pre-Veterinary

*Major and minor available

2019–20 TUITION, ROOM, BOARD, FEES

$39,592 (Commuter)
$54,112 (Resident)

FINANCIAL AID

Approximately 99% of Monmouth incoming students receive some form of financial aid. Those packages typically include scholarships, grants, student loans, and work-study that may be applied toward tuition and fees, room and board or living expenses, books, and other personal expenses.

Here are some facts to consider about the financial aid packages created for Monmouth's undergraduates last year:

- About 98% received a scholarship or grant (federal, state, or University).
- The average scholarship/grant package was $24,192.
- The average financial aid package, including student loans and work-study, was approximately $34,400.
- More than $68 million in University grants and scholarships was awarded; this places Monmouth among the more affordable private universities in New Jersey.

STUDENT ORGANIZATIONS AND ACTIVITIES

The University is proud to host a successful NCAA Division I intercollegiate athletics program that fields 23 teams for men and women. The University's basketball and track and field teams compete in the 153,200-square-foot OceanFirst Bank Center. All Monmouth students have access to the arena, which also houses a 200-meter, six-lane indoor track; fitness center; conference space; the University Store; and luxury suites. The University's football, men's/women's lacrosse and outdoor track and field programs play in Kessler Stadium. This new stadium, adjacent to the OceanFirst Bank Center, accommodates 4,200 fans and features state-of-the-art media facilities and end zone to end zone seating.

Beyond athletics, students have an assortment of extracurricular activities to choose from, including more than 110 student-run clubs and organizations, as well as sororities and fraternities that engage in service work on behalf of the University and the community. Students can also get involved with the Student Government Association, the campus newspaper (The Outlook), the student-run online news portal (The Verge), the FM radio station (WMCX), the television station (Hawk TV), the yearbook (Shadows), and the literary magazine (Monmouth Review).

ADMISSIONS PROCESS

The early action deadline for first-time, full-time students is December 1, and for regular decision it is March 1.

Students applying to the spring semester must do so by December 1.

If you're applying as a part-time student, applications for the fall semester are due by July 15, and for the spring semester they are due by December 1.

Applicants to the Bachelor of Science in Nursing (BSN) program must submit their applications by December 1 for the fall start term only.

An application includes the application form, a non-refundable $50 application fee, all official transcripts, standardized test scores, at least one letter of recommendation, and a personal essay of 250 to 500 words.

NAZARETH COLLEGE

AT A GLANCE

Nazareth provides a comprehensive education with a proactive approach to career and life readiness. Nazareth's Center for Life's Work pairs students with a personal career coach to guide experience-based learning and build skills, confidence, and career-launching connections. Nazareth students demonstrate readiness for academic rigor and eagerness to make their mark in the world. Admission is based primarily on academic achievement. The College seeks students with a high level of competency and recommends applicants complete a rigorous college-preparatory curriculum in high school that includes English, a foreign language, math, science, and social studies. Successful completion of Advanced Placement and International Baccalaureate courses are looked upon favorably. An audition or portfolio review is required for applications to art, dance, music, and theatre programs. Co-curricular activities, the essay, and letters of recommendation are also considered. A campus visit is highly recommended. Information sessions and campus tours are available Mondays through Saturdays.

LOCATION AND ENVIRONMENT

Nazareth is situated on 150 acres in the charming town of Pittsford, seven miles from Rochester, New York state's third largest city. Classic and modern buildings are interspersed amongst expansive lawns, shady woodland groves, and landscaped gardens. Cultural, co-curricular, and entertainment opportunities include: music, dance, and theatrical presentations at the Nazareth College Arts Center and newly constructed Glazer Music Performance Center, 27 Golden Flyer Division 3 athletic teams, 50+ clubs and organizations representing students' academic, cultural, interfaith, and athletic interests, and presentations from national and international scholars and performers. The Golisano Training Center opened in fall 2019 featuring 120,000 square foot athletic training space that includes an indoor track, training fields, courts, and fitness and recreation facilities.

CAMPUS FACILITIES AND EQUIPMENT

In recent years, Nazareth College has invested nearly $47 million to provide enhanced learning and research facilities including: Peckham Hall Integrated Center for Math and Sciences, York Wellness and Rehabilitation Institute, renovated nursing labs and learning spaces, and the Glazer Music Performance Center, and the newly constructed Golisano Training Center.

OFF-CAMPUS OPPORTUNITIES

Nazareth is known for its civic engagement—locally, regionally, nationally, and globally, as detailed at naz.edu/civic-engagement.

ACADEMIC PROGRAMS

The College offers a broad spectrum of 60 undergraduate majors, including education, foreign languages, health and human services, pre-professional fields, sciences and math, business and leadership, and visual and performing arts. Nazareth's student-centered community includes small class sizes and an environment committed to providing students with research, hands-on learning, and professional skill-building opportunities that prepare them for their life's work. The College is nationally recognized for its Fulbright global student scholars and national recognition for commitment to civic engagement. Nazareth is coeducational and is an inclusive religiously independent comprehensive college. The Nazareth student experience includes a liberal arts education, as well as local, national, and global service learning opportunities to prepare students to live peacefully in a diverse world that's increasingly interconnected.

MAJORS AND DEGREES OFFERED

Biological and Biomedical Sciences
  Biochemistry
  Biology/Biological Sciences
  Biomedical Sciences

Business, Management, Marketing and Related

Accounting
  Business Management
  Finance
  Marketing
  Music Business

Communication, Journalism

English
  Communication and Media
  Communication Sciences and Disorders

Education
  Art Teacher Education
  Biology Teacher Education
  Business Teacher Education
  Chemistry Teacher Education
  Education, General
  Elementary Education and Teaching
  English/Language Arts Teacher Education
  Environmental Science and Sustainability Education
  Foreign Language Teacher Education
  French Language Teacher Education
  Global Studies Teacher Education
  History Teacher Education
  Junior High/Intermediate/Middle School (Adolescence) Education and Teaching
  Mathematics Teacher Education
  Music Teacher Education
  Secondary Education and Teaching
  Spanish Language Teacher Education
  Special Education and Teaching, Other
  Speech Teacher Education
  Teacher Education, Multiple Levels
  Theatre Arts Education

English Languages, Literatures, and Linguistics

English Language and Literature

Foreign Languages, Literatures, and Linguistics
  Foreign Languages, Literatures, and Linguistics, Other
  Chinese Language, Literature
  French Language and Literature
  Italian Language and Literature
  Spanish Language and Literature

Health Professions and Related Clinical Sciences
  Art Therapy/Therapist
  Clinical Laboratory Sciences
  Communication Disorders Sciences
  Music Therapy/Therapist
  Nursing/Registered Nurse (RN, ASN, BSN, MSN)
  Occupational Therapy (BS, MS)
  Physical Therapy/Therapist (BS, DPT)
  Pre-Dentistry Studies (4+4)
  Pre-Medicine/Pre-Medical Studies (3+4 or 4+4)
  Pre-Veterinary Studies
  Public Health
  Social Work
  Speech-Language Pathology/Pathologist

History
  American Studies
  History, General
  Museums, Archives, and Public History

Mathematics
  Mathematics

Natural Resource and Conservation

Environmental Science and Sustainability

Philosophy and Religious studies
  Philosophy
  Religious Studies

Physical Sciences
  Chemistry
  Toxicology

Psychology
  Psychology

Public Administration and Social Service Professions
  Community Youth Development
  Public Health
  Social Work

Social Sciences
  American Studies
  Anthropology
  Legal Studies
  Peace and Justice
  Philosophy
  Social Science
  Women and Gender Studies

Political Science and Government, General
  Political Science

Religious Studies

Social Science
  Sociology

Visual and Performing Arts
  Acting
  Art Education
  Art History
  Art Studio/ General
  Dance Studies
  Design
  Music Education
  Music History, Literature, and Theory
  Music Performance
  Musical Theatre
  Music Theory and Composition
  Music, General
  Technical Theatre/Theatre Design and Technology
  Theatre Arts
  Visual Communication Design

Multi/Interdisciplinary studies

Community Youth Development

Global Studies

3 + 3 Law Degree with Syracuse University College of Law and University at Buffalo Law

Music Business

Pre-Med, Pre-Dental, Pre-Vet Programs

Women and Gender Studies

TUITION, ROOM, BOARD, FEES
The College offers merit-based awards for excellence in academics, art, music, and drama, as well as need-based aid.

FINANCIAL AID
Students seeking aid complete the Free Application for Federal Student Aid (FAFSA). Full cost and financial aid details: go.naz.edu/tuition-aid

STUDENT ORGANIZATIONS AND ACTIVITIES
Under the guidance of faculty, students frequently find themselves working with peers (including students from other disciplines) in clinical and lab settings, and on projects and productions. As one student recently mentioned: *"There's a community feeling on campus and the surrounding area of Rochester is welcoming to students. The school offers variety and diversity and I believe the school is dedicated to their students' wholeness, health, and overall wellbeing. It's not ALL about your academic success but your overall growth along with personal maturity and life preparation. The advisors are truly dedicated to insuring you are on the right path and advise instead of tell."* Professors and advisors encourage students to link their studies with practical experiences, including study abroad, service-learning, research, and internships. Students can support or discover their varied interests through involvement in over 50 clubs and organizations ranging from academic clubs, athletics, culture and entertainment, and interfaith groups. It's common for a math major to be a member of the dance team, a physical therapy major to minor in music, or a biochemistry major to minor in legal studies.

All campus clubs are initiated and led by students. Current campus clubs and organizations include Art Club; Art Therapy Club; ASL Club; Association of Social Work Students; Badminton Club; Ballroom Club; Best Buddies Club; Black Student Union; Capoeira Club; Campus Activities Board; Center for Spirituality Council; Chinese Club; Communications, Sciences and Disorders Association; Club Italianissimo; Community Youth Development Collective; Crew Club; Dare2Dance; Diversity Council; French Club; German Club; Gerontology Club; Golden Creative Marketing Agency, Golden Gazette; Habitat for Humanity, Inc.; International Club; Lambda Association; LASMA-Spanish Club; Marketing Club; Math Club; Millennial Action Council, Mind Over Matter; Music Business Club; Music Therapy Club; National Association of Black Accountants; National Association for Music Education; Nazareth College Law Club; Nazareth Commuter Association; Nazareth Crew Club; Nazareth Dance Organization; Naz Ultimate; Nursing Club; Philosophy Club; Physical Therapy Club; Pre-Health Professionals Club; Psychology; Public Health Club; Quidditch Club; Racquetball Club; Residence Hall Council; Science Club; Student Athlete Mentors; Student Occupational Therapy Association; Student Veterans of America; Theatre League; and WNAZ Campus Radio Station. The Undergraduate Association provides student advocacy. For more: naz.edu/student-activities.

Division 3 Varsity Athletics include: basketball, cross country, equestrian, field hockey, golf, ice hockey, lacrosse, rugby, rowing, soccer, softball, swimming & diving, tennis, track, volleyball.

ADMISSIONS PROCESS
Nursing and 3+3 law program applicants are required to submit standardized test scores (SAT, ACT, or both). For all other programs, test scores are helpful, but not required. Approximately 75% of applicants submit scores. For admissions details: naz.edu/admissions, email admissions@naz.edu, or call (585) 389-2860. Nazareth offers merit-based awards for excellence in academics, art, dance, music, and theatre, as well as need-based aid. Students seeking aid complete the Free Application for Federal Student Aid (FAFSA). For cost and financial aid details: go.naz.edu/tuition-aid.

Nazareth uses the Common Application. In addition, applicants must submit an official high school transcript, an essay, and a letter of recommendation. Test scores are optional except for nursing and 3+3 Law programs. An audition or portfolio review is required for applications to art, dance, music, and theatre programs: naz.edu/auditions. A campus visit is highly recommended: naz.edu/visit International students should consult the website for application guidelines: naz.edu/international.

In addition to Regular Decision (RD), Nazareth offers two Early Decision (ED) application tracks. Application deadlines are: November 15 for ED 1, January 10 for ED 2, and February 1 for RD. The College seeks students with a high level of competency and recommends applicants complete a rigorous college-preparatory curriculum in high school that includes English, a foreign language, math, science, and social studies. Successful completion of Advanced Placement and International Baccalaureate courses are looked upon favorably. Co-curricular activities are also considered.

For admissions details: naz.edu/admissions, email admissions@naz.edu, or call (585) 389-2860 or (800) 462-3944. Nazareth offers merit-based awards for excellence in academics, art, dance, music, and theatre, as well as need-based aid. Students seeking aid complete the Free Application for Federal Student Aid (FAFSA). For cost and financial aid details: go.naz.edu/tuition-aid.

NEW YORK UNIVERSITY

AT A GLANCE

New York University is the largest independent research university in the United States and is unlike any other institution of higher education. NYU has degree-granting campuses in New York, Abu Dhabi, and Shanghai, and 11 global academic centers around the world.

NYU's more than 20,000 undergraduates come from all 50 states and over 130 countries. NYU is both the No. 1 sender and receiver of students studying internationally, and we believe our global network raises the level of discourse in the classroom and provides a modern education for our global society. NYU's global sites are entirely owned, operated, and staffed by NYU, creating a seamless experience for students.

The energy and resources within New York City, Abu Dhabi, and Shanghai serve as extensions of our campuses, which, by design, are in and of their cities, providing unique opportunities for research, internships, and job placement. Within our New York campus, NYU has ten undergraduate schools and colleges, nine of which surround Washington Square and one, our school of engineering, in downtown Brooklyn.

Students choose from thousands of courses in over 230 areas of study. Despite our size, we have a remarkably intimate academic environment on our campuses. Our student to faculty ratio in New York is 10:1, and our average class size is fewer than 30 students.

A faculty of renowned scholars, researchers, and artists teach our students who take courses both inside and outside a chosen major, providing breadth across different disciplines and depth in a chosen area of concentration. NYU's urban locations enable us to attract stunning diversity in academic talent, with faculty who have won awards ranging from the Pulitzer Prize and Abel Prize in Mathematics to the Grammys and Tony's. Being in some of the largest cities in the world enables us to offer students thousands of internship opportunities and comprehensive career preparation during their undergraduate studies. For the class of 2018, over 96% of students were employed or enrolled in graduate school within six months of graduation.

LOCATION AND ENVIRONMENT

At NYU, we believe that where you learn is just as important as what you learn. Our university was founded without walls to allow for an exchange of ideas to flow freely, not only on campus but within the cities we call home. Our location in New York City draws energy from the cultural and artistic traditions of Greenwich Village and the enthusiasm and entrepreneurial spirit of Brooklyn's Tech Triangle. Our campus in Shanghai sits at the intersection of the rich history and technological innovation of China, and our campus in Abu Dhabi allows for students to ignite their passions for diplomacy, language, and improving the world in the growing United Arab Emirates.

CAMPUS FACILITIES AND EQUIPMENT

NYU offers an exceptional range of facilities and student services, including a variety of residence halls, meal plans, and dining locations on each campus. Academic facilities include nine libraries and institutes renowned for their research in applied mathematics, physics, neural science, and fine arts. Foreign language and cultural centers offer lectures, films, and concerts. Students may also access NYU's Wasserman Center for Career Development and student support offices addressing almost every need, from health and wellness to academic support and enrichment. The Kimmel Center for Student Life houses dining facilities, student lounges, computers, club spaces, and the Skirball Center for the Performing Arts, lower Manhattan's largest performance space.

OFF-CAMPUS OPPORTUNITIES

Students have access to NYU's extensive global network, within which they can pursue their studies and explore new cultures and perspectives while remaining connected to all of the University's academic resources. They may choose from 11 global academic centers: Accra, Ghana; Berlin, Germany; Buenos Aires, Argentina; Florence, Italy; London, England; Madrid, Spain; Paris, France; Prague, Czech Republic; Sydney, Australia; Tel Aviv, Israel; and Washington, DC. Or one of the many exchange programs NYU has with outstanding research universities around the world. Each location provides a rich curriculum in which students—whose financial aid will travel with them—can complete some of their general degree requirements and, in many fields, take courses in their major. Some of NYU's schools, colleges, and programs (like the Global Liberal Studies program and the major in Business and Political Economy) offer specific curricula and majors with an international focus. With all of these opportunities, it's no surprise that NYU is #1 for the number of students who study abroad (per the most recent IIE Open Doors report).

ACADEMIC PROGRAMS

At NYU in New York City, students enroll into one of the University's undergraduate schools, colleges, or programs: The College of Arts and Science; the Core Program in Liberal Studies; the Global Liberal Studies Program; the Leonard N. Stern School of Business; the Steinhardt School of Culture, Education, and Human Development; the Tisch School of the Arts; the Gallatin School of Individualized Study; the Silver School of Social Work; the Meyers College of Nursing; the School of Professional Studies; and the Tandon School of Engineering.

NYU Abu Dhabi is NYU's second degree-granting campus and a major research center. Located in the United Arab Emirates, it draws students from around the world, preparing them for the challenges and opportunities of our interconnected world. It offers degrees in the liberal arts and sciences as well as engineering. It is also, the first comprehensive liberal arts college in the Middle East to be operated by and integrated into an American private research university.

NYU Shanghai is NYU's third degree-granting campus in China. NYU Shanghai offers students an immensely cross-cultural, close-knit learning community, along with a strong foundation in the liberal arts and sciences with an emphasis on science, technology, engineering, and mathematics, as well as Chinese language and culture. It supports world-class academic research and graduate and professional education.

NYU faculty are among the world's leading scholars and have received Nobel, Crafoord, and Pulitzer Prizes; MacArthur, Guggenheim, and Fulbright Fellowships; and Oscar and Emmy Awards. Faculty members teach undergraduate and graduate courses, allowing undergraduate students to become directly involved in research projects with internationally renowned professors and experts in their fields.

MAJORS AND DEGREES OFFERED

NYU students begin their studies at one of NYU's three urban locations: New York City, Abu Dhabi, UAE, or Shanghai, China. No matter where their home campus is, all students graduate with an NYU degree, and may travel throughout the NYU global network as they complete their majors.

In New York, students enroll directly into one of the aforementioned undergraduate schools, colleges, or programs, all of which have earned national recognition in their respective fields.

Among the more than 230 areas of study offered by NYU's three campuses are Anthropology, Arab Crossroads Studies, Biochemistry, Economics, Dance, Education, Engineering, Environmental Science, Film and Television, Finance, Global Public Health, Hospitality and Tourism Management, Individualized Study, Integrated Digital Media, Marketing, Metropolitan Studies, Nursing, Real Estate, Social Work, Theatre, and Recorded Music.

TUITION, ROOM, BOARD, FEES

On average, tuition and fees are approximately $53,000 for two semesters; room and board cost approximately $18,000 per year. Most NYU students receive one or more forms of financial aid to support contributions made by them and their families. (Financial aid information is subject to change; please visit admissions.nyu.edu/faexplained for the most up-to-date information.)

FINANCIAL AID

The vast majority of financial aid awarded at NYU is need-based. Low-interest education loans are available for both students and parents. NYU also offers or participates in a variety of payment plans, ranging from interest-free prepayment plans to extensive loan programs that allow families to finance the cost of a college education over many years. A financial aid package might include any combination of scholarships, loans, or work-study programs. The average scholarship/grant for incoming first-year students in New York is approximately $37,000.

To be considered for financial aid, students must submit the Free Application for Federal Student Aid (FAFSA)* and the CSS/Financial aid PROFILE (and CSS Noncustodial Parent PROFILE, if applicable), administered by the College Board.

Financial aid information is subject to change; visit admissions.nyu.edu/faexplained for the latest deadlines and more specific details about financial aid for each NYU campus.

*NYU Abu Dhabi applicants, and any non-US citizens or US permanent residents are not required to complete the FAFSA.

STUDENT ORGANIZATIONS AND ACTIVITIES

With 21 varsity sports teams that compete at the NCAA Division III level, as well as intramural sports, club athletics, over 400 student clubs, and numerous volunteer activities, NYU students are actively involved both on and off-campus.

Student-run clubs are as varied as the student body. Whether their interests lie in world languages, politics, ballroom dancing, writing for the Washington Square News, or working at NYU's radio station, students will find something (or more likely, a dozen things!) they love to do.

Hundreds of students annually serve communities across the city, country, and world through the Center for Student Life's C-Team, Alternative Breaks Program, student OutReach Program, greek life, and student grassroots organizations. Students deliver meals to the needy and homebound, tutor children, paint public schools, clean up parks, rebuild areas devastated by natural disasters, provide healthcare services in underdeveloped areas, and more.

NYU is anything but cookie-cutter, that's one of the best things about being a part of a large, global university. The culture of openness, opportunity, and inclusion allows NYU students to thrive. There are so many choices here about what to do that no two students make the same selection.

ADMISSIONS PROCESS

When choosing a new entering class, the Admissions Committee conducts a holistic review, carefully considering many significant factors, including a comprehensive review of the applicant's academic background, standardized test scores, extracurricular activities, personal statement, and recommendation letters. Several performing or visual art programs also require the applicant to audition or submit creative materials. Applicants who have completed a broad range of challenging course work throughout high school are the most desirable candidates. Also considered are your unique talents, personal attributes, and future goals.

Applicants should demonstrate their talents and mastery of subject matter to support their applications and to make their best case for admission. As a result, NYU accepts a wide range of national examinations in addition to the SAT, ACT, SAT Subject Tests, AP exams, and IB scores. International students may be required to submit TOEFL, IELTS, or PTE Academic results as proof of English language proficiency. More information about NYU's complete standardized testing requirements can be found online at admissions.nyu.edu/apply.

NYU accepts applications in three separate rounds: Early Decision I, Early Decision II, and Regular Decision.

Prospective students are strongly encouraged to visit campus and attend an information session. The admissions staff also visits high schools and hosts receptions worldwide. For dates and times, and for reserving a space at our information sessions and campus tours, go to admissions.nyu.edu/visit.

OCCIDENTAL COLLEGE

AT A GLANCE

Founded in 1887, Occidental College fully integrates the liberal arts and sciences with the cultural and intellectual resources of one of the world's great cities. Situated on a 120-acre residential campus in the heart of Los Angeles, our location serves as a springboard for putting theory into practice and ideas into action. At Oxy, students spend as much time in the lab, the field, the community and the studio as they do in the classroom. Oxy is a place for talented, hard-working, curious students to explore their current passions—and discover new ones. They benefit from our small-classroom environment and demanding yet supportive faculty, who are as dedicated to teaching and mentorship as their research. Our distinctive interdisciplinary and global approach gives students the chance to explore new ideas and perspectives, and connect with the world. With more than 40 majors and minors, one-of-a-kind programs like the Kahane United Nations Program and Campaign Semester and our emphasis on research through the Undergraduate Research Center and senior comprehensives, Occidental lays the groundwork for a compelling intellectual adventure. And the academic rigor on campus is enhanced by internships and partnerships across L.A., Southern California and beyond. Our graduates are strategic thinkers and effective communicators. Uncommonly inclusive and consciously collaborative, our students seek to embrace difference and make a difference in the world. Occidental is reinventing the liberal arts and sciences for a new generation of problem solvers, creators and thinkers. It's an education that is distinctly Oxy.

LOCATION AND ENVIRONMENT

Nestled in the hills of Los Angeles' Eagle Rock community and replete with natural beauty, the Occidental campus is both peaceful and a place of palpable energy. Though downtown Los Angeles is mere miles away, our picturesque campus defies the stereotype of an urban college. We reside on 120 acres studded with century-old oak and eucalyptus trees, graceful arches, and halls built in the Spanish Colonial style. Planned in 1911 by noted California architect Myron Hunt, the Oxy campus reflects a rich history; today, state-of-the-art science facilities are just down the path from beautifully preserved historic buildings.

At Oxy, you get the best of both worlds: the intimacy of a picturesque, residential campus plus access to the educational, cultural and recreational resources of a global city. Our location in one of the most vibrant, dynamic cities in the world makes an Oxy education like no other. L.A. lives up to its laid-back reputation, but under the surface the city is a hotbed of activity. The world's third-largest metropolitan economy, it's also the entertainment capital of the world, an international trade center, and home to the 2028 Olympics. And when it comes to career exploration, the possibilities for internships and other professional and post-graduate opportunities are endless.

Engaging with L.A. is an important aspect of the Oxy experience. Our curriculum gets you actively involved in addressing real-world issues, often with one of our many community partners. You might spend a day on the Pacific Ocean trawling for fish eggs, tutoring young students in urban schools, or conducting geology fieldwork in the Mojave Desert. And professors tap into the city's wealth of expertise by bringing guests from a variety of fields into the classroom. L.A. is also home to world-class museums, theaters and music venues; scenic hiking trails; impactful volunteer opportunities; and restaurants from every country on the map. Quite literally, there's something for everyone.

CAMPUS FACILITIES AND EQUIPMENT

The European-style 400-seat Keck Theater and attached shop is the main venue for Theater Department productions. (All stage sets and costumes are produced in-house.) Art students have access to multiple studio spaces, including printmaking, printing and sculpture studios, and three galleries.

In addition to standard science labs, Oxy has a superconducting magnet, a world-class paleomagnetic laboratory, a complete geochemical/environmental lab with an inductively-coupled plasma spectrometer, and a fission track lab.

Occidental's internationally known natural history collections, including the Moore Bird Collection and the Cosman Shell Collection, provide cutting-edge opportunities for genomic research.

Special Collections in the Library is home to one of the world's leading collections of material relating to the poet Robinson Jeffers (Oxy Class of 1905), a World War II Japanese-American relocation archive, and the 16,000-volume Guymon collection of mysteries and detective fiction.

Los Angeles weather allows for year-round use of outdoor athletic facilities, including Kemp Stadium, a practice venue for the 1984 Olympics. The new De Mandel Aquatics Center, featuring a 25-yard by 34-meter pool and an attached recreational pool, is designed to foster the highest level of competition at Oxy.

OFF-CAMPUS OPPORTUNITIES

Whether you hail from five miles away or 5,000, Oxy will challenge you to explore your academic interests in contexts beyond the classroom and Los Angeles. Three-quarters of our students pursue Oxy's multiple routes to global citizenship: traditional study abroad, and research, internships, and fellowships on six continents.

Oxy offers the country's only residential undergraduate United Nations program. Students of all disciplines can spend a semester in New York City, taking classes and working as interns at UN-related organizations. Every two years, students get the chance to participate in Campaign Semester, spending the term working on key elections all while earning course credit.

InternLA is a unique summer internship program that funds more than 35 students to intern in Los Angeles based organizations and companies in six broad sectors: business, policy, media, research, advocacy, and the arts. Students intern full-time for 10 weeks over the summer while also enrolling in a weekly on-campus educational component.

Occidental has a strong history of producing winners of national fellowships and scholarships, a reflection of our rigorous undergraduate preparation. These highly sought after and extremely competitive awards give Oxy students opportunities to pursue advanced study and research at home and abroad.

ACADEMIC PROGRAMS

The foundation of our commitment to a liberal arts and science education is embodied in the Core Program, an interdisciplinary set of courses required of all students. Core courses provide the intellectual foundation for Oxy's commitment to its mission of equity, excellence, community and service. They explore the big questions that we believe all students should address in order to participate fully in their college education, vocations and lives.

Research opportunities are possible for students in every discipline. For more than 15 years, we've offered a full-time Summer Research Program, an experience that often results in co-authored publications and positions students to win prestigious awards and gain entrance to graduate programs. As scholars equally committed to teaching and research, our professors open doors and champion student work. They drive an approach to the liberal arts at Oxy that encourages students to venture outside of their comfort zones. With a class size averaging 19 students, and a 10:1 student-faculty ratio, students get to know their professors and their classmates, engage in critical discussion, and learn from and about one another.

Every Oxy student completes a Senior Comprehensive Project, a project reflecting Oxy's educational philosophy of learning deeply and independently. Comps take a variety of different forms: projects, fieldwork, theses, exams, presentations, or creative works. Each discipline defines its comps expectations differently, and they all challenge and inspire students in unexpected ways. Many of our students draw senior comps inspiration from their multicultural surroundings in Los Angeles as well as research and exploration abroad.

MAJORS AND DEGREES OFFERED

Occidental offers 45 majors, minors and programs across our departments, as well as countless opportunities for independent research and experiential learning.

Majors Offered:
American Studies
Art and Art History
Biochemistry
Biology
Black Studies
Chemistry
Chinese Studies
Classical Studies*
Cognitive Science
Comparative Studies in Literature & Culture
Computer Science
Critical Theory & Social Justice

Diplomacy & World Affairs
East Asian Studies
Economics
Education*
English
Food Studies*
French
Gender, Women, & Sexuality Studies*
Geology
German*
Group Language
History
Independent Pattern of Study
Interdisciplinary Writing*
Japanese Studies
Kinesiology
Latino/a and Latin American Studies
Linguistics*
Mathematics
Media Arts & Culture
Music
Neuroscience*
Philosophy
Physics
Politics
Psychology
Public Health*
Religious Studies
Russian*
Sociology
Spanish
Theater
Urban & Environmental Policy

* Minor only

TUITION, ROOM, BOARD, FEES

Cost of attendance for 2019–20:
Tuition: $55,980
Room & Board: $16,034
Required Fees: $596
Total: $72,610

FINANCIAL AID

We extend financial aid through merit scholarships, need-based grants and scholarships, work-study and student loans to meet the various needs and circumstances of our students. Our aid programs often make Oxy's cost comparable to those of public institutions.

If you are interested in Oxy, we encourage you to apply for financial aid—regardless of your financial circumstances. The New York Times has consistently ranked Occidental as one of the country's most economically diverse colleges. The financial aid Office is committed to meeting 100% of the demonstrated need of every enrolled student.

STUDENT ORGANIZATIONS AND ACTIVITIES

Students come to our residential campus from all over the world, each contributing their unique perspective to our ongoing conversation. Oxy students come from 49 states and 64 countries; international students make up 7% of the student body. From academic initiatives to a thriving network of student clubs and multicultural living communities, Oxy is a place for nuanced, sophisticated discussions about our differences, our similarities and where we can go from here.

About 20% participate in the Greek system, more than 25% are varsity NCAA Division III athletes, and hundreds more compete in year-round club and intramural sports.

Residence life is the heart of the student experience at Oxy. More than three-quarters of all students live on campus in one of 13 coed residence halls, including four reserved for first-year students.

Students consistently give Oxy's on-campus dining high marks. Not only is the food delicious, but Oxy's Dining Services is also environmentally friendly, taking part in the Real Food Challenge by providing local, organic food in the dining facilities.

Oxy students don't just take classes. They take charge and create new opportunities for innovation and learning. Oxy students thrive in their extracurricular pursuits, running over 100 clubs and organizations.

Dance Production, which features the work of student choreographers and dancers, is the largest student club on campus and sells out each of its three annual performances. For the vocally inclined, Glee Club has been a central part of the Oxy community since 1906. With L.A. being the home to a large portion of world media, it's no surprise that our students show interest in these areas. KOXY radio and the student newspaper *The Occidental* give students avenues for expression. (*The Occidental* alumni include two Pulitzer Prize-winning journalists.)

As the hub for community-based arts at Occidental, Oxy Arts promotes a socially-conscious, interdisciplinary conversation about contemporary arts practices on campus and in the community. Oxy Arts also serves as a comprehensive source of information for arts events and cultural happenings, including music, theater, film, the visual arts, literature, and art history.

Oxy students are running small businesses and departments on campus every day. From the student-run Green Bean Coffee Lounge to Oxy Design Service and the Bengal Bus shuttle service, student initiatives provide essential services and job opportunities that have led to post-graduation jobs.

Reaching out and supporting other areas of L.A. is important to Oxy students. From tutoring and mentoring to preparing meals for those in need, Oxy has a rich tradition of students partnering with the local community.

Sustainability is a passion for many Oxy students, and food plays a big part in that. That's why the Oxy campus has a student-run organic garden and a student-managed bike-sharing and repairing program. The student government Renewable Energy & Sustainability Fund supports student sustainability projects that make Oxy a better place to study and live.

ADMISSIONS PROCESS

Occidental is committed to admitting and enrolling a highly qualified and diverse student body. To that end, the admission committee evaluates each applicant individually and holistically. Academic preparation is paramount, so we will closely examine your high school transcript, focusing on your performance and course rigor. We also give serious consideration to qualities such as motivation, intellectual curiosity, leadership ability, and distinctive talents. Your personal statement, short answer responses, extracurricular activities, and letters of recommendation offer us valuable insight into these areas.

Whether you are applying as a first-year or transfer student, the following materials must be submitted by the appropriate application deadline with a non-refundable application processing fee of $65 or a fee waiver:

- Completed Common Application
- Short answer responses
- High school transcript
- Standardized test scores (SAT or ACT)
- Personal statement
- Letters of recommendation

To learn more about the application process, visit oxy.edu/admission-aid/apply.

OGLETHORPE UNIVERSITY

AT A GLANCE

Founded in 1835, Oglethorpe University is Atlanta's only co-educational small private college, providing a superior education in which liberal arts and sciences and professional programs complement each other in this small-college environment within a dynamic urban setting.

2019 marked the opening of the I.W. "Ike" Cousins Center for Science and Innovation and the Q. William Hammack, Jr. School of Business. Other recent additions have included an award-winning campus center, a residential complex with six state-of-the-art classrooms and the expansion of arts and athletic facilities.

In 2018, Oglethorpe launched Flagship 50, a groundbreaking merit tuition scholarship that matches all 50 states' flagship tuition for qualified students.

LOCATION AND ENVIRONMENT

Imagine life at Hogwarts with the world at your doorstep. Oglethorpe's historic gothic architecture is situated in a safe, enclosed 100-acre wooded oasis. Brookhaven, our hometown, is ranked as the safest city in metro Atlanta.

CAMPUS FACILITIES AND EQUIPMENT

Oglethorpe's gothic architecture has earned designation on the National Register of Historic Places. Old meets new with the Turner Lynch Campus Center, opened in 2013, and the cutting-edge Cousins Center for Science and Innovation, opened in 2019. The 7,000 sq. ft. Oglethorpe University Museum of Art hosts internationally recognized exhibits throughout the year. The 511-seat Conant Performing Arts Center is home to the Oglethorpe theatre and music departments, where students join professionals in performances by the Tony-winning Alliance theatre, Georgia Ensemble Theatre, Capitol City Opera and many more. In addition to our eight traditional, suite and apartment-style residence halls, students can experience luxury on-campus apartment living in Gables Brookhaven, which includes a pool, gym, clubhouse and six Oglethorpe classrooms.

OFF-CAMPUS OPPORTUNITIES

Outside our green campus is a thriving metropolis. Oglethorpe students build their professional network and on-the-job skills through internships in Atlanta, home to one of the largest concentrations of Fortune 500 corporations in the US. They volunteer in our campus-wide days of service and take on active roles in community engagement, helping feed the hungry at soup kitchens, tend the vegetables in community gardens, mentor school children, and so much more. They also take advantage of our international study opportunities to travel abroad, whether for a semester or a two-week trip. Then they return to our multicultural campus—and our global city—with new experiences, new friends, and new perspectives about the world.

ACADEMIC PROGRAMS

Nearly 60% of students at Oglethorpe major in STEM or business fields and new programs in fields such as filmmaking and public health have recently been added. Through a unique partnership with Georgia Tech, Auburn and Kennesaw State, we offer a dual-degree engineering program where students can earn two degrees, one in physics from OU and one in engineering from our partner school, in as little as 5 years. In fall 2019, Oglethorpe's business programs were expanded with the launch of the new Hammack School of Business, funded by a record $50 million gift from an Oglethorpe alumnus. Oglethorpe joins theory and practice in its A_LAB (Atlanta Laboratory for Learning), an incubator for experiential learning through internships, study abroad, civic engagement, and undergraduate research.

MAJORS AND DEGREES OFFERED

Renowned for its groundbreaking Core program, Oglethorpe's academically rigorous programs emphasize intellectual curiosity, individual attention, close collaboration among faculty and students, and active learning in relevant field experiences. Students choose from more than 60 areas of study—or invent their own major with the Individually Planned Major.

TUITION, ROOM, BOARD, FEES

Estimated 2020–2021 cost of attendance

Tuition: $40,880
Room and board: $13,600
Activity fee: $280
Orientation fee: $250
Total: $55,010

FINANCIAL AID

Named one of only 20 Best Buy Colleges in the nation by the 2020 Fiske Guide to Colleges, Oglethorpe awards over $27 million in financial aid each year. In 2018, Oglethorpe introduced Flagship 50—a scholarship program that matches the in-state flagship tuition for every state in the country for qualified students, allowing students from any state the opportunity to attend Oglethorpe for the same price as a huge state school. Students can also compete for prestigious full-tuition scholarships for academic excellence, business, civic engagement or theatre. 99% of Oglethorpe students receive financial aid.

STUDENT ORGANIZATIONS AND ACTIVITIES

Oglethorpe students are bright, curious, and engaged. They aren't looking to hide from their professors, but to really learn from them. They're independent, individual, and involved. They're willing to work with everything they've got—in the classroom, on the job, in the community. They're entrepreneurial thinkers who aren't afraid to explore new ideas. A quarter of them are the first in their families to attend college. Some are athletes. Some are artists. Some are all of the above. Some are unconventional. Some are a bit quirky. Some are just plain weird, and proud of it! They're personable and friendly. They're liberal and conservative. They come from the city, the suburbs, and the country—or another country altogether. They're confident in who they are, no matter who that might be. They know that leaders are born in the most unexpected places. They're free spirits and fierce competitors. They come here with open minds and open hearts. They work to build an accepting community where differences are embraced. Where cliques are absent.

Where "an active Greek life" means "everyone is welcome." In short? There is no "typical" Oglethorpe student. There's no standard to conform to and no background to blend into.

- 1,385 students
- 51% identify as non-white
- 59% female
- 10% international
- 28% are student-athletes
- 38% are the first in their families to attend college
- 21% Greek
- 56% live on-campus

Oglethorpe offers everything you expect from college life—championship athletics, Greek life, music, art, theatre, and more than 60 student clubs and organizations. The Oglethorpe Stormy Petrels' 16 women's and men's teams compete in the Southern Athletic Association, an NCAA Division III conference comprised of the top private liberal arts colleges in the South.

ADMISSIONS PROCESS

We're looking for students who present strong evidence of purpose, maturity, academic ability, integrity, good conduct and the potential for success at Oglethorpe. The admission process is selective, but unlike some other schools, we are looking for reasons to include you, not exclude you. Can you demonstrate academic achievement in your high school courses, including appropriate courses in English, social studies, mathematics and science? Does your involvement in your school, your job and your community reflect your potential to make a life, make a living and make a difference?

We'll determine your admission by evaluating:

- Completed application form
- Official transcript of high school work
- SAT or ACT scores (Our SAT code is 5521. Our ACT code is 0850.)
- Recommendation Form and/or Letter of Reference
- Application Essay
- Portfolios & Videos (optional)
- Interviews (optional)

Applications are accepted on a rolling basis. Early action deadline is November 15. Apply early action and we will waive the $50 application fee.

ORAL ROBERTS UNIVERSITY

AT A GLANCE

Oral Roberts University was founded to educate the whole person—spirit, mind and body. With over 77 undergraduate majors, 65 undergraduate minors, 14 master's, and four doctoral degree programs, ORU is the world's leading interdenominational, Spirit-empowered university. Learn more at oru.edu.

WHOLE PERSON EDUCATION

Oral Roberts University was founded to educate the whole person—spirit, mind and body—and after five decades of being the first university of its kind, ORU is still the world's leading interdenominational, Spirit-empowered university. Its vibrant Christ-centered community and unique whole person education equip students to become Whole Leaders for the Whole World, reaching and exceeding their academic and professional goals… all while empowering them on their quest for wholeness through an environment that challenges them to be spiritually alive, intellectually alert, physically disciplined, socially adept, and professionally competent.

ORU is accredited by the Higher Learning Commission of the North Central Association of Colleges and Schools (HLC), and a member of the Council for Christian Colleges and Universities (CCCU), the Oklahoma Independent Colleges and Universities (OICU) and the Council of Independent Colleges (CIC).

"MAKE NO LITTLE PLANS HERE"

This powerful challenge from ORU's founder has inspired more than 50,000 ORU alumni and associates to impact over 145 nations around the globe, permeating every area of society—business, education, medicine, politics, media, science, engineering, ministry, and much more.

ORU has been recognized for its excellence annually by US News and World Report, Princeton Review, and Forbes, and was ranked fourth in the nation in student engagement by Times Higher Education. In addition to housing one of the world's most respected colleges for theology and ministry, it is also one of the leading liberal arts universities in the U.S., with educational opportunities spanning every interest and stage of learning.

- Six unique colleges with bachelor's, master's and doctoral degree programs
- 135+ undergraduate majors and minors
- 14 master's programs
- Four doctoral programs
- 100% online bachelor's, graduate, diploma, and certificate programs
- On-campus and online dual-enrollment programs for high school students

LOCATION AND ENVIRONMENT

TAKE A VIRTUAL TOUR

ORU's beautiful 385-acre campus can now be experienced on your phone, tablet or computer. Visit oru.edu/info/virtual-tour to experience it today.

TULSA, OKLAHOMA

ORU's campus is located in the vibrant and opportunity-rich city of Tulsa, Oklahoma. If a future ORU student were to describe a perfect college town, it might go something like this: growing city, great job opportunities, entertainment options, and plenty of places of worship. That describes Tulsa perfectly!

This flourishing city, settled in the heartland of the U.S., has the friendliness and close-knit attitude of a much smaller town, but with almost 1 million residents in the metropolitan area, it's the second largest city in the state of Oklahoma.

CAMPUS FACILITIES AND EQUIPMENT

EXPLORE ORU FOR YOURSELF

Schedule a campus visit today at oru.edu/visit or experience a virtual tour of ORU's campus, including buildings, classrooms and facilities. Visit oru.edu/info/virtual-tour/ today.

ACADEMIC PROGRAMS

ORU has built a network of programs and resources to prepare every student for success in the classroom and after graduation. The following are key programs and services that ORU offers:

- Advantage Program: online and on-campus dual enrollment courses for high school students (advantage.oru.edu)
- Bridges for Success Program: assists students who do not fully meet admissions criteria to successfully adjust to the University
- Career Services: helps students and graduates to find and secure a career
- Chaplain Program: consists of student chaplains who oversee and encourage spiritual community in the dorms
- Disability Service Center: assures that no qualified individual with a disability will be denied reasonable accommodations in modification of policies, practices, and procedure
- Eli Center: provides services and resources for student athletes
- Enrollment Counselors: help all students develop their semester schedules
- Freshman Leadership Program: allows freshman students opportunities for leadership development
- Graduate Quest Fellowship and Scholarship Program: opportunities for incoming graduate students to receive full-tuition coverage or annual scholarships (oru.edu/quest/graduate-quest/)
- Honors Program: provides exceptional opportunities and scholarships up to $20,000 per year for students with extraordinary intellectual talents
- International Student Center: helps ORU's growing international community adjust to student life at ORU and navigate Tulsa
- Intramural Sports: recreational and competitive sports leagues for students
- Missions and Outreach: provides opportunities for students to serve alongside partner ministries and organizations on a weekly basis or on short-term mission trips across the globe
- One-on-One Tutoring Program: caters to the individual academic and tutoring needs of each student at ORU
- ORU Worship Center: an artistic community of ORU students who lead the student body during times of worship
- Prayer Movement: teams of students who work with prayer and worship leaders to arrange and facilitate times of prayer throughout the week
- Quest Whole Person Scholarship Program: opportunities for incoming undergraduate students to receive additional scholarships worth up to $20,000 per year (quest.oru.edu)
- Resident Advisor Program: student leaders who assist with the development of the residents on a wing by providing daily support, accountability and helping with maintenance or emergency situations
- Residual ACT: offers multiple on-campus ACT testing dates throughout the year
- Student Association: students elected and assigned by ORU students who represents the student body and facilitates events and activities throughout the year
- Study Abroad Trips: semester or summer-long opportunities for students who want to combine the adventure of traveling with the benefits of taking classes in a new environment

In addition to personable 16:1 classroom sizes, ORU professors are leaders within their respective fields; and with a deep conviction to equip the next generation of Spirit-empowered leaders, they invest one-on-one with students through mentoring relationships.

ORU faculty members want their students to succeed and change the world. This reflects in their commitment to excellence in the classroom; their guidance and friendship outside the classroom; and their continued advice, networking, and counsel even after students graduate.

MAJORS AND DEGREES OFFERED

ORU is committed to providing excellent academics through its matchless Whole Person Education, whether that's to students on ORU's Tulsa campus or to online students around the globe. Grounded in a conviction to send Spirit-empowered leaders into every person's world, ORU houses six unique colleges offering 77 undergraduate majors, 65 undergraduate minors, 14 master's, and four doctoral degree programs that span every interest, dream, and calling:

- College of Arts & Cultural studies
- College of Business
- College of Education
- College of Nursing
- College of Science and Engineering
- College of Theology and Ministry

The following list covers degree programs according to their respective college, then department. For details about specific degree programs, visit oru.edu/academics.

COLLEGE OF ARTS AND CULTURAL STUDIES
COMMUNICATION AND MEDIA

Public Relations and Advertising/Cinema, Television and Digital Media/Media Production/Communication (BS or BA)/Convergence Journalism

THEATRE, DANCE AND VISUAL ARTS

Drama, TV, Film Performance/Dance Performance/Graphic Design/Art Education/Studio Art/BSA in Theatre/BA in Theatre/BSA in Art/BA in Art/BA in Dance

ENGLISH AND MODERN LANGUAGES

English with Professional Education Concentration/English Literature/French/French with Professional Education Concentration/Spanish/Spanish with Professional Education Concentration/Translation and Interpreting/Writing

HISTORY, HUMANITIES AND GOVERNMENT

Global Studies/History/History with a Professional Education Concentration/International Community Development/International Relations/Leadership Studies (on-campus or online)/Liberal Studies/Political Science (on-campus or online)

MUSIC

Music Arts/Music Composition/Music Education/Music Performance/Music Production/Music Therapy/Worship Arts

COLLEGE OF BUSINESS
BUSINESS

Accounting/Business Administration (on-campus or online)/Finance/International Business/International Business and Ministry (on-campus or online)/Management (on-campus or online)/Marketing/Quantitative Business Administration

GRADUATE SCHOOL OF BUSINESS

Master of Business Administration and Leadership (online)/Master of Business Administration

COLLEGE OF EDUCATION
EDUCATION

Early Childhood Education/Elementary Education/English Language Teaching in the Global Classroom/Special Education, Mild-Moderate Disabilities

GRADUATE SCHOOL OF EDUCATION

Master of Education in School Administration Public/Christian (modular program or online)/Master of Education in Curriculum and Instruction (modular program) /Master of Arts in Teaching (modular program)/Master of Arts Teaching with Alternative Licensure/Education Specialist/Doctor of Education in Educational Leadership (modular program)

COLLEGE OF NURSING
NURSING

BSN/RN to BSN Program (online)

GRADUATE PROGRAMS

Master of Science in Nursing/Doctor of Nursing Practice

COLLEGE OF SCIENCE AND ENGINEERING
BEHAVIORAL SCIENCES

Psychology (on-campus or online)/Social Justice /Social Work

BIOLOGY AND CHEMISTRY

Biology/Biomedical Chemistry/Chemistry/Global Environmental Sustainability/Medical Molecular Biology/Science Education with Biology Emphasis

COMPUTING AND MATHEMATICS

Computer Information Technology/Computer Science/Mathematical Finance/Mathematics/Mathematics Pre-Health/Mathematics Pre-Medicine/Mathematics Preactuary

ENGINEERING

Biomedical Engineering/Engineering /Engineering Physics

HEALTH, LEISURE AND SPORT SCIENCES

Health and Exercise Science /Health, Physical Education/Sports Management/Recreation Administration

COLLEGE OF THEOLOGY AND MINISTRY
THEOLOGY AND MINISTRY

Biblical Literature (on-campus or online)/Christian Caregiving and Counseling (on-campus or online)/Global Ministry and the Marketplace/Ministry and Leadership (on-campus or online)/Theological, Historical Studies

GRADUATE SCHOOL OF THEOLOGY AND MINISTRY

Master of Arts in Biblical Literature/Master of Arts in Professional Counseling/Master of Arts in Intercultural Studies/Master of Arts in Practical Theology (on-campus or modular program)/Master of Arts in Theological and Historical Studies/Master of Divinity (on-campus or modular program)/Doctor of Ministry, Ph.D. in Theology

TUITION, ROOM, BOARD, FEES

Visit http://www.oru.edu/financial-assistance/ for the most up-to-date cost of education.

FINANCIAL AID

Visit http://www.oru.edu/financial-assistance/ for the most up-to-date scholarships and financial aid offerings.

STUDENT ORGANIZATIONS AND ACTIVITIES

ORU is a diverse yet unified community with students from more than 115 nations and every corner of the US. Students create lasting relationships with peers and professors who have a rich variety of backgrounds and experiences. In fact, Huffington Post ranked ORU as one of the top friendliest universities.

ORU students are known in Tulsa and across the globe for being Whole Leaders for the Whole World. Companies pursue ORU graduates because they embody the whole person lifestyle, carrying integrity, skill, and excellence into every area of life, especially their careers.

ADMISSIONS PROCESS

ORU operates with a rolling admission policy for most programs. For specific questions, please visit oru.edu/admissions, or contact ORU's Office of Admissions at 918.495.6518 or admissions@oru.edu. Note: ORU's $35 application fee is waived if applications are completed online at apply.oru.edu.

QUINNIPIAC UNIVERSITY

AT A GLANCE

An education at Quinnipiac embodies the University's commitment to developing enlightened global citizens, prepared for evolving 21st century careers. A survey of recent graduates indicated that close to 98 percent were either employed or enrolled in graduate school within six months of graduation.

Quinnipiac, founded in 1929, is a private, co-educational, non-sectarian university located in a uniquely attractive New England setting in Hamden, Connecticut and nearby North Haven. Quinnipiac's mission is to provide a supportive and stimulating environment for the intellectual and personal growth of its approximately 7300 undergraduate and 3000 graduate, law and medical students.

The university offers broadly-based undergraduate programs together with graduate programs in selected professional fields. At the undergraduate level, through integrated liberal arts and professional curricula, programs in the Schools of Business, Engineering, Communications, Education, Health Sciences, Nursing, and the College of Arts and Sciences prepare students for career entry or advanced studies. Graduate programs are designed to provide professional qualifications for success in business, education, health professions, nursing, communications, social work, medicine, law and related fields.

LOCATION AND ENVIRONMENT

Hamden, Connecticut: 8 miles north of New Haven, midway between Boston and New York City. Quinnipiac is a suburban campus with 600 acres on three sites. The Mount Carmel Campus is adjacent to Sleeping Giant State Park, with 1,700 acres of trails for hiking and walking. A picturesque setting provides an enjoyable academic and residential campus experience for students. Ninety-five percent of freshmen choose to live on campus. A campus shuttle system provides easy access to theaters, shopping, museums, sports, recreation and a variety of area dining and entertainment options. The nearby York Hill Campus is home to the People's United Center with 3500-seat twin arenas for basketball and ice hockey, a lodge-like student/recreation center, plus suite-style residence halls with single and double rooms, kitchens and common living areas. The North Haven Campus, about five miles away, provides upper-level and graduate students in health sciences, nursing, education, social work, medicine and law with a state-of-the-art setting on 100 acres.

Driving time to Quinnipiac from Boston or New York City is about two hours. Metro-North and Amtrak provide train service to New Haven's Union Station, which is 15 minutes from campus. Airline service is available through Bradley International Airport, about 30 minutes from campus, and through John F. Kennedy, LaGuardia and Newark airports serving the New York City area. Ground transportation is available from all airports to New Haven.

CAMPUS FACILITIES AND EQUIPMENT

The Bernhard Library is the centerpiece of academic life and is open 24/7 during the fall and spring semesters. Automated library systems, wireless technology, and individual study carrels and team study rooms provide an ideal setting for studying and relaxing.

The Learning Commons offers academic support with free tutoring as well as sessions to improve study techniques, writing skills and research methods. Quinnipiac's Writing Across the Curriculum initiative is designed to help students develop strong critical thinking and communication skills through writing. Essential Learning Outcomes have been identified that broaden students' knowledge and engage them in the educational process.

The University Honors Program fosters the needs and interests of the most academically talented and committed students. Service Learning courses integrate meaningful community service with instruction and reflection to enrich the learning experience, teach civic responsibility and strengthen communities.

OFF-CAMPUS OPPORTUNITIES

Quinnipiac is a suburban campus with easy access to nearby shopping, restaurants and activities offered in Hamden, New Haven and North Haven. Students, faculty and staff are involved in community service through the "Big Event" held each April. Local community service opportunities also include Habitat for Humanity and tutoring in the elementary schools.

ACADEMIC PROGRAMS

School of Business majors: accounting, applied business, biomedical marketing, business analytics, computer information systems, computer information systems & accounting, entrepreneurship and small business management, finance, human resource management, international business, marketing and supply chain management. The Lender School of Business Center offers case method classrooms, a financial technology center, center for innovation and entrepreneurship, a software application development classroom and team study rooms for project work. An innovative 3+1 BS/MBA invites academically strong students to complete two degrees in four years. A five-year BA/MBA 'fast track' option offers the MBA to students from all majors in the University. (AACSB accredited)

School of Engineering majors: computer sciences and ABET accredited programs in civil, industrial, mechanical and software engineering. The school offers state-of-the-art labs, including a thermodynamics workshop, environmental and hydraulics workshop, geotechnical lab, and an advanced automation and production lab.

School of Health Sciences and School of Nursing majors: athletic training, biomedical sciences, diagnostic medical sonography, health science studies, microbiology and immunology, nursing, occupational therapy (5-and-a-half-year BS/MOT master's program), physician assistant (6-year BS/MHS master's program), physical therapy (6-or 7-year BS/DPT doctorate) and radiologic sciences (accelerated 3-year BS). Dual-degree options include a BS athletic training/Doctor of physical therapy (4+3) and a BS radiologic sciences/MHS in advanced medical imaging & leadership (3+1). Health Science Studies offers dual-degrees, including the BS/DPT (3+3 and 4+3); BS/MOT (4+1.5); BS/MHS physician assistant (4+27 mos.) and accelerated BS/MSW (3+2). The North Haven facility offers state-of-the-art labs including a diagnostic imaging suite, orthopedics lab, adaptive model apartment, clinical skills labs, intensive care unit, clinical simulation labs, and biomechanics lab.

College of Arts and Sciences majors: behavioral neuroscience, biochemistry, biology, chemistry, criminal justice, economics, English, game design and development, gerontology, history, independent majors, interdisciplinary studies, law in society, mathematics, philosophy, political science, psychology, sociology, Spanish language and literature, and theater as well as more than 30 minors. Also offered are accelerated dual-degrees, including the BA or BS/MSW (3+2); BA or BS/Juris Doctor (3+3); BA theater/MBA or MSA (3+1); BA theater/MS Communications (3+1); BS biochemistry or biology/MS molecular & cell biology (3+1) to academically strong students. Also, offered are the 4+1 BA or BS/MBA, BA or BS/Master of Arts in Teaching and BS biology/MS molecular & cell biology.

School of Communications majors: advertising and integrated communications, communications /media studies, film, television and media arts, graphic and interactive design, journalism, and public relations. Resources include a new podcast studio as well as the Ed McMahon Center for Mass Communications, which provides a professional-grade facility with a digital high-definition television production studio, media innovation classroom, audio production studio, 4k editing room, and more. An innovative 3+1 BA/MS degree offers academically talented students the opportunity to complete two degrees in four years. Students across all majors can experience a semester in Los Angeles, combining classes with an internship in the fall, spring or summer in the QU in LA program which provides cohort housing and an on-site director.

For those interested in teaching (K–6 or 7–12), completion of an undergraduate major in a liberal arts or natural sciences discipline, combined with courses in the **School of Education** plus, a fifth year as a full-time graduate education student, culminates in the Master of Arts in Teaching degree.

pre-med program is designed to provide the undergraduate student interested in a career as a health professional the appropriate background necessary to meet the entrance requirements of a variety of medical schools. Students interested in Law are guided by a pre-law advisor. Academically talented students may consider the 3+3 BA or BS/JD combined degree with the **Quinnipiac School of Law.**

All programs at Quinnipiac offer an ideal combination of classroom learning with internships or clinical experiences. Students in business, engineering, communications, and liberal arts and sciences intern at nearby corporations, health care agencies, or media outlets. Students in health sciences and nursing are placed in a wide variety of clinical settings as part of their learning experience.

Students can take advantage of study abroad opportunities during the academic year or summer months. Program sites include: Ireland, Australia, Austria, Czech Republic, England, France, Spain, Italy, Netherlands and South Africa and through affiliates such as AIFS, API, and Semester at Sea, to name a few.

Career Development services within each academic division provide students with assistance with resume writing, interview skills and job placement. Each year about half of students in internships are offered permanent jobs as a result of their work.

Quinnipiac University educates students to be valued and contributing members of their communities through a vital, challenging and purposeful educational program. Students engage in real-world issues through practice and the consideration of different perspectives.

Quinnipiac is where professors who want to know students by name come to teach, and where students who want a personal, challenging education come to learn. Quinnipiac's approximately 400 full-time faculty members are experts in their respective fields and include published authors, health care practitioners and researchers. Generous with their time and eager to share their knowledge with students, Quinnipiac faculty also lend their expertise to the public forum through op-ed pieces, newspaper articles and television discussions.

MAJORS AND DEGREES OFFERED

Undergraduate students can choose from almost 60 majors through the College of Arts and Sciences and the Schools of Business, Engineering, Education, Communications, Health Sciences and Nursing. About 30% of all entering freshmen remain at Quinnipiac through their graduate degree program. Several innovative combined undergraduate/graduate degree programs benefit students with fixed tuition and graduation at least a year ahead of their peers in business, communications, law, social work and biology/molecular cell biology.

Graduate students specialize in law, medicine, business, organizational leadership, health management, computer information systems, journalism, interactive media and communications, sports journalism, public relations, education, social work, and health science programs for physician assistant, pathologists' assistant, medical laboratory sciences, molecular and cell biology, cardiovascular perfusion, radiologist assistant and nursing. Several programs are offered online.

TUITION, ROOM, BOARD, FEES

Costs for 2020–21: Tuition & Fees $50,020; Technology Fee $740, Room and Board $15,440.

FINANCIAL AID

The Office of financial aid works with all applicants to ensure they receive the maximum state and federal aid for which they are eligible. Families are encouraged to file the FAFSA for federal student aid (code: 001402) after Oct. 1. The university also offers merit-based scholarships to incoming freshmen (fall semester). No additional application is necessary for scholarship consideration; recipients are notified by the admissions office. If you have any questions, please contact the Office of financial aid at (203) 582-8750 or (800) 462-1944, or e-mail: finaid@qu.edu.

STUDENT ORGANIZATIONS AND ACTIVITIES

Quinnipiac University offers more than 150 student clubs and organizations including student government, newspaper, yearbook, radio station, service organizations, community activities, religious fellowships, diversity awareness (Black Student Union, Latino Cultural Society, Asian Student Alliance, International Student Association), dance and drama productions, and Greek life, along with numerous recreation activities, providing a balanced college experience. An active intramural program has team competition in more than 30 sports and activities, as well as 10 club sports.

Quinnipiac's 10,000-plus undergraduate, graduate, law and medical students hail from 46 states and 61 countries. Housing options include traditional residence halls, suites, and suites with kitchens. Freshmen and sophomores generally live on the Mt. Carmel campus; juniors and seniors live on the York Hill campus and in university-owned houses.

Quinnipiac Bobcats: www.gobobcats.com

The NCAA Division I athletic program in 21 sports includes Men: basketball, baseball, cross-country, lacrosse, ice hockey, tennis, and soccer. Women: acrobatics & tumbling, basketball, softball, cross-country and track (indoor and outdoor), field hockey, golf, ice hockey, lacrosse, rugby, soccer, tennis and volleyball. Quinnipiac competes in the MAAC in most sports, the ECAC (ice hockey, acrobatics and tumbling), Rugby Northeast (rugby) and the Big East (field hockey.)

Athletic and recreation facilities include a gymnasium, two fully-equipped fitness centers, a spinning studio, dance/yoga studios, tennis courts, a 24,000-square-foot recreation center with an indoor track, and a sports center with twin 3500-seat arenas for ice hockey and basketball.

ADMISSIONS PROCESS

High school students should begin applying for admission early in the fall of their senior year. Visit www.qu.edu/apply for application information. Quinnipiac is a member of the Common Application. A completed application consists of the application form which includes an essay, followed by official high school transcript, first-quarter senior grades, and one letter of recommendation. Students applying to the Schools of Health Sciences or Nursing must submit official SAT (QU code-3712) and/or ACT (QU code-0582) test scores. International and homeschooled students, as well as athletes playing a Division I sport (per NCAA rules) also must submit official test scores. For all other majors, files will be reviewed for an admission decision as well as consideration for scholarships based on overall academic work. If test scores are received, the highest critical reading and math scores or the highest ACT composite score will be chosen.

Quinnipiac reviews applications on a 'regular admissions' basis and also offers Early Decision and Early Action options for freshman applicants. Early Decision candidates must file their application by November 1 with a notification date of mid-December. Early Action candidates must file their application by November 15, with a notification date of mid-January. Students applying for the 6-year BS/MHS Physician Assistant program, the BS/DPT in physical therapy, BS/MOT occupational therapy and BSN nursing programs are encouraged to apply Early Action by November 15. For all other applicants, Quinnipiac offers Regular Decision I, which candidates must file their application by January 1, with a notification date of early February and Regular Decision II, which requires candidates to file an application by February 1 and has a notification date of mid-March.

All programs subscribe to the nationally recognized candidate reply date of May 1. Waitlisted students who indicate an interest in being considered for admission if spaces become available are notified as soon after May 1 as possible.

Transfer students who have or will receive an associate degree prior to entrance are not required to provide high school transcripts and SAT results. Official transcripts of all courses taken at other colleges must be provided to the admissions office. The entry-level physician assistant and physical therapy programs are not available to transfer students.

To schedule an interview, campus tour, group information session or register for a spring or fall open house, go to www.qu.edu/visit. For questions, email admissions@qu.edu or call 800-462-1944 or 203-582-8600. www.qu.edu.

RAMAPO COLLEGE OF NEW JERSEY

AT A GLANCE

Established in 1969, Ramapo College is New Jersey's Public Liberal Arts College, dedicated to providing students a strong foundation for a lifetime of achievement and preparing them to be successful leaders for a changing world.

Ramapo College offers bachelor's degrees in the arts, business, humanities, social sciences and the sciences, as well as in professional studies, which include nursing, social work, and teacher certification at the elementary and secondary levels. Ramapo College also offers eight graduate programs, with 4 of the 8 programs, having 4+1 accelerated completion options as well as articulated programs with other reputable institutions.

Ramapo College of New Jersey is sometimes mistaken for a private college. This is, in part, due to its unique interdisciplinary academic structure, its size of approximately 6,100 students and its pastoral setting in the foothills of the Ramapo Mountains on the New Jersey/New York border. Ramapo College students receive an elite education at the cost of a public college.

The College is committed to academic excellence through interdisciplinary and experiential learning, and international and intercultural understanding. The international mission is accomplished through a wide range of study abroad and student exchange links with institutions all over the world. Additional experiential programs include internships, co-ops and service learning.

The College's interdisciplinary commitment helps students push intellectual boundaries; our commitment to experiential, hands-on learning allows students to push personal and professional boundaries as well. The devotion of our faculty to attentive teaching and mentoring empowers students to learn actively and attain the skills they will need to succeed professionally and to become lifelong learners.

Ramapo College is committed to maintaining strength and opportunity through diversity of age, race, gender, sexual orientation, ethnicity, and economic background among faculty, staff, and students. Barrier-free, the College maintains a continuing commitment to persons with disabilities.

LOCATION AND ENVIRONMENT

Ramapo College is spread across 300 acres, resting within the foothills of the Ramapo Mountains in Mahwah, New Jersey. Enhancing these tranquil surroundings is the knowledge that the campus is approximately 32 miles from the nation's cultural mecca, New York City.

Campus is located just five minutes from major highways such as I-287, the New York State Thruway, and Route 17, making it very easy to bring you right to Ramapo's doorstep.

CAMPUS FACILITIES AND EQUIPMENT

A campus-wide building program during recent years has resulted in the renovation of the G-wing building and completion of the Adler Center for Nursing Excellence, a central feature of the main entrance to the campus. The renovations include expanded classrooms as well as a research and simulation laboratory space. This 36,000 square-foot facility is connected by an overhead walkway to the College's science/social science building. Students engage in new experiences that build and grow their whole being through programming offered at the recently renovated Padovano Commons. In addition, a campus-wide photovoltaic installation project is complete, supplementing power resources to campus.

Construction has begun on a new Learning Commons, which will add 18,000 square feet of space to the existing 62,000 square feet of the George T. Potter Library that is under renovation. Anticipated completion date is mid-year 2021. Construction will include the Library collection, meeting spaces, study space, classrooms and state-of-the-art research capabilities.

Within the Anisfield School of Business academic facility is a real-time Global Financial Markets Trading Laboratory, which features 32 workstations, ticker displays inside and outside the lab, and 3 LCD television screens.

The Bill Bradley Sports and Recreation Center features a 2,200-seat arena, fitness center, 24 foot high Edelman climbing wall, as well as track and dance/aerobics studios.

The Angelica and Russ Berrie Center for Performing and Visual Arts houses performance theaters, art galleries and specialized spaces devoted to fine arts, computer art, photography, theater, dance and music.

The campus also boasts the Sharp Sustainability Education Center, an environmentall friendly building which embodies the concepts of Green building. The Salameno Spiritual Center provides the College community a place to self reflect and enhance their wellness

Our dining services includes two main dining halls (one with late night options), th Atrium if you're on the go, a quick convenience store, a café that brews Starbucks, an one of the first "next gen" Dunkin's.

Housing at Ramapo College offers students convenient, modern amenities within the eigh residence halls on campus, including air conditioning, cable television, complimentar laundry, and semi-private bathrooms within each suite.

The campus features new and upgraded facilities that enhance all areas of campus life including a library with electronic research facilities; a student life building with an FM radio station, student offices, cafeterias, and entertainment and meeting rooms; housin for more than 3,000 students; modern academic buildings with 24-hour computer labs and a fully wireless access campus, including academic buildings and residence halls.

OFF-CAMPUS OPPORTUNITIES

Ramapo College encourages students to take advantage of experiences outside of the classroom, such as internships, co-ops, and study abroad opportunities.

Ramapo College has developed a diverse selection of more than 400 individual study abroad program options in more than 60 countries. Opportunities exist for ALL major and range from one-week to a full year.

Being only 32 miles away from New York City makes it easy for Ramapo Colleg students to take advantage of internship opportunities with over 200 NYC companie and even more in New Jersey. Students in the past have completed a co-op or internship at companies like Google, Madison Square Garden, Yahoo!, BMW of North America Deloitte, and Sony.

Students are able to purchase discounted bus tickets from Roadrunner Central and take a bus service that leaves from campus and takes them to The Port Authority of NY & NJ station in Manhattan. The College recently launched Ramapo Roadrunner Express a new transit link - free service to and from the Westfield Garden State Plaza in Paramus with a stop at Bergen Community College. The new shuttle offers direct links to buses from many areas including Hackensack, Union City, Weehawken, Fort Lee, Paterson, Passaic, Clifton, Bloomfield, Rutherford and more (bus routes 709, 163, 770, 758).

ACADEMIC PROGRAMS

Undergraduate students can choose from more than 40 academic programs. Ramapo College boasts an average student/faculty ratio of 16:1 and average class size of 21 affording students the opportunity to develop close ties to the College's exceptional faculty.

95 percent of our faculty members hold terminal degrees in their field, allowing them to be excellent mentors to students inside and outside of the classroom.

Undergraduate students have the opportunity to engage in faculty-guided research, present papers at national conferences, and take advantage of over 200 different internship and co-op opportunities in nearby New York City companies and many more in New Jersey.

To strengthen the student's college background before concentrating on major courses for a degree, students are required to complete an all-college general education program consisting of courses in English, Mathematics, the Humanities, Social Sciences, and Natural Sciences.

All students are assigned an academic advisor during their first semester, allowing the choice of major to be made by the end of the sophomore year (with the exception of Nursing and Biology). There is ample time to explore several fields of interest before selecting a major.

MAJORS AND DEGREES OFFERED

Ramapo College offers the following undergraduate degree programs, which are hosted within our five academic schools on campus:

ANISFIELD SCHOOL OF BUSINESS

Accounting (BS) | Economics (BA) | Finance (BS) | Information Technology Management (BS) | International Business (BA) | Management (BS) | Marketing (BS) |

SCHOOL OF CONTEMPORARY ARTS

Communication Arts/Digital Filmmaking (BA) | Communication Arts/Global Communication and Media (BA) | Communication Arts/Journalism (BA) | Communication Arts/Visual Communication Design (BA) | Communication Arts/Writing (BA) | Contemporary Arts (BA) | Music/Music Education (BA) | Music/Industry (BA) | Music/Performance (BA) | Music/Production (BA) | Music Studies (BA) | Theater/Acting (BA) | Theater/Design & Technical Theater (BA) | Theater/Directing & Stage Management (BA) | Theater Studies (BA) | Visual Arts/Art History (BA) | Visual Arts/Drawing & Painting with Art Therapy (BA) | Visual Arts/Electronic Art & Animation (BA) | Visual Arts/Photography (BA) | Visual Arts/Sculpture (BA) | Visual Arts/Sculpture with Art Therapy (Joint) (BA) |

SCHOOL OF HUMANITIES AND GLOBAL STUDIES

Africana Studies (BA) | American Studies (BA) | History (BA) | International Studies (BA) | Liberal Studies (BA) | Literature (BA) | Literature/Creative Writing (BA) | Philosophy (BA) | Political Science (BA) | Spanish Language Studies (BA) |

SCHOOL OF SOCIAL SCIENCE AND HUMAN SERVICES

Elementary Education (BA) | Environmental Studies (BA) | Law and Society (BA) | Psychology (BA) | Social Science/Community Mental Health (BA) | Social Science/Education Studies (BA) | Social Science/Society and Culture (BA) | Social Science/Ethnicity & Race Studies (BA) | Social Science/Gender & Sexuality Studies (BA) | Social Science/Labor, Work & Organization (BA) | Social Work (BSW) | Sociology (BA) | Sociology/Crime and Justice Studies (BA) | Sociology/Public Sociology (BA) | Sustainability (BA) |

SCHOOL OF THEORETICAL AND APPLIED SCIENCES

Biochemistry (BS) | Bioinformatics (BS) | Biology (BS) | Chemistry (BS) | Clinical Lab Science (BS) | Computer Science (BS) | Data Science (BS) | Engineering Physics (BS) | Environmental Science (BS) | Integrated Science Studies (BS) | Mathematics (BS) | Medical Imaging Science (BS) | Nursing (BSN) |

TUITION, ROOM, BOARD, FEES

The approximate tuition and fees for undergraduates in the 2018–2019 academic year are as follows:

In-state tuition and fees: $14,678.40
Out-of-state tuition and fees: $24,228.80
Room and board (all students): $12,310.00

FINANCIAL AID

Because Ramapo College is a state institution, the cost of attending is affordable compared to many other institutions. About 77 percent of Ramapo's students receive some form of financial assistance, including grants and loans. Students may also be eligible for Federal work-study funding that allows a student to find a job on campus where they can earn money to help pay for school.

To apply for financial aid at Ramapo College, students should complete the Free Application for Federal Student Aid (FAFSA) by March 1. No other application forms are required. By complying with this priority deadline, students will be notified by April 1 about their expected aid package. The FAFSA is available after October 1 at www.fafsa.ed.gov. Applicants should use Ramapo's school code (009344) when filing.

Transfer students must initiate a school code change on the Student Aid Report (SAR) to ensure that their account will be appropriately credited. Students should begin this process at the time of application. Contact Ramapo's Financial Aid Office at (201)-684-7549 and finaid@ramapo.edu.

STUDENT ORGANIZATIONS AND ACTIVITIES

At Ramapo College, student clubs and organizations are recognized as important parts of the total learning experience. Students are urged to take advantage of the many opportunities available that allows for learning experiences beyond class time.

There are more than 100 groups including cultural, academic, religious, recreational, entertainment, political, social and special interest groups. Clubs and organizations at Ramapo College are run by students under the general supervision of the Center for Student Involvement. Each group operates under its own constitution, according to the interests and enthusiasm of its membership. All welcome new members, new ideas and new directions. Many groups can provide valuable experience and connections to the job market.

Ramapo College offers intramural sports, club sports, 18 NCAA Division III sport teams, 30 honor societies, and 21 fraternities and sororities.

ADMISSIONS PROCESS

Every year, Ramapo College welcomes more than 1000 freshmen primarily from New Jersey, the Mid-Atlantic and Northeast regions of the United States and from many foreign countries. In addition, Ramapo College receives over 7,000 applications from all 21 counties in New Jersey, 33 different states and 34 foreign countries.

A complete application to Ramapo College includes:

- Application (Apply at www.ramapo.edu/apply, www.commonapp.org, or at https://www.mycoalition.org/)
- $65 application fee
- Official high school transcripts
- One letter of recommendation (two preferred)
- Essay
- Official SAT or ACT scores

The Test of English as a Foreign Language (TOEFL) is required of all international students and is recommended for all students who have resided in the United States fewer than four years.

Ramapo College practices a holistic review process. Each application is evaluated individually with emphasis placed on academic achievement in high school and standardized test scores, however, successful applicants also present a record of extracurricular activities that reflect maturity, responsibility and commitment.

Ramapo College seeks the very best students for its Educational Opportunity Fund (EOF) Program. If you qualify, you will join a community of achievers who are supported by a partnership between the College and EOF that is outstanding not only in financial assistance to cover your college cost, but also in personal and academic counseling, career planning, and leadership training. Your admission to the Ramapo College EOF program depends upon meeting financial eligibility requirements and academic standards.

The Ramapo College Honors Program is a community of faculty and students dedicated to intellectual, creative, and moral engagement. Honors students seek excellence through continual guidance and a distinctive curriculum of critical thinking, intercultural and international understanding, experiential learning, service, and interdisciplinary studies.

Fall Application Deadlines:

Ramapo College offers binding Early Decision for students who know Ramapo College is their number one choice. Early Decision applicants must apply by November 1 and will receive their decision by December 5. Ramapo offers Early Action applicants must apply by December 15 and will receive their decision by February 1. Additionally Ramapo offers Regular Decision applicants must apply by February 1 and will receive their decision by March 1.

Students who are applying to the Nursing or Biology program must apply by December 15. The priority deadline for merit scholarship consideration for all majors is also December 15. The supporting documents and credential deadline (date by which Ramapo College must receive your documents, including transcript, test scores, recommendation letters, and EOF questionnaire, if applicable) is January 15.

The final deadline for all other majors outside of the Nursing and Biology program is February 1. All decisions for completed applications will be sent by March 1.

Scholarships:

Ramapo College offers scholarships that are merit based opportunities. This means they are offered to students based on their academic and personal achievements, not financial need. Students who apply by December 15 and submit all required credentials by January 3 and are in the top 10 percent of their high school class with SAT scores of at least a 1280 total or at least a 27 ACT score will be considered for a merit based scholarship.

Unfortunately, due to an increase in applications and limited funding, the College may be unable to offer every student that fits the above criteria a merit based scholarship.

Awards are continued for four years provided that students maintain the required number of credits and grade point average. No separate application is necessary.

If you have any questions, please email us admissions@ramapo.edu or 201-684-7300.

REED COLLEGE

AT A GLANCE

Intellectual. Free-thinking. Classical. Curious. Paradoxical. This constellation of features only begins to describe Reed: one of the most distinctive colleges in the nation.

Reed attracts serious scholars who don't take themselves too seriously. Always engaged and often engrossed in a demanding, exhilarating educational adventure, "Reedies" thrive on a mix of classical study, critical analysis, and guided inquiry that rewards creativity, independence, and reflection. Classes are small, faculty members are highly accessible, and students adhere to an honor principle both inside and outside the classroom.

Reed students hail from 48 states in the nation and Reedies travel the farthest to attend Reed out of any school in the nation. The student body is also composed of 11 percent international students. Reed is ranked number one in the nation in the percentage of STEM majors who go on to earn PhDs in STEM fields, second among U.S. liberal arts colleges in the percentage of graduates going on to earn doctoral degrees, and fourth among all institutions of higher education. The breadth, depth, and rigor of the curriculum provide great preparation for nearly any career. Many Reed alumni found or lead companies and organizations, earn medical or law degrees, write books or create works of art, and work to make life on the planet better for all.

LOCATION AND ENVIRONMENT

Located in a quiet, residential neighborhood is a 116-acre campus of verdant lawns, winding paths, statuesque trees, a wooded natural wetland preserve, and a spring-fed lake frequented by migratory birds and other wildlife. Reed is a short bicycle, bus, and light rail ride from the energy and excitement of downtown Portland, which is widely cited as the nation's most livable urban center. Portland boasts a wealth of diverse cultural, entertainment, shopping, and dining opportunities in an environment characterized by a combination of youthful exuberance and Pacific Northwest nonchalance. The Oregon Coast is 90 minutes to the west and Mt. Hood 90 minutes to the east where Reed has its own ski cabin that is free of charge for students to use.

On the campus itself, century-old brick Tudor gothic buildings are interspersed with newer traditionally designed and remodeled facilities. The library, classrooms, and laboratories resonate with the history of decades of inquiry and discovery, supported with modern technology.

CAMPUS FACILITIES AND EQUIPMENT

The Reed College campus was established on a tract of land known in 1910 as Crystal Springs Farm. In a park-like setting near the heart of the city, the rolling lawns and open spaces of Reed's 116-acre campus include some of the largest and finest specimen trees in the Portland area.

The social center of the college is the Gray Campus Center. It includes a commons building, student union, kitchen, dining room, private meeting rooms, student activities offices, bookstore, and mail services.

At the physical center of campus is the canyon, a beautiful wooded upland surrounding a spring-fed lake and emergent marsh. A walking trail around the lake provides numerous opportunities to observe migratory birds and other woodland wildlife. The college recently built a fish passageway that creates a link from the upper Reed Lake area to the Crystal Springs stream below.

In fall 2013, Reed opened a new Performing Arts Building, representing a major step forward in the College's commitment to the important role the arts have played throughout Reed's first 100 years. For the first time in Reed's history, the departments of music, dance, and theatre are housed in one building that includes rehearsal and performance space, offices, scene and costume studios, collaborative spaces, and a multimedia lab.

Housing at Reed includes traditional residence halls, as well as theme dorms, co-ops, and language houses. Reed's newest residence hall, Trillium, opened in 2019 and has earned a LEED Platinum certification.

OFF-CAMPUS OPPORTUNITIES

Reed undergraduates may participate in a number of domestic exchange and study abroad opportunities. Domestic programs include: Howard University in Washington, D.C.; Sarah Lawrence College in New York; and Sea Education Association in Massachusetts. In addition, Reed provides study-abroad opportunities for students in Argentina, Australia, China, Costa Rica, Cuba, Czech Republic, Ecuador, Egypt, France, Germany, Greece, Hungary, Ireland, Israel, Italy, Kenya, Lebanon, Morocco, Palestine, Russia, South Africa, Spain, Tanzania, Taiwan, Turks and Caicos, Turkey, and the United Kingdom. Students may also arrange independent study plans in consultation with appropriate faculty members.

ACADEMIC PROGRAMS

The curriculum at Reed is both demanding and wide-ranging. Through required studies, Reed students receive a solid grounding in the liberal arts and sciences.

All first-year students must complete Humanities 110, which introduces students to academic life at Reed and provides rigorous instruction in research and writing. Distribution requirements set a substantial portion of a student's curriculum for the first two years at Reed. Students must complete courses in each of the three major divisions of the college. Beyond Humanities 110, no specific courses are required; students are free to pursue their interests.

Reed juniors take a comprehensive qualifying exam in their major to allow faculty members the chance to evaluate and assist in the student's readiness for his or her senior thesis project. The required senior thesis is the capstone experience of a Reed education. Every senior produces an original independent research project over the course of the final year.

Reed strongly believes that learning should be undertaken for its own sake, not for the sake of letter grades. Accordingly, students do not receive grade reports unless they wish to. A student's transcript does include letter grades for all courses taken, but students can better gauge their progress through professors' written evaluations of their work and one-on-one meetings with faculty. Most prefer this system, which greatly reduces competition among students and allows them to focus on the content of their academic work.

MAJORS AND DEGREES OFFERED

Reed confers the bachelor of arts degree in 41 traditional academic departments and interdisciplinary combinations across a wide selection of fields. Approval of an interdisciplinary program (linking two or more disciplines) is reviewed by the student's adviser and the departments concerned.

Reed offers a number of 3-2 (dual degree) programs; these allow undergraduates to earn a three-year bachelor's degree from Reed, then earn a professional degree in engineering, computer science, or forestry from a cooperating institution (Caltech, Columbia, Duke, RPI) in two additional years.

TUITION, ROOM, BOARD, FEES

Tuition for the 2019–2020 Academic year is $58,130. Room and board is $14,210. The student body fee is $310.

FINANCIAL AID

Reed College meets 100% of the demonstrated need for incoming and continuing students. The college maintains a need-based assistance program that allows students of all economic backgrounds to attend the college. For the incoming class of 2023, the average financial aid package including grants, loans, and work opportunities was approximately $45,490. Reed students' average graduating loan debt for all four years is $21,081, well below the national average. The college is the primary source of grant money for its students. Reed also administers federal sculptor grants and a number of other awards. Campus employment and work-study programs also figure into many aid packages. Over half of Reed undergraduates receive financial aid.

STUDENT ORGANIZATIONS AND ACTIVITIES

Reed maintains inclusivity in all organizations and activities, so the college has no fraternities or sororities and no NCAA or NAIA athletic teams (more about sports below). All campus organizations are student-created and student-run. Student organizations must lobby the Student Senate for funding annually, after which the Senate oversees a vote in which the entire student body decides what organizations should be funded. Thus, the number and nature of campus organizations at Reed changes every year to meet current student interests. Instead of NCAA or NAIA competition, students participate in sports on an informal basis. Intramural sports and club sports proliferate in basketball, fencing, rugby, sailing, soccer, squash and ultimate Frisbee. A three-semester physical education requirement underscores the importance of physical fitness and the balance of healthy mind and body.

ADMISSIONS PROCESS

Reed seeks students who demonstrate a commitment to learning and to the ideals embodied by a rigorous and stimulating liberal arts education. First-year and transfer applications are welcome. The ideal incoming class is diverse in its range of talents, interests, ethnic and socioeconomic backgrounds, and perspectives, and comprised of students who share a common passion for academic inquiry. Successful applicants have pursued a rigorous secondary school curriculum that includes honors and advanced courses. Reed recommends that students take 4 or 5 core academic courses per year which typically includes 4 years of English, at least 3 years of a foreign or classical language, 3 to 4 years of mathematics, 3 to 4 years of science, and 3 to 4 years of history or social studies. Because secondary school curricula vary widely in quality and content, Reed sets no fixed requirements in this area. The admissions committee sets no "cutoff points" for high school grades, college grades (for transfer students), or standardized test scores. Reed seeks candidates who demonstrate excellence of character, motivation, intellectual curiosity, individual responsibility, and social consciousness. The admission committee recognizes the importance of creating a diverse community in which individual differences contribute to the vitality of the campus and enhance the learning opportunities for students. Reed recommends a personal interview but an interview is not required. Early Decision applicants should apply to Reed by November 15 (ED 1) or December 20 (ED 2). Early Decision at Reed is binding: students who are admitted under Early Decision are expected to matriculate. Early Action applications should arrive at Reed by November 15. The deadline for regular first-year admission applications is January 15. Transfer candidates seeking admission for the spring semester should apply no later than November 1 and for the fall semester, March 1.

RHODES COLLEGE

AT A GLANCE

Rhodes is a nationally-ranked, four-year, private, coeducational, residential college committed to the liberal arts and sciences. Our highest priorities are intellectual engagement, service to others, commitment to diversity and inclusion, and honor among ourselves. Our students live and learn on one of the country's most beautiful campuses in the heart of Memphis, an economic, medical, and cultural center, making Rhodes one of a handful of prominent liberal arts colleges located in a major metropolitan area.

The Rhodes experience combines the best of the classroom and the real world—through internships, service, research and other opportunities in Memphis and far beyond. Students learn, explore, and serve others with a determination to grow personally and to improve the quality of life within their communities.

Rhodes aspires to graduate students with a life-long passion for learning, a compassion for others, and the ability to translate academic study and personal concern into effective leadership and action in their communities and the world.

The classroom experience at Rhodes is intimate and challenging. We value the type of engaging dialogue that arises when students and professors work together to investigate questions and problems they care about. In this environment, students are expected to formulate and articulate big ideas and contribute in major ways to the critical discussions and debates that take place in our classrooms and laboratories.

LOCATION AND ENVIRONMENT

Rhodes' Collegiate Gothic campus sits on a 123-acre, wooded site in the heart of historic Midtown Memphis, Tennessee. Our walkways, quadrangles, residence halls, common areas and classrooms are all intentionally designed to encourage intimate conversation, the exchange of ideas, and life-changing connections.

CAMPUS FACILITIES AND EQUIPMENT

In this beautiful, supportive environment, our students and faculty comprise a community unmatched in its dedication to learning and a life of honor.

Our walkways, quadrangles, residence halls, common areas and classrooms are all intentionally designed to encourage intimate conversation, the exchange of ideas and life-changing connections.

The original buildings, including Southwestern Hall (1925), Kennedy Hall (1925), and Robb and White dormitories (1925), were designed by Henry Hibbs in consultation with Charles Klauder, who designed many buildings at Princeton University, alma mater of former Rhodes president Charles Diehl.

Later buildings were designed by H. Clinton Parrent, a young associate of Hibbs. His buildings include the Catherine Burrow Refectory (1957), which was an expansion of the original dining hall. Parrent also added Halliburton Tower (1962) to Palmer Hall. The 140-foot bell tower was named in honor of explorer Richard Halliburton. The Paul Barret, Jr. Library holds a collection of Halliburton's papers.

With each new expansion, Rhodes has maintained its Collegiate Gothic architecture. The Paul Barret Jr. Library (2005), which was designed by the firm of Hanbury Evans Wright and Vlattas, has been ranked among the country's most beautiful libraries.

In 2012, Rhodes opened the expanded Catherine S. Burrow Refectory and the West Village Residence Hall, both of which were designed by Hanbury Evans Wright and Vlattas and maintain the Collegiate Gothic style.

In September of 2017 Rhodes opened its most recent expansion, Robertson Hall. It is a $30 million, 55,000-square-foot science facility that features state-of-the-art research and teaching labs and smart classrooms.

In addition, Briggs Hall underwent extensive renovation in 2017. The recent renovation provided the campus a much-needed computer science facility with classrooms, computer labs, offices, and a virtual reality lab. In addition, the building is fortunate to house the Spence Wilson Commons and the Spence Wilson Multi-Purpose Room.

OFF-CAMPUS OPPORTUNITIES

Memphis is our home. Here, Rhodes students are helping researchers at St. Jude Children's Research Hospital discover cures for childhood cancers, addressing the ills of urban poverty through education and health care, launching new businesses and nonprofit organizations, and focusing on environmental issues from an urban perspective. They are immersed in a culture where academic growth and social action go hand in hand, and where their ideas and actions make an impact in the real world.

ACADEMIC PROGRAMS

Rhodes offers more than 50 majors, interdisciplinary majors, minors, and academic programs. Rhodes students sometimes design their own majors to suit their specific goals, and the college provides pre-professional advising for students who plan to work in the health professions, law, engineering, ministry, and education. Through partnerships with other universities, Rhodes also offers dual-degree programs in engineering, education and nursing.

Majors may be directly related to a student's anticipated vocation, but that is not the primary purpose in a liberal arts curriculum. The qualities of mind and abilities that will serve students best in their careers are developed within the curriculum as a whole. The major is a refinement of intellectual discipline and a deepening of understanding of an area of study. The academic enrichment gained through a major affords access to other disciplines as well as an appreciation of the complexity of other fields of study. Students should consider carefully how all of the courses they select can enrich and complement work done in the major.

MAJORS AND DEGREES OFFERED

- Africana Studies
- Anthropology & Sociology
- Archaeology *
- Art
- Art History
- Art & Art History
- Asian Studies *
- Biochemistry & Molecular Biology
- Biology
- Biomathematics
- Business (Concentrations in General Business & International Business)
- Chemistry
- Chinese Studies
- Computer Science
- Economics
- Economics/Business
- Economics & International Studies
- Educational Studies
- English (Concentrations in Literature and Literature & Creative Writing)
- Environmental Science
- Environmental Studies
- Film & Media Studies *
- French & Francophone Studies
- Gender & Sexuality Studies *
- German Studies
- Greek & Roman Studies (Concentrations in Classical Studies, Greek, Latin & Material Culture)
- History
- History & International Studies
- International Studies
- Jewish, Islamic & Middle East Studies
- Latin American and Latinx Studies

- Mathematics
- Mathematics & Economics
- Modern Languages & Literatures
- Music
- Music & Psychology
- Neuroscience
- Philosophy
- Physics
- Political Economy
- Political Science
- Political Science & International Studies
- Psychology
- Religious Studies
- Russian Studies
- Russian & International Studies
- Self-Designed Interdisciplinary Majors
- Spanish Studies
- Theatre
- Urban Studies

* Available only as a minor

TUITION, ROOM, BOARD, FEES

The cost for tuition and fees at Rhodes is among the lowest of the national liberal arts colleges. Still, we understand that financing a college education is a big task, and we are here to help. We carefully consider every student's circumstances and do our best to help make it possible for every accepted student to attend.

2020–2021 Fees

Resident Students
Tuition: $50,600
Fees: $310
Room/Board (21 meals/per week, standard multiple occupancy): $11,750
Total: $62,660

The good news is that many of the "extras" at other colleges are included in your fees:

- Internet access, cable TV and telephones with individual voicemail
- Free laundry facilities
- State-of-the-art computer labs running Microsoft Office Suite, Adobe Photoshop, etc.
- 1,000 pages of laser prints per year
- Unlimited use of campus fitness facilities and swimming pool
- Incidental first-aid and health supplies (band aids, aspirin, etc.) from the campus health center
- Meal plans in 7-, 15-and 21-meal/week increments
- Free parking

Students should allow approximately $1,125 for books and supplies. You should also allow for transportation and personal expenses. In addition, evidence of health insurance is required in order to enroll at Rhodes.

FINANCIAL AID

Thanks to scholarships, grants, loans, and work-study, there are many ways to afford a Rhodes education. The Office of financial aid will work closely with you to explore all available funding resources.

Our goal is to remove cost as the primary determinant for applying to Rhodes. The financial aid and scholarship programs offered by Rhodes make it possible for qualified students from all walks of life to attend.

STUDENT ORGANIZATIONS AND ACTIVITIES

Approximately 2,000 students.

It's no accident that Rhodes students are involved in more than 100 student organizations on campus. We intentionally seek students who are involved in the world around them, and desire to learn from and contribute to their community.

Rhodes is well known for student involvement that makes a real-world impact in the Memphis community. We're also famous for excellence in the arts, commanding enthusiastic audiences for student plays, choral and instrumental performances, and art openings. To help you find your niche at Rhodes, we put on the SACK Fair at the beginning of each term to introduce you to our campus organizations.

ADMISSIONS PROCESS

The college application allows you to show the Admission committee that you are ready and excited to transform yourself, the college, and the community. We use a holistic approach to evaluate every facet of your application to get a better sense of the whole you.

When examined together, your transcript, test scores (optional to submit), extracurricular activities, recommendations, and personal statement can paint a bigger picture of your ability to contribute to Rhodes as a classmate, roommate, teammate, and community member.

We recommend that applicants be active throughout their college search and personally engaged with the college. We want to get to know you and to help you get to know Rhodes! Come for a campus visit, meet your Admission counselor when they visit your school, or connect with us through an interview. You may also demonstrate your interest by contacting your Admission counselor.

First year students can choose from three application options:

- Early Decision (ED) applicants make a commitment to Rhodes as their first-choice institution and agree that, if admitted, they will enroll and withdraw all other applications. It's perfect for students who are ready to say, "If we can make Rhodes possible, Rhodes is where I will be."
- Early Action (EA) applicants submit their application early but are not making a binding commitment. It's great for students who want to apply early but aren't yet ready to make their final college choice.
- Regular Decision (RD) applicants send in their application in January. This plan is ideal for students who find Rhodes a little later during senior year or want to wait for new transcripts or test scores to become available.

RIPON COLLEGE

AT A GLANCE

Established in 1851, Ripon College is a national leader in liberal arts and sciences education and Wisconsin's best-value private college, devoted to ensuring every student realizes their unique potential. Students receive a top-notch private education at a net price similar to a public state school. Ripon's five-course Catalyst curriculum is designed to provide the essential skills sought after by today's employers while allowing maximum freedom to choose their own path of study.

The core requires only 20 credits and upon completion each student earns a Concentration in Applied Innovation. This one-of-a-kind academic flexibility offers the opportunity to complete multiple majors and minors, engage in experiential study, play sports and hold internships—all in four years. Students are overwhelmingly satisfied with the amount of personalized attention they receive from devoted faculty and staff throughout their time on campus. Within six months of graduation, 98 percent of alumni are employed, in graduate school or student teaching.

Ripon is a member of the prestigious Associated Colleges of the Midwest (ACM). We compete athletically as part of the Midwest Conference and offer 21 NCAA Division III varsity teams. Our new $23.5 million Willmore Center provides students with state-of-the-art facilities to train and work out, and it boasts the best NCAA indoor track in Wisconsin. To find out more, visit ripon.edu/willmore-center.

Ripon has a student-to-faculty ratio of 14 to 1, and the average class size is fewer than 20 students. As a matter of fact, 76 percent of classes at Ripon have fewer than 20 students and 92 percent of classes have fewer than 30 students.

LOCATION AND ENVIRONMENT

The College is located in the historic city of Ripon, Wisconsin—a friendly, safe community of just under 8,000 people 80 miles northwest of Milwaukee, 70 miles southwest of Green Bay, 73 miles northeast of Madison, 180 miles northwest of Chicago and 255 miles southeast of the Twin Cities in Minnesota. The nearest airport is 40 minutes away in Appleton, Wisconsin.

The campus spans 250 tree-lined acres and includes 27 buildings, 10 of which are listed on the National Register of Historic Places. A sustainable campus, Ripon is home to the Ceresco Prairie Conservancy with 130 acres of native prairie, oak savanna and wetland habitat in the making.

CAMPUS FACILITIES AND EQUIPMENT

The Ripon campus is adjacent to downtown Ripon and includes tree-lined walkways and 27 buildings, 10 of which are listed on the National Register of Historic Places. Historic limestone buildings are complemented with more modern structures and continual updates, such as an apartment-style residence hall, a $23.5 million renovation and expansion of athletics, health and wellness facilities, and upgrades to the student union, dining facilities, and career and professional development.

The athletics, health and wellness facilities feature new high-tech classrooms, a cutting-edge fitness center, an NCAA indoor track, performance courts, fitness studios, athletic training center and other enhancements.

Ripon College provides a secure, high-speed (802.11ac) WiFi network in every building on campus. In addition, a state-of-the-art fiber optic network (10 Gb/s) connects all academic buildings, administrative buildings and residence halls. Connectivity to the internet and Internet2 is provided by WiscNet at a speed of 1 Gb/s.

Members of the student body, faculty and staff are issued a G Suite account that offers a variety of productivity tools (Gmail, Calendar, Drive, Docs, Hangouts) to enhance campus collaboration and communication. Multi-functional devices (MFDs) are located in every academic and administrative building to service the campus printing, copying and scanning needs. The College also has new 3D printers that several faculty have incorporated into their course curricula.

Open-use computer labs are located across campus, offering both Windows and Mac OS devices, projectors and MFDs.

Ripon College has partnered with Apogee to provide a cutting-edge cable TV/video solution. With the revolutionary IPTV service, Stream2, students can view HD content live, on demand or recorded (20 hours of DVR storage per user) on their laptops, tablets and smartphones.

Library staff provide friendly, efficient circulation, reference, instruction and interlibrary loan services that aid in research. The library also houses the College archives, a computer lab, digital media stations and more than 25 online databases. Library holdings include access to more than 300,000 physical and electronic books, as well as 55,000 periodicals.

C.J. Rodman Center for the Arts is home to a theater with an advanced computerized lighting system, a newly renovated recital hall with one of only 50 existing Bedient organs, an art gallery, a high-tech lab and a sculpture garden.

OFF-CAMPUS OPPORTUNITIES

Ripon College offers three-week Liberal Arts In Focus courses in May and August. Taught in short, intensive blocks, In Focus courses are designed as immersion experiences to provide a bridge between the theory and content of disciplines. Recent courses have included history lessons in Italy; intensive biology field studies in Costa Rica and the Wilderness Field Station near Ely, Minnesota; and a unique English course in Great Britain covering children's fantasy literature from Beatrix Potter to Harry Potter.

ACADEMIC PROGRAMS

Our innovative five-course curriculum, Catalyst, began rolling out to the first-year class during the fall semester of 2016. Catalyst is designed to provide the essential skills sought after by today's employers while allowing maximum freedom to choose your own path of study. This one-of-a-kind academic flexibility gives Ripon students the opportunity to complete multiple majors and minors, engage in experiential study, play sports and hold internships—all in four years

Ripon's liberal arts curriculum introduces students to a wide variety of disciplines. About 40 percent of our students complete double or triple majors, while some create special self-designed majors. Hallmarks of a Ripon education are excellent communications skills, both written and oral; critical-thinking and problem-solving skills; and the opportunity to explore serious research pursuits alongside faculty as an undergraduate, no matter what your major.

A Ripon education will take you anywhere! You could study psychology and play basketball at Ripon, and then become a seven-time Grammy Award winner like jazz singer Al Jarreau (1962). You could become a Nobel Prize winner in economics like Oliver Williamson (1954). You could guide the space shuttle into orbit like Jeff Bantle (1980), a chief flight director with NASA, or become an international opera star like Gail Dobish (1976). Perhaps you'll set records in medical science like neonatologist Dr. John Muraskas (1978), who is on record for saving the world's smallest premature baby, or cover world events, like Richard Threlkeld (1959), former Moscow correspondent for CBS News. You could make your mark in the world of entertainment like Harrison Ford (1964), Spencer Tracy (1924) or Justin Neibank (1978). Or perhaps you'll end up studying at University of Oxford in Great Britain as a Rhodes Scholar like Zach Morris (2002), who also found time to play touch football with former President Bill Clinton and spend an evening at Buckingham Palace with Queen Elizabeth II.

MAJORS AND DEGREES OFFERED

Ripon College offers a four-year graduation guarantee with 31 majors and 42 minors, including a variety of fast-track pre-professional programs. Every student graduates with a concentration in Applied Innovation upon completing the innovative five-course Catalyst curriculum.

Majors include Anthropology, Art History (Cultural Criticism, Museum Studies), Biology, Business Management, Chemistry, Chemistry-Biology, Communication, Computer Science, Economics, Educational Studies, English, Environmental Studies, Exercise Science (Athletic Training, Human Performance, Physical Education, Sports Management), Finance, Foreign Languages , Global Studies, History, Mathematics, Music, Music Education, Philosophy, Physical Science, Physics, Politics and Government, Psychobiology, Psychology, Religion, Self-Designed, Sociology, Spanish, Studio Art and Theatre.

Minors include Adapted Physical Education, American Studies, Ancient, Renaissance & Medieval Studies, Anthropology, Art History, , Biology, Business Management, Chemistry, Classical Studies, Coaching, Communication, Computer and Data Sciences, Criminal Justice, Economics, Educational Studies,, English, Entrepreneurship, Environmental Biology, Francophone Studies, French, Health, History, Latin American and Caribbean Studies, Law and Society, Mathematics, Military Leadership, Museum Studies, Music, National Security Studies, Nonprofit Management, Philosophy, Physics, Politics and Government, Psychology, Religion,, Sociology, Spanish, Strength and Conditioning, , Theatre and Women's and Gender Studies.

Ripon College offers fast-track programs that allow students to get professional degrees sooner in engineering, law and osteopathic medicine. We currently have affiliations with Washington University in St. Louis (engineering); Marquette University, American University, Mitchell Hamline School of Law and the University of St. Thomas (law); and Lake Erie College of Osteopathic Medicine (osteopathic medicine). Ripon also offers pre-professional advising in: health professions (including medicine, nursing, chiropractic medicine, dentistry, optometry, sports medicine, pharmacy, physical therapy, podiatry, veterinary medicine), criminal justice, government service, journalism, military leadership, museum studies, national security studies and social work.

Teacher certification is offered in Early Childhood, Elementary, Middle/Junior High, Secondary and ESL. In addition, Ripon offers licensure in 21 subject areas. Teacher certification programs approved by the Wisconsin Department of Public Instruction prepare students for licensure at the early childhood/middle childhood level (grades PK through 5), the middle childhood/early adolescence level (grades 1 through 8), and the early adolescence/adolescence level (grades 6 through 12). The educational studies department also offers PK-12 certification programs in art, foreign language (French and Spanish), music, physical education, physical education and health, and theatre.

TUITION, ROOM, BOARD, FEES

Pursuing a college degree is an important investment in your future. That's why at Ripon College your family's financial circumstances will never affect our admission decision. We provide 100 percent of our students with the financial assistance necessary to graduate and make it our mission to ensure a great economic value per every dollar spent. Tuition is $46,823, room and board is $8,653, and fees are $300, for a total cost of $55,776.

Average cost for books and supplies: $900

FINANCIAL AID

We are proud to offer our students competitive packages with funding from many sources: merit-based scholarships, need-based grants, educational loans, work-study and scholarships from outside organizations. Academic scholarships range from $23,000 to $36,000 per year.

STUDENT ORGANIZATIONS AND ACTIVITIES

From pre-professional programs to paintballing, Ripon College hosts more than 60 student-run clubs and organizations. Students at Ripon are encouraged to lead the programs, supported by the Student Senate's activity fee. This allows students to collaborate together in conceiving, organizing, marketing and developing unique activities.

In addition, Ripon offers a variety of intramural sports throughout the year, including: kickball, dodgeball, flag football, indoor soccer, inner tube water polo, basketball, bowling, volleyball and aerobics.

Ripon's NCAA Division III Intercollegiate Teams compete in the Midwest Conference:

Men's varsity sports: baseball, basketball, cross-country, cycling, football, soccer, swimming and diving, tennis, and indoor and outdoor track and field.

Women's varsity sports: basketball, cross-country, cycling, dance, soccer, softball, swimming and diving, tennis, indoor and outdoor track and field, and volleyball.

ADMISSIONS PROCESS

The faculty committee on academic standards establishes the criteria for admission. The school considers a variety of factors. An admission application and secondary school record are required for admission while standardized test scores (SAT or ACT), recommendations, a written essay, and extracurricular or community service activities also may be considered. Ripon's admission process reflects the personal attention students can expect to receive during their college careers, and applicants are encouraged to provide any additional information that they consider helpful.

Ripon encourages applications from those students who are best prepared to benefit from and contribute to the academic and extracurricular programs that it offers. In evaluating applications, attention is paid to evidence of academic achievement, as indicated both by the distribution of courses taken in secondary school and by performance in those courses.

The faculty committee on academic standards establishes the criteria for admission. Ripon is test-optional. We will consider test scores if you elect to submit them.

For more information contact:

Admission Office
Ripon College
300 Seward Street
Ripon, WI 54971
Telephone: 920-748-8709
E-mail: adminfo@ripon.edu

ROCHESTER INSTITUTE OF TECHNOLOGY

AT A GLANCE

At RIT, we empower a kaleidoscope of engaged, socially conscious, and intellectually curious minds to collaborate through creativity and innovation. We blend technology, the arts, and design to inspire a diverse community of problem solvers. Together, we find new and meaningful ways to move the world forward. We provide exceptional individuals with a wide range of academic pathways, including expansive experiential learning opportunities, a leading research program, and internationally recognized education and access services for deaf and hard-of-hearing students. Beyond our main campus in Rochester, New York, RIT has international campuses in China, Croatia, Dubai, and Kosovo. And with more than 19,000 students and more than 125,000 graduates from all 50 states and over 100 nations, RIT is driving progress in industries and communities around the world.

LOCATION AND ENVIRONMENT

RIT's 1,300-acre campus is located in the suburbs, about six miles from downtown Rochester, NY. More than 7,100 diverse, creative, ambitious students live on campus in residence halls or apartments, and the self-contained, suburban location gives the campus a safe, residential atmosphere. RIT also maintains locations in China, Croatia, Dubai, and Kosovo.

CAMPUS FACILITIES AND EQUIPMENT

RIT is comprised of nine colleges and two additional degree-granting units. The campus is filled with the latest equipment, software, laboratories, and conveniences to give students the tools they need to excel. RIT offers academic facilities that are rarely matched on other university campuses.

A selected list of facilities includes:

- American Packaging Corporation Center for Packaging Innovation;
- Artificial Intelligence Lab
- Center for Sustainable Packaging
- Center for Accessibility and Inclusion Research
- Entertainment Lab for 3D modeling, game, and interactive media development
- Mobile Computing and Robotics Lab
- William G. McGowan Center for Telecommunications, Innovation, and Collaborative Research
- REDCOM Telecommunications Systems Laboratory
- Integrated circuit design center,
- Computer labs with industry-standard CAD software packages
- A Class-1000 clean-room laboratory space for the fabrication of integrated circuits
- A machining and manufacturing center equipped with state-of-the-art CNC machinery
- 3D printing equipment
- Center for Applied Psychophysiology and Self-regulation
- Center for Bioscience Exploration and Technology
- 30 fully equipped photographic studios,
- 20 fully equipped b/w and color darkrooms
- Image Permanence Institute

OFF-CAMPUS OPPORTUNITIES

Rochester provides a perfect setting—it's large enough to provide the dining, shopping, and night life opportunities found in a bigger city, yet small and friendly enough to be inviting and accessible. In fact, Rochester was ranked 10th best among large cities in the Northeast in a recent Money magazine Best Places to Live in America survey. The greater Rochester area is home to more than 1 million people, making it the third-largest metropolitan area in New York State. Rochester's reputation as an active and inventive community is supported by extensive cultural and intellectual opportunities.

ACADEMIC PROGRAMS

At RIT, some of the world's most talented, ambitious, and creative students find a remarkable array of academic programs; diverse, talented and accessible faculty; sophisticated facilities; an unusual emphasis on experiential learning; and a vibrant, connected community that is home to students from more than 100 countries. Excelling in teaching and research, RIT's faculty are passionate about their role in the classroom and in their field. RIT's faculty are diverse, innovative and resourceful, and engage students in the process of personal and professional discovery. RIT's nine colleges and two academic units offer more than 90 undergraduate programs. To complement their specialized field of study, students select from more than 80 minors available at RIT. Students can also complete a master's degree in five years through one of the university's accelerated BS/MS or 4+1 MBA programs.

Experiential Learning

Since 1912, the hallmark of an RIT has been experiential education. RIT was among the first universities in the world to offer cooperative education, and its co-op program is now one of the largest in the world. Last year more than 4,400 students completed nearly 6,000 co-op work assignments by alternating periods of study on campus with paid employment in more than 2,300 firms across the United States and overseas. Experiential learning also includes internships, study abroad, and undergraduate research.

MAJORS AND DEGREES OFFERED

Art, Design and Visual Communications

- 3D Digital Design
- Advertising and Public Relations
- Digital Humanities and Social Sciences
- Film and Animation
- Graphic Design
- Illustration
- Industrial Design
- Interior Design
- Media Arts and Technology
- Medical Illustration
- Motion Picture Science
- New Media Design
- New Media Interactive Development
- Photographic and Imaging Arts (options in Advertising Photography, Fine Art Photography, Photojournalism, Visual Media)
- Photographic Sciences (options in Biomedical Photographic Communications, Imaging and Photographic Technology)
- Studio Arts (options in Ceramics, Expanded forms, Furniture Design, Glass, Metals and Jewelry Design, Painting, Printmaking, and Sculpture)

Business and Management

- Accounting
- Economics
- Finance
- Hospitality and Tourism Management
- International Business
- Management
- Marketing
- Management Information Systems
- Supply Chain Management

Computing and Information Sciences

- 3D Digital Design
- Bioinformatics
- Computational Mathematics
- Computer Science
- Computing and Information Technologies
- Computing Security
- Game Design and Development
- Human-Centered Computing
- Management Information Systems
- New Media Interactive Development
- Software Engineering
- Web and Mobile Computing

Engineering and Engineering Technology

- Biomedical Engineering
- Chemical Engineering
- Civil Engineering Technology
- Computer Engineering
- Computer Engineering Technology

- Electrical Engineering (options in Computer Engineering, Clean and Renewable Energy, and Robotics)
- Electrical Engineering Technology
- Electrical Mechanical Engineering Technology
- Industrial Engineering (with options in Ergonomics, Lean Six Sigma, Manufacturing, and Supply Chain)
- Manufacturing Engineering Technology
- Mechanical Engineering (options in Aerospace, Automotive, Bioengineering, and Energy and environment)
- Mechanical Engineering Technology
- Microelectronic Engineering
- Packaging Science
- Software Engineering

Health Sciences and Technology

- Biomedical Sciences
- Diagnostic Medical Sonography (Ultrasound)
- Dietetics and Nutrition
- Exercise Science
- Nutritional Sciences
- Physician Assistant BS/MS

Science, Mathematics, and Imaging Science

- Applied Mathematics
- Applied Statistics and Actuarial Science
- Biochemistry
- Bioinformatics
- Biology
- Biomedical Sciences
- Biotechnology and Molecular Bioscience
- Chemistry
- Computational Mathematics
- Diagnostic Medical Sonography (Ultrasound)
- Environmental Science
- Environmental, Health and Safety Management
- Imaging Science
- Physics

Social Sciences and Humanities

- Applied Modern Language and Culture (options in Chinese, Japanese, and Spanish)
- ASL-English Interpretation
- Communication
- Criminal Justice
- Environmental Science
- International and Global Studies
- Journalism
- Museum Studies
- Philosophy
- Political Science
- Psychology
- Public Policy
- Sociology and Anthropology

TUITION, ROOM, BOARD, FEES

For 2019–20, tuition and fees cost $51,240; room and board averaged $13,976; and books, transportation, and other expenses averaged $2,088.

FINANCIAL AID

RIT's Office of Financial aid and Scholarships assists students and their families in identifying sources of financial aid to help meet the cost of a quality education. Currently, more than 12,000 RIT undergraduate and graduate students receive over $340 million dollars in financial assistance from federal, state, and institutional resources, in the form of scholarships, grants, loans, and part-time employment.

STUDENT ORGANIZATIONS AND ACTIVITIES

The backgrounds and interests of RIT students contribute in many ways to the quality of campus life. With students from all 50 states and more than 100 countries, RIT is a living-learning environment rich in diversity in classrooms, residence halls, and everywhere else on campus. RIT attracts students from every state and approximately 2,700 international students from more than 100 countries. Embodying our commitment to diversity, nearly 3,200 students of color have elected to study at RIT. Adding a social and educational dynamic not found at any other university are nearly 1,000 deaf and hard-of-hearing students supported by RIT's National Technical Institute for the Deaf.

Students take their academic pursuits seriously, but they'll be the first to tell you that they are passionate about life outside of the lectures, labs and studios. RIT is alive with energy and excitement-24/7. A number of campus organizations and student services focus on the unique needs and interests of minority, deaf, and international students at RIT. You'll have plenty of opportunity to interact with a mind expanding mix of people. More than 7,100 full-time students live on campus in residence halls or apartments, and our self-contained, suburban location creates a safe and secure atmosphere. Clubs and organizations exist to bring students of similar interest together and provide them with opportunities to become effective leaders. These groups enhance the quality of student life by fostering social interaction, leadership development, school spirit and an affinity to RIT. Clubs and Organizations promote activities, diversity, service and learning outside of the classroom. Currently there are approximately 300 active clubs, 10 Major Student Organizations, and 30 Greek Organizations on campus. Last year, clubs and organizations held nearly 1,300 events on campus.

RIT's intercollegiate teams have a history of excellence, recording many impressive seasons and capturing a number of conference and national championships. The men's and women's hockey teams are Division I. The remainder of the intercollegiate teams competes at Division III. RIT teams are members of the National Collegiate Athletic Association (NCAA), the Eastern College Athletic Conference (ECAC), the Atlantic Hockey Association, the College Hockey America, the Liberty League, and the New York State Women's Collegiate Athletic Association.

ADMISSIONS PROCESS

RIT seeks a diverse and multicultural student body. Entering students come from a variety of geographic, social, cultural, economic, and ethnic backgrounds. Admission to RIT is competitive, but the admission process is a personal one. The university is interested in learning about students' interests, abilities, and goals in order to provide the best information and guidance as they select the college that is right for them. Factors considered in our admission decisions include, but are not limited to, past high school and/or college performance (particularly in required academic subjects), admission test scores, competitiveness of high school or previous college, and academic program selected.

Students applying for freshman admission for the fall semester (September) may apply through an Early Decision Plan or Regular Decision Plan. The Early Decision Plans are designed for students who consider RIT their first-choice college and wish to make an early commitment regarding admission. Early Decision I requires that candidates file their applications and supporting documents by November 1; the Early Decision II deadline for applications and supporting documents is January 1. Regular Decision applicants should file the required application materials by January 15.

SACRED HEART UNIVERSITY

AT A GLANCE

Sacred Heart University (SHU), the second-largest independent Catholic university in New England, offers more than 80 undergraduate, graduate, doctoral and certificate programs on its main campus in Fairfield, Conn., and satellites in Connecticut, Luxembourg and Ireland. Over 9,0000 students attend the University's six colleges: Arts & Sciences; Health Professions; Dr. Susan L. Davis, RN, & Richard J. Henley College of Nursing; the AACSB-accredited Jack Welch College of Business & Technology; St. Vincent's College and the Isabelle Farrington College of Education.

Distinguished by the personal attention it provides its students, SHU is recognized for its commitment to academic excellence, award-winning advisement program, cutting-edge technology, championship Division I athletic teams, and nationally recognized community service programs. Situated in Fairfield, Connecticut, the main campus is ideally located one hour north of New York City and 2.5 hours south of Boston in proximity to world-class hospitals, nationally ranked elementary and secondary schools, a high concentration of Fortune 500 corporations and access to the employers in Connecticut's creative corridor. SHU also has international campuses in Dingle, Ireland and the European business center of Luxembourg, a partner campus in Rome, and study abroad options worldwide. Students may spend their freshman fall semester abroad program or participate in short-term and semester programs throughout their four years. Within the six colleges and School of Computer Science & Engineering, School of Social Work and School of Communication, Media & the Arts, students in all majors engage in hands-on education both in and outside of the classroom. Cutting-edge technology in West Campus allows students to apply their skills in real world settings such as the finance lab and trading floor, the iHub, IDEA Lab, incubator space and AI lab. The Center for Healthcare Education features the latest technology available to health professions students. Students in the sciences utilize recently renovated laboratories and state-of-the-art computer labs. A hallmark of a SHU education is the strong connection between students and faculty beginning in the freshman year. Faculty connect with students in interactive, innovative spaces in our academic buildings; through online communities; in joint research projects; in advising sessions and through many academic clubs, organizations and activities. Faculty lead students on study trips across the globe. The University's commitment to experiential learning incorporates concrete, real-life study for students in all majors including research, internships, clinical placements, independent study, service learning and work-study. Drawing on the rich resources in New England and New York City, students are connected with research and internship opportunities ranging from full-time internships at sought-after sites such as Madison Square Garden to research with faculty on marine life in the Long Island Sound. These opportunities help pave the way for a 99.2 percent placement rate for graduating seniors in full-time jobs and graduate study. SHU's experiential learning opportunities are complemented by a rich student life program offering more than 100 student organizations, including Greek life; leadership programs, media organizations such as the TV station, radio station and newspaper; academic clubs and multicultural organizations. The University has a well-respected Division I athletic program and a robust club sports program with more than 1,500 athletes who compete in 32 varsity sports and more than 25 competitive club sports teams. The University's strong performing arts program, led by a Tony-and-Grammy-nominated producer, includes the theatre arts program (also available as an academic major), a choir program with various ensembles, an instrumental music program including marching band, pep band and concert band among other ensembles and a dance program with a variety of ensembles. The campus has a lively atmosphere with over 90 percent of freshmen living on campus and many school spirit, cultural and social events offered throughout the year.

LOCATION AND ENVIRONMENT

Sacred Heart University comprises more than 300 acres of land, including an 18-hole golf course and the former global headquarters of General Electric, named West Campus.

The University-owned golf course is located in Milford/Orange, Conn. It is a signature Tommy Fazio-designed facility that has been ranked fourth-best in Connecticut by Golf.com.

SHU's dining hall, JP's Diner, is a '50s-style diner and the first on-campus diner in all of New England. Named for SHU President John J. Petillo, JP's is located on SHU's newly-constructed Upper Quad.

The University maintains satellite campuses for graduate students in the physician assistant program in Stamford, CT and for graduate education students in Griswold, CT.

CAMPUS FACILITIES AND EQUIPMENT

The Edgerton Center for Performing Arts; Frank and Marisa Martire Center for the Liberal Arts, which features smart classrooms with multimedia technology, interactive labs, a motion capture lab, and two large television studios for TV, video and film production; The Center for Healthcare Education containing an audiology suite, motion analysis and human performance labs, driving simulator, pediatrics clinic, medical gym, an immersive acute care simulation lab with video and data capture capability, a simulated outpatient suite, high-fidelity manikins, home-care suite, cadaver lab, and many more learning resources featuring the latest technology; West Campus includes AI Lab, IDEA Lab, iHub, incubator space, finance lab, state-of-the-classrooms; Jandrisevits Learning Center includes spaces and technologies to provide academic support to students, including those with disabilities; The Bobby Valentine Health & Recreation Center includes state-of-the-art work out equipment for student use, an indoor track, indoor basketball courts, a smoothie bar and much more; The William H. Pitt Center is for SHU's Division I student-athletes.

OFF-CAMPUS OPPORTUNITIES

SHU offers programs in countries around the world, including two of our own global campuses in Ireland and Luxembourg. International experiences are available to SHU and visiting students—with study abroad programs that support a broad range of educational, professional, and personal goals. Looking at New England liberal arts colleges to study business? SHU has the only American-accredited MBA program in Luxembourg.

Through service abroad, students learn about a new culture, generosity, and the value of serving others. With our Office of Volunteer Programs & Service Learning, opportunities to volunteer abroad in Latin America and the Caribbean include helping to build homes, schools or medical facilities for those in need.

SHU also offers undergraduate and graduate nursing and health professions students the opportunity to complete clinical service hours, capstone projects or service learning hours in Guatemala, Haiti, Jamaica, Uganda, India and the Cheyenne River Sioux Tribe Reservation in S. Dakota, as well as experience the local healthcare systems in each nation.

ACADEMIC PROGRAMS

The University offers undergraduate, graduate, doctoral and certificate programs including online degree programs.

Upon introducing the new undergraduate Core Curriculum in Fall 2007, the University was invited to become a member of the Association of American Colleges & Universities (AAC&U) Core Commitments Leadership Consortium. AAC&U has recognized SHU's Core Curriculum as a national model of values education. A newly revised core curriculum was launched in Fall 2015.

MAJORS AND DEGREES OFFERED

At the undergraduate level, SHU offers two baccalaureate degrees: bachelor of arts or bachelor of science depending upon the nature of the discipline of the major. SHU also offers associate in arts and associate in science degrees. A central component of undergraduate study is the University's Core Curriculum, the Human Journey, which embodies the University's commitment to academic excellence, social responsibility, and ethical awareness. All candidates for the baccalaureate degree must complete at least 120 credits, with a minimum of 30 credits taken at SHU. A minimum cumulative GPA 2.0 is required.

Majors include: Accounting, Art and Design, Biochemistry, Biology, Business Administration, Business Economics, Business Economics & Finance, Business Analytics, Broadcast Journalism & Media Production, Chemistry, Coastal & Marine Science, Communication Studies, Communication Disorders, Computer Engineering, Computer Science, Computer Science & Information Technology, Cybersecurity, Criminal Justice, CT Literacy Specialist Program, Digital Communication, Economics, Electrical Engineering, English, Exercise Science, Fashion Marketing & Merchandising, Finance, Game Design & Development, Global Studies, General Studies, Health Science, History, Hospitality, Resort & Tourism, Information Technology, Interdisciplinary Studies, Management, Marketing, Mathematics, Media Arts, Media Studies, Molecular & Cellular Biology, Neuroscience, Nursing Completion Programs (RN-to-BSN and Accelerated RN-to-BSN-to-MSN Program), Nursing, Philosophy, Political Science, Pre-Occupational Therapy, Pre-Physical Therapy, Pre-Physician Assistant Studies, Pre-Speech-Language Pathology, Psychology, Social Work, Sociology, Spanish, Sport Management, STEM, Theatre Arts, Theology & Religious Studies

TUITION, ROOM, BOARD, FEES

Tuition for the 2019–20 school year is $42,800. Room and board is $15,960.

FINANCIAL AID

SHU works with all students throughout the financial aid process. There are a wide variety of aid types SHU including need-based scholarships and grants, loans and student and University employment.

STUDENT ORGANIZATIONS AND ACTIVITIES

The entire mood here is very upbeat, gushes one Sacred Heart student, and another adds that "door holding symbolizes us because we care about those around us and are very genuine people." When it comes to school spirit, Sacred Heart has it in spades. As one student puts it, "Sacred Heart University exemplifies school spirit and hospitality to every single student that walks [through] our campus." To sum it up, "The entire student body is one giant family." Much of the student body from the Tri-State area but students stress that Sacred Heart is "all about embracing diversity and cultivating a caring, safe, and academically prosperous environment." The school is a "tightly-knit community where people are excited to try new things and professors encourage students to branch out."

ADMISSIONS PROCESS

Students heap praise on this small Catholic university located in Fairfield, Connecticut, a place where "academics meet real-world experiences." Sacred Heart University is a Catholic school, but students underscore that "we do not force religious teachings upon the student body; rather, we offer a helping hand in times of despair as well as times of fortune." One of Sacred Heart's points of pride is being known as a "door-holding" school: "We all hold doors for each other, help each other out, and look out for one another." With an undergraduate population of a little over 6,000, students say, "The student body is one of the most tight-knit groups of people [they] have ever been a part of." The school's proximity to New York City, Hartford, and Stamford provide opportunities for real-world experiences outside the classroom, and students say the "internship and job opportunities we have here are unique and amazing." Specific programs of note for students include the "business, nursing, and health professions programs," with one student declaring that the choice to attend SHU was down to the school's "fantastic nursing program." Professors are "enthusiastic, encouraging, and helpful" on the whole, and students appreciate that some "also allow students to engage with their research which then will allow kids to get published." Beyond the coursework, one student says that professors at Sacred Heart have "opened my eyes to how the world works."

SAINT ANSELM COLLEGE

AT A GLANCE

Founded in 1889, Saint Anselm College is a Benedictine, Catholic, liberal arts college dedicated to undergraduate education. The third oldest Catholic college in New England, Saint Anselm enrolls just over 2,000 students and prepares students for life beyond college. Saint Anselm encourages its students to not only be challenged academically, but also to lead a life that is both creative and generous. Graduates are CEOs, doctors, engineers, teachers, marketers, and researchers. They are humanitarians, healers, and philanthropists. They graduate Saint Anselm with the drive to achieve, empowered to make the world a better place.

LOCATION AND ENVIRONMENT

Located on 380 acres of land overlooking Manchester, New Hampshire, Saint Anselm College boasts a peaceful, suburban campus just minutes from the downtown area.

CAMPUS FACILITIES AND EQUIPMENT

There's much to see and do on campus from open skate nights at Sullivan Arena to spring concerts on the quad. Academic buildings including the Goulet Science Center and Gadbois Hall house innovative labs where remarkable research happens every day. There are cell culture labs, climate controlled environmental chambers, a green house, a sleep lab, SimMan labs in Nursing, and more. In the library, students have access to a range of workspaces for individuals and groups in addition to technological advances.

The Roger & Francine Jean Student Center, opened in 2018, is a one-stop shop for student life. Home to offices such as Student Engagement and Leadership, Campus Ministry, the Intercultural Center, the Career Development Center, the Academic Resource Center, and the Meelia Center for Community Engagement, it has become a hub of activity, community, and opportunity. Students can also get the latest Saint Anselm gear in the bookstore or pick up a coffee from Starbucks in the Gallo Café.

Recreational facilities include the Carr Center with basketball courts and a 9,000-square-foot, three-level fitness center. Many of the college's 17 intercollegiate athletic teams compete on some of the top athletic facilities in the Northeast-10 Conference, including Grappone Stadium, Stoutenburgh Gymnasium, Sullivan Ice Arena, or Melucci Field.

Ninety-one percent of Saint Anselm students live on campus in traditional residence halls, suites, townhouses, or apartments. Whether students live on campus or commute, everyone has access to Saint Anselm College's amazing food, consistently ranked within the top 20 in the nation by the Princeton Review.

Saint Anselm is home to the New Hampshire Institute of Politics & Political Library (NHIOP), which offers unparalleled opportunities for students to be in the front row of the democratic process. Its auditorium, West Wing, TV-studio, and classrooms are where students meet today's most prominent political policy thinkers and researchers, journalists and authors, scientists, industry executives, global leaders and presidential candidates. The Institute, nationally known to political scholars and strategists, is an essential campaign stop for presidential candidates offering unparalleled opportunities for students to be in the front row of the democratic process. In fact, every United States president in the last 60 years has visited Saint Anselm College.

OFF-CAMPUS OPPORTUNITIES

Saint Anselm College is situated just 3 miles from downtown Manchester, which is the biggest city in the state of New Hampshire. One can find a diverse array of restaurants and shops in Manchester, along with museums, concert venues, a minor league baseball team, and the largest taco tour in the Northeast. The campus is also an hour from the White Mountains, seacoast New Hampshire, and Boston, Massachusetts and the Manchester-Boston Regional Airport is just four miles away.

ACADEMIC PROGRAMS

The core curriculum focuses on humanities, college writing, and learning outcomes. It is a balance between common courses that foster academic community and elective courses that allow for individual choice. Students can learn in intimate academic environments and engage with faculty and peers.

All first-year students engage in the Conversatio program, a shared-learning experience designed to integrate the liberal arts into each student's education. Students will meet in groups made up of all types of majors and backgrounds in seminar-style classes to promote debate and discussion. Over the course of the year, they will read diverse texts, debate topics from numerous perspectives, develop research skills, hear from guest speakers, and polish writing and public speaking abilities.

An emphasis is placed on experiential learning at Saint Anselm. Students are encouraged to take on opportunities such as service, internships, and studying abroad. As a campus that is consistently ranked for community service engagement, students can fuel their academic experience with volunteer opportunities including service-based learning. With thousands of internships made available through the Career Development Center, they can gain real-world working experience and discover future careers. Students interested in studying abroad will find there is an abundance of locations and timelines to choose from. Saint Anselm College operates a satellite campus in Orvieto, Italy, approximately an hour from Rome. Students can take Saint Anselm faculty taught courses in a gorgeous European setting. They have also studied abroad in over 50 different countries on 5 different continents.

MAJORS AND DEGREES OFFERED

At Saint Anselm College, students may pursue a Bachelor of Arts degree in the following academic programs and majors: Accounting, American Studies, Behavioral Neuroscience, Biochemistry, Biology, Business, Chemistry, Classical Archaeology, Classics, Communication, Computer science (including concentrations with business or mathematics), Criminal Justice, Cyber Criminology, Economics, Education (secondary and elementary), Engineering (3-2 program), English, Environmental Science, Environmental Studies, Finance, Fine Arts, Forensic Science, French, German Studies, Great Books, History, International Business, International Relations, Mathematics, Mathematics with Economics, Marketing, Natural Science, Peace and Justice Studies, Philosophy, Physics, Politics, Psychology, Social Work, Sociology, Spanish, and Theology. The college also offers a Bachelor of Science in Nursing (BSN).

Saint Anselm students may pursue pre-professional programs in dentistry, law, medicine, theology, veterinary medicine, and other allied health fields, such as pharmacy, physical therapy, and physician assistant.

The engineering physics (3-2 program) partners with the University of Notre Dame, University of Massachusetts-Lowell, Catholic University of America, and Manhattan College.

TUITION, ROOM, BOARD, FEES

The 2020–2021 school year tuition and fees is $42,840 and room and board costs are $15,120. The total cost is $57,960.

FINANCIAL AID

Saint Anselm provides students with financial aid opportunities through both private and federal aid programs. The college provides financial aid to offset the reasonable monetary investment that the student and family are expected to contribute.

99% of the college's undergraduates receive some degree of financial aid. Saint Anselm's financial aid opportunities include grants, loans, scholarships, and employment positions. Outstanding students may also be eligible for merit scholarships through the Office of Admission.

Two forms are required in applying for institutional need-based aid; the student must submit the CSS/Financial aid PROFILE and the Free Application for Federal Student Aid (FAFSA) by February 15.

Average Freshman Total Need-Based Gift Award: $26,500

Average total financial aid offer: $29,940

STUDENT ORGANIZATIONS AND ACTIVITIES

With more than 50 clubs and organizations, 17 varsity athletic teams, a performing arts center, and an art gallery, Saint Anselm students have plenty of activities to explore. From Rugby to the Broadcast Club to the Multicultural Student Coalition, there is a club for every interest, cultural to academic.

Students interested in service will be right at home volunteering through the Meelia Center for Community Engagement or through Campus Ministry. Saint Anselm students volunteered more than 52,000 hours last year doing everything from teaching English to new Americans to working the crisis hotline at the YWCA to raising over $110,000 for the American Cancer Society with the Relay for Life. Every winter and spring break, Saint Anselm students travel to organizations around the country to volunteer at service sites through Service & Solidarity Mission Trips.

Saint Anselm College with over 2,000 enrolled students, is part of the Division II Northeast-10, ECAC, and NEWHA Conferences with 17 varsity teams: men's intercollegiate sports in baseball, basketball, cross-country, football, golf, ice hockey, lacrosse, and soccer and women's sports in basketball, cross-country, field hockey, ice hockey, lacrosse, soccer, softball, tennis, and volleyball. For students interested in club or intramurals, Saint Anselm has a variety of club, recreational, and intramural sports teams.

ADMISSIONS PROCESS

In reviewing applicants for the first-year class, admission considers each prospective student carefully. Counselors assess each applicant's secondary school performance, SAT I or ACT scores (optional for non-nursing majors, nursing majors must submit scores and should apply Early Action or Early Decision), recommendation letters, extracurricular involvement, and the written essay. Of highest priority is the applicant's secondary school transcript, with a specific focus on both the rigor of course study and the marks received. Saint Anselm invites transfer and international students to apply.

Saint Anselm College has the following admission deadlines:

Early Action, November 15
Nursing Majors, November 15 or December 1
Early Decision, December 1
Regular Decision, February 1

Saint Anselm College invites students and families to visit campus for a tour, information session and/or interview.

For more information, students should contact:

Office of Admission
Saint Anselm College
100 Saint Anselm Drive
Manchester, NH 03102
Telephone: 603-641-7500 or 888-426-7356 (toll-free)
Email: admission@anselm.edu
Website: www.anselm.edu

SAINT FRANCIS UNIVERSITY (PA)

AT A GLANCE

Saint Francis is a private, Catholic, co-educational liberal arts university. Established in 1847, the University is among America's first Franciscan institutions and is the nation's 12th-oldest Catholic institution of higher education. Saint Francis operates under the conventions of the Franciscan Friars of the Third Order Regular. The University is dedicated to providing each student with top-rated academics, a vibrant student life, opportunities for leadership, and unflagging attention from a distinguished faculty. For the past century and a half, Saint Francis University's commitment to academics and student life has embodied two important values: high-quality education and respecting students as individuals.

LOCATION AND ENVIRONMENT

Saint Francis University is located on a 600-acre mountaintop campus in the town of Loretto, Pennsylvania. Just 80 miles east of Pittsburgh and 60 miles west of State College, the campus has its own lake, nature trails, ski tubing park and championship golf course. Near to campus are three state parks, four biking/ walking trails and four ski resorts. The beautiful campus has an impressive suite of academic and research facilities as well as 19 residence halls to offer students a comprehensive experience. Student recreational, athletic, eateries and a student union provide each student a robust campus living experience.

CAMPUS FACILITIES AND EQUIPMENT

Saint Francis offers a totally wireless campus, computer labs, a Macintosh-based computer lab, and numerous Smart Classrooms. The cost of attendance at Saint Francis includes a laptop computer as well as technical support. Other facilities that complement student learning include well-equipped science labs, on-campus radio and television stations, and the Southern Alleghenies Museum of Art.

A recently completed state-of-the-art Science Center sits at the center of campus. The facility houses highly competitive science, technology, engineering and mathematics programs. The DiSepio Institute for Rural Health and Wellness education and research center features the DiSepio Center for Rehabilitation, Student Health Services, Fitness Center, Spiritual Wellness Center, Human Performance Laboratory, and Ernest J. Scharpf Family Conference Center. A complete renovation of Schwab Hall was recently completed in an effort to house the Shields School of Business.

OFF-CAMPUS OPPORTUNITIES

Saint Francis University's Office for Study Abroad offers a truly unique semester abroad program in the beautiful village of Ambialet, in southern France. Students can experience the adventure, beauty, and history of Europe in the halls of a centuries-old Franciscan monastery. Travel and research abroad are components of many academic programs at Saint Francis University. Students are encouraged to engage in the multitude of semester long or condensed travel abroad experiences facilitated by the Office for Study Abroad.

ACADEMIC PROGRAMS

Bachelor degrees are typically earned within eight semesters. To graduate, each student is required to complete a course of study that meets with approval from the University Provost. The University operates on a two-semester academic calendar, with three sessions in the summer. The University offers students over 45 academic programs of study and a wide variety of minors and concentrations to choose. Among the most competitive academic offerings are 2 entry-level Masters health science majors (Occupational Therapy and Physician Assistant Science) and an entry-level Doctoral program in Physical Therapy. The institution is well known for the cooperative student-faculty research that occurs within the School of Science, Technology, Engineering, Arts and Mathematics (STEAM). Petroleum & Natural Gas Engineering and Environmental Engineering are among the most recent program additions to the School of STEAM. In the School of Health Sciences & Education, Early Childhood Education students may complete dual certification in Special Education in four years. Saint Francis University also has an extensive list of minors and concentrations available for students to complement their academic program of study.

MAJORS AND DEGREES OFFERED

Saint Francis University students may earn bachelor (BA, BS) degrees, master degrees and doctoral degrees. The Division of Adult Degree & Continuing Studies offers certificate, associate and bachelor degree programs in a flexible, on-line learning environment.

SHIELDS SCHOOL OF BUSINESS

Accounting
  Entrepreneurship
Business Analytics
  Entrepreneurship
Communications
  Digital Media, Integrated Marketing Communications
Criminal Justice
Economics
  Entrepreneurship, Ph.D. Track
Finance
  Entrepreneurship
Management
  Healthcare Management
Management Information Systems
  Entrepreneurship
Marketing
  Entrepreneurship
Sociology

SCHOOL OF HEALTH SCIENCES & EDUCATION

American Sign Language (*minor*)
Education–Early Childhood and Special Education option
Education–Middle Childhood and Special Education option
Education–Secondary Education in subject specific areas
Exercise Physiology
  (C)Fitness Professionals, Graduate/Research, Pre-Allied Health, Pre-Medicine
Healthcare Studies
  (C)Pre-Allied Health, Pre-Occupational Therapy, Pre-Physician Assistant
Nursing
Occupational Therapy
Physical Therapy (3+3 Accelerated Option and 4+3 Traditional Option)
Physician Assistant Sciences
Psychology
Public Health
  (C)Biostatistics, Education, Environmental Science, Epidemiology, Health Policy Administration, Psychology
Social Work

SCHOOL OF SCIENCE, TECHNOLOGY, ENGINEERING, ARTS, & MATHEMATICS

Aquarium & Zoo Science
Biochemistry
   (C)Pre-Medicine
Biology
   (C)Ecology and Environmental Biology, Marine Biology, Molecular Biology,
      Pre-Medicine, Pre-Pharmacy, Secondary Education
Chemistry
   (C)Environmental Chemistry, Forensic, Nanotechnology, Pre-Medicine, Pre-Pharmacy,
      Secondary Education
Computer Science
   (C)Gaming/New Media Design and Production, General, Information Technology and
      Security, Software Development
CyberSecurity Administration
Engineering (General and 3-2 options)
   (C)Aeronautics, Computational Modeling, Innovation and Entrepreneur, Mechanical,
      Robotics
English
   (C)Literature, Media Studies, Secondary Education, Secondary Education
Environmental Engineering
   (C)Ecological Engineering, Renewable Energy
Environmental Studies
Fine Arts (minor)
History
   (C)American Studies, Pre-Law, Secondary Education
Mathematics
   Actuarial Science, Applied Mathematics, Computer Science, Secondary Education
Medical Laboratory Science
Petroleum & Natural Gas Engineering
Philosophy minor
Political Science
   (C)International Studies, Political Communications, Pre-Law, Public
      Administration/Government Service, Secondary Education
Pre-Law (available through multiple degree paths)
Pre-Medicine (available through multiple degree paths)
Religious Studies minor
Spanish
   Secondary Education
Women's Studies

(C) denotes concentration

TUITION, ROOM, BOARD, FEES
2020–21

Tuition: $38,078
Room: $6148
Board: $6200
Technology Program Fee: $1300

FINANCIAL AID

Saint Francis University awards financial aid to greater than 90 percent of its student body. Need-based federal and state awards are awarded based on information obtained from the Free Application for Federal Student Aid (FAFSA). In order to qualify for financial aid students must apply for admission and complete a FAFSA.

Saint Francis University has a generous merit-based scholarship program. Students who have been accepted for admission are awarded merit-based scholarships solely based upon their academic performance. Academic performance is measured by credentials submitted upon application including high school grade point average, SAT/ACT scores and class rank.

Saint Francis University participates in NCAA Division I athletics in the Northeast Conference. Athletic scholarships may be granted in all 24 athletic teams. Students may also receive scholarship money in Pep Band, Marching Band, Cheerleading, and Dance.

STUDENT ORGANIZATIONS AND ACTIVITIES

Saint Francis University is a diverse campus community with approximately 2,600 students. Our students arrive at Saint Francis University from over 30 states and 25 countries.

The University provides students many opportunities to exercise their interests and talents. Over 60 on-campus clubs and organizations representing a wide range of interests are available to students. These range from departmental clubs to volunteer organizations, and include social and service sororities and social, service, and business fraternities. Student-run activities on campus include theatre productions, SFU singers, Greek life opportunities for men and women as well as Club Baseball, Ice Hockey and Rugby. Each year, the Student Activities Organization brings a lively docket of comedians, concerts, films, and lectures to campus. The University is a NCAA Division I member institution and maintains a comprehensive program that consists of men's and women's teams. Students may also participate in cheerleading, pep band, and marching band.

ADMISSIONS PROCESS

The undergraduate application for admission operates under a rolling admission policy except for the Physician Assistant Science program, which has a Priority Application Date of **November 15th.** The Occupational Therapy and Physical Therapy program have a Priority Application Date of **January 15th.** All students must submit the application for admission, official high school transcripts and official standardized test scores (SAT or ACT). A writing sample (minimum of 250) is required for students applying to the Occupational Therapy, Physical Therapy and Physician Assistant Science majors.

SAINT LOUIS UNIVERSITY

AT A GLANCE

Saint Louis University was founded in 1818 as the first university west of the Mississippi River. At the core of this diverse community of scholars is SLU's service-focused mission, which prepares students to make the world a better, more just place.

WORLD-CLASS: SLU is a Catholic, Jesuit research university, highly ranked by the Princeton Review and by U.S. News & World Report.

SLU boasts 15 academic programs in the top 50 in their fields, along with accolades for campus sustainability efforts, military-friendliness and as a "best value" in private education. SLU is also the first Jesuit university to receive the Higher Education Excellence in Diversity Award.

URBAN AND INTERNATIONAL: With two dynamic, urban campuses—in St. Louis, Missouri, and Madrid, Spain—the university is home to nearly 13,000 students from 50 states and 82 countries. SLU's international focus and 50+ study abroad programs invite students to engage with and learn from the global community. The St. Louis campus is a welcoming residential oasis located steps from some of the region's top art and culture venues, while SLU-Madrid puts students in the heart of one of Europe's most vibrant, history-rich cities.

HANDS-ON: One of only nine Catholic universities with a "higher" or "highest" research activity designation, SLU empowers students to collaborate with faculty mentors on groundbreaking research and gain hands-on experience. From developing systems to filter arsenic pollution out of water to exploring innovative ways to get fresh produce into low-income neighborhoods, students don't just contemplate solutions to the day's most challenging problems—they actively work to make those solutions reality.

SERVICE-MINDED: Jesuit tradition inspires the SLU community's commitment to service and social justice. Designated a "character-building college," SLU was also the first institution named to the President's Higher Education Community Service Honor Roll for nine consecutive years. Students cook meals in the Campus Kitchen, volunteer at student-run medical and law clinics, and work alongside dozens of community organizations to serve their neighbors.

A SLU education gives graduates not only the skills to succeed in their careers but also the wisdom to lead lives of meaning and purpose. SLU alumni have become mayors of major cities, helped put men on the moon, directed Hollywood blockbusters and worked side-by-side with Mother Theresa.

LOCATION AND ENVIRONMENT

At Saint Louis University, students are in the center of everything, whether studying at SLU's Midtown St. Louis campus or SLU's international campus in Madrid, Spain.

ST. LOUIS: SLU's beautiful urban campus in Midtown St. Louis stretches across more than 230 acres of lush greenery, flowers and fountains. Students and visitors alike appreciate the unique vibe of a close-knit community nestled in the middle of a dynamic city.

The St. Louis metro region boasts nearly 3 million people. The city's mix of Midwestern friendliness and large-city amenities has helped St. Louis garner its ranking as one of the best cities for young professionals. In 2019, St. Louis grabbed the No. 1 spot on 'Forbes' "Happiest Cities for Job-Seeking Grads" list. The city also is home to the iconic Gateway Arch and a variety of cultural, historical and sporting attractions.

Students love cheering on the SLU Billikens. The only NCAA Division I school in town, SLU fields teams in 11 different sports, and the Billikens have earned many accolades, including 10 NCAA men's soccer championships—more than any other team in the United States.

MADRID: In 1967, SLU became one of first American universities to establish a foreign campus. Each semester, 800+ students from about 50 countries pursue their studies at SLU-Madrid. Southern Europe's greenest city, Madrid offers refreshing parks and a beautiful riverside promenade. The historic central district is easy to cross on foot, and the barrios popular among students are only a few metro stops away—Madrid's mass transit system is among the best in the world.

CAMPUS FACILITIES AND EQUIPMENT

During the past three decades, Saint Louis University improvements and expansions have totaled approximately $850 million. In recent years, the University completed some of the most significant building projects in its history, including the $82 million Edward A. Doisy Research Center, which offers SLU's innovative researchers a world-class facility.

SLU's on-campus housing options include two residence halls, reflecting a nearly $115 million investment in student housing. On track for a 2020 completion, the University is adding 10,000 square feet of new state-of-the-art research space to campus in the Interdisciplinary Science and Engineering Building.

Also on campus is the 10,600-seat Chaifetz Arena, which is the home of Billiken basketball and also hosts many of the country's top entertainment acts, and SLU's 70,000-square-foot Center for Global Citizenship. Students can enjoy countless recreational activities at the university's 120,000-square-foot Simon Recreation Center, which features indoor basketball and handball courts, a bouldering wall and an indoor pool.

OFF-CAMPUS OPPORTUNITIES

ST. LOUIS: Midtown St. Louis offers access to affordable living as well as the excitement of the Grand Center arts district, the cultural heart of St. Louis. The booming performing arts neighborhood features opportunities to experience world-class art, theater, dance and music just steps away from SLU's campus.

Minutes away by car, bus or light rail train, students can explore Forest Park, the 1904 World's Fair site that's larger than even New York City's Central Park and home to the city's world-class art museum, zoo, science center and history museum—all free to the public. Check out the Delmar Loop, one of the "10 Great Streets in America," or head to "The Hill," a nationally noted neighborhood for authentic Italian cuisine, including St. Louis' famous toasted ravioli. Then go downtown to catch a game. St. Louis is noted for being one of the nation's best sports cities, and residents root for the St. Louis Cardinals baseball team, St. Louis Blues hockey team, and a bevy of independent sports teams.

MADRID: The city of Madrid is home to 230,000 university students. It's a cosmopolitan capital, a metropolis alive with learning and all that Spanish life has to offer, from flamenco shows to late-night tapas.

Madrid offers cultural experiences to rival any city in Europe, including a Royal Palace, a train station designed by Eiffel, countless theaters, museums and glorious churches. Gorgeous fountains with splashing waters can be found at the intersections of the city's grand, tree-lined avenues, and the city's beautiful parks are ideal for weekend picnics or morning runs.

ACADEMIC PROGRAMS

High-achieving young men and women come from around the globe to pursue a world-class education at Saint Louis University. SLU offers nearly 90 undergraduate programs of study and more than 100 graduate and professional programs, with many ranked among the nation's top 50 programs in their respective disciplines.

For the most up-to-date selection of majors and programs offered, visit slu.edu/majors-and-programs.

UNDERGRADUATE PROGRAMS

- Accounting *
- Aeronautics ^
- Aerospace Engineering ^
- African American Studies
- American Studies *
- Analytics and Enterprise Systems
- Anthropology
- Art History
- Athletic Training *
- Biochemistry * ^
- Bioethics and Health Studies
- Biology * ^
- Biomedical Engineering ^
- Biostatistics * ^
- Chemical Biology and Pharmacology * ^
- Chemistry * ^
- Civil Engineering ^
- Classical Humanities
- Communication *
- Communication Sciences and Disorders *
- Computer Engineering ^
- Computer Science *
- Criminology and Criminal Justice *
- Data Science ^
- Economics
- Education *
- Electrical Engineering ^
- Engineering Physics ^
- English *
- Entrepreneurship
- Environmental Science ^
- Environmental Studies ^
- Finance
- Forensic Science ^
- French *
- Geology
- Geophysics ^
- German Studies
- Greek and Latin Languages and Literature
- Health Information Management

- Health Management
- Health Sciences
- History *
- Information Technology Management
- International Business *
- International Studies
- Investigative and Medical Sciences
- Italian Studies
- Leadership and Human Resource Management
- Magnetic Resonance Imaging
- Marketing
- Mathematics * ^
- Mechanical Engineering ^
- Medical Laboratory Science ^
- Medieval Studies
- Meteorology *
- Music
- Neuroscience
- Nuclear Medicine Technology
- Nursing *
- Nutrition and Dietetics *
- Occupational Science and Occupational Therapy *
- Philosophy *
- Philsophy for Ministry
- Physical Therapy *
- Physics ^
- Political Science *
- Psychology
- Public Health *
- Radiation Therapy
- Russian Studies
- Social Work *
- Sociology *
- Spanish *
- Sports Business
- Studio Art
- Theatre
- Theological Studies *
- Women's and Gender Studies *

ADDITIONAL GRADUATE PROGRAMS

- Anatomy
- Applied Analytics
- Applied Behavior Analysis
- Applied Financial Economics
- Aviation
- Biochemistry and Molecular Biology
- Bioinformatics and Computational Biology
- Business Administration
- Curriculum and Instruction
- Dentistry
- Educational Foundations
- Educational Leadership
- Family Therapy
- Geographic Information Sciences
- Geoscience
- Health Administration
- Health Care Ethics
- Health Data Science
- Health Outcomes Research and Evaluation Science
- Higher Education Administration
- Integrated and Applied Sciences
- International Business and Marketing
- Law
- Leadership and Organizational Development
- Medicine
- Molecular Imaging and Therapeutics
- Molecular Microbiology and Immunology
- Occupational Therapy
- Pathology
- Pharmacological and Physiological Science
- Physician Assistant
- Public Administration
- Public and Social Policy
- Public Health, Biosecurity and Disaster Preparedness
- Public Health Studies
- Software Engineering
- Special Education
- Supply Chain Management
- Sustainability
- Urban Planning and Development

* Indicates graduate program offered

^ Indicates designated STEM degree by the U.S. Department of Homeland Security

MAJORS AND DEGREES OFFERED

Academics at Saint Louis University are rigorous, ambitious, enriching and worthwhile. SLU ranks amount the nation's top 100 research universities and offers over 80 different majors stemming from the humanities and liberal arts to engineering and flight to health care and biology. SLU also offers a robust array of professional and graduate programs for those students seeking to further their education.

TUITION, ROOM, BOARD, FEES

Annual tuition for full-time undergraduate students is $44,700. Room and board amounts to approximately $12,832 per student (depending on specific residence hall and board plan). Fees average $724 per year.

FINANCIAL AID

Saint Louis University remains committed to keeping its one-of-a-kind education within reach and understands the sacrifices students and families make for quality education. SLU is dedicated to serving others, in part, by providing financial access to an unparalleled and life-changing educational experience.

In 2019, 97 percent of SLU's first-time freshmen received some sort of scholarship or financial assistance.

Scholarships are awarded based on academic merit, talents, service, leadership and financial need. In addition to SLU's financial aid programs, the state of Missouri and the federal government also provide assistance.

Contact SLU's Office of Student Financial Services at 314-977-2350, 800-SLU-FOR-U or sfs@slu.edu.

STUDENT ORGANIZATIONS AND ACTIVITIES

Students participate in more than 175 clubs, honor societies and service organizations; 18 NCAA Division I teams; intramural sports; and community service efforts that see 85 percent of SLU students volunteering at least once during the academic year.

Talent and commitment matter at SLU, and high levels of energy and dedication exist in everything Saint Louis University students pursue: academic societies, athletics, performing arts and media groups, student government, cultural and political organizations, and fraternities and sororities. SLU's multicultural organizations highlight and celebrate the diversity of the University community, and a variety of faith-based organizations support and challenge students as they explore their own faith traditions.

ADMISSIONS PROCESS

For information about the admission process at Saint Louis University or to schedule a campus visit, call the office of admission at 800-SLU-FOR-U, email admission@slu.edu, or check out slu.edu/visit.

SAINT MARY'S COLLEGE OF CALIFORNIA

AT A GLANCE

Saint Mary's College of California is distinctive for all the right reasons. With nationally renowned faculty, a tight-knit community, and rigorous academics, Saint Mary's stands out from the pack. We see things differently. Enter to Learn. Leave to Serve. For 150 years, we've transformed education into a platform for the common good. We stand up for the silenced and speak out against injustice. It's been our mission since the start–and the motivation that moves us forward.

Our graduates are leaders in both public and private sectors. They find their niche and make a difference. State and national government positions, courtroom benches, and corner offices in companies like Microsoft all belong to our alumni. Gaels make an impact. No doubt you'll do the same.

It's no wonder Saint Mary's College has been named one of the Top 5 Western Regional Universities and in the Top 10 Percent Nationwide for Return on Investment. Bottom line: Value is important, and Saint Mary's provides it.

So, leave behind the expectations of who you ought to be. Let go of what the world says you're supposed to be. Your voice is uniquely your own: Claim it boldly. Saint Mary's tightly knit community, focus on student research and real-world experience, and highly ranked academic programs help you find your true self.

LOCATION AND ENVIRONMENT

Our campus, established in 1928, is located in a beautiful, bustling community in the Bay Area east of San Francisco.

CAMPUS FACILITIES AND EQUIPMENT

Saint Mary's students have access to state-of-the-art facilities. For example, our Museum of Art is the only accredited art museum in Contra Costa County. Young actors find their passion at the LeFevre Theatre and book professional roles even before graduation. Students pursuing careers in medicine and health science will find unique opportunities in our anatomy lab, where advanced classes give undergraduates access to hands-on dissection, 3-D imaging software, and live telesurgery.

Outside of the classroom, there's something for everyone at the Joseph L. Alioto Recreation Center. The center offers multiple gymnasiums and exercise rooms, studio fitness classes, personal trainers, a swimming pool, hydrotherapy spa, and rock climbing wall, in addition to being the campus hub for intramural and club sports.

OFF-CAMPUS OPPORTUNITIES

The San Francisco Bay Area is a thriving metropolis that offers easy access to museums and art galleries; live theater and outdoor concerts; restaurants and local coffee shops; beaches, parks, hiking trails; and more. We are also close to Yosemite, Lake Tahoe, and Napa Valley. As a Saint Mary's student, you are only a short ride from Bay Area Rapid Transit (BART), a highly efficient rail system that provides easy connections throughout the Bay Area. You'll also receive the student-only perk of free bus service to and from campus. Whichever way you choose to get there, you'll easily discover all that the San Francisco Bay Area has to offer.

ACADEMIC PROGRAMS

Specialized programs include:

3+2 Engineering–Earn a BA and BS in five years with Washington University in St. Louis.

Teachers for Tomorrow—Earn a BA and a Preliminary Multiple Subject (MSTE) or Education Specialist Teaching Credential (SPED) in four years, or a BA/BS and a Preliminary Single Subject Teaching Credential (SSTE) with an optional Master of Arts in Teaching (MAT) in five years.

The Integral Great Books Program—Discover the interconnected nature of broad fields through a classic liberal arts approach.

Pre-Professional Curricula—Work toward your future with Saint Mary's pre-law, pre-med, pre-vet, pre-dental, pre-counseling, and pre-allied health professions curricula.

MAJORS AND DEGREES OFFERED

Saint Mary's College sees academic majors as flexible pathways that lead to intentional and customized careers. Pick a path reflective of your strengths, and take some inventive courses for a spin. Get feedback from faculty, determine your goals, then work together to choose a program where you'll thrive.

Just ask Academy Award winning actor and alumnus Mahershala Ali. What starts as a passion can expand into an unexpected and rewarding career.

Saint Mary's offers more than 40 majors and minors across the schools of Liberal Arts, Science, Education, and Economics. Some of our most popular majors include: Communications; Biology; Business Administration; Justice, Community, and Leadership; Psychology; Performing Arts; and Spanish and Latin American Studies.

TUITION, ROOM, BOARD, FEES

Undergraduate tuition for 2020–2021: $50,460
Room & Board: $15,706
Student Activity Fee: $200
Total: $66,366

FINANCIAL AID

Saint Mary's mission is to make education accessible to all, and we use federal, state, and institutional funds to ensure that you can afford a Saint Mary's education. Saint Mary's awards $20 million in grants and scholarships to new incoming students, and 90 percent of new students who apply for financial aid receive it. Saint Mary's scholarship awards for first-year students range from $7,000 to full tuition. Awards consider GPA, standardized test scores, college prep curriculum rigor, and class standing. Students who complete the federal financial aid application may also qualify for California state and federal grants. All Saint Mary's scholarships are renewed annually for four years.

STUDENT ORGANIZATIONS AND ACTIVITIES

Student Body at a Glance:

- Undergraduate Student Body: 2,675
- Male: 43%
- Female: 57%
- Hispanic/Latino: 29%
- Black or African American: 5%
- White: 42%
- Asian: 17%
- Native Hawaiian or other Pacific Islander: 1%
- Other or unspecified: 3%
- International: 4%

At Saint Mary's, students can join one of the 40+ student organizations, suit up for one of our intramural leagues, or sit in on the School of Economics and Business Administration's Global Economic Forum. First-year students will find all the support they need at orientation and the Weekend of Welcome, and from faculty advisors and success coaches throughout each year. The first six weeks are packed with activities and events where students get to know each other and build their community.

ADMISSIONS PROCESS

To apply to Saint Mary's, you'll need:

- Completed Common Application
- Official high school transcripts
- Official ACT or SAT test scores
- A letter of recommendation from a teacher or counselor

Saint Mary's seeks candidates with a high level of intellectual preparation, seriousness of purpose, and moral integrity. The student's school record is considered the most reliable measure of potential college ability. Extra-curricular accomplishments, however, may strengthen an application insofar as they indicate special talents, perseverance, and maturity. All successful applicants are expected to complete at least 16 units of secondary school coursework that will include the following:

- 4 years of English
- 3 years of Mathematics (algebra, advanced algebra or the equivalent, and geometry)*
- 2 years of the same foreign language
- 2 years of science (at least one laboratory)*
- 2 years of social studies (at least 1 year of U.S. history)

*Students who plan to major in a science or mathematics are expected to show particular strength in their scientific and mathematical preparation.

SCHOOL OF VISUAL ARTS

AT A GLANCE

School of Visual Arts, located in the heart of New York City, has been a leader in the education of artists, designers and creative professionals for over seven decades. With a faculty of more than 1,000 distinguished working professionals, a dynamic curriculum and an emphasis on critical thinking, SVA is a catalyst for innovation and social responsibility. Comprising 7,000 students at its Manhattan campus and 38,000 alumni in 75 countries, SVA also represents one of the most influential artistic communities in the world.

Bachelor of Fine Arts degrees are offered in Advertising; Animation; Cartooning; Computer Art, Computer Animation and Visual Effects; Design, Film; Fine Arts; Illustration; Interior Design: Built Environments; Photography and Video; and Visual & Critical Studies.

Master of Arts degrees are offered in Art Education; Curatorial Practice; and Design Research, Writing and Criticism.

Master of Fine Arts degrees are offered in Art Practice; Computer Arts; Design; Design for Social Innovation; Fine Arts; Illustration as Visual Essay; Interaction Design; Photography, Video and Related Media; Products of Design; Social Documentary Film; and Visual Narrative.

Master of Professional Studies degrees are offered in Art Therapy, Branding, Digital Photography; Directing and Fashion Photography.

A Master of Arts in Teaching degree is offered in Art Education.

SVA also offers workshops, continuing education classes, studio residencies, international student programs, summer programs abroad, and a pre-college program for high school students.

For more information on the College and its offerings, visit sva.edu.

LOCATION AND ENVIRONMENT

SVA's urban-style campus comprises 16 buildings with state-of-the-art studio facilities, workshops, residence halls, and gallery spaces. As the creative capital of the world, New York City is home to more artists than any other U.S. city, with a creative workforce of 300,000. It is also home to over 14,000 creative businesses and non-profits. Students come here to be immersed in real-world experience, not the insulated experience of other schools. Surrounded by a thriving and artistic urban environment during their years at SVA, students are able to transition to the working world with ease, finding unique opportunities for internships and mentorships.

MAJORS AND DEGREES OFFERED

Bachelor of Fine Arts degrees are offered in Advertising; Animation; Cartooning; Computer Art, Computer Animation & Visual Effects; Design; Film; Fine Arts; Illustration; Interior Design: Built Environments; Photography and Video; and Visual and Critical Studies.

Master of Arts degrees are offered in Art Education; Curatorial Practice; and Design Research, Writing and Criticism.

Master of Fine Arts degrees are offered in Art Practice; Computer Arts; Design; Design for Social Innovation; Fine Arts; Illustration as Visual Essay; Interaction Design; Photography, Video and Related Media; Products of Design; Social Documentary Film; and Visual Narrative.

Master of Professional Studies degrees are offered in Art Therapy, Branding, Digital Photography; Directing and Fashion Photography.

A Master of Arts in Teaching degree is offered in Art Education.

TUITION, ROOM, BOARD, FEES

Expenses for 2020–2021

Application fee: $50

Tuition: $43,400 per year for undergraduate programs; for Graduate program tuition, please visit https://sva.edu/students/financial-resources/tuition-and-fees

Departmental fees: $640 to $1,465 per semester depending on undergraduate major

Estimated Supplies: $1,050 to $3,150

Housing Charges: range from $16,000 to $19,950 per year

FINANCIAL AID

Currently, 43% of SVA first-time freshmen receive some form of financial aid. Undergraduate merit scholarships are also available through Admissions. A payment plan is available.

STUDENT ORGANIZATIONS AND ACTIVITIES

The Student Engagement and Leadership Office provides a diverse range of programming designed to enrich the SVA student's experience. Students are offered the opportunity to tap into a multitude of social, cultural, educational and recreational activities. Students are encouraged to take advantage of all New York City has to offer.

The Visual Arts Student Association (VASA), the student government, represents the students' point of view at SVA. Participating in VASA gives students the opportunity to develop leadership skills by coordinating events and activities. VASA funds and supports a number of clubs and activities that are organized by students.

ADMISSIONS PROCESS

Undergraduate Application Deadlines:

Deadline for freshman and transfers: rolling

Deadline for Early Action: December 1

Deadline for all application materials to be submitted for the Silas H. Rhodes Scholarship Program: February 1 for first-time freshman applicants and March 1 for transfer applicants. There is no separate application for the Silas H. Rhodes Scholarship Program.

Undergraduate Requirements:

- Application for Undergraduate Admission
- A nonrefundable $50 application fee
- Official transcripts from all high schools and colleges attended
- Results of the SAT or ACT
- Statement of intent
- Portfolio
- Demonstration of English proficiency (required of all international applicants whose primary language is not English)

SETON HALL UNIVERSITY

AT A GLANCE

As one of the nation's leading Catholic universities, Seton Hall provides over 90 rigorous academic programs that are highly ranked by *The Princeton Review, U.S. News & World Report* and *Bloomberg Businessweek*. We offer all the advantages of a large research university: challenging academic programs, notable alumni, state-of-the-art facilities, renowned faculty, extensive opportunities for internships, research and scholarships with all the benefits of a small, supportive and nurturing environment. Our 14:1 student-to-faculty ratio and average class size of 21 students means faculty know more than just your name.

Our accomplished faculty include Fulbright Scholars, prominent researchers, authors, artists, filmmakers, former school superintendents and principals, leaders in nursing, former ambassadors, analysts and lawmakers-all of whom are dedicated to their fields and their students. We have graduates that have pursued further studies at some of the nation's leading institutions, including Seton Hall, Harvard, Columbia, Yale, Princeton and Dartmouth. Each day, our faculty members shine in the lecture halls and on the national stage. We meet regularly with students outside the classroom and help them develop great minds.

Seton Hall offers more than 17,000 internship opportunities, and over 80 percent of our students have an internship or two on their resume before graduation, this is just one of the reasons our students have a 93% employment rate after graduation and mid-career earnings 50% higher than the national average. In fact, Seton Hall was recently ranked top 5 in the nation for providing internship opportunities. Our national reputation and stellar academic programs draw over 550 employers to campus each year just to recruit our graduates. Seton Hall has also been rated as one of the best schools for a return on your investment and for having the highest paid graduates for the investment and Forbes has rated Seton Hall one of America's Best Value Colleges.

Seton Hall is a Catholic university with over a 160-year tradition of educational excellence. A welcoming community, Seton Hall embraces students of all faiths and inspires students to become servant leaders who make a difference in the world. That's why our community performs over 40,000 hours of community service annually. You'll feel at home on our campus, where it's easy to make friends and get involved.

LOCATION AND ENVIRONMENT

Nestled in the suburban village of South Orange, New Jersey, Seton Hall provides small-town charm combined with big-city opportunities. The University's suburban, 58-acre park-like campus sits proudly within this picturesque town with tree-lined streets; historic, gracious homes; and quaint shops just 14 miles from New York City close to all the action, yet not engulfed by it.

Just a five-minute walk from campus lands you in the middle of a bustling town center where you'll find diners and pizzerias, banks, pharmacies, Starbucks, Cold Stone Creamery, a gourmet marketplace, South Orange Performing Arts Center, a movie theatre, and so much more. You might not ever want to leave this quiet suburbia, but if you do, the train station, right in the center of town, is your direct link to NYC's Penn Station just 30 minutes away.

We take full advantage of all the Big Apple has to offer-where the worlds of entertainment, art, publishing, global finance, international diplomacy and fashion collide. NYC is also one of the world's largest job markets, brimming with internship and job placement opportunities in a variety of companies. Over 80% of Seton Hall students have an internship or two on their resume before graduation at leading companies like Goldman Sachs, American Express, CNN, the Secret Service, Merck, Lincoln Center, The New York Mets, the United Nations, The New York Times, NBC, Prudential, Sony Music, JP Morgan Chase and more.

And if all the advantages and opportunities of the Big Apple aren't enough, New Jersey's got you covered. One of the wealthiest states in the nation, New Jersey is brimming with opportunity. Seton Hall's backyard boasts a powerhouse corporate corridor of more than 50 Fortune 500 companies, pharmaceutical giants and major corporations. For you this means networking, internships and career opportunities.

CAMPUS FACILITIES AND EQUIPMENT

Seton Hall places a strong emphasis on the use of state-of-the-art technology, facilities and support services to aid in its students' development. Many investments have been made to the campus infrastructure, including the recent construction of a new academic classroom building, a new medical campus, and a new state of the art recreation and fitness center. In addition the campus boasts a state-of-the-art research library complete with a computerized catalog and 200 computer terminals. The Science and Technology Center, is home to state-of-the-future biology and chemistry labs, an atrium and auditorium, as well as an observatory and greenhouse. The campus also offers many unique learning labs like our Mock Trading Room, Patient Simulation Laboratory, Market Research Center, Sport Polling Center and WSOU, the number 1 ranked college radio station in the nation.

Seton Hall recently opened a new Interprofessional Health Sciences campus, located in Clifton & Nutley, NJ. The IHS campus creates a forward-thinking approach to healthcare education, bringing together future doctors, nurses and health professionals in the fields of medicine, nursing, physical therapy, physician assistant, occupational therapy, athletic training and speech language pathology. This innovative team-based training reflects the future of healthcare delivery; Seton Hall is one of only a few universities using this model. This new approach will vastly improve cooperation and communication among health professionals and greatly strengthen patient care.

ACADEMIC PROGRAMS

Seton Hall offers over 90 rigorous academic programs in seven undergraduate colleges. We have excellent programs in business, education, communication, diplomacy and International relations, nursing, humanities, social sciences, biology, chemistry, physics as well as direct admission joint degree programs in medicine, physical therapy, athletic training, occupational therapy, physician assistant and speech language pathology. Our state-of-the-art Interprofessional Health Sciences campus, located in Clifton & Nutley, NJ, houses our School of Health and Medical Sciences and College of Nursing, which is ranked in the top 5% of Nursing programs nationwide. The IHS campus is also home to the Hackensack Meridian School of Medicine which, in partnership with Seton Hall University, offers direct admission to a seven-year Joint Bachelor's/M.D. program.

Seton Hall's Stillman School of Business has the number one rated leadership program in the country and has AACSB accreditation, the most rigorous accreditation a business school can hold, putting them in the top 10% of business schools in the world and their accounting program in the top 1% in the world. Graduates of the business school, along with graduates of the College of Communication and the Arts, The College or Education and the School of Diplomacy and International Relations have 100% admit rates into graduate school and nearly a 100% employment rate for students within six months of graduation. Seton Hall also has a 93% admit rate into medical school for its pre-med students.

MAJORS AND DEGREES OFFERED

Accounting•
Accounting (5-year B.S./M.S. dual-degree∞)
Africana Studies•
American Humanics√
Ancient Greek†
Anthropology•
Applied Scientific Mathematics†
Arabic†
Archaeology†
Art (Art History•, Fine Arts•, Graphic Interactive and Advertising Design•)
Art (BA/MA in Museum Professions)♠
Asian Studies•
Athletic Training (5-year B.S./M.S. or B.A./M.S. dual-degree)∞

Biochemistry
Biology (B.A. or B.S.)
Broadcasting and Visual Media•
Business Administration•‡
Catholic Studies•‡
Catholic Theology•
Chemistry•
Classical Culture†
Classical Languages†
Classical Studies•
Communication Studies (B.A./M.A. in Communication or Public Relations)∞
Computer Graphics√
Computer Science•
Creative Writing
Criminal Justice•

Cybersecurity√
Data Visualization and Analysis√
Digital Media and Video√
Digital Media Production for the Web√
Diplomacy and International Relations•
Early Childhood Education (integrated with elementary and special education)
Elementary Education (integrated with early childhood and special education)
Education with Speech Language Pathology (6-year B.S.E./M.S. dual degree)∞
Economics (B.A. or B.S.)
Engineering (Biomedical, Chemical, Civil, Computer, Electrical, Industrial, Mechanical)♠
English•
Entrepreneurial Studies‡
Entrepreneurship
Environmental Sciences†
Environmental Studies•
Ethics and Applied Ethics†
Finance
French•
Gerontology√
Graphic, Interactive and Advertising Design
History•
Information Technologies√
Information Technology Management‡
International Business†
International Relations
Italian•
Italian Studies†
Journalism•
Latin†
Latin America and Latino/Latina Studies•
Law (3+3 Seton Hall Law J.D. with B.S. in International Relations, or B.S. in Business, or B.A. in Political Science)∞
Legal Studies in Business†
Liberal Studies
Management
Marketing
Mathematical Finance
Mathematics•
M.B.A. (5-year B.S./M.B.A. or B.A./ M.B.A. dual-degree)∞

Medicine (Joint Bachelor's/M.D. Program)
Modern Languages
Music (Comprehensive Music/Music Education, Music Performance•)
Music History†
Music Technology†
Musical Theatre†
Nonprofit Studies†
Nursing
Occupational Therapy (6-year B.A./M.S. dual-degree)∞
Online Course Development and Management√
Philosophical Theology√
Philosophy•
Physical Therapy (6-year B.S./D.P.T. dual-degree)∞
Physician Assistant (6-year B.S./M.S. dual-degree)∞
Physics (B.A. or B.S.)•
Political Science•
Pre-Dental*
Pre-Law*
Pre-Medical*
Pre-Optometry*
Pre-Veterinary*
Psychology (B.A. or B.S.)•
Public Relations
Religion•
Russian†
Russian and East European Studies†√
Secondary Education (optional integration with special education)
Social and Behavioral Sciences
Social Work•
Sociology•
Spanish•
Special Education (integrated with early childhood, elementary, and secondary education)
Speech Language Pathology (6-year 4+2 Bachelor's in Psychology or Education/ M.S. dual degree)
Sport Management•
Supply Chain Management√
Theatre and Performance•
Web Design√
Women and Gender Studies†
Writing†
Undecided

• Minor also available
† Minor only
√ Certificate program only
‡ Certificate program also available
♠ Dual-degree Program with NJIT
∞ Seton Hall dual-degree program (please contact the Office of Admissions for details)
* Pre-professional programs (you must also select a major)

TUITION, ROOM, BOARD, FEES

Seton Hall offers a flat-tuition rate for students taking between 12–18 credit hours. The 2019–2020 tuition and fees are $44,080. Room and Board fees range depending on meal plans; however, an average cost is $15,222.

FINANCIAL AID

Paying for college is a major investment. Seton Hall University is committed to providing students with the resources needed to make your dreams a reality. The University gives over $96 million in aid each year and 98 percent of our students receive some form of financial aid with 97 percent receiving scholarships or grants directly from the University. Seton Hall University has been rated as one of the best schools in the nation for a return on your investment. Most scholarships are automatically awarded upon admission and do not require a separate application. However there are also several special scholarships for which students can apply, learn more at www.shu.edu/scholarships. Seton Hall also provides need-based aid to eligible students who complete the Free Application for Federal Student Aid (FAFSA) form by November 1.

STUDENT ORGANIZATIONS AND ACTIVITIES

On campus, Great minds learn to put their ideas into action; discover something new; become part of a community; and build trust, spirit and lasting friendships. Here, you'll find activities galore, over 130 clubs and organizations and 26 Greek societies. You can audition for one of the nearly dozen theatre performances cast each year or broadcast at the #1 ranked college radio station in the nation, WSOU-FM, which attracts more than 120,000 listeners a week from the NYC area. Join the Brownson Speech and Debate Team, ranked in the Top 20 college and university forensic teams for years or write for one of our three student newspapers. You'll not only make lots of new friends and have fun, you'll also learn about your leadership style. More than two-thirds of our students participate in clubs and organizations.

You don't have to be a superstar athlete to be part of the game at Seton Hall. Our athletic programs include competition on varsity, intramural and club levels. In fact, almost 50 percent of our students participate in club or intramural sports. Even if you don't know a handball from a handoff, you'll be decked out in blue and cheering your heart out when you attend any one of Seton Hall's 14 NCAA division I Big East athletic events. So grab your friends and catch some Pirate fever!

ADMISSIONS PROCESS

At Seton Hall, we take a holistic approach to reviewing your application. When we receive your application, we start by considering your academic performance in high school, your grades and the rigor of your curriculum, as well as your standardized SAT and/or ACT scores. These are essential indicators of your ability to succeed at Seton Hall. We also will consider your personal essay, recommendations and extracurricular activities.

The typical student who entered Seton hall last year had an average GPA of 3.6 (B+) and an average SAT score of 1235 and 27 on the ACT.

Visit

The best way to experience Seton Hall is to visit in person. We offer tours Mon-Fri at 10 am and 2 pm and on Saturdays at 10 am, noon and 2 pm. Open Houses are offered in mid-October, mid-November mid-February and late April. To schedule a visit or sign up for Open House visit www.shu.edu/visiting

For more information, contact the Office of Undergraduate Admission:

Website: admissions.shu.edu

Telephone: 1-800-THE-HALL (843-4255)

E-mail: thehall@shu.edu

Instagram and Facebook #halladmissions

SKIDMORE COLLEGE

AT A GLANCE

Founded in 1903, Skidmore College is an independent, coeducational, liberal arts college in Saratoga Springs, New York, that prides itself on its creative approaches to just about everything. Creativity powers the way we think, communicate and do. We boldly declare that, here, at Skidmore, more than anything, Creative Thought Matters. With a diverse student body of 2,500 students from 40 states and 70 countries and a faculty of 304 dedicated teacher-scholars, Skidmore offers 43 majors in the arts, humanities, sciences and social sciences, as well as in pre-professional fields. Forty percent of our students are men, 60% women, 24% domestic students of color, 12% international and 15% first-generation collegians.

We are known for our interdisciplinary approach to learning, faculty-student collaborative research, funded research opportunities, off-campus study and the prominence of the performing and visual arts. The College's rigorous academic program begins with the foundational First-Year Experience, which integrates the curricular and cocurricular and gets students involved in the life of the community from day one. Students enjoy close relationships with faculty members who have earned recognition through Guggenheim, Pulitzer, and Emmy awards, and fellowships and grants from Fulbright, MacArthur, the National Science Foundation and others. About half of our students carry two majors or add a related minor to their major, and nearly 60% are attending graduate or professional school or have completed advanced degrees within five years of graduation.

LOCATION AND ENVIRONMENT

Skidmore truly offers the best of both worlds—a beautiful campus and a thriving hometown in Saratoga Springs, one of the most vibrant small cities in the US. Famed for its "health, history, and horses," Saratoga Springs is a popular year-round cultural and tourist destination. The Saratoga Performing Arts Center is summer home to the New York City Ballet, Philadelphia Orchestra and Opera Saratoga, and is a performing venue for top rock and jazz musicians. Downtown Saratoga is brimming with galleries, museums, shops, coffeehouses, bistros and restaurants. No wonder Travel & Leisure named it the sixth-best college town in the nation. The city's location near the foothills of the Adirondack Mountains puts an abundance of outdoor recreational opportunities within an hour's drive, including great downhill and Nordic skiing. Boston, New York City and Montreal are each approximately 180 miles from campus.

CAMPUS FACILITIES AND EQUIPMENT

The beautiful 1,000-acre campus—300 acres of which consists of the recreation- and research-rich North Woods—has been upgraded in recent years with renovations to dining and residential facilities. The new Center for Integrated Sciences is slated for partial completion in Fall 2020. Skidmore's Zankel Music Center is a 54,000-square-foot facility with a spectacular 600-seat recital hall and state-of-the art recording studio. In addition, the Northwoods Apartments, opened in 2007 for upperclassmen, feature "green" apartments that use geothermal heating and cooling systems. The similar Sussman Village Apartments opened six years ago. And the Tang Teaching Museum and Art Gallery, opened in 2000, has earned a national reputation through exhibitions that feature contemporary art but also address disciplines such as the natural and social sciences.

In recent years, our Community Garden has produced thousands of pounds of organic food for the dining hall and through our student-run composting program we've saved about 100,000 pounds of food waste from the landfill. We've also cut 45% of greenhouse gas emissions since 2000, thanks to renewable energy and efficiency efforts. In all, 19% of campus electricity is generated by our hydroelectric dam (8%) and solar field (11%). And 35% of campus is geothermally heated and cooled, with 45% projected in the near future.

ACADEMIC PROGRAMS

Skidmore offers numerous pre-professional and cooperative programs: pre-law advising; pre-medical/health professions advising; 4+1 M.B.A. programs (Clarkson, RIT); Whitman M.B.A. Advantage Program, 4+1 M.S.A. and 4+1 M.S.F. (Syracuse); dual-degree engineering programs (Clarkson, Dartmouth, RPI); B.S.N. (NYU School of Nursing); dual-degree programs in occupational therapy and physical therapy (Sage Graduate School); M.S. in Accountancy (Wake Forest); M.S. in Teaching (Clarkson); internships (academic credit, funded summer programs); applied civic-engagement courses; Periclean Honors Forum; faculty-student collaborative research (academic year and summer program); international and domestic off-campus study options; and the Moore Documentary Studies Collaborative.

Off-campus study: With about 60% of students studying abroad at some point during their college years, Skidmore is perennially ranked in the top five nationally on a list of top 40 baccalaureate institutions for number of students studying abroad for a semester. Students can choose from 118 programs in 45 countries, including Skidmore-run programs in England, France, New Zealand and Spain.

MAJORS AND DEGREES OFFERED

Skidmore offers bachelor degrees in the following 43 majors: American studies, anthropology, art (studio), art history, Asian studies, biology, business (business-French, business-German, business-Spanish, and business-political science), chemistry, classics, computer science, dance, economics, education studies, English, environmental science, environmental studies, exercise science, French, gender studies, geosciences, German, history, international affairs, mathematics, music, neuroscience, philosophy, physics, political science (political science-French, political science-German, and political science-Spanish), psychology, religious studies, a self-determined major, social work, sociology, Spanish, and theater.

Most majors have minors. Others include arts administration, Black studies, Chinese, intergroup relations, Italian, Japanese, Latin American and Latinx studies, statistics, and media and film studies.

TUITION, ROOM, BOARD, FEES

Skidmore 2019–2020 costs: $56,172 tuition and fees; $8,868 dorm-double room; and $6,132 board.

FINANCIAL AID

Skidmore annually provides $53 million in financial aid on the basis of demonstrated financial need. The most recent first-year aid package was $44,000, ranging from $2,000 to $65,000; 47% of students received need-based grants; 50% received some form of financial aid; and 50% took advantage of the opportunity to work on campus. Average post-college student debt (just under $23,000) is well below the national average.

Aid is provided in the form of a student-aid package that usually includes a grant, campus job and loan. We encourage any student interested in applying for admission to do so regardless of his or her intention to seek financial aid. A great place to start is our Skidmore student aid calculator, which will give you an idea for where you stand. A Free Application for Federal Student Aid (FAFSA), a copy of the federal income tax form and the CSS Profile must be filed each year.

Skidmore also hosts an annual Filene Music Scholarship Competition to award four to six $60,000 ($15,000 per year) scholarships on the basis of musical ability without regard to financial need. Twelve to fourteen $15,000 Porter-Wachenheim Presidential Scholarships in Science and Mathematics scholarships are also awarded annually ($60,000 over four years). In addition, up to eight Skidmore Scholars in Science and Mathematics—students with demonstrated financial need—annually receive financial aid packages with no loan component in the first two years and with reduced loans in years three and four.

STUDENT ORGANIZATIONS AND ACTIVITIES

Student clubs/organizations/leadership: Whether you engage in one of Skidmore's nearly 120 student clubs or serve as a residential advisor, a varsity athlete or intramural participant, a student gardener, or a volunteer in a local school, you will find opportunities to use your creativity and round yourself out while giving back to the larger community.

Varsity sports: A founding member of the highly competitive NCAA, Division III Liberty League, Skidmore offers 19 varsity sports: baseball, basketball (men and women), field hockey, golf, ice hockey, lacrosse (men and women), riding, rowing (men and women), soccer (men and women), softball, swimming/diving (men and women), tennis (men and women), and volleyball. Liberty League members are Bard, Clarkson, Hobart & William Smith, Ithaca, RPI, RIT, Rochester, St. Lawrence, Skidmore, Union, and Vassar.

Student Academic Services (SAS) serves all Skidmore students interested in strengthening their academic performance or skills by organizing peer tutoring, study groups, and drop-in tutoring and by offering professional one-on-one and small-group academic support. SAS collaborates with other campus offices and faculty to support Skidmore students with specific responsibility for international students, English Language Learners, students of color, student-athletes and students with disabilities.

ADMISSIONS PROCESS

In 2018–19, Skidmore received more than 11,000 applications for a first-year class of 740 (including 35 students spending their first semester in London); 30% were offered admission; nearly half enrolled through Early Decision.

Those seeking admission to Skidmore's first-year class should complete a secondary-school curriculum that includes at least 16 credits in college-preparatory courses. The Admissions Committee also considers applications from qualified high school juniors who plan to accelerate and enter college early. Applicants typically have completed four years of English, a foreign language, mathematics, and social studies and three to four years of laboratory science. Applicants must provide a secondary school transcript, letters of recommendation from two teachers of academic subjects and a report from their guidance counselor. Skidmore encourages a campus visit and interview.

Skidmore is test-optional when it comes to standardized testing (SAT, ACT), though the college does require standardized test results from international students who have not attended an English language-based school for at least three years, homeschooled students and students attending secondary schools offering written evaluations without accompanying grades. Applicants for the Porter-Wachenheim Presidential Scholarships in Science and Mathematics are encouraged to submit SAT/ACT and any SAT subject tests in math and science. Of course, students may submit either the SAT or ACT if they feel their standardized testing results best represent their academic potential.

Through its participation in the Higher Education Opportunity Program (HEOP), Skidmore enrolls capable and ambitious New Yorkers who, because of their academic and financial situations, would not otherwise gain admission to the college under traditional requirements. Skidmore's Academic Opportunity Program (AOP) enrolls similar students who reside out of state and/or whose family income slightly exceeds HEOP guidelines. Together, HEOP and AOP are referred to as the Opportunity Program (OP). About 180 OP students are enrolled at Skidmore.

An applicant for admission must complete the Common Application or the Coalition for Access, Affordability and Success Application and submit it with a $65 fee (or a fee-waiver request supported by your guidance counselor). All information for Regular Decision applicants should be postmarked by January 15. Applications from Early Decision applicants should be submitted by November 15 for the Round I Early Decision plan or by January 15 for the Round II Early Decision plan. Regular Decision applicants can convert their applications to Early Decision until February 1. Transfer applicants must submit their applications by November 15 for January admission or by April 1 for September admission.

International students are given special attention throughout the Admissions Process. Applicants whose first language is not English are encouraged to submit the results of the Test of English as a Foreign Language (TOEFL). There are a limited number of need-based financial-aid awards available for outstanding international students.

CAREER SERVICES AND PLACEMENT

Thanks in part to the College's strong internship, student-faculty summer research and off-campus study programming, some 95% of Skidmore students report being employed or pursuing further education one year after graduating. Close to 60% complete or are enrolled in advanced-degree programs within five years of graduation. Career Development offers one-on-one career counseling (in person and virtual) for life; off-campus job and internship interviewing fairs in New York, Boston, Washington, D.C. and Los Angeles; internship openings reserved for Skidmore students; a graduate and professional school expo (nearly 50 institutions); several summer funded internship awards programs, and networking events such as Career Jam and Creative Thought (Net)Works.

FACULTY

277 full-time (304 FTE), 87% with doctoral or highest degree in their field. National and international recognitions include Guggenheim, MacArthur, Pulitzer, and Emmy awards and major fellowships and grants from Fulbright, Getty, NEH, NIH, NSF, and the Andy Warhol Foundation.

SOUTHERN ILLINOIS UNIVERSITY—CARBONDALE

AT A GLANCE

Southern Illinois University Carbondale is: students who are ready to hit the ground running and begin working toward their future career right away; faculty mentors who turn their creative and research experience into classroom learning and mentoring opportunities; staff dedicated to clearing the path for students; alumni who remain dedicated to their alma mater. That's SIU; that's what it means to be a Saluki.

Chartered in 1869, SIU is a comprehensive, state-supported institution with nationally and internationally recognized instructional, research and service programs, and is fully accredited by the North Central Association of Colleges and Schools. SIU offers more than 200 undergraduate majors, minors and specializations; three associate degree programs; nearly 100 baccalaureate degree programs; approximately 80 master's degree programs; more than 30 doctoral programs; and professional degrees in law and medicine. The top 10 majors of new freshman and transfer students are: animal science, automotive technology, aviation flight, biological sciences, business, criminology and criminal justice, mechanical engineering, psychology, radiologic sciences and zoology.

During the 2019–20 academic year, SIU's enrollment was 11,695, which included 8,466 undergraduate students and 3,229 graduate and professional students. Approximately 25% percent of students are minority, and international students account for about 8% of SIU's total enrollment. SIU is a multi-campus university that includes the Carbondale campus as well as the SIU School of Medicine at Springfield.

LOCATION AND ENVIRONMENT

Love at first sight is a common reaction from potential students and their families during a campus visit. SIU is a beautiful, bicycle-friendly, pedestrian-dominated Tree Campus USA. Most freshmen live in residence halls, either next to our 40-acres spring-fed lake or in the Towers. Campus apartments and family housing are also available.

Carbondale is a city of 26,000 with downtown shops, an active live music scene, art galleries, theater and international eateries as well as a shopping mall, strip mall and box stores.

Southern Illinois is a unique geographic area, boasting four large recreational lakes, two great rivers (the Mississippi and the Ohio) and the 270,000-acre Shawnee National Forest—all within easy reach of campus. Numerous unique small towns as well as bike trails, hiking trails and the Shawnee Hills Wine Trail make exploring the region easy and fun. The mid-South climate is ideal for year-round outdoor activities.

CAMPUS FACILITIES AND EQUIPMENT

Hands-on learning, the hallmark of an SIU education, takes place all over campus, including University Farms, art and natural history museums, Shryock Auditorium, three theaters, dozens of outdoor and indoor laboratories with millions of dollars of specialized equipment, 3D printing maker space, art, architecture and design studios, teaching and research greenhouses, Morris Library, Touch of Nature Environmental Center, the Kraft Trading Floor, and the Transportation Education Center.

The SIU Student Center is a hub of student activity, while the Student Recreation Center is the place to go to get fit, with facilities appropriate to the beginner or the fitness expert. The Student Health Center helps keep students healthy in mind and body with wellness programs, doctors' offices and counseling and more.

Coming soon—extensive remodeling to the Communication Building, home of the student newspaper the Daily Egyptian, the WSIU-TV public television station, the student-run River Region Evening News and more.

OFF-CAMPUS OPPORTUNITIES

Southern Illinois University Carbondale is committed to serving statewide, national and international needs. This commitment is reflected in SIU Extended Campus, which offers educational opportunities located off campus and online. SIU Extended Campus is present at 15 military installations and 15 nonmilitary locations across 13 states, offering 27 online degree programs, 8 off-campus programs and 3 military programs.

Off-campus credit programs are designed to meet the educational needs of adults wishing to pursue a degree but who are unable to travel to the Carbondale campus. Faculty members who teach off-campus courses travel to distant sites to teach SIU courses.

All credit courses offered through these programs and those available online carry full SIU academic credit and are taught by faculty members appointed by the academic departments of the university.

ACADEMIC PROGRAMS

SIU emphasizes mentored and independent research and creative activity as integral to hands-on learning. The Research Enriched Academic Challenge (REACH) program offers grants for undergraduate research or creative projects, and the Student Creative Activities Research Forum each year as a place to showcase the results of months of dedicated work. Several departments offer opportunities for students to publish their research or display their art or design projects.

The University Honors Program offers seminar-style courses that promote in-depth study of specific subject areas, from pop culture to physical science—including travel courses to England, Costa Rica and other destinations. All eligible students can participate in study abroad opportunities, and several departments offer field schools.

SIU's Center for Learning Support Services offers tutoring, academic coaching, group study sessions, GRE test prep and more, and anyone on campus, including faculty, can use the Writing Center resources. Disability Support Services offers a wide range of accommodations, including note taking services, test conversion and accessible course materials.

MAJORS AND DEGREES OFFERED

In Agricultural, Life and Physical Sciences, SIU offers courses in: agribusiness economics; animal science; forestry; plant, soil and agricultural systems; biological sciences; chemistry and biochemistry; microbiology; physics; plant biology; zoology; earth systems and sustainability; geology; geography and environmental resources.

In Business and Analytics, SIU offers courses in: accounting; analytics; finance; economics; information systems technologies; management; marketing; hospitality and tourism administration; and public administration.

In Health and Human Services, SIU offers courses in communication disorders and sciences; dental hygiene; health care management; mortuary science and funeral service; nursing; physical therapist assistant; radiologic sciences; rehabilitation services; food and nutrition; kinesiology; public health; recreation professions; social work; psychology; behavior analysis therapy; criminology and criminal justice; paralegal studies; and public safety management.

In Education, SIU offers courses in counseling; quantitative methods; special education; curriculum and instruction; educational administration and higher education; workforce education and development; elementary education; early childhood; and sport administration. Teacher education programs include courses in: agricultural education; art education; biological science education; English teacher education; foreign languages; history teacher education; mathematics education; and physical education teacher education.

In Engineering, Technology and Transportation, SIU offers courses in technology; electronic systems technologies; technical resource management; computer science; mathematics; civil and environmental engineering; electrical and computer engineering; mechanical engineering; energy processes; mining and mineral resources; aviation management and flight; aviation technologies; and automotive technologies.

In Social Sciences, Humanities and Arts, SIU offers courses in art; design; interior design; fashion design; architectural studies; Africana studies; English; history; languages, cultures and international trade; philosophy; cinema and photography; communication studies; music; theater; anthropology; linguistics; political science; and sociology.

In Mass Communication and Media Arts, SIU offers courses in journalism; and radio, TV and digital media.

Many majors are also available as minors, and SIU offers several additional minors and many specializations. Online courses, degree completion and degree programs are increasingly available at SIU. Students who are ready to start college but not ready to commit to a specific major can enroll in SIU's Exploratory Student-Undeclared (EXPU) program. Advisers and career counselors help these students plan their education and careers.

TUITION, ROOM, BOARD, FEES
SIU has eliminated out-of-state tuition. All domestic students pay the same rate. Tuition and fee charges for the 2019–2020 academic year (fall and spring) for students enrolled in 15 or more semester hours were $14,904, and approximately $30,000 for international students. Room and board totaled $10,622. (All costs are subject to change.) The cost of books and school supplies varies among programs. The average cost is $1,100 per academic year.

FINANCIAL AID
More than $222 million in financial aid was distributed to 13,541 SIU students in fiscal year 2018–19 through federal, state and institutionally funded financial aid programs.

To apply for financial aid at SIU, students should complete the Free Application for Federal Student Aid (FAFSA). Applications that are filed before April 1 receive priority consideration for campus-based aid. The FAFSA can be completed electronically at the U.S. Department of Education's website (fafsa.ed.gov). SIU's Federal School Code is 001758.

An important part of student financial aid is on-campus student employment. SIU has one of the largest student employment programs in the country, with about 4,000 students employed each year in a wide variety of job classifications, many of them related to students' career goals.

STUDENT ORGANIZATIONS AND ACTIVITIES
SIU intercollegiate sports teams compete at the NCAA Division I level (football is Division I-FCS). Conference affiliations include the Missouri Valley Conference and the Missouri Valley Football Conference. Intercollegiate sports teams include men's and women's basketball, cross-country, diving, golf, swimming, and track and field; men's baseball and football; and women's softball, soccer and volleyball. The campus has various playing fields, several tennis courts, and a campus lake with a beach and boat dock. SIU's Student Recreation Center offers an Olympic-size pool; indoor tracks; handball/racquetball and squash courts; a climbing wall; weight rooms; basketball, volleyball and tennis courts; outdoor equipment rental; an aerobic area; wallyball; martial arts; and dance and cardio studios.

The Student Center is one of the largest in the United States without a hotel. It holds a bookstore, several restaurants, a craft shop, facilities for bowling and billiards, headquarters for more than 275 student organizations and the student government office, four ballrooms and an auditorium.

SIU makes student involvement easy by supporting more than 200 Registered Student Organizations (RSOs). RSOs include: Greek fraternities and sororities, SIU chapters of national organizations, honors organizations, career and major affiliated groups, political and religious groups, special interest groups, inter- and intramural sports groups, student government and more. Living Learning Communities, on-campus residence halls reserved for students in similar majors, enhance undergraduate campus life.

ADMISSIONS PROCESS
SIU no longer requires submission of SAT and ACT scores for future undergraduate students with a high school GPA of 2.75 or above who have met course pattern requirements. Students enrolling for summer or fall 2021 with a 2.75 or above GPA will be eligible for consideration for most scholarships without submitting standardized test scores.

Course pattern requirements for freshmen are: four years of English, three years of mathematics, three years of laboratory science, three years of social science and two years of electives.

Transfer applicants must have an overall grade point average of at least 2.0 on a 4.0 scale, based on work attempted at all institutions and calculated by SIU grading policies. Transfer applicants must also be eligible to continue at the last institution attended. Some programs have higher admission requirements or require additional screening for admission. Undergraduates can apply online at admissions.siu.edu.

Admission is granted on a rolling basis. Application priority deadlines for freshmen and transfer students are May 1 for the summer term and fall semester, and Dec. 1 for the spring semester. The application fee is $40. For more information, prospective students should contact:

Undergraduate Admissions
Mail Code 4710
1263 Lincoln Drive
Southern Illinois University Carbondale
Carbondale, IL 62901
Phone: 618/536-4405
Email: admissions@siu.edu
Website: www.siu.edu
Facebook: http://www.facebook.com/SouthernIllinoisUniversityCarbondale
Twitter: twitter.com/siuc

SOUTHWESTERN UNIVERSITY

AT A GLANCE

Founded in 1840 and located in scenic Georgetown just 45 minutes north of Austin, Southwestern University was the first institution of higher education in Texas. Today, we are a nationally ranked private university that is home to 1,500 students and 110 faculty from across the U.S. and 13 other countries.

At SU, students learn how to discover, collaborate, communicate, adapt, and problem-solve from multiple perspectives through a rigorous liberal arts and sciences curriculum. These lifelong skills will enrich your life *and* prepare you for 21st-century careers. And because of our students' commitment to community engagement and alumni satisfaction in finding meaningful careers, Southwestern is the only school in Texas included on the Princeton Review's list of Best Schools for Making an Impact, ranking #3 nationally.

Our curriculum incorporates the humanities, fine arts, social sciences, and natural sciences. Our 26 academic departments range from biochemistry and business to foreign languages and computer science. In addition, SU offers seven pre-professional pathways, including pre-engineering, pre-law, and pre-medicine.

Complementing our model of inquiry-based learning, SU students participate in transformative experiences such as study abroad, community-engaged learning, internships, and faculty-mentored research projects. The majority of SU students live on campus and are actively involved in one or more of our 100 student organizations. Students are civic-minded and have volunteered more than 204,000 service hours since 2004. Athletically, the Pirates compete in 20 different varsity sports at the NCAA Division III level, with many more involved in club or intramural sports.

> "My *Southwestern Experience* has been one great opportunity to discover my true passions, hone my strengths, and learn from my weaknesses—all while being part of a community that not only supports me but encourages me to be the best person I can be."
>
> —Taylor Lewis '18

Office of Admission
Southwestern University
1001 E. University Avenue
Georgetown, TX 78626
Telephone: 800.252.3166
E-mail: admissions@southwestern.edu
Website: www.southwestern.edu

LOCATION AND ENVIRONMENT

Southwestern's campus is filled with history and tradition. Located on 700 acres in the heart of Georgetown, SU's towering oak trees, limestone buildings, and lush lawns add to its picturesque feel. It has a strong commitment to sustainability: the campus boasts two LEED-certified buildings, and a student-led initiative earned SU recognition as the first university in the state and one of the first in the nation to be 100% powered by renewable (wind) energy.

Students excel at Southwestern, but they don't compete in a cutthroat atmosphere. Instead, students thrive in a genuinely warm, welcoming environment, in part because the majority of SU students live on campus. All first-year students live in one of four residence halls (one female, one male and two coed dorms). The central dining hub on campus, Mabee Commons, features a variety of meal, snack, and drink choices while the nearby Cove houses a coffee bar and grill that's open late for playing pool or simply hanging out with friends.

Southwestern's location just 30 miles north of Austin provides the best of both worlds for its students. The city of Georgetown, with its historic downtown and the flowing San Gabriel River, provides small-town charm while the capital city is known for its live music, Austin City Limits, SXSW, and world-famous BBQ. Austin was also recently dubbed the "Silicon Valley of the South" for its tech focus and innovation.

CAMPUS FACILITIES AND EQUIPMENT

Southwestern's campus is dotted with a harmonious mix of historic edifices—such as the Cullen Building and Mood–Bridwell Hall, which date back to 1898 and 1908, respectively—and cutting-edge facilities, such as the Fondren–Jones Science Center (FJSC).

Completed in 2019, the Science Center was designed to mirror SU's commitment to interdisciplinary learning and boasts state-of-the-art equipment and facilities, including 20 research labs, a nuclear magnetic resonance spectroscope, a molecular biology center, a kinesiology human performance lab, a plant-growth facility, and a cell-culture facility.

The Alma Thomas Fine Arts Center is our world-class arts education facility. SU students put on major productions in either the Thomas Theater, which seats 750, or the Jones Theater, which features a state-of-the-art rotating stage. Our public art gallery hosts exhibitions by students, alumni, and internationally known artists.

The Robertson Center is where our student–athletes train and where all students can take fitness and recreational classes. Students, faculty, and staff enjoy access to our basketball courts, indoor pool, and recently renovated running track and workout room.

The Academic Mall is the central outdoor gathering place for the Southwestern community. When the weather is nice, which is most of the school year, you'll find students studying in the Adirondack chairs, socializing, or even napping in the hammocks. Faculty will sometimes hold their classes under the oaks, and throughout the year, you can experience music festivals, picnics, and other events on the lawn.

ACADEMIC PROGRAMS

Southwestern promotes lifelong learning through an integrated liberal arts and sciences program that incorporates the humanities, fine arts, social sciences, and natural sciences. All students take a first-year seminar that sets the stage for critical thinking and innovative learning across the disciplines. Other requirements include social justice, foreign language and culture, and fitness. SU's Paideia philosophy encourages students to make connections between courses, culminating in a capstone experience. The curriculum allows for increased student agency, allowing individuals to pursue their passions and explore subjects outside their major. As a sociology and English double major explains, "It's nice to be able to get a taste of how others may see and understand the world in various other disciplines."

One of the unique advantages at SU is the opportunity to conduct faculty-mentored research. It's not uncommon for students to collaborate on or coauthor with their professors conference presentations or publications in scholarly journals.

The Sarofim School of Fine Arts provides a world-class arts education, with alumni going on to careers in performance and production but also in education, medicine, and law. History and political science majors benefit from the school's proximity to Austin, the state capital. In addition, students in our seven pre-professional pathways are accepted into top graduate programs; over the past 10 years, 68% of our pre-health graduates have been accepted to medical, dental, and veterinary school.

SU provides many experiential opportunities, such as community-engaged learning, study abroad, internships, and undergraduate research. The King Creativity Fund provides grants to support "innovative and visionary projects" each academic year. The Research and Creative Works Symposium provides an annual opportunity for students to present original research and creative work in an academic conference setting. SU faculty lead academic programs in England, Spain, Peru, and Argentina as well as a service-learning program in Jamaica. The University also sponsors internships in Washington, DC; arts apprenticeship programs in New York City; and other countless other opportunities for hands-on learning.

MAJORS AND DEGREES OFFERED

Southwestern faculty balance the highest level of scholarship with a dedication to teaching and collaboration with students. Professors intentionally create opportunities for students to think broadly and make connections between different subjects, preparing them for future innovation and leadership. SU's 26 academic departments offer 37 majors, 41 minors, and seven pre-professional pathways that prepare students for success in any professional or personal endeavor.

MAJORS & MINORS

- Animal Studies*
- Anthropology
- Applied Physics
- Architecture & Design Studies*
- Art (Studio)
- Art History
- Biochemistry

- Biology
- Business
- Chemistry
- Chinese*
- Classics
- Communication Studies
- Computational Mathematics
- Computer Science
- Data Science*
- Design Thinking*
- Early Modern Studies*
- Economics
- Education
- English
- Environmental Studies
- Exercise & Sports Studies*
- Feminist Studies
- Financial Economics
- French
- German
- Greek
- Health Studies*
- History
- Independent Major
- International Studies
- Kinesiology
- Latin
- Latin American & Border Studies
- Mathematics
- Music
- Philosophy
- Physics
- Political Science
- Psychology
- Race & Ethnicity Studies*
- Religion
- Sociology
- Spanish
- Theatre

* Indicates Minor Only

PRE-PROFESSIONAL PATHWAYS

- Pre-Dentistry
- Pre-Engineering
- Pre-Law
- Pre-Medicine
- Pre-Ministry
- Pre-Physical Therapy
- Pre-Veterinary Medicine

TUITION, ROOM, BOARD, FEES

Costs for the 2020–2021 Academic Year
Tuition (full-time, 12–19 hours per semester): $45,120
Room and Board (approximate): $11,760

Other Fees:

Part-Time Tuition (per credit): $1,880
Fine Arts Music Fee/Applied Music Lessons (per credit): $180
Vehicle Registration Fee (per semester): $100
Lab Fee (per applicable class): $75

FINANCIAL AID

For a world-class liberal arts and sciences education at one of the best schools in the country, Southwestern provides an excellent return on investment. Scholarships, grants, and work–study help to offset the cost of college, with 98% of SU students receiving financial aid from the University.

Entering students are evaluated for merit scholarships through a holistic review of the admission application. Need-based financial aid is awarded annually and requires the submission of a FAFSA, which is available beginning October 1 prior to the year in which the student will enroll.

STUDENT ORGANIZATIONS AND ACTIVITIES

Southwestern's Center for Career and Professional Development (CCPD) is ranked #1 in Texas and #6 nationally by The Princeton Review. Students begin using career services during their first year to develop the skills needed to obtain a job or to continue their education after graduation. In 2018, Southwestern introduced PirateConnect, in which students develop their professional networks and receive advice about their career interests through connections with alumni. In addition, SU's Alumni Network Mentoring Program matches students and mentors based on their shared academic pursuits and cocurricular activities. At least two-thirds of all students participate in at least one internship for academic credit, and 91% of graduates are employed or in graduate school within 10 months.

The University is home to 100 student organizations ranging from Greek life and intramural sports to honor societies and special-interest groups. Our students discover new passions and develop their skills through engagement and leadership on campus, and our Mosaic initiative helps students reflect on and articulate the value of these cocurricular experiences.

Faculty

Southwestern's faculty truly set the University apart. This diverse and dynamic group consists of innovative leaders and award-winning researchers in their respective fields. Professors often work side by side with students, collaborating on research and even publication.

Southwestern classes are taught by professors, not teaching assistants, and all tenured or tenure-track faculty hold a doctorate or the highest degree in their respective fields. As educators, SU faculty excel at teaching in an intimate and engaged environment: the student–faculty ratio is 12:1, with an average class size of 19 students. The University provides multiple development and training opportunities for its faculty, keeping them on the cutting edge of the latest scholarship.

ADMISSIONS PROCESS

In looking for engaged learners, we consider academic performance—both grades earned and challenging courses in areas of interest—above all else. In addition, strength and depth of writing samples, participation and demonstrated leadership in extracurricular activities, cogency and content of recommendations, and recognition or achievement in national programs allow us to determine how a student will fit within our community. In fall 2020, SU implemented a test-optional admission policy. We also value the opportunity to get to know students better through an optional interview.

Our mission is to treat all applicants fairly and with respect. In all cases, our decisions are reached by multiple individuals reviewing the application and voting in a manner they believe is in the best interest of both the student and the University. We take this responsibility seriously and recognize that we are helping to shape the futures of our applicants.

Students may choose to apply Early Decision (binding), Early Action, or Regular Decision based on the time frame that works best for the student. Students may apply by submitting a Common Application, an Apply Texas application, or Southwestern's application.

Transfer students—students who have completed at least one semester (12 hours or more) following high-school graduation—are welcomed during the fall and spring semesters and may apply using either the Common Application or Apply Texas. Students should submit an essay, an official high-school transcript, official college transcripts from all schools attended, official SAT/ACT scores, and a college official's report. An individual interview allows transfer students to ask questions regarding course transferability.

To learn more, visit southwestern.edu/admission.

ST. JOSEPH'S COLLEGE

AT A GLANCE

Ready. Set. Joe's

Inspire the next you at St. Joseph's College (SJC) with innovative programs developed by industry leaders to give you the competitive edge you're looking for.

Students choose SJC for its small, hands-on classes, meaningful faculty interaction, vibrant student life, commitment to leadership and compassionate service to others. With a 12:1 student-to-faculty ratio, SJC faculty serve as mentors, valued advisers and leaders for more than 5,000 learners who comprise SJC's diverse student body.

With one of the lowest tuition rates of independent colleges and universities in the metropolitan area and a network of more than 42,000 successful alumni, it's no wonder *U.S. News & World Report* consistently names SJC as an outstanding college in the "Regional Universities—Northeast" category in its annual Best Colleges issue.

CAMPUS FACILITIES AND EQUIPMENT

SJC Brooklyn

Since its founding, SJC Brooklyn has been at the center of one of the nation's most diverse academic and cultural cities. Campus amenities include the Dillon Child Study Center, McEntegart Hall Library and the 40,000-square-foot Hill Center that features a 270-seat, NCAA-regulation basketball and volleyball court. SJC Brooklyn also offers off-campus housing for students at the St. George/Clark Residence, New York's leading resource for student housing.

SJC Long Island

SJC Long Island is located on a 32-acre lakeside campus in Patchogue, which was recently named a Great Place in America by the American Planning Association. Campus amenities include the Clare Rose Playhouse, Callahan Library, John A. Danzi Athletic Center and a state-of-the-art 24.8-acre outdoor field complex that is home to several NCAA Division III teams. SJC Long Island is just minutes from the Great South Bay, L.I. MacArthur Airport, Orient Point and many of Long Island's ocean beaches.

SJC Online

Ranked by U.S. News & World Report as one of the nation's "Best Online Bachelor's Programs," SJC Online—the College's fully online campus—offers more than 25 online degree programs for students interested in furthering their academic, personal and professional education goals while taking advantage of the College's resources, discounted tuition rate and generous transfer credit system for online learning.

Service

The SJC community is dedicated to hands-on service and improving the lives of others —you can participate in numerous service projects and fundraising efforts on a local, regional or global level. In addition, the College offers opportunities to participate in an ever-expanding number of mission trips. In recent years, SJC students have traveled to Texas, Washington, D.C., Oklahoma, North Carolina, South Carolina, New Jersey and abroad to Nicaragua, to serve those in need.

Experiential Learning

SJC believes that the college experience isn't limited to its own classrooms. The Office of Career Services facilitates internship opportunities to introduce you to the workforce in locations such as federal, state and local politicians' offices, as well as employers like Microsoft, Google, NASA, Brookhaven National Laboratory, Viacom/MTV and Grant Thornton LLP. The College also provides its students with the opportunity to explore the world via its study abroad programs.

SJC Military and Veteran Affairs

A proud participant in the Post-9/11 GI Bill® Yellow Ribbon Program, SJC has been named a "Best College for Veterans" by Military Times for its excellence in providing opportunities to America's veterans and active military. The College offers special tuition rates for current service members (active duty, guard and reserve) enrolled in undergraduate studies for up to 10 credits per semester. With a dedicated Office of Military and Veteran Services, SJC staff are equipped to provide veteran and military students with support that leads to academic success.

ACADEMIC PROGRAMS

Undergraduate Majors

- Accounting
- Biology
- Biology—Secondary Education
- Business Administration
- Chemistry
- Chemistry—Secondary Education
- Child Study
- Criminal Justice
- Computer Information Technology
- English
- English—Secondary Education
- General Studies
- Health Administration
- History
- History, Social Studies—Secondary Education
- Hospitality and Tourism Management
- Human Relations
- Human Resources
- Human Services
- Journalism and New Media Studies
- Leisure Services Management
- Marketing
- Mathematics
- Mathematics—Secondary Education
- Medical Technology
- Nursing
- Philosophy
- Philosophy and Religious Studies
- Political Science
- Psychology
- Spanish
- Spanish—Secondary Education
- Speech Communication
- Sociology
- Studio Art
- Therapeutic Recreation

Dual Degree/Five-Year Programs

- Accounting, B.S./M.B.A.
- Computer Information Technology, B.S./M.S. Forensic Computing
- Criminal Justice, B.S./M.S. Forensic Computing
- Health Administration/Health Care Management, B.S./M.B.A.
- Human Services, B.S./M.S. Human Services Leadership
- Mathematics Adolescence Education, B.A./B.S. & M.A.
- Mathematics/Computer Science, B.S./Forensic Computing, M.S.
- Organizational Management and Management, Human Resources Management Concentration, B.S./M.S.
- Organizational Management, B.S./M.B.A.
- Psychology, B.A./M.B.A.

Minors

- Accounting
- American Studies
- Art History
- Fine Arts (LI)
- Studio Art
- Biology
- Business Administration
- Chemistry
- Computer Information Technology
- Computer Science
- Criminal Justice
- Digital Design
- Economics
- English
- Environmental Studies
- Film/Media
- History
- Hospitality and Tourism Management
- Human Relations
- Human Resources
- Journalism and New Media Studies
- Labor, Class, Ethics
- Latino Studies
- Marketing
- Mathematics
- Mindfulness and Contemplative Living
- Music (LI)
- Music History
- Peace and Justice Studies
- Philosophy
- Political Science
- Psychology
- Religious Studies
- Sociology
- Speech
- Spanish
- Theatre
- Therapeutic Recreation
- Women's Studies

Graduate Programs

- Childhood or Adolescence Special Education with an Annotation in Severe and Multiple Disabilities, M.A.
- Educational Leadership with Critical Consciousness, M.A.
- Infant/Toddler Early Childhood Special Education, M.A. (SJC Long Island)
- Literacy and Cognition, M.A.
- Literacy/Cognition and Special Education, M.A.
- Creative Writing, M.F.A. (SJC Brooklyn)
- Forensic Computing, M.S.
- Accounting, M.B.A.
- Health Care Management, M.B.A.
- Health Care Management-Health Information Systems Concentration, M.B.A.
- M.B.A.
- Management, Health Care Management Concentration, M.S.
- Management, Human Resources Management Concentration, M.S.
- Management, Organizational Management Concentration, M.S.
- Human Services Leadership, M.S.
- Mathematics Education, M.A. (SJC Long Island)
- Nursing, Adult Gerontology Clinical Nurse Specialist, M.S.
- Nursing, Adult Gerontology Primary Care Nurse Practitioner, M.S.
- Nursing, Nursing Education Concentration, M.S.

CERTIFICATE PROGRAMS

In addition to our undergraduate programs, SJC offers credit-bearing certificates that part-time students can complete in less than a year. These certificates may be earned individually or as part of an undergraduate degree. Certificate programs enable you to delve deeper into your specific interests, help you focus on your career goals and give you a head start when entering the work world. We offer certificate programs (undergraduate and professional studies) in:

- Alcoholism and Addictions Counseling
- Applied Sociology
- Care Management
- Counseling
- Criminology/Criminal Justice
- Gerontology
- Health Care Management
- Home Care Administration
- Hospice
- Human Resources
- Human Services
- Information Technology Applications
- Industrial Organizational Psychology
- Leadership and Supervision
- Management
- Marketing, Advertising, and Public Relations
- Nursing Home Administrator
- Religious Studies
- Training and Staff Development

A Service Members Opportunity College

As a core member of the Service Members Opportunity College Degree Network System, SJC is committed to the transfer of relevant course credits, flexible academic residence requirements and credit learning from appropriate military training and work experience. SJC also offers online, on-and off-site class schedules for its military and veteran students, including class offerings at Fort Hamilton in Brooklyn and Fort Wadsworth in Staten Island, New York. In addition, SJC is an active participant in the Post-9/11 GI Bill® Yellow Ribbon Program, offering veteran students financial support, a monthly housing allowance and an annual stipend for books and school supplies.

TUITION, ROOM, BOARD, FEES

SJC is committed to providing quality education while maintaining one of the lowest private college tuition rates in New York. To supplement the cost of education, scholarships, loans and work-study programs are some of the financial aid options available. Currently, more than 80 percent of SJC students receive some form of financial aid. SJC offers generous scholarships and financial aid packages to students who qualify.

FINANCIAL AID

SJC offers generous scholarships and financial aid packages to students who qualify. For a listing of scholarships available at SJC Long Island, visit http://www.sjc.edu/long-island/admissions/financial-aid/sjc-scholarships. For a listing of scholarships available at SJC Brooklyn, visit http://www.sjcny.edu/brooklyn/admissions/financial/sjc-scholarships.

STUDENT ORGANIZATIONS AND ACTIVITIES

SJC students have an abundance of extracurricular opportunities within reach through the Office of Student Involvement, Leadership and Multicultural Programming. Students can join clubs, athletic teams, organizations and committees that emphasize leadership, community service and effective communication.

ADMISSIONS PROCESS

What are the admissions requirements?

St. Joseph's College is a selective institution. Applicants are evaluated on an individual basis. The College enrolls students who are academically talented and diverse. Successful admissions candidates typically have:

- A high school diploma or its equivalent, or postsecondary transcripts.
- A personal statement or essay of recommendation.
- Standardized test scores that demonstrate the promise of success in college-level courses.
- Two letters of recommendation and a personal essay.

Students can obtain a copy of our application or also apply online, by visiting sjcny.edu/applynow.

When should I apply? When is the application deadline?

SJC admits students on a rolling basis, but there are scholarship priority dates. For the fall semester, the scholarship priority date is March 15 for freshmen and August 1 for transfer students. For the spring semester, the priority date is January 1 for both freshmen and transfer students.

What do I need to submit as a transfer student?

Applications can be submitted by mail or online. Transfer students should request that official transcripts from all former colleges, and a listing of courses in progress, be sent to our Office of Admissions. You are not required to submit a high school transcript if you have an A.A. degree or have successfully completed 24 or more credits from an accredited college. You may transfer a maximum of 64 credits if you have an A.A. degree; certain A.A.S. degrees are also transferable.

ST. LAWRENCE UNIVERSITY

AT A GLANCE

The mission of St. Lawrence University is to provide an inspiring and demanding undergraduate education in the liberal arts to students selected for their seriousness of purpose and intellectual promise.

Nestled in the small upstate New York town of Canton, St. Lawrence is a liberal arts school where students seek insight and knowledge through an education that empowers them to ask better questions, magnify understanding, and put their boldest ideas to the test. For one history major, St. Lawrence is "a university that pushes me to pursue my dreams," a place where "it felt like I was coming home, not leaving home." With roughly 2,400 students and a student-to-faculty ratio of 11:1, St. Lawrence prides itself on a community of faculty and alumni who give everything they have in order to empower and inspire students to make the world a better place. Interdisciplinary studies are encouraged here, and the most popular majors at St. Lawrence include economics, business in the liberal arts, biology, government, and psychology. Even though its location might be considered remote, the school's proximity to the Adirondacks is a huge draw and, as one anthropology major says, "St. Lawrence manages to be a place with countless opportunities and things going on despite being in the middle of nowhere."

LOCATION AND ENVIRONMENT

St. Lawrence University provides a distinctive learning environment, offering 69 majors, 41 minors, and a graduate program in educational leadership. Its First-Year Program has become a national model as a living-learning environment that transitions students successfully out of high school and into college life. Just 80 miles from Ottawa, St. Lawrence is the closest liberal arts college to another country's capital and is only 100 miles from Montréal. St. Lawrence welcomes and celebrates diversity in the widest sense, welcoming students from nearly 60 countries. It also boasts the Collegiate Science and Technology Entry Program, the Ronald E. McNair Scholars Program, and is a partner with the New York State Higher Education Opportunity Program.

CAMPUS FACILITIES AND EQUIPMENT

St. Lawrence University has two libraries, the Owen D. Young Library and Launders Science Library, containing more than 850,000 print and digital volumes, as well as a writing center, a Bloomberg terminal, and ample space for reading, digital scholarship, and research.

Students also enjoy a performing arts center with a recital hall and two theaters as well as an art gallery containing a 7,000-piece art collection and a state-of-the-art, interdisciplinary arts technology facility.

With a commitment to sustainability, St. Lawrence's Johnson Hall of Science was the first LEED Gold certified science building in New York State. In 2014, the University opened Kirk Douglas Hall, a 155-bed residence hall that features 24 geothermal heating/cooling wells and was built to LEED Gold standards. There's also the 15,000-square-foot Sullivan Student Center, which includes space for student activities and meetings, studying, staff offices, and a popular dining facility.

Recreational facilities include a network of trails available for running and cross-country skiing; a 133-station fitness center; a three-story climbing wall; indoor and outdoor tennis courts; and two gymnasium/fieldhouse complexes, one with a 9-lane/400-meter track and five tennis/basketball courts and the other with a 200-meter track, three tennis courts, and 10 squash courts. There's also a pool, equestrian center, golf course, indoor golf facility, AstroTurf field, baseball, soccer and softball fields, and a boathouse for rowing teams located on the St. Lawrence River. The recently-renovated Appleton Arena is home to St. Lawrence's only NCAA Division I sport teams, men's and women's hockey.

OFF-CAMPUS OPPORTUNITIES

St. Lawrence University offers 30 off-campus program sites in over 21 countries, including Australia, Austria, Canada, China, Costa Rica, Czech Republic, Denmark, England, France, Germany, India, Italy, Japan, Jordan, Kenya, Nepal, New Zealand, Spain, Sweden, Thailand, and Trinidad. Students can also direct-enroll at foreign universities through the International Student Exchange Program (ISEP).

The University also offers five off-campus study programs within the United States: Washington, D.C. through The Washington Center; an exchange program with Fisk University in Nashville, Tennessee; the Liberal Arts in New York City, the Adirondack Semester, and a Sustainability Program located just five miles from campus.

ACADEMIC PROGRAMS

The University offers the following degrees: Bachelor of Arts, Bachelor of Science, and Master of Education.

There are 69 majors, which include a number of combined major programs in areas such as environmental studies, economics and biology. Students can even design their own major with faculty approval. The University also offers 41 minors and 61 interdisciplinary programs (see MAJORS AND DEGREES OFFERED.)

St. Lawrence has a number of affiliations, giving students the opportunity to pursue a five-year program in business administration (this program leads to the MBA) and engineering, combining coursework at St. Lawrence with work at other institutions.

Students can also enter a number of affiliate programs leading to degrees in data science, pharmacy, nursing, physician assistance, and physical therapy. There are also tracks for pre-med, pre-vet, pre-dental, and pre-law.

The St. Lawrence distribution requirements involve coursework in seven areas: the arts, social sciences, humanities, natural sciences, human diversity, quantitative/logical reasoning, and environmental literacy. All students are expected to demonstrate writing competence before graduating. The University provides extensive opportunities for honors projects and independent work.

MAJORS AND DEGREES OFFERED

Students have the following major/minors to explore:

African Studies, African-American Studies, Anthropology, Arabic Studies, Art & Art History, Asian Studies, Biochemistry, Biology, Biology-Physics, Business in the Liberal Arts, Canadian Studies, Caribbean, Latin American, and Latino Studies, Chemistry, Chinese Studies, Computer Science, Conservation Biology, Economics, Economics-Mathematics, Education, English, Environmental Studies, Estudios Hispanicos (Spanish), European Studies, Film and Representation Studies, Francophone Studies (French), Gender and

Sexuality Studies, Geology, Geology-Physics, German Studies, Global Studies, Government, History, International Economics, International Studies, Italian Studies, Mathematics, Modern Languages and Literatures, Multifield (self-designed), Music, Native American Studies, Neuroscience, Outdoor Studies, Peace Studies, Performance and Communication Arts, Philosophy, Physics, Psychology, Public Health, Religious Studies, Sociology, Sports Studies and Exercise Science, Statistics.

TUITION, ROOM, BOARD, FEES

2019–20

Tuition:	$ 56,360
Room:	$ 77,880
Board:	$ 6,750
Fees:	$ 405
Total:	$ 71,395

FINANCIAL AID

St. Lawrence awards both merit scholarships and need-based financial aid. More than a third of accepted students receive a merit scholarship, and nearly 59 percent receive need-based aid. St. Lawrence is committed to assisting as many students as possible and recognizes academic and personal achievement in making financial aid decisions. To apply for need-based financial aid, students must file the Free Application for Federal Student Aid (FAFSA) between October 1 and February 1 and request that the results be sent directly to St. Lawrence.

STUDENT ORGANIZATIONS AND ACTIVITIES

All first-year undergraduate students are enrolled in St. Lawrence's nationally-recognized First-Year Program, which places approximately 30 first-year students in small communities that live and learn together while honing critical communication and research skills needed for their academic career

With housing guaranteed all four years, upper-level students may choose to live in traditional residence halls, interest-based theme suites, theme cottages, Greek houses, apartment-style rooms, or senior townhouses.

St. Lawrence provides a full range of services to students, including academic support, counseling, comprehensive career planning, and graduate and professional school guidance.

Students seeking co-curricular activities can choose from over 150 organizations, including everything from student government to interest groups, to arts and culture.

St. Lawrence boasts 34 intercollegiate teams including NCAA Division I teams in men's and women's ice hockey. Most other teams compete in the NCAA's Division III. Club sports are also available, as is participation in a broad range of popular intramural sports.

ADMISSIONS PROCESS

St. Lawrence seeks undergraduates with the capacity to manage a demanding academic regimen successfully. In addition, the ideal student contributes substantially to the quality of community life. The University strives to enroll students who represent the broadest possible range of economic, ethnic, geographic, and social backgrounds. The admissions committee values academic achievement, but ability in athletics, community service, leadership, and the creative arts is also considered a strong indicator of a student's capacity to benefit from his or her time at St. Lawrence. The University is test optional for all domestic students, so students may choose to submit the results of their SAT, ACT, both SAT and ACT, or none. Any submitted tests will be used during the evaluation process. Students are strongly encouraged to plan a campus visit; interviews may be scheduled to occur on campus. In certain areas, off-campus interviews are also an option.

The University makes no requirement of applicants' high school curricula; however, successful applicants generally demonstrate extensive preparation in the humanities, mathematics, the natural sciences, and the social sciences. Advanced Placement, IB, and honors work are looked upon favorably, as they demonstrate the applicant's intellectual curiosity and maturity. These are qualities that are highly sought by the admissions committee.

St. Lawrence uses the Common Application exclusively. The application processing fee is $60, which is waived with an official campus visit. Applicants pursuing Regular Decision should submit all materials by February 1 and will be notified in mid-March of the University's decision. Students whose first choice is St. Lawrence may apply for Early Decision: the priority deadline for Early Decision applications begins on November 1 and goes until February 1. Notification of the early decision is sent approximately two weeks after the application folder is complete.

To request additional information, students should contact:

Office of Admissions and Financial aid
St. Lawrence University
Canton, NY 13617
Visit www.stlawu.edu/admissions

STATE UNIVERSITY OF NEW YORK—COLLEGE OF ENVIRONMENTAL SCIENCE AND FORESTRY

AT A GLANCE

Founded in 1911, the College of Environmental Science and Forestry is a premier environmental college focused on building a sustainable future through research and degree programs in the environmental sciences, engineering, design and management fields.

ESF inspires tomorrow's environmental leaders through discovery and the development of innovative solutions. The college strives to actively inform and involve the greater society on the environmental challenges of our time.

As a small, doctoral granting institution, ESF attracts top-notch faculty who push the boundaries of knowledge in their academic fields. Working side by side with these highly acclaimed faculty on research ranging from restoring polluted lakes to developing new sources of biofuels, our students push those boundaries too. Unlike many research institutions, experience and outstanding teaching is our top priority. This close-knit community of faculty and students share interests and work together to improve the world around them. Together, they learn and work in labs, classrooms, forests and wetlands across ESF campuses and field stations. Other research and educational opportunities take place nationally, internationally, and through our study-abroad programs.

Every ESF major requires some type of experiential learning. Career-related internships provide invaluable work experience and often pave the way to a permanent position after graduation. The College has an extensive internship program to help students with those connections.

These connections include over 40 internships through the New York Department of Environmental Conservation (NYDEC) reserved specifically for ESF students. Alumni have had great success in the NYDEC, notably among them is the former commissioner, Joe Martens. In Martens' words, "ESF is poised like no other College to put people in positions of critical importance around the world." Alumnus, Ana Maria Menezes of the class of 2008, is a perfect example of that. Menezes works as an environmental consultant on adaption to climate change for the U.N. Alumni have been presidents of the Union of Concerned Scientists (UCS), chemists at Georgia-Pacific and Proctor & Gamble, engineers at Bristol Meyer Squibb and Kimberly-Clark, lawyers, forest rangers, hydrologists, podcasters, cartographers and countless other exciting positions.

Students at our main campus enjoy the benefits of a unique partnership with neighboring Syracuse University (SU). These benefits include the ability to take courses at SU, participate in academic and cultural events, the use of athletic and recreational facilities, dining and religious services, discounted tickets to SU NCAA Division 1 sports events and a club offering of over 350 student organizations between both campuses.

What makes ESF truly unique is the strong sense of community between students, faculty, and Alumni. It is a sense of pride, family, and belonging that travels far beyond graduation. "I experience this wherever I go. People are proud to tell me they went to ESF when I see them," says alumnus Joe Martens. Students arrive on campus as first-years and transfers, all eager to change the world for the better. They leave as skilled professionals ready to make a difference. Most start making that difference before they ever leave. It is a tradition of good will, positive energy, creativity and community that threads us together.

LOCATION AND ENVIRONMENT

ESF's main campus is in Syracuse, New York, immediately adjacent to the Syracuse University campus. This offers students a unique "small and large school" environment, where students benefit from small classes and personal attention from faculty on the ESF campus while also having access to the academic facilities, diverse student population, and active social life offered by Syracuse University.

CAMPUS FACILITIES AND EQUIPMENT

ESF campuses include both the urban setting found on our main campus and more than 25,000 acres of forest and wetlands at seven regional campuses and field stations throughout the state. The College features a number of sustainability projects including a LEED platinum-rated Gateway Center housing the trailhead cafe and LEED gold-rated dorms. Computing, library, dining and sports facilities are available at ESF and neighboring Syracuse University.

OFF-CAMPUS OPPORTUNITIES

Syracuse is a medium-size city and a "college town" featuring many cultural and entertainment options. Students often attend NCAA Division I sports events at the Syracuse University Carrier Dome. The downtown area is a five-minute shuttle bus ride from campus, and the city culture is student-friendly. The largest shopping mall in the northeast (Destiny USA) is in Syracuse. Students with vehicles enjoy hiking in local and regional parks nature preserves and trail systems. Among these are Green Lakes State Park, Onondaga County Park and Clark Reservation. For those looking for winter sports recreation, there are several downhill and cross-country skiing locations within a forty-five minute drive of campus. Trips are frequently scheduled to the Adirondack State Park through student organizations for camping, rock climbing, hiking, biking and canoeing excursions among others.

SUNY: ENVIRONMENTAL SCIENCE AND FORESTRY COLLEGE

ACADEMIC PROGRAMS

The faculty at ESF are leaders in their fields as both professors and accomplished researchers. A highly selective Honors Program is offered, focused on undergraduate research opportunities. Study-abroad programs take students to a variety of countries, providing opportunities to conduct research in a range of ecosystems. ESF's long-standing partnership with SU provides students with the opportunity to take classes there as part of their ESF degree program with access to hundreds of elective courses in the liberal arts and management fields among many others.

MAJORS AND DEGREES OFFERED

ESF offers more than 50 associate's, bachelor's, master's and doctoral degree programs focused on sustainability and the science, design, engineering and management of our environment and natural resources. All degree programs offer research and experiential learning opportunities. Popular programs include wildlife science, forestry and natural resources management, environmental science and conservation biology. Our engineering programs include environmental resource engineering, biochemistry, biotechnology, bioprocess engineering and paper engineering. Communication around the environment is also very important to us. Environmental studies, environmental interpretation and landscape architecture all focus on telling the story of our environment in different ways ranging from multimedia, to traditional interpreter positions to designing the sustainable parks and cities of the present and future. Our environmental health program prepares students to address challenges to human health from toxins, and pollution among other byproducts of modern society. We prepare students to address almost every issue related to the environment, its protection, the health of the plants, animals and humans living in it, and planning for a sustainable future.

TUITION, ROOM, BOARD, FEES

Tuition, room, board and fees for the 2019–20 academic year total $27,635 for New York state residents and $37,745 for out-of-state residents.

FINANCIAL AID

ESF has been ranked among the top 50 "Best Buy" colleges in the nation. ESF National Scholarships offset out-of-state costs up to $8,000 per year for qualified applicants. The College awards approximately half of its scholarships based on academic potential and half based on financial need. Last year, undergraduates received more than $18 million from all sources, including more than $7 million in scholarships and grants. Students file the Free Application for Federal Student Aid (FAFSA) for financial aid consideration, with a priority deadline of Feb. 1. Admissions applications must be submitted by Feb. 1 for academic (merit) scholarship consideration.

STUDENT ORGANIZATIONS AND ACTIVITIES

Students can participate in over 350 clubs and organizations jointly offered between ESF and SU. ESF offers intercollegiate athletics teams in basketball, soccer, golf, cross country, track, fishing and timber sports. Community service is an important part of the student culture at ESF. Many student activities focus on outdoor recreation and travel.

ADMISSIONS PROCESS

Admission is selective and the College attracts a diverse and academically qualified entering class. An Early Decision (first choice) application plan is offered. See www.esf.edu/admissions. Students apply to the specific major that interests them and most programs require strong grades in high school mathematics and science. SAT/ACT scores are also important, along with a demonstrated interest in sustainability and the environment.

ESF attracts a large number of transfer students (more than 250 per year) in addition to the entering first-year class, and a minimum college GPA of 2.80 or higher is generally required for transfer admission.

Students most often use the Common Application when applying, and a campus visit is strongly encouraged.

SWARTHMORE COLLEGE

AT A GLANCE

Swarthmore College is a highly selective college of liberal arts and engineering located about a half an hour outside of Philadelphia, in a charming suburb of Pennsylvania. The college is founded on the value of striving towards the greater good and empowers students to intertwine their academic curiosity with social responsibility and a sense of purpose.

Swarthmore's faculty and staff are fully behind this mission, from the world-class professors who engage directly with students in meaningful ways, to the staff in the dining hall, coffee bars, and libraries who can come to feel like friends. Close relationships with community members fuel life at Swarthmore. Many students collaborate with their professors on joint research projects, and the exchange of intellectual ideas between students and faculty is enhanced by small class sizes. The College's Honors Program extends the depth of free and critical discussion of ideas via small-group seminars.

One trademark of a "Swattie" is the desire to learn for the sake of knowledge and the pursuit of interests inside and outside the classroom. Swatties can be astrophysicists who write poetry, economists who love to code, and athletes with a passion for choreography. Almost half of the student body enjoys playing sports, whether it's at the competitive Division III level, or in more casual club and intramural sports teams.

LOCATION AND ENVIRONMENT

The beauty of Swarthmore's 425-acre campus is immediately striking. Students draw inspiration from the meticulously-tended gardens, stunning arboretum specimen trees, and variety of woodsy trails. Each fall, *The Graduate* is screened on the lawn in front of Parrish Hall, allowing students to contemplate life beyond Swarthmore. Swatties enjoy connecting to the wider world, with Philadelphia less than 30 minutes away, and New York City and Washington, D.C. within a 90-minute train ride. The close-knit campus community allows all students to access the college's wide array of opportunities. The bottom line: Swarthmore's sense of place prepares you for anything and everything. Our alumni are equipped to make the most of where they've been—and make sense of what they haven't yet seen.

CAMPUS FACILITIES AND EQUIPMENT

Swarthmore provides a dynamic array of arts spaces for students to enjoy or stage a performance—including professional theater facilities. Students explore their interests across campus by learning a new dialect through immersion in the Language Center, making sense of the stars in the Peter Van de Kamp Observatory, and connecting their studies to their communities through the Lang Center for Civic & Social Responsibility. The new Maxine Frank Singer Hall brings together the Biology, Engineering, and Psychology Departments, featuring cutting-edge labs and collaborative work spaces. The Matchbox fitness facility offers a multifaceted, modern approach to wellness, recreation, and community. Whether students are teaming up to design a prototype in the MakerSpace, or chatting with friends about summer research over a meal at Sharples, the abundance of campus resources permeates life at Swarthmore.

OFF-CAMPUS OPPORTUNITIES

Swarthmore belongs to the tri-college consortium, which links to nearby Bryn Mawr and Haverford Colleges both academically and socially. In addition, students can take courses at the University of Pennsylvania, a short train ride away. These extensions of the Swarthmore experience allow students to expand their intellectual and social capital, such as watching a play at Haverford, connecting with a Penn professor about an internship, or practicing with an a capella group at Bryn Mawr. The College offers shuttle vans to the other tri-co schools, community service sites, local restaurants and shops, and more. The train station on campus invites students to explore the rich cultural tapestry of center city Philadelphia. In addition, students who are interested in becoming physicians with expertise in health policy, population health, and community engagement benefit from Swarthmore's early acceptance program with Thomas Jefferson University's Sidney Kimmel Medical College Scholars Program. An integral part of the partnership allows students to work alongside Jefferson faculty engaged in a variety of local and global health issues.

ACADEMIC PROGRAMS

The interdisciplinary nature of the college's curriculum allows unique opportunities for academic discovery. For example, Swarthmore offers a wide array of courses in distinct and intersecting disciplines, with courses such as *Race, Gender, Class and Environment* which draws from multiple departments and programs, including Black Studies, Sociology/Anthropology, Gender and Sexuality Studies, Global Studies, and Environmental Studies. Students have the chance to craft special majors, including recent examples such as Medical Anthropology, Behavioral Economics, and Sustainable Development Studies. Swarthmore's Educational Studies Program leads to Pennsylvania secondary school certification. All students have significant undergraduate research opportunities in the natural sciences, social sciences, humanities, and engineering.

One hallmark of the college's academic program is that first-year students take their fall semester courses pass-fail. Swarthmore encourages its students, many of whom spent their high school careers concerned about their GPA, to focus on learning for the sake of knowledge. The pass-fail semester provides a true sense of discovery for students, as they are empowered to experiment with new fields. Many students identify potentially life-changing passions, while knowing that they're free to make academic mistakes in the process. Swarthmore recognizes that adjusting to college is a learning process, and achieving a balance between engaging in the campus community both inside and outside of the classroom is vital.

Some Swatties decide to take a deep dive into their area of interest. Those students find their intellectual home in Swarthmore's distinctive Honors Program. Honors seminar classes feature small groups of students working collaboratively with faculty to explore topics through spirited debate and thoughtful exploration of ideas. At the close of their senior year, Honors Program candidates are evaluated by visiting examiners, such as Federal Reserve economists and directors of world-class theater companies. You know you've truly mastered a topic when it's time to discuss your ideas with brilliant strangers.

MAJORS AND DEGREES OFFERED

Swarthmore College awards two degrees, the Bachelor of Arts and the Bachelor of Science. The College offers the following courses of study:

- Art and Art History
- Asian Studies
- Astronomy
- Biology
- Black Studies
- Chemistry and Biochemistry
- Classics
- Cognitive Science
- Comparative Literature
- Computer Science
- Dance
- Design Your Own Major
- Economics
- Educational Studies
- Engineering
- English Literature
- Environmental Studies
- Film and Media Studies
- Gender and Sexuality Studies
- Global Studies
- History
- Interpretation Theory
- Islamic Studies
- Latin American and Latino Studies
- Linguistics
- Mathematics and Statistics
- Medieval Studies
- Modern Languages and Literatures (including Arabic, Chinese, French, German, Japanese, and Russian)
- Music
- Peace and Conflict Studies
- Philosophy
- Physics
- Political Science
- Psychology
- Religion
- Sociology and Anthropology
- Spanish
- Theater

TUITION, ROOM, BOARD, FEES

For 2019–2020, the College charges, including tuition, room, board, and student activity fee, amount to $70,744. The average aid award for the Class of 2023 was $56,326. The College's Quaker roots manifest themselves in a cash-free campus; the annual activity fee covers not only the usual student services—health, library, laboratory fees, for example—but everything from digital printing and laundry to sporting events, campus movie screenings, and dance performances.

Tuition: $56,256

On-Campus Room and Board: $16,088

FINANCIAL AID

Swarthmore's commitment to financial aid and access is at the core of our educational mission. We understand that students are admitted from a variety of economic backgrounds. The College strives to make it possible for all admitted students to attend Swarthmore, regardless of their ability to pay, and meets 100% of determined need for all admitted students. If you are a U.S. citizen, permanent resident, or undocumented/DACA student graduating from a U.S. high school, the decisions about your admission to Swarthmore and your financial aid eligibility are made independently.

Nearly 60 percent of the student body received need-based Swarthmore Scholarship aid from an overall financial aid budget of more than $43 million. Our financial aid offers consist of grants (which do not need to be repaid) and the expectation that students will work in a part-time, campus-based job. Although Swarthmore financial aid awards are loan-free, some families choose to borrow a loan to pay a portion of the educational expenses.

STUDENT ORGANIZATIONS AND ACTIVITIES

With more than 100 student clubs and organizations on campus, dozens of community service groups, 22 Division III varsity athletic teams, free lectures and performances occurring daily on campus, and full course loads, Swarthmore students actively engage in pursuits that matter to them.

ADMISSIONS PROCESS

First-year applicants may apply to Swarthmore via Common Application, Coalition Application, or QuestBridge Application. Swarthmore does not have a preference among any of our application options. Please submit only one application in an application year.

Required Materials

- Common Application, Coalition Application, or Questbridge Application
- Swarthmore College Short Answer
  - As part of the Common or Coalition Application, you will be asked to submit no more than 250 words in response to the following short answer question (Questbridge applicants are asked this question on our Questbridge Conversion Form): "Please write about why you are interested in applying to and attending Swarthmore."

- $60 application fee or fee waiver
- School report
- Guidance counselor recommendation
- High school transcript
- Midyear grades: If your school does not have midyear grades, please provide a mid-year progress report from your teachers.
- Self-reported or official standardized test scores
- Two academic-subject teacher evaluations

Optional Materials

- You may request an on-campus or off-campus interview. You may interview before submitting your application.
- You may submit a creative supplement with art, music, dance, theater, or creative writing materials. We accept supplements exclusively through SlideRoom, which provides instructions for submitting materials online, including a video tutorial. Please use the SlideRoom link that matches your choice of application. Submitting additional materials is strictly optional, and is at no additional charge.
- Please review financial aid application instructions and deadlines for first-year applicants.

TEMPLE UNIVERSITY

AT A GLANCE

Temple University attracts some of the most diverse and motivated minds from across the nation and around the world. The unstoppable energy of our students and faculty defines Temple and generates success in our academic and athletic programs, research efforts, and contributions to the arts. Temple's real-world impact is driven by innovative approaches to admissions and affordability; a campus transformation; plentiful creative and research opportunities; rigorous academic programs; an indelible bond with the city of Philadelphia; and groundbreaking work in science, research and technology.

As Philadelphia's public research university, Temple is home to nearly 40,000 students; and offers more than 570 academic programs in 17 schools and colleges, on eight campuses, including locations in Japan and Italy.

More than 3,800 distinguished faculty members; top art, business, dental, law and medical schools; five professional schools; and dozens of renowned programs make Temple an academic powerhouse. Students enjoy the advantages and atmosphere of a large urban, public research university with the individualized attention that comes from a 13-1 student-faculty ratio.

The majority of first-year students live on campus, where they are steps away from class; a state-of-the-art TECH Center; Charles Library; fitness and recreation facilities; dining options such as cafés, dining halls and food trucks; and the many arts, cultural, sports and scholarly events that happen daily at Temple and throughout the city.

Temple's ongoing physical transformation ensures students have all that they need on campus. The newest living and learning residence, the 27-story Morgan Hall, offers unparalleled views of the Philadelphia skyline. The 247,000-square-foot Science Education and Research Center supports student and faculty opportunities for discovery and innovation.

Located at the heart of Main Campus, the new, state-of-the-art Charles Library is a four-story testament to innovation and excellence. A 21st-century collaboration space that features a robotic book retrieval system as well as technology-enhanced spaces devoted to data visualization and 3D printing, the library is a place where students can learn, connect and develop lifelong skills.

In 2015, Temple achieved the R1 Carnegie Classification of Institutions of Higher Education, placing it among the most active research universities in the nation.

Temple's influence also extends around the globe, with long-standing campuses in Tokyo and Rome; programs in London, Beijing and other locations; and a worldwide alumni network of more than 320,000. Our 3,000 international students at Temple's Main Campus hail from more than 127 countries.

No matter their background, Temple students—nicknamed Owls—are drawn to the university's vibrant location in the heart of Philadelphia. The professional world is a walk or subway ride away, and countless possibilities exist for hands-on learning and internships in business, healthcare, education, the arts and beyond.

By living and learning in an urban environment, Temple students are well prepared for the world. Employers laud Owls for their tenacity, teamwork and talent. Students also have access to an immense alumni network for guidance, job opportunities and mentoring.

LOCATION AND ENVIRONMENT

Temple students enjoy a striking, modern campus in one of the country's liveliest urban centers. Philadelphia—the first World Heritage City in the U.S.—is home to history, arts and culture, technology and innovation, healthcare, and many other fields and interests. Opportunities for learning, whether through a class, an internship or a research project, abound.

Nearly 75% of first-year students live on campus. They walk to class, relax on the grass surrounding the Bell Tower, catch a film at our on-campus movie theater, get lunch at one of the many food trucks, and workout at several different fitness facilities. Temple's campus has many residence halls, and students can choose a living and learning community tailored to their major or interest.

CAMPUS FACILITIES AND EQUIPMENT

Whether in the glass-blowing studio or the virtual balance lab, Temple students are immersed in world-class facilities. The Science Education and Research Center is one of the university's newest buildings and home to 68 research and teaching labs and leading-edge technologies such as clean rooms, powerful supercomputers and a scanning tunneling microscope that allows scientists to study matter on the nanoscale.

In the TECH Center—one of the largest student computing labs in the country—students can collaborate in breakout rooms, edit video in specialized labs, get assistance from the 24-hour help desk or work on one of 700 computers. There are also more than 200 other computer labs on campus.

Temple's libraries host intrepid, curious students and scholars. With the equivalent of more than four million bound volumes and an extensive special collection of rare books and archives, Temple's libraries are among the top research libraries in North America. Our brand-new Charles Library hosts cutting-edge makerspaces like the Scholars Studio, which features 3-D printing capabilities, high-end computing and a virtual reality studio.

In addition, the university always has an eye toward building a premier student life experience through facilities such as the Aramark STAR (Student Training and Recreation Complex). The facility, which opened in fall 2017, includes recreation space, a 70-yard turf field and a juice bar, as well as classrooms and clinical training areas for the College of Public Health.

OFF-CAMPUS OPPORTUNITIES

Temple's Main Campus is located 1.5 miles from the center of Philadelphia. For Temple students, the city blends seamlessly with their studies. Those studying stormwater management work hands-on with the water department, art students restore fading historical signs on older buildings, and political science majors learn from civic leaders.

As much as the city is a classroom, it's also a place of adventure. Students can explore more than 100 museums, a thriving restaurant scene, numerous professional sports teams and the largest landscaped urban park in the nation.

Owls interested in experiencing different languages and cultures by studying abroad have dozens of options. They can study at Temple campuses in Tokyo or Rome or join summer programs in Brazil, South Africa, Spain and beyond. Many of the programs tie in to areas of study, like business students studying real markets in hubs such as Paris and Mumbai, or art and architecture students studying among the masterpieces in Rome.

ACADEMIC PROGRAMS

Temple has a long tradition of self-made success. The university started in 1884 as a night school so students who worked during the day could keep their jobs. Though much has changed, Temple's heritage still drives the work ethic of its students. Owls turn opportunities into accomplishments. World-class labs are the staging areas for world-changing ideas. A classroom doubles as a tech startup's boardroom. Professors mentor students through graduate school and beyond. And it's all because of the uncommon drive Temple students and faculty share.

Students customize their college life in numerous ways: living and learning communities, an immersive honors program, interdisciplinary majors, creative and research grants, internships, and career preparation and placement.

Temple encourages the spirit of entrepreneurship universitywide, so Owls know how to thrive no matter their course in life. To help foster such skills, annual innovation and business idea competitions are open to the entire Temple community, and all students have access to mentors, resources and guidance to develop their business ideas and plans.

Temple also propels students into top graduate programs through challenging academic work, research opportunities and close partnerships with professors.

MAJORS AND DEGREES OFFERED

Students passionate about learning are attracted to Temple because of its variety of academic programs: More than 570 are offered, including more than 140 bachelor's degree programs. Students who need time to decide on a major work with advisors and professors to discover their strengths and options.

TUITION, ROOM, BOARD, FEES

Tuition and fees for the 2019–2020 academic year were approximately $16,970 for Pennsylvania residents and $29,882 for out-of-state residents (tuition rates vary by school or college). Room and board for the same period was about $12,188, on average.

FINANCIAL AID

Temple is known for its innovation in student loan debt reduction and college affordability. Each year, the university awards more than $100 million in scholarships. A variety of programs are available and 70% of first-year students receive need-based financial aid. No separate application is necessary.

Applicants for need-based aid must file the Free Application for Federal Student Aid, also called FAFSA. Transfer students must file a financial aid transcript, even if they have received no aid from their previous school.

Each year, 93% of first-year students sign up for Temple's Fly in 4 program, which helps students limit their debt by graduating in four years. As a part of Fly in 4, Temple awards four-year grants to 500 eligible students to reduce their need to work for pay. Temple also helps Owls understand their finances through courses, workshops and a money management website.

STUDENT ORGANIZATIONS AND ACTIVITIES

Temple's student body is known for its diversity: over 127 countries are represented at the university. Students come from all over the world and with different interests, but find at Temple corners all their own thanks to a wide range of programs and perspectives. It's with that experience that students gain a global understanding that prepares them for the world that awaits them after college.

With more than 300 student clubs and organizations on campus, students have no shortage of opportunities to explore their interests and champion their beliefs. The university also hosts 18 Division I sports teams and 30 intercollegiate sports clubs.

The Temple marching band's renditions of popular songs have earned the team national attention. In 2017, the Temple Student Government was ranked among the "most active" student governments in the country. And if students seek an organization that doesn't exist, they're encouraged to create their own.

Throughout the year, students can attend academic talks and panels, art exhibits, cultural events, films, music and dance performances, theater productions, and sports. There are several large venues for concerts and shows in the city and on campus, including the historic Temple Performing Arts Center and the university's 10,200-seat entertainment complex, which also hosts its NCAA Division I basketball games.

To keep students healthy and strong, Temple offers multiple indoor and outdoor sports, recreation, and fitness facilities, including an outdoor volleyball court, a rock-climbing wall, running tracks, pools, and several locations for weightlifting and classes.

ADMISSIONS PROCESS

Temple Option is an innovative admissions path for talented students who may not perform well on standardized tests. If students choose to apply through Temple Option, they answer brief essay questions instead of submitting SAT or ACT scores. Temple Option reflects the university's commitment to provide talented, motivated students of all backgrounds opportunities for high-quality college experiences.

Temple's admissions process is holistic: Every aspect of a student's academic history is considered. For first-year student admissions, high school grades, standardized test scores (sent directly from the appropriate testing agencies) or Temple Option responses, and other factors (such as a required essay, recommendations, extracurricular activities, work or leadership experience, and other personal circumstances) are considered.

Typically, students with B+ averages or better in strong, college-preparatory curricula in grades nine through 12 and in the top 30 percent of their graduating classes are accepted. For students submitting test scores, admitted students in fall 2019 averaged a 27 composite on the ACT, and a 1238 SAT score.

Temple has Regular Decision and Early Action plans for the fall semester. The Early Action deadline is Nov. 1, with notifications scheduled for mid-January (or earlier). The Regular Decision deadline is Feb. 1.

Those who apply as first-year students are automatically considered for merit-based scholarships and honors.

The application fee is $55, and most students apply online through Temple or the Common Application.

Temple University welcomes transfer applicants. Applicants are considered transfer students if they have attempted 15 or more college-level credits after high school.

Apply to Temple at admissions.temple.edu/apply or via the Common Application. If you have questions, visit admissions.temple.edu; email askanowl@temple.edu; or find Temple Admissions on Twitter, Instagram or Snapchat: @admissionsTU.

TROY UNIVERSITY

AT A GLANCE

Troy University, based in Alabama, is a public university founded in 1887. Through a network of locations and a robust online offering, TROY serves both traditional students and adult learners.

Troy University, based in Alabama, is a public university founded in 1887. Through a network of locations and a robust online offering, TROY serves both traditional students and adult learners with a worldwide enrollment of more than 20,000. TROY operates four campuses in Alabama—Troy, Dothan, Montgomery and Phenix City-and locations in 7 states, in both Japan and Korea and partnerships with universities in China, Vietnam and Malaysia.

TROY is accredited by the Southern Association of Colleges and Schools Commission on Colleges, and offers degree programs at the Associate's, Bachelor's, Master's and Doctoral level.

Founded as a college to train teachers, Troy University has today grown into a thriving international university that enrolls more than 1,000 international students, representing more than 76 countries. Also highlighting the University's international focus, TROY is home to Alabama's only Confucius Institute that maintains a statewide mission of educating about the Chinese language, culture and history and forging economic development ties between the state and China.

Troy University offers degree programs in high-demand fields across its five colleges—the College of Arts and Sciences; the Sorrell College of Business; the College of Communication and Fine Arts; the College of Education; and, the College of Health and Human Services.

Troy University has more than 160,000 alumni worldwide and the University's Alumni Association has 65 local alumni chapters throughout the United States and international chapters in China, Russia and Vietnam.

LOCATION AND ENVIRONMENT

The complete university experience may be found at Troy University's beautiful, historic campus in Troy, Ala. The Troy, Ala. campus provides top-notch academic programs as well as experiences that shape careers and lives. Students on the Troy Campus enjoy more than 200 clubs, Greek organizations and philanthropic groups, as well study abroad programs, Division I athletics, an honors program and more.

The Troy Campus also offers a wide variety of residence halls, including apartment style units. The surrounding city of Troy is a charming Southern city with a picturesque town square featuring unique boutiques and food options.

Troy's Dothan Campus is located between Dothan and Fort Rucker and serves primarily adult learners through day, evening and weekend classes. The campus is home to R. Terry Everett Hall, named in honor of the longtime Alabama Congressman from the state's Wiregrass region, and includes in its library collection Everett's Congressional papers. The Wiregrass Archives, featuring historical photos and documents from the region, is also located at the campus.

The University's Montgomery Campus is located in the heart of the state's capital city, and has been a catalyst to revitalization within the downtown area. The campus' administrative offices are located in the former Whitley Hotel, which was renovated to include office and classroom space in what is now known as Whitley Hall. Another revitalization project that is a centerpiece of the campus is the Davis Theatre for the Performing Arts, a 1,200-seat theatre and performing arts venue which features performing groups from throughout the region. The campus is also home to the Rosa Parks Library and Museum, which is located on the site of Mrs. Parks' 1955 arrest that sparked the Montgomery Bus Boycott. The museum pays tribute to Mrs. Parks' legacy of courage and celebrates the people and events of the 381-day boycott, which led to the integration of the city's public transportation system.

The Phenix City Campus, includes a location on the banks of the Chattahoochee River, which has served as a catalyst for development along the East Alabama city's riverfront. The Phenix City campus serves primarily adult learners from East Alabama and neighboring Columbus, Georgia.

CAMPUS FACILITIES AND EQUIPMENT

The Troy Campus offers a full complement of facilities for students, including numerous on-campus computer labs and study facilities, a dining hall complete with numerous dining options; the Trojan Student Center, which includes activity space for events, bookstore, and food court, a student fitness and wellness center, a comprehensive library; numerous residence halls that provide a variety of living options; fraternity and sorority houses; athletic facilities, including the 30,000-seat Veterans Memorial Stadium and Trojan Arena, which is home to men's and women's basketball.

Students also can take advantage of opportunities that will help them hone their skills and enhance their academic success. The John W. Schmidt Center for Student Success provides programs and services that enhance students' academic achievement, personal and social growth, campus and civic engagement and persistence to graduation.

ACADEMIC PROGRAMS

Academic programs include a range of options in business, management and accounting, human resource management, criminal justice, education, psychology and counseling, social work, nursing, public administration and political science, athletic training, theatre and dance, art and design, and sport, tourism and hospitality management, among many others.

MAJORS AND DEGREES OFFERED

Troy University offers more than 225 undergraduate and graduate academic programs and concentrations. Accredited by the Southern Association of Colleges and Schools Commission on Colleges to award associate, baccalaureate, master's, education specialist and doctoral degrees.

With a student-first philosophy, Troy University continues to serve both traditional college-aged students and adult learners with quality academic programs, in high-demand fields, through its five colleges—the Sorrell College of Business, the College of Communication and Fine Arts, Arts and Sciences, Education and Health and Human Services.

TUITION, ROOM, BOARD, FEES

Undergraduate tuition for the 2019–2020 academic year is $325 per credit hour for in-state students, and $650 per credit hour for out-of-state students. Graduate tuition for the 2019–2020 academic year is $425 per credit hour for in-state students and $850 per credit hour for out-of-state students.

Fees charged each semester include:

- General University fee—$42 per credit hour
- Registration fee—$50 per semester
- Registration fee (Phenix City, Montgomery and Dothan)—$25 per term
- Student Facility fee (Troy Campus only)—$100 per semester in fall and spring semesters and $50 in summer semester.

FINANCIAL AID

Troy University is committed to providing exceptional service to students and their families who apply for financial assistance. The Office of Financial Aid offers a variety of services and programs designed to help you find ways to meet the costs of education. Additional information on the various types of financial aid and their requirements can be found at www.troy.edu/financialaid.

A number of scholarship opportunities are also available through the University that can help students finance their education. For more information on available scholarships and their requirements, visit www.troy.edu/scholarships.

STUDENT ORGANIZATIONS AND ACTIVITIES

The University's Troy Campus is home to a diverse student population, including students from across the United States and more than 1,000 international students representing more than 76 countries.

Students on the Troy Campus have a variety of opportunities to enrich their college experience. Troy students have nearly 200 student organizations from which to choose, including fraternities and sororities, academic/professional clubs, honor societies, leadership and service groups, political and special interest organizations, religious groups, performing groups and campus publications.

One of the campus' largest student organizations is the Sound of the South Marching Band, which includes students from each of the University's five colleges. A variety of performing ensembles are also available through the John M. Long School of Music.

Leadership opportunities are available through participation in the Student Government Association, the Freshman Forum, Trojan Ambassadors, and IMPACT orientation leaders, among others.

In addition, the Office of Service Learning and Civic Engagement, a part of the John W. Schmidt Center for Student Success, connects Troy University students to applied learning opportunities where students can develop skills in leadership, project management and civic action, while making a difference in the local community. Current student Service Learning and Civic Engagement initiatives include: poverty and hunger, sustainability, healthy futures and community action and outreach.

ADMISSIONS PROCESS

Undergraduate Admission: High School graduates may be admitted as Freshmen to Troy University on the basis of acceptable high school records (a 2.0 Grade Point Average) and scores achieved on the American College Testing Program (minimum composite of 20 on the ACT) or the Scholastic Aptitude Test (minimum composite of 950 or 1030 if taken since March 2016). Applicants who are 25 years of age or older are not required to submit ACT/SAT scores for admission to the university. All applicants who are graduates of accredited high schools must submit an official transcript showing graduation and a minimum of fifteen Carnegie units, with three or more units in English. Of the units presented, eleven must be in academic courses. Applicants who are graduates of non-accredited secondary schools may be admitted provided they meet the same requirements as students from accredited schools. Pending judgment of the Admissions Committee, these students are expected to complete satisfactory academic work.

Undergraduate students applying to Troy University will be charged a $30 application fee.

Graduate Admission: Those students wishing to apply to Troy University to pursue graduate degrees must submit a letter of recommendation and final official transcripts from all colleges/universities attended, including the degree granted and award date. Graduate students must submit official test score results for the GRE, the MAT or the GMAT.

Graduate students applying to Troy University will be charged a $50 application fee.

Apply online today at troy.edu/admissions.

UNION COLLEGE

AT A GLANCE

Union College is one of the nation's oldest and most distinguished liberal arts colleges. Chartered by the state of New York in 1795, Union is a leader in offering an innovative, integrated liberal arts education that fully embraces STEM and emphasizes collaboration with students and faculty through small classes, undergraduate research, interdisciplinary and international study, and service learning. We provide a rigorous, holistic, and immersive residential education guided by our mission: "to develop every student to lead with wisdom, empathy and courage, in ways large and small, now and across multiple tomorrows."

LOCATION AND ENVIRONMENT

Designed by Joseph-Jacques Ramée, the campus includes the 16-sided Nott Memorial, a historic landmark, and Jackson's Garden, a certified natural wildlife habitat. Union is located on 130 acres in the revitalized city of Schenectady, part of New York's Capital Region. Steps from campus, the city features a lively mix of restaurants, cafés, shops, theaters and a popular weekly greenmarket. The region's rich cultural heritage, thriving high-tech industry and diverse economy offer opportunities for student/faculty research, internships and jobs. Union is a 20-minute drive from Albany International Airport and a short walk or drive from the Schenectady bus and train stations. It is within easy reach of New York City (a 3-hour drive), Boston (3 hours), Montreal (4 hours), and rural and wilderness areas.

CAMPUS FACILITIES AND EQUIPMENT

Union recently completed the largest and most ambitious project in its history—a $100 million makeover and expansion of its science and engineering center. A centerpiece of the striking new Integrated Science and Engineering Complex is Ainlay Hall, an arc-shaped building featuring floor-to-ceiling glass walls and a four-story lightwell that allows individuals to glimpse the work of various disciplines. It is home to labs and classrooms for biology, chemistry, engineering (biomedical, computer, electrical and mechanical), physics and astronomy, and psychology.

The Peter Irving Wold Center, an interdisciplinary hub, offers leading-edge programs in biochemistry and environmental studies. Housed here are a robotics lab with high-speed, high-precision 3D motion capture system; an aerogel lab; and our research-oriented Makerspaces, where students innovate through 3D design, printing, modeling and scanning. The Imagine Lab is stocked with virtual, augmented and mixed reality tools for student and faculty use across all disciplines. The Castrucci Gallery displays artworks and objects at the intersection of visual arts and science.

The Center for Neuroscience in Butterfield Hall brings together computer and research labs, classrooms and collaborative spaces. The F.W. Olin Center houses the Union Observatory and the Geology Department.

The Nott Memorial is used for study, exhibits and special events, including the annual Study Abroad Fair, the Lothridge Festival of Dance, and guest lectures by such noted figures as U.S. Sen. Kirsten Gillibrand, architect Maya Lin, environmentalist Bill McKibben, activist Cornel West and journalist Bob Woodward.

Schaffer Library has over 1 million print and electronic volumes and more than 11,000 current print and electronic serial titles. Union also participates in the ConnectNY consortium, giving users access to the holdings of 14 other member libraries. The College Archives, Language Lab, Special Collections and Writing Center are also housed at Schaffer Library.

Karp Hall houses the departments of English, and Modern Languages and Literature. Lippman Hall is home to the Social Sciences, including Economics, History, Political Science and Sociology. Lamont House is home to Anthropology, Classics and Philosophy, and the Religious Studies program.

The Feigenbaum Center for Visual Arts includes studios for drawing, painting, sculpture, printmaking, 2D and 3D design, and metal-working, as well as a media lab, traditional dark room, public galleries and classrooms. Other arts facilities include the Mandeville Gallery and Wikoff Student Gallery, both in the Nott Memorial; the all-Steinway Taylor Music Center; the Yulman Theater, home to Mountebanks, the nation's oldest student performing group; and the Henle Dance Pavilion. Union's Kelly Adirondack Center in nearby Niskayuna houses one of the largest research collections focused on the Adirondack region.

Residential options for students include traditional dorms, apartment-style housing, theme houses, Minerva Houses, Greek houses, College Park Hall and Garnet Commons. Reamer Campus Center includes dining facilities, the bookstore and offices for student activities.

Among the athletic facilities are Alumni Gymnasium, which features the Breazzano Fitness Center, a swimming/diving pool, and exercise and yoga studios. Other recreational and sports facilities include the 3,000-seat Messa Rink at Achilles Center, home of Union's Div. I hockey teams, and the Travis J. Clark '00 Strength Training Facility for varsity athletes. The men's and women's crew teams train at the College's boathouse on the Mohawk River. The Wicker Wellness Center offers professional health, wellness and counseling services and is the home of the campus therapy dogs.

The Becker Career Center helps students align their personal passions with their academic and professional pursuits, and it works with employers and alumni to guide students in competing effectively in today's job market. Students can connect with alumni in all fields through the Union Career Advisory Network (UCAN). Handshake, the center's comprehensive career services platform, is the hub for all things college to career—internship and job postings, career fairs, events, career center appointments and more. Students regularly meet potential employers at campus career and internship fairs and other events. Ninety-eight percent of new Union graduates are employed or pursuing an advanced degree or fellowship.

OFF-CAMPUS OPPORTUNITIES

Union offers more than 40 terms and mini-term programs in 30 countries. Students can conduct anthropological research in Fiji, learn about Italian Renaissance architecture in Florence, study engineering in Turkey or visit alternative energy sites in New Zealand. There are many opportunities for internships and service. Students also may design their own study abroad program, as well as participate in non-Union and exchange programs. In addition to full-term programs, three-week mini-terms are offered during winter and summer breaks in various U.S. cities and other countries. The unique Minerva Fellows program gives young alumni a chance to travel abroad their first year after leaving Union, instilling in them the power of an entrepreneurial approach to addressing poverty in developing countries.

ACADEMIC PROGRAMS

Union is committed to integrating the humanities and social sciences with science and engineering while emphasizing the practical application of ideas through experience. Students gain deep knowledge within their majors and also experience ideas and insights from multiple disciplines.

Students must complete a minimum of 36 courses (up to 40 for engineering degrees) and satisfy departmental and Common Curriculum requirements, including the First-Year Preceptorial and Sophomore Research Seminar, which promote reading, writing, research and critical thinking skills. Distribution requirements in the humanities, literature, social sciences, linguistic and cultural competency, quantitative mathematical reasoning and the sciences promote a breadth of knowledge about the social and natural world, and key skills in analysis, literacy and numeracy. Writing Across the Curriculum requires students to take five designated courses from at least two divisions and one Senior Writing Experience.

Union encourages student research in all disciplines. Three-quarters of students actively engage in research. They work one-on-one with professors and have access to sophisticated instrumentation often reserved for graduate students at large universities. At Steinmetz Symposium each spring, some 500 students present their research, scholarship and creative work. Approximately 140 students participate in summer research. Many students co-author publications with faculty and present at major conferences. Union consistently ranks among the top of its peer institutions in National Science Foundation awards.

Academic advisors help students select the right coursework, develop research topics, and pursue internships and service in accord with their interests and future plans. In addition, class deans support students academically and personally throughout their four years. Students participate in internships at more than 500 organizations worldwide, gaining real-world experience in such fields as businesses, health care, government, science, social service, technology and the arts. Union also sponsors the Silicon Valley Internship on Innovation and Creativity, which combines internships in Bay Area startups and NGOs with courses in culture and entrepreneurship. There is faculty advising for business, law, medical and graduate school, and students also receive encouragement and support in applying for prestigious national and international scholarships and fellowships.

MAJORS AND DEGREES OFFERED

Union offers more than 58 majors and minors. Students may choose double majors; combine majors and minors; or pursue interdepartmental and multidisciplinary programs, such as ethnic and cultural studies. Some students design their own Organizing Theme major. Most students take three courses in each of the three 10-week terms that comprise Union's academic calendar. The average introductory class has 21 students; the average upper level class, 14.

Union also offers numerous joint programs leading to advanced degrees. These include: a 3+3 accelerated law program (B.A. plus J.D.); a 4+1 master of arts in teaching (B.A. or B.S., plus MAT); a 4+1 health care management program (B.A. or B.S., plus M.B.A.); and an 8-year leadership in medicine program (B.S. plus M.S. or M.B.A., plus M.D.)

TUITION, ROOM, BOARD, FEES

Union's comprehensive fee, which includes tuition, room, board, and mandatory fees, is $71,385 for the 2019–20 academic year. The estimated cost for books and personal expenses is $2,000.

FINANCIAL AID

Union is committed to admitting an economically diverse student body and to meeting the full demonstrated need of all admitted students. Its comprehensive financial aid program includes more than $75 million in aid from Union's own resources and from federal, state, institutional and other agencies. The College offers more than $53 million annually in the form of grants and scholarships that do not need to be repaid. Scholarship awards are based on academic performance and financial need. The average need-based financial aid package is $46,200; need-based aid is evaluated annually. First-year applicants are automatically considered for merit scholarships. These scholarships are awarded to top applicants each year based on academic credentials. The average merit package is $14,500. Students who demonstrate financial need are offered a financial aid package that generally consists of a grant, loan and work opportunity. More than 60 percent of students receive financial assistance from the College. Candidates for aid must file the Free Application for Federal Student Aid (FAFSA) and the College Scholarship Service's PROFILE form by Jan. 15; Early Decision (ED) candidates must file by the ED application deadline.

In addition, the College offers Making U Possible grants to students who apply for financial aid but who otherwise would not qualify for need-based aid or would qualify for only minimal amounts. Families who have an EFC—as measured through the CSS Profile—up to $50,000 (average family income of $100,000) can expect a minimum of $30,000 in grant and scholarship assistance. Families with an EFC between $50,000 and $90,000 (incomes as high as $250,000) would be eligible for a minimum of $20,000.

STUDENT ORGANIZATIONS AND ACTIVITIES

Union's approximately 2,200 full-time undergraduates come from 40 U.S. states and territories and 36 other countries. International students make up 10 percent of the student body, and 22 percent of domestic students identify themselves as members of a multicultural group.

Union has more than 130 campus clubs, including arts and cultural groups; the student newspaper, *Concordiensis*, and radio station, WRUC; sports clubs; academic societies; service and political interest groups; 9 residential fraternities and sororities; and 13 theme houses (devoted to arts, civil liberties, the LGBTQ community, sustainability, technology and more). Cultural events include concerts, theater, dance, film and exhibits. Union's comprehensive athletics program offers 26 varsity intercollegiate sports, organized intramurals, club sports, and recreational and fitness activities. Union is a member of the NCAA, Liberty League and ECAC Hockey. Men's and women's ice hockey compete in NCAA Division I programs; other teams are Division III. Union triumphed in the Frozen Four to capture the national men's hockey title in 2014.

The Minerva House system is a vibrant community and launch pad for an array of college experiences. All students and faculty members belong to one of seven on-campus houses, where they contribute in distinct ways to Union's social, cultural, academic and intellectual life. Student-run Minerva programs range from book clubs and barbecues to language tables, current events discussions and cooking dinner with professors. The longest running Minerva program, Green House jams, brings together students and faculty for musical jam sessions every Friday afternoon.

Union encourages students to engage with the local and global community through meaningful volunteer work and charitable projects. Some 1,200 students each year are involved in more than 30 programs and other opportunities for service and leadership. The Kenney Community Center is a hub that connects students with Big Brothers Big Sisters, Habitat for Humanity, tutoring programs and many civic projects. Many student groups, athletic teams and Greek organizations also sponsor community service activities.

ADMISSIONS PROCESS

More than 7,000 applicants typically seek first-year class positions. Admissions counselors look at grades, rigor of courses taken, class rank, letters of recommendations and extracurricular involvement. Typically, 16 units of secondary school preparation are required for admission. These should include credits in such fundamental subjects as English, foreign language, mathematics, social studies and science. It is strongly recommended that students visit Union for an interview and student-guided tour. Alumni interviews may be requested online. A student can choose not to submit his or her SAT or ACT scores for review, except for accelerated programs, which require applicants to submit the SAT and two SAT Subject Tests.

Union offers early action admission. The deadline to apply is Nov. 1. Early decision (ED) candidates have two options. The application deadline (including all supporting credentials) for Option I is Nov. 15, with notification by Dec. 15. Option II has a Jan. 15 deadline (including all supporting credentials) and Feb. 15 notification. Applications for regular decision (RD) admission must be filed by Jan.15; decisions are mailed by April 1. Applications to the Leadership in Medicine program are due no later than Nov. 15, and for Law and Public Policy, by Jan. 15. Accepted students (with the exception of ED) have until May 1 to commit.

THE UNIVERSITY OF CENTRAL FLORIDA

AT A GLANCE

The University of Central Florida is a comprehensive research university with over 69,500 students. As one of the nation's fastest growing and largest universities, UCF enrolls a diverse student body representing all 50 states and 149 countries. The University offers educational and research programs that complement the economy, with strong components in engineering, business, education, science, film, health, nursing, social sciences, and hospitality management. UCF's programs in communication and the fine arts help to meet the cultural and recreational needs of a growing metropolitan area. The University also offers many graduate programs leading to masters and doctoral degrees.

UCF has established extensive partnerships with businesses and industry in the central Florida area and beyond that provide students with exceptional research and learning experiences. These partnerships bring practical learning environments to UCF students through co-op and internship programs. Joint curriculum development strategies are used throughout the university.

The on-campus and campus-affiliated housing facilities include traditional residence halls, apartment-style options, and Greek housing that accommodates approximately 12,140 students. Several thousand students live in apartments located within walking distance of the campus.

LOCATION AND ENVIRONMENT

The University of Central Florida: Competitive Advantages

A Focus on Undergraduate Education: We're committed to teaching and providing advising and academic support services for all students. Our undergraduates have access to state-of-the-art wireless buildings, high-tech classrooms and research labs, Web-based classes and an undergraduate research and mentoring program.

A Talented Student Body: As one of the fastest growing universities, total enrollment has reached over 69,500; 59,483 are undergraduates. Our emphasis on excellence in undergraduate education has produced many rewarding results: a Goldwater Scholarship awardee, a Rhodes Scholarship finalist, a Clarion awardee in Radio/Television, a Zonta International Amelia Earhart fellowship awardee, and internationally ranked Computer Science programming and Cyber Defense teams.

Career Opportunities: Our Career Services professionals help students gain practical experiences at NASA, schools, hospitals, high-tech companies, local municipalities, and the entertainment industry. UCF faculty sit on boards and planning committees, and our graduates make their mark in engineering, business, computer science, education, health care, science, tourism, film and public service.

An International Presence: With an international focus to our curricula and research programs, we currently enroll international students from 149 nations. Our study abroad programs and other study and research opportunities are available in Europe, Asia, Africa, Australia/Pacific Islands, South America, Latin America, and the Middle East.

A Spacious, Modern Campus, plus Orlando: UCF's 1,415-acre Main Campus in East Orlando provides a safe and serene setting for learning, with natural lakes and woodlands. Other campuses include the Rosen College of Hospitality Management Campus, UCF Downtown Campus, and the Health Sciences Campus. The university provides housing for approximately 12,140 students on campus and through affiliated housing. The many attractions of Orlando lie a short distance away: the Orlando Magic, the Orlando City Soccer Club, the Kennedy Space Center, major film studios, Walt Disney World, Universal Orlando, Sea World, and sandy beaches are all nearby.

CAMPUS FACILITIES AND EQUIPMENT

In addition to the academic programs offered on the Main Orlando campus, the Rosen College of Hospitality Management campus, the UCF Downtown campus, and the Health Sciences campus, upper division students can work toward a degree at 11 UCF Connect Campuses around the central Florida area. These campuses work cooperatively with local state colleges to provide all four years of course work in many academic areas. The library houses over 1.8 million print volumes and subscribes to more than 50,000 periodicals and journals (49,000 in electronic format). Students have access to an online computer catalog that provides information on the collections of the State University System libraries. An extensive online network of more than 500 computer PC's, laptops and iPads cover the campus. The Institute for Simulation and Training gives students the opportunity to pursue undergraduate research. The College of Optics and Photonics allows faculty members and students to work directly with industrial personnel in conducting basic and applied research at the regional and national level. The Central Florida Research Park, located next to the UCF campus, houses more than 145 high-technology firms and agencies with approximately 10,000 employees. This proximity fosters relationships between industry and the University, which strengthens the academic programs at UCF.

OFF-CAMPUS OPPORTUNITIES

Career Services and Experiential Learning provides comprehensive and coordinated career development, enhances academic study, and builds ongoing partnerships with employers and the community. UCF is a participant in the National Student Exchange Consortium.

ACADEMIC PROGRAMS

The University offers the degrees of Bachelor of Arts, Bachelor of Design, Bachelor of Fine Arts, Bachelor of Music, Bachelor of Music Education, Bachelor of Science, Bachelor of Science in Business Administration, Bachelor of Science in Education, Bachelor of Science in Engineering, Bachelor of Science in Nursing, Bachelor of Social Work, and Bachelor of Science in Social Sciences.

MAJORS AND DEGREES OFFERED

These degrees are available in the colleges listed below, with majors or areas of specialization as indicated.

The College of Arts and Humanities offers degrees in art, architecture, emerging media, English, French and Francophone Studies, history, humanities and cultural studies, Latin American Studies, music, music education, philosophy, photography, religion and cultural studies, Spanish, studio art, theatre, theatre studies, and writing and rhetoric.

The College of Business Administration offers degrees in accounting, business economics, economics, finance, integrated business, management, real estate and marketing.

The College of Community Innovation and Education offers degrees in criminal justice, early childhood development and education, elementary education, emergency management, exceptional student education, health informatics and information management, health services administration, legal studies, nonprofit management, public administration, secondary education, teacher education, and technical education and industry training.

The College of Engineering and Computer Science offers degrees in aerospace engineering, civil engineering, computer engineering, computer science, construction engineering, electrical engineering, environmental engineering, industrial engineering, information technology and mechanical engineering.

The College of Health Professions and Sciences offers degrees in communication sciences and disorders, health sciences, kinesiology, and social work.

The College of Medicine and the Burnett School of Biomedical Sciences offers degrees in biotechnology, medical laboratory sciences, and biomedical sciences.

The College of Nursing offers degrees in nursing.

The College of Optics and Photonics offers degrees in photonic science and engineering.

The College of Sciences offers degrees in actuarial science, anthropology, biology, chemistry, forensic science, international and global studies, mathematics, physics, political science, psychology, social sciences, sociology, and statistics.

The College of Undergraduate Studies offers degrees in environmental studies, integrative general studies, and interdisciplinary studies.

The Rosen College of Hospitality Management offers degrees in hospitality management, event management, entertainment management, restaurant and foodservice management, and senior living management.

The Nicholson School of Communication and Media offers degrees in advertising/public relations, communication and conflict, digital media, film, human communication, journalism, radio/television.

Pre-professional programs are offered in chiropractic, medicine (allopathic medicine (M.D.) and osteopathic medicine (D.O.)), occupational therapy, optometry, pharmacy, physician assistant, physical therapy, podiatry, public health, dentistry, veterinary and law.

TUITION, ROOM, BOARD, FEES

Approximate Tuition, Health Fee, Room and Board Annual Rates 2019–20:

Florida Resident	Florida	Non-Resident
Tuition and Fees	$6,368	$22,466
Room and Board	$10,010	$10,010
Books (estimate)	$1,200	$1,200
Approximate Total / Annual Cost	$17,578	$33,676

Based on 15 credit hours per semester, double room and meal plan.

FINANCIAL AID

Financial aid is awarded according to each student's demonstrated need in relation to college costs and may include grants, loans, scholarships and part-time employment. Programs based on need include the Federal Pell Grant, Florida Student Assistance Grant, Federal Work-Study, Florida College Career Work-Study Program, and Federal Stafford Student Loan. To qualify for these programs, students must complete the Free Application for Federal Student Aid (FAFSA). The priority application deadline is December 1. Approximately 76 percent of UCF students receive some form of financial aid.

STUDENT ORGANIZATIONS AND ACTIVITIES

Students participate in over 650 organizations, including special interest clubs, multi-cultural associations, fraternities and sororities, honor societies, and academic and pre-professional organizations. The Office of Student Involvement schedules a wide array of extracurricular programs, including concerts, movies, and guest speakers. The innovative LEAD Scholars Academy fosters leadership and service commitment through a comprehensive student development program for freshman. The Major Exploration Program (MEP) helps entering freshmen define their career goals and develop an academic strategy to reach their goals. UCF offers Air Force and Army ROTC programs.

The University of Central Florida is a member of the NCAA and the American Athletic Conference. All teams compete on the NCAA Division 1 Level. UCF's men's teams compete in intercollegiate baseball, basketball, football, golf, soccer, and tennis. Women's teams compete in basketball, cross-country, golf, rowing, soccer, softball, tennis, track and field, and volleyball. Intercollegiate coed club activities include championship cheerleading, crew, and waterskiing teams. The university offers an extensive intramural sports program.

ADMISSIONS PROCESS

A freshman applicant is a student with fewer than 12 hours of college coursework after high school graduation. The most important criteria in the admission decision for these applicants is the high school academic record, rigor of coursework, grade point average, grade trends, and SAT I or ACT test scores. UCF operates on a rolling admission basis. Students are generally notified of their initial admission decision within two to three weeks after receipt of the application and all supporting documents. If the number of qualified applicants exceeds the number that the university is permitted to enroll, a waiting list will be established.

All applicants must have earned a minimum of 18 high school academic units (yearlong courses that are not remedial in nature). These include 4 units of English (3 must include substantial writing), 4 units of mathematics at or above algebra I, 3 units of natural science (2 must include a laboratory), 3 units of social science, 2 units of one world language, and 2 units of academic electives. Grades in honors courses, International Baccalaureate, Advanced Placement, AICE and dual enrollment courses are given additional weight in the GPA computation. Students must meet the Florida Board of Governors minimum eligibility to be considered for admission. Applicants should understand that the satisfaction of minimum requirements does not automatically guarantee admission to UCF.

Admission requirements for Transfer applicants vary by the number of college credit hours the student has successfully completed prior to enrolling at UCF. For complete details, go to http://admissions.ucf.edu/apply/transfer/. A transfer credit summary evaluation is provided to students once they are offered admission to UCF.

Students are encouraged to apply several months in advance. Transfers can apply online at http://admissions.ucf.edu/ and Freshmen can apply online at http://admissions.ucf.edu/ or through the Common Application. It is recommended that freshman students apply early during the fall semester of their senior year. Applications are accepted up to one year prior to the start of the term for which entry is desired. Priority application deadlines are May 1 for the fall term (July 1 for transfers), November 1 for the spring term, and March 1 for the summer term.

UNIVERSITY OF MAINE

AT A GLANCE
UMaine: Define Tomorrow

The University of Maine (UMaine) offers extensive academic opportunities expected from a flagship research university, with the close-knit feel of a small college. Founded in 1865, UMaine is a land and sea grant institution and the flagship campus of the University of Maine System. UMaine offers the most comprehensive academic experience in the state. There are nearly 100 majors and academic programs, 75 graduate degree programs and 30 doctoral programs. Top students are invited to join the Honors College, one of the oldest and most prestigious honors college in the nation. UMaine is also the state's only public research university, housing facilities with international reputations for excellence. UMaine students have extraordinary opportunities to gain real-world experience through research and experiential learning. Our undergraduates have the opportunity to collaborate with faculty, conduct fieldwork, and participate in internships around the world. Wildlife ecology studies learn about animal behavior by working with wildlife biologists and baby black bears. Many engineering students secure co-ops that typically lead to employment immediately upon graduation and are global leaders in deepwater offshore wind energy research. Education majors have the opportunity to take advantage of urban, rural, and international student teaching opportunities, and our marine science students have the opportunity to spend a semester by the sea at our world renowned Darling Marine Center. There are over 200 student organizations such as SPIFFY, the student investment club that manages a $3.2 million real money portfolio, Greek Life, Division I athletics, and many more.

LOCATION AND ENVIRONMENT
There's no place like Maine. Located in Orono, Maine, students are surrounded by the great outdoors and ample opportunity to explore everything that Maine has to offer. Orono is nestled between the Stillwater and Penobscot rivers and the campus has a traditional New England feel with ivy-covered brick buildings, towering pines, and beautiful fall foliage that is second to none. Some of the best skiing in the northeast is within easy driving distance. Beautiful tourist attractions such as Bar Harbor, Acadia National Park, Baxter State Park, and the northern terminus of the Appalachian Trail are just a short drive from campus. UMaine is also only 10 minutes from the city of Bangor, Maine's third largest city which is consistently ranked as one of the most desirable places to live for its natural beauty, safety, quality of life and affordability.

CAMPUS FACILITIES AND EQUIPMENT
UMaine is home to state-of-the-art research facilities, classrooms and teaching laboratories.

Fogler Library is the state's largest library and located right in the center of campus. It houses more than 3.6 million print volumes, including government documents, as well as 1.6 million microforms. The library provides access to more than 615,000 e-books, 104,000 online serials, 380 online databases, and 154,000 media titles.

Students will also have access to the Capital Markets Training Laboratory with state-of-the-art technology and 12 Bloomberg Terminals that allow for hands-on learning in financial education.

Engineering students get the opportunity to work alongside professors and research scientists in the internationally recognized, Advanced Structures and Composite Center. Students have assisted on projects for NASA, off shore wind resources, the United States Military and "Bridge in a Backpack." The Advanced Structures and Composite Center has partnered with more than 500 national and international companies and is home to the world's largest 3D printer.

The Virtual Environment and Multimodal Interaction Laboratory (VEMI) is a research facility that combines fully immersive virtual reality with augmented reality technologies in an integrated research and development environment. Students from all interest and majors collaborate in projects in the VEMI Lab on the latest research in areas such as aging research, vision impairment research and virtual realities.

OFF-CAMPUS OPPORTUNITIES
There are also many ways to explore Maine off campus as well. There is outdoor recreation, music and food festivals, museums and much more. Bangor, a 10-minute drive from campus, hosts Waterfront Concerts, the State Fair, and traveling Broadway Shows. Take a trip to Maine's famous Lobster Festival in Rockport or to Acadia National Park on Mount Desert Island. There are over 120 miles of hiking trails to explore. You don't need to go far for trails, as there are 15 miles of hiking right behind UMaine's campus!

Students at UMaine also have many opportunities to travel abroad. Through our study abroad programs, students will be able to explore globally while enhancing their education by taking courses, volunteering, or researching. Students have traveled to China to study emerging financial markets, to Italy to learn about Renaissance art history, to Turkey to study film, and to Brazil to look at our world's diverse ecosystem. Students will have the opportunity to enhance their education and experience at UMaine with fun, enriching, on and off-campus activities.

THE UNIVERSITY OF NEW ENGLAND

ACADEMIC PROGRAMS

UMaine offers nearly 100 majors and programs across six colleges at the undergraduate level: The College of Education and Human Development; College of Engineering; College of Liberals Arts and Sciences; College of Natural Sciences, Forestry and Agriculture; the Maine Business School and the School of Engineering Technology. UMaine also offers the Explorations program which is designed to help undecided students identify a major best fit for a degree program to pursue. The Division of Lifelong Learning offers online classes, Summer University session, and distance-learning opportunities for students who need a flexible class schedule.

Undergraduate research is a major component of the learning atmosphere. UMaine offers students true hands on research experience, as early as their first year on campus. UMaine is the state's largest research university providing rich and diverse opportunities to publish findings, travel around the globe, and work alongside UMaine's world-class scholars and researchers. The Center of Undergraduate Research connects students with faculty projects applicable to their academic interests and future careers. The abundance of research opportunities also provides students with great mentoring connections between faculty and students that carry benefits beyond the classroom. The skills students develop through research creates applicants who are much more competitive for the workplace and graduate school placement.

UMaine is also host to one of the country's oldest and most prestigious Honors College. The Honors College provides an in-depth, academically challenging curriculum for qualified students across all majors. Honors College student take part in unique research, academic and cultural opportunities, and have the option for exclusive housing.

STUDENT ORGANIZATIONS AND ACTIVITIES

Students get a full and enriching college experience at UMaine, which hosts many on-campus programs and opportunities for students to explore and meet new people. Students can kayak, ski, snowshoe, canoe, hike, and much more. 15 miles of walking, biking, and cross country ski trails surround UMaine's beautiful campus. There are also over 200 clubs and organizations for students to get involved in, such as Greek Life, The Woodsmen's Club, Robotics Club, Spanish Club and countless more. The Campus Activities and Student Engagement puts on free events during the school year including movies, karaoke, game nights, and astronomy shows. You can join an athletic team or cheer on the UMaine Black Bears Division I teams to victory for free during the year. In fact, the Wall Street Journal names UMaine's Alfond Arena the best atmosphere in college hockey.

ADMISSIONS PROCESS

Admission to UMaine is a highly competitive and selective process. Successful applicants are those whose scholastic achievement, intellectual curiosity, and established study habits promise success in a comprehensive university environment. Applicants may apply using the University of Maine System application, the Common Application, or UMaine's Mobile-Friendly Application. UMaine uses a holistic process. This process looks at the strength of high school curriculums, grades achieved, class rank, counselor recommendation, SAT or ACT score, student essay, and extracurricular involvement to evaluate for admission consideration. UMaine also recognizes Advance Placement tests, honors, and higher education courses. Student who pass examinations may be exempt from certain courses at UMaine.

UMaine has an Early Action deadline of December 1. Early Action candidates are given first consideration for the Honors College and merit scholarships awarded by the Admissions Office. All other applicants are encouraged to submit their applications and all supporting documents by March 1, and are notified by rolling admission.

Students should also submit their Free Application for Federal Student Aid (FAFSA) by March 1st to be considered for the maximum possible financial aid eligibility. UMaine's School Code for the FAFSA is 002053.

Overview:	Applicants	Acceptance Rate	Average GPA
	15,000	90%	3.31 (on 4.0 scale)
Testing Policies:	Superscore ACT YES	Superscore SAT YES	ACT Writing Policy: ACT with or without Writing accepted
			SAT Writing Policy: SAT with or without Writing accepted
Deadlines:	Early Action: December 1		
	Regular Admission: March 1		

THE UNIVERSITY OF NEW ENGLAND

AT A GLANCE

The University of New England is a private, top-ranked university offering flagship programs in the health and life sciences, as well as degrees in business, education, the social sciences and the liberal arts. UNE's three beautiful campuses in Biddeford and Portland, Maine, and Tangier, Morocco, are home to an active and close-knit student community engaged in rigorous academic experiences.

Innovation drives UNE each day. In state-of-the-art facilities in Maine, Morocco and around the world, research, hands-on learning, interdisciplinary engagement and global awareness empower the next generation of leaders for New England and beyond.

LOCATION AND ENVIRONMENT

BIDDEFORD CAMPUS

UNE's campus in Biddeford, Maine offers more than 4,000 feet of scenic shoreline where the Saco River flows into the Atlantic Ocean. From surfing and swimming to kayaking and running along the shore, the ocean is never more than a short walk away. The campus is also home to a 363-acre forest with beautiful trails to wander and vernal pools to explore. With Boston just a short 90-minute drive away, southern Maine is an ideal place to study and live.

PORTLAND CAMPUS

A rustic brick port sets the stage for a thriving buy-local economy and dynamic cultural scene with outdoor adventure all around. UNE's Portland Campus, a classic, century-old New England quad just a short drive from the waterfront, anchors UNE's tight-knit, engaged community within this exciting city.

TANGIER CAMPUS

UNE's Tangier, Morocco campus features state-of-the-art labs and classrooms, as well as easy access to beaches, downtown adventures and cultural attractions. The campus includes a residence hall, an on-site café, fitness areas, and plenty of outdoor spaces to soak up the sun. Many opportunities exist beyond the serenity of the campus, including excursions in Morocco and nearby countries.

CAMPUS FACILITIES AND EQUIPMENT

Both the Biddeford and Portland Campuses feature buildings with a variety of uses to support the needs of the University community.

BIDDEFORD CAMPUS

The Biddeford Campus includes undergraduate student housing, graduate and undergraduate classrooms, labs, the Ketchum Library and a makerspace; dining, innovative study and gathering spaces in Danielle N. Ripich Commons; and various athletic facilities and fields, including an NHL-size hockey arena, two blue turf fields, performance courts and a gymnasium, and much more. Several research facilities are on campus, including the Arthur P. Girard Marine Science Center and the Harold Alfond Center for Health Sciences, with biology and chemistry labs as well as lecture halls, classrooms, a gross anatomy lab, and UNE's medical school facilities. This campus is also home to the Pickus Center for Biomedical Research and the Peter and Cécile Morgane Hall, a science center providing additional classrooms and an undergraduate teaching laboratory.

PORTLAND CAMPUS

This campus houses Maine's only College of Dental Medicine, the College of Pharmacy, and the Westbrook College of Health Professions, which offers undergraduate and graduate programs in several allied health fields. The campus also includes the Center for Global Humanities, Art Gallery and Maine Women Writers Collection. The Blewett Science Center consists of science labs and classrooms. UNE's Interprofessional Simulation and Innovation Center, which provides customized training and education for students and health professionals, is also on the Portland Campus.

OFF-CAMPUS OPPORTUNITIES

On any given weekend at UNE, thrilling adventures await. Students can ride countless miles of mountain bike trails and scenic rural roads, kayak and sail on Casco Bay, camp and hike at hundreds of great parks, or just take in some sun at UNE's own Freddy Beach. With more than 90 clubs and organizations on UNE's campuses, students discover many opportunities to get involved. Whether an academic club, an arts club, student government, a cultural organization or an outdoor recreation group, it's easy to find others who are ready to welcome new students aboard.

UNE also fosters global citizenship by providing the opportunity for all students to study abroad. In fact, UNE students study abroad at five times the national average. Students can study at our very own campus in Morocco, or our partner institutions in Spain, France and Iceland. Plus, UNE offers faculty-led travel courses in many exciting locations. Opportunities include studying coral reefs in Belize, volunteering at a local elementary school in Cuba, providing health services in Ghana, and much more.

ACADEMIC PROGRAMS

At UNE, experiential education goes beyond training, beyond the classroom and beyond comfort zones. Through research, internships, interprofessional opportunities, community involvement, and even our own clinical simulation lab, students gain real-world experience right from the start. In fact, 92% of our undergraduates participate in clinical rotations, fieldwork, or internship experiences.

Undergraduate programs offered in: Animal Behavior, Applied Exercise Science, Applied Mathematics, Applied Social and Cultural Studies, Aquaculture and Aquarium Science, Art and Design Media, Art Education, Athletic Training, Biochemistry, Biological Sciences, Business, Chemistry, Communications, Data Science, Dental Hygiene, Elementary/Middle Education, English, Environmental Science, Environmental Studies, Global Studies, Health, Wellness and Occupational Studies, History, Interdisciplinary Studies in the Humanities (including Pre-Law), Laboratory Science, Marine Affairs, Marine Entrepreneurship, Marine Sciences, Medical Biology (Pre-Dental Medicine, Pre-Medicine, Pre-Optometry, Pre-Physician Assistant, and Pre-Veterinary Medicine), Neuroscience, Nursing, Nutrition, Political Science, Pre-Pharmacy, Pre-Physical Therapy, Psychology, Public Health, Secondary Education, Social Work, Sociology, Sport and Recreation Management, and Sustainability and Business.

Master's programs offered in: Applied Nutrition, Athletic Training, Biological Sciences, Education, Health Informatics, Marine Sciences, Nurse Anesthesia, Occupational Therapy, Physician Assistant, Ocean Food Systems, Public Health, and Social Work.

Doctorate programs offered in: Dental Medicine (D.M.D.), Education (Ed.D.), Osteopathic Medicine (D.O.), Pharmacy (Pharm.D.), and Physical Therapy (D.P.T.).

TUITION, ROOM, BOARD, FEES

Tuition: $37,390
Required Fees: $1,360
On Campus Room & Board: $14,410
Total: $53,160

FINANCIAL AID

Ninety-eight percent of all full-time undergraduate students receive merit-based scholarships up to $20,000. The average total award package for UNE students is $24,000. $42 million is awarded annually in institutional scholarships. To learn more about financial aid, visit: https://www.une.edu/sfs/undergraduate.

STUDENT ORGANIZATIONS AND ACTIVITIES

Students feel right at home in our welcoming and vibrant community. Many say UNE is "just the right size," giving opportunities for all students to find their own special role, inside and outside the classroom.

The personal attention students receive from faculty both in and out of class, and the quality of faculty as experts in their fields are key strengths of the UNE experience. Students appreciate their faculty members as mentors and trust them as accomplished scholars who impact their fields. From designing coastal trails and restoring wetlands on campus to caring for patients in need, UNE faculty members work side-by-side with their students and are recognized by their peers and other leaders for their expertise. UNE faculty members are national award recipients, Fulbright scholars, authors and world-class researchers, and they share their knowledge with their students.

UNE offers a variety of cultural and social events and encourages students to become involved in activities, clubs and sports. Popular interests include scuba diving, skiing, hiking, biking, varsity and intramural sports, swimming, surfing, music, theater, community service and student leadership development programs.

UNE athletes—called Nor'easters after one of the nastiest storms in Mother Nature's arsenal—strive for success on and off the field. With 15 conference championships in the last five years, the Nor'easters athletics teams are a serious source of pride at UNE and have a history of blowing through the competition. UNE's intercollegiate teams compete at the Division III level in men's basketball, cross country, football, golf, ice hockey, lacrosse and soccer. Varsity women's sports include basketball, cross country, field hockey, ice hockey, lacrosse, rugby, soccer, softball, swimming and volleyball. Starting in Spring 2021, women's outdoor track and field will compete at the varsity level.

ADMISSIONS PROCESS

Students applying for admission should submit a Common Application, a Coalition application or a UNE application, a $40 nonrefundable application fee, and transcripts of all academic work (high school and college if applicable). UNE does not require submission of ACT/SAT scores to apply for undergraduate admission. UNE's test-optional policy excludes the following:

- Applicants for Nursing
- Applicants for Medical Biology/Pre-Dental Medicine 3+4 or Medical Biology/Pre-Medicine 3+4
- Homeschooled applicants
- Some international applicants
- Applicants with unweighted GPAs less than 2.5 (on a 4.0 scale)
- Applicants with narrative or non-letter grade transcripts

UNE's application requirements, including the test-optional policy and exceptions, as well as international applicant requirements, are available at: https://www.une.edu/admissions.

UNE's nonbinding Early Action deadline for fall term admission is November 15. The regular decision deadline is February 15. Applications received after the deadline are reviewed on a space-available basis. Applications for the spring term are accepted through December 1.

All prospective students are encouraged to visit UNE. Campus tours are offered most weeks Monday-Saturday with additional visit opportunities available, including program-specific information sessions, high school junior preview events, personalized visits and group tours. More information is available at: https://www.une.edu/visit.

UNIVERSITY OF NEW HAVEN

AT A GLANCE

The University of New Haven, founded on the Yale campus in 1920, is a private, coeducational university situated on the coast of southern New England. It's a diverse and vibrant community of nearly 6,800 students hailing from across the country and around the world.

Within its five colleges and schools, students immerse themselves in a transformative, career-focused education across the liberal arts and sciences, health sciences, business, engineering and computer sciences, and public safety and public service. More than 100 academic programs are offered, all grounded in a long-standing commitment to collaborative, interdisciplinary, project-based learning.

At the University of New Haven, the experience of learning is both personal and pragmatic, guided by a distinguished faculty who care deeply about individual student success. As leaders in their fields, faculty provide the inspiration and recognition needed for students to fulfill their potential and succeed at whatever they choose to do.

LOCATION AND ENVIRONMENT

The University of New Haven is located in suburban West Haven, Connecticut. The campus is conveniently situated 75 miles from New York City and 135 miles from Boston. Only minutes away from the beautiful beaches along Long Island Sound, the university offers a shuttle to downtown New Haven and other local areas, including two nearby train stations.

CAMPUS FACILITIES AND EQUIPMENT

Over $500 million has been invested in facilities and academic programs at the university in just the past few years. Some of these include: a first-year student residence hall (Westside Hall) and new student dining area (Food on Demand); the 58,000-square-foot David A. Beckerman Recreation Center; the $48 million Celentano Residence Hall, with apartment-style housing for upperclassmen; Ralph A. DellaCamera Stadium, featuring our blue and gold turf field; and a STEM-based magnet high school on the university's campus. Standout academic facilities include: the Henry C. Lee Institute of Forensic Science; the National Crime Scene Training and Technology Center, the Cyber Forensics Research and Education Lab; the Laurel Vlock Center for Convergent Media; the Samuel S. Bergami Jr. Cybersecurity Center; a TV and film production studio; digital and analog recording studios; MIDI and sound synthesis lab; engineering makerspace, Dental Center, the Health Sciences Simulation Laboratory, and the Hazell Nut Café (student-run coffee shop). Currently, new projects include: the Robert M. Lee and Linda M. Wilkins Center for Marine Sciences, right on the water in the greater New Haven area; a college village within walking distance to campus with new commercial and residential properties; and the 40,000-square-foot Bergami Center for Science, Technology, and Innovation.

ACADEMIC PROGRAMS

The University of New Haven mixes traditional degrees along with many unique programs across five academic colleges and schools. A new multidisciplinary degree— B.S. in Esports and Gaming—will be offered beginning in the fall of 2020, with opportunities to specialize in concentrations such as Corruption and Gambling, Esports Performance and Health, and Game Studies. The university also offers more than 60 graduate programs and certificates, with options for a variety of dual degree programs for popular career tracks that enable students to easily transition from a bachelor's degree to a master's degree.

MAJORS AND DEGREES OFFERED

College of Arts and Sciences

The College of Arts and Sciences offers traditional majors such as Art, Biology, Chemistry, Communication, English, History, Mathematics, Psychology, and Political Science as well as unique majors in the areas of Environmental Science, Genetics & Biotechnology, Global Studies, Graphic Design, Graphic Design-Digital Art and Design, Interior Design, Interior Design-Pre-Architecture, Legal Studies, Marine Biology, Marine Affairs, Music, Music Industry, Music & Sound Recording, Psychology-Forensic Psychology, and Theater Arts. The university also offers minors in languages such as Arabic, Chinese, Italian, Russian, and Spanish.

College of Business

The College of Business offers degrees in Accounting, Business Analytics, Business Management, Business Management-Esports Management, Economics, Esports and Gaming, Finance, Hospitality and Tourism Management, International Business, Marketing, and Sport Management. The College offers students an accelerated degree program making it possible to complete a three-year bachelor's degree with the option to tack on a one-year master's degree.

Henry C. Lee College of Criminal Justice and Forensic Sciences

The Henry C. Lee College of Criminal Justice and Forensic Sciences offers degrees in Criminal Justice, Fire Protection Engineering, Fire Science, Forensic Science, Homeland Security & Emergency Management, International Affairs, National Security, and Paramedicine. The university offers separate Criminal Justice concentrations in Investigative Services, Crime Analysis, Police Science, Correctional Rehabilitation and Supervision, Crime Victim Services, and Juvenile Justice and Delinquency Prevention. The Henry C. Lee College of Criminal Justice and Forensic Sciences also contains two distinct degrees in the area of Fire Science-Arson Investigation and Fire Science- Administration.

School of Health Sciences

Though the university has a long-standing tradition of offering degrees preparing students for jobs in the healthcare industry, a standalone School of Health Sciences was created to better train students in this fast-growing field. The University's School of Health Sciences offers degrees in Dental Hygiene, Exercise Science, Health Sciences, Medical Laboratory Science, Nutrition Sciences, and Paramedicine.

Tagliatela College of Engineering

The Tagliatela College of Engineering offers degrees in Chemistry, Computer Science, and Cybersecurity and Networks in addition to an array of engineering disciplines, including Chemical Engineering, Civil Engineering, Computer Engineering, Electrical Engineering, Engineering, Industrial and Systems Engineering, and Mechanical Engineering.

Accreditations and Recognitions

Many of our academic programs have earned further distinction through high-level private accrediting bodies in the respective fields:

- AACSB (The Association to Advance Collegiate Schools of Business) accredits six of our undergraduate business degree programs: Accounting, Business Management, Finance, International Business, Marketing, and Sport Management.
- FEPAC (Forensic Science Education Programs Accreditation Commission) accredits our Forensic Science program. Only a select number of programs have earned this level of distinction through the American Academy of Forensic Science (A.A.F.S.).
- ABA (American Bar Association) approves our undergraduate degree in Legal Studies, one of only a few such programs at the undergraduate level in the entire country.
- ABET (Accreditation Board of Engineering and Technology) accredits seven of our undergraduate academic degree programs in the Tagliatela College of Engineering: Chemical Engineering, Civil Engineering, Computer Engineering, Computer Science, Electrical Engineering, Industrial and Systems Engineering, and Mechanical Engineering.
- ACEND (Accreditation Council for Education in Nutrition and Dietetics) of the American Academy of Nutrition and Dietetics accredits our very popular undergraduate degree in Nutrition and Dietetics, leading many of our students to become Registered Dietitians (R.D.). The university also has a master's degree with integrated supervised practice designed to fulfil ACEND-required competencies.
- ACS (American Chemical Society) accredits our Chemistry program.
- ADA (American Dental Association) accredits our Dental Hygiene program.
- NASAD (National Association of Schools of Art and Design) accredits our B.F.A. programs in Graphic Design, Illustration and Interior Design as well as our B.A. program in Art.

The CAE-CO (Center of Academic Excellence in Cyber Operations) stamp of approval was granted by the NSA (National Security Agency) to pathways in our Cybersecurity & Networks and Computer Science with a concentration in Cybersecurity programs. The University of New Haven is one of only two schools in New England—and 21 in the country—to earn this distinction.

Marvin K. Peterson Library

The Marvin K. Peterson Library offers over 240,000 volumes, 1,400 print journal and newspaper subscriptions, and electronic access to over 19,000 full-text journal and newspaper titles as well as approximately 550,000 pieces of microfiche, 12,000 volumes of microfilm, e-books, 33,000 e-journals, and 162,000 paper U.S. Government documents. Students have 24/7 access to popular research databases and can take a break from their studies in the library's lounge area and coffee shop.

TUITION, ROOM, BOARD, FEES

Cost for the 2020–2021 academic year is tuition and fees, $41,654; room and board, $16,630.

FINANCIAL AID

Students are automatically considered for merit-based academic scholarships by simply applying for full-time admission to the University of New Haven. Merit-based scholarships range from $10,000 to $24,000 per academic year for students who qualify.

To file for need-based aid, students must fill out the Free Application for Federal Student Aid (FAFSA), which is available online at http://fafsa.gov. The priority deadline to file FAFSA is March 1 for the fall semester and December 1 for the spring semester.

STUDENT ORGANIZATIONS AND ACTIVITIES

The Undergraduate Student Government Association (USGA) oversees all aspects of undergraduate life, organizing campus social and cultural activities, supporting the student-run radio station and student-produced publications, and overseeing the budget for all undergraduate organizations. There are more than 200 campus clubs and organizations, including chapters of several professional societies, religious groups, social clubs, student councils, cultural clubs, and national fraternities and sororities.

Study Abroad

The University of New Haven opened its satellite campus in Prato, Italy (Tuscany region) in the fall of 2012. The course offerings at the Tuscany campus change from semester to semester. Students can take a total of 15 credits (five courses) during the semester, including one mandatory Italian language course. Each semester, the university sends full-time faculty to teach courses alongside Italian faculty. Students can study abroad at our Prato, Italy campus as early as the first semester of their first year. The University of New Haven is a leading provider of study abroad education, offering students more than 300 options worldwide. One such option is an intensive study abroad program that features two-week abroad sessions with a University of New Haven faculty member during intersession. Locations include London, Dubai, Rome, and other exciting areas of the world. The two-week study abroad program earns six credits.

Athletics

As a member of the Northeast 10 Conference, the University of New Haven competes in 17 Division II varsity sports (7 men's and 10 women's), including baseball, basketball, cross-country, field hockey, football, lacrosse, soccer, softball, tennis, track, and volleyball. The university also has a number of club sports, which compete at the intercollegiate level, including: men's baseball, women's softball, esports (co-ed), field hockey (co-ed), golf (co-ed), gymnastics (co-ed), ice hockey (men's and women's), lacrosse (men's and women's), rugby (men's and women's) running (co-ed), soccer (co-ed), swimming, (co-ed), tennis (co-ed), ultimate frisbee (co-ed), volleyball (men's and women's), and wrestling (co-ed). Spirit organizations include both the cheerleading team and the dance team. The 58,000-square-foot David A. Beckerman Recreation Center adds another dimension to athletic opportunities at the University of New Haven. It features a fitness center with aerobic equipment, weights, and televisions; multi-purpose rooms for yoga, aerobics, Pilates, spinning, and other wellness activities; two basketball/volleyball courts; a multi-sport court for in-line skating, floor hockey, indoor soccer, and other activities; an elevated indoor running track; and lounge areas, including a juice bar/café.

Residential Life

The university has 13 on-campus and six off-campus housing options, ranging from a traditional residence hall to apartment-style housing with suites of two or more bedrooms. The university is also in the process of building a college village adjacent to campus, which will add apartments for upperclass and graduate students. In 2005, the university started a Living Learning Community (LLC) program which enables students to enhance their overall living experience by combining academic and personal interests through field trips, guest lectures, unique and individualized academic support, and service-learning projects. A number of LLCs are offered each year. Some popular examples include Forensic Science, Engineering, Marine Biology, Honors, and ROTC.

ADMISSIONS PROCESS

The University of New Haven has an Early Decision and Early Action admissions policy; we begin to review applications on September 1 and continue until programs are filled. The university offers one binding and three non-binding admission programs for fall admission. To be considered for certain programs, applicants must follow the established timelines and important dates: Early Decision Applications are due by December 1; Early Action applications are due by December 15; Early Action II applications are due by February 15; Regular Decision applications are due after December 15, with a priority deadline of March 1; and Spring Admission Applications are due no later than January 15.

Students may apply using the Common Application. To be considered for admission, candidates must complete the application and submit it along with a non-refundable $50 application fee. In addition to the Common Application and a 250- to 650-word essay, candidates must also submit an official high school transcript and one letter of recommendation from an academic source. Submitting standardized test scores such as the SAT or ACT is optional.

Beginning with applicants for the fall 2020 semester, the university instituted a test optional policy that allows candidates to apply for admission without submission of the SAT or ACT—except for candidates applying for Forensic Science, the Honors Program, or a dual degree program; students who are homeschooled; and students from countries where English is not the official language. Prospective student-athletes can apply test-optional to the university but must submit their test scores to the NCAA Eligibility Center.

Visiting Campus

We encourage all prospective students and their families to visit us and see what the University of New Haven has to offer. The university offers a variety of campus visits for students and their families, seven days a week. Visits include daily information sessions and tours, Open Houses, major-specific Enhanced Visits, Accepted Student Days, and much more. To view our campus-visit calendar and register for an event, go to www.newhaven.edu/visit

For further information about the University of New Haven and to schedule a campus visit or personal interview, students may contact:

Office of Undergraduate Admissions
Phone: 203-932-7319
Fax: 203-931-6093
Email: admissions@newhaven.edu
Visit our website: www.newhaven.edu

THE UNIVERSITY OF PITTSBURGH—BRADFORD

AT A GLANCE

The University of Pittsburgh at Bradford takes students beyond. Students will go beyond smart by having real-world experiences that will take them beyond the intellectual aspects of college and give them skills they need to succeed; beyond fun by participating in an active student life, a friendly residence-life environment, excellent athletic and cultural facilities, and a wide range of recreational opportunities; beyond borders by being exposed to the world through many study-abroad opportunities; beyond expectations by having a college experience that will transform them; and beyond success by achieving a life that has impact and one in which they are happy, healthy, productive members of society.

Students at Pitt-Bradford live and learn on a safe, welcoming and inclusive campus, where they receive personalized attention from committed professors who work side by side with them. And, because Pitt-Bradford is a regional campus of the University of Pittsburgh, students earn a degree from the University of Pittsburgh, which commands respect around the world.

Learn more at http://www.upb.pitt.edu/About/

LOCATION AND ENVIRONMENT

Pitt-Bradford is located in Northwestern Pennsylvania. The 319-acre campus is nestled in the foothills of the Allegheny Mountains and is only steps away from the Allegheny National Forest.

Pitt-Bradford also is a short drive from larger cities such as Buffalo, N.Y., 80 miles to the north; Pittsburgh, 160 miles to the southwest; and Erie, PA, 90 miles to the west. Pitt-Bradford can also be reached easily by car and plane.

CAMPUS FACILITIES AND EQUIPMENT

The CSI House enables criminal justice students to solve mock crime scenes in a realistic setting, using professional investigative tools. Nursing students can practice their skills in the simulation lab using electronic mannequins. Students studying computer information systems and technology have a lab where they can set up a server room, install and update software, and create virtual machines to back up and protect data; and a new virtual reality lab, which includes 13 new VR-ready, high-performance laptops and 13 sets of Oculus Rift viewers with touch-control bundles.

Students can work out in a state-of-the-art fitness center or swim in the six-lane swimming pool in the Richard E. and Ruth McDowell Sport and Fitness Center. The building also houses facilities for intercollegiate and intramural athletic events. Pitt-Bradford competes in Division III of the NCAA and fields seven men's (baseball, basketball, golf, soccer, swimming, tennis and wrestling) and seven women's teams (basketball, bowling, soccer, softball, swimming, tennis and volleyball).

The Frame-Westerberg Commons gives students a place to eat, gather and participate in campus life. The building houses the dining hall, where students can help themselves to a wide assortment of meals; a bookstore, which features an after-hours convenience store; offices for many student clubs and organizations; and areas for students to read or relax.

Blaisdell Hall, the university's fine arts and communication arts building, houses the communication arts, theater and music programs and features state-of-the-art equipment. The building also houses a multi-purpose theater, where students can participate in dramatic and musical performances. The building also serves as the cultural center for the region by housing plays, concerts, lectures and other arts-related events.

Hanley Library has more than 150,000 print books access to more than 700,000 ebooks. Since Pitt-Bradford is a regional campus of the University of Pittsburgh, you can also borrow materials from Pitt's other four campuses through interlibrary loan.

OFF-CAMPUS OPPORTUNITIES

Because of Pitt-Bradford's location, students have many opportunities to participate in unique academic and extracurricular activities. Students may collect and examine specimens in the creek that runs through campus or set up easels along the edge of the surrounding woods. After class, they may cross-country or downhill ski, snowboard or snowshoe, ice skate, kayak, bike, fish, explore caves, go rock climbing, hike and hunt.

ACADEMIC PROGRAMS

The academic programs stress critical-thinking skills and communication and encourage hands-on learning through field experience, internships, and faculty-student collaboration on research. A Pitt-Bradford bachelor's degree requires 120-128 credit hours (requirements differ slightly among programs). Students must complete between 60 and 70 credit hours to earn an associate degree.

The biology program prepares students for careers in health-related professions; education; research; field work; with companies that produce food, pharmaceuticals, chemicals, and biotechnology; and technical positions with governmental agencies. Most students interested in medicine, dentistry, optometry, pharmacy, osteopathy, optometry, physical therapy, occupational therapy, podiatry, chiropractic medicine, veterinary medicine, pre-clinical dietetics and nutrition, and a variety of careers in health and rehabilitation sciences, are biology majors.

Students in the broadcast communications, English and writing programs broadcast over the college radio station, WDRQ: and publish original works in the award-winning student literary magazine, Baily's Beads. Students also have access to a state-of-the-art radio studio, television studio, and video editing room with analog and digital technology.

Students who choose to major in computer information systems and technology will get a broad IT background and gain hands-on lab experiences. Students will learn programming applications, network development, systems design and analysis, web technologies, multimedia applications, database development, and systems administration.

The criminal justice program provides opportunities for hands-on learning through the Crime Scene Investigation House, where students can solve mock crime scenes using many of the same tools as professional law enforcement agents; and internships with local and regional police departments, county courts and probation offices, and a federal prison.

The Early Level Education Pre K-4 and secondary education majors prepare students for careers as teachers in a world of rapid political, economic, scientific and cultural change. The Education Department seeks to graduate students who have general knowledge and specific content knowledge, as well as sound theory and practice.

The nursing program at Pitt-Bradford offers an associate of science degree that can be completed in two years and the bachelor of science in nursing that requires two more years. Students may commence this program on completion of the ASN. Students may also pursue both degrees in a unique 1+2+1 program.

In psychology, students gain knowledge in the scientific and theoretical aspects of psychology as well as the application of this knowledge. The major prepares students for graduate work in psychology and related disciplines and for employment in social service agencies, mental health centers, industries, and not-for-profit and governmental agencies.

Students may relocate to another university campus to complete academic programs not offered at Pitt-Bradford. They may earn no more than 70 credits before transferring. All students in the arts and sciences may relocate provided they are students in good standing with a minimum GPA of 2.5. Engineering students may relocate if they maintain a GPA of at least 3.0.

To learn more about our academic programs, visit http://www.upb.pitt.edu/academicprograms.

MAJORS AND DEGREES OFFERED

Students at Pitt-Bradford may pursue four-year degrees in Accounting; Applied Mathematics; Biology; Biology Education 7-12; Broadcast Communications; Business, Computer and Information Technology Education K-12; Business Management; Chemistry; Chemistry Education 7-12; Communications; Computer Information Systems and Technology; Criminal Justice; Early Level Education Pre-K–4; Economics; Energy Science and Technology; English; English Education 7-12; Environmental Studies; Exercise Science; Forensic Science; General Studies; Health and Physical Education; History/Political Science; Hospitality Management; Interdisciplinary Arts; International Affairs; Mathematics Education 7-12; Nursing; Physical Sciences; Psychology; Radiological Science; Social Studies Education 7-12; Sociology; Sport and Recreation Management; and Writing.

Students may pursue associate degrees in Engineering Science, Nursing (RN), Liberal Studies, Information Systems, and Petroleum Technology.

Students may study engineering for up to two years at Pitt-Bradford then complete a program at the Pittsburgh campus in bioengineering, chemical and petroleum engineering, civil and environmental engineering, electrical and computer engineering, industrial engineering, materials science and engineering, or mechanical engineering.

Students may pursue programs offered in conjunction with the University of Pittsburgh School of Dental Medicine and the Pennsylvania College of Optometry. Undergraduates begin their studies at Pitt-Bradford and, after three years, transfer to the appropriate graduate school to complete four more years of study.

Pitt-Bradford also offers the first two years of study leading to the doctorate in pharmacy. Students must complete the program at the Pittsburgh campus, where admission is competitive. The Pittsburgh School of Pharmacy pre-admits some qualified high school seniors, pending completion of the first two years of the pre-professional program at Pitt-Bradford.

TUITION, ROOM, BOARD, FEES

Full-time tuition for the two-term academic year in 2019–20 was $13,198 for Pennsylvania residents and $24,666 for out-of-state students. Tuition for students in the nursing program was $16,908 for Pennsylvania residents and $31,454 for nonresidents.

A double-occupancy room for the year was $5,826. A full meal plan per year was $3,786. Students must also pay yearly fees: $200 activity fee, $350 computer fee, $150 wellness fee, a $180 recreation fee, and an $80 parking and transportation fee. On average, students spend about $500 per term on books and supplies.

FINANCIAL AID

Our tuition and housing fees are competitive compared to other area institutions, and our room and board rates are among the top five most affordable for public colleges in Pennsylvania.

On top of that, we offer generous merit and need-based scholarships to qualified students. More than 94% of our students receive some form of financial aid through grants, loans, work study, or scholarships. For the 2019–20 academic year, the average financial aid award was $19,171 for Pennsylvania students and $24,102 for out-of-state students.

All aid applicants must submit the Free Application for Federal Student Aid (FAFSA) by March 1 to receive priority consideration. Pennsylvania residents who complete the FAFSA by March 1 are also eligible for Pennsylvania Higher Education Assistance Agency (PHEAA) grants. Non-Pennsylvania students should contact their state agency to learn more about the prerequisites for grants.

The university awards merit-based scholarships, which range from $1,000 to $12,700, to those who demonstrate exceptional academic achievement. The university ROTC program is another possible source of financial aid. The university encourages veterans to contact the VA about educational benefits.

Additionally, students who receive a Federal Pell Grant will have their grant matched dollar for dollar by the university.

Contact the financial aid Office or visit http://www.upb.pitt.edu/financialaid to learn more about financial assistance.

STUDENT ORGANIZATIONS AND ACTIVITIES

There are about 1,400 students enrolled Pitt-Bradford, who, along with the faculty and staff, form a diverse, friendly and caring campus community. Students come from 21 different countries, including Burkina Faso, Bangladesh, Bahamas, Canada, China, Cameroon, Germany, Ethiopia, Nigeria, Italy and Pakistan; 27 states, from California and Alaska to Massachusetts and Florida; and 57 of the 67 counties in Pennsylvania.

There are more than 60 clubs and organizations, ranging from the African-American Student Union and Gamers United, to academic clubs, honor societies, fraternities and sororities.

Because Pitt-Bradford is a personalized campus, opportunities for leadership are plentiful. Many students become campus leaders as early as their sophomore year. Regardless of your background or interests, you will find many places to become involved as a student at Pitt-Bradford.

The Student Activities Council schedules many activities, including comedy performances, lectures, art exhibits, movies, and trips to many places, including Toronto, Canada; Niagara Falls, N.Y.; and New York City. To learn more about clubs and organizations, visit http://www.upb.pitt.edu/clubs.

ADMISSIONS PROCESS

The Admissions committee primarily looks at three factors in evaluating applicants: high school achievement; standardized test results (SAT I or ACT), and letters of recommendation from teachers and/or a counselor at their high school. Class rank, extracurricular activities, personal qualifications, and potential role in the school community are also considered.

Pitt-Bradford accepts applicants on a rolling basis, which means applications are welcome at any time. The Admissions committee notifies candidates as soon as a decision has been made on their application.

Applicants must complete and submit the application online, which is free.

An official high school transcript and an official standardized test score report (SAT I or ACT) are also required. Transfer applicants must also submit official copies of all college transcripts, which must reflect a GPA of at least 2.0. Students and their families are welcome to visit our campus. The Office of Admissions schedules interviews and tours Monday through Friday, 9 a.m. to 4 p.m. all year long, as well as on selected Saturdays during the school year. Contact the Office of Admissions to arrange a visit.

Students seeking more information should contact:

The Office of Admissions
The University of Pittsburgh at Bradford
300 Campus Drive
Bradford, PA 16701-2898
Telephone: 814-362-7555
800-872-1787 (toll free)
Fax: 814-362-5150
http://www.upb.pitt.edu
Email: admissions@upb.pitt.edu

UNIVERSITY OF REDLANDS

AT A GLANCE

The University of Redlands is a private, nonprofit university that connects students to a world of opportunity, geared toward their passions and potential.

Centrally located near the beaches, mountains and desert in the heart of Southern California, the University offers more than 50 undergraduate programs, as well as 20 graduate programs in business, communication sciences and disorders, education, geographic information systems, and music—blending liberal arts and professional programs, applied and theoretical study, traditional majors and self-designed curricula.

For undergraduates, the University has one of the highest study-abroad participation rates among its peers; an NCAA Division III athletic program contributes to the many extracurricular opportunities available; and students complete more than 120,000 hours of community service annually. The distinctive Johnston Center for Integrative Studies enables self-motivated undergraduates to negotiate their own interdisciplinary course of study with a faculty/peer committee.

The University has its main campus in Redlands, six regional locations throughout Southern California, and an international campus in Austria. Since 1960, more than 3,000 Redlands students have taken part in the Salzburg Semester, living in a castle built in the 16th century. Surveys show that generations of alumni have found that the University, established in 1907, prepared them well for career success and lifelong learning.

LOCATION AND ENVIRONMENT

The main 160-acre residential campus in Redlands features orange groves, stunning architectural landmarks, and more than 1,700 trees. The University's six other regional locations provide innovative programs for working professionals.

CAMPUS FACILITIES AND EQUIPMENT

To create the fully immersive University of Redlands experience, most college students reside on campus in one of 15 residential communities during their course of study.

Other notable facilities include:

- A multimillion-dollar athletic facility with an Olympic-size pool and state-of-the-art weight and exercise rooms.
- The Redlands cogeneration and chiller plant, which enables the University to produce a majority of its energy.
- A "makerspace" within the Fletcher Jones Computer Center, where students can work and collaborate using state-of-the-art technology, such as 3D printers, Autocad, and Virtual Reality, to work on physical and virtual projects.
- The Irvine Commons, which offers spacious seating, a casual food-court layout, and a fresh, Californian menu.
- A counseling and health center that supports physical and mental health.
- Tutoring and writing lab services.

OFF-CAMPUS OPPORTUNITIES

Redlands was recently named a "Great So Cal College Town" by *AAA Westways Magazine*. Historic homes, America's longest continuously running free summer music festival and beautiful parks make the city of Redlands a one-of-a-kind gem in the Southern California region. The University's close ties to nonprofit organizations and local businesses, including Amazon and Esri, the world's largest geographic information systems mapping software company, make it a great place to land an internship or get involved with community service.

ACADEMIC PROGRAMS

Guided by a philosophy of liberal arts inquiry, a Redlands education seeks to cultivate relevant skills that can be transferred to many professional contexts. Programs such as the First-Year Seminar and First-Year Journeys bridge high school and college, helping students develop essential academic skills.

With the Redlands Promise, the University guarantees it will provide the opportunity for college students to graduate in four years, otherwise it will cover the cost of any additional courses necessary.

Redlands' award-winning faculty conduct research and creative endeavors that have helped shape the world, even as they teach and mentor students. Professors' scholarly and artistic accomplishments infuse Redlands' teaching and curriculum, impact students both in and outside the classroom, and contribute to the collective energy, wisdom, innovation, and creativity of the University.

The University also offers undergraduate business degree completion and graduate degree programs in business and education for working professionals.

MAJORS AND DEGREES OFFERED

The University offers more than 50 undergraduate programs, as well as 20 graduate programs, including Accounting, Biochemistry and Molecular Biology, Business Administration and Management, Computer Science, Communication Sciences and Disorders, Creative Writing, Economics, Music, Psychology, Political Science, Biology/Prehealth, and more.

TUITION, ROOM, BOARD, FEES

On average, tuition and fees are approximately $50,630 for fall, spring, and May terms; room and board cost approximately $14,670 per year. More than 90 percent of Redlands students receive financial aid to offset contributions made by them and their families. (Financial aid information is subject to change; please visit https://www.redlands.edu/admissions-and-aid/undergraduate for the most up-to-date information.)

FINANCIAL AID

At Redlands, students are automatically considered for need-based financial aid and merit scholarships based on their academic record. Redlands also offers talent scholarships in art, creative writing, music, and theatre.

Financial aid is available to all undergraduate students who are citizens or permanent residents of the United States. Students wishing to be considered for financial aid must submit the Free Application for Federal Student Aid (FAFSA). Forms can be found online at U.S. Department of Education website.

California residents must also complete a Cal-Grant GPA Verification Form by March 2. Generally, students' current high school or college will submit this form on their behalf. For more information on the qualification for the Cal-Grant, please contact the California Student Aid Commission (CSAC).

Financial aid information is subject to change; visit https://www.redlands.edu/admissions-and-aid/student-financial-services/student-financial-services-undergraduate/apply-for-aid for the latest deadlines and more specific details pertaining to financial aid.

STUDENT ORGANIZATIONS AND ACTIVITIES

The University of Redlands College of Arts and Sciences has an undergraduate population of more than 2,400 and a graduate population of more than 1,700. Our student population size translates to a stronger campus community; students, faculty, and staff are on a first-name basis. Most students live on campus in halls, apartments, or organizational houses.

Students at the U of R are engaged; they transform and impact their communities on campus, in Redlands, and around the world. A majority of the student body is involved in some type of leadership activity. Community service is a requirement; in 2017, U of R students collectively put in more than 120,000 community service hours.

There are more than 125 clubs and organizations on campus, and more than 450 events are organized (mostly by students) per year. A Club and Organization Advisory Board oversees and supports each group. The Greek system is local-only (not belonging to national groups) and involves about 28 percent of the student population. U of R's 21 Division III athletic teams regularly compete at championship levels. On average, Redlands' scholar-athletes achieve a 3.5 GPA or higher along with active involvement in their sport.

Many students are involved in intramurals and club sports. Outdoor programs, in which students go on trips catering to different interests and skill levels, offer classes such as May Term Outdoor Adventure; this monthlong course helps students develop outdoor skills, competence, leadership, and community. First-Year Journeys offer students adventure and the chance to make friends and learn about life at Redlands before the school year starts; activities include rock climbing, camping, bungee jumping, canoeing, biking, scuba diving, surfing, volunteering and more.

Redlands' academic emphasis is reflected in the many academic clubs and honor/professional societies, which foster faculty and student networking and encourage exploration and service.

The Associated Students of the University of Redlands (ASUR) is the University's student government organization that represents students on issues including academics, University policy, student life, and other areas. The ASUR also works to provide high-quality programming and special events, hosting speakers such as activist Angela Davis, soccer star Landon Donovan, author Sandra Cisneros, and more.

ADMISSIONS PROCESS

At the University of Redlands, our commitment is to support those who seek to expand their mind and skills, find their passion, contribute to society and the world, and ensure a safe, productive future for themselves and their families.

When selecting a new entering class, the Admissions Committee carefully considers many significant factors, including reviewing the applicant's academic background, standardized test scores, extracurricular activities, personal statements, member questions, and recommendation letters.

Talent-based scholarships also require the applicant to audition or submit creative materials. Students' unique talents, personal attributes, and future goals are also considered.

International students may be required to submit TOEFL or iELTS results as proof of English language proficiency. More information about admission requirements can be found at https://www.redlands.edu/admissions-and-aid/undergraduate/.

Application Checklist

- The Common Application, including the personal essay and University of Redlands questions
- $50 application fee
- Official transcripts from all secondary schools attended
- One letter of recommendation from a guidance/college counselor and/or the Common Application Secondary school report
- One letter of recommendation from a teacher who can speak to academic ability.
- SAT or ACT scores

Deadlines

Applications must be submitted through the Common Application on the deadline indicated below:

November 15 Early Decision
November 15 Early Action
January 15 Regular Decision

Supporting documents may be submitted after the deadline to complete a student's application. However, an application cannot be reviewed until all documents have been received by the admissions office.

Applications received after the Regular Decision deadline will be considered on a space-available basis.

UNIVERSITY OF RICHMOND

AT A GLANCE

The University of Richmond, a private, liberal arts university, provides a collaborative learning and research environment unlike any other in higher education, offering students an extraordinary combination of the liberal arts with law, business, leadership studies, and continuing education.

LOCATION AND ENVIRONMENT

With its 350 acre campus in the city of Richmond, it is characterized by a distinctly integrated student experience—a rich and innovative life for students inside and outside the classroom—and a welcoming spirit that prizes diversity of experience and thought. It is rooted in a determination to engage as a meaningful part of our community and our world. It is committed to ensuring its opportunities are accessible to talented students of all backgrounds.

OFF-CAMPUS OPPORTUNITIES

Every traditional undergraduate student is guaranteed funding of up to $4,000 for one summer research or internship experience before they graduate. Faculty-mentored research experiences allow students to pursue original intellectual discovery while also providing them with the laboratory, field, or archival experience that positions them to compete successfully for admission and fellowships to elite graduate programs.

Internships in fields ranging from healthcare to nonprofits are essential avenues to jobs after graduation, and the search begins with Career Services. In the case of unpaid internships, UR Summer Fellowships enable students to pursue those opportunities that, taken early in their academic career, position them to secure subsequent paid internships and gain traction in the professional world.

ACADEMIC PROGRAMS

Richmond integrates a liberal arts core with a top-ranked school of business and the nation's first school of leadership studies, as well as schools of law and professional and continuing studies—a combination you won't find anywhere else. But it goes deeper than that. When an undergraduate can take a first-year seminar with a law professor, or seamlessly pair an economics major with a minor in art history, that's when you will know you are at Richmond.

FINANCIAL AID

The University of Richmond meets 100% of demonstrated financial need for all admitted students. Richmond is need-blind in admission for U.S. citizens and permanent residents and need-aware when reviewing admission applications from non-U.S. citizens. Also, Richmond reserves the right to be need-aware for transfer applicants. For more information, visit http://financialaid.richmond.edu/prospective/index.html.

First year students should apply by December 1 for consideration for the Richmond Scholars program. Richmond Scholar awards range from tuition to tuition, room, and board. All first year applicants are considered for Presidential Scholarships which is one-third tuition for up to four years. To be considered, submit the admission application and supporting application documents by the stated deadline.

STUDENT ORGANIZATIONS AND ACTIVITIES

90% of undergraduates live on campus all four years with a variety of housing opportunities including gender flexible options. Dining Services is consistently ranked for "best campus food" with numerous eateries across campus and one central dining hall. With more than 190 student clubs and organizations, there are a wide range of ways Richmond students connect with the campus and local communities.

As the only Spiders in the NCAA, Richmond fields 17 Division I sports and 30 sport club teams, winning 47 conference championships since 2000. The Richmond Rowdies cheer on our athletes year round.

ADMISSIONS PROCESS

The University of Richmond offers non-binding Early Action, binding Early Decision I and II, and Regular Decision plans for the fall term for first year applicants. Students interested in transferring may apply for spring or fall admission. To be eligible to transfer, you must complete or be in progress to complete at least 24 credit hours before the intended enrollment term.

First Year Application Deadlines

- Early Decision I–November 1
- Early Action–November 1
- Richmond Scholars consideration–December 1
- Early Decision II–January 1
- Regular Decision–January 1

Transfer Application Deadlines

- Fall Priority–February 15
- Fall Space Available–April 15
- Spring–November 1

For more information about application requirements and deadline details, visit http://admissions.richmond.edu/process/index.html.

UNIVERSITY OF SAN FRANCISCO

AT A GLANCE

The University of San Francisco—a private, Jesuit university—reflects the energy, diversity, and opportunities of the city that surrounds it. USF gives students from all backgrounds an education that is intensely personalized, intellectually inspiring, and designed expressly to help them change the world for the better.

The university enrolls 6,577 undergraduate and 4,059 graduate students, offers over 100 undergraduate and graduate degree programs, and boasts a network of more than 110,000 alumni worldwide. The school's campus, in the geographic center of the city, puts students in the middle of everything San Francisco has to offer.

LOCATION AND ENVIRONMENT

Our 55–acre campus in the geographic center of San Francisco offers big grassy lawns, panoramic views of the city and the Pacific Ocean, and a classic college feel, with residence halls next to labs and libraries. First–year students are guaranteed on–campus housing, and many students have views of the Golden Gate Bridge, Marin Headlands, and Farallon Islands from their dorm rooms. The campus is small enough to walk across in ten minutes, but large enough to offer plenty of space to learn, study, and relax.

CAMPUS FACILITIES AND EQUIPMENT

USF offers six on-campus and one off–campus residence halls, with meal plans and common areas. The Lone Mountain Residence Hall, with anticipated completion in fall 2021, will have 600 additional beds, event spaces, and a new dining commons.

Gleeson Library offers spaces for individuals and group study, computer labs, and the Learning, Writing, and Speaking Centers that provide free academic support to students. It also houses the Thacher Gallery, which curates exhibitions by emerging artists from campus and across California.

Across from the library is the Lo Schiavo Center for Science and Innovation, which houses a lecture halls, spaces for collaborative learning, and labs for chemistry, toxicology, and mathematics. Harney Science Center's new biotechnology laboratory is equipped with the latest technologies used by Bay Area life science and biotech companies. The Innovation Hive, currently under construction, is scheduled for completion in summer 2020 and will offer all students use of 3D printers, power tools, and heavy equipment for wood and metal work.

Many programs have dedicated spaces as well. Our Nursing Skills Laboratory is exclusively for nursing students, and our Hospitality Management students enjoy the use of a demonstration industrial kitchen. Kalmanovitz Hall houses all programs in the humanities and social sciences, and features a rooftop sculpture garden and seventeen laboratories for language, writing, media, and psychology. The 281 Masonic building houses the Performing Arts and Social Justice department and the Leo T. McCarthy Center for Public Service and the Common Good, while the Presentation Theater and Lone Mountain Studio Theater offer space for theatrical productions and guest speakers.

University Center, in the heart of campus, is home to the USF bookstore, the Center for Academic and Student Achievement, the Career Services Center.

The Koret Health and Recreation Center provides three floors of exercise equipment, court games, weight training, massage, personal training, fitness classes, and an Olympic–size pool. In late 2019 and with ongoing improvements in 2020, the Sobrato Center will offer premium seating at athletic events, a hall of fame, and expanded practice and weight–training facilities. It will also serve as a concert and event venue.

OFF-CAMPUS OPPORTUNITIES

Our campus is just minutes from the Financial District, Golden Gate Park, and the Pacific Ocean. Students enjoy the city's natural beauty, 36 unique neighborhoods, cultural attractions, sporting events from the Bay Area's seven professional teams, and unlimited access to research, internship, and employment opportunities at the Bay Area and Silicon Valley's most successful companies. At USF, everything in San Francisco is only a walk, bike, bus, or BART ride away.

In San Francisco, professors immerse students in projects throughout the city. Whether you're partnering with a local nonprofit for a sociology class, designing a housing project down the street for an architecture class, or testing water samples in a lake for environmental science, you'll get one–of–a–kind practical experiences as a college student in San Francisco.

Through USF's Center for Global Education, students also have access to more than 100 study abroad opportunities in 47 countries. Some programs offer internships to gain valuable work experience abroad or field study programs with research opportunities and experiential learning.

In addition, many professors organize trips with their own classes locally and internationally to supplement the class curriculum.

ACADEMIC PROGRAMS

Whatever your interests, you'll find programs that will encourage you to step up, speak up, and challenge your assumptions.

- More than 100 undergraduate majors, minors, and interdisciplinary concentrations.
- A Core Curriculum that will push you to explore new passions and communicate your beliefs on complex questions in humanities, science, ethics, and the arts.
- A tight–knit and supportive learning community with an average class size of 23.
- The Honors College, which includes interdisciplinary forum courses and special lectures from scholars and artists in different fields.
- Dual–degree and credential programs for business, nursing, psychology, economics, teaching, and more.
- A new engineering program that develops engineers who are humane, responsive, and inclusive.

Our Living–Learning Communities offer an opportunity for deeper connected learning. Together with your peers, you can enroll in a common set of courses and live together in shared housing:

- Black Living–Learning Community: Explore the intellectual and political history of Black Americans and engage with the local Black community in the Bay Area.
- Erasmus Community: Explore ethics, service, and justice at local and global levels.
- Martín–Baró Scholars: Examine social justice issues in San Francisco through classroom assignments and a service–learning project.
- St. Ignatius Institute: A blend of rigorous academics and spiritual expression and growth, open for students of any (or no) religious affiliation.
- Esther Madríz Diversity Scholars: Analyze the 40-year culture of hip-hop to explore issues of diversity and inequality.

While our professors are accomplished scholars and researchers—96% hold the highest degree in their academic disciplines—they're at USF because they put teaching first. You'll find them next to your desk, not behind a microphone. They're mentors as well as teachers, and they'll look for opportunities to put you to work helping them with research and pointing you toward internships.

MAJORS AND DEGREES OFFERED

Undergraduate students choose USF for a whole range of reasons: The small, rigorous classes (average size 23) taught by professors, not teaching assistants. The warm and vibrant campus community with students from 50 states and 98 countries. Our location in the heart of a city known for its optimism, energy, and opportunity. Or, our Jesuit values that encourage students to use their education to change the world for the better.

We have 43 majors and 70+ minors through the College of Arts and Sciences, School of Management, School of Nursing and Health Professions, and our new School of Engineering. Students can pursue special certificates on top of their major or minor to boost their understanding in a particular area. There are also dual–degree programs in health, business, and science, as well as a teacher credential program for undergraduate students. In 2019, the top 10 most popular programs were:

1. Business/marketing
2. Health professions and related programs
3. Social sciences
4. Communication/journalism
5. Psychology
6. Biological/life sciences
7. Visual and performing arts
8. Computer and information sciences
9. Natural resources and conservation
10. English

TUITION, ROOM, BOARD, FEES

Estimated cost of attendance for 2020–21:
Undergraduate tuition: $51,930
Mandatory Fees: $552
Housing: $10,930
Standard Meal Plan: $5,060
Total estimated cost of attendance: $68,472

This estimate does not include books, supplies, transportation, or personal items.

FINANCIAL AID

Almost 90% of the fall 2019 class received some form of financial aid, with an average aid package of nearly $36,000. The FAFSA is required to receive a financial aid package.

Domestic first-year students who want to receive full consideration for financial aid must file the Free Application for Federal Student Aid (FAFSA) by the January 15 priority deadline.

We encourage all students and families to estimate their net price—the amount students will pay after scholarships and grants. Our Net Price Calculator can be found online at https://www.usfca.edu/admission/financial-aid/net-price-calculator

STUDENT ORGANIZATIONS AND ACTIVITIES

In 2019, USF was ranked #3 in student ethnic diversity among all national universities (U.S. News and World Report). True to our Jesuit values, USF welcomes students from all backgrounds, which we believe leads to a stronger educational experience and richer ideas. The campus serves as a space for complex conversations and a meeting place for perspectives from all walks of life. While Catholic students make up approximately one fifth of the student body, the rest identify with other religious groups, or with no religion at all.

The fall 2019 incoming class was 33% first–generation students, 15% international, 33% Pell Grant recipients, and came from 46 states and 47 countries.

At USF, you'll always have things to do and communities to join:

- More than 100 clubs spanning academic honor clubs, student government, media, business, performance, politics, recreational, spiritual, service, and Greek organizations
- The Culturally Focused Clubs Council encourages collaboration among the 20+ cultural organizations
- 22 intramural and club sport teams and 17 Division I sports teams
- Muscat Scholars Program: An intensive academic program to support incoming, first–year, first–generation students in their transition to college life
- Magis Emerging Leaders Program: A year–long fellowship for first–year students to become socially responsible leaders
- Black Achievement Success and Engagement (BASE) initiative: Creating an academically challenging and personally supportive educational experience for Black–identified students, including a four–year Black Scholars Program, a Black Living–Learning Community, and a Black Resource Center
- The University Ministry supports the spiritual, religious, and pastoral needs of students from all religious backgrounds with retreats, immersion trips, mass, meditation, and more.

Our Career Services Center supports students to secure at least three internships before graduation. We take students on exclusive visits to local companies and bring top employers on campus to meet you. Best of all, our alumni working at those companies regularly come back to campus to tell you how to ace the interview, what to wear, and how to write the perfect follow–up email. Here's a partial list of where our students intern, and get hired: Apple, Berkshire Hathaway, Cisco, Deloitte, DWA Media, Gap Inc., Golden State Warriors, Google, Fine Arts Museums of San Francisco, Federal Reserve Bank, Kiva, Marriott, Nike, Peace Corps, Pixar, San Francisco Mayor's Office, San Francisco Unified School District, Silicon Valley Bank, Stanford Hospital, Square, Teach for America, Tesla, Uber, University of California—San Francisco.

ADMISSIONS PROCESS

We're looking for students who are sincerely interested in pursuing a rigorous, meaningful education and who hope to make a positive difference in the world. We welcome students of all races, nationalities, and religious beliefs (or no religious belief) to apply. Eligibility is based on high school coursework and GPA, the application essay(s), an academic recommendation, and extracurricular involvement. We do not require standardized test scores for admission. If you choose to enroll, we'll need your test scores for advising and course placement.

If you've taken college coursework after your high school graduation, you must apply as a transfer student, regardless of the number of units/semesters you've taken.

International applicants are required to submit TOEFL or IELTS test scores. This requirement can be waived with sufficient SAT or ACT scores.

For more information on our application process, visit https://www.usfca.edu/undergraduate.

THE UNIVERSITY OF SCRANTON

AT A GLANCE

The University of Scranton is a Catholic and Jesuit institution that delivers a transformative education, grounded in the liberal arts, to over 3,800 undergraduate students.

With a rich tradition of academic excellence, our programs are taught in small classes and led by faculty who are experts in their fields. Every aspect of a Scranton education exists to help our students succeed. Scholars are challenged here, and supported.

Here, you'll have many choices. With 68 majors and 47 minors across three colleges, faculty and staff work with students to choose a combination of majors and minors that suit them as individuals.

Our graduates are known for their devotion to the welfare of other human beings and by their special commitment to the pursuit of social justice. The University, made up of over 3,800 undergraduates, is one of just 361 colleges in the nation that earned the 2015 Community Engagement Classification designated by the Carnegie Foundation for the Advancement of Teaching, which recognizes Scranton for success in curricular engagement and outreach partnerships.

Scranton develops leaders in every sense through rigorous preparation in students' chosen fields coupled with a commitment to educating the whole person, or *cura personalis*. We challenge students morally, spiritually and intellectually. Students extend their academic experience through participation in honors programs, internships, faculty-student research and study abroad, and the University provides excellent preparation for medical and other health professions doctoral programs, law school, graduate school, and post-graduate fellowships and scholarships.

In addition to conducting high-level research alongside professors, our students find abundant opportunities to apply classroom learning in the real world. We encourage all students to gain experience and make connections through internships. And they regularly collaborate on professional projects within the local community and beyond.

Year after year, Scranton is recognized among the top tier of universities in the nation for the outstanding quality of its education. According to *U.S. News and World Report*, Scranton is sixth among master's universities in the North. We are also ranked among the "Best Colleges for Veterans." Our Kania School of Management was ranked among the "Best Graduate Schools," as was our online graduate programs in education and nursing. We're also among the nation's top colleges according to Forbes and The Princeton Review.

According to PayScale's most recent salary report, Scranton is in the top 15% of universities listed by the median salaries of their alumni. This is just one of several "best value" rankings for the University.

LOCATION AND ENVIRONMENT

Our 58-acre campus offers the best of both worlds—the city and the mountains. We are located in Pennsylvania's Pocono Northeast in the heart of the city of Scranton, a vibrant college town, home to five colleges and universities. In the city and surrounding area, there are coffeehouses, eateries, festivals, shops and minor-league sports teams, as well as a nearby outdoor concert venue and ski mountain.

We're close to New York City, Philadelphia and Washington, D.C. so Scranton students have unique access to professional learning experiences with many of the world's leading companies and organizations.

CAMPUS FACILITIES AND EQUIPMENT

In recent years, we have invested more than $260 million in campus improvements. Ninety-eight percent of the University's housing is new or renovated and our dining facilities are ranked among the very best in the nation.

In 2011 and 2012, we opened the state-of-the-art Loyola Science Center, a 200,000-square-foot, Gold LEED certified science facility featuring 22 class and seminar rooms, 34 laboratories and a multistory atrium.

In fall 2015, we dedicated the new Leahy Hall, which houses our physical therapy, occupational therapy and exercise science departments and features 25 laboratories and multiple simulation environments including a hospital patient room for acute and long-term care and a streetscape for rehabilitation education.

Most recently, we dedicated the new $14 million Kevin P. Quinn, S.J., Athletics Campus, now home to the University's soccer, lacrosse, field hockey, baseball and softball Division III NCAA teams.

ACADEMIC PROGRAMS

We offer five unique options for honors programs. First, each year Scranton selects approximately 50 of the most qualified first-year students to join the Special Jesuit Liberal Arts Honors Program (SJLA). As an alternative approach to satisfying general education requirements, this unique, four-year program pairs selected students with designated faculty in a curriculum that is deeply rooted in philosophy and dedicated to serving the common good.

Second, our Business Honors Program is geared toward students interested in pursuing academic excellence in business. Students engage in four years of honors studies in the areas of economics, entrepreneurship, operations management, accounting, finance, international business, marketing and management. Students also focus on their personal development through a series of extracurricular activities in the areas of service and career building.

Third, open to students from all majors, our Business Leadership Honors Program allows students to explore basic theories and concepts of leadership through special seminars and courses in management, ethics, strategy and analysis. This highly selective program accepts 15 sophomores each spring.

Next, the Magis Honors Program in STEM provides our undergraduate students with a more intense, interdisciplinary experience of research in STEM fields. Participants are enrolled in a special first year seminar and a series of 1.5-credit seminar courses culminating in a senior thesis project.

Finally, open to all majors, the Honors Program each year accepts between 40 and 50 of our most able sophomores, giving them the opportunity to take seminars together and to work one-on-one with professors both in tutorials and on projects.

Additionally, we offer opportunities to participate in research and other creative projects with faculty mentors through the Faculty/Student Research Program, which students can begin participating in as early as their first year.

Scranton has connections to programs across the globe, helping students in nearly every major study abroad. Since 2015, our students have studied in 37 countries. In many cases, their studies have included internships and community service.

We offer a variety of services to help our students succeed both academically and personally, including a Center for Teaching and Learning Excellence, Counseling Center, Center for Career Development and Center for Health Education and Wellness, to name a few.

MAJORS AND DEGREES OFFERED

Scranton offers more than 90 undergraduate and graduate academic programs of study through three colleges and schools. Scranton's 68 undergraduate programs of study will match your interests and prepare you to meet the future with confidence. Scranton also offers 47 minors, 19 combined or accelerated bachelor's and master's programs, more than 35 master's degree programs either on-line or on-campus, including Doctor of Business Administration, Doctor of Physical Therapy and Doctor of Nursing Practice degrees.

The Gerard R. Roche Center for Career Development helps students focus on career decisions that are consistent with their unique talents, aspirations and vision for living. Professional counselors help students discover links between their personal traits and career options through individual counseling, workshops, and many other resources.

All students can receive training in resume and cover letter writing as well as interview and job search techniques. They are also able to participate in employer on-campus recruiting visits, employment fairs, and the annual Graduate School Fair.

99% of the Class of 2019 were employed, continuing their education or engaging in service within six months of graduating. Over the past 20 years, an average of 80% of our applicants to doctoral health professions schools were accepted to schools of medicine, dentistry, veterinary medicine, pharmacy, podiatry and optometry.

Since 1972, 158 of our graduates have earned a Fulbright or other international fellowship.

Our professors are not only highly regarded researchers and teachers; they are caring involved mentors as well. They attend student plays, games and concerts. They lead study and service trips. They serve as club and team advisors. They invest in the lives of their students.

When it comes to scholarly activity, Scranton professors rival the best. Their works are published widely in prestigious scholarly journals. They are featured in national media and are frequent presenters at national and international conferences. Their research projects, many of which are conducted with the assistance of students, are often supported by competitive grants. Faculty members hold degrees from 289 universities in 25 countries on five continents, and 89% of full-time, instructional faculty members hold doctoral or other terminal degrees.

Majors are available in:

Accounting
Advertising/Public Relations
Applied Computing
Applied Mathematics
Biochemistry
Biochemistry, Cell & Molecular Biology
Biology
Biomathematics
Biophysics
Business Administration
Business Analytics
Business Communication
Chemistry
Chemistry/Business
Communication
Community Health Education
Computer Engineering
Computer Science
Counseling and Human Services
Criminal Justice
Economics (Business)
Economics (Social Science)
Education
Early and Primary Teacher Education
Middle Level Teacher Education
Secondary Education
Electrical Engineering
Engineering Management
English
Entrepreneurship
Environmental Science
Finance
Forensic Chemistry
Health Administration
History
Human Resources Studies
Information Technology
International Business
International Language/Business
International Studies
Journalism & Electronic Media
Kinesiology
Languages & Cultures
French & Francophone Cultural Studies
German Cultural Studies

Greek Studies
Hispanic Studies
Italian
Latin Studies
Latin American Studies
Management
Marketing
Mathematics (BS or BA)
Mechanical Engineering
Military Science
Neuroscience
Nursing
Occupational Therapy (Master's)
Operations Management
Philosophy
Physical Therapy (DPT)
Physics
Physiology
Political Science
Pre-Engineering
Psychology
Social Media Strategies
Sociology
Theatre
Theology/Religious Studies
Women's & Gender Studies

Accelerated Graduate Programs

Accountancy (4 or 5-year)
BS/MBA in Accounting
BS/MBA in Finance
BS/MBA in Marketing
BS/MBA in Operations Management
BS or BA/MBA in many majors
BS/MS in Special Education (5-year)

Pre-Professional

Dentistry
Law
Medicine
Optometry
Pharmacy
Physician Assistant
Podiatry
Veterinary Medicine

TUITION, ROOM, BOARD, FEES

Undergraduate tuition and fees for freshmen in the 2019–20 academic year is $45,790, and room and board charges are $15,310.

FINANCIAL AID

Of the freshman aid applicants who were enrolled for the fall semester, 96% were offered funding from University scholarships and need-based grants. The average freshman aid package for 2019–20, not including private and parent loans, was $34,500.

There are full-and partial-tuition academic scholarships available, which are awarded on a merit basis, taking into consideration academic achievement and standardized test scores.

STUDENT ORGANIZATIONS AND ACTIVITIES

As part of our mission, Scranton is committed to advancing the Jesuit tradition of forming men and women for and with others. Service experiences enable our students to put their learning and values into practice as they work and collaborate with others, develop interpersonal and leadership skills and shape lives of meaning and selfless service.

The University offers a 24/7 college experience. Our students are involved, helping to plan and guide more than 900 events each year. They participate in leadership programs and workshops and engage in extensive co-curricular activities. Through experiences geared toward personal and professional development, they grow into capable confident, lifelong leaders.

The University also provides opportunities to participate in an array of social, educational, wellness and retreat activities. There are more than 80 active clubs and organizations, from Urban Beats Crew to rugby to Habitat for Humanity.

Scranton fields NCAA Division III varsity teams in eleven sports for men and twelve sports for women. Nearly all of our teams compete in NCAA Division III's Landmark Conference. In addition, more than 1,500 students are involved in recreational sports and intramurals, including leagues, tournaments and weekend special events.

ADMISSIONS PROCESS

Scranton welcomes students of all races, national origins and religious beliefs. We look for high-achieving students who have shown that they are prepared for a challenging college program through their high school course selection and level, grades, class rank and SAT/ACT scores. Also important are involvement in activities, athletics and service, and work experience. A campus visit with a personal appointment or group presentation is encouraged.

We offer an Early Action Application program with a Nov. 15 deadline. Students who apply early will receive notification of admission on Dec. 15. For students who choose not to apply for Early Action, we operate on a rolling admissions basis, with a preferred application deadline of March 1 and an undergraduate program confirmation deadline of May 1.

Students may apply without submitting SAT/ACT scores if they are in the top 30% of their graduating class. If their high school does not rank, students must have a GPA of at least 3.0 on a 4.0 scale. In addition, students may be asked to schedule an on-campus interview.

The SAT/ACT Optional application is not available to students applying for the following programs: Master of Accountancy, BS/MBA in various majors, BA/MBA in various majors, Education, Nursing, Occupational Therapy, Doctor of Physical Therapy, or the Pre-Medical and Pre-Health Professions Program. Students may apply online for free using the Common Application. Visit scranton.edu/apply for more information.

UNIVERSITY OF TAMPA

AT A GLANCE

The University of Tampa is a private, medium-sized, comprehensive university in the heart of Tampa. UT offers students an exciting combination of challenging coursework and real-world learning experience in more than 200 areas of study. Situated on a beautiful 110-acre campus, the University is adjacent to the Hillsborough River and downtown Tampa. Students enjoy a traditional, self-contained campus only steps away from the professional and cultural opportunities of a bustling city. At the center of campus lies Plant Hall, once a luxurious hotel for the rich and famous. This historical landmark is complemented by modern surroundings and excellent facilities including a student union, art studios and gallery, theaters, computer resource centers, athletic facilities, science labs and new residence halls. Approximately 9,600 students (8,600 full-time undergraduates) are enrolled at UT. With students from all 50 states and 132 countries, UT provides a diverse and dynamic environment. Students may choose from 300 clubs and organizations, including honor societies, student media, fraternities and sororities, community service groups and intramural sports. The University of Tampa has one of the top NCAA Division II sports programs in the nation, winning 18 national championships, including recent championships in baseball (2019, 2015, 2013, 2007, 2006), women's volleyball (2018, 2014, 2006) and women's soccer (2007).

LOCATION AND ENVIRONMENT

Located on the west central coast of Florida, Tampa has far more to offer than beautiful beaches and a pleasant climate. The Tampa Bay area is one of the fastest growing regions in the United States and is a leading center for the arts, international business, law, education, media and health and scientific research. Forbes and Newsweek consistently pick Tampa Bay as one of the nation's best places to live.

CAMPUS FACILITIES AND EQUIPMENT

UT has invested approximately $650 million in new academic facilities, technology and residence halls since 1998, making this national historic landmark the model of a modern university. 93% of residence halls are new within the past 15 years and most others have been renovated recently. (For residence hall video tours, visit www.ut.edu/residencelife/videos.) The Vaughn Center and residence hall complex serves as the hub of student life. Here students find food courts, recreational areas, a theater, student office space, the Barnes & Noble campus store and a ninth-floor conference center with incredible views of Tampa Bay. Morsani Hall offers state-of-the-art amenities and eight separate dining venues. Other outstanding facilities and resources include the Sykes College of Business, a waterfront Marine Science Field Station and research vessels, Ferman Music Center, Reeves Theater, the 1,000-seat Falk Theatre, R.K. Bailey Art Studios and Sykes Chapel and Center for Faith and Values. The newly renovated Martinez Athletics Center, Naimoli Family Softball Complex and Naimoli Family Athletics and Intramural Complex represent some of the best athletic facilities in the country. Students also enjoy a 21st-century fitness center, completed in fall 2016.

OFF-CAMPUS OPPORTUNITIES

Across the river in downtown is the Tampa Museum of Art, Straz Center for the Performing Arts, Florida Aquarium, Amalie Arena and an outstanding public library. Students are able to walk to the dynamic Sparkman Wharf, which includes 15 dining venues and a beautiful bayside view. Busch Gardens is several miles from campus, and Walt Disney World and Universal Studios are only 90 minutes away. Tampa International Airport is 5 miles from campus.

ACADEMIC PROGRAMS

The University of Tampa's undergraduate curriculum is designed to give students a broad academic and cultural background as well as a concentrated study in a major. Students complete a comprehensive core curriculum known as the Baccalaureate Experience, which is highlighted by the unique and innovative First-Year Seminar—an academic orientation program that encourages student development via exploration of global issues, career possibilities and critical thinking and communication skills. International experience is an important focus at The University of Tampa. Through globally oriented courses and study abroad opportunities, students are prepared to live and work internationally. In 2019 there were more than 24 faculty-led travel courses to countries such as Costa Rica, Ghana, Cuba, Morocco and China. For qualifying students, UT offers a rigorous and rewarding Honors Program of expanded instruction, student research, internships and the opportunity to study at Oxford University.

MAJORS AND DEGREES OFFERED

The University of Tampa offers bachelor's degrees in accounting, actuarial science, advertising and public relations, allied health, animation, art, athletic training, biochemistry, biology, business information technology, chemistry, communication, criminology and criminal justice, cybersecurity, dance, digital arts, economics, education (elementary and secondary certification), English, entrepreneurship, environmental science, film and media arts, finance, financial enterprise systems, forensic science, graphic design, history, human performance, international business, international studies, journalism, liberal studies, management, management information systems, marine science (biology and chemistry), marketing, mathematical programming, mathematics, music, music education, music performance, musical theatre, new media, nursing, philosophy, physical education, physics, political science, psychology, public health, sociology, Spanish, sport management, theatre and writing. Minors and concentrations are offered in advertising, aerospace studies, applied sociology, art history, art therapy, Asian studies, biology/business, biology/molecular, biology/organismal and evolutionary, business administration, business analytics, criminal investigation, exercise physiology, French, international studies, law, justice and advocacy, leadership studies, military science, naval science, professional and technical writing, recreation, speech/theatre and women's and gender studies. Pre-professional programs offered include pre-dentistry, pre-law, pre-medicine, pre-veterinary science, allied health and chemistry. An undergraduate School of Continuing Studies offers 30 degree programs designed for adults who want to study part-time. Four summer sessions also offer excellent learning and professional advancement opportunities. At the graduate level, the business school offers an MBA (full time and part time), 4+1 MBA and M.S. degrees in accounting, business analytics, cybersecurity, entrepreneurship, finance and marketing. An M.S. in Nursing, Doctor of Nursing Practice, Master of Physician Assistant Medicine, M.S. in Exercise and Nutrition Science, M.S. in Criminology and Criminal Justice, M.A. in Professional Communication, M.Ed. in Curriculum and Instruction, M.Ed. in Educational Leadership, 4+1 M.Ed. and M.S. in Instructional Design and Technology are also offered. For a full list of programs, visit www.ut.edu/degrees.

TUITION, ROOM, BOARD, FEES

The average cost for the 2020–2021 academic year is $30,790 for tuition and fees and $11,468 for room and board. 95% of UT students students receive financial assistance.

FINANCIAL AID

The high-quality, private education offered by The University of Tampa is not as difficult to finance as some students may think. Each family's situation is evaluated individually for need-based assistance. Academic achievements, leadership potential, athletic skills and other special talents are also recognized, regardless of need. Academic scholarships are awarded to most entering first-year students with a 3.0 unweighted GPA or above. Transfer, leadership, departmental, Phi Theta Kappa, International Baccalaureate and ROTC scholarships are also available. Learn more at www.ut.edu/financialaid.

STUDENT ORGANIZATIONS AND ACTIVITIES

UT offers 300 clubs, organizations and teams, making it easy for students to get involved in campus life. Options include academic and social clubs, leadership groups and student government, amongst many others. For a full list, visit www.ut.edu/studentorgs.

ADMISSIONS PROCESS

The University of Tampa is an academically competitive institution that offers several non-binding early action admission dates. Visit www.ut.edu/admissions for more details.

UNIVERSITY OF TULSA

AT A GLANCE

The University of Tulsa (TU) is a private, comprehensive doctoral-degree-granting university that provides education of the highest quality in the arts, humanities, sciences, engineering, business, education, applied health sciences and law. TU features four undergraduate colleges: the Kendall College of Arts and Sciences, the Collins College of Business, the College of Engineering and Natural Sciences and the Oxley College of Health Sciences, as well as the College of Law and Graduate School.

TU's 11:1 student/faculty ratio, average class size of 20, and emphasis on individual attention anchor an educational culture where students are rigorously challenged and comprehensively supported.

The university is fully accredited by the North Central Association of Colleges and Universities, and is an NCAA Division IA participant in the American Athletic Conference. TU maintains a covenant relationship with the Presbyterian Church (USA).

Extracurricular opportunities include intramural sports, special-interest clubs, preprofessional organizations, national fraternities and sororities, community service organizations, an active student government, departmental honorary organizations and campus ministry groups.

Total fall 2019 enrollment was 4,380, with 3,269 undergraduates and 1,111 graduate and law students. The ratio of men to women is 54:46 and 33% are multicultural students. Over half the students are from out of state and international students make up 14% of the student population, with 68 countries represented.

The University of Tulsa is Oklahoma's top university.

LOCATION AND ENVIRONMENT

TU's 216-acre residential campus is in Tulsa, Oklahoma (961,561 MSA). The city's prominent industries include energy, telecommunications, high technology, manufacturing, health care, aerospace and education which present opportunities for internships and employment after graduation. Tulsans enjoy Broadway shows in the Performing Arts Center and pop concerts in the BOK Center (arena) as well as acclaimed ballet and opera companies, symphony, Philbrook Museum, Gilcrease Museum, Tulsa Arts District and cultural festivals. Local professional sports include minor league baseball, hockey and soccer. The popular River Parks area features jogging and bicycling trails, while Guthrie Green is a popular arts, music and food truck destination. Tulsa's world-class riverfront park, Gathering Place, was voted USA Today's Best New Attraction of 2018.

CAMPUS FACILITIES AND EQUIPMENT

Since 2002, The University of Tulsa has added one million square feet of building space and a stunning entrance.

Hardesty Hall, TU's newest building, houses 300 residents and houses the offices of Career Services, Center for Global Education, Multicultural Affairs, Greek Life and the English Institute for international students.

The Lorton Performance Center, which houses the School of Music and the Department of Film Studies, features a 700-seat concert hall, specialized rehearsal and practice rooms and a film production suite with post-production editing and scoring capabilities.

In 2012, the College of Engineering & Natural Sciences added two new buildings: J. Newton Rayzor Hall, which features 24 integrated classrooms and state-of-the-art teaching/research laboratories. Rayzor houses the Tandy School of Computer Science and the Department of Electrical and Computer Engineering. Stephenson Hall is home to the McDougall School of Petroleum Engineering and the Department of Mechanical Engineering. Additional research facilities are located in Keplinger Hall and at TU's North Campus where government and industry-funded research consortia foster student learning while exploring innovations and solving petroleum industry problems.

The historic McFarlin Library and the Mabee Legal Information Center house more than 5 million items. McFarlin holdings include 991,000 volumes, more than 680,000 titles, 54,000 electronic journals, 450,000 electronic books, and more than 1,000 collections of electronic reference sources and databases as well as print resources. McFarlin's Department of Special Collections and University Archives' rare book holdings are internationally recognized, particularly in Native American history and law. The department includes one of the five largest collections in the world on James Joyce, the life archive of Nobel Laureate Sir V.S. Naipaul and holdings in nineteenth and twentieth century Irish, British and American Literature. The library's Academic Technology Center annex includes computer labs, a coffee shop and reading rooms.

Helmerich Hall, which houses the Collins College of Business, was renovated to include innovative learning spaces such as the Williams Student Services Center and Studio Blue. Academic centers include the Schools of Accounting and CIS; Energy Economics, Policy and Commerce and Finance, Operations Management and International Business; as well as the Departments of Economics and Management and Marketing.

The Mary K. Chapman Center for Communicative Disorders, part of the university's Oxley College of Health Sciences, serves the community in its clinical facility and is the learning center for the Department of Communication Disorders. The department has the latest equipment for research, diagnostic and therapy activities.

The Kendall College of Arts and Sciences features the Alexandre Hogue Gallery in the School of Art, Design and Art History, TUTV Media Lab, as well as psychology and anthropology labs.

Renovated in 2014, the Allen Chapman Student Union includes a food court with nine eateries and a convenience store. It also houses an ATM, offices for student organizations, lecture and meeting rooms, the Faculty Club, post office and the Hurricane Hut sports bar.

The TU College of Law received an "A" from National Jurist magazine for Best Law School Facility with more than 110,000 square feet.

The Oxley College of Health Sciences, housed at 1215 S. Boulder Avenue in downtown Tulsa, occupies floors 1 through 5 of remodeled space that encompasses 52,000 square feet. The college includes state-of-the-art classrooms and the Lawson Family Nursing Simulation Center and Skills Laboratory.

The Donald W. Reynolds Center is TU's arena and convocation center. This facility, home for the intercollegiate basketball and volleyball programs, has cutting-edge facilities for video editing and training.

The university's sports and recreation complex features the Collins Fitness Center, Michael D. Case Tennis Center (which has hosted NCAA Finals), track, intramural and NCAA-grade soccer fields and softball fields.

In partnership with the City of Tulsa, the university manages Gilcrease Museum as well as the Zarrow Center for Art and Education, which provides gallery space, classes and studio space in the city's Tulsa Arts District.

TU students have the option of hundreds of attractive and convenient on-campus apartments and residence halls.

OFF-CAMPUS OPPORTUNITIES

The university strongly supports studying abroad, and the Center for Global Engagement helps students locate the perfect program, whether it is for TU credit or as an intern/volunteer. Students have hundreds of options through direct exchange with an international university, through an affiliate-sponsored program or as part of a faculty-led course.

Many students take advantage of the internship opportunities afforded by Tulsa's business and industry community, as well as in the arts, social services and government agencies.

ACADEMIC PROGRAMS

The Tulsa Curriculum links a broad, humanities-based core and writing for all students across all disciplines. TU students can receive a personalized education that is well rounded. Candidates for graduation must complete at least 124 semester hours of coursework.

The Honors Program engages students in a critical examination of the major epochs and ideas of Western thought and culture through careful study of primary texts. A separate application is required. The Tulsa Undergraduate Research Challenge (TURC) program combines advanced research, scholarship, and community service.

TU's Global Scholars Program engages students in global issues from the perspective of their particular major. Students take a set of classes that explore the big questions affecting the world today and participate in monthly programming on campus and an international study, research or intern experience.

The one-year Presidential Leaders Fellowship program prepares students to maximize their college experience through various service opportunities, in addition to weekly classes and special projects.

The TU Center for Information Security is developing defenses against cyber-terrorist attacks and information warfare. The center supports TU's National Security Agency (NSA)-accredited certificate program in information assurance and a curriculum that integrates information security with computer law and policy issues. TU has been designated a Center of Excellence in Information Assurance by the NSA and is one of six pioneer institutions selected by the National Science Foundation for the Federal Cyber Service Initiative (Cyber Corps).

Air Force ROTC is available through a satellite program.

Students may receive credit through Advanced Placement testing. Depending on their test scores, students who complete the International Baccalaureate diploma can receive up to 30 college credits.

The University of Tulsa operates on a semester calendar. The fall term begins in late August, the spring term in mid-January, and the summer session in late May.

MAJORS AND DEGREES OFFERED

The Kendall College of Arts and Sciences grants the Bachelor of Arts or Bachelor of Science degree in anthropology, art, art history, arts management, creative writing, economics, education, elementary education, English, environmental policy, film studies, French, German, history, media studies, music, organizational studies, political science, psychology, sociology, Spanish, women's and gender studies, and a self-designed major. The college also grants the Bachelor of Fine Arts in art and the Bachelor of Music Education degrees. Minors include most disciplines as well as advertising, African American studies, Chinese, creative writing and Medieval and early modern studies.

The Collins College of Business awards the Bachelor of Science in Business Administration degree in accounting, business and law, computer information systems (CIS), economics, energy management, finance, international business and languages, management and marketing. Minors are available in most disciplines plus business administration (for non-majors), business analytics, innovation and entrepreneurship, international business, and sport management. The college is home to several specialized centers, including the Energy Management Program, the Family Owned Business Institute, the Risk Management Center and Studio Blue.

The College of Engineering and Natural Sciences offers the Bachelor of Arts degree in biology and chemistry, earth and environmental sciences, geology, mathematics and physics and the Bachelor of Science degree in mathematics and physics. The College also offers the Bachelor of Science in Biological Science (with pre-med option), Bachelor of Science in Chemical Engineering, Bachelor of Science in Biochemistry, Bachelor of Science in Chemistry, Bachelor of Science in Computer Science, Bachelor of Science in Computer Simulation and Gaming, Bachelor of Science in Electrical and Computer Engineering, Bachelor of Science in Electrical Engineering, Bachelor of Science in Geosciences (with environmental science, geology, and petroleum engineering options), Bachelor of Science in Applied Mathematics, Bachelor of Science in Mechanical Engineering, Bachelor of Science in Petroleum Engineering, and Bachelor of Science in Engineering Physics (with bioengineering, electrical engineering, and mechanical engineering options) degrees. Minors are available in most disciplines as well as bioinformatics, computational sciences, cyber security, high performance computing, geology, and biomedical engineering. The college features state-of-the-art research facilities, including the Center for Information Security. Since 1995, more than 50 TU engineering students have received the prestigious Barry M. Goldwater Scholarship, the nation's premier award for undergraduate students studying engineering, math, or science.

The Oxley College of Health Sciences, TU's newest college, offers Bachelor of Science in Exercise and Sports Science, the Bachelor of Science in Nursing and the Bachelor of Science in Speech-language Pathology degrees. The College also offers a R.N. to B.S.N. program for licensed R.N.s with associate's degrees. Minors are available in early intervention, health sciences, coaching, exercise and sports science and speech-language pathology. The college, which houses TU's Faculty of Community Medicine, will advance the university's strong partnership with the Laureate Institute for Brain Research. The Early Careers in Community Medicine Program offers qualified students provisional acceptance into the University of Oklahoma's School of Medicine after completing an undergraduate degree at TU. A separate application is required.

The Graduate School offers the Master of Accountancy (M.Acc.) degree; the Master of Arts (M.A.) degree in anthropology (with archaeology or cultural anthropology track), clinical psychology, education, English language and literature, industrial-organizational psychology and museum science and management; the Master of Athletic Training (M.A.T.) degree; the Master of Science (M.S.) degree in applied mathematics, biological science, computer science, cyber security, geosciences and speech-language pathology; the Master of Business Administration (M.B.A.); the Master of Science in Business Analytics (M.S.B.A.); the Master of Engineering (M.E.) in chemical engineering, computer engineering, electrical engineering, mechanical engineering, and petroleum engineering; the Master of Science in Engineering (M.S.E.) in chemical engineering, computer engineering, mechanical engineering, and petroleum engineering; the Master of Energy Business (M.E.B.); the Master of Science in Mathematics and Science Education (M.S.M.S.E.); the Master of Teaching Arts (M.T.A.); the Doctor of Philosophy (Ph.D.) in biological science, chemical engineering, clinical psychology, computer engineering, computer science, English language and literature, industrial-organizational psychology, mechanical engineering and petroleum engineering; and Doctor of Nursing Practice (D.N.P.) (with adult gerontology acute care, post-master's to D.N.P. completion or family nurse practitioner option); degrees are offered by the Graduate School.

The College of Law awards the Juris Doctor (J.D.) degree.

TUITION, ROOM, BOARD, FEES

Estimated costs for the 2020–21 academic year are as follows: the typical cost for students living on campus is $55,012 including $42,950 for tuition, $12,062 for room and board, and $1,035 fees. Additional miscellaneous expenses (including books) average about $4,500 per year.

TU invested more than $21,000,000 via scholarships to the freshman class of 2017. The average combined financial aid and scholarship package offered to Tulsa students in 2017 is approximately $29,300.

FINANCIAL AID

In 2019, 96 percent of entering students received some form of financial aid (including grants, scholarships, work-study, and loans). TU offers a limited number of highly competitive Presidential Scholarships that cover full tuition, room, and board. All applicants may be considered for a range of university scholarships based on academic merit. Performance scholarships are available in music and theater by audition. The University of Tulsa participates in National Merit and National Achievement Scholarship Corporation's Finalist program, and the National Hispanic Scholar Program. Applicants for aid should submit the Free Application for Federal Student Aid (FAFSA) as soon as possible after October 1 for priority consideration.

EXPENSES PER ACADEMIC YEAR—Tuition $42,950; Room and Board $12,062; Required Fees $1,035

STUDENT ORGANIZATIONS AND ACTIVITIES

TU hosts more than 200 student organizations and societies that appeal to a wide range of student interests-from professional to recreational. (For the complete listing, see https://utulsa.edu/campus-life/student-activities/student-organizations/.) Students can participate in a variety of activities on and off campus including intramural sports, special interest clubs, trips to Tulsa's museums, parks, shopping malls, cultural events, etc.

ADMISSIONS PROCESS

The University of Tulsa seeks students whose academic background indicates potential for success in the university's rigorous academic environment. Performance in high school college-preparatory subjects and scores on the SAT or ACT are key factors in the admission evaluation, but each applicant is reviewed holistically. The counselor recommendation, extracurricular activities, and indicators of leadership, creativity, and focus are all taken into consideration. Campus visits and interviews are highly recommended.

TU has a non-binding, Early Action freshman admission plan with an application deadline of November 1. Decisions are mailed within three weeks. Applications received after November 1 are reviewed under a Rolling Admission process with notifications made on an ongoing basis after mid-December.

An official high school transcript, ACT or SAT score results, and a guidance counselor recommendation are required of freshman applicants. TU accepts the Common Application or TU's application online. TU adheres to the national Candidate's Reply Date of May 1.

For additional information, students should contact:

The University of Tulsa
Office of Admission
800 South Tucker Drive
Tulsa, Oklahoma 74104-3189

Telephone: 918-631-2307 (in Tulsa),
800-331-3050 (toll-free)
Fax: 918-631-5008
E-mail: admission@utulsa.edu
Web: www.utulsa.edu/admission

UNIVERSITY OF UTAH

AT A GLANCE

EAE offers a truly unique academic experience. We've brought together a diverse faculty with expertise in every facet of game development, and consulted with top industry professionals to create a one-of-a-kind learning experience in game development. Students studying games in the EAE program are typically interested in careers in interactive entertainment, and our curriculum is built with this goal in mind. Not only do we offer students a world-class education from a leading research university, but we also offer the opportunity to develop and enhance a professional game portfolio through our "studio simulation" projects courses.

LOCATION AND ENVIRONMENT

The University of Utah is set on the eastern edge of Salt Lake City. Campus is just minutes away from a vibrant downtown—the epicenter of SLC's restaurants, theaters, pubs, and civic events—and burgeoning neighborhoods, like the coffee-and movie-art-house hub, 9th and 9th district.

Salt Lake City is the capital of Utah, is home to about 190,000 residents, and covers 84,900 square miles, making it the 11th largest state in the U.S. There are 21 national parks and monuments in the state, including Zion National Park, Dinosaur National Monument, Arches National Park and the Golden Spike National Historic Site. Salt Lake is about a 6 hour drive from Las Vegas; 5 hours from Yellowstone National Park; and 6 hours from the Grand Canyon.

The city is home to a large international airport (the western most hub of Delta Airlines), and is easily accessed by multiple freeways. The University of Utah sits at the base of the Wasatch Mountain range, which—together with the rest of the Utah mountains—are on average the tallest in the United States, enjoying an average snowfall of 500 inches per year.

CAMPUS FACILITIES AND EQUIPMENT

EAE is centrally located on the beautiful University of Utah campus in a newly redesigned space. We are constantly improving our students learning spaces by providing access to a motion capture lab, games user research lab, streaming studio, eSports team practice facilities, classrooms equipped with Cintiq tablets at each work station, a 3D scan lab and more. The University of Utah campus has many additional resources to offer through student groups and clubs, recreation, community engagement and housing.

ACADEMIC PROGRAMS

The B.S. in Games (BSG) degree is intended specifically for students who aspire to hold careers within the professional games industry or a related field, such as simulation, edutainment, or visualization, and is designed to prepare our students to compete in an increasingly complex industry. The BSG prepares students with skills applicable to the development of entertainment software, games-based learning environments for K-12 students, professional task-training tools, serious games for health, and scientific collaboration or other contexts addressing compelling societal needs. This degree provides a technical grounding in mathematics and computational skills, core knowledge in the design and production of digital playable experiences, and specialization options that prepare students for technical supervision, tools development and overall game design.

The B.S. in Computer Science, Entertainment Arts and Engineering emphasis is offered in conjunction with the School of Computing, and a key characteristic of the program is its interdisciplinary nature. As the digital entertainment industry continuously grows, employers are focusing on students who understand both sides of the industry, whether it is computer science students with additional game arts skills, game artists with computing skills, or game producers with varying specializations. This EAE specialization offers cutting edge courses designed for undergraduate students interested in pursuing careers as video game engineers and expressing themselves using digital media, including courses covering video game design and development, 3D animation, and computer-generated special effects, in addition to the full Computer Science curriculum.

TUITION, ROOM, BOARD, FEES

Your college education is one of the best investments you'll ever make—but it doesn't have to be the biggest. A degree at the U is a phenomenal value. Recent rankings by The Economist and Brookings about the economic value of a college degree place the U in the top 7% in the nation, and #1 among Utah, PAC-12 and Big Ten public institutions.

Utah Resident Tuition, Room and Board, Books and Fees Per year: $24,000

Non-Utah Resident Tuition, Room and Board, Books and Fees Per year: $42,000

FINANCIAL AID

https://financialaid.utah.edu/

ADMISSIONS PROCESS

Students interested in applying to any of the undergraduate degree programs offered by the EAE Program must first be accepted into The University of Utah. Once accepted to the university students can begin taking the necessary courses required to declare their major. For additional details on The University of Utah undergraduate Admissions Process, visit this link: https://admissions.utah.edu/apply/undergraduate/.

UNIVERSITY OF VERMONT

AT A GLANCE

Since 1791, the University of Vermont has worked to move humankind forward. Today, UVM is a Public Ivy and top 100 research university of a perfect size, large enough to offer a breadth of ideas, resources, and opportunities, yet small enough to enable close faculty-student mentorship across all levels, from bachelor's to M.D. programs, in nearly every field of study. Here, students' educational experience and activities are enriched by our location—from the energy and innovation of Burlington to the forests, farms, and independent spirit of Vermont. UVM provides students endless ways to explore the world, challenge ideas, and dig in on the most pressing issues of our time.

LOCATION AND ENVIRONMENT

Students reap educational as well as recreational rewards from our location in Burlington, a city lauded for business innovation, arts, food, and outdoor recreation. It's an easy walk from campus to downtown restaurants, coffee spots, retail shops, music, and other arts venues. A short stroll from the city center leads to Waterfront Park, a skate park, sailing center, and 10-mile bike path along Lake Champlain, with panoramic views of the Adirondack Mountains. Some of the best skiing/riding, hiking, biking, and paddling trails in the Northeast are less than an hour's drive from campus. Burlington itself is easily reached by car, bus, or plane; Burlington International Airport (BTV) is 3 miles from campus daily direct flights from several major cities.

CAMPUS FACILITIES AND EQUIPMENT

The UVM Campus has undergone transformation in the last few years with completion of several major building projects: our new STEM center, comprising Discovery and Innovation Halls; Ifshin Hall, expanding the Grossman School of Business; the Michele and Martin Cohen Hall for the Integrative Creative Arts; and a new residence hall for 695 first-year students connected to the main library with several dining options, including a teaching kitchen.

OFF-CAMPUS OPPORTUNITIES

Area businesses and agencies offer internships and job experience in fields ranging from food science to finance, snowboard manufacturing to biotech. The Vermont landscape is a vast laboratory for geology, biology, and natural sciences. Vermont's conscientious communities and government also offer exceptional opportunities for research and involvement.

ACADEMIC PROGRAMS

The University of Vermont offers study in disciplines spanning business, STEM, humanities, education, social services, food systems, health sciences, environmental studies, medicine and more (view all program offerings at uvm.edu/academics).

Academics at UVM are supplemented and deepened by a world of hands-on learning opportunities, from travel-study to service learning, and a wide array of internships in locations ranging from Vermont to China. Undergraduate research opportunities are plentiful; students assist faculty with their groundbreaking research in state-of-the-art facilities across campus, including UVM's highly-ranked medical school and affiliated University of Vermont Medical Center, and in our new STEM facility.

The university's Honors College enrolls students from the full spectrum of academic programs at the university, providing a rigorous, multi-disciplinary academic challenge that complements and enriches the entire undergraduate experience.

MAJORS AND DEGREES OFFERED

UVM's 100+ undergraduate majors are offered through its seven undergraduate colleges: College of Agriculture & Life Sciences, College of Arts & Sciences, College of Education & Social Services, College of Engineering & Mathematical Sciences, College of Nursing & Health Sciences, Grossman School of Business, and Rubenstein School of Environment & Natural Resources.

UVM undergraduates have access to 35 accelerated master's degree programs. In total, the university offers 54 master's and 25 doctoral programs through its Graduate College and an M.D. program through the Larner College of Medicine.

TUITION, ROOM, BOARD, FEES

Vermont Resident

Tuition: $16,392

Comprehensive Student Fee: $2,670

Average Room and Board: $13,354

TOTAL: $32,416

Out-of-State Resident

Tuition: $41,280

Comprehensive Student Fee: $2,670

Average Room and Board: $13,354

TOTAL: $57,304

RSP Tuition Break Program

FINANCIAL AID

The FAFSA is the only application required to be considered for federal and university financial aid.

Scholarships: Prospective, first-time, undergraduate students are automatically considered for merit based scholarships when they apply for admission.

Please note that some scholarships require a separate application for consideration.

STUDENT ORGANIZATIONS AND ACTIVITIES

UVM students are known for being active in service and in sports and as social progress and environmental health defenders. They are national and international contenders in competitions ranging from debate to skiing to alternative race car design. There are countless ways for UVM students to get involved on campus, in the Burlington community, beyond borders—and they do.

Catamount pride swells for the university's 18 Division I sports programs. Enthusiastic crowds come out for soccer, hockey, and basketball games. Many of UVM's 50+ club sports also compete nationally and bring home trophies.

All first-year students live in residential learning communities, where they engage with others who share their particular interests in areas spanning art and creativity, wellness, leadership, outdoor experience, innovation and entrepreneurship, and global citizenry.

ADMISSIONS PROCESS

UVM welcomes applications from talented students. Through a holistic admissions review, we select students with strong potential for academic success who will contribute to our community. The rigor of an applicant's academic program; grades; standardized test results; and trends in performance are considered. Essays, recommendations, and other evidence of each student's life experience also assist our evaluation. We also offer a number of optional essay questions should a student wish to express their interest further. Admission decisions are made without regard to family financial circumstances. All applicants must complete the following requirements prior to enrolling at UVM.

Students applying for admission may choose between the following applications: Coalition Application or Common Application. There is a $65 (U.S.) nonrefundable application fee (Vermont first-year applicants who apply by November 1 under Early Action will have their application fee waived).

VANCOUVER FILM SCHOOL

AT A GLANCE

In 1987, Vancouver Film School introduced the world's first true immersion film program. Today, VFS is Canada's premier post-secondary entertainment arts institution, offering an immersive curriculum in film, animation, video game production, VR/AR development, motion and interactive design, programming, art/production foundation, and other related programs. VFS is known for providing high-quality education in accelerated timeframes. VFS alumni are consistently credited on the most successful products in the entertainment economies

LOCATION AND ENVIRONMENT

Located in the heart of Vancouver's Gastown district, Vancouver Film School is an integral component of Western Canada's most beautiful city. Situated among leading global tech and media companies, VFS's eight campus buildings house more than 250,000 square feet of studio and production facilities, connecting students to industry professionals and instructors, with modernized equipment in well-appointed learning spaces. At VFS, students are immersed in Vancouver's arts and culture, with the North Shore Mountains on one side and the Georgia Strait on the other. It's no surprise that some of the world's most creative talents have emerged from VFS over the past three decades.

CAMPUS FACILITIES AND EQUIPMENT

Vancouver Film School's commitment to innovative and emerging technologies is apparent in each of their eight modernized campus buildings. The facilities mirror those found in leading studios and production houses around the world. This ranges from a massive 280° green screen space to the LG UltraWide Monitor Academy Lab, and our unique partnership with Beyond Capture, a signature, 32,000 square foot performance capture studio available to students and used by some of the most advanced industry projects in film, television, and video games.

OFF-CAMPUS OPPORTUNITIES

Vancouver provides the perfect blend of nature, arts and culture, and exposure to the industry in which VFS alumni will work. Students and graduates can hit the slopes in the morning and take a ride on Vancouver's scenic seawall in the afternoon, and drop in any of Vancouver's museums, theatres, and eclectic arts spaces in the evening. The creative economy in Vancouver is thriving, helping students and alumni connect to shoots, projects, and industry insiders in their field through a wide range of VFS-run and third-party events.

ACADEMIC PROGRAMS

Graduating students receive a diploma.

Upon completing a one-year diploma programs, students can obtain an accelerated bachelor's degree through Pathway programs at the universities listed below:

- Royal Roads University (Victoria, BC)
- Capilano University (North Vancouver, BC)
- Wilfrid Laurier University (Waterloo, ON)
- University of the Fraser Valley (Fraser Valley, BC)
- BCIT (Metro Vancouver, BC)
- Regent's University in London (London, UK)

Diplomas Offered

- Game Design
- Programming for Games, Web & Mobile
- 3D Animation & Visual Effects
- Classical Animation
- Animation Concept Art
- Foundation Visual Art & Design
- Digital Design
- Acting Essentials
- Acting for Film & Television
- Writing for Film, Television & Games
- Film Production
- Sound Design for Visual Media
- Makeup Design for Film & Television
- VR/AR Design & Development
- English for Creative Arts

TUITION, ROOM, BOARD, FEES

VFS tuition is all-inclusive. All school supplies (books, equipment, and incidentals) are included in your tuition fees. The rates listed below are in Canadian dollars.

- Game Design: https://vfs.edu/programs/game-design
  - Domestic: C$32,750 (current); C$32,950 (Aug. 31, 2020 and later start dates)
  - International: C$49,250 (current); C$49,750 (Aug. 31, 2020 and later start dates)
- Programming for Games, Web & Mobile: https://vfs.edu/programs/programming
  - Domestic: C$32,050
  - International: C$49,050
- 3D Animation & Visual Effects: https://vfs.edu/programs/3D-animation-vfx
  - Domestic: C$35,750 (current); C$35,950 (Aug. 31, 2020 and later start dates)
  - International: C$53,250 (current); C$53,750 (Aug. 31, 2020 and later start dates)
- Classical Animation: https://vfs.edu/programs/classical-animation
  - Domestic: C$25,500 (current); C$25,950 (Aug. 31, 2020 and later start dates)
  - International: C$30,500 (current); C$30,750 (Aug. 31, 2020 and later start dates)
- Animation Concept Art: https://vfs.edu/programs/animation-concept-art
  - Domestic: C$25,500 (current); C$25,950 (Aug. 31, 2020 and later start dates)
  - International: C$33,500 (current); C$33,750 (Aug. 31, 2020 and later start dates)

- Foundation Visual Art & Design: https://vfs.edu/programs/foundation
  - Domestic: C$20,500 (current); C$20,950 (Aug. 31, 2020 and later start dates)
  - International: C$30,500 (current); C$30,750 (Aug. 31, 2020 and later start dates)
- Digital Design: https://vfs.edu/programs/digital-design
  - Domestic: C$27,750 (current); C$27,950 (Aug. 31, 2020 and later start dates)
  - International: C$42,250 (current); C$42,750 (Aug. 31, 2020 and later start dates)
- Acting Essentials: https://vfs.edu/programs/acting-essentials
  - Domestic: C$7,500 (current); C$7,750 (Aug. 31, 2020 and later start dates)
  - International: C$10,500 (current); C$10,750 (Aug. 31, 2020 and later start dates)
- Acting for Film & Television & Games: https://vfs.edu/programs/acting
  - Domestic: C$20,500
  - International: C$30,500
- Writing for Film, Television & Games: https://vfs.edu/programs/writing
  - Domestic: C$20,750 (current); C$20,950 (Aug. 31, 2020 and later start dates)
  - International: C$28,250 (current); C$28,750 (Aug. 31, 2020 and later start dates)
- Film Production: https://vfs.edu/programs/film-production
  - Domestic: C$36,750 (current); C$36,950 (Aug. 31, 2020 and later start dates)
  - International: C$53,250 (current); C$53,750 (Aug. 31, 2020 and later start dates)
- Sound Design for Visual Media: https://vfs.edu/programs/sound-design
  - Domestic: C$28,750 (current); C$28,950 (Aug. 31, 2020 and later start dates)
  - International: C$43,250 (current); C$43,750 (Aug. 31, 2020 and later start dates)
- Makeup Design for Film & Television: https://vfs.edu/programs/makeup
  - Domestic: C$32,250 (current); C$33,950 (Aug. 31, 2020 and later start dates)
  - International: C$46,750
- English for Creative Arts: https://vfs.edu/programs/english-creative-arts
  - Domestic & international: C$6,720
- VR/AR Design & Development: https://vfs.edu/programs/vrar
  - Domestic: C$22,000
  - International: C$33,000

ROOM AND BOARD

VFS offers a robust housing and homestay placement service. Renting in Vancouver is expensive. VFS aims to provide convenient accommodation that makes it easier for students to focus on their academic and personal growth.

VFS's Housing Coordinator has well-established connections with landlords in Vancouver and will help students find accommodation that best meets their individual and budgetary needs. Whether you want to rent your own apartment, share with roommates, or live in a homestay, VFS's Housing Coordinator can offer students a variety of excellent options.

https://vfs.edu/accommodation

FINANCIAL AID

Vancouver Film School's programs are recognized by all Federal and Provincial loan providers in Canada. VFS regularly offers a variety of scholarship programs offering full or partial tuition funding, with partners that have included writer/director/producer Kevin Smith, animator Michal Makarewicz (Pixar), actor Emily Bett Rickards, and video game developers Blackbird Interactive and The Coalitions (Gears 5).

Past and current creative scholarship programs offered by VFS can be found here:

https://vfs.edu/scholarships-overview

For international students, VFS has a team dedicated to assisting with payment plans and can work with a student's local loan providers to assist with tuition and other costs.

STUDENT ORGANIZATIONS AND ACTIVITIES

The iconic Vancouver Film School backpack is a ubiquitous sign that VFS's diverse Canadian and international student body is everywhere in Vancouver. Some are attending VFS as their first post-secondary stop, while others are changing directions and pursuing a longtime creative passion. No matter what stage they're at, all are immersed in industry production experience on their first day of class.

VFS students engage in a broad range of activities both in and outside school. A passionate commitment to the arts means that most students are connected not only to their own projects, but to those of fellow students as well, as they collaborate throughout their intensive one-year programs. A number of opportunities for activism, volunteer work, and other pursuits keep VFS students engaged every day.

ADMISSIONS PROCESS

Over the years, VFS Advisors have helped thousands of individuals through the application process. Advisors encourage applicants to be well-informed about their educational options and help ensure there is a strong fit between program choice and desired career outcomes. Advisors also assist prospective students in putting together the components needed to satisfy specific portfolio requirements when applicable.

Application Process & Criteria

1. Students can apply to VFS at any time, from grade 11 and up. However, before attending classes, students must either be 19 years old or have completed grade 12.
2. C$100 non-refundable application fee
3. Photo ID copy
4. Two Reference Letters—Preferably, these should be from someone who can comment on your passion and abilities in the area for which you are applying. Please note that family members are not eligible as references.
5. Transcript from High School or University
6. Online Application Form (https://vfs.edu/admissions)
7. Applicants may be asked to submit a program-specific portfolio, when applicable.

VANDERBILT UNIVERSITY

AT A GLANCE

In 1873, on the heels of the Civil War, "Commodore" Cornelius Vanderbilt gave $1 million to the university that now bears his name, with the hope that it would "contribute to strengthening the ties which should exist between all sections of our common country." Since then, Vanderbilt has consistently enrolled highly talented students and challenged them daily to expand their intellectual horizons in an inclusive environment based on open inquiry and respect. Vanderbilt's comprehensive interdisciplinary approach to education allows students to pursue a wide array of academic and curricular interests outside of their main focus of study, and the university's Opportunity Vanderbilt financial aid program ensures that it is often cited among the country's best values. Consistently ranked among the top 20 universities in the country by U.S. News & World Report, Vanderbilt is a private research university that features ten schools, four of which have undergraduate programs. Each year, 1,600 first-year students join the university, bringing the total undergraduate population to approximately 6,900 students, more than half of whom collaborate with professors on research across disciplines. The university's 7:1 student-faculty ratio gives students access to faculty members of prominence in every area of academic study. Faculty members provide a challenging, comprehensive education that encourages broad perspectives and critical thinking.

LOCATION AND ENVIRONMENT

Located in the heart of Nashville, TN, Vanderbilt offers the best of both worlds: a beautiful park-like campus surrounded by a vibrant city filled with live music, food, and exciting events.

CAMPUS FACILITIES AND EQUIPMENT

Vanderbilt University is located 1.5 miles southwest of downtown Nashville on a 330-acre, park-like campus that has been officially recognized as an arboretum by the American Public Gardens Association since 1988. The university shares a name with and enjoys close collaboration with the separate, nonprofit Vanderbilt University Medical Center. The university comprises 178 buildings, including the Jean and Alexander Heard Library, home to over 8 million items. All first-year students live on The Martha Rivers Ingram Commons, a living-learning community that fosters collaboration among student communities and resident faculty members. Additional residential colleges include Warren and Moore and E. Bronson Ingram, living-learning communities for upper-division students. The university's planned expansion will bring the addition of three more residential colleges for upper-division students by 2023—the first of these, the Nicholas S. Zeppos College, is slated to open in 2020. The campus is also home to a 230,000-square-foot state-of-the-art Engineering and Science Building and a cross-disciplinary creative and makerspace called the Wond'ry, the campus epicenter for innovation and entrepreneurship.

OFF-CAMPUS OPPORTUNITIES

Study abroad programs allow students to immerse themselves in languages and cultures around the world. More than 150 programs are offered in 40 countries including Argentina, Australia, Austria, Brazil, Chile, China, Cuba, the Czech Republic, Denmark, the Dominican Republic, England, France, Israel, India, Italy, Japan, Nepal, New Zealand, Russia, Singapore, South Africa, and Spain, among others. Students receive direct credit for courses, and the cost of tuition is usually the same as for study on campus in Nashville. In addition, any scholarships, grants, or loans a student has been awarded apply to Vanderbilt study abroad programs. Students may also work with an adviser to participate in programs sponsored by other universities.

Students also take advantage of internships in many industries located in Nashville, including entertainment, business, health care, government, publishing, and education.

ACADEMIC PROGRAMS

Students apply directly to one of Vanderbilt's four undergraduate schools: the College of Arts and Science, School of Engineering, Peabody College of Education and Human Development, or Blair School of Music. In all four schools, honors programs and opportunities for research, independent study, and internships are available. About 30 percent of undergraduate students pursue double majors within or across the four undergraduate schools, and about half add an optional minor. The College of Arts and Science (A&S) offers a wide spectrum of courses in the humanities, social sciences, and natural sciences along with majors in 50 departments and interdisciplinary areas. The core curriculum, AXLE (Achieving eXcellence in Liberal Education), fosters critical thinking, analytical expertise from diverse perspectives, and effective writing and oral communication skills. The Blair School of Music offers the Bachelor of Music degree in composition, integrated studies, integrated studies/teacher education, jazz studies, and performance. Instruction is available in every instrument of the orchestra as well as piano, euphonium, saxophone, and voice. Unlike many schools of music, Blair has no graduate students. The curriculum combines intensive musical training with liberal arts studies. The Blair School also offers music minors and a wide variety of courses, private instruction, and performing organizations for non-majors.

For more than 125 years, the School of Engineering has educated engineers for careers in industry, government, consulting, teaching, and research. In addition to technical courses, each student's program includes a complement of course work in the humanities and social sciences, resulting in a balanced foundation for future achievement. All programs leading to a Bachelor of Engineering degree are ABET-accredited, and students can earn the Bachelor of Science degree while majoring in computer science or engineering science.

Ranked one of the top ten graduate schools of education (according to U.S. News & World Report) for twenty-five consecutive years, Peabody College offers majors leading to teacher certification in early childhood and elementary education, secondary education, special education. Other Peabody College majors include human and organizational development, child development, child studies, and cognitive studies. The Peabody degree reflects a strong liberal arts foundation combined with a solid program of pre-professional courses and a multitude of internship and practicum opportunities. All undergraduates must complete requirements in communications, the humanities, mathematics, the natural sciences, and the social sciences. Students gain an abundance of field experiences throughout their four years.

All first-year students entering Vanderbilt in summer or fall 2018 and beyond (and all transfer students entering summer or fall 2019 and beyond) will complete an immersion experience as part of their graduation requirements. Immersion Vanderbilt provides undergraduate students with the opportunity to pursue their passions and cultivate intellectual interests through experiential learning. This intensive learning experience takes place in and beyond the classroom and culminates in the creation of a final project. Students will engage in a civic and professional, creative expression, international, or research immersion experience.

MAJORS AND DEGREES OFFERED

Degrees are offered in African American and Diaspora studies; American studies; anthropology; art; Asian studies; biochemistry and chemical biology; biological sciences; biomedical engineering; chemical engineering; chemistry; child development; child studies; cinema and media arts; civil engineering; classical and Mediterranean studies; cognitive studies; communication of science and technology; communication studies; computer engineering; computer science; earth and environmental sciences; ecology, evolution, and organismal biology; economics; economics and history; education (early childhood and elementary, secondary, and special education); electrical engineering; engineering science; English; environmental sociology; European studies; European studies: Russia and Eastern Europe; French; French and European studies; German studies; German and European studies; history; history of art; human and organizational development; Italian and European studies; jazz studies, Jewish studies; Latin American studies; Latino and Latina studies; law, history, and society; mathematics; mechanical engineering; medicine, health, and society; molecular and cellular biology; music composition; music integrated studies; music integrated studies/teacher education; music performance; neuroscience; philosophy; physics; political science; psychology; public policy studies; religious studies; Russian; sociology; Spanish; Spanish and European studies; Spanish and Portuguese; theatre; women's and gender studies.

TUITION, ROOM, BOARD, FEES

The estimated costs for 2019–2020 include: tuition, $53,086; housing, $11,542; meals, $6,130; books and supplies, $1,194; student service fees, $1,328; personal expenses allowance, $3,022; travel allowance varies; first-year experience fee, $874; new student transcript fee. For engineering students only: engineering lab fee, $1,000; and engineering laptop allowance, $1,600. First-year engineering students are required to provide their own computer that meets published requirements.

FINANCIAL AID

Through Opportunity Vanderbilt, the university makes three important commitments to ensure that students from many different economic circumstances can enroll as undergraduates at Vanderbilt: the admissions process is need-blind for all U.S. citizens and eligible non-citizens; Vanderbilt meets 100 percent of demonstrated need for all admitted students; and Vanderbilt's financial aid packages do not include loans. This initiative does not involve income bands or income cutoffs that limit eligibility. Need-based aid is awarded according to the evaluation of the FAFSA and the CSS/Financial aid PROFILE.

Vanderbilt also awards approximately 250 merit-based scholarships to select first-year applicants who demonstrate exceptional accomplishment and intellectual promise. Three signature scholarships comprise the majority of these merit scholarships: the Ingram Scholarship Program, the Cornelius Vanderbilt Scholarship, and the Chancellor's Scholarship.

In the 2019/2020 school year, 65 percent of the university's undergraduate students received some type of financial assistance.

STUDENT ORGANIZATIONS AND ACTIVITIES

Vanderbilt undergraduates come from all 50 states and 63 countries, 51% are female, 49% are male, 41.0% are students of color, and 9.7% are international students. Vanderbilt is recognized for an active campus life, where students balance their academic lives with enriching experiences outside the classroom. Students can select from among 420+ student-run organizations, including pre-professional, cultural, religious, political, recreational, and social clubs. Elected representatives of Vanderbilt Student Government work in conjunction with other student leaders and faculty to bring noted speakers, events, and musicians to campus. Vanderbilt also has a thriving college athletics program. A founding member of the SEC, Vanderbilt has 16 Division I teams that have won five national championships and 34 individual and team league championships since 2000.

ADMISSIONS PROCESS

Vanderbilt seeks students with high standards of scholarship and character who are significantly engaged in their community. Admission is based on a holistic review of academic and personal credentials. The typical applicant will have completed 20 or more units in a challenging high school curriculum, including at least two years of a foreign language. It is highly recommended that School of Engineering applicants have taken calculus and calculus-based physics.

Generally, applicants who are admitted to Vanderbilt have exceptional academic credentials and are highly engaged in their communities, often serving in leadership roles. Admissions decisions are based on strength of high school transcript, standardized test results (either the SAT or ACT), personal essays, official recommendations, and extracurricular activities. SAT Subject Tests are not required.

Students may apply to Vanderbilt through Early Decision I or II, or Regular Decision. Early Decision I and II are binding decision plans, and may be appropriate for students who are committed to attending Vanderbilt if they are admitted. The application deadline is November 1 for Early Decision I and January 1 for Early Decision II; admissions decisions are available by mid-December for Early Decision I and by mid-February for Early Decision II. Regular Decision applications are due January 1 and admissions decisions are available by late March.

To apply, applicants must submit official standardized test scores and all required parts of the Common Application, Coalition Application, or QuestBridge Application, including two academic teacher letters of recommendation, a counselor letter of recommendation, an official high school transcript, and a $50 application fee, or fee waiver for qualified students. In addition to completing standard application materials, applicants to the Blair School of Music must submit a Blair School of Music application, which includes a pre-screening video. Selected applicants will be invited to audition in person.

Campus visits are encouraged although a student's demonstrated interest in Vanderbilt is not considered in admissions decisions. Students should visit vu.edu/visit to learn about group information sessions, campus tours, and half- and full-day visit programs. To visit Vanderbilt without traveling, take the virtual tour at vu.edu/virtualtour. Vanderbilt does not conduct on-campus interviews, but optional alumni interviews are available to first-year applicants in many locations.

WASHINGTON COLLEGE

AT A GLANCE

"Washington College is all about the student experience. Their happiness reflects our student-centric focus, which is the cornerstone of who we are and the positive impact we have on a student's personal and professional life."

—Kurt Landgraf, President of Washington College

A Washington College education affords students unmatched opportunities to work closely with an exceptional faculty on projects they are passionate about. We believe that a diverse liberal arts education is both academically rewarding and the most effective way to prepare for a future in anything you want to do. From studying on the Chesapeake Bay to interning at The White House, there's something for everyone at Washington College.

In their first two years on campus, WC students are encouraged to explore their interests, examine different perspectives, and challenge their old ways of thinking. There is no one-size-fits-all education at Washington College: from double-majoring to internships to study abroad and semester-long interdisciplinary programs, we encourage our students to think outside the box and shape a college experience that is right for them.

Founded in 1782, Washington College was the first college chartered in the sovereign United States of America. General George Washington lent us his name, donated 50 guineas to our founding, and served on our first Board of Visitors and Governors. Our goal back then was to cultivate responsible, educated citizen-leaders who could nurture the new democracy. That founding purpose still holds true today.

LOCATION AND ENVIRONMENT

Where we are is who we are. Our 120-acre campus in Chestertown, Md., is an integral part of Maryland's Eastern Shore, but still close enough to Washington, D.C., Baltimore, and Philadelphia that our students benefit from a wealth of distinguished speakers, internship opportunities, and institutional partnerships. Our River and Field Campus grants students from all disciplines unprecedented access to 4,700 acres of waterfront, meadows, untouched hardwood forests, ponds, grasslands, marshes and riverine habitat.

Local life in Chestertown is deeply-rooted in community and tradition. The town dates back to 1706, when it was established as a major port town on the Chester River. Beloved for its historic homes, brick walkways, and close-knit feel, Chestertown warmly welcomes the students of Washington College each year. There's always room for students-take a walk down High Street on First Fridays, or visit the Farmer's Market in Fountain Park on Saturday mornings!

CAMPUS FACILITIES AND EQUIPMENT

With some buildings as old as the mid-nineteenth-century and others still under construction, Washington College seamlessly combines the old with the new. Our pathways might be red brick reminiscent of colonial times, but our Hodson Dining Hall is award-winning, our Cain Gymnasium received a new floor in 2017, and our Miller library contains a state-of-the-art Makerspace with a 3-D printer, one-button recording studio, and all the latest technology to bring your ideas to life.

We are committed to sustainability. Many buildings on campus incorporate alternative energy sources like solar and geothermal, and our Campus Garden is a growing experiment in permaculture, with plenty of edible plants and even our own beehives. Additionally, our River and Field Campus provides access to a diverse collection of Eastern Shore ecosystems, a bird banding laboratory, 2.5 miles of Chester River waterfront, and 4,700 acres of living laboratory for students of all majors to study.

Our science centers provide majors with state-of-the art lab equipment, and our research vessels *Callinectes* and *Lookdown* give science students access to all the equipment they need to scan the bed of the Chester River and chemically test water and sediment samples.

The Chester River is an essential part of Chestertown, and our students have taken advantage of the unique opportunities it offers, from developing competitive varsity programs in rowing and sailing and club sport programs for waterskiing and wakeboarding, to learning to sail in class and enjoying recreational activities such as kayaking.

OFF-CAMPUS OPPORTUNITIES

There's something special about small-town life, and Chestertown delivers: grab a coffee at the local Play It Again Sam's or Evergrain Bakery, visit the shops on High Street, or head down to the water and rent a kayak for a day on the Chester River. For the more adventurous, campus is close enough to Baltimore, Philadelphia, Annapolis, and Washington, D.C. to make daytripping simple. The College offers a weekend shuttle to metro stations for those without individual transportation.

ACADEMIC PROGRAMS

Washington College celebrates the relationship between student and professor. Our diverse array of fellowships, internships, off-campus programs, and research opportunities provide chances for students to pursue their own interests and conduct research at a graduate level.

The Douglass Cater Society of Junior Fellows provides competitive grants to support self-directed undergraduate research and scholarship anywhere in the world. Additionally, our Presidential Fellows program puts high-achieving freshmen on the fast track to academic distinction, including the chance to work with full Cater Fellows as an apprentice, and provides multiple scholarships, including a chance for a full-tuition scholarship.

Other programs include: the Explore America Fellowships, which place students in paid summer internships at prestigious institutions including the Library of Congress, National Constitution Center, and the Smithsonian American Art Museum; the Alex. Brown Fund, which tasks students with managing an equities portfolio of $500,000; the Washington to Wall Street Program, which offers internships to students pursuing careers in business or financial sector; and the John S. Toll Science Fellows and Hodson Science Fellows programs, which enable students to conduct in-depth research with faculty while earning a stipend and a housing allowance.

Our three Signature Centers position students at a dynamic intersection of academics and hands-on learning in the "real world." Each Center provides programming, events, internships, and coursework in a singular area of focus: the environment (the Center for Environment & Society), literature and writing (the Rose O'Neill Literary House), and history (the Starr Center for the Study of the American Experience).

The Center for Environment & Society offers internships and fellowships in the great outdoors. The Center is also home to the Chester River Watershed Observatory and the Chester River Field Research Station. CES's interdisciplinary academic programs promote the integration of environmental issues, social values, and good old river mud.

The Starr Center for the Study of the American Experience is dedicated to fostering innovative approaches to the American past and present. Through educational programs, scholarship and public outreach, and a special focus on written history, the Starr Center seeks to bridge the divide between the academic world and the public at large.

The Rose O'Neill Literary House provides literary programming across disciplines, a diverse array of lecturers and writers each year, and training in new and antique printing technologies. Lit House students grow as artists under professional mentorship, and each year, one graduating senior is awarded the Sophie Kerr Prize, the largest undergraduate literary award in the world (the 2019 winner won $63,912).

Washington College also offers an extensive study abroad program with both short-term and long-term study opportunities. Our students have traveled to places like the Galapagos Islands, Ecuador, Germany, Israel, Japan, Peru, Turkey, and the United Kingdom.

MAJORS AND PROGRAMS
- American Studies
- Anthropology
- Art and Art History
- Biochemistry and Molecular Biology
- Biology
- Business Management
- Chemistry
- Communication and Media Studies

- Computer Science
- Economics
- Education
- English
- Engineering
- Environmental Science and Studies
- History
- Human Development
- Humanities
- International Literature and Culture
- International Studies
- Mathematics
- Music
- Nursing
- Pharmacy
- Philosophy and Religion
- Physics
- Political Science
- Pre-Law
- Premedical
- Psychology
- Related Health Professions
- Sociology
- Teacher Certification Programs
- Theatre
- World Languages and Cultures

MINORS, CONCENTRATIONS, AND AREAS OF EMPHASIS

- Accounting and Finance
- African Studies
- Archaeology
- Art History
- Asian Studies (Concentration)
- Asian Studies (Minor)
- Behavioral Neuroscience
- Biophysics and Biological Chemistry
- Black Studies
- Cell/Molecular Biology and Infectious Disease
- Chesapeake Regional Studies
- Clinical Counseling
- Creative Writing
- Dance
- Earth and Planetary Sciences
- Ecology and Evolution
- Ethnomusicology
- European Studies
- Gender Studies
- Global Business Studies
- Greener Materials Science
- Justice, Law and Society
- Information Systems
- Latin American Studies
- Marketing
- Near Eastern Studies
- Organic and Medicinal Chemistry
- Peace and Conflict Studies
- Physical and Instrumental Chemistry
- Physiology and Organismal Biology
- Public Health
- Secondary Education
- Social Welfare
- Studio Art

Interdisciplinary programs of study, advanced degree programs, partnerships:

- Elementary and Secondary education certification
- Engineering dual-degree program with Columbia University
- Environmental management (MEM) program with Duke University
- Forestry (MF) dual-degree program with Duke University
- Environmental management (MEM) program with Duke University
- Nursing dual-degree program with University of Maryland
- Pharmacy dual-degree program with University of Maryland
- Premedical and Pre-Law programs

TUITION, ROOM, BOARD, FEES

Basic educational fees for 2020–2021
Tuition (full-time) $48,678
Mandatory Student Fees $1,090
Standard Dormitory $6,365
Standard Meal Plan $6,673
Total $62,806

FINANCIAL AID

Washington College is committed to providing educational excellence and equity for all students; 90% of our students receive need-based financial aid and/or merit-based scholarships. We develop financial packages that include tuition scholarships, tuition grants, work/study, and low-interest loans, in addition to federal, state, and independent aid programs for eligible students. With the investment of funds for scholarships and grants from donors and benefactors, the College provides more than $20 million annually in scholarships and grants to help make it possible for students to get an education here. More than 50% of all Washington College students qualify for merit-based tuition scholarships averaging from $18,000 to $30,000 per year.

STUDENT ORGANIZATIONS AND ACTIVITIES

Washington College supports more than 80 clubs, from the nationally recognized Habitat for Humanity Club to wakeboarding, sailing, and entrepreneurial activism through Enactus.

As a Division III member of the NCAA, our 18 intercollegiate teams compete in the Centennial Conference, the Middle Atlantic Intercollegiate Sailing Association, and the Mid-Atlantic Rowing Conference (MARC). Nearly a third of WC students are varsity athletes, and 60% participate in varsity, intramural, or club sports.

Our Student Events Board is always hard at work putting together amazing opportunities for students, from festivals and quiz nights to the semi-formal George Washington's Birthday Ball, which also welcomes back alumni.

ADMISSIONS PROCESS

Washington College is a selective institution. In order to assess an applicant's "fit" with the College, the Admission Committee requires the submission of all relevant academic records and test scores, an essay/personal statement, and a letter of recommendation. In some cases, an on-campus interview may also be required.

Prospective applicants are strongly encouraged to come to campus for an information session and tour. These visits should be scheduled in advance by calling 410-778-7700 or visiting washcoll.edu/visit.

Prospective students may apply online using the Common Application or via washcoll.edu/apply. Application deadlines are: November 15 for early decision; December 1 for early action; February 15 for regular decision. Admitted applicants must pay a $700.00 enrollment deposit by May 1. For details, visit www.washcoll.edu/admissions.

WELLS COLLEGE

AT A GLANCE

For more than 150 years, Wells College has made it our mission to help you to think critically, reason wisely and act humanely as you cultivate a meaningful life. You will always feel at home on our beautiful lakeside campus in Aurora, New York, as you gain the knowledge, skills and experience to create your own unique path. From day one as a member of our closely connected campus community, you will develop personal relationships with faculty mentors and successful alumni around the world. Every Wells student graduates with at least one professional internship, so you can immediately benefit from a purposeful education that combines the liberal arts and sciences with real-world experience.

LOCATION AND ENVIRONMENT

Wells College sits on 300 acres of land on the shore of Cayuga Lake in Aurora, a historic village in the heart of the scenic Finger Lakes Region of New York State. Wells is an hour's drive from Syracuse, 1.5 hours from Rochester, and 4.5 hours from New York City and Philadelphia.

CAMPUS FACILITIES AND EQUIPMENT

The Wells College campus is an eclectic mix of history and modernity. As a Wellsian, you can live in residence halls built as stately 19th century mansions, enjoy an all-you-can-eat buffet in our gothic dining hall, and attend science classes in laboratories personally designed by professors. Feel at the top of your game on the all-weather, multi-sport turf field or indoor gym; put your smartphone down to experience our 20th century iron letterpress, then develop models with 3D printers. Take out a kayak or sail Cayuga Lake from the College Boathouse to conduct environmental testing for class, or just for your own enjoyment!

OFF-CAMPUS OPPORTUNITIES

Wells College offers over 20 study abroad locations (your financial aid goes with you) and operates a nationally renowned study abroad program in Lorenzo de' Medici, at the Italian International Institute in Florence, Italy.

ACADEMIC PROGRAMS

Exploratory (if you are still deciding what to study), Individualized Major (create your own), Biochemistry & Molecular Biology, Biology, Business, Chemistry, Computer Science, Criminal Justice, Economics & Management, Education: Inclusive Childhood, English (Literature, Creative Writing), Environmental Science, Health Sciences, History, Mathematics, Physics, Political Science, Psychology, Sociology & Anthropology, Spanish, Theatre, Visual Arts (Art History, Book Arts, Studio Art), Women's & Gender Studies

MAJORS AND DEGREES OFFERED

Wells College offers a modern, flexible undergraduate curriculum rooted in the liberal arts. Our students are aspiring doctors, lawyers, health care professionals, poets, activists, pharmaceutical scientists, entrepreneurs and change-making leaders of the world. Interdisciplinary dialogue and hands-on experience are part of every academic program. Students benefit from one-on-one guidance by faculty mentors, and often partner with professors to conduct original research that leads to presentations at national conferences and publication in peer-reviewed scholarly journals. Advising for professional careers such as medicine and law is available. Fast track or round out your education with one of Wells' partnerships that include cross-registration, dual degree and accelerated programs with other institutions such as Clarkson University, Cornell University, Columbia University, Syracuse University and the University of Rochester.

TUITION, ROOM, BOARD, FEES

For the 2020–2021 year:

Tuition: $30,300
Fees: $1,500
Room and Board: $14,500
TOTAL: $46,300

FINANCIAL AID

All admitted students are considered for one of Wells College's many merit-based scholarships, and every incoming first-year student is guaranteed a minimum of $32,000 in institutional aid over the course of their four years of undergraduate study. The average net cost for students is $16,000.

STUDENT ORGANIZATIONS AND ACTIVITIES

Wells College has over 400 students from 30 states and 7 countries. Most students live on campus. The female-to-male ratio is roughly 6:4. In Fall 2018, 46% of new students were awarded top-level scholarships that required a 3.5 GPA or higher.

With 150 years of vibrant campus traditions, over 40 student organizations, 13 NCAA Division III teams, social clubs, community service projects, student government, religious affiliations and theatre and performance groups, you will find every day at Wells is a new adventure.

ADMISSIONS PROCESS

Apply to Wells College using the Common Application or the Wells Application. We are test-optional, and there is no application fee.

Deadlines

Early Decision: November 15
Early Action: December 15
Regular Admission: March 15
Recommended FAFSA Filing: December 1

Applicants should submit:

- Official high school transcripts and school report
- One teacher recommendation from an 11th and/or 12th grade teacher in academic subject areas
- Supplemental Material: To help us better understand your achievements and potential, we welcome you to submit any material that showcases your unique personality and talents. This can be a personal statement or essay, résumé, creative portfolio, and/or video recording of a musical performance. Feel free to submit more than one!
- International students only: Test scores that demonstrate English proficiency, such as TOEFL (80), IELTS (6.5), PTE Academic (55), or the Duolingo English Test (100).
- Students applying for first-year admission should pursue a secondary school program with a minimum of four academic subjects each year, including:
  - four years of English
  - three or more years of mathematics
  - three or more years of social science
  - two or more years of laboratory science
  - one or more years of a foreign language

WENTWORTH INSTITUTE OF TECHNOLOGY

AT A GLANCE

Wentworth Institute of Technology is an independent, co-educational, nationally ranked institution located in the Fenway neighborhood of Boston, MA offering 19 bachelor's degree programs in the fields of applied mathematics, applied sciences, architecture, business management, computer science and networking, construction management, design, and engineering.

LOCATION AND ENVIRONMENT

Small school benefits, big city resources.

This private, coeducational college is located on 31 acres in Boston's historic Fenway, a diverse, dynamic neighborhood famous for arts, culture, sports, and fun. With over 4,000 students, it provides the friendliness of a small school, alongside the resources and excitement of the ultimate college town.

The original center of higher education in the U.S., it hosts 50 colleges and universities and draws a quarter of a million students every year, with nearly 20,000 of those students coming from outside the country. Boston is a city with exceptional character. In addition to its rich history, it's also a hub for science, technology, and startup scenes, giving Wentworth students access to educational and career opportunities they would not find elsewhere.

CAMPUS FACILITIES AND EQUIPMENT

The Wentworth campus is well-appointed to deliver the top-notch education and living conditions demanded by today's students. Our modernized laboratories are at the vanguard of technology; the equipment mirrors that found in the leading employers in industry. The Institute has spent millions of dollars to upgrade its information technology infrastructure.

The latest addition to campus, the Center for Engineering, Innovation, and Science, is designed to meet the next evolution in the collegiate study of several engineering disciplines by providing modern academic space for Wentworth's existing student body and to enhance the campus experience in a new "state-of-the-art" building.

At approximately 64 feet in height and approximately 78,000 gross square feet, the Center for Engineering, Innovation and Sciences contains laboratories, student learning and group meeting space, offices, and support/storage space on floors two through four, and a first-floor maker-space, manufacturing, and gathering space intended to invite the campus population to experience first-hand displays of Wentworth's engineering capabilities and teachings. The Center for Engineering, Innovation and Sciences will accommodate Wentworth's transition from providing engineering technology programs.

And the facilities for sleeping are just as impressive as the ones for studying. The Institute operates seven residence halls: Evans Way/Tudbury Hall, Edwards/Rodgers Hall, Baker Hall, Louis Prang/Vancouver Apartments, 610 Huntington Avenue, 555 Huntington Avenue and the Apartments at 525 Huntington.

Whether you're looking for state-of-the-art computing resources, healthcare you can rely on, or one of several other services that make campus life better, you can rest assured that Wentworth is working hard to meet your needs.

The Flanagan Campus Center is the hub of student life at Wentworth. The campus center is home to the bookstore, the cafeteria, the Schumann Fitness Center, the Center for Diversity & Social Justice, Wentworth Internet Radio Experience (WIRE), a recreation room, study areas, and the Office of Campus Life.

The Center for Academic Excellence provides students with academic support services such as peer and faculty tutoring, computer-based tutorials, and subject study groups. We are dedicated to preparing students for academic success.

Wentworth is committed to helping you make the best use of computers. We offer a range of computing resources including: a wireless campus; labs equipped with the latest hardware and software; and a full-time Office of Information Technology. The result is a highly connected academic and social community where advanced computing is accessible and convenient.

Wentworth subscribes to the policies set forth in the Americans with Disabilities Act and in Section 504 of the Federal Rehabilitation Act of 1973, which mandate equal opportunity in educational programs and activities for students with disabilities.

At Wentworth, we work hard to provide the very best health services. In addition to expert primary medical care, we also offer specialized services including counseling, disability services and comprehensive health education.

In order to make the transition for international students as smooth as possible, Wentworth employs a full-time international student advisor who has extensive experience with international students, and assists them in their personal, social and academic adjustment to Wentworth and the U.S.

Conveniently located at the center of campus, the Douglas D. Schumann Library & Learning Commons is a valuable resource. The online catalogue includes the holdings of nine other libraries all available for use by Wentworth students. And, membership in the 14-institution Fenway Library Consortium provides access to more than 2,900,000 volumes and 13,000 periodical titles. Various services are also available through the Alumni Library.

OFF-CAMPUS OPPORTUNITIES

Honoring our tradition of out-of-classroom learning, all undergraduate students are required to spend a minimum of two semesters in a co-op program, regardless of the college or their major. This multifaceted academic approach stems from our commitment to the tenets of EPIC Learning (Externally collaborative, Project-based, Interdisciplinary Culture). Co-op experiences are directly related to your field of study, allowing you to tie your coursework to concrete knowledge developed in the workplace. During your co-op experiences, you earn income and not pay tuition, allowing you to save toward future semesters. If your co-op is local, you can choose to live on campus during it, maintaining close connections to friends and Wentworth activities. However, you may also complete your co-op wherever you would like whether it is near home, another part of the country or abroad. We attract nearly 350 unique organizations to Wentworth's two annual co-op and career fairs, resulting in 2,000 full-time jobs for our graduates, And our top-tie services in areas such as resume and cover letter prep, interviewing, and networking have earned us a #3 ranking in the Northeast for career preparation from *The Wall Street Journal* and *Times Higher Education*.

As part of the five-member Colleges of the Fenway (COF) consortium (representing more than 12,000 undergraduate students, comprising 16.2% of the total Boston population of undergraduates attending four-year colleges, more than 700 full-time faculty and 2,300-course offerings), Wentworth offers students both the intimacy of a small college community and the vast resources of a major university. Students at any of the member institutions can cross-register for classes and gain access to social events, intramural teams, dance and theater troupes, a chorus and orchestra, professional activities, libraries, dining halls, and campus facilities at the four other schools—all of which are within walking distance of one another.

ACADEMIC PROGRAMS

Undergraduate Majors: Applied Mathematics, Applied Sciences, Architecture, Biological Engineering, Biomedical Engineering, Business Management, Civil Engineering, Computer Engineering, Computer Information Systems, Computer Sciences, Computer Networking, Construction Management, Cybersecurity, Electromechanical Engineering, Electrical Engineering, Engineering, Facility Management (through College of Professional and Continuing Education), Project Management (through College of Professional and Continuing Education), Industrial Design, Interior Design, Mechanical Engineering

Undergraduate Minors: Aerospace Engineering, Applied Mathematics, Architectural Studies, Bioinformatics, Biology, Business Analytics, Business Management, Chemistry, Civil Engineering, Computer Networking, Computer Science, Construction Management, Cybersecurity Management, Data Science, Electrical Engineering, Environmental Engineering, Financial Mathematics, Manufacturing, Performing Arts, Media, Culture and Communications Studies, Physics, Surveying

Graduate Majors: Master of Architecture, Master of Engineering in Civil Engineering, Master of Science in Applied Computer Science, Master of Science in Construction Management, Master of Science in Facility Management, Master of Science in Project Management, Master of Science in Technology Management

Associate Degrees/Certificates: Construction Management (AS), Building Information Modeling (Certificate), Construction (Certificate), Professional Land Surveying (Certificate), Facilities Management (Certificate), Managing Construction Projects (Certificate), Project Management (Certificate)

MAJORS AND DEGREES OFFERED

Associates, Bachelors, Masters, Certificates

TUITION, ROOM, BOARD, FEES

Tuition: $35,970

Room & Board: $14,970

FINANCIAL AID

Average financial aid Award in 2018: $20,683

STUDENT ORGANIZATIONS AND ACTIVITIES

4,516 students, 3,940 undergraduate full-time students from 37 states and 64 countries

Wentworth participates in 18 NCAA-sponsored varsity sports. Students can also participate in any of more than 65 clubs and organizations dedicated to activities such as competitive video gaming, sustainability, cycling, rugby, ultimate Frisbee, and many more. Students can also build their resumes and networking skills by participating in student government; cultural organizations; event programming; Wentworth Internet Radio + Entertainment (W.I.R.E.), and a range of professional associations for every major. And if students can't find what they're looking for on the Wentworth campus, they simply visit one of the four neighboring Colleges of the Fenway institutions with which the Institute is affiliated. In addition to Wentworth, the Colleges of the Fenway consist of the Massachusetts College of Art, Massachusetts College of Pharmacy, Emmanuel College, and Simmons University.

ADMISSIONS PROCESS

Wentworth practices rolling admissions, which means we review applications as they are received. The priority deadline for completed applications is December 15. Apply early as some programs may reach capacity. If applying after December 15, we invite you to contact the Admissions Office for space availability in your area of interest.

In order to apply, Wentworth requires the following:

An Application

We accept any of the following online submissions:

- Wentworth Application
- Common Application

Your Official Transcripts

Please note that transcripts are considered official only if sent directly from your high school.

Standardized Tests

Wentworth does not require the ACT/SAT for admission. However, we will still accept SAT or ACT scores if the applicant chooses to submit them. Official scores should be sent to us directly from College Board or ACT. Wentworth's College Board code is 3958 and ACT code is 1928. Scores may also be submitted directly from your guidance office. In addition, please note:

- We encourage students to sit for the SAT no later than January of each year.
- If you are applying for Fall 2017 or later, you may submit scores from the old SAT *if the exam was completed prior to March 2016.*
- If you take both the old and the new SAT, both exams may be submitted.
- If you did not complete the SAT prior to March 2016, you must submit the new SAT scores.

Recommendation Letters

We require at least one recommendation from a guidance counselor or teacher.

Personal Statement/Essay

You can submit your essay with your application, or send it separately by mail or email. The required length is 250–500 words. Please make sure your name is included on your essay.

Extracurricular Activities

Be sure to include your participation in community service activities, athletic teams, employment and involvement in clubs and organizations.

Prerequisites

You must complete a mathematics course of study through the Algebra II level, at least one laboratory science course (e.g., Biology, Chemistry, or Physics), and four years of English.

- Students applying for Applied Mathematics, Applied Sciences, Computer Science, Cybersecurity, or Electromechanical, Civil, Computer, Biomedical, Electrical or Mechanical Engineering must also have taken a minimum of Precalculus.

WEST VIRGINIA WESLEYAN COLLEGE

AT A GLANCE

Discover Your Every Potential. West Virginia Wesleyan is a private four-year co-educational residential college that is affiliated with The United Methodist Church. Wesleyan creates a unique learning environment enabling our students to develop the skills, values, relationships, and perspectives needed for them to obtain employment, enhance their careers, and demonstrate leadership throughout their lives. Wesleyan graduates are well prepared to be successful and respected citizens in a rapidly changing world. 95% of the class of 2018 graduates obtained a job in their field or were attending graduate school within 6 months of graduation (with 85% of the class reporting).

The college's student to faculty ratio is 13:1 with an average class size of 19. The College offers over 40 majors and over 40 minors of study, and several additional master's programs spanning Athletic Training, Business Administration, English (Creative Writing), and Nursing. Last year, the College launched its first doctoral program: Doctorate Nurse Practitioner (DNP).

West Virginia Wesleyan is accredited by the Commission on Institutions of Higher Education of the North Central Association of Colleges and Schools and approved by the University Senate of The United Methodist Church. It is a member of the National Association of Schools of Music and is approved by the West Virginia Department of Education and the National Council for the Accreditation of Teacher Education. The College participates in the Interstate Certification Project whereby several states certify teachers graduating from Wesleyan's Department of Education. The athletic training program is accredited by the Commission on Accreditation of Allied Health Education Programs. Degree programs offered in business and economics, including the Master of Business Administration program, are accredited by the International Assembly for Collegiate Business Education.

All academic programs either require or strongly encourage the completion of an internship experience. Wesleyan's academic calendar is 4-4-1 that includes an optional May Term in which students pursue unique study abroad courses or intensive study curricular offerings. The Advising and Career Center assists students with course scheduling, academic advising, internships and study abroad, resume writing, job searches, and graduate and professional school placement. The Learning Center provides tutoring services as well as comprehensive services for students with diagnosed learning disabilities.

Of the more than 1,250 students, 53 percent are from West Virginia, while the other 47 percent originate from 39 states and 19 countries. 16 percent of Wesleyan's American students are minority students. Over 90 percent of Wesleyan's new students live on-campus and the College guarantees four years of on-campus housing for all undergraduate students. Housing options include double and single rooms, suites, and apartments. Campus dining is provided and prepared by a contracted professional catering service.

LOCATION AND ENVIRONMENT

Situated in the foothills of the Allegheny Mountains, Wesleyan's beautiful 100-acre campus is located in the quaint, residential town of Buckhannon, West Virginia. Buckhannon has been included in Norman Crampton's book, The Top 100 Best Small Towns in America, a Random House Publication. Many students are drawn to this personal and picturesque setting and the numerous outdoor opportunities located near campus. The local community offers movie theatres, coffee houses, department stores, and a wide selection of local and chain restaurants. Wesleyan is a short two-hour drive from Pittsburgh, Pennsylvania, and 90 minutes from Charleston, West Virginia, the state capital.

CAMPUS FACILITIES AND EQUIPMENT

Wesleyan's 23 buildings include 10 modern residence hall units, including two suite style halls renovated or newly built in the last eight years. Located in the center of campus is Wesley Chapel, which chapel serves as a focal point of campus and houses many campus events, both religious and cultural. Benedum Campus and Community Center houses a convenience store, bookstore, swimming pool, campus radio station, student development offices, study lounges, and a cabaret-style restaurant, recently renovated for 2020. The Rockefeller Physical Education Center includes a main arena that seats 3,700 spectators, an intramural gymnasium, training rooms, and an indoor turf training area. The multimillion-dollar Reemsnyder Research Center was opened in 2009 and boasts state of the art laboratory space for the sciences. Other vital buildings on campus include Christopher Hall of Science; Middleton Hall, which houses the Nursing Department and region-renowned simulation facilities; and the Lynch-Raine Administration Building. In addition, the multimillion-dollar Virginia Thomas Law Center for the Performing Arts, opened in 2009, offers the most advanced performing arts facility of its kind in the region. Most recently, a completely renovated student wellness center was opened in 2012 along with a new multi-sport stadium project in phase one in 2015. Since 2015 more than 50 learning spaces have been completely updated and renovated.

Wesleyan's Annie Merner Pfeiffer Library re-opened in Fall 2019 after a 2.2-million-dollar renovation including new 24 hour access, food market, lounge and study spaces, technology, and incredible enhancements to make it the academic hub of campus with facilities to rival any library in the region.

The entire campus has been outfitted with a ubiquitous campus-wide wireless network ensuring access to all students, faculty, and staff from all major campus buildings and every residence hall room. Network speeds are improved yearly and rival any private college in the region.

OFF-CAMPUS OPPORTUNITIES

Wesleyan encourages all students to expand their education beyond the traditional classroom. Many students have studied abroad in such places as England, Ireland, Wales, Germany, Spain, Kenya, Scotland, and Australia. Professional internships are available in the Buckhannon area, Charleston, WV, Washington, D.C.; New York, NY; Pittsburgh, PA; and other states and countries.

ACADEMIC PROGRAMS

Wesleyan's liberal arts curriculum begins with a broad base view in a variety of core courses designed to enrich the student's whole view. The classes range from the humanities to contemporary issues and can be intermingled with the courses in the individual's major throughout the four-year program.

Wesleyan's Honors Program is offered for superior students who meet the specific requirements and demonstrate a high quality of academic excellence. Challenging, yet rewarding, classes, along with culturally enriching outings, offer Honors students a diverse and unique educational experience.

MAJORS AND DEGREES OFFERED

West Virginia Wesleyan offers four undergraduate degrees: The Bachelor of Arts; the Bachelor of Music Education; Bachelor of Science; and the Bachelor of Science in Nursing. The most popular programs of study are in the sciences (biology, physics / engineering, pre-professional studies, etc.); education; business; athletic training; and nursing. Wesleyan also offers several master's degree programs.

TUITION, ROOM, BOARD, FEES

The 2020–2021 total direct costs at Wesleyan are $31,074 for tuition, $9,576 for standard room and board, and $1,178 for student fees, which includes a student activity fee, facility fee, and a technology fee. These costs do not include books, travel, clothing, the laptop computer, medical insurance, or other personal expenses. Wesleyan offers an interest-free monthly payment plan during the academic year.

FINANCIAL AID

The College offers financial aid based on a variety of criteria: scholastic achievements, special talents and abilities, and financial need. Several scholarships are available including awards for academics, athletics, performing arts, leadership, community service, and visual arts. Student employment is available in most areas of the College community, financed through a blend of institutional and federal funds. Students may apply for low-cost federal loans. All students should file the Free Application for Federal Student Aid. Currently, more than 95 percent of all students receive grants or scholarships from Wesleyan.

STUDENT ORGANIZATIONS AND ACTIVITIES

Wesleyan has a balanced and diverse student life program that includes more than 70 campus organizations. Included among these are a campus radio station, newspaper, student government, departmental clubs, national fraternities and sororities, and religious organizations. Over 84 percent of Wesleyan students of those reporting in the NSSE survey participate in community service activities that include the complete administration of a youth basketball program to Special Olympics, to tutoring, mentoring, and educational activities to senior citizens programs to more global programs such as hurricane relief and international service trips.

Wesleyan features 22 varsity programs in NCAA Division II. Wesleyan competes in the Mountain East Conference. Our newest sports include Women's Lacrosse and Women's Acrobatics and Tumbling.

In fall of 2018, WVWC launched varsity e-sports including an eSports arena and scholarships for participants.

ADMISSIONS PROCESS

Students are selected by the Office of Admission based on ability, interests, academic preparation, character, and promise, as indicated by their own statements on the application, as well as by high school or college records, recommendations, and standardized test results. Open without discrimination to all qualified students, the College reserves the right to refuse to admit any applicant who, because of low scholarship or citizenship record, is deemed by the Admission and Academic Standing Council to be unlikely to succeed within the standards the College seeks to maintain.

Persons wishing to be admitted directly from high school should present an application for admission with (no paper application fee); a transcript from an accredited high school; and a record of either SAT or ACT scores. Applicants from non-accredited high schools or completing General Educational Development may be considered for admission if satisfactory ability and achievement are demonstrated. Students are encouraged to apply for free online (www.wvwc.edu) or via the Common Application (www.commonapp. org). Neither of these applications require a fee.

Persons seeking to transfer from another accredited college or university may be admitted to advanced standing upon presentation of an application for admission; an official transcript showing all credits attempted at all post-secondary institutions previously attended; a high school transcript certifying graduation and showing courses pursued and grades earned and, if the cumulative grade point average is less than 2.5, either the SAT I or ACT scores. Wesleyan will accept transfer credit courses compatible with its academic program. Grades and hours so earned shall count toward graduation. The College accepts no more than 60 semester hours of credit from a junior or community college.

Students who transfer to Wesleyan with an associates degree from a regionally accredited community or junior college may be admitted with the degree credited as fulfilling Wesleyan's general studies requirements when the total educational background, including high school record, shows compatibility with Wesleyan's general studies requirements. Deficiencies in general studies requirements, as determined by the Admission and Academic Standing Council, must be satisfied after enrollment at Wesleyan.

Wesleyan participates in the Advanced Placement Program of the College Entrance Examination Board and the International Baccalaureate Diploma Program. Students who have successfully completed AP or IB programs should contact the Office of Admission for credit transfer policies.

WILLAMETTE UNIVERSITY

AT A GLANCE

Think beyond

Think beyond the conventional classrooms and standard textbooks and step into a learning environment that stimulates your intellect, stirs your heart and prepares you for the world of tomorrow.

At Willamette, you'll collaborate with the nation's top professors on innovative studies that span the sciences, arts and humanities. You'll create knowledge that transforms lives and builds bridges of understanding. And you'll put your ideas to work in learning opportunities that encompass the globe.

Things are changing fast. Many of today's careers will diminish in importance or vanish entirely. You need the perspective, agility and foresight to stay one step ahead in a dynamic landscape—and those are the qualities you'll develop at Willamette.

Learn without limits

As a university with a rich tradition of intellectual curiosity and social awareness, Willamette will empower you as a thought leader and an agent of positive change. We do this by building a bridge that connects the lessons of the past, the challenges of the present and the possibilities of the future.

You'll immerse yourself in courses that teach you how to think creatively across multiple disciplines. You'll share your ideas with classmates and faculty who open your mind to diverse perspectives and emerging trends. And you'll master the latest technology and research tools in professional settings on and off campus.

Get the full college experience

Willamette is intellectually challenging, but it's also a lot of fun. With more than 90 student organizations, 19 NCAA Division III teams and dozens of intramural sports to choose from, you'll find all kinds of ways to tap your talents and make the most of your time.

You can get involved in Greek life, DJ for KWU Radio, celebrate your heritage in one of our multicultural clubs or bring big-time acts to campus for the Willamette Events Board. And when it's time for a break, you'll always find good food and great conversation at The Bistro, our student-run coffeehouse.

Make lifelong connections

There are no walls at Willamette. This is a place where you can dine with the dean at Goudy Commons, collaborate with an anthropology major on a theatrical performance and play Ultimate Frisbee with your thesis advisor on a sweeping expanse of lawn we call "The Quad." It's a place where the lives of community members blend seamlessly to form bonds that aren't easily broken.

What's more, the connections you make at Willamette won't be limited to your classmates and professors. The Willamette community is expansive and inclusive, with traditions that stretch back more than 175 years. If you're looking for a learning opportunity, a word of advice or an entry point into your profession, our alumni will be there for you.

Lead the way

Willamette has been a place for emerging leaders since the Oregon Legislature held its first meeting here in the 1850s. That tradition continues to this day, and the location of the state Capitol across the street gives our students a ready-made platform to shape public policy while they're pursuing their degrees.

But our concept of leadership extends well beyond the political realm. We encourage our students to cast a vision that encompasses every academic discipline, and they're on the forefront of breakthroughs in the realms of medicine, environmental science, social justice issues—the list goes on. At Willamette, you'll have the freedom to define leadership on your terms, and your experiences will prepare you for life as a difference maker.

Be a citizen of the world

An interconnected world demands an education that knows no boundaries. Willamette will give you every chance to immerse yourself in a different culture, starting with Tokyo International University. This unique partnership brings more than 100 international students a year to campus and gives you the option of taking classes at our sister school in Japan.

You'll also have access to more than 60 study abroad programs at Willamette, and your travels won't be limited to the first semester of your junior year. Many of our students travel to multiple countries to explore their interests, and sometimes these experiences incorporate cutting-edge research and prestigious internships. The same thing can happen to you.

LOCATION AND ENVIRONMENT

Willamette University is located in downtown Salem, Oregon. The residential campus is set on 60 acres of land and situated between the state Capitol and Salem Hospital. Oregon's scenic mountains and coastline, as well as Portland, the state's largest city, are all an hour from campus.

CAMPUS FACILITIES AND EQUIPMENT

Willamette has outstanding athletic and academic facilities. These include a laser laboratory, greenhouse, cadaver laboratory and a large telescope at the 305-acre outdoor learning laboratory and forest at Zena. Willamette also features acoustically exceptional music venues, a digital media and music lab, a flexible theatre space, the Hallie Ford Museum of Art and a state-of-the-art campus theatre for film studies.

OFF-CAMPUS OPPORTUNITIES

Willamette offers a robust outdoor program that allows you to choose from more than 120 excursions throughout the year. You also can spend time at our 305-acre forest laboratory at Zena just a few miles from campus, and you'll have easy access to coffee shops, restaurants, malls and movie theaters right down the street. Internships and research opportunities with public, private and non-profit organizations are readily available as well.

ACADEMIC PROGRAMS

You can select more than one undergraduate major or minor and create a program that reflects your passions and interests. Willamette also offers dual-degree programs that allow you to earn a BA and an MBA in five years or a BA and JD in six years. You can pair the best of a liberal arts experience with advanced professional degrees at Willamette's Atkinson Graduate School of Management or College of Law.

MAJORS AND DEGREES OFFERED

Willamette offers more than 50 academic programs and provides a broad-based liberal arts and sciences curriculum with countless opportunities for original research and artistic expression. You also can put your ideas to work in professional internships and study abroad experiences that speak directly to your interests.

TUITION, ROOM, BOARD, FEES

Tuition: $51,750
Room and Board: $12,938
Fees: $860
Books and supplies (estimated): $1,012

FINANCIAL AID

Our average annual financial aid package is $37,658. The financial aid process is influenced by the quality of your academic record and the extent of your financial resources. If you're a strong student, you'll receive scholarship recognition from us regardless of whether you qualify for need-based aid. If you have demonstrated financial need, academic standing is a strong factor in how much gift aid (scholarships and grants) you'll receive.

Average financial aid package: $37,658
Students who receive financial aid: 99%
Average amount students borrow: $26,643

STUDENT ORGANIZATIONS AND ACTIVITIES

More than 75% of Willamette's students come from California, Washington and Oregon. Dozens of other states are represented as well, and students from Tokyo International University of America add a cultural dimension to the campus community. Students are passionate about pursuing their academic interests across disciplines and being civically engaged. Thirty-one percent of the student population is racially or ethnically diverse.

There are more than 90 clubs and organizations on campus, including the Outdoor Club, Ultimate Frisbee, Men's and Women's Rugby, Willamette Events Board, Black Student Union, Willamette Dance Company, Hawaii Club, Rainbow Alliance, Zena Farm Club and the Bearcat Pantry.

ADMISSIONS PROCESS

Willamette is a Common Application exclusive institution. We use the Common Application because it collects a broad range of academic and extracurricular information about potential Bearcats and simplifies the process for our applicants. Counselors submit official transcripts through the Common Application. To ensure adequate academic preparation for success in Willamette's rigorous curriculum, we recommend the following pattern of secondary school coursework:

- Four years of English
- Three years of mathematics (including algebra, geometry and trigonometry)
- Four years of social science coursework
- Three to four years of lab-based science coursework
- Two to four years of a foreign language

Counselors may submit School Report Forms and Recommendations through the Common Application. Willamette offers test-optional admission with the completion of a supplemental essay question as part of the Common Application.

If you decide to include standardized test scores, make sure you send your official score reports from either the SAT or the ACT. If students take the SAT or ACT more than once, the Admission Committee will review your highest scores from each section, resulting in what is widely known as a superscore. Letter(s) of recommendation may be submitted by your teachers through the Common Application.

WORCESTER POLYTECHNIC INSTITUTE

AT A GLANCE

Here, you don't just learn—you do. Everything about Worcester Polytechnic Institute (WPI) is designed to stimulate your curiosity, challenge you, and support you so that you can imagine anything and innovate everything.

WPI is a nationally renowned, private research university focused on science, technology, engineering, and math. WPI's founding motto, "Theory and Practice," provides a distinctive approach to education by balancing rigorous academics with hands-on learning. At WPI, students go above and beyond traditional classroom education.

WPI's unique project-based education converts classroom concepts into real-world impact. The WPI Plan (wpi.edu/wpi-plan) will set you apart in the world first as a student, then as a sought-after young professional, and ultimately across your career and life. Fifty years after its implementation, the Plan continues to help WPI students succeed in college and in their careers.

All WPI students complete at least two projects that allow them to tackle issues they feel passionate about and make a lasting difference on the world around us—from improving access to clean water in rural communities, to developing robots for underwater research, to building human heart tissue scaffolding from spinach leaves. Through the Plan, you learn how to learn by applying your classroom experiences to projects that challenge you from a proficiency, social, and global perspective.

WPI consistently receives high rankings as one of America's Best Colleges, according to the *U.S. News & World Report*. The university has earned praise and attention for its project-based curriculum, small class sizes, robust career services, study abroad opportunities, return on investment, and ability to create futures. Find out more at wpi.edu/+formula.

LOCATION AND ENVIRONMENT

Founded in 1865, WPI's 95-acre campus is located in a residential area of Worcester (Wus-tah), Massachusetts, the second largest city in New England. With its beautiful architecture and green spaces, WPI has a classic New England feel. Ranked ninth on Forbes' "America's Most Livable Cities," the up-and-coming city offers the charm and ease of a college town with the convenience of urban living.

CAMPUS FACILITIES AND EQUIPMENT

These three buildings spotlight WPI and its cutting-edge equipment available in labs and classrooms all across campus:

The Foisie Innovation Studio serves as a hub for WPI's project-based curriculum. Makerspaces, high-tech active learning classrooms, an Innovation & Entrepreneurship Center, and Global Impact Lab support the "hands-on" aspect of the WPI curriculum.

The Life Sciences & Bioengineering Center at Gateway Park is a state-of-the-art research center housing faculty from four departments. The Fire Science Laboratory enables students and faculty to evaluate fire safety measures in actual fire simulations. The recently opened PracticePoint facility is a membership-based development and testing facility in which academics, industry, healthcare professionals, and patients will help advance medical devices and healthcare technologies. The new Lab for Education & Application Prototypes supports the growing integrated photonics manufacturing sector. Laser holography labs, computer music labs, medical imaging labs, a bioprocess lab—they're all here, and lots more.

WPI's Sports and Recreation Center, one of the greenest in the nation, includes a four-court gymnasium, indoor jogging track, 14,000 sq. ft. of fitness space, racquetball and squash courts, competition pool, workout studios, and rowing tanks.

OFF-CAMPUS OPPORTUNITIES

Worcester boasts over 38,000 college students attending nine universities. Along with a robust college population, the city offers world-class restaurants, cultural sights, concerts and sporting events, beautiful parks, and affordable cost of living. Area transportation allows easy access to regional amenities such as skiing and hiking, plus quick travel to Boston, Cape Cod, and New York City.

ACADEMIC PROGRAMS

WPI's academic program is built to be flexible. Students take the equivalent of three courses (as courses or project work) during each of four seven-week terms (two in the fall and two in the spring). As part of the WPI Plan, you have the freedom and the responsibility to choose the courses and experiences that best suit your goals and interests.

In addition, WPI does not have failing grades, so the focus is on learning, teamwork, and collaboration, not on competing. You earn A, B, C, or NR (No Record). This unique grading system encourages you to branch out, experiment, and cross disciplines—that's where amazing things happen at WPI, and ultimately, in your career.

Ranked No. 1 as the best study abroad program by the Princeton Review in 2016 and referred to as "life changing," the majority of WPI students travel to one of more than 50 off-campus locations, and every student receives a one-time global scholarship of up to $5,000 toward the experience. Students make a difference to communities and organizations around the globe by bringing thoughtful approaches to an astounding array of societal and technological challenges. Past projects have included using community engagement to reduce flood rise in Albania's Shkoder region, the development of an interactive data portal for rural electrification in Namibia, and an interactive museum exhibit featuring pueblo influence on New Mexican contemporary architecture.

MAJORS AND DEGREES OFFERED

WPI's 50+ areas of study include engineering, science, management, and the liberal arts leading to undergraduate degrees of the bachelor of science (BS) or bachelor of arts (BA). The university also has strong graduate degree programs. Exciting interdisciplinary programs, driven by real-world demand, include interactive media and game development, environmental engineering, architectural engineering, and the nation's first undergraduate program in robotics engineering.

WPI also offers pre-professional programs (law, medicine, dentistry, and veterinary) and a four- and five-year BS/MS program. You can even create your own major or minor program and go out on co-op. Its academic advising program and comprehensive academic support services help students make the right choices to reach their goals.

TUITION, ROOM, BOARD, FEES

Tuition for the 2020–21 academic year is set at $53,410 and approximate on-campus room and board is $15,838. There is a required fee of $736 to cover student life and health charges.

WPI has an excellent ROI, and our graduates earn 38% higher starting salaries than the national average. Graduates are able to move quickly up the ranks to positions of influence as a result of the opportunities they have to gain real work experiences before graduation.

Top-tier employers seek out WPI graduates for their real-world experience and ability to work collaboratively. With more than 95 percent of graduates in jobs or attending graduate school within several months of graduation, students are recruited by leading organizations such as Pfizer, General Electric, Fidelity Investments, Tesla, and Google. Each year, WPI graduates are accepted at many prestigious graduate schools, including MIT, Yale University, Princeton University, Johns Hopkins University, and Tufts University School of Medicine.

FINANCIAL AID

All admitted applicants are considered for merit-based scholarships based upon academic performance, leadership, extracurricular involvement, and community service—there is no separate application required.

Students may indicate if they wish to be considered for need-based aid. About 97 percent of WPI students receive merit or need-based aid to attend the university, not including federal aid. Most applicants will receive a financial aid package within two weeks of their acceptance.

Students applying for need-based aid are required to file the FAFSA and CSS Profile no later than February 1. By filing before the deadline, you will receive notification of your aid much sooner, allowing you to make informed decisions.

WPI boasts a 98.9% loan repayment rate—showing that WPI graduates earn strong salaries and are able to pay off their loans in a reasonable amount of time.

STUDENT ORGANIZATIONS AND ACTIVITIES

The WPI community is welcoming and close-knit, with a robust support system ready to help academically, emotionally, physically, and culturally. The university prioritizes inclusiveness and acceptance.

The student community of innovators and explorers who thrive here make their own decisions and set their own course; they want to be leaders and not followers; they are eager to tackle the issues that will make the world a better place; they work in teams to get things done; and they love math and science but feel just as passionate about other subjects.

There's lots to do here at WPI and in the surrounding Worcester area to complement the skills you'll gain from the classroom with different academic, professional, social, and athletic organizations. You can volunteer your time at a number of local nonprofit organizations, join a fraternity or sorority, offer your talents to over 235 student life groups, such as an a cappella group or theatre production, or channel your inner *Saturday Night Live* performer and participate in a sketch comedy group—and that's just the beginning.

Twenty varsity sports and 41 club sports and intramural teams are sponsored by WPI, supporting a wide range of athletic interests and abilities. Our Sports & Recreation Center (opened in 2013) is one of the finest higher education athletic facilities in the Northeast.

ADMISSIONS PROCESS

WPI is a member of the Common Application, the exclusive method by which to apply to WPI. A $65 application fee is required for all applicants. (WPI endorses the fee waiver policy of the College Board, as well as accepts fee waivers from guidance or college counselors.) Seniors in high school should interview before December 15 of their senior year. Interviews are optional but are highly encouraged.

The regular decision deadline is February 1, while the two early-action deadlines are November 1 and January 1, respectively. The deadline for transfer students to apply for fall admission is April 15 on a rolling notification.

WPI is test-optional; SAT/ACT scores are accepted, but not required, and official scores do not need to be sent until deciding to enroll. Academic requirements include four years of math (including pre-calculus), four years of English, and two years of lab science.

Other requirements:

- High school transcript, including most recent senior grades
- Teacher recommendation (preferably in math or science)
- Guidance counselor recommendation
- Personal essay
- TOEFL, IELTS, or Pearson's Test of English (PTE) scores for international students whose first language is not English

INDEXES

INDEXES

ALPHABETICAL INDEX

For more free content, visit PrincetonReview.com

University of Florida	696	University of Montevallo	735	University of Southern California	774
University of Georgia	697	University of Mount Union	735	University of Southern Indiana	775
University of Great Falls	698	University of Nebraska—Omaha	736	University of Southern Maine	776
University of Hartford	699	University of Nebraska—Lincoln	737	University of Southern Mississippi	777
University of Hawaii—Hilo	699	University of Nebraska Medical Center	738	University of South Florida	777
University of Hawaii—Manoa	700	University of Nevada, Las Vegas	738	University of South Florida—St. Petersburg	778
University of Hawaii—West Oahu	700	University of New England	739, 1040	University of Tampa	778, 1054
University of Houston	701	University of New Hampshire	739	University of Tennessee—Chattanooga	779
University of Houston—Clear Lake	702	University of New Haven	740, 1042	University of Tennessee—Knoxville	780
University of Houston—Downtown	702	University of New Mexico	741	University of Tennessee—Martin	781
University of Houston—Victoria	703	University of New Orleans	742	The University of Texas at Arlington	781
University of Idaho	703	The University of North Carolina—Asheville	742	The University of Texas at Austin	782
University of Illinois—Chicago	704	University of North Carolina—Chapel Hill	743	The University of Texas at Brownsville	783
University of Illinois—Springfield	705	University of North Carolina—Charlotte	744	The University of Texas at Dallas	783
University of Illinois—Urbana-Champaign	705	University of North Carolina—Greensboro	745	The University of Texas at El Paso	784
University of Indianapolis	706	The University of North Carolina—Pembroke	745	The University of Texas at Medical	
University of Iowa	707	University of North Carolina—Wilmington	746	Branch at Galveston	784
University of Jamestown	708	University of North Dakota	747	The University of Texas at Rio Grande Valley	785
University of Kansas	708	University of Northern Colorado	748	The University of Texas at San Antonio	785
University of Kentucky	709	University of Northern Iowa	748	The University of Texas at Tyler	786
University of King's College	710	University of North Florida	749	University of the Arts	786
University of La Verne	710	University of North Georgia	750	University of the Incarnate Word	787
The University of Lethbridge	711	University of North Texas	751	University of the Ozarks	788
University of Louisiana at Lafayette	711	University of Notre Dame	751	University of the Pacific	788
University of Louisville	712	University of Oklahoma	752	University of the Sciences in Philadelphia	789
University of Lynchburg	713	University of Oregon	753	University of Toronto	790
University of Maine	713, 1038	University of Pennsylvania	754	University of Tulsa	790, 1056
University of Maine—Augusta	714	University of Phoenix	755	University of Utah	791, 1058
University of Maine—Farmington	715	University of Pikeville	755	University of Vermont	792, 1060
University of Maine—Fort Kent	715	University of Pittsburgh—Bradford	756, 1044	University of Virginia	793
University of Maine—Machias	716	University of Pittsburgh—Greensburg	756	University of Virginia's College at Wise	794
University of Maine—Presque Isle	716	University of Pittsburgh—Johnstown	757	University of Washington	794
University of Mary Hardin-Baylor	717	University of Pittsburgh—Pittsburgh Campus	758	University of Washington—Bothell	795
University of Maryland, Baltimore County	718	University of Portland	758	University of Washington—Tacoma	795
University of Maryland, College Park	719	University of Puget Sound	759	University of West Alabama	796
University of Mary Washington	719	University of Redlands	760, 1046	University of West Florida	796
University of Massachusetts—Amherst	720	University of Rhode Island	761	University of West Georgia	797
University of Massachusetts—Boston	721	University of Richmond	761, 1048	University of Windsor	798
University of Massachusetts—Dartmouth	722	University of Rio Grande	762	University of Wisconsin—Eau Claire	798
University of Massachusetts—Lowell	723	University of Rochester	763	University of Wisconsin—Green Bay	799
The University of Memphis	723	University of St. Francis (IL)	764	University of Wisconsin—La Crosse	800
University of Miami	724	University of St. Francis (IN)	764	University of Wisconsin—Madison	800
University of Michigan—Ann Arbor	725	University of Saint Joseph	765	University of Wisconsin—Milwaukee	801
University of Michigan—Dearborn	726	University of Saint Mary (KS)	765	University of Wisconsin—Oshkosh	802
University of Michigan—Flint	726	University of Saint Thomas (MN)	766	University of Wisconsin—Platteville	802
University of Minnesota—Crookston	727	University of St. Thomas (TX)	767	University of Wisconsin—River Falls	803
University of Minnesota—Duluth	728	University of San Diego	767	University of Wisconsin—Stevens Point	804
University of Minnesota—Morris	728	University of San Francisco	768, 1050	University of Wisconsin—Stout	804
University of Minnesota—Twin Cities	729	University of Science & Arts of Oklahoma	769	University of Wisconsin—Superior	805
University of Mississippi	730	The University of Scranton	770, 1052	University of Wisconsin—Whitewater	806
University of Missouri	731	The University of the South	770	University of Wyoming	806
University of Missouri—Kansas City	731	University of South Alabama	771	Upper Iowa University	807
University of Missouri—Saint Louis	732	University of South Carolina—Aiken	772	Ursinus College	808
University of Mobile	733	University of South Carolina—Beaufort	772	Ursuline College	808
The University of Montana—Missoula	733	University of South Carolina—Columbia	773	Utah State University	809
The University of Montana—Western	734	The University of South Dakota	774	Utica College	810

INTERNATIONAL

CANADA

EGYPT

IRELAND

MEXICO

UNITED KINGDOM

For more free content, visit PrincetonReview.com

INDEX BY SIZE

1,000—2,000 STUDENTS

For more free content, visit PrincetonReview.com

Rollins College	539	University of Pittsburgh—Greensburg	756	Augustana College (IL)	44
Russell Sage College	543	University of Rio Grande	762	Aurora University	46
St. Bonaventure University	550	University of St. Francis (IL)	764	Babson College	50, 890
Saint Francis University (PA)	553, 1006	University of Saint Francis (IN)	764	Baldwin Wallace University	51
Saint Martin's University	561	University of St. Thomas (TX)	767	Barnard College	54, 894
Saint Mary-of-the-Woods College	562	The University of the South	770	Barry University	55
Saint Mary's College (IN)	563	University of South Carolina—Beaufort	772	Belhaven University	60
St. Mary's College of Maryland	564	University of the Arts	786	Bellarmine University	61
Saint Mary's University of Minnesota	565	University of Virginia's College at Wise	794	Bemidji State University	63
Saint Michael's College	566	Ursinus College	808	Benedict College	64
St. Norbert College	567	Vaughn College of Aeronautics and		Benedictine University	65
St. Thomas Aquinas College	569	Technology	814	Bentley University	67, 900
St. Thomas University (FL)	570	Vermont Technical College	814	Berkeley College	69
Saint Vincent College	570	Virginia Military Institute	817	Berklee College of Music	69
Sarah Lawrence College	579	Virginia Wesleyan University	819	Bethel University (MN)	73
Schreiner University	582	Viterbo University	820	Biola University	74
Scripps College	583	Wagner College	821	Bob Jones University	78
Seton Hill University	586	Walla Walla University	823	Bradley University	83
Shaw University	587	Wartburg College	826	Brandeis University	84
Shorter University	590	Washington & Jefferson College	827	Brigham Young University—Hawaii	89
Simmons University	592	Washington and Lee University	828	Bryant University	92, 904
Southern New Hampshire University	604	Washington College	829, 1066	Bucknell University	94, 906
Southern Wesleyan University	607	Waynesburg University	832	Butler University	96
Southwestern College (KS)	608	Western Colorado University	842	California Lutheran University	100
Southwestern University	609, 1020	Westminster College (PA)	849	California University of Pennsylvania	110
Spring Hill College	611	Westminster College (UT)	850	Calvin University	112
State University of New York—College of		Westmont College	851	Campbellsville University	113
Environmental Science and Forestry	617, 1026	West Virginia Wesleyan College	854, 1072	Campbell University	113
State University of New York—		Wheaton College (MA)	855	Canisius College	114
Maritime College	621	Whitman College	857	Capital University	115
State University of New York—		Whittier College	857	Carleton College	116
Polytechnic Institute	623	Willamette University	861, 1074	Carroll University (WI)	118
Swarthmore College	635, 1028	William Peace University	864	Carthage College	119
Taylor University	638	William Penn University	864	The Catholic University of America	123
Texas A&M University—Texarkana	643	Wilmington College (OH)	866	Cedarville University	125
Texas Lutheran University	644	Wisconsin Lutheran College	869	Central Ohio Technical College	129
Thiel College	647	Wittenberg University	870	Champlain College	133
Thomas More College	650	Wofford College	870	Christopher Newport University	138, 910
Tusculum College	661	Woodbury University	871	The Citadel, The Military College of	
Union Institute & University	664			South Carolina	138
University of Advancing Technology (UAT)	668	## 2,001—5,000 STUDENTS		Clark Atlanta University	147
University of Charleston	686			Clarkson University	148
University of Dallas	691	Abilene Christian University	10	Clark University	149
University of Dubuque	694	Acadia University	11	Colgate University	158
University of Hawaii—West Oahu	700	Alabama A&M University	14	College of Saint Benedict/	
University of King's College	710	Albany State University	16	Saint John's University	163
University of Lynchburg	713	Alcorn State University	19	The College of Saint Rose	165
University of Maine—Farmington	715	Alvernia University	23	The College of Saint Scholastica	165
University of Maine—Fort Kent	715	Anderson University (SC)	28	College of the Holy Cross	167
University of Minnesota—Crookston	727	Arcadia University	32	Colorado College	170
University of Minnesota—Morris	728	Arizona State University at the West campus	34	Colorado School of Mines	171
University of Mobile	733	Arizona State University Polytechnic campus	35	Colorado State University-Pueblo	172
The University of Montana—Western	734	Art Center College of Design	38	Columbia University School of	
University of Mount Union	735	The Art Institute of Atlanta	39	General Studies	177
University of Pikeville	755	Ashland University	40	Concordia University (St. Paul, MN)	181
University of Pittsburgh—Bradford	756, 1044	Auburn University at Montgomery	43	Concordia University (WI)	182
		Augsburg University	44		

St. Thomas University (Canada)	570
Saint Xavier University	571
Salve Regina University	573
Samford University	574
School of the Art Institute of Chicago	580
School of Visual Arts	581, 1012
Seattle Pacific University	583
Seattle University	584
Shawnee State University	586
Shenandoah University	587
Shepherd University	588
Siena College	590
Siena Heights University	591
Skidmore College	593, 1016
Smith College	594
South Dakota School of Mines and	
Technology	596
Southeastern Oklahoma State University	598
Southeastern University	599
Southern Adventist University	600
Southern Maine Community College	603
Southern Oregon University	605
Southwest Baptist University	608
Spelman College	610
Spring Arbor University	610
State University of New York—	
Alfred State College	612
State University of New York—Cobleskill	615
State University of New York—Fredonia	619
State University of New York—Potsdam	624
State University of New York—	
Purchase College	625
Stetson University	630
Stevens Institute of Technology	630
Stevenson University	631
Stonehill College	632
Suffolk University	633
Susquehanna University	634
Tiffin University	651
Trevecca Nazarene University	653
Trine University	654
Trinity College (CT)	655
Trinity University	657
Truman State University	659
Tuskegee University	662
Union College (NY)	663, 1034
Union University	664
United States Air Force Academy	665
United States Military Academy	666
United States Naval Academy	667
University of Arkansas at Pine Bluff	673
University of Baltimore	675
University of Bridgeport	675
University of Detroit Mercy	694
University of Evansville	695
The University of Findlay	696

University of Hartford	699
University of Hawaii—Hilo	699
University of Houston—Clear Lake	702
University of Houston—Victoria	703
University of Illinois—Springfield	705
University of Indianapolis	706
University of La Verne	710
University of Maine—Augusta	714
University of Mary Hardin-Baylor	717
University of Mary Washington	719
University of Montevallo	735
University of New England	739, 1040
University of New Haven	740, 1042
University of North Carolina—Asheville	742
University of Pittsburgh—Johnstown	757
University of Portland	758
University of Puget Sound	759
University of Redlands	760, 1046
University of Richmond	761, 1048
The University of Scranton	770, 1052
University of South Carolina—Aiken	772
University of South Florida—St. Petersburg	778
University of the Pacific	788
University of the Sciences in Philadelphia	789
The University of Tulsa	790, 1056
University of Washington—Tacoma	795
University of West Alabama	796
University of Wisconsin—Superior	805
Upper Iowa University	807
Utica College	810
Valparaiso University	811
Vassar College	813
Virginia State University	818
Walsh University	824
Washburn University	826
Wayland Baptist University	832
Wayne State College	833
Webster University	836
Wellesley College	837
Wentworth Institute of Technology	838, 1070
Wesleyan University	840
Western Connecticut State University	842
Western New England University	845
Western Oregon University	846
Westfield State University	848
West Virginia State University	852
West Virginia University Institute of	
Technology	853
Wheaton College (IL)	855
Whitworth University	858
Widener University	859
Wilkes University	860
Williams College	865
Wilmington College (DE)	866
Wingate University	867
Winthrop University	868

Worcester Polytechnic Institute	872, 1076
Worcester State University	872
Xavier University of Louisiana	875
Yeshiva University	876
York College of Pennsylvania	877

5,001—10,000 STUDENTS

Academy of Art University	10, 882
Adelphi University	12
American University	25
American University in Cairo	26
Angelo State University	28
Arizona State University at the	
Downtown Phoenix campus	34
Arkansas State University	36, 884
Arkansas Tech University	36
Augusta State University	46
Austin Peay State University	48
Azusa Pacific University	49
Belmont University	62, 896
Bloomsburg University of Pennsylvania	76
Boston College	79
Bridgewater State University	88
Brown University	91
California Baptist University	98
California State University, East Bay	103
California State University, Monterey Bay	107
California State University, Stanislaus	110
Carnegie Mellon University	117
Case Western Reserve University	121
Central Connecticut State University	128, 908
Central Washington University	130
Chapman University	133
City University of New York—	
Lehman College	142
City University of New York—	
Medgar Evers College	142
Clarion University of PA	146
Clayton State University	150
Coastal Carolina University	154
College of Charleston	159, 914
The College of New Jersey	161, 916
Colorado Mesa University	170
Columbia College Chicago (IL)	173
Columbia University	176
Columbus State University	178
Duke University	209
Duquesne University	210
Eastern Connecticut State University	213
East Stroudsburg University of Pennsylvania	217
Edinboro University of Pennsylvania	221
Elon University	223
Embry Riddle Aeronautical University (FL)	225
Emory University	228
Fashion Institute of Technology,	
State University of New York	235

10,001—15,000 STUDENTS

Baylor University	58
Bowling Green State University	82
California State University, Dominguez Hills	103
California State University, San Marcos	109
Central Michigan University	128
City University of New York—Baruch College	139
City University of New York— Brooklyn College	140
City University of New York—City College	140
City University of New York— Kingsborough Community College	141
City University of New York— The College of Staten Island	144
Cleveland State University	153
Cornell University	186
DePaul University	198
Eastern Kentucky University	214
Eastern Washington University	217
East Tennessee State University	218
Embry Riddle Aeronautical University— Worldwide	225
Ferris State University	236
Florida Gulf Coast University	241
Fort Hays State University	246
The George Washington University	261, 932
Kean University	332
Liberty University	360
Loyola University of Chicago	375, 964
Minnesota State University, Mankato	419
Montana State University	427
New Mexico State University	451
North Dakota State University	457
Northern Illinois University	461
Northern Kentucky University	461
Rochester Institute of Technology	536, 1000
St. John's University (NY)	556
Savannah College of Art and Design	580
Southeastern Louisiana University	598
Southern Illinois University—Edwardsville	602
State University of New York— Binghamton University	613
State University of New York— Empire State College	618
State University of New York— University at Albany	626
Syracuse University	636
Tarleton State University	638
Trinity College Dublin	656
Troy University	658, 1032
The University of Alabama—Birmingham	669
University of Alaska Anchorage	671
University of Central Oklahoma	685
University of Hawaii—Manoa	700
University of Houston—Downtown	702

University of Louisiana at Lafayette	711
University of Louisville	712
University of Maryland, Baltimore County	718
University of Massachusetts—Boston	721
University of Massachusetts—Lowell	723
University of Miami	724
University of Nebraska—Omaha	736
University of New Hampshire	739
University of North Carolina—Wilmington	746
University of North Florida	749
University of Pennsylvania	754
University of Rhode Island	761
University of South Alabama	771
University of Southern Mississippi	777
University of Tennessee—Chattanooga	779
The University of Texas at Brownsville	783
University of Vermont	792, 1060
University of West Georgia	797
University of Windsor	798
University of Wisconsin—Oshkosh	802
Valdosta State University	810
West Chester University of Pennsylvania	840
Western Kentucky University	844
Wichita State University	859
Wright State University	873

15,001—25,000 STUDENTS

Appalachian State University	30
Auburn University	42, 888
Ball State University	52
Boise State University	79
Boston University	81, 902
Brock University	90
California Polytechnic State University	101
California State University, Chico	102
California State University, Fresno	104
California State University, Los Angeles	106
California State University, San Bernardino	109
City University of New York— Hunter College	141
City University of New York— New York City College of Technology	143
City University of New York— Queens College	143
Clemson University	152
Drexel University	208
East Carolina University	212
Eastern Michigan University	215
Florida Atlantic University	240
Georgia Institute of Technology	262
Georgia Southern University	264
Grand Valley State University	273
Illinois State University	309
Indiana University—Purdue University Indianapolis	315
James Madison University	322

Kansas State University	331
Kent State University—Kent Campus	335
Louisiana State University—Baton Rouge	371
Miami University	408
Middle Tennessee State University	412, 974
Mississippi State University	421
Montclair State University	429
North Carolina State University	456
Northeastern University	459
Oakland University	471
Ohio University—Athens	479
Oklahoma State University	482
Old Dominion University	483
Portland State University	512
Rowan University	542
Sam Houston State University	575
State University of New York— Stony Brook University	625
State University of New York— University at Buffalo	627
Thomas Edison State University	649
Towson University	652
The University of Akron	668
University of Arkansas—Fayetteville	674
University of California—Riverside	680
University of California—Santa Barbara	682
University of California—Santa Cruz	683
University of Connecticut	690
University of Delaware	692
University of Georgia	697
University of Illinois—Chicago	704
University of Iowa	707
University of Kansas	708
University of Kentucky	709
University of Massachusetts—Amherst	720
The University of Memphis	723
University of Mississippi	730
University of Missouri	731
University of Nebraska—Lincoln	737
University of Nevada, Las Vegas	738
University of New Mexico	741
University of North Carolina—Chapel Hill	743
University of North Carolina—Charlotte	744
University of North Carolina—Greensboro	745
University of North Georgia	750
University of Oklahoma	752
University of Oregon	753
University of Pittsburgh—Pittsburgh Campus	758
University of Southern California	774
University of Tennessee—Knoxville	780
The University of Texas at Dallas	783
The University of Texas at El Paso	784
The University of Texas at Rio Grande Valley	785
University of Utah	791, 1058
University of Virginia	793
University of Wisconsin—Milwaukee	801

Utah State University	809
Virginia Commonwealth University	816
Wayne State University	834
Weber State University	836
Western Michigan University	844
Western University	846
Western Washington University	847
West Virginia University	853

OVER 25,000 STUDENTS

American Public University System	25
Arizona State University	33
Athabasca University	42
Brigham Young University (UT)	89
California State Polytechnic University, Pomona	101
California State University, Fullerton	105
California State University, Long Beach	105
California State University, Northridge	108
California State University, Sacramento	108
Colorado State University	172
Excelsior College	232
Florida International University	243
Florida State University	244
George Mason University	259, 930
Georgia State University	266

Indiana University—Bloomington	312
Iowa State University	319
Kennesaw State University	334
McGill University	399
Michigan State University	409
New York University	453, 982
Northern Arizona University	460
The Ohio State University—Columbus	475
Oregon State University	485
Penn State University Park	502
Purdue University—West Lafayette	518
Rutgers University—New Brunswick	545
San Diego State University	576
San Francisco State University	577
San Jose State University	577
Tecnológico de Monterrey	639
Temple University	639, 1030
Texas A&M University—College Station	641
Texas A&M University—Galveston	642
Texas State University	645
Texas Tech University	646
The University of Alabama—Tuscaloosa	670
University of Arizona	673
The University of British Columbia	676
University of California—Berkeley	676
University of California—Davis	677
University of California—Irvine	678

University of California—Los Angeles	679
University of California—San Diego	681
University of Central Florida	684, 1036
University of Cincinnati	687
University of Colorado—Boulder	688
University of Florida	696
University of Houston	701
University of Illinois—Urbana-Champaign	705
University of Maryland, College Park	719
University of Michigan—Ann Arbor	725
University of Minnesota—Twin Cities	729
University of North Texas	751
University of Phoenix	755
University of South Carolina—Columbia	773
University of South Florida	777
The University of Texas at Arlington	781
The University of Texas at Austin	782
The University of Texas at San Antonio	785
University of Toronto	790
University of Washington	794
University of Wisconsin—Madison	800
Virginia Tech	818
Washington State University	830
York University	878

INDEX BY TUITION & REQUIRED FEES

LESS THAN $10,000

Sam Houston State University	575
San Diego State University	576
San Francisco State University	577
San Jose State University	577
Shawnee State University	586
Shepherd University	588
Sonoma State University	595
South Dakota State University	597
Southeastern Louisiana University	598
Southeastern Oklahoma State University	598
Southeast Missouri State University	599
Southern Connecticut State University	601
Southern Oregon University	605
Southern University and A&M College	606
Southern Utah University	606
State University of New York— Alfred State College	612
State University of New York— Binghamton University	613
State University of New York— Buffalo State College	614
State University of New York—Cobleskill	615
State University of New York— The College at Brockport	615
State University of New York— The College at Old Westbury	616
State University of New York—College of Environmental Science and Forestry	617, 1026
State University of New York—Cortland	617
State University of New York— Empire State College	618
State University of New York— Farmingdale State College	619
State University of New York—Fredonia	619
State University of New York—Geneseo	620
State University of New York— Maritime College	621
State University of New York—New Paltz	621
State University of New York—Oswego	623
State University of New York— Polytechnic Institute	623
State University of New York— Purchase College	625
State University of New York— Upstate Medical University	627
Tennessee State University	640
Tennessee Technological University	641
Texas A&M University—Kingsville	643
Texas A&M University—San Antonio	643
Texas Woman's University	647
Thomas Edison State University	649
Truman State University	659
The University of Alabama—Huntsville	670
University of Alaska Anchorage	671
University of Alaska Fairbanks	672
University of Arkansas at Pine Bluff	673

University of Arkansas—Fayetteville	674
University of Baltimore	675
University of Central Florida	684, 1036
University of Central Missouri	685
University of Central Oklahoma	685
University of Colorado—Denver	689
University of Florida	696
University of Hawaii—Hilo	699
University of Hawaii—West Oahu	700
University of Houston—Clear Lake	702
University of Idaho	703
University of Iowa	707
The University of Lethbridge	711
University of Maine—Augusta	714
University of Maine—Farmington	715
University of Maine—Fort Kent	715
University of Maine—Machias	716
University of Maine—Presque Isle	716
University of Mississippi	730
University of Missouri—Kansas City	731
The University of Montana—Missoula	733
University of Nebraska—Omaha	736
University of Nebraska—Lincoln	737
University of Nebraska Medical Center	738
University of New Orleans	742
University of North Carolina—Asheville	742
University of North Carolina—Chapel Hill	743
University of North Carolina—Charlotte	744
University of North Carolina—Greensboro	745
University of North Carolina—Pembroke	745
University of North Carolina—Wilmington	746
University of North Dakota	747
University of Northern Iowa	748
University of North Florida	749
University of North Georgia	750
University of North Texas	751
University of South Alabama	771
The University of South Dakota	774
University of Southern Indiana	775
University of Southern Maine	776
University of Southern Mississippi	777
University of South Florida	777
University of South Florida—St. Petersburg	778
University of Tennessee—Chattanooga	779
University of Tennessee—Martin	781
The University of Texas at Arlington	781
The University of Texas at El Paso	784
The University of Texas at Rio Grande Valley	785
The University of Texas at San Antonio	785
University of Toronto	790
University of Utah	791, 1058
University of West Florida	796
University of West Georgia	797
University of Windsor	798
University of Wisconsin—Eau Claire	798
University of Wisconsin—Green Bay	799

University of Wisconsin—Madison	800
University of Wisconsin—Milwaukee	801
University of Wisconsin—Oshkosh	802
University of Wisconsin—Platteville	802
University of Wisconsin—River Falls	803
University of Wisconsin—Stevens Point	804
University of Wisconsin—Stout	804
University of Wisconsin—Superior	805
University of Wisconsin—Whitewater	806
University of Wyoming	806
Utah State University	809
Valdosta State University	810
Virginia State University	818
Walsh College	823
Washburn University	826
Weber State University	836
Western Carolina University	841
Western Oregon University	846
Western University	846
West Texas A&M University	852
West Virginia State University	852
West Virginia University	853
West Virginia University Institute of Technology	853
Wichita State University	859
Wilmington College (DE)	866
Winona State University	868
Wright State University	873
York University	878
Youngstown State University	878

$10,000–$19,999

Allen College	22
Antioch University Santa Barbara	30
Arizona Christian University	32
Arizona State University	33
Arizona State University at the Downtown Phoenix campus	34
Arizona State University at the West campus	34
Arizona State University Polytechnic campus	35
Auburn University	42, 888
Baptist College of Florida	53
Belmont Abbey College	61
Benedict College	64
Bennett College	66
Berkeley College	69
Bethany College (KS)	70
Blackburn College	75
Bloomsburg University of Pennsylvania	76
Bob Jones University	78
Bowling Green State University	82
Brescia University	85
Bridgewater State University	88
Bryn Athyn College of the New Church	93
California State University, Maritime Academy	106
California University of Pennsylvania	110

Hope International University	300	Roberts Wesleyan College	535	Wilmington College (OH)	866
Howard University	302	Rockford University	536	Wilson College	866
Huntington University	305	Rocky Mountain College	538	Xavier University of Louisiana	875
Immaculata University	311	Roosevelt University	540		
Indiana Wesleyan University	318	St. Andrews University	548		

$30,000–$39,999

John Brown University	324	Saint Anthony College of Nursing	550	Abilene Christian University	10
Kansas City Art Institute	331	St. Joseph's College	556, 1022	Academy of Art University	10, 882
Kentucky Wesleyan College	337	St. Joseph's College, New York (Patchogue)	557	Adelphi University	12
Keuka College	338	Saint Leo University	560	Alfred University	20
La Sierra University	351	St. Louis College of Pharmacy	560	Alvernia University	23
Lesley University	357	Saint Mary-of-the-Woods College	562	American International College	24
Liberty University	360	Saint Xavier University	571	Anderson University (IN)	27
LIM College	361, 962	School of Visual Arts	581, 1012	Antioch College	30
Limestone College	362	Siena Heights University	591	Augsburg University	44
Lincoln Memorial University	363	Sierra Nevada College	591	Augustana University	45
Lubbock Christian University	375	Southern California Institute of Architecture	601	Averett University	48
Lyme Academy College of Fine Arts	378	Southern Wesleyan University	607	Azusa Pacific University	49
Lyon College	379	Spring Arbor University	610	Baker University	50
Maharishi University of Management	381	Sterling College (KS)	628	Baldwin Wallace University	51
Malone University	381	Stevenson University	631	Belmont University	62, 896
Marymount University	392	Sweet Briar College	636	Berry College	70
Maryville College	392	Thomas Aquinas College	648	Bethel University (MN)	73
Maryville University of Saint Louis	393	Thomas Jefferson University	649	Birmingham-Southern College	74
The Master's University and Seminary	397	Thomas More College	650	Bradley University	83
McMurry University	400	Tiffin University	651	Brenau University	85
Methodist University	407	Toccoa Falls College	651	Bridgewater College	87
MidAmerica Nazarene University	410	Trevecca Nazarene University	653	Buena Vista University	95
Missouri Valley College	423	Trinity International University	657	California Baptist University	98
Mitchell College	424	Tuskegee University	662	California Institute of the Arts	99
Morehouse College	431	Union College (KY)	662	California Lutheran University	100
Morningside College	432	Unity College	667	Calvin University	112
Mount Mary University	435	University of Bridgeport	675	Capital University	115
Mount Mercy University	436	University of Detroit Mercy	694	Carlow University	116
Mount St. Joseph University	437	University of Dubuque	694	Carthage College	119
Multnomah University	441	University of Indianapolis	706	Catawba College	122
Muskingum University	442	University of Jamestown	708	Cazenovia College	124
Naropa University	443	University of Rio Grande	762	Cedar Crest College	124
Nebraska Wesleyan University	445	University of Saint Mary (KS)	765	Cedarville University	125
Neumont College	446	University of Tampa	778, 1054	Centenary College of Louisiana	126
New England Institute of Technology	448	University of the Ozarks	788	Chatham University	134
North Park University	464	Upper Iowa University	807	Chestnut Hill College	135
Northwest Nazarene University	467	Utica College	810	The College of Idaho	160
Northwood University	467	VanderCook College of Music	813	College of Mount Saint Vincent	161
Nova Southeastern University	470	Vaughn College of Aeronautics and Technology	814	College of Saint Elizabeth	163
Oklahoma Baptist University	480	Walla Walla University	823	The College of Saint Rose	165
Otterbein College	486	Walsh University	824	The College of Saint Scholastica	165
Ouachita Baptist University	487	Waynesburg University	832	Concordia College (Moorhead, MN)	179
Our Lady of the Lake University (OLLU)	488	Webber International University	834	Concordia University (NE)	180
Pacific Union College	490	Webster University	836	Corcoran College of Art and Design	185
Patrick Henry College	493	Wesleyan College	839	Cornish College of the Arts	188
Piedmont College	505	Westminster College (MO)	848	Covenant College	188
Point Park University	508	Wheeling Jesuit University	856	Curry College	191
Quincy University	519	William & Mary	861	Dallas Baptist University	193
Randolph College	522	William Peace University	864	Defiance College	196
Regent University	524	William Penn University	864	DigiPen Institute of Technology	202, 920
Rivier University	533			Doane University	203

Becker College	60	Luther College	376	Transylvania University	653
Bellarmine University	61	Lycoming College	377	Trinity University	657
Biola University	74	Manhattan College	383	University of Dallas	691
Bryant University	92, 904	Manhattanville College	383	University of Dayton	692
Butler University	96	Marist College	387	University of Portland	758
California College of the Arts	98	Marlboro College	388	University of Redlands	760, 1046
The Catholic University of America	123	Marquette University	388	University of Saint Joseph	765
Centre College	131	McDaniel College	399, 972	University of Saint Thomas (MN)	766
Champlain College	133	Menlo College	403	The University of Scranton	770, 1052
Clark University	149	Merrimack College	406	The University of the South	770
The Cleveland Institute of Art	152, 912	Millsaps College	416	University of the Pacific	788
Coe College	154	Milwaukee School of Engineering	417	The University of Tulsa	790, 1056
College of Performing Arts at The New School	162	Minneapolis College of Art and Design	418	Valparaiso University	811
College of Saint Benedict/		Moravian College	430	Wabash College	821
Saint John's University	163	Mount St. Mary's University (MD)	439	Wagner College	821
College of the Atlantic	166	New York Institute of Technology	451	Wartburg College	826
The Cooper Union for the Advancement		North Central College	457	Washington & Jefferson College	827
of Science and Art	184	Ohio Wesleyan University	480	Washington College	829, 1066
Cornell College	186	Otis College of Art and Design	486	Whittier College	857
Creighton University	189	Pace University	488	Whitworth University	858
Delaware Valley University	197	Pacific Lutheran University	489	Widener University	859
DePaul University	198	Pacific University	491	Wittenberg University	870
Dominican University of California	205	Polytechnic Institute of New York University—		Wofford College	870
Drake University	206	Brooklyn	510	Woodbury University	871
Drew University	207	Quinnipiac University	520, 990	Xavier University (OH)	874
Duquesne University	210	Randolph-Macon College	523		
Earlham College	211	Rhode Island School of Design	528		
Eckerd College	219	Rhodes College	529, 996		
Emerson College	226, 926	Rice University	529		
Emmanuel College	227	Rider University	531		
Eugene Lang College of Liberal Arts at		Ripon College	532, 998		
The New School	231	Roanoke College	533		
Fairfield University	233	Rochester Institute of Technology	536, 1000		
Florida Institute of Technology	242	Rose-Hulman Institute of Technology	541		
Gonzaga University	268, 936	Sacred Heart University	546, 1002		
Goucher College	270	Saint Anselm College	549, 1004		
Gustavus Adolphus College	278	St. Edward's University	552		
Hampden-Sydney College	281	St. John's University (NY)	556		
Hartwick College	286	Saint Joseph's University (PA)	558		
Hofstra University	296, 942	Saint Mary's College (IN)	563		
Hood College	299	Saint Michael's College	566		
Hult International Business School	303	St. Norbert College	567		
Illinois Institute of Technology	309, 944	St. Olaf College	568		
Illinois Wesleyan University	310	Salve Regina University	573		
Iona College	318	School of the Art Institute of Chicago	580		
Ithaca College	320	School of the Museum of Fine Arts	581		
John Carroll University	324	Seattle Pacific University	583		
The Juilliard School	329	Seattle University	584		
Juniata College	329	Siena College	590		
Kettering University	338	Simmons University	592		
Lake Forest College	345, 952	Southwestern University	609, 1020		
Lawrence University	353	Stetson University	630		
Lebanon Valley College	353	Stonehill College	632		
Linfield College	366	Suffolk University	633		
Loyola University New Orleans	374	Susquehanna University	634		
Loyola University of Chicago	375, 964	Texas Christian University	644		

OVER $50,000

Allegheny College	21
American University	25
Amherst College	26
Babson College	50, 890
Bard College	53
Bard College at Simon's Rock	54, 892
Barnard College	54, 894
Bates College	57
Beloit College	63, 898
Bennington College	66
Bentley University	67, 900
Boston College	79
Boston University	81, 902
Bowdoin College	82
Brandeis University	84
Brown University	91
Bryn Mawr College	94
Bucknell University	94, 906
California Institute of Technology	99
Carleton College	116
Carnegie Mellon University	117
Case Western Reserve University	121
Chapman University	133
Claremont McKenna College	145
Clarkson University	148
Colby College	156
Colgate University	158
College of the Holy Cross	167
The College of Wooster	168

Colorado College 170
Columbia University 176
Columbia University School of General Studies 177
Connecticut College 183
Cornell University 186
Dartmouth College 194
Davidson College 195
Denison University 197
DePauw University 199
Dickinson College 200
Drexel University 208
Duke University 209
Emory University 228
Fordham University 246
Franklin & Marshall College 250
Franklin W. Olin College of Engineering 252
Georgetown University 260
The George Washington University 261, 932
Gettysburg College 266, 934
Grinnell College 276
Hamilton College 279
Hampshire College 281
Harvard College 286
Harvey Mudd College 287
Haverford College 288
Hobart and William Smith Colleges 295
Johns Hopkins University 325, 946
Kalamazoo College 330
Kenyon College 337
Knox College 341, 950
Lafayette College 343
Landmark College 348
Lehigh University 355
Lewis & Clark College 358, 960
Loyola University Maryland 373, 966
Macalester College 379, 968
Maryland Institute College of Art 390
Massachusetts Institute of Technology 396
Middlebury College 412
Mount Holyoke College 434
Muhlenberg College 440
New York University 453, 982
Northeastern University 459
Northwestern University 466
Oberlin College 472
Occidental College 473, 984
Parsons School of Design at The New School 492
Pepperdine University 505
Pitzer College 506
Pomona College 511
Pratt Institute 513
Princeton University 515
Reed College 523, 994
Rensselaer Polytechnic Institute 527
Rollins College 539
St. Lawrence University 559, 1024
Saint Mary's College of California 563, 1010
Santa Clara University 578
Sarah Lawrence College 579
Scripps College 583
Skidmore College 593, 1016
Smith College 594
Southern Methodist University 603
Stanford University 612
Stevens Institute of Technology 630
Swarthmore College 635, 1028
Syracuse University 636
Trinity College (CT) 655
Tufts University 660
Tulane University 660
Union College (NY) 663, 1034
The University of Chicago 686
University of Denver 693
University of Miami 724
University of Notre Dame 751
University of Pennsylvania 754
University of Puget Sound 759
University of Richmond 761, 1048
University of Rochester 763
University of San Diego 767
University of San Francisco 768, 1050
University of Southern California 774
Ursinus College 808
Vanderbilt University 812, 1064
Vassar College 813
Villanova University 815
Wake Forest University 822
Washington and Lee University 828
Washington University in St. Louis 831
Wellesley College 837
Wesleyan University 840
Wheaton College (MA) 855
Whitman College 857
Willamette University 861, 1074
Williams College 865
Worcester Polytechnic Institute 872, 1076
Yale University 875

TUITION-FREE SCHOOLS

Berea College 68
College of the Ozarks 168
Deep Springs College 196
United States Air Force Academy 665
United States Coast Guard Academy 665
United States Merchant Marine Academy 666
United States Military Academy 666
United States Naval Academy 667
Webb Institute 835

INDEX BY SELECTIVITY

84

Albright College	18
Appalachian State University	30
Bay Path University	58
Bethel University (MN)	73
Bluffton University	78
Bradley University	83
Brescia University	85
Clayton State University	150
Concordia University (CA)	180
Concord University	182
Dakota State University	193
Eastern Illinois University	213
Elon University	223
Flagler College	238
Florida Institute of Technology	242
Ithaca College	320
John Brown University	324
Marian University (IN)	385
Maryland Institute College of Art	390
Miami University	408
Michigan State University	409
Northwest Nazarene University	467
Regis University	525
Saint Vincent College	570
Salem State University	572
Sam Houston State University	575
Slippery Rock University of Pennsylvania	593
Stonehill College	632
Tuskegee University	662
The University of Alabama—Tuscaloosa	670
University of Baltimore	675
University of Central Oklahoma	685
University of Massachusetts—Lowell	723
University of Michigan—Dearborn	726
University of North Georgia	750
University of Saint Mary (KS)	765
University of Tennessee—Knoxville	780
University of Wisconsin—La Crosse	800
Warner Pacific College	824

83

Alderson Broaddus University	19
Alma College	22
Anderson University (SC)	28
Arcadia University	32
Arizona Christian University	32
Auburn University	42, 888
Berry College	70
Buena Vista University	95
California Lutheran University	100
California State University, Chico	102
California State University, Fresno	104
Cedar Crest College	124
Central Connecticut State University	128, 908

Central State University	129
Cheyney University of Pennsylvania	136
Christopher Newport University	138, 910
Concordia College (Moorhead, MN)	179
Drexel University	208
Eckerd College	219
Endicott College	229
Faulkner University	236
Five Towns College	238
Florida College	241
Florida Southern College	243, 928
Francis Marion University	249
Georgia College & State University	262
Graceland University	272
Gustavus Adolphus College	278
Hollins University	298
King University	340
LaGrange College	343
Lewis & Clark College	358, 960
Louisiana State University—Baton Rouge	371
Lycoming College	377
Lyon College	379
Missouri University of Science and Technology	422
Mount Aloysius College	434
New College of Florida	447
North Park University	464
Northwestern College (IA)	465
Ohio Northern University	475
Ouachita Baptist University	487
Reinhardt University	526
St. Catherine University	551
St. Joseph's College, New York (Patchogue)	557
Southern University and A&M College	606
State University of New York—Maritime College	621
State University of New York—Potsdam	624
Stephens College	628
Stevenson University	631
The University of Alabama—Huntsville	670
University of Arkansas—Fayetteville	674
University of Cincinnati	687
University of Great Falls	698
University of Louisville	712
University of Nebraska—Omaha	736
University of Nebraska—Lincoln	737
University of Puget Sound	759
The University of Scranton	770, 1052
University of the Ozarks	788
University of Wisconsin—River Falls	803
University of Wisconsin—Superior	805
Wagner College	821
Westmont College	851
Winona State University	868
Youngstown State University	878

82

Alfred University	20
Anderson University (IN)	27
Arkansas State University	36, 884
California Baptist University	98
Campbellsville University	113
Claflin University	145
Clearwater Christian College	151
College of Saint Elizabeth	163
Duquesne University	210
Fontbonne University	245
Georgia Southwestern State University	265
Idaho State University	307
James Madison University	322
Lebanon Valley College	353
Lenoir-Rhyne University	356
Lyme Academy College of Fine Arts	378
Marymount California University	391
Methodist University	407
Minnesota State University, Mankato	419
Mount Mary University	435
New York Institute of Technology	451
Northland College	463
Oral Roberts University	484, 988
Penn State Shenango	502
Saint Charles Borromeo Seminary	551
Salisbury University	572
School of Visual Arts	581, 1012
Seattle University	584
Shenandoah University	587
Simmons University	592
Spring Arbor University	610
State University of New York—Fredonia	619
Texas State University	645
University of Arizona	673
University of Denver	693
University of Evansville	695
University of Iowa	707
University of Jamestown	708
University of Mary Washington	719
University of Michigan—Flint	726
University of Missouri	731
University of North Florida	749
University of Rhode Island	761
University of Saint Joseph	765
University of Science & Arts of Oklahoma	769
University of the Pacific	788
University of West Georgia	797
Western Illinois University	843

81

The Art Institute of Boston at Lesley University	39
Baldwin Wallace University	51
Bowling Green State University	82
Briar Cliff University	86

DeSales University 200, 918
Eugene Lang College of Liberal Arts at
   The New School 231
Frostburg State University 254
Houston Baptist University 301
Indiana University Northwest 314
Indiana University South Bend 316
Indiana Wesleyan University 318
Kansas City Art Institute 331
Kentucky Wesleyan College 337
Le Moyne College 355, 958
Malone University 381
Marywood University 394
McNeese State University 401
Millikin University 415
Northern Michigan University 462
Shaw University 587
Siena Heights University 591
Spring Hill College 611
Susquehanna University 634
Tarleton State University 638
The University of Alabama—Birmingham 669
The University of Findlay 696
University of Idaho 703
University of Saint Thomas (MN) 766
Xavier University (OH) 874

77

Alverno College 24
Antioch College 30
Arizona State University Polytechnic campus 35
Assumption College 41, 886
Averett University 48
Becker College 60
Belmont Abbey College 61
Bloomfield College 76
Bob Jones University 78
California State University, San Marcos 109
Canisius College 114
The Catholic University of America 123
Champlain College 133
Clarke University 147
College of Saint Benedict/
   Saint John's University 163
The College of Saint Scholastica 165
Colorado Mesa University 170
Colorado State University 172
Concordia University (NE) 180
Cornerstone University 187
Covenant College 188
Dominican University of California 205
D'Youville College 211
East Carolina University 212
Eastern Kentucky University 214
Eastern Michigan University 215
Edinboro University of Pennsylvania 221

Elizabethtown College 221
Emory and Henry College 227
Framingham State University 248
Georgian Court University 263
Goucher College 270
Grand Valley State University 273
Hanover College 283
Hardin-Simmons University 285
Hastings College 288
Hawai'i Pacific University 289
Heidelberg University 290
Holy Family University 298
Illinois State University 309
Indiana University—Purdue University
   Indianapolis 315
Indiana University Southeast 317
John Carroll University 324
Judson College (AL) 328
Lee University 354
Lesley University 357
Lincoln Christian College and Seminary 362
Linfield College 366
Long Island University 368
Longwood University 369
Loras College 369
Lourdes University 372
Maryville University of Saint Louis 393
Massachusetts Maritime Academy 396
Mercyhurst University 405
Millersville University of Pennsylvania 413
Molloy College 424, 976
Monmouth University (NJ) 426, 978
Montana State University 427
Montana Tech of the University of Montana 428
Mount St. Mary's University (MD) 439
Muskingum University 442
Nebraska Wesleyan University 445
Nicholls State University 454
Northwood University 467
Oglethorpe University 474, 986
Ohio Dominican University 474
Ohio University—Athens 479
Park University 492
Penn State Mont Alto 500
Penn State New Kensington 500
Penn State Schuylkill 501
Purdue University—Northwest 517
Queens University of Charlotte 518
Rhode Island College 527
St. Joseph's College 556, 1022
St. Mary's College of Maryland 564
Saint Michael's College 566
Saint Peter's University 568
San Francisco State University 577
Seton Hall University 585, 1014
Southeastern Louisiana University 598

Southern Connecticut State University 601
Southern Illinois University—
   Carbondale 602, 1018
Southern Utah University 606
Thiel College 647
Thomas College 648
Tiffin University 651
Transylvania University 653
Union College (KY) 662
University of Bridgeport 675
University of California—Merced 680
University of Charleston 686
University of Dubuque 694
University of Hartford 699
University of Hawaii—Manoa 700
University of Massachusetts—Boston 721
University of Massachusetts—Dartmouth 722
University of Minnesota—Crookston 727
University of Mount Union 735
University of North Carolina—Greensboro 745
University of North Dakota 747
University of Redlands 760, 1046
The University of South Dakota 774
University of Tennessee—Chattanooga 779
University of Wisconsin—Eau Claire 798
University of Wisconsin—Whitewater 806
Walsh University 824
Wartburg College 826
Watkins College of Art, Design & Film 831
Wentworth Institute of Technology 838, 1070
Western Connecticut State University 842
West Virginia University 853
West Virginia University Institute of
   Technology 853
West Virginia Wesleyan College 854, 1072
Whitworth University 858
Wisconsin Lutheran College 869
Wittenberg University 870

76

Arkansas Tech University 36
Aurora University 46
Bennett College 66
Biola University 74
Bloomsburg University of Pennsylvania 76
Boise State University 79
California Institute of the Arts 99
California State University, Maritime Academy 106
California State University, Monterey Bay 107
California State University, Sacramento 108
Calvary Bible College and Theological
   Seminary 111
Carroll University (WI) 118
Central Washington University 130
Columbia College Chicago (IL) 173
Columbus College of Art and Design 177

Notes

Notes

Notes

Notes

Notes

Notes

Notes